# THE PUBLISHER'S PAGE

Our research this year has delved more deeply into the next generation of lawyers. To the lists of ranked attorneys and those who are 'up-and-coming' we have added 'senior associates to watch'. These associates, often the unsung heroes of the most complex cases and biggest deals, guarantee the future of the law firms recommended in *Chambers USA*. They clearly deserve recognition.

We have also doubled the number of national tables, which rank the top law firms across the USA. We have added several new practice areas, such as Financial Services, Government Relations & Political Law and Wealth Management.

Within each state, we have added practice areas that clients have requested as being important in their day-to-day business operations – specialisms such as ERISA and employee benefits, healthcare, tax litigation and medical malpractice defense.

This fourth edition, therefore, increases our coverage in breadth and depth. We welcome readers' feedback, both positive and negative, which will help us to improve the quality of the next edition.

*Michael Chambers*

Published by **Chambers & Partners Publishing**
(a division of Orbach & Chambers Ltd)
23 Long Lane, London EC1A 9HL
**Tel** +44 207 606 1300
**Fax** +44 207 606 3191

**ISBN** 0-85514-423-8
Copyright © 2006 Michael Chambers and Orbach and Chambers Ltd

**Publisher** Michael Chambers
**Managing Editor** Fiona Boxall
**Editor** Rieta Ghosh
**Contributing Editors** Ross Cogan, Anna Williams
**Assistant Editor** Miranda Clow
**Editorial Assistant** Joanne Grote
**Profiles Editor** Richard Pettet
**Profiles Assistants** Jill Tugwell, Fiona Tulloch, Rebecca Denn, Stephen Beckett

**Production Team** Jasper John, John Osborne, Paul Cummings
**Business Development Manager** Brad Sirott
**Business Development Team** Richard Ramsay, Neil Murphy, Janene Warren
**Distribution** Marli Enslin

Orders to: Chambers & Partners Publishing
Printed in the USA by R R Donnelley

# Contents

## NATIONAL RANKINGS

## STATE RANKINGS

# Contents

**Rieta Ghosh (Editor)**
Graduated in Ancient History at University of Durham. Former Client Information Manager with European market research agency. Previously worked at a leading business advisory company.

**Pippa Grèze (Deputy Editor)**
Solicitor. Graduated in Law at UCW Aberystwyth. LL.M in European and International Trade Law from Leicester University. Trained with a major law firm, subsequently qualifying into commercial property law. Previously worked as a translator and guide in Poitiers, France.

**James Cowdell (Deputy Editor)**
Barrister. Graduated in Modern History at The Queen's College, Oxford. Practiced at the Criminal Bar for five years and was a fee-earner in the family department of a leading London law firm.

**Michael Leigh (Deputy Editor)**
Gained a First in Philosophy from Bristol University, where he also completed a doctorate in modern social contract theory. Has taught ethics and political philosophy and undertaken freelance satire for local newspapers.

**Sarah Brown (Research Manager)**
Solicitor. Graduated in Law at Newnham College, Cambridge. Trained and practiced at a magic circle firm. Specialized in corporate finance and insolvency law.

---

**Abby Rochford** Graduated with a Masters in American Studies from the University of Edinburgh. Previously worked for an independent publisher and travelled extensively before going into research.

**Robert Wainwright** Solicitor. Graduated in Law and English at University of Queensland, Australia. Trained at leading niche litigation firm and wrote for a national legal journal. Has also written for Chambers Student Guide.

**Catherine Rodgers** Graduated from King's College London with a First in English Language and Literature. Completed two mini-pupillages with sets of barristers, gaining experience in aspects of criminal law.

**Kate Fitzgerald** Solicitor. Graduated in Law and English at the University of New South Wales, Australia. Worked in human rights and international relations in Geneva and Australia.

**Louise Carr** Graduated in American and English Studies at the University of Nottingham. Previously worked in consumer magazine publishing and in information management for the insurance and financial services industry.

**Romila Chowdhury** Graduated in Law at the School of Oriental and African Studies.

**Edward Bannell** Graduated in Law at London School of Economics. Worked as a Legal Executive for a leading Australian law firm. Has worked in legal publishing and legal recruitment.

**Ifeyinwa Okoye** Solicitor. Graduated in Jurisprudence at Balliol College, Oxford. LL.M in child and family law-related subjects from King's College London. Trained with a top-50 London law firm before working in paralegal recruitment and legal publishing.

**Jacob Aitken** Graduated in Hispanic Studies from the University of Birmingham and Universidad de Salamanca in Spain. Worked as an English teacher in a school in Chile. Fluent in Spanish and Portuguese.

**Marion Volondat** Solicitor admitted to the New York and Paris Bars. Graduated in Law at The University of Paris 1 - Sorbonne and earned a master's degree in Law from the University of Texas at Austin. Has worked for several international law firms in Paris and New York. Fluent in French.

**Alexandra Quilici** Graduated in Politics at the American University in Paris. Completed a Master's in Modern History and a Master's in Political and Social Communications at Université Paris 1 Panthéon-Sorbonne. Has worked in business research, and financial information. Bilingual.

**Richard James** Graduated in English Literature at the University of Wales, Cardiff. Former paralegal and recently published author.

**Eleni Chalkidou** MA in Journalism from Westminster University. Worked as a journalist for BBC News Online, International Financial Law Review and Corporate Finance magazine. Also journalist for Commercial Lawyer magazine. Fluent in Greek, German, Spanish and Krio (spoken in Sierra Leone).

**Karen Williams** Graduated in Politics at Glasgow University. Previously worked as a parliamentary researcher at the House of Commons and as a paralegal at a New York law firm.

**Joanna Mason** Awarded first-class honours in English Literature from University of East Anglia. Graduated from King's College, Cambridge with an M.Phil in Eighteenth-Century British Literature.

**Jessica Culpan** Studied English and Law at the University of Otago in New Zealand. Has worked as a press officer and private secretary in the New Zealand House of Representatives, and subsequently as a researcher in both the public and private sector.

**Christine Yung** Graduated in Law from Christ's College, University of Cambridge.

**Louise Popplewell** Graduated with a Master of Arts (first class honours) from the University of Auckland, New Zealand. Has written for various magazines and newspapers.

**Abigail Andersen** Read English at the University of Nottingham and graduated from the University of Birmingham with an MA in International Relations, including studies in International Law. Previously worked in the Office of Government Commerce, an independent office of the Treasury.

**Jessica Owen** Graduated in Law at the University of Bristol. Subsequently awarded a Diploma in Legal Practice with Distinction from the College of Law. Has worked as a researcher and as a paralegal at a City law firm.

**Steven Sharman** Graduated with first-class honours in Law from the University of Greenwich, London. Subsequently awarded a Diploma in Legal Practice with Commendation from the College of Law and has worked for a solicitors firm in South London.

**Helen Lyle** Barrister. Graduated in English Literature at the University of Bristol with a First. Awarded the Roy Littlewood Prize for best performance in the dissertation unit. Completed the PgDL and the BVC at BPP Law School. Currently studying for an LL.M in Criminology and Criminal Justice. Will be commencing pupillage at 2 Bedford Row in 2006.

**Tom Wicker** Graduated in English Language and Literature at Corpus Christi College, Oxford. Worked in the editorial department of a London-based literary magazine after completing an MPhil in British Studies at Cambridge. Has also been involved in the research for a biography published in 2005.

**Adam Betts** Graduated in Chemistry at King's College London. Completed the Graduate Diploma in Law and Legal Practice Course at BPP Law School, London. Commencing training contract at a City law firm in 2006.

**Hannah McCarthy** Graduated with a First in English and Philosophy from University College Cork, Ireland. Completed an MA in Modernism from Warwick University. Also studied and researched at the University of Massachusetts, Smith College, and Harvard University, Massachusetts, USA.

**Anish Shonpal** Graduated in Law at Girton College, University of Cambridge.

**Edward Shum** Graduated in Law at Magdalene College, Cambridge. Previously worked at a South London law firm.

**Lydia Boos** Studied Law at the University of Tübingen in Germany before transferring to the University of Westminster. Completed the LPC at the College of Law. Fluent in German and French.

**Pue San Lam** Graduated in Law at University College London where she also completed a Corporate and Commercial Law LL.M. Awarded a Distinction for the LPC from the College of Law, London.

**Aoife Clifford** Barrister. Graduated with a First in Drama from the University of East Anglia. Worked as a writer, director and intern in various west end and fringe theatre venues including the Young Vic, the Etcetera and the Orange Tree. Had a play produced by BBC Radio 4.

**Amanda Howe** Graduated from University of Leeds with a First in German and Russian and is currently studying for Graduate Diploma in Law. Previously worked in the conference industry, organizing and producing business seminars in Moscow.

**John Daniel** Graduated with a Master's in Russian from the University of Edinburgh. Previously worked as a teacher in Russia and the UK, as well as a freelance translator/interpreter, musician and chef. Fluent in Russian and French.

**Victoria Howitt** Graduated with a degree in Law and History from Sidney Sussex College, Cambridge in 2003 and then passed with Distinction the Graduate Diploma in Law and the Legal Practice Course at the College of Law. Commencing a training contract with a City firm in 2006.

**Ruby Fasten** Graduated in law at Leiden University in the Netherlands. Previously worked as a clerk in the magistrate's court. Fluent in Dutch and French.

**Ignacio Abella** BA in English Language and Literature from Universidad de Oriente in Cuba. Freelance translator/interpreter, worked as project manager for a local branch of the Ministry of Culture. Started an MA in Caribbean Studies before relocating to the UK. Extensive experience in market research having worked for an Information and Communication Technology advisory company and for a major data analysis group in London.

**Giles Thomas** Graduated in International Relations from the University of Sussex in 2005.

**Melisa Thomas** Graduated in English and History at Nottingham Trent University, and has completed the Graduate Diploma in Law, at BPP Law School in London.

**Katie Cooke** Graduated in English and French at King's College London. Worked in Marseille, France as an English teacher before becoming a journalist. Was previously deputy editor of a leading City reinsurance magazine.

**Alice Woudhuysen** Graduated in English Language and Literature (European) at University of Leeds. Gained NCTJ pre-entry level qualification at Lambeth College, South London. Previously worked as an English language teacher in Bolivia and Spain. Fluent in Spanish.

**Lee Saunders** Graduated in French and History at University of Leeds. Worked as an English teacher in Paris, France and subsequently as a research analyst in London for an American media company.

**Christopher Nichols** Graduated from The University of Sheffield with a First in Law. Fluent in Spanish.

**Daniel Kidd** Graduated in History from the University of Warwick in 2001. Spent three years studying and working in Japan. Fluent in Japanese.

**Lori Jay Frecker** Graduated in Law at Nottingham University.

**Rav Casley Gera** Achieved a First in History from the University of Sheffield and studied at Harvard University as a Kennedy Scholar. He has worked as a communications officer for a national disability charity.

**Russell Bramley** Graduated in History at the University of East Anglia. Completed the Graduate Diploma in Law at The College of Law in 2004.

**Daniela Nadj** Studied English and European Law at Queen Mary College, University of London. Completed a master's degree (LL.M.) in International Law at Cornell Law School (USA). Previously worked as paralegal and legal translator in the US and as an English language teacher in Italy. Fluent in German, Serbo-Croatian, Italian, Spanish and French.

**Annett Herzog** German lawyer. Graduated in Law from Leipzig University, Germany. Trained at Zwickau District Court in Germany and several German law firms in London. Has worked in financial publishing.

**Shivali Chaudhry** Graduated in Law at University College, London. Completed the LPC at the College of Law. Has studied in Singapore.

**Maite Usoz de la Fuente** Graduated with first-class honours in German from the University of the Basque Country (Spain); MA in European Theory and Culture from Royal Holloway College (University of London). Fluent in Spanish, German and French.

**Tracey Sinclair** Graduated with a joint First in English Literature and Philosophy from Glasgow University. Has worked as a business editor and researcher for non-profit organizations and a national broadcasting company. Is a published author and has written for several magazines and business websites. Spent four years working as a subtitler for the BBC.

**Adam Harrison** Graduated with a First in French and Russian from Gonville and Caius College, Cambridge. Previously worked in Moscow both as a researcher for a polling organization and a translator in a cinema. Also taught English in Bosnia.

V

## The Four Additional Categories

*Chambers USA* is one of a series of guides to the legal profession, the other publications being *Chambers Global*, *Chambers UK*, *Chambers Student* and the forthcoming *Chambers Europe*. The guides are independent and research-based – not simply a collection of paid-for entries. No lawyers will be mentioned unless they have strong recommendations from the market. No one – in other words – can 'buy their way in'.

In addition to the six tier rankings in the Chambers' tables, there are four additional categories in which attorneys are ranked. They are as follows:

### 1. Senior Statesman

How should we rank those distinguished older partners – often name partners – who are admired throughout the profession and who are still, in their senior years, the principal point of contact with major clients? In the very top band? But they are no longer seen around so much on everyday transactions. Their role has changed. As leading practitioners doing the deals they are being overtaken by the next generation. Logically, then, they should be demoted to the band below. But given their immense prestige, this would look wrong. It would also be inaccurate.

They are not exactly 'declining': their contribution is as valuable as ever. We resolved this dilemma with the 'senior statesman' category. They are the sages of their particular legal markets and beyond. Among them is Marty Lipton, one of the global giants of M&A and the main architect of the 'poison pill' defense. Another legal virtuoso is Jack Levin, hailed for his contribution to the development of private equity law, not just in Illinois but across the world.

### 2. Star

These players are the first names that roll off everyone's lips, the standard by which others are judged. Beyond that, these attorneys operate in a 'right here, right now' mode, immersing themselves in the most significant work around. At the top of their game, they also bring to the negotiating table a certain degree of gravitas – the kind of influence that sends shivers down the spine of the opposing side. The star category is reserved for those individuals whose profile is far ahead of the pack.

This marketplace authority is cultivated through a long history of excellence, and it usually manifests in the research process through the sheer weight of recommendations compared with their peers. Additionally, they've also managed to change the legal landscape in dramatic ways. For example, rainmaker Larry Sonsini of Wilson Sonsini Goodrich & Rosati is not only a catalyst in the success of his own firm, but also consistently sets industry records for the number of IPOs to his name.

### 3. Up-and-Coming Individual

If the senior statesmen are the brains of a firm, then this 'bubbling-under' set is its added brawn. Yet, while these individuals do not make or break a firm, they do fuel the firm's growth. This next generation of talent doesn't necessarily have the industry reputation to warrant a numeric ranking, which is reserved for those with an already established profile. But what they lack in experience, they make up for in energy.

They are the young dynamos that give an operation extra edge. More importantly, they bridge the practice's present and its future. These operators range in age, but are generally in their 30s and early 40s, partly depending on their areas of specialty; certain fields require more 'seasoning' than others.

### 4. Senior Associates to Watch

These lawyers, often the unsung heroes of the most complex cases and biggest deals, are the future of the law firms recommended in Chambers USA and so worthy of recognition. While our up-and-coming partners can often be found as headliners on matters, these senior associates have been spotted by clients as they beaver away in the background.

They are the young dynamos that give an operation extra edge. More importantly, they bridge the practice's present and its future. These operators range in age, but are generally in their 30s and early 40s, partly depending on their areas of specialty; certain fields require more 'seasoning' than others.

## The Chambers Award Ceremonies

The Chambers legal guides celebrate excellence in the profession – across the world. Our researchers and editors (see their details on page iv-v) speak to a vast range of clients, industry experts and lawyers in order to select the nominations for these awards.

## The Global Awards

The Chambers Global Awards has become the most prestigious event in the legal calendar and attracts over 800 of the cream of the legal profession from around the world. The champagne reception and gala dinner provide outstanding net-working opportunities and the chance to catch up with colleagues from overseas. For the past two years it has been hosted by Ms Cherie Booth QC, an eminent barrister and wife of the British Prime Minister.

The Chambers Global awards have been an outstanding success not just because of the huge turnout of leading lawyers from around the world, but also because — in the words of one guest — it's a damn fine party.

## The USA Awards

Following the success of the annual Chambers Global Awards in London, we are proud to announce the first Chambers USA Awards for Excellence ceremony in New York. At this event, we are honouring the achievements of outstanding lawyers across the USA.

## The Bar Awards

Held each year in September, the Chambers Bar Awards recognize the achieve-ments of England's most outstanding barristers. The event, held in London, has become the most prestigious awards for the Bar. Over 400 of the profession's leading individuals attend.

# Abbreviations

| | |
|---|---|
| AAA | American Arbitration Association |
| ABA | American Bar Association |
| ACREL | American College of Real Estate Lawyers |
| ADA | Americans with Disabilities Act |
| ADEA | Age Discrimination in Employment Act |
| AMA | American Medical Association |
| CAA | Clean Air Act |
| CERCLA | The Comprehensive Environmental Response, Compensation, and Liability Act |
| CRM | Customer Relationship Management |
| CWA | Clean Water Act |
| DEP | Department of Environmental Protection |
| DMCA | Digital Millennium Copyright Act |
| D&O | directors and officers (insurance) |
| ERISA | Employee Retirement Income Security Act of 1974 |
| EU | European Union |
| FCC | Federal Communications Commission |
| FDA | Food and Drug Administration |
| FERC | Federal Energy Regulatory Commission |
| FLSA | Fair Labor Standards Act |
| FMLA | Family and Medical Leave Act |
| FTC | Federal Trade Commission |
| GATT | General Agreement on Tariffs and Trade |
| ICC | International Criminal Court |
| ICSID | International Centre for Settlement of Investment Disputes |
| IFA | International Fiscal Association |
| IP | Intellectual Property |
| IPL | Intellectual Property Law |
| IPP | Independent Power Producer |
| IRS | Internal Revenue Service |
| ITC | International Trade Commission |
| LCIA | London Court of International Arbitration |
| MSHA | Mine Safety and Health Administration |
| NAFTA | North American Free Trade Agreement |
| NEPA | National Environmental Policy Act |
| NLRA | National Labor Relations Act |
| NLRB | National Labor Relations Board |
| OECD | Organisation for Economic Co-operation and Development |
| OFCCP | Office of Federal Contract Compliance Programs |
| OSHA | Occupational Safety and Health Act/Administration |
| PTO | Patent and Trademark Office |
| RCRA | Resource Conservation and Recovery Act |
| REIT | Real Estate Investment Trust |
| REOC | Real Estate Operating Company |
| RICO | Racketeer-Influenced and Corrupt Organizations Act |
| RIC | Regulated Investment Companies |
| SEC | Securities and Exchange Commission |
| SLAPPs | Strategic Lawsuits against Public Participation |
| UNCITRAL | United Nations Commission on International Trade Law |
| WIPO | World Intellectual Property Organization |
| WTO | World Trade Organization |

NATIONAL

# BUSINESS PROCESS OUTSOURCING

## Band 1

### Mayer, Brown, Rowe & Maw LLP

See firm details p.876

**The Firm:** Interviewees praised this practice for its "*unparalleled depth*," its large volume of ITO and BPO deals, and its terrific relationship with technology consultants TPI in particular. According to clients: "*The dollar-for-dollar value that you get with them is completely unmatched – the only way they could improve would be to clone individuals and get even more of them!*"

**The Lawyers:** Clients believe that **Dan Masur** (see p.118) is a pioneer in this field, bringing as he does "*a lot of poise and direction*" to all his negotiations. He also impresses by being "*passionate about driving through to solutions, but willing to consider the other side's position.*" He recently represented Wachovia in the outsourcing to Hewitt Associates of human resources, employment, benefit administration, payroll, and other business process functions – one of the largest employee services outsourcing transactions ever attempted. Chicago-based **Brad Peterson** (see p.125) has a "*focused, common-sense approach*" and clear presentation skills. He "*clearly and concisely conveys his position so all parties understand.*" He recently advised Whirlpool, the world's leading manufacturer and marketer of major home appliances, on entering into a ten-year human resources outsourcing agreement with Convergys. Especially rated by peers for his ITO expertise, **David Hudanish** (see p.109) is "*hard-working and thoughtful*" and a trusted negotiator who seeks sensible solutions. He

represented Sun Microsystems in a global five-year BPO transaction in which Hewitt Associates will provide human resources services to the company and its employees. **Nigel Howard** (see p.108) has developed a broad technology practice. He "*stays in command, understands objectives and communicates issues well.*" Clients also appreciated **Paul Roy**'s (see p.131) confident approach: he is "*good at coaching on the key issues*" and has knowledge of the right contractual protections which means he "*considers all the important factors in reaching conclusions.*" The "*intelligent, focused and pragmatic*" **Rebecca Eisner** (see p.98) is a patient negotiator who brings the important issues to the fore; she has "*an ability to get the results we're looking for without antagonizing the other party.*" She has been representing a leading provider of back office services in the development of a proprietary servicing platform that assists finance vehicles in managing their portfolios. **Sonia Baldia** (see p.86) is a "*consummate professional*" according to clients, while **Kevin Rang** (see p.128) is a definite asset in negotiations because of his "*logical brain and unflappable approach – he builds trust on all sides of the deal.*" The detail-oriented **Geoff Master** (see p.117) displays a phenomenal base of knowledge. According to one client: "*There are few lawyers I've met who can so instantly and confidently win clients' trust while at the same time driving totally hard bargains by charming the other side.*"

**Clients/Work Highlights:** Sun Microsystems; TXU; Procter & Gamble; Fifth Third Bank; Whirlpool; The Williams Companies; Gillette; US Airways; United Technologies and Kodak.

### Milbank, Tweed, Hadley & McCloy LLP

**The Firm:** This dedicated team has long been a market leader in the most significant BPO transactions. Clients value the expertise of its pioneering attorneys and believe the whole team is "*really plugged into what's going on in the marketplace.*" The range of experience within the group means that the attorneys "*add an extra dimension with their common-sense approach to the intersection of the legal and business perspective.*" The firm has been especially active in HRO deals in recent times.

**The Lawyers:** Universally considered to be "*one of the godfathers of the industry,*" practice head **John Halvey** brings "*star power, connections, common sense, personality and excellent drafting skills*" to the table, reported sources. His recent work includes leading the team advising on human resources outsourcings for clients including PepsiCo, Omnicom, DuPont and VNU. He has also advised on BPO transactions for clients such as Home Depot and TXU. **Rob Finkel** employs his "*polished, sharp and economic mind*" to the most complex of transactions. His recent work includes advising Tyco International in an outsourcing deal with ADP involving employer-related functions. He also advised Master-Card on a call center agreement with Convergys. Younger partner **Debra White** is "*smart, easy to deal*

*with and amazing with clients,*" and possesses a deep understanding of business strategy.

**Clients/Work Highlights:** General Atlantic Partners; Prudential Financial; Home Depot; AT&T; DuPont; Cendant; Pepsi Bottling Group; MasterCard and Tyco International (US).

### Pillsbury Winthrop Shaw Pittman LLP

See firm details p.1550

**The Firm:** Bolstered by its merger with Pillsbury Winthrop, this "*formidable technology practice*" is rated by commentators for its ITO expertise in particular. Despite recent departures, it possesses a tremendous depth of experience, fielding attorneys who have a "*heavy knowledge base*" across a broad range of hi-tech issues.

**The Lawyers:** Clearly one of the first players in the field, **Bob Zahler** (see p.143) is "*a real personality – always innovative, he understands the nature of business.*" A top-notch marketer and strategist, **Trevor Nagel** (see p.123) in DC has continued to advise Ahold on its global ITO agreements, and PepsiCo on its global network outsourcing. Especially noted for his ITO expertise, **Michael Murphy** (see p.122) in Los Angeles won plaudits for being "*creative and collaborative.*" According to one source: "*He does an excellent job representing his clients and helped build relationships with service providers that stand the test of time.*" He recently represented PG&E in the negotiation of a comprehensive agreement with Accenture concerning the provision of business transformation services. The BPO team can also call on the support of technology specialists such as Aaron Oser, Jim Alberg and Harry Glasspiegel, the latter recently rejoining the firm after eight years as a business leader and investor in the sourcing and technology markets.

**Clients/Work Highlights:** A highlight for the practice involved assisting Dun & Bradstreet in the global outsourcing of a number of back office data collection, finance and accounting, and inbound/outbound call center services to various vendors, particularly IBM. Other clients include Capital One; GE Consumer Finance; Stop & Shop Supermarket and Educational Testing Service.

## Band 2

### Alston & Bird LLP

See firm details p.728

**The Firm:** Clients commended this practice for its success in fostering "*tireless lawyers with outstanding technical knowledge.*" Their experience of both the practical business and legal aspects of outsourcing is appreciated. The firm acts for clients in a range of sectors, including financial services, insurance, transportation and retail. Its recent activities include the renegotiation of existing deals. It is also becoming increasingly engaged in developments arising out of the energy sector, as well as in healthcare and pharmaceuticals.

## Business Process Outsourcing
### Leading Individuals

### Up-and-coming individuals

### Associates to watch

**The Lawyers:** Clients believe that **Chris Ford** (see p.100) brings a wealth of experience to the table and has a *"well-prepared, measured approach"* that ensures the smooth running of deals. He is *"steadfast on the most important points, with a good feel for the direction negotiations are likely to go in."* With a customer-biased practice, his recent work includes advising on an insurance claims processing deal with IBM. **Bob Reynolds** (see p.129) is particularly commended for his work for ACS. He has also advised on a large supply chain outsourcing for a Fortune 50 company. Senior associate **Todd McClelland** (see p.119) is making a name for himself as a *"motivated, smart and hard-working attorney."*

## Brown Raysman Millstein Felder & Steiner LLP
See firm details p.1521

**The Firm:** Commentators believe this firm has earned its seat at the table through building on its strong technology and IP transactional background to form a *"pioneering"* outsourcing practice. It has a range of clients on both the customer and vendor sides, but remains best known for its work with key client AT&T. Especially active in the HRO sphere of late, the group's expertise also includes IT operations, tax compliance and logistics transactions.

**The Lawyers:** Clients described **Julian Millstein** (see p.121) as the *"shining star"* of the practice and a highly skilled deal negotiator. With clients on both sides of the fence, his recent work includes advising on the restructuring of a large HRO. **Richard Raysman** (see p.128) possesses *"pure technology expertise,"* which has attracted a broad clientele of investment banks, insurance companies, hospitals and data management companies. His recent BPO workload has featured transactions for overseas companies, primarily Indian clients, in addition to IT-related work for domestic companies, such as co-location agreements and renegotiating existing agreements.

**Clients/Work Highlights:** Clients include Wall Street investment banks; Fortune 50 entertainment and media companies; leading financial services and insurance firms; top-tier software and technology infrastructure vendors and well-known e-commerce concerns.

## Jones Day
See firm details p.570

**The Firm:** The most notable development for this practice has been the recent arrival of David Guedry from Hughes & Luce. The prevailing market consensus is that the addition of his expertise will *"move the practice up a notch,"* particularly on the vendor side. Clients endorsed the whole team, and appreciated that these attorneys *"know the right answers and help us to understand the issues with a balanced view of the world."*

**The Lawyers:** **John Funk** (see p.100) has cultivated a *"huge depth of knowledge of the marketplace,"* especially on the customer side. Clients are attracted by his international experience and value his *"measured, reserved, but effective approach – he's a gentleman in*

negotiations, but doesn't give any ground."* His recent work includes representing Sprint in its F&A outsourcing deal with ACS, and acting for Dana in its HRO with IBM. Recently moved from Hughes & Luce, **David Guedry** (see p.104) has built up a respected supplier-side practice. Clients spoke of his long track record of excellent advice and his *"nonconfrontational way of making a point – he determines what's important and what he can let go of."* His recent work includes advising EDS in the negotiation of a seven-year IT master services agreement with Black & Veatch, a global engineering, consulting and construction company.

**Clients/Work Highlights:** Clients include Washington Mutual, Hewitt Associates and Sprint.

## King & Spalding LLP
See firm details p.1933

**The Firm:** The firm's relationship with Accenture is widely recognized as providing strong foundations to this practice. The firm is best known for its BPO and ITO advice on the vendor side. Clients endorsed the high-caliber service provided by these attorneys: *"They go above and beyond to meet our needs."*

**The Lawyers:** **Bill Roche** (see p.130) is recommended for his work with Accenture, although this does not limit his practice. Of late he has advised TSYS on a five-year definitive agreement with Capital One to provide processing services for its North America portfolio of consumer and small business credit card accounts. The *"forthright"* **Ellen Ray** (see p.128) has recently advised Sprint on several technology and BPO transactions including the negotiation and consummation of a strategic BPO with IBM. Technology transactions practice head **Steve de Groot** (see p.95) is an excellent drafter who is *"fair, but tough when he has to be."* Clients also value his responsiveness and *"great sense of humor, which can help in negotiations!"* He recently represented ING North America Insurance in connection with various BPOs.

**Clients/Work Highlights:** Sprint; Belk Department Stores; ChoicePoint; Crawford & Company; EDS; GE; Home Depot; SAIC and UPS.

## Latham & Watkins LLP

**The Firm:** This firm's depth of experience and expertise on both the West and East Coasts has impressed many clients and peers. The practice has developed strong institutional relationships and is *"increasingly moving up the food chain"* because of the broad expertise of its attorneys. In recent times, the group has been progressively active for clients in the healthcare and life insurance sectors, in addition to financial institutions and brokerage houses.

**The Lawyers:** **Dan Mummery** in the firm's Menlo Park office has *"negotiated with all the big players"* said clients, who pointed to his *"professionalism and integrity – he avoids ego, doesn't get caught up in the heat of arguments, but wins the necessary battles."* Peers credit him with increasing the Latham brand value in this sector. His recent work includes representing a Fortune 500 apparel retailer in the negotiation of an HRO with Accenture, and representing a

Fortune 500 energy services company in its renegotiation of an HRO agreement with ADP. **Allen Klein** in DC won praise from clients for his *detail-oriented drafting skills and his fantastic negotiating.* He recently represented F&G Life in an amendment of its insurance applications and claims processing transaction with TAG. Chair of the firm's technology transactions practice group, Los Angeles-based **Michael Shockro** recently represented WellPoint in the negotiation of a BPO of its claims processing services to India-based Daksh eServices and US-based Accenture.

**Clients/Work Highlights:** CGI-AMS; Charles Schwab; F&G Life; Hawaiian Telecom and Valeant Pharmaceuticals.

## Morgan, Lewis & Bockius LLP
See firm details p.1758

**The Firm:** Clients respect this team of efficient lawyers for their *excellent, practical negotiating style, and for bringing innovative and workable solutions to problems that arise.* Its lawyers have big-deal experience and *bring a lot of firepower to the table.* The group has seen increased activity in the HRO sector in recent times, leveraging off the firm's preeminent labor and benefits practice.

**The Lawyers:** The ITO experience and *incredible market knowledge* of **Akiba Stern** (see p.136) ensures his market prominence. According to clients: *His words have three times the impact!* His recent work has included advising an international confectionery and beverages company in relation to an F&A and HR outsourcing. Endorsed for her vendor-side work the *knowledgeable and articulate* **Barbara Melby** (see p.120) is a tough negotiator who can *keep all the pieces in line during complicated deals – she never drops a detail.* Her recent work includes a multitower BPO for a large pharmaceutical company. **Ed Hansen**'s (see p.105) caseload has included a facilities management outsourcing in the healthcare field and HRO in the entertainment field. With a *practical sensibility,* **Michael Pillion** (see p.125) takes a balanced approach to deal negotiations, particularly those that entail the management of volumes of documents. He is *credible, holds his ground and understands a range of legal issues.* The pharmaceutical and healthcare fields are current areas of activity with issues such as logistics and human resources.

**Clients/Work Highlights:** Clients include pharmaceutical companies; chemical and gas companies; insurance companies; healthcare providers; electric utilities; manufacturing companies; food and beverage companies; and financial services companies.

## Sonnenschein Nath & Rosenthal LLP
See firm details p.884

**The Firm:** The firm's work on the sell side is particularly respected; however, this should not diminish its increasing prominence in the customer sphere. Clients spoke of *nimble and technology-aware* lawyers, who understand both the legal and business issues.

**The Lawyers:** A *professional, smart and articulate lawyer,* **Ross Docksey** (see p.96) has been especially engaged in F&A outsourcings in recent times. For example, he advised OPI in Durant's outsourcing of its F&A services. He also acted in the F&A outsourcing by one of the Big Four accounting firms. **Rosemary Gullikson**'s (see p.104) recent work includes representing ACS in Delta Air Line's outsourcing of its human resources functions. She also advised a major global consulting firm in relation to an ITO and F&A outsourcing involving a large credit card provider.

**Clients/Work Highlights:** Aon; Hyrian; DSC Logistics; PwC and Accenture.

# Band 3

## Baker & McKenzie
See firm details p.866

**The Firm:** An international footprint has been established through the activity of the firm's global IT and communications department. This geographic reach is coupled with a breadth of resources that clients value for product development and the negotiation of global agreements. Clients also rated the practice for its deep understanding of both technical issues and legal liability. In a significant market development, the team has been joined by George Kimball from Arnold & Porter; a move that many predict will increase the group's market share.

**The Lawyers:** Widely recognized for his work on the supplier side, **George Kimball** (see p.113) is heavily involved in HRO and applications outsourcing work. National practice head and *chief architect* in the practice's expansion, **Michael Mensik** (see p.120) won plaudits from clients: *He is an expert in a variety of topics, and knows the best person in every office around the world for your situation – people listen to him.* Clients also believe that **Sam Kramer** (see p.113) has *the ability to look at complicated issues and provide panoramic options from both a legal and consulting perspective.* An excellent strategist, he assisted ESPN Mobile in the establishment of a mobile virtual network operator (MVNO), which included carrier, data platform, billing platform and call center agreements. He also advised Turtle Wax on a multivendor strategy for the outsourcing of all the manufacturing services relating to the company's consumer product lines. Younger partner **Peter George** (see p.101) impresses clients as he is in *complete command of documents and issues.*

**Clients/Work Highlights:** The group assisted Rohm and Haas in a long-term multijurisdiction HRO transaction involving the outsourcing of payroll, call centers, benefits administration and employee relocation assistance. Other clients include Bank of America; Thomson; Hewlett-Packard; CSG Systems and Siemens.

## Baker Botts LLP
See firm details p.1922

**The Firm:** Clients praised this practice's lawyers for being *thorough, practical and attentive to our needs,* highlighting their deep knowledge of law and common market practice across the industry. The firm has experience on both sides of the fence, but is best known for its expertise on the vendor side. In recent times, the team has been engaged in customer care work, particularly in the utilities industry, and call center work in the telecom industry. Human resources, benefits administration and F&A outsourcings complete the picture.

**The Lawyers:** Dallas-based practice head **John Martin** (see p.117) adopts a *firm but collaborative style,* said clients. He understands the dynamics of a transaction and can *help parties reach a compromise, particularly during deadlocks.* **Brian Henchey**'s (see p.106) depth of experience means he brings a creative approach to complex negotiations.

**Clients/Work Highlights:** Recent major transactions for the practice include a $1 billion outsourcing by a US state government of integrated eligibility and enrolment functions for health and human service programs. The team also advised on an HRO of management functions by an international restaurant and beverage chain. Further clients include Accenture; Affiliated Computer Services; Cisco Systems; Dell; Deloitte Consulting; EDS; Liberty Media; Nokia Networks; OpenTV and Perot Systems.

## Hughes & Luce LLP

**The Firm:** The firm's representation of long-term client EDS, and its broader expertise on the vendor side have won it a following in the market. Clients spoke of the firm's development of *a tenure in the industry that is difficult to match.* Its lawyers *could not be better at understanding our business and issues – you know you're going to get a top-quality end product.*

**The Lawyers:** Hugely experienced **John Howell** has been in the field *from day one,* reported clients, who appreciated his *responsive, relaxed, nonconfrontational style* and drafting skills. His recent work has included advising Hewitt Associates in the renegotiation of a human resources services agreement with Duke Energy. He has also been advising Pacific Investment Management and its foreign subsidiaries on regulatory compliance for various outsourcing contracts.

**Clients/Work Highlights:** Clients include Pacific Investment Management, BearingPoint and Worldspan.

## Hunton & Williams LLP
See firm details p.1989

**The Firm:** According to sources, these attorneys *raise issues in an intelligent, non-offensive way, and they focus on getting transactions closed.* The caseload of late has included a range of BPO, ITO and HRO deals, particularly those arising out of the utilities sector. The group has also advised clients in the consumer products, credit reporting and online data industry. It has recently benefited from the arrival of veteran outsourcing attorneys Jim Harvey from Alston & Bird and Jim Meadows from Duane Morris.

**The Lawyers:** The "*diligent*" **Randy Parks** (see p.125) is a skilled negotiator, who "*knows both the issues and the reasons behind the issue.*" His recent work includes representing Duke Energy in a multifunction HRO, and handling a data center deal for Altria and Philip Morris. Also noted for his work on the customer side, **Jim Harvey** (see p.105) "*stays abreast of changes*," particularly in the technology field, and has "*amazing creativity*" in his approach to the structuring of agreements. He recently acted on a $300 million store operations outsourcing for a large retailer, and advised another client on an IT infrastructure and human resources outsourcing. The "*technically expert*" **Jim Meadows** (see p.120) has a user-side technology and outsourcing practice for a number of Fortune Global 250 companies. Clients believe he has "*good commercial instincts*" and "*really knows the industry hands down with his eyes closed!*"
**Clients/Work Highlights:** The team has advised on an HRO for Rolls-Royce North America, and represented GE's insurance subsidiary on the restructuring of its outsourcing work. Other clients include Genworth Financial and General Dynamics UK.

## Kirkland & Ellis LLP
See firm details p.875
**The Firm:** The firm's institutional client base and its wealth of experience in the M&A market has attracted a wide clientele seeking its ITO expertise in particular. Its client base includes a heavy component of financial services institutions and manufacturers on the customer side. On the service provider side, the team has recently advised an IT consulting company, a Big Four accounting firm, a supply chain management software company and a global real estate services company.
**The Lawyers:** Chicago-based **Gregg Kirchhoefer** (see p.113) is head of the firm's IP and technology practice group. His recent work includes a broadbased outsourcing initiative for a financial services company, involving call centers, F&A and human resources aspects. He has also been acting for a manufacturing client in an ITO involving a variety of support functions, such as putting in place a new ERP system.
**Clients/Work Highlights:** Accenture; Affiliated Computer Services; Allstate Insurance; Hewitt Associates; Morgan Stanley; News Corporation; PwC; Sun Microsystems; USG; Vertex Outsourcing and WW Grainger.

## O'Melveny & Myers LLP
See firm details p.336
**The Firm:** This thriving practice has developed a broad caseload featuring human resources, F&A, ITO, procurement and the outsourcing of legal services. Much of its work of late has come from the financial services and automotive manufacturing sectors. Clients endorsed the group's attorneys for being "*conscientious, client-oriented, smart and thor-*

*ough negotiators.*"
**The Lawyers:** **Bill Peters** (see p.125) is a "*bright, energetic guy*," and a real force in the marketplace. Clients believe "*he holds all the cards in negotiations because he's used to doing this all the time*," and is experienced in both the vendor and the corporation perspective.
**Clients/Work Highlights:** Recent highlights include representing Federal-Mogul in its full global F&A outsourcing and advising Marriott International in its domestic HRO with Hewitt/Exult. The team also represented Safeco Insurance in the outsourcing of its human resources functions to ACS.

## Skadden, Arps, Slate, Meagher & Flom LLP
See firm details p.1557
**The Firm:** This practice has benefited from its institutional client base and status as a corporate powerhouse, which has ensured a steady flow of M&A-related outsourcings. Clients appreciate that its "*fantastically responsive*" lawyers turn documents around quickly and "*don't give legal advice in the abstract – they often outsmart the opposition without being confrontational.*" The practice has recently been active in the renegotiation of existing outsourcing arrangements, as well as outsourcing projects involving telecom carriers or associated systems.
**The Lawyers:** Head of the firm's IT and e-commerce practice is **Stu Levi** (see p.115). Clients benefit from his broad experience and his background in computer science and the IT industry. **Rita Rodin** (see p.130) displays "*presence and poise while negotiating.*" She recently represented Capgemini in its agreements with TXU Energy and ONCOR to form a joint venture for the provision of IT and other BPO services to TXU.
**Clients/Work Highlights:** Other recent work for the practice includes handling an insourcing for a major US insurance company and representing a key US retailer in outsourcing different aspects of its back office financial infrastructure. Clients are drawn from a range of sectors including financial services, insurance, telecom, energy, consulting, travel, media and publishing.

## Band 4

## Arnold & Porter LLP
See firm details p.560
**The Firm:** This practice is best known for its ITO work on the customer side. Its expertise includes mainframe and database administration, voice and data network management, and application maintenance and development. Its attorneys are also well versed in HRO and F&A outsourcings.
**The Lawyers:** The Los Angeles-based practice head **Matt Maccoby** (see p.117) is particularly active in the shipping and transportation fields. Clients value the "*personable, knowledgeable and calm way he presents things*," and his ability to see the business issues. He represented IndyMac Bank, the country's

tenth largest thrift, in the renegotiation of a major contract to outsource core retail banking functions. He also represented California State University in the outsourcing of its financial, human resources and student information systems. In addition, he represented US Airways in the outsourcing of maintenance for its aircraft, engines and components.
**Clients/Work Highlights:** Other clients include Herbalife International and clients from industries such as aviation, banking, brewing, education, nutritional supplements and transportation.

## Bierce & Kenerson, PC
**The Firm:** This practice's recent workload has included human resources administration outsourcings, in addition to F&A, ITO and accounting functions. The group acts both on the customer side and for midmarket service providers.
**The Lawyers:** The "*gentlemanly*" practice head **Bill Bierce** is respected for his work with financial institutions and commercial consumer-related transactions.
**Clients/Work Highlights:** Clients come from a range of sectors including financial services, insurance, real estate, manufacturing, mining, pharmaceuticals and healthcare.

## DLA Piper Rudnick Gray Cary US LLP
See firm details p.870
**The Firm:** The firm has established a substantial presence in both Europe and on the West Coast following its recent merger. This has been a significant boost to its technology practice, and sources believe it has a "*formidable stable of lawyers doing a great job.*" The group is well known through its work for Accenture, and has attracted a range of customers involved in the outsourcing of their real estate portfolios, human resources, F&A, and supply chain management.
**The Lawyers:** Chicago-based Vincent Sanchez co-heads the practice with Palo Alto-based Mark Radcliffe.
**Clients/Work Highlights:** Accenture; Starbucks; Marriott Hotels; Polo Ralph Lauren and Sears.

## Hogan & Hartson LLP
See firm details p.568
**The Firm:** Clients praised this group's lawyers for being "*cost-conscious, timely and practical in advice and contract negotiations.*" This is a sizable practice group, but clients feel that the service levels remain strong: "*They care about the quality of advice and are exceptionally quick at understanding issues from the company's perspective.*"
**The Lawyers:** Leader of the firm's outsourcing practice group, **Phil Porter** (see p.127) "*brings practical solutions to negotiations.*" He combines an understanding of technology law with a great business sense and "*an ability to explain complex deals in layman's terms.*" He led the team advising Textron, one of the USA's largest multi-industry companies, on a global IT infrastructure outsourcing deal worth $1.1 billion with Computer Sciences.
**Clients/Work Highlights:** The team advised long-

term client British Telecom on the absorption of the worldwide telecom infrastructure of Bristol-Myers Squibb. The practice also advised a large international consulting company on the co-sourcing of IT management functions for a large regional banking company. Additional clients include Accenture; CV Therapeutics; GE; Graduate Management Admission Council; Textron and Sodexho.

### Morrison & Foerster LLP
See firm details p.335
**The Firm:** This firm is best known for its work in the media field, assisting clients with ITO and other outsourcing agreements.
**The Lawyers:** Sources believe **John Delaney** (see p.95) *"understands the technology as well as the business practice – a great combination."*
**Clients/Work Highlights:** A&E Television Networks; The Harry Fox Agency; Hertz; Time Warner Cable; Yahoo!; HotJobs and EMI Music Publishing.

### Weil, Gotshal & Manges LLP
See firm details p.1565
**The Firm:** *"Increasingly making a splash in the area,"* said sources, who pointed to the firm's New York office in particular. The group has leveraged off the firm's sizable IT capability to act in a number of ITOs as well as in the outsourcing of title insurance and back office operations.
**The Lawyers:** A skilled technology lawyer, Jeffrey Osterman recently advised GE in the sale of a majority interest in its captive offshore outsourcing business, GE Capital International Services.
**Clients/Work Highlights:** Clients include MGM and Fidelity National Information Systems.

### Other Notable Practitioners
**Scott Hobby** (see p.107) has recently moved from Hunton & Williams to the Atlanta office of Paul, Hastings, Janofsky & Walker LLP. Clients believe he *"knows the important points to protect our business"* and takes a common-sense approach to negotiation: *"He puts things to the other side in a way that makes it hard for them to argue with him."* Clients believe that Kilpatrick & Stockton LLP's technology team chair **Jim Steinberg** (see p.136) *"knows the law inside out."* He is a calm and professional attorney who delivers swift and creative solutions. Experienced on both the customer and vendor side, he recently advised a large financial institution in the outsourcing of its IT functions. Peers believe the *"thorough and experienced"* **Bill Tanenbaum** (see p.137) at Kaye Scholer LLP in New York is *"good at communicating with clients"* and *"an effective negotiator."* His recent caseload includes call center work in the Philippines and Latin America, in addition to a procurement outsourcing and offshore project concerning custom software development. **Mike Brito** (see p.90) at Fulbright & Jaworski LLP is noted by interviewees for his ITO and BPO expertise on the service-provider side, particularly for key client ACS. He is described by clients as having *"a proven track record of success"* and a *"collaborative approach."*

# CAPITAL MARKETS                              DEBT & EQUITY

| Capital Markets: Debt & Equity (excludes West Coast) Leading Firms | | |
|---|---|---|
| **1** | CLEARY GOTTLIEB STEEN & HAMILTON LLP | |
| | CRAVATH, SWAINE & MOORE LLP | |
| | DAVIS POLK & WARDWELL | |
| | SIMPSON THACHER & BARTLETT LLP | |
| | SULLIVAN & CROMWELL LLP | |
| **2** | LATHAM & WATKINS LLP | |
| | SHEARMAN & STERLING LLP | |
| | SKADDEN, ARPS, SLATE, MEAGHER & FLOM | |
| **3** | CAHILL GORDON & REINDEL LLP | |
| | DEBEVOISE & PLIMPTON LLP | |
| | FRIED, FRANK | |
| | SIDLEY AUSTIN LLP | |
| **4** | DECHERT LLP | |
| | DEWEY BALLANTINE LLP | |
| | MAYER, BROWN, ROWE & MAW LLP | |
| | PAUL, WEISS | |
| | VINSON & ELKINS LLP | |
| | WEIL, GOTSHAL & MANGES LLP | |

| Capital Markets: High Yield Products Leading Firms | | |
|---|---|---|
| **1** | CAHILL GORDON & REINDEL LLP | |
| | LATHAM & WATKINS LLP | |
| **2** | CRAVATH, SWAINE & MOORE LLP | |
| | SHEARMAN & STERLING LLP | |
| | SIMPSON THACHER & BARTLETT LLP | |
| | SKADDEN, ARPS, SLATE, MEAGHER & FLOM | |
| **3** | DAVIS POLK & WARDWELL | |
| | FRIED, FRANK | |
| | SULLIVAN & CROMWELL LLP | |
| | WEIL, GOTSHAL & MANGES LLP | |

## Cleary Gottlieb Steen & Hamilton LLP

See firm details p.1525

**The Firm:** The "*breadth of knowledge and constructive approach to the deals*" displayed by this "*splendid*" team of attorneys has won a loyal following among the market's major issuers and underwriters. Lately, the firm has significantly raised its profile on the domestic capital markets and carved itself "*a fair share of the national IPO market,*" commentators said. On the debt side, the firm also enjoys an enviable reputation, regularly advising on large-scale high-yield bond offerings, such as a $1.15 billion high-yield offering made by Elan Finance. The firm's international resources have provided it with additional scope and depth. The team here is "*responsive to the increasing globalization of the capital markets*" and offers "*by far the most impressive cross-border capacities.*" It is particularly dominant in Latin America, where it represents some of the largest corporates and sovereigns in their capital markets transactions. It notably represented the underwriters on the IPO

of the Brazilian low-fare airline company Gol Transportes. In addition to transactional counsel, clients rely on the team for the most current advice on securities regulatory issues and reforms.

**The Lawyers:** According to industry experts, the "*absolutely remarkable*" **Les Silverman** (see p.134) always "*brings a distinctive excellence*" to the deals. In 2004, he was particularly visible on the IPO market. A notable highlight was representing Morgan Stanley and Bear Stearns as underwriters' leads in the International Securities Exchange IPO. He is also the "*go to person for convertible or exchangeable problems*" and was strongly recommended for his "*well-crafted*" advice on the new SEC's Securities Offering Reform. The "*exceptionally talented*" **Allan Sperling** (see p.136) maintains strong ties with Citigroup, for which he provides a wide range of transactional and regulatory advice. He represented this client as underwriter of a $400 million preferred share issuance by Southern California Edison. **Carmen Corrales** (see p.93) is becoming an important name in the field of sovereign securities offerings and debt restructuring. She is particularly active in the Latin American markets and was notably retained as lead partner for the Republic of Argentina's $80 billion debt restructuring. Sources also singled out **Craig Brod** (see p.90), who is "*equally brilliant for issuer and underwriter representation;*" and **Nicolas Grabar** (see p.103), described as "*absolutely outstanding for cross-border deals,*" especially international IPOs. **Jeffrey Karpf** (see p.112) is the "*rising star*" of the group, who was endorsed by observers for his creativity and his broad experience of the capital markets.

**Clients/Work Highlights:** Citigroup; Goldman Sachs; Morgan Stanley; American Express; Bank of America; Bear Stearns and CSFB.

## Cravath, Swaine & Moore LLP

See firm details p.1527

**The Firm:** An "*obvious leader*" in the market, this "*utterly wonderful*" practice provides advice across the full range of offerings to a client base essentially composed of major underwriters. The team of "*tremendously skilled securities lawyers*" is prized for its "*dynamic and perfectionist*" approach as well as its strong working relationship with the SEC. In 2004, the group made the best of an improved domestic IPO market, representing the underwriters on the $855 million Lazard IPO and on the $600 million Seaspan IPO. On the debt side, the team has acted on a significant volume of investment-grade offerings, including for JPMorgan as underwriter and IBM as issuer. The group also belongs to the handful of firms demonstrating exceptional skills in high-yield offerings, and was consistently described as a major player in the field.

**The Lawyers:** **Kris Heinzelman** (see p.106) is consistently recognized as "*the finest high-yield specialist out there.*" According to commentators, he is a "*real delight to work with,*" as he demonstrates a "*pragmatic, solution-oriented and pleasant attitude.*"

Clients added that he "*offers great perspective and judgment on the most challenging matters.*" **William Whelan** (see p.142) is a "*wonderfully experienced lawyer,*" who represents investment banks and issuers in high-yield offerings, IPOs and follow-on equity offerings. **Marc Rosenberg** (see p.130) regularly represents underwriters on a variety of debt offerings, and is also recommended for his "*great regulatory knowledge.*" **Stephen Burns** (see p.91) also earned high marks for his exemplary work for clients such as CSFB and JPMorgan, while the "*smart and impressive*" **Paul Michalski** (see p.121) is particularly esteemed for his regulatory knowledge. The group is also home to young partner **Andrew Pitts** (see p.126) who led the Seaspan IPO and was also instrumental in the PanAmSat Holdings $900 million IPO. After spending his entire career developing Cravath's preeminent securities practice, the "*amazingly smart*" John White has recently taken on the important position of Director of the Divison of Corporation Finance at the SEC.

**Clients/Work Highlights:** CSFB; Citigroup; Goldman Sachs; JPMorgan Chase; IBM; Lehman Brothers; Morgan Stanley and DreamWorks Animation.

## Davis Polk & Wardwell

See firm details p.1528

**The Firm:** The firm's "*extraordinary breadth and depth of experience*" ensures that it remains at the forefront of both the East and West Coast markets. Clients had nothing but great things to say about the "*highly professional*" team, and peers declared they were "*always pleased to see this bunch of brilliant securities lawyers on the other side.*" The group is a clear leader in the equities field, where it works on a healthy diet of straight equity and equity-linked products. Recently, it notably assisted IHS on a $625 million IPO and represented the lead managers on a $2.1 billion secondary offering of Genworth Financial shares by GE Financial. On the debt side, the group's profile in the investment-grade debt arena is aided by long-standing relationships with major underwriters and some of the most active debt issuers, such as GE Capital, GMAC and Morgan Stanley. Issuers and underwriters of high-yield debt also seek counsel from this firm; recent highlights include a $400 million offering of senior notes by E*Trade Financial.

**The Lawyers:** "*Outstanding in every respect,*" **Richard Sandler** (see p.132) commands great respect from peers and clients. According to observers, he "*definitely belongs to the elite*" and is also "*a pleasure to work with.*" Clients frequently turn to him for innovative transactions that present unique regulatory issues. **Jeffrey Small** (see p.135) was endorsed for both his "*constructive approach to transactions and awesome personality.*" According to clients, **Wit Conrad** (see p.93) possesses the "*years of experience and judgment to inspire total trust;*" while **Sarah Beshar** (see p.88) is a highly capable lawyer, whose practice covers public and private debt and equity offerings by US and foreign companies. Also

## Capital Markets: Debt & Equity (excludes West Coast)
### Leading Individuals

#### Senior Statesmen

| | |
|---|---|
| MALLOW Matthew *Skadden, Arps* | WILLIAMS JR William *Sullivan & Cromwell* |
| [1] DAVENPORT Kirk *Latham & Watkins* | HARTNETT William *Cahill Gordon & Reindel* |
| HEINZELMAN Kris *Cravath, Swaine & Moore* | SANDLER Richard *Davis Polk & Wardwell* |
| SILVERMAN Leslie *Cleary Gottlieb* | |

| | |
|---|---|
| [2] BOSTELMAN John *Sullivan & Cromwell* | BUCKHOLZ JR Robert *Sullivan & Cromwell* |
| EVANS III Robert *Shearman & Sterling* | KORFF Phyllis *Skadden, Arps* |
| REITER Glenn *Simpson Thacher & Bartlett* | SLONAKER Norman *Sidley Austin LLP* |
| SMALL Jeffrey *Davis Polk & Wardwell* | SPERLING Allan *Cleary Gottlieb* |

| | |
|---|---|
| [3] BRITTENHAM David *Debevoise & Plimpton* | BROD Craig *Cleary Gottlieb Steen & Hamilton* |
| BURSKY Daniel *Fried, Frank* | CLARK James *Cahill Gordon & Reindel* |
| CONRAD JR Winthrop *Davis Polk* | FORD JACOB Valerie *Fried, Frank* |
| GOLDSCHMIDT David *Skadden, Arps* | GRABAR Nicolas *Cleary Gottlieb Steen* |
| HARMS David *Sullivan & Cromwell LLP* | JAFFE Marc *Latham & Watkins LLP* |
| KROUSE JR George *Simpson Thacher* | LOBRANO John *Simpson Thacher & Bartlett* |
| MCLAUGHLIN Cathleen *Allen & Overy* | PISANO Vincent *Kirkland & Ellis LLP* |
| SCHAFFZIN Jonathan *Cahill Gordon & Reindel* | SOUSSLOFF Andrew *Sullivan & Cromwell* |
| TEHAN John *Simpson Thacher & Bartlett LLP* | TRUESDELL Richard *Davis Polk & Wardwell* |
| WEERASINGHE Rohan *Shearman & Sterling* | |

| | |
|---|---|
| [4] BARSAMIAN Bonnie *Dechert LLP* | BESHAR Sarah *Davis Polk & Wardwell* |
| BURNS Stephen *Cravath, Swaine & Moore* | CORRALES Carmen *Cleary Gottlieb* |
| DOWNES Robert *Sullivan & Cromwell LLP* | GANNETT William *Cahill Gordon & Reindel* |
| GIOVE Stephen *Shearman & Sterling LLP* | HOGAN Adele *Linklaters* |
| KANTER Stacy *Skadden, Arps* | KEOGH Kevin *White & Case LLP* |
| LEFKOWITZ David *Weil, Gotshal & Manges* | |
| MICHALSKI Paul *Cravath, Swaine & Moore* | MICHETTI Michael *Cahill Gordon & Reindel* |
| PALEY Alan *Debevoise & Plimpton LLP* | ROSENBERG Marc *Cravath, Swaine & Moore* |
| TOLLEY III Edward *Simpson Thacher & Bartlett* | WHELAN III William *Cravath, Swaine & Moore* |

#### Up-and-coming individuals

| | |
|---|---|
| CLAYTON Walter *Sullivan & Cromwell LLP* | KARPF Jeffrey *Cleary Gottlieb* |
| LIN Raymond *Latham & Watkins LLP* | PITTS Andrew *Cravath, Swaine & Moore LLP* |
| SLUTZKY Steven *Debevoise & Plimpton LLP* | |

strongly recommended is **Richard Truesdell** (see p.138), a *"terrific lawyer,"* whose very broad skill set includes high-yield debt financings, convertible offerings and IPOs. **Bruce Dallas** (see p.94), based in the Menlo Park office, is a leading light on the West Coast. His practice encompasses IPOs, high-yield and convertible debt offerings in the hi-tech and biotech industries. A recent highlight was representing biopharmaceutical company XenoPort in its $52.6 million IPO. *"Young but immensely gifted"* **Alan Denenberg** (see p.95), also based in Menlo Park, is making a name for himself on the debt side, especially for his work in convertible and high-yield offerings.

**Clients/Work Highlights:** The firm's underwriter and client base includes Banc of America Securities; Citigroup Capital Markets; CSFB; Deutsche Bank Securities and JPMorgan Securities. Its issuer clients include Aetna; Air China; Comcast; Oracle; RBS; and Westar Energy.

### Simpson Thacher & Bartlett LLP
See firm details p.1555
**The Firm:** *"A huge player and definitely up there among the best,"* reported one observer, echoing the widespread view that this firm has developed one of the most impressive and comprehensive capital markets practices. The attorneys here are *"outstanding from associate to partner level,"* and are consistently praised for their *"great business savvy and ability to think ahead."* The firm's leading private equity practice gives the capital markets team a clear advantage in the market, making it preferred counsel to a myriad of private equity houses and blue-chip corporates in buyout financings, high-yield securities offerings, IPOs and convertible and exchangeable securities offerings. Highlights among the firm's issuer representation include advice to Warner Music in a $465 million high-yield offering. The team has also forged enduring relationships with major financial institutions such as JPMorgan Securities, Lehman Brothers and CSFB, advising them on large high-yield offerings and IPOs.

**The Lawyers:** **John Tehan** (see p.137) is *"one of the cleverest lawyers around"* and displays a *"strong business sense of what is worth fighting for."* He regularly advises KKR and its portfolio companies on their high-yield debt and IPOs. A highly accomplished lawyer, **Glenn Reiter** (see p.129) continues to impress with his *"extremely diversified skill set."* A key figure at Simpson Thacher, **George Krouse's** (see p.114) low-key profile in the capital markets arena is due to his managerial commitments. He oversees the firm's key relationship with major underwriters such as Lehman Brothers. Observers described him as *"extremely bright and well organized."* Clients also singled out **John Lobrano** (see p.116) as an *"extremely careful, thoughtful lawyer – he has great judgment."* The *"intellectually gifted"* **Edward Tolley** (see p.138) represents several leading private equity sponsors in their high-yield financings. **William Hinman** (see p.107) in the Palo Alto office continues to impress clients and peers as *"a major brain in the equity sphere."* *"Dean of the profession"* Paul Ford, included in *Chambers'* tables for many years, retired this year.

**Clients/Work Highlights:** Banc of America Securities; Barclays Capital; Citigroup; Merrill Lynch; UBS Investment Bank; KKR and The Blackstone Group.

### Sullivan & Cromwell LLP
See firm details p.1558
**The Firm:** The securities group has established its place at the forefront of the market because, according to commentators, it has been *"exposed to every novel and sophisticated product and shown exceptional creativity and forward-thinking abilities."* Its attorneys are *"very cooperative and excellent deal-doers, who never compromise on quality."* The team is renowned for its thriving straight equity and equity-linked products practice, but it is also gaining *"admirable strength"* in investment-grade debt offerings. For example, it recently represented AIG Bank on a $1.5 billion debt offering. Of late, the firm's high-yield practice has also experienced increased activity. Highlights in this field include representing EchoStar Communications in several billion dollars worth of high-yield offerings. Clients are appreciative of the firm's international reach and its ability to *"efficiently manage large-scale, cross-border offerings."* In particular, the firm is regularly involved in financings by sovereign issuers, especially in Latin America.

**The Lawyers:** A *"great mind, and a legend of the profession,"* **Bill Williams** (see p.142) continues to garner praise from clients and peers alike. Now of counsel to the firm, he remains very active and *"at the forefront of anything new."* The *"extremely talented"* **John Bostelman** (see p.89) is renowned for his ability to *"answer thorny questions in a split second."* Observers expressed great respect for his judgment and value his academic contribution to the industry. **David Harms** (see p.105) is *"quite a star"* and stands among the *"best to advise on difficult disclosure issues."* **Robert Buckholz** (see p.90) is the go-to partner for complex high-yield bond offerings. He also has extensive experience of equity derivatives. **Andrew Soussloff** (see p.136) is a major player in the field of sovereign finance and has been the lead partner on numerous SEC-registered global bond offerings by Argentina, Brazil, Panama and Peru. New to the table this year are **Robert Downes** (see p.89), a high-yield specialist, and **Jay Clayton** (see p.92) a *"very talented junior partner,"* reported clients.

## Capital Markets: Debt & Equity (West Coast)
### Leading Firms

**1** DAVIS POLK & WARDWELL
LATHAM & WATKINS LLP
SIMPSON THACHER & BARTLETT LLP
WILSON SONSINI GOODRICH & ROSATI

**2** GIBSON, DUNN & CRUTCHER LLP
PILLSBURY WINTHROP SHAW PITTMAN LLP
SKADDEN, ARPS, SLATE, MEAGHER & FLOM
SULLIVAN & CROMWELL LLP

**3** COOLEY GODWARD LLP
MILBANK, TWEED, HADLEY & MCCLOY
MORRISON & FOERSTER LLP
O'MELVENY & MYERS LLP
ORRICK, HERRINGTON & SUTCLIFFE LLP
SIDLEY AUSTIN LLP

### Leading Individuals

**1** DALLAS Bruce *Davis Polk & Wardwell*
DAVIDSON Gordon *Fenwick & West*
EDMONSON Tracy *Latham & Watkins*
HINMAN JR William *Simpson Thacher*
SAGGESE Nicholas *Skadden, Arps*
SAPER Jeff *Wilson Sonsini*

**2** DEL CALVO Jorge *Pillsbury*
DENENBERG Alan *Davis Polk & Wardwell*
FORE John *Wilson Sonsini*
KILB Brian *Gibson, Dunn & Crutcher*
POHLEN Patrick *Latham & Watkins LLP*
RESSLER Alison *Sullivan & Cromwell*
SNYDER David *Pillsbury*
WOLFE Scott *Latham & Watkins LLP*

**3** BARONSKY Kenneth *Milbank, Tweed*
MOTTESI Marcelo *Milbank, Tweed*
PRINGLE Paul *Sidley Austin LLP*
STEGEMOELLER Mark *Latham & Watkins*

On the West Coast, **Alison Ressler** (see p.129) regularly crosses over from M&A to capital markets and provides well-structured advice on a variety of debt and equity transactions.

**Clients/Work Highlights:** The firm boasts a balanced client base of issuers and underwriters including Cablevision Systems; Computer Associates; France Télécom; Deutsche Bank; Goldman Sachs; JPMorgan; UBS and Wachovia.

## Latham & Watkins LLP

**The Firm:** Market observers repeatedly endorsed the firm's first-rate capital markets practice and spoke admiringly of the "*amazing combination of technical proficiency and clear understanding of the market*" displayed by this group. Clients particularly rated the partners' "*professionalism and amenable personalities,*" and added that they "*truly take client service to the highest level.*" They also appreciated the excellent communication and cooperation throughout the firm's international network of offices. The group remains an indisputable leader for high-yield finance, enjoying a colossal market share for both issuers' and underwriters' representation. For example, the group recently advised on a $1.2 billion high-yield debt offering as part of Texas Genco's multibillion LBO financing. The team's capital markets expertise goes far beyond high-yield though, and its vast experience encompasses convertibles and investment-grade debt offerings as well as IPOs and follow-on offerings. Observers reported that over recent years the group has become "*a big dog in the equity capital markets,*" with a significant part of the work for issuers originating from its West Coast offices, while work for underwriters is handled in the East Coast offices. High-profile deals of late include representing Las Vegas Sands in its global IPO. The healthcare, energy, communication and defense industries have also been fruitful sources of work.

**The Lawyers: Kirk Davenport** remains "*everyone's favorite on the high-yield market.*" Investment bank clients are fond of his "*engaging personality, practical solutions, and ability to manage his team efficiently.*" Lately he has been increasingly visible in the IPO market, advising on the Las Vegas Sands IPO and the Rockwood Holdings $470 million IPO. Also highly rated is **Marc Jaffe**, a talented high-yield and leveraged finance adviser. He recently represented Bear Stearns and Lehman Brothers on a bridge financing and secondary offering by Elvis Presley Enterprises (CKX). Young partner **Ray Lin** also stands out as a "*very responsive, dedicated and solution-oriented lawyer.*" **Tracy Edmonson**, based in San Francisco, ranks among the stars of the West Coast debt capital markets. She commands respect from observers for her "*tremendous experience of complex high-yield transactions.*" She recently assisted pharmaceutical company Amgen in debt offerings and exchange offers worth $4 billion. The "*wonderfully experienced*" **Scott Wolfe** is a key player in the San Diego area. He has attracted an impressive biopharmaceuticals client base, which he represents in IPOs and follow-on offerings. He advised SkinMedica in its IPO. Silicon Valley is home to **Patrick Pohlen** a specialist in the equity financing of hi-tech companies. He represented Goldman Sachs in the $36 million IPO by Volterra Semiconductor. **Mark Stegemoeller**, based in Los Angeles, rounds out the picture with his focus on debt offerings.

**Clients/Work Highlights:** Bear Stearns; The Carlyle Group; CSFB; Dex Media; Goldman Sachs; Harrah's Entertainment; Jefferies; KKR; Lehman Brothers and UBS Investment Bank.

## Shearman & Sterling LLP
See firm details p.1554

**The Firm:** This broad-based securities practice is, according to interviewees, a "*great choice to tackle complex, fast-paced transactions*" and to execute them smoothly. The group remains "*particularly strong and visible in the high-yield arena,*" where it represents a pool of major underwriters in sizable offerings. Important work in the field includes representing Bank of America, Citigroup and Merrill Lynch as managers in the $700 million high-yield bond issue by Rayovac. The group has also further strengthened its presence in the equity markets, acting for both underwriters and issuers on several IPOs. For example, it represented Banc of America Securities as lead underwriter of the MWI Veterinary Supplies IPO and acted for issuer Lincoln Educational Services on its recent IPO. With the benefit of its multijurisdictional network, the firm is also nurturing a reputation for complex international securities offerings and is particularly sought after for its experience of the Latin American markets. A view commonly shared by market sources, however, is that the group may suffer a slight setback due to the recent loss of several partners.

**The Lawyers:** The "*remarkably skilled*" **Rohan Weerasinghe** (see p.141) is best known for his underwriters' representation in high-yield transactions. He is an "*intellectually gifted adviser,*" who displays "*excellent business acumen,*" although some clients perceive that his new functions as managing partner of the firm may distract him from hands-on capital markets work. **Robert Evans** (see p.98), the firm's lead securities partner, is strongly endorsed for his "*wonderful expertise on convertible and preferred stock.*" Clients also spoke of his "*helpful judgment on risk management and tough securities regulation issues.*" **Stephen Giove** (see p.102) focuses on issuer representation. He acts for a variety of major public companies and recently represented Viacom in its separation into two publicly traded companies ('New' Viacom and CBS Corporation), and acted for WebMD Health in its IPO.

**Clients/Work Highlights:** The firm represents major investment banks and public companies including Merrill Lynch; CSFB; Citigroup; Banc of America Securities; Morgan Stanley; Wachovia; UBS; Lincoln Educational Services; Nash Finch and Viacom.

## Skadden, Arps, Slate, Meagher & Flom LLP
See firm details p.1557

**The Firm:** This M&A powerhouse has secured an enviable position in the capital markets, acting as issuers' counsel for its huge corporate client base. On the debt side, the group is a popular choice for high-yield offerings. Major assignments in this field include representing IAAI Finance in a $150 million high-yield offering. On the equity side, the group offers "*considerable experience in IPOs,*" and in spite of a slow market the group continues to advise on blockbuster transactions. One such example is its advice on the multibillion-dollar China Construction Bank IPO. This high-profile transaction also shows the firm's "*remarkable penetration*" into the burgeoning Chinese capital markets. The group has significantly increased its underwriter representation capacity and now frequently acts for Lehman Brothers, CSFB and Morgan Stanley. In addition, commentators identified the group as a major player in the real estate capital markets, especially for REIT representation. A small shadow cast on the overall picture was the concern expressed by clients about discrepancies in the consistency of the quality of work delivered by the group.

**The Lawyers:** The "*wonderfully experienced*" **Matthew Mallow** (see p.117) heads the firm's corporate finance group. He is a "*well-respected figure*" of the IPO market and remains the trusted adviser of corporations such as American Express and NASDAQ. **Phyllis Korff** (see p.113) continues to impress with her "*technical excellence and formidable understanding of the IPO market.*" She also operates in the high-yield arena. **David Goldschmidt**'s (see p.94) practice focuses on representing issuers and underwriters of debt and equity offerings by Israeli companies; he is also one of the few income deposit securities (IDS) specialists in the market. Making a big impression in the REIT capital markets is **Stacy Kanter** (see p.111), a "*smart and dedicated attorney.*" Based in Los Angeles, **Nick Saggese** (see p.132) is "*a terrific lawyer – with an empowering presence.*" Clients describe him as "*extremely practical, never dogmatic,*" and proclaimed him "*the best to advise on M&A-driven debt deals;*" he demonstrated this combination of talent when advising on the acquisition of MGM by Providence Equity Partners and Texas Pacific Group, which involved a $4 billion debt financing.
**Clients/Work Highlights:** American Express; NASDAQ; Revlon; Kuwait Petroleum; Bank of America; CSFB; Citigroup; Goldman Sachs; Merrill Lynch and JPMorgan Chase.

## Cahill Gordon & Reindel LLP

**The Firm:** The representation of underwriters in high-yield financings lies at the foundation of this capital markets practice. The firm has dedicated "*fantastic resources*" to the domestic high-yield market, and fields attorneys whose "*great negotiating skills and deep knowledge*" has secured the loyalty of many clients. The team demonstrated such expertise when representing Deutsche Bank, Citigroup and JPMorgan in a $1.6 billion high-yield offering by Solar Capital in connection with the LBO financing of SunGard Data. The group is also increasingly present in the international equity capital markets, where it concentrates on specific industries such as the telecom and media sectors. Recent work in the field includes representing the underwriters in the IPO of Golden Telecom, a telecom operator in Russia; and representing the Canadian company 360networks in its IPO and high-yield financings.
**The Lawyers:** A major figure in the high-yield bond arena, **Bill Hartnett** is an "*effective counselor, truly in touch with the market,*" who "*gets involved from day one and focuses on getting the deal done,*" said clients. **James Clark** is praised for his "*willingness to try new things and ability to always spot the pitfalls.*" Observers added: "*Complex transactions are his forte.*" Also commended were partners **William Gannett**, "*a talented debt finance lawyer,*" and the high-yield expert **Jonathan Schaffzin**. Sources also pointed to **Michael Michetti** as a "*great negotiator for both secured bank financings and high-yield debt offerings.*"
**Clients/Work Highlights:** The firm represents many of the largest investment banks including Banc of America Securities; CIBC World Markets; CSFB; Deutsche Bank Securities; Goldman Sachs; JPMor-

gan Chase; Lehman Brothers; Merrill Lynch; Salomon Smith Barney and UBS Warburg.

## Debevoise & Plimpton LLP
See firm details p.1529
**The Firm:** This team earned high marks from clients for its "*efficiency, creativity and consistent high level of quality throughout.*" It has gained "*a great deal of experience*" over recent years, and firmly established itself as a leading issuer-led practice. A significant portion of the team's work, including high-yield finance, derives from its impressive client base of private equity houses. In addition, the group has devoted increasing resources to underwriter representation and is regularly instructed by Citigroup, JPMorgan and Morgan Stanley. The firm also calls upon the support of its leading insurance practice to advise issuers and underwriters on insurance-related offerings. For example, it recently represented Swiss Re in a $245 million offering secured by a portfolio of health and life insurance businesses. Commentators also acclaimed the premium put by the firm on client service. One client reported that the team "*always allocates proper resources to the deals and delivers high-quality work within the assigned time frame;*" another added: "*One could not make a better choice of firm regarding depth of expertise and value for money.*"
**The Lawyers:** Observers described **Alan Paley** as an "*efficient and savvy securities expert.*" Clients praise his "*non-obstructive approach and success in bringing about the solutions.*" His practice focuses on representing major domestic or foreign issuers. For example, he regularly represents Australian bank Westpac on a wide variety of offerings in the USA. **David Brittenham** is a "*well-regarded, high-yield finance expert,*" who recently represented Rexel in obtaining $2.4 billion of credit facilities from a syndicate of banks led by JPMorgan. **Steven Slutzky** is a "*highly skilled young partner,*" who concentrates on underwriter representation. According to observers, he really distinguished himself in the representation of the lead underwriters in B&G Foods' $300 million IPO. He was involved in another noteworthy transaction, DSW's $307 million common stock IPO, where he advised Lehman Brothers as underwriter.
**Clients/Work Highlights:** American Airlines; BNP Paribas; The Carlyle Group; China Life Insurance; Goldman Sachs; Kelso & Company; Lehman Brothers; Merrill Lynch; MetLife; Pinault-Printemps-Redoute and Prudential Financial.

## Fried, Frank, Harris, Shriver & Jacobson LLP
See firm details p.1532
**The Firm:** This capital markets practice continues to attract accolades from clients because it is "*intensely customer-focused.*" The attorneys here are "*excellent deal-makers,*" and their experience in advising issuers, sponsors and underwriters gives them a "*unique ability to reach the consensus much needed in high-yield transactions.*" Recently, the group caught the market's attention when representing long-term client Merrill Lynch as lead arranger of the cross-

border $1.2 billion high-yield offering by the Jean Coutu Group, which was related to the acquisition of the Eckerd drugstores. Another important part of the team's work consists of advising large LBO and private equity investor clients on acquisition finance involving high-yield offerings. On the equity side the team has also advised on a significant number of IPOs. It represented Merrill Lynch, CSFB, Citigroup and Morgan Stanley and other lead managers in the NASDAQ IPO.
**The Lawyers:** Managing partner **Valerie Ford Jacob** (see p.100) is "*tremendously loved by her clients,*" not least because of her "*technical excellence, drive and enthusiasm.*" A "*formidable lawyer,*" **Daniel Bursky** (see p.91) is another key practitioner at the firm. He represented Bank of America in providing innovative debt and equity financing for Blackstone Crystal Holdings Capital Partners.
**Clients/Work Highlights:** Community Health Systems; Deutsche Bank; Dow Jones; Goldman Sachs; Bank of America; Jefferies & Co; National Bank of Canada and Wachovia Securities.

## Sidley Austin LLP
See firm details p.883
**The Firm:** Although better known for its structured finance prowess, the firm has increasingly raised its profile in the debt and equity marketplaces. Observers admired the team's "*immense talent for underwriter representation,*" illustrated by long-standing relationships with major institutions such as Merrill Lynch and Morgan Stanley. The group also undertakes issuer work and shows particular skill in its advice to corporate and private equity clients on IPOs, convertible, exchangeable and trust preferred securities offerings, MTN and CP programs. Its work in the real estate capital markets and REIT sector has also impressed sources. Important instructions for 2004 include representing Fannie Mae in a $5 billion issuance of convertible and straight preferred stock.
**The Lawyers:** Based in the New York office, **Norman Slonaker** (see p.135) is widely recognized as "*one of the most experienced securities practitioners in the country.*" His areas of strength include investment-grade debt securities, MTN programs, convertible and exchangeable securities. **Paul Pringle** (see p.127), who works from the San Francisco and Los Angeles offices, is commended for his wide experience of corporate and securities transactions. Of late, his practice has included a large number of transactions involving REITs.
**Clients/Work Highlights:** Dolby Laboratories; Hilton Hotels; Nike; Occidental Petroleum; Safeway; Sempra Energy; Southern California Gas; Disney; Wells Fargo; healthcare Property Investors; KKR Financial and Nationwide Health Properties.

## Dechert LLP
See firm details p.1752
**The Firm:** According to market sources, this group "*possesses all the ingredients for success, including a growing client base and balanced diet of debt and equity deals.*" The team particularly distinguishes itself for issuer representation when acting for its

corporate and private equity clients in sizable IPOs and high-yield debt offerings. For example, it recently represented MWI Veterinary Supply on its $74 million IPO and advised B&G Foods in its $300 million IPO. The group's recent efforts to attract top-tier underwriters have also been rewarded. Recently, the group represented Lehman Brothers in a $450 million high-yield offering by Spanish Broadcasting System, the largest Hispanic-controlled broadcast company in the USA.

**The Lawyers:** Commentators identified **Bonnie Barsamian** (see p.88) as "*the key element*" in the recent achievements of the firm's capital markets practice.

**Clients/Work Highlights:** Bear Stearns; JPMorgan Securities; Merrill Lynch; Wachovia; Jefferies Capital Partners; MagnaChip Semiconductor; Crown Holdings; Remy International and Intersil.

## Dewey Ballantine LLP
See firm details p.1530

**The Firm:** The firm is renowned in the marketplace for its tremendous healthcare capital markets practice, providing expert advice to major underwriters of equity offerings originating from this industry. In addition, it is increasingly focusing on transactions derived from other industries such as energy and insurance. Recent successes include representing Citigroup as lead underwriter of Conor Medsystems $78 million IPO, as well as advising on the financing for LifePoint Hospitals' acquisition of Province Healthcare. Commentators reported that the team has also made an impact on the convertible securities scene, where it notably represented UBS as initial purchaser in a $125 million issuance by CONMED.

**The Lawyers:** Clients highly rated the team's "*in-depth technical knowledge of highly regulated industries.*" Frederick Kanner is the contact partner here.

**Clients/Work Highlights:** LifePoint Hospitals; Citigroup Capital Markets; Triad Hospitals and UBS Securities.

## Mayer, Brown, Rowe & Maw LLP
See firm details p.876

**The Firm:** Clients endorsed the firm's attorneys as "*exceptionally responsive and knowledgeable, especially when dealing with innovative issues.*" The group has made great advances in the debt and equity capital markets, representing both issuers and underwriters on a broad array of transactions, especially in the gaming and telecom industries. In 2005, it represented TAL International Group in its $207 million IPO. The team is also developing a high-yield finance practice and is building ties with major high-yield debt issuers and underwriters. For example, it represented Dobson Communication in an $825 million offering, and assisted iPCS in a $165 million high-yield offering, while the company was in bankruptcy.

**The Lawyers:** The firm boasts teams of capital markets attorneys based in Chicago and New York. Lawyers here attract accolades from clients because they are "*very effective at dealing with straight legal issues while bearing in mind the overall commercial and even the political context.*"

**Clients/Work Highlights:** GSI Group; Isle of Capri Casinos; Merrill Lynch; Morgan Stanley; Jefferies roup and Wachovia.

## Paul, Weiss, Rifkind, Wharton & Garrison LLP
See firm details p.1548

**The Firm:** The firm has won market recognition for its success in developing a "*comprehensively talented and hard-working capital markets group.*" The team shows a healthy record of debt and equity transactions, acting for both issuers and underwriters. It routinely represents Lehman Brothers, CIBC World Markets and Merrill Lynch in their underwriting engagements and notably acted for the latter two in connection with a $2.5 billion secondary offering by Petro-Canada. Its work on prestigious cross-border transactions, particularly in the Canadian and Asian markets, has impressed many. For example, it provided US securities law advice to Mitsubishi Tokyo Financial Group in its proposed merger with UFJ Holdings, a transaction valued at $42.7 billion.

**The Lawyers:** Mark Bergman and Edwin Maynard co-head the firm's capital markets and securities team.

**Clients/Work Highlights:** CSFB; RBC Capital Markets; Nexen; Las Vegas Sands; Canadian Natural Resources; PetroKazakhstan; Revlon; Universal American Financial and Terasen.

## Vinson & Elkins LLP
See firm details p.1938

**The Firm:** According to clients and peers, the firm has "*built up a significant presence in the national capital markets.*" It is renowned for its "*unparalleled experience of the energy markets,*" and has acted for both issuers and underwriters on many of the major offerings in this industry. It has also benefited from the recent upsurge of activity in the shipping industry, representing several shipping and tankers companies in high-profile transactions. Recent highlights include advising Seaspan in its $600 million IPO and Teekay LNG Partners in its $151.8 million IPO. The firm's enviable roster of traded limited partnership clients is also an important source of instructions.

**The Lawyers:** The Texas powerhouse has teams of securities lawyers operating from its Houston headquarters and from its New York office.

**Clients/Work Highlights:** Goldman Sachs; Lehman Brothers; Chesapeake Energy; Hunstman; The Shaw Group; Sunoco Logistics Partners; Riverstone Holdings and Complete Energy Holdings.

## Weil, Gotshal & Manges LLP
See firm details p.1565

**The Firm:** The firm is consistently endorsed for its "*fantastic expertise*" in offerings of high-yield debt securities. The practice has attracted a strong base of corporate clients, including private equity funds and their portfolio companies. The group also enjoys deep relationships with some of the world's leading investment banks. A particular highlight in 2005 was acting for Citigroup as financial adviser to Koch

Industries in its $13.2 billion proposed acquisition of Georgia-Pacific. The firm's traditional strength in bankruptcy also makes it a "*first choice to engineer exit financings*" for companies emerging from bankruptcy.

**The Lawyers:** Co-head of the capital markets practice **David Lefkowitz** (see p.115) is a key driver in the firm's relationship with Citigroup. In addition to his high-yield expertise, he has established a strong track record in equity transactions such as the $3 billion Genworth Financial IPO.

**Clients/Work Highlights:** Bear Stearns; Bain Capital Partners; Citigroup; CSFB; Estée Lauder; Lehman Brothers; JPMorgan Chase; Merrill Lynch; GE and Genworth Financial.

## Wilson Sonsini Goodrich & Rosati
See firm details p.344

**The Firm:** Market sources are unanimous in proclaiming that this group is the "*obvious leader in Northern California equity capital markets.*" Over recent years, and despite the sluggish IPO environment, it has represented a substantial number of hi-tech and emerging life science companies in their IPO and subsequent offerings. Indeed, observers reported: "*Not only has it handled the largest number of NASDAQ listings, it has also been involved in the loudest successes,*" such as Google's $2.7 billion IPO and the $460 million Dolby Laboratories IPO. The group scored high marks with clients because it has also developed strong debt capabilities, advising on both investment-grade and high-yield debt offerings. This is also a popular choice for cross-border deals, as illustrated by its advice on the $1 billion secondary offering for Infosys, the Indian IT outsourcing giant.

**The Lawyers:** Few lawyers are more experienced in IPOs than **Jeff Saper** (see p.132). Clients pledged their loyalty to this high-profile lawyer for his "*intrinsic understanding of Silicon Valley.*" He has been involved in many of the market's most prominent and complex domestic and cross-border transactions. **John Fore** (see p.100) undertakes the debt finance work at the firm. Clients simply described him as "*one of the best debt capital markets lawyers on the West Coast.*"

**Clients/Work Highlights:** Check Point Software Technologies; Harmonic; McAfee; Microchip Technology; BackWeb; ClickSoftware Technologies; Banc of America Securities; Deutsche Bank Securities; Lehman Brothers; Merrill Lynch; Morgan Stanley; Thomas Weisel Partners and UBS Securities.

## Gibson, Dunn & Crutcher LLP
See firm details p.328

**The Firm:** The firm has cultivated a strong reputation for debt capital markets work across California, where it chiefly represents seasoned and first-time issuers in substantial high-yield and investment-grade offerings. Issuer clients are appreciative of the fact that the team "*really endeavors to know our business intimately,*" and are happy to entrust the firm with all of their corporate finance work. A noteworthy deal in 2005 was the representation of Entravision Communication in a $650 million high-yield offering. The firm also undertakes significant underwriter work and recently represented Banc of America Securities and Bear Stearns in a $170 million high-yield offering by the Greenbrier Companies. Although it enjoys a better market profile on the West Coast, the firm handles an eclectic caseload of equity and debt offerings from its New York and Washington, DC, offices.

**The Lawyers: Brian Kilb** (see p.113) is based in Los Angeles and stands out as an *"excellent leveraged finance expert,"* agreed interviewees.

**Clients/Work Highlights:** JF Shea Company; MGM; Hilton Hotels; Pacific Life Insurance; Tenet Healthcare; K2; CSFB and UBS.

## Pillsbury Winthrop Shaw Pittman LLP
See firm details p.1550

**The Firm:** The February 2005 merger has brought together Pillsbury Winthrop's renowned capital markets experience in the technology and life sciences industries, and Shaw Pittman's acclaimed REIT and real estate capital markets practice. According to observers, the merger has *"tremendously increased the firm's geographical coverage and client base."* Equities form the backbone of this practice. It provides *"top-quality"* advice on IPOs and follow-on offerings to California-based corporate issuers. For example, the team was instructed by MediciNova, a San Diego-based pharmaceutical company in the first Japanese IPO by a US company. A highlight in the real estate field was to represent Crescent Real Estate in the reorganization and financing of Canyon Ranch. In addition, the team is well versed in representing private equity funds in their offerings and assisting hedge funds with product development.

**The Lawyers:** The *"immensely talented"* **Jorge del Calvo** (see p.95) advises technology companies in venture capital and securities transactions. His diverse caseload also includes acting for major underwriters such as Goldman Sachs, Deutsche Bank and Lehman Brothers. **David Snyder** (see California profiles) concentrates on cross-border equity work for life science companies and was instrumental in the MediciNova IPO.

**Clients/Work Highlights:** Biogen Idec; McKesson; Detwiler, Mitchell & Co; Onex; Chevy Chase Bank and Western Inventory Services.

## Cooley Godward LLP
**The Firm:** The Silicon Valley-based firm is a *"giant on the IPO scene."* Observers spoke of a *"cluster of exceptional lawyers, with a fantastic combination of financing expertise and technology industry knowledge."* The group is among the busiest on the West Coast for IPO and secondary offerings. It is particularly popular among biotech and life sciences companies, as illustrated by its representation of gene discovery company Diversa in its $174 million IPO. A substantial portion of the firm's public offering work also derives from the emerging and growth technology industry, particularly the hardware, software and semiconductor businesses. Highlights in this sector of activity include representing Alteon

WebSystems, an Internet infrastructure company, in a $517 million secondary offering.

**The Lawyers:** Lawyers in the Palo Alto and San Diego offices handle much of the firm's IPO work.

**Clients/Work Highlights:** Abgenix; Active Network; Applied Micro Circuits; Blue Martini Software; COR Therapeutics; Diversa; FirstWorld Communications; Gilead Sciences; InterMune; Metricom; Nektar Therapeutics and Vitria Tech.

## Milbank, Tweed, Hadley & McCloy
**The Firm:** The West Coast capital markets practice is best known for its work in Southern California, where it principally engages in debt financings originating from the gaming and energy industries. It is particularly rated for the outstanding advice it gives to issuers and underwriters on high-yield debt offerings. Examples include acting for Station Casinos in over $350 million of high-yield offerings in 2004. Recently, the firm successfully combined its capital markets capabilities and its renowned toll-road project finance experience to advise Citigroup and Goldman Sachs as initial purchasers of the $1.4 billion high-yield offering by Chicago Skyway Concession. The firm's New York practice is also strongly recommended for its advice on investment-grade debt offerings.

**The Lawyers:** Active in New York and California, **Marcello Mottesi** is a *"well-known figure in the national debt capital markets."* His colleague **Kenneth Baronsky** is described as a *"prominent debt capital markets lawyer, very commercial and easy to work with."*

**Clients/Work Highlights:** Lehman Brothers; CSFB; BNP Paribas Securities; Deutsche Bank; Highbridge Capital Management; TWC and Wildflower Energy.

## Morrison & Foerster LLP
See firm details p.335

**The Firm:** The firm's West Coast offices are equally adept at advising both underwriters and issuers in investment-grade debt offerings. The team also earns high marks for its advice on convertible and high-yield debt offerings. An impressive record sheet for 2004-2005 includes representing Deutsche Bank in a $200 million convertible offering by Powerwave Technologies. On the equity side, hi-tech companies increasingly approach the group to guide them in their IPOs and secondary offerings. For example, attorneys here represented the main selling stockholder in the Dolby Laboratories $495 million IPO. Another distinguishing strength of the firm is its enviable presence in the Chinese and Japanese markets. It recently represented Linktone, a Chinese mobile wireless company, in its $86 million IPO.

**The Lawyers:** With offices in Los Angeles, Orange County, Palo Alto, Sacramento, San Diego and San Francisco, the firm enjoys the most comprehensive coverage of the West Coast market. A significant capital markets team is also based in the New York office.

**Clients/Work Highlights:** WR Hambrecht; JMP Securities; Syneron Medical; Mindspeed Technolo-

gies; The Clorox Company; Boyd Gaming; Westcorp and InterDent Service.

## O'Melveny & Myers LLP
See firm details p.336

**The Firm:** The firm's finance practice has a long-standing reputation for excellence in the West Coast equity markets. Securities lawyers here are said to provide *"vision, hard work and a high level of commitment to the deals."* The team has assisted countless companies, chiefly in the technology sector, through the process of their IPOs and secondary offerings. The group is involved in offerings of all types of equity securities, ranging from standard common stock to perpetual preferred stock and the more complex preferred stock securities, such as Dutch auction rate transferable securities (DARTS), money market preferreds (MMPs) and various types of convertible securities. Attorneys also advise major national and regional underwriters.

**The Lawyers:** Karen Dreyfus, managing partner of the Silicon Valley office, and Peter Healy based in San Francisco, are the primary contacts.

**Clients/Work Highlights:** The Macerich Company; Meade Instruments; New Century Financial; PowerOne; CSFB; Lehman Brothers; Morgan Stanley and SSSB.

## Orrick, Herrington & Sutcliffe LLP
See firm details p.337

**The Firm:** The firm ranks among the Bay Area's top debt practices for its experience in representing issuers in investment-grade debt offerings. The team advises on a broad array of financings, and is especially rated for its advice on convertible notes offerings. The team enjoys fruitful relationships with large corporate issuers such as PG&E Corp and Caterpillar Financial Services. Recent highlights include advising Caterpillar on a $9 billion MTN program. Of late, the firm has also been particularly active completing accelerated stock buyback programs for its corporate client base. For example, it recently acted for PG&E in stock repurchase programs valued at $317 million and $1.05 billion.

**The Lawyers:** The firm's key capital markets lawyers are based in San Francisco, Silicon Valley and New York. The firm also continues to grow its capital markets practice in Asia.

**Clients/Work Highlights:** Knight Ridder; Trident Resources; Micrus Endovascular; Gentium; Nomura Capital & Credit; Banc of America Securities and Deutsche Bank Securities.

## Other Notable Practitioners
**Cathleen McLaughlin** (see p.120) co-heads the international capital practice at Allen & Overy LLP. Clients described her as their *"first choice"* to advise on cross-border deals, particularly in the Latin American markets. She advised the managers on the European legal aspects of the $80 billion global exchange offer by the Republic of Argentina. **Vincent Pisano** (see p.126) of Kirkland & Ellis LLP continues to raise the profile of the firm's New York office and has developed the underwriter representation

side of the practice. A particular highlight of his was to represent Goldman Sachs on a $2 billion debt offering by News Corporation. The "*highly esteemed*" **Adele Hogan** (see p.107) has left Cravath, Swaine & Moore LLP to reinforce Linklaters' securities law capabilities on the US domestic market. She is renowned for the depth of her experience and excellent understanding of the telecom, oil and gas, and healthcare industries. **Kevin Keogh** (see p.112) recently advised WellPoint in its $1.6 billion debt offering. He is described as a "*very responsive, extremely knowledgeable lawyer always aware of clients' time and cost constraints.*" **Gordy Davidson** (see p.95) of Fenwick & West LLP is a "*landmark of the West Coast legal scene,*" and he "*comes top of the list*" for many hi-tech and biotech companies for advice on IPOs and follow-on offerings.

# CAPITAL MARKETS CDOS, REPACKAGING & OTHER SYNTHETIC PRODUCTS

| Capital Markets: CDOs, Repackaging & Other Synthetic Products |
| --- |
| Leading Firms |
| **1** CADWALADER, WICKERSHAM & TAFT LLP |
| CLEARY GOTTLIEB STEEN & HAMILTON LLP |
| SIDLEY AUSTIN LLP |
| **2** CLIFFORD CHANCE US LLP |
| FRESHFIELDS BRUCKHAUS DERINGER LLP |
| MCKEE NELSON LLP |
| MILBANK, TWEED, HADLEY & MCCLOY LLP |
| ORRICK, HERRINGTON & SUTCLIFFE |
| SCHULTE ROTH & ZABEL LLP |
| SKADDEN, ARPS, SLATE, MEAGHER & FLOM LLP |
| **3** ALLEN & OVERY |
| LATHAM & WATKINS LLP |
| LINKLATERS |
| MAYER, BROWN, ROWE & MAW LLP |

## Band 1

### Cadwalader, Wickersham & Taft LLP
See firm details p.1522

**The Firm:** According to market sources, the firm has maintained an "*undeniable hegemony*" in the CDO market since its inception. The interdisciplinary nature of the practice surely explains its success, as the group also provides "*top-quality service*" in the related areas of real estate securitization and derivatives. The team has assisted clients in hundreds of CDO transactions involving a broad range of asset types including mortgage-related assets, ABS, distressed debt and emerging market obligations. Commentators reported that the group has "*fully mastered this evolving market and always stays on top of new products.*" In particular, it has developed a taste for synthetic CDO transactions, and receives a significant number of instructions from AIG Capital Partners and CSFB in this field. CBO and CLO transactions are also high on the agenda. The group is extremely active in the asset-repackaging market, where it frequently acts for Lehman Brothers and Banc of America Securities on hedge fund-repackaging transactions.

**The Lawyers:** "*In a class of his own,*" **Richard Schetman** (see p.133) has played a critical role in the successful development of the CDO and repackaging practice at the firm. His wide-ranging practice also encompasses ABS and derivatives expertise. Another "*outstanding choice to advise on derivatives-based, cutting-edge work*" is **Ira Schacter** (see p.132),

while young partner **Ray Shirazi** (see p.134) is largely regarded as the "*rising star of the profession.*" His practice focuses on repackaging, derivatives-related CDOs and hedge fund-linked products.

**Clients/Work Highlights:** The group represents major investment banks including AIG Capital Partners; Lehman Brothers; CSFB; Goldman Sachs; RBS Greenwich Capital and UBS.

### Cleary Gottlieb Steen & Hamilton LLP
See firm details p.1525

**The Firm:** "*By far the most talented group out there,*" commentators regard the firm's structured finance team as "*setting the standard others aspire to.*" Key to the group's success is the presence of "*highly skilled and seasoned attorneys,*" who have "*pioneered most of the groundbreaking structures in the field.*" The group offers a "*clever, integrated approach*" and draws on superb derivatives, securitization, tax and secured transactions practices to provide comprehensive advice on a variety of CDO transactions. The team routinely advises on cash flow transactions and has recently built up strong capacities on the synthetic side. For example, the team advised Citigroup on the $500 million TESS deal, the first US-managed CDO squared transaction involving a fully synthetic portfolio. The team is also specifically recommended to execute CLO transactions. It demonstrated expertise in this field when it represented Morgan Stanley and JPMorgan as manager and placement agents in the KKR Financial CLO 2005-1 transaction valued at more than $1 billion. A respected practice in the repackaging of fixed income securities and derivatives rounds out the picture.

**The Lawyers:** Commentators strongly recommended the "*consistently excellent*" **Mike Mazzuchi** (see p.118) for his expertise on synthetic CDOs embedding credit derivatives. Clients value his "*amazing analytical skills on new products.*" Also based in Washington, DC, **Mitch Dupler** (see p.97) is similarly commended, particularly for his advice on synthetic CLO transactions and repackaging. In New York, **Ray Check** (see p.91) is a lawyer who is "*able to think through novel structures faster than many.*" He recently represented Citigroup and INVESCO in the $400 million Skytop synthetic CLO.

**Clients/Work Highlights:** Citigroup Global Markets; CSFB; INVESCO Institutional; JPMorgan Securities and Morgan Stanley.

### Sidley Austin LLP
See firm details p.883

**The Firm:** Commentators shared respect and admiration for this "*exceptional outfit.*" The group has a strong tradition of excellence in the area of structured finance, and possesses the depth of expertise and geographical reach to secure a top-flight reputation. It is home to a team of "*tremendously talented partners,*" who are "*genuinely involved in the deals.*" Clients also endorsed their "*creativity and well-crafted advice.*" The group's leadership in the field of real estate securitization and its deep experience of the commercial loan asset class give it an "*excellent vision for CLO transactions.*" The group demonstrated such expertise when representing Deutsche Bank on its cross-border Craft CLO 2004-1, a $1.5 billion synthetic CLO transaction. The team also shines on CBO transactions and arbitrage CDOs. This expertise extends to cash flow, market value and synthetic structures, as well as hybrids.

**The Lawyers:** The "*superstar of the practice,*" **Renwick Martin** (see p.117) received countless tributes from peers and clients, who dubbed him "*the world's best structured finance expert.*" This "*tireless worker*" is particularly sought after for his advice on complex and innovative deals. Also highly thought of is **Rob Robinson** (see p.130), "*a great lawyer, retained from all corners of the country.*" He is adviser to Deutsche Bank on the Craft and the Gate CLO series. **Cathy Kaplan** (see p.111) remains "*one of the very best for CLO transactions*" and **Samir Gandhi** (see p.101) stands out as a "*multitalented young partner.*" In Chicago, **Mark Greenberg** (see p.274344) was strongly recommended for the breadth of his expertise regarding a variety of derivative products, in particular total return and credit default swaps used in connection with synthetic CLOs and other structured finance transactions.

**Clients/Work Highlights:** The group represents prominent investment banks including Banc of America Securities; Calyon; Deutsche Bank and RBS.

## Band 2

### Clifford Chance US LLP
See firm details p.1526

**The Firm:** Observers reported that this structured products group has built a successful practice handling a large volume and wide variety of CDO transactions. The practice of this "*hungry, successful and result-oriented*" team spans MBS and ABS CDOs, CBOs, CLOs, repackaging and offers

| Capital Markets: CDOs, Repackaging & Other Synthetic Products |
| --- |
| **Leading Individuals** |

**1** ISAACSON Laurence *McKee Nelson*
MARTIN Renwick *Sidley Austin LLP*
MAZZUCHI Michael *Cleary Gottlieb*
RAFF Joshua *Orrick, Herrington & Sutcliffe*
SCHETMAN Richard *Cadwalader*
WATTERSON Paul *Schulte Roth & Zabel*

**2** BARNETT Gary *Linklaters*
CHECK Raymond *Cleary Gottlieb*
CURTIS Susan *Skadden, Arps*
DUPLER Mitchell *Cleary Gottlieb*
GLASS Adam *Linklaters*
KAPLAN Cathy *Sidley Austin LLP*
KOLYER Steve *Clifford Chance US LLP*
PULEO Frank *Milbank, Tweed, Hadley*
RANCE Brian *Freshfields Bruckhaus Deringer*
ROBINSON Robert *Sidley Austin*
SCHACTER Ira *Cadwalader*
STEIN Craig *Schulte Roth & Zabel*
WAINER David *Allen & Overy*

**3** FELSENTHAL David *Clifford Chance US LLP*
RAE Mark *Stroock & Stroock & Lavan LLP*
SAWYERS Al *Orrick, Herrington & Sutcliffe*
STRINGFELLOW James *Skadden, Arps*
UTLEY Frederick *Clifford Chance US LLP*
VILLANI Robert *Thacher Proffitt & Wood*

**Up-and-coming individuals**
AZZOLLINI Phillip *Schulte Roth & Zabel*
FERRER Eugene *McKee Nelson LLP*
GANDHI Samir *Sidley Austin LLP*
GREENBERG Mark *Sidley Austin LLP*
SHIRAZI Ray *Cadwalader, Wickersham & Taft*

expertise on synthetic, cash flow and market value structures. A particular strength of the team is its real estate CDO practice. For example, it recently represented Deutsche Bank, Citigroup and Wachovia in a $400 million commercial real estate CDO. Hedge fund-linked CDO products are also a specialty of the group. In 2004, it notably represented Morgan Stanley on the Black River CFO, a US-based securitization of hedge fund interests. Clients also appreciate the firm's "*ability to reach out for amazing international resources when needed.*"

**The Lawyers:** **Steve Kolyer** is extolled for his cutting-edge work on REIT-sponsored CDOs. Interviewees also endorsed **David Felsenthal** as a "*great deal-doer,*" who provides "*learned advice*" on related derivatives matters. Clients also singled out **Fred Utley** for his negotiation skills, particularly "*when a constructive approach is needed.*"

**Clients/Work Highlights:** Ambac Financial Group; Bank of America; Barclays; HypoVereinsbank; FGIC; Merrill Lynch; Morgan Stanley; Standard & Poor's; Swiss Re; RBS; UBS and Wachovia.

## Freshfields Bruckhaus Deringer LLP

**The Firm:** Over recent years, the structured finance team has made a "*very big impression*" on the market, particularly with its expertise in CDO transactions. They are admired for the uncompromising quality of their documentation. Clients also regard the firm's international reach as a distinct advantage.

**The Lawyers:** The highly knowledgeable **Brian Rance** is the leading figure at the firm. He is well acquainted with all forms of structured financings.

**Clients/Work Highlights:** Merrill Lynch; CIBC World Markets; Citigroup; Lehman Brothers; RBS Greenwich Capital; UBS and Barclays Capital.

## McKee Nelson LLP

See firm details p.574

**The Firm:** Established in 2003, the firm's CDO practice has swiftly grown into a "*preeminent*" force with a team of attorneys that "*operates in accord with the highest professional standards.*" Clients also appreciate that they are "*excellent at interpreting clients' business imperatives.*" Transactions handled by the team include project finance CDOs, CDOs squared, emerging market CBOs, CDOs, market value transactions and static CDOs. Observers also noted that the group's extensive expertise in credit derivatives and securitization adds significant value to their advice. Recent highlights include acting as transaction counsel to Deutsche Bank on the Start CDO 2005-1 deal, one of the first to utilize pay-as-you-go credit default swap confirmation.

**The Lawyers:** **Larry Isaacson** (see p.109) received accolades for his "*technical excellence, extraordinary responsiveness and civil, deal-focused negotiations.*" Also strongly recommended, **Eugene Ferrer** (see p.99) was described as a "*brilliant and promising young partner.*"

**Clients/Work Highlights:** The group represents major Wall Street banks including CSFB; Deutsche Bank; Goldman Sachs; JPMorgan Chase; Merrill Lynch and UBS, among others.

## Milbank, Tweed, Hadley & McCloy LLP

**The Firm:** The firm's structured finance group advises a clientele of investment banks, hedge funds and private equity firms in a variety of CDO-related transactions. The team focuses predominantly on applying cash flow CDO techniques to the securitization of novel asset classes, such as project finance loan CLOs or distressed loans CLOs. The group is also tracking the burgeoning synthetic market and has recently represented Citibank as swap counterparty in the Palmyra II CDO Fund, a synthetic CDO involving a $500 million notional portfolio.

**The Lawyers:** Finance guru **Frank Puleo** is increasingly involved in the firm's CDO practice. He is described as an "*extremely smart lawyer,*" who rolls up his sleeves in negotiations and brings his valuable banking, securitization and derivatives expertise to the table.

**Clients/Work Highlights:** CIBC World Markets; Citibank; JPMorgan; Lehman Brothers and Goldman Sachs.

## Orrick, Herrington & Sutcliffe

See firm details p.337

**The Firm:** This "*impressive group*" represents issuers, placement agents and managers in CDO transactions securitizing a variety of assets including high-yield bonds, bank loans, ABS and project loans. Its talented attorneys have gained particular market recognition for their "*undeniable strength on the cash CDO side*" and are also recommended to handle mortgage-related CDO transactions. Recently, the group pooled these areas of expertise to advise WestLB on the Blue Heron cash flow ABS/MBS CDO series. Repackagings are also a significant source of work for the group.

**The Lawyers:** "*Very impressive on all accounts,*" **Joshua Raff** (see p.128) is a versatile lawyer, who combines tremendous CMBS and mortgage-related CDO expertise. Clients also commended **Al Sawyers** (see p.132) as a "*quality operator,*" respected for his work at the intersection of structured finance and derivatives.

**Clients/Work Highlights:** Bear Stearns; Deutsche Bank; Goldman Sachs; GMAC; Citigroup; Franklin Templeton and Mizuho Bank.

## Schulte Roth & Zabel LLP

See firm details p.1552

**The Firm:** Observers agree that this "*top-notch*" team has "*an excellent perception of where the market is going*" and understands the crucial interaction between structured products, securitization and derivatives. Accordingly, the firm has coordinated these areas of practice to provide "*excellent thought-through advice*" on synthetic CLOs and CBOs. Attorneys here have also acted as deal counsel on a number of cash flow and market value CDOs. It is no surprise, considering the make-up of this firm's client base, that the attorneys have also been engaged in the development of CFOs backed by hedge fund portfolios.

**The Lawyers:** Clients spoke of **Paul Watterson**'s "*excellent judgment, focus and talent*" and all agreed that his "*first-rate reputation*" is well deserved. Also strongly endorsed were **Craig Stein**, who is "*technically very impressive,*" and **Phillip Azzollini**, a "*very talented newcomer.*"

**Clients/Work Highlights:** The firm represents sponsors, issuers, placement agents, counterparties, managers and collateral managers in connection with a wide variety of cash and synthetic CDO transactions, including CIT Group, Merrill Lynch and Witherspoon Funding.

## Skadden, Arps, Slate, Meagher & Flom LLP

See firm details p.1557

**The Firm:** According to commentators, Skadden is "*a great choice for cutting-edge work and added-value service.*" The group's reputation for operating at the high end of the CDO market is reflected in the transactions it handles. Major Wall Street banks, acting as underwriters or managers, frequently instruct the team in cash flow, market value and synthetic CDO, CLO and CBO offerings. A particular highlight was to act for iStar Financial on its innovative CMO offerings valued at $740 million. The team is also well versed at handling hybrid structures and recently advised on the Tourmaline CDO, underwritten by Morgan Stanley, which involved the combination of a synthetic bucket and cash assets. Hedge funds also regularly turn to the firm for advice on their CDO investments.

**The Lawyers:** Sources described **Susan Curtis** (see p.94) as a "*distinguished leader*" in the CBO market, while "*real deal-doer*" **James Stringfellow** (see p.137) stands out for his work on CBO and CLO transactions. **Clients/Work Highlights:** Morgan Stanley; Goldman Sachs; CIBC; Highbridge Capital Hedge Fund; JPMorgan Securities and Bankers Trust.

## Band 3

### Allen & Overy
See firm details p.1516
**The Firm:** The firm is building up a serious structured finance practice to complement its leading derivatives practice. This has not gone unnoticed by competitors who spoke of a "*blooming practice, getting great client-wins*." A popular choice with Wall Street banks to advise on synthetic transactions, the team receives repeat instructions from Bear Stearns on synthetic ABS CDOs. Another distinguishing feature of the group is its global reach, allowing it to advise on the most complex multijurisdictional matters. One such transaction was its work with RBS as arranger of the Lansdowne synthetic CDO, of which notes were sold in the USA, Europe and Asia. **The Lawyers: David Wainer** (see p.140) is a key player in the development of the New York-based structured finance practice and has done "*exemplary work in the field,*" according to sources. CDO transactions embedding derivatives form a staple of his

diet. For example, he advised HSBC on the first synthetic CDO transaction completed in Thailand since Thai investors were allowed to purchase CDO securities.
**Clients/Work Highlights:** Citigroup; CSFB; Deutsche Bank; Goldman Sachs; JPMorgan Chase; Merrill Lynch; Morgan Stanley and UBS.

### Latham & Watkins LLP
**The Firm:** This firm houses structured finance capabilities in both its Los Angeles and New York offices. Many major financial institutions favor the group because it is "*always abreast of CDO market developments.*" The group is regularly instructed to act as deal counsel, collateral manager counsel, as well as adviser to investors in a variety of CLO, CBO and CDO transactions.
**The Lawyers:** Laura DeFelice chairs the structured finance practice.
**Clients/Work Highlights:** Bear Stearns; Deutsche Bank; JPMorgan; Merrill Lynch and Morgan Stanley.

### Linklaters
See firm details p.255
**The Firm:** High-quality recruits and a "*strategic approach to the market*" show the firm's determination to increase its share of the CDO market, and, according to observers, it is "*heading in the right direction.*" The team has established a thriving practice for cash, synthetic and hybrid CDOs, CLOs and CBOs. Attorneys are also very well versed in derivative structured finance products. A particular highlight for the group was its advice to Deutsche Bank on the Stack Ltd transaction, one of the first US-managed synthetic ABS CDOs using credit derivatives technology.
**The Lawyers: Adam Glass** (see p.102) has been an important hire in the strategic development of the group. His diversified practice also encompasses

synthetic securitization and credit derivative transactions. **Gary Barnett** (see p.87) has a reputation for innovation in the fields of international securitization, sophisticated financings and other structured finance and derivative matters.
**Clients/Work Highlights:** WestLB and Deutsche Bank are among the representative clients of the firm.

### Mayer, Brown, Rowe & Maw LLP
See firm details p.876
**The Firm:** Market sources reported that this group has "*significantly increased its presence in the CDO market.*" Combining strengths from the New York, Charlotte, Los Angeles and Chicago offices, the group represents a diverse clientele of sponsors, arrangers, managers, financial guarantors, trustees and rating agencies. It has acted for such clients in arbitrage, cash flow, market value and synthetic CDOs, in connection with various types of underlying collateral pools. The group also excels at utilizing credit-linked notes, credit default and total return swaps in connection with synthetic CDOs.
**The Lawyers:** Jason Kravitt supervises the firm's CDO practice group.
**Clients/Work Highlights:** The group regularly represents Banc of America Securities; Citigroup; CSFB; Merrill Lynch; CALYON Securities; Wachovia Securities; Lehman Brothers; GE Capital and Carlyle Investment Management.

### Other Notable Practitioners
At Stroock & Stroock & Lavan LLP, **Mark Rae** is responsible for the structured finance work. Sources described him as a "*very intelligent and unflappable adviser.*" **Robert Villani** (see p.140) from Thacher Proffitt & Wood LLP has been instrumental in the development of the firm's synthetic CDO practice.

---

# CAPITAL MARKETS

# DERIVATIVES

| Capital Markets: Derivatives |
|---|
| Leading Firms |
| [1] ALLEN & OVERY |
| CLEARY GOTTLIEB STEEN & HAMILTON LLP |
| [2] CADWALADER, WICKERSHAM & TAFT LLP |
| DAVIS POLK & WARDWELL |
| SULLIVAN & CROMWELL LLP |
| [3] MORRISON & FOERSTER LLP |
| SCHULTE ROTH & ZABEL LLP |
| SKADDEN, ARPS, SLATE, MEAGHER & FLOM |
| STROOCK & STROOCK & LAVAN LLP |
| [4] MAYER, BROWN, ROWE & MAW LLP |
| SIDLEY AUSTIN LLP |

## Band 1

### Allen & Overy
See firm details p.1516
**The Firm:** The firm's privileged relationship with the ISDA gives it an "*unrivaled understanding of market developments and new products,*" securing its preeminent position in the market. The talented group of "*fine lawyers*" continues to represent the ISDA on a variety of documentation and legislation projects. Recent instructions include the substantial task of preparing the 2005 ISDA Commodity Definitions and a project for the regulation of energy derivatives. The team's expertise is not limited to ISDA representation; according to interviewees, this team is "*firmly established as a leading transactional practice for credit derivatives.*" A particular highlight was representing Fortis Bank in a total return swap on a portfolio of hedge funds. Another important

feature of the firm's practice is derivatives litigation work, for example representing JPMorgan in a dispute regarding ISDA documentation.
**The Lawyers:** "*The first name to come to mind for the toughest regulatory matters,*" **Daniel Cunningham** (see p.94) is "*among the most impressive and influential practitioners around.*" He commands the "*highest respect*" for his work and contribution to the industry. He notably represented the ISDA in connection with Title IX provisions implementing important changes to the US Bankruptcy Code to clarify the termination netting of derivatives. "*High-caliber lawyer,*" **Joshua Cohn** (see p.93) is praised for his ability to "*combine faultless legal advice and the highest level of market awareness.*" He assisted in the creation of the ISDA protocol to adjust the novation process and ease backlogs of credit derivatives transfer agreements.
**Clients/Work Highlights:** ISDA; CSFB; Deutsche

## Capital Markets: Derivatives
### Leading Individuals

Bank; HSBC; JPMorgan Chase and Highbridge Capital Management.

## Cleary Gottlieb Steen & Hamilton LLP
See firm details p.1525

**The Firm:** "*A definite leader and a model for other players,*" the firm's derivatives practice is "*simply fantastic,*" reported sources. The firm fields some of the "*strongest derivatives lawyers in the country,*" who are widely recognized for their expertise in designing "*uniquely innovative techniques on big-ticket transactions.*" The well-rounded team is equally skilled in advising on equity, credit or commodities-linked products and provides expertise on the most complex derivatives-related transactions and litigation to loyal clients such as Citigroup, Goldman Sachs, CSFB and Barclays Capital. Another major feature of the group's practice is its "*indisputable influence*" when it comes to shaping financial derivatives legislation and regulations. For example, the team negotiated new provisions of the Bankruptcy Code on behalf of several industry associations, "*reaching excellent results for the enforcement of derivatives in insolvency proceedings,*" agreed sources. The group also proves adept at employing its derivatives knowledge across a wider range of structured finance transactions including CLO, CDO and repackagings, as well as securities offerings. On the litigation front, the team is representing Lehman Brothers in a dispute involving equity derivatives transactions with Enron.

**The Lawyers:** The "*terrific*" **Ed Rosen** (see p.130) is "*simply unbeatable for top-level regulatory advice on*

derivatives trading." He recently represented the Bond Market Association (BMA), the ISDA and the Securities Industry Association (SIA) in responding to the guidance principles on responsibilities of financial institutions engaged in complex structured finance activities proposed by regulators, including the SEC and the Federal Reserve. He is also a recognized expert for derivatives-related internal investigations and enforcement issues. The "*absolutely magnificent*" **Seth Grosshandler** (see p.104) received accolades from commentators for "*service rendered to the industry.*" He played a critical role for the ISDA and the BMA in the negotiation of the new provisions to the insolvency legislation, and is said by peers to be "*the most visible and popular member of the profession.*" The "*exceptional*" **Michael Dayan** (see p.95) is described as "*an impressive expert for equity and credit derivatives transactions alike.*" He represented CDS IndexCo LLC in the development of the new CDX Emerging Markets Diversified Index and the CDX Crossover index.

**Clients/Work Highlights:** The group represents major financial institutions including Morgan Stanley; Banc of America Securities; Merrill Lynch; Lehman Brothers and Bear Stearns. The group's client base also comprises commercial banks, swap dealers, exchanges, clearinghouses, financial trade associations, sovereigns and corporate users.

## Band 2

## Cadwalader, Wickersham & Taft LLP
See firm details p.1522

**The Firm:** The firm's derivatives practice is a popular choice among clients "*when practical and creative answers are needed.*" The team of "*formidable lawyers*" is prominent in the field of credit derivatives and "*second to none*" in the municipal swaps market. Other products on the team's agenda include fixed income, equity, currency and fund-linked derivatives. Recent highlights include advising the private equity firm The Blackstone Group in the proposed purchase of the New York Mercantile Exchange. The group is also actively involved in the representation of industry associations and was retained by the ISDA to develop a new template for credit default swaps. Clients are also appreciative of the support provided by strong tax, insolvency and derivatives litigation practices. "*A major player for derivatives CDO-linked work,*" the group has successfully integrated its derivatives practice with its structured products and securitization practices.

**The Lawyers: Lary Stromfeld** (see p.137) is a "*leading figure*" in the derivatives field. He was retained by the ISDA to head the committee developing credit default swaps on municipal debt. According to clients, he is "*the authority in municipal derivatives markets.*" **David Mitchell** (see p.121) is an "*extremely versatile derivatives lawyer,*" providing the full range of regulatory, transactional and litigation advice. He is an "*expert for getting clearance approvals,*" advising on fund-linked products and handling derivatives litigation in the context of insolvency proceedings.

For example, he was chosen to act as special counsel in the Enron case.

**Clients/Work Highlights:** The group acts for dealers, hedge-fund end users, issuers and investment banks, including Ambac Financial Group; Goldman Sachs; Morgan Stanley; Lehman Brothers; Merrill Lynch; Deutsche Bank and UBS. Industry associations are also part of the firm's client base, and include the BMA, the SIA and the Association of Financial Guaranty Insurers, among others.

## Davis Polk & Wardwell
See firm details p.1528

**The Firm:** Davis Polk maintains its "*unrivaled position as the finest firm*" in the field of equity derivatives. It boasts a team of "*sharp and clear-thinking derivatives lawyers,*" who are "*always perceptive of the latest trends.*" The group is highly regarded for its integrated approach to OTC products, equity-linked securities, convertible and exchangeable offerings. The team demonstrated its expertise in the field when representing Citigroup as purchaser in the $862.5 million Rule 144A convertible note offering by Charter Communication, a US broadband communication company. Sources also recognized the firm as "*a clear leader*" in advice to hedge funds on complex equity-related transactions. Clients further praise the group's ability to mobilize skills in other relevant disciplines such as tax, bankruptcy and accounting.

**The Lawyers:** According to peers, **John Brandow** (see p.89) has become a "*real inspiration*" for his work on convertible and exchangeable securities offerings. He is the "*guru of equity derivatives.*" Recently, he advised Goldman Sachs as dealer manager on Getty Images' SEC-registered offer to exchange an aggregate of up to $265 million of its convertible subordinated debentures. **Daniel Budofsky** (see p.90) is praised for his ability to "*quickly get to grips with complex issues and swiftly come up with a solution.*" Recent highlights include advising Deutsche Bank as underwriter on an SEC-registered $736 million offering of contingent convertible notes by Calpine. He also dedicates a significant part of his time advising hedge fund clients. **James Rothwell** (see p.131) is another key partner in the group. He is "*thoughtful, inventive and hard working.*" Recently, Rothwell advised Merrill Lynch and Morgan Stanley as underwriters of a $275 million mandatorily exchangeable securities offering by Nuveen Investments.

**Clients/Work Highlights:** The group acts for major financial institutions, including Banc of America Securities; Deutsche Bank Securities; CSFB; JPMorgan Securities; Morgan Stanley and UBS Securities. It also regularly represents corporations, hedge funds and individuals as end users of equity derivatives.

## Sullivan & Cromwell LLP
See firm details p.1558

**The Firm:** The respected commodities, futures and derivatives group maintains a key position in the market for the "*depth and breadth of its expertise across all areas of the derivatives markets.*" These include transactional, advisory and litigation services. On the transactional side, the group is *"top of the tree"* for the development of new derivatives products linked to energy commodities. Lately, it has handled derivatives work for hedge funds clients and acted as advisory counsel to a group of large hedge fund managers in the development of a report entitled 'Sound Practices for Hedge Fund Managers.' Another distinguishing feature of the group is its involvement in the structuring and development of electronic exchanges and on the use of new technologies for derivatives-related activities. For example, it assisted in establishing the Archipelago Exchange, the first completely open electronic stock market in the USA.

**The Lawyers:** *"A terrific lawyer and a very personable adviser,"* **Kenneth Raisler** (see p.128) is *"the first port of call for sophisticated regulatory advice"* for many commentators. He played a major role in the creation and approval of the Chicago Climate Futures Exchange (CCFE) for emissions derivatives trading. He was equally recommended for his tremendous expertise on equity derivatives. **David Gilberg** (see p.102) is another leading figure at the firm, who is described as *"extremely efficient"* and highly rated for his deep knowledge of the equity derivatives market. Another skilled adviser, **Robert Reeder** (see p.129), was particularly commended for his *"responsiveness and the degree to which he gets involved in the transactions;"* while younger partner **Rebecca Simmons** (see p.134) is rapidly building a profile as a *"respected credit derivatives expert,"* reported sources.

**Clients/Work Highlights:** Bear Stearns; Chicago Climate Futures Exchange; Goldman Sachs and Wachovia are among the firm's clients.

## Band 3

### Morrison & Foerster LLP
See firm details p.335

**The Firm:** Clients strongly recommended the firm for its expertise on bespoke and highly structured transactions. Derivatives attorneys work as part of the firm's financial transactions team, and are *"very quick to grasp concepts and recognize the business implications,"* clients said. The group's broad remit encompasses credit and equity derivatives, energy, metal and foreign exchange derivatives and insurance-related derivatives. In addition, attorneys here have extensive experience with all aspects of equity-linked note programs, having served as designated underwriters' counsel on all of the Banc of America Securities note programs.

**The Lawyers:** The *"extremely smart"* **Anna Pinedo** (see p.126), who joined from Stroock & Stroock & Lavan, has reinforced the ranks of the derivatives and structured products team. She brings with her *"invaluable experience"* in the field of structured preferred securities offerings.

**Clients/Work Highlights:** Clients include the derivatives groups of numerous investment and commercial banks, commodity dealers and users,

insurance companies, mutual funds, hedge funds and other financial institutions.

### Schulte Roth & Zabel LLP
See firm details p.1552

**The Firm:** The firm is consistently described as a *"sturdy player"* in the derivatives market. Its tremendous funds client base affords the group a preeminent position in the burgeoning field of hedge fund-linked derivatives. The group also acts for structured finance vehicles, investment banks, commercial banks and monoline insurance companies. It has been involved in a broad variety of derivatives transactions, including credit derivatives, equity derivatives, interest rate and currency swaps and foreign exchange. The team is also retained for a variety of unusual and specialized projects, such as advising the liquidator of an insolvent hedge fund that had entered into a variety of complex derivatives. Its experience in CDO transactions completes the picture.

**The Lawyers:** Partner **Craig Stein**, a *"superb deal-oriented lawyer,"* is part of the firm's well-rounded finance team. He provides particular expertise on structured hedge fund products.

**Clients/Work Highlights:** The group represents a diverse client base including investment funds; structured finance vehicles; investment banks and commercial banks.

### Skadden, Arps, Slate, Meagher & Flom LLP
See firm details p.1557

**The Firm:** The firm takes a coordinated, international approach to the areas of OTC derivatives, futures, options and traditional commodities transactions. In particular, sources pointed to it as a *"major force in the field of energy derivatives,"* with work originating from the New York, Washington, DC and Houston offices. The group is also well known for its convertible bonds expertise, and has recently developed the credit derivatives side of the practice. A particular feature on the firm's agenda is its catastrophe bonds work, largely resourced from its first-rate insurance practice. For instance, attorneys recently completed such transactions for Swiss Re and Goldman Sachs. Clients highlighted the firm's renowned derivatives-related tax advice and the litigation practice as a distinguishing feature.

**The Lawyers:** **John Osborn** (see p.124) commands a great deal of respect from his peers, and is considered a *"fully trusted adviser"* by his clients. **Philip McBride Johnson** (see p.110) stands out with his *"top-quality technical advice"* on futures regulations.

**Clients/Work Highlights:** The firm advises numerous commercial and investment banks and other dealers as well as major corporations, insurance companies and other end users of derivatives.

### Stroock & Stroock & Lavan LLP

**The Firm:** The firm's commodities and derivatives group has *"a fantastic sense of how trading of derivatives should be done."* It remains a leading force in the physical markets, particularly those of energy and

metals. Lately, the team has also been engaged in the field of credit derivatives, engineering new credit default swaps structures. The team of derivatives litigators has scored what many see as an *"impressive record of victories."* It recently obtained a $156 million arbitration award for its client Liberty Electric Power, in a case arising out of the breach of a tolling agreement. On the documentation side, the group helped develop ISDA templates for ABS credit default swaps transactions. Another characteristic of this practice is its ability to advise clients with respect to derivatives techniques embedded in structured finance transactions. For example, the firm recently represented a major financial guarantor in the structuring and documentation of a $720 million synthetic CDO.

**The Lawyers:** **Marvin Goldstein** is an *"astute lawyer,"* whose particular skill in advising on risk management issues, among other things, has won him a loyal client following. Interviewees also reserved special praise for **Thomas Heftler**'s *"thoroughness and enthusiasm."*

**Clients/Work Highlights:** The firm's client base includes Goldman Sachs; J Aron & Company; Hess Energy Trading and Sempra Energy Trading.

## Band 4

### Mayer, Brown, Rowe & Maw LLP
See firm details p.876

**The Firm:** Based in Chicago, New York and Washington, DC, the firm's derivatives practice provides comprehensive advice on all aspects of its clients' transactional, regulatory and derivatives litigation matters. Derivatives transactions handled here include the representation of Merrill Lynch in its acquisition of the execution and clearing unit of ABN AMRO, and in its acquisition of a stake in the Philadelphia Stock Exchange. On the litigation side, the group successfully resolved federal and state court claims brought against client Credit Lyonnais Rouse, alleging its involvement in a conspiracy to manipulate worldwide physical and futures copper markets. The attorneys practicing in this area include a number of former advisers to regulatory bodies, and according to clients this gives them a *"unique and privileged perspective on regulatory matters."*

**The Lawyers:** **Joseph Collins** (see p.93) divides his time equally between New York and Chicago. He is endorsed for his broad experience of derivatives matters, spanning transactional aspects as well as *"first-rate regulatory advice."* His expertise on the Chinese futures market is particularly sought after.

**Clients/Work Highlights:** Merrill Lynch; Société Générale; CIBC and Morgan Stanley.

## Sidley Austin LLP

See firm details p.883

**The Firm:** The firm is probably better known for applying its credit derivatives expertise to its distinguished securitization and structured finance practice, however it also operates in the pure derivatives market. Attorneys in the firm's Chicago and New York offices advise clients on a broad range of domestic and international transactions and regulatory matters involving investment funds, securities, futures, options and swaps. The firm also has a particularly active commodity pool practice. Another distinguishing strength of the group rests in its hedge funds-related expertise. It provides ongoing representation to hundreds of hedge funds and their managers in a wide variety of investment strategies executed in the equities, fixed income and derivatives markets.

**The Lawyers:** **Joseph Harrison** (see p.105) is widely respected for his advisory work. He advised the Ministry of International Trade and Industry of Japan, the Government of the People's Republic of China and the Government of Indonesia on futures matters. **David Sawyier** (see p.132) advises on futures, commodity pools and hedge fund-related products.

**Clients/Work Highlights:** Société Générale, Dresdner Bank and Deutsche Bank are among the firm's clients.

### Other Notable Practitioners

**Jerrold Salzman** from Freeman, Freeman & Salzman P.C is a *"great advisory lawyer with good judgment."* He remains favourite external counsel to the Chicago Mercantile Exchange.

---

# CAPITAL MARKETS

# SECURITIZATION

| Capital Markets: Securitization |
|---|
| Leading Firms |
| [1] CADWALADER, WICKERSHAM & TAFT LLP<br>SIDLEY AUSTIN LLP |
| [2] MAYER, BROWN, ROWE & MAW LLP<br>MCKEE NELSON LLP<br>ORRICK, HERRINGTON & SUTCLIFFE<br>SKADDEN, ARPS, SLATE, MEAGHER & FLOM<br>THACHER PROFFITT & WOOD LLP |
| [3] CLEARY GOTTLIEB STEEN & HAMILTON LLP<br>DECHERT LLP<br>HUNTON & WILLIAMS LLP<br>SIMPSON THACHER & BARTLETT LLP |
| [4] CRAVATH, SWAINE & MOORE LLP<br>DEWEY BALLANTINE LLP<br>KIRKLAND & ELLIS LLP<br>LATHAM & WATKINS LLP<br>WEIL, GOTSHAL & MANGES LLP |

## Band 1

### Cadwalader, Wickersham & Taft LLP

See firm details p.1522

**The Firm:** According to market sources, the attorneys at Cadwalader have *"really mastered the art of securitization."* The group stands as *"a distinct domestic and international leader,"* with sizable teams of *"sharp and highly intelligent lawyers"* throughout its ranks and across its New York, DC and Charlotte offices. Such dedication has allowed this group to capture one of the largest market shares in the field of real estate-related securitization and sources agreed that this is *"the world's best CMBS practice."* It also excels for RMBS transactions due to privileged relationships with government-sponsored enterprises such as Freddie Mac, Ginnie Mae and Fannie Mae. Asset-backed securitization (ABS) is, of course, high on the agenda, including credit cards, auto loans, student loans and commercial paper. Recently, the practice has focused on a range of emerging asset classes such as construction loans and healthcare receivables. The team continues to represent a balanced client base of issuers and underwriters, who complimented its ability to *"effectively manage volume and sophistication."* This base of traditional securitization expertise has also allowed the firm to develop a busy structured finance practice, handling CDOs, CLOs, repackagings and synthetic products.

**The Lawyers:** Head of practice **Anna Glick** (see p.102) is described as a *"leading light"* of the profession and is regarded by clients as *"the best lawyer for miles around"* for commercial mortgage-backed deals. Recently, she advised RBS Greenwich Capital on a $5 billion CMBS transaction. **Richard Schetman** (see p.133) has a *"tremendous ABS practice"* and has played a critical role in the successful development of the CDO and repackaging practice at the firm. The *"terrific"* **Michael Gambro** (see p.101) provides first-rate advice on a diversified range of asset classes. In a recent highlight, he acted for Bear Stearns on the largest single borrower CMBS transaction to date. **Jordan Schwartz** (see p.133) is highly respected for his RMBS practice and expertise on home equity ABS. Of late, he has been busy advising his clients on the implications of Regulation AB. A *"first-class lawyer,"* **James Croke** (see p.94) has returned from the London office and brings to the team his invaluable expertise on asset-backed commercial paper. The *"consistently excellent"* **Charlie Bryan** (see p.90) is based in Washington, DC and his practice focuses on mortgage pass-throughs, CMOs and real estate mortgage investment conduits (REMICs). A team based in Charlotte completes the firm's impressive set of experts. **James Carroll** (see p.91) is widely recognized for his expertise on all aspects of real estate finance, while **Steven Cohen** (see p.93) divides his time between Charlotte and New York, and has a varied structured finance practice. **Stuart Goldstein** (see p.103) remains a favorite among Charlotte's premier banks for advice on CMBS, CDO and CLO transactions. Younger partner **Patrick Quinn** (see p.128) was also strongly endorsed for his *"extraordinary work"* on real estate-related securitizations. He recently advised CSFB on the first securitization of condominium conversion loans.

**Clients/Work Highlights:** CSFB; Countrywide Financial; RBS Greenwich Capital; Morgan Stanley; Deutsche Bank; CWCapital; Goldman Sachs; UBS; IXIS Corporate and Investment Bank; Barclays Capital; GE Capital; Société Générale; Wachovia and Prudential.

### Sidley Austin LLP

See firm details p.883

**The Firm:** Industry experts were unanimous in endorsement of this *"magnificent"* securitization group: *"It has always been, and remains, a leader."* With its *"intellectually superb attorneys"* based in New York, Chicago, DC, Los Angeles and San Francisco, this team has the resources and expertise to manage a high volume of transactions, as well as to design and execute sophisticated, esoteric deals. The group is experienced in virtually every traditional asset class and has been a trendsetter in the securitization of emerging classes, such as life insurance settlement, film revenue and taxi licenses. A competitor also conceded: *"No one beats Sidleys for asset-backed CP programs."* The group is also at the forefront of the international emerging markets. It notably advised Merrill Lynch as manager in a $600 million future flow securitization of coal export receivables by major Indonesian energy group, PT Bumi Resources. This transaction heralded the reopening of the Asian capital markets. The firm is also a recognized leader in the arena of cash, synthetic or hybrid CDO, CBO and CLO transactions.

**The Lawyers:** *"The best, the finest, the greatest"* are just a few of the superlatives used to describe **Renwick Martin** (see p.117). He is a lawyer who *"simply cannot be faulted"* and a *"welcome sight across the deal table,"* commentators reported. Much of his workload of late has been focused on the CDO market. Also based in New York, the *"absolutely terrific"* **Butch Cullen** (see p.94) is consistently described as an *"exceptional CMBS expert,"* while **Arthur Hickok** (see p.106) continues to impress with his aptitude in the field of CP conduits. Entering the table this year is **Janet Barbiere** (see p.87), a *"very efficient"* younger partner who is particularly distinguished by the depth of her expertise on CMBS transactions. Based in the Chicago office, the *"outstanding"* **Tom Albrecht** (see p.84) co-heads the global securitization and structured finance practice. He is a national expert for whole business securitization and also garners respect for his tremendous

## Capital Markets: Securitization
### Leading Individuals

#### Senior Statesman
KRAVITT Jason *Mayer, Brown, Rowe & Maw*

[1] ALBRECHT Thomas *Sidley Austin LLP*
COWAN Cameron *Orrick, Herrington & Sutcliffe*
DE SEAR Edward *McKee Nelson LLP*
GLICK Anna *Cadwalader, Wickersham & Taft*
HUGI Robert *Mayer, Brown, Rowe & Maw*
KUNZ C Thomas *Skadden, Arps*
MARTIN Renwick *Sidley Austin LLP*
STERN Gary *Sidley Austin LLP*

[2] ARNHOLZ John *McKee Nelson LLP*
AUERBACH Reed *McKee Nelson LLP*
BRADY Christopher *Mayer, Brown, Rowe & Maw*
BUCKLEY Kevin *Hunton & Williams LLP*
CARROLL James *Cadwalader, Wickersham & Taft*
CULLEN William *Sidley Austin LLP*
GOLDSTEIN Stuart *Cadwalader, Wickersham & Taft*
KUDENHOLDT Stephen *Thacher Proffitt & Wood LLP*
PALMA Laura *Simpson Thacher & Bartlett LLP*
SCHETMAN Richard *Cadwalader, Wickersham & Taft*
WIPPERMAN Robert *McKee Nelson LLP*

[3] BLAUCH Kevin *Latham & Watkins LLP*
CHECK Raymond *Cleary Gottlieb*
COHEN Steven *Cadwalader, Wickersham & Taft*
CROKE James *Cadwalader, Wickersham & Taft*
CROST Katharine *Orrick, Herrington & Sutcliffe*
DUPLER Mitchell *Cleary Gottlieb*
EISENBERG David *Simpson Thacher & Bartlett LLP*
FAULKNER Andrew *Skadden, Arps*
GAMBRO Michael *Cadwalader, Wickersham & Taft*
HAHN Robert *Hunton & Williams*
HITSELBERGER Carol *Mayer, Brown, Rowe & Maw*
HOROWITZ Richard *Thacher Proffitt & Wood LLP*
JORISSEN Paul *Mayer, Brown, Rowe & Maw*
LITWIN Stuart *Mayer, Brown, Rowe & Maw*
MORRISON Kenneth *Kirkland & Ellis LLP*
PECOULAS George *Mayer, Brown, Rowe & Maw*
SCHWARTZ Jordan *Cadwalader, Wickersham & Taft*

[4] BANNON Eileen *Dewey Ballantine LLP*
BRYAN Charles *Cadwalader, Wickersham & Taft*
BUCK Willis *Sidley Austin LLP*
DORRIS Malcolm *Dechert LLP*
FONTAINE Mary *Mayer, Brown, Rowe & Maw*
GAINOR Edward *McKee Nelson LLP*
GALAINENA M David *Winston & Strawn LLP*
HICKOK Arthur *Sidley Austin LLP*
HOCHBERG Kevin *Sidley Austin LLP*
KADLICK Richard *Skadden, Arps*
MITCHELL Michael *Orrick, Herrington & Sutcliffe*
MOLITOR Steven *Dechert LLP*
MURPHY Paul *Moore & Van Allen, PLLC*
NEDZBALA Michael *Hunton & Williams*
NOCCO Frank *Weil, Gotshal & Manges LLP*
OBERKFELL Keith *Mayer, Brown, Rowe & Maw*
SUGERMAN David *Cleary Gottlieb*
VAN GORP Jon *Mayer, Brown, Rowe & Maw*

#### Up-and-coming individuals
BARBIERE Janet *Sidley Austin LLP*
QUINN Patrick *Cadwalader, Wickersham & Taft*

---

international practice. **Skip Stern** (see p.136), also based in Chicago, is said to be *"an indisputable leader in the film finance industry."* One of his highlights was to represent Merrill Lynch in the financing of Marvel Studios through the securitization of film revenue. **Willis Buck** (see p.90) is *"thorough, enthusiastic and amenable,"* qualities that make him a *"true pleasure to work with."* His practice focuses on credit card and auto loan securitization. **Kevin Hochberg's** (see p.107) practice encompasses the widest range of asset classes such as shipping containers, railcars, utility stranded costs and relocation company receivables.

**Clients/Work Highlights:** Barclays Capital; Citigroup; CSFB; Deutsche Bank; DZ Bank; MBIA Insurance; Lehman Brothers; Merrill Lynch and Nomura.

### Band 2

#### Mayer, Brown, Rowe & Maw LLP
See firm details p.876

**The Firm:** The firm's *"outstanding"* securitization practice spreads across New York, Chicago and Charlotte and enjoys a stellar reputation even beyond national borders. According to clients, the *"partners at Mayer Brown are just excellent and the associates are fantastic too, always on top of their subject."* The group has monumental resources and is geared to act on all traditional asset classes, giving clients the assurance that *"they can always deliver a smooth product in the assigned time frame."* Areas of strength include MBS, auto loans, credit card and trade receivables securitizations. The firm is also highly recommended for asset-backed CP work. A recent highlight was the securitization of Banco do Brasil's rights to receive current and future dollar-denominated payments relating to payment orders from US banks.

**The Lawyers:** Senior Statesman **Jason Kravitt** (see p.114) in New York is a *"landmark"* of the industry. Still active on the transactional side, he regularly advises on private trade receivables financings. He also concentrates on regulatory matters and, according to interviewees, is *"second to none to advise on Regulation AB and Basel II."* In the Chicago office, the *"charismatic"* **Robert Hugi** (see p.109) is praised for *"using his technical brilliance in a practical way."* Credit card and equipment contract-backed securities make up the bulk of his practice. **Carol Hitselberger** (see p.107) continues to impress by her technical excellence. Clients described her as *"focused and committed,"* while peers said she is *"sensible and thoughtful."* **George Pecoulas** (see p.125) is the CP expert here: commentators reported that he *"understands diplomacy and knows what issues are worth fighting for."* **Stuart Litwin** (see p.116) specializes in auto loans and equipment cross-border securitization. He notably represented Volkswagen in the first-ever true sale-funded securitization of German assets using the True Sale Initiative Program. The *"most impressive young partner one can hope to come across"* is **Jon Van Gorp** (see p.139), claim clients. They also

report that he *"surpasses his clients' very high expectations."* He recently acted for Bank of America in a $55 billion auto loan transaction with GMAC. Observers commended **Mary Fontaine** (see p.100) as a *"charming negotiator"* with *"exceptional intellectual abilities."* Based in New York, **Paul Jorissen** (see p.110) is a *"fine lawyer"* with a broad practice encompassing mortgage-backed securitization, with an emphasis on mortgage warehouse finance, as well as asset-backed securitization, particularly equipment loans and leases. In the Charlotte office, **Keith Oberkfell** (see p.124) has a broad structured finance practice encompassing CDOs, CLOs and derivatives, while **Christopher Brady** (see p.89) is heavily engaged in the representation of two of the country's largest CMBS servicers.

**Clients/Work Highlights:** ABN AMRO; Bank of America; Citigroup; CSFB; Deutsche Bank; Lehman Brothers; Volkswagen; Goldman Sachs and JPMorgan Chase.

#### McKee Nelson LLP
See firm details p.574

**The Firm:** According to observers, the firm's securitization group has *"recruited intelligently and done extremely well ever since it started."* It has grown rapidly into a major national and international player. The team of attorneys here is said to be *"exceptional"* and received accolades for its mortgage-related work. For example, it represented Lehman Brothers in the first securitization of home equity lines of credit structured as a REMIC. Credit card receivables securitization is another specialty and the group demonstrated its expertise in this field when it helped Providian National Bank implement an innovative credit card master trust. The team is also able to advise on more esoteric deals and notably represented MBNA in its inaugural securitization of loans to dentists and other healthcare practitioners. In addition, the team's lawyers are experienced in all aspects of the cash and synthetic collateralized debt market. In 2004 the group formed an alliance with the capital markets team at leading European law firm Ashurst, in order to extend its global reach.

**The Lawyers:** Industry experts only have goods things to say about **Ed De Sear** (see p.95), who is widely recognized as *"the guru"* of credit card receivables securitization. His wide-ranging practice features dealer floor plan receivables, tobacco settlement payment and legal fees. The *"brilliant"* **Reed Auerbach** (see p.86) is commended for his *"true appreciation of the commercial side of the deals,"* while **Robert Wipperman** (see p.142) is *"effortlessly good"* on a very broad array of structured products. The highly respected **John Arnholz** (see p.86) is particularly rated for his advice on cross-border and global offerings, while **Edward Gainor** (see p.100) has been heavily involved in the real estate-related securitization arena.

**Clients/Work Highlights:** ABN AMRO; Banc of America Securities; Banc One Capital Markets; Bear Stearns; Citigroup; Countrywide Securities; CSFB; Deutsche Bank Securities; Goldman Sachs; RBS Greenwich Capital; JPMorgan; Lehman Brothers;

Merrill Lynch; Morgan Stanley; UBS Investment Bank; Wachovia Securities and Washington Mutual.

## Orrick, Herrington & Sutcliffe
See firm details p.337

**The Firm:** With offices spanning the USA, the firm can boast one of the largest securitization groups in the country. The attorneys here are commended for their *"intelligent, constructive manners"* and their *"refusal to play fast and loose."* Clients reserved particular praise for the partners' *"responsiveness and true dedication."* Enduring relationships with MBNA and Capital One secure the firm's preeminence in the field of credit card receivables securitization. The group's experience of ABS also encompasses auto, lease and trade receivables, as well as the most recent trends such as securitization of utilities receivables, catastrophe bonds and tobacco litigation settlement payments. Another forte of the group is its MBS expertise, which includes single-family residential mortgage loans, home equity loans and manufactured housing contracts securitization. The team is also renowned for delivering *"excellent service"* on both cash and synthetic CDO transactions.

**The Lawyers:** The *"extremely bright"* **Cam Cowan** (see p.93) remains the trusted adviser of the American Securitization Forum, for which he notably drafted the comment letter regarding Regulation AB in response to the SEC proposal. On the transactional side, he continues to represent Capital One on most of its credit card and unsecured consumer loans securitizations. **Katharine Crost** (see p.94) also won respect for her work on a wide variety of asset classes. In particular, she is said to demonstrate *"sheer excellence"* on mortgage loans ABS, an area of expertise shared with the *"very smart and cooperative"* **Mike Mitchell** (see p.121).

**Clients/Work Highlights:** American Securitization Forum; Bear Stearns; Capital One; Citigroup; CSFB; GMAC; Merrill Lynch; Providian National Bank; Wachovia and Washington Mutual.

## Skadden, Arps, Slate, Meagher & Flom LLP
See firm details p.1557

**The Firm:** Rather than amassing a large volume of instructions, the firm has made the strategic choice to target challenging deals. Market commentators endorsed this strategy, pointing to the firm as *"extremely good for unique high-profile transactions."* Attorneys in the structured finance group particularly stand out for the securitization of certain types of assets such as credit card receivables, automobile loan contracts and trade receivables. The team was notably selected to handle most of Ford's auto lease securitization work. Another distinguishing feature is its expertise in designing insurance products-backed securities, such as funding agreements-backed securities. The firm advised on the implementation of such programs for John Hancock, Allstate, Principal, Nationwide and New York Life. Several members of the group have extended their horizons and established a very successful CDO practice.

**The Lawyers:** The *"admirable"* **Thomas Kunz** (see p.114) is said to have *"a thirst for the challenging and cutting-edge transactions."* The *"devoted and conscientious"* **Andrew Faulkner** (see p.98) remains highly ranked for his well-regarded credit card securitization practice, while **Richard Kadlick** (see p.110) is said to be *"an excellent choice for avant-garde deals."*

**Clients/Work Highlights:** Caterpillar; JPMorgan Chase; Bank of America; Cendant; NatWest; CSFB; Fleet Bank; Sumitomo Bank and Bank of Tokyo-Mitsubishi.

## Thacher Proffitt & Wood LLP
See firm details p.1560

**The Firm:** The firm remains *"at the forefront"* of the RMBS market, in recognition of the sheer volume of instructions it successfully attracts from a variety of market participants. This busy group, lead by 23 partners, demonstrates its proficiency in the field when handling transactions involving manufactured housing loans, home equity loans, interest only loans or subprime mortgages. The team is also very active in the CMBS arena, where it has recently experimented with new types of products such as B notes and mezzanine participations. In addition, the team frequently represent REITs as issuers. A particular highlight was representing American Home in a $5.6 billion MBS offering. Asset-backed work includes student loan, credit card, healthcare, export and municipal receivables securitization. Recent lateral hires have also bolstered the firm's CDO and derivatives expertise.

**The Lawyers:** **Stephen Kudenholdt** (see p.114) is commended as a *"highly versatile and intelligent"* lawyer, able to advise on a broad array of transactions as well as the latest regulatory issues, as demonstrated by his advice to the Bond Market Association on Regulation AB. **Richard Horowitz** (see p.108) is renowned for his wealth of expertise in mortgage-backed securitization, particularly involving residential and multifamily loans.

**Clients/Work Highlights:** Bear Stearns; Citigroup; Goldman Sachs; Merrill Lynch; Nomura; UBS; NorthStar Realty Finance; MortgageIT; Newcastle Investment; New Century Financial and Hanover Capital Mortgage Holdings.

## Band 3

## Cleary Gottlieb Steen & Hamilton LLP
See firm details p.1525

**The Firm:** Clients described this *"elite"* securitization team as one that possesses the *"best resources to act on the US as well as the global financial markets."* Domestically, the Washington, DC office offers particular expertise in RMBS transactions having served as counsel on more than $100 billion of MBS offerings by Ginnie Mae, Fannie Mae and Freddie Mac in recent times. The group is *"at the top of the game"* with its advice on REMIC transactions in particular, while CMBS deals form a staple diet of the New York team. A recent highlight in this area was represent-

ing Goldman Sachs in the securitization of a $1.7 billion loan secured by the New York City landmark Rockefeller Center. In addition, the group is prominent on cross-border securitizations and recently represented Korea First Bank in a €500 million RMBS offering. It is also counsel to sovereign debtors in numerous significant securitizations in the emerging markets. Finally, the group boasts the *"most fantastic CDO practice"*, and the lawyers here are cross-trained in all areas of structured finance.

**The Lawyers:** The *"very impressive"* **Mitch Dupler** (see p.97), based in Washington, DC, is the preferred counsel for numerous underwriters of offerings by Freddie Mac, Ginnie Mae and Fannie Mae, while **Ray Check** (see p.91) in New York was singled out for his *"eclectic"* practice and the *"uncompromising quality of his documentation."* **David Sugerman** (see p.137), also based in New York, is said to be *"immensely talented"* for MBS and has a related expertise in the field of synthetic CDOs.

**Clients/Work Highlights:** Barclays; Bear Stearns; Citigroup; Deutsche Bank Securities; JPMorgan Securities; Lehman Brothers; Morgan Stanley; Nomura; CSFB; KKR Financial Advisors; UBS; INVESCO and Korea First Bank.

## Dechert LLP
See firm details p.1752

**The Firm:** This group has enjoyed an excellent deal flow, placing it among the busiest firms in recent times. This *"efficient and resourceful team"* has built up a particular expertise in real estate securitization. On the residential side, the firm handles transactions involving prime and subprime mortgage loans, Alt-A mortgage loans, home equity line of credit (HELOCs) and manufactured housing contracts. On the commercial side, the team has acted on virtually all the CMBS transactions rated by Standard & Poor's. The firm also occasionally handles more novel structures such as the securitization of prescription drugs royalties. The team's *"constant high quality of work"* attracted the praise of clients, who agreed that *"at Dechert, the premium is always placed on client service."*

**The Lawyers:** **Malcolm Dorris** (see p.96) is considered the *"driving force"* of this successful practice. Clients also strongly endorsed **Steven Molitor** (see p.121), appreciating his *"high degree of involvement and responsiveness."*

**Clients/Work Highlights:** Bank of America; CSFB; Deutsche Bank; GE Capital; RBS Greenwich Capital; Jefferies & Company; JPMorgan Chase; Lehman Brothers; MBIA Insurance; Merrill Lynch; MFS Investment Management and Wachovia Securities.

## Hunton & Williams LLP
See firm details p.1989

**The Firm:** The firm is widely recognized as a *"rising star"* in the national securitization market. With experienced finance lawyers in Richmond, Charlotte, New York, DC and Miami offices, the group has, in the eyes of many, taken on the mantle of a *"direct challenger"* to the largest New York players. In 2004, it represented a wide variety of participants in securities offerings totaling more than $1 trillion. The group offers special expertise in MBS transactions and REMICs in particular. The team is particularly sought after by REITs to implement mortgage securitization programs and is also very popular with major Wall Street underwriters including CSFB, JPMorgan and Merrill Lynch in MBS offerings.

**The Lawyers:** The "*incredibly skilled,*" **Kevin Buckley** (see p.90) is based in Richmond from where he co-heads the firm's asset securitization group. Clients described him as "*exceptionally insightful – he has excellent judgment,*" and added: "*His great personality makes the deal process a smooth one.*" His fellow co-head of practice, **Michael Nedzbala** (see p.123) is based in Charlotte. He possesses an "*enormous breadth of experience*" on MBS and asset-backed CP transactions. **Robert Hahn** (see p.104) was also singled out for his "*ability to provide concise and well-structured advice.*"

**Clients/Work Highlights:** The group's client base includes major residential mortgage REITs such as Fieldstone Investment and New York Mortgage Trust. Other financial institution clients include Wells Fargo and Third Federal Savings & Loan Association of Cleveland.

### Simpson Thacher & Bartlett LLP
See firm details p.1555

**The Firm:** The firm's securitization team has fewer resources than some of its competitors and is nurturing a practice that many described as best suited to "*unique, technical and very complex*" transactions. According to commentators, the key to the group's success is that it has "*high-class lawyers, who are committed to excellence.*" The practice is a specialist player in auto fleet securitization and regularly acts for the largest originators in the field. Bank credit card receivables securitization is another important feature here, along with aircraft leases, airline ticket receivables and future revenue streams. Recent highlights include representing JPMorgan in the first offering of securities secured by a revolving pool of commercial fleet leasing assets of a subsidiary of Cendant.

**The Lawyers:** A key figure in the group is "*hard-hitting lawyer*" **Laura Palma** (see p.124), who is widely recognized as "*a top name*" in the field of car rental fleet financings. A "*real genius,*" **David Eisenberg** (see p.98) gained the admiration of his peers and clients for his expertise in the fields of credit card receivables and dealer floor plan loans securitization. His practice also extends to CLO and CDO transactions.

**Clients/Work Highlights:** JP Morgan Chase; Lehman Brothers; MBIA Insurance; Avis; Hertz and Vanguard Car Rental.

## Band 4

### Cravath, Swaine & Moore LLP
See firm details p.1527

**The Firm:** The firm fields a dedicated team of attorneys, smaller than its direct competitors and, accordingly, does not handle a huge volume of transactions. Rather, it is renowned for engineering highly complex structures involving niche asset classes. Clients described the firm as "*a scout – always on the look for new, esoteric products.*" Regardless of its size, the group is the trusted adviser to major financial institutions. For example, it is the designated underwriter counsel in connection with Citigroup Credit Card Issuance Trust's issuance of ABS.

**The Lawyers:** David Mercado and Neil Westreich are the key members of the securitization practice.

**Clients/Work Highlights:** Ambac Assurance; Canada Mortgage and Housing; Citibank; Hertz; Providian National Bank and Vitro America.

### Dewey Ballantine LLP
See firm details p.1530

**The Firm:** This healthy practice continues to "*successfully compete with bigger fish in the market,*" agreed sources. The "*remarkably skillful*" team of lawyers provides advice to a variety of issuers, underwriters, placement agents and credit enhancers in all types of structured finance transactions. These include traditional mortgage, auto loans and credit card receivables as well as novel asset types such as insurance premium loans and stranded utility costs. The firm is also experienced in cross-border structured financings involving assets originated in a wide variety of emerging markets. In recent times, attorneys represented Merrill Lynch as initial purchaser of notes issued by Brazil Foreign Diversified Payment Rights Finance Company and backed by existing and future US dollar electronic inter-bank payments.

**The Lawyers:** **Eileen Bannon** (see p.86) stands out with her broad securitization and derivatives expertise. In 2004, she led the team advising Household Finance in the creation of a $4 billion single-seller CP conduit.

**Clients/Work Highlights:** AmeriCredit; Household Finance; Ameriquest Mortgage; CSFB; Barclays Capital; Morgan Stanley; Ambac Assurance; UBS and Fannie Mae.

### Kirkland & Ellis LLP
See firm details p.875

**The Firm:** The firm continues to attract praise for its "*wonderful*" auto loan securitization practice. In recent years, it has handled offerings by GMAC totaling over $100 billion of notes backed by pools of retail auto loan receivables and dealer floor plan receivables. Other asset classes in which the group has particular experience are mainstream categories such as credit cards, trade receivables, and equipment leases. Emerging asset classes such as charged-off credit cards, structured settlements and healthcare receivables are also found in the caseload here.

**The Lawyers:** **Kenneth Morrison** (see p.122) is highly esteemed for his experience in the auto

finance arena. Interviewees endorsed his "*great attention to detail,*" adding: "*He is very good at recognizing the commercial parameters within which clients operate.*" Recently, he led the team on a $55 billion whole loan sale of retail auto loans by GMAC.

**Clients/Work Highlights:** GTCR Golder Rauner, Goldman Sachs Private Equity Group and GMAC are among the clients.

### Latham & Watkins LLP

**The Firm:** This "*dynamic*" group, based in New York, Chicago and Los Angeles, is "*definitely on the rise.*" Commentators indicated that over recent years the team has shown "*great abilities*" in the securitization field and significantly increased its market share in the CMBS arena. The team is particularly popular among Wall Street investment banks. The group's experience in structured financings also involves a full array of non-real estate assets such as equipment leases, credit card receivables and automobile loans. It has also fortified its experience in the CDO and CLO market.

**The Lawyers:** Head of the MBS team, **Kevin Blauch** is said to be one of the "*very best*" lawyers to advise on CMBS transactions.

**Clients/Work Highlights:** Morgan Stanley; JPMorgan; Deutsche Bank; Bear Stearns; Merrill Lynch and CSFB.

### Weil, Gotshal & Manges LLP
See firm details p.1565

**The Firm:** The firm has combined its "*distinguished*" securitization and derivatives practices to provide clients with integrated structured finance advice. Issuers, underwriters, credit enhancers and trustees routinely call upon these "*deeply experienced*" lawyers to advise on the most complex and innovative transactions. Examples of groundbreaking structures include acting on the first asset-backed MTN offering to be effected by a bankrupt company. The group also advised on the first securitization of airline ticket receivables as well as assisting in the securitization of auto, student and equipment loans.

**The Lawyers:** **Frank Nocco** (see p.123) heads the structured finance and derivatives practice. He is said to have "*excellent judgment*" and an effective, deal-focused approach to negotiations.

**Clients/Work Highlights:** Lehman Brothers; MBIA Insurance; Rabobank; Wachovia and WestLB.

### Other Notable Practitioners

**Paul Murphy** from Moore & Van Allen, PLLC remains a leading figure in Charlotte's securitization marketplace; his practice includes RMBS, CMBS and healthcare receivable transactions. **David Galainena** (see p.101) at Winston Strawn LLP in Chicago receives praise for his "*can-do attitude and exemplary commercial drive.*" His practice focuses on asset-backed and MBS.

# ERISA LITIGATION

| ERISA Litigation Leading Firms |
| --- |
| 1 MORGAN, LEWIS & BOCKIUS LLP |
| O'MELVENY & MYERS LLP |
| PROSKAUER ROSE LLP |
| STEPTOE & JOHNSON LLP |
| 2 ALSTON & BIRD LLP |
| GIBSON, DUNN & CRUTCHER LLP |
| MCDERMOTT WILL & EMERY |
| 3 COVINGTON & BURLING |
| GROOM LAW GROUP |
| KILPATRICK STOCKTON LLP |
| VEDDER, PRICE, KAUFMAN & KAMMHOLZ |

| Leading Individuals | |
| --- | --- |
| 1 ECCLES Bob | *O'Melveny & Myers LLP* |
| ONDRASIK Paul | *Steptoe & Johnson LLP* |
| SHAPIRO Howard | *Proskauer Rose LLP* |
| 2 BRADEN Gregory | *Alston & Bird LLP* |
| KALLSTROM D Ward | *Morgan, Lewis & Bockius LLP* |
| KILBERG William | *Gibson, Dunn & Crutcher LLP* |
| ORTELERE Brian | *Morgan, Lewis & Bockius LLP* |
| ROSS Nancy | *McDermott Will & Emery* |
| 3 BAKER James | *Jones Day* |
| BOIES Bill | *McDermott Will & Emery* |
| HINSON H Douglas | *Alston & Bird LLP* |
| HUVELLE Jeffrey | *Covington & Burling* |
| SACHER Steven | *Kilpatrick Stockton LLP* |
| SCALLET Edward | *Groom Law Group* |
| WOLF Charles | *Vedder, Price, Kaufman & Kammholz* |

## Band 1

### Morgan, Lewis & Bockius LLP
See firm details p.1758

**The Firm:** *"Outstanding in terms of expertise, results and responsiveness,"* Morgan Lewis boasts the largest ERISA litigation taskforce in the USA. Spread across San Francisco, Chicago, New York, Pennsylvania, Washington DC and Dallas, the team is representing high-profile clients in many of the current 'stock drop' cases, where employees who invested company stock in a 401k plan incurred financial losses as the stock suffered. It has acted for US Airways, Freddie Mac and Touch America among others and, in line with the national trend, has been busy with cash balance claims, handling a major case for CIGNA. The firm has also witnessed an increase in fiduciary litigation against investment managers. More established forms of ERISA litigation center around retiree medical benefits. Here the team is spearheading a case for Unisys connected with the company's early retirement incentive programs. The firm also offers clients a specialized ESOP transactional unit that enhances its overall capabilities in this arena and complements its impressive labor and employment practice.

**The Lawyers:** *"One of the foremost experts in the area,"* **Brian Ortelere** (see p.124) cochairs the ERISA litigation practice alongside his equally talented partner, **Ward Kallstrom** (see p.111). Clients regard Philadelphia-based Ortelere as *"a substantive expert, who is comfortable handling the technical and esoteric aspects of ERISA."* Recent successes include acting for ABB in a cash balance claim, and representing Vanguard, the directed trustee in the Dynergy case. Leading the charge on the West Coast, Kallstrom is providing the ERISA input on a double class action for Health Net, a medical insurance provider. The presence of employee benefits specialist, Steve Spencer, adds considerable value to the practice.

### O'Melveny & Myers LLP
See firm details p.336

**The Firm:** This *"top-notch"* national player is said to have *"terrific bench strength"* when it comes to ERISA litigation. According to clients it has proven trial experience and the tactical skills to master the most complex disputes. Examples include acting as lead defense attorneys in US Trust v Keach, a case concerning an ESOP that acquired a major share in Foster & Gallagher, which then went bankrupt. The team is also currently handling several cases on behalf of directed trustees, institutions that have been increasingly swept into ERISA class actions since the Enron and WorldCom cases. Other clients include employers, fiduciaries and service providers embroiled in any kind of ERISA litigation at both the state and federal level, and the firm continues to uphold a reputation for representing major managed care companies.

**The Lawyers:** **Bob Eccles** (see p.97) is lauded by his clients as *"the all-encompassing ERISA expert, who is equally capable of trying any case and of being the tactical negotiator."* They also admire his *"wonderful facility for taking complex issues and distilling them in such a way that they make sense."* Much of the credit for the group's high profile can be laid at the feet of this seasoned practitioner, who successfully transferred the skills and experience gained as former head ERISA attorney at the DOL into private practice.

### Proskauer Rose LLP
See firm details p.1551

**The Firm:** With the acquisition of Howard Shapiro's team from Shook, Hardy & Bacon in October 2004, this firm has *"leveraged itself into a high position,"* from where it attracts the enthusiastic praise of the market. The team *"provides incredible customer service,"* according to interviewees, tackling a diverse range of challenging instructions. As one client put it: *"They have all the tools."* A 13-strong group, located in Florida, New Orleans and New York, focuses on ERISA litigation, handling a large number of 401k cases. Notable examples include Langbecker v EDS, which is pending before the Fifth Circuit Court of Appeals. The team is also working on a cash balance case for a prominent financial services company.

**The Lawyers:** The *"masterful and charismatic"* **Howard Shapiro** (see p.134) *"knows ERISA like the back of his hand,"* according to clients. He was warmly recommended to researchers as a *"top-class national player"* who enjoys an *"excellent practice with both breadth and depth."* Though the team is centered on Shapiro, he is said to be *"good at developing people"* and *"willing to share his expertise"* with a group of ERISA litigators that also includes Myron Rumeld and Robert Rachal.

### Steptoe & Johnson LLP
See firm details p.576

**The Firm:** *"At the top of the list"* for ERISA and employee benefits, this firm is home to a prestigious group of former government officials with almost unrivaled experience in the industry. It represents plan sponsors, fiduciaries and service providers in cases relating to the investment of 401k plan assets in company stock, recently settling a major class action on behalf of Dynegy. Other highlights include representing the directed trustee, Deutsche Bank, in the case against Qwest. Outside the 'stock drop' arena, the team advised on a high-profile matter brought by the DOL against the trustees of the Plumbers and Pipefitters National Pension Fund. This concerned the plan's investment in the Diplomat Resort and Country Club in Florida. It also took part in the United Airlines bankruptcy case, representing the independent fiduciary appointed to the company's pension plan.

**The Lawyers:** **Paul Ondrasik** (see p.124) was described to researchers as the *"elder statesman"* of the ERISA litigation Bar. According to clients, *"there are not too many people who can carry his briefcase,"* while his experience as a legal clerk in the highest circles *"gives him an enormous step up in terms of insider knowledge."* Market sources also note that, as an experienced litigator, he shows *"good judgment in terms of separating the primary from the secondary issues."*

## Band 2

### Alston & Bird LLP
See firm details p.728

**The Firm:** This dedicated unit is home to a group of *"knowledgeable and determined"* ERISA litigators, who are equally comfortable advising on the esoteric details of ERISA law as they are fighting for a client in the courtroom. The department handles all forms of benefits litigation, acting for every type of defendant. Many of its instructions arrive on a standalone basis. Among the team's stellar clients are companies like Goodyear, ChoicePoint and Coca-Cola, and it is currently acting for AIG American General in multidistrict litigation concerning the termination of benefits. The firm also brings its weight to bear in lobbying the US regulatory agencies for changes in the law, most recently in connection with cash balance litigation.

The Lawyers: **Greg Braden** (see p.89) is renowned as "*a talented and aggressive litigator*," who brings an extremely high level of expertise to his casework. He is part of a growing team that is increasingly attracting nationwide litigation. Much of the credit for its development falls to group head, **Doug Hinson** (see p.107), a "*calm lawyer who doesn't over react but is passionate about winning*." Hinson handles both ERISA and securities litigation, a combination that is helpful to clients who describe him as an attorney who can "*hit the ground running*."

## Gibson, Dunn & Crutcher LLP

See firm details p.328

The Firm: This "*litigation powerhouse*" earns a place in the table due to its "*tactical skills in ERISA and its litigation capabilities*." The team is said to be "*especially well versed in the law*," a claim given flesh by its involvement in many of the benchmark ERISA cases since its enactment in 1974. These include the WorldCom bankruptcy, in which the team scored a decisive victory for Merrill Lynch Trust Company, the directed trustee of the company's 401k plan. The firm boasts a long-established reputation in the managed care arena. Here, it successfully represented Aetna before the US Supreme Court, in a case that established that participants cannot sue under state law for coverage decisions.

The Lawyers: **Bill Kilberg** (see p.113) "*is the kind of guy you want in your corner if you are facing major litigation*," say clients. The leader of the practice, his years of experience at the DOL give him "*extra insight*" and ensure that clients receive a value-added service. The group can also call upon appellate lawyer Miguel Estrada.

## McDermott Will & Emery

See firm details p.878

The Firm: According to clients, this team brings "*substantive knowledge to the table*" and has a "*jumpstart as far as experience goes*." Interviewees were quick to point to the firm's depth of resources as a major advantage, especially in the employee benefits arena. As one stated: "*It has the horsepower and the back-up required*." Significant victories include a favorable ruling for the defendant in Berger v AXA Network, a case concerning the benefits rights of life insurance sales agents, who were classified as 'independent contractors' rather than 'employees'. The firm is also attracting an impressive share of 'stock drop' cases from prominent corporates, such as GM. In the retiree health insurance space, the team successfully advised Equitable Life Assurance in a class action involving 5,000 insurance agents.

The Lawyers: "*Steeped in the law*," **Nancy Ross** (see p.130) is a "*creative and zealous advocate*" capable of running highly complex litigation. A recent jewel in her crown was representing the board chairman of Foster & Gallagher in the Keach v US Trust case. She devotes her practice full-time to ERISA disputes, where she is supported by **Bill Boies** (see p.89). Clients readily turn to Boies for 'bet the ranch' type cases and hail him as a "*top-notch, well-seasoned litigator in the ERISA arena*." He has built his reputation acting for financial institutions in weighty cases centered on securities and fraud issues.

## Band 3

## Covington & Burling

See firm details p.563

The Firm: With the support of a "*premier*" ERISA tax and counseling group, this team is well positioned to tackle benefits litigation from its DC base. A string of high-profile cases for national clients, such as Verizon, GE Capital Mortgage Services and Union Pacific, demonstrates this. Notable examples include Cooper v IBM, a hotly contested piece of litigation examining whether or not cash balance plans are age discriminatory. The firm also found itself in the spotlight in Re: Schering-Plough, a significant 'stock drop' case that is still awaiting a verdict. Overall, clients deem the firm to be "*excellent from both a procedural and a substantive perspective*."

The Lawyers: **Jeffrey Huvelle** (see p.109) spearheads the firm's ERISA litigation efforts. A "*creative*" lawyer who provides "*good analysis of the matter in hand*," he is leading the defense for IBM.

## Groom Law Group

The Firm: Clients facing potential lawsuits are drawn to this boutique employee benefits firm because of its "*expertise in the field, coupled with its litigation experience*." It handles a variety of disputes under ERISA, including 'stock drop' litigation, cash balance matters and cases concerning employee classification. The group is especially well known for representing service providers, such as insurers, actuarial consulting firms and law firms that work for benefit plans, and it has carved a niche for itself in professional malpractice cases. The firm also acts for individuals, handling benefit claims for members of large institutional disability and pension plans, such as the National Football League Players Association.

The Lawyers: Head of litigation **Ted Scallet** is a "*client-oriented*" adviser who is part of a troop of DOL alumni at this prestigious firm. He focuses on employer stock and investment litigation.

## Kilpatrick Stockton LLP

See firm details p.735

The Firm: Clients rely on this firm's specialist knowledge of ERISA to see them through all forms of litigation involving pension and welfare plans. The firm has invested in an "*excellent cadre of ERISA lawyers*" who practice full time in the area, counseling and defending plan sponsors throughout the country. High-level appointments include acting for Xerox in a securities fraud case relating to a drop in the company's stock. The firm is also acting for Delta Air Lines in a 'stock drop' case that was filed before the airline entered Chapter 11 proceedings. Unusually, it is currently handling another case where a rise in company stock is the point of contention.

The Lawyers: "*One of the leading ERISA practitioners in the country*," **Steve Sacher** (see p.132) is recognized by market commentators as "*responsive, thoughtful and extremely good at what he does*." His forte lies in complex fiduciary responsibility matters and his experience includes representing clients in federal courts and before the DOL.

## Vedder, Price, Kaufman & Kammholz

See firm details p.885

The Firm: Home to "*extremely sharp litigators who get to the core issues quickly*," this firm represents clients around the country in a variety of employee benefits matters. The team's close cooperation with its employment and labor law group is said to give it an advantage over competitors, particularly in relation to multiemployer plan issues. The firm boasts an impressive group of European clients, such as Syngenta and Diageo, and is currently representing Novartis in a case pertaining to the company's pension plan benefit accrual scheme. Current challenges for the group include the redesign of healthcare programs, in order to make them more affordable for plan sponsors as the cost of healthcare in the US has risen.

The Lawyers: **Chuck Wolf** "*has a good understanding of ERISA and can translate that into advice that addresses client concerns*." A talented lawyer, his practice encompasses ERISA litigation as well as other labor and employment, and employee benefit issues.

## Other Notable Practitioners

"*Hands-on and practical*," **James Baker** (see p.86) has devoted 20 years of practice to ERISA litigation. His move to Jones Day, a preeminent litigation outfit, provides him with the platform to develop the firm's national practice in this arena. Notable cases include City of Eugene v State Public Employees Retirement Board, where a 'win-win' settlement was reached in a $2 billion dispute.

# FINANCIAL SERVICES

## Cleary Gottlieb Steen & Hamilton LLP

See firm details p.1525

**The Firm:** The firm's financial institutions advisory practice is generally perceived to be "*the greatest in the country.*" A "*most comprehensively talented group,*" it spans the entire range of regulatory, transactional and enforcement issues that confronts its "*prestigious financial house clients*" in their daily activities or their business expansion strategies. With an equally strong presence in New York and Washington, DC the firm is ideally positioned to fully service its clients, while maintaining close ties with the regulatory agencies. Financial institutions M&A is its forte as illustrated by its involvement in the highest-profile deals in recent years. A small sample of the firm's caseload for 2005 includes representing Banc of America in its $35 billion acquisition of MBNA and its $3 billion investment in China Construction Bank. The team brings to bear decades of exceptional depth and breadth of corporate and capital markets expertise and, as such, is particularly rated for its advice on compliance with federal and state securities laws and regulations. The firm's international reach also ensures its popularity among foreign banks; it has been selected to represent the Institute of International Bankers before US financial policy-makers. The practice also includes the handling of investigations and enforcement matters. For example, the DC team acted as counsel to the nonmanagement directors of Riggs Bank regarding various regulatory investigations.

**The Lawyers:** Clients and peers have "*immense respect* for **Bob Tortoriello**'s (see p.138) "*unsurpassed*" securities regulations expertise. Also recognized as a bank M&A expert, he recently advised Sherman Financial Group in its acquisition of Marin National Bancorp and its credit card bank operation, First National Bank of Marin. Also strongly endorsed is **Jack Murphy** (see p.122), a "*formidable, straightforward and personable adviser.*" Clients swear by him for "*first-class advice on financial institution M&A and business expansion.*" He recently represented Capital One in its acquisition of Hibernia Bank. **Michael Ryan** (see p.132) possesses "*tremendous experience of bank M&A,*" and works with the next generation of "*spectacular young partners*" such as **Paul Glotzer** (see p.102) (based in New York) and **Derek Bush** (see p.91) (located in DC). These two have developed respected practices advising private equity and hedge funds on the regulatory implications of their minority investments in US banks.

**Clients/Work Highlights:** Banco de Chile; Capital One; CSFB; BBVA Bancomer; Bank of America; Goldman Sachs; HSBC; Laredo National Bank; Barclays; Wells Fargo; Crédit Agricole; Calyon; Texas Pacific Group; Citigroup; BNP Paribas and Riggs Bank. The client base also includes other bank holding companies, investment banks, swaps dealers, clearinghouses, investment managers, hedge funds and private equity firms.

## Sullivan & Cromwell LLP

See firm details p.1558

**The Firm:** Characterized by "*an extraordinary breadth of expertise and the highest professional standards,*" the firm's financial institutions group belongs to the elite of regulatory practices. The group, which fields experts in New York and Los Angeles, is home to "*legendary practitioners*" and is geared to advise its stellar client base across the full spectrum of regulatory, transactional and enforcement issues. The team "*distances many of its competitors*" in the bank M&A field and has been involved in the largest deals in US banking history. Recent highlights include advising the board of JPMorgan regarding its $60 billion acquisition of Bank One. The team also represented major South African retail lender Absa Group, in the sale of 60% of its stake to Barclays for $5.5 billion. Its extensive experience in the securities industry and its strength in derivatives markets complements this group's advice on federal and state securities laws and regulations. A highly skilled litigation practice is on hand to provide representation in proceedings before the regulators.

**The Lawyers:** When asked to name the most respected member of the profession, observers invariably mentioned the "*exceptional*" **Rodgin Cohen** (see p.92). This outstanding bank M&A expert has been involved in most of the major bank acquisitions in the USA and abroad and has also worked on a significant number of cross-industry acquisitions. Clients prize the fact that "*his name is a synonym for credibility and authority in the regulators' minds.*" Clients can also call upon the "*extremely able, thorough and professional*" **Michael Wiseman** (see p.142). He commends immense respect for his experience in bank M&A and capital markets regulatory matters. His practice also encompasses enforcement issues. Younger partner **Mark Menting** (see p.120) is getting a "*seriously enviable reputation,*" said sources in the field of bank M&A. In 2005 he had a prolific year, as he advised Cullen/Frost Bankers in its $107 million acquisition of Horizon Capital Bank, its $31 million acquisition of Texas Community Bank and Trust and its $87 million acquisition of Alamo Bank. Also recommended was **Mitchell Eitel** (see p.98), an impressive young partner, "*technically as good as it gets and very client-friendly.*" **Stanley Farrar** (see p.98) oversees the financial services work in the Los Angeles office. He is a "*distinguished and respected dean of the profession.*"

**Clients/Work Highlights:** The firm's client base includes AIG; Bank of New York; Bankers Trust New York; Barclays; Dresdner Bank; The New York Clearing House; UBS and Wachovia. The team also represents some of the largest US and foreign insurance companies and investment management companies.

## Arnold & Porter LLP

See firm details p.560

**The Firm:** "*Historical dedication to regulatory matters and wealth of experience*" naturally put this group among the leading financial services practices in the country. The team is chiefly based in Washington, DC but represents a broad cross-section of US and international financial services clients. Among its strengths are the assistance provided to firms in entering new lines of business and structuring new products, as well as expanding banking activities internationally through the establishment of foreign branches. Bank M&A regulatory advice is also a major focus of the team, and according to observers, it is particularly renowned for its advice on the antitrust implications of financial institutions M&A and strategic alliances. The team's recent caseload includes advising BB&T on all the regulatory implications of its acquisition of First Virginia Bank. Attorneys also played a prominent role in the most significant federal banking litigation of the past decades and the group is recognized as one of the strongest to advise on the Bank Secrecy Act, privacy matters and discriminative lending, among other issues.

**The Lawyers:** The team includes several attorneys who have held senior positions at the key federal regulatory agencies. Among them is **John Hawke** (see p.106), founder of the practice and a "*highly respected pioneer of the profession.*" **Richard Alexander** (see p.84) is an exceptional supervisory counselor, strongly endorsed for his "*excellent bedside manners and pragmatic advice.*" According to clients, he "*actually listens to his clients and is extremely fast at getting to grips with the issues.*" **Michael Mierzewski** (see p.121) is a "*premier regulatory enforcement lawyer,*" particularly rated for his antitrust expertise.

**Clients/Work Highlights:** State Farm; BB&T; Texas Pacific Group; JPMorgan; Bank of America and HSBC.

## Morrison & Foerster LLP
See firm details p.335

**The Firm:** The firm is established as one of the largest and finest financial services regulatory practices in the USA. With teams of "*intellectually superb lawyers*" based in San Francisco, Los Angeles, New York and Washington, DC it is "*everywhere its clients need it to be*" and provides the broadest array of services. According to commentators, the group is "*indisputably the strongest in the field of consumer financial services and retail banking.*" It provides well-crafted advice on the regulatory and compliance requirements for credit cards, debit cards and other payment products, as well as privacy and electronic payment matters. Expertise in financial institutions M&A is another string to the group's bow. In 2005, the team represented Union Bank of California in the sale of its International Banking Group's operations and acted for the same client in its acquisition of the corporate trust business of Bank of Tokyo-Mitsubishi Trust Company. Rounding out the picture is a team of financial services litigators, who provide clients with advice regarding consumer class actions and regulatory enforcement proceedings.

**The Lawyers:** Based in San Francisco, **Roland Brandel** (see p.89) enjoys a national reputation as a "*landmark of the profession*" and the "*driving force*" in the field of consumer financial services. He particularly focuses on electronic payment systems issues. In Los Angeles, **Henry Fields** (see p.99) is an internationally respected bank M&A expert. Clients praise his "*experience, dedication and enthusiasm*" and see him as the "*first port of call when creative structures are needed.*" Of late he has been extremely active in Asia and notably represented SinoPac Financial Holdings on the US regulatory matters arising from its acquisition of International Bank of Taipei. The excellent **Richard Fischer** (see p.99), who is based in DC, also commands respect for his "*unequaled expertise of retail banking regulatory issues,*" while **Oliver Ireland** (see p.109) is extremely knowledgeable on all matters of financial regulatory compliance. Ireland's former position with the Federal Reserve "*gives him a unique understanding of the regulations*" and "*excellent working relations with the regulators.*"

**Clients/Work Highlights:** Clients includes both domestic and foreign banks and other financial services organizations, as well as their holding companies and affiliates. These include GBC Bancorp; The Bank of East Asia; Chinatrust Commercial Bank; Bank of America; JPMorgan Chase; Japan Bank for International Cooperation; Providian Financial; Société Générale; Travelers; Visa and Wells Fargo.

## Sidley Austin LLP
See firm details p.883

**The Firm:** Commentators recommended this "*incredibly talented*" group for the representation of retail financial services institutions. Clients, who "*have total confidence in the team's legal knowledge and skills,*" were particularly impressed by the "*exceptional quality of work at associate level.*" This group concentrates on representing US and foreign banks, with an emphasis on savings associations and depository institutions, as well as other diversified financial services companies in the full range of consumer financial services regulations. In particular, the team provides first-rate advice on financial privacy issues. And, through advice to financial institutions, e-commerce startups and payments networks, the team is intimately involved in all aspects of Internet financial services. Building on its historical funds expertise, the firm acts for bank clients in obtaining regulatory approval for, and in helping implement, programs involving pooled investment vehicles such as commodity funds, bank common trust funds and collective investment funds.

**The Lawyers:** **William Eckland** (see p.97) focuses on federal regulatory issues governing the operations of depository institutions and is also actively involved in M&A and restructuring of financial institutions. **Michael McEneney** (see p.119), a "*very able regulatory lawyer, excellent for advice on privacy issues,*" provides assistance on the regulatory issues affecting retail banking.

**Clients/Work Highlights:** The group advises US and foreign banks, bank holding companies, savings associations and payment systems, as well as securities, insurance, finance, mortgage and other diversified financial services companies.

## Simpson Thacher & Bartlett LLP
See firm details p.1555

**The Firm:** This financial institution group is one of the "*most authoritative and respected practices*" in the USA, proclaimed sources. The team's lawyers regularly advise on banking, securities and corporate law issues affecting commercial and investment banks as well as private equity clients. These "*deeply experienced, trustworthy lawyers*" are well equipped to act on the development of new products and activities, provide ongoing regulatory advice and also assist clients in regulatory investigations. M&A involving banks and other financial institutions stands out amid the broad workload; peers endorsed the firm's involvement in the most prestigious transactions of recent years. For example, it counseled JPMorgan Chase in each of its major merger transactions and the related regulatory approvals. Capitalizing on its dominance of the private equity sector, the group is also often found counseling private equity funds on their minority investments in financial institutions.

**The Lawyers:** Originally trained as an M&A lawyer, **Lee Meyerson** (see p.121) has "*developed into one of the finest financial institutions M&A regulatory experts over the years.*" He heads the firm's financial institutions practice and his caseload for 2005 included representing Washington Mutual in its $6.6 billion acquisition of Providian Financial and advising The Toronto-Dominion Bank in its $3.8 billion acquisition of a majority interest in Banknorth. He also assisted Federated Department Stores in the sale of its credit card portfolio to Citigroup for $7.4 billion. Also strongly recommended are **Gary Rice** (see p.129) ("*exceptional expert on bank M&A and capital markets regulations*") and **John Walker** (see p.140), who was particularly rated for his first-class advice on business growth and expansion of financial services institutions.

**Clients/Work Highlights:** The firm's client base includes Mizuho Financial Group, Greenwich Capital Markets and Shinsei Bank among many others.

### Skadden, Arps, Slate, Meagher & Flom LLP & Affiliates

See firm details p.1557

**The Firm:** The firm is famed for the high caliber of its advice on financial institutions M&A and related regulatory issues. The financial services group works hand in hand with the firm's powerful M&A practice in order to provide savings banks, mortgage companies, investors and investment banks with all the necessary assistance to complete such transactions. This includes assisting its prestigious client base in getting authorizations from the relevant regulatory agencies, organizing proxy contests or acquiring controlling stock position and finally structuring and executing M&A transactions. According to observers, a distinctive strength of the team resides in its "*unparalleled expertise on antitrust considerations in connection with M&A and joint ventures.*" The group counts many of the country's largest financial institutions among its clients. Foremost among these are JPMorgan, which the team advised in its acquisition of Bank One's corporate trust business, and Citigroup, which it advised on the acquisition of Sears Roebuck's credit card business. In the regulatory arena, the group has also become increasingly active in investigations and regularly represents clients in various types of civil and criminal matters. Largely recognized as a "*full-scale practice,*" the group is also chosen to advise on the full array of federal and state regulations affecting financial institutions, particularly capital markets regulations.

**The Lawyers:** **Bill Sweet** (see p.137) earned the highest marks for his "*full-blown regulatory expertise,*" which includes financial institutions M&A, regulatory and enforcement experience. His practice concentrates chiefly on representing major investment banks and mutual funds in M&A matters. **William Rubenstein** (see p.131) is also a regulatory bank M&A adviser. "*He is an excellent business generator, and very practical deal-maker.*" Co-head of the firm's financial institutions M&A practice, **Fred White** (see p.142) is described as a "*hugely talented and knowledgeable bank M&A expert.*"

**Clients/Work Highlights:** Lone Star Funds; Citigroup; US Trust; Dresdner Bank; Charles Schwab; Franklin Resources; Travelers; First Nationwide Holdings and Bank of Boston Corporation.

### Covington & Burling

See firm details p.563

**The Firm:** Best known for its work in the regulatory compliance and enforcement spheres, this team of "*extremely knowledgeable lawyers*" provides assistance to banks, thrifts and other financial services providers across the USA. Its caseload features M&A, tax and securities matters, privacy and consumer protection issues. Of late, the team has been particularly busy handling significant litigation for financial services providers. One particular highlight was representing Freddie Mac in the ongoing resolution of the issues surrounding its $5 billion restatement and in the defense of a securities law class action. Observers added that the team provides high-quality advice on preemption litigation and has the capacity to represent clients in legislative proposals pending before lawmakers. For example, it is currently working with Congress on a reform to modify the status of government-sponsored enterprises (GSEs). Another source of work originates from foreign-based clients seeking advice on the acquisition of US financial institutions and other ongoing operations, as well as assisting domestic clients with activities abroad.

**The Lawyers:** **Stuart Stock** (see p.136) has "*successfully translated his banking knowledge into the most fantastic regulatory expertise,*" agreed sources. His practice is extremely versatile and includes regulatory enforcement and litigation, ongoing regulatory compliance advice and M&A expertise. "*A brilliant young partner,*" **Mark Plotkin** (see p.126) is seen by many as the "*natural successor to Stuart Stock.*" His experience includes advice on regulatory security and technology issues as well as enforcement representation. **Jean Veta**'s (see p.139) practice focuses exclusively on enforcement and litigation matters. Observers were impressed by her "*ability to come up with creative ways to present her clients' cases.*" A former member of the DOJ, she enjoys "*invaluable credibility with the regulators.*" Her experience includes safety and soundness, anti-money laundering and lending discrimination matters.

**Clients/Work Highlights:** Abbey; American Bankers Association; American Council of Life Insurers; Bank of America; Farm Credit Council and Farm Credit Banks; Freddie Mac; Financial Services Sector Coordinating Council; Microsoft; Mortgage Electronic Registration System; The Northern Trust Company; Riggs Corporation; UBS Warburg and Wilmington Trust.

### Davis Polk & Wardwell

See firm details p.1528

**The Firm:** According to market participants, the firm has a "*long tradition and legacy of excellence for bank regulatory work.*" The financial institutions group concentrates on providing bank and broker-dealer regulatory advice in M&A and capital markets activities. In the bank M&A field, the group particularly distinguishes itself on sophisticated cross-border transactions; it provided regulatory advice to UBS regarding its minority investment in the recently privatized Bank of China. Clients appreciated that the group "*delivers the full package.*" Beyond regulatory advice, it also possesses the faculties to execute the transactions. In the field of securities regulations, the team is "*second to none*" in the eyes of some clients when it comes to derivatives products marketing and energy contract trading. The firm's litigators also routinely handle investigations of bank fraud and money laundering, and are acclaimed for their representation of insurance companies.

**The Lawyers:** The "*creative and intellectually gifted* **Randall Guynn** (see p.104) *possesses the strategic insight that gives his clients an edge in any situation.*" He is currently focusing on the burgeoning Chinese institutional market.

**Clients/Work Highlights:** Industrial and Commercial Bank of China; RBS; ABN AMRO; JPMorgan; Citigroup; BSCH; CSFB; Deutsche Bank; Lehman Brothers and Rabobank.

## Debevoise & Plimpton LLP

See firm details p.1529

**The Firm:** The market consensus is that the firm has "*no match in the regulatory representation of insurance companies and private equity funds.*" Teams based in both New York and Washington, DC work for major insurers on the full range of regulatory, transactional, enforcement and litigation matters. A recent highlight was its representation of AXA Financial in its $2.3 billion acquisition of the MONY Group, an insurance and thrift holding company. Another major matter was to advise UFJ Holdings in the proposed management integration of Mitsubishi Tokyo Financial Group. The firm also extensively advises investment companies and preeminent private equity or hedge funds on the regulatory implications of cross-industry activities. A "*wonderful team of litigators*" also manages enforcement issues, internal reviews and litigation matters.

**The Lawyers:** **Paul Lee** is a dominant figure in the firm's financial institutions group. He offers a "*fantastic range of skills in the regulatory banking and insurance fields,*" said clients.

**Clients/Work Highlights:** UFJ Bank; Bank of China; HSBC; NuVerse Advisors and Promontory Financial Group.

## Pillsbury Winthrop Shaw Pittman LLP

See firm details p.1550

**The Firm:** One of the broadest practices in the country, it fields approximately 30 attorneys across offices in New York, California and Washington, DC. The April 2005 merger has brought together Pillsbury Winthrop's renowned financial services transactional expertise, particularly in the M&A field, and Shaw Pittman's acclaimed expertise on regulatory matters for foreign financial institutions. Work here spans the full range of strategic, regulatory, compliance and enforcement matters, in particular obtaining regulatory approvals for M&A, expanding banking operations and new product launches. A recent transactional highlight was the team's advice to BNP Paribas and its subsidiary BancWest Corporation in their $1.3 billion acquisition of Community First BancShares and their $245 million acquisition of USDB Bancorp. When the situation warrants, the team also conducts comprehensive internal investigations, and defends clients in regulatory investigations and enforcement proceedings. A major success in this field was to negotiate favorable consent agreements and civil money penalty for Banco de Chile in the context of money laundering and related investigations.

**The Lawyers:** Based in the San Francisco office, **Rodney Peck** (see p.125) is a "*deeply experienced*" attorney, particularly in the M&A field, a specialism he shares with **Robert Webster** (see p.141) in New York. Observers especially highlighted Webster's recent enforcement caseload.

**Clients/Work Highlights:** The group represents a diverse client base of financial services organizations from around the world including banks, thrifts, insurance and reinsurance firms, broker-dealers, investment advisers and private equity funds. The most important clients include Institute of International Bankers; Bank Hapoalim; The Bank of New York Company; Chevy Chase Bank; Dresdner Bank; Fortis Bank and Wells Fargo.

## Shearman & Sterling LLP

See firm details p.1554

**The Firm:** The largest domestic financial institutions are the province of this practice. The team provides "*well thought-through, practical and commercial advice*" on regulatory issues principally relating to wholesale and retail businesses, but is also visible in the broker-dealer, insurance and investment management industries. It counsels clients on day-to-day matters; with an emphasis on money laundering, facilitation payments, consumer legislation and data protection regulations. Attorneys here are also routinely approached by the most dynamic financial institutions to assist and facilitate their development of new products, and are engaged in legislative lobbying. The structuring, regulation and execution of financial institutions M&A is among the group's strengths. For example, it represented Citigroup in the acquisition of Washington Mutual Finance Corporation.

**The Lawyers:** **Brad Sabel** (see p.132) impresses clients as a "*bright, thorough and creative adviser.*" His recent experience includes representing UFJ Holdings in its merger with Mitsubishi Tokyo Financial Group.

**Clients/Work Highlights:** Alex.Brown; BHF Securities; Citigroup; CSFB; CyberCorp; Deutsche Bank; Goldman Sachs; Merrill Lynch; Industrial Bank of Japan; NASD and Prudential Real Estate.

## Wachtell, Lipton, Rosen & Katz

See firm details p.1561

**The Firm:** "*Wachtell is the place to go for the highest quality bank M&A regulatory advice.*" A substantial team of attorneys is dedicated to advising clients on the regulatory and antitrust implications of their M&A and other strategic alliances. Over recent years, the team has been involved in high-caliber deals, such as its representation of MBNA in its acquisition by Bank of America. It also acted for Hibernia in its acquisition by Capital One. Clients also value the fact that the firm assists them "*from start to finish – after advising on the regulatory issues it also provides the resources to execute the transaction.*" In a political environment prone to regulatory scrutiny and investigations, the firm has also recently developed internal investigation and enforcement capacities in order to fully service its clients.

**The Lawyers:** **Ed Herlihy** (see p.106) is "*just about the best around*" for bank M&A. He specializes in the largest and most complex bank and financial institution M&A and recapitalizations throughout the USA and abroad. **Craig Wasserman** (see p.141) also enjoys a fantastic reputation in the field. His practice extends to complex corporate governance, securities, regulatory and compliance matters. **Richard Kim** (see p.113) combines "*technical proficiency and strong business sense.*" He specializes in representing banks, thrifts, credit card issuers and insurance companies.

**Clients/Work Highlights:** The group represents major domestic financial institutions including Hibernia and MBNA.

## WilmerHale

See firm details p.580

**The Firm:** Its ability to "*combine genuinely first-rate expertise in both regulatory and enforcement fields*" ensures this financial services practice a national prominence. Hailed as "*the champions*" of consumer financial services and retail banking, the group's attorneys routinely advise on compliance with the privacy and information security legislation, the Fair Credit Reporting Act, Equal Credit Opportunity Act and Electronic Funds Transfer Act, among others. The firm also allocates significant resources to the lobbying of federal rulemakers and has been influential in matters involving consumer credit. On the enforcement and litigation side, it is "*exceptionally strong*" in investigations related to securities regulations, working closely with the securities group in enforcement actions concerning disclosure issues. Notable assignments in 2005 include representing the nonmanaging directors of Riggs Bank in investigation and litigation proceedings. The firm is also increasingly visible in the transactional arena and recently represented HSBC in business expansion matters, including its acquisition of a $3.5 billion mortgage financing business.

**The Lawyers:** **Russell Bruemmer** (see p.90) chairs the firm's financial institutions department. Clients value his "*consummate professionalism.*" He acted as lead counsel for Fannie Mae in regulatory proceedings leading to an accounting restatement and corporate restructuring. **Gregory Baer** (see p.86) was also strongly endorsed for his "*wide-ranging experience*" of banking regulatory and consumer credit matters. Commentators identified **William McLucas** (see p.120) and **Harry Weiss** (see p.141) as "*two of the most charismatic figures*" in the securities enforcement and litigation field.

**Clients/Work Highlights:** AOL; Morgan Stanley; Capital One; Merrill Lynch; TransUnion; Citibank; American Express; MBNA and Juniper Bank.

## Alston & Bird LLP

See firm details p.728

**The Firm:** Sources spoke of the firm's successful representation of major banks and their officials in investigation and enforcement proceedings, as well as ongoing regulatory and transactional matters. Attorneys based in the Atlanta and Washington, DC offices display "*clear-thinking abilities and provide sophisticated yet practical advice.*" The group's "*excellent credentials*" for enforcement representation particularly impressed market observers. Work in the field includes advising a senior officer of a major national bank in an Office of the Comptroller of the Currency (OCC) allegation regarding money laundering and representing a large regional bank in alleged violations of the Fair Lending Act. Instructions on the transactional side include representing Global Payments in its $200 million acquisition of DolEx Dollar Express, the largest US-to-Latin America money transfer business.

**The Lawyers:** **John Douglas** (see p.96) is chair of

the financial services and products group and practices in both the Atlanta and Washington, DC offices. He is generally recognized as a major player for financial institutions M&A.

**Clients/Work Highlights:** American Express Financial Advisors; American Home Mortgage Investment; CheckFree Corporation; Juniper Financial; Silicon Valley Bank; Sumitomo Mitsui Banking; UBS; Wachovia and Wells Fargo.

## Bingham McCutchen LLP
See firm details p.1110

**The Firm:** A major presence on the West Coast, this dedicated group of attorneys has developed a *"vibrant advisory practice"* for financial institutions corporate and regulatory matters. Companies in the financial sector seek out the firm for advice on transactional matters. Highlights for 2005 include representing Calnet Business Bank in its sale to the Irvine Bank and representing Westamerica Bank in its acquisition of Redwood Bank. General advice on bank regulatory and securities law compliance matters is also on the agenda here. Of late, the team has been increasingly busy advising on anti-money laundering issues and on the application of the Bank Secrecy Act.

**The Lawyers:** **James Rockett** (see p.130), a bank M&A expert and *"one of the most respected lawyers in Northern California,"* cochairs the firm's financial institutions corporate and regulatory group.

**Clients/Work Highlights:** Union Bank of California; Premier Valley Bank; First Financial Bancorp; Cathay Bancorp; UnionBanCal Corporation and LandAmerica Financial Group.

## Dechert LLP
See firm details p.1752

**The Firm:** The firm's work in the insurance and funds market, in relation to both transactional and regulatory matters, has secured it a high profile. Capitalizing on its broader investment management industry expertise, the team has been particularly active in the M&A of investment advisers and other financial services companies. For example, it recently acted on the integration of JPMorgan and Bank One's asset management businesses. The firm also displayed its knowledge of the funds industry when advising the Association for the Advancement of Retired Persons on the merits of implementing its own mutual fund. For insurance companies, the team has been instrumental in creating and marketing some of the most innovative investment products. It also represents financial services clients in examinations, inspections, investigations and formal proceedings by the SEC.

**The Lawyers:** Joseph Fleming and Paul Huey-Burns are the main contacts at the firm.

**Clients/Work Highlights:** JPMorgan; Bank One; AIG Global Investment Group; Legg Mason; Nationwide; Pacific Life and Sun America.

## Fried, Frank, Harris, Shriver & Jacobson LLP
See firm details p.1532

**The Firm:** According to observers, the firm's financial institutions group is *"doing an excellent job on the more sophisticated regulatory matters."* Although the team routinely acts for a variety of financial institutions in dealing with corporate and transactional matters, it is better known for its advice on day-to-day regulatory compliance and its enforcement prowess. Its effective representations in the area of contested financial institutions transactions are widely recognized, such as bank litigation, including the defense of fair lending challenges and lawsuits. Observers also noted that the group particularly distinguishes itself in the federal home loan industry and has built a top-flight reputation for GSE defense. In 2005 attorneys represented the former chief operating officer of Freddie Mac in regulatory investigations regarding the GSE's accounting scandal. Other successes include negotiating the first-ever enforcement agreements issued by the Federal Housing Finance Board on behalf of the Federal Home Loan Banks of Chicago and Seattle.

**The Lawyers:** Clients described **Thomas Vartanian** (see p.139) as an *"extremely genial character,"* and *"a preeminent name in the enforcement field."* He is the trusted adviser of many participants in the federal home loan market and provides expert advice on electronic payment systems regulatory compliance.

**Clients/Work Highlights:** American Express; Federal Home Loan Bank of New York; National City Corporation; PNC Bank and Wells Fargo.

## Mayer, Brown, Rowe & Maw LLP
See firm details p.876

**The Firm:** The firm's financial regulatory practice is generally recognized as a prominent domestic player. The team chiefly advises large US financial services institutions on all aspects of their organization and governance, transactions, product development and compliance activities. A particular strength of the team lies in its expertise on capital markets regulatory compliance; it provides ongoing advice to Wachovia relating to its capital markets and asset management activities. The team recently made *"important strides"* in the cross-border financial institutions M&A market. For example, it represented Northern Trust on the US regulatory aspects of its $500 million acquisition of the Channel Islands based Barings Financial Services Group.

**The Lawyers:** Based in Washington, DC **Charles Horn** (see p.108) is the *"most visible member of the group."* His *"good judgment and problem-solving attitude"* attracted praise from clients. His practice focuses chiefly on securities regulatory matters.

**Clients/Work Highlights:** ShoreBank Corporation; Federal Home Loan Banks (Seattle, Indianapolis, Cincinnati and Atlanta); Charles Schwab Corporation; Associated Bancorp and American Bankers Association.

## White & Case LLP
See firm details p.1566

**The Firm:** The firm's financial services group is particularly rated for its expertise on investigations and enforcement matters. The team works routinely with its clients to evaluate and strengthen their internal controls, risk management processes, and compliance programs. The group also has extensive experience with investigation proceedings and is said to have an *"impressive track record of successful negotiations for the settlement of enforcement actions"* by banking and securities regulators. On the litigation front, the team is notably instructed by long-standing client Deutsche Bank to defend the bank in various claims arising from the collapse of Enron, including securities class action. The practice's noncontentious work also includes advising US and foreign financial institutions with respect to regulatory compliance in their day-to-day operations, business expansion and M&A transactions.

**The Lawyers:** **Kevin Barnard** (see p.87) is the global head of the bank advisory practice group. This preeminent practitioner is said to belong to a *"tiny community of lawyers able to advise on complex cross-border investigations."* He has advised the Iraqi Board of Supreme Audit in the investigations of fraud, waste and abuse related to the UN Oil-for-Food Program.

**Clients/Work Highlights:** ABN AMRO; Apple Bank; Banco Central de Venezuela; Bank of America; BNP Paribas; Citigroup; Royal Bank of Canada and US Trust.

## Willkie Farr & Gallagher LLP
See firm details p.1567

**The Firm:** Advice to mutual funds, hedge funds, investment advisers and insurance companies on questions arising from their relationships with financial institutions forms the foundations of this practice. In particular, the team is well known for advising hedge funds with respect to investments by banking organizations as well as representing companies in the sale of their credit card portfolios to banking entities. For example, it recently represented Alliance & Leicester Commercial Bank on the US bank regulatory implications of the sale of its credit card processing business to US Bank National Association. The team also advises on regulatory matters and the creation of new lines of business.

**The Lawyers:** Tim McTaggart is the main contact at the firm.

**Clients/Work Highlights:** Banca Intesa; Bank of America; Bank of Thailand; Federal Home Loan Bank of San Francisco and Bank of Tokyo-Mitsubishi.

## Morgan, Lewis & Bockius LLP
See firm details p.1758

**The Firm:** This *"wonderful, sizable and dedicated"* group is recognized as a national leader in the field of securities regulatory investigation, enforcement and litigation. It is particularly renowned for its experience in representing broker-dealers and investment advisers in investigations led by the SEC,

NASD or NYSE. Clients were impressed by the team's abilities to *"get outstanding results for its clients in the negotiation of formal or informal enforcement agreements."* Recently the group reached a favorable outcome for Lehman Brothers in investigations before the NYSE regarding their trading practices. The team also routinely provides counsel in traditional regulatory matters such as the formation of new entities, the raising of capital and the acquisition or sale of financial institutions.

**The Lawyers: Robert Mendelson** (see p.120) and **Robert Romano** (see p.130) are renowned litigators, particularly recommended for their *"incomparable experience of securities regulations."*

**Clients/Work Highlights:** Alliance Capital; Merrill Lynch; Citibank; Fidelity Investments; Jefferies & Co; Ameritrade; E*TRADE and Deutsche Bank.

## Venable LLP

**The Firm:** This group has a diversified national financial institutions practice, representing banks, thrifts, insurance companies, financial institution holding companies as well as securities firms. While the group provides a wide range of advice, it is best known for successfully handling the defense of enforcement proceedings before regulatory agencies. In 2005, attorneys achieved a global settlement for a leading insurance company in claims by the OCC arising from alleged mortgage frauds. This was the first time a federal banking agency entered into a global settlement with any commercial company. The group also conducts internal investigations of several major banking organizations at the request of their boards of directors as well as advising bank and thrift boards of directors on regulatory and transactional matters.

**The Lawyers:** Chair of the financial services group, **Ronald Glancz** is respected for his successes in the regulatory enforcement field.

**Clients/Work Highlights:** The firm represents banks; saving associations; thrifts; insurance companies; financial institution holding companies and securities firms.

## Cadwalader, Wickersham & Taft LLP

See firm details p.1522

**The Firm:** Clients are impressed by the group's performance before regulatory agencies such as the SEC, NASD, NYSE and the OCC. Audit committees frequently call upon these attorneys to conduct internal investigations and compliance reviews to ensure that their regulatory policies and procedures are sufficient to meet federal standards. The group's practice also focuses on securities regulatory defense and litigation, and serves a variety of market participants, including major financial institutions and their directors, as well as broker-dealers and investment advisers. It combines this enforcement expertise with a straight regulatory practice and provides day-to-day compliance advice on its clients' capital markets activities.

**The Lawyers: Bruce Hiler** (see p.106) is based in Washington, DC from where he chairs the firm's securities and financial institutions regulation department. Having served in the investigation and litigation divisions of the SEC, he enjoys *"a unique perspective and understanding of how securities litigation must be handled."*

## Williams & Connolly LLP

**The Firm:** The renowned litigation firm was strongly recommended for its wide-ranging experience in securities, derivatives and financial services litigation. This practice handles all types of proceedings from class actions involving large financial institutions to individual actions involving smaller companies and private sales. The caseload includes pre-complaint investigations and, when cases require, trial representation.

**The Lawyers: John Villa** is the *"first name to come to mind for financial services litigation matters."* Clients turn to him when caught up in banking scandals and describe him as *"the last resort when the cause seems irremediably compromised."*

**Clients/Work Highlights:** The group represents banks, a variety of corporations, directors and officers, underwriters and auditors as well as law firms in securities actions.

## Other Notable Practitioners

**Frank Puleo** is the cochair of the global finance group at Milbank, Tweed, Hadley & McCloy LLP. A respected figure, his broad finance practice contains a significant strand of bank and bank holding company regulatory and securities advice. **Alan Kaplinsky** (see p.111) of Ballard Spahr Andrews & Ingersoll LLP in Philadelphia was described as a *"guru"* of consumer financial services on both the regulatory and litigation sides. He earned his *"well-deserved national reputation"* when successfully defending the very first class actions brought against financial institutions.

# GOVERNMENT

# GOVERNMENT CONTRACTS

**OVERVIEW:** *Chambers USA*'s new Governmental section encompasses three distinct areas at the intersection between business and government. This year we have introduced new tables for Government Relations and Political Law to accompany the existing rankings for Government Contracts. The first of these new tables principally focuses on lobbying and appropriation work. Many law firms undertake this work, but it should be emphasized that they face sturdy competition from leading lobby shops such as Barbour Griffiths & Rogers, Cassidy & Associates, Quinn Gillespie & Associates, Van Scoyoc Associates, Podesta Mattoon and The Federalist Group. As these outfits are not law firms, they cannot appear in our tables; however, it must be acknowledged that they are also leaders in the field. In a similar vein, law firms hire prominent government officials or former elected members who are not legally qualified to work in their government relations departments. As *Chambers USA* remains a guide of leading business lawyers, we have limited ourselves to ranking qualified lawyers; however, we acknowledge that the non-lawyers are an important part of the market, and considered their influence when ranking the firms. The Political Law table covers the law regulating election campaigning and the conduct of elected members and government officials. As such, it remains firmly in the realm of qualified lawyers.

| Government: Government Contracts |
|---|
| Leading Firms |
| [1] CROWELL & MORING LLP |
| DLA PIPER RUDNICK GRAY CARY |
| MCKENNA LONG & ALDRIDGE LLP |
| [2] FRIED, FRANK, HARRIS, SHRIVER |
| JENNER & BLOCK LLP |
| ROGERS JOSEPH O'DONNELL & PHILLIPS |
| VENABLE LLP |
| WILEY REIN & FIELDING LLP |
| [3] GARDERE WYNNE SEWELL LLP |
| GIBSON, DUNN & CRUTCHER LLP |
| HOGAN & HARTSON LLP |
| HOLLAND & KNIGHT LLP |
| MAYER, BROWN, ROWE & MAW |
| SHEPPARD, MULLIN, RICHTER & HAMPTON |
| SMITH PACHTER MCWHORTER PLC |
| THELEN REID & PRIEST LLP |
| VINSON & ELKINS LLP |

## Band 1

### Crowell & Moring LLP

See firm details p.564

**The Firm:** Yet again, one of the discipline's original superstar firms impresses the market with its "*deep bench strength*" and "*uniformly good people who know their stuff.*" The team of 18 partners and 20 associates remains "*absolutely the best*" in the field, according to many; rivals acknowledge that the firm has "*kept its core together*" and clients particularly rely on the fact that the firm can advise on all manner of transactional and advisory work as well as tackling major litigation. The quality of its work matches the scale of some of the matters taken on. The team recently represented Pratt & Whitney in a defective pricing claim against the Air Force to the tune of $299 million, arising from the infamous Great Engine War between Pratt & Whitney and GE.

**The Lawyers: Stan Johnson** (see p.110) is named as "*one of the premier litigators of all time in this business*" and has become firmly established as "*the great dean of the Bar.*" A "*wonderful scholar and a great analyst of the law,*" he also excels in the courtroom, where he is said to be "*bright and well prepared.*" **Terry Albertson** (see p.84) is recognized as "*one of*

the very best" in the sphere of cost accounting. He is moving towards resolving more issues through alternative dispute resolution. Working primarily on bid protests, **Thomas Humphrey** (see p.109) was recommended by a number of interviewees as a "*strong, younger lawyer.*" Interviewees mentioned **Kent Morrison** (see p.122) in the same breath, pointing to him as another future leader in the field. **Clients/Work Highlights:** The firm is known for its representation of large aerospace companies such as Lockheed Martin; United Technologies; Boeing; Raytheon; General Dynamics and BAE Systems. Other clients include the Department of Trade and Industry in the UK; Blue Cross and Blue Shield Association; SBC; Blackwater and Newport News.

### DLA Piper Rudnick Gray Cary US LLP

See firm details p.870

**The Firm:** Almost unanimously cited by peers as their "*strongest competition,*" since its merger the international giant now boasts a "*broad-based*" practice of 18 lawyers who mainly serve clients selling general commercial products to the government. It undertakes a considerable amount of "*high-quality*" counseling and transactional work, and has particular expertise on the General Services Administration's Multiple Award Schedule Program. The firm also gets involved in large-scale litigation and last year filed a bid protest for Neopost, manufacturer of Post-It notes.

**The Lawyers: Carl Vacketta** (see p.139) has "*a very strong pedigree.*" Having learnt his trade with the finest in the business, he now holds a position as a "*stand-up person*" among the current generation of government contracts specialists and continually provides "*first-rate*" work. **Greg Smith** (see p.135) leads the government contracts department and is another impressive practitioner, particularly in the costs area. **Richard Rector** (see p.128) concentrates on litigation, especially bid protests. Clients appreciate his "*good judgment*" and know him as "*a hard-working and genuinely nice guy.*" **Clients/Work Highlights:** The team has done a considerable amount of work for 3M and Smiths Aerospace, among others.

### McKenna Long & Aldridge LLP

See firm details p.737

**The Firm:** It was at this firm that Gilbert Cuneo and others created the first government contracts practice, and ever since then McKenna has maintained its preeminence in the field. While the kudos of being the original player undoubtedly aids the firm in its quest to remain "*the number one,*" this does not detract from the combined skill of more than 50 government contracts specialists, stretching from Los Angeles, through San Diego and Denver, all the way to Washington, DC and Philadelphia. With resources of such magnitude, it is unsurprising that the firm covers every aspect of the discipline and particularly thrives on large litigation matters. For example, it represented GM in a massive Qui Tam case which lasted for more than six years until it was finally dismissed in 2005. Lawyers also won summary judgment for client United Defense which became embroiled in a defamation and unfair business practices case following the cancellation of a military procurement. The firm represents eight of the ten largest defense companies in the USA.

**The Lawyers:** Interviewees declared great respect for seasoned Washington, DC practitioner **Stanley Dees** (see p.95): "*He is undoubtedly a senior statesman and has the poise and experience to prove it.*" The firm's West Coast team is led by yet another "*big name,*" **Jay Gallagher** (see p.101), who offers clients more than 30 years of experience in this area and is renowned for his work with aviation companies. Commentators assert that he is "*undoubtedly a premier lawyer.*"

**Clients/Work Highlights:** Lockheed Martin; Boeing; GMH Military Housing; sanofi-aventis and Sanofi Pasteur.

## Band 2

### Fried, Frank, Harris, Shriver & Jacobson LLP

See firm details p.1532

**The Firm:** Fried Frank is best known for its "*big footprint*" in the bid protests area. It has had yet another notable year, working on two high-profile protests. Firstly, the team represented SAIC in a successful bid protest at the Government Accountability Office (GAO), concerning a $700 million procurement of a

| Government: Government Contracts |
| Leading Individuals |

**Senior Statesman**

DEES Stanley *McKenna Long & Aldridge*
DOKE JR Marshall *Gardere Wynne Sewell*
JOHNSON W Stanfield *Crowell & Moring*

[1] ALLEN Rand *Wiley Rein & Fielding LLP*
JOSEPH Allan *Rogers Joseph O'Donnell*
VACKETTA Carl *DLA Piper*

[2] ALBERTSON Terry *Crowell & Moring*
CHIERICHELLA John *Sheppard, Mullin*
CHURCHILL David *Jenner & Block*
GALLAGHER James *McKenna Long*
MADDEN Thomas *Venable LLP*
MADSEN Marcia *Mayer, Brown*
MCCULLOUGH James *Fried, Frank*
O'DONNELL Neil *Rogers Joseph*

[3] CHARNESS Michael *Vinson & Elkins*
DEVECCHIO Jay *Jenner & Block*
MANOS Karen *Gibson, Dunn & Crutcher*
NIBLEY Stuart *Thelen Reid & Priest*
PACHTER John *Smith Pachter McWhorter*
RECTOR Richard *DLA Piper*
SMITH Gregory *DLA Piper*
WEST Joseph *Gibson, Dunn & Crutcher*

[4] HUMPHREY Thomas *Crowell & Moring*
MCCALEB Scott *Wiley Rein & Fielding*
MCGOVERN III Thomas *Hogan & Hartson*
MORRISON Kent *Crowell & Moring*

systems engineering services contract by the EPA. Secondly, it was successful in a bid protest for Hunt Building Company at the Court of Federal Claims regarding a $1.3 billion military family housing project in Hawaii. The firm actually has a varied diet of cases involving numerous agencies from military agencies to the Department of the Interior, the Department of Housing and Urban Development, and the FAA. It also devotes a considerable amount of time to compliance and fraud investigations. The Washington, DC practice regularly assists the firm's New York lawyers on M&A transactions involving companies with government contracts.
**The Lawyers:** Litigator **James McCullough** (see p.119) heads the Washington, DC-based government contracts practice. He is described as a "*very well-respected, active and capable*" member of the Bar. McCullough's experience on bid protests, contractual disputes and general advisory work renders him a top choice for major-name clients.
**Clients/Work Highlights:** Northrop Grumman; Boeing; SAIC and Computer Sciences Corporation.

## Jenner & Block LLP
See firm details p.873
**The Firm:** This "*quality*" practice was kick-started five years ago with the recruitment of David Churchill and has "*a reputation for doing a good job.*" Since its beginnings the firm has gone from strength to strength and now has 15 lawyers, including some

recent additions from Miller & Chevalier. Operating from Washington, DC and Texas, the firm is best known for advising aerospace and defense clients, particularly General Dynamics, but is also expanding into the healthcare sector. The past year was notable for the number of large bid protests in which the team was involved, both prosecuting and defending. It was also involved in a number of contractor claims for equitable adjustment.
**The Lawyers:** Chair of the department **David Churchill** (see p.92) is resoundingly recommended as a "*very sound and knowledgeable*" lawyer with an "*understated*" style – "*he doesn't talk at the top of his lungs; he's very rational.*" **Jay DeVecchio** (see p.96) recently joined the team from Miller & Chevalier and is judged to be a "*very smart*" addition to the practice.
**Clients/Work Highlights:** General Dynamics, Lockheed Martin and MCI are on the client roster.

## Rogers Joseph O'Donnell & Phillips
**The Firm:** This boutique firm has government contracts at the heart of its practice. Distinguished as "*far and away the best government contracts lawyers on the West Coast,*" despite being small in size, this is a "*spectacular*" team that is frequently "*chosen for the most challenging work.*" The group handles complex contract disputes involving subcontracts and teaming agreements, Qui Tam cases and bid protests as well as general counseling. For example, it defended contract awardees Gateway in a bid protest with a value of $400 million.
**The Lawyers:** "*Thorough*" **Allan Joseph** is "*a real scholar*" with specialist knowledge in several different areas, including termination for convenience cases. He is "*highly experienced*" and "*a big name*" in the field. **Neil O'Donnell** has a construction slant to his practice. Peers regard this "*smart and bright*" lawyer as both "*a formidable adversary*" and "*a really pleasant guy to work with.*"
**Clients/Work Highlights:** Lockheed Martin Space Systems; United Defense; Accenture and Northrop Grumman.

## Venable LLP
See firm details p.78998
**The Firm:** Venable has a "*leading and well-respected*" full-service government contracts practice with a particular niche in cases involving IP. Illustrative of this is its role for Lockheed Martin in Honeywell v USA and Lockheed Martin. This case arose from Honeywell's claim that the defendants have infringed one of its patents. It is also highly visible in the realm of bid protests, where the core group of 20 lawyers has the resources to "*do an extremely good job.*" Corporate governance advice is the other key component of the practice.
**The Lawyers:** **Thomas Madden** heads the group and is "*a really well-known force.*" Rated "*a strong litigator,*" Madden has built a great name for himself in bid protests. He is also said to be "*highly capable*" on cost issues.
**Clients/Work Highlights:** Other clients include US Foodservice and Securitas Services.

## Wiley Rein & Fielding LLP
See firm details p.579
**The Firm:** Of all the firms in the second tier, this is generally considered to be the one that is "*nipping at the heels of the top group.*" It has built up a "*substantial and broad-based*" practice that especially excels at bid protests, and interviewees consistently praised the "*impressive quality of their work*" in this area. Compliments were also reserved for the high standard of the associates within the team.
**The Lawyers:** **Rand Allen** (see p.85) chairs the government contracts practice group, and commentators report that he has done a "*laudable*" job of building it up. A "*bright and broadly skilled*" litigator, Allen provides a very "*thoughtful*" service to clients. Interviewees also pointed out that **Scott McCaleb** (see p.118) is "*a real standout among the younger generation.*" He is especially active in bid protests, where he does a "*terrific*" job.

### Band 3

## Gardere Wynne Sewell LLP
See firm details p.1901
**The Firm:** This Dallas-based firm has a skilled and knowledgeable group with an undoubtedly national practice. It has recently handled a large matter involving an extensive review of contracts and subcontracts, evaluating the performance of the client and subcontractors and negotiating a settlement to a dispute. The team has also been involved in a substantial false claims case in Florida, which it managed to have dismissed. Although Marshall Doke is by far the best-known lawyer here, he draws upon a sizable and experienced team.
**The Lawyers:** **Marshall Doke** (see p.96) is "*absolutely terrific,*" commentators say. He is "*a top-of-the-list lawyer who owns the southwest.*" Hugely experienced, peers regard him as "*definitely one of the people I'd go to if I had a really difficult problem.*" Doke is one of only two private lawyers appointed to the Acquisition Advisory Panel by the US government, the purpose of which is to recommend improvements to the procurement system.
**Clients/Work Highlights:** The group represents a number of large national bodies as well as smaller companies and startups doing government work. It has strong support in the engineering and aerospace markets.

## Gibson, Dunn & Crutcher LLP
See firm details p.328
**The Firm:** The reputation of this small but well-regarded practice group is centered on key lawyer Joseph West, who is backed up by three further partners. Together they handle compliance and investigation work, primarily representing mainstream commercial companies with incidental government contracts rather than defense companies and weapons manufacturers. A highlight of the past year was acting as litigation counsel in a series of high-stakes bid protest controversies concerning the nine-year 'winner takes all' award for a contract to provide

integrated, automated reservation services for all federal recreation facilities. The engagements included two matters at the GAO and two cases at the Court of Federal Claims. The lawyers have also represented IT and professional services firms in contract disputes and/or negotiations, including negotiations for complex IT contracts with California.

**The Lawyers:** A "*solid and trustworthy*" lawyer, **Joseph West** (see p.142) is the lynchpin of the practice. Originally a construction lawyer, he is felt to have made the transition with ease and to be "*a smart operator who scores good points.*" **Karen Manos** (see p.117) is a recent arrival from Howrey. She is regarded by commentators as "*an absolutely top-class costs lawyer.*" She is highlighted as "*the expert's expert, with great knowledge and a great attitude.*" Strong on regulations and federal grants, Manos is seen as particularly good in her representation of trade associations.

**Clients/Work Highlights:** Computer Sciences Corporation; GKN North America; Deloitte Consulting; Deloitte & Touche; BMC Software; Express Services; MCI; ITT Educational Services; Lockheed Martin; Mellon Bank; Northrop Grumman; SBC; Sprint; Supersonic Aerospace International; Hawthorne & York International; Aurora Capital and Ticketmaster.

## Hogan & Hartson LLP
See firm details p.568
**The Firm:** New to this year's rankings, Hogan & Hartson won market support as "*a small but quality group.*" It is particularly known for its representation of companies in federal research issues, IT and healthcare, and its lawyers are busiest in the defense/aerospace sector. They recently represented a corporate client in a misappropriation of trade secrets case relating to a multibillion-dollar procurement of satellite launch vehicles. Although not a great size, the team is felt to have "*a surprising breadth of knowledge*" and to be "*a strong competitor.*"

**The Lawyers:** **Thomas McGovern** (see p.120) is applauded as "*a smart and capable lawyer*" who is particularly hailed for his work in bids protests.

## Holland & Knight LLP
See firm details p.1534
**The Firm:** "*A committed practice with good quality control*" was the verdict of one commentator on Holland & Knight. The group impresses with the reach and the depth of its work, experienced as it is across the board in contract and dispute matters. The team enjoys a strong following in construction, defense and aerospace, healthcare, manufacturing and homeland security.

**The Lawyers:** Dave Metzger in northern Virginia is the best-known member of the team.

## Mayer, Brown, Rowe & Maw LLP
See firm details p.876
**The Firm:** This respected protest practice is based around esteemed partner Marcia Madsen and is seen as a smart and growing group. It boasts a good client base and has been active in some high-profile matters, including the representation of GM in a complex pension cost accounting case regarding claims that the Department of Defense had underpaid the pensions of GM employees since the 1950's. The case resulted in a successful $253 million verdict for GM.

**The Lawyers:** "*Superb protest lawyer*" **Marcia Madsen** (see p.117) is regarded as "*a strong attorney who makes a good impression.*" She is skilled across the board on bid protests, claims and disputes, as well as on issues relating to cost accounting and conflicts between contractors and subcontractors. Madsen is one of only two private practice lawyers appointed to the Acquisition Advisory Panel by the US government, the purpose of which is to recommend improvements to the procurement system.

**Clients/Work Highlights:** Clients include Verizon and Bechtel National.

## Sheppard, Mullin, Richter & Hampton LLP
**The Firm:** The new kid on the block, this firm is felt to have invested astutely in the field and to be building up an expert practice. Its 20 lawyers are split between LA and Washington, DC, and as well as a large amount of bid protest work, they take on false claims litigation (especially cases arising from cost accounting) and most other types of contract claims. The firm has a strong capability concerning IP rights in government contracts, and experience in the area of multiple awards schedule contracts is reflected in the fact that lawyers have written a book on the subject. There is a further specialism in export control matters. The group recently settled a dispute between a client and the Russian government, which involved the termination of a contract following actions by the US government.

**The Lawyers:** **John Chierichella** is regarded as "*one of the best lawyers in the field.*" He is portrayed as "*hardworking and energetic with a great mind that comes up with truly innovative solutions to problems.*" Chierichella has recently achieved summary judgment in the federal court in a case involving the modification of a contract relating to the modernization of the travel system for the Department of Defense.

**Clients/Work Highlights:** The group's client base is particularly strong in the defense and aerospace sectors, but the firm represents a wide range of commercial entities involved in government contracting.

## Smith Pachter McWhorter PLC
**The Firm:** This north Virginia boutique is hailed as "*expert and experienced.*" It is active in all matters relating to government contracts, though it is recognized most for its protest work. The group boasts a diverse client base and represents clients in defense and aerospace, construction, telecommunications and professional services.

**The Lawyers:** **John Pachter** "*gives a quality service to clients,*" researchers were told. One client said: "*I've observed his practice for over 20 years and the comments he makes and the positions he takes are wonderful.*" He is seen to be at his best when working to resolve disputes.

## Thelen Reid & Priest LLP
See firm details p.342
**The Firm:** Although this is a relatively new practice, it is felt to be making strides, particularly following the recruitment of Stuart Nibley. Its clientele reflects the fact that this is a combined construction and government contracts practice, and it is currently representing a large company in a False Claims Act investigation being brought by the DOJ. Lawyers also handle more traditional work, and are active for Lockheed Martin, especially in relation to its satellite and missile programs.

**The Lawyers:** After having taken time off to teach, experienced **Stuart Nibley** (see p.123) is making an impression on his return to practice. He is known as "*a smart lawyer who is great at presentation.*"

## Vinson & Elkins LLP
See firm details p.1938
**The Firm:** The DC office of this Texas-based firm has a substantial presence in the market. It is skilled in the area of contract procurement as well as bid protests and other contract-related litigation. The lawyers are additionally active in outsourcing and privatization, representing companies in construction, architecture and engineering. They also work closely with colleagues specializing in international trade. A highlight from the past year was successfully defending a company in a bid protest relating to a large defense contract.

**The Lawyers:** **Michael Charness** (see p.91) wins peer approval as "*a talented and capable lawyer.*" He is hailed for his skills in construction matters and is proficient in issues relating to Export Administration Regulations and the Foreign Corrupt Practices Act.

## GOVERNMENT

## GOVERNMENT RELATIONS

### Government: Government Relations

**Leading Firms**

1. AKIN GUMP STRAUSS HAUER & FELD LLP
   PATTON BOGGS LLP
2. DLA PIPER RUDNICK GRAY CARY US LLP
   HOGAN & HARTSON LLP
3. ARNOLD & PORTER LLP
   BLANK ROME LLP
   HOLLAND & KNIGHT LLP
   SONNENSCHEIN NATH & ROSENTHAL
   WILLIAMS & JENSEN PLLC
4. ALSTON & BIRD LLP
   BINGHAM MCCUTCHEN LLP
   COVINGTON & BURLING
   DICKSTEIN SHAPIRO MORIN & OSHINSKY
   GREENBERG TRAURIG LLP
   MAYER, BROWN, ROWE & MAW LLP

**Leading Individuals**

1. BOGGS JR Thomas *Patton Boggs*
   HART J Steven *Williams & Jensen PLLC*
   HOUSE W Michael *Hogan & Hartson*
   JANKOWSKY Joel *Akin Gump*
   MERRIGAN John *DLA Piper*

## Band 1

### Akin Gump Strauss Hauer & Feld LLP

See firm details p.559

**The Firm:** Revered as *"one of the oldest and most mature public policy practices in town,"* this group has been going for over 25 years and continues to dominate the top end of the market. It was originally set up by prominent Democrats, but it has consciously sought to develop a bipartisan stance and now has high-profile personalities from both sides of the aisle. For example, it is home to former Republican member of Congress for New York Bill Paxon, as well as Tom Foley, former speaker of the House of Representatives and a prominent Democrat. In addition to boasting a fine mix of real politicians with *"connections into virtually every branch of government,"* this large law firm can also offer regulatory experts in every possible industry. Indeed, the level of resources and *"amazing depth"* available to clients is a real standout feature of the firm; some 50 lawyers in the policy group make this the largest team in town. It represents clients before federal branches of government, state government and even has the international capability to lobby Geneva and Brussels. It is most frequently to be found working for large commercial clients, and during the past year has been advising AT&T on federal and state issues arising from its proposed merger with SBC. The firm undertakes work for Native American tribes: it helped the Gila River Indian Community in Arizona achieve the largest water settlement in US history. **The Lawyers:** Chair of the policy department **Joel Jankowsky** (see p.109) is *"excellent, just superb,"* and

one of the longest established figures on the scene. Clients proudly state that *"the best advice on how to get things done ethically and effectively in Washington, DC always comes from him."* He is also described as *"smart, dynamic and one of the best strategists in the game."*

**Clients/Work Highlights:** Motion Picture Association; Mortgage Insurance Companies of America; Liberty Mutual; Dow Chemical; The State University of New York; Pfizer; PG&E Corporation and Grocery Manufacturers Association.

### Patton Boggs LLP

**The Firm:** A name to roll quickly off market commentators' tongues, Patton Boggs has one of the country's *"premier"* government relations practices and is *"the major lobbying force"* in Washington, DC. As one of the first firms to realise the potential of this field, it is cited as *"the original and the best"* and impresses on both revenue and reputation. Patton Boggs is a full-service firm with 400 lawyers, but its administrative and lobbying department is the real crown jewel. It has some *"real heavy hitters"* on the staff roster, including Rodney Slater, the Secretary of Transportation during Clinton's presidency, and former congressman John Breaux. These big names ensure that the firm has *"fantastic connections"* in Washington, DC; indeed, it is especially influential with the Democratic Party. It represents a wide range of clients, from municipal authorities, universities and major corporations to foreign sovereigns. Over the past year, the team has been influential in pushing for the Native Hawaiian Government Reorganization Act on behalf of the Office of Hawaiian Affairs. This bill will ensure that native Hawaiians will receive special treatment in order to protect the islands' unique heritage.

**The Lawyers:** It is not often that a lawyer is described as *"a legend,"* but this sobriquet seemed to spring straight to interviewees' minds when they talked about the group's central personality, **Thomas Boggs** (see p.89). He is named *"the dean of the lobbying Bar"* and is *"extremely influential"* in Washington, DC, especially within the Democratic Party.

**Clients/Work Highlights:** The firm represents more clients than can be listed here, but some examples include the Republic of Kazakhstan; 1-800 Contacts; Hoffmann-La Roche; The Association of Trial Lawyers of America and Mars.

## Band 2

### DLA Piper Rudnick Gray Cary US LLP

See firm details p.870

**The Firm:** The changes that this firm has undergone in recent years has created *"a growing juggernaut"* within the government relations field. Specialist lobby firm Verner Lipford joined Piper Rudnick, and subsequent mergers with Gray Cary and DLA have created considerable regulatory depth and an international platform. It is worth noting that there are

also strong teams based in London and Brussels. In addition, the firm's alliance with former Secretary of Defense William Cohen's consulting firm, The Cohen Group, is seen as a *"great asset."* The firm now has a highly impressive list of practitioners and the prestige of being the only practice with three former Congress majority leaders, including Senator George Mitchell. This ensures *"a good-quality lobbying operation with strong connections"* and a strong congressional investigation practice. As a large litigation firm, it has been extraordinarily well placed to work on the reform of the tort and judicial system. In this context, it has been retained by Equitas to represent it in the restructure of asbestos liability. Real estate is another sweet spot. This year, the firm was hired by the State of Florida to defend military bases that were earmarked for closure.

**The Lawyers:** The team is led by **John Merrigan** (see p.121), who is *"very smart and aggressive"* and has *"done a superb job of growing the practice."*

**Clients/Work Highlights:** Northwest Airlines; GM; Wal-Mart; Boeing; The Kingdom of Spain; Merrill Lynch and Diageo.

### Hogan & Hartson LLP

See firm details p.568

**The Firm:** This traditional powerhouse on the DC legal scene has harnessed its regulatory capability to work in tandem with its lobbying group, thereby creating a practice that is *"seamless, substantive and dynamic."* The team contains *"top-caliber"* attorneys with government experience, as well as high-profile personalities such as Bob Michel, former Republican leader of the House of Representatives, and Clayton Yeutter, former US Secretary of Agriculture and national chairman of the Republican National Committee. Clients speak highly of the *"diversity of knowledge"* available at the firm, and although it is particularly strong in healthcare and international trade, its work stretches far beyond this. For example, the group is advising FM Policy Focus, a financial services organization lobbying for the regulation of government-sponsored enterprises. It has had some *"great successes"* over the years, and clients particularly enjoy working with the team because *"it gets really passionate about our issues and always gives 110%."*

**The Lawyers:** **Michael House** (see p.108) is the director of the legislative group. Clients have nothing but exuberant praise for him, focusing in particular on his *"excellent strategic mind, which helps us achieve our goals."*

**Clients/Work Highlights:** DTE Energy; Nissan; Michelin; Milton S Eisenhower Foundation and Northwestern University.

## Band 3

### Arnold & Porter LLP
See firm details p.560

**The Firm:** This solid regulatory law firm is now building up its government relations capability by developing a wide practice covering lobbying, congressional investigations and government contracts. It is especially strong on national security issues and has a group dedicated to this work. The team is led by the former general counsel to the CIA, Jeffrey Smith, who now counsels In-Q-Tel, a panel using venture capital to develop technology used by the intelligence community. He has recently completed the five-year review of its operations. The team is also advising Microsoft and Altria on national security issues. Heralding further expansion, the firm recently recruited former Congressman Jim Turner from Texas.

### Blank Rome LLP
See firm details p.1747

**The Firm:** It may not be as long established as the firms at the top of the list, but this team has "*excellent political connections.*" Though a bipartisan firm, it is particularly known for its "*strong Republican credentials*" and strong ties with the Bush administration. With one of the largest political action committees of any law firm, Blank Rome has little trouble opening doors on Capitol Hill. It advises a number of large corporations such as Aramark on pending legislation, and is also tried and tested when it comes to proactive lobbying. For example, it is representing Take 2, makers of Grand Theft Auto, during Congress's investigation into regulating the video game industry. In addition, the team is representing American Financial Group on the reform of the asbestos tort system. While the firm concentrates on federal work, it is also notable for its strong links with state governors. Chairman of the firm David Girard-diCarlo is the practice's key practitioner.

### Holland & Knight LLP
See firm details p.1534

**The Firm:** Holland & Knight has grown exponentially from a principally Florida-based state practice into a thriving presence in numerous states and a real competitor at the federal level. It now has 105 professionals working on legislative matters, from local to federal level, and a client base ranging from large Fortune 50 companies, such as DuPont and Hartford Insurance, to small emerging companies and municipal entities, of the likes of the Cities of Cleveland and San Antonio. During the passage of a major transportation bill last year, the team secured $1 billion of funding for its clients, including $72 million to widen Interstate 80 in California. The practice benefits from "*years of experience*" and has "*invested heavily*" in the area. Rich Gold heads up the public policy and regulation group.

### Sonnenschein Nath & Rosenthal
See firm details p.884

**The Firm:** The arrival of the "*energetic and sparky*" Elliott Portnoy three years ago was absolutely in keeping with the "*aggressive growth*" plan of the public law and policy strategies group. The group now has 25 full-time practitioners with a reputation for "*high technical competence*" and is regarded as a "*top-notch*" addition to the scene. It works on high-profile matters and has been appointed by the Federal-Mogul Unsecured Creditors Committee to try and delay the reform of the asbestos tort reform until after the company has emerged from bankruptcy. It has met with success in the appropriation field, and has long experience in the healthcare sector, where it assists charities such as the Lance Armstrong Foundation and Christopher Reeve Paralysis Foundation in gaining government funding. The firm has a subspecialism in what it calls political intelligence; for example, it has helped the financial services industry predict what Congress may do in the future. To give a satisfied client the final word, the firm provides "*insightful political and legal counsel and is a delight to work with.*"

### Williams & Jensen PLLC
See firm details p.116287

**The Firm:** This boutique government relations firm is "*the place to go if you want to work with leading Republicans.*" It is a "*heavily political*" practice which has developed an "*outstanding*" reputation for "*knowing how to read the Hill.*" Williams & Jensen may be small but it is certainly successful in terms of both revenue and market standing. Among the non-lawyer professionals, Susan Hirschmann is particularly recommended due to the contacts she developed as chief of staff to Tom DeLay. **Steven Hart** is frequently cited as the star lawyer in the practice.

## Band 4

### Alston & Bird LLP
See firm details p.728

**The Firm:** This "*powerhouse*" Georgia firm is "*making a very aggressive run of it*" in Washington, DC and is famous as the base for former Republican presidential candidate Senator Bob Dole. The high-profile recruitment campaign continues apace, and the practice now has Senator Tom Daschle and Tom Scully, Administrator of the Centers for Medicare & Medicaid Services, on board. As these appointments would suggest, the firm is particularly good for healthcare lobbying.

### Bingham McCutchen LLP
See firm details p.1110

**The Firm:** At the time of going to press, Swidler Berlin's government affairs practice was set to join Bingham McCutchen following the recently announced merger of the two firms. The Swidler practice is best known as the representative of the Asbestos Study Group, the consortium of major US corporations involved in asbestos litigation. As such, it is the chief proponent of the bill to reform the system and establish an asbestos compensation fund. Peers confess that it has "*a very good team of lawyers,*" ably led by Barry Direnfeld. It is also a strong regulatory firm and can provide substantive government relations support for clients in many industries. By way of example, it excels in the telecom area and is representing clients such as Vonage in pushing for greater competition in the industry.

### Covington & Buriing
See firm details p.563

**The Firm:** This premier regulatory firm is "*raising its profile considerably*" in the government relations field. It already had substantive legal and regulatory knowledge, and now it has built up an impressive roster of former government officials to consolidate the lobbying side of its business. The well-known personalities here include Roderick DeArment, Deputy Secretary of Labor in the first Bush administration, and Stuart Eizenstat, former Deputy Secretary of the Treasury Department and US Ambassador to the EU.

### Dickstein Shapiro Morin & Oshinsky LLP
See firm details p.565

**The Firm:** No list would be complete without the inclusion of the traditional Washington, DC law firm of Dickstein Shapiro. It does not have an enormous policy practice but it does "*good work*" in the field and its presence is growing year on year. The firm is seen to have been particularly successful in its representation of tobacco companies, and it has been heavily involved in attempts by Congress to pass regulatory legislation affecting the tobacco industry.

### Greenberg Traurig LLP
See firm details p.664

**The Firm:** This Florida firm has "*aggressively expanded*" its government relations practice to cover nine separate states, including a thriving presence in New York. In addition, it has achieved "*great successes*" at the federal level, where it represents cities and counties such as the City of Oakland in California and Miami-Dade County in Florida. The firm parted company with its most high-profile lobbyist, Jack Abramoff, following controversy surrounding his representation of Indian tribes. Some commentators raised questions about how the firm would recover from this, while others maintained that it was strong enough to recover.

### Mayer, Brown, Rowe & Maw LLP
See firm details p.876

**The Firm:** Mayer Brown has developed a government relations practice that concentrates more on policy rather than politics, thereby playing on its strength as an excellent Supreme Court and appellate firm. It has excellent public policy advocates and a deep knowledge of the litigation system, hence it is "*the best and most experienced*" when it comes to civil justice reform. In the past, the group was involved in the Securities Litigation Reform Act on behalf of the accounting profession; now it is advising on a push to reform the class action system by moving it up to the federal court. The group is led by James Wootton.

# GOVERNMENT

# POLITICAL LAW

## Band 1

### Perkins Coie LLP

**The Firm:** Not only is Perkins Coie the largest political law group in the country, it is also the Democratic Party's firm of choice, as illustrated by its representation of the Kerry presidential campaign. A giant in the field, as well as advising political parties and candidates, the team also helps corporations, trade associations, nonprofit organizations and wealthy individuals keep on the right side of the law with their political activity. Of late, the firm has been particularly busy advising clients on the implementation of the McCain-Feingold campaign finance law.

**The Lawyers: Robert Bauer** is the chair and lynchpin of the political law group. He has *"a really high, national profile"* as the long-time attorney for various Democratic organizations, including the Democratic National Committee and Senatorial and Congressional Campaign Committees.

### Wiley Rein & Fielding LLP

See firm details p.579

**The Firm:** The Republican Party's favored firm, Wiley Rein is another dominant force in the sector. The election law and government ethics department advises clients on federal and state laws dealing with campaign finance, lobbying and ethics. It also represents them in formal proceedings before the Federal Election Commission (FEC), House or Senate Ethics Committees, or in court when required. This is a large team with the resources to provide expertise on laws passed by every state in the country. Although most work is done for large corporations such as Microsoft and GM, its role for the Republican Party, including the Republican National Committee, is not to be underestimated.

**The Lawyers: Jan Baran** (see p.86) is widely recognized as *"the leading Republican practitioner"* and hailed as *"one of the best election lawyers in the US with the most comprehensive knowledge of the law at both state and federal level."* He recently acted as co-counsel to Senator Mitch McConnell in the landmark McConnell v FEC case, which challenged the new McCain-Feingold campaign finance law.

## Band 2

### Arent Fox PLLC

**The Firm:** Arent Fox is an emerging name in the field, advising corporations as well as both committees and candidates from the Republican Party. The practice is heavily centered around the work of **Craig Engle** (see p.98), former official at the FEC and general counsel to the National Republican Senatorial Committee. Peers admire his *"encyclopedic knowledge of FEC"* and reveal that he is *"indispensable for remembering how arcane rules have been applied in the past."*

### McDermott Will & Emery

See firm details p.878

**The Firm:** This firm is known for its significant political litigation experience, especially since it recruited **Bobby Burchfield** (see p.90) from Covington & Burling. Although a general litigator, Burchfield has tried many cases in the area of political law, including representing the Republican National Committee at the Supreme Court in its constitutional challenge to the McCain-Feingold campaign finance law. Interviewees had nothing but praise for his advocacy skills, describing him as *"a superb and knowledgeable litigator."*

### Patton Boggs LLP

**The Firm:** As well as an excellent government relations team, Patton Boggs can boast a well-regarded political law group. **Ben Ginsberg** (see p.102) is the most visible member of this team, his fame being due in no small part to his position as general counsel to the Bush-Cheney presidential campaign. He has also done a considerable amount of work for the Republican National Committee and Republican Governors Association. Peers respect Ginsberg's *"many years of practice"* and recommend him as a sound representative.

### Pillsbury Winthrop Shaw Pittman LLP

See firm details p.1550

**The Firm:** As most of the team is based in California, its state laws naturally feature heavily in the day-to-day business of this political law practice. Nevertheless, its lawyers work throughout the country including at the federal level. Most of their work involves advising corporations, such as Chevron, on building compliance systems to ensure their political activity stays within the law. Clients report that the team fulfills its duties with *"tenacity, discipline and focus."* Head of the group **Fred Lowell** (see p.116) represented the Bush-Cheney presidential campaign within California. He is an *"honest and tireless worker"* who has *"good judgment and a thorough knowledge of the law."*

### Ryan Phillips Utrecht & MacKinnon

**The Firm:** This boutique firm is dedicated wholly to legislative, administrative and political law, and serves a wide range of clients from corporations to political candidates. **Lyn Utrecht** is its best-known political law specialist and she is famous in the market for representing the Clintons. She gained her *"extensive knowledge and experience"* from her time at the FEC, and has continued to thrive as one of the most *"capable"* lawyers in private practice.

### Sandler Reiff & Young

**The Firm:** This small five-lawyer outfit focuses all its resources in this sphere. It is a very political practice which is proud to be *"in the trenches"* for the Democratic Party. As such it handles a great deal of ballot disputes. **Joseph Sandler** is particularly notable as the general counsel of the Democratic National Committee. Feedback indicates that he is an *"extremely capable"* lawyer who is *"very seasoned in election law."*

### Skadden, Arps, Slate, Meagher & Flom LLP & Affiliates

See firm details p.1557

**The Firm:** Unsurprisingly for this top-level corporate firm, 90% of its political law practice involves advising large companies on their political contributions and lobbying activities. It has a firm grip on the loyalties of the largest investment banks and represents Citigroup, Morgan Stanley, UBS, among others. The practice additionally represents political candidates and, almost uniquely, counsels both Democrats and Republicans. For example, the team advises the Republican Mayor of New York, Mike Bloomberg, and also the Democrat contender for governor of New York, Eliot Spitzer. Whether representing companies or candidates, the team always displays a *"great focus on dotting the i's and crossing the t's, and ensuring we stick to all the regulations,"* say clients. **Ken Gross** (see p.104) leads the group. His is *"a very big name"* in the field and he is firmly ensconced as *"a real expert on US election law."* Gross worked at the FEC for many years and is consequently *"very knowledgeable and connected."*

# INTERNATIONAL ARBITRATION

| International Arbitration |
| --- |
| Leading Firms |
| **1** DEBEVOISE & PLIMPTON LLP |
|     SULLIVAN & CROMWELL LLP |
|     WHITE & CASE LLP |
| **2** COVINGTON & BURLING |
|     FULBRIGHT & JAWORSKI LLP |
|     HUGHES HUBBARD & REED L.L.P. |
|     SIDLEY AUSTIN LLP |
|     SIMPSON THACHER & BARTLETT LLP |
|     SKADDEN, ARPS, SLATE, MEAGHER & FLOM |
| **3** CLEARY GOTTLIEB STEEN & HAMILTON LLP |
|     CLIFFORD CHANCE US LLP |
|     FRESHFIELDS BRUCKHAUS DERINGER LLP |
|     KING & SPALDING LLP |
|     MAYER, BROWN, ROWE & MAW LLP |
|     O'MELVENY & MYERS LLP |
|     SHEARMAN & STERLING LLP |
|     WINSTON & STRAWN LLP |
| **4** ASTIGARRAGA DAVIS |
|     BAKER & MCKENZIE |
|     BOIES, SCHILLER & FLEXNER |
|     FRIED, FRANK, HARRIS, SHRIVER & JACOBSON |
|     GREENBERG TRAURIG LLP |
|     HOGAN & HARTSON LLP |
|     KIRKLAND & ELLIS LLP |
|     MORGAN, LEWIS & BOCKIUS LLP |
|     VINSON & ELKINS LLP |
|     WEIL, GOTSHAL & MANGES LLP |
|     WILMERHALE |

## Band 1

### Debevoise & Plimpton LLP
See firm details p.1529

**The Firm:** Under the guiding hand of Robert von Mehren, this *"Tiffany's of a practice"* became one of the first New York firms to focus on international arbitration. Now, with von Mehren's protégés at the helm, it *"dominates the upper end of the spectrum"* and is seen to be going from strength to strength. As well as working on a myriad of commercial arbitrations, the team displays considerable expertise and experience in public international law, including investment treaty disputes. As a result, clients regularly boast about *"the sheer depth and diversity"* of the practice. New York is seen as its nerve center although strong teams are also to be found in London and Paris where Mark Friedman and Bart Legum lead the respective teams. Whatever the type of case and regardless of the country involved, commentators enthuse that *"you can practically touch the quality on offer here."*

**The Lawyers:** **Donald Donovan** and **David Rivkin**, as the practice's brand-name lawyers, form a highly effective team. Donovan is *"an energetic visionary with creative flair"* whose strong background in public international law is evidenced by

his regular appearances at the ICJ. Within the arbitration field, he succeeded in gaining one of the largest ever treaty-based monetary awards ($500 million) for client First Eagle Funds, in its case against the Bank for International Settlements at the Hague Tribunal. Rivkin is a *"highly technical and zealous advocate"* who has been occupied recently with the long-standing Occidental Petroleum v Ecuador UNCITRAL arbitration. Having won $75 million for Occidental, he is now standing firm against attempts to overturn the award. Despite spending most of their time as counsel, both attorneys are in extremely high demand as arbitrators because of their *"deep understanding of the intricacies of international arbitration procedure."* Fred Davis is a new boon to the firm, having recently joined the Paris office from Shearman & Sterling.

### Sullivan & Cromwell LLP
See firm details p.1558

**The Firm:** Sullivan & Cromwell is consistently praised for its *"breadth and depth of talent"* and involvement in *"a huge quantity of high-end cases."* Clients spoke enthusiastically of the *"tremendous sense of confidence"* they have in its lawyers who *"really get involved and fight wholeheartedly for the cause."* Although it does have experience in investment treaty disputes, the firm is best known for commercial arbitrations, including problems arising out of large joint ventures. This work is led from New York but the practice certainly operates on a worldwide basis, especially following the bolstering of its London office. Wherever a dispute takes place, clients revel in the presence of *"smart and energetic"* lawyers who have the *"ability to carry a tremendous workload and deliver results in a number of competing cases at the same time."*

**The Lawyers:** Named as *"a founding father of the discipline in New York,"* **James Carter** (see p.91) is revered as an *"erudite and lawyerly character"* who excels at advocacy. He presents his cases in a *"calm, rational but also very sharp"* manner and *"always provides a strong counterpoint to the other party's argument."* He has served as counsel on a number of ICC cases lately, including representing Swedish investors in a dispute arising out of a Russian company's takeover of a Turkish cell phone business. Carter is also *"one of the top arbitrators in the country"* and sat on the ICC tribunal that awarded $125 million to claimant Bechtel in a dispute arising out of the Dabhol power project in India. **Joseph Neuhaus** (see p.123) maintains a Latin American focus and has been involved in both commercial and ICSID arbitrations in the region recently. A seasoned litigator, he is also *"extremely knowledgeable about arbitration law."* One commentator declared: *"He is the most effective and proactive counsel I've worked with in an arbitration."*

### White & Case LLP
See firm details p.1566

**The Firm:** Few other US firms are as internationally

entrenched as White & Case. It comes as little surprise, therefore, that it possesses a *"terrific"* international arbitration practice that stands as a *"leader in the field."* Its quality is enhanced by the profile of its *"impressive core of well-known experts"* in Washington DC, New York and Paris. These are experienced in all manner of arbitrations. However, the legacy of Charles Brower's public international law focus continues to prevail such that the firm's reputation shines particularly brightly when it comes to investor-state disputes. Clients confirmed the team's strong standing and waxed lyrical about the *"depth of talent"* on offer and the firm's *"plugged-in and extremely well-prepared"* lawyers.

**The Lawyers:** **Carolyn Lamm** (see p.114) is *"a recognized expert in the area of investment disputes."* She is *"thoroughly immersed in her work"* and impresses commentators with her display of *"tenacity and quiet determination."* She has recently been representing Tenex in an interesting case arising from the Swords to Plowshares agreement between the USA and Russia, whereby Russia has agreed to break down its nuclear warheads into uranium that can be used for energy. The case was brought by Globe Nuclear Services and Supply who claimed that Tenex breached the contract to supply it with chemicals to break down the uranium. Lamm succeeded in getting the case against her client dismissed. Interviewees frequently claimed that **Paul Friedland** (see p.100) *"has a more extensive technical knowledge of arbitration than any other lawyer out there - you can go to him with any conceivable question."* Clients also praised his *"quickness of mind"* and *"the seriously impressive speed at which he outpaces opponents or witnesses."* He is currently handling investor-state arbitrations for both Bulgaria and Indonesia. **Abby Cohen Smutny** (see p.135) is renowned for her *"thorough and technical"* preparation, as well as her *"vigorous and energetic"* advocacy. Admirers confidently stated that *"you can't go to a better practitioner, especially on cutting-edge cases."* She has had a very notable past year due to her secural of an $877 million award for CSOB in its ICSID case brought against the Slovak Republic.

## Band 2

### Covington & Burling
See firm details p.563

**The Firm:** While some firms make their name due to excellence in specific types of arbitration, Covington & Burling's claim to fame lies with the breadth of its practice. Among its notable cases, it has represented investors in a number of investor-state disputes and is currently working on the high-profile LG&E Energy v Argentina case. Its work here is being eagerly watched by the market as this is the next case in line following the landmark decision won by CMS against Argentina. The practice is generally in the public law sphere and has a strong reputation for state versus state and boundary disputes. It further complements this with work on behalf of corporate litigators whom it has represented in various matters, making its biggest impact in insurance disputes.

Despite straddling so many subject areas, clients were quick to comment on the *"consistency of quality"* on offer. This was felt to be the practice's trump card along with its *"highly sophisticated approach to teamwork."*

**The Lawyers:** **Oscar Garibaldi** (see p.101) specializes in investor-state relations, with his Argentinean roots making him particularly well suited to Latin American cases. Commentators noted that he has a *"polished Ivy League style"* and that he offers *"convincing and clearly thought-through analysis."* Clients particularly turn to him, when they require a *"bigger picture approach,"* confident in the knowledge that he has a *"full understanding of all cultural and international issues."* **Eugene Gulland** (see p.104) is an experienced trial lawyer who is highly prized for his advocacy skills. Described as *"a torpedo smashing through the other party's hull,"* he has *"great energy and focus"* and is *"excellent at winning cases."* As well as using these skills in the arbitration field, he also handles litigation relating to the enforcement of arbitration awards. **Thomas Johnson** (see p.110) has an *"exceptionally brilliant"* international public law background – as well as having worked on many cases at the Iran-USA Claims Tribunal, he is also representing Eritrea in its boundary dispute with Ethiopia. Clients enjoy his *"relaxed and informal"* style and also point to his *"sheer persuasiveness"* when on his feet. **Mitchell Dolin** (see p.96) specializes in arbitrations in the insurance field. He represents Fortune 500 clients such as Cardinal Health, in high-value disputes regarding asbestos and pharmaceutical mass tort claims or large property losses. A lawyer with a *"very dignified"* presence, Dolin is a big client favorite and as one interviewee said: *"Some attorneys have a smart mouth but not a smart head; Dolin has both."*

## Fulbright & Jaworski L.L.P.
See firm details p.1928

**The Firm:** Fulbright heads a contingent of Texas firms that is increasingly playing a key role in the international arbitration market. Its practice has been built up on the back of its oil and gas expertise and it continues to consistently win impressive mandates in that field. For example, it is currently representing YUKOS in a $16.5 billion claim against the shareholders of OAO Siberian Oil Company, following a failed merger between the companies. Being one of the largest commercial arbitrations in the world at the moment, this matter seems certain to ensure the firm a high profile for some time to come. Its core team is based in Houston but the practice is also notable for the exponential growth of its international presence. The team in London has expanded dramatically and it also has a nascent practice in Hong Kong. Its strength in Latin American cases should be emphasized; it recently represented Duke Energy in an ICSID case against Peru in relation to that country's reacquisition of former state-owned electric companies that had gone into private hands. This case is particularly interesting as it will be the first ICSID case to consider issues relating to legal stability agreements. All in all, a year of growth

and high-profile appointments, and one that confirms Fulbright's position as a *"top of the pile"* practice.

**The Lawyers:** **Mark Baker** (see p.86) is revered as an *"exemplary front lawyer for a case,"* a claim backed up by his role in the YUKOS case. He has become *"extremely well known in the community"* and is credited for much of the firm's recent successes. He is complemented by cochair **John Bowman** (see p.89) who is a *"thoroughly prepared, considered and competent"* advocate. **Arif Ali** (see p.85), working from the DC office, is predicted to be *"on his way to becoming a prominent star in the area."* A producer of *"quality, detailed and thorough work,"* clients report that he *"doesn't over-delegate and has his fingerprints all over every case."*

## Hughes Hubbard & Reed LLP
See firm details p.1535

**The Firm:** Hughes Hubbard houses an impressive number of *"top-flight lawyers handling top-flight cases."* Clients have nothing but good things to say about these attorneys, noting that they are *"experienced, knowledgeable and fully cognizant with the rules of international arbitration."* *"A definite leader in the field,"* the firm's clear dedication to the sector is demonstrated by the fact that it deploys more than 50 lawyers to its practice. The work is largely centered around commercial arbitration, servicing a strong client list in a wide range of industries, but NAFTA cases also feature frequently. The US team's reputation is such that it is admired throughout the world. When teamed with its very strong sister group in Paris, Hughes Hubbard has an international position it can be proud of.

**The Lawyers:** **John Townsend** (see p.138) heads the arbitration practice and is well known as counsel in complex international contract disputes and as an arbitrator in his own right. Clients admire him as an *"elder statesman"* and value his *"experience and reliability when it comes to predicting outcomes."* Peers state that he is *"a real stand-out"* whose *"generosity with his time in training the next generation is an example to all."* **Steven Hammond** (see p.105) is highly recommended by both clients and peers. He is especially rated as an arbitrator as he is *"effective at managing parties and is organized and fair in procedural orders."* **John Fellas** (see p.99) is a younger lawyer who has impressed the market with his *"strategic understanding"* and *"deep and creative mind."* One seasoned client went so far as to say that he is *"one of the best lawyers I've ever dealt with."* Similarly talented, **Daniel Weiner** (see p.141) is becoming more prominent as he handles more and more of Hughes Hubbard's New York cases. He is hailed as *"the best of the younger generation."*

## Sidley Austin LLP
See firm details p.883

**The Firm:** This practice has an unparalleled place in the market when it comes to investor-state disputes, since both of its leading arbitration lawyers have extensive experience of negotiating investment treaties on behalf of their home countries. This expe-

## International Arbitration: Arbitrators

1 **AKSEN Gerald** *Sole Practitioner*
**BERMANN George** *Sole Practitioner*
**BROWER Charles** *20 Essex Street*
**CARON David** *Sole Practitioner*
**CARTER James** *Sullivan & Cromwell LLP*
**DONOVAN Donald** *Debevoise*
**GARFINKEL Barry** *Skadden, Arps*
**GRIGERA NAÓN Horacio** *Sole Practitioner*
**HAMMOND Steven** *Hughes Hubbard*
**LOWENFELD Andreas** *Sole Practitioner*
**PARK William** *Sole Practitioner*
**PLANT David** *Sole Practitioner, Sole Practitioner*
**REISMAN W Michael** *Sole Practitioner*
**RENFREW Charles** *Sole Practitioner*
**RIVKIN David** *Debevoise & Plimpton LLP*
**SCHWEBEL Stephen** *Sole Practitioner*
**TOWNSEND John** *Hughes Hubbard*
**VON MEHREN Robert** *Sole Practitioner*

rience extends to representing both investors and states, a fact amply demonstrated by this year's deal roster. On the investor side, the group has represented Fireman's Fund in an arbitration against Mexico. This is the first-ever claim to be brought under the financial services chapter of NAFTA. On the state side, it has defended Peru in an ICSID case brought by Duke Energy. Impressed clients stress that they would *"unreservedly recommend"* the firm to anyone, primarily due to the level of experience on offer and *"the meticulous and exhaustive preparation and follow-up that goes into every case."*

**The Lawyers:** Chair of the practice **Daniel Price** (see p.127) is an *"important practitioner who is prominently involved in large high-profile cases."* Researchers were informed that he is *"about the most deft and natural advocate out there"* and, as a former negotiator for the US government, is *"very knowledgeable on the law of bilateral investment treaties."* As well as the cases described above, he has been handling a Chapter 11 NAFTA case against Mexico for Tate & Lyle. This relates to the tax being raised on soft drinks containing high fructose syrup. **Stanimir Alexandrov** (see p.85) is a former Vice Minister of Foreign Affairs of Bulgaria. In that capacity he gained considerable knowledge of bilateral investment treaties (BITs) during negotiations he handled on behalf of the government. Interestingly enough, Alexandrov negotiated opposite colleague Dan Price in talks leading to the US-Bulgarian BIT. He is a *"scholarly"* lawyer who offers *"excellent analytical"* insights. His caseload in the past year has included acting as co-counsel to GE and Bechtel in the UNCITRAL arbitration against India arising from the collapse of the Dabhol power plant.

### Simpson Thacher & Bartlett LLP

See firm details p.1555

**The Firm:** Simpson Thacher has a wide caseload that covers a thriving insurance arbitration practice and plenty of purchase price adjustment cases on behalf of investment banks. It is probably best known, however, for its periodical involvement in massive high-profile cases. In the past year, the Dabhol case, in particular, has been hogging the headlines for the firm. Its team has been representing GE and Bechtel in four arbitrations arising from this massive power project in India, including two investment treaty arbitrations at UNCITRAL. The group is chosen for such matters because it *"excels in developing strategy"* and can be *"aggressive"* when required. As one client put it: *"There are certain cases where only a first-class firm with a strong reputation will do and Simpson Thacher fits the bill admirably."*

**The Lawyers:** **John Kerr** (see p.112) is popularly regarded as a *"top person"* in the field who is *"smart, creative and knowledgeable."* **Robert Smit** (see p.135) is *"already a star despite being fairly young"* and has impressed commentators with his *"deep, specialized knowledge."*

### Skadden, Arps, Slate, Meagher & Flom LLP

See firm details p.1557

**The Firm:** Skadden's towering presence in the corporate and commercial world guarantees it a high profile in the commercial arbitration sphere. The practice refuses to rest on its laurels, however, and continues to grow and expand. For example, the London office is thriving and its lawyers generally are becoming more and more involved in investor-state arbitrations. Its team is most frequently found in the thick of the most complex and high-value cases such as its representation of the Indonesian telecom company, PT Telekomunikasi, in a $1.5 billion ICC arbitration concerning a breach of contract with a foreign-controlled operator. Commentators point to the presence of *"a bevy of lawyers with strong reputations"* and agree that it is one of the best practices in the USA.

**The Lawyers:** **Dana Freyer** (see p.100) was frequently recommended by clients and peers alike as a *"very experienced and able"* lawyer. She works alongside **Barry Garfinkel** (see p.101), *"one of the pioneers in international arbitration in New York."* *"Smart, fair and organized,"* he is representing CEMEX in an ICSID case against Indonesia but is spending more and more time as an arbitrator. **John Gardiner** (see p.101) climbs the ranks this year due to the sheer volume of commentators who regard him as *"extremely capable."* He *"always delivers as good a job as you could possibly hope for."* **Marco Schnabl** (see p.133) was also singled out as a lawyer with a strong practice.

### Band 3

### Cleary Gottlieb Steen & Hamilton LLP

See firm details p.1525

**The Firm:** This highly international firm is particularly well known in the market for its representation of foreign sovereigns in major arbitrations and has strong teams in New York, DC, Paris and Rome. Indeed, the Paris office is representing the Russian Federation in one of the highest value matters currently ongoing ($30 billion), defending the sovereign in three parallel UNCITRAL arbitrations brought by various shareholders of YUKOS. The US offices are equally busy having represented Indonesia in the arbitration concerning the Karaha Bodas geothermal project. Presently they are involved in litigation to block the arbitration award granted to the plaintiffs. This high-profile work for sovereigns does not, however, eclipse its role in the commercial arbitration world – the firm represented Citibank in an ICC arbitration with Telecom Italia in a dispute over the control of Brasil Telecom.

**The Lawyers:** The firm can draw on a team of approximately 30 lawyers experienced in arbitration cases. **Lawrence Friedman** (see p.100) was particularly recommended as a lawyer who *"excels at managing court relations."* He represented the Carlyle Group in an ICC arbitration where the client won the right to sell its investment in a Chinese retail venture.

### Clifford Chance US LLP

See firm details p.1526

**The Firm:** Despite the New York office having just two partners working full-time in international arbitration, the practice can draw on the resources of a highly respected global arbitration team led from the London office. This means it competes with the best when it comes to appointments on major cases. Thus it is acting as counsel to AES in the much talked about ICSID case the company is bringing against Argentina. Most of the team's work has historically been in the energy sector, however, it has started to expand beyond its traditional core strength and is now representing many international banks. For example, it is representing a US fund manager in a dispute arising from a joint venture investment in Argentina.

**The Lawyers:** **David Lindsey** is an active presence in international conferences and a regular sight on high-profile cases. Peers contend that he is a *"go-to person if you ever have a problem with anything."*

### Freshfields Bruckhaus Deringer LLP

**The Firm:** The New York outpost has thoroughly established itself as a key component of the group, complementing the work undertaken by the Paris office. The firm has developed one of the busiest treaty-based arbitration practices in the world and is particularly experienced in representing claimant companies in these cases. Commentators believe that its success in such an important case speaks volumes about the level of skill inherent in this practice.

**The Lawyers:** **Lucy Reed** is a great advocate and has been one of the leaders of the international arbitration Bar for a long time.

### King & Spalding LLP

See firm details p.1933

**The Firm:** According to interviewees, one would be *"hard pushed to find another US firm involved in as many significant international arbitrations."* The firm has certainly made an impact in the energy sector and is representing an impressive list of major Houston-based oil companies and oil company service providers on international disputes. For example, clients include Chevron, Shell and Kellogg Brown & Root. As well as working on many commercial disputes, the team has a significant practice in investor-state arbitrations. In this field, it is representing both Sempra Energy and Enron in cases brought against Argentina at ICSID. While Houston is the lightning rod for work, due to the presence of Doak Bishop, the Atlanta, New York, London and DC offices are also heavily involved in international arbitration.

**The Lawyers:** **Doak Bishop** (see p.89) has carved a real niche as an expert in investor-state disputes and has handled countless cases in Latin America. Clients enjoy his *"understated and informal style"* and also count on him for *"dependable advice."* Others commented on the *"clarity of his presentation and ability to highlight issues that really matter."* **William Russell** (see p.131) has also made a name for himself through working alongside Bishop and is increasingly running his own cases.

## Mayer, Brown, Rowe & Maw LLP
See firm details p.876

**The Firm:** This firm's profile in the arbitration world has shot through the roof since it was appointed to represent the Republic of Argentina in a number of high-profile ICSID cases, arising from the privatization of its utilities in the 1990's and the subsequent abolition of the fixed exchange rate. The firm fields a *"terrific team"* from Chicago and Houston that benefits from a deep historic knowledge of Latin America. The practice stretches beyond this key appointment, however, and enjoys a *"high reputation for advocacy"* among other clients. These include BellSouth, Diners Club International and the Chicago Mercantile Exchange.

**The Lawyers:** Fluent Spanish speaker **Javier Rubinstein** (see p.131) is leading the team in the Argentina cases. Commentators were particularly impressed with his presentation skills, and noted that he is *"a forceful advocate who always remains deferential to the panel and never gets aggressive."* He is also *"a very sophisticated cross-examiner"* and equally *"effective with the written word."* **William Knull** (see p.113) works from the Houston office and is a *"well-prepared"* practitioner with *"a good book of business."* As well as helping with the Argentina cases, he is representing the Republic of Turkmenistan in a series of ICC arbitrations arising out of failed oil and gas ventures.

## O'Melveny & Myers LLP
See firm details p.336

**The Firm:** Despite being a relative newcomer to the practice area, O'Melveny & Myers is already renowned as a *"highly competent outfit on the way up."* Boasting teams based in New York, San Francisco and Asia, the group is truly international in scope and capable of tackling any matter, however large or Byzantine. Its US team successfully arbitrated a case on behalf of two financial institutions

at the ICC in the past year against Uruguay. More recently, it filed a related arbitration claiming another breach of contract. With such successful outcomes, the firm's star is set to continue rising.

**The Lawyers:** **Louis Kimmelman** (see p.113) is *"an engaging performer who knows how to connect with arbitrators."* He leads the New York team and is acknowledged as *"one of the city's true experts"* in the field. The team in San Francisco is led by Steve Smith.

## Shearman & Sterling LLP
See firm details p.1554

**The Firm:** Shearman & Sterling is universally acknowledged as a global force in the international arbitration sphere. The Paris team, led by Emmanuel Gaillard, is spoken of in awed tones, but the New York team represents a further key contributor to the firm's international reputation. The focus in New York is mainly on cross-border investment disputes, many of which concern Latin America. For example, the practice recently represented Ameriven in a $900 million dispute with Fluor Daniels regarding the construction of the Hamaca project in Venezuela. Clients report particular benefits in choosing this firm above others, citing its *"bright, experienced and effective team players"* as a particular asset.

**The Lawyers:** **Henry Weisburg** (see p.141) is admired for his *"intellectual"* capabilities and his *"experienced and practical"* approach. He has had a high-profile year successfully representing CSFB and Dresdner Bank in two arbitrations against Uruguay. These concerned the failure of Uruguay's largest commercial bank. Fred Davis has left the firm for Debevoise & Plimpton in Paris.

## Winston & Strawn LLP
See firm details p.886

**The Firm:** The absorption of a group of White & Case lawyers in 2004 means Winston & Strawn now has the US capability to complement its strong Geneva and Paris-based arbitration practices. Indeed, many commentators feel it has acquired *"the best Latin American-focused arbitration practice in the US."* Ten full-time, Spanish-speaking lawyers work on international arbitration matters, involving themselves in an impressive list of ICSID cases. The team represents many sovereign nations and is currently acting for Venezuela in a $1.2 billion arbitration brought by Canadian mining company Vannessa Ventures. It has also handled many cases for Chile. Demonstrating its versatility, the group is frequently found on the other side of the fence and is representing EDF in the ICSID case against Argentina.

**The Lawyers:** Former White & Case lawyer **Ronald Goodman** heads the US branch of the international arbitration practice. He is *"an exceptionally capable fellow"* blessed with the talent of being able to offer both *"broad and specialized"* advice. **Paolo Di Rosa** (see p.96) has been helping Goodman with ICSID cases against Argentina and the market reports that there is *"a good buzz about him and his work."*

## Band 4

## Astigarraga Davis
See firm details p.658

**The Firm:** This small boutique in Miami specializes in litigation and arbitration matters and has developed a fine reputation for work in the Latin American market. Its team of 15 lawyers is attributed with putting Miami on the map for international arbitration work. It has handled a broad range of arbitrations, ranging from commercial AAA and ICC cases to investor-state disputes at ICSID.

**The Lawyers:** **José Astigarraga** (see p.86) is *"at the forefront of the bicultural North American and South American practice spheres."* He is *"one of the top practitioners in the country and, truly, one of the experts on arbitration in Latin America."*

## Baker & McKenzie
See firm details p.866

**The Firm:** With offices throughout the world and 200 dedicated lawyers to call upon, Baker & McKenzie's international commercial arbitration group can boast a global reach most firms can only dream of. The US side of the operation is like a microcosm of the overall practice as the lawyers are spread across the continent from San Francisco and Houston to New York and DC. The group combines arbitration work with extensive litigation experience and can handle any dispute resolution problems a client may face.

**The Lawyers:** New York-based **Lawrence Newman** is viewed as a *"senior statesman who knows this area of law intellectually as well as anyone else in the USA."* He has worked throughout the world but is particularly interested in Latin American cases.

## Boies, Schiller & Flexner
See firm details p.1520

**The Firm:** Despite its small size, this boutique has a huge reputation as a litigation powerhouse. It is experienced in every form of dispute resolution and, by extension, international arbitration is well to the fore. Known for its polished service, it was succinctly summarized by one interviewee: *"It does a lot of arbitration work and it does it to a very high standard."* The firm has a chain of offices along the East Coast, as well as a base over in California. It has experience in ICC, LCIA, UNCITRAL, ICSID and AAA arbitrations.

**The Lawyers:** The arbitration practice is headed by managing partner **Jonathan Schiller** (see p.133). He is a well-known name in the field who has effectively adapted his inestimable skills as a trial lawyer to his arbitration practice. Interviewees say he *"presents an effective case"* and has *"a sound understanding of the arbitral process."* Colleague **William Isaacson** (see p.109) is *"a very smart thinker"* and a *"fantastic writer."*

## Fried, Frank, Harris, Shriver & Jacobson LLP

See firm details p.1532

**The Firm:** *"A good choice when the stakes are high,"* this firm is not only *"knowledgeable on the arbitral process"* but also *"takes the time to get to know the client's business and needs."* It appears in many commercial arbitrations at both the ICC and International Center for Dispute Resolution (ICDR) and has developed considerable expertise in IP issues. For example, the team has been representing a French aerospace company in a patent infringement dispute against a US space company. Insurance and reinsurance disputes form another important part of the practice. The team is currently representing underwriters at Lloyd's of London in multiple arbitrations commenced by Century Indemnity Company.

**The Lawyers:** The team is led by **Elliot Polebaum** (see p.126), who is admired by clients as a *"calm personality who is able to explain what to expect along the way."* He is fluent in French and hence is a particularly popular choice with French clients. The market is also watching the arrival of William Taft with interest. As a former legal adviser at the Department of State, Taft has represented the USA in NAFTA arbitrations and is expected to make an impact in private practice.

## Greenberg Traurig LLP

See firm details p.664

**The Firm:** The heart of this firm's international arbitration practice is to be found in its Miami office. From here, a team of 15 attorneys work on a range of international commercial arbitration matters, proving particularly strong in the Latin American market. The skills it has gained there, however, have proved eminently transferable and the group has triumphed in many other countries including Italy and Germany. Recently, it represented an Israeli company in an ICDR arbitration against a Brazilian distribution company in relation to a breach of contract.

**The Lawyers:** **Pedro Martinez-Fraga** (see p.117) is the practice's best-known name and is renowned as an *"aggressive advocate"* who delivers *"an excellent performance."* He has had a very noteworthy year having represented the Republic of Chile in a number of court cases brought against Augustin Pinochet.

## Hogan & Hartson LLP

See firm details p.568

**The Firm:** This firm has a *"first-rate"* global arbitration practice with 48 lawyers and continues to expand, having opened offices in Geneva and Caracas. Within the USA, the core of the practice is based in Miami and its team is especially active in Latin America. Clients enjoy working with these lawyers as they *"exude calmness and never get angry"* while also demonstrating the *"ability to bridge the more technical side of arbitration."* The practice is broad and encompasses disputes involving development and infrastructure projects, the energy industry and the telecommunications industry. One highlight of the

past year saw the practice representing News Holdings in a massive $1 billion dispute with a minority shareholder of DIRECTV Latin America. The case is currently filed at state courts in both New York and Florida and is also in arbitration.

**The Lawyers:** Seasoned trial lawyer **Daniel González** (see p.103) is deemed by some to be *"one of the leading lawyers in arbitration in the western hemisphere."* Clients appreciate his *"customer service-orientation"* and report that he has an *"approachable and accommodating personality."*

## Kirkland & Ellis LLP

See firm details p.875

**The Firm:** The distinguished litigation practice at Kirkland & Ellis has approximately 25 lawyers who are also very experienced in international arbitration matters. The bulk of this work is handled from Chicago and London and is centered on ICC and ICDR commercial disputes. It has handled major cases for such household names as GM, Morgan Stanley, SC Johnson and Lucent Technologies. Illustrative of the firm's typical caseload, it represented BellSouth in a dispute with a minority owner of a Venezuelan telephone company.

**The Lawyers:** James Schink leads the work from Chicago.

## Morgan, Lewis & Bockius LLP

See firm details p.1758

**The Firm:** Robert Hornick garners considerable name recognition for this firm. He is, however, but part of a much broader practice that takes in six offices across the world – New York, DC, Philadelphia, Miami, San Francisco and London. The team works on a wide range of commercial arbitrations but is particularly strong in the firm's traditional areas of expertise such as IP, securities and purchase price adjustments in connection with acquisitions. For example, it has defended Merrill Lynch in numerous arbitrations brought by foreign investors who have bought stock on the US Stock Exchange. In the IP arena, the firm represented Neurochem in an ICC arbitration brought by Immtech International relating to alleged breaches of contract, fraud and misappropriation of trade secrets.

**The Lawyers:** **Robert Hornick** (see p.108) is a *"terrific advocate"* with *"a great nose for strategy"* and *"exemplary presentation and writing skills."* He is particularly experienced in IP arbitration but has, this year, also served as the claimant's Indonesian expert in the Karaha Bodas v Pertamina case regarding the cancellation of a geothermal project in Indonesia.

## Vinson & Elkins LLP

See firm details p.1938

**The Firm:** The firm's reputation as a leader in the energy world ensures that it gets involved in many of that industry's high-stakes arbitrations. Most of the work is undertaken from the Houston office but the London office is growing apace as it increasingly concerns itself with the Asia and Middle East markets. Despite the retirement of key lawyers Ben

Sheppard and Platt Davis, there remains a strong team of lawyers which clients say *"leaves no stone unturned."* In a busy year, the firm has represented El Paso in an UNCITRAL arbitration against Petrobras concerning a power plant in Macaé. It also acted for F-W Oil in an ICSID case against Trinidad following the withdrawal of an award of an oil field redevelopment project.

**The Lawyers:** **James Loftis** (see p.116) now heads up the arbitration practice along with Stephen Douglas York in London. Commentators agree that Loftis can be relied upon to keep the practice thriving as he is a *"thorough and competent"* lawyer.

## Weil, Gotshal & Manges LLP

See firm details p.1565

**The Firm:** The firm's global dispute resolution group works on both litigation and arbitration matters, with satisfied clients asserting that *"the lawyering is very strong across the board."* Its commercial workload includes acting for LV Finance Group in an arbitration in Zurich against IPOC International Growth Fund. Commentators also highlighted this as *"a firm to watch for investor-state cases."* The group has represented Ecuador in a number of arbitrations including the case brought by Occidental Petroleum.

**The Lawyers:** **Eric Ordway** (see p.124) spends the majority of his time on arbitration matters and, as a fluent Spanish speaker, is very popular for cases in Latin America. He is well regarded in the market for being *"a smart and talented lawyer who is building up a strong practice."*

## WilmerHale

See firm details p.580

**The Firm:** WilmerHale is renowned as a powerhouse for international arbitration work, largely due to the reputation of its London office. Alive to change, however, it has successfully built up its US presence, centering a strong practice around its New York office. The team here works closely with the London office on complex commercial disputes. Examples of this include representing a major US capital goods manufacturer in an ICC arbitration against two Colombian companies claiming unpaid commission. The firm is now also beefing-up a DC office increasingly renowned for its commercial and investor-state disputes.

**The Lawyers:** New York-based **John Pierce** (see p.125) is a general litigator who has worked on numerous arbitrations. He is considered as *"a real up-and-comer in the field"* and a *"very knowledgeable"* practitioner.

## Other Notable Practitioners

Clients compare **Stephens Clay** (see p.92) from Kilpatrick Stockton LLP to a *"highly skilled chess player who keeps an eye on the current situation but is also looking three or four moves down the line."* They are also enamored of his presentation skills, describing how he *"engages the panel with his words"* before using a *"velvet hammer"* approach to ram his point home. This year, Clay represented BellSouth in an arbitration arising from a Latin American joint venture that was dissolved. **Christopher Dugan** (see p.97) of Paul, Hastings, Janofsky & Walker LLP has a high profile as he succeeded in gaining a $261 million award for the Karaha Bodas Company following Indonesia's decision to close down the client's geothermal project. He is now litigating on the enforcement of this award. **Wilfredo Rodriguez** (see p.130) of Holland & Knight LLP is a Latin American specialist working from Miami. Commentators say he is *"very prepared, hard-working, creative, aggressive and knows what he's doing – a combination it's hard to find in just one practitioner."* **George von Mehren** (see p.140) of Squire, Sanders & Dempsey L.L.P. has had a notable year working on two enormous arbitrations on behalf of the Czech Republic. Both arbitrations, namely Saluka v The Czech Republic and National Property Fund of the Czech Republic v Nomura, relate to a $1.25 billion claim arising out of the failure of one of the largest Czech commercial banks.

## Other Notable Arbitrators

Enthralled commentators describe **Gerald Aksen** as *"an enormously experienced arbitrator and an exceptional authority on the law."* That Aksen garners such praise is due to the fact that he adopts a *"fair and unbiased"* approach and has a *"wonderful sense of the arbitration process, what works and how to keep it going."* **George Bermann** has a profound knowledge of arbitration law as he is also a full-time professor of law at Columbia University. Counsel that have appeared before him report that he is *"very sharp and effective – an excellent arbitrator."* Having now retired

from White & Case, **Charles Brower** splits his time between Washinton DC, London and The Hague, where he is a judge on the Iran-US Claims Tribunal. He is known for his work in investment treaty disputes, and is currently appointed to six ICSID cases, but he remains equally busy with commercial arbitrations. He is *"the classic American statesman"* and *"clearly miles ahead of the rest of the field."* Various lawyers were particularly awed by his ability to *"master the record better than anyone I know."* As a professor of law at Berkeley University and an author of a commentary on the UNCITRAL rules, **David Caron** is a good choice for arbitrations that relate to his area of scholarship. He is presiding over the ICSID tribunal in the Aguas del Tunari v Bolivia case, an investment arbitration which arose out of the famous water wars in Bolivia in 2000. He is rated as *"a first-class academic"* and a *"very able"* arbitrator. **Horacio Grigera Naón** left White & Case and set up a sole practice this year. He continues to be a leading choice for cases relating to Latin America and is also *"hugely experienced in the ICC"* as he was the secretary general of that particular institution for a while. He is variously described as *"terrific,"* *"simply wonderful,"* *"very conscientious"* and one who *"assumes control with grace."* **Professor Andreas Lowenfeld** from the New York University School of Law is *"a founder of the American arbitration scene and as active as ever."* Commentators view him as *"one of the leading professors in the field"* and also a *"go-to guy"* for complex cases. As a professor at Boston University Law School and one of the leading authors in this subject area, **William Park** (see p.124) *"knows the field inside out."* On top of his

academic credentials, interviewees also emphasized that he is *"very practical and doesn't over-pontificate despite his deep knowledge."* He also displays the utmost dedication and *"treats every case as if it were his last."* Retired Fish & Neave partner **David Plant** is recommended as a well-known and highly respected choice for arbitrations relating to IP. He *"can tackle the difficult technical questions"* and is *"sharp and organized"* on every case he does. Yale University law professor **Michael Reisman** is *"one of the stars of international law"* and is a top choice for investor-state arbitrations. Counsel were extremely complimentary about his *"exceptional legal imagination and drive,"* finding that his *"wonderful intellectual horsepower brings huge benefits during arbitrations."* **Charles Renfrew** is *"very well received"* as both a domestic and international arbitrator. Commentators report that he can be relied upon to deliver a *"very good job"* as he is a *"thoughtful and judicious gentleman."* The *"preeminent"* **Judge Stephen Schwebel** is *"absolutely wonderful"* for public international disputes. Unsurprisingly, he has been chosen to act as arbitrator in the largest financial claim for many a moon – the $34 billion YUKOS v Russian Federation case. As well as being a *"true scholar of international law,"* he is also known for his *"mastery of procedure and ability to study the record closely."* **Robert von Mehren** is described as *"one of the grand old men of arbitration"* and *"the most distinguished arbitrator in New York."* His experience and knowledge of procedure go without saying, but he is also singled out as an *"unbelievably talented scholar."*

# INTERNATIONAL TRADE

## Band 1

### Steptoe & Johnson LLP
See firm details p.576

**The Firm:** Few competitors can match Steptoe & Johnson when it comes to providing a *"truly comprehensive"* international trade service. It represents both petitioners and respondents in trade litigation, and offers experts in all aspects of both import and export matters. Unsurprisingly for such a broad practice, it has a large group of lawyers, and interviewees consistently highlighted the quality of the operation. As one peer remarked: *"It is a top-flight practice across the board, and every lawyer I have worked with in the team has been more than capable."* Consistent with its high profile in the market, it is representing the British Columbia Lumber Trade Council (BCLTC), the largest trade association in the Canadian lumber sector, in the highest-value trade remedy case of recent times. It has been a key player in all aspects of this softwood lumber case, and is largely credited for winning the injury case at NAFTA.

**The Lawyers:** **Richard Cunningham** (see p.94) is *"the dean of the Bar"* when it comes to antidumping work. Peers admit that he is in *"a class of his own"* due to his *"strategic capability and ability to see the whole chess board."* Clients also admit to being dazzled by his *"wide-ranging intellect."* **Edward Krauland** (see p.114) is one of the most *"versatile"* practitioners on the export side and can cover the gamut of export control and sanctions issues. Interviewees stated that he is *"at the top of the field, and offers just the right combination of experience and talent."* **Susan Esserman** (see p.98) is highly recommended for trade policy issues, not least because of the extensive experience of high-level WTO negotiations she acquired as Deputy United States Trade Representative (USTR). **George Grandison** (see p.103) is coordinating the softwood lumber injury case for the BCLTC, and has been invaluable as the *"ever-steady hand at the helm."* The other key lawyer in this high-profile case is **Mark Moran** (see p.122), who is credited as *"the principal strategist for the lumber industry."* Special praise was reserved for his *"incisive, creative intelligence,"* and *"big-picture viewpoint."* **Sheldon Hochberg** (see p.107) is yet another big name for trade and countervailing duties cases. He cut his teeth in the State Department, and has been involved in many high-profile cases since turning to private practice. Younger lawyer **Eric Emerson** (see p.98) is *"making a name for himself"* and is touted as *"one of the stars of the future."*

**Clients/Work Highlights:** Canadian Wheat Board; Corn Refiners Association; National Association of Animal Breeders; Corus; Bechtel; Mitsubishi Heavy Industries; Norsk Hydro; Reliance Industries; Occidental Chemical; Outokumpu; Raytheon; BAT; New Skies Satellites; Syngenta; Yahoo!; Electronic Data Systems; Elementis; Harley-Davidson; Homer Laughlin China and Ispat Mexicana/Caribbean Ispat.

### WilmerHale
See firm details p.580

**The Firm:** WilmerHale offers a full international trade service with plenty of resources in each specialist area, and commentators frequently praised the outfit's *"terrific constellation of lawyers,"* not to mention its *"sheer depth."* The raft of former government officials that feature in the team means that, above all, it is recognized as being home to the field's leading policy experts. It can truly be said that the firm offers *"a depth of understanding of the inner workings of the US government that is unsurpassed."* This has come to the fore during its representation of Boeing in the famous WTO dispute with Airbus concerning subsidies. Its trade remedies practice is also among the best, and was given significant credit for winning the softwood lumber case at the Supreme Court on behalf of the Government of Canada.

**The Lawyers:** Former USTR **Charlene Barshefsky** (see p.88) is said to *"know all the senior officials worldwide,"* as a result of her government experience, and is regarded as *"simply the best for market access issues."* **Gary Horlick** (see p.108) is representing Peru in its FTA negotiations, and is also an acknowledged leader in antidumping matters. Clients report that he is *"a great person to have on your side when you're going in to battle,"* as he *"has a good brain and knows this stuff cold."* **Robert Novick** (see p.124) works closely with Barshefsky and also has considerable experience as general counsel to the Office of the USTR. Clients like him because *"it's not just that he knows the law, he has an acute sense of strategy that is invaluable in complex matters."* **John Greenwald** (see p.103) is the firm's key trade remedies lawyer and he has been heavily involved in the Chinese furniture case. He has *"lots of experience of negotiations involving the US government"* and is also popular as an *"extremely insightful big-picture person."* **Robert Cassidy** (see p.91) is renowned as an *"analytical"* lawyer who produces *"very precise and detail-oriented"* work. He spends most of his time on customs issues but also has experience in trade remedy cases. Having worked in the field for many years, **Charles Levy** (see p.115) has developed *"a sound understanding of the workings of government."* He works with many trade associations, such as the Business Round Table and Computer Group, on trade policy issues.

**Clients/Work Highlights:** DuPont; Arch Chemicals; Cisco Systems; ASML Holding; Wolfson Microelectronics; Danaher and Parker Hannifin.

## Band 2

### Akin Gump Strauss Hauer & Feld LLP
See firm details p.559

**The Firm:** This firm climbs up the ranks this year following effusive client feedback and involvement in high-profile cases. In the words of one satisfied client: *"I've had to go through many lawyers to reach*

| International Trade: Trade Remedies Trade Policy Leading Individuals | |
|---|---|
| **1** ANDERSON M Jean *Weil, Gotshal & Manges LLP* | BARSHEFSKY Charlene *WilmerHale* |
| CUNNINGHAM Richard *Steptoe & Johnson LLP* | HORLICK Gary *WilmerHale* |
| PRICE Daniel *Sidley Austin LLP* | WOLFF Alan *Dewey Ballantine LLP* |
| **2** BARRINGER William *Willkie Farr & Gallagher LLP* | CAMERON JR Donald *Kaye Scholer LLP* |
| EIZENSTAT Stuart *Covington & Burling* | ESSERMAN Susan *Steptoe & Johnson LLP* |
| GRANDISON W George *Steptoe & Johnson LLP* | KANTOR Michael *Mayer, Brown, Rowe & Maw* |
| MCCONNELL Mark *Hogan & Hartson LLP* | MORAN Mark *Steptoe & Johnson LLP* |
| NOVICK Robert *WilmerHale* | ROSENTHAL Paul *Kelley Drye Collier Shannon* |
| SHOYER Andrew *Sidley Austin LLP* | |
| **3** ARCHIBALD Jeanne *Hogan & Hartson LLP* | CLARK Matthew *Arent Fox PLLC* |
| CONNELLY Warren *Akin Gump Strauss Hauer & Feld* | DEMPSEY Kevin *Dewey Ballantine LLP* |
| GREENWALD John *WilmerHale* | GRIFFITH Spencer *Akin Gump Strauss Hauer & Feld* |
| LEIBOWITZ Lewis *Hogan & Hartson LLP* | LIGHTHIZER Robert *Skadden, Arps* |
| MENDOZA Julie *Kaye Scholer LLP* | READE Claire *Arnold & Porter LLP* |
| ROH Charles *Weil, Gotshal & Manges LLP* | ROSEN Stuart *Weil, Gotshal & Manges LLP* |
| SCHER Peter *Mayer, Brown, Rowe & Maw LLP* | SLATER Valerie *Akin Gump Strauss Hauer & Feld* |
| STEWART Terence *Stewart & Stewart* | |
| **4** ADDUCI II V James *Adduci, Mastriani & Schaumberg* | APPLEBAUM Harvey *Covington & Burling* |
| BERG Gracia *Gibson, Dunn & Crutcher LLP* | CASSIDY JR Robert *WilmerHale* |
| CORR Christopher *White & Case LLP* | DORN Joseph *King & Spalding LLP* |
| DURLING James *Willkie Farr & Gallagher LLP* | FELDMAN Elliott *Baker & Hostetler LLP* |
| HARTQUIST David *Kelley Drye Collier Shannon* | HOUSE Michael *McDermott Will & Emery* |
| KAPLAN Gilbert *King & Spalding LLP* | LEVY Charles *WilmerHale* |
| MASTRIANI Louis *Adduci, Mastriani & Schaumberg* | MOYER JR E Homer *Miller & Chevalier* |
| PIERCE Kenneth *Willkie Farr & Gallagher LLP* | PLAINE Daniel *Gibson, Dunn & Crutcher LLP* |
| SCHNEIDER Lawrence *Arnold & Porter LLP* | SPAK Walter *White & Case LLP* |
| **5** CLARK Harry *Dewey Ballantine LLP* | CLINTON William *White & Case LLP* |
| CURTISS Catherine *Hughes Hubbard & Reed LLP* | DUNN Christopher *Willkie Farr & Gallagher* |
| HOCHBERG Sheldon *Steptoe & Johnson LLP* | KAPLAN H Deen *Hogan & Hartson LLP* |
| LEVINE David *McDermott Will & Emery* | MANGAN John *Skadden, Arps* |
| PORGES Amelia *Sidley Austin LLP* | PORTER Daniel *Willkie Farr & Gallagher LLP* |
| SAMET Andrew *Sandler, Travis & Rosenberg* | SCHAGRIN Roger *Schagrin Associates* |
| SHOR Michael *Arnold & Porter LLP* | SPAK Gregory *White & Case LLP* |
| VERRILL JR Charles *Wiley Rein & Fielding* | WARD Bradford *Dewey Ballantine LLP* |
| Up-and-coming individuals | |
| EMERSON Eric *Steptoe & Johnson LLP* | NICELY Matthew *Willkie Farr & Gallagher LLP* |
| SHAPIRO Hal *Miller & Chevalier Chartered* | |

such a good international trade group." Commentators speak highly of the *"depth of industry knowledge to be found in the practice,"* which covers the full gamut, including trade policy to customs as well as trade litigation and export control. In each of these disciplines, the team displays *"strong technical knowledge combined with political know-how."* Typical of its high-profile mandates was its representation of Unocal following the takeover attempt by Chinese oil company CNOOC – the firm advised the company on all Exxon-Florio issues. It is also representing the Government of British Columbia in the Canadian softwood lumber case, where it is *"doing an excellent job."* Another highlight was enticing Grant Aldonas to join the firm from the Commerce Department, where he carved out a strong reputation for himself as undersecretary for international trade. The market waits with interest to see how his career in private practice develops.

**The Lawyers: Edward Rubinoff** (see p.131) is one of the leading practitioners in the export and sanc-

tions fields, as he *"has significant expertise and a practical approach, both of which are necessary when counseling business clients in these areas."* This year, he successfully obtained a license from the Office of Foreign Assets Control (OFAC), enabling Archer Daniels Midland to import a drug from Cuba for clinical testing. This is particularly notable as it is only the third license to have been granted in the 40 years during which the embargo on Cuba has been in place. **Warren Connelly** (see p.93) is a well-known trade litigator and he is advising the American Seafood Distributors Association, along with exporters from Ecuador, Thailand and India, in the shrimp antidumping case. Clients all agree that his *"knowledge base, experience and work product are excellent."* **Spencer Griffith** (see p.103) has a high profile in the market as he is representing the Government of British Columbia in the subsidies part of the Canadian softwood lumber antidumping case, where he is praised for *"managing a large portfolio just fine."* **Val Slater** (see p.135) specializes in

trade remedies and principally acts for claimants. She is busy working for the nitrogen industry with regard to energy pricing in Russia.

**Clients/Work Highlights:** Baker Hughes; Dresser; Siemens; Fujitsu; Mittal Steel; Disney; Pier 1 Imports and UPS.

### Dewey Ballantine LLP

See firm details p.1530

**The Firm:** Consensus remains strong that this is *"the premier petitioners firm."* The team represents a range of domestic trade associations in antidumping cases and has been involved in countless steel cases. Advising the Coalition for Fair Lumber Imports in the Canadian softwood lumber controversy, involving 24 different pieces of litigation, has won the firm further kudos of late. Most recently, it upped the stakes in the case by filing a constitutional challenge to Chapter 19 of NAFTA. Commentators say that members of the firm are doing a *"fabulous job,"* especially in terms of sustaining political support for the domestic industry. Additionally, the firm is also heavily involved in market access work relating to China on behalf of clients such as the Semiconductor Industry Association.

**The Lawyers: Alan Wolff** (see p.143) *"heads any list of top trade lawyers"* because *"he has worked in the field forever."* He heads the group and is repeatedly named as a key lawyer in the Canadian softwood lumber case. Commentators describe him as *"an outstanding strategist for US industries"* because he *"puts the pieces together and keeps the pressure on."* **Clark McFadden** (see p.119) is another *"senior and well-known"* name in the practice. He concentrates on export work, and is currently working on compliance and enforcement issues relating to sanctions and the Foreign Corrupt Practices Act (FCPA). The *"terrific"* **Kevin Dempsey** (see p.95) is leading on the injury side of the softwood lumber case, and peers report that he has *"great credibility."* **Harry Clark** (see p.92), who is leading the team's Supreme Court challenge in the lumber case, enters the table this year. He is also recommended for his expertise in export matters. **Bradford Ward** (see p.140) was identified as the firm's leading trade remedies litigator.

**Clients/Work Highlights:** Other clients include the American Council of Life Insurers (ACLI), Southern Shrimp Alliance and the American Petroleum Institute.

### Hogan & Hartson LLP

See firm details p.568

**The Firm:** Hogan & Hartson's *"excellent"* reputation in the market stems largely from its prowess in trade policy work. The team is experienced in WTO, NAFTA and Free Trade Agreement (FTA) negotiations, and this year secured a Pharmaceuticals Annex to the US-Australia FTA for the industry trade association, PhRMA. This specialty is part of a much broader public policy practice, and the group is also renowned for advising foreign governments on major policy issues with the USA. The firm also handles a steady flow of antidumping cases, generally opposing the imposition of duties. The DC group works alongside teams in Brussels and Geneva, while its lawyers in Beijing and Shanghai are becoming increasingly involved as the Chinese market grows.

**The Lawyers:** **Mark McConnell** (see p.119) is the real *"cream of the crop"* when it comes to international trade lawyers, and he has really shown his caliber while representing Ontario in the Canadian softwood lumber dispute. **Jeanne Archibald** (see p.86) is a *"first-rate"* trade policy lawyer, not least because of the knowledge she gained during her tenure as general counsel to the Department of the Treasury. *"Thoughtful and intelligent"* **Lewis Leibowitz** (see p.115) is recommended for both policy and litigation work. **Deen Kaplan** (see p.111) also impressed as one of the brighter next-generation trade lawyers.

**Clients/Work Highlights:** The team represents many foreign governments including Japan; The Bahamas; China and Haiti. Other clients include Accenture; University of Southern California; Amgen; Becton Dickinson and GE Medical Systems.

### Sidley Austin LLP
See firm details p.883

**The Firm:** When clients begin their appraisal of a firm with *"on a scale of one to ten I would give it 100,"* you know this is going to be a pretty special practice. The firm has won an *"exceptional"* reputation for being at the *"cutting edge"* when it comes to applying international treaty law to international commerce. The knowledge of WTO case law on offer is hugely impressive and the operation's global platform in DC, Brussels and Geneva means that members of the group *"know everyone who matters – you can do no better if access to government is what's required."* Recent highlights include working with Goldman Sachs to develop WTO rules on government regulation in the securities industry, and winning a WTO case against Mexico on behalf of the Corn Refiners Association. This case arose from Mexico's decision to impose a 20% tax on soft drinks sweetened with anything except cane sugar in order to protect its domestic sugar industry.

**The Lawyers:** Head of practice **Dan Price** (see p.127) is hugely respected for his *"sheer brilliance."* Clients gush that *"governments listen to Dan"* and also rave about *"the breadth and range of his experience and the quality of his intellect."* **Andy Shoyer** (see p.134) gained considerable experience during his time at the Office of the USTR. In particular, he spent four years as the representative of the US government in Geneva, so his WTO knowledge is second to none. Clients reveal that he is *"invaluable when you get into the nitty-gritty of trade agreements,"* and is *"steady, skilled and thoughtful"* in guiding them through negotiations. **Amelia Porges** (see p.126) also offers *"exceptional government experience"* and is *"able to explain exceedingly complex issues in easy to understand language."*

**Clients/Work Highlights:** Other high-profile matters this year include representing the Government of Canada in its challenge to the US govern-

ment's distribution of duties collected on Canadian imports to US companies at the US Court of International Trade; advising Monsanto and the US biotechnology industry in a case where the USA, Canada and Argentina are challenging the EU regarding its refusal to approve certain new biotech products; acting for the Government of Colombia in FTA negotiations with the USA; and acting as counsel to Airbus in its WTO dispute with Boeing. Other clients include Caterpillar; UPS; the National Thoroughbred Racing Association; PhRMA and the US Business Alliance for Customs Modernization.

### Band 3

### Arnold & Porter LLP
See firm details p.560

**The Firm:** Arnold & Porter handles a wide range of international trade litigation, including antidumping, countervailing duty and Section 337 cases. Clients report that they turn to the firm when faced with high-level policy issues, and it has a fine reputation for representing sovereigns. Indeed, the Government of China appointed the firm in the wooden furniture antidumping case, and the team advised Panama in negotiations for a bilateral FTA with the USA. A proportion of export matters involving export control, trade sanctions and FCPA issues rounds out this *"expert and experienced"* group's workload.

**The Lawyers:** **John Barker** (see p.87) heads up the export team and peers particularly commend him for his expertise relating to International Traffic in Arms Regulations (ITAR). He is *"really thorough and knows everything there is to know about the practice area,"* and won further praise for being *"practical and extremely responsive."* Equally attractive to clients is the fact that he *"has built up a great rapport with the agencies."* Meanwhile, **Claire Reade** (see p.128) heads up the import team and is highly recommended by peers and clients alike. She was said to have put in a *"strong performance"* representing the Government of Alberta in the Canadian softwood lumber case. He may be low-key, but **Lawrence Schneider** (see p.133) keeps winning high-profile appointments. He has been busy representing importers of chemicals used in the manufacture of tires in the largest Section 337 action currently pending against China. **Michael Shor** (see p.134) works closely with Schneider and the duo recently won an antidumping case for South African company Hulett Aluminium.

**Clients/Work Highlights:** Other sovereign clients include Israel and Venezuela.

### Gibson, Dunn & Crutcher LLP
See firm details p.328

**The Firm:** Considered an *"outstanding"* player in the market, this practice has a keenly felt presence in import disputes relating to dumping or countervailing duties. It represents a wide variety of respondents, most frequently in the steel industry, where it acts for Nippon Steel. Acting for West Fraser Timber in litigation arising out of the Canadian softwood

lumber antidumping controversy further reinforces its profile. Unusually for a major international firm, it also boasts a sophisticated customs practice. Export control and foreign sanctions work constitute another important component of the practice. Clients spoke highly of Gibson Dunn's style of lawyering, explaining that its attorneys *"always offer several good alternatives with detailed pros and cons to ensure that we make a fully informed decision."*

**The Lawyers:** **Gracia Berg**'s (see p.88) impressive credentials include a stint as deputy general counsel at the US ITC, and she was commended for providing a *"very high-quality"* service. The *"hard-working"* **Daniel Plaine** (see p.126) splits his practice between import disputes and export regulatory work. The esteemed Joseph Price has retired.

**Clients/Work Highlights:** Honda; Occidental Chemical; Nissan North America; Saab; Princess Cruises; First Data; Tolko Industries and Cadence Design Systems.

### Kaye Scholer LLP
See firm details p.1536

**The Firm:** Kaye Scholer is credited with a preeminent antidumping practice, particularly in the steel and lumber industries. As such, it can be proud of an *"excellent reputation"* for doing a *"consistently first-rate job."* It is representing over 60 clients in the Canadian softwood lumber case, consisting of a mix of Canadian producers and trade associations. Elsewhere, the team notched up a significant victory for Nucor, a Korean producer of cold rolled steel, in defeating a challenge by domestic producers to the US ITC's negative injury determination. China is emerging as another key market for the firm, and its Shanghai office has recently expanded in response to an increased demand for services.

**The Lawyers:** **Donald Cameron** (see p.91) is well known as a lawyer who is more than prepared to *"shoot from the hip."* His forthrightness is reinforced by *"years of experience"* and *"great skill as an advocate."* His colleague **Julie Mendoza** (see p.120) is also rated as a *"superb lawyer,"* and commended by clients for her *"comprehensive advice and responsiveness."*

**Clients/Work Highlights:** POSCO; Korea Iron & Steel Association; Pusan Pipe America; Terminal Forest Products; Industrias Unicon; Independent Lumber Association and Pope & Talbot.

### Kelley Drye Collier Shannon

**The Firm:** Representing US petitioners in antidumping cases is the firm's true forte. Peers view its team as an awesome opponent, members of which are described as *"resourceful and persistent - they keep hammering away at you, and skillfully utilize every legal advantage they can."* This year has been as busy as ever and it is representing the Specialty Steel Industry of North America, a coalition of wire rod producers, in a large case. It has also worked on a large number of sunset reviews of antidumping duties, including one for NACCO Materials Handling regarding imports from Japan. At the time of going to press, Collier Shannon Scott had announced its intention to merge with Kelley Drye & Warren to form Kelley Drye Collier Shannon in DC.

**The Lawyers:** Firm chairman and group head **Paul Rosenthal** received a torrent of praise from commentators. He is described as a *"formidable advocate"* who is *"seasoned and knowledgeable"* and has *"the ability to really zone in on the key issues."* **David Hartquist** works alongside him, and focused this year on advising the China Currency Coalition in its campaign to persuade the Chinese government to revalue its currency.

**Clients/Work Highlights:** In addition to many steel industry clients, the firm acts for a wide range of entities in agriculture, such as honey and garlic growers. It also handles market access issues for the Plasma Protein Therapeutics Association and SC Johnson.

## Weil, Gotshal & Manges LLP

See firm details p.1565

**The Firm:** It was unanimously agreed that those members of the firm acting for the Canadian government in the softwood lumber case are *"excelling themselves."* Interviewees remarked that the largest ever dumping and countervailing proceeding, where approximately $5 billion is at stake, is in safe hands. The firm's involvement in the dispute with the USA has involved coordinating all of the various parties on the Canadian side and juggling 28 different pieces of litigation. With several former senior government officials on board, it has a strong trade policy practice that offers substantial experience of representing sovereigns in negotiations. For example, the group represented Canada during the NAFTA negotiations, and advised Chile during their free trade negotiations with Canada and then the USA.

**The Lawyers:** **Jean Anderson** (see p.85) enjoys a towering presence in the field. As chief counsel for international trade at the Department of Commerce, she helped negotiate the US-Canada FTA and was responsible for developing Chapter 19 of NAFTA dealing with dispute resolution. She commands *"great respect"* among commentators, especially with regard to her work for the Government of Canada. **Charles Roh** (see p.130) worked at the Office of the USTR for many years and received a torrent of praise from commentators, who variously described him as *"savvy and unassuming," "very smart and very sharp"* and *"highly regarded by everyone."* **Stuart Rosen** (see p.130) had a highly successful year, which included victory on behalf of French uranium company COGEMA in a dumping case brought by USEC, where it was established that antidumping rules do not apply to services.

**Clients/Work Highlights:** The team is defending the North American Millers' Association in antidumping litigation following allegations relating to subsidies to the Canadian wheat industry. It also represents many sovereigns including Ecuador, El Salvador and Australia.

## White & Case LLP

See firm details p.1566

**The Firm:** This firm is traditionally strong in trade litigation and continues to work on major cases on this front. For example, it is defending GCC (Grupo Cementos de Chihuahua) in the cement antidumping dispute between Mexico and the USA, where $250 million is at stake. However, the practice has now broadened to include Section 337 disputes and WTO trade policy work. Indicative of its growing reputation in these areas is its appointment by Taiwan Semiconductor Manufacturing in a Section 337 case against SMIC. In addition, impressed commentators avow: *"This is one of the few law firms I've encountered that has a better grasp of WTO than even the government."* Clients also pointed to the benefits of having access to a network of offices all over the world.

**The Lawyers:** **Christopher Corr** (see p.92) works on both antidumping and Section 337 cases. Clients agree that he *"intuitively grasps complex issues"* and also *"takes into consideration both the short and long-term implications of all available options."* **Walter Spak** (see p.136) won praise for his *"extensive knowledge, attention to detail and prompt service."* **William Clinton** (see p.92) is currently advising Saudi Aramco on the implications of Saudi Arabia's accession to the WTO. Rounding off the strong bench is fluent Spanish speaker **Gregory Spak** (see p.136). He has *"good technical knowledge"* and takes a *"fair and reasoned approach to the matter in hand."*

**Clients/Work Highlights:** Buchanan Group; FedEx; Fuji Photo Film; Industrias Monterrey; Novartis; Tenaris; Siderca; Unisource Worldwide/ Georgia-Pacific; Ministry of Commerce (Government of Thailand); Ministry of Finance (Government of Thailand); JETRO; Duferco; Minebea; NMB Singapore; SICARTSA; Yieh United Steel; Tubería Nacional and Deacero.

## Willkie Farr & Gallagher LLP

See firm details p.1567

**The Firm:** Rarely does a major antidumping case take place without the *"effective"* team at Willkie Farr representing the respondents. Recent highlights include successfully acting for Yamaha in an antidumping case regarding the import of outboard engines from Japan. The team represented the company in both the dumping and the injury investigations, and successfully achieved a negative determination of injury from the US ITC. In addition, the team represents foreign governments in WTO negotiations, including both China and Japan of late. Known for providing *"assertive and focused"* advice, the team is a good choice for tough battles.

**The Lawyers:** **William Barringer** (see p.87) heads up the team and, despite his senior status, is frequently to be found *"in the thick of things."* Commentators concur that he *"knows how to organize and argue a case"* and has the *"highest reputation"* at the international trade Bar. **James Durling** (see p.97) received his fair share of recommendation, while **Kenneth Pierce** (see p.125) sustains his profile by taking the lead in representing the Thai exporters

in a large antidumping case concerning imported shrimps from Asia. **Christopher Dunn** (see p.97) won plaudits for his expansive knowledge of trade remedy matters, especially those with an Asian or Latin American element. Another *"impressive"* member of the team is **Daniel Porter** (see p.126), who successfully represented Japanese steel producers in an antidumping case at court of appeal level. **Matthew Nicely** (see p.123) also received a substantial portion of positive feedback.

**Clients/Work Highlights:** The team has also been working for the Manitoba Pork Council in the antidumping and countervailing duty investigation of swine from Canada. Other clients include Boston Scientific and Hynix Semiconductor.

## Band 4

### Adduci, Mastriani & Schaumberg LLP

See firm details p.558

**The Firm:** This 28-lawyer boutique specializes in international trade regulation, and boasts a niche practice relating to the adjudication of US intellectual property rights. Clients exclaim that the lawyers here *"simply know the US ITC inside out,"* and are frequently found both defending and prosecuting Section 337 cases. For example, on behalf of 3M the team obtained a general exclusion order relating to the import of foam masking tape.

**The Lawyers:** **James Adduci** (see p.84) is cited as *"the big name"* at the firm, while clients said of **Louis Mastriani** (see p.117): *"He is an incredible guy – so knowledgeable and dynamic, and got it all."*

**Clients/Work Highlights:** Further active clients include Korea Kumho Petrochemical, Carsem and Tohatsu.

### Covington & Burling

See firm details p.563

**The Firm:** The *"excellent quality"* of this firm's work on both import and export fronts greatly impressed clients. It has *"a lot of depth"* when it comes to export control and sanctions, and can be relied upon to provide *"skilled and knowledgeable"* advice. On the import side, it is experienced in WTO negotiations, trade disputes and customs work.

**The Lawyers:** One of the younger lawyers to make the top tier of the tables, **Peter Flanagan** (see p.99) is frequently described as an *"outstanding"* export controls specialist. According to sources, this is in large part due to him being *"incredibly sharp and therefore able to impart an understanding of complex issues to clients."* He works with senior partner **Peter Trooboff** (see p.138), who is best known as an *"extremely experienced"* practitioner, particularly where issues relating to the Office of Foreign Assets Control are concerned. Interviewees agreed that his *"advanced knowledge of the field is much in demand."* The *"talented"* **Stuart Eizenstat** (see p.98) heads the group and concentrates on the import side. He is a senior and distinguished practitioner whose government posts include Deputy Treasury Secretary, Under Secretary of Commerce for International Trade and

Ambassador to the European Union. **Harvey Applebaum** (see p.85) is another *"long-standing"* figure in the field. Despite focusing his practice on antitrust cases, he has taken a considerable interest in international trade over the years and is rated as a *"significant"* addition to the Bar.

**Clients/Work Highlights:** Boeing; BT; Canon; Council of the European Union; Global Crossing; Medtronic; Microsoft; Pacific Telecom and Vodafone.

## King & Spalding LLP
See firm details p.1933

**The Firm:** The firm offers a full range of international trade expertise, but is particularly well known for representing domestic petitioners in trade remedy cases. The work is led by lawyers in Washington, DC and London offices, and involves clients from a wide range of industries and many different countries.

**The Lawyers:** **Joseph Dorn** (see p.96) splits his time between London and Washington, DC. He is heavily involved in acting for petitioners bringing antidumping cases, but is also experienced in representing foreign companies. Peers view him as a strong practitioner and a *"tough competitor."* Also well known for his appearances in trade remedy cases is **Gilbert Kaplan** (see p.111).

**Clients/Work Highlights:** GE; Lockheed Martin; DuPont Dow; Boise Cascade; US Magnesium; Dow AgroSciences; American Forest & Paper Association; Southern Tier Cement Committee; USA Rice Federation and Bassett Furniture Industries.

## Mayer, Brown, Rowe & Maw LLP
See firm details p.876

**The Firm:** The expansion of Mayer Brown's international trade practice has made waves in the market as it adds to the number of former senior government officials who have entered private practice. This has created a group that is perfectly placed to provide market access, trade remedy and export control advice. Trade policy is naturally a key focus area, particularly where US-China trade is concerned. It is also winning work in Europe, especially since scooping up the former Coudert Brothers international trade practice in Brussels. Advising several chemical and agriculture biotech companies on new EU regulations is a case in point.

**The Lawyers:** Recruiting the former US Secretary of Commerce and former USTR **Michael Kantor** (see p.111) has really put the Mayer Brown practice on the map. He joins former US Special Trade Negotiator **Peter Scher** (see p.132), who has already made his name in private practice.

**Clients/Work Highlights:** Agrium; Alberta Beef Producers; Arch Chemicals; Caterpillar; Dow Chemical; DuPont; FMC Corporation; International Custom Products; Monsanto; Morgan Stanley; Pfizer; PriceSmart; Time Warner; Retail Industry Leaders Association; Renewable Fuels Association; Target; UBS and Weldbend.

## McDermott Will & Emery
See firm details p.878

**The Firm:** McDermott Will & Emery prides itself on the breadth of its practice, and it does indeed cover the whole gamut, taking in WTO matters, trade remedies, export control and customs. Its niche experience of representing agricultural clients distinguishes the firm further, and it has advised a number of Latin American producers in the WTO action relating to bananas. All in all, interviewees discerned a *"deep, expert and sophisticated"* practice.

**The Lawyers:** Known as *"a particularly capable practitioner,"* **Michael House** (see p.108) is currently representing the Chinese interest in the US-China safeguarding action regarding textiles. **David Levine** (see p.115) is a *"sophisticated"* lawyer with an eclectic practice, encompassing import relief, customs and export control.

**Clients/Work Highlights:** The team is also handling trade litigation on behalf of Renesas Technology, a joint venture formed by Hitachi and Mitsubishi.

## Miller & Chevalier Chartered
See firm details p.575

**The Firm:** This operation is said to excel at both the import and export sides of international trade. It mainly advises defense, technology or energy companies in export control and sanctions issues. On the import side it is most frequently seen in trade remedy cases, which recently involved representing Weyerhauser in the Canadian softwood lumber case. The team is also experienced in handling Section 337 cases and trade policy issues, and advised the Government of Morocco in its FTA negotiations with the USA.

**The Lawyers:** **Bill McGlone** (see p.119) is the firm's lead lawyer on the export side. Clients declare that *"his advice is always on target, he is well connected and he has an excellent reputation; he is also responsive, friendly and customer-focused."* **Homer Moyer** (see p.122) is an experienced trade litigator, and one of the few practitioners to have argued several NAFTA Chapter 19 cases. **Hal Shapiro** (see p.134) leads the trade policy work. He is a former general counsel at the Office of the USTR and was a trade policy adviser to President Clinton.

**Clients/Work Highlights:** Intel; Motorola; Nikon and Eton Company.

## Paul, Hastings, Janofsky & Walker LLP
See firm details p.339

**The Firm:** The trade remedies sphere was the firm's historical focus, though its practice has broadened of late to encompass export control and sanctions, as well as Section 337 cases. The three-partner team was described as *"sophisticated and experienced,"* and has handled many major cases, which recently included defending SMIC at the US ITC in a Section 337 case brought by a Taiwanese semiconductor company. Clients appreciate the *"crisp and to-the-point advice"* they received from members of the firm.

**The Lawyers:** **Behnam Dayanim** (see p.95) focuses on export control and trade sanctions. He is *"extraordinarily helpful, not to mention capable of providing innovative new solutions."*

**Clients/Work Highlights:** The Government of Québec; the Chinese Ministry for Commerce; Hitachi; Tokio Marine & Nichido Fire Insurance; Broadcom and GE.

## Skadden, Arps, Slate, Meagher & Flom LLP & Affiliates
See firm details p.1557

**The Firm:** The firm's strong reputation for acting on behalf of petitioners in trade remedy cases is key to its overall profile. Historically, cases involving the US steel industry were a mainstay for the practice, and although there are now far fewer such matters than in the past, the team continues to work on many related sunset reviews. It also assists US companies in overseas jurisdictions, whether with trade litigation or with securing market access.

**The Lawyers:** **Robert Lighthizer** (see p.116), head of the firm's international trade department, has been a stalwart of the discipline for many years. Meanwhile, **John Mangan** (see p.117) is an invaluable member of the team who clients rely upon for his deep knowledge of the steel sector and of litigating trade remedy cases relating to the industry.

**Clients/Work Highlights:** The team represents large US corporations and industry coalitions.

## Stewart & Stewart

**The Firm:** This boutique trade practice is able to compete with its larger rivals when it comes to representing petitioners in trade remedy litigation. Despite the small size of the team, market observers agree that it *"produces a quality product."* Steel companies account for a large portion of the client base, and it has been doing a lot of work recently for Mittal Steel.

**The Lawyers:** **Terence Stewart** is the firm's best-known name, and he impresses as a *"tough opponent"* who is *"excellent"* at representing petitioners.

## Vinson & Elkins LLP
See firm details p.1938

**The Firm:** A team of eight attorneys concentrates solely on export work, and has developed into *"one of the strongest practices in this discrete and complex area of law."* While its practitioners are particularly knowledgeable in International Traffic in Arms Regulations (ITAR) issues, expertise in Foreign Corrupt Practices Act and sanctions matters is also offered.

**The Lawyers:** **Kathleen Little** (see p.116) is *"a big name in export controls"* and is singled out as *"one of the handful of the most effective advisers in the field."* She is particularly well known for providing ITAR advice to defense companies.

**Clients/Work Highlights:** Northrop Grumman; Honeywell; United Defense; ITT Industries; 3M and Caterpillar.

## Band 5

### Crowell & Moring LLP

See firm details p.564

**The Firm:** This *"good-quality, solid"* practice covers the full gamut of international trade work. It has a wide-ranging export practice, members of which have advised non-US parties on transactions under the Iran and Libya Sanctions Act. The team also successfully represented DuPont in securing the dismissal of an antidumping case relating to polyvinyl alcohol from Taiwan. The group is aided by an affiliation with C&M International, a non-lawyer consulting business specializing in international trade.

**The Lawyers:** **Jeffrey Snyder** (see p.135), chair of the international trade group, can turn his hand to both export and import issues. Clients appreciate his *"sophisticated long-term experience in the field,"* as well as his *"good client rapport skills."*

**Clients/Work Highlights:** DuPont; NSK Americas; AstraZeneca; Avecia; SAP America; Tomen; TDK USA; Elementis; Metal One America (formerly Mitsubishi International Steel); Hitachi Metals America; General Dynamics; Arysta LifeScience; Valeo and Levi Strauss.

### Davis Polk & Wardwell

See firm details p.1528

**The Firm:** Frequently cited as the first choice for sanctions work, the Davis Polk practice entered the spotlight when it recruited former general counsel of the Office of Foreign Assets Control, William Hoffman. He has been at the firm since 2004 and is building up a practice covering the full range of export issues.

**The Lawyers:** *"Spectacular"* practitioner **William Hoffman** (see p.107) specializes in sanctions and embargoed countries. His years in government ensure that he has a vast bank of knowledge and provides an *"absolutely wonderful"* service to clients.

### O'Melveny & Myers LLP

See firm details p.336

**The Firm:** In combination with the firm's international arbitration outfit, the international trade practice at O'Melveny & Myers provides clients with a truly comprehensive service. It has good geographic reach, with teams based in Washington, Brussels and Beijing. Of late, Office of Foreign Assets Control

(OFAC) issues have featured heavily in the workload.

**The Lawyers:** *"Thoughtful and extremely smart,"* **Greta Lichtenbaum** (see p.116) leads the OFAC work. She won commendation for being *"ultra-organized and therefore always on top of what the client needs."*

**Clients/Work Highlights:** ConocoPhillips; Amerada Hess; Marathon Oil; Occidental Petroleum; Goldman Sachs; Nippon Steel; Macsteel International; Cargill; Nachi-Fujikoshi; Böhler-Uddeholm and GlobalSantaFe.

### Sandler, Travis & Rosenberg

**The Firm:** This boutique retains its position in the table due to the *"outstanding"* quality of its customs practice. It is particularly strong in the textiles industry, and also benefits from its relationship with a subsidiary international trade consultancy, Sandler & Travis Trade Advisory Services.

**The Lawyers:** Benefiting from years of government experience, **Andrew Samet** is a fine choice for representing international clients in their dealings with federal agencies.

### Wiley Rein & Fielding LLP

See firm details p.579

**The Firm:** The team here covers regulatory, market access and trade disputes work. It sustains a high profile in trade remedy litigation, having built a favorable reputation for itself in the steel sector. The team also offers expertise in national security issues.

**The Lawyers:** **Charles Verrill** (see p.129) chairs the international trade practice, and advises on import and export matters as well as trade policy. **John Reynolds** (see p.129) is regarded as an *"outstanding"* OFAC practitioner who has *"worked in the field for years and therefore has a tremendous sense of how it has evolved."* While he has a general practice, he is particularly recommended for munitions and sanctions regulations.

## Other Notable Practitioners

**Export Controls Economic Sanctions**

Described as *"the current dean in the area"* and *"a true scholar who is ahead of the rest,"* **Evan Berlack** (see p.88) from Baker Botts LLP is clearly admired as one of the country's leading export control experts. **Benjamin Flowe** (see p.99) of Berliner, Corcoran & Rowe, LLP is recommended as the foremost expert in the field as it relates to the technology sector,

particularly with regard to areas such as encryption. Nobody doubts his commitment to his work as he is billed as *"a real export control junkie who has an encyclopedic knowledge of when issues have cropped up and how they were resolved."* **Chris Wall** (see p.140) from Pillsbury Winthrop Shaw Pittman LLP has a strong reputation for handling the full range of export issues, including those relating to International Traffic in Arms Regulations and the Office of Foreign Assets Control. Clients say: *"The quality, thoughtfulness and timeliness of his work make for a terrific service."* Having spent many years as in-house counsel at GE, **Bill Clements** (see p.92) of Foley & Lardner LLP obviously has *"a great depth of business experience,"* in addition to which he is credited with the knack of being *"practical, and boiling things down to simple terms."* He has also held prominent positions within government, which gives his practice yet another dimension. **Scott Maberry** (see p.116) at Fulbright & Jaworski L.L.P. is rated for *"his ability to handle a huge workload,"* and is also *"very resourceful and full of interesting ideas."* These qualities have been brought to the fore this year during his representation of major corporations in the multijurisdictional investigation into the United Nations Oil for Food program.

**Trade Remedies Trade Policy**

**Matthew Clark** (see p.92) of Arent Fox PLLC has one of the most highly respected practices in terms of trade remedy litigation. In particular, the whole market commends the work he is doing for the Québec government in the Canadian softwood lumber antidumping and countervailing case. He is a *"thoughtful and detail-oriented"* practitioner, and offers *"a full understanding of the subject area, including the underbelly of international trade."* **Elliott Feldman** of Baker & Hostetler LLP also has a prominent role in the same lumber case, representing a group of lumber trade associations from Ontario. He has made a *"significant contribution"* to the Canadians' arguments and is praised for being *"very creative, so that he is able to draw attention to issues that might otherwise go unnoticed and come up with ideas on how to pursue them."* Also recommended for trade remedy matters is **Catherine Curtiss** (see p.94) from Hughes Hubbard & Reed LLP. Meanwhile, **Roger Schagrin** of Schagrin Associates is much in demand among petitioners.

# NATIVE AMERICAN LAW

**OVERVIEW:** The interest in Native American law has grown in line with the increased commerciality surrounding the nation's tribes. As a result, some states require an Indian law component in the Bar exams and many law firms have diversified their practices to accommodate the needs of a broad range of clients in this area. While casino developments on Native American land remain a key facet of this market, the trend has slowed. At the same time, tribes have expanded economically and geographically with wind energy projects, resorts, golf courses, hotels and other real estate developments as areas of particular activity. In the course of this expansion, some tribes have entered into joint ventures with other tribes as well as with private entities. Native American law experts have become more involved in environmental and natural resources issues due to the high levels of coal, uranium and water found on the reservations. Additionally, disputes over these resources have led to tribal sovereignty clashes with the government and the DOI. This trend is especially seen in the southwestern states of the USA. While only a small portion of law firms have established a dedicated Native American law department, the number of specialists is increasing steadily as the need for expertise in this arena continues to gather pace.

---

### Native American Law
#### Leading Firms

1. AKIN GUMP STRAUSS HAUER & FIELD LLP
   BRACEWELL & GIULIANI LLP
   DORSEY & WHITNEY LLP
   HOGAN & HARTSON LLP
   HOLLAND & HART LLP
   HOLLAND & KNIGHT LLP
   HUGHES HUBBARD & REED LLP
   LATHAM & WATKINS LLP
   MILLER, CANFIELD, PADDOCK AND STONE
   ORRICK, HERRINGTON & SUTCLIFFE LLP

#### Leading Individuals

1. APPLEBY Nancy *Bracewell & Giuliani, LLP*
   HYATT Townsend *Orrick*
   JARBOE Mark *Dorsey & Whitney LLP*
   KING Carol *Hogan & Hartson LLP*
   LEVINE Jerome *Holland & Knight LLP*
   LIN Raymond *Latham & Watkins LLP*
   MCSLOY Steven *Hughes Hubbard & Reed LLP*
   MOODY Kevin *Miller, Canfield, Paddock and Stone*
   PONGRACE Donald *Akin Gump*
   SHERIDAN Mark *Holland & Hart LLP*

#### Up-and-coming individuals

SWANICK Christine *Dorsey & Whitney LLP*

---

## Band 1

### Akin Gump Strauss Hauer & Feld LLP

See firm details p.559

**The Firm:** This well-established firm was among the first to create a Native American law practice group and its wealth of experience and the dedication of its attorneys have impressed clients. The ten-strong team works mainly on the Native American side, where it represents tribes, their corporations and other entities. With tribes expanding economically and geographically, the group's workload contains complex business and financing matters, such as capital raising, energy projects and infrastructure development. The group is also well equipped to advise on gaming, land acquisitions and hotel and resort development. For instance, it assisted the Kiowa Casino Operations Authority in a $37 million mezzanine debt facility to finance the construction of the tribe's initial gaming and resort facility. It also advised Seneca Gaming on a $200 million 144A senior notes offering. Further expertise is provided in environment and land use, homeland security, and IP as well as federal legislative advocacy and strategic policy. Recently, the group represented the Hopi Tribe in federal issues before the Congress and the executive branch, and acted for the Gila River Indian Community in the negotiation and Congressional ratification of the largest Indian water rights settlement in US history.

**The Lawyers:** Head of the department **Don Pongrace** (see p.126) resides in the firm's Washington, DC office and won praise from clients for his excellent knowledge of American Indian law. Skilled in gaming, financing and construction matters, clients "*trust him implicitly and feel comfortable with his legal and strategic advice.*"

**Clients/Work Highlights:** The firm's client roster includes the Gila River Indian Community, Seneca Gaming and the Hopi Tribe as well as other tribes and tribal enterprises across the USA.

### Bracewell & Giuliani LLP

See firm details p.1924

**The Firm:** This respected firm serves tribes, investors and lenders in a diverse range of matters linked to Native American law. Its attorneys are experienced in business and finance, real estate, tax, and government relations issues, and can call on the support of attorneys across the firm's national and international offices. The oil and gas sector, and projects connected to wind farms, have also proved to be a key part of the recent workload. The group has represented clients in credit and equity financings for the development of oil and gas resources and advised on the development of electricity-generating facilities on tribal land. Advice is also provided on telecom, retail, housing and title insurance issues.

**The Lawyers:** An "*enthusiastic and conscientious lawyer*," **Nancy Appleby** (see p.86) has developed a broad practice encompassing transactional and lending work, dispute resolution and regulatory issues connected to tribal and nontribal land. She has a wealth of experience in advising lenders, real estate and energy developers, and other businesses on Native American law matters. One interviewee summed up the market consensus: "*I have never known a better lawyer. She is detailed, critical and knowledgeable and knows the Indian law backward and forward.*"

**Clients/Work Highlights:** The firm represents institutional lenders; developers; traditional and alternative energy companies; tribal consultants; contractors; and mortgage loan and resort management companies among others.

### Dorsey & Whitney LLP

See firm details p.1169

**The Firm:** This "*premier all-rounded player*" handles an array of Native American law matters including Indian and Alaska tribal issues. The group's workload contains employment, tax, gaming and litigation matters. Attorneys advise the tribes, their commercial entities and those engaged in business in this sector on issues of diversification, reservation financing, environmental matters and regulatory compliance. Intergovernmental relations and social services complete the picture.

**The Lawyers:** Minneapolis-based **Mark Jarboe** (see p.109) is a "*smart, well-prepared and tremendously experienced attorney.*" Chairman of the firm's Indian law and gaming department, he represents both tribal and nontribal clients in transactional, regulatory and gaming work and has built up a national profile in the sector. He is supported by up-and-comer **Christine Swanick** (see p.137), who resides in the firm's New York offices. Sources singled her out as a "*very capable adviser with an excellent understanding of the law.*" She primarily represents lenders in Indian reservation infrastructure financings, economic developments and gaming matters.

**Clients/Work Highlights:** Tribes and their enterprises; commercial and investment banks; developers; manufacturers; distributors and other businesses are among the firm's clients.

### Hogan & Hartson LLP

See firm details p.568

**The Firm:** This group primarily represents tribes in real estate, land use and environmental issues. For example, it acted for the Lower Elwha Klallam Tribe on the Elwha River restoration project, which included the removal of two large dams in order to restore salmon runs to the river. As tribes expand and enter into joint ventures, the group provided further advice on transactional and economic developments. Its attorneys also assist clients on policy advocacy, lobbying and litigation. Clients value the breadth of expertise at this firm and appreciate that the attorneys "*go out of their way to provide advice on the big picture.*" The firm's offices located all over the USA and across the globe ensure a huge spread of resources.

**The Lawyers: Carol Weld King** (see p.523) is primarily a commercial real estate lawyer but also represents tribes in real estate developments and financings, such as casinos, shopping centers and golf courses. She has acted as principal transactional counsel to a prominent Native American tribe in a large gaming and hospitality project, and represented a tribe and its gaming authority in a $391 million bank credit facility and the issuance of more than $900 million of publicly traded debt.

**Clients/Work Highlights:** The firm's client roster contains the Lower Elwha Klallam Tribe, the Mohegan Tribe of Connecticut and various investment banks.

## Holland & Hart LLP
See firm details p.369

**The Firm:** With offices throughout the USA, this large firm advises tribes, organizations and individuals on a broad range of Native American law sovereignty, litigation and transactional matters. Finance, tax, gaming, land acquisition, natural resources and environmental law are all on the agenda here. On the litigation side, the team has represented clients on natural resources, gaming, employment and PI issues at trial and appellate level, as well as in the jurisdiction of Indian tribes.

**The Lawyers: Mark Sheridan** (see p.134) advises on trial and appellate matters in connection with water rights and natural resources and provides preventive counseling to clients. Additionally, he draws support from natural resources experts in other offices, namely William Myers and Thomas Sansonetti.

**Clients/Work Highlights:** The firm serves tribal and nontribal businesses and individuals on a nationwide basis.

## Holland & Knight LLP
See firm details p.1534

**The Firm:** This prominent firm represents tribal governments and enterprises in an array of affairs, such as project financing, real estate and natural resources development, gaming and employment law issues. The team is equally strong in litigation encompassing environmental issues, water rights and the protection and recovery of burial, sacred and historic sites and artefacts. With its significant federal legislative and regulatory presence in Washington DC, the firm assists clients on matters relating to the tribal revenue taxation and the Indian Child Welfare Act. Its attorneys are also experienced in dealing with the Bureau of Indian Affairs, the DOJ and Indian Health Service budgets, and the Congressional Native American Caucus.

**The Lawyers:** With a wealth of experience under his belt, **Jerome Levine** (see p.115), director of the national Indian law practice group was described as "*the godfather of Indian law.*" According to commentators, he "*understands the wider business issues and has excellent technical skills.*" His areas of expertise include government-related litigation and regulation as well as business and financing transactions.

**Clients/Work Highlights:** The firm advises tribes, tribal governments and businesses throughout the USA.

## Hughes Hubbard & Reed LLP
See firm details p.1535

**The Firm:** The main components of this "*truly excellent and well-established*" team's Indian law practice are gaming, development, high-yield and tax-exempt financing, and syndicated lending. For example, the group acted for the Oneida Indian Nation of New York in a $310 million combined high-yield, tax-exempt and secured bank loan facility connected to the Turning Stone Resort & Casino's expansion. The casinos, hotels, resorts and golf courses market has also been an important area of activity. Recently, it represented the Native American Casino in its $16 million purchase of video gaming terminals and related licensed IP. Clients spoke of the "*timely and strong support*" the group provides, and its ability to draw on additional expertise from specialists across the firm's departments.

**The Lawyers:** "*Brilliant, hugely talented and very focused*" **Steven McSloy** (see p.120) specializes in transactional Native American law, where he "*knows all the tribes, is on good terms with the investment banks and has a lot of good business contacts.*" Clients also appreciate that he is "*very focused – he adopts a high sense of urgency to all his cases.*"

**Clients/Work Highlights:** River Rock Entertainment Authority; Chumash Casino and Resort Enterprise; Upstream Point Molate and investment and commercial banks are among the firm's clients.

## Latham & Watkins LLP

**The Firm:** According to interviewees, this "*great and highly professional*" group excels in casino finance. It represents tribes, developers and banks in high-yield bond work and entertainment financing on a national scale. The team sports further expertise such as transactional and legislative advice on irrigation and power projects, fish and wildlife, and land and water settlements. Its national and worldwide office network allows the firm to provide a huge level of resources to its transactional caseload.

**The Lawyers:** "*Very balanced, smart and business-minded*" corporate attorney **Raymond Lin** acts for Indian tribes, developers and financial institutions in gaming issues across the USA. Clients describe him as one of the most in-demand casino experts in the USA: according to one, he is "*a very suave legal wizard who always plays his cards right.*"

**Clients/Work Highlights:** The firm represents Native American tribes, developers and banks.

## Miller, Canfield, Paddock and Stone, P.L.C.
See firm details p.1148

**The Firm:** The firm's environmental and regulatory group advises tribes and corporations on a variety of Native American law matters. Its workload includes gaming, health and safety, tribal sovereignty and government relations. Related litigation and arbitration advice is also provided and the group represents tribes as well as their counterparts. The group's national spread of resources is attractive to clients.

**The Lawyers: Kevin Moody** (see p.122) earned applause for his deep understanding of Native American law and his "*strong analytical skills.*" He concentrates on gaming and healthcare matters related to Native American law.

**Clients/Work Highlights:** The firm serves tribes, state and local governments, businesses, individuals, and private and public organizations.

## Orrick, Herrington & Sutcliffe LLP
See firm details p.337

**The Firm:** The key focus of this dedicated group is on finance issues. The Indian tribal finance practice group assists tribes, Alaska native enterprises and financial institutions and corporations in a range of financing transactions. The group's expertise is broad: casinos, hotels and resorts, transportation, housing projects and the utilities sector are all areas of activity. The 11-strong team has acted as bond counsel on the first publicly offered tribal governmental bonds. It represented the Cabazon Band of Mission Indians in the financing of the Fantasy Springs hotel and resort, and assisted the Oneida Indian Nation in the financing of the Turning Stone Resort & Casino. Attorneys also served the Confederated Tribes of the Warm Springs Reservation of Oregon in their acquisition of the Warm Springs power hydroelectric dam.

**The Lawyers:** Leader of the Indian tribal finance practice **Townsend Hyatt** (see p.109) is based in the Portland office. A popular port of call for tribes, he is "*an excellent business adviser and a highly skilled lawyer.*" He advises tribes on a nationwide level on financings and land acquisitions, water rights and other infrastructure development, and casinos and resorts.

**Clients/Work Highlights:** Yavapai-Apache Nation; the Klamath Tribes; Swinomish Indian Tribal Community; Upper Skagit Indian Tribe; Robinson Rancheria of Pomo Indians of California; Seminole Tribe of Florida; Pascua Yaqui Tribe of Arizona; Chukchansi Economic Development Authority; St. Croix Chippewa Indians of Wisconsin and Salt River Pima-Maricopa Indian Community.

# PRODUCTS LIABILITY

| Products Liability Leading Firms | |
|---|
| **1** ARNOLD & PORTER LLP |
| DECHERT LLP |
| JONES DAY |
| KING & SPALDING LLP |
| KIRKLAND & ELLIS LLP |
| SKADDEN, ARPS, SLATE, MEAGHER & FLOM |
| **2** KAYE SCHOLER LLP |
| O'MELVENY & MYERS LLP |
| ORRICK, HERRINGTON & SUTCLIFFE |
| SHOOK, HARDY & BACON LLP |
| SIDLEY AUSTIN LLP |
| **3** DLA PIPER RUDNICK GRAY CARY US LLP |
| FULBRIGHT & JAWORSKI L.L.P. |
| GIBSON, DUNN & CRUTCHER LLP |
| HOLLAND & KNIGHT LLP |
| HUGHES HUBBARD & REED LLP |
| LATHAM & WATKINS LLP |
| MAYER, BROWN, ROWE & MAW LLP |
| REED SMITH LLP |
| SIMPSON THACHER & BARTLETT LLP |
| WHEELER TRIGG KENNEDY LLP |
| WILLIAMS & CONNOLLY LLP |
| **4** BUTLER, SNOW, O'MARA, STEVENS & CANNADA |
| CHADBOURNE & PARKE LLP |
| HOGAN & HARTSON LLP |
| MCDERMOTT WILL & EMERY |
| NELSON MULLINS RILEY & SCARBOROUGH |
| PEPPER HAMILTON LLP |
| WINSTON & STRAWN LLP |

## Band 1

### Arnold & Porter LLP
See firm details p.560

**The Firm:** Boasting more than 100 attorneys with experience of products liability issues, this DC-based firm has achieved considerable prominence in recent years. Interviewees applaud a *"smart and creative"* ethos that has enabled the firm to develop its acclaimed FDA practice into a major market force. It now offers pharmaceutical expertise, reinforced by unimpeachable regulatory credentials, to a *"tremendous network of national clients."* As an example, more than 40 of the firm's lawyers are currently serving as national coordinating counsel for Wyeth in its enormous phen-fen diet drug litigation. This requires an astute understanding of epidemiological and clinical data, and compliance with FDA new drug and adverse event reporting strictures in almost every state in the country. The firm has also performed a national role for Hoffmann-La Roche and Pfizer in cases involving prescription drugs and artificial heart valves. Commentators heartily commend the *"superlative, strategic and analytical skills"* on display in these and similar matters. It would be a mistake, however, to assume that a lofty position in the pharmaceutical industry circumscribes the reach of this *"top-notch"* group; observers also draw attention to its enviable track record in tobacco litigation. The firm's ongoing representation of Philip Morris in numerous state class action lawsuits, brought by plaintiffs seeking to recover for alleged tobacco-related illnesses, testifies to its excellence in this area. Elsewhere, its lawyers have also acted for a variety of companies with regard to lead pigment litigation.

**The Lawyers:** Senior litigator and former head of the firm's litigation group, **Peter Grossi** (see p.104) receives bountiful praise for his *"brilliance when it comes to the medical aspects of pharmaceutical litigation."* He has served as national counsel for Wyeth since 1997 and has represented Philip Morris in tobacco products liability litigation for more than 15 years. He is a favorite among clients, and one acolyte reports: *"He's fantastic. I get e-mails from him at every possible hour of the day and he obtains amazing results in trial."* **Robert Weiner** (see p.141) oversees the litigation practice at the firm and is well known to market authorities as a peerless tactician and theorist. He adopts an *"innovative and thoughtful"* approach to cases relating to diet drugs, heart valves and lead paint fumes, which clients regard as highly effective. Based in New York, **Peter Zimroth** (see p.143) has made his mark as a result of participation in the phen-fen litigation. *"A superb intellect and a great litigator,"* he has also represented Pfizer in lawsuits connected with welding rod fumes. **Ellen Reisman** (see p.129) is co-head of the firm's product liability practice – a standing that comes as no surprise to those who observe, approvingly: *"If she sets a direction, people follow it."* One of the lead partners in the diet drug litigation, she continues to be the principal architect of Wyeth's ongoing defense strategy.

**Clients/Work Highlights:** Other clients include American Red Cross and ARCO.

### Dechert LLP
See firm details p.1752

**The Firm:** Observers are in no doubt that this *"national firm with great regional presence"* will emerge unscathed, even strengthened, from the heat of the legal and media crucible that is the current Vioxx litigation. Boasting *"many weapons at its disposal,"* including 18 full-time members assisted by an additional six litigation partners, the firm's mass tort and products liability practice is certainly positioned for success. Always strong in tobacco, the group's appointment by Merck as one of four national coordinating counsels is indicative of the firm's impressive *"dedication to growth"* in the health and pharmaceutical sector. The team has also been involved in Wyeth's ongoing diet drug litigation, defending the company before the Philadelphia Court of Common Pleas against claims by two plaintiffs that phen-fen had caused their heart injuries. In other matters, the firm is acting for Nutraquest in more than 100 cases in which the claimants allege personal injury as a consequence of ingestion of products used for weight loss or energy gain. It has not, however, forgotten its roots, representing a variety of major tobacco manufacturers in over 1,000 cases relating to lung cancer and heart disease brought by residents of West Virginia. A *"creative approach and good client communication"* provides the icing on a cake that is fast proving irresistible.

**The Lawyers:** **Diane Sullivan** (see p.137) is renowned for her pharmaceutical work and is at ease defending clients such as Merck and Wyeth in either mass torts or individual suits. Peers approve of a *"dogged"* attitude that translates into a formidable success rate – *"she gets in there and fights hard for her clients."* She has also found time to serve as a member of the International Association of Defense Counsel. Sources describe **Robert Limbacher** (see p.116), responsible for coordinating the team involved in the Philadelphia Wyeth litigation, as someone *"willing to push limits on behalf of his clients while remaining utterly professional."* He has also served as national counsel for GlaxoSmithKline, defending the company against thousands of lawsuits and class actions across the country relating to the cholesterol-lowering drug Baycol. Interviewees agree that head of department **Sean Wajert** (see p.140) is largely responsible for the firm's rapid ascent to prominence in the products liability market: *"Calm and organized, you know that work within his purview will be completed efficiently and well."* He represents companies such as Wyeth, Baxter Healthcare and Philip Morris in toxic torts and class actions throughout the USA.

**Clients/Work Highlights:** Johnson & Johnson; York International; Amerisource Bergen; VF Corporation; West Pharmaceutical Services; PLAC; Cardinal Health; Airgas; BP Amoco; Stryker; Medtronic; sanofi-aventis; Delta; Kraft; Elan; Interline Brands and Rhodia.

### Jones Day
See firm details p.570

**The Firm:** In recent years this firm has blazed a trail through corporate America, garnering heartfelt praise for the excellence of its products liability practice and eliciting glowing epithets as *"the best in the country for sheer breadth and depth."* Traditionally, the group has focused on cases connected with durable products, a fact confirmed by its settlement of more than 100 putative class actions filed after Firestone recalled approximately 14 million Firestone ATX and Wilderness AT tires. Observers link the firm's success in defending automobile manufacturers to the strength of a Washington-based issues and appeals practice that conducts a substantial amount of work. One client placed a high premium on lawyers' *"conceptualization and tailoring of strategy to reflect the differing legal requirements of multiple jurisdictions."* Increasingly, these talents have attracted a wider audience. Commentators agree that the 45-strong group now *"walks the walk"* in tobacco litigation, acting for key client RJ Reynolds in a diverse range of precedent-setting matters. It won a defense verdict for the company in the first smoking and health jury trial in Manhattan, and triumphed in an appellate decision relating to the extent to which RICO could be used to claim against legitimate business. The US Court of Appeals for DC rejected the government's proposed $280 billion disgorgement remedy. The firm's striking out into virgin legal territory is further illustrated by its representation of airplane parts manufacturer Parker Hannifin in litigation connected with a Boeing 737-300 crash in the Red Sea. While the group is not readily associated with the pharmaceutical industry, involvement in numerous breast implant lawsuits and continuing work for TAP Pharmaceutical suggest that this is a situation soon to be remedied. Certainly, parlaying its reputation as the first port of call for companies *"if survival is in doubt,"* the future looks bright.

**The Lawyers:** In the midst of a *"cast of extremely bright lawyers,"* first and foremost, sources assert, **Daniel Reidy** (see p.129) is an excellent trial lawyer: *"He knows when to bluff, and when to fold his cards."* A pivotal role in the firm's national coordination of products liability defense falls within the ambit of his prestigious civil litigation practice. Robert Weber has recently left the firm to go in-house at IBM.

**Clients/Work Highlights:** The firm represented Pfizer and others before the Ohio Supreme Court in a trial court and appellate decision reversal relating to an asbestos settlement agreement. Additional clients include Textron; Norton Company; Xcel Energy; Sherwin-Williams; Brown & Williamson Holdings and Brush Engineered Materials.

## King & Spalding LLP

See firm details p.1933

**The Firm:** King & Spalding has formed adamantine bonds with the upper echelon of drug companies as a consequence of its impressive FDA practice. In conjunction with a strong track record for litigation (sources report that the firm is *"highly regarded by the courts"*) and extensive experience of Congressional hearings, the seven-partner group is flourishing in the currently febrile state of the pharmaceutical industry. Among its successes, it represented Purdue Pharma as national coordinating and trial co-counsel in more than 600 individual and class action suits in 32 states arising from the marketing of the painkiller OxyContin. The group's subsequent dismissal of approximately 300 of these headline cases caused ripples in the market and has become a focal point for peer comment and admiration. The firm also achieved victory for major client GlaxoSmithKline in the similarly attention-grabbing Paxil litigation: team members employed a vigorous *Daubert* defense to achieve summary judgment in 350 claims alleging suicidal and violent tendencies following the drug's discontinuation. It would be strange, however, if a firm noted by observers for its *"adaptability and flexibility"* was not equally proficient in other sectors. Accordingly, the group's endeavors have ensured it a prominent position in the automotive and tobacco industries, representing, for example, Brown & Williamson Tobacco in hundreds of smoking class actions across the country. A powerful toxic tort practice further ensures a wide geographical coverage.

**The Lawyers:** An assortment of interviewees value **Chilton Varner** (see p.139) as *"thoughtful, professional, polite – and as tough as nails."* She combines an active national trial practice with singular appellate expertise, as evidenced by recurrent descriptions of a *"terrific legal theorist and strategist who establishes a great rapport with clients."* In a field dominated by male attorneys, Varner's well-earned reputation as *"one of the best trial lawyers in the USA"* is a source of deep satisfaction to many of her contemporaries.

**Clients/Work Highlights:** The group also successfully represented Purdue Pharma in a whistle-blower case relating to the alleged violation of FDA regulations. In other matters, team members acting for GM in its appeal of a design defect verdict won a $122 million reversal. The firm's broad range of clients also includes Chevron; Dow Chemical; Exxon Mobil Corporation; Home Depot; RJ Reynolds; Shell and UPS.

## Kirkland & Ellis LLP

See firm details p.875

**The Firm:** *"Good and extremely aggressive in court,"* this firm's products liability and mass tort attorneys are standard bearers for an illustrious litigation practice that enjoys a reputation as one of the best in the USA. Observers were particularly complimentary about matters conducted from the Chicago office. Customarily retained in bet-the-company situations, team members demonstrate what one client identifies as Kirkland's *"philosophy of litigation,"* which emphasizes *"speed of response, pragmatism and a single-minded commitment to success."* The group has mined a rich seam of work in recent years, involving itself in complex disputes relating to breast implants, asbestos and tobacco. Peers highlight its virtuoso performance on behalf of Brown & Williamson Tobacco in United States v Philip Morris USA, the federal government's $280 million RICO suit against the tobacco industry. The firm's scene-stealing appearances in cases with far-reaching implications extend to the asbestos arena where it has been instrumental in restructuring litigation and appellate procedures. The group also represents key players in the pharmaceutical industry. It obtained summary judgment for Abbott Laboratories in a series of individual and class action lawsuits alleging that Meridia, a drug used in the treatment of obesity, was responsible for plaintiffs' cardiovascular disease. Team members have also been centrally involved in litigation relating to the Hanford Nuclear Reservation. Renowned for the influx of *"quality people"* who pass through its doors and the *"terrific training"* they receive, the firm's synonymy with cases of this magnitude seems assured for years to come.

**The Lawyers:** Very few attorneys currently practicing have made the same impact on the shifting plates of the legal landscape as **David Bernick** (see p.88), a lawyer whose *"name you hear over and over again."* Responsible for the administration of the general commercial litigation practice, he has focused on mass tort matters since the 1980's. Competitors laud his knowledge of complex medical and damage modeling issues and happily concede that he displays a *"remarkable ability to get his arms around the science, filter the details and apply it in the best possible way."* Closely associated with tobacco and asbestos litigation, he took the lead in the Brown & Williamson government lawsuit. Onlookers ascribe his high success rate to exemplary people skills: he *"gets to the heart of what makes juries tick, presenting arguments in a clear and comprehensible manner."* A variety of sources agree that *"bright and capable"* **Stephen Patton**'s (see p.125) key role in the Sanders v Lockyer tobacco litigation has guaranteed him an enviable place on the product liability map. He and Andrew McGaan represented Brown & Williamson in this case, which pivoted on claims that the $206 billion Master Settlement Agreement between the company, three other cigarette manufacturers and the attorney general was an illegal output cartel violating federal antitrust laws.

**Clients/Work Highlights:** In other matters, the firm achieved a complete defense verdict for GM in highly publicized litigation arising from the death of All-Pro linebacker Derrick Thomas. This concerned alleged design defects in the roofs of Chevrolet Suburbans. Other clients include 3M; Allstate; BP America; ARCO Products Company (now part of BP America); UNC Incorporated; Dow Corning; Motorola and UAL.

## Skadden, Arps, Slate, Meagher & Flom LLP
See firm details p.1557

**The Firm:** Skadden Arps boasts a *"long history in this particular field."* Evolving from its origins acting for automobile companies such as Ford and Chrysler, the firm now handles a diverse mix of mass tort and products liability cases from a national coordination perspective. Its emphasis on analysis and strategic planning has resulted in its acquiring a reputation for *"applying top-notch brain power to thorny legal issues."* Market observers point to extraordinary settlement, class certification and appellate expertise as a three-fold explanation for continuing client loyalty. No other matter in recent times provides a better example of this than the firm's much-envied representation of State Farm before the Illinois Supreme Court in a $1 billion class action. The group's reversal and dismissal of this claim (the largest ever made against an insurance company) culminated in a judgment prescribing the extent of punitive damages awards. Team members also won court approval of a class action settlement relating to a train derailment in South Carolina that resulted in multiple casualties and mass evacuation – a further illustration of the firm's aptitude for successfully resolving complex matters. A significant proportion of the group's current workload stems from the pharmaceutical industry where attorneys represent major players such as Pfizer in litigation relating to prescription drugs and medical devices.

**The Lawyers:** *"Legendary figure"* **Sheila Birnbaum** (see p.89) is a *"settlement guru"* with unparalleled experience of the coordination of mass torts and asbestos litigation. The firm's practice in these areas greatly benefits from her *"respected, academic*

approach to advocacy that is well received by judges and deeply appreciated by defendants."* Sources confirm this observation, identifying Birnbaum as *"one of the very best in the country at making rain."* Her skill at forming enduring client relationships guarantees repeat business while also attracting a steady stream of important cases. Taking the lead in the State Farm matter, her distinctive presence looks set to determine the upward motion of the firm's products liability practice for some time to come. Partner in the Chicago office **Ryan Stoll** (see p.137) fields a reputation for excellence in complex torts defense and offers extensive trial and appellate experience.

**Clients/Work Highlights:** The team was instrumental in the dismissal of a putative class action in Chicago brought against Anheuser-Busch and another brewer. This was the first of five class actions pending in state and federal courts against distillers and brewers, all of which seek to censor the content and placement of alcohol advertisements. Other clients include Intel; Compaq; Norfolk Southern and a raft of Fortune 500 companies.

## Band 2

## Kaye Scholer LLP
See firm details p.1536

**The Firm:** The undoubted jewel in the crown of this firm's products liability litigation and counseling practice is its status as Pfizer's national counsel, a role that has guaranteed it prominence in a slew of landmark matters in recent years. The 60-strong team continues to defend the company in litigation connected with the diabetes drug Rezulin, defeating an attempt at class certification in a medical monitoring suit. It also provides advice on claims arising from hormone replacement therapy. Nine defense verdicts in 11 cases since 2002 confirm the firm's *"reputation for excellence"* in the life sciences arena. In addition to pharmaceutical expertise, the team impresses observers with its sure grasp of complex medical device and biotech issues. In this environment, clients relish a *"thoughtful and creative"* approach that reassures them they are in safe hands.

**The Lawyers:** Cochair of the practice **Steven Glickstein** (see p.102) is an invaluable resource to clients seeking strategy advice. Fielding vast experience of products varying from the mainstream to the esoteric – including artificial heart valves, pharmaceuticals, blood products and penile prostheses – he is deemed *"great at generating ideas."* He is Pfizer's primary contact at the firm. Fellow cochair **Jay Mayesh**'s (see p.118) universally recognized trial skills are the perfect complement to Glickstein's strategic insight. Peers cite his visibility in the automobile industry, where he represents powerful manufacturers like DaimlerChrysler and Navistar, as evidence of his success in propelling the firm into new products liability terrain. Clients find him never less than *"bright and capable."*

**Clients/Work Highlights:** The firm's clientele also includes Novartis, Boston Scientific and American Medical Systems.

## O'Melveny & Myers LLP
See firm details p.336

**The Firm:** Renowned for the *"top-notch legal analysis"* its attorneys offer, this firm has made the most of corollary corporate nous to recast itself as a potent force in mass tort class actions. Its reputation as *"one of the premier firms in the country"* for this work was given an undoubted boost in the pharmaceutical market as a consequence of its appointment by Merck to coordinate Vioxx proceedings in New Jersey and California. Lawyers persuaded the New Jersey state court to dismiss a class action seeking to establish a nationwide medical monitoring program for millions of former users. Interviewees lavished praise on the team for the skillful management perceived to be responsible for this successful outcome. *"A bunch of smart lawyers who can think through a complicated case, identify the issues and position it in a way that plaintiffs can stomach,"* is how one competitor described the firm's composition and approach. Another lightning rod for peer approbation is the group's involvement in highly publicized litigation currently facing the welding industry. It achieved a defense verdict in Presler et al. v Lincoln Electric, which culminated in the jury's rejection of plaintiff claims that the neurological disorders he suffered were the result of fumes he had inhaled while using welding rod products.

**The Lawyers:** Head of O'Melveny's firmwide class action defense practice and managing partner of the DC office, **John Beisner** (see p.88) is a *"superb tactician"* whose profile in the market has grown exponentially following his *"creative and aggressive"* participation in the welding rod cases. He displays an ability to *"marshal all the diverse elements of a problem and mark out a route"* that distinguishes him from many of his contemporaries. Clients jump at the chance to hire **Randy Oppenheimer** (see p.124). *"He's fabulous – smart and easy to work with."* Based in Century City, his practice centers on national trial litigation and counseling for the business community.

**Clients/Work Highlights:** The firm represents a host of pharmaceutical companies and manufacturers.

## Orrick, Herrington & Sutcliffe
See firm details p.337

**The Firm:** products liability is an important component of this firm's litigation practice, with 93 *"top-quality"* attorneys devoting their time to this fertile area. Peers concede the group's dominance in New York and California and observe that it has aimed for more distant horizons in recent years. Traditionally associated with large-scale tobacco and asbestos disputes, it now puts together punitive damage models for clients from the pharmaceutical industry and represents them in a variety of class actions. One index of the firm's rapid ascent to prominence in this market came with its appointment by Wyeth in a multidefendant lawsuit brought by plaintiffs on behalf of themselves and millions of children who allegedly suffered injuries from FDA-approved vaccines containing the preservative thimerosal. An equally successful performance on behalf of Dow

Chemical in ongoing breast implant litigation led to instruction that returned the group to its roots: Kelly-Moore Paint sued Dow subsidiary Union Carbide to recover $6 billion costs connected with all past and future asbestos claims. The firm obtained a defense verdict, demonstrating a *"real team effort"* that impressed competitors.

**The Lawyers:** New York-based **James Stengel** (see p.136) earns his stripes for the *"outstanding judgment and strong strategic thinking"* he demonstrates in national asbestos and pharmaceutical litigation. *"There are certain lawyers who have a collective body of experience, style and results that make them phenomenal trial lawyers. He falls into this category."* **Peter Bicks** (see p.89) tried the Union Carbide case, winning the respect of observers for his success in a state, Texas, commonly regarded as inhospitable to corporate defendants. Bicks was also praised for his awareness, and utilization in court, of new technologies: *"One of his fortes is state-of-the-art graphics; it isn't enough anymore to put up a flip chart and scrawl some things down for the jury."*

**Clients/Work Highlights:** The firm also provided Dow Chemical with strategy advice and developed arguments regarding international law in a lawsuit brought by the Vietnam Association for Victims of Agent Orange/Dioxin claiming that the company had committed a war crime by supplying the US government with Agent Orange during the Vietnam war. The case was dismissed after ten days.

### Shook, Hardy & Bacon LLP
See firm details p.1218

**The Firm:** From its Kansas stronghold, this firm has extended outward to lay claim to national territory for products liability work. This is due, in part, to a string of stellar performances on behalf of the tobacco industry and market perception that it is Philip Morris' main resource for advice and representation in litigation. A *"huge role"* in the tobacco world is not, however, the end of the story for this continually evolving practice: peers note that it has engendered an equally distinctive reputation in the pharmaceutical market. This was most recently demonstrated by an impressive showing in Merck's Vioxx litigation, but the team is kept just as busy defending cases involving acne drugs, heart valves and bone screws. A significant volume of work in the alcohol and automobile sectors further illustrates the firm's receptivity to shifting market dynamics and bodes well for the future. Varied expertise, combined with low rates and a thoughtful fee structure, presents clients with an extremely attractive package.

**The Lawyers:** **Harvey Kaplan** (see p.111) oversees the firm's pharmaceutical and medical device litigation division. In addition to being *"great at arranging teams who can meet any problem,"* he is described by grateful beneficiaries of his expertise as *"one of the premier pharmaceutical lawyers in the country."* **Timothy Pratt** (see p.127) focuses on the defense of major pharmaceuticals in toxic tort matters. *"Outstanding by any measure,"* onlookers reserved particular acclaim for his sensitivity to the jury: *"He understands that if you can't tell the company's story in*

*court, you're dust."* Partner and vice chairman of the national products liability litigation group, **William Allinder** (see p.85) is a *"conscientious and tenacious"* attorney held in high esteem by clients throughout the tobacco industry.

### Sidley Austin LLP
See firm details p.883

**The Firm:** Boasting a *"nice combination of aggression and strategic thinking,"* this firm allures companies *"looking for assistance with the toughest of cases."* More than 20 partners operating out of Chicago and Los Angeles sustain a reputation for excellence within the connected spheres of pharmaceutical and medical device litigation. The firm is, for example, national coordinating counsel for AstraZeneca in class actions relating to the cholesterol-reducing drug Crestor. Work in this area goes hand in glove with a *"superb appellate practice,"* commentators report. The team can also claim experience of a range of other products, including breast implants, vinyl chloride and cell phones. It continues to be heavily involved in litigation connected with lead paint poisoning and recently defeated a medical monitoring suit brought by Chicago that, if successful, would have resulted in the establishment of a victims fund to be compulsorily supported by members of the lead industry.

**The Lawyers:** *"Tough-minded and displaying great leadership skills,"* **Sara Gourley** (see p.103) is based in Chicago and acts as national counsel for a producer of blood products in the AIDS and hepatitis C litigation. Conducting a practice dealing with similarly sensitive issues, she *"protects her clients and avoids unnecessary flashiness."*

**Clients/Work Highlights:** The firm obtained a defense verdict for GE in Madison County in a claim relating to ongoing asbestos class actions. The firm's pharmaceutical clients also include sanofi-aventis and Pfizer.

### Band 3

### DLA Piper Rudnick Gray Cary US LLP
See firm details p.870

**The Firm:** Piper Rudnick's consolidation of its presence in the products liability market has been given a major boost by its merger with Gray Cary. This union has provided attorneys with unprecedented geographic reach and opened the gates to a host of new clients such as Cisco Systems. Commensurate with this expansion, it has had greater involvement in a range of controversial and highly visible class actions: the firm's impressive performance as national counsel to Pfizer, in the company's turbulent Bextra and Celebrex litigation, was mirrored by its successful representation of Wyeth in 120 individual lawsuits filed by New York residents claiming heart valve injuries due to the ingestion of diet drugs. Marking an interesting intersection between products liability and antitrust concerns, DLA Piper's lawyers are also defending Merck against claims brought by consumers alleging they have paid too much for Vioxx.

**The Lawyers:** *"Extremely well thought of"* in the pharmaceutical arena, **Amy Schulman** (see p.133) founded the practice and sits on the firm's global board. She has acted for Wyeth both at home and abroad, appearing for the company in the New York phen-fen collective action and traveling as far afield as Scotland in pursuit of the client's needs.

**Clients/Work Highlights:** The firm successfully dismissed a suit backed by the National Justice League that alleged aspartame was unsafe and that Altria Group had induced consumers to purchase the product. Other clients include KONE; UPS; Nissan and Michelin.

### Fulbright & Jaworski L.L.P.
See firm details p.1928

**The Firm:** Purveying a wealth of experience at state and federal level accumulated since the inception of manufacturer's liability in the 1960's, Fulbright & Jaworski retains its pole position in the market. This reputation is largely due to the caliber of the firm's Austin, Dallas and Houston offices, out of which the majority of products liability and mass tort matters are handled. Very often, these are test cases: at present, attorneys are defending Cooper Tire & Rubber in Texas against a number of actions relating to alleged design defects in tire retreads. The firm's advocacy on US soil of Dutch aircraft manufacturer Fokker also illustrates a dedication to international representation that has paid dividends in providing it with a global profile. It has not, however, neglected other industries, supplementing *"highly regarded"* participation in Merck's Vioxx litigation with the defense of numerous clients located in the health sciences sector.

**The Lawyers:** **Jonathan Skidmore** (see p.135) is an *"excellent"* litigator who *"steps up to whatever is placed in front of him,"* commentators observe. He is currently shining in the media glare of the Vioxx trials following his star turn in the Baycol litigation. An *"intelligent lawyer who can really craft an argument,"* **Otway Denny** (see p.95) is acting for BP Products North America in civil litigation arising from an explosion that occurred at its Texas plant resulting in hundreds of injuries and the deaths of 15 people. Co-head of the products liability team and former law professor **Vincent Walkowiak** (see p.140) receives applause as a *"very bright guy"* with a broad range of expertise.

**Clients/Work Highlights:** Additional clients include GlaxoSmithKline (for whom the firm is acting in litigation arising from alleged dependency on over-the-counter laxatives) and Biedermann Motech and its US distributor. Attorneys are representing the latter in 150 multidistrict lawsuits connected with bone screws.

### Gibson, Dunn & Crutcher LLP
See firm details p.328

**The Firm:** Given Gibson Dunn's formidable West Coast heritage in environmental litigation and toxic tort cases, its ascendancy in this field is far from surprising. A continuing affinity with contaminated community matters sees lawyers at the firm defending Redlands residents before the California Supreme Court in a claim connected with two contaminants produced by a former rocket manufacturing facility; the team has mirrored its success in court with victory in seven appeals showcasing its celebrated skills at appellate level. It receives equal acclaim for punitive damages expertise, particularly in relation to the automotive industry where it is currently representing DaimlerChrysler in litigation totaling $98 million. Along the same industry lines, lawyers acting for Ford in claims arising from alleged Explorer design defects persuaded the Supreme Court to reject plaintiffs' attempts to apply aggregate disgorgement theory to the claims process.

**The Lawyers:** *"Creative, articulate and persuasive,"* Los Angeles-based **Theodore Boutrous** (see p.89) specializes in high-stakes appeals and the formation of appellate strategies. Raymond Ludwiszewski is partner in the DC office and fields cases with an environmental tinge.

## Holland & Knight LLP
See firm details p.1534

**The Firm:** This firm acts for a wide array of businesses in the products area, boasting particular capability in the tire industry. National counsel to Firestone/Bridgestone in the aftermath of its Ford Explorer recalls, it represented the manufacturer in congressional hearings and, ultimately, before a grand jury investigation. It continues to handle and coordinate about 100 cases relating to this litigation. More than 150 connected claims involving accidents in foreign jurisdictions have also provided attorneys with the opportunity to hone their appellate skills. This association with big names and newsworthy prosecutions continues, with the firm acting for GlaxoSmithKline in ongoing vaccine litigation and defending a major producer of petroleum products against a series of claims alleging a link between groundwater contamination and a gasoline additive.

**The Lawyers:** Bringing considerable legal muscle to complex toxic tort litigation – particularly claims connected with water contamination – the *"aggressive and successful"* **Kathleen Strickland** (see p.137) also serves as national trial counsel in food and drug cases. Chair of the appellate group, **Laurie Webb Daniel**'s (see p.94) *"undoubted excellence"* in addressing class action medical liability issues makes her an invaluable asset to the firm.

**Clients/Work Highlights:** Other prominent clients include BAE Systems, Texas Instruments and Exxon-Mobil.

## Hughes Hubbard & Reed LLP
See firm details p.1535

**The Firm:** This practice, consisting of 75 partners specializing in toxic torts and product issues, is riding high in the market at the moment. The team has followed a scene-stealing performance in multistate contaminated blood litigation by assuming center stage in the national defense of Merck's Vioxx lawsuits. A broad approach to the products liability arena ensures, however, that the pharmaceutical industry is not the only one to benefit from Hughes

Hubbard's careful attentions. It has also flourished in toxic exposure matters, providing Viacom with strategy advice and representation in 1,500 claims alleging illness as a consequence of contact with mercury, lead and beryllium. Much of this work is founded on the group's thorough knowledge of asbestos litigation, learning that has prompted a major chemical company to engage it on a national level. The firm's reputation for doing *"an excellent job in regard to the factual development of a case"* is borne out by repeated forays into technologically complex cases on behalf of various members of the automotive industry, including Ford.

**The Lawyers:** *"Tireless when it comes to identifying the issues and coordinating strategy,"* **Theodore Mayer** (see p.118) began his career acting for car manufacturers. His practice has now moved to more pharmaceutical climes and he is currently participating in Merck's defense. **Norman Kleinberg** (see p.113) has also devoted much of his time to the Vioxx litigation. Elsewhere, he has applied his experience of insurance coverage issues to the representation of the American Bureau of Shipping in claims brought by the Government of Spain seeking compensation for the cleanup costs entailed by the sinking of the oil tanker 'Prestige'. Observers respect his efficiency in difficult situations: *"There is no wasted emotion. The questions are addressed, the course of action decided and he proceeds."*

**Clients/Work Highlights:** The firm's impressive client roster also includes Rockwood Specialties whom it acted for in defeating a class certification connected with the chemical effects of wood treatment.

## Latham & Watkins LLP

**The Firm:** Latham brings together teams that cut across every geographical and departmental line. *"Well managed, with wonderful lawyers,"* it is a familiar sight in beauty contests. Although *"faultless"* white-collar expertise continues to set the tone of the firm's acclaimed litigation practice, a huge environment group, combined with established appellate excellence, guarantees it prominence in major toxic tort matters. Attorneys defended Kuhlman Electric in multiple actions in which plaintiffs sought more than $1 billion in damages. Ultimately, the cases were settled for less than five percent of the original amount. The firm's aptitude in this environment translates well into other circumstances. This past year, the group has been immersed in tobacco litigation, obtaining a second defense verdict for Philip Morris in the California Superior Court – the conclusion of a seven-week trial arising from a fraudulent concealment claim worth $17 million. Peers drew further attention to the firm's expansive sphere of influence by highlighting its impressive showing in a series of lawsuits that have been brought against the alcohol industry.

**The Lawyers:** Peter Winik, global co-chair of the firm's products liability and mass torts practice group, is deputy managing partner of the DC office. A wearer of several hats, he has expertise in products safety and crisis management and does a lot of work

for European companies under investigation. This has led to involvement in a variety of class actions, defending industry heavyweights such as GE. He is currently representing a number of alcohol companies embroiled in allegations of improper advertising relating to underage drinking.

**Clients/Work Highlights:** On behalf of Monsanto, the firm won the dismissal of a toxic tort class action filed against it and other US chemical companies by four million Vietnamese nationals, including North Vietnamese soldiers and Viet Cong. The firm's pharmaceutical clientele includes Pfizer.

## Mayer, Brown, Rowe & Maw LLP
See firm details p.876

**The Firm:** This firm *"offers an advocacy package of the highest level"* containing attorneys who evince a *"fundamental understanding of products liability law nationwide."* Its development and effective management of national mass tort strategies is apparent in the relationships it has formed in the pharmaceutical industry. Whether it is marshaling evidence to create sophisticated science defenses or utilizing a strong appellate practice to overturn previous verdicts, much of the firm's heavy lifting in this arena is directed toward defeating class certification. During the past couple of years, SCHWARZ PHARMA has been subject to eight claims alleging deficiencies in its Reglan labeling – raising the question of whether a brand-name manufacturer is responsible for injuries caused by a generic product that uses the same label. So far, a team led by Peter Liaskos has obtained the dismissal of all but one of these lawsuits. The firm is also involved in the third wave of asbestos litigation currently sweeping the country. Expertise in silica, tools and heavy metals cases rounds off the workload of a practice firing on all cylinders.

**The Lawyers:** Clients bring in *"big-picture strategist"* **Herbert Zarov** (see p.143) to break logjammed cases. The main contact at the firm for Dow Chemical, he was national counsel in the company's multistate breast implant litigation – a role ideally suited to a man who, according to peers, *"works well in a team setting."* Demonstrating an *"orderly mind that goes right to the heart of the issue,"* **Peter Liaskos** (see p.115) shines in a courtroom setting. He is handling all of the Reglan products liability litigation for SCHWARZ.

**Clients/Work Highlights:** The firm represented Eli Lilly in litigation relating to diethylstilbestrol (DES). Other clients include Novartis, BASF and Abbott Laboratories.

## Reed Smith LLP
See firm details p.1762

**The Firm:** Since the absorption of Crosby Heafey in 2003 – an outfit greatly respected for the savvy it displayed in pharmaceutical litigation – Reed Smith's efforts to expand beyond Pittsburgh have really taken wing. The firm, which began life as local counsel, has built upon its enviable court connections and reputation for *"quality all the way through"* to secure a place on a national platform. Counting among its staff a number of medical doctors and epidemiologists, it is ideally suited to the contours of the life sciences market, staking out its territory through the representation of heavyweights such as Eli Lilly. The firm's assured performance on behalf of Wyeth in thousands of phen-fen cases consolidated in the first district of Pennsylvania elicited sincere praise from rivals. It also acts as national counsel for a manufacturer of implantable cardiac devices.

**The Lawyers:** The *"sound and highly regarded"* **Michael Brown** (see p.90) came to Reed Smith following the firm's merger with Crosby Heafey. Formerly chair of the latter's complex litigation group, sources observe that in court he is *"extremely comfortable on his feet."* **Michael Scott** (see p.134) *"sets the tone for the practice."* His experience runs the gamut of pharmaceutical and medical device matters. Judges respect him and clients attest to the fact that he *"tries cases beautifully."*

**Clients/Work Highlights:** A small selection from the firm's broad range of clients includes American Crane & Equipment, Cirrus Design and St. Jude Medical.

### Simpson Thacher & Bartlett LLP
See firm details p.1555

**The Firm:** Simpson Thacher assumes a national coordinating role for companies dealing with lawsuits arising from their products liability issues and those of their subsidiaries. While the litigation department covers a variety of areas, interviewees for the most part associate the practice with claims arising from coverage disputes. Its involvement in this market began in the sixties with representation of GM in New York-based litigation. The Big Apple continues to be a stronghold for the firm, out of which it conducts a substantial amount of asbestos litigation – much of it stemming from insurance disputes. Recently, the team has transferred skills acquired in this arena to the pharmaceutical industry. It also takes full advantage of the firm's adjacent international expertise to advise BAT on jurisdictional matters and remove European claims against the company from US courts. The group's current representation of a major beer company in nationwide class actions is typical of the breadth, depth and sector reflexivity that defines Simpson Thacher as a whole.

**The Lawyers:** The *"fabulous"* **Roy Reardon** (see p.128) is a legend in litigation circles. He deploys his considerable talents in products cases before state and federal trial courts across the country.

**Clients/Work Highlights:** The group acts for Wyeth, Heineken and a diverse range of other manufacturers drawn from a variety of industries.

### Wheeler Trigg Kennedy LLP

**The Firm:** This Denver-based firm may be small but it is a major force in products liability, deploying its *"exceedingly fine trial lawyers"* to great effect in pharmaceutical and medical device matters. Currently, the firm is representing Guidant Endovascular Solutions in claims relating to coronary devices; with characteristic tenacity and diligence it has had ten of

these class actions dismissed. Many interviewees, however, locate the backbone of the practice in the automotive arena – an industry association that has existed since the firm's original entrance into the market. For the past ten years, attorneys have enjoyed a close relationship with manufacturers such as Ford and DaimlerChrysler, defending them in multidistrict litigation stemming from alleged design defects. This *"superlative"* work has not prevented the group from pushing the envelope in other sectors and it has defended a host of companies in mining, heavy metals and industrial equipment cases. One client attributed his loyalty to the firm to the fact that *"they never short-change me – I'm never passed around and they always obtain great results."* This is a sentiment that resounds throughout the marketplace.

**The Lawyers:** **Malcolm Wheeler** is *"a prodigious worker who crosses industry lines, as all the best lawyers do."* There is very little in the products liability arena that falls outside this national leader's purview and in the area of punitive damages he is unparalleled. The *"one you parachute in when in trouble,"* his *"relentlessness"* when seeking out and pressing home defense strategy warrants him the regard of all those who have opposed him. **John Trigg** acts as national trial counsel for automobile companies in substantial claims arising from alleged design and manufacturing defects. The pharmaceutical community also benefits from the *"intelligence and legal acumen"* he reveals in trial. Recently he defended Merck in Vioxx litigation that took place in Louisiana. Individually, Wheeler and Trigg prove formidable presences; as a duo, they are unstoppable.

**Clients/Work Highlights:** Other clients include DaimlerChrysler, Whirlpool and Pfizer.

### Williams & Connolly LLP

**The Firm:** The products liability environment provides a natural habitat for a firm where immense trial capability lies deep in the fabric of its litigation department. Involved in national mass tort coordination for decades, this practice's upward trajectory began with tractor fire proceedings in the 1970's, before moving on to asbestos claims and, currently, class actions leveled at the pharmaceutical industry. The firm is joint national coordinating counsel for Merck in the Vioxx disputes and national counsel for Wyeth in its hormone replacement litigation. While the team suffered disappointment in the Texas Vioxx trial, this has not dented its reputation. Interviewees describe a cadre of *"smart, aggressive and nononsense"* attorneys who *"promote their clients' interests rather than themselves."* The defense of Bayer in scores of lawsuits relating to the cholesterol-reducing drug Baycol presents yet another feather in the cap for the firm. *"If you have to win a case, use them,"* one commentator said.

**The Lawyers:** **David Kiernan**'s medical background lends considerable authority to his practice and makes him the first choice for clients such as Merck, for whom he acts as national coordinating counsel in the Vioxx litigation. *"Very important behind-the-scenes guy"* **Lane Heard** also dedicates a large percentage of his time to the defense of mass

tort pharmaceutical claims. He continues to work closely with Wyeth.

**Clients/Work Highlights:** Additional clients include GE, Bell Sports and American Cyanamid.

## Band 4

### Butler, Snow, O'Mara, Stevens & Cannada, PLLC
See firm details p.1189

**The Firm:** Building on *"enormous power and presence"* in the Southeast, where it is a familiar fixture in the Texas Supreme Court, this firm has radiated outward to foster client relationships throughout the country. Sources ascribe the reason for this transition from regional to national representation to sheer, unambiguous quality; the team may not be as large as some in terms of resources but a raft of *"outstanding lawyers with tremendous insight"* provides ample compensation. Particularly strong in the pharmaceutical and medical device arenas, the team is conducting regional Vioxx litigation as well as defending a major client against claims relating to Accutane, a drug used in the treatment of acne. The firm boasts equal proficiency in asbestos, silica and environmental chemical matters and leverages talent drawn from its well-regarded agricultural practice to provide clients with national claims and regulatory advice.

**The Lawyers:** Chair of the litigation department **Christy Jones** (see p.110) plays a leading role in the health litigation subdivision. Presenting clients with *"the whole package – intelligence, presence and trial experience,"* she has broad experience of prescription medication, vaccine, herbicide, asbestos and plastics-related lawsuits. Jones' skillful and successful negotiation of the complexities inherent in the Vioxx litigation has impressed her contemporaries.

**Clients/Work Highlights:** The firm is national counsel for a machine and tool manufacturer that has been sued in Missouri, Illinois and Kentucky as a consequence of injuries allegedly resulting from the design of tools used in the formation of plastic items.

### Chadbourne & Parke LLP
See firm details p.1524

**The Firm:** This *"client-driven"* practice, headquartered in New York, has always had an advantage over other firms in the tobacco arena, having represented many of the leading brands since the infancy of interstate prosecutions. It is currently acting for BAT (Investments) in litigation involving individual class action and medical reimbursement matters. The pharmaceutical skill evinced in the successful resolution of these and similar lawsuits achieves its fullest expression in Chadbourne's role as co-national counsel to the Purdue Pharma consortium, producers of the opioid analgesic OxyContin. To date, a significant number of claims arising from defective design allegations have been defeated on motion or withdrawn.

**The Lawyers:** As well as participating in the defense of BAT, Donald Strauber is co-national counsel for

the Purdue defendants in the OxyContin litigation.
Clients/Work Highlights: Other clients include Jim Beam, Gallagher and Brown & Williamson Tobacco.

## Hogan & Hartson LLP
See firm details p.568

The Firm: Hogan's *"depth of experience and years of knowing the market"* guarantee it a potency in the products liability field. While some observers question the extent to which its *"top-notch"* attorneys focus their energies in this direction, others point to the firm's thriving relationship with DaimlerChrysler as conclusive proof of its continuing relevance and impact. The Delaware Superior Court recently granted the group's motion to exclude expert testimony in an action brought against the motor company; a Supreme Court dismissal of the plaintiff's subsequent appeal of summary judgment provides verification of the firm's much-admired strength at appellate level. In addition to ties with the automobile industry, carefully pitched FDA expertise has also granted the practice many a happy marriage in the pharmaceutical arena. Illustrative of this, attorneys won an important victory on behalf of Amgen in June 2005, when the District Court for the Southern District of New York denied a motion for preliminary injunction filed by two participants in a failed clinical trial sponsored by the company.

The Lawyers: Mark Gately is Hogan's primary contact. A member of the products liability Advisory Council (PLAC), he is national counsel for a major pharmaceutical company.

Clients/Work Highlights: The firm was instrumental in obtaining a denial by the New Jersey Supreme Court of an application to designate all pending and future litigation relating to Enbrel, Celebrex and Remicade as mass torts. Other clients include Bristol-Myers Squibb and Mercedes-Benz USA.

## McDermott Will & Emery
See firm details p.878

The Firm: A new entry to *Chambers* this year, McDermott received marketwide endorsement as a firm *"rapidly gaining ground"* in products liability circles. Beginning with national representation of a major producer of GM corn recalled in 2000 following the discovery of corn DNA in human food products, a trickle of cases has become a deluge. *"Knowledgeable and responsive"* in the face of complex claims, the firm's attorneys specialize in latter-stage intervention in high-profile matters such as the phen-fen litigation, while also defending a host of companies embroiled in asbestos class actions. This ever-broadening remit further encompasses assisting heavy equipment manufacturers with design defect issues and leading the charge in agricultural mass torts. Clients also applauded the quality of the firm's RICO and health insurance-related advice.

The Lawyers: A partner in the Chicago office, **Michael Pope** (see p.126) chairs the firm's international products liability practice. Famed for his

assured handling of complex class actions, he has been instrumental in effecting procedural reforms and revising electronic evidence regulations. Presently, he is acting for State Farm in Illinois-based litigation and representing 17 Blue Cross and Blue Shield Association plans in multidistrict claims. **Peter Resnik** (see p.129) operates out of the Boston office and is in charge of the pharmaceutical and biotech products liability group. *"Creative, smart and excellent in trial,"* a pivotal role in the theophylline litigation provided a fitting prelude to his current participation in the phen-fen diet drug litigation as national counsel for two phentermine defendants.

## Nelson Mullins Riley & Scarborough LLP
See firm details p.1758

The Firm: Recently chosen by Pfizer as one of its 24 go-to firms, Nelson Mullins is highly regarded in the pharmaceutical arena. It has *"the utmost credibility"* in a variety of product liability suits, including claims associated with asbestos, blood product and breast implant matters. The firm's expertise in claim prevention and the development of procedures to mitigate future litigation make it an ideal candidate for those companies, such as Wyeth, seeking regional representation in media-friendly, complex class actions. While sources concur that the group has yet to achieve comprehensive national presence, they readily concede that the portents for its achievement of this aim seem favorable.

The Lawyers: The *"utterly phenomenal"* **Stephen Morrison** chairs the firm's litigation group and is based in the Columbia office. products liability is an important facet of a practice that also covers technology law, business liability and securities litigation. Clients give him their backing for being *"everything a lawyer should be – brilliant and extremely down-to-earth."*

Clients/Work Highlights: Hoffmann-La Roche; Ford; Honda; Isuzu Motors America; Kawasaki Motors and Mazda.

## Pepper Hamilton LLP
See firm details p.1760

The Firm: Pepper Hamilton is a familiar face in the pharmaceutical world. Excelling at case preparation, the firm's attorneys undertake a substantial amount of discovery work on behalf of heavyweight manufacturers involved in major litigation relating to experimental drugs, including gene therapies. It has been involved in Prozac litigation and represented Eli Lilly. The group does not, however, neglect medical device issues, boasting experience of a constellation of claims arising from cranial drills, bone screws, cardiac pacemakers and other surgical implants. While these matters frequently take the firm into national territory, where it coordinates federal multi-district litigation proceedings, interviewees reserve much praise for its tremendous showing in Philadelphia. Lawyers operating out of this office also tackle asbestos claims and toxic tort litigation stemming from state and federal environmental enforcement activity.

The Lawyers: A *"born leader"* in the estimation of market observers, **Nina Gussack** (see p.104) combines an executive position at the firm with responsibility for the health effects litigation practice group. Her renown as a *"brilliant strategist and excellent communicator"* makes her the perfect choice for multidistrict pharmaceutical defense.

## Winston & Strawn LLP
See firm details p.886

The Firm: Winston Strawn *"can do it all: they have appellate people, trial people and the muscle to handle a big case."* Carving a sizable niche in tobacco litigation through the representation of major players such as Philip Morris, competitors also regularly encounter the Chicago-based firm in the alcohol litigation presently dominating the market. Interviewees did not restrict their praise to these areas, extolling *"general excellence"* in the national and international defense of claims relating to diet products, asbestos, construction equipment and an assortment of drugs and delivery systems.

The Lawyers: Chairman of the firm's litigation department, **Dan Webb** is praised as *"one of the most sought-after, big case trial lawyers"* in the USA. *"He can connect with juries and judges in virtually every part of the country and he's not afraid to tell clients the truth."* Credited by peers for putting Winston & Strawn on the map in the region of products liability, he has tried a series of key federal tobacco cases. He also undertakes civil, regulatory and white-collar criminal matters.

## Other Notable Practitioners

Snell & Wilmer LLP's **Warren Platt** (see p.126) attracts plaudits for being *"as tough as nails, yet utterly charming."* He specializes in defending national and international manufacturers in complex class actions, demonstrating a capacity for work that often daunts competitors: *"He can dive in and be ready to go at the drop of a hat."* His stellar clientele includes Ford, DaimlerChrysler and Caterpillar. The *"very capable"* **Edward Weltman** (see p.142), chair of Goodwin Procter LLP's products liability group, reflects in his own caseload the firm's pronounced emphasis on pharmaceutical matters. He has been lead counsel to Teva Pharmaceutical Industries for more than 20 years, handling class actions in jurisdictions extending as far as Israel. His involvement in the phen-fen litigation provoked admiring comment from peers. DC-based **Theodore Voorhees** (see p.140) of Covington & Burling earns recognition for his long-standing defense of alcohol and beverage-related claims. Exercising *"good judgment"* and displaying *"great organizational and writing skills,"* his position as chair of the products liability and toxic tort practice entails the strategic shaping and management of incipient mass tort actions.

# PROJECTS

## Band 1

### Latham & Watkins LLP

**The Firm:** This "*absolutely first-class*" team has enjoyed another impressive year, working on a swath of deals that highlight its all-round capability and geographic reach. The firm's reputation for projects work stems from its ability to cater to a range of both international and domestic clients drawn from the sponsor and lender fields. The firm possesses unrivaled depth among its ranks. Clients report: "*Of course there are real stars in the team, but I am always amazed at the number and quality of associates backing them up.*" The Washington, DC office provides support to the multilateral banks, and is complemented by a thoroughbred finance practice in New York. The highly respected California team is noted for its power prowess. On the international front, the firm closed the groundbreaking Qatargas II project for US Ex-Im Bank, and reinforced its reputation for Middle East gas matters by advising the borrowers and sponsors on RasGas II/3. The team enjoys a fine reputation in Latin America, and recently advised Inter-American Development Bank in the financing of a 1,200 MW electricity transmission line in Brazil. Closer to home, the team has flexed its transactional muscle, advising the joint arrangers in the acquisition of La Paloma Generating Company. Top finance houses, and particularly the increasingly acquisitive private equity funds, regularly seek counsel here. Commentators were united in their praise for the consistently high-quality advice provided by the group and its commitment to adapting quickly to industry developments. The departure of Andy Singer, a huge client draw, was naturally noted by the market; however, there is little doubt that Singer has left a legacy of a finely tuned team with depth and breadth that remains the envy of many.

**The Lawyers:** This team has developed a reputation for producing lawyers who are "*committed, responsive, know the business and quite simply are a pleasure to deal with.*" Clients sing the praises of **David Gordon**, managing partner of the New York office: "*He's a terrific guy – personable and enthusiastic – we just love him.*" He has extensive experience in guiding clients from soup to nuts in a range of projects. Global chair of projects, **William Voge** "*is everything and more,*" according to clients. He displays superb client skills and his stocks are high following his work on RasGas II/3. **Jonathan Rod** co-heads the projects team and is noted for his capital markets expertise. He is "*a considered attorney with huge commercial understanding.*" **John Sachs** is based in Washington, DC and is the key relationship partner with multilaterals. Clients were quick to point out his keen eye for detail.

**Clients/Work Highlights:** ABN AMRO; Lehman Brothers; JPMorgan; Morgan Stanley; WestLB; Deutsche Bank Securities; Mobil Producing Nigeria; Citigroup Global Markets; CSFB and Goldman Sachs.

### Milbank, Tweed, Hadley & McCloy LLP

**The Firm:** The market was united in its recommendation of this firm, pointing to its depth of experience across a number of infrastructure fields and its broad-based finance practice. "*They're most definitely a player and so diverse in their expertise,*" agree clients. The team has leveraged its strong relationships with finance houses and banks, particularly from the New York and Los Angeles offices, to harness the momentum in the hedge fund and private equity arena. The Washington, DC-based team adopts a greater focus on sponsors. A key drawing card here is the integrated nature of the practice, with clients praising the geographic and cross-practice coordination offered. Energy naturally features prominently in the team's showcase, but its dedication to the renewables sector has distinguished it from competitors. Transportation is another area where the firm has consolidated its position in the market; it represents key industry players on toll road projects across the country and in Latin America. The team made its mark representing Macquarie Bank and Cintra as acquirers on the Chicago Skyway transaction and recently represented the underwriters on the partial refinancing of debt and floated bonds. The group has established a reputation for handling the financing and refinancing of complex and multiple-party transactions, such as its recent refinancing of KGen's senior credit facility for a number of gas-powered facilities from Duke Energy. Latin America is a key market, particularly with the firm's stellar mining and minerals practice and its recognized strength in emerging markets. In Brazil, the team completed a complex refinancing of $571 million debt of Light Serviços de Electricidade.

**The Lawyers:** **Edwin Feo** has forged a distinct presence in the market. Cochairing the firm's global project finance practice, he has spearheaded the firm's renewables and greenfield practice. Clients report that his commercial acumen keeps them coming back: he is "*very bottom-line-oriented and will do anything to get the deal done.*" **Jonathan Green** "*is a force to be reckoned with*" and has developed a reputation for expertise in the Latin American market as well as domestic projects. **Richard Brach** is "*extremely sound in his judgment, pragmatic and has a deep well of experience,*" said clients. **Douglas Harris** garnered strong praise from the market for his client-friendly approach to negotiations. He is "*technically excellent and zealously represents our interests without being overly aggressive,*" remarked clients.

**Clients/Work Highlights:** WestLB; Citigroup; Macquarie Bank; Cintra; Dexia; DEPFA BANK; OPIC; US Ex-Im Bank; CSFB; ANZ and Mitsubishi.

### Skadden, Arps, Slate, Meagher & Flom LLP

See firm details p.1557

**The Firm:** Truly an established heavyweight in the market, Skadden has devoted resources to building up its enviable projects practice, leveraging its renowned transactional and restructuring capability. Clients heaped praise on this outfit; this is the group clients turn to when the stakes are high in "*bet the company*" deals. "*They're our first choice because the quality of their advice is exceptional and the availability and total dedication of senior partners is second to none.*" Projects work is driven by offices in New York, Washington, DC and Houston. Internationally, the firm's footprint is firmly planted in the Middle East. Securing plum advisory roles for Ras Laffan II and III and Qatargas II are examples of recent headline deals. Domestically, the firm has built on its historical strength in the utilities market, with Edison Mission Energy, as well as key financial players such as CSFB and RBS, seeking the team's counsel.

**The Lawyers:** **Hal Moore** (see p.122) is "*a spectacularly talented attorney,*" credited with being the driving force in establishing Skadden as a serious

projects force, particularly in the Middle East. He recently advised the Egyptian General Petroleum Corporation in a Rule 144A financing of floating rate notes. **Marty Klepper** (see p.113) drives the Washington, DC capability and is well liked by peers and clients. The latter report he is particularly skilled in dealing with his own clients as well as those across the table: "*He is very diplomatic, he diffuses rather than creates situations.*"
**Clients/Work Highlights:** A snapshot of clients includes NRG Energy; Wisconsin Energy; RBS; CSFB; Goldman Sachs; KBC Bank; Sumitomo Bank; BNP Paribas; Lehman Brothers and Mizuho Bank.

### White & Case LLP
See firm details p.1566

**The Firm:** This firm's profile in the projects sector has continued to rise as it forges a presence in the domestic market, complementing its well-established international practice. It is "*an extremely active team of savvy operators,*" according to market sources, with a deal list that features a healthy share of the year's top matters and most active clients. The team has developed a reputation for serving commercial banks and multilaterals from the New York and Washington, DC offices in particular. Illustrating its domestic energy capability and its extending reach into renewables, the team advised the underwriters, led by CSFB, in their offering of senior secured bonds of FPL Energy National Wind. In the transport sector, the firm counseled Skyway Concession in its refinancing of the Chicago Skyway. Internationally, the firm has become synonymous with transport projects in Latin America, with the Miami and Mexico City offices providing key sector and local know-how. The Washington, DC office recently advised the Inter-American Development Bank on an 880 MW hydroelectric power plant in Brazil. The Middle East provides a platform for the firm, in conjunction with its London office, to really make its mark. Advice to Saudi Aramco in its joint venture with Sumitomo Chemical in the upgrade of the Rabigh refinery has certainly attracted attention.
**The Lawyers: Victor DeSantis** (see p.95) is based in the Washington, DC office and is an expert in representing commercial and multilateral lenders, sponsors and export credit agencies. "*I can't stop raving about him,*" enthused one client, reflecting the endorsement of many sources. **Art Scavone** (see p.132) is "*always a favorite of clients and other lawyers.*" Clients appreciate his personable manner and value his broad experience. **Troy Alexander** (see p.85) has built up a reputation as one of the finest lawyers to the multilaterals. According to clients, "*he sees the bigger picture and focuses in on our commercial interests.*"
**Clients/Work Highlights:** Abu Dhabi Water & Electricity; Deutsche Bank; US Ex-Im Bank; IFC; JBIC; MACH Gen; Qatar Petroleum; Quiport and Société Générale.

## Band 2

### Sullivan & Cromwell LLP
See firm details p.1558

**The Firm:** "*One of the finest firms in the world*" according to clients, who recognized its vision of providing the highest quality advice rather than the largest quantity of work. The projects practice has lent its formidable expertise to some of the most complicated and technically difficult deals in the market. A key player in Latin America, the team acted for the project company, borrower and sponsors of the Los Pelambres mining project in Chile. This involved the equity sale of an interest and project financing, which also underlines the team's stellar reputation for financing projects in the extractive industry. Large, complex, multiparty deals are the specialty of this firm, with clients reporting there is no cultural, language or technical issue it cannot overcome. In Europe, the team is international finance counsel to Tengizchevroil (TCO), assisting in the expansion of its upstream operations in Kazakhstan.
**The Lawyers:** The commitment of the firm to quality is reflected in its personnel, one client said: "*I've always had the sense that from partner through associate, they bring a real quality capability to the table and frankly lift the burden from us as clients. I can't speak highly enough about them.*" **Frederic Rich** (see p.129) "*is amazing, absolutely first class and has built a team of equally competent people around himself,*" clients reported. **Sergio Galvis** (see p.101) coordinates the Spain and Latin America practice and is "*business-focused and pragmatic – he doesn't over-lawyer and knows how to get the deal done.*"
**Clients/Work Highlights:** Palabora Mining; Sumitomo Metal Mining; Sumitomo; BP Exploration (Alaska); ConocoPhillips Alaska; ExxonMobil Alaska; Eskom; Citibank and Pacific Hydro.

### Vinson & Elkins LLP
See firm details p.1938

**The Firm:** This firm is synonymous with top-quality domestic oil and gas projects work. The range of work undertaken here is truly diverse, covering upstream, downstream and a host of matters in between. The team is best known as sponsors counsel, serving international majors, but its lenders practice is flourishing too. Houston is the hub of the projects practice and is complemented by a highly regarded Washington, DC office as well as finance specialists based in New York. In addition to its traditional energy expertise, the firm is carving itself a healthy slice of the power and renewables sector. In one of the banner deals of the year, it advised Complete Energy Holdings in the financing of its acquisition of La Paloma Generating, which owns the 1,000 MW power project. According to clients, "*through the entire deal process, they can be trusted to be on the look-out for any potential issues and they deal with them before they become a problem.*" An innovative approach to financing has become the team's signature, and for the Bank of Nova Scotia the team undertook a highly structured

financing of the Medusa Spar in Mexico.
**The Lawyers: Bruce Bilger** (see p.89) handles complex international and domestic projects in the oil and gas sector. Clients report: "*He knows how to get a deal done – when he is on the deal I don't have to worry.*"
**Clients/Work Highlights:** WestLB sought the firm's counsel for the financing of the 750 MW El Cajon hydroelectric power project. Other clients include BG Group; JPMorgan Chase; PSEG Global; Calyon; Bank of Montreal; AIG and Allied Irish Banks.

## Band 3

### Baker Botts LLP
See firm details p.1922

**The Firm:** A market leader for oil and gas work, with a particularly strong reputation in LNG, this firm impressed both peers and clients with its quality advice. There has been a push by this group to strengthen its projects capability, and client feedback confirms that it is paying off: "*The team is led by outstanding partners but what is also important is that the associates are of a high caliber, too.*" From key offices in Houston and Washington, DC, the practice undertakes development work as well as acquisition and divestitures for some of the most active sponsors in the market. The firm's international work has certainly captured the attention of the market. It recently closed the Peru LNG deal on behalf of Hunt Oil, establishing the first liquefaction project in South America. Advice on the Tangguh LNG project in Indonesia and Qatargas III has also impressed market commentators.
**The Lawyers: David Asmus** (see p.86) generates high praise from the industry for his work, which encompasses development from upstream to midstream. He is "*one of the best in the business, very knowledgeable and a pleasure to work with.*"
**Clients/Work Highlights:** BP; ExxonMobil; Marathon and ConocoPhillips are clients of the firm.

### Chadbourne & Parke LLP
See firm details p.1524

**The Firm:** With deep roots in the projects industry, this firm maintains its presence in the market thanks to expertise across a number of sectors, particularly power. Historically the team has been seen as a developer's counsel, but increased lender work has given the team balance, with top-class banks seeking its counsel. Bilateral and multilateral clients also enjoy this group's service. Commentators were impressed by the team's ability to take its expertise in the electricity market and transpose it onto oil and gas and make a real mark, especially in LNG. This capability is underlined by the firm's representation of Freeport LNG in its development of an LNG storage facility. The New York and Washington, DC offices are long established, and the Houston office is developing increasing capacity. There is strong integration with the team based in London, which facilitates this firm's incredible penetration into the Eastern Europe and East African markets. Renewables, ethanol and biodiesel projects form a growing area of expertise for the team, which clients say consists of "*good, strong projects lawyers – it's a great team of people who work well together.*"

**The Lawyers: Peter Fitzgerald** (see p.99) is responsible for directing the firm's work in emerging markets. He is "*incredibly well respected as a multilateral attorney and from a client's perspective he is great to work with,*" said one client. He is also noted for his experience advising lenders. **Keith Martin** (see p.117) injects his specialized tax expertise into the projects practice and is "*a safe pair of hands.*" **Chaim Wachsberger** is "*a true luminary in the field*" and represents sponsors across the energy and transport sectors. He is noted also for his acquisition and divestitures work.

**Clients/Work Highlights:** El Paso; CSFB; RBS; GE Energy; AES; Citibank; Union Bank of California; Duke Energy; Tractebel; IFC; Inter-American Development Bank; Sovereign Risk Insurance; Greka Energy and Interconexión Eléctrica (ISA) Bolivia.

## Shearman & Sterling LLP
See firm details p.1554

**The Firm:** A frequent presence on deals, particularly in Latin America, this team punches above its weight in projects arising out of the power, transport and mining sectors. Clients report that it is the level of consistency in attorneys and accessibility of partners that keep them coming back. This firm's finance pedigree sees it serving a who's who of bank and finance clients in international projects, such as advice to the lead arrangers on the Mexico City Airport expansion financing. The service offered is broad and also encompasses sponsors, underwriters, export credit agencies and off-take purchasers. Clients agree: "*They're good people, with great depth. They're a great choice for international projects work.*"

**The Lawyers: Cynthia Urda Kassis** (see p.139) co-heads the project development group and received warm reviews from clients and peers. "*She's a great lawyer, always accessible and has great business acumen,*" report clients. She is supported by Jeanne Olivier who specializes in multiple-risk insurance.

**Clients/Work Highlights:** The firm enjoys strong relationships with Japanese finance clients such as Mizuho Bank, Javic, Mitsui and Mitsubishi Trading. Other clients include Marubeni; CSFB; Citigroup; ABN AMRO; Barclays; Crédit Lyonnais; Central American Bank for Economic Integration (CABEI); Deutsche Investitions- und Entwicklungsgesellschaft (DEG); BNP Paribas; PSEG Global and Placer Dome.

## Other Notable Practitioners
**John Cogan** (see p.92) of Akin Gump Strauss Hauer & Field LLP is "*a superstar attorney and fantastically personable – for such a heavyweight he is always available,*" said clients. He is based in the Houston office and is recognized for his oil and gas work. **Richard Shutran** (see p.134) attracts clients to Dewey Ballantine LLP and is described as "*tremendously capable, good to work with, is creative and has a great sense of humor.*" Spearheading Freshfield Bruckhaus Deringer LLP's projects practice from New York, **Ted Burke** commands respect for his "*immense knowledge and business understanding.*" **Timothy Unger** of Andrews Kurth LLP is "*a consistent performer who you can trust to get the best results for clients.*"

# SPORTS LAW

| Sports Law Leading Firms | |
|---|---|
| 1 | COVINGTON & BURLING |
| | PROSKAUER ROSE LLP |
| | SKADDEN, ARPS, SLATE, MEAGHER & FLOM |
| 2 | DEWEY BALLANTINE LLP |
| 3 | BINGHAM MCCUTCHEN LLP |
| | FOLEY & LARDNER LLP |
| | MAYER, BROWN, ROWE & MAW LLP |
| | MILLER, CANFIELD, PADDOCK AND STONE |
| | WEIL, GOTSHAL & MANGES LLP |
| 4 | DEBEVOISE & PLIMPTON LLP |
| | HOGAN & HARTSON LLP |
| | WHITE & CASE LLP |

| Leading Individuals | |
|---|---|
| 1 | GANZ Howard *Proskauer Rose LLP* |
| | GOLDFEIN Shepard *Skadden, Arps* |
| | KESSLER Jeffrey *Dewey Ballantine LLP* |
| | LECCESE Joseph *Proskauer Rose LLP* |
| | LEVY Gregg *Covington & Burling* |
| | MISHKIN Jeffrey *Skadden, Arps* |
| 2 | ALKALAY Peter *McLaughlin & Stern LLP* |
| | ANDREOZZI Bradley *Mayer, Brown, Rowe & Maw* |
| | FEHER David *Dewey Ballantine LLP* |
| | FRIEDMAN Andrew *Covington & Burling* |
| | GOLDBERG Daniel *Bingham McCutchen LLP* |
| | HOLBREICH Curt *Howard, Rice* |
| | QUINN James *Weil, Gotshal & Manges LLP* |
| | RUSKIN Bradley *Proskauer Rose LLP* |
| 3 | ABRAMS Lee *Mayer, Brown, Rowe & Maw* |
| | BATTERMAN Robert *Proskauer Rose LLP* |
| | BERNSTEIN Jonathan *Bingham McCutchen* |
| | BRAZA Mary *Foley & Lardner LLP* |
| | CURTNER Gregory *Miller, Canfield, Paddock* |
| | GIBSON Douglas *Covington & Burling* |
| | KATZ Wayne *Proskauer Rose LLP* |
| | KLEPPER Martin *Skadden, Arps* |
| | LEVINSTEIN Mark *Williams & Connolly* |
| | WILSON Bruce *Covington & Burling* |

## Band 1

### Covington & Burling
See firm details p.563

**The Firm:** Hailed as a group at the vanguard of sports work, clients describe this team as *"smart and business-focused, with an understanding of the history of the discipline."* As one impressed interviewee stated: *"A lot of things don't appear rational if you take a step back and look at sports law, but Covington know how we got here."* The firm offers *"sage counsel"* and is rated for its skills in the areas of litigation, corporate, antitrust, tax and financing. Clients recommend it as having *"the kind of experience which gives you the utmost confidence."*
**The Lawyers:** *"A formidable bench strength"* means

that, as one client put it, *"no matter what the problem, there'll be someone there who can solve it."* *"Hot shot"* **Gregg Levy** (see p.115) is touted as *"a top-dollar, second-to-none litigator – there is no one who can beat him for experience."* He has acted on a number of matters for the NFL including cases concerning the Oakland Raiders and a number of antitrust claims. He is currently advising it on the negotiations for its new collective bargaining agreement. **Andy Friedman** (see p.100), *"undeniably the expert's expert,"* is rated as having *"taken the niche of sports tax work and made it his own."* He has acted on tax issues for all four of the major leagues (including matters relating to the end of the National Hockey League strike) and has also advised the US Tennis Federation on setting up a number of tournaments in the run-up to the US Open. Clients praise **Bruce Wilson** (see p.142) as *"a smart lawyer with excellent experience of financings."* Recommended for his skills in stadium deals, he has acted for the DC Sports and Entertainment Commission in relation to an agreement with the Montreal Expos regarding relocation and stadium development. He also advised on the renegotiation of the NFL's television contracts, deals which were reported to be in excess of $4 billion. Working with Wilson on the media deals was **Douglas Gibson** (see p.102). He is endorsed by clients as *"a sharp, commercially astute lawyer who really understands sports law."*
**Clients/Work Highlights:** The group handles a range of matters for all four of the major leagues, as well as commercial and litigation issues for individual teams.

### Proskauer Rose LLP
See firm details p.1551

**The Firm:** *"A simply outstanding group"* according to clients, *"it can just wheel out experts in labor, corporate and litigation matters and has quality from top to bottom."* Another successful year saw it representing the NHL over the conclusion of its lengthy and high-profile dispute with its players; this was a convoluted matter that led to involvement in the renegotiation of numerous media and advertising contracts relating to the sport. The breadth of the team's abilities is something frequently commented upon by clients. One opined that *"they are never baffled and can quite genuinely turn their hand to anything."*
**The Lawyers:** The *"terrific"* **Howard Ganz** (see p.101) wins client plaudits as *"a guy you can rely on to get you results."* He is highly rated for his skills in employment and labor and represented the NHL in its recent dispute. He has also handled matters for the National Basketball Association and Major League Baseball. **Robert Batterman** (see p.88) is praised for his skills in labor matters, with clients asserting that *"he's a sharp guy who can think on his feet."* *"Super-star"* **Joe Leccese** (see p.115) is hailed as *"one of the top transactional lawyers."* He is seen as *"a must-have on large corporate deals and capital projects"* and has recently acted for one of the prospective buyers of the new Washington, DC football team. He works closely with **Wayne Katz** (see p.112) who is endorsed

as *"sharp, dedicated and committed."* **Brad Ruskin** (see p.131) heads up the litigation side of the sports group and was said by clients to be *"not just a guy for the big disputes, but a smart and thoughtful adviser who it's always good to just pick up the phone to."* He is recommended for his work at league level and also for his representation of clubs, ownership groups and media companies in court matters and arbitrations.
**Clients/Work Highlights:** The group handles a range of commercial, corporate, employment, litigation and media advice for the NHL, NBA and MLB. It also acted for the New York Jets in its headline-grabbing new stadium project. Other clients include the ATP Tour and Major League Soccer.

### Skadden, Arps, Slate, Meagher & Flom LLP & Affiliates
See firm details p.1557

**The Firm:** One of the triumvirate of top sports law firms, Skadden Arps boasts *"a quality, knowledgeable and versatile team which is results-driven."* Clients particularly recommend it as *"a great source of advice. The lawyers tell us what we need in a clear and practical way, neither sugarcoating the issue nor drowning it in legal jargon."* The group boasts strong league experience, having carried out extensive work for the NBA, NFL and NHL. It has further represented individual teams and intercollegiate sports associations. It wins plaudits for its abilities in antitrust and litigation and is rated as having *"a terrific transactional understanding of the sports market."*
**The Lawyers:** The *"outstanding"* **Jeff Mishkin** (see p.121) is praised for his skills in antitrust and litigation matters. Formerly in-house at the NBA, he is said to be *"hot-wired to sport. He understands the culture, knows the history and has a great eye for the target."* He remains closely linked to the NBA and acted on disputes arising from a brawl between the Detroit Pistons and the Indiana Pacers. As part of this he defended a challenge relating to the league commissioner's powers to suspend players. **Shep Goldfein** (see p.102) is *"an astute adviser, a sharp litigator and someone who really impresses in the courtroom."* He was particularly active in the last year on the conclusion of the NHL's dispute with its players – this included negotiating a new drafting agreement and examining issues relating to profit sharing and salary caps. He also advised on media and advertising issues. New to this year's guide is **Martin Klepper** (see p.113). He wins plaudits for his skills in transactional and facilities and was praised by clients for being *"a quick, responsive lawyer who knows the ins and outs."*
**Clients/Work Highlights:** The group represented the football-playing schools of the Big East Conference in their high-profile dispute with the Atlantic Coast Conference, relating to the defection of a number of teams. It has also counseled the United States Tennis Association and provided antitrust advice to the Professional Golf Association and the Collegiate Licensing Company.

## Band 2

### Dewey Ballantine LLP
See firm details p.1530

**The Firm:** Recommended to researchers as "*the top firm on sports labor matters,*" this group continues to draw a strong following from across the various players' associations. Particularly known for its skills in collective bargaining agreements and unionwide disputes, it also wins plaudits for its representation of the interests of individuals and teams. Interviewees commended it for being "*a strong and forthright competitor in litigation*" and a firm with great breadth of knowledge and experience.

**The Lawyers:** The "*magnificent*" **Jeff Kessler** (see p.113) is recommended as "*absolutely the best lawyer for players' organizations.*" He has represented the National Basketball Players Association in relation to a new collective bargaining agreement and assisted it on matters arising from a brawl between the Detroit Pistons, and Indiana Pacers' players in Michigan. He is also rated for his skills in antitrust, with one commentator saying: "*If there's a sports antitrust case anywhere, someone will call Jeff.*" He recently acted for the Metropolitan Intercollegiate Basketball Association in its dispute with the National Collegiate Athletic Association. **David Feher** (see p.99) is also rated for his skills in collective bargaining agreements and salary cap issues. He was praised as "*a smart lawyer with a definite can-do attitude.*"

**Clients/Work Highlights:** The group's clients include the National Football League Players Association; National Basketball Players Association; MIBA; Adidas; Women's Tennis Players Benefit Association; NHL Coaches Association and SFX.

## Band 3

### Bingham McCutchen LLP
See firm details p.1110

**The Firm:** Although best known for handling work from its Boston base, this firm's presence continues to grow so that it is now recognized as a truly national player. It represents entities across the country and advises individual teams on the full spectrum of sports law matters, including merchandising and litigation. Particularly lavish praise was reserved by interviewees for its transactional and financing capabilities where "*a savvy business sense*" is clearly on show. This multioffice team is also seen as offering strong experience in the representation of leagues. **The Lawyers:** **Daniel Goldberg** (see p.102) is the best-known member of the team and is rated by peers as "*a thoughtful and combative litigator,*" and by clients as "*a guy who radiates experience and enthusiasm.*" He has acted on various matters for the New England Patriots and the New England Revolution and is also advising the NFL and Major League Soccer on a number of issues. **Jonathan Bernstein** (see p.88) joins *Chambers*' tables this year. He is rated as "*a top guy on corporate matters*" and excels on the finance side as well as on issues of merchandising and promotion.

**Clients/Work Highlights:** The group has acted for the NFL in its drawn-out dispute with the Oakland Raiders. In the past year this has entailed getting an appellate court decision in the league's favor.

### Foley & Lardner LLP
See firm details p.2007

**The Firm:** "*The experts on baseball,*" according to clients, this group wins plaudits for being "*a dedicated and innovative practice.*" It is best known for its representation of the MLB, acting on litigation, antitrust, real estate and IP issues. The group also acts for individual sports teams and is particularly rated for its handling of the financing, construction and political sides of complex stadium matters.

**The Lawyers:** Head of the team **Mary Braza** (see p.90) was praised by clients as "*a smart problem solver.*" A litigator, she is busiest for the MLB and acts on a range of issues including structuring and ownership matters. She has been particularly active in disputes arising from the relocation of the Montreal Expos to Washington, DC. This has involved a challenge brought by some of the limited partners of the former owners, as well as disputes involving territorial rights and broadcasting rights.

**Clients/Work Highlights:** Although the MLB is the group's biggest client, it further acts on media matters for MLB Advanced Media. The group has also represented the Green Bay Packers and the Milwaukee Brewers on stadium matters.

### Mayer, Brown, Rowe & Maw LLP
See firm details p.876

**The Firm:** This busy international team is said by clients to "*understand the nitty-gritty of sports law.*" It is well known for its work for USA Track & Field and has acted on matters relating to disabled athletes and disputes involving failed drugs tests. The group also represents individual athletes on regulatory, sponsorship and IP issues. It further represents leagues, teams and various entities on a range of commercial and litigation advice.

**The Lawyers:** Clients rate **Brad Andreozzi** (see p.85) as "*a lawyer who stays calm while all around are losing their heads.*" He is praised as "*an utter gentleman who chooses his words carefully and gives a sensible perspective.*" He is best known for his work for USATF and recently represented it on various matters concerning the failure of a drug test by the runner Jerome Young. The highly regarded **Lee Abrams** (see p.84) is best known for his work for the United States Golf Association.

**Clients/Work Highlights:** The group's client base encompasses broadcasters, manufacturers, financiers and leagues.

### Miller, Canfield, Paddock and Stone, P.L.C.
See firm details p.1148

**The Firm:** This highly rated team is endorsed for its work for the National Collegiate Athletic Association (NCAA). Recommended for its skills in litigation, the team has handled all manner of disputes including sports injury matters, equipment disputes and large antitrust cases. It acted in a major matter last year, representing the NCAA in a high-profile dispute with the National Invitation Tournament (NIT). This involved the rights of teams to play in the NIT rather than the NCAA and resulted in the NCAA buying the preseason and postseason National Invitation tournaments for $56.5 million.

**The Lawyers:** The team is headed up by **Gregory Curtner** (see p.94) who wins praise as "*a conscientious and smart lawyer.*"

**Clients/Work Highlights:** The group represented the NCAA in the continuing litigation relating to preseason and early season basketball contests. The dispute related to the 'two-in-four' rule, which restricts teams from entering certain preseason tournaments more than twice in four years.

### Weil, Gotshal & Manges LLP
See firm details p.1565

**The Firm:** Although still best known for its work for players' associations, this "*small but weighty*" team continues to be active in a range of sporting matters. As well as representing individual teams and team owners, it is also felt to be strong in media and IP matters. For example, the group represented ESPN in a number of disputes including a complex global matter and a high-profile defamation claim. It also wins plaudits for handling IP rights for individual players in domain-naming disputes.

**The Lawyers:** **Jim Quinn** (see p.127) is deemed by clients to be "*a guy with million-dollar experience.*" He is "*a great negotiator and litigator with a quick legal mind and sure touch*" who regularly represents the NFL Players Association. Currently, he is acting for the association in negotiating the new collective bargaining deal with the league.

**Clients/Work Highlights:** The group successfully represented the majority owners of the Atlanta Hawks in a dispute with the minority owner.

## Band 4

### Debevoise & Plimpton LLP
See firm details p.1529

**The Firm:** This strong media group was recommended to researchers for its skills in IP and media disputes for sporting entities. The team has represented the NFL regarding various Internet matters and in a case concerning counterfeit shirts. The lawyers have also represented the NHL on a range of sponsorship and broadcast issues. Clients rate the group as "*razor-sharp on IP; the guys really understand our needs.*"

**The Lawyers:** Lorin Reisner, Bruce Keller and David Bernstein are all active in this area.

**Clients/Work Highlights:** The group's client base draws primarily upon the leagues.

### Hogan & Hartson LLP
See firm details p.568

**The Firm:** "*A talented, good-to-work-with team,*" according to clients. The firm is primarily known for its expertise in the representation of teams and the owners of teams. A particular specialty is stadium development. By way of illustration, it acted for Kroenke Sports Enterprises and the Colorado Rapids on the development of a 20,000-seat outdoor stadium.

**The Lawyers:** Denver-based Craig Umbaugh heads up the team.

**Clients/Work Highlights:** The group won praise for its litigation and media skills and acted for the NFL in litigation over IP rights concerning the Baltimore Ravens' original team logo. It also acted for News International on a $1 billion restructuring that had aspects of sports law attached to it.

## White & Case LLP
See firm details p.1566

**The Firm:** This *"responsive, high-quality"* group is seen as having taken its IP skills and applied them expertly to the sports market. The group has a long history of representing the NFL and is currently acting for the body on three disputes. These concern the IP rights of the league and member clubs the Washington Redskins, Baltimore Ravens and Cleveland Browns. It has also acted for the NHL and Major League Soccer on the management of their global brands.

**The Lawyers:** Robert Raskopf heads up the practice.

**Clients/Work Highlights:** The group has represented ESPN on various trademark and litigation issues.

## Other Notable Practitioners
The *"incredibly good"* **Peter Alkalay** of McLaughlin & Stern LLP continues to win favor for his skill in all matters relating to athletics. Clients say he is equally strong as a litigator or arbitrator and that he has *"superb depths of knowledge."* Similarly gifted in this specific arena, **Curt Holbreich** of Howard, Rice, Nemerovski, Canady, Falk & Rabkin is especially good on drugs cases. One client stated: *"There are few people as knowledgeable on drugs matters. His insight really does give you the edge."* He has also been busy in matters concerning horse racing. **Mark Levinstein** of Williams & Connolly LLP wins market respect for the strength of his sports dispute practice. He represents a range of athletes, teams and leagues and boasts experience in copyright, labor and a variety of antitrust matters.

# TAX LITIGATION

| Tax Litigation |
|---|
| Leading Firms |
| [1] BAKER & MCKENZIE |
| MAYER, BROWN, ROWE & MAW LLP |
| MCKEE NELSON LLP |
| MILLER & CHEVALIER CHARTERED |
| SKADDEN, ARPS, SLATE, MEAGHER & FLOM LLP |
| [2] FULBRIGHT & JAWORSKI LLP |
| KRONISH LIEB WEINER & HELLMAN LLP |
| LATHAM & WATKINS LLP |
| MCDERMOTT WILL & EMERY |
| [3] KIRKLAND & ELLIS LLP |
| PILLSBURY WINTHROP SHAW PITTMAN LLP |
| SHEARMAN & STERLING LLP |

| Leading Individuals |
|---|
| [1] GARDNER Stephen *Kronish Lieb Weiner & Hellman* |
| GIDEON Kenneth *Skadden, Arps* |
| GOLDBERG JR Fred *Skadden, Arps* |
| HALL Charles *Fulbright & Jaworski LLP* |
| KAFKA Gerald *Latham & Watkins LLP* |
| MAGEE John *McKee Nelson LLP* |
| MOORE Robert *Miller & Chevalier Chartered* |
| TURKUS Albert *Skadden, Arps* |
| WILLIAMS B John *Shearman & Sterling* |
| WILLIAMSON Joel *Mayer, Brown* |
| [2] BONANO William *Pillsbury* |
| LEMEIN Gregg *Baker & McKenzie* |
| NELSON William *McKee Nelson LLP* |
| OATES Mark *Baker & McKenzie* |
| SALTZMAN Michael *White & Case LLP* |
| SWENSON David *Baker & McKenzie* |
| TAYLOR Jasper *Fulbright & Jaworski LLP* |
| [3] BORDERS Thomas *McDermott Will & Emery* |
| DURHAM Thomas *Mayer, Brown* |
| HELTZER Harold *Crowell & Moring LLP* |
| HILL Lawrence *Dewey Ballantine LLP* |
| HOROWITZ Alan *Miller & Chevalier Chartered* |
| KARTER Philip *Miller & Chevalier Chartered* |
| STEWART Scott *Mayer, Brown* |

| Up-and-coming individuals |
|---|
| PAKENHAM Kathleen *White & Case LLP* |

| Associates to watch |
|---|
| VASQUEZ Juan *Chamberlain, Hrdlicka* |

## Band 1

### Baker & McKenzie

See firm details p.866

**The Firm:** This bunch of *"conversant and creative"* players takes any tax litigation matter in its stride. Commentators describe a *"classy team"* that handles sophisticated work, notably in the field of transfer pricing. It offers *"global potency"* and the *"fantastically bright attorneys"* are heavily involved in both national and international disputes.

**The Lawyers:** The *"absolutely first-rate"* **Gregg**

Lemein (see p.115) commands deep respect for his transfer pricing work. His cooperative manner is a hit with all parties, and clients declare him a *"savvy"* operator who instinctively *"knows the right way to prepare and present a case."* **Mark Oates** offers *"excellent judgment and superb client skills."* His varied workload has both international and domestic elements, and he is singled out for partnership, financial product, and penalty expertise. **David Swenson** (see p.137) *"delights and impresses non-stop."* He is predominantly involved in corporate tax planning and tax controversies relating to domestic and international transactions.

**Clients/Work Highlights:** Cisco Systems; Dell; Merck; Microsoft and Seagate Technology.

### Mayer, Brown, Rowe & Maw LLP

See firm details p.876

**The Firm:** Housing some of the *"best trial lawyers money can buy,"* this group pioneered tax controversy representation and acts for some of the premier businesses in the country. The team is prominent in the market and fields *"analytical, resourceful and thoughtful"* lawyers. Commentators attribute the group's success in part to *"its superior communication skills in dealing with clients,"* and to its track record of hiring *"astonishing talent."* The *"tremendously deep bench"* offers expertise across the board, and its trial expertise is *"outrageously sought after."* Rivals envy the firm's *"huge network of contacts"* while clients commend its *"high level of strategic insight."* The team recently handled trial litigation for the Tribune Company before the US Tax Court.

**The Lawyers:** Leading the ranks is *"the don,"* **Joel Williamson** (see p.142). Regarded as *"at the top of his game,"* his clients extol him as a *"great listener"* and an *"objective analyst,"* whose *"responsive and thoughtful"* approach harnesses peerless technical expertise and a deep understanding of business issues. Similarly *"analytical and insightful,"* **Thomas Durham** (see p.97) is a *"one of a kind"* controversy strategist who *"listens to what clients have to say and is always prepared."* **Scott Stewart** (see p.136) is recommended for his spot-on judgment and analysis, and his *"ability to anticipate issues before they arise."*

**Clients/Work Highlights:** Akzo Nobel; Altera; Tribune Company; Dole Food Company; Health-South; Intel; Cargill; Galderma Laboratories; Nestlé Holdings; Tenneco Automotive; UPS; Pfizer; Tyco; Goodrich; Boeing and Abbott Laboratories.

### McKee Nelson LLP

See firm details p.574

**The Firm:** *"Nationally, you can't beat this dynamic firm,"* according to observers. The talented DC team impresses clients with its *"attentive, methodical and alert"* approach to a solid diet of tax litigation, transfer pricing and partnership matters. Commentators point to *"simply tremendous depth and resources"* at the firm, and clients are attracted by the *"legal acumen, excellent atmosphere and healthy level of thought and debate between lawyers."* The group

recently represented GlaxoSmithKline to contest allegations of tax deficiencies of more than $4.5 billion, and counseled Dow Chemical in a case that sustained the company's entitlement to federal income tax benefits arising from its corporate-owned life insurance policies.

**The Lawyers:** Among *"some of the most insightful attorneys in the business,"* **John Magee** (see p.117) is the most highly celebrated. Closely linked to Glaxo-SmithKline, he is *"a creative and energetic player with an international flair."* His practice includes transfer pricing, income tax planning and IRS administrative proceedings as well as tax litigation. IRS connoisseur **William Nelson** (see p.123) *"distills complex information into language that non-experts can understand,"* say clients. He has a flair for dealing with senior management and comes across as *"a level-headed guy who knows his audience and does not panic."* He handles a healthy flow of large litigation and enforcement matters.

**Clients/Work Highlights:** GE Capital, Glaxo-SmithKline and Dow Chemical are among the clients.

### Miller & Chevalier Chartered

See firm details p.575

**The Firm:** Clients flock here for the team's *"gift of pulling the unattainable out of the hat"* and its historical strength in federal tax litigation, controversy and planning. At the forefront of hotly contested issues, the team successfully represented the taxpayer in *Black & Decker v USA*, to establish whether a taxpayer is entitled to capital loss from the sale of stock in a contingent liability healthcare subsidiary. The breadth and quality of the team is summed up in clients' observations that *"even the younger people assigned to us over the years have always been first rate."* It recently represented long-standing client ExxonMobil on several different tax litigation matters and represented a high-end plumbing manufacturer in *Kohler v USA*.

**The Lawyers:** *"The consummate authority"* in the field, **Robert Moore** (see p.122) enjoys a national reputation for his courtroom performance. Clients observe: *"The firm is full of remarkable tax litigators, but if you want just one person to try a case he is at the top of the list."* The *"brilliant"* **Alan Horowitz** (see p.108) focuses on appellate litigation, with a particular line in federal tax appeals. This *"analytical and succinct"* attorney is *"great at taking intricate concepts and putting them in a form that is easy to comprehend,"* say clients. For *"raw intelligence,"* **Philip Karter** (see p.112) *"is worth his weight in gold."*

### Skadden, Arps, Slate, Meagher & Flom LLP

See firm details p.1557

**The Firm:** This *"substantial group"* has effectively secured a national reputation for tax litigation excellence. With a *"highly skilled trial department and unparalleled connections"* behind it, the group is *"ready for any rumble."* Interviewees commend the *"talented and forceful"* team, which recently earned victory for FedEx before the Sixth Circuit Court of Appeals.

**The Lawyers: Kenneth Gideon**'s (see p.102) *"keen brain power"* and *"imposing presence,"* combined with *"generosity of character,"* appeal to clients and rivals alike. Clients are drawn to him by sophisticated government experience and a *"formidable courtroom track record."* Former IRS commissioner **Fred Goldberg** (see p.102) has *"enviable government contacts"* and represents clients on tax controversies and IRS administrative and regulatory proceedings. This *"extremely sharp"* player is also a *"top referral"* for tax legislation matters, note clients. **Albert Turkus** (see p.138) impresses clients with his *"powerful intellect and superb trial expertise."*

## Band 2

### Fulbright & Jaworski L.L.P.

See firm details p.1928

**The Firm:** Offering *"rock solid strength in trial work,"* this group has a rapacious appetite for complex tax litigation. Clients commend the *"terrific individuals,"* who are prominent in the most intricate and high-profile cases. The practice focuses almost exclusively on tax controversy and tax litigation, delivering *"sophisticated and consistently excellent"* advice.

**The Lawyers:** The *"astonishingly successful"* **Charles Hall** (see p.104) *"really pays attention to clients and understands their needs."* He combines *"superb tactics"* with *"a common-sense style that works well with judges,"* according to sources, and possesses the *"knack of establishing a fantastic rapport with clients."* The *"extremely professional"* **Jack Taylor** (see p.137) is *"a wonderful investigator and great at laying the foundations and raising all the facts,"* say clients. Regarded as a pillar of the firm, he is *"tremendous at getting down to what is really important and articulating it simply."*

**Clients/Work Highlights:** The team has acted in matters involving Shell Oil, Schering-Plough, Dart Management, Texas Medical Center and Ernst & Young tax shelters. It also represented the interests of Joe L Allbritton and the Blaffer and Hubbard families.

### Kronish Lieb Weiner & Hellman LLP

**The Firm:** Putting this firm in a nutshell, clients describe a troupe of *"dedicated and first-class"* attorneys renowned for *"thoroughly marvelous work."* It has a glittering track record in tax litigation and clients commend its *"flawless, practical interpretation of the law."* All in all, this is a group that can *"handle even the most complicated"* matters *"energetically and decisively."*

**The Lawyers:** *"The man is a genius, intelligent beyond imagining,"* say sources of *"stellar trial*

*attorney"* **Stephen Gardner**. He is known for his complex tax controversy and litigation work, and exhibits *"a remarkably deep understanding of the issues at hand."*

**Clients/Work Highlights:** American Express; Coltec Industries; ConocoPhillips; Entergy; Goodrich; HSBC; ITT Industries; Shell Oil; Starwood Hotels and Walter Industries.

### Latham & Watkins LLP

**The Firm:** This *"refined and proficient"* firm leverages its international network of offices to serve clients on a global scale. Sources declare that it has just the right mixture of expertise, nous and sheer endurance. Recent highlights include the representation of DaimlerChrysler, Cardinal Health and HCA before the IRS and on federal income tax controversies.

**The Lawyers:** The *"genuinely decent"* **Gerald Kafka** is enthusiastically placed at the *"top of the tree"* for his *"pragmatism, professionalism and level-headedness."*

**Clients/Work Highlights:** Aon Group; Mitsubishi Motors North America; Ernst & Young and CIGNA.

### McDermott Will & Emery

See firm details p.878

**The Firm:** Commentators unite in praise of this *"extraordinarily effective"* firm. The *"highly responsive"* attorneys *"know controversy law like the backs of their hands."* According to clients, the expertise runs deep and is consistent all through the ranks, with even the junior team members demonstrating *"confidence and straightforward strength."*

**The Lawyers:** *"Fast thinker"* **Thomas Borders** (see p.89) focuses on federal tax controversies involving audits, administrative appeals, litigation and criminal investigations. Commentators appreciate his expertise and note: *"He is fantastic on his feet, and grasps and explains complex issues effortlessly."*

**Clients/Work Highlights:** Abbott Laboratories; Archer Daniels Midland; Motorola; RR Donnelley and SBC Communications.

## Band 3

### Kirkland & Ellis LLP

See firm details p.875

**The Firm:** A *"powerful name nationwide,"* this firm impresses sources with the strength and depth of its *"second to none"* litigation practice. Interviewees endorse this *"well-rounded and well-connected"* group, agreeing that its top-quality litigation combined with its tax expertise makes a momentous impact on the market.

**The Lawyers:** Todd Maynes is a key contact at the firm and concentrates on tax litigation.

**Clients/Work Highlights:** Representative clients include United Airlines, Conseco and Alcoa.

### Pillsbury Winthrop Shaw Pittman LLP

See firm details p.1550

**The Firm:** Clients assert that this *"terrifically high-caliber nationwide group can be put up against anyone."* The team has benefited from the April 2005 merger of two respected firms, and the new combined offering had a key victory recently in a case for Beneficial. Clients are drawn particularly to the *"profundity of its knowledge."*

**The Lawyers: William Bonano** (see p.89) *"works around the clock to keep clients happy,"* and sources appreciate his fast response time and *"forthcoming demeanor."*

**Clients/Work Highlights:** Intel; Cisco Systems; DIRECTV; Applied Materials and Apple.

### Shearman & Sterling LLP

See firm details p.1554

**The Firm:** This *"significant national force"* is devoted to controversy and general tax litigation. According to sources, the *"dynamic"* team *"thinks through matters to get to a practical resolution."* The lawyers display *"great judgment"* and a profound sense of the business stakes, say interviewees.

**The Lawyers:** *"If* **John Williams** (see p.142) *is on the other side you know you are in trouble,"* admit rivals. Clients praise this *"terrifically tenacious"* lawyer for his *"down-to-earth approach, pragmatism and astute judgment."*

### Other Notable Practitioners

White & Case LLP's tax *"genius,"* **Michael Saltzman** (see p.132), is considered *"the authority in tax procedure."* This *"outstanding litigator"* advises clients such as Time Warner, El Paso and Verizon. *"Excellent communicator"* **Kathleen Pakenham** (see p.124), also at White & Case, *"gives good business advice without spending hours arguing about angels on pinheads."* Crowell & Moring LLP's **Harold Heltzer** (see p.106) is a *"straight shooter"* who is *"able to advise on the pitfalls of any given course of action,"* according to clients. Dewey Ballantine LLP's *"champion,"* **Lawrence Hill** (see p.106), is *"service-oriented and always on the ball."* Associate **Juan Vasquez** at Chamberlain, Hrdlicka, White, Williams & Martin represents clients in disputes with federal, state and local taxing authorities and is praised by sources as *"diligent and with-it."*

# TRANSPORTATION

### Transportation: Aviation: Finance
#### Leading Firms

1. MILBANK, TWEED, HADLEY & MCCLOY LLP
2. HOLLAND & KNIGHT LLP
   PILLSBURY WINTHROP SHAW PITTMAN LLP
   VEDDER, PRICE, KAUFMAN & KAMMHOLZ
3. CADWALADER, WICKERSHAM & TAFT
   FULBRIGHT & JAWORSKI L.L.P.
   SHEARMAN & STERLING LLP
   SIMPSON THACHER & BARTLETT LLP
   WHITE & CASE LLP
4. DEWEY BALLANTINE LLP
   HUGHES HUBBARD & REED LLP
   PAUL, HASTINGS, JANOFSKY & WALKER LLP
   SIDLEY AUSTIN LLP

#### Leading Individuals

1. FINE Drew *Milbank, Tweed, Hadley & McCloy*
   GERBER Dean *Vedder, Price*
   GEWIRTZ Elliot *Milbank, Tweed, Hadley*
   HONG Ji Hoon *Shearman & Sterling LLP*
   PRITCHARD John *Holland & Knight LLP*
   SCHEINBERG Ronald *Vedder, Price*
2. ABORN Richard *Cadwalader*
   BOWERS William *Pillsbury*
   COLEMAN Payson *Pillsbury*
   JACOBSON Martin *Simpson Thacher & Bartlett*
   PIELS William *Holland & Knight LLP*
   ROBERTSON Elihu *Milbank, Tweed, Hadley*
   SMITH Michael *White & Case LLP*
   SMITH JR Richard *White & Case LLP*
   TUSSING James *Fulbright & Jaworski*
3. BASS Fredric *Dewey Ballantine LLP*
   BOGAARD Jonathan *Vedder, Price*
   HOWITT John *Paul, Hastings*
   HOYNS John *Hughes Hubbard & Reed LLP*
   KELLEHER Rory *Sidley Austin LLP*
   SCHUMAECKER Michael *Pillsbury*
   SCHWARZ Helfried *Milbank, Tweed, Hadley*
   VEBER Jeffrey *Vedder, Price*

#### Up-and-coming individuals
GENTNER Joshua *Vedder, Price*
LEONG Alvin *Milbank, Tweed, Hadley*

#### Associates to watch
SEHGAL Zarrar *Milbank, Tweed, Hadley & McCloy*

## Band 1

### Milbank, Tweed, Hadley & McCloy LLP

**The Firm:** According to many commentators, Milbank Tweed dominates the aircraft finance sector. Clients praised the depth of the 25-attorney transportation group, which primarily represents the financing parties on aircraft lease portfolio securitizations and structured finance transactions. "*The Milbank team has always delivered the goods,*" said

one. Peers agree that the team sets high standards: "*They have the creativity required to come up with a solution that works for everyone.*" Recent highlights include representing Cerberus in the financing of its acquisition of debis AirFinance, which called upon a cross-disciplinary team of seven M&A, structured finance and transportation partners.

**The Lawyers:** Chair of Milbank's global transportation finance group is **Elliot Gewirtz**. Clients described him as a true leader in his field; he is "*incomparable in his knowledge of this sector and the structures used to finance it.*" Clients attested that **Drew Fine** "*can take on just about anything.*" Lead partner in the Cerberus transaction, his industry knowledge and expertise is "*unparalleled – he makes you believe that you are the only client he has, and his professionalism and dedication is unmatched.*" Recently promoted to head of global finance, **Hugh Robertson** maintains a strong client base in the aircraft finance sector. His practice encompasses leveraged acquisition work and reflects an increased emphasis on private equity investors in the aircraft sector. **Helfried Schwarz** recently returned to the New York office after four years spent establishing Milbank's Frankfurt office. He is best known for his focus on foreign banks in air finance restructurings, and clients praise his "*pragmatic grasp of deals*" and his ability to "*lead a difficult negotiation with calm temper.*" **Alvin Leong** has also recently returned from a stint in Hong Kong. "*Incisive, diligent and philosophical, he anticipates issues and is proactive in trying to resolve them.*" Clients also appreciated his negotiation skills and his ability to maintain cordial relations with opposing parties in conflicting situations. **Zarrar Sehgal** works closely with Elliot Gewirtz on securitization matters. He is "*constructive and proactive, dedicated and informed*" and has recently worked with investment banks such as Lehman Brothers and Wachovia.

**Clients/Work Highlights:** The team recently represented Calyon Securities as underwriters' counsel in the financing of 89 spare engines for American Airlines. It has also advised on issues arising from the bankruptcies of Delta, Northwest and United Airlines. Other clients include Asiana Airlines; Banca Intesa; Citigroup; EastMerchant/Landesbank Sachsen; Lehman Brothers and Tenenbaum Capital.

## Band 2

### Holland & Knight LLP

See firm details p.1534

**The Firm:** Holland & Knight's national team excels in all aspects of aviation law, housing both a structured finance practice and aircraft accident and litigation specialists. The nine-partner structured finance group is best known for the international dimension of its work, particularly its expertise in operating leases. The team is highly regarded for its work for major international airline clients, and has wide experience in large-scale fleet acquisitions and

tax leasing work. Clients spoke of the high quality of advice provided by these attorneys and the cost-effective, responsive service.

**The Lawyers:** Head of structured finance **John Pritchard** (see p.127) is "*one of the deans*" of the aircraft finance community. Respected for his academic workload, he is a personable deal-doer and "*one of the best contract negotiators around.*" He is currently advising on the continued restructurings arising from the US airline bankruptcies. San Francisco-based **Bill Piels** (see p.125) is also commended as a "*very bright, knowledgeable operating leases attorney.*" His clients include aircraft operating lessors and international financial institutions.

**Clients/Work Highlights:** Recent highlights include involvement in the major repossession of aircraft and workout activity related to the ECA/Ex-Im Bank financing of Pan American Airways. The group also represented Cargolux in the financing of two 747-400 freighters using operating leases from Pegasus Aviation. Clients include Air Canada; GE Commercial Aviation Services (Gecas); Singapore Airlines and UT Finance.

### Pillsbury Winthrop Shaw Pittman LLP

See firm details p.1550

**The Firm:** Pillsbury's national team is recognized by clients for the depth of its broad-based aviation expertise, in addition to its competitive pricing. Clients are able to refer to Pillsbury for "*a full-scope service*" of equipment finance in addition to regulatory and litigation expertise. The 21-lawyer strong equipment finance group is currently working primarily on restructuring matters, predominantly representing financial institutions as creditors, lessors and trustees. The team have substantial positions in the Air Canada and Delta Air Lines bankruptcies.

**The Lawyers:** Clients praise the technical capability, industry expertise and personal service provided by equipment finance practice group leader **Payson Coleman** (see p.93). They describe him as "*very focused, capable and easy to work with.*" He recently represented BayernLB and nine other bank syndicates as agent during the Air Canada bankruptcy and advised on the restructuring of $1 billion of loans secured by Boeing 747-400, 767-300ER, Canadair Regional Jets, Airbus A321 and other aircraft leased to Air Canada. Coleman is also a member of the Aviation Working Group appointed by Boeing and Airbus to advise on the implementation of the Cape Town Convention. Clients "*just can't say enough good things about*" **Bill Bowers** (see p.89). "*Fabulous on the legal side,*" his advice is laced with valuable business experience. He recently represented Willis Lease Finance in a first-of-its-kind securitization of a portfolio of leased aircraft engines that also provided term financing and a $114 million warehouse credit facility. The "*terrific*" **Mike Schumaecker** (see p.133) brings to the negotiating table a "*great depth of experience.*" He is recognized for his work with foreign banks and his role in the VARIG restructuring.

**Clients/Work Highlights:** Airbus SAS; BayernLB;

Citibank; Deutsche Bank; DVB Bank; Mitsubishi; TUI AG; VARIG Brazilian Airlines and Willis Lease Finance.

## Vedder, Price, Kaufman & Kammholz

See firm details p.885

**The Firm:** Clients praised the "*great depth of expertise*" and competitive pricing of the Chicago-based Vedder Price. The 25-strong team is widely respected for the depth of its practice, particularly its work in the midmarket for operating and financing of leases. The group has also developed a loyal following among banks for its smooth handling of commercial aviation transactions. Sources spoke of the group's efficiency and detail-oriented advice; these are "*very thorough, smart guys, who know how to get a business deal done without being tedious.*"

**The Lawyers:** Vedder Price's dedicated 14-partner aviation team is headed by Chicago-based equipment finance group chair **Dean Gerber**. Clients endorsed his personable nature and "*steady unruffled approach,*" which makes him a good deal-maker with a "*developed understanding of the most technical aspects of aircraft finance transactions.*" Gerber has been chief aircraft counsel on United Airlines' recent restructuring and bankruptcy, heading the restructuring of all but eight of United's 450-aircraft fleet. Competitors have the highest respect for chair of the New York office's equipment and institutional finance practice, **Ron Scheinberg**. Best known for representing lenders, his is "*a very wide network of contacts,*" agree clients. **Jonathan Bogaard** is commended for his "*unique talent for breaking down complex issues in order to explain them to clients.*" Best known for his well-developed understanding of tax structurings, he is working alongside Dean Gerber for United Airlines. **Jeff Veber** stands out for his work on US Ex-Im Bank matters, while new partner **Josh Gentner** is "*one of the bright young folks who will make it big.*" Clients maintain that his concentrated experience in the sector enables him to "*add value*" to any discussion.

**Clients/Work Highlights:** The team is singled out in the marketplace for its pervasive industry expertise; clients include both airlines and financiers, a broad range of lower-level operating lessors, major carriers, banks, export credit agencies and underwriters. Examples include DVB Bank; US Ex-Im Bank; JetBlue; Goldman Sachs; Fortress; Lehman Brothers and Q Aviation.

## Band 3

### Cadwalader, Wickersham & Taft LLP

See firm details p.1522

**The Firm:** The past year has been particularly eventful for the team; on 14 September 2005 Northwest Airlines and Delta Air Lines, both long-term clients, filed for bankruptcy within half an hour of each other. The team has been involved in aircraft financing and restructuring matters for Northwest for many years and is representing the airline in its recent bankruptcy. Although the team carried out

the Enhanced Equipment Trust Certificate (EETC) work for Delta, due to conflict issues, it has not advised on its bankruptcy. The team also works on general corporate matters with an emphasis on leveraged lease, aircraft, vessel and other equipment and project financings.

**The Lawyers:** This small but highly efficient group is led by **Richard Aborn** (see p.84). Commentators appreciate that he is both a "*smart and tough adviser*" and a seasoned aircraft finance specialist. He displays excellent client-handling skills: "*He has a way of making people feel comfortable.*" Aborn has carried out Northwest's financing and restructuring matters for the past 18 years.

**Clients/Work Highlights:** Delta Air Lines Northwest Airlines and JetBlue are examples of the firm's client base.

### Fulbright & Jaworski L.L.P.

See firm details p.1928

**The Firm:** While the firm is also recognized for its expertise in regulatory and litigation matters, asset finance remains the key drawing card here. The New York-based aviation team is able to call on the considerable capability of the firm's bankruptcy and tax practice. Clients recognise the firm's experience in aircraft leasing, financing and taxation matters: "*They are practical, they take positions that are commercially reasonable, and they get the deal done.*"

**The Lawyers:** Head of the firm's equipment finance practice group **Jim Tussing** (see p.138) is praised by clients for his "*proactive and practical*" nature and his solution-focused approach. His unassuming nature wins over clients, who refer to him as "*concise and precise – a rarity among US lawyers – and knowledgeable of the current market.*"

**Clients/Work Highlights:** The team recently negotiated a $400 million warehouse facility for Pegasus Aviation to finance aircraft acquisitions. It represented Mizuho Corporate Bank, NIB Capital Bank NV, ORIX Corporation, Pegasus Aviation and others in workouts and new financings with airlines in South America, Central America, the USA, Canada, Asia and Europe. Over the past year, it also negotiated purchase contracts for five 747-200 aircraft, spare engines and parts, and service contracts for a startup airline.

### Shearman & Sterling LLP

See firm details p.1554

**The Firm:** Capital markets, structured finance and sovereign debt restructuring form the backbone of this respected finance firm's aviation practice. Attorneys here have represented the underwriters in offerings of EETCs by numerous airlines, including Delta Air Lines, Northwest Airlines and JetBlue Airways.

**The Lawyers:** **Ji Hoon Hong** (see p.107) is described as "*a wonderful, tremendous technical lawyer*". He is greatly admired by clients and competitors for his intellectual capability and skill in the structured finance arena, particularly on complex capital markets deals.

**Clients/Work Highlights:** The team has recently acted as underwriters' counsel in two offerings by

JetBlue. It also represented Merrill Lynch in a convertible debt offering by Pinnacle Airlines.

### Simpson Thacher & Bartlett LLP

See firm details p.1555

**The Firm:** Market sources commended the securitizations and broader capital markets expertise provided by this team. Its attorneys come together as part of a large interdisciplinary group which has won acclaim from clients for its "*deep and experienced bench.*"

**The Lawyers:** Clients singled out **Martin Jacobson** (see p.109) as "*a technically brilliant lawyer, very responsive and creative.*" They also spoke of the thoroughness of Jacobson and his team's background research and legal knowledge.

**Clients/Work Highlights:** The team is widely recognized as long-term counsel to Airbus, and recently represented it in financing arrangements with US Airways and America West Airlines upon the emergence of US Airways from bankruptcy and its merger with America West. The team also represented RBS in its predelivery payment and long-term financing of 12 Boeing 737-7BD aircraft with AirTran Airways.

### White & Case LLP

See firm details p.1566

**The Firm:** Clients spoke of this group's responsiveness, partner-led service and the quick turnaround time of its attorneys. The respected finance team recently represented Aviation Capital Group in all aspects of its $2.65 billion acquisition of Boullioun Aviation from WestLB, which included the acquisition of 102 commercial aircraft, 11 Airbus airplanes, management contracts and other assets.

**The Lawyers:** New York-based **Mike Smith** (see p.135) is "*detail-oriented, client-oriented and very practical.*" He focuses on aircraft finance and equipment leasing work and heads up the aviation capital group team. Los Angeles-based **Rick Smith** (see p.135) is best known for his ongoing work with Babcock & Brown, including operating leases, sale/leaseback transactions and residual value guarantees involving more than 100 aircraft. Clients refer to him as "*extremely commercial, he knows the business inside out*".

**Clients/Work Highlights:** Aeromexico; Aerolitoral; Aviation Capital Group; Babcock & Brown and CIT Group.

## Band 4

### Dewey Ballantine LLP

See firm details p.1530

**The Firm:** The four-partner New York and Los Angeles-based practice traditionally has its roots in representation for the lessor in leveraged lease and operating lease work. Its expertise in the tax arena has also ensured a loyal following among clients. Recently, the firm's involvement in the Delta, United Airlines and Independence Air pre-bankruptcy restructurings and transactions arising out of the bankruptcies has signaled a greater focus on the debt side of the market.

**The Lawyers:** Clients value **Fred Bass**' (see p.88) firm negotiation style and thorough understanding of leveraged lease documentation, and refer to him as "*energetic, enthusiastic, driven,*" and overall "*a fantastic lawyer.*" He is commended in particular for his tax-based leasing work, and bankruptcy-related matters on leveraged leases, and pre-bankruptcy restructuring of leveraged leases. Bass is involved in lease, debt and project financings, and represents both investors and lenders.

**Clients/Work Highlights:** The team recently represented the lessor in the leveraged leases for 24 Canadair Regional Jets leased to air carriers including Air Canada and Delta Air Lines. It also represented the lending syndicate in the refinancing of loans secured by aircraft leased to Alitalia.

## Hughes Hubbard & Reed LLP
See firm details p.1535

**The Firm:** Clients endorsed this firm for its success in developing a "*first-rate team of attorneys with a terrific knowledge of aircraft finance.*" The group is widely recognized as Continental Airlines' counsel on aircraft finance, capital markets deals and litigation matters. The group has also been involved in the recent restructurings facing the airline industry; it has been retained by Northwest Airlines to handle

certain matters in its Chapter 11 bankruptcy case, and recently acted for DaimlerChrysler Capital Services as lessor of aircraft in restructuring transactions by Independence Air.

**The Lawyers:** The "*extremely detail-oriented, hard-working and pragmatic*" **John Hoyns** (see p.108) has acted as Continental Airlines' regular outside counsel for the past 20 years. His caseload includes aircraft financings, leasings and financing issues related to routes, gates and slots. Sources also appreciated his "*attentive and astute advice*" and his wealth of deal experience.

**Clients/Work Highlights:** The team recently represented Continental Airlines in a major debt placement of $350 million of notes by Merrill Lynch secured by assets of Continental's subsidiaries Air Micronesia and Continental Micronesia. It also represented Republic Airline in the purchase from US Airways of 28 Embraer ERJ-170 aircraft.

## Paul, Hastings, Janofsky & Walker LLP
See firm details p.339

**The Firm:** Multinational aircraft leasing and financing forms the foundation of this practice. Its small but highly effective team excels in the representation of operating lessors, including Gecas, among others. Recent highlights have included the representation of international aircraft leasing companies in restruc-

turing issues.

**The Lawyers:** Clients concur that **John Howitt** (see p.108) is "*knowledgeable, hands on, accessible, and down-to-earth.*" He is praised for his excellent business sense and "*tendency not to over-lawyer the transaction.*"

**Clients/Work Highlights:** The group recently advised on a 100-plus aircraft lease restructuring and a multi-hundred million dollar lease and loan finance commitment for additional aircraft.

## Sidley Austin LLP
See firm details p.883

**The Firm:** The team advises on a broad range of aircraft financing and leasing matters, including securitization, restructuring and regulation issues. Clients described the group as "*responsive, knowledgeable, diplomatic and very focused on client relations.*"

**The Lawyers:** Clients have great confidence in **Rory Kelleher** (see p.112), who is "*dedicated, reliable, and gets good results for his clients in a timely and professional manner.*" He represents clients in domestic and international finance transactions, leveraged and cross-border lease transactions, and other structured financings.

**Clients/Work Highlights:** AT&T Capital; Boeing; Boullioun Aviation Services; BFGoodrich; CS Aviation Services and General Electric Aircraft Engines.

# AVIATION

## Band 1

## Condon & Forsyth LLP
**The Firm:** An aviation boutique with a worldwide reputation, this firm operates from offices in New York, DC and Los Angeles. The aviation and aerospace group is widely commended for its expertise in major commercial airline disaster cases, in which it acts primarily for airlines and their insurers. The New York-based team is continuing its work on the property claims arising from the 9/11 terrorist attack, in addition to working on the liability issues arising out of the November 2001 American Airlines crash. The Los Angeles-based team recently successfully secured the dismissal of litigation on forum non conveniens grounds against China Airlines in relation to a 747 accident involving Taiwanese litigants. Financing and commercial matters are also on the agenda here.

**The Lawyers:** Clients state that **Desmond Barry**'s (see p.87) work is "*of the highest quality.*" His specialty is in disaster work and major liability cases, and he is currently acting as lead counsel for American Airlines in 9/11-related litigation. He is "*vastly experienced and a big-picture person,*" who adopts a "*tenacious, practical and versatile approach.*" He displays strong client-handling skills and is respected by both plaintiff and defendant lawyers for his problem-solving abilities. **Rod Margo** is "*extremely academic, with*

*unparalleled knowledge in this sector.*" Like Barry, he also principally represents airlines and their insurers, and wins praise for his expertise in insurance defense matters.

**Clients/Work Highlights:** American Airlines; Aon; China Airlines; VARIG Brazilian Airlines; Marsh and Swiss International Airlines.

## Crowell & Moring LLP
See firm details p.564

**The Firm:** Clients refer to this three-partner DC-based team as "*one of the best aviation regulatory teams in Washington.*" It is heavily endorsed for its airline regulatory enforcement work before the US Department of Transportation (DOT) and FAA, foreign governments and the US Court of Appeals. Clients report: "*They are exceptionally talented and have the appropriate contacts in DC.*" The firm acts as external regulatory counsel to Continental Airlines, and recently represented the airline in the US-Argentina route and Houston-Buenos Aires route proceedings. Litigation, environmental, air space and airport access issues also form an important part of the workload.

**The Lawyers:** Head of the aviation group **Bruce Keiner** (see p.104) is a "*professional straight shooter.*" Clients praised his responsiveness and high-quality advice; he is "*on the ball, up to date, with the right networks.*" He carries out a broad range of airline-

# REGULATORY & LITIGATION

related economic and regulatory counseling, but is best known for his work as regulatory counsel for Continental Airlines. He recently advised on operating authority issues surrounding a new route to Beijing for this client. **Lorry Halloway** (see p.104) is "*outstanding – she delivers consistently high-quality advice and service levels.*" Her broad-ranging regulatory expertise includes export control advice.

**Clients/Work Highlights:** Continental Airlines; Southern Air; Regional Airline Association; Aer Lingus and First Choice Holidays.

## Hogan & Hartson LLP
See firm details p.568

**The Firm:** This aviation practice has long been heralded as one of the most prestigious in DC, and in spring 2005 it recruited three attorneys from Shaw Pittman (Bob Cohn, Sacha Van der Bellen and Sheryl Israel) to cement this reputation. The core aviation team now numbers seven attorneys. It possesses a particular expertise in FAA regulatory matters and also advises on a range of related commercial litigation and aircraft financings. The team can also draw upon the firm's broad-based experience in corporate, commercial litigation, antitrust, international and immigration law.

**The Lawyers:** Head of transportation group **George Carneal** (see p.91) recently advised the Government of the Bahamas on the operation and

| Transportation: |
| --- |
| **Aviation: Regulatory & Litigation** |
| Leading Firms |
| [1] CONDON & FORSYTH LLP |
| CROWELL & MORING LLP |
| HOGAN & HARTSON LLP |
| HOLLAND & KNIGHT LLP |
| PERKINS COIE LLP |
| PILLSBURY WINTHROP SHAW PITTMAN |
| [2] GAROFALO GOERLICH HAINBACH |
| LORD, BISSELL & BROOK |
| MILLER, CANFIELD, PADDOCK AND STONE |
| WILMERHALE |
| ZUCKERT, SCOUTT & RASENBERGER, LLP |

| Leading Individuals |
| --- |
| [1] BARRY JR Desmond *Condon & Forsyth* |
| CRAFT Randal *Holland & Knight LLP* |
| DAMERIS Thad *Pillsbury* |
| KEINER JR R Bruce *Crowell & Moring* |
| QUINN Kenneth *Pillsbury* |
| [2] CARNEAL George *Hogan & Hartson* |
| COHN Robert *Hogan & Hartson LLP* |
| DILLOW John *Perkins Coie LLP* |
| ELLETT E Tazewell *Hogan & Hartson* |
| [3] COSTELLO Frank *Zuckert, Scoutt* |
| GAROFALO Gary *Garofalo Goerlich* |
| HALLOWAY Lorraine *Crowell & Moring* |
| KATZ Donald *Miller, Canfield, Paddock* |
| MARGO Roderick *Condon & Forsyth* |
| RABINOVITZ Bruce *WilmerHale* |
| VAN DER BELLEN Alexander *Hogan & Hartson* |
| WESTERBERG Gary *Lord, Bissell & Brook* |
| Associates to watch |
| HARRINGTON David *Holland & Knight* |

development of its civil aviation oversight, airports system, and air traffic management structure. He is a trusted adviser, who is commended for his deep knowledge of the sector. Formerly with Shaw Pittman **Bob Cohn** (see p.93) is *"attentive, focused on details, and a very good businessman,"* said clients. He is counsel to Delta Air Lines and represented this client in the first-ever bid for antitrust immunity for an international alliance involving two US carriers. **Ted Ellett** (see p.98) is *"extremely well versed in aviation law,"* and has a wealth of experience with regulatory issues and the regulators themselves. Clients also admire his persuasive advocacy style. As long-term aviation regulatory counsel for NetJets, Ellett recently assisted the company in obtaining DOT economic authority for NetJets Europe program to fly into the USA. In connection with this matter and advice given to a consortium of fractional ownership program managers, the team took a leading role in the FAA's Fractional Ownership Aviation Rulemaking Committee concerning safety regulation. The *"experienced and smart"* **Sacha Van der Bellen** (see p.139) works alongside Bob Cohn as a representative of Delta Air Lines, focusing particularly on route

cases.

**Clients/Work Highlights:** Delta Airlines; Rolls-Royce North America; NetJets Aviation; Pogojet; Government of the Commonwealth of the Bahamas and Wexford Capital.

## Holland & Knight LLP
See firm details p.1534

**The Firm:** The firm's aircraft accident investigation and litigation practice focuses primarily on the representation of airlines, aircraft manufacturers and component part manufacturers in the defense of claims brought before the US National Transportation Safety Board (NTSB), the FAA and Congress. The group is respected for its liability work; a recent success has been its privacy litigation victory for client JetBlue. The group has also recently successfully settled almost all of the 300 lawsuits in federal multidistrict litigation arising out of the November 2001 American Airlines crash near Belle Harbor, New York. The 25-partner litigation team also advises on general products liability, space work and other transportation matters.

**The Lawyers:** Commentators agree that *"rainmaker"* **Bob Craft**'s (see p.93) *"knowledge of the sector is encyclopedic."* Craft works primarily on crash litigation and NTSB investigatory work. He recently acted as lead counsel for Air France in connection with the Concorde crash, and acted as lead counsel for TWA in the Flight 800 investigation and litigation. A former navy F14-B pilot, **David Harrington** (see p.105) is *"a bright energetic lawyer"* and a rising star in the sector. Alongside colleague Alan Reitzfeld, Harrington led the team representing American Airlines in the Belle Harbor litigation.

**Clients/Work Highlights:** Air France; American Airlines; BAE Systems; JetBlue and TWA.

## Perkins Coie LLP

**The Firm:** The stronghold of this 15-partner national aviation group lies in Seattle. Its enduring relationship with Boeing, on both transactional and liability matters, has ensured the firm takes a leading role in the sector. Attorneys have recently represented Boeing in the Hawaiian Air, US Airways, Delta Air Lines and Northwest Airlines bankruptcies. The team is also counsel to a number of other domestic and foreign entities on the negotiation and structuring of cross-border transactions, a recognized area of strength being on the liability side.

**The Lawyers:** Head of the eight-partner practice is **John Dillow**. A respected liability lawyer, he is *"competent, responsive and thorough, with excellent business sense,"* said clients.

**Clients/Work Highlights:** Boeing; Bouillion; Google and PacifiCorp.

## Pillsbury Winthrop Shaw Pittman LLP
See firm details p.1550

**The Firm:** Clients praised Pillsbury's aviation, aerospace and transportation group for its depth of industry expertise and broad capabilities. Key strengths of the practice are accident investigation and litigation, regulatory and products liability.

Clients spoke of a *"lean team of thoroughly engaged lawyers,"* high-quality advice and *"responsiveness to requirements."* The team is heavily involved in regulatory work, and challenging decisions made by the FAA. Recent highlights for the group include representing the City of Chicago in the modernization of O'Hare International Airport, led by Kenneth Quinn.

**The Lawyers:** Co-leaders of the aviation, aerospace and transportation group are former FAA chief counsel **Kenneth Quinn** (see p.127) and **Thad Dameris** (see p.94), chair of the ABA's tort, trial and insurance practice section on aviation and space law. DC-based Quinn is regulatory and litigation counsel to aerospace and aviation service companies, airports and airlines. He is currently working on the post-9/11 regulation and transportation security administration issues, and is the *"dean of the Bar here on FAA issues,"* reported clients. Houston-based Dameris is recognized as a skilled trial lawyer, particularly in insurance defense matters. According to clients, he is *"devoted and proactive."* He serves as national trial counsel for Airbus SAS.

**Clients/Work Highlights:** Allianz Marine & Aviation; American Airlines; Corsair; GE; Rolls-Royce North America and Sabre Inc/Travelocity.

## Band 2

### Garofalo Goerlich Hainbach PC

**The Firm:** This nine-strong boutique punches well above its weight in DOT and FAA regulatory work, primarily representing airlines in regulatory matters. The team has recently obtained operating licenses for a number of clients in relation to private 9-14-seater business jets. It also recently settled several large enforcement cases in addition to advising on a substantial amount of trade association work.

**The Lawyers:** Former FAA lawyer **Gary Garofalo**'s (see p.101) specialty is in foreign on-demand air taxis, and larger aircraft airlines flying into the USA. He is also well versed in economic regulatory issues before the FAA and DOT. Clients appreciate his common-sense approach and ability to *"think outside the box;"* he is *"professional, practical, efficient and very creative, with excellent business sense."*

**Clients/Work Highlights:** The team represents a variety of clients including major foreign airlines, corporations, fractional ownership providers and owners, and jet car suppliers.

### Lord, Bissell & Brook

**The Firm:** Based in the Chicago and Atlanta offices, the 18-strong group is best known for its litigation expertise and works primarily on major international airline accidents and multiparty products liability litigation. Corporate, finance and leasing advice are also provided to clients.

**The Lawyers:** Sources describe **Gary Westerberg** as *"an effective adviser"* on aviation liability; he is *"immensely experienced, and can handle himself in any litigation."* Clients also endorsed his handling of complex cases. Recent highlights include representing the security company which conducted the pre-board passenger screening for American Airlines Flight 11 on 9/11 in proceedings before the federal court in New York.

**Clients/Work Highlights:** Clients include aircraft product manufacturers, airlines, aviation operators and insurers.

## Miller, Canfield, Paddock and Stone, P.L.C.

See firm details p.1148

**The Firm:** This Michigan-based team's core focus is on transactional work for corporations buying and operating business jets. Its workload features the counseling of clients on tax liabilities and regulatory issues. The team also acts for municipalities on the building of airports and other related commercial considerations. A recent highlight was the team's work with long-term client Aerodynamics on aviation regulations and labor issues regarding its pilots and crews for the operations of all of Intel's aircraft assets.

**The Lawyers:** **Don Katz** (see p.112) is the whole business lawyer, agreed clients, who believe he "*adds immediate value*" to any discussion with his "*informed, focused and precise counsel.*" His broad practice includes operational and regulatory issues arising from the acquisition and usage of business jets.

**Clients/Work Highlights:** Clients include Aerodynamics; Comerica Bank; General Dynamics; Kellogg; National City Bank, amongst other banks and lending companies.

## WilmerHale

See firm details p.580

**The Firm:** The eight-lawyer core aviation regulatory practice is concentrated in the DC office; however the team is able to draw on the extensive resources of the firm as a whole. This proves to be a particular attraction for clients as the group works closely with their counterparts in the London and Berlin offices on airline regulatory matters. The team combines this broad regulatory practice with aircraft finance and joint ventures work.

**The Lawyers:** Chair of the firm's aviation practice **Bruce Rabinovitz** (see p.128) impresses with his work on administrative and enforcement matters before the DOT and the FAA. He is "*thorough and understands the detail of the law,*" reported sources. He advised on the formation of the Star Alliance network, obtaining immunity from antitrust for clients United Airlines and Lufthansa. The team has subsequently obtained authority to add SAS, Austrian Airlines and bmi to the immunized alliance.

**Clients/Work Highlights:** The team recently filed an application with the DOT for immunity from US antitrust laws for an alliance among eight Star Alliance member carriers. It also recently advised on a significant change in DOT regulations governing the disclosure of code-sharing arrangements in airline advertising. Examples of the firm's client base include United Airlines; DHL; Lufthansa and Boeing.

## Zuckert, Scoutt & Rasenberger, LLP

**The Firm:** This DC-based aviation boutique is held in high regard by interviewees for its regulatory expertise, particularly its handling of complaint and enforcement matters before the DOT and the FAA. The firm also carries out a broad range of finance and operating lease transactions on behalf of airlines, financial institutions and leasing companies.

**The Lawyers:** Sources endorsed **Frank Costello** as a "*very thorough and very thoughtful lawyer,*" who has a broad base of experience. He is chair of the Aviation Committee of the ABA.

**Clients/Work Highlights:** The team regularly advises clients such as foreign airlines and other aviation interests on ways to structure transactions in accordance with Federal Aviation Act requirements. Recent highlights include US Airways' sale of stock to British Airways and the purchase of stock in Continental Airlines by Air Canada and Air Partners. The team also regularly acts as special counsel in matters involving the registration of aircraft and issues of security interests in aircraft with the FAA.

---

# TRANSPORTATION                                    RAIL

**OVERVIEW:** The rail sector continues to search for solutions to its greatest challenge: capacity. Projected growth over the next few decades has led many practitioners to question whether the USA currently has the ability to handle such growth. In addition to advice on day-to-day needs and disputes concerning the reasonableness of rates, clients now demand counsel on enhancing improved operations and infrastructure, as well as private sector financing. Furthermore, the post-9/11 climate has brought new issues to greater prominence, especially those concerning the transportation of potentially hazardous materials by rail. The tussle between government bodies and the rail companies will continue for some time yet, and many clients expect firms advising on rail work to be able to work with them on all of these issues.

## Band 1

### Covington & Burling

See firm details p.563

**The Firm:** This dependable rail mainstay utilizes many different entry points into the sector, so as to provide a broad coverage of traditional litigation, regulatory issues and policy matters. The firm's core, wholly dedicated rail group is relatively small, but links up as a matter of course with experts in other practice groups whenever required. Famed for its assistance to Union Pacific, the Washington, DC and New York teams advise other railroads, as well as providing assistance to industry associations, counseling on appearances before federal agencies and on all aspects of the legislative process. The firm also provides antitrust counsel – an area in which it has an excellent reputation – and advises on a broad array of issues related to the safety and security of hazardous materials transportation.

**The Lawyers:** **Linda Morgan** (see p.122) is chair of the transportation practice group and is held in the highest regard by all corners of the market. Her industry experience is without equal, having previously been the chairman of both the former Interstate Commerce Commission and the current Surface Transportation Board (STB). Her practice focuses on a broad range of railroad and other transportation matters as well as general legislative, governmental, and policy issues. Her workload of late has included counsel on safety policies concerning hazardous material in America's post-9/11

climate. *"First-rate to deal with"* and highly professional, she also works with individual railroads, principally Union Pacific, and the industry as a whole on agency matters including new changes, infrastructure issues and rate cases. This includes an ongoing investigation of pricing actions by Union Pacific and another western railroad. She further acted for Union Pacific putting forward proposals to possible changes to the Staggers Rail Act of 1980. **David Meyer** (see p.121) advises on government investigations and antitrust matters. *"Bright and meticulous"* with a well-appreciated writing style, he impresses sources with his refined and balanced advocacy style. He advised Union Pacific in a major rate reasonableness challenge, successfully achieving the dismissal of the complaint.
**Clients/Work Highlights:** The team assisted TTX's flatcar pooling application in a major case involving the pool that provides most of the flatcars used by North American railroads to handle vital intermodal traffic. It argued before the STB and successfully achieved a ten-year reauthorization of the TTX flatcar pool. It is also working with a group of investors interested in the development of a high-speed rail passenger line between Las Vegas and Southern California.

## Sidley Austin LLP
See firm details p.883
**The Firm:** A long-time leader in the rail sector, this team's *"willingness to subordinate its own ego for a team effort"* was well received by the market. This goal-oriented practice is a popular choice when it comes to railroad disputes, and it has most recently advised on several preemption litigation cases concerning hazardous material transportation. In a similar vein, it advised a regional railroad on litigation in the District Court of New Jersey concerning new regulations on loading facilities that handle construction and demolition materials debris. Real estate and environment lawyers in New York and labor experts in Chicago complement the central rail team in Washington, DC.
**The Lawyers:** **Paul Moates** (see p.121) is the firm's most experienced rail practitioner. An *"intelligent man with a good sense of judgment,"* interviewees warmed to his *"aggressive but effective pursuit of his clients' interests"* in litigation and *"passionate but*

*sincere arguments,"* sourced from his deep experience. One competitor commented: *"He utilizes the sort of adversarial relationship you want to see."* Much of his caseload relates to eastern railroads, working regularly with Norfolk Southern and CSX on litigious matters, although this should not overshadow his respected transactional work. He successfully assisted CSX before the STB in protracted litigation with the District of Columbia regarding its ordinance banning the transportation of certain types of hazardous chemicals within a 2.2-mile radius of the Capitol. His colleague Carter Phillips assisted on the appellate aspects of the case.
**Clients/Work Highlights:** The group assisted key client Norfolk Southern on a joint venture with Kansas City Southern to invest in a line between Mississippi and Louisiana, in a creative attempt to deal with the current capacity constraints. The team advised the plaintiffs on the Norfolk Southern Railway Company v Kirby case, which involved the interpretation of the Carriage of Goods by Sea Act regarding the extent of liability for damage to goods. It represented Canadian Pacific Railway on the sale to the Indiana Rail Road Company of its 350-mile line between Chicago and Louisville. Consolidated Rail Corporation (Conrail) and Norfolk Southern also successfully used the firm's Chicago branch on a major federal court employment case.

## Band 2

## Arnold & Porter LLP
See firm details p.560
**The Firm:** The firm handles rail transportation matters in concert with trucking as a single, intermodal focus. In 2005, the emphasis for this chiefly DC-based team was on homeland security measures; for which the firm is well suited, as its members include former general counsels of the CIA and NSA. It is working on a greater number of environmental matters than it has in the past, including matters concerning contaminated property and the release of pollutants. The team has assisted key client CSX for many years and also advises contractors and consultants to the government.
**The Lawyers:** Richard Baltz works with CSX on a variety of corporate and securities representations. Steven Kaplan focuses more on the M&A side, while Mary Gay Sprague counsels on regulatory and some environmental issues.
**Clients/Work Highlights:** Of central importance to the firm's rail work in 2005 was its assistance to CSX on a major preemption case, following an ordinance from the District of Columbia prohibiting the transport through the district of certain hazardous materials. The firm sought a declaration of invalidity of the DC law in the district court and continues to advise CSX on other potential legislation elsewhere in the USA. The team also represented CSX on the sale of its global port facilities business, CSX World Terminals, to Dubai Ports International for $1.15 billion.

## Mayer, Brown, Rowe & Maw LLP
See firm details p.876
**The Firm:** A national practice with trusted specialist attorneys was the verdict of market sources on Mayer Brown's rail transportation work. This sister strand of transportation expertise runs alongside the firm's well-established road group. Frequently working for BNSF Railway, its involvement in the sector also incorporates regular representation of the Association of American Railroads.
**The Lawyers:** **Robert Jenkins** (see p.110) brings his wide knowledge and experience of government contracts and arbitration to bear on rail transportation. He is fluent in all aspects of economic regulation, working with both corporate and trade association clients on disputes and appellate proceedings. Interviewees also noted the involvement of this *"top-flight advocate with good judgment"* on issues relating to the transportation of hazardous materials and the area of preemption. He challenges states and localities in an effort to prevent them from passing ordinances banning such transportation. Although still an expert in economic regulation and mergers within the rail sector, Erika Jones currently spends the majority of her time on road and related matters.

## Slover & Loftus
**The Firm:** The first choice of America's coal shipping clients throughout the country, this DC-based boutique advises on an increased number of service issues and clients' rights under their common carrier arrangements. While coal-related matters form the bulk of the workload here, the team also assists clients with other commodities. It is one of the main firms appearing opposite the big rail groups on regulatory matters, representing utilities on technical rate cases and related disputes. In this sphere, the firm is respected as an aggressive litigator on behalf of its clients' interests. It further advises on arbitrations concerning disputes arising under rate readjustment provisions, the application of fuel surcharges and service performance stipulations.
**The Lawyers:** Several commentators spoke of **Michael Loftus'** sound judgment and adversarial method, describing their *"highest regard for his ethics and high level of courtesy and professional dialog."* He frequently advises on the phasing-in of rail rate increases and their reasonableness. For example, he was lead counsel for Duke Energy and Progress Energy on their eastern coal rate actions against CSX and Norfolk Southern, where the STB was asked to phase in the rate increases over a period of time. He is additionally working with Arizona Public Service and PacifiCorp in similar claims against BNSF Railway.
**Clients/Work Highlights:** The firm has represented several utilities' interests on cases before the STB relating to the application of its stand-alone cost methodology in coal rate cases and also on possible changes to the Staggers Rail Act of 1980. It set up a new railroad in Nebraska via the STB on behalf of a utility group and is regularly involved in FERC. The team shows no sign of slowing its pursuit of coal rate

cases, filing two new actions for both Western Fuels Association and Kansas City Power & Light Co, with another still undecided on behalf of AEP (Texas North) involving rail rates for coal transportation from Powder River Basin. It has also worked with Dyno Nobel on proceedings regarding the rates it has been charged by a pipeline company to transport anhydrous ammonia in the USA. Other clients include Arizona Public Service; Columbus & Ohio River Railroad Company; Duke Energy; Reliant Energy and Saginaw Bay Southern/J&JG Holding.

## Steptoe & Johnson LLP

See firm details p.576

**The Firm:** Intermodal advice and coal work are the drivers of this nationwide rail team. From its DC base, it advises western giant BNSF Railway on a range of transportation issues. It also advises other groups, such as CSX. In addition to the commercial and regulatory litigation work, attorneys here have developed a special expertise representing railroad clients in large-verdict personal injury appeals.

**The Lawyers:** Sources commended **Samuel Sipe** (see p.135) as an *"extremely capable professional with a charming manner."* He undertakes a fair amount of appellate work and provides advice on economic regulatory matters and policy issues. He led the firm's successful action on an arbitration between a major freight railroad and its trucking company intermodal service partner. Sipe's transportation and appellate specialist colleague **Betty Jo Christian** (see p.92) remains a well-known name in the sector. Interviewees pointed to her key role in developing the firm's rail practice. There is a great diversity to the practice, as illustrated by the workload of David Coburn, and this breadth of experience is also important to the group's success.

**Clients/Work Highlights:** The group mounted a successful challenge on behalf of BNSF Railway in the US Court of Appeals for the District of Columbia Circuit to an STB decision in a rail rate case involving the transportation of coal to a Texas power plant. It currently represents BNSF in a major commercial dispute in California involving its intermodal business and further advised the group on an appeal of a $7 million verdict awarded to the family of a man killed in a grade crossing accident. In addition to BNSF, regular rail clients include the Association of American Railroads and CSX.

### Band 3

## DeOrchis Hillenbrand & Wiener LLP

**The Firm:** This small yet highly experienced transportation group advises on road, rail, maritime and some aviation matters. In 2005, much of the firm's rail work was undertaken by its Florida office, although its offices in New York and elsewhere also assist the firm's national clients.

**The Lawyers:** Over a third of **Hyman Hillenbrand**'s wide-ranging transportation work involves defending railroads, principally CSX and, to a lesser extent, Norfolk Southern. He remains a widely respected attorney with a *"terrific aptitude for analyzing issues and the legal and factual details that can make a case,"* said clients. He negotiated a settlement on behalf of CSX prior to mediation on four shipments of perishables, where the railroad's records did not show good handling.

**Clients/Work Highlights:** The team worked with CSX in its claim for the disappearance of part of a shipment of electronics in transit; on three lawsuits for thefts of parts of shipments of expensive car parts; and on a case concerning a used transformer transported by rail, which was damaged in a derailment by another carrier to whom CSX had interchanged the shipment so it could travel to its destination.

## Thompson Hine LLP

See firm details p.1651

**The Firm:** A regular champion of shippers and railroad freight customers that bring actions against the railroads on both individual matters and issues of national policy. Its extensive knowledge of intermodal transportation is also brought to bear on behalf of national associations on rail mergers and rulemakings before the STB. The team advises Holcim on its efforts to construct a new rail line directly adjacent to the existing line of competitor CSX, and on CSX's property, due to environment issues in the desired construction area. It is also working with ALSTOM in a dispute with Norfolk Southern concerning damages for delayed rail deliveries and premium transportation services.

**The Lawyers:** **Nick DiMichael**'s (see p.96) work on behalf of trade associations and others against the railroads is well respected in the market. His practice incorporates advice on transportation rates, terms and conditions and the negotiation of rail and motor transportation contracts. He counsels on regulatory matters involving hazardous materials and assists utilities on their coal supply and transportation rate

issues. DiMichael acts for the State of North Dakota and is currently assisting it on a complaint against railroad grain shipping rates. Jeffrey Moreno in the Washington, DC office is also on hand to advise utilities and coal producers on regulatory rates challenges and disputes.

**Clients/Work Highlights:** ALSTOM; Basell USA; Cargill; DuPont; Fortune Brands; GE; Hasbro; Holcim; Mittal Steel; The National Industrial Transportation League; Otter Tail Power Company and Pier 1 Imports.

## Zuckert, Scoutt & Rasenberger, LLP

**The Firm:** The transportation group advises on a variety of transactions and disputes between its clients and other railroad groups and shippers. This includes litigation over car hire and trackage rights, rail line ownership and labor disputes. Chief among its successes was the rearrangement of railroad operations in the northeast and Canada between its client Norfolk Southern and Canadian Pacific Railway and one of its subsidiaries. As well as assisting the sector's larger players, the team also works with regional and short line railroads on their sales and real estate concerns, as well as trackage rights and other disputes.

**The Lawyers:** **Richard Allen**'s DC-based practice is primarily concerned with regulatory and commercial disputes in the rail sector, although he does also assist on maritime matters.

**Clients/Work Highlights:** The group is general counsel to the Texas Mexican Railway Company.

## Other Notable Practitioners

Based within the firm's projects group, rail specialist **Michael McBride** (see p.118) of LeBoeuf, Lamb, Greene & MacRae LLP also assists on general litigation, environmental and regulatory matters. His recent caseload has featured issues relating to the transportation of goods within the chemicals sector. He represented BP Amoco against Norfolk Southern at the STB in the first so-called 'small shipment rate case', where the petroleum group challenged common carrier rates for the transportation of paraxylene. His nationwide practice is located in Washington, DC, a feature of the federal nature of his work, but covers an impressively large range of rail work nationwide, including litigation on reasonable rates. He has worked with electric utilities such as the Edison Electric Institute, and advised shipping clients regarding the practicalities of the movement of their goods relating to common carrier obligations.

# TRANSPORTATION

# ROAD (CARRIAGE/COMMERCIAL)

**OVERVIEW:** The burgeoning toll road and infrastructure market now occupies the largest slice of the road carriage sector in terms of value. State budgetary shortfalls and aging infrastructures have led those lacking the funds necessary to undertake improvements to seek alternative ways of structuring their assets. The Chicago Skyway transaction is the yardstick for these efforts, kick-starting a tremendous growth in interest in the privatization of existing roads and extension projects and project financing for new roads. Ongoing counsel on safety regulation and manufacturers' compliance now frequently incorporates antitrust issues. In addition, concerns regarding the transportation of hazardous materials continue to occupy a significant place in the market, ensuring that several specialties co-exist beneath the wide umbrella terminology of road carriage.

---

**Transportation:**
**Road (Carriage/Commercial)**
**Leading Firms**

**[1]**
HUNTON & WILLIAMS LLP
MAYER, BROWN, ROWE & MAW LLP
MILBANK, TWEED, HADLEY & MCCLOY LLP
ORRICK, HERRINGTON & SUTCLIFFE

**[2]**
DENNIS, CORRY, PORTER & SMITH LLP
DEORCHIS HILLENBRAND & WIENER LLP
HOGAN & HARTSON LLP
MCGUIREWOODS LLP
THOMPSON HINE LLP

**Leading Individuals**

**[1]**
FEO Edwin *Milbank, Tweed*
JONES Erika *Mayer, Brown*
MATHEWS Daniel *Orrick*
PULLEY III J Waverly *Hunton & Williams*

**[2]**
CHUSED Wesley *Looney & Grossman LLP*
COGBILL III John *McGuireWoods LLP*
DIMICHAEL Nicholas *Thompson Hine*
HILLENBRAND Hyman *DeOrchis Hillenbrand*
MARKS Allan *Milbank, Tweed*
PORTER R Clay *Dennis, Corry, Porter & Smith*
RAHER Patrick *Hogan & Hartson LLP*
SCHMIDT John *Mayer, Brown*

---

## Band 1

### Hunton & Williams LLP
See firm details p.1989

**The Firm:** The firm enjoys a strong reputation in Virginia for its work that is also spreading out nationally, with a transportation infrastructure footprint that primarily targets private but also some public ventures. Its road practice is combined with a robust international project finance practice and a significant investment in statutory reform. Virginia's Public Private Transportation Act (PPTA) has intensified the interest in toll road investments by private sector companies on not only tax-exempt financing but also greater involvement from foreign companies following the Chicago Skyway success. This has led to the firm's involvement in matters such as the Dulles Toll Road (and five related projects) and Interstate 81 project. Clients highlighted the firm's experience of the appropriate legislation and knowledge of how the government agencies think. Sources believe that the group has *"some real quality individuals in the taxation arena and in public finance,"* many of whom were *"instrumental in drafting the transportation act that Virginia uses,"* a model that other states are following. It is also working on procurement issues in the post-Hurricane Katrina clear-up.

**The Lawyers: Waverly Pulley**'s (see p.127) practice has moved toward transportation infrastructure in preference to his real estate work. Clients spoke of an *"excellent lawyer with a good manner and him, able to deal with difficult problems – and clients!"* Others repeatedly referred to his professional demeanor, problem-solving attitude and *"understanding of what the problems are and how to act in our best interests."* While some of the firm's most noteworthy transactions took place in Virginia in 2005, its overall transportation infrastructure group includes attorneys in Atlanta, New York and even London.

**Clients/Work Highlights:** The team represents an international consortium in a proposal to improve, maintain and operate the Dulles Toll Road under a concession arrangement pursuant to the PPTA. An international consortium also used the firm in its proposal to the Virginia Department of Transportation to finance, construct and operate the Route 495 high-occupancy toll (HOT) lanes under the Virginia PPTA. It also continues to assist Kellogg, Brown & Root on the Interstate 81 corridor improvements project.

### Mayer, Brown, Rowe & Maw LLP
See firm details p.876

**The Firm:** Advice to existing and potential manufacturers of motor vehicles and equipment remains central to this firm's road practice. Partners with significant pedigree within the industry – including two former chief counsels of the National Highway Traffic Safety Administration (NHTSA) – form a formidable presence in the marketplace. The firm advises clients on the regulatory issues that they may encounter nationwide, including compliance with federal regulations and whether a vehicle contains safety defects and may need recalling. Related advice includes cooperative agreements, appellate litigation and the defense of punitive damages cases. The firm also attracts a wealth of transactional matters, particularly auto loan securitizations and tax advice as well as outsourcing and internal development contracts. The trucking side of the industry looks to the firm for advice on a number of areas, including regulatory advice on pending regulations and related litigation. The firm is also well known for its expertise in project finance and was called upon by the City of Chicago to advise on the landmark $1.83 billion Chicago Skyway toll road privatization, the first US public toll road to be turned over to a private firm.

Competitors agree that the firm has developed the whole package and a prominent brand name for projects in the automotive, trucking and toll road sectors.

**The Lawyers: Erika Jones** (see p.110) in Washington, DC is focused on road safety work. Clients enthused about her ability *"to give plain English advice, often on the fly, because she knows it so well."* She represents clients in front of the two federal regulatory agencies on issues of recalls and proposed regulation changes, in addition to a share of consumer safety advice. A further dimension to her practice concerns working with manufacturing clients on their private products liability litigation when regulatory issues arise, including preemption cases. She and her Los Angeles colleague Philip Recht are former chief counsels of the NHTSA, with Kenneth Weinstein in DC joining the firm in February 2005 from the Department of Transportation for issues of road safety. **John Schmidt** (see p.133) assists public entities on major projects and led the firm's advice to the City of Chicago on the Chicago Skyway transaction. He provides *"straightforward and smart advice"* and his practical approach to negotiations with local government entities was commended by sources.

**Clients/Work Highlights:** The team is representing the Alliance of Automobile Manufacturers in a challenge to an NHTSA regulation on tire pressure monitorings. It is advising this client on regulations regarding the treatment and evaluation of confidential business information and where it is entitled to be protected. It is also conducting an environmental litigation in Maine on behalf of an industry association relating to the disposal of mercury switches, and is representing a major automaker in litigation involving California's effort to impose fuel economy standards on motor vehicles in the state.

### Milbank, Tweed, Hadley & McCloy LLP

**The Firm:** The firm has built on the tremendous growth in interest in the privatization of existing road projects and those proposing extensions, as well as project financing for new roads. This increased caseload has followed on naturally from its advice to the Cintra-Macquarie consortium on the successful Chicago Skyway deal. Large toll road projects such as the Dulles Greenway Toll Road are a key part of the team's activity in the sector, working the line where projects and transportation meet. It is also conducting refinancing and M&A on the transfer of existing private roads, as well as on early stage development of greenfield toll roads and other new road projects in Texas, Oregon and Virginia. The firm's strong focus on the Latin American market has led to similar infrastructure projects. Capable of assisting both investors and lenders, this well-rounded practice also deals with the restructuring of existing but troubled projects.

**The Lawyers:** Los Angeles-based **Edwin Feo**'s successes on the SR 125 South toll road in California and the Chicago Skyway project led him to assist sponsors Macquarie Infrastructure Group on its $533 million investment in the Dulles Greenway (14-mile) Toll Road. Sources view the cochair of the firm's global project finance group as a *"smart, practical lawyer, professional and even-keeled,"* who has adapted his work with the times. Like Feo, project finance partner **Allan Marks** operates from a Los Angeles base. He regularly advises on complex infrastructure projects worldwide, such as the MXN2.2 billion bond financing for the Monterrey-Cadereyta toll road in Mexico.

**Clients/Work Highlights:** The firm regularly advises domestic and foreign sponsors, such as Cintra and Transurban, on their projects. It also works with lenders and underwriters such as Citigroup on secured bond financings for toll roads. Recent examples include its advice to WestLB on a Mexican rail project and DEPFA BANK on a venture in Virginia.

## Orrick, Herrington & Sutcliffe

See firm details p.337

**The Firm:** Acquisition financing within transportation is this firm's specialty, particularly for toll roads and also within the aviation sector. Clients speak of *"one of the leading firms on negotiations for toll road concession deals."* It is involved on behalf of both lenders and sponsors in many developing and ongoing road-related matters, such as the Indiana Toll Road and Dulles Toll Road. This follows on from its assistance to the mandated lead arrangers in the $1.2 billion financing of the Cintra/Macquarie Infrastructure Group's joint purchase of a concession for the Chicago Skyway. The firm also represented the same clients in the bond refinancing for the deal in August 2005. Commentators noted the group's well-maintained relationships with foreign banks keen to invest in the sector.

**The Lawyers:** **Dan Mathews** (see p.118) played a lead role on the firm's Chicago Skyway representations. *"Flexible and commercially oriented,"* interviewees warmed to his *"patient and thoughtful"* solutions-driven approach and *"effective negotiation skills."* Mathews is also appearing on behalf of a consortium consisting of Transurban and DEPFA BANK negotiating for the proposed purchase of Pocahontas Parkway, a toll road in Virginia.

**Clients/Work Highlights:** As well as the Pocahontas Parkway deal, the firm's work in Virginia includes working with senior debt underwriters for the Macquarie Infrastructure Group/John Laing and Autostrade bid for the acquisition of the Dulles Toll Road. Lead arrangers NordLB and DEPFA BANK also employed the firm on the proposed financing of the Okanagan Lake Bridge, a PPP project sponsored

by the Ministry of Transportation of British Columbia, Canada. Other clients include BSCH; BayernLB; BBVA; Calyon; HSH Nordbank; NordLB and Transurban.

## Band 2

## Dennis, Corry, Porter & Smith LLP

**The Firm:** The defense of motor carriers and assistance on truck insurance issues have been the focus of this Atlanta firm for two decades. Accordingly, its members are much in demand for a wide range of automotive advisory and trial needs, particularly regarding the federal regulations applicable to motor carriers. The team also advises on claims for cargo loss and damage, including claims involving air, motor, ocean and railroad carriers.

**The Lawyers:** Interviewees referred to **Clay Porter** as one of the leading lawyers for motor carrier defense, advising on personal injury trials and truck casualty litigation. He serves as general outside counsel to leading transportation and logistics group Schneider National and its related companies.

## DeOrchis Hillenbrand & Wiener LLP

**The Firm:** Although by no means the largest firm in the table, DeOrchis occupies a strong position as a result of its experience of intermodal issues. Alongside its aviation, maritime and railroad work, attorneys here advise on both the defense of and subrogation of cargo claims for surface transportation. This is in addition to its capabilities in cargo security compliance, bills of lading and service contracts.

**The Lawyers:** Managing partner **Hyman Hillenbrand** has developed a well-respected practice for both railroad and motor carrier defense, with the emphasis slightly on the latter. His wide range of expertise allows him to advise on the relationship between transportation modes. One interviewee summarized the thoughts of several: *"He is like a walking encyclopedia, with tons of experience relating to the ins and outs and intricacies of transportation law."* His detail-oriented analysis led others to suggest that *"he may know more about truckers' tariffs than the truckers do!"*

**Clients/Work Highlights:** The team defended two lawsuits (in Houston and Denver) on behalf of Palletized Trucking, one of which concerned the defendant's ability to limit its liability for damages. It also won a case in the Third District Court of Appeal in Florida on behalf of a motor carrier insurer, determining issues of coverage in motor cargo policies.

## Hogan & Hartson LLP

See firm details p.568

**The Firm:** Truck transportation within the USA is a key element of this firm's road transportation practice. The team focuses on the transportation of hazardous materials, often involving national security issues that place greater limitations on clients. It advises on the transportation of vehicles themselves, especially from Mexico and Canada, and counsels on

homeland security concerns in relation to container shipments. In the aftermath of Hurricane Katrina, the firm has been working with the trucking industry and its engine manufacturers, striving to ensure that proper fuel is available to keep the new engines and vehicles that they have purchased in operation, and to ensure that no hidden costs are passed on. Attorneys also appear on a large number of motor vehicle safety matters, for which the practice enjoys a good reputation among peers.

**The Lawyers:** **Patrick Raher** (see p.128) in Washington, DC assists primarily on homeland security issues, for example those relating to cargo containers and the transportation of hazardous materials. With a background in emissions and safety advice, he is highly regarded by leading contemporaries for his *"significant abilities and talent."* He also advises on truck safety standards.

## McGuireWoods LLP

**The Firm:** The group aims to bring together parties interested in road and transport infrastructure matters, including work with local governments and sophisticated contractors. Historically, products liability has formed a major strand in this transportation group's workload; however the corporate practice has grown in importance, attracting finance and M&A-related work. The majority of the firm's work is located in the Virginia area, one of the most active US markets for road projects at present, with the rest coming from international work. In this latter area, its continuing assistance on a toll road in Bulgaria has also provided work on a gas pipeline matter.

**The Lawyers:** **John Cogbill** structures master transport agreements between prospective developers and local governments and agencies from his Richmond base. He prepared the master contract for the Star Solutions 1-81 scheme – the widening of Route 81 through Virginia, restricted to tolled truck traffic. He is also involved in regional transportation advisory matters looking at possible improvements and how to fund them.

**Clients/Work Highlights:** The firm negotiated on the structuring of a transaction for the construction of a new interchange on Route 64, incorporating a major shopping center and office complex. It is also advising Clark Construction on the Dulles Toll Road extension and continues to work with Shirley Contracting Company on the HOT lanes project.

## Thompson Hine LLP

See firm details p.1651

**The Firm:** This team advises motor carriers, intermediaries and shippers on broker and freight forwarder contracts and claims for loss, damage or delay. It also advises clients on safety and licensing matters from its DC base. This includes counsel on compliance with hazardous materials regulations, where the firm has advised on rulemaking proceedings before regulatory bodies. It further advises on antitrust immunity for motor carrier rate bureaus, and its attorneys have participated on the committee that created a motor carrier through bill of lading for NAFTA freight shipments.

**The Lawyers:** Nick DiMichael (see p.96) assists a wide range of clients on their motor carrier issues, including contracts negotiation, the development of effective service arrangements and regulatory matters involving hazardous materials. As well as roads work, he also counsels on rail and maritime matters, and acts as general counsel to the National Industrial Transportation League.

**Clients/Work Highlights:** The group's workload included involvement in a rulemaking before the Federal Motor Carrier Safety Administration to change the hours of service requirements for over-the-road truck drivers. The group has also helped to develop model contracts for use in the trucking industry. Clients include ALSTOM; Basell USA; Cargill; DuPont; Fortune Brands; GE; Hasbro; Holcim; Mittal Steel; National Industrial Transportation League; Otter Tail Power Company and Pier 1 Imports.

**Other Notable Practitioners**

The majority of **Wesley Chused**'s practice at Looney & Grossman LLP comprises truck and road transportation assistance to trucking companies and insurers, primarily in New England. He defends cargo loss and damage matters, as well as some personal injury liability cases. He successfully represented a household goods van line in a cargo case concerning the determination of a sufficient claim under new federal regulations aimed at broadening consumer protection.

# TRANSPORTATION

# SHIPPING (NEW YORK)

**OVERVIEW:** Consolidation within the sector has continued apace, as steamship lines and insurance companies buy up or align with their contemporaries. Furthermore, several major casualty cases reached conclusions and there were fewer large, new cases. Consequently, many firms working within the maritime field have engaged in work beyond their traditional admiralty advice. The activity of private equity groups investing in the sector, and the growing attraction of companies going public, have ensured a steady flow of transactional matters. Moreover, intermediaries can now go direct to shippers and offer long-term contracts, which may take business away from the steamship carriers. The result is an industry where international corporate and finance advice is as much a factor as litigation or arbitration in charter party and pollution matters.

| Transportation: Shipping (New York) Leading Firms |
|---|
| **1** FREEHILL HOGAN & MAHAR LLP |
| HEALY & BAILLIE LLP |
| HOLLAND & KNIGHT LLP |
| **2** BURKE & PARSONS |
| HILL RIVKINS & HAYDEN LLP |
| SEWARD & KISSEL LLP |
| **3** CARTER LEDYARD & MILBURN |
| DEORCHIS & PARTNERS LLP |
| GILMARTIN, POSTER & SHAFTO |
| NICOLETTI HORNIG CAMPISE |
| NOURSE & BOWLES LLP |
| WATSON, FARLEY & WILLIAMS |
| **4** BADIAK WILL & RUDDY |
| CICHANOWICZ, CALLAN, KEANE |
| CLARK, ATCHESON & REISERT |
| CRAVATH, SWAINE & MOORE LLP |
| DONOVAN PARRY MCDERMOTT & RADZIK |
| KENNEDY LILLIS SCHMIDT & ENGLISH |
| THACHER PROFFITT & WOOD LLP |

## Band 1

## Freehill Hogan & Mahar LLP

**The Firm:** Chief among this impressive and dynamic firm's successes in 2005 was a major victory in the 'DG Harmony' explosion and fire litigation on behalf of the vessel owners and their hull and P&I insurers. The case found that shipper PPG Industries was liable for the explosion and fire that destroyed the vessel and its cargo. Its leading experience in the criminalization of maritime casualties in cases such as the 'Bow Mariner' makes the firm an immediate option to assist in similar matters, such as its work in the Staten Island ferry crash. Its leading position in the market is cemented by the ethics and integrity of its "*intelligent, hard-working and dedicated players.*" Interviewees repeatedly underlined their moderated approach and balanced negotiation, with clients highlighting the team's "*foresight to cut through matters to get to solutions.*" The firm provides regular advice on oily water separator (OWS) cases and on the drafting of a number of shipping companies' electronic bill of lading agreements. It provides "*excellent quality, thoroughness and speed*" to clients concerning the US requirement that non-tank vessels have a qualified individual on board, in the event of an oil spill incident in US waters. In a similar vein, it has advised on new FDA regulations requiring the tracking of the origins of food cargoes. The caseload here stretches internationally to encompass major casualties in Taiwan, Oman and the Gulf of Mexico.

**The Lawyers:** Peter Gutowski (see p.104) acted on the 'DG Harmony' litigation for the ship's owners and insurers. An "*energetic, hands-on guy*" capable of handling large cases simultaneously, this thorough and experienced practitioner is at the forefront of a well-balanced team. Clients said he "*can usefully build the confidence of a shipowner, cutting through all the mist and targeting what's needed.*" He has undertaken numerous cases seeking security for clients' claims via Rule B attachments, a security device available under US law only in maritime cases. Wayne Meehan's (see p.120) steep rise in profile has continued. Clients respect this "*incredibly talented, clear-thinking ship collision lawyer,*" who approaches cases with "*a high level of energy*" and the talent to "*rapidly grasp the important issues and what's needed.*" As well as advising the New York City Department of Transportation on substantial criminal and civil matters relating to the 2003 crash of the ferry 'Andrew J Barberi', he also represented the owner of the product tanker 'Tradewind Sunrise' following an explosion of the vessel in Trinidad that resulted in four deaths. Managing partner **Bill Juska** (see p.110) impresses with his appearance on cargo defense and charter party dispute cases. His "*pleasing character is linked to an enormous depth of experience*" and the ability to read circumstances well, such that one interviewee believed: "*You can introduce him to anyone under the sun and he will respond effectively.*" **Michael Fernandez** (see p.99) has made a strong impression on the market through his representations of crew members in two major OWS cases over the past year, both of which included US Coast Guard investigations and related criminal prosecutions. Clients commended his regular dialog and methodology, with one saying: "*I make sure that he understands the mechanics in a claim, and he makes sure that I understand the legal implications!*" A vessel owner assigned **Don Murnane** (see p.122) to an onboard investigation in Oman concerning a serious shipboard burn case. The Kings Point graduate illustrates the firm's success in attracting attorneys with significant, non-legal maritime expertise.

**Clients/Work Highlights:** The firm is engaged on a major casualty on behalf of the owners and insurers of a double-hulled tank barge carrying 120,000 barrels of black oil that ran over a submerged offshore oil platform off the coast of Texas. In the wake of the severe disruption caused by Hurricanes Katrina and Rita, the firm is also advising numerous

## Transportation:
## Shipping Litigation (New York)
### Leading Individuals

**1** GUTOWSKI Peter *Freehill Hogan & Mahar*
HOOPER Chester *Holland & Knight LLP*
KIMBALL John *Healy & Baillie LLP*

**2** BURKE JR Raymond *Burke & Parsons*
HAYDEN Raymond *Hill Rivkins & Hayden*
HEARD Keith *Burke & Parsons*
MEEHAN Wayne *Freehill Hogan & Mahar*
NOURSE David *Nourse & Bowles LLP*

**3** BURRELL Lizabeth *Levy Phillips & Konigsberg*
COHEN Michael *Nicoletti Hornig*
DEORCHIS Vincent *DeOrchis & Partners*
GREENBAUM Jack *Healy & Baillie LLP*
HONAN III William *Holland & Knight LLP*
JUSKA William *Freehill Hogan & Mahar LLP*
KEANE Paul *Cichanowicz, Callan, Keane*
KENNEDY Donald *Carter Ledyard*
LAMBERT LeRoy *Healy & Baillie LLP*
PARÉ Jay *Nourse & Bowles LLP*
PRUZINSKY Anthony *Hill Rivkins & Hayden*
STARER Brian *Holland & Knight LLP*

**4** CLARK Peter *Clark, Atcheson & Reisert*
ENGLISH Craig *Kennedy Lillis Schmidt*
FERNANDEZ Michael *Freehill Hogan & Mahar*
FRANCE II William *Healy & Baillie LLP*
GINOS Geoffrey *Nicoletti Hornig Campise*
MURNANE Don *Freehill Hogan & Mahar LLP*
RADZIK Edward *Donovan Parry McDermott*
SHIRLEY James *Holland & Knight LLP*
SWEENEY III James *Nicoletti Hornig Campise*
WOODS John *Thacher Proffitt & Wood LLP*

## Transportation:
## Shipping Finance (New York)
### Leading Individuals

**1** HENGEN Nancy *Holland & Knight LLP*
RUTKOWSKI Lawrence *Seward & Kissel LLP*
WOLFE Gary *Seward & Kissel LLP*

**2** CHANG Leo *Watson, Farley & Williams*
POSTER Robert *Gilmartin, Poster & Shafto*
TENEV Jovi *Holland & Knight LLP*
WHALEN Thomas *Carter Ledyard & Milburn*

shipowning and terminal operator clients on their rights and liabilities.

## Healy & Baillie LLP

See firm details p.1533

**The Firm:** This traditional marine firm is perennially consulted by a clientele that comprises shipowning groups and P&I clubs. A leading competitor in terms of resources and structure alone, its traditionally defense and transactional work now also includes corporate and nonmaritime work. One example of this is its increased involvement in capital markets transactions, tracking the activity of a changing market. The industrious and well-regarded group occupies an established seat in the New York marine market, where its largest office is located.

**The Lawyers:** Interviewees regard **John Kimball** (see p.113) as the team's *"premier talent."* Opponents admit: *"If anybody has succeeded in playing things close to his chest, it's him – he is extremely smart and you can't figure out where he is going!"* Yet, in the same breath, they comment that he is always willing to sit down and rationalize a case. His low-key, composed manner led the team defending the 'Kariba' on the 'Tricolor' case. **Jack Greenbaum's** (see p.103) similarly understated approach is said to *"just focus on the key issues in a case."* A litigator with an *"insightful intellect,"* he engenders much respect among peers, who claim that they can *"always walk away from cases with him feeling clean."* **LeRoy Lambert** (see p.114) continues to impress market observers with his commercial sense and *"understanding of the client's needs and desires,"* as well as the ability to reach a solution within these parameters without necessarily resorting to contentious action. He was lead counsel for the prevailing party on the 'Aqua Stoli' case, an important decision concerning the use of Rule B attachments, whereby assets can be seized other than the vessel that gave rise to a claim – provided it is an asset of the debtor. **William France** (see p.100) maintains a fine reputation based upon his maritime design and naval architecture expertise.

**Clients/Work Highlights:** The group successfully represented Marathon Ashland Petroleum in a major lawsuit against Equili Company concerning the termination of two long-term bareboat charters. It also represented Columbus Line in achieving the settlement of a major litigation arising out of the derailment of a train owned and operated by BNSF Railway.

## Holland & Knight LLP

See firm details p.1534

**The Firm:** The sizable New York office of this national firm concentrates on significant casualty and related issues, in preference to more commonplace matters. For example, its successful representation of the owners of the 'Tricolor' in the large, long-running case in federal court found that its client was without fault, even though the ship was moving at the time. It is the only firm in *Chambers'* top band with a combined finance and disputes expertise that the market recognizes in equal measure. Its overall size enables a greater degree of specialization. Its *"iconic"* Haight, Gardner, Poor & Havens legacy lingers, in the opinion of many commentators, as a result of a perceived movement away from its traditional maritime background. However, other observers counter that it has blazed a trail in targeting finance and corporate-led elements of major maritime issues. Furthermore, its *"tremendous experience"* across the whole sector is undisputed, as are its considerable, partner-led resources in maritime and its leading related practice areas.

**The Lawyers:** Business law partner **Nancy Hengen** (see p.106) maintains her leading position for finance-related maritime work at the firm, where competitors praise her *"smart and accomplished"* representations. Typical advice includes assistance to a US Jones Act NYSE-listed shipowner in a $155 million revolving credit line and several secured loans. She also represented a shipowner in restructuring the Marshall Islands aspects of several tanker joint ventures. **Jovi Tenev's** (see p.138) practice covers aviation as well as high-level maritime work. He assisted Citibank on a number of large syndicated financings, primarily in the offshore sector, and also advises Nordea on its activities in the specialized reefer sector. M&A and complex tax issues form a key part of his practice, and he assists US and foreign shipowning clients in negotiating substantial shipbuilding contracts across the globe. **Chet Hooper** (see p.108) leads the firm's disputes caseload. A well-respected maritime authority, his *"thorough and innovative"* adversarial manner and *"tireless hard work"* is brought to bear not only in an active cargo practice, but also in the drafting of the new UNCI-TRAL transport convention. An *"able and straightforward litigator who does not get distracted by tangents and will cooperate to bring a matter to a conclusion,"* he represented the owners of the 'Tricolor'. **Bill Honan's** (see p.107) greatest reputation lies in charter party disputes and arbitrations. He represented a Norwegian vessel owner in an arbitration concerning their future, long-term continued use. Senior partner **Brian Starer's** (see p.136) *"zealous advocacy for his clients"* continues to be applied through his lead counsel to the Kingdom of Spain. He is advising this client on its efforts to recover damages as a result of the oil spillage from the motor vessel 'Prestige' that caused billons of dollars' worth of damage. A major part of **James Shirley's** (see p.134) practice concerns vessel casualty, with a particular emphasis on assistance to salvors, although he is not limited to this area. Interviewees affirmed that his *"laid-back and effective"* style *"will do the job quickly and courteously."* He is representing ExxonMobil in a US Coast Guard investigation and hearings arising out of a petroleum barge explosion in Chicago that resulted in deaths and pollution damage.

**Clients/Work Highlights:** Public Service Enterprise Group (PSEG) employed the firm to provide an opinion and recover damages after the 'Athos I' tanker struck a submerged object in the Delaware River, which led in part to the temporary shut-down of two reactors at its Salem nuclear power plant. The firm was also retained by Lafarge North America for an opinion on a class action regarding Barge 4827 (the construction vessel that was ripped from its moorings during Hurricane Katrina), as to whether it was responsible for breaking the levee. Other clients include Expedo Ship Management (Canada); ExxonMobil; Kingdom of Spain; Skuld P&I Club and Standard Club.

## Band 2

### Burke & Parsons

**The Firm:** Casualty and defense work remain the key areas for this acclaimed firm, such as its victory on appeal in the 'MSC Carla' case for Hyundai Mipo Dockyard, the shipyard that built the vessel. The appeal ruled that Korean rather than US law should have applied to the dispute and that, as a result, the claims were time-barred. As well as these core areas, the firm is also advising on an increasing proportion of finance-related matters. It has counseled on a number of attachments of funds to obtain security for claims in foreign proceedings. This broadening of its expertise extends into the IPO field. The team is assisting the Overseas Shipholding Group (OSG) in both its IPO for double-hulled tankers, and also in bareboat, time charters and other contracts relating to a new deal for Kvaerner Philadelphia Shipyard. The firm also continues to assist on several major OWS investigations.

**The Lawyers:** Interviewees report that **Raymond Burke** "*continues to enjoy a well-deserved reputation as an excellent attorney.*" He retains his high profile for casualty work, although he also appears on charter party arbitrations. He appeared on the 'MSC Carla' matter and has advised OSG on transactional matters. **Keith Heard**'s regular portfolio includes casualty work, charter party disputes and advice on the attachment of funds in the banking system. It was a commonly held view among interviewees that this talented performer is "*an excellent analyst, able and acute thinker and quick on the uptake,*" utilizing a style that penetrates to the heart of the matter.

**Clients/Work Highlights:** The firm continues to advise the bareboat charterer on the South African grounding of the 'Sealand Express' and has represented some of the cargo interests in the long-running 'Tricolor' case. It also acted, with others, for the purchaser in the acquisition of bulk carrier operator Navios, and advised three lenders on ongoing financing for the McAllister Towing fleet for the acquisition of new equipment.

### Hill Rivkins & Hayden LLP

**The Firm:** This sizable team does not specifically target financing; instead, it is best recognized by market observers as the go-to firm for cargo-related disputes work, frequently appearing on the underwriters' side. With many major industry clients consolidating and merging, this focus on increasingly valuable cargo issues has continued to stand the firm in good stead. It also carries out charter party work on behalf of trading companies.

**The Lawyers:** **Raymond Hayden** led on behalf of the cargo of luxury cars aboard the 'Tricolor' in that long-running case. He is also acting for the defendants in litigation arising out of the 2001 sinking of the P36 oil platform, at that time the world's largest oil production platform. Much of his activity is sourced from areas outside New York, including the Channel Islands and Japan. Sources praised his broad knowledge and ability to react quickly when required. **Anthony Pruzinsky** is an able litigator,

who impresses many observers with his assured handling of major matters, such as his role as lead cargo lawyer in the 'DG Harmony' case.

**Clients/Work Highlights:** The firm has undertaken considerable work on the 'Prestige' litigation in conjunction with other firms, representing the American Bureau of Shipping. It also represented the cargo interest in a state Supreme Court matter concerning a warehouse fire in premises owned by the Port Authority of New York and New Jersey.

### Seward & Kissel LLP

See firm details p.1553

**The Firm:** The firm has been the quickest and most successful in responding to the marked boost in equity transactions within the maritime sector, according to interviewees, despite being one of the smaller firms in *Chambers*' tables. Such deals have increased in both size and sophistication, requiring a greater depth of knowledge and experience that this "*strong and practical*" team is able to provide – over half its shipping activity in 2005 was devoted to this area. It appeared as issuer's counsel on a large number of IPOs for shipping and transportation clients, many of whom have been foreign-based issuers accessing the US capital markets. The firm is also a regular presence in maritime transactions that involve substantial elements of US and international taxation. For example, it advised on the US tax, financing and commercial aspects of the formation of an $80 million private equity fund investing in shipping opportunities between major Dutch and US offshore shipping equity fund groups and a Kuwaiti investor group.

**The Lawyers:** **Larry Rutkowski**'s (see p.131) practice encompasses transactions with a strong banking aspect. This much-praised attorney also practices structured finance work. **Gary Wolfe**'s (see p.143) "*incredible industry perspective*" and "*pragmatic and patient*" manner assist the smooth running of transactions involving first-time issuers in offerings.

**Clients/Work Highlights:** The team represented bank syndicates in the $350 million financing for the construction of ten tankers for the US Jones Act trade at Kvaerner Philadelphia Shipyard. A major Norwegian operator hired the firm to advise on the tax aspects of the formation of a $750 million joint venture to construct three LNG vessels. It additionally represented Export Finance Insurance Corporation (EFIC) of Australia and the Australian branch of ABN AMRO on the mortgage foreclosure proceedings involving 'Spirit Of Ontario 1', a 775-passenger high-speed catamaran ferry that operated between Rochester and Toronto. Other clients include Aries Maritime Transport; Diana Shipping; DryShips; DVB Bank; Genco Shipping & Trading; Sealift and Top Tankers.

## Band 3

### Carter Ledyard & Milburn LLP

See firm details p.1523

**The Firm:** This varied and experienced New York stalwart advises clients on many maritime and related public and corporate finance issues, as well as securities and arbitration. Antitrust too features prominently, with the firm's continued involvement on the Stolt-Nielsen restructuring. Indeed, the mainstay of the firm lies in nontraditional maritime matters such as passenger ferry restructuring cases, including its representation to New York Cruise Lines. It is also active on behalf of clients trading forward freight agreements.

**The Lawyers:** The firm's most prominent finance attorney is **Thomas Whalen**. He assisted in the restructurings of New York Cruise Lines and Sea Containers. Arbitration and disputes expert **Don Kennedy** frequently represents foreign interests. He worked with the Government of Guyana on the privatization of its mining interests, as well as on litigation arising out of its existing shipping agreements, and the negotiation of new agreements for shipping and transportation.

**Clients/Work Highlights:** The group has a notable foreign client caseload. It acted on litigation for Norwegian Hull Club, representing its interests in the USA, and also conducted an arbitration for a Polish steamship company.

### DeOrchis & Partners LLP

**The Firm:** A smaller group with a strong following, this traditional maritime firm deals chiefly in insurance and cargo defense. A key aspect of its work is its ability to advise not only on maritime matters, but also on the next stages of transportation, whether it be rail, road or air, through its intermodal and freight-forwarding expertise. Its office network covering Massachusetts, Connecticut and Florida is a distinct advantage in this regard.

**The Lawyers:** **Vincent DeOrchis**' (see p.95) highly experienced and "*low-key but tenacious approach*" won plaudits from peers. He worked with the MSC Group on the 'MSC Carla' case.

### Gilmartin, Poster & Shafto

**The Firm:** This boutique is well equipped to advise on transactions arising out of the shipping arena. It counsels major national and multinational corporations, as well as successful entrepreneurs, on long-term charters and bank lending. It regularly acts as special counsel on admiralty and general maritime matters and possesses noted expertise in the more multinational aspects of shipping. Attorneys are able to advise on matters arising under Liberian, Panamanian and Marshall Islands law.

**The Lawyers:** Ship finance is **Robert Poster**'s (see p.127) primary stock in trade. *Chambers*' research indicates that he is the New York ship finance market's go-to attorney when other leading shipping contemporaries find themselves in conflict situations. His "*constructive approach and commercial, knowledgeable advice*" drew consistent praise. He continues to represent the Official Committee of Creditors as maritime counsel in the bankruptcy of Navigator Gas.

**Clients/Work Highlights:** The team acted on the acquisition and financing of eight new building container ships for European/South American joint ventures. It also advised on the reorganization of maritime shipping companies from Brazil, Chile and Uruguay.

### Nicoletti Hornig Campise and Sweeney

**The Firm:** Strong cargo recovery work and international insurance coverage assistance are areas of particular strength at this firm. Attorneys are also well versed in PI cases and those concerning injuries and death to seamen and other maritime casualties. As a consequence of this focus, the firm maintains an alert awareness of the overlap between specifically marine and insurance considerations, and related regulations, treaties and conventions, both in the USA and internationally.

**The Lawyers:** The forthright and assertive **Michael Marks Cohen** impressed interviewees with his arbitration expertise and *"knowledge of the law and history of charter party forms, including how they developed."* He represented charterer Morgan Stanley and its cargo underwriters against the owners of the 'Vicky' in a New York arbitration seeking reimbursement of salvage and other expenses incurred when the vessel became stranded on the wreck of the 'Tricolor' in the English Channel. **Geoffrey Ginos** is especially known for environmental concerns and for his skillful handling of disputes. **James Sweeney** specializes in cargo recovery work for underwriters. His practical approach – *"always looking for an amicable resolution, while still being an advocate for his clients' position"* – was frequently recommended. He represented cargo underwriters in their continuing insurance coverage lawsuit against pharmaceutical group Merck.

**Clients/Work Highlights:** The team acted for the underwriters in a large insurance coverage lawsuit that questioned whether BP had timely and properly declared 28 of its offshore oil construction projects under the insurance policies covering those undertakings. The group assists charterer Petróleos Mexicanos and its cargo insurer in a long-running New York arbitration of cargo contamination claims against the owners of the 'Tbilisi.' Other clients include American International; Arcelor; Celanese; Chubb Group; Fireman's Fund Insurance; Lufthansa; MacSteel International; Morgan Stanley; Reinauer Transportation and St. Paul Travelers.

### Nourse & Bowles LLP

**The Firm:** This relatively small but vastly experienced firm acts mainly for the defense in national and especially international admiralty disputes. It further counsels in charter party and casualty claims. **The Lawyers:** **David Nourse** sets high standards for the group with his *"calm, gentlemanly and knowledgeable approach."* Observers comments that the firm's founding partner excels at *"organizing a case*

*and presenting it in a way that is effective."* He appeared opposite the Norwegian owners of two vessels in an arbitration concerning their future long-term continued use. **Jay Paré** is a similarly well-seasoned performer who is endorsed for his often firm opinions and aggressive stance. As well as his maritime expertise, he is also able to counsel on related insurance and international trade concerns.

### Watson, Farley & Williams
See firm details p.1564

**The Firm:** This finance specialist is an increasingly active presence in the maritime sector, although not from traditional perspectives. It is heavily involved in the LNG sector and uses its international network, such as its offices in Hamburg, London and Singapore, to complement its shipping advice and capabilities. It also runs a leasing group in New York, led by two tax partners, that provides the team with greater depth. As well as its ability to assist clients in their IPOs, commentators also recognize the firm's knowledgeable work on the chartering of vessels, ship mortgages and related filings.

**The Lawyers:** **Leo Chang** (see p.91) represents shipowners and financial institutions providing credit for the maritime industry. He advised lenders, including RBS, on a series of shipping company IPOs. Interviewees describe his style as relatively reserved but highly commercial and effective. Chang is the highest-profile name in a team that boasts several talented attorneys with growing caseloads.

**Clients/Work Highlights:** The firm acted for RBS and for Bank of America in loan facilities to Eagle Bulk Shipping and TBS International respectively. It appeared as maritime counsel to Nordea in the refinancing of General Maritime and advised a syndicate of Scandinavian banks on their financing of five US-flag car carriers. Its broader caseload has also included assistance to DVB Bank in the sale and leaseback of 1,300 reefer containers to a South American shipping company.

### Band 4

### Badiak Will & Ruddy

**The Firm:** This compact and primarily defense firm assists insurance companies on both cargo loss and PI matters.

**The Lawyers:** Name partner Roman Badiak is a key contact for insurance-related work, while his colleague James Paul Krauzlis is an experienced plaintiff's cargo recovery attorney.

### Cichanowicz, Callan, Keane, Vengrow & Textor, LLP

**The Firm:** Attorneys at this firm advise intermediaries such as container operators and other clients nationwide and internationally. For example, it drafted and negotiated a major alliance agreement between multiple carriers to cover worldwide trade to and from the USA. Similarly, the group has represented numerous container and bulk carrier members, on behalf of P&I clubs, in filing petitions

to remit or mitigate US Customs penalties regarding the seizure of drugs.

**The Lawyers:** **Paul Keane** represented an international marine transport group following a major fire on board a container ship in an arbitration with the vessel's time charterer in New York. He acts for leading container operators in disputes and undertakes corporate leasing and contractual work on behalf of stevedores and some railroads.

**Clients/Work Highlights:** The firm is working on a claim by a major steamship carrier against the Government of Iraq, a major French bank and a Swiss surveying firm in regard to cargoes fraudulently misdelivered under the Oil For Food Program. It is also representing a major container operator in an investigation and plea agreement concerning government charges relating to OWS and MARPOL Convention violations.

### Clark, Atcheson & Reisert

**The Firm:** Technical and engineering issues are the forte of this leading maritime boutique. A coterie of naval architects and engineers counsels on engineering cases and engine performance issues for a clientele of P&I clubs and vessel owners. Partly as a result of a reduction in the number of new, major oil spill or weather-related cases in 2005, the firm also appears on charter party disputes and arbitrations and some collision cases.

**The Lawyers:** **Peter Clark** advises on engineering matters, as well as charter party matters and arbitrations.

**Clients/Work Highlights:** As well as the firm's representations to a group of non vessel-owning common carriers (NVOCCs) on the 'MSC Carla' case, it continues to represent a multitude of similar clients on the 'DG Harmony' matter, assisting on motions to recover their indemnity from PPG Industries.

### Cravath, Swaine & Moore LLP
See firm details p.1527

**The Firm:** A new entrant to the table and far from the traditional admiralty firm, this strong team of corporate and finance partners are trained as generalists, but with a focus on shipping within transportation. It is especially prominent on corporate finance and M&A matters for issuer and other clients, exemplified by its representation of OSG in its $1.3 billion purchase of Stelmar Shipping, creating the second largest tanker company in the world. In addition, its *"excellent quality of service"* is applied on behalf of a large number of investment banks operating in the shipping sector and has assisted in IPOs and sophisticated public financings in this area, often representing underwriters.

**The Lawyers:** **John Gaffney** works mainly for issuers, dealing with their corporate finance and M&A concerns and filings. **Andy Pitts** assists underwriters in shipping transactions.

**Clients/Work Highlights:** The firm represented the underwriters, led by Citigroup and Merrill Lynch, on the IPO and NYSE listing of international container ship company Seaspan. It also counseled newly formed Marshall Islands group Double Hull Tankers on its $192 million IPO. Other clients include CSFB and Morgan Stanley.

## Donovan Parry McDermott & Radzik

**The Firm:** Primarily a litigation-focused group, it also conducts deal work, such as advising on contracts of carriage and representing banks on financings for major ship-purchasing programs. Its disputes portfolio incorporates wake damage incidents and collision cases, as well as the provision of opinions on insurance coverage and cargo hull and machinery P&I policies. Maritime arbitrations of charter party disputes and cargo loss and damage claims also feature regularly.

**The Lawyers:** Eponymous partner **Edward Radzik** has advised cargo interests on the 'MSC Carla' case, petitioning for a panel re-hearing, and worked with charterers and cargo owners on the 'San Sebastian' matter. Additionally, he successfully acted on behalf of underwriters for PepsiCo in the Second Circuit Court of Appeals, reversing an earlier dismissal relating to contamination during transit of a shipment of Pepsi liquid concentrate.

**Clients/Work Highlights:** The firm assisted barge owners and a marine construction company in an incident involving a Manhattan sightseeing vessel that lost its rudder while on the Harlem River. It also defended hull and machinery underwriters in a lawsuit, commenced by a gas pipeline company, against claims arising from an anchor drag incident affecting a power transmission cable in Long Island Sound.

## Kennedy Lillis Schmidt & English

**The Firm:** In addition to defense and cargo matters, this group's primary clients remain New York marine insurers, which it assists in liability and policy interpretation.

**The Lawyers:** The *"experienced, knowledgeable, absolutely ethical and honest"* **Craig English** is the firm's leading light. Sources appreciate his good advice to clients and tendency not to overwork a case. The City of New York engaged him to defend several crew members aboard the Staten Island ferry 'Andrew J Barberi' who were sued personally for the deaths and numerous PI claims following the crash of the ferry in October 2003.

**Clients/Work Highlights:** The team acted for one of the parties in a $40 million insurance coverage dispute and also assisted on a $6 million cargo claim against a major carrier. It was also involved in the 'DG Harmony' and 'MSC Carla' major cargo cases.

## Thacher Proffitt & Wood LLP

See firm details p.1560

**The Firm:** Although not a traditional admiralty mainstay, this firm continues to make its presence felt counseling marine insurance underwriters and other clients on general finance, refinancings and leasebacks. It is also increasingly engaged in arbitrations, in preference to litigation, and provides opinions relating to environmental and political risk matters. For example, the firm represented a pool of major insurance groups insuring against liabilities arising from oil and hazardous substance spills in the navigable waters of the USA. It is also representing a group of US and English war risk insurers in an action to recover unpaid premiums on crude oil shipments from Iran.

**The Lawyers:** **John Woods** (see p.143) continues to predominantly represent the US and London insurance markets in maritime matters, notably acting for hull and liability insurers, major marine insurers and pools or syndicates.

**Clients/Work Highlights:** Recently the firm was involved in a significant matter that allowed disputes relating to cargo damage to be heard in foreign arbitration forums, even if the carriage of the goods was to and from the USA. It also provided an amicus brief on the Norfolk Southern Railway v Kirby Engineering case, extending the breach of limitations in bills of lading to the inland carriage of goods that have a sea component to their transportation. The decision has limited the liability of carriers in subsequent litigation. The group also advises marinas and shipyards concerning sail and motor yachts.

## Other Notable Practitioners

**Lizabeth Burrell** at Levy, Phillips & Konigsberg LLP is widely recognized as the industry's leading appellate maritime specialist, having carved out a prominent niche in this crossover area. The current first vice president of the Maritime Law Society, she is praised for her oral advocacy and especially for her *"beautiful, cogent and clear"* writing skills on all aspects of maritime law, for which companies and other attorneys frequently flock to her. She also advises on ocean policy matters, consulting on charter and broker issues and some PI work.

---

# TRANSPORTATION

# SHIPPING (OUTSIDE NEW YORK)

**OVERVIEW:** Without doubt the after-effects of Hurricanes Katrina and Rita in 2005 will be felt by oil and shipping clients for many years, not only in the Gulf region but nationwide. Clients have sought advice on contracts and financing for rebuilding and redrilling transactions from admiralty practices already dealing with cargo and collision defense, pollution concerns and the demands of fisheries. Several firms outside of New York have underlined their leading expertise in maritime subsectors, while others have begun to emerge as pan-regional experts in the changing market.

## Band 1

## Akerman Senterfitt

See firm details p.657

**The Firm:** This traditional charter party practice also undertakes a degree of transactional work for tug companies and shipping lines. The firm's state-based work focuses mainly on Florida matters, although it also maintains a profile in the DC market and referral relationships with other firms nationwide.

**The Lawyers:** Tampa-based **Anthony Cuva** (see p.94) advises domestic and foreign engine manufacturers working within the maritime sector on negligent repair and products liability claims in southern Florida and elsewhere. He continues to advise on Jones Act defense cases, representing domestic insurers, as well as PI cases. Recently, he acted on behalf of a tug company in a complicated maritime lien case concerning the arrangement of ship financing for the addition of a new tractor tug to its fleet, and persuaded the court that this would be an unnecessary extension of US maritime lien law.

**Clients/Work Highlights:** The team continues to counsel Marine Towing of Tampa on collisions, allisions and license issues. It appears in administrative hearings concerning charges brought by the US Coast Guard against mariners' licenses, and deals with a smaller number of cargo disputes.

## Blank Rome LLP

See firm details p.1747

**The Firm:** This well-known government relations firm has fostered a DC-based maritime group that advises on legislative and regulatory work for a nationwide and global clientele. Such work includes environmental compliance and citizenship issues, enabling foreign companies to act in the USA. It also regularly works with P&I clubs and hull underwriters, as well as some claimants, on disputes relating to collisions and environmental concerns, cargo loss and PI. Interviewees spoke of the firm's talented lawyers with broad experience, who *"cover a wide variety of subjects that might come up – whether it's finance, environment or government contracts – while staying closely attuned to developments."*

**The Lawyers:** Jon Waldron obtained a Bureau of Customs and Border Protection ruling, allowing a major US chemical company to offload chemicals at a US port without violating the Jones Act and thus providing substantial cost savings. His colleague James Ellis advises on transactional and finance matters, working with the Aker Philadelphia Shipyard on its large tanker-building program. The team also comprises several former US Coast Guard officers, as well as names drawn from leading administrative positions and environmental experts.

**Clients/Work Highlights:** The firm represented one of the largest US shipyards in its $850 million deal for the construction and operation of ten Jones Act product tankers. It resolved a case on behalf of a major cruise line concerning government attempts to revoke corporate probation for alleged environmental violations. It also negotiated an emergency contract with the Military Sealift Command for three ships to provide six months' berthing and transportation to assist in Hurricane Katrina relief activities. Clients include Carnival Cruise Lines, Dow Chemical and Heerema Marine Contractors.

## DeOrchis Hillenbrand & Wiener LLP

**The Firm:** A multifaceted group with a leading reputation for its assistance in intermodal matters, the firm incorporates both rail and road carriage advice into an overall practice with a strong foundation in maritime transport. A substantial insurance department also assists in related maritime matters.

**The Lawyers:** Hyman Hillenbrand is the managing partner of the firm's Florida office and remains a key name for the firm, acting on matters spread across maritime, rail and road, although it is in the latter areas where his focus currently lies. Also in Miami, Vincent O'Brien advises on marine and other litigated matters such as boat accidents in marinas, cruise ship work for passengers and assistance to insurance groups, especially in pleasure boats and marina matters. David Farrell is a part of the DeOrchis & Partners office in Boston, where he conducts the firm's maritime work (frequently insur-

ance defense) in New England.

**Clients/Work Highlights:** The firm emerged victorious in the Third District Court of Appeal in Florida on behalf of an insurer of a motor carrier, determining the issues of coverage in motor cargo policies. It conducts a substantial amount of work for Icelandic steamship company Eimskip, successfully suing for unpaid freight on 32 containers of frozen herring shipped from Boston to Estonia. Attorneys at the firm also brought a successful resolution before the Maritime Law Association to support a Congressional amendment eliminating maritime liens on federal fishing permits.

## Fowler White Burnett PA (FowlerWhite)

**The Firm:** This full-service firm, operating out of Miami and Fort Lauderdale, is historically associated with litigation in the maritime sector. Its advice to international P&I clubs remains a core part of its practice, although the group also works with nondomestic groups and insurers. In addition, and in response to market demands, the firm is increasingly active in issues relating to the cruise industry, defending crew and passenger injury claims. It further assists on environmental claims involving vessels, such as groundings in protected coral areas, and runs complementary aviation and motor carrier departments.

**The Lawyers:** Litigator Charles De Leo focuses not only on matters arising out of Florida, but also Central and South America and the Caribbean.

**Clients/Work Highlights:** The team appeared on a major PI matter relating to a Polish seafarer, which included arbitration elements. Several international P&I clubs also employed the firm on a serious environmental claim in South America, and on the detention of a vessel in the Dominican Republic, which involved a serious allegation by a stowaway. It also acted on a major charter party arbitration for a cruise line. Clients include British Marine Managers; Compañía SudAmericana de Vapores (CSAV); CP Ships; Gard; Maersk; Seaboard Ship Management; SeaDream Yacht Club; Steamship Mutual Underwriting Association and Trimar Defense Services.

## Garvey Schubert Barer

**The Firm:** This broad-based admiralty practice provides long-term assistance to Alaska's fishing industry, among its several areas of practice. It advises both purchasers and sellers regularly on the acquisition of shipping companies, tug and barge operators and factory trawler fleets, while also negotiating charter party and other contracts. Furthermore, it has a fully fledged ship-financing practice that incorporates ship mortgage assistance, equipment finance and the securitization of freight receivables on behalf of domestic and foreign financial institutions. In common with several contemporaries, it also works with clients on transactions in which US-flag vessels, planning to operate in the US fisheries or coastwise trade, are purchased by foreign or loaned funds. These clients require cross-border income tax advice among other considerations.

**The Lawyers:** Interviewees commend **Bruce King** for his financing expertise on "*anything from fishing boat contracts to cruise ships, mega yachts to complicated business deals.*" Peers praised his intelligence and excellent writing skills.

**Clients/Work Highlights:** The firm acts as general US counsel to China Ocean Shipping and its US subsidiaries, work which includes significant securitization financings involving global assets.

## Holland & Knight LLP

See firm details p.1534

**The Firm:** A powerhouse that maintains a strong presence in transportation and especially in maritime matters, even outside of New York. Although some interviewees drew attention to the firm's closure of several offices in its sizable national network, it remains one of the few major maritime players with a demonstrable multistate capacity. It is buoyed by a large number of talented attorneys "*with tremendous experience in various maritime areas.*" Its offices adjacent to the Gulf of Mexico act as a correspondent for the P&I clubs in the region, representing the clubs themselves and also shipowners. On the West Coast, the maritime group works closely with specialists in aviation, logistics and ground transportation. It acts on natural resource damage cases and works with non-vessel operating common carriers (NVOCCs) on all aspects of their business, including regulatory hurdles on the carriage of goods by sea, assigning bills of lading and service contracts. It also uses its environmental knowledge to advise on regulatory concerns relating to air pollution from ships.

**The Lawyers:** Jacksonville executive partner George Gabel has worked with a prominent international multimodal transport group investing in the region. Matthew Vafidis assists in maritime and transportation logistics matters from San Francisco, where he heads up the firm's West Coast litigation practice group. Also in San Francisco, transactional attorney Audrey Sung works closely with the firm's maritime experts in New York.

**Clients/Work Highlights:** The firm represented Standard P&I Club in successful resistance to a claim for loss of cargo and other expenses following the loss of the vessel 'MAR' when she sank after leaving Gibraltar from St Martin under tow. It was retained by a construction company to advise on the maritime aspects of a wrongful death, arising out of the placement of a construction barge. Clients include Charles Taylor P&I Management, Standard Steamship Owners' Protection & Indemnity Association and Steamship Mutual Underwriting Association.

## Keesal Young & Logan PC

**The Firm:** This West Coast firm's offices in California, Alaska and Hong Kong continue to cement its leading reputation for always dependable advice in the Pacific region. It enjoys equally strong recognition in eastern states and Washington, DC for its "*personal service, prompt and professional*" advice on behalf of international P&I clubs and other clients.

Interviewees commend the firm's regulatory counsel on the interstate and international transportation of goods and passengers. Attorneys also represent several major international oil and transportation groups on their varied oil pollution matters.

**The Lawyers:** Skip Keesal is a leading trial lawyer with an active civil as well as maritime practice.

**Clients/Work Highlights:** The firm's prominent position in the West Coast market is indicated by an extensive client portfolio that includes American President Lines; BHP Transport; Blue Star Line; Chevron Shipping; Cunard Line; Fairmont Shipping; International Tanker Indemnity Association; Maersk; Mobil Shipping; North of England P&I Association; UK P&I Club; West of England Shipowners Mutual Assurance Association and Yang Ming Marine Transport.

## Lau, Lane, Pieper, Conley & McCreadie

**The Firm:** This maritime boutique is praised for the uniform high quality of its team members and their advice on casualty and insurance-related matters and a variety of niche areas. Interviewees endorsed this fine firm for its focus on Jones Act cases, pollution, PI and wrongful death claims.

**The Lawyers:** Interviewees singled out David McCreadie as the firm's most senior practitioner for maritime matters. His colleague, maritime expert Nathaniel Pieper, now acts primarily as a mediator.

## Moseley Prichard Parrish Knight & Jones

**The Firm:** The main P&I club correspondent firm in Jacksonville, this boutique is widely recommended for its capable work in and around the port region, as well as further south. In addition to maritime work, the firm assists on other, related transportation matters, including those incorporating insurance aspects.

**The Lawyers:** Trial lawyer James Moseley Jr advises on maritime and complex civil litigation, with an accent on insurance and PI matters. James Moseley Sr is a key figure in the Florida marketplace and one of the main contacts for the P&I clubs in the region.

## Phelps Dunbar LLP

See firm details p.997

**The Firm:** The group provides a broad spectrum of admiralty capabilities across the whole Gulf of Mexico, from Texas to Florida. Its assistance on pollution matters has increased markedly since the departure of Hurricanes Katrina and Rita in 2005, which caused a significant number of ongoing problems for oil and shipping clients. The firm is advising on their attempts to bring facilities and oil production back up to speed via a series of contracts and deals. Regulatory, labor and employment advice complement these main areas of focus. However, the team has also established a niche advising on gaming matters with maritime aspects, such as floating casi-

nos. For example, it appeared as maritime counsel in a $3 billion merger of two public companies and in a related credit facility. Away from the Gulf region, the firm has cultivated a national and international profile.

**The Lawyers:** Based in the firm's maritime center of New Orleans, George Gilly is advising on contracts for oil field service companies and other oil clients. He also conducts litigation, as do the majority of the firm's members. Clients spoke of a team with pragmatic and down-to-earth members.

**Clients/Work Highlights:** The team has advised on a ship fire case in which its client allegedly negligently installed a fuel override system on the vessel that led to the fire. It further worked on a construction company's risk insurance dispute claim, and has assisted in a number of M&A and credit facilities for deals in the maritime domain. In addition, the firm was involved as maritime counsel in a claim for wreck removal arising from the negligent sinking of a floating casino.

## Sher & Blackwell

**The Firm:** This predominantly DC-based firm represents groups of container carriers on antitrust and regulatory matters and is best known in the market for its traditional Federal Maritime Commission (FMC) focus. Attorneys counseled on the renewal of the maritime subsidy program for carriers, and are also active in maritime security issues before Congress and the Department of Homeland Security. The team also deals with insurance companies on legislative or policy issues, making good use of the firm's government relations experience. The group's clients are drawn from across America.

**The Lawyers:** Founding partner Stanley Sher frequently appears on behalf of international ocean carriers, as well as for other clients, before federal agencies, the courts and Congress. He advises on their negotiations, financing transactions and civil disputes.

**Clients/Work Highlights:** The team represented a leading trade association of global liner shipping companies before the US Supreme Court in a case with significant implications for cargo liability claims arising from international intermodal transportation. It acted for an NYSE-listed company in issuing government-guaranteed ship-financing obligations for the construction of new oil-drilling platforms, and also on the sale of two other oil-drilling rigs. The firm advised the lender in the $140 million construction financing for two coastwise eligible vehicle and passenger ferries to be built in the US for employment in Hawaii.

## Troutman Sanders LLP

**The Firm:** This DC-based group focuses on trade and transportation, targeting intermodal issues. It runs a heavy caseload of trial and appellate litigation concerning federal safety regulation of maritime activity and marine environmental regulation. Attor-

neys often assist shipowners in cases between states and local authorities on the one hand, and the federal government on the other, which sometimes involves international treaty obligations. Such work regularly leads to ancillary matters such as import/export control and customs. Much of the activity involves the West Coast of the USA. In addition, the group has picked up substantial work in the marine terminal area, as well as cruise ship work relating to passenger claims against cruise lines. It rounds off a broad and substantial portfolio by providing legislative advice to P&I clubs for their activities in the USA.

**The Lawyers:** Jonathan Benner heads the firm's transportation section. Sources endorsed his "*considerable success*" in assisting national and international shipowners before federal courts and agencies on matters affecting vessel safety and marine environmental protection, as well as on antitrust considerations. He also advises clients subject to investigations or complaints before the Federal Maritime Commission (FMC) and Surface Transportation Board (STB).

**Clients/Work Highlights:** The firm is conducting a major piece of litigation in federal court involving constitutional challenges to Massachusetts' regulation of tank vessels, on behalf of a wide range of maritime industry trade organizations. It provides counseling on citizenship restrictions to the ownership of vessels that engage in point-to-point work along the US coast, and is representing a major container operator in appellate work regarding rates and practices in the Pacific trades.

## Winston & Strawn LLP

See firm details p.886

**The Firm:** In common with many of its contemporaries in the capital, a large proportion of this firm's maritime endeavors involves governmental issues. However, it also undertakes a proportion of more traditional maritime work, including advice on pollution.

**The Lawyers:** Charlie Papavizas (see p.124) worked with Liberty Global Logistics on a joint venture with a Swedish group to bring a new car carrier into the US-flag fleet, including advice on federal government and corporate aspects. The well-respected partner is regularly involved on similar administrative and legislative matters.

**Clients/Work Highlights:** In 2005, the team completed a long-term dispute between client US Ship Management and Maersk relating to the operation of 15 US-flag vessels, comprising multiple federal actions and maritime arbitrations. It advised French Groupe Bourbon on the defense of its financing of ten offshore supply vessels constructed in the US and acted for OMI on the implementation of its environmental compliance program. Clients include Energía Costa Azul; Great Lakes Dredge & Dock; Liberty Global Logistics; Liberty Shipping Group and Sempra LNG.

# WEALTH MANAGEMENT

**OVERVIEW:** In this edition of *Chambers USA*, we have considered private client work across the USA, an immense market that is home to both large firms with offices nationwide and boutiques, whose smaller size belies their great influence. While New York, of course, remains the hub of private client activity, there are centers of significant wealth across the country. For this reason, the National Wealth Management table also features those powerful regional players that have not – and need not – establish a national reach.

It is also worth noting that the vast majority of the work undertaken by these practitioners is for US clients; while most firms undertake a portion of international work, only a few have committed resources to building a truly international practice. Due to the confidential nature of the work carried out in the wealth management sector, in most cases we are unable to give details of work or clients.

| Wealth Management |
| --- |
| Leading Firms |
| **1** HOLLAND & KNIGHT LLP |
| KATTEN MUCHIN ROSENMAN LLP |
| MCDERMOTT WILL & EMERY |
| MCGUIREWOODS LLP |
| MILBANK, TWEED, HADLEY & MCCLOY LLP |
| WEIL, GOTSHAL & MANGES LLP |
| **2** BLANK ROME LLP |
| CADWALADER, WICKERSHAM & TAFT LLP |
| CARTER LEDYARD & MILBURN LLP |
| DAY, BERRY & HOWARD LLP |
| DEBEVOISE & PLIMPTON LLP |
| GREENBERG TRAURIG LLP |
| KIRKLAND & ELLIS LLP |
| MOSES & SINGER LLP |
| PAUL, WEISS |
| PILLSBURY WINTHROP SHAW PITTMAN LLP |
| PROSKAUER ROSE LLP |
| SCHIFF HARDIN LLP |
| SCHULTE ROTH & ZABEL LLP |
| SHEARMAN & STERLING LLP |
| SIDLEY AUSTIN LLP |
| SONNENSCHEIN NATH & ROSENTHAL LLP |
| SULLIVAN & CROMWELL LLP |
| WHITE & CASE LLP |
| WILLKIE FARR & GALLAGHER LLP |
| WITHERS BERGMAN |

## Band 1

### Holland & Knight LLP
See firm details p.1534

**The Firm:** This firm has *"a large national practice with very good depth,"* reported interviewees. The private wealth services group is spread across several offices, with particular strength in Florida. It handles the full scope of trusts and estates work, including estate, gift and generation-skipping transfer tax planning, international taxation and business succession planning. The group is also well equipped to advise on the establishment of charitable organizations and private foundations. Attorneys can also call on the support of the dispute resolution group, which has extensive experience of probate and IRS litigation as well as federal estate and gift tax disputes.

**The Lawyers:** **Ed Koren** (see p.113) is a *"real star,"* who practices principally out of the firm's Florida offices. A *"fabulous technician,"* he has an impressive

reputation that extends beyond the state. *"He has built his career to a point where if he's involved, you know it's a significant matter,"* said sources.

### Katten Muchin Rosenman LLP
See firm details p.874

**The Firm:** The firm's private client group consists of around 45 lawyers and is spread across its US offices, with the strongest concentration of attorneys in New York. The group handles a broad range of trusts and estates work, including the administration of trusts, estate planning and litigation. It also advises clients in contested tax matters and surrogate's court proceedings.

**The Lawyers:** The *"remarkable"* **Josh Rubenstein** (see p.131) is *"one of the top practitioners in New York State."* He is *"smart, in control and knows the law well."* Clients also appreciate that *"he is interactive, not reactive, comes up with innovations and new ideas,"* and delivers advice with an *"absolutely phenomenal response time."* His practice focuses on trusts and estate work for international clients and litigation.

### McDermott Will & Emery
See firm details p.878

**The Firm:** *"This superb firm is really committed to the sector,"* agree interviewees. The private client department consists of around 40 lawyers, with the bulk of the work handled out of the firm's well-regarded Chicago office. A leading firm for trusts and estates matters, the group won particular praise for being *"thorough, responsive and able to team well with clients and other advisers."* *"They have the breadth, depth and brightest people,"* enthused one interviewee. The firm handles the full range of trusts and estates work for clients, who include individuals and families, foundations, closely held businesses and investment management entities both in the USA and overseas.

**The Lawyers:** The *"outstanding"* **Carol Harrington** (see p.105) works out of the firm's Chicago office. A *"smart, practical and hard-working attorney,"* she is considered by many interviewees to be *"the nation's expert on generation-skipping transfer tax."* Her practice also covers trust and estate administration and contested trust and tax matters. Another well-regarded partner is **Judith McCue** (see p.119), incumbent president of the American College of Trust and Estate Counsel (ACTEC) and a respected player in the Chicago market. Her practice focuses on estate planning and trust and estate administration for US residents. Head of the private client

department, **George Heisler** (see p.106) is *"an excellent leader who has developed strong and enduring relationships with his clients,"* reported sources. Also based in Chicago, he is *"up there with the best on a national basis,"* with particular expertise in all areas of taxation, including fiduciary income taxation. He is admired as a *"direct, thorough and thoughtful"* attorney.

### McGuireWoods LLP
**The Firm:** The firm's private wealth group consists of around 30 lawyers spread across four offices, with the largest concentration in Virginia. This broad-reaching practice focuses on representing high net worth individuals as well as trustees who manage assets for beneficiaries. Work includes developing tax-efficient wealth transfer plans, creating charitable foundations and advising on succession issues. The bulk of the firm's private wealth clients are based in the USA.

**The Lawyers:** Based in Virginia, the *"thoughtful"* **Dennis Belcher** is a *"wonderful lawyer who thinks outside the box but understands the law."* His practice covers estate and trust administration, planning, and fiduciary litigation. In the same office, another respected partner is **Louis Mezzullo**. His practice has a niche specialty in retirement benefits. Over in the firm's McLean office, **Ronald Aucutt** commands an impressive reputation for his work with the IRS. An *"articulate attorney who is up to date on the legislative scene,"* he specializes in representing clients who are either in dispute with the IRS or who require advance guidance. He is also known as an effective speaker on this subject.

### Milbank, Tweed, Hadley & McCloy LLP
**The Firm:** This *"highly respected and efficient"* team works out of New York. Comprising around 12 attorneys, the group works closely with other departments in the firm to offer a comprehensive range of trusts and estates services. It has advised some of America's most famous families on the formation of family trust companies, including the Getty, Rockefeller and Dart families. It also serves as counsel to institutions such as Neuberger Berman Trust Company, the Rockefeller Trust Company, Chase Domestic and International Private Bank, and JPMorgan. The group represented the children of J Seward Johnson in contesting his will, and successfully defended against the contest of the will of Charles Shipman Payson.

## Wealth Management
### Leading Individuals

#### Senior Statesman
KURZ Theodore *Debevoise & Plimpton LLP*

★ MCCAFFREY Carlyn *Weil, Gotshal & Manges*

**[1]** BLATTMACHR Jonathan *Milbank, Tweed*

CHRISTENSEN III Henry *Sullivan & Cromwell*

HARRINGTON Carol *McDermott Will & Emery*

KALIK Mildred *Simpson Thacher & Bartlett*

ROTHSCHILD Gideon *Moses & Singer LLP*

RUBENSTEIN Joshua *Katten Muchin*

WHITAKER G Warren *Day, Berry & Howard*

ZABEL William *Schulte Roth & Zabel LLP*

**[2]** ADAMS Roy *Sonnenschein Nath & Rosenthal*

BELCHER Dennis *McGuireWoods LLP*

DETZEL Lauren *Dean, Mead, Egerton*

HALPERIN Alan *Paul, Weiss*

HARRISON Ellen *Pillsbury*

KOREN Ed *Holland & Knight LLP*

LAWRENCE III Robert *Cadwalader*

PERRY JR C Jones *Shearman & Sterling*

PLAINE Lloyd *Sutherland Asbill*

RUTHERFURD JR Winthrop *White & Case*

SCHNEIDER Pam *Gadsden Schneider*

SLADE Georgiana *Milbank, Tweed*

**[3]** AUCUTT Ronald *McGuireWoods LLP*

BRODY Lawrence *Bryan Cave LLP*

DADAKIS John *Schiff Hardin LLP*

DUBREUIL Francis *Wilson Sonsini*

ELIAS John *Greenberg Traurig LLP*

FRIMMER Paul *Irell & Manella LLP*

GORTZ Albert *Proskauer Rose LLP*

HANDLER David *Kirkland & Ellis LLP*

HARRISON Louis *Harrison & Held*

HEISLER Quentin *McDermott Will & Emery*

KAVOUKJIAN Michael *White & Case LLP*

MCCABE David *Willkie Farr & Gallagher LLP*

MCCALL Jennifer *Pillsbury*

MCCUE Judith *McDermott Will & Emery*

MCCUE III Howard *Mayer, Brown, Rowe & Maw*

MEZZULLO Louis *McGuireWoods LLP*

MOORE Malcolm *Davis Wright Tremaine LLP*

REDD Charles *Sonnenschein Nath & Rosenthal*

REGAN Andrew *Shearman & Sterling LLP*

RICHMAN Lawrence *Neal, Gerber & Eisenberg*

ROSS Bruce *Luce, Forward*

SUGARMAN Myron *Cooley Godward LLP*

TESCHER Donald *Tescher Gutter Chaves*

VALENTE Peter *Blank Rome LLP*

WAGNER Theodore *Carter Ledyard & Milburn*

WALLACE John *King & Spalding LLP*

WAXENBERG Jay *Proskauer Rose LLP*

WELCH Lyman *Sidley Austin LLP*

**The Lawyers:** A key figure in the practice, **Jonathan Blattmachr** is *"brilliant but controversial,"* reported sources. Known for his *"aggressive strategies"* and willingness to *"push the envelope hard,"* he is one of the most high-profile attorneys in this area. He has a reputation for using his *"top-level intellect"* to create *"dynamic and imaginative"* strategies for clients. The *"thorough and dedicated"* **Georgiana Slade** is *"extremely bright and well versed in the work that she is doing."* Clients appreciate that she *"really understands her clients' objectives and family dynamics before making any recommendations."* She is also respected for her expertise on generation-skipping transfer tax.

## Weil, Gotshal & Manges LLP
See firm details p.1565

**The Firm:** This relatively small but highly regarded group is based in the firm's New York office. It advises clients on the creation of family trusts, income tax planning, annual gift tax exclusion, overseas trust creation and generation-skipping transfer tax. The team also has experience in litigation and handles contested tax and probate proceedings.

**The Lawyers:** To many in the market, **Carlyn McCaffrey** (see p.118) is *"quite simply number one."* She secures her place in the star category due to the exceptional level of feedback from across the USA. *"She's one of the finest lawyers in the universe,"* raved one peer. The bulk of her practice is focused on estate and tax planning, with a niche specialty in generation-skipping transfer tax. She also has a reputation for international expertise. *"A truly outstanding lawyer,"* she is *"a brilliant estate planner who comes up with innovative techniques but always exercises discretion."* Across the table, she is considered *"very thoughtful and an engaging person."*

## Band 2

### Blank Rome LLP
See firm details p.1747

**The Firm:** This respected practice handles sophisticated estate planning for high net worth individuals in the USA and abroad. The group fields attorneys from its offices in Philadelphia, Florida and Pennsylvania, but the bulk of the work is handled from New York. The practice has a heavy emphasis on tax, advising clients in issues such as generation-skipping transfer tax, charitable giving and post-mortem tax planning. Attorneys here are also well versed in contested probates and accounting procedures, IRS audits and litigation in surrogate's courts.

**The Lawyers:** Clients say there is *"no one better"* than **Peter Valente** (see p.139). The chair of the firm's private client group, his practice covers estate planning, trusts administration and trusts and estates litigation. He also has experience of proceedings before New York's surrogate's courts. He is *"very ethical, very protective of clients"* and admired for being *"accurate, up to date and knowledgeable."* Clients also appreciate his straightforward approach and the fact that *"he's not a yes-man."*

### Cadwalader, Wickersham & Taft LLP
See firm details p.1522

**The Firm:** This small, New York-based private client department handles trusts and estates work for clients in the USA and overseas. The team works closely with the firm's banking, corporate and litigation lawyers, and advises clients on personal, financial, charitable and tax planning. As well as counseling individual private clients, the department also represents institutions such as banks, museums, nonprofit entities and charities.

**The Lawyers:** Chairman of the private client department, **Robert Lawrence** (see p.114) has developed a truly international practice. An *"extremely impressive"* attorney, his client roster includes high net worth individuals from Europe, the Middle East and Latin America. He also enjoys good working relations with tax, and trusts and estates specialists in a number of jurisdictions. His practice covers structuring and planning for inbound and outbound investments, succession planning and the transfer of wealth to families, trusts and charities.

### Carter Ledyard & Milburn LLP
See firm details p.1523

**The Firm:** This New York-based trusts and estates group continues to maintain an impressive reputation established by the legendary Richard Covey. Boasting *"a number of talented lawyers,"* the group offers tax, trust and estate planning for national and international clients. It has a specialization in taxation and regularly acts as special counsel in tax audits and litigation. It also offers particular expertise in art law and advises clients on the income and estate tax implications of lifetime gifts, establishing art foundations and the role of art collections in estate planning.

**The Lawyers:** Head of the group **Theodore Wagner** concentrates his practice on advising US individuals and families. Respected for his experience and expertise in trusts and estates work, he handles a broad and diverse range of matters for clients, who include entrepreneurs, entertainment and art industry figures and business executives.

### Day, Berry & Howard LLP
See firm details p.386

**The Firm:** This firm's individual clients department consists of around 30 lawyers, focused primarily in Boston, Hartford and New York. The practice encompasses the whole range of trusts and estates matters including estate and tax planning, business succession planning, charitable giving, guardianships and trust and estate-related litigation. The group has developed expertise in a number of niche specialties, such as same-sex couples and special needs and disabilities planning. The firm represents high net worth US individuals and families, as well as a significant number of major international clients.

**The Lawyers:** **Warren Whitaker** (see p.142) is *"one of the leading lights in international estate planning."* A *"very thorough"* attorney, he *"looks at the whole picture to see what fits best for clients."* He is particularly praised for his client service. *"He doesn't only answer the questions that are asked, he asks questions until he really understands the clients' objectives,"* reported sources.

## Debevoise & Plimpton LLP

See firm details p.1529

**The Firm:** This New York-based trusts and estates group works closely with the firm's tax, corporate and litigation teams to enable it to provide a comprehensive range of services. These include designing and administering trusts and representing clients in administrative and judicial proceedings. One particular area of focus is estate planning for the principals of private equity funds and hedge fund managers. As well as acting for individuals, the firm also advises corporate fiduciaries, private foundations, public charities and major universities.

**The Lawyers:** **Ted Kurz** is a "*careful, thoughtful attorney with his feet on the ground.*" Clients appreciate his experience and "*deep insight.*" According to one source: "*He's a go-to guy when we need some really wise advice.*"

## Greenberg Traurig LLP

See firm details p.664

**The Firm:** The "*excellent*" trusts and estates department has attorneys in most of the firm's offices, with a particularly strong reputation in Florida. The practice covers the full range of trusts and estates work, including all aspects of wealth transfer and estate planning. It is experienced in IRS administrative and court proceedings and coordinates with the litigation department to handle contested matters. The arrival of John Elias from Gibbons has seen the firm increase its focus on private client work in the New York and New Jersey areas. As well as acting for individual clients, the firm has represented institutions such as Bessemer Trust, JPMorgan, Northern Trust and Mellon Financial.

**The Lawyers:** Based in the firm's New Jersey office, **John Elias** (see p.98) is "*able to articulate technicalities to laymen in simple language and enable them to understand.*" His expertise includes estate and charitable planning, trust and estate administration and tax controversy work.

## Kirkland & Ellis LLP

See firm details p.875

**The Firm:** The trusts and estates group advises individuals and families on wealth preservation, transfer and management. The client roster here consists primarily of private investors, entrepreneurs, highly compensated business executives and wealthy families. The firm also counsels individual and corporate fiduciaries on trust and estate planning and administration, and assists both public and private charities. Litigation, such as will challenges, contested accountings and contested tax matters is also part of the portfolio here.

**The Lawyers:** **David Handler** (see p.105) focuses his practice on trust and estate planning and administration. Reflecting the firm's strong private equity practice, he also undertakes a significant amount of work for the principals of venture capital and LBO firms.

## Moses & Singer LLP

**The Firm:** As well as covering the traditional areas of estate administration, and drafting trusts and wills, this trusts and estates and wealth preservation group has expertise in wealth preservation strategies such as the use of children's or offshore trusts. The firm also represents clients in estate-related litigation and surrogate's court proceedings.

**The Lawyers:** Although he handles all aspects of estate planning, **Gideon Rothschild** is also "*one of the leading authorities on asset protection.*" Enjoying an enviable national reputation, he is a "*very smart, practical lawyer who knows what his clients want.*"

## Paul, Weiss, Rifkind, Wharton & Garrison LLP

See firm details p.1548

**The Firm:** This small but respected personal representation group handles the full range of trusts and estates work. Alongside its traditional roster of cases, the firm also advises on estate and gift tax audits and tax controversies. It has experience of handling contested surrogate's court proceedings such as will challenges and contested accounting procedures. Close working relations with the litigation department enable the group to handle estate and trust-related litigation.

**The Lawyers:** The "*unflappable*" **Alan Halperin** (see p.105) is "*a great listener who is very client-oriented.*" Building an impressive reputation in the market, he won praise for being "*very effective, responsive and accommodating.*" Clients also appreciated that he was "*sensitive to people and clearly had technical mastery over the subject matter.*"

## Pillsbury Winthrop Shaw Pittman LLP

See firm details p.1550

**The Firm:** The individual client services team offers an extensive range of services for individuals and families, including estate administration and planning, gift transfer and tax planning. The firm also handles litigation and contested probate proceedings.

**The Lawyers:** Based in DC, the "*terrific*" **Ellen Harrison** (see p.105) is "*a first-rate estate planning lawyer with a lot of experience in cross-border transactions,*" agreed sources. She is also known for her tax expertise. **Jennifer Jordan McCall** (see p.119) splits her practice between Silicon Valley and New York. She "*communicates and connects with clients and doesn't hide behind jargon.*" She has the ability to "*take a plan, augment it and help tailor it to the client in a collaborative manner.*" One satisfied client declared that she "*worked magic.*"

## Proskauer Rose LLP

See firm details p.1551

**The Firm:** This personal planning practice is concentrated in New York and Florida, with a smaller presence in California. The teams work closely together, offering a similar range of expertise and often providing valuable continuity and local expertise for those New York clients who wish to retire to Florida. Accordingly, the client roster in Florida

includes a significant proportion of retirees and the work is tailored to reflect this, with the "*very sharp, boutique-style team*" there having particular expertise in advising on the tax implications of change of domicile and Florida residency. Both the New York and Florida offices handle trusts and estates litigation work.

**The Lawyers:** **Albert Gortz** (see p.103), "*the consummate professional,*" enjoys a strong reputation in South Florida. He is "*a man of integrity and a pleasure to work with,*" who "*keeps his clients' best interests at heart and has sound judgment when it comes to evaluating risk,*" reported clients. According to one: "*The work he does is personalized, tailored and implemented with clients in mind.*" **Jay Waxenberg** (see p.141) is "*a real people person who can adapt his style to fit his audience,*" who is also "*ahead of the crowd on technical ability.*" Based in New York, his practice covers the whole range of trusts and estates work. He also has experience of handling will contests and other trust-related litigation work.

## Schiff Hardin LLP

See firm details p.881

**The Firm:** Spread across the firm's Illinois, New York and Florida offices, this estate planning and administration group advises clients on wealth preservation, management and transfer. It is well equipped to advise on the full scope of regulations affecting high net worth individuals, including those covering income, gift and generation-skipping transfer tax, charitable giving, and business succession. The group also advises a number of corporate fiduciaries and has experience in corporate fiduciary litigation.

**The Lawyers:** **John Dadakis** (see p.94) represents high net worth individuals, acting as private general counsel to many Fortune 500 executives and business entrepreneurs. Based in New York, he handles a range of private wealth issues including asset protection, wealth transference and tax minimization.

## Schulte Roth & Zabel LLP

See firm details p.1552

**The Firm:** The individual client services practice of this New York firm is one of the most respected in the USA, thanks in large part to the presence of industry stalwart and founding partner William Zabel. The group offers a comprehensive range of trusts, estates and wealth preservation services to some of the country's best-known families and individuals. Its areas of expertise include estate and trust administration and planning, charitable giving, surrogate's court matters and matrimonial representation.

**The Lawyers:** One of the most established names in this area, **William Zabel** is a "*tremendous rainmaker,*" who continues to play an active role in his firm's private wealth practice. He has represented some of the most well-known names in America, including the Vanderbilt, Rockefeller and Chrysler families. His current client roster includes George Soros and hedge fund manager Michael Steinhardt. Unlike many of the attorneys in this field, Zabel also undertakes matrimonial work. He represented Jane

Beasley Welch in her high-profile divorce from General Electric CEO Jack Welch.

## Shearman & Sterling LLP
See firm details p.1554

**The Firm:** This relatively small but well-regarded group offers "*expertise delivered in a professional, friendly manner by lawyers who aren't verbose or impressed by themselves,*" reported sources. Close working relations with colleagues, who specialize in corporate, tax and real estate matters, enable the team to advise clients on an extensive range of personal and business issues.

**The Lawyers:** **Jones Perry** (see p.125) is "*extremely knowledgeable and understands all the issues.*" Clients appreciate that he "*is able to articulate solutions in understandable language and never wastes your time.*" He has significant expertise in the international arena and is "*respected in countries across the world.*" The "*outstanding*" **Andrew Regan** (see p.129) represents both domestic and international clients on estate planning and tax matters. His areas of expertise include offshore trusts and multijurisdictional estate planning.

## Sidley Austin LLP
See firm details p.883

**The Firm:** Working out of the firm's New York and Chicago offices, this group of "*highly regarded, expert lawyers*" has a particularly high profile in the Chicago market. The private client, trusts and estates group advises individuals and families as well as banks, charities and a range of other organizations. Trust and estate administration, tax and estate planning and charitable giving are all areas of expertise in this group. Attorneys also advise on trust and estate litigation and the New York office also has a particular niche specialty in art-related wealth.

**The Lawyers:** **Lyman Welch** (see p.141) in Chicago is "*thorough, thoughtful and creative*" said interviewees. A "*very bright and capable*" attorney, he is involved in drafting legislation proposals and is widely recognized as principal draftsman in both the Illinois Prudent Investor Act and the Illinois Total Return Trust Act.

## Sonnenschein Nath & Rosenthal LLP
See firm details p.884

**The Firm:** This firm's trusts and estates practice group is spread across the USA. The practice areas are roughly divided into four areas of specialization: estate planning, trusts and estates administration, trusts and estates-related litigation and public law. Clients include entrepreneurs, owners of closely held businesses, corporate executives, real estate investors, families and corporations such as charities.

**The Lawyers:** Senior chairman of the trusts and estates practice group, **Roy Adams** (see p.84) practices out of the firm's New York office. A "*nationally renowned attorney,*" his clients include wealthy families and individuals, public charities and private foundations. Over in St. Louis, **Charles Redd** (see p.128) wins praise for his "*integrity, disciplined approach and meticulous attention to detail.*" An

"*outstanding communicator,*" he is "*extremely smart and super to work with.*" His practice covers a broad range of trusts and estates matters as well as estate and trust-related litigation.

## Sullivan & Cromwell LLP
See firm details p.1558

**The Firm:** This firm's estates and personal clients group represents domestic and international clients in a range of matters including trust and planning and related litigation, charitable gifts and the establishment of family partnerships. It also advises clients on prenuptial/postnuptial agreements, personal wealth planning and the sale and purchase of high-value items such as artworks, aircraft and yachts. The group also advises many non-US families and individuals, working closely with overseas counsel to provide effective representation in clients' US affairs.

**The Lawyers:** A practitioner with a strong international focus, **Terry Christensen** (see p.92) is "*technically miles ahead.*" According to sources, he is "*urbane, highly intelligent, very charming and extremely wise.*"

## White & Case LLP
See firm details p.1566

**The Firm:** This "*high-quality team*" has developed an impressive practice advising individuals and their families as well as banks, charitable foundations, multinational corporations and their executives. Its workload features compensation and retirement planning, business counseling, fiduciary administration and related litigation. In a recent highlight, the team acted for the founder and controlling shareholder of a $1 billion closely held manufacturing company in developing an estate plan.

**The Lawyers:** **Winthrop Rutherfurd** (see p.131) is a "*people person who can explain complex legal matters to a client and have them understand.*" He is appreciated for his calming ability to deal with "*both critical legal issues and critical personal issues.*" **Michael Kavoukjian** (see p.112) is "*extremely thorough and creative.*" He is a "*proactive and bright lawyer who is good at anticipating possible problems and ensuring they don't arise.*" He won plaudits for his client-friendly service. "*I want him to shepherd my family through the generations,*" enthused one interviewee.

## Willkie Farr & Gallagher LLP
See firm details p.1567

**The Firm:** The firm's private clients group is concentrated in New York, where a significant number of its clientele consist of individuals from the financial services industry. It provides sophisticated estate planning advice to both US and international clients, including lifetime planning, healthcare planning and charitable giving. The estate administration practice encompasses both individuals and fiduciaries. The department also handles estate and trust litigation and contested matters in surrogate's courts.

**The Lawyers:** **David McCabe** (see p.118) is "*the man you would want on your side in trusts and estates litigation.*" He is "*a good decision-maker and a good*

counselor,*" who employs "*a very practical approach to dealing with families of substantial wealth and navigating the difficulties that those families can encounter.*" As well as handling traditional trusts and estates work, he represents clients in litigation in surrogate's courts and the Supreme Court of the State of New York.

## Withers Bergman

**The Firm:** Offering a unique, firmwide focus on private client work, Withers Bergman is building on its merger of 2002 to strengthen its presence in the US and international market. The firm offers expertise in trust, estate and income planning, administration and the structuring and managing of closely held enterprises. The firm also advises on the purchase, transfer and sale of property and items such as works of art, yachts and aircraft. As well as acting for individuals and families, it represents banks and trust companies on fiduciary matters and advises business organizations on estate planning for their principals. The firm has a strong international practice, with particular expertise on the tax and estate implications of UK-US relocation.

## Other Notable Practitioners

The "*terrific*" **Mildred Kalik** (see p.111) at Simpson Thacher & Bartlett LLP in New York is particularly well known for her expertise on tax issues. Head of the firm's personal planning department, she is a "*very bright, capable and well-regarded*" attorney with a national reputation. Based in Florida, **Lauren Detzel** (see p.96) is head of the wealth transfer and estate planning department at Dean, Mead, Egerton, Bloodworth, Capouano & Bozarth PA. She enjoys a strong local reputation for her tax expertise and her practice covers the entire gamut of trusts and estates work, including contested tax matters. **Pam Schneider**, founding partner of the Pennsylvania trusts and estates boutique Gadsden Schneider & Woodward LLP is "*a terrific all-around estate planning lawyer.*" "*Extremely bright and creative,*" she has particular expertise in generation-skipping transfer tax. **Lawrence Brody** in the St Louis office of Bryan Cave LLP is an "*experienced and well-qualified practitioner.*" Based in the Palo Alto office of Wilson Sonsini Goodrich & Rosati, **Frank Dubreuil** (see p.97) is "*terrific,*" agreed interviewees. His wealth management practice covers company founders, entrepreneurs and private equity investors. Dubreuil "*earns his stripes when dealing with technology;*" and his focus in this area reflects the firm's overall business practice. Los Angeles-based **Paul Frimmer** of Irell & Manella LLP drew endorsement from interviewees across the country. "*A highly talented lawyer,*" he has a niche specialty in the estate planning aspects of owning art collections. He is head of the firm's personal planning workgroup. "*I have tremendous respect for* **Lloyd Leva Plaine** (see p.126)," enthused one interviewee, echoing the sentiments of others. Based in the Washington, DC office at Sutherland Asbill & Brennan LLP, Plaine heads the individual tax planning practice group. She particularly focuses on estate and wealth transfer planning. **Lawrence Richman** (see p.129) of Neal, Gerber & Eisenberg LLP in Chicago has "*the ability to work with all parties in creating a plan that satisfies everyone's goals*." A "*thorough, meticulous and conscientious*" attorney, he is "*kind and generous with his time*." "*He made me feel like I was his most important client*," enthused one satisfied interviewee. **Louis Harrison** is the founding partner of the Chicago firm Harrison & Held. A "*well-rounded and respected practitioner*," he "*does big-firm work at a smaller firm*." He is also a highly regarded writer and speaker in the trusts and estates field. Based in the Chicago office of Mayer, Brown, Rowe & Maw LLP, the "*wonderful and smart*" **Scott McCue** (see p.119) has a particular focus on counseling

nonprofit organizations including public charities and community foundations. As well as handling the usual range of trusts and estates work, he also handles related litigation. At the Seattle office of Davis Wright Tremaine LLP, **Malcolm Moore** "*has wonderful judgment on when to try new things and when to stay on the safe side*" said sources. He focuses on trusts and estates work for wealthy clients in the Washington area and has served as an expert witness in cases across the USA. Based in the Atlanta office of King & Spalding LLP, **John Wallace** (see p.140) is respected for his wealth of experience in the trusts and estates sector. Admired for his "*extraordinary practice*," he is also a frequent speaker on the tax

aspects of estate planning. **Myron Sugarman** at the San Francisco office of Cooley Godward LLP commands a strong reputation. An "*exceptional practitioner*," his typical clients include technology entrepreneurs and venture capitalists. At Tescher Gutter Chaves Josepher Rubin Ruffin & Forman PA in Boca Raton, **Donald Tescher** is "*a true leader in estate planning*." He was praised for his "*integrity and knowledge*." **Bruce Ross** is among the ten trust and estate attorneys that Luce, Forward, Hamilton & Scripps LLP has snatched from Holland & Knight's Los Angeles office. He is particularly well regarded for his litigation and tax controversy work.

# National Leaders

## ABORN, Richard A
Cadwalader, Wickersham & Taft LLP, New York 212 504 6188
richard.aborn@cwt.com
*Recommended in Transportation*
**Practice Areas:** Focuses on leveraged lease, aircraft, vessel and other equipment and project financings. Primary aircraft clients have included Northwest Airlines, Delta Air Lines and JetBlue Airways. Also represented equity investors and lenders in aircraft financing transactions with major air carriers. Since 1984, has participated in aircraft financing transactions aggregating more than $20 billion. **Personal:** JD, Boston College (1969); BA Williams College (1965). Member, Boston College Industrial and Commercial Law Review, Order of the Coif. Chosen as a 'Recommended High Flyer' in Aviation Counsel's elite peer-group survey of the world's leading aviation law practitioners. Member, Association of the Bar of the City of New York and New York State Bar Association.

## ABRAMS, Lee N
Mayer, Brown, Rowe & Maw LLP, Chicago 312 782 0600
*Recommended in Antitrust, Sport*
*Please see Illinois for profile*

## ADAMS, Roy M
Sonnenschein Nath & Rosenthal LLP, New York 212 768 6726
rmadams@sonnenschein.com
*Recommended in Wealth Management*
**Practice Areas:** National and international practice in the areas of estate and tax planning, advising wealthy families, private foundations, public charities as well as individuals whose assets often include substantial business interests; renowned estate planning lecturer and prolific author; conducts professional education seminars at universities, banks and trust organizations nationwide and

hosts monthly telephone conferences and satellite broadcasts on sophisticated and practical planning techniques; frequent expert witness in high profile trusts and estates litigations.
**Prof. Memberships:** American College of Trusts and Estates Counsel; licensed to practice in New York and Illinois.
**Personal:** Northwestern University School of Law, LLM Taxation, Chicago-Kent School of Law, JD, University of Delaware, BA; Board Chair, Trusts and Estates Magazine; Professor Emeritus of Estate Planning and Taxation Northwestern University School of Law; listed in Best Lawyers in America and New York's Best Lawyers.

## ADDUCI II, V James
Adduci, Mastriani & Schaumberg LLP, Washington, DC 202 467 6300
adduci@adduci.com
*Recommended in International Trade*
**Practice Areas:** International trade regulation and intellectual property litigation.
**Prof. Memberships:** Federal Circuit Bar Association, DC Bar, ABA, Customs and International Trade Bar, AIPLA, ITCTLA, Washington International Trade Association, US Council for International Business.
**Career:** Participated in nearly 40 § 337 cases at the ITC. Counsels clients on trade policy issues. Served as legal counsel with the ITC from 1975 to 1979. In 1977, appointed by the US Trade Representative to the Multilateral Trade Negotiations (Tokyo Round) in Geneva.
**Publications:** 'Everybody Comes to the ITC', Legal Times.
**Personal:** JD John Marshall Law School.

## AKSEN, Gerald
Gerald Aksen - Sole Practitioner, New York 212 249 4499
*Recommended in Arbitration*

## ALBERTSON, Terry
Crowell & Moring LLP, Washington, DC
202 624 2635
talbertson@crowell.com
*Recommended in Government Contracts*
**Practice Areas:** Partner in Crowell & Moring's Government Contracts Group. Focuses on government procurement law, including contract cost accounting, pricing and termination issues. Has tried numerous important cases concerning defective pricing, Cost Accounting Standards, the allowability of costs, multiple award contracts, terminations, and more.
**Career:** Selected by Legal Times as a leading Washington government contracts lawyer; received Bronze Star for service in Vietnam War for service in US Army. Bachelor's Degree from Georgetown University, magna cum laude,1968; MA from Yale University, 1969; JD from Harvard Law School, cum laude, 1974.

## ALBRECHT, Thomas W
Sidley Austin LLP, Chicago
312 853 7213
talbrecht@sidley.com
*Recommended in Capital Markets*
**Practice Areas:** Partner in Chicago office of Sidley Austin LLP. Practice includes domestic and international securitizations and structured finance. Co-Head of firm's Securitization Practice Area. Member of the firm's Management and Executive Committees and Chair of firm's International Operations. Frequent lecturer at securitization industry conferences.
**Prof. Memberships:** Member, American Bar Association. Member, American College of Commercial Finance Lawyers.
**Publications:** Co-author, 'Corporate Loan Securitization: Selected Legal and Regulatory Issues' (Duke Journal of Comparative and International Law, Spring 1998).
**Personal:** University of Dayton, BA,

1975; University of Chicago Law School, JD, 1979. Admission: Illinois, 1979.

## ALEXANDER, Richard M
Arnold & Porter LLP, Washington, DC
202 942 5728
Richard.Alexander@aporter.com
*Recommended in Financial Services*
**Practice Areas:** Richard Alexander represents financial services companies and their corporate directors and officers, in a variety of regulatory, compliance, and governance matters. He has conducted many internal and other special investigations into possible accounting fraud, money laundering, legal, ethical and internal control violations, self-dealing and other wrongdoing on behalf of management and boards of directors. Since the passage of the Sarbanes-Oxley Act, he has handled a number of so-called 'whistleblower complaints'. Mr Alexander frequently represents financial services companies, as well as accountants, attorneys, and other professionals, in enforcement or investigative proceedings brought by federal or state regulatory agencies.
**Publications:** Trends in Data Security: Business Risk and Legal Exposure - appeared in the 2005-06 (10th Edition) issue of Global Banking and Financial Policy Review. Managing Crises by Conducting Internal Investigations - appeared in the September 2005 issue of Financier Worldwide's Managing Risk and Resolving Crisis Review. Recent Developments in Anti-Money Laundering Enforcement - appeared in the August 2005 issue of Euromoney. Recent Developments in US Anti-Money Laundering Initiatives Affecting Financial Institutions - appeared in 2004-05 issue of Network and Correspondent Banking Review, a Euromoney publication. 'Big Price for Lax Anti-Laundering' appeared in the October 22, 2004 issue of American Banker.

## ALEXANDER, Troy
White & Case LLP, New York
212 819 8200
*Recommended in Projects*
*Please see New York for profile*

## ALEXANDROV, Stanimir A
Sidley Austin LLP, Washington, DC
202 736 8115
salexandrov@sidley.com
*Recommended in International Arbitration*
**Practice Areas:** Focuses on international arbitration, in particular on investor-state disputes under investment treaties. Has represented both private-sector claimants and government respondents in international arbitration, and has advised private parties and governments in WTO disputes. Serves as a Member of the Panel of Arbitrators of the World Bank's International Centre for Settlement of Investment Disputes. Has provided expert testimony in international arbitration on the interpretation of investment treaties. Professorial lecturer of law at The George Washington University Law School teaching courses on dispute settlement and foreign investment.
**Prof. Memberships:** American Bar Association, American Society of International Law.
**Publications:** 'The "Baby Boom" of Treaty-Based Arbitrations and the Jurisdiction of ICSID Tribunals', 4 The Law And Practice Of International Courts And Tribunals 19 (2005); 'Breaches of Contract and Breaches of Treaty: The Jurisdiction of Treaty-Based Arbitration Tribunals to Decide Breach of Contract Claims', 5(4) Journal Of World Investment And Trade 555 (2004).
**Personal:** Served as Vice Minister of Foreign Affairs of Bulgaria and negotiated trade agreements and bilateral investment treaties. Holds Russian and US Law Degrees, including Doctor of Juridical Science. Admissions: New York and District of Columbia.

## ALI, Arif H
Fulbright & Jaworski L.L.P.,
Washington, DC 202 662 4547
aali@fulbright.com
*Recommended in International Arbitration*
**Practice Areas:** Cross-border dispute resolution through arbitration, ADR and litigation; international investment risk management; international war claims and reparations; private and public international law.
**Prof. Memberships:** International Bar Association (Committee D); American Bar Association; American Society of International International Law; International Law Association; International Arbitration Institute; Advisory Board, Institute of Transnational Arbitration; Houston International Arbitration Club; panel arbitrator for various arbitral insti-

tutions (AAA/ICDR, WIPO, CRCICA, HKIAC).
**Career:** Mr Ali is a Partner in the International Arbitration Group and an Adjunct Professor of Law at Georgetown University, where he teaches international commercial and investment arbitration. He has represented private and state parties in ICSID, ICC, LCIA, UNCITRAL, AAA (domestic and international) arbitrations involving thermal, nuclear and hydro power plants, oil and gas pipeline construction and concession-related matters, tourism projects, project finance and development agreements, patents and trademarks, and information technology, including under multilateral and bilateral investment treaties. He has also represented parties before inter-governmental tribunals, including the United States-Iran Claims Tribunal and the United Nations Compensation Commission. Before joining the firm, he held positions as a Section Chief at the United Nations Compensation Commission and Senior Legal Counsel at the WIPO Arbitration and Mediation Center.
**Publications:** 'Best Practices Series No.7: Best Practices in Drafting International Arbitration Clauses', UNITAR: Training and Building Programmes in Legal Aspects, Financial Management and Negotiations, December 2003; 'Risk Management in International Commercial Transactions: Arbitration and Alternative Dispute Resolution', International Quarterly, Vol 15, No 2, April 2003; 'A Cross-Comparison of Institutional Mediation Rules', American Arbitration Association Dispute Resolution Journal, Vol 57, No 2, May-July 2002; 'Disputas en Materia de Tecnologias de Informacion y Comunicaciones: Arbitraje y Mediacion Como Alternativas a los Litigios Judiciales, Derecho de la Alta Tecnologia', Vol No 147, November 2001 (Buenos Aires, Argentina).
**Personal:** JD, New York University School of Law (1990), recipient of the Vanderbilt Medal. BA, summa cum laude, Columbia University (1986). Member, Phi Beta Kappa. Working languages: English, Spanish, French, Hindi, Urdu and Bengali. Recipient of the Order of Bahrain (II).

## ALKALAY, Peter
McLaughlin & Stern LLP, New York
212 448 1100
*Recommended in Sport*

## ALLEN, Rand L
Wiley Rein & Fielding LLP, Washington, DC, 202 719 7329
rallen@wrf.com
*Recommended in Government Contracts*
**Practice Areas:** Chairs firm's 25-attorney Government Contracts Practice, representing many of the nation's largest government contractors, and is the 'go-to'

counsel for the industry on some of the highest-profile matters. Named the Washington, DC area's Top Government Contracts Lawyer by Legal Times. Handles full range of contracting issues, including bid protests, contract claims and disputes litigation, terminations, mergers and acquisitions, procurement fraud and False Claims Act investigations and suspensions/debarments.
**Prof. Memberships:** American Bar Association, Past Chair, Section of Public Contract Law.
**Personal:** Georgetown University Law Center (JD); United States Military Academy at West Point (BS).

## ALLEN, Richard
Zuckert, Scoutt & Rasenberger, LLP, Washington, DC 202 298 8660
*Recommended in Transportation*

## ALLINDER, William
Shook, Hardy & Bacon LLP, Kansas City
816 474 6550
wallinder@shb.com
*Recommended in Products Liability*
**Practice Areas:** Specializes in defending major products liability litigation and has extensive experience in complex litigation in state and federal courts, including individual claims, class actions and other consolidated mass tort proceedings. Has served as national coordinating counsel for various types of industry-liability claims, including tobacco, alcohol beverage and silica litigation.
**Prof. Memberships:** Kansas City Metropolitan Bar Association, The Missouri Bar, the Missouri Organization of Defense Lawyers, and the American Bar Association.
**Career:** Joined Shook, Hardy & Bacon, 1987; became Partner, 1991.
**Personal:** JD, University of Missouri-Columbia School of Law, 1979; BS, United States Military Academy, 1974.

## ANDERSON, M Jean
Weil, Gotshal & Manges LLP, Washington, DC 202 682 7000
jean.anderson@weil.com
*Recommended in International Trade*
**Practice Areas:** Jean Anderson, a senior Partner in Weil Gotshal's International Trade practice, is a trade policy strategist and litigator for companies and governments around the world. She provides strategic and substantive advice in international trade negotiations, litigates antidumping and subsidies cases, represents clients in WTO and other trade and investment disputes, and advises on trade legislation, market access, economic sanctions, export controls, the Foreign Corrupt Practices Act and other trade and regulatory issues.
**Personal:** Northwestern University, BA, 1965; Georgetown University Law Center, JD, 1975.

## ANDREOZZI, Bradley J
Mayer, Brown, Rowe & Maw LLP, Chicago 312 701 8564
bandreozzi@mayerbrown.com
*Recommended in Sport*
**Practice Areas:** Represents sports federations and athletes in litigation and international arbitration concerning governance issues, drug testing, eligibility, regulatory compliance, and other matters, including before the Court of Arbitration for Sport (CAS) in Lausanne, Switzerland. Represents corporations, banks, insurance companies and accounting firms before trial and appellate courts throughout the US, including class action defense, and claims involving securities, accountant liability, lender liability, and constitutional law issues. Conducts internal investigations and advises clients regarding remedial measures to avoid or limit claims and strategies for dealing with federal enforcement and administrative agencies.
**Career:** Mayer, Brown, Rowe & Maw LLP, Chicago, 1998 to date; Partner, 2000; Counsel, 1998. Mayer, Brown, Rowe & Maw LLP, New York, 1991-98. Reboul, MacMurray, Hewitt, Maynard & Kristol, New York, 1986-91. Hughes, Hubbard & Reed, New York, 1983-86.
**Publications:** 'Arbitration and Dispute Resolution in the Olympics', 2005 Annual Winter Sports Law Symposium, DePaul University College of Law; co-author: 'Lender's 'Right to be Wrong' on Material Adverse Change Affirmed', Lender Liability News, August 11, 1995.
**Personal:** JD, University of Chicago Law School, 1983. BA (magna cum laude), Yale College, 1980.

## APPLEBAUM, Harvey M
Covington & Burling, Washington, DC
202 662 5626
happlebaum@cov.com
*Recommended in International Trade*
**Practice Areas:** Partner in Covington's Antitrust and International Trade practices. His antitrust practice includes DOJ and FTC investigations and litigation; private antitrust litigation; and a diverse counseling practice. His international trade practice involves ITC, Commerce Department and USTR proceedings. He has an active practice in customs law matters including trade law and customs law judicial appeals.
**Career:** Former Chairman, ABA Antitrust Law Section; First Chairman, Editorial Board of ABA Antitrust Law Developments; Former Chairman, Section's Robinson-Patman Act Committee; Current Member, Section's International Antitrust Advisory Committee.
**Personal:** Harvard University, (JD, 1962, magna cum laude); Yale University (BA, 1959, summa cum laude).

## APPLEBY, Nancy J
Bracewell & Giuliani LLP,
Washington, DC 202 828 5891
nancy.appleby@bracewellgiuliani.com
*Recommended in Native American Law*
**Practice Areas:** Focuses on Indian law
including representation of lenders, contractors, real estate and energy developers, vendors, telecommunication companies, and other business clients. Board
certified in real estate law, her practice
includes construction and permanent
lending for commercial projects; government-guaranteed loan programs; acquisitions, development and sales; commercial and retail leasing; entitlements and
proffers; joint use agreements; negotiating contracts; dispute resolution; and regulatory and agency matters related to
both tribal and non-tribal transactions.
**Personal:** JD, with honors, The University of Texas School of Law, 1977; MLA,
with honors, Southern Methodist University, 1973; BA, with honors, Southern
Methodist University, 1970.

## ARCHIBALD, Jeanne S
Hogan & Hartson LLP, Washington, DC
202 637 5740
jsarchibald@hhlaw.com
*Recommended in International Trade*
**Practice Areas:** Jeanne Archibald is the
Director of Hogan & Hartson's International Trade Group and has more than 25
years of experience in a broad range of
international trade law matters. Her practice focuses on international trade negotiations and dispute settlement under the
World Trade Organization, North American Free Trade Agreement, and other
international trade agreements; compliance counseling and enforcement proceedings with respect to economic sanctions and export controls; national security reviews relating to foreign direct
investment in the United States; customs
and legislative proposals affecting trade;
and strategic trade counseling for multinational companies.
**Career:** Before joining Hogan & Hartson
Jeanne served as general counsel of the
US Department of the Treasury, where
she served as the Chief Legal Officer of
the department and all of its 10 subordinate bureaus. She provided legal and policy advice to the secretary of the treasury
and other senior officials on the full range
of issues under the department's jurisdiction. Before joining the department,
Jeanne served in the Office of the US
Trade Representative. She also served on
the staff of the Ways and Means Committee of the US House of Representatives.
**Personal:** Georgetown University Law
Center (JD).

## ARNHOLZ, John
McKee Nelson LLP, Washington, DC
202 775 4138
jarnholz@mckeenelson.com
*Recommended in Capital Markets*

**Practice Areas:** Securitization and
structured finance, corporate/securities.
Represents issuers and underwriters in
securitization transactions with an
emphasis on cross-border offerings.
Works with broad range of financial
assets, including residential mortgage
loans, debt obligations, home equity
loans, auto loans, franchise loans, and
high LTV loans. Has represented under-
writers and issuers in many significant
securitization programmes.
**Career:** Heads the DC office's Structured
Finance Group. Prior to joining McKee
Nelson, was a Partner at Sidley Austin
Brown & Wood.
**Publications:** Co-authored the treatise
'Offerings of Asset-Backed Securities'.
**Personal:** JD, Georgetown University
Law Center, 1985.

## ASMUS, David
Baker Botts LLP, Houston
713 229 1234
*Recommended in Energy, Projects*
*Please see Texas for profile*

## ASTIGARRAGA, José I
Astigarraga Davis, Miami
305 372 8282
jia@astidavis.com
*Recommended in International
Arbitration*
**Career:** Astigarraga, founding shareholder at Astigarraga Davis, litigates in
courts in the US and in arbitral tribunals
in the US and abroad. Astigarraga has
supervised legal proceedings throughout
Latin America in his 27 year career. He
serves on the 35-member London Court
of International Arbitration and was
recently appointed Vice President. He has
served as Arbitrator, Co-Arbitrator or
Chair before the ICC, AAA, among oth-
ers; is Vice-Chair of the International Bar
Association's worldwide International
Arbitration; Vice-Chair of the National
Law Center for Inter-American Free
Trade; and member of the Executive
Council of the American Law Institute,
Restatements of Law publishers.

## AUCUTT, Ronald
McGuireWoods LLP, McLean
703 712 5000
*Recommended in Wealth
Management*

## AUERBACH, Reed
McKee Nelson LLP, New York
917 777 4400
rauerbach@mckeenelson.com
*Recommended in Capital Markets*
**Practice Areas:** Practice focused on
structured finance and derivative transactions. Represents underwriters and
issuers in connection with public and private offerings of asset-backed and mortgage-backed securities and related interim warehouse financings, whole loan
purchases, repurchase agreements and
residual financings. Has broad-based

experience with a wide variety of assets,
including student loans, prime and non-
prime auto loans, auto leases, equipment
leases, royalty streams and other intellectual property rights, dealer floor plan
receivables, telecommunication receivables, litigation settlement fees, Australian
mortgage loans, manufactured housing
contracts, recreational vehicle loans, boat
loans, home equity loans, credit card
receivables, and insurance premium
finance agreements.
**Career:** Managing Partner of the firm's
New York office. Prior to joining McKee
Nelson, was a Partner at the New York
office of Stroock & Stoock & Lavan LLP.
**Personal:** JD, Columbia University
School of Law, 1985, Harlan Fiske Stone
Scholar, editor for The Journal of Trans-
actional Law, Certificate with honors
from the Parker School of International
and Comparative Law. MA, International
Affairs, Columbia University's School of
International Affairs, 1982, International
Fellow. BA (magna cum laude), Franklin
& Marshall College, 1980, Phi Beta
Kappa.

## AZZOLLINI, Phillip
Schulte Roth & Zabel LLP, New York
212 756 2000
*Recommended in Capital Markets*

## BAER, Gregory A
WilmerHale, Washington, DC
202 663 6859
gregory.baer@wilmerhale.com
*Recommended in Financial Services*
**Practice Areas:** Partner, Financial Institutions and Securities Departments. Represents clients in enforcement actions
before Federal Reserve Board, OCC, SEC.
Counsels domestic and foreign banking
clients on general bank regulatory issues;
advises on bank powers and preemption
issues; advises on legislative issue; provides representation in chartering and
application process.
**Career:** Former assistant secretary for
financial institutions at US Department
of the Treasury; co-ordinated Treasury
policy on Gramm-Leach-Bliley Act. Former managing senior counsel at Federal
Reserve Board.
**Personal:** JD, cum laude, Harvard Law
School, 1987; managing editor, Harvard
Law Review; AB, University of North
Carolina at Chapel Hill, 1984.

## BAKER, James P
Jones Day, San Francisco
415 875 5721
jpbaker@jonesday.com
*Recommended in ERISA Litigation*
**Practice Areas:** Recognized by The
National Law Journal as one of the 40
best ERISA/employee benefit attorneys in
the US and has written and lectured
extensively on ERISA litigation topics.
Successfully defended clients in ERISA
class action lawsuits, including Ogden v.
Americredit Corp. (motion to deny class

certification granted); In Re Administrative Committee ERISA Litigation (case
dismissed as class representative lacked
standing); Braden v LSI Logic Corp.
(obtained summary judgment in class
action severance plan case); Henderson v
State of Oregon Public Employees Retirement Board (won summary judgment in
$1.6 billion pension plan benefit calcula-
tion dispute).

## BAKER, Mark
Fulbright & Jaworski L.L.P., Houston
713 651 5151
*Recommended in Energy, International
Arbitration*
*Please see Texas for profile*

## BALDIA, Sonia
Mayer, Brown, Rowe & Maw LLP,
Washington, DC 202 263 3000
*Recommended in Business Process
Outsourcing, Technology*
*Please see District of Columbia for
profile*

## BANNON, Eileen
Dewey Ballantine LLP, New York
212 259 6190
ebannon@deweyballantine.com
*Recommended in Capital Markets*
**Practice Areas:** Ms Bannon has represented participants in a wide variety of
domestic and international transactions.
She has been involved in structuring and
documenting, among other things, asset-
backed commercial paper programs,
derivative product transactions, market
value, cash flow and synthetic CBOs and
CDOs, repackaged securities transactions, securities arbitrage programs, and
warehouse financing programs. Ms Bannon has also represented participants in
numerous public and private securitization transactions backed by a variety of
asset types.
**Career:** Structured finance, derivatives
and corporate finance.
**Personal:** MS, Seton Hall University,
1979. JD, New York University School of
Law, 1982.

## BARAN, Jan W
Wiley Rein & Fielding LLP,
Washington, DC 202 719 E7330
jbaran@wrf.com
*Recommended in Government:
Political Law*
**Practice Areas:** Chairs nation's premier
Election Law and Government Ethics
Practice. Named by Washingtonian mag-
azine as a 'Top Campaign and Elections
Lawyer' and one of Washington, DC's
'Top 50 Lawyers'. Advises clients and liti-
gates on federal, state and local campaign
finance laws, government ethics require-
ments and lobbying laws.
**Prof. Memberships:** American Bar
Association, Special Advisor, Standing
Committee on Judicial Independence;
Member, Commission to Review Model
Code of Judicial Conduct.

**Career:** Former General Counsel, Republican National Committee; Member, President's Commission on Federal Ethics Law Reform; Executive Assistant, Federal Election Commission.
**Personal:** Vanderbilt University School of Law (JD); Ohio Wesleyan University (BA).

## BARBIERE, Janet A
Sidley Austin LLP, New York
212 839 5922
jbarbiere@sidley.com
*Recommended in Capital Markets*
**Practice Areas:** Janet A Barbiere is a securitisation Partner in the New York office, representing issuers, underwriters, loans sellers and institutional investors in the primary and secondary market. She concentrates on the securitization of commercial mortgage loans and other structured financings of mortgage-related assets.
**Prof. Memberships:** Member, New York City Bar Association.
**Personal:** Fordham University School of Law, JD, 1983 (Law Review); Columbia University, MA, 1976; Brooklyn College, BA, 1975. Admissions: New Jersey, 1985; New York, 1984.

## BARKER, John
Arnold & Porter LLP, Washington, DC
202 942 5328
John.Barker@aporter.com
*Recommended in International Trade*
**Practice Areas:** Mr Barker's practice focuses on national security matters including export controls, international technology transfers, trade sanctions administered by the Office of Foreign Assets Control at the US Treasury (OFAC), as well as compliance with the Foreign Corrupt Practices Act (FCPA). He helps companies and institutions establish compliance plans, obtain export authorizations and provides representation in enforcement proceedings. Mr Barker came to the firm from the US Department of State, where he served as the Deputy Assistant Secretary for Nonproliferation Controls and prior to that as Deputy Assistant Secretary for Export Controls.
**Career:** In his most recent position at the State Department, Mr Barker supervised the development and implementation of US policy on multilateral nonproliferation and security regimes, and nonproliferation sanctions. As the Deputy Assistant Secretary for Export Controls, he supervised the US munitions licensing and defense trade compliance system including imposing sanctions on companies for violation of US export control law and overseeing the US government's nonproliferation review of dual-use exports. Mr Barker testified frequently before Congress on export control matters including trade sanctions, preventing the transfer of arms and dual-use tech-

nology to state sponsors of terrorism, the Export Administration Act, export licensing and compliance, and regulation of the aerospace industry.
**Publications:** Co-author, Stanford University study on ballistic missile proliferation; author of article on regulation of brokers of defense articles.
**Personal:** Mr Barker received his JD from the University of Michigan Law School in 1986, where he was managing editor of the Journal of Law Reform.

## BARNARD, Kevin
White & Case LLP, New York
212 819 8483
kbarnard@whitecase.com
*Recommended in Financial Services*
**Practice Areas:** Heads the firm's Bank Advisory Practice. Represents leading global banking organizations concerning the application of US laws to their worldwide activities. Practice emphasizes helping clients structure acquisitions, develop new products, resolve complex regulatory matters and address internal management and organizational issues. Also represents clients negotiating and settling litigation and administrative enforcement actions brought by federal and state banking authorities.
**Career:** Was an attorney at the US Treasury Department, Office of the Comptroller of the Currency (1976-78) and Deputy Superintendent of Banks and General Counsel of the New York State Banking Department (1982-83). Joined White & Case in 1983.

## BARNETT, Gary
Linklaters, New York
212 903 9025
gary.barnett@linklaters.com
*Recommended in Capital Markets*
**Practice Areas:** Partner in the Structured Finance and Derivatives Practice, has a reputation for innovation in the fields of securitization and other sophisticated financings, and specializes in cash and synthetic CDOs, derivatives, structured products (including repackagings), SIVs (structured investment vehicles) and domestic and international securitizations of a wide variety of asset types.
**Publications:** Published numerous articles on securitization and derivatives in the publications of The Practising Law Institute and other publications.
**Personal:** Received his LLM from New York University School of Law in 1986, his JD from the University of Tulsa College of Law in 1981 and his BS from the University of Tulsa in 1978. Has been Chairman of the Practising Law Institute's annual conference on New Developments in Securitization since 1995.

## BARONSKY, Kenneth
Milbank, Tweed, Hadley & McCloy LLP, Los Angeles 213 892 4000
*Recommended in Capital Markets*

## BARRINGER, William H
Willkie Farr & Gallagher LLP, Washington, DC
202 303 1101
wbarringer@willkie.com
*Recommended in International Trade*
**Practice Areas:** Partner and Chair of the International Trade Department, specializing in all aspects of international trade law, with particular emphasis on defending antidumping and countervailing duty investigations and advising on international trade negotiations and trade policy disputes. He has significant experience defending Japanese and other foreign interests in trade disputes with the United States and representing clients in WTO dispute settlement proceedings. Has been involved in some of the most significant international trade disputes over the last several decades, including, among others, disputes between the US and Japan involving autos, film, and steel. He has been the lead counsel on more than 60 antidumping investigations, more than a dozen safeguards investigations, and numerous investigations under Section 301 of US trade law. Most recently he successfully defended Chinese pipe and tube producers in a product specific safeguard proceeding arising out of China's accession to the WTO, a proceeding generally perceived as ending the use of product specific safeguards against China. Frequently advises foreign industries and governments on bilateral and multilateral trade issues, was actively involved in this capacity during the Uruguay Round negotiations, and is presently involved in advising on the rules negotiations in the Doha Round. His work on WTO disputes contributed to the termination of US safeguards on steel, eventually led to legislation ending the US practice of payment of antidumping duties to petitioning parties under the Byrd Amendment, and was instrumental in the near elimination of Section 301 as a tool of trade policy for the US Government.
**Prof. Memberships:** Member of the American Bar Association.
**Career:** Admitted to the Bar of the District of Columbia.
**Publications:** Has lectured and written extensively on a wide variety of trade law and trade policy issues, including issues relating to the intersection of trade and competition policy. He recently authored a book published under the auspices of the American Institute for International Steel, entitled Paying the Price for Big Steel: 30 Years of the Integrated Steel Companies' Capture of US Trade Policy.
**Personal:** Received an LLM in 1976 and a JD in 1973 from Georgetown University Law Center, and an AB from Brown University in 1970.

## BARRY JR, Desmond T
Condon & Forsyth LLP, New York
212 894 6770
dbarry@condonlaw.com
*Recommended in Transportation*
**Practice Areas:** Complex and multidistrict aviation, products liability and insurance litigation.
**Prof. Memberships:** Fellow, American College of Trial Lawyers; International Association of Defense Counsel (Member, Executive Committee, 1997-2001; Dean, Corporate Counsel College, 2003; Chairman, Aviation and Space Law Committee, 1995-97); IADC Foundation (Board Member, 2001-present); Defense Research Institute; Association of Insurance Attorneys; Association of Defense Trial Attorneys; American Arbitration Association; The Association of the Bar of the City of New York (Member, Aeronautical Committee, 1986-present); New York State Bar Association; American Bar Association (Chairman, Aviation and Space Law Committee, Tort and Insurance Practice Section, 1996-97).
**Career:** Major Aircraft Accident Litigation Experience: In Re DC-10 Accident Near Paris, France on March 3, 1974; In Re B-747 Collision at Tenerife on March 27, 1977; In Re B-737 Accident Near Washington, D.C. on January 13, 1982; In Re Air Crash Near Warsaw, Poland on March 12, 1980; In Re Korean Air Lines Flight 007 Shootdown on September 1, 1983; In Re LOT Polish Airlines Accident Near Warsaw, Poland on May 9, 1987; In Re SAHSA B-727 Acident Near Tegucigalpa, Honduras on October 22, 1989; Compania Panamena de Aviacion (COPA) Accident in Panama on June 6, 1992; In Re September 11, 2001 Terrorist Attack Litigation; In Re Air Crash at Belle Harbor, New York on November 12, 2001.
**Publications:** 'Legislative Response to the September 11, 2001 Terrorism Attack on the United States: The Air Transportation Safety and System Stabilization Act'. IADC Newsletter (Nov 2001, co-authors, Stephen R Stegich, III and Noreen G Carroll); 'Litigating the Aviation Case From Pretrial to Closing Argument', second edition. American Bar Association, 1998. (editor); 'Recent Cases Under Article 17 of the Warsaw Convention Defining 'Accident' and Bodily Injury', IADC Newsletter (July 2001); 'Recoverability of Pre-Impact Fear Damages in Aircraft Disaster Cases', Defense Counsel Journal (April 1998); 'Unlimited Liability: The New Ball Game in International Transportation By Air', 64 Defense Counsel Journal 381 (July 1997, co-author Thomas Whalen); 'A Practical Guide to the Ins and Outs of Multidistrict Litigation', 64 Defense Counsel Journal 58 (Jan 1997); 'Aviation Insurance. New York Insurance Law (Chapter 46: 1995); Recoverable Damages in Wrongful Death

Actions Governed by the Warsaw Convention' (Feb. 1995); 'Foreign Corporations: Forum Non Conveniens and Change of Venue', 61 Defense Counsel Journal 543 (Oct. 1994); 'Forum Non Conveniens: The Arguments for and Against Dismissal/ Transfer of the Foreign Corporation', International Association of Defense Counsel (July 1994); 'Certain Particulars of Article 8 of the Unamended Warsaw Convention and the Particular Specter of Potential Unlimited Liability' (June 1994); 'The Proof of Foreign Damage Law Under the Federal Rules of Civil Procedure,' The Defense Research Institute Damages Seminar (March 1994); 'Punitive Damages in Domestic and Foreign Mass Disaster Cases: The Defense View', ABA National Institute on Litigation in Aviation (Oct. 1990); 'The Defense of Airlines in Major Air Crash Litigation', Association of Defense Trial Attorneys (April 1989); 'Solving Choice of Law Problems in Foreign Sovereign Immunities Act Cases', Defense Counsel Journal (July 1988); 'The Evolution of Warnings: The Liberal Trend Toward Absolute products liability', 20:1 The Forum (Fall 1984).
**Personal:** Born March 26, 1945; Fordham University School of Law (JD, 1973); Princeton University (AB, 1967); United States Marine Corps (1967-70). Wife: Patricia M Barry. Children: Kate Barry and Todd Barry.

### BARSAMIAN, Bonnie A
Dechert LLP, New York
212 698 3520
bonnie.barsamian@dechert.com
*Recommended in Capital Markets*
**Practice Areas:** Ms Barsamian is a Partner in the Corporate and Securities and Mergers and Acquisitions Groups. She focuses her practice in corporate transactional and securities law, representing issuers and investment banks in public and private securities offerings and other corporate finance transactions, including US and cross-border mergers and acquisitions. Many of her clients are in the media and entertainment, real estate investment trust, and manufacturing and consumer products sectors.
**Prof. Memberships:** Member, New York, Massachusetts, District of Columbia Bars.
**Personal:** Amherst College, BA, 1986; University of Chicago, JD, 1989, member of the University of Chicago Law Review.

### BARSHEFSKY, Charlene
WilmerHale, Washington, DC
202 663 6130
charlene.barshefsky@wilmerhale.com
*Recommended in International Trade*
**Practice Areas:** Senior International Partner. Practice centers on international business transactions, the structuring and negotiation of commercial agreements and the removal of trade and regulatory

impediments to exporting to or investing in markets throughout Asia, Europe and Latin America.
**Prof. Memberships:** Board, Council on Foreign Relations; board, America-China Society; member, American Academy of Diplomacy; member the Trilateral Commission; Boards of Directors of American Express Company, The Estee Lauder Companies Inc., Intel Corporation and Starwood Hotels & Resorts Worldwide, Inc.
**Personal:** Catholic University, Columbus School of Law (JD 1975); University of Wisconsin, 1972.

### BASS, Fred
Dewey Ballantine LLP, New York
212 259 6330
fbass@deweyballantine.com
*Recommended in Transportation*
**Practice Areas:** Mr Bass focuses his practice in the areas of lease, debt and project financings and has extensive experience in aviation finance transactions. He regularly represents lessors and lenders in a wide range of financings of aircraft, engines and related equipment, including operating leases, leveraged leases, secured debt financings, EETC transactions, cross-border financings, predelivery deposit facilities, transactions with third-party support arrangements, aircraft and portfolio purchases and sales, like-kind exchanges and restructurings.
**Career:** Bank and Institutional Finance, Leasing and Tax-Advantaged Financing, Project Finance and Corporate Finance.
**Personal:** BA, Cornell University, 1978. JD, Columbia Law School, 1981.

### BATTERMAN, Robert
Proskauer Rose LLP, New York
212 969 3010
rbatterman@proskauer.com
*Recommended in Sport*
**Practice Areas:** Labor and employment law, including negotiation of collective bargaining agreements; advice re: corporate campaigns; serves as labor counsel to the National Hockey League and Major League Soccer; Member of Proskauer's Lodging and Gaming Practice Group.
**Prof. Memberships:** ABA, ABCNY (Chair of Personnel Policy Committee and Member of the Executive Committee); Governing board of the NYU Center for Labor and Employment Law.
**Career:** Partner since 1974.
**Personal:** New York University School of Law-Law Review (1966).

### BAUER, Robert
Perkins Coie LLP, Washington, DC
202 628 6600
*Recommended in Government:
Political Law*

### BEISNER, John
O'Melveny & Myers LLP, Washington, DC
202 383 5370
jbeisner@omm.com
*Recommended in Products Liability*

**Practice Areas:** John Beisner heads O'Melveny & Myers LLP's 120-attorney Class Action Defense Practice and focuses on the defense of purported class actions, mass tort matters, and other complex litigation in both federal and state courts. John also serves as the Managing Partner for the Washington, DC office. Over the past 20 years, he defended numerous major US and foreign corporations in upwards of 500 purported class actions filed in the federal and state courts of 40 states at both the trial court and appellate level. John is a frequent writer and lecturer on class action and complex litigation issues, and has been an active participant in litigation reform initiatives before Congress, state legislatures, and judicial committees. In recent years, he has frequently testified on class action and claims aggregation issues before the US Senate and House Judiciary Committees (particularly regarding the Class Action Fairness Act of 2005) and before state legislative committees.

### BELCHER, Dennis
McGuireWoods LLP, Richmond
804 775 1000
*Recommended in Wealth
Management*

### BENNER, C Jonathan
Troutman Sanders LLP, Washington, DC
202 274 2950
*Recommended in Transportation*

### BERG, Gracia M
Gibson, Dunn & Crutcher LLP, Washington, DC 202 887 3644
gberg@gibsondunn.com
*Recommended in International Trade*
**Practice Areas:** Extensive experience in international trade and customs law, including trade disputes under the antidumping and countervailing duty laws, the escape clause, Section 301, and general fact-finding investigations. Represents domestic and multinational companies on trade matters before US administrative agencies and Congress.
**Prof. Memberships:** Past Chair, ABA Administrative Law and Practice Section's Committee on International Trade Regulation.
**Career:** Served as Deputy General Counsel and Assistant General Counsel for Antidumping and Countervailing Duty Investigations at the International Trade Commission.
**Personal:** JD, University of Notre Dame, 1980, year in London and diploma from Institute Internationale des Droits de L'Homme, Strasbourg, France.

### BERLACK, Evan R
Baker Botts LLP, Washington, DC
202 639 7771
evan.berlack@bakerbotts.com
*Recommended in International Trade*
**Practice Areas:** Evan Berlack's practice primarily involves international trade

regulatory matters, with a background in international transactions.
**Prof. Memberships:** District of Columbia Bar; New York State Bar; United States Court of International Trade.
**Career:** Regulatory expertise includes Commerce, State, and Defense export controls, Treasury and State Department economic sanctions, Exon-Florio proceedings, FCPA issues, anti-dumping proceedings and Customs, including NAFTA-related, issues. Transactional experience includes LNG and OPIC projects.
**Publications:** Co-editor since 1985 of annual Practicing Law Institute volumes on 'Coping with US Export Controls'.
**Personal:** JD, Harvard Law School, 1962; AB (magna cum laude), government, Harvard University, 1956.

### BERMANN, George
George A Bermann - Sole Practitioner, New York 212 854 2680
*Recommended in Arbitration*

### BERNICK, David M
Kirkland & Ellis LLP, Chicago
312 861 2000
*Recommended in Litigation, Products Liability*
*Please see Illinois for profile*

### BERNSTEIN, Jonathan K
Bingham McCutchen LLP, Boston
617 951 8630
jon.bernstein@bingham.com
*Recommended in Sport*
**Practice Areas:** Serves as Co-Chair of the firm's Bank, Commercial and Structured Finance Group. Represents some of the most sophisticated US lenders. Practice focuses on general corporate and corporate finance, including debt financings, structured financings, workouts and bankruptcies. Clients include the Ottawa Senators NHL franchise, the Buffalo Sabres NHL franchise and the New England Patriots NFL football club.
**Personal:** University of Pennsylvania Law School, JD, 1987; Brandeis University, BA, summa cum laude, 1984.

### BESHAR, Sarah
Davis Polk & Wardwell, New York
212 450 4000
sarah.beshar@dpw.com
*Recommended in Capital Markets*
**Practice Areas:** Member of Davis Polk & Wardwell's Corporate Department and represents clients in equity, debt and other securities offerings, and advises on corporate governance and general securities and disclosure issues. She has taken a leading role in the initial public offerings and other financing transactions on behalf of many companies. Also, has represented investment banks in a variety of roles, including capital markets and structured products transactions and general compliance matters. Advises companies on governance and general

corporate issues.

### BICKS, Peter A
Orrick, Herrington & Sutcliffe LLP,
New York 212 506 3742
pbicks@orrick.com
*Recommended in Products Liability*
**Practice Areas:** Extensive trial success
nationwide in mass torts, contracts, intellectual property, corporate governance,
and bankruptcy. Lead trial counsel for
Orrick team acting as National Counsel
to Union Carbide Corporation in
asbestos-related personal injury lawsuits,
including biggest defense verdict of 2004.
**Prof. Memberships:** State Bar of New
York.
**Career:** Managing Partner, Orrick's New
York office; previously, Partner, Donovan
Leisure Newton & Irvine LLP (1995-98).
**Publications:** 'Defending a Company in
a Punitive Damages Case, a Comprehensive Approach to Defeating Punitive
Damages in light of Present-Day Juror
Attitudes', Aspatore, Inc., 2005.
**Personal:** JD, Georgetown University
Law, 1986; BA, Pomona College, 1982.

### BIERCE, William
Bierce & Kenerson, P.C., New York
212 840 0080
*Recommended in Business Process
Outsourcing, Technology*

### BILGER, Bruce
Vinson & Elkins LLP, Houston
713 758 2222
*Recommended in Energy, Projects
Please see Texas for profile*

### BIRNBAUM, Sheila L
Skadden, Arps, Slate, Meagher & Flom
LLP & Affiliates, New York
212 735 3000
*Recommended in Insurance, Products
Liability
Please see New York for profile*

### BISHOP, Doak
King & Spalding LLP, Houston
713 751 3200
*Recommended in Energy, International
Arbitration
Please see Texas for profile*

### BLATTMACHR, Jonathan
Milbank, Tweed, Hadley & McCloy LLP,
New York 212 530 5000
*Recommended in Wealth
Management*

### BLAUCH, Kevin
Latham & Watkins LLP, New York
212 906 1200
*Recommended in Capital Markets*

### BOGAARD, Jonathan
Vedder, Price, Kaufman & Kammholz,
Chicago 312 609 7500
*Recommended in Transportation*

### BOGGS JR, Thomas Hale
Patton Boggs LLP, Washington, DC
202 457 6040
tboggs@pattonboggs.com
*Recommended in Government
Relations*
**Practice Areas:** Advises on many legislative/regulatory matters, including tax,
healthcare, trade, and telecommunications. Unrivaled experience in policy-
making proceedings before Congress, the
White House, and federal agencies.
**Prof. Memberships:** American Judicature Society; Federal Bar Associations;
past/present Board Member for numerous organizations/universities.
**Career:** Partner; Executive Committee
Chairman. Named to The National Law
Journal's top 100 US lawyers list every
year since its inception. Made firm
national leader in joint government-business matters. Served as Joint Economic
Committee economist, among other government positions.
**Publications:** Co-author, 'Corporate
Political Activity' and 'Private Trade Barriers in the Atlantic'.
**Personal:** Georgetown University (LLB,
1965); Georgetown University (AB,
1961).

### BOIES, Bill
McDermott Will & Emery, Chicago
312 372 2000
*Recommended in Employment, ERISA
Litigation
Please see Illinois for profile*

### BONANO, William E
Pillsbury Winthrop Shaw Pittman LLP,
San Francisco
415 983 1248
william.bonano@pillsburylaw.com
*Recommended in Tax Litigation*
**Practice Areas:** Mr Bonano advises on
international and domestic tax issues and
represents taxpayers involved in IRS controversy matters before Examinations,
Appeals and in litigation. He has litigated
over 25 tax controversy matters, including the only Tax Court arbitration of a
transfer pricing issue; has extensive experience in representing taxpayers and
resolving transfer pricing and other issues
at Examinations and Appeals; and assists
clients with international planning,
including in obtaining advance pricing
agreements and in Competent Authority
proceedings.
**Career:** International Special Trial Attorney with the Office of Chief Counsel,
Internal Revenue Service, at San Francisco, California.

### BORDERS, Thomas
McDermott Will & Emery, Chicago
312 372 2000
*Recommended in Tax, Tax Litigation
Please see Illinois for profile*

### BOSTELMAN, John T
Sullivan & Cromwell LLP, New York
212 558 4000
bostelmanj@sullcrom.com
*Recommended in Capital Markets*
**Practice Areas:** Co-ordinates S&C's

Global Securities Practice. Broad securities experience includes public and private securities offerings for issuers in a
broad range of industries, corporate governance, investment management, commodities and derivatives and broker-
dealer regulation.
**Prof. Memberships:** ABA (Chair, Securities Registration Subcommittee, Federal
Regulation of Securities Committee);
ABCNY; NYSBA.
**Career:** Partner since 1986.
**Publications:** 'The Sarbanes-Oxley
Deskbook' (Practising Law Institute,
2003); 'PLI's Guide to the Sarbanes-Oxley
Act for Business Professionals '(Practising
Law Institute, 2005).
**Personal:** Yale University (BA, 1975);
Columbia Law School (JD, 1979).

### BOUTROUS JR, Theodore J
Gibson, Dunn & Crutcher LLP,
Los Angeles 213 229 7000
*Recommended in Media &
Entertainment, Products Liability
Please see California
for profile*

### BOWERS, William C
Pillsbury Winthrop Shaw Pittman LLP,
New York 212 858 1106
william.bowers@pillsburylaw.com
*Recommended in Transportation*
**Practice Areas:** Mr Bowers works in
transportation structured finance, representing arrangers, issuers, lenders and liquidity providers in securitizations, loans,
leases and other financings involving aircraft, ships, rolling stock and aircraft
engines. He has represented issuers,
arrangers and liquidity providers in asset-
backed commercial paper financings and
portfolio securitizations of aircraft and
other transportation assets. Most recently, he represented Willis Lease Finance
Corporation in the first ever securitization of a portfolio of leased aircraft
engines through Willis Engine Securitization Trust (WEST), named Airfinance
Journal 2005 overall deal of the year.
**Personal:** JD, Emory University, 1975
(with distinction); AB, Princeton University, 1968.

### BOWMAN, John
Fulbright & Jaworski L.L.P., Houston
713 651 5151
*Recommended in Energy, International
Arbitration
Please see Texas for profile*

### BRACH, Richard
Milbank, Tweed, Hadley & McCloy LLP,
New York 212 530 5000
*Recommended in Projects*

### BRADEN, Gregory C
Alston & Bird LLP, Atlanta
404 881 7497
gbraden@alston.com
*Recommended in ERISA Litigation*
**Practice Areas:** ERISA litigation;
employee benefits and executive com-

pensation; ESOP transactions.
**Prof. Memberships:** Fellow, American
College of Employee Benefits Counsel;
Member, American Bar Association (Tax
and Labor sections), State Bars of Georgia and Wisconsin, ESOP Association,
Southern Employee Benefits Conference
(Treasurer).
**Career:** Represented defendants in several major ERISA class action lawsuits;
extensive courtroom experience in
ERISA cases; represented clients on benefits issues in corporate transactions.
**Publications:** Published and lectured
extensively, including in Benefits Law
Journal and Journal of Compensation,
Planning and Compliance.
**Personal:** BA, with honors, University of
Wisconsin-Milwaukee (1979); JD, with
honors, University of Wisconsin-Madison (1982).

### BRADY, Christopher
Mayer, Brown, Rowe & Maw LLP,
Charlotte 704 444 3500
*Recommended in Capital Markets
Please see North Carolina for profile*

### BRANDEL, Roland E
Morrison & Foerster LLP, San Francisco
415 268 7093
rbrandel@mofo.com
*Recommended in Financial Services*
**Practice Areas:** Active in the field of
consumer financial services and financial
institution regulation. In addition to regularly advising clients in this field, has
been directly involved in many federal
legislative and regulatory efforts affecting
the field in the past 30 years. Has had primary responsibility for joint efforts in the
financial services industry in development of products such as bankcards, electronic fund transfer systems and other
innovative lending and value transfer services.
**Prof. Memberships:** Charter Member,
Consumer Advisory Council, Federal
Reserve Board.
**Career:** Admitted to practice in California. Lifetime Achievement Award, American College of Consumer Financial Services Lawyers, 2004.
**Personal:** BS, Illinois Institute of Technology, 1960; JD, University of Chicago
Law School, 1966.

### BRANDOW, John M
Davis Polk & Wardwell, New York
212 450 4000
john.brandow@dpw.com
*Recommended in Capital Markets*
**Practice Areas:** Member of Davis Polk
& Wardwell's Corporate Department and
heads the firm's Equity Derivatives
Group. The group advises a wide variety
of market participants - commercial and
investment banks, issuers, hedge funds
and institutional and individual holders
of equity positions - on a complex array
of equity-related transactions. Has been
actively involved in the design of

exchangeable securities containing imbedded options or forward contracts on the underlying equities, the development of mandatory and optional convertible securities that are issued in tax- or accounting-driven capital-raising transactions, and the structuring of public and private hedging transactions using collars and variable prepaid forward contracts.

### BRAZA, Mary K
Foley & Lardner LLP, Milwaukee
414 297 5505
mbraza@foley.com
*Recommended in Sport*
**Career:** Mary K Braza, a Partner in the Milwaukee office of Foley & Lardner LLP, is the leader of Foley's Sports Industry Team. Ms Braza serves as outside counsel to Major League Baseball in a wide variety of issues including strategic planning, employment, taxation, technology and consulting agreements, licensing, trademark and antitrust litigation. In addition to her sports practice, Ms Braza has extensive experience in litigating commercial disputes in federal and state courts, involving such areas as environmental law, bankruptcy, distribution, insurance coverage, reinsurance and healthcare. Ms Braza received her JD Degree from Cornell University.

### BRITO, Michael James
Fulbright & Jaworski L.L.P., Dallas
214 855 8125
mbrito@fulbright.com
*Recommended in Business Process Outsourcing*
**Practice Areas:** Corporation, banking and business; technology and emerging companies.
**Prof. Memberships:** State Bar of Texas.
**Career:** A Partner in Fulbright's Dallas office, Michael Brito has a broad range of experience representing clients in a wide variety of technology transactions, in the US, Europe, Latin America, and Asia Pacific. He has significant expertise in structuring, negotiating, and drafting information technology outsourcing agreements, business process outsourcing arrangements, domestic and international distribution agreements, software development agreements, licensing and marketing agreements, joint ventures, strategic alliances and teaming relationships. In addition, Michael has been actively involved in various e-commerce transactions, with an emphasis on business to business (B2B) transactions, web hosting, e-applications (ASP), and data mining and warehousing transactions.
**Personal:** JD, Stanford University School of Law (1987); BA, Georgetown University (1984).

### BRITTENHAM, David
Debevoise & Plimpton LLP, New York
212 909 6000
*Recommended in Banking & Finance, Capital Markets*

### BROD, Craig B
Cleary Gottlieb Steen & Hamilton LLP, New York 212 225 2650
cbrod@cgsh.com
*Recommended in Capital Markets*
**Practice Areas:** General US and international issuer representation, corporate governance, corporate finance and securities law. Represents corporate issuers, investment banks and investors and has extensive experience in initial public offerings for domestic and foreign issuers, public and private debt and equity financings for companies, and financings related to corporate restructurings. International securities practice involves global and cross-border financings and exchange listings for issuers domiciled in a wide variety of jurisdictions.
**Career:** Joined firm, 1980; became Partner, 1989. JD, Yale Law School (1980). editor, The Yale Law Journal. BA, summa cum laude, Phi Beta Kappa, Columbia University, Columbia College (1977). Member, Securities Advisory Committee of the Ontario Securities Commission (1995-99). Admitted in New York and New Jersey.

### BRODY, Lawrence
Bryan Cave LLP, St Louis
314 259 2000
*Recommended in Wealth Management*

### BROWER, Charles
20 Essex Street, London
+44 20 7842 1200
*Recommended in Arbitration*

### BROWN, Michael K
Reed Smith LLP, Los Angeles
213 457 8018
mkbrown@reedsmith.com
*Recommended in Products Liability*
**Practice Areas:** Litigation and trial practice focuses on complex products liability and commercial matters, including class actions, Multi-District Litigations, mass torts, and claims for unfair business practices under California Business and Professions Code Section 17200. Member of Executive Committee.
**Prof. Memberships:** Board of Governors, Association of Business Trial Lawyers (LA Chapter); products liability Defense Council.
**Career:** Managing Partner of Crosby Heafey's Los Angeles office; combined with Reed Smith, 2003.
**Publications:** Author of dozens of articles for various publications.
**Personal:** University of San Francisco (JD, 1982); Georgetown University (AB, 1978); 'International Who's Who of Product Liability Defense Lawyers'.

### BRUEMMER, Russell
WilmerHale, Washington, DC
202 663 6804
Russell.Bruemmer@wilmerhale.com
*Recommended in Financial Services*

**Practice Areas:** Chair, Financial Institutions Department. Focus: corporate and financial services areas; negotiation and documentation of acquisitions, divestitures, and financing transactions; corporate governance and corporate structuring matters; trasactions, national security issues.
**Prof. Memberships:** Former Chair of two ABA banking law subcommittees, Vice-Chair of subcommittee corporate compliance; Advisory Board of UNC Banking Law Institute; American Law Institute.
**Career:** CIA's General Counsel; Special Counsel to Director of Central Intelligence; Chief Counsel-Congressional Affairs, Assistant to the Director for the FBI.
**Personal:** JD, University of Michigan Law School; BA, Luther College.

### BRYAN, Charles E
Cadwalader, Wickersham & Taft LLP, Washington, DC 202 862 2212
charlie.bryan@cwt.com
*Recommended in Capital Markets*
**Practice Areas:** Concentrates in securities, structured finance, financings and commercial transactions. Has acted as issuer's or underwriter's counsel on several thousand securitized offerings, involving both mortgage and asset-backed securities. Has extensive experience with mortgage pass-throughs, CMOs and REMICs, as well as ABS backed by student loans, auto loans and other financial instruments. Represents investment banks, banks, government-sponsored enterprises and other financial institutions. Has supervised and participated in acquisitions, divestitures and reorganizations.
**Personal:** JD, Yale Law School (1974); BA, with highest distinction, University of Virginia (Phi Beta Kappa) (1970).

### BUCK, Willis
Sidley Austin LLP, Chicago
312 853 7819
wbuck@sidley.com
*Recommended in Capital Markets*
**Practice Areas:** Specializes in securitization and structured finance. His practice includes term and conduit executions involving a variety of assets, including trade receivables, credit card receivables (including private label), automobile loans and leases, floorplan loans, residential mortgages, home equity loans, taxi medallion loans and aircraft leases. Transaction structures have included, among others, direct asset purchases, master trusts and master note trusts (including de-linked structures) and 'repo' structures. He has been involved in the structuring and formation of several asset-backed commercial paper conduits, including conduits issuing extendible and callable paper and eurocommercial paper. Clients include Bank of America,

Barclays Capital, Citigroup, ING, JPMorgan Chase, MBIA, Societe Generale and Wheels, Inc. (a national automobile fleet leasing company).
**Personal:** The University of Chicago Law School, JD, 1984; Yale University, MPhil, 1979; Williams College, BA, 1973; Oxford University, BA, 1975. Clerked for Judge Milton I Shadur of the Northern District of Illinois from 1984-85. Admission: Illinois, 1985.

### BUCKHOLZ JR, Robert E
Sullivan & Cromwell LLP, New York
212 558 4000
buckholzr@sullcrom.com
*Recommended in Capital Markets*
**Practice Areas:** Head of the firm's Corporate and Finance Group, specialising in capital markets transactions. Has handled a wide range of public and private debt and equity financings for US and foreign issuers and their underwriters, including initial public offerings, privatisations, and investment grade and high-yield financings. Also has extensive experience advising on equity derivatives matters, in both the capital markets and over-the-counter contexts.
**Prof. Memberships:** ABA; ABCNY; NYSBA.
**Career:** Partner since 1987.
**Personal:** Columbia Law School (JD, 1979); Dartmouth College (AB, 1976).

### BUCKLEY, Kevin
Hunton & Williams LLP, Richmond
804 788 8200
*Recommended in Capital Markets, Corporate/M&A*
*Please see North Carolina for profile*

### BUDOFSKY, Daniel
Davis Polk & Wardwell, New York
212 450 4000
daniel.budofsky@dpw.com
*Recommended in Capital Markets*
**Practice Areas:** Member of Davis Polk & Wardwell's Derivatives and Hedge Fund Groups. Advises financial institutions, corporations, hedge funds and individuals on innovative financial products in domestic and international transactions and has worked on numerous convertible, exchangeable and private equity derivatives transactions. Also advises underwriters, issuers and end-users on fund derivatives transactions.

### BURCHFIELD, Bobby
McDermott Will & Emery, Washington, DC 202 756 8000
*Recommended in Government: Political Law, Litigation*
*Please see District of Columbia for profile*

### BURKE, Ted
Freshfields Bruckhaus Deringer LLP, New York 212 277 4000
*Recommended in Projects*

## BURKE JR, Raymond
Burke & Parsons, New York
212 354 3800
*Recommended in Transportation*

## BURNS, Stephen
Cravath, Swaine & Moore LLP, New York
212 474 1146
sburns@cravath.com
*Recommended in Capital Markets*
**Practice Areas:** Represents investment banking firms and issuers in connection with public and private offerings of securities. Represents various corporations on general corporate matters.
**Career:** Partner since 1998.
**Personal:** University of Texas School of Law (JD, with honors, 1990; associate editor of the Law Review; Chancellors); University of Oklahoma (BBA, with distinction, 1987).

## BURRELL, Lizabeth
Levy Phillips & Konigsberg LLP,
New York 212 605 6200
*Recommended in Transportation*

## BURSKY, Daniel
Fried, Frank, Harris, Shriver & Jacobson LLP, New York
212 859 8428
Daniel.Bursky@FriedFrank.com
*Recommended in Capital Markets*
**Practice Areas:** Corporate Partner. Concentrates his practice in corporate finance and the US securities law representing both issuers and underwriters in a variety of financing transactions, including equity offerings, high-yield debt, mezzanine and bridge financings, and acquisition financings.
**Career:** Joined Fried Frank in 1993. Became a Partner in 2001.
**Personal:** JD (1993), Columbia University Law School, Harlan Fiske Stone Scholar. BA (1990), Yale University.

## BUSH, Derek M
Cleary Gottlieb Steen & Hamilton LLP,
Washington, DC 202 974 1526
dbush@cgsh.com
*Recommended in Financial Services*
**Practice Areas:** US bank regulatory matters affecting domestic and international financial institutions and foreign sovereigns. Corporate transactions involving financial institutions, including mergers and acquisitions, asset sales, privatizations and capital markets transactions. Internal investigations and enforcement proceedings by the US federal banking agencies, including representation of financial institutions, their boards of directors, employees and shareholders.
**Prof. Memberships:** Member of the Bar in the District of Columbia.
**Career:** Joined firm, 1995; became Partner, 2003. JD, with honors, Law Review comment editor, University of Chicago (1994); AB, cum laude, Princeton University (1989).

## CAMERON JR, Donald B
Kaye Scholer LLP, Washington, DC
202 682 3630
dcameron@kayescholer.com
*Recommended in International Trade*
**Practice Areas:** Don Cameron is Co-Chair of Kaye Scholer LLP's International Trade Group. During his career of more than 25 years, Mr Cameron has represented foreign manufacturers, foreign governments, trade associations and US importers in various trade actions arising under the US countervailing duty law, the anti-dumping law, Sections 201 and 301, and various provisions of the customs laws and the export control law. Mr Cameron has represented foreign producers and importers in a number of product sectors including footwear, lumber, textiles, electronic products, and steel products. He regularly practices before the US Department of Commerce, the US International Trade Commission, the Office of the US Trade Representative, the US Court of International Trade and the US Court of Appeals for the Federal Circuit. In addition, Mr Cameron advises clients on World Trade Organization (WTO) proceedings and has participated in WTO Panel and Appellate Body proceedings on behalf of clients and their member governments.
**Prof. Memberships:** District of Columbia Bar, US Court of International Trade, US Court of Appeals for the Federal Circuit, Court of International Trade Advisory Committee, American Bar Association.
**Career:** LLM, Program on International Legal Cooperation, Vrije Universiteit Brussels, 1975. JD, Vanderbilt University, 1974. BA, Kenyon College, 1971.

## CARNEAL, George U
Hogan & Hartson LLP, Washington, DC
202 637 6546
gucarneal@hhlaw.com
*Recommended in Transportation*
**Practice Areas:** Aviation, all segments.
**Prof. Memberships:** General Counsel, National Aeronautic Association; ABA (Forum Committee on Air and Space Law); Aero Club of Washington (past President); Princeton Club of Washington, DC (past President); Board of Governors (past), Flight Safety Foundation.
**Career:** 1961-62, Law Clerk, Honorable E Barrett Prettyman, US Court of Appeals for the District of Columbia Circuit; 1962-68, Hogan & Hartson, associate; 1969-70, Special assistant, Secretary of Transportation; 1970-72, General Counsel, Federal Aviation Administration; 1973-present Hogan & Hartson, Partner.
**Personal:** University of Virginia School of Law (LLB, Order of the Coif, 1961); Princeton University (AB, 1957).

## CARON, David
David D Caron - Sole Practitioner,
Berkeley 510 642 7249

*Recommended in Arbitration*

## CARROLL, James
Cadwalader, Wickersham & Taft LLP,
Charlotte 704 348 5100
*Recommended in Capital Markets*
*Please see North Carolina for profile*

## CARTER, James
Sullivan & Cromwell LLP, New York
212 558 4000
carterj@sullcrom.com
*Recommended in Arbitration, International Arbitration*
**Practice Areas:** Coordinator, Arbitration Practice. Principal focus is on international arbitration, as counsel and arbitrator, in ICC, LCIA, AAA, CPR, ICSID, CAS, ad hoc proceedings and other fora. Typical cases: international joint venture, investment and intellectual property licensing disputes.
**Prof. Memberships:** AAA Chairman of the Board. Member, AAA and CPR Arbitration Rules Revisions committees; CAS; Japan Commercial Arbitration Association Arbitrator Panel; Swiss Arbitration Association; former member, LCIA Court; International Arbitration Institute; President, ASIL.
**Career:** Partner since 1977.
**Publications:** 30 arbitration articles and chapters.
**Personal:** Graduate, Yale College and Yale Law School; Fulbright Scholar, Cambridge University.

## CASSIDY JR, Robert C
WilmerHale, Washington, DC
202 663 6740
Robert C.Cassidy Jr.@wilmerhale.com
*Recommended in International Trade*
**Practice Areas:** Partner, International Trade, Investment and Market Access Department. Focus: cross-border business transactions including antidumping and countervailing duty proceedings, economic sanctions, export controls, customs issues. Devises strategies using trade law procedures to achieve business objectives and resolve disputes between companies and the US government concerning sanctions, export controls, customs laws.
**Career:** General Counsel, Office of the US Trade Representative; International Trade Counsel to US Senate Committee on Finance; a primary architect of modern antidumping and countervailing duty statutes enacted in Trade Agreements Act of 1979.
**Personal:** LLM, Georgetown University; JD, University of Pennsylvania Law School; BA, Johns Hopkins University

## CHANG, Leo
Watson, Farley & Williams, New York
212 922 2210
lchang@wfw.com
*Recommended in Transportation*
**Practice Areas:** Partner specialising in shipping, ship finance and general corporate and commercial transactions; acting for financial institutions and operating companies involved in US and international shipping.
**Prof. Memberships:** Vice Chairman of the Subcommittee on Coastguard Documentation, US Citizenship and Related Matters, and to the Committee on Marine Financing of the Maritime Law Association of the United States.
**Career:** Associate and then Partner at Burlingham, Underwood & Lord in New York for a total of 12 years; Partner, Watson, Farley & Williams,1990.

## CHARNESS, Michael
Vinson & Elkins LLP, Washington, DC
202 639 6780
mcharness@velaw.com
*Recommended in Government Contracts*
**Practice Areas:** Government contracts.
**Career:** University of Pennsylvania, BA, 1976; Georgetown University, JD, 1979. Admitted to practice: District of Columbia, 1979; District Court of Maryland; US Court of Federal Claims; US Courts of Appeal for the District of Columbia and the Federal Circuit. Extensive experience with domestic and international government claims and disputes; due diligence in mergers and acquisitions; bid protests; defense of qui tam actions; and internal investigations involving false claims and statements and Foreign Corrupt Practices Act violations.
**Publications:** Numerous articles on government contracts, privatization and outsourcing, and construction law. Frequent lecturer on government and international procurement issues.

## CHECK, Raymond B
Cleary Gottlieb Steen & Hamilton LLP,
New York 212 225 2122
rcheck@cgsh.com
*Recommended in Capital Markets*
**Practice Areas:** Broad experience in capital markets and other financings: domestic and international public and private debt and equity offerings, asset-backed securities and securitizations. Particular expertise in offerings of convertible and mandatorily exchangeable securities (e.g. Credit Suisse exchangeable into Equinix) and other innovative or complex structures (e.g. Berkshire Hathaway negative interest rate units), synthetic and cash-flow CDO programs.
**Career:** Joined firm, 1986; became Partner 1995. JD, magna cum laude, Order of the Coif, University of Michigan Law School (1986); BS, cum laude, Wharton School of the University of Pennsylvania (1983).

## CHIERICHELLA, John
Sheppard, Mullin, Richter & Hampton LLP, Washington, DC
202 218 0000
*Recommended in Government Contracts*

## CHRISTENSEN III, Henry
Sullivan & Cromwell LLP, New York
212 558 4000
christensenh@sullcrom.com
*Recommended in Wealth Management*

**Practice Areas:** Senior Partner, Estates and Personal Clients Group. Represents high-profile individuals and wealthy families throughout the world. Active Surrogate's Court and Tax Court Litigation Practice. Helps many well-known families with international tax and estate planning. Active Dispute Resolution Practice.
**Prof. Memberships:** Chair, International Estate Planning Committee and Regent (elected 2005), ACTEC; Vice President, IAETL; ABA; ABCNY.
**Career:** Partner since 1977.
**Publications:** Adjunct faculty member, University of Miami Law School, NYU Law School (Spring, 2006). Author, 'International Estate Planning' (Matthew Bender, Second Edition 1999).
**Personal:** Yale University (BA, 1966); Harvard Law School (JD, 1969).

## CHRISTIAN, Betty Jo
Steptoe & Johnson LLP, Washington, DC
202 429 8113
bchristian@steptoe.com
*Recommended in Transportation*

**Practice Areas:** Practices extensively before the US Supreme Court, US Courts of Appeals, State Supreme Courts and federal regulatory agencies, primarily in cases involving railroads and other regulated industries. Recent cases include Commerce Clause and other federal constitutional issues, federal preemption, statutory interpretation, and administrative procedure issues. Also represents transportation companies in connection with the regulatory aspects of a wide variety of transactions, including railroad mergers and acquisitions, tender offers, railroad construction projects, railroad abandonments, and equipment financing.
**Personal:** LLB, University of Texas, 1960; BA, University of Texas, 1957.

## CHURCHILL, David A
Jenner & Block LLP, Washington, DC
202 639 6056
dchurchill@jenner.com
*Recommended in Government Contracts*

**Practice Areas:** David A Churchill is a Partner in Jenner & Block's Washington, DC office. He is Chair of the firm's Government Contracts Practice, Co-Chair of the Defense and Aerospace Practice, and a Member of its Arbitration: Domestic and International Practice. Mr Churchill practices before the major forums for resolution of federal contract award and performance disputes, including the Court of Federal Claims, the agency boards of contract appeals and the Gov-

ernment Accountability Office. He also counsels in matters involving the award and performance of international public contracts under the US Foreign Military Sales and Foreign Military Finance programs. He has experience in conducting domestic and international arbitration proceedings and various types of alternative dispute resolution techniques. Mr Churchill has an active counseling practice in proposal and award-related matters involving government contracts, including domestic preference requirements, such as Buy American and Trade Agreements Acts, gratuities and procurement integrity issues, Truth in Negotiations Act requirements, and suspension and debarment of prime and subcontractors. He counsels regularly on issues arising during performance of government contracts and subcontracts, such as changes, delays and claims preparation. Mr Churchill is Immediate Past President of the US Court of Federal Claims Bar Association. In 1998-99, he was Chair of the Public Contract Law Section of the American Bar Association. In November 2004, he was named a 'leading lawyer' in Government Contracts by the editors of Legal Times.
**Personal:** Cornell University, JD, 1979, cum laude.

## CHUSED, Wesley
Looney & Grossman LLP, Boston
617 951 2800
*Recommended in Transportation*

## CLARK, Harry L
Dewey Ballantine LLP, Washington, DC
202 429 2359
hclark@deweyballantine.com
*Recommended in International Trade*

**Practice Areas:** International trade, litigation, white-collar crime and government investigations.
**Career:** Harry Clark is a Member of Dewey Ballantine's International Trade Group. He leads major international trade legal and policy initiatives, including work on behalf of the US lumber industry relating to trade in softwood lumber. He is an expert on international trade and national security-related measures such as export controls, economic sanctions, the Foreign Corrupt Practices Act, the Exon-Florio Amendment, anti-money laundering provisions, industrial security requirements and other government procurement rules, and anti-boycott regulations.
**Personal:** BA, University of North Carolina, 1985. JD, University of Virginia Law School, 1989.

## CLARK, James
Cahill Gordon & Reindel LLP, New York
212 701 3900
*Recommended in Capital Markets*

## CLARK, Matthew J
Arent Fox PLLC, Washington, DC
202 828 3435
clark.matthew@arentfox.com
*Recommended in International Trade*

**Practice Areas:** Head of the firm's International Trade Group and Member of the firm's Executive Committee. More than 20 years of practice focused on adversarial trade proceedings, particularly complex antidumping and countervailing duty proceedings, including dispute resolution under the NAFTA and the WTO Agreements. Practice includes a long history of trade policy advice and import regulatory matters including Customs penalty proceedings and investigations, and compliance.
**Publications:** 'Inside the Minds': International Trade Law Best Practices', Aspatore Books (2006); 'Trade and The Environment: Law, Economics, and Policy', Colorado Journal of International Law and Policy 6 (1) (Review) 157; 'Regulating International Trade, Global Law and Business' (October 1995).
**Personal:** JD Catholic University of America, 1983; BA Villanova University, 1980.

## CLARK, Peter
Clark, Atcheson & Reisert, New York
212 297 0257
*Recommended in Transportation*

## CLAY, A Stephens
Kilpatrick Stockton LLP, Atlanta
404 815 6500
*Recommended in International Arbitration, Litigation*
*Please see Georgia for profile*

## CLAYTON III, Walter J (Jay)
Sullivan & Cromwell LLP, New York
212 558 3445
claytonwj@sullcrom.com
*Recommended in Capital Markets*

**Practice Areas:** Extensive cross-border experience in public/private M&A and capital markets transactions, including equity and leveraged finance transactions. Jay regularly counsels several global financial institutions on securities trading issues. He also has advised multinational companies and their boards in connection with investigations involving the SEC, Department of Justice and the Federal Reserve Bank of New York.
**Prof. Memberships:** IBA; ABA; ASIL.
**Career:** Partner since 2001.
**Publications:** Active in preparing comments of industry groups on proposed US and EU securities laws and regulations.
**Personal:** University of Pennsylvania (BSE, 1988); University of Cambridge (BA, 1990); University of Pennsylvania Law School (JD, 1993).

## CLEMENTS, William L
Foley & Lardner LLP, Washington, DC
202 295 4615
wclements@foley.com
*Recommended in International Trade*

**Career:** William L Clements is a Partner with the Washington, DC office of Foley & Lardner LLP. A Member of the White Collar and Corporate Compliance Practice Group and the International Practice, he counsels foreign and domestic parties regarding international business regulatory matters, particularly export controls, economic sanctions and the Foreign Corrupt Practices Act. He leads internal investigations of potential violations of the US Export Administration Regulations, the International Traffic in Arms Regulations, Office of Foreign Assets Control regulations and the Foreign Corrupt Practices Act. He received his JD from Suffolk University Law School.

## CLINTON, William J
White & Case LLP, Washington, DC
202 626 3620
wclinton@whitecase.com
*Recommended in International Trade*

**Practice Areas:** A recognized authority on legal developments related to the WTO, NAFTA and other multilateral trade arrangements. Has extensive experience in representing parties in import trade investigations under the antidumping, countervailing duty, safeguards and customs laws of many jurisdictions. Also advises sovereign governments on multilateral dispute settlements and negotiations related to these laws.
**Prof. Memberships:** District of Columbia Bar, US Court of International Trade, US Court of Appeals for the Federal Circuit.
**Career:** Speaks and reads Chinese; taught writing at Tunghai University and Tamkang University in Taiwan.
**Personal:** JD, Georgetown University, 1982; BS, Georgetown University, 1976.

## COGAN JR, John P
Akin Gump Strauss Hauer & Feld LLP, Houston 713 220 5800
*Recommended in Energy, Projects*
*Please see Texas for profile*

## COGBILL III, John
McGuireWoods LLP, Richmond
804 775 1000
*Recommended in Real Estate, Transportation*

## COHEN, H Rodgin
Sullivan & Cromwell LLP, New York
212 558 4000
*Recommended in Corporate/M&A, Financial Services*
*Please see New York for profile*

## COHEN, Michael
Nicoletti Hornig Campise and Sweeney, New York 212 220 3830
*Recommended in Transportation*

## COHEN, Steven
Cadwalader, Wickersham & Taft LLP,
Charlotte 704 348 5100
*Recommended in Capital Markets*
*Please see North Carolina for profile*

## COHN, Joshua
Allen & Overy LLP, New York
212 610 6428
joshua.cohn@allenovery.com
*Recommended in Capital Markets*
**Practice Areas:** Highly diverse transactional and advisory derivatives practice (including as counsel to the International Swaps and Derivatives Association).
**Career:** Partner at Allen & Overy LLP since 2001. Previously, he was Derivatives Counsel at Cravath, Swaine & Moore, Senior Vice President and General Counsel of DKB Financial Products, and First Vice President and Counsel of Security Pacific National Bank.
**Personal:** NYU School of Law (JD, 1980); Columbia College (BA, 1972).

## COHN, Robert
Hogan & Hartson LLP, Washington, DC
202 637 4999
recohn@hhlaw.com
*Recommended in Transportation*
**Practice Areas:** Counseling and representation of airlines and airports on regulatory and transactional matters, including licensing, certification, compliance, safety, security, environmental, airport rates and charges and revenue use issues, aircraft acquisitions/finance/leasing, airport use and lease agreements, domestic and international air service development, FAA funding, legislation, litigation before federal courts, international trade, mergers and acquisitions.
**Prof. Memberships:** American Bar Association; Federal Bar Association; International Aviation Club; Aero Club.
**Career:** Mr Cohn has specialized in aviation law for over 35 years. Prior to joining Hogan & Hartson, Mr Cohn was Chairman of the Aviation Practice Group of a major Washington DC law firm and was outside general counsel to one of the largest post-deregulation airlines. Prior to entering private practice he held a number of senior policy positions at the Civil Aeronautics Board, including executive assistant to three Board Members, including the Chairman and Vice Chairperson of the CAB.
**Personal:** Georgetown University Law Center (JD, 1969); Syracuse University (BA, 1966).

## COLEMAN, Payson
Pillsbury Winthrop Shaw Pittman LLP,
New York 212 858 1426
payson.coleman@pillsburylaw.com
*Recommended in Transportation*
**Practice Areas:** Mr Coleman is the leader of the firm's Equipment Finance Practice Team. He represents equipment financiers, lessor and manufacturers in a broad range of domestic and cross-border lease, finance, acquisition, repossession and remarketing activities. Recent assignments include representation of significant creditor groups in the Air Canada, Delta, Northwest and United Airlines bankruptcies, and commercial and corporate aircraft sales financing, operating leasing and securitization transactions. Mr Coleman is a Member of the Legal Advisory Panel of the Aviation working Group appointed by Boeing and Airbus for implementing the Cape Town Convention and of the ABA Sub-Committee on Aircraft Financing.

## COLLINS, Joseph P
Mayer, Brown, Rowe & Maw LLP,
Chicago 312 701 8353
jcollins@mayerbrownrowe.com
*Recommended in Capital Markets*
**Practice Areas:** Practice Leader, Futures and Derivatives Law Practice. Represents brokerage firms, investment management clients, trading and investment advisors, hedge fund operators, investment companies, banks, and pension plans. Practice encompasses financial services acquisitions and regulatory counseling on securities, futures, forwards, swaps, options, and hybrid securities. Lead attorney in Refco Group's acquisitions including Cargill Investor Services; Ameritrade's acquisitions including Datek, and Merrill Lynch's acquisition of Bear Stearns' ISE operations, ABN's securities clearing businesses, Pax Clearing, and investment in PHLX.
**Prof. Memberships:** Member and past Chair, ABA Committee on Regulation of Futures and Derivatives Instruments; Member and past Chair, Chicago Bar Association and Association of the Bar of the City of New York, Futures Regulation Committees.
**Career:** Mayer, Brown, Rowe & Maw LLP as Partner in 1994 following 19 years with Schiff Hardin & Waite.
**Publications:** ABA Committee on Regulation of Futures and Derivatives Instruments Conferences, SIA and FIA Law and Compliance Conferences, and various other panels and workshops regarding derivative instruments and securities.
**Personal:** JD, New York University School of Law, 1975; Root-Tilden Scholar. AB (magna cum laude), College of the Holy Cross, 1972. Former Circuit Secretary, NYU School of Law Root-Tilden Scholarship Programme.

## CONNELLY, Warren E
Akin Gump Strauss Hauer & Feld LLP,
Washington, DC 202 887 4046
wconnelly@akingump.com
*Recommended in International Trade*
**Practice Areas:** Warren Connelly represents clients in proceedings before the Department of Commerce, International Trade Commission, Office of the US Trade Representative, Customs Service, Court of International Trade and US Court of Appeals for the Federal Circuit. He handles a wide variety of import- and export-related matters, including trade policy, WTO dispute resolution proceedings, export controls, import licensing, sanctions, antiboycott and customs. He has been extensively involved in a variety of administrative and civil court litigation.
**Personal:** AB, Dartmouth College (1968); JD, Georgetown University Law Center (1973).

## CONRAD JR, Winthrop B
Davis Polk & Wardwell, New York
212 450 4000
winthrop.conrad@dpw.com
*Recommended in Capital Markets*
**Practice Areas:** Member of Davis Polk & Wardwell's Corporate Department. Has extensive experience in securities offerings of all types, as well as mergers and acquisitions. Recent experience includes numerous initial public offerings representing underwriters, including Morgan Stanley, Bank of America Securities, and CSFB; and issuers, such as Canadian National Railway and Pepsi Bottling Group. Represented PepsiCo in its $13.5 billion acquisition of Quaker Oats. Has also worked on numerous restructuring transactions, including high-yield financings, debt tender offers and exchange offers, as well as cross-border transactions.

## CORR, Christopher F
White & Case LLP, Washington, DC
202 626 3613
ccorr@whitecase.com
*Recommended in International Trade*
**Practice Areas:** International trade matters, including antidumping, countervailing duty and intellectual property actions before the ITC and DOC; trade litigation before US Federal Courts; Section 337 investigations; WTO and NAFTA rules governing goods, services, investment and intellectual property; export control; national security controls; customs matters; Section 301; and GSP proceedings. He has served as counsel in numerous trade cases including those concerning semiconductors, computers and other electronics, steel products, lumber, seafood, agricultural products, chemicals, pharmaceuticals and technology transfer, as well as the negotiation of government-to-government agreements.

## CORRALES, Carmen Amalia
Cleary Gottlieb Steen & Hamilton LLP,
New York 212 225 2982
ccorrales@cgsh.com
*Recommended in Capital Markets*
**Practice Areas:** Sovereign transactions, including securities offerings by sovereign issuers and sovereign debt restructuring. Represented Argentina in one of the largest sovereign debt restructurings in history, the Dominican Republic in its debt restructurings and financings, Perú in its financings as well as various underwriters in financings by Costa Rica, El Salvador, Guatemala and various state-owned entities. International finance transactions, including representing public and private issuers and underwriters in equity and debt offerings in international markets and in the legal structuring and documentation of derivative transactions and complex commercial bank lending transactions.
**Prof. Memberships:** Member of the Bar in New York and New Jersey.
**Career:** Joined firm, 1990; became Partner, 1998. JD, Harvard Law School (1989); BA, University of Pennsylvania (1986).

## COSTELLO, Frank
Zuckert, Scoutt & Rasenberger, LLP,
Washington, DC 202 298 8660
*Recommended in Transportation*

## COWAN, Cameron
Orrick, Herrington & Sutcliffe LLP, Washington, DC
202 339 8488
ccowan@orrick.com
*Recommended in Capital Markets*
**Practice Areas:** Represents financial institutions, investment banks, and companies with particular expertise in the structuring, issuance, and purchase of asset-backed, mortgage-backed, and derivative products.
**Prof. Memberships:** American Securitization Forum: Member, Board of Directors and Executive Committee; Chair, Legal, Regulatory, Tax and Accounting Committee.
**Career:** Founder, Orrick's Washington office (1993); Member, Executive Committee (2001-present); Managing Director, Finance (2001-04); Managing Partner, East Coast offices (1998-2000).
**Publications:** Co-author, 'Mortgage-Backed Securities: Developments and Trends in the Secondary Mortgage Market'.
**Personal:** JD, University of Virginia School of Law, 1981; MBA, Columbia University Graduate School of Business; BS, magna cum laude, Syracuse University.

## CRAFT, Randal Robert
Holland & Knight LLP, New York
212 513 3200
randal.craft@hklaw.com
*Recommended in Transportation*
**Practice Areas:** Partner in the Litigation Section, his practice is devoted primarily to providing advice and conducting litigation concerning aviation, product liability, mass disaster, and insurance matters. He has been lead counsel to airlines and manufacturers of aircraft, engines, and components, especially in major air crash cases and NTSB investigations. Craft has extensive experience as lead counsel in product liability cases, including mass disaster cases, for manufacturers

of various products, including industrial machinery, chemicals, railroad cars, electrical equipment, engines, and consumer products. He has also advised and represented insurers on the interpretation of policies, coverage issues, and claims settlement procedures.

## CROKE, James
Cadwalader, Wickersham & Taft LLP, New York 212 504 6139
james.croke@cwt.com
*Recommended in Capital Markets*
**Practice Areas:** Represents underwriters and issuers in public offerings and private placements of funded and synthetic asset-backed securities, including pass-through certificates, asset-backed notes, credit-linked notes, medium-term notes, commercial paper notes. Structured finance experience includes funded and synthetic securitizations of credit card receivables, high-yield bonds, hedge funds, collateralized debt obligations, leveraged and synthetic lease debt, project finance debt, mortgage loans, commercial loans, equipment leases, government receivables, interests in mortgage warehouse lines of credit, trade receivables of various types and numerous other assets. Practice involves both US offerings and offerings in the Euromarkets; also global underwriting facilities involving simultaneous offerings in the US and Euromarkets. Has acted as counsel to banks, insurance companies and other sponsors, commercial paper dealers and placement agents in connection with establishment of over 130 asset-backed commercial paper conduits and structured investment vehicles.
**Prof. Memberships:** New York and California Bars; Member, Board of Directors, Asset Securitization Forum.
**Personal:** JD, University of Notre Dame Law School (1983); BS, University of Kentucky (cum laude) (1980).

## CROST, Katharine I
Orrick, Herrington & Sutcliffe LLP, New York 212 506 5070
kcrost@orrick.com
*Recommended in Capital Markets*
**Practice Areas:** Represents issuers, underwriters, servicers, institutional purchasers, and credit enhancers in securitization transactions involving a wide variety of assets, including all types of mortgage loans. She has helped develop innovative structures for the securitization of assets such as mortgages, tobacco litigation settlement funds, tax liens, utility stranded costs, and student loans.
**Prof. Memberships:** State Bar of New York.
**Career:** Co-Head of Orrick's Structured Finance Group (2003-06); Executive Committee member (1993-99).
**Personal:** JD, University of Virginia School of Law, 1978; BM, cum laude, Michigan State University, 1974.

## CULLEN, William J
Sidley Austin LLP, New York 212 839 7376
wcullen@sidley.com
*Recommended in Capital Markets*
**Practice Areas:** Partner in the New York office in the Securitization Group. His practice is focused on securities and corporate finance, with an emphasis on securitization of financial assets and, in particular, commercial mortgage assets.
**Personal:** University of Pennsylvania Law School, JD, 1985; Colgate University, BA, 1982. Admission: New York, 1986.

## CUNNINGHAM, Daniel
Allen & Overy LLP, New York 212 610 6427
daniel.cunningham@allenovery.com
*Recommended in Capital Markets*
**Practice Areas:** Involved in all types of capital markets transactions, and has particular expertise in the fields of structured finance and derivatives. He has been US Counsel to ISDA since its inception. He has also worked at the very highest level in M&A.
**Career:** Partner at Allen & Overy LLP since 2001. Previously, he was a Partner at Cravath, Swaine & Moore.
**Personal:** Harvard Law School (JD, magna cum laude, 1975); Princeton University (AB, cum laude, 1971).

## CUNNINGHAM, Richard
Steptoe & Johnson LLP, Washington, DC 202 429 6434
rcunningham@steptoe.com
*Recommended in International Trade*
**Practice Areas:** Senior Partner, Steptoe & Johnson LLP, Washington, DC. Focuses on US import relief laws, trade policy issues, WTO matters, and international trade strategies. Advises and represents foreign and domestic clients in matters involving market access negotiations, US antidumping and countervailing duty laws, bilateral and multilateral trade negotiations, and trade-related IP policy and litigation. Represented clients in the Tokyo Round and the Uruguay Round of Multilateral Trade Negotiations, and governments and corporations in WTO dispute resolution proceedings. Advised Congressional committees and governmental agencies on trade issues.
**Personal:** JD, George Washington University, 1968; AB, George Washington University, 1964.

## CURTIS, Susan M
Skadden, Arps, Slate, Meagher & Flom LLP & Affiliates, New York 212 735 2119
scurtis@skadden.com
*Recommended in Capital Markets*
**Practice Areas:** Represents underwriters, placement agents, issuers and banks in asset-backed securities transactions and other financings. Acts as counsel in public offerings and private placement and Regulation S transactions involving

the issuance of asset-backed notes, asset-backed certificates, preferred stock, commercial paper and medium-term notes. Has represented underwriters and collateral managers in the collateralized bond obligation market from its inception. Acts as deal counsel in cash-flow CBOs and market value CBOs and in the repackaging of bonds, asset-backed securities, swaps and other derivative instruments.
**Career:** JD, Vanderbilt University, 1981; BA, University of Tennessee, 1977 (summa cum laude; Phi Beta Kappa).

## CURTISS, Catherine
Hughes Hubbard & Reed LLP, Washington, DC 202 721 4660
curtiss@hugheshubbard.com
*Recommended in International Trade*
**Practice Areas:** Countervailing duty; antidumping; customs; NAFTA; WTO Agreement.
**Career:** Partner, Washington, DC since 1997. Private practice since 1981, Partner since 1990.
**Publications:** 'Against the Grain: US-Canada Wheat Trade Dispute', in The First Decade of NAFTA (2004); 'US Customs Law and Compliance', in Corporate Legal Departments (2004); 'Agreement on Trade-Related Investment Measures: A Five-Year Review', in The Comparative Law Yearbook of International Business (2003); 'Antidumping As An International Corporate Strategy', Canadian International Lawyer (2001).
**Personal:** Born 1950. University of Michigan BA (1972), MA (1973 cum laude), Georgetown University Law Center JD (1980 cum laude).

## CURTNER, Gregory
Miller, Canfield, Paddock and Stone, P.L.C., New York 212 704 4400
*Recommended in Litigation, Sport*
*Please see Michigan for profile*

## CUVA, Anthony J
Akerman Senterfitt, Tampa 813 209 5049
anthony.cuva@akerman.com
*Recommended in Transportation*
**Career:** Anthony Cuva is a Board Certified Specialist in Admiralty and Maritime Litigation by the Florida Bar. He has extensive experience representing maritime clients in federal courts, Florida state courts, arbitrations and administrative hearings. For the past 15 years, he has been actively involved in traditional maritime litigation pertaining to collisions, personal injuries, cargo damage and salvage cases. A complete biography can be found at www.akerman.com.

## DADAKIS, John D
Schiff Hardin LLP, New York 212 745 0860
JDadakis@schiffhardin.com
*Recommended in Wealth Management*
**Practice Areas:** Wealth management.

**Prof. Memberships:** American Bar Association, Attorneys for Family-Held Enterprises, Family Firm Institute.
**Career:** Concentrates in representing high net worth individuals. Acts as 'Personal General Counsel' for numerous Fortune 500 executives and successful private business entrepreneurs. Practice focuses on asset protection, tax minimization, and wealth transference, and he has developed individual client mission statement programs to help his clients manage and achieve these goals. Also works with financial advisers and financial institutions to devise and implement wealth preservation strategies.
**Personal:** Johns Hopkins University (BA, 1973), Fordham University School of Law (JD, 1976)

## DALLAS, Bruce
Davis Polk & Wardwell, Menlo Park 650 752 2000
bruce.dallas@dpw.com
*Recommended in Capital Markets*
**Practice Areas:** Member of Davis Polk & Wardwell's Global Technology Group. Advises clients in public and private securities offerings, including equity derivatives, convertible debt, high-yield debt and initial public offerings. Also advises clients on general corporate matters, including SEC and Sarbanes-Oxley compliance. Has been the primary capital markets Partner for Comcast, E*Trade, Gateway and Oracle, among others, regularly represents Morgan Stanley and J.P. Morgan, among others, as underwriters' counsel, and has been lead Partner on a number of technology, telecommunications and biotechnology securities offerings.

## DAMERIS, Thad
Pillsbury Winthrop Shaw Pittman LLP, Houston 713 425 7322
thad.dameris@pillsburylaw.com
*Recommended in Transportation*
**Practice Areas:** Mr Dameris is co-leader of Pillsbury's Aviation, Aerospace and Transportation Team. He has handled a variety of complex business disputes, including disputes relating to aviation, breach of contract, fiduciary duty, fraud, international arbitration, oil and gas, partnership, and shareholder agreements. He has vast experience in multi-party litigation centering on international disputes and particular experience in dealing with issues such as jurisdiction of US courts, foreign sovereign immunity, forum non conveniens, and multidistrict litigation.
**Prof. Memberships:** Member, American Board of Trial Advocates.
**Personal:** JD, University of Texas School of Law, 1986 (with honors); BBA, Southern Methodist University, 1982.

### DANIEL, Laurie Webb
Holland & Knight LLP, Atlanta
404 817 8500
*Recommended in Litigation, Products
Liability
Please see Georgia for profile*

### DAVENPORT, Kirk
Latham & Watkins LLP, New York
212 906 1200
*Recommended in Capital Markets*

### DAVIDSON, Gordon
Fenwick & West LLP, Mountain View
650 988 8500
*Recommended in Capital Markets,
Corporate/M&A
Please see California
for profile*

### DAYAN, Michael D
Cleary Gottlieb Steen & Hamilton LLP,
New York
212 225 2382
mdayan@cgsh.com
*Recommended in Capital Markets*
**Practice Areas:** Structuring and docu-
menting complex over-the-counter and
capital markets derivative products; regu-
latory analysis of securities, margin, com-
modities, banking and insolvency issues
relating to derivative products.
**Prof. Memberships:** Member, New York
Bar; Global Documentation Steering
Committee; ISDA Equity Derivatives and
Credit Derivatives Committees.
**Career:** Joined firm, 1993; became Part-
ner, 2003. Law clerk, Honorable Jon O
Newman, US Court of Appeals, Second
Circuit (1992-93). JD, magna cum laude,
Law Review, Harvard Law School (1992);
BS, summa cum laude, Wharton School,
University of Pennsylvania (1986).
**Publications:** 'Raising Capital Through
OTC Equity Derivatives: The Goldman,
Sachs & Co. Interpretive Letter', FDLR;
Securities Reporter.

### DAYANIM, Behnam
Paul, Hastings, Janofsky & Walker LLP,
Washington, DC
202 551 1737
bdayanim@paulhastings.com
*Recommended in International Trade*
**Practice Areas:** Advises on international
trade, export controls and technology
transfer issues, representing clients in
enforcement investigations, counseling
and developing compliance programs.
Also advises in privacy and information
security; electronic financial services, gaming and commerce; IT outsourcing; and
false advertising and intellectual property.
His work in each area includes counseling,
compliance, litigation, licensing and related transactional representations.
**Prof. Memberships:** American Bar
Association; Computer Law Association.
**Publications:** He has published extensively in law reviews, magazines and
newspapers on trade, information technology and public international law

issues.
**Personal:** Harvard Law School, JD cum
laude 1993; Yeshiva University, BA
summa cum laude 1989.

### DE GROOT, Steven
King & Spalding LLP, Atlanta
404 572 3412
SdeGroot@KSLAW.com
*Recommended in Business Process
Outsourcing*
**Practice Areas:** Private equity and intellectual property with substantial experience in publicly and privately held companies in connection with a wide variety
of corporate and technology matters,
including the acquisition, sale, development, licensing and distribution of technology assets; the formation of technology ventures and marketing alliances; various information technology and business
process outsourcing transactions; and a
variety of merger and acquisition and
financing transactions.
**Prof. Memberships:** American Bar
Association; Atlanta Bar Association;
New Jersey Bar Association; State Bar of
Georgia.
**Personal:** BA, University of Notre Dame,
1981; JD, Notre Dame Law School,1988.

### DE SEAR, Edward
McKee Nelson LLP, New York
917 777 4565
edesear@mckeenelson.com
*Recommended in Capital Markets*
**Practice Areas:** Asset-backed securities,
both in the US and overseas. Particular
expertise in securitisation of credit card
receivables, auto dealer floorplan loans,
life settlements, future flows, mutual fund
fees, distressed assets, tobacco litigation
settlement payments, tobacco quota payments and entertainment-related assets.
Represents issuers, underwriters, credit
enhancers and placement agents.
**Career:** Before joining McKee Nelson,
was a Partner at Orrick, Herrington &
Sutcliffe LLP. Earlier in his career, he
helped to structure the earliest asset-
backed transactions, initially as an investment banker and later as a Partner at Milbank, Tweed, Hadley & McCloy.
**Personal:** JD, University of Virginia
School of Law.

### DEES, C Stanley
McKenna Long & Aldridge LLP,
Washington, DC 202 496 7628
sdees@mckennalong.com
*Recommended in Government
Contracts*
**Practice Areas:** Practice encompasses
counseling and litigation in the field of
government contracts and related areas,
including: contract formation and negotiation; bid protests; issues in commercialization and privatization; rights in
technical data; schedule contracts; claims
preparation under supply, construction,
and shipbuilding contracts; debarment
and suspension proceedings; procure-

ment fraud investigations and qui tam
cases; contractor self-governance and
compliance programs; defective pricing;
cost recovery under contracts and grants;
equitable adjustments; and remedies
under illegal contract provisions.
Authored articles on antitrust in government contracts, defective specifications,
contract interpretation, delays, recovery
of unabsorbed overhead, recovery of
attorneys' fees, disputes and remedies,
competition in service contracting, contract financing, and contractor self-governance.
**Prof. Memberships:** Member and officer of: Public Contract Law Section of
American Bar Association (Chair 1987-
88); District of Columbia Bar; National
Contract Management Association;
Council of Defense and Space Industry
Associations; honorary faculty member,
US Army JAG School.
**Personal:** University of Virginia (LLB,
1963, Order of the Coif); Princeton University (AB, 1960, with honors).

### DEL CALVO, Jorge
Pillsbury Winthrop Shaw Pittman LLP,
Palo Alto 650 233 4500
*Recommended in Capital Markets,
Corporate/M&A
Please see California
for profile*

### DELANEY, John
Morrison & Foerster LLP, New York
212 468 8000
*Recommended in Business Process
Outsourcing, Technology
Please see New York for profile*

### DEMPSEY, Kevin M
Dewey Ballantine LLP, Washington, DC
202 862 3676
kdempsey@deweyballantine.com
*Recommended in International Trade*
**Practice Areas:** Kevin Dempsey handles
a wide variety of international trade matters, with a focus on US and foreign
antidumping and countervailing duty
investigations, safeguards actions, WTO
and NAFTA dispute settlement, trade
policy and international negotiations. He
has considerable experience in US law
and international agreements related to
subsidies, trade remedies, market access,
trade-related aspects of intellectual property, product standards, foreign investment, and e-commerce, as well as US legislative procedures for authorizing and
implementing international trade agreements.
**Career:** Partner, Dewey Ballantine LLP.
**Personal:** AB, honors, Washington University, 1984. JD, cum laude, Harvard Law
School, 1987.

### DENENBERG, Alan
Davis Polk & Wardwell, Menlo Park
650 752 2000
alan.denenberg@dpw.com
*Recommended in Capital Markets*

**Practice Areas:** Member of Davis Polk
& Wardwell's Global Technology Group.
Has extensive experience in capital markets and mergers and acquisitions transactions. Practice includes general corporate representations, as well as a broad
range of public and private financings,
including convertible debt, high-yield
debt, equity and initial public offerings,
representing both domestic and foreign
issuers and underwriters. In the mergers
and acquisitions area, has represented
both acquirer and target companies in a
variety of public and private transactions.

### DENNY, Otway
Fulbright & Jaworski L.L.P., Houston
713 651 5151
*Recommended in Litigation, Products
Liability
Please see Texas for profile*

### DEORCHIS, Vincent M
DeOrchis & Partners LLP, New York
212 344 4700, Ext. 233
vdeorchis@marinelex.com
*Recommended in Transportation*
**Practice Areas:** Maritime, transportation, commercial, and insurance. Defence
of shipowners, charterers, P&I clubs, forwarders, and others in maritime, land
and air transportation. Has handled litigation and arbitration in areas involving
cargo, hull, charterparties, salvage, environmental, personal injury. Drafting of
documentation used in the transportation field. Acts for carriers and P&I
including Zim Lines, MSC and ACL.
Presently advisor to US State Department
on transportation law.
**Prof. Memberships:** US Maritime Law
Association (Member, retired Board of
Directors; Ex-Chairman Carriage of
Goods), NY County Bar (Committee on
Maritime and Admiralty law), Defence
Association, Propeller Club; Director,
NYMAR.
**Career:** Fordham College, 1971; Ford-
ham Law School 1974; admitted New
York Bar 1975; admitted to practice
before the US Supreme Court 1985; US
Court of Appeal for the Second (1975),
Third (1989) and Fourth (1996) Circuits,
and before the Southern and Eastern Dis-
trict of New York and Southern District
of Texas 1975.
**Publications:** Contributing Author,
'Attorney's Practice Guide to Negotia-
tions', Callaghan Press.
**Personal:** Born 25 August 1949 in New
York. Director, South Street Seaport
Museum, Maritime Heritage Council.
Interests include sailing. Lives in Manhat-
tan and East Hampton.

### DESANTIS, Victor
White & Case LLP, Washington, DC
202 626 3600
*Recommended in Projects
Please see District of Columbia for
profile*

**DETZEL, Lauren**
Dean, Mead, Egerton, Bloodworth,
Capouano & Bozarth PA, Orlando
407 841 1200
*Recommended in Tax, Wealth
Management
Please see Florida for profile*

**DEVECCHIO, Jay W**
Jenner & Block LLP, Washington, DC
202 639 6893
jdevecchio@jenner.com
*Recommended in Government
Contracts*
**Practice Areas:** W Jay DeVecchio is a
Partner in Jenner & Block's Washington,
DC office. He is a Member of the firm's
Government Contracts, Defense and
Aerospace, and Litigation and Dispute
Resolution Practices. Mr DeVecchio represents clients in all facets of government
procurement law, from bid protests, to
complex claims and disputes, through
suspension and debarment. He also represents clients in related issues such as
criminal and civil fraud, qui tam actions,
and internal investigations. His litigation
practice has encompassed the largest
defective pricing appeal tried to date, the
leading case on latent defects, and the
Eleventh Circuit's decision on false claims
immunity for Medicare contractors. His
clients are primarily from the aerospace,
healthcare, and technology sectors. Mr
DeVecchio has been a guest instructor at
the University of Virginia and the George
Washington University Law School Government Contracts Program. He is a recognized leader in the field of intellectual
property rights in government contracts,
lecturing nationwide on the subject for
Federal Publications Seminars, LLC. He
also conducts seminars on diverse subjects such as Contract Pricing, Compliance Programs, Qui Tam Litigation,
Claims, Rights in Data and Software, and
Teaming Agreements. Similarly, Mr
DeVecchio developed and appeared in a
series of training videotapes, used by over
100 companies, addressing Labor Charging, Materials Charging, and Procurement Integrity.
**Personal:** The Catholic University
School of Law, JD, 1978; casenote editor
of the Law Review. Duke University, BA,
1974, cum laude.

**DI ROSA, Paolo**
Winston & Strawn LLP, Washington, DC
202 282 5000
pdirosa@winston.com
*Recommended in International
Arbitration*
**Practice Areas:** International arbitration and litigation; public international
law. Specializes in disputes between
investors and sovereign States, particularly pursuant to Bilateral Investment
Treaties, and represents both Claimants
and Respondent States in arbitral fora
such as the International Centre for Set-

tlement of Investment Disputes (ICSID).
Extensive experience in public interna-
tional law and sovereign representation
**Prof. Memberships:** President, Chilean-
American Chamber of Commerce
(Washington DC); Member, Internation-
al Bar Association; International Law
Association; American Society of Inter-
national Law; Inter-American Bar Associ-
ation; American Bar Association; District
of Columbia Bar Association.
**Career:** Partner at Winston & Strawn
since 2004. Former Head of Office of
Legal Adviser for Western Hemisphere
Affairs, US Department of State; Chief
US negotiator for numerous treaties and
international agreements.
**Publications:** Speaker/panelist at confer-
ences sponsored by, inter alia, Interna-
tional Chamber of Commerce (ICC),
American Arbitration Association
(AAA), ICSID, Institute of Transnational
Arbitration (ITA); New York State Bar
Association. Author, 'The Recent Wave of
Arbitrations Against Argentina Under
Bilateral Investment Treaties: Back-
ground and Principal Legal Issues' (U. of
Miami Inter-American Law Review, vol
36 no 1 (Fall 2004)).
**Personal:** Harvard Law School, JD cum
laude (1991); Harvard College, BA
magna cum laude (1987). Languages:
English and Spanish (native fluency).

**DILLOW, John**
Perkins Coie LLP, Seattle
206 583 8888
*Recommended in Transportation*

**DIMICHAEL, Nicholas**
Thompson Hine LLP, Washington, DC
202 263 4103
Nick.DiMichael@ThompsonHine.com
*Recommended in Transportation*
**Career:** Nick assists companies in satisfying domestic and international transportation needs and complex transportation-related litigation. He represents utilities and industrial concerns, including
companies in the chemical, steel, forest
products, automobile, mining, recycling,
and other industries, as well as agricultural interests. Nick serves as counsel to The
National Industrial Transportation
League, the nation's largest association
representing shippers, and is transportation counsel to The Fertilizer Institute
and other trade associations. He has participated in numerous proceedings before
the Surface Transportation Board,
Department of Transportation, Federal
Maritime Commission, and other agencies; in international transportation
negotiations; and in litigation and arbitration on transportation matters.

**DOCKSEY, Ross**
Sonnenschein Nath & Rosenthal LLP,
Chicago 312 876 8000
*Recommended in Business Process
Outsourcing, Technology
Please see Illinois for profile*

**DOKE JR, Marshall J**
Gardere Wynne Sewell LLP, Dallas
214 999 4733
mdoke@gardere.com
*Recommended in Government
Contracts*
**Practice Areas:** Government contracts
litigation and counseling.
**Prof. Memberships:** US OMB Acquisi-
tion Advisory Panel for Federal Procure-
ment established by federal law; American Bar Association (former Board of
Governors, House of Delegates, Chairman of Section of Public Contract Law,
Co-Chair of National Conference of
Lawyers and Certified Public Accountants, and Standing Committee on
Audit); Board of Governors and former
President of both US Court of Federal
Claims Bar Association and Boards of
Contract Appeals Bar Association; Board
of Governors of Federal Circuit Bar Association; American Arbitration Association's Commercial Panel of National Roster of Neutrals.
**Career:** Marshall Doke represents clients
in counseling and litigation involving
federal, state, and local public contracts,
including procurement protests, changes
and termination claims, defective pricing,
cost and accounting issues, compliance
matters, and false claims allegations. He
also has extensive experience in international transactional issues related to government contracts, including the Buy
American and Trade Agreements Acts,
foreign military sales agreements, the
Foreign Corrupt Practices Act, license
agreements, and export controls.
**Publications:** 'Government Procurement
Chapter', American Bar Association's International Lawyer's Desk Book
2003; 'The Business of Government Contracts', Winning Legal Strategies for Government Contracts (Aspatore Books,
2005); and numerous periodical publications.
**Personal:** LLB with high honors, Southern Methodist University School of Law,
1959; BA magna cum laude, Hardin Simmons University.

**DOLIN, Mitchell**
Covington & Burling, Washington, DC
202 662 6000
*Recommended in Insurance,
International Arbitration
Please see District of Columbia for
profile*

**DONOVAN, Donald**
Debevoise & Plimpton LLP, New York
212 909 6000
*Recommended in Arbitration,
International Arbitration*

**DORN, Joseph W**
King & Spalding LLP, Washington, DC
202 626 5445
jdorn@kslaw.com
*Recommended in International Trade*
**Practice Areas:** International trade reg-

ulation, customs law and complex business litigation. Substantial experience in
trade remedy actions on behalf of US
industries against imports from other
countries. Extensive experience in
NAFTA and WTO dispute settlement
proceedings, appeals before the US Court
of International Trade and the US Court
of Appeals for the Federal Circuit.
**Prof. Memberships:** American Bar
Association; ITC Trial Lawyers Association; International Bar Association; State
Bar of Georgia; The District of Columbia
Bar; US Court of International Trade, US
Court of Appeals for the Federal Circuit.
**Personal:** BA, University of North Carolina, 1970; JD, University of Virginia,
1973.

**DORRIS, Malcolm S**
Dechert LLP, New York
212 698 3519
malcolm.dorris@dechert.com
*Recommended in Capital Markets*
**Practice Areas:** Mr Dorris, a Partner in
the Finance and Real Estate Group, is
Chair of the Bank Financing and Securitization Group. He focuses on legal issues
connected with structured financings,
including CDOs, commercial paper conduit facilities, and the securitization of a
range of assets. He also serves as outside
counsel to a ratings agency and advises
borrowers, banks, and guarantors on
securitization issues.
**Publications:** Frequent author and lecturer on issues affecting the securitization
industry.
**Personal:** Colgate University, AB, 1976;
Washington and Lee University School of
Law, JD, 1980, executive editor of the
Washington and Lee University Law
Review.

**DOUGLAS, John**
Alston & Bird LLP, Atlanta
404 881 7000
*Recommended in Banking & Finance,
Financial Services
Please see Georgia for profile*

**DOWNES, Robert W**
Sullivan & Cromwell LLP, New York
212 558 4312
downesr@sullcrom.com
*Recommended in Capital Markets*
**Practice Areas:** Co-Coordinator, High
Yield Financing Group. Has extensive
experience advising issuers and underwriters in public and private offerings of
debt and equity securities, including
securities issued in structured finance
transactions. Also counsels US and foreign clients in mergers, acquisitions and
joint ventures. Active advisor to domestic
issuers on corporate governance matters.
**Career:** Partner since 2000. Prior to
returning to law school in 1987, was a
certified public accountant with Coopers
& Lybrand in Washington, DC.
**Personal:** University of Virginia (BS,
1985); George Washington Law School

(JD, 1991).

## DUBREUIL, Francis W
Wilson Sonsini Goodrich & Rosati, Palo Alto 650 493 9300
fdubreuil@wsgr.com
*Recommended in Wealth Management*
**Practice Areas:** Chairman of the firm's Tax Services Practice, which includes the employee benefits and compensation, tax, funds services, and estate planning and wealth management practices. Focuses on the representation of company founders and other entrepreneurs, venture capitalists, and private and public company executives and investors. Assists such clients, as well as other high-net-worth individuals, on a broad range of personal planning matters, with an emphasis on wealth transfer and the other planning opportunities and sophisticated strategies available.
**Personal:** JD, (cum laude) Harvard Law School, 1974; MS, Stanford University Graduate School of Business, 1990; BA, (summa cum laude) Boston College, 1970.

## DUGAN, Christopher F
Paul, Hastings, Janofsky & Walker LLP, Washington, DC
202 551 1723
chrisdugan@paulhastings.com
*Recommended in International Arbitration*
**Practice Areas:** International arbitrations, both commercial and treaty-based; international litigation, such as enforcement of arbitration awards and foreign judgments; and complex civil litigation. Mr Dugan is the Chair of Paul Hastings' International Arbitration Practice and the Litigation Department in Washington.
**Prof. Memberships:** American Society of International Law, International Bar Association.
**Career:** Prior to joining Paul Hastings in 2003, Mr Dugan was a Partner at Jones Day, where he practiced for 22 years. Mr Dugan is also an Adjunct Professor at Georgetown University Law Center.
**Publications:** 'International Investment Treaties and Investor-State Arbitration' (textbook/treatise to be published in 2006); 'NAFTA Chapter 11 Arbitral Tribunal: Ethyl Corporation v. The Government of Canada (Decision Regarding The Place Of Arbitration)', American Journal of International Law (1999); 'The FCPA in Russia and Other Former Communist Countries', American Journal of International Law (1997); and 'Foreign Privileges in US Litigation', Journal of International Law and Practice (1996).
**Personal:** Mr Dugan received his BA Degree from Johns Hopkins University and his JD Degree, cum laude, from Georgetown University Law Center in 1980. From 1980–81, Mr Dugan was a law

clerk to the Hon John Lewis Smith, Jr, Chief Judge, United States District Court for the District of Columbia.

## DUNN, Christopher A
Willkie Farr & Gallagher LLP, Washington, DC 202 303 1108
cdunn@willkie.com
*Recommended in International Trade*
**Practice Areas:** Partner in the International Trade Department, specializing in antidumping, subsidies, and 'safeguards' cases as well as customs matters. With a client base that includes Asian and Latin American governments and companies, he has significant experience representing actions before the World Trade Organization. Recent significant matters include the high-profile antidumping defense of outboard motors from Japan, shrimp from Thailand, and orange juice from Brazil.
**Prof. Memberships:** Member of the Bar Association of the District of Columbia and the American Bar Association.
**Career:** Admitted to the District of Columbia Bar.
**Publications:** Author of 'The Buy American Act and Other Buy National Programs', A Lawyer's Guide to International Transactions, ALI/ABA, 1977 and 'Antidumping and Countervailing Duty Investigations Under the Trade Agreements Act of 1979', George Washington Journal of Law and Economics, 1979. He is the co-author of 'Trade Agreement Program of the United States', A Lawyer's Guide to International Business Transactions, ALI/ABA, 1977, and a treatise entitled International Trade Practice, Clark Boardman Callaghan, 1977.
**Personal:** Received a JD from the Georgetown University Law Center in 1975, where he served as student Editor-In-Chief of The Tax Lawyer, and an AB from Brown University in 1972.

## DUPLER, Mitchell S
Cleary Gottlieb Steen & Hamilton LLP, Washington, DC 202 974 1630
mdupler@cgsh.com
*Recommended in Capital Markets*
**Practice Areas:** Corporate and financial matters, especially structured financings. Specializes in securities offerings backed by mortgages, other financial assets and derivatives. Leads team that brought to market over $1.5 trillion of mortgage-backed securities in last 10 years. Outside mortgage area, representative matters include 'synthetic treasuries', repackagings of fixed-income securities and derivatives, and collateralized debt obligations backed by high-yield securities, emerging market debt, asset-backed securities and interests in private equity funds, along with securities, banking and other related regulatory advice.
**Prof. Memberships:** Member of the Bar in the District of Colombia.
**Career:** JD, cum laude, Harvard Law

School (1979); AB, cum laude, Harvard College (1976).
**Publications:** Mr Dupler is widely published on structured finance, securities and banking law, including the 1995 text International Asset Securitization, which he co-edited.

## DURHAM, Thomas C
Mayer, Brown, Rowe & Maw LLP, Chicago 312 701 7216
tdurham@mayerbrownrowe.com
*Recommended in Tax Litigation*
**Practice Areas:** Representation of taxpayers before the Internal Revenue Service and various state and local taxing authorities, including litigation in US Tax Court, US Court of Federal Claims, and all levels of the federal court system. Particular experience in litigation of foreign issues, leasing, including LILOs and sales-leasebacks, appellate litigation, section 482, tax-advantaged investments and economic substance, summons enforcement litigation, and tax shelter registration and promoter issues. Also experienced in not-for-profit and natural resources tax law.
**Career:** Mayer, Brown, Rowe & Maw LLP, Chicago, 1980 to date.
**Publications:** 'Mrs Gregory's Great-Grandchildren: The Lost Generation', Journal of Taxation of Global Transactions (Summer 2002) (with Joel V Williamson and Stuart E Thiel). Author: 'The IRS Audit Process – Counsel to Counsel', published by Arthur Andersen & Co., Spring 1993.
**Personal:** New York University, JD, 1980; research editor, New York University Review of Law and Social Change. Cornell College, BA, magna cum laude, 1977, Phi Beta Kappa.

## DURLING, James P
Willkie Farr & Gallagher LLP, Washington, DC 202 303 1109
jdurling@willkie.com
*Recommended in International Trade*
**Practice Areas:** Partner in the International Trade Department, specializing in defending foreign companies and governments in antidumping, countervailing duty and other trade remedy investigations, and providing advice on parties' obligations under World Trade Organization agreements. Additionally, he has significant experience litigating WTO disputes and trade policy disputes between the US and foreign parties. Handles a wide range of customs matters, export control issues, including transfer pricing issues, and regularly works with economic experts. He has a significant practice representing Asian, particularly Japanese and Korean, companies and has also worked with clients in Thailand, Malaysia, Singapore, Taiwan, Indonesia, and the Philippines. Has worked with clients on a wide range of high-profile trade policy disputes, including the trade

policy battles over automobiles, semiconductors, and color film, and has been actively involved in the related WTO proceedings arising out of these trade policy battles. His recent major matters include defending foreign steel companies in dumping and safeguard actions, prosecuting several WTO challenges to US trade remedies, and coordinating the presentation of complex economic expert testimony. He has also been called upon to provide advice on launching a new round of WTO trade talks and on negotiating strategies for the round.
**Prof. Memberships:** Member of the American Bar Association, the DC Bar Association and the American Economics Association.
**Career:** Admitted to the District of Columbia Bar.
**Publications:** Regularly writes and has spoken frequently at trade association groups around the world about US international trade laws, transfer pricing laws, and trade policy issues. He authored the following books: 'A Business Guide to US Trade Remedy Laws' (2003); 'Understanding the WTO Antidumping Agreement: Negotiating History and Subsequent Interpretation' (2002, co-author), and 'Anatomy of a Trade Dispute: A Documentary History of the Kodak-Fujifilm Dispute' (2000).
**Personal:** Received a JD from New York University School of Law in 1984, where he was an articles editor of the New York University Law Review, an MPA from the Woodrow Wilson School at Princeton University in 1984, where he studied applied microeconomics and international economics, and a BA from Haverford College in 1980, where he was elected to Phi Beta Kappa.

## ECCLES, Bob
O'Melveny & Myers LLP, Washington, DC 202 383 5300
*Recommended in Employee Benefits, ERISA Litigation*
*Please see District of Columbia for profile*

## ECKLAND, William S
Sidley Austin LLP, Washington, DC 202 736 8267
weckland@Sidley.com
*Recommended in Financial Services*
**Practice Areas:** Practice focuses primarily on financial institutions, with particular emphasis on federal regulatory issues governing the operations of depository institutions and their holding companies. A significant portion of his practice involves the representation of diversified or nontraditional financial services holding companies. A key aspect of his practice relates to the development of new products and services for financial services entities, as well as regulatory aspects associated with mergers, acquisitions and restructuring activities of

financial institutions. He also represents financial institutions and officers and directors in regulatory enforcement matters.

**Personal:** The George Washington University Law School, JD, 1979; University of Maryland BA, 1976. Admissions: District of Columbia, 1979; New York, 1989.

## EDMONSON, Tracy
Latham & Watkins LLP, San Francisco
415 391 0600
*Recommended in Capital Markets*

## EISENBERG, David
Simpson Thacher & Bartlett LLP,
New York 212 455 2000
deisenberg@stblaw.com
*Recommended in Capital Markets*
**Practice Areas:** A Partner at Simpson Thacher & Bartlett and Member of the firm's Corporate Department, concentrating on banking and corporate law and asset-backed securities transactions.
**Prof. Memberships:** Association of the Bar of the City of New York.
**Career:** Member of the firm since 1984.
**Personal:** Received a BA, summa cum laude, in 1974 from Duke University and a JD in 1977 from Duke University School of Law.

## EISNER, Rebecca S
Mayer, Brown, Rowe & Maw LLP, Chicago 312 782 0600
*Recommended in Business Process Outsourcing, Technology*
*Please see Illinois for profile*

## EITEL, Mitchell S
Sullivan & Cromwell LLP, New York
212 558 4000
eitelm@sullcrom.com
*Recommended in Financial Services*
**Practice Areas:** Practice focused principally on mergers and acquisitions involving banks, thrifts, broker-dealers, investment managers and other financial institutions. Mr Eitel also advises on bank regulatory, commercial lending and securities matters.
**Prof. Memberships:** ABA (former Co-Chair, International Banking and Finance Committee); Fellow, ABF.
**Career:** Partner since 1996.
**Personal:** Columbia University (AB, 1984); Columbia Law School (JD, 1987).

## EIZENSTAT, Stuart
Covington & Burling, Washington, DC
202 662 5745
seizenstat@cov.com
*Recommended in International Trade*
**Practice Areas:** Heads Covington's International Practice.
**Career:** Ambassador to the EU; Deputy Treasury Secretary; Under Secretary of State for Economic, Business and Agricultural Affairs; Under Secretary of Commerce for International Trade; Chief Domestic Policy Adviser and Executive Director of the White House Domestic Policy Staff. During the Clinton adminis-

tration he participated in negotiations of the Transatlantic Agenda with the European Union; EU agreements regarding the Helms-Burton Act and the Iran-Libya Sanctions Act; the Japan Port Agreement; the Kyoto Protocol on global warming; and the development of the Transatlantic Business Dialogue among European and US CEOs.
**Personal:** Harvard University (JD, 1967).

## ELIAS, John M
Greenberg Traurig LLP, Florham Park
973 360 2354
eliasj@gtlaw.com
*Recommended in Wealth Management*
**Practice Areas:** Wealth management, trusts and estates.
**Prof. Memberships:** Madison, New Jersey Borough Council, 2004-present; Madison, New Jersey Area YMCA Board of Directors, 1997-2003; Museum of Early Trades and Crafts, Madison, New Jersey, Board of Directors, 1994-present; Clergy Partnership on Domestic Violence, Madison, NJ, Board of Directors, 1996-2002; Chair, 2000-02.
**Career:** 2005 New Jersey Super Lawyer, Trusts and Estates.
**Publications:** Author, 'Protecting Assets of Elder Clients with Living Trusts', New Jersey Business, 11/04.
**Personal:** LLM, Taxation, New York University School of Law, 1989; JD, The Catholic University of America Columbus School of Law, 1980; AB, cum laude, Boston College, 1977.

## ELLETT, E Tazewell
Hogan & Hartson LLP, Washington, DC
202 637 8644
etellett@hhlaw.com
*Recommended in Transportation*
**Practice Areas:** Aircraft airworthiness regulation; airline and airport regulation; aviation accident investigation; business aviation regulation; aerospace manufacturers, aviation service and maintenance companies, aircraft leasing and financial organizations, and state and local governments; airport privatization and public-private partnerships.
**Prof. Memberships:** Past President, VBA; DCBA; ABA; IBA; FBA; Lawyer Pilots Bar Association; American Counsel Association; Former Chairman, FBA's Transportation Law Section and VBA's Transportation Law Section; Founding Member, National Transportation Safety Board Bar Association, Former GC, Airport Consultants Council; Board of Governors, Past President, Aero Club of Washington; Former Member of Aviation Advisory Board, University of Southern California.
**Career:** Hogan & Hartson: Partner since 1988; FAA: 1985-88, chief counsel; FAA: 1984, Special Counsel to the administrator; NTSB: 1982-84, Special Assistant to Member Donald D Engen.

**Personal:** University of Virginia School of Law (JD, 1977); Davidson College (BA, 1974).

## EMERSON, Eric
Steptoe & Johnson LLP, Washington, DC
202 429 8076
eemerson@steptoe.com
*Recommended in International Trade*
**Practice Areas:** Partner, Steptoe & Johnson LLP, Washington, DC. Focuses on international trade regulation and trade policy, with particular emphasis on US antidumping and countervailing duty law. Represents US and foreign companies across a wide range of industries. Appears before US government agencies and federal courts in trade litigation proceedings. Assists clients in developing pricing strategies to minimize antidumping risks. Experienced with both market and non-market economy based antidumping investigations. Counsels clients on their rights and obligations under the WTO agreements. Participated in Steptoe's export control and immigration practices.
**Personal:** JD, University of Virginia, 1991; BA, University of Iowa, 1986.

## ENGLE, Craig
Arent Fox PLLC, Washington, DC
202 775 5791
engle.craig@arentfox.com
*Recommended in Government: Political Law*
**Practice Areas:** Joined Arent Fox's Government Relations Practice after a distinguished career on Capitol Hill. He has extensive experience advising corporations, trade associations, tax exempt and ideological groups, candidates and political committees on legal, legislative, political and communications issues. In 2003, Craig was chosen by 14 state governments to author a Supreme Court amicus brief in the McCain-Feingold litigation. Craig served as General Counsel to the National Republican Senatorial Committee from 1995-2000 where he was responsible for the legal matters of a $90 million National Party Committee. Elected Partner to the firm in 2005.
**Personal:** Georgetown University Law Center, JD 1985; University of Cincinnati, BA (summa cum laude) 1982.

## ENGLISH, Craig
Kennedy Lillis Schmidt & English,
New York 212 430 0800
*Recommended in Transportation*

## ESSERMAN, Susan
Steptoe & Johnson LLP, Washington, DC
202 429 6753
sesserman@steptoe.com
*Recommended in International Trade*
**Practice Areas:** Heads Steptoe & Johnson LLP's International Department. Advises on expanding access to foreign markets, WTO policy, trade litigation and dispute resolution. Former Deputy US

Trade Representative (with ambassadorial rank) responsible for trade policy and negotiations with Europe, India, Russia, the former Soviet Union, Africa, the Middle East, and in the WTO. Served as USTR General Counsel devising US litigation strategy in the early years of WTO dispute resolution. Decision maker in hundreds of antidumping and countervailing duty cases as Assistant Secretary of Commerce for Import Administration.
**Personal:** JD, University of Michigan Law School, 1977; BA, Wellesley College, 1974.

## EVANS III, Robert
Shearman & Sterling LLP, New York
212 848 8830
revans@shearman.com
*Recommended in Capital Markets*
**Practice Areas:** Co-Head of Shearman & Sterling's Capital Markets-Americas Group. Specializes in corporate and securities law. Works extensively with investment banks as underwriters in securities offerings, particularly involving complex transactions such as convertible securities issuances, initial public offerings and tender/exchange offers. Advises corporate clients on offerings and corporate and securities law matters.
**Prof. Memberships:** American Bar Association, New York State Bar Association, New York County Lawyer's Association, admitted to the New York Bar.
**Career:** Joined Shearman in 1990 and became Partner in 1996.
**Personal:** AB, cum laude, Harvard College (1982); JD, cum laude, Boston University School of Law (1985).

## FARRAR, Stanley F
Sullivan & Cromwell LLP, Los Angeles
310 712 6600
*Recommended in Banking & Finance, Financial Services*
*Please see California for profile*

## FAULKNER, Andrew M
Skadden, Arps, Slate, Meagher & Flom LLP & Affiliates, New York
212 735 2853
afaulkne@skadden.com
*Recommended in Capital Markets*
**Practice Areas:** Represents issuers, underwriters, credit enhancers and lenders in asset-backed securities transactions and credit-enhanced securities issuances. Has a broad securitization practice with emphasis on credit card transactions. Helped establish credit card master trusts for many major issuers, and has represented issuers and the underwriters of securities backed by bank VISA and MasterCard receivables and retailer private label credit card receivables. Worked on the first public trade receivables securitization as well as many other innovative structured transactions.
**Career:** JD, Columbia University School of Law, 1985 (Harlan Fiske Stone Schol-

ar); BA, Cornell University, 1981 (magna cum laude).

## FEHER, David G
Dewey Ballantine LLP, New York
212 259 8070
dfeher@deweyballantine.com
*Recommended in Sport*
**Practice Areas:** Mr Feher is one of the leading sports lawyers in the country. He is one of the principal negotiators of the CBAs in the NFL, NBA and AFL, and is an expert on the Salary Cap in each of those sports. He's litigated numerous matters in those and other sports, including the Terrell Owens proceeding, the Pacers/Pistons arbitration and the Joe Smith circumvention case.
**Prof. Memberships:** Sports Lawyers Association, ABA Antitrust Section.
**Career:** Partner, Dewey Ballantine LLP. Admitted to practice 1984, New York.
**Personal:** AB, magna cum laude, Georgetown University, 1980. JD, Duke University School of Law, 1984.

## FELDMAN, Elliott
Baker & Hostetler LLP, Washington, DC
202 861 1621
*Recommended in International Trade*

## FELLAS, John
Hughes Hubbard & Reed LLP, New York
212 837 6075
fellas@hugheshubbard.com
*Recommended in International Arbitration*
**Practice Areas:** International arbitration and litigation. Has acted as Counsel, and served as sole arbitrator, co-arbitrator or Chair, in cases under, eg, ICC, AAA and UNCITRAL Rules. Has been retained to act as expert witness on US law in foreign courts, most recently by the US Department of Justice. Regularly represents foreign clients involved in litigation in US courts and advises foreign and US clients on global litigation strategy.
**Prof. Memberships:** American Law Institute; American Society for International Law; International Bar Association; London Court of International Arbitration.
**Career:** Admitted in New York; Solicitor of Supreme Court of England and Wales.
**Publications:** Numerous publications on issues on international arbitration and litigation, including, Transatlantic Commercial Litigation and Arbitration (Oceana 2004, editor).
**Personal:** University of Durham, BA (Hons) (Law), 1983; Harvard Law School, LLM, 1985; SJD 1989.

## FELSENTHAL, David
Clifford Chance US LLP, New York
212 878 3452
david.felsenthal@cliffordchance.com
*Recommended in Capital Markets*
**Practice Areas:** Engaged in structured finance and derivatives transactions. Experience includes advising issuers and

arrangers on a range of structured finance arrangements, including synthetic CDOs, credit linked notes, repackagings, and a variety of other structures. Advises on a range of derivative and trading transactions, including credit, equity and interest rate derivatives, repurchase agreements and securities lending transactions. Serves on the Advisory Board of the Journal of Risk Finance.
**Career:** Partner since 1997; Harvard Law School (JD); Princeton University (BA).

## FEO, Edwin
Milbank, Tweed, Hadley & McCloy LLP, Los Angeles 213 892 4000
*Recommended in Energy, Projects, Transportation*

## FERNANDEZ, Michael
Freehill Hogan & Mahar LLP, New York
212 425 1900
fernandez@freehill.com
*Recommended in Transportation*
**Practice Areas:** Maritime claims and litigation involving casualties, fires, collisions, oil spills, investigations (civil and criminal), containership losses, hazardous cargoes, terminal liability for cargo loss/damage. Also, routinely involved in providing advises to carriers, operators and shore based terminals. Holds an Unlimited Master's License issued by the US Coast Guard. Bar Admissions: New York (State and Federal); New Jersey (State and Federal).
**Prof. Memberships:** New York State Bar Association.
**Career:** Joined Freehill Hogan & Mahar as an associate in 1990 and became a Partner in 1999.
**Personal:** Born 1959; United States Merchant Marine Academy at Kings Point, BS, 1981; Rutgers Law School, JD, 1990.

## FERRER, Eugene
McKee Nelson LLP, New York
917 777 4354
eferrer@mckeenelson.com
*Recommended in Capital Markets*
**Practice Areas:** Concentrates on structured finance and securitization matters, with a principal focus on cash and synthetic collateralized debt obligation transactions and other structured credit products. Representative transactions include CLOs, CBOs, CFOs, CDOs of ABS, securities repackagings and credit-linked note offerings. Regularly represents investment banks, underwriters, placement agents, issuers and investment advisors in this area. Also experienced in advising swap providers and end users in the negotiation and documentation of OTC derivatives.
**Career:** Before joining McKee Nelson, was a Partner at Weil, Gotshal & Manges.
**Personal:** JD, University of San Francisco, 1992. BS, University of the Pacific, 1986.

## FIELDS, Henry M
Morrison & Foerster LLP, Los Angeles
213 892 5275
hfields@mofo.com
*Recommended in Financial Services*
**Practice Areas:** Has advised on banking issues for over 30 years. Engaged in a general corporate and banking practice, including domestic and international mergers and acquisitions and capital market transactions.
**Prof. Memberships:** Member, Board of Directors, International Financial Institutions Association of California; Member (and former Chair), Board of Directors, Institute for Corporate Counsel.
**Career:** Admitted to practice in California, New Jersey, and New York. Named a 'World's Leading Banking Lawyer', International Financial Law Review. One of only four California attorneys to receive the highest individual rating in banking and finance by 'Global Counsel 3000' (7th edition).
**Personal:** BA, Harvard College, 1968, Phi Beta Kappa; JD, Yale Law School, 1972, managing editor, Yale Law Journal; Federal Clerkship, 1972-73, Honorable Leonard I Garth.

## FINE, Drew
Milbank, Tweed, Hadley & McCloy LLP, New York 212 530 5000
*Recommended in Transportation*

## FINKEL, Robert
Milbank, Tweed, Hadley & McCloy LLP, New York 212 530 5000
*Recommended in Business Process Outsourcing, Technology*

## FISCHER, L Richard
Morrison & Foerster LLP, Washington, DC 202 887 1566
lfischer@mofo.com
*Recommended in Financial Services*
**Practice Areas:** For over 30 years, has advised a wide variety of financial institutions and other companies across the United States on the full range of financial services, payment system, and retail banking issues. In particular, practice has a special emphasis on privacy, e-commerce, technology, and joint venture issues.
**Career:** Admitted to practice in California and the District of Columbia.
**Publications:** Author, 'The Law of Financial Privacy' (Third Edition), published by AS Pratt & Sons. Editor-in-Chief, Privacy & Information Law Report, Glasser LegalWorks.
**Personal:** BA, University of San Francisco, 1965; JD, University of California, Hastings College of the Law, 1970

## FITZGERALD, Peter
Chadbourne & Parke, London
+44 207 337 8000
*Recommended in Projects*
*Please see District of Columbia for profile*

## FLANAGAN, Peter L
Covington & Burling, Washington, DC
202 662 5163
pflanagan@cov.com
*Recommended in International Trade*
**Practice Areas:** Focuses on compliance requirements involving national security, including export controls, economic sanctions constraints, defense trade limitations, implications of related non-US requirements and international regulatory requirements. Clients include leading companies in oil and gas, software and high-technology, pharmaceuticals and biotechnology, defense contractors, manufacturing, financial institutions, and university-affiliated laboratories.
**Career:** Co-Vice-Chair of Covington's International Trade and Finance Group. Prior employment with Federal Reserve Board's International Finance Division.
**Personal:** Former Term Member of the Council on Foreign Relations. NYU (JD, 1993, magna cum laude, Order of the Coif); Princeton University (MPA, 1993); and University of Wisconsin (BA, 1987, with distinction).

## FLOWE JR, Benjamin H
Berliner, Corcoran & Rowe, LLP, Washington, DC 202 293 6117
Bflowe@BCR-DC.com
*Recommended in International Trade*
**Practice Areas:** Export controls, embargoes and sanctions, antiboycott laws, Exon-Florio CFIUS reviews of mergers, FCPA, cross-border business transactions, asset acquisitions, software licensing. For 25+ years has counseled and represented non-US and US clients on compliance and enforcement matters before agencies including Commerce, State, Treasury's Office of Foreign Assets Controls, Justice, and DHS's Customs, established and audited company compliance programs, and worked to improve applicable laws.
**Prof. Memberships:** Commerce Department Regulations and Procedures Technical Advisory Committee (Vice-Chair 2001-02), ABA (Vice-Chair or Chair for 10 years of Export Controls and Economic Sanctions Committee), AeA Export Controls Committee (Co-Chair 2002-03), US Supreme Court Bar, DC Bar, WITA, SIA, NCITD.
**Career:** Partner since 1997; Partner Verner, Liipfert and prior; associate Arent, Fox 1981-83.
**Publications:** 'Export Compliance Guide' (1995 Treatise), and has spoken and written extensively on export control and sanctions matters, testified before congress and agencies.
**Personal:** JD high honors (top five) UNC CH 1981, Order of the Coif, Executive Editor, NC J Int'l L and Com Reg, NCL Rev; AB Sociology/Psychology 1978 Duke University.

**FONTAINE, Mary C**
Mayer, Brown, Rowe & Maw LLP,
Chicago 312 701 7106
mfontaine@mayerbrownrowe.com
*Recommended in Capital Markets*
**Practice Areas:** Represents banks,
issuers, and insurance companies in
structured finance transactions in the
term and commercial paper markets:
synthetic risk transfer products, including
credit derivatives and insurance arrangements; CDO transactions; establishment
of single-seller and multi-seller asset
securitization conduits; domestic and
cross-border medium-term note
issuances in the public and private markets; securitization workouts; secured
and unsecured lending. Foreign and
domestic assets financed include insurance risk, equipment leases, credit cards,
trade receivables, premium finance loans,
timeshare loans, franchise loans, corporate and asset-backed bonds, other commercial and consumer debt, e-commerce
receivables, future cash flows and operating assets.
**Prof. Memberships:** New York State Bar
Association, Section on Business Law.
**Career:** Joined Mayer, Brown, Rowe &
Maw LLP, Chicago, in 1981; became Partner, 1988; served at Tokyo affiliate office,
April-May 1987 and London affiliate
office, September 1985-March 1986.
**Publications:** Frequent speaker at securitization industry conferences.
**Personal:** University of Chicago Law
School, JD, 1981. Syracuse University, BA
summa cum laude, 1978.

**FORD, Christopher D**
Alston & Bird LLP, Washington, DC
202 756 3371
cford@alston.com
*Recommended in Business Process
Outsourcing*
**Practice Areas:** Business process outsourcing, information technology outsourcing, technology, telecommunications, electronic commerce
**Prof. Memberships:** State Bar of Georgia; District of Columbia Bar; Executive
Committee, Potomac Counsel of the
American Electronics Association
**Career:** Extensive experience advising
clients on technology transactions,
including information technology outsourcing, business process outsourcing,
strategic alliances, and joint ventures. Frequent speaker on outsourcing and technology-related legal issues.
**Publications:** Authored numerous articles in such publications as TPI's 'Journal
of Sourcing Leadership', Finance Today,
and the Sourcing Interest Group's 'Inside
Sourcing Newsletter'.
**Personal:** BS, University of Virginia
(1987); JD, Emory University (1993).

**FORD JACOB, Valerie**
Fried, Frank, Harris, Shriver & Jacobson
LLP, New York 212 859 8158

Valerie.Jacob@FriedFrank.com
*Recommended in Capital Markets*
**Practice Areas:** Corporate Partner.
Chairperson of firm and Head of Global
Capital Markets Group. Acts as counsel to
issuers and underwriters in domestic and
international financings. Represents
clients in all types of securities offerings,
including initial public offerings, secondary offerings, high-yield offerings,
mezzanine and bridge financings, investment-grade debt offerings, acquisition
financings and recapitalizations. Counsels corporations on corporate governance and securities regulation.
**Career:** Joined Fried Frank in 1978.
Became a Partner in 1986.
**Personal:** JD (1978), Cornell University.
BS (1975), Boston University.

**FORE, John A**
Wilson Sonsini Goodrich & Rosati, Palo
Alto 650 493 9300
jfore@wsgr.com
*Recommended in Capital Markets*
**Practice Areas:** Extensive experience
with a variety of debt transactions,
including secured/unsecured bank
financings, private placements, acquisition finance, project finance, leveraged
leasing, senior, subordinated and convertible note sales, multicurrency loans, letter
of credit facilities, interest rate caps, collars and swaps, off-balance sheet financings, 144A and Regulation S transactions
and public offerings of investment grade
and non-investment grade notes and
convertible subordinated debt securities.
**Prof. Memberships:** Admitted to practice in California and New York.
**Career:** Became WSGR Partner, 1991.
**Personal:** JD, New York University
School of Law, 1983; BA (cum laude),
Yale University, 1979.

**FRANCE II, William N**
Healy & Baillie LLP, New York
212 709 9226
wfrance@healy.com
*Recommended in Transportation*
**Practice Areas:** All maritime casualty
and related commercial litigation and
arbitration with focus on naval architec-
ture, marine engineering, design, safety,
surveying, classification, construction,
and operational liabilities, and cargo
claims of any kind.
**Prof. Memberships:** Society of Naval
Architects and Marine Engineers; ASME;
Maritime Law Association.
**Career:** Naval architect/marine engineer,
Esso International 1972-76; admitted NY
Bar 1978; joined Healy & Baillie 1977,
Partner 1983; licensed professional engi-
neer.
**Publications:** 'An Investigation of Head-
Sea Parametric Rolling and its Influence
on Container Lashing Systems', 40
Marine Technology 1 (SNAME 2003).
**Personal:** BSc, NA and ME, Webb Insti-
tute 1972; JD NYU Law School 1977.

**FREYER, Dana H**
Skadden, Arps, Slate, Meagher & Flom
LLP & Affiliates, New York
212 735 2506
dfreyer@skadden.com
*Recommended in International
Arbitration*
**Practice Areas:** Heads the firm's Arbitration and Alternative Dispute Resolution Practices and is a Member of the
firm's International Arbitration Group.
Represents clients in all types of US and
international commercial litigation and
arbitration, including international arbitrations under the ICC, ICSID, AAA
International, UNCITRAL, Stockholm
Chamber of Commerce and other arbitration rules, and in mediations and
other ADR proceedings. Serves as arbitrator Chair and Member of arbitration
panels. Also heads the firm's Corporate
Compliance Program Practice. Advises
clients on the development and implementation of ethics, compliance and corporate governance programs.
**Career:** JD, Columbia University, 1971;
BA, Connecticut College, 1965.

**FRIEDLAND, Paul**
White & Case LLP, New York
212 819 8917
pfriedland@whitecase.com
*Recommended in International
Arbitration*
**Practice Areas:** Co-Head of firm's
International Arbitration Practice Group.
Counsel/arbitrator in international com-
mercial arbitrations.
**Prof. Memberships:** NYS Bar; Paris Bar;
US District Courts for Southern and
Eastern Districts of NY; US Court of
Appeals for the Second Circuit; US
Supreme Court; AAA Arbitration Prac-
tice Committee (Chairman); AAA
(Board of Directors); Institute for
Transnational Arbitration (Executive
Committee, Board of Trustees, Programs
Co-Chair); US Council for International
Business (Board of Trustees, Arbitration
Committee); World Arbitration and
Mediation Reporter (international edi-
tor).
**Publications:** Include 'Arbitration Claus-
es for International Contracts' (2000).
**Personal:** Yale University (BA, 1976);
Columbia Law School (JD, 1980), Law
Review, Kent Scholar.

**FRIEDMAN, Andrew**
Covington & Burling, Washington, DC
202 662 5466
afriedman@cov.com
*Recommended in Sport*
**Practice Areas:** Primary tax counsel to
all US major professional sports leagues
MLB, NBA, NFL, NHL; also the USTA
and clubs such as the Boston Red Sox.
Lead industry representative in dealings
with the IRS sports audit task force.
**Career:** Highlights include John Henry's
sale of the Florida Marlins and purchase

of the Boston Red Sox and related entities; established NFL Network, World
Baseball Classic, US Open Series, and
regional sports networks; NFL's expansion to Cleveland and Houston; NFL and
NHL credit facilities; Buffalo Bills v US.
**Personal:** Harvard University (JD, 1980,
cum laude); Trinity College (BA, 1977, as
valedictorian).

**FRIEDMAN, Lawrence B**
Cleary Gottlieb Steen & Hamilton LLP,
New York 212 225 2840
lfriedman@cgsh.com
*Recommended in International
Arbitration*
**Practice Areas:** International and
domestic commercial litigation and arbi-
tration, involving joint venture and
license agreements, mergers and acquisi-
tions, international banking and securi-
ties regulation, and patent, trademark,
copyright and trade secret disputes.
Recent clients include sanofi-aventis, Cit-
igroup, Credit Lyonnais, the Carlyle
Group, Ricoh, Gucci, and the Guggen-
heim Museum.
**Prof. Memberships:** Past Chairman,
Association of the Bar of the City of New
York International Commercial Dispute
Resolution Committee.
**Career:** Partner since 1991. JD, cum
laude, Harvard Law School; BS, summa
cum laude, Georgetown University
School of Foreign Service. Law clerk for
US District Judge Charles P Sifton.

**FRIMMER, Paul**
Irell & Manella LLP, Los Angeles
310 277 1010
*Recommended in Wealth
Management*

**FUNK, John**
Jones Day, Dallas
214 220 3939
*Recommended in Business Process
Outsourcing, Technology*
*Please see Texas for profile*

**GAINOR, Edward E**
McKee Nelson LLP, Washington, DC
202 775 4137
egainor@mckeenelson.com
*Recommended in Capital Markets*
**Practice Areas:** Practice focuses on
securitization. Experience includes securitization of single family residential,
multifamily and commercial mortgage
loans; HELOCs; reverse mortgage loans;
auto and recreational vehicle loans; boat
loans; franchise loans; servicing advance
receivables; dealer floorplan receivables;
unguaranteed portions of SBA 7(a)
loans; government obligations; previously issued securities; and other assets. He
has represented issuers, underwriters and
investors in domestic and cross-border
public offerings and private placements
of securities.
**Career:** Before joining McKee Nelson,
was a Partner at Brown & Wood LLP.

**Publications:** Co-authored the treatise 'Offerings of Asset-Backed Securities', and has written articles for a variety of publications.
**Personal:** JD, with highest honors, George Washington University Law School, 1990.

## GALAINENA, M David
Winston & Strawn LLP, Chicago
312 558 7442
dgalainena@winston.com
*Recommended in Capital Markets*
**Practice Areas:** Partner in the firm's Corporate Department. His practice concentrates in asset securitization/structured finance including the asset-backed markets, inclusive of CLOs and CBOs.
**Career:** Admitted to Illinois Bar in 1983. Joined Winston & Strawn LLP, 1995 as Partner. Member, Diversity Committee. Member, firm's Executive Committee.
**Personal:** Born November 11, 1957. Received BA, magna cum laude, Phi Beta Kappa 1980, Tulane University; JD from University of Notre Dame 1983.

## GALLAGHER, James J
McKenna Long & Aldridge LLP, Los Angeles 213 688 6165
jgallagher@mckennalong.com
*Recommended in Government Contracts*
**Practice Areas:** Has represented government contractors, including many of the largest aerospace companies, for over three decades. Experience includes the full range of government contract financial issues, including civil and criminal fraud investigations and litigation, defective pricing, terminations, claims, breach of contract and cost allowability. Has served as lead counsel in more than 20 False Claims Act cases, most of which were qui tam matters. Five of those cases have been heard by the United States Court of Appeals for the Ninth Circuit, including the highly publicized US ex rel Schumer v Hughes case. Has also argued more than a dozen cases at the federal appellate courts.
**Prof. Memberships:** Public Contract Law Section of the American Bar Association; District of Columbia Bar; Federal Bar Association; National Contract Management Association; State Bar of California.
**Personal:** Georgetown University Law Center (LLB, 1965); University of Notre Dame (BBA, 1961).

## GALVIS, Sergio
Sullivan & Cromwell LLP, New York
212 558 4000
*Recommended in Projects*
*Please see New York for profile*

## GAMBRO, Michael S
Cadwalader, Wickersham & Taft LLP, New York 212 504 6825
michael.gambro@cwt.com
*Recommended in Capital Markets*

**Practice Areas:** Primarily represents financial institutions in the financing, purchase and sale, and securitization of financial assets. Has represented some of the largest financial institutions in the country in noteworthy securitization transactions, including: Lehman Brothers and Goldman Sachs as underwriters for the largest single borrower commercial mortgage loan securitization, for General Growth Properties; Confederation Life Insurance Company (US) in Rehabilitation and the underwriters in Confederation Life's securitization of commercial mortgage loans, at the time the largest CMBS transaction in history and one of the Institutional Investor deals of the year; The Prudential Insurance Company of America in a securitization of loans secured by life insurance policies, the only transaction of its kind and recognized as one of the Investment Dealer's Digest deals of the year.
**Personal:** JD, Columbia (1980) (Harlan Fiske Stone Scholar); BS, Tufts University, summa cum laude and Phi Beta Kappa. Frequently lectures and writes articles on numerous business law topics.

## GANDHI, Samir A
Sidley Austin LLP, New York
212 839 5684
sgandhi@sidley.com
*Recommended in Capital Markets*
**Practice Areas:** Partner in the New York office whose practice focuses on structured finance, private equity, capital markets offerings and cross-border investments, with particular emphasis on India. He has devoted a substantial portion of his practice to the areas of corporate finance and the development of new financial products. He has represented domestic and foreign issuers and underwriters in a broad range of capital markets activities, with particular emphasis on structured corporate finance transactions. He has extensive experience in complex financial structures, domestic and international Tier-1 capital raising transactions, convertible securities, debt- and equity-linked products and preferred securities products. He also represents underwriters in a variety of securities offerings by US government sponsored entities and multilateral development banks. He also advises US companies with operations in India, including advising on outsourcing issues, joint ventures and foreign direct investment. He has represented India-based companies on acquisitions and joint ventures in the US and regularly advises investment funds in their investment activities in India.
**Prof. Memberships:** Serves on the Board of Directors of Lawyers Alliance for New York.
**Personal:** The George Washington University Law School (JD, 1993), University of Chicago (AB, 1990). Admission: New York, 1994.

## GANNETT, William
Cahill Gordon & Reindel LLP, New York
212 701 3900
*Recommended in Capital Markets*

## GANZ, Howard
Proskauer Rose LLP, New York
212 969 3000
*Recommended in Employment, Sport*
*Please see New York for profile*

## GARDINER, John L
Skadden, Arps, Slate, Meagher & Flom LLP & Affiliates, New York
212 735 2442
jgardine@skadden.com
*Recommended in International Arbitration*
**Practice Areas:** Represents clients in commercial disputes before international arbitration tribunals under the auspices of the International Chamber of Commerce, American Arbitration Association and ad hoc UNCITRAL rules, and before federal and state courts in the US. Representative cases involve allegations of fraud, breach of contract, theft of trade secrets and other related matters as both plaintiff's and defendant's counsel. Has advised clients in corporate litigations including takeover contests, related shareholder litigation, and class actions involving state and federal securities laws. Has acted as mediator and arbitrator in various domestic and international disputes.
**Career:** Admitted: New York, 1988; Roll of Solicitors, Republic of Ireland, 1988; Roll of Solicitors, England and Wales; LLB, University College, Dublin, 1984.

## GARDNER, Stephen
Kronish Lieb Weiner & Hellman LLP, New York
212 479 6000
*Recommended in Tax Litigation*

## GARFINKEL, Barry
Skadden, Arps, Slate, Meagher & Flom LLP & Affiliates, New York
212 735 2500
bgarfink@skadden.com
*Recommended in Arbitration, International Arbitration*
**Practice Areas:** Heads Skadden's International Litigation and Arbitration Practice. Lead many of the firm's more significant appeals and major international arbitrations. Acted as arbitrator in ICC, UNCITRAL, and AAA arbitrations. Advises major US and foreign companies on transnational arbitration matters.
**Prof. Memberships:** Fellow, College of Commercial Arbitrators; former Chairman and trustee, Practising Law Institute; Advisory Committee, Institute for Transnational Arbitration; International Arbitration Committee, American Arbitration Association; American Arbitration Association (Complex Cases), London Court of International Arbitration and ICC; Fellow, American College of

Trial Lawyers.
**Career:** LLB, Yale University, 1955 (Managing Editor, Yale Law Journal); BSS, College of the City of New York, 1950.

## GARIBALDI, Oscar M
Covington & Burling, Washington, DC
202 662 5624
ogaribaldi@cov.com
*Recommended in International Arbitration*
**Practice Areas:** International arbitration (investor-state and international commercial arbitration); international litigation; international trade; public and private international law.
**Prof. Memberships:** Member, ICSID Panel of Conciliators (appointed by the United States).
**Career:** Trained in civil-law and common-law systems; taught public international law at the Cornell and Virginia Law Schools; clients include ExxonMobil Corporation; LG&E Energy LLC; MTD Equity Sdn. Bhd.; Bacardi Ltd.; Newmont Mining Company; Southern Peru Copper Corporation; and Amoco Oil Company.
**Personal:** University of Buenos Aires Law School (Procurador [LLB], 1971, Abogado [JD], 1972, Diploma de Honor); Harvard Law School (LLM, 1975); Studied at Harvard towards SJD.

## GAROFALO, Gary B
Garofalo Goerlich Hainbach PC, Washington, DC 202 776 3970
ggarofalo@ggh-airlaw.com
*Recommended in Transportation*
**Practice Areas:** Aviation regulatory, transactional and enforcement matters.
**Prof. Memberships:** National Business Aviation Association, American Bar Association Forum on Aviation Law, International Aviation Club.
**Career:** Managing Partner since 1984.
**Publications:** 'Aviation Drug Testing Handbook'.
**Personal:** University of Virginia School of Law (LLB, 1965); Rensselaer Polytechnic Institute (BS Aeronautical Engineering, 1962).

## GENTNER, Joshua
Vedder, Price, Kaufman & Kammholz, Chicago 312 609 7500
*Recommended in Transportation*

## GEORGE, Peter
Baker & McKenzie, Chicago
312 861 8800
*Recommended in Business Process Outsourcing, Technology*
*Please see Illinois for profile*

## GERBER, Dean
Vedder, Price, Kaufman & Kammholz, Chicago 312 609 7500
*Recommended in Banking & Finance, Transportation*

### GEWIRTZ, Elliot
Milbank, Tweed, Hadley & McCloy LLP,
New York 212 530 5000
*Recommended in Transportation*

### GIBSON, Douglas G
Covington & Burling, Washington, DC
202 662 5483
dgibson@cov.com
*Recommended in Sport*
**Practice Areas:** Corporate counsel to
the leading US professional sports
leagues, including the NFL, NHL, MLB,
NASCAR and the US Tennis Association.
Advise with respect to corporate, finance,
governance and media matters, including
league-wide financing arrangements, stadium financing, ownership transfers,
television broadcast agreements, sponsorship arrangements and internet, wireless and other new media matters. He
also represents corporate clients, including Fortune 100 companies in a broad
array of M&A, finance and governance
matters.
**Career:** Former General Counsel and
member of Executive Committee of Bacardi Limited.
**Personal:** JD, cum laude, Harvard Law
School (1990); BS with honors, The
Johns Hopkins University (1987).

### GIDEON, Kenneth
Skadden, Arps, Slate, Meagher & Flom
LLP & Affiliates, Washington, DC
202 371 7000
*Recommended in Tax, Tax Litigation*
*Please see District of Columbia for*
*profile*

### GILBERG, David J
Sullivan & Cromwell LLP, New York
212 558 4000
gilbergd@sullcrom.com
*Recommended in Capital Markets*
**Practice Areas:** Practice involves broad
range of derivatives and related matters,
including development of electronic
trading facilities for trading of securities
and derivatives; structuring of indexed
products, over-the-counter derivatives
and other financial instruments; and
development of structured transactions,
hedge funds and other private funds and
other managed trading vehicles. Also
advises clients on legal and regulatory
issues related to the trading of securities
and derivatives.
**Career:** Partner since 1996.
**Personal:** University of Pennsylvania
(BA, MA, 1978) and Harvard Law School
(JD, 1981).

### GINOS, Geoffrey
Nicoletti Hornig Campise and Sweeney,
New York 212 220 3830
*Recommended in Transportation*

### GINSBERG, Benjamin L
Patton Boggs LLP, Washington, DC
202 457 6405
bginsberg@pattonboggs.com
*Recommended in Government:*

*Political Law*
**Practice Areas:** Represents numerous
candidates, parties, members of Congress, corporations, etc, participating in
the political process. Served as national
counsel in 2000 and 2004 presidential
campaigns, playing central role in 2000
Florida recount. Advises on major election law issues. Represents clients on
Capitol Hill regarding appropriations,
healthcare, and other matters.
**Career:** Partner. Newspaper reporter
for five years, including The Boston
Globe and Philadelphia Evening Bulletin. Frequent television appearances
commenting on law/politics; previously
Georgetown University Adjunct Law
Professor.
**Personal:** Fellow - Institute of Politics,
Kennedy School of Government, Har-
vard University (Fall 2005); Georgetown
University (JD, 1982); University of
Pennsylvania (AB, 1974).

### GIOVE, Stephen
Shearman & Sterling LLP, New York
212 848 7325
sgiove@shearman.com
*Recommended in Capital Markets*
**Practice Areas:** Co-Head of the Capital
Markets – Americas Group of Shearman
& Sterling. Represents issuers and underwriters in initial public offerings and
offerings of common and preferred
stock, convertible securities, high yield
and investment grade debt and commercial paper.
**Career:** Joined the firm in 1987 and
became a Partner in 1993.
**Personal:** BS, State University of New
York at Binghamton (1981); MBA, Cornell University (1985), JD, Cornell University (1985).

### GLANCZ, Ronald
Venable LLP, Washington, DC
202 962 4800
*Recommended in Financial Services*

### GLASS, Adam W
Linklaters, New York
212 903 9033
adam.glass@linklaters.com
*Recommended in Capital Markets*
**Practice Areas:** Head of US Structured
Finance and Derivatives Practice. Practice
includes cash and synthetic CBOs, CLOs
and CDOs; credit derivatives transactions;
and derivatives structured finance products, including hedge fund-linked notes.
Worked on 'synthetic securities' created by
packaging asset-backed securities or corporate debt with swap agreements, and on
total return swaps used to create off-balance sheet financing vehicles. Represented
underwriters in SEC-registered 'resecuritizations' of corporate debt securities since
documenting the first such transaction in
1994. Also, experienced in term and commercial paper-funded financing of securities, net lease properties, franchise and
mortgage loans, and trade receivables.

**Publications:** Published numerous articles on structured finance and derivatives
on www.legalmediagroup.com, on
www.linklaters.com, in IFLR and in other
publications.
**Personal:** Received his JD from Stanford
Law School in 1981 and his AB from
Harvard University in 1978.

### GLICK, Anna
Cadwalader, Wickersham & Taft LLP,
New York 212 504 6309
anna.glick@cwt.com
*Recommended in Capital Markets*
**Practice Areas:** Concentrates in multi-
class securitisation of commercial mortgage loans, mezzanine debt and other
financings of mortgage-related assets,
federal securities laws issues particular to
securitisations, and related securities
compliance matters. Also works in CBOs
(particularly those backed by asset and
mortgage securities). Represents issuers,
underwriters and institutional investors
active in the primary and secondary capital markets. Works closely with real estate
attorneys to advise on rating agency and
securitisation issues (origination of large
and conduit-size mortgage loans pending
securitisation). Concentrates on federal
securities law, registration of public securities, financings, and other business
arrangements for closely-held corporations.
**Career:** JD, New York University School
of Law (1982); Member, Law Review and
Order of the Coif.

### GLICKSTEIN, Steven
Kaye Scholer LLP, New York
212 836 8485
sglickstein@kayescholer.com
*Recommended in Products Liability*
**Practice Areas:** Partner and Co-Chair,
Product Liability Group. Has vast experience in product liability mass torts and
class actions. Has been National Counsel
in cases involving pharmaceuticals
(Rezulin, Viagra, Trovan, homone
replacement therapy), medical devices
(heart valves, penile protheses, hip
implants, incontinence devices), agricultural pesticides (Galecron), and fire
alarms (San Juan Dupont Plaza hotel
fire). Has published extensively, and was a
consultant to the City of New York on
class action issues.
**Prof. Memberships:** Board of Editors,
Product Liability Law and Strategy;
American Bar Association (Co-Chair of
Class Action Subcommittee, Product Lia-
bility Committee, Litigation Section);
Defense Research Institute; International
Association of Defense Counsel.
**Career:** JD, Columbia Law School, 1976,
Harlan Fiske Stone Scholar; BA (magna
cum laude), Lehigh University, 1973.
**Publications:** 'The Restatement Sections
Specifically Applicable to Pharmaceutical
and Medical Device Cases in State Court:
A 50-State Survey', American Bar Associ-

ation, 2004. 'Circuits Split on Trying
Product Liability Class Actions in Federal
Court', Product Liability Law and Strate-
gy, December 2001. 'High Court's 'Fraud
on the Agency' Preemption Ruling May
Have Broad Product Liability Implica-
tions', Product Liability Law and Strategy,
April 2001. '50 State Survey of Medical
Monitoring', American Bar Association,
2001. 'Do Class Actions Toll Product Lia-
bility Statutes of Limitations?', Product
Liability Law and Strategy, October 2000.

### GLOTZER, Paul E
Cleary Gottlieb Steen & Hamilton LLP,
New York 212 225 2314
pglotzer@cgsh.com
*Recommended in Financial Services*
**Practice Areas:** US and international
corporate and regulatory matters, including mergers and acquisitions, cross-border transactions, joint ventures and
restructurings, as well as derivatives and
capital markets transactions and internal
investigations. Has extensive experience
representing US and non-US banks and
bank holding companies before, among
others, the Federal Reserve Board, Office
of the Comptroller of the Currency,
FDIC and various state banking regulators.
**Prof. Memberships:** Member of the Bar
in New York.
**Career:** Joined firm, 1990; became Partner, 1999. JD, cum laude, University of
Michigan (1990); MS and BS, Public
Management and Policy, Carnegie-Mellon University (1983 and 1982).
**Publications:** Mr Glotzer lectures and is
widely published on a variety of banking
issues.

### GOLDBERG, Daniel
Bingham McCutchen LLP, Boston
617 951 8000
*Recommended in Antitrust, Sport*
*Please see Massachusetts for profile*

### GOLDBERG JR, Fred T
Skadden, Arps, Slate, Meagher & Flom
LLP & Affiliates, Washington, DC
202 371 7000
*Recommended in Tax, Tax Litigation*
*Please see District of Columbia for*
*profile*

### GOLDFEIN, Shepard
Skadden, Arps, Slate, Meagher & Flom
LLP & Affiliates, New York
212 735 3000
*Recommended in Antitrust, Sport*
*Please see New York for profile*

### GOLDSCHMIDT, David J
Skadden, Arps, Slate, Meagher & Flom
LLP & Affiliates, New York
212 735 3574
dgoldsch@skadden.com
*Recommended in Capital Markets*
**Practice Areas:** Represents investment
banks and US and international issuers in
a variety of financing matters, including
public offerings and private placement of

debt and equity securities, and international securities offerings. Focuses primarily on offerings for technology companies as well as REITs. Involved in developing new products, such as the Income Deposit Security.
**Career:** JD, New York University School of Law, 1987 (Member, Review of Law and Social Change); BA, New York University, 1984 (magna cum laude).

### GOLDSTEIN, Marvin
Stroock & Stroock & Lavan LLP, New York 212 806 5400
*Recommended in Capital Markets*

### GOLDSTEIN, Stuart
Cadwalader, Wickersham & Taft LLP, Charlotte 704 348 5100
*Recommended in Capital Markets*
*Please see North Carolina for profile*

### GONZÁLEZ, Daniel E
Hogan & Hartson LLP, Miami
305 459 6649
degonzalez@hhlaw.com
*Recommended in International Arbitration*
**Practice Areas:** Director of the firm's International Litigation and Arbitration Practice. Practices principally in international complex commercial litigation and arbitration, having tried and arbitrated cases in English and Spanish throughout the United States, Latin America and Europe.
**Prof. Memberships:** Member, American Bar Association; International Bar Association; International Chamber of Commerce; American Arbitration Association.
**Career:** With his common and civil law experience and financial background, he represents multinational clients involved in all aspects of commercial disputes, including securities, project finance, infrastructure construction, product defects, insurance coverage, distributorships and environmental liability.
**Personal:** University of Miami School of Law (JD, summa cum laude).

### GOODMAN, Ronald
Winston & Strawn LLP, Washington, DC
202 282 5000
*Recommended in International Arbitration*

### GORDON, David
Latham & Watkins LLP, New York
212 906 1200
*Recommended in Projects*

### GORTZ, Albert
Proskauer Rose LLP, Boca Ratón
561 995 4700
agortz@proskauer.com
*Recommended in Wealth Management*
**Practice Areas:** Has built an extensive pratice counseling individuals and families of high net worth regarding estate, personal, charitable and financial plan-

ning including guidance in areas of gift, estate and generation-skipping tax planning. In depth experience in the administration of complicated estates and trusts. Extensive experience in representing charitable organizations and has worked with public charities in setting up planned giving programs.
**Prof. Memberships:** Member of both New York and Florida Bars.
**Career:** Resident Partner in the firm's Florida office since it was established in 1977. Member of the firm's six-person Executive Committee.
**Personal:** Yale Law School (1970); Williams College (1967). Vice Chairman and a Member of the Board of the Jewish Federation of South Palm Beach County, Inc.; Vice President and Member of the Board of The American Jewish Committee.

### GOURLEY, Sara J
Sidley Austin LLP, Chicago
312 853 7694
sgourley@sidley.com
*Recommended in Products Liability*
**Practice Areas:** Litigation Partner in the Chicago office. Ms Gourley has substantial experience in pharmaceutical and blood products liability litigation, as well as in aviation litigation. Her practice is concentrated in the areas of pharmaceutical and medical device defense, especially multi-jurisdictional coordination and defense of class actions. She is national counsel for a producer of blood products in AIDS and Hepatitis C litigation and represents manufacturers in multidistrict and related state litigation and class actions.
**Prof. Memberships:** American Bar Association and the Defense Research Institute.
**Personal:** University of Illinois College of Law, JD, 1980; Ripon College AB, 1977. Admissions: US Court of Appeals, 4th Circuit; US Court of Appeals, 7th Circuit; US Court of Appeals, 8th Circuit; US Court of Appeals, 11th Circuit; US District Court, District of Arizona; US District Court, ND of Illinois - General; Illinois, 1980.

### GRABAR, Nicolas
Cleary Gottlieb Steen & Hamilton LLP, New York 212 225 2414
ngrabar@cgsh.com
*Recommended in Capital Markets*
**Practice Areas:** International capital markets, securities regulation and representation of large reporting companies. Extensive experience in international financings in public and private markets, US securities law and regulations applicable to foreign issuers, and regulation of financial reporting. Specializes in telecommunication and natural resource sectors, and advises on acquisitions, joint ventures, privatizations and debt restructurings.

**Prof. Memberships:** ABCNY and ABA.
**Career:** Joined firm, 1984; became Partner, 1991. JD, cum laude, Harvard Law School (1982); BA, magna cum laude, Harvard College (1978).
**Publications:** Articles on various topics, including securities regulation, privatizations and legal opinions.

### GRANDISON, W George
Steptoe & Johnson LLP, Washington, DC
202 429 6447
wgrandison@steptoe.com
*Recommended in International Trade*
**Practice Areas:** Partner, International Trade Group, Steptoe & Johnson LLP, Washington, DC. Work has encompassed major cases under the antidumping and countervailing duty laws, WTO agreements, and the customs and export control laws. Represented and advised clients in matters involving a variety of products from agricultural and forestry products to high technology equipment and materials. Extensive experience in cases involving the valuation and pricing of natural resources, subsidy aspects of export restrictions and imports of complex, high technology equipment and high volume commercial products.
**Personal:** JD, Yale Law School, 1972; BS, United States Military Academy, 1966.

### GREEN, Jonathan
Milbank, Tweed, Hadley & McCloy LLP, New York 212 530 5000
*Recommended in Projects*

### GREENBAUM, Jack A
Healy & Baillie LLP, New York
212 943 3980
jgreenbaum@healy.com
*Recommended in Transportation*
**Practice Areas:** Maritime law; commercial law; litigation; maritime arbitration; best known for charter party and bill of lading disputes, as advocate and arbitrator, but experience extends to litigation involving commodity contracts, letters of credit, and general commercial disputes. Clients include P&I and FD&D associations, shipowners, operators, charterers, brokers, and commodity traders. Admitted 1971, New York; 1983, New Jersey.
**Prof. Memberships:** The Maritime Law Association of the United States.
**Career:** Joined Healy & Baillie 1971; became Partner 1977; Executive Committee 1990 to present.
**Personal:** Born: Brooklyn, New York, October 26, 1947. Brooklyn Law School, 1971, JD Brooklyn College, 1967, BS.

### GREENBERG, Mark I
Sidley Austin LLP, Chicago
312 853 4149
mgreenberg@sidley.com
*Recommended in Capital Markets*
**Practice Areas:** A Partner in the Chicago office, Mr Greenberg represents money-center commercial and investment banks, insurance companies and

other financial institutions participating in US domestic and international securitization and structured finance transactions. Recently, Mr Greenberg has advised clients in connection with the establishment of structured investment vehicles and credit derivative product companies, as well as a variety of insurance-related and other risk-transfer products, including insurance embedded cost securitizations, total return swaps and credit derivatives, catastrophe bonds and weather derivatives. Mr Greenberg's experience also includes the securitization of various traditional and non-traditional assets, including loans and securities (CDOs), real estate and real estate leases, residential mortgage loans, equipment and motor vehicle finance receivables, credit card receivables, small business mortgage loans and trade receivables. At recent industry conferences, he has spoken on CDOs, risk securitization, structured investment vehicles and ISDA documentation.
**Prof. Memberships:** American Bar Association; Illinois State Bar Association; Chicago Bar Association.
**Publications:** Co-author, 'Key Issues in Structuring a Synthetic Securisation Transaction', Securitisation and Structured Finance Guide 2001.
**Personal:** The University of Chicago Law School, JD, 1991; Harvard University, AB, 1987. Admission: Illinois, 1991.

### GREENWALD, John D
WilmerHale, Washington, DC
202 663 6743
john.greenwald@wilmerhale.com
*Recommended in International Trade*
**Practice Areas:** Represents clients in matters arising under trade laws of US, Commission of European Communities and other foreign jurisdictions. Advises and represents various clients on trade legislation in Congress and/or trade policy issues under review in executive branch of US government.
**Career:** Attorney, Office of US Trade Representative from 1974, then served as Deputy General Counsel of that USTR. From 1980-81 served as first Head of Import Administration at Department of Commerce, responsible for administration of US antidumping and countervailing duty laws.
**Personal:** Columbia University School of Law (JD); University of North Carolina at Chapel Hill (BA).

### GRIFFITH, Spencer S
Akin Gump Strauss Hauer & Feld LLP, Washington, DC 202 887 4575
sgriffith@akingump.com
*Recommended in International Trade*
**Practice Areas:** Partner, International Trade Practice. Handles international trade litigation in US and international fora. Handles countervailing duty, antidumping and other trade remedy

matters, and provides trade policy advice. Regularly appears before US agencies and courts handling trade remedy proceedings, including Office of the United States Trade Representative, US Department of Commerce and US International Trade Commission. Routinely handles complex appeals to US courts and to international tribunals, including NAFTA and WTO Panels. Also provides advice on WTO matters and WTO litigation.

**Personal:** AB (honors), Brown University; JD, New York University School of Law.

## GRIGERA NAÓN, Horacio

Horacio A Girgera Naon - Independent Arbitrator, Washington, DC
202 337 1832
*Recommended in Arbitration*

## GROSS, Kenneth A

Skadden, Arps, Slate, Meagher & Flom LLP & Affiliates, Washington, DC
202 371 7007
kgross@skadden.com
*Recommended in Government: Political Law*

**Practice Areas:** Advises clients on matters relating to the regulation of political activity; noted authority on campaign law compliance, gift and gratuity rules, lobby registration provisions, securities laws regulating political activity and municipal securities transactions, and counsels numerous Fortune 500 corporations/political candidates at the state and federal level. As former associate general counsel of the Federal Election Commission (FEC), headed the general counsel's Enforcement Division and supervised the legal staff charged with the review of the FEC's Audit Division.

**Prof. Memberships:** Co-Chairs, Practising Law Institute's annual seminar on 'Corporate Political Activities'. Member, American Bar Association's Standing Committee on Election Law Chaired, Election Law Committee for the Federal Bar Association. On the board of trustees of the Campaign Finance Institute and is a Member of the Executive Committee, and the American Council of Young Political Leaders.

**Career:** JD, Emory University School of Law, 1975, BA, University of Bridgeport, 1972 (cum laude), Faculty Member, George Washington University (1993-98), Faculty Member, New York University (2003-05), Associate General Counsel, Federal Election Commission (1980-86), Member, Federal Judicial Screening Committee for New York (1996-2000).

**Publications:** Co-author, 'Ethics Handbook for Entertaining and Lobbying Public Officials', Stanford, Law and Policy Review and the Yale Law and Policy Review regarding the regulation of campaign finance. Co-author, 'BNA Corporate Political Activity'.

## GROSSHANDLER, Seth

Cleary Gottlieb Steen & Hamilton LLP, New York 212 225 2542
sgrosshandler@cgsh.com
*Recommended in Capital Markets*

**Practice Areas:** Creditors' rights, derivative products, securities transactions, financial institutions and structured finance, with particular emphasis on risks to counterparties and investors in the event of insolvency.

**Prof. Memberships:** Member of the Bar in New York.

**Career:** Joined firm,1983; became Partner, 1992. JD, Law Review, Editorial Board, cum laude, Order of the Coif, Northwestern University School of Law (1983); BA, Phi Beta Kappa, Reed College (1979).

**Publications:** Mr Grosshandler lectures and is widely published on various aspects of creditors' rights and derivative products and securities transactions.

## GROSSI, Peter

Arnold & Porter LLP, Washington, DC
202 942 5670
Peter.Grossi@aporter.com
*Recommended in Products Liability*

**Practice Areas:** Peter Grossi, who joined Arnold & Porter in 1974, is former Head of the firm's Litigation Group. Since 1997, he has served as national counsel for Wyeth in its diet drug cases. He has tried more of the Wyeth cases to verdict – and obtained more defense verdicts – than any other member of the trial teams. Mr Grossi has also had extensive involvement over the past 15 years representing Philip Morris in tobacco product liability and related litigation, including as its principal counsel in its effort to void the FDA's assertion of regulatory jurisdiction over the tobacco industry - a case culminating in the Supreme Court's decision invalidating the FDA regulations.

**Career:** Prior to joining Arnold & Porter, Mr Grossi clerked for Judge J Joseph Smith on the United States Court of Appeals for the Second Circuit.

**Publications:** 'Litigation Driven Medial Screenings: Diagnosis for Dollars', 33 BNA Product Safety and Liability Reporter 1027 (October 2005).

**Personal:** Mr Grossi is ranked in the International Who's Who of Leading Product Liability Defense Lawyers for 2006.

## GUEDRY, David

Jones Day, Dallas
214 220 3939
*Recommended in Business Process Outsourcing, Technology*
*Please see Texas for profile*

## GULLAND, Eugene D

Covington & Burling, Washington, DC
202 662 5504
egulland@cov.com
*Recommended in International Arbitration*

**Practice Areas:** Extensive experience in international and domestic commercial arbitration, and in judicial actions seeking or resisting enforcement of arbitration awards. Includes cases before the ICC, LCIA, ICSID, AAA, CPR, CAS, and disputes under UNCITRAL Rules.

**Prof. Memberships:** Member of the District of Columbia and Virginia Bars, the US Supreme Court, 10 federal courts of appeals, and many federal district courts. Member of the LCIA, the American Judicature Society, USCIB (arbitration committee), and Faculty Member of the National Institute for Trial Advocacy (NITA).

**Personal:** Born 27 August 1947. JD Yale Law School (1972) and AB Princeton University (1969).

## GULLIKSON, Rosemary

Sonnenschein Nath & Rosenthal LLP, Chicago 312 876 8000
*Recommended in Business Process Outsourcing, Technology*
*Please see Illinois for profile*

## GUSSACK, Nina M

Pepper Hamilton LLP, Philadelphia
215 981 4950
gussackn@pepperlaw.com
*Recommended in Products Liability*

**Practice Areas:** Partner; Chair, Health Effects Litigation Group; past Vice-Chair, Executive Committee. Experienced in: defense of pharmaceutical and medical device companies regarding marketed products, investigational new drugs, medical devices, professional labeled, and over-the-counter drug products; counseling companies and physicians regarding clinical trial compliance.

**Prof. Memberships:** Product Liability Advisory Council. International Association of Defense Counsel. Women's Pharmaceutical Network. Member, Drug and Medical Device Steering Committee and Former Chair, Drug and Medical Device Committee, Defense Research Institute.

**Career:** JD 1979 Villanova University School of Law; MS 1976 University of Pennsylvania; BA 1976 University of Pennsylvania.

## GUTOWSKI, Peter

Freehill Hogan & Mahar LLP, New York
212 425 1900
gutowski@freehill.com
*Recommended in Transportation*

**Practice Areas:** Areas of expertise are charter party disputes, the defence of cargo damage and cargo contamination claims and commercial litigation. Has a significant amount of experience in the exercise of provisional remedies such as arrest and attachment, both domestic and foreign. Has tried cases in State and Federal Courts in New York, as well as Federal Courts in various other states, and has argued cases before the Courts of Appeals for the Second, Third and Ninth Circuits. Bar Admission: New York

**Prof. Memberships:** Maritime Law Association of the United States; New York Bar Association.

**Career:** Joined Freehill, Hogan & Mahar as an associate in 1981 and became a Partner in 1988.

**Personal:** Born 1956, New Jersey; Columbia University, BA, 1978; Tulane University, JD, cum laude, 1981.

## GUYNN, Randall

Davis Polk & Wardwell, New York
212 450 4000
randall.guynn@dpw.com
*Recommended in Financial Services*

**Practice Areas:** Head of Davis Polk & Wardwell's Financial Institutions Group. His practice focuses on providing bank regulatory advice, and on M&A and capital markets transactions when the target or issuer is a banking organization or other financial institution. He also advises on corporate governance and internal controls, enforcement actions, cross-border collateral transactions, securities settlement systems and payment systems.

## HAHN, Robert

Hunton & Williams, Charlotte
704 378 4700
*Recommended in Capital Markets*
*Please see North Carolina for profile*

## HALL, Charles

Fulbright & Jaworski L.L.P., Houston
713 651 5151
*Recommended in Tax, Tax Litigation*
*Please see Texas for profile*

## HALLOWAY, Lorraine B

Crowell & Moring LLP, Washington, DC
202 624 2538
lhalloway@crowell.com
*Recommended in Transportation*

**Practice Areas:** Partner in Aviation and International Groups of Crowell & Moring LLP and specializes in aviation law and export control matters. In aviation practice, represents airlines/air freight forwarders/charter operators/aviation manufacturers/ shippers/aviation trade associations in proceedings before the Department of Transportation/ Federal Aviation Administration/ Transportation Security Administration/ federal courts/ foreign governments. In international practice, represents clients before the Department of Commerce/ Directorate of Defense Trade Controls (State Department)/Office of Foreign Assets Control (Treasury Department)/ Department of Homeland Security. Advises on licensing and embargo issues/drafts export control compliance programs/conducts audits/ prepares voluntary disclosures. Represents clients in enforcement proceedings involving alleged violations of customs/ export control/ embargo laws/ regulations.

**HALPERIN, Alan S**
Paul, Weiss, Rifkind, Wharton & Garrison LLP, New York 212 373 3313
ahalperin@paulweiss.com
*Recommended in Wealth Management*
**Practice Areas:** Co-Chair of Personal Representation Department. Counsels clients on estate planning and related tax work, estate and trust administration, tax and succession planning for family corporations and partnerships and charitable giving. Works closely with entrepreneurs, corporate executives, investment bankers, real estate developers, family offices and philanthropists to identify objectives and provide creative, pragmatic solutions designed to meet specific goals. Fellow of The American College of Trust and Estate Counsel. Adjunct Professor at NYU School of Law, teaching Advanced Estates and Gift Taxation and Income Taxation of Trusts and Estates. Selected for 2006 edition of The Best Lawyers of America.

**HALVEY, John**
Milbank, Tweed, Hadley & McCloy LLP, New York 212 530 5000
*Recommended in Business Process Outsourcing, Technology*

**HAMMOND, Steven A**
Hughes Hubbard & Reed LLP, New York 212 837 6253
hammond@hugheshubbard.com
*Recommended in Arbitration, International Arbitration*
**Practice Areas:** Specializes in international arbitration and litigation, with service as counsel or arbitrator in dozens of international commercial arbitrations under ICC, UNCITRAL, AAA, and IACAC rules, including proceedings conducted in English, Spanish and French. Also experienced in sovereign claims and defense, extraterritorial application of US laws, foreign discovery, parallel proceedings, and enforcement of foreign arbitral awards and judgments.
**Prof. Memberships:** Union Internationale des Avocats (President d'Honneur); International Bar Association; American Bar Association; The Association of the Bar of the City of New York; Judicial Conference of the US Court of Appeals for the Second Circuit (Executive Secretary, Planning Committee) (1992-99).
**Career:** Partner since 1986.
**Publications:** Published work has appeared in The Journal of International Arbitration and Graham & Trotman's 'Pre-Trial and Pre-Hearing Procedures Worldwide.'
**Personal:** Honors graduate: Free University of Brussels (LLM, 1979); Maine Law School (JD, 1977); Bowdoin College (AB, 1974). Institut d'Etudes Sciences Politique, Faculté de Droit, Paris 1 (1972-73). Fluent in French, Spanish.

**HANDLER, David A**
Kirkland & Ellis LLP, Chicago
312 861 2477
dhandler@kirkland.com
*Recommended in Wealth Management*
**Practice Areas:** Trust and estate planning, representation of owners of closely-held businesses, executives and families of significant wealth, and establishment and administration of tax-exempt entities.
**Publications:** Mr Handler is often interviewed for prominent trade and news periodicals, frequently lectures at professional education seminars, and regularly writes for leading estate planning and taxation journals, magazines and newsletters. He writes the monthly tax update column in Trusts and Estates Magazine and co-authored a treatise and formbook on estate planning, 'Drafting the Estate Plan: Law and Forms (CCH)'.
**Personal:** University of Illinois, BS (Finance), 1989; Northwestern University School of Law, JD, 1992.

**HANSEN, Edward**
Morgan, Lewis & Bockius LLP, New York
212 309 6000
*Recommended in Business Process Outsourcing, Technology*
*Please see New York for profile*

**HARMS, David B**
Sullivan & Cromwell LLP, New York
212 558 4000
harmsd@sullcrom.com
*Recommended in Capital Markets*
**Practice Areas:** Co-Head, General Practice Group, overseeing all practices except litigation, tax and estates/personal. Handles a wide variety of securities and corporate law matters, advising on capital markets transactions (representing both underwriters and issuers), SEC requirements, corporate governance and securities trading. Also advises financial institutions regarding broker-dealer regulation and SEC, NASD and NYSE inquiries. Deputy Coordinator, Securities Finance Practice, and Coordinator, Broker-Dealer Regulation Practice.
**Career:** Partner since 1992.
**Publications:** Co-Chairman, PLI's 38th Annual Institute on Securities Regulation (2006).
**Personal:** SUNY Purchase (BA, 1978); NYU Law School (JD, 1984; Editor-in-Chief, NYU Law Review).

**HARRINGTON, Carol A**
McDermott Will & Emery, Chicago
312 984 7794
charrington@mwe.com
*Recommended in Wealth Management*
**Practice Areas:** Advises clients on a variety of matters, including estate, gift and generation skipping tax issues, trust and estate administration, and contested trust and tax matters. As a national authority on the federal generation skipping tax, advised attorneys, tax professionals, executors, trustees and other individuals nationwide on this issue.
**Publications:** Co-author of a tax treatise, Generation-Skipping Transfer Tax (Harrington, Plaine & Zaritsky) and has published many articles on the federal generation-skipping tax.
**Personal:** University of Illinois College of Law (JD, summa cum laude with University Honors Bronze Table); University of Illinois (BS, summa cum laude).

**HARRINGTON, David J**
Holland & Knight LLP, New York
212 513 3200
david.harrington@hklaw.com
*Recommended in Transportation*
**Practice Areas:** Member of the Litigation Section, practice primarily focuses on aviation law, including accident investigation and litigation. In addition to his aviation experience, he is well versed in handling all types of complex civil litigation, including multi-district mass tort and product liability litigation. Harrington has represented numerous companies, including foreign and domestic air carriers, aircraft manufacturers, corporate aviation departments, and fixed-based operators in complex civil litigation, in cases involving claims for wrongful death and personal injury, premises liability, breach of contract and breach of warranty. He also has significant experience handling FAA enforcement actions and other aviation regulatory matters.

**HARRIS, L Douglas**
Milbank, Tweed, Hadley & McCloy LLP, New York 212 530 5000
*Recommended in Projects*

**HARRISON, Ellen K**
Pillsbury Winthrop Shaw Pittman LLP, New York 202 663 8316
ellen.harrison@pillsburylaw.com
*Recommended in Wealth Management*
**Practice Areas:** Ms Harrison's practice covers a broad range of tax issues, including estate planning and administration, tax controversies, and income, gift and estate tax planning for individuals, businesses and charitable organizations. Ms Harrison has significant experience drafting wills, trusts, powers of attorney, prenuptial agreements, buy-sell agreements, a variety of corporate documents, and family partnership agreements. Her tax controversy and estate litigation experience includes Internal Revenue Service (IRS) audits, IRS appeals, refund claims, and US Tax Court litigation.
**Personal:** JD, Harvard Law School, 1971 (cum laude); BA, University of Michigan, 1968 (with highest honors).

**HARRISON, Louis**
Harrison & Held, Chicago
312 332 1111
*Recommended in Wealth Management*

**HARRISON, JR, Joseph H**
Sidley Austin LLP, Chicago
312 853 7043
jharrison@sidley.com
*Recommended in Capital Markets*
**Practice Areas:** Joseph Harrison advises and represents clients in futures-related regulatory and litigation matters and with respect to alternative investment funds. He has advised the Ministry of International Trade and Industry of Japan, the government of the People's Republic of China and government of Indonesia. He has extensive experience in structuring and documenting complex investment funds both in United States and offshore and was involved in the first futures sold in Japan, and the first multi-asset alternative strategy funds sold on a retail basis in Japan.
**Prof. Memberships:** Founding Vice President, Secretary and General Counsel of National Futures Association, 1982-87; former Director of the Futures Industry Association and member of its Executive Committee; a former Executive Council Member of the American Bar Association Futures Regulation Committee and former Chairman of the Chicago Bar Association, Futures Regulation Committee.
**Personal:** Northwestern University School of Law, JD, 1979; Northwestern University, MA, 1976; Princeton University, AB, 1973. Admission: Illinois, 1979.

**HART, J Steven**
Williams & Jensen PLLC, Washington, DC 202 659 8201
*Recommended in Government Relations*

**HARTNETT, William**
Cahill Gordon & Reindel LLP, New York
212 701 3900
*Recommended in Capital Markets*

**HARTQUIST, David**
Collier Shannon Scott, Washington, DC 202 342 8400
*Recommended in International Trade*

**HARVEY, James A**
Hunton & Williams, Atlanta
404 888 4160
jaharvey@hunton.com
*Recommended in Business Process Outsourcing*
**Practice Areas:** Jim's practice focuses on sourcing and technology, particularly representation of customers in multi-shore IT and business process sourcing transactions.
**Prof. Memberships:** Former Chair, Technology Law Section, Georgia Bar; Member, Sourcing Interests Group and Board of Editors, The Internet and Computer Lawyer.
**Publications:** Numerous publications including The Privacy and Information Law Report, The Electronic Commerce and Banking Law Report, EuroWatch, and Computer and Internet Litigation

Journal.

**Personal:** Phi Beta Kappa, University of Arkansas; JD, with honors, University of North Carolina.

### HAWKE JR, John D
Arnold & Porter LLP, Washington, DC
202 942 5908
John.Hawke@aporter.com
*Recommended in Financial Services*
**Practice Areas:** Jerry Hawke has rejoined Arnold & Porter LLP's financial Services Practice after nine and a half years of government service, spanning two administrations, in the area of financial institutions policy and regulation.
**Career:** Mr Hawke first joined Arnold & Porter as an associate in 1962 and became a Partner in 1967. He left the firm in 1975 to serve as General Counsel to the Board of Governors of the Federal Reserve System, returning in 1978. From 1995-98 he served as Under Secretary of the Treasury for Domestic Finance, and from 1998-2004 as Comptroller of Currency. As Comptroller, he was a Member of the Basel Committee on Banking Supervision, the Board of Directors of the Federal Deposit Insurance Corporation, and the Federal Financial Institutions Examination Council. As Under Secretary of the Treasury, he chaired the Advanced Counterfeit Deterrence Steering Committee and served as a director of the Securities Investor Protection Corporation. In 2001, he was given the Alexander Hamilton Award, the highest award conferred by the Department of the Treasury.
**Publications:** Mr Hawke has published extensively on matters relating to the regulation of financial institutions.
**Personal:** He has taught federal regulation of banking at the Georgetown University Law Center and at the Morin Center for Banking Law Studies at Boston University School of Law, where he serves as Chairman of the Board of Advisors.

### HAYDEN, Raymond
Hill Rivkins & Hayden LLP, New York
212 669 0600
*Recommended in Transportation*

### HEARD, Keith
Burke & Parsons, New York
212 354 3800
*Recommended in Transportation*

### HEARD III, F Lane
Williams & Connolly LLP, Washington, DC 202 434 5000
*Recommended in Products Liability*

### HEFTLER, Thomas
Stroock & Stroock & Lavan LLP, New York 212 806 5400
*Recommended in Capital Markets*

### HEINZELMAN, Kris
Cravath, Swaine & Moore LLP, New York
212 474 1336
kris.heinzelman@cravath.com
*Recommended in Capital Markets*

**Practice Areas:** Head of the Corporate Department. Domestic and international corporate finance transactions, including public and private offering of debt and equity securities. Routinely represents underwriters and has extensive experience representing issuers in IPOs. Has served as Recruiting Partner, Corporate, and Managing Partner, Corporate.
**Prof. Memberships:** ABA; NYSBA; ABCNY.
**Career:** Partner since 1983.
**Personal:** Yale Law School (JD, 1976); Brown University (MA, AB, magna cum laude, 1973; Phi Beta Kappa).

### HEISLER, Quentin G
McDermott Will & Emery, Chicago
312 984 7606
qheisler@mwe.com
*Recommended in Wealth Management*
**Practice Areas:** Head of firm's Private Client Department. Practices estate and business planning, with particular emphasis on the succession and transfer tax problems of families that control public and closely-held companies. Engaged in structuring of family business control and valuation devices, insurance planning to facilitate the retention of family businesses, multi-generational tax and estate planning for wealthy families. Clientele includes public and private corporations and their executives and shareholders, professionals, individual investors, trust beneficiaries, trusts, estates and foundations.
**Career:** Member of the Florida Bar (1977), Illinois Bar (1968).
**Personal:** Harvard Law School (JD); Harvard College (AB, magna cum laude).

### HELTZER, Harold J
Crowell & Moring LLP, Washington, DC
202 624 2565
hheltzer@crowell.com
*Recommended in Tax Litigation*
**Practice Areas:** Partner and Chair of Crowell & Moring LLP's Tax Group. Represents corporate, partnership, and individual clients in tax matters. Specializes in tax planning for acquisitions/partnership formation/divestitures, and other transactions. Represents clients in tax litigation and administrative practice before the IRS and state tax agencies.
**Career:** Served in the Office of Tax Legislative Counsel for the US DOT; trial attorney in Tax Division of the US DOJ.
**Personal:** JD from New York University; Master of Laws Degree from Georgetown University. Adjunct Professor in the LLM Tax Program at the Georgetown University Law Center. Author of 'Coping with IRS Audits'.

### HENCHEY, Brian
Baker Botts LLP, Dallas
214 953 6576
brian.henchey@bakerbotts.com
*Recommended in Business Process*

*Outsourcing*
**Practice Areas:** Experienced in information technology and business process outsourcing transactions for both customers and service providers. Extensive experience in other types of technology-related commercial transactions, including joint ventures, licensing and distribution agreements, marketing alliances, and mergers and acquisitions involving significant intellectual property components. Active practice in public company representation in day-to-day securities matters.
**Career:** Baker Botts LLP (1999 to present).
**Personal:** Cornell Law School (JD cum laude, 1999); University of North Carolina (BS, 1992).

### HENGEN, Nancy
Holland & Knight LLP, New York
212 513 3200
nancy.hengen@hklaw.com
*Recommended in Transportation*
**Practice Areas:** Partner in firm's Business Law Section. She represents clients in secured and unsecured financing transactions in connection with commercial vessels and other 'big ticket' equipment financing, including leveraged and single-investor leases, synthetic leases, loan agreements and related security documentation, ship mortgages, Title XI financing, and other US governmental financing programs and vessel construction contracts. She has represented US and foreign banks, financial institutions and other investors, as well as borrowers and lessees in loan and leasing transactions involving equipment and facilities. Her practice includes mergers and acquisitions in the shipping industry and corporate transactions.

### HERLIHY, Edward
Wachtell, Lipton, Rosen & Katz, New York 212 403 1000
*Recommended in Corporate/M&A, Financial Services*
*Please see New York for profile*

### HICKOK, Arthur
Sidley Austin LLP, New York
212 839 5318
ahickok@sidley.com
*Recommended in Capital Markets*
**Practice Areas:** Practice focuses on the representation of commercial and investment banks, monoline insurers and other financial institutions participating in securitisation and structured finance transactions as underwriters, placement agents, providers of credit enhancement and investors. Transactions include the securitization of corporate loans and bonds (CLOs and CBOs), mortgage loans, premium finance loans, trade receivables, commodities, guaranteed investment contracts, intellectual property and other financial assets, financed through a variety of means including the

issuance of term securities and commercial paper. Mr Hickok has also assisted clients in establishing commercial paper conduits and other investment vehicles.
**Personal:** The University of Chicago Law School, JD, 1994; Princeton University, AB, 1990. Admissions: Illinois, 1994; New York, 2001.

### HILER, Bruce A
Cadwalader, Wickersham & Taft LLP, Washington, DC 202 862 2256
bruce.hiler@cwt.com
*Recommended in Financial Services*
**Practice Areas:** Chairman, Securities and Financial Institutions Regulation Department. Concentrates on securities regulatory defense, regulatory and corporate counseling, internal investigations and securities litigation. Has represented public companies, broker-dealer firms, investment advisors, and individuals in investigations before the Securities and Exchange Commission, the Department of Justice, state securities agencies, the National Association of Securities Dealers, the New York Stock Exchange, the Office of the Comptroller of the Currency, and other regulatory agencies. Has conducted internal investigations for the Audit Committees and Boards of Directors of US public companies in connection with on-going government investigations; counsels corporations on disclosure and corporate compliance issues. Author of numerous articles on securities law cited by Federal Courts including the US Supreme Court.
**Prof. Memberships:** Illinois and District of Columbia bars.
**Personal:** JD, University of Michigan Law School (cum laude) (1977); BA, University of Notre Dame (magna cum laude) (1974). Former Associate Director, SEC Division of Enforcement; former Adjunct Professor of Securities Law, Georgetown University Law Center LLM Program.

### HILL, Lawrence
Dewey Ballantine LLP, New York
212 259 8330
lhill@dbllp.com
*Recommended in Tax Litigation*
**Practice Areas:** Partner and Chair, Tax Controversy and Litigation Group.
**Career:** Mr Hill represents multinational corporations, investment banks, professional service firms and wealthy individuals in tax litigation, IRS controversies, white-collar and corporate internal investigations and other complex litigation. He also represents clients in tax shelter investigations commenced by the IRS, Department of Justice and US Senate, including the largest criminal tax investigation in US history and is lead nationwide counsel to an international bank in over 100 related lawsuits brought by investors.
**Personal:** BA, State University of New York at Binghamton, JD, 1981. LLM Tax-

ation, 1989. George Washington University.

### HILLENBRAND, Hyman
DeOrchis Hillenbrand & Wiener LLP, Miami 305 571 9200
*Recommended in Transportation*

### HINMAN JR, William
Simpson Thacher & Bartlett LLP, Palo Alto 650 251 5000
whinman@stblaw.com
*Recommended in Capital Markets*
**Practice Areas:** Corporate Partner at Simpson Thacher & Bartlett. His area of concentration is corporate finance, advising both issuers and underwriters in capital-raising transactions with a particular emphasis on public and private financings and initial public offerings. He has been involved with debt and equity offerings of high technology, healthcare, and biopharmaceutical companies as well as a variety of offerings and general corporate work for a wide range of issuers and underwriters. His practice has had a strong international focus. He also has significant experience regarding convertible offerings, derivatives, novel securities, and private placements. Has represented boards of directors and their audit committees on a number of governance matters.
**Prof. Memberships:** Member, Bar Association of the State of California, Association of the Bar of the City of New York; Advisory Board Member, Latin American Law and Business Report edited by WorldTrade Executive, Inc.
**Career:** Joined the firm in 2000 as a Partner. Prior to coming to Simpson Thacher, he was the Managing Partner of Shearman & Sterling's San Francisco and Menlo Park offices.
**Personal:** Cornell University Law School, JD, 1980; Editorial Board, Cornell Law Review. Michigan State University, BA (with honors), 1977.

### HINSON, H Douglas
Alston & Bird LLP, Atlanta
404 881 7590
dhinson@alston.com
*Recommended in ERISA Litigation*
**Practice Areas:** Concentrates on ERISA litigation; securities litigation; complex commercial, insurance and transaction-based litigation; class action defense.
**Prof. Memberships:** State Bar of Georgia, Atlanta Bar Association, American Bar Association (Vice-Chair, Employee Benefits Committee of Tort and Insurance Practice Section).
**Career:** Leads the firm's ERISA Litigation Group; member of Securities Litigation Group. Frequent lecturer for the Institute for Applied Management and Law.
**Personal:** BA, magna cum laude, Emory University (1982); JD, cum laude, Georgetown University (1986).

### HITSELBERGER, Carol A
Mayer, Brown, Rowe & Maw LLP, Chicago 312 701 7740
chitselberger@mayerbrownrowe.com
*Recommended in Capital Markets*
**Practice Areas:** Specializes in securitization and other structured finance products, including structuring domestic and cross-border commercial paper and extendible note funded securitization vehicles and SIVs and securitizing trade receivables, credit card receivables, aircraft, leases, franchise portfolios, government contracts, trademark licenses, and various other financial assets, as well as synthetic leases and synthetic securitizations; experience includes representation of program sponsors, underwriters, placement agents, advisors, liquidity providers, credit enhancers and issuers in private placements, public offerings and Rule 144A/Regulation S executions.
**Prof. Memberships:** Membership Committee, American Securitization Forum.
**Career:** Joined Mayer, Brown, Rowe & Maw LLP, Chicago, 1989; Partner, 1998.
**Publications:** Is a contributing author to the two-volume treatise, 'Securitization of Financial Assets', Aspen Law and Business (2nd ed 2004). Regularly speaks at professional seminars and conferences, including at the American Securitization Forum and Information Management Network industry conferences.
**Personal:** University of Pennsylvania Law School, JD cum laude, 1989. Bryn Mawr College, AB magna cum laude, 1986.

### HOBBY, Scott M
Paul, Hastings, Janofsky & Walker LLP, Atlanta 404 815 2214
scotthobby@paulhastings.com
*Recommended in Business Process Outsourcing*
**Practice Areas:** Scott Hobby's practice focus is in four areas: multinational business process, information technology and application service provider outsourcing arrangements; enterprise resource platform level systems development and integration transactions; multinational procurement and off-shore captive corporate subsidiary arrangements; and corporate finance including public and private offerings, mergers, acquisitions and corporate governance. Listed in Best Lawyers in America 2003-04 and 2005-06, named one of Georgia's 2005 and 2006 Legal Elite in Georgia Trend Magazine, December 2005 and December 2006, named a Corporate Finance Super Lawyer in Atlanta Magazine and Georgia Super Lawyers magazine, March 2005 and March 2006.

### HOCHBERG, Kevin J
Sidley Austin LLP, Chicago
312 853 2085
khochberg@sidley.com
*Recommended in Capital Markets*

**Practice Areas:** Kevin Hochberg's practice focuses on structured finance, asset securitization, merger and acquisition financing, restructurings and bankruptcies, and other secured and unsecured lending transactions. He represents issuers, monoline insurance companies, underwriters and investors in both public and private offerings of asset-backed securities, including commercial paper conduit transactions, Rule 144A and public offerings. His practice has covered a wide range of asset classes, including trade receivables, auto loans, equipment leases, rental car fleets, shipping containers, container chassis, railcars, utility stranded costs and relocation company receivables.
**Prof. Memberships:** Member of the Chicago and American Bar Associations and the American College of Commercial Finance Lawyers.
**Personal:** The University of Chicago Law School, JD, 1984; University of Chicago, MA, 1978; University of Maryland, BA, 1977. Admission: Illinois, 1984.

### HOCHBERG, Sheldon
Steptoe & Johnson LLP, Washington, DC
202 429 6218
shochberg@steptoe.com
*Recommended in International Trade*
**Practice Areas:** Partner in the Washington office of Steptoe & Johnson LLP. Focuses on international trade and administrative law matters, particularly judicial review of federal agency determinations. Has extensive experience on some of the most complex and important issues related to countervailing duty and antidumping laws. He also has expertise in the Real Estate Settlement Procedures Act, the Fair Credit Reporting Act, and privacy issues relating to financial/insurance institutions. Clients include foreign and domestic industries in trade matters, as well as the title, and property/casualty, insurance industries.
**Personal:** LLB, Harvard University, 1967; AB, Columbia College, 1964.

### HOFFMAN, William
Davis Polk & Wardwell, Washington, DC
202 962 7000
william.hoffman@dpw.com
*Recommended in International Trade*
**Practice Areas:** Counsel in Davis Polk & Wardwell's Washington office, advising financial institutions and other clients on economic sanctions issues and certain money laundering, terrorist financing and other regulatory matters.

### HOGAN, Adele
Linklaters, New York
212 903 9195
adele.hogan@linklaters.com
*Recommended in Capital Markets*
**Practice Areas:** Partner in the Corporate Group with a broad capital markets practice, having advised issuers and underwriters on numerous debt and

equity offerings across a range of industries, including financial, telecommunications, oil and gas, and healthcare. Played a key role in the development of numerous novel structures, and regularly counsels participants in the capital markets on transactional, regulatory and related issues. Presented more than 50 seminars in the last three years, including co-chairing PLI's 'Understanding the Securities Laws' and chairing the New York City Bar's 'Annual Corporate and Securities Laws: A Practical Overview of the Rules', 'Hedge Funds' and 'Annual Corporate and Securities Laws Update: Keeping Current in Legal and Business Developments'.
**Prof. Memberships:** Securities Regulations Committees of the American Bar Association and the New York State Bar Association.
**Personal:** Received her JD from Cornell University in 1985 and her BA from Cornell University in 1982.

### HOLBREICH, Curt
Howard, Rice, Nemerovski, Canady, Falk & Rabkin, San Francisco
415 434 1600
*Recommended in Sport*

### HONAN III, William J
Holland & Knight LLP, New York
212 513 3200
bill.honan@hklaw.com
*Recommended in Transportation*
**Practice Areas:** Partner in the Litigation Section with extensive experience in arbitration, mediation and maritime law, especially in maritime contracts. Mr Honan is Chairman of the Board of New York Maritime Inc., an organization formed to promote New York, and is Vice-Chairman of the Documentary Committee of Intertanko, an entity that represents most of the privately owned tanker owners in the world. He is also a member of the Arbitration Committee of the ABA Section of Dispute Resolutions, the Committee on Arbitration and ADR of the International Bar Association and the Committee on Maritime Arbitration of the Maritime Law Association.

### HONG, Ji Hoon
Shearman & Sterling LLP, New York
212 848 7417
jhong@shearman.com
*Recommended in Transportation*
**Practice Areas:** Of Counsel in the Capital Markets Group at Shearman & Sterling. Experience includes structured finance transactions, capital markets transactions, sovereign debt restructurings and general corporate practice.
**Career:** Joined Shearman in 1986, became Partner in 1996 and became of counsel in 2005.
**Personal:** Mr Hong is a native speaker of Korean and studied at Seoul National University in 1977 before immigrating to the United States. SB in economics, Mass-

achusetts Institute of Technology, (1983); JD, Harvard Law School (1986)

## HOOPER, Chester D
Holland & Knight LLP, New York
212 513 3200
chester.hooper@hklaw.com
*Recommended in Transportation*
**Practice Areas:** Partner in the Litigation Section, practice involves defense of vessel interests against claims for cargo damage, collisions, advice on multimodal carriage of cargo, drafting bills of lading and other shipping documents. Has tried numerous cases. Was President of The Maritime Law Association of the United States from 1994-96 and is a Titulary Member of the Comité Maritime International. He is a Member of the United States delegation to the United Nations Commission on International Trade Law Working Group that is drafting a new treaty to govern the international carriage of goods that includes an international sea leg.

## HORLICK, Gary N
WilmerHale, Washington, DC
202 663 6050
gary.horlick@wilmerhale.com
*Recommended in International Trade*
**Practice Areas:** Provides global business, investment, regulatory and negotiating advice to US and international clients. Has handled antidumping and countervailing duty cases in the US and Europe and 10 other countries; GATT and WTO cases; and GATT, WTO and FTA negotiations for governments and businesses.
**Prof. Memberships:** ABA International Section Committee on International Trade, the Executive Council of the American Branch of the International Law Association, the Council on Foreign Relations and the Trade Policy Subcouncil of the Competitiveness Policy Council.
**Personal:** Yale Law School (JD 1973); Cambridge University (MA); Cambridge University (BA 1970); Dartmouth College (AB 1968).

## HORN, Charles M
Mayer, Brown, Rowe & Maw LLP, Washington, DC 202 263 3219
chorn@mayerbrown.com
*Recommended in Financial Services*
**Practice Areas:** Represents domestic and foreign financial services firms on regulatory and transactional issues affecting organization, structure, governance/management, operations, compliance and regulatory supervision. Extensive experience in the development of new capital markets and other financial products and services. Routinely counsels on transactions and activities involving the convergence of financial services sectors (banking, securities, insurance).
**Career:** Mayer, Brown, Rowe & Maw LLP, Washington, DC, 1992 to date. Stroock & Stroock & Lavan, Washington,

DC, 1989-92. Securities and Corporate Practices Division, Office of the Comptroller of the Currency, US Department of Treasury, Washington, DC: Director, 1986-89; Assistant Director, 1983-86; Senior Attorney, 1983. Securities and Exchange Commission, Washington, DC: Branch Chief, 1982-83; Senior Counsel, 1980-82; Attorney, Division of Enforcement, 1978-82; Attorney, Division of Market Regulation, 1976-78.
**Publications:** Recent writings: 'Trends in Federal Securities Regulation of Banking Organizations', The Review of Banking and Financial Services (2005). 'In Defense of Moderation: Avoiding Overregulation of 'Special Purpose Entities', The Legal Backgrounder (Wash. Legal Foundation), Vol 17, No 39, Sept. 2002. 'Financial Services Privacy at the Start of the 21st Century: A Conceptual Perspective', 5 North Carolina Banking Institute 89, April 2001.
**Personal:** Cornell Law School, JD, 1976. Harvard College, AB magna cum laude, 1973.

## HORNICK, Robert
Morgan, Lewis & Bockius LLP, New York
212 309 6945
rhornick@morganlewis.com
*Recommended in International Arbitration*
**Practice Areas:** Robert Hornick is a Partner in the Litigation Practice. He concentrates on international commercial arbitration, with special emphasis on Asia. His arbitration work has included representation both of investors and governments, including the foreign investors in the four Amco arbitrations against the Government of Indonesia during the 1980s and early 1990s and a South Asian government in the first ICSID claim ever brought under a bilateral investment treaty. His other cases have involved inter alia disputes about power projects, international distributorships and joint ventures, engineering, procurement and construction contracts, licenses, patents and other intellectual property, acquisition agreements and services agreements.

## HOROWITZ, Alan
Miller & Chevalier Chartered, Washington, DC 202 626 5839
ahorowitz@milchev.com
*Recommended in Tax Litigation*
**Practice Areas:** US Supreme Court and Appellate Litigation, with special emphasis on tax litigation. Has argued 28 cases in US Supreme Court, plus many others in federal courts of appeals. Has represented major corporations and individuals at all levels of federal court litigation.
**Prof. Memberships:** American Bar Association; Bar Association of DC.
**Career:** Member, Miller & Chevalier Chartered (1990-present); tax assistant to the Solicitor General, US Department of Justice (1986-90); assistant to the Solicitor General, US Department of Justice

(1979-86); associate, Covington & Burling (1977-79). '
**Publications:** 'Foreign Tax Violations May Be Prosecuted Here as With Fraud', ABA International Law News (Summer 2005) (with Philip West and Keith Sleveding). 'The Supreme Court's 'Dim' View of the Bright-Line Test in INDOPCO', Tax Notes (January 1992).
**Personal:** JD, Columbia Law School, 1977, (Articles and Book Reviews Editor), Columbia Law Review; BS, Massachusetts Institute of Technology, 1974.

## HOROWITZ, Richard M
Thacher Proffitt & Wood LLP, New York
212 912 7828
rhorowitz@tpw.com
*Recommended in Capital Markets*
**Practice Areas:** Mr Horowitz concentrates in mortgage-backed securities. He has represented various investment banking firms as issuers and underwriters, sellers, servicers and financial guarantors, among others, in public offerings and private placements of pass-through and debt transactions. Mr Horowitz has experience in residential, multifamily and commercial loan securitizations.
**Career:** Mr Horowitz graduated from Hamilton College in 1983 and the University of Pennsylvania Law School in 1986.

## HOUSE, Michael
McDermott Will & Emery, Washington, DC 202 756 8626
mhouse@mwe.com
*Recommended in International Trade*
**Practice Areas:** Import relief measures, multilateral trade disputes, WTO and customs. Represents multinational clients in trade actions arising under unfair trade and import practices laws, safeguards proceedings, GSP program and export controls. Represents clients before US Department of Commerce, US Trade Representative, US International Trade Commission, Customs and Border Protection.
**Career:** Appears before US Court of International Trade and Federal Circuit Court of Appeals for various industry sectors, including such major industries as semiconductors, steel, consumer electronics, chemicals and textiles.
**Personal:** University of Texas School of Law (JD, magna cum laude); Southern Methodist University (BFA, magna cum laude).

## HOUSE, W Michael
Hogan & Hartson LLP, Washington, DC
202 637 5636
wmhouse@hhlaw.com
*Recommended in Government Relations*
**Practice Areas:** Mike House, Director of the firm's Legislative Group, concentrates on legislative and regulatory matters before the US Congress, White House, and various departments and

independent agencies of the executive branch. He represents national and multinational corporations, trade associations, and coalitions.
**Prof. Memberships:** Member, Society of International Business Fellows; Member, The Council on Excellence in Government; Board of Directors, Washington Project for the Arts; Trustee, Farrah Law Society, University of Alabama School of Law; The President's Council, University of Alabama.
**Career:** Prior to joining the firm in 1991, Mike's career included serving as administrative assistant, Chief of Staff to Sen Howell Heflin of Alabama and legislative assistant to Congressman James M Collins of Texas, where he was responsible for legislative matters involving the House Committee on Energy and Commerce.
**Personal:** University of Alabama School of Law (JD); Auburn University (BS).

## HOWARD, Nigel
Mayer, Brown, Rowe & Maw LLP, New York 212 506 2500
*Recommended in Business Process Outsourcing, Technology*
*Please see New York for profile*

## HOWELL, John
Hughes & Luce LLP, Dallas
214 939 5500
*Recommended in Business Process Outsourcing, Technology*

## HOWITT, John P
Paul, Hastings, Janofsky & Walker LLP, New York 212 318 6005
johnhowitt@paulhastings.com
*Recommended in Transportation*
**Practice Areas:** General finance practice, specializing in aircraft finance, including securitisations; leveraged and single-investor leases; operating leases; purchases and sales; loans secured by aircraft, engines, parts; enhanced equipment trust certificate financings; airline restructurings; airline bankruptcies; and manufacturer support arrangements.
**Prof. Memberships:** Admitted to practice in New York and California.
**Career:** Paul, Hastings, Janofsky & Walker (1978-present; Partner, 1986-present; seconded to Nagashima & Ohno, Tokyo, Japan 1981-83).
**Publications:** Spoken and written on aircraft leasing, aircraft financing and operating leases.
**Personal:** UCLA (BA 1975, magna cum laude, Phi Beta Kappa); UCLA (JD 1978, Order of the Coif).

## HOYNS, John K
Hughes Hubbard & Reed LLP, New York
212 837 6767
hoyns@hugheshubbard.com
*Recommended in Transportation*
**Practice Areas:** Aviation industry matters, including debt and lease financings, public and private securities offerings,

code-share arrangements, workouts, recapitalizations and mergers and acquisitions.
**Prof. Memberships:** Member, American Bar Association and the Bar of the City of New York.
**Career:** Partner, New York since 1986.
**Publications:** Author or co-author of three chapters in treatise 'Securities Law Techniques' and various other articles. Lectures at Practising Law Institute and other seminars.
**Personal:** Colgate University (BA, 1976, cum laude); University of Michigan (JD, 1979, magna cum laude).

### HUDANISH, David
Mayer, Brown, Rowe & Maw LLP, New York 212 506 2500
*Recommended in Business Process Outsourcing, Technology*
*Please see New York for profile*

### HUGI, Robert F
Mayer, Brown, Rowe & Maw LLP, Chicago 312 701 7121
rhugi@mayerbrownrowe.com
*Recommended in Capital Markets*
**Practice Areas:** Represent issuers, underwriters and conduit administrators in public and private issuances of asset-backed securities, principally backed by credit card and equipment contract receivables. Represent the American Securitisation Forum and other industry groups in commenting on various accounting and bank regulatory proposals.
**Prof. Memberships:** Admitted: Illinois, 1986.
**Career:** Mayer, Brown, Rowe & Maw LLP, Chicago, 1991 to date; 1986-89; London, 1989-91.
**Publications:** Co-author: 'Registration Under the Investment Company Act of 1940', Securitization of Financial Assets, Prentice Hall Law and Business, 1993. 'Hidden Liens: A Trap for the Unwary', Banking Law Journal, 1989. 'Recent Regulatory Developments Affecting Sales of Strip Participations', Journal of International Banking Law, 1988.
**Personal:** University of Chicago, JD cum laude, 1986. Northwestern University, BS with highest distinction, 1980.

### HUMPHREY, Thomas P
Crowell & Moring LLP, Washington, DC 202 624 2633
thumphrey@crowell.com
*Recommended in Government Contracts*
**Practice Areas:** Partner in Crowell & Moring's Government Contracts Group. Represents clients in a wide variety of government contracts matters, including bid protests/False Claims Act/qui tam litigation/investigations of potential criminal matters. Specializes in handling computer, telecommunications, and healthcare bid protest litigation before the GAO and various trial and appellate courts.

**Prof. Memberships:** Active in the Bid Protest Committee of the Public Contract Law Section of the American Bar Association; served for many years as a Vice-Chair of a committee of the Litigation Section of the American Bar Association.

### HUVELLE, Jeffrey
Covington & Burling, Washington, DC 202 662 6000
JHuvelle@cov.com
*Recommended in ERISA Litigation*
**Practice Areas:** A Partner who concentrates on ERISA litigation, employment litigation and employment advice. Has handled individual and class-action ERISA litigation for IBM, GE, the NFL and Verizon, including the defense of nation-wide class-action litigation challenging the design of cash balance plans. Won 15 consecutive victories in jury and non-jury employment cases tried to a verdict. These include verdicts in jury trials for the World Football League, IBM and Computer Associates in race discrimination cases.
**Personal:** Columbia Law School (JD); Harvard College (BA).

### HYATT, Townsend
Orrick, Herrington & Sutcliffe LLP, Portland 503 943 4820
thyatt@orrick.com
*Recommended in Native American Law*
**Practice Areas:** Leads Orrick's Indian Tribal Finance Practice. Works nationally as bond counsel, lender's counsel or other on financing transactions by Indian tribes, including gaming, lodging and entertainment projects, land acquisitions, health clinics, schools, government buildings, sewer, water and infrastructure development, parks and recreation facilities, manufacturing plants, and more. Substantial experience in both taxable and tax exempt markets, commercial loans, bonds, notes and other securities offerings by Indian tribes.
**Publications:** 'An Introduction to Indian Tribal Finance', and 'Doing Business with Indian Tribes'.
**Personal:** JD and LLM, Duke University, 1989; BA, University of North Carolina, 1984.

### IRELAND, Oliver I
Morrison & Foerster LLP, Washington, DC 202 778 1614
oireland@mofo.com
*Recommended in Financial Services*
**Practice Areas:** Focuses primarily on retail financial services including electronic commerce, compliance with Federal Reserve regulations, including Regulations Z and E, compliance with the Gramm-Leach-Bliley Act privacy provisions, the Fair Credit Reporting Act, E-SIGN, the US Patriot Act, and telemarketing rules. His practice also includes all types of payment transactions, including compliance with NACHA rules, bank

regulatory issues and other aspects of banking, securities and commodities markets, including margin lending.
**Career:** Admitted to practice in Illinois, Massachusetts, and the District of Columbia.
**Personal:** BA, Yale University, 1970; JD, The University of Texas School of Law, 1974.

### ISAACSON, Laurence B
McKee Nelson LLP, New York 917 777 4500
lisaacson@mckeenelson.com
*Recommended in Capital Markets*
**Practice Areas:** Concentrates practice in structured finance, particularly in complex securitisations involving the structuring and offering of collateralized debt obligations. Transactions have included both cash and synthetic CDOs, CLOs, CDOs of CDOs, CFOs, ABS CDOs and MBS CDOs. Has participated in the structuring of other investments, including structured investment vehicles, future oil receivables, emerging-market receivables, risk transfer swap transactions and credit-linked offerings.
**Career:** Prior to joining McKee Nelson, was the Head of Structure Finance Practice at Fried, Frank, Harris, Shriver & Jacobson LLP.
**Personal:** JD, Duke University, 1987. BA, Cornell University, 1984.

### ISAACSON, William
Boies, Schiller & Flexner, Washington, DC 202 237 5607
wisaacson@bsfllp.com
*Recommended in International Arbitration*
**Practice Areas:** In the field of arbitration, Mr Isaacson has won major trials and enforcement proceedings. He served as lead counsel in a federal court action to enforce an international arbitration award under the New York Convention, obtaining a $261 million judgment that was affirmed on appeal. In a London ICC arbitration in which he was counsel, Claimant won $39.5 million, with a 300-page award upholding claims for fraud and breach of fiduciary duty. More recently, Mr Isaacson won an $8 million award in a three-week AAA arbitration. Mr Isaacson has also successfully prosecuted claims in arbitration against AOL worth over $60 million and successfully defended a respondent against a claim for $30 million in lost profits. In addition, Mr Isaacson specializes in antitrust class actions against international price-fixing cartels. He has won jury verdicts of $148.5 million against foreign vitamin manufacturers and $23 million against scrap metal dealers in conspiracy cases. In 2005 and 2006, Mr Isaacson filed the first class actions against Chinese cartels involving products exported to the United States, including vitamin C, magnesite and bauxite.

**Career:** Mr Isaacson has been a Partner at Boies, Schiller & Flexner LLP since its inception in 1997. He was formerly a Partner at Kaye Scholer Fierman Hays & Handler LLP, and served as a law clerk to Chief Judge Harrison L Winter of the US Court of Appeals for the Fourth Circuit (1986-87).
**Personal:** BA (1982) University of Redlands, California; JD (1986), University of Virginia School of Law. Mr Isaacson has lectured at Georgetown University Law School and in ABA seminars.

### JACOBSON, Martin
Simpson Thacher & Bartlett LLP, New York 212 455 2000
*Recommended in Projects, Transportation*
*Please see New York for profile*

### JAFFE, Marc
Latham & Watkins LLP, New York 212 906 1200
*Recommended in Capital Markets*

### JANKOWSKY, Joel
Akin Gump Strauss Hauer & Feld LLP, Washington, DC 202 887 4082
jjankowsky@akingump.com
*Recommended in Government Relations*
**Practice Areas:** Mr Jankowsky chairs Akin Gump's Policy Department. He represents numerous clients on a variety of public policy matters, with an emphasis on entertainment and telecommunications issues.
**Prof. Memberships:** Chairman, Board of Directors, Close Up Foundation; Member, Board of Governors, Bryce Harlow Foundation; Member, Board of Directors, National Rehabilitation Hospital; Member, Board of Advisors, Carl Albert Center, University of Oklahoma.
**Personal:** BBA, University of Oklahoma (1965); JD, University of Oklahoma Law School (1968).

### JARBOE, Mark A
Dorsey & Whitney LLP, Minneapolis 612 340 2686
jarboe.mark@dorsey.com
*Recommended in Native American Law*
**Practice Areas:** Represents Indian tribal governments, tribal businesses and entities doing business with tribes across the country in connection with financings of reservation infrastructure, economic development and other activities; contractual, regulatory, gaming, economic development and other matters; and governmental and tribal court structuring and jurisdiction issues.
**Prof. Memberships:** Minnesota State Bar Association; Minnesota American Indian Bar Association.
**Publications:** 'Recourse and Limited Recourse in Casino Financings', Indian Gaming, April 2004; 'Financing Alternatives for Tribal Gaming Facilities', Indian

Gaming, April 2003.
**Personal:** Harvard Law School (JD, 1975); University of Michigan (AB, 1972).

## JENKINS III, Robert M
Mayer, Brown, Rowe & Maw LLP, Washington, DC 202 263 3261
rmjenkins@mayerbrown.com
*Recommended in Transportation*
**Practice Areas:** Substantial experience in railroad regulatory and transactional matters. Represents major US railroads and principal US railroad trade association in rulemaking and complaint proceedings before the federal Surface Transportation Board, and its predecessor the Interstate Commerce Commission. Handles court litigation, appellate proceedings, and arbitrations involving railroad regulation and transactions. Advises on rate reasonableness and revenue adequacy regulation; preemption of state and local railroad regulation; rail construction permitting and environmental reviews; major railroad mergers and line acquisitions; crossings, abandonments, and condemnations of rail lines and other facilities; claims of monopolization, predation, discrimination, foreclosure, and unreasonable practices; deregulation of previously regulated services; and disputes involving trackage rights, access rights, line sale contract conditions, regulated merger conditions, interchange and routing requirements, and the railroad common carrier obligation.
**Career:** Mayer, Brown, Rowe & Maw LLP, Washington, DC, 1998 to date. Harkins Cunningham, 1992-98. Pepper, Hamilton & Scheetz, 1980-92. Covington & Burling, 1975-80. Law Clerk to the Honorable Malcolm R Wilkey, US Court of Appeals for the DC Circuit, 1974-75. Peace Corps Volunteer (Peru), 1969-71.
**Personal:** JD (honors), University of California at Berkeley, 1974; Order of the Coif; editor, Law Review. BA (honors), Harvard College, 1969.

## JOHNSON, Philip McBride
Skadden, Arps, Slate, Meagher & Flom LLP & Affiliates, Washington, DC
202 371 7340
pjohnson@skadden.com
*Recommended in Capital Markets*
**Practice Areas:** Served as Chairman of the US Commodity Futures Trading Commission in Reagan Administration, author of the dominant US legal treatise on derivatives regulation (Derivatives Regulation, 3 vol Aspen Law and Business 2004), founded the derivatives law committees for both American and International Bar Associations, served on five CFTC advisory committees, New York Stock Exchange Regulatory Advisory Committee, first public director of Futures Industry Association, heads exchange-traded derivatives law practice at Skadden with extensive international

practice.
**Career:** LLB, Yale University, 1962 (managing editor, Yale Law Journal); BA, Indiana University, 1959 (with honors).

## JOHNSON, W Stanfield
Crowell & Moring LLP, Washington, DC
202 624 2520
wjohnson@crowell.com
*Recommended in Government Contracts*
**Practice Areas:** Served four times as Crowell & Moring's Chairman. A senior member of the firm's Government Contracts Group, focuses on counseling/litigation/resolution of contract issues. Helped secure a victory in the 'Great Engine War', a dispute between United Technologies Corp's Pratt & Whitney and the Air Force over a jet engine contract awarded in the 1980s. Has negotiated settlements of numerous government claims-cost disallowances/defective pricing/false claims allegations. Counseled and represented a substantial portion of the defense industry and other contractors.
**Personal:** Undergraduate with great distinction, Stanford University,1960; JD, Harvard Law School, 1963. Member of Phi Beta Kappa.

## JOHNSON JR, O Thomas
Covington & Burling, Washington, DC
202 662 5170
ojohnson@cov.com
*Recommended in International Arbitration*
**Practice Areas:** International litigation; dispute resolution concerning land and maritime boundaries, international trade, claims by and against foreign governments, commercial arbitrations; advise on Foreign Corrupt Practices Act. Counsel to Eritrea in negotiating peace treaty that ended border war with Ethiopia. Represented Amoco in claim against Iran before the Iran-US Claims Tribunal (1990), resulting in that tribunal's largest award.
**Career:** Appointed by President Bush to US Panel of Arbitrators for ICSID (2003); Office of the Legal Adviser, US Department of State (1971-75); special assistant to the Legal Adviser (1973-75).
**Personal:** Stanford University (JD, 1971; AB, 1968).

## JONES, Christy
Butler, Snow, O'Mara, Stevens & Cannada, PLLC, Jackson 601 948 5711
*Recommended in Litigation, Products Liability*
*Please see Mississippi for profile*

## JONES, Erika Z
Mayer, Brown, Rowe & Maw LLP, Washington, DC
202 263 3232
ejones@mayerbrownrowe.com
*Recommended in Transportation*
**Practice Areas:** Represents clients

before federal regulatory agencies, including: National Highway Traffic Safety Administration, Federal Motor Carrier Safety Administration, Surface Transportation Board; US Consumer Product Safety Commission and others. Counsels on federal safety laws governing motor vehicles and consumer products. Handles issues related to federal information laws, including Freedom of Information Act; Privacy Act; Federal Advisory Committee Act; Paperwork Reduction Act; and protection of confidential business information from public disclosure. Assists clients in federal regulatory proceedings, including drafting comments and providing strategic advice on the regulatory process. Represents clients in litigation involving direct review of federal decision, federal regulatory issues in product liability or class action litigation, and federal preemption.
**Career:** Mayer, Brown, Rowe & Maw LLP, Washington, DC, 1989 to date; Partner, 1991. National Highway Traffic Safety Administration, US Department of Transportation, Washington, DC: Chief Counsel, 1985-89; Special Counsel to the Administrator, 1981-85. Attorney/Regulatory Policy Analyst, Office of Management and Budget, Washington, DC, 1980-81. Staff, Federal Communications Commission, Washington, DC, 1976-80.
**Personal:** JD, Georgetown University Law Center, 1980; BA (magna cum laude), Georgetown University, 1976; Phi Beta Kappa.

## JORISSEN, Paul A
Mayer, Brown, Rowe & Maw LLP, New York 212 506 2555
pjorissen@mayerbrownrowe.com
*Recommended in Capital Markets*
**Practice Areas:** Broad and varied asset and mortgage-backed related practice, including structuring numerous single seller conduits and related deriviative transactions for leading domestic and foreign mortgage loan originators as well as extendible note funded repurchase facilities for large real estate investment trusts; working with credit default and other derivatives and unusual asset types including defaulted and reperforming loans, servicing rights and servicing advances; experience in workouts of securitized franchise loans and other troubled and non-performing debt; representing subordinated bond investors and master, primary and special servicers of mortgage-backed securities; representing sellers and commercial paper conduits in transactions involving various asset types; and extensive experience representing issuers and underwriters of securities backed by commercial and residential mortgages and home equity loans, equipment loans and leases, auto loans, and franchise loans.
**Career:** Mayer, Brown, Rowe & Maw LLP, New York, 2001 to date; Chicago,

1993-2001. Hopkins and Sutter, Chicago, 1991-93. Ernst & Whinney, Senior Tax Consultant, Detroit, 1985-88. Certified Public Accountant, Michigan, 1985.
**Personal:** Loyola University of Chicago School of Law, JD magna cum laude, 1991; articles editor, Law Journal. Walsh College, Masters in Taxation with honors, 1990. Certified Public Accountant, Michigan, 1985. University of Michigan, BBA with distinction, 1984.

## JOSEPH, Allan
Rogers Joseph O'Donnell & Phillips, San Francisco 415 956 2828
*Recommended in Government Contracts*

## JUSKA, William L
Freehill Hogan & Mahar LLP, New York
212 425 1900
juska@freehill.com
*Recommended in Transportation*
**Practice Areas:** Experienced in maritime litigation and arbitration. Areas of expertise are all types of cargo claims and charter party disputes. Also has considerable experience in oil pollution, marine contracts, general average, regulatory matters and provisional remedies, such as arrest and attachment. Bar Admission: New York.
**Prof. Memberships:** Maritime Law Association of the United States; New York State Bar Association.
**Career:** Joined Freehill Hogan & Mahar as an associate in 1969 and became a Partner in 1976.
**Personal:** Born 1944, New Jersey; College of the Holy Cross, AB, 1966; Fordham University School of Law, JD, 1969.

## KADLICK, Richard F
Skadden, Arps, Slate, Meagher & Flom LLP & Affiliates, New York
212 735 2716
rkadlick@skadden.com
*Recommended in Capital Markets*
**Practice Areas:** Represents principally underwriters, financial institutions, banks and borrowers in mortgage-backed and asset-backed securities transactions, and credit enhancers in credit-enhanced securities issuances. Has acted as counsel in a variety of public offerings, private placements and transactions in which structured securities instruments have been backed by single-family and commercial mortgage loans, credit card receivables, under-performing and non-performing assets, home equity loan receivables, auto loan receivables, boat loan receivables, federal agency securities, auto and equipment leases and various other assets.
**Career:** JD, Georgetown University, 1982; BA, Hamilton College, 1979 (summa cum laude; Phi Beta Kappa).

## KAFKA, Gerald
Latham & Watkins LLP, Washington, DC
202 637 2200
*Recommended in Tax Litigation*

## KALIK, Mildred
Simpson Thacher & Bartlett LLP, New
York 212 455 2778
mkalik@stblaw.com
*Recommended in Wealth
Management*
**Practice Areas:** Mildred Kalik is a Partner with Simpson Thacher & Bartlett
LLP where she is Head of the firm's Personal Planning Department. She advises
clients on estate planning and trust and
estate administration, as well as other
personal financial matters. The focus of
the estate planning practice is sophisticated techniques designed to facilitate the
transmission of wealth to younger generations in a tax efficient manner. The trust
and estate administration practice
includes sophisticated tax planning and
counsel related to rights of beneficiaries
and obligations of fiduciaries.
**Prof. Memberships:** Ms Kalik is a Member of the American Bar Association,
where she has served on the Council of
the Probate and Trust Law Section; The
American College of Trust and Estate
Counsel; The Association of the Bar of
the City of New York, member of the
Estate and Gift Tax Committee; The
International Academy of Estate and
Trust Law; and the New York State Bar
Association.
**Personal:** BA, University of Wisconsin
(1969); JD, George Washington Law
School (1972), elected to Order of the
Coif; LLM in Taxation, New York Univer-
sity School of Law (1982).

## KALLSTROM, D Ward
Morgan, Lewis & Bockius LLP, San Francisco 415 442 1308
dwkallstrom@morganlewis.com
*Recommended in ERISA Litigation*
**Practice Areas:** D Ward Kallstrom is a
Partner in the Labor and Employment
Practice Group, focusing on class and
other complex employee benefits litiga-
tion and fiduciary counseling. He is a
nationally known labor and employment
attorney, named in 1998 by The National
Law Journal as one of the top manage-
ment side benefits litigators in the nation.
Mr Kallstrom lectures and publishes fre-
quently on all aspects of ERISA fiduciary
law and litigation.
**Prof. Memberships:** Governor and
Charter Fellow, American College of
Employee Benefits Counsel. Fellow, Col-
lege of Labor and Employment Lawyers.
Management Member, Council of the
ABA Section of Labor and Employment
Law.

## KANTER, Stacy J
Skadden, Arps, Slate, Meagher & Flom
LLP & Affiliates, New York
212 735 3497

skanter@skadden.com
*Recommended in Capital Markets*
**Practice Areas:** Represents corporate
clients and investment banks in a variety
of transactions, including public and private offerings of equity and debt securities (both high-yield and investment
grade), initial public offerings, exchange
offers, consent solicitations, restructurings and mergers and acquisitions. Counsels corporate clients on an ongoing basis,
advising on disclosure and corporate
governance issues.
**Career:** JD, Brooklyn Law School, 1984
(cum laude; Managing Editor, Brooklyn
Law Review); BS, State University of New
York at Albany, 1979 (magna cum laude).

## KANTOR, Michael
Mayer, Brown, Rowe & Maw LLP,
Washington, DC 202 263 3295
mkantor@mayerbrownrowe.com
*Recommended in International Trade*
**Practice Areas:** Corporate and international transactions. Market access issues –
expanding client activities in foreign
markets through trade, direct investment,
joint ventures and strategic business
alliances. Directorships: CB Richard Ellis;
ING USA (Advisory Board); Internation-
al Advisory Board, Fleishman-Hillard;
Board of Councilors, Annenberg School
USC; Board of Visitors, Georgetown Uni-
versity Law Center; Drug Strategies;
Commission on Capital Markets.
**Prof. Memberships:** Admitted: California, 1974; District of Columbia, 1972;
Florida, 1968.
**Career:** Mayer, Brown, Rowe & Maw
LLP, Washington, 1997 to date. Senior
Advisor, Morgan Stanley & Co., Inc.,
1997 to present. Distinguished lecturer,
Annenberg School of Communications
at the University of Southern California,
1997 to present. United States Secretary
of Commerce, 1996-97. United States
Trade Representative, Washington, 1993-
96. Manatt, Phelps, Phillips & Kantor, Los
Angeles, 1976-93.
**Personal:** Georgetown University, JD,
1968. Vanderbilt University, BA, 1961.
United States Naval Officer, 1961-65.
Order of the Southern Cross Award by
The Government of Brazil, 2001. William
O Douglas Award by the Constitutional
Rights Foundation. Thomas Jefferson
Distinguished Public Service Medal from
the Center for the Study of the Presiden-
cy. The Albert Schweitzer Leadership
Award from the Hugh O'Brien Youth
Foundation. Elihu Root Distinguished
Lecturer, Council on Foreign Relations.

## KAPLAN, Cathy
Sidley Austin LLP, New York
212 839 5531
ckaplan@sidley.com
*Recommended in Capital Markets*
**Practice Areas:** Co-Head of the New
York office's Securitization Practice, a
Member of the firm's Executive Commit-

tee and Co-Chair of the firm's Accounting and Finance Committee. Ms Kaplan's
practice focuses on asset backed securitizations, with particular concentration on
cross border transactions, CLOs and
CDOs, synthetic securitizations and
insurance linked securitizations.
**Personal:** Columbia University School
of Law, JD, 1977; Yale University, BA,
1974. Admission: New York, 1978.

## KAPLAN, Gilbert
King & Spalding LLP, Washington, DC
202 661 7981
gkaplan@kslaw.com
*Recommended in International Trade*
**Practice Areas:** International trade and
trade policy issues focusing on
antidumping (price discrimination),
countervailing duties (subsidies), Section
337, (intellectual property infringement),
and other trade matters. Substantial
experience with international transactions, market access, trade negotiation,
export matters, and legislative and trade
policy matters. Extensive work in connection with WTO matters.
**Prof. Memberships:** Massachusetts Bar
Association; District of Colombia Bar
Association.
**Personal:** BA, Harvard College, 1973; JD,
Harvard Law School, 1977.

## KAPLAN, H Deen
Hogan & Hartson LLP, Washington, DC
202 637 5799
hdkaplan@hhlaw.com
*Recommended in International Trade*
**Practice Areas:** Deen Kaplan's areas of
concentration include World Trade Organization policy and dispute resolution,
subsidy law policy, homeland security
and trade, antidumping and countervailing duty litigation, customs, specialized
trade sector analysis, immigration, and
trade in technology products.
**Prof. Memberships:** Member, International Law & Practice Section, ABA.
**Career:** Prior to joining Hogan & Hartson, Deen worked with a series of international non-profits, and served as an
executive with computer hardware, software development and consulting businesses. He lectures regularly on international trade issues and teaches international trade law at the University of
Maryland School of Law as a member of
the adjunct faculty. Deen is the associate
editor of the Kluwer Law International
ITA Monthly Report, an international
arbitration law journal published in association with the Institute for Transnational Arbitration.
**Publications:** Co-author, 'World Customs Organization Commits to Global
Trade Security and Facilitation Standards', Customs & International Trade
Update, Hogan & Hartson L.L.P.
(December 2004). Co-author, 'Final Rule:
Advance Electronic Presentation of
Cargo Manifest Information', Interna-

tional Trade and US Homeland Security
Update, Hogan & Hartson L.L.P.
(December 2003).
**Personal:** Georgetown University Law
Center (JD, magna cum laude, Order of
the Coif). Member, District of Columbia
and Virginia Bars.

## KAPLAN, Harvey
Shook, Hardy & Bacon LLP, Kansas City
816 474 6550
*Recommended in Litigation, Products
Liability*
*Please see Missouri for profile*

## KAPLINSKY, Alan S
Ballard Spahr Andrews & Ingersoll LLP,
Philadelphia 215 864 8544
kaplinsky@ballardspahr.com
*Recommended in Financial Services*
**Practice Areas:** Chair, Consumer
Financial Services Group. More than 35
years of experience in: counseling financial institutions with respect to regulatory
and transactional matters, particularly
consumer financial services law and arbi-
tration, and defending financial institu-
tions in consumer lawsuits (particularly
class actions) and government enforce-
ment proceedings.
**Prof. Memberships:** First President and
Member of the American College of Consumer Financial Services Lawyers. Former
Chair and Member of the Consumer
Financial Services Committee and its
Interest Rate Regulation and Alternative
Dispute Resolution subcommittees of the
American Bar Association, Section of Busi-
ness Law. Member of the Litigation and
Alternative Dispute Resolution Sections of
the American Bar Association. Chair,
Lawyers Committee, National Home Equi-
ty Mortgage Association. Member, Lawyers
Committee, Consumer Bankers Associa-
tion. Named as 'top banking lawyer' in
Philadelphia on two occasions by Philadel-
phia Magazine and as a 'Pennsylvania
Super Lawyer' by that magazine.
**Career:** Admitted to Pennsylvania Bar
(1971). Former law clerk to Judge John
Biggs, Jr, United States Court of Appeals
for the Third Circuit. Former Adjunct
Professor at the University of Pennsylvania and Temple Law Schools (taught
banking law).
**Publications:** Chair, Practicing Law Institute Annual Institute on 'Consumer
Financial Services Litigation', eleventh
year. Author of annual article on consumer arbitration developments for The
Business Lawyer, a law review published
by the Business Law Section of the American Bar Association. Frequent lecturer at
programs sponsored by the American Bar
Association, American Law Institute and
trade association conferences and meetings. Financial Services Advisor, Consumer Financial Services Law Report.
**Personal:** JD, cum laude, Boston College
Law School (1970), Member of Order of
the Coif and Editor of law review; BS,

cum laude, University of Pennsylvania, Wharton School of Business (1967).

## KARPF, Jeffrey D

Cleary Gottlieb Steen & Hamilton LLP, New York 212 225 2864
jkarpf@cgsh.com
*Recommended in Capital Markets*

**Practice Areas:** Corporate and financial transactions, including representation of investment banks and issuers in a variety of SEC-registered and private debt and equity offerings and liability management transactions. Has extensive experience in developing new financial instruments and structured equity derivatives products. Advises on securities regulatory and corporate governance matters. Also has significant experience representing sovereign governments in debt restructurings and capital markets transactions.
**Prof. Memberships:** Member of the Bar in New York.
**Career:** Joined firm, 1994. JD, Order of the Coif, Stanford University Law School (1994); BA, Political Science, magna cum laude, Yale University (1989).
**Publications:** Co-author of PLI's Guide to the Securities Offering Reforms (2005); 'The SEC's Securities Offering Reform Proposals: Will this Ship Sail?', The Review of Securities & Commodities Regulations (March 2005).

## KARTER, Philip

Miller & Chevalier Chartered, West Conshohocken 610 617 7530
pkarter@milchev.com
*Recommended in Tax Litigation*

**Practice Areas:** Tax; tax audits and administrative appeals; tax litigation and judicial appeals.
**Prof. Memberships:** American Bar Association: Tax and Litigation Sections; International Tax Institute.
**Career:** Member, Miller & Chevalier Chartered (2000-present); Partner, Odell & Partners LLP (1997-2000); Barrister, J Edgar Murdock Inn of Court – US Tax Court (1994-97); Trial Attorney, Tax Division, US Department of Justice (1986-92). Admitted to practice WI (1982), CT (1984), NY (1987), DC (1991), PA (1997).
**Publications:** The Corporate Counselor, 'The Role Of Economic Substance In Tax Shelter Controversies' (January 2005). 'Transfer Pricing for Services', 'Transfer Pricing Methods – An Applications Guide', John Wiley & Sons (2004). Journal of International Tax Planning, 'US Officials' Latest Proposals to Curb 'Abusive Tax Shelters' Could Affect Legitimate Cross-Border Transactions' (March 2000). Journal of Taxation, 'IRS Access to Computerized Records of Corporate Taxpayers' (September 1997).
**Personal:** LLM, New York University School of Law, 1984; JD, University of Wisconsin, 1982; BA, Emory University, 1979. Barrister, J Edgar Murdock Inn of

Court – US Tax Court (1994-97). Department of Justice – Outstanding Attorney (1987).

## KATZ, Donald L

Miller, Canfield, Paddock and Stone, P.L.C., Detroit 313 496 8476
katz@millercanfield.com
*Recommended in Transportation*

**Practice Areas:** Practice involves business planning, mergers and acquisitions, and commercial transactions in aviation and automotive marketplace. Strong background in taxation, particularly sales and use taxes, federal excise and fuel taxes, business and transactional tax planning, and real and tangible property taxes. Past experience includes fixed income portfolio management and municipal bond sales and trading for several Wall Street firms.
**Prof. Memberships:** American Bar Association, State Bar of Michigan, National Business Aviation Association, Michigan Business Aviation Association.
**Career:** Senior Attorney, 2003-present; Deputy Director, Aviation and Transportation Practice Group.
**Personal:** JD, Michigan State University College of Law; BA, Hobart College.

## KATZ, Wayne D

Proskauer Rose LLP, New York
212 969 3071
wkatz@proskauer.com
*Recommended in Sport*

**Practice Areas:** A Partner in Proskauer's Corporate Department specializing in sports and media. He represents leagues and teams in their various corporate matters. League matters include the NBA's and NHL's approval of team ownership transfers and financings; the NBA's grant of expansion franchises to Toronto, Vancouver and Charlotte; the NHL's grant of expansion franchises to Nashville, Atlanta, Columbus and Minnesota; the NBA's $1.3 billion league-wide credit facility; the formation of the WNBA and NBDL; and the NBA's temporary relocation of the New Orleans Hornets to Oklahoma City. Team matters include acquisitions and financings of several NFL, MLB and MLS teams and facilities, including Jeffrey Lurie's purchase of the Philadelphia Eagles; Robert Wood Johnson's purchase of the New York Jets; Jeffrey Loria's purchase of the Montreal Expos; the simultaneous sale of the Expos and purchase of the Florida Marlins; the financing for Lincoln Financial Field; and Red Bull's recent purchase of the MetroStars. He is in the Sports Business Journal's Hall of Fame after being named one of its '40 under 40' in 2000, 2001 and 2002.
**Personal:** University of Michigan Law School, JD, cum laude. University of Michigan, BBA, Phi Beta Kappa.

## KAVOUKJIAN, Michael E

White & Case LLP, Miami
305 371 2700
mkavoukjian@whitecase.com
*Recommended in Wealth Management*

**Practice Areas:** Advises high-net-worth individuals and families worldwide in all aspects of estate planning, including tax-advantaged transfers of assets, multigenerational planning, the taxation of trusts and estates, charitable giving, pre-nuptial and post-nuptial planning, and issues relating to change of residence. Has counseled a broad range of clients, including those with inherited wealth, owners of closely-held businesses and international clients with multijurisdictional contacts. In his planning practice, he works closely with investment advisors, insurance planners and accountants to ensure a coordinated approach to his clients' needs. Also has broad experience in the administration of trusts and estates.

## KEANE, Paul

Cichanowicz, Callan, Keane, Vengrow & Textor, LLP, New York
212 344 7042
*Recommended in Transportation*

## KEESAL JR, Samuel

Keesal, Young & Logan PC, Long Beach
562 436 2000
*Recommended in Transportation*

## KEINER JR, R Bruce

Crowell & Moring LLP, Washington, DC
202 624 2615
rbkeiner@crowell.com
*Recommended in Transportation*

**Practice Areas:** Chair of Crowell & Moring's Aviation Group. Since 1970, his practice has focused on domestic and international aviation matters. Advises clients on matters involving international passenger and cargo aviation, air cargo, fares and rates, regulation of air freight forwarders, airline charters, enforcement issues, and ownership and control relationships involving the airline industry. Represented numerous large and small airlines. Serves as Washington regulatory counsel for Continental Airlines and general counsel for the Regional Airline Association.
**Personal:** Bachelor of Laws, University of Virginia Law School, Editorial Board, Virginia Journal of International Law, 1966-67. BA, Dickinson College, 1964.

## KELLEHER, Rory

Sidley Austin LLP, New York
212 839 7385
rkelleher@sidley.com
*Recommended in Transportation*

**Practice Areas:** Partner in the New York office. His practice focuses on aircraft finance, portfolio securitizations, equipment leasing and structured finance. Mr Kelleher has represented major manufac-

turers of aircraft, aircraft engines and rail transportation products and US finance and leasing companies in both domestic and international finance transactions, single investor, leveraged and cross-border lease transactions, other structured financings and securitizations.
**Prof. Memberships:** Association of the Bar of the City of New York, Member of the Legal Advisory Panel of the Aviation Working Group.
**Personal:** Columbia University School of Law, JD, 1972; Fordham University, BA, 1969. Admissions: US District Court, SD of New York; New York, 1973.

## KENNEDY, Donald

Carter Ledyard & Milburn LLP, New York
212 732 3200
*Recommended in Transportation*

## KEOGH, Kevin

White & Case LLP, New York
212 819 8227
kkeogh@whitecase.com
*Recommended in Capital Markets*

**Practice Areas:** Securities offerings, corporate governance, corporate counseling and strategic advice. Representation of issuers, private investors and underwriters from several countries in global and domestic public offerings, 144A offerings, venture capital investments and private placements.
**Career:** Partner at White & Case since 1988.
**Publications:** Regular speaker on securities law programs presented by Practising Law Institute, most recently: 'Preparation of Annual Disclosure Documents 2006', 'New Developments in Securities Law' and 'Risk Factors and Forward-Looking Statements in SEC Filings'
**Personal:** AB, College of the Holy Cross, 1963, History and Philosophy, with honors JD, Harvard Law School, 1966.

## KERR, John

Simpson Thacher & Bartlett LLP, New York 212 455 2000
jkerr@stblaw.com
*Recommended in International Arbitration*

**Practice Areas:** Partner, member of Litigation Department and Head of Arbitration Group. Advises clients in general litigation before state courts of New York, federal courts nationwide and the US Supreme Court (recently, New Jersey v. New York). Advises clients in all major arbitration systems, including ICC, AAA and UNCITRAL, cases, and serves as arbitrator.
**Prof. Memberships:** American Arbitration Association (Director); American Bar Association (Litigation Section and International Litigation Committee; former Chair, Jury Trials Committee; International Bar Association (Business Section and Arbitration/ADR Committees), Federal Bar Council, Association of the Bar of the City of New York and Ameri-

can Foreign Law Association (Vice President); Member, Columbia Law School Board of Visitors.
**Career:** Joined firm 1978; became Partner 1983. Law clerk to Honourable Gus J Solomon, US District Court (District of Oregon).
**Publications:** Author, 'Court Jurisdiction and Arbitration over Misrepresentation in US Securities Transactions' (Sweet & Maxwell, London, 1999); 'A Chart Comparing International Commercial Arbitration Rules', published in collaboration with Parker School of Comparative Law, Columbia Law School (Juris Publishing, 1998; 2d ed 2003).
**Personal:** Boston College (AB, 1972, summa cum laude); Columbia Law School (JD, 1976), (Stone Scholar; International Fellow; National Scholar (7th Circuit); Editor-in-Chief, Columbia Journal of Environmental Law).

**KESSLER, Jeffrey**
Dewey Ballantine LLP, New York
212 259 8000
*Recommended in Antitrust, Sport*
*Please see New York for profile*

**KIERNAN, David C**
Williams & Connolly LLP, Washington, DC 202 434 5000
*Recommended in Products Liability*

**KILB, Brian**
Gibson, Dunn & Crutcher LLP, Los Angeles 213 229 7000
*Recommended in Banking & Finance, Capital Markets*
*Please see California for profile*

**KILBERG, William J**
Gibson, Dunn & Crutcher LLP, Washington, DC 202 955 8500
*Recommended in Employee Benefits, Employment, ERISA Litigation*
*Please see District of Columbia for profile*

**KIM, Richard K**
Wachtell, Lipton, Rosen & Katz, New York
212 403 1354
RKim@wlrk.com
*Recommended in Financial Services*
**Practice Areas:** Specializes in representing banks, thrifts, insurance companies, credit card issuers and other financial institutions in connection with mergers and acquisitions and regulatory matters.
**Prof. Memberships:** Member of the Association of the Bar of the City of New York and of the American Bar Association where he currently serves as Chair of Mergers and Acquisitions on the Banking Law Committee.
**Career:** Partner in the Corporate Department at Wachtell, Lipton, Rosen & Katz. Previously, he was a staff attorney with the Board of Governors of the Federal Reserve System where he worked on a wide range of regulatory matters,

including mergers and acquisitions involving bank holding companies, banks and investment banks. He was also Assistant General Counsel with NationsBank Corporation.
**Personal:** Graduated from Stanford University (AB, 1983) and from Columbia Law School (JD, 1986).

**KIMBALL, George**
Baker & McKenzie, San Diego
619 236 1441
*Recommended in Business Process Outsourcing, IT Outsourcing*
*Please see California for profile*

**KIMBALL, John D**
Healy & Baillie LLP, New York
212 709 9241
jkimball@healy.com
*Recommended in Transportation*
**Practice Areas:** Chairman. Main area of work is maritime law, including casualties, charterparty disputes, insurance, creditors rights, insolvency. Adjunct Professor of Law at NYU Law School (1986-present).
**Prof. Memberships:** Maritime Law Association of the United States; Fellow of the American Bar Association; Federal Bar Council; Comité Maritime International.
**Career:** Joined Healy & Baillie in 1975. Graduate of Duke University (BA 1971); Georgetown University Law School (1975).
**Publications:** Co-author, 'Time Charters' (5th ed. 2003); co-author, 'Voyage Charters' (2d ed. 2001); co-author, 'The Law of Salvage, 3A Benedict on Admiralty' (2005).

**KIMMELMAN, Louis B**
O'Melveny & Myers LLP, New York
212 326 2036
bkimmelman@omm.com
*Recommended in International Arbitration*
**Practice Areas:** Louis B Kimmelman's practice focuses on the arbitration and litigation of complex commercial and construction disputes. He represents US and foreign parties, as well as sovereign entities, in international disputes before arbitral tribunals and courts. Mr Kimmelman has arbitrated before various arbitral institutions, including the ICC International Court of Arbitration, the American Arbitration Association, and the Kuala Lumpur Regional Centre for Arbitration, and has litigated proceedings to confirm arbitral awards. He serves as Chair of the Arbitration Committee of the United States Council for International Business and is an Adjunct Professor of Law at Brooklyn Law School.

**KING, Bruce**
Garvey Schubert Barer, Seattle
206 464 3939
*Recommended in Transportation*

**KING, Carol Weld**
Hogan & Hartson LLP, Washington, DC
202 637 5600
*Recommended in Native American Law, Real Estate*
*Please see District of Columbia for profile*

**KIRCHHOEFER, Gregg**
Kirkland & Ellis LLP, Chicago
312 861 2000
*Recommended in Business Process Outsourcing, Technology*
*Please see Illinois for profile*

**KLEIN, Allen**
Latham & Watkins LLP, Washington, DC
202 637 2200
*Recommended in Business Process Outsourcing, Technology*

**KLEINBERG, Norman**
Hughes Hubbard & Reed LLP, New York
212 837 6680
kleinber@hugheshubbard.com
*Recommended in Products Liability*
**Practice Areas:** Product liability, insurance coverage litigation.
**Prof. Memberships:** Fellow, American College of Trial Lawyers; Chairman, Sub-Committee on Federal Judicial Center; Member of Center for Public Resources ('CPR') Regional Panel of Distinguished Neutrals; Various Bar Associations including the International Bar Association.
**Career:** Partner since 1980.
**Personal:** Tufts University (BA, 1968); Columbia University School of Law (JD, 1972); Harlan Fiske Stone Scholar.

**KLEPPER, Martin**
Skadden, Arps, Slate, Meagher & Flom LLP & Affiliates, Washington, DC
202 371 7000
*Recommended in Projects, Sport*
*Please see District of Columbia for profile*

**KNULL, William H**
Mayer, Brown, Rowe & Maw LLP, Houston 713 546 0528
wknull@mayerbrownrowe.com
*Recommended in International Arbitration*
**Practice Areas:** Extensive experience in transnational disputes involving oil and gas, mergers and acquisitions, contracts, corporate governance, lending practices; ICC, ICDR, ICSID, AAA, UNCITRAL and NASD arbitrations. Lead counsel in multi-billion dollar disputes in transnational and domestic oil and gas projects.
**Prof. Memberships:** LCIA. Advisory Board, Institute of Transnational Arbitration. Member, Chartered Institute of Arbitrators.
**Career:** Joined Mayer, Brown, Rowe & Maw LLP, Houston, 1986; Partner 1987. Sullivan & Cromwell, New York, 1977-86. US Navy, 1970-74.
**Publications:** 'Bridas v. Turkmenistan: A Case Study in Arbitration as an Instrument of Risk Management', presented at

Managing Risk – Dispute Avoidance & Resolution, London, April 2004;' with Noah Rubins, Betting the Farm on International Arbitration: Is it Time to Offer an Appeal Option?' 11 Am. Rev. Int'l. Arb. 531 (2002). 'Uncertainty in the Courts: Split in US Appellate Courts on Expanded Judicial Review by Agreement of Parties' presented at Barriers to Free Movement of Civil Justice, CILS, Salzburg, Austria, November 2001.
**Personal:** University of Virginia, JD, 1977; Order of the Coif; Virginia Law Review, Member, 1975-77; notes editor, 1976-77. Yale University, BA, magna cum laude, 1970; Departmental Honors in Political Science.

**KOLYER, Steve**
Clifford Chance US LLP, New York
212 878 8000
*Recommended in Capital Markets*

**KOREN, Edward**
Holland & Knight LLP, Lakeland
813 227 8500
ed.koren@hklaw.com
*Recommended in Wealth Management*
**Practice Areas:** Partner in the Business Section, his practice is heavily involved in estate planning and probate matters for business owners, including the use of life insurance and other vehicles to plan for needed estate liquidity, and GRATs (or similar vehicles), family limited partnerships and S corporations to minimize estate taxes. A considerable portion of his practice is related to succession planning for closely held business interests, as well as the determination of the value of entities. He often handles tax controversies involving succession and income taxes, and is involved in various forms of probate and trust litigation.

**KORFF, Phyllis G**
Skadden, Arps, Slate, Meagher & Flom LLP & Affiliates, New York
212 735 2694
pkorff@skadden.com
*Recommended in Capital Markets*
**Practice Areas:** Represents US and international issuers, and investment banks in a variety of financing matters. Has worked on equity and debt financings, both investment grade and high-yield, in the US and international markets. Has worked on numerous initial public offerings and other offerings registered with the Securities and Exchange Commission, as well as offerings exempt from SEC registration pursuant to Rule 144A and Regulation S. Has extensive experience in representing Israeli and Canadian companies.
**Career:** JD, New York University School of Law, 1981 (notes editor, NY University Law Review); EdM, Boston University, 1967; BA, Brooklyn College, 1964.

**KRAMER, Samuel**
Baker & McKenzie, Chicago
312 861 8800
*Recommended in Business Process Outsourcing, Technology*
*Please see Illinois for profile*

**KRAULAND, Edward**
Steptoe & Johnson LLP, Washington, DC
202 429 8083
ekrauland@steptoe.com
*Recommended in International Trade*
**Practice Areas:** Partner in Steptoe & Johnson LLP's Washington office. 23 years of experience. Advises on requirements in export control, economic sanctions, anticorruption, counter money laundering, and foreign investment/national security (NISPOM) restrictions in the US (transactions, corporate structures, mergers and acquisitions, and intra-corporate supply relationships). Handles internal investigations, enforcement actions by US government authorities, and compliance programs enhancements. Represents US and non-US multinationals, businesses, and individuals in aerospace and defense, energy, oil field services, information management, electronics, telecommunications, consumer products, e-commerce, engineering, professional services, chemicals, industrial equipment, and financial services.
**Personal:** JD, University of Michigan, 1980; AB, Princeton University, 1976.

**KRAVITT, Jason H P**
Mayer, Brown, Rowe & Maw LLP, New York 212 506  2622
jkravitt@mayerbrownrowe.com
*Recommended in Capital Markets*
**Practice Areas:** Founder of the firm's Securitisation Practice and Senior Partner in that practice. Variety of finance and regulatory related practices. Represents industry groups with regard to securitisation regulatory initiatives, including the Bank for International Settlements' risk-based capital consultative papers, the FFIEC's risk-based capital projects, FASB's Standards on Securitization and Consolidation, SEC initiatives.
**Prof. Memberships:** Adjunct Professor of Law at Northwestern University Law School, an Adjunct Professor of Finance at the Kellogg Graduate School of Management of Northwestern University, and a Fellow in the American College of Commercial Finance Lawyers. One of three founding Members, secretary, and Chair of Legal, Regulatory, Accounting and Tax Committee, American Securitization Forum and Executive Committee Member, European Securization Forum.
**Career:** Joined Mayer, Brown, Rowe & Maw LLP, 1973; became Partner, 1979. Co-Chairman of the firm in 1998-2001.
**Publications:** Editor of, and contributing author to, 'Securitization of Financial Assets', Aspen Law & Business, 1996 (2nd Ed).

**Personal:** Born 19 January 1948. Phi Beta Kappa graduate of The Johns Hopkins University (Member of the Advisory Board to the Dean of School of Arts & Sciences). JD, cum laude, Harvard Law School, 1972; diploma in comparative law, Cambridge University, 1973. Chairman, The Cameron Kravitt Foundation.

**KROUSE JR, George R**
Simpson Thacher & Bartlett LLP, New York 212 455 2730
gkrouse@stblaw.com
*Recommended in Capital Markets*
**Practice Areas:** A Partner at Simpson Thacher & Bartlett LLP, specialising in corporate governence, securities law and mergers and acquisitions. From 1991 through 2002, served as Head of the firm's Corporate Department. Also a member of the Executive Committee, the firm's management body, and the firm's Senior Administrative Partner. Has principal responsibility for some of the firm's most important client relationships, including Lehman Brothers, which the firm represents as issuer of its own securities, underwriter or placement agent for offerings in the domestic and international capital markets, financial advisor and principal in merchant banking transactions.
**Prof. Memberships:** Association of the Bar of the City of New York; the New York State and American Bar Associations.
**Career:** Has been a member of the firm since 1979. Received AB Degree cum laude from Brown University in 1967 and graduated with distinction in 1970 from Duke University School of Law, where he was articles editor of the Duke Law Journal and elected to Order of the Coif. Admitted to practise law in New York in 1971. Currently holds an appointment as Senior Lecturing Fellow at the law school.

**KUDENHOLDT, Stephen S**
Thacher Proffitt & Wood LLP, New York 212 912 7450
skudenholdt@tpw.com
*Recommended in Capital Markets*
**Practice Areas:** Mr Kudenholdt serves as Chairman of Thacher Proffitt's Structured Finance Practice Group. His practice includes residential and commercial mortgage-backed securities, and other asset-related securities (ABS), primarily focusing on residential mortgage loan securitization as well as resecuritization transactions involving various classes of MBS. He has helped develop many transaction structures and formats that have become industry standards, including shifting interest subordination techniques. He represents issuers, underwriters, loan sellers and other entities in public offerings and private placements and has represented several major investment banks in a variety of mortgage securitization transactions, including subprime

and home equity loans, commercial and multifamily mortgage loan securitizations and in connection with new product and structure development and joint ventures.
**Prof. Memberships:** American Bar Association: Federal Regulation of Securities, Structured Finance Subcommittee; Bond Market Association: MBS/ABS Legal Advisory Committee; American Securitization Forum: Executive Committee, Legal and Regulatory Subcommittee, and Chair of Legislative and Judicial Subcommittee.
**Career:** Recently, Mr Kudenholdt served as counsel to the Bond Market Association and prepared their letter to the SEC regarding new regulations proposed for asset-backed securities. Mr Kudenholdt also is a member of the Executive Committee of the American Securitization Forum. He received his JD in 1980 from the University of Michigan Law School, cum laude, and his BA in 1977 from the University of Illinois.
**Publications:** Structured Finance Notes – SEC's Regulation AB: Major Changes for the Securitization Industry (January 12, 2005); 'The Impact of Regulation AB and Securities Offering Reform on US Public ABS', Global Securitization and Structured Finance 2005 (May 01, 2005); Structured Finance Notes: SEC's Securities Offering Reform – Impact on the ABS Markets (August 05, 2005); Structured Finance Notes: EU Prospectus Directive – Effect on US. ABS Offerings (September 28, 2005).

**KUNZ, C Thomas**
Skadden, Arps, Slate, Meagher & Flom LLP & Affiliates, New York
212 735 3240
ckunz@skadden.com
*Recommended in Capital Markets*
**Practice Areas:** Represents underwriters, issuers, depository institutions and credit enhancers in asset-backed securities transactions and credit-enhanced securities issuances. Counsels in public offerings and private placement transactions involving the issuance of pass-through certificates, asset-backed notes and bonds, commercial paper notes and participation certificates. Worked on transactions in which structured finance techniques were utilized to enable non-traditional financings to access the capital markets.
**Career:** JD, Cornell University, 1975 (magna cum laude; Order of the Coif; Phi Kappa Phi; editor, Cornell Law Review); BA, Colgate University, 1972 (magna cum laude; Phi Beta Kappa).

**KURZ, Theodore**
Debevoise & Plimpton LLP, New York
212 909 6000
*Recommended in Wealth Management*

**LAMBERT, LeRoy**
Healy & Baillie LLP, New York
212 709 9274
llambert@healy.com
*Recommended in Transportation*
**Practice Areas:** Maritime (charter parties, bills of lading, liens, arrests, attachments); multimodal transportation; commercial litigation; arbitration; international law; bankruptcy.
**Prof. Memberships:** American Bar Association, New York State Bar Association, Maritime Law Association of the United States.
**Career:** Joined Healy & Baillie 1984; Partner 1991. Member, Executive Committee, 2001-present.
**Publications:** Co-author, 'Voyage Charters' (2d ed 2001); 'Damages Arising from Breach of Contract, Loss of Revenue, and 'Indirect' Damages', 72 Tulane Law Review, 759 (1997), among others.
**Personal:** Born 13 April 1954. JD, 1983, Tulane University School of Law; University of Tuebingen, Germany, 1976-78; BA, Louisiana State University, 1976. Foreign language: German.

**LAMM, Carolyn**
White & Case LLP, Washington, DC
202 626 3605
clamm@whitecase.com
*Recommended in International Arbitration*
**Practice Areas:** Concentrates on international arbitration (counsel or arbitrator) or litigation, including ICSID, AAA, ICC, LCIA and Stockholm chamber arbitration. Co-Chair of International Arbitration Group in Washington DC offfice. Lead counsel representing foreign corporations and sovereigns.
**Prof. Memberships:** ABA, Board of Governors (2002-05); State Delegate, DC; DC Bar, President (1997-98); US Secretary of State's Advisory Committee on Private International Law; American College of Trial Lawyers, Fellow and Member, International Committee; American Law Institute, Council Member; AAA Executive Committee; NAFTA 2022 Committee; ICSID Panel of Arbitrators; American Society of International Law, Co-Chair International Dispute Resolution Interest Group.

**LAWRENCE III, Robert C**
Cadwalader, Wickersham & Taft LLP, New York 212 504 6211
robert.lawrence@cwt.com
*Recommended in Wealth Management*
**Practice Areas:** Chairman, Private Client Department. Advises wealthy individuals and families on international and domestic tax-efficient structures for US and global holdings emphasizing taxation minimization, management and transfer of holdings to family members, entities, trusts and/or charities. Leading authority in international and domestic

tax, trust personal planning matters.

**Prof. Memberships:** New York, New Jersey bars; United States District Courts (SDNY, DNJ); United States Tax Court; United States Court of Appeals (2d Cir); United States Supreme Court; International Academy of Estate and Trust Law (past President); American College of Trust and Estate Counsel (International Estate Planning Committee); Society of Trust and Estate Practitioners (International Committee); ABA Tax Section (past Chair, International Estate Planning Subcommittee); New York State Bar Association (International Estate and Tax Planning Committee); Association of the Bar of the City of New York (past Chairman, Committee on Recruitment of Lawyers); Editorial Board, Journal of International Trust and Corporate Planning; Museum of Modern Art, Planned Giving Group Advisory Committee.

**Personal:** LLB, LLM (Taxation), New York University School of Law; BA, Government, Cornell University.

## LECCESE, Joseph M
Proskauer Rose LLP, New York
212 969 3238
jleccese@proskauer.com
*Recommended in Sport*

**Practice Areas:** A Partner in Proskauer Rose LLP's Corporate Department, he has a broad-based corporate practice with particular emphasis on the representation of professional sports leagues and teams, financial institutions providing funds to sports properties and companies engaged in various media and communications businesses, including numerous matters for the National Basketball Association, the National Hockey League, ATP Tour and WTA Tour, as well as a number of individual sports teams and other sports-related entities, including the NBA's $1.4 billion League-wide credit facility; the NBA's expansion in 2002 to Charlotte, North Carolina, and the related arena lease and development negotiations; the lease, development and financing of the Philadelphia Eagles' new football-based stadium and New Jersey Devils' new hockey arena; the ATP Tour's $1.2 billion transaction with ISL relating to the worldwide television and marketing rights to the ATP World Championships and Super 9 Tournaments; the formation and structuring of the Women's National Basketball Association. His media and communications experience includes numerous acquisitions, dispositions and private and public financings relating to cable television systems, television stations, radio stations and magazines.

**Personal:** University of Virginia Law School, JD, 1985 Member, Virginia Law Review, 1983-85. Georgetown University, BA, cum laude, 1982.

## LEE, Paul
Debevoise & Plimpton LLP, New York
212 909 6000
*Recommended in Financial Services*

## LEFKOWITZ, David
Weil, Gotshal & Manges LLP, New York
212 310 8850
david.lefkowitz@weil.com
*Recommended in Capital Markets*

**Practice Areas:** David Lefkowitz is Co-Head of Weil Gotshal's global Capital Markets Practice. He represents issuers and investment banks in a range of public and private equity and debt offerings and bridge financings, and has worked on offerings with total proceeds in excess of $30 billion. He was selected as a 'Dealmaker of the Year' for 2004 by The American Lawyer and at age 35, he was selected by The National Law Journal for its '40 Under Forty' listing of 40 rising stars in the law under age 40.

**Personal:** Northwestern University, BS, 1982; Georgetown University Law Center, JD, 1986.

## LEIBOWITZ, Lewis E
Hogan & Hartson LLP, Washington, DC
202 637 5638
leleibowitz@hhlaw.com
*Recommended in International Trade*

**Practice Areas:** Lewis Leibowitz practices in the areas of international trade law, customs law, and international commercial transactions. He is active in matters before Congress, agencies, courts, and international organizations dealing with international trade matters, including the US Department of Commerce, the office of the US Trade Representative, the International Trade Commission, US Customs and Border Protection, US courts, NAFTA tribunals, and the World Trade Organization.

**Prof. Memberships:** Board Member, Consumers for World Trade; Counsel, Consuming Industries Trade Action Coalition; Member, National Foreign Trade Council; American Association of Exporters and Importers; Customs and International Trade Bar Association, National Association of Foreign Trade Zones.

**Career:** Lewis has been practicing international trade law since the 1970s. As a leading attorney in trade law matters under US and international law, Lewis advises and assists clients in actual and potential antidumping and countervailing duty proceedings. In addition, he works with clients on proceedings under Section 201 and 301 of the Trade Act of 1974 and Section 337 of the Tariff Act of 1930. He is also active in dispute settlement activities involving the WTO, and advising clients in private industry and government on all these matters. Lewis specializes in representing downstream industries in trade cases.

**Personal:** University of Maryland School

of Law (JD, with honors, Order of the Coif).

## LEMEIN, Gregg
Baker & McKenzie, Chicago
312 861 8800
*Recommended in Tax, Tax Litigation*
*Please see Illinois for profile*

## LEONG, Alvin
Milbank, Tweed, Hadley & McCloy LLP, New York 212 530 5000
*Recommended in Transportation*

## LEVI, Stuart
Skadden, Arps, Slate, Meagher & Flom LLP & Affiliates, New York
212 735 3000
*Recommended in Business Process Outsourcing, Technology*
*Please see New York for profile*

## LEVINE, David J
McDermott Will & Emery, Washington, DC 202 756 8153
dlevine@mwe.com
*Recommended in International Trade*

**Practice Areas:** Trade and regulatory practices before international trade organizations, federal agencies and courts. Represents numerous industries in antidumping and countervailing duty cases and related federal appellate litigation, foreign market access matters, NAFTA procedures, World Trade Organization disputes, legislative and rulemaking proceedings, and trade negotiations. Counsels clients on import relief, customs, export controls, trade sanctions, Foreign Corrupt Practices Act, antiboycott and regulatory compliance matters.

**Prof. Memberships:** Advisory Board, Washington University Global Studies Law Review; NAFTA Chapter 19 Panelists Roster.

**Personal:** Washington University School of Law (JD); University of Denver Graduate School of International Studies (MA); Colorado College (BA).

## LEVINE, Jerome L
Holland & Knight LLP, Los Angeles
213 896 2400
jerry.levine@hklaw.com
*Recommended in Native American Law*

**Practice Areas:** Partner in the Government Section and Head of the firm's Indian Law Practice Group. For more than 20 years, he has been a leading attorney nationally in the field of Indian law, representing tribes throughout the country in matters ranging from internal constitutional and governance issues, land in trust matters, fee to trust issues, economic development projects, natural resource protection and development, sacred sites protection, artifacts recovery, and gaming and hotel development and regulation. He also has a broad range of experience in complex business, commercial and government litigation and regulation, business and financing transactions.

## LEVINSTEIN, Mark
Williams & Connolly LLP, Washington, DC 202 434 5000
*Recommended in Sport*

## LEVY, Charles S
WilmerHale, Washington, DC
202 663 6400
charles.levy@wilmerhale.com
*Recommended in International Trade*

**Practice Areas:** Advises corporations and business associations on international trade, financial and investment issues, including the Business Roundtable, the Coalition of Service Industry / Financial Services Group, the Intellectual Property Committee, Burlington Industries, and the Information Technology Industry Council (ITIC). Was Counsel to USA*NAFTA and GATT*NOW, the national coalitions that successfully supported implementation of NAFTA and the Uruguay Round of Multilateral Trade Agreements by the Congress.

**Prof. Memberships:** Board of Directors of Transparency International USA, a non-governmental organization dedicated to combating bribery and corruption in international business transactions.

**Personal:** George Washington University Law School (JD 1970); Boston College (BA 1967).

## LEVY, Gregg
Covington & Burling, Washington, DC
202 662 5292
glevy@cov.com
*Recommended in Sport*

**Practice Areas:** Co-Chair of Covington's Litigation Group, he has extensive experience with complex, multi-party litigation, including trial-level, appellate, and arbitral proceedings, and substantial expertise with respect to legal issues affecting amateur and professional sports leagues.

**Career:** He has been the NFL's principal outside counsel for over a decade and played a lead role in each of the NFL's major trial and appellate victories during that period, including Brown v Pro-Football, Inc., decided by the US Supreme Court, and Clarett v NFL, upholding the NFL's draft eligibility rules.

**Personal:** Harvard Law School (JD, 1977); Harvard College (AB, 1974).

## LIASKOS, Peter S
Mayer, Brown, Rowe & Maw LLP, New York 212 506 2609
pliaskos@mayerbrownrowe.com
*Recommended in Products Liability*

**Practice Areas:** Represent Fortune 500 companies in variety of commercial cases. Products liability litigation, complex mass tort cases and pharmaceutical disputes. Expertise in real estate litigation, securities cases, employment disputes and professional misconduct matters. Currently national counsel in series of pharmaceutical products liability cases. Represented major pharmaceutical company in complex litigation over best-selling prescription drug; successful result: financial impact of $100+ million. Currently Partner in charge of litigation training in New York. Notable published decisions: Rubel v. Eli Lilly and Co., 160 FRD 458 (SDNY 1995); Guimond v. Wyndham Hotels & Resorts, 1996 WL 281959 (SDNY 1996); Zimring v. Coinmach Corporation, 2000 US District Lexis 19701 (ED Mo 2000). **Career:** Mayer, Brown, Rowe & Maw LLP, New York, 1997 to date. Beatie, King & Abate, New York, associate, 1993-97. Brown & Wood, New York, associate, 1992-93. **Personal:** The College of William and Mary Law School, JD, 1992; Member, ABA Administrative Law Review, Moot Court Team. State University of New York at Albany, BS cum laude, 1989. Products Liability Committee of the Association of the Bar of the City of New York (1994 -97).

### LICHTENBAUM, Greta
O'Melveny & Myers LLP, Washington, DC
202 383 5249
glichtenbaum@omm.com
*Recommended in International Trade*
**Practice Areas:** Greta Lichtenbaum's practice principally relates to regulations governing international business transactions and trade. Greta represents and advises clients in matters related to US export controls, economic sanctions, antiboycott, foreign investment ('Exon-Florio'), customs, the Foreign Corrupt Practices Act, as well as various international agreements that apply to international business transactions. She also represents clients before the US Bureau of Customs and Border Protection, International Trade Commission, the Department of Commerce, and the Court of International Trade in antidumping investigations and procedures as well as in connection with other matters implicating US trade laws.

### LIGHTHIZER, Robert E
Skadden, Arps, Slate, Meagher & Flom LLP & Affiliates, Washington, DC
202 371 7770
rlighthi@skadden.com
*Recommended in International Trade*
**Practice Areas:** Leads the firm's International Trade Department. Clients include large US corporations and coalitions. Represents heavy manufacturing, agricultural and hi-tech companies, as well as financial services institutions. Has been lead counsel in scores of antidumping and countervailing duty cases during the last several years and is currently active in numerous pending cases and administrative reviews. Also focuses on market-opening trade actions on behalf of US companies seeking access to foreign markets. **Career:** JD, Georgetown University Law Center, 1973; BA, Georgetown University, 1969.

### LIMBACHER, Robert A
Dechert LLP, Philadelphia
215 994 2977
robert.limbacher@dechert.com
*Recommended in Products Liability*
**Practice Areas:** Mr Limbacher is a Partner and the former Chair of the Mass Torts and Product Liability Group. He focuses on product liability and complex commercial litigation. He has litigated high-profile pharmaceutical and tobacco cases, defending his clients against individual personal injury and class action lawsuits nationwide. **Prof. Memberships:** Member of the Product Liability Advisory Council, the Federation of Insurance and Corporate Counsel, the Defense Research Institute, and the Philadelphia Association of Defense Counsel. **Personal:** Texas A&M University, BA, cum laude, 1977; University of Texas, JD, 1981, Member of the University of Texas Law Review.

### LIN, Raymond
Latham & Watkins LLP, New York
212 906 1200
*Recommended in Capital Markets, Native American Law*

### LINDSEY, David
Clifford Chance US LLP, New York
212 878 8000
*Recommended in International Arbitration*

### LITTLE, Kathleen C
Vinson & Elkins LLP, Washington, DC
202 639 6663
klittle@velaw.com
*Recommended in International Trade*
**Practice Areas:** Export controls (ITAR and EAR), OFAC sanctions, FCPA, Foreign Military Sales and Foreign Military Financed Direct Sales, Government Contracts. Work includes criminal and civil enforcement matters, compliance, counseling, training and audits. Represents both domestic and foreign companies. **Prof. Memberships:** ABA, SIA. **Career:** Partner since 1988. **Publications:** Has lectured and written extensively on export controls and related topics.

### LITWIN, Stuart M
Mayer, Brown, Rowe & Maw LLP, Chicago 312 701 7373
slitwin@mayerbrownrowe.com
*Recommended in Capital Markets*
**Practice Areas:** Co-Head of firm's global Securitization Group. Among leading lawyers in representing originators, investment banks, ABCP conduit sponsors, commercial banks and investors in structuring, negotiating and documenting US and international asset-backed and other securities transactions. Emphasis on auto loan, auto lease, equipment lease, cross border, synthetic risk transfer and transactions in which auto and

equipment finance, leasing, structured finance and the capital markets come together. Substantial experience representing lessees, equity investors and debt investors in leveraged and synthetic lease transactions. Experienced in securitization of virtually all asset types. Recognized expert in the securitization and financing of equipment and auto leases, auto loans, dealer floorplan receivables, synthetic risk transfers and the creation of asset-backed securities for money market funds. **Prof. Memberships:** Former Chairman of the Securities Law Committee of the Chicago Bar Association. **Career:** Mayer, Brown, Rowe & Maw LLP, 1985-present; Partner, 1994. **Publications:** Frequent lecturer on securitization. Author: 'Equipment and Auto Lease Financing: Securitization, Leveraged Leasing and Titling Trusts', Aspen Law and Business. **Personal:** JD, University of Chicago Law School. MBA, University of Chicago Graduate School of Business. Certified Public Accountant.

### LOBRANO, John D
Simpson Thacher & Bartlett LLP, New York 212 455 2890
jlobrano@stblaw.com
*Recommended in Capital Markets*
**Practice Areas:** A Partner in the firm's Corporate Department and member of the Capital Markets and Mergers and Acquisitions Practice Groups. Regularly represents investment banking clients, such as JP Morgan Securities, Lehman Brothers and Bear Stearns, and issuers in domestic and international securities offerings, with a particular specialization in offerings of convertible securities and high yield debt securities. These activities are complemented by his liability management practice, representing dealer managers and issuers in tender offers and consent solicitations, as well as merger and acquisition representations. **Prof. Memberships:** Association of the Bar of the City of New York, New York Bar Association, American Bar Association, International Bar Association. **Career:** Member of the firm since 1990. A member of the firm's International Practice Group and practiced in the firm's London office for seven years. Has advised on securities offerings and corporate matters all over the world. **Personal:** Graduate of New York University School of Law (JD, 1983) and Amherst College (BA, magna cum laude, 1979).

### LOFTIS, James
Vinson & Elkins LLP, Houston
713 758 1024
jloftis@velaw.com
*Recommended in International Arbitration*
**Practice Areas:** Arbitration of interna-

tional disputes, particularly state contracts, investment agreements, foreign investment laws and treaties. Has handled arbitrations under all major arbitration rules and in most major venues. Represents a broad range of clients in oil, gas and energy, construction, technology, environment, and finance. **Prof. Memberships:** ICC Commission on Arbitration; LCIA; Chartered Institute of Arbitrators; Chair, International Law Section, Texas Bar. **Career:** Partner since 2000. Senior Legal Officer, UN Compensation Commission, Geneva, 1997-2000. **Publications:** Co-editor, International Litigation Quarterly; 'Advocacy Before International Claims Resolution Bodies', 'The Art of Advocacy in International Arbitration'. **Personal:** University of Texas (BBA 1983; JD 1990).

### LOFTUS, C Michael
Slover & Loftus, Washington, DC
202 347 7170
*Recommended in Transportation*

### LOWELL, Frederick K
Pillsbury Winthrop Shaw Pittman LLP, San Francisco 415 983 1585
frederick.lowell@pillsburylaw.com
*Recommended in Government: Political Law*
**Practice Areas:** Mr Lowell is the Leader of the firm's Political Law Group, which advises on campaign finance, lobbying and conflict of interest laws; as well as legislation, ballot initiatives, reapportionment and enforcement litigation. **Prof. Memberships:** Member, California Republican State Central Committee; past President, California Political Attorneys Association; past Chair and current Chair of The Lincoln Club of Northern California; California delegate to the 1992, 1996, 2000 and 2004 National Republican Conventions; Volunteer California counsel, Bush-Cheney 2000 and 2004 campaigns. **Personal:** JD, University of Virginia School of Law, 1975; BA, Columbia University, 1971

### LOWENFELD, Andreas
Prof Andreas F Lowenfeld - Sole Practitioner, New York
212 998 6208
*Recommended in Arbitration*

### MABERRY, John Scott
Fulbright & Jaworski L.L.P., Washington, DC 202 662 4693
smaberry@fulbright.com
*Recommended in International Trade*
**Practice Areas:** International law; international trade; sanctions; export controls; anti-bribery; white-collar crime; and government investigations and enforcement. **Prof. Memberships:** New York, District of Columbia, and American Bar Associations; ABA Export Controls & Economic

Sanctions Committee, Chairman.
**Career:** J Scott Maberry is a Partner in Fulbright's International Law Department. Prior to entering private practice he was law clerk to Arlin M Adams, US Independent Counsel.
**Personal:** BS, Northwestern University (1988); MS, Georgetown University (1993); JD, Georgetown University (1993).

### MACCOBY, Matthew
Arnold & Porter LLP, Los Angeles
213 243 4000
*Recommended in Business Process Outsourcing, IT Outsourcing*
*Please see California*
*for profile*

### MADDEN, Thomas
Venable LLP, Washington, DC
202 962 4800
*Recommended in Government Contracts*

### MADSEN, Marcia G
Mayer, Brown, Rowe & Maw LLP, Washington, DC 202 263 3274
mgmadsen@mayerbrownrowe.com
*Recommended in Government Contracts*
**Practice Areas:** Advises on government contract formation, teaming and strategic alliances, contract and subcontract negotiations, performance disputes, audits, terminations, cost accounting and allowability, technical data rights and trade secrets, and fraud/false claims investigations. Litigates bid protests and claims and disputes before the GAO, the Boards of Contract Appeals, the Court of Federal Claims, and other courts. Numerous ADR and mediation proceedings. Areas of concentration: aerospace and defense contracts, systems integration, information systems and telecommunications contracts, healthcare and bio-technology, homeland security contracts; environmental remediation, and research and development contracts.
**Prof. Memberships:** Chair, Federalist Society Government Contracts Committee; past Chair, ABA Section of Public Contract Law; past President, Board of Contract Appeals Bar Association.
**Career:** Mayer, Brown, Rowe & Maw LLP, Washington, DC, 2001 to date (Chair, Homeland Security Practice Group). Miller & Chevalier, 1996-2001 (Chair, Government Contracts Department). Morgan, Lewis & Bockius, 1980-96.
**Publications:** Published numerous articles on government contracts issues in Government Contract Litigation Reporter, BNA Federal Contracts, West Briefing Papers Series, and many similar publications.
**Personal:** JD, American University, Washington College of Law, 1976. LLM, Georgetown University Law Center, 1980. BA, University of Utah, 1972.

### MAGEE, John B
McKee Nelson LLP, Washington, DC
202 775 1880
*Recommended in Tax, Tax Litigation*
*Please see District of Columbia for profile*

### MALLOW, Matthew J
Skadden, Arps, Slate, Meagher & Flom LLP & Affiliates, New York
212 735 3930
mmallow@skadden.com
*Recommended in Capital Markets*
**Practice Areas:** Head of firm's Corporate Finance Department. Represents investment banks, issuers and corporations in a variety of financing matters, including initial public offerings and insurance company offerings.
**Prof. Memberships:** Board of Trustees, Brown University, Member (1990-present), Treasurer (1999-present).
**Career:** LLM, New York University, 1968; LLB, New York University, 1967; AB, Brown University, 1964.

### MANGAN, John J
Skadden, Arps, Slate, Meagher & Flom LLP & Affiliates, Washington, DC
202 371 7775
jmangan@skadden.com
*Recommended in International Trade*
**Practice Areas:** Focuses on antidumping and countervailing duty matters. A part of his practice has been in the legislative arena. Has testified before key congressional committees, including the Senate Finance Committee and the Senate Judiciary Committee, on various trade bills. Other areas of his practice include customs matters, Section 301 cases and the Generalized System of Preferences program. Has represented respondents in antidumping proceedings in Europe and in Mexico.
**Career:** JD, Cornell University, 1967; B Civil Eng, Cornell University, 1964.

### MANOS, Karen
Gibson, Dunn & Crutcher LLP, Washington, DC 202 955 8536
kmanos@gibsondunn.com
*Recommended in Government Contracts*
**Practice Areas:** Extensive experience on a broad range of government contracts issues, including complex claims preparation/ litigation, civil and criminal fraud investigations/litigation, qui tam suits under the False Claims Act, defective pricing, cost allowability, the Cost Accounting Standards, suspension and debarment, bid protests, corporate compliance.
**Prof. Memberships:** Council Member, ABA Section of Public Contract Law. Managing editor, 'Public Contract Law Journal'. Chair, National Defense Industrial Council Contract Finance Committee.
**Publications:** 'Government Contract Costs & Pricing' (Thomson-West 2004), over 30 government contract articles.
**Personal:** JD (highest honors), Duke

University School of Law, 1986, note editor, Duke Law Journal.

### MARGO, Roderick
Condon & Forsyth LLP, Los Angeles
310 557 2030
*Recommended in Transportation*

### MARKS, Allan
Milbank, Tweed, Hadley & McCloy LLP, Los Angeles 213 892 4000
*Recommended in Projects, Transportation*

### MARTIN, John
Baker Botts LLP, Dallas
214 953 6500
*Recommended in Business Process Outsourcing, Technology*
*Please see Texas for profile*

### MARTIN, Keith
Chadbourne & Parke LLP, Washington, DC 202 974 5600
*Recommended in Projects*
*Please see District of Columbia for profile*

### MARTIN, Renwick
Sidley Austin LLP, New York
212 839 5319
rmartin@sidley.com
*Recommended in Capital Markets*
**Practice Areas:** Renwick D Martin is Co-Head of the Global Securitization Practice and a member of the firm's Management and Executive Committees. Mr Martin has worked in the mortgage backed area since 1977 when he participated in the Bank of America pass through transaction, which was the first publicly-offered conventional pass through transaction. Since 1984, Mr Martin has concentrated on mortgage backed and asset backed financings of all types.
**Personal:** Harvard Law School, JD 1972; Stanford University, AB, 1969. Admission: New York, 1974.

### MARTINEZ-FRAGA, Pedro J
Greenberg Traurig LLP, Miami
305 579 0595
martinep@gtlaw.com
*Recommended in International Arbitration*
**Practice Areas:** International litigation.
**Prof. Memberships:** ICC Approved Arbitrator; Board Member and Secretary, United States-Mexico Chamber of Commerce, Inter-American Chapter; Board of Directors, Editorial Cubana, Inc.; Member, London Court of International Arbitration (LCIA), 2005.
**Career:** Listed, Best Lawyers in America, 2005-06; Listed, Chambers & Partners USA Guide, 2004-06; listed, Florida Legal Elite, Florida Trend Magazine, 2004-06; listed, 'Top Lawyers in South Florida', South Florida Legal Guide, 2001-06; recipient, 'Most Effective Lawyer Award for International Law', Daily Business Review, 2005.

**Personal:** JD, Columbia University School of Law, 1987; BA, with high honors, St John's College, Annapolis, 1984.

### MASTER, Geoffrey L
Mayer, Brown, Rowe & Maw LLP, Washington, DC 202 263 3270
gmaster@mayerbrownrowe.com
*Recommended in Business Process Outsourcing*
**Practice Areas:** Broad experience in outsourcing and procurement transactions, including the outsourcing and offshoring of information technology and services as well as of business processes. IT procurement experience includes transactions involving infrastructure, applications maintenance, development and support, network management, telecommunications services and help desk functions, as well as implementation and integration of major enterprise applications and systems. Outsourcing of business processes experience includes the outsourcing of human resources, finance and accounting, procurement, customer relationship management and other business functions. Clients include financial services, healthcare, insurance, consumer products, telecommunications, advertising and publishing, airline, manufacturing, chemical, energy, information technology and forestry products industries, as well as governmental entities.
**Career:** Mayer, Brown, Rowe & Maw LLP, Washington, DC, 2001 to present. The Capital Markets Company, General Counsel and Secretary. Electronic Data Systems Corporation.
**Personal:** University of Texas, Austin, JD, 1979; Order of the Coif; Texas Law Review. New York University, LLM in Taxation, 1983. University of Texas, Austin, BA with high honors, 1975; Phi Beta Kappa. University of Texas, Austin, MPA, 1979.

### MASTRIANI, Louis S
Adduci, Mastriani & Schaumberg LLP, Washington, DC
202 467 6300
mastriani@adduci.com
*Recommended in International Trade*
**Practice Areas:** International trade regulation and intellectual property litigation.
**Prof. Memberships:** DC Bar, Federal Circuit Bar Association, ABA, ITCTLA.
**Career:** Participated in more than 50 § 337 cases at the ITC. Assists clients in worldwide enforcement programs for intellectual property rights. Served as legal counsel and an investigative attorney with the ITC. Appointed by the US Trade Representative, served as both a panelist and Chairman on bi-national panels convened pursuant to the North American Free Trade Agreement.
**Publications:** 'Antidumping Law: Issues and Applications in High Technology Industries', The Licensing Journal.
**Personal:** JD Whittier College.

## MASUR, Daniel
Mayer, Brown, Rowe & Maw LLP,
Washington, DC 202 263 3000
*Recommended in Business Process
Outsourcing, Technology*
*Please see District of Columbia for
profile*

## MATHEWS, Daniel A
Orrick, Herrington & Sutcliffe LLP,
New York 212 506 5050
dmathews@orrick.com
*Recommended in Transportation*
**Practice Areas:** Represents lenders,
developers and investors in the development, construction, and financing of
complex infrastructure projects, focusing
on the transportation, energy, and
telecommunications sectors. In over 25
years of practice, he has acted as lead
counsel on numerous project financings,
acquisitions, divestitures, privatizations
and restructurings, including representation of the mandated lead arrangers for
Project Finance Magazine's North American Transport Deal of the Year for 2003,
2004 and 2005. He is experienced in corporate and asset acquisitions and other
investment-related transactions, debt
restructurings, and commercial finance.
**Personal:** JD, University of California,
Hastings College of Law, 1975; AB, Occidental College.

## MAYER, Theodore VH
Hughes Hubbard & Reed LLP, New York
212 837 6888
mayer@hugheshubbard.com
*Recommended in Products Liability*
**Practice Areas:** Mr Mayer leads a Product Liability Practice Group at Hughes
Hubbard that includes over 75 lawyers.
Mr Mayer and his partners in the group
serve as national coordinating counsel for
major US corporations in litigation
involving pharmaceuticals, welding rods,
treated wood, and asbestos-containing
heat transfer machinery. These include
some of the most active and well-publicized individual and class action litigations pending in the United States.
**Publications:** Co-author with Robb W
Patryk of the treatise Product Liability
(Law Journal Seminars-Press); numerous
published articles on product liability and
complex litigation topics.
**Personal:** Harvard Law School (JD,
1977); Yale College (BA, magna cum
laude 1974).

## MAYESH, Jay
Kaye Scholer LLP, New York
212 836 7606
jmayesh@kayescholer.com
*Recommended in Products Liability*
**Practice Areas:** Partner, litigation; Co-
Chair, Product Liability. Jay P Mayesh is a
noted product liability defense lawyer
with extensive jury trial experience. In
addition to serving as trial counsel to The
Upjohn Company in DES litigation, Baxter Healthcare in silicone breast implant
litigation, Pfizer in pharmaceutical litigation, Warner-Lambert in Rezulin litigation and DaimlerChrysler and Navistar
in automotive litigation, Mr Mayesh has
served as counsel for American Motors in
Jeep rollover litigation, for Niagara
Mohawk Power in electromagnetic field
(EMF) litigation and for the welding
industry in cases alleging occupational
exposure to asbestos. Examples of his
trial successes include: the defense of
Baxter Healthcare in a breast implant
case; the defense of DaimlerChrysler in
the first child air bag case to be tried in
the United States; and the defense of Pfizer in a phase III clinical trial case. In addition to litigation, Mr Mayesh has particular experience in conducting audits to
evaluate the potential product-related liabilities in proposed corporate acquisitions and reorganizations.
**Prof. Memberships:** Board of Editors,
Products Liability Law and Strategy;
Product Liability Advisory Council;
American Bar Association; Defense
Research Institute.
**Career:** JD, Columbia Law School, 1972,
Harlan Fiske Stone Scholar; BA, Universi-
ty of Wisconsin, 1969, Phi Beta Kappa.
**Publications:** Mayesh, Jay P, Wendy
Dowse and Steven Glickstein – 'Recent
Decision Provides Guidance on Admissi-
bility of Expert Testimony', LJN's Product
Liability Law & Strategy (December
2004): 3, 4. Mayesh, Jay P and Mary F
Scranton. 'Legal Aspects of Biomaterials',
'Biomaterials Science: An Introduction to
Materials in Medicine', San Diego: Elsevi-
er Inc., 2004. Mayesh, Jay P, Jonathan
Englander and Victoria Haje. 'An Unex-
pected Evidentiary Battleground: The
'Causation' Element in Consumer Pro-
tection Claims', LJN's Product Liability &
Strategy (October 2003): 1, 2, 4, 5, 8.
Mayesh, Jay P, 'Product Liability Law –
Where the Rubber Meets the Road',
'Inside the Minds: Leading Product Lia-
bility Lawyers', Boston: Aspatore, Inc.,
2003. Mayesh, Jay P, Alan E Rothman and
Mark A Beckman. 'Advances in Protect-
ing Defendants' Right to Remove from
State to Federal Court', LJN's Product Lia-
bility Law & Strategy (May 2002): 1-4.

## MAZZUCHI, Michael A
Cleary Gottlieb Steen & Hamilton LLP,
Washington, DC
202 974 1572
mmazzuchi@cgsh.com
*Recommended in Capital Markets*
**Practice Areas:** Corporate and securities matters, particularly domestic and
international structured finance and
derivatives matters. Has extensive experience in mortgage and asset securitizations, collateralized bond obligation
transactions, synthetic debt securities and
repackagings, credit derivative transactions and interest rate, currency and equity derivatives.
**Prof. Memberships:** Member of the Bar

in the District of Columbia.
**Career:** Joined firm, 1992; became Partner, 2001. JD, magna cum laude, member
of Law Review's Editorial Board, University of Michigan Law School (1992); BA,
Political Science, Phi Beta Kappa, University of Michigan (1989).

## MCBRIDE, Michael F
LeBoeuf, Lamb, Greene & MacRae LLP,
Washington, DC
202 986 8050
mfmcbrid@llgm.com
*Recommended in Transportation*
**Practice Areas:** Counsel to utilities and
other railroad customers involved in litigation at the Interstate Commerce Commission (now known as Surface Transportation Board) and in court cases concerning transportation of nuclear materials, coal and oil. As special assistant attorney general of the Commonwealth of
Massachusetts, he litigated at the STB and
courts on railroad-related transportation
matters.
**Prof. Memberships:** Association of
Transportation Law Professionals (President, 1994-95, 2004-05).
**Career:** Joined LeBoeuf Lamb in 1976;
Oak Ridge National Laboratory, Environmental Sciences Division, Research Associate 1972.
**Personal:** University of Wisconsin,
Madison (JD)1976; California Institute of
Technology (MS)1973; University of Wis-
consin, Milwaukee (BS)1972.

## MCCABE, David J
Willkie Farr & Gallagher LLP, New York
212 728 8723
dmccabe@willkie.com
*Recommended in Wealth
Management*
**Practice Areas:** Partner in the Private
Clients Group, specializing in all aspects
of estate planning and administration,
with emphasis on the development of
sophisticated plans for high-net-worth
individuals and their families. His practice includes the preparation of complex
wills, trust agreements and related instruments, the representation of clients in
estate tax and gift tax audits, and general
counseling of clients in all phases of the
administration of decedents' estates. He
represents non-resident aliens regarding
US tax aspects of their plans as well as US
persons establishing trusts off shore. He
also represents banks and trust companies and has counseled bank trust departments on trusts and estates matters. He
has advised trust companies located in
other states on offering trust services to
residents of New York and has represented clients in the establishment of offshore
trust companies. He also advises fiduciaries and beneficiaries in estate and trust
litigation matters in Surrogate's Courts
and the Supreme Court of the State of
New York. Additionally, his practice
includes the representation of national

public charities, private foundations and
charitable trusts. He has advised directors
and trustees of eleemosynary organizations on a variety of corporate and tax
issues and has formed numerous private
foundations and public charitable entities.
**Prof. Memberships:** He was elected
Chair of the Committee on Trusts,
Estates and Surrogate's Courts of the
Association of the Bar of the City of New
York and is a Fellow of the American College of Trusts and Estates Counsel. He is
also a Member of the New York State Bar
Association and a member of Trusts &
Estates magazine's Estate Planning and
Taxation Committee and has authored
articles for the magazine.
**Career:** Admitted to the Bar of the State
of New York.
**Publications:** He has written and lec-
tured on estate tax planning for high-net-
worth individuals and small business
owners, and has co-authored 'Is Estate
Planning Expensive?', Trusts & Estates
Magazine (2004), 'There But for the
Grace...', Trusts & Estates Magazine
(2002), 'Transfer of Wealth', New York
State Bar Association (1993) and 'New
York Limited Liability Companies: A
Guide to Law and Practice', West Publish-
ing Company (1995).
**Personal:** Received a JD from Fordham
University School of Law in 1983 and a
BA in Economics (magna cum laude)
from Iona College in 1980.

## MCCAFFREY, Carlyn
Weil, Gotshal & Manges LLP, New York
212 310 8136
carlyn.mccaffrey@weil.com
*Recommended in Wealth
Management*
**Practice Areas:** Carlyn McCaffrey is
Co-Head of Weil, Gotshal's Trusts &
Estates Department. She is a Fellow and a
past President of the American College of
Trust & Estate Counsel, a Fellow and
regent of the American College of Tax
Counsel and a Member of the Interna-
tional Academy of Trust & Estate Coun-
sel. She is a Member of the Tax Section of
the New York State Bar Association and
the Co-Chair of the Section's Estates and
Trusts Committees.
**Personal:** George Washington University, BA, 1963; New York University School
of Law, JD, 1967; New York University
School of Law, LLM, 1974.

## MCCALEB, Scott M
Wiley Rein & Fielding LLP, Washington,
DC 202 719 3193
smccaleb@wrf.com
*Recommended in Government
Contracts*
**Practice Areas:** Represents clients on
procurement matters including bid
protests, contract disputes and termination litigation, appellate litigation, audits
and cost allowability, government investi-

gations, suspensions/debarments, False Claims Act actions and mergers and acquisitions.

**Prof. Memberships:** American Bar Association, Section of Public Contract Law, Co-Chair, Federal Procurement Division and Vice-Chair, Regulatory Coordinating Committee; Federal Circuit Bar Association: Member, Board of Governors and Co-Chair, Government Contracts Committee; Member, Court of Federal Claims Bar Association, Board of Governors.

**Career:** Adjunct Professor, George Washington University School of Law; Instructor, US Army Judge Advocate General's School.

**Personal:** Georgetown University Law Center (JD); Brown University (BA).

**MCCALL, Jennifer Jordan**
Pillsbury Winthrop Shaw Pittman LLP, Palo Alto 650 233 4020
jmccall@pillsburylaw.com
*Recommended in Wealth Management*

**Practice Areas:** Ms McCall is the Leader of the firm's Individual Client Services Practice Section. She represents individuals, families, foundations, museums and charities regarding domestic and international gift and estate planning. She advises clients on estate, gift/generation-skipping transfer taxes, complex estate administration, estate-related litigation, and the integration of these matters with the client's business objectives. Her clients have included internationally renowned museums and corporations, as well as domestic and foreign individuals and fiduciaries of estates and trusts.

**Personal:** LLM, New York University Law School, 1988; JD, University of Virginia School of Law, 1982; BA, Princeton University, 1978 (cum laude).

**MCCLELLAND, Todd S**
Alston & Bird LLP, Atlanta
404 881 4789
tmcclelland@alston.com
*Recommended in Business Process Outsourcing*

**Practice Areas:** IP and technology transactional matters with an emphasis on IT and business process outsourcing, software licensing, stategic IP-related issues in large-scale corporate transactions, wireless transactions, strategic alliances, licensing and transfer of IP rights. Advising on open source matters including procurement, management, development, distribution and risk assessment.

**Career:** Registered US Patent and Trademark Office. Former engineer for Factory Automation Systems; software and hardware designer for Coca-Cola and Ford.

**Personal:** BME, Georgia Institute of Technology (1994); JD, Florida State University (1998), Member, Florida State University Law Review and Executive

Editor, Journal of Land Use and Environmental Law.

**MCCONNELL, Mark S**
Hogan & Hartson LLP, Washington, DC
202 637 5796
msmcconnell@hhlaw.com
*Recommended in International Trade*

**Practice Areas:** Mark McConnell represents and advises clients in international trade litigation, disputes, and foreign policy issues, with a particular focus on representing coalitions formed to achieve policy and legislative change. He frequently assists clients on strategic matters that involve a blend of litigation, policy, and diplomatic activity.

**Career:** Mark joined Hogan & Hartson in 1979 and is one of the founders of the firm's international Trade Practice. He served on President-elect Reagan's Presidential Transition Team in 1980-81, and in 2000-01 served President-elect Bush as a member of his Transition Advisory Committee for the US Trade Representative.

**Publications:** Mark has written a number of articles on international trade and investment regulation, and speaks frequently on US trade policy and political developments.

**Personal:** Stanford Law School (JD, associate editor of the Law Review, 1979); Stanford Graduate School of Business, (MBA). He is admitted to practice in the District of Columbia.

**MCCREADIE, David**
Lau, Lane, Pieper, Conley & McCreadie, Tampa 813 229 2121
*Recommended in Transportation*

**MCCUE, Judith W**
McDermott Will & Emery, Chicago
312 984 7515
jmccue@mwe.com
*Recommended in Wealth Management*

**Practice Areas:** Practices estate planning and trust and estate administration.

**Prof. Memberships:** President of American College of Trust and Estate Counsel (2005-06), an association of distinguished trust and estate attorneys. Past Chair of College's State Laws Committee and Elder Law Committee. Past President of Chicago Estate Planning Council and winner of its distinguished service award (2002). Chaired the Chicago Bar Association's Probate Practice Committee and Estate and Gift Tax Division of its Federal Tax Committee.

**Personal:** Harvard Law School (JD); University of Pennsylvania (BA, cum laude). Admitted to Illinois Bar (1972). Vice-Chair and Trustee of the Chicago Symphony Orchestra.

**MCCUE III, Howard M**
Mayer, Brown, Rowe & Maw LLP, Chicago 312 701 7102
hmccue@mayerbrownrowe.com

*Recommended in Wealth Management*

**Practice Areas:** Not-for-profit organizations: counsel to more than 20 private foundations ranging in asset size from less than $1 million to more than $1 billion; counsel to public charities, community foundations and healthcare organizations. Estate planning: corporate executives and individuals, including preparation and implementation of wills, trusts, partnerships, asset freezes, private foundations, split-interest trusts. Estate and trust advice and litigation, representing charitable organizations, fiduciaries and individuals in litigation.

**Career:** Mayer, Brown, Rowe & Maw LLP, Chicago, 1975 to date. Navy, Judge Advocate General's Corps, 1972-75. Hale and Dorr, Boston, 1971-72.

**Publications:** Numerous reviews, tax institutes, books, law journals and popular publications. Charitable Governance Issues, Chicago Estate Planning Council (2004). 'Tax Exempt Organization 'Reform': The Struggle to Cure the Bad Actors Without Hurting the Good Guys' (with Sara R Stadler, New Haven, Connecticut), American College of Trust and Estate Counsel (2005).

**Personal:** Harvard University, JD cum laude, 1971. Princeton University, AB, 1968; Princeton University Scholar; Phi Beta Kappa.

**MCCULLOUGH, James**
Fried, Frank, Harris, Shriver & Jacobson LLP, Washington, DC 202 639 7130
James.McCullough@FriedFrank.com
*Recommended in Government Contracts*

**Practice Areas:** Litigation Partner. Head of Fried Frank's Government Contracts Practice. Practice in pre-award protest litigation and counseling, post-award disputes and litigation, alternative dispute resolution, and representation of government contractors in various civil proceedings and enforcement matters involving suspension and debarment.

**Career:** Joined Fried Frank in 1980. Became a Partner in 1985. Chair of National Defense Industrial Association's Procurement Division; Co-Chair ABA Public Contract Law ADR Committee.

**Personal:** JD (1976), University of Virginia School of Law. BA (1969), cum laude, Villanova University.

**MCENENEY, Michael F**
Sidley Austin LLP, Washington, DC
202 736 8368
mmceneney@sidley.com
*Recommended in Financial Services*

**Practice Areas:** Practice focuses primarily on regulatory and legislative issues impacting financial institutions, with special emphasis on retail banking. He advises banks, savings associations, finance companies, trade associations and others on the full range of issues that

affect day to day retail banking operations. He spends much of his time concentrating on issues pertaining to privacy, payment systems, consumer loan and deposit products and consumer bankruptcy. Mr McEneney is a frequent speaker and writer on financial services issues and has testified before Congress on behalf of a diverse group of financial services organizations.

**Personal:** Boston University School of Law, JD, 1986; Manhattan College, BS, 1980. Admissions: Connecticut, 1986, District of Columbia, 1989.

**MCFADDEN II, W Clark**
Dewey Ballantine LLP, Washington, DC
202 429 2333
cmcfadden@deweyballantine.com
*Recommended in International Trade*

**Practice Areas:** W Clark McFadden II represents corporate clients in international trade, encompassing work in litigation, regulation and legislation. He has conducted numerous international investigations and defended clients in enforcement proceedings. He also specializes in international corporate transactions, especially the formation of joint ventures and consortia. Mr McFadden has a broad background in foreign affairs and international trade, having experience with Congressional committees, the US Department of Defense and the National Security Council.

**Career:** Partner, Dewey Ballantine LLP.

**Personal:** BA, Williams College, 1968. MBA, Harvard Business School, 1972. JD, Harvard Law School, 1972.

**MCGLONE, William M**
Miller & Chevalier Chartered, Washington, DC 202 626 5833
wmcglone@milchev.com
*Recommended in International Trade*

**Practice Areas:** Export controls and defense trade controls; trade and economic sanctions; FCPA and international corruption; antiboycott.

**Prof. Memberships:** American Bar Association's International Law and Practice Section – Committee on Export Controls and Economic Sanctions (former Chair); American Electronics Association/ Bar Association of DC.

**Career:** Member, Miller & Chevalier Chartered (1995-present), associate (1987-94).

**Publications:** 'Avoiding Problems Under the US Foreign Corrupt Practices Act, US Antiboycott Laws, OFAC Sanctions, Export Controls, and the Economic Espionage Act', International Quarterly (January 2004); 'International Legal Developments in Review: Economic Sanctions and Export Controls', The International Lawyer (Summer 2001); 'International Legal Developments in Review: Economic Sanctions and Export Controls', The International Lawyer (Summer 2000); 'Learning All the Lessons of Export Con-

trols', The Journal of Commerce (March 2000); 'Creeping Extraterritorial Reach of US Trade Laws Catches Many Foreign Companies By Surprise' (Sept 1999); 'Expanding Use of Encryption Poses New Challenges for Businesses and Government Regulators', Corporate Legal Times (April 1999).
**Personal:** JD; Georgetown University Law Center, 1987; BA, Harvard University, 1982.

## MCGOVERN III, Thomas L
Hogan & Hartson LLP, Washington, DC
202 637 5784
tlmcgovern@hhlaw.com
*Recommended in Government Contracts*
**Practice Areas:** Tom McGovern is a litigator with extensive experience in all types of government contracts matters, including protests, contract claims, misconduct investigations, and suspension/debarment cases.
**Career:** Tom has more than 25 years of government contracts and grants experience in both government and private practice. With Hogan & Hartson since 1987, Tom has handled high-stakes cases for major defense/aerospace contractors, information technology companies, and research institutions. He is the current Co-Chair of the ABA Contract Claims and Disputes Committee.
**Publications:** Tom is an in-demand speaker and writer on topics in his areas of particular expertise, such as privatization and outsourcing, bid protest rules, and past performance issues.
**Personal:** Stanford Law School (JD, with distinction); Babson College (MBA, with distinction); US Air Force Academy (BS). Colonel, US Air Force Reserve, assigned to Air Force Senate Liaison Office.

## MCLAUGHLIN, Cathleen
Allen & Overy LLP, New York
212 610 6320
cathleen.mclaughlin@allenovery.com
*Recommended in Capital Markets*
**Practice Areas:** Varied transactional and advisory securities experience related to SEC-registered and Rule 144A debt and equity offerings by US, Latin American and other non-US issuers. She recently has concentrated on restructurings for corporations and sovereigns, and sovereign bond offerings. She founded the Latin America Group.
**Career:** Joined Allen & Overy LLP in 1997 as senior counsel. Partner since 1999.
**Personal:** University of Pennsylvania (JD, Order of the Coif, cum laude, 1988; BA, magna cum laude, Phi Beta Kappa, 1984).

## MCLUCAS, William
WilmerHale, Washington, DC
202 663 6000
*Recommended in Financial Services, Securities*
*Please see District of Columbia for profile*

## MCSLOY, Steven
Hughes Hubbard & Reed LLP, New York
212 837 6614 or 917 446 7834
mcsloy@hugheshubbard.com
*Recommended in Native American Law*
**Practice Areas:** American Indian Law and complex financing transactions.
**Prof. Memberships:** NNABA; Indian Law Section, Federal Bar Association; NABA of Washington, DC; Commercial Law Committee, USET; OIBA; NCAI; NNALSA.
**Career:** Co-Chair, Native American Practice since 2004; previously General Counsel, Oneida Indian Nation of New York; Professor of American Indian Law.
**Publications:** Articles on American Indian Law appear in Indian Country Today, American Indian Law Review, Harvard Civil Rights-Civil Liberties Law Review, and NYU Journal of International Law and Politics, among others.
**Personal:** Harvard Law School JD (1988, cum laude); New York University BA (1985; Phi Beta Kappa, magna cum laude).

## MEADOWS, James E
Hunton & Williams, Atlanta
404 888 4161
jmeadows@hunton.com
*Recommended in Business Process Outsourcing*
**Practice Areas:** Jim Meadows' practice focuses on strategic technology matters and multinational business process, information technology and application service provider outsourcing arrangements, including business process transactions involving human resources, customer care, finance and accounting, engineering and construction, and supply chain functions.
**Prof. Memberships:** Past Chair, Technology Law Section, State Bar of Georgia; Appointee, Information Technology Law Committee, Association of the Bar of the City of New York.
**Publications:** Numerous articles including: 'Business Continuity...Yours and Theirs: Contingency Planning Can Minimize Disruptions in Offshore Deals', Offshore Business Sourcing.

## MEEHAN, Wayne D
Freehill Hogan & Mahar LLP, New York
212 425 1900
meehan@freehill.com
*Recommended in Transportation*
**Practice Areas:** Areas of expertise are collisions and all types of marine casualties, including groundings, allisions, sinkings, explosions and fires. Is well-versed in casualty-related issues such as limitation of liability, general average and navigation. Holds US Coast Guard Unlimited Chief Mate's license. Has considerable experience in cargo loss and damage cases and in charter party disputes. Has tried cargo, collision and total loss cases in various Federal Courts. Bar Admissions: New York and New Jersey.
**Prof. Memberships:** Maritime Law Association of the United States; Association of Average Adjusters of the United States; New York State Bar Association.
**Career:** Joined Freehill Hogan & Mahar as an associate in 1984 and became a Partner in 1992.
**Personal:** Born 1954, New York; United States Merchant Marine Academy at Kings Point, BS, with honors, 1976; Boston University, JD, 1984.

## MELBY, Barbara Murphy
Morgan, Lewis & Bockius LLP, Philadelphia 215 963 5053
bmelby@morganlewis.com
*Recommended in Business Process Outsourcing*
**Practice Areas:** Ms Melby is a Partner in the Global Outsourcing Practice focusing on US based and international outsourcing and technology-related transactions, including information technology, human resources, finance and accounting, logistics, call center, claims processing and various other business process outsourcing; offshore outsourcing; licensing and hosting agreements; joint ventures and strategic alliances. Ms Melby has authored several books on outsourcing, including information technology outsourcing transactions and business process outsourcing transactions.
**Prof. Memberships:** Editor, Boston University Law Review Distinguished Scholar.

## MENDELSON, Robert C
Morgan, Lewis & Bockius LLP, New York
212 309 6303
rmendelson@morganlewis.com
*Recommended in Financial Services*
**Practice Areas:** Robert C Mendelson is Co-Chair of the firm's Securities Interdisciplinary Practice. Mr Mendelson is a recognized authority on securities. Mr Mendelson's practice focuses on securities and derivatives markets, broker-dealer regulation and enforcement defense, public offerings and private placements. Mr Mendelson has extensive experience in all aspects of broker-dealer regulation, representing bulge bracket investment banks in derivatives and securities trading as well as securities offerings and general commercial issues.
**Prof. Memberships:** Member IPO Process Committee of NASD and NYSE. Member National Association of Securities Dealers, Corporate Finance Committee; Member, American Bar Association, Settlement of Market Transactions, Advisory Committee.

## MENDOZA, Julie C
Kaye Scholer LLP, Washington, DC
202 682 3640
jmendoza@kayescholer.com
*Recommended in International Trade*
**Practice Areas:** Julie Mendoza is Co-Chair of Kaye Scholer LLP's International Trade Group. She practices before all the agencies responsible for administering US trade laws, as well as the US Court of International Trade and the US Court of Appeals for the Federal Circuit. Ms Mendoza has significant experience litigating antidumping, countervailing duty and safeguard cases on behalf of foreign respondents, governments and US importers. As counsel to foreign manufacturers, she has advised foreign governments on a variety of bilateral and multilateral trade negotiations including the Uruguay Round, negotiations related to the WTO's Agreement on Safeguards, bilateral subsidies agreements, framework agreements on trade and investment and the negotiation of Voluntary Restraint Arrangements on steel. Active in the area of WTO dispute resolution, Ms Mendoza has argued on behalf of clients before WTO panels and the Appellate Body. Ms Mendoza frequently speaks at conferences and seminars sponsored by the WTO Secretariat in Member countries on topics of international trade practices and remedies. She also has presented numerous seminars and conducted a variety of training sessions on international trade issues in various parts of the world. Ms Mendoza is fluent in Spanish and has worked extensively in Latin America on a wide variety of trade matters.
**Prof. Memberships:** District of Columbia Bar, US Court of International Trade, US Court of Appeals for the Federal Circuit.
**Career:** JD, University of Chicago. BA (summa cum laude), Tufts University. Harvard University. Universidad Nacional Autónoma de México.

## MENSIK, Michael S
Baker & McKenzie, Chicago
312 861 8800
*Recommended in Business Process Outsourcing, Technology*
*Please see Illinois for profile*

## MENTING, Mark J
Sullivan & Cromwell LLP, New York
212 558 4000
mentingm@sullcrom.com
*Recommended in Financial Services*
**Practice Areas:** Partner, Financial Institutions and M&A Groups. Expertise in M&A, securities, corporate and regulatory matters for US and non-US financial institutions and broad experience in general corporate and securities law matters. Regularly advises on M&A transactions involving banks and thrifts, investment management firms, brokers-dealers, mortgage banking companies, and insurance companies, and on US securities offerings by banks and their holding companies.
**Prof. Memberships:** ABA; ABCNY; NYSBA.
**Career:** Partner since 1994.

**Publications:** Frequent speaker on various topics for financial institutions.
**Personal:** University of Wisconsin (BS, 1979); University of Pennsylvania Law School (JD, 1983).

## MERRIGAN, John A
DLA Piper Rudnick Gray Cary US LLP, Washington, DC
202 861 6455
john.merrigan@dlapiper.com
*Recommended in Government Relations*
**Practice Areas:** Governmental affairs; federal affairs and legislative; legislative financial services.
**Career:** Co-Chair of the Federal Affairs practice, he has extensive political and legal experience and has played a leading role in building one of the nation's premier law and lobbying practices, formulating and executing successful strategies to advance or protect clients' interests. These clients include numerous Fortune 100 corporations, domestic and foreign governments, and other entities. He provides strategic planning that integrates the firm's capabilities in the legislative, regulatory, judicial, and political arenas.
**Personal:** JD, Loyola University Chicago; AB, Georgetown University 1970.

## MEYER, David L
Covington & Burling, Washington, DC
202 662 5582
dmeyer@cov.com
*Recommended in Transportation*
**Practice Areas:** Vice-Chair of Covington's Antitrust Practice Group. Broad and deep experience in antitrust (counseling, litigation, government investigations) and railroad matters (including control cases, rate regulation, contract arbitration, and others). Represents the Association of American Railroads, Union Pacific Railroad Company, and TTX Company. Counsels clients on all manner of antitrust issues and successfully defends them in antitrust litigation and government investigations.
**Prof. Memberships:** ABA Antitrust Section Leadership – associate editor, Antitrust Magazine.
**Career:** Special Assistant to the Assistant Attorney General, Antitrust Division, US DOJ.
**Personal:** Yale University (JD, 1986); Amherst College (BA, 1983, magna cum laude).

## MEYERSON, Lee
Simpson Thacher & Bartlett LLP, New York 212 455 2000
*Recommended in Corporate/M&A, Financial Services*
*Please see New York for profile*

## MEZZULLO, Louis
McGuireWoods LLP, Richmond
804 775 1000
*Recommended in Wealth Management*

## MICHALSKI, Paul
Cravath, Swaine & Moore LLP, New York
212 474 1868
PMichalski@cravath.com
*Recommended in Capital Markets*
**Practice Areas:** Broad-based experience, encompassing corporate finance transactions (including bank financings and public and private debt and equity issuances, representing both borrowers/issuers and lenders/underwriters), mergers and acquisitions, restructurings and joint ventures. He also advises on securities law and corporate governance matters. As a resident Partner in London for several years, he has been involved in numerous international and cross-border transactions advising US and non-US clients.
**Prof. Memberships:** ABA; NYSBA; ABCNY; IBA; New York Law Institute: Board Member.
**Career:** Partner since 1994.
**Personal:** Harvard Law School (JD, mcl, 1986); Harvard College (AB, mcl, 1983).

## MICHETTI, Michael
Cahill Gordon & Reindel LLP, New York
212 701 3900
*Recommended in Capital Markets*

## MIERZEWSKI, Michael B
Arnold & Porter LLP, Washington, DC
202 942 5995
Michael.Mierzewski@aporter.com
*Recommended in Financial Services*
**Practice Areas:** Michael Mierzewski specializes in financial institutions and corporate governance and securities law. In addition to bank merger and acquisition counseling, Mr Mierzewski routinely counsels clients on fair lending, Community Reinvestment Act, payment systems, enforcement, and general regulatory issues. In addition, Mr Mierzewski frequently conducts internal investigations on behalf of Boards of Directors, Audit Committees and other special purpose committees.
**Prof. Memberships:** Mr Mierzewski is a past Vice-Chair of American Bar Association's Section of Antitrust Law Committee on Financial Markets and Institutions.
**Career:** Prior to joining Arnold & Porter, he was a law clerk with the Office of the Comptroller of the Currency, 1978.
**Publications:** He is a frequent author and lecturer on bank regulatory and bank antitrust issues. For example, Mr Mierzewski wrote 'New Redlining Settlement Shows DOJ's Commitment to Fair Lending Compliance' which ran in Volume 16 of the Banking Policy Report. Most recently, Mr Mierzewski served as Co-Chair with respect to the drafting of The Bank Merger Book published in 2006 by the Antitrust Section of the American Bar Association.

## MILLSTEIN, Julian
Brown Raysman Millstein Felder & Steiner LLP, New York 212 895 2000
*Recommended in Business Process Outsourcing, Technology*
*Please see New York for profile*

## MISHKIN, Jeffrey A
Skadden, Arps, Slate, Meagher & Flom LLP & Affiliates, New York
212 735 3230
jmishkin@skadden.com
*Recommended in Sport*
**Practice Areas:** Practice centers on all aspects of sports law, and includes antitrust, intellectual property, labor and a wide range of trial and appellate business litigation. Formerly its Chief Legal Officer, now serves the NBA as its chief outside counsel. Has participated in every major legal decision that has affected the NBA in the past 30 years. Has been involved in every round of collective bargaining between the NBA and the NBA Players Association. Has acted as lead litigation counsel in numerous major sports litigations.
**Career:** JD, Cornell Law School, 1972; BA, State University of New York at Albany, 1969.

## MITCHELL, David S
Cadwalader, Wickersham & Taft LLP, New York 212 504 6285
david.mitchell@cwt.com
*Recommended in Capital Markets*
**Practice Areas:** Concentrates on all aspects of the derivatives markets, including providing regulatory, transactional and litigation advice relating to sales and trading activities and formation of funds. Represents a diverse group of clients, including broker-dealers, commercial banks, trading companies, fund sponsors, investment managers, and corporate and institutional end-users of derivative products. Practice includes the development and documentation of complex structured products and private investment funds, including fund of funds and master/feeder structures. Has authored numerous articles on derivatives law issues and is a frequent speaker at industry conferences.
**Prof. Memberships:** Member, American Bar Association, Association of the Bar of the City of New York, New York State Bar Association, and Board of Directors, Futures Industry Association.
**Personal:** JD, New York Law School (1979) (magna cum laude); LLM, New York University School of Law (1980); BA, City College (1976) (summa cum laude, Phi Beta Kappa); admitted 1980, New York.

## MITCHELL, Michael H
Orrick, Herrington & Sutcliffe LLP, Washington, DC 202 339 8479
mhmitchell@orrick.com
*Recommended in Capital Markets*
**Practice Areas:** Transactional practice:

represents issuers and underwriters in public offerings and private placements for a variety of asset-backed securities. Advisory practice: provides guidance on a range of issues under the federal securities laws relating to both structured finance and corporate finance.
**Prof. Memberships:** California State Bar Association; District of Columbia Bar Association.
**Career:** Before joining Orrick, Mr Mitchell was Special Counsel with the Securities and Exchange Commission in the Chief Counsel's Office for the Division of Corporation Finance.
**Personal:** JD, Georgetown University Law Center, 1986; BS, Finance, magna cum laude, Siena College, 1983; First in Class, School of Finance.

## MOATES, G Paul
Sidley Austin LLP, Washington, DC
202 736 8175
pmoates@sidley.com
*Recommended in Transportation*
**Practice Areas:** Paul Moates leads the firm's Transportation Practice, is a member of Sidley's Executive Committee, and Co-Chair of the firm's Accounting and Finance Committee. His practice includes representation of large railroads, railroad holding companies, and the railroad industry's national trade association. He has tried contract and antitrust cases in the federal courts, argued appeals of decisions of federal regulatory agencies in a number of the United States Courts of Appeals, represented railroads in numerous rate cases and commercial disputes, and has served as lead litigation counsel in many of the largest railroad merger and intermodal consolidation cases before the Surface Transportation Board of the Department of Transportation. He has played a prominent role in cases testing the scope of federal preemption of attempts by States and local jurisdictions to regulate various aspects of railroad operations, including the transportation of hazardous materials.
**Publications:** He has written numerous transportation-related articles in professional journals and is a respected speaker at conferences and symposia relating to developments in the transportation industry.
**Personal:** Admissions: US Supreme Court; DC; Illinois.

## MOLITOR, Steven J
Dechert LLP, New York
215 994 2777
steven.molitor@dechert.com
*Recommended in Capital Markets*
**Practice Areas:** Mr Molitor is a Partner in the Finance and Real Estate Practice who focuses on the securitization of financial assets. He has acted as issuer's counsel in connection with hundreds of public mortgage-backed securitization transactions and represents issuers, origi-

nators, underwriters, and servicers in transactions involving the securitization of non-mortgage assets. He also has an active practice in asset-backed commercial paper transactions.
**Prof. Memberships:** Member, Pennsylvania and New York Bars.
**Personal:** Franklin and Marshall College, BA, 1984; Cornell Law School, JD, 1987.

## MOODY, Kevin J
Miller, Canfield, Paddock and Stone, P.L.C., Lansing 517 483 4989
moody@millercanfield.com
*Recommended in Native American Law*
**Practice Areas:** Practice is concentrated in regulatory law, insurance law, Gaming (State law and American Indian Gaming law), and commercial litigation.
**Prof. Memberships:** American Bar Association; State Bar of Michigan.
**Career:** Joined firm 1985; Principal, 1991; Leader, Insurance Practice.
**Personal:** JD, cum laude, University of Detroit Law School, 1981; BA, Kalamazoo College, 1978.

## MOORE, Harold
Skadden, Arps, Slate, Meagher & Flom LLP & Affiliates, New York
212 735 3000
*Recommended in Projects*
*Please see New York for profile*

## MOORE, Malcolm
Davis Wright Tremaine LLP, Seattle
206 622 3150
*Recommended in Wealth Management*

## MOORE, Robert
Miller & Chevalier Chartered, Washington, DC 202 626 5800
rmoore@milchev.com
*Recommended in Tax Litigation*
**Practice Areas:** Tax litigation and judicial appeals; tax audits and administrative appeals; taxation of natural resources; exempt organizations; transfer pricing; tax reduction transactions.
**Prof. Memberships:** American Bar Association; Bar Association of DC.
**Career:** Member, Miller & Chevalier Chartered (1971-present); associate (1967-71).
**Publications:** International Tax Review's 'World Tax 2006' (November 2005). Tax Practice & Procedure, 'New Rules for Tax Opinions and Penalty Protection: Proposed Revisions to Circular 230 and Final Penalty Regulations' (February-March 2004).
**Personal:** LLB, University of Virginia School of Law, 1964; BA, Davidson College, 1961.

## MORAN, Mark
Steptoe & Johnson LLP, Washington, DC
202 429 6292
mmoran@steptoe.com
*Recommended in International Trade*
**Practice Areas:** International Partner,

Steptoe & Johnson LLP, Washington, DC. Litigation-based trade practice concentrating on US antidumping, countervailing duty, and safeguards actions, and WTO dispute resolution proceedings. Advises on WTO agreements, market access issues, and negotiation of bilateral trade agreements. Represents trade associations, governments, and domestic and foreign corporations in the forest products, steel, agricultural, semiconductor, and uranium sectors. Diverse international arbitration experience under ICC, AAA, Stockholm, and UNCITRAL Rules involving turnkey construction projects, oil and gas concession agreements, aircraft services agreements, telecommunications joint ventures, and electric power projects.
**Personal:** JD, University of Michigan, 1986; BS, University of Michigan, 1979.

## MORGAN, Linda
Covington & Burling, Washington, DC
202 662 5214
lmorgan@cov.com
*Recommended in Transportation*
**Practice Areas:** Transportation Practice Group Chair and Legislative Practice Group core member. Railroad and other transportation regulatory and legislative matters, including general governmental and policy issues. 25 years of in-depth experience with the transportation sector.
**Career:** Appointed Chairman of the former Interstate Commerce Commission by President Clinton in 1995, and then of the successor agency, the Surface Transportation Board. Served for 15 years as counsel with the Senate Committee on Commerce, Science, and Transportation, including seven years as General Counsel.
**Personal:** Georgetown University (JD); Vassar College (AB); Harvard's John F Kennedy School of Government Senior Managers Program.

## MORRISON, Kenneth P
Kirkland & Ellis LLP, Chicago
312 861 2347
kmorrison@kirkland.com
*Recommended in Capital Markets*
**Practice Areas:** Mr Morrison is Partner in charge of Kirkland's growing Asset Securitisation Practice. Since 1990, he has handled securitisations involving a variety of asset classes on behalf of originators, underwriters, and conduit sponsors. He is particularly known for his work with auto finance companies and first time issuers and his handling of novel transactional structures. He speaks on securitization topics, and has written widely acclaimed pieces like 'A Letter to a First Time Issuer' and 'Glossary of Terms Used in Asset Securitization'.
**Personal:** Yale University, BA, 1977; Massachusetts Institute of Technology, MSM, 1983; Boston University School of Law, JD, 1983.

## MORRISON, Kent R
Crowell & Moring LLP, Washington, DC
202 624 2610
kmorrison@crowell.com
*Recommended in Government Contracts*
**Practice Areas:** Partner in Crowell & Moring's Government Contracts Group. Practice focuses on government contracts claims counseling and litigation/defense of procurement fraud allegations/counseling and litigation regarding defective pricing and related cost issues/counseling regarding foreign sales and relations with foreign sales representatives/internal investigations/compliance reviews.
**Prof. Memberships:** Council of the American Bar Association's Section of Public Contract Law, Co-Chair of the Section's Federal Division, Chair of the Section's Federal Claims and Remedies Committee, and Vice-Chair of the Section's Judicial Remedies and Truth in Negotiations Act Committees.
**Personal:** Phi Beta Kappa graduate of Rice University; Law Degree from Yale Law School.

## MORRISON, Stephen
Nelson Mullins Riley & Scarborough LLP, Columbia 803 799 2000
*Recommended in Litigation, Products Liability*

## MOSELEY JR, James
Moseley Prichard Parrish Knight & Jones, Jacksonville
904 356 1306
*Recommended in Transportation*

## MOTTESI, Marcelo
Milbank, Tweed, Hadley & McCloy LLP, New York 212 530 5000
*Recommended in Capital Markets*

## MOYER JR, E Homer M
Miller & Chevalier Chartered, Washington, DC 202 626 6020
hmoyer@milchev.com
*Recommended in International Trade*
**Practice Areas:** International; FCPA and international corruption; trade policy and disputes; corporate compliance and internal investigations; export controls and economic sanctions; investment disputes and international arbitration; Supreme Court and appellate litigation; white-collar crime litigation.
**Prof. Memberships:** American Bar Association; Bar Association of DC; CEELI (Central and East European Law Initiative); Center for American International Law; Council for Excellence in Government; Council on Foreign Relations.
**Career:** Member, Miller & Chevalier Chartered (1994-present); General Counsel; Counselor to the Secretary; Deputy General Counsel – US Department of Commerce (1976-81); associate, Covington & Burling (1972-75); LCDR – Office of the Judge Advocate General of

the US Navy (1967-71).
**Publications:** 'Audit Committees and FCPA', Directors Monthly (February 2006). 'DOJ Turns Up Heat on FCPA', Legal Times (June 2005). 'Voluntary Disclosure and Independent Compliance Monitors', Metropolitan Corporate Counsel (June 2005). 'Provide Clearer Guidance', National Law Journal (May 2005). 'FCPA: Keeping Enforcement and Policy Objectives Aligned', Washington Legal Foundation (May 2005).
**Personal:** LLB, Yale Law School, 1967; BA, Emory University, 1964.

## MUMMERY, Dan
Latham & Watkins LLP, Menlo Park
650 328 4600
*Recommended in Business Process Outsourcing, IT Outsourcing*

## MURNANE, Don P
Freehill Hogan & Mahar LLP, New York
212 425 1900
murnane@freehill.com
*Recommended in Transportation*
**Practice Areas:** Areas of expertise are maritime litigation and arbitration of contractual and tort disputes including cargo, charter party, collisions and casualties. Has significant experience with cases involving bulk and product tanker disputes including product contamination and loss. Has also handled major cases involving vessel purchase and sale, liner service contract disputes and issues involving electronic bills of lading. Bar Admissions: New York (State and Federal); District of Columbia.
**Prof. Memberships:** Maritime Law Association of the United States (Arbitration Committee Member); Society of Maritime Arbitrators – MLA Liaison Committee Member; New York State Bar Association.
**Career:** Joined Freehill Hogan & Mahar as a Partner in 1997 having been associated with Haight, Gardner, Poor & Havens from 1986-97.
**Personal:** Born 1960; United States Merchant Marine Academy at Kings Point, BS, 1982 (Salutatorian); Georgetown University Law Center, JD, 1986.

## MURPHY, Michael
Pillsbury Winthrop Shaw Pittman LLP, San Francisco 415 983 7446
*Recommended in Business Process Outsourcing, IT Outsourcing*
*Please see California for profile*

## MURPHY, Paul
Moore & Van Allen, PLLC, Charlotte
704 331 1000
*Recommended in Capital Markets*

## MURPHY JR, John C
Cleary Gottlieb Steen & Hamilton LLP, Washington, DC 202 947 1580
jmurphy@cgsh.com
*Recommended in Financial Services*
**Practice Areas:** Represents domestic

and foreign financial institutions and boards of directors on mergers, acquisitions and restructurings, regulatory and enforcement matters, new powers and corporate governance issues. Frequently involved in major domestic and international bank transactions and investments.
**Career:** General Counsel, FDIC (1984-87); Special Counsel, SEC (1975-77); Partner, Cleary Gottlieb (1982-84 and 1987-preent).
**Personal:** JD, cum laude, University of Pennsylvania (1972); AB, cum laude, Georgetown University (1967).

### NAGEL, Trevor
Pillsbury Winthrop Shaw Pittman LLP, Washington, DC 202 663 8417
Trevor.Nagel@pillsburylaw.com
*Recommended in Business Process Outsourcing*
**Practice Areas:** He has advised both public and private sector clients on legal and commercial issues on a wide-range of large-scale global outsourcing and complex technology transactions. He represents clients in structuring, negotiating and implementing IT infrastructure projects, business process outsourcing, innovative co-marketing arrangements and other strategic alliances.
**Prof. Memberships:** International Bar Association, Vice-Chair, Committee on Technology and e-Commerce; American Bar Association, Section of International and Practice.
**Personal:** Harvard Law School (SJD, 1984); Chicago Law School (LLM, 1981); University of Adelaide (LLB (Hons)), 1980; Dip Ed, 1974; BA(Hons), 1973; Knox Fellow, Harvard Law School, 1981-84.

### NEDZBALA, Michael
Hunton & Williams, Charlotte
704 378 4700
*Recommended in Capital Markets*
*Please see North Carolina for profile*

### NELSON, William
McKee Nelson LLP, Washington, DC
202 775 1880
*Recommended in Tax, Tax Litigation*
*Please see District of Columbia for profile*

### NEUHAUS, Joseph E
Sullivan & Cromwell LLP, New York
212 558 4000
neuhausj@sullcrom.com
*Recommended in International Arbitration*
**Practice Areas:** International commercial litigation in arbitral and court settings.
**Prof. Memberships:** Vice-Chair, Institute for Transnational Arbitration; NYSBA (Chair, Professional Ethics Committee); ABCNY (Member, Professional and Judicial Ethics Committee).
**Career:** Partner since 1992. Law clerk, Justice Lewis F Powell, Jr, US Supreme Court and Judge Carl McGowan, DC

Circuit Court of Appeals; Legal Assistant, Iran-United States Claims Tribunal.
**Publications:** Guide to the UNCITRAL Model Law on International Commercial Arbitration: Legislative History and Commentary (Kluwer, 1989).
**Personal:** Dartmouth College (1979); Columbia University Law School (1982).

### NEWMAN, Lawrence
Baker & McKenzie, New York
212 626 4100
*Recommended in International Arbitration*

### NIBLEY, Stuart B
Thelen Reid & Priest LLP, Washington, DC 202 508 4334
snibley@thelenreid.com
*Recommended in Government Contracts*
**Practice Areas:** Mr Nibley's practice includes representation of defense and civilian contractors before Boards of Contract Appeals, federal and state courts, administrative agencies and international arbitration forums. He represents all aspects of the procurement process, from contract negotiation and proposal preparation through claims and dispute resolution. Mr Nibley's practice increasingly involves representation of clients in international arbitration. He has expertise in handling complex technical disputes and has developed practical techniques for employing electronic organization and presentation of documents in connection therewith. Mr Nibley's specific expertise include: alternative dispute resolution, bid protests, commercial item and GSA schedule contracting, contract formation and negotiation issues, contract performance issues/ claims and changes, contract pricing, ethics compliance/white-collar criminal law, international arbitration, litigation and dispute resolution, socioeconomic requirements, state and local government contracts, technical data/intellectual property and terminations.
**Prof. Memberships:** American Bar Association, Section of Public Contract Law; Vice-Chair, Privatization and Competitive Sourcing Committee; Vice-Chair, Contract Claims and Disputes Resolution Committee; past Chair, Acquisition Reform Committee; past Vice-Chair, Bid Protest Committee; past Vice-Chair, International Procurement Committee; past Vice-Chair, Environmental Committee; International Bar Association; American Arbitration Association; National Defense Industrial Association, past Chair, Legal Subcommittee, Procurement Planning Committee; Thomson-West Publishing, The Government Contractor Advisory Board (2004-present); National Contract Management Association National Board of Advisors (1996-2002); Federal Contracts Report, BNA Board of Advisors (1985-2000); US Geospatial

Intelligence Foundation, Member; London Court of International Arbitration.
**Career:** Partner of Thelen Reid & Priest LLP's Construction and Government Contracts Group. Admitted to practice in the District of Columbia and Virginia. Speaking engagements include: Panel Chair, Improving The Government Contracts Dispute Process, National Defense Industrial Association Annual Education Conference (March 2005); Speaker and Paper, 'Government Contracting Risks: New Potholes On The Road To Profitability', American Bar Association/ NCMA 11th Annual Procurement Institute (February 2005); Speaker and Paper, 'The Governmental Administrative Hammer: Suspension And Debarment From Federal, State And Local Contracting And Not Participating In Certain Governmental Programs', Thelen Reid & Priest LLP Business CLE (February 2005); Panel Chair, 'Managing Sensitive Information After 9/11, The Contracting Challenges of Combating Nuclear, Biological and Chemical Threats', American Bar Association (May 2002); Keynote Speaker, 'The Use of New Technologies in Commercial Arbitration – A Practical Example of an "Electronic File"', Deutsche Institute Fur Schiedsgerichtsbarkeit E.V. (German Arbitration Institute) (April 2002).
**Publications:** 'Companies Called Up, The Defense Production Act: An Old and Rusty Procurement Tool Is Now Seeing Considerable Action', Legal Times of Washington (April 2002); 'Forming Strategic Alliances' (lead article), Contract Management Magazine (NCMA), with Joseph Dyer (December 2001); 'Think Globally: International Ventures Will Lead Contractors to More International Arbitration', Legal Times (March 5, 2001); 'Disputes for Government Contractors', West Publishing (February 2001); co-author, 'The Government Contract Compliance Handbook', West Publishing (1988-2002); 'Cost Issues in the A-76 Process: Comparing Apples to Apples', Government Contract Audit Report, with Joseph Dyer (April 2001); 'Affirmative Action: The New Rules', Contract Management (NCMA), with Joseph Dyer (May 2001); 'Protesting Orders Under Federal Supply Schedule and Multiple Award Contracts', Government Contract Audit Report, with Michael Garson (May 2000); 'Just A Little Oversight: Calls for More Review Suggest We're Not Ready for Laissez-Faire Government', Legal Times, with Michael Garson (March 2000).
**Personal:** Graduate of Washington and Lee University School of Law, JD, cum laude (1979), National Moot Court Team, Burkes Scholar. Graduate of Washington and Lee University, BA, magna cum laude (1975), Majors in English and Philosophy Phi Beta Kappa, Rhodes

Scholar Nominee, Young Scholarship (Outstanding Senior Philosophy Major).

### NICELY, Matthew R
Willkie Farr & Gallagher LLP, Washington, DC 202 303 1113
mnicely@willkie.com
*Recommended in International Trade*
**Practice Areas:** Special Counsel in the International Trade Department, specializing in trade remedy laws, WTO dispute settlement, and other trade policy disputes. He regularly represents respondents in antidumping (AD), countervailing duty (CVD), Section 201 safeguards, and Section 301 market access litigation before US agencies, US courts, and the European Commission. He has managed all aspects of the defense in investigations/reviews before the US Department of Commerce (DOC) and International Trade Commission (ITC) on behalf of producers, exporters, importers, and users of steel, agricultural, and other products from various countries including Australia, Brazil, Canada, Korea, Japan, Thailand, and Vietnam. He also advises governments on WTO agreements compliance and dispute settlement, with a focus on trade remedy matters. Recently represented the Thai and Vietnamese shrimp industries in high-profile antidumping actions.
**Prof. Memberships:** A Member of the American Bar Association.
**Career:** Admitted to the District of Columbia Bar.
**Publications:** Publications include 'Understanding the WTO Anti-Dumping Agreement: Negotiating History and Subsequent Interpretation' (2002) (co-author); 'Textiles and Apparel: The New Protectionism — Primer on Antidumping Duties, Countervailing Duties, and Safeguard Measures' (January 2001, co-author); 'International Legal Developments in Review: 2000 — International Trade', The International Lawyer (Summer 2001); 'Thailand's Application of Post-Uruguay Round Antidumping Procedures', Trade Balance, a legal journal of the Royal Thai Government, Ministry of Justice (April-June 1997, co-author).
**Personal:** Received a JD (cum laude) from the American University Law School in 1991 and a BA from Oberlin College in 1987.

### NOCCO, Frank
Weil, Gotshal & Manges LLP, New York
212 310 8918
frank.nocco@weil.com
*Recommended in Capital Markets*
**Practice Areas:** Frank Nocco is Head of Weil Gotshal's Structured Finance/Derivatives Practice, and concentrates in representing issuers, underwriters and credit enhancers in structured and corporate securities offerings. Mr Nocco has participated in the securitizations of various types of loans, credit card receivables,

trade receivables, equipment and vehicle leases, high-yield and other non-conventional assets. He is experienced in structuring single-seller and multi-seller commercial paper vehicles, owner trusts, master trusts, grantor trusts, REMICs and special purpose corporation vehicles that can issue a variety of debt and equity securities.
**Personal:** Columbia College, BA, 1985; Columbia University School of Law, JD, 1988.

## NOURSE, David
Nourse & Bowles LLP, New York
212 952 6200
*Recommended in Transportation*

## NOVICK, Robert T
WilmerHale, Washington, DC
202 663 6140
robert.novick@wilmerhale.com
*Recommended in International Trade*
**Practice Areas:** Chair of the firm's Trade Department; member of Wilmer-Hale's Management Committee. Represents clients in international business, trade, negotiation and WTO dispute resolution matters, with particular emphasis on developing and implementing market penetration strategies and securing market access opportunities. Representations include companies and associations in the aerospace, agriculture, hi-tech, consumer goods and services sectors.
**Career:** Counselor and General Counsel in the Office of the US Trade Representative from 1997 to 2001.
**Personal:** American University, Washington College of Law (JD 1983); Bucknell University (BA 1980).

## OATES, Mark
Baker & McKenzie, Chicago
312 861 8800
*Recommended in Tax Litigation*

## OBERKFELL, Keith F
Mayer, Brown, Rowe & Maw LLP, Charlotte 704 444 3500
*Recommended in Capital Markets*
*Please see North Carolina for profile*

## O'DONNELL, Neil
Rogers Joseph O'Donnell & Phillips, San Francisco 415 956 2828
*Recommended in Government Contracts*

## ONDRASIK, Paul
Steptoe & Johnson LLP, Washington, DC
202 429 3000
*Recommended in Employee Benefits, ERISA Litigation*
*Please see District of Columbia for profile*

## OPPENHEIMER, M Randall
O'Melveny & Myers LLP, Los Angeles
310 246 6722
roppenheimer@omm.com
*Recommended in Products Liability*
**Practice Areas:** Randy Oppenheimer is a Partner in O'Melveny & Myers' Century

City office and Co-Chair of the Entertainment, Sports and Media Practice. He emphasizes national trial practice, litigation and counseling involving the business community, the entertainment industry, intellectual property issues, environmental issues, and antitrust and regulatory matters.

## ORDWAY, Eric
Weil, Gotshal & Manges LLP, New York
212 310 8609
eric.ordway@weil.com
*Recommended in International Arbitration*
**Practice Areas:** Mr Ordway co-chairs Weil Gotshal's Global Dispute Resolution Practice. He specializes in international commercial and investor state arbitration, representing companies and foreign governments in disputes concerning various sectors such as nuclear power, oil and gas, real estate, financial services and banking and others. Mr Ordway has handled international arbitrations before the ICC, AAA, LCIA, International Arbitration Center of Austrian Federal Economic Chamber, Arbitration Court of Hungarian Chamber of Commerce, and investor-state arbitrations under UNCITRAL rules.
**Personal:** Institut d'Etudes Politiques, CEP, 1970; Princeton University, AB, 1971; New York University, MA, 1982; Brooklyn Law School, JD, cum laude, 1986.

## ORTELERE, Brian T
Morgan, Lewis & Bockius LLP, Philadelphia 215 9635150
bortelere@morganlewis.com
*Recommended in ERISA Litigation*
**Practice Areas:** Brian T Ortelere is a Partner in the Labor and Employment Law Practice and is Co-Chair of the ERISA Litigation Practice. Mr Ortelere's practice covers the full range of employee benefit defense litigation matters, including a number of ERISA class actions. He has particular expertise in defending class action claims challenging the administration of 401(k) savings plans, cash balance plans and ESOPs.
**Prof. Memberships:** Member, Advisory Board of BNA's ERISA Compliance & Enforcement Library.

## OSBORN, John W
Skadden, Arps, Slate, Meagher & Flom LLP & Affiliates, New York
212 735 3270
josborn@skadden.com
*Recommended in Capital Markets*
**Practice Areas:** Head of Derivative Financial Products Practice. In OTC derivatives practice represents commercial and investment banks and other dealers as well as major corporations, hedge funds, high net worth individuals and other end-users of the products; and has analyzed, developed, negotiated and documented full range of transaction types. In securities-related financial products

practice represents issuers, underwriters, placement agents and other parties in a wide range of convertible securities, equity securities units and other complex debt and equity securities. Strong new product development focus.
**Career:** JD, University of Pennsylvania School of Law, 1975; BA, Michigan State University, 1972.

## PACHTER, John
Smith Pachter McWhorter PLC, Vienna
703 847 6300
*Recommended in Government Contracts*

## PAKENHAM, Kathleen M
White & Case LLP, New York
212 819 8324
kpakenham@whitecase.com
*Recommended in Tax Litigation*
**Practice Areas:** Partner in the Tax Litigation and Controversy Group; experienced litigator in matters involving complex questions of federal tax law and procedure. Extensive experience representing clients involved in all types of government and internal investigations, as well as related trial and appellate matters.
**Prof. Memberships:** ABA, Section on Taxation; Chair of Subcommittee on alternate dispute resolution.
**Career:** Partner since 2004.
**Publications:** Extensive writings on US tax matters; regular contributor to Tax Notes and State Tax Notes.
**Personal:** New York University School of Law (LLM, 1998); Brooklyn Law School (JD, 1995); State University of New York at Albany (BA, 1992).

## PALEY, Alan
Debevoise & Plimpton LLP, New York
212 909 6000
*Recommended in Capital Markets, Corporate/M&A*

## PALMA, Laura
Simpson Thacher & Bartlett LLP, New York 212 455 2000
lpalma@stblaw.com
*Recommended in Capital Markets*
**Practice Areas:** Partner and member of the firm's Corporate Department. Concentrates on general corporate finance matters, with a focus on the representation of sponsors, underwriters and credit enhancement providers in a variety of structured finance transactions, including rental car fleet financings, whole business securitizations, intellectual property securitizations, aircraft portfolio securitizations, auto loan and lease securitizations, equipment lease securitizations and other receivable financings.
**Prof. Memberships:** Bar Association of the City of New York.
**Career:** Partner at firm since 1995.
**Personal:** BA, magna cum laude, Dartmouth College (1980); Phi Beta Kappa. JD, Columbia University Law School (1983).

## PAPAVIZAS, Constantine G
Winston & Strawn LLP, Washington, DC
202 282 5732
cpapavizas@winston.com
*Recommended in Transportation*
**Practice Areas:** Corporate finance, including leasing and securities, litigation, administrative/regulatory and legislative.
**Prof. Memberships:** Editorial Board, J Maritime Law & Commerce (2003 -); Board of Governors, DC Port, Propeller Club (1996-2002); frequent speaker at conferences.
**Publications:** Publications include: '2003-04 US Maritime Legislative Developments', J Maritime Law & Commerce (July 2005); 'The Jones Act Foreign Mortgage Debate', Marine Log (April 2005); 'Lease Financing Goes Another Round', Benedict's Maritime Bulletin (4th Quarter 2004); 'New Developments in US-Flag Vessel Financing and Citizenship Requirements', Tulane Maritime LJ (Winter 1999).
**Personal:** Georgetown (BA, 1978); Columbia (MIA, 1981); George Washington (JD, 1984 with honors).

## PARÉ, Jay
Nourse & Bowles LLP, New York
212 952 6200
*Recommended in Transportation*

## PARK, William W
William W. Park - Sole Practitioner, Boston 617 353 3149
wwpark@bu.edu
*Recommended in Arbitration*
**Practice Areas:** Chairman, sole arbitrator and party-nominated arbitrator in ICC, AAA, ICSID, LCIA, UNCITRAL and IACAC arbitrations, concerning inter alia joint ventures, expropriation, insurance coverage disputes, corporate acquisitions, political risk policies, LNG pricing, construction, financial transactions, securities, biotech licenses, letters of credit, technology transfer, agency and distribution contracts. Arbitrator and Senior Claims Judge, Claims Resolution Tribunal for Dormant Accounts in Switzerland. Appeals Tribunal, International Commission on Holocaust Era Insurance Claims.
**Prof. Memberships:** General editor, Arbitration International. Vice President, London Court of International Arbitration. NAFTA Financial Services Roster. Co-Chairman, ABA International Commercial Dispute Resolution Committee. Fellow, College of Commercial Arbitrators. Chartered Arbitrator and Fellow, Chartered Institute of Arbitrators. Admitted to Bar, Massachusetts (1972) and DC (1980).
**Career:** Practised in Paris from 1972-79. Since 1979, Professor of Law at Boston University. Director of Boston University Centre for Banking and Financial Law Studies (1989-93). Other academic

appointments have included Cambridge University, Fletcher School of Law and Diplomacy, University of Dijon, Geneva's Institut Universitaire de Hautes Etudes Internationales and University of Hong Kong.
**Publications:** Published works include Arbitration of International Business Disputes, 'International Chamber of Commerce Arbitration' (with Craig and Paulsson), 'International Commercial Arbitration' (with Reisman, Craig and Paulsson), 'International Forum Selection', 'Arbitration in Finance and Banking' and 'Income Tax Treaty Arbitration' (with Tillinghast).
**Personal:** Yale, BA; Columbia, JD; Cambridge, MA. Fluent in written and spoken French.

### PARKS, Randall S
Hunton & Williams LLP, Richmond
804 788 7375
rparks@hunton.com
*Recommended in Business Process Outsourcing*
**Practice Areas:** Mr Parks' outsourcing practice focuses on large-scale business process and IT outsourcings for Global 2000 firms. Transactions in the last 18 months include human resources, finance and accounting and data center outsourcings for large consumer products, defense, energy and media companies with a total contract value in excess of $4.5 billion. He is author of the Virginia Business Trust Act and Vice-Chairman of the Virginia Bar Association's Section of Business Law.

### PATTON, Stephen
Kirkland & Ellis LLP, Chicago
312 861 2000
*Recommended in Litigation, Products Liability*
*Please see Illinois for profile*

### PECK, Rodney R
Pillsbury Winthrop Shaw Pittman LLP, San Francisco
415 983 1516
Rodney.Peck@pillsburylaw.com
*Recommended in Financial Services*
**Practice Areas:** Mr Peck practices in the corporate, securities, finance and banking law areas, including mergers and acquisitions, bank transactional and regulatory matters and corporate and securities transactions. Industry groups emphasized in Mr Peck's practice include financial services, energy and telecommunications.
**Prof. Memberships:** Board of Trustees, Dominican University of California; Financial Institutions Committee, California State Bar; Committee on Banking Law, American Bar Association.
**Career:** Admitted to practice: California; District of Columbia; New York.
**Personal:** JD, Columbia University School of Law, 1970. AB, Stanford University, 1967.

### PECOULAS, George A
Mayer, Brown, Rowe & Maw LLP, Chicago 312 701 7956
gpecoulas@mayerbrown.com
*Recommended in Capital Markets*
**Practice Areas:** Specialises in representing commercial banks, issuers, underwriters and placement agents in structured securities offerings. Participation in the securitisation of trade receivables and retail installment contracts, including auto loans and equipment loans, credit card receivables, equipment and vehicle leases, commercial loans, insurance premium finance contracts and intellectual property. Experience structuring single-seller and multi-seller commercial paper vehicles, owner trusts, master trusts, grantor trusts, and domestic special purpose corporation vehicles that can issue a variety of debt and equity securities.
**Career:** Joined Mayer, Brown, Rowe & Maw LLP, Chicago, 1990; Partner, 1996. Schiff Hardin & Waite, Chicago, 1987-90.
**Personal:** The John Marshall Law School, JD summa cum laude, 1987; first in class; Law Review. Southern Illinois University, BA, 1971; Dean's List.

### PERRY JR, C Jones
Shearman & Sterling LLP, New York
212 848 8854
jperry@shearman.com
*Recommended in Wealth Management*
**Practice Areas:** Partner in the Private Client Group, representing both domestic and international clients in a broad range of estate planning and tax matters, including pre-immigration tax planning, establishment of cross-border trusts and multi-jurisdictional estate and expatriation tax planning.
**Prof. Memberships:** American Bar Association and New York State Bar Association.
**Career:** Joined the firm in 1987 and became a Partner in 1995.
**Personal:** BA, University of North Carolina (1980); JD, University of North Carolina (1984); LLM in Taxation, New York University (1988).

### PETERS, William
O'Melveny & Myers LLP, Los Angeles
213 430 6000
*Recommended in Business Process Outsourcing, IT Outsourcing*
*Please see California for profile*

### PETERSON, Brad
Mayer, Brown, Rowe & Maw LLP, Chicago 312 782 0600
*Recommended in Business Process Outsourcing, Technology*
*Please see Illinois for profile*

### PIELS, William
Holland & Knight LLP, San Francisco
415 743 6900
william.piels@hklaw.com

*Recommended in Transportation*
**Practice Areas:** Partner in the firm's Structured Finance Group, he has a broad range of experience in general corporate, partnership and securities law matters, as well as more than 20 years of experience in asset-based financing. His practice is focused on aviation finance and includes representation of financial institutions, airlines, shipping lines, manufacturers and investors in a variety of domestic and cross-border equipment financing transactions, operating leases, joint ventures, workouts and repossessions. He is a Member of the State Bar of California and the American Bar Association. He is an author and frequent lecturer on commercial law topics.

### PIERCE, John V H
WilmerHale, New York
212 230 8829
john.pierce@wilmerhale.com
*Recommended in International Arbitration*
**Practice Areas:** Has a diverse practice focusing on international arbitration and litigation, complex commercial litigation, securities enforcement and litigation, and internal corporate investigations.
**Prof. Memberships:** American Bar Association; International Bar Association; Association of the Bar of the City of New York; Council on Foreign Relations.
**Publications:** 'The Haitian Crisis and the Future of Collective Enforcement of Democratic Governance', 27 Law and Policy in International Business 477 (1996); co-author, 'Trade Finance Fraud: Understanding the Threats and Reducing the Risk', ICC Commercial Crime Services, April 2002.
**Personal:** Georgetown University Law Center (JD 1996); Georgetown University, School of Foreign Service (BSFS 1992).

### PIERCE, Kenneth J
Willkie Farr & Gallagher LLP, Washington, DC 202 303 1114
kpierce@willkie.com
*Recommended in International Trade*
**Practice Areas:** Partner in the International Trade Department, specializing in the full range of US unfair trade actions, such as antidumping and countervailing duty, and Sections 301 and 201 actions. He has extensive experience in customs matters including audits, valuation and classification investigations, and Foreign Trade Zones applications, operations, and audits. Regularly handles the litigation and policy aspects of such matters at the agency, legislative, and judicial levels. Additionally, he represents clients in connection with World Trade Organization complaints and in antidumping investigations by European and other non-US national authorities. Clients include major foreign manufacturers (including their US-based operations), foreign gov-

ernments, trading houses, and US importers. Has recently been active in seeking to revoke antidumping and countervailing duty orders through new sunset review procedures, particularly concerning steel products. He represents the Thai, Vietnamese, and Indian shrimp industries in the recent high profile antidumping actions and has been lead counsel for respondents in dozens of other anti-dumping and countervailing duty investigations and reviews in the United States and other countries.
**Prof. Memberships:** Member of the American Bar Association and the International Trade Steering Committee.
**Career:** Admitted to the Bar of the District of Columbia. He is also admitted to practice before the United States Court of International Trade, the United States Court of Appeals for the Federal Circuit, and various other federal courts. Legislative assistant to US Senator Patrick Leahy, 1978-81.
**Publications:** Writes and lectures frequently on international trade law issues in diverse forums in the United States and abroad.
**Personal:** Received a JD (cum laude) from Cornell Law School in 1984, where he was a lead editor for the Cornell International Law Journal and was awarded the 1984 Earl Warren Prize for writing, and a BA (magna cum laude) from the University of Vermont in 1978, where he was elected to Phi Beta Kappa and received several scholastic awards.

### PILLION, Michael L
Morgan, Lewis & Bockius LLP, Philadelphia 215 963 5554
mpillion@morganlewis.com
*Recommended in Business Process Outsourcing*
**Practice Areas:** Michael Pillion is a Partner in the Global Outsourcing Group and is a member of the firm's Technology Steering Committee. Mr Pillion's practice focuses on US based and international outsourcing and technology-related transactions including: human resources, finance and accounting, logistics, claims and data processing and various other business process outsourcing transactions; information technology outsourcing transactions; offshore outsourcing transactions; licensing and hosting agreements; joint ventures and strategic alliances. Mr Pillion advises and represents clients in a broad range of industries, including the pharmaceutical and life sciences, financial services, software and telecommunications industries.
**Prof. Memberships:** Member, Philadelphia Bar Association; Member, Pennsylvania Bar Association; Member, New Jersey Bar Association.

**PINEDO, Anna**
Morrison & Foerster LLP, New York
212 468 8179
apinedo@mofo.com
*Recommended in Capital Markets*
**Practice Areas:** Concentrates on securities and derivatives, representing issuers, investment banks and financial intermediaries in financings, including public and private offerings of equity and debt securities, as well as structured products and innovative financial products. Works with foreign private issuers in their US and Euro offerings. In the derivatives area, counsels major financial institutions acting as dealers and participants in the derivatives markets. Advises on structuring issues, as well as on regulatory issues, monetization and hedging techniques. A regular speaker on new financial instruments and other aspects of the securities laws; frequently publishes on these topics. Active participant in various Bar and other professional associations.
**Personal:** BSFS, Georgetown University, 1990; University of Chicago Law School, 1993. Bar admission: New York.

**PISANO, Vincent**
Kirkland & Ellis LLP, New York
212 446 4980
vpisano@kirkland.com
*Recommended in Capital Markets*
**Practice Areas:** Extensive experience structuring public and private offerings of debt, equity and hybrid securities. Clients include all major US investment banks, as well as private equity funds, and major US and foreign corporations. Representative clients include Merrill Lynch, JP Morgan Securities, Bear Stearns Merchant Banking, The News Corporation and Cendant Corporation.
**Personal:** Vassar College, BA, 1975; St John's University, JD, 1978.

**PITTS, Andrew J**
Cravath, Swaine & Moore LLP, New York
212 474 1620
apitts@cravath.com
*Recommended in Capital Markets*
**Practice Areas:** Public and private securities offerings for investment banking clients and issuers. Represents investment banking clients in connection with liability management transactions, including debt tender and exchange offers and consent solicitations.
**Prof. Memberships:** ABA; ABCNY.
**Career:** Partner since 2003.
**Personal:** Boston University (MBA, 1995); Boston University (JD, summa cum laude, 1994); Trinity College (BA, 1988). Boston University Alumni Achievement Award.

**PLAINE, Daniel**
Gibson, Dunn & Crutcher LLP, Washington, DC 202 955 8286
dplaine@gibsondunn.com
*Recommended in International Trade*
**Practice Areas:** Extensive experience in international law, including trade disputes, anti-dumping – countervailing duty cases, and matters involving economic sanctions, Foreign Corrupt Practice Act issues, anti-boycott law compliance and US export control regulation. Represents clients in foreign sovereign claims litigation and antitrust issues. Advises both domestic and overseas clients in establishing transnational mergers, acquisitions and joint ventures.
**Prof. Memberships:** Member, American Society of International Law; Washington Institute of Foreign Affairs. Former Chair, ABA Business Law Section, International Business Committee.
**Personal:** JD, Yale Law School, 1970; LLB International Law, Marshall Scholar, Cambridge University, 1967; BA, magna cum laude, Williams College, 1965.

**PLAINE, Lloyd Leva**
Sutherland Asbill & Brennan LLP, Washington, DC 202 383 0155
lloyd.plaine@sablaw.com
*Recommended in Wealth Management*
**Practice Areas:** Partner-in-charge, Individual Tax Planning Practice Group; practice encompasses income, estate, gift and generation-skipping transfer tax planning, drafting wills and trusts, handling estate and trust administrations, representing taxpayers in income and estate tax audits and business planning for owners of closely-held businesses.
**Prof. Memberships:** Past President, District of Columbia Estate Planning Council; former member of the National Conference of Lawyers and CPAs; former member of the National Conference of Lawyers and Corporate Fiduciaries; Fellow of the American Bar Foundation; Fellow and former Regent of the American College of Trust and Estate Counsel; Fellow of the American College of Tax Counsel; academician of the International Academy of Estate and Trust Law; member of the Estate Planning & Taxation Committee of the Trusts & Estates magazine Editorial Advisory Board; member of the Advisory Committee of the University of Miami Law Center Philip E Heckerling Institute on Estate Planning.
**Publications:** Co-authored, 'Generation-Skipping Transfer Tax: Analysis with Forms – a Treatise' (RIA/Warren Gorham & Lamont, 2001 with 2005 supplement).
**Personal:** JD, Georgetown University Law Center, 1975; an editor of the Georgetown Law Journal; BA, cum laude, with distinction, University of Pennsylvania, 1969.

**PLANT, David**
David W Plant - Sole Practitioner, New London 603 526 2653
*Recommended in Arbitration*

**PLATT, Warren**
Snell & Wilmer LLP, Phoenix
602 382 6000
*Recommended in Litigation, Products Liability*
*Please see Arizona for profile*

**PLOTKIN, Mark E**
Covington & Burling, Washington, DC
202 662 5656
mplotkin@cov.com
*Recommended in Financial Services*
**Practice Areas:** Counsels banks, thrifts and holding companies, as well as non-banking organizations such as retailers and technology companies, on financial services regulation, bank secrecy, privacy, security and technology issues; represents clients before US and foreign government agencies in connection with major transactions as well as significant enforcement and regulatory matters.
**Career:** Clients have included Bank of America, Brown Brothers Harriman, Expedia, JPMorgan Chase, General Electric, Home Shopping Network, Microsoft, NFL, New York Life, Patagonia, Sun Life Financial, Wilmington Trust Company, Yahoo!, others.
**Publications:** Books and numerous articles.
**Personal:** Yale (BA, summa cum laude, Phi Beta Kappa), Harvard (JD, honors).

**POHLEN, Patrick**
Latham & Watkins LLP, Menlo Park
650 328 4600
*Recommended in Capital Markets*

**POLEBAUM, Elliot E**
Fried, Frank, Harris, Shriver & Jacobson LLP, Washington, DC 202 639 7067
Elliot.Polebaum@FriedFrank.com
*Recommended in International Arbitration*
**Practice Areas:** Partner. Leads Fried Frank's International Arbitration Practice. Specializes in international arbitration (throughout the world) and complex civil litigation in US courts.
**Career:** Joined Fried Frank in 1986. Became a Partner in 1989. Listed in Euromoney's Guide to the World's Leading Experts in Commercial Arbitration. Adjunct Professor of Law at Georgetown, teaching International Commercial Arbitration. Law clerk to Supreme Court Justice William Brennan.
**Personal:** JD(1977), cum laude, New York University School of Law. MPA(1975), Harvard University. AB(1972), magna cum laude, Middlebury College.

**PONGRACE, Donald R**
Akin Gump Strauss Hauer & Feld LLP, Washington, DC 202 887 4466
dpongrace@akingump.com
*Recommended in Native American Law*
**Practice Areas:** Don Pongrace chairs Akin Gump's American Indian Law and Policy Practice and advises clients on domestic and foreign public policy issues.
**Prof. Memberships:** District of Columbia Bar.
**Personal:** BA (magna cum laude and Phi Beta Kappa), Bates College (1979); JD (magna cum laude), American University (1985); law clerk, Honorable H E Widener Jr, US Court of Appeals for the 4th Circuit (1985-86). Mr Pongrace is fluent in French.

**POPE, Michael**
McDermott Will & Emery, Chicago
312 372 2000
*Recommended in Litigation, Products Liability*
*Please see Illinois for profile*

**PORGES, Amelia**
Sidley Austin LLP, Washington, DC
202 736 8361
aporges@sidley.com
*Recommended in International Trade*
**Practice Areas:** Advises businesses, trade associations and governments on how to use trade and investment rules to solve market access problems. She counsels clients in WTO disputes and advises on international negotiations, US legislation and bilateral agreements on trade in goods, services and technology.
**Prof. Memberships:** ABA International Law Section International Trade Steering Committee; program Co-Chair, Georgetown University International Trade Update; Trade Policy Forum; US Dispute Settlement Panelist Roster, NAFTA Chapter 19.
**Career:** As USTR's Senior Counsel for Dispute Settlement and Head of Enforcement, she argued WTO cases, guided US litigation efforts in over 120 government-to-government trade disputes, and negotiated on WTO dispute settlement rules. She earlier served as Senior Legal Officer and Counsellor for Legal Affairs at the GATT Secretariat, advising on trade disputes, negotiations and drafting of the WTO Agreement. Principal author of the leading current work on GATT law, the 'Guide to GATT Law and Practice' published by the WTO.
**Personal:** Teaches WTO law at Johns Hopkins School of Advanced International Studies. Harvard Law School, JD, 1980; Kennedy School of Government, MPP, 1980; Cornell University, BA, 1973. Admitted to US Court of International Trade and DC Bars. Languages: Japanese, French.

**PORTER, Daniel L**
Willkie Farr & Gallagher LLP, Washington, DC 202 303 1115
dporter@willkie.com
*Recommended in International Trade*
**Practice Areas:** Partner in the International Trade Department, specializing in a variety of US laws that affect the cross-border shipment of goods, including antidumping, countervailing duty, market access (Section 301), escape clause

relief (Section 201), customs, and the various US laws imposing economic sanctions. His practice also includes assisting exporters and governments in World Trade Organization (WTO) Panel proceedings. Has developed particular expertise representing the interests of foreign exporters in US antidumping proceedings. On behalf of foreign exporters, he appears regularly before the US Commerce Department, the US International Trade Commission (ITC), the US Court of International Trade, the US Court of Appeals, and NAFTA Bi-National Panels. In antidumping cases he has represented clients from a wide variety of industries such as various steel products, semiconductors, and consumer goods, and from diverse economies such as Japan, China, Thailand, Korea, Brazil, Thailand, Canada, and India. He has significant expertise in preparing defenses for ITC injury proceedings and minimizing the dumping margin in Commerce Department proceedings. Recent significant matters include successfully defending the Chinese steel industry in an antidumping case against steel wire rod and a safeguard case against steel pipe, representing Hynix Semiconductor in the US countervailing duty (anti-subsidy) proceeding, and assisting Hynix's defense efforts in similar proceedings initiated by the European Union and Japan, representing pig farmers in Manitoba, Canada in their successful efforts to convince the US government not to impose anti-dumping and countervailing duties on live swine from Canada, representing the Japanese steel industry in their efforts to terminate antidumping duties on tin mill steel from Japan and advising the Korean International Trade Association on trade policy issues.
**Career:** Admitted to the Bars of Maryland, Virginia and the District of Columbia.
**Publications:** Co-author of a book-length treatise entitled 'US Trade Remedies: A Guide for Foreign Businesses', (2002) (up-date new version expected soon), among other publications.
**Personal:** Received a JD (with a specialization in international legal affairs) from Cornell Law School in 1985, where he was an articles editor for the Cornell International Law Journal, and a BA from Columbia University in 1982.

## PORTER, Philip
Hogan & Hartson LLP, McLean
703 610 6100
*Recommended in Business Process Outsourcing, Intellectual Property*
*Please see Virginia for profile*

## PORTER, Clay
Dennis, Corry, Porter & Smith LLP, Atlanta 404 365 0102
*Recommended in Transportation*

## POSTER, Robert L
Gilmartin, Poster & Shafto, New York
212 425 3220
rlposter@lawpost-nyc.com
*Recommended in Transportation*
**Practice Areas:** Ship and equipment financing, sales, and leasing.
**Career:** Past Vice-Chair, Admiralty & Maritime Law Committee of the Section of International Law and Practice, American Bar Association; past Chair, Admiralty Committee, The Association of the Bar of the City of New York; past Chair, Subcommittee on US Coast Guard Documentation, US Citizenship and Related Matters, Marine Finance Committee, Maritime Law Association of the United States.
**Publications:** 'The Uniform Commercial Code and Bankruptcy', 59 Tulane Law Review, No 5 and 6, p1361; 'Case Note, Shipping Statutes', Journal of Maritime Law and Commerce, Vol 27, No 3, July, 1996; principal author, 'Unnecessary Citizenship Requirements Imposed on Maritime Industries', by the Committee on Admiralty, The Record, Association of Bar of City of New York, Vol 49, No 6.
**Personal:** AB Princeton University 1962, JD Harvard Law School 1065, LLM Harvard Law School 1966.

## PRATT, Timothy
Shook, Hardy & Bacon LLP, Kansas City
816 474 6550
tpratt@shb.com
*Recommended in Products Liability*
**Practice Areas:** Concentrates his practice in the defense of pharmaceutical and medical device litigation and toxic tort cases. Also regularly consults on preventative litigation issues. Has served as national and regional trial counsel for manufacturers of numerous pharmaceutical products, and has also defended manufacturers of a number of medical devices.
**Prof. Memberships:** Admitted to practice before the state courts of Missouri, Texas and Iowa. Also admitted to practice before the US District Courts for the Western District of Missouri, the District of Colorado and the Eastern District of Wisconsin; the Missouri Court of Appeals; and the Fourth, Fifth, Sixth, Eighth, Ninth, and Tenth Circuits of the US Court of Appeals. Vice President of Federation of Defense and Corporate Counsel, faculty member of National Institute for Trial Advocacy and member Defense Research Institute.
**Career:** Joined Shook, Hardy & Bacon, 1977; became Partner, 1981.
**Personal:** JD, Drake University School of Law, 1975; BA, Tarkio College 1971.

## PRICE, Daniel M
Sidley Austin LLP, Washington, DC
202 736 8226
dmprice@sidley.com
*Recommended in International*

*Arbitration, International Trade*
**Practice Areas:** Chairs the firm's International Trade and Dispute Resolution Practice. Counsels multinational companies, financial institutions and trade associations on market access, services, investment and sanctions issues, and matters arising in intergovernmental negotiations. Advises parties in disputes under international trade agreements and investment treaties. Served as counsel or arbitrator in disputes under the UNCITRAL, AAA, ICC, ICSID, and Stockholm Chamber rules. Appointed by President George W Bush to the ICSID Panel of Arbitrators.
**Prof. Memberships:** Department of State's Advisory Committee on International Economic Policy, the Council on Foreign Relations, Advisory Board of the European Institution, Advisory Board of Georgetown University Law Center's Institute of International Economic Law, Advisory Board of the Canada-United States Law Institute, Executive Council of the ABA Section on International Law, Executive Committee of The American Society of International Law, and Advisory Board of the British Institute of International and Comparative Law.
**Career:** Served as USTR Principal Deputy General Counsel, negotiating trade and investment agreements with the former Soviet Union, Eastern Europe and Latin America; served as USTR's lead negotiator on investment issues in the NAFTA talks and as legal advisor on the GATT Uruguay Round investment agreement. Earlier served as deputy agent to the Iran-US. Claims Tribunal in The Hague, representing the US government and advising US business in arbitrating multi-million dollar claims against Iran stemming from the Iranian revolution.
**Personal:** Harvard Law School, JD, 1981; University of Cambridge, Diploma in Law, 1979; Haverford College, BA, 1977. Admissions: US Supreme Court; DC; PA.

## PRINGLE, Paul C
Sidley Austin LLP, San Francisco
415 772 1249
ppringle@sidley.com
*Recommended in Capital Markets*
**Practice Areas:** Paul C Pringle is the Managing Partner of the San Francisco office and practices in corporate securities and REIT transactions. He has served as underwriters' counsel on financings by: Beverly Enterprises, Inc.; Del Monte Foods Company; Dolby Laboratories, Inc.; Finisar Corporation; Hilton Hotels Corporation; KB Home; Nektar Therapeutics; Nike, Inc.; Occidental Petroleum Corporation; Plantronics, Inc.; Questar Gas Company; Questar Market Resources, Inc.; Questar Pipeline Company; Robert Half International, Inc.; Safeway Inc.; Sempra Energy; San Diego Gas & Electric Company; Southern California Gas Company; The Walt Disney Compa-

ny; URS Corporation and Wells Fargo & Company. Mr Pringle's REIT representations include numerous financings by Bedford Property Investors, Inc., healthcare Property Investors, Inc.; KKR Financial Corp.; Nationwide Health Properties, Inc.; Plum Creek Timber Company, Inc.; and Realty Income Corporation.
**Personal:** The University of Michigan Law School (JD, 1968); Dartmouth College (AB, 1965). Admissions: California, 1972; New York, 1969.

## PRITCHARD, John F
Holland & Knight LLP, New York
212 513 3233
john.pritchard@hklaw.com
*Recommended in Transportation*
**Practice Areas:** Partner in the firm's Business Law Section, concentrates on the representation of lessees, lessors, lenders, borrowers, and government guarantors in domestic and cross-border financings, securitizations, workouts and foreclosures. He has over 20 years experience in aircraft, equipment and facility finance and is knowledgeable in all areas of asset-based financing. He has given many speeches on aircraft and equipment financing. Pritchard is an active member of the American Bar Association and served as Chairman of the Subcommittee on Aircraft Financing from 1987-94. He is also a Member of the American College of Finance Lawyers.

## PRUZINSKY, Anthony
Hill Rivkins & Hayden LLP, New York
212 669 0600
*Recommended in Transportation*

## PULEO, Frank
Milbank, Tweed, Hadley & McCloy LLP, New York 212 530 5000
*Recommended in Capital Markets, Financial Services*

## PULLEY III, J Waverly
Hunton & Williams LLP, Richmond
804 788 8200
*Recommended in Real Estate, Transportation*
*Please see Virginia for profile*

## QUINN, James
Weil, Gotshal & Manges LLP, New York
212 310 8000
*Recommended in Litigation, Sport*
*Please see New York for profile*

## QUINN, Kenneth P
Pillsbury Winthrop Shaw Pittman LLP, Washington, DC
202 663 8898
kquinn@pillsburylaw.com
*Recommended in Transportation*
**Practice Areas:** Co-leader of Pillsbury's Aviation Practice; General Counsel of the Flight Safety Foundation. Mr Quinn represents a wide variety of aviation companies in regulatory, litigation, certification, enforcement, international, legislative, and criminal matters.

**Career:** Chief Counsel, Federal Aviation Administration (1991-93); Counselor to the Secretary, US Department of Transportation (1989-91); senior advisor, Office of the President-elect (1988). Editor-in-Chief, American Bar Association 'The Air & Space Lawyer'. Fellow, Royal Aeronautical Society. Director, DePaul International Aviation Law Institute. **Personal:** JD, DePaul University College of Law, 1985 (with honors; editor, DePaul Law Review; editor, ASILS International Law Journal; BS, Northern Illinois University (Finance), 1982.

## QUINN, Patrick T
Cadwalader, Wickersham & Taft LLP, New York 212 504 6067
pat.quinn@cwt.com
*Recommended in Capital Markets*
**Practice Areas:** Concentrates in mortgage and asset securitisation and finance, representing issuers, underwriters, and investors in both public and private securities and financing transactions. Broad experience in structuring public and private residential and commercial mortgage securitisation transactions, including traditional pass-through structures, debt structures and offshore structures. Significant expertise in structuring mezzanine debt and preferred equity real estate transactions. Represents clients in acquisitions and sales of subordinate interests in mortgage loans and mezzanine loans, as well as financings thereof. **Personal:** JD, University of Virginia School of Law (1988); BA, Fordham University (1985).

## RABINOVITZ, Bruce H
WilmerHale, Washington, DC
202 663 6960
bruce.rabinovitz@wilmerhale.com
*Recommended in Transportation*
**Practice Areas:** Chair, Aviation Department. Represents US and foreign air carriers in administrative, adjudicatory and enforcement matters before the Department of Transportation, Federal Aviation Administration, and Transportation Security Administration. Counsels US and foreign air carriers regarding compliance with US antitrust laws and unfair competition laws administered by the Department of Transportation. Advises clients on aircraft sale, lease, and financing transactions, including negotiating operating, finance and cross-border lease agreements; purchase agreements with airframe and engine manufacturers; product support and maintenance agreements; and corporate aircraft transactions. **Personal:** JD, George Washington University Law School; BA, Washington University in St Louis.

## RADZIK, Edward
Donovan Parry McDermott & Radzik, New York 212 376 6400
*Recommended in Transportation*

## RAE, Mark
Stroock & Stroock & Lavan LLP, New York 212 806 5400
*Recommended in Capital Markets*

## RAFF, Joshua E
Orrick, Herrington & Sutcliffe LLP, New York 212 506 5090
jraff@orrick.com
*Recommended in Capital Markets*
**Practice Areas:** Represents issuers, underwriters, institutional investors, investment advisors, credit enhancement providers, and others in the structuring, issuance, distribution, and purchase of asset-backed and mortgage-backed securities. He has experience in transactions involving a wide variety of structures and asset types, including residential and commercial mortgage loans, home equity loans and lines of credit, high yield bonds, bank loans, auto and truck loans, trade receivables, lease receivables, credit card receivables, perpetual floating rate notes. He focuses on CBOs, CLOs and commercial mortgage-backed securities. **Personal:** JD, with honors, Order of the Coif, University of Maryland School of Law, 1977; BA, Columbia University.

## RAHER, Patrick
Hogan & Hartson LLP, Washington, DC
202 637 5600
*Recommended in Environment, Transportation*
*Please see District of Columbia for profile*

## RAISLER, Kenneth M
Sullivan & Cromwell LLP, New York
212 558 4000
raislerk@sullcrom.com
*Recommended in Capital Markets*
**Practice Areas:** Head, Commodities, Futures and Derivatives Group, which renders regulatory, transactional and litigation advice in the commodities, securities and banking areas to brokerage, hedge fund, investment banking, banking and commercial clients. **Prof. Memberships:** ABA; ABCNY (Chairman, Committee on Futures Regulation, 1988-91). **Career:** Judicial clerk to Hon Lee P Gagliardi, US District Court (SDNY) Asst US Attorney DC 1977-82. General Counsel, Commodity Futures Trading Commission 1983-87. **Personal:** Yale University (BS, 1973); NYU School of Law (JD, 1976). Board of Directors, Futures Industry Association.

## RANCE, Brian
Freshfields Bruckhaus Deringer LLP, New York
212 277 4000
*Recommended in Capital Markets*

## RANG, Kevin A
Mayer, Brown, Rowe & Maw LLP, Chicago 312 701 8798
krang@mayerbrownrowe.com
*Recommended in Business Process*

*Outsourcing*
**Practice Areas:** Corporate/information technology/outsourcing: Kevin represents clients in transactions involving the outsourcing of business process functions, including collections, benefits, accounts payable, and facilities management; and the outsourcing of technology functions, including network management, help desk, call center, telecommunications and application hosting. He advises clients on issues associated with software licenses, the purchase/sale of hardware, consulting agreements, alliance agreements, ASP agreements, software development agreements, and various technology-related service agreements. Mr Rang has also represented clients in matters involving copyright and trademark litigation and general commercial litigation. **Career:** Mayer, Brown, Rowe & Maw LLP, Chicago, 2000 to date. Kupelian, Ormond, and Magy, P.C., 1994-2000. Consumers Energy, 1990-93. **Personal:** University of Michigan Law School, JD cum laude, 1995. Michigan State University, BA, 1990.

## RAY, Ellen
King & Spalding LLP, Atlanta
404 572 2885
eray@kslaw.com
*Recommended in Business Process Outsourcing*
**Practice Areas:** Private equity with extensive experience in technology and business process outsourcing transactions, licensing transactions and the formation of strategic alliances. The types of licensing transactions include traditional software licenses, together with maintenance and support, content licenses and ASP agreements. **Prof. Memberships:** American Bar Association (Member, Intellectual Property Section); State Bar of Georgia. **Personal:** BBA, Emory University, 1980; JD, Emory University, 1983; LLM, University of Alabama, 1985.

## RAYSMAN, Richard
Brown Raysman Millstein Felder & Steiner LLP, New York 212 895 2000
*Recommended in Business Process Outsourcing, Technology*
*Please see New York for profile*

## READE, Claire E
Arnold & Porter LLP, Washington, DC
202 942 5566
Claire.Reade@aporter.com
*Recommended in International Trade*
**Practice Areas:** Claire Reade represents foreign and domestic clients on international trade, customs, legislative, and business issues. Her work includes NAFTA and WTO-related matters and 'trade-plus' questions, including labor, environment, and international business practices. **Publications:** She is the author of numerous articles addressing interna-

tional trade questions, including '1995-96 Developments in International Trade Disputes', 'Fair Value Investigations Under the Antidumping Statute', and an article on NAFTA dispute settlement in Mexico. **Personal:** Sheldon Fellow, Harvard University, 1979-80; MALD, Fletcher School of Law and Diplomacy, 1979; JD, Harvard Law School, 1979, cum laude; BA, Wesleyan University, 1973, magna cum laude.

## REARDON, Roy
Simpson Thacher & Bartlett LLP, New York 212 455 2000
*Recommended in Litigation, Products Liability*
*Please see New York for profile*

## RECTOR, Richard
DLA Piper Rudnick Gray Cary US LLP, Washington, DC
202 861 6426
richard.rector@dlapiper.com
*Recommended in Government Contracts*
**Practice Areas:** Government contracts; government affairs. **Career:** His practice is focused on federal and state procurement issues, including IT contracts and transactions, homeland security, entry to the federal market, state procurement laws and issues, terminations for convenience, US Postal Service procurement, and compliance with procurement integrity and ethics laws. He has litigated contract actions and bid protests before various courts and other jurisdictions and has represented prime contractors and subcontractors in breach-of-contract and protest actions, as well as prepared contract claims and requests for equitable adjustment. **Personal:** JD, University of Maryland; BA, University of Maryland.

## REDD, Charles A
Sonnenschein Nath & Rosenthal LLP, St Louis 314 259 5819
credd@sonnenschein.com
*Recommended in Wealth Management*
**Practice Areas:** Estate planning, estate and trust administration and estate and trust-related litigation. Experience and expertise in: (a) drafting estate planning documents; (b) pre- and post-death tax planning; (c) estate tax returns, gift tax returns and fiduciary income tax returns; (d) representation of fiduciaries; and (e) litigation. **Prof. Memberships:** Member: American Bar Association; Missouri Bar; Illinois State Bar Association; Bar Association of Metropolitan St Louis; Fellow, American College of Trust and Estate Counsel (Estate and Gift Tax Committee and Fiduciary Litigation Committee); Adjunct Professor, Northwestern University School of Law. **Personal:** Saint Louis University, JD, 1979; BA, summa cum laude, 1976.

**REED, Lucy**
Freshfields Bruckhaus Deringer LLP,
New York 212 277 4000
*Recommended in International
Arbitration*

**REEDER III, Robert W**
Sullivan & Cromwell LLP, New York
212 558 4000
reederr@sullcrom.com
*Recommended in Capital Markets*
**Practice Areas:** Co-Head, Corporate
Group. Acts as corporate counsel to a
number of issuers, including AIG, The
Goldman Sachs Group and Prudential
Financial. Has experience in a wide array
of securities and derivatives matters,
including establishing three AAA-rated
derivative products companies and advis-
ing on 'restricted' and 'control' securities.
**Prof. Memberships:** ABA; ABCNY;
NYSBA.
**Career:** Partner since 1993. Judicial clerk
to Hon Anthony J Celebrezze, US Court
of Appeals (6th Circuit), 1984-86.
**Personal:** Youngstown State University
(BS, 1981); Ohio State University Law
School (JD, 1984).

**REGAN, Andrew W**
Shearman & Sterling LLP, New York
212 848 8793
awregan@shearman.com
*Recommended in Wealth
Management*
**Practice Areas:** Partner in the Private
Client Group, representing both domes-
tic and international clients in a broad
range of estate planning and tax matters,
including the administration of estates
and trusts, charitable organizations, offshore trust and multi-jurisdictional estate
planning.
**Prof. Memberships:** American Bar
Association- Real Estate, Probate and
Trust Law Section; New York State Bar
Association: Tax Section; Trust and
Estates Law Section; Committee on International Estate and Tax Planning; Society
of Trust and Estate Practitioners.
**Personal:** College of St Columba,
Dublin, Ireland, 1969; BBS, Trinity College, Dublin (1973); JD, Fordham University (1976).

**REIDY, Daniel**
Jones Day, Chicago
312 782 3939
*Recommended in Litigation, Products
Liability*
*Please see Illinois for profile*

**REISMAN, Ellen**
Arnold & Porter LLP, Los Angeles
213 243 4111
Ellen.Reisman@aporter.com
*Recommended in Products Liability*
**Practice Areas:** Ms Reisman's main area
of practice involves representing pharmaceutical and medical device companies in
connection with product liability litigation and US and international regulatory

matters. Since 1997, while at both Arnold
& Porter and AHP, she has been one of
the lead lawyers for the defense in the diet
drug litigation and was one of the negotiators of the National Diet Drug Class
Action Settlement. Ms Reisman has also
represented Pfizer in product liability and
regulatory matters involving the Bjork-
Shiley Heart Valve, including the implementation of a class action settlement,
and served as national counsel for Hoffmann-La Roche in the Versed litigation
and Pfizer in the Feldene litigation.
**Career:** Ellen Reisman joined the Washington, DC office of Arnold & Porter in
1984. She became a Partner in 1992 and
relocated to the Los Angeles office in
1993. In May 1999, Ms Reisman joined
American Home Products (AHP, now
Wyeth) as Associate General Counsel of
AHP and Vice President, Legal Division
of Wyeth-Ayerst Pharmaceuticals. She
returned to Arnold & Porter in 2001.
Personal: The January 2003, American
Lawyer magazine ranked Ms Reisman as
one of the '45 under 45', a group that the
editors have noted "as the rising stars of
the private bar". The National Law Journal also ranked her as one of the top 50
women litigators in 2001.

**REISMAN, W Michael**
W. Michael Reisman - Sole Practitioner,
New Haven
*Recommended in Arbitration*

**REITER, Glenn M**
Simpson Thacher & Bartlett LLP, New
York 212 455 3358
greiter@stblaw.com
*Recommended in Capital Markets*
**Practice Areas:** Corporate Partner at
Simpson Thacher & Bartlett LLP. Advises
clients on a broad range of capital markets transactions, including domestic US
securities offerings, cross-border securities offerings and international corporate
finance transactions. Has significant
experience in merger and acquisition
transactions. Represents US and non-US
corporations, government-related entities and leading investment banks in
equity offerings (including IPOs and follow-on offerings), debt offerings (including investment grade, high-yield, Yankee
bond, Eurobond and sovereign bond
offerings), structured financings, liability
management transactions, merger and
acquisition transactions, outsourcing
transactions and other types of corporate
transactions. In recent years, active in
transactions involving Latin America, the
Caribbean, Canada and Europe in addition to the United States.
**Prof. Memberships:** American Bar
Association, Association of Bar of The
City of New York and International Bar
Association.
**Career:** Joined the firm 1978; became
Partner 1984. Managing Partner of London office, 1986-90.

**Personal:** BA, Yale College, 1973
(summa cum laude, Phi Beta Kappa). JD,
Yale Law School, 1976 (note editor of Yale
Law Journal). Law clerk, 1976-77, The
Honorable Arlin M Adams, United States
Court of Appeals, Third Circuit.

**RENFREW, Charles**
Law Offices of Charles B. Renfrew, San
Francisco 415 397 3933
*Recommended in Arbitration*

**RESNIK, Peter L**
McDermott Will & Emery, Boston
617 535 4075
presnik@mwe.com
*Recommended in Products Liability*
**Practice Areas:** Head, firm-wide Pharmaceutical and Biotech Products Liability
Practice. Focus – pharmaceutical and
agricultural biotech products liability,
multicase and complex business litigation.
**Career:** National counsel and co-lead
counsel- phentermine manufacturer for
phentermine group in federal multidistrict consolidated diet drug litigation
(MDL); lead counsel for StarLink™
genetically modified (GMO) corn producer in federal MDL and state class and
individual case litigation, national products liability counsel for asthma and cold
prescription products for major pharmaceutical company; lead counsel in trade
secret technology misappropriation jury
trials.
**Personal:** Boston University School of
Law (JD, cum laude), Yale University
(BA); editor, Boston University Law
Review.

**RESSLER, Alison S**
Sullivan & Cromwell LLP, Los Angeles
310 712 6600
*Recommended in Capital Markets,
Corporate/M&A
Please see California
for profile*

**REYNOLDS, Robert C**
Alston & Bird LLP, Atlanta
404 881 7560
rreynolds@alston.com
*Recommended in Business Process
Outsourcing*
**Practice Areas:** Technology, outsourcing, information systems, business model
innovation activities, privacy, M&A.
**Prof. Memberships:** American Bar
Association; State Bar of Georgia.
**Career:** Frequent speaker at professional
seminars on such topics as strategic
alliances, outsourcing arrangements, and
emerging business models.
**Personal:** BA, University of Virginia
(1981); JD, Vanderbilt University (1984).

**REYNOLDS III, John B**
Wiley Rein & Fielding LLP, Washington,
DC 202 719 7342
jreynolds@wrf.com
*Recommended in International Trade*
**Practice Areas:** Advises corporations,

financial institutions and defense, technology and consumer products companies on privacy, security and regulatory
issues including foreign investment
transactions, economic sanctions, export
controls, anti-boycott compliance and
compliance with the FCPA. Represents
clients before the US Departments of
State, Treasury, Commerce, Defense and
Homeland Security and the Office of the
US Trade Representative.
**Prof. Memberships:** American Bar
Association: former Chair, Committee on
Export Controls and Economic Sanc-
tions; Co-Chair, Committee on Senior
International Appointments; Co-Chair,
Committee on National Security and
International Law.
**Career:** Attorney-advisor, US Depart-
ment of State.
**Personal:** Yale Law School (JD);
Williams College (BA).

**RICE, Gary**
Simpson Thacher & Bartlett LLP,
New York 212 455 7345
grice@stblaw.com
*Recommended in Financial Services*
**Practice Areas:** Gary Rice is a Partner in
the firm's Corporate Department, regu-
larly advising clients on bank regulation,
bank mergers and acquisitions, and pri-
vate securities offerings.
**Prof. Memberships:** Association of the
Bar of the City of New York, the Business
Law Section of the American Bar Associ-
ation and the Foreign Banking Lawyers
Association.
**Career:** Mr Rice joined Simpson
Thacher in 1985 and became a Partner in
1992. Prior to joining the firm, he served
in the Legal Department of the Federal
Reserve of New York from 1982-85.
**Publications:** 'Federal Deposit Insurance
Reform', Banking and Financial Services
Report, June 2002; 'US Banking Regula-
tion and the Internet', The Review of
Banking and Financial Services, March
2000.
**Personal:** He received his BA summa
cum laude in 1977 from Northeastern
University and his JD from Harvard Law
School in 1982.

**RICH, Frederic**
Sullivan & Cromwell LLP, New York
212 558 4000
*Recommended in Projects
Please see New York for profile*

**RICHMAN, Lawrence I**
Neal, Gerber & Eisenberg LLP, Chicago
312 269 8070
lrichman@ngelaw.com
*Recommended in Wealth
Management*
**Practice Areas:** Advises entrepreneurs,
tax-exempt organizations, fiduciaries and
high net worth families on estate, gift and
charitable planning issues, including
business succession, tax-efficient ownership structures, sophisticated tax-exempt

structures, trust and estate administration, executive benefits, life insurance and international estate planning issues.
**Prof. Memberships:** Chairman, Trust Law Committee, Chicago Bar Association.
**Career:** Partner; Private Wealth Services Chair.
**Publications:** Author and lecturer on various private wealth management topics; estate and succession planning columnist for the CCH Journal of Passthrough Entities.
**Personal:** University of Chicago Law School (JD, 1977); Columbia University (BA, 1974).

### RIVKIN, David
Debevoise & Plimpton LLP, New York
212 909 6000
*Recommended in Arbitration, International Arbitration*

### ROBERTSON, Elihu
Milbank, Tweed, Hadley & McCloy LLP, New York 212 530 5000
*Recommended in Transportation*

### ROBINSON, Robert J
Sidley Austin LLP, New York
212 839 5762
rrobinson@sidley.com
*Recommended in Capital Markets*
**Practice Areas:** Synthetic securitizations, structured credit derivative products and alternative risk transfer transactions. Primary focus at present is on synthetic CLOs and related credit derivative products, synthetic (and hybrid cash-synthetic) ABS CDOs and related credit derivative products and synthetic mortgage loan securitizations.
**Prof. Memberships:** Derivatives & Structured Products Committee, Section on Business Law, New York State Bar Association.
**Career:** 1987-91: private practice in New York and London. 1991-98: attaché (1991-94) and official (1994-98), Legal Service, Bank for International Settlements (BIS), Basel, Switzerland. 1998-present: Private practice in New York (Sidley Austin LLP or predecessor firm since 1999).
**Personal:** Harvard Law School, JD, 1987; Swarthmore College, BA, 1982. Admission: New York, 1988.

### ROCHE, William G
King & Spalding LLP, Atlanta
404 572 4936
broche@kslaw.com
*Recommended in Business Process Outsourcing*
**Practice Areas:** Private equity and intellectual property focusing primarily on the computer software and telecommunications industries. Extensive experience in transactions involving intellectual property and technology-based assets and services, including information technology outsourcing transactions. Sub-

stantial experience in acquisition, development, marketing and protection of intellectual property and technology assets through merger and acquisition transactions, development agreements, licensing, joint ventures, strategic alliances and other arrangements.
**Prof. Memberships:** American Bar Association; State Bar of Georgia.
**Personal:** BA, Notre Dame, 1980; JD, Stanford University, 1983.

### ROCKETT, James M
Bingham McCutchen LLP, San Francisco
415 393 2025
james.rockett@bingham.com
*Recommended in Financial Services*
**Practice Areas:** Has more than 30 years of experience representing banking and financial services clients. Practice includes M&A, corporate governance and bank regulation, regulatory compliance and operations, and de novo bank and holding company formation. Served as lead counsel in over a dozen sales or acquisitions of financial services companies in the last two years.
**Career:** Served as assistant general counsel to First Interstate Bank of California. Received Frandzel Award from California Bankers Association for superior legal assistance to the California banking industry.
**Personal:** University of San Francisco School of Law, JD, 1969; University of San Francisco, BA, 1966.

### ROD, Jonathan
Latham & Watkins LLP, New York
212 906 1200
*Recommended in Projects*

### RODIN, Rita A
Skadden, Arps, Slate, Meagher & Flom LLP & Affiliates, New York
212 735 3000
*Recommended in Business Process Outsourcing, Technology*
*Please see New York for profile*

### RODRIGUEZ, Wilfredo A
Holland & Knight LLP, Miami
305 374 8500
fred.rodriguez@hklaw.com
*Recommended in International Arbitration*
**Practice Areas:** Partner in the Litigation Section, specializing in international litigation and arbitration. Rodriguez serves as the firm's Chair of the International Litigation Team consisting of more than 25 specialized legal practitioners. With over 20 years of experience, Rodriguez has defended, prosecuted and tried numerous complex international business disputes in various courts. He also routinely acts as advocate and legal counsel in a wide variety of international arbitrations conducted in the United States and in several foreign jurisdictions. Rodriguez is a Member of the Advisory Board of the Institute for Transnational

Arbitration and is a regular speaker on international litigation.

### ROH, Charles E
Weil, Gotshal & Manges LLP, Washington, DC 202 682 7100
chip.roh@weil.com
*Recommended in International Trade*
**Practice Areas:** Chip Roh concentrates his practice in international trade and international investment matters. He advises companies, associations and governments in international dispute settlement proceedings, international arbitrations and negotiations. He has served as party counsel in four investor-state treaty arbitrations and in more than 25 dispute settlement proceedings under the WTO and GATT. He has counseled businesses, associations and governments in numerous international trade and investment negotiations, and he advises and represents businesses regarding economic sanctions, export controls, anti-bribery, investment review and similar US international economic regulatory laws.
**Personal:** Princeton University, BA, 1969; Harvard Law School, JD, 1973.

### ROMANO, Robert M
Morgan, Lewis & Bockius LLP, New York
212 309 7083
rromano@morganlewis.com
*Recommended in Financial Services*
**Practice Areas:** Robert M Romano is a Partner in the Litigation Practice. His practice focuses on a variety of securities regulatory litigation matters, including the defense of individuals and companies under investigation by the Securities and Exchange Commission, the New York Stock Exchange, NASD Regulation and state securities regulators for securities fraud, trading and sales violations and related supervisory issues.
**Prof. Memberships:** Member, American Bar Association, Litigation Section; Member, Bar Association of the City of New York.

### ROSEN, Edward J
Cleary Gottlieb Steen & Hamilton LLP, New York 212 225 2820
erosen@cgsh.com
*Recommended in Capital Markets*
**Practice Areas:** Structuring and regulatory analysis of complex securities and derivatives transactions and US securities and commodities law regulation. Clients include Securities Industry Association, International Swaps and Derivatives Association and Futures Industry Association, The Bond Market Association, major commercial and investment banks, exchanges, and clearinghouses.
**Prof. Memberships:** Member ISDA Regulatory Advisory Committee, FIA Board of Directors, CFTC Technology Advisory Committee. Chair, Practicing Law Institute Annual Conference on Swaps and Derivatives.
**Career:** JD, Columbia University School

of Law (1982) (Stone Scholar); BA, MA (hon), Oxford University (1975).
**Publications:** Co-author 'US Regulation of the International Securities and Derivatives Markets' (eighth edition, 2005).

### ROSEN, Stuart M
Weil, Gotshal & Manges LLP, New York
212 310 8660
stuart.rosen@weil.com
*Recommended in International Trade*
**Practice Areas:** Stuart M Rosen heads Weil Gotshal & Manges' International Trade Practice in New York. He specializes in regulatory and commercial matters, and in international trade, customs, and financial services areas. He has extensive international experience, and has been actively involved in all types of trade proceedings, including anti-dumping, countervailing duty, escape clause and other proceedings, customs valuation, classification and penalty/enforcement matters, as well as commercial transactions and other regulatory matters involving international trade, retailing and distribution, insurance, credit and finance.
**Personal:** Dickinson College, BA, 1962, Phi Beta Kappa; Harvard Law School, JD, 1965, magna cum laude.

### ROSENBERG, Marc S
Cravath, Swaine & Moore LLP, New York
212 474 1676
mrosenberg@cravath.com
*Recommended in Capital Markets*
**Practice Areas:** Securities, mergers and acquisitions. Counseling boards of directors, audit committees and senior management in connection with SEC investigations, governance issues and other special situations.
**Prof. Memberships:** ABCNY.
**Career:** Partner since 1990. Clerkship: Hon Walter R Mansfield (US Court of Appeals for the Second Circuit).
**Personal:** Harvard Law School (JD, magna cum laude, 1983; Sears Prize; editor, Law Review); Princeton University (AB, summa cum laude, 1980; Phi Beta Kappa).

### ROSENTHAL, Paul
Collier Shannon Scott, Washington, DC
202 342 8400
*Recommended in International Trade*

### ROSS, Bruce
Luce, Forward, Hamilton & Scripps LLP, Los Angeles
213 892 4992
*Recommended in Wealth Management*

### ROSS, Nancy
McDermott Will & Emery, Chicago
312 372 2000
*Recommended in Employment, ERISA Litigation*
*Please see Illinois for profile*

## ROTHSCHILD, Gideon
Moses & Singer LLP, New York
212 554 7800
*Recommended in Wealth Management*

## ROTHWELL, James T
Davis Polk & Wardwell, New York
212 450 4000
james.rothwell@dpw.com
*Recommended in Capital Markets*
**Practice Areas:** Member of Davis Polk & Wardwell's Corporate Department. Represents investment banks, corporations, and individuals regarding equity derivatives and other structured equity financial products. Has been involved in the original design of many innovative financial products that have become staples of the equity derivatives marketplace. Also advises underwriters and issuers in securities offerings, specializing in convertible and equity-linked securities in the public, Rule 144A and Regulation S capital markets.

## ROY, Paul J N
Mayer, Brown, Rowe & Maw LLP, Chicago 312 782 0600
*Recommended in Business Process Outsourcing, Technology*
*Please see Illinois for profile*

## RUBENSTEIN, Joshua
Katten Muchin Rosenman LLP, New York 212 940 7150
joshua.rubenstein@kattenlaw.com
*Recommended in Wealth Management*
**Practice Areas:** Joshua S Rubenstein handles a wide variety of private client matters on a local, national, and international level, including personal and estate planning, the administration of estates and trusts, and contested Surrogate's Court and tax proceedings for high net worth individuals, professionals, entrepreneurs, artists and others with unique intellectual property interests, and is a frequent lecturer and author on these topics.
**Prof. Memberships:** Mr Rubenstein is an academician and Executive Council Member of the International Academy of Estates and Trusts Law, a Fellow and Regent of the American College of Trusts and Estates Counsel and a Member of the Society of Trusts and Estates Practitioners. He is a former Chair of the NYSBA Trusts & Estates Law Section and of the International Committee of the ABA Real Property and Probate Section.
**Career:** Mr Rubenstein received his BA, magna cum laude, Phi Beta Kappa, from Columbia University (1976), and his JD from Columbia University Law School (1979), Harlan Fiske Stone Scholar. He is admitted to the New York and New Jersey Bars. He is an Adjunct Professor at Brooklyn Law School and is the author of the LexisNexis AnswerGuide on New York Surrogate's Court Practice.

## RUBENSTEIN, William S
Skadden, Arps, Slate, Meagher & Flom LLP & Affiliates, New York
212 735 2642
wrubenst@skadden.com
*Recommended in Financial Services*
**Practice Areas:** Co-Head of Financial Institutions Mergers and Acquisitions Group, advises on all kinds of transactions involving financial institutions. Extensive experience in negotiated and contested mergers and acquisitions, proxy fights, privately negotiated investments and restructuring transactions.
**Career:** JD, Benjamin N Cardozo School of Law, 1981 (cum laude; note and comment editor, Cardozo Law Review); BA, Fairleigh Dickinson University, 1978.

## RUBINOFF, Edward L
Akin Gump Strauss Hauer & Feld LLP, Washington, DC
202 887 4026
erubinoff@akingump.com
*Recommended in International Trade*
**Practice Areas:** Heads firm's Export Trade Practice. Is a recognized authority on US export controls, trade embargoes, economic sanctions, antiboycott regulations, CFIUS reviews and foreign corrupt practices. Advises domestic, foreign and multinational companies in all business sectors on compliance with US export control and sanctions laws; structures export compliance programs; performs audits and internal investigations; conducts international trade due diligence for mergers, acquisitions and joint ventures; and represents clients in civil and criminal export enforcement cases.
**Prof. Memberships:** President's Export Council Subcommittee on Export Administration; ABA, Section of International Law.
**Personal:** BA, University of Pennsylvania; JD, George Washington University.

## RUBINSTEIN, Javier H
Mayer, Brown, Rowe & Maw LLP, Chicago 312 701 7781
jrubinstein@mayerbrownrowe.com
*Recommended in International Arbitration*
**Practice Areas:** Represents clients from Latin America, Europe, North America and Asia in international commercial arbitrations before the world's leading arbitral institutions, including the ICC International Court of Arbitration, the International Centre for the Settlement of Investment Disputes, the Court of Arbitration for Sport, the International Center for Dispute Resolution (AAA), and the London Court of International Arbitration.
**Career:** Mayer, Brown, Rowe & Maw LLP, Chicago, 1989 to date; Partner, 1998; Chicago Litigation Practice Leader, 2003 to date. University of Chicago Law School, Lecturer in Law, 1996 to date. Teaching courses in International Com-

mercial Arbitration and Litigation and US Supreme Court Litigation.
**Publications:** 'International Commercial Arbitration: Reflections at the Crossroads of the Common Law and Civil Law Traditions', 5 Chi J Intl L 303 (2004). 'The Attorney-Client Privilege and International Arbitration', 18 J Intl Arb 587 (Dec 2001).
**Personal:** JD (cum laude), Georgetown University Law Center, 1989; Dean's List; Member, Law and Policy in International Business; Member, National Moot Court Team. Master of Public Policy, Harvard University, John F Kennedy School of Government, 1986. BA (magna cum laude; Dean's List), University of Michigan, 1984. Born, Buenos Aires, Argentina. Native fluency in Spanish.

## RUSKIN, Bradley I
Proskauer Rose LLP, New York
212 969 3465
bruskin@proskauer.com
*Recommended in Sport*
**Practice Areas:** A Partner in Proskauer Rose LLP's Litigation and Dispute Resolution Department and a member of the firm's Executive Committee. A significant portion of his practice is dedicated to litigating issues and counseling clients active in the sports business. Among the league clients for whom he performs services are the National Hockey League, Major League Soccer, the National Basketball Association, the ATP, and the WTA. In addition, he has represented ownership groups and clubs in each of the major US sports (including the Florida Marlins, the New York Jets, the Philadelphia Eagles and the New Jersey Devils), and media companies in sports-related disputes. He also regularly handles a wide range of litigated complex commercial matters throughout the country in various federal and state courts and in domestic and international arbitral forums, and has handled proceedings (along with foreign co-counsel) before the European Commission and the Office of Fair Trading.
**Publications:** Bi-monthly 'Letter from America' column in Sports Law Administration and Practice.
**Personal:** New York University School of Law, JD, 1981. Brown University, AB (with honors), 1978.

## RUSSELL, William
King & Spalding LLP, Houston
713 751 3237
wrussell@kslaw.com
*Recommended in International Arbitration*
**Practice Areas:** Fluent in Spanish with extensive experience in international litigation and arbitration, complex commercial litigation and professional liability.
**Prof. Memberships:** State Bar of Texas, Grievance Committee; advisory board of the Southwest Legal Foundation's Institute for Transnational Arbitration; Hous-

ton International Arbitration Club.
**Personal:** BA, Southern Methodist University, 1992; JD, South Texas College of Law, 1995.

## RUTHERFURD JR, Winthrop
White & Case LLP, New York
212 819 8700
wrutherfurd@whitecase.com
*Recommended in Wealth Management*
**Practice Areas:** Practices in Trusts and Estates Department, advising individuals and families on all aspects of estate planning, including charitable giving, tax-motivated transfers of property and taxation of estates and trusts. Also advises charitable organizations and trusts, and has extensive experience in audit and appellate proceedings with federal and state taxing authorities.
**Prof. Memberships:** American College of Trust and Estate Counsel; American Bar Association, section on real property, probate and trust law; The Association of the Bar of the City of New York; New York State Bar Association.
**Personal:** University of Virginia Law School (LLB, 1967); Princeton University (BA, 1964).

## RUTKOWSKI, Lawrence
Seward & Kissel LLP, New York
212 574 1200
*Recommended in Transportation*
**Practice Areas:** Mr Rutkowski is Head of the firm's Transportation Finance Group, a cross section of attorneys within the firm from the Corporate Finance, Corporate Securities, Litigation and Tax Departments with expertise on matters of interest to clients in the transportation industry. In such capacity, Mr Rutkowski has worked on matters ranging from the formation of joint ventures, asset finance transactions, registered and unregistered securities transactions and cross-border leases to restructurings and bankruptcy. In addition to representing clients in the transportation industry, Mr Rutkowski's practice has included considerable experience in equipment finance and in the energy and mining fields.
**Prof. Memberships:** Mr Rutkowski is a Member of the Association of the Bar of the City of New York (former Chair, Maritime Law Committee), the American Bar Association (the Air and Space Law Forum, Business Law Section, International Law and Practice Section), the City Bar Association Committee on Aeronautics, the Maritime Law Association of the United States (Maritime Finance Committee), the Executive Vice President and a member of the Board of the Norwegian-American Chamber of Commerce, the Secretary and a board member of New York Maritime, Inc., and the President and board member of the Holy Cross Lawyers Association, a group of alumni of the College of the Holy Cross

engaged in the practice of law.

**Career:** Mr Rutkowski received a BA Degree, magna cum laude, from College of the Holy Cross, in 1975, and a JD Degree, from Columbia University in 1978. Mr Rutkowski is a Partner in Seward & Kissel's Corporate Finance group. Mr Rutkowski has practiced law since 1979. He joined Seward & Kissel as a Partner in 1992.

### RYAN, Michael
Cleary Gottlieb Steen & Hamilton LLP, New York 212 225 2000
*Recommended in Corporate/M&A, Financial Services*
*Please see New York for profile*

### SABEL, Bradley K
Shearman & Sterling LLP, New York 212 848 8410
bsabel@shearman.com
*Recommended in Financial Services*
**Practice Areas:** Partner of Shearman & Sterling specializing in bank and financial regulation.
**Prof. Memberships:** Member of the New York Bar; Chair, Banking Law Committee, New York City Bar Association.
**Career:** Federal Reserve Bank of New York, 1975-94; Shearman & Sterling, 1994-present.
**Publications:** Author, 'Federal Reserve's Reserve Requirements', and co-author, 'Securities Activities of Foreign Banks in the US', in Regulation of Foreign Banks (Gruson & Reisner, eds, 4th ed 2003).
**Personal:** BA, cum laude, Vanderbilt University (1970); JD, Cornell Law School (1975); MSBP, Columbia Business School (1984).

### SACHER, Steven
Kilpatrick Stockton LLP, Washington, DC 202 508 5800
*Recommended in Employee Benefits, ERISA Litigation*
*Please see District of Columbia for profile*

### SACHS, John
Latham & Watkins LLP, Washington, DC 202 637 2200
*Recommended in Projects*

### SAGGESE, Nicholas
Skadden, Arps, Slate, Meagher & Flom LLP & Affiliates, Los Angeles 213 687 5000
*Recommended in Capital Markets, Corporate/M&A*
*Please see California for profile*

### SALTZMAN, Michael I
White & Case LLP, New York 212 819 8938
msaltzman@whitecase.com
*Recommended in Tax Litigation*
**Practice Areas:** Co-ordinates firm's Tax Litigation and IRS Procedure Practice. Represents clients on substantive and procedural tax issues in civil trials, and in IRS audits and administrative appeals.

Represents taxpayers in administrative proceedings and trials before state and local tax tribunals. Expertise in white-collar and criminal tax cases.
**Prof. Memberships:** Association of the Bar of the City of New York; New York State Bar; American College of Tax Counsel.
**Career:** Former trial attorney in tax division US Department of Justice.
**Publications:** IRS Practice & Procedure.
**Personal:** Georgetown University (LLM, 1968); Columbia Law School (LLB, 1964); Colgate University (BA, 1961).

### SALZMAN, Jerrold
Freeman, Freeman & Salzman, Chicago 312 222 5100
*Recommended in Capital Markets*

### SAMET, Andrew
Sandler, Travis & Rosenberg, Washington, DC 202 216 9307
*Recommended in International Trade*

### SANDLER, Joseph
Sandler Reiff & Young, Washington, DC 202 479 1111
*Recommended in Government: Political Law*

### SANDLER, Richard J
Davis Polk & Wardwell, New York 212 450 4000
richard.sandler@dpw.com
*Recommended in Capital Markets*
**Practice Areas:** Head of Davis Polk & Wardwell's Global Capital Markets Practice, with extensive experience advising on corporate governance matters, securities regulatory matters and all aspects of public and private securities offerings, including initial public offerings, high-yield debt securities, derivatives, venture capital and leveraged investments, spin-offs, restructurings, exchange offers and new financial products. Regularly represents Aetna, CSFB, JPMorgan Chase, Horizon Blue Cross Blue Shield of New Jersey, IHS Inc. (a company controlled by the Thyssen family), MCI, Montpelier Re, Morgan Stanley and PartnerRe, as well as representing other corporate and investment banking clients on domestic and international matters and transactions.

### SAPER, Jeff
Wilson Sonsini Goodrich & Rosati, Palo Alto 650 493 9300
*Recommended in Capital Markets, Corporate/M&A*
*Please see California for profile*

### SAWYERS, Al B
Orrick, Herrington & Sutcliffe LLP, New York 212 506 5041
asawyers@orrick.com
*Recommended in Capital Markets*
**Practice Areas:** Focuses on the creation of complex derivative securities; structured financial products; repackaged asset-backed, corporate, and municipal

securities; credit-linked notes; collateralized bond obligations; synthetic convertible bonds, and synthetic money market eligible securities. He represents issuers, investment banks, insurance companies and other institutional investors and participants in the structured finance market. He has particular expertise in the area of swap agreements and derivative securities, including credit default, currency, equity and interest rate swaps.
**Career:** Co-Chair, Orrick's Structured Finance Group.
**Personal:** JD, University of Chicago, 1986; MBA, University of Chicago, 1986; BA, magna cum laude, Vanderbilt University, 1982.

### SAWYIER, David R
Sidley Austin LLP, Chicago 312 853 7261
dsawyier@sidley.com
*Recommended in Capital Markets*
**Practice Areas:** Partner in the Commodities and Financial Litigation Practice in Chicago. Advises and represents clients in investment advisory, hedge fund and futures-related corporate and regulatory matters, including the organization and offering of interests in commodity pools and hedge funds and investments in advisory and trading firms.
**Prof. Memberships:** American Bar Association.
**Personal:** Educated at Cambridge University, England, Diploma in Law, 1979; Oxford University, England, MA, 1974; Harvard College, AB, 1972; Harvard University, JD, 1977. Admissions: District of Colombia, 1978; Illinois, 1977.

### SCALLET, Edward
Groom Law Group, Washington, DC 202 857 0620
*Recommended in ERISA Litigation*

### SCAVONE, Arthur
White & Case LLP, New York 212 819 8200
*Recommended in Projects*
*Please see New York for profile*

### SCHACTER, Ira
Cadwalader, Wickersham & Taft LLP, New York 212 504 6035
ira.schacter@cwt.com
*Recommended in Capital Markets*
**Practice Areas:** Practice consists principally of creating and structuring complex financial solutions and the formation, acquisition and capital raising activities of businesses that issue, underwrite, trade or invest in financial products. Frequently called upon to develop unique financial solutions for corporate and financial institutions that bridge traditional finance with structured finance. Involved in virtually all aspects of the structured finance business and with almost every type of securitization including insurance risk, whole-company and CDOs and

with assets from the traditional to the varied, including corporate loans, swap receivables, repo and other financial assets, as well as a variety of other unique assets, such as franchise royalties and shipping containers. Has extensive experience counseling monolines and representing them in their transactions.
**Personal:** JD, Nova Center for the Study of Law; LLM, Corporations Law, New York University School of Law; BA, Economics, State University of New York at Stony Brook.

### SCHAFFZIN, Jonathan
Cahill Gordon & Reindel LLP, New York 212 701 3900
*Recommended in Capital Markets*

### SCHAGRIN, Roger
Schagrin Associates, Washington, DC 202 223 1700
*Recommended in International Trade*

### SCHEINBERG, Ronald
Vedder, Price, Kaufman & Kammholz, New York 212 407 7700
*Recommended in Transportation*

### SCHER, Peter L
Mayer, Brown, Rowe & Maw LLP, Washington, DC 202 263 3360
pscher@mayerbrown.com
*Recommended in International Trade*
**Practice Areas:** Represents companies on a worldwide basis, assisting clients in addressing regulatory and other governmental issues and expanding their business activities in foreign markets. Specialises in market access issues – expanding client activities in foreign markets through trade and strategic business alliances. Provides advice and counsel on federal legislative and regulatory affairs in international trade, tax policy, environmental policy, copyright and intellectual property.
**Career:** Mayer, Brown, Rowe & Maw LLP, Washington, DC, 2000 to date; Partner 2000. Practice Leader, Government and Global Trade Practice, 2002 to Date. United States Special Trade Negotiator, 1997-2000. Chief of Staff, United States Department of Commerce, 1996-97. Chief of Staff, Office of the United States Trade Representative, 1995-96. Staff Director, US Senate Committee on Environment and Public Works, 1993-95. Chief of Staff to US Senator Max Baucus, 1991-93. Keck, Mahin & Cate, Washington, DC, 1989-91.
**Publications:** Author: 'The WTO and America's Agricultural Trade Agenda', Minnesota Journal of Global Trade, Winter 2000, Volume 9, Issue 1. Atlantic Council of the United States, Working Group on US-EU Trade and Economic Issues, 2000-01. German Marshall Fund, Guest Lecturer, 2000.
**Personal:** JD, American University, Washington College of Law, 1987. BA,

The American University, 1983.

## SCHETMAN, Richard
Cadwalader, Wickersham & Taft LLP,
New York 212 504 6906
richard.schetman@cwt.com
*Recommended in Capital Markets*
**Practice Areas:** Concentrates in structured finance, derivative products, and other types of financial products. Extensive experience in structuring commercial paper vehicles and CDOs, synthetic CDOs and vehicles for repackaging corporate, asset-backed and non-US securities. Represents underwriters, issuers, institutional investors, and swap counterparties in a wide range of matters, including the securitization of cash flows from such assets as credit card receivables, auto, trade and lease receivables. Speaker at various conferences on CDOs, repackagings and other securitization issues.
**Prof. Memberships:** Member, American Bar Association and Association of the Bar of the City of New York.
**Personal:** JD, The University of Pennsylvania School of Law (1983) (Member, Moot Court Board); BA, Brown University (1980).

## SCHILLER, Jonathan D
Boies, Schiller & Flexner, Washington,
DC 202 237 2727
jschiller@bsfllp.com
*Recommended in International Arbitration*
**Practice Areas:** Jonathan Schiller is a co-founder and Managing Partner of Boies, Schiller & Flexner LLP. He has 30 years of experience in trying cases before juries and judges throughout the United States, and is recognized as a leading practitioner in the field of international arbitration. Mr Schiller's practice covers a full range of complex commercial matters including securities, corporate governance and antitrust. His clients include Aetna, CBS, The Republic of France, Goldman Sachs, Guardsmark, The New York Yankees, Yankees Entertainment & Sports Network, Monsanto, National Geographic, Philip Morris, Qwest Communications International, Siemens, and Westinghouse. In the past year, Mr Schiller has: led the defense of Qwest in federal class action securities litigation and 'opt out' state court cases across the country; led Qwest's defense in parallel proceedings in Europe and the US arising out of the KPNQwest bankruptcy; represented the Board of Directors of RenaissanceRe Holdings, a Bermuda reinsurer, in government investigations of securities law matters; and successfully defended Goldman Sachs against New York Stock Exchange seat holders who sought to enjoin NYSE's merger with Archipelago Holdings.
**Career:** Mr Schiller serves as an arbitrator in ICC, UNCITRAL, AAA and ad hoc arbitrations. He was elected as Fellow of

the American Bar Foundation and appointed to the Milan Chamber of Commerce National and International Arbitration Club of Arbitrators. He served as a law clerk to the Honorable Charles R Richey, US District Court, District of Columbia (1973-74).
**Personal:** BA (1969) and JD (1973), Columbia University. Recipient of 2006 Columbia University John Jay Award for distinguished professional achievement. Member, Judicial Conference of the District of Columbia Circuit (1976-81 and 1983-2004); Standing Committee on Pro Se and Pro Bono Matters of the Judicial Conference of the District of Columbia (1984-90); Director of Washington Tennis and Education Foundation.

## SCHMIDT, John R
Mayer, Brown, Rowe & Maw LLP,
Chicago 312 701 8597
jschmidt@mayerbrownrowe.com
*Recommended in Transportation*
**Practice Areas:** Corporate mergers and acquisitions and other large-scale transactions. Federal and state regulation. Appellate practice. Served as Lead Partner in the $1.8 billion lease of the Chicago Skyway, the first ever privatization of a tollway complex in the United States.
**Career:** Mayer, Brown, Rowe & Maw LLP, Chicago, 1998 to present; 1967-84. Visiting scholar, Northwestern University School of Law, 1997-98. Associate attorney General of the United States, Department of Justice, 1994-97 (responsible for Civil, Antitrust, Civil Rights, Environment and Tax Divisions). Ambassador and Chief US Negotiator for the Uruguay Round under the General Agreement on Tariffs and Trade, 1993-94. Skadden, Arps, Slate, Meagher & Flom, Chicago, 1984-93. Transition Chief and Chief of Staff to Chicago Mayor Richard M Daley, 1989. Named by American Lawyer as an 'All-Star of the 90s' and a 2004 'Dealmaker of the Year'.
**Publications:** Articles on infrastructure privatization, corporate and securities law, mental health, election laws and constitutional issues in the Harvard Law Review, Northwestern Law Review, Journal of Criminal Law and other publications.
**Personal:** Harvard Law School, JD cum laude, 1967; editor, Harvard Law Review. Harvard College, BA magna cum laude, 1964.

## SCHNABL, Marco E
Skadden, Arps, Slate, Meagher & Flom LLP & Affiliates, New York
212 735 2312
mschnabl@skadden.com
*Recommended in International Arbitration*
**Practice Areas:** Handles international litigations and arbitrations. Also acts as plaintiff or defendant counsel in US domestic commercial litigations. Has

arbitrated at all major arbitral institutions including the ICC, ICSID, LCIA, ICDR and AAA. Has handled domestic and international hostile M&A litigations and international arbitrations concerning changes in corporate control. Worked on securities class actions for US and foreign clients, contested proceedings before administrative agencies, SEC investigations, contract disputes and other commercial litigations. As a native of Argentina, he is fluent in Spanish and has conducted arbitral proceedings where both English and Spanish were working languages.
**Career:** JD, Columbia University School of Law, 1981; MPhil, Economics, Columbia University, 1977; MS, Management, Sloan School of Management, Massachusetts Institute of Technology, 1973; Lic, Economics, University of Buenos Aires, 1971.

## SCHNEIDER, Lawrence
Arnold & Porter LLP, Washington, DC
202 942 5694
Lawrence.Schneider@aporter.com
*Recommended in International Trade*
**Practice Areas:** Lawrence Schneider is a Senior Partner who heads the firm's International Trade Practice. He handles a full range of international trade, customs, legislative, and policy matters, including disputes under import laws. He has more than two decades' experience representing companies, trade associations, and governments in anti-dumping, countervailing duty, and other international trade proceedings before administrative agencies, courts, and international dispute settlement panels.
**Prof. Memberships:** He has served as President and Member of the Board of Directors of the Washington Council of Lawyers.
**Personal:** JD, Harvard Law School, 1974, cum laude; BA, Yale University, 1971, cum laude.

## SCHNEIDER, Pam
Gadsden Schneider & Woodward LLP,
King of Prussia 484 683 2600
*Recommended in Wealth Management*

## SCHULMAN, Amy
DLA Piper Rudnick Gray Cary US LLP,
New York 212 835 6108
amy.schulman@piperrudnick.com
*Recommended in Products Liability*
**Practice Areas:** Product liability and toxic torts; class action; drug and medical device; employment.
**Career:** A Litigation Practice Group leader, she has an extensive product liability practice concentrating in drug and medical device litigation. Acts as national coordinating counsel and trial counsel; designs and implements alternative resolution programs for Fortune 500 companies; has handled nearly 750 mediations. Her practice includes employment issues

and substantial international litigation. She appears frequently in federal courts throughout the country and writes and speaks on litigation, resolution strategies, and women in the legal profession.
**Personal:** JD, Yale University Law School; BA, Wesleyan University.

## SCHUMAECKER, Michael
Pillsbury Winthrop Shaw Pittman LLP,
New York 212 858 1000
*Recommended in Transportation*
**Practice Areas:** Section Leader, firm's Finance Practice. Advises clients on the legal and structural aspects of cross-border asset-based and asset-backed financings. Particular focus on highly structured transactions involving credit enhancement and liquidity support, aircraft finance and corporate debt restructuring. Assignments have included representing international airlines in de-leveraging of balance sheets; representing issuers, underwriters, credit enhancers and liquidity support providers in Rule 144A offerings; structuring US Government-guaranteed export financings; and securitizing power purchase contracts, leases, receivables and other financial assets.
**Personal:** LLM, New York University Law School, 1976; JD, Brooklyn Law School, 1972 (Editor-in-Chief, Brooklyn Law Review); BA, Georgetown University, 1966.

## SCHWARTZ, Jordan
Cadwalader, Wickersham & Taft LLP,
New York 212 504 6136
jordan.schwartz@cwt.com
*Recommended in Capital Markets*
**Practice Areas:** Served as lead counsel in hundreds of public and private securitization transactions involving over $250 billion in securities and a wide array of asset classes. Clients include major mortgage banks, investment banks, commercial banks, insurance companies and institutional investors. Over 20 years experience as corporate lawyer and business advisor with participation in a variety of corporate transactions, including mergers and acquisitions, leveraged buyouts, initial public offerings, leveraged aircraft leasing, and computer hardware and software development, acquisition and licensing arrangements.
**Personal:** JD, University of Chicago Law School (1981); BA, Stanford University (1978); Member, American Bar Association and the Secondary and Capital Markets Committee of the Mortgage Bankers Association.

## SCHWARZ, Helfried
Milbank, Tweed, Hadley & McCloy LLP,
New York 212 530 5000
*Recommended in Transportation*

## SCHWEBEL, Stephen
Judge Stephen M. Schwebel,
Washington, DC 202 736 8328
*Recommended in Arbitration*

**SCOTT, Michael**
Reed Smith LLP, Philadelphia
215 851 8100
*Recommended in Litigation, Products Liability*
*Please see Pennsylvania for profile*

**SEHGAL, Zarrar**
Milbank, Tweed, Hadley & McCloy LLP,
New York 212 530 5000
*Recommended in Transportation*

**SHAPIRO, Hal S**
Miller & Chevalier Chartered,
Washington, DC 202 626 6052
hshapiro@milchev.com
*Recommended in International Trade*
**Practice Areas:** International; government affairs; international trade policy and international trade agreements; WTO and NAFTA dispute settlement; import, export and customs; federal civil litigation; litigation; appellate litigation; customs; domestic and international arbitration.
**Prof. Memberships:** American Bar Association; Bar Association of District of Columbia; Council on Foreign Relations.
**Career:** Member, Miller & Chevalier Chartered (2000-present); The Hill, Top 10 Washington Trade Lobbyists (September 2004); senior advisor for International Economic Policy, National Economic Council, Executive Office of the President (2000); Counsel, Miller & Chevalier Chartered (1998-2000); Associate General Counsel, Office of the United States Trade Representative (1996-98); trial attorney, US Department of Justice (1993-96); associate, Cravath, Swaine & Moore (1991-93).
**Publications:** 'Fast Track: A Legal, Political and Historical Analysis', Transnational Publishers, (2006). 'The Elimination of Counter-Ambition in US International Trade Policy-Making: Is There a Role for the States and Localities?' Ius Gentium, (2003).
**Personal:** JD, Columbia University School of Law, 1991; BA, Columbia College, 1988.

**SHAPIRO, Howard**
Proskauer Rose LLP, New Orleans
504 310 4085
howshapiro@proskauer.com
*Recommended in ERISA Litigation*
**Practice Areas:** Partner at Proskauer Rose LLP. National ERISA Litigation Practice focuses on defending matters raising sophisticated preemption issues; fiduciary issues; fiduciary misrepresentation claims; ESOP litigation issues; 401(k) plan issues; blackout period cases; plan asset diversification issues; prohibited transaction allegations; directed trustee issues; cash balance cases; independent contractor litigation; 'serious consideration' cases; retiree rights litigation; severance pay cases; executive compensation/'top hat' litigation; Section 510 cases; benefit claims cases; ERISA class actions; and

class-wide challenges to plans that do not offer contraception benefits. He has appeared in federal courts from coast to coast, maintaining an active national ERISA litigation practice.
**Prof. Memberships:** Past Chair of the Section of Labor and Employment Law, American Bar Association and the Joint Committee on Employee Benefits (ABA). Also past Chair of the Employee Benefits Committee, Section of Labor and Employment Law (ABA).
**Personal:** BA Tulane University, New Orleans, LA, May 1972; MA History, McGill University, Montreal, Quebec, November 1975; JD Loyola University of New Orleans, LA, May 1979.

**SHER, Stanley**
Sher & Blackwell, Washington, DC
202 463 2500
*Recommended in Transportation*

**SHERIDAN, Mark F**
Holland & Hart LLP, Santa Fe
505 988 4421
*Recommended in Native American Law*
*Please see New Mexico for profile*

**SHIRAZI, Ray**
Cadwalader, Wickersham & Taft LLP,
New York 212 504 6376
ray.shirazi@cwt.com
*Recommended in Capital Markets*
**Practice Areas:** Concentrates in structured products and derivatives encompassing a wide range of financial assets, including equity-linked products, hedge-fund linked products, credit-linked products and repackaging of financial assets. Active practice in derivatives, particularly equity derivatives and all related documentation, trading and regulatory issues. Advises on, structures and handles execution on credit derivatives, asset swaps, leverage and arbitrage products. Primary client base is is leading dealers and end users of derivative products.
**Prof. Memberships:** ISDA North American Committee on Equity Derivatives.
**Personal:** BS, University of California-Riverside (cum laude, 1984); JD, University of California Los Angeles School of Law (1988).

**SHIRLEY, James**
Holland & Knight LLP, New York
212 513 3200
jim.shirley@hklaw.com
*Recommended in Transportation*
**Practice Areas:** Partner in the firm's Litigation Section, his practice primarily involves maritime casualties. He has investigated and tried a wide range of matters concerning marine casualties and pollution response, both in the US and abroad. He is a master mariner, marine salvage master, and deep sea diver. Prior to becoming a lawyer, he held command at sea, and participated on-scene in more than 100 marine salvage and wreck removal operations. He has lectured to

industry groups and military units on marine salvage and harbor clearance work, and frequently writes and speaks on maritime legal issues.

**SHOCKRO, Michael**
Latham & Watkins LLP, Los Angeles
213 485 1234
*Recommended in Business Process Outsourcing, IT Outsourcing*

**SHOR, Michael T**
Arnold & Porter LLP, Washington, DC
202 942 5732
Michael.Shor@aporter.com
*Recommended in International Trade*
**Practice Areas:** Michael Shor has over 20 years experience representing private companies, trade associations, and foreign governments in international trade matters, including antidumping and countervailing duty investigations, reviews and appeals, sunset reviews, WTO disputes, and US Customs proceedings. Mr Shor also has extensive experience with appeals of trade cases, including involvement as counsel in some 40 decisions issued by courts and binational panels. He has also assisted foreign governments in dispute settlement proceedings before the World Trade Organization.
**Career:** Legal assistant, Iran-United States Claims Tribunal, 1984-86.
**Personal:** JD, Harvard Law School, 1983; AB, Dartmouth College, 1980.

**SHOYER, Andrew W**
Sidley Austin LLP, Washington, DC
202 736 8326
ashoyer@sidley.com
*Recommended in International Trade*
**Practice Areas:** Andrew Shoyer focuses on the implementation and enforcement of international trade and investment agreements. He advises companies, trade associations and governments on the use of WTO, NAFTA and other treaty-based rules to address market access barriers and unfair conditions of competition. Mr Shoyer spent seven years at the Office of the US Trade Representative, serving most recently as Legal Advisor in the US Mission to the World Trade Organization in Geneva. He was the principal negotiator for the United States of the rules implementing the WTO Dispute Settlement Understanding, and briefed and argued numerous WTO cases before dispute settlement panels and the WTO Appellate Body. In Washington, he served as Assistant General Counsel at USTR where he was principal legal counsel in the negotiation of the market access rules of the NAFTA. He worked on numerous trade policy issues with Congress and the economic agencies of the Executive Branch.
**Personal:** Georgetown University Law Center, JD, 1986; Georgetown University School of Foreign Service, MS in Foreign Service, 1986; University of Pennsylvania,

BA, 1981. Admission: District of Columbia, 1987.

**SHUTRAN, Richard**
Dewey Ballantine LLP, New York
212 259 8000
*Recommended in Projects*
*Please see New York for profile*

**SILVERMAN, Leslie N**
Cleary Gottlieb Steen & Hamilton LLP,
New York 212 225 2380
lsilverman@cgsh.com
*Recommended in Capital Markets*
**Practice Areas:** Domestic and international capital markets, particularly cross-border offerings and development of new financial products, and corporate counseling regarding compliance with the Sarbanes-Oxley Act and related governance matters.
**Prof. Memberships:** Member of the Bar in New York. Admitted to practice before US Court of Appeals (Second Circuit) and US District Court (Southern District of New York).
**Career:** Joined firm, 1974; became Partner, 1982. JD, Law Journal editor, Yale Law School (1973); BS, summa cum laude, Wharton School of the University of Pennsylvania (1969).
**Publications:** Co-author of 'US Regulation of the International Securities and Derivatives Markets' (Eighth edition, 2006); 'PLI's Guide to the Securities Offering Reforms' (Practising Law Institute 2005); 'The Sarbanes-Oxley Act: Analysis and Practice (2003)'; 'Director Diligence After WorldCom, The Review of Securities and Commodities Regulation' (January 2006); and 'Raising Capital Through OTC Equity Derivatives: The Goldman, Sachs & Co. Interpretive Letter, Futures and Derivatives' (January 2004).

**SIMMONS, Rebecca J**
Sullivan & Cromwell LLP, New York
212 558 3175
simmonsr@sullcrom.com
*Recommended in Capital Markets*
**Practice Areas:** Advises on structuring and development of financial products, novel securities and structured transactions, and regulated transactions. Practice includes: derivatives structuring and regulation; US securities, banking and commodities laws and regulation; bankruptcy and insolvency issues; and capital markets transactions. Developed first synthetic AAA-rated derivatives products program for an insured US bank and first synthetic securitization of swaps receivables. Employs broad range of credit risk transfer and mitigation techniques. Advises clients regarding US disclosure and corporate governance requirements.
**Prof. Memberships:** ACBNY (secretary, Business Law Section); NYSBA.
**Career:** Partner since 2000.
**Personal:** Harvard University (AB, 1991); Columbia Law School (JD, 1984).

**SIPE JR, Samuel M**
Steptoe & Johnson LLP, Washington, DC
202 429 6486
ssipe@steptoe.com
*Recommended in Transportation*
**Practice Areas:** Partner and Transportation Practice Group Leader in the Washington office of Steptoe & Johnson LLP. Represents railroads in regulatory proceedings, including rate cases and mergers before the Surface Transportation Board as well as in commercial litigation in federal and state courts and in arbitration proceedings. Advises non-railroad clients, including municipalities and port authorities, regarding commercial and regulatory issues arising from dealings with railroads. Extensive background in antitrust law and economic regulation encompassing various network industries.
**Personal:** JD, Yale University, 1978; PhD, State University of New York-Buffalo, 1973; AB, Princeton University, 1967.

**SKIDMORE, Jonathan B**
Fulbright & Jaworski L.L.P., Dallas
214 855 8038
jskidmore@fulbright.com
*Recommended in Products Liability*
**Practice Areas:** Products liability; litigation.
**Prof. Memberships:** American Bar Association; State Bar of Texas; Dallas Bar Association.
**Career:** Admitted to practice in Texas. Recognized as a 'Texas Super Lawyer', 2003, 2004 and 2005.
**Personal:** JD, with honors, The University of Texas School of Law (1983); BA, Accounting, The University of Texas at Austin (1980).

**SLADE, Georgiana**
Milbank, Tweed, Hadley & McCloy LLP, New York
212 530 5000
*Recommended in Wealth Management*

**SLATER, Valerie A**
Akin Gump Strauss Hauer & Feld LLP, Washington, DC 202 887 4112
vslater@akingump.com
*Recommended in International Trade*
**Practice Areas:** Extensive experience in prosecuting and defending anti-dumping, countervailing duty, safeguard and other trade remedy investigations; particular expertise with suspension agreements and non-market economy cases. Handles appeals before Court of International Trade and Court of Appeals for the Federal Circuit. Practices before Office of the US Trade Representative and other federal agencies in connection with trade policy and WTO matters, including accessions and dispute settlements. Experienced with NAFTA panel proceedings.
**Prof. Memberships:** Member, Advisory Committee on Rules, US Court of International Trade.

**Personal:** BA, Allegheny College (magna cum laude, Phi Beta Kappa); JD, Catholic University of America.

**SLONAKER, Norman**
Sidley Austin LLP, New York
212 839 5356
nslonaker@sidley.com
*Recommended in Capital Markets*
**Practice Areas:** Norman D Slonaker is Co-Head of the Corporate Securities Practice in New York and is a Member of the firm's Executive Committee. He has extensive experience in all aspects of capital markets transactions, with particular emphasis on structured securities, investment grade debt securities, convertible and exchangeable securities, medium-term note programs and Rule 144A offerings. Mr Slonaker was a member of the ABA Task Force on Sellers' Due Diligence and Similar Defenses under the Federal Securities Laws and is currently a Member of the Financial Reporting Committee of the Association of the Bar of the City of New York. He has been a speaker at seminars on new financial instruments and techniques and other aspects of the federal securities laws.
**Personal:** Harvard Law School, LLB, 1965; University of Washington, BS, 1962. Admission: New York, 1966.

**SLUTZKY, Steven**
Debevoise & Plimpton LLP, New York
212 909 6000
*Recommended in Capital Markets*

**SMALL, Jeffrey**
Davis Polk & Wardwell, New York
212 450 4000
jeffrey.small@dpw.com
*Recommended in Capital Markets*
**Practice Areas:** Co-Head of Davis Polk & Wardwell's global Capital Markets Group. Advises US and non-US clients on a variety of transactions, including initial public offerings, spinoffs, other securities underwritings, corporate finance, foreign asset privatisations, and international corporate and sovereign offerings. Advises numerous US companies in conjunction with capital-raising transactions and corporate governance, and has been a principal legal advisor to Morgan Stanley for many years. Also a principal advisor to Telefonica, Banco Santander Central Hispano, Repsol YPF and Burger King.

**SMIT, Robert H**
Simpson Thacher & Bartlett LLP, New York 212 455 2000
rsmit@stblaw.com
*Recommended in International Arbitration*
**Practice Areas:** Litigation Partner at Simpson Thacher & Bartlett LLP specialising in international arbitration and litigation. Represents clients and serves as arbitrator in a wide range of complex commercial arbitrations, concentrating

in the areas of bilateral investment treaty arbitrations, joint venture, agency, distributorship and construction disputes as well as insurance matters. Recent engagements include counsel to General Electric Capital Corporation and Bechtel in various arbitrations arising out of India's expropriation of the Dabhol Power Plant in Maharashtra, India, and counsel to Andersen Consulting in one of the largest ever ICC arbitrations, based in Geneva, Switzerland.
**Prof. Memberships:** US member of ICC Court of Arbitration, and Chair of CPR Arbitration Committee.
**Career:** Has been a Partner at the firm since 1997.
**Personal:** JD from Columbia Law School; DEA in private international law and international arbitration from the Sorbonne in Paris; clerked in the SDNY Federal courts; taught US Commercial Law at the Sorbonne.

**SMITH, Gregory A**
DLA Piper Rudnick Gray Cary US LLP, Reston 703 773 4074
gregory.smith@dlapiper.com
*Recommended in Government Contracts*
**Practice Areas:** Government contracts, government affairs, international trade, aerospace and defense.
**Career:** Chair of the Government Contracts Group, he focuses on federal procurement counseling, dispute resolution, claim analysis and preparation, and litigation. He represents domestic and international clients negotiating with government agencies; counsels on defective pricing and cost-accounting and termination disputes; represents subcontractors and prime contractors before the US Court of Federal Claims, US district courts, and appeals courts; has tried complex cases involving major claims before boards of contract appeals; has litigated contract award disputes before the GAO and federal courts.
**Personal:** JD, University of Virginia; AB, Miami University.

**SMITH, Michael W**
White & Case LLP, New York
212 819 8968
msmith@whitecase.com
*Recommended in Transportation*
**Practice Areas:** Practice is focused on aircraft finance and equipment leasing. Aircraft finance experience includes cross-border leveraged operating leases, finance leases, US Ex-Im Bank and ECA supported lease transactions, sales of lease receivables, portfolio purchases, restructuring and bankruptcy matters and a variety of vendor finance matters.
**Prof. Memberships:** New York State Bar, 1981.
**Personal:** BBA, University of Iowa, 1977; JD, Duke University School of Law, 1980.

**SMITH JR, Richard K**
White & Case LLP, Los Angeles
213 620 7788
rsmith@whitecase.com
*Recommended in Transportation*
**Practice Areas:** Executive Partner of the Los Angeles office and has a transactional and corporate practice with an emphasis on leasing and equipment finance, lending transactions and municipal securities. Has represented and advised lessors, lessees, lenders, intermediaries and equity interests in a wide variety of equipment leasing transactions. Significant experience in aircraft leasing and finance transactions and airline restructurings and bankruptcies.
**Prof. Memberships:** State Bar of California; United States District Court for the Central District of California; American Bar Association.
**Personal:** BA, cum laude, University of Illinois, 1977; JD, magna cum laude, University of Illinois, 1980.

**SMUTNY, Abby Cohen**
White & Case LLP, Washington, DC
202 626 3600
asmutny@whitecase.com
*Recommended in International Arbitration*
**Practice Areas:** International dispute resolution through arbitration or litigation; disputes involving state parties, disputes under investment treaties, claims of expropriation and political risk insurance. Counsel in ICSID, ICSID additional facility, ICC, UNCITRAL and other ad hoc proceedings, and cases before US courts.
**Prof. Memberships:** NY State Bar, 1990; Washington DC Bar, 1992; Member of Executive Council and Executive Committee, American Society of International Law; Chair, International Law Section of DC Bar; ABA; IBA; LCIA; Institute for Transnational Arbitration; International Law Association.
**Personal:** AB, cum laude, Vassar College; London School of Economics; Université de Grenoble; JD, University of Chicago.

**SNYDER, David**
Pillsbury Winthrop Shaw Pittman LLP, San Diego 619 234 5000
*Recommended in Capital Markets, Corporate/M&A*
*Please see California for profile*

**SNYDER, Jeffrey L**
Crowell & Moring LLP, Washington, DC
202 624 2790
jsnyder@crowell.com
*Recommended in International Trade*
**Practice Areas:** Chair of Crowell & Moring's International Group and focuses on the US regulation of international trade. With clients in the chemical, electronics, pharmaceuticals, and insurance industries, he advises on Customs law, antidumping, and other import laws.

Creating strategies to eliminate, minimize, or manage the burden on imports is a feature of his practice. Has developed approaches for multinationals to manage the impact of US extraterritorial regulations, such as sanctions administered by the Office of Foreign Assets Control.
**Personal:** BA from American University, 1980; JD from American University, 1983; LLM from Columbia University, 1984.

## SOUSSLOFF, Andrew D
Sullivan & Cromwell LLP, New York
212 558 3681
soussloffa@sullcrom.com
*Recommended in Capital Markets*
**Practice Areas:** Domestic and international corporate finance experience representing clients from the US, Latin America, Canada and Europe in hundreds of securities offerings, acquisitions and other commercial transactions. Has represented major corporations, financial institutions and sovereign governments in their capital-raising activities in the US and international markets, and regularly advises multinational companies on public disclosure, securities law and corporate governance issues.
**Prof. Memberships:** Legal Practice Division Council and Chair, Capital Markets Forum, IBA.
**Career:** Partner since 1986.
**Personal:** University of Pennsylvania (BA, MA, 1975); University of Pennsylvania Law School (JD, 1979).

## SPAK, Gregory J
White & Case LLP, Washington, DC
202 626 3641
gspak@whitecase.com
*Recommended in International Trade*
**Practice Areas:** International trade regulation at all levels, including national administrative bodies, reviewing courts, regional arbitral panels, and all levels of WTO dispute resolution.
**Prof. Memberships:** American Bar Association.
**Career:** Partner since 1995.
**Publications:** Multiple publications on international business and trade regulation.
**Personal:** Georgetown University (BSFS, 1984); Georgetown University Law Center (JD, 1987).

## SPAK, Walter J
White & Case LLP, Washington, DC
202 626 3606
wspak@whitecase.com
*Recommended in International Trade*
**Practice Areas:** Practice emphasizes the US and third country trade proceedings, customs issues, bilateral and multilateral trade negotiations, dispute resolution under NAFTA and the WTO and sector specific trade policy issues. Has been involved in over 100 original investigations and reviews under the US trade laws and the trade laws of third countries.

His experience in customs law includes criminal and civil customs fraud investigations, valuation issues, classifications issues, customs audit, country-of-origin matters, marking requirements and general customs advice.
**Personal:** JD, Georgetown University, 1977; BA, University of Notre Dame, 1973; Sophia University (Japan), 1971.

## SPERLING, Allan G
Cleary Gottlieb Steen & Hamilton LLP, New York
212 225 2260
asperling@cgsh.com
*Recommended in Capital Markets*
**Practice Areas:** Securities, financial, and corporate matters. Extensive experience representing underwriters, issuers and investors in public and private debt and equity financings, advising financial institutions on securities law and counseling businesses on corporate legal matters.
**Prof. Memberships:** Bar in New York. Admitted to practice before US Court of Appeals (Second Circuit), US District Court (Southern and Eastern Districts of New York), Member of New York State Bar Association.
**Career:** Joined firm, 1968; became Partner, 1976. LLB, Law Journal editor, Order of the Coif, Yale Law School (1967); AB, cum laude, Phi Beta Kappa, Columbia University (1964).

## STARER, Brian
Holland & Knight LLP, New York
212 513 3200
brian.starer@hklaw.com
*Recommended in Transportation*
**Practice Areas:** Partner and Head of the Rapid Response Team for Holland & Knight. Over 30 years experience in admiralty practice focused primarily on marine casualties including groundings, sinkings, fires, collisions and environmental pollution. Starer regularly advises ship owners, international Protection and Indemnity Clubs and hull underwriters on worldwide basis. Starer has investigated and advised on all aspects of maritime and environmental casualties, including property damage, cargo loss, personal injury and death claims, natural resource and other environmental damage. Starer has served as casualty counsel on more than 100 ship disasters worldwide including Exxon Valdez and Prestige.

## STEGEMOELLER, Mark
Latham & Watkins LLP, Los Angeles
213 485 1234
*Recommended in Capital Markets*

## STEIN, Craig
Schulte Roth & Zabel LLP, New York
212 756 2000
*Recommended in Capital Markets*

## STEINBERG, James
Kilpatrick Stockton LLP, Atlanta
404 815 6283
JSteinberg@KilpatrickStockton.com
*Recommended in Business Process Outsourcing*
**Practice Areas:** Complex commercial transactions, including business process and IT outsourcing, strategic alliances, enterprise system development/implementation, hardware and system procurement, and joint ventures, focusing on telecommunications, healthcare, financial institutions and technology. Recent transactions include Transformation Outsourcing and Pan-European IT outsourcing.
**Prof. Memberships:** American Bar Association (Business Law and Science and Technology Sections); State Bar of Georgia (Corporate and Banking Law Section).
**Career:** Chair, firm's Technology and Communications Team.
**Publications:** Frequent speaker on structuring and negotiating business process and IT outsourcing transactions.
**Personal:** Harvard Law School (JD, magna cum laude, 1989); Emory University (BA, 1986).

## STENGEL, James L
Orrick, Herrington & Sutcliffe LLP, New York 212 506 3775
jstengel@orrick.com
*Recommended in Products Liability*
**Practice Areas:** Represents clients in large, complex, and multi-party class action litigation. He has handled significant actions involving the chemical, tobacco, and medical device industries.
**Prof. Memberships:** State Bar of New York; US Court of Appeals for the Second and Sixth Circuits; US District Courts for the Southern, Eastern, and Northern Districts of New York and Eastern District of Michigan; United States Supreme Court.
**Career:** Managing Director of all Orrick's Litigation Practices; previously, Mr Stengel was a Partner at Donovan Leisure Newton & Irvine LLP (1988-98).
**Personal:** JD, cum laude, University of Michigan, 1980; BA, University of Illinois, 1977.

## STERN, Akiba
Morgan, Lewis & Bockius LLP, New York
212 309 6000
*Recommended in Business Process Outsourcing, Technology*
*Please see New York for profile*

## STERN, Gary
Sidley Austin LLP, Chicago
312 853 7267
gstern@sidley.com
*Recommended in Capital Markets*
**Practice Areas:** Partner in the Banking and Securitization Group in Chicago. Represents investors, issuers, placement agents, credit enhancers and liquidity providers in securitization transactions

involving a variety of asset types, including, credit cards, auto loans, equipment leases, student loans, consumer loans, trade receivables, sports related revenue streams and entertainment royalties and revenue streams, with a particular emphasis on transactions in the motion picture industry. Transaction structures include multi-seller and single-seller commercial paper conduit deals, private placements and 144A issuances.
**Prof. Memberships:** American and Chicago Bar Associations.
**Personal:** Northwestern University School of Law, JD, 1982; University of Michigan, BA, 1979. Admission: Illinois, 1982.

## STEWART, Scott M
Mayer, Brown, Rowe & Maw LLP, Chicago 312 701 7821
sstewart@mayerbrownrowe.com
*Recommended in Tax Litigation*
**Practice Areas:** Represents taxpayers at all levels of federal tax controversy, including audit, administrative appeals before the Internal Revenue Service, mediation involving the Appeals division of the IRS, and litigation before the United States Tax Court. Experienced in all aspects of international transfer pricing, including planning cross-border movement of tangible and intangible property, advance pricing agreements, Section 6662 documentation, and transfer pricing litigation. Other areas of substantive expertise include deductibility of interest expense relating to debt-versus-equity characterization, taxation of insurance, reinsurance and annuity contracts, acquisition-related issues including valuation of assets, and 'sham transaction' and 'economic substance' issues.
**Career:** Mayer, Brown, Rowe & Maw LLP, Chicago, 1989 to date.
**Publications:** Recent publications: 'Litigating Transfer Pricing Cases and Tax-Advantaged Transactions', co-author, Practicing Law Institute, 2001-04. 'Intercompany Debt-Equity Classification, Organization for International Investment', Sonoma, California, April 2004.
**Personal:** Harvard University School of Law, JD, 1989. Cornell University, MBA with distinction (accounting and finance), 1986. Creighton University, BS cum laude, 1984.

## STEWART, Terence P
Stewart & Stewart, Washington, DC
202 785 4185
*Recommended in International Trade*

## STOCK, Stuart C
Covington & Burling, Washington, DC
202 662 5384
sstock@cov.com
*Recommended in Financial Services*
**Practice Areas:** Represents financial institutions regarding governance matters, financial services regulation, regulatory enforcement, litigation, and mergers

and acquisitions.

**Career:** Law clerk, US Supreme Court Justice Marshall; and law clerk, Chief Judge Friendly, US Court of Appeals, Second Circuit.

**Publications:** 'Federal and State Regulation of Insurance after the Gramm-Leach-Bliley Act', The Review of Banking & Financial Services; 'Barnett Bank Opens New Opportunities for Banks', Int'l Financial Law Review 21; and 'The Reigle-Neal Interstate Banking and Branching Efficiency Act of 1994', 9J Int'l Banking Law 402.

**Personal:** BS in Engineering, with highest distinction, Purdue University; JD, magna cum laude, Harvard Law School.

### STOLL, R Ryan
Skadden, Arps, Slate, Meagher & Flom LLP & Affiliates, Chicago
312 407 0780
rstoll@skadden.com
*Recommended in Products Liability*
**Practice Areas:** Concentrates in complex litigation, complex torts defense, white-collar criminal defense and domestic and international arbitration. Has extensive trial and appellate experience and previously served in the office of the US Attorney for the Northern District of Illinois, where he handled a wide variety of cases, including complex racketeering, public corruption and fraud prosecutions. Has been involved in a number of significant civil litigation matters, including federal multidistrict proceedings and other complex state and federal litigations.
**Career:** JD, Harvard Law School, 1990 (editor, Harvard Law Review); MA, Stanford University, 1987; BA, Stanford University, 1987 (Phi Beta Kappa).

### STRICKLAND, Kathleen
Holland & Knight LLP, San Francisco
415 743 6900
kathleen.strickland@hklaw.com
*Recommended in Products Liability*
**Practice Areas:** Partner in the Litigation Section, practice focuses on complex litigation and mass torts. She has served as national trial counsel for mass litigation, such as asbestos litigation, breast implant litigation, drinking and groundwater litigation. She also handles class action litigation. Her mass tort litigation practice has included defending large multinational corporations in mass tort and 'putative class' cases involving hundreds of plaintiffs seeking to recover for personal injury, medical monitoring and punitive damages. She has tried to defense verdicts over 30 civil jury trials. She has authored 25 published articles on mass torts and complex litigation management.

### STRINGFELLOW, James S
Skadden, Arps, Slate, Meagher & Flom LLP & Affiliates, New York
212 735 3405

jstringf@skadden.com
*Recommended in Capital Markets*
**Practice Areas:** Represents issuers, underwriters, placement agents, lenders, agents, managers, investors and other participants in a variety of public and private structured finance transactions. Experience includes credit card, auto loan and other receivable securitizations; collateralized debt obligation issuances (including cash flow, market value, synthetic and hybrid type transactions) and other investment funds; commercial and residential mortgage loan securitizations; asset-backed commercial paper transactions; and resecuritizations and repackagings of various securities and other financial assets and derivative products.
**Career:** JD, New York University School of Law, 1987; AB, Columbia College, 1983.

### STROMFELD, Lary
Cadwalader, Wickersham & Taft LLP, New York 212 504 6291
lary.stromfeld@cwt.com
*Recommended in Capital Markets*
**Practice Areas:** Expertise in OTC fixed income products, credit derivatives, and municipal finance. Represents numerous commercial banks, bond insurers, derivative product companies, broker-dealers, hedge funds, and other financial institutions. Also advises The Bond Market Association and the International Swaps and Derivatives Association. Develops, negotiates and documents a wide variety of complex financial products. Extensively involved in developing and utilizing financial products in the primary and secondary municipal markets.
**Personal:** JD, University of Pennsylvania Law School (1981); BA, Brandeis University (1977). Credit Derivatives and General Documentation Committees of the International Swaps and Derivatives Association, Inc.; National Association of Bond Lawyers.

### SUGARMAN, Myron
Cooley Godward LLP, San Francisco
415 693 2000
*Recommended in Wealth Management*

### SUGERMAN, David L
Cleary Gottlieb Steen & Hamilton LLP, New York 212 225 2890
dsugerman@cgsh.com
*Recommended in Capital Markets*
**Practice Areas:** Corporate finance, securities offerings, domestic and international structured finance. Regularly advises investment and commercial banks on principal investment activities. Bank financing work for Morgan Stanley, Texas Pacific Group and Goldman Sachs. Collateralized debt obligations for Bank of America and Goldman Sachs. Numerous cross-border and domestic structured equity investments for Citigroup and other financial institutions.

**Career:** Joined firm, 1986; became Partner, 1994.
**Personal:** JD, New York University School of Law (1980); BA, Dartmouth College (1974).

### SULLIVAN, Diane P
Dechert LLP, Princeton
609 620 3200
*Recommended in Litigation, Products Liability*
*Please see New Jersey for profile*

### SWANICK, Christine L
Dorsey & Whitney LLP, Minneapolis
212 415 9315
swanick.christine@dorsey.com
*Recommended in Native American Law*
**Practice Areas:** Practices in the area of commercial financing and other credit transactions, including commercial loans, syndicated credit facilities and note purchase transactions. Also represents commercial lenders, investors and borrowers in connection with financings of Indian reservation infrastructure, economic development and other activities; and contractual, gaming, regulatory, and economic development matters.
**Career:** Prior to joining Dorsey, practiced as an 'on reservation' attorney for tribes in Michigan, Arizona and Colorado.
**Personal:** University of Arizona, James E Rogers College of Law (JD, 1995); Boston College (BA, 1990).

### SWEENEY III, James
Nicoletti Hornig Campise and Sweeney, New York 212 220 3830
*Recommended in Transportation*

### SWEET, William J
Skadden, Arps, Slate, Meagher & Flom LLP & Affiliates, Washington, DC
202 371 7030
wsweet@skadden.com
*Recommended in Financial Services*
**Practice Areas:** Focuses on financial institution merger and acquisition, regulatory and enforcement matters. Represents US and non-US banks, thrifts, insurance, securities and investment companies in connection with the acquisition of banks, savings and loan associations, savings banks, investment managers, securities firms, mutual funds, credit card issuers and other financial institutions. Counseled numerous non-US banking and investment banking clients engaged in various joint ventures with US financial institutions, especially in the securities, investment management, derivatives and leasing fields.
**Career:** JD, Georgetown University Law Center, 1978; BA, Bucknell University, 1974.

### SWENSON, David
Baker & McKenzie, Washington, DC
202 452 7011
c.david.swenson@bakernet.com
*Recommended in Tax Litigation*

**Practice Areas:** Mr Swenson has specialized in the domestic and international taxation of multinational corporations for more than 20 years. His practice involves corporate tax planning and tax controversies relating to domestic and international transactions, with focus on: organization of multinational corporate structures, including joint ventures, mergers, acquisitions, and divestitures; intercompany pricing; international tax planning involving Subpart F, Foreign Tax Credit, hybrid entities, derivative financial products, insurance matters, PFICs, foreign currency issues; competent authority matters; tax controversies; Advance Pricing Agreements; and implementation of global tax minimization strategies.
**Career:** Mr Swenson is a graduate of Georgetown University Law Center where he was associate editor of The Tax Lawyer and he is currently an Adjunct Professor, having taught international tax courses continuously since 1987. He has presented outlines and speeches at conferences sponsored by the University of Chicago, Georgetown University, George Washington University, the World Trade Institute, the Tax Executives Institute, the International Fiscal Association, the ABA, the DC Bar, and other institutes, associations, and universities. In addition, he has published numerous articles and papers on international tax issues.
**Personal:** BA and JD with honours, University of Mississippi, LLM, Taxation, Georgetown University Law Center. Mr Swenson is a Partner in the Washington, DC office of Baker & McKenzie, is Chairman of the Washington Office Tax Group, and is Chairman of the North American Transfer Pricing Practice Group. Mr Swenson has served as a Member of the firm's Worldwide Financial Committee, the North American Tax Group Management Committee, and the Washington Office Management Committee. Mr Swenson has served as Chairman of the Section 482 (Transfer Pricing) Subcommittee of the ABA Tax Section Committee on Foreign Activities of United States Taxpayers, Chairman of the International Tax Committee of the District of Columbia Bar, and Chairman of the International Tax and Finance Forum.

### TANENBAUM, William
Kaye Scholer LLP, New York
212 836 8000
*Recommended in Business Process Outsourcing, Technology*
*Please see New York for profile*

### TAYLOR, Jasper
Fulbright & Jaworski L.L.P., Houston
713 651 5151
*Recommended in Tax, Tax Litigation*
*Please see Texas for profile*

**TEHAN, John**
Simpson Thacher & Bartlett LLP, New
York 212 455 2000
jtehan@stblaw.com
*Recommended in Capital Markets*
**Practice Areas:** Corporate Partner at
Simpson Thacher & Bartlett LLP and
Chairman of the firm's Opinions Committee. Concentrates in corporate finance
advising both issuers and underwriters in
capital raising transactions with emphasis
on public and private high-yield financings and initial public offerings. Also designated by investment grade and other
corporate issuers to act as underwriters
counsel on an ongoing basis in connection with the offering by such issuers of
their debt and equity securities. Regularly
advises KKR and its portfolio companies
in connection with their high-yield debt
and initial public offerings. On the
underwriting side, primarily represents
Lehman Brothers, Credit Suisse, JP Morgan Chase, Merrill Lynch, Morgan Stanley and Goldman Sachs. Acts as underwriters counsel for corporate issuers such
as, Textron, MBNA Corporation, Halliburton Corporation, Georgia-Pacific
Corporation, The Ryland Group and
Owens-Illinois.
**Prof. Memberships:** Member of the Association of the Bar of the City of New York.
**Career:** Member of the firm since 1982.
Admitted to the New York Bar in 1974.
**Personal:** Received AB from LeMoyne
College in 1970 and JD from Catholic
University School of Law in 1973 where
he was the Recent Developments Editor
of The Catholic University Law Review
from 1972 to 1973.

**TENEV, Jovi**
Holland & Knight LLP, New York
212 513 3200
jovi.tenev@hklaw.com
*Recommended in Transportation*
**Practice Areas:** Partner in the firm's
Business Law Section. He has extensive
experience representing financial institutions, investment banks, foreign and
domestic companies, and airlines in a
wide variety of transactions. He practices
in all areas of corporate finance, including finance projects in the US and international aerospace, shipping, offshore
drilling and rail industries, utilizing complex syndicated loan, leveraged and single-investor leasing structures, and capital
markets. He has been involved in domestic and foreign mergers and acquisitions,
portfolio purchases, workouts, bankruptcies, restructurings, enforcement and
foreclosures, and in US regulatory proceedings.

**TESCHER, Donald**
Tescher Gutter Chaves Josepher Rubin
Ruffin & Forman PA, Boca Ratón
561 998 7847
*Recommended in Tax, Wealth
Management*

**TOLLEY III, Edward P**
Simpson Thacher & Bartlett LLP, New
York 212 455 3189
etolley@stblaw.com
*Recommended in Capital Markets*
**Practice Areas:** Partner in the Corporate Department. Represents several of
the country's largest private equity spon-
sors in connection with their securities
financing matters. Recent experience
includes representing sponsors in con-
nection with high-yield debt financings
and/or bridge financings for the acquisi-
tions of: the semi-conductor unit of Agi-
lent (KKR/Silver Lake); SunGard Data
Systems (seven member consortium);
Chart Industries (First Reserve); Team
Health (Blackstone); Foundation Coal
(Blackstone/First Reserve); Celanese
(Blackstone); Warner Music (T.H.
Lee/Bain/Providence) Ondeo Nalco
(Blackstone/Apollo); Houghton Mifflin
(T.H. Lee/Bain/Blackstone); and Sealy,
Wincor, Willis and Rockwood (KKR).
Equity experience includes representing
Dresser-Rand, Warner Music, Celanese,
Nalco, Alpha Natural Resources, Founda-
tion Coal, Premcor and Willis Group in
their IPOs and underwriters in various
IPOs, including the $8.6 billion IPO of
Kraft Foods in 2001.
**Career:** Joined Simpson Thacher 1990;
became Partner in January 1999.
**Personal:** BA, 1984, Dartmouth College
(Phi Beta Kappa, magna cum laude); JD,
1990, University of Virginia School of
Law.

**TORTORIELLO, Robert L**
Cleary Gottlieb Steen & Hamilton LLP,
New York 212 225 2390
rtortoriello@cgsh.com
*Recommended in Financial Services*
**Practice Areas:** Bank capital markets
and regulatory, securities and compliance
matters; financial institution mergers,
acquisitions, joint ventures and restructurings; derivative products; activity
expansion; and securities offerings. Regulatory counseling to US and foreign
banking organizations and industry participants concerning the Gramm-Leach-
Bliley Act, the Bank Holding Company
Act/Change in Bank Control Act, the
National Bank Act, the Glass-Steagall Act
and the International Banking Act.
**Career:** Joined firm, 1974; became Partner, 1982. JD, magna cum laude, Harvard
Law School (1974); BA, summa cum
laude, St. Peters College, New Jersey
(1971).
**Publications:** 'Guide to Bank Underwriting, Dealing and Brokerage Activities'
(Thomson LegalWorks, Tenth edition,
2005). 'The Federal Reserve Board's Pro-
posed Interpretation of the Anti-tying
Provisions of the Bank Holding Company Act Amendments of 1970' (Banking
Law Journal, 2003). 'Financial Modernization in the United States: the Gramm-
Leach-Bliley Act' (Journal of Internation-

al Financial Markets, 2000). Other scholarly and professional journals.

**TOWNSEND, John**
Hughes Hubbard & Reed LLP,
Washington, DC 202 721 4640
townsend@hugheshubbard.com
*Recommended in Arbitration,
International Arbitration*
**Practice Areas:** Partner; Chair, Arbitra-
tion and ADR Group. International dis-
putes; competition law.
**Prof. Memberships:** Board of Directors,
Chairman of Executive Committee,
American Arbitration Association;
Trustee, Arbitration and Competition
Law Committees, US Council for Inter-
national Business; Chair, Mediation
Committee, International Bar Associa-
tion; Challenge Review Board, CPR Insti-
tute for Dispute Resolution; American
Law Institute; College of Commercial
Arbitrators.
**Career:** Hughes Hubbard & Reed since
1971, New York, Paris and Washington.
Admitted New York 1972; District of
Columbia 1990.
**Publications:** Include 'Revised AAA-
ABA Code of Ethics for Arbitrators
Explained' (with Bruce Meyerson), Dis-
pute Resolution Journal, Feb/April 2004;
'Drafting Arbitration Clauses: Avoiding
the 7 Deadly Sins', Dispute Resolution
Journal, Feb/April 2003; 'Arbitration
Across the Civil Law – Common Law
Divide' (with Siegfried Elsing), Arbitra-
tion International, Feb 2002; 'The Case
for Site Licenses', ECLR, March 1999;
'Nonsignatories and Arbitration', ADR
Currents, Sept 1998.
**Personal:** Born 21 March, 1947. BA Yale
University 1968; JD Yale University 1971.
Fluent French.

**TRIGG, John**
Wheeler Trigg Kennedy LLP, Denver
303 292 2525
*Recommended in Products Liability*

**TROOBOFF, Peter D**
Covington & Burling, Washington, DC
202 662 5512
ptrooboff@cov.com
*Recommended in International Trade*
**Practice Areas:** Foreign investment,
foreign trade and export controls, foreign
trade sanctions, international investments, foreign assets control, and international litigation and arbitration.
**Career:** Counsel, Grand Duchy of Luxembourg, Whitehead v. Grand Duchy of
Luxembourg, et al, US District Court,
Eastern District of Virginia; arbitrator in
a claim before the International Centre
for the Settlement of Investment Disputes, Compañía de Aguas del Aconquija,
S.A. & Compagnie Générale des Eaux v.
Argentine Republic.
**Personal:** Harvard University (LLB, cum
laude); London School of Economics
(LLM); Hague Academy of International
Law, (Diploma, cum laude); Columbia

University (AB, cum laude); Institut d'
Études Européennes.

**TRUESDELL, Richard**
Davis Polk & Wardwell, New York
212 450 4000
richard.truesdell@dpw.com
*Recommended in Capital Markets*
**Practice Areas:** Member of Davis Polk
& Wardwell's Corporate Department.
Represents clients in US and international capital markets transactions and advises on corporate governance and securities
market regulation. Has extensive experience with a wide variety of both public
and private debt and equity offerings by
US and non-US issuers, including high-
yield debt financings, convertible offerings and initial public offerings.

**TURKUS, Albert H**
Skadden, Arps, Slate, Meagher & Flom
LLP & Affiliates, Washington, DC
202 371 7360
aturkus@skadden.com
*Recommended in Tax Litigation*
**Practice Areas:** Specializes in tax litigation and complex civil litigation. Extensive experience in trial of complex tax
matters in US Tax Court and District
Courts throughout the country, and in
appellate representation before the vari-
ous US Courts of Appeals. Trials have
included corporate tax matters, partner-
ship tax matters, and significant individ-
ual tax matters, including gift and estate
tax matters.
**Prof. Memberships:** Fellow, American
College of Trial Lawyers.
**Career:** JD, Harvard Law School, 1971;
BS in Economics, Wharton School of
Finance and Commerce, University of
Pennsylvania, 1967 (cum laude); assistant
United States attorney for the District of
Columbia, 1972-78.

**TUSSING, James D**
Fulbright & Jaworski L.L.P., New York
212 318 3024
jtussing@fulbright.com
*Recommended in Transportation*
**Practice Areas:** Aviation and equipment finance.
**Prof. Memberships:** Mr Tussing is the
Chairman of the Aircraft Financing Subcommittee of the American Bar Association. He joined the US Civil Aeronautics
Board in Washington, DC, in 1976 and
served as trial attorney and senior trial
attorney from 1977-82.
**Career:** James D Tussing is a Partner in
the New York office of Fulbright and
heads the firm's Equipment Finance
Practice Group. He has more than 30
years of experience in financing aircraft
and other equipment. He has been in private practice in New York since 1982.
From 1977 to 1982, he was with the US
Civil Aeronautics Board serving as trial
attorney and senior trial attorney.
**Personal:** BA, cum laude, Yale University
(1973); JD, Boston University School of

Law (1976). Mr Tussing is admitted to practice in Massachusetts, Washington, DC, and New York.

## UNGER, Timothy
Andrews Kurth LLP, Houston
713 220 4200
*Recommended in Energy, Projects*

## URDA KASSIS, Cynthia
Shearman & Sterling LLP, New York
212 848 4000
*Recommended in Projects*
*Please see New York for profile*

## UTLEY, Frederick
Clifford Chance US LLP, New York
212 878 8356
Frederick.Utley@cliffordchance.com
*Recommended in Capital Markets*
**Practice Areas:** Since founding the firm's US Structured Finance Group in the 1980s, Mr Utley has structured transactions involving nearly every type of security, mortgage and receivable securitized to date, both domestically and in cross-border markets. He represents leading financial guaranty insurers, issuers, underwriters and investment managers in ABS and MBS offerings. A pioneer in the development of CDOs and CMBS securities, he continues to be involved with new products such as private equity and insurance securitzations.
**Career:** Partner since 1987; Harvard Law School (JD); Cambridge University (BA, MA); Yale University (BA, magna cum laude).

## UTRECHT, Lyn
Ryan Phillips Utrecht & MacKinnon, Washington, DC 202 293 1177
*Recommended in Government: Political Law*

## VACKETTA, Carl Lee
DLA Piper Rudnick Gray Cary US LLP, Washington, DC
202 861 6460
carl.vacketta@dlapiper.com
*Recommended in Government Contracts*
**Practice Areas:** Government affairs; government contracts.
**Career:** He has more than 39 years of experience in government contracts law. He has represented companies selling information technology, telecommunications equipment, and professional and technical services to the government. He has also led teams of attorneys, accountants, and engineers in the investigation and preparation of multi-million dollar claims for major shipyards, aerospace, power generating, electronics, and telecommunication companies. He has in-depth experience in the General Services Administration's Multiple Award Schedule Contract (MASC) program.
**Personal:** JD, University of Illinois at Urbana-Champaign; BS, University of Illinois at Urbana-Champaign.

## VALENTE, Peter C
Blank Rome LLP, New York
212 885 5320
pvalente@blankrome.com
*Recommended in Wealth Management*
**Practice Areas:** Mr Valente concentrates his practice on estate planning, estate and trust administration and litigation pertaining to trusts and estates. He has extensive experience in preparing wills and trust agreements, the administration of estates and trusts, the settlement of trust accountings (many of which involved litigation) and judicial proceedings in the Surrogates' Courts of the State of New York. He has been appointed, on numerous occasions, by the Surrogates' Courts in New York City to act as guardian ad litem to protect the interests of persons under a disability in various court proceedings.
**Prof. Memberships:** Fellow, American College of Trust and Estate Counsel; Association of the Bar of the City of New York; New York State Bar Association; American Bar Association; New York County Lawyers' Association.
**Career:** Partner and Practice Group Leader, Private Client Group, Blank Rome LLP, 2003-present; formerly Co-Chair; Tax and Fiduciary Department, Blank Rome LLP and Chair, Trusts and Estates Department, Tenzer Greenblatt LLP.
**Publications:** Mr Valente co-authors the column 'Wills, Estates and Surrogate's Practice', which appears thrice yearly in the New York Law Journal.
**Personal:** New York University, Master of Laws; Columbia University School of Law, JD; Bowdoin College, BA, Phi Beta Kappa.

## VAN DER BELLEN, Alexander
Hogan & Hartson LLP, Washington, DC
202 637 5600
sascha.vanderbellen@hhlaw.com
*Recommended in Transportation*
**Practice Areas:** Airlines, airports and civic parties and aviation manufacturers on matters including DOT and FAA regulation and certification; international aviation policy and bilateral negotiations; contested route proceedings; antitrust, codesharing; air service development; airport rates and charges; noise regulation and environmental issues; enforcement actions; hazardous materials transportation; and FAA maintenance and airworthiness requirements. Negotiated numerous aircraft purchase and lease transactions, aircraft management agreements, and assists private jet operators and charter companies with compliance issues.
**Prof. Memberships:** ABA Forum on Air and Space Law, American Bar Association; Aircraft Owners and Pilots Association.
**Career:** Brings a pilot's perspective to the firm's Aviation Practice Group as a com-

mercial pilot, instrument flight instructor, and the owner-operator of a Grumman Tiger aircraft.
**Personal:** Tulane University School of Law (JD, 1994); Hamiltion College (BA, 1988).

## VAN GORP, Jon D
Mayer, Brown, Rowe & Maw LLP, Chicago 312 701 7091
jvangorp@mayerbrownrowe.com
*Recommended in Capital Markets*
**Practice Areas:** Concentrates on structured finance transactions, with an emphasis on asset-backed securities offerings in the capital markets. Experience securitizing virtually all types of financial assets, and is a recognized expert in the securitization of mortgage loans and auto receivables.
**Prof. Memberships:** New York, 2004. Illinois, 1998. Texas, 1994.
**Career:** Mayer, Brown, Rowe & Maw LLP, Chicago, 1997 to date; Partner, 2003. Thompson & Knight, LLP, associate, Dallas, 1994-97.
**Publications:** Recent articles: 'Securitizations After Securities Offering Reform', Journal of Structured Finance, Winter 2006 (co-author with Chris Horn); 'The Impact of Regulation AB on Auto Loan and Auto Lease Securitizations', Journal of Structured Finance, Spring 2005 (co-author with Chris Horn); 'Funding Mortgage Loans With Extendible Note Funding Facilities', Journal of Structured Finance, Fall 2004 (co-author with Laura Turnquest). Recent Presenations: 'IMN ABS West', Phoenix, Arizona, 2005, 2004, 2003. 'IMN ABS East', Boca Raton, Florida, 2004, 2005. 'Structured Finance Institute Introduction to Securitization Transactions', Chicago, Illinois, June and October 2004.
**Personal:** JD (cum laude), Southern Methodist University School of Law, 1994; staff editor, The International Lawyer. BA, Calvin College, 1991. Member, 2005 Leadership Greater Chicago Fellows Class.

## VARNER, Chilton
King & Spalding LLP, Atlanta
404 572 4600
*Recommended in Litigation, Products Liability*
*Please see Georgia for profile*

## VARTANIAN, Thomas
Fried, Frank, Harris, Shriver & Jacobson LLP, Washington, DC
202 639 7200
Thomas.Vartanian@FriedFrank.com
*Recommended in Financial Services*
**Practice Areas:** Chairman of Financial Institutions and Electronic Commerce Transactions Groups. Nationally recognized counselor, litigator, dealmaker and regulatory expert in financial services industry. Specializes in friendly and unsolicited mergers and acquisitions, bank enforcement, complex financial

crises and the regulation of government sponsored entities, failing bank scenarios, bank litigation, boardroom counseling, development and delivery of electronic network and payment systems.
**Career:** Joined Fried Frank in 1983 as a Partner. General Counsel, Federal Home Loan Bank Board and FSLIC (1981-83); special assistant to the Chief Counsel, Office of the Comptroller of the Currency (1978-81).

## VASQUEZ, Juan
Chamberlain, Hrdlicka, White, Williams & Martin, Houston 713 658 1818
*Recommended in Tax Litigation*

## VEBER, Jeffrey
Vedder, Price, Kaufman & Kammholz, New York 212 407 7700
*Recommended in Transportation*

## VERRILL JR, Charles Owen
Wiley Rein & Fielding LLP, Washington, DC 202 719 7323
cverrill@wrf.com
*Recommended in International Trade*
**Practice Areas:** Chairs the firm's International Trade Practice. Counsels clients on trade law and policy, including import and export regulation, import trade remedies, international bilateral and multilateral negotiations, international arbitration, mediation in commercial disputes and regulation of foreign investments. Represents clients before the International Trade Commission, the US Department of Commerce, the Court of International Trade and the US Court of Appeals for the Federal Circuit.
**Career:** Senior Lecturing Fellow, International Business Transactions, Duke University School of Law; Adjunct Professor, International Trade Law and Regulations, Georgetown University Law Center.
**Personal:** Duke University School of Law (JD); Tufts University (BA).

## VETA, D Jean
Covington & Burling, Washington, DC
202 662 5294
jveta@cov.com
*Recommended in Financial Services*
**Practice Areas:** Civil and regulatory enforcement matters, white-collar crime, corporate and congressional investigations, e-commerce, cybersecurity, and privacy issues. Provided congressional testimony on cyber-jurisdiction issues.
**Career:** Deputy associate attorney general, US DOJ; Deputy GC, US Dept of Education; and Co-Chair, Task Force on the Judiciary, ABA Section of Litigation. Law clerk, Hon Harold H Greene of the US District Court (DC). Member of the DC bar.
**Personal:** Tulane Law School (magna cum laude, Order of the Coif); Editor-in-Chief, Tulane Law Review; Thomas J Watson Fellowship award; and Tulane University Newcomb College (summa cum laude, Phi Beta Kappa, with honors).

## VILLA, John
Williams & Connolly LLP,
Washington, DC 202 434 5000
*Recommended in Financial Services,
Litigation*

## VILLANI, Robert A
Thacher Proffitt & Wood LLP, New York
212 912 7817
rvillani@tpw.com
*Recommended in Capital Markets*
**Practice Areas:** Robert Villani concentrates his structured finance practice in structured products, derivatives and asset-backed securitization, with a primary focus on: collateralized debt obligations backed by bonds, loans, asset-backed and real estate securities and real estate loans, synthetic CDOs and other risk transfer products, securitizations of loans and leases backed by automobiles, equipment and other vehicles and trade and healthcare receivable securitization. Mr Villani has represented various investment banking firms as issuers and underwriters, as well as other issuers, investors, bond insurers, collateral managers and asset-backed commercial paper conduits.
**Career:** Mr Villani has lectured at the American Bar Association, Strategic Research Institute, International Management Network, American College of Investment Counsel and Capital Markets Credit Analyst conferences. He received his JD in 1989 from the University of California, Los Angeles School of Law, and his BS, magna cum laude, in 1986 from the Wharton School of the University of Pennsylvania.
**Publications:** 'The Impact of Regulation AB and Securities Offering Reform on US Public ABS', Global Securitization and Structured Finance 2005 (May 01, 2005).

## VOGE, William
Latham & Watkins LLP, New York
212 906 1200
*Recommended in Projects*

## VON MEHREN, George M
Squire, Sanders & Dempsey LLP,
Cleveland 216 479 8614
gvonmehren@ssd.com
*Recommended in International
Arbitration*
**Practice Areas:** Partner and co-leader of the firm's international Dispute Resolution Practice Group with an established record of working with counsel in Europe and Asia. More than 25 years experience in complex international commercial arbitration and litigation. Arbitration caseload involves representing clients with multi-million to multi-billion US dollar damage claims. Experienced in World Bank debarment and arbitration based on bilateral and multilateral investment treaty claims. Named in 'Who's Who in America'. Frequent commentator on arbitration-related topics.
**Prof. Memberships:** International

Chamber of Commerce Task Force Amiable Composition and Ex Aequo et Bono principles in International Arbitration.

## VON MEHREN, Robert
Robert B von Mehren - Sole Practitioner,
New York
212 909 6588
*Recommended in Arbitration*

## VOORHEES JR, Theodore
Covington & Burling, Washington, DC
202 662 5236
tvoorhees@cov.com
*Recommended in Products Liability*
**Practice Areas:** Partner, Chair of Product Liability and Toxic Tort Practice Group. Represents clients in software, mining, medical devices, construction equipment, pharmaceutical, chemical, food, and beverage alcohol industries. Serves or has served as national coordinating counsel for clients involved in mass tort litigation over chemical exposures, welding fumes exposures, alcohol products and hip implants. Clients include: Air Products & Chemicals Co., American Welding Society, American Chemistry Council, Distilled Spirits Council and The Toxicology Forum.
**Personal:** Ted received his AB Degree in 1971 from Harvard University and his JD Degree in 1974 from Catholic University.

## WACHSBERGER, Chaim
Chadbourne & Parke LLP, New York
212 408 5100
*Recommended in Projects
Please see New York for profile*

## WAGNER, Theodore
Carter Ledyard & Milburn LLP, New York
212 732 3200
*Recommended in Wealth
Management*

## WAINER, David
Allen & Overy LLP, New York
212 610 6380
david.wainer@allenovery.com
*Recommended in Capital Markets*
**Practice Areas:** US and UK qualified, Head of New York's Capital Markets Practice, who specializes in a broad range of derivatives, CDOs and other structured products. He advised on balance-sheet CLO transactions for the Japanese 'mega-banks' while based in the Tokyo office, and more recently led the team on the development of the North American credit derivatives indexed products.
**Career:** Joined Allen & Overy LLP in 1993 as an associate. Partner since 2000.
**Personal:** The College of Law, Chancery Lane, London (1991); London School of Economics and Political Science (LLB, honors, 1990).

## WAJERT, Sean P
Dechert LLP, Philadelphia
215 994 2387
sean.wajert@dechert.com
*Recommended in Products Liability*

**Practice Areas:** Mr Wajert, a Partner, chairs the Mass Torts and Product Liability Group. He advises clients in the pharmaceutical and chemical industries, among others, on product liability and toxic tort matters.
**Prof. Memberships:** Member, Pennsylvania Bar; admitted to practice before US Court of Appeals, Third Circuit, and US District Court, EDPA; member, Defense Research Institute.
**Career:** Lecturer, University of Pennsylvania Law School, (1990-2000); clerkship, Honorable Arlin M Adams, US Court of Appeals, Third Circuit.
**Publications:** Frequent author on litigation topics.
**Personal:** Harvard University, AB, magna cum laude, 1981; University of Pennsylvania Law School, JD, cum laude, 1984.

## WALKER, John
Simpson Thacher & Bartlett LLP, New York 212 455 2000
jwalker@stblaw.com
*Recommended in Financial Services*
**Practice Areas:** Simpson Thacher Partner practicing banking and corporate law. Represents domestic and foreign commercial banks, investment banks and private equity firms, including JP Morgan Chase, Toronto-Dominion Bank, Mizuho Financial Group, Greenwich Capital Markets and Shinsei Bank. Practice also focuses on the convergence of commercial banking and investment banking businesses and the consolidation of financial institutions. Advises financial institutions regarding banking law and regulatory matters, including with respect to merchant banking, capital, securitization and insolvency issues.
**Prof. Memberships:** Association of the Bar of the City of New York (past Chairman, Banking Law Committee); Committee of Counsel of The Clearing House; Institute of International Bankers. Member, Council on Foreign Relations. Vice Chairman of Financial Services Volunteer Corps, a not-for-profit organization that channels expertise of financial sector professionals to assist in strengthening the financial infrastructure in transition and developing countries.
**Career:** Joined firm in 1979 and became Partner in 1984. Early in career, attorney at the Board of Governors of the Federal Reserve System.
**Publications:** Include 'Guiding Principles and Core Requirements for a Legal System in a Market Economy' (Aspen Institute).
**Personal:** JD, Duke Law School, 1977.

## WALKOWIAK, Vincent
Fulbright & Jaworski L.L.P., Dallas
214 855 8037
vwalkowiak@fulbright.com
*Recommended in Products Liability*
**Practice Areas:** Product liability; litiga-

tion; class actions.
**Prof. Memberships:** American Bar Association; State Bar of Texas; College State Bar of Texas.
**Career:** Admitted to practice in Texas, US Court of Appeals (Fifth Circuit), US District Courts (Northern, Southern, Eastern and Western Districts of Texas). Vincent co-heads Fulbright & Jaworski L.L.P's Product Liability Litigation Practice Group, which is comprised of more than 50 attorneys in seven offices.
**Publications:** 'Preserving Corporate Privilege Takes Planning', The National Law Journal, April 25, 2005; Attorney Client Privilege in Civil Litigation (ABA 2004).

## WALL, Christopher
Pillsbury Winthrop Shaw Pittman LLP,
Washington, DC 202 775 9850
cwall@pillsburylaw.com
*Recommended in International Trade*
**Practice Areas:** Mr Wall is the firm's senior international trade Partner. His practice focuses on export controls, foreign investment, international trade proceedings and policy. He advises clients on commercial and military export licensing and enforcement; economic sanctions; national security reviews; anti-boycott compliance and enforcement; the Foreign Corrupt Practices Act; import relief proceedings and appeals; market access; bilateral investment treaties; complex customs matters; and trade policy and legislation. Mr Wall has extensive NAFTA and WTO dispute resolution experience.
**Personal:** BA, Yale College, 1974 (summa cum laude, Phi Beta Kappa); BA, Oxford University, 1976; JD, University of Virginia Law School, 1979.

## WALLACE, John A
King & Spalding LLP, Atlanta
404 572 4932
jwallace@kslaw.com
*Recommended in Wealth
Management*
**Practice Areas:** Tax concentrating in trusts and estates.
**Prof. Memberships:** American Bar Association (Council Member, 1980- and Chair, 1992-93, Real Property, Probate and Trust Section); American Bar Foundation; American College of Tax Counsel.
**Personal:** AB, Princeton University, 1960; JAW, Harvard Law School, 1963.

## WARD, Bradford L
Dewey Ballantine LLP, Washington, DC
202 429 2342
bward@deweyballantine.com
*Recommended in International Trade*
**Practice Areas:** Bradford Ward has specialized in international trade law and particularly anti-dumping matters since 1984. His recent activities have included litigation before NAFTA panels, advising the US government in WTO litigation, management of numerous anti-dumping proceedings before US government agen-

cies, litigation before the US Court of International Trade, preparation of extensive antidumping, analyses for use during consideration of the Uruguay Round Agreements Act and implementing regulations, and client counseling regarding business negotiations and public and political relations.
**Career:** Partner, Dewey Ballantine LLP.
**Personal:** BS, University of Oregon, 1980. JD, American University, 1983.

## WASSERMAN, Craig
Wachtell, Lipton, Rosen & Katz, New York 212 403 1000
*Recommended in Corporate/M&A, Financial Services*
*Please see New York for profile*

## WATTERSON, Paul N
Schulte Roth & Zabel LLP, New York 212 756 2563
paul.watterson@srz.com
*Recommended in Capital Markets*
**Practice Areas:** Collateralized debt obligation and other securitization transactions, derivative products and capital markets regulation.
**Prof. Memberships:** Association of the Bar of the City of New York.
**Career:** Schulte Roth & Zabel; law clerk to Judge Leonard I Garth, US Court of Appeals, Third Circut; assistant to the Mayor of the City of New York; Chase Manhattan Bank, London and New York.
**Publications:** Has written extensively on capital markets, structured products and derivatives. Served as an editor of the Harvard Law Review.
**Personal:** Harvard Law School, JD, magna cum laude; Princeton University, AB, cum laude.

## WAXENBERG, Jay D
Proskauer Rose LLP, New York 212 969 3606
jwaxenberg@proskauer.com
*Recommended in Wealth Management*
**Practice Areas:** He has been with the Proskauer Rose LLP Personal Planning Department since 1984 and is currently Chair of the Department. He is on the firm's Policy Committee and is a former member of the firm's Executive Committee. The focus of his practice is estate and tax planning and estate and trust administration. He is involved in the full range of his clients' economic and personal concerns including closely held businesses, real estate holdings, artistic collections and philanthropy. He has been involved in will contests and other estate- and trust-related litigations. In addition, he has handled family matters such as the preparation of prenuptial agreements. He regularly counsels individuals concerning charitable giving and advises private foundations and public charities on tax issues.
**Prof. Memberships:** Fellow, American College of Trust and Estate Counsel; list-

ed in Best Lawyers in America; Committee on Estate and Gift Taxation of the Association of the Bar of the City of New York (Past Chair); Committee on Estate Planning – New York State Bar Association; Trusts and Estates Committee, UJA-Federation of New York (past Chair); Member, Planned Giving Advisory Committees of Columbia University Health Sciences, Museum of Modern Art, New York-Presbyterian Hospital, New York Public Library and Memorial Sloan-Kettering Cancer Center.
**Publications:** Has written and lectured extensively on estate planning topics. He is regularly quoted in publications.
**Personal:** New York University School of Law (LLM in Taxation, 1987); Boston University School of Law (JD, 1981); State University of New York at Stony Brook (BA, 1978).

## WEBB, Dan
Winston & Strawn LLP, Chicago 312 558 5600
*Recommended in Litigation, Products Liability*

## WEBSTER, Robert
Pillsbury Winthrop Shaw Pittman LLP, New York 212 858 1303
Robert.Webster@pillsburylaw.com
*Recommended in Financial Services*
**Practice Areas:** Represents financial institutions in the US, Europe and Asia with particular emphasis on the effect of governmental regulation on both the ordinary conduct of their business and their acquisition and new product development activities. Advises clients on diverse governmental actions, such as capital adequacy directives, restrictions on geographic and functional expansion, and anti-money laundering initiatives and sanctions in response to international crises; and represents clients subject to supervisory examinations and compliance proceedings.
**Personal:** LLB, Harvard Law School, 1962 (cum laude); AB, Colgate University, 1959 (magna cum laude; Phi Beta Kappa).

## WEERASINGHE, Rohan
Shearman & Sterling LLP, New York 212 848 7088
rweerasinghe@shearman.com
*Recommended in Capital Markets*
**Practice Areas:** Shearman & Sterling's Senior Partner. Practices in Capital Markets Group. Specializes in corporate and securities law. Regularly represents both underwriters and issuers in public offering transactions, especially complex transactions such as those involving leveraged buyouts, high-yield debt issuances, initial public offerings and cross-border offerings.
**Prof. Memberships:** Member, New York State Bar Association.
**Career:** Joined Shearman in 1977 and became Partner in 1985.

**Personal:** BA, summa cum laude, Harvard College (1972); MBA, Baker Scholar, Harvard Business School (1977); JD, Harvard Law School (1977).

## WEINER, Daniel H
Hughes Hubbard & Reed LLP, New York 212 837 6874
weiner@hugheshubbard.com
*Recommended in International Arbitration*
**Practice Areas:** Partner, New York. Concentrates on international and domestic arbitration and litigation. Dan has served as counsel in numerous arbitrations under ICC and AAA rules including matters involving joint ventures, licensing and other contractual disputes.
**Career:** Partner since 1993. Admitted in New York 1985. Deputy Special Counsel, United States Senate Judiciary Committee, Subcommittee on Terrorism, Technology and Government Information, Fall 1995-Summer 1996.
**Personal:** Born January 20, 1960. Princeton University AB cum laude 1981; New York University JD 1984.

## WEINER, Robert N
Arnold & Porter LLP, Washington, DC 202 942 5855
Robert.Weiner@aporter.com
*Recommended in Products Liability*
**Practice Areas:** Robert Weiner is Head of the Business Litigation Group at Arnold & Porter in Washington, DC. He has experience as a trial lawyer and appellate advocate in criminal and civil cases. He has served as national counsel in product liability and toxic tort cases involving, among other things, diet drugs, heart valves, pharmaceutical products, and lead paint. He has also represented clients in high profile Congressional investigations and regulatory inquiries. He is uniquely positioned to handle problems spanning multiple forums.
**Prof. Memberships:** Mr Weiner is a Member of the American Law Institute and the Product Liability Advisory Council (PLAC). He was President of the District of Columbia Bar and, before that, General Counsel of the Bar. Currently President of the DC Bar Foundation, he has served on many charitable boards and received numerous awards for public service.
**Career:** In 1997-98, Mr Weiner was Senior Counsel in the White House Counsel's Office. In that position, he handled the legal aspects of major policy issues confronting the nation, including civil rights, privacy, financial reform, bankruptcy, telecommunications, and the internet. In the mid-1980s, he served as an Associate Independent Counsel. Mr Weiner clerked for Judge Henry Friendly of the Second Circuit Court of Appeals and Supreme Court Justice Thurgood

Marshall. He has taught Mass Torts at the University of Virginia School of Law and Complex Criminal Litigation at the Georgetown University Legal Center.
**Personal:** Mr Weiner is ranked in International 'Who's Who of Leading Product Liability Defense Lawyers for 2006; Who's Who in American Law'; 'The Best Lawyers in America 2005-06' (Commercial Litigation); Legal Media Group's Expert Guide's 'Guide to the Leading United States Litigation Lawyers 2005'; 'Who's Who Legal – The International Who's Who of Business Lawyers 2005'; and Washingtonian Magazine, Top Lawyers in DC.

## WEISBURG, Henry
Shearman & Sterling LLP, New York 212 848 4193
hweisburg@shearman.com
*Recommended in International Arbitration*
**Practice Areas:** Partner at Shearman & Sterling specializing in international arbitration and litigation, particularly in the area of international financial, investment and insolvency disputes; also active in handling complex international insurance matters, particularly involving political risk insurance.
**Prof. Memberships:** Member of the Committee on International Commercial Dispute Resolution, the Association of the Bar of the City of New York; Member of the American Bar Association; Member of the American Society of International Law.
**Career:** Joined Shearman in 1977 and became Partner in 1986.
**Personal:** BA, Trinity College (1973); JD, New York University School of Law (1977).

## WEISS, Harry J
WilmerHale, Washington, DC 202 663 6000
*Recommended in Financial Services, Securities*
*Please see District of Columbia for profile*

## WELCH, Lyman W
Sidley Austin LLP, Chicago 312 853 4165
lwelch@sidley.com
*Recommended in Wealth Management*
**Practice Areas:** Partner in the Chicago office who concentrates in all phases of trust and estate work, with special interests in advanced estate planning techniques, estate planning for executive and family business owners. He serves as counsel to bank trust departments, closely held corporations and charitable organizations.
**Prof. Memberships:** Advisor to the Restatement of the Law of Trusts project of the American Law Institute, Fellow of the American College of Trust and Estate Counsel, Member of the American Bar

Association's Federal Tax Section Committee on Fiduciary Income Tax and the Committee on Partnerships.

**Publications:** Among his publications are 'New Alternatives in Trust Design: How to Structure Beneficial Ownership and Trusteeship for Intergenerational Wealth', FOX CEO Forum (2003); 'When and How to Use a Total Return Trust', CPA Estate and Gift Tax Conference (2003); 'Implementing the New Total Return Trust Law', Illinois Institute for Continuing Legal Education (2003); 'Implementing Sophisticated Trust and Tax Structures'.

**Personal:** Harvard Law School, JD, 1967; Knox College, BA, (1964). Admissions: US Tax Court, 1976, Florida, 1978, Illinois, 1968.

## WELTMAN, Edward S
Goodwin Procter LLP, New York
212 813 8800
eweltman@goodwinprocter.com
*Recommended in Products Liability*

**Practice Areas:** Mr Weltman specializes in the areas of products liability, toxic torts and environmental law, with a particular emphasis in pharmaceutical products and medical devices. He has been involved, both as company counsel and as insurer-appointed counsel, in some of the nation's largest litigated mass tort controversies. Mr Weltman has served as National Counsel in the 'Fen-Phen' litigation, as well as court-appointed Lead Counsel for the group of phentermine defendants in the federal Diet Drugs multidistrict litigation (MDL).

**Prof. Memberships:** International Association of Defense Counsel: Member; The National Judicial College: Member.

**Personal:** JD, Washington University School of Law; BA, Brandeis University (cum laude).

## WEST, Joseph D
Gibson, Dunn & Crutcher LLP,
Washington, DC 202 955 8500
*Recommended in Construction,*
*Government Contracts*
*Please see District of Columbia for*
*profile*

## WESTERBERG, Gary
Lord, Bissell & Brook, Chicago
312 443 0700
*Recommended in Transportation*

## WHALEN, Thomas
Carter Ledyard & Milburn LLP, New York
212 732 3200
*Recommended in Transportation*

## WHEELER, Malcolm
Wheeler Trigg Kennedy LLP, Denver
303 292 2525
*Recommended in Litigation, Products*
*Liability*

## WHELAN III, William J
Cravath, Swaine & Moore LLP, New York
212 474 1644
wwhelan@cravath.com
*Recommended in Capital Markets*

**Practice Areas:** High-yield offerings, initial public offerings and follow-on equity offerings. Managing Partner, administration.

**Prof. Memberships:** ABA (Negotiated Covenant Task Force of the Trust Indenture Subcommittee); ABCNY (Securities Regulation Committee).

**Career:** Partner since 1998. Clerkship: Hon William H Timbers (US Court of Appeals for the Second Circuit). Head of Cravath's internal continuing legal education program for corporate lawyers, 1998-2005.

**Publications:** Chair, 'Securities Offerings 2006: Operating Under the New Rules', Practising Law Institute, April 2006.

**Personal:** Fordham University School of Law (JD, cum laude, 1983; managing editor, Fordham Law Review); University of Virginia (BA, with distinction, 1980).

## WHITAKER, G Warren
Day, Berry & Howard LLP, New York
212 829 3602
gwwhitaker@dbh.com
*Recommended in Wealth*
*Management*

**Practice Areas:** International trust and estate planning, business succession planning, estate planning, estate administration, planning for entrepreneurs, representation of fiduciaries, tax-exempt organizations and charitable giving, trust services, international tax.

**Prof. Memberships:** Member of the American College of Trusts and Estates Counsel (ACTEC) and its International Estate Planning Committee; Chair of the New York Branch of the UK-based Society of Trusts and Estates Practitioners (STEP); Member of the Estate and Gift Tax Committee of the Association of the Bar of the City of New York.

## WHITE, Debra
Milbank, Tweed, Hadley & McCloy LLP,
Washington, DC 202 835 7500
*Recommended in Business Process*
*Outsourcing, Technology*

## WHITE III, Fred B
Skadden, Arps, Slate, Meagher & Flom LLP & Affiliates, New York
212 735 2144
fwhite@skadden.com
*Recommended in Financial Services*

**Practice Areas:** Partner, New York. Co-Head, Skadden's financial institutions M&A Practice. Represents bank holding companies, commercial banks, acquirers, investors, savings and loan associations, savings banks, consumer finance companies, mortgage banking companies and related services entities. Advises numerous investment banking firms concerning regulatory issues, mergers and acquisitions and public offerings. Represents various institutions before federal banking agencies and consults with major corporations concerning investments in financial institutions and new products in the financial services industry.

**Prof. Memberships:** Admitted in New York, Delaware, DC, Massachusetts and New Jersey.

**Personal:** JD, The George Washington University National Law Center, 1972 (with honours); BA, Wheaton College, 1969.

## WILLIAMS, B John
Shearman & Sterling, Washington, DC
202 508 8150
bjwilliams@shearman.com
*Recommended in Tax Litigation*

**Practice Areas:** Partner, Shearman & Sterling's Tax Group. Represents clients in Internal Revenue Service examinations and appeals and before federal trial and appeals courts in tax litigation.

**Prof. Memberships:** American College of Tax Counsel, American Law Institute, American Bar Association's Tax Section.

**Career:** Rejoined Shearman after 18 months as Chief Counsel for the IRS. Formerly a Judge of the US Tax Court, Deputy Assistant Attorney General in the Tax Division of the Justice Department and Special Assistant to Chief Counsel of the IRS.

**Personal:** BA with honors, George Washington University (1971); JD with distinction, George Washington University Law School (1974).

## WILLIAMS JR, William J
Sullivan & Cromwell LLP, New York
212 558 3722
williamsw@sullcrom.com
*Recommended in Capital Markets*

**Practice Areas:** Extensive experience in international securities offerings by European, Japanese and Latin American issuers. Helped to develop SEC Regulation S, Rule 15a-6, Regulation M, and Securities Act public offering reforms. Represented SIA in SEC's consideration of fixed price offerings, shelf registration, Securities Act Concept Release, 'Aircraft Carrier' and Regulation FD.

**Prof. Memberships:** Member, NYSE Legal Advisory Committee; Chair, Task Force on Review of the Federal Securities Laws, Federal Regulation of Securities Committee, ABA; former Member, NASD Legal Advisory Board.

**Career:** Partner since 1969. Of Counsel since 2005.

**Personal:** College of Holy Cross (AB, 1958); NYU Law School (LLB, 1961).

## WILLIAMSON, Joel
Mayer, Brown, Rowe & Maw LLP,
Chicago 312 782 0600
*Recommended in Tax, Tax Litigation*
*Please see Illinois for profile*

## WILSON, Bruce S
Covington & Burling, Washington, DC
202 662 5400
bwilson@cov.com
*Recommended in Sport*

**Practice Areas:** Practice includes corporate finance, mergers, acquisitions, and licensing transactions. He advises all of the major US sports leagues, including the NFL, NHL, NBA, and NASCAR on acquisitions, over-the-air and digital media development and licensing, entity structures, corporate governance, finance, and securities matters.

**Career:** Joined Covington in 1987. 1993-97, General Counsel, Bacardi Limited. 1986-87, law clerk to Judge Pasco M Bowman, US Court of Appeals for the Eighth Circuit. 1981-83, legislative assistant to Rep Steven L Neal, US House of Representatives.

**Personal:** University of Virginia, JD, (1986), Order of the Coif; BA (1981), Phi Beta Kappa.

## WIPPERMAN, Robert
McKee Nelson LLP, New York
917 777 4600
rwipperman@mckeenelson.com
*Recommended in Capital Markets*

**Practice Areas:** Since 1986 has concentrated exclusively in structured finance transactions. Represents originators, servicers, issuers, purchasers, and underwriters in public offerings and private placements of mortgaged-backed and asset-backed securities, as well as originators in both on-balance-sheet and off-balance sheet warehouse arrangements. Established and maintained securitization programs for several issuers. Is experienced in prime and subprime residential mortgage loans; home equity lines of credit; auto loan receivables; manufactured housing contracts; and agricultural loans.

**Career:** Heads the firm's Structured Finance Group. Prior to joining McKee Nelson, was a Partner at Stroock & Stroock & Lavan LLP.

**Personal:** JD, Boston College Law School, 1979.

## WISEMAN, Michael M
Sullivan & Cromwell LLP, New York
212 558 4000
wisemanm@sullcrom.com
*Recommended in Financial Services*

**Practice Areas:** Specialises in banking and financial institutions law, representing domestic and foreign commercial banks, investment banks and insurance companies. Practice encompasses regulatory and enforcement issues, mergers and acquisitions, capital markets, new products initiatives, derivative products, payment system issues, and corporate governance and counseling.

**Prof. Memberships:** ABA; ABCNY (former Chair, Banking Law Committee); NYSBA (Banking Law Committee); ABF;

ALI.

**Career:** Partner since 1985. Managing Partner, Financial Institutions Group.
**Personal:** Harvard College (AB, 1975); Harvard Law School (JD, 1978; editor, Harvard Law Review).

### WOLF, Charles
Vedder, Price, Kaufman & Kammholz, Chicago 312 609 7500
*Recommended in Employment, ERISA Litigation*

### WOLFE, Gary
Seward & Kissel LLP, New York
212 574 1223
wolfe@sewkis.com
*Recommended in Transportation*
**Practice Areas:** Securities, capital markets, corporate finance, shipping and environmental, cross-border transactions and maritime lease finance.
**Prof. Memberships:** Association of the Bar of the City of New York (Admiralty Committee); New York County Lawyers Association (former Chairman, Maritime Law Committee); US Business Council for Southeastern Europe (former President).
**Career:** Mr Wolfe specializes in corporate securities and capital market transactions. He represents foreign and domestic issuers and investment banks and money managers in mergers and acquisitions, joint ventures, commercial transactions, private placements, initial and secondary United States and offshore public offerings and consent solicitations, domestic and foreign lenders in United States based financings, and investors and issuers in restructurings to limit environmental liability risk. Mr Wolfe has acted as counsel to issuers and underwriters in groundbreaking offerings by companies in the international transportation industry, involving structured transactions, equity offerings, debt placements and finance leases, global listings, publicly traded warrants, passive foreign investment companies and establishment and termination of American Depositary Receipt programs.

**Personal:** Mr Wolfe received an AB Degree from Cornell University in 1971, Phi Beta Kappa, and a JD Degree in 1975 from Yale Law School. He was a Post-Doctoral Fulbright Scholar at the University of Ljubljana and University of Belgrade and was a recipient of an IREX Fellowship. His languages are English, Croatian, Slovenian, Russian and French.

### WOLFE, Scott
Latham & Watkins LLP, San Diego
619 236 1234
*Recommended in Capital Markets*

### WOLFF, Alan Wm
Dewey Ballantine LLP, Washington, DC
202 429 2352
awolff@deweyballantine.com
*Recommended in International Trade*
**Practice Areas:** Alan Wolff is a member of Dewey Ballantine's Management Committee and Managing Partner of the firm's Washington, DC office. He also leads Dewey Ballantine's International Trade Practice Group.
**Career:** Partner, Dewey Ballantine LLP. Mr Wolff served as United States Deputy Special Representative for Trade Negotiations (1977-79) in the Carter Administration, holding the rank of ambassador, after having served as General Counsel of the agency from 1974-77.
**Personal:** BA, Harvard College, 1963. LL.B, Columbia Law School, 1966.

### WOODS, John
Thacher Proffitt & Wood LLP, New York
212 912 7672
jwoods@tpw.com
*Recommended in Transportation*
**Practice Areas:** John Woods concentrates his practice in maritime law and insurance and reinsurance litigation and arbitration. He principally represents US and foreign insurers (and their assureds) in the areas of maritime hull, liability, cargo, pollution, war risk, loss of earnings, general average and environmental law. His practice also includes arbitration and mediation of maritime disputes, handling of offshore and onshore energy claims and losses, and review and advis-

ing on shipbuilding contracts and related disputes. Mr Woods has handled litigations involving major maritime casualties and claims in courts across the United States, and has counseled clients involved in litigations in foreign courts, principally in Europe. He has argued appeals in the New York appellate courts (including the New York Court of Appeals) and five of the US Courts of Appeal.
**Prof. Memberships:** Association of the Bar of the City of New York; American Bar Association; and Maritime Law Association: member of the Board of Directors, Chair of the Hull and P&I Insurance Subcommittee, Marine Insurance Committee.
**Publications:** Mr Woods was the author of 'Third-Party Liability Under OPA 90: Have the Courts Veered Off Course?', published in 73 Tul L Rev 1863 (May/June, 1999). He has also been a contributing editor to chapters in two standard texts: the 'Marine Insurance' chapter of Business Insurance Guide; and the 'Pollution by Recreational Craft' chapter in Recreational Boating Law, published in Benedict on Admiralty.

### ZABEL, William
Schulte Roth & Zabel LLP, New York
212 756 2000
*Recommended in Wealth Management*

### ZAHLER, Robert
Pillsbury Winthrop Shaw Pittman LLP, Washington, DC 202 663 8000
*Recommended in Business Process Outsourcing, Technology*
*Please see District of Columbia for profile*

### ZAROV, Herbert
Mayer, Brown, Rowe & Maw LLP, Chicago 312 782 0600
*Recommended in Litigation, Products Liability*
*Please see Illinois for profile*

### ZIMROTH, Peter L
Arnold & Porter LLP, New York
212 715 1010
Peter.Zimroth@aporter.com
*Recommended in Products Liability*
**Practice Areas:** Peter Zimroth, a Senior Partner in the New York office of Arnold & Porter, serves as the Lead National Counsel for the defendant pharmaceutical manufacturer in In Re Diet Drugs Products Liability Litigation, (MDL No. 1203). He is a recognized leading litigator in products liability, civil, commercial, securities and white-collar crime matters. He has tried jury and non-jury cases and arbitrations, argued appeals (including in the United States Supreme Court), and represented clients before regulatory and other government agencies, congressional committees (eg Whitewater), and disciplinary panels.
**Career:** Prior to joining Arnold & Porter, he served as an Assistant United States Attorney for the Southern District of New York (securities fraud unit), as the Chief Assistant District Attorney in Manhattan, and as the Corporation Counsel of the City of New York, where he supervised major litigations and provided counsel on employment issues, major economic development projects, city contract and procurement policies, environmental issues, tort and product liability and legislation.
**Publications:** He has been published on a wide variety of subjects in the Yale Law Journal, The New York Times and The New York Law Journal and is the author of 'Perversions of Justice', published by the Viking Press.
**Personal:** Mr Zimroth is ranked in the International Who's Who of Leading Product Liability Defense Lawyers for 2006.

STATE BY STATE

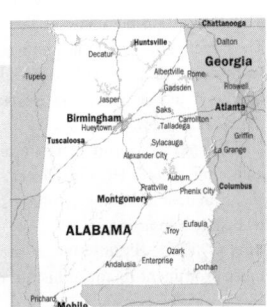

## How lawyers are ranked

Every year we carry out thousands of in-depth interviews with clients and lawyers in order to assess the reputations and expertise of business lawyers across the USA. Chambers rankings and editorial are referred to extensively by General Counsel and other purchasers of legal services who look to our recommendations when choosing their lawyers.

# BANKING & FINANCE

| Banking & Finance |
| --- |
| Leading Firms |
| 1 BALCH & BINGHAM *Birmingham* |
| BRADLEY ARANT ROSE & WHITE LLP *Birmingham* |
| 2 BURR & FORMAN LLP *Birmingham* |
| MILLER HAMILTON SNIDER & ODOM LLC *Mobile* |
| 3 ADAMS AND REESE LLP *Birmingham* |
| JOHNSTON BARTON PROCTOR *Birmingham* |
| MAYNARD, COOPER & GALE, P.C. *Birmingham* |

| Leading Individuals |
| --- |
| 1 COMPTON Paul *Bradley Arant Rose* |
| VINSON Laurence *Bradley Arant Rose* |
| 2 BAINS Kay *Bradley Arant Rose* |
| DRESHER David *Bradley Arant Rose* |
| GIBBENS Ray *Burr & Forman LLP* |
| JONES Haskins *Johnston Barton Proctor* |
| MILLER JR John *Miller Hamilton Snider* |
| MILLS Gail *Burr & Forman LLP* |
| MIXSON Dwight *Burr & Forman LLP* |
| MORROW Randall *Maynard, Cooper & Gale* |

| Banking & Finance: Mainly Regulatory |
| --- |
| Leading Individuals |
| 1 BOLES H Hampton *Balch & Bingham* |
| 2 SHEVIN Maurice *Sirote & Permutt PC* |

## Band 1

### Balch & Bingham
See firm details p.161

**The Firm:** This vibrant banking practice is "*a definite winner*" and offers a full range of services. Areas of expertise include advising on the formation of banks, banking-related M&A and regulatory advice. The team specializes in litigation for financial institutions, covering class actions, lender liability claims and consumer fraud. Advising banks and financial institutions all over the state, the firm has gained an inevitable reputation for expertise in the industry. Appreciative clients praise the "*professional and attentive*" team for its service-oriented approach, saying: "*They anticipate our needs.*"

**The Lawyers:** Regulatory expert **Hampton Boles**

(see p.155) chairs the financial services and transactions group. His practice is devoted to the banking industry, and clients report: "*He does his homework and understands the issues.*"

**Clients/Work Highlights:** Compass Bank; Wachovia; AmSouth Bank and Regions Bank.

### Bradley Arant Rose & White LLP
See firm details p.162

**The Firm:** Market sources agree that this group "*can handle any complicated issue.*" The banking and financial services group advises financial institutions on a broad spectrum of matters including capital markets. Over the past year the team has advised an active clientele on three bank formations including the Bryant Bank of Tuscaloosa. It advises institutions of all sizes across the Southeast. The lawyers are perceived as "*beyond reproach: extremely professional, knowledgeable and personable.*"

**The Lawyers:** Commentators extol "*top-flight*" **Paul Compton**'s (see p.156) prowess in banking matters, particularly when it comes to the formation of institutions. Clients endorse his "*innovative*" business plans. Clients go to **Laurence Vinson** (see p.160) "*when the chips are down,*" declaring: "*He instills confidence.*" He advises on regulatory compliance, consumer law and credit leases. The "*phenomenal and professional*" commercial lending expert **Kay Bains'** (see p.154) clients respect her skillful advice. **David Dresher** (see p.156) is another favorite and represents banks in a range of lending matters.

**Clients/Work Highlights:** Clients include Wachovia, AmSouth Bank and Regions Bank.

## Band 2

### Burr & Forman LLP

**The Firm:** The banking and financial services team here is flourishing and winning clients throughout the region. Finance transactions are the core of the firm's work. The team handles all aspects of a deal including asset-based and commercial lending elements. It joins forces with the litigation team to offer a formidable package of expertise to clients.

**The Lawyers:** Commercial lending expert **Ray Gibbens'** knowledge of the industry is held in high

esteem. **Gail Mills** is characterized as "*gregarious, friendly and completely on the ball*" by clients. Her practice encompasses commercial real estate transactions for banks. **Dwight Mixson**'s clients enthuse: "*He develops intelligent solutions to our problems.*" Representing lenders and advising on permanent financing are two key aspects of his practice.

**Clients/Work Highlights:** The firm's client list includes financial institutions such as Wachovia.

### Miller Hamilton Snider & Odom LLC

**The Firm:** This "*superb*" full-service firm originally specialized in banking and regulatory law, and it is for this that the team is still best known. With headquarters in Mobile and five other offices across the Southeast, the firm is a considerable force in the region.

**The Lawyers:** Mobile native **John Miller** advises on banking, government relations, strategic planning and litigation.

**Clients/Work Highlights:** The firm has an active client base including local and national financial institutions.

## Band 3

### Adams and Reese LLP
See firm details p.989

**The Firm:** This firm has built a strong reputation in the southeastern region for solid banking and finance advice. The sizable team handles loans, public finance and leasing deals. Lawyers are equally at home on routine and complex deals. The team also advises on compliance with federal and state laws.

**The Lawyers:** Key members of the group are Joe Joseph, Richard Carmody and Charles Pinckney. They act for a diverse clientele, including financial institutions, on commercial, debt recovery, bankruptcy and other business matters.

**Clients/Work Highlights:** The firm has an active practice advising banks and financial institutions.

### Johnston Barton Proctor & Powell LLP

**The Firm:** This firm's banking and finance capability is strengthening well, say commentators. The team was bolstered recently by the arrival of Kurt Miller, former general counsel at AmSouth Bank. The practice covers both lending and regulatory work and has an established litigation offering. Sources note that the team is *"responsive, highly efficient and knowledgeable."*

**The Lawyers:** Commentators praise *"true thinker and professional"* **Haskins Jones**. He represents clients in their technology, commercial, lending and real estate transactions.

**Clients/Work Highlights:** Some of the region's most prominent financial institutions are on this firm's client list, including AmSouth Bank, Bank One and First Commercial Bank.

## Maynard, Cooper & Gale, P.C.
See firm details p.165

**The Firm:** This group represents a diverse bunch of financial institutions, large and small, public and private. It assists these institutions in all aspects of their business, including regulatory compliance, M&A, privacy issues and product development. It also advises new banks, managing them from inception through to subsequent expansion.

**The Lawyers:** The respected **Randall Morrow** (see p.158) is *"bright and easy to work with."* He represents both lenders and borrowers in transactions including structured finance and multistate deals.

**Clients/Work Highlights:** The firm acts for financial institutions across the region.

## Other Notable Practitioners
The *"skilled"* **Maurice Shevin** of Sirote & Permutt PC has a national reputation. He is corporate counsel for several financial institutions, advising them on regulatory and commercial concerns.

# CORPORATE/COMMERCIAL

| Corporate/Commercial |
|---|
| **Leading Firms** |
| [1] **BALCH & BINGHAM** *Birmingham* |
| **BRADLEY ARANT ROSE & WHITE LLP** *Birmingham* |
| **BURR & FORMAN LLP** *Birmingham* |
| [2] **MAYNARD, COOPER & GALE, P.C.** *Birmingham* |
| [3] **BAKER, DONELSON** *Birmingham* |
| **JOHNSTON BARTON PROCTOR** *Birmingham* |
| **SIROTE & PERMUTT PC** *Birmingham* |

| Leading Individuals |
|---|
| **Senior Statesman** |
| **CARRUTHERS Thomas** *Bradley Arant Rose* |
| [1] **CURRAN Gregory** *Maynard, Cooper & Gale, P.C.* |
| **GRENIER John** *Bradley Arant Rose* |
| **HUGHEY JR James** *Balch & Bingham* |
| **KUSHNER Harold** *Bradley Arant Rose* |
| **PRICE Gene** *Burr & Forman LLP* |
| **THUSTON Lee** *Burr & Forman LLP* |
| [2] **BEALE JR Walter** *Balch & Bingham* |
| **BROCKMAN Richard** *Johnston Barton Proctor* |
| **COOPER John** *Sirote & Permutt PC* |
| **DREW Mark** *Maynard, Cooper & Gale* |
| **HARMON Christopher** *Maynard, Cooper & Gale* |
| **MINISMAN JR B G** *Baker, Donelson* |
| **ROSE JR J William** *Johnston Barton Proctor* |
| **STEPHENSON Jack** *Burr & Forman LLP* |
| **TRACY Timothy** *Balch & Bingham* |
| **WARE Paul** *Bradley Arant Rose* |

## Band 1

### Balch & Bingham
See firm details p.161

**The Firm:** Commentators *"cannot praise it highly enough"* when speaking of this full-service outfit. It divides its efforts across a broad front covering everything from corporate and securities to M&A and corporate governance matters. For example, lawyers successfully acted for HealthSouth on securities issues arising out of fraud and accounting problems. The group has a strong practice advising publicly traded companies and utility businesses such as Nevada Power. Commenting on the firm's ethos, clients observe: *"They have a strong ethical approach to the law and provide us with straight interpretations of the situation we are in."*

**The Lawyers:** **James Hughey**'s (see p.157) fans assert: *"He has a firm grasp of the law and understands all the implications."* He advises on corporate and securities transactions and represents a variety of business entities. He has been acting for a lot of public companies recently. **Walter Beale**'s (see p.155) clients are full of praise for his 30 years plus of experience in the field. He has a solid practice representing issuers in IPOs. Another key member of the team is **Timothy Tracy** (see p.160), recently involved in a large corporate restructuring transaction for Sherman Industries.

**Clients/Work Highlights:** Vesta Insurance; AmSouth Bank; Wolverine Tube and Alabama Power.

### Bradley Arant Rose & White LLP
See firm details p.162

**The Firm:** This group is popular with clients and admired by peers; all agree that it fields *"excellent attorneys who offer an outstanding service."* There has been a notable increase in workload over the past year, which has led to team growth: for example, Harold Kushner, formerly of Baker, Donelson, Bearman, Caldwell & Berkowitz, has joined the group. The practice covers all aspects of corporate and securities advice for both private and public companies. It recently represented MOBIS Alabama, a supplier to Hyundai, in negotiations for a $65 million expansion of its existing plant in Montgomery. It also advised Thompson Plastics on the $25 million sale of assets and lease of facilities to Charlotte Pipe & Foundry Company.

**The Lawyers:** **Thomas Carruthers** (see p.155) enters the category of senior statesman this year. A veteran in the field, he has a deep knowledge of everything from M&A to estate planning and corporate taxation. The *"brilliant and detailed"* **John Grenier** (see p.157) chairs the firm's executive committee and spends much of his time managing the corporate group. He remains accessible to clients, who aver: *"We use him on the most complex transactions."* New member **Harold Kushner** (see p.157) is *"one of the most exceptional lawyers in the state,"* according to clients. He represents businesses in a range of industries including software, steel and manufacturing. He is experienced in startup ventures and private equity transactions. *"Talented young guy"* **Paul Ware** (see p.160) debuts this year: his reputation was significantly boosted by his involvement in Wachovia's purchase of SouthTrust.

**Clients/Work Highlights:** HealthSouth; Wachovia; Ready Mix USA; Boyd Bros. Transportation; MAP Pharmaceuticals and The Birmingham News.

### Burr & Forman LLP

**The Firm:** This large and active corporate group has an enviable profile in the state. M&A is at the heart of the practice, but the team is adept across the range of commercial work. It is renowned for representing automotive industry clients, as when the team advised parts manufacturer Gestamp Automoción on its $100 million acquisition of a local manufacturing facility. It also advises clients outside Alabama, notably in Florida and Texas. Clients are particularly impressed with the lawyers' business sense and practicality; as one typical interviewee avowed: *"They are our firm of choice – we wouldn't go anywhere else."*

**The Lawyers:** Clients appreciate **Gene Price**'s directness and depth of understanding, declaring: *"He gets straight to the essence of what we are trying to achieve."* He heads the general corporate group and advises on a wide variety of matters, notably in the technology and healthcare sectors. The *"exceptional"* **Lee Thuston** has a reputation that extends beyond Alabama. He is renowned for his specialist knowledge of the automotive industry, in particular plant relocations. Senior securities attorney **Jack Stephenson** advises a range of regional clients from real estate developers to nursing homes.

**Clients/Work Highlights:** ProAssurance; USX; Citation Corporation; Honda; Vulcan Engineering and Wachovia.

## Band 2

### Maynard, Cooper & Gale, P.C.
See firm details p.165
**The Firm:** This Birmingham-based firm is one of the best in the region according to clients, who assert: *"They are excellent from top to bottom."* It is a full-service outfit that advises across the board on corporate and commercial law. The *"responsive and intelligent"* lawyers *"do a great job"* in any situation, according to commentators. The team's cross-border capability is illustrated by its ongoing advice to mining giant Drummond, enabling coal mined in Colombia to be imported into the USA.
**The Lawyers:** Clients endorse the *"bright and professional"* **Greg Curran** (see p.156), who is well known in the area of private investment fund formation. Recent transactions include a fund formation project for Highland Associates. **Mark Drew**'s (see p.156) clients value his expertise and versatility. **Christopher Harmon** (see p.157) is particularly known for his securities compliance work. He also handles M&A, venture capital and general corporate and securities matters.
**Clients/Work Highlights:** AmSouth Bank; Baptist Health Systems; Momentum Telecom; Southern Research Institute and Torchmark.

## Band 3

### Baker, Donelson, Bearman, Caldwell & Berkowitz, PC
See firm details p.1819
**The Firm:** *"The depth of knowledge marks it out,"* say commentators of this significant regional player. The team advises on the gamut of corporate matters and is no stranger to M&A, venture capital or corporate governance. It acts for private and public companies and was associated with several major IPOs over the past year.
**The Lawyers:** **B G Minisman** (see p.158) is sought out for his public companies and securities expertise. Harold Kushner recently left the firm.
**Clients/Work Highlights:** The client list includes The Colonial Company, Bayer Properties and Southern Pipe and Supply Co.

### Johnston Barton Proctor & Powell LLP
**The Firm:** This firm is an undoubted *"leader in Birmingham,"* according to observers. The sizable corporate and securities group covers all aspects of business activity, and sources report a marked increase in M&A work recently. Quite apart from its considerable local credibility, the team has been active nationally. Clients describe the lawyers as *"extremely knowledgeable and skilled at what they do."*
**The Lawyers:** **Richard Brockman** has a broad corporate/commercial practice and is particularly noted for work related to nursing homes. **William Rose**'s work for healthcare giant HealthSouth ensures a prominent profile.
**Clients/Work Highlights:** The team advises private and public companies from a range of industries, including healthcare.

### Sirote & Permutt PC
**The Firm:** From offices throughout Alabama this group advises on a wide range of corporate and commercial matters, including M&A, restructuring, joint ventures and securities. It is particularly well regarded throughout the Southeast for its work in tax, advising on the gamut of related issues such as maximizing tax benefits, risk reduction and general compliance.
**The Lawyers:** **John Cooper** advises both public and private businesses at all stages of their development. His skills are deployed in many industry sectors, including healthcare, real estate and retail.
**Clients/Work Highlights:** The firm has a substantial list of local and regional clients

# EMPLOYMENT

# MAINLY DEFENDANT

| Employment: Mainly Defendant Leading Firms |
| --- |
| 1  BRADLEY ARANT ROSE & WHITE LLP *Birmingham* |
|    LEHR MIDDLEBROOKS PRICE *Birmingham* |
| 2  BURR & FORMAN LLP *Birmingham* |
|    MAYNARD, COOPER & GALE, P.C. *Birmingham* |
| 3  CABANISS, JOHNSTON, GARDNER *Birmingham* |
|    CONSTANGY, BROOKS & SMITH, LLC *Birmingham* |
|    OGLETREE, DEAKINS, NASH, SMOAK *Birmingham* |
| 4  ADAMS AND REESE LLP *Birmingham* |
|    BAKER, DONELSON *Birmingham* |
|    BALCH & BINGHAM *Montgomery* |
|    JOHNSTON BARTON PROCTOR *Birmingham* |

## Band 1

### Bradley Arant Rose & White LLP
See firm details p.162
**The Firm:** This team is seasoned in all aspects of employment law and is especially recommended for *"outstanding"* traditional labor advice: expertise in the prevention of unionization and the progressive defense of large-scale class actions in and outside Alabama are the lawyers' stock-in-trade. The team defended Family Dollar Stores in a $98 million collective action brought by over 1,000 employees, a precedent-poor area requiring sure and careful handling. Clients applaud the team's depth, saying: *"They are large enough to handle anything, but they still deliver personal service and attention to detail."*
**The Lawyers:** *"The best in the Southeast,"* according to sources, **James Alexander** (see p.154) has an active trial practice in both federal and state courts. One client summed up the consensus: *"I have a world of respect for him."* His broad practice includes working as a mediator and arbitrator, and offering risk assessments to employers. Sources describe **James May** (see p.158) as *"one of the reasons the firm is so good."* He is expert in large and complex class actions and advises on a variety of discrimination cases, including equal opportunity indictments. **Jay St Clair** (see p.160) is a hit with clients for his habit of getting *"right down to the roots"* of a matter and his flair for rendering highly complex information intelligible. Also valued were his regular seminars on developments in labor law. Client favorite **Abdul Kallon** (see p.157) was identified as *"the complete package – he does it all."*
**Clients/Work Highlights:** Hunt Refining Company; Marriott International; University of Alabama Health Services Foundation; Vulcan Materials and Goodyear.

### Lehr Middlebrooks Price & Vreeland, P.C.
**The Firm:** This boutique's enthusiastic clients agree: it is *"one of the finest labor crews in the southern USA."* Acting for management, exclusively on labor and employment law, the team offers a range of services including litigation and collective bargaining. The appellate practice is also highly regarded. With a reputation that extends beyond the state, the group has a nationwide presence and an impressive client list. It was appointed negotiator for BP's North America Alaska Business Unit, guiding the company through an eight-month strike until agreement was reached and staff replacements were found. In a nutshell, according to a typical client: *"They're a tremendous asset – they meet and exceed all our expectations."*
**The Lawyers:** **Richard Lehr**'s clients and peers award him the accolade *"Best in Class."* He brings a weighty knowledge of traditional labor issues to the table, and counsels employers on workplace strategies. **David Middlebrooks** has an active discrimination practice. Clients applaud his *"high ethics, conscientiousness, and pleasant and easy manner."* Managing partner **Albert Vreeland**'s objectivity and affability are popular with clients.
**Clients/Work Highlights:** BAE Systems; Alyeska Pipeline Service; Wal-Mart; Xerox; Dean Foods and JVC America.

## Band 2

### Burr & Forman LLP
**The Firm:** This is a *"top of the line"* firm that offers clients a full service. On the employment front the team practices across the Southeast, representing employers before government agencies including federal and state courts. High-profile discrimination cases stud the workload and the team successfully defended Mercedes-Benz US International against

| Employment: Mainly Defendant |
| --- |
| **Leading Individuals** |
| **Senior Statesman** |
| GARDNER William *Cabaniss, Johnston, Gardner* |
| INGRAM Fredric *Burr & Forman LLP* |
| POWELL III Charles *Johnston Barton Proctor* |
| [1] ALEXANDER James *Bradley Arant Rose & White LLP* |
| LEHR Richard *Lehr Middlebrooks Price* |
| MAY James *Bradley Arant Rose* |
| MIDDLEBROOKS David *Lehr Middlebrooks Price* |
| [2] LEE Jeffrey *Maynard, Cooper & Gale* |
| MITCHELL Chris *Maynard, Cooper & Gale* |
| SINGER Fern *Baker, Donelson, Bearman* |
| SMITH David *Maynard, Cooper & Gale* |
| VREELAND Albert *Lehr Middlebrooks Price & Vreeland* |
| [3] BROWN Stephen *Maynard, Cooper & Gale* |
| COLEMAN John *Burr & Forman LLP* |
| DAVIS Thomas *Constangy, Brooks & Smith* |
| DEBRUGE Marcel *Burr & Forman LLP* |
| DOBBS Tammy *Constangy, Brooks & Smith* |
| FRAZIER Sydney *Cabaniss, Johnston, Gardner, Dumas* |
| HANCOCK William *Adams and Reese LLP* |
| LACY JR Peyton *Ogletree, Deakins, Nash, Smoak* |
| LUCAS Michael *Burr & Forman LLP* |
| NELSON Carol Sue *Maynard, Cooper & Gale, P.C.* |
| ST CLAIR Jay *Bradley Arant Rose & White LLP* |
| STARLING III M Jefferson *Balch & Bingham* |
| **Up-and-coming individuals** |
| KALLON Abdul *Bradley Arant Rose & White* |

claims of sexual harassment. The experienced attorneys' track record attracts clients who also appreciate special services such as seminars and training sessions.

**The Lawyers:** Senior statesman **Fredric Ingram** *"makes the firm tick,"* according to market sources. His credentials are impressive, and he is regarded as a formidable force in the region. **John Coleman** is recommended for his trial and counseling expertise. Clients praise **Marcel Debruge**'s insistent litigation style and appreciate his dedication to his work. **Michael Lucas** was described as *"one of the most effective employment lawyers around."*

**Clients/Work Highlights:** Sara Lee; Honda; United HealthCare Services and Sears Roebuck.

## Maynard, Cooper & Gale, P.C.

See firm details p.165

**The Firm:** This sizable Alabama firm has a highly regarded labor and employment team. It includes a number of effective jury trial attorneys who handle the full range of cases in both federal and state courts. The firm demonstrated its strength recently when it defended mining company Jim Walter Resources against government allegations after 13 miners died in an explosion. The team is deemed *"professional and a pleasure to work with."*

**The Lawyers:** **Jeffrey Lee** (see p.158) focuses on employment litigation and is hailed for his string of court successes. He defends management against

labor action and handles some commercial plaintiff work. The *"terrific"* **Chris Mitchell** (see p.158) represents management as both a litigator and arbitrator and practices before federal and state courts. **David Smith** (see p.159) *"has done a particularly excellent job"* this year, according to clients. Seasoned practitioner **Stephen Brown** (see p.155) heads the group. **Carol Sue Nelson** (see p.159) has defended a variety of discrimination cases.

**Clients/Work Highlights:** Merrill Lynch; Tyson Foods; AmSouth Bank; Pemco Aviation Group and BellSouth.

## Band 3

### Cabaniss, Johnston, Gardner, Dumas & O'Neal

**The Firm:** As one of Alabama's most venerable outfits, this firm has worked long and hard to secure its excellent reputation in this field. The team advises management on the gamut of employment matters including state, federal and antidiscrimination laws. The discrimination caseload is up these days, particularly on national origin matters and often involving plaintiffs originating from the Middle East. One recent case featured a plaintiff alleging that a business transaction failed to materialize because the plaintiff was from Pakistan.

**The Lawyers:** **William Gardner** *"knows the law better than anyone,"* according to interviewees. His *"unlimited talent,"* hard work, and intelligence draw approbation from all sides, and his courtroom skills inspire a deep respect in peers. **Sydney Frazier** is experienced in traditional labor matters and has a strong litigation practice.

**Clients/Work Highlights:** The firm's client list includes major national and international companies.

### Constangy, Brooks & Smith, LLC

**The Firm:** Clients of this boutique declare: *"We get whatever we need from them; they're a real one-stop shop."* The team advises management on both ERISA and EEOC issues, and counsels clients on policy changes. The growing clientele is often from outside the state, drawn here by the uncompromising standards of service. Clients observe: *"They are more than just a law firm – they know us, they are business partners."*

**The Lawyers:** According to his clients, litigator **Thomas Davis** *"always exceeds expectations – you ask and he delivers."* **Tammy Dobbs** *"offers good solid advice,"* by all accounts.

**Clients/Work Highlights:** Target; Alfa Insurance Company; Winn-Dixie; The Bank and Northeast Alabama Regional Medical Center.

### Ogletree, Deakins, Nash, Smoak & Stewart, PC

See firm details p.738

**The Firm:** The recent merger with Haynsworth Baldwin Johnson & Greaves was calculated to enhance this firm's strengths and widen its client

base. It also opened an office in Phoenix, thus becoming one of the largest specialty firms in the USA. The Birmingham office serves a wide client base including many smaller, owner-managed businesses. The team acts for management and deals with an assortment of labor concerns. Recent highlights have included finalizing collective bargaining agreements.

**The Lawyers:** Experienced advocate **Peyton Lacy** (see p.157) is praised as *"one of the good guys"* by interviewees.

**Clients/Work Highlights:** University of North Alabama; Vulcan Group; Regions and Mercedes-Benz.

## Band 4

### Adams and Reese LLP

See firm details p.989

**The Firm:** This full-service firm has offices across the Southeast and debuts in *Chambers'* tables this year on the strength of praise for its *"superb, responsive and experienced"* team. It offers a broad and versatile practice covering the usual employment and labor issues, as well as nuanced human rights and discrimination advice. Recent work has included an increasing number of collective actions.

**The Lawyers:** Sources have only good things to say of **William Hancock** (see p.157), an experienced advocate who has represented management in the region for years.

**Clients/Work Highlights:** The firm acts for an established management client list.

### Baker, Donelson, Bearman, Caldwell & Berkowitz, PC

See firm details p.1819

**The Firm:** This nationwide firm enters the table this year with enthusiastic endorsements from clients and peers. The team provides general advice on employment and labor law. It has an established track record in traditional union work and a renowned mediation practice. An active client-training program complements the team's litigation avoidance expertise. Clients declare: *"They can handle any type of business."*

**The Lawyers:** **Fern Singer** (see p.159) is a recognized mediation and arbitration expert. Clients describe her as a *"tenacious and smart lawyer."*

**Clients/Work Highlights:** Adesa; Arcade Marketing; AT&T Wireless; Delta Air Lines; Northwest Airlines and King Pharmaceuticals.

### Balch & Bingham

See firm details p.161

**The Firm:** This firm advises private and public management clients on a wide range of employment and labor matters. Its counseling service helps employers navigate new regulatory developments as well as traditional issues like attempted union organization. The group is expert in key areas such as employee benefits and labor-management relations, and offers a respected litigation capability.

The Lawyers: The *"marvelous"* **Jefferson Starling** (see p.160) is a young lawyer with a great reputation for advising on traditional labor law.
Clients/Work Highlights: The firm represents a number of high-profile clients in Alabama and nationally.

## Johnston Barton Proctor & Powell LLP

The Firm: This Birmingham-based outfit maintains its strong reputation despite the departure of Barry Johnson. The group advises clients on avoiding and resolving litigation, recently handling a noticeable upsurge in discrimination cases. The team successfully represented RPH Management, a franchisee of

McDonald's, against allegations that it violated the ADA.
The Lawyers: **Charles Powell**'s clients value him so highly because he has *"seen and done it all."* He has a long and distinguished history in this field and advises on the range of labor and employment law.
Clients/Work Highlights: The client list includes O'Charley's and Delphi.

# LITIGATION

| | |
|---|---|
| **Litigation: General Commercial** | |
| Leading Firms | |

**1**   BRADLEY ARANT ROSE & WHITE LLP *Birmingham*
    CUNNINGHAM, BOUNDS, YANCE *Mobile*
    HARE, WYNN, NEWELL & NEWTON LLP *Birmingham*
    LIGHTFOOT, FRANKLIN & WHITE, LLC *Birmingham*
    STARNES & ATCHISON LLP *Birmingham*

**2**   BALCH & BINGHAM *Birmingham*
    HELMSING, LEACH, HERLONG *Mobile*
    RUSHTON, STAKELY, JOHNSTON *Montgomery*

**3**   BEASLEY, ALLEN, CROW, METHVIN *Montgomery*
    LANIER FORD SHAVER & PAYNE P.C. *Huntsville*
    MAYNARD, COOPER & GALE, P.C. *Birmingham*

**4**   BAINBRIDGE, MIMS, ROGERS *Birmingham*
    CABANISS, JOHNSTON, GARDNER *Birmingham*
    CHRISTIAN & SMALL LLP *Birmingham*
    MCDOWELL KNIGHT ROEDDER *Mobile*

## Band 1

### Bradley Arant Rose & White LLP

See firm details p.162
The Firm: To its devotees, this Birmingham-based group is *"absolutely top in Alabama."* The team fields experienced lawyers that handle some of the most complex and high-profile work in the state. It recently represented Walter Industries in a suit questioning the ownership of the company's strip-mining resources in the Warrior Coal Basin area. The litigation group encompasses a wide range of sectors from general commercial work to products liability and pharmaceutical. This scope fuels a growing department that works throughout the Southeast region. The team is a favorite with clients: *"They can communicate their ideas well and are always available when we call."*
The Lawyers: The seasoned **Hobart McWhorter** (see p.158) is *"top-flight"* by any standard. His practice includes complex litigation in both federal and state courts. *"Wily old fox"* **John Morrow** (see p.158) has unparalleled experience in diverse litigation matters. He is particularly expert in civil and commercial litigation including both products liability and personal injury work. **James Gewin** (see p.156) *"is right at the top in business litigation,"* according to commentators. Sources describe him as *"the whole package,"* and he is especially recommended for defending corporate clients in insurance

and products liability cases. **Michael McKibben** (see p.158) is an *"excellent fellow,"* in the words of commentators, and popular with clients. Construction guru **Mabry Rogers** (see p.159) is lauded across the nation as *"a star."*
Clients/Work Highlights: Jim Walter Resources; Wachovia; Dryvit Systems; Pfizer; Torchmark; Synovus; HealthSouth; Bayer; Cooper Tire & Rubber Company; 3M and University of Health Services Foundation.

### Cunningham, Bounds, Yance, Crowder & Brown, LLC

The Firm: This Mobile-based boutique specializes in representing plaintiffs and has gained a national reputation. It covers national and state litigation in a range of areas including medical malpractice, products liability, white-collar crime and personal injury. The team is also expert in class actions. This expertise was recently mobilized in a case against the US government brought by National Guardsmen seeking compensation for time spent taking correspondence courses.
The Lawyers: Sources describe **Robert Cunningham** as *"the premier plaintiff lawyer in Alabama."* **Gregory Breedlove** has an impressive string of successful verdicts to his name.
Clients/Work Highlights: The firm has a long list of notable local and national clients.

### Hare, Wynn, Newell & Newton LLP

The Firm: This *"phenomenal"* firm is one of the oldest in Alabama and the proud possessor of one of the best reputations in the region. The team represents plaintiffs in diverse areas including general business litigation and commercial disputes. It has built an unrivaled practice in niche areas such as whistle-blower and nursing home abuse and neglect cases. For example, lawyers represented the family of a deceased Arkansas man against a nursing home that had allegedly caused his death, winning a $2.98 million verdict for the plaintiff.
The Lawyers: **Leon Ashford** is *"an honorable and respected man,"* according to sources, who add: *"You just know he's not going to make a mistake."* His practice ranges from complex litigation to truck and automobile accidents.
Clients/Work Highlights: The firm represents many notable companies as plaintiffs, but its clients are predominantly private individuals.

### Lightfoot, Franklin & White, LLC

The Firm: This is a very credible regional player operating throughout the Southeast. Interviewees suggest that it may be *"unique in its ability to hire and retain top-level talent."* The team is characterized as deep and broad, with experts in everything from business litigation and antitrust to white-collar criminal defense and environmental work. It acted for GE in a range of multiplaintiff toxic tort cases. The firm has a strong appellate practice. Interviewees praise the team as resolute and adroit, noting: *"They are willing to try the cases that no one else will touch."*
The Lawyers: A one-time president of the American College of Trial Lawyers, **Warren Lightfoot** is lauded as *"a great success and extremely well connected."* **Samuel Franklin** garners praise for a varied practice that includes general business litigation, environmental and toxic torts as well as appellate work. Clients admire his courtroom dexterity, commenting: *"He is amazingly smart when the going gets tough."* **Jere White** practices a range of litigation and is considered *"a natural winner."*
Clients/Work Highlights: Freightliner; Dupont; Monsanto; AIG; GM; ExxonMobil; Hyundai and USX.

### Starnes & Atchison LLP

See firm details p.166
The Firm: Fans of this boutique litigation outfit declare: *"If you are looking for a defense firm in the Southeast, not just Alabama, call these guys first."* The lawyers are admired for their courtroom prowess. The team represented The University of Alabama in recent trademark litigation against a portrait artist. It is adept at general business and securities matters, and has a celebrated medical malpractice offering.
The Lawyers: **Stancil Starnes** (see p.160) is *"the kind of lawyer you turn to when the chips are down and you need the best,"* according to commentators. His clients avow: *"He embodies the 'if it's important to you it's important to me' strategy."* Medical malpractice expert **Randal Sellers** (see p.159) is *"smart, industrious and wins cases,"* say sources. **Michael Atchison** (see p.154) recently obtained the dismissal of a major class action for Caremark. **Walter Bates** (see p.155) joins the *Chambers* ranks this year for his medical malpractice and personal injury litigation practice; also making his *Chambers* debut is the *"thoughtful, likable and jury-friendly"* **Michael Florie** (see p.156). **Rik Tozzi**'s (see p.160) clients value his expertise in various areas, including class actions.

## Litigation: General Commercial
### Leading Individuals

### Senior Statesmen

**LIGHTFOOT Warren** *Lightfoot, Franklin & White, LLC*
**MCWHORTER Hobart** *Bradley Arant Rose & White LLP*
**MORROW John** *Bradley Arant Rose & White LLP*

[1]
**ASHFORD Leon** *Hare, Wynn, Newell Bounos*
**CUNNINGHAM Robert** *Cunningham, Bounds, Yance*
**FRANKLIN Samuel** *Lightfoot, Franklin & White*
**GEWIN James** *Bradley Arant Rose & White*
**KEENE Thomas** *Rushton, Stakely, Johnston & Garrett*
**MARSH David** *Marsh, Rickard & Bryan P.C*
**MCGIVAREN Crawford** *Cabaniss, Johnston, Gardner*
**STARNES Stancil** *Starnes & Atchison LLP*

[2]
**ATCHISON W Michael** *Starnes & Atchison LLP*
**BEASLEY Jere** *Beasley, Allen, Crow, Methvin, Portis*
**EDWARDS Michael** *Balch & Bingham*
**NOVAK Tabor** *Ball, Ball, Matthews & Novak*
**WHITE JR Jere** *Lightfoot, Franklin & White, LLC*

[3]
**BAINS Lee** *Maynard, Cooper & Gale, P.C.*
**BOYD David** *Balch & Bingham*
**BREEDLOVE Gregory** *Cunningham, Bounds, Yance*
**CHRISTIAN Thomas** *Christian & Small LLP*
**GILL Richard** *Copeland, Franco, Screws & Gill*
**HELMSING Frederick** *Helmsing, Leach, Herlong*
**KNIGHT Michael** *McDowell Knight Roedder*
**LEACH JR John** *Helmsing, Leach, Herlong, Newman*
**MCDOWELL Jerry** *McDowell Knight Roedder*
**MCKIBBEN Michael** *Bradley Arant Rose & White LLP*
**RODGERS W Stanley** *Lanier Ford Shaver & Payne P.C.*
**ROGERS Alan** *Balch & Bingham*
**ROGERS Bruce** *Bainbridge, Mims, Rogers*
**TOZZI Rik** *Starnes & Atchison LLP*

## Litigation: Construction
### Leading Individuals

[1]
**ROGERS E Mabry** *Bradley Arant Rose & White*

## Litigation: Medical Malpractice Defense
### Leading Individuals

[1]
**SELLERS Randal** *Starnes & Atchison LLP*

[2]
**BATES Walter** *Starnes & Atchison LLP*
**FLORIE Michael** *Starnes & Atchison LLP*

**Clients/Work Highlights:** Citigroup; Medical Assurance/ProNational; GE Capital; Protective Life; Honda and Drummond.

## Band 2

### Balch & Bingham
See firm details p.161

**The Firm:** This is one of the largest full-service outfits in the state and it makes its presence felt throughout the region. Clients praise the team's customer service and declare the lawyers *"responsive and sensitive to our needs."* The practice covers litiga-

tion in many areas including general business, casualty, environmental, and healthcare. The firm has a particularly strong energy practice and acts as lead counsel to Nevada Power, for which it successfully resolved a number of lawsuits relating to the Western power market crisis.

**The Lawyers:** Former litigation chair **Michael Edwards** (see p.156) is a fund of knowledge, according to commentators, and *"does an excellent job of training others."* **David Boyd** (see p.155) divides his time between commercial, employment and constitutional and civil rights litigation. **Alan Rogers** (see p.159) is said to be *"a good guy who knows how to make a stand."*

**Clients/Work Highlights:** ExxonMobil, Compass Bank and Regions are all on the client roster.

### Helmsing, Leach, Herlong, Newman & Rouse, PC
See firm details p.164

**The Firm:** *"Mobile's finest"* offers a range of legal services and enjoys a particularly strong reputation in litigation. The team has successfully tried many high-profile cases in both federal and state courts, and it is expert in large and complex matters. Its litigation capabilities include business, personal injury, property damage and tax. White-collar crime is something of a specialty.

**The Lawyers:** **Frederick Helmsing** is praised for his diverse litigation practice, as is the effective **John Leach**.

**Clients/Work Highlights:** Alabama Power; Montgomery Aviation; Hunt Petroleum and Glaxo-SmithKline.

### Rushton, Stakely, Johnston & Garrett

**The Firm:** This *"formidable"* Montgomery-based firm has a strong business and antitrust practice and its healthcare litigation wins fulsome praise. The team also advises on professional and products liability and has a renowned appellate practice.

**The Lawyers:** **Thomas Keene** is *"outstanding – period,"* according to sources. He is primarily involved in the defense of professional liability and medical matters.

**Clients/Work Highlights:** The firm offers advice to local, national and international clients.

## Band 3

### Beasley, Allen, Crow, Methvin, Portis & Miles, PC

**The Firm:** This Montgomery team is held in high repute for its cutting-edge plaintiff work. It is expert in many areas including consumer fraud, products liability, personal injury, and toxic torts. It recently acted for the City of Columbus (Georgia), Action Marine, and two individuals in an air pollution suit brought against Continental Carbon alleging property damage, loss of income and physical and emotional damage caused by carbon black emission.

**The Lawyers:** The *"formidable"* **Jere Beasley** is *"powerful in the community,"* according to sources.
**Clients/Work Highlights:** The State of Alabama and the City of Columbus, Georgia, are two of the firm's clients.

### Lanier Ford Shaver & Payne P.C.

**The Firm:** This is the largest firm in Huntsville and it offers its clients a full and rounded service. Lawyers offer expertise in many areas, including professional malpractice, products liability, healthcare and insurance litigation. This adds depth to the solid general business and commercial practice.

**The Lawyers:** **Stanley Rodgers** is deemed *"an exceptionally smart lawyer."* He specializes in products liability litigation in federal and state courts.

**Clients/Work Highlights:** The firm's client list includes public and private, local and national clients.

### Maynard, Cooper & Gale, P.C.
See firm details p.165

**The Firm:** This broad practice is noted for *"outstanding standards and positive results."* The team handles an interesting cross-section of commercial disputes and environmental torts. It has particular strength in insurance, securities and products liability litigation. Appreciative clients observe: *"They go out of their way to help you."*

**The Lawyers:** **Lee Bains** (see p.155) enters the *Chambers* tables this year, recommended by sources who applaud his *"imaginative way and good tactics."*

**Clients/Work Highlights:** Merrill Lynch and HealthSouth are on the firm's client list.

## Band 4

### Bainbridge, Mims, Rogers & Smith, LLP

**The Firm:** This is a small but effective team that attracts fierce loyalty for its expert, quality advice and enjoys a solid reputation in the community. It undertakes both plaintiff and defense work.

**The Lawyers:** **Bruce Rogers** is the man that catches clients' eyes.

**Clients/Work Highlights:** The firm's clients include individuals and businesses such as Health-South, First Commercial Bank and Dow Chemical.

### Cabaniss, Johnston, Gardner, Dumas & O'Neal

**The Firm:** This is one of Birmingham's elder practices and it is a fixture of the local landscape. The versatile team turns its hand to many things, notably general commercial, environmental, and intellectual property work. It is also renowned for complex litigation involving derivative and class actions.

**The Lawyers:** **Crawford McGivaren** is *"at the pinnacle of the field,"* according to interviewees. His immense expertise spans such areas as antitrust, products liability and medical malpractice. He is a persistent litigator with a proven track record in court.

**Clients/Work Highlights:** The firm acts for public and private companies.

## Christian & Small LLP

See firm details p.163

**The Firm:** Putting this Birmingham boutique in a nutshell, commentators describe it as *"a fine firm full of fine lawyers."* The firm is a credible operator in many areas of the law, but it is litigation that garners the most enthusiastic praise from clients. The team handles work on a national scale without compromising its dedication to clients in the Southeast.

**The Lawyers:** Interviewees singled out **Thomas Christian** (see p.155) for his extensive experience in litigation matters.

**Clients/Work Highlights:** Clients include local and national businesses such as AstraZeneca, St Vincent's Hospital and Caremark.

## McDowell Knight Roedder & Sledge LLC

**The Firm:** This Mobile stalwart has a fine reputation throughout the Southeast for litigation. As well as the usual cases, lawyers have niche expertise in areas such as railroad and drug liability. Clients and peers aver: *"They are a pillar of the litigation community."*

**The Lawyers:** The seasoned **Michael Knight** defends corporate clients in a variety of matters, especially personal injury and products liability claims. Alabama native **Jerry McDowell** is another client favorite.

**Clients/Work Highlights:** The firm has a substantial list of local and national clients.

## Other Notable Practitioners

Many describe **David Marsh** of Marsh, Rickard & Bryan P.C as *"the single best lawyer in the state right now,"* particularly for personal injury work. His *"remarkable ability to cut through any situation and identify the important issues"* is like catnip to clients. **Tabor Novak** of Ball, Ball, Matthews & Novak receives plaudits for his wealth of litigation experience. *"On top of the game,"* commentators describe him as *"polished, smart, and savvy."* **Richard Gill** of Montgomery-based Copeland, Franco, Screws & Gill has a broad practice that ranges from antitrust to motor vehicle accidents.

# REAL ESTATE

## Real Estate
### Leading Firms

1. **BRADLEY ARANT ROSE & WHITE** *Birmingham*
   **BURR & FORMAN LLP** *Birmingham*
2. **BALCH & BINGHAM** *Birmingham*
   **LEITMAN, SIEGAL & PAYNE, PC** *Birmingham*
3. **BAKER, DONELSON** *Birmingham*
   **CORRETTI, NEWSOM & HAWKINS** *Birmingham*
   **MAYNARD, COOPER & GALE, P.C.** *Birmingham*
   **SIROTE & PERMUTT PC** *Birmingham*

### Leading Individuals

#### Senior Statesman
**POWELL Fred** *Burr & Forman LLP*

1. **BEAVERS JR Charles** *Bradley Arant Rose & White*
   **ISOM Chervis** *Baker, Donelson*
   **SIEGAL Don** *Leitman, Siegal & Payne*
2. **BAINS Kay** *Bradley Arant Rose & White*
   **LANIER Randolph** *Balch & Bingham*
   **MIXSON Dwight** *Burr & Forman LLP*
   **MONK Stephen** *Bradley Arant Rose & White*
   **SEXTON Robert** *Maynard, Cooper & Gale*
3. **BRICKMAN Steven** *Sirote & Permutt PC*
   **CLARK Thomas** *Maynard, Cooper & Gale*
   **DRESHER David** *Bradley Arant Rose & White*
   **HELD Jerry** *Sirote & Permutt PC*
   **MILLS Gail** *Burr & Forman LLP*
   **SIEGAL Bradley** *Leitman, Siegal & Payne, PC*
   **SMITH Felton** *Balch & Bingham*
   **STEWART Carol** *Burr & Forman LLP*
   **SYLVESTER William** *Walston, Wells, Anderson*

## Band 1

### Bradley Arant Rose & White LLP

See firm details p.162

**The Firm:** This team offers services that run the gamut of commercial real estate including lending, finance, land use, acquisition and development. Clients turn to the lawyers here *"when we have to get the job done, any job."* The workflow has recently exploded with resort development work, such as the rezoning of property in Orange Beach for a 30-story resort condominium tower. Pleased with the consistently high-quality service, clients are further reassured by the lawyers' *"vast knowledge."*

**The Lawyers:** Veteran attorney **Charles Beavers** (see p.155) is *"one of the kings of the Southeast,"* according to clients and peers. His practice covers everything to do with the acquisition, sale and development of properties. **Kay Bains'** (see p.154) *"efficient and professional"* manner is a hit with clients. She is recognized throughout the region for her skills in commercial lending. **Stephen Monk** (see p.158) specializes in the representation of real estate developers and in the past year has worked extensively on developments in and around Alabama. **David Dresher**'s (see p.156) appreciative clients declare him *"competent and caring."*

**Clients/Work Highlights:** Daniel Realty; Hyundai; HealthSouth; Graham & Company; EBSCO Properties; Wachovia; Regions; Jim Wilson & Associates; Stonegate Realty and The Birmingham News.

### Burr & Forman LLP

**The Firm:** This firm is associated with high-profile work, and its real estate development and financing practices are flourishing. The team was lead counsel to a national shopping center developer in a series of precedent-setting transactions with local boroughs. It concentrates on the southern states. Clients observe: *"With the diverse range of services they offer our needs are always met."*

**The Lawyers:** **Fred Powell**'s has been a long and distinguished career, and he is one of the most *"prominent and unbelievably knowledgeable"* lawyers in the state. **John De Buys'** unparalleled knowledge of zoning and land use law earns him a move up *Chambers'* tables this year, according to clients. The *"extremely bright and knowledgeable"* **Dwight Mixson** mostly represents lenders but he also covers the leasing, sale and acquisition of properties. **Gail Mills'** clients recognize her as *"a deal-maker not a deal-breaker."* Described as *"gregarious and friendly,"* she *"doesn't have that 'my way or the highway' attitude."* She concentrates on commercial transactions advising lenders. Condominiums specialist **Carol Stewart** maintains an active litigation practice.

**Clients/Work Highlights:** Wachovia; D R Horton; Colonial Properties Trust; Eason; Graham & Sandner; Ingram and Associates; Southpace Properties and CSFB Mortgage Capital.

## Band 2

### Balch & Bingham

See firm details p.161

**The Firm:** This regional player is particularly strong in Mississippi and Alabama. The team advises clients across a broad spectrum of real estate matters including sales and acquisitions, lending, leasing and land use, as well as development and finance. The real estate group is integrated within the financial services department and has grown a solid reputation for its aptitude in the field.

**The Lawyers:** Commercial lending and development expert **Randolph Lanier** (see p.157) is *"practical, reasonable and easy to work with,"* according to market sources. **Felton Smith** (see p.159) is especially admired for his expertise on the financial side of transactions.

**Clients/Work Highlights:** The firm's active client list includes regional banks and financial institutions.

## Leitman, Siegal & Payne, PC

**The Firm:** *"They are the nicest folks, a great group of people,"* enthuse clients about this Birmingham-based outfit. The firm has a real commitment to this sector and nearly a third of its attorneys focus on real estate. The team advises on all manner of real estate matters and works on some of the largest transactions in the region. It recently advised on all real estate aspects of Colonial Property Trust's merger with Cornerstone Realty Income Trust.

**The Lawyers: Don Siegal** is acknowledged to be *"very experienced and great at what he does."* His practice incorporates general business law as well as real estate. **Bradley Siegal** represents buyers and sellers in a range of commercial transactions.

**Clients/Work Highlights:** The firm acts for local and regional clients.

## Band 3

## Baker, Donelson, Bearman, Caldwell & Berkowitz, PC

See firm details p.1819

**The Firm:** This significant regional player has an established reputation in real estate and its lawyers

are expert in development law and corporate transactions. The team also represents tenants, landlords and lenders. Lawyers recently acted in a transaction involving the sale of 40 acres of a 75-acre project in Nashville to a retail developer.

**The Lawyers:** The *"accomplished"* **Chervis Isom** (see p.157) has a healthy practice advising developers on various commercial ventures including shopping centers and industrial and warehouse facilities. His insistent style has gained him fans across the region.

**Clients/Work Highlights:** Key clients include Bayer Properties and Daniel Realty Company.

## Corretti, Newsom & Hawkins

**The Firm:** Based in Birmingham, this boutique fields an effective and well-regarded team dedicated to real estate issues. Its niche land practice is particularly noteworthy, and sources also praise the finance and transactional capability here.

**The Lawyers:** Seasoned campaigner **Douglas Corretti** is *"one of the deans of real estate in Alabama"* and seen as a guru on zoning and land use issues. A commentator opines: *"He knows more than everyone else put together."*

**Clients/Work Highlights:** Clients include Grimmer Realty, Wal-Mart and the City of Hoover.

## Maynard, Cooper & Gale, P.C.

See firm details p.165

**The Firm:** Clients appreciate this team's diverse expertise, saying: *"We need a group to get their arms around all the different disciplines in real estate, and they have that wealth of knowledge."* Demonstrating

its flair, the team recently acted for a developer in a condemnation case involving part of a 400-acre property in Alabaster.

**The Lawyers: Robert Sexton** (see p.159) is *"an experienced and well-rounded professional"* who, according to clients, *"doesn't just come up with the obvious answers but a complete strategy."* Debuting in the tables this year is the *"super"* **Thomas Clark** (see p.156). Clients remark: *"He is creative and has good vision."*

**Clients/Work Highlights:** American Cancer Society; Baptist Health Systems; Citigroup; Boy Scouts of America; Colonial Pipeline Company; Drummond Company; MetLife; Skye Realty and US Steel.

## Sirote & Permutt PC

**The Firm:** This respected group carries clients through every stage of a project from planning to financing and development. The sizable team advises on a wide range of developments including retail buildings, offices and industrial facilities.

**The Lawyers:** The *"methodical"* **Steven Brickman** has forged a strong reputation representing clients in all stages of real estate development. **Jerry Held** handles all stages of commercial transactions.

**Clients/Work Highlights:** The firm has clients across the region.

## Other Notable Practitioners

**William Sylvester** of Walston, Wells, Anderson & Bains is admired as *"a talented guy."* His capabilities include business and tax planning for real estate and commercial developments.

# Leaders in Alabama

### ALEXANDER, James P
Bradley Arant Rose & White LLP, Birmingham 205 521 8348
jalexander@bradleyarant.com
*Recommended in Employment*

**Practice Areas:** Defends employment discrimination cases; advises employers on efficacious policies and practices to manage risks; also handles traditional management labor disputes.

**Prof. Memberships:** Admitted to practice in Alabama (1969); Adjunct Professor of law at the University of Alabama School of Law teaching employment discrimination (1981-2003); Member of American and Alabama Bars; Arbitrator, American Arbitration Association; Employment Disputes and Commercial Panels.

**Career:** Joined Bradley Arant Rose & White LLP in 1969; became a Partner in 1975.

**Personal:** Born 14 October 1944, JD Duke University 1969; AB Duke University 1966.

### ASHFORD, Leon
Hare, Wynn, Newell & Newton LLP, Birmingham 205 328 5330
*Recommended in Litigation*

### ATCHISON, W Michael
Starnes & Atchison LLP, Birmingham 205 868 6015
matchison@starneslaw.com
*Recommended in Litigation*

**Practice Areas:** He has been Lead Defense Counsel in a wide variety of civil trials and appeals spanning more than 35 years of practice. Included are cases involving securities; anti-trust; ERISA; legal, accounting and medical malpractice; commerical airline crashes; products liability; complex civil litigation; class actions; copyright infringement and prescription drugs.

**Prof. Memberships:** Fellow, American College of Trial Lawyers; Advocate, American Board of Trial Advocates; Member, Birmingham, Alabama and American Bar Associates; Federation of

Insurance and Corporate Counsel.

**Career:** Admitted 1968. Law clerk, US District Court 1968-69, Partner at Starnes & Atchison LLP; Adjunct Professor, University of Alabama School of Law, 2003 to present.

**Publications:** Co-author, 'Proving Damages in Mass Tort Litigation', 1982; co-author, 'Alabama Damages', 1985; co-author, 'Medical Practice in Alabama', 1986; author, 'Medical Malpractice: A Defense Attorney's Perspective', 1994; co-author, 'The Professional Liability of Attorneys in Alabama', 2000.

**Personal:** Born April 13, 1941. Graduated with an AB Degree from Birmingham Southern College in 1965 and Juris Doctorate Degree from Cumberland School of Law Samford University in 1968; Recipient Honorary LLD Birmingham-Southern College in 2000.

### BAINS, Kay K
Bradley Arant Rose & White LLP, Birmingham 205 521 8220
kbains@bradleyarant.com
*Recommended in Banking & Finance, Real Estate*

**Practice Areas:** Commercial real estate, including advice regarding title issues, access, zoning, permitting and usage. Representation of national lenders in loans secured by real estate in multiple states. Representation of regional banks in acquiring and disposing sites in multi-state market.

**Prof. Memberships:** ABA; Alabama Bar Association; Member, American College of Mortgage Attorneys

**Career:** Private practice, concentrating in commercial real estate, for over 25 years.

**Personal:** Auburn University, magna cum laude, 1969; Cumberland School of Law, summa cum laude, 1980.

## BAINS, JR, Lee E
Maynard, Cooper & Gale, P.C.,
Birmingham 205 254 1022
lbains@maynardcooper.com
*Recommended in Litigation*
**Practice Areas:** Complex litigation;
class action litigation; insurance sales
practice litigation; general litigation;
antitrust and trade regulation; appellate
and post-verdict practice. Focuses primarily on complex civil litigation with an
emphasis on class action litigation,
antitrust litigation and business tort and
commercial litigation.
**Prof. Memberships:** American Bar
Association. Alabama State Bar Association, Former Chairman of the Business
Torts and Antitrust Law Section. Birmingham Bar Association.
**Career:** Admitted to practice in Alabama
in 1980. Joined Maynard Cooper when it
started in 1984.
**Personal:** Harvard University (AB, 1977
cum laude); Harvard University School
of Law (JD, 1980 cum laude).

## BATES, Walter
Starnes & Atchison LLP, Birmingham
205 868 6059
bbates@starneslaw.com
*Recommended in Litigation*
**Practice Areas:** He has been Lead
Defense Counsel in a wide variety of civil
trials and appeals spanning 25 years of
practice. Included are cases involving
medical professional liability, products
liability, pharmaceutical, insurance and
bad faith litigation.
**Prof. Memberships:** Advocate, American Board of Trial Attorneys (President-Elect, State Chapter); International Association of Defense Counsel; Birmingham,
Alabama, and American Bar Association.
**Career:** Admitted in 1981. Partner at
Starnes & Atchison LLP.
**Personal:** Born October 22, 1956. Graduated from University of Alabama with
BS Degree in Business Administration in
1978 and Cumberland School of Law in
1981.

## BEALE JR, Walter M
Balch & Bingham, Birmingham
205 226 3436
mbeale@balch.com
*Recommended in
Corporate/Commercial*
**Practice Areas:** Corporate and securities; energy regulation and transactions;
mergers and acquisitions; corporate governance.
**Prof. Memberships:** Birmingham Bar
Association; Alabama State Bar; American Bar Association.
**Career:** Mr Beale's practice is devoted
primarily to corporate finance transactions and advising publicly held corporations. He has over 30 years experience in
these areas and has represented issuers in
both initial and secondary public offerings, public and private offerings of debt

securities and offerings of 'hybrid' securities, such as trust preferred securities. Mr
Beale also advises publicly held corporations regarding compliance with federal
and state securities laws and regularly
advises boards of directors of publicly
held corporations on their duties and
responsibilities. Mr Beale represents corporations with securities listed on the
New York Stock Exchange and the NASDAQ National Market System. In addition to his corporate and securities practice, Mr Beale serves as a Member of the
Executive Committee. Mr Beale is listed
in The Best Lawyers in America, 2003
Edition-present.
**Personal:** Born: October 30, 1945. Education: Cumberland School of Law (JD,
1970); Auburn University (BS, 1967).

## BEASLEY, Jere
Beasley, Allen, Crow, Methvin, Portis &
Miles, PC, Montgomery
334 269 2343
*Recommended in Litigation*

## BEAVERS, JR, Charles AJ
Bradley Arant Rose & White LLP,
Birmingham 205 521 8620
cbeavers@bradleyarant.com
*Recommended in Real Estate*
**Practice Areas:** Real estate practice concentrated in the acquisition, sale and
development of commercial, office, residential and mixed-use properties. Experienced in representing developers and
neighborhood associations in the rezoning and subdivision of real properties.
**Prof. Memberships:** Admitted to practice in Alabama (1977). Member, Alabama Law Institute, American College of
Mortgage Attorneys, American Bar Association, Alabama State Bar and Birmingham Bar Association.
**Career:** Has practiced law in Birmingham, Alabama for the past 28 years. He
joined Bradley Arant Rose & White LLP
as a Partner in 1985.
**Personal:** Born 19 June 1952; JD, University of Alabama School of Law, 1977.

## BOLES, H Hampton
Balch & Bingham, Birmingham
205 226 3471
hboles@balch.com
*Recommended in Banking & Finance*
**Practice Areas:** Banking law; commercial and residential lending and closings
law; real estate-commercial law.
**Career:** H Hampton Boles is Chairman
of the Financial Services and Transactions section. Mr Boles' practice consists
primarily of advising banks and other
creditors, insurance companies and real
estate developers in corporate, financial
and regulatory matters. Mr Boles is a
Member of the American College of Real
Estate Lawyers, and has served on the
Alabama Law Institute UCC Articles 2A,
3, 4, 4A and Revised Article 9 Committees. He has been listed in The Best
Lawyers in America, 1995 Edition-pre-

sent.
**Personal:** Born: November 27, 1942.
Education: Tulane University School of
Law (JD, 1967); Auburn University (BS,
1965). Military: US Navy Reserve, active
duty 1968-71.

## BOYD, David R
Balch & Bingham, Birmingham
205 226 3485
dboyd@balch.com
*Recommended in Litigation*
**Practice Areas:** Business litigation; civil
rights litigation; class action litigation;
education; financial services litigation;
labor and employment litigation; state
governmental relations; state and local
government litigation; appellate.
**Prof. Memberships:** Alabama Board of
Bar Examiners, Former Chairman;
Alabama Law Institute, Executive Committee; American Bar Foundation, Fellow; Alabama Law Foundation, Fellow;
Multistate Bar Examination Committee,
Chairman; National Conference of Bar
Examiners, Chair of Board of Trustees.
**Career:** Mr Boyd's practice focuses primarily on commercial litigation, employment law, and constitutional and civil
rights litigation, where he has extensive
trial and appellate experience in the state
and federal courts. Mr Boyd's practice
also includes education law and state government matters. Among other state and
national professional involvements, he is
a Member of the Lawyers' Advisory
Committee in the Middle District of
Alabama, Chair of the National Conference of Bar Examiners, and Chair of the
Multistate Bar Examination Committee.
Mr Boyd has been listed for the last 10
years in the Best Lawyers in America.
**Personal:** Born: October 2, 1950. Education: University of Alabama (JD, 1976);
University of Alabama (BA, 1973).

## BREEDLOVE, Gregory
Cunningham, Bounds, Yance, Crowder &
Brown, LLC, Mobile 251 471 6191
*Recommended in Litigation*

## BRICKMAN, Steven
Sirote & Permutt PC, Birmingham
205 930 5100
*Recommended in Real Estate*

## BROCKMAN, Richard
Johnston Barton Proctor & Powell LLP,
Birmingham
205 458 9400
*Recommended in
Corporate/Commercial*

## BROWN, Stephen E
Maynard, Cooper & Gale, P.C.,
Birmingham
205 254 1023
sbrown@maynardcooper.com
*Recommended in Employment*
**Practice Areas:** Labor and employment.
**Prof. Memberships:** American Bar
Association; Alabama State Bar Associa-

tion; Birmingham Bar Association; College of Labor and Employment Attorneys.
**Career:** Since 1974, Mr Brown's practice
has focused exclusively on labor and
employment law, where he regularly represents management and employers in all
aspects of labor and employment law,
including labor and employment litigation in both federal and state courts and
before various federal, state and/or local
administrative agencies. Admitted to
practice in Alabama.
**Personal:** Dartmouth College (AB,
1971); Tulane School of Law (JD, 1974).

## CARRUTHERS, Thomas Neely
Bradley Arant Rose & White LLP,
Birmingham 205 521 8263
tcarruthers@bradleyarant.com
*Recommended in
Corporate/Commercial*
**Practice Areas:** Specializes in M&A,
estate planning and corporate taxation.
**Prof. Memberships:** Named 2001 Outstanding Lawyer of the Year, Birmingham
Bar Association, President of Birmingham Legal Aid Society, American Law
Institute, American Bar Association,
American College of Tax Counsel, Alabama Bar Foundation Fellow, International
Law Association, Birmingham Rotary
Club, Children's Hospital Board,
Lakeshore Foundation Trustee, Chairman Alabama Academy of Honor, Past
Chairman Birmingham Museum of Art.
Awarded Spain-Hickman Award, Medal
of Honor Birmingham-Southern College.
**Career:** Partner and former Managing
Partner of Bradley Arant. Graduate of
Princeton University and Yale Law
School.

## CHRISTIAN, Thomas W
Christian & Small LLP, Birmingham
205 250 6611
twchristian@csattorneys.com
*Recommended in Litigation*
**Practice Areas:** Accomplished litigation
attorney, representing an extensive list of
clients in most areas of tort litigation,
government contract litigation and construction litigation. His practice is primarily devoted to the defense of physicians and hospitals charged with medical
malpractice and the defense of manufacturers and insurance companies in products liability cases.
**Prof. Memberships:** Admitted to the
Alabama State Bar, 1965. Admitted to
practice in all state and federal trial courts
in Alabama, the Supreme Court of Alabama, the Courts of Appeals for the Fifth
and Eleventh Circuits and the Supreme
Court of the United States. Fellow of the
American College of Trial Lawyers, the
International Academy of Trial Lawyers,
the American Board of Trial Advocates,
and the American Bar Foundation.
Member of the American Bar Associa-

tion, Birmingham Bar Association (President, 1984), and Alabama State Bar. Member of the Alabama Defense Lawyers Association (President, 1978); International Association of Defense Counsel.
**Career:** Associate and Partner with Balch & Bingham, 1965-81; Partner with Rives & Peterson, 1981-2000; a founding Partner of Christian & Small LLP, 2000-present.

## CLARK, Thomas C
Maynard, Cooper & Gale, P.C., Birmingham 205 254 1072
tclark@maynardcooper.com
*Recommended in Real Estate*
**Practice Areas:** Real estate; commercial lending; economic development and incentives; general corporate. Mr Clark's practice focuses on all aspects of the representation of buyers, sellers, developers, landlords and tenants in all types of real estate matters, including acquisition, development, financing and leasing matters. In addition, Mr Clark focuses on all aspects of the representation of lenders and borrowers in secured and unsecured transactions and multi-state transactions.
**Prof. Memberships:** American, Alabama State and Birmingham Bar Associations.
**Career:** Admitted in Alabama.
**Personal:** Duke University (BS, 1988 cum laude); University of Pennsylvania School of Law (JD, 1991).

## COLEMAN, John
Burr & Forman LLP, Birmingham 205 251 3000
*Recommended in Employment*

## COMPTON, Paul
Bradley Arant Rose & White LLP, Birmingham 205 521 8381
pcompton@bradleyarant.com
*Recommended in Banking & Finance*
**Practice Areas:** Bank and financial services industry capital markets activities; denovo bank and insurance company formation; federal and state income tax credit related financing.
**Prof. Memberships:** Alabama State Bar; State Bar of Georgia; Counsel, Alabama Consumer Finance Association; Alabama Chair, ABA Forum on Affordable Housing and Community Development.
**Career:** Partner since 1996.
**Publications:** Low Income Housing Tax Credits and the Community Reinvestment Act: The Perfect Complement; Frequently lectures on ancillary bank products and low income housing tax credits.
**Personal:** University of Virginia (JD 1989); London School of Economics and Political Science; University of Alabama (BS 1985); Harry S Truman Scholar.

## COOPER, John
Sirote & Permutt PC, Birmingham 205 930 5100
*Recommended in Corporate/Commercial*

## CORRETTI, Douglas
Corretti, Newsom & Hawkins, Birmingham 205 251 1164
*Recommended in Real Estate*

## CUNNINGHAM, Robert
Cunningham, Bounds, Yance, Crowder & Brown, LLC, Mobile 251 471 6191
*Recommended in Litigation*

## CURRAN, Gregory S
Maynard, Cooper & Gale, P.C., Birmingham 205 254 1098
gcurran@maynardcooper.com
*Recommended in Corporate/Commercial*
**Practice Areas:** Securities; mergers and acquisitions; executive compensation; venture capital and private equity investment; general corporate; corporate governance and compliance. Mr Curran provides general legal and strategic business advice to companies and their boards and management, including matters of corporate governance, crisis response, dispute resolution, strategic planning and communications. Mr Curran also regularly represents clients in a variety of business acquisitions, venture capital and private equity transactions and corporate finance transactions.
**Prof. Memberships:** American, Alabama State and Birmingham Bar Associations.
**Career:** Admitted in Alabama.
**Personal:** Vanderbilt University (BA, 1985); University of Alabama School of Law (JD, 1989).

## DAVIS, Thomas
Constangy, Brooks & Smith, LLC, Birmingham 205 252 9321
*Recommended in Employment*

## DE BUYS JR, John
Burr & Forman LLP, Birmingham 205 251 3000
*Recommended in Real Estate*

## DEBRUGE, Marcel
Burr & Forman LLP, Birmingham 205 251 3000
*Recommended in Employment*

## DOBBS, Tammy
Constangy, Brooks & Smith, LLC, Birmingham 205 252 9321
*Recommended in Employment*

## DRESHER, J David
Bradley Arant Rose & White LLP, Birmingham 205 521 8605
ddresher@bradleyarant.com
*Recommended in Banking & Finance, Real Estate*
**Practice Areas:** Real estate: transactional work involving real property (purchase, sale, leasing and financing); refinancings and conduit borrowings; and development. Banking: real estate and commercial lending; workouts and restructurings; and residential mortgage lender compliance/consulting.
**Prof. Memberships:** ABA, Alabama Bar,

MBA, Alabama Consumer Finance Association (Counsel).
**Career:** Practice group leader for Banking and Finance Group; Partner since 1990; Best Lawyers in America since 2000.
**Personal:** Samford University (JD, summa cum laude, 1983); Auburn University (BS, Economics, 1977); Editor -in-Chief: Cumberland Law Review.

## DREW, Mark
Maynard, Cooper & Gale, P.C., Birmingham 205 254 1031
mdrew@maynardcooper.com
*Recommended in Corporate/Commercial*
**Practice Areas:** Emerging businesses; financial institutions; general corporate; mergers and acquisitions; venture capital and private equity investment. Mr Drew focuses primarily in the areas of mergers and acquisitions, venture capital financings and related corporate activities and transactions. He regularly represents both public and private companies in a variety of matters and also has significant experience representing financial institutions.
**Prof. Memberships:** American Bar Association, past Cabinet Member , past Director of the ABA/YLD. Alabama State and Birmingham Bar Associations.
**Career:** Admitted in Alabama.
**Personal:** Wake Forest University (BS, 1983); Wake Forest University School of Law (JD, 1988).

## EDWARDS, Michael L
Balch & Bingham, Birmingham 205 226 3401
medwards@balch.com
*Recommended in Litigation*
**Practice Areas:** Banking; business litigation; financial services litigation; alternative dispute resolution.
**Prof. Memberships:** Fellow, American College of Trial Lawyers; Master, Birmingham Inns of Court (President, 2001-03); Birmingham Bar Association; Birmingham Bar Foundation; Alabama State Bar; Fellow, Alabama Law Foundation; American Arbitration Association, Arbitrator – Commercial Panel; Mediator.
**Career:** Michael L Edwards' practice is concentrated in business litigation. He has represented financial institutions, accounting firms, manufacturing, mining and energy companies, as well as individuals. He also has experience in trademark, patent, trade secret, and computer litigation. Mr Edwards has written and lectured on a variety of legal topics, including trial of complex cases, appellate practice, enforcement of agreements to arbitrate, class actions, lender liability, securities litigation, accountants' liability, shareholder liability for corporate debt, covenants not to compete, and the attorney-client privilege. Mr Edwards is listed in The Best Lawyers in America.
**Personal:** Born: September 10, 1942. Education: University of Alabama (LLB,

1966); University of Alabama (AB, 1964). Military: United States Army, Judge Advocate General's Corps, 1966-71.

## FLORIE, Michael A
Starnes & Atchison LLP, Birmingham 205 868 6045
mflorie@starneslaw.com
*Recommended in Litigation*
**Prof. Memberships:** Fellow, American College of Trial Lawyers; Advocate, American Board of Trial Advocates (Alabama State President, 2002); Member, Birmingham, Alabama, Louisiana and American Bar Associations; listed – Best Lawyers in America.
**Career:** Admitted Alabama 1976, Louisiana, 1977; associate, Phelps Dunbar (New Orleans), 1977-78; Partner, Burge & Florie (Birmingham), 1978-85; Senior Partner, Starnes & Atchison, 1985-present.
**Personal:** Born April 27, 1950. Tulane University, BA, 1972; Tulane Law School, JD, 1976.

## FRANKLIN, Samuel
Lightfoot, Franklin & White, LLC, Birmingham 205 581 0700
*Recommended in Litigation*

## FRAZIER, Sydney
Cabaniss, Johnston, Gardner, Dumas & O'Neal, Birmingham 205 716 5200
*Recommended in Employment*

## GARDNER, William
Cabaniss, Johnston, Gardner, Dumas & O'Neal, Birmingham 205 716 5200
*Recommended in Employment*

## GEWIN, James
Bradley Arant Rose & White LLP, Birmingham 205 521 8352
jgewin@bradleyarant.com
*Recommended in Litigation*
**Practice Areas:** General civil litigation. Extensive experience centering around representation of corporate defendants, including clients who are claimants in commercial disputes.
**Prof. Memberships:** Admitted, Alabama (1966). Member, American College of Trial Lawyers; Alabama Law Foundation; Fellow, American Bar Foundation; Alabama Bar Association, Board of Bar Examiners (1976-80), Bar Commissioners (1991-2000); United States Court of Appeals (11th Circuit), Lawyers Qualifications and Conduct Committee.
**Career:** Joined Bradley Arant, 1967; Partner, 1973; The Best Lawyers in America; Chambers USA
**Personal:** Born 9 November 1940. LLB, University of Alabama School of Law, 1966, AB, Editor-in-Chief, Alabama Law Review; Princeton University, 1963.

## GIBBENS, Ray
Burr & Forman LLP, Birmingham 205 251 3000
*Recommended in Banking & Finance*

## GILL, Richard
Copeland, Franco, Screws & Gill, Montgomery 334 834 1180
*Recommended in Litigation*

## GRENIER, John B
Bradley Arant Rose & White LLP, Birmingham 205 521 8355
bgrenier@bradleyarant.com
*Recommended in Corporate/Commercial*
**Practice Areas:** Practices in general corporate and securities law, corporate finance, and mergers and acquisitions. Responsible Partner for the public and private offering of securities and acquisitions and divestitures in various industries.
**Prof. Memberships:** Admitted to practice in Alabama (1982). Member, American and Birmingham Bar Associations. Planning Committee, Southeastern Corporate Law Institute.
**Career:** Joined Bradley Arant in 1983; became Partner in 1990; Chairman of the Executive Committee, 2001 to present.
**Personal:** Born 28 April 1956. JD, Vanderbilt University, 1982; BA, with high distinction, University of Virginia, 1978. Phi Beta Kappa. Editor-in-Chief, Vanderbilt Law Review, 1981-82.

## HANCOCK, William K
Adams and Reese LLP, Birmingham 205 250 5007
will.hancock@arlaw.com
*Recommended in Employment*
**Practice Areas:** Partner: Special Business Services Practice Group; labor and employment; management counseling.
**Prof. Memberships:** Alabama Bar Association; American Bar Association.
**Career:** Represents management in the labor and employment field and has handled ERISA litigation matters since 1989, assisting healthcare, telecommunications, poultry processing and other clients plan, implement, and defend employment policies and procedures.
**Personal:** JD Cumberland School of Law, Alabama, 1989, Dean's Scholar and Editor of the Cumberland Law Review; BA University of the South, Sewanee, Tennessee in 1986.

## HARMON, Christopher B
Maynard, Cooper & Gale, P.C., Birmingham 205 254 1090
charmon@maynardcooper.com
*Recommended in Corporate/Commercial*
**Practice Areas:** Securities; mergers and acquisitions; emerging businesses; executive compensation; corporate governance and compliance; healthcare; financial institutions; venture capital and private equity investment; intellectual property and technology. Mr Harmon handles mergers and acquisitions, private equity, general corporate and securities matters for private and publicly held companies with a nonexclusive concentration in

transactions relating to healthcare and financial institutions. His practice also involves advising companies on corporate governance.
**Prof. Memberships:** American Bar, Alabama State Bar and Birmingham Bar Associations.
**Career:** Admitted in Alabama.
**Personal:** University of Alabama (BS, 1985); University of Alabama School of Law (JD, 1991).

## HELD, Jerry
Sirote & Permutt PC, Birmingham 205 930 5100
*Recommended in Real Estate*

## HELMSING, Frederick
Helmsing, Leach, Herlong, Newman & Rouse, PC, Mobile 251 432 5521
*Recommended in Litigation*

## HUGHEY JR, James F
Balch & Bingham, Birmingham 205 226 3469
jhughey@balch.com
*Recommended in Corporate/Commercial*
**Practice Areas:** Corporate and securities; employee benefits and executive compensation; wills, trusts, estates and wealth management; tax; healthcare; mergers and acquisitions; corporate governance.
**Prof. Memberships:** Alabama Board of Bar Examiners; American Bar Foundation, Fellow; Alabama Law Foundation, Fellow; Alabama Law Institute, Member.
**Career:** James F Hughey, Jr's practice relates primarily to corporate and securities transactions and general representation of business entities, including wealth preservation planning for business owners and executives. He has extensive experience advising both private and publicly held companies regarding corporate governance matters, business planning, mergers and acquisitions, compliance with federal and state securities laws and general corporate matters. In addition to his Corporate and Securities Practice, Mr Hughey serves as Chairman of the firm's Executive Committee. Mr Hughey is listed in The Best Lawyers in America.
**Personal:** Born: August 15, 1945. Education: New York University (LLM in Taxation, 1972); University of Alabama (JD, 1970); University of Alabama (BA, 1967).

## INGRAM, Fredric
Burr & Forman LLP, Birmingham 205 251 3000
*Recommended in Employment*

## ISOM, Chervis
Baker, Donelson, Bearman, Caldwell & Berkowitz, PC, Birmingham 205 250 8302
cisom@bakerdonelson.com
*Recommended in Real Estate*
**Practice Areas:** Former Chair of Baker Donelson's Real Estate Group. Practice concentrated in real estate and capital

finance, with emphasis on the legal aspects of the development, leasing and financing of commercial real estate including retail, office, industrial and apartment properties.
**Prof. Memberships:** Member, American College of Mortgage Attorneys. Member, American and Birmingham Bar Associations. Associate Member, International Council of Shopping Centers.
**Career:** Licensed in Alabama since 1967.
**Personal:** Birmingham-Southern College, BA, 1962. Cumberland School of Law of Samford University, JD, 1967. Member, Curia Honoris.

## JONES, Haskins
Johnston Barton Proctor & Powell LLP, Birmingham 205 458 9400
*Recommended in Banking & Finance*

## KALLON, Abdul
Bradley Arant Rose & White LLP, Birmingham 205 521 8294
akallon@bradleyarant.com
*Recommended in Employment*
**Practice Areas:** Practices labor and employment. Litigates claims on behalf of employers, provides comprehensive advice to employers on labor and employment issues, and provides legal assistance during affirmative action compliance proceedings.
**Prof. Memberships:** Admitted to practice in Alabama (1995); American Bar Association; Legal Aid Society, Birmingham Board of Trustees, Big Brothers/Big Sisters, Board of Directors; Children's Village, Board of Directors.
**Career:** Joined Bradley Arant in 1994; Partner in 2001.
**Personal:** Born 5 April 1969. AB Dartmouth College (History) 1990; JD University of Pennsylvania Law School, 1993.

## KEENE, Thomas
Rushton, Stakely, Johnston & Garrett, Montgomery 334 834 8480
*Recommended in Litigation*

## KNIGHT, Michael
McDowell Knight Roedder & Sledge LLC, Mobile 251 432 5300
*Recommended in Litigation*

## KUSHNER, Harold
Bradley Arant Rose & White LLP, Birmingham 205 521 8600
hkushner@bradleyarant.com
*Recommended in Corporate/Commercial*
**Practice Areas:** Practice concentrated in the areas of tax and corporate law, including mergers and acquisitions, securities, estate and trust planning and employer resources. Represents clients in diverse industries including steel, manufacturing, retail, technology and software, real estate development and healthcare, with an emphasis on representation of closely held corporations.
**Prof. Memberships:** Chair, Alabama Securities Commission. Member, Ameri-

can and Birmingham Bar Associations. Member, American Bar Association Personal Services Organizations Committee. Past Representative of the Alabama Bar Association to the Internal Revenue Service Practitioners Council. President of the Community Real Estate Foundation.
**Career:** Licensed in Louisiana 1971; Alabama 1975.

## LACY JR, Peyton
Ogletree, Deakins, Nash, Smoak & Stewart, PC, Birmingham 205 328 1900
peyton.lacy@ogletreedeakins.com
*Recommended in Employment*
**Practice Areas:** Labor relations and employment law.
**Prof. Memberships:** Alabama, American and District of Columbia Bar Associations. National Association of College and University Attorneys.
**Career:** Admitted to practice in Alabama, District of Columbia, US Supreme Court, US Court of Appeals (Fifth, Eighth and Eleventh Circuits), and US District Courts (Western District of Louisiana; Northern, Middle and Southern Districts of Alabama; Northern District of Mississippi; and Northern District of Florida). Adjunct Professor of labor law at the University of Alabama (1987-88).
**Publications:** Co-authored the 'Alabama Employers Handbook'.
**Personal:** University of Alabama (BA, 1962), University of Alabama School of Law (LLB, 1965).

## LANIER, Randolph H
Balch & Bingham, Birmingham 205 226 3487
rlanier@balch.com
*Recommended in Real Estate*
**Practice Areas:** Construction; real estate; finance, lending and leasing.
**Prof. Memberships:** Birmingham Bar Association; Alabama State Bar; American Bar Association; International Council of Shopping Centers; National Association of Industrial and Office Properties.
**Career:** Randolph H Lanier is an attorney with over 25 years experience practicing in the real estate and financial services industries, with emphasis on commercial lending and commercial real estate development. His work includes issues relating to financing, zoning, land use controls, street and subdivision regulations, environmental matters, restrictive covenants, owner and commercial associations, title reviews, utilities, regulatory concerns, purchase and sale agreements, construction and architects' contracts, building and other permitting matters, NPDES storm water permits, bonding, surveys, flood insurance regulations, annexation issues, common area maintenance, and other construction, development and leasing issues. Mr Lanier has also been listed in The Best Lawyers in America from the 1987 edition-present.

**Personal:** Born: August 26, 1949. Education: Vanderbilt University (JD, 1974); University of Alabama (BS, 1971).

### LEACH JR, John
Helmsing, Leach, Herlong, Newman & Rouse, PC, Mobile 251 432 5521
*Recommended in Litigation*

### LEE, Jeffrey
Maynard, Cooper & Gale, P.C., Birmingham 205 254 1987
jlee@maynardcooper.com
*Recommended in Employment*
**Practice Areas:** Labor and employment. Mr Lee's practice is focused primarily on employment litigation. In the past 10 years, Mr Lee has tried 11 cases to a jury verdict. In two of those cases, he represented plaintiffs in commercial disputes where his clients received verdicts of $7,546,515.00 and $3,400,000.00. In the other cases, Mr Lee represented the defendant in various employment lawsuits. His clients received defense verdicts in seven of the cases. In the other two, the plaintiffs received verdicts of $3,000.00 and $5,000.00.
**Personal:** Auburn University (BS, 1998); University of Alabama School of Law (JD, 2001).

### LEHR, Richard
Lehr Middlebrooks Price & Vreeland, P.C., Birmingham 205 326 3002
*Recommended in Employment*

### LIGHTFOOT, Warren
Lightfoot, Franklin & White, LLC, Birmingham 205 581 0700
*Recommended in Litigation*

### LUCAS, Michael
Burr & Forman LLP, Birmingham 205 251 3000
*Recommended in Employment*

### MARSH, David
Marsh, Rickard & Bryan P.C., Birmingham 205 879 1981
*Recommended in Litigation*

### MAY, James
Bradley Arant Rose & White LLP, Birmingham 205 521 8324
jmay@bradleyarant.com
*Recommended in Employment*
**Practice Areas:** Practices labor and employment. Extensive experience in individual and major class action employment discrimination cases, collective actions under the FLSA. Defends EEOC charges and OFCCP proceedings.
**Prof. Memberships:** Admitted to Practice in Alabama (1980). Past Chair of the Alabama Bar's Labor Section. Has appeared in a leading legal publication in America since 1995-96 and Member of the College of Labor and Employment Lawyers.
**Career:** Joined Bradley Arant in 1980; Partner in 1987.
**Personal:** Born 7 Jan 1949. BS University of Mississippi (Mathematics), 1971; JD

University of Virginia 1980. LT, USN 1971-77.

### MCDOWELL, Jerry
McDowell Knight Roedder & Sledge LLC, Mobile 251 432 5300
*Recommended in Litigation*

### MCGIVAREN, Crawford
Cabaniss, Johnston, Gardner, Dumas & O'Neal, Birmingham 205 716 5200
*Recommended in Litigation*

### MCKIBBEN, Michael D
Bradley Arant Rose & White LLP, Birmingham 205 521 8421
mmckibben@bradleyarant.com
*Recommended in Litigation*
**Practice Areas:** Chairs firm's Litigation Group. Represents clients in a variety of areas, including medical, manufacturing, and computer industries. Subject matters include contracts and business torts, professional negligence, and products liability disputes.
**Prof. Memberships:** ABA; DRI; International Association of Defense Counsel (Drug and Medical Device and Medical Defense Committees); Alabama Defense Lawyers Association. Alabama State Bar (Character & Fitness Committee); Birmingham Bar (Medical Liaison Committee).
**Publications:** 'The Resale Price Maintenance Compromise', 38 Vand. L. Rev. 163.
**Personal:** JD (Patrick Wilson Scholar), Vanderbilt University, 1985; BS (magna cum laude), Spring Hill College, 1981. Associate Editor, Vanderbilt Law Review.

### MCWHORTER, Hobart
Bradley Arant Rose & White LLP, Birmingham 205 521 8241
hmcwhorter@bradleyarant.com
*Recommended in Litigation*
**Practice Areas:** Senior Partner, general civil litigation. Extensive experience securities fraud, commercial litigation, construction, environmental, products liability, and insurance defense.
**Prof. Memberships:** Admitted, Alabama (1958). Fellow, American College of Trial Lawyers; International Association of Defense Counsel; International Association of Railroad Trial Counsel; American Board of Trial Advocates; American Bar Association; Fellow, Alabama Law Foundation.
**Career:** Joined Bradley Arant Rose & White LLP, 1958; Partner, 1963; Litigation Practice Group.
**Personal:** Born 24 December 1931. LLB, University of Virginia Law School 1958; BA, Yale University, 1953.

### MIDDLEBROOKS, David
Lehr Middlebrooks Price & Vreeland, P.C., Birmingham 205 326 3002
*Recommended in Employment*

### MILLER JR, John
Miller Hamilton Snider & Odom LLC, Mobile 251 432 1414
*Recommended in Banking & Finance*

### MILLS, Gail
Burr & Forman LLP, Birmingham 205 251 3000
*Recommended in Banking & Finance, Real Estate*

### MINISMAN JR, B G
Baker, Donelson, Bearman, Caldwell & Berkowitz, PC, Birmingham 205 250 8305
bminisman@bakerdonelson.com
*Recommended in Corporate/Commercial*
**Practice Areas:** Practice concentrated in corporate, securities and health law. Extensive experience in representing public companies regarding compliance with proxy solicitation and periodic reporting requirements of the Securities Exchange Act of 1934, tender offers, corporate governance, going-private transactions and mergers and acquisitions. Practice also includes representation of a variety of closely-held companies, including private placements of equity securities.
**Prof. Memberships:** Member, American, Alabama and Birmingham Bar Associations. Member, Order of the Coif.
**Career:** Licensed in Alabama since 1970.
**Personal:** University of North Carolina, BA, 1967. Emory University School of Law, JD, 1970, with distinction.

### MITCHELL, Chris
Maynard, Cooper & Gale, P.C., Birmingham 205 254 1160
cmitchell@maynardcooper.com
*Recommended in Employment*
**Practice Areas:** Labor and Employment. Mr Mitchell represents management in a wide variety of labor, EEO and employment matters. His experience includes advising management on union organizing issues, negotiating union contracts and handling labor-management arbitrations. In addition, he has tried over thirty employment discrimination cases to successful jury verdicts and has extensive experience in appellate courts.
**Career:** Admitted before the federal courts in Alabama and Georgia, the US Supreme Court and the Federal Courts of Appeal in several major US cities.
**Personal:** Georgia Tech (BS, 1970 summa cum laude); University of Alabama School of Law (JD, 1973).

### MIXSON, Dwight
Burr & Forman LLP, Birmingham 205 251 3000
*Recommended in Banking & Finance, Real Estate*

### MONK, Stephen
Bradley Arant Rose & White LLP, Birmingham 205 521 8429
smonk@bradleyarant.com
*Recommended in Real Estate*
**Practice Areas:** Partner in Birmingham office specializing in representation of real estate development clients. Extensive experience in large-scale residential, retail, office, golf and mixed-use developments, including annexation and planned unit development matters and formulation of restrictive covenants and residential, office and mixed use Condominiums.
**Prof. Memberships:** Admitted to practice in Alabama (1980). Member, American, Alabama and Birmingham Bar Associations.
**Career:** Joined Bradley Arant Rose & White LLP in 1996 as Partner; 1983-96: General Counsel of Daniel Corporation, Birmingham, Alabama.
**Personal:** Born 28 February 1955; JD (cum laude), Cumberland School of Law (Birmingham, Alabama) (1980); BS (Accounting), Auburn University (1977).

### MORROW, John H
Bradley Arant Rose & White LLP, Birmingham 205 521 8212
jmorrow@bradleyarant.com
*Recommended in Litigation*
**Practice Areas:** General civil litigation, including commercial litigation, product and personal injury defense.
**Prof. Memberships:** Member, American College of Trial Attorneys; listed: Chambers USA 2003, 2004 and 2005, Alabama, leading general commercial litigation attorneys; listed: The Best Lawyers in America, Business Litigation, Personal Injury Litigation, First Amendment Law, since inception; Birmingham Bar Association, President, 1981.
**Career:** Joined Bradley Arant Rose & White LLP, 1958; became Partner, 1963.
**Personal:** Born July 15, 1931. Order of the Coif, JD, University of Michigan Law School, 1958; AB, Princeton University, (magna cum laude), Phi Betta Kappa, 1953.

### MORROW, Randall H
Maynard, Cooper & Gale, P.C., Birmingham 205 254 1047
rmorrow@maynardcooper.com
*Recommended in Banking & Finance*
**Practice Areas:** Commercial lending; real estate; financial institutions; energy and natural resources. Mr Morrow's commercial lending practice focuses on all aspects of the representation of lenders and borrowers in secured and unsecured transactions, structured financing transactions and multistate transactions. His real estate practice focuses on the representation of sellers and purchasers in real estate acquisitions, development, financing and leasing matters.

**Prof. Memberships:** American, Alabama State and Birmingham Bar Associations. Fellow in the American College of Mortgage Attorneys.
**Career:** Admitted in Alabama.
**Personal:** Vanderbilt University (BA, 1985 magna cum laude); Vanderbilt University School of Law (JD; 1988).

## NELSON, Carol Sue
Maynard, Cooper & Gale, P.C., Birmingham 205 254 1119
cnelson@maynardcooper.com
*Recommended in Employment*
**Practice Areas:** Labor and employment. Practice focuses on employment litigation, advising and counseling clients on employment issues, and affirmative action and OFCCP. Representative Cases: defending nationwide retailer in race discrimination class action. Defending nationwide retailer in class action regarding time keeping and wage practices. Defending healthcare institutions, insurance companies, financial institutions, manufacturers, retailers, and municipalities in discrimination actions, FMLA, ADEA, ADA FLSA, and retaliatory discharge.
**Prof. Memberships:** American, Alabama State and Birmingham Bar Associations.
**Career:** Law clerk to Judge James H Hancock.
**Personal:** Auburn University (BA, 1974 summa cum laude); Cumberland School of Law (JD, 1977 magna cum laude).

## NOVAK, Tabor
Ball, Ball, Matthews & Novak, Montgomery 334 387 7680
*Recommended in Litigation*

## POWELL, Fred
Burr & Forman LLP, Birmingham 205 251 3000
*Recommended in Real Estate*

## POWELL III, Charles
Johnston Barton Proctor & Powell LLP, Birmingham 205 458 9400
*Recommended in Employment*

## PRICE, Gene
Burr & Forman LLP, Birmingham 205 251 3000
*Recommended in Corporate/Commercial*

## RODGERS, W Stanley
Lanier Ford Shaver & Payne P.C., Huntsville 256 535 1100
*Recommended in Litigation*

## ROGERS, Alan T
Balch & Bingham, Birmingham 205 226 3486
arogers@balch.com
*Recommended in Litigation*
**Practice Areas:** Energy and utility litigation; insurance industry litigation; financial services litigation; business litigation; appellate.
**Prof. Memberships:** Federation of

Insurance and Corporate Counsel; Alabama State Bar; Alabama Defense Lawyers Association; Louisiana State Bar; American Bar Association; Rotary International; Newcomen Society; American Inns of Court.
**Career:** Alan T Rogers is Chairman of the firm's Litigation Section. He has substantial experience presenting cases to juries, arbitrators and appellate courts. His cases and legal counseling work have involved the energy industry, the commercial insurance industry, the financial services industry and others. Mr Rogers also has experience in representing a variety of other businesses and professionals in civil litigation. Alan is also listed in The Best Lawyers in America, 2005-06 Edition.
**Personal:** Born: March 10, 1954; education: Tulane University School of Law (JD, cum laude, 1980); Birmingham-Southern College (BA, 1977).

## ROGERS, Bruce
Bainbridge, Mims, Rogers & Smith, LLP, Birmingham
205 879 1100
*Recommended in Litigation*

## ROGERS, E Mabry
Bradley Arant Rose & White LLP, Birmingham
205 521 8225
mrogers@bradleyarant.com
*Recommended in Litigation*
**Practice Areas:** Construction contract negotiation, advice and litigation, all over the world. Familiar with virtually all ADR methods, US and international. Frequent speaker on construction topics.
**Prof. Memberships:** American College of Construction Lawyers; American Bar Association; Forum on the Construction Industry.
**Career:** Partner since 1980.
**Publications:** Frequently published on various construction topics.
**Personal:** JD, (cum laude, class secretary), Harvard Law School, 1974; BA (cum laude, honors English), Yale University, 1969.

## ROSE JR, J William
Johnston Barton Proctor & Powell LLP, Birmingham 205 458 9400
*Recommended in Corporate/Commercial*

## SELLERS, Randal H
Starnes & Atchison LLP, Birmingham 205 868 6019
rsellers@starneslaw.com
*Recommended in Litigation*
**Practice Areas:** 24 years of experience dedicated to civil litigation in state and federal courts.
**Prof. Memberships:** Fellow, American College of Trial Lawyers; Advocate, American Board of Trial Advocates; Member, Defense Lawyers Association; Member, Birmingham, Alabama and

American Bar Association; Listed Best Lawyers in America.
**Career:** Admitted to practice in 1981 and has since tried cases in state and federal courts throughout Alabama.
**Personal:** Graduated from Vanderbilt University, cum laude, with a BA degree in 1978. Graduated from Vanderbilt University, School of Law in 1981.

## SEXTON, Robert
Maynard, Cooper & Gale, P.C., Birmingham 205 254 1032
rsexton@maynardcooper.com
*Recommended in Real Estate*
**Practice Areas:** Commercial lending; real estate. Mr Sexton's lending practice focuses on representing lenders in loan transactions secured primarily by real estate. His real estate practice focuses on representing sellers and purchasers in the acquisition, development, financing and leasing of income producing properties.
**Prof. Memberships:** American College of Mortgage Attorneys, Fellow. American, Alabama State and Birmingham Bar Associations.
**Career:** Admitted in Alabama. Listed in Best Lawyers in America since 1995 in Real Estate. Listed in Chambers since 2003 in Real Estate.
**Personal:** Birmingham-Southern College (BA, 1974); University of Alabama School of Law (JD, 1974).

## SHEVIN, Maurice
Sirote & Permutt PC, Birmingham 205 930 5100
*Recommended in Banking & Finance*

## SIEGAL, Bradley
Leitman, Siegal & Payne, PC, Birmingham 205 251 5900
*Recommended in Real Estate*

## SIEGAL, Don
Leitman, Siegal & Payne, PC, Birmingham 205 251 5900
*Recommended in Real Estate*

## SINGER, Fern H
Baker, Donelson, Bearman, Caldwell & Berkowitz, PC, Birmingham 205 250 3801
fsinger@bakerdonelson.com
*Recommended in Employment*
**Practice Areas:** Chair of Baker Donelson's Labor & Employment Group. Practice concentrated in labor and employment, alternative dispute resolution, commercial litigation, and fair housing litigation.
**Prof. Memberships:** Charter Member, Alabama Academy of Mediators. Former Adjunct Faculty Member, University of Alabama School of Law. Former Chair, Employment Law Section of the Alabama Defense Lawyers Association. Member, American Bar Association and National Association for Women Lawyers.
**Career:** Licensed in New York since 1981 and Alabama since 1987.
**Personal:** State University of New York

at Stony Brook, BA, 1973. St John's University School of Law, JD, 1980.

## SMITH, David M
Maynard, Cooper & Gale, P.C., Birmingham 205 254 1059
dsmith@maynardcooper.com
*Recommended in Employment*
**Practice Areas:** Labor and employment. Mr Smith's primary practice area is in representing management or the employer in employment cases. Mr Smith has 23 years experience and is the original Member of the firm's 16-member Labor Practice Group. Mr Smith has an active non-litigation practice in advising clients on discipline, contracts, policies, arbitrations, RIFs and benefits in all types of employment and labor relations matters.
**Prof. Memberships:** American and Alabama State Bar Associations.
**Career:** Law clerk to Federal District Judge Robert B Propst, 1982-83.
**Personal:** Birmingham-Southern College (BA, 1979 magna cum laude); Vanderbilt University School of Law (JD, 1982).

## SMITH, Felton W
Balch & Bingham, Birmingham 205 226 3458
fsmith@balch.com
*Recommended in Real Estate*
**Practice Areas:** Real estate; finance, lending and leasing; real property/title insurance litigation; condemnation, land use and water rights.
**Prof. Memberships:** American Bar Association; Alabama State Bar; Birmingham Bar Association.
**Career:** Felton Smith practices primarily in the areas of real estate and finance and representing a range of clients from large corporations to individual owners and investors. The largest part of Mr Smith's practice is acquisitions, sales, operation, management and leasing of commercial and industrial real estate for users and investors. He also represents lenders and borrowers in various types of in-state and multi-state financing transactions. Prior to joining Balch & Bingham LLP, Mr Smith worked as a banker for a number of years in the areas of branch banking, investment services, correspondent banking and commercial lending and is a graduate of the Stonier Graduate School of Banking.
**Personal:** Born: March 29, 1955; education: University of Alabama (JD, 1990); Colorado University (BA, 1977).

**ST CLAIR, Jay D**
Bradley Arant Rose & White LLP,
Birmingham 205 521 8344
jstclair@bradleyarant.com
*Recommended in Employment*
**Practice Areas:** Labor and employment.
**Prof. Memberships:** ABA, Sections on Labor and Employment and Litigation.
**Career:** Partner since 1990. Adjunct Professor, Cumberland School of Law, 1999 to present.
**Publications:** Has lectured and written extensively on labor and employment matters.
**Personal:** Yale Law School (JD, 1983), University of Tennessee (BA, 1980).

**STARLING III, M Jefferson**
Balch & Bingham, Birmingham
205 226 3406
jstarling@balch.com
*Recommended in Employment*
**Practice Areas:** Labor and employment.
**Prof. Memberships:** American Bar Association, Labor & Employment, Litigation Sections; Birmingham Bar Association; State Bar of Georgia; Alabama State Bar.
**Career:** Mr Starling is the Chair of the firm's Labor & Employment Practice Group. His practice is devoted to the representation of employers in employment litigation, preventive advice and counselling and labor relations. Mr Starling is a regular speaker and has conducted numerous training sessions across the United States for diverse clients, including some of the nation's largest employers.
**Personal:** Born December 2, 1966; education: University of Arkansas School of Law (JD with honors, 1992); Vanderbilt University (BA 1989).

**STARNES, Stancil**
Starnes & Atchison LLP, Birmingham
205 868 6014
sstarnes@starneslaw.com
*Recommended in Litigation*
**Practice Areas:** For over 30 years, he has represented local and national clients in a wide range of civil trials, appeals and litigation in state and federal courts, including antitrust, securities, defense of major law firms, professional liability, RICO, insurance and complex civil litigation.
**Prof. Memberships:** Fellow, American College of Trial Lawyers; Advocate, American Board of Trial Attorneys; Chair, Alabama Supreme Court Advisory

Committee on Alabama Rules of Civil Procedure; Member, Alabama Law Institute.
**Career:** Admitted in 1972. Formed current firm in 1975, specializing in civil litigation. Firm has grown from two lawyers in 1975 to over 50 lawyers in 2006.
**Personal:** Graduated from University of Alabama with BS in Business Administration in 1969 and Cumberland School of Law at Samford University, summa cum laude, in 1972.

**STEPHENSON, Jack**
Burr & Forman LLP, Birmingham
205 251 3000
*Recommended in
Corporate/Commercial*

**STEWART, Carol**
Burr & Forman LLP, Birmingham
205 251 3000
*Recommended in Real Estate*

**SYLVESTER, William**
Walston, Wells, Anderson & Bains,
Birmingham 205 244 5200
*Recommended in Real Estate*

**THUSTON, Lee**
Burr & Forman LLP, Birmingham
205 251 3000
*Recommended in
Corporate/Commercial*

**TOZZI, Rik S**
Starnes & Atchison LLP, Birmingham
205 868 6088
rtozzi@starneslaw.com
*Recommended in Litigation*
**Practice Areas:** His practice involves representing a wide range of commercial entities and financial institutions including national banks, state chartered banks, broker-dealers, mortgage companies, mortgage servicing companies and insurance companies in both state and federal litigation throughout the country. He has served as Lead Counsel in numerous class, mass and individual actions involving FCRA, FDCPA, FCBA, HOLA, RESPA, privacy claims, identity theft, RICO, unfair competition, state UDTPA laws and allegations of fraud or bad faith. A significant portion of his practice focuses on enforcing arbitration agreements and arbitrating before the NASD, AAA, JAMS and NAF.
**Prof. Memberships:** Member, Birmingham, Alabama, Fifth Circuit Court of Appeals, Sixth Circuit Court of Appeals, Eleventh Circuit Court of Appeals and American Bar Associations.

**Career:** Admitted 1993. Burr & Forman, associate, 1993-95; Deputy Attorney General, State of Alabama, 1995; Starnes & Atchison LLP, Partner and associate, 1995-present.
**Publications:** He is a regular speaker on class action issues and removal/trial strategy in dangerous jurisdictions.
**Personal:** Graduated with honors degree from Oxford University (Mansfield College) with a BA/MA in 1990; JD cum laude from Tulane University School of Law in 1993. Certificate in Environmental Law from Tulane University School of Law in 1993. Editor, Tulane Environmental Law Journal.

**TRACY, Timothy J**
Balch & Bingham, Birmingham
205 226 3456
ttracy@balch.com
*Recommended in
Corporate/Commercial*
**Practice Areas:** Corporate and securities; tax; mergers and acquisitions.
**Prof. Memberships:** Birmingham Bar Association; Alabama State Bar; American Bar Association.
**Career:** Timothy J Tracy's practice is devoted primarily to mergers and acquisitions, corporate and project finance, and corporate and partnership taxation. He has structured, negotiated and documented numerous acquisitions of stock and assets of both public and private companies, project finance transactions for independent power production facilities, steel production facilities and pulp and paper facilities, leveraged lease financings of equipment and industrial facilities, and secured and unsecured corporate borrowings. Mr Tracy also regularly advises and counsels companies regarding a variety of federal and state taxation matters, including obtaining from the Internal Revenue Service private letter rulings on tax issues and consequences of multi-party business transactions.
**Personal:** Born: Alabama, September 1, 1956; education: New York University (LLM in Taxation, 1985); Cumberland School of Law (JD, cum laude, 1984); University of Alabama (BS, 1979).

**VINSON, Laurence D**
Bradley Arant Rose & White LLP,
Birmingham 205 521 8607
lvinson@bradleyarant.com
*Recommended in Banking & Finance*
**Practice Areas:** Bank regulation, consumer credit compliance, and commercial transactions, including interstate branching, exportation of interest rates and fees, permissible activities of banks, and international trade finance.
**Prof. Memberships:** ABA; Alabama State Bar; Birmingham Bar Association; Alabama Law Institute (Council Member; Chair of revision committees on UCC Articles 3 and 4, Article 4A, Article 9, and Articles 1 and 7); former Member, State Board of Bar Examiners; Conference on Consumer Finance Law.
**Career:** Partner since 1979.
**Publications:** Has written and lectured on a wide range of banking and UCC topics.
**Personal:** University of Alabama (BS, 1969; JD, 1973).

**VREELAND, Albert**
Lehr Middlebrooks Price & Vreeland,
P.C., Birmingham 205 326 3002
*Recommended in Employment*

**WARE, Paul**
Bradley Arant Rose & White LLP,
Birmingham 205 521 8624
pware@bradleyarant.com
*Recommended in
Corporate/Commercial*
**Practice Areas:** Practices in general corporate and securities law, corporate finance, and mergers and acquisitions. Has been the responsible Partner for the public and private offering of securities and acquisitions and divestitures in various industries, including specifically financial institutions.
**Prof. Memberships:** Admitted to practice in Alabama (1987). Member, American Bar Association.
**Career:** Joined Bradley Arant Rose in 1986, became Partner in 1993.
**Personal:** Born December 3, 1960. JD, Washington & Lee University, 1986, cum laude; Ottenheimer Brothers Scholar, 1984-86; Lead Articles Editor, Washington & Lee Law Review, 1985-86; BA, University of the South, 1982; Georgia M Wilkins Scholar.

**WHITE JR, Jere**
Lightfoot, Franklin & White, LLC,
Birmingham 205 581 0700
*Recommended in Litigation*

# BALCH & BINGHAM LLP

## THE FIRM

**Managing Partner & Chairman, Executive Committee:** James F Hughey, Jr

**Number of partners:** 136
**Number of other lawyers:** 109

## AREAS OF PRACTICE:

Litigation . . . . . . . . . . . . . . . . . . . . . . . . . . . . . . . . . . . . . . . . . . . . 30%
Financial Services & Transactions . . . . . . . . . . . . . . . . . . . . . . . . . . . . 19%
Utility, Legislative & Regulatory . . . . . . . . . . . . . . . . . . . . . . . . . . . . 18%
Corporate, Tax & Finance . . . . . . . . . . . . . . . . . . . . . . . . . . . . . . . . . 17%
Labor & Employment . . . . . . . . . . . . . . . . . . . . . . . . . . . . . . . . . . . . 9%
Environmental & Natural Resources . . . . . . . . . . . . . . . . . . . . . . . . . . 7%

**FIRM OVERVIEW:** Founded in 1922, Balch & Bingham LLP is one of the largest law firms in Alabama with offices in Birmingham, Montgomery, and Huntsville, Alabama, Gulfport and Jackson, Mississippi, and Washington, DC, Balch & Bingham LLP serves a diverse group of clients in business and litigation matters.

## MAIN AREAS OF PRACTICE:

**Litigation:** Attorneys in this group handle trial and appellate practice before federal and state courts, administrative agencies and arbitration panels. The litigation attorneys handle cases in the areas of antitrust, professional liability, consumer finance, insurance, personal injury and property damage, securities, accounting, construction, products liability, intellectual property and trade secrets, computers and technology, First Amendment and media. This group supports the litigation needs of the firm's other practice groups, including banking, healthcare, ERISA and managed care litigation, environmental, labor and commercial disputes.

**Financial Services & Transactions:** The firm represents financial institutions in bank and bank holding formations, mergers and acquisitions, establishing branches, interstate banking, and compliance with state and federal regulatory matters. In the area of commercial real estate, developers, owners and mortgage lenders are represented in the many aspects of project development. The firm has played a major role in significant real estate projects throughout the State of Alabama. The firm's Bankruptcy Practice is devoted to creditors' rights, debt restructuring, workouts, debt collection and bankruptcy.

**Utility, Legislative & Regulatory:** The Utility, Legislative and Regulatory Practice handles legal issues associated with every energy option. In addition to being active in the field of utility regulation and rate making, these attorneys handle contract work, including drafting, negotiation and administration and have particular expertise with contracts relating to the purchase, sale and transportation of coal, natural gas and other energy resources. Attorneys are also actively involved in the drafting and evaluating of proposed federal and state legislation and regulations.

**Corporate, Tax & Finance:** The firm's Corporate and Securities Practice provides business planning and counseling services to corporations, partnerships and individuals, including structuring and restructuring business organizations and preparing agreements for corporate and partnership governance, shareholder and partnership relationships and employment arrangements. The firm assists clients with public and private securities offerings, corporate transactions and finance, project finance, intellectual property, and antitrust matters. This group also includes attorneys practicing in the following areas: (1) general taxation, including tax planning and representation in complex business transactions involving publicly traded and closely held corporations, general and limited partnerships, joint ventures, proprietorships, and charitable and other tax-exempt organizations, tax litigation, and representation before the Internal Revenue Service and state and local administrative bodies; (2) estate planning and administration, including preparation of wills and trusts and counseling and representation in gift and estate tax matters; and (3) governmental and public authority finance, in which area the firm's attorneys serve as bond counsel,

## HEAD OFFICE

**ALABAMA**
1710 Sixth Avenue North, **Birmingham**, AL 35203
**Tel:** 205 251 8100  **Fax:** 205 226 8798
**Email:** nyardley@balch.com
**Website:** www.balch.com

## BRANCH OFFICES

**ALABAMA**
105 Tallapoosa Street, Suite 200, **Montgomery**, AL 36104
**Tel:** 334 834 6500  **Fax:** 334 269 3115

655 Gallatin Street, **Huntsville**, AL 35801
**Tel:** 256 551 0171  **Fax:** 256 512 0119

**DISTRICT OF COLUMBIA**
1275 Pennsylvania Avenue, NW, **Washington, DC** 20004
**Tel:** 202 347 6000  **Fax:** 202 347 6001

**GEORGIA**
14 Piedmont Center, Suite 1100, 3535 Piedmont Rd, NE, **Atlanta, GA** 30305
**Tel:** 404 261 6020  **Fax:** 404 261 3656

**MISSISSIPPI**
1310 Twenty Fifth Avenue, **Gulfport**, MS 39501
**Tel:** 228 864 9900  **Fax:** 228 864 8221

401 East Capitol Street, Suite 200, **Jackson**, MS 39201
**Tel:** 601 961 9900  **Fax:** 601 961 4466

## CONTACTS

Litigation . . . . . . . . . . . . . . . . . . . . . . . . . . . . . . . . . . . . . . . Alan T Rogers
**Financial Services & Transactions** . . . . . . . . . . . . . . . . . H Hampton Boles
**Utility, Legislative & Regulatory** . . . . . . . . . . . . . . . . . . . DH McCrary
. . . . . . . . . . . . . . . . . . . . . . . . . . . . . . . . . . . . . . . . M Stanford Blanton
**Labor & Employment** . . . . . . . . . . . . . . . . . . . . . . . M Jefferson Starling, III
**Environmental & Natural Resources** . . . . . . . . . . . . . . Steven G McKinney

underwriter's counsel and issuer's counsel in tax-exempt and taxable financing on behalf of the State of Alabama, agencies and departments of the State, municipalities and counties and numerous public authorities, boards and corporations at the State and local levels.

**Labor & Employment:** Attorneys in this group advise clients on employment and labor issues and represent clients in administrative proceedings, elections, arbitrations, and jury and non-jury trials in state and federal forums. Development of effective employment policies, testing and other employee selection procedures, employee manuals, and programs to control drug and alcohol abuse are among the services offered. Industries served by the firm's labor and employment attorneys include utility, construction, manufacturing, retail, banking and financial organizations as well as municipalities, school boards and universities.

**Environmental & Natural Resources:** The Environmental and Natural Resources Group provides representation and counseling on environmental and natural resource issues to clients ranging from individuals and small businesses to large corporations. Attorneys are actively engaged in state and federal legislation processes and the related administrative rulemaking proceedings. Using their knowledge of the laws, regulations and political climate, the attorneys provide direction on compliance issues, applications for environmental permits, and the appeal and litigation defense of state and federal environmental issues.

**INTERNATIONAL WORK:** The firm has assisted its clients from time to time in transactions in foreign countries.

# BRADLEY ARANT ROSE & WHITE LLP

## THE FIRM

**Executive Committee Chairman:** John B Grenier

**Number of partners:** 138
**Number of other lawyers:** 104

**FIRM OVERVIEW:** More than 240 Bradley Arant Rose & White LLP lawyers resident in six offices located in the Southeastern United States provide clients with a broad range of legal experience and business resources. Since its founding in Birmingham, Alabama, in 1871, the firm has remained committed to providing the highest quality legal services to its clients, understanding and addressing their needs, and doing so in a timely and cost-effective manner. The firm's offices are located in Birmingham, Huntsville and Montgomery, Alabama, Jackson, Mississippi, Charlotte, North Carolina and Washington, DC.
Bradley Arant's practice groups work closely together, sharing information and lending expertise as needed. This team approach ensures that each matter is handled by the lawyers whose skill and experience are best suited for the clients' particular needs.

**MAIN AREAS OF PRACTICE:** Practice areas include alternative dispute resolution; antitrust and trade regulation; appellate litigation; banking and financial services; bankruptcy, reorganization, restructuring and insolvency; complex and multi-district litigation; construction and procurement and government contracts; corporate and securities; energy; environmental law and litigation; ERISA and ERISA litigation; general litigation; governmental affairs; healthcare; healthcare fraud and abuse; intellectual property (copyrights, patents, trademarks and trade secrets); international law and transactions; labor and employment; media law; mergers and acquisitions; partnership law; private equity, venture capital and investment funds; products liability; public finance; public utility law; real estate law, finance and development; tax exempt entities; taxation (federal, state and local) and tax litigation; trusts and estates and white-collar crime.

**CLIENTS:** Aker Kvaerner; Alabama Municipal Electric Authority; AmSouth Bancorporation; Associated Builders and Contractors, Inc.; Associated Grocers of Alabama, Inc.; AT&T; Auburn University; Bayer Corporation; BE&K, Inc.; BioCryst Pharmaceuticals; BP/Amoco; Brasfield & Gorrie, LLC; Bridgestone / Firestone, Inc.; Champion International Corporation; Chevron/Texaco; Chicago Bridge & Iron Company; Children's Health System of Alabama; Coca-Cola Bottling Company United, Inc.; ComFrame Software Corporation; Cooper Tire & Rubber Company; Daniel Realty; Ductile Iron Pipe Research Association; EBSCO Industries, Inc.; EBSCO Realty; Energen/Alagasco; Express Oil Change, LLC; Financial Investors of the South; First Commercial Bank; Graham & Company, Inc.; B.L. Harbert LLC; HealthSouth Corporation; Hunt Refining Co.; Hyundai Motor Manufacturing of Alabama, LLC; Jim Walter Resources, Inc.; MeadowBrook Healthcare, Inc. and its subsidiaries; Michelin Tire Corp.; MONY Life Insurance Co.; National Cement; Pfizer, Inc.; Principal Life Insurance Co.; Progressive Casualty Insurance; Randall Publishing Company; Regions Financial Corporation; Retirement Systems of Alabama; Russell Corporation; Shoney's; Southern Applied Technologies, Inc.; Southern BioSystems, Inc.; Southern Pipe & Supply Company, Inc.; Southern Progress Corporation; Sprint; Synovus Financial Corp.; The Clark Construction Group; The Goodyear Tire & Rubber Co.; The Huntsville Times; The New York Times; 3M Company; Torchmark Corporationl; U.S. Pipe and Foundry Co.; University of Alabama; University of Alabama at Birmingham; University of Alabama Health Services Foundation, P.C.; University of South Alabama; Vulcan Materials Company; Wachovia Bank, N.A..

## HEAD OFFICE

**ALABAMA**
One Federal Place, 1819 Fifth Avenue North, **Birmingham**, 35203-2119
**Tel:** 205 521 8000   **Fax:** 205 521 8800
**Email:** info@bradleyarant.com
**Website:** www.bradleyarant.com

## BRANCH OFFICES

**ALABAMA**
200 Clinton Avenue West, Suite 900, **Huntsville**, AL, 35801-4900
**Tel:** 256 517 5100   **Fax:** 256 517 5200

Alabama Center for Commerce, 401 Adams Avenue, Suite 780,
**Montgomery**, AL, 36104
**Tel:** 334 956 7700   **Fax:** 334 956 7701

**MISSISSIPPI**
188 East Capitol Street, Suite 450, **Jackson**, MS, 39201
**Tel:** 601 948 8000   **Fax:** 601 948 3000

**DISTRICT OF COLUMBIA**
1133 Connecticut Avenue NW, **Washington**, DC, 20036
**Tel:** 202 393 7150   **Fax:** 202 347 1684

**NORTH CAROLINA**
Bank of America Corporate Center, 100 N Tyron Street, Suite 2690,
**Charlotte**, NC 28202
**Tel:** 704 338 6000   **Fax:** 704 332 8858

## CONTACTS

| | |
|---|---|
| **Birmingham Office** | John B Grenier |
| **Charlotte Office** | John D Bond |
| **Huntsville Office** | Hall B Bryant |
| **Montgomery Office** | Philip H Butler |
| **Jackson Office** | Margaret O Cupples |
| **Washington, DC Office** | Douglas L Patin |

| | |
|---|---|
| **Appellate Litigation** | Matthew H Lembke (Birmingham) |
| **Banking & Financial Services** | J David Dresher (Birmingham) |
| **Competitive Practices & IP** | Thad G Long (Birmingham) |
| **Construction & Procurement** | Walter J Sears (Birmingham) |
| **Corporate & Securities** | Virginia C Patterson (Birmingham) |
| **Emerging Business & Tevhnology** | Revelle S Gwyn (Huntsville) |
| **Energy** | John G Harrell (Birmingham) |
| **Environmental** | Sid J Trant (Birmingham) |
| **Government Affairs** | Luther J Strange (Birmingham) |
| **Healthcare** | Deane K Corliss (Birmingham) |
| **Labor & Employment** | James P Alexander (Birmingham) |
| **Litigation** | Michael D McKibben (Birmingham) |
| **Public Finance** | P Nicholas Greenwood (Birmingham) |
| **Real Estate** | J Keith Windle (Birmingham) |
| **Bankruptcy, Restructuring & Reorganization** | |
| | J Patrick Darby (Birmingham) |
| **Tax, Trusts & Estates, & ERISA** | K Wood Herren (Birmingham) |
| **Venture Capital and Private Equity** | James W Childs (Birmingham) |
| **White Collar Criminal Defense** | Jack W Selden (Birmingham) |

Bradley Arant
BRADLEY ARANT ROSE & WHITE LLP

# CHRISTIAN & SMALL LLP

## THE FIRM

**Managing Partner:** Richard E Smith

**Number of partners:** 18
**Number of other lawyers:** 16

## AREAS OF PRACTICE:

Litigation . . . . . . . . . . . . . . . . . . . . . . . . . . . . . . . . . . . . . . . . . . . . . . 80%
Corporate & Business Transactions . . . . . . . . . . . . . . . . . . . . . . . . . . . 15%
Mediation . . . . . . . . . . . . . . . . . . . . . . . . . . . . . . . . . . . . . . . . . . . . . . 5%

**FIRM OVERVIEW:** Christian & Small is a full-service law firm representing a diverse clientele throughout Alabama, the southeast and across the nation. Founded in July 2000 by partners Thomas W Christian and Clarence M Small, formerly with Rives & Peterson, the firm has a solid foundation and an impressive history. Four partners are Fellows of the American College of Trial Lawyers; four are Fellows of the International Academy of Trial Lawyers; four are members of the American Board of Trial Advocates; four are Fellows of the American Bar Foundation; and two have served as President of the Alabama State Bar. Each of the firm's lawyers is committed to providing the most vigorous, effective and cost-efficient representation available, with a continual focus on building enduring client relationships and exceeding client expectations. Christian & Small has proven itself as a leader among Birmingham law firms, offering the high quality of legal representation expected from the larger firms and the client focused attention that distinguishes the best boutique firms. The firm's team approach, recruitment of top level lawyers, and investment in the most advanced technology enhances their success and efficiency. Zealous client advocacy tempered by a commitment to the highest ethical standards has secured the superior reputation in every representation the firm undertakes. These guiding principles have earned the firm a distinguished place among Alabama's elite law firms.

**MAIN AREAS OF PRACTICE:** Christian & Small's diverse practice enables the firm to provide the broad range of capabilities that clients expect from a full-service law firm. By working in practice teams, the lawyers are able to deliver innovative solutions to the legal and business problems facing their clients. The firm's practice groups are primarily divided into the areas of litigation, corporate and business transactions, and mediation.

**Litigation:** Christian & Small's trial lawyers have an impressive history of earning defense verdicts. Extensive experience in a variety of state and judicial forums nationwide combined with the firm's reputation for creative and zealous client advocacy has earned Christian & Small a distinguished place in Alabama's Trial Bar. The firm matches highly experienced litigators with specific client needs so that the most innovative, effective and efficient solutions can be achieved. The firm assists clients in all stages of litigation from preventative strategies to avoid potential liability, pre-transaction counseling, and alternative dispute proceedings, trial and, if necessary, appeal. Christian & Small's litigation practice encompasses virtually every area of the law including: labor and employment; medical/professional malpractice defense; product liability; business and commercial; transportation, including trucking and aviation; bankruptcy; environmental and toxic tort; construction; white-collar criminal defense; domestic relations; insurance and first party insurance defense; bad faith and fraud; briefing and appellate.

## HEAD OFFICE

**ALABAMA**
505 North 20th Street, Suite 1800, **Birmingham**, AL 35203
**Tel:** 205 795 6588  **Fax:** 205 328 7234
**Website:** www.csattorneys.com

## CONTACTS

Litigation . . . . . . . . . . . . . . . . . . . . . . . . . . . . . . . . . . . . . . . . . Duncan Y Manley
Corporate & Business Transactions . . . . . . . . . . . . . . . . . . Steven A Benefield
Mediation . . . . . . . . . . . . . . . . . . . . . . . . . . . . . . . . . . . . . . . . Kenneth O Simon

**Corporate & Business Transactions:** The corporate and business lawyers at Christian & Small handle all aspects of a business' operations through all stages of development, including real estate acquisition. They also have substantial experience managing the legal needs of individuals with small business, estate planning and tax needs. The firm's corporate and business lawyers routinely handle legal matters in the following areas: business and tax planning; business organization and reorganization; corporate and business transactions; contract disputes; employer/employee relationship agreements; real estate; wills, estate and trust planning.

**Mediation:** The firm has several attorneys who routinely participate in a variety of ADR proceedings as mediators and arbitrators. Consistently recognized by their peers for the strength and effectiveness of their mediation skills, the firm's attorney mediators' comprehensive knowledge of litigation, claims and the judicial process allows them to provide meaningful insight and assessment to the involved parties throughout the negotiation.

**CLIENTS:** Christian & Small represents a diverse clientele, ranging from individuals and closely-held businesses to Fortune 500 corporations. The firm's list of clients includes manufacturers, banks and financial institutions, hospitals, nursing homes and assisted living facilities, physicians, accountants, retail companies, technology companies, insurance companies, and trucking companies.

# HELMSING, LEACH, HERLONG, NEWMAN & ROUSE, PC

## THE FIRM

**Managing Partner:** James B Newman
**Senior Partner:** Frederick G Helmsing
**Number of partners:** 11
**Number of other lawyers:** 5

## AREAS OF PRACTICE:

Commercial Litigation . . . . . . . . . . . . . . . . . . . . . . . . . . . . . . . . . . . . . . . 60%
Banking & Finance . . . . . . . . . . . . . . . . . . . . . . . . . . . . . . . . . . . . . . . . 20%
M&A. . . . . . . . . . . . . . . . . . . . . . . . . . . . . . . . . . . . . . . . . . . . . . . . . . . . . 20%

**FIRM OVERVIEW:** The firm was founded in 1976 when successful partners of large firms joined forces to create a firm that could offer a diverse array of legal services with enthusiasm, expertise, and confidence. As a full service firm of medium size, Helmsing, Leach, Herlong, Newman & Rouse, PC combines the characteristics of smaller firms' vigor and personality with the quality and efficiency attributed to larger groups. Since 1976, the firm has been dedicated to providing quality legal services to business, professionals, families and individuals.

## MAIN AREAS OF PRACTICE:

**Banking & Finance:** The firm is routinely involved in all phases of banking and financial transactions as counsel for both borrowers and lenders. Its representation of banks, other financial institutions and borrowers includes negotiating and structuring loans, analyzing loan terms and conditions, and developing and drafting loan documents and agreements.

**Bankruptcy:** The firm has engaged in the active practice of all creditors' rights, workouts and insolvency litigation. This practice group offers a comprehensive array of services regarding the protection and enforcement of creditors' interests in bankruptcy and non-bankruptcy workouts. The firm has extensive experience in representing asset-based lenders and financial service institutions, including local, regional and national banks. The firm also has significant experience involving representation of bankruptcy trustees, examiners and other fiduciaries. The firm represents both creditors and corporate debtors faced with the numerous issues that accompany business insolvencies.

**Business & Corporate Matters:** The firm regularly performs the functions involved in modern corporate law. It creates, maintains, reorganizes, liquidates and dissolves corporations, partnerships, limited liability companies, joint ventures, and professional corporations and associations. The firm has significant experience in the resolution and litigation of business and corporate disputes. It administers corporate acquisitions and mergers, and works out corporate structural changes among stockholders, partners, and other business owners.

**Taxation & Tax Planning:** Several of the firm's lawyers have received advanced training in taxation. The firm regularly advises its clients on individual and corporate tax matters spanning the total spectrum of State and Federal taxation.

**White Collar Criminal Defense:** The firm has broad experience in white collar criminal practice, including tax crimes, fraud, health fraud, RICO, anti-trust, bank and credit charges, embezzlement and other economic crimes. The firm provides representation for those undergoing criminal investigation by the Internal Revenue Service and other governmental agencies, as well as grand jury investigation. The firm handles the case in every phase of investigation, trial and appellate proceedings.

**Litigation:** The firm conducts a substantial Litigation Practice. It has tried major cases in all surrounding State and Federal courts and has handled appeals to the highest levels of the State and Federal judicial systems. The firm is known for successfully handling complicated and significant cases and disputes. The firm has extensive experience in virtually all types of business litigation, whether involving breach of contract, tortious conduct, equitable or extraordinary remedies, or statutory relief.

## HEAD OFFICE

**ALABAMA**
150 Government Street, Suite 2000, **Mobile**, AL 36602
**Tel:** 251 432 5521   **Fax:** 251 432 0633
**Website:** www.helmsinglaw.com

## CONTACTS

**Banking & Financing** . . . . . . . . . . . . . . . . . . . . . . . . . . . . . Robert H Rouse
**Litigation/White Collar Criminal Practice** . . . . . . . . Frederick G Helmsing
**M&A** . . . . . . . . . . . . . . . . . . . . . . . . . . . . . . . . . . . . . . . . . . . . . Robert H Rouse

**Eminent Domain & Condemnation:** For more than 20 years the firm has engaged in the practice of eminent domain law. It represents landowners and condemning agencies throughout the State of Alabama in a wide variety of takings, both direct and inverse, at the local, state, and federal level in administrative, trial and appellate proceedings.

**Product Liability:** The firm has extensive and significant experience in representing manufacturers, component part suppliers, distributors, and individuals in product liability cases. Products the firm has defended include aircraft, aviation equipment, aircraft engines, helicopters, automobiles, automobile parts, seatbelts, boats, marine products, chainsaws, household appliances, power tools, drugs, pharmaceutical products, medical devices and equipment, surgical supplies, tires, motor homes, water heaters, paper-making machinery, wire rope and other steel products and heavy machinery and engines. The firm has also represented manufacturers and distributors of chemicals and other products in toxic tort cases and class actions. Recently, a team of its lawyers successfully represented Kumho Tire Company in the United States Supreme Court landmark decision clarifying that the trial court's gatekeeping duty under Federal Rule of Evidence 702 applies to all experts and not just scientific experts (Kumho Tire Co. v Carmichael), 119 S.CT.1167 (1999).

**Real Estate Law:** The firm has a broad Real Estate Practice, representing clients engaged in all areas of the real estate industry. Its clients include residential and commercial buyers and sellers, shopping center owners and tenants, apartment complex and condominium owners and developers, brokerage companies, residential and commercial contractors, real estate investment trusts, title companies, and banks and other financial institutions who lend money secured by real estate.

**Government Relations:** The firm has full scale capability in handling matters arising from the regulation of business affairs by the government at all levels. Such activities include the regulation of pharmaceutical products, the environment, healthcare facilities, public utilities, zoning and matters involving the licensure of businesses, professions and contractors.

**Health Law:** The firm maintains an active Health Law Section dedicated to serving the healthcare community in administrative, regulatory and compliance matters. The firm has represented clients' interests in matters involving Medicare, Medicaid, HCFA, the United State Department of Justice and the Alabama Attorney General's office, in successfully defending clients accused of Medicare and Medicaid fraud and abuse.

**Employment Law:** The firm is engaged, primarily by employers, in employment-related transactions and disputes. The firm's attorneys assist its business clients in dealing with a wide range of employment matters, including employment contracts, arbitration agreements, day-to-day employment issues with the goal of avoiding or minimizing conflicts, and responses to EEOC or other complaints. The firm also has an extensive Litigation Practice in this area of law.

# MAYNARD, COOPER & GALE, P.C.

## THE FIRM

**Managing Partner:** Fournier J Gale, III
**Number of partners:** 90
**Number of other attorneys:** 55

**FIRM OVERVIEW:** Founded in 1984, Maynard, Cooper & Gale, P.C. is a full-service law firm, with 145 attorneys. The firm's client base ranges from numerous Fortune 500 companies to a broad range of closely held companies, partnerships, professional associations, charities and individuals. In just two decades, Maynard Cooper has emerged as one of the Southeast's leading firms, offering services encompassing nearly the entire spectrum of legal practice. Maynard Cooper regularly represents clients in litigation and regulatory matters across the country. The firm also serves as regional counsel for a number of Fortune 500 companies throughout the Southeast. Maynard Cooper serves a variety of local, national and international business entities, as well as charities and individuals. The firm's services include litigation, corporate law, banking and commercial law, real estate law, antitrust, public finance, estates and trusts, taxation, intellectual property, healthcare, securities law, labor law, environmental law and bankruptcy law.

Maynard Cooper's attorneys have held numerous leadership positions in varying professional organizations. One of the firm's partners is a past President of the 400,000-member American Bar Association, and another is the immediate past Chairman of the ABA's House of Delegates, the ABA's second highest office. Maynard Cooper also has three former Chairs of the 74,000-member litigation section of the ABA. At the state and local level, Maynard Cooper's attorneys include a former Chief Justice of the Alabama Supreme Court and a Special Counsel to the former Governor of Alabama. Another Maynard partner is the President-elect of the Alabama Bar Association for 2005-2006 and will then resume the presidency in July of 2006. Other Maynard Cooper attorneys have been elected President of both the Birmingham Bar Association and the Alabama Bar Association's Young Lawyer's Section. Maynard Cooper attorneys have also served in various positions on the American Judicature Society's Board of Directors, as Director of the Lawyers' Committee for Civil Rights, as Chair of the ABA Katrina Task Force, on the Rand Institute for Civil Justice Board of Overseers, and as Chair of several Sections of the Alabama State Bar, including Antitrust, Environmental, Labor & Employment and Workers Compensation. Maynard Cooper attorneys have been recognized in various publications for their expertise in their area of practice. In Chambers USA 2005, America's Leading Lawyers for Business, Maynard Cooper is listed as a leading law firm in Alabama in all four rated categories: corporate/M&A, labor and employment, real estate and general commercial. In addition, Maynard Cooper has ten attorneys touted in Chambers USA 2005 as leaders in these areas of practice. In Best Lawyers in America® 2006, the firm has thirty attorneys noted for their legal excellence in their areas of practice. Also, in the Birmingam Business Journal's Inaugural Best of the Bar, Maynard Cooper had ten attorneys recognized for their leadership in the local market-- the largest number of any firm in the city.

## CLIENTS:

**Automotive:** Briggs & Stratton; Concours Mold Alabama, Inc.; Eissmann Manufacturing North America, Inc.; Ford Motor Co.; General Motors; Hanil Tube Corporation/Hanil USA L.L.C.; Heil Environmental Industries, Ltd.; Honda North America, Inc.; Kia Motors America Inc.; Nissan Motors; TI Group Automotive Systems, L.L.C..

**Banking & Financial Services:** A. G. Edwards & Sons, Inc.; Alabama National Bancorporation; American General Securities Inc.; AmSouth Bancorporation; Bank of America; Bear, Stearns & Co. Inc.; Collateral Mortgage, Ltd.; Fleet Finance, Inc.; GE Capital Corporation; H&R Block, Inc.; J.P. Morgan Chase Bank; McGraw-Hill, Inc. (Standard & Poors); Merrill Lynch; Morgan Stanley DW, Inc., Morgan, Keegan & Co., Inc.; PricewaterhouseCoopers, LLP; Raymond James Financial Services, Inc.; Regions Bank, Robinson-Humphrey/American Express; Salomon Smith Barney, Inc.; Sterne, Agee & Leach, Inc.; UBS Financial Services Inc.

### HEAD OFFICE

**ALABAMA**
1901 Sixth Avenue North, 2400 AmSouth/Harbert Plaza,
**Birmingham**, AL 35203-2618
**Tel:** 205 254 1000 **Fax:** 205 254 1999
**Website:** www.maynardcooper.com

### BRANCH OFFICE

**ALABAMA**
201 Monroe Street, Ste 1650, **Montgomery**, AL 36104-3720
**Tel:** 334 262 2001 **Fax:** 334 262 2043

**Biotechnology/Pharmaceutical:** Abbott Laboratories, Inc.; Brookwood Pharmaceuticals, Inc.; Glaxo, Inc.; Hoffman La-Roche, Inc.; Neurorecovery, Inc.; Southern Research Institute; Wyeth-Ayerst Pharamceuticals.

**Consumer Products:** AutoZone, Inc.; ADT Security Services, Inc.; Borden, Inc.; Gulf States Paper Corporation; Harley-Davidson Motor Company; Mattel-Fisher Price, Michelin North America, Inc.; Movie Gallery, Inc.; Nintendo; Philip Morris Companies, Inc. (Kraft, Inc./Miller Brewing); Royal Cup, Inc.; Tyson Foods; U-Haul International; Wal-Mart, Inc..

**Energy & Utilities:** Amoco Production Co.; Colonial Pipeline Co.; ConocoPhillips Petroleum Co.; Crown Central Petroleum; Drummond Company, Inc.; El Paso Energy Corporation (Southern Natural Gas Company); Equiva, Inc.; ExxonMobil; General Electric Co.; Jim Walter Resources, Inc.; Plantation Pipeline Company; Shell Oil Company.

**Governmental Entities & Non-Profit:** American National Red Cross; Birmingham Airport Authority; Birmingham Water Works Board; Business Council of Alabama; City of Birmingham; Jefferson County Commission; Retirement Systems of Alabama; The University of Alabama.

**Healthcare:** Baptist Health System, Inc.; Baxter Healthcare Corp.; CardioThoracic Surgeons, P.C.; Cardiovascular Associates, P.C.; East Alabama Medical Center; HealthSouth Corporation; Northeast Alabama Regional Medical Center.

**Insurance:** AIG Life Insurance Co.; American General Life Companies; AXA Equitable Life Insurance Company; Blue Cross and Blue Shield of Alabama; Cigna Companies; Connecticut Mutual Life Insurance Company; The Hartford Companies; Life Insurance Company of Georgia; Lloyd's; Metropolitan Life Ins. Co.; New York Life Insurance Co.; Protective Life Corp.; Torchmark Corporation; U.S. Auto Holdings, Inc.; U.S. Life Ins. Co.; Western Southern Life Assurance Company.

**Industrial/ Manufacturing/Distribution:** AIG Aviation; American Cast Iron Pipe Company; Amerex, Inc.; Armstrong International Inc.; Atofina Chemicals, Inc.; Borden Chemical, Inc.; Bush Hog, L.L.C.; Ciba Geigy Corporation; Chemical Waste Management; Clow Water Systems; Continental Carbon Company; International Paper Co.; Jim Walter Resources, Inc.; McWane, Inc.; Manchester Tank and Equipment Co., Inc.; MeadWestvaco, Inc.; Pemco Aviation Group, Inc.; Sloss Industries; Southern Energy Homes, Inc.; Takata, Inc.; TRW, Inc.; The Dow Chemical Company; Tyco International Inc.; United Rentals, Inc.; U.S. Pipe & Foundry; U.S. Fertilizer Corporation; U.S. Steel Corporation; Waste Management, Inc.; Weil Brothers Cotton; Wise Alloys.

**Intellectual Property/Technology:** AT&T; BellSouth Telecommunications, Inc.; GTE/Verizon; Integrated Medical Solutions, Inc.; Intercom Consulting, Inc.; Intermark; Inter-tel Corporation; Microsoft Corporation; Momentum Telecom, Inc.; Qwest; Raycom Media, Inc.; Source Medical Solutions, Inc.; Southern Research Institute.

**Real Estate:** AIG Baker Shopping Center; Alabama Real Estate Holdings, Inc.; American Government Services; Chicago Title Insurance Company; Dantract, Inc.; Hubbard Properties; Johnson Development, LLC; PCH Hotel & Resorts, Inc; Ratliff Partners, LLC; Skye Realty, LLC; Taylor & Mathis, Inc; Thompson Realty Co., Inc..

# STARNES & ATCHISON LLP

## THE FIRM

**Managing Partner:** W Stancil Starnes

**Number of partners:** 32
**Number of other attorneys:** 24

**FIRM OVERVIEW:** Since its inception over 30 years ago, Starnes & Atchison LLP has become one of the largest law firms in Alabama devoted exclusively to litigation. Over 55 attorneys strong, the firm continues to be committed to a varied civil litigation practice. The firm's distinguished list of clients includes physicians, attorneys, architects, accountants and other professionals, as well as corporations, hospitals, long-term care facilities, municipalities and insurance companies. Starnes & Atchison LLP has its principle office in Birmingham, with a second office in Mobile. The firm handles litigation matters throughout Alabama and serves as lead counsel in a number of cases pending around the United States. The attorneys who comprise Starnes & Atchison LLP consistently try more complex civil jury trials each year than any other firm in the state, and are recognized as ranking among the most experienced trial lawyers in the state - four of the firm's partners are Fellows of the American College of Trial Lawyers, seven of its partners are members of the American Board of Trial Advocates and four of its attorneys are listed in the Best Lawyers in America. The firm places great emphasis on maintaining state of the art technology and substantial legal and medical libraries. Starnes & Atchison LLP is a young and energetic firm which holds a respected position in the legal community.

## CLIENTS:

**Corporations & Institutions:** University of Alabama; Salomon Smith Barney, Inc.; General Electric Capital Corporation; City of Mountain Brook; ACE USA; First American Bank; UBS Securities, LLC; Burk-Kleinpeter, Inc.; Gold-Cup Coffee Services, Inc.; SPX Corporation; Primerica; AT&T Universal Card Services; Citigroup, Inc.; Bancorp South, Inc.; Alabama National Bancorporation; Verizon; Verizon Wireless; International Paper; Capital One; Caremark RX, Inc.; American Mining, Co.; National Service Industries; Murphy Oil USA, Inc.; Lowes; Drummond Company, Inc.; American Arbitration Association; American Honda; GTE Mobilnet; Mercedes Benz of North America, Inc.; Home Depot; Kohlberg, Kravis, Roberts & Co; Fluke Corp.; Aero-Global, Inc.; Hennessy Industries, Inc.; Bonds Development Co.; Ocwen Loan Servicing, LLC; Intervect USA, Inc.; DuPont Corporation; Asset Acceptance, LLC., Atlas-Copco.

**Medical:** ProNational Inc; ProAssurance Inc; American Health Insurance Company; Brookwood Medical Center, Inc.; Glaxo Wellcome, Inc.; HealthPartners of Alabama, Inc.; Hoffman-LaRoche, Inc.; Med Partners, Inc.; Medical Assurance, Inc.; Podiatry Insurance Company of America; St. Vincent's Hospital; University of Alabama at Birmingham; University of Alabama Health Services Foundation; Tenet Health Systems; Woodcrest Service, Inc.; Ascension Health Care; Caronia Corp.

**Insurance:** Protective Life Insurance Co.; Alabama Municipal Insurance Corp.; Markel Insurance Co.; American National Insurance Company; American Heritage Insurance Company; Associated Aviation Underwriters; Attorneys Insurance Mutual; Attorneys Liability Assurance Society; Chubb Group Insurance; CNA Insurance Company; Farmers Insurance Company; Fidelity and Deposit Company of Maryland; The Fidelity and Casualty Company of New York; Great American Insurance Company; International Fidelity Insurance Company; J. C. Penney Life Insurance Company; Reliance Insurance Company; St. Paul Fire and Marine Insurance Company; State Farm Insurance Company; Travelers Insurance Company; Western Surety Company; Zurich Insurance Company; Kemper Insurance Co.; PMA Insurance Co.; AIG; Allstate Insurance Co.; Meadowbrook ASI Insurance Group.; Robinson Adams Insurance.

### HEAD OFFICE

**ALABAMA**
100 Brookwood Place, 7th Floor, P.O. Box 598512, **Birmingham**, AL 35259
**Tel:** 205 868 6000 **Fax:** 205 868 6099
**Website:** www.starneslaw.com

### BRANCH OFFICES

**ALABAMA**
Riverview Plaza, Suite 1106, 63 S. Royal Street, **Mobile**, AL 36602
**Tel:** 251 433 6049

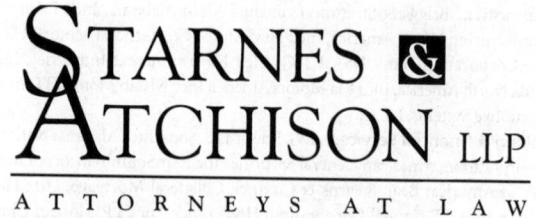

STARNES & ATCHISON LLP
ATTORNEYS AT LAW

**CONTENTS: Bankruptcy/Restructuring p.167; Corporate/M&A p.167; Employment p.168; Environment, Natural Resources & Regulated Industries p.169; Litigation p.171; Real Estate p.172; Individuals' Profiles p.173.**

## How lawyers are ranked

Every year we carry out thousands of in-depth interviews with clients and lawyers in order to assess the reputations and expertise of business lawyers across the USA. Chambers rankings and editorial are referred to extensively by General Counsel and other purchasers of legal services who look to our recommendations when choosing their lawyers.

# BANKRUPTCY/RESTRUCTURING

| Bankruptcy/Restructuring |
| --- |
| **Leading Firms** |
| [1] CHRISTIANSON, BOUTIN *Anchorage* |
| [2] DAVIS WRIGHT TREMAINE LLP *Anchorage* |
| DORSEY & WHITNEY LLP *Anchorage* |

| Leading Individuals |
| --- |
| [1] BUNDY David *David H Bundy PC* |
| CHRISTIANSON Cabot *Christianson, Boutin & Spraker* |
| MILLS Michael *Bankston, Gronning, O'Hara, PC* |
| PARISE Michael *Birch, Horton, Bittner & Cherot* |
| SIEMERS John *Burr, Pease & Kurtz, PC* |
| SNEED Spencer *Dorsey & Whitney LLP* |
| [2] DAWSON Jon *Davis Wright Tremaine LLP* |
| OESTING David *Davis Wright Tremaine LLP* |
| SPRAKER Gary *Christianson, Boutin & Spraker* |
| TRAVOSTINO Joan *Preston Gates & Ellis LLP* |

## Band 1

### Christianson, Boutin & Spraker

**The Firm:** This group garners praise for its *"decisive and intelligent"* responses to a broad range of bankruptcy-related matters. The team is dedicated to this area of law and sources especially compliment its track record in business reorganizations and Chapter 7 and 11 matters.

**The Lawyers: Cabot Christianson**'s experience and *"unparalleled gravitas"* are potent attractants. He counseled the trustee in SEC v Raejean Bonham, World Plus. The *"powerful"* **Gary Spraker** is considered an able assistant to Christianson, with a practice that is suffused with *"relentless enthusiasm and dedication."*

**Clients/Work Highlights:** Clients include both debtors and creditors.

## Band 2

### Davis Wright Tremaine LLP

**The Firm:** This national firm has a prominent practice and a dedicated following in Alaska. With the capacity to call upon a deep pool of specialist knowledge, the prestigious bankruptcy team attracts a large and varied clientele.

**The Lawyers:** Litigator **David Oesting** serves a loyal client base and regularly acts for secured and unsecured creditors. He recently represented contractors in the reorganization of a steel company following bankruptcy proceedings. **Jon Dawson** is recommended for his litigation skills and business acumen.

**Clients/Work Highlights:** The client base includes some of the largest companies in the USA and worldwide; the team represents both creditors and debtors.

### Dorsey & Whitney LLP

See firm details p.1169

**The Firm:** Since opening its Anchorage office in 1999 this firm has worked successfully to win strong market endorsement for its bankruptcy litigation offering. With an impressive client base, including both national and international companies operating within Alaska, the bankruptcy group acts for debtors, creditors and boards of directors.

**The Lawyers:** Clients and peers agree that **Spencer Sneed** (see p.174) is an *"effective negotiator"* whose commercial nous lends his bankruptcy litigation practice great depth. He acts mainly for creditors.

## Other Notable Practitioners

The *"sophisticated"* **David Bundy** of David H Bundy PC is a byword for expertise and reliability. He is adept at acting for both creditors and debtors, and regularly handles workouts. **Michael Mills** of Bankston, Gronning, O'Hara, PC is lauded for his *"extensive experience,"* particularly in Chapter 11 matters. Birch, Horton, Bittner & Cherot's **Michael Parise** wins plaudits from clients who respect his *"attention to detail."* He works exclusively for creditors, recently advising on Chapter 11 reorganization for a major steel company. He also plays a significant role appraising changes in local bankruptcy rules in the light of recent federal legislation. **John Siemers** of Burr, Pease & Kurtz, PC is renowned as an *"erudite and effective"* attorney. His clients are mostly creditors and he is experienced in advising trustees and creditors' committees on US Bankruptcy Code issues. **Joan Travostino** of Preston Gates & Ellis LLP is regarded as an adroit lawyer with genuine commercial sensitivity. She recently represented Gunderboom in out-of-state bankruptcy proceedings.

# CORPORATE/M&A

## Band 1

### Birch, Horton, Bittner & Cherot

**The Firm:** Successfully cross-marketing between states, this team enjoys a sterling reputation for its experience and flexibility, particularly within the oil, gas and regulated industries. The firm's notable DC presence provides an extra dimension to the Anchorage offering, and constitutes an important draw for large corporations. The team recently represented an investment bank in the refinancing by a California company of a hotel in Hawaii.

**The Lawyers:** The *"stellar"* **Kathryn Black** epitomizes the dexterity of the attorneys here and is sought out for complex matters. She recently handled the delicate purchase by a religious organization of a $25 million seafood-processing unit owned by a state agency. Black also handles a prodigious workload for nonprofit organizations.

**Clients/Work Highlights:** The clients are a healthy mix of financial institutions, corporations and nonprofit entities.

### Davis Wright Tremaine LLP

**The Firm:** This firm's transactional group draws on a rich pool of talent throughout its nationwide network. Clients warmly praise the attorneys' responsiveness to their short and long-term needs. It is renowned for work in the energy, healthcare and defense sectors.

**The Lawyers: Jon Dawson** is admired for doing *"a fantastic job for his clients."* He practices in the fertile territory of corporate and real estate crossover. He represented Yukon Fuel in commercial real estate

## Corporate/M&A

### Leading Firms

[1] BIRCH, HORTON, BITTNER *Anchorage*
DAVIS WRIGHT TREMAINE LLP *Anchorage*
DORSEY & WHITNEY LLP *Anchorage*

[2] DURRELL LAW GROUP, PC *Anchorage*
HUGHES BAUMAN PFIFFNER GORSKI *Anchorage*
LANDYE BENNETT BLUMSTEIN LLP *Anchorage*
PRESTON GATES & ELLIS LLP *Anchorage*

### Leading Individuals

[1] BLACK Kathryn *Birch, Horton, Bittner & Cherot*
BLUMSTEIN Philip *Landye Bennett Blumstein LLP*
DAWSON Jon *Davis Wright Tremaine LLP*
DURRELL Brian *Durrell Law Group, PC*
KRAFT Barbara *Davis Wright Tremaine LLP*
ROSSTON Richard *Dorsey & Whitney LLP*

[2] ODSEN Frederick *Hughes Bauman Pfiffner Gorski*
RECKMEYER Peter *Heller Ehrman LLP*
REECE Joseph *Davis Wright Tremaine LLP*

matters, and successfully defended a prominent service provider in the restaurant industry in a state investigation of predatory pricing allegations. **Barbara Simpson Kraft** *"adds depth"* to the team, and frequently acts as counsel on acquisitions requiring local agency approvals. **Joseph Reece** is an *"excellent and responsive"* attorney whose advice is *"always solid."* He recently represented the owner of an insurance agency brokerage in an asset sale.

**Clients/Work Highlights:** Clients include notable healthcare, energy and industrial companies.

## Dorsey & Whitney LLP

See firm details p.1169

**The Firm:** A power in the USA and beyond, this firm's corporate group acts on the full range of business transactions from acquisitions and joint ventures to restructurings and contracts. The team also draws on a potent range of support from experienced sector specialists.

**The Lawyers:** **Richard Rosston**'s (see p.174) clients choose him for his *"ability to grasp the crux of an issue and explain all the ramifications of a proposed solution."* He is prized as a good man to have on board in negotiations.

## Band 2

## Durrell Law Group, PC

**The Firm:** This *"small yet effective"* practice operates out of Anchorage and rests on the three pillars of transactions, business organization and estate planning.

**The Lawyers:** **Brian Durrell** serves a solid client base and wins respect for his *"exacting standards."* He is an acknowledged tax-planning specialist. He recently oversaw the $50 million merger of a family-owned airline with an out-of-state airline.

**Clients/Work Highlights:** Clients are drawn from various sectors, including transportation, construction and tourism.

## Hughes Bauman Pfiffner Gorski & Seedorf LLC

**The Firm:** Popular with large Alaskan corporations, this small, established team *"punches above its weight"* across the board in transactions, and is noted for its finance expertise.

**The Lawyers:** **Fred Odsen**'s professionalism wins the respect of those that work with him. His transactional services include a niche expertise in 'corporate divorces'.

**Clients/Work Highlights:** Clients include corporations and financial institutions.

## Landye Bennett Blumstein LLP

See firm details p.1689

**The Firm:** Renowned for its commitment to the highest standards of service, this firm draws on its deep experience of native corporations to handle many of the major development projects in Alaska.

**The Lawyers:** **Phil Blumstein** has an unbeatable grasp of Native American law and a solid reach across the transactional spectrum. Much of his practice involves real estate transactions, including commercial developments and a large-scale military housing privatization project.

**Clients/Work Highlights:** The clientele includes prominent Native American businesses.

## Preston Gates & Ellis LLP

**The Firm:** With offices in key cities across the USA and Asia, this firm offers services to a range of businesses, especially where the financing of growth and new ventures is concerned.

**The Lawyers:** Christopher Cyphers has left the group. Inquiries should be directed to Robert Jaffe.

## Other Notable Practitioners

Heller Ehrman LLP's **Peter Reckmeyer** (see p.174) is *"adept at complex issues"* and clients underline his *"responsiveness and attention to detail."* His varied practice frequently involves out-of-state transactions and he regularly represents native corporations.

# EMPLOYMENT

# MAINLY DEFENDANT

## Employment: Mainly Defendant

### Leading Firms

[1] DAVIS WRIGHT TREMAINE LLP *Anchorage*
PERKINS COIE LLP *Anchorage*
PRESTON GATES & ELLIS LLP *Anchorage*

[2] BIRCH, HORTON, BITTNER & CHEROT *Anchorage*
DORSEY & WHITNEY LLP *Anchorage*
TINDALL BENNETT & SHOUP PC *Anchorage*
TURNER & MEDE, PC *Anchorage*

## Band 1

## Davis Wright Tremaine LLP

**The Firm:** Renowned for its serious and expert attorneys, this team is *"thoroughly recommended"* by clients. It handles collective bargaining, discrimination and wrongful termination matters with aplomb, generally acting for management.

**The Lawyers:** **Parry Grover** is recognized as a *"superb attorney"* who is realistic and a polished communicator. Bullish unions caused an increase in his traditional labor workload over the past year, and he recently renegotiated a labor agreement for Bartlett Regional Hospital. **James Juliussen** assists employers in all things employment or labor. He is counsel to Anchorage Municipal Employee Relations Board and has defended clients in retaliatory actions in both state and federal courts. **Robert Stewart** has a healthy employment practice and expertise in construction.

**Clients/Work Highlights:** Usibelli Coal Mine; Central Peninsula General Hospital; Chugach Electric Association; CSK Auto and Valley Hospital Association.

## Perkins Coie LLP

**The Firm:** In the course of a busy year the team has been involved in a cross-section of employment issues, including wrongful dismissals and discrimination actions. The firm's wider network of offices,

with Seattle at its heart, is a valuable resource. The team handled a major class action for Hageland Aviation Services, and volumes of traditional labor work for UPS.

**The Lawyers:** The *"astute and dynamic"* **Thomas Daniel** has been active over the past year in litigation concerning wrongful discharge, family leave disputes and discrimination. The *"accomplished and reliable"* **Helena Hall** provides able support to Thomas Daniel.

**Clients/Work Highlights:** NANA Development; Norton Sound Health; Era Aviation; Northwest Airlines; Tanana Chiefs Conference; University of Alaska; Princess Cruises; Southcentral Foundation; Alutiiq and UPS.

## Preston Gates & Ellis LLP

**The Firm:** This firm has the resources, experience and local knowledge to assist clients in employment issues including employee termination, disability accommodation and discrimination. Attorneys also counsel clients on wage and hour law, traditional labor law, and business strategy.

**The Lawyers:** Group chair **Doug Parker**'s practice covers the gamut of employment matters. He is adept at representing clients before state and federal courts, and has extensive experience of administrative proceedings before labor boards at all levels, EEOC agencies and OSHA. Associate **Amy Limeres** is admired for her work in the area of retirement and welfare benefits.

**Clients/Work Highlights:** The clientele includes national corporations as well as Alaska businesses and state entities.

## Band 2

### Birch, Horton, Bittner & Cherot

**The Firm:** This team represents employers in all forms of employment dispute resolution, including arbitration, mediation and state and federal litigation. Attorneys also offer training and strategic advice to clients. Careful attention to detail is a trademark of the team, according to commentators.

**The Lawyers:** **Jennifer Alexander** represents employers in all areas of labor and employment law.

**Clients/Work Highlights:** The firm represents local and national companies and Alaskan native corporations.

### Dorsey & Whitney LLP

See firm details p.1169

**The Firm:** The employment and labor capabilities here are backed powerfully by the firm's corporate and commercial experience. Commentators are warm in their praise of attorneys' intellectual prowess. The team has acted in a number of high-profile employment cases in recent years.

**The Lawyers:** The group's linchpin, **William Evans** (see p.173), provides support to management on traditional labor law issues. Commentators agree that he "*delivers a robust defense*" in employment litigation.

**Clients/Work Highlights:** The firm represents a broad range of local, national and international companies.

### Tindall Bennett & Shoup PC

**The Firm:** This group advises employers on personnel policies, discrimination cases and contracts, as well as on traditional labor matters.

**The Lawyers:** At the heart of the team is **Wilfred Bennett**, a tried and tested labor and employment attorney.

**Clients/Work Highlights:** The clientele includes notable Alaska institutions and businesses.

### Turner & Mede, PC

**The Firm:** This team offers employers advice on the full range of employment matters, and has a long and creditable track record in traditional labor matters.

**The Lawyers:** **William Mede** advises his public and private sector employers on all their employment and labor matters, in or out of court.

**Clients/Work Highlights:** The firm advises a number of Alaska businesses and institutions.

### Other Notable Practitioners

**Kimberlee Colbo** of Hughes Bauman Pfiffner Gorski & Seedorf, LLC is experienced in employment litigation and has defended clients against numerous allegations of sexual harassment, discrimination, and wrongful terminations. She also provides preventive advice, acting primarily for Alaska-based businesses and nonprofit organizations. **Andrew Behrend** (see p.173) of Heller Ehrman LLP impresses commentators with his "*great intellectual prowess.*" He defends employers against a broad range of claims including discrimination claims and allegations of violations of wage and hour laws. Guess & Rudd PC's **Joan Rohlf** is a skilled litigator and adept across the board of employment and labor issues.

# ENVIRONMENT, NATURAL RESOURCES & REGULATED INDUSTRIES

## Band 1

### Dorsey & Whitney LLP

See firm details p.1169

**The Firm:** Clients testify to the impact this national firm has had since it strode into the Alaskan arena. The combination of deep national resources and market-leading local experts cements the firm's position in *Chambers'* top tier. Attorneys offer a broad service to its clients, and are particularly recommended for utilities matters.

**The Lawyers:** Commentators express the "*highest possible regard*" for **Heather Grahame** (see p.173). She is a public utilities expert and also heads the firm's telecommunications group. She represents public utilities before state legislatures on public utility issues, and has drafted numerous amendments that have subsequently become law. **James Reeves** (see p.174) is described as "*incredibly talented, and simply one of the best litigators in the state.*" He focuses on natural resources law, including public lands, mining, and environmental regulation. He is the firm's managing partner in Anchorage.

**Clients/Work Highlights:** United Utilities; Waste Management; TelAlaska; Safeway; Ketchikan Public Utilities and BP.

### Guess & Rudd PC

**The Firm:** This is a long-established player in the natural resources area and it enjoys an unsurpassed reputation and enviable client base. The team is well regarded for its environmental insurance expertise.

**The Lawyers:** **James Linxwiler** handles issues such as permitting and large native land exchanges. He regularly represents oil companies and large native corporations, and is general counsel to an electric utility company. **George Lyle**'s practice has notable strength in environmental insurance issues as they relate to mining, oil and gas. **Joseph Perkins** is a nationally recognized natural resources attorney, adept at handling Alaska's somewhat archaic and complex land use laws and an acknowledged expert in mining law. **Louis Veerman** is involved almost exclusively with regulatory work and is an accomplished performer before administrative and judicial bodies. He has been heavily involved in the TransAlaska Pipeline System.

**Clients/Work Highlights:** The firm acts for diverse clients involved in exploring, acquiring, developing, producing and promoting Alaska's natural resources.

### Perkins Coie LLP

**The Firm:** Oil and gas work forms a prominent part of the team's workload. It has developed particular expertise in project development and compliance counseling for industry clients such as BP Exploration. This development work is followed seamlessly by ongoing permitting and strategy services.

## Environment, Natural Resources & Regulated Industries
### Leading Individuals

**Senior Statesman**

MASON III Julian *Ashburn & Mason, PC*

[1] FJELSTAD Eric *Perkins Coie LLP*

GRAHAME Heather *Dorsey & Whitney LLP*

REEVES James *Dorsey & Whitney LLP*

TORGERSON James *Heller Ehrman LLP*

[2] BAUMAN Carl *Hughes Bauman Pfiffner Gorski*

HARTIG Lawrence *Hartig Rhodes Hoge & Lekisch PC*

REEVES Susan *Rubini & Reeves LLC*

ROZELL William *Sole Practitioner*

SAUPE A William *Ashburn & Mason, PC*

STOLLER Robert *Sole Practitioner*

[3] GROVIER Tina *Birch, Horton, Bittner & Cherot*

LINXWILER James *Guess & Rudd PC*

LYLE George *Guess & Rudd PC*

MORAN Joseph *DeLisio Moran Geraghty & Zobel, P.C.*

PERKINS Joseph *Guess & Rudd PC*

REGES Robert *Reges & Boone LLC*

SERDAHELY Douglas *Patton Boggs LLP*

VEERMAN Louis *Guess & Rudd PC*

---

Two full-time lawyers run the practice area, backed by colleagues in other disciplines and the firm's network across the USA.

**The Lawyers:** **Eric Fjelstad** has built up a strong practice on the strength of his high-profile clients. He has represented a number of companies in contamination proceedings.

**Clients/Work Highlights:** BP Exploration; Flint Hills Resources Alaska; Ketchikan Pulp Company; Cook Inlet Region; Ketchikan Public Utilities and NANA.

## Band 2

### Ashburn & Mason, PC

**The Firm:** The team is primarily associated with public utility work, in which attorneys offer unbeatable collective experience. It provides a wide range of regulatory services to a variety of clients, including the state and companies in such sectors as fisheries and real estate.

**The Lawyers:** The *"peerless"* **Julian Mason** is described as a *"benchmark for excellence,"* and his clients agree that he is indispensable in the rarefied atmosphere of Alaskan regulated industries advice. Litigator **William Saupe** provides clients with *"assured performances"* before the courts. He is renowned as an expert in public utilities and telecom.

---

**Clients/Work Highlights:** AT&T Alascom; Crowley Maritime; Prince William Sound Aquaculture and Semco Energy.

### Hartig Rhodes Hoge & Lekisch PC

**The Firm:** The team acts for a stable of business clients to secure permits and offer strategic advice in natural resource development projects. Attorneys also provide solid representation before state and federal administrative authorities.

**The Lawyers:** **Lawrence Hartig**'s clients describe him as *"extremely competent, dedicated and responsive."* His prominence is in part due to his success handling complex environmental issues for companies such as Teck Cominco.

**Clients/Work Highlights:** Teck Cominco; Coeur d'alene Mines; Placer Dome US; ConocoPhillips; Alpine Pipeline Company; Anadarko Petroleum; Kuparuk Pipeline Company and Taiga Mining.

### Heller Ehrman LLP
See firm details p.329

**The Firm:** This experienced team of four attorneys represents high-profile utility, oil and gas clients at both state and federal level. It has an active environmental litigation practice and provides advice to financial institutions and companies.

**The Lawyers:** The *"calm and collected"* **James Torgerson** (see p.174) *"empathizes effectively with the client,"* according to sources, and is a master of finding solutions to tricky situations. He recently handled cases before the Superior Court for clients including Chugach Electric.

**Clients/Work Highlights:** Chugach Electric Association; Deloitte Touche Tohmatsu; NANA Regional; CenturyTel of the Northwest and Peak Oilfield.

### Hughes Bauman Pfiffner Gorski & Seedorf LLC

**The Firm:** This is a highly esteemed local outfit offering broad services in the state to business clients from around the world. Attorneys are experienced in oil and gas matters, contamination and waste.

**The Lawyers:** Commentators recommend **Carl Bauman**, who advises clients on oil and gas law and defends them in environmental litigation.

**Clients/Work Highlights:** The clientele includes local businesses of all shapes and sizes as well as clients from the rest of the USA, Asia and Europe.

### Patton Boggs LLP

**The Firm:** With its commanding presence in DC and tight connections with the regulatory community, this team provides its clients with first-rate advisory and defense services in all areas of environment and regulated industries law. Attorneys also offer a deep experience of defending criminal litigation.

---

**The Lawyers:** **Douglas Serdahely** (see p.174) is a respected and astute litigator, handling complex environmental and antitrust issues for companies in sectors such as energy and transportation.

**Clients/Work Highlights:** The clientele is studded with oil and gas clients large and small, as well as transportation and energy companies.

### Reges & Boone LLC

**The Firm:** This small team has offices in Juneau and Wasilla, and enjoys the unwavering support of individual and corporate clients. The practice has a pronounced real estate flavor. Attorneys advise on compliance matters and issues arising in the context of resource extraction.

**The Lawyers:** **Robert Reges** has a long and reputable history in environmental law, which has grown to encompass all aspects of land use. He is the man to go to for permitting and litigation assistance.

**Clients/Work Highlights:** Clients include developers, local businesses, municipalities and large corporations.

### Rubini & Reeves LLC

**The Firm:** After nearly a decade of affiliation, this outfit has severed its links to Seattle's Foster Pepper. It is active across the waterfront of environmental and natural resources issues, acting on a rich diversity of projects. It guides clients from conception to completion, securing permits and providing strategic advice as needed. It is an attractive package that has secured an enviable list of clients such as Northern Dynasty Mines and Crawley Maritime.

**The Lawyers:** Clients describe **Susan Reeves** as a *"thorough and astute lawyer."* Her reputation is founded on many years of experience, and she is a figure by which practitioners in this field gauge themselves. All the lawyers here have litigation experience.

**Clients/Work Highlights:** The firm acts for local, national and international clients.

### Other Notable Practitioners

Sole practitioner **William Rozell** is based in Juneau and is an accomplished litigator at home in courts all the way up to the Supreme Court. **Robert Stoller** is a universally well-regarded utilities attorney who brings *"masses of experience"* to the table. Birch, Horton, Bittner & Cherot's **Tina Grovier** acts for telecom public utilities in disputes and regulatory proceedings. Sources admire her *"careful dedication."* **Joseph Moran** of DeLisio Moran Geraghty & Zobel, P.C. enjoys a sterling reputation as a corporate adviser, particularly in the banking sector. He is also known for representing public utilities in the telecom and waste sectors, and handles their regulatory needs with aplomb.

# LITIGATION

## Litigation: General Commercial

### Leading Firms

**1** ASHBURN & MASON, PC *Anchorage*

DORSEY & WHITNEY LLP *Anchorage*

FELDMAN ORLANSKY & SANDERS *Anchorage*

**2** ATKINSON, CONWAY & GAGNON *Anchorage*

BANKSTON, GRONNING, O'HARA, PC *Anchorage*

BIRCH, HORTON, BITTNER & CHEROT *Anchorage*

PATTON BOGGS LLP *Anchorage*

**3** LANE POWELL PC *Anchorage*

### Leading Individuals

**1** ASHBURN Mark *Ashburn & Mason, PC*

BUNDY Robert *Dorsey & Whitney LLP*

FELDMAN Jeffrey *Feldman Orlansky & Sanders*

GAGNON Bruce *Atkinson, Conway & Gagnon*

**2** BANKSTON William *Bankston, Gronning, O'Hara, PC*

GILMORE Patrick *Atkinson, Conway & Gagnon*

OESTING David *Davis Wright Tremaine LLP*

ORLANSKY Susan *Feldman Orlansky & Sanders*

PETUMENOS Timothy *Birch, Horton, Bittner & Cherot*

SNEED Spencer *Dorsey & Whitney LLP*

SPAAN Michael *Patton Boggs LLP*

**3** COUGHLIN Jennifer *Preston Gates & Ellis LLP*

DICKSON Robert *Atkinson, Conway & Gagnon*

HUTCHINGS Stephen *Birch, Horton, Bittner & Cherot*

JAMIESON Brewster *Lane Powell PC*

SERDAHELY Douglas *Patton Boggs LLP*

TORGERSON James *Heller Ehrman LLP*

## Litigation: Construction

### Leading Individuals

**1** DICKSON Robert *Atkinson, Conway & Gagnon*

HUTCHINGS Stephen *Birch, Horton, Bittner & Cherot*

KREGER Michael *Perkins Coie LLP*

WATTS Grant *Holmes Weddle & Barcott*

## Band 1

### Ashburn & Mason, PC

**The Firm:** This prestigious group offers a deep bench of commercial litigation and advisory services, and is particularly well regarded for highly complex cases and antitrust matters.

**The Lawyers:** At the heart of the practice is **Mark Ashburn**, whose "*incisive*" mind is a hit with clients. He continues to act in litigation and arbitration for the University of Alaska, and has been handling a significant antitrust case.

**Clients/Work Highlights:** Clients include major businesses, financial institutions and public entities.

### Dorsey & Whitney LLP

See firm details p.1169

**The Firm:** Litigation is a key plank of this heavyweight's offering. A stable of impressive trial lawyers attracts a strong institutional client base. The team is versatile, and acts in a wide range of cases and sectors, drawing on the firm's nationwide and overseas resources at need.

**The Lawyers:** "*Surefooted*" civil litigator **Robert Bundy** (see p.173) enjoys a high profile as a trial lawyer with a broad range. He also has a great track record in insurance and public sector cases. **Spencer Sneed** (see p.174) has strong finance credentials and a thriving practice in business litigation and antitrust disputes.

**Clients/Work Highlights:** The top-drawer client base includes banking and insurance institutions and major corporations.

### Feldman Orlansky & Sanders

**The Firm:** This small, focused and effective firm "*never puts a foot wrong*," according to clients. The team is high profile and offers sophisticated services in complex civil and criminal cases, acting at all court and administrative levels. Attorneys have a knack for resolving disputes before they actually hit the courts. The defense of corporations and their officers in major environmental cases is something of a specialty. Attorneys also undertake significant pro bono work.

**The Lawyers:** **Jeffrey Feldman** has "*an unfailing hunter's instinct*" and is regarded as an exemplary trial lawyer. His practice is diverse, and tends toward intricate cases. The "*extraordinarily talented*" **Susan Orlansky** has an equally high-octane practice, and is often found side by side with Feldman on high-level cases.

**Clients/Work Highlights:** The group's bespoke services are sought out by some of the world's most prestigious corporations, as well as local private and public businesses.

## Band 2

### Atkinson, Conway & Gagnon

**The Firm:** This team combines deep talent with experience and commercial drive, winning a loyal following of Alaska-based companies. Attorneys are traditionally strong in insurance-related matters. The recent workload includes sizable class actions arising out of a housing dispute.

**The Lawyers:** **Bruce Gagnon** is one of the foremost litigators in the state and brings a wealth of experience to the table. **Patrick Gilmore** serves an impressive clientele that includes a number of independent state corporations. **Robert Dickson** is an acknowledged authority in construction and is an experienced performer before Alaska's Supreme Court.

**Clients/Work Highlights:** Ahtna; Alaska Telecom; Alaska Industrial Development and Export Authority; Baugh Construction; Cook Inlet Region; Crowley Maritime; Doyon; Holland America Line; Providence Hospital and Wells Fargo.

### Bankston, Gronning, O'Hara, PC

**The Firm:** This compact group offers "*a strong defense capability*" and acts in diverse commercial matters. Attorneys are experienced in class actions, and the team is well versed in construction disputes.

**The Lawyers:** **William Bankston** has a broad commercial practice with a construction and real estate investor/developer twist. He is an accomplished litigator.

**Clients/Work Highlights:** The clientele includes large and small Alaskan businesses, and large outside companies active in the state. Lawyers also serve a considerable number of the rural school districts of Alaska.

### Birch, Horton, Bittner & Cherot

**The Firm:** This firm fields trial experts out of its Anchorage and DC offices, acting across the country in both administrative and courtroom arenas. It provides services to a diverse clientele across a wide range of commercial areas, and has notable strength in the transportation, energy and telecom sectors.

**The Lawyers:** **Timothy Petumenos**' trial experience makes him a favorite with clients involved in high-profile and complex proceedings. He also spearheads the firm's contingent fee practice. **Stephen Hutchings** defends key Alaskan clients from all manner of sectors in criminal and civil proceedings. He is particularly noted for his construction expertise.

### Patton Boggs LLP

**The Firm:** The Anchorage office is part of a national network geared to the needs of business clients, providing dependable state and federal advocacy services and litigation. Clients recommend it particularly as being "*plugged into the whole government thing at every level.*" Attorneys are entirely at home in the corridors and regulatory agencies of Washington, and the team has relationships with firms across the globe.

**The Lawyers:** **Michael Spaan** (see p.174) is a polished litigator with years of trial experience under his belt. His practice centers on commercial, civil and white-collar criminal cases, and he also assists clients in internal investigations. **Douglas Serdahely** (see p.174) manages the Anchorage office and "*really knows his stuff.*" His practice focuses on cases involving environmental or antitrust issues.

**Clients/Work Highlights:** Representing the interests of international trade, the firm serves business clients from around the world.

## Band 3

### Lane Powell PC

See firm details p.2009

**The Firm:** Acting for its robust stable of business clients, this team handles commercial matters of all types, including trials and appeals. Attorneys are versed in the niceties of securities, insurance and employment litigation.

The Lawyers: **Brewster Jamieson**'s broad practice exhibits particular strength in employment and insurance matters.

Clients/Work Highlights: The firm represents emerging businesses as well as some of the biggest corporate names on the block.

### Other Notable Practitioners

The "*quick-witted*" **David Oesting** leads the Anchorage office of Davis Wright Tremaine LLP. He recently defended a client against allegations of pollution following an oil spillage, and defended a software company in a commercial contract dispute with the state. He has a strong reputation for handling partnership dissolutions. **James Torgerson** (see p.174) of Heller Ehrman LLP represents clients from a range of industries and is well regarded for his appellate, environmental and white-collar crime experience. The market recognizes **Jennifer Coughlin** of Preston Gates & Ellis LLP for her commercial litigation work, and especially for real estate and class actions. Construction specialist **Michael Kreger** of Perkins Coie LLP is also known for his representation of design professionals and handling of government contract cases. Holmes Weddle & Barcott's **Grant Watts** is particularly recommended for construction expertise and his representation of design professionals, contractors and suppliers.

# REAL ESTATE

| Real Estate | |
|---|---|
| Leading Firms | |
| 1 | ASHBURN & MASON, PC *Anchorage* |
| 2 | ATKINSON, CONWAY & GAGNON *Anchorage* |
| | DAVIS WRIGHT TREMAINE LLP *Anchorage* |
| | DORSEY & WHITNEY LLP *Anchorage* |
| 3 | PRESTON GATES & ELLIS LLP *Anchorage* |
| | RUBINI & REEVES LLC *Anchorage* |
| | TINDALL BENNETT & SHOUP PC *Anchorage* |

| Leading Individuals | |
|---|---|
| 1 | CHEROT Suzanne *Birch, Horton, Bittner & Cherot* |
| | MCCLINTOCK Donald *Ashburn & Mason, PC* |
| | ROSSTON Richard *Dorsey & Whitney LLP* |
| | TINDALL John *Tindall Bennett & Shoup PC* |
| 2 | CUMMINGS William *Ashburn & Mason, PC* |
| | HEAPHEY Christopher *Bankston, Gronning, O'Hara* |
| | MCCOLLUM James *Law Offices of James McCollum* |
| | REECE Joseph *Davis Wright Tremaine LLP* |
| | STANLEY James *Rubini & Reeves LLC* |
| | TRAVOSTINO Joan *Preston Gates & Ellis LLP* |

## Band 1

### Ashburn & Mason, PC

The Firm: This Anchorage thoroughbred's position is unassailable, thanks to a strong bench across day-to-day real estate law backed by "*genuine depth on the finance side*" and close ties to the Alaska realty industry. It brings construction and litigation expertise to bear as needed.

The Lawyers: The "*vastly experienced*" **Donald McClintock** acts for a diverse clientele on all manner of real estate concerns, including finance, zoning, land use and construction issues. He is described as an attorney of "*great integrity*" who excels in complex cases. The "*bright, ethical and careful*" **William Cummings** has a healthy transactional real estate practice and is an adroit courtroom performer.

Clients/Work Highlights: Clients include developers, landlords and landowners, agencies, contractors and design professionals.

## Band 2

### Atkinson, Conway & Gagnon

The Firm: This broad-based Anchorage firm offers legal services in a range of commercial areas including real estate. Generally acting for developers, attorneys are expert in finance and able to draw on the firm's potent construction and litigation capabilities. Bruce Gagnon is the main contact for real estate matters.

### Davis Wright Tremaine LLP

The Firm: As one expects from a smart commercial group, the team here understands the real estate market in all its forms. Attorneys offer transactional advice across the board, and are particularly recommended where complex permitting issues arise. The team has been growing its residential development practice and remains engaged in work for Anchorage Global Logistics Airpark Development.

The Lawyers: M&A specialist **Joseph Reece** is an accomplished real estate attorney, advising on acquisitions, developments and leases.

Clients/Work Highlights: Eklutna is a key client.

### Dorsey & Whitney LLP

See firm details p.1169

The Firm: This national powerhouse is transactional adviser to a discerning clientele. The team is especially recommended for developments and financings.

The Lawyers: "*Intellectually agile*" **Richard Rosston** (see p.174) grasps points quickly and explains even the subtlest ramifications lucidly and concisely, according to clients. He has acted on loans and leases for clients such as the Ketchikan Indian Corporation and the Union Bank of California.

Clients/Work Highlights: The diverse clientele includes banks, developers, contractors and design professionals.

## Band 3

### Preston Gates & Ellis LLP

The Firm: Relations between Seattle and Alaska are deep and strong, and the Anchorage office of this national player is a testimony to this. The versatile and talented real estate team is adept in all areas of real estate law, and particularly well regarded for strength in finance and insolvency matters, attracting enviable lender clients. The team has useful environmental and litigation capability.

The Lawyers: **Joan Travostino**'s practice is a rewarding mix of real estate and bankruptcy, generally acting for buyers and creditors respectively.

### Rubini & Reeves LLC

The Firm: After nearly a decade of affiliation, this outfit has severed its links to Seattle's Foster Pepper. It offers a full service – including sophisticated transactional advice – in the real estate sector, and has been busy handling land transactions for national businesses. As well as land use, regulatory and zoning issues, attorneys advise on the finance aspects of deals.

The Lawyers: The "*fast and dependable*" **James Stanley** is a committed real estate attorney and a luminary of the Alaska market. He represents clients in both transactional and contentious matters.

### Tindall Bennett & Shoup PC

The Firm: The growing trend toward real estate-based joint ventures is driving this healthy transactional practice along nicely. The team has been active in residential development projects, and picks up lucrative acquisition work from oil and gas exploration businesses and European clients buying real estate in Alaska.

The Lawyers: **John Tindall**'s M&A expertise enables him to serve the interests of a wide range of acquisitive clients. He is identified with developer clients, and businesses in the oil and gas and telecom sectors.

### Other Notable Practitioners

Birch, Horton, Bittner & Cherot's **Suzanne Cherot** maintains a thriving practice that weaves real estate, corporate and banking law into a sophisticated commercial offering. She frequently acts for developers, banks and financial institutions. **Christopher Heaphey** of Bankston, Gronning, O'Hara, PC is a seasoned litigator who cut his teeth on real estate, construction and environmental law disputes. His practice increasingly encompasses acquisitions and commercial contracts, especially in the development sector. **James McCollum** of the Law Offices of James McCollum LLC is a recognized condominiums expert. He acts for developers and financial institutions on a range of real estate issues

# Leaders in Alaska

**ALEXANDER, Jennifer**
Birch, Horton, Bittner & Cherot,
Anchorage 907 276 1550
*Recommended in Employment*

**ASHBURN, Mark**
Ashburn & Mason, PC, Anchorage
907 276 4331
*Recommended in Litigation*

**BANKSTON, William**
Bankston, Gronning, O'Hara, PC,
Anchorage 907 276 1711
*Recommended in Litigation*

**BAUMAN, Carl**
Hughes Bauman Pfiffner Gorski &
Seedorf LLC, Anchorage
907 274 7522
*Recommended in Environment*

**BEHREND, Andrew**
Heller Ehrman LLP, Anchorage
907 263 8412
andrew.behrend@hellerehrman.com
*Recommended in Employment*
**Practice Areas:** Labor and employment, energy.
**Prof. Memberships:** Alaska Bar Association; American Bar Association.
**Career:** Mr Behrend represents employers in matters relating to employment contracts, non-competition agreements, the development of employment policies and procedures, and compliance with employment laws. He has defended employers against claims alleging employment discrimination based on gender, age, race and disability; violation of federal and state wage and hour laws; violation of the Family Medical Leave Act; wrongful discharge; employer retaliation; defamation; and breach of employment contracts.
**Personal:** University of California, Boalt Hall School of Law (JD, 1993).

**BENNETT, Wilfred**
Tindall Bennett & Shoup PC, Anchorage
907 278 8533
*Recommended in Employment*

**BLACK, Kathryn**
Birch, Horton, Bittner & Cherot,
Anchorage 907 276 1550
*Recommended in Corporate/M&A*

**BLUMSTEIN, Philip**
Landye Bennett Blumstein LLP,
Anchorage 907 276 5152
*Recommended in Corporate/M&A*

**BUNDY, David**
David H Bundy PC, Anchorage
907 248 8431
*Recommended in Bankruptcy*

**BUNDY, Robert C**
Dorsey & Whitney LLP, Anchorage
907 257 7853
bundy.robert@dorsey.com
*Recommended in Litigation*

**Practice Areas:** Civil litigation in the areas of commercial and business litigation, environmental, personal injury, healthcare and professional malpractice, and criminal litigation in the areas of white-collar and environmental matters.
**Prof. Memberships:** Alaska Bar Association, Chair, Rules of Professional Conduct Committee; Member, Ethics Committee; Co-Chair, Gender Equality Section. Anchorage Bar Association.
**Career:** Partner since 2001. United States Attorney for the District of Alaska from 1994 to 2001.
**Personal:** University of California, Berkeley School of Law (Boalt Hall), JD, 1971. University of Southern California, BA, 1968, cum laude.

**CHEROT, Suzanne**
Birch, Horton, Bittner & Cherot,
Anchorage 907 276 1550
*Recommended in Real Estate*

**CHRISTIANSON, Cabot**
Christianson, Boutin & Spraker,
Anchorage 907 258 6016
*Recommended in Bankruptcy*

**COLBO, Kimberlee**
Hughes Bauman Pfiffner Gorski & Seedorf LLC, Anchorage 907 274 7522
*Recommended in Employment*

**COUGHLIN, Jennifer**
Preston Gates & Ellis LLP, Anchorage
907 276 1969
*Recommended in Litigation*

**CUMMINGS, William**
Ashburn & Mason, PC, Anchorage
907 276 4331
*Recommended in Real Estate*

**DANIEL, Thomas**
Perkins Coie LLP, Anchorage
907 279 8561
*Recommended in Employment*

**DAWSON, Jon**
Davis Wright Tremaine LLP, Anchorage
907 257 5300
*Recommended in Bankruptcy,
Corporate/M&A*

**DICKSON, Robert**
Atkinson, Conway & Gagnon, Anchorage
907 276 1700
*Recommended in Litigation*

**DURRELL, Brian**
Durrell Law Group, PC, Anchorage
907 258 3224
*Recommended in Corporate/M&A*

**EVANS, William J**
Dorsey & Whitney LLP, Anchorage
907 257 7871
evans.william@dorsey.com
*Recommended in Employment*
**Practice Areas:** Employment litigation defense as well as traditional management-side labor law. Construction-based litigation and general commercial litigation.
**Prof. Memberships:** Alaska Bar Association.
**Publications:** Has written on labor and employment law for regional and national publications. Also a frequent presenter on these topics.
**Personal:** University of Michigan Law School, JD, 1992, cum laude. Cleveland State University, BA, History and Political Science, 1988, cum laude.

**FELDMAN, Jeffrey**
Feldman Orlansky & Sanders,
Anchorage 907 272 3538
*Recommended in Litigation*

**FJELSTAD, Eric**
Perkins Coie LLP, Anchorage
907 279 8561
*Recommended in Environment*

**GAGNON, Bruce**
Atkinson, Conway & Gagnon, Anchorage
907 276 1700
*Recommended in Litigation*

**GILMORE, Patrick**
Atkinson, Conway & Gagnon, Anchorage
907 276 1700
*Recommended in Litigation*

**GRAHAME, Heather H**
Dorsey & Whitney LLP, Anchorage
907 257 7822
grahame.heather@dorsey.com
*Recommended in Environment*
**Practice Areas:** Public utility law and civil litigation. Significant experience representing telecommunications, refuse, water and wastewater, and oil and gas companies in major adjudicatory and rulemaking proceedings before state public utility commissions, the Federal Communications Commission, and in state and federal court litigation.
**Prof. Memberships:** Member, Alaska Bar Association, Intellectual Property Section and Administrative Law Section. Member, American Bar Association, General Litigation Section and Public Utility, Communications and Transportation Law. Member, Federal Communications Bar Association, Pacific Northwest Chapter.
**Personal:** University of Oregon School of Law, JD, 1984. Stanford University, BA, Human Biology, 1978.

**GROVER, Parry**
Davis Wright Tremaine LLP, Anchorage
907 257 5300
*Recommended in Employment*

**GROVIER, Tina**
Birch, Horton, Bittner & Cherot,
Anchorage 907 276 1550
*Recommended in Environment*

**HALL, Helena**
Perkins Coie LLP, Anchorage
907 279 8561
*Recommended in Employment*

**HARTIG, Lawrence**
Hartig Rhodes Hoge & Lekisch PC,
Anchorage 907 276 1592
*Recommended in Environment*

**HEAPHEY, Christopher**
Bankston, Gronning, O'Hara, PC,
Anchorage 907 276 1711
*Recommended in Real Estate*

**HUTCHINGS, Stephen**
Birch, Horton, Bittner & Cherot,
Anchorage 907 276 1550
*Recommended in Litigation*

**JAMIESON, Brewster**
Lane Powell PC, Anchorage
907 277 9511
*Recommended in Litigation*

**JULIUSSEN, James**
Davis Wright Tremaine LLP, Anchorage
907 257 5300
*Recommended in Employment*

**KRAFT, Barbara Simpson**
Davis Wright Tremaine LLP, Anchorage
907 257 5300
*Recommended in Corporate/M&A*

**KREGER, Michael**
Perkins Coie LLP, Anchorage
907 279 8561
*Recommended in Litigation*

**LIMERES, Amy**
Preston Gates & Ellis LLP, Anchorage
907 276 1969
*Recommended in Employment*

**LINXWILER, James**
Guess & Rudd PC, Anchorage
907 793 2200
*Recommended in Environment*

**LYLE, George**
Guess & Rudd PC, Anchorage
907 793 2200
*Recommended in Environment*

**MASON III, Julian**
Ashburn & Mason, PC, Anchorage
907 276 4331
*Recommended in Environment*

**MCCLINTOCK, Donald**
Ashburn & Mason, PC, Anchorage
907 276 4331
*Recommended in Real Estate*

**MCCOLLUM, James**
Law Offices of James McCollum LLC,
Anchorage 907 770 7773
*Recommended in Real Estate*

**MEDE, William**
Turner & Mede, PC, Anchorage
907 276 3963
*Recommended in Employment*

**MILLS, Michael**
Bankston, Gronning, O'Hara, PC,
Anchorage 907 276 1711
*Recommended in Bankruptcy*

**MORAN, Joseph**
DeLisio Moran Geraghty & Zobel, P.C.,
Anchorage 907 279 9574
*Recommended in Environment*

**ODSEN, Frederick**
Hughes Bauman Pfiffner Gorski &
Seedorf LLC, Anchorage 907 274 7522
*Recommended in Corporate/M&A*

**OESTING, David**
Davis Wright Tremaine LLP, Anchorage
907 257 5300
*Recommended in Bankruptcy,
Litigation*

**ORLANSKY, Susan**
Feldman Orlansky & Sanders,
Anchorage 907 272 3538
*Recommended in Litigation*

**PARISE, Michael**
Birch, Horton, Bittner & Cherot,
Anchorage 907 276 1550
*Recommended in Bankruptcy*

**PARKER, Douglas**
Preston Gates & Ellis LLP, Anchorage
907 276 1969
*Recommended in Employment*

**PERKINS, Joseph**
Guess & Rudd PC, Anchorage
907 793 2200
*Recommended in Environment*

**PETUMENOS, Timothy**
Birch, Horton, Bittner & Cherot,
Anchorage 907 276 1550
*Recommended in Litigation*

**RECKMEYER, Peter R**
Heller Ehrman LLP, Anchorage
907 263 8411
peter.reckmeyer@hellerehrman.com
*Recommended in Corporate/M&A*
**Practice Areas:** Life sciences, information technology, intellectual property
transactions.
**Prof. Memberships:** Alaska Bar Association, State Bar of Wisconsin.
**Career:** Mr Reckmeyer has substantial
experience negotiating and drafting contracts for complex commercial transactions, with particular experience in the
life sciences industry. He has previous
experience as in-house counsel and negotiated licenses, technology transfer agreements, supply agreements, OEM agreements and distribution agreements for
domestic and international transactions.
He also counsels senior management on
day to day commercial issues, regulatory
compliance issues, contract interpretation matters, and conflict resolution and
negotiation strategies for commercial disputes.
**Personal:** Loyola University School of
Law (JD, 1989).

**REECE, Joseph**
Davis Wright Tremaine LLP, Anchorage
907 257 5300
*Recommended in Corporate/M&A,
Real Estate*

**REEVES, James N**
Dorsey & Whitney LLP, Anchorage
907 257 7825
reeves.jim@dorsey.com
*Recommended in Environment*
**Practice Areas:** Civil litigation, commercial disputes, administrative law, real
estate and natural resources law including
public lands, mining, and environmental
regulation. Served as primary counsel in
over 25 civil appeals and in civil trials conducted throughout the State of Alaska.
**Prof. Memberships:** Alaska Bar Association. American Bar Association (Section
of Natural Resources, Energy and Environmental Law and Section of Administrative Law). Rocky Mountain Mineral
Law Foundation.
**Personal:** East-West Center, Honolulu,
Hawaii, Senior Fellow, Multi-National
Environmental Policy, 1977. University of
Minnesota Law School, JD, 1970. Dartmouth College, AB, 1967.

**REEVES, Susan**
Rubini & Reeves LLC, Anchorage
907 222 7104
*Recommended in Environment*

**REGES, Robert**
Reges & Boone LLC, Juneau
907 790 2777
*Recommended in Environment*

**ROHLF, Joan**
Guess & Rudd PC, Anchorage
907 793 2200
*Recommended in Employment*

**ROSSTON, Richard**
Dorsey & Whitney LLP, Anchorage
907 257 7837
rosston.dick@dorsey.com
*Recommended in Corporate/M&A,
Real Estate*
**Practice Areas:** Commercial, corporate,
finance, merger and acquisition, Alaska
Native, real property, state securities and
telecommunications law.
**Prof. Memberships:** Alaska Bar Associa-
tion. American Bar Association; Business
Law Section, Real Estate Section, Health
Law Section.
**Career:** Partner in Dorsey's Corporate
Group since 1999.
**Personal:** University of California,
Berkeley School of Law (Boalt Hall), JD,
1977. Dartmouth College, AB, 1973,
summa cum laude.

**ROZELL, William**
William Rozell - Sole Practitioner, Juneau
907 586 0142
*Recommended in Environment*

**SAUPE, A William**
Ashburn & Mason, PC, Anchorage
907 276 4331

*Recommended in Environment*

**SERDAHELY, Douglas J**
Patton Boggs LLP, Anchorage
907 263 6310
dserdahely@pattonboggs.com
*Recommended in Environment,
Litigation*
**Practice Areas:** Complex civil litigation
involving environment/antitrust. Repre-
sented ExxonMobil in Exxon Valdez Oil
Spill. Has advised Marathon Oil, Travel-
ers Insurance, Crowley Maritime Ser-
vices, Inc., and various energy/trans-
portation/fuel distribution companies.
Represents companies in major M&A.
Liaison counsel in $1 billion class action.
Has served as settlement mediator in civil
actions.
**Prof. Memberships:** Alaska Bar Associa-
tion; DC Bar Association.
**Career:** Anchorage Managing Partner.
Former litigation Partner, Bogle & Gates.
Alaska Superior Court Judge (1981-89),
presiding judge of Third Judicial District.
Pro tem panelist on Alaska Appeals Court
and Alaska Supreme Court.
**Personal:** Harvard Law School (JD
1972); Northwestern University (BA,
1968).

**SIEMERS, John**
Burr, Pease & Kurtz, PC, Anchorage
907 276 6100
*Recommended in Bankruptcy*

**SNEED, Spencer**
Dorsey & Whitney LLP, Anchorage
907 257 7819
sneed.spencer@dorsey.com
*Recommended in Bankruptcy,
Litigation*
**Practice Areas:** Financing transactions
and commercial/bankruptcy litigation.
**Prof. Memberships:** Alaska Bar Associa-
tion, Bankruptcy Law Section. American
Bar Association Member, Business Law
Section. American Bankruptcy Institute.
**Career:** Partner in Dorsey's Trial Group
since 2000.
**Personal:** Williamette University College
of Law, JD, 1978. Arizona State Universi-
ty, BA, Philosophy, 1975, magna cum
laude.

**SPAAN, Michael**
Patton Boggs LLP, Anchorage
907 263 6305
mspaan@pattonboggs.com
*Recommended in Litigation*
**Practice Areas:** Litigation issues involving complex commercial, civil, and
white-collar criminal cases. Helps companies conduct internal corporate investigations. Has successfully defended
numerous officers/companies in grand
jury matters and jury cases.
**Prof. Memberships:** ABA, Litigation and
Criminal Law Sections; Alaska Inns of
Courts (former President, 1992-96);
National Association of Former United
States Attorneys (former Board Member).

**Career:** Partner. United States Attorney
for District of Alaska (1981-89).
**Publications:** Numerous speeches and
presentations before professional and Bar
Associations.
**Personal:** University of California -
Davis (JD, 1972); Chico State College
(BS, 1968).

**SPRAKER, Gary**
Christianson, Boutin & Spraker,
Anchorage 907 258 6016
*Recommended in Bankruptcy*

**STANLEY, James**
Rubini & Reeves LLC, Anchorage
907 222 7104
*Recommended in Real Estate*

**STEWART, Robert**
Davis Wright Tremaine LLP, Anchorage
907 257 5300
*Recommended in Employment*

**STOLLER, Robert**
Robert Stoller - Sole Practitioner,
Anchorage 907 522 2299
*Recommended in Environment*

**TINDALL, John**
Tindall Bennett & Shoup PC, Anchorage
907 278 8533
*Recommended in Real Estate*

**TORGERSON, James**
Heller Ehrman LLP, Anchorage
907 263 8404
james.torgerson@hellerehrman.com
*Recommended in Environment,
Litigation*
**Practice Areas:** Consumer litigation,
energy, insurance recovery, white-collar
criminal defense, product liability.
**Career:** Mr Torgerson's practice focuses
on complex trial and appellate litigation
in accounting, energy, insurance, transportation and related industries. He has
extensive experience litigating environmental, False Claims Act, Native American, and white-collar criminal disputes in
federal courts. Previous experience
includes eight years in the United States
Attorney's Office for the District of Alaska. He served as Chief of the Civil Division for four years and as Chief of the
Criminal Division for two years.
**Personal:** University of Washington
School of Law (JD, 1984).

**TRAVOSTINO, Joan**
Preston Gates & Ellis LLP, Anchorage
907 276 1969
*Recommended in Bankruptcy, Real
Estate*

**VEERMAN, Louis**
Guess & Rudd PC, Anchorage
907 793 2200
*Recommended in Environment*

**WATTS, Grant**
Holmes Weddle & Barcott, A Professional Corporation, Anchorage
907 274 0666
*Recommended in Litigation*

**CONTENTS:**

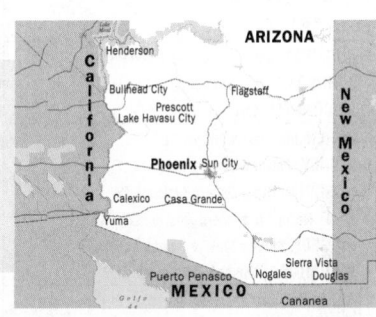

## How lawyers are ranked

Every year we carry out thousands of in-depth interviews with clients and lawyers in order to assess the reputations and expertise of business lawyers across the USA. Chambers rankings and editorial are referred to extensively by General Counsel and other purchasers of legal services who look to our recommendations when choosing their lawyers.

# CORPORATE/M&A

| Corporate/M&A Leading Firms | |
| --- | --- |
| 1 | FENNEMORE CRAIG *Phoenix* |
| | OSBORN MALEDON PA *Phoenix* |
| | SNELL & WILMER LLP *Phoenix* |
| 2 | BRYAN CAVE LLP *Phoenix* |
| | GREENBERG TRAURIG LLP *Phoenix* |
| | SQUIRE, SANDERS & DEMPSEY LLP *Phoenix* |
| 3 | JENNINGS, STROUSS & SALMON, PLC *Phoenix* |
| | QUARLES & BRADY STREICH LANG LLP *Phoenix* |
| 4 | LEWIS AND ROCA *Phoenix* |
| | PERKINS COIE LLP *Phoenix* |
| | RYLEY CARLOCK & APPLEWHITE *Phoenix* |
| | TITUS, BRUECKNER & BERRY PC *Scottsdale* |

## Band 1

### Fennemore Craig

See firm details p.197

**The Firm:** Having carefully nurtured its young, dynamic group, Fennemore Craig has established itself as a leader in business law. Clients particularly appreciate its high-service standards, praising the proactive approach and "*time taken to learn about our needs and our company.*" Indeed, one self-confessed 'demanding client' stated: "*They never fail to meet my demands and needs, which really says something.*" Operating from three offices in Arizona, the corporate team regularly handles M&A for private and public companies, as well as securities issues, ERISA and tax. Its considerable size and presence across the region has helped the corporate group to consistently win high-caliber deals, such as the Giant Industries sale of one million shares of common stock, in a public offering underwritten by Banc of America Securities.

**The Lawyers:** **Karen McConnell** (see p.192) "*inspires tremendous client loyalty*" with her easy manner, integrity and diligent approach. Known as a "*can-do*" lawyer who leads well and delegates effectively, she was enthusiastically praised by peers as a "*bright and creative deal lawyer*" who is "*even-handed and a pleasure to work with.*" **Sarah Strunk** (see p.195) has a knack of "*handling difficult situations brilliantly,*" which has earned her the implicit trust of colleagues and clients alike. According to intervie-

wees, she possesses a refreshing talent for achieving the right result for her client without unnecessary aggression.

**Clients/Work Highlights:** The firm handled the sale of assets of Landmark Interiors to Floorworks, a division of Home Depot. Other clients include Allied Waste Industries; City of Glendale; Giant Industries and Phelps Dodge.

### Osborn Maledon PA

See firm details p.198

**The Firm:** Clients who walk through this boutique firm's door "*wouldn't dream of going anywhere else.*" The "*outstanding*" group has won its leading position in the market through developing a culture that is versatile, responsive and keen to understand business objectives. While the team is large and broad enough to cover all aspects of corporate M&A, its real forte is said to lie in the area of venture capital and angel financings for entrepreneurial companies and investors. Here it has represented Grayhawk Venture Partners and Montage Holdings on the investor side, and Andigilog, GoalCentrix and Intesource on the company side. However, the firm takes more traditional transactions in its stride, as demonstrated by the central role Osborn Maledon plays in WL Gore's global strategy. In the past year, for example, it advised the maker of GORE-TEX on the acquisition of three medical device technology companies.

**The Lawyers:** There was praise from all sides for **Tom Curzon** (see p.189), who gives "*crisp, clear advice*" and has a "*great gut-feel*" when it comes to difficult issues. Peers agree that he is "*undeniably one of the best,*" while clients appreciate his "*ability to sense our needs rather than impress his own opinions.*" "*Gentleman*" **William Hardin** (see p.191) is admired by clients for his "*incredible intellect*" and knack of "*zeroing in on key issues and the dynamics of a deal.*" Undisputedly at the top of their game, this pair are supported by a team of rising stars, who should ensure that Osborn Maledon remains at the top of this field for the foreseeable future. Chief among them are **Andrew Kelly** (see p.192) and **Jonathan Ariano** (see p.187). Kelly is said to be "*well versed in the technical legal issues,*" yet realizes the importance of sound, practical advice. He has already assisted in a number of multimillion-dollar transactions. Ariano, who is known as Tom Curzon's protégé, was

praised for his creativity and intellect.

**Clients/Work Highlights:** WL Gore & Associates; Andigilog; Cox Communications; Arizona Diamondbacks; Intesource and MedAire.

### Snell & Wilmer LLP

See firm details p.200

**The Firm:** This corporate powerhouse is "*undisputedly a top-ranking firm,*" according to market sources. Clients expressed their appreciation of a team of "*well-versed*" attorneys providing "*economic and timely*" services. The group focuses on sophisticated midmarket transactions but also boasts an impressive track record in the larger deals. Recent examples include advising on the $143 million acquisition by Encore Capital Group of Jefferson Capital assets and portfolios, and the pending $250 million sale of Action Performance to an entity jointly owned by International Speedway and Speedway Motorsports. Despite handling multimillion-dollar transactions on a day-to-day basis, the firm also counsels and promotes emerging entrepreneurial businesses.

**The Lawyers:** "*Skilled adversary*" **Jon Cohen** (see p.189) can be "*counted on to give the opposition a hard time*" where necessary. A talented corporate lawyer, he was consistently recommended by market sources. **Matthew Feeney** (see p.190) is a "*great adviser*" with a "*superb intellect,*" according to clients. His dedication and commitment were particularly appreciated: as one source noted, he "*always has his clients' interests at heart.*" **Steven Pidgeon** (see p.194) is considered an aggressive lawyer with a confident approach and a will to win. His key strength is held to be securities law, where he has built one of the largest and most impressive practices in the state. **Terry Roman**'s (see p.194) forte, meanwhile, lies in her ability to deal with difficult situations, her "*sound business judgment*" and her "*excellent risk analysis.*"

**Clients/Work Highlights:** Pinnacle West; APS (Arizona Public Service); The Tech Group; Bank of America; Ford and Meritage Homes.

## Band 2

### Bryan Cave LLP

**The Firm:** The corporate team in Arizona benefits from the support of a national – indeed international

175

## Corporate/M&A
### Leading Individuals

**1**  CURZON Thomas *Osborn Maledon PA*
   JOHNSON Christopher *Squire, Sanders*
   MCCONNELL Karen *Fennemore Craig*

**2**  COHEN Jon *Snell & Wilmer LLP*
   FEENEY Matthew *Snell & Wilmer LLP*
   HARDIN William *Osborn Maledon PA*
   KANT Robert *Greenberg Traurig LLP*
   PIDGEON Steven *Snell & Wilmer LLP*
   RICHARDSON Joseph *Bryan Cave LLP*

**3**  BLANEY Brian *Greenberg Traurig LLP*
   BROPHY James *Ryley Carlock & Applewhite*
   HACKETT Robert *Jennings, Strouss*
   HOFFMANN Christian *Quarles & Brady*
   LAUSE Christopher *Bryan Cave LLP*
   MOYA Bob *Quarles & Brady*
   PLACENTI Frank *Bryan Cave LLP*
   ROMAN Terry *Snell & Wilmer LLP*
   STRUNK Sarah *Fennemore Craig*
   WILLIAMS Quinn *Greenberg Traurig LLP*

**4**  BERRY Charles *Titus, Brueckner*
   CRABB Joseph *Quarles & Brady*
   DEWALD Scott *Lewis and Roca*
   EMERICK Steven *Quarles & Brady*
   MACDONOUGH Bruce *Greenberg Traurig LLP*
   WEISS Judith *Perkins Coie LLP*

### Up-and-coming individuals
   ARIANO Jonathan *Osborn Maledon PA*
   HALL Gregory *Squire, Sanders*
   KELLY Andrew *Osborn Maledon PA*

– team of M&A lawyers, helping it to consistently win mandates in the largest and most sophisticated deals in the state. A highly visible player in the market, Bryan Cave has taken on individuals from the SEC, expanding its experience and resources in securities law. Clients appreciate the effort that has gone into building up long-term relationships – one even said that with such a level of responsiveness and support *"it almost feels as if the team is part of us."* The *"one-stop-shop"* approach, with a broad range of services available under one roof, also proved popular.

**The Lawyers: Joe Richardson**'s *"mellow, thorough"* and quietly diligent style, coupled with his excellent technical skills and flair for securities work, earned him the respect of peers and clients alike. Market sources also rated the *"impressive and extraordinarily capable"* **Christopher Lause** for his *"meticulous and detailed"* approach. An important figure in the local legal community, his profile is felt to be on the up at present. **Frank Placenti** is a masterful *"front man"* for the group, whose *"excellent client skills"* have played a great role in its development. Clients were impressed by his responsiveness, pragmatism and *"ability to see the big picture."*

**Clients/Work Highlights:** Viad Corp; Medicis Pharmaceutical; MoneyGram International; Dial Corporation; AMERCO; Ben & Jerry's Homemade; VistaCare and the FINOVA Group.

## Greenberg Traurig LLP
See firm details p.664

**The Firm:** Though Greenberg Traurig has not been in Arizona as long as some of its competitors, the international firm deserves great credit for the speed with which it has grown a *"terrific, diverse, thorough and professional"* corporate practice. Great emphasis is placed on service standards; as one client noted, the team delivers *"consistently high quality – even down to the paralegals."* As part of an expanding global firm, the group in Arizona contributes to a 1,400-strong corporate team, allowing it to call upon an unparalleled wealth of expertise located across the world.

**The Lawyers: Robert Kant** (see p.192) remains the firm's outstanding name in this field. His success has been built on the combination of an informed legal mind and considerable business acumen, while his direct style is said to make him a force to be reckoned with. Following in his footsteps is the aggressive and energetic **Brian Blaney** (see p.187). Armed with a strong work ethic and a client-focused approach, he is known as a *"solid business partner"* who provides *"well-balanced, knowledgeable counsel."* **Quinn Williams** (see p.196) is the firm's *"public persona in the venture capital area."* A *"community leader in promoting Phoenix capital,"* he is admired by all for his well-honed business instincts. **Bruce Macdonough** (see p.192) concentrates on M&A, public and private securities offerings, and sophisticated corporate finance transactions, utilizing his collaborative skills and flair for creative deal-making. Clients particularly appreciate his honesty: *"He doesn't hide the picture from you, however bleak!"*

**Clients/Work Highlights:** Recent highlights include representing MarineMax in a $107.7 million public offering underwritten by JPMorgan and Raymond James & Associates. It also counseled Directed Electronics on a proposed IPO to be lead managed by Goldman Sachs. Other clients include Brillian; GameTech; Smith & Wesson Holding; Synaptics and Vodavi Technology.

## Squire, Sanders & Dempsey LLP
See firm details p.1650

**The Firm:** With 15 different locations in North America and a rapidly growing international network, Squire Sanders offers its regional clients access to an outstanding level of resources and expertise from its Phoenix office. Over the years, it has built and nurtured strong working relationships with local, state, national and international clients and governmental bodies. The *"experienced, confident and skilled"* attorneys handle a wide range of matters, including restructuring debtor companies for creditor clients, private investments and public equity transactions.

**The Lawyers: Christopher Johnson** (see p.192) is celebrated as Arizona's *"most experienced securities lawyer in public offerings."* His stellar negotiating skills and *"sound analytical writing"* earn him a top-band ranking once again. **Gregory Hall** (see p.190) is identified as a younger lawyer on the cusp of great things. His *"quiet confidence"* and willingness to go

the extra mile for his clients make him one to watch in this arena.

**Clients/Work Highlights:** Clients range from chemicals producers and aircraft systems manufacturers to the USA's largest energy provider.

## Band 3

### Jennings, Strouss & Salmon, PLC

**The Firm:** This well-established firm boasts experts in a broad array of industries, from utilities and healthcare, to telecom and the Internet. However, what particularly distinguishes Jennings, Strouss & Salmon is its edge in biotech and life sciences transactions. Here, the firm has pioneered a cross-disciplinary approach, giving the corporate group valuable support from deal-focused IP colleagues. Other strengths include securities law, where the firm handles a wide variety of private and public offerings.

**The Lawyers: Robert Hackett** brings with him vast experience of East Coast investment banking and highly respected expertise in the corporate area.

**Clients/Work Highlights:** Clients range from Fortune 500 companies to local emerging businesses.

### Quarles & Brady Streich Lang LLP
See firm details p.2039

**The Firm:** It has been another busy year for this 400-strong national team. In Arizona, the corporate group has expanded in response to a thriving market. Work is largely focused on M&A and SEC reporting, and the firm has a particular niche in advising emerging and small-cap growth companies. These clients highlighted the firm's *"exemplary"* service, and particularly appreciated an intelligent approach to staffing deals that *"assigns the right person with the right level of experience to the job."*

**The Lawyers: Christian Hoffmann** (see p.191) continues to excel in a broad spectrum of deals, including M&A, vencap and private equity transactions, and public offerings of equity and debt securities. Market sources highlighted his *"excellent judgment."* **Bob Moya** (see p.193) was heartily welcomed back into the fold by peers and clients, having spent the last few years as chief administrative officer, executive vice president, general counsel and corporate secretary at Insight Enterprises. *"He is said to have the knack of making all his clients feel like his top priority."* **Joseph Crabb** (see p.189) impressed the market with his vast breadth of knowledge that spans, inter alia, M&A, stock asset acquisitions and commercial lending transactions. He has already built up an impressive track record in a number of industries, including transportation, financial services, software and manufacturing. **Steven Emerick** (see p.189), meanwhile, is admired by clients for his *"ability to see the wood for the trees"* and *"get quickly to the heart of the matter."*

**Clients/Work Highlights:** Recent work has included the sale of a medical device company, a deal valued in the region of $50-100 million.

## Band 4

### Lewis and Roca

**The Firm:** Lewis and Roca has an emphasis on transactional work, which includes securities offerings, M&A, public finance and corporate structuring, as well as advice on the venture capital needs of emerging companies. An eclectic client base is drawn from a number of industries, including software, computer data services, healthcare, plastics manufacturing, electronics and airlines.

**The Lawyers:** "*Solid performer*" **Scott DeWald** was applauded by interviewees for his straightforward, practical approach. He is said to have won considerable client loyalty, especially among hi-tech and emerging growth companies.

### Perkins Coie LLP

**The Firm:** The firm's arrangement into nationwide practice groups offers its clients the necessary depth and breadth of experience to handle sizable transactions across the country and internationally. Indeed, market commentators highlight Perkins Coie for its huge clients and global capabilities. Both of these were recently demonstrated by its involvement in an $850 million mine expansion in Peru. Typical work for the group in Arizona includes banking, M&A and corporate finance.

**The Lawyers:** **Judith Weiss** was recommended for her "*focus on the details*," sensitivity to clients' needs and understanding of the legal implications of business transactions. Her key areas include M&A and private offerings.

### Ryley Carlock & Applewhite

See firm details p.199

**The Firm:** A busy year for this developing group has seen it involved in the creation of several small independent banks. It also handles a rich diet of finance work driven by the booming real estate market. The firm has been working in recent years to build up a national practice in the corporate arena, and has focused on broadening its experience to the point where it can handle most issues thrown at it. These include M&A, stock compensation issues, securities law, insurance and most varieties of corporate lending.

**The Lawyers:** The "*understated but effective*" **James Brophy** (see p.188) was enthusiastically recommended by interviewees for his wealth of experience and "*wonderful, easy manner.*"

### Titus, Brueckner & Berry PC

**The Firm:** This boutique transactional firm prides itself on providing a high level of personal attention to clients, who tend to be smaller entrepreneurial companies. Based in Scottsdale – a current hothouse for the real estate market – Titus, Brueckner & Berry combines its M&A work with an emphasis on real estate financing. In addition, it handles a steady stream of securities law and commercial litigation.

**The Lawyers:** According to clients, **Charles Berry** combines "*substantial experience*" in securities law and transactional work with a "*personable manner*" that makes him good to deal with.

## EMPLOYMENT

## MAINLY DEFENDANT

| Employment: Mainly Defendant |
|---|
| Leading Firms |
| **1** STEPTOE & JOHNSON LLP *Phoenix* |
| **2** FENNEMORE CRAIG *Phoenix* |
| GREENBERG TRAURIG LLP *Phoenix* |
| LEWIS AND ROCA *Phoenix* |
| OGLETREE, DEAKINS *Phoenix* |
| RYLEY CARLOCK & APPLEWHITE *Phoenix* |
| **3** PERKINS COIE LLP *Phoenix* |
| QUARLES & BRADY STREICH LANG LLP *Phoenix* |
| SNELL & WILMER LLP *Phoenix* |
| STINSON MORRISON HECKER LLP *Phoenix* |

## Band 1

### Steptoe & Johnson LLP

See firm details p.576

**The Firm:** The national and international reach of this group, coupled with its reputation for giving "*truthful and practical advice*," have earned them a position as "*simply the best and most comprehensive firm in town*" for employment work. The massive firm is further distinguished by its extensive experience in all aspects of employment law. These include the range of discrimination cases, wrongful termination claims and whistle-blowing, to name but a few. Its expertise in litigation extends from pretrial hearings all the way to appellate proceedings, before a variety of courts and bodies. However, the team is equally adept at counseling on the avoidance of liability and conducting HR audits.

**The Lawyers:** Longtime leader of the employment law department **Lawrence Katz** (see p.192) makes each of his clients feel like his top priority. They also greatly appreciate his "*ability to distill issues down into small, digestible pieces.*" Peers, meanwhile, admire his extensive knowledge, "*intelligent, articulate brief-writing skills*" and "*practical problem solving.*" **Monica Goebel**'s (see p.190) focus includes multiplaintiff and class action lawsuits, wage and hour matters and sexual harassment claims. She is recognized as an ethical and talented adviser and a skilled problem solver.

**Clients/Work Highlights:** Over the past twelve months, the firm has been kept busy with significant trade secrets work for Wal-Mart. Allied Waste, Motorola and Microchip also feature in its impressive client roster.

## Band 2

### Fennemore Craig

See firm details p.197

**The Firm:** Fennemore Craig is committed to developing strategies designed to improve employee relations and reduce the likelihood of costly litigation. This proactive approach is reflected in the firm's popular seminar program, intended to introduce new areas of law and alert clients to legislative changes. Initiatives like this have proved a hit with clients, who repeatedly stressed the excellence of the team's advice and its friendly, collegiate atmosphere. However, a constructive approach and an emphasis on litigation avoidance have not prevented the group building an impressive track record in litigation. In the past year, this includes successfully defending Robson Communities against claims of pregnancy discrimination, breach of contract and tortuous interference.

**The Lawyers:** With his "*great combination of technical and interpersonal skills*," **Ronald Stolkin** (see p.195) was rated by clients as "*one of the best in Tucson.*" His many highlights of late include obtaining a summary judgment, injunctive relief and monetary payment for a client in a complex action relating to restrictive covenants. Phoenix-based **Donald Gilbert** (see p.190) is one of the "*real sages of this area*," according to at least one client. He recently obtained two summary judgments on behalf of Phelps Dodge. **Janice Proctor-Murphy** (see p.194) was hailed as instrumental to the success of the Robson Communities case. Her exceptional written work is said to ensure that she "*regularly wins cases on the strength of her pleadings.*"

**Clients/Work Highlights:** Avnet; Wick Communications; The Lyle Anderson Company; PSS/World Medical; Phelps Dodge; Robertson Aviation and Southwest Airlines.

### Greenberg Traurig LLP

See firm details p.664

**The Firm:** This eight-strong team possesses a wealth of resources, not least of which is the ability to access the firm's extensive national and international network. With the group's long-standing position in this sphere, it can offer clients a comprehensive range of services, from cutting-edge discrimination and harassment cases, to traditional labor disputes, negotiations and organizing campaigns. Clients include some of the largest employers in the USA, though the team also acts for up-and-coming local businesses: both ends of the spectrum find the team consistently "*wonderful.*"

**The Lawyers:** Known for his ability to "*turn a case over on a dime*," **John Doran** (see p.189) impresses both in the courtroom and in negotiations. Clients repeatedly cite him as "*the main reason we stay with Greenberg.*" Recent successes include obtaining preliminary and permanent injunctions, followed by a summary judgment on behalf of a plaintiff. In addition, clients appreciate **Mary Bruno**'s (see p.188) obvious *"dedication to our case,"* and **Lawrence Rosenfeld**'s (see p.194) *"strategic and focused"* approach.

Clients/Work Highlights: Clients are drawn from a diverse array of industries, such as healthcare, hospitality, construction, entertainment and insurance. Of particular note recently was the team's successful defense against a large union-organizing drive. This involved more than 40 unfair labor practice charges before the NLRB.

## Lewis and Roca

The Firm: This is among the largest – possibly the largest – employment groups in the Southwest. Lewis and Roca offers an across-the-board service, handling a steady stream of wrongful termination, health and safety, and wage and hour disputes. Where the team is felt to particularly excel, however, is in the field of employment discrimination, where top-end courtroom skills are complemented by an expanding alternative dispute resolution practice. Clients were particularly impressed by the group's mixture of experience, with excellent partners supported by talented attorneys at every level.

The Lawyers: A *"consummate professional,"* **Richard Cohen** is acclaimed by a number of sources as the *"best defense lawyer in town."* His position is said to be based upon a combination of *"top-notch"* courtroom skills coupled with an *"encyclopedic knowledge"* of the law. **Jane Reddin** was recommended as his solid successor. She was said to have strong interper-

sonal skills, which are invaluable in counseling clients to prevent employment disputes.

## Ogletree, Deakins, Nash, Smoak & Stewart, PC
See firm details p.738

The Firm: One of the most exciting developments in the market last year was the move of a substantial quantity of key staff, including new managing partner Joseph Clees, from Bryan Cave to launch the Arizona branch for this national employment and labor firm. The team has clearly hit the ground running, and market sources agree that it is *"really set to make a mark."* While at Bryan Cave, the team had developed experience of representing major employers at a variety of labor and employment tribunals, with a particular name for handling large class actions. This is now complemented by Ogletree Deakins' vast store of specialist expertise and national network.

The Lawyers: **Joseph Clees** (see p.189) was recommended as a *"practical and experienced"* lawyer and an *"excellent client counselor."* His dedication to his clients has rewarded him with a client base that is the envy of his peers – as one competitor claimed: *"I'd love him to work here."*

Clients/Work Highlights: An impressive client base comprises a number of Fortune 500 companies, including Ford; Verizon; Procter & Gamble; Morgan Stanley; Chevron and JPMorgan Chase.

## Ryley Carlock & Applewhite
See firm details p.199

The Firm: Peers express their *"great admiration"* for this group, admiring in particular the constructive, collegiate atmosphere. As one said, remarking on its growing profile and impressive track record: *"It's good to see them get their due credit."* The 12-strong group handles every facet of employment law, including arbitration and litigation, before a variety of bodies, collective bargaining, union relations, benefits law, immigration and noncompete agreements. The team also emphasizes proactive counseling to avoid expensive litigation.

The Lawyers: *"Skilled academic"* **Michael Moberly** (see p.192) has forged a strong presence as an advocate who also *"writes prolifically and beautifully."* **Nathan Niemuth** (see p.193) is pinpointed as *"among the top traditional labor lawyers"* in the state. He won plaudits for achieving *"phenomenal results"* for his clients. Clients also appreciate **Charles Chester**'s (see p.188) wise yet *"down-to-earth approach and personable manner."* His experience in age and race discrimination is said to make him a good choice to train managers in harassment and discrimination law.

Clients/Work Highlights: The team represents an array of banks; technology companies; builders; public utilities and government entities. Clients include Knight Transportation; PETsMART; Thames Water; City of Glendale and Colombian Chemicals.

## Band 3

## Perkins Coie LLP

The Firm: This fine firm's strength is said to lie in its commitment to preventing costly litigation wherever possible. However, if litigation is needed, the team is more than up to the task: notable assets include its experience in class actions and unusual employment issues. Following last year's merger, the team has been able to adopt a more collective approach to litigation, utilizing the strengths of the network to assign groups of experts to cases.

The Lawyers: **Michael Berman** divides his time between labor and employment litigation, and alternative dispute resolution. Sources note his considerable experience, identifying him as *"extremely bright and well-informed."*

Clients/Work Highlights: The team's clients are drawn from a range of industries and sectors, such as manufacturing, retail and construction, and also includes public utilities and school districts.

## Quarles & Brady Streich Lang LLP
See firm details p.2039

The Firm: Clients appreciate the consistently *"fantastic"* quality of the lawyers at this full-service firm. The group covers the breadth of employment law, including trade secrets, employee benefits, discrimination, harassment, unfair dismissal and OSHA cases. It also enjoys a strong name for traditional labor law issues, conducting union negotiations and representing employers in hearings before a range of courts and bodies.

The Lawyers: **Jon Pettibone** (see p.193) is referred to by market sources as a *"walking encyclopedia"* for his exceptional knowledge and understanding of traditional labor law. He focuses on advising management on collective bargaining and union-organizing campaigns, and representing them in disputes before a variety of federal and state bodies. Although better known as a general litigator rather than an employment law specialist, **Lonnie Williams'** (see p.196) *"superb trial skills"* earn him a high place in the rankings once again. **Charles Herf** (see p.191) was recommended as a *"real asset to Quarles."* In particular, he is said to bring an unparalleled expertise in education and public sector issues to the table.

## Snell & Wilmer LLP
See firm details p.200

The Firm: This corporate powerhouse has undeniably suffered some attorney losses from its employment team in recent years. However, Snell & Wilmer remains a major player in the state, particularly for its strong employee benefits practice. Lawyers work from both the Tucson and Phoenix offices, handling a variety of cases, including discrimination and harassment, wrongful discharge, breach of contract, wage and hour, and OSHA matters, before a variety of tribunals and courts.

The Lawyers: *"Bright and knowledgeable"* **William Hayden** (see p.191) is highly regarded by market sources for both labor and employment work. He has been busy of late working on a large class action for alleged misclassification of employees in connection with overtime payments. **Rebecca Winterscheidt** (see p.196) advises employers on a range of matters connected with personnel administration. Peers described her as having "*really blossomed*" in the past couple of years, and praised her "*poised, well-spoken and comfortable demeanor*" in court. Rising star **Tibor Nagy** (see p.193) is hailed as an excellent all-rounder, with an emphasis on workers' compensation. Peers flagged him up as "*extremely intelligent, confident and ethical.*"

## Stinson Morrison Hecker LLP
See firm details p.1220
**The Firm:** "*Small yet strong,*" Stinson Morrison's flair for OSHA cases is especially well regarded. The firm acts for an impressive roster of clients, who range from Fortune 500 companies to small local employers. Recent highlights include a high-profile wrongful termination case involving alleged plagiarism, and a sexual harassment case for a hospital.
**The Lawyers:** "*Cerebral professor-type*" **David Selden** (see p.194) offers incredible knowledge

coupled with a tenacious style of litigation, earning him respect across the board.

## Other Notable Practitioners
Interviewees were quick to mention **Amy Gittler** of Frazer Ryan Goldberg Arnold & Gittler LLP. Her "*great capacity for the full spectrum of employment matters*" impressed clients so much that they would "*recommend her to anyone.*"

# ENVIRONMENT      (INCLUDING WATER RIGHTS)

## Environment (including water rights)

### Leading Firms

| | |
|---|---|
| 1 | **FENNEMORE CRAIG** *Phoenix* |
| | **GALLAGHER & KENNEDY PA** *Phoenix* |
| 2 | **BRYAN CAVE LLP** *Phoenix* |
| | **MOYES STOREY** *Phoenix* |
| | **QUARLES & BRADY STREICH LANG LLP** *Phoenix* |
| | **RYLEY CARLOCK & APPLEWHITE** *Phoenix* |
| | **SNELL & WILMER LLP** *Phoenix* |
| | **SQUIRE, SANDERS & DEMPSEY LLP** *Phoenix* |
| 3 | **LEWIS AND ROCA** *Phoenix* |
| | **STEPTOE & JOHNSON LLP** *Phoenix* |

### Leading Individuals

| | |
|---|---|
| 1 | **BROPHY Michael** *Ryley Carlock & Applewhite* |
| | **DEROUIN James** *Steptoe & Johnson LLP* |
| | **FERLAND Roger** *Quarles & Brady Streich Lang LLP* |
| | **KIMBALL David** *Gallagher & Kennedy PA* |
| | **NARDUCCI Lucas** *Bryan Cave LLP* |
| | **PORTER Amy** *Lewis and Roca* |
| 2 | **CASTER Lauren** *Fennemore Craig* |
| | **CURRY J Stanton** *Gallagher & Kennedy PA* |
| | **FARGOTSTEIN Phillip** *Fennemore Craig* |
| | **STOREY Lee** *Moyes Storey* |
| | **THOMAS Christopher** *Squire, Sanders* |
| 3 | **ANDERSON Robert** *Withey Anderson* |
| | **DAY Barton** *Bryan Cave LLP* |
| | **HAMULA James** *Gallagher & Kennedy PA* |
| | **MOELLENBERG Dalva** *Gallagher & Kennedy PA* |
| | **MOYES Jay** *Moyes Storey* |
| | **PEARCE John** *Fennemore Craig* |
| | **WOLF G Van Velsor** *Snell & Wilmer LLP* |

### Up-and-coming individuals

| | |
|---|---|
| | **BELLAMY Fredric** *Steptoe & Johnson LLP* |
| | **WALLWORK Nicholas** *Steptoe & Johnson LLP* |

## Band 1

### Fennemore Craig
See firm details p.197
**The Firm:** Fennemore Craig attracts enthusiastic praise for its "*excellent and broad-based*" environmental practice. A sizable team regularly advises on hazardous waste, air quality, grazing permits, pollu-

tion prevention, underground storage tanks and toxic torts. However, it is its market-leading position in sophisticated water law matters and issues connected to the Endangered Species Act that are repeatedly singled out by clients and peers. The group's impressive transactional and compliance counseling capabilities are complemented by a considerable track record of success in the courtroom. Here, recent battles have involved alleged pulmonary damage from air pollutants; groundwater contamination involving polychlorinated biphenyls, petrochemicals and other industrial solvents; and an alleged violation of the Republican River Compact.
**The Lawyers:** Creativity is the key to **Lauren Caster**'s (see p.188) success in the area of water rights. Described by sources as "*low key and soft spoken,*" his quiet diligence and ability to focus on the details make him an "*extraordinary and excellent*" adviser. **Phillip Fargotstein** (see p.190), in contrast, directs his energies toward cutting a dash in the courtroom, where he is "*top quality on contamination law suits.*" Fargotstein is widely admired as a more general environment practitioner, whose "*strong and effective presence*" enables him to turn his hand to a range of disputes. **John Pearce**'s (see p.193) impressive client list includes several major oil companies – testament to his status as the leader in issues involving underground storage tanks.
**Clients/Work Highlights:** DMB Associates; The Lyle Anderson Company; National Association of Home Builders; Arizona Cattle Growers' Association; Nebraska Public Power District and Florida Department of Environmental Protection.

### Gallagher & Kennedy PA
**The Firm:** Market sources highlighted this group's diversity and depth, factors that allow it to handle a number of substantial matters simultaneously. Rivals, meanwhile, acknowledge it as "*tough competition,*" holding the team in particularly high regard for its experience in environmental quality matters. However, its constructive approach ensures it success in the full range of environmental work connected with air and water quality, solid and hazardous waste, or compliance with federal and state environmental laws and regulations. Recent highlights include complex settlements arising out of the Pinal Creek

site contamination, and ongoing negotiations over a program for regulating hazardous air pollutants in the state.
**The Lawyers:** **David Kimball** is devoted to his clients and possesses the necessary "*drive and determination*" to get them top-notch results. The head of the environmental and natural resources team at Gallagher & Kennedy, he is actively involved in the legislative arena. His practice encompasses water issues, mining, waste and other natural resources work. **Stan Curry** focuses on air quality and Superfund matters, but also commands an impressive multistate compliance and auditing practice. Peers appreciate his experience, creativity and "*positive personality.*" "*Bright and talented*" **James Hamula** focuses on strategic planning, compliance counseling, toxic substance matters, permitting and natural resource damage. Clients value his sound understanding of their operational needs and his calm, articulate manner. **Dalva Moellenberg** was also highlighted by clients as a "*level-headed, strategic thinker*" with a "*highly credible presence.*"
**Clients/Work Highlights:** Apache Nitrogen Products; APS; Arizona Rock Products Association; El Paso; The Fertilizer Institute; Freescale Semiconductor; Goodrich; Motorola and Phelps Dodge.

## Band 2

### Bryan Cave LLP
**The Firm:** Gaining in prominence in the Arizona market, Bryan Cave's environmental team provides comprehensive nationwide coverage of the core areas: air, water and waste. The firm has nurtured a collaborative, collegial approach to build a respected interstate practice. Clients particularly value the opportunity to tap into a network of "*excellent lawyers at the senior level nationwide,*" whose expertise can be called upon in complex litigation or regulatory matters.
**The Lawyers:** Managing partner **Lucas Narducci** is the envy of peers for his stellar client relationship skills. Research confirmed this, as satisfied clients queued up to heap praise on a talented adviser and "*decent human being.*" One even went as far as to dub him a "*saint*" for his attention to their interests and conscientious approach. **Barton Day** is universally

admired for his "*significant expertise*" in underground injection and hazardous waste matters.

Clients/Work Highlights: BHP Copper, Inspiration Mining and Phelps Dodge feature in the firm's client roster.

## Moyes Storey

The Firm: Although one of the smaller firms on the list, this Phoenix-based environmental boutique enjoys a large profile in the market. Interviewees were full of admiration for the group's "*superb attorneys*," who are focused in particular on water law and natural resources. The group provides creative solutions at a low cost for clients.

The Lawyers: Interviewees recommended **Lee Storey** as a "*likeable and trustworthy*" attorney who is "*strong and experienced*" in water issues. **Jay Moyes** is also highly respected for his expertise in natural resources and water law.

## Quarles & Brady Streich Lang LLP

See firm details p.2039

The Firm: Although Quarles & Brady houses only a handful of environment lawyers in its Phoenix office, the firm's 400-strong national presence gives it a wealth of expertise across the network that few local competitors can rival. The group was praised for its practical appreciation of clients' business issues, and can call upon attorneys from many practice areas to supplement the core environmental team where necessary. Its expertise encompasses toxic torts, water regulations, environmental insurance and natural resources, among other issues.

The Lawyers: "*Outgoing and larger than life*," **Roger Ferland** (see p.190) is at the top of his game, according to market sources. Among the weapons in his armory is a style of "*highly effective advocacy*" based on a "*fantastic presence*" in the courtroom. His pragmatic advice also wins him respect: as one source commented, he has a knack of "*knowing when to hold 'em and when to fold 'em.*"

Clients/Work Highlights: Clients are drawn from a wide range of industries, including chemicals; mining; financial services and healthcare.

## Ryley Carlock & Applewhite

See firm details p.199

The Firm: The focus of this team lies squarely in the area of water rights, where its top-class team advises on acquisition, transfer and protection strategies related to this most valuable resource. Fueled by the current boom in Arizona's real estate market, the past twelve months have seen Ryley Carlock's environmental group expand considerably.

The Lawyers: **Michael Brophy** (see p.188) enjoys a "*fantastic reputation as a leading water rights lawyer*" with a practice spanning many states. Clients partic-

ularly recommended him for his "*pragmatism and superior ability.*" He has been a major force in the development of water banking rights, including the enactment of federal legislation and advice on evaluating the effects of interstate decrees.

Clients/Work Highlights: Maricopa Water District, Roosevelt Irrigation District and Buckeye Water Conservation and Drainage District are among the firm's environmental clients.

## Snell & Wilmer LLP

See firm details p.200

The Firm: Snell & Wilmer's strong regional presence ensures that it is a regular player in the most important environmental cases issuing from the southwestern states. Sources earmarked this group as one of the most likely to challenge for market leadership in the near future, and peers acknowledge it as a "*major competitor across the board.*" The seasoned team has been successfully developing its water resources practice in recent months to meet the rising demand to support real estate developments.

The Lawyers: **Van Velsor Wolf** (see p.196) is the trump card and major attraction in this group. Among his many talents are remarkable academic skills, a considerable breadth of experience and great strategic planning expertise. Recent successes have included a summary judgment awarded in favor of Huron Valley Fritz West, a recycler of airplane parts.

Clients/Work Highlights: The team acts for companies from a variety of sections, including mining; recycling; real estate; manufacturing; electric utilities; healthcare; financial services and technology.

## Squire, Sanders & Dempsey LLP

See firm details p.1650

The Firm: Longevity in this field and highly developed expertise have earned Squire Sanders an enviable client base, enabling the group to grow both nationally and on a global scale. For example, a number of major cities have instructed the firm in complex environmental cases, involving waste, air or water quality matters. The Phoenix office recently suffered the loss of Karen Peters, however it retains considerable expertise and the group is not expected to be adversely affected.

The Lawyers: **Christopher Thomas**' (see p.195) practice encompasses hazardous waste, groundwater contamination, industrial compliance and environmental permitting, among other things. Peers were swift to highlight his skill as a Superfund litigator, rating him as "*one of the best*" in the field, while his "*tough yet reasonable*" negotiating style also attracted praise.

Clients/Work Highlights: Oglebay Norton; City of Phoenix; MeadWestvaco and OM Group.

## Band 3

## Lewis and Roca

The Firm: This "*small but highly regarded group*" operates out of both Tucson and Phoenix. It has been kept busy this past year with a stream of mining, permitting and air quality issues for existing clients. However, like many in Arizona, the group's most important cases recently have concerned water quality and rights matters.

The Lawyers: **Amy Porter**'s expertise in air quality matters has earned her a reputation as Arizona's leading authority in this niche. Interviewees were full of praise for her tough and determined advocacy.

Clients/Work Highlights: Clients come from a range of industries, including financial services; real estate; healthcare; manufacturing; mining; construction and energy.

## Steptoe & Johnson LLP

See firm details p.576

The Firm: Setting this group apart is its strength in toxic torts – particularly in the realm of personal injury resulting from groundwater contamination. The team also thrives on the challenge of handling unique and difficult 'spotted cow cases.' This year has seen the 17-strong group fight to preserve the historic downtown area of Tucson, as well as representing the City of Peoria in a fatal toxic tort case involving a rare parasite. The firm's record of using sophisticated technology also attracted the attention of commentators.

The Lawyers: Environmental practice group leader **James Derouin** (see p.189) is the most "*brilliant and respected*" member of the team. His litigation and strategic planning skills, coupled with 35 years of experience in the area, earn him a top ranking once again. Although he has been the sole visible player in the Phoenix team of late, growth has clearly been a priority and the firm has taken on two more partners in a bid to raise its profile. Recent addition **Fredric Bellamy** (see p.187) impresses many as a "*deep and creative thinker*" with a natural analytical ability. Fellow newcomer **Nicholas Wallwork** (see p.195) brings experience to the table, along with "*impeccable personal and professional credentials.*"

Clients/Work Highlights: DuPont; Dow Chemical; City of Tucson; Rohm and Haas; Exxon Minerals; Sentry Insurance; Parker Pen; City of Peoria and Gillette.

## Other Notable Practitioners

**Robert Anderson** of Withey Anderson & Morris PLC focuses on environmental work. His expertise includes endangered species law and environmental quality issues.

# LITIGATION

## Osborn Maledon PA

See firm details p.198

**The Firm:** The outstanding success of this boutique firm is attributed to its *"uniformly great litigators"* and their *"excellence in client service."* Clients also expressed their appreciation for the team's mindful approach to staffing litigation, *"ensuring every dime is well spent."* A broad spectrum of matters are covered, from commercial to criminal litigation. Recent successes in the commercial arena include defending Continental Airlines in a securities fraud class action, achieving a summary judgment. Repre-senting PGA Tour, the group managed to get allega-tions that a player had contracted a rare disease during a PGA Tour event dismissed on a summary judgment. It is now acting for the client on an appeal over the same matter. The firm's criminal work is equally wide-ranging, and includes cybercrime, healthcare fraud and industrial accidents.

**The Lawyers:** **Bill Maledon** (see p.192) has *"all the things a good litigator should have: integrity, intelli-gence and an analytical temperament."* Clients raved about his *"poise, terrific advice and extremely good examination skills in court,"* and he is universally acclaimed as *"the cream of the crop."* Indeed, one source even went so far as to say that he *"walks on water."* Having represented clients like PGA Tour and WL Gore & Associates in sophisticated disputes, he is without a doubt a first choice for large complex cases. *"Positively brilliant"* **David Rosenbaum** (see p.194) is appreciated by clients for his *"calm, smooth demeanor,"* ability to *"cut to the key issues"* and deter-mination to *"leave no stone unturned."* His recent victory for Continental Airlines in a securities fraud class action is testament to his talent as a *"super commercial litigator."* **Mark Harrison** (see p.191) has recognized experience in representing professionals in disciplinary disputes, and is seen as *"top dog"* in ethical responsibility cases. His low-key style and common-sense, practical approach make him popu-lar with judges, according to the market. **Diane Johnsen** (see p.191) focuses on environmental liti-gation, insurance coverage actions and commercial contract and tort cases. She was described by peers as *"excellent, capable, businesslike, thorough and ethi-cal,"* as well as a *"real pleasure to work with."* In the realm of criminal defense, **Larry Hammond** (see p.190) is the *"dean."* He has gained enormous credi-bility with the courts for his extensive experience and *"dedication to clients and principles."* Well versed in all aspects of the field, his *"immense intelligence"* has earned him a reputation as *"the best in town."* He is also renowned for his active role in serious criminal litigation, including two recent federal death penalty cases.

**Clients/Work Highlights:** American Express; Arizona State University; Boeing; Continental Airlines; Honeywell; PGA Tour; Pinnacle West and WL Gore & Associates.

## Snell & Wilmer LLP

See firm details p.200

**The Firm:** Its sheer volume of commercial litigation distinguishes this as the *"big gorilla in town."* Often likened to the larger, East Coast practices, Snell & Wilmer's 40-strong team is organized into specialist groups to cater to its clients' every need: business commercial; products liability; healthcare and employment. Clients appreciate the *"broad, diverse areas of expertise,"* which include, among others, antitrust, employee benefits, professional malprac-tice, real estate, securities and trade secrets cases. Especially adept at managing large and complex disputes, the team has recently handled a multimil-lion-dollar professional liability case. It also tried a class action alleging negligence against its client – a healthcare company – for the theft of confidential information. Here, the firm succeeded in obtaining a summary judgment. The enviable client base is testament to the firm's unswervingly first-rate service.

**The Lawyers:** Managing partner **John Bouma** (see p.188) is hailed as a *"gentle giant of the litigation Bar."* Contemporaries marvel at his *"incredible ability to manage cases"* and *"phenomenally long list of accom-plishments,"* while more junior lawyers cite him as a tremendous influence, particularly for his strategic skills and effective, low-key style. **James Condo** (see p.189) has spent a substantial amount of his year on professional negligence cases, including taking the position of national trial counsel for a major truck company. A talented litigator, he is particularly skilled in products liability and general commercial cases. Good things were said of *"rising star"* **David Rauch** (see p.194), who is earning the respect of clients and courts with his creative and personable approach. Hot on his heels comes *"hugely energetic and committed"* **Warren Platt** (see p.194), whose incredible capacity for hard work has already given him a *"sterling track record."*

**Clients/Work Highlights:** The team's client base ranges from emerging entrepreneurs to Fortune 500 companies. Examples include Del Webb Corpora-tion; Edelson Technology Partners; Perini Building Company; Arizona Public Service Company; Pinna-cle West Capital Corporation; Meredith Corpora-tion; DMG-Maximus; Prudential Real Estate Affiliates and Bank of America.

## Fennemore Craig

See firm details p.197

**The Firm:** According to clients, this firm really places them at the center of things, providing creative, alter-native solutions wherever possible to avoid expensive litigation and preserve business relationships. This approach has helped it to build a loyal following, with clients of the caliber of Allied Waste, for whom it recently won a favorable settlement in a major antitrust lawsuit. The team handles a workload that includes business and PI torts, as well as bankruptcy, environmental, labor and employment, and white-collar litigation. Indeed in this latter field, Fennemore Craig is widely considered the out-and-out market leader, with a track record that includes many of the largest and most sophisticated white-collar cases in the region. This year has also seen it expand its portal process, allowing clients fully interactive access to information in an efficient way.

**The Lawyers:** Sources highlighted **Jordan Green** (see p.190) as the *"preeminent lawyer in the realm of white-collar crime."* His vast experience, *"high personal standards"* and honesty have earned him unquestionable respect, and have made him a first port of call for conflict referrals. *"Industrious"* **Bates Butler** (see p.188) is *"the anchor for Fennemore in Tucson,"* according to commentators. He was

commended for his commitment to *pro bono* work and admired for his thorough understanding of complex issues. Despite a deceptively *"folksy demeanor,"* **Kenneth Sherk** (see p.195) is viewed as an authority due to his vast knowledge, *"refreshing decency and common sense."* He has earned his place as dean of the Arizona Bar, and one of the best legal malpractice lawyers in the state, through an unparalleled ability to *"charm the birds out of the trees"* in the courtroom. *"Top-notch"* **John Everroad** (see p.189) is a hard-hitting commercial litigator who brings *"skill, experience and wisdom to the table."* **Timothy Berg** (see p.187) impressed with his vast appellate practice and *"bright professional"* manner. Chairing the commercial litigation group is rainmaker **Andrew Federhar** (see p.190). A power in the courtroom, he is rated as *"likeable, but hard-nosed and quick."* **Douglas Northup** (see p.193) chairs the PI and business torts group. An *"impressive strategist,"* according to clients, he is receptive and quick to grasp business needs. **William Thorpe** (see p.195) excels in both products liability and high-stakes commercial litigation where he remains *"focused and gregariously charming"* in pressure situations.
**Clients/Work Highlights:** Recent successes include a six-week jury trial in a multidistrict litigation case involving a pharmaceutical company. The firm also tried a huge insurance coverage action following a groundwater contamination incident by a steel manufacturing plant, and obtained both a preliminary and a permanent injunction for a lace provider against undermining competitors.

## Lewis and Roca

**The Firm:** Lewis & Roca is seen by many as *"one of the most capable firms in the city"* when it comes to high-stakes litigation. While it undoubtedly fields its share of stars, the firm's emphasis on mentoring younger associates has helped ensure it a reputation for housing *"sensible, mature litigators, who look to resolve issues reasonably and cost-effectively"* at every level. Recent successes include obtaining summary judgment in two cases involving agents' breaches of nonsolicitation agreements with farmers. The small but top-class white-collar crime practice can point to involvement in the high-profile Baptist Foundation case, among other highlights. Further representative work includes a number of Native American tribe investigations, including federal and state investigations of internal tribe matters. The recent loss of Scott Bales, who became a Justice of the Supreme Court, may be a setback, but it is also testament to the high caliber of the group's lawyers.
**The Lawyers:** **Peter Baird**'s many positive attributes include being *"an exceptional and prolific writer,"* a *"brilliant thinker"* and a *"strong, articulate advocate."* He remains the firm's standout litigation name. *"Bright and persistent"* **Dale Danneman** has experience in both the prosecution and defense side of civil litigation, representing corporations, directors and officers, and employees. **James Belanger**'s work ranges from FTC and consumer fraud investigations to advising boards on compliance procedures. However, he is best known for his involvement in some of the largest death penalty cases in Arizona. Peers applaud his *"wonderful courtroom instincts,"* his skill in identifying critical issues and his *"comprehensive understanding of the process."* Sources also identified **Fred Petti** as a leading light, highlighting his *"knowledge and gravity"* and strong courtroom presence.
**Clients/Work Highlights:** Clients range from individuals to Fortune 500 companies and include United States Postal Service, a multinational natural gas company and an Alaskan airline.

## Perkins Coie LLP

**The Firm:** Benefiting from being part of a 300-strong nationwide litigation team, members of this group frequently appear in the federal and state trial and appellate courts. Lawyers represent clients under investigation by state and federal agencies, such as the IRS and SEC, and act for large national and international clients in complex, cross-jurisdictional cases. The firm was praised for its sophisticated approach to case management, ensuring cost efficiency for the client and paperless visits to the courtroom through the use of advanced technology.
**The Lawyers:** **Paul Eckstein** is a well-seasoned and broad-based civil litigator, whose practice encompasses appellate, antitrust, media and Native American law. His insight into the process and his *"cool instincts, marvelous judgment and poise"* are said to make him a *"stellar guide"* for the next generation of litigators. *"Talented"* **Howard Cabot** is viewed by some as a *"star"* on the horizon. His extensive experience of IP, class actions, securities, and complex financial disputes was noted by market sources.

Recent recruit **Lee Stein** has already proved a valuable asset to the team, putting it on the map for white-collar defense litigation and government investigations. Interviewees point to him as a *"bright spark"* with extensive knowledge.
**Clients/Work Highlights:** Vitesse Semiconductor Corporation; Google; UPS; Starbucks; Boeing; Phelps Dodge Corporation and Qwest.

## Gallagher & Kennedy PA

**The Firm:** Having begun as a litigation boutique over 25 years ago, Gallagher & Kennedy certainly has not forgotten its roots. Market sources confirm that it maintains an *"excellent focus"* on litigation, while evolving into a more wide-ranging, full-service firm. Areas of expertise include tortious business disputes, commercial construction, financial fraud and professional malpractice cases. Interviewees particularly admired the criminal defense practice and the *"fluid"* management of cases.
**The Lawyers:** **Michael Kennedy**'s impressive client base ranges from Fortune 500 companies to professional sports teams; he acts for the Phoenix Suns, the Arizona Diamondbacks and the Arizona Cardinals. He was recommended as an *"ethical, honorable, serious player"* who commands the attention and respect of any court. Heading up the litigation team is *"high-energy, high-emotion"* **Kevin O'Malley**, who is reported to *"grasp details easily and throw down hard."* Peers envied his *"stunning"* successes of the past year and described him as a *"real star."* **Tom Henze** is an *"incredible, savvy, persuasive and fearless lawyer"* who communicates issues well and whose *"storytelling skills"* help him to establish a good rapport with any jury. As one peer stated: *"His people skills are unsurpassed – I'd hire him to represent my family."* Up-and-comer **Barry Mitchell** is a *"solid A-plus lawyer"* who has *"earned his spurs,"* say peers. His practical and diligent approach are said to make him a dangerous opponent for even the most seasoned litigator.
**Clients/Work Highlights:** Phoenix Suns; Arizona Diamondbacks; Arizona Cardinals; Phelps Dodge Corporation; Motorola and Arizona Public Service.

## Mariscal, Weeks, McIntyre & Friedlander PA

**The Firm:** In keeping with the firm's overall rapid growth, the past year has seen the litigation team expand substantially, with the addition of four senior litigators. The emphasis still remains on the group's *"truly fine"* real estate practice, where the client base includes a number of major regional and national home builders and title insurers. However, the team is also well versed in litigation in the areas of securities, antitrust, construction and professional liability.
**The Lawyers:** **Gary Birnbaum** is hailed as an *"intense, tenacious and tactical"* litigator, whose skills extend to mediation where he is considered to be a leading light.
**Clients/Work Highlights:** During the past twelve months, the firm successfully defended a multimillion-dollar jury trial arising out of a business sale, and successfully represented a home health agency in a wrongful death jury trial.

## Quarles & Brady Streich Lang LLP

**The Firm:** This firm makes good use of its national network and ample resources to gain a role in some of the larger work in the state. It has the breadth to cope with almost any contentious matter, from construction disputes to commercial contract matters, real estate and IP litigation. Arizona is well served by the regional powerhouse and its litigators act from two offices, Phoenix and Tucson.

**The Lawyers:** **Lonnie Williams** (see p.196) *"turns the cerebral into the understandable,"* according to market sources, and has *"a golden touch with the jury".* His reputation as a preeminent employment lawyer is matched by his ability in a variety of commercial settings. **Edward Novak** (see p.193) has made his mark in white-collar and criminal defense litigation. Interviewees described him as *"one of the strongest lawyers in town for accounting firms,"* a claim which is supported by his recent defense of a Big Four accounting firm in multiple simultaneous proceedings.

**Clients/Work Highlights:** The team serves government agencies; major national and multinational corporations; charitable organizations; and educational and research institutions.

## Haralson, Miller, Pitt, Feldman & McAnally PLC

**The Firm:** This smaller firm is focused on all aspects of business law and PI litigation. On the business side, attorneys are well equipped to deal with disputes involving contracts, business partners, stockholders, unfair competition, consumer fraud, IP, antitrust and condemnation. Its presence is felt in both Phoenix and Tucson, where peers hold the team's commercial litigation practice in especially high esteem.

**The Lawyers:** **Gerald Maltz** was described to researchers as an *"able and aggressive"* litigator who stands out as *"quick on his feet and tenacious"* in the courtroom. Sources consider him among the finer litigators in the southern part of the state.

## Rusing & Lopez PLLC

**The Firm:** Interviewees recommended this outfit for its responsiveness and impressive grasp of the ins and outs of general civil and business litigation. The commercial litigation team represents clients in a range of disputes involving employment, business torts, real estate, contracts and trade secrets. In addition, the firm also covers wrongful deaths and PI litigation, representing plaintiffs, defendants and insurers. Its experience includes work for a variety of internationally-known companies as well as local clients.

**The Lawyers:** **Michael Rusing** is no stranger to multimillion-dollar disputes. He was enthusiastically praised by the market for his *"hard-headed"* approach in the courtroom and high-quality client care.

**Clients/Work Highlights:** Clients of the team include University of Arizona and Bank of America.

## Ryley Carlock & Applewhite

See firm details p.199

**The Firm:** Though not the highest-profile outfit in the commercial litigation arena, Ryley Carlock & Applewhite has won mandates in a number of impressive multimillion-dollar disputes. Interviewees put the team's success down to its business acumen and in-depth understanding of risk assessment.

**The Lawyers:** The 25-strong litigation team includes such well-respected names as Charles Chester, who particularly excels in employment litigation.

## Piccarreta & Davis PC

**The Firm:** This smaller firm is not shy of sizable cases, with the result that it boasts an impressive track record of success in complex, high-value jury trials. A commitment to criminal defense has carved the team a reputation as a sharp white-collar player, helping to win it a mandate in the recent mammoth Baptist Foundation case, where many millions of dollars were lost by investors.

**The Lawyers:** **Michael Piccarretta**'s name is inextricably linked to high-profile white-collar cases involving fraud, money laundering and other complex corporate crimes. He is renowned for his *"excellent knowledge and judgment"* and *"savvy style"* in the courtroom.

## Other Notable Practitioners

Peers endorse **Donald Bivens** as a *"terrific, energetic and hard-working"* litigator. He remains a major force in the market, and his progress at his new firm, Bivens & Nore PA, will be watched with interest. **Ed Hendricks** is a firm favorite and a *"premier lawyer."* Indeed, for some sources he is simply *"as good as it gets."* Together with his son and three other lawyers, he established the firm Meyer Hendricks this year. **Michael Meehan** of Meehan LLP is noted for his vigorous litigation style. *"A real force to be reckoned with,"* **Leo Beus** of Beus Gilbert PLLC has a sharp and *"relentless"* style, which is testament to his unswerving commitment in his clients' cause. On the white-collar criminal side, sources admired the *"polite, professional and industrious"* **Marc Budoff** of Budoff & Ross PC, particularly pointing to his client care. Having left Bryan Cave LLP to set up a new firm, **Stephen Dichter** remains a respected presence and attracts praise as a bright and experienced courtroom lawyer. Kimerer & Derrick PC's **Mike Kimerer** attracted recommendations for his *"honesty, integrity"* and steadfast focus on criminal litigation. Colleagues admired his diverse practice, decades of experience and genuine desire to help clients. Market sources also expressed a lot of faith in **Stephen Weiss** of Karp, Heurlin & Weiss PC and his 37 years' experience in criminal litigation.

# REAL ESTATE

| | Real Estate Leading Firms | |
|---|---|---|
| 1 | FENNEMORE CRAIG | *Phoenix* |
| | MARISCAL, WEEKS, MCINTYRE | *Phoenix* |
| 2 | GALLAGHER & KENNEDY PA | *Phoenix* |
| | GREENBERG TRAURIG LLP | *Phoenix* |
| | SNELL & WILMER LLP | *Phoenix* |
| 3 | LEWIS AND ROCA | *Phoenix* |
| | QUARLES & BRADY STREICH LANG LLP | *Phoenix* |
| | SQUIRE, SANDERS & DEMPSEY LLP | *Phoenix* |
| 4 | OSBORN MALEDON PA | *Phoenix* |
| | PERKINS COIE LLP | *Phoenix* |
| | SACKS TIERNEY PA | *Scottsdale* |

## Band 1

### Fennemore Craig

See firm details p.197

**The Firm:** This large and important firm has reached the summit of Arizona's real estate market, securing a range of sophisticated deals. More than 30 top-notch real estate attorneys operate from three offices in the state. They offer clients advice on a spectrum of real estate matters, including acquisitions and disposals, property finance, development schemes and leasing, as well as related services such as environmental and tax issues.

**The Lawyers:** **Jay Kramer** (see p.192) was praised for his experience of working on planned residential and mixed-use communities. Peers particularly admire his *"wonderful work ethic,"* which sees him handling many deals simultaneously. Chairing the real estate finance practice, **Robert Robinson** (see p.194) is hailed as incredibly *"accomplished and experienced."* *"People go to"* **Gregg Hanks** (see p.191) *"for both his manner and his expertise,"* say interviewees. His broad practice spans many areas but he is especially visible in real estate syndications, master-plan projects and joint ventures, where his *"knowledge and diligence"* are valued.

**Clients/Work Highlights:** The past year has seen the team represent a sports authority in the process of building a national league football stadium, and assist a client with the acquisition of 18 major

| Real Estate |
|---|
| **Leading Individuals** |
| [1] **LANSKY David** *Mariscal, Weeks* |
| **MAST Gregory** *Gallagher & Kennedy PA* |
| **POKORSKI Jody** *Snell & Wilmer LLP* |
| **STOREY Lesa** *Greenberg Traurig LLP* |
| [2] **BISKIND Neil** *Biskind, Hunt & Taylor plc* |
| **FATHE Fred** *Mariscal, Weeks* |
| **HALLER Diane** *Quarles & Brady Streich Lang* |
| **KRAMER Jay** *Fennemore Craig* |
| **LISKER Steven** *Lisker & Associates PLLC* |
| **VAN WINKLE Kenneth** *Lewis and Roca* |
| **WRIGHT Joyce** *Snell & Wilmer LLP* |
| [3] **BROADFOOT Alexander** *Valenzuela & Broadfoot* |
| **BURNHAM Beckey** *Greenberg Traurig LLP* |
| **HIRSCH Stephen** *Bryan Cave LLP* |
| **MAY Bruce** *Jennings, Strouss & Salmon* |
| **ROBINSON Robert** *Fennemore Craig* |
| **SORENSON Derek** *Quarles & Brady Streich Lang* |
| **STOKES Randall** *Lewis and Roca* |
| **WINKLER Peter** *Mariscal, Weeks* |
| [4] **BATES Robert** *Snell & Wilmer LLP* |
| **DYEKMAN Donald** *Mariscal, Weeks* |
| **HANKS Gregg** *Fennemore Craig* |
| **HINK John** *Ryley Carlock & Applewhite* |
| **LOWE Ronald** *Perkins Coie LLP* |
| **OSBORN II Jones** *Osborn Maledon PA* |
| **SACKS Seymour** *Sacks Tierney PA* |
| **WILEY Jay** *Snell & Wilmer LLP* |

shopping centers. It also acts for railroad companies; mining companies; public utilities; ranchers and farmers as well as large landowners.

## Mariscal, Weeks, McIntyre & Friedlander PA

**The Firm:** Real estate advice is a cornerstone of this full-service firm's practice. The sizable team was recommended by clients of all sorts for the *"excellent quality"* of its advice and documentation. Typical work includes the acquisition and sale of land and buildings, leasing, mortgage lending and redevelopment, and the firm can also assist clients with any related environmental issues they may face.

**The Lawyers:** **David Lansky** was hailed as the *"preeminent figure in retail"* in the state. He has been visible this year in a variety of luxury lifestyle mall developments and retail leasing projects. Peers recommended him as an *"exceptionally diligent"* attorney with a creative approach well tailored to finding solutions. **Fred Fathe** is affectionately known as *"the professor"* for his sharp intellect and technical skill. Experience in the corporate commercial realm has served him well, enabling him to swiftly pinpoint the key issues in any transaction. Also recommended is **Peter Winkler**, whose efficient and practical style is appreciated by peers. The bulk of his caseload is comprised of bare land work but he also handles lending and landlord and tenant issues, among other things. *"Big-picture lawyer"* **Donald Dyekman** is respected for his

expertise in condominiums and work with homeowners associations.

**Clients/Work Highlights:** The firm acts for major developers, builders, lenders and investors. This year it has been handling planning, negotiations and documentation connected with the parcel of over 2,000 acres which now comprises the Spur Cross Ranch Conservation Area.

## Band 2

### Gallagher & Kennedy PA

**The Firm:** Gallagher & Kennedy's real estate team has grown in response to the thriving market, adding two new partners this year. The group focuses primarily on development and land use entitlement work, and has been at the forefront of some important deals. These include work on the leasing development, financing and disposition of Scottsdale Promenade Shopping Center, as well as representing the developers of luxury residential condominiums and apartments across Arizona.

**The Lawyers:** **Gregory Mast** heads the real estate group and focuses on large projects for major developers. Peers invariably acknowledge him as a player at the top of his game and the top of the field.

**Clients/Work Highlights:** Opus West; The Pederson Group; SunCor; TW Lewis; Toll Brothers; Grayhawk Development; Globe Corporation; Shea Homes and Arizona Cardinals.

### Greenberg Traurig LLP

See firm details p.664

**The Firm:** The international giant's dramatic merger with *"exceptional boutique"* Storey & Burnham looks set to radically change its profile in the Arizona real estate market. Combining Storey's *"fabulous substantive quality"* with Greenberg's ample resources allows the group to offer clients a comprehensive package of real estate coverage. This includes advice on land acquisition and development, the leasing of state trust land, land use entitlements, infrastructure planning, construction and compliance, along with any ancillary environmental or tax issues. Sources predict that the newly formed group will have a particular impact in the area of master-planned communities, as its individuals already bring exceptional experience to the table. For example, they advised on the DC Ranch 8,400-acre master-planned community, which includes residential, retail, commercial, resort and golf components.

**The Lawyers:** **Lesa Storey** (see p.195) focuses on the acquisition, entitlement, financing, development and disposition of mixed-use developments and master-planned communities. Her reputation as *"an absolutely incredible, honest and fair dealdoer"* has secured her a loyal client following, including DMB Realty who are moving with her to her new home. **Beckey Burnham** (see p.188) chairs the new team. She concentrates on development, with a focus on master-planned communities, state trust lands and infrastructure finance. A *"highly energetic lobbyist,"* she also represents real estate

industry associations in legislative and public policy matters.

**Clients/Work Highlights:** Ryland Homes; DMB Realty; Schuler Homes; Home Builders Association of Central Arizona; TW Lewis; McDowell Mountain Ranch and Canyon Trails.

## Snell & Wilmer LLP

See firm details p.200

**The Firm:** The breadth of Snell & Wilmer's real estate department is reflected by its varied, and much admired, client base. The team breaks down into four main groups, covering traditional real estate, real estate finance, environmental issues and natural resources and utilities law. Its lawyers were warmly recommended for their skill in work related to large master-planned communities, retail developments, condominium projects, and property acquisitions, among other things.

**The Lawyers:** *"Real star"* **Jody Pokorski** (see p.194) was singled out by clients as the team's outstanding name. In the words of one: *"She is professional, personable, tenacious and an all-around class act – I am so glad she sits on my side of the table,"* while another highlighted her as *"phenomenal, dedicated and with the critical skill of dealing professionally with a disparate range of personalities."* Market sources also identified **Joyce Wright** (see p.196) as *"an extremely smart and tough attorney,"* who manages to combine this toughness with being *"a delight to deal with."* Another real estate generalist, her broad practice means that she is well versed in all aspects of the field. **Robert Bates** (see p.187) picked up strong endorsements for his excellent work on the finance side, while **Jay Wiley** (see p.195) is said to be an *"experienced, thoughtful"* all-rounder.

**Clients/Work Highlights:** Mayo Clinic Hospital; American Express; T-Mobile USA; University of Phoenix; American West Arena; Civano Community; Tucson Airport Authority; Powdr Corp and Sheraton Wildhorse Pass Resort & Spa.

## Band 3

### Lewis and Roca

**The Firm:** Lewis and Roca benefits from a strong regional presence, including two offices in Arizona, helping it to maintain a first-class knowledge of the southwest market. The team advises on the range of real estate law and boasts expertise in development projects, sales and acquisitions, commercial leasing, land use, master-planned communities, finance transactions and restructurings. Recent highlights have included a major role in a multimillion-dollar property acquisition. The firm boasts a growing national presence and is representing one of the country's largest insurance companies on the national stage.

**The Lawyers:** Managing partner and *"talented gentleman"* **Kenneth Van Winkle** focuses on the transactional side of the field. He is well regarded for his expertise in acquisitions and disposals, leasing and equity and debt financing, which is typically employed on behalf of banks, insurance companies and REITs. Commentators also singled out **Randall Stokes** for his *"broad experience"* and *"ability to solve issues,"* especially in the areas of planned residential, commercial and mixed-use communities, condominiums and shopping centers.

**Clients/Work Highlights:** The firm acts for leaders in real estate development, investment and lending. Clients are drawn from a variety of sections, including the retail, hospitality and airline industries.

## Quarles & Brady Streich Lang LLP

**The Firm:** This larger, full-service firm has a strong nationwide presence, which carries with it the ability to handle sizable and complex real estate transactions along with any ancillary issues. The group's ethos of matching the project to the specific expertise of each lawyer demonstrates a commitment to keeping costs down, which is popular with clients. Peers too, were swift to mention the team's particular strengths, especially in residential and commercial development transactions.

**The Lawyers:** *"Deep in her knowledge and thorough in her approach,"* **Diane Haller** (see p.190) is admired for her skill in real estate lending, her commitment to clients and her ability to resolve issues in an easygoing style. Reacting to the fast pace of the Arizona real property market, the team has this year welcomed **Derek Sorenson** (see p.195) on board. He brings with him a wealth of experience as well as a healthy client base.

**Clients/Work Highlights:** Clients include local and national developers of commercial and residential property, contractors, brokerage firms and property managers.

## Squire, Sanders & Dempsey LLP

See firm details p.1650

**The Firm:** Squire Sanders is not as well known in Arizona's real estate circles as some of its competitors. However, following a series of successful mergers, the increasing international focus and reach of the group earns it a place in the tables. It has also earned it a central role in complex multimillion- dollar transactions for large public company clients, hotel resorts, sports facilities and construction companies. A strong finance firm, its real estate finance capabilities are another draw for clients, as is the capacity it has in specialist areas such as environmental work.

**The Lawyers:** Richard Ross, whose practice is largely focused outside of Arizona, cochairs the team. He has especially impacted on the development of the hotel business in the real estate sector.

**Clients/Work Highlights:** The firm assists a client base comprising developers; owners; operators; hotels; theaters; stadiums; clubs and others. Consistent with its increasingly international profile, many of these are companies with global interests.

## Band 4

## Osborn Maledon PA

See firm details p.198

**The Firm:** Once again, Osborn Maledon's commitment to client care shines through as the real estate group consistently won high praise from happy customers. The team has experience in a range of work, including advice on leasing, financing, development, zoning and land use issues. These skills were recently on show in work for Host Marriott relating to the conversion of an aging resort and golf course valued in excess of $60 million.

**The Lawyers:** Among his many skills, **Jones Osborn** (see p.193) is appreciated by clients for his knack of spotting the strengths and weaknesses of a case, as well as his ability to *"combine practical knowledge and business needs with legal advice."* His integrity, reliability and clear presentation of arguments ensure that he is routinely recommended.

**Clients/Work Highlights:** Acacia Mortgage; De Rito Partners; Saul Diskin Real Estate Services; Salt River Pima-Maricopa Indian Community and Matrix Capital Markets Group.

## Perkins Coie LLP

**The Firm:** Perkins Coie has recently introduced a national practice group structure, which plugs the Phoenix office more closely into a 600-strong, full-service outfit spanning the nation. As such, clients have access to the expertise to handle virtually any real estate matter, no matter how large or complex. Recent examples include acting in Optima DCH Development's acquisition and development of a 230-unit condominium, and a 711-unit condominium project. It also assisted with a 20,000-acre master-planned development for LKY Development.

**The Lawyers:** **Ronald Lowe** is never shy of rolling up his sleeves and getting stuck in, and has forged a reputation as one of the most *"hard-working, diligent and committed"* figures in this arena. Clearly his dedication has paid off, as peers were swift to acknowledge his *"strength and technical proficiency."*

**Clients/Work Highlights:** Optima DCH Development and LKY Development feature in the group's client roster.

## Sacks Tierney PA

**The Firm:** This Scottsdale-based firm is respected in the market for its *"well-rounded"* practice and impressive client base. Despite being smaller than many of its competitors, the team impressed interviewees with its comprehensive coverage of the real estate field. Typical work spans planning, construction, environment and real estate development issues, making this a one-stop shop for its clients. Interviewees particularly highlighted the group's ability to handle real property litigation.

**The Lawyers:** **Seymour Sacks** was affectionately described by peers as *"a real entertaining character."* *"One of the deans of the Arizona real estate Bar,"* he is particularly admired for his *"ability to see the big picture."*

## Other Notable Practitioners

**Neil Biskind** of boutique firm Biskind, Hunt & Taylor plc is *"good at getting to the finishing line,"* say sources. His knowledge of home building and financial structuring, and his dedication to client needs and goals, are widely admired. **Steven Lisker**, formerly of Bryan Cave, has channeled his *"brilliant knowledge"* of real estate into setting up his own firm, Lisker & Associates PLLC. The four-strong boutique focuses on real estate, lending and commercial transactions. Having left Gallagher & Kennedy, **Alexander Broadfoot** has also set up a new firm, Valenzuela & Broadfoot, PLC. Sandy is recommended as a *"terrific, broadly experienced guy"* who is *"a pleasure to work with."* At Bryan Cave LLP, **Stephen Hirsch** has a broad practice spanning commercial litigation, zoning and land use, as well as real estate. In the latter sphere, he handles valuation, construction and utility litigation, and particularly excels in condemnation work. **Bruce May** chairs the real estate group at Jennings, Strouss & Salmon, PLC and possesses comprehensive knowledge of the development process, be it at a local, regional or national level. Sources expressed their appreciation of his *"great service, efficiency and impressive thoroughness."* **John Hink** (see p.191) of Ryley Carlock & Applewhite is admired for his knowledge of real estate financing, acquisition and development, and experience with master-planned communities, as well as his *"delightful"* personality.

# REAL ESTATE

# ZONING/LAND USE

## Beus Gilbert PLLC

**The Firm:** Though far from the largest firm in the state, Beus Gilbert manages a vast workload on a day-to-day basis. Its high-caliber attorneys are enormously respected in the field of zoning and land use for their ability to "*represent doggedly and deliver results.*" Sources pointed in particular to a well-established and successful zoning practice, and also highlighted the firm's good connections with government bodies. Although the departure of John Berry will not be easily shrugged off, there have been no signs that the quality of service has diminished, and the group is acknowledged to be heading the pack once more.

**The Lawyers:** Commonly recognized as "*the busiest land use lawyer in the valley,*" **Paul Gilbert** impresses peers with his consistently high-quality representation and seemingly limitless appetite for work. The veteran lawyer is highly regarded by elected officials, peers and clients alike for his "*integrity and tenure in the industry,*" and his extensive experience as the state's "*preeminent zoning attorney*" means that he has built a track record of success in some of the most controversial cases in the region.

## Gammage & Burnham, PLC

**The Firm:** This group prides itself on establishing a solid rapport between parties in order to improve the chances of successful mediation. Its clients range from developers and property owners to neighborhood associations, community groups, homeowners and municipalities. The team has a niche in work related to state-owned land, however it has also won mandates connected with master-planned communities, campuses, shopping centers, schools and power centers among others.

**The Lawyers:** **Grady Gammage** brings some 30 years of experience to the table. An adjunct professor at the Arizona State University, where he lectures on land use regulation and historic preservation planning, he remains an active private practitioner. Interviewees dub him an "*excellent adviser with an outstanding reputation.*" Also attracting plaudits is **Stephen Anderson**, who began as Gammage's protégé but has since developed a reputation of his own. His work includes the zoning of office parks, neighborhood commercial projects and subdivisions, as well as advice on development agreements, annexations, use permits and certificate of occupancy issuance. Peers praised his thorough, well-researched and constructive approach.

## Withey Anderson & Morris PLC

**The Firm:** Although it is a comparatively youthful outfit, this "*fabulous firm*" impresses sources with its unswerving dedication to the field. Not afraid to take on controversial matters, the team was endorsed by commentators for its ability to handle a wide range of work, including complex and high-profile cases. The firm also handles a variety of related matters, most notably environmental and water issues.

**The Lawyers:** "*Rock solid*" **Michael Withey** was highlighted by interviewees as "*brilliant – not flashy, he just focuses on the job and gets it done.*" His "*down-to-earth*" people skills earned him particularly positive feedback from peers and clients who appreciate his ability to complete work "*without causing any stress or ruffling any feathers.*"

# Band 2

## Burch & Cracchiolo

**The Firm:** This group can service the client's every need in this arena and offers experience in a wide range of matters, including advice on zoning applications, infrastructure development agreements, construction contracts, environmental implications, and use permits and amendments. Peers expressed their admiration for the group, which is said to be a popular choice for referrals. Typical clients include commercial developers, home builders, master-planned community developers, investors and golf course developers.

**The Lawyers:** President of the firm and a "*prince among men,*" **Edwin Bull** was recommended as "*a man of intellect, integrity and substance.*" He practices in, inter alia, land use, zoning, use permits, site plan approvals and development projects.

## Earl, Curley & Lagarde, PC

**The Firm:** This "*fantastic*" boutique offers dedicated expertise in the fields of zoning and subdivision, development agreements and coordination with planning commissions and neighborhood bodies. Sources were impressed with the attorneys' focus and commitment to the field, which has helped them to develop an outstanding record of success in the area.

**The Lawyers:** **Stephen Earl** possesses a "*full set of skills*" and a vast breadth of experience, making him "*the number-one guy*" in the field for a number of sources. Interviewees were particularly impressed with his zoning practice.

## Fennemore Craig

See firm details p.197

**The Firm:** This general practice firm boasts an established zoning and land use practice that has grown rapidly in recent months. Although the group's experience spans the entire field, it has a particular emphasis on government and state-owned land, which accounts for more than 80 percent of the land in Arizona. Clients spoke highly of the team's "*strength, depth and diversity.*"

**The Lawyers:** Sources admire **Michael Phalen** (see p.194) for his "*superior understanding of state issues and solid technical foundation.*" In addition, clients found him to possess "*a strong chemistry with people*" and impressive problem-solving skills. He represents clients – including master-planned community developers, commercial and industrial developers, utilities, municipalities, investors and school districts – in issues surrounding the acquisition, development, zoning and use of land.

## Gallagher & Kennedy PA

**The Firm:** Despite already housing quite a sizable team in this area, growth has been a priority for the firm of late, in response to an ever-increasing demand. The group serves clients in the full range of zoning and land use work, as well as handling any ancillary issues, making it a one-stop shop for clients. The past twelve months have seen the group busy with two major master-plan communities.

**The Lawyers:** **Robert Kerrick** is singled out by interviewees as a "*litigation specialist and an effective mediator.*" He has a clear focus on eminent domain issues, and his impressive resume boasts involvement in some of the largest condemnation verdicts ever seen in the state.

## Lewis and Roca

**The Firm:** Lewis and Roca covers the spectrum of land use and zoning matters, from representing companies in litigation to advising on legislative changes and the administrative aspects of the field. According to clients, this highly regarded group stands out for the "*efficiency, availability and creative thinking*" of its attorneys, and several commented on the ease with which they have developed "*solid relationships with their staff.*"

**The Lawyers:** **Frank Bangs** represents clients in rezoning, subdivision, variance, development agreements and other matters. According to commentators, this "*knowledgeable, experienced and practical*" attorney is among the leaders in Tucson.

### Snell & Wilmer LLP
See firm details p.200

**The Firm:** The firm boasts a sizable presence in the southwestern states, which inevitably extends to zoning and land use matters. According to peers, however, a steady focus on the area is paying dividends in terms of increasing profile. Experienced attorneys handle a variety of work involving subdivisions, land acquisition, title review, zoning analysis, development entitlements, conditional and special-use permits, rezoning and general plan amendments. Other work includes advice on master plans, vested rights applications and non-conforming uses, and the team appears for clients in hearings and appeals.

**The Lawyers: Marc Simon** (see p.195) concentrates on all aspects of real estate including land use, where he is frequently retained to analyze existing zoning arrangements. Recently he has been busy handling contested cases involving multifamily issues, as well as advising on master-planned residential projects.

### Other Notable Practitioners
**John Berry** of Berry & Damore LLC is not only "*a great people person*" but also "*a creative thinker and a sound adviser who understands the political component more than anyone.*" Clients cite his strengths as "*collaboration, strategizing, public speaking, problem solving and advocating.*" He recently won a mandate on what could be considered the highest-profile land

use change case in Scottsdale – the former location of Rawhide, a western theme park in operation for 35 years. Clients choose **Larry Lazarus** of Lazarus & Associates Limited for his "*super reputation, excellent communication skills and strategic thinking.*" His long tenure has given him exceptional experience in Arizona's zoning and development issues, which earns him client confidence from the outset. As one satisfied customer remarked: "*Because of that confidence, I do not have to micro-manage him – I know he'll get the job done in an effective and timely manner.*" **Lawrence Schubart** of Stubbs & Schubart PC was also highlighted as an important player in the Tucson market, particularly as a condemnation lawyer.

# Leaders in Arizona

### ANDERSON, Robert
Withey Anderson & Morris PLC, Phoenix
602 230 0600
*Recommended in Environment*

### ANDERSON, Stephen
Gammage & Burnham, PLC, Phoenix
602 256 0566
*Recommended in Real Estate*

### ARIANO, Jonathan F
Osborn Maledon PA, Phoenix
602 640 9311
jariano@omlaw.com
*Recommended in Corporate/M&A*
**Practice Areas:** Business Transactions Practice representing growth-oriented and entrepreneurial clients, often in connection with the firm's outside general counsel practice, focusing on intellectual property and technology related matters such as licensing, distribution, procurement and trademark prosecution and protection. Practice also includes representing companies in business transactions and corporate governance matters, including mergers and acquisitions, venture capital, private equity financing and securities offerings.
**Prof. Memberships:** State Bar of Arizona: Internet, E-Commerce, and Technology Section, Intellectual Property Section; American Bar Association: Intellectual Property Law Section; United States Patent and Trademark Office.
**Career:** Associate, Osborn Maledon, PA since 2003; Senior Counsel, ConocoPhillips (formerly Tosco Corporation), 2000-03.
**Publications:** Co-author, 'California Disclosure Law Reaches Out to Touch Arizona Companies', The Business Journal of Phoenix, June 9, 2003; lectures frequently on intellectual property issues for small businesses.
**Personal:** JD, Rutgers University, School

of Law, 1999; BS, with distinction, Cornell University, College of Engineering, 1993.

### BAIRD, Peter
Lewis and Roca, Phoenix 602 262 5311
*Recommended in Litigation*

### BANGS, Frank
Lewis and Roca, Tucson 520 622 2090
*Recommended in Real Estate*

### BATES, Robert
Snell & Wilmer LLP, Phoenix
602 382 6263
bbates@swlaw.com
*Recommended in Real Estate*
**Practice Areas:** A Certified Arizona Real Estate Law Specialist engaged in all areas of real estate practice, including municipal development agreements; master planning strategy; acquisitions and sales of large tracts of undeveloped property; sale leaseback transactions; development, financing and leasing of shopping centers, office buildings and industrial, warehouse and office parks; representation of major resort hotels and international clients regarding real estate.
**Prof. Memberships:** Admitted to practice in Arizona and Colorado. Memberships include the State Bar of Arizona, the American Bar Association, and the Maricopa County Bar Association. Is also a Founding Fellow of the Arizona Bar Foundation.

### BELANGER, James
Lewis and Roca, Phoenix
602 262 5311
*Recommended in Litigation*

### BELLAMY, Fredric D
Steptoe & Johnson LLP, Phoenix
602 257 5204
fbellamy@steptoe.com
*Recommended in Environment*

**Practice Areas:** Partner, Phoenix office of Steptoe & Johnson LLP. Represents clients in environmental, natural resources and toxic tort litigation, including matters relating to groundwater contamination, hazardous and solid wastes, toxic exposure, administrative matters, and all levels of appeals. Member: Environmental and Natural Resources Law Section (ENRLS), State Bar of Arizona; Former Editor in Chief, Former Contributing Editor, Toxic Tort and Insurance Update, ENRLS Update. Litigated environmental and toxic tort matters involving CERCLA, RCRA, CWA and FIFRA issues, representing mining, oil, chemical, waste management and real estate companies, and municipalities.
**Personal:** JD, Harvard Law School, 1986; AB, Harvard College, 1983.

### BERG, Timothy J
Fennemore Craig, Phoenix
602 916 5421
tberg@fclaw.com
*Recommended in Litigation*
**Practice Areas:** Appeals, utilities.
**Prof. Memberships:** Officer, Director, American Academy of Appellate Lawyers; Executive Committee, NCCUSL; Member, ACUSL.
**Career:** Chair, Management Committee. Numerous appeals before the United States Courts of Appeals, the Supreme Court of Arizona, and the Arizona Court of Appeals on state constitutional and public law, contract and commercial disputes, natural resources, employment, medical malpractice, product liability, state and local taxation, business torts, real property, mineral rights, and public utilities. Frequently appears before the Arizona Corporation Commission for electricity, water and telecommunications corporations.

**Personal:** JD, University of Arizona, 1975; BA, Arizona State University, 1972; Best Lawyers in America.

### BERMAN, Michael
Perkins Coie LLP, Phoenix
602 351 8000
*Recommended in Employment*

### BERRY, Charles
Titus, Brueckner & Berry PC, Scottsdale
480 483-9600
*Recommended in Corporate/M&A*

### BERRY, John
Berry & Damore LLC, Scottsdale
480 385 2727
*Recommended in Real Estate*

### BEUS, Leo
Beus Gilbert PLLC, Scottsdale
480 429 3000
*Recommended in Litigation*

### BIRNBAUM, Gary
Mariscal, Weeks, McIntyre & Friedlander PA, Phoenix 602 285 5000
*Recommended in Litigation*

### BISKIND, Neil
Biskind, Hunt & Taylor plc, Phoenix
602 955 3452
*Recommended in Real Estate*

### BIVENS, Donald
Bivens & Nore PA, Phoenix
602 604 2200
*Recommended in Litigation*

### BLANEY, Brian H
Greenberg Traurig LLP, Phoenix
602 445 8322
blaneyb@gtlaw.com
*Recommended in Corporate/M&A*
**Practice Areas:** Corporate and securities.
**Prof. Memberships:** Planning Committee Member, Arizona Angel Investment Conference; Executive Council Member,

State Bar of Arizona, Securities Regulation Section; Member, State Bar of Arizona, Business Law and Securities Regulation Sections; Board of Directors, Desert Voices Oral Learning Center. **Publications:** Co-author, 'Agency Authority in LLC Statutes (Part I): Uniformity and Peculiarity', 4 J. Ltd. Liab. Cos. 139 (1998); co-author, 'Agency Authority in LLC Statutes (Part II): Hypothetical Situations and Practical Suggestions', 5 J. Ltd. Liab. Cos. 11 (1998). **Personal:** JD, magna cum laude, University of Notre Dame Law School, 1998; BBA, University of Michigan, 1990.

## BOUMA, John J
Snell & Wilmer LLP, Phoenix
602 382 6216
jbouma@swlaw.com
*Recommended in Litigation*

**Practice Areas:** Practice concentrated in complex commercial litigation, including antitrust, commercial and business torts, financial institutions, professional malpractice defense and alternative dispute resolution. **Prof. Memberships:** Admitted in Arizona, Iowa, Wisconsin, US Supreme Court; US Court of Appeals, Ninth, Tenth and District of Columbia Circuits. Memberships include American College of Trial Lawyers, Fellow; American Bar Association - Board of Governors (1998-2001), House of Delegates (1989-present); Attorneys' Liability Assurance Society (ALAS), Board of Directors (1986-present), Chairman (2002-04); State Bar of Arizona, President (1983-84); National Conference of Bar Presidents, President (1989-90); Maricopa County Bar Association, President (1977-78); Phoenix Association of Defense Counsel, President (1970-71).

## BROPHY, James E
Ryley Carlock & Applewhite, Phoenix
602 440 4807
jbrophy@rcalaw.com
*Recommended in Corporate/M&A*

**Practice Areas:** James E Brophy has practiced as an attorney with Ryley Carlock & Applewhite since 1974, primarily in the areas of business transactions, securities, mergers and acquisitions, insurance and banking regulation, and related tax and fiduciary matters. Mr Brophy has experience in public and private securities offerings, preparation of periodic securities reports, and has advised boards of directors concerning their fiduciary and legal obligations, including Sarbanes-Oxley compliance. Mr Brophy was the lead counsel in Trans City Life Insurance Co. v Commissioner, 106 T.C. 274 (1996), a seminal case in which the taxpayer prevailed, involving the Internal Revenue Service's application of Section 845(b) of the Internal Revenue Code to disregard reinsurance agreements. **Prof. Memberships:** Mr Brophy is a

Member of the American Bar Assocation, the Arizona State Bar, and the Tax and Securities Sections of the Arizona State Bar. Mr Brophy is past President and a Director of the Men's Arts Council of the Phoenix Art Museum, a founder and past Director of the Phoenix Chapter of the Western Pension Conference, a past Director of the Phoenix Tax Workshop, a member of the Board of Directors and the Chairperson of the Finance and Human Relations Committee of The Foundation for Senior Living, and a member of the Executive Committee of Ryley Carlock & Applewhite. **Publications:** Mr Brophy has lectured at various programs for the Arizona State Bar, including serving as an instructor for the State Bar's Professionalism course. Mr Brophy's publications include 'Securities Aspects of Real Estate Syndication, Real Estate Syndication Syllabus, Realty Seminar Institution'; 'Selected Tax Aspects of Real Estate Transactions'; 'Fiduciary Responsibility Under ERISA — An Update'; the 'Sarbanes-Oxley Act of 2002 and Intellectual Property'; and 'Problems with Stock Option Exercises'. **Personal:** BA, cum laude, University of Arizona (1968); JD magna cum laude, Arizona State University (1974); Articles Editor, Arizona State Law Journal, (1974). The Best Lawyers in America, 2006.

## BROPHY, Michael J
Ryley Carlock & Applewhite, Phoenix
602 440 4811
mbrophy@rcalaw.com
*Recommended in Environment*

**Practice Areas:** Natural resources, with an emphasis on water rights. Extensive experience in strategic water rights planning, major water rights acquisitions and dispositions, and the negotiated or litigated resolution of federal, state and local water rights disputes in the Southwest. **Prof. Memberships:** Admitted to practice in Arizona in 1977. Admitted to practice before United States District Court for the District Court of Arizona (1977); United States Court of Appeals for the Ninth Circuit (1977); and the United States Supreme Court (1983). Past Chairman of the Western States Water Council. **Career:** Joined Ryley Carlock & Applewhite in 1977. Became a shareholder in 1982 and has served on the firm's Management Committee and as the firm's Managing Shareholder. **Publications:** Editor-in-Chief, Arizona State University Law Journal: 'Statutes of Limitations in Civil Rights Litigation.' Numerous publications on water rights for CLE programs. **Personal:** Born on May 8, 1949. BA (magna cum laude), University of Arizona (1971). JD (with distinction), Arizona State University (1977). Phi Beta Kappa.

## BRUNO, Mary E
Greenberg Traurig LLP, Phoenix
602 445 8505
brunom@gtlaw.com
*Recommended in Employment*

**Practice Areas:** Labor and employment. **Prof. Memberships:** Member of the Membership, Training and Awareness Taskforce of EADV (Employers Against Domestic Violence) Taskforce of the Maricopa Association of Governments; Member, State Bars of Arizona and California; Member, American Bar Association, Labor and Employment Law Section. **Publications:** Presenter, 'Managing the Workplace, Problems of Employee Theft and Financial Manipulation', Sterling Education Services, February 2005; Presenter, 'Labor and Employment Law Eye for the Non-Labor and Employment Law Guy', Maricopa County Bar Association, November 2004. **Personal:** JD, University of California, Hastings College of Law, 1986; BA, with high honors, University of Arizona, 1983.

## BUDOFF, Marc
Budoff & Ross PC, Phoenix
602 253 9110
*Recommended in Litigation*

## BULL, Edwin
Burch & Cracchiolo, Phoenix
602 234 9913
*Recommended in Real Estate*

## BURNHAM, Beckey
Greenberg Traurig LLP, Phoenix
602 445 8251
burnhamr@gtlaw.com
*Recommended in Real Estate*

**Practice Areas:** Real estate. **Prof. Memberships:** Member, Crisis Nursery Foundation Board; member, ASU Foundation Advisory Board; Chairman of the Program Committee, ASU Foundation Women and Philanthropy Program; member, ASU Economic Club. **Career:** Listed, Chambers & Partners USA Guide, 2005-06; Listed, Best Lawyers in America, 1998-2005; listed, 'Leading Lawyers', Phoenix Business Journal, 2006. **Personal:** JD, University of California at Los Angeles, School of Law, 1980; BS, magna cum laude, Arizona State University, 1977.

## BUTLER III, A Bates
Fennemore Craig, Tucson
520 879 6804
bbutler@fclaw.com
*Recommended in Litigation*

**Practice Areas:** White collar criminal defense; civil litigation. **Prof. Memberships:** Arizona Attorneys for Criminal Justice, National Association of Former US Attorneys, National Association of Criminal Defense Lawyers, Trial Lawyers for Public Justice. **Career:** Former county prosecutor and

US Attorney for Arizona. Over 24 years as a defense attorney. Participated in numerous multi-party complex trials. Conducts internal corporate investigations. Recently successfully defended physician charged with illegally prescribing controlled substances. Representative clients include defense contractors, accountants, economists, small businesses and business leaders. **Personal:** JD, National Law Center, George Washington University, 1969; BA, Trinity University, 1966; Best Lawyers in America; Rated 'AV', Martindale-Hubbell.

## CABOT, Howard Ross
Perkins Coie LLP, Phoenix
602 351 8000
*Recommended in Litigation*

## CASTER, Lauren
Fennemore Craig, Phoenix
602 916 5367
lcaster@fclaw.com
*Recommended in Environment*

**Practice Areas:** Environmental; natural resources; water. **Prof. Memberships:** Chair-Elect, Section of Environment, Energy, and Resources, American Bar Association. **Career:** Practices in the area of water rights. Represents clients in the general stream adjudications in Arizona courts, and in interstate stream conflicts and other water right litigation pending in federal courts. Also represents clients in proceedings before the Arizona Department of Water Resources, and advises clients on water matters generally. **Personal:** JD, with distinction, Order of the Coif, University of Nebraska, 1976; BA, University of Nebraska, 1973; Best Lawyers in America; Rated 'AV', Martindale-Hubbell.

## CHESTER, Charles L (Rusty)
Ryley Carlock & Applewhite, Phoenix
602 440 4806
cchester@rcalaw.com
*Recommended in Employment*

**Practice Areas:** Mr Chester's practice emphasizes employment practices and complex civil litigation. Historically, his practice has involved civil litigation, representing clients in employment, antitrust, securities, product liability, commercial contract, franchise and common law business and personal injury litigation. Mr Chester has tried cases ranging from multi-million dollar products liability computer chip jury trials to Perishable Agricultural Commodities Act trials to the Court. Mr Chester's practice focuses on employee and labor relations law. His labor and employee relations practice is devoted to defense of individuals and companies against the claims of employees, unions and the government. He has defended collective and class action claims, pattern and practice claims, OFCCP and EEOC claims, state civil rights agency claims, union and employ-

ee claims in virtually all areas of employment law. Mr Chester serves as a certified arbitrator for the United States District Court for the District of Arizona.
**Prof. Memberships:** Mr Chester first was licensed in 1970 and currently is a Member of the State Bar of Arizona (past Chair of Labor and Employment section), Texas and Missouri. He is admitted to practice before the United States Supreme Court and the Courts of Appeal for the Fifth, Ninth and Tenth Circuits. Mr Chester also is licensed to practice in the corresponding District Courts. He remains a Member of the ABA antitrust section and its Sherman Act 1 and 2, and Robinson-Patman Act committees. He has been elected to the prestigious American College of Labor and Employment Lawyers and is also a Member of the American Employment Law Council, Defense Research Institute, and Equal Opportunity Committee of the Labor Section of the American Bar Association.
**Publications:** Contributing author, Schlei & Grossman, 'Employment Discrimination Law' (2d ed. Five-Year Cumulative Supplement, 1989). Contributing author, 'Employment-at-Will: A 1989 State-by-State Survey' (D Cathcart & M Dichter, eds).
**Personal:** Born August 9, 1945, in Kansas City, Missouri. BA University of Arizona (1967). JD (cum laude) University of Houston (1970).

## CLEES, Joseph T
Ogletree, Deakins, Nash, Smoak & Stewart, PC, Phoenix 602 778 3701
joe.clees@ogletreedeakins.com
*Recommended in Employment*
**Practice Areas:** Labor and employment, litigation.
**Prof. Memberships:** Chair, Arizona State Bar Labor Section, Metro Phoenix Human Resources Association (SHRM).
**Career:** Admitted to practice in Arizona, Arizona Court of Appeals, Arizona Supreme Court, US District Court for the District of Arizona, US Court of Appeals (Ninth Circuit), US Supreme Court, Apache Tribal Court. Ranked top employment law attorney in Chambers USA 2005-06. 2006 Best Lawyers in America. AV Rated.
**Publications:** 'Arizona Employment Law Handbook' (editor), Arizona Labor Letter (member, editorial board).
**Personal:** Dickinson College (BA, 1981), Villanova University (JD, 1984).

## COHEN, Jon
Snell & Wilmer LLP, Phoenix
602 382 6247
jcohen@swlaw.com
*Recommended in Corporate/M&A*
**Practice Areas:** General corporate practice concentrated in the area of securities offerings, mergers and acquisitions, venture capital, and corporate compliance.
**Prof. Memberships:** Admitted to prac-

tice in Arizona. Memberships include the State Bar of Arizona and the American Bar Association. Board of Directors Memberships include: the Arizona Science Center, the Arizona Technology Council, Kronos Longevity Research Institute, and Vika Corporation.

## COHEN, Richard
Lewis and Roca, Phoenix
602 262 5311
*Recommended in Employment*

## CONDO, James
Snell & Wilmer LLP, Phoenix
602 382 6353
jcondo@swlaw.com
*Recommended in Litigation*
**Practice Areas:** Trial practice concentrated in complex commercial, professional liability and product liability litigation.
**Prof. Memberships:** State Bar of Arizona; Maricopa County Bar Association; State Bar of Colorado; American Bar Association; Defense Research Institute; Judge Pro Tempore, Maricopa County Superior Court, Arizona. Admitted in Arizona, Colorado, District of Columbia, US Supreme Court, US Court of Appeals, Sixth, Ninth, Tenth and District of Columbia Circuits.
**Personal:** Member, Lehigh University National Leadership Council; Member and Chairman-Elect, Arizona Town Hall.

## CRABB, Joseph
Quarles & Brady Streich Lang LLP, Phoenix 602 229 5742
jcrabb@quarles.com
*Recommended in Corporate/M&A*
**Practice Areas:** Corporate services; mergers and acquisitions; corporate finance/securities; private equity/venture capital; commercial financial services; financial institutions.
**Prof. Memberships:** State Bar of Arizona.
**Career:** Partner since 2001.
**Personal:** University of Iowa (JD, 1992; BA, 1989).

## CURRY, Stanton
Gallagher & Kennedy PA, Phoenix
602 530 8000
*Recommended in Environment*

## CURZON, Thomas H
Osborn Maledon PA, Phoenix
602 640 9308
tcurzon@omlaw.com
*Recommended in Corporate/M&A*
**Practice Areas:** Serves as outside general counsel to emerging, growth-oriented companies; entrepreneurial transactions, including venture capital and other private placements of securities, entity formation and transaction structuring, mergers, acquisitions and divestitures, initial public offerings, corporate governance, licensing and distribution of software and other products, employee matters, and executive compensation.

**Career:** MS Shell Dlg; Partner, Osborn Maledon, PA (and predecessor firm) since 1986; recognitions include: 'The Best Lawyers in America', editions 1995-2006; Best of the Bar (Business Journal), 2004; Chambers USA, American's Leading Business Lawyers, 2003-2006; Marquis' 'Who's Who in American Law'; Marquis' 'Who's Who in America'.
**Publications:** Arizona Legal Forms, Business Organizations (Corporations), Volumes 8 and 9, West Publishing, Second Edition, 2001-02; Presenter: 'Show Me the Money: Lecture on Intellectual Property in Business Models' (Thunderbird, the Garvin School of International Management, 2004); Presenter: 'Venture Capital Financing Recent Trends and Developments' (Enterprise Network Business Seminar Series, 2003; Presenter: 'Venture Capital Financing - Standard Terms and Recent Developments', (Financial Executives Institute, 2002); Presenter: 'Getting Ready for the Dance: Preparing to Raise Venture Capital - A Coaching Primer' (The Seminar Group, 2001).
**Personal:** JD, magna cum laude, University of Texas, 1979; BA, summa cum laude, University of Kansas, 1976; Third Degree Black Belt, Taekwon-do (ITF).

## DANNEMAN, Dale
Lewis and Roca, Phoenix
602 262 5311
*Recommended in Litigation*

## DAY, Barton
Bryan Cave LLP, Phoenix
602 364 7000
*Recommended in Environment*

## DEROUIN, James
Steptoe & Johnson LLP, Phoenix
602 257 5237
jderouin@steptoe.com
*Recommended in Environment*
**Practice Areas:** Partner, Phoenix office of Steptoe & Johnson LLP. Represents clients on environmental and natural resource issues including groundwater contamination, surface water discharges, hazardous waste, toxicology, endangered species, groundwater contaminant fate and transport modeling, civil and criminal enforcement and complex project permitting. Member: EPA's NACEPT Superfund Subcommittee (2002-02). Member, CDC Board of Scientific Counselors, United States Department of Heath and Human Services (2003-05). Negotiated laws involving surface water quality, solid and hazardous waste, air quality, PCBs, dioxin, pesticides, fluorocarbons, mining reclamation and groundwater quality.
**Personal:** JD, University of Wisconsin Law School, 1968; BA, University of Wisconsin-Eau Claire, 1967.

## DEWALD, Scott
Lewis and Roca, Phoenix
602 262 5311
*Recommended in Corporate/M&A*

## DICHTER, Stephen M
Bryan Cave LLP, Phoenix
602 364 7000
*Recommended in Litigation*

## DORAN, John Alan
Greenberg Traurig LLP, Phoenix
602 445 8507
doranj@gtlaw.com
*Recommended in Employment*
**Practice Areas:** Labor and employment; litigation; appellate.
**Prof. Memberships:** Chair, Arizona Association of Industries, HR Subcommittee; Chairman, State Bar of Arizona Employment and Labor Executive Council; National Council of Appellate Attorneys; Charter Member, Management Labor and Employment Roundtable.
**Career:** Listed, Chambers & Partners USA Guide, 2005-06; The Phoenix Business Journal's 'Best of the Bar Award' for Labor and Employment Law, 2003, 2004 and 2005.
**Personal:** JD, Vanderbilt University Law School, 1988; BA, magna cum laude, Loyola Marymount University, 1985.

## DYEKMAN, Donald
Mariscal, Weeks, McIntyre & Friedlander PA, Phoenix 602 285 5000
*Recommended in Real Estate*

## EARL, Stephen
Earl, Curley & Lagarde, PC, Phoenix
602 265 0094
*Recommended in Real Estate*

## ECKSTEIN, Paul
Perkins Coie LLP, Phoenix
602 351 8000
*Recommended in Litigation*

## EMERICK, Steven P
Quarles & Brady Streich Lang LLP, Phoenix 602 230 5517
emerick@quarles.com
*Recommended in Corporate/M&A*
**Practice Areas:** Corporate services, corporate finance/securities, mergers and acquisitions, private equity/venture capital, commercial financial services.
**Prof. Memberships:** State Bar of Wisconsin; State Bar of Arizona; Maricopa County Bar Association; American Bar Association.
**Career:** Partner since 1991.
**Personal:** Lewis & Clark College (JD, 1984); Oregon State University (BS, 1981).

## EVERROAD, John
Fennemore Craig, Phoenix
602 916 5302
jeverroad@fclaw.com
*Recommended in Litigation*
**Practice Areas:** Alternative dispute resolution; business and personal injury torts; litigation.

**Prof. Memberships:** Fellow, American College of Trial Lawyers; Member, American Board of Trial Advocates; Member, National Board of Trial Advocates; Fellow, American Bar Association.
**Career:** Primarily practices in the area of general civil litigation dealing with personal injury and wrongful death, professional negligence, complex commercial litigation and insurance issues.
**Personal:** JD, Vanderbilt University, 1969; Best Lawyers in America; Certified Personal Injury and Wrongful Death Specialist; Rated 'AV', Martindale-Hubbell; USMC Retired.

## FARGOTSTEIN, Phillip F
Fennemore Craig, Phoenix
602 916 5453
pfargots@fclaw.com
*Recommended in Environment*
**Practice Areas:** Environmental; litigation.
**Prof. Memberships:** State Bar of Arizona, Environmental and Natural Resources Law Section; American Bar Association, Section of Environment, Energy, and Resources; Arizona Association of Industries; Rocky Mountain Mineral Law Institute.
**Career:** Member, firm management committee. Former editor of State Bar environmental newsletter. Represents business and property owners relating to state and federal air quality, Superfund, underground storage tanks and waste laws.
**Personal:** JD, Harvard University, 1977; Best Lawyers in America; Rated 'AV', Martindale-Hubbell, Colonel (USMCR Retired).

## FATHE, Fred
Mariscal, Weeks, McIntyre & Friedlander PA, Phoenix 602 285 5000
*Recommended in Real Estate*

## FEDERHAR, Andrew M
Fennemore Craig, Phoenix
602 916 5301
afederhar@fclaw.com
*Recommended in Litigation*
**Practice Areas:** Commercial litigation; product liability; professional liability; insurance coverage; government relations.
**Prof. Memberships:** Chairman, Supreme Court's Committee on Complex Civil Litigation and Supreme Court's Business Roundtable; Lawyer's Committee, National Center for State Courts.
**Career:** Chair, commercial litigation practice. Notable recent cases include: Maher v DeConcini, 124 P.3d 770 (App. 2005); ChartOne v Bernini, 83 P.3d 1103 (App. 2004); Manistee Town Center v City of Glendale, 227 F.3d 1090 (9th Cir. 2000).
**Personal:** JD, University of Arizona, 1980; Rated 'AV', Martindale-Hubbell.

## FEENEY, Matthew
Snell & Wilmer LLP, Phoenix
602 382 6239
mfeeney@swlaw.com
*Recommended in Corporate/M&A*
**Practice Areas:** General corporate practice concentrated in the area of securities, including public offerings, private placements, and mergers and acquisitions.
**Prof. Memberships:** State Bar of Arizona; American Bar Association (Commission on Interest on Lawyer Trust Accounts, 1998-2002, and Co-Chair, Committee on Prototype Limited, Liability Company Legislation 1991-92); Board Member for the Arizona Foundation for Legal Services and Education.

## FERLAND, Roger
Quarles & Brady Streich Lang LLP, Phoenix 602 229 5607
rferland@quarles.com
*Recommended in Environment*
**Practice Areas:** Environmental.
**Prof. Memberships:** State Bar of Arizona; Chair, Arizona Association of Industries (Air Quality Subcommittee); Former Chair, Governor's Air Quality Strategies Task Force; Former Chair, Arizona Chamber of Commerce Air Quality Subcommittee; State Bar of Arizona (Administrative Law Committee).
**Career:** Partner since 1984.
**Publications:** 'Air Pollution Regulation', Enforcement and Investigation Methods, Arizona State University ETM 502 Regulatory Framework Course; 'Preparing for and Responding to Government Investigations', SHE Conference.
**Personal:** Duke University (JD, 1974); Lewis & Clark College (BA, 1968).

## GAMMAGE JR, Grady
Gammage & Burnham, PLC, Phoenix
602 256 0566
*Recommended in Real Estate*

## GILBERT, Donald R
Fennemore Craig, Phoenix
602 916 5306
dgilbert@fclaw.com
*Recommended in Employment*
**Practice Areas:** Labor and employment; litigation.
**Prof. Memberships:** State Bar of Arizona; State Bar of California.
**Career:** Co-Chair, Labor and Employment Practice. Represents clients with employment-related issues in both state and federal courts including disputes over restrictive covenants, contract interpretation and discrimination. Also represents clients before the NLRB, EEOC, Department of Labor, and the Arizona Civil Rights Division. Has tried more than 100 labor arbitrations. Counsels clients on employment issues and policies. Designs and implements employment audits to assist clients in identifying and correcting high-risk employment practices.
**Personal:** JD, University of California,

1971; BA, Stanford University, 1968; Rated 'AV', Martindale-Hubbell.

## GILBERT, Paul
Beus Gilbert PLLC, Scottsdale
480 429 3000
*Recommended in Real Estate*

## GITTLER, Amy
Frazer Ryan Goldberg Arnold & Gittler LLP, Phoenix 602 277 2010
*Recommended in Employment*

## GOEBEL, Monica
Steptoe & Johnson LLP, Phoenix
602 257 5218
mgoebel@steptoe.com
*Recommended in Employment*
**Practice Areas:** Managing Partner of Steptoe & Johnson LLP's Phoenix office. Practices employment and employee benefits law, emphasizing multi-plaintiff and class action lawsuits, discrimination and sexual harassment claims, whistleblower litigation, wage-and-hour matters, non-compete agreements, trade secret protection, and defending benefits plans and fiduciaries in ERISA litigation. Advises and defends retailers, manufacturers, and insurance companies in connection with union-avoidance efforts, union elections, matters before the National Labor Relations Board, and investigations or litigation by the EEOC and Department of Labor's Wage and Hour Division and OFCCP.
**Personal:** JD, Arizona State University, 1988; BS, Grand Canyon University, 1985.

## GREEN, Jordan
Fennemore Craig, Phoenix
602 916 5426
jgreen@fclaw.com
*Recommended in Litigation*
**Practice Areas:** White collar criminal defense; internal investigations; commercial litigation.
**Prof. Memberships:** Fellow, American College of Trial Lawyers; Fellow, International Academy of Trial Lawyers; Member, National Association of Criminal Defense Lawyers; Arizona Attorneys for Criminal Justice.
**Career:** Represents businesses and individuals in criminal investigations and prosecutions in matters involving, among others, the Environmental Protection Agency, Securities and Exchange Commission, Sarbanes-Oxley, Internal Revenue Service, Medicare/Medicaid, antitrust and the Department of Defense.
**Personal:** JD, DePaul University College of Law, 1965; Best Lawyers in America (1983-2006); Rated 'AV', Martindale-Hubbell.

## HACKETT, Robert
Jennings, Strouss & Salmon, PLC, Phoenix 602 262 5911
*Recommended in Corporate/M&A*

## HALL, Gregory
Squire, Sanders & Dempsey LLP, Phoenix 602 528 4134
ghall@ssd.com
*Recommended in Corporate/M&A*
**Practice Areas:** Partner in firm's Capital Markets Group. Practices in the area of corporate and securities law and has acted as transactional and securities counsel to New York Stock Exchange and Nasdaq-listed companies, startups, mid-cap and large public and private entities, and regional and national investment banks. Counsels clients in securities law compliance, corporate governance and general corporate matters in a variety of industries including technology, biotech, telecommunications, transportation, manufacturing, oil and gas and gaming.
**Prof. Memberships:** Arizona Business Leadership; Securities Regulation Section of the State Bar of Arizona; Association of Corporate Growth; Arizona Technology Council; ASU Technopolis; Enterprise Network.

## HALLER, Diane
Quarles & Brady Streich Lang LLP, Phoenix 602 229 5625
dhaller@quarles.com
*Recommended in Real Estate*
**Practice Areas:** Real estate.
**Prof. Memberships:** Member: State Bar of Arizona; Maricopa County Bar Association; American Bar Association.
**Career:** Partner since 1993.
**Publications:** 'Subleasing Commercial Property in Arizona' (co-author), Arizona Journal of Real Estate and Business, 1995; 'Breach of a Real Estate Contract,' Arizona Journal of Real Estate and Business, 1995; Contributing Editor to Commercial Real Estate Transactions Practice Manual, Arizona State Bar Association, 1988-89 (First Edition).
**Personal:** University of Notre Dame (JD, 1986); University of Utah (BS, 1983).

## HAMMOND, Larry A
Osborn Maledon PA, Phoenix
602 640 9361
lhammond@omlaw.com
*Recommended in Litigation*
**Practice Areas:** Criminal defense (including both white collar and major felony, especially capital defense); also engages in complex commercial litigation and False Claims Act litigation.
**Prof. Memberships:** President, American Judicature Society (2003-05); Chair, Justice Project of Arizona Attorneys for Criminal Justice (Arizona's project related to questions of actual innocence); Chair, Arizona State Bar Indigent Defense Task Force; Officer, Arizona Capital Representation Project.
**Career:** Mr Hammond has practiced law for 36 years; five of those years were spent with the United States Department of Justice both as an Assistant Watergate Special Prosecutor and as the First

Deputy Assistant Attorney General in the Office of Legal Counsel during the Carter Administration. His practice has always included both complex commercial litigation and criminal defense. Throughout his career he has devoted substantial time to cases, projects and programs designed to improve the administration of justice.
**Publications:** Mr Hammond has written extensively on issues associated with convictions of the wrongfully accused. A sampling of his numerous publications can be found at the website for Osborn Maledon.
**Personal:** Mr Hammond considers himself the most knowlegeable baseball fan in his law firm. While the claim is often disputed, it has yet to be disproved. He is also extremely proud to be able to say that all of his children have devoted their careers to public service; his eldest daughter has been a social worker for an immigrant and refugee rights project; his son is a Phoenix police officer; and his youngest daughter after returning from the Peace Corps is now a law student in her last semester at the University of Colorado and has plans to become a public defender.

### HAMULA, James
Gallagher & Kennedy PA, Phoenix
602 530 8000
*Recommended in Environment*

### HANKS, Gregg
Fennemore Craig, Phoenix
602 916 5309
ghanks@fclaw.com
*Recommended in Real Estate*
**Practice Areas:** Real estate, tax.
**Prof. Memberships:** American Bar Association, State Bar of Arizona, Maricopa County Bar Association.
**Career:** Practices primarily in the area of real estate, but has significant experience with limited liability companies, joint ventures and taxation. Has written articles on tax matters and lectured at seminars on various partnership, limited liability company and tax issues.
**Personal:** JD, Brigham Young University, 1984; BA, Brigham Young University, 1979; Best Lawyers in America; Rated 'AV', Martindale-Hubbell.

### HARDIN, William M
Osborn Maledon PA, Phoenix
602 640 9322
whardin@omlaw.com
*Recommended in Corporate/M&A*
**Practice Areas:** Business Transactions Practice, including outside general counsel services, mergers and acquisitions, venture capital and private equity financings, securities, intellectual property transactions and executive compensation matters.
**Prof. Memberships:** State Bar of Arizona; Enterprise Network Board of Directors.
**Career:** Partner, Osborn Maledon, PA (and predecessor firm) since 1988. Co-

Chair, Governor's Council on Innovation and Technology, 2004-06. Recognitions include: Chambers USA, American's Leading Business Lawyers, 2003-05; 'The Best Lawyers in America', editions 1995-2006; 'Best of the Bar' (Business Journal), 2004. Law clerk to Judge Thomas Gibbs Gee, United States Court of Appeals for the Fifth Circuit, 1982-83.
**Publications:** Arizona Legal Forms, Business Organizations, (Corporations), Volumes 8 and 9, West Publishing, 2nd Edition, 2001-02. Presenter: 'Venture Capital Financing Recent Trends and Developments' (Enterprise Network Business Seminar Series, 2003); Presenter: 'Venture Capital Financing - Standard Terms and Recent Developments', (Financial Executives Institute, 2002); Presenter: 'Getting Ready for the Dance: Preparing to Raise Venture Capital - A Coaching Primer' (The Seminar Group, 2001).
**Personal:** JD, with honors, University of Chicago Law School, 1982. Associate editor, University of Chicago Law Review; Order of the Coif.

### HARRISON, Mark I
Osborn Maledon PA, Phoenix
602 640 9324
mharrison@omlaw.com
*Recommended in Litigation*
**Practice Areas:** Professional ethics and professional liability; consulting and testifying as an expert in matters involving legal ethics, professional liability and law firm risk management; appellate litigation; complex commercial and tort litigation; service as a mediator and arbitrator.
**Prof. Memberships:** Member and past President, State Bar of Arizona and Arizona Bar Foundation; Member and past President, Maricopa County Bar Association; Member and past President, Association of Professional Responsibility Lawyers; Fellow and past President, American Academy of Appellate Lawyers; ABA (Member and Chair, Standing Committees on Professional Discipline and Professionalism; Member, Standing Committee on Ethics; Chair, American Bar Association Commission to Evaluate the Code of Judicial Conduct.
**Career:** Law clerk to former Chief Justice Lorna E Lockwood, Supreme Court of Arizona; Harrison, Harper, Christian & Dichter (and predecessor firms), 1966-93; Partner, Bryan Cave LLP (1993-2004); Member, Osborn Maledon, P.A. (2004-present).
**Publications:** Co-author, Arizona Appellate Practice; 'An Overview: The New Arizona Rules of Professional Conduct', 20 Arizona Bar Journal 8 (1985); 'LLPs Are Just Another Star Wars!' 39 S.Tex. L.R. 633 (1998); Co-author, 'Ethical Implications of Partnerships and Other Associations Involving American and Foreign Lawyers', 22 Penn State Internat'l L.R. 639 (Spring 2004).

**Personal:** Adjunct Professor, University of Arizona College of Law (1994-97), Arizona State University Law School (Legal Ethics), 2000-present; Antioch College (BA 1957); Harvard Law School (LLB, 1960).

### HAYDEN, William
Snell & Wilmer LLP, Phoenix
602 382 6329
bhayden@swlaw.com
*Recommended in Employment*
**Practice Areas:** Advises management clients regarding all phases of personnel administration and avoidance of personnel-related litigation. Represents management clients before state and federal regulatory agencies including, the Equal Employment Opportunity Commission, the Arizona Civil Rights Division, the National Labor Relations Board, and the Department of Labor. Defends management clients in personnel-related litigation, including employment discrimination, wrongful discharge, breach of contract, restrictive covenants.
**Prof. Memberships:** Memberships include the State Bar of Arizona; the American Bar Association; Maricopa County Bar Association; District of Columbia Bar Association; the American Arbitration Association, National Panel of Arbitrators, specializing in employment dispute resolution.

### HENDRICKS SR, Ed
Meyer Hendricks, Phoenix
602 604 2200
*Recommended in Litigation*

### HENZE, Tom
Gallagher & Kennedy PA, Phoenix
602 530 8000
*Recommended in Litigation*

### HERF, Charles
Quarles & Brady Streich Lang LLP, Phoenix 602 230 5581
cwh@quarles.com
*Recommended in Employment*
**Practice Areas:** Labor and employment, litigation, school.
**Prof. Memberships:** State Bar of Arizona; Maricopa County Bar Association; American Bar Association (Labor Relations and Litigation Section); State Bar of California; State Bar of Wisconsin; Illinois State Bar.
**Career:** Partner since 1974.
**Publications:** 'Prosecuting and Defending Temporary Restraining Order and Injunctive Litigation', National School Boards Association, November 2000; 'Early Retirement Plans and Age Discrimination', Arizona School Boards Association, 2000.
**Personal:** University of Wisconsin (JD, 1968; BS, 1965).

### HINK, John
Ryley Carlock & Applewhite, Phoenix
602 440 4835
jhink@rcalaw.com

*Recommended in Real Estate*
**Practice Areas:** Real estate finance, acquisition and development, including acquisitions and sales of undeveloped property and developed property; residential subdivisions and condominiums; development, financing and leasing of shopping centers, office buildings, and apartment projects.
**Prof. Memberships:** Admitted to practice in Arizona. Memberships include the State Bar of Arizona; Maricopa County Bar Association; Arizona Town Hall; Scottsdale Charros; Scottsdale Area Chamber.
**Personal:** JD, Arizona State University (1988); BA (Economics), University of Arizona (1984).

### HIRSCH, Stephen
Bryan Cave LLP, Phoenix
602 364 7000
*Recommended in Real Estate*

### HOFFMANN, Christian
Quarles & Brady Streich Lang LLP, Phoenix 602 229 5336
choffman@quarles.com
*Recommended in Corporate/M&A*
**Practice Areas:** Corporate services, corporate finance/securites, mergers and acquisitions, private equity/venture capital.
**Prof. Memberships:** State Bar of Arizona (Securities Law Section); American Bar Association; Maricopa County Bar Association.
**Career:** Partner since 1979.
**Personal:** Georgetown University (JD, 1973); Georgetown University (BS, BA, 1969).

### JOHNSEN, Diane M
Osborn Maledon PA, Phoenix
602 640 9327
djohnsen@omlaw.com
*Recommended in Litigation*
**Practice Areas:** Diane practices general commercial litigation, specializing in complex contract, business tort and environmental matters. She also has prosecuted and defended insurance coverage actions, particularly where the loss at issue involves environmental damages. Before becoming an attorney, Diane was a political reporter for the Arizona Daily Star in Tucson. She has represented a local television station in defamation and privacy issues, and successfully defended a national television news organization in a hidden camera, invasion of privacy and defamation case. Her other clients include Honeywell International, Cox Communications, Arizona Public Service and PGA Tour. Diane is a pro tem Superior Court Judge and sits on the board of the Children's Action Alliance. She is also a board member and past President of Arizona Center for Law in the Public Interest.
**Prof. Memberships:** Arizona Center for Law in the Public Interest, Board of

Directors, 1993- , Vice President, 1997-98, President 1998-2002; Children's Action Alliance, Member, Board of Directors, 2004-present; Stanford Law School Board of Visitors, Member, 2003-present.
**Career:** The Best Lawyers in America, Commercial Litigation, edition 2006; Judge Pro Tempore, Superior Court of Arizona, Maricopa County, 1993-present; political reporter and an editor, Arizona Daily Star, 1975-79; law clerk to Judge Ben C Duniway, US Court of Appeals, Ninth Circuit, 1982-83.
**Personal:** JD, Stanford University, 1982; Stanford Law Review, associate editor 1981-82; BA summa cum laude, University of Arizona, 1975; Phi Beta Kappa.

## JOHNSON, Christopher D
Squire, Sanders & Dempsey LLP, Phoenix 602 528 4046
cjohnson@ssd.com
*Recommended in Corporate/M&A*
**Practice Areas:** Partner with more than 25 years experience in the corporate and securities areas, with significant experience in initial and subsequent public offerings, private placements, M&A, corporate reorganizations and restructurings, public company securities law compliance, venture capital finance and corporate governance. Listed in 'The Best Lawyers in America'. Frequent author/lecturer on corporate and securities law topics.
**Prof. Memberships:** State Bar of Arizona, Securities Regulation Section, Executive Council 1979-95, Chair 1994-95; Enterprise Network and the Arizona Technology Incubator, Board of Directors; Arizona Venture Capital Conference and the Arizona Technology Council's Investing in Innovation Conference, planning committees.

## KANT, Robert
Greenberg Traurig LLP, Phoenix 602 445 8302
kantr@gtlaw.com
*Recommended in Corporate/M&A*
**Practice Areas:** Corporate and securities/M&A.
**Prof. Memberships:** Member, State Bar of Arizona, Small Business Capital Formation Subcommittee of Committee on Securities Regulation.
**Career:** Listed, Chambers & Partners USA Guide, 2003-06; Listed, Best Lawyers in America, 2003-06; Listed, 'Best of the Bar', Securities Law, Phoenix Business Journal, February 2004; 'Best Lawyer in Valley', Phoenix Business Journal, January 2005; Listed, 'Best of the Bar', Corporate Law, Phoenix Business Journal, February 2003.
**Publications:** Co-author: 'Presumptive Merit-A New Era for Arizona Securities Law', 45 Bus Law, 1347, 1990.
**Personal:** JD, Villanova University School of Law, 1970; BA, University of Pennsylvania, 1966.

## KATZ, Lawrence
Steptoe & Johnson LLP, Phoenix 602 257 5211
lkatz@steptoe.com
*Recommended in Employment*
**Practice Areas:** Head of the Labor Relations and Employment Practice Group and Partner in the Phoenix office of Steptoe & Johnson LLP. Practice involves state and federal court litigation representing management in the defense of lawsuits alleging violations of employment discrimination statutes, contracts, or various common-law employment rights. Further assists clients in union-avoidance efforts and represents employers in union elections, unfair labor practice proceedings, litigation related to union organizational activities, and other matters before the National Labor Relations Board. Handles matters involving trade secrets, unfair competition, and executive compensation.
**Personal:** JD, Boston College Law School, 1967; BA, Harvard University, 1960.

## KELLY, Andrew P
Osborn Maledon PA, Phoenix 602 640 9329
akelly@omlaw.com
*Recommended in Corporate/M&A*
**Practice Areas:** Commercial Transactions Practice including mergers and acquisitions, software licensing, entity formation, employment matters, securities and general counsel services with an emphasis on transactional and regulatory aspects of Indian gaming.
**Prof. Memberships:** State Bar of Arizona; Greater Phoenix Economic Council Ambassador Steering Committee, 2004.
**Career:** Member, Osborn Maledon, PA since 2000.
**Personal:** JD, magna cum laude, Arizona State University, 1994; Arizona State Law Journal, editor, 1993-94; Order of the Coif; BA, cum laude, History, Williams College, 1988.

## KENNEDY, Michael
Gallagher & Kennedy PA, Phoenix 602 530 8000
*Recommended in Litigation*

## KERRICK, Robert
Gallagher & Kennedy PA, Phoenix 602 530 8000
*Recommended in Real Estate*

## KIMBALL, David
Gallagher & Kennedy PA, Phoenix 602 530 8000
*Recommended in Environment*

## KIMERER, Mike
Kimerer & Derrick, P.C., Phoenix 602-279-5900
*Recommended in Litigation*

## KRAMER, Jay
Fennemore Craig, Phoenix 602 916 5341

jkramer@fclaw.com
*Recommended in Real Estate*
**Practice Areas:** Real estate; finance.
**Prof. Memberships:** Member, State Bar of Arizona; Member, Maricopa County Bar Association; President, Fennemore Craig Foundation; Board Member, Kivel Campus of Care; Board Member, Arizona Work Force Housing Task Force.
**Career:** Practice encompasses real estate transactions and corporate finance, including real estate acquisition, entitlements, infrastructure development and financing, and disposition, and real estate and other asset-based financing.
**Personal:** JD, Vanderbilt University, 1984; MBA, Vanderbilt University, 1984; BA, Georgetown University, 1980; Certified Real Estate Specialist, 1995; Best Lawyers in America; Rated 'AV', Martindale-Hubbell.

## LANSKY, David
Mariscal, Weeks, McIntyre & Friedlander PA, Phoenix 602 285 5000
*Recommended in Real Estate*

## LAUSE, Christopher
Bryan Cave LLP, Phoenix 602 364 7000
*Recommended in Corporate/M&A*

## LAZARUS, Larry
Lazarus & Associates, Phoenix 602 340 0900
*Recommended in Real Estate*

## LISKER, Steven
Lisker & Associates PLLC, Phoenix 602 778 4300
*Recommended in Real Estate*

## LOWE, Ronald
Perkins Coie LLP, Phoenix 602 351 8000
*Recommended in Real Estate*

## MACDONOUGH, Bruce E
Greenberg Traurig LLP, Phoenix 602 445 8305
macdonoughb@gtlaw.com
*Recommended in Corporate/M&A*
**Practice Areas:** Corporate and securities; mergers and acquisitions; public and private equity and debt offerings.
**Personal:** JD, University of Virginia School of Law, 1981; AB, Stanford University, 1978.

## MALEDON, William J
Osborn Maledon PA, Phoenix 602 640 9331
wmaledon@omlaw.com
*Recommended in Litigation*
**Practice Areas:** Complex commercial litigation, with an emphasis on antitrust, trade regulation, securities, product liability, insurance bad faith, and sports litigation.
**Prof. Memberships:** A Member of various state and federal Bar associations, a Founding Fellow of the Arizona Bar Foundation and a Life Member of the American Bar Foundation, a former

Chairman of the Antitrust Section of the Arizona State Bar, and a member of various Arizona State Bar Committees.
**Career:** University of Notre Dame (JD 1972); Law Clerk to the Honorable William J Brennan, Jr, United States Supreme Court (1972-73).
**Publications:** Has lectured extensively on trade regulation matters, complex litigation, and jury trial reform issues.
**Personal:** Adjunct Professor of Sports Law, Arizona State University Law School.

## MALTZ, Gerald
Haralson, Miller, Pitt, Feldman & McAnally PLC, Tucson 520 792 3836
*Recommended in Litigation*

## MAST, Gregory
Gallagher & Kennedy PA, Phoenix 602 530 8000
*Recommended in Real Estate*

## MAY, Bruce
Jennings, Strouss & Salmon, PLC, Phoenix 602 262 5911
*Recommended in Real Estate*

## MCCONNELL, Karen C
Fennemore Craig, Phoenix 602 916 5307
kmcconne@fclaw.com
*Recommended in Corporate/M&A*
**Practice Areas:** Securities; mergers and acquisitions; business law.
**Prof. Memberships:** Member, Securities and Business Law Sections, State Bar of Arizona; Subcommittees on 1933 Act Registration and 1934 Act Reporting Companies and Committee on Federal Regulation of Securities, Business Law Section, American Bar Association.
**Career:** Chair, Business and Finance Practice. Represents buyers and sellers in asset and stock-based transactions, private equity and venture capital transactions, mergers, leveraged buyouts and other business acquisitions and reorganizations. Represents issuers in public offerings and private placements of debt and equity securities.
**Personal:** JD, University of Notre Dame, 1984; Best Lawyers in America; Rated 'AV', Martindale-Hubbell.

## MEEHAN, Michael
Meehan LLP, Tucson 520 622 8855
*Recommended in Litigation*

## MITCHELL, Barry D
Gallagher & Kennedy PA, Phoenix 602 530 8000
*Recommended in Litigation*

## MOBERLY, Michael D
Ryley Carlock & Applewhite, Phoenix 602 440 4821
mmoberly@rcalaw.com
*Recommended in Employment*
**Practice Areas:** Former Practice Leader of firm's Labor and Employment Group.

Has extensive experience in employment and civil rights litigation, EEOC, NLRB and other agency representation, labor arbitration, and strike contingency and other employment planning issues.
**Prof. Memberships:** Admitted to practice in Arizona (1983). Member of College of Labor & Employment Lawyers; Defense Research Institute; American Bar Association, Section of Labor and Employment Law; State Bar of Arizona, Employment and Labor Law Section; Arizona Industrial Relations Association. Appointment; Chairman, Arizona Agricultural Employment Relations Board.
**Career:** Joined Ryley Carlock & Applewhite, 1983; became shareholder, 1989. Serves as a Chairman of Ryley Carlock & Applewhite Executive Committee.
**Publications:** Contributing author 'Arizona Employment Law Handbook' (1998). Author of more than 30 law review articles addressing litigation and labor-related topics, including 'Striking a Happy Medium: The Conversion of Unfair Labor Practice Strikes to Economic Strikes', 22 Berkeley Journal of Employment & Labor Law 131 (2001).
**Personal:** Born 21 November 1956. JD (with high distinction), University of Iowa (1983); BBA (with high distinction), University of Iowa (1979).

### MOELLENBERG, Dalva
Gallagher & Kennedy PA, Phoenix
602 530 8000
*Recommended in Environment*

### MOYA, Bob
Quarles & Brady Streich Lang LLP, Phoenix 602 230 5580
prmoya@quarles.com
*Recommended in Corporate/M&A*
**Practice Areas:** Corporate services, corporate finance/securities, international business, mergers and acquisitions.
**Prof. Memberships:** State Bar of Arizona (Member, Securities Regulation Committee, 1973-83; Member, 1983- and Chairman, 1984-86, Securities Law Section; Member, 1996- and Chairman, 1998-99, Law Practice Management Section); American Bar Association; Maricopa County Bar Association; Los Abogados/Hispanic Bar Association; Hispanic National Bar Association.
**Career:** Partner since 1973.
**Personal:** Stanford University (JD, 1969); Princeton University (AB, 1966).

### MOYES, Jay
Moyes Storey, Phoenix
602 604 2141
*Recommended in Environment*

### NAGY, Tibor
Snell & Wilmer LLP, Tucson
520 882 1228
tnagy@swlaw.com
*Recommended in Employment*
**Practice Areas:** Primary area of practice in employment law representing employ-

ers in matters including wrongful discharge, employment discrimination, anti-competition covenants and employer trade secrets, wage and hour law, NLRB law, labor arbitration, drafting of employment contracts, employee handbooks, manuals and policies. Other areas of emphasis include workers' compensation and unemployment compensation proceedings.
**Prof. Memberships:** State Bar of Arizona, State Bar of Arizona Labor and Employment Law Section (Past Chairman), American Bar Association.
**Publications:** Arizona Employment Law Handbook, Editor and Writer. Arizona Labor Letter, Editorial Review Board (past member).
**Personal:** Born October 23, 1957. Married; two children. Foreign languages: Hungarian.

### NARDUCCI, Lucas
Bryan Cave LLP, Phoenix
602 364 7000
*Recommended in Environment*

### NIEMUTH, Nathan R
Ryley Carlock & Applewhite, Phoenix
602 440 4810
nniemuth@rcalaw.com
*Recommended in Employment*
**Practice Areas:** Labor and employment. Has extensive experience in National Labor Relations Board representation and unfair labor practice proceedings, collective bargaining negotiations, strikes and lockouts, grievance and arbitration cases, union avoidance strategy, equal employment opportunity matters, wage and hour issues, drug and alcohol testing, and related federal and state labor and employment issues.
**Prof. Memberships:** Admitted to practice in Arizona (1976) and Wisconsin (1976). Admitted to practice before US Supreme Court, US Court of Appeals for the Fifth Circuit, US Court of Appeals for the Ninth Circuit, and US District Court, District of Arizona. Member of American Bar Association, Labor and Employment Law Section and International Law Section; State Bar of Arizona, Employment and Labor Law Section and International Law Section; Outstanding Lawyers of America; The Best Lawyers in America; Industrial Relations Research Association; Arizona Industrial Relations Association.
**Career:** Joined Evans, Kitchel, & Jenckes, 1976; became Partner, 1982. Joined Ryley Carlock & Applewhite as a shareholder, 1989. Member, Ryley Carlock & Applewhite 401(k) Plan Trustee Committee.
**Publications:** 'Constitutional Law - Prejudgment Garnishment', Wisconsin Law Review.
**Personal:** Born 2 October 1951. JD (cum laude), University of Wisconsin, 1976; BA, University of Wisconsin, 1973.

### NORTHUP, Douglas C
Fennemore Craig, Phoenix
602 916 5362
dnorthup@fclaw.com
*Recommended in Litigation*
**Practice Areas:** Business and personal injury torts, complex commercial litigation.
**Prof. Memberships:** Arizona Association of Defense Counsel, Defense Research Institute, American Bar Association.
**Career:** Chair, Business and Personal Injury Torts Practice. Focuses on commercial, tort, personal injury, and professional liability litigation. Represents clients in complex commercial disputes. Handles complex product liability matters and has represented manufacturers of firearms, forklift equipment, pharmaceutical drugs, tires, and heavy mining equipment. Assists clients with avoiding and minimizing the risk of litigation through contractual indemnity clauses.
**Personal:** JD, Oklahoma City University, 1991; BA, New Mexico State University, 1984; Best Lawyers in America; Rated 'AV', Martindale-Hubbell.

### NOVAK, Edward F
Quarles & Brady Streich Lang LLP, Phoenix 602 229 5400
enovak@quarles.com
*Recommended in Litigation*
**Practice Areas:** White-collar criminal and governmental investigations.
**Prof. Memberships:** State Bar of Arizona (Board of Governors, 1999-present; Criminal Rules Committee, Chairman 1993-97; Criminal Justice Section, Chairman 1986-87); American Bar Association (Criminal Justice; Antitrust Law and Litigation Sections); Maricopa County Bar Association; National Association of Criminal Defense Lawyers; Arizona Attorneys for Criminal Justice.
**Career:** Partner since 1983.
**Publications:** 'Staying Out of the Headlines', AZ CPA, February 2004.
**Personal:** DePaul University (JD, 1976); Knox College, Illinois (BA, 1969).

### O'MALLEY, Kevin
Gallagher & Kennedy PA, Phoenix
602 530 8000
*Recommended in Litigation*

### OSBORN II, Jones
Osborn Maledon PA, Phoenix
602 640 9338
josborn@omlaw.com
*Recommended in Real Estate*
**Practice Areas:** Commercial real estate including transactions, leasing, secured transactions, financing and entitlements; entity formation and joint ventures; development; and general corporate and business law.
**Career:** Founding Partner and President, Osborn Maledon, P.A.; member, Phoenix Planning Commission, 1981-85; Chairman, City of Phoenix Peripheral Plan-

ning Committee, 1986-88; and member and past President of CoreNet Arizona (organization of corporate real estate executives).
**Publications:** Author of book, 'Arizona Real Estate Law'; and numerous articles in various business and legal publications.
**Personal:** Adjunct Professor, Commercial Real Estate Law, Arizona State University Law School; University of Arizona (JD, 1970); law clerk to Justice James Duke Cameron, Arizona Supreme Court (1970-71).

### PEARCE, John
Fennemore Craig, Phoenix
602 916 5376
jpearce@fclaw.com
*Recommended in Environment*
**Practice Areas:** Environmental; litigation; real eestate.
**Prof. Memberships:** Member, State Bar of Arizona, State Bar of Nevada, and State Bar of Washington. Past Chairperson, Environmental and Natural Resources Law Section, State Bar of Arizona.
**Career:** Practices in the areas of environmental and natural resources litigation, regulatory compliance, and regulatory interface, including waste facilities, Underground Storage Tanks, and pipelines, and actions under CERCLA, RCRA, toxic tort, indemnity, contribution, nuisance and trespass. Extensive experience in real estate transactions and litigation pertaining to convenience store/motor fuels facilities.
**Personal:** JD, University of Oregon, 1988; BA, Washington State University, 1985; Rated 'AV', Martindale-Hubbell.

### PETTI, Fred
Lewis and Roca, Phoenix
602 262 5311
*Recommended in Litigation*

### PETTIBONE, Jon E
Quarles & Brady Streich Lang LLP, Phoenix 602 230 5572
jpettibone@quarles.com
*Recommended in Employment*
**Practice Areas:** Labor and employment.
**Prof. Memberships:** State Bar of Arizona (Labor and Employment Section; Chair, 1980-83); American Bar Association (Labor and Employment Section, Individual Rights Committee); Fellow, Arizona Bar Foundation; Arizona Industrial Relations Association (Executive Board, 1990-94).
**Career:** Partner since 1982.
**Publications:** 'Bannering Neutrals - Coercive Secondary Boycott or Free Speech?', The Labor Lawyer, Winter/Spring 2003; 'Advising Private-Sector Clients', Arizona Attorney, May 2003.
**Personal:** Arizona State University (JD, 1976; BS, 1973).

**PHALEN, Michael**
Fennemore Craig, Phoenix
602 916 5415
mphalen@fclaw.com
*Recommended in Real Estate*
**Practice Areas:** Real estate; zoning; government lands.
**Prof. Memberships:** Member, Real Property Section, Executive Council, Treasurer, State Bar of Arizona; Member, State Bar of California; American Bar Association; Member, Urban Land Institute.
**Career:** Focuses on all aspects of land development, such as land use entitlements, zoning, and governmental relations, with a specialization in transactions that involve state and other government lands. Former Assistant Attorney General, Land and Natural Resources Section, Arizona Attorney General's Office (1988-94) and Former Planning Director, Arizona State Land Department (1994-99).
**Personal:** JD, University of the Pacific, McGeorge School of Law, 1984; BA, University of Arizona, 1980.

**PICCARRETA, Michael**
Piccarreta & Davis PC, Tucson
520 622 6900
*Recommended in Litigation*

**PIDGEON, Steven**
Snell & Wilmer LLP, Phoenix
602 382 6252
spidgeon@swlaw.com
*Recommended in Corporate/M&A*
**Practice Areas:** Practice concentrated on securities offerings, mergers and acquisitions, and venture capital investments involving clients in a wide variety of industries including technology, financial services, healthcare, manufacturing, transportation, homebuilding and consumer goods, as well as the representation of underwriters, venture capital firms and other financial intermediaries in their underwriting, investment and advisory activities.
**Prof. Memberships:** Best Lawyers in America; Who's Who in American Law; National Registry of Who's Who; State Bar of Arizona; American Bar Association; Maricopa County Bar Association.

**PLACENTI, Frank**
Bryan Cave LLP, Phoenix
602 364 7000
*Recommended in Corporate/M&A*

**PLATT, Warren**
Snell & Wilmer LLP, Phoenix
602 382 6292
wplatt@swlaw.com
*Recommended in Litigation, Products Liability*
**Practice Areas:** Practice is concentrated in civil litigation matters with principal emphasis on defense of major product liability claims for manufacturers with interests in the United States and abroad; complex commercial litigation; and

defense of accounting malpractice litigation for national and regional public accounting firms.
**Prof. Memberships:** American Bar Association; State Bar of Arizona; State Bar of California; State Bar of Texas; American College of Trial Lawyers, Fellow; Phoenix Association of Defense Counsel, President (1984-85); Superior Court of Arizona Civil Rules Study Committee (1982-83); State Bar Civil Jury Instructions Committee (1984-85).

**POKORSKI, Jody**
Snell & Wilmer LLP, Phoenix
602 382 6399
jpokorski@swlaw.com
*Recommended in Real Estate*
**Practice Areas:** Practice primarily in the area of real estate transactions, finance and regulatory matters, including work relating to commercial purchase and sale transactions, real estate financing, master planned communities, subdivision matters and leasing.
**Prof. Memberships:** Memberships include the State Bar of Arizona; American Bar Association; Maricopa County Bar Association; Arizona Commercial Real Estate Women; Arizona Women Lawyers Association; Lambda Alpha; Urban Land Institute, full member.

**PORTER, Amy**
Lewis and Roca, Phoenix
602 262 5311
*Recommended in Environment*

**PROCTOR-MURPHY, Janice**
Fennemore Craig, Phoenix
602 916 5331
jpmurphy@fclaw.com
*Recommended in Employment*
**Practice Areas:** Appeals, labor and employment.
**Prof. Memberships:** American Bar Association, State Bar of Arizona.
**Career:** Practices in the areas of civil appeals and labor and employment law. Has been involved in numerous appellate matters covering a wide range of business related topics. Counsels and trains employers and their management personnel on EEO and compliance issues. Represents and defends exclusively employers in litigation and administrative proceedings involving discrimination, breach of contract, wrongful discharge, wage and hour issues, violations of restrictive covenants and unfair labor practices.
**Personal:** JD, University of Michigan, 1988; BA, University of Michigan, 1985; Rated 'AV', Martindale-Hubbell.

**RAUCH, David**
Snell & Wilmer LLP, Phoenix
602 382 6294
drauch@swlaw.com
*Recommended in Litigation*
**Practice Areas:** Practice concentrated in general commercial litigation, franchise

litigation, professional malpractice defense and media law.
**Prof. Memberships:** Arizona Liaison For Franchise Business Network; Sandra Day O'Connor Inn of Court American Bar Association, President, 2002-03; American Bar Association, Chairman, Young Lawyer Division Corporate Counsel Committee, 1997; State Bar of Arizona; Maricopa County Bar Association.

**REDDIN, Jane**
Lewis and Roca, Phoenix
602 262 5311
*Recommended in Employment*

**RICHARDSON, Joseph**
Bryan Cave LLP, Phoenix
602 364 7000
*Recommended in Corporate/M&A*

**ROBINSON, Robert P**
Fennemore Craig, Phoenix
602 916 5355
rrobinson@fclaw.com
*Recommended in Real Estate*
**Practice Areas:** Commercial and real estate finance; real estate; business law.
**Prof. Memberships:** Fellow, American College of Mortgage Attorneys; Past Chair, Business Law Section, State Bar of Arizona; Past Chair, Real Property Section, State Bar of Arizona.
**Career:** Practice focuses on new corporate, asset-based and real estate finance, as well as workouts of troubled loans and the acquisition, development and sale of real estate. Certified Public Accountant. Certified Real Estate Specialist.
**Personal:** JD, University of Arizona, 1966; MS, Arizona State University, 1963; Best Lawyers in America; Rated 'AV', Martindale-Hubbell.

**ROMAN, Terry**
Snell & Wilmer LLP, Phoenix
602 382 6293
troman@swlaw.com
*Recommended in Corporate/M&A*
**Practice Areas:** Experience in advising corporate clients in various business transactions, including healthcare and insurance regulatory issues (including captive insurance issues), securities offerings, mergers and acquisitions, and contract negotiations.
**Prof. Memberships:** Memberships include the State Bar of Arizona, Securities Council, Committee on Corporate, Banking and Business Law; the American Bar Association, Health Law Section; Maricopa County Bar Association; Arizona Women Lawyers Association; Arizona Health Lawyers Association; and Arizona Captive Insurance Association.

**ROSENBAUM, David**
Osborn Maledon PA, Phoenix
602 640 9345
drosenbaum@omlaw.com
*Recommended in Litigation*
**Practice Areas:** Complex commercial litigation in US federal and state courts.

He has represented public companies and their officers and directors in numerous securities fraud class actions and represented Fortune 50 companies in a wide range of complex commercial litigation. He has handled intellectual property litigation and large sales and use tax disputes.
**Prof. Memberships:** ABA; AZBA; DAZ; 9thCir; Former President, Federal Bar Association Phoenix Chapter; Fellow, American Bar Foundation; Charter Fellow, Vice President, Foundation of Federal Bar Association.
**Career:** Partner since 1990.
**Publications:** He lectures frequently on litigation topics.
**Personal:** Georgetown Law School (JD, 1983); University of Pennsylvania (BA 1979).

**ROSENFELD, Lawrence**
Greenberg Traurig LLP, Phoenix
602 445 8501
rosenfeldl@gtlaw.com
*Recommended in Employment*
**Practice Areas:** Labor and employment; litigation.
**Prof. Memberships:** Member and General Counsel, Maricopa County Bar Association.
**Career:** Listed, Marquis Who's Who in America, 2006; listed, Marquis Who's Who in the West, 2006; Listed, Chambers & Partners USA Guide, 2005-06; listed, Best Lawyers in America, 2003-06; listed, 'Who's Who in Law', The Phoenix Business Journal, 2006.
**Publications:** Co-author: 'When Mary Fires Joe: Defending Wrongful Termination Lawsuits', Arizona Journal, 1999 State Bar Convention Supplement, June 1999.
**Personal:** JD, Yale Law School, 1975; BA, magna cum laude, City University of New York at Queens College, 1972.

**RUSING, Michael**
Rusing & Lopez PLLC, Tucson
520 792 4800
*Recommended in Litigation*

**SACKS, Seymour**
Sacks Tierney PA, Scottsdale
480 425 2600
*Recommended in Real Estate*

**SCHUBART, Lawrence**
Stubbs & Schubart, Phoenix
520 623 5466
*Recommended in Real Estate*

**SELDEN, David**
Stinson Morrison Hecker LLP, Phoenix
602 212 8566
dselden@stinsonmoheck.com
*Recommended in Employment*
**Practice Areas:** Represents management in discrimination, wrongful discharge, employment contracts, workplace torts, OSHA, DOL, restrictive covenants, trade secrets, litigation, counseling, training, etc.

**Prof. Memberships:** Chairman, Arizona Chamber of Commerce Employment Committee, 1989-present; Board of Directors, Arizona Chamber and Phoenix Symphony; Management Labor and Employment Roundtable.
**Career:** Congressional aide, Washington, DC, 1971-1982. Author of and lobbied to enactment several landmark Arizona employment laws to reduce employment litigation.
**Publications:** Editor-in-Chief, 'Arizona and Federal Employment Law'; Board of Editors, 'Arizona Employment Law Handbook' and 'Arizona Labor Letter'.
**Personal:** JD, magna cum laude, Georgetown University, 1982; MA, 1976, BA, 1973, George Washington University.

### SHERK, Kenneth J
Fennemore Craig, Phoenix
602 916 5383
ksherk@fclaw.com
*Recommended in Litigation*
**Practice Areas:** Civil litigation.
**Prof. Memberships:** Past Member, Board of Directors, Arizona Bar Foundation; Fellow, American College of Trial Lawyers and American Academy of Appellate Lawyers; past President, State Bar of Arizona and Maricopa County Bar Association.
**Career:** Has extensive experience, including trial experience, in personal injury and business litigation as well as products liability, lawyer discipline, professional liability and insurance coverage matters. Recipient of the Walter E Craig Distinguished Service Award, Arizona Bar Foundation (1999).
**Personal:** JD, with distinction, George Washington University, 1961; BSC, University of Iowa, 1955; Best Lawyers in America; Rated 'AV', Martindale-Hubbell.

### SIMON, Marc
Snell & Wilmer LLP, Tucson
520 882 1233
msimon@swlaw.com
*Recommended in Real Estate*
**Practice Areas:** Areas of practice concentration include real estate, subdivision and development, title insurance, general commercial and corporate, and construction law and water law.
**Prof. Memberships:** American Bar Association (Business Law Section; Real Property, Probate and Trust Section); State Bar of Arizona, Member: Arizona Real Property Section, and Certified Specialist, real estate law, Arizona Board of Legal Specialization; Pima County Bar Association; Arizona Planning Association.

### SORENSON, Derek L
Quarles & Brady Streich Lang LLP, Phoenix 602 229 5320
derek.sorenson@quarles.com
*Recommended in Real Estate*
**Practice Areas:** Real estate; Privately Held Business Group.

**Prof. Memberships:** Member, Arizona State Bar Association; American Bar Association; Valley Partnership.
**Career:** Partner since 1992.
**Personal:** University of Minnesota (JD, 1985); Colgate University (BA, 1982).

### STEIN, Lee
Perkins Coie LLP, Phoenix
602 351 8000
*Recommended in Litigation*

### STOKES, Randall
Lewis and Roca, Phoenix
602 262 5311
*Recommended in Real Estate*

### STOLKIN, Ronald J
Fennemore Craig, Tucson
520 879 6801
rstolkin@fclaw.com
*Recommended in Employment*
**Practice Areas:** Labor and employment; litigation.
**Prof. Memberships:** Member and Past Chairman, Labor and Employment Section, State Bar of Arizona; Member, Labor and Employment Section, American Bar Association; Judge Pro Tem, Arizona Superior Court, Pima County; Member, Defense Research Institute.
**Career:** Co-Chair, Labor and Employment Practice. Counsels management on personnel practices, employee discipline and labor relations. Defends employers in litigation alleging employment discrimination, breach of contract, wrongful discharge and other employment-related torts. Practices in education law and complex commercial litigation.
**Personal:** JD, University of Arizona, 1970; BA, University of Arizona, 1967; Best Lawyers in America, 1983-2006; Rated 'AV', Martindale-Hubbell.

### STOREY, Lee
Moyes Storey, Phoenix
602 604 2141
*Recommended in Environment*

### STOREY, Lesa J
Greenberg Traurig LLP, Phoenix
602 445 8239
storeyl@gtlaw.com
*Recommended in Real Estate*
**Practice Areas:** Real estate.
**Prof. Memberships:** Member, Board of Governors, Banner Health Foundation; Member, Board of Governors, Safeway International LPGA Tournament; Member, Executive Women's Golf Association; Chair, The Heather Farr Golf Tournament; Member, Valley Partnership.
**Career:** Listed, Chambers & Partners USA Guide, 2005-06; listed, Best Lawyers in America, 2000 to present.
**Personal:** JD, cum laude, Arizona State University College of Law, 1986; BS, magna cum laude, Miami University, 1981.

### STRUNK, Sarah A
Fennemore Craig, Phoenix
602 916 5327
sstrunk@fclaw.com
*Recommended in Corporate/M&A*
**Practice Areas:** Securities; mergers and acquisitions; business law.
**Prof. Memberships:** Member, American Bar Association, State Bar of Arizona, State Bar of New York, State Bar of California, State Bar of Connecticut, and State Bar of Kansas; Member, Phoenix Committee on Foreign Relations; Member, Rocky Mountain Mineral Law Foundation.
**Career:** Member, firm management committee. Practice includes securities, complex corporate transactions, mergers and acquisitions, and general contracts, corporate law and governance. Experienced in derivative or commodities hedging agreements.
**Personal:** LLM, New York University, 1987; JD, University of Kansas School of Law, 1985; BA, Wichita State University, 1982; Rated 'AV', Martindale-Hubbell.

### THOMAS, Christopher
Squire, Sanders & Dempsey LLP, Phoenix 602 528 4044
cthomas@ssd.com
*Recommended in Environment*
**Practice Areas:** Partner in environmental litigation; represents corporate, industrial and municipal clients. Focuses on hazardous substances and waste, groundwater contamination, industrial compliance, environmental permitting for new and expanded facilities, the environmental aspects of real estate and corporate transactions and covering the major federal environmental statutes.
**Prof. Memberships:** American Bar Association, Litigation and Environment, Energy and Resources Sections; State Bar of Arizona, Environmental and Natural Resources Law Section; Arizona Governor's Regulatory Review Council, member; Arizona Supreme Court, disciplinary hearing officer; and on the boards of The Nature Conservancy, Arizona Chapter, and the Upward Foundation School for special needs children.

### THORPE, William L
Fennemore Craig, Phoenix
602 916 5350
wthorpe@fclaw.com
*Recommended in Litigation*
**Practice Areas:** Business and personal injury torts; product liability; litigation.
**Prof. Memberships:** Member, Executive Committee, National Association of Railroad Trial Counsel.
**Career:** Chair, litigation section. Has extensive personal injury and product liability experience representing railroads, interstate trucking companies, and manufacturers of rough terrain forklifts, aerial work platforms, tires, earth-moving equipment, automobiles, child restraint

seats and consumer products. Has extensive commercial litigation experience, including the areas of securities, professional negligence, employment law and insurance bad faith.
**Personal:** JD, Boston College, 1978; BA, Stanford University; Best Lawyers in America; Rated 'AV', Martindale-Hubbell.

### VAN WINKLE, Kenneth
Lewis and Roca, Phoenix
602 262 5311
*Recommended in Real Estate*

### WALLWORK, Nicholas J
Steptoe & Johnson LLP, Phoenix
602 257 5202
nwallwork@steptoe.com
*Recommended in Environment*
**Practice Areas:** Partner, Phoenix office of Steptoe & Johnson LLP. Represents clients in environmental, mass tort and complex civil litigation. Co-Chair, ALI-ABA Advanced Toxic Tort & Environmental Litigation (1995-); Past Liaison, ABA Standing Committee on Environmental Law; Member, International Association of Defense Counsel; Member, National Conference of Bar Presidents; past President, State Bar of Arizona; Member and Budget Committee Chair, Arizona State Superfund (WQARD) Advisory Board.
**Personal:** JD, University of Virginia School of Law, 1983; (Executive Editor, 'Virginia Journal of Natural Resources Law'); BA University of Utah, 1980.

### WEISS, Judith
Perkins Coie LLP, Phoenix
602 351 8000
*Recommended in Corporate/M&A*

### WEISS, Stephen
Karp, Heurlin & Weiss PC, Tucson
520 325 4200
*Recommended in Litigation*

### WILEY, Jay
Snell & Wilmer LLP, Phoenix
602 382 6261
jdwiley@swlaw.com
*Recommended in Real Estate*
**Practice Areas:** Practice areas focus on real estate and real estate finance, including the representation of buyers, sellers, investors, landlords and tenants. Representation of developers of multi-use projects and planned communities, office, retail, industrial and distribution centers and facilities, resort, recreational and hospitality projects and multi-family and single family housing projects in all phases of such development, including preparation of CC&Rs and condominium documents. Representation of contractors and architects; and representation of lenders in acquisition, development, construction, bridge and permanent loans.
**Prof. Memberships:** State Bar of Arizona; American Bar Association; Maricopa County Bar Association; Arizona Bar Foundation (Founding Fellow).

**WILLIAMS, Quinn**
Greenberg Traurig LLP, Phoenix
602 445 8343
williamsq@gtlaw.com
*Recommended in Corporate/M&A*
**Practice Areas:** Corporate and securities; franchising.
**Prof. Memberships:** Board Member, Governor's Council on Innovation and Technology; Board Member, Arizona Technology Council Executive Committee; Board Member, Scottsdale Chamber of Commerce; Founding Chair, Governor's Small Business Executive Council.
**Career:** Listed, Chambers & Partners USA Guide, 2005-06; Listed, The Best Lawyers in America, 1995-2006; The Business Journal's 'Best of the Bar Award' for Corporate Financing, 2005; Most Influential Business Leaders, Phoenix Business Journal, 2003.
**Publications:** Numerous articles and presentations on venture capital and financing entrepreneurial companies
**Personal:** JD, University of Arizona James E Rogers College of Law, 1975; BBA, University of Wisconsin, Madison.

**WILLIAMS JR, Lonnie**
Quarles & Brady Streich Lang LLP, Phoenix 602 229 5300
lwilliam@quarles.com
*Recommended in Employment, Litigation*
**Practice Areas:** Labor and employment; litigation; commercial transactions litigation; real estate, land use and condemnation litigation.
**Prof. Memberships:** National Conference of Bar Presidents (President); American College of Trial Lawyers (Fellow); National Bar Association (Member); American Bar Foundation (Fellow); Arizona Women Lawyers Association (Member); Maricopa County Bar Association (Past President); American Bar Association (Past Delegate).
**Career:** Partner since 1985.
**Personal:** Yale University (JD, 1979); University of Arizona (BS, 1976).

**WINKLER, Peter**
Mariscal, Weeks, McIntyre & Friedlander PA, Phoenix 602 285 5000
*Recommended in Real Estate*

**WINTERSCHEIDT, Rebecca**
Snell & Wilmer LLP, Phoenix
602 382 6343
bwinterscheidt@swlaw.com
*Recommended in Employment*
**Practice Areas:** Advises employers concerning all aspects of employment law, including discrimination, harassment, wrongful discharge, breach of contract, wage and hour disputes, disability accommodation issues, family and medical leave issues, etc.
**Prof. Memberships:** American Bar Association; State Bar of Arizona; American Immigration Lawyers Association; American Bar Association, Labor and Employment Law Sections, Member; Committee on Immigration Law; Arizona Women Lawyers Association; National Association of Women Business Owners, Phoenix Chapter (President 1998-99).

**WITHEY, Michael**
Withey Anderson & Morris PLC, Phoenix
602 230 0600
*Recommended in Real Estate*

**WOLF, G Van Velsor**
Snell & Wilmer LLP, Phoenix
602 382 6201
vwolf@swlaw.com
*Recommended in Environment*

**WRIGHT, Joyce**
Snell & Wilmer LLP, Phoenix
602 382 6000
www.swlaw.com
*Recommended in Real Estate*
**Practice Areas:** Certified real estate law specialist engaged in all areas of real estate practice including: master planned developments; resort and golf course developments; subdivisions; leases; options; restrictive covenants and easements; purchase, sale and development transactions involving undeveloped land, energy and telecommunication facilities, retail, office, industrial, residential and mixed-use projects, hotel properties, farm and ranch land; state and federal land; title examinations and insurance; real estate finance; joint venture and entity agreements; condemnation matters, nonprofit owners associations; and development agreements.
**Prof. Memberships:** State Bar of Arizona; American Bar Association; Maricopa County Bar Association; Arizona Women Lawyers Association.

# FENNEMORE CRAIG, P.C.

## THE FIRM

**Chairman, Management Committee:** Timothy J Berg
**Number of partners:** 102
**Number of other lawyers:** 60

**FIRM OVERVIEW:** Fennemore Craig is one of the largest and oldest law firms in the Southwest with over 160 attorneys. The firm recognizes that both complex challenges and straightforward legal issues require and deserve the best possible legal advice, provided as efficiently as possible. Fennemore Craig offers clients a full range of quality legal services in both litigation and commercial transactions.

## MAIN AREAS OF PRACTICE:

**Bankruptcy & Creditors' Rights:** This practice group represents secured creditors, unsecured creditors, financial institutions, bankruptcy committees, debtors, bankruptcy trustees and purchasers of financially distressed businesses.

**Business & Finance:** Firm attorneys have substantial experience in a variety of corporate, commercial and securities-related transactions, including public offerings, private placements, 1934 Act reporting, corporate reorganizations, mergers and acquisitions, venture capital financing, leveraged lease financing, leveraged buyouts, and syndications.

**Business & Personal Injury Torts:** Fennemore Craig represents litigants in personal injury and business tort actions ranging from individual negligence actions to complex multi-party litigation.

**Commercial Litigation:** Fennemore Craig represents business parties in commercial disputes in federal and state courts, including cases involving white collar crime, fraud, derivative claims, lender liability, securities, corporate control, contracts, consumer statutes, insurance coverage, the UCC and eminent domain.

**Estate Planning & Probate:** Fennemore Craig attorneys represent individuals, business owners, nonprofit organizations, charitable foundations, and trust companies in trust, estate, probate, guardianship/conservatorship, and taxation matters.

**Government Relations:** For more than a century, Fennemore Craig has been deeply involved in developing and defining local and state laws affecting many of the state's major industries.

**Intellectual Property:** Fennemore Craig counsels clients on intellectual property protection, including patent prosecution, transactions, and enforcement.

**Labor & Employment:** The firm defends management in virtually all aspects of the employment relationship and counsels employers on employment practices. This includes employment-related immigration issues, personnel policies and manuals, supervisor training, employee discipline, drug and alcohol testing and sexual harassment policies, and compliance with state and federal statutes and regulations. It also counsels clients on issues relating to unions, including collective bargaining, contract interpretation and administration.

**Natural Resources & Environmental:** This practice includes environmental, water, mining, timber, oil and gas, energy, Indian and public land law. The firm consults with and represents clients on all aspects of permitting, planning and compliance as well as in transactions and due diligence investigations.

**Real Estate:** The practice encompasses all aspects of real estate investment, from acquisition and finance, through development, leasing and sale. The firm represents developers of master-planned communities, condominiums, apartment complexes, hotels, resorts, clubs, office buildings, industrial parks, shopping centers, golf courses, and other residential and commercial projects.

**Tax:** The firm handles tax planning for individuals, partnerships, and corporations, and represents clients before the Internal Revenue Service and the courts. It also has a significant practice involving Arizona income taxation, and state and local excise and property taxation.

**Utilities:** Fennemore Craig represents several utilities in the telecommunications, water, sewer, and natural gas industries.

## HEAD OFFICE

### ARIZONA
3003 North Central Avenue, Suite 2600, **Phoenix**, AZ 85012-2913
**Tel:** 602 916 5000   **Fax:** 602 916 5999
**Website:** www.fennemorecraig.com

## BRANCH OFFICES

### ARIZONA
420 West Mariposa Road, Suite 200, **Nogales**, AZ 85621-1074
**Tel:** 520 761 4215   **Fax:** 520 761 3505

One South Church Avenue, Suite 1000 **Tucson**, AZ 85701-1627
**Tel:** 520 879 6800   **Fax:** 520 879 6899

### NEBRASKA
206 South 13th Street, Suite 1400, **Lincoln**, NE 68508-2019
**Tel:** 402 323 6200   **Fax:** 402 323 6210

## BRANCH OFFICE CONTACTS

| | |
|---|---|
| **Nogales, AZ** | Hector G Arana, Kimberly A Arana |
| **Tucson, AZ** | Richard T Coolidge |
| **Lincoln, NE** | Donald G Blankenau |

## CONTACTS

| | |
|---|---|
| **Bankruptcy & Creditors' Rights** | Cathy L Reece |
| **Business & Finance** | Karen C McConnell |
| **Business & Personal Injury Torts** | Douglas C Northup |
| **Commercial Litigation** | Andrew M Federhar |
| **Estate Planning & Probate** | Neil H Hiller |
| **Government Relations** | Michael Preston Green |
| **Intellectual Property** | Ray K Harris |
| **Labor & Employment** | Donald R Gilbert, Ronald J Stolkin |
| **Natural Resources & Environmental** | Robert J Kramer |
| **Real Estate** | Don J Miner |
| **Tax** | Paul J Mooney |
| **Utilities** | Norman D James |

**CLIENTS:** 7-Eleven Inc.; Allied Waste Industries, Inc.; America West Arena; Arizona-American Water Company; Arizona Cattlegrowers' Association; Arizona Sports & Tourism Authority; Avnet, Inc.; Banner Health Arizona; Blue Cross Blue Shield of Arizona; Bridgestone/Firestone, Inc.; The Burlington Northern and Santa Fe Railway Company; Catholic Healthcare West; Cendant Corporation; City of Glendale; ConocoPhillips Company; Crescent Real Estate Equities Limited Partnership; DMB Associates, Inc.; D.R. Horton-Continental Series; Eurofresh, Inc.; GIANT Industries, Inc.; The Goodyear Tire & Rubber Company; Harvard Investments; Hensley & Company; Home Builders Association of Central Arizona; Lennar Communities Development, Inc.; The Lyle Anderson Co., Inc.; Microchip Technology; National Association of Home Builders; Northern Trust Bank, N.A.; Nucor Corporation; Phelps Dodge Corporation; Phoenix Suns Limited Partnership; PSS World Medical; Qwest Corporation; Robson Communities; Robertson Aviation L.L.C.; Ryan Companies U.S., Inc.; Southern Arizona Home Builders Association; Southwest Airlines Co.; Standard Insurance Company; Standard Pacific; State of Florida; State of Nebraska; Sturm, Ruger & Co.; Summit Builders; SunAmerica Securities Inc.; Trammell Crow Company; United Auto Group Inc.; Wachovia Corporation; Wells Fargo Bank, N.A.; Wick Communications Co.; Wyndham International Inc.; Z Gallerie, Inc.

## FENNEMORE CRAIG
### A HISTORY TO LEVERAGE

# OSBORN MALEDON, P.A.

## THE FIRM

**Managing Partner:** Jones Osborn II

**Number of Members:** 27
**Number of other lawyers:** 19

**FIRM OVERVIEW:** A leading law firm based in Phoenix, Arizona, Osborn Maledon is recognized by its clients and peers for its smart and creative litigation, business and general counsel solutions to complex problems. The firm represents a wide range of clients from sophisticated international companies in major litigation to start-up enterprises requiring all manner of counsel in launching a new venture.

## MAIN AREAS OF PRACTICE:

**Administrative and Regulatory:** Osborn Maledon is at the forefront of administrative and regulatory work involving the telecommunications and cable industries and represents major clients in these areas before the Arizona Corporation Commission.

**Antitrust & Trade Regulation:** The firm provides comprehensive antitrust litigation and counseling services to its clients and has been heavily involved in a majority of the significant antitrust and trade regulation cases in Arizona and throughout the US.

**Bankruptcy:** The firm represents debtors, creditors, trustees, creditors' committees and purchasers of bankruptcy estate assets in commercial Chapter 11 bankruptcy reorganizations.

**Corporate:** Osborn Maledon's Corporate Practice serves clients ranging from venture capital-backed start-ups to publicly-held corporations. The firm has made a significant commitment to assist emerging ventures in the technology, life sciences and media industries in the Southwest and has extensive experience in the software and internet industries. The firm provides counsel and general counsel services in the areas of corporate governance, public and private equity financing, venture capital and angel financings, debt financing, mergers, acquisitions and strategic transactions, technology licensing, distribution and transactions, compliance with state and federal securities laws, public and private securities offerings, equity compensation and executive employment, compensation and severance agreements.

**Employment & Labor:** The firm defends employers and executives in litigation involving a wide variety of employment issues before administrative agencies such as the EEOC and in state and federal court. The firm has an extensive employment counseling practice focusing on preventative practices.

**Environmental:** The firm's environmental practice focuses on contamination issues in class action cases, regulatory agency proceedings, and CERCLA allocations. The firm handles investigations of historical site operations and defends against citizens' suits and litigates insurance coverage actions.

**Ethics and Professional Liability:** The firm's professional responsibility lawyers counsel clients in matters relating to complex ethics questions, Sarbanes-Oxley laws, and risk management. The firm defends lawyers and law firms and provides expert testimony in legal discipline and malpractice claims.

**Indian Law:** The firm represents Indian tribes in litigation, employment, business, and real estate and development matters. The firm's Indian law practice also involves assisting non-Indian clients in business dealings with Indian tribes

**Intellectual Property & Technology:** Osborn Maledon's Intellectual Property and Technology Practice assists clients in acquiring, exploiting and transferring proprietary assets and businesses, and in aggressively defending proprietary positions.

**Litigation & Appellate:** The firm represents clients throughout the country in complex and major litigation in class actions and multi-district matters in state and federal court and in regulatory agencies. Osborn Maledon's appellate services include pre-trial counsel on surviving appellate scrutiny, special action petitions and appeals in state and federal courts, including the United States Supreme Court. The firm has represented clients in numerous significant appeals.

## HEAD OFFICE

**ARIZONA**
2929 North Central Avenue, Suite 2100, **Phoenix**, AZ 85012-2794
**Tel:** 602 640 9000 **Fax:** 602 640 9050
**Email:** webmaster@omlaw.com
**Website:** www.omlaw.com

## CONTACTS

| | |
|---|---|
| **Administrative & Regulatory** | Joan Burke |
| **Antitrust & Trade Regulation** | William J Maledon |
| **Bankruptcy** | James E Cross |
| | Brenda K Martin |
| **Corporate & Mergers & Acquisitions** | Thomas H Curzon |
| | William M Hardin, Randall C Nelson |
| **Ethics & Professional Liability** | Mark I Harrison |
| **Environmental** | Diane M Johnsen |
| **Indian Law** | Thayne Lowe |
| **Intellectual Property & Technology** | Brent L Dunkelman |
| | Jonathan F Ariano |
| **Labor & Employment** | Scott W Rodgers |
| **Litigation & Appellate** | William J Maledon, Diane M Johnsen |
| | David B Rosenbaum, Thomas L Hudson |
| **Real Estate** | Jones Osborn II |
| **White Collar Criminal** | Larry A Hammond |

**Real Estate:** The firm's real estate lawyers provide extensive real estate services involving real estate transactions, development, financing, zoning and land use regulations, joint ventures, leasing, brokerage, taxation and public and Indian lands.

**White Collar Criminal:** Osborn Maledon represents corporations and individual officers, directors or employees in matters involving securities fraud, cybercrime, health care fraud, industrial accidents, environmental crimes and financial frauds in Federal and State criminal investigations, Grand Jury inquiries and in all manner of pre-trial, trial and appellate proceedings. The firm also handles complex criminal defense matters involving non-violent and violent crimes.

**INTERNATIONAL WORK:** Osborn Maledon represents a wide variety of international clients in litigation and transactions in the United States and maintains collaborative relationships with premier firms outside the Untied States to service the intermittent needs of the firm's clients.

**CLIENTS:** Altria Group, Inc.; American International Group; AT&T Communications, Inc.; AAA Arizona, Inc.; Arizona State University; Arizona Public Service Co.; The Boeing Co.; Colliers International; Cox Communications; DeRito Partners, Inc.; Grand Canyon Railroad, Inc.; Grayhawk Venture Partners; Heska Corporation; Honeywell International, Inc.; Hopi Indian Tribe; MCO Properties, Inc.; Microchip Technology, Inc.; Microsoft Corporation; myGeek.com, Inc.; NetPro Computing, Inc.; PGA Tour, Inc.; Philosophy, Inc.; Pinnacle West; Quality Care Solutions, Inc.; Salt River Maricopa Indian Community; Schaller Anderson, Inc.; SunCor Development; Wells Fargo Bank; WL Gore & Associates.

OSBORN MALEDON

A PROFESSIONAL ASSOCIATION
ATTORNEYS AT LAW

# RYLEY CARLOCK & APPLEWHITE

## THE FIRM

**Executive Committee Chairman:** Michael D Moberly

**Number of shareholders:** 42
**Number of other lawyers:** 29

**FIRM OVERVIEW:** Since being founded in Phoenix in 1948, the Ryley Carlock & Applewhite law firm has been a major player in the development of Arizona. In response to the expanding needs of its clients, the firm and its services have grown substantially. The firm now has more than 70 lawyers in Arizona and Colorado, serving clients throughout the West and beyond. The firm's Phoenix office represents all segments of the Arizona business community, and some of the firm's practices take its attorneys far beyond the Arizona border. The firm's Denver office, like the Phoenix office, is home to some of the most experienced natural resources and lending lawyers in the West. RC&A lawyers pride themselves on understanding clients' businesses and the business implications of legal advice. Many of the firm's lawyers have worked in-house for clients. All understand the importance of providing sound legal advice and the need to complement this advice with imagination, innovation, and creative solutions. The firm knows its clients' businesses and has helped them achieve their goals, taking them from an emerging company to listing the company on national stock exchanges. In today's environment, businesses expect their lawyers to solve problems and create value. This is where Ryley Carlock & Applewhite delivers, and that is why clients trust and rely on the firm.

## MAIN AREAS OF PRACTICE:

**Corporate:** Banks, corporations, municipalities, partnerships, and high wealth individuals turn to RC&A for advice on business planning, formation, financing, mergers, acquisitions, securities, bonds, estate planning, wills, taxation, and intellectual property matters. The firm also has an active practice in all aspects of public finance and municipal law.

**Creditors' Rights & Bankruptcy:** RC&A represents a wide array of creditors, creditors committees, and trustees in bankruptcy matters. Financial institutions regularly tap into the firm's broad experience in defaults, restructuring, liquidations and reorganizations.

**Environmental & Natural Resources:** The firm's Environmental and Natural Resources Practice is widely-known throughout the region. RC&A has extensive experience in all aspects of water law, and is involved in water rights litigation, transactions, legislation and rule-making efforts in Arizona, Colorado and throughout much of the Southwest. RC&A also provides services ranging from assistance with regulatory compliance and permitting issues associated with the handling and use of hazardous materials, water quality, hazardous and solid waste disposal, underground storage tanks and air quality to contamination cleanup, asbestos abatement and environmental real estate due diligence.

**Labor & Employment:** RC&A advises employers and management throughout the Southwest and nationally on a comprehensive range of labor and employment law issues. The firm also maintains an active immigration law practice.

**Litigation:** The firm's Litigation Practice is devoted primarily to complex commercial disputes and other matters involving business interests. The diverse backgrounds of the litigators result in a diversity of substantive expertise and industry knowledge. The bulk of RC&A's trial practice is in complex litigation, with an emphasis on intellectual property, business torts and complex business transactions. RC&A's litigators collectively have conducted more than 400 civil and criminal trials.

## HEAD OFFICE

**ARIZONA**
One North Central Avenue, Suite 1200, **Phoenix**, AZ 85004-4417
**Tel:** 602 258 7701  **Fax:** 602 257 9582
**Website:** www.rcalaw.com

## BRANCH OFFICES

**COLORADO**
1775 Sherman Street, 21st Floor, **Denver**, CO 80203
**Tel:** 303 863 7500  **Fax:** 303 595 3159

## CONTACTS

Corporate ...................................................Phillip P Guttilla
Creditors' Rights & Bankruptcy ...........................John J Fries
Environmental & Natural Resources ..............L William Staudenmaier
Labor & Employment ...............................Carolann E Cervetti
Litigation.................................................Rodolfo Parga
Real Estate & Lending ...............................Thomas W Rouse

**Real Estate & Lending:** RC&A is actively involved in the real estate industry, a key driver of Arizona's economy. The firm provides comprehensive legal services in all aspects of real estate development, ownership, construction and financing. RC&A is conversant with the numerous federal, state and local laws and regulations affecting real estate, including those relating to water, mineral and other property rights, commercial leases, land use controls, condemnation, duties and liabilities of landlords and real property owners, subdivisions and lot sales, business planning and ownership, entity structuring, federal, state and local taxation, environmental issues, construction law, and title insurance.

**CLIENTS:** The firm's clients include: Arizona Public Service, Bank of America, Banner Health Arizona, Del Webb Corporation, Knight Transportation, The Industrial Authority of the County of Maricopa, PETsMART, Phelps Dodge, Pinnacle West Capital, Pulte Homes, and U-Haul International.

ATTORNEYS
Ryley Carlock & Applewhite
A PROFESSIONAL ASSOCIATION

# SNELL & WILMER LLP

## THE FIRM

**Chairman:** John J Bouma

**Number of partners:** 189
**Number of other lawyers:** 226

**FIRM OVERVIEW:** Snell & Wilmer has grown to become one of the largest full-service law firms in the Western United States, with more than 400 attorneys in six offices located throughout the region. Since being established in 1938 the firm's diverse client base of *Fortune* 500 companies, publicly-held companies, small businesses, emerging organizations, and entrepreneurs has grown to more than 10,000 businesses and individuals. Over the years, Snell & Wilmer has earned a reputation for providing clients what they value - exceptional legal skills, quick response and practical solutions with the highest level of professional integrity. Snell & Wilmer is most renowned nationally for its extensive experience in product liability litigation concentrated in the automotive and marine industries, as well as its business litigation, intellectual property and employee benefits practice groups. The long-standing relationships that the firm has established with its clients can be attributed to their practice of providing customized legal strategies to achieve their goals, through cost-effective and practical solutions.

The firm's industry teams offer businesses legal insight into issues that are typically faced by a particular industry. The firm's attorneys focus their efforts in a wide variety of industries, staying abreast of developments in the law and pending legislation, as well as economic trends through industry association memberships and conference presentations. These industry teams include real estate, retail and franchising services, bioscience, heathcare, pharmaceutical and medical device, construction, transportation, public utilities and hospitality.

Snell & Wilmer has been recognized for its legal skills and ethical business practices with various distinguished awards, including having the most attorneys of any Arizona law firm listed in The Best Lawyers in America (Woodward/White, Inc., of Aiken, S.C.); being named a winner of the 2003 Better Business Bureau's Business Ethics Awards; and named the best law firm in Phoenix and Salt Lake City to do business with by Corporate Board Member magazine. The firm's attorneys have been recognized as SuperLawyers in both California and Colorado, and the firm was recently named The Best Place to Work in California for mid-level associates by The American Lawyer magazine. The firm is a co-founder and member of LEX MUNDI, a leading association of independent law firms. Through LEX MUNDI and other international contacts, Snell & Wilmer clients have access to attorneys and law firms practicing throughout the World network.

**MAIN AREAS OF PRACTICE:** General practice, including trials and appeals before state and federal courts. As well as administrative law, alternative dispute resolution, airport, antitrust, appellate, banking, bankruptcy insolvency and business reorganization, biotechnology, commercial finance, commercial litigation, construction, corporate finance, corporate and securities, copyrights, emerging business, employee benefits and executive compensation, employee relations, environmental and natural resources, ERISA, estate planning and probate, financial institutions, financial services, franchising and licensing, gaming, government contracts, immigration, investment, insurance company regulation, insurance defense litigation, intellectual property and technology, international law, labor, legislation and government affairs, media, mergers and acquisitions, municipal finance, natural resources, partnerships, patents, probates and trusts, product liability litigation, professional liability litigation, real estate, securities regulation, taxation, telecommunications, water law, venture capital and zoning and land use.

## US OFFICES

### ARIZONA
400 East Van Buren, One Arizona Center, **Phoenix**, AZ 85004-2202
**Tel:** 602 382 6000  **Fax::** 602 382 6070

One South Church Avenue, Suite 1500, **Tucson**, AZ 85701-1630
**Tel:** 520 882 1200  **Fax::** 520 884 1294

### CALIFORNIA
600 Anton Blvd. Suite 1400, **Costa Mesa**, CA 92626-7689
**Tel:** 714 427 7000  **Fax::** 714 427 7799

### COLORADO
1200 Seventeenth Street, Suite 1900, **Denver**, CO 80202-5854
**Tel:** 303 634 2000  **Fax::** 303 634 2020

### NEVADA
3800 Howard Hughes Parkway, Suite 1000, **Las Vegas,** NV 89109-0925.
**Tel:** 702 784 5200  **Fax::** 702 784 5252

### UTAH
15 West South Temple, Suite 1200, **Salt Lake City**, UT 84101-1531
**Tel:** 801 257 1900  **Fax::** 801 257 1800

**CLIENTS:** Allergan; Arizona Public Service Co.; Bank of America; Chase; CIGNA Healthcare, Inc.; Cold Stone Creamery; Del Webb/Pulte Corp.; Emerson Electric Company; Ford Motor Co.; Honeywell, Inc.; Mayo Clinic; Mutual Insurance Company of Arizona; Perini Building Company; Pinnacle West; Scottsdale HealthCare; Sea Ray Boats; U-Haul International; Wells Fargo, N.A.

**INTERNATIONAL WORK:** For more than 30 years, Snell & Wilmer has been a leader in providing international legal services to businesses and individuals involved with transactions or investments in the United States and internationally. Over the years, the firm has represented clients in a wide variety of international legal matters. The firm's attorneys regularly work with clients to attract foreign capital to the Western United States and in facilitating and structuring investments and corporate transactions on behalf of international businesses and investors in foreign regions including Asia, Canada, Europe, and Latin America.

Snell & Wilmer
L.L.P.
LAW OFFICES
Character comes through.®

## How lawyers are ranked

Every year we carry out thousands of in-depth interviews with clients and lawyers in order to assess the reputations and expertise of business lawyers across the USA. Chambers rankings and editorial are referred to extensively by General Counsel and other purchasers of legal services who look to our recommendations when choosing their lawyers.

# CORPORATE/COMMERCIAL

### Corporate/Commercial
#### Leading Firms

1. FRIDAY, ELDREDGE & CLARK *Little Rock*
   MITCHELL, WILLIAMS, SELIG, GATES *Little Rock*
2. KUTAK ROCK LLP *Little Rock*
   ROSE LAW FIRM *Little Rock*
3. JACK, LYON & JONES, PC *Little Rock*
   WILLIAMS & ANDERSON PLC *Little Rock*
   WRIGHT, LINDSEY & JENNINGS *Little Rock*

#### Leading Individuals

1. BUFORD JR C Douglas *Mitchell, Williams, Seli*
   GREGORY H Watt *Kutak Rock LLP*
   SELIG John *Mitchell, Williams, Selig*
2. BENHAM III Paul *Friday, Eldredge & Clark*
   CLARK Ronald *Rose Law Firm*
   FLETCHER John *Kutak Rock LLP*
   GARDNER Price *Friday, Eldredge & Clark*
   JACK JR Donald *Jack, Lyon & Jones, PC*
   TISDALE John *Wright, Lindsey & Jennings LLP*

### Corporate/Commercial: Tax
#### Leading Individuals

##### Senior Statesman
EISEMAN Byron *Friday, Eldredge & Clark*

1. CLARK Ronald *Rose Law Firm*
   EBEL Walter *Friday, Eldredge & Clark*
   GRUNDFEST Jack *Mitchell, Williams, Selig*
   TISDALE John *Wright, Lindsey & Jennings LLP*

## Band 1

### Friday, Eldredge & Clark

**The Firm:** Held up as "*the standard of excellence in the state*," the Little Rock and Fayetteville firm's dominance of the Arkansas corporate market has been reinforced by increased activity in tax and a variety of corporate transactions, as well as more traditional M&A. In direct response to an economic shift in the state, driven by the boom in its northwest corner, the firm's clients are growing through corporate acquisitions and its practice has developed accordingly. Consistently hailed as "*sophisticated*," in the past year Friday Eldredge lawyers advised on the $500 million sale and acquisition of a healthcare company and represented a seller in the $250 million disposal of stocks in a publicly traded company. It undertakes bond work and other financing activity for Entergy, whose service area was affected by Hurricane Katrina in August 2005. Tax and municipal finance are noted as strengths.

**The Lawyers:** Paul Benham's "*fine reputation*" was apparent to researchers after speaking to peers and clients. They say his "*upfront and straightforward*" manner, coupled with expertise in corporate finance and municipal bonds, has enabled him to corner the market. **Price Gardner**'s practice focuses on M&A, real estate and healthcare matters. He acted in the recent $15 million sale of an insurance company to a publicly traded company. Now the firm's managing partner, "*senior statesman in tax*" **Byron Eiseman** is multitalented. He also litigates and is well known for commercial transactions, estate planning and probate. In the field of litigation he has represented Union Pacific and a number of insurance companies in various disputes, and recently won a case on behalf of a bank alleged to have distorted information about the value of a business it had acquired. Known for "*top-notch transactions work*," **Walter Ebel** is recognized as another "*strong tax guy*" with "*great negotiation skills*" and the ability "*to hold on to his clients.*"

**Clients/Work Highlights:** Entergy Arkansas; Union Pacific; Regions Bank; Stephens; ALLTEL and Acxiom.

### Mitchell, Williams, Selig, Gates Woodyard, PLLC

**The Firm:** Viewed by the market as an unmitigated success for this "*high-quality*" firm, the recruitment of Doug Buford and Walter May in 2004 set in motion a broadening and deepening of this substantial Little Rock and Rogers firm. Its corporate and commercial offering now spans banking, M&A, tax and securities. Clients are impressed with the firm's strength in numbers, saying: "*There are always enough attorneys to deal with the work we give the firm;*" furthermore, they are "*consistently capable.*" The team undertook work on the demutualization of an insurance company, the first of its kind in Arkansas, involving 15,000 shareholders in 27 different states. It acted on the takeover of nursing home owner and operator Beverley Enterprises, and participated in several bank acquisitions and stock offerings. On the tax side, clients describe the firm as "*professional, prompt and reasonably priced,*" and confirm that "*it exceeds all expectations.*"

**The Lawyers:** **Doug Buford** "*has increased the quality of the work coming out of the firm.*" Clients rate his ability to "*build up strong relationships,*" and report that he is "*extremely competent.*" In his role as general counsel for JB Hunt Transport, his work centers on Sarbanes-Oxley implementation and compliance, and he spends an increasing amount of time on shareholder initiatives as a result. Clients are also enthusiastic in their support for the "*wonderful and meticulous*" **John Selig**, who they say has an impressive ability to "*isolate and button down the issues and come up with a solution.*" A "*clear leader,*" Selig is a securities expert with "*great intelligence and an aptitude for communication with people at all levels.*" Tax advice is dispensed primarily by **Jack Grundfest**, who has "*work and a client list of New York standards.*" He is recognized as "*a wonderful and very personable manager,*" and his "*intelligence and professionalism*" are matched by his "*hard-working and thorough*" approach. Work in the past twelve months has included a number of multimillion-dollar transactions, some of which have been worth several hundred million dollars.

**Clients/Work Highlights:** JB Hunt Transport; First Electric Cooperative; American Management Corporation and Bank of the Ozarks.

## Band 2

### Kutak Rock LLP

**The Firm:** The only national firm operating from Little Rock is known as "*a strong player in the corporate field.*" Handling significant M&A transactions from inside and outside the state, for both public and private entities, its lawyers recently acted in the state's largest ever capital raise of $45 million for a startup bank. Another highlight involved a $6 billion transaction between ALLTEL and Western Wireless, with $3 billion registered in common stock. The firm is recognized for its "*ethical and accommodating*" approach to serving clients.

**The Lawyers:** "*Guru*" **Watt Gregory** was singled out by market observers for his "*wealth of knowledge and broad experience.*" Heading up a six-strong corporate team, his work over the past year included a high-profile, high-value transaction in which a private education company sold to a private equity buyer. According to peers: "*He does an excellent job.*" **John Fletcher**'s recent highlights include refinancing a $1 billion credit facility for Tyson Foods. The view of the market is that he is "*a good technician and a steady performer.*"

**Clients/Work Highlights:** Bank of the Ozarks; ALLTEL; Acxiom; Insight America; Dillard's; Tyson Foods; Wal-Mart; Beverley Enterprises; Back Yard Burgers; Stephens; Arkansas Bio Ventures and ContourMed.

## Rose Law Firm

**The Firm:** Having consolidated its practice over the past few years, Hillary Clinton's erstwhile firm has impressed the market and risen in *Chambers*' tables. Recent corporate activity includes stock purchases, reviews and dispositions. Clients are reassured by the firm's reputation for "*top-quality expertise.*"

**The Lawyers:** Commentators label **Ron Clark** an "*outstanding tax and corporate lawyer.*" His work is deemed to be "*New York or DC standard,*" but with "*lower fees and shorter turnaround time.*" Recent transactions include the disposal of an oil and gas company, negotiating for the acquisition of a pet store chain, and representing a Hot Springs-based client acquiring a Mexico-based manufacturing company. Clients appreciate that he is "*detail-focused, efficient and honest,*" and always "*mindful of clients' interests.*"

**Clients/Work Highlights:** Clients include advertising agencies; pet distributors; investment banks and poultry suppliers.

## Band 3

### Jack, Lyon & Jones, PC

**The Firm:** A stalwart of the Arkansas corporate and M&A market, this "*well-known and well-respected*" firm secured an impressive client in the form of First Security Bancorp. It is advising this holding company on its statewide expansion, in addition to handling hospital finance work, securities and municipal finance on behalf of other clients. Despite the firm's relatively small size, peers are impressed by its diverse strengths.

**The Lawyers:** Heading up a seven-strong team, **Donald Jack** is "*extremely smart*" and noted for "*paying close attention to detail.*"

**Clients/Work Highlights:** Clients include private and publicly held companies in industries including insurance, banking and healthcare.

### Williams & Anderson PLC

See firm details p.213

**The Firm:** With an emphasis on financing and municipal bond work, the corporate practice at Williams & Anderson has close ties with its real estate operations. It represents borrowers and lenders in real estate transactions across the South, and recently acted in the acquisition of the largest office block in downtown Little Rock. It regularly undertakes work involving finance for ski resorts, golf clubs, shopping centers, churches and office buildings in many

southern states, and has the monopoly on infrastructure financing in addition to undertaking half of the state's water and sewage work.

**The Lawyers:** David Menz acted in the $23 million financing of North West Arkansas Community College, while Paul Hoover was the lead lawyer in the development and construction of the Little Rock Convention Center and Arkansas' Excelsior Hotel.

**Clients/Work Highlights:** Doyle Rogers; North West Arkansas Community College; Morgan Keegan and American Municipal Securities.

### Wright, Lindsey & Jennings LLP

See firm details p.214

**The Firm:** "*Multispecialty and high quality,*" this firm compensated for the departure of Doug Buford by buttressing its strengths in corporate matters through drawing on the expertise of others in the firm. It represented E Ritter Communications in the acquisition of a cable TV franchise, and First Arkansas BancShares in the acquisition of assets of a bank holding and operating company. It regularly handles M&A transactions in the $1-30 million bracket.

**The Lawyers:** "*Talented and sharp*" **John Tisdale** (see p.210) leads the practice and is a recognized force in both regular M&A work and tax-related issues. Noted by clients to be "*skilled and thorough in all areas of tax law,*" he is also viewed as "*not being afraid to raise difficult issues.*" He is supported by Sean Hatch, a loans and borrowing specialist.

**Clients/Work Highlights:** E Ritter Communications; West Tree Service; Terra Renewal Service and First Arkansas BancShares.

# EMPLOYMENT

## MAINLY DEFENDANT

| Employment: Mainly Defendant |
|---|
| **Leading Firms** |
| [1] **CROSS, GUNTER, WITHERSPOON** *Little Rock* |
| [2] **FRIDAY, ELDREDGE & CLARK** *Little Rock* |
| **KAPLAN, BREWER, MAXEY & HARALSON** *Little Rock* |
| **MITCHELL, WILLIAMS, SELIG, GATES** *Little Rock* |
| **WRIGHT, LINDSEY & JENNINGS LLP** *Little Rock* |
| [3] **GILKER AND JONES PA** *Mountainburg* |
| **QUATTLEBAUM, GROOMS, TULL** *Little Rock* |
| **RAMSAY, BRIDGFORTH, HARRELSON** *Pine Bluff* |
| **ROSE LAW FIRM** *Little Rock* |

## Band 1

### Cross, Gunter, Witherspoon & Galchus, PC

See firm details p.211

**The Firm:** With the largest number of lawyers in any firm in the state engaged purely in labor and employment defense work, it is unsurprising that testaments to this firm's expertise echo across the market. "*Highly professional, competent and efficient*" was the consen-

sus of clients; one peer commented: "*The perception is that if you work there you must be brilliant.*" Recent developments have seen the firm branch into immigration law insofar as it relates to employment, and develop training programs for clients and small businesses. The firm convinced the Governor of Arkansas to sign an executive order that requires individual contractors to sign a project labor agreement with the union. This is the first of its kind in the USA and may be used as a model for other states.

**The Lawyers:** "*Rainmaker*" **Carolyn Witherspoon** focuses much of her practice on public entities. Recent work saw her involved in the representation of the Islamic Center of Little Rock which fired its imam for allegedly acting outside the Islamic faith under the First Amendment freedom of religion laws. The imam is attempting to sue the center's executive committee and the case is on appeal at the Arkansas Supreme Court. Witherspoon also worked on employment disputes at a large nonprofit organization concerned with hunger in Africa. The market's perception is that "*she is exceptionally intelligent and experienced,*" making her "*one of the best lawyers in Arkansas.*" **Russell Gunter** is best known

for labor and NLRB work, a domain in which his authority is undisputed. His "*levelheadedness and knowledge are unsurpassed.*" Clients appreciate **Bruce Cross**' "*diligence and willingness to keep everyone informed.*" He has a reputation for being "*unafraid and efficient,*" and having the ability to "*take control, like he's preparing you for war.*" Cross was responsible for the signing of the executive order by the Governor of Arkansas, and his practice has seen an increase in pre-labor matters and contract negotiations that put the firm's "*proactive and preventative*" approach to the test. **Donna Galchus**' specialty in the immigration arena has continued to develop over the past year, while race, sex and age discrimination cases have also generated a substantial volume of work. One significant case involved her representing the City of Fayetteville in a wage and hour matter brought by its firefighters. The case raised issues on compensation for Fayetteville employers. Based in the firm's Fort Smith office, **Benjamin Shipley** works in all areas of labor and employment law.

**Clients/Work Highlights:** North Little Rock Police Department; Nabholz Construction; Heifer International; ABC of Arkansas; Mountain Mechanical

Contractors; Regions Bank; Whirlpool; ALLTEL; Arkansas Pizza Group and Ace Glass.

## Band 2

### Friday, Eldredge & Clark

**The Firm:** The eight-strong labor and employment team at the state's largest firm provides a full service to its impressive public and private sector client base. Over the past year, it defended clients involved in ADA and FMLA litigation at federal level, with EEOC and NLRB investigation work also undertaken. It advises the HR departments of many Arkansas employers, and with the largest employee benefits practice in the state, it represents more than 900 retirement plans, including all the employers, fiduciaries, service providers and investment managers involved in the process.

**The Lawyers:** **Michael Moore** specializes in discrimination cases, and recently won a pivotal race discrimination jury trial. Known for being "*a great trial lawyer without being too aggressive,*" his reputation is also tied to his "*great experience and knowledge.*" Working across multiple states, "*expert*" **Oscar Davis** focuses on OSHA and labor matters. In 1972, he became the first lawyer in the USA to try an OSHA case and is therefore regarded as an authority on the subject. In addition to regular employment litigation work, **Daniel Herrington** undertakes trade secrets litigation and recently defended a breach of covenant noncompete case. Clients warm to his

"*effective and direct*" style, which in turn helps "*juries respond well to him.*" Although Herrington undertakes some employee benefits work, the only attorney at the firm whose practice focuses purely on it is **Wyckliff Nisbet**. Heading up a ten-strong team, he is "*fluent in all aspects of employee benefits work,*" having begun his career 32 years ago, on the day after ERISA was enacted in Washington, DC.

**Clients/Work Highlights:** The firm received summary judgment in the Eighth Circuit Court of Appeals in a discrimination case involving a local television station. Additional clients include St. Paul Travelers; Entergy Arkansas; Union Pacific; ConAgra Foods; Liberty Mutual; Federated Rural Electric Insurance; Rebsamen Medical Center and Acxiom.

### Kaplan, Brewer, Maxey & Haralson

**The Firm:** Having formerly been exclusively an employee adviser, in a somewhat unusual move the firm has diversified such that employers are also catered for. This broadening of its practice has impressed not only clients but also peers. They view Kaplan Brewer as "*a small but excellent firm with some high-profile cases.*" Recent highlights include the representation of a national brokerage firm, A G Edwards & Sons, in an age discrimination case, and a lengthy race discrimination trial involving the termination of a basketball coach's contract.

**The Lawyers:** "*A very special guy,*" **Phil Kaplan** is described in a variety of superlative terms. "*Extremely classy*" in his approach, he is seen as "*probably the best labor lawyer in the whole of Arkansas.*" Rivals credited him with "*a tremendous command of the English language, enabling him to communicate with people at all levels without intimidating them;*" clients appreciated his "*incredible intelligence.*" Handling work of a similar nature and providing backup to Kaplan, **JoAnn Maxey** is also rated highly. "*Very capable in her own right,*" her expertise straddles all aspects of employment law.

**Clients/Work Highlights:** A G Edwards & Sons; Arkansas Oklahoma Gas; Cingular Wireless; University of Arkansas; Wal-Mart; Stephens; Green Bay Packaging and Carlton-Bates.

### Mitchell, Williams, Selig, Gates Woodyard, PLLC

**The Firm:** Boosted by the arrival of Kathlyn Graves in 2004, this "*excellent*" employment practice is becoming increasingly active in an array of discrimination cases. It recently defended a pregnancy-related discrimination case heard before a state court jury. It was also successful in representing a company and its new employee concerning a temporary restraining order regarding information protected by the Arkansas Trade Secrets Act.

**The Lawyers:** With a background in employment litigation and labor advice, "*first-rate attorney*" **Kathlyn Graves** has made a considerable impact on the practice. She is highly respected by the market, which views her as having "*the kind of experience that really counts.*" **Byron Freeland** drew positive comments; he is "*a top-notch individual*" with "*a wonderful ability to deal with any type of person.*" A

new addition to the tables, **Leigh-Anne Shults** "*really knows how to try a case.*" She is team leader of both the labor and employment practice and the ERISA and employee benefits practice.

**Clients/Work Highlights:** Baptist Health; Southwestern Bell; First Electric Cooperative and MetLife.

### Wright, Lindsey & Jennings LLP
See firm details p.214

**The Firm:** With a ten-strong team working on labor and employment cases, this "*superior*" practice has weathered the departure of Kathlyn Graves. Clients believe the firm has "*exceptionally broad and deep*" legal expertise, coupled with "*a high degree of visibility across the state.*" In the alternative dispute resolution field, many of its attorneys are recognized as arbitrators and mediators; in employment litigation, they have seen a rise in the number of discrimination and trade secrets cases being filed. The firm has also expanded its capability with regard to ERISA, union organization and more traditional labor law matters.

**The Lawyers:** Labor law specialist **John Davis** (see p.208) represents employers in negotiations with unions. A substantial portion of his work takes him out of state and he has, over the course of his 25-year career, built up a reputation as "*a very ethical and knowledgeable lawyer.*" Recent work includes advising a client on union issues prior to setting up an operation in Australia. Employment litigator **John Lile** (see p.209) recently defended a bank in a trial concerning gender, ADA and age claims while **Stuart Jackson** (see p.209) acted in a noncompete trial and an arbitration relating to the termination of an employee's contract. Clients appreciate his "*wonderful listening skills*" and his "*willingness to make himself available.*"

**Clients/Work Highlights:** Central Arkansas Water; St Joseph's Mercy Health Center; IC Corporation; The Price Companies; QualChoice and Youth Home.

## Band 3

### Gilker and Jones PA

**The Firm:** Located in the boom area of Northwest Arkansas, this boutique firm is experiencing an increase in demand for its services. Undertaking both defendant and plaintiff work, this "*truly excellent*" firm regularly tries discrimination and labor cases in the federal and state courts, and boasts an impressive array of high-profile clients. Regular work such as wage and hour, and Title VII cases are undertaken in addition to more complex litigation. Sources note that the firm has "*healthy relationships with the unions and expertise in all employment matters.*"

**The Lawyers:** A four-strong team is led by **Michael Jones**, who market commentators are confident "*can turn his hand to anything – and does.*"

**Clients/Work Highlights:** Tyson Foods; Southwestern Energy; Rheem Manufacturing; Razorback Foundation and University of Arkansas.

## Quattlebaum, Grooms, Tull & Burrow PLLC

See firm details p.212

**The Firm:** This firm handles wrongful termination claims; allegations of age, race, sex and disability discrimination; claims of retaliation; hostile workplace allegations; covenants not to compete; confidentiality issues and contract negotiations.

**The Lawyers:** Chip Chiles is the contact partner for employment work.

**Clients/Work Highlights:** Clients include America's Car-Mart, AT&T Wireless and Concurrent Computer.

## Ramsay, Bridgforth, Harrelson & Starling LLP

**The Firm:** This Pine Bluff-based firm stands out thanks to its "well-connected and capable" lawyers. With a focus on pure labor relations work, both in and out of state, it represents companies involved with unions and has noted an upturn in union orga-

nization. Lawyers also undertake employment litigation and recently represented an individual fired by his employer after allegations of sexual harassment. The jury found in favor of the employee. Clients say the firm is "knowledgeable and pleasant to deal with."

**The Lawyers:** Attracting praise from commentators in all corners of the market, "seasoned lawyer" **Spencer Robinson** "can get to the essence of a case." With a traditional labor and litigation practice, he is viewed as "a true expert in his field," and one who is "always honest and forthright." In court, he comes across as "smooth and well prepared."

**Clients/Work Highlights:** Washington International Group; Levi Strauss; Riceland Foods and Simmons First National.

## Rose Law Firm

**The Firm:** The firm defends corporate clients in state and federal court litigation involving claims under Title VII of the Civil Rights Act, ADA, OSHA and FMLA. Recently it represented L'Oréal in a race

discrimination and retaliation claim, in which the plaintiff's claims were dismissed and summary judgment obtained. It also undertakes mediations and arbitrations, and has significant experience of advising clients on restrictive covenants and breaches of confidentiality agreements.

**The Lawyers:** "First-rate" **Tim Boe** has a "smooth, accurate" style; he earns peer endorsements for his "experience and competence," while clients appreciate that he can "arrive at conclusions quickly and is also quick to respond." Described as an "excellent attorney," **David Martin** has secured an impressive number of victories on behalf of his clients recently.

**Clients/Work Highlights:** Denver Roller; Pat Salmon & Sons; L'Oréal; JA Riggs Tractor and HealthSCOPE Benefits.

# LITIGATION

| | Litigation: General Commercial |
|---|---|
| | **Leading Firms** |
| 1 | FRIDAY, ELDREDGE & CLARK *Little Rock* |
| | QUATTLEBAUM, GROOMS, TULL *Little Rock* |
| | WILLIAMS & ANDERSON PLC *Little Rock* |
| | WRIGHT, LINDSEY & JENNINGS LLP *Little Rock* |
| 2 | EVERETT LAW FIRM *Fayetteville* |
| | KAPLAN, BREWER, MAXEY *Little Rock* |
| | MITCHELL, WILLIAMS, SELIG, GATES *Little Rock* |
| 3 | ALLEN LAW FIRM *Little Rock* |
| | ROSE LAW FIRM *Little Rock* |
| | SHEMIN & HENDREN, PLLC *Fayetteville* |
| | SHULTS LAW FIRM, LLP *Little Rock* |

## Band 1

### Friday, Eldredge & Clark

**The Firm:** This distinguished and well-established law firm is comprised of "fine, well-connected lawyers." Its litigation team is one of the largest in Arkansas, and is considered "the premier business litigation unit in the state." Recent highlights include acting for Capital One in a nationwide class action concerning its credit cards; representing an insurance company in a class action relating to the use of a computer program, and counseling Regions Bank in a 21-day arbitration in connection with its purchase of an insurance company.

**The Lawyers:** "Top-notch trial lawyer" **William Sutton** is now of counsel. His "towering reputation" has not been diminished by his retirement from the partnership in July 2005, and he still has a hand in important cases. "Experienced and conscientious" **Kevin Crass** combines the courtroom style of "a bulldog litigator" with that of "a real gentleman." He displays "careful judgment and quick thinking,"

recently representing Cargill in a case concerning its agricultural business in which plaintiffs claim they have sustained personal injury from the disposal of poultry litter, which they allege contains arsenic. Described as "extraordinarily bright and meticulous," **William Waddell** ascends *Chambers*' tables this year following praise for his "ability to think outside the box" and his "phenomenally thoughtful" manner. Clients confirm that "he strives to protect our interests at all times," while peers comment: "He is truly a pleasure to work with and as decent a human being as you could hope to find." Waddell has been involved in several class actions, defending entities such as farm bureaux, insurers and the Lenders Title Company. In medical malpractice defense, **Laura Smith** is widely viewed as "the market leader." She recently defended a gastrointestinal clinic in a case that attained summary judgment at the Supreme Court at appellate level. The case turned on whether the clinic had a duty to warn a patient against driving after a procedure.

**Clients/Work Highlights:** Lawyers represented Tyson Foods in a case brought by hog producers who alleged that Tyson had committed fraud when it decided to terminate its pork division in Southwest Arkansas. Other clients include Capital One Bank; Regions Bank; Southern Farm Bureau Casualty Insurance; Cargill; Acxiom and Lenders Title Company.

## Quattlebaum, Grooms, Tull & Burrow PLLC

See firm details p.212

**The Firm:** In spite of its comparative youth, this firm is a favorite in Arkansas. A "well-orchestrated and talented" unit, the 18-strong litigation practice is "on a par with big city firms in terms of quality," and clients enthuse over its "top-notch people." Working

across the full range of business litigation, toxic torts, environmental and employment cases, Quattlebaum has secured recent victories for a client base that includes several Fortune 200 companies.

**The Lawyers:** "Honest and ethical" **Steven Quattlebaum** (see p.210) retains his spot at the top of the tables largely due to clients' admiration of his "sharp and articulate" style. He is said to come into his own in front of a jury and is viewed as "a good conceptualizer" who can "think on his feet." Quattlebaum recently represented a real estate developer in a land contamination action, and also acted on behalf of a family in the successful defense of a fraud and breach of contract case that arose from the sale of a steel fabrication company. "Excellent litigator" **John Tull** (see p.210) has "an unfussy, down-home style" that affords him strong relationships with judges and juries. **Chip Chiles** (see p.208) rises in the tables this year in response to growing recognition of his "practical and thorough" approach to cases. Clients value his corporate law expertise, and say he is a "great lawyer who is always accessible and well prepared." Working alongside Quattlebaum, he represents AstraZeneca in the defense of a putative class action. Alone, he has been working on the defense of a disability discrimination claim. Described as "smart and pleasant," **Kris Baker** (see p.208) is a newcomer to *Chambers*' tables this year. She has a "very accommodating" nature, which she successfully combines with a "tough-as-nails" manner.

**Clients/Work Highlights:** Recent cases include the successful dismissal of an alleged race discrimination claim against a client, acting for AT&T Wireless in a deceptive trade practices case, and defending a well-known retailer in a wrongful death action. Other clients include Schering-Plough, AstraZeneca and Cingular Wireless.

## Litigation: General Commercial
### Leading Individuals

**Senior Statesmen**

ANDERSON Philip *Williams & Anderson PLC*
SUTTON William *Friday, Eldredge & Clark*

**1** EVERETT John *Everett Law Firm*
KAPLAN Philip *Kaplan, Brewer, Maxey & Haralson*
QUATTLEBAUM Steven *Quattlebaum, Grooms, Tull*
RATHER JR Gordon *Wright, Lindsey & Jennings LLP*
SHEMIN Kenneth *Shemin & Hendren, PLLC*

**2** CRASS Kevin *Friday, Eldredge & Clark*
LOWTHER JR Edwin *Wright, Lindsey & Jennings LLP*
WADDELL JR William *Friday, Eldredge & Clark*

**3** ALLEN William *Allen Law Firm*
KUMPE Peter *Williams & Anderson PLC*
LILE John *Wright, Lindsey & Jennings LLP*
TULL III John *Quattlebaum, Grooms, Tull & Burrow*

**4** ASKEW III Jess *Williams & Anderson PLC*
CHILES IV EB *Quattlebaum, Grooms, Tull*
COULTER Nate *Wilson, Engstrom, Corum & Coulter*
DEERE Beth *Williams & Anderson PLC*
DONOVAN Richard *Rose Law Firm*
HENDREN Jennifer *Shemin & Hendren, PLLC*
POWELL David *Williams & Anderson PLC*
SHULTS Steven *Shults Law Firm, LLP*

**Up-and-coming individuals**

BAKER Kristine *Quattlebaum, Grooms, Tull & Burrow*
VINES J Andrew *Wright, Lindsey & Jennings LLP*

## Litigation: Environmental
### Leading Individuals

**1** GATES Allan *Mitchell, Williams, Selig*
NESTRUD Charles *Chisenhall, Nestrud & Julian*
PERKINS G Alan *Perkins & Trotter PLLC*

## Litigation: Medical Malpractice Defense
### Leading Individuals

**1** BEARD III RT *Mitchell, Williams, Selig*
SMITH Laura *Friday, Eldredge & Clark*

## Williams & Anderson PLC
See firm details p.213

**The Firm:** Replete with *"fine and capable"* lawyers, this ten-strong business litigation team is active in high-value statewide cases. It recently engineered a multimillion-dollar settlement between the City of Fort Smith and the South Sebastian County Water Users Association achieved via a state court action, a federal court action and an administrative action. As defense counsel for a nursing home, the firm obtained a temporary stay of a $20 million interlocutory bond in a putative class action case from the Arkansas Supreme Court. Expertise in media law led it to the representation of Arkansas' state newspaper in an action to protect its copyright in unpublished photographs. Experienced litigators have *"a wealth of court expertise,"* but also *"do their utmost to help clients avoid litigation."* Clients say the firm *"does an outstanding job, and never takes shortcuts."*

**The Lawyers:** A former president of the ABA, *"formidable lawyer"* **Philip Anderson** (see p.208) is dubbed *"the epitome of the Southern gentleman."* His expertise is recognized across the state; peers say he is *"extremely intelligent and refined,"* while clients label him *"a paragon of availability."* As a reflection of his long and distinguished career, he ascends *Chambers'* tables this year to take up a spot in the coveted Senior Statesman category. **Peter Kumpe** (see p.209) is well versed in libel and antitrust law. This renowned appellate lawyer recently led several class actions and a state-based pricing litigation on behalf of an out-of-state company. Peers acknowledge he is *"bright and well prepared."* Construction law expert **David Powell** (see p.210) has been active in an increasing number of arbitrations and mediations of construction and commercial disputes. He is defending Simon Property Group in a trial concerning University Mall in Little Rock, and has built up a reputation as *"a great, careful litigator."* **Jess Askew** (see p.208) handles a broad range of commercial litigation for both plaintiff and defendant. Researchers were told of this *"astute and hard-working"* lawyer's ability to *"see things that aren't readily apparent in a case and get to the heart of a matter."* **Beth Deere** (see p.208) represents news and broadcast media in business litigation, recently defending a national broadcast news corporation in a defamation claim brought by the subject of a news story aired on national television.

**Clients/Work Highlights:** Arkansas Development Finance Authority; Arkansas Democrat Gazette; GE Capital; Metropolitan National Bank; MSF Financial Group; Potlatch; Roman Catholic Diocese of Little Rock; Scholastic; University of Arkansas and Wells Fargo Financial Leasing.

## Wright, Lindsey & Jennings LLP
See firm details p.214

**The Firm:** One of Arkansas' pedigree law firms, this outfit has a *"fine, long-standing tradition"* of maintaining *"the highest level of integrity and honor."* It is elevated to the top tier of the tables based on the volume and nature of positive feedback from market commentators. The firm counts more litigators under its roof than any other in the state, with 22 lawyers undertaking commercial, employment, bankruptcy, toxic torts, construction and products liability litigation. It has attracted a high-caliber clientele and represents Ford throughout the State of Arkansas.

**The Lawyers:** *"Simply one of the best lawyers in town,"* **Gordon Rather** (see p.210) ascends the tables on the strength of his ability to *"connect and communicate with jurors and win the respect of the judges."* Outside the courtroom, he is said to *"exude credibility"* and is *"a true gentleman."* Sources attest to his modest and ethical nature, saying he is *"very civil and humble despite his accomplishments."* Somewhat unusually for an attorney in a landlocked state, he is involved in admiralty and maritime law, and recently settled a case for Maersk. *"A terrific trial lawyer"* and the firm's managing partner, **Edwin Lowther** (see p.209) secured an important defense verdict for Ford

recently. Lowther is *"a consummate professional"* who is *"smart, skilled and can relate well to juries."* He recently branched into medical malpractice litigation. In addition to his renowned employment practice, *"extremely talented and experienced"* **John Lile**'s (see p.209) general litigation work is viewed with similarly high regard. A *"confident"* operator, he recently represented a firework manufacturer in a case relating to a factory explosion. Making his debut in *Chambers'* tables this year, **Andrew Vines** (see p.210) is tipped to become *"a great trial lawyer,"* according to market observers.

**Clients/Work Highlights:** Notable work includes contaminated land litigation on behalf of an El Dorado-based oil company. Also represented are Ford; Chubb Group; Maersk and Lion Oil.

## Band 2

### Everett Law Firm

**The Firm:** Everett Law Firm is a blossoming group of trial lawyers in the northwestern corner of the state. The headcount has grown over the past year with the addition of two new trial attorneys, taking the total to five. It handles commercial and criminal litigation and is also becoming increasingly active in alternative dispute resolution.

**The Lawyers:** *"One of the best all-around lawyers in Arkansas,"* **John Everett**'s éclat extends beyond the locale into the rest of the state, where peers recognize that he is *"very capable and courageous."* *"He's sharp, funny and has a wonderful reputation,"* they report. Meanwhile, clients are impressed by his *"high standards of integrity and honesty."*

**Clients/Work Highlights:** The firm acts for several big-name clients in addition to local companies and individuals. Recent casework includes a patent infringement action involving soybean seeds as well as a capital murder case.

### Kaplan, Brewer, Maxey & Haralson

**The Firm:** In addition to undertaking employment litigation, this firm is widely recognized for its general litigation capabilities. Although a small outfit, Kaplan has handled an impressive workload over the past year and is consistently viewed as *"one of the premier litigation firms in the state."* Recent highlights include a lengthy arbitration for the state's largest insurance broker and a successful trial on behalf of information management firm Experian. It also defended a law firm in two malpractice cases.

**The Lawyers:** *"Top of the ladder,"* **Phil Kaplan** is universally fêted for his *"gentlemanly yet tough"* courtroom manner and *"good-natured"* demeanor. Clients and peers rate him *"up there with any of the great litigators."* His recent work includes representing regional electric utility Entergy, and involvement in some significant employment cases.

**Clients/Work Highlights:** Sonnenschein, Nath & Rosenthal; Rebsamen Insurance; Dover Dixon Horne; General Properties; AG Edwards & Sons and BKD.

## Mitchell, Williams, Selig, Gates Woodyard, PLLC

**The Firm:** Environmental and personal injury litigation are the cynosure of this *"honest and fair"* practice, which is comprised of *"exceptionally talented individuals."* Lawyers also handle medical malpractice cases on behalf of a cadre of corporate clients.

**The Lawyers: Allan Gates'** name is synonymous in the market with *"authority and tenacity"* in environmental litigation and regulatory advice. Fellow partner **RT Beard** has a practice that focuses primarily on nursing home defense and medical malpractice. Valued for his *"effectiveness in front of a jury,"* he is considered by peers to be one of the state's *"standout practitioners"* in his field.

**Clients/Work Highlights:** Beverly Enterprises; CNA Insurance Companies; Medical Assurance; State Volunteer Mutual Insurance and United Insurance.

## Band 3

## Allen Law Firm

**The Firm:** Soon to be boosted to a four-attorney firm, by the arrival of an IP specialist, this multi-skilled boutique practice is renowned for a strength that belies its size. Covering a medley of complex corporate litigation matters, it successfully defended Wells Fargo in the Eighth Circuit Court of Appeal, and represented a land developer in a dispute with the property owners' association over an area of land. In an 11-state class action, it is acting as co-counsel with a Washington, DC firm in defending a pharmacy benefit management company against a regional accounting firm. Clients recognize that what the firm may lack in numbers, it makes up for in the quality of its service, saying: *"It makes sure it never takes on too much work so it can devote enough attention to existing clients."*

**The Lawyers:** *"Splendid"* **Bill Allen** has the marketwide profile of *"an intelligent, capable and honorable lawyer."* Clients admire him being *"plain-spoken and down to earth"* and having *"an excellent attitude to communication,"* emphasizing that he

*"writes one hell of a brief."* Peers celebrate him as an *"outstanding lawyer's lawyer."*

**Clients/Work Highlights:** Clients include Wells Fargo, Millennium Marketing Group and J Michael Sentell Living Trust.

## Rose Law Firm

**The Firm:** Raising its profile again following a tumultuous period in the wake of the Clintons' departure, this venerable firm is a permanent fixture on the Arkansas litigation landscape. It recently represented RentWay in a pending consumer class action and Fidelity National Insurance in a class action.

**The Lawyers:** *"Capable and effective"* **Richard Donovan** is rated by his peers as *"a smart guy and great lawyer."*

**Clients/Work Highlights:** The firm's clients include Griffin Chipping; Murphy Oil; Bank of the Ozarks and Acxiom.

## Shemin & Hendren, PLLC

**The Firm:** Making its debut in the tables this year on the back of marketwide recognition, this three-attorney boutique handles a spectrum of complex litigation matters for an impressive list of commercial clients. Its size does not preclude it from taking on larger cases as it *"fosters good relationships with other firms in the state,"* yet its attorneys avoid spreading themselves too thinly by *"knowing when to say no."* Complex commercial litigation and white-collar criminal work are handled alongside banking and securities work.

**The Lawyers:** An *"extraordinarily talented trial lawyer,"* **Kenneth Shemin** is hailed for his *"unique abilities to understand people,"* which enable him to *"engage well with judges and juries."* Clients were unreserved in their praise for Shemin, confirming that one of his many talents is the ability to *"take a vast array of confusing facts and sort them into an argument that is persuasive and effective."* They also value the fact he *"continually maintains his clients' interests over his own."* Shemin has an enviable courtroom style that combines *"empathy, courteousness and toughness."* **Jennifer Hendren** is gaining a name

as a *"detail-oriented, bright and diligent"* lawyer.

**Clients/Work Highlights:** The firm has worked on cases across the USA on behalf of clients such as JB Hunt Transport and USA Drug. Other clients include Moore Stephens Frost, Tyson Foods and Wal-Mart.

## Shults Law Firm, LLP

**The Firm:** Another addition to the rankings this year, Shults Law Firm is quite simply a *"nice boutique practice with some great clients."* It has gained visibility on the strength of the commercial cases it has taken on: over the past year these have included asbestos claims, insurance coverage litigation, and two real estate suits.

**The Lawyers:** Son of highly respected senior partner Robert Shults, the *"very thorough and precise"* **Steven Shults** has earned a reputation in his own right as an *"eminently capable"* practitioner.

**Clients/Work Highlights:** Abbott Laboratories; BASF; Fina Oil & Chemical; Utica Mutual Insurance and Winthrop Rockefeller Foundation.

## Other Notable Practitioners

*"Experienced and hard-working"* **Nate Coulter**, name partner of Little Rock-based Wilson, Engstrom, Corum & Coulter was rated *"an outstanding litigator"* by competitors. An environment litigation specialist, *"tenacious and dogged"* **Charles Nestrud** of Chisenhall, Nestrud & Julian, PA is also highly respected. Peers say he is *"a brilliant and effective lawyer,"* while clients appreciate his *"common-sense and skilled approach,"* adding that *"he cuts to the chase."* As one of only a handful of environment litigators in the state, his caseload includes property damage and contamination matters. Another environment specialist, **Alan Perkins** of Perkins & Trotter PLLC enjoys a reputation as *"an excellent litigator who does a good job for his clients."* He has been instrumental in the South Arkansas oil field damage litigation and has represented cities across this state, and in Tennessee, in cases relating to CAA and ozone non-attainment.

# REAL ESTATE

## Band 1

## Friday, Eldredge & Clark

**The Firm:** Since its formation, the firm's real estate practice has gone from strength to strength. Favorable conditions arising from continuing low interest rates have given rise to an explosion of work, especially in the sellers' market. Lawyers have advised on a diverse range of transactions, including several sales in the $5-10 million range, and some valued at $30-40 million. In addition to everyday real estate work, the practice handles debt and equity financing, partnerships, joint ventures and other investment vehicles. The firm is highly regarded for the level of its

expertise in securities and has acted in projects in which investors have pooled resources to take advantage of Section 1031 exchange rules. Clients recognize the depth of expertise here, flagging up the firm as *"one of the best in the state in its understanding of complex financial real estate transactions."*

**The Lawyers:** **James Saxton** is *"capable and experienced"* in real estate matters and has considerable tax expertise. Saxton recently worked with a major retail client, assisting it with an expansion program. Colleague **Jay Taylor** is *"very smart and reasonable,"* and clients appreciate *"his good grasp of bonds and financing, and his ability to understand the nuances of deals."* One source referred to his *"nonconventional* *approach to real estate;*" another described him as "*creative and understanding.*" Bringing corporate expertise to the table, **Price Gardner** enters the rankings to reflect increasing recognition of his activity on the development side. Peers view him as "*an excellent performer.*"

**Clients/Work Highlights:** The firm acts for a number of banks, retailers and developers.

## Mitchell, Williams, Selig, Gates Woodyard, PLLC

**The Firm:** With offices in Little Rock and Rogers, this "*small but excellent*" practice is rated as "*one of the best in Arkansas, if not the whole of the Southeast.*" At its core lie "*trustworthiness and impeccable ethical standards.*" Its real estate repertoire comprises financing, acquisitions, disposals, leasing and development in the public and private sectors. It represents every bank in central Arkansas and a considerable number of other lending institutions. Reflecting the demand for commercial properties in Northwest Arkansas, the firm also represents developers and purchasers of land. Clients attest to the firm's "*extreme depth in all areas*" and appreciate the fact that "*it takes care of everything, right down to the last detail.*"

**The Lawyers:** Less active in transactional work, but still "*an icon among Arkansas attorneys,*" **Maurice Mitchell** "*really has been there and done that.*" Other lawyers call him "*a prince of a guy and the epitome of a gentleman.*" **Christopher Barrier**'s "*scholarly, thoughtful*" approach is valued by clients because "*he can take on complex issues and make them work.*" According to peers, he is "*respected for his intellect and careful manner,*" which he combines with "*a dry wit and great attention to detail.*" Rising through *Chambers'* tables this year amid a flurry of plaudits, **Harry Hamlin** is viewed as "*one of the finest, nicest people you can imagine working with.*" Possessing "*a deep knowledge of real estate law,*" he is "*erudite and efficient*" and "*keeps his clients out of trouble.*" Heading up the real estate practice in the Rogers office is **Alan Lewis**, who was the subject of many positive comments in this year's research. Peers credit him with being "*easy to work with and extremely knowledgeable,*" and were impressed with his clientele. He represents real estate developers and lenders, working in commercial projects in Arkansas and neighboring states.

**Clients/Work Highlights:** Recent highlights include closing an $11 million real estate loan, and several other high-value financing packages. Bank of the Ozarks; Bailey Properties; Bank of America; BancorpSouth; MetLife and Arkansas Teacher Retirement System feature on the client list.

## Quattlebaum, Grooms, Tull & Burrow PLLC

See firm details p.212

**The Firm:** A seven-lawyer practice, expanding with the addition of an office in Northwest Arkansas, this "*high-quality*" unit covers the full range of real estate work and displays "*impressive depth of expertise in zoning.*" Lawyers have been engaged by several high-profile national retailers for development work, and in one important retail sector project it is representing the developers of what will become one of Arkansas' largest shopping malls. The team was also instrumental in changing state legislation, having been involved in amending the Arkansas Tax Increments Financing (TIF) that will benefit developers and municipalities across the state.

**The Lawyers:** **Tim Grooms** (see p.209) specializes in the financing of real estate transactions and is "*a top-notch attorney with considerable experience.*" Although he undertakes other types of real estate work, **Randy Frazier** (see p.209) is known first and foremost for his zoning and land use expertise. In this field, he is "*head and shoulders above anyone else.*" Frazier acts for major retailers and successfully represented a developer in connection with a referendum attempting to overturn a zoning decision made by a local city.

**Clients/Work Highlights:** The firm represents national retailers, lenders, developers and building associations within the State of Arkansas and in its surrounding regions.

## Wright, Lindsey & Jennings LLP

See firm details p.214

**The Firm:** This six-partner real estate practice is described as "*conscientious and client-oriented.*" Labeled "*one of the finest firms around,*" it represents national banks, lenders and insurance companies involved in real estate syndication, acquisitions and dispositions, while assisting developers with contract negotiations, zoning, land use approval and financing work. It also represents landlords and tenants in commercial lease negotiations and renegotiations. Its bankruptcy attorneys and commercial litigators deal with foreclosure and insolvency involving various types of properties. Clients appreciate that it "*does all it can to help you accomplish what you want without getting you into trouble.*"

**The Lawyers:** "*More than competent,*" **John Spivey** (see p.210) is highly regarded as "*the foremost expert in public finance.*" His connections are as valuable in clients' eyes as his "*detail-oriented, problem-solving approach.*" Other lawyers acknowledge his "*smooth yet low-key*" mastery of complex bond work.

**Clients/Work Highlights:** The firm recently helped Deltic Timber to obtain the public financing on the infrastructure for a major commercial shopping center in West Little Rock. Other clients include Cooper Realty Investments; Central Arkansas Library System; City of Little Rock; Irwin Partners; Plunkett, Boerner & Associates; The Webster Corporation; Pathfinder and Bank of America.

## Band 2

## Dover Dixon Horne

**The Firm:** Experienced in the transactional and tax aspects of real estate work, this firm earns its place in *Chambers'* tables. It offers expertise in acquisitions, development, leasing, title issues, loan transactions and tax-deferred exchanges.

**The Lawyers:** Veteran attorney **Darrell Dover** has "*a wealth of experience*" built up during "*a long and distinguished career.*" He is the only lawyer in Arkansas to be a fellow of the American College of Real Estate Lawyers, and this contributes to people's "*enormous respect for him.*"

**Clients/Work Highlights:** The firm's client roster includes many developers and lenders.

## Hankins & Hicks

**The Firm:** A niche practice with an impressive clutch of clients, Hankins & Hicks takes on a variety of work, including acquisitions, sales, commercial leases and real estate litigation. It has a special interest in retail developments.

**The Lawyers:** "*Competent and confident*" **Stuart Hankins** has a "*good head for business*" and significant finance expertise. He is also very comfortable on regulatory issues and has real estate litigation experience.

**Clients/Work Highlights:** Ashley Development; Twin City Bank; Community Bank; Apartment House Builders; National Coatings; Maumelle Water Management; Red Apple Enterprises and Aromatique.

## Kutak Rock LLP

**The Firm:** A "*small but powerful*" outpost in Kutak Rock's multistate operation, the Little Rock office conducts work that emanates from Arkansas and beyond. Its prowess in corporate transactions gives it "*an extra edge*" in real estate financing, acquisitions, disposals and investments. The firm recently strengthened its smaller Fayetteville practice with the addition of noted real estate lawyer Terry Pool.

**The Lawyers:** Recognized as "*a dominant force*" in real estate, **Scott Schallhorn** impresses others with an "*outstanding grasp of bond work.*" He is also experienced in the development of family housing projects, with all their ancillary financing issues. **Clients/Work Highlights:** The firm's clientele includes Beverly Enterprises and Fairfield Corporation.

## Other Notable Practitioners

The state's "*zoning virtuoso*" is **Hal Kemp** (see p.209). In the past year he represented Arkansas Water in a case against a real estate developer seeking to condemn a section of land. His "*ability and experience*" are known throughout the market.

# Leaders in Arkansas

**ALLEN, William**
Allen Law Firm, Little Rock
501 374 7100
*Recommended in Litigation*

**ANDERSON, Philip S**
Williams & Anderson PLC, Little Rock
501 372 0800
PSA@williamsanderson.com
*Recommended in Litigation*
**Practice Areas:** Philip S Anderson has broad experience in trial and appellate practice as well as in acquisitions, mergers and general corporate matters. He represents local and national news media, including the Arkansas Democrat-Gazette, Arkansas's statewide newspaper. In addition to trying cases in federal and state courts throughout Arkansas, he regularly appears before the United States Court of Appeals for the Eighth Circuit and the Arkansas Supreme Court.
**Prof. Memberships:** Mr Anderson is a Member of the American Law Institute and its governing Council.
**Career:** Mr Anderson was President of the American Bar Association from 1998 until 1999. He was Chair of the House of Delegates in 1992-94. He served for 35 years on the Arkansas Supreme Court Committee on Jury Instructions. He was appointed by President Carter to the United States Circuit Judge Nominating Commission in 1978 and 1979. He has served as a Member and Co-Chair of the Federal Advisory Committee for the United States Court of Appeals for the Eighth Circuit.
**Publications:** Arkansas section for the annual 50-State Libel Survey published by Media Law Resource Center.
**Personal:** Mr Anderson received BA and LLB degrees from the University of Arkansas. He served as Editor-in-Chief of the Arkansas Law Review.

**ASKEW III, Jess**
Williams & Anderson PLC, Little Rock
501 372 0800
jaskew@williamsanderson.com
*Recommended in Litigation*
**Practice Areas:** Business and commercial litigation and media law.
**Prof. Memberships:** Mr Askew is a Member of the American Bar Association, Litigation and Business Law Sections. He chaired the Arkansas Bar Association's Litigation Section upon its formation in 2002.

**Career:** Law clerk to Judge Richard Sheppard Arnold of the United States Court of Appeals for the Eighth Circuit.
**Personal:** Graduated from Harvard University, with honors, in 1982. Graduated magna cum laude from the University of California, Hastings College of the Law, in 1986, where he was Order of the Coif and Senior Review Editor of the Hastings Constitutional Law Quarterly.

**BAKER, Kristine G**
Quattlebaum, Grooms, Tull & Burrow PLLC, Little Rock 501 379 1704
kbaker@qgtb.com
*Recommended in Litigation*
**Practice Areas:** Primary areas of practice include complex business, employment, securities, and products liability litigation and media law.
**Prof. Memberships:** American, Eighth Circuit, Arkansas, and Pulaski County Bar Associations; William R Overton Inn of Court.
**Career:** Admitted to Arkansas Bar (1996). A Partner of Quattlebaum, Grooms, Tull & Burrow PLLC. Law clerk to Judge Susan Webber Wright, US District Court, ED Arkansas (1996-98).
**Publications:** 'BB&B Construction Co v. FDIC Mechanics' and Materialmen's Liens in Arkansas: Priority as a Function of Removability', 48 Arkansas Law Review 783 (1995).
**Personal:** Received a JD (with high honors) from the University of Arkansas School of Law in 1996, attended Washington University School of Law (1993-94), and received a BA (summa cum laude) from Saint Louis University in 1993.

**BARRIER, W Christopher**
Mitchell, Williams, Selig, Gates Woodyard, PLLC, Little Rock 501 688 8800
*Recommended in Real Estate*

**BEARD III, RT**
Mitchell, Williams, Selig, Gates Woodyard, PLLC, Little Rock 501 688 8800
*Recommended in Litigation*

**BENHAM III, Paul**
Friday, Eldredge & Clark, Little Rock
501 376 2011
*Recommended in Corporate/Commercial*

**BOE, Tim**
Rose Law Firm, Little Rock
501 375 9131
*Recommended in Employment*

**BUFORD JR, C Douglas**
Mitchell, Williams, Selig, Gates Woodyard, PLLC, Little Rock 501 688 8800
*Recommended in Corporate/Commercial*

**CHILES IV, EB (Chip)**
Quattlebaum, Grooms, Tull & Burrow PLLC, Little Rock 501 379 1734
cchiles@qgtb.com
*Recommended in Litigation*
**Practice Areas:** Primary areas of practice include business, employment, and products liability litigation.
**Prof. Memberships:** Chair, Federal Practice Committee, ED Ark, DRI, Eighth Circuit Bar Association, and William R Overton Inn of Court.
**Career:** Admitted to Arkansas and Tennessee Bars, Eighth and Sixth Circuits, and US Supreme Court. A Partner of Quattlebaum, Grooms, Tull & Burrow PLLC.
**Publications:** 'A Hand to Rock the Cradle: Transracial Adoption, the Multiethnic Placement Act and a Proposal for the Arkansas General Assembly', 49 Arkansas Law Review 501 (1996).
**Personal:** Received a JD (cum laude) from Harvard Law School in 1996 and BA (summa cum laude) from Hendrix College in 1993.

**CLARK, Ronald**
Rose Law Firm, Little Rock,
501 375 9131
*Recommended in Corporate/Commercial*

**COULTER, Nate**
Wilson, Engstrom, Corum & Coulter, Little Rock 501 375 6453
*Recommended in Litigation*

**CRASS, Kevin**
Friday, Eldredge & Clark, Little Rock
501 376 2011
*Recommended in Litigation*

**CROSS, J Bruce**
Cross, Gunter, Witherspoon & Galchus, PC, Little Rock 501 371 9999
*Recommended in Employment*

**DAVIS, John D**
Wright, Lindsey & Jennings LLP, Little Rock 501 212 1373
jddavis@wlj.com
*Recommended in Employment*
**Practice Areas:** Representation of management in all areas of labor and employment law and workers' compensation defense.
**Prof. Memberships:** American Bar Association (Labor and Employment Law Section); Arkansas Bar Association; Pulaski County Bar Association; Arkansas Human Resources Association.
**Career:** Engaged in the practice of labor and employment law and workers' compensation defense since 1980. Listed in 'The Best Lawyers in America' (1997-2006).
**Personal:** University of Arkansas School of Law (JD 1980); Auburn University (BS 1975).

**DAVIS, Oscar**
Friday, Eldredge & Clark, Little Rock
501 376 2011
*Recommended in Employment*

**DEERE, Beth M**
Williams & Anderson PLC, Little Rock
501 372 0800
BDeere@williamsanderson.com
*Recommended in Litigation*
**Practice Areas:** Ms Deere practices business and commercial litigation, media law, and employment law.
**Prof. Memberships:** Ms Deere is a Member of the Arkansas Bar Association's House of Delegates; the American, Eighth Circuit, Arkansas, and Pulaski County Bar Associations; the Henry Woods Inn of Court; and Scribes – the American Society of Writers on Legal Subjects. She is a Fellow of the Arkansas Bar Foundation.
**Career:** Ms Deere clerked for US District Judge Henry Woods and has taught as an Adjunct Professor both at the undergraduate and law school levels.
**Publications:** Ms Deere is co-author of 'Comparative Fault', 3rd edition, published by Thomson West in 1996, and continues to publish yearly supplements. She also has published articles in law reviews of both Arkansas law schools.
**Personal:** She graduated summa cum laude from Henderson State University and graduated with honors from UALR School of Law in 1986, where she served as assistant editor of the UALR Law Journal.

**DONOVAN, Richard**
Rose Law Firm, Little Rock
501 375 9131
*Recommended in Litigation*

**DOVER, Darrell**
Dover Dixon Horne, Little Rock
501 375 9151
*Recommended in Real Estate*

**EBEL, Walter**
Friday, Eldredge & Clark, Little Rock
501 376 2011
*Recommended in Corporate/Commercial*

**EISEMAN, Byron**
Friday, Eldredge & Clark, Little Rock
501 376 2011
*Recommended in Corporate/Commercial*

**EVERETT, John**
Everett Law Firm, Fayetteville
479 443 0292
*Recommended in Litigation*

**FLETCHER, John**
Kutak Rock LLP, Little Rock
501 975 3000
*Recommended in Corporate/Commercial*

**FRAZIER, Randal B**
Quattlebaum, Grooms, Tull & Burrow
PLLC, Little Rock, 501 379 1771
rfrazier@qgtb.com
*Recommended in Real Estate*
**Practice Areas:** Primary areas of practice include banking law, real estate acquisitions and financing and zoning law.
**Career:** Admitted to the Arkansas Bar (1984).
**Personal:** Received a JD from University of Oklahoma School of Law in 1984 and a BA from Olivet Nazarene University (summa cum laude) in 1981.

**FREELAND, Byron**
Mitchell, Williams, Selig, Gates Woodyard, PLLC, Little Rock 501 688 8800
*Recommended in Employment*

**GALCHUS, Donna Smith**
Cross, Gunter, Witherspoon & Galchus, PC, Little Rock 501 371 9999
*Recommended in Employment*

**GARDNER, Price**
Friday, Eldredge & Clark, Little Rock
501 376 2011
*Recommended in Corporate/Commercial, Real Estate*

**GATES, Allan**
Mitchell, Williams, Selig, Gates Woodyard, PLLC, Little Rock 501 688 8800
*Recommended in Litigation*

**GRAVES, Kathlyn**
Mitchell, Williams, Selig, Gates Woodyard, PLLC, Little Rock 501 688 8800
*Recommended in Employment*

**GREGORY, H Watt**
Kutak Rock LLP, Little Rock
501 975 3000
*Recommended in Corporate/Commercial*

**GROOMS, Timothy**
Quattlebaum, Grooms, Tull & Burrow
PLLC, Little Rock 501 379 1713
tgrooms@qgtb.com
*Recommended in Real Estate*
**Practice Areas:** Primary areas of practice are banking law, real estate, acquisitions and financing, and he serves as General Counsel to the Arkansas REALTORS Association, Arkansas Homebuilders Association and the Arkansas Community Bankers.
**Prof. Memberships:** American, Arkansas and Pulaski County Bar Associations; American College of Real Estate Lawyers; International Council of Shopping Centers.
**Career:** Admitted to the Arkansas Bar (1984). A founding Partner of Quattlebaum, Grooms, Tull & Burrow PLLC. Licensed real estate broker, Arkansas, 1979.
**Personal:** Received a JD (with high honors) from the University of Arkansas at Little Rock Law School in 1984 and a BBA (magna cum laude) from the University of Arkansas at Little Rock in 1981.

**GRUNDFEST, Jack**
Mitchell, Williams, Selig, Gates Woodyard, PLLC, Little Rock 501 688 8800
*Recommended in Corporate/Commercial*

**GUNTER, Russell**
Cross, Gunter, Witherspoon & Galchus, PC, Little Rock 501 371 9999
*Recommended in Employment*

**HAMLIN, Harold**
Mitchell, Williams, Selig, Gates Woodyard, PLLC, Little Rock
501 688 8800
*Recommended in Real Estate*

**HANKINS, Stuart**
Hankins & Hicks, Little Rock
501 371 9226
*Recommended in Real Estate*

**HENDREN, Jennifer**
Shemin & Hendren, PLLC, Fayetteville
479 973 4442
*Recommended in Litigation*

**HERRINGTON, Daniel**
Friday, Eldredge & Clark, Little Rock
501 376 2011
*Recommended in Employment*

**JACK JR, Donald**
Jack, Lyon & Jones, PC, Little Rock
501 375 1122
*Recommended in Corporate/Commercial*

**JACKSON, William Stuart**
Wright, Lindsey & Jennings LLP, Little
Rock 501 371 0808
wjackson@wlj.com
*Recommended in Employment*
**Practice Areas:** Federal/state court litigation and appeals, including claims under Title VII, ADA, FMLA, ADEA, and 42 USC Sec 1981 and 1983, and state law claims involving trade secrets, non-compete agreements, arbitration agreements, the Arkansas Civil Rights Act, and wrongful discharge.
**Prof. Memberships:** American Bar Association (Labor and Employment Law Section); Arkansas Bar Association; Pulaski County Bar Association.
**Career:** Partner since 1998.
**Personal:** Duke Law School (JD 1992); Hendrix College (BA 1989, magna cum laude with distinction). Hendrix College Alumni Board (2005-present); American Diabetes Association (Chair/Central Arkansas Council 2003-04; Member 2001-present); Rotary Club of Little Rock.

**JONES, Michael**
Gilker and Jones PA, Mountainburg
479 369 4294
*Recommended in Employment*

**KAPLAN, Philip**
Kaplan, Brewer, Maxey & Haralson, Little Rock 501 372 0400
*Recommended in Employment, Litigation*

**KEMP, Hal**
Hal Joseph Kemp PA, Little Rock
501 372 7243
*Recommended in Real Estate*

**KUMPE, Peter G**
Williams & Anderson PLC, Little Rock
501 372 0800
pkumpe@williamsanderson.com
*Recommended in Litigation*
**Practice Areas:** Mr Kumpe has handled numerous complex litigation matters including multi-party and class action litigation in both federal and state courts. He has substantial substantive knowledge in the areas of securities regulation and antitrust. In addition to his litigation practice, he has experience in governmental enforcement actions and governmental investigations into business matters.
**Prof. Memberships:** Member of the American Bar Association, the Arkansas Bar Association, and the American Law Institute. He is a Fellow of the Arkansas Bar Foundation.
**Career:** Mr Kumpe was admitted to the both the Arkansas Bar and the Texas Bar in 1972. He clerked for Judge G Thomas Eisele, US District Court for the Eastern District of Arkansas, from 1972-74. As an adjunct faculty member at the University of Arkansas at Little Rock School of Law, Mr Kumpe taught securities regulation from 1975 until 1978 and antitrust law from 1980-91. Mr Kumpe served as Chairman of the Arkansas Supreme Court Committee on Jury Instructions-Civil from 1999-2004.
**Publications:** Mr Kumpe, with others, authored the Arkansas section of 'State Antitrust Practice and Statutes', second edition (2004), published by the Antitrust section of the American Bar Association.
**Personal:** Mr Kumpe received a JD, with honors in 1972 from the University of Texas School of Law. He was a member of Order of the Coif and Managing Editor of the Texas Law Review from 1971-72.

**LEWIS, John Alan**
Mitchell, Williams, Selig, Gates Woodyard, PLLC, Rogers 479 273 9561
*Recommended in Real Estate*

**LILE, John G**
Wright, Lindsey & Jennings LLP, Little Rock 501 212 1260
jlile@wlj.com
*Recommended in Employment, Litigation*
**Practice Areas:** Business and commercial litigation (including employment discrimination) and product liability.
**Prof. Memberships:** American Bar Association (Litigation and Labor and Employment Law Sections); Arkansas Bar Association (Chair, Professional Ethics Committee 2002-04; Chair, Young Lawyers Section 1971-72); Pulaski County Bar Association; Jefferson County Bar Association (President 1973); Fellow, American College of Trial Lawyers; Fellow, American Bar Foundation; Arkansas Association of Defense Counsel.
**Career:** Coleman, Gantt & Ramsay (1962-65); Ramsay, Cox, Lile, Bridgforth, Gilbert, Harrelson and Starling (1965-87); Partner, Wright, Lindsey & Jennings LLP since 1990.
**Personal:** Hendrix College (BA 1959); Duke University (LLB 1962).

**LOWTHER JR, Edwin L**
Wright, Lindsey & Jennings LLP, Little Rock 501 371 0808
elowther@wlj.com
*Recommended in Litigation*
**Practice Areas:** General litigation (including product liability), legal and medical malpractice, toxic tort, and employment litigation.
**Prof. Memberships:** American Bar Association (Tort and Insurance Practice and Litigation Sections); Arkansas Bar Association; Pulaski County Bar Association; American College of Trial Lawyers; American Board of Trial Advocates; Arkansas Association of Defense Counsel; International Association of Defense Counsel; Fellow, Arkansas Bar Foundation.
**Career:** Partner since 1987. Managing Partner (2005-present).
**Personal:** Ouachita Baptist University (BA, 1975, cum laude); University of Arkansas at Little Rock (JD 1981, with honors); UALR Law Journal (1980-81).

**MARTIN, David**
Rose Law Firm, Little Rock
501 375 9131
*Recommended in Employment*

**MAXEY, JoAnn**
Kaplan, Brewer, Maxey & Haralson,
Little Rock 501 372 0400
*Recommended in Employment*

**MITCHELL, H Maurice**
Mitchell, Williams, Selig, Gates Wood-
yard, PLLC, Little Rock 501 688 8800
*Recommended in Real Estate*

**MOORE, Michael**
Friday, Eldredge & Clark, Little Rock
501 376 2011
*Recommended in Employment*

**NESTRUD, Charles**
Chisenhall, Nestrud & Julian, PA,
Little Rock 501 372 5800
*Recommended in Litigation*

**NISBET, A Wyckliff**
Friday, Eldredge & Clark, Little Rock
501 376 2011
*Recommended in Employment*

**PERKINS, G Alan**
Perkins & Trotter PLLC, Little Rock
501 603 9000
*Recommended in Litigation*

**POWELL, David M**
Williams & Anderson PLC, Little Rock
501 372 0800
dmpowell@williamsanderson.com
*Recommended in Litigation*
**Practice Areas:** Mr Powell practices
construction law, business litigation, professional liability, arbitration, and banking and real estate law.
**Prof. Memberships:** Mr Powell is a
Member of the Panel of Arbitrators of the
American Arbitration Association and
the International Association of Defense
Counsel. He is a Fellow of the Arkansas
Bar Foundation and the Defense
Research Institute.
**Career:** Mr Powell has spoken at national and local seminars on defending claims
against professionals, representing financial institutions in litigation and real
estate transactions. As an adjunct instructor at the University of Arkansas at Little
Rock School of Law, he has taught classes
on the Uniform Commercial Code and
real estate.
**Personal:** Mr Powell graduated cum
laude from Davidson College, where he
was elected to Phi Beta Kappa. He
received a JD, with high honors, from
Duke University, where he was a Member
of the Order of the Coif.

**QUATTLEBAUM, Steven**
Quattlebaum, Grooms, Tull & Burrow
PLLC, Little Rock
501 379 1707
quattlebaum@qgtb.com
*Recommended in Litigation*
**Practice Areas:** Primary areas of prac-

tice include business, products liability,
environmental and toxic tort litigation.
**Prof. Memberships:** International Academy of Trial Lawyers, American Board of
Trial Advocates, Products Liability Advisory Council, William R Overton Inn of
Court.
**Career:** Admitted to the Arkansas Bar
(1984). A founding Partner of Quattlebaum, Grooms, Tull & Burrow PLLC.
**Publications:** 'Defending the Institution
of Trial by Jury', Voir Dire, Fall 2001;
'Effective Video Presentations at Trial',
Arkansas Lawyer, Spring and Summer
1993.
**Personal:** Received a JD from the University of Arkansas in 1983 and a BA
from Western State College of Colorado
in 1981.

**RATHER JR, Gordon S**
Wright, Lindsey & Jennings LLP,
Little Rock 501 371 0808
grather@wlj.com
*Recommended in Litigation*
**Practice Areas:** Litigation (including
product liability, toxic tort, commercial
issues, and maritime personal injury
defense).
**Prof. Memberships:** American Board of
Trial Advocates (National President 1996;
President, Arkansas Chapter 1987-88);
American College of Trial Lawyers (Fel-
low); International Academy of Trial
Lawyers (Fellow and State Chair);
Arkansas Association of Defense Coun-
sel; Maritime Law Association of the
United States (Proctor); American Bar
Association (Litigation Section);
Arkansas Bar Association; Pulaski Coun-
ty Bar Association; Arkansas Bar Founda-
tion (Fellow); Arkansas Chapter of The
Fellows of the American Bar Foundation.
**Career:** Partner since 1972.
**Personal:** Vanderbilt University (BA
1961, cum laude), Phi Beta Kappa; Duke
University (JD 1968).

**ROBINSON, Spencer**
Ramsay, Bridgforth, Harrelson & Starling
LLP, Pine Bluff 870 535 9000
*Recommended in Employment*

**SAXTON, James**
Friday, Eldredge & Clark, Little Rock
501 376 2011
*Recommended in Real Estate*

**SCHALLHORN, Scott**
Kutak Rock LLP, Little Rock
501 975 3000
*Recommended in Real Estate*

**SELIG, John**
Mitchell, Williams, Selig, Gates Wood-
yard, PLLC, Little Rock 501 688 8800
*Recommended in
Corporate/Commercial*

**SHEMIN, Kenneth**
Shemin & Hendren, PLLC, Fayetteville
479 973 4442
*Recommended in Litigation*

**SHIPLEY III, Benjamin**
Cross, Gunter, Witherspoon & Galchus,
PC, Fort Smith 479 783 8200
*Recommended in Employment*

**SHULTS, Leigh-Anne**
Mitchell, Williams, Selig, Gates Wood-
yard, PLLC, Little Rock 501 688 8800
*Recommended in Employment*

**SHULTS, Steven**
Shults Law Firm, LLP, Little Rock
501 375 2301
*Recommended in Litigation*

**SMITH, Laura**
Friday, Eldredge & Clark, Little Rock
501 376 2011
*Recommended in Litigation*

**SPIVEY III, John William**
Wright, Lindsey & Jennings LLP,
Little Rock 501 212 1310
jspivey@wlj.com
*Recommended in Real Estate*
**Practice Areas:** Banking and finance,
commercial real estate, zoning and land
use, acquisitions, municipal bonds, and
property tax appeals.
**Prof. Memberships:** American Bar
Association (Urban, State and Local Gov-
ernment Law and Real Property Sec-
tions); Arkansas Bar Association; Pulaski
County Bar Association; National Associ-
ation of Bond Lawyers; Fellow, American
College of Mortgage Attorneys.
**Career:** Partner since 1983.
**Personal:** Hendrix College Alumni Loy-
alty Fund (past Chair); Hendrix College
Alumni Association (past Member, Board
of Governors); Arkansas Territorial
Restoration Foundation (past President,
Board Member); Camp Aldersgate, Inc.
(past Treasurer, Board of Directors);
Board Member, City Parks Conservancy;
Board Member, Camp Aldersgate Foun-
dation.

**SUTTON, William**
Friday, Eldredge & Clark, Little Rock
501 376 2011
*Recommended in Litigation*

**TAYLOR, Jay**
Friday, Eldredge & Clark, Little Rock
501 376 2011
*Recommended in Real Estate*

**TISDALE, John**
Wright, Lindsey & Jennings LLP, Little
Rock 501 212 1256
jtisdale@wlj.com
*Recommended in
Corporate/Commercial*
**Practice Areas:** Taxation (including
tax-exempt financing, corporate and
partnership issues), corporate law, health
law and real estate.
**Prof. Memberships:** American Bar
Association (Taxation and Business Law
Sections); Arkansas Bar Association;
Pulaski County Bar Association; National
Association of Bond Lawyers; Fellow,
Arkansas Bar Foundation.

**Career:** Partner since 1980.
**Personal:** Rhodes College (BA 1968,
with honors); Washington University (JD
1975), Managing Editor, Washington
University Law Quarterly (1974-75). Our
House (Board of Directors 1998-pre-
sent); Chancellor, Episcopal Diocese of
Arkansas; Moderator American Institute
of Certified Public Accountants seminars;
advisor, Tobacco Settlement Task Force-
Arkansas House of Representatives.

**TULL III, John E**
Quattlebaum, Grooms, Tull & Burrow
PLLC, Little Rock 501 379 1705
jtull@qgtb.com
*Recommended in Litigation*
**Practice Areas:** Mr Tull's primary areas
of practice are commercial litigation,
media law and products liability.
**Prof. Memberships:** American,
Arkansas and Pulaski County Bar Associations, ABOTA, DRI and MLRC.
**Career:** Admitted to the Arkansas Bar
(1984). A founding Partner of Quattlebaum, Grooms, Tull & Borrow PLLC.
**Personal:** Received a JD (with high honors) from the University of Arkansas in
1984 and a BA from Vanderbilt University in 1980.

**VINES, J Andrew**
Wright, Lindsey & Jennings LLP,
Little Rock 501 212 1237
javines@wlj.com
*Recommended in Litigation*
**Practice Areas:** General litigation; com-
mercial litigation; construction law;
insurance defense; product liability
defense; trucking defense; pharmaceuti-
cal defense; mass tort defense.
**Prof. Memberships:** American Bar
Association; Arkansas Bar Association;
Pulaski County Bar Association; Defense
Research Institute; William R Overton
Inn of Court.
**Career:** Joined firm 1998; became Part-
ner 2004.
**Personal:** Education: University of
Arkansas (BA 1995, JD 1998, with hon-
ors), Note and Comment Editor –
Arkansas Law Review; Civic: Advisory
Board – Westside YMCA, Foundation
Board – Little Rock Catholic High
School; Honors: WA Eldredge Jr, Out-
standing Young Trial Lawyer Award
(2005), Arkansas Association of Defense
Counsel.

**WADDELL JR, William**
Friday, Eldredge & Clark, Little Rock
501 376 2011
*Recommended in Litigation*

**WITHERSPOON, Carolyn**
Cross, Gunter, Witherspoon & Galchus,
PC, Little Rock 501 371 9999
*Recommended in Employment*

# CROSS, GUNTER, WITHERSPOON & GALCHUS, P.C.

## THE FIRM

**Managing Partner:** Richard 'Rick' Roderick
**Number of directors:** 15
**Number of associates:** 4
**Number of counsel:** 2

**FIRM OVERVIEW:** The law firm of Cross, Gunter, Witherspoon & Galchus, P.C., represents union and non-union companies, locally, regionally and nationally, in almost every industry. From trucking to banking, manufacturing to health care, retailing to hospitality, and many others, with 250 plus years of cumulative experience, the firm's lawyers intertwine legal expertise with practical hands-on knowledge of business operations to provide its clients with successful and economical strategies.

## MAIN PRACTICE AREAS:

**Labor & Employment:** Listed as the largest management labor/employment law firm in Arkansas, the firm is well recognized with emphasis on union avoidance and NLRB matters; EEOC charges and lawsuits; arbitration, contract interpretation/negotiation of DOL-OFCCP/affirmative action matters, and general employment advice.

**Employee Relations:** The firm has worked for many years with a broad cross-section of companies to develop effective employee relations programs designed to attract, maintain and motivate high-quality employees. CGWG works with clients to design and implement employee compensation and benefits programs, management development programs, communications and employee motivation programs, personnel policies and practices, and seminars/training. With its extensive knowledge of labor and employment issues, CGWG also advises and counsels multinational corporations, United States corporations doing business oversees, and foreign employers with operations in the United States regarding labor and employment issues.

**Construction Law:** The firm handles materialman's and laborer's liens, licensing, payment and performance bond claims, construction contract drafting interpretation and disputes, and Miller Act claims.

**Immigration:** The firm works with employers and individuals to offer assistance in obtaining non-immigrant visas and immigrant status. It also offers employers strategic planning advice and counseling on compliance issues, including Forms I-9 and Social Security documentation.

**General Litigation:** CGWG handles a wide spectrum of cases in a number of diverse areas of law. Active in state and federal courts at the trial and appellate levels, the firm's lawyers are able to fully and aggressively address the litigation needs and concerns of its clients. CGWG lawyers are experienced and skilled in: products liability, professional liability, general insurance defense, commercial litigation, credit card fraud, and bankruptcy litigation.

**Healthcare:** The firm represents healthcare providers, including hospitals, nursing homes, and clinics in matters involving medical staff membership and credentialing; employee benefits; administrative and regulatory matters, including permits of approval, licensing and reimbursement; development of policies and procedures, including corporate compliance programs and HIPAA compliance; and general corporate matters including personal services and employment agreements, recruitment agreements, and joint ventures between providers.

**Products Liability:** CGWG represents insurers, manufacturers and suppliers in the defense of products liability actions involving such items as motor vehicles, heavy equipment, home appliances and medical devices, as well as other industrial and consumer products. The firm serves as local counsel for several national and international manufacturers.

**Corporate & Business:** Significant experience in business and corporate law matters including: incorporating businesses; establishing limited liability companies, partnerships and joint ventures; drafting and reviewing various types of business and commercial contracts including leases, contracts of sale, and noncompete agreements; handling all legal matters related to the acquisition and sale of businesses; and advising clients regarding debt collection methods and procedures.

## HEAD OFFICE

**ARKANSAS**
500 President Clinton Avenue, Suite 200, **Little Rock,** Arkansas 72201
**Tel:** 501 371 9999   **Fax:** 501 371 0035
**Website:** www.cgwg.com

## BRANCH OFFICES

**ARKANSAS**
5401 Rogers Avenue, Suite 200, **Fort Smith,** AR 72903
**Tel:** 479 783 8200   **Fax:** 479 783 8265

101 West Mountain Street, Suite 200, **Fayetteville,** AR 72701
**Tel:** 479 443 6978   **Fax:** 479 443 7697

**CLIENTS:** Categories of clients: trucking companies; retailers; banks; builders and construction companies; hospitality employers; manufacturers; retail, non-profits; utilities; municipalities; information technology companies; hospitals (general medical/surgical and behavioral); physician clinics and offices; home health agencies; hospices; nursing homes; nursing home development companies; durable medical equipment suppliers; and community mental health centers.

# QUATTLEBAUM, GROOMS, TULL & BURROW PLLC

## THE FIRM

**Number of partners:** 6
**Number of other lawyers:** 18

**FIRM OVERVIEW:** Quattlebaum, Grooms, Tull & Burrow PLLC provides a full range of business-related legal services. The firm represents individuals, sole proprietorships, partnerships, limited liability companies, corporations, and government organizations. Its practice encompasses a wide variety of transactions, litigation, regulatory work, and estate planning.

## MAIN AREAS OF PRACTICE:

**Corporate & Commercial:** The firm has extensive experience in litigating complex business and commercial cases, including class actions. It has been involved in numerous matters involving multiple parties and claims pending in multiple jurisdictions. These cases have included antitrust litigation, business and commercial disputes, construction disputes, securities disputes, franchise disputes, employment discrimination and related disputes, real estate litigation, toxic tort claims, products liability claims, professional malpractice claims, libel and First Amendment claims, constitutional law claims, and insurance coverage litigation. The firm has represented corporate and individual clients, as both plaintiffs and defendants. It also has extensive litigation experience in trial and appellate courts on both the state and federal levels.

**Banking & Finance:** The firm has extensive experience in a wide range of banking issues for state and national banks and bank holding companies, including bank formation, holding company formation, loan transactions, representation of the bank as creditor, as well as regulatory and compliance issues involving the FDIC, the OCC, and the Federal Reserve Board. It is frequently called upon to prepare loan documentation and provide legal opinions in the areas of usury, enforceability of security interests, and choice of law issues. The firm has advised clients on issues involving financing for public and private entities. It has acted as bond counsel and trustee counsel in Arkansas Development Finance Authority bond issues. The firm has counseled issuers in numerous corporate securities offerings, including initial and secondary capital offerings for financial institutions, offerings for bank holding companies, and restricted offerings pursuant to Regulation D. Frequently in connection with securities offerings, the firm is called upon to offer professional advice on ancillary issues in securities offerings, such as taxation, real estate, banking and environmental issues.

**Real Estate:** The firm represents, among others, developers, lenders, investment banks, pension funds, domestic investors and major corporations in connection with real estate-related transactions involving the purchase, sale, construction, financing, development, management and operation of commercial, industrial and residential projects throughout Arkansas and the United States; the public and private offering of various types of real estate securities; securitized lending transactions; leasing on behalf of landlords and major tenants; real estate litigation; and debt restructuring transactions on behalf of lenders and borrowers.

**CLIENTS:** Acxiom Corporation; Arkansas Community Bankers; Arkansas Press Association; Arkansas REALTORS® Association; AT&T Wireless, Inc.; BASF Corporation; Building & Utility Contractors, Inc.; CenterPoint Energy; DaimlerChrysler Corporation; Eagle Bank & Trust; Entergy Corporation; H&R Block, Inc.; Kohler Co.; The Phillips Companies; Koppers Industries, Inc.; MBC Holdings, LLC; Simmons First National Bank; Uniroyal; Multi-Purpose Civic Center Facility Board for Pulaski County (Alltel Arena); Moses Tucker Real Estate, Inc.; Regions Bank; Salomon Smith Barney, Inc.; Schering-Plough Corp.; Summit Bank; US Bank; The Lincoln Electric Company; Tyson Foods, Inc., and Waste Management, Inc..

## HEAD OFFICE

**ARKANSAS**
111 Center Street, Suite 1900, **Little Rock**, Arkansas 72201
**Tel:** 501 379 1700 **Fax:** 501 379 1701
**Website:** www.qgtb.com

5305 Village Parkway, Suite 7, **Rogers**, Arkansas 72758
**Tel:** 479 254 3662 **Fax:** 479 254 3664

## CONTACTS

**Banking & Finance** ...................................................Patrick A Burrow
**Commercial Property** ...........................................Timothy W Grooms
**Environmental** .................................................................Al Eckert
**Litigation**...........................................................Steven W Quattlebaum
................................................................................John E Tull III
...............................................................................Kristine G Baker
.............................................................................EB (Chip) Chiles, IV
.......................................................................Charles L Schlumberger

QUATTLEBAUM, GROOMS, TULL & BURROW, PLLC

# WILLIAMS & ANDERSON PLC

## THE FIRM

**Number of partners:** 14
**Number of attorneys:** 24

**FIRM OVERVIEW**: Williams & Anderson PLC is a twenty-four lawyer firm established in 1988 to handle sophisticated business transactions and complex commercial litigation. The firm's statewide practice is limited to business-related matters. The firm strives to attain the highest level of professional performance. It is recognized for its competence throughout the Arkansas business and legal communities, including state and federal trial and appellate courts. Six of the firm's lawyers are listed in The Best Lawyers in America. Williams & Anderson is pleased to represent successful business organizations and individuals in furtherance of their business interests.

## MAIN AREAS OF PRACTICE:

**Banking Law:** The firm has substantial experience in representing banks and other financial institutions in the full range of banking activities, including lending agreements, secured transactions, regulatory matters, and related litigation.

**Business Litigation:** Litigation experience includes antitrust, business torts, construction, defamation, employment matters, and intellectual property. The firm has established a track record for successfully litigating the "big case" with a team approach to litigation, combining subject matter competence with management and advocacy skills. The experience extends to class action litigation; lawyers in the firm have handled major class actions on behalf of plaintiffs as well as defendants. The firm has an appellate practice before both the state appellate courts and the United States Court of Appeals for the Eighth Circuit. The firm's experience has been that the most certain strategy for satisfactory results in litigation is vigorous and determined advocacy.

**Construction Law:** The firm's Construction Law Practice includes contract preparation and review, construction-related litigation, as well as alternative dispute resolution. With respect to both public and private projects, the firm represents owners, contractors, subcontractors, suppliers and design professionals, and it also handles licensing matters.

**Corporate & Securities:** The firm advises and represents public and private companies, lenders, borrowers, broker-dealers and other participants in the securities markets in transactions with compliance and regulatory issues, and in litigation matters. It also represents issuers, underwriters, placement agents and investors in public and private offerings of securities, proxy solicitations, and going private transactions.

**Intellectual Property:** The firm is experienced in the protection and licensing of trademarks and copyrights, in addition to the preparation and negotiation of technology licensing agreements. It handles both patent advice and prosecution.

**Media Law:** The firm is experienced in First Amendment and access issues. It defends defamation actions and prosecutes suits brought pursuant to the Arkansas Freedom of Information Act. It represents print and electronic media.

**Mergers & Acquisitions:** The firm has represented both sellers and purchasers in transactions involving large and small business enterprises, local and regional franchisees, major media properties and agricultural and manufacturing entities.

**Public Finance:** The firm is a nationally recognized public finance firm and has served as bond counsel to the State of Arkansas, the Arkansas Student Loan Authority and the Arkansas Development Finance Authority, as well as many local governmental entities. The firm handles municipal bond transactions from inception to closing.

**Tax and Estate Planning:** The firm's tax clients are businesses and individuals. The firm provides tax planning and administration advice for charitable and other nonprofit organizations.

## HEAD OFFICE

**ARKANSAS**
111 Center Street, Suite 2200, **Little Rock**, AR 72201
**Tel:** 501 372 0800   **Fax:** 501 372 6453
**Website:** www.williamsanderson.com

**CLIENTS**: Arkansas Development Finance Authority; Arkansas Democrat-Gazette, Inc.; Arkansas Department of Economic Development; Arkansas Short Line Railroad; Arkansas Student Loan Authority; Baldwin and Shell Construction Company; BITEC, Inc.; Citizens Bank; General Electric Capital Corporation; GMAC Mortgage Corporation; Home Bancshares, Inc.; Hot Springs Sentinel-Record, Inc.; Technisource, Inc.; McLane Company, Inc.; Metrocentre Improvement District No. 1; Metropolitan National Bank; MSF Financial Group; Potlatch Corporation; Pulaski Tax Company; Roman Catholic Diocese of Little Rock; Scholastic, Inc.; The Doyle Rogers Companies; University of Arkansas; WEHCO Media, Inc.; Wells Fargo Financial Leasing, Inc.

**WILLIAMS & ANDERSON** PLC

# WRIGHT, LINDSEY & JENNINGS LLP

## THE FIRM

**Managing Partner:** Edwin L Lowther, Jr
**Number of partners:** 37
**Number of other attorneys:** 19

**FIRM OVERVIEW:** Wright, Lindsey & Jennings LLP is a full service law firm with offices in Little Rock and Rogers, Arkansas, from which legal services are provided to clients based in Arkansas and across the country. Founded in 1900, the firm now consists of some 56 lawyers. Interaction among the practice groups enables the firm's members to address legal issues while remaining sensitive to the business considerations inherent in every legal matter. They strive to understand each client's particular needs and to address them in a cost-efficient and timely manner.

## MAIN AREAS OF PRACTICE:

**Banking & Finance:** Among the firm's clients are a number of national, regional and state banking associations, investment banking firms and other affiliated banking and investment companies. Members of the firm regularly represent banks in a variety of lending, investment, trust, workout and other general commercial transactions. In addition, members of the firm's Business Team represent bank clients in the acquisition of and merger with other banks and the sale of bank related assets.

**Bankruptcy & Creditors' Rights:** The firm practices in all chapters and aspects of bankruptcy cases. The Bankruptcy Practice includes the representation of secured and unsecured creditors, creditor committees, trustees, and reorganizing and liquidating debtors. Firm members also specialize in creditors' rights issues, including 'out-of-court' restructuring and workouts, lender liability cases, replevin, foreclosure, and commercial and consumer banking matters.

**Corporate & Securities:** The firm advises a wide array of business clients on commercial transactions, business planning and regulatory matters. Firm members currently serve as regular counsel to a number of large multinational corporations headquartered in the state of Arkansas and work closely with management in all areas of SEC reporting, acquisitions and sales of companies, negotiation and documentation of contracts and debt facilities, debt and stock offerings, and management compensation plans.

**Intellectual Property:** The firm handles various aspects of intellectual property, including patents, trademarks, copyrights, trade secrets and unfair competition. Firm members litigate infringement cases in both state and federal courts and practice before the relevant administrative bodies, including the United States Patent and Trademark Office.

**Labor & Employment:** The firm has a management-oriented labor and employment practice covering all aspects of employee-employer relations. The firm has extensive experience in litigation of employment claims and also represents clients in labor arbitrations, union contract negotiations and in administrative investigations.

**Litigation:** The firm provides experienced representation in all areas of tort and commercial litigation, including medical, engineering, architect, legal and professional malpractice, environmental law, franchise and construction issues, admiralty and maritime, railroad, personal injury, transportation, and insurance defense. Firm members represent and defend a broad range of clients, including insurance carriers, product manufacturers, professionals, individuals and businesses. The firm is widely recognized as one of the premier defense firms in Arkansas.

**Municipal Finance:** Service as bond counsel and issuer's counsel to Arkansas state, county, municipal and other local issuers of municipal debt is a major part of the firm's practice. The firm has delivered opinions in connection with both general obligation and revenue bond issues for major public facilities including public buildings, jails, municipal buildings, community centers, convention centers, hospitals, schools, parks, and numerous municipal utilities including electric, water and sewer facilities. The firm has served as bond counsel to state agencies, public facilities boards, public water authorities and a variety of special improvement districts. In addition the firm regularly serves as counsel to underwriters and corporate trustees in the origination of municipal debt.

**Products Liability:** The firm serves as statewide counsel for one of the US 'big three' domestic automobile manufacturers and a number of the major foreign automobile manufacturers, as well as several other manufacturers and suppliers of automobiles, trucks, and recreational vehicles. Firm members also regularly defend a broad array of manufacturers and suppliers of other products. In addition, the firm is active in the defense of toxic tort, environmental, and chemical exposure cases.

**Real Estate:** The firm offers a wide range of real estate related legal services and has been recognized as being one of the leading real estate law firms in the state. The practice focuses primarily upon commercial real estate and real estate finance; however, firm members also provide services for the owners of residential properties.

**Regulated Industries:** Many of the firm's clients are engaged in businesses or professions that are regulated by state or federal agencies and commissions. The firm offers broad expertise in the area of public utility regulation, particularly including electricity, natural gas, telecommunications and transportation. Additionally, firm members are experienced in regulatory matters involving the environment, occupational safety, labor relations and health care.

**Tax Practice:** The Tax Practice of the firm includes both state and federal tax matters. The firm handles federal tax issues for corporations, partnerships, trusts and individuals in areas such as income taxes, mergers, acquisitions, tax planning, real estate, decedents' estates and estate tax planning, audits and tax litigation. The practice also includes advice to and planning for tax exempt organizations and tax exempt bond and lease financing transactions. Tax practitioners in the firm have experience in state tax matters including income, sales and use, ad valorem, audits and appeals and litigation.

**CLIENTS:** The firm's corporate clients include Acxiom Corp.; Amerisure Cos.; AT&T Communications, Inc.; Bank of America Securities LLC; Bank of America N.A.; Central Arkansas Water; Chubb Group of Insurance Cos.; CNA Insurance Co.; Cooper Realty Investments, Inc.; Deltic Timber Corp.; Direct Insurance Company; E.I. Du Pont de Nemours and Co.; Entergy Corp.; First Arkansas Bank & Trust; Ford Motor Co.; General Electric Capital Corp.; Georgia Pacific Corp.; Government Employees Insurance Group; Hartford Insurance Cos., Helena Chemical Co.; Hyundai Motor America; Ingersoll-Rand Company; John Deere & Co.; Kemper Insurance Group; Landstar Transportation Group; Lion Oil Co.; Mazda Motors of America, Inc.; Medmarc, Inc.; Ryder Systems, Inc.; Schneider National Carriers Inc.; Sisters of Mercy Health System, St. Louis; Stephens Inc.; Suzuki Motor Corp.; Synthes, Inc.; Toyota Motor Sales USA, Inc.; University of Arkansas; Vanderbilt Mortgage & Financial, Inc.; Virco Manufacturing Co.; Wal-Mart Stores, Inc.; Weyerhaeuser Co.; and Xerox Corp.

### HEAD OFFICE

**ARKANSAS**
200 West Capitol Avenue, Suite 2300, **Little Rock,** AR 72201-3699
**Tel:** 501 371 0808  **Fax:** 501 376 9442
**Website:** www.wlj.com

### BRANCH OFFICE

**ARKANSAS**
903 North 47th Street, Suite 101, **Rogers,** AR  72756
**Tel:** 476 986 0888   **Fax:** 479 986 8932

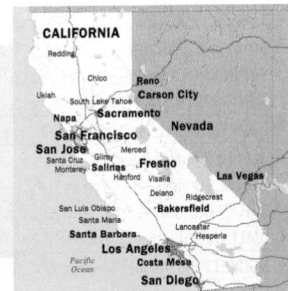

## How lawyers are ranked

Every year we carry out thousands of in-depth interviews with clients and lawyers in order to assess the reputations and expertise of business lawyers across the USA. Chambers rankings and editorial are referred to extensively by General Counsel and other purchasers of legal services who look to our recommendations when choosing their lawyers.

# ANTITRUST

## Antitrust
### Leading Firms

1. **GIBSON, DUNN & CRUTCHER LLP** *Los Angeles*
   **LATHAM & WATKINS LLP** *Los Angeles*
2. **BINGHAM MCCUTCHEN LLP** *San Francisco*
   **BLECHER & COLLINS** *Los Angeles*
   **HELLER EHRMAN LLP** *San Francisco*
   **JONES DAY** *Los Angeles*
   **O'MELVENY & MYERS LLP** *Los Angeles*
3. **COOLEY GODWARD LLP** *San Francisco*
   **HOWREY LLP** *Los Angeles*
   **MORRISON & FOERSTER LLP** *San Francisco*
   **MUNGER, TOLLES & OLSON LLP** *Los Angeles*
   **SHEPPARD, MULLIN,** *San Francisco*
   **TOWNSEND AND TOWNSEND** *San Francisco*
   **WILSON SONSINI** *San Francisco*

## Band 1

### Gibson, Dunn & Crutcher LLP
See firm details p.328

**The Firm:** This is *"one of the preeminent firms in the country,"* say clients, who spoke of the antitrust team's *"talent and depth"* on both West and East coasts. Its national presence means that it is able to draw on resources in DC when necessary, to complement its *"outstanding"* capacity in California. *"Why would you use anyone else?"* mused one client. Litigation is the mainstay of the practice, and the group has been involved in a number of high-profile matters. On behalf of leading organizations of copyright owners, the team recently submitted an amicus brief to the US Supreme Court arguing that a presumption of market power should not be applied in antitrust cases based on IP ownership. The group also assisted Flexsys with obtaining dismissals of indirect purchaser price-fixing lawsuits. The team's remit does not stop at litigation – M&A review and joint venture matters further contribute to the workload, although it is the East Coast practice that undertakes the lion's share of this work.

**The Lawyers: Robert Cooper** (see p.284) is *"the prototypical gentleman lawyer,"* and *"has attracted most of the major cases in the last few years."* Peers applaud his ability to *"zero in on what matters to the court, and predict which way a lawsuit is going to turn."* His expertise is currently being put to use on behalf of Intel, in its defense of litigation brought by AMD alleging the company monopolized the market for computer chips. Peers agree he has a *"terrific reputation for bet-the-company matters."* *"Straight-shooter"* **Gary Spratling** (see p.315) is *"certainly a superstar"* in criminal antitrust issues, a field in which many clients would turn to him in preference to any other practitioner. His wealth of experience at the DOJ means that he is adept at *"anticipating the reactions of government bodies,"* and therefore *"if you want to make a deal with the government, he's the person to make the deal for you."* **Daniel Swanson** (see p.317) is credited with *"a level of understanding of the rationale behind antitrust laws and policies that very few practitioners even begin to approach,"* clients insisted. This, combined with *"fresh ideas"* and a PhD in economics, makes him a *"tough opponent"* in civil and criminal litigation, alleged cartel matters and IP-related issues. He acts on behalf of an international clientele. **Joel Sanders** (see p.311) has a *"great client manner,"* say interviewees, who appreciate his *"good solid advice and great judgment."* He has both a civil and a criminal litigation portfolio. **Peter Sullivan** (see p.316) is heavily involved in antitrust matters relating to the automotive industry, where he is involved in ongoing price-fixing litigation on behalf of Nissan.

**Clients/Work Highlights:** Hewlett-Packard; ExxonMobil; Sempra Energy; American Airlines; Ticketmaster; Nissan; DaimlerChrysler; Wal-Mart and Sony.

### Latham & Watkins LLP

**The Firm:** Rivals acknowledge this as *"clearly a top firm"* in the antitrust field, and admit it's *"hard to choose"* between the state's top two players. Latham's transactional might is illustrated by the team's antitrust advice to Reebok during its acquisition by adidas-Salomon. Such *"phenomenal exposure"* places the firm squarely in the first tier, *"purely on the strength of work."* Technology companies feature heavily in the client base, and the firm advises biotech, hardware and software clients on a range of technology and IP-related disputes. Since last year's successful defense of attempts to enjoin Oracle's takeover of PeopleSoft on antitrust grounds, the firm has continued to advise Oracle on all antitrust matters, including those relating to its $5.85 billion acquisition of Siebel Systems. The group can also count manufacturing, healthcare and retail companies as clients, and is increasingly active on the international stage. Commentators from outside the state insist the team is *"every bit as up to speed as those in DC."*

**The Lawyers:** Tom Rosch's status as *"one of the most knowledgeable antitrust lawyers in every respect"* was confirmed by his recent appointment as a commissioner at the FTC. **Daniel Wall**'s *"star has risen"* following his victory in the Oracle-PeopleSoft matter, and since then interviewees have heard *"nothing but good things"* about his practice. He enjoys a reputation as a *"prominent"* antitrust litigator, although he is involved in the full range of issues, and was active on the matter for Reebok. Meanwhile, **Charles Samel** won praise for being *"right on the mark in terms of judgment and efficiency,"* and is experienced in antitrust class action work. Observers note **Karen Silverman** for her work on merger-related antitrust matters, and she also acts in litigation and cartel defense.

**Clients/Work Highlights:** Integrated Device Technology; KKR, Silver Lake Partners; Wells Fargo; Apple; Avery Dennison; McKesson and Toshiba.

## Band 2

### Bingham McCutchen LLP
See firm details p.1110

**The Firm:** Clients have had *"very positive"* experiences working with the group, acknowledged as an active player in the antitrust market, not least because of the *"clear vision"* of its practitioners and able up-and-comers. A significant portion of the practice concerns IP-related antitrust issues, as well as single-firm conduct issues and class actions. Highlights include advising DSL provider Covad Communications Group in antitrust litigation against SBC, resulting in a $750 million settlement. Team members also represented Intel in over 50 antitrust class actions connected with AMD.

**The Lawyers:** Commentators *"think the world"* of litigation chair **Christopher Hockett** (see p.295). An *"energetic"* practitioner, his *"thoughtful and*

## Antitrust
### Leading Individuals

**Senior Statesmen**

POPOFSKY Laurence *Heller Ehrman LLP*
THUMANN Henry *O'Melveny & Myers LLP*

★ COOPER Robert *Gibson, Dunn & Crutcher LLP*

[1]
BLECHER Maxwell *Blecher & Collins*
BOMSE Stephen *Heller Ehrman LLP*
SPRATLING Gary *Gibson, Dunn & Crutcher LLP*
WALL Daniel *Latham & Watkins LLP*

[2]
HOCKETT Christopher *Bingham McCutchen LLP*
LEVEE Jeffrey *Jones Day*
MARKHAM Jesse *Morrison & Foerster LLP*
PHILLIPS Bradley *Munger, Tolles & Olson LLP*
PICKETT Donn *Bingham McCutchen LLP*
PREOVOLOS Penelope *Morrison & Foerster LLP*
ROSENFELD Robert *Heller Ehrman LLP*
SWANSON Daniel *Gibson, Dunn & Crutcher LLP*
TAYLOR Robert *Howrey LLP*
TUBACH Michael *O'Melveny & Myers LLP*

[3]
ALEXIS Geraldine *Bingham McCutchen LLP*
BAKER Tyler *Fenwick & West LLP*
COMPTON Charles *Wilson Sonsini*
CREW Eugene *Townsend and Townsend*
GOLDMAN Melvin *Morrison & Foerster LLP*
HALLING Gary *Sheppard, Mullin*
HUNT James *Bingham McCutchen LLP*
NOLAN Thomas *Skadden, Arps*
POMERANTZ Glenn *Munger, Tolles & Olson*
PRINGLE Robert *Thelen Reid & Priest LLP*
SAMEL Charles *Latham & Watkins LLP*
SANDERS Joel *Gibson, Dunn*
SILVERMAN Karen *Latham & Watkins LLP*
STORK Anita *Cooley Godward LLP*
SULLIVAN Peter *Gibson, Dunn*
VARNER Carlton *Sheppard, Mullin*

*analytical"* approach makes him a hit in the marketplace. He represented AT&T Wireless in the DOJ's investigation of its $41 million merger with Cingular Wireless. Vice chairman of the firm **Donn Pickett** (see p.307) is popular among clients for his *"reassuring"* manner, and *"successful"* track record of appearances at trial. **James Hunt** (see p.295) is a *"very, very able"* trial lawyer, known for his *"good common sense"* and representation of clients such as the NFL. **Geraldine Alexis** (see p.276) *"takes great pains to understand clients' needs,"* and is valued for the analytical approach she employs in solving problems. She cochairs the firm's antitrust and trade regulation group and her clients include First Data.

**Clients/Work Highlights:** T-Mobile; Knight Ridder; ExxonMobil; Ciena; Adaptec; IKON Office Solutions; Pay By Touch; Hyundai Space & Aircraft; LVMH; Mitsui; First Data and the International Code Council.

## Blecher & Collins
See firm details p.325

**The Firm:** Interviewees extolled this *"fabulous"* firm's strength in plaintiff antitrust cases. In particular, clients highlighted the group's skill in media-related matters, which was recently on display in a class action against a group of record companies and mass merchandisers. The case centered on a challenge to a price policy where it is alleged that major retailers benefited from favorable pricing arrangements. Other highlights included a case against SBC challenging its practices in making DSL services available to ISPs. Although plaintiff work is the mainstay of the firm's reputation, the group also undertakes defense work.

**The Lawyers:** The *"courageous"* **Max Blecher** (see p.279) is a long-standing leader on the plaintiff side at the antitrust Bar: *"There is no one else of his caliber,"* according to sources. Said to be *"truly dedicated to his field,"* Blecher's *"rigorous and creative"* approach has made him a *"particularly tough adversary."* He acted in a case against a motion picture studio, concerning a joint venture in the view-on-demand industry.

**Clients/Work Highlights:** The County of Los Angeles and Intertainer are both active clients.

## Heller Ehrman LLP
See firm details p.329

**The Firm:** With offices in Los Angeles, San Francisco and Silicon Valley, the firm boasts *"a strong and well-established antitrust presence"* in California. As clients point out, it also offers *"first-rate"* antitrust expertise *"all over the country."* The outfit's *"great strength at the top"* is supported by *"terrific junior to mid-level attorneys,"* so that the team *"gives nothing away"* to competitors in the state. It is representing one of the defendants in worldwide price-fixing litigation filed against four manufacturers of vitamin C, and defending Visa against claims involving interchange fees made against Visa and MasterCard.

**The Lawyers:** **Larry Popofsky** (see p.308) is *"a legend"* among antitrust experts in California, having enjoyed *"a brilliant career"* in the field, where he remains *"an eminent practitioner,"* in addition to running a successful appellate practice. Taking the reins is *"big gun"* **Stephen Bomse** (see p.280), who co-heads the antitrust and trade regulation group. A *"litigation warhorse,"* he is also *"a seasoned trial lawyer"* who applies a *"thoughtful approach"* to the full gamut of antitrust matters. **Robert Rosenfeld** (see p.311) is a particular hit with clients, who applaud his *"excellent management of the litigation process."* A *"brilliant tactician,"* he is *"always thinking ahead,"* and his *"ever reasonable"* stance means *"he oozes credibility before both judge and jury."* He is particularly active on behalf of Microsoft.

**Clients/Work Highlights:** Philip Morris; 3M; Weyerhaeuser; Del Monte Foods; Black & Decker; SunTrust Banks; Kohler; Sony and QUALCOMM.

## Jones Day
See firm details p.570

**The Firm:** This group attracts commendation nationally from interviewees who note its East Coast strength, but it is also perceived to be *"emerging"* as a key competitor in California, where it is said to have *"attracted a lot of business."* The group is busiest in healthcare and retail sector antitrust matters, where contentious matters have occupied members of the team of late. The group also acted for Federated Department Stores in its acquisition of The May Department Stores Company.

**The Lawyers:** *"Smooth operator"* **Jeffrey LeVee** (see p.300) stands out as a *"super"* antitrust attorney. He has been active in price-fixing litigation, and recently advised Sutter Health, Banner Health and Presbyterian Healthcare against allegations that uninsured patients in the USA are paying unreasonable prices for healthcare.

**Clients/Work Highlights:** The group's client base includes ICANN, Procter & Gamble and a number of hospitals throughout the West Coast.

## O'Melveny & Myers LLP
See firm details p.336

**The Firm:** The team is perceived to have grown in significance, according to interviewees, thanks to its *"superb stable of talent"* and involvement in high-profile litigation.

**The Lawyers:** **Henry Thumann** (see p.317) is a long-standing member of the antitrust community, and is considered a *"fine lawyer"* by peers. **Michael Tubach** (see p.318) caught the eye of sources as someone who *"is winning an extremely good reputation for himself in white-collar antitrust defense."* His practice has included a significant number of criminal antitrust matters.

## Band 3

## Cooley Godward LLP

**The Firm:** Though less visible in the antitrust arena of late, the team produced a favorable reaction among clients. It covers the full range of antitrust issues, and this year represented NC Interactive in pursuing unfair competition counterclaims in a trademark and copyright infringement case concerning its online game 'City of Heroes'. Other successes include advising Siebel Systems in its acquisition by Oracle.

**The Lawyers:** Above all, interviewees rate **Anita Stork** for her communication skills in litigious settings. Contentious matters account for the bulk of her workload, though counseling and some merger-related activity also contribute. She represented a lawyer from another firm in a malpractice claim arising from an antitrust matter.

**Clients/Work Highlights:** PacifiCare; SanDisk; Dillard's; LSI Logic and LeapFrog Enterprises.

## Howrey LLP

**The Firm:** *"Historically a very proud name in the antitrust arena,"* the firm has weathered firmwide departures and maintained a *"world-class"* antitrust group, in the eyes of clients. The California group can draw on the resources of a significant national antitrust practice, encompassing both merger and litigation matters. As one client commented: *"I'd be surprised if Howrey was far outside the top five antitrust firms nationwide."* Highlights have included acting for a Japanese semiconductor manufacturing equipment company in a case involving patent claims and an antitrust counterclaim. The group also represented a foreign company that was the target of a grand jury investigation.

**The Lawyers: Robert Taylor** is *"a giant of a lawyer,"* said clients, who dub him *"one of the best on the interface between IP and antitrust."* His litigation prowess won market support, and sources called him *"a good person to have in your corner when you have a fight: if he can't talk his way out of it, he can brawl with the best of them."* He is acting as an expert witness for the defendant on patent and antitrust issues in the case of Specialty Minerals Inc v Omya AG et al.

**Clients/Work Highlights:** The group's client base cuts across a wide range of industries, and includes companies such as Tokyo Semitsu.

## Morrison & Foerster LLP
See firm details p.335

**The Firm:** Clients approve of this *"wonderful group of lawyers,"* and identify the firm as a *"definite leader"* in the state's antitrust market. The team is experienced in providing antitrust advice to clients in the life sciences, medical devices, pharmaceuticals, financial services, energy and transportation sectors. In the paper industry, the team acted for NorskeCanada in multidistrict antitrust litigation. It also acted for NTT DoCoMo and Panasonic in the case of Golden Bridge Technology v Nokia, which involved antitrust claims against the world's leading wireless companies, challenging the standard-setting process for wireless technology.

**The Lawyers: Jesse Markham** (see p.302) chairs the antitrust practice group, and is *"just excellent,"* according to clients. His *"results-oriented"* approach impresses interviewees, and he is particularly active in technology and life sciences matters, although this year has seen him involved in the paper industry as well. He was lead antitrust counsel to JPMorgan Chase in re ATM Fee Antitrust Litigation, and in class actions against the STAR ATM system and six US banks, involving an antitrust challenge to the interchange fees set by the STAR ATM system. **Penelope Preovolos** (see p.308) is a *"really wonderful lawyer"* according to peers, who deem her particularly capable in unfair competition matters. She acted for Barnes & Noble in the case of American Booksellers Association v Barnes & Noble, concerning Robinson-Patman and state unfair practices claims involving alleged discrimination against independent booksellers. The result was summary judgment in a published opinion on all damages claims, and a favorable settlement of remaining claims. **Melvin Goldman** (see p.291) also enjoys a loyal client following, and splits his time between antitrust and securities litigation.

**Clients/Work Highlights:** Bank of America; UPS; JDS Uniphase and Medtronic.

## Munger, Tolles & Olson LLP

**The Firm:** Its *"sensational"* litigation department makes for a strong contentious antitrust practice, staffed by *"a lot of very talented lawyers."* Beyond antitrust litigation, the team provides corporate support during mergers in addition to day-to-day counseling. Industries covered include entertainment, pharmaceuticals and defense contracting. Acting for Microsoft in antitrust litigation brought by RealNetworks was a recent work highlight.

**The Lawyers: Bradley Phillips** *"has all the attributes to make him a highly convincing operator,"* said competitors, who believe he combines *"smart"* with *"savvy."* **Glenn Pomerantz** is another *"prominent"* member of the antitrust community, thanks to his depth of experience and varied caseload. With regard to antitrust, he advises primarily on issues arising in the media and entertainment sectors.

**Clients/Work Highlights:** Microsoft; Abbott Laboratories; Shell and NBC Universal.

## Sheppard, Mullin, Richter & Hampton LLP

**The Firm:** Competitors pinpointed newspaper and media-related antitrust matters as being this group's true forte, although it also covers mergers and structural issues, criminal grand jury proceedings, class actions based on federal statutes and state unfair competition laws. Other areas of specialization include pricing practices, product distribution and international antitrust enforcement.

**The Lawyers: Gary Halling** is considered an *"accomplished"* antitrust specialist, while **Carlton Varner** is another *"go-to guy"* in the field.

**Clients/Work Highlights:** The firm's client base spans the healthcare, pharmaceutical, financial services, aerospace, energy, technology, publishing, distribution, courier and food services sectors.

## Townsend and Townsend and Crew LLP

**The Firm:** This *"has got to be considered a top antitrust plaintiff's firm,"* insisted opponents, who cited the group's *"great results"* in the field. The firm focuses on the nexus between antitrust and IP matters, which has resulted in a high volume of technology-related cases. Highlights include ongoing involvement in litigation against Microsoft on behalf of two major competitors of the company. Additional successes have included achieving a jury verdict against News America, attaining treble and punitive damages.

**The Lawyers:** *"Fantastic lawyer"* **Gene Crew** is a

*"true star of the Bar,"* say peers, in admiration of his plaintiff-oriented practice.

**Clients/Work Highlights:** Among the group's clients are Novell and Go Computer Inc.

## Wilson Sonsini Goodrich & Rosati
See firm details p.344

**The Firm:** This well-known California firm was commended for its merger review work and handling antitrust aspects of transactions under investigation by the FTC, the DOJ and other agencies. On the counseling front, lawyers were heavily involved in hybrid antitrust/IP issues, as might be expected from a group with a predominantly technology-focused client base. In terms of litigation, the firm enhanced its capabilities with the hire of two attorneys in the New York office and involvement in antitrust and patent-related disputes. Acting for Plantronics in its acquisition of Altec Lansing and for Sun Microsystems in its acquisition of Storage Technology were two major highlights of recent times.

**The Lawyers: Charles Compton** (see p.284) heads the antitrust group, and is a recognized face in merger review matters.

**Clients/Work Highlights:** Ameritrade; Business Objects; Gartner Group; Juniper Networks and Network Appliance.

## Other Notable Practitioners

Fenwick & West LLP's **Tyler Baker** (see p.277) continues to enjoy a *"terrific"* profile for his technology-oriented antitrust advice, which often dovetails with the group's IP practice. He focuses on the litigation aspects of antitrust, and has argued an appeal for Leegin Creative Leather Products relating to antitrust standards for vertical pricing agreements. **Tom Nolan** (see p.305) of Skadden, Arps, Slate, Meagher & Flom LLP & Affiliates *"can try any type of case,"* according to sources, and antitrust is an area in which he continues to shine. He is acting for TRL Group against claims by the California Attorney General, alleging deceptive sales practices. According to clients, the *"exceptionally bright"* **Robert Pringle** (see p.308) is particularly strong in counseling and antitrust matters. He chairs Thelen Reid & Priest LLP's practice group and his broad experience takes in a slew of litigation, M&A and Second Request matters. Cartel work has been a focus of late for Pringle, and he acted for two companies involved in the DOJ grand jury investigation and the EU investigation of the DRAM industry, and appeared in related civil litigation in federal and state courts. His clients include NEC; TXU Energy; Bechtel; Elpida Memory and Mirant.

# BANKING & FINANCE

## Band 1

### Bingham McCutchen LLP

See firm details p.1110

**The Firm:** Making significant inroads into California's banking and finance market, this outfit is definitely "*making noise.*" It operates for the most part out of Northern California offices, but has a growing presence in the southern part of the state. Lender representation is the focus, and the diverse client base is a combination of money-center banks, nonbanking financial institutions such as insurance companies, and hedge funds. The team also acts for a smaller number of borrowers. Key representations have included acting for the lender in a $300 million loan to restructure a family real estate operation. The group has also seen a number of transactions involving asset-based lending to foreign borrowers.

**The Lawyers:** Clients favor "*fabulous*" **George Hisert** (see p.295) for his "*tremendous breadth of experience in bank finance.*" This is particularly evident in letter of credit and UCC issues, where clients appreciate his "*knowledgeable and business-focused manner – not at all pretentious.*" A typical client avows: "*he is the most responsive outside counsel I've ever worked with.*"

**Clients/Work Highlights:** JPMorgan Chase; GE Capital; Silicon Valley Bank; Merrill Lynch Capital; BNP Paribas; Pacific Life Insurance; Prudential; Wells Fargo and CapitalSource Finance.

### Gibson, Dunn & Crutcher LLP

See firm details p.328

**The Firm:** This "*premier midmarket corporate counsel*" regularly acts for Fortune 100, 500 and 1000 clients. It is best known for its work on behalf of borrowers and issuers. Rivals are "*happy to work on the other side*" of the team, finding its members "*deal-oriented and practical.*" The group is focused in and around Los Angeles, and its deal flow is heavily weighted toward leveraged acquisition finance for private equity groups and other corporate clients, although the group engages in a range of other financing transactions. A key success was the group's advice to MGM, Sony and a consortium of private equity firms regarding a secured syndicated bank credit agreement to finance the $4 billion acquisition of MGM. The group also represented Hilton Hotels in a $1 billion amended and restated credit facility.

**The Lawyers:** "*Smart, knowledgeable and thorough*" **Brian Kilb** (see p.298) "*will focus on the major point,*" winning approval from market sources. He concentrates on borrower-side transactions, particularly leveraged acquisition finance, although he also does periodic work for lenders such as Wells Fargo, Bank of America and Citibank. His highlights have included advising Tenet Healthcare on a $1.2 billion syndicated credit facility. Peers earmarked "*impressive and practical*" associate **Cromwell Montgomery** (see p.303) for future prominence.

**Clients/Work Highlights:** Entravision Communications; Avnet; Banc of America Securities; JF Shea; Pacific Life Insurance; healthcare Property Investors and K2.

### Latham & Watkins LLP

**The Firm:** A "*unique*" group that opponents are "*pleased to have on the other side of the table,*" this heavyweight of the large-cap market is "*a force in high-yield and subordinated debt.*" The group is also regarded as "*one of the leaders in the complicated areas of structured finance, such as CDOs.*" Leveraged finance is a focus, but the group also has expertise in areas such as aircraft finance, project finance and tax-exempt work. It has also been involved in a number of cross-border transactions. Successes have included acting for UBS and its affiliates in providing credit facilities, and leading the Odin synthetic CDO. In all areas, attorneys are characterized by their "*care and attention to detail.*"

**The Lawyers:** Interviewees are full of praise for LA's **John Mendez.** Leveraged finance is his strongest suit; he acts mainly for investment banks, but takes on sponsors as well. He is an authority in cross-border transactions and entertainment-related work for clients such as Village Roadshow. "*Not only does she know her material,*" say clients of **Vicki Marmorstein,** but "*she's incredibly easy to work with and gives great service.*" She has an active securitization practice, and acted recently for Black Diamond CLO in the global offering of $1 billion collateralized loan obligations.

**Clients/Work Highlights:** AIG Global Investment; Ameriprise Financial (formerly American Express); Deutsche Bank; Morgan Stanley; Goldman Sachs and UBS Warburg.

### O'Melveny & Myers LLP

See firm details p.336

**The Firm:** Despite "*tremendous*" veteran James DeMeules' recent retirement, clients are confident in the group's "*excellent*" work in structured deals on behalf of banks. It is known for large-cap work, and offers "*a lot of depth*" still. Commentators aver that the group is "*clearly at the top in commercial lending,*" and remains "*one of the stronger banking firms around.*" Attorneys are experienced in structuring and documenting leveraged acquisition financings on behalf of agent and lender clients. The practice also takes instructions in debt underwriting and placements, derivatives, securitization and international transactions. Its finance practice covers clients in a huge range of sectors, including entertainment, broadcasting, healthcare, real estate, project and infrastructure finance.

**The Lawyers:** **Matt Kirby** (see p.298) is a "*terrific lawyer,*" and sought out for lending work. He cochairs the finance and restructuring group, and concentrates on leveraged acquisition financing, restructuring and media finance. "*Sensible*" **Jill Matichak** (see p.302) "*focuses on the important stuff and is easy to work with,*" according to sources. Her broad lending experience encompasses secured and unsecured arrangements, leveraged acquisitions, project financings, and restructurings. Clients "*think the world of*" **Christine Olsen** (see p.305) for her "*user-friendliness and proactivity,*" extolling her knack of coming up with solutions to complicated problems. She offers a breathtaking range of services to clients such as commercial and investment banks and insurance companies.

**Clients/Work Highlights:** The team has acted for CSFB, BNP Paribas and Wells Fargo.

## Orrick, Herrington & Sutcliffe LLP

See firm details p.337

**The Firm:** This group "*dominates the public finance space,*" according to sources. The past year has brought a rise in acquisition finance instructions and financings for European banks in their US activities. The team has a significant slice of Indian Native finance work for the gaming industry. Team members advise on aircraft finance and leasing and insurance company finance. Key client Wells Fargo yields a substantial workflow; one highlight was representing the bank in $225 million syndicated senior secured credit facilities for the Sycuan Band of the Kumeyaay Nation. It also acted for JPMorgan Chase in more than $200 million syndicated senior secured credit facilities for Morongo Band of Mission Indians. Clients enthusiastically commend the team's "*unsurpassed understanding of the law,*" relying on it to give "*not only a legal view, but a business one.*"

**The Lawyers:** **Alan Benjamin** (see p.278) heads the banking and commercial finance group and is a great favorite with clients. He is especially active in acquisition finance, but also advises on Indian Native finance and the occasional corporate borrower. He acted for HypoVereinsbank to provide $93 million credit facilities for the acquisition of Legoland California. **Thomas Coleman** (see p.284) enjoys a solid reputation among banks and other financial institutions in such areas as secured and unsecured syndicated and single-lender credit agreements, project finance, public finance, and lease arrangements.

**Clients/Work Highlights:** Bank of America; Calyon; WestLB; Union Bank of California; Colony Capital; Pacific Gas and Electric; John Hancock; CIGNA and Prudential.

---

## Band 2

## Morrison & Foerster LLP

See firm details p.335

**The Firm:** This team is strong across the state and has a healthy upper and midmarket practice, which is powerfully supported by its recognized strength in regulatory matters. Debt transactions are a focus, and the group is active in Rule 144A debt offerings and syndicated loans. The team also has a growing practice in asset-based lending. Lending clients are the mainstay of the practice, although borrowers also feature. Successes have included an acquisition of stock financing for InterDent, involving a Rule 144A offering through asset-based lender Foothill.

**The Lawyers:** LA-based Kathryn Johnstone cochairs the financial transactions practice.

**Clients/Work Highlights:** Wells Fargo Foothill; Bank of America; John Hancock; Bank of the West; IXIS Financial and Standard Chartered Bank.

## Paul, Hastings, Janofsky & Walker LLP

See firm details p.339

**The Firm:** This team "*gets the ball across the goal line,*" according to observers. Based in LA, attorneys represent investment banks and hedge funds in lending transactions. Highlights have included a $240 million first-lane leveraged loan for New World Pasta, and acting for Florida Digital Network in a $15 million telecom revolver. The group also acted for Wells Fargo Foothill in a $547 million senior credit facility for Key Energy Services.

**The Lawyers:** **John Hilson** (see p.294) has a "*formidable*" reputation, particularly in asset-based and leveraged lending, where he enjoys "*a tremendous following.*" A "*thoughtful and dedicated*" attorney, he is expert in "*developing business products within a safe legal playing field.*" He acted for Aozora Bank in its purchase of notes to finance the take-private acquisition by Cerberus Capital Management of LNR Property.

**Clients/Work Highlights:** GE Capital; Wells Fargo Foothill; Goldman Sachs; Allied Holdings; Chrysalis Capital; Ableco Finance and Silver Point Capital.

## Pillsbury Winthrop Shaw Pittman LLP

See firm details p.1550

**The Firm:** With great regulatory depth and committed attorneys throughout the state, this team "*has what it takes*" to handle transactions in the upper to midmarket. It serves financial institutions from the USA and abroad in a varied range of lending and complex finance deals – there is hardly an asset class or project type with which attorneys are not thoroughly au fait.

**The Lawyers:** Jan Harris Cate leads the firm's bank finance practice.

**Clients/Work Highlights:** The client base is mostly domestic and foreign banks, other financial institutions and insurance companies. The team also handles borrower-side work for corporate clients.

## Sheppard, Mullin, Richter & Hampton LLP

**The Firm:** Sources endorse this "*force*" in banking and finance, particularly for specialized lending in the gaming and REIT arenas. The bulk of the practice is lender-oriented, acting for financial institutions on all kinds of loans and financings, including plant leasings and real estate lending.

**The Lawyers:** **William Scott** is prominent in the gaming area and regarded as "*one of the very best bank lawyers in Los Angeles;*" rivals "*would love to lure him away.*" A smart and careful attorney, clients appreciate that he is "*cognizant of borrowers' needs and never adopts a dogmatic, form-driven approach.*" He recently acted on a number of multibillion-dollar loan facilities for gaming and resort companies. **John Berchild** acts for lenders on asset-based finance matters, leveraged acquisitions, bankruptcy and secured and unsecured loans.

**Clients/Work Highlights:** Bank of America; CIT Group; Citicorp; Farm Credit Bank; CoBank; Honda Finance; LaSalle Business Credit; Toyota Motor

Credit; Pitney Bowes Credit; US Bank; Wells Fargo and Union Bank of California.

## White & Case LLP

See firm details p.1566

**The Firm:** "*An excellent global network,*" say satisfied clients, complements this "*well-supervised, diligent and thoughtful*" team. Asset finance and leasing are key areas, and commentators repeatedly drew attention to the group's "*sophistication within aircraft financing.*" Attorneys have acted for clients such as Babcock & Brown in leasing matters involving commercial aircraft and airlines, including a range of Japanese operating lease transactions and other leveraged operating lease transactions in Europe, Asia, and North and South America. The team is also experienced in credit and liquidity support for state and municipal instruments, as well as sovereign debt issues. Additional highlights have included advising the Global Committee of Argentina Bondholders in connection with the restructuring of more than $100 billion of external debt on which Argentina defaulted in 2001, and acting for Bank of America in the purchase of short-term debt securities of the City of San Diego.

**The Lawyers:** Asset finance specialist **James Cairns** (see p.281) is closely involved in aircraft finance work, handling cross-border structures for aircraft transactions, as well as the restructuring and bankruptcies of domestic and foreign air carriers. His clients have included Boeing and CIT Group. "*Incredibly diligent*" **Neil Rust** (see p.311) "*goes above and beyond what it takes to get the deal done,*" according to clients. He co-heads the practice, and was the principal attorney in the City of San Diego matter.

**Clients/Work Highlights:** Allied Irish Banks; Bank of New York; Commerzbank: Delta Air Lines; Deutsche Bank; ECA; GM; Mizuho Bank; Nord/LB; Pegasus Aviation; Rhodes Homes; Sumitomo Trust & Banking Co; WestLB and Union Bank of California.

---

## Band 3

## Buchalter Nemer Fields & Younger

**The Firm:** Known in the California market for its varied finance practice, the group is also praised for the strength of its client relationships. Acting for its largely lender base, the team has experience of arranging financing in a great variety of sectors, including aerospace, healthcare, media and communications, and gaming.

**The Lawyers:** Matthew Kavanaugh is a key contact for the group.

**Clients/Work Highlights:** The client base includes banks of all shapes and sizes, mortgage companies and equipment lessors. It also features Bank of America; CIT Group; Union Bank of California; Wells Fargo Foothill; Comerica; Silicon Valley Bank and Bank of the West.

## DLA Piper Rudnick Gray Cary US LLP

See firm details p.870

**The Firm:** The growing national footprint of this global giant increasingly takes in banking, especially following the recent acquisition of four partners from Winston & Strawn. The practice now has presence across the state, with finance attorneys in Los Angeles, San Francisco, San Diego and Palo Alto. Midmarket commercial finance is the order of the day, with substantial volumes of private equity transactions for both borrowers and lenders. Lender finance, negotiating key creditor issues connected to Term B loans, and venture finance are all focus areas. Successes have included representing GE Capital in a multitranche arrangement with OMNI Energy Services, and acting for a private equity fund in a bridge loan facility by JPMorgan Chase.

**The Lawyers:** The arrival of **Gary Rosenbaum** (see p.310) from Winston & Strawn spells "*all good news*" for the practice, according to competitors who "*would hire him in a heartbeat.*" He chairs the finance group nationally, and has acted on behalf of lender clients such as Union Bank of California and GE Capital, as well as borrowers such as private equity fund Pacific Partners.

**Clients/Work Highlights:** Comerica; Silicon Valley Bank; Wells Fargo Foothill and Square One Bank.

## Manatt Phelps & Phillips LLP

**The Firm:** This group receives particular recognition for its work on behalf of community banks. It is active across the board on such matters as capital markets and structured finance, commercial lending, bank regulation and corporate governance. Highlights of the year have included electronic commerce agreements and legislative matters.

**The Lawyers:** Ellen Marshall cochairs the banking and financial services industry group.

**Clients/Work Highlights:** California National Bank; Comerica; Union Bank of California and Citibank.

## Mayer, Brown, Rowe & Maw LLP

See firm details p.876

**The Firm:** Clients applaud this "*consultive and customer-friendly*" LA-based group for doing an "*exceptional job in potentially nightmarish scenarios.*" Above all, the team's "*terrific understanding of structured finance*" draws them to the firm. The practice is national and international in scope, attorneys undertaking matters with a California connection. These have included revolver work, acquisition finance, asset-based lending and senior leveraged finance. The year's highlights include representing JPMorgan Chase as agent in a $325 million senior debt financing to a distributor of regulated consumer products in the USA and Canada. Attorneys advised the agent and arranger in a $131 million secured term loan facility for the acquisition of companies operating port facilities in Mexico.

The Lawyers: Marshall Stoddard and Don Weaver are key members of the team.

**Clients/Work Highlights:** Wells Fargo Foothill; Babcock & Brown; Bank of America; Chase Business Credit; GECC; LaSalle Bank; PNC; Wachovia Securities; Wachovia Capital Finance and Goldman Sachs.

## McDermott Will & Emery

See firm details p.878

**The Firm:** M&A finance is a key focus for this group, which generally acts for private equity clients. It also has a nice line in debtor finance. The emphasis is on borrower-side representation, though the group undertakes work on behalf of lenders as well. The team represented JW Childs in its $110 million financing of the acquisition of Summit Medical Holdings. It also acted for Vector Group in the $82 million private offering of notes to institutional investors.

**The Lawyers:** Eric Reimer (see p.310) divides his time between the firm's Los Angeles and New York offices. He heads the project finance group and vice chairs the corporate finance practice.

**Clients/Work Highlights:** Oaktree Capital Management; CIT Group; CMS Energy; JPMorgan Chase; Bayside Capital; Metagenics; Seadrift; Fidelity Capital Investors; Super Center Concepts; Health Net and Tenet Healthcare.

## Milbank, Tweed, Hadley & McCloy LLP

**The Firm:** With a strong profile in project finance and bankruptcy-related lending work, this team is often involved in matters with a restructuring flavor. Activities include structuring work for hedge funds interested in acquiring or making equity or debt investments in distressed companies. Highlights have included acting for CSFB in a $295 million secured financing for Krispy Kreme.

**The Lawyers:** Greg Bray is a key member of the team that represented Wachovia in its $1 billion unsecured letter of credit exposure in the Mirant bankruptcy.

**Clients/Work Highlights:** Wachovia; Ares Management; American Restaurant Group; Oaktree Capital Management and Tennenbaum Capital Partners.

## Shearman & Sterling

See firm details p.1554

**The Firm:** San Francisco is an important outpost of this New York banking power-player, and it makes a significant impact in the California market. The team provides advice to financial institutions on acquisition finance, and also represents corporate clients in financing matters. Key representations have included leveraged buyout work for Wells Fargo, and advising Bank of America in connection with loans to Michael Jackson.

**The Lawyers:** **Steven Sherman** (see p.313) heads the firm's West Coast private finance and bankruptcy group, and is principally active in acquisition finance and restructuring. He also undertakes some bankruptcy matters. His client base has been company-focused this past year, although he acts for lenders as well.

**Clients/Work Highlights:** Bank of America; Wells Fargo; Citibank; CSFB and Levi Strauss.

## Skadden, Arps, Slate, Meagher & Flom LLP & Affiliates

See firm details p.1557

**The Firm:** This firm offers stellar acquisition practices on both coasts. The LA group's prominence is attributed in large part to the firm's "*tremendous corporate contacts.*" On the company side, the team focuses on representing low investment grade entities on leveraged finance matters. It also acts for banks and private equity companies, and is developing a real estate finance offering. Successes have included representing Penn National Gaming in a $2.725 billion credit facility to finance its acquisition of Argosy Gaming. On the lender side, the group acted for CSFB as lead arranger of a $1.275 billion senior secured credit facility for Regal Cinemas.

**The Lawyers:** The "*thoughtful, goal-oriented and pragmatic*" **David Reamer** (see p.309) has been visible in real estate-related work over the past year.

**Clients/Work Highlights:** CSFB; Penn National Gaming; Fox Paine & Company; Vulcan and Apollo Advisors.

## Sullivan & Cromwell LLP

See firm details p.1558

**The Firm:** The California arm of this East Coast leviathan is stacked with quality attorneys focused on debt and equity capital markets, financial institutions M&A, and work for community banks and insurers. Highlights have included acting for Lehman Brothers as the lead underwriter for Zions Bancorp in the $600 million financing of its acquisition of Amergy. A smattering of smaller bank M&A financing deals has also kept the team busy.

**The Lawyers:** "*Nobody equals*" **Stanley Farrar** (see p.288) in the bank M&A area, according to sources. A "*first-rate attorney,*" he "*has full understanding of the various issues,*" making him "*wonderful to deal with.*" Regulatory matters have been a major component of his practice recently. To pigeonhole **Hydee Feldstein** (see p.288) for her undoubted bankruptcy expertise would be a mistake according to sources who point to her "*really big deals for muscular clients.*" Her skills in leveraged and structured finance, acting for lenders and acquirers, attract whole-hearted admiration. She has recently joined the firm from Paul, Hastings.

**Clients/Work Highlights:** Goldman Sachs; Zions Bancorp; Centennial and First Community Bancorp.

# BANKRUPTCY/RESTRUCTURING

| Bankruptcy/Restructuring |
|---|
| **Leading Firms** |
| **1**   KLEE, TUCHIN, BOGDANOFF & STERN *Los Angeles* |
|     MILBANK, TWEED, HADLEY & MCCLOY *Los Angeles* |
|     STUTMAN, TREISTER & GLATT *Los Angeles* |
| **2**   HENNIGAN, BENNETT & DORMAN LLP *Los Angeles* |
|     LATHAM & WATKINS LLP *Los Angeles* |
|     O'MELVENY & MYERS LLP *Los Angeles* |
|     PACHULSKI, STANG, ZIEHL, YOUNG *Los Angeles* |
|     SIDLEY AUSTIN LLP *Los Angeles* |
| **3**   ALSCHULER GROSSMAN STEIN *Santa Monica* |
|     GIBSON, DUNN & CRUTCHER LLP *Los Angeles* |
|     HELLER EHRMAN LLP *San Francisco* |
|     HOWARD, RICE *San Francisco* |
|     IRELL & MANELLA LLP *Los Angeles* |
|     KIRKLAND & ELLIS LLP *Los Angeles* |
|     LEVENE, NEALE, BENDER, RANKIN *Los Angeles* |
|     ORRICK, HERRINGTON & SUTCLIFFE *San Francisco* |
|     PAUL, HASTINGS *San Francisco* |
|     PEITZMAN, WEG & KEMPINSKY LLP *Los Angeles* |
|     SHEPPARD, MULLIN *Los Angeles* |
|     SKADDEN, ARPS *Los Angeles* |
|     WHITE & CASE LLP *Los Angeles* |
|     WINSTON & STRAWN LLP *San Francisco* |

## Band 1

### Klee, Tuchin, Bogdanoff & Stern LLP

See firm details p.332

**The Firm:** This nationally rated insolvency boutique enjoys *"a phenomenal share of the market,"* according to sources. It offers a full service in the reorganization and insolvency fields; in particular, the team's *"creative specialists"* and its potent reputation for debtor work attract clients. It serves debtors' and creditors' committees with equal aplomb, and attorneys act in and out of court in restructurings, Chapter 11 cases, acquisitions and investments and bankruptcy-related litigation.

**The Lawyers:** Undisputed *"dean of the national bankruptcy Bar,"* **Kenneth Klee**'s (see p.298) *"remarkable"* career has included acting as one of the chief drafters of the 1978 Bankruptcy Code. He is well known for his academic work and recognized on all sides as a *"star"* in the field. *"Great technician"* **Lee Bogdanoff** (see p.279) receives commendations as *"a straight shooter."* Commentators declare him *"supersmart but also superpractical."* Meanwhile, interviewees speak highly of the *"wonderful"* **Michael Tuchin**'s (see p.318) *"great manner."* He enjoys a rising reputation in the field and *"is really blossoming,"* according to admirers. **Thomas Patterson** (see p.306) *"is, refreshingly, not a windbag,"* and sources stress: *"He's easy to deal with and a terrific guy all-around."*

**Clients/Work Highlights:** Crescent Jewelers; Adelphia Communications Unsecured Creditors' Committee; The Century Trust and Paramount Studios/Viacom.

### Milbank, Tweed, Hadley & McCloy LLP

**The Firm:** A popular choice for *"big-ticket work,"* this group is said to have *"an unbelievable lock on the market for public debt."* It undertakes a large chunk of work for bondholders, including investments related to distressed bond funds and work for troubled bondholding institutions. Other substantial sources of work include hedge funds, for which the team handles structuring work on the acquisition of distressed companies, banks and debtors. Recent highlights include acting for two groups of bondholders in the bankruptcy of Trump Casino Holdings, and representing the official creditors' committee in EaglePicher's bankruptcy. It's all in a day's work for this *"colossus of the field."*

**The Lawyers:** Clients regard **Paul Aronzon** as *"an outstanding talent,"* and rivals express frank envy of his *"wonderful practice,"* national prominence and *"wealth of knowledge."* He cochairs the financial and restructuring group. Sources also praise the *"unfailingly impressive"* **Robert Moore** for his *"professionalism"* and ability to *"keep fractious clients together."* **Thomas Kreller** is acknowledged as a solid specialist.

**Clients/Work Highlights:** Trust Company of the West; Oaktree Capital Management; Cerberus Capital Management; AIG; SunAmerica; Tennenbaum Capital Partners; Wachovia NA; CSFB; JPMorgan and ABM AMRO.

### Stutman, Treister & Glatt Professional Corporation

See firm details p.341

**The Firm:** This boutique has been *"the preeminent debtor firm in California for 30 years or more."* It is admired for its *"huge depth,"* and is *"stuffed with first-rate lawyers from top to bottom."* The practice covers Chapter 11 reorganizations and workouts, distressed M&A and related litigation and tax matters. Interviewees concur that this team is *"as good as it gets"* in the bankruptcy arena.

**The Lawyers:** **Robert Greenfield** has a long and honorable history in this area, and sources agree: *"He is still at the top."* He was recently appointed lead reorganization counsel for Falcon Products. **Isaac Pachulski** is singled out for his *"genius,"* and at least one respondent declared him *"the smartest lawyer I know."* He is visible representing the holders of more than $1.6 billion of Enron's unsecured debt. **Alan Pedlar** is *"unbelievably good,"* and also a *"well-rounded attorney"* in the eyes of interviewees.

**Clients/Work Highlights:** The team represents distressed businesses and creditors' and bondholders' committees, as well as shareholders' and investors' interests.

## Band 2

### Hennigan, Bennett & Dorman LLP

See firm details p.330

**The Firm:** For big-ticket bankruptcy litigation *"there's no better bet,"* researchers were assured. The expertise offered here is well rounded and encompasses the gamut of reorganization and bankruptcy matters.

**The Lawyers:** *"Brains plus business equals* **Bruce Bennett**,*"* according to interviewees. He enjoys a high profile and is a favorite *"hired gun"* in matters requiring litigation prowess.

**Clients/Work Highlights:** The client base includes all kinds of interested parties, including debtors and creditors, committees of all stamps and potential acquirers.

### Latham & Watkins LLP

**The Firm:** This *"dynamite"* offering wins tremendous approval for its debtor-focused Chapter 11 and bankruptcy-related M&A work. It acts for clients across a spectrum of industry sectors. Representations have included Trump Hotels and Casino Resorts and 28 subsidiaries/affiliates in its $2 billion debt restructuring. The group also acted for Yucaipa and Aloha Aviation Investment Group as plan investors in Aloha Airlines' reorganization proposals; it represented Comtel Investments as the successful purchaser of the assets of VarTec Telecom and its 16 subsidiaries.

**The Lawyers:** Experts applaud national figure **Michael Lurey** for his *"level-headed, consensus-building"* approach. A *"bright, brilliant"* lawyer, he is *"a counselor to counselors,"* and a *"phenomenal attorney."* He represented the liquidation trust in the bankruptcy of Consolidated Freightways. **Robert Klyman** is *"imaginative and good with the judge,"* say sources. He acted in the Trump Hotels and Casino Resorts and Aloha Airway matters.

**Clients/Work Highlights:** Consolidated Freightways; Aloha Airlines; Comtel Investments and IdeaSphere.

### O'Melveny & Myers LLP

See firm details p.336

**The Firm:** This group of *"absolutely first-rate attorneys"* is highly visible in creditor representations, and enjoys a reputation for being *"capable, easy to deal with and honest."* Acting for syndicated senior bank groups is a major focus, alongside an increasing client base of funds at all levels of the capital structure. The team also acts for debtors and has been particularly noted for work in the retail sector. It successfully concluded Protocol Communications' Chapter 11 proceedings, acting for the senior secured lenders' agent. The group also acted for Cerberus to acquire a large chain of fast-food franchises through a Chapter 11 plan.

**The Lawyers:** *"Exceptional"* **Ben Logan** (see p.301) has a growing profile in Chapter 11 cases both in and out of court, and out-of-court restructuring advice.

He has been active recently on inter-creditor and subordinated debt issues. **Robert White** (see p.320) has *"been around the block"* and has a national profile in the bankruptcy arena.

Clients/Work Highlights: Clients include CIBC; Bank of America; Deutsche Bank; Watershed Asset Management and Post Advisory Group, as well as a number of debtors on a more episodic basis, such as Tower Records and Ormet.

## Pachulski, Stang, Ziehl, Young, Jones & Weintraub P.C.

See firm details p.338

**The Firm:** This boutique has a national imprint and an *"edge,"* according to commentators, which has made it a force in bankruptcy litigation. The debtors' practice also draws acclaim. Attorneys handle business reorganizations and out-of-court workouts, including Chapter 11 cases, and are active in related business litigation and commercial and real estate transactions.

**The Lawyers:** *"Powerhouse"* **Richard Pachulski** is a noted business generator and admired as *"a consensus-builder."* He is *"exceedingly sharp,"* according to commentators, and *"a cut above the rest."* His practice covers reorganizations and litigation, acting for debtors and creditors' committees in and out of court. **Brad Godshall** enjoys regional standing for his corporate restructuring work under Chapter 11. Finance and workouts are also areas of expertise.

Clients/Work Highlights: Direct TV Latin America; Equitable Life Assurance Society of America; Executive Life Insurance Company; Farmers Insurance Group; First Capital Holdings; Gateway Educational Products; Hilton Hotels and Six Continents Hotels; Orange County; PG&E and Zenith Electronics.

## Sidley Austin LLP

See firm details p.883

**The Firm:** This *"tremendous"* group operates along national lines. The California team has been involved in a number of Chapter 11 cases, acting for shareholders, secured and unsecured creditors. Out-of-court settlements are a focus, and work has included representing the parent company and shareholders in a Chapter 11 case involving Asarco, and involvement in the Federal-Mogul reorganization.

**The Lawyers:** **Richard Havel** (see p.293) heads the LA team and has a solid Chapter 11 practice, often acting for equity groups and hedge funds. **Sally Neely** (see p.304) is universally acclaimed as a *"wonderful"* bankruptcy attorney. Her recent caseload has included ongoing work on the asbestos-related Chapter 11 reorganization of Flintkote.

Clients/Work Highlights: Canyon Partners; Fortress Investment Group; Meridian Auto Parts; CIBC and GE.

## Band 3

## Alschuler Grossman Stein & Kahan LLP

See firm details p.323

**The Firm:** This three-lawyer Santa Monica group primarily represents creditors or buyers of assets, and it is particularly strong in handling bankruptcies for the healthcare and food service industries. The members of this solid team are *"proactive, rather than waiting to react to whatever is happening."* The firm handled two bankruptcy cases involving film distributors, protecting the interests of the director and the primary actor. Another highlight was its representation of the liquidator of SNIC against the insurers' affiliates.

**The Lawyers:** The *"tenacious"* **Henry David** (see p.285) has taken on an increasing volume of cases filed locally by midsized companies. Clients appreciate his personal involvement, adding: *"He communicates as to what is feasible and what is not – he is truly on their team and not just showing up for a paycheck."* He represented Sun Dunes Villas Vacation Plan Owners Association in the bankruptcy of TNT Management.

Clients/Work Highlights: The team represented Epson America in several preference claims; Heritage Provider Network; Baker & Taylor and Marubeni-Itochu Steel.

## Gibson, Dunn & Crutcher LLP

See firm details p.328

**The Firm:** This team is well known for its out-of-court workouts practice. The group is ably supported by its corporate colleagues and its workload is very much congruent with the firm's corporate practice. It represents a wide variety of parties, including debtors, creditors' committees and secured creditors. The senior lawyers are highly regarded and, with the firm's resources behind them, they are able to staff cases on a national basis.

**The Lawyers:** **Kathryn Coleman** (see p.284) is *"just so organized and clear."* She tends to be involved in workouts, concentrating on the transactional, acquisition and finance side of bankruptcies. She has been representing Scotia Pacific in a potential restructuring of outsourcing notes. She also had great success helping Citibank with the restructuring of a $100 million debt for Brobeck, Phleger & Harrison. *"Creative and easy to deal with,"* **Oscar Garza** (see p.290) is a *"smart and super hard-working"* attorney more involved on the litigation side. He was appointed debtor's counsel to House2Home and EMSolutions, and counsel to the Chapter 7 trustee in the Commercial Money Center and Commercial Servicing Company cases in San Diego. **Craig Millet** (see p.303) undertakes debtor and creditor representations in Chapter 11 reorganizations, asset acquisition and litigation. He successfully obtained judgment in New York for Flag Telecom in its Chapter 11 reorganization plan. He also represented Solutia in a $500 million claim filed by Calpine, and is involved in ongoing mediation work arising out of the Enron bankruptcy.

Clients/Work Highlights: The group negotiated on behalf of James Hardie with the Government of New South Wales regarding alleged asbestos liability, and represented aerospace manufacturers in an out-of-court restructuring.

## Heller Ehrman LLP

See firm details p.329

**The Firm:** This national firm is focused on all aspects of complex bankruptcy, reorganizations and debt restructurings. Its standing is secured by the excellent reputation in Northern California of its *"strong individuals."*

**The Lawyers:** *"The most impressive guy in town,"* **Peter Benvenutti** (see p.278) handles both transactions and litigations in bankruptcy and creditors' rights matters. He frequently represents financial institutions in workout negotiations involving real estate and commercial loans, bringing *"excellent technical knowledge and a very constructive attitude"* to the table. He has been representing Chapter 11 debtors-in-possession in the Jomed and Worldcom cases.

## Howard, Rice, Nemerovski, Canady, Falk & Rabkin

**The Firm:** A "*talented group*" of five lawyers operates out of San Francisco, representing a varied bunch of clients including debtors, creditors (individuals and committees) and Chapter 11 trustees. Its high-profile representation of PG&E is the benchmark against which the firm continues to increase its presence in this field.

**The Lawyers:** **James Lopes** chairs the bankruptcy and reorganization group and "*did a superb balancing act*" in the PG&E case. Commentators extol him because he "*knows how to really engage to resolve disputes.*"

**Clients/Work Highlights:** Banc of America Securities; Chapter 11 Estate of Gateway Educational Products; Creative Labs; Hartford Accident and Indemnity; Imaginarium; Insurance Commissioner of the State of California; PG&E; The Charles Schwab Corporation; The Oakland Tribune and The Wine Group.

## Irell & Manella LLP

**The Firm:** Based in Los Angeles and Orange County, this firm gets involved in major cases. In the past year the team has been active for the hospitality and restaurant industries in matters involving government regulations, real estate and gaming and casinos. For instance, the lawyers counseled the creditors' committee in the Chevys case. Four partners are involved in bankruptcy work on a full-time basis, and are supported by tax specialists and litigators. In addition to its national reputation in bankruptcy tax issues the team has a strong debtor practice. Its lawyers acted for five debtors in the bankruptcy of Numair Pirzada.

**The Lawyers:** Debtor lawyer **William Lobel** enjoys an "*extraordinary reputation and stature*" in the community. He has "*an energetic and creative*" practice that is recognized nationwide. He has been acting as debtors' counsel in a variety of pending Chapter 11 cases, involving a gaming casino in Colorado, a national fast-food chain and an apartment complex in Texas. **Jeffrey Reisner** is "*one of the best debtor lawyers in the state,*" and also represents creditors' committees. He handles cases throughout the country. He has had successes reorganizing and disposing of the assets of troubled restaurants, and has been representing a debtor in the First Alliance Mortgage bankruptcy.

## Kirkland & Ellis LLP

See firm details p.875

**The Firm:** Backed by a highly integrated national practice, the Californian restructuring practice has been expanding ever since it merged with a local bankruptcy boutique; it now has 15 lawyers practicing bankruptcy law in Los Angeles. Attorneys served as Chapter 11 trustee for Ritter Ranch Development, selling it at auction to SunCal for $57.2 million. The group also represented the Reed Slatkin creditors' committee, being later appointed as special counsel to the trustee. It investigated Slatkin's Ponzi scheme, handling 101 fraudulent transfer cases, obtaining judgments for 21 and settling eight. It also sued the group of banks who allegedly aided the fraud, obtaining a $26.5 million settlement for investors.

**The Lawyers:** The "*knowledgeable and pragmatic*" **Richard Wynne** (see p.321) "*is someone you can get along with,*" according to interviewees. His high-profile caseload included representing Clifford Chance and Tower Snow against allegations of causing the demise of Brobeck Phleger & Harrison. A thoroughly versatile attorney, he was instrumental in the Chapter 11 sale of Chevys for more than $90 million.

**Clients/Work Highlights:** Cable & Wireless; The Fleming Companies; Slatkin Creditors' Committee and Adelphia.

## Levene, Neale, Bender, Rankin & Brill

**The Firm:** This 16-lawyer boutique spends half of its time handling debtor work in the midmarket and the rest representing creditor committees, buyers, sellers and equity holders. The firm is praised for its "*practical-minded, business-oriented restructuring practitioners who are open to considering solutions beyond bankruptcy.*" Due to the developments in the state's malpractice laws, the team often represents creditors' committees or acts as debtors' counsel in the hospital and healthcare industry. It also has a niche IP bankruptcy practice, representing movie studios. It has been dealing with the US assets of Kirsch Media.

**The Lawyers:** Craig Rankin is a key bankruptcy contact at the firm.

**Clients/Work Highlights:** The firm represents a broad spectrum of businesses and individuals involved in the entertainment, healthcare, food and beverage, manufacturing, energy, real estate, retail and technology industries.

## Orrick, Herrington & Sutcliffe LLP

See firm details p.337

**The Firm:** With eight lawyers in California focusing on bankruptcy and related matters, this international heavyweight enjoys an excellent reputation in the San Francisco legal community for restructuring and bankruptcy expertise. It successfully represented Quickturn Design Systems in a recent Chapter 11 case, and has been defending Squire, Sanders & Dempsey from a $30 million claim by the trustee of Graham & James.

**The Lawyers:** **Frederick Holden** (see p.295) has been building up an international practice, particularly in Asia. He continues to act as debtor's counsel to Philippine Airlines, working through the claims and issues of creditors based in the USA. Given the increased focus on reducing medical and pension obligations to retirees, he increasingly represents retirees' committees and New York bondholder committees. He is advising the Official Committee of Retirees in the Kaiser Aluminum Chapter 11 case.

**Clients/Work Highlights:** The group principally acts in Chapter 11 cases, representing diverse creditor clients such as Electronic Arts and Gap. It also acts for technology and electronics companies such as NVIDIA and American President Lines, and takes on debtor work.

## Paul, Hastings, Janofsky & Walker LLP

See firm details p.339

**The Firm:** This team acts regularly for money sources such as investment banks, hedge funds and other lenders. The practice includes a large volume of restructuring work. Highlights have included closing a $230 million debtor-in-possession financing for Allied Holdings, and advising Chrysalis Capital Partners in the case of American Business Financial Services.

**The Lawyers:** John Hilson is the contact for the banking as well as the bankruptcy group.

## Peitzman, Weg & Kempinsky LLP

**The Firm:** This boutique commands the admiration of peers. It focuses on business reorganizations under Chapter 11, out-of-court workouts and a significant amount of bankruptcy-related litigation. The client base is mainly debtors' and creditors' committees, although the team also acts for trustees as part of a well-balanced bankruptcy offering. As befits a Los Angeles-based operation, a substantial portion of the workload is related to the entertainment industry, where the team has acted for prominent debtors and bank groups. The group has also had successes in the power industry, which have included representing toy manufacturer Applause in its Chapter 11 case, and advising Warner Bros. in connection with the bankruptcy of Franchise Pictures.

**The Lawyers:** **Lawrence Peitzman** is "*the type of person who exudes an aura of confidence,*" according to sources. **Howard Weg** is experienced in the interplay of bankruptcy and energy regulatory issues.

**Clients/Work Highlights:** DreamWorks SKG; Sony Pictures; BC Hydro and The Regents of the University of California.

## Sheppard, Mullin, Richter &Hampton LLP

**The Firm:** This group of "*great workout lawyers*" typically represents creditors, creditors' committees and trustees, although the San Francisco group and some Los Angeles members act for debtors as well. The focus is firmly on lender representation, however, and the practice has included insolvencies and restructurings in sectors as diverse as agricultural products, telecom, shipping and hotels. Attorneys also act in matters with international aspects, and have a line in representing buyers of distressed assets. They were involved in the PG&E bankruptcy, and have been successful in a string of asbestos cases, on behalf of credit groups.

**The Lawyers:** San Francisco-based **Michael Ahrens** is esteemed for his "*intelligent point of view and persuasive arguments.*" He has acted for secured creditors, creditors' committees, trustees, debtors and receivers in a full range of insolvency matters and loan workouts, and is expert in advising potential acquirers in the purchase and sale of distressed assets.

**Clients/Work Highlights:** Clients include Bank of America; Union bank of California; CoBank; US Bank and CoAmerica Bank, as well as smaller banks, diverse industrial companies and creditors' committees.

## Skadden, Arps, Slate, Meagher & Flom LLP & Affiliates

See firm details p.1557

**The Firm:** Despite Richard Levin's departure to New York, commentators still see this group as home to a *"dynamite"* bankruptcy practice and lawyers that are *"made for debtor work."* The staple of the practice involves acting for private equity companies and their distressed portfolio companies. The team is experienced in representing public companies in Chapter 11 cases in and out of court, and is expert in the airline, retail and auto-manufacture industries. Highlights include representing Friedman's as creditor in the Crescent Jewelers Chapter 11 case. Attorneys also appeared in the Chapter 11 proceedings of debtors such as Fujita USA, Kmart and US Airways Group.

**The Lawyers:** Van Durrer is a key contact in the Los Angeles team.

**Clients/Work Highlights:** Vulcan; First Virtual Communications; Brentwood Associates and UnitedGlobalCom.

## White & Case LLP

See firm details p.1566

**The Firm:** Sources singled out this group's quality and consistency, reporting an enviable bench made up of *"star-quality and business-savvy"* attorneys. The team acts for parties of all kinds, and excels in the energy, hi-tech and airline sectors. As one should expect from a firm with such a global footprint, attorneys have a penchant for cross-border matters and are particularly experienced in dealing with Latin America. For example, the team acted for Corporación Durango SA de CV and its affiliates under Mexico's Business Reorganization Act, restructuring the company's $800 million unsecured debt. Other highlights include advising Mirant and 82 direct and indirect subsidiaries in pending Chapter 11 cases involving over $20 billion in assets and around $11.4 billion in debts.

**The Lawyers:** Brian Holman heads the group.

**Clients/Work Highlights:** Automated Power Exchange; Bank of America (and affiliates); Bank of New York; Enpower; Montecito Bank & Trust; Official Committee of Excel Independent Representatives and RBS.

## Winston & Strawn LLP

See firm details p.886

**The Firm:** At the heart of this respected San Francisco outfit is a cadre of experienced attorneys handling bankruptcies, restructurings, workouts and distressed asset purchases and sales. The transactional capability is supported by litigation expertise, and attorneys are adept on the international stage.

**The Lawyers:** Patrick Murphy (see p.304) is a long-standing member of the group, and experienced in cross-border matters.

**Clients/Work Highlights:** Clients include institutional lenders, corporations, partnerships, and limited liability companies.

## Other Notable Practitioners

*"Exceptionally talented"* **Hydee Feldstein** (see p.288) has recently joined Sullivan & Cromwell LLP from Paul, Hastings. She is a gifted banking and finance lawyer with strong bankruptcy capabilities, and acts for lenders and acquirers in restructurings and bankruptcy-related acquisitions. Kaye Scholer LLP's **Marc Cohen** (see p.283) is *"a workhorse,"* say sources, and *"the guy to go to if you want something done."* He chairs the business reorganization and creditors' rights practice in Los Angeles, and has expertise in representing bondholders, secured creditors, creditors' committees and debtors-in-possession.

# CONSTRUCTION

| Construction | |
|---|---|
| Leading Firms | |
| [1] THELEN REID & PRIEST LLP *San Francisco* | |
| [2] FARELLA BRAUN & MARTEL LLP *San Francisco* | |
| GIBBS, GIDEN, LOCHER & TURNER *Los Angeles* | |
| [3] BINGHAM MCCUTCHEN LLP *San Francisco* | |
| COX CASTLE & NICHOLSON LLP *Los Angeles* | |
| HANSON, BRIDGETT, MARCUS *San Francisco* | |
| MILLER, MORTON, CAILLAT & NEVIS *San Jose* | |
| MONTELEONE & MCCRORY, LLP *Los Angeles* | |

## Band 1

### Thelen Reid & Priest LLP

See firm details p.342

**The Firm:** This worldwide giant is *"as big a firm as you're going to see in construction law;"* its long tradition in the field and historical roots in California enable it to offer broad services and deep resources with the expertise and market savvy of a local firm. Its 40 construction attorneys, split between the San Francisco and Los Angeles offices, make up what clients called *"the deepest pool of talent they had seen"* in construction law. Attorneys here serve a range of major state and national property owners, contractors and designers. Over the past year, the firm has been particularly active in litigation: it represented Clark Construction Group in disputes arising from the $100 million renovation of the Cook Convention Center in Memphis. It also represents Fireman's Fund in the closing out of projects worth over $200 million for the firm's former client, JA Jones Construction, including the related litigation. Clients highlighted the sound advice, excellent thorough representation and attentive service of these attorneys, who have the ability to *"make things happen without waiting for instructions."*

**The Lawyers:** *"Tough but professional"* and *"easy to get along with,"* **David Buoncristiani** (see p.281) is a litigator first and foremost, but his practice focuses ever more closely on construction disputes. In particular, he has represented a major contractor in litigation concerning a large gas-fired energy plant in eastern USA. He leads the firm's work on disputes arising out of the building of the Tacoma Narrows Bridge in Washington. **John Clark** (see p.283) is the team's senior trial specialist. Like Buoncristiani, he is active in matters concerning the energy industry, and this year won $30 million in a jury trial for Modern Continental Construction in litigation concerning the La Paloma power plant in McKittrick. **Robert Thum** (see p.317) has devoted much of his time of late to work on the University of California's new Merced campus. His approach may be aggressive, but he has the ability to resolve disputes. The University of California is also a key client of **John Heisse** (see p.293). Now chair of construction at the firm, Heisse maintains a varied practice, combining litigation with contract counseling, and is *"more than competent at both negotiation and trials."* He repre-

sents the regents of the university in issues arising out of the development of its Mission Bay campus in San Francisco. *"Tenacious"* **Stephen O'Neal** (see p.306) now combines his respected construction law practice with his new role as the chair of Thelen Reid.

**Clients/Work Highlights:** The firm represents major contractors, subcontractors, design professionals and owners, including Clark Construction and Bechtel.

## Band 2

### Farella Braun & Martel LLP

**The Firm:** This San Francisco firm houses a *"dream team"* of 13 lawyers, who *"do a damn fine job"* protecting their clients' interests. Well versed in all aspects of construction law, it has a particular niche in PPPs, especially in counseling clients in drawing up engineering, procurement and construction (EPC) contracts. In this regard, the healthcare, energy and transportation sectors have proved to be areas of activity. With a reputation for *"getting results,"* the group has recently provided contract counsel to Acciona on one of its first US projects, an alternative power plant in Nevada. Its *"highly personable"* lawyers are also acknowledged for their interactive approach to lobbying.

**The Lawyers:** An *"excellent adviser and litigator,"* **Alan Harris'** vast experience puts him at the top of many clients' lists. He is involved in disputes across the country and beyond, including a recent matter concerning a nitrogen plant in Mexico. He possesses substantial industry knowledge, with peers noting: "*He knows what can go wrong.*" Though skilled in alternative dispute resolution, he "*can try cases when he needs to*" and is increasingly called on as an arbitrator. "*Well-grounded and knowledgeable,*" **Charles Sink** is greatly respected in the legal community for his results-focused approach. A "*highly articulate*" attorney with "*lots of class,*" he pushes for resolution outside of trial but is also a capable and experienced litigator. Recently he has been involved in EPC contracts for three traditional coal-fired plants in Kansas. As well as dealing with EPC contractors, he also represents private owners and public entities, engineers and architects. Although **Deborah Ballati** (see p.277) has an increasingly broad litigation practice, she remains active in construction matters. Her clients include the University of California, representing them in litigation and related claims regarding their new building in Santa Cruz. She has been active this year in complex litigation concerning landfill conversion, with the attendant environmental issues.

**Clients/Work Highlights:** Acciona; InterGen; University of California; Black & Veatch; Stewart & Stevenson Services and Bechtel.

## Gibbs, Giden, Locher & Turner
See firm details p.327

**The Firm:** This team of 45 attorneys possesses a wide range of expertise and the ability to "*understand business decisions as well as legal ones.*" Known for its skill in resolving disputes quickly, this team has established a practice that stretches to Arizona and Nevada. Recently, it has represented Mortenson in the $50 million dispute surrounding the Walt Disney Concert Hall. With a "*high work ethic,*" it is a "*responsive, client-oriented*" firm, accomplishing "*great results.*"

**The Lawyers:** "*Hard-working and easy to deal with,*" **Kenneth Gibbs** (see p.290) is endorsed by clients for his excellent customer service. His "*persuasive demeanor*" underpins his advocacy and he displays "*insight into the quirky intricacies of Californian construction law.*" An "*astute adviser,*" he is also a leading figure in the field of mediation. A "*superb litigator,*" **Glenn Turner** (see p.318) is highly valued by clients for his ability to present complex legal issues in an accessible way. He has recently defended the Southern California Public Power Agency in a $15 million dispute concerning an electrical power plant.

**Clients/Work Highlights:** Centex Construction, University of California and Mortenson are among the major contractors and owners who instruct the firm.

## Band 3

### Bingham McCutchen LLP
See firm details p.1110

**The Firm:** This San Francisco firm, "*one of the premier teams in the city,*" focuses on representing owners in both litigation and contract negotiations. A key client is Stanford University, a relationship enhanced by the firm's recent opening of a small Palo Alto office. This demonstrates the firm's commitment to customer service, with clients appreciating that these attorneys are responsive: "*They get you answers to your questions, in short order.*" Despite their long-standing reputation in the San Francisco market, the team is not willing to ride a reputation and clients respect and value the extra levels of service: "*They really earn our business.*"

**The Lawyers:** "*The man for construction disputes,*" **Stephen Zovickian** (see p.321) combines a litigation background with an extensive construction knowledge that sees him as active in counseling as in disputes. "*Organized, prepared and well-documented*" in court, he adopts a trial manner that is "*matter-of-fact, clear and convincing.*" Whether before a court or a client, he "*does his research and gets his facts straight.*"

**Clients/Work Highlights:** Madison Marquette; Episcopal Homes Foundation; Stanford University; Lousiana-Pacific; CNA Insurance and Wausau Insurance.

### Cox Castle & Nicholson LLP

**The Firm:** This midsized Los Angeles firm continues to impress clients with its "*strong and aggressive*" construction litigation practice. It has recently combined this specialism with its growing real estate practice in order to provide clients with a well-rounded service. Litigation head Larry Teplin has been particularly active in real estate this year.

**The Lawyers:** **Tim Truax** impresses with his skillful handling of construction litigation, alternative dispute resolution and contract counseling. He acts on a variety of public and private developments, ranging from residential to infrastructure.

**Clients/Work Highlights:** The firm has an extensive developer client base.

## Hanson, Bridgett, Marcus, Vlahos & Rudy, LLP

**The Firm:** A core team of 12 construction attorneys are supplemented by additional support from other teams at this San Francisco general practice firm. Active in both litigation and counseling, the team is also involved in project formation and financing work for owners, developers and contractors, as well as design professionals. It focuses on infrastructure projects, such as highways and waste treatment.

**The Lawyers:** **Howard Ashcraft** has been involved in projects as varied as a University of California laboratory in Berkeley and a nitrogen plant in Mexico. He is also involved in litigation concerning the seismic rehabilitation of the Golden Gate Bridge. He combines "*good technical knowledge*" with a "*pragmatic*" approach that leaves clients and jurors alike convinced that he "*really knows what he's doing.*"

**Clients/Work Highlights:** Compañia de Nitrógeno de Cantarell; BOC Gases; Marubeni; CH2M HILL; URS; HDR; ROMA Design Group; University of California; Golden Gate Bridge Highway & Transportation District; San Mateo County Transit District; California Department of Corrections and Rehabilitation; Terra Insurance and Kingston Constructors.

### Miller, Morton, Caillat & Nevis

**The Firm:** This 20-attorney general practice has a dedicated team of seven construction attorneys, representing contractors, owners and particularly homebuilders, in litigation as well as counseling. It has recently developed a strong practice negotiating contracts for the building of casinos in Native American land in central California.

**The Lawyers:** **Frank Hughes**' litigation and counseling practice is statewide, and in 2005 he negotiated three contracts of more than $100 million in Los Angeles. "*A great communicator,*" he "*has a knack for taking complex issues and making them understandable,*" said clients. He combines this ability with an impressive "*depth of skill and judgment*" and excellent customer service.

**Clients/Work Highlights:** The firm's clients range from construction firms to casino developers.

### Monteleone & McCrory, LLP

**The Firm:** This 15-strong firm focuses primarily on construction law. Its "*high-quality team*" represents contractors, designers and owners in most kinds of dispute. The projects in which it has been involved range from commercial developments to major infrastructure schemes, and its "*sharp legal minds*" have been particularly active in mass transit systems.

**The Lawyers:** **Michael Minchella** has a "*good practical mind*" that enables him to "*quickly pick up on the issues.*" He has established "*good contacts in the industry and great credibility*" in the market.

**Clients/Work Highlights:** The firm's client base is broad, but is weighted towards contractors such as Granite Construction.

## Other Notable Practitioners

**Peter Ippolito** (see p.296), a partner in the San Diego office of McKenna Long & Aldridge LLP, has a *"rough 'n' tumble style that's very effective."* *"Very knowledgeable"* about all sides of construction law, he focuses on representing contractors in litigation, contract negotiations and administrative hearings. **Dan McMillan** (see p.303) heads up the construction practice in Jones Day's Los Angeles office. Clients expressed *"a lot of confidence in his legal abilities and judgment."* The scope of his practice was illustrated recently when he represented Genentech and its Spanish affiliate in litigation concerning the design and construction of a pharmaceutical factory in Spain. Though *"extremely competent and thorough"* in and out of trial, he is *"particularly effective on his feet."*

# CORPORATE/M&A

### Corporate/M&A: Northern California
#### Leading Firms

1. **LATHAM & WATKINS LLP** *Menlo Park*
   **WILSON SONSINI** *Palo Alto*
2. **COOLEY GODWARD LLP** *Palo Alto*
   **DAVIS POLK & WARDWELL** *Menlo Park*
   **FENWICK & WEST LLP** *Mountain View*
   **SKADDEN, ARPS** *San Francisco*
3. **DLA PIPER RUDNICK GRAY CARY US** *Palo Alto*
   **GIBSON, DUNN & CRUTCHER LLP** *San Francisco*
   **GUNDERSON DETTMER STOUGH** *Menlo Park*
   **HELLER EHRMAN LLP** *Menlo Park*
   **MORGAN, LEWIS & BOCKIUS LLP** *San Francisco*
   **MORRISON & FOERSTER LLP** *San Francisco*
   **O'MELVENY & MYERS LLP** *Menlo Park*
   **PILLSBURY WINTHROP SHAW PITTMAN** *Palo Alto*
   **SIMPSON THACHER & BARTLETT LLP** *Palo Alto*

### Corporate/M&A: Southern California
#### Leading Firms

1. **GIBSON, DUNN & CRUTCHER LLP** *Los Angeles*
   **LATHAM & WATKINS LLP** *Los Angeles*
   **SKADDEN, ARPS** *Los Angeles*
2. **O'MELVENY & MYERS LLP** *Los Angeles*
   **SHEPPARD, MULLIN** *Los Angeles*
   **SIDLEY AUSTIN LLP** *Los Angeles*
3. **DLA PIPER RUDNICK GRAY CARY** *San Diego*
   **IRELL & MANELLA LLP** *Los Angeles*
   **MUNGER, TOLLES & OLSON LLP** *Los Angeles*
   **PAUL, HASTINGS** *Los Angeles*
   **SULLIVAN & CROMWELL LLP** *Los Angeles*

## Latham & Watkins LLP

**The Firm:** This Californian stalwart dominates a market from which it elicits *"immense respect."* With its broad footprint across the state and nationally, clients cite its *"tremendous resources"* as a major draw, and rivals acknowledge its *"broad range and capability."* Clients value the attorneys as *"business lawyers as opposed to theoreticians – good at reaching decisions."* The Northern California practice is technology-focused and the team is credited with *"an interesting biotech practice."* In Southern California the team has a broader base, covering private equity and midmarket industrial work, as well as technology. Clients gladly declare the firm *"absolutely the top in the USA in capital markets, securities and financing."* The group advised KKR and Silver Lake Partners on the $2.66 billion acquisition of Agilent Technologies' semiconductor products group.
**The Lawyers:** Menlo Park's **Alan Mendelson** is a byword for quality life sciences and biotech work – *"there is no question but he has substantial influence"* in these sectors. LA-based **Paul Tosetti** is a *"dealmaker"* with the *"judgment, temperament, and desire to bring things to a successful conclusion,"* say sources. He advised Intermix Media in its $580 million cash acquisition by News Corporation. As part of his tech-focused Silicon Valley practice **Kit Kaufman** represented Aviza Technology in its $50 million acquisition of Trikon Technologies. From Orange County, **Charles Ruck** represented Morgan Stanley, financial adviser to PacifiCare in its $8.1 billion merger with UnitedHealth Group. At Menlo Park, **Michael Hall** is active on behalf of both public and private emerging growth companies and handles venture capital financing, M&A and public securities.
**Clients/Work Highlights:** Amgen Ventures; Beckman Coulter; Harrah's and Leonard Green & Partners.

## Wilson Sonsini Goodrich & Rosati

See firm details p.344
**The Firm:** This Silicon Valley landmark's market share and name recognition are legendary. Rivals encounter its attorneys *"all over"* the hi-tech industry, often acting for venture-backed companies. The firm's architecture is geared to the needs of emerging growth companies; these are typical of the client base and attorneys represent them all the way through to maturity. Crystallizing the group's global aspirations, there are plans to open a Shanghai office. Highlights include acting for Seagate in its $1.9 billion acquisition of Maxtor, and advising Google in its acquisition of a 5% stake in AOL.
**The Lawyers:** Despite his decision to step down as chief executive last year, **Larry Sonsini's** (see p.315) *"incredible reputation and contacts"* mean that he is still *"the one that drives that shop,"* according to commentators. He is undoubtedly *"a force of nature,"* and remains *"the most recognizable name in Silicon Valley."* Commentators extol rainmaker and Palo Alto-based **Jeff Saper** (see p.311) for his *"ability to develop relationships with emerging companies."* A corporate and securities attorney first and foremost, he spends a considerable part of his time in New York. His clients include public companies, financial institutions, private equity firms and venture capitalists. M&A head **Martin Korman** (see p.298) is *"among the best the firm has to offer,"* claim sources, and **Mario Rosati** (see p.310) is admired for the strength of his client relationships. **Mark Bertelsen** (see p.279) enjoys a healthy profile in corporate, finance and securities law, while **Kenneth Clark** (see p.283) receives recommendations on the strength of his representation of venture-backed companies in the biotech and nanotechnology industries. He is particularly active in partnering and technology transactions. Sources pinpointed **Casey McGlynn's** (see p.303) proficiency in life sciences, and he also enjoys a profile in the IT and telecom sectors.
**Clients/Work Highlights:** Ameritrade Holding; Google; Juniper; Wind River; Eontec; McAfee; Lehman Brothers; Apple; Hewlett-Packard; Infosys; Checkpoint; Merrill Lynch; Trident Capital and Warburg Pincus.

## Cooley Godward LLP

**The Firm:** This group excels in life sciences and technology, offering *"a pack of excellent corporate lawyers"* to Silicon Valley clients. Sources point particularly to the firm's M&A capability, much in evidence on a number of significant deals this year. These have included representing Adobe Systems in its $3.4 billion acquisition of Macromedia, and eBay in its $3.9 billion acquisition of Skype Technologies. A thriving cross-border practice included advising BEI Technologies on its sale to Schneider Electric.
**The Lawyers:** *"Extraordinary M&A attorney"* **Richard Climan** is credited with building the group's M&A practice; he remains at the forefront of the market nationally. Clients are delighted with his *"exceptional engagement with the business team."* He acted for Verity in its $500 million sale to UK-based Autonomy. Rivals recognize **Keith Flaum** as a solid player in the M&A market, where he focuses on work for technology companies. He has handled a significant amount of work for eBay recently, as well as representing Siebel Systems in its $5.8 billion sale to Oracle. Sources have *"never run across a client who didn't have a favorable impression of"* **Bob Jones**. His *"creative yet unflappable"* manner wins him fans, particularly in the life sciences arena. National group head **Barbara Kosacz** is skilled in complex strategic partnering and joint ventures for companies ranging from startups to public giants. She also handles private financings, spinouts, public offerings and M&A for companies and investors. In Southern California, **Fred Muto** heads up the San Diego office and handles a generalist corporate and securities law practice, acting for emerging and public technology companies, venture capital investors and investment banking firms. Palo Alto's **Mark Tanoury** is a *"terrific lawyer and a great business adviser,"* according to

## Corporate/M&A
### Leading Individuals

★ **SONSINI Larry** *Wilson Sonsini*

[1] **BOGEN Andrew** *Gibson, Dunn & Crutcher LLP*
**MCCARTHY Brian** *Skadden, Arps*
**TOSETTI Paul** *Latham & Watkins LLP*

**DAVIDSON Gordon** *Fenwick & West LLP*
**MENDELSON Alan** *Latham & Watkins LLP*

[2] **CLIMAN Richard** *Cooley Godward LLP*
**GALLO Greg** *DLA Piper*
**KING Kenton** *Skadden, Arps*
**SAPER Jeff** *Wilson Sonsini*

**COBEN Jerome** *Skadden, Arps*
**KAUFMAN Christopher** *Latham & Watkins LLP*
**SAGGESE Nicholas** *Skadden, Arps*

[3] **BELLAH MAGUIRE Jennifer** *Gibson, Dunn*
**DEL CALVO Jorge** *Pillsbury*
**KENNEDY Mike** *O'Melveny & Myers LLP*
**LARSON John** *Morgan, Lewis & Bockius LLP*
**ROSATI Mario** *Wilson Sonsini*

**CAMAHORT Steve** *O'Melveny & Myers LLP*
**GUNDERSON Bob** *Gunderson Dettmer*
**KORMAN Martin** *Wilson Sonsini*
**LAYNE Jonathan** *Gibson, Dunn & Crutcher LLP*
**RUCK Charles** *Latham & Watkins LLP*

[4] **ADLER Robert** *Munger, Tolles & Olson LLP*
**BRAUN Lawrence** *Sheppard, Mullin*
**COGEN Douglas** *Fenwick & West*
**DETTMER Scott** *Gunderson Dettmer*
**GIUNTA Joseph** *Skadden, Arps*
**HALL Michael** *Latham & Watkins LLP*
**JENETT Bruce** *Heller Ehrman LLP*
**KELLER Don** *Orrick, Herrington & Sutcliffe*
**KNAUSS Robert** *Munger, Tolles & Olson LLP*
**KUPIETZKY Moshe** *Sidley Austin LLP*
**LESSER Henry** *DLA Piper*
**MILLER Robert** *Paul, Hastings*
**RESSLER Alison** *Sullivan & Cromwell LLP*
**SEGEL Alvin** *Irell & Manella LLP*
**SINGER Gary** *O'Melveny & Myers LLP*
**SMITH Gregory** *Skadden, Arps*
**STEVENS Mark** *Fenwick & West LLP*
**TONSFELDT Steven** *Heller Ehrman LLP*
**VETTER Jeff** *Fenwick & West LLP*

**BERTELSEN Mark** *Wilson Sonsini*
**CLARK Kenneth** *Wilson Sonsini*
**DENHAM Robert** *Munger, Tolles & Olson LLP*
**FLAUM Keith** *Cooley Godward LLP*
**GREEN Josh** *Heller Ehrman LLP*
**HARTIGAN John** *Morgan, Lewis & Bockius LLP*
**JONES Robert** *Cooley Godward LLP*
**KELLY William** *Davis Polk & Wardwell*
**KOSACZ Barbara** *Cooley Godward LLP*
**LAZAROW Warren** *O'Melveny & Myers LLP*
**MCGLYNN Casey** *Wilson Sonsini*
**MUTO Fred** *Cooley Godward LLP*
**SANCHEZ Carl** *Paul, Hastings*
**SIMONS III Laird** *Fenwick & West LLP*
**SMITH Douglas** *Gibson, Dunn*
**SNYDER David** *Pillsbury Winthrop*
**TANOURY Mark** *Cooley Godward LLP*
**TOWNSEND Robert** *Morrison & Foerster LLP*
**VILLENEUVE Tom** *Gunderson Dettmer*

sources. He is particularly recommended for representing emerging growth companies; he is involved in corporate, partnership and securities matters.
**Clients/Work Highlights:** Applied Materials; Gilead Sciences; Quest Software; Synopsys; WR Hambrecht + Co; NVIDIA and Borland Software.

### Davis Polk & Wardwell
See firm details p.1528
**The Firm:** With its California operations based in Menlo Park, this firm is well positioned for higher end transactions. Technology-related instructions are a key focus for the office, which is also the headquarters of the firm's global technology group. Its prominence is assured by its representation of Oracle, including the latter's infamous hostile acquisition of PeopleSoft. Attorneys also acted on the company's acquisition of Retek, its purchase of a $900 million controlling interest in i-flex solutions, and its $5.85 billion acquisition of Siebel Systems. Attorneys also represent private equity firms in M&A, and a mix of companies and underwriters in capital markets and corporate finance and governance issues. Clients are drawn to the *"spectacular"* group by attorneys who can be *"trusted implicitly."*
**The Lawyers:** William Kelly (see p.298) *"under-stands the complexity of an organization"* and provides *"even-tempered"* advice. He acts for technology companies in all their corporate and finance needs, and was a key figure in Oracle's conquest of PeopleSoft.
**Clients/Work Highlights:** Oracle; Mercury Interactive; Aximetrix; KLA-Tencor; Francisco Partners; Morgan Stanley and CSFB.

### Fenwick & West LLP
See firm details p.326
**The Firm:** Operating out of offices in Silicon Valley and San Francisco, this California native is *"one of the state's most credible"* corporate and M&A players. Technology sector M&A has been a major driver of the practice. Key deals in this area include acting for Macromedia in its merger with Adobe Systems. Outside the M&A arena, the group represented DexCom and Diamond Foods in their respective IPOs, and also took Shopping.com public before its sale to eBay. Venture-backed startups are a significant portion of the team's workload.
**The Lawyers:** Firm chairman Gordy Davidson (see p.285) stands out as *"the cream of the crop"* and *"a real force in this marketplace,"* in the opinion of commentators. Sources applaud his preparedness to

*"roll up his sleeves"* on matters ranging from M&A, corporate governance, public offerings and startups; he was involved in both the aforementioned IPOs. San Francisco-based **Douglas Cogen** (see p.283) garners recognition for his role in the Adobe-Macromedia deal. He cochairs the firm's M&A group and leads the M&A team for key client Cisco Systems. Managing partner **Laird Simons** (see p.314) has an active public offerings practice. **Mark Stevens'** (see p.316) *"knowledge of the technology industry and operational experience"* have secured his reputation as a *"fantastic corporate lawyer"* in the eyes of interviewees. Complex transactions are his bailiwick, and he has represented a range of private and public companies, venture capitalists and investment banks. **Jeff Vetter** (see p.319) has a prominent M&A, public and private offerings, counseling and securities practice.
**Clients/Work Highlights:** Symantec; VeriSign; Cisco Systems; Intuit and Macromedia.

### Skadden, Arps, Slate, Meagher & Flom LLP & Affiliates
See firm details p.1557
**The Firm:** Interviewees agree that this firm has *"effectively extended its corporate muscle to the West Coast,"* underscoring its profile as *"a truly national operation with international projection."* M&A and corporate finance are the staples of the practice; the team offers expertise in private equity acquisitions and finance, transactional advice for public and private corporations and financial advice to investment banks. It acted for Skype Technologies in its acquisition by eBay. It also advised Wynn Resorts on a strategic alliance with Société des Bains de Mer et du Cercle des Étrangers à Monaco, and on its $2.3 billion refinancing of Wynn Las Vegas.
**The Lawyers:** Based in Los Angeles, **Brian McCarthy** (see p.302) has high visibility in M&A transactions, corporate governance matters and restructurings. He recently represented Advanced Medical Optics in its $1.3 billion acquisition of VISZ. Also in Los Angeles, the *"talented"* **Jerome Coben** (see p.283) has a sterling reputation in private equity and M&A, and took a lead role in the work for Wynn Resorts. **Kenton King** (see p.298) runs the Northern California side of the practice, and his *"considerable deal flow"* is the envy of peers. **Nicholas Saggese** (see p.311) has a following in securities, private equity, M&A and high-yield financing transactions. He advised Providence Equity Partners, Texas Pacific Group and DLJ Merchant Banking Partners on their interests in a consortium with Sony and Comcast to acquire MGM for $4.8 billion. **Joseph Giunta** (see p.290) has an enviable reputation for M&A in the Los Angeles market, and Palo Alto's **Gregory Smith** (see p.314) is experienced in all manner of corporate transactions and finance, including restructurings. Smith generally acts for technology and life science companies, as well as underwriters and investors.
**Clients/Work Highlights:** Vulcan; Advanced Medical Optics; Texas Pacific Group; Oaktree Capital Management; Jefferies & Co and CSFB.

## DLA Piper Rudnick Gray Cary US LLP

See firm details p.870

**The Firm:** Its national spread ensures that this firm occupies *"a comfortable position in the midmarket,"* and last year's merger with Europe's DLA strengthens claims to a global reach and allows it to engage in new markets. The technology sector remains a focus for the Silicon Valley office, which represents businesses ranging from startups to large companies. The offering is broad, ranging from finance, including venture capital and leveraged transactions, through to the whole corporate life cycle, including M&A. Highlights include representing Protein Design Labs in its $660 million acquisition of ESP Pharma by auction. The group also acted for Maxtor in its $300 million Rule 144A offering. The firm has a strong base in San Diego and a significant presence in Los Angeles and Sacramento. Successes for the practice in the southern part of the state include acting for QUALCOMM in its acquisition of Flarion Technologies.

**The Lawyers:** Palo Alto-based **Greg Gallo**'s (see p.289) management responsibilities do not detract from his practice representing startups and vigorous technology companies. He acted for Pinnacle Systems in its merger with Avid Technology. According to peers, **Henry Lesser** (see p.300) is a technology lawyer who *"understands the issues and the hostile takeover environment better than anybody."*

**Clients/Work Highlights:** The group's client base includes public and private companies, banks, finance companies, venture capital and private equity funds, insurance companies, pension funds and other institutional lenders. Examples include Accredited Home Lender; Dr Seuss Enterprises; Invitrogen and Jack in the Box.

## Gibson, Dunn & Crutcher LLP

See firm details p.328

**The Firm:** This established Southern California player enjoys historic relationships with Californian corporations, winning praise from clients as a *"spectacular"* group offering *"practical and timely advice,"* attorneys are deemed to have a real flair for making difficult deals look effortless. The diet here is mainly M&A, capital markets and general corporate transactions; a burgeoning Northern California team is experienced in hi-tech matters. The group acted for Aurora Capital in its $1.6 billion acquisition of K&F Industries, and also for the special committee of the board of directors of Hollywood Entertainment in a $1.2 billion sale to Movie Gallery.

**The Lawyers:** In a turbulent year, **Andy Bogen**'s (see p.279) preeminence as an M&A practitioner is undiminished, and rivals acknowledge him as *"one of the best attorneys in the business."* Clients endorse *"terrific"* **Jennifer Bellah Maguire** (see p.278), and are happy to place matters in her *"capable hands."* She has a thriving corporate and securities practice and is experienced at raising leveraged buyout, venture and other funds. She advised Phoenix Scientific on its sale to IVAX by Green Equity Investors. Commentators pick out **Jonathan Layne** (see p.299) as an effective rainmaker: *"He's a smooth quarterback*

who hands the ball to terrific people, and stays involved."* His practice centers on M&A, private equity and capital markets work for his clientele of predominantly publicly held corporations. He represented Churchill Downs in the $257.5 million sale of Hollywood Park racetrack and surrounding acreage to Bay Meadows Land. *"Diligent and thoughtful"* **Douglas Smith** (see p.314) wins clients' praise for his *"fine demeanor."* The core of his practice is advising public companies on securities law, public debt and equity offerings and M&A.

**Clients/Work Highlights:** A clientele of hi-tech companies, private equity houses and investment banks is studded with names such as Camco; Morgan Stanley; Goldman Sachs; UBS Investment Bank; JPMorgan; Bear Stearns; Lehman Brothers; Merrill Lynch; Banc of America Securities; Green Equity Investors III; Cadence Design Systems; Transamerica and St Jude Medical.

## Gunderson Dettmer Stough Villeneuve Franklin & Hachigian

**The Firm:** This smaller firm stands out in Silicon Valley for its work for startups and in fund formation. Since the heyday of the tech boom, it has stuck to its model of representing fast-growing technology companies and investors into that sector. The caseload ranges from launching early-stage companies and financings to public offerings and strategic alliances. The team represented Equinix in a series of transactions.

**The Lawyers:** **Bob Gunderson** is a renowned dealmaker. He advises tech companies, leading venture funds and other venture investors. Another *"leading light"* in the group is **Scott Dettmer**, who acts for public and private companies in the IT, Internet, telecom and life sciences markets, as well as advising institutional investors and venture funds. **Tom Villeneuve** completes the trilogy of high-end corporate attorneys.

**Clients/Work Highlights:** Aruba; Theravance; iDirect and Ariba.

## Heller Ehrman LLP

See firm details p.329

**The Firm:** This firm's best-known claim to fame lies in the litigation arena, but it also hosts the Heller Ehrman venture law group, which has a solid profile in Northern California for startup and emerging growth company work. The group's reach also extends to San Diego, and it counts some tech giants among its key clients. The practice is focused on IT, life sciences, financial services and some defense contractor work. Highlights have included advising SAIC in the $1.4 billion sale of its Telcordia division, and in the ongoing process of taking the company public. The team also acted in the sale of Aspect Communications to a private equity group.

**The Lawyers:** **Josh Green** (see p.291) advises emerging growth companies and venture capital concerns in a variety of corporate matters including strategic partnerships, finance, IPOs and licensing. Life sciences are a focus for **Bruce Jenett** (see p.296), who is active on behalf of hi-tech businesses domes-

tically and internationally. **Steven Tonsfeldt** (see p.318) chairs the M&A group and cochairs the corporate/venture law practice group. He is closely identified with the representation of IT and life sciences clients.

**Clients/Work Highlights:** Pelikan Technologies; Jazz Pharmaceuticals; Digital Theater Systems; Symantec; Seattle Genetics; RedEnvelope; Threshold Pharmaceuticals; IronPort Systems; Concept Therapeutics; Depomed; At Road; Menlo Ventures; US Venture Partners; Kleiner, Perkins, Caufield & Byers; New Enterprise Associates; Sequoia Capital Partners; Embarcadero Technologies; InfoUSA and Yahoo!

## Morgan, Lewis & Bockius LLP

See firm details p.1758

**The Firm:** Growing beyond its solid base in the Bay Area, this group has an expanding footprint in Southern California. In the North, much of its workload consists of representing venture-backed companies, often in the biotech or life sciences industries, in the full life cycle of corporate development. In the southern part of the state the practice is dominated by private equity and has a healthy flow of energy transactions. The team acted for Autonomy in its $500 million acquisition of Verity.

**The Lawyers:** **John Larson** (see p.299) enjoys a *"huge reputation"* for his corporate and M&A practice for hi-tech companies of all sizes. The *"pragmatic and smart"* **John Hartigan** (see p.293) wins fans with his superb business judgment.

**Clients/Work Highlights:** Nanogen; SanDisk; Kleiner, Perkins, Caufield & Byers; Elevation Partners and Apollo Management.

## Morrison & Foerster LLP

See firm details p.335

**The Firm:** Clients extol this *"fantastic firm"* for its *"great mix of national and international capability."* Attorneys offer a well-rounded corporate service with particular strength in the technology, media, financial services and life sciences industries. The *"seasoned and credible"* team acted for MarketWatch in its $528 million acquisition by Dow Jones, and advised McKesson in its $105 million acquisition of Medcon.

**The Lawyers:** *"One of the best,"* **Robert Townsend** (see p.318) co-heads the group and is admired as an *"accomplished and pragmatic"* attorney. As well as representing US clients at home and abroad, he handles cross-border transactions for European and Japanese businesses. He represented Fujikura in the dissolution of its joint venture with Alcoa, and also acted for Thomson in its $285 million acquisition of PRN Corporation.

**Clients/Work Highlights:** VISX; Dubai Investment Group; JDS Uniphase; McKesson; Global Cash Access; ACCESS Co; BEA Systems; Redfire; American Pacific; Scharffen Berger; Sterling Stamos Capital; Westcorp; UnionBanCal; Quantum; Beech Street; Amana Group; Cogent Systems and BofI Holdings.

## O'Melveny & Myers LLP

See firm details p.336

**The Firm:** This traditional California player fields a team of talented attorneys on the corporate/M&A field. Last year's recruits from Wilson Sonsini have been neatly integrated into the San Francisco office, where the emphasis is on the technology market. The group is building a diverse base of corporate clients, financial sponsors and buyout funds. It acted for Francisco Partners in the raising of capital for its second fund. The Newport Beach team has a diverse general corporate practice for a varied client base, while the Los Angeles and Century City offices offer strong M&A expertise. Highlights have included advising Vicuron Pharmaceuticals in its $1.9 billion acquisition by Pfizer.

**The Lawyers:** San Francisco's **Steve Camahort** (see p.282) is admired as *"an outstanding lawyer"* by rivals, while **Mike Kennedy** (see p.298) is *"as prominent as anyone in the M&A area."* In Silicon Valley, **Warren Lazarow** (see p.299) is *"a pleasure to deal with"* thanks to his *"dedication to his clients and wonderful talent."* Venture capital, funds and finance are the mainstays of his practice. In Orange County, **Gary Singer** (see p.314) is especially active on behalf of public companies.

**Clients/Work Highlights:** Vector Capital; Sun Microsystems; Intuit; Deutsche Bank Securities and Thomas Weisel Partners.

## Pillsbury Winthrop Shaw Pittman LLP

See firm details p.1550

**The Firm:** Clients appreciate this team's ability to *"effectively drive the process"* in a transaction, while maintaining quality that is *"first-class"* throughout. Acting across the state, lawyers handle M&A and public offerings for a client base that features hi-tech, life sciences and old economy businesses. A recent high point was advising Chevron on its $18.1 billion stock and cash merger with Unocal. Other successes included acting for Fox Interactive Media in its $580 million acquisition of Intermix Media.

**The Lawyers:** Palo Alto-based **Jorge del Calvo** (see p.285) has a *"strong following"* and specializes in nurturing companies from inception to value realization; he is active in public offerings. In San Diego **David Snyder** (see p.315) is described as *"knowledgeable, efficient and fair."* His practice is an even balance of M&A, public offerings and securities work. Clients laud his habit of *"going straight to the bullet point,"* adding confidently: *"He's always there for us."* He represented Excel Pharmaceuticals in its $280 million acquisition by Valeant Pharmaceuticals International.

**Clients/Work Highlights:** Biogen Idec; BNP Paribas; Detwiler, Mitchell & Co; PRN Corporation; Tenaska; Potlatch; MediciNova; McKesson and WebEx.

## Simpson Thacher & Bartlett LLP

See firm details p.1555

**The Firm:** This firm has caught the eye of rivals in Northern California, who see its *"sharp and problem-solving M&A attorneys"* as worthy competitors for high visibility deals. Despite its comparatively modest presence in the state, the firm has a vibrant practice focused on capital markets and M&A, and a substantial private equity load. Key transactions have included advising VERITAS Software on its merger with Symantec, and representing Morgan Stanley and CSFB on Google's IPO. The group also acted for Agilent Technologies in the sale of its semiconductor group.

**The Lawyers:** Richard Capelouto heads the M&A section from the Palo Alto office.

**Clients/Work Highlights:** CB Richard Ellis; Silver Lake Partners; Hellman & Freeman; Bond Capital and Elevation Partners.

## Sheppard, Mullin, Richter & Hampton LLP

**The Firm:** Sources watch this *"growing force"* with interest, recognizing its stock of *"fine lawyers"* and robust activity in the marketplace. The team has a lot to offer across the corporate front, from M&A and finance to corporate governance issues. The client base includes both public and privately held companies. The team acted for JAMDAT Mobile in its $680 million acquisition by Electronic Arts.

**The Lawyers:** Corporate chair **Lawrence Braun** is a well-known figure in midmarket M&A.

**Clients/Work Highlights:** The clientele includes private and public companies, ranging from startups and emerging businesses to international corporations.

## Sidley Austin LLP

See firm details p.883

**The Firm:** This is a much-respected and very capable team. It is visible in capital markets transactions, and has been active in the financing, recapitalization and purchase and sale of companies. Structured finance and high-yield debt are also a focus, and in the past year the group has expanded its real estate finance capabilities. Recent highlights have been transactions with KKR and Meridian.

**The Lawyers:** The *"technically adept"* **Moshe J Kupietzky** (see p.299) manages the office and also heads the corporate and finance practice there. He has a particularly strong reputation for private equity work.

**Clients/Work Highlights:** Merrill Lynch; Goldman Sachs; Bank of America; Wachovia; Morgan Stanley; Starwood Hotels & Resorts; Century Park Capital Partners and Canyon Capital.

## Irell & Manella LLP

**The Firm:** Based in Century City and Newport Beach, this group is best known as an IP powerhouse. It has firmly established its credentials in the corporate/M&A sphere, however, and is particularly visible acting for private equity clients. The versatile lawyers act in a great range of matters.

**The Lawyers:** **Alvin Segel** is *"skilled"* for corporate securities and business law. He counts Vulcan and Charter Communications among his clients.

**Clients/Work Highlights:** The client base includes startups and emerging growth companies, as well as public companies, venture capital funds and individual investors.

## Munger, Tolles & Olson LLP

**The Firm:** This group offers *"fine lawyers who don't play games"* in the corporate arena, in addition to a stellar litigation practice. The clientele includes such prestigious entities as Berkshire Hathaway. Attorneys are active in corporate governance, M&A, private equity, venture capital and securities offerings.

**The Lawyers:** The *"superb"* **Robert Adler** is experienced in the full range of corporate matters, including governance, and is renowned for his restructuring work in the electricity industry. **Robert Denham** advises clients on strategic and financial issues, while *"ten-time excellent"* **Robert Knauss** is active in general corporate law, principally M&A, corporate finance and securities, for clients such as Merrill Lynch and Salomon Smith Barney.

**Clients/Work Highlights:** City National Bank; Edison International and Southern California Edison; International Creative Management; KB Home; Oaktree Capital Management; United Talent Agency; Universal Music Group and The Yucaipa Companies.

## Paul, Hastings, Janofsky & Walker LLP

See firm details p.339

**The Firm:** The group has a great position in the Southern California market and a *"wonderful investment fund practice."* The workload spans the entire spectrum of corporate representation, including M&A and securities. Key recent matters have included advising Citigroup in the $1.2 billion sale of its affiliate Associate Housing Finance to 21st Mortgage. The team also represented Micromuse in its sale to IBM.

**The Lawyers:** Los Angeles-based **Robert Miller** (see p.303) concentrates on corporate finance and M&A, seasoned with securities work. His clients include public and private entities and private equity firms and their portfolio companies. San Diego-based **Carl Sanchez** (see p.311) chairs the M&A practice group, acting both buy-side and sell-side for companies and private equity funds. He acted for Citigroup in its acquisition of the Diners Club Europe franchise.

**Clients/Work Highlights:** Biomarin Pharmaceutical; Optical Communication Products; Blue Capital; Dow Chemical; Amgen; Siemens; Bear Stearns; NorthWestern Corporation; Charter Communications; State Street and Time Warner.

## Sullivan & Cromwell LLP

See firm details p.1558

**The Firm:** This East Coast powerhouse attracts particular praise for its banking practice, but the corporate team is also valued by clients for its *"tremendous depth of expertise"* and *"firm answers, not couched in ambiguities and carve-outs."* The group is driven by M&A and private equity activity, and the group enjoys strong relationships with investment banks. Highlights have included repre-

229

senting the chairman, CEO and controlling shareholder of Westcorp in its acquisition by Wachovia, and also acting for Occidental Petroleum in its acquisition of Vintage Petroleum.

**The Lawyers:** Commentators acclaim **Alison Ressler** (see p.310) as "*a fine lawyer with terrific clients.*" As well as coordinating the California prac-

tice and co-heading the private equity group, she has an active M&A practice. She led the team advising on the acquisition of Chiron by Novartis.

**Clients/Work Highlights:** Hilton Hotels; Lehman Brothers; Goldman Sachs; Cerberus Capital Management and Hershey Foods.

## Other Notable Practitioners

At Orrick, Herrington & Sutcliffe LLP, **Don Keller** (see p.297) is focused on emerging company work, as well as representing public companies, investment banks and venture capital firms. He acted recently on a significant transaction for eHarmony.

# EMPLOYMENT

| Employment: Mainly Defendant |
| --- |
| Leading Firms |
| [1] PAUL, HASTINGS *Los Angeles* |
| [2] GIBSON, DUNN & CRUTCHER LLP *Los Angeles* |
| MORGAN, LEWIS & BOCKIUS LLP *San Francisco* |
| ORRICK, HERRINGTON & SUTCLIFFE *Los Angeles* |
| SEYFARTH SHAW LLP *Los Angeles* |
| [3] LATHAM & WATKINS LLP *Los Angeles* |
| MORRISON & FOERSTER LLP *Los Angeles* |
| O'MELVENY & MYERS LLP *Los Angeles* |
| [4] HELLER EHRMAN LLP *San Francisco* |
| LITTLER MENDELSON, PC *San Francisco* |
| MUNGER, TOLLES & OLSON LLP *Los Angeles* |
| SHEPPARD, MULLIN *Los Angeles* |
| WILSON SONSINI *San Francisco* |
| [5] LIEBERT CASSIDY WHITMORE *Los Angeles* |
| PROSKAUER ROSE LLP *Los Angeles* |

## Band 1

### Paul, Hastings, Janofsky & Walker LLP

See firm details p.339

**The Firm:** This responsive and results-oriented firm sets "*the gold standard,*" in the opinion of commentators. Clients extol it as "*the best of the best,*" and congratulate themselves on choosing a team that delivers "*unparalleled service.*" The group offers a common-sense approach to complex matters and leads the way in class actions. It recently acted for Wal-Mart in Dukes v Wal-Mart, a colossal class action involving 1.6 million employees. Another highlight was representing UPS in Marlo v UPS, a high-profile wage and hour case. Associate training is taken seriously, and clients note that a Paul Hastings team always bears the hallmark of quality.

**The Lawyers:** **Nancy Abell** (see p.276) chairs the 92-strong employment "*powerhouse.*" Clients say she is "*driven and focused*" with an "*aggressive edge*" in litigation and negotiation. She led on the Wal-Mart case and acts for a variety of blue-chip clients on the full range of employment issues, including audits and class actions. **Paul Grossman** (see p.292) is "*assiduous and gentlemanly,*" and regarded as having "*literally written the book*" on employment law. He successfully defended Disney in a notable wage and hour class action. **Kirby Wilcox** achieves "*phenomenal results*" in his wage and hour practice. In his recent work for UPS he defeated several class certifi-

cations. **Paul Cane** is described as an "*exceptional thinker and superior communicator.*" Demonstrating his creative abilities both in the courtroom and in written briefs, he gives clients the impression that he can "*walk on water.*" The "*affable*" **Jeffrey Wohl** combines deep legal expertise with practical advice, leading clients to declare him "*highly responsive and a great technician.*" Palo Alto's rising partner **Brad Newman** (see p.305) represents various technology companies and entrepreneurs in Silicon Valley, and dedicates much of his time to trade secrets work. **Ethan Lipsig** (see p.300) founded the employee benefits team and elicits warm endorsements from clients who value his "*real law brain power.*" He acted recently as fiduciary counsel to a large pension fund.

**Clients/Work Highlights:** Wal-Mart; UPS; Cintas; Ford; Bank of America; SBC; Disney; GE; Northwest Airlines and Target Stores.

## Band 2

### Gibson, Dunn & Crutcher LLP

See firm details p.328

**The Firm:** This outfit maintains its "*stellar reputation*" in this arena. Clients applaud the "*highly sophisticated*" team and the breadth of its resources: "*They can arrange immediate contact with specialists in any area.*" Backed by the prodigious litigation department, the team is well placed to handle substantial class actions. Recent engagements have included wage and hour suits, noncompetition matters and cases brought under the new Sarbanes-Oxley whistle-blower provision.

**The Lawyers:** "*Bright star*" **Pamela Hemminger** (see p.294) is "*as good as it gets,*" according to Fortune 500 clients who value her extensive OSHA defense experience. **William Claster** (see p.283) is "*smart and efficient.*" Clients appreciate his levelheaded judgment, and a typical commentator added: "*I go out of my way to use him.*" He recently represented Dole Food in a million-dollar class action alleging violations of the Worker Adjustment and Retraining Notification Act. **David West**'s (see p.320) astonishing efficiency leaves clients "*wondering how he juggles everything.*" An employee benefits expert, he recently represented a large technology company in the negotiation of its executive severance agreement. Employee benefits attorney **Stephen Fackler** (see p.287) recently joined the firm and brings "*a good sense of the dynamics*" to the table. Clients declare him an "*original thinker*" and a clever negotiator.

**Clients/Work Highlights:** Toyota Financial Services; Decurion; UPS; Tenet Healthcare; Dole Food; Mitsubishi and Standard Pacific.

### Morgan, Lewis & Bockius LLP

See firm details p.1758

**The Firm:** This prestigious group's distinguished reputation is attributed to its "*proactive rather than reactive*" approach. The sophisticated practice is split into five specialized subgroups including regulatory and employment counseling. Commentators point to outstanding litigation expertise, a potent US and overseas network and an "*expert and efficient team that resolves matters quickly.*" Lawyers recently handled a multimillion-dollar insurance industry litigation settlement.

**The Lawyers:** The "*sharp, skillful and strategic*" **Rebecca Eisen** (see p.287) "*doesn't get ruffled*" by her opponents. A "*bright and collaborative*" wage and hour expert, her latest work includes a high-profile case concerning the entitlement of financial advisers to overtime payment. Executive compensation expert **Jim DiBernardo**'s (see p.286) clients declare him "*head and shoulders above everyone else.*" He has been advising them on the implications for compensation plans of Section 409(A) of the Internal Revenue Code. The "*amazing*" **Zaitun Poonja** (see p.308) also specializes in employee benefits, particularly the international aspects of equity compensation. Her clients "*feel lucky to use her.*" She recently advised executives of a prominent company undergoing a leveraged buyout on how to structure the equity. **Mark Boxer** (see p.280) advises on a range of employee benefits matters.

**Clients/Work Highlights:** Clients are drawn from a range of industries including financial services, pharmaceuticals, media, transportation and retail. Foot Locker and Blockbuster are on the list.

### Orrick, Herrington & Sutcliffe

See firm details p.337

**The Firm:** This outfit is recommended for its "*expert command of the subtleties*" of employment law, and for lawyers who are "*terrific to work with.*" It has impressive depth in the financial services arena, and close relationships with high-profile financial institutions. Notable highlights include handling a wage and hour class action for two leading software providers.

**The Lawyers:** Clients are confident in the judgment of the "*polished*" **Gary Siniscalco** (see p.314); and **Lynne Hermle** (see p.294) is respected as an

## Employment: Mainly Defendant
### Leading Individuals

**1** ABELL Nancy *Paul, Hastings*
GROSSMAN Paul *Paul, Hastings*
WILCOX Kirby *Paul, Hastings*

**2** CANE Paul *Paul, Hastings*
HERMLE Lynne *Orrick*
SINISCALCO Gary *Orrick*

**3** ALVAREZ Fred *Wilson Sonsini Goodrich & Rosati*
DIEKMANN JR Gilmore *Seyfarth Shaw LLP*
DRAPKIN Steven *Law Offices of Steven Drapkin*
GILLETTE Patricia *Heller Ehrman LLP*
HEMMINGER Pamela *Gibson, Dunn & Crutcher LLP*
HOWARD JR George *Pillsbury*
KADUE David *Seyfarth Shaw LLP*
KRISCHER Gordon *O'Melveny & Myers LLP*
WHEELER Raymond *Morrison & Foerster LLP*

**4** BERKOWITZ Alan *Bingham McCutchen LLP*
BERMAN Jeffrey *Sidley Austin LLP*
CLASTER William *Gibson, Dunn & Crutcher LLP*
COLE William *Mitchell, Silberberg & Knupp LLP*
EISEN Rebecca *Morgan, Lewis & Bockius LLP*
EMANUEL William *Littler Mendelson, PC*
FRIEDMAN Alan *Munger, Tolles & Olson LLP*
KEYES Judith *Morrison & Foerster LLP*
MATHIASON Garry *Littler Mendelson, PC*
ONCIDI Anthony *Proskauer Rose LLP*
SANCHEZ Terry *Munger, Tolles & Olson LLP*
SAXE Deborah *Jones Day*
SIEGEL Robert *O'Melveny & Myers LLP*
SIMMONS Richard *Sheppard, Mullin*
THOMPSON Tracy *Cook & Roos LLP*
VIRJEE Framroze *O'Melveny & Myers LLP*
WOHL Jeffrey *Paul, Hastings*

### Up-and-coming individuals

NEWMAN Bradford *Paul, Hastings*

"*extremely smart and aggressive*" litigator. Clients attest that "*she can handle anything and gets fantastic results.*" She recently handled a notable wage and hour class action for Countryside Mortgage. **Jon Ocker** (see p.305) chairs the compensation and benefits group and is pronounced an "*extremely confident and effective communicator.*" His recent work includes drafting company stock plans for several technology companies.

Clients/Work Highlights: MetLife; Morgan Stanley; Apple; Electronic Arts; Northwest Airlines; Advanced Microdevices; UBS; Citigroup; JPMorgan Chase; Intel; Cisco Systems; Barclays Bank and Goldman Sachs.

### Seyfarth Shaw LLP
See firm details p.882

The Firm: This firm draws on a national network, tailoring teams to the job in a way that causes clients to comment: "*They manage to make us feel like their top priority.*" Commentators describe a reliable and sophisticated group that ensures consistent quality through attention to training. The varied workload

includes litigation, traditional union work and employer training. Recent key projects include the successful representation of the Los Angeles Times in a large wage and hour class action.

The Lawyers: **David Kadue** is a "*thoughtful and well-rounded*" attorney who commands clients' respect by virtue of his "*scholarly and sharp*" advice. "*Intelligent and able,*" he has handled a series of major glass ceiling cases for international retailers. A "*fine litigator with a style that really works,*" **Gilmore Diekmann** is respected as one of the most "*innovative*" thinkers in this area. Clients declare him a "*truly exceptional lawyer.*" He has been representing Costco in a large sex discrimination case.

Clients/Work Highlights: Costco; Bosley; the Los Angeles Times; Jiffy Lube; IKON Office Solutions; FedEx; Aramark; Intel; Safeway; Sun Microsystems and Levi Strauss.

## Band 3

### Latham & Watkins LLP

The Firm: This 50-strong California employment team has been inundated with class action work in the last year. Thomas Pfister's retirement is naturally lamented, but the remaining lawyers ("*they're superb*") are as busy as ever on behalf of the prominent clientele. Recent examples of work include the ongoing representation of Arthur Andersen in appeal cases alleging discrimination, harassment and defamation. The firm is also defending Consolidated Freightways against a $200 million class action by employees alleging violations of the federal Worker Adjustment and Retraining Notification Act.

The Lawyers: "*Intelligent and fun to deal with,*" **James Barrall** heads the benefits and compensation group and is acknowledged "*a class act*" in that area. He handled the employee benefits aspect of Sony's acquisition of MGM Entertainment. Clients regard the up-and-coming **Joseph Yaffe** as an "*outstanding technical adviser.*" He led on KKR's $2.6 billion acquisition of Agilent Technologies, which entailed negotiations in many different countries. Joel Krischer and Wayne Flick are key contacts for straight employment work.

Clients/Work Highlights: Rent-a-Center; Arthur Andersen; ChevronTexaco; Allstate; Consolidated Freightways; Guthy-Renker; Infornet; MGM; Harrah's and Intramix.

### Morrison & Foerster LLP
See firm details p.335

The Firm: Clients marvel at the "*consistent top quality and professionalism*" across the board at this firm, from attorneys to administrative assistants. Its collaborative character is a hit with clients, resulting in strong and broad relationships. Lawyers demonstrate a hands-on approach that results in clients being "*thrilled to work with them.*" The team is full service and especially strong in harassment issues. Lawyers have been defending a leading financial services client in a multimillion-dollar employee raiding and unfair competition case.

The Lawyers: **Raymond Wheeler** (see p.320) is a pragmatic lawyer who goes "*far beyond pure black letter law*" and possesses an uncanny sense of the political climate in the companies he acts for. Clients recommend him "*without reservation*" for his "*terrific judgment.*" He defended an electronic equipment manufacturer against employees alleging breaches of Sarbanes-Oxley legislation. The "*effective and able*" **Judith Keyes**' (see p.298) clients regard her as a "*diplomatic and thoughtful*" attorney who "*truly engages with issues and brings credibility to the table.*" She successfully negotiated a settlement for S.Com in a nationwide class action. The "*fantastic*" **Patrick McCabe** (see p.302) is the leading executive compensation lawyer at the firm. He recently advised Scharffen Berger Chocolate Maker on its merger with Hershey's.

Clients/Work Highlights: Hitachi; Korn/Ferry International; Robert Half; Oracle; Coca-Cola; Intel; Lucasfilm and Fireman's Fund.

### O'Melveny & Myers LLP
See firm details p.336

The Firm: This is a "*vibrant*" firm with a "*fabulous*" team of lawyers, according to sources. It attracts large volumes of discrimination and wage and hour work. Lawyers represent several financial investment companies. Clients appreciate their efforts to add value, observing: "*Their advice is always appropriate.*" The employment team regularly handles prominent Hollywood cases, and has been working for a TV industry client on an age discrimination class action. Lawyers also represent large corporations targeted by defamatory labor campaigns alleging violations of RICO legislation.

The Lawyers: **Gordon Krischer**'s (see p.299) extensive practice includes heading efforts to respond to defamatory labor union campaigns. "*Capable, articulate and courteous,*" he has an excellent reputation both in California and nationwide. Industry clients regard **Robert Siegel** (see p.314) as the "*guru of airline work.*" He acts for major airlines such as United Airlines and US Airways. The "*extremely bright and dedicated*" **Framroze Virjee** (see p.319) handles wage and hour work. Peers applaud his "*genuinely caring and gentlemanly approach*" and "*enviable*" client service skills. The "*superb*" **Linda Griffey** (see p.292) is said to be "*as proficient an attorney as you will find anywhere.*" She cochairs the employee benefits and executive compensation group.

Clients/Work Highlights: Cintas; Lockheed Martin; Columbia Pictures; Ford; US Airways; General Dynamics; California Institute of Technology; Korn/Ferry International; Citigroup; Sony; Verizon and Warner Bros.

## Band 4

### Heller Ehrman LLP
See firm details p.329

The Firm: This firm specializes in class actions by consumers. Clients seek the team out for strategic

## Employment: Employee Benefits

### Leading Individuals

**1** DIBERNARDO S James *Morgan, Lewis & Bockius LLP*
LIPSIG Ethan *Paul, Hastings*

**2** BARRALL James *Latham & Watkins LLP*
FACKLER Stephen *Gibson, Dunn & Crutcher LLP*
GRIFFEY Linda *O'Melveny & Myers LLP*
LAWSON Michael *Skadden, Arps*
SPECTOR Scott *Fenwick & West LLP*
TRUCKER Lee *Trucker Huss PC*
WEST David *Gibson, Dunn*

**3** AGUIRRE John *Wilson Sonsini*
BURMEISTER Edward *Baker & McKenzie*
KIRSCHBAUM Thomas *Irell & Manella LLP*
NIEHANS Daniel *Gunderson Dettmer*
POONJA Zaitun *Morgan, Lewis & Bockius LLP*

**4** BOXER Mark *Morgan, Lewis & Bockius LLP*
HENDRICKS Sharon *Heller Ehrman LLP*
MCCABE Patrick *Morrison & Foerster LLP*
OCKER Jonathan *Orrick*
STERN Roger *Wilson Sonsini*

### Up-and-coming individuals

YAFFE Joseph *Latham & Watkins LLP*

---

counsel and applaud its management of complex issues. Lawyers "*shine in large litigation*" and will also take on single plaintiff cases. Clients declare the firm to be one of the "*highest quality litigation outfits ever seen.*"

**The Lawyers:** **Patricia Gillette** (see p.290) is a "*polished and tough litigator*" who is renowned for her work in the financial service industry. She has negotiated lucrative settlements for major clients in several large class actions. The "*technically competent and smart*" **Sharon Hendricks** (see p.294) is an accomplished employee benefits attorney who represents numerous technology clients. A "*capable*" communicator, she recently worked with a large public company to design and implement its equity compensation plans.

**Clients/Work Highlights:** The client roster lists a range of financial and consumer credit institutions including Bank of America.

## Littler Mendelson, PC

See firm details p.333

**The Firm:** This specialist employment and labor boutique brings "*high quality of expertise to the table.*" Helpful and "*fantastically experienced,*" the lawyers cover 42 subspecialties. The different offices work closely together to ensure that the right skills are brought to bear on a case. Commentators extol the team's "*tremendous client communication*" and "*extremely responsive*" ethos. With its history of traditional labor law, the firm has deep and strong union expertise.

**The Lawyers:** **William Emanuel** (see p.287) "*knows what he's doing,*" according to interviewees. He is a calm and measured negotiator who puts clients at their ease, prompting one to comment: "*I would use him again in a second.*" The "*tenacious*" **Garry**

Mathiason (see p.302) is a "*well-rounded and knowledgeable*" attorney and responsible for the strategy and coordination of the firm. Despite his managerial duties he remains a litigator and recently won a jury trial for a major US airline.

**Clients/Work Highlights:** The firm advises many clients from a variety of industries.

## Munger, Tolles & Olson LLP

**The Firm:** The lawyers at this well-regarded outfit enjoy close relations with an extensive array of clients. Sources admire the caliber of the attorneys here, and the "*bright and focused*" team advises clients on sophisticated issues arising out of both federal and state law.

**The Lawyers:** **Alan Friedman**'s "*expertise and excellent judgment*" attracts clients from diverse industries. He advises, negotiates and litigates on an assortment of labor and employment issues. **Terry Sanchez** is described as a "*fantastic trial lawyer.*" Clients express confidence in his "*excellent record and litigation capability.*"

**Clients/Work Highlights:** The client list includes major entities from the financial, pharmaceutical, media and retailing industries.

## Sheppard, Mullin, Richter & Hampton LLP

**The Firm:** Consistently exceeding clients' expectations, this group has handled a number of high-profile wage and hour actions in the past year. The lawyers provide "*nothing but superlative representation,*" according to clients, who appreciate their willingness to "*go all the way.*" Despite its considerable size, this "*well-organized*" group adopts a friendly and concerted approach that ensures clients "*never feel lost.*" The team is active in litigation, covering wage and hour class actions and the representation of numerous trade associations.

**The Lawyers:** Renowned as the expert of wage and hour work, **Richard Simmons**' clients agree he is "*one of the most capable individuals you could ever meet with.*" A "*hero*" with an "*insightful*" mind, he tackles the most challenging wage and hour cases.

**Clients/Work Highlights:** The firm's clientele is drawn from a range of industries and includes 55 companies from the Fortune 100 list.

## Wilson Sonsini Goodrich & Rosati

See firm details p.344

**The Firm:** This group's "*knowledge of California law is second to none,*" according to clients who cheerfully assert its status as preferred experts in the field. Focusing on high-profile work for technical clients, the practice has developed a "*deep mastery*" of litigation in this area. Lawyers provide invaluable advice in "*strategizing and choosing the right option,*" say interviewees, and always "*deliver what they promise.*" The team recently handled a series of multimillion-dollar discrimination cases for Google, and has been defending an international law firm in a national origin case.

**The Lawyers:** **Fred Alvarez** (see p.276) is a talented advocate. Describing him as "*mature, and a careful*

thinker,*" clients believe he brings "*balance and perspective*" to any situation. He represented Abercrombie & Fitch in a nationwide discrimination class action. **John Aguirre** (see p.276) is "*a superior player*" on the employee benefits team. His clients value his "*calm and reassuring*" demeanor. He recently achieved a favorable severance agreement for the CEO of a multinational technology company. To his fans, **Roger Stern** (see p.316) "*is the energy*" of the employee benefits group. "*Practically minded,*" he is noted for his subtle structuring of compensation and benefit programs.

**Clients/Work Highlights:** Broadcom; Sybase; Google; Juniper Networks; Network Appliances; McAfee; Sun Microsystems and PMC-Sierra.

## Band 5

## Liebert Cassidy Whitmore

**The Firm:** Building on the firm's strong public sector tradition, this 50-strong team trains and advises a number of public entities on employment issues. It has litigated numerous wage and hour actions for entities such as police departments. This is not the end of the story, however: the group does handle work in the private arena.

**The Lawyers:** Brian Walter is an experienced litigator and the key contact for this area.

**Clients/Work Highlights:** Clients include public entities and private employers throughout California.

## Proskauer Rose LLP

See firm details p.1551

**The Firm:** This firm has a solid track record in keeping its clients out of the courtroom. Clients extol the lawyers' "*reliably good results,*" and the high standards of service they deliver.

**The Lawyers:** The "*credible and confident*" **Anthony Oncidi** (see p.305) provides a "*spot-on*" service. Clients celebrate his "*know-how and ability to get to the point quickly.*" He has worked for a number of entertainment industry clients and Fortune 500 businesses. He recently represented a Hollywood studio in a suit alleging disability discrimination and harassment.

**Clients/Work Highlights:** Clients include Fortune 500 companies and high-profile entertainment industry entities.

## Other Notable Practitioners

A "*deep thinker,*" **Steven Drapkin** of the Law Offices of Steven Drapkin is a "*brave and aggressive counselor.*" His "*relentless*" representation has cemented his relationships with a notable clientele. Pillsbury Winthrop Shaw Pittman LLP's **George Howard** (see p.295) is a "*thoughtful*" and versatile litigator "*at the top of his game.*" He recently represented two professional sports franchises in their labor union relations. **Alan Berkowitz** (see p.278) of Bingham McCutchen LLP is "*experienced and strong,*" say interviewees, and recommended for his management of national union matters. At Sidley Austin Brown & Wood LLP, **Jeffrey Berman** (see p.279) is acclaimed as a "*fabulous*" mentor with "*excellent business acumen.*" Clients regard **William Cole** of Mitchell, Silberberg & Knupp LLP as the "*master of guild issues.*" Without this accomplished labor specialist they would feel "*at a complete loss.*" "*Smart, practical, aggressive and creative,*" **Deborah Saxe** joined Jones Day from Heller Ehrman in January this year and is a familiar face at the employment Bar. **Tracy Thompson**, who just joined Cook & Roos LLP from Morgan Lewis, "*always hits a home run.*" Analytical and decisive, she "*leaves no stone unturned*" and delivers a wide-ranging service that clients label "*nothing short of excep-*

*tional.*" At Fenwick & West LLP, **Scott Spector** (see p.315) works hard at his "*terrific*" employee benefits practice. His mixture of technical expertise and client service makes him a leading light in executive compensation. **Lee Trucker** at Trucker Huss PC has a distinguished 25-year track record in employee benefits and "*exudes expertise.*" The "*godfather*" of Baker & McKenzie's international stock options practice, **Edward Burmeister** (see p.281), is admired for his "*great bedside manner.*" Heading up the employee benefits practise at Skadden, Arps, Slate, Meagher & Flom LLP & Affiliates, Los Angeles,

**Michael Lawson** (see p.299) is a "*focused*" attorney whose fans "*think the world of him.*" His carefully balanced perspective is sought on many issues, and especially on pension planning. Gunderson Dettmer Stough Villeneuve Franklin & Hachigian LLP's **Daniel Niehans** is a "*capable and dedicated*" employee benefits practitioner. **Thomas Kirschbaum** at Irell & Manella LLP has a notable executive compensation workload. Commentators declare him "*technically strong and delightful to work with.*"

# ENERGY & NATURAL RESOURCES

## Energy & Natural Resources
### Leading Firms

| | |
|---|---|
| 1 | **MILBANK, TWEED, HADLEY & MCCLOY** *Los Angeles* |
| | **ORRICK, HERRINGTON & SUTCLIFFE** *San Francisco* |
| | **WHITE & CASE LLP** *Los Angeles* |
| 2 | **GOODIN MACBRIDE SQUERI RITCHIE** *San Francisco* |
| | **LATHAM & WATKINS LLP** *San Diego* |
| | **MORRISON & FOERSTER LLP** *Walnut Creek* |
| | **PILLSBURY** *San Francisco* |
| 3 | **DAVIS WRIGHT TREMAINE LLP** *San Francisco* |
| | **DOWNEY, BRAND, SEYMOUR** *Sacramento* |
| | **ELLISON SCHNEIDER & HARRIS** *Sacramento* |
| 4 | **BINGHAM MCCUTCHEN LLP** *Los Angeles* |
| | **MUNGER, TOLLES & OLSON LLP** *Los Angeles* |

### Leading Individuals

| | |
|---|---|
| 1 | **BLOOM** Jerry *White & Case* |
| | **FEO** Edwin *Milbank, Tweed* |
| | **MALKIN** Joseph *Orrick* |
| 2 | **DAY** Michael *Goodin MacBride* |
| | **ELLISON** Christopher *Ellison Schneider* |
| | **GREENWALD** Steven *Davis Wright Tremaine LLP* |
| | **HANSCHEN** Peter *Morrison & Foerster LLP* |
| | **KARP** Joseph *White & Case LLP* |
| 3 | **BOOTH** William *Law Offices of William H Booth* |
| | **ERSPAMER** Gordon *Morrison & Foerster LLP* |
| | **FESSLER** Daniel *Holland & Knight LLP* |
| | **MACK** Joel *Latham & Watkins LLP* |
| | **O'NEILL** Edward *Davis Wright Tremaine LLP* |
| | **WEISSMANN** Henry *Munger, Tolles & Olson LLP* |
| | **YANNEY** Fred *Fulbright & Jaworski L.L.P.* |

## Band 1

### Milbank, Tweed, Hadley & McCloy LLP

**The Firm:** The firm is generally perceived to have "*the last word in high-end project financing,*" particularly on the lender side. Milbank's finance capability, combined with its national and international reach, guarantees it a position at the top of the table. Major energy industry players remark: "*We insist that the banks we deal with use the firm – it just makes every-*

*thing run smoothly.*" The firm astutely identified renewables as an important sector, and the Los Angeles team has predictably forged an enviable presence in this market. The standout deal was advising enXco on its disposition of the 150 MW Shiloh wind project in Northern California.

**The Lawyers:** "*The first name that comes to mind in the field,*" **Ed Feo** has an almost legendary status as an energy sector project finance lawyer, particularly where renewables are concerned. He recently lent his considerable talents to represent the lenders and lead arrangers in the $822 million credit facility to finance the construction of an LNG terminal in Louisiana.

**Clients/Work Highlights:** Key clients include ANZ; Fortis Bank; Dexia; BayernLB and BNP Paribas. Private equity ventures and sponsor companies are increasingly seeking the firm's services.

### Orrick, Herrington & Sutcliffe LLP

See firm details p.337

**The Firm:** The San Francisco office has built its reputation in the energy sector on representing key utility clients such as PG&E. The team's regulatory expertise is complemented by Orrick's finance strength, and peers remark: "*It really does offer a full service.*" It has continued to represent PG&E in negotiations relating to issues arising from the California energy crisis, and recently advised on the acquisition of the Contra Costa 8 electricity-generating facility. Elsewhere, the team appeared before the California Public Utilities Commission on behalf of key client Sempra Energy. Finance highlights include advising AES on a number of wind projects, amid increased interest in the renewables sector.

**The Lawyers:** Partner-in-charge at the San Francisco office, **Joseph Malkin** (see p.301) is a "*highly respected*" litigator and regulatory expert who comfortably retains his top-tier status.

**Clients/Work Highlights:** PG&E and Sempra Energy head the firm's client roster.

### White & Case LLP

See firm details p.1566

**The Firm:** Peers and clients alike are impressed with this finance powerhouse's ability to bring genuine regulatory knowledge and understanding to transactions and, when they arise, disputes. Its much-

envied reputation stems from acting for independent power producers, including before the California Public Utilities Commission and the California Energy Commission. Clients report that the team has "*a great understanding of policy and business issues.*" Mirant is a long-standing client and has sought the group's advice on settling disputed claims relating to the California energy crisis, as well as on negotiations with PG&E over the transfer of the partially constructed Contra Costa 8 power plant. Further highlights include representing US Borax in settling its dispute with Delta Power by establishing a new structure for the continued operation of the Delta Power cogeneration plant. The team's ability to manage complex matters is highly valued by clients, who deem it "*absolutely fantastic for multiparty and multi-issue matters.*"

**The Lawyers:** Practice head **Jerry Bloom** (see p.279) is a favorite among clients for his "*patience and excellent negotiating skills.*" He embodies the team's capacity to combine policy and commercial ability and is described as "*very practical and cerebral at the same time.*" **Joseph Karp** (see p.297) spearheads the firm's renewables work and is "*a truly fine lawyer who gets it right away – he knows exactly what we need.*"

**Clients/Work Highlights:** Calpine is another important client for the team, which it represented in California and Louisiana in the settlement of payment rates and refund portion matters. Other significant clients include the California Cogeneration Council and AES.

## Band 2

### Goodin MacBride Squeri Ritchie & Day LLP

**The Firm:** This "*knowledgeable and experienced*" energy team boasts a good proportion of attorneys who have worked at the California Public Utilities Commission. While natural gas work is considered one of the firm's key fortes, its presence in power infrastructure matters has attracted considerable attention of late. While the team's policy know-how is beyond dispute – "*they really are the go-to firm for government and legislative advice*" – it is increasingly utilizing its regulatory expertise in transactional settings. Its advice to the Warren Buffet affiliate MidAmerican Energy Holdings on the Californian regulatory aspects of its acquisition of PacifiCorp is a case in point.

**The Lawyers:** **Michael Day** is "*an attorney of the highest caliber*" who has recently lent his skills to energy infrastructure developments such as the Transbay Cable project.

**Clients/Work Highlights:** In addition to MidAmerican Energy Holdings, Babcock & Brown is another new client, complementing long-standing clients such as EnCana and the California Retailers Association.

## Latham & Watkins LLP

**The Firm:** This "*super-active*" firm continues to increase its national footprint in the energy sector. Its notable financing expertise has led to heavy involvement in the development of energy projects, but peers and clients note that the group has cultivated capacities that go beyond finance and is "*increasingly expansive.*" An increasing number of appearances before the California Public Utilities Commission, including its representation of PG&E in recovery proceedings, would suggest that it is making a name for itself on the regulatory front. Market sources also complimented the firm's handling of other matters, including environmental impact statements. Meanwhile, the diversity of projects covered was noted, especially with regard to renewables, and wind projects in particular.

**The Lawyers:** Clients branded **Joel Mack** an "*outstanding*" lawyer who can "*get projects up and running with considerable ease.*"

**Clients/Work Highlights:** Anchor client Sempra Energy sought the firm's expertise in its development of an LNG terminal in Baja and various LNG projects in Latin America. Other clients include Edison Mission Energy and TransAlta.

## Morrison & Foerster LLP

See firm details p.335

**The Firm:** "*Always a solid performer,*" the Walnut Creek-based team is universally considered a "*safe pair of hands*" for energy work, especially where top-notch litigation and regulatory services are required. Power consumers constitute the mainstay of the practice, and the team is heavily involved in resolving residual energy crisis issues, which often involves handling briefs for multiple defendants at appeal. Key client Calpine has also kept the team busy in relation to its service contract dispute with Western Area Power Administration. Members of the firm are renowned for their sophisticated handling of matters before state and federal regulatory bodies, whether in relation to power, oil, gas or renewables. Advising clients on solar, hydro and wind projects accounts for a growing proportion of the team's output. Meanwhile, in cooperation with the Washington, DC office, it advised the State of Alaska on regulatory issues surrounding the trans-Alaska pipeline.

**The Lawyers:** **Peter Hanschen** (see p.292) is credited with "*extraordinary regulatory knowledge and experience.*" He recently advised on a transmission control dispute, in addition to representing an oil pipeline in proceedings to establish new pipeline rates. **Gordy Erspamer** (see p.287) heads the litigation team and is noted for his relentless defense of client interests. One commentator remarked: "*If you're at war with Attila the Hun, he's the one you want.*"

**Clients/Work Highlights:** Further clients include IDACORP, Genentech and El Paso.

## Pillsbury Winthrop Shaw Pittman LLP

See firm details p.1550

**The Firm:** Following last year's merger, this firm has continued to cement its profile as a one-stop shop for energy clients that now offers additional expertise in key energy markets in Washington, DC and Houston. In addition to offering "*far-sighted strategic vision*" to its institutional client base of power operators and owners, the group increasingly attracts clients from all sides, including high-profile players in the capital markets arena. The big-ticket deal of the past year was advising Chevron on the corporate/commercial aspects of its acquisition of Unocal. Key client PacifiCorp called upon the group's regulatory expertise with regard to the development of a gas-fired power plant in Utah, where the group handled all air, land and water rights issues. Clients report that the team is "*incredibly diligent in protecting their clients' interests*" and that its commercial focus ensures "*deals are closed as soon as is humanly possible.*"

**The Lawyers:** Rob James is the corporate and securities attorney who heads up the energy team. Michael Hindus and Terry Kee are also key contacts.

**Clients/Work Highlights:** Dynegy; Chevron Energy Solutions; Duke Energy; Valero Refining; Headwaters; GE and Hanson.

## Band 3

## Davis Wright Tremaine LLP

**The Firm:** In combining a full service that compares favorably with that of its larger rivals on the one hand, with the client service and quick turnaround of a boutique on the other, this firm is said to offer clients "*absolutely the best of both worlds.*" Its lawyers cover regulatory, finance, litigation and corporate/commercial fronts, all the while "*running fast in order to get things done.*" The group sustains its stellar reputation for assisting with the development and operation of power plants, and offering clients such as Calpine the advantages of its significant depth of experience before the California Public Utilities Commission. Natural gas, water and, increasingly, renewables also feature as core practice areas. Recent highlights include providing finance and regulatory advice to FPL Energy in connection with major wind and solar-generating facilities on the West Coast. FERC expertise constitutes an important element of the firm's national armory, and clients remarked favorably on the outfit's integrated energy and litigation expertise, which it has used to full

effect this year in several large-scale disputes against public utilities.

**The Lawyers:** Regulatory expert **Steve Greenwald** offers clients "*good common sense*" and is "*able to move things forward in a constructive way.*" A number of clients reported that he is "*very creative in his approach.*" **Ed O'Neill** is thought to benefit from his years of experience as chief federal solicitor at the California Public Utilities Commission, and recently represented citizens' groups at the Commission in proceedings concerning the location of transmission facilities. Rivals report that he has an "*absolutely first-class mind.*"

**Clients/Work Highlights:** The team also represents the Bay Area Rapid Transport District (BART) and Modesto Irrigation District.

## Downey, Brand, Seymour & Rohwer LLP

**The Firm:** This Sacramento outfit is another firm offering regulatory expertise and in-depth knowledge of the California Public Utilities Commission, the California Energy Commission and FERC. It combines the provision of services on the ground in California with federal capabilities. Recent work includes representing large industrial electric and gas consumers in public utility rate proceedings.

**The Lawyers:** Natural resources partner James Day is the principal contact in this six-strong team.

**Clients/Work Highlights:** Industrial energy clients are at the core of this firm's client base.

## Ellison Schneider & Harris

**The Firm:** Based in Sacramento, this "*slick outfit*" concentrates on providing an enviable client roster with state and federal regulatory expertise. The team's reputation has historically rested on acting for non-utility generators such as Calpine, which it represented this year in licensing issues surrounding its Los Esteros critical energy facility. However, the client base also includes independent power producers, municipal utilities and trade organizations from the power and, increasingly, the renewables sectors. Flexing its policy muscle, the team successfully represented the American Wind Energy Association in a campaign to persuade FERC to adopt wind-specific rules for electricity transmission systems.

**The Lawyers:** **Christopher Ellison** heads up the team and is "*the firm's preeminent regulatory lawyer.*" He works on both state and federal levels and, as peers concede, "*clients either use him, or to their disappointment, are conflicted from using him.*"

**Clients/Work Highlights:** Duke Energy; Independent Energy Producers; East Bay Municipal Utility District; Stanford University and the Western Electricity Coordinating Council.

## Band 4

## Bingham McCutchen LLP

See firm details p.1110

**The Firm:** This firm enters the table thanks to its extensive involvement in post-energy crisis litigation.

Antitrust and dispute resolution are key areas of focus for the firm, and it has leveraged these strengths to serve utilities in a range of contentious matters. Sources report that the team "*sustains a consistently high quality of service and is very proactive.*"

**The Lawyers:** Terry Houlihan is a key contact where contentious matters relating to regulated industries, including energy, are concerned.

**Clients/Work Highlights:** Reliant Energy is an important client for the group.

## Munger, Tolles & Olson LLP

**The Firm:** This California-based firm has built its reputation in the energy sector on its representation of anchor client Southern California Edison, whether in matters before the California Public Utilities Commission or in transactional settings. Recently it advised Edison International on the sale of most of its international operations.

**The Lawyers:** Henry Weissman "*does a fine job and is a high-quality lawyer.*" In addition to being the key partner responsible for acting for Southern California Edison, he acts for oil majors such as Shell and Occidental Petroleum in litigation.

### Other Notable Practitioners

Sole practitioner **William Booth** is "*a very sophisticated advocate,*" according to sources, and an expert on electricity utilities. He successfully settled a revenue allocation matter as part of a PG&E case, and also acts for PacifiCorp and the California Large Energy Consumers Association. **Daniel Fessler** (see p.288) of Holland & Knight LLP is highly respected in industry circles, having served as president of the California Public Utilities Commission for five years. He uses his regulatory knowledge and contacts to advance policy initiatives on behalf of clients such as San Diego Gas & Electric and Southern California Edison. **Fred Yanney** (see p.321) heads up Fulbright & Jaworski L.L.P.'s energy team. He represents independent power producers, marketers, investors and publicly owned utilities in state and federal regulatory matters. Clients raved that he is "*an exceptional lawyer who is both responsive and accommodating.*" He has been heavily involved in the Magnolia power plant project, one of the first major power plants to be built in Southern California since the energy crisis.

# ENVIRONMENT

| Environment |
|---|
| **Leading Firms** |
| 1 **BINGHAM MCCUTCHEN LLP** *Los Angeles* |
| **LATHAM & WATKINS LLP** *Los Angeles* |
| 2 **MORRISON & FOERSTER LLP** *San Francisco* |
| **PILLSBURY** *San Francisco* |
| 3 **FARELLA BRAUN & MARTEL LLP** *San Francisco* |
| **GIBSON, DUNN & CRUTCHER LLP** *Los Angeles* |
| **WESTON BENSHOOF ROCHEFORT** *Los Angeles* |
| 4 **MORGAN, LEWIS & BOCKIUS LLP** *San Francisco* |
| **PAUL, HASTINGS** *San Francisco* |

## Band 1

### Bingham McCutchen LLP

See firm details p.1110

**The Firm:** This fast-growing national firm boasts several high-profile names, but is also highly rated by observers for the consistency of talent on offer throughout its ranks. Interviewees noted that its 40 "*methodical, meticulous and very effective*" lawyers offer "*tremendous expertise,*" while others commented that the firm "*hires good people and trains them well.*" Active across the USA, the team has recently represented the City of Denver in challenging the EPA's proposed cleanup plan for a former municipal and industrial landfill site. The group has also been busy advising on the growing area of military base conversions. As well as offering "*incredibly good advice,*" the team won praise for its customer service ethos. Clients noted that the team provides a timely service and that the lawyers "*put in long hours and treat our work as a priority.*"

**The Lawyers:** Patricia Shanks (see p.313) is a seasoned environment attorney who specializes in negotiating scientific remedies to regulatory problems ranging from Proposition 65 to Superfund matters. She is "*a quick learner who can grasp the issues,*" and was a popular choice among clients who described her as a "*zealous advocate who is nonetheless*" sympathetic to the business realities." She also impressed interviewees with her ability to clearly outline complex science in layman's terms. This skill came to the fore when she negotiated a complex and urgent cleanup of a property in El Segundo, which had been contaminated by industrial activity on neighboring sites. **James Dragna** (see p.286) focuses on complex multiparty litigation. Twenty-five former customers of an abandoned landfill in suburban Los Angeles recently chose him to negotiate a settlement with the state for the interim and long-term maintenance of the site. He also handles CWA disputes and recently represented Southern Californian water suppliers and regulators in litigation challenging the structure of the multibillion-dollar California State Water Project. Clients also call on him for support in Superfund disputes and described him as "*an excellent negotiator who is tough but always looking for solutions.*" Despite his youth, **Trent Norris** (see p.305) was recommended to researchers as "*possibly the top lawyer in California*" in the niche areas of vaccines and toxic chemicals, and handles both product liability and IP-related disputes. Clients appreciate his diligent, professional and creative approach and note that he "*does a terrific job of keeping us informed of developments.*" This year he has attracted attention for his role in Proposition 65 litigation concerning the alleged toxic qualities of acrylamide, a chemical found in many foods. Here he is defending one of the major snack food manufacturers in the case, which involves all three branches of the California state government as well as the EPA.

**Clients/Work Highlights:** The firm's client base ranges from local governments to multinational companies, particularly chemical and electronics manufacturers.

### Latham & Watkins LLP

**The Firm:** This giant firm's stable of 60 "*highly qualified*" environment attorneys includes "*some of the smartest lawyers in the state.*" Clients appreciate the team's commitment to customer service, and reported: "*The lawyers are judicious with their time, responsive to our suggestions and will work until the early hours to meet deadlines.*" Boasting five offices across California, the team represents multinationals including Chevron and Toyota, alongside state-based businesses and trade associations. The group's prowess in clean air matters was demonstrated when, on behalf on International Truck and Engine, it successfully repelled regulation proposed by the South Coast Air Quality Management District relating to natural gas engines in school buses. In addition to air-related work, the team is highly visible in water, contamination and cleanup matters and is often the first port of call for clients requiring support in compliance counseling and enforcement litigation. In one of its headline cases, the team successfully represented a coalition of California builders, in defending a ruling by the State Water Resources Control Board regarding runoff from construction sites against challenges by environmental groups.

**The Lawyers:** Although one of the group's leading lights, BJ Kirwan, retired this year, the team has "*great people coming up through the ranks.*" One of these is **Gene Lucero**, a former head of enforcement at the EPA who is famed for his top-level experience in Superfund and hazardous waste matters. He is currently representing GE in administrative proceedings relating to the chemical contamination in San Francisco Bay. The case raises jurisdictional questions about the relationship between Superfund and the CWA. Clients warmly recommended him because "*he's politically astute and provides advice we can rely on. He's great to work with and is effective in negotiations.*" Interviewees nominated **Robert Wyman** as "*the go-to person*" for air matters. He is currently advising the Maritime Goods Movement Coalition on developing a low-cost solution to the emissions problems of Southern California's ports and freight infrastructure. Along with **Michael Carroll**, Wyman is counsel to the Western States

## Environment
### Leading Individuals

[1] **BARR Michael** *Pillsbury Winthrop Shaw Pittman*
**BRUEN James** *Farella Braun & Martel LLP*
**CORASH Michèle** *Morrison & Foerster LLP*
**LUCERO Gene** *Latham & Watkins LLP*
**WYMAN JR Robert** *Latham & Watkins LLP*

[2] **DENNIS Patrick** *Gibson, Dunn & Crutcher*
**HERNANDEZ Jennifer** *Holland & Knight LLP*
**RUBALCAVA Sharon** *Weston Benshoof*
**SHANKS Patricia** *Bingham McCutchen LLP*
**ZISCHKE Michael** *Morrison & Foerster LLP*

[3] **DRAGNA James** *Bingham McCutchen LLP*
**SCHMALL Deborah** *Farella Braun & Martel LLP*
**STEEL Michael** *Pillsbury Winthrop Shaw Pittman*
**THOMPSON Jocelyn** *Weston Benshoof*
**WEINER Peter** *Paul, Hastings, Janofsky & Walker*

[4] **CARROLL Michael** *Latham & Watkins LLP*
**GARVIN Anthony** *Morgan, Lewis & Bockius LLP*
**HANSEN John** *Pillsbury Winthrop Shaw Pittman*
**HART Gordon** *Paul, Hastings, Janofsky & Walker*
**HOWARD Robert** *Latham & Watkins LLP*
**ROSEGAY Margaret** *Pillsbury Winthrop Shaw Pittman*

### Up-and-coming individuals
**DINTZER Jeffrey** *Gibson, Dunn & Crutcher LLP*
**NORRIS Trenton** *Bingham McCutchen LLP*

---

Petroleum Association on its emission reductions strategy. Carroll is a "*thoughtful, knowledgeable and practical*" attorney who also focuses on air issues; he "*knows the local Air Quality Management Districts inside and out.*" He successfully represented ConocoPhillips in challenges to permits issued by the South Coast Air Quality Management District for the modification of a Los Angeles refinery. Interviewees also endorsed him as an "*articulate lawyer who is excellent in dealing with politicians and regulators.*" Though he chairs the firm's environment team in San Diego, **Robert Howard**'s litigation and compliance practice sees him involved in matters as far afield as Texas and the East Coast. "*Intelligent, creative and an excellent strategist*," he is "*extremely knowledgeable, both on the status of the law and of trends in similar matters.*" A "*first-class communicator*" and "*great at dealing with people*," he has recently been active on the latest round of military base conversions.

**Clients/Work Highlights:** ConocoPhillips; Chevron; National Steel and Shipbuilding; Building Industry Association of California; Western States Petroleum Association; PG&E; Edison International; Fluor; Montrose Chemical; Playa Capital; Toyota and Sempra Energy.

## Band 2

### Morrison & Foerster LLP
See firm details p.335
**The Firm:** Interviewees recommended this team of around 30 attorneys as a "*preeminent force in the market.*" Although it offers a spectrum of environmental law advice, Proposition 65 work remains a key focus for the group. It is currently representing five snack food manufacturers and fast food restaurants in the high-profile Proposition 65 case regarding the presence of acrylamide in foods. In addition, the team has been boosted by the arrival of well-regarded Edgar Washburn who has acknowledged experience in wetlands and logging issues. The team also picked up praise for its burgeoning California Environmental Quality Act (CEQA) practice.

**The Lawyers:** **Michèle Corash** (see p.284) is a high-profile player who observers believe is well deserving of her reputation as "*the Proposition 65 guru.*" In addition to leading the firm's efforts in the acrylamide case, she is currently representing a coalition of meat producers in challenging state labeling requirements for their products. However, her practice is not solely limited to Proposition 65: this year she also obtained a $5 million award for Kerr-McGee from the federal government in a challenge to an EPA order requiring the cleanup of an abandoned uranium mine. **Mike Zischke**'s (see p.321) practice bridges environmental and land use law although he won most applause for his "*great knowledge of CEQA*" and his extensive lobbying experience. Interviewees also consider him "*one of the top people in the state for environmental impact reports*" and point to his catalog of precedent-setting cases. In one of the first cases of its kind in California, he successfully challenged regulation prepared by the California State Lands Commission that sought to affect the operation of plants in Mexico belonging to the North Baja Pipeline. He also represents the California Department of Transportation in an appellate case assessing the jurisdiction of CEQA's Environmental Impact Review in relation to the development of sovereign tribal lands.

**Clients/Work Highlights:** The firm boasts a client base that includes major public companies and associations such as Hershey Foods; TransCanada Pipelines; Grocery Manufacturers Association and Coca-Cola.

### Pillsbury Winthrop Shaw Pittman LLP
See firm details p.1550
**The Firm:** This expanding international firm houses a team of around 20 "*outstanding*" environment lawyers in its California offices. Interviewees pointed to the consistency of the team, from its leading partners down to its "*go-getting associates who work hard to please their clients.*" The group's "*straightforward*" approach to law also met with approval and clients said: "*They are not afraid to tell it like it is and can break things down into simple terms.*" The team has recently advised Union Pacific and BNSF Railway in negotiating reductions in diesel emissions with the state Air Resources Board. It also represented Los Angeles Unified School District in securing and defending the approval for a major new learning center in Mid-Wilshire, which involves the redevelopment of the historic Ambassador Hotel, the site of Robert Kennedy's assassination.

**The Lawyers:** **Michael Barr** (see p.277) was warmly recommended as "*the guru of environmental law in the Bay area,*" and is also widely regarded as "*one of the preeminent air experts*" in the state. Recent examples of his work in this area include representing Union Pacific in negotiations for a groundbreaking agreement with state air authorities to reduce diesel emissions. He is a firm favorite among clients, who remarked: "*He can explain issues without resorting to alphabet soup and is an extraordinary strategic thinker who drives cases to a resolution in a cost-effective manner.*" As one source noted: "*He's the epitome of a trusted adviser.*" **Michael Steel** (see p.315) brings "*substantial regulatory experience*" to his enforcement defense practice. Peers also praised him for his "*huge amount of scientific expertise,*" and his strong presentation skills in negotiations and in court. He is defending a major public company in an action brought by the Attorney General and 17 District Attorneys involving alleged violations relating to the storage of petroleum underground. **John Hansen**'s (see p.293) environmental practice ranges from enforcement defense to compliance counseling. Clients believe that his "*even-tempered and thoughtful*" approach makes him ideally suited to controversial matters. He has been busy negotiating Title V permits for several major oil refineries and has represented a medical waste processor in the defense of a permit to build a major waste disposal facility in Tehama County. "*One of the top water lawyers in California,*" **Margaret Rosegay** (see p.310) boasts an "*encyclopedic knowledge*" of water regulations. She is also active in the related area of hazardous waste work and is currently representing the former owners of a refinery in Bakersfield in complex and high-value litigation regarding residual cleanup duties. Commentators told us that Rosegay "*knows the players,*" and that her "*unflappable*" approach stands her in good stead in litigation and in administrative hearings.

**Clients/Work Highlights:** The group's clients include major state enterprises and government bodies, in addition to some of the USA's largest oil refining companies. Key clients include 3M; Imation; Sempra Energy; Association of American Railroads; Golden Gate National Parks Conservancy; Medtronic and Union Pacific.

## Band 3

### Farella Braun & Martel LLP
**The Firm:** This San Francisco-based team of around 20 "*highly experienced*" attorneys offers comprehensive environmental law advice ranging from air and water compliance to military base and brownfield redevelopment issues. The team scored highly with clients who were impressed with its level of responsiveness and its consistency in providing "*strong support and excellent legal advice.*" Its roster of clients includes several major public companies such as GE, which it represented in large-scale litigation concerning chemical exposure in the manufacture of welding rods.

**The Lawyers:** Interviewees warmly endorsed **James Bruen** as "*one of the great environment litigators*" in the state. He manages a broad caseload that encompasses toxic torts, natural resources damages litigation, and enforcement defense, and frequently acts in nationwide cases. He is a popular figure among peers, who conceded: "*He has a great down-to-earth approach and you often don't realize how brilliant he is.*" **Deborah Schmall**'s "*tremendous*" practice includes regulatory counseling and litigation, particularly in the areas of hazardous waste and brownfields development. She is currently advising Genentech on the acquisition and permitting of 100,000 sq ft of office space in downtown San Francisco. She is gifted at expressing and absorbing complex information and can "*explain fine points of law in plain English.*" Clients particularly appreciate her "*tireless, dedicated and extraordinarily responsive*" customer service and believe that "*she never gives less than 100%.*"

**Clients/Work Highlights:** The group acts for a range of major state and national companies. Key clients include Union Pacific; GE; University of California and Levi Strauss.

## Gibson, Dunn & Crutcher LLP

See firm details p.328

**The Firm:** This giant firm's Los Angeles-based environment team has a Southern California-focused practice and acts for both national and state enterprises. It is currently representing the California Farm Bureau at the appellate level in long-running litigation challenging the conversion of agricultural land into habitat. Another key client is Lockheed Martin, which the team acted for in relation to the cleanup of a variety of facilities in the West, including a former rocket-testing site. The team of around 28 attorneys won plaudits for the consistent caliber of its leading lawyers, down to its "*smart, knowledgeable*" associates.

**The Lawyers:** **Pat Dennis** (see p.285) chairs the firm's environmental group but continues to maintain his own substantial caseload. Recent highlights include acting as environment counsel on the $260 million sale of Hollywood Park. This historic racetrack sits over an oil and gas field, raising complex environmental concerns involving several state and regional agencies. "*A wonderful representative,*" sources said he can shape strategy in line with clients' wider business aims. One interviewee revealed: "*He can be tough and hang on in there but also knows when it's a good time to cut a deal.*" Another noted: "*You hire him for his specific expertise, but you stay with him for the quality of the entire service.*" **Jeff Dintzer**'s (see p.286) "*passion for his clients' cause and dedication to their best interests*" set him apart from some of his competitors in the field. He represented the Los Angeles Conservancy in opposing Los Angeles Unified School District's redevelopment of the Ambassador Hotel and helped secure a $5 million settlement in relation to other conservation projects around the city. His roster of clients also includes household names such as Wal-Mart and Pioneer and he is widely regarded as a "*charming and decent*"

attorney who is nevertheless "*a real bulldog who is not afraid to get his hands dirty.*"

**Clients/Work Highlights:** Kerr-McGee; Pacific Gulf Properties; Northrop Grumman; Lockheed Martin; General Growth Properties and Proficiency Capital.

## Weston Benshoof Rochefort Rubalcava MacCuish LLP

See firm details p.343

**The Firm:** Environmental law is a key focus of this well-regarded local firm, and it has built a sizable team of 20 environment specialists who also work closely with the firm's litigation department. The group has long-standing experience of California's complex environmental laws but is also tuned into the workings of the regulators and governmental bodies. As a result, major companies such as Boeing, ConocoPhillips and BP turn to the firm for help in obtaining permits for local projects. The group also has a strong client base of local businesses and state bodies, including San Diego County Regional Airport Authority, which it is currently representing in a federal action regarding soil and groundwater contamination on sites surrounding the airport. Clients choose the team for its "*professional and trustworthy*" approach and believe the lawyers here "*understand we have a goal and can shape their strategy around it.*"

**The Lawyers:** With her "*complete experience of environmental law,*" **Sharon Rubalcava** (see p.311) has a knack of obtaining permits for clients in the face of public opposition and difficult circumstances. "*Well connected and respected,*" she "*knows the issues in and out*" and excels at presenting them clearly and persuasively. She is currently representing Browning-Ferris Industries on the expansion of Sunshine Canyon Landfill in northern Los Angeles, which requires permits from a wide range of different regulators, under state and federal water and waste laws. She is also an expert in air matters and was recently selected by the Mayor of Los Angeles to serve on a task force aimed at identifying means of reducing emissions at the city's massive port. **Jocelyn Thompson** (see p.317) combines permitting and compliance counseling with environmental litigation. She assisted Flying J on environmental review and permitting matters in relation to the Bakersfield refinery, recently acquired from Shell. On behalf of Mitsubishi Cement she is also involved in negotiations with both state and federal air quality authorities, seeking to identify ways of reducing the emissions of ships visiting the ports.

**Clients/Work Highlights:** Browning-Ferris Industries; Pacific Energy Partners; FPL Energy; Mitsubishi Cement; Stonebridge Holdings; Western States Petroleum Association; Boeing; BP; ConocoPhillips; San Diego County Regional Airport Authority; QUIKRETE and Rockwell Collins.

## Band 4

### Morgan, Lewis & Bockius LLP

See firm details p.1758

**The Firm:** This sophisticated environmental group operates from San Francisco and Los Angeles. Its team of ten dedicated environment attorneys focuses on environmental disputes where it can draw on support from the firm's wider litigation team. In particular, it won recognition for its skill in hazardous waste disputes.

**The Lawyers:** **Anthony Garvin** (see p.290) divides his time between environmental counseling, litigation and enforcement defense. He is a "*personable, responsive and user-friendly*" lawyer who has "*a detailed understanding of all the applicable regulations and statutes.*" His ability to "*take the initiative*" makes him excellent at dealing with the regulators and as a result, clients "*never hesitate to call him.*" His recent highlights include defending an enforcement action brought by the EPA concerning alleged violations of pesticide regulations.

**Clients/Work Highlights:** Clear Channel, Fresh Del Monte and Chevron are among the group's major clients.

### Paul, Hastings, Janofsky & Walker LLP

See firm details p.339

**The Firm:** This firm's San Francisco office is home to around ten environmental attorneys who are supported by members of the litigation department. The team's specialties include brownfield development, military base conversions and hazardous waste matters. One of its major clients is Dow Chemical, which it represents on clean air matters, including Title V permits in California, and on Superfund matters across the country. The group also acts as national environment counsel to Vanguard Car Rental USA, the owner of Alamo Rent A Car.

**The Lawyers:** **Peter Weiner**'s (see p.320) highlights include securing a preliminary approval for Hopkins Real Estate Group's precedent-setting plan to build a residential development on a former hazardous waste landfill. One of his other key clients is Market Street Investors, which he advises on a range of brownfield developments across the country. **Gordon Hart** specializes in the growing area of military base conversions. He assisted one of his key clients, Lennar, on the $650 million purchase of El Toro Marine Corps Air Station, which was one of the largest public auction purchases of a former military base. Other areas of his practice include Superfund work, where he represents both businesses and local government entities.

**Clients/Work Highlights:** The group's major clients include Dow Chemical, Lennar and The Dewey Group.

### Other Notable Practitioners

Market observers viewed **Jennifer Hernandez**'s (see p.294) decision in 2005 to quit Beveridge & Diamond in favor of Holland & Knight LLP as an astute move. Her practice combines land use work with environmental counseling, including base conversions, urban infill and greenfield development. Interviewees described her as a lawyer who is "*aggressive, but in a positive, strategic way.*" She received staunch support from clients who reported: "*She sees the whole chessboard, not just the next move.*"

# HEALTHCARE

## Healthcare
### Leading Firms

**1** FOLEY & LARDNER LLP *Los Angeles*
HOOPER LUNDY & BOOKMAN INC *Los Angeles*
LATHAM & WATKINS LLP *Los Angeles*
MCDERMOTT WILL & EMERY *Los Angeles*

**2** DAVIS WRIGHT TREMAINE LLP *San Francisco*
FULBRIGHT & JAWORSKI L.L.P. *Los Angeles*
MANATT PHELPS & PHILLIPS LLP *Los Angeles*
PAUL, HASTINGS *San Francisco*

**3** HASSARD BONNINGTON LLP *San Francisco*
JONES DAY *San Francisco*
SONNENSCHEIN NATH & ROSENTHAL *Los Angeles*

### Leading Individuals

#### Senior Statesmen

MEMEL Sherwin *Manatt Phelps & Phillips LLP*
WEISSBURG Carl *Foley & Lardner LLP*

**1** DEMETRIOU Andrew *Fulbright & Jaworski L.L.P.*
HIGGINS Daniel *Paul, Hastings*
HOOPER Patric *Hooper Lundy & Bookman Inc*
KADZIELSKI Mark *Fulbright & Jaworski L.L.P.*
MANCINO Douglas *McDermott Will & Emery*
PETERS Gerald *Latham & Watkins LLP*
ROOT JR George *Foley & Lardner*
SCHWARTZ James *Manatt Phelps & Phillips LLP*
STROMBERG Ross *Jones Day*

**2** BOOKMAN Lloyd *Hooper Lundy & Bookman Inc*
DEMURO Paul *Latham & Watkins LLP*
GIRARD Robert *Sonnenschein Nath & Rosenthal*
GOLDMAN Donald *McDermott Will & Emery*
HELLOW John *Hooper Lundy & Bookman Inc*
HINKLEY Gerry *Davis Wright Tremaine LLP*
LANDSBERG Barry *Manatt Phelps & Phillips LLP*
LIPTON M Steven *Davis Wright Tremaine LLP*
LUNDY Robert *Hooper Lundy & Bookman Inc*
RODRIGUEZ Denise *Foley & Lardner LLP*
SETTLEMAYER Daniel *Latham & Watkins LLP*
STANTON W Clark *Davis Wright Tremaine LLP*

**3** BLANCHARD Timothy *McDermott Will & Emery*
GOLDBERG Phillip *Hassard Bonnington LLP*
GORDON Eric *McDermott Will & Emery*
HIRSCH Reece *Sonnenschein Nath & Rosenthal*
LISET J Robert *Musick Peeler & Garrett*
PIMSTONE Gregory *Manatt Phelps & Phillips LLP*
SCHUCHARD Robert *Sonnenschein Nath & Rosenthal*
SEIDEN Richard *Foley & Lardner LLP*
SMITH Paul *Davis Wright Tremaine LLP*
THOMPSON Martin *Manatt Phelps & Phillips LLP*
TULLY W Bradley *Hooper Lundy & Bookman Inc*
YOOD Kenneth *Paul, Hastings*

## Band 1

### Foley & Lardner LLP
See firm details p.2037
**The Firm:** "*For expertise and knowledge of the unique nature of western USA healthcare, you'd be hard pressed to match Foley,*" clients believe. Its national reach goes some way to explain its prominence but it is ultimately the diversity of its practice and systemwide expertise that impresses clients and observers. With "*more troops on the ground*" than many of its competitors and still growing, the group is able to offer counseling, advice and litigation services across the discipline. The fact that healthcare accounts for one of the firm's six departments further demonstrates the firm's commitment to the industry. Its expertise includes long-term care, acting for specialty or community hospitals and physicians groups, and Medicare and Medicaid reimbursement matters. Commentators say that the team "*always comes right up to the mark to meet the high expectations of clients*" in this demanding marketplace. The firm's representation of a host of trade associations ensures that it keeps abreast of current trends.
**The Lawyers:** A mentor to many budding healthcare attorneys, **Carl Weissburg** (see p.320) is the principal founder of Weissburg & Aronson, which merged with Foley & Lardner in 1996. Naturally considered a dean of the California healthcare Bar, his involvement spans the gamut of health issues, including M&A, structured integrated delivery systems and managed care issues. "*High in stature and nationally renowned,*" **George Root** (see p.310) has cut a swath in healthcare law that is matched by few. Clients view him as "*a remarkable lawyer whose breadth of understanding across all the components of healthcare is phenomenal.*" His portfolio includes both transactional and specialty matters, where recent work includes a significant compliance investigation concerning a dialysis company that was settled for over $300 million. **Denise Rios Rodriguez** (see p.310) is "*California's leading big-hitter on Medicare and Medicaid funding*" according to interviewees, who point to the depth of her experience in the field and her diverse client base. Much of her time has been taken up with the financing aspects of the Medicaid programme. The "*responsive and well-informed*" **Richard Seiden** (see p.313) is retained as outside general counsel by numerous hospitals, nursing homes and surgeries. His business practice received praise for its attention to the complex funding and licensing issues surrounding M&A, joint ventures and real estate in the healthcare arena.
**Clients/Work Highlights:** The firm represents hospitals, physician groups, HMOs and trade associations, including Gambro Healthcare; Children's Hospital of Orange County; CalOptima; California Hospital Association and Blue Cross and Blue Shield Association.

### Hooper Lundy & Bookman Inc
**The Firm:** Upheld by market commentators as the "*premier boutique reimbursement firm,*" this outfit reaches out to compete across California and nationwide. Clients are impressed by the firm's "*outstanding presence*" and note that it is home to a "*deep pool of strong and focused attorneys,*" who tackle the most complex of healthcare issues. Its overarching experience includes acting for hospitals, physician practices, associations and the long-term care industry, providing advice on the acquisitions, business transactions, financing options and litigation. The group continues to be involved in Tenet Healthcare's divestiture of hospitals across the United States.
**The Lawyers:** The eminent **Pat Hooper** "*does a superb job*" on Medicare appeals and is cited as "*one of the best*" on fraud and kickback issues. In fact, "*his experience and craftsmanship across healthcare counseling and litigation are unmatched,*" according to commentators. He is also recognized as a driving force in terms of drawing in business and "*getting the right people on the job.*" **Lloyd Bookman** stands out as "*one of the brightest reimbursement lawyers there is,*" often acting on top-level matters. His 25 years of experience in the field have seen him build up a deep understanding of Medicaid and Medicare financing programs. **John Hellow** is nationally regarded for his leading practice in Medicare and Medicaid reimbursement and regulatory procedure. He has represented hospitals in payment disputes and advised clients on the reimbursement implications of their business transactions. **Robert Lundy** is cited to be "*extremely successful in healthcare business transactions.*" He has brought his experience to bear on a myriad of joint ventures, the structuring of physician organizations and licensing and certification matters. He is particularly active in the multifaceted area of hospital finance and acquisitions. **Bradley Tully** has "*a strong reputation and a solid book of business in the fraud and abuse arena.*" He is skilled in guiding hospitals, physicians and health providers through the maze of transactional and regulatory issues in this complex field.
**Clients/Work Highlights:** The firm acts for healthcare providers, from hospitals to individual physician practices, including Tenet Healthcare and HCA.

### Latham & Watkins LLP
**The Firm:** This firm has forged a sterling reputation in California and beyond, fielding a "*high-end practice*" that is driven by a "*tremendously strong bench.*"

Clients report that quality is consistently high across the firm's global platform and note that the team is often at the forefront of industry developments. The preeminent white-collar defense practice continues to play a key role in governmental investigation and whistle-blower actions, thereby enhancing the efforts of the healthcare and life sciences groups. The firm represents a number of major hospital systems alongside a broad range of physician organizations, pharmaceutical companies, hospices and medical device manufacturers. The department's "*prime players*" are ably assisted by a host of rising stars who are experienced in various specialties such as tax exemption, compliance, FDA regulation, medical staff issues and fraud and abuse.

**The Lawyers:** "*A creative lawyer and a high-end deal-maker,*" **Gerald Peters** enjoys a national reputation and spearheads the group's development. His broad experience in business, transactional and regulatory affairs marks him out to clients as a valuable adviser. **Paul DeMuro** is respected as a "*knowledgeable and comprehensive transactional lawyer who really knows his stuff.*" He remains committed to reimbursement and fraud and abuse matters, acting for managed care organizations, health systems, physicians and ancillary providers. Clients highlight **Daniel Settelmayer** as a "*creative and cutting-edge lawyer who thoroughly understands the healthcare industry.*" One of the cochairs of the firm's global healthcare practice group, he focuses on transactional and regulatory issues and is commended for his compliance expertise. He acted for HCA on matters before the IRS in regard to federal income tax controversies.

**Clients/Work Highlights:** HCA; Tenet Healthcare; Blue Cross and Blue Shield Association; Cedars-Sinai Medical Center; Fortress Investment Group and NorthBay Healthcare.

## McDermott Will & Emery
See firm details p.878
**The Firm:** This firm's "*commanding national reputation*" is derived from over 50 years' history at the forefront of the healthcare industry. Fielding "*more geographic diversity and more healthcare lawyers than anyone else in the country,*" the firm is a force to be reckoned with. In California, particular strengths lie in M&A, Health Insurance Portability and Accountability Act (HIPAA) privacy, product regulation and class action litigation. The group has been active in the acquisition and disposal of Tenet Healthcare hospitals as well as in running compliance programs and finding regulatory solutions for other healthcare providers. In all cases, clients are impressed by the seamless service on offer and the team's ability to transfer expertise on a cross-departmental basis. "*Wherever they are,*" commentators noted, "*they are very good at getting in touch.*"

**The Lawyers:** Master of a nationally renowned tax practice, **Doug Mancino** (see p.301) is recognized as a "*spectacular lawyer and a real star at McDermott Will & Emery.*" Clients describe him as "*the best in the USA in terms of tax-exempt healthcare providers*" and note that "*he has a handle on the practical application*

*of his deep knowledge.*" He recently litigated an HMO tax-exempt case for Intermountain Healthcare. Earning a "*wide and loyal following,*" **Donald Goldman** (see p.291) concentrates on high-profile fraud and abuse cases as well as counseling hospitals in relation to medical staff matters. He acted for a large national hospital chain in a wide-ranging series of government, regulatory and compliance matters. In addition, he represented a leading supplier of dialysis services in its successful appeal regarding Medicare payments involving approximately $60 million. "*Standout player*" **Timothy Blanchard** (see p.279) focuses on healthcare regulatory issues including Medicare and Medicaid billing and payment, HIPAA privacy, managed care and compliance programs. He takes an active role in the American Health Lawyers Association and is a frequent industry writer and speaker. "*Rising star*" **Eric Gordon** (see p.291) is said to "*distill extremely complex issues to their essence.*" He operates on a myriad of healthcare issues, including Stark self-referral, kickback, corporate governance and healthcare transactions.

**Clients/Work Highlights:** Clients include major health systems, medical centers, physician organizations and pharmaceutical companies.

## Band 2

## Davis Wright Tremaine LLP
**The Firm:** The "*one-stop shop*" approach taken by this prominent firm chimes well with clients. It operates a cohesive and well-structured practice across its offices in Los Angeles and San Francisco, and further afield in Washington, DC and New York, leaving the firm well placed to serve its high-profile healthcare clients. The innovative group has been at the forefront of the nationwide growth in providing integrated health information systems and the associated compliance and privacy issues. As a mark of its success in the area, clients consider the firm "*head and shoulders above the rest in HIPAA health information privacy.*" It is often found acting at the intersection of HIPAA, state law and enforcement. Other hot spots include kickback matters, fraud and abuse and managed care. Market sources praise the group's "*expert facilitation skills and impressive availability.*"

**The Lawyers:** "*Knowledgeable and client-focused*" **Gerry Hinkley** heads up the health information and technology practice. He is involved in health information technology provision and compliance and the wider implications of HIPAA. Additional strengths include assisting hospitals with their strategic affiliations, creating and maintaining relationships between different providers. **Steven Lipton** impresses as "*a leading light*" in Emergency Medical Treatment and Active Labor Act (EMTALA) interpretation. Clients comment that "*he is well researched and well grounded in the opinions and advice he gives.*" Meanwhile, the "*extremely congenial*" **Clark Stanton** is a strong draw for clients with technical and regulatory healthcare issues. His breadth of expertise covers medical staff matters, HIPAA and governance

matters and in these complex areas his "*responsive, timely and candid*" approach is much appreciated. With "*tremendous experience in HIPAA,*" **Paul Smith** is a popular choice for a range of clients including hospitals, hospital associations, medical groups and other organizations.

**Clients/Work Highlights:** The group acts on behalf of a substantial number of hospitals – both nonprofit and profit organizations – including California Hospital Association and Children's Hospital Central California.

## Fulbright & Jaworski L.L.P.
See firm details p.1928
**The Firm:** The market holds that this "*excellent practice*" owes a lot to its "*responsive, thorough and efficient people.*" The group operates on an interdepartmental basis, fielding five dedicated partners in California who are supported by a further 80 attorneys nationwide. One of the first general practice firms to establish a healthcare practice in the 1970's, "*it has a great deal of expertise and by virtue of its size and depth it has every area well covered.*" A thriving transactional practice is complemented by medical malpractice and professional liability matters, torts and commercial litigation, and administrative and regulatory representation. The group has been handling the repercussions of the growth of large-scale physician organizations, dealing with kickback issues and providing solutions to the challenges posed by mergers and divestitures.

**The Lawyers:** **Andrew Demetriou** (see p.285) has consolidated his "*fine*" reputation after his recent move to the firm. He focuses on the business aspects of healthcare from M&A and project finance to regulatory counseling and compliance. Sources say he is "*excellent at finding practical solutions.*" Clients liken **Mark Kadzielski** (see p.297) to a "*chess player, who thinks several steps ahead.*" Head of the West Coast health law practice, he is well practiced in medical staff issues, such as credentialing and peer review and in policy development, including risk management and patient safety issues. He is a well-known industry writer and speaker.

**Clients/Work Highlights:** The group represents healthcare providers from hospital centers to community health clinics.

## Manatt Phelps & Phillips LLP
**The Firm:** This "*strong and influential*" law firm features a dynamic healthcare practice, comprising highly regarded healthcare lawyers and litigators. Its national footprint (anchored by its four offices in California) enables the group to ably serve a broad spectrum of clients. These number industry leaders such as Tenet Healthcare and Trinity Health alongside nonprofit healthcare systems and academic medical centers. The group is singled out by market sources for its particular strength in litigation and in nonprofit conversion transactions. Commentators also praised the firm's active presence in the charitable trust field.

**The Lawyers:** The influential **Sherwin Memel** is hailed as one of the founders of modern healthcare law. A powerful mentor and an impressive practitioner, he remains a substantive force at the firm. **James Schwartz** (see p.312) is described as "*a rare individual who has made the successful transition from being a career government lawyer to a go-to practitioner.*" His experience as California deputy attorney general is invaluable to clients who see him as "*an expert on the representation of nonprofit organizations – there are very few who have his knowledge and professional relationships.*" His considerable experience lies in charitable trusts, corporate governance, distribution of funds and regulatory proceedings. Identified by the market as the "*go-to guy for litigation,*" **Barry Landsberg** commands a robust trial and appellate practice. He acts in the main for healthcare provider clients, who reap the benefit of his experience in unfair competition, false claims, medical staffing issues, and fraud and abuse. **Gregory Pimstone** acts as lead counsel for a variety of healthcare entities. He handles a diverse range of matters from consumer class actions, unfair competition, fraud and abuse, compliance and HIPAA to all forms of commercial disputes. **Martin Thompson** enjoys a solid practice that encompasses the representation of multihospital systems and healthcare providers. According to sources he "*stands out on antitrust matters as they relate to healthcare.*"

Clients/Work Highlights: Blue Shield of California; Tenet Healthcare; Catholic Healthcare West; Elizabeth Glaser Pediatric AIDS Foundation; University of California and Trinity Health.

## Paul, Hastings, Janofsky & Walker LLP

See firm details p.339

The Firm: Enhanced by a full-service international network, this firm has an impressive statewide presence and proves a top choice for many a Fortune 500 company. The "*robust*" California-based group represents an array of businesses across the healthcare sector, including providers and payors, investors and lenders, biotechnology and pharmaceutical companies and Internet healthcare organizations. The team focuses on high-end projects, and ongoing work includes internal investigations (pertaining to white-collar crime, fraud and abuse, and compliance), financing, Medicaid and Medicare reimbursement, and M&A. The team acted in a tax-exempt financing for a large hospital system in California, in the region of $500 million.

The Lawyers: Cochair of the firm's healthcare group, **Daniel Higgins** is credited with the title "*lion of the healthcare Bar.*" Clients continue to say: "*He's a top-tier lawyer and a close professional adviser to many significant organizations.*" His experience spans public finance transactions, fraud and abuse, and white-collar crime. He has also represented numerous clients in investigations before the DOJ, the IRS

and the FTC. "*Effective and talented,*" **Kenneth Yood** (see p.321) is experienced in Medicaid and Medicare reimbursement and takes a lead role in developing compliance programs for clients. His practice also runs the gamut of transactional work including acquisitions and restructurings as well as fraud and abuse in the sale and marketing of pharmaceuticals.

Clients/Work Highlights: Clients typically include major health systems and providers across the United States.

## Band 3

### Hassard Bonnington LLP

The Firm: This San Francisco-based firm has played a role in defending medical malpractice claims since the beginning of the twentieth century, and is considered a "*sophisticated litigation outfit.*" Its particular expertise lies in physician liability cases, often acting as outside counsel to medical malpractice insurance companies. Counseling professional groups and hospital staff on regulatory and compliance requirements is another important component of the practice. The firm also represents health service plans and health insurers.

The Lawyers: **Phillip Goldberg** acts on business transactions and consultations for medical groups, health plans, physicians and professional organizations. His expertise covers self-referral and antikickback laws, M&A and contracting matters.

Clients/Work Highlights: Clients include major hospitals and medical groups, along with health plans, physicians and professional associations.

### Jones Day

See firm details p.570

The Firm: The firm's impressive geographic reach is matched by its breadth and depth of experience. Following its internal restructuring this year, healthcare is now officially one of the firm's 22 practice groups, though it has been practicing in this area for many years. The group takes on complex business transactions, advising boards and senior managers of healthcare organizations on strategy. Physician joint ventures have also proved popular, and in other matters the team advised health plans in establishing strategic alliances with academic centers. Recently, the group represented Community Memorial Hospital of San Buenaventura in its joint venture with Grossman Imaging Center medical group. Clients view the firm as a one-stop shop which can compete on an international basis.

The Lawyers: An "*outstanding lawyer,*" **Ross Stromberg** (see p.316) is a nationally renowned figure who has over 30 years of experience in the field. His name is closely associated with the firm's San Francisco practice and he represents health

systems, hospitals and physician groups on the full run-down of corporate healthcare matters. He has acted for Loma Linda Medical Center on joint ventures and physician integration matters and for Capital BlueCross on major transactions.

Clients/Work Highlights: Clients include Cottage Health System, Sutter Health and TMC Healthcare.

### Sonnenschein Nath & Rosenthal

See firm details p.884

The Firm: The firm's steady expansion within the healthcare market does not go unnoticed by commentators, who point to its national reputation and "*deep knowledge base.*" It is committed to serving healthcare delivery systems and is well positioned to act for providers, hospitals and pharmaceutical companies. The team has built up a range of experience that encompasses M&A, regulatory and compliance issues and reimbursement matters. It has also made a name for itself acting in the healthcare technology sector and advising on bioethics, including compliance and regulatory matters as they relate to pharmaceutical manufacturers.

The Lawyers: A "*smart lawyer who is on top of his game,*" **Robert Girard** (see p.290) spends a significant amount of his time advising on corporate governance issues in the health arena. Keenly interested in the new forms of integrated delivery systems that are emerging in the healthcare market, he has assisted clients in joint ventures between physicians and hospital organizations. The "*talented*" **Reece Hirsch** (see p.295) enjoys a broad practice with a niche in privacy and HIPAA issues. He is well informed in the current privacy issues surrounding IT and data exchange between providers. In addition, he serves as general counsel to a range of hospitals. **Robert Schuchard** (see p.312) is a transactional lawyer with a "*terrific business mind,*" who is able to bring his experience to bear on both corporate and commercial matters. His "*far-ranging expertise*" includes acting for tax-exempt organizations, hospitals and health systems across the state.

Clients/Work Highlights: Clients include healthcare systems, hospitals, physician organizations, insurance companies and pharmaceutical suppliers.

### Other Notable Practitioners

"*Tenacious litigator*" **Robert Liset** of California firm Musick Peeler & Garrett is known for his expertise in medical staff issues. His previous experience as a federal prosecutor with the DOJ "*gives him an edge in medical staff administrative hearings,*" according to sources. Other matters include administration litigation, fraud and abuse, and corporate compliance.

# IMMIGRATION

| Immigration |
| --- |
| Leading Firms |
| 1 BERRY APPLEMAN & LEIDEN LLP *San Francisco* |
| 2 BERNARD P WOLFSDORF PC *Pacific Palisades* |
| LARRABEE & ZIMMERMAN LLP *San Diego* |
| PAPARELLI & PARTNERS LLP *Irvine* |
| 3 GONZALEZ & HARRIS PC *Pasadena* |
| LITWIN & ASSOCIATES *San Francisco* |
| MAUTINO & MAUTINO *San Diego* |
| OFFICES OF CARL SHUSTERMAN *Los Angeles* |
| 4 FRAGOMEN *Santa Clara* |
| IVENER & FULLMER LLP *Los Angeles* |
| LAWLER & LAWLER LAW OFFICES *San Francisco* |
| PEARL LAW GROUP *San Francisco* |

| Leading Individuals |
| --- |
| 1 LEIDEN Warren *Berry Appleman & Leiden LLP* |
| PAPARELLI Angelo *Paparelli & Partners LLP* |
| WOLFSDORF Bernard *Bernard P Wolfsdorf PC* |
| 2 GONZALEZ Josie *Gonzalez & Harris PC* |
| LANGE Cynthia *Fragomen* |
| LARRABEE Peter *Larrabee & Zimmerman LLP* |
| LITWIN Edward *Litwin & Associates* |
| SHUSTERMAN Carl *The Law Offices of* |
| 3 APPLEMAN Jeff *Berry Appleman & Leiden LLP* |
| BERRY David *Berry Appleman & Leiden LLP* |
| HAIGHT Catherine *The Law Office of Catherine Haight* |
| IVENER Mark *Ivener & Fullmer LLP* |
| LAWLER Martin *Lawler & Lawler Law Offices* |
| MAUTINO Robert *Mautino & Mautino* |

| Up-and-coming individuals |
| --- |
| PEARL Julie *Pearl Law Group* |

## Band 1

### Berry Appleman & Leiden LLP

**The Firm:** As "*one of the top practices in the country*," this devoted immigration firm has a reputation for providing a high-quality service that has attracted major Silicon Valley clients. Peers hold the attorneys here in high esteem, describing them as "*capable, courteous and extraordinarily gracious.*" "*Excellent*" case management skills underwrite a "*bold, strategic*" approach to the full range of corporate immigration issues, including the growing trend of outbound immigration. Aside from a vast array of activity in the technology sector, the firm's profile has attracted clients from a variety of other sectors, such as finance, manufacturing and health.

**The Lawyers:** "*Cream of the crop*" **Warren Leiden** is an immigration lawyer whom peers say deserves to be recognized for his work in the field. As the firm's principal strategist, much of the credit for the firm's success is attributed to him. Leiden is also considered a "*leader in groundbreaking litigation*," and works extensively with technology and software companies. Clients drew attention to his knowledge of Congressional issues as a further asset. Meanwhile, **Jeff Apple-man** is seen as the "*legal genius*" behind the practice. Peers describe the "*well-known*" **David Berry** as a "*fine lawyer*" who focuses on domestic and international nonimmigrant business visas. In addition, his abilities in counseling clients with regard to complex immigration issues are also much in demand.

**Clients/Work Highlights:** A variety of technological, scientific research, engineering, health, media and finance companies comprise the client base.

## Band 2

### Bernard P Wolfsdorf PC

**The Firm:** "*A force to be reckoned with*," this 17-lawyer operation is one of the larger boutique firms in the state. Specializing exclusively in immigration law, clients say it is "*hard to fault it on anything.*" The firm has been able to cultivate a strong national reputation and a "*fantastic*" client list. In addition to its two coastal offices, the opening of a Shanghai branch promises to enhance the outfit's capacity to deal with outbound issues, an area in which it already has a thriving practice. Its diverse range of expertise is perceived as being central to the firm's capacity to build an "*excellent rapport*" with a variety of clients.

**The Lawyers:** "*Superstar*" **Bernard Wolfsdorf** is an attorney who clearly "*knows what he's doing.*" At the "*cutting edge of practice*," clients and lawyers alike hold him in the highest regard. A leading light in the American Immigration Lawyers Association, Wolfsdorf's outstanding reputation is said to hinge on his "*integrity and incredibly thorough approach.*" He is further renowned for his "*exceptional*" consular practice, which focuses on niche areas such as third country national processing in Mexico and Canada.

**Clients/Work Highlights:** The firm represents individuals and Fortune 500 companies from a range of industries including healthcare, education and entertainment.

### Larrabee & Zimmerman LLP

**The Firm:** Formed over ten years ago, this boutique has developed a canny ability to "*draw the clients in*," and has duly gone from strength to strength. It is based in San Diego and handles a range of complex contentious matters on behalf of over 380 clients from across the nation, largely concentrating on the technology sector. Market commentators praised its "*excellent advocates*" for their handling of inbound immigration matters as well as outbound visa requirements, where the team utilizes favorable working relationships with firms overseas.

**The Lawyers:** Peter Larrabee's "*true can-do attitude*" has attracted a loyal client following. Praise for him ranged from "*a fabulous lawyer*" to "*a winner,*" and he maintains a great practice reinforced by excellent advocacy skills and a polished manner with clients. He is perceived as the driving force behind the firm that is "*making it happen,*" as well as being recommended for his handling of contentious matters.

**Clients/Work Highlights:** Business entities in software, telecom, electronics and Internet technology industries can all be counted as clients.

### Paparelli & Partners LLP

**The Firm:** A substantial portion of this "*successful*" boutique's caseload involves acting on behalf of corporations. A range of issues are covered, including the immigration consequences of M&A. As such, this "*brilliant*" firm is a favorite of several clients.

**The Lawyers:** A "*perfectionist*" in every respect, **Angelo Paparelli** is a lawyer who submits nothing but the best. He is said to possess a "*brilliant legal mind,*" and clients remark his case analysis and preparation are "*excellent,*" while peers admit to calling him whenever they "*have a tough question.*" In terms of advising on the immigration aspects of M&A, he is seen as "*one of the best in the field.*"

**Clients/Work Highlights:** The firm acts for Fortune 500 companies in several industries, including the automobile and technology sector.

## Band 3

### Gonzalez & Harris PC

**The Firm:** Immigration law has been the exclusive focus area of this Los Angeles-based boutique for almost 30 years. The firm provides an extensive range of employment services including the acquisition of temporary and permanent visas, and I-9 and Immigration Reform and Control Act (IRCA) compliance work.

**The Lawyers:** A popular immigration attorney, **Josie Gonzalez** is perceived as an "*active*" lawyer with an extensive track record, who is "*near the top*" of her profession. This "*excellent*" lawyer uses her renowned analytical skills to strategize and generate the best outcome for her clients. She is a leading authority on labor certifications.

**Clients/Work Highlights:** The firm's clients hail from, inter alia, finance, technology, education and health sectors. In addition, the firm services several nonprofit and religious organizations.

### Litwin & Associates

**The Firm:** The team of immigration lawyers at this boutique firm in South San Francisco deals with an assortment of work but primarily secures visas on behalf of corporate clients. It enjoys a national reputation in the area of labor certification and represents a range of Fortune 500, technology and startup companies.

**The Lawyers:** The founder of the firm **Edward Litwin** has practiced immigration law for 30 years and peers bill him as an "*A-plus quality lawyer.*" His niche labor certification expertise constitutes one of the firm's core assets.

**Clients/Work Highlights:** The client list includes a range of Fortune 500 companies including Philips, AMD and Novellus Systems.

## Mautino & Mautino

See firm details p.114186

**The Firm:** This "*strong*" boutique is primarily run by father and daughter. Its three attorneys have forged a leading reputation in the area of citizenship both statewide and nationally. The practice also covers permanent and temporary residence requests, deportation and asylum.

**The Lawyers:** **Robert Mautino** is celebrated as a "*nationally recognized expert in citizenship.*" He has been working in immigration for over 25 years.

## The Law Offices of Carl Shusterman

See firm details p.113749

**The Firm:** Established in 1979, peers identify the firm as a "*leading name*" when it comes to immigration issues relating to the healthcare sector.

**The Lawyers:** "*Well-known*" attorney **Carl Shusterman** anchors the five-attorney firm and was characterized as a man who "*means business.*" While he is perceived as having done much to influence the firm's focus on the healthcare sector, he is also experienced in servicing clients from a range of industries.

## Band 4

## Fragomen, Del Rey, Bernsen & Loewy, LLP

**The Firm:** A strong national network and affiliated global offices mark this firm out; indeed one commentator likened its immigration practice to an "*empire.*" The depth of expertise offered by its "*fine*"

lawyers came in for praise among clients. This technically accomplished operation is particularly well renowned for its handling of outbound immigration work.

**The Lawyers:** **Cynthia Lange** has long been a familiar name in the field in California. A "*dynamic and calm*" attorney, she manages the firm's Northern Californian team while handling a range of immigration work. Peers admit that she "*takes work away*" from them, while clients say she has "*made an excellent impression*" in the immigration arena.

## Ivener & Fullmer LLP

**The Firm:** Business immigration is the order of the day here, an area in which clients profess this boutique has "*done some incredible work.*" In addition to assisting corporations with obtaining visas, the team tackles numerous EB5 cases. Commentators admire the "*personable*" approach of members of the firm and commend their ability to provide "*creative solutions to difficult problems.*"

**The Lawyers:** During his 35 years in practice **Mark Ivener** has developed a reputation as an attorney who "*never ceases to impress.*" Focusing on the entertainment industry, clients "*go out of their way to use him.*" He recently acted for several major studios in order to ensure the presence of certain actors and directors for the production of films and television serials.

**Clients/Work Highlights:** Advising clients in the publishing, technology, hotel and mining sectors further contributes to the workload.

## Lawler & Lawler Law Offices

**The Firm:** This renowned San Francisco-based boutique handles immigration work for both businesses and individuals. Obtaining business visas accounts for a large proportion of the caseload, and the firm has served athletes and high-profile entertainment industry clients among others.

**The Lawyers:** Peers view **Martin Lawler** as an "*excellent*" attorney. Renowned for his intellectual capacity, he writes extensively and is held to be a "*guru*" on H1B visas. He is also acknowledged as "*a highly successful federal court litigator.*"

**Clients/Work Highlights:** The firm represents large international corporations and smaller national firms in a range of sectors, including engineering, technology, pharmaceuticals and manufacturing.

## Pearl Law Group

**The Firm:** An "*excellent and well-run*" firm, this boutique was established over a decade ago and has continued to flourish ever since. Its five-attorney team deals with a range of work, from acquiring visas and green cards, to advising and training clients on immigration issues.

**The Lawyers:** CEO of the firm **Julie Pearl** (see p.307) is a "*dynamic*" attorney under whose guidance the practice has flourished.

## Other Notable Practitioners

Clients admire **Catherine Haight** as a "*fantastic*" attorney who "*goes that extra mile.*" She has a broad experience of immigration issues, having represented companies in engineering, technology, sport and entertainment sectors.

# INSURANCE

# INSURER FIRMS

## Band 1

## Duane Morris LLP

See firm details p.1753

**The Firm:** California insurance giant Hancock Rothert & Bunshoft announced its merger with full-service, national firm Duane Morris as of January

2006. The combined firm provides Hancock with deeper bench strength and an enhanced national reach. The group will have more than 100 lawyers involved in insurance coverage work across the USA. During research, commentators consistently praised the "*terrific*" group of Hancock lawyers for remaining a "*significant force in London market coverage.*" Hancock attorneys have long represented Lloyd's entities as well as other European, US and Bermudian insurance and reinsurance companies, some of which are existing Duane Morris clients. The group's prominence in litigation in this market is also well documented: it continues to impress following its involvement in the long-running Kaiser Aluminum dispute, numbering landmark coverage cases among its defense verdicts. Outside the remit of London market insurers, the team maintains a distinguished cadre of top-drawer clients. Yahoo! has retained the group in significant coverage matters regarding commercial disputes and data security. Clients high-

lighted the team's "*detail-oriented*" stance and "*impressive turnaround times*" with many appreciating its ultimate commitment in "*going all out to defend with professionalism and integrity.*"

**The Lawyers:** The inimitable **Philip Matthews** (see p.302) "*gets right to the heart of coverage issues*" and has been involved in some of the most significant insurance trials and appeals in California, notably the Kaiser Aluminum asbestos litigation. Peers describe him as "*an honorable opponent*" with expert facilitation and management skills who is "*quite remarkable in his ability to settle seemingly intractable cases.*" According to commentators, the "*calm, thoughtful*" **Richard Seabolt** (see p.313) "*always thinks three or four chess moves ahead to maximize clients' options.*" He is lauded for his work on major matters concerning environmental pollution, toxic tort and asbestos litigation. His "*first-rate courtroom presence*" and wealth of professional connections contribute to the high regard in which peers and clients alike hold him. He has cemented his reputation with his appointment as chair of the executive committee of the litigation section of the State Bar of California. "*Heavyweight litigator*" **Andrew Gordon** (see p.291) scales the rankings through garnering "*great respect for his adversarial skills.*" He is prominent in complex multiparty insurance litigation and environmental coverage. **Deborah Pitts** (see p.307) draws praise from commentators as a "*smart, hard-driving lawyer.*" She is recognized as a formidable opponent in insurance coverage and technology matters and is said to be "*terrific on her feet at trial.*" "*Respected and intelligent,*" **Ray Wong** (see p.320) features strongly in this strong and cohesive team, impressing through his settlement expertise and results-driven practice. Clients/Work Highlights: Equitas; Lloyd's; Yahoo!; Liberty Mutual and Kraft.

## Band 2

### Barger & Wolen

The Firm: This firm scores highly on the back of its corporate and regulatory work for insurance companies and is said to be a "*major thorn in the side*" of its competitors. Its expertise encompasses insurance company formations, compliance, M&A and representation in administrative proceedings. In addition, its standing in reinsurance litigation, arbitration and dispute resolution and its ability to act as an "*appellate specialist*" have both brought prestige to the firm. This "*effective group of well-respected lawyers*" takes advantage of robust industry connections to operate with ease throughout the United States, Canada, Europe and Asia.

The Lawyers: **Royal Oakes** stands out to commentators as "*one of the best insurance company coverage*

lawyers in the state,*" making waves with his "*creative yet practical and client-oriented*" stance. Sources were particularly impressed by his "*ability to think on his feet*" in the area of bad faith and punitive damages litigation. As well as his legal and courtroom expertise, he is known for his role as on-air legal commentator for a number of radio and television networks. **Kent Keller**, managing partner of the Los Angeles office, has a "*striking regulatory practice,*" according to sources. In addition, interviewees underlined his "*excellent abilities as a trial lawyer.*"
Clients/Work Highlights: The firm represents insurance and business clients across the state and beyond.

### O'Melveny & Myers LLP

See firm details p.336

The Firm: The "*talented, accomplished*" lawyers at O'Melveny & Myers form an impressive team generating, according to sources, a "*skilled, smart and all-round effective service.*" Building on its position at the forefront of benchmark asbestos litigation proceedings, the firm has maintained its coverage profile by taking on unusual and complex claims for insurers. Alongside environmental and toxic tort matters, the full-service practice boasts expertise in consumer class actions, reinsurance and bad faith law. This work is undertaken on a nationwide scale and includes the London markets. Regarding all its efforts, interviewees were quick to stress the strong and comprehensive relationships the team forms with its noteworthy clients.
The Lawyers: Venerated by sources for his "*always intelligent, high-powered work,*" **Martin Checov** (see p.282) represents major insurance carriers in coverage disputes. He continues as the firm's "*bright and respected*" risk manager and brings his experience to bear on some weighty matters. Peers cite **Mark Wood** (see p.320) as having "*qualities to aspire to: he can simplify information to make a clear, strong point then stick the knife in and turn it five times.*" He controls major litigation and arbitration for insurance and reinsurance clients in both California and New York, in the latter working on 9/11-associated litigation.
Clients/Work Highlights: CIGNA; ACE; American Re and Zurich North America.

### Sonnenschein Nath & Rosenthal

See firm details p.884

The Firm: The firm earns considerable market respect for its twin strengths in litigation and regulatory work. It handles the full gamut of insurance-related litigation and enjoys a "*striking success at trial level*" in matters ranging from coverage disputes to class actions and constitutional cases. The regulatory practice group operates countrywide but has a marked standing in California. It covers formation, licensing, asset transfer and compliance issues. Across the board, peers highlight the effective manner in which it has augmented its "*distinguished reputation*" in the marketplace, citing in particular, its strong presence in the San Francisco area.
The Lawyers: **Paul Glad** (see p.290) impresses as a "*first port of call for insurance company representa-

tion.*" With his "*focus and talent,*" he is "*hands down the premier choice*" for big-ticket litigation. He saw recent success in the insurance coverage trial relating to the State of California's alleged $750 million liability for the Stringfellow Acid Pits. Counseling the London market on IPO laddering cases also forms a substantial component of his practice. **Kara Baysinger's** (see p.278) growing practice testifies to her expertise in the regulatory arena. She counts boards of directors, insurance companies, agents and regulators among her clientele. Servicing these, she negotiates on regulatory settlements and counsels on compliance and market conduct procedures. "*Highly regarded*" **Gary Hernandez** (see p.294), formerly deputy insurance commissioner, enjoys market repute for his regulatory practice. He handles state regulatory compliance, administrative law matters and company setups. He also numbers insurance insolvency expertise among his skills. "*Straight shooter*" **Ronald Kent** (see p.298) is described as a "*major league player*" in insurance company representation. An increasing dynamic of his work involves first and third-party coverage issues arising out of commercial and personal lines policies. Long-term care and health insurance also make up a large volume of his caseload. He continues to be national coordinating counsel for ACE entities and has recently been working on complex claims at the interface of insurance and bankruptcy law.
Clients/Work Highlights: St. Paul Travelers; Allstate; Prudential Financial; AIG; State Fund Insurance and Crum & Forster.

## Band 3

### Alschuler Grossman Stein & Kahan LLP

See firm details p.323

The Firm: Commentators endorsed the "*depth of experience*" in this long-standing Los Angeles firm. Offering the full range of insurance legal services, the group stood out to peers for its "*broad industry knowledge*" and its ability to handle multimillion-dollar exposures. The group, in its ongoing representation of California's Insurance Commissioner, is acting on D&O litigation arising from the case of insolvent insurer Fremont Indemnity Company. On an environmental tack, the firm has been retained by AIG on pollution coverage polices. The group continues to orient toward providing practical solutions to this type of complex insurance issue.
The Lawyers: "*Talented*" **Bruce Friedman** (see p.289), currently serving as managing partner of the firm, focuses his expertise on coverage matters and related business litigation. He has been especially active in D&O representation and employment, media and entertainment issues. As a recent example of his work, he has been dealing with professional liability matters for Arch Insurance Group. **Frank Kaplan** (see p.297) wins support for his "*commitment and expertise*" and his efficient handling of complex cases. He is retained on matters for the California Insurance Commissioner.

**Clients/Work Highlights:** AIG; CNA; California Department of Insurance; Royal & SunAlliance; Employers Reinsurance Corporation and Arch Insurance Group.

## Berkes Crane Robinson & Seal, LLP

**The Firm:** This efficacious firm has been "*an influencing and initiating force*" in the realm of insurance defense for many years. Its standout work has been in the fields of asbestos and environment law, toxic tort, product liability and reinsurance and underwriting advice. Within this, the group demonstrates depth and breadth in trial, mediation, alternative dispute resolution and appellate procedures. Peers and clients recognize the attorneys to be "*strong supporters in complex matters*," pointing to their authoritative presence in many prominent cases in California.

**The Lawyers:** Interviewees regard **Steven Crane** as a "*smart, talented lawyer who does a great job for his clients*," most typically working "*hand in glove*" on complex matters. Sources also highlight his strength in leadership and "*well-organized, thoughtful*" outlook. **Robert Berkes** is generally agreed to be a "*great person to have on your team when it matters*." His experience is often sought on multilayered proceedings, an area in which he excels.

**Clients/Work Highlights:** CNA; Farmers; Federal Deposit Insurance Company; Reliance Insurance Company and Great American.

## Gibson, Dunn & Crutcher LLP

See firm details p.328

**The Firm:** Boasting a "*good-quality offering*" in insurance defense, this "*upper echelon firm*" stands tall in the market due to its work on coverage and bad faith investigations. Its "*strong back catalog of experience*" takes in such issues as trigger of coverage, number of occurrences, broker liability and contribution and allocation issues for insurance carriers. "*Always diligent*," its recent matters include the cross-state representation of a large insurance company in asbestos products and premises liability. Furthermore, its healthcare representation remains prominent and respected in the California marketplace.

**The Lawyers:** The "*energetic and respected*" **Gary Justice** (see p.297) represents a large reinsurer in weighty matters covering a number of jurisdictions. He is also involved in a significant environmental coverage matter tried before the Ohio federal court.

**Clients/Work Highlights:** The firm represents insurer and reinsurer clients in issues relating to insurance coverage and alleged bad faith.

## Band 4

## Sedgwick, Detert, Moran & Arnold

**The Firm:** This well-coordinated practice group is known for carrying out "*fine work*" in insurance coverage, across all areas of the industry. The "*efficient and*

*practical team*" tackles matters for clients who range from multinational insurers to specialty line carriers. It merits a place in *Chambers*' tables for its wealth of experience and skill in representing the industry both domestically and internationally, with competitors praising its "*deep and thorough knowledge*."

**The Lawyers:** **Bruce Celebrezze** "*would be on any insurer's list*," according to commentators. He combines "*good instincts with a real understanding of insurer and policyholder concerns*" to carve out a solid following in the insurance arena.

**Clients/Work Highlights:** Clients include major insurers and reinsurers across the USA, London markets and internationally.

## Other Notable Practitioners

**Patrick Cathcart** (see p.282) of the newly formed Cathcart, Collins & Kneafsey LLP is acknowledged by peers to be a "*superb, skilled litigator*" in commercial matters. "*Smart and talented*," he "*defines reasonableness and inspires confidence in his clients*." His skills are facilitating the rapid evolution of a practice that encompasses insurance coverage, business litigation, products liability and a significant amount of business litigation. The "*well-organized, analytically minded*" **David Babbe** (see p.277) of Morrison & Foerster LLP handles a broad range of coverage work, environmental matters, toxic tort and bad faith claims. He holds St. Paul Travelers among his cadre of clients. Peers call him a "*fine lawyer, a great writer and a good thinker*."

---

# INSURANCE

# POLICYHOLDER

## Band 1

## Heller Ehrman LLP

See firm details p.329

**The Firm:** With "*depth and star quality*" and a reputation in the market second to none, this firm is "*right at the top of plaintiff representation*," according to peers and clients. Its network of offices across California and the world is staffed with "*bright, can-do attorneys*" who are "*plugged in and always ready to step up to the mark*." As an illustration of its standing, the firm handles major coverage action for Kaiser Aluminum. In addition, the firm has inter-

ested itself in World Trade Center litigation and has continued to act on business interruption and property liability claims for company groups at the heart of the proceedings. As a unit, it is held to be "*exceptionally thorough and knowledgeable, acting on all matters with an outstanding degree of skill and foresight*."

**The Lawyers:** **David Goodwin** (see p.291), "*top of the table on the policyholder side*," holds the reins of a practice marked by its geographical scope and breadth of concentration. His is, to a large extent, an international practice: peers note his involvement on "*complex, high-stakes cases*" from London to Beijing, Vietnam and all points in between. He is known as "*thorough and analytical with good strategic sense*" and impresses by effectively walking the line between being "*aggressive on behalf of clients while maintaining credibility with insurance carriers*." Clients are impressed by his "*encyclopedic knowledge and first-class, expeditious advice*." Interviewees rate **Stephen Goldberg** (see p.290) as an "*expert facilitator*," able to bring all parties together to meet the crux of the matter. In achieving this, he is "*detail-oriented with the ability to quickly grasp multilayered concepts*," according to peers. Recently, he has been engaged in two complex cases: one, a business interruption claim from a leisure facility adjacent to the WTC; and

the other, an insurance coverage claim relating to a construction matter at a hotel in Las Vegas. "*He does a first-class job in the preparation and submission of legal documents*," competitors said. The "*exceptional*" **Lawrence Hobel** (see p.295) is recognized as a "*thoughtful, creative advocate and a case strategist who provides clear-headed and calm guidance in all situations*." Peers acknowledge his "*well-developed ethical compass*" and his "*excellent ability to articulate issues and options*," both of which enable him to find his way through what is often a mass of litigation involving multiple insurers. He pilots Kaiser Aluminum's coverage action, handling asbestos product liability and the associated premises coverage cases in this multibillion-dollar action. **Barry Levin** (see p.300) has returned to active practice, where he is expected to thrive, after a successful spell as the firm's chair: "*He is a great lawyer whatever he does*," say industry sources. "*Standout attorney*" **Nancy Cohen** (see p.284) marshals a broad-based insurance practice that covers D&O liability, comprehensive general liability issues, property damage and environmental remediation. Included in this is a lead role in the ongoing World Trade Center coverage litigation. She has also represented a mining company in business interruption claims resulting from an explosion.

**Clients/Work Highlights:** Other clients include

| Insurance: Policyholder |
| --- |
| Leading Individuals |

**Senior Statesman**

SHERNOFF William *Shernoff, Bidart & Darras LLP*

[1] BROWN Donald *Covington & Burling*

GOODWIN David *Heller Ehrman LLP*

HALBREICH David *Morgan, Lewis & Bockius LLP*

LERMAN Cary *Munger, Tolles & Olson LLP*

PASICH Kirk *Dickstein Shapiro*

STEUBER David *Howrey LLP*

[2] BIDART Michael *Shernoff, Bidart & Darras LLP*

GOLDBERG Stephen *Heller Ehrman LLP*

HOBEL Lawrence *Heller Ehrman LLP*

HORTON Michel *Morgan, Lewis & Bockius LLP*

LEVIN Barry *Heller Ehrman LLP*

LEVINE Harvey *Levine, Steinberg, Miller & Huver*

LUNDBERG G Andrew *Latham & Watkins LLP*

[3] CHILDRESS Tyrone *Howrey LLP*

COHEN Nancy *Heller Ehrman LLP*

CRAIG CALKINS Mary *Howrey LLP*

FRIEDRICH William *Farella Braun & Martel LLP*

MCCUTCHEON Mary *Farella Braun & Martel LLP*

MOONEY Ann *Cooley Godward LLP*

MULLIKEN David *Latham & Watkins LLP*

PORTERFIELD Curtis *Howrey LLP*

ROSEN Peter *Latham & Watkins LLP*

Hewlett-Packard, BP and Freeport-McMoRan Copper & Gold.

## Band 2

### Covington & Burling

See firm details p.563

**The Firm:** Traditionally having a *"heavyweight national reputation,"* the firm's San Francisco office individually enjoys strong positive endorsement from market sources. Its policyholder work is *"always top of the tree,"* according to commentators, and covers a range of policies including D&O, business interruption, product liability and mass torts and environmental cleanup liability. The London market forms a significant percentage of this output. The firm is representing McDonald's against its insurance companies and the claims of false advertising brought against it. The *"top-notch"* group also represents Adelphia in substantial claims to coverage under D&O liability insurance policies.

**The Lawyers:** **Donald Brown** (see p.280), a *"terrifically smart lawyer"* held in the highest regard, is credited with the rise of this burgeoning California practice. He is known for his *"fully rounded presence in court"* and for his *"high intellect - he can cite cases straight off and writes beautifully."*

**Clients/Work Highlights:** McDonald's; Morgan Stanley; Adelphia; Imperial Oil and ExxonMobil.

### Howrey LLP

**The Firm:** A *"deep bench"* and a pool of *"bright, talented people"* raise this firm to the upper echelons of the insurance recovery market. Described as *"client-friendly, affable and staffed with consummate professionals,"* the group has a national and international reputation for dispute resolution and the enforcement of coverage rights. Its presence in such high-profile and labyrinthine areas as toxic tort, terrorism risk insurance and D&O liability in the light of Sarbanes-Oxley points to its credibility in the market. Clients believe the group is *"effective at counseling and protecting clients before they know they have a problem"* and appreciate its ability to staff a case with *"fierce litigators"* once the need arises.

**The Lawyers:** **David Steuber** is described as an *"exceptional coverage attorney used on the most complex of matters."* As an indication of his status, he has been representing the primary lessees of the World Trade Center in the enforcement of coverage rights. This involves $1 billion of liability insurance policies arising out of the events of 9/11. In addition, he is special insurance counsel for WorldCom (now MCI), advising the company on its existing and ongoing insurance needs. Peers recognize him to be a *"great team player; productive and facilitative with a high level of integrity."* **Tyrone Childress** specializes in insurance coverage advice and related coverage litigation, along with general business and tort litigation. He takes a lead role on insurance issues related to the World Trade Center action. Clients raved about his well-rounded skill set, holding him out to be *"analytical and knowledgeable with great negotiation skills."* *"When it comes to the crunch,"* they said, *"you can rely on him to get results."* **Mary Craig Calkins** *"brings the entire package to the table."* She *"commands respect with her intellect"* and clients appreciate her ability to *"authoritatively convey complex ideas and make a difficult situation much more manageable."* She operates at the cutting edge of insurance coverage issues, in entertainment (reality TV, feature film, video and distribution), e-commerce and technology (including issues pertaining to peer-to-peer technology sharing) and IP D&O liability claims. The *"articulate, polished and sharp"* **Curtis Porterfield** stands out to commentators, who report: *"He's got the knowledge and is always looking out for the client."* As a representation of his multifarious practice, he has handled insurance issues relating to allegations of international human rights violations in Myanmar. He also represented United Space Alliance against American Home Assurance Company over coverage issues relating to the termination of a subcontractor.

**Clients/Work Highlights:** FMC; Lockheed Martin; Unocal; FremantleMedia North America and others on the Fortune 500 list.

### Latham & Watkins LLP

**The Firm:** In what is recognized as a *"truly global practice,"* the lawyers of Latham & Watkins possess the *"outstanding resources and knowledge"* necessary to take control of some of the most significant insurance coverage cases. The team ably handles insurance disputes arising out of the firm's corporate client base: interviewees claim they *"achieve tremendous results with nice strategic moves."* In a reflection of the post-Enron climate, clients increasingly look to the firm for up-front preventive legal counseling, particularly on D&O renewals and replacement. In addition, alternative dispute resolution remains a key means of addressing differences. A greater emphasis on first-party property and business interruption has led to the representation of a major international energy company in claims arising out of damage to oil pipelines and infrastructure. These totaled more than $100 million in value. In a separate incident, the group secured over $200 million in insurance coverage for Fluor to resolve a claim against it arising from its design and engineering of a nickel-cobalt refinery project in Australia.

**The Lawyers:** **Andrew Lundberg** is a *"brilliant thinker, able to try complex cases with integrity and substantial skill."* Commentators believe him to be a *"smart guy and an integral part of the team on large matters."* Acting as insurance coverage counsel on clergy-related sexual abuse cases resulting in a $100 million settlement, he enhanced an already fine reputation through a strong showing. He also presided over the rehearing of the RemedyTemp case. This resulted in the overturn of the court's original ruling, leading to a decision in favor of the client. Observers state: *"He is a tremendous appellate lawyer with exceptional oral advocacy skills."* The *"talented and committed"* **David Mulliken** has been at the forefront of the consideration and development of new forms of insurance coverage, made necessary in the wake of corporate financial scandals and the implementation of the Sarbanes-Oxley legislation. Although D&O actions form a large part of his work, his practice mirrors that of the firm's in its geographical spread and variety. At the time of press, his role is changing as he begins his relocation to the firm's London office to oversee its rapidly growing European and Asian controversy practice. **Peter Rosen** takes a *"no holds barred"* approach to coverage representation in his comprehensive and respected policyholder practice. He acted for the retail leaseholder at the World Trade Center in seeking a court decision on whether the terrorist attacks constituted two events for insurance purposes. Separately, he represents URS on disputes and litigation involving damage claims in excess of $350 million worldwide.

**Clients/Work Highlights:** Campbell Industries; City of Beverly Hills; Fluor; County of San Diego and Westfield Group.

### Morgan, Lewis & Bockius LLP

See firm details p.1758

**The Firm:** This firm constitutes a *"robust and confident"* presence on the West Coast and has an insurance practice widely regarded as being *"on an up-tick."* Commentators state that the arrival of partners from Zevnik Horton, so soon after the absorption of lawyers from what was the firm Brobeck, has meant that the team is now of a *"tremendous quality."* The group is known for its actions on a range of insurance matters and, in particular, for having achieved some of the largest settlements and jury verdicts in insurance history, having taken a lead role in asbestos-related bankruptcies and toxic tort claims. Satisfied clients speak of being "*confident of the back-up this well-connected firm brings to complex proceedings.*"

**The Lawyers:** **David Halbreich** (see p.292) continues to impress following his much-publicized role in the landmark Western MacArthur case which resulted in a settlement totaling over $2 billion. Described as an "*outstanding*" litigator, he is focused on insurance recovery and takes a lead role in asbestos and toxic tort claims, environmental waste and product liability actions. Quite simply, peers report, he is a "*tremendously tenacious lawyer with a knack for digging out information from the most unlikely places.*" **Michel Horton** (see p.295) "*has got quite a resumé,*" market sources agree. Clients who have followed him from Zevnik Horton praise his "*assured, practical and efficient style.*" As one put it: "*He is always available with clear and practical advice.*"

**Clients/Work Highlights:** Policyholder clients are drawn from financial services organizations and the banking, real estate, technology, securities, telecommunications, construction and energy sectors.

## Shernoff, Bidart & Darras LLP

**The Firm:** This firm "*simply cannot be matched on plaintiff bad faith cases,*" competitors concede. Its effective group of four partners operates with a full bench of talented associates and covers all areas of insurance law from health and disability, homeowner and automobile matters to catastrophic injury and products liability. "*Tough cookies*" they may be, but peers agree these lawyers use their strength to secure best results for a client base made up of individuals, private businesses and corporations. The firm operates on a contingency fee basis and is known for its "*ability to achieve David v Goliath victories.*"

**The Lawyers:** **William Shernoff** "*pioneered the development of bad faith law in California*" and has advanced it ever since. As well as being a significant consumer law expert, he is known for his skills as "*an incredible trial lawyer - one of the best at figuring out how to play it to the jury.*" He takes credit for numerous landmark cases including Holocaust-era life insurance litigation against many of Europe's most prominent insurance companies. The highly respected **Michael Bidart** is "*a major driving force in the firm*" who has cemented an already high-flying reputation by adding cutting-edge class actions to his standard repertoire. Dubbed a "*creative, law-in-motion attorney,*" he has developed the firm's health insurance practice by successfully prosecuting bad faith disputes against insurers and HMOs.

**Clients/Work Highlights:** AJ Industries; City of Los Angeles; Buenavision; Kenco Construction; Time Warner and MGM.

## Band 3

## Dickstein Shapiro Morin & Oshinsky LLP

See firm details p.565

**The Firm:** The integration of Pasich & Kornfeld into this established multiservice law firm has given rise to a substantially "*bulked-up competitor,*" according to industry sources. The group has a predilection for entrepreneurial activity and innovation and is focused on developing new initiatives in the insurance coverage arena. Lately, this has included electronic and website security and the insurance issues related thereto. This cutting-edge remit sits well with the group's representation of a large proportion of the entertainment industry in insurance coverage and IP matters. The firm handles cases on behalf of policyholders in courts throughout the United States and also offers alternative dispute resolution as part of its arsenal of coverage advice.

**The Lawyers:** The arrival of top-flight lawyer **Kirk Pasich** (see p.306) from the merger with Pasich & Kornfeld solidifies the firm's position on the West Coast. His "*smart, fearless and energetic*" style wins him the undying support of clients. "*He is one of the first places I would send anyone,*" said one admirer; "*he knows the area inside out and his work rate is second to none.*"

**Clients/Work Highlights:** The firm represents many Fortune 500 policyholders as well as small and privately held companies.

## Farella Braun & Martel LLP

**The Firm:** This "*high-quality policyholder practice*" contains a number of experienced litigators who bring their experience to bear on a variety of coverage disputes. The group's "*significant reputation*" in such areas as construction liability, D&O and environmental exposures is clear. For example, on the D&O front, the firm advises companies on the placement of policies and the scope of coverage and exclusions. The demand for construction insurance and pollution liability also remains high, with the group demonstrating a leaning towards complex risk transfer projects. The practice is also at the forefront of coverage disputes involving property contamination and asbestos bodily injury claims.

**The Lawyers:** Clients say **William Friedrich** is "*a great litigator - strategic, creative and appropriately aggressive.*" He acts on disputes arising from multiparty civil litigation and represents clients on both first and third-party liability claims. His mediation skills are also in great demand in negotiation and arbitration. **Mary McCutcheon** "*stays on top of cutting-edge issues*" and marshals a broad practice covering pollution liability, construction insurance,

IP and employment matters. Her expertise further includes D&O coverage issues, securities fraud and derivative actions.

**Clients/Work Highlights:** Insurance coverage clients include Dow Chemical; Chiron Corporation; US Borax; Levi Strauss and Napster.

## Munger, Tolles & Olson LLP

**The Firm:** Known to have been "*up there on pure talent*" since the precedent-setting asbestos insurance cases of the 1980's, this firm continues to score highly with observers. With offices in San Francisco and Los Angeles, the insurance team inside the litigation department is well placed to serve its raft of prominent clients across California and further afield. Matters for these clients include business interruption and first-party property damage policies (environmental liability, construction litigation and mass tort personal injury amongst them), along with D&O policies, general liability and fidelity insurance. The firm has the reputation of "*operating more with a scalpel than a sledgehammer,*" and uses common sense and analysis to maximize the advantage to its clients.

**The Lawyers:** **Cary Lerman** enjoys high visibility at the firm due to an assured style that generates considerable market respect. "*He is a spectacular lawyer,*" peers enthused, "*with the intelligence and common sense needed to get the best for his clients,*" many of whom are national companies. An increase in London market arbitrations has been a feature of his practice recently and he has lately acted on behalf of a corporate policyholder in a pollution claim.

**Clients/Work Highlights:** Shell; General Reinsurance; Ameron International; Quanex and Mattel.

## Other Notable Practitioners

The "*smart, talented*" **Harvey Levine** of Levine, Steinberg, Miller & Huver is known for his litigation prowess and the mark he has made across the country by taking on huge bad faith cases. Peers collectively agree he is an "*accomplished speaker who does a great job of making his point.*" **Ann Mooney**, partner in the litigation department and head of the insured's rights practice group of Cooley Godward LLP, is credited as a "*terrific writer and counselor.*" A good part of her time has been spent on claims and policy placement counseling for public and private companies looking for D&O insurance. Clients have included both venture capital funds and emerging companies in the tech industry. "*Great on her feet,*" she displays the ability to handle complex cases of all sizes.

# INTELLECTUAL PROPERTY

## Band 1

### Irell & Manella LLP

**The Firm:** This firm of *"hard-working, high-caliber practitioners"* is renowned for taking on and winning high-profile cases for leading clients in the electronics, medical device, semiconductor, computer software, IT and entertainment industries. Its strong, resourceful team has a rich technology practice and a supremely successful track record that interviewees say stems in large part from a policy of hiring talented young lawyers. Patent infringement cases are perceived as being where the team appears most frequently though, as market commentators repeatedly pointed out; its lawyers are feared as tough opponents armed with *"the resources and tactics to deal with any case."* Over the past year the group once again highlighted its ability to represent clients in technically diverse cases, achieving favorable verdicts for semiconductor manufacturer ASML and the City of Hope National Medical Center. It won $82 million in damages for technology manufacturer Immersion, a client who

successfully sued Sony over patent infringement of touch-based technologies.

**The Lawyers: Morgan Chu** is frequently cited as a giant in the IP field who consistently delivers *"staggering results for clients"* in some of the state's biggest cases. His *"passionate and tenacious"* courtroom style spells success for clients across the board, and he took the lead role for Immersion in its dispute with Sony. Interviewees spoke warmly of the way in which *"he treats everybody with respect"* and say he is second to none in dealing with trial cases. Described as a *"great strategist,"* **Jonathan Steinberg** covers a range of cases dealing with copyright, trade secrets, trademark and patent infringement litigation. Sources claim that he possesses a powerful courtroom style, and agree he is potentially a star in the making within this leading firm.

**Clients/Work Highlights:** The team has been involved in a number of high-profile cases for Texas Instruments; Hewlett-Packard; Stac Electronics; Lucas Digital; Western Digital; St Jude Medical; Novellus Systems; Affymetrix and Elan.

### Keker & Van Nest LLP

See firm details p.331

**The Firm:** Competitors describe the IP team here as *"one of the most feared in the courtroom."* It manages to achieve an *"unparalleled level of cooperation"* and sustain an *"unrivaled work ethic"* that clients find deeply appealing. The firm's dedicated IP litigators have contributed much to its profile by dealing with top clients on patent, trade secrets and copyright cases. Market sources stated that the combination of an *"excellent reputation"* and *"unwavering efforts to operate cost-efficiently"* guarantees Keker & Van Nest its position in the top tier. The firm is currently working on a number of high-profile cases awaiting trial or on appeal, and recently forced summary judgment in favor of BlueArc in a patent infringement case involving computer file servers.

**The Lawyers:** The *"terrifically talented"* **John Keker** (see p.297) is recommended for his willingness to *"roll up his sleeves and tackle any case that comes his way."* Keker is regarded as one of the best trial lawyers in the field, not least due to his *"fearless and creative"* style. High-profile patent infringement and trade secrets cases have come to the fore in Keker's practice of late. **Daralyn Durie** (see p.286) is another of the firm's practitioners to have fostered a formidable reputation in the courtroom, and is applauded by clients as an articulate speaker and a great writer. She is considered something of a rising star who is fast making her name as a strong IP litigator, having acted for both plaintiff and defense parties such as Genentech and Speedera. Following his involvement in the successful defense of file-sharing online music provider Grokster, **Michael Page** (see p.306) was recently hired by Hummer Winblad Venture Partners to defend claims of liability for copyright infringement by users of Napster, a music provider in which they have invested. Market sources report

that his *"highly innovative approach"* and *"incisive mind gives him an edge,"* particularly where copyright and trademark infringement cases are concerned. **Robert Van Nest** (see p.319) has established a strong reputation as *"an exceptional trial lawyer who gets to the heart of the matter every time."* He specializes in handling patent infringement cases on behalf of technology firms of all sizes, including Intel and BlueArc. The tenacious **Jeffrey Chanin** (see p.282) has worked on several patent infringement and trade secrets misappropriation cases. Recent successes include obtaining a substantial settlement for Taiwan Semiconductor Manufacturing. His colleague **Jon Streeter** (see p.316) is another IP litigator renowned for being *"hard-hitting and talented."*

**Clients/Work Highlights:** Cadence Design Systems; Comcast; Google; Genentech; Intel and Grokster.

### Morrison & Foerster LLP

See firm details p.335

**The Firm:** Morrison & Foerster boasts one of the largest and best-established IP teams in the industry. Its *"intellectually and technically accomplished"* practitioners are said to have *"developed a taste for success at an international level."* The outfit is also acclaimed for its first-rate trial lawyers. Portfolio management; the prosecution, defense and appeal of patent litigation; and the handling of copyright and trademark disputes all contribute to the workload, along with trade secrets and adversarial licensing matters. The firm strengthened its reputation as litigators of choice within the biomedical industry by successfully invalidating a technology patent for assay component manufacturer Scantibodies Laboratory, and has successfully litigated patent claims on behalf of Charter Communications and Macronix America.

**The Lawyers:** Clients highlight the quality of service provided by **Michael Jacobs** (see p.296), a *"strategic thinker"* who is always *"willing to go the extra mile."* He recently applied his *"impeccable reputation"* in the courtroom to handling a number of important cases for companies in the biotech and electronics fields. **Harold McElhinny** (see p.302) is a popular choice of attorney at both trial and appellate levels, and is widely admired as an *"amazingly successful litigator."* He defended EchoStar before the ITC in a patent infringement case. **Gerald Dodson** (see p.286) is well known for acting on behalf of plaintiffs and is heavily involved in high-profile patent infringement cases, where he represents clients in the biotech, semiconductor and silicon materials industries. He is currently preparing to represent Regents of the University of California in a patent infringement case against Monsanto. A leading light in the field of biotech litigation, **Kate Murashige** (see p.304) has a *"capable and competent"* style and is perceived as *"a magnet"* when it comes to winning work for the firm. She is well known for representing Genentech. Meanwhile, the *"powerful scientific mind"* of **Rachel Krevans** (see p.299) has impressed clients in the life sciences industry.

## Intellectual Property
### Leading Individuals

★ **CHU Morgan** *Irell & Manella LLP*

[1] **DAY Lloyd** *Day Casebeer Madrid & Batchelder*    **KEKER John** *Keker & Van Nest LLP*
**KRUPKA Robert** *Kirkland & Ellis LLP*    **MCMAHON Terry** *McDermott Will & Emery*
**POWERS Matthew** *Weil, Gotshal & Manges LLP*

[2] **ANTHONY William** *Orrick, Herrington & Sutcliffe LLP*    **BUNSOW Henry** *Howrey LLP*
**JACOBS Michael** *Morrison & Foerster LLP*    **MCELHINNY Harold** *Morrison & Foerster LLP*
**PASAHOW Lynn** *Fenwick & West LLP*    **QUINN John** *Quinn Emanuel*

[3] **DESMARAIS John** *Kirkland & Ellis LLP*    **DODSON Gerald** *Morrison & Foerster LLP*
**DURIE Daralyn** *Keker & Van Nest LLP*    **ELACQUA James** *Dechert LLP*
**FLAGEL Mark** *Latham & Watkins LLP*    **GARTMAN John** *Fish & Richardson P.C.*
**GOLDMAN Robert** *Ropes & Gray LLP*    **GUY III G Hopkins** *Orrick, Herrington & Sutcliffe*
**HASLAM Robert** *Heller Ehrman LLP*    **HAYES David** *Fenwick & West LLP*
**JOHNSON JR Daniel** *Morgan, Lewis & Bockius LLP*    **JOHNSTON Ronald** *Arnold & Porter LLP*
**LORIG Frederick** *Quinn Emanuel*    **MARTENS Don** *Knobbe Martens Olson & Bear*
**MURASHIGE Kate** *Morrison & Foerster LLP*    **NEWCOMBE George** *Simpson Thacher & Bartlett LLP*
**PAGE Michael** *Keker & Van Nest LLP*    **POOLEY James** *Pooley & Oliver*
**PRETTY Laurence** *Hogan & Hartson LLP*    **PRUETZ Adrian** *Quinn Emanuel*
**REINES Edward** *Weil, Gotshal & Manges LLP*    **SHULMAN Ron** *Wilson Sonsini Goodrich & Rosati*
**STEINBERG Jonathan** *Irell & Manella LLP*    **STERN Claude** *Quinn Emanuel*
**VAN NEST Robert** *Keker & Van Nest LLP*

[4] **ABEL Sally** *Fenwick & West LLP*    **ABRAMS William** *Pillsbury Winthrop Shaw Pittman*
**ALLCOCK John** *DLA Piper Rudnick Gray Cary*    **BARSKY Wayne** *Gibson, Dunn & Crutcher LLP*
**BOHLER William** *Townsend and Townsend and Crew*    **BRIDGES Andrew** *Winston & Strawn LLP*
**CHANIN Jeffrey** *Keker & Van Nest LLP*    **COATS William** *White & Case LLP*
**COOPER John** *Farella Braun & Martel LLP*    **DE ALCUAZ Anthony** *McDermott Will & Emery*
**ELSON Vera** *McDermott Will & Emery*    **FELDMAN Robert** *Wilson Sonsini Goodrich & Rosati*
**FRAM Robert** *Heller Ehrman LLP*    **HEMMINGER Steven** *White & Case LLP*
**KREVANS Rachel** *Morrison & Foerster LLP*    **NEAL Stephen** *Cooley Godward LLP*
**OTTENWELLER Chris** *Orrick, Herrington & Sutcliffe*    **RANDALL Jeff** *Skadden, Arps*
**SAMUELS Mark** *O'Melveny & Myers LLP*    **SAVIKAS Victor** *Jones Day*
**SEKA J Georg** *Townsend and Townsend and Crew*    **SMITH Neil** *Sheppard, Mullin, Richter & Hampton*
**STREETER Jon** *Keker & Van Nest LLP*    **VERHOEVEN Charles** *Quinn Emanuel*
**VISCOUNTY Perry** *Latham & Watkins LLP*

### Up-and-coming individuals
**CHATTERJEE I Neel** *Orrick, Herrington & Sutcliffe*

### Associates to watch
**BROWN Nicholas** *Weil, Gotshal & Manges LLP*

**Clients/Work Highlights:** Novell; Fujitsu; EchoStar; Nikon; Apple; SiGen; University of Rochester; Ecast and Jenoptiks.

## Weil, Gotshal & Manges LLP
See firm details p.1565

**The Firm:** Its *"focused and committed"* group of talented experts is armed with an *"enviable pool of resources,"* making Weil, Gotshal & Manges a certain leader in the field. The team regularly takes on complex, high-profile cases that set the standard for competitors, with recent highlights including a $460 million settlement for electronics manufacturer Lexar Media, and the defense of Cisco Systems against a damages claim where more than $1 billion was at stake. A commitment to client satisfaction has yielded a loyal client following that includes some of the giants of the entertainment and IT sectors. The practice is further lauded for its investment in a broad pool of younger attorneys. Members of the firm advise both

plaintiffs and defendants in patent infringement, trade secrets, trademark and copyright litigation.

**The Lawyers:** Peers regularly describe **Matthew Powers** (see p.308) as being a *"dominant force in the market"* after a series of impressive victories that have clients queuing up to demand his services. Powers' corporate connections and in-depth knowledge of patent law have elevated him to the status of a *"maestro and a leader"* who is *"well liked by judges and genuinely feared as a courtroom opponent."* He recently took a lead role in defending Cisco Systems against a large claim for damages and has worked with many industry-leading clients across the country. Commentators describe his colleague **Edward Reines** (see p.310) as a highly accomplished writer of briefs and an effective advocate. His reputation as a *"creative and hard-working"* IP expert was bolstered of late by acting for Applera and Applied Biosystems in patent infringement and unjust enrichment matters. Commentators also note **Nicholas Brown**

(see p.281) as a *"tremendous young lawyer"* who is one to watch, having assisted Genus with the defense of a summary judgment order dismissing claims of patent infringement.

**Clients/Work Highlights:** Applera; Bertelsmann; Yeda Research; McGraw-Hill; Lexar Media; Procter & Gamble; National Geographic Society; Samsung; Microsoft and the Radio Music License Committee.

## Band 2

## Day Casebeer Madrid & Batchelder LLP

**The Firm:** Loyal clients declare the relatively small but much admired IP group here *"a fantastic outfit of outstanding lawyers."* The team deals with patent, copyright and trademark claims for a variety of high-profile clients in the biotech, IT and communications industries. Sources praise its *"strategic capabilities"* and its *"total commitment to the demands of clients."* That it can count the likes of Amgen, QUALCOMM and Sun Microsystems as clients is testament to the quality of its lawyers' workload.

**The Lawyers:** Interviewees applaud **Rusty Day** for his great advocacy skills, with which he *"lights up the courtroom."* He is the go-to lawyer for a number of hi-tech companies in the region and highly respected for his appearances in patent infringement, copyright and trademark disputes as well as trade secrets litigation. Day acts for the likes of Sun Microsystems and has international experience of litigating claims.

**Clients/Work Highlights:** QUALCOMM; Amgen; Ciphergen Biosystems; Angiotech Pharmaceuticals; Lilly ICOS; Symantec and SAP.

## Fenwick & West LLP
See firm details p.326

**The Firm:** Rivals admire Fenwick & West's commitment to fostering *"strong talent across the board"* and its constant involvement in cutting-edge matters. The team draws on the *"diverse technical backgrounds"* of each of its attorneys in providing a full service to its deep corporate client base. The practice covers a range of matters, from patent litigation through software licensing to copyright and trademark protection.

**The Lawyers:** Championed as a *"thoughtful guy who has a great ability to simplify complex cases,"* **Lynn Pasahow** (see p.306) has carved out a reputation for himself that spans the bioscience, Internet and software industries, and he is described on all sides as an *"excellent choice of counsel."* Sources report that **David Hayes** (see p.293) is a *"copyright whizz kid"* and a *"bright, well-informed"* lawyer who is capable of dealing with all aspects of patent prosecution, licensing of technologies, trademark disputes and trade secrets litigation. **Sally Abel** (see p.276) is regularly cited as an acclaimed trademark lawyer with a talent for her chosen specialization.

**Clients/Work Highlights:** Apple; Electronic Arts; Cisco Systems; Logitech; Sun Microsystems; Informatica; VIA Technologies and Fannie Mae.

## Kirkland & Ellis LLP

See firm details p.875

**The Firm:** The presence of Apple and International Gaming Technology in this firm's client base gives some indication of the status of its IP practice. It is said to field "*a superb cast of lawyers with formidable legal skills*," who are experienced in handling a huge range of cases. The team of IP litigators is accustomed to both prosecuting and defending clients from various industries involved in such actions as licensing, marketing alliances and outsourcing arrangements. The outfit is also understood to be one of the most successful locally active offshoots from a firm that operates on a global scale.

**The Lawyers:** Sources consistently branded **Bob Krupka** (see p.299) a "*tremendous success,*" and he is credited with a "*highly client-oriented approach.*" He is renowned for having settled a patent infringement case on behalf of Dr Gary Michelson for $1.35 billion, the fourth-largest verdict of its kind in the field of IP litigation. Krupka was repeatedly labeled as being among the best patent litigators in the USA, and he has a wealth of experience appearing in courts across the country, including the ITC and the Federal Court of Appeals. Rivals expect this first-rate attorney to taste success yet again as partner of choice for such clients as Apple, ConocoPhillips and Boston Scientific in a number of pending cases. **John Desmarais** (see p.284) commands respect in the courtroom as a "*dogged cross-examiner,*" especially in patent infringement cases, and trademark and copyright disputes.

**Clients/Work Highlights:** Honeywell; Amgen; Motorola; Pioneer Electronics and Schering-Plough.

## McDermott Will & Emery

See firm details p.878

**The Firm:** Having captured a significant share of the IP litigation market at an international level, this powerful group maintains three offices in California representing clients across a spectrum of industries including biotech, electronics and entertainment. Patent prosecution is discerned as being a key strength for the team, though it also provides an integrated service across the board, including where trademark and copyright disputes are concerned. Sources enthusiastically embraced the firm's "*great working culture and depth of talent,*" a combination that has generated high expectations of the firm for the future. Rivals laud the team for doing "*a brilliant job*" for the likes of Fox Entertainment Group, Paramount, Univision Communications, Motorola, Hitachi and Panasonic.

**The Lawyers:** The IP litigation team is said to revolve around **Terry McMahon** (see p.303), who "*inspires a great deal of client confidence*" and has delivered a series of terrific victories for hi-tech companies nationwide. Market sources confirm this "*charismatic professional*" as one of the state's premier trial lawyers and he has nearly 30 years of experience under his belt. He recently secured significant damages for medical device manufacturer Medtronic for patent infringement of equipment used in detecting brain tumors. Landing a

large settlement for Extreme Networks was another highlight. **Anthony de Alcuaz** (see p.285) is renowned for successes on behalf of several large electronics firms and was recently hired by Intel in a large lawsuit. He is well respected for the "*breadth of his knowledge.*" With "*a mind like a steel trap,*" **Vera Elson** (see p.287) is an acknowledged specialist in hi-tech IP litigation and has an advanced degree in electronic engineering, not to mention a wealth of experience working as a digital circuit designer.

**Clients/Work Highlights:** Intergraph; Seagate Technology; Comcast; Silicon Image; EMC; Medtronic; AMD; Sony and Cisco Systems.

## Orrick, Herrington & Sutcliffe

See firm details p.337

**The Firm:** This "*fine firm*" of "*leading talent*" has established a strong IP boutique that offers a full range of legal services from patent prosecution and defense to trademark and copyright litigation to specialist counseling. Drawing upon its reputation as a successful leader in the field and working on a large volume of high-profile cases, the Orrick team is famed for having represented clients in the electronics, hi-tech and semiconductor industries including Compal Electronics in several patent infringement disputes. With a depth of international experience to call upon and a client list that spans both domestic and foreign companies working across the country, this outfit operates five offices in California and deservedly handles cases as a result of the "*sensational quality*" of its work.

**The Lawyers:** Researchers were told that "*being at the top of his game throughout his long career*" has led to **William Anthony** (see p.276) being able to offer a depth of expertise and "*a fantastic trial presence.*" He achieved summary judgment dismissal of patent infringement cases brought against hi-tech firms Compal Electronics and Cisco Systems. "*A lion of the Bar,*" who has become a key name in IP law, Anthony primarily acts as counsel to biotech, IT and semiconductor companies. Sources were also keen to draw attention to the "*bright and effective*" **Hopkins Guy** (see p.292) as a leading light in IP circles. Peers envy the "*methodical approach*" and outstanding experience of **Chris Ottenweller** (see p.306). He is developing an impressive reputation in the state as the IP litigator of choice for EMC, a client for whom he successfully counter-sued Hewlett-Packard over patent infringement of a number of technologies. "*An outstanding trial lawyer,*" he acts for the likes of Intel and SBC. At the forefront of the generation of talented young IP lawyers, **Neel Chatterjee** (see p.282) made a lasting impression on interviewees as an "*effective communicator with a sharp and creative mind, who understands all the angles.*"

**Clients/Work Highlights:** Cadence Design Systems; Applied Materials; Lucasfilm; Cisco Systems; General Surgical Innovations; Foundry Networks; Yahoo!; Xerox and eBay.

## Quinn Emanuel Urquhart Oliver & Hedges, LLP

See firm details p.340

**The Firm:** The firm's team of "*excellent and aggressive*" young lawyers is said to have established a "*hell of a litigation shop*" within a relatively short period of time, so that it already boasts a significant book of clients in California. With several offices across the state, Quinn Emanuel has made great progress by attracting giants such as AOL, Bancorp Services and GM, and is known for taking on high-risk cases in all areas of IP. This includes patent litigation, trade secrets, copyright and trademark disputes.

**The Lawyers:** Partner **John Quinn** (see p.309) was the subject of impressive feedback from peers, who described him as a "*quintessential litigator*" and a leading trial lawyer who devotes a significant proportion of his time to cases concerning IP disputes. Increasingly found alongside him on IP cases is **Adrian Pruetz** (see p.309), whose confident style and reservoir of knowledge means she is "*on everybody's shortlist*" when it comes to dealing with trademark litigation. Patent prosecution and defense, as well as trade secrets misappropriation cases, further contribute to her workload. Clients praised **Claude Stern** (see p.316) as a "*strategic and responsive*" lawyer, not to mention an "*all-around likable guy.*" He is a popular choice for trademark, copyright and trade secrets litigation, and is recognized in Silicon Valley for his success with hi-tech firms such as Medo Industries and Intuit. The "*remarkable and exceptionally successful*" **Fred Lorig** (see p.301) has joined the firm from his own intellectual boutique Bright & Lorig. He is "*great in front of a jury,*" and focuses on patents, antitrust and trade secrets. **Charles Verhoeven** (see p.319) is a perennial performer in IP disputes who supplements his caseload with complex litigation in a number of other fields, including entertainment and antitrust.

**Clients/Work Highlights:** Avery Dennison; Apple; Mattel; Genentech; Johnson & Johnson; Nike; Shell and Time Warner.

## Band 3

## Cooley Godward LLP

**The Firm:** Clients are reassured by the group's consistent quality: "*The entire team is exceptional and you can always get hold of a lawyer in an emergency.*" In a recent patent infringement case against Microsoft, the Federal Court of Appeals ruled in favor of the firm's client, AT&T, in a noteworthy decision concerning the application of US patent law to the export of infringing software.

**The Lawyers:** **Stephen Neal** was adjudged a smart and able attorney. A talented general litigator, he covers patents, trade regulation, trade secrets and copyright cases.

**Clients/Work Highlights:** Excel; eBay; Flyswat; National Semiconductor; NVIDIA; PETsMART; QUALCOMM; Gilead and Siebel Systems.

## Finnegan Henderson Farabow Garrett & Dunner LLP

See firm details p.567

**The Firm:** This respected firm has continued to grow its IP litigation practice, and peers paid tribute to its younger lawyers in particular "*who are truly excellent on their feet.*" Areas covered include copyright, patent, trademark and trade secrets. This large IP boutique impressed market commentators with its "*hands-on, concrete and thorough*" service and high level of partner participation. Clients also counted its lawyers' "*knack of putting complex issues in layman's terms*" in the firm's favor.

**The Lawyers:** Paul Barker is the firm's principal contact for all IP matters.

**Clients/Work Highlights:** Dyax; Akzo Nobel; Guidant; Home Diagnostics; Agilent Technologies; GlaxoSmithKline; Beckman Coulter; Biosynexus; Dade Behring Marburg; Wyeth; Elan; Eli Lilly and Novogen.

## Fish & Richardson P.C.

See firm details p.1113

**The Firm:** The firm is credited with "*enormously knowledgeable and responsive*" attorneys who "*get to the heart of the matter without running up unreasonably large legal fees.*" They are particularly well regarded for their "*ability to master complex technology sector cases.*" The team can rely on backup from its national network of offices as required.

**The Lawyers:** "*Devoted, bright and tremendously skilled,*" **John Gartman** (see p.289) knows how to impress clients and peers. He handles all manner of IP issues but is renowned above all for his "*extraordinary impact at trial,*" particularly in the context of cases relating to software, telecom and semiconductors.

**Clients/Work Highlights:** Microsoft; Princo; Gigastorage; Adaptec; Marconi; Suzuki; Sensormatic; ADE; Intel; Callaway Golf and Autodesk.

## Heller Ehrman LLP

See firm details p.329

**The Firm:** Long-standing clients saw no need for improvement, and enthusiastically endorsed the firm for its "*prompt counsel, superior IP experts and understanding of clients' needs.*" Complex copyright, trade secrets, trademarks and licensing disputes are all covered, along with patent infringement cases and ITC investigations. Peers recognize a serious competitor in this firm, with its "*quality resources and successful track record.*"

**The Lawyers:** The "*gentlemanlike*" **Robert Haslam** (see p.293) garnered considerable client approval for his patent litigation skills. **Robert Fram** (see p.289) enjoys a stellar reputation in patent, trade secrets and licensing matters. Clients love working with this "*extremely smart, hard-working and imaginative individual.*"

**Clients/Work Highlights:** Chips & Technologies; AMATI; Unitrode; Philip Morris; Merck; Allergan; Genentech; Superconductor Technologies; ActivCard and Atmel.

## Howrey LLP

**The Firm:** "*Its relationship-oriented method and out-and-out meticulousness*" continue to impress. The team offers the full gamut of legal services from patent prosecution and defense to trademark and copyright litigation. The interface between IP and antitrust is an important focus area for the practice.

**The Lawyers:** "*Formidable talent*" **Henry Bunsow** was pinpointed by peers as "*truly outstanding on heavy-duty IP matters.*" He is active in cases relating to biotech, technology patents, consumer goods and medical devices. As one client remarked: "*Not many attorneys can put up a case as effectively and quickly as he can.*" That Bunsow has a degree in electrical engineering further enhances his technical understanding.

## Knobbe Martens Olson & Bear

**The Firm:** This IP boutique maintains its spot in the tables following wholehearted client commendation for "*the technical expertise of its lawyers, who always manage to keep the business fundamentals of even the most intricate matters in focus.*" A demonstrably "*deep knowledge of various technologies*" aids the firm in producing superior work in patent, trademark, copyright and trade secrets litigation.

**The Lawyers:** **Don Martens** is "*a remarkable force in the IP world,*" say clients. According to leading market sources this "*well-rounded lawyer deserves to get top marks for integrity.*"

**Clients/Work Highlights:** Nobel Biocare; Masimo; Bausch & Lomb and Mustek Systems.

## Latham & Watkins LLP

**The Firm:** Clients have "*no qualms whatsoever*" about hiring "*this formidable team for highly complex cases.*" The group's "*resourcefulness, common sense and super legal skills*" were all mentioned during research as drivers of client loyalty. National and international clout has reaped the firm impressive rewards, and the team recently secured summary judgment for Genentech in an antitrust and patent infringement lawsuit brought by MedImmune.

**The Lawyers:** Clients praised the "*effective and highly skilled*" cochair of the firm's national IP and technology team, **Mark Flagel**, as being "*exceptionally good on his feet.*" He is renowned for litigating patent, copyright, trademark, trade secrets and false advertising cases. Outstanding trademark specialist **Perry Viscounty** has pleased clients with his "*practical and personable approach.*"

**Clients/Work Highlights:** Cross Medical Products; Playtex; Gap; Allergan and Sony Pictures.

## Ropes & Gray LLP

See firm details p.1117

**The Firm:** Its 2004 merger with Fish & Neave, an outfit that enjoyed an excellent reputation as one of California's leading IP boutiques, has benefited the team by supplying it with greater resources and geographical reach. A strong focus on patent litigation relating to areas such as medical devices and electronics is a defining feature of the practice.

**The Lawyers:** "*Matter of fact lawyer*" **Robert Goldman** (see p.291) enjoys a fantastic reputation and "*makes complex issues understandable,*" clients say. Commentators agreed that his forte lies in IP litigation with an IT, pharmaceuticals or medical devices focus.

**Clients/Work Highlights:** Hewlett-Packard; Ampex; Harrah's and Linear Technologies.

## Skadden, Arps, Slate, Meagher & Flom LLP & Affiliates

See firm details p.1557

**The Firm:** This corporate powerhouse channels a large part of its IP resources into transactional support and strategic advice. However, its involvement in IP litigation, counseling, outsourcing and technology transfer did not go unnoticed. Clients praise attorneys at the firm, saying: "*No matter what they touch, they turn it into gold.*" The team is also well known for its high-profile advice concerning patent prosecution, trademark and copyright.

**The Lawyers:** **Jeff Randall** (see p.309) is highly respected simply for "*going in there and doing the job.*" He counsels numerous technology companies on issues concerning semiconductors, cellular telephony and infrastructure, disk drives and PCs, enterprise and database software, and servers.

**Clients/Work Highlights:** Applied Materials; eBay; McKesson and Intel.

## Townsend and Townsend and Crew LLP

**The Firm:** With more than 170 attorneys, this firm is constantly boosting its patent expertise with new additions, and "*shines as bright as ever,*" clients note. The team recently advised California consumers in the $1.1 billion Microsoft settlement, Lingo v Microsoft, which consolidated a sequence of class action lawsuits alleging that Microsoft violated California's antitrust and unfair competition laws.

**The Lawyers:** **Georg Seka** is considered "*one of the best*" for prosecuting patent applications in the areas of electromechanics, optics, hydraulics and industrial developments. He received further praise for counseling startups and for his trademark know-how. New to the tables and a fellow client favorite is the "*creative and diligent*" **William Bohler**, who offers expertise in patent preparation and prosecution, licensing and litigation.

**Clients/Work Highlights:** Intergraph; Affymetrix; Altera; Bechtel; Boeing; Dolby Laboratories and NVIDIA.

## Wilson Sonsini Goodrich & Rosati

See firm details p.344

**The Firm:** This "*powerful indigenous contender*" boasts profound technology and business expertise, and its IP team is correspondingly strong in providing corporate support and counseling. It also boasts a respectable track record in complex, high-profile IP litigation. The firm is envied for being "*amazingly successful in generating business,*" a facet that ensures its IP department a lucrative stream of work.

**The Lawyers:** Patent litigator **Ron Shulman** (see

p.314) is a long-standing figure in the field and the "*star of the show*" at Wilson Sonsini. Clients commend the "*creative and tactical methods*" he applies to both contentious and noncontentious matters, whether concerning patents or wider IP issues. Possessing a "*courtroom style second to none,*" **Robert Feldman** (see p.288) is "*a wonderful examiner of witnesses who comes complete with a wry wit,*" clients enthuse. He "*thinks through complex problems swiftly and effortlessly,*" and focuses his practice on IP litigation and white-collar crime.

**Clients/Work Highlights:** Amkor Technology; Google; Williams-Sonoma; Echelon and Yodlee.

## Band 4

### Arnold & Porter LLP
See firm details p.560

**The Firm:** Arnold and Porter is perceived to be gaining distinction as a growing force in patent litigation via a thriving network of 100 attorneys practicing IP in offices across the country. Clients value this internationally renowned firm for the experience it has gained across various industries, including through involvement in high-profile biotech and IT cases. The firm acts for the likes of Intel and 3M, and since many of its lawyers have advanced degrees in computer and natural sciences, as well as electrical engineering, they bring a wealth of technical expertise to the table. An integrated approach to cases with a multinational dimension means the firm offers the full range of IP legal services throughout the USA and beyond.

**The Lawyers: Ronald Johnston** (see p.297) has a long track record of success as a "*creative and effective*" litigator with a robust understanding of the interface between IT and IP. He covers patent infringement, trademark and copyright disputes, antitrust and trade secrets. A "*trustworthy and discreet*" partner at the firm, Johnston has represented companies in the entertainment sector, as well as in IT and Internet services industries.

**Clients/Work Highlights:** AtheroGenics; Micron Technology; AOL; Dell and Microsoft.

### Dechert LLP
See firm details p.1752

**The Firm:** Dechert has advised KLA-Tencor, Synopsys, Intersil and Sony, as well as medical devices companies Datascope and Boston Scientific, on complex patent and trade secret litigation matters. The group was boosted recently by the arrival of seven partners and several associates from Dewey Ballantine, who bring extensive experience of trying cases before the ITC and of trials before federal district courts. This was discerned as a distinguishing factor for their practice. The group is currently handling pending litigation for key IT players, such as computer giant Gateway.

**The Lawyers: James Elacqua** (see p.287) has gained a wealth of experience before both trial and appellate courts, which has led to him being hired by Intel and Biogen Idec in complex cases.

**Clients/Work Highlights:** Microsoft; Nomai; Com21; 3M and Edwards Lifesciences.

### Dewey Ballantine LLP
See firm details p.1530

**The Firm:** Despite its recent loss of IP experts from several of its US offices, this outfit can draw on the skills of several lawyers across the country and covers cases pertaining to both hard and soft IP matters. Sources were impressed by the firm's success in attracting up-and-coming, technically adept attorneys, and cited this as further enhancing the team's in-depth knowledge of the electronics and IT industries.

**The Lawyers:** Jeannine Sano is the key contact at the firm for issues relating to IP.

**Clients/Work Highlights:** Rambus, Matsushita Electric Industrial and Intel are examples of clients.

### DLA Piper Rudnick Gray Cary US LLP
See firm details p.870

**The Firm:** Commentators praised this firm for providing clients with a team of talented and technically sound IP attorneys who combine a "*holistic*" approach with "*cost-effectiveness.*" Copyright and trademark disputes, patent litigation, trade secrets misappropriation and licensing matters are all handled at the practice, and it was remarked that a "*good understanding of each client's business*" is always kept in sight. Clients found the "*attention paid to small details*" by these hard-working attorneys particularly praiseworthy. In the past twelve months, the firm has represented Hewlett-Packard in a patent infringement case, and managed an anticounterfeiting campaign relating to wristbands on behalf of the Lance Armstrong Foundation.

**The Lawyers:** There was effusive praise for **John Allcock** (see p.276), in which he was branded an excellent strategist and prized for his "*business-savvy*" outlook. An established partner within the firm, Allcock specializes in patent litigation and has acted in more than 150 cases before both federal and state courts, as well as the ITC.

**Clients/Work Highlights:** Hewlett-Packard; Agilent Technologies; Intel; Samsung and Toshiba.

### Farella Braun & Martel LLP

**The Firm:** Sources recommended this small yet growing San Francisco-based firm for its "*gifted and reliable*" lawyers. They are renowned for handling complex case material with ease and representing clients in local industries such as entertainment, wine-making and IT. The team takes pride in forging lasting relationships with high-profile corporations including Dolby Laboratories, Genentech and Visa. In addition to offering the full range of patent litigation services, the firm has channeled significant resources into niche areas that include licensing and litigation relating to digital technology, where it boasts a wealth of trial experience.

**The Lawyers:** Clients love **John Cooper**, in equal measure, for both his "*eloquent advocacy*" and his "*dexterity in tackling tough cases.*"

**Clients/Work Highlights:** Universal Studios;

Disney; Chiron; Opus One Winery; Applied Biosystems; Robert Mondavi; Macromedia; Reader's Digest and Micron Technology.

### Gibson, Dunn & Crutcher LLP
See firm details p.328

**The Firm:** The breadth of resources available at the four offices operated by this fine firm throughout California impressed interviewees, who agreed patent infringement and technological product licensing constituted the two key focus areas for the practice. It continues to represent Columbia University in its defense of an action brought by a group of biotech corporations seeking the invalidation of technology patents covering the manufacture of widely used protein material. It has, furthermore, strengthened its reputation as the go-to firm for video game litigation as it prepares to represent a cluster of clients including Electronic Arts and Ubisoft Entertainment against claims of patent infringement.

**The Lawyers: Wayne Barsky** (see p.277) is much admired for balancing an "*aggressive and fearless*" courtroom approach with a reputation for remaining "*fair and even-handed.*" He was recently hired by a biotech corporation in a patent infringement case over rheumatoid arthritis treatments.

**Clients/Work Highlights:** Columbia University; Serono; Electronic Arts; LucasArts; Atari; Ubisoft Entertainment; Activision; Vivendi Universal; SEGA; Stac Electronics; Nortel Networks; GE and Johnson & Johnson.

### Jones Day
See firm details p.570

**The Firm:** The firm's global reach has ensured the growth of an enviable client roster, especially when it comes to patent litigation. One client, who summed up the general feeling about the team in the market, described it as "*responsive and thorough*" with an "*excellent grasp of the issues and details.*" Many of the lawyers here are experienced in technical areas such as electrical engineering, biotech and computer science. The full spectrum of services is covered, including trademark and copyright litigation, appeals, patent prosecution, product licensing advice and technology transactions.

**The Lawyers:** The "*effective, no-nonsense*" approach of **Victor Savikas** (see p.311) in handling complex patent litigation cases won him great respect among commentators. He has been chosen to represent DIRECTV in two cases of alleged patent infringement of digital technology.

**Clients/Work Highlights:** Micron Technology; Soverain Software; Advanced Fibre Communications; Baptist Health System; Beckman Coulter; Motorola; Hughes Aircraft; Mattel and Toyota.

### O'Melveny & Myers LLP
See firm details p.336

**The Firm:** More than 70 attorneys throughout California are involved in the field, and the operation comes highly recommended for its work in trademark and copyright litigation. Peers note that members of the firm have worked hard to establish themselves with clients across the board, but especially in the semiconductor, computer software, life sciences and medical devices sectors. Relatively rapid expansion and a *"good depth of experience"* have led to it becoming a force to be reckoned with. Two subdivisions of the IP practice, dealing with IT disputes and healthcare technology litigation respectively, supplement the team's traditional strengths.

**The Lawyers:** **Mark Samuels'** (see p.311) practical attitude and *"terrific presence"* in the courtroom were repeatedly commented upon. Cases involving an antitrust element are a recurring theme for him and he has represented hi-tech firms such as Top Victory Electronics and Achtel in patent infringement lawsuits.

**Clients/Work Highlights:** AMD; Apple; Gemstar-TV Guide; International Game Technology; Lockheed Martin; News Corporation; Honda and Magma Design Automation.

## Paul, Hastings, Janofsky & Walker LLP

See firm details p.339

**The Firm:** This full-service IP litigation practice has done tremendous work in bolstering its reputation over the past few years and is tipped for the top in the near future. It is commended by peers for a strong team that handles patent litigation and prosecution, trademark and copyright issues, trade secrets and licensing affairs. The team can tap into international experience supplied through its worldwide network of offices and handles IP matters for clients from an array of industries including manufacturers of computer software, semiconductors, pharmaceuticals, agricultural products, integrated circuits and consumer electronics. In the past year, it has built upon its representation of SICOR Pharmaceuticals through the handling of further medical technology disputes.

**The Lawyers:** John Phillips in San Francisco is involved in complex litigation that often has an IP strand running through it.

**Clients/Work Highlights:** The firm's key highlight was the development of a strategy for financing and patenting a new medical device for Cameron Health.

## Simpson Thacher & Bartlett LLP

See firm details p.1555

**The Firm:** Simpson Thacher fields an excellent IP practice that covers patent litigation, trade secrets issues, copyright and trademark disputes and product licensing in any number of fields, ranging from the manufacture of fiber optics to the biotech and medical device industries. The group's ability to maneuver the client through technical minefields associated with IP litigation is much celebrated. Juggling several high-profile cases at once has defined the practice of late: a patent litigation matter for Daiichi Pharmaceutical and a lawsuit alleging infringement of copyright protection over user interfaces on behalf of Lotus Development being prominent examples. Further highlights include representing Intel in patent litigation filed by Patriot Scientific against five of Intel's largest customers.

**The Lawyers:** A key player in IP circles, **George Newcombe** (see p.305) is said to possess a *"fine level of expertise."* He is known for attracting and retaining clients in the hi-tech industries of Silicon Valley including NEC and Intel.

**Clients/Work Highlights:** Avistar Communications; UMC; Verizon; 3Com; Daiichi Pharmaceutical; Accenture; JDS Uniphase and Johnson & Johnson.

## White & Case LLP

See firm details p.1566

**The Firm:** The firm's California IP practice has seen strong growth over the past year and prides itself on possessing the resources to litigate cases at an intercontinental level. It has particularly profited from a strategic focus on lawsuits featuring a mixture of entertainment and technology elements, which has led to the firm representing established names such as LucasArts, In-Three and Industrial Light & Magic. It is looking to build on its growing reputation within the sector as a go-to boutique for patent infringement cases involving clients based in Asia, and recently achieved a $175 million settlement on behalf of Taiwan Semiconductor Manufacturing for patent infringement.

**The Lawyers:** Interviewees were keen to recommend the *"clever and respected"* **William Coats** (see p.283), who spends a great deal of time representing clients in litigation relating to copyright, trademark and trade secrets disputes. He is renowned for acting for Lucasfilm and has also worked with the DVD Copy Control Association. Sources report that

**Steven Hemminger** (see p.294) is sought after for his *"aggressive and hard-working"* approach, not to mention his in-depth technical knowledge. He has increasingly taken a lead role in representing Taiwan Semiconductor Manufacturing of late.

**Clients/Work Highlights:** Cirrus Logic; DVD Copy Control Association; In-Three; LucasArts; Mesa Boogie; Pioneer Electronics and Trek.

## Other Notable Practitioners

**Daniel Johnson** (see p.296) of Morgan, Lewis & Bockius LLP proves to be *"enormously good on his feet and delivers first-class results,"* clients say. Rivals find him *"very articulate and charismatic but dangerous to have on the other side."* His recent representation of Compuware in a five-week jury trial against IBM did not go unnoticed. Johnson dealt with claims of theft regarding trade secrets, antitrust claims, and claims for copyright and patent infringement, eventually settling the case in Compuware's favor for $400 million. *"Trade secrets devotee"* **James Pooley** (see p.308) has set up Pooley & Oliver in Palo Alto following his departure from Milbank. He is considered an *"effective and tenacious"* attorney who is nationally renowned for his abilities. Pooley is also au fait with patent litigation and software copyright issues. *"Tip-top"* **Laurence Pretty** (see p.308) of Hogan & Hartson LLP knows how to *"separate the important issues from the rest and is scholarly without being stuffy,"* clients say. He represents clients including Beckman Coulter; Catalytic Solutions; MediaTek; Sichuan Changhong Electric and United Microelectronics.

Billed as *"a wizard of the patent Bar,"* **William Abrams** (see p.276) of Pillsbury Winthrop Shaw Pittman LLP is a *"courageous litigator who understands both the broader picture and the social context surrounding issues,"* say clients. He represents the following clients in IP matters: Intel; Stanford University; Marvell; Everypath; PostX and Positive Light. The *"admirable"* **Andrew Bridges** (see p.280) of Winston & Strawn LLP was singled out for his *"practical and resourceful"* handling of soft IP work, and proficiency in trademark issues. **Neil Smith** recently left Howard, Rice, Nemerovski, Canady, Falk & Rabkin for Sheppard, Mullin, Richter & Hampton LLP. He received plaudits from clients for his *"astounding trademark expertise."*

# IT & IT OUTSOURCING

## IT & IT Outsourcing
### Leading Firms

1. **LATHAM & WATKINS LLP** *Los Angeles, Menlo Park*
2. **COOLEY GODWARD LLP** *Palo Alto*
   **DLA PIPER RUDNICK GRAY CARY US** *Palo Alto*
   **FENWICK & WEST LLP** *Mountain View*
   **MORRISON & FOERSTER LLP** *San Francisco*
   **PILLSBURY** *San Francisco*
   **WILSON SONSINI** *San Francisco*
3. **ARNOLD & PORTER LLP** *Los Angeles*
   **O'MELVENY & MYERS LLP** *Los Angeles*

### Leading Individuals

#### Senior Statesman
**SHOCKRO Michael** *Latham & Watkins LLP*

1. **BELL Suzanne** *Wilson Sonsini Goodrich & Rosati*
   **KIMBALL George** *Baker & McKenzie*
   **MUMMERY Dan** *Latham & Watkins LLP*
   **RADCLIFFE Mark** *DLA Piper Rudnick Gray Cary US LLP*
2. **HAYES David** *Fenwick & West LLP*
   **KLEIN Anthony** *Latham & Watkins LLP*
   **MOORE Gary** *Cooley Godward LLP*
   **MURPHY Michael** *Pillsbury Winthrop Shaw Pittman LLP*
   **NASH Glenn** *Latham & Watkins LLP*
   **PETERS William** *O'Melveny & Myers LLP*
   **VILLENEUVE Tom** *Gunderson Dettmer Stough Villeneuve*
3. **COX Evan** *Covington & Burling*
   **JAHN Paul** *Morrison & Foerster LLP*
   **MACCOBY Matthew** *Arnold & Porter LLP*
   **PASS Brian** *Brown Raysman*
   **SCHWARTZ William** *Morrison & Foerster LLP*

#### Up-and-coming individuals
**BEBAWY Adel** *Latham & Watkins LLP*
**BROCKLAND John** *Cooley Godward LLP*
**SHARRON Stephanie** *Wilson Sonsini*

## Band 1

### Latham & Watkins LLP
**The Firm:** This cosmopolitan outfit has built a strong, customer-oriented group in California, widely recognized as *"the best team in the area."* Clients were impressed by the depth of experience its lawyers possess in terms of working with the major players in outsourcing, which allows them to *"provide clients with an informed perspective."* Of particular note, the team represented WellPoint in an $800 million IT infrastructure outsourcing deal with IBM. Elsewhere, its much-praised *"international footprint"* was put to good use assisting Valeant Pharmaceuticals in the negotiation of an IT outsourcing agreement spanning 30 countries. Members of the firm were also praised for *"internalizing clients' concerns"* and adopting a sensitive approach to outsourcing negotiations. Other areas in which the group is active include licensing, e-commerce hosting and telecommunications. Clients appreciated the *"ability to think proactively about*

hidden pitfalls" and provide *"prompt thoughtful responses"* to difficult problems.

**The Lawyers:** Founder and chair of the firm's technology transactions practice group, clients described **Michael Shockro** as *"bright, thorough and calming, and therefore adept at building professional relationships."* He advises on complex technology transactions in the energy industry and on telecom outsourcings. *"Bright star of outsourcing"* **Dan Mummery** led the team in its largest IT outsourcings. In addition to WellPoint and Valeant Pharmaceuticals, he served as lead counsel to a number of Fortune 500 companies and represented Levi Strauss in the negotiation of an offshore application development and management outsourcing. Clients made reference to his *"good, calm manner of resolving issues and ability to negotiate contracts in clients' favor."* In addition, he was praised for his *"outstanding knowledge and experience in the area"* and his *"bright and creative approach to transactions."* **Anthony Klein** was described as *"strategically brilliant, tactically flawless and very responsive."* His work typically straddles IP and outsourcing, and he advised Silver Lake on both areas in connection with the KKR/Silver Lake acquisition of the semiconductor products group Agilent. Furthermore, he represents a number of startups, including the nanotech company Intermolecular. *"Outstanding"* **Glenn Nash** focuses on complex technology transactions in a number of areas, including the software, e-commerce, media and communications industries. His impressive client list includes Yahoo! which he advised on a number of Internet access partnerships and software and technology licensing arrangements. **Adel Bebawy** is *"moving up the ladder from minder to finder and will become a good relationship attorney in time."* He is said *"never to be ruffled by anything,"* and recently led the team in a number of deals, including several major software license deals for United Online.

**Clients/Work Highlights:** Adobe Systems; American Express; AT&T; Blue Shield of California; BT; Chevron; DuPont; Epson America; Gateway; GM; Intermolecular; Miller Brewing Company; Sun Microsystems; The TriZetto Group; United Airlines and UnitedHealthcare.

## Band 2

### Cooley Godward LLP
**The Firm:** The firm's five-partner team focuses exclusively on IT and outsourcing work, and is deemed to be *"always up to speed with the latest developments in the technology sector."* Its lawyers won praise for *"going out of their way to understand a client's business"* and cover the full spectrum of work, including licensing, outsourcing and the IT and IP aspects of M&A. Highlights include handling the IP, licensing and technology aspects of Adobe's acquisition of Macromedia. The group also has a long-standing relationship with Applied Materials, which

it recently advised on a joint venture with IBM and Albany NanoTech to create a research partnership for nanotechnology development.

**The Lawyers:** Peers and clients alike recognize **Gary Moore** as a *"prominent player"* in technology transactions. His practice covers software and patent licensing as well as strategic alliances and IP issues in the IT sector. He was lead counsel in the Applied Materials/IBM/Albany NanoTech joint venture and advised Cymer in its joint venture with Zeiss. On the outsourcing front, **John Brockland** received much praise from satisfied clients: *"He is just terrific,"* remarked one. An enviable list of clients includes PacifiCare and Yahoo! which he represented in significant IT outsourcing transactions.

**Clients/Work Highlights:** AOL; Borland Software; BroadSoft; Cisco Systems; Cymer; eBay; Owens Corning; Quest Software and Time Warner.

### DLA Piper Rudnick Gray Cary US LLP
See firm details p.870

**The Firm:** Clients were full of praise for a team which is *"active in all aspects of IT, has impressive international reach and boasts a great supporting cast."* Such attributes have been cemented by the alliance of Gray Cary with Piper Rudnick and DLA. The team offers expertise in a wide range of technology industries, from semiconductors, software and new media, through to biotech. It is well integrated with the corporate group and *"has great depth of experience in venture work and complex transactions involving corporate and IP matters."* An impressive client roster includes companies such as Sony and NEC, as well as a number of startups.

**The Lawyers:** Interviewees were full of praise for the *"well-established"* **Mark Radcliffe** (see p.309). He *"really understands the intricacies of the technology sector"* and has a broad practice, covering software and Internet licensing, copyright and trademark issues and strategic IP advice. As the general outside counsel of the Open Source Initiative, he is particularly active in the open source space. He benefits from having *"a good early-detection radar for danger"* and *"clearly has a passion for what he does."*

**Clients/Work Highlights:** Eastman Chemical Company; Magnum Semiconductors; Sun Microsystems and SugarCRM.

### Fenwick & West LLP
See firm details p.326

**The Firm:** This large California-based firm is widely recognized by commentators as one of the premier firms in the state for IT and licensing. It focuses on providing a comprehensive service to technology and life science companies. Clients appreciated the fact that the firm *"hires more attorneys from technical backgrounds than any other firm in the Bay area."* Internet entertainment companies have featured heavily in the workload of late.

**The Lawyers:** *"IP guru"* **David Hayes** (see p.293) is a prominent lawyer in IT transactions. *"He has a good reputation and deserves it,"* according to interviewees, who reserved special praise for his expertise in software copyright infringement. This is an area in which he acted as counsel in precedent-setting cases, including A & M Records v Napster.

**Clients/Work Highlights:** The firm represents a range of clients across the advertising, software, ISP and hardware sectors. That it has acted for the likes of Apple, Macromedia and Amazon.com gives an indication of its stature in the field.

## Morrison & Foerster LLP

See firm details p.335

**The Firm:** The firm boasts a sizable team of *"superb experts in software-related areas and IP."* While the development and licensing of technology is clearly the team's forte, interviewees were quick to note its increased visibility in outsourcing. Working closely with the firm's Tokyo office, it has a strong track record in Asia. Members of the firm frequently act for Fujitsu, notably in the restructuring of its FASL joint venture with AMD, concerning the development and manufacture of EPROM chips and flash memory. Clients praised the group for being *"adaptable"* to the needs of clients.

**The Lawyers:** The *"personable"* **Paul Jahn** (see p.296) impressed clients with his IT and IP expertise, which he put to good use in advising Thomson on the IP and licensing aspects of its acquisition of the retail television network PRN. **William Schwartz** (see p.312) has a similar focus and was billed as an *"experienced and creative lawyer who is excellent at bridging seemingly insurmountable chasms during negotiations."* Recent highlights for him include advising Novell on open-source related issues surrounding its dispute over UNIX copyrights.

**Clients/Work Highlights:** AIG Technologies; Ask Jeeves; Bank One; Chiron; EchoStar; Hertz; Hitachi; Nikon and Tanox.

## Pillsbury Winthrop Shaw Pittman LLP

See firm details p.1550

**The Firm:** Following the merger of Shaw Pittman and Pillsbury Winthrop, the practice now centers on a 12-strong team of lawyers and nonlegal consultants based in San Francisco. Clients appreciate the added value offered by practitioners who are able to *"provide structured legal advice with a commercial edge"* and offer seamless legal and nonlegal support. Notable highlights include acting for PG&E Corporation in a multibillion-dollar IT outsourcing transaction involving five separate vendors.

**The Lawyers:** **Michael Murphy** (see p.304) leads the firm's global sourcing group on the West Coast and has a wealth of experience in IT outsourcing transactions, whether domestic or international in scope. He acted as lead counsel to PG&E Corporation, and represented Stanford University Hospital in a full IT outsourcing project. *"He is very good at coordinating his own team, in-house counsel and business people to the best effect,"* say commentators.

**Clients/Work Highlights:** The team has advised a number of Fortune 500 companies from a wide variety of industries.

## Wilson Sonsini Goodrich & Rosati

See firm details p.344

**The Firm:** Interviewees say the technology transactions practice group at this corporate powerhouse *"certainly features among the usual suspects."* Integrated advice is considered key to the firm's success in the field: *"The firm's goal is to act as general counsel and provide all the services you need as a client,"* remarked one commentator. Clients paid homage to the training ethic at the firm, which breeds *"practical and street-smart attorneys capable of picking a case up and running with it."* A growing IT outsourcing practice has also attracted some high-profile customers, including Dolby Laboratories and DaimlerChrysler.

**The Lawyers:** For market observers, it is **Suzanne Bell** (see p.278) who generates *"the buzz about this department."* As co-manager of the practice she has overseen the group's growth from five to over 40 attorneys firmwide. She advises both emerging and mature technology companies on strategic alliances, distribution and development agreements, IP issues and outsourcing. Her colleague **Stephanie Sharron** (see p.313) impressed many clients with her work on outsourcing transactions. One remarked: *"I couldn't imagine anyone more supportive."*

**Clients/Work Highlights:** The firm advises companies from an array of industries, including semiconductors, media and entertainment, life science, energy, software and hardware.

## Band 3

## Arnold & Porter LLP

See firm details p.560

**The Firm:** Despite the departure of George Kimball, the firm remains home to *"really good people in its LA office."* A team of four attorneys devotes substantial time to outsourcing transactions, and recently represented California State University, the largest state university system in the USA, in the outsourcing of its student information systems. Elsewhere it represented Herbalife International in the development and outsourcing of a new e-commerce platform for online ordering.

**The Lawyers:** **Matt Maccoby** (see p.301) is the partner charged with heading the group since the departure of George Kimball. He focuses primarily on outsourcing transactions and *"his expertise and experience compares favorably with that of any other lawyer in the field."*

**Clients/Work Highlights:** Further highlights include representing IndyMac Bank in the renegotiation of a major contract to outsource core retail banking functions.

## O'Melveny & Myers LLP

See firm details p.336

**The Firm:** The outsourcing expertise at this large international firm is concentrated in California, where *"the continually expanding"* team currently comprises around ten attorneys and counsel. It focuses exclusively on outsourcing transactions, on which it has advised a number of Fortune 500 companies. Typical work includes advising a Japanese automobile manufacturer on the outsourcing of its data center operations across three continents to IBM.

**The Lawyers:** Outsourcing expert **William Peters** (see p.307) impressed clients by combining his *"total grasp of the industry"* with *"excellent people skills and a good sense of humor."* His *"reserved yet confrontational style"* in negotiations *"wears the opposition down like a constant drum beat."* He leads the team in all of its larger transactions and is perceived as the dynamo behind its expansion.

## Other Notable Practitioners

**Evan Cox** (see p.284) of Covington & Burling is credited with a strong reputation in digital rights management matters, having acted as counsel to Microsoft in relation to the digital media aspects of its core operating system. *"He has a keen appreciation for the international dimensions of technology transactions,"* say sources. Commentators were quick to applaud the IT outsourcing work of **George Kimball** (see p.298), now of Baker & McKenzie. He primarily represents suppliers, although his *"ample experience with major players on both sides of the table means he can swiftly adapt and take the middle road in almost any context."* It remains to be seen what effect his move will have on the local presence of a firm already boasting a very strong international outsourcing practice. Brown Raysman Millstein Felder & Steiner LLP, one of the leading technology firms on the East Coast, is considered well represented in California by **Brian Pass** (see p.306). *"He is fantastic at dealing with opposition counsel and has great technical capability,"* according to clients. He has worked at the forefront of new technology, including on such matters as the Music Genome Project. One of the founders of Gunderson Dettmer Stough Villeneuve Franklin & Hachigian, **Tom Villeneuve** impressed clients with his *"deep knowledge and brilliant ideas as to how to handle complex and novel areas."* Predominantly representing small to medium-sized technology companies in strategic alliances with larger companies, his *"unmatched thoroughness"* and pragmatic negotiation skills *"don't allow the opposition much room in which to throw their weight around."* Notable highlights for him include representing 2Wire in a joint venture with SBC.

# LITIGATION

## Gibson, Dunn & Crutcher LLP
See firm details p.328

**The Firm:** A national litigation giant. Clients particularly approve of the firm's ability to smoothly coordinate its East and West Coast operations. The California-based team has established a superb track record across a range of commercial disputes. Highlights included defending Janus in multidistrict litigation proceedings, in which hundreds of lawsuits against the company and other mutual fund complexes have been consolidated. The team is also acting for another Janus entity, Janus Capital, in the resolution of parallel investigations by the New York attorney general, the SEC, the Colorado attorney general and the Colorado Division of Securities concerning alleged market timing. A favorable settlement was achieved. In the white-collar sphere, clients admire the manner in which "*the group's talents come together.*" Healthcare, public corruption and education-related issues have been on the agenda, as well as tax and mail fraud.

**The Lawyers:** Commercial litigator **Robert Cooper** (see p.284) remains "*at the top of his game*" in a range of disputes, displaying particular expertise in the antitrust field. Sources also highlighted the practice of **James Clark** (see p.283): "*He has that rare combination of excellent jury skills and solid written work.*" One observer insisted that in trial he gave "*one of the finest performances that I've seen.*" His caseload encompasses high-stakes commercial litigation, entertainment, IP and white-collar matters. He recently successfully acted for French entrepreneur François Pinault and his holding company Artemis, as well as two of its affiliates, in claims arising out of the collapse of Executive Life Insurance. The "*enormously experienced*" **Thomas Holliday** (see p.295) has long held a successful practice in white-collar crime, resulting in a "*very firm grasp of this area of law.*" Clients described him as "*resourceful and creative – he has the type of personality that motivates and inspires others.*"

**Clients/Work Highlights:** American Airlines; Ticketmaster; Intel; Hewlett-Packard; Nissan; Daimler-Chrysler; Wal-Mart; ExxonMobil; General Mills; Best Best & Krieger and ITT Educational Services.

## Heller Ehrman LLP
See firm details p.329

**The Firm:** "*It is this group's client service levels and great communication skills that set it apart,*" enthused one client. Others spoke of the "*extremely strong work product*" and expertise "*across a matrix of complex matters.*" Among these are antitrust, IP, insurance coverage and securities litigation. One example of the latter is the group's advice to a number of officers and directors in the Yahoo! shareholder derivatives litigation. Attorneys here also acted for Visa in several pieces of litigation.

**The Lawyers:** **Larry Popofsky** (see p.308) is "*a grandfather of the business*" in the eyes of many competitors, who see him as "*particularly dangerous in court.*" Although his practice now revolves largely around antitrust issues, he remains "*one of the most brilliant people around*" and a pillar of the litigation practice. Securities litigator **Sara Brody** (see p.280) is a popular figure in the market, thanks to her "*organized and diligent approach.*" **Norman Blears** (see p.279) is also active in securities-related matters, covering a range of stockholder suits, coordinated investor matters, regulatory proceedings and securities fraud. In this regard, some predict him to be "*the future of the firm*" thanks to his "*great results, excellent written work and appreciation of the impact on a business generally.*" **Stephen Bomse** (see p.280) has earned an impressive reputation in commercial litigation, especially in the antitrust arena; while the "*brilliant*" **Douglas Schwab** (see p.312) is able "*to make the most out of any legal position,*" said clients. They particularly appreciated his expert handling of securities-related cases.

**Clients/Work Highlights:** Microsoft; Philip Morris; Siliconics; Symantec; Mentor Graphics; PwC; Alliance Semiconductor and Deloitte & Touche.

## Keker & Van Nest LLP
See firm details p.331

**The Firm:** Commentators "*think the world*" of this renowned litigation boutique, which has attracted a caseload that ranges across commercial litigation, white-collar criminal matters and IP issues. A propensity to handle high-stakes litigation has made this firm a popular port of call for securities, class action, malpractice defense and trade secrets litigation. Recent highlights are its defense of class actions against clients of the caliber of AT&T Wireless. The group has also been engaged on behalf of Electronic Arts in a stockholder class action concerning financial disclosures, including state and federal derivatives actions. On the white-collar side, the team flexes its muscles on behalf of clients involved in SEC and grand jury investigations and internal corporate investigations.

**The Lawyers:** "*The star of the firm and of the market,*" **John Keker** (see p.297) is a favorite among peers and clients for both commercial litigation and white-collar matters. In the latter field, he is deemed "*the dean of the Bar right now,*" for his street-fighter courtroom tactics. Not to be overshadowed is "*gentleman scholar*" **Robert Van Nest** (see p.319), whose practice also spans civil and white-collar matters. He is currently representing the owners of 31% of the Oakland Raiders against Al Davis, who is alleged to have sought to misappropriate their limited partner interest by stripping them of voting and inspection rights. Commentators are "*extremely impressed*" with the work of **Jan Nielsen Little** (see p.300), a "*smart and capable*" white-collar specialist. **Elliot Peters** (see p.307) is another figure who has "*stepped out from the shadows*" into a prominent white-collar criminal practice.

**Clients/Work Highlights:** Commentators drew attention to the firm's client list, which was deemed to be "*as blue-chip as you get.*" Names include Google, American Honda Motor, American Honda Finance and a slew of major law firms.

## Morrison & Foerster LLP
See firm details p.335

**The Firm:** Clients were delighted by the performance of this "*highly accomplished group of excellent litigators.*" The group's depth of talent and broad expertise places it at the forefront of the market. Among its caseload can be found securities, IP, antitrust and products liability disputes, as well as matters arising from the financial services sector. A particular field of activity of late has been internal investigations and cases with regulatory components. Highlights have included representing The Hartford in connection with regulatory and investigative matters.

**The Lawyers:** "*Classic war-horse and marquee litigator,*" **James Brosnahan** (see p.280) attains "*the gold standard*" with his trial practice. Equally well regarded in both civil and white-collar cases, he is a legendary figure among peers. He recently achieved a $340,000 jury verdict for an Oakland Raiders football player in an assault case. The "*outstanding*" **Melvin Goldman** (see p.291) is "*one of the old guard*" said sources, and a real force in the courtroom with his securities and antitrust litigation at the cornerstone of his practice. Rivals envied his "*superb job in depositions and sound judgment.*" Clients admire securities specialist **Jordan Eth** (see p.287) for his "*creativity and ability to structure a strategic approach based on developing facts and judicial approaches.*" His "*completely honest and straightforward attitude*" also wins him fans among peers. National cochair of the securities litigation and white-collar defense group, he represented Yahoo! in its defense of a derivative action against its officers and directors, regarding the alleged improper allocations of stock in IPOs from Yahoo!'s underwriters. **James Bennett** (see p.278) is "*highly talented and a great courtroom performer,*" bringing his impressive courtroom skills to bear in his broad, general commercial litigation caseload. Clients have been thrilled with **Arturo González**'s (see p.291) "*smart and aggressive*" approach to litigation. Chair of the firm's trial practice group, he is acting for Universal Corporation in a federal suit alleging insurance fraud, which stems from a fire at a nut-processing plant. Universal Corporation has cross-claimed against the insurance company for bad faith.

**Clients/Work Highlights:** Bank of America; UPS; Nikon; Chiron; EchoStar and Capital One.

## Munger, Tolles & Olson LLP

**The Firm:** Clients placed this team as among "*the brightest collection of lawyers seen in California.*" A "*smart and efficient*" approach, combined with "*even quality throughout*" has made this a high-powered litigation outfit. SEC and accounting issues, legal malpractice claims and IP issues are all areas of expertise. Highlights have included advising Boeing in a dispute with Lockheed Martin concerning allegations of theft of trade secrets. The matter was settled with a joint venture between the two companies, which is awaiting approval by US and European authorities. The team is also acting for a law firm that gave advice concerning tax shelters, which is now the subject of litigation.

**The Lawyers:** **Brad Brian** is very much in demand for both commercial and white-collar litigation. His "*engaging and gregarious*" personality makes him a popular choice for both types of work, and his "*tenacity and grasp of the issues*" cement his reputation. He has litigated in the entertainment and securities arenas, as well as in matters arising from government investigations and disputes surrounding government contracts. Sources also commended

**Ronald Olson** as an "*intelligent and good-natured litigator,*" while **John Spiegel** is "*one of the best oral advocates around.*" He impressed with his experience in securities, stockholder derivative cases and investigations. **Mark Epstein** has caught the eye of the market this past year following his "*terrific*" performances in court.

**Clients/Work Highlights:** Berkshire Hathaway; Northrop Grumman; Universal Studios; Warner Bros; Time Warner; Verizon; Archer Daniels Midland; Abbott Laboratories; Merrill Lynch and News Corporation.

## O'Melveny & Myers LLP

See firm details p.336

**The Firm:** Clients spoke of "*a top-stratum firm with a deep bench*" particularly in the class action arena. Here, the group employs its "*strong strategic approach*" to full effect, particularly when assisting clients in investigations and disputes arising out of the securities market. The white-collar criminal practice is also commended, and in this sphere attorneys advise on a range of matters, from internal investigations and healthcare fraud to environmental disputes. The team successfully represented BP in multiple-state and federal investigations arising from alleged noncompliance with environmental laws regulating underground storage tanks for retail gas stations. It also obtained the dismissal of a False Claims Act suit for Caltech concerning patents related to a DNA sequencer that enabled mapping of the human genome. In the healthcare sector, the group is defending the Alvarado Hospital owned by Tenet Health System Hospitals, in allegations concerning fraudulent agreements to relocate new doctors into existing medical practices that referred patients to the hospital.

**The Lawyers:** Managing partner of the Los Angeles office, **Seth Aronson** (see p.277) chairs the securities litigation practice and is a popular choice for complex class actions. He acted for Lockheed Martin in the Ninth Circuit Court of Appeals in a securities class action. Rainmaker **Daniel Petrocelli** (see p.307) is held in high regard for his entertainment and commercial trial work. His skillful handling of high-profile cases led some to describe him as "*a master of manipulating the media to protect his clients.*" This past year has seen a departure from his predominantly civil practice as much of his time has been devoted to the representation of Jeffrey Skilling, a former executive of Enron. This has involved criminal charges, several Congressional investigations, a DOL inquiry and a number of civil lawsuits filed across the country. Sources endorsed **James Asperger** (see p.277) as "*a first-class securities lawyer.*" Chair of the firm's global enforcement and criminal defense group, he acted on the Alvarado Hospital matter. **Daniel Bookin**'s "*top-flight analytical abilities*" and "*no-nonsense approach to litigation*" have made him a strong contender in the marketplace. White-collar and related administrative proceedings occupy his time, in addition to complex civil litigation. **Mark Holscher** (see p.295) "*has come into his own as a force to be reckoned with,*" which is under-

lined by his involvement in the Skilling case; while **Michael Tubach** (see p.318) also stands out as a "*highly effective*" white-collar practitioner, reported sources.

**Clients/Work Highlights:** Fannie Mae; Merck; Johnson & Johnson; Franklin Templeton; Martha Stewart; Alaska Air and Hynix Semiconductor.

## Quinn Emanuel Urquhart Oliver & Hedges, LLP

See firm details p.340

**The Firm:** "*It is hard not to notice Quinn Emanuel's rise,*" observed peers. Its "*aggressive and fast-growing*" practice is "*more willing and more able*" than many other firms to take cases to trial, gaining it a name as "*a hot firm*" in the California market. The group has witnessed an explosive growth in the patent litigation field, and increased activity in the field of corporate fraud. The firm is acting for Enrico Bondi, the bankruptcy administrator responsible for the reorganization of Parmalat, Italy's largest food-processing company, which allegedly misused company money. Other highlights include achieving a $126 million jury verdict on behalf of Freedom Wireless.

**The Lawyers:** **John Quinn** (see p.309) is a "*smart, tough and persuasive*" trial lawyer, who is skilled in cross-examination. His engagements of late have included acting in the Parmalat litigation, and representing Bank of New York in a separate suit against Citigroup, surrounding its sale of Enron credit-linked notes. **William Urquhart** (see p.319) is also a forceful courtroom performer. Complex litigation is his forte, and he has lately advised Royal Dutch Shell in a number of antitrust suits involving alleged fixing of the California natural gas market. **John Potter** (see p.308) joined the San Francisco office recently from Covington & Burling, and is spearheading the white-collar practice in the Bay area. Together with the team, he represents pharmaceutical companies and large energy suppliers in matters such as antitrust and SEC investigations. Highlights include acting for the president of a global company under investigation for antitrust price-fixing.

**Clients/Work Highlights:** In the white-collar arena the firm acts for Fortune 100 companies as well as individuals, while its commercial litigation clients include IBM; Shell; Mattel; Electronic Arts; Micron and Nike.

## Hennigan, Bennett & Dorman LLP

See firm details p.330

**The Firm:** Clients endorsed this trial boutique for its deep expertise in handling bet-the-company litigation. The emphasis here has been securities cases and other disputes related to investment firms, banks and insurance companies. The "*team of highly skilled and intellectual lawyers*" has acted for a group of investors who purchased Enron-related securities. Other key representations this past year have included advising the Archdiocese of Los Angeles in connection with more than 500 civil sex abuse cases.

**The Lawyers:** Clients endorsed "*intellectual strategist*" **Michael Hennigan** (see p.154629) as a highly skilled commercial litigator. His "*theatrical courtroom*"

## Litigation: General Commercial
### Leading Individuals

**Senior Statesmen**

POPOFSKY Laurence *Heller Ehrman LLP*
QUINN John *Arnold & Porter LLP*

[1] BRIAN Brad *Munger, Tolles*
BROSNAHAN James *Morrison & Foerster LLP*
COTCHETT Joseph *Cotchett, Pitre, Simon & McCarthy*
KEKER John *Keker & Van Nest LLP*
NOLAN Thomas *Skadden, Arps*

[2] BLECHER Maxwell *Blecher & Collins*
COOPER Robert *Gibson, Dunn*
FELDMAN Boris *Wilson Sonsini*
GOLDMAN Melvin *Morrison & Foerster LLP*
GROSSMAN Marshall *Alschuler Grossman*
HENNIGAN J Michael *Hennigan, Bennett*
LERACH William *Lerach Coughlin Stoia Geller*
NEAL Stephen *Cooley Godward LLP*
OLSON Ronald *Munger, Tolles & Olson LLP*
QUINN John *Quinn Emanuel*
SPIEGEL John *Munger, Tolles & Olson LLP*
YOUNG Douglas *Farella Braun & Martel LLP*

[3] ARONSON Seth *O'Melveny & Myers LLP*
BRODY Sara *Heller Ehrman LLP*
ETH Jordan *Morrison & Foerster LLP*
FELDMAN Larry *Kaye Scholer LLP*
PETROCELLI Daniel *O'Melveny & Myers LLP*
RUBY Allen *Ruby & Schofield*
RUTHBERG Miles *Latham & Watkins LLP*
SACKS Robert *Sullivan & Cromwell LLP*
SIEGEL David *Irell & Manella LLP*
URQUHART A William *Quinn Emanuel*
VAN NEST Robert *Keker & Van Nest LLP*
VANYO Bruce *Katten Muchin Rosenman*

[4] BALABANIAN David *Bingham McCutchen LLP*
BENNETT James *Morrison & Foerster LLP*
BLEARS Norman *Heller Ehrman LLP*
BOMSE Stephen *Heller Ehrman LLP*
CARUSO Joanne *Howrey LLP*
CLARK James *Gibson, Dunn & Crutcher LLP*
COUGHLIN Patrick *Lerach Coughlin Stoia Geller*
DAVIDSON Jeffrey *Kirkland & Ellis LLP*
DAWES Paul *Latham & Watkins LLP*
DUNCAN Helen *Fulbright & Jaworski L.L.P.*
EPSTEIN Mark *Munger, Tolles & Olson LLP*
FELDMAN Robert *Wilson Sonsini*
GLASER Patricia *Christensen, Miller, Fink*
GONZÁLEZ Arturo *Morrison & Foerster LLP*
JOHNSON Edward *Mayer, Brown, Rowe & Maw*
JOHNSTON Ronald *Arnold & Porter LLP*
LYONS James *Skadden, Arps*
MALLORY Robert *McDermott Will & Emery*
MCKNIGHT Frederick *Jones Day*
REDING John *Paul, Hastings*
SCHULMAN Alan *Bernstein Litowitz Berger*
SCHULMAN Robert *Fulbright & Jaworski L.L.P.*
SCHWAB Douglas *Heller Ehrman LLP*
STURGEON John *White & Case LLP*
SULLIVAN William *Paul, Hastings*
WOODS Daniel *White & Case LLP*

*performances"* ensure he is a formidable opponent, and peers are left in no doubt that he is a *"hardened trial lawyer."* He acts in major trials across a range of practice areas such as securities fraud and breach of contract. He is currently representing a major utility in energy litigation against the State of California.

**Clients/Work Highlights:** Rabobank; Trust Company of the West; Oaktree Capital Management; Principal Insurance Group; AEGON USA and Maguire Partners.

### Irell & Manella LLP

**The Firm:** The team's expertise in the IP arena is well documented; but in addition to housing a great stable of patent litigators, this is one of California's *"outstanding business trial firms,"* reported sources. The group's experience spans securities class actions, media and entertainment cases, antitrust matters and corporate control disputes. Tax matters, real estate and insurance disputes are a feature of the practice. The team successfully defended NBC Studios against a breach of contract claim for contingent compensation arising out of an executive producer agreement for the television program 'Profiler'. In the white-collar sphere, the group has undertaken a significant volume of SEC grand jury work, involving allegations of securities fraud and insider trading, primarily for executives of corporations, as well as corporations themselves.

**The Lawyers:** **David Siegel** is the firm's managing partner, who has established a *"dominant securities litigation practice."* His workload includes defending securities class and stockholder claims against corporations and their directors and officers, as well as advising on SEC enforcement proceedings and disputed corporate takeovers. Sources endorsed **Brian Hennigan**, whose *"gregarious and engaging personality"* coupled with strong trial skills make him a hit in the marketplace. His is a diet of securities, government, defense contractor and healthcare fraud, as well as tax and political corruption cases.

**Clients/Work Highlights:** Among the group's client base are manufacturers and retailers, venture capitalists and financial institutions drawn from the energy, airline, media, real estate and education sectors, as well as governmental bodies.

### Jones Day
See firm details p.570

**The Firm:** Clients are impressed with this firm's penetration of the California market and its nationwide resources, which can ensure a *"work product that is beyond compare."* Its attorneys produce *"commanding courtroom performances"* across a range of commercial and white-collar disputes. The Los Angeles office forms the hub of this California practice, supported by attorneys in Irvine, San Diego and a burgeoning San Francisco office. Highlights include defending Chevron in a class action brought by Unocal stockholders challenging a proposed merger between the two companies. The group's white-collar criminal experience includes matters related to price-fixing, accounting fraud and managed earnings. In this regard, the team has

acted for clients in the electronics and computer industries.

**The Lawyers:** Head of the Los Angeles office, **Rick McKnight** (see p.303) has a long list of complex commercial trials under his belt. These have included successfully representing Dole Food in defense of an enforcement action brought in the USA, following claims by 466 Nicaraguan nationals for alleged exposure to the pesticide DBCP. Clients of the white-collar practice approved of **Brian O'Neill** (see p.306), because *"when you have a messy problem, he will sort it out."* Rivals, meanwhile, admire **Brian Sun's** (see p.317) *"unique ability to come up with a solution that everyone can live with."*

**Clients/Work Highlights:** Mellon Financial; Unocal; County of Los Angeles; Lehman Brothers; Applied Medical Resources; Verizon; Experian; Gap; Marvell; Philippine Airlines; NVIDIA; Helm Financial; Sacramento Kings; IBM and DIRECTV.

### Latham & Watkins LLP

**The Firm:** This *"stable of thoroughbreds"* is attractive to clients for its *"variety of really talented litigators in different arenas."* The team fields experienced attorneys in securities litigation, professional liability, mass torts, white-collar and government investigations. Recent successes included securing a jury verdict for DIRECTV, Hughes Network Systems and Hughes Electronics, against allegations made by plaintiff NNWS that it had negotiated an oral contract with Hughes Network Systems to purchase a $58 million convertible promissory note. Additional highlights included successfully defending Ernst & Young in a federal securities fraud class action.

**The Lawyers:** Accountants' liability matters are the forte of Los Angeles-based **Miles Ruthberg**. He has cultivated a robust securities and professional liability caseload. Peers deemed **Paul Dawes** an *"outstanding trial lawyer,"* particularly for securities litigation. His practice also covers complex corporate, IP and regulatory matters. **Steven Bauer** *"is really hitting his stride"* in the white-collar arena, said commentators. They pointed to his *"great judgment and great caseload,"* which principally features white-collar and IP matters. **David Schindler** is an *"incredibly talented trial lawyer"* with a white-collar, IP and business litigation practice.

**Clients/Work Highlights:** Oracle; Philip Morris; Ernst & Young; Tenet Healthcare; Genentech; Arthur Andersen; Broadcom and Roche Molecular.

### Lerach Coughlin Stoia Geller Rudman & Robbins LLP

**The Firm:** *"The masters of taking plaintiff cases and extracting the value from them,"* claimed sources. Attorneys at this firm take a key role in many of the market's leading securities class actions. Clients credit them with first-rate knowledge, and point to their *"sensitivity where client matters are concerned."* The team acts on behalf of large union pension funds and municipalities whose pension funds have been the alleged victims of securities fraud. Highlights have included achieving a $7.1 billion settlement with

Enron, in addition to settling claims with Qwest and AT&T among others.

**The Lawyers:** Rivals approach securities specialist **William Lerach** with trepidation in view of his *"aggressive litigation style"* and track record of success. **Patrick Coughlin** also enjoys a powerful reputation for his trial work.

**Clients/Work Highlights:** The group's clients include California Public Employees' Retirement System, Teachers' Retirement Fund and Central States Teamsters. It has also advised states such as New Mexico, Ohio and Montana in connection with retirement fund issues.

## Alschuler Grossman Stein & Kahan LLP

See firm details p.323

**The Firm:** An aggressive approach to litigation and a wealth of experience have placed this firm at the forefront of the market. Its caseload spans the media and entertainment fields, professional malpractice, insurance coverage and securities disputes. The group recently acted as lead counsel for Arthur Andersen in disputes arising from the restatement of HBOC's earnings following its acquisition by McKesson. Arthur Andersen had been the auditor for HBOC prior to the acquisition. Attorneys also acted in the case of Harris v County of Los Angeles involving a preliminary injunction against the reduction of beds at Los Angeles County Hospital and Rancho Los Amigos.

**The Lawyers:** **Marshall Grossman** (see p.292) is a central figure within this commercial litigation practice. A lawyer of *"considerable reputation and skill,"* he has recently been occupied with professional malpractice defense, particularly for accounting firms, in defense of securities fraud litigation. Among his recent caseload has also been the representation of Chabad in a suit against the Russian Federation to retrieve religious writings seized by the Nazis during the Second World War, then captured by the Russians at the end of the war.

**Clients/Work Highlights:** Blockbuster; AIG; Deloitte & Touche; Cendant; NRT; Coldwell Banker Residential Brokerage; L-3 Titan; New Century; Epson America; Heritage Provider Network; Baker & Taylor; Marubeni-Itochu Steel; Aames Investment and the California Insurance Commissioner.

## Arnold & Porter LLP

See firm details p.560

**The Firm:** Although the DC-based practice tends to attract much of the limelight, its California counterpart is home to *"astute litigators,"* whose expertise across a range of disputes should not be overshadowed. Technology, products liability, entertainment and IP-related litigation are all found on the agenda here. High-profile examples include acting for VeriSign subsidiaries Jamster! and Jamba! in the defense of international class actions and other disputes concerning trade practices in the downloadable entertainment content for cell phones. In another key case of the past year, the group acted for Allianz Global Risks US Insurance in connection with childhood sexual abuse claims against the Roman Catholic Archbishop of Los Angeles and Orange County.

**The Lawyers:** **John Quinn** (see p.309) is undoubtedly the star of the group. Opponents cite his *"spectacular courtroom demeanor"* coupled with an *"elegant litigation style"* that attracts respect from clients, peers and the bench. **Ron Johnston** (see p.297) is largely focused on litigation arising out of the technology and entertainment sector, often appearing in issues connected to IP.

**Clients/Work Highlights:** Microsoft; VeriSign; Oakland Raiders; Wyeth; Bank of America; BP companies (such as BP America, BP West Coast Products and Atlantic Richfield); Honeywell; Hopi Indian Tribe of Arizona and ICL/Fujitsu, UK.

## Bingham McCutchen LLP

See firm details p.1110

**The Firm:** Clients were satisfied that this group was *"everything you'd expect of a top-flight litigation firm,"* highlighting its ability to marshal resources as a key attraction. Securities, antitrust, corporate governance and regulatory litigation form much of this firm's diet. From its San Francisco base, the group applies its *"high-quality skill set"* to a range of matters. It recently successfully advised the runner-up bidder for assets of Executive Life on allegations that its bid was wrongfully defeated by a consortium that was later found to have engaged in illegal conduct. The team was also involved in the high-profile dispute between Oracle and PeopleSoft, in defense of Oracle's hostile takeover bid.

**The Lawyers:** Clients were full of praise for **David Balabanian** (see p.277), a long-standing presence in the litigation community. *"He brings great judgment to litigation strategy,"* and is a creative courtroom performer.

**Clients/Work Highlights:** The group's clients include Mitsui, JPMorgan Chase and McKesson.

## Cooley Godward LLP

**The Firm:** Distinguished in the northern part of the state for its vibrant Silicon Valley practice, this is a group valued by clients for its *"incredibly practical approach – their attorneys don't beat around the bush."* Among the firm's recent cases, attorneys represented PG&E in its contested bankruptcy, in which the bankruptcy court confirmed a plan of reorganization. The group also acted as lead counsel for all asbestos personal injury matters in the USG bankruptcy, successfully moving to disqualify the original District Court judge on grounds of improper ex parte contacts with opponents and because of the appointment of advisers with conflicts of interest.

**The Lawyers:** Peers are convinced that the pivotal member of the group is *"fantastic trial lawyer"* **Steve Neal.** If you have him on your side *"you're in great shape,"* they agreed. Chairman and CEO, his caseload has ranged across civil and criminal matters; he acted for AT&T in a patent infringement case against Microsoft, involving voice encoding or compression technology.

**Clients/Work Highlights:** The team's client base has included numerous corporations and individuals, as well as audit committees and special committees of boards. Companies include Ronald A Katz Technology; Stanford University; NVIDIA and Brunswick.

## Cotchett, Pitre, Simon & McCarthy

**The Firm:** Commentators endorsed this firm's skillful handling of complex litigation, citing its particular reputation for plaintiff representation. The group's current workload encompasses IP, natural gas, prescription drugs, fraud and whistle-blowing disputes. Recent achievements have included obtaining settlement of a false advertising class action concerning the battery life of Apple iPods.

**The Lawyers:** A *"true character,"* **Joseph Cotchett** is *"a remarkable trial lawyer,"* said sources. His civil rights work and plaintiff representation are widely recommended.

**Clients/Work Highlights:** The team's client base includes individuals, corporations, profit and nonprofit organizations, municipalities and public entities, unions, representatives and banks.

## Farella Braun & Martel LLP

**The Firm:** Commercial disputes and white-collar crime are handled with equal aplomb by this committed and effective litigation department. Securities, antitrust, construction and employment matters have occupied the team on the defense side. The group has also developed a thriving insurance defense practice, acting for corporate insureds. On the criminal side, the team has represented a former officer of McKesson in criminal securities litigation, and has advised on a number of theft of trade secrets disputes. Antitrust matters arising out of the computer chip industry have also been an area of focus.

**The Lawyers:** According to sources, **Douglas Young**'s *"unassuming and mild-mannered"* approach to litigation makes him a *"credible"* force in the courtroom. His *"calm and balanced"* view means he *"brings great perspective to a case."*

**Clients/Work Highlights:** Among the firm's commercial litigation clients are Dolby International; Veritas; Samsung and Safeway. On the white-collar side, the group's clientele includes a number of officers of corporations as well as boards of directors. The team has also represented the City and County of Los Angeles in a construction case.

## Howrey LLP

**The Firm:** This team of effective litigators *"is not afraid to try a case,"* reported appreciative clients. Its experience spans mass torts, consumer class actions, securities and liability litigation. The white-collar criminal practice has recently been dealing with securities, tax, healthcare and antitrust law violations, as well as matters pertaining to the use of mail and wire communications. The group has successfully acted for a major auto manufacturer in a breach of contract case arising from an agreement with a software development firm shortly before the firm filed for bankruptcy. Other successes include achieving a verdict that the California Voting Rights Act of 2001 is unconstitutional.

**The Lawyers:** **Joanne Caruso**, John McDermott, Joanne Lichtman and Michael Turrill lead the commercial litigation group. Caruso has recently been involved in substantial contract disputes,

including a number of trials involving insurance coverage issues. **Jan Handzlik** has cultivated a thriving practice in white-collar criminal matters. He defended Homestore against allegations of securities law violations.

**Clients/Work Highlights:** Caterpillar; Lockheed Martin; World Trade Center; Unocal (now Chevron); International Paper; WorldCom (now MCI); Dole Food; Occidental Petroleum; Boeing; Verizon; Avery Dennison; Union Pacific; Nestlé and United Space Alliance. White-collar clients include publicly traded companies and their officers and directors.

## McDermott Will & Emery

See firm details p.878

**The Firm:** Clients place their trust in this firm's considerable depth at partner level, its *"strong support at associate level"* and the fact that these lawyers are able to provide *"interesting and novel solutions."* The group's caseload includes white-collar crime, securities disputes, corporate governance issues and employment litigation. Among recent highlights, the team successfully defended Perot Systems in a consumer class action concerning allegations that the company conspired with Enron and other energy suppliers to manipulate the California electricity market. White-collar criminal matters are also undertaken, and investigations by the SEC and issues arising out of the healthcare sector have proved to be key areas of late.

**The Lawyers:** Clients are confident that **Robert Mallory** (see p.301) *"won't be out-maneuvered by anyone."* He combines a *"forthright yet careful"* approach to complex litigation and has a *"great courtroom manner,"* claimed admirers. He represented Chiquita Brands International in a dispute with Dole Food concerning importation rights. The *"talented"* **Gordon Greenberg** (see p.292) *"works behind the scenes to make problems go away."* He also employs his *"charming and affable"* manner to good effect in the courtroom.

**Clients/Work Highlights:** Crédit Lyonnais; First National Bank; KB Toys; Northrop Grumman; Walgreen; California Tan; CMS Energy; John Paul Mitchell Systems and Telemac.

## Skadden, Arps, Slate, Meagher & Flom LLP & Affiliates

See firm details p.1557

**The Firm:** Clients value the *"consistently high-quality work product"* this firm is able to provide, while peers noted the strongly national caseload, drawing on the support of its New York attorneys. Antitrust, securities fraud and mass torts bolster the general commercial litigation caseload. Recent successes include acting for Mercury Insurance in defeating an attempt to assert a class action challenging the company's practice of charging an installment fee on premium payments. The team also successfully acted for Activision in a suit alleging securities fraud.

**The Lawyers:** Interviewees agreed that respected trial lawyer **Thomas Nolan** (see p.305) is a powerful force in boosting the firm's West Coast profile.

*"Anything he does turns to gold"* claimed rivals, while clients were in awe of his *"ability to draw an analogy that changes the paradigm of thinking in the room, at the right moment in the discussion."* He acted as co-lead counsel for 17 investment banks in a consolidated federal class action and nearly 200 related individual actions. The matter concerned $13 billion of WorldCom bonds. **James Lyons** (see p.301) is also known for his prominent caseload, with an emphasis on securities and corporate issues, D&O liability and international arbitration. The team has increased its white-collar profile with the recruitment of former Proskauer Rose attorneys **Richard Marmaro** (see p.302) (*"a very, very effective litigator"*) and **Jack Dicanio** (see p.286). Their caseload includes SEC enforcement and white-collar criminal defense work.

**Clients/Work Highlights:** Clients include Farmers; Mercury Insurance; Chiron; AmerUS Group and TRL Group.

## Wilson Sonsini Goodrich & Rosati

See firm details p.344

**The Firm:** This *"formidable"* set of litigators is widely acclaimed for its securities litigation practice. Highlights have included representing Google in SEC actions, and acting for Guidant in stockholder litigation. The firm is a leading player in the technology market, particularly in Silicon Valley, and has carved out a respected profile through its work in technology-related litigation and IP.

**The Lawyers:** The *"charming"* **Boris Feldman** (see p.288) is a *"brilliant securities tactician"* according to clients. Stockholder actions, derivative suits and financial restatement cases are his bailiwick. **Robert Feldman**'s (see p.288) work on complex commercial matters has won him a loyal following.

**Clients/Work Highlights:** Business Objects; Sun Microsystems; Genentech and Krispy Kreme.

## Fulbright & Jaworski L.L.P.

See firm details p.1928

**The Firm:** This team's ability to *"get ahead of the game, shape the issues and come up with industry standards"* has made it a hit with clients. Class actions across a range of sectors have occupied the group recently, and its attorneys are well equipped to handle a range of issues, such as tax and securities fraud and IP disputes.

**The Lawyers:** *"Fabulous trial lawyer"* **Helen Duncan** (see p.286) *"is afraid of nothing,"* reported sources. She takes a robust approach to litigation, displaying integrity and *"an almost zealous devotion"* to client representation. Her securities expertise was widely endorsed, and she enjoys a profile for her work on behalf of investment banks. She is the lead counsel in an appeal of a class action jury trial in which Lehman Brothers was found to have aided and abetted a commercial client in defrauding its borrowers. At issue is whether a commercial lender can be held liable for its provision of financial services to an allegedly fraudulent company. The *"persuasive"* **Robert Schulman** (see p.273550) is *"gentlemanly and articulate,"* said clients. They approved of his "*big book of contacts in this field*," and his status as a skilled courtroom performer.

**Clients/Work Highlights:** CNA Surety; BDO Seidman; USI Holdings; Lincoln National Life Insurance; California Dairies; Staples; Federated Department Stores; Disney; JC Penney Company; Farmers and CB Richard Ellis Investors.

## Orrick, Herrington & Sutcliffe
See firm details p.337

**The Firm:** This growing practice acts for clients in the energy, telecom and computer hardware and software sectors. Its work for the former CFO of McKesson has been a talking point in the marketplace of late. The defendant was acquitted on all counts of criminal conspiracy and securities fraud. The team has also been involved with criminal antitrust investigations of international cartels. Although best known for white-collar work, the team has enjoyed success in noncriminal matters, including acting for Nike, achieving summary judgment in a business discrimination case. The plaintiffs claimed Nike rejected their application to be an authorized dealer for Nike footwear and apparel because they are black.

**The Lawyers:** According to observers, **Walt Brown** (see p.281) has "*an informal, low-key style; but if negotiations break down, his fact-based cross-examination and tight presentation*" make him a respected trial lawyer. He represented a former executive who was held in contempt of court following his refusal to produce documents in response to a grand jury subpoena. The Ninth Circuit Court of Appeals reversed the district court's ruling, and rejected the government's argument that the defendant's act of production conveyed a foregone conclusion. His colleague **Melinda Haag** (see p.292) "*gets the truth out on the table*" and enjoys the respect of the judge, said sources.

## Paul, Hastings, Janofsky & Walker LLP
See firm details p.339

**The Firm:** This litigation department is stocked with attorneys who "*leave no stone unturned*," said clients. Clients have access to firmwide resources from its base in Los Angeles, which ensures "*great support in tricky litigation.*" A recent highlight was appearing in the Supreme Court on behalf of the defendants in Dura Pharmaceuticals, against Broudo.

**The Lawyers:** The "*smart and driven*" **John Reding** (see p.309) chairs the litigation department. He is a hit among clients for his ability to "*handle many complex matters simultaneously.*" His "*strategic, nonformulaic*" attitude provides a roadmap for litigation, and ensures "*collaboration and understanding, not confrontation.*" Chair of the securities litigation group, **William Sullivan** (see p.316) is "*a gentleman in the courtroom*," but behind the scenes he "*pushes hard for the clients' interests.*" He is an attorney who "*always has control,*" and is "*extremely skilled at managing disparate groups of clients.*" He defends public companies in securities class actions and regulatory proceedings.

**Clients/Work Highlights:** Boeing; SBC; Dell; Wal-Mart and Ligand Pharmaceuticals.

## Pillsbury Winthrop Shaw Pittman LLP
See firm details p.1550

**The Firm:** The April 2005 merger of Pillsbury Winthrop with Shaw Pittman has brought further "*energy and expertise*" to the firm, agree clients, who also appreciate the firm's continued commitment to the California market. The litigation team is composed of more than 120 attorneys in offices throughout the state who possess a range of experience, including white-collar, securities, insurance and regulatory matters. Attorneys recently defended Pacific Bell against allegations of monopolization in violation of the Sherman Act.

**The Lawyers:** Patrick Marshall heads the firm's national litigation team.

**Clients/Work Highlights:** Chevron; Dynegy; Xerox; SBC; PostX and Wells Fargo.

## Sidley Austin LLP
See firm details p.883

**The Firm:** Sources commended this firm's substantial presence in the state, particularly noting its work in the arena of securities litigation, products liability and accountants' liability. Attorneys based in San Francisco and Los Angeles advise on complex commercial litigation such as securities, IP, healthcare disputes and issues relating to the telecom, technology and energy sectors.

## Sullivan & Cromwell LLP
See firm details p.1558

**The Firm:** The Los Angeles office of this "*outstanding firm*" is acclaimed by clients for its clear, strategic advice. Complex securities, antitrust and M&A-related litigation are areas of focus for the group. The team is defending EnCana in a number of class actions relating to alleged manipulations of the price of natural gas in California and Nevada and a related commodities manipulation case in New York.

**The Lawyers:** Client favorite **Robert Sacks** (see p.311) "*out-lawyers*" the competition with his "*calm and certain cadence in court*" and "*savvy business sense.*"

**Clients/Work Highlights:** Thomas Weisel Partners; Goldman Sachs; Morgan Stanley; SOFTBANK and Philips.

## White & Case LLP
See firm details p.1566

**The Firm:** Clients endorsed this litigation department, linking its profile to "*talent at the top*" and "*effective communication across the state.*" The Los Angeles team possesses an international caseload with a number of foreign entities on its roster, alongside domestic clients bringing actions against non-US organizations. Complex business litigation is the heart of the practice, and this has included banking and financial services, insurance and liability matters. Highlights have included acting for Cirrus Logic in a products liability matter concerning allegedly defective disk drives used in desktop personal

computers. The matter settled on terms favorable to Cirrus Logic.

**The Lawyers:** Clients commended the "*deep experience in formulating strategy*" that **John Sturgeon** (see p.316) brings to the table. He has represented Mirant in class actions brought by power consumers, and related actions filed by the California attorney general. Practice head **Daniel Woods**' (see p.321) "*practical and down-to-earth*" manner won him fans among clients, who admire his confident trial skills and knack for "*always being right.*"

**Clients/Work Highlights:** Bank of America; Bank of New York; BDO Seidman; Bimbo Bakeries USA; BNP Paribas; Crédit Lyonnais; International Lease Finance; Northern Trust Bank of California; The Salvation Army and Wells Fargo.

## Beck, De Corso, Daly, Kreindler & Harris
See firm details p.324

**The Firm:** Known for its "*highly professional*" work in white-collar cases and investigations, this group's client base features both companies and senior executives. Criminal highlights have recently included representing an international PR company against allegations of alleged unlawful activity among its employees.

**The Lawyers:** **Mark Beck** is an "*impressive figure in the market,*" agree peers, as are his partners **Bryan Daly** and **Marc Harris**. The latter focuses on matters pertaining to the False Claims Act, RICO and federal securities laws.

**Clients/Work Highlights:** Clients of the firm have included Evergreen Shipping and senior executives at Columbia Healthcare; Tenet Healthcare; Boeing; Teledyne Technologies; Infineon Technologies; Samsung; Matson; Texaco and Merrill Lynch.

## Bird, Marella, Boxer & Wolpert PC

**The Firm:** This team is frequently visible in white-collar matters in the state, winning "*nothing but respect*" from clients. Cases involving defense contractors, export control, investment and healthcare fraud and environmental matters have all been on the agenda of late. The group is currently defending the City of Los Angeles against a suit brought by the estate of a murdered rap star. It has also secured a favorable settlement on behalf of the CFO of Qwest. Clients are assured the team conducts litigation "*without aggravating the opposition.*"

**The Lawyers:** The "*talented and strategic*" **Vincent Marella** "*just knows how to put together a defense,*" said rivals. **Terry Bird** "*has been a leader at the white-collar Bar for many years*" and, as a result, he has "*a good deal of wisdom when it comes to assessing a case.*" Furthermore, "*if he doesn't get a satisfactory resolution from negotiations, the other side knows they will face a formidable opponent.*" **Ronald Nessim** can "*see right through to the heart of the matter,*" so that he "*knows when to be nice and knows when to be tough,*" claimed sources. Healthcare fraud is a specialty of his white-collar practice. Sources predict even greater things for the increasingly prominent practice of **Gary**

Lincenberg. He continues to be well known in environmental criminal matters.

Clients/Work Highlights: The team's wide-ranging client base has also included major healthcare providers and wealthy individuals.

## Clarence & Dyer LLP

The Firm: From its San Francisco base, this firm has built a terrific reputation for matters ranging across securities fraud, antitrust and environmental cases. A current highlight is the representation of a large publicly traded energy company indicted, along with three electricity traders, in a case alleging the defendants manipulated the California energy market, and precipitated the California energy crisis in 2000.

The Lawyers: Nanci Clarence is a prominent member of the criminal Bar, thanks to her commitment and skill in defense matters. She represented Lea Fastow, wife of the former CFO of Enron, in tax-related charges.

Clients/Work Highlights: The firm's client base consists typically of officers or directors of corporate entities facing criminal charges or investigation.

## Lightfoot, Vandevelde, Sadowsky, Medvene & Levine

The Firm: This criminal defense firm focuses on white-collar crime, civil rights litigation, appeals and related civil proceedings. The group counts foreign and domestic corporations, governmental entities and individuals among its client roster.

The Lawyers: Former federal public defender Janet Levine is deemed "a first-rate lawyer" by opponents. Her experience encompasses securities, healthcare, tax and public corruption matters. "You meet him, you trust him," claimed admirers of John Vandevelde. His combination of "smarts and hard work" led some interviewees to dub him "one of the most trusted in the market." Michael Lightfoot is also held in high regard by market sources, who place him among the white-collar Bar's star players.

## Stevens & O'Connell LLP

The Firm: Commentators named this the top firm in Sacramento for white-collar work. The practice is especially involved in matters pertaining to healthcare, government contract and securities fraud and environmental matters. Highlights included representing a major healthcare provider in a criminal investigation and civil False Claims Act case, resulting in a favorable settlement before charges were brought.

The Lawyers: George O'Connell and Charles Stevens have attracted the respect of both peers and clients. O'Connell focuses on white-collar matters, whereas Stevens is involved in a range of cases, spanning white-collar, civil fraud and general litigation work.

Clients/Work Highlights: The client base tends to consist predominantly of corporate clients, but the team does act for individuals as well.

## Swanson & McNamara LLP

The Firm: The group is staffed with "highly credible" lawyers possessed of "great judgment and impressive understanding of technical issues." The past year has seen the team working closely with the SEC in investigations relating to securities fraud, while computer fraud and energy disputes have proved to be other areas of activity. High-profile representations have included advice to Victor Conte in the steroid abuse scandal linked to the Bay Area Laboratory Co-Operative. The case concerns allegations that Conte and others supplied steroids and other performance-enhancing substances to athletes.

The Lawyers: Sources endorsed Mary McNamara's "thoroughness and professionalism" in complex cases.

Clients/Work Highlights: The team is known for its representation of individuals, and this has included executives of companies charged or investigated for alleged securities violations.

## Topel & Goodman PC

The Firm: A firm known for the broad range of its trial work, its expertise in white-collar, administrative and related civil matters, as well as international extradition, is widely commended. Ongoing representation includes advising Reliant Energy in a pending case arising out of the California energy crisis. The team is also acting for a Taiwanese company in a price-fixing investigation.

The Lawyers: The "astute" William Goodman (see p.291) is a top-flight trial attorney, noted for his "excellent judgment." He is largely occupied with the representation of corporations and individuals who are the subject of criminal investigations. In addition to his white-collar caseload, he has also litigated a number of death penalty cases.

Clients/Work Highlights: The client base includes corporate clients and their employees, often officers or directors of corporations. The client roster includes Mosel Vitelic, and the largest egg producer in Northern California.

## Other Notable Practitioners

"Star trial lawyer" Allen Ruby of Ruby & Schofield "commands the courtroom," claimed observers. He "knows how to capture the attention and imagination of the jury," leading to success in both the commercial and white-collar domains. Max Blecher (see p.279) of Blecher & Collins is a stellar commercial litigator with great powers of persuasion in the courtroom. "Talented securities litigator" Bruce Vanyo (see p.319) is now a significant drawing card at Katten Muchin Rosenman LLP having recently joined from Wilson Sonsini. Larry Feldman (see

p.288) at Kaye Scholer LLP applies his "common sense and strong litigation skills" to a wide range of civil cases, both for plaintiffs and defendants. He successfully represented a client in a suit brought by Univision attempting to prevent the client's ratings service from existing. Christensen, Miller, Fink, Jacobs, Glaser, Weil & Shapiro LLP's Patricia Glaser is counted among the top litigators in the state, by peers. A "tough trial lawyer," she co-heads the firm's commercial litigation practice. Ward Johnson (see p.296), at Mayer, Brown, Rowe & Maw LLP is "an accomplished litigator," clients said. Articulate in the courtroom, he is "aggressive yet polite," with "the unique ability to get inside the other parties' strategy." A general litigator, he has been involved in technology, telecom and media-related disputes, and recently achieved a $14 million jury verdict for Philips Semiconductors against a supplier of a defective plastic molding compound. Alan Schulman (see p.312) of Bernstein Litowitz Berger & Grossmann LLP is best known for his work in the field of securities litigation. He heads the firm's West Coast office in San Diego. At Kirkland & Ellis LLP, highly regarded Los Angeles partner Jeffrey Davidson's (see p.285) varied business trial practice has taken in securities, antitrust, IP and mass torts. From Arguedas, Cassman & Headley LLP, Cristina Arguedas is consistently named as "one of the most respected practitioners in the Bay area." Peers noted: "In every instance she proves that she is one of the most effective lawyers in the state." With Corbin & Fitzgerald LLP's Robert Corbin "you really get your bang for your buck." He handles cases for individual defendants utilizing his "uncanny ability to assist folks in a way that makes them feel comfortable." At the same time, however, "he sizes up the predicament they face with great acuity." Stephen Miller of the Law Offices of Stephen D Miller PC has a thriving practice in the white-collar field. He defends corporations, political figures and others against federal and state criminal investigations and indictments. At McKenna Long & Aldridge LLP, Robert Brewer (see p.280) represented Alvarado Hospital in a four-month trial alleging healthcare violations. He acts for officers and companies in all aspects of federal grand jury investigations, allegations of unauthorized conduct, and internal investigations and audits. George Cotsirilos, of Cotsirilos & Campisano LLP combines outstanding written briefs with "masterful trial lawyer's perception" of the courtroom. Akin Gump Strauss Hauer & Feld LLP's Stephen Mansfield (see p.301) is "extraordinarily bright and a terrific tactical thinker," said peers. He manages the San Francisco office as well as being resident in Los Angeles, and enjoys a wide-ranging white-collar criminal and civil practice. Sole practitioner Donald Re is a "terrific trial practitioner," according to observers who "love watching him work."

# MEDIA & ENTERTAINMENT

## LITIGATION

## Band 1

### Alschuler Grossman Stein & Kahan LLP

See firm details p.323

**The Firm:** The incredibly dedicated lawyers at Alschuler Grossman have earned the firm a position at the forefront of the talent market, both in terms of domestic and international representation. Members advise "*an extremely prestigious clientele*" that hails from the TV, music and film industries. The team's outstanding service and successful track record right across the board is believed to rest upon its "*zealous and aggressive representation of clients.*" As one commentator remarked: "*It has one speed. Full speed ahead.*" The outfit represents A-list stars, producers, directors, writers, agents and independent production companies in mediation, arbitration and litigation. The team recently filed a claim on behalf of RDF Media, the producers of Wife Swap, alleging that Fox Broadcasting infringed its copyright in creating the show Trading Spouses. This is widely heralded as an important test case for how the courts will deal with the widespread theft of programming in the reality TV arena.

**The Lawyers:** The formidable **Larry Stein** (see p.315) was billed as "*one of the most feared litigators in LA.*" As one market observer remarked, "*the man is brilliant.*" This "*sophisticated bulldog*" has been involved in a series of vertical integration cases on behalf of television stars, including David Duchovny and Alan Alda, challenging sweetheart deals that cheated talent out of their profit participation. Although recognized predominantly as a general commercial litigator, **Marshall Grossman** (see p.292) regularly advises on complex entertainment disputes. His "*no-nonsense approach and impeccable*

*grasp of the fundamental issues at hand*" drew plaudits from clients. Exceptional entertainment litigator **Michael Plonsker** (see p.307) enters the table having recently been at the forefront of several major developments concerning idea submission, defamation, copyright infringement, Internet disputes, right of privacy and right of publicity.

**Clients/Work Highlights:** Celador International; William Morris Agency; Castaway Television Productions; Village Roadshow; Mary-Kate and Ashley Olsen; Paris Hilton; Rick Dees; Jodie Foster; Billy Bob Thornton; Meg Ryan; Lucy Lawless; Kevin Sorbo; Sean Hayes; Rosa Blasi; Sugar Ray Leonard; Stephanie Seymour; Aisha Tyler; Estate of John Ritter; Seth MacFarlane; Michael Jackson; Prince; Harrison Ford; Tony Hawk; Madonna; Mel Gibson; Jennifer Lopez; Jennifer Love Hewitt; RJ (Robert) Wagner; Clint Eastwood; Rob Lowe and Mariah Carey.

### Christensen, Miller, Fink, Jacobs, Glaser, Weil & Shapiro, LLP

**The Firm:** Clients return time and again to this team of "*creative trouble shooters*" for first-class expertise and support. They emphasize that its attorneys "*never lose their composure, even in the midst of the most intricate entertainment matters.*" Another commentator summed the group up as a "*bunch of tough litigators with a great breadth of resources to draw upon.*" The firm recently filed suit on behalf of the Saul Zaentz Company against New Line Cinema, alleging that New Line had failed to pay Zaentz over $19 million owed from exploitation of the first Lord of the Rings film and, further, that New Line was in a similar position with regard to the two Lord of the Rings sequels. Elsewhere, this top-quality operation defended a former officer and director of Gemstar-TV Guide in an action filed by the SEC relating to shareholder litigation against Gemstar's former management. It successfully negotiated a complex settlement agreement with the SEC and a separate agreement with Gemstar resolving all allegations against its client.

**The Lawyers:** "*Highly intelligent gunslinger*" **Patricia Glaser** "*does not take any prisoners,*" rivals say with admiration. Observers describe this incredibly hard worker as being "*among the most honorable and loyal attorneys going.*" According to clients, she is able to "*resolve multiple issues promptly, is persuasive in court and has a larger-than-life personality.*" The "*exceedingly professional*" **Joie Marie Gallo** received accolades from all quarters for her hard work and comprehensive expertise.

**Clients/Work Highlights:** Sony Pictures Entertainment; Sony Electronics; Rod Stewart; Kelsey Grammer; Nick Nolte; Bob Barker; Barbra Streisand; Elton John; Don Felder; Sean Connery and Paula Abdul.

### Davis Wright Tremaine LLP

**The Firm:** This is a "*professional and highly accomplished*" First Amendment team with considerable depth and an impressive client base that is nationwide in scope. According to clients the firm is "*full of exceptionally bright, strategic litigators who can deal with matters effortlessly.*" Interviewees acknowledged this group's "*broad industry knowledge and exposure,*" and appreciated its intelligent use of resources. Its lawyers represented a plaintiff class of more than 27,000 songwriters and music publishers in one of the most talked-about cases of the year, Metro-Goldwyn-Mayer Studios et al v Grokster et al. The case related to the copying of music on Internet peer-to-peer file-sharing services. Moreover, the team co-counseled the defendants in SB Beach Properties v Berti, which involved the application of California's anti-SLAPP statute. This is an ongoing dispute between plaintiff SB Beach Properties and some of its limited partners for breach of fiduciary duty, breach of contract and breach of the covenant of good faith and fair dealing.

**The Lawyers:** "*Razor-sharp*" **Kelli Sager** is "*amazingly quick on her feet, a tireless worker and has one of the best minds in the market.*" This skilled advocate focuses on defending cases relating to areas such as defamation, privacy, copyright and trademark, misappropriation, court access and reporter's privilege. One interviewee noted: "*If she's on the other side, run for your life because she could squash you like a bug.*" The "*level-headed*" **Thomas Burke** has "*a permanent sense of calmness about him that inspires confidence,*" say clients. This "*enthusiastic and bright player*" is no stranger to representing Internet publishers and new media players in cutting-edge media cases, though he also represents more traditional clients including newspapers, TV networks, movie studios and journalists. Defense of libel actions and cases concerning privacy, rights of publicity and news gathering issues all contribute to his caseload. Clients report that the insightful **Alonzo Wickers** mixes "*intelligence and charm with a genuine passion for the practice area.*" He has advised on First Amendment and IP issues surrounding Comedy Central programs at the pre-production and pre-broadcast stage, including South Park, Drawn Together, Reno 911, Con, Weekends at the DL, Mind of Mencia, Distractions and The Showbiz Show.

**Clients/Work Highlights:** CNN; the Los Angeles Times; ANG Newspapers; The Associated Press; Metro Publishing; The McGraw-Hill Companies; The New York Times; Paramount Pictures; Condé Nast Publications; Courtroom Television Network; MTV Networks; Warner Bros.; Fox Entertainment Group; CBS Broadcasting; ABC and NBC.

### Greenberg Glusker Fields Claman Machtinger & Kinsella LLP

**The Firm:** The firm's elite media and entertainment group with its "*first-rate partners and strong supporting cast*" comfortably retains a place in the

## Media & Entertainment: Litigation
### Leading Individuals

**1** FIELDS Bertram *Greenberg Glusker Fields Claman*
  GLASER Patricia *Christensen, Miller, Fink*
  SAGER Kelli *Davis Wright Tremaine LLP*
  SINGER Martin *Lavely & Singer PC*
  STEIN Larry *Alschuler Grossman Stein*

**2** BOSTWICK Gary *Sheppard, Mullin*
  CUMMINS Guylyn *Sheppard, Mullin*
  FRACKMAN Russell *Mitchell, Silberberg*
  GROSSMAN Marshall *Alschuler Grossman Stein*
  HEINKE Rex *Akin Gump Strauss Hauer*
  KENDALL Richard *Irell & Manella LLP*
  LAVELY JR John *Lavely & Singer PC*
  OLSON Ronald *Munger, Tolles*
  PETRICH Louis *Leopold, Petrich*

**3** ALEXANDER Judith *Winn & Alexander LLP*
  BASICH Anthony *Hogan & Hartson LLP*
  BOUTROUS JR Theodore *Gibson, Dunn*
  BURKE Thomas *Davis Wright Tremaine LLP*
  EDELMAN Scott *Gibson, Dunn*
  FELDMAN Larry *Kaye Scholer LLP*
  KENYON Charity *Riegels Campos*
  MARENBERG Steven *Irell & Manella LLP*
  MEISINGER Louis *Sheppard, Mullin*
  POMERANTZ Glenn *Munger, Tolles*
  QUINN John *Quinn Emanuel*
  SCHWARTZ Robert *O'Melveny & Myers*
  STEINTHAL Kenneth *Weil, Gotshal*
  WHITE Andrew *White O'Connor Curry*
  WICKERS IV Alonzo *Davis Wright Tremaine LLP*

**4** BERGMAN Michael *Weissmann, Wolff*
  CHADWICK James *DLA Piper Rudnick*
  CRAVEN Erica *Levy, Ram & Olson*
  GALLO Joie Marie *Christensen, Miller*
  GOODKIND Jim *Loeb & Loeb LLP*
  GREENSPAN Eric *Myman, Abell*
  KINSELLA Dale *Greenberg Glusker*
  LITVACK Sanford *Hogan & Hartson LLP*
  MAYER Patricia *Mitchell, Silberberg*
  MYERS Roger *DLA Piper Rudnick*
  OLSON Karl *Levy, Ram & Olson*
  PLONSKER Michael *Alschuler Grossman Stein*
  TITLE Gail *Katten Muchin Rosenman LLP*

top tier. "*High-level expertise and counsel who know how to drive a hard bargain*" mean that, according to clients, this practice is "*nationally known as one of the best, a reputation that it undoubtedly lives up to.*" The team is renowned for its representation of sophisticated clientele including high-profile individual talent, major studios and recording companies.

**The Lawyers:** The heart and soul of the practice is "*godfather*" **Bertram Fields**. One client went so far as to say: "*If you don't know Bert you have not lived. The man is a genuine Californian success story.*" Under his strong leadership, the firm is said to have won an incredible client roster, making him one of the most sought-after attorneys in the state. New entry **Dale**

Kinsella impressed clients as "*a tough and tenacious litigator.*"
**Clients/Work Highlights:** Paramount; Joel Silver; Twentieth Century Fox; MGM; Tom Cruise; Mike Nichols; James Cameron; Dustin Hoffman and Warren Beatty.

## Lavely & Singer PC

**The Firm:** The long-established entertainment litigation boutique has met with "*huge success and respect*" in representing individual talent, according to interviewees. As such, its much-envied practice is considered part of the fabric of the entertainment industry. The workload includes a range of media and new media work, relating to defamation, rights of publicity and privacy, IP, Internet issues, contract disputes and labor and employment law.

**The Lawyers:** Leading talent litigator **Martin Singer** is renowned for "*coming out with all guns blazing,*" an approach that clients find works exceptionally well. He is believed to have "*one of the best client lists in the business*" and combines "*an aggressive approach with amazing judgment.*" The "*intellectually astute and hard-working*" **John Lavely** is described as an "*incredibly diligent practitioner,*" and perceived as naturally belonging to the upper echelons of entertainment litigators.

**Clients/Work Highlights:** The firm represents among others actors, directors, recording artists, producers and writers.

## Band 2

### DLA Piper Rudnick Gray Cary US LLP
See firm details p.870

**The Firm:** Clients credit the firm with an outstanding reputation and first-class resources for serving media and entertainment interests. Special praise was reserved for its thriving First Amendment practice, members of which were described as being "*finely attuned to the nuances of the practice area and not too aggressive.*" A wide range of clients includes television companies, key newspapers and radio networks as well as online and book publishers. Complex privacy and defamation matters have come to the fore of late. According to interviewees, the firm has gone from strength to strength despite the loss of partner Ed Davis, who joined the litigation department of Orrick in San Francisco. It recently represented the defendant in Barrett v Rosenthal before the California Supreme Court, a case expected to determine the scope of ISP immunity in California from defamation under Section 230 of the federal Communications Decency Act. In addition, the team advised the California First Amendment Coalition in CFAC v Schwarzenegger, a case arising from a lawsuit under the California Public Records Act where access to the records of the Governor's top aides was sought.

**The Lawyers:** The widely admired **James Chadwick** (see p.282) has an excellent track record, particularly where issues concerning the First Amendment, trademark, privacy and white-collar crime are

concerned. Another First Amendment lawyer to have impressed the market is former newspaper reporter **Roger Myers** (see p.304), who was dubbed "*bright, thorough and ethical.*"

**Clients/Work Highlights:** The New York Times Company; Knight-Ridder and its California flagship publication The San Jose Mercury News; Lee Enterprises; MediaNews Group; Ottaway Newspapers; Gannett; Associated Press; Time Warner; Newsweek; Mother Jones; Business Wire; CNET; NBC; HBO; John Wiley & Sons and Courthouse News.

## Irell & Manella LLP

**The Firm:** Above all, this firm is considered the "*best in the business*" for IP copyright and trademark litigation, though the firm's entertainment litigation group was praised for its ambition and strength, not to mention its handling of complex, high-stakes media litigation. In Threshold v Osbournes it defended MTV Networks against claims concerning the rights to a show about the Osbourne family. The firm also took a lead role in Ransohoff v Paramount, where it defended Paramount against a producer's claim that Paramount allegedly broke an oral promise to make a film.

**The Lawyers:** Interviewees cited the "*professionalism and energy*" of nationally renowned **Richard Kendall** as key to the team's success. He recently wrapped up a victory for Viacom Outdoor against plaintiffs who sued for $80 million. Kendall turned the tables and won compensatory and punitive damages from the plaintiffs. Hot on his heels is the "*simply fantastic*" **Steven Marenberg**, who successfully represented Universal Music Group before the California Supreme Court in HLC Properties v MCA Records, a case concerning the scope of the attorney-client privilege in California. He was also successful in his defense of Mark Burnett, Donald Trump and NBC Universal in Bethea v Burnett, concerning a copyright infringement case involving the NBC television series 'The Apprentice'.

**Clients/Work Highlights:** CBS Broadcasting; Infinity Broadcasting; MTV Networks; Paramount Pictures; Showtime Networks; UPN and Viacom Outdoor.

## Mitchell, Silberberg & Knupp LLP

**The Firm:** Clients were united in praising this "*excellent group of entertainment lawyers, who know exactly how to get things done.*" It is perceived as having genuine strength on both transactional and regulatory fronts, where it advises music companies, major producers, distributors, and video game and Internet companies. Expertise relating to the involvement of financial institutions in the entertainment sector is also on offer. With regard to individual talent, it advises actors, directors, producers and musical artists.

**The Lawyers:** Clients were impressed by **Russell Frackman**'s determination to "*get the job done properly.*" This "*extraordinarily well-versed*" litigator is considered "*a true great*" in the media and entertainment field. The understated **Patricia Mayer** "*always does a fine job for her clients.*"

**Clients/Work Highlights:** Motion Picture Association of America; Recording Industry Association of America; BMG and Arista Records.

## Munger, Tolles & Olson LLP

**The Firm:** According to sources the team here is renowned for its "*awe-inspiring success in high-profile trials.*" It mainly advises studios and networks involved in complex disputes.

**The Lawyers:** Interviewees identified **Ronald Olson** as a "*big-shot trial lawyer*" who comes across as "*thoroughly credible on every issue.*" One client spoke of Olson's "*gift of being able to inspire confidence in anyone; I would trust him with my life.*" **Glenn Pomerantz** won his fair share of praise as a "*hard-working and straight-forward attorney.*"

**Clients/Work Highlights:** Universal Music Group; NBC Universal; Twentieth Century Fox; Warner Bros.; Activision; Brillstein-Grey Entertainment and House of Blues.

## O'Melveny & Myers LLP

See firm details p.336

**The Firm:** O'Melveny & Myers maintains its position in the table upon receiving substantial market approval for its "*amazing breadth and depth*" in the media and entertainment arena. It is deemed to be strengthening its position in California and nationally, via a cadre of "*resourceful, business-minded and proficient*" lawyers. Clients spoke enthusiastically about the firm's capacity to offer "*fresh spirit, solid, rigorous advice and a whole heap of new ideas.*"

**The Lawyers:** **Robert Schwartz** (see p.312) was described in research as the cornerstone of this group, and widely hailed as "*an exceedingly influential player.*" A "*consummate entertainment lawyer,*" he provides superior advice to record companies, motion picture studios, TV and cable networks and individual producers on complex contractual issues.

**Clients/Work Highlights:** Clients include New Line Cinema, Time Warner and Sony Pictures.

## Sheppard, Mullin, Richter & Hampton LLP

**The Firm:** There was agreement among market sources that this firm has cultivated the best connections in the market when it comes to representing motion picture studios and independent production companies. This supportive team, which offers a choice of "*talented attorneys who complement each other well,*" is proficient in areas including TV, publishing, sports, music, home video, licensing and branded entertainment. Clients state that it is "*deeply committed to building an even stronger practice,*" with media sector activity being the focus of recent growth.

**The Lawyers:** Clients discern "*a truly diligent practitioner and excellent performer*" in **Gary Bostwick**, who concentrates on First Amendment cases. **Guylyn Cummins** impresses peers and clients alike with her "*in-depth knowledge of cutting-edge issues.*" Another standout practitioner is rainmaker **Louis Meisinger**, who offers clients "*unquestionably sound judgment.*"

**Clients/Work Highlights:** Disney; Paramount Pictures; Sony; New Line Cinema and The Marketing Store Worldwide.

## White O'Connor Curry & Avanzado LLP

**The Firm:** A well-deserved reputation for all-around competence and exceptional media and entertainment representation ensures this firm its place in the table. Commentators note its close ties with key client CBS, and admire the "*first-rate work*" conducted by the firm's attorneys. Its trial attorneys offer alternative dispute resolution services, "*but are more than willing*" to litigate complex entertainment and business matters.

**The Lawyers:** The tenacious **Andrew White** elicits praise from clients for his "*superb ability to try any case.*" As one client remarked: "*He does not play any games, he simply goes in and does what he has to.*"

**Clients/Work Highlights:** Viacom, MTV Networks and CBS Broadcasting can all be counted as clients.

## Band 3

## Gibson, Dunn & Crutcher LLP

See firm details p.328

**The Firm:** Clients appreciate the structure of this group, saying: "*Here is a cohesive team that makes the best possible use of resources at the same time as allowing lawyers to work independently where necessary.*" It is renowned for its handling of contentious defamation, copyright and trademark issues. The firm was involved in the representation of a coalition of key media organizations including, among others, NBC, CBS and Fox News, in a case to secure access to the records and proceedings associated with the Michael Jackson criminal trial. In a different case, Matthew Cooper and Time Inc v United States, the firm took a lead role in representing Time magazine reporter Matthew Cooper and Time in proceedings relating to the disclosure of Valerie Plame as a CIA operative.

**The Lawyers:** **Theodore Boutrous** (see p.280) is an "*esteemed appellate lawyer, who is enormously dogged,*" say clients. He has been at the forefront of some of the highest-profile cases in the country and has carefully defended his client's interests. The "*smart, talented and professional*" **Scott Edelman** (see p.287), who cochairs the media and entertainment group, is perceived as "*a dominant figure in the area.*" In Merchant v Columbia Tri-Star Home Entertainment et al, he was lead counsel for Columbia. The case concerned a lawsuit brought by independent video retailers against the major studios and Blockbuster challenging the revenue-sharing model applied to the distribution of videotapes to the major video chains.

**Clients/Work Highlights:** Sony Entertainment; Fox Broadcasting; Dow Jones; The Wall Street Journal; Sony Music; Warner Bros. Records; NBC Universal; Intertainment; Evergreen Studios; CNN; the Los Angeles Times and The New York Times.

## Hogan & Hartson LLP

See firm details p.568

**The Firm:** Clients value the "*upfront approach*" of its lawyers and their ability to convert "*high-caliber skills into legal victories.*" Interviewees applaud the firm for its breadth and depth, particularly with regard to regulatory and antitrust issues in media and entertainment contexts. Recent highlights include obtaining a favorable arbitration award for Buena Vista Home Entertainment in a dispute with Blockbuster arising out of a November 1997 revenue sharing agreement. The group also represented Disney before the federal court in Los Angeles, in Marvel v Disney.

**The Lawyers:** The highly tactical **Anthony Basich** (see p.278) is "*attuned to the strategic business interests of clients,*" and is described as "*bright, practical and assiduous.*" **Sanford Litvack** (see p.300) enters the table having been showered with praise by clients who find him to be "*ultra alert, brilliantly calculating and very thorough.*"

**Clients/Work Highlights:** News Corporation; Fox Entertainment Group; Fox Cable Networks; Disney; Sony Corporation of America; Gemstar-TV Guide International and DIRECTV.

## Levy, Ram & Olson

**The Firm:** Clients praise this significant player for "*providing precise guidance and being quick to respond if we have a problem.*" It is held in particularly high regard for acting on behalf of newspapers in media litigation, especially where First Amendment and public records issues are involved. The team represented The Modesto Bee and the Los Angeles Times in successfully vacating a trial court's gag order that prohibited all parties from speaking about a criminal prosecution relating to a farm worker's exposure to dangerous pesticides.

**The Lawyers:** **Erica Craven** is referred to as a "*diligent and thorough attorney,*" and enjoys an expanding practice in the field. Meanwhile, the "*super-smart and effective*" **Karl Olson** is a pleasure to deal with. He represented the Contra Costa Times in seeking access to the names and salary information of highly paid government employees. Having won at the Superior Court and Court of Appeal, the case is currently pending before the California Supreme Court.

**Clients/Work Highlights:** The San Francisco Chronicle, a Hearst Corporation publication; Contra Costa Times, a Knight-Ridder publication; The Sacramento Bee and The Modesto Bee, McClatchy Corporation publications; the Los Angeles Times and Bloomberg Media.

## Loeb & Loeb LLP

See firm details p.334

**The Firm:** This outfit is renowned for the "*fantastic judgment of its attorneys.*" The firm's client-friendly and service-oriented approach in dealing with media and entertainment matters also wins accolades from clients.

**The Lawyers:** The "*outstandingly smart*" **Jim Goodkind** (see p.291) enters the table as the firm's standout entertainment lawyer.

**Clients/Work Highlights:** Woody Allen; William Morris Agency; Bertelsmann; Poppe Tyson; Dixie Chicks; Oprah Winfrey and Regis Philbin.

## Quinn Emanuel Urquhart Oliver & Hedges, LLP

See firm details p.340

**The Firm:** This contender, which *"can hit hard when it needs to,"* won endorsement from all quarters for its outstanding trial work. One client went as far as to say: *"Be it IP, general litigation or media and entertainment law – the firm impresses in all of these areas."* It is renowned for advising the Academy of Motion Picture Arts and Sciences, the National Academy of Recording Arts and Sciences and the Academy of Television Arts and Sciences. Production companies, major talent, networks and studios also feature as clients, which the firm represents in a broad array of contract and IP disputes.

**The Lawyers:** When commenting on **John Quinn** (see p.309), peers and clients concurred that *"not many people take him on and come out victorious."*

**Clients/Work Highlights:** CBS Broadcasting; HBO; Warner Bros.; DIRECTV and Fox Entertainment Group.

## Riegels Campos & Kenyon

**The Firm:** First Amendment matters are considered to be where this firm's true forte lies. The media and entertainment outfit maintains its market position in light of affirmative client feedback for its *"creative and intelligent outlook."*

**The Lawyers:** *"Unflappable and determined,"* **Charity Kenyon** provides clients with *"a superior service and enjoys a great deal of credibility in the market."* According to rivals, *"she is deceptively easy-going; but don't underestimate her."*

**Clients/Work Highlights:** The firm has a number of newspaper clients and local television stations on its books.

## Winn & Alexander LLP

**The Firm:** According to clients, this firm's name has true gravitas in the media and entertainment sphere, particularly with regard to First Amendment matters. Highlights include involvement in International Federation of Professional & Technical Engineers v Superior Court of Alameda County. This is a California Public Records Act case that is expected to decide whether the public has a right to know the name and salary of public employees in the State of California. The firm's clients in this matter comprise most of the major California newspaper chains supporting Contra Costa Newspapers and names such as the California Newspaper Publishers Association and the Los Angeles Times.

**The Lawyers:** For many clients interviewed, **Judith Alexander** *"commits 100% to every case she works on."*

**Clients/Work Highlights:** The Monterey County Herald; the Santa Cruz Sentinel; the Spartan Daily; Capital Cities/ABC; NBC; Fox Television; Ingonish Films; San Francisco magazine; Mother Jones magazine and The Stanford Daily.

## Other Notable Practitioners

The *"smart and rock-solid"* **Rex Heinke** (see p.293) of Akin Gump Strauss Hauer & Feld LLP is held in high esteem throughout the state for his media work and is acknowledged as a *"tremendous appellate lawyer."* First Amendment, general media and IP issues feature in his demanding workload and he is applauded for his representation of newspapers, magazines, motion picture studios, TV networks and Internet clients. *"Highly skilled"* **Louis Petrich** of

Leopold, Petrich & Smith is seen as *"a bright, competent and professional"* entertainment litigator who is *"honorable and true to his word."* Peers agree that *"nobody can question the high quality of his work"* for the likes of DreamWorks SKG; MGM; Paramount Pictures; Sony; Twentieth Century Fox; Universal Studios and Motion Picture Association of America. **Larry Feldman** (see p.288) at Kaye Scholer LLP is *"a superb commercial litigator"* and a *"fantastic trial lawyer,"* whose practice has expanded to encompass general business law and legal malpractice as well as entertainment cases. *"Top-drawer"* trial attorney **Kenneth Steinthal** (see p.316) at Weil, Gotshal & Manges LLP co-heads the firm's IP and media practice. He concentrates on the music sector as well as the broader entertainment and television industries, both in the United States and internationally. His clients include AOL; Yahoo!; MTV Networks; Real-Networks; Listen.com; MusicNet; Disney/ABC; Viacom's cable and satellite services; ESPN; Discovery Communications; USA Networks; The WB Network; Lodgenet Entertainment; Univision Communications and WorldSpace. The *"highly competent and incredibly tenacious"* **Michael Bergman** of Weissmann, Wolff, Bergman, Coleman, Grodin & Evall, LLP concentrates on complex IP matters and business disputes within the entertainment industry. **Eric Greenspan** of Myman, Abell, Fineman, Greenspan & Light LLP sustains his position in the table and is best known for his presence in music industry matters. New entry **Gail Title** (see p.317) of Katten Muchin Rosenman LLP is held in high regard for doing a *"fabulous job for her clients."* High-profile clients of hers include NBC Universal; Miramax; Imagine Entertainment and MGM.

---

# MEDIA & ENTERTAINMENT TRANSACTIONAL

## Band 1

### Akin Gump Strauss Hauer & Feld LLP

See firm details p.559

**The Firm:** Clients agree that the attorneys at this firm can both *"talk the talk and walk the walk"* where sophisticated matters are concerned. It wins promotion in the tables having received a shower of praise from market sources, not least as an *"amazing outfit that offers knowledge and expertise second to none."* Members of the group are perceived to be *"unafraid of tackling any case and capable of always producing high-quality work."* Recent highlights include representing Deutsche Bank in connection with a portion of the $500 million financing for Legendary Pictures' Production Financing Distribution Agreement with Warner Bros. It also assisted Mobius Entertainment with the acquisition of Capitol Films and represented 2929 Entertainment in negotiations with Steven Soderbergh relating to a Production Financing Distribution Agreement. Further proof of its incredible versatility is to be found in the firm's representa-

tion of Yahoo! in connection with all Internet, film, television, music and other entertainment products, and in its counseling of Bob Dylan with respect to his music, entertainment and business transactions. Clients enjoy working with the group's attorneys because *"they are proactive problem solvers who get the deal done."*

**The Lawyers:** **John Burke** takes a *"pragmatic approach"* and provides high-quality advice that is sensitive to client needs. Indeed, clients sang his praises for *"always being available, and protecting our position in a professional and fearless manner."* According to peers, he is *"conservative by nature but proactive in getting deals done and has a finely tuned understanding of the industry."* Meanwhile, *"clients who want diligent representation should hire the astonishing"* **Steve Fayne** (see p.288), say sources. He deals with complex motion picture and television finance transactions and is *"incredibly creative and resourceful."* The highly responsive **Marissa Román** (see p.310) was also credited with making a significant contribution to the team's success.

**Clients/Work Highlights:** 2929 Entertainment; Bob Dylan; Bank of Ireland; Clear Channel Communications; Union Bank of California; Comerica Bank; Deutsche Bank; DrKW; MGM and Yahoo!

## Gang Tyre Ramer & Brown

**The Firm:** Billed as a "*rich practice that puts other firms in the shade*," this well-established Beverly Hills entertainment boutique is celebrated as a magnet for stage, motion picture, screen and music talent. It has a particularly strong track record in transactional and corporate cases, leading market sources note. According to clients, it boasts "*classy, smart and creative lawyers*" who provide first-class advice.
**The Lawyers:** There was some consensus among interviewees that **Donald Passman** has something of the genius about him, while one commentator branded him "*the best music lawyer in America: he hits everybody's top note.*" The "*gentlemanly*" **Bruce Ramer** is a definite leader, who is widely trusted and respected, according to clients. "*A genuinely accom-*

plished technical lawyer" with a "*brain the size of a planet*," he came in for further praise for his "*honesty, diplomacy and professionalism.*" **Harald Brown** is highly rated as an absolutely superb entertainment lawyer, who interviewees admire for his "*decency, great ability and brilliant sense of humor.*"
**Clients/Work Highlights:** Clint Eastwood; Janet Jackson; Steven Spielberg; Tina Turner; REM; Robert Zemeckis; Milos Forman and Ben Stiller.

## Hansen Jacobson Teller Hoberman Newman, Warren, Sloane & Richman, LLP

**The Firm:** This high-flying outfit frequently deals with complicated issues in which it represents "*sophisticated*" producers, writers and artists. Its attorneys are much in demand for their great business sense, and observers noted a growing emphasis on the corporate arena. Clients regard the team as "*incredibly responsive, methodical and always willing to go the extra mile to achieve success.*" According to leading market commentators, this firm is ever more visible in terms of advising on reality TV issues.
**The Lawyers:** "*If Superman were real, he would be*" **Tom Hansen**, one client enthused. He is said to have met with phenomenal success in matters relating to TV and motion pictures by "*combining stunning proficiency with a lethal intellect.*" The energetic **Craig Jacobson** enters the tables upon receiving positive feedback from clients who say: "*He knows the TV business like the back of his hand.*" Clients simply love **Jeanne Newman**, who is "*cooperative and keen to go above and beyond the call of duty to win a case for her clients.*" She is best known for advising Hollywood producers and TV companies.
**Clients/Work Highlights:** The firm is known for acting as counsel to prominent individual talents and significant companies on film and commercial matters.

## O'Melveny & Myers LLP

See firm details p.336
**The Firm:** Sources had nothing but praise for this "*very classy group of individuals,*" which is considered to have secured a statewide and national reputation for excellence. Its diligent partners are renowned for their involvement in large financing transactions, M&A and joint ventures within the entertainment field. A happy marriage of "*acute attention to detail in fact gathering and creativity*" was deemed to be the signature of this team's work product.
**The Lawyers:** Throughout his involvement in large media sector joint ventures and M&A, **Joseph Calabrese** (see p.281) has proven himself to be "*constantly on the ball.*" "*Technical whizz kid*" **Christopher Murray** (see p.304) is "*simply great to deal with on the other side,*" say rivals. A "*fantastically smart*" attorney, he sustains a multifaceted practice centering on the production, financing and distribution of motion pictures and TV programs. Also new to the tables is the seasoned **Stephen Scharf** (see p.312) who is "*on the shortlist of all the big clients,*" according to interviewees.
**Clients/Work Highlights:** Hyundai; TeleImage and

M6 Television (France); Convergence PLC (UK); Japan Broadcasting Corporation; Korakuen (Tokyo Dome International); Marubeni; NHK Enterprises and Tokyo Broadcasting System.

## Ziffren Brittenham Branca Fischer Gilbert-Lurie & Stiffelman LLP

**The Firm:** The "*great strategic advisers*" at this firm provide "*high-quality global business advice,*" clients say. Clearly a top-tier player, this pure entertainment boutique receives accolades for the lengths to which its "*resourceful and assiduous*" attorneys go on behalf of clients. These include eminent talent and companies within multimedia, TV, motion picture and music industries.
**The Lawyers:** "*Masterful deal-maker*" **Skip Brittenham** was identified as the "*principal driving force*" at the outfit. Having been repeatedly cast as a power broker among major players in TV, music and motion picture industries, researchers were left in no doubt that he is "*on top of everybody's list.*" Sources concurred that **Kenneth Ziffren** is "*trusted implicitly by everyone in the industry,*" and entertainment clients have the highest possible regard for this "*simply brilliant über counsel.*" **John Branca** is admired as a distinguished and highly experienced music specialist, while **Samuel Fischer** "*channels his aggression perfectly into his first-class representation of clients.*" The "*passionate and dedicated*" **Melanie Cook** works hard to protect her clients' interests, while **David Nochimson** is described as "*a bright and affable, gentlemanlike lawyer.*"
**Clients/Work Highlights:** Liberty Media; Bruce Willis; Céline Dion; Harrison Ford; Eddie Murphy and DreamWorks SKG.

## Band 2

### Irell & Manella LLP

**The Firm:** This firm's "*meticulous and highly effective attorneys*" were noted by sources as "*enjoying a great, nationwide reputation in the entertainment industry.*" The team advises clients on virtually all issues in the field, whether transactional or contentious in nature, and offers stellar expertise in related areas such as IP. Its high-profile clientele includes financial institutions and individual financiers as well as studios, actors, talent agencies, producers and writers. Vastly qualified practitioners represent a number of studios, including Paramount Pictures, MTV Networks, MGM, Nickelodeon and LucasFilm. The firm won plaudits for its extensive involvement in the reality TV arena, including shows such as 'The Apprentice', 'Survivor', 'Contender' and 'Rockstar'.
**The Lawyers:** Clients acknowledge the "*exceptionally bright*" **Clark Siegel** as having "*blossomed in recent years,*" and he is said to have accrued "*extensive knowledge*" of advising parties on the finance aspects of sophisticated matters. Meanwhile, **Juliette Youngblood** is said to never fail in "*simply making clients happy.*" She provides "*wonderful entertainment and IP advice*" to motion picture, TV, mobile media and advertising clients.

**Clients/Work Highlights:** Paramount Pictures; Pixar; NBC Universal; LucasFilm; Nickelodeon; MTV Networks; ABC; CBS Broadcasting; NEC; Universal Music Group; Recording Industry Association of America (RIAA); Activision; THQ; Charter Communications; Classic Media; Broadway Video and Technicolor.

## Loeb & Loeb LLP

See firm details p.334

**The Firm:** The firm's top-caliber lawyers make for a particularly powerful entertainment team, which clients rate highly for its commitment to their businesses. As one remarked: "*This is a genuinely impressive operation, with lawyers who really understand our goals.*" Entertainment finance, film and TV production and distribution, as well as music and theater matters all contribute to the workload. Special praise was reserved for its involvement in complex international co-production and co-financing transactions. In this respect, banks, funds and bond companies all feature as clients.

**The Lawyers:** **Michael Mayerson** (see p.302) is an "*excellent attorney, who is good at pinpointing and dealing with issues.*" His client roster includes names such as Diana Ross, Glenn Close, Anthony Hopkins, Gary Oldman, the Dixie Chicks and the Grateful Dead. **John Frankenheimer** (see p.289) "*brings masses of ideas to the table*" when it comes to music advice, clients say.

**Clients/Work Highlights:** Lakeshore Entertainment Group; Media Monster; Merrill Lynch; MySpace; Newmarket Capital Group; Platinum Studios; Robert Rodriguez; Ryan Seacrest Productions; Saban Capital Group; Spectacor; Union Bank of California; X-Filme Creative Pool; Woody Allen; Anthony Hopkins; Bavaria Media; Carsey-Werner; Citibank; Digimax and HSBC.

## Manatt Phelps & Phillips LLP

**The Firm:** "*A firm with great breadth*" is how clients summed up this offering. Observers cited the team's "*industrious and effective approach*" as being key to its ability to form robust client relations on a state and national level. Its lawyers attracted further praise for their "*intelligence, creativity and integrity.*" Clients include major recording artists and composers, record companies and publishing companies.

**The Lawyers:** Music specialist **Lee Phillips** is respected throughout the state. Clients noted that he brings a "*mature, rational viewpoint*" to cases.

**Clients/Work Highlights:** The Eagles; Glenn Frey; Kenny Loggins; Lisa Marie Presley; Tracy Chapman; Josh Groban; Yanni; Cher and the Rolling Stones.

## Sheppard, Mullin, Richter & Hampton LLP

**The Firm:** The firm's entertainment group received plenty of accolades for its "*competence, timeliness and quality of service.*" It represents prominent TV networks, motion picture studios and independent production companies, as well as other institutional entertainment and media clients. Characterized as "*tough and versatile,*" the team covers a broad

mixture of issues concerning the development, production and worldwide distribution of motion pictures, music videos, TV programs and video games.

**The Lawyers:** Clients applaud new entry **Robert Darwell** for "*immersing himself in the case until he gets to the heart of it.*" One client noted: "*He knows how to deal with matters successfully and is always available.*" The calm and collected **Thomas Leo** is "*a thoughtful lawyer who is thorough without getting bogged down in details.*"

**Clients/Work Highlights:** Société Générale; Paramount Pictures; Sony and MGM.

## Band 3

## Bloom, Hergott and Diemer LLP

**The Firm:** Clients admire this boutique for "*its highly developed talent expertise.*" They look to the firm for the "*diversity and quality*" of services on offer as well as its "*highly specialized entertainment practitioners.*" Even though it is comparatively small in size, it attracts some of the most prominent clientele in the state, in terms of directors and actors.

**The Lawyers:** Commentators were effusive in their praise for the assertive **Jacob Bloom** and his depth of experience. This talented lawyer has "*a larger than life personality and simply invaluable industry contacts.*"

**Clients/Work Highlights:** Clients include Brian Grazer, Nicolas Cage and Ron Howard.

## Gibson, Dunn & Crutcher LLP

See firm details p.328

**The Firm:** There is a strong consensus that this national player has a "*credible and noteworthy*" team that has attracted a robust entertainment caseload. Several clients were keen to point out that they enjoy the support of a "*well-balanced and enormously talented team of attorneys who are well respected in the community.*" The lawyers here won further praise for their terrific hands-on experience in negotiating financing deals for major studios and for both traditional and nontraditional entertainment companies. Highlights include advising Vivendi Universal Games on its acquisition of games developer Swordfish Studios, and representing video retailer Special Committee of Hollywood Entertainment in its sale to Movie Gallery. Furthermore, members of the firm assisted DaimlerChrysler with a product placement in the film 'Sahara' and dealt with licensing matters relating to the Chrysler Million Dollar Film Festival.

**The Lawyers:** **Lawrence Ulman** (see p.318) is considered a serious force in the market, not least due to his 30 years of experience in advising some of the most prominent clients around. High-end finance work in the entertainment arena is the order of the day for Ulman.

**Clients/Work Highlights:** Universal Pictures; Twentieth Century Fox; New Line Cinema; Volkswagen and Activision.

## Katten Muchin Rosenman LLP

See firm details p.874

**The Firm:** The media and entertainment practice at Katten Muchin Rosenman is said to "*always produce classy work on behalf of an elite group of clients.*" It mostly advises companies in an assortment of complex transactions including M&A, licensing and joint ventures. A prime example involved the firm acting as special entertainment counsel to Sony in the Sony Consortium acquisition of MGM, which meant advising on film, TV and IP assets. In a different matter, it represented a provider of feature film visual effects, The Orphanage, in the formation of Orphanage Animation Studios, a new CG animation studio. Another highlight was advising CBS Paramount International Television on a deal with CanWest Global Communications to create a Canadian version of the US television show 'Entertainment Tonight'.

**The Lawyers:** The skilled and popular **Rik Toulon** (see p.318) stands out as an "*exceptionally hard-working practitioner who is passionate about helping his clients.*"

**Clients/Work Highlights:** Some of the firm's key clients over the past year included CBS; Paramount Pictures; Sony Pictures Entertainment; Sony Computer Entertainment and The Orphanage.

## Kaye Scholer LLP

See firm details p.1536

**The Firm:** This highly respected team handles a steady diet of entertainment and media work. It is renowned for representing record companies, actors, writers, TV and motion picture production companies, new media, talent agencies, directors, publishers and software developers.

**The Lawyers:** **Sheri Jeffrey** (see p.296) "*will do everything possible to get the best deal for her clients,*" according to market sources.

## Lichter Grossman Nicholas Adler & Goodman

**The Firm:** The firm's compact team "*gives as good as it gets,*" say clients. Leading market sources left researchers in no doubt that this individual talent boutique is well regarded for providing clients with quality advice.

**The Lawyers:** Rivals said of **Linda Lichter:** "*Once you have her on the other side, you can't help but be unbelievably impressed by how driven she is as an advocate.*" "*Diligence, professionalism and excellence*" were only a few of the qualities that clients mentioned when commenting upon this leading talent lawyer.

## Weissmann, Wolff, Bergman, Coleman, Grodin & Evall, LLP

**The Firm:** A respected talent practice makes the firm "*a force to be reckoned with*" in the media and entertainment field, according to interviewees. Its lawyers advise writers, directors, producers, distributors, financiers, software designers, recording artists and print publishers.

**The Lawyers:** A former head of worldwide business affairs at Warner Bros, **Eric Weissmann** is respected for his straightforward manner, and *"excels at making complex issues understandable to the layman,"* say clients.

**Clients/Work Highlights:** Clients include Warner Bros, Lehman Brothers and City National Bank.

## Other Notable Practitioners

Based in Santa Monica, the *"terrific"* **Jay Cooper** (see p.284) of Greenberg Traurig LLP received plaudits from all quarters for his proficiency in advising *"high-profile music clientele."* He also acts for entities involved in motion pictures, TV and multimedia. The *"brilliant"* **Barry Hirsch** of Hirsch Wallerstein Hayum Matlof & Fishman LLP cuts a *"colossal figure"* in the entertainment world, interviewees say. His

former colleague **James Jackoway** of Jackoway Tyerman Wertheimer Austen Mandelbaum & Morris was praised for his *"bright and keen insight in the context of complex entertainment issues."* Clients adore talent lawyer **Deborah Klein** of Barnes Klein Mark Yorn Barnes & Levine for *"the unending effort"* she puts in on their behalf. At Kleinberg, Lopez, Lange, Brisbin & Cuddy LLP, the *"top-notch"* **Kenneth Kleinberg** was widely acknowledged as a leader in the field.

# PROJECTS

| Projects |
|---|
| Leading Firms |
| [1] **LATHAM & WATKINS LLP** *Los Angeles* |
| **MILBANK, TWEED, HADLEY & MCCLOY** *Los Angeles* |
| [2] **MORGAN, LEWIS & BOCKIUS LLP** *Los Angeles* |
| **ORRICK, HERRINGTON & SUTCLIFFE** *Los Angeles* |
| **PAUL, HASTINGS** *Los Angeles* |
| **THELEN REID & PRIEST LLP** *San Francisco* |

| Leading Individuals |
|---|
| [1] **FEO Edwin** *Milbank, Tweed, Hadley & McCloy LLP* |
| [2] **SHORTZ Richard** *Morgan, Lewis & Bockius LLP* |
| **SPIELBERG David** *Thelen Reid & Priest LLP* |
| **WEITZEL Mark** *Thelen Reid & Priest LLP* |
| [3] **BARAJAS Dino** *Paul, Hastings, Janofsky & Walker LLP* |
| **GALE Kelley** *Latham & Watkins LLP* |
| **GLASCOCK Thomas** *Thelen Reid & Priest LLP* |
| **GREENBERG Jeffrey** *Latham & Watkins LLP* |
| **MARKS Allan** *Milbank, Tweed, Hadley & McCloy LLP* |
| **WONG Karen** *Milbank, Tweed, Hadley & McCloy LLP* |

## Band 1

### Latham & Watkins LLP

**The Firm:** This firm has established one of the finest reputations for projects work in California, based largely on long-established relationships with banks who serve as arrangers on the market's major deals. One of the highlights in the past year was representing the joint arrangers for the acquisition by Complete Energy Holdings of La Paloma Generating Company and its 1,022 MW gas-fired combined-cycle facility in Kern County. The quality of the team across the board also attracts project developers. *"The Latham brand of lawyer is very distinctive and runs deep in its California practice,"* said clients, who pointed to the team's *"diligence, flexibility and great manner"* as key draws. Andy Singer's departure has left large boots to fill but sources were confident that he has built up a quality team as his legacy.

**The Lawyers:** According to clients, **Kelley Gale** *"does an amazing job every time"* and is a reputable developer's counsel. **Jeffrey Greenberg** was singled out for his strong lender expertise and recently advised JPMorgan as lead arranger in the $400

billion financing of a crude oil refinery for HOVENSA, a joint venture of Amerada Hess and PDVSA.

**Clients/Work Highlights:** Lenders such as CSFB; Goldman Sachs; Société Générale and ING are key clients.

### Milbank, Tweed, Hadley & McCloy LLP

**The Firm:** The Los Angeles office is largely responsible for the firm's formidable reputation in the renewables sector and provides a key platform for its work in both the domestic and international markets across the energy and transport sectors. In the USA, the team is advising lenders on toll road projects in Virginia and Texas. Latin America is a significant market for the firm and it is advising the lenders on a rail project in Mexico in addition to representing the former senior lenders on the partial refinancing of the Brazilian oil and gas field Barracuda. Clients point to the team's integrated approach as a real attraction: *"I know when I deal with one office I have the entire firm's resources at my fingertips."*

**The Lawyers:** The *"absolutely legendary"* **Ed Feo** (see p.54468) has secured himself a reputation as an eminent renewables attorney. *"A true powerhouse,"* according to clients, he led on the Chicago Skyway 144A bond offering. **Allan Marks** (see p.159885) is a respected figure in the market and is noted for his work in the ethanol sector. **Karen Wong** (see p.194744) won plaudits for her expertise in the Asian and Latin American markets.

**Clients/Work Highlights:** WestLB; HSH; Citigroup; Macquarie Bank; CINTRA; Dexia and DEPFA BANK number among the team's clients.

## Band 2

### Morgan, Lewis & Bockius LLP

See firm details p.1758

**The Firm:** This firm's projects practice is grounded in its work for utilities, however, its work in the renewables sector – particularly wind – is attracting the most attention lately. The team has made a concerted push into this area and can boast a client roster of key industry players. For example, it recently advised Clipper Windpower on the sale of a number of wind project assets, and Caithness Energy on its

development activities. Advice to developers is viewed as the firm's specialty but it is increasing its capacity to serve a number of equity investor clients. The utilities practice has attracted key clients such as Edison Mission Energy and Black Hills.

**The Lawyers:** **Richard Shortz** (see p.314) has developed a very high profile in this area. *"His reputation stems from his dedication to the industry and commitment to serving his clients,"* say sources.

**Clients/Work Highlights:** The team advises enXco on the development of a number of projects in the USA. Other clients include Diamond Generating, Sempra Energy and TXU.

### Orrick, Herrington & Sutcliffe

See firm details p.337

**The Firm:** Forming a key component of Orrick's national projects practice, the California offices make up part of a highly integrated national network. The coordination of this office with its New York and Washington DC-based counterparts is considerable, providing clients with enhanced financial and regulatory expertise. The firm has developed a high profile in the energy market and serves key domestic players such as PG&E. The wind sector is another key area for the group and AES has sought its counsel in the development of a number of wind projects.

**The Lawyers:** Joe Malkin is based in San Francisco and co-heads the energy and project finance group.

**Clients/Work Highlights:** Eurus Energy, UPC Wind and Osaka Gas Power America.

### Paul, Hastings, Janofsky & Walker LLP

See firm details p.339

**The Firm:** Entering *Chambers'* table this year, this firm has certainly made a big push into the projects sector, making both clients and peers take notice. Energy is the industry and Latin America the region where this team is making its mark. Advising developers and lenders, this fully bilingual team has impressed the market with a list of impressive transactions. *"The short answer for using them is that they are the best,"* claim clients. The group's work on deals of such caliber as the 495 MW Tuxpan V project (in which it advised Mitsubishi and Kyushu Electric Power on development and financing issues) have helped cement this reputation.

The Lawyers: **Dino Barajas** (see p.277) is the key contact here. He is highly regarded for his work for sponsors and lenders and for his expertise in Latin American markets. According to clients, "*he speaks the language, understands the culture and his legal skills are superb.*"

Clients/Work Highlights: Clipper Windpower; CSW International; Grupo Alfa, SA; AES; Tampa Electric; Central and South West Corporation; CSFB and Sithe Energies are among the firm's key clients.

### Thelen Reid & Priest LLP

See firm details p.342

The Firm: This firm continues to build a solid profile in the market, predominantly through its advice to sponsors in the energy sector. This caseload is complemented by a growing number of lender clients. The San Francisco office houses "*a dedicated team of industry-oriented attorneys who make themselves available all the time,*" say clients, and it forms part of a highly integrated projects practice along with the New York and Washington, DC offices. Work in the domestic market is concentrated in the energy sector, in which Calpine is a key client. For international work, Central America and North Africa have proved to be fertile markets.

The Lawyers: **David Spielberg** (see p.315) joined the team this year from Stoel Rives and clients report he is "*one of the strongest energy project attorneys in the country.*" **Mark Weitzel** (see p.320) is an industry stalwart and is recognized for his expert tax advice. **Thomas Glascock** (see p.290) is a "*tenacious negotiator who will defend his clients' interests to the hilt.*"

Clients/Work Highlights: Orion Power Holdings; Bechtel; Southern Energy and Duke Energy are among the firm's clients.

# REAL ESTATE

## Band 1

### Allen Matkins Leck Gamble & Mallory LLP

See firm details p.322

The Firm: With more than 100 "*incredible attorneys*" working directly on real estate matters, plus support from dedicated tax and litigation teams, this venerable California firm continues to stand head and shoulders above both local and national competitors. The team was said by clients to offer "*great service across the board,*" with "*lots of high-level partners*" and associates "*of a very high standard.*" The firm has recently established a toehold in the expansive market for military base conversions. For example, it represented Heritage Fields, a joint venture led by Lennar and LNR Property, in the $649 million acquisition of the El Toro Marine Corps Air Station in Irvine, and is continuing to assist in the permitting and development of a major mixed-use project there. It also represented Chadmar and its finance partner in the acquisition of 250 acres of Fort Ord in Monterey, and the planning and development of

1,000 housing units on the site. A different aspect of its expertise in this field was demonstrated when it represented ProLogis (formerly Catellus) in a PPP to modernize Los Angeles Air Force Base, in order to prevent its closure. Offering "*excellent responsiveness and quick turnaround time,*" the firm was also praised for its constructive approach to disputes and "*ability to deal with the other side and stay out of the gutter.*"

The Lawyers: With his "*wealth of knowledge*" and "*phenomenal expertise,*" **Rick Mallory** is "*the guru of commercial leasing*" in California. He boasts a "*friendly, low-key style*" that enables him to "*get things done without pursuing a scorched-earth policy.*" His effectiveness is enhanced by "*national connections at all levels.*" Mallory combines his practice with a role as head of the firm's San Francisco office. Like Mallory, **Michael Matkins** was a founding partner of the firm; he is now its managing partner. A senior attorney, he remains hands-on, benefiting from a good sense of perspective that years of experience bring and an ability to put the pieces of a transaction together. Matkins has a reputation for taking a line that is fair to both sides. A "*businessman's lawyer,*" he is appreciated by clients for his ability to "*put into English in five minutes what others take weeks to explain.*" His skills are matched by "*excellent customer service that sets the tone for the rest of the firm.*" "*Fantastic*" **Tony Natsis** is "*AAA-plus, as a lawyer and a person.*" Offering a transactional and leasing practice, he represented Kilroy Realty in one of the biggest bespoke leases of the past year in California, leasing more than 400,000 sq ft in San Diego to Intuit. Praised for his "*creative*" approach, he has recently been retained by the City of Anaheim to negotiate the building of a new football stadium with the NFL. "*An excellent younger lawyer,*" **Kevin Ehrhart** debuts in the tables following his recent elevation to partner. Specializing in complex commercial acquisitions, particularly in hotels, greenfields and golf courses, he has gained the attention of peers for his "*top-flight*" work.

Clients/Work Highlights: Hillwood; DLJ Real Estate Capital Partners; AEW; CB Richard Ellis; ProLogis; Beacon Capital Partners; Sumitomo Realty & Development; Boston Properties; Tishman Speyer Properties and Colony Properties.

## Band 2

### Cox Castle & Nicholson LLP

The Firm: This growing real estate firm comprises around 125 "*superb lawyers*" based in offices in Los Angeles, Orange County and San Francisco, making one of the largest real estate teams in California. It has managed to hold its own against increasing competition from national firms, working both with California-based developers and locally for national companies, including many major shopping center operators. Although the firm is primarily associated with the development side of the market, it also acts as local counsel for major financiers, including MassMutual and Wells Fargo.

The Lawyers: "*One of the top choices*" for commercial finance transactions, **Ira Waldman** boasts extensive experience in all aspects of real estate law, particularly in ground lease work. "*Smart, diligent and detail oriented,*" Waldman is active in the burgeoning redevelopment of Marina Del Rey, recently working on the lease for a new mixed-use development in Fisherman's Village. Head of the litigation department, **Lawrence Teplin** was acclaimed by clients as a "*superb counselor, adviser and attorney*" who is "*efficient and responsive.*" Clients also appreciated Teplin's hands-on approach, enabling him to deliver a "*high quality of service.*" A former chair of the firm's 15-strong land use group, **Kenneth Bley** is "*one of the best thinkers*" in the area. "*A terrific litigator,*" he is "*one of the eminent names of the real estate Bar.*" A former leading light of the practice, the "*brilliant*" **Phillip Nicholson** is a prominent name in the marketplace, boasting a wealth of experience.

Clients/Work Highlights: MassMutual; California National Bank; Fremont Investment and Wells Fargo.

### DLA Piper Rudnick Gray Cary US LLP

See firm details p.870

The Firm: This mammoth firm's growing real estate team boasts "*some of the top real estate lawyers*" in California, with "*solid quality*" throughout its 40-strong ranks. The firm covers all aspects of real estate, recently expanding to include opportunity funds and land banking. Recent additions have made it "*a particularly strong competitor*" in the leasing field.

The team's practice crosses the western USA: the firm was involved in one of the largest land acquisitions deals in Arizona history when it represented the Newland Communities in its acquisition of Estrella Mountain Ranch planned community. It also represented the Bank of Nova Scotia in a $1.62 billion refinance of the Venetian Hotel in Las Vegas, and is representing the State of California in the lease of the Los Angeles Coliseum to the NFL.

**The Lawyers:** *"The father of Los Angeles real estate,"* **Alan Wayte** (see p.319) proved a significant gain for the team when he joined in late 2004. Focusing on finance, he is instructed by major banks, pension funds, REITs and insurance companies, most notably Washington Mutual. Boasting *"energy and clout,"* **Michael Meyer** (see p.303) is regarded by clients and peers alike as *"one of the finest leasing attorneys the States has to offer."* One of the pioneers of leasing law in California, he boasts *"unparalleled"* knowledge of the area and can *"understand its unique intricacies."* His clients include Bank of America and City National Bank. *"Great practitioner"* **Richard Mendelson** (see p.303) is *"one of the best financial lawyers"* in California. He represents financial institutions, pension funds and major developers, and recently represented New York Life Insurance in negotiating a $100 million loan on office property in San Francisco; as well as LBA Realty in its purchase of Los Angeles' SBC Tower.

**Clients/Work Highlights:** The Prudential Insurance Company of America; Macerich; Morgan Stanley; VEF Advisors; Equity Office Properties; Citigroup and New York Life Insurance.

## Gibson, Dunn & Crutcher LLP

See firm details p.328

**The Firm:** This firm's global stature gives it *"a grasp of national and worldwide issues"* and *"a high level of commercial sensibility,"* while nationally the firm boasts a 30-strong team of real estate lawyers based in three offices across California. Active in development, transactions and financings, the team represented Rockpoint Group in the joint venture acquisition of the El Toro airbase, one of the largest of the latest crop of military base conversions, and Hilton Hotels in the development of a 1,200-room convention center hotel in San Diego. Gibson operates at the higher end of the market, but clients were quick to note that it offers *"excellent value for excellent services"* and *"great support staff."*

**The Lawyers:** *"One of the top real estate lawyers in Los Angeles,"* **Jesse Sharf** (see p.313) is *"the complete package: bright, extraordinarily hard-working and an effective negotiator."* Focusing on high-end financing, he recently represented Rockpoint Group and Stellar Management in the acquisition of Parkmerced, one of the largest residential rental projects in San Francisco. Sharf was also praised for his negotiation style, which was said to be constructive, while still keeping a hard enough edge to be effective. *"Lawyer's lawyer"* **Dennis Arnold** (see p.276) has an *"exceptional ability to communicate with counterparts, assuaging them of their fears."* With extensive experience in all aspects of commercial and residential real estate, Arnold has a

*"nimble mind,"* and is recognized for his *"attention to detail and incredible depth of knowledge of the law."* Enjoying a stellar reputation, **Michael Sfregola** (see p.313) is a *"consummate attorney,"* lauded by clients as *"creative and insightful,"* with his *"intellect, real estate acumen and good counsel"* as well as his ability to seize upon the key business issues and be both legal and business counselor. Sfregola has a wide range of experience in real estate, tax and partnership funds and recently represented Sunstone in connection with various hotel portfolios financing and refinancing in excess of $1 billion. A new addition to the directory, **Amy Forbes** (see p.289) impresses clients and market commentators with the *"incredible accuracy of her predictions and timeframes."* A *"creative problem solver,"* her practice focuses on land use and planning issues, representing some of the largest investors in the real estate arena.

**Clients/Work Highlights:** Rockpoint Group; Hilton Hotels; Wachovia; Normandy Real Estate Partners; Pacific Coast Partners; CSFB; Sunstone Hotel Properties and Lehman Brothers.

## Latham & Watkins LLP

**The Firm:** A national and international giant, this *"highly professional"* team was praised by clients for its *"top talent"* and *"substantial expertise,"* particularly in relation to REIT transactions. The team is especially active in developments, acquisitions and financing and has been involved in more than $10 billion of transactions in the past year; it recently represented Maguire Properties in its $1.5 billion acquisition of a portfolio of office properties in Southern California. In addition, the firm has an active land use practice; it represented the developers of the Playa Vista project, an $8 billion, 1,000-acre mixed-use project in San Francisco.

**The Lawyers:** Specializing in land use, **George Mihlsten** is credited for being *"strategic and analytically minded,"* illustrated by his ability to come up with alternative options when confronted with a problem. One client concluded: *"He can bat back a fast curveball like no one else."* Emerging into the limelight, **Cindy Starrett** is a *"superb land use lawyer"* whose practice includes land use entitlements for infrastructure projects and real estate development. *"Politically plugged in,"* counterparts admire her and clients *"love her to death."* *"User-friendly, constructive and an accomplished problem solver,"* **Don Berger** is said to possess an excellent base in corporate real estate law. He recently represented Deutsche Bank in its acquisition of Wilmorite with regard to more than $1 billon in financing. Berger also represented Deutsche Bank and Goldman Sachs in connection with a $2.35 billion financing for the acquisition of LNR Property.

**Clients/Work Highlights:** CSFB; Deutsche Bank; Goldman Sachs; JMB Realty and Playa Capital.

## Paul, Hastings, Janofsky & Walker LLP

See firm details p.339

**The Firm:** This international giant, headquartered in San Francisco, boasts *"a terrific team"* of 57 real estate attorneys in its Los Angeles, San Francisco and Orange County offices. "*A real powerhouse*," it leans toward the higher end of the market and specializes in the financing of complex transactions. It recently represented Lehman Brothers in its $500 million financing of the acquisition of the El Toro Marine Corps Air Station by Heritage Fields. Debt restructuring is another key area for the team, and the hospitality industry is a key aspect of the client base. Peers note that the firm's major infrastructure "*gives it the edge*" over smaller rivals, enabling it to offer a "*high quality of service.*"

**The Lawyers:** Specializing in finance acquisitions, real estate loan workouts and reconstructing, **Philip Feder** (see p.288) is a "*top-notch attorney*" who brings a wealth of relevant experience to the table. Regarded by his clients as a "*pragmatic, issue-focused deal-closer*," Feder recently counseled Urban Partners on its purchase of the long-term ground lease and joint venture to develop a large dormitory complex on the University of Southern California campus. "*Smooth like silk*," **Charles Thornton** (see p.317) is "*a real gentleman*" who many onlookers admire for his skills as a lawyer and his loyal client base. He concentrates on joint ventures, development, acquisitions and financing, and representing institutional real estate investors and larger developers.

**Clients/Work Highlights:** Lehman Brothers; Oaktree Capital Management; Rockpoint Group; KOR Group and Urban Partners.

### Pircher, Nichols & Meeks

**The Firm:** Peers note that this "*business savvy*" team of around 60 attorneys has "*the wherewithal to expand and increase its influence*," should it so choose. Boasting strong expertise in the financing arena, the firm concentrates exclusively on real estate and related matters. The firm has "*successfully carved out a niche*" representing the real estate sections of major opportunity funds. The firm recently assisted The Blackstone Group in a joint venture acquisition and development of a student housing complex for the University of Southern California. Although leading partners at the firm were singled out for praise, observers noted: "*Everyone at the firm knows what they are doing.*"

**The Lawyers:** **Stevens Carey** (see p.158690) specializes in transactional law and is a "*phenomenal*" business attorney who "*knows when and when not to negotiate*," according to clients. An "*even-tempered*" attorney, Carey is described as one of the most knowledgeable joint venture specialists in the sector, and praised for his dedication to the cause and meticulous drafting. **Phillip Nichols** (see p.155439) represents investors, particularly opportunity funds, in complex transactions. He recently represented Walton Street Capital in the $560 million acquisition of eight hotels across the country from CTF Holdings, to be managed by Marriot Hotels. A "*deal-doer*," he is described as a strong transactional lawyer who is adept at the real estate aspects of a deal, as well as joint venture and tax issues. Nichols represented Walton Street Capital in the acquisition of a portfolio of Renaissance hotels, a transaction including the

Mayflower Hotel in DC as well as hotels in other states. Celebrated as "*one of the deans of Los Angeles real estate*," **Leo Pircher** (see p.155441) is an "*awesome name*" in the sector, and held in the highest regard by clients and peers alike.

**Clients/Work Highlights:** Walton Street Capital; AIG Global Real Estate; Farallon Capital Management; Apollo Real Estate Advisors; JMB Realty and Starwood Capital Group.

### Morrison & Foerster LLP
See firm details p.335

**The Firm:** This team's "*tremendous*" attorneys offer "*first-rate quality*" on transactions and financing. It has built up substantial credibility in the market over the years with peers noting that the firm has the ears of the market. It is an international firm boasting around 40 real estate attorneys across the state, primarily in the San Francisco head office. A major client is Hines Interests, which the firm recently represented on the purchase of four office properties in the Bay area for more than $300 million. The consistent quality of the team led observers to conclude that the firm "*doesn't hire anyone who isn't a shining light.*"

**The Lawyers:** **Kim Seneker** (see p.313) was lauded by clients for offering "*incredibly thorough and exacting*" counsel with "*an unbelievably quick turn-around*," a knack attributed to his willingness to "*work day and night*" for his clients. He recently counseled Peery/Arrillaga on the sale of the Westport office complex in San Mateo. A "*great communicator*," Seneker will "*always be able to articulate a well-thought-out position.*" **Mike Zischke**'s (see p.321) land use practice benefits from his status as "*the recognized expert*" on the California Environmental Quality Act (CEQA). This background helps him secure and defend approval for sensitive matters. He successfully defended the Town of Mammoth Lakes' proposal for expansion of its local airport, an issue that focused on the environmental impact report accompanying the proposal. Experienced in dealing with planners, municipal governments and antagonistic groups, Zischke can "*put together deals to get things done.*" **Tom Fileti** (see p.288) debuts in the tables after client recommendation for his "*pragmatic and creative*" approach to his financing-focused practice. Although "*detail-oriented*," he also "*understands the dynamics of deals*," particularly in his core area of lease financings.

**Clients/Work Highlights:** Pacific Energy Group; UBS Realty Advisors; Bank of America; Deutsche Bank; Goldman Sachs and University of California.

### Munger, Tolles & Olson LLP

**The Firm:** This well-established California firm can boast an involvement in some of Los Angeles' most notable recent developments, including the Walt Disney Concert Hall and Our Lady of the Angels Cathedral. Its "*excellent lawyers*" assist developers such as Maguire Properties in financing and devel-

opment. A key client is Tishman Speyer Properties, who the firm represented on the £240 million purchase of O'Melveny and Myers' Los Angeles head office from that firm's pension fund.

**The Lawyers:** **Edward Hagerott**'s "*soft-spoken but tough*" style stands him in good stead in a practice that encompasses transactions, financing and workouts. He recently represented CSFB and WCB Properties on the $185 million sale of Sorrento South Corporate Center in San Diego, a 650,000 sq ft office and retail development. Noted for his constructive style, Hagerott "*avoids beating up the other side*," while his forward planning "*ensures there are no last-minute crises.*" "*Brilliant*" **O'Malley Miller**'s "*breadth of knowledge*," not just depth, allows him to offer a broad service encompassing finance, land use, development and transactions, enhanced by his practical approach.

**Clients/Work Highlights:** Maguire Properties; Catholic Archdiocese of Los Angeles; Disney; Tishman Speyer Properties; CSFB; Beacon Capital Partners and Hines Interests.

### Orrick, Herrington & Sutcliffe LLP
See firm details p.337

**The Firm:** This international firm's San Francisco and Los Angeles offices boast more than 20 real estate attorneys between them, with "*excellent associates*" supporting the leading lights. The firm's most significant US clients are investment funds and managers such as RREEF, who the team advised on sales, investments and acquisitions with a combined value of more than $1 billion. Another key client is Colony Capital, who the firm advised on the $72 million sale of Dulles Airport Hotel. However, the team's strength comes largely from its rapidly expanding global real estate practice. In collaboration with the Tokyo office, the firm has tapped the lucrative Asian market and is active in both exporting and importing capital. It recently advised a Japanese affiliate of Colony Capital in a $1 billion financing, and clients note that it "*understands how to get deals done in Japan.*" The Tokyo office also adds to the full-service capacity of the California offices, allowing them to offer round-the-clock work on difficult matters. Clients noted that the firm seemed "*more transparent than other large firms*," with cross-office communications deemed to be first rate.

**The Lawyers:** In addition to leading the firm's work for RREEF, **Michael Liever** (see p.300) has an extensive practice representing foreign and domestic investors. He recently closed several hundred million dollars in acquisitions across the country for AMB Property, a San Francisco-based REIT. Liever's "*intense*" demeanor and "*no-frills*" approach make him "*an effective advocate*" for his clients. **William Murray**'s (see p.304) work focuses on private equity financing. In recent years he has shepherded Equinix, a leading network infrastructure provider, in rapid expansion that has seen it doubling its real estate use. "*Professional*" and extremely knowledgeable, Murray melds his "*great business perspective*," with a nonadversarial manner that builds trust with the other side. A former chair of the real estate practice, "*terrific*" **Noel Nellis** (see p.304) now focuses on spearheading the team's move into international markets.

**Clients/Work Highlights:** CalWest Industrial Properties; Colony Capital; Los Angeles County Employees' Retirement Association; University of California; Fidelity Partners; Equinix; AMB Property; RREEF; Westbrook Partners and Prime Group.

## Pillsbury Winthrop Shaw Pittman LLP
See firm details p.1550

**The Firm:** Operating primarily out of the firm's San Francisco office, this team is active in transactions, financing and development and land use. It recently represented Fifth Street Properties in one of the largest real estate transactions in the state, the $1.5 billion portfolio sale of 14 office buildings in California, Colorado and Texas, including Los Angeles' famous 777 Tower. Noted for a "*strong work ethic*," the team offers "*superior service*" to its clients, who also note that attorneys "*know how to strike a balance between protecting clients' interests and facilitating the deal.*" After some high-profile departures in recent years, the team now stands to benefit from its parent's mammoth merger, and clients note that the team is highly integrated with the firm as a whole, enabling it to call upon a wealth of resources.

**The Lawyers:** **James Rishwain** (see p.310) "*works tirelessly,*" both as co-leader of real estate for the entire firm and in his own role that encompasses financing, acquisitions and development. He "*can understand all the business aspects of a deal*" and can "*respond to challenging matters rapidly and effectively.*" In addition to leading the firm's work with Fifth Street Properties, Rishwain closed more than $150 million of acquisitions of office and hotel portfolios for his clients. "*Pleasant and charming,*" and "*cool under pressure,*" **Lewis Feldman** (see p.288) makes "*a good representative for contentious issues.*" He recently attracted attention for his work on LA Live, the enormous convention center and hotel project planned by Anschutz Entertainment for downtown Los Angeles. He negotiated a unique PPP for the project with the City of Los Angeles, establishing an entire new city district exclusively for the project area. Feldman also tackled the related litigation from rival hotel operators. The "*enormously talented*" **Robert Herr** (see p.294) brings a "*calm, thoughtful demeanor*" to his work, representing commercial real estate developers and investors. A key client is Shorenstein, which he advised on the $1 billion recapitalization of one of San Francisco's major high-rise office buildings, 555 California Street, and on dispositions and acquisitions totaling more than $1.5 billion. Combining "*terrific judgment*" with "*strong transactional skills,*" clients give him "*high marks on all aspects of effective representation.*"

**Clients/Work Highlights:** Emerald Venture Group; ClubCorp; Anschutz Entertainment; Stark Investments; SunCal; Shorenstein and SKS Investments.

## Band 4

### Coblentz, Patch, Duffy & Bass LLP
**The Firm:** Clients point to a team of 18 real estate attorneys who combine "*skill with a down-to-earth approach*" that ensures advice is delivered in a user-friendly format. Primarily known for land use, this midsized Bay area firm also maintains an active development practice focused on the City of San Francisco. It is currently assisting the San Francisco 49ers on development and permitting matters for their planned new stadium. The "*real team approach*" means its "*excellent associates*" make a full contribution to the practice.

**The Lawyers:** With "*an intellect only surpassed by her humor and wit,*" **Pamela Duffy** is highly skilled in the complex permitting climate of San Francisco. Possessed of a "*nonconfrontational and understated*" style, Duffy combines "*political sense*" with "*exemplary knowledge*" of the crucial CEQA.

**Clients/Work Highlights:** ProLogis; eBay; California Pacific Medical Center; San Francisco 49ers; Fairmont Hotels; Hearst and Gap.

### Dechert LLP
See firm details p.1752

**The Firm:** Clients noted that this team offers "*experience, accountability and responsiveness,*" seeing it as "*ideal for those used to the service of a New York firm.*" The firm is an East Coast giant that has carved out a West Coast niche in mortgage, mezzanine and preferred equity financing. Its San Francisco office boasts "*terrific*" attorneys and high-caliber clients, including Merrill Lynch. The team acted for the latter on a $629 million mortgage financing of 61 shopping centers, and a mortgage and mezzanine financing package for an institutional real estate owner totaling more than $1 billion. The team was also responsible for a mortgage and mezzanine package secured by 650 hotels worth over $5.5 billion.

**The Lawyers:** **Joseph Heil** (see p.293) is a man who "*knows everybody in the industry*" and "*understands the nuances of documents, and of loan structure.*" His personal practice focuses on mortgage financing and capital markets while he has carved out a niche in representing lenders in dealing with CMBS rating agencies. This expertise means clients "*can trust him to act on high-stakes issues with minimal supervision;*" while his precise use of language ensures that he can "*explain complex matters to lawyers and nonlawyers alike.*"

**Clients/Work Highlights:** Merrill Lynch; Prudential; Countrywide Commercial Real Estate Finance; Wells Fargo; Barclays and Hypo Real Estate Capital.

### Heller Ehrman LLP
See firm details p.329

**The Firm:** This national firm boasts around 30 real estate attorneys in its several California offices working closely with sister offices across the country. Clients pointed to the "*diplomacy and creativity*" of the group, as well as its efficiency, and noted: "*It achieves more in less time than most firms, at similar rates.*" The team represents hotel owners and

investors in transactional work, and represents banks and private equity funds in investments. The team's specific expertise makes it "*good for tricky, one-off transactions,*" a skill illustrated when it represented the owners of Century Plaza in Los Angeles in its sale for almost $300 million to an owner-manager partnership of Sunstone Hotel Investors and Hyatt. The team also recently set up a series of large portfolio loans for Wells Fargo.

**The Lawyers:** Highly respected in the marketplace, **Brian Smith** (see p.314) represented the Government of Singapore on its setting up of a $800 million REIT. He is noted for his constructive but tough approach to negotiations: "*He's a deal-maker not a deal-breaker,*" concluded one client. **Peter Benudiz** (see p.278) debuts in the tables in a year that saw him emerge from the shadow of his senior partner Smith. Focusing on hotel financing, he is a "*terrific deal-maker*" who is noted by peers for his ability to "*just get things done.*" "*Aggressive in a positive way,*" Benudiz is said to boast a "*broad skill set*" ranging from traditional loans to mezzanine and securitized financings.

**Clients/Work Highlights:** The firms' clients include major investors, investment managers and developers such as Warburg Pincus; Lehman Brothers; Starwood Hotels and the Government of Singapore.

### Mayer, Brown, Rowe & Maw LLP
See firm details p.876

**The Firm:** This massive firm boasts a small but "*top-notch*" team, which works closely with the firm's other US offices and its litigation, tax and ERISA teams. Its transactional practice sees it involved in purchases as far afield as London. A key client is TIAA-CREF, which the firm represented in several large sales and purchases nationwide. Clients noted that the firm offers "*great value*" and is "*careful not to overstaff matters.*"

**The Lawyers:** "*A true gentleman*" **Louis Eatman** (see p.287) leads the firm's work with TIAA-CREF. "*On anyone's dream team*" for real estate financing, he increasingly specializes in joint ventures. He is currently representing CB Richard Ellis on the development of two high-profile luxury condominiums: One Rincon Hill in San Francisco and Allure in Las Vegas. Eatman "*combines knowledge of the law with a sense of how to get things done.*"

**Clients/Work Highlights:** CB Richard Ellis and Bank of Nova Scotia are among the firm's financial clients.

### O'Melveny & Myers LLP
See firm details p.336

**The Firm:** This giant international firm boasts a real estate team that focuses on the higher end of the market, representing developers and investors on major projects. It is counseling Anschutz Entertainment on the leasing, transactions and development of LA Live, a $1 billion convention and entertainment center project in downtown Los Angeles. The group has a strong team approach with clients noting that "*if one member is unavailable, another can always step in.*" It also calls on expertise from the firm's wide range of other practices, including litigation and tax. Clients felt that the firm is good value for complex matters. One general counsel noted: "*I had to fight to get them hired but, now we have, everyone's glad we got them.*"

**The Lawyers: Steve Edwards** (see p.287) heads the firm's real estate matters from its Newport Beach office. Noted by clients for his business focus, he "*takes time to understand our goals,*" and "*reduces matters quickly to a dollar-and-cents question.*" Specializing in complex developments, he recently conducted an intricate process of acquisition and entitlement of the remaining undeveloped land around Ontario Airport. In addition to defeating environmental challenges to the entitlements, he also negotiated the sale of the residential section of the development to a major home builder with substantial profit returns to his client on future sales. Edwards leaves clients "*amazed at his range of capabilities: from pitbull to white kid gloves, as needed.*"

**Clients/Work Highlights:** Anschutz Entertainment; California Polytechnic State University; Resmark Equity Partners and Kennecott Land are just some of the large state developers, owners and investors represented by the firm.

### Sheppard, Mullin, Richter & Hampton LLP

**The Firm:** This midsized San Francisco office has developed a strong reputation for real estate. This reputation was boosted through its extensive involvement in the redevelopment of the city's waterfront, and is currently involved in plans for a new cruise ship terminal. The firm is also active in the growing area of military base redevelopment.

**The Lawyers:** "*Steady and calm,*" but "*able to step it up when he needs to,*" **Robert Thompson** heads the firm's real estate team. Active in development, and particularly in land use, he has been the driving force behind much of the firm's success in the city. He is a "*superb draughtsman*" with "*personal integrity.*" **James Lonergan**'s practice encompasses development, lending and leasing. Clients consider him "*deal-oriented*" and "*super bright.*"

**Clients/Work Highlights:** The firm represents major state and national owners such as University of California and Presidio Trust, as well as major developers.

### Other Notable Practitioners

Although he is considered the "*godfather of mezzanine and securitized financing,*" **Paul Walker** (see p.319) "*understands the entire spectrum of real estate financing.*" Clients note that he is balanced and reasonable in his dealings, and "*unparalleled as a negotiator.*" He recently moved from Dewey Ballantine LLP to Sidley Austin LLP, a move that peers felt would increase his visibility still further. **Susan Diamond** (see p.286), of Morgan, Lewis & Bockius LLP, focuses on land use. Working primarily on San Francisco matters, she "*knows city politics as well as state laws.*" "*Anticipatory,*" she "*knows the exposures, good and bad, from each course of action;*" however, she is also a "*self-starter*" who clients trust to "*move things forward.*" "*Dean of the real estate Bar*" **Howard Ellman**, of Ellman Burke Hoffman & Johnson, now focuses primarily on land use and the related litigation. He recently represented landowners on obtaining approvals for sales to major developers including Lennar and Pulte Homes. **Mary Murphy**, of San Francisco's Farella Braun + Martel LLP, "*knows the land use laws off the top of her fingers.*" "*Extremely competent and bright,*" she has obtained permits for the redevelopment of historic buildings across the waterfront of the city. **Paul Rutter**, of Gilchrist & Rutter Professional Corporation, is "*the landlord guy*" in California's high-end leasing market. Peers noted: "*He's so knowledgeable that, once everyone decides they want to make a deal, he immediately knows all the issues.*" **Cecily Talbert** (see p.317) "*brings a combination of skills*" to her land use practice at Bingham McCutchen LLP. "*An excellent negotiator*" with "*great persuasive skills,*" she boasts "*a remarkable understanding of project economics*" that allows her to "*place land use negotiations in the context of a client's wider goals.*" Specializing in complex projects, including military base conversions, she is noted by clients for her skill at navigating California's unique approvals environment.

# TAX

| Tax | |
|---|---|
| **Leading Firms** | |
| [1] BAKER & McKENZIE *Palo Alto* | |
| IRELL & MANELLA LLP *Los Angeles* | |
| LATHAM & WATKINS LLP *Los Angeles* | |
| [2] FENWICK & WEST LLP *Mountain View* | |
| GIBSON, DUNN & CRUTCHER LLP *Los Angeles* | |
| LOEB & LOEB LLP *Los Angeles* | |
| MORRISON & FOERSTER LLP *San Francisco* | |
| ORRICK, HERRINGTON & SUTCLIFFE *San Francisco* | |
| WILSON SONSINI GOODRICH & ROSATI *Palo Alto* | |
| [3] COOLEY GODWARD LLP *Palo Alto* | |
| McDERMOTT WILL & EMERY *Los Angeles* | |
| MUNGER, TOLLES & OLSON LLP *Los Angeles* | |
| O'MELVENY & MYERS LLP *Los Angeles* | |
| PAUL, HASTINGS *Los Angeles* | |
| PILLSBURY *San Francisco* | |

## Band 1

### Baker & McKenzie

See firm details p.866

**The Firm:** "*Simply superb,*" this firm has over 550 lawyers in the global tax practice group, which spans 38 countries. International tax law is one of the key drawing cards for major national and multinational clients; however this should not overshadow the group's transactional work or its prominence on domestic matters.

**The Lawyers:** "*The dean of the tax Bar,*" **John Peterson** (see p.307) "*is so on the ball it is unbelievable.*" A terrific international tax attorney, he brings to the deal table nearly 30 years of experience and his background as a certified public accountant.

### Irell & Manella LLP

**The Firm:** A stalwart of the West Coast market, this firm is renowned for its substantial expertise in tax matters and the commercial and practical advice provided by its high-quality attorneys. The group undertakes federal and state tax issues as well as complex international matters. For example, it recently advised Broadcom on various issues including its recent acquisitions and debt recoveries.

**The Lawyers: Milt Hyman** is the "*go-to guy for his deep technical understanding*" and his appreciation of clients' needs in business planning for corporations and partnerships. Hyman also possesses extensive experience in handling tax controversies and federal and state issues. **Elliot Freier** is an "*astute lawyer who stays up to date with the law and is good at keeping his clients informed.*" He is particularly commended for his bankruptcy work. Formerly with the ITC, **Joel Rabinovitz** is a "*master of international tax*" according to sources. A "*personable, thoughtful and technically sharp*" attorney, he represents foreign investors in their transactions in the USA, as well as American companies in their international tax planning.

### Latham & Watkins LLP

**The Firm:** The attorneys based in California form a cohesive, international practice group spanning 21 offices in ten countries. Illustrating its unified approach, attorneys in San Francisco, Los Angeles, Silicon Valley and New York acted for KKR as part of the investment group that acquired Toys 'R' Us in a transaction valued at $6.6 billion (plus assumption of debt). The tax team is also large enough to have niche specialties, such as project finance, land use and taxation issues arising out of environment law issues. The team packs a punch in the transactional arena, and controversy and compensation benefits are also key strands of the caseload.

**The Lawyers: John Clair** is an extremely talented attorney whose "*sheer experience makes his advice so trusted.*" His clientele includes a broad mix of industrial and retails clients; he acted for KKR on the Toys 'R' Us deal and assisted KKR and Silver Lake Partners on their acquisition of Agilent Technologies' semiconductor product group for $2.66 billion. **Karen Bryan** works within the team's growing controversy practice. Her advice is practical and "*straight down the line.*" She advised Amgen on its $2.36 billion note offering and debenture modification. A creative and intelligent attorney, **Samuel Weiner** acted for Bright Now! Dental on its sale to Freeman Spogli for $350 million. Global chair of the tax department, **Laurence Stein**, provides valuable counseling to clients on corporate tax, financial products and related matters before the IRS.

## Band 2

## Fenwick & West LLP
See firm details p.326

**The Firm:** Housing 250 attorneys in its Silicon Valley and San Francisco offices, this firm is focused on providing tailored advice to clients within the life sciences and hi-tech industries. Its specialization is clearly reaping dividends with a huge Fortune 500 client base (over 100 corporations) turning to the firm for advice on a range of matters. International tax law, federal tax litigation, state taxation and employee benefit taxation are handled by a "*practice boutique*" praised for its commitment to the field. With two full-time litigators, the firm has represented corporate clients in nearly 60 federal tax court cases including Xilinx v Commissioner in which the US Tax Court ruled that Xilinx's allocations met the

arm's length standard.

**The Lawyers:** Group chair **James Fuller** (see p.289) is an "*institution in the market*" due to the authority ascribed to his opinions. He wins high marks for his practical, solutions-focused advice. A highly experienced attorney, **David Forst** (see p.289) focuses on international corporate and partnership taxation.

## Gibson, Dunn & Crutcher LLP
See firm details p.328

**The Firm:** The firm, which has long-established roots within the California market, has successfully adopted a multioffice approach to service a national and international client base. This strategy is clearly reaping dividends as New York-based clients such as JF Lehman now instruct the Los Angeles team direct. It is also adept at advising international clients on both inbound and outbound international transactions. The three-partner tax team echoes the firmwide tradition of hiring quality people with expertise in niche areas. "*Always a pleasure to work with,*" the trio are "*thoughtful, client-focused and respectful in the way they deal with people.*" These partners act on a substantial amount of M&A, ranging from the formation of new entities to joint ventures as well as related areas such as real estate.

**The Lawyers:** **Hatef Behnia** (see p.278) is "*a cut to the chase kind of guy,*" appreciative clients reported. He provided the tax advice to Computer Sciences Corporation in the sale of its DynCorp International unit to Veritas Capital for $850 million. Well versed in both federal income and California taxation, **Stephen Tolles** (see p.318) is "*client-focused and a pragmatic adviser on transactions.*" He acted for Transamerica Finance in the $1.2 billion sale of Transamerica Maritime Containers to TAL International, an entity controlled by The Jordan Company and Klesch & Company.

**Clients/Work Highlights:** New clients to the firm include Charter Communications, while other clients include Qwest, Hollywood Entertainment Corporation and Pitney Bowes. The Williams Companies also provide a steady stream of work.

## Loeb & Loeb LLP
See firm details p.334

**The Firm:** This "*quick and effective team*" of 12 attorneys has carved out a profile as "*the best in California for tax-related entertainment work.*" Nationally respected for its work in this sector, the group is well equipped to handle controversy matters and international taxation as well as general tax planning for limited liability companies and partnerships.

**The Lawyers:** According to interviewees, **Terry Cuff** (see p.284) "*is one of the very top people in the field of partnership matters.*" He also focuses on key areas such as real estate and energy. A "*meticulous and sophisticated lawyer,*" **Paul Sczudlo** (see p.313) is an attorney who is "*so thorough, he will never get anything wrong,*" clients believe. His practice centers on tax matters with an international element. For example, he is advising a California-based industry group on international real estate planning in France, Eastern Europe and China. On the private

client side, Sczudlo represents famous entertainment figures residing offshore.

## Morrison & Foerster LLP
See firm details p.335

**The Firm:** Clients draw upon the services of over 40 tax attorneys based in 19 offices across the globe. Although the firm is renowned for its strengths within the finance, life science and technology sectors, sources also pointed to the team's dominance across the USA for local and state taxation arising out of a broad mix of transactions, planning and litigation.

**The Lawyers:** With "*an impressive combination of practical skills and a great knowledge of tax and corporate law,*" **Stuart Offer** (see p.305) is one of the most experienced tax lawyers in the state. He divides his practice between tax litigation and international taxation, and recently advised McGrath RentCorp in the acquisition of the US and Canadian-based equipment rental business of CIT Group.

## Orrick, Herrington & Sutcliffe LLP
See firm details p.337

**The Firm:** The reach of this firm continues to spread beyond the USA; the recent opening of an office in Taiwan is an indication of its commitment to the international arena. Sources endorsed the practical and businesslike approach of this "*knowledgeable and efficient*" team of lawyers. The tax practice is large enough to have diversified; for instance, it fields a large municipal finance team and several partners work on structured finance. There is also a sizable litigation capability.

**The Lawyers:** "*Superb in tax controversy,*" **Paul Sax** (see p.312) is one the most knowledgeable tax litigators on the West Coast. He devotes his time to dealing with tax planning for domestic and multinational corporations, and handles IRS disputes and litigation. **Grady Bolding** (see p.279) is highly experienced in the venture fund arena, and works closely with colleagues in New York on client matters.

**Clients/Work Highlights:** A range of clients particularly in the energy and entertainment sectors.

## Wilson Sonsini Goodrich & Rosati
See firm details p.344

**The Firm:** This team offers a "*high level of expertise and responsiveness,*" according to clients, who also noted that it has the depth of resources to ensure the appropriate level of coverage. These attorneys "*use their experience to ensure they address the right issues rather than wasting time.*" Focusing mainly on transactional matters, the group recently acted on major acquisitions and spin-offs including the $4.1 billion acquisition by Sun Microsystems of StorageTek. The team also acted for Forstmann Little on the 24 Hour Fitness Worldwide deal worth $1.6 billion.

**The Lawyers:** M&A specialist **Ivan Humphreys** (see p.295) impresses as "*he is the future of the tax team,*" due to his mix of "*attention to detail and good business perspective.*"

## Band 3

### Cooley Godward LLP

**The Firm:** This premier Silicon Valley firm is at the forefront of several emerging industries including technology and life sciences. Accordingly, the team enjoys a strong reputation in the venture capital and startup arenas. The tax team has a transactional focus and as such has benefited from the resultant upswing in the M&A market. eBay is a client.

**The Lawyers:** Susan Philpot is recommended as a *"top-notch attorney with a strong practice, great experience and thoroughness."* Clients can also call upon the wealth of federal and state tax expertise and emerging markets knowledge of **Bill Morrow.**

### McDermott Will & Emery

See firm details p.878

**The Firm:** This strong national practice continues to make its presence felt on the West Coast. The team advises on a broad range of tax matters encompassing state, local, federal and international matters. A steady flow of M&A work keeps the transactional team busy.

**The Lawyers:** Having developed a broad tax practice **Edwin Schuck** (see p.312) advises on federal and state tax law from billion-dollar M&A transactions to federal government tax litigation. His international work has included the restructuring of an international jeans factory in Switzerland. The *"personable and hard-working"* **Frederick Chilton** (see p.282) won plaudits for his outstanding knowledge of rules for outbound investments.

### Munger, Tolles & Olson LLP

**The Firm:** The team fields *"a number of great partners and juniors that show promise."* Although litigation is a traditional strong suit of the firm, it is increasingly regarded as one of the leading transactional practices in the state. An enviable client roster ensures that the transactional, litigation and tax controversy attorneys receive a steady flow of work.

**The Lawyers:** **Stephen Rose** is *"quite a talent,"* agree sources; he is a *"superb tax practitioner who is knowledgeable and great to deal with."*

### O'Melveny & Myers LLP

See firm details p.336

**The Firm:** The strong suits of this large and well-established firm are banking and finance, litigation and bankruptcy. Complementary to these areas, the tax practice has more than 50 attorneys residing in a dedicated department, which works closely with clients from a range of sectors worldwide including motion picture companies and hotel chains. These attorneys are *"great people - easy to deal with and responsive."* The team undertakes state, federal and international tax matters and has made strides across the USA and abroad recently with a string of key lateral hires.

**The Lawyers:** Based in the Century City office, **Robert Blashek** (see p.279) is not only a *"terrific guy, who takes real care of his clients,"* he was also deemed a great resource for the firm because of his broad expertise in the entertainment arena. His practice encompasses private equity fund formation, corporate acquisitions and reorganizations, and bankruptcy and workouts. A *"high-quality lawyer,"* **Robert Rizzi** splits his time between California and DC. The chair of the firm's tax department, he is a well-rounded attorney and a trusted port of call for referrals in conflict situations.

**Clients/Work Highlights:** Representative clients include California Institute of Technology; Hilton Hotels; Wells Fargo; Lockheed Martin and Motion Picture Industry Pension Plan.

### Paul, Hastings, Janofsky & Walker LLP

See firm details p.339

**The Firm:** The global footprint of this firm sets it apart from rivals. With over 17 offices across the world, including three in China, the firm's strongly international client base is provided with a seamless cross-border service. Domestically, the California operation was recently bolstered by the opening of an office in Palo Alto, which is designed to service the needs of the area's entrepreneurial clients. This balances nicely with San Francisco's more traditional banking environment. The offices field dedicated tax teams experienced in the controversy arena and tax planning strategy. Highlights include successfully resolving matters pre-litigation for a large Chinese multinational. The group also advises on joint venture work between pension plans and advising corporates on structuring issues.

**The Lawyers:** **Nancy Iredale** (see p.296) brings a wealth of experience to all her cases. Renowned as *"extremely capable and competent,"* tax controversy is her primary focus. Tom Wisialowski is newly ensconced in the firm's Palo Alto office and acts on matters such as REITs.

### Pillsbury Winthrop Shaw Pittman LLP

See firm details p.1550

**The Firm:** Clients spoke of an efficient group, whose attorneys are *"cooperative, extremely responsive and leave no stone unturned in the attempt to get results."* The firm possesses a number of former government people among its ranks. Now that the dust has settled on the April 2005 merger, the tax group can display a broader and deeper service across 16 locations. The resultant deal flow illustrates this. For example, the team represented BancWest in its cash acquisition of Commercial Federal for $1.36 billion.

**The Lawyers:** Corporate and partnership work dominates the work roster of **Julie Divola** (see p.286). A *"thorough and creative lawyer,"* she engenders confidence in clients.

**Clients/Work Highlights:** Intel; Cisco Systems; Bank of America and Sun Microsystems.

### Other Notable Practitioners

**Larry Langdon** (see p.299) of Mayer, Brown, Rowe & Maw has *"a great tax mind."* Formerly of the IRS, Langdon is based in the Palo Alto office and deals with tax controversy and planning.

# Leaders in California

## ABEL, Sally
Fenwick & West LLP, Mountain View
650 335 7212
sabel@fenwick.com
*Recommended in Intellectual Property*
**Practice Areas:** Chair of firm's Trademark Group. International trademark/domain protection, selection/acquisition, registration, litigation/dispute resolution, internet issues and trade dress.
**Prof. Memberships:** Member, Board of Directors of International Trademark Association (INTA), 1998-2000; chaired INTA's Internet Subcommittee, 1996-98; recently chaired INTA's Issues and Policy Committee. Served as INTA's representative on 11 member International Ad Hoc Committee (IAHC), international body organized by Internet Society at behest of Internet Assigned Numbers Authority to develop enhancements to Internet Domain Name System. Participated in World Intellectual Property Organization's (WIPO) First Meeting of Consultants on Trademarks and Internet Domain Names, 1997.
**Career:** In 2001, named one of the top three most frequently nominated trademark lawyers in the world in Euromoney's 'Best of the Best' Global Guide to the World's Best Lawyers and included in Euromoney's 'Guide to the World's Leading Trademark Law Practitioners' for the past five years (2000-05); also included in Law Business Research Limited's 'International Who's Who of Business Lawyer' for the past five years (2000-05).
**Personal:** University of California Los Angeles School of Law, JD, 1984; University of California, Davis, BA in History summa cum laude, 1977.

## ABEL, Nancy L
Paul, Hastings, Janofsky & Walker LLP, Los Angeles 213 683 6162
nancyabell@paulhastings.com
*Recommended in Employment*
**Practice Areas:** Chair, Employment Law Department. Represents employers in employment class actions and individual discrimination/harassment/retaliation/wrongful discharge lawsuits, OFCCP and EEOC proceedings, labor negotiations and arbitrations.
**Prof. Memberships:** Fellow of the College of Labor and Employment Lawyers; Daily Journal 2005: one of California's Top 100 lawyers.
**Publications:** 'An Employer's Guide for Preparing Affirmative Action Programs'; 'An Employer's Guide to the Americans with Disabilities Act (1991)'; 'Employment Discrimination Law' Federal Contractor chapter.
**Personal:** Pitzer College of the Clare-

mont Colleges, 1972, first in class; UCLA School of Law, 1979, Order of the Coif and Order of the Barristers.

## ABRAMS, William
Pillsbury Winthrop Shaw Pittman LLP, San Francisco 650 233 4668
william.abrams@pillsburylaw.com
*Recommended in Intellectual Property*
**Practice Areas:** Mr Abrams has extensive experience in trials, arbitrations, mediations and appeals involving IP, business torts, constitutional law, employment, contracts and complex litigation throughout the US and abroad. He has represented clients in a wide range of industries and fields, including software/hardware companies; universities and research institutions; biotech; financial institutions; and wineries and alcoholic beverage companies. Additionally, Mr Abrams has defended management in wrongful termination, 'whistle-blowing', harassment, discrimination and other employment matters, and fraud, racketeering and misappropriation claims.
**Personal:** JD, University of Santa Clara Law School (1979, Managing Editor, Santa Clara Law Review); AB, Stanford University (1976, with honors).

## ADLER, Robert
Munger, Tolles & Olson LLP, Los Angeles 213 683 9100
*Recommended in Corporate/M&A*

## AGUIRRE, John E
Wilson Sonsini Goodrich & Rosati, Palo Alto 650 493 9300
jaguirre@wsgr.com
*Recommended in Employment*
**Practice Areas:** His practice encompasses all aspects of employee benefits and executive compensation, including tax, the Employee Retirement Income Security Act (ERISA), and federal and state securities law. He helps clients design and administer a wide array of plans, including tax-qualified retirement programs (for example, 401(k) plans), health and disability programs, equity-based compensation plans, and all kinds of executive compensation arrangements. He also has significant experience in the employee benefits and executive compensation aspects of mergers, acquisitions and spin transactions.
**Prof. Memberships:** Admitted to practice in Cailfornia.
**Personal:** JD, Stanford Law School, 1987; BA, University of California, Berkeley, 1984.

## AHRENS, Michael
Sheppard, Mullin, Richter & Hampton LLP, San Francisco 415 434 9100
*Recommended in Bankruptcy*

## ALEXANDER, Judith
Winn & Alexander LLP, Capitola
831 479 3490
*Recommended in Media & Entertainment*

## ALEXIS, Geraldine
Bingham McCutchen LLP, San Francisco 415 393 2054
geraldine.alexis@bingham.com
*Recommended in Antitrust*
**Practice Areas:** Serves as Co-Chair of the firm's Antitrust and Trade Regulation Practice Group. Represents clients before the US Department of Justice, the Federal Trade Commission and state antitrust enforcement agencies in mergers, acquisitions, joint ventures and other government antitrust investigations, with an emphasis on obtaining accelerated clearances from the relevant government agency. Counsels companies on the antitrust aspects of B2B electronic marketplaces.
**Career:** Served as attorney-advisor in the Justice Department's Office of Legal Counsel.
**Personal:** Northwestern University School of Law, JD, cum laude, 1976; Northwestern University, MBA, with distinction, 1975; University of Rochester, BA, magna cum laude, 1971.

## ALLCOCK, John
DLA Piper Rudnick Gray Cary US LLP, San Diego 619 699 2828
john.allcock@dlapiper.com
*Recommended in Intellectual Property*
**Practice Areas:** Intellectual property, patent litigation, life sciences.
**Career:** Focusing on patent litigation, he has extensive experience handling patent cases through trial and appeal to the Federal Circuit. In intellectual property litigation, he has tried 22 patent cases. In general litigation, he has extensive jury trial experience (Lead Counsel in excess of 50 cases tried to juries to verdict), arbitration experience (Lead Counsel in excess of 100 arbitrations), as well as extensive experience in court trials, International Trade Commission hearings, various forms of alternate dispute resolution, and management of complex litigation.
**Personal:** JD, Harvard Law School; AB, Boston College.

## ALVAREZ, Fred
Wilson Sonsini Goodrich & Rosati, Palo Alto 650 493 9300
falvarez@wsgr.com
*Recommended in Employment*
**Practice Areas:** Heads Employment Law Litigation Practice.
**Prof. Memberships:** Admitted to practice in California. Member, House of Delegates of the ABA; Equal Employment Opportunity Law Committee of the ABA

Labor and Employment Law Section; and Advisory Committee of the American Law Institute Restatement of Employment Law. Management Chair of the Employment Sub-Committee of the Class Actions and Derivative Suits Committee of the ABA Section of Litigation.
**Career:** Joined WSGR as Partner, 1997. Partner, Pillsbury Madison Sutro, 1989-97. Commissioner, US EEOC, 1984-87. Assistant Secretary of Labor of the US Department of Labor, 1987-89.
**Personal:** BA, Stanford, 1972; JD, Stanford, 1975.

## ANTHONY, William
Orrick, Herrington & Sutcliffe LLP, Menlo Park 650 614 7453
wanthony@orrick.com
*Recommended in Intellectual Property*
**Practice Areas:** Focuses his practice exclusively on technology and high-stakes patent litigation. Tried a substantial number of cases, to both jury and bench, involving semiconductors, computers, and biotechnology. Appeared numerous times before the Court of Appeals for the Federal Circuit.
**Prof. Memberships:** Admitted to practice before the Patent Office and in Connecticut, Michigan and California. Serves on the Santa Clara University School of Law Dean's High Tech Advisory Council.
**Publications:** Lectures for organizations like the American Intellectual Property Association and Intellectual Property Section of the California State Bar.
**Personal:** JD, University of Connecticut, 1966; BS, Worcester Polytechnic Institute, 1961.

## APPLEMAN, Jeff
Berry Appleman & Leiden LLP, San Francisco 415 398 1800
*Recommended in Immigration*

## ARGUEDAS, Cristina
Arguedas, Cassman & Headley, LLP, Berkeley 510 845 3000
*Recommended in Litigation*

## ARNOLD, Dennis
Gibson, Dunn & Crutcher LLP, Los Angeles 213 229 7864
darnold@gibsondunn.com
*Recommended in Real Estate*
**Practice Areas:** He has extensive experience in all aspects of commercial and residential real estate, commercial law, banking and finance law, as well as workouts, bankruptcy and debt restructuring and is a nationally recognized expert in real estate finance, insolvency and commercial law. He is a noted authority on secured transactions, the law of guaranties, letters of credit, and California's one action and anti-deficiency laws.
**Prof. Memberships:** Member, American College of Real Estate Lawyers.

**Publications:** Drafted California Civil Code Section 2856.
**Personal:** JD, Yale Law School, 1975.

## ARONSON, Seth
O'Melveny & Myers LLP, Los Angeles
213 430 7486
saronson@omm.com
*Recommended in Litigation*
**Practice Areas:** Seth Aronson is Head of O'Melveny & Myers' Los Angeles office and Chair of the firm's Securities Litigation Practice Group. He has significant trial and appellate experience in state and federal courts defending corporations, their directors, officers and professionals in securities class actions, shareholder derivative actions, mergers and acquisitions litigation, RICO, unfair competition, and consumer class actions under the California Business and Professions Code.

## ARONZON, Paul
Milbank, Tweed, Hadley & McCloy LLP, Los Angeles 213 892 4000
*Recommended in Bankruptcy*

## ASHCRAFT, Howard
Hanson, Bridgett, Marcus, Vlahos & Rudy, LLP, San Francisco
415 777 3200
*Recommended in Construction*

## ASPERGER, James
O'Melveny & Myers LLP, Los Angeles
213 430 6491
jasperger@omm.com
*Recommended in Litigation*
**Practice Areas:** Jim Asperger, Chair of O'Melveny & Myers' Global Enforcement and Criminal Defense Practice, specializes in civil and criminal trials, white-collar criminal defense, internal corporate investigations, and civil RICO and fraud actions. Jim has extensive trial experience, including 20 jury trials and well over 100 court trials and contested evidentiary hearings. He is a Fellow of the prestigious American College of Trial Lawyers. Jim has been recognized by the Los Angeles Business Journal as one of the top trial lawyers in Southern California and by Los Angeles Magazine as a 'Super Lawyer' in Southern California.

## BABBE, David B
Morrison & Foerster LLP, Los Angeles
213 892 5549
dbabbe@mofo.com
*Recommended in Insurance*
**Practice Areas:** Focused on advising and representing insurance companies in connection with coverage disputes. Has handled a broad range of coverage matters, including first party and third party claims, environmental, asbestos, toxic tort, mold, construction defect, and bad faith claims. Has represented insurers in coverage litigation in both state and federal courts throughout the western United States, as well as in arbitrations and mediations.

**Prof. Memberships:** Member, Litigation Section, American Bar Association. Member, Association of Business Trial Lawyers.
**Career:** Admitted to practice in California.
**Personal:** BA Degree, magna cum laude, University of California, Irvine, 1978; JD Degree, University of California, Los Angeles School of Law, 1981, Order of the Coif.

## BAKER, Tyler A
Fenwick & West LLP, Mountain View
650 335 7624
tbaker@fenwick.com
*Recommended in Antitrust*
**Practice Areas:** Chair of firm's Antitrust and Unfair Competition Group. Complex litigation, with primary emphasis on antitrust and intellectual property law. Extensive experience in all aspects of antitrust law, representing plaintiffs and defendants in civil antitrust trials, as well as individuals and companies that were targets in state and federal antitrust investigations. Has provided antitrust advice to clients on issues including distribution practices, joint ventures, pre-merger notification, and substantive merger reviews by the Department of Justice and Federal Trade Commission. Involved in numerous appeals in state and federal courts. Has argued in the United States Court of Appeals for the Fifth Circuit and several Texas state courts of appeal.
**Career:** Law clerk to US Judge Charles Renfrew, Northern District of California, and to Justice Lewis F Powell, Jr, United States Supreme Court, 1976. Law Professor, University of Virginia School of Law, 1978-81. Special Assistant to William F Baxter, Assistant Attorney General, Antitrust Division, United States Department of Justice, 1981-82.
**Personal:** Stanford Law School, JD with highest honors, 1975; Oxford University, BA in jurisprudence with first class honors (Rhodes Scholar), 1972; Southern Methodist University, BA in Economics with highest honors, 1969.

## BALABANIAN, David M
Bingham McCutchen LLP, San Francisco
415 393 2170
david.balabanian@bingham.com
*Recommended in Litigation*
**Practice Areas:** Has more than 35 years of experience in complex commercial litigation, representing a broad cross section of Fortune 100 clients ranging from financial institutions to international trading companies to software giants. Representative matters include People-Soft v Oracle, Sierra National Insurance Co. v Crédit Lyonnais, WWII forced labor cases, Reilly v The Hearst Corp. and Chemical Bank v S.C. Johnson Co. Has lectured in more than 150 courses on various litigation subjects.
**Personal:** Harvard Law School, LLB, cum laude, 1965; University of Oxford, Bachelor of Philosophy, 1962; Harvard

University, BA, magna cum laude, 1960.

## BALLATI, Deborah
Farella Braun & Martel LLP, San Francisco 415 954 4400
dballati@fbm.com
*Recommended in Construction*
**Practice Areas:** Senior Partner in Complex Litigation Department. Over 30 years of commercial litigation experience, specializing in construction and insurance coverage.
**Prof. Memberships:** Admitted to California Bar, 1975. ABA Forum on the Construction Industry (Chair, 2002-03). Thomson West Construction Group Advisory Board. AGC Legal Advisory Committee. CPR Construction Advisory Board, 2005-06. Fellow, American College of Construction Lawyers, 1997-present.
**Career:** Joined Farella, Braun + Martel LLP, 1977; Partner since 1983. Arbitrator, American Arbitration Association. Judge Pro Tem, SF Superior Court.
**Publications:** 'Privatizing Governmental Functions', Editor (Law Journal Press, 2001); 'State False Claims Acts: Expanding the Federal Model' (ABA, 1996); 'California's Experience with MBE/WBE/DBE Preference Programs after Croson' (AGC Legal Advisory Committee, 1995); 'Proving and Calculating Owner Damages' (Construction Business Review Magazine, 1991). Various construction and insurance seminars.
**Personal:** Born July 30, 1950. JD, Hastings College of Law, University of California, 1975 (Order of the Coif, Thurston Society). BA, Stanford University, 1972.

## BARAJAS, Dino
Paul, Hastings, Janofsky & Walker LLP, Los Angeles 213 683 6130
dinobarajas@paulhastings.com
*Recommended in Projects*
**Practice Areas:** Mr Barajas has extensive experience representing lenders, investors, and developers in a wide range of domestic and international project financings in the energy, power, infrastructure and commercial sectors, as well as traditional banking, structured finance, mergers and acquisitions, corporate finance, asset finance and joint ventures. His clients include commercial lenders, institutional investors, investment funds and project sponsors. Mr Barajas has worked on transactions in Argentina, Brazil, Chile, Colombia, Costa Rica, El Salvador, Guam, Guatemala, Honduras, Mexico, Nicaragua, the United States, Yemen and elsewhere.
**Career:** Mr Barajas was recognized by California Lawyer Magazine as 'Attorney of the Year (Energy)' in 2004. Additionally, Project Finance Magazine awarded the Tuxpan V Project and the Altamira II Project in Mexico, transactions for which Mr Barajas was lead attorney, the Latin American Deal of the Year (Power) 2004

and the Latin American Deal of the Year (Power) 2002, respectively. The Choloma III Project in Honduras, for which Mr Barajas was lead attorney, was first runner-up for the Latin American Deal of the Year (Power) 2004. Mr Barajas is recognized (one of only four California lawyers) in 'The International Who's Who of Project Finance Lawyers', 2005 (3rd Edition) for his accomplishments.
**Personal:** Mr Barajas is a Member of the State Bar of California. He received his JD from Harvard Law School and holds a Bachelor of Arts Degree summa cum laude in Communication Studies and the Business Emphasis Program from the University of California, Los Angeles. Mr Barajas is fluent in Spanish.

## BARR, Michael R
Pillsbury Winthrop Shaw Pittman LLP, San Francisco 415 983 1151
michael.barr@pillsburylaw.com
*Recommended in Environment*
**Practice Areas:** Mr Barr is the Co-Leader of Pillsbury's Environment, Land Use and Natural Resources Practice Section. He practices in the administrative, commercial and corporate law fields and has extensive experience assisting established and emerging ventures in the transportation, communications, computer, chemical, food products, energy, mining and manufacturing industries. Mr Barr focuses on emerging issues and innovative solutions to complex regulatory, commercial and corporate matters.
**Career:** Admitted to practice: State of California.
**Personal:** JD, Harvard University, 1973; BS, University of Washington at Seattle, 1970.

## BARRALL, James
Latham & Watkins LLP, Los Angeles
213 485 1234
*Recommended in Employment*

## BARSKY, Wayne
Gibson, Dunn & Crutcher LLP, Los Angeles 310 557 8183
wbarsky@gibsondunn.com
*Recommended in Intellectual Property*
**Practice Areas:** Co-Chair of the firm-wide Intellectual Property Practice Group. Practices exclusively in the area of patent litigation for clients in the biotech, computer, electronics and medical industries. Representative clients include Johnson & Johnson, Serono, Electronic Arts, Vivendi Universal, Neutrogena and Sega.
**Prof. Memberships:** American Intellectual Property Law Association, Federal Circuit Bar Association, American Bar Association.
**Publications:** Numerous publications and speaking engagements; frequent participant in Practising Law Institute programs on patent trial practice.
**Personal:** JD, UC Berkeley, Boalt Hall School of Law, 1983.

**BASICH, Anthony M**
Hogan & Hartson LLP, Los Angeles
310 785 4626
ambasich@hhlaw.com
*Recommended in Media & Entertainment*
**Practice Areas:** Extensive experience in commercial and general business litigation, with a focus on entertainment-related matters. Has successfully litigated copyright, trademark and contract-based actions involving idea submission, accounting, vertical integration, guild, product placement, employment and rights claims on behalf of major movie studios, television production companies and television networks.
**Prof. Memberships:** Member, Los Angeles County Bar Association.
**Career:** Former Member, Executive Committee, California State Bar Litigation Section; Former Chairman, Litigation Section, California Bar Education Committee; Former Chairman, Litigation Section, California Bar Trial Symposium Committee.
**Personal:** Stanford University (BS); The George Washington University (JD; Member, The George Washington Law Review).

**BAUER, Steven**
Latham & Watkins LLP, San Francisco
415 391 0600
*Recommended in Litigation*

**BAYSINGER, Kara**
Sonnenschein Nath & Rosenthal LLP, San Francisco 415 882 2475
kbaysinger@sonnenschein.com
*Recommended in Insurance*
**Practice Areas:** Insurance Practice Vice-Chair. Represents national insurance and reinsurance companies, insurance-related service companies and state governments in matters of market conduct (pro-active and reactive), compliance, government/regulatory relations, privacy, security, e-business, regulatory licensing and approvals, insurance entity transactions (including reinsurance), reinsurance and product and market development.
**Prof. Memberships:** Illinois and California Bar Associations, California State Bar Insurance Law Committee; Past Chair, California State Bar Group Insurance Programs Committee; Chairperson, California Advisory Counsel, BizWorld.
**Personal:** Loyola University School of Law, JD; University of Michigan, BA, Political Science.

**BEBAWY, Adel**
Latham & Watkins LLP, Los Angeles
213 485 1234
*Recommended in IT Outsourcing*

**BECK, Mark**
Beck, De Corso, Daly, Kreindler & Harris, Los Angeles 213 688 1198
*Recommended in Litigation*

**BEHNIA, Hatef**
Gibson, Dunn & Crutcher LLP, Los Angeles 213 229 7534
hbehnia@gibsondunn.com
*Recommended in Tax*
**Practice Areas:** Specializes in tax aspects of mergers and acquisitions, spin-offs and separations, debt and equity financings, derivative securities, partnership transactions, and taxation of financial institutions. Has successfully represented taxpayers before the Internal Revenue Service in cases involving significant audit adjustments. Representative clients include Washington Mutual, Technicolor, The Williams Companies, Herbalife, IAC, Qwest, BCBG Max Azria Group and Computer Sciences Corporation.
**Personal:** JD, University of Southern California, 1981, Order of the Coif, Note and Article Editor, University of Southern California Law Review. MBA, Stanford University Graduate School of Business, 1977. BA in Mathematics, Reed College, 1975.

**BELL, Suzanne Y**
Wilson Sonsini Goodrich & Rosati, Palo Alto 650 493 9300
sbell@wsgr.com
*Recommended in IT Outsourcing*
**Practice Areas:** Co-manages WSGR's Technology Transactions Practice. Handles technology and IP-related transactions, with an emphasis on strategic alliances for high technology and life sciences companies. Also counsels such clients with respect to new business models and IP issues.
**Prof. Memberships:** Admitted to practice in California.
**Career:** Joined WSGR, 1988. Became Partner, 1995. Co-Chair, Nominating Committee, WSGR. Former member, WSGR's Operations Committee, Executive Committee, Management Committee and Strategic Planning Committee.
**Personal:** JD (with distinction), Stanford Law School, 1988; MS, Columbia University, 1982; BA (cum laude), Middlebury College, 1980.

**BELLAH MAGUIRE, Jennifer**
Gibson, Dunn & Crutcher LLP, Los Angeles 213 229 7986
jbellah@gibsondunn.com
*Recommended in Corporate/M&A*
**Practice Areas:** Extensive experience in corporate transactions and securities work, with an emphasis on mergers and acquisitions and private equity matters, representing equity fund sponsors and investors in diverse fund formation matters. Recently represented Leonard Green & Partners in the pending acquisition of The Sports Authority.
**Career:** Joined Gibson, Dunn & Crutcher after clerking for the Ninth Circuit Court of Appeals and has practiced in the firm's Los Angeles offices and Paris office. Speaks fluent French and handles cross-border transactions.

**Personal:** JD, University of California, Boalt Hall School of Law, 1982, Order of the Coif, Associate Editor, Law Review.

**BENJAMIN, Alan**
Orrick, Herrington & Sutcliffe LLP, Los Angeles 213 612 2431
abenjamin@orrick.com
*Recommended in Banking & Finance*
**Practice Areas:** Mr Benjamin heads Orrick's Banking and Commercial Finance Group worldwide. He concentrates his practice on complex financial transactions, including secured and unsecured loan transactions, project financings, leveraged buyouts and major debt restructurings. He has particular expertise in lending to the gaming industry, including lending to Native American tribes.
**Career:** Orrick, Herrington & Sutcliffe LLP; Partner, 1994-present; Managing Director, 2001; Executive Committee Member, 1997-2001; Private Finance Group Chair, 1996-2000. Morrison & Foerster LLP, Partner, 1983-94; associate 1977-83.
**Personal:** JD, UCLA Law School, 1977; MBA in Finance, UCLA School of Management, 1977; AB in Economics, UCLA, 1974.

**BENNETT, Bruce**
Hennigan, Bennett & Dorman LLP, Los Angeles 213 694 1200
*Recommended in Bankruptcy*

**BENNETT, James P**
Morrison & Foerster LLP, San Francisco
415 268 7169
jbennett@mofo.com
*Recommended in Litigation*
**Practice Areas:** Commercial practice encompasses all manner of complex actions and IP matters, including patent infringement, misappropriate of trade secrets, insurance coverage and bad faith, securities and RICO cases, plus actions for breach of contract and business torts. Tried over 30 civil and criminal cases. Record includes four plaintiffs' cases in which verdicts and judgments obtained had a collective value in excess of $150 million. Has argued in the California Supreme Court, California Courts of Appeal and the Ninth Circuit.
**Prof. Memberships:** Associate Member, American Board of Trial Advocates; Fellow, American College of Trial Lawyers. Chair, Litigation Department, 1999-2003
**Career:** Admitted to practice in California.
**Personal:** BA, University of California, Berkeley, 1972; JD, UC Hastings College of the Law, 1975.

**BENUDIZ, P Peter**
Heller Ehrman LLP, Los Angeles
213 689 7513
peter.benudiz@hellerehrman.com
*Recommended in Real Estate*
**Practice Areas:** Real estate and finance, hospitality, debt finance, structured

finance.
**Prof. Memberships:** International Society of Hospitality Consultants, State Bar of California, Los Angeles County Bar Association.
**Career:** Mr Benudiz has been the lead on financings, acquisitions and dispositions of billions of dollars of real estate and hospitality assets, including land assemblages; development of office projects, shopping centers, multi-use developments; acquisitions, dispositions and financings of limited service hotels, five star luxury resorts, golf courses and spas. He has also managed partnership and corporate securities issues, tax issues, workouts, bankruptcies and litigation, and management agreements and franchise agreements.

**BENVENUTTI, Peter J**
Heller Ehrman LLP, San Francisco
415 772 6403
peter.benvenutti@hellerehrman.com
*Recommended in Bankruptcy*
**Practice Areas:** Restructuring and insolvency.
**Prof. Memberships:** State Bar of California; American Bar Association; Bar Association of San Francisco; American College of Bankruptcy.
**Career:** Mr Benvenutti has engaged in a Bankruptcy and Creditors' Rights Practice since 1974. In the bankruptcy courts, he has represented secured and unsecured institutional lenders, reorganization trustees, debtors in possession, creditors' committees, real and personal property lessors, asset acquirers, and venture capital investors in reorganization cases, and parties in litigation.
**Personal:** Harvard College (BA, cum laude, 1971); University of California, Berkeley, Boalt Hall School of Law (JD, 1974); Order of the Coif.

**BERCHILD, John**
Sheppard, Mullin, Richter & Hampton LLP, Los Angeles 213 620 1780
*Recommended in Banking & Finance*

**BERGER, Don**
Latham & Watkins LLP, Los Angeles
213 485 1234
*Recommended in Real Estate*

**BERGMAN, Michael**
Weissmann, Wolff, Bergman, Coleman, Grodin & Evall, LLP, Beverly Hills
310 858 7888
*Recommended in Media & Entertainment*

**BERKES, Robert**
Berkes Crane Robinson & Seal, LLP, Los Angeles 213 955 1150
*Recommended in Insurance*

**BERKOWITZ, Alan R**
Bingham McCutchen LLP, San Francisco
415 393 2636
alan.berkowitz@bingham.com
*Recommended in Employment*

**Practice Areas:** Has extensive experience in labor/management issues, including union election campaigns, picketing, unfair labor practice proceedings, labor arbitrations and collective bargaining. Focuses on wrongful termination, discrimination, sexual harassment, unfair competition, and wage and hour matters. With a 95 percent win rate, has tried more than 50 cases, including civil jury and non-jury matters in state court; civil and criminal contempt cases in US District Court; and administrative trials before the NLRB.
**Career:** Served in various roles as an attorney with the National Labor Relations Board.
**Personal:** American University, Washington College of Law, JD, 1967; Drake University, BA, 1964.

### BERMAN, Jeffrey
Sidley Austin LLP, Los Angeles
213 896 6655
jberman@sidley.com
*Recommended in Employment*
**Practice Areas:** Partner in the Labor and Employment Practice. Has represented management in a wide variety of industries, including major medical centers, universities, newspaper publishers, airlines, banks, motion picture and television producers, insurance companies, retailers and manufacturers. Mr Berman has been involved in almost every aspect of labor and employment law. He has represented employers in nearly all of the National Labor Relations Board's regional offices in the Western United States.
**Prof. Memberships:** Legal Committee of the Employers Group, as well as the Chair of its Amicus Committee, Fellow of The College of Labor and Employment Lawyers, Labor Relations Advisory Committee.
**Personal:** University of California at Los Angeles, JD, 1971; University of California, Santa Barbara BA, 1968. Admissions: US Court of Appeals, Ninth Circuit; US District Court, ED of California; US District Court, ND of California; US District Court, CD of California; US District Court, SD of California; California, 1972.

### BERRY, David
Berry Appleman & Leiden LLP,
San Francisco 415 398 1800
*Recommended in Immigration*

### BERTELSEN, Mark A
Wilson Sonsini Goodrich & Rosati,
Palo Alto 650 493 9300
mbertelsen@wsgr.com
*Recommended in Corporate/M&A*
**Practice Areas:** Corporate law and governance, M&A, international and cross-border transactions.
**Prof. Memberships:** Admitted to practice in California.
**Career:** Joined WSGR, 1972; became Partner, 1977. Member, WSGR Policy Committee and Executive Management

Committee. Former Managing Partner, 1990-96. Prior to joining firm, served two years as an officer in the US Army. Serves on a number of boards of directors and is currently a Director of Autodesk and a Trustee of The UCSB Foundation.
**Personal:** JD, Boalt Hall School of Law, University of California (Berkeley), 1969; BA, high honors, University of California (Santa Barbara), 1966.

### BIDART, Michael
Shernoff, Bidart & Darras LLP,
Claremont 909 621 4935
*Recommended in Insurance*

### BIRD, Terry
Bird, Marella, Boxer & Wolpert PC,
Los Angeles 310 201 2100
*Recommended in Litigation*

### BLANCHARD, Timothy P
McDermott Will & Emery, Los Angeles
310 551 9320
tblanchard@mwe.com
*Recommended in Healthcare*
**Practice Areas:** Healthcare regulatory compliance and payment issues, including Medicare and Medicaid coverage and billing rules, payment appeals, HIPAA privacy, fraud and abuse audits and investigations, false claims act defense, certification and licensing, and utilization review.
**Prof. Memberships:** Member of Board of Directors of American Health Lawyers Association (AHLA); Co-Chair of AHLA's Annual Institute on Medicare and Medicaid Payment Issues; Fellow, Healthcare Financial Management Association.
**Personal:** Saint Louis University (JD, cum laude, MHA); Oklahoma State University (BS, with honors).

### BLASHEK, Robert D
O'Melveny & Myers LLP, Los Angeles
310 246 6790
rblashek@omm.com
*Recommended in Tax*
**Practice Areas:** Rob Blashek's practice covers a broad range of federal and California income tax matters, with particular emphasis on private equity fund formation, corporate acquisitions, reorganizations, and financings; bankruptcy and workouts; partnerships/joint ventures; and general business tax planning. In recent years, Rob has handled the tax aspects of numerous mergers and acquisitions of major companies, as well as bankruptcies and workouts. He has also formed or assisted in the formation of numerous private equity partnerships.

### BLEARS, Norman J
Heller Ehrman LLP, Menlo Park
650 324 7017
norman.blears@hellerehrman.com
*Recommended in Litigation*
**Practice Areas:** Securities litigation, corporate governance.
**Prof. Memberships:** American Bar

Association; State Bar of California; Santa Clara County Bar Association; Law Foundation Board of Directors.
**Career:** Mr Blears has represented corporations, officers, outside directors and accountants in class actions, shareholder derivative actions and complex co-ordinated investor lawsuits in both state and federal courts, as well as in government regulatory proceedings. He has led successful defense efforts in all aspects of securities litigation, including jury trial and appeal. Mr Blears has served as a court-appointed special master and arbitrator in both state and federal court.
**Personal:** Stanford Law School (JD, 1980).

### BLECHER, Maxwell M
Blecher & Collins, Los Angeles
213 622 4222
mblecher@blechercollins.com
*Recommended in Antitrust, Litigation*
**Practice Areas:** Antitrust litigation; complex business litigation; intellectual property litigation; professional malpractice litigation; class actions.
**Prof. Memberships:** American Bar Association; State Bar of California; Los Angeles County Bar Association; American College of Trial Lawyers (Fellow); American Board of Trial Advocates (Fellow); American Judicature Society; Chancery Club; Association of Business Trial Lawyers.
**Career:** Maxwell M Blecher, the founding Partner of Blecher & Collins, is renowned for his expertise in the antitrust field. He has litigated significant cases resulting in many precedent-setting decisions in state and federal courts and the Supreme Court. He has testified before Congressional hearings; authored numerous articles on antitrust and civil litigation; and lectures extensively on antitrust and trial practice at programs sponsored by federal, state and local bar associations.

### BLEY, Kenneth
Cox Castle & Nicholson LLP, Los Angeles
310 277 4222
*Recommended in Real Estate*

### BLOOM, Jacob
Bloom, Hergott and Diemer LLP,
Beverly Hills 310 859 6800
*Recommended in Media & Entertainment*

### BLOOM, Jerry
White & Case LLP, Los Angeles
213 620 7707
jbloom@whitecase.com
*Recommended in Energy*
**Practice Areas:** Engages in a broad-based regulatory, infrastructure and project finance practice, emphasizing the development and operation of independent energy projects in the United States and abroad, and electric industry restructuring and privatization. Represents an

amalgam of energy-related clients, including power generation developers and sponsors, wholesalers, marketers, end-users and foreign governments. Also continues to be a leading advocate of diversified and competitive electric markets. Chair of White & Case's Energy Practice, which integrates firm-wide energy-related services across firm practice areas, such as bankruptcy, mergers and acquisitions, project and structured finance, and litigation.

### BOGDANOFF, Lee R
Klee, Tuchin, Bogdanoff & Stern LLP,
Los Angeles 310 407 4070
lbogdanoff@ktbslaw.com
*Recommended in Bankruptcy*
**Practice Areas:** Is a member and Co-Manager of Klee, Tuchin, Bogdanoff & Stern LLP. He has represented debtors in and out-of-court, often in very large and complex cases, as well as parties interested in acquiring assets from debtors. Recent debtor representations include Sun World International and Crescent Jewelers. He has also represented creditors' committees, including serving as counsel to the official noteholders' committee in National Energy and Gas Transmission. Has served as lead counsel in some of the largest chapter 11 cases pending at the time. Recent representations include Sun World International and Crescent Jewelers. He has represented many acquirers and post-petition lenders, including in Read Rite International and International Industrial Services, Inc.

### BOGEN, Andrew E
Gibson, Dunn & Crutcher LLP,
Los Angeles 213 229 7159
abogen@gibsondunn.com
*Recommended in Corporate/M&A*
**Practice Areas:** Advises clients on matters involving corporate transactions and securities law, mergers and acquisitions, and insolvency issues. Represented special board committees and corporations in matters involving corporate governance, finance, and restructuring. Recent successes include his representation of Allergan Corporation in its tender offer for Inamed and Northrop Grumman in its acquisitions of TRW and Litton Industries.
**Prof. Memberships:** Member of firm's Executive Committee 1990-2004.
**Personal:** LLB, Harvard University, 1966, cum laude.

### BOHLER, William
Townsend and Townsend and Crew LLP,
Palo Alto 650 326 2400
*Recommended in Intellectual Property*

### BOLDING, Grady
Orrick, Herrington & Sutcliffe LLP,
San Francisco 415 773 5716
gbolding@orrick.com
*Recommended in Tax*
**Practice Areas:** Practices in the area of

federal income tax and fund formation. Emphasizes corporate transactions - including acquisitions, divestitures and spin-offs, partnership and limited liability company transactions, real estate transactions, and REITs.
**Prof. Memberships:** State Bar of California; Best Lawyers in America.
**Career:** Prior to joining Orrick, Mr Bolding had devoted his career to the firm of Brobeck Phleger & Harrison, where he served on the firm's Executive Committee and as Chair of the Tax Group.
**Personal:** JD, cum laude, Harvard University Law School, 1977; BA, cum laude, Harvard University, 1973.

### BOMSE, Stephen
Heller Ehrman LLP, San Francisco
415 772 6142
steve.bomse@hellerehrman.com
*Recommended in Antitrust, Litigation*
**Practice Areas:** Antitrust and trade regulation; appeals and strategy; international arbitration and ADR.
**Prof. Memberships:** American Bar Association; State Bar of California; Bar Association of San Francisco; American Law Institute; American Bar Foundation.
**Career:** Mr Bomse's practice emphasizes antitrust litigation, although he has tried complex cases in a number of areas. He has written and lectured extensively in the antitrust field. He has tried cases involving multi-billion dollar claims in several states while also maintaining a significant appellate practice.
**Personal:** Stanford University (AB, with honors, 1964); Yale Law School (LLB, 1967).

### BOOKIN, Daniel
O'Melveny & Myers LLP, San Francisco
415 984 8700
*Recommended in Litigation*

### BOOKMAN, Lloyd
Hooper Lundy & Bookman Inc,
Los Angeles 310 551 8111
*Recommended in Healthcare*

### BOOTH, William
Law Offices of William H Booth,
Walnut Creek 925 296 2460
*Recommended in Energy*

### BOSTWICK, Gary
Sheppard, Mullin, Richter & Hampton LLP,
Los Angeles 213 620 1780
*Recommended in Media & Entertainment*

### BOUTROUS JR, Theodore J
Gibson, Dunn & Crutcher LLP,
Los Angeles 213 229 7804
tboutrous@gibsondunn.com
*Recommended in Media & Entertainment, Products Liability*
**Practice Areas:** Co-Chair of Media and Entertainment and Appellate Groups. Represents media organizations and reporters in First Amendment, access,

subpoena, libel, and prior restraint matters. Clients include NBC, CNN, Fox, Wall Street Journal, Time Inc. and Martin Bashir. Also represents businesses appealing large jury verdicts. Persuaded US Supreme Court to vacate largest ever personal injury award on behalf of Ford. Persuaded federal court to overturn largest ever libel verdict on behalf of Wall Street Journal.
**Personal:** JD, University of San Diego School of Law, 1987, summa cum laude, valedictorian, Editor-in-Chief, Law Review.

### BOXER, Mark H
Morgan, Lewis & Bockius LLP,
San Francisco 415 442 1695
mboxer@morganlewis.com
*Recommended in Employment*
**Practice Areas:** Mr Boxer is a Partner in the San Francisco office in the Employee Benefits Practice Group. He advises employers on all aspects of employee benefit matters. Practice emphasis is on the design and drafting of qualified retirement plans and welfare plans, advising clients as to their fiduciary duties under Title I of ERISA and the design and funding of executive deferred compensation arrangements.

### BRANCA, John
Ziffren Brittenham Branca Fischer
Gilbert-Lurie & Stiffelman LLP,
Los Angeles 310 552 3388
*Recommended in Media & Entertainment*

### BRAUN, Lawrence
Sheppard, Mullin, Richter & Hampton LLP,
Los Angeles 213 620 1780
*Recommended in Corporate/M&A*

### BREWER JR, Robert S
McKenna Long & Aldridge LLP,
San Diego 619 595 5400
rbrewer@mckennalong.com
*Recommended in Litigation*
**Practice Areas:** Managing Partner of San Diego office. Represents officers, directors and employees in complex civil and criminal litigation cases including government contract procurement fraud; fraud and false claims and qui tam; intellectual property; securities/shareholder disputes; trade secrets; professional negligence; corporate compliance; corporate investigations; class action defense.
**Prof. Memberships:** Fellow of the American College of Trial Lawyers; Member of American Bar Association, Association of Business Trial Lawyers; San Diego County Bar Association; Master of Enright Inn of Court (President in 2005-06); Member of Board of Directors of Federal Defenders, Inc.; Deputy District Attorney 1975-77; Assistant United States Attorney, Criminal Division, 1977-81.
**Publications:** Numerous Bar Publications re: 'Business Crimes and Evidentiary Issues'.

**Personal:** St Lawrence University, BA, 1968; University of San Diego, JD, 1975; Captain, US Army, Infantry, active duty, 1968-72.

### BRIAN, Brad
Munger, Tolles & Olson LLP, Los Angeles
213 683 9100
*Recommended in Litigation*

### BRIDGES, Andrew
Winston & Strawn LLP, San Francisco
415 591 1482
abridges@winston.com
*Recommended in Intellectual Property*
**Practice Areas:** Complex trial and appellate litigation and litigation-risk counseling, especially in trademark, copyright, advertising, publicity, trade secret, unfair competition, consumer protection, and license disputes.
**Prof. Memberships:** Early Neutral Evaluator, US District Court, Northern District of California. Domain Name Panelist, WIPO Arbitration and Mediation Center. Trustee, Copyright Society of the USA. Issues Council, Emerging Issues Committee of International Trademark Association.
**Career:** Law clerk to US District Judge Marvin Shoob, Atlanta, 1983-85. Previously Partner and Head of Trademarks and Advertising Practices Group, Wilson Sonsini Goodrich & Rosati; to Winston & Strawn as Partner, 2004. Cases include the landmark 1999 victory defending Diamond Multimedia's Rio MP3 music player against the recording industry; victory for MasterCard in a contributory copyright/trademark lawsuit by a publisher based on processing of internet merchant transactions; and victory for ClearPlay, maker of DVD playback filtering technology, in trademark and copyright claims brought by Hollywood studios and directors. Other notable representations include Netscape, Napster, Digital Media Association, StreamCast Networks (MGM v Grokster) and Google.
**Publications:** Frequent lecturer on internet law and litigation topics. Taught classes at Stanford, Columbia, Michigan and other law schools. Addressed conferences for Federal Judicial Center, Copyright Office of the United States, Copyright Society of USA, ABA, University of Amsterdam, International Trademark Association, and Practising Law Institute.
**Personal:** AB (with distinction), Phi Beta Kappa, Stanford Univ, 1976; BA(Hons.) and MA, Univ. of Oxford, 1980 and 1985; JD (cum laude) Harvard Law School, 1983. Board Member, Ronald McDonald House at Stanford. Languages: Modern Greek, French, Italian.

### BRITTENHAM, Harry
Ziffren Brittenham Branca Fischer
Gilbert-Lurie & Stiffelman LLP,
Los Angeles 310 552 3388
*Recommended in Media & Entertainment*

### BROCKLAND, John
Cooley Godward LLP, Palo Alto
650 843 5000
*Recommended in IT Outsourcing*

### BRODY, Sara
Heller Ehrman LLP, San Francisco
415 772 6475
sara.brody@hellerehrman.com
*Recommended in Litigation*
**Practice Areas:** Securities litigation; corporate governance.
**Prof. Memberships:** State Bar of California; American Bar Association; San Francisco Bar Association.
**Career:** Ms Brody has extensive experience in securities litigation, defending issuers, officers, directors, underwriters and venture capital firms in shareholder class actions and derivative actions in state and federal courts throughout the United States. She has extensive experience representing companies and individuals in matters involving Securities and Exchange Commission and self-regulatory organizations such as the National Association of Securities Dealers.
**Personal:** University of California, Berkeley (BA, 1982); Emory University School of Law (JD, 1987).

### BROSNAHAN, James
Morrison & Foerster LLP, San Francisco
415 268 7189
jbrosnahan@mofo.com
*Recommended in Litigation*
**Practice Areas:** Civil and criminal trial attorney. Approximately 139 jury cases. Argued both civil and criminal appeals in state and federal court, including two cases in the United States Supreme Court.
**Career:** Admitted to practice in Arizona and California. Practiced five years as Assistant US Attorney in Arizona and San Francisco. Associate Member, Office of Independent Counsel: Iran-Contra. Lead prosecutor, US v. Caspar Weinberger (1992). Inducted into: Trial Lawyers Hall of Fame, State Bar of California, 1996. Received: Trial Lawyer of the Year, ABTA 2001; Legend of the Law, San Francisco Lawyers' Club 2002; Top 100 Most Influential Attorneys, Daily Journal newspaper 2003; 500 Leading Lawyers in America, Lawdragon 2005.
**Personal:** BSBA, Boston College, 1956; LLB, Harvard Law School, 1959.

### BROWN, Donald W
Covington & Burling, San Francisco
415 591 7063
dwbrown@cov.com
*Recommended in Insurance*
**Practice Areas:** Trial lawyer representing policyholders with substantial claims to coverage under all types of policies, including directors and officers liability claims, false advertising and other media/advertiser liability claims, consumer fraud and unfair business practices claims, mass tort, errors and omissions, patent infringement, construction defect,

and catastrophic property damage claims. Major clients include Adelphia, Anschutz Company, Exxon Mobil, Fibreboard, Home Shopping Network, Imperial Oil, McDonald's, McKesson, Morgan Stanley, Vail Resorts and Vulcan Materials Company.

**Publications:** 'Business and Commercial Litigation in Federal Courts' (West 2005) (Insurance chapter co-author).

**Personal:** JD, Yale Law School, 1978; AB, Ohio University, summa cum laude, 1975.

## BROWN, Harald
Gang Tyre Ramer & Brown, Beverly Hills
310 777 4800
*Recommended in Media & Entertainment*

## BROWN, Nicholas A
Weil, Gotshal & Manges LLP, Redwood Shores 650 802 3100
nicholas.brown@weil.com
*Recommended in Intellectual Property*

**Practice Areas:** Nicholas Brown is a senior associate in Weil Gotshal's Patent Litigation Group and specializes in intellectual property litigation, particularly patent litigation involving complex technology. Mr Brown has experience in cases involving semiconductor manufacturing, DNA sequencing and biotechnology, digital media, software, and medical devices. Mr Brown has trial experience representing companies such as Applied Materials, Applera, and Samsung, and has litigated in federal courts across the country, the 9th and Federal Circuits, and California state courts.

**Personal:** Harvard Law School, JD magna cum laude, 1998; Princeton University, AB, 1995.

## BROWN, Walt
Orrick, Herrington & Sutcliffe LLP, San Francisco 415 773 5995
wbrown@orrick.com
*Recommended in Litigation*

**Practice Areas:** Focuses on white-collar criminal defense and complex business litigation. Represents companies and individuals in connection with criminal and regulatory investigations, as well as parallel civil and administrative proceedings. Extensive experience in cases involving securities fraud, antitrust offenses, mail and wire fraud, computer crimes, healthcare fraud, defense contractor fraud, public corruption, environmental crimes, tax evasion and money laundering.

**Career:** Brown was an Assistant United States Attorney in the Criminal Division of the US Attorney's Office for the Central District of California from 1989-94.

**Personal:** JD, University of Notre Dame, 1985; AB, UC Berkeley, 1982.

## BRUEN, James
Farella Braun & Martel LLP, San Francisco 415 954 4400
*Recommended in Environment*

## BRYAN, Karen
Latham & Watkins LLP, Los Angeles
213 485 1234
*Recommended in Tax*

## BUNSOW, Henry
Howrey LLP, San Francisco
415 848 4900
*Recommended in Intellectual Property*

## BUONCRISTIANI, David
Thelen Reid & Priest LLP, San Francisco
415 369 7227
dbuoncristiani@thelenreid.com
*Recommended in Construction*

**Practice Areas:** Mr Buoncristiani has more than 34 years of commercial litigation experience with primary emphasis on construction industry related disputes, including all facets of public and private construction works of improvement; representation of contractors in bid protest disputes arising under competitively-bid contracts; claim preparation and claim evaluation; prosecution and defense of contractor claims before both state and federal courts and before arbitration tribunals and governmental administrative panels, such as the Board of Contract Appeals. He is experienced in all phases of discovery and pre-trial/pre-hearing procedures and adversarial hearings and in the preparation and use of both manual and computerized document/ information indexing and retrieval systems and computer-generated graphics and evidence. He also has extensive experience with mediation and other forms of alternative dispute resolution.

**Prof. Memberships:** Fellow, American College of Construction Lawyers; American Bar Association, Forum on the Construction Industry and Public Contracts and Litigation Sections; Associated General Contractors Legal Advisory Committee, 1984-98; Bar Association of San Francisco; State Bar of California (1972); Member, Thurston Honor Society; Member, The Olympic Club.

**Career:** Partner of Thelen Reid & Priest LLP. Admitted to practice before all California Courts and US Court of Federal Claims, (1976). Speaking Engagements include: ADR Superconference, 1998; Practicing Law Institute, 'Delay v. Disruption v. Inefficiency Claims', 2003; Panel Member, Practicing Law Institute Program on Handling Construction Risks, April 2004; Panel Member, International Bar Association Program on Energy and Resource Law, May 2004.

**Personal:** Received his JD from the University of California, Hastings College of the Law in 1971, where he was a member of Thurston Honor Society and the Order of the Coif. Received his BA from University of San Francisco in 1968. Recognized as one of the leading construction attorneys in the United States, '2003-04 Chambers USA Guide to America's Leading Business Lawyers'; named Super

Lawyer 9/2004 issue of San Francisco Magazine.

## BURKE, P John
Akin Gump Strauss Hauer & Feld LLP, Los Angeles 310 229 1038
jburke@akingump.com
*Recommended in Media & Entertainment*

**Practice Areas:** Represents financial institutions, producers, high net worth individuals, studios and distributors in production, financing and distribution matters, with emphasis on complex financing and co-production arrangements worldwide.

**Prof. Memberships:** Officer and Corporate Counsel, American Film Institute; Co-Chair, Advisory Committee, UCLA Entertainment Law Symposium (2002-04); Advisory Board Member, AFI International Film Festival (2000-03); Member, Board of Directors, Japan America Society (1988-92); Member, Intellectual Property and Entertainment Law Section, Los Angeles County Bar Association; Member, Entertainment Law Section, Beverly Hills Bar Association.

**Personal:** BA, University of Southern California (1973); JD, Southwestern University School of Law (1976), LLM, New York University (1977).

## BURKE, Thomas
Davis Wright Tremaine LLP, San Francisco 415 276 6500
*Recommended in Media & Entertainment*

## BURMEISTER, Edward
Baker & McKenzie, San Francisco
415 576 3029
edward.d.burmeister@bakernet.com
*Recommended in Employment*

**Practice Areas:** Assisting multinational companies in extending their stock plans to employees outside the United States including option exchange programs, implementation of global stock purchase plans, implementation of restricted stock unit plans, stock appreciation rights plans, tax chargeback arrangements, social security minimization projects, and tax 'audits' of global equity plan compliance.

**Prof. Memberships:** Past Chairman of the State Bar of California – Taxation Section. Listed in The Best Lawyers of America, Member of the Advisory Board of the National Association of Stock Plan Professionals, Advisory Board of the Certified Equity Professional Institute, Santa Clara University, Board of the Global Equity Organization, International Foundation of Employee Benefit Plans, and the Western Pension and Benefits Conference.

**Career:** Principal shareholder, Baker & McKenzie LLP since January, 1988, Head of Global Equity Services Practice; Gray, Cary, Ames & Frye; Landels, Ripley & Diamond; O'Melveny & Myers.

**Publications:** Frequent lecturer on international equity issues. Presentations to the National Association of Stock Plan Professionals, the Tax Executive Institute, the Global Equity Organization, the National Center for Employee Ownership and the Foundation for Enterprise Development. Authored an article, published in the Spring 2001 edition of the WorldatWork Journal, entitled 'Top 10 Mistakes in Implementing a Global Stock Plan'.

**Personal:** Stanford University (AB); Stanford Law School (JD) Order of the Coif and Managing Editor of the Stanford Law Review; admitted to practice in California and before the US Tax Court and Claims Court.

## CAIRNS, James
White & Case LLP, Los Angeles
213 620 7739
jcairns@whitecase.com
*Recommended in Banking & Finance*

**Practice Areas:** Has a Bank Finance Practice with an emphasis on leasing and equipment finance. Represents and advises lessors, lessees, lenders, intermediaries and equity interests in a wide variety of equipment leasing transactions and has particular experience in domestic and cross-border aircraft leasing and financing. Recent aircraft transactions have involved many jurisdictions, including the US, Canada, India, Indonesia and Russia. Other lease transactions have involved railcars, and telecommunications, manufacturing and gas production equipment. Also represents US-based commercial paper conduits in making investments and in acquiring liquidity.

## CALABRESE, Joseph
O'Melveny & Myers LLP, Los Angeles
310 246 6743
jcalabrese@omm.com
*Recommended in Media & Entertainment*

**Practice Areas:** Joe Calabrese chairs O'Melveny & Myers' Entertainment and Media Practice and heads their Century City office. His practice includes general entertainment/media/sports counsel and specialized entertainment and media acquisitions and finance counsel. Joe represents major producers, studios, independent film, television and music companies, video game publishers, sports licensing organizations and financial institutions in all aspects of their business, including complex distribution and licensing transactions, mergers and acquisitions, structured financing and the formation of joint ventures. Joe regularly advises American companies doing business overseas and global media companies seeking to establish or expand their presence in the United States.

## CAMAHORT, Steve L

O'Melveny & Myers LLP, San Francisco
415 984 8930
scamahort@omm.com
*Recommended in Corporate/M&A*

**Practice Areas:** Steve Camahort has extensive experience in mergers and acquisitions and related corporate governance issues. He has worked for corporate clients, private equity funds and financial advisors in negotiated and hostile transactions in the technology, healthcare, entertainment and media, consumer products, aerospace, real estate, utility and other industries. Since 1999, Steve has advised principals in 25 transactions with an announced value of at least $1 billion, as well as numerous smaller transactions. Steve has also advised numerous investment banks in their capacity as financial advisor in M&A transactions.

## CANE, Paul

Paul, Hastings, Janofsky & Walker LLP, San Francisco 415 856 6000
*Recommended in Employment*

## CAREY, Stevens

Pircher, Nichols & Meeks, Los Angeles
310 201 8900
*Recommended in Real Estate*

## CARROLL, Michael

Latham & Watkins LLP, Costa Mesa
714 540 1235
*Recommended in Environment*

## CARUSO, Joanne

Howrey LLP, Los Angeles
213 892 1800
*Recommended in Litigation*

## CATHCART, Patrick

Cathcart, Collins & Kneafsey LLP,
Los Angeles 213 225 6600
pcathcart@cckllp.com
*Recommended in Insurance*

**Practice Areas:** Founding Partner of Cathcart Collins & Kneafsey LLP in Los Angeles, California, in 2005. Partner and Co-Chair of Business Litigation Practice Group at Hancock Rothert & Bunshoft LLP through December 2004. Concentrates on complex, multi-party business litigation. Has been lead defense counsel, or trial counsel, in the following cases: Pintlar v Aetna (the Bunker Hill litigation) (US District Court, Idaho); Martin Marietta et al v Aetna Casualty & Surety Co. (Los Angeles) (two jury trials); FMC Corporation v Liberty Mutual, et al (San Jose, California) (three month jury trial); Rockwell International Corporation v Aetna Cas. & Surety Co., et al (Los Angeles); Southern California Gas Co. v AEGIS, Ltd., et al (Los Angeles); McColl-Frontenac Inc. v Adriatic Insurance Company et al (Los Angeles); Armstrong v Aetna (six week arbitration in 1998, before retired US District Judge Nicholas Bua, Chicago, Illinois); Golden Eagle v Associated International Ins. Co., et al

(Los Angeles) Highlands Ins. Co. v Powerine Oil Company and related cross actions (Los Angeles); Fuller-Austin v Fireman's Fund (Los Angeles). Is involved in litigation on behalf of clients against Del Monte Corporation (litigation pending in Hawaii), I C Industries, Southern Pacific Transportation Company. Has represented clients before appellate courts on a variety of issues (see Certain Underwriters at Lloyd's, London v Superior Court 24 Cal 4th 945 (2001)), most recently in Hool and Meeker v Village Roadshow Pictures (unpublished opinion). Has litigated intellectual property disputes, beginning with litigation between PC Magazine and PC World Magazine over trade name infringement in 1983 and in connection with a trademark copyright dispute against the Walt Disney Company. Has represented a major contractor in two arbitrations in the Hague, Netherlands, in connection with construction disputes involving pipeline and pumping station contracts with the government of Iran, and motion picture producers in a suit against Village Roadshow Pictures (an Australian motion picture production, distribution and exhibition company). Trial counsel in Fuller-Austin v Highlands Ins. Company, the subject of a just published Court of Appeal decision in California. Extensive experience in handling professional liability claims against lawyers and law firms.

**Prof. Memberships:** American Bar Association; State Bar of California; Association of Business Trial Lawyers, Los Angeles (Member of Board of Governors, currently President); Los Angeles County Bar Association. Formerly, International Bar Association (Chair, Committee 13).

**Career:** Admitted to California Bar (1975). Law clerk to US District Court Judge Spencer Williams (N D Cal) (1975-77). Partner at Hancock Rothert & Bunshoft LLP (1982), and founded the firm's Los Angeles office in 1989. Partner at Cathcart Collins & Kneafsey LLP (2005 to present).

**Personal:** JD from University of California Hastings College of Law (1975); AB from Stanford University (1968); graduate, Phillips Academy, Andover (1964). Member, US Peace Corps/Iran (1969-71).

## CELEBREZZE, Bruce

Sedgwick, Detert, Moran & Arnold,
San Francisco 415 781 7900
*Recommended in Insurance*

## CHADWICK, James

DLA Piper Rudnick Gray Cary US LLP,
Palo Alto 650 833 2293
james.chadwick@dlapiper.com
*Recommended in Media & Entertainment*

**Practice Areas:** Media and new media.
**Career:** He focuses on media law and media defense litigation, First Amend-

ment and privacy law, trademark and copyright law, civil litigation, and white-collar criminal defense.

**Personal:** JD, Santa Clara University; MA, San Francisco State University; BA, University of California, Santa Cruz.

## CHANIN, Jeffrey R

Keker & Van Nest LLP, San Francisco
415 391 5400
jchanin@kvn.com
*Recommended in Intellectual Property*

**Practice Areas:** Jeff Chanin's practice spans the range of complex IP, commercial litigation and white-collar criminal defense, with a specialization in trade secret misappropriation. Jeff also represents companies and individuals in copyright and patent infringement cases, and in civil and criminal False Claims Act, securities fraud, and Foreign Corrupt Practices Act investigations and prosecutions.

**Prof. Memberships:** Fellow of the American Bar Foundation; member of the San Francisco Bay Area Intellectual Property Inns of Court; former chair of the ABA Subcommittee on Uniform Trade Secrets Act/Federal Protection for Trade Secrets.

**Career:** Recognized by Best Lawyers in America and by San Francisco Magazine Superlawyers in intellectual property litigation. Notable trade secret, patent, and copyright cases include Microsoft v Google (Wash); Taiwan Semiconductor Manufacturing v Shanghai Manufacturing Int'l (ND Cal, Cal ITC); Nuance Communications v Yahoo! (Cal); LSI Logic v Broadcom (Colo); Cadence Design Systems v Avant!, 125 F 3d 824 (9th Cir 1997) (The American Lawyer, Jan/Feb 1998 and Nov 1999); Target Therapeutics v Cordis Endovascular Systems 113 F 3d 1256 (Fed Cir, 1997); Ventritex v Intermedics, 822 F Supp 634 (ND Cal 1993) (listed in 5 National Law Journal, No 28, March, 1993, 'Top Ten Defense Verdicts'); Informix v Oracle Corp. (Or). Other notable cases include Jordache Enterprises v Brobeck, Phleger & Harrison (legal malpractice) 18 Cal 4th 739 (Cal 1998); Tolhurst v Johnson & Johnson (product liability) (5 Mealey's Emerging Toxic Torts, No 17 (Dec 1996)); United States v Hilger (admiralty, manslaughter) 867 F 2d 566 (9th Cir 1989). Partner, Keker & Van Nest 1985-present. Law clerk to the Honorable Richard Posner, US Court of Appeals for the Seventh Circuit (1981-82), law clerk to the Honorable Patrick Higginbotham, US District Court Judge for the Northern District of Texas, (1980-81). Director, Rhode Island Bail Project (Rhode Island Governor's Justice Commission, US Law Enforcement Assistance Administration 1976-77).

**Publications:** 'Judicial Practices and Decision-Making in Pretrial Release: A Study of Bail Administration in Rhode

Island', Rhode Island Governor's Justice Commission, 1977.

**Personal:** JD, University of Chicago, cum laude, Order of the Coif (1980); AB, Brown University, magna cum laude (1976).

## CHATTERJEE, I Neel

Orrick, Herrington & Sutcliffe LLP,
Menlo Park 650 614 7356
nchatterjee@orrick.com
*Recommended in Intellectual Property*

**Practice Areas:** Concentrates on complex litigation for technology companies. Recognized expertise in patent litigation, internet liability litigation, trade secrets litigation, and technology transactions litigation. Significant experience litigating extremely complex disputes where simplifying difficult technical concepts and effective case management are a key to success. Focuses on computer, semiconductor, networking and telecommunications, data storage, internet and computer software technologies.

**Career:** Heads Community Responsibility and Diversity Committee for Orrick's Silicon Valley office. Board Member, Law Foundation of Silicon Valley and Bar Association of San Francisco. Lawyer Representative for the Northern District of California.

**Personal:** JD, Vanderbilt University, 1994; BA, Dartmouth College, 1991.

## CHECOV, Martin S

O'Melveny & Myers LLP, San Francisco
415 984 8700
mchecov@omm.com
*Recommended in Insurance*

**Practice Areas:** Martin Checov is a Partner in the firm's San Francisco office and currently serves as General Counsel of O'Melveny & Myers LLP firm-wide. He has extensive experience in complex trial matters. He is active in the representation of major domestic and foreign insurance carriers and reinsurers in disputes concerning coverage, financial, regulatory, and related matters. He has litigated scores of bad faith claims and questions of coverage for construction defect claims, patent infringement, trademark infringement, and other intellectual property claims, product liability claims, first-party property losses, and securities fraud and consumer class action cases.

## CHILDRESS, Tyrone

Howrey LLP, Los Angeles
213 892 1800
*Recommended in Insurance*

## CHILTON, Frederick

McDermott Will & Emery, Palo Alto
650 813 5121
fchilton@mwe.com
*Recommended in Tax*

**Practice Areas:** Partner in the firm's Tax Department. Focuses on the representation of high technology, biotechnology and other companies on complex tax matters.

**Career:** Law clerk for Judge Leo H Irwin, US Tax Court and a Tax Law Specialist in the Foreign Rulings Group of the Internal Revenue Service. Often speaks and serves as Chair for seminars on behalf of the ATLAS, Practicing Law Institute and the Tax Executives Institute. Has written a number of articles on a variety of federal income tax issues.

**Personal:** Fresno State College (BA); Hastings College of Law (JD); New York University (LLM).

### CHU, Morgan
Irell & Manella LLP, Los Angeles
310 277 1010
*Recommended in Intellectual Property*

### CLAIR, John
Latham & Watkins LLP, Los Angeles
213 485 1234
*Recommended in Tax*

### CLARENCE, Nanci
Clarence & Dyer LLP, San Francisco
415 749 1800
*Recommended in Litigation*

### CLARK, James P
Gibson, Dunn & Crutcher LLP,
Los Angeles 213 229 7941
jclark@gibsondunn.com
*Recommended in Litigation*

**Practice Areas:** Member of firm's Litigation, Intellectual Property, Antitrust, Media and Entertainment and White-Collar Crimes Practice Groups. Specializes in complex commercial litigation and counseling in pricing and distribution practices, mergers and acquisitions, securities regulation, parallel civil and criminal government investigations and litigation, trademark, trade name, trade dress and trade secret, copyright, theft of ideas, Lanham Act violations, nationwide class actions, and unfair competition.

**Publications:** Co-Editor, Desk Edition of 'von Kalinowski's Antitrust Laws and Trade Regulation'.

**Personal:** JD, New York University School of Law, 1973, Root-Tilden Scholar, Note and Comment Editor, Law Review; law clerk, Judge John Minor Wisdom.

### CLARK, John
Thelen Reid & Priest LLP, Los Angeles
213 576 8040
jbclark@thelenreid.com
*Recommended in Construction*

**Practice Areas:** Mr Clark is a trial lawyer who has specialized for many years in a wide variety of construction disputes involving a range of projects from power and chemical plants to buildings, highways, refineries, hospitals, waste water treatment plants and airports. He has tried numerous cases before juries, judges, arbitrators and boards of contract appeals, has resolved many cases through mediation, and has acted as a mediator and as an arbitrator in disputes arising

from construction projects. Mr Clark is a member of the American College of Construction Lawyers and has written, lectured and spoken extensively on a variety of topics related to construction including basic construction law, proof and defense of claims and the use of the California False Claims Act in defending against public agencies. Mr Clark represents owners, contractors, subcontractors and design professionals throughout the United States and abroad.

**Prof. Memberships:** American Bar Association, Public Contract Law Section and Forum Committee on the Construction Industry; Fellow, American College of Construction Lawyers; Board of Editors, Stanford Law Review, 1960-61.

**Career:** Partner of Thelen Reid & Priest LLP. Admitted to practice in New York (1962), California (1966) and Colorado (1991).

**Publications:** 'The AGCC Handbook of California Construction Law' (Associated General Contractors of California), 1992; 'California Construction Law' (Federal Publications), 1980-present; 'Understanding the Government Procurement Process' (Engineering News Record); 'Claims and the Project Schedule' (Federal Publications), 1983.

**Personal:** Received his LLB from Stanford University in 1961 and a BS in General Engineering from Stanford University in 1958.

### CLARK, Kenneth A
Wilson Sonsini Goodrich & Rosati,
Palo Alto 650 493 9300
kclark@wsgr.com
*Recommended in Corporate/M&A*

**Practice Areas:** Specializes in intellectual property, particularly technology transactions involving products and/or technology, from strategic alliances to license, development, supply and distribution arrangements. Regularly represents companies in M&As, spin-outs and core technology licenses.

**Career:** Joined WSGR as Partner, 1993. Member, WSGR Policy Committee and Executive Management Committee. Negotiated more than 50 major strategic alliance transactions in both the life sciences and information technology industries. Served as Vice President, general counsel and secretary of Maxtor Corporation, 1992-93.

**Personal:** JD (highest honors), University of Texas, 1985. Order of the Coif; BA (magna cum laude), Vanderbilt University, 1980. Phi Beta Kappa.

### CLASTER, William D
Gibson, Dunn & Crutcher LLP, Irvine
949 451 3804
wclaster@gibsondunn.com
*Recommended in Employment*

**Practice Areas:** Advises management in a wide array of labor and employment matters, including class actions, employ-

ment discrimination, wrongful termination, negotiations and arbitrations under collective bargaining agreements, executive employment agreements, unfair competition, ERISA, and proceedings before state and federal agencies such as EEOC, OSHA and NLRB. Tried numerous cases in jury and non-jury settings and argued significant cases before appellate courts.

**Publications:** Frequent lecturer on labor and employment law. Contributing author, 'Wrongful Employment Termination Practice', 'California Practice Guide: Employment Litigation' and 'Developing Labor Law'.

**Personal:** JD, UCLA, 1976, Managing Editor of UCLA Law Review; BA, Stanford University, 1973.

### CLIMAN, Richard
Cooley Godward LLP, Palo Alto
650 843 5000
*Recommended in Corporate/M&A*

### COATS, William S
White & Case LLP, Palo Alto
650 213 0343
wcoats@whitecase.com
*Recommended in Intellectual Property*

**Practice Areas:** Focuses his Intellectual Property Practice on cases involving software copyrights and patents, copyrights for movies and music, trademark and trade secret disputes, and bankruptcy issues. Represents leading business, computer, and entertainment hardware and software companies in complex intellectual property matters.

**Prof. Memberships:** ABA; UNCITRAL Working Group on Electronic Commerce.

**Career:** White & Case since 2005.

**Personal:** University of San Francisco (AB 1972); University of California, Hastings College of the Law (JD 1980).

### COBEN, Jerome L
Skadden, Arps, Slate, Meagher & Flom LLP & Affiliates, Los Angeles
213 687 5010
jcoben@skadden.com
*Recommended in Corporate/M&A*

**Practice Areas:** Mr Coben is one of the founding partners of Skadden's Los Angeles office. He has a broad-based corporate and securities law practice, representing both issuers and investment banks in a variety of corporate finance, merger and acquisition, and general corporate matters. Mr Coben has regularly represented, among other public companies, Oakley Inc., Occidental Petroleum Corporation, and Wynn Resorts, Limited.

**Prof. Memberships:** Member, American and Los Angeles County Bar associations; Board Member, Constitutional Rights Foundation; Board Member, Bet Tzedek Legal Services.

**Career:** JD, New York University School of Law, 1969 (Root-Tilden-Kern Scholar); AB, Brown University 1966 (cum laude).

### COGEN, Douglas N
Fenwick & West, San Francisco
415 875 2409
dcogen@fenwick.com
*Recommended in Corporate/M&A*

**Practice Areas:** Co-Chair of the firm's Mergers and Acquisitions Group. Practice focuses on mergers and acquisitions, strategic and commercial transactions, corporate counseling and financings. Mr Cogen's practice also includes advising publicly traded and privately held companies with respect to corporate, securities, commercial and intellectual property licensing matters generally.

**Career:** Mr Cogen's transactional experience includes over $30 billion of completed mergers, acquisitions and divestitures, including cross-border transactions in the networking, software, telecommunications, biotechnology, semiconductor, internet and computer hardware industries; public company tender offers; and private placements of equity and debt securities. Mr Cogen also counsels companies on takeover defenses, corporate governance matters and strategic partnering arrangements. Mr Cogen has lectured on transactional law at Columbia University Law School, Stanford University Law School and the Stanford Graduate School of Business.

**Personal:** Mr Cogen received his BA magna cum laude with academic honors in Architecture and Society from Brown University, where he was elected Phi Beta Kappa. He attended the University of Michigan Law School, receiving his JD cum laude.

### COHEN, Marc S
Kaye Scholer LLP, Los Angeles
310 788 1223
marccohen@kayescholer.com
*Recommended in Bankruptcy*

**Practice Areas:** Partner and Chair, Business Reorganization and Creditors' Rights Group in Los Angeles. He has 30 years' experience in bankruptcy law and corporate reorganization, with particular emphasis representing bondholders, secured creditors, creditors' committees, and debtors-in-possession in both in- and out-of-court restructurings and asset sale transactions. He has counseled and represented clients in a variety of industries, including energy, healthcare, transportation and entertainment.

**Prof. Memberships:** Member of the Bars of the States of California and Ohio and admitted to practice before the Federal Courts in California; Fellow in the American College of Bankruptcy.

**Career:** JD, New York University School of Law, Law Review, Order of the Coif; BA, Cornell University; Clerkship: Southern District of New York, J Robert L Carter, US District Court.

**Publications:** 'The Aftermath and Jurisdictional Quagmire Following California's Energy Crisis', Business Law News, Spring Edition, Issue 2, 2005.

## COHEN, Nancy
Heller Ehrman LLP, Los Angeles
213 689 7689
nancy.cohen@hellerehrman.com
*Recommended in Insurance*
**Practice Areas:** Insurance recovery, consumer litigation, product liability.
**Career:** Ms Cohen practices insurance coverage litigation, mass tort, class actions, products liability, and general commercial litigation. Her practice includes prosecution of claims against insurers seeking insurance coverage for products and toxic tort and the representation of various manufacturing companies in state and federal courts in mass tort and class actions. Ms Cohen has experience in all aspects of product liability litigation representing a wide variety of manufacturers.
**Personal:** Loyola Law School of Los Angeles (JD, cum laude, 1978).

## COLE, William
Mitchell, Silberberg & Knupp LLP, Los Angeles 310 312 2000
*Recommended in Employment*

## COLEMAN, Kathryn A
Gibson, Dunn & Crutcher LLP, San Francisco 415 393 8265
kcoleman@gibsondunn.com
*Recommended in Bankruptcy*
**Practice Areas:** Practices business restructuring and reorganization. Has extensive experience in workouts, troubled loans, creditors' rights and all phases of bankruptcy cases. Represents debtors, creditors' committees, secured creditors, and acquirers in bankruptcy cases, preparation and prosecution of creditors' plans of reorganization, and complex loan restructurings.
**Career:** Former clerk for the Honorable C Martin Pence, US District Judge for the District of Hawaii.
**Publications:** Frequent lecturer on bankruptcy law and problem loans.
**Personal:** JD, UC Berkeley-Boalt Hall School of Law, 1983, Senior Articles Editor of the California Law Review and a Member of the Order of the Coif.

## COLEMAN, Thomas
Orrick, Herrington & Sutcliffe LLP, San Francisco 415 773 5870
tycoleman@orrick.com
*Recommended in Banking & Finance*
**Practice Areas:** Represents banks and other financial institutions in a variety of transactions, including syndicated and single-lender credit agreements; both secured and unsecured; project financings; public finance transactions; and 'synthetic' and other lease arrangements. Frequently participates in seminars addressing topics related to commercial transactions sponsored by such organizations as the California Bankers Association, the Banking Law Institute, Prentice Hall Law & Business, and the International Bankers Association in California.

**Career:** Before joining Orrick, Mr Coleman was Vice President and Counsel at California First Bank (now Union Bank of California) in San Francisco.
**Personal:** JD, University of Virginia, 1975; BA, 1971.

## COMPTON, Charles T
Wilson Sonsini Goodrich & Rosati, Palo Alto 650 493 9300
ccompton@wsgr.com
*Recommended in Antitrust*
**Practice Areas:** Antitrust counseling.
**Prof. Memberships:** Admitted to practice in California and DC, as well as in several United States District Courts, the US Court of Appeals for the Ninth Circuit, the US Court of Military Appeals and the United States Supreme Court.
**Career:** Partner, WSGR. Overseen the antitrust regulatory work in nearly 700 M&As and joint ventures. Handled antitrust suits involving alleged price discrimination, refusals to deal, distributor terminations, group boycotts, monopoly, state law Cartwright Act claims, grand jury investigations, and price fixing.
**Personal:** JD, NYU School of Law, 1968. BS (with honors), United States Air Force Academy, 1965.

## COOK, Melanie
Ziffren Brittenham Branca Fischer Gilbert-Lurie & Stiffelman LLP, Los Angeles 310 552 3388
*Recommended in Media & Entertainment*

## COOPER, Jay L
Greenberg Traurig LLP, Santa Monica 310 586 7888
cooper@gtlaw.com
*Recommended in Media & Entertainment*
**Practice Areas:** Entertainment; intellectual property; technology, media and telecommunications.
**Prof. Memberships:** Former President, National Academy of Recording Arts and Sciences; Member, Los Angeles Copyright Society; Co-Chairman, Alliance of Artists & Recording Companies.
**Career:** Listed, The Best Lawyers in America, continuously since 1987; Listed, Chambers & Partners USA Guide, 2004-06; listed, 'Southern California Super Lawyers, 2004-06'; awarded, Entertainment Lawyer of the Year for 2006, Century City Bar Association.
**Publications:** Author, 'Withol v. Crow: Fair Use Revisited', UCLA Law Review; Author, 'Use of Fair Use', Los Angeles Bar Bulletin, Publishing Entertainment, Advertising Law Quarterly.
**Personal:** JD, DePaul University College of Law.

## COOPER, John
Farella Braun & Martel LLP, San Francisco 415 954 4400
*Recommended in Intellectual Property*

## COOPER, Robert E
Gibson, Dunn & Crutcher LLP, Los Angeles 213 229 7179
rcooper@gibsondunn.com
*Recommended in Antitrust, Litigation*
**Practice Areas:** Co-Chair of firm's Antitrust and Trade Regulation Practice Group. Extensive experience trying major antitrust and business cases to a verdict before a jury. Achieved a series of trial victories in antitrust cases for major companies such as Pfizer, American Airlines and Hewlett-Packard. Other representative clients include Intel, Ticketmaster, Northrop, Allergan, Callaway Golf and Sempra Energy.
**Prof. Memberships:** Fellow, American College of Trial Lawyers.
**Publications:** Frequent lecturer on antitrust laws and trial of complex litigation.
**Personal:** LLB, Yale University School of Law, 1964, Order of the Coif, Article and Book Review Editor, Yale Law Journal.

## CORASH, Michèle B
Morrison & Foerster LLP, San Francisco 415 268 7124
mcorash@mofo.com
*Recommended in Environment*
**Practice Areas:** Specializes in environmental law and defense of enforcement actions and class actions relating to food and consumer products. Represents companies in mining and petrochemicals, real estate transactions and land development. One of the nation's leading experts on Proposition 65.
**Career:** Served as General Counsel, US Environmental Protection Agency (EPA)(1979-82) and, before that, as Deputy General Counsel, US Department of Energy. Founded Environmental Section of the Inter-Pacific Bar Association. Recent honors include being named: 100 Most Influential Lawyers in California and Top 50 Women Litigators, Daily Journal newspaper; and Go-To Environmental Defense Lawyer, The Recorder newspaper. Heads the firm's Environmental Practice Group.
**Personal:** BA, Economics, Mount Holyoke College, 1967; JD, cum laude, New York University School of Law, 1970.

## CORBIN, Robert
Corbin & Fitzgerald LLP, Los Angeles 213 612 0001
*Recommended in Litigation*

## COTCHETT, Joseph
Cotchett, Pitre, Simon & McCarthy, Burlingame 650 697 6000
*Recommended in Litigation*

## COTSIRILOS, George
Cotsirilos & Campisano LLP, San Francisco 415 397 2373
*Recommended in Litigation*

## COUGHLIN, Patrick
Lerach Coughlin Stoia Geller Rudman & Robbins LLP, San Francisco 415 288 4545
*Recommended in Litigation*

## COX, Evan R
Covington & Burling, San Francisco 415 591 7073
ecox@cov.com
*Recommended in IT Outsourcing*
**Practice Areas:** IP transactional and antitrust practices – emphasis on representation of technology companies in structuring and negotiation of licensing, distribution, joint ventures, standards and other IP-driven relationships. Works with leading companies and trade associations in software, hardware and pharmaceutical industries on internet anti-piracy, anti-counterfeiting, and DRM strategies and enforcement.
**Prof. Memberships:** Berkeley Center for Law and Technology, ABA.
**Career:** Recent representations: Boeing in ATA eBusiness Program; Microsoft in AACS consortium developing/licensing content protection system for HD-DVD and BluRay optical disk formats; Greenpoint Mortgage in outsourcing agreement with Fidelity Information Services.
**Personal:** Berkeley (JD 1987), Michigan State (BA 1982).

## CRAIG CALKINS, Mary
Howrey LLP, Los Angeles 213 892 1800
*Recommended in Insurance*

## CRANE, Steven
Berkes Crane Robinson & Seal, LLP, Los Angeles 213 955 1150
*Recommended in Insurance*

## CRAVEN, Erica
Levy, Ram & Olson, San Francisco 415 433 4949
*Recommended in Media & Entertainment*

## CREW, Eugene
Townsend and Townsend and Crew LLP, San Francisco 415 576 0200
*Recommended in Antitrust*

## CUFF, Terence
Loeb & Loeb LLP, Los Angeles 310 282 2181
tcuff@loeb.com
*Recommended in Tax*
**Practice Areas:** Concentrates on partnership and real estate tax problems. Principal clients include REITs, real estate investors, energy companies, large corporations and financial institutions.
**Prof. Memberships:** ABA; California State Bar Association; LA County Bar Association; Board of Advisors, NYU Institute on Federal Taxation.
**Career:** Partner since 1986.
**Publications:** Speaks frequently at tax seminars. Authored hundreds of articles about partnership, real estate taxation,

like-kind exchanges and drafting partnership and LLC agreements. Editorial Boards: Journal of Real Estate Taxation and Business Entities.
**Personal:** NYU Law School (LLM 1979); USC Law School (JD, 1977); University of California, Santa Cruz (BA, 1974).

### CUMMINS, Guylyn
Sheppard, Mullin, Richter & Hampton LLP, San Diego 858 720 8900
*Recommended in Media & Entertainment*

### DALY, Bryan
Beck, De Corso, Daly, Kreindler & Harris, Los Angeles 213 688 1198
*Recommended in Litigation*

### DARWELL, Robert
Sheppard, Mullin, Richter & Hampton LLP, New York 212 332 3800
*Recommended in Media & Entertainment*

### DAVID, Henry S
Alschuler Grossman Stein & Kahan LLP, Santa Monica 310 255 9167
hdavid@agsk.com
*Recommended in Bankruptcy*
**Practice Areas:** Practices complex commercial litigation concentrating on bankruptcy, insurance insolvency, creditor's rights, corporate and partnership dissolutions, and international arbitration matters.
**Prof. Memberships:** Member, American Bankruptcy Institute; Association of Insolvency and Restructuring Advisors; Financial Lawyers Conference; International Association of Insurance Receivers; Los Angeles Bankruptcy Forum. Co-founder of the Remedies Section of the Los Angeles County Bar Association (served as Chair of its Executive Committee).
**Career:** A Partner of Alschuler Grossman Stein & Kahan LLP. Has undertaken leadership in numerous complex matters in state, federal and bankruptcy courts, as well as before various arbitration associations. Such matters include prosecution of a $254 million preference and fraudulent transfer action on behalf of the California Insurance Commissioner; successful representation of the New York Superintendent of Insurance in obtaining a stay of litigation in California due to the New York rehabilitation proceedings; repossession of DC10s and L1011s from failing airlines; general representation of debtors, bankruptcy trustees, and creditors' committees in Chapter 11 cases in a variety of industries, including windfarms, timeshare projects, retailers, healthcare, and oil; representation of major global technology company in the bankruptcy aspects of patent infringement disputes with various debtors; successful representation of minority equityholders in various debtors; representation of purchasers of assets out of bankruptcy,

including hospitals, refineries, and technology. Has tried over 50 matters to judgment or arbitral award; has handled many appeals.
**Personal:** Mediator, Bankruptcy Mediation Panel and the Attorney Settlement Officer Panel for the Central District of California. Co-author of the chapter regarding 'Seller's Performance' in California UCC Sales and Leases (CEB 1993). California Institute of Technology (BS with honors, 1976). New York University School of Law (JD cum laude, Order of the Coif, 1979). Law Review, New York University School Law. Admitted in California and Florida.

### DAVIDSON, Gordon K
Fenwick & West LLP, Mountain View 650 988 8500
gdavidson@fenwick.com
*Recommended in Capital Markets, Corporate/M&A*
**Practice Areas:** Firm Chairman. Start-up companies, venture capital financings, public securities offerings, mergers and acquisitions and strategic alliances. Advises technology companies, including networking, computer software and electronics companies, as well as medical technology companies. Also advises investors and investment banks. Clients range from start-ups to Fortune 1000 companies. Has worked on more than 30 public offerings and has acted as Lead Counsel on more than 100 mergers and acquisitions valued at more than $50 billion.
**Career:** Recognized by Forbes Magazine in February 2001 as one of the 50 Most Powerful Venture Capital Dealmakers; by Upside Magazine in October 2001 as one of '100 People Who Changed Our World'; by California Lawyer Magazine in August 2004 as one of the 10 best corporate lawyers in California; by San Francisco Magazine in August 2004 as one of the 10 best lawyers in Northern California; and by Forbes Magazine in February 2005 as one of the top 100 venture capital deal makers in 2004. He is one of only two lawyers in the United States to be named by BTI Consulting to its All Star Team for each of the last five years for outstanding client service based on a survey of Fortune 1000 companies.
**Personal:** Stanford Law School, JD, Order of the Coif, 1974; Stanford University, MS in Electrical Engineering, Computer Systems, National Science Foundation Fellow, 1971; Stanford University, BS in Electrical Engineering, Phi Beta Kappa, 1970.

### DAVIDSON, Jeffrey S
Kirkland & Ellis LLP, Los Angeles 213 680 8422
jdavidson@kirkland.com
*Recommended in Litigation*
**Practice Areas:** Mr Davidson is an accomplished trial lawyer whose cases

involve contracts, securities, antitrust, mergers and acquisitions, insurance coverage, intellectual property, products liability, toxic tort, and environmental matters in state and federal courts, in federal administrative proceedings, before AAA and NASD arbitration panels, and before the London Court of International Arbitration. He has tried over 40 cases.
**Personal:** Wabash College (AB, 1970); Columbia University (BS, 1970); Indiana University School of Law (JD, 1973).

### DAWES, Paul
Latham & Watkins LLP, Menlo Park 650 328 4600
*Recommended in Litigation*

### DAY, Lloyd
Day Casebeer Madrid & Batchelder LLP, Cupertino 408 255 3255
*Recommended in Intellectual Property*

### DAY, Michael
Goodin MacBride Squeri Ritchie & Day LLP, San Francisco 415 392 7900
*Recommended in Energy*

### DE ALCUAZ, Anthony
McDermott Will & Emery, Palo Alto 650 813 5193
adealcuaz@mwe.com
*Recommended in Intellectual Property*
**Practice Areas:** Partner and Head of the Silicon Valley Office, focused on intellectual property and complex commercial disputes and trials, and IP transactions. 28 years' experience in IP matters successfully representing parties in patent, copyright, trademark, trade secret and unfair competition disputes. Industry experience includes integrated circuits, gaming, I/O products, consumer electronics, disk drives, resource recovery, internet commerce, search engine and network administration software and medical devices.
**Career:** Member of the California, Texas (inactive), Ninth Circuit, Federal Circuit and US Supreme Court Bars.
**Personal:** University of California – Hastings College of Law (JD); University of California-Santa Cruz (BA)

### DEL CALVO, Jorge
Pillsbury Winthrop Shaw Pittman LLP, Palo Alto 650 233 4537
jorge@pillsburylaw.com
*Recommended in Capital Markets, Corporate/M&A*
**Practice Areas:** Co-Chair, firm's Silicon Valley Business Group. Mr del Calvo's practice focuses primarily on representation of technology companies in securities and venture capital transactions, including public offerings, private placements, mergers and acquisitions, and joint ventures. He has represented issuers and underwriters in hundreds of private and public offerings of equity securities, including IPOs, and merger and acquisition transactions.
**Personal:** JD, Harvard Law School (cum

laude), 1981. MA, Harvard University (Public Policy), 1981. MA, University of California at Los Angeles (Latin American History), 1978. BA, Stanford University (Phi Beta Kappa, with distinction), 1977. ND, University of the Philippines, 1982.

### DEMETRIOU, Andrew James
Fulbright & Jaworski L.L.P., Los Angeles 213 892 9338
ademetriou@fulbright.com
*Recommended in Healthcare*
**Practice Areas:** Mergers and acquisitions, healhcare, and corporate and securities law.
**Prof. Memberships:** Mr Demetriou is Vice-Chair of the Health Law Section of the American Bar Association. He has held various leadership positions on committees and sections of the State Bar of California, the Los Angeles County Bar Association and American Health Lawyers Association.
**Career:** Andrew Demetriou joined the Los Angeles office of Fulbright & Jaworski L.L.P as Partner in 2004 with more than 25 years of experience in representing a range of domestic and foreign enterprises on corporate and strategic matters. Since 1991 he has concentrated on the representation of entities that provide and finance healthcare services. He was named one of 15 Outstanding Healthcare Transaction Lawyers for 2003 by Nightingale's Healthcare Law News.
**Personal:** AB, University of California, Los Angeles (1976); JD, University of California, Berkeley, Boalt Hall School of Law (1979).

### DEMURO, Paul
Latham & Watkins LLP, Los Angeles 213 485 1234
*Recommended in Healthcare*

### DENHAM, Robert
Munger, Tolles & Olson LLP, Los Angeles 213 683 9100
*Recommended in Corporate/M&A*

### DENNIS, Patrick
Gibson, Dunn & Crutcher LLP, Los Angeles 213 229 7567
pdennis@gibsondunn.com
*Recommended in Environment*
**Practice Areas:** Chair of firm's Environment and Natural Resources Practice Group. Represents clients in matters including litigation, due diligence, compliance counseling, defense of environmental enforcement actions, private citizen suit claims, private party cleanup cost recovery and toxic tort lawsuits, and permit requirements. Deals extensively with administering agencies for air quality, hazardous waste and water quality. Represents buyers and sellers of major industrial facilities worldwide and contaminated real estate for redevelopment. Lead litigation counsel for numerous remediation cost recovery, toxic tort and Super-

fund matters, including one of the few natural resource damage actions brought by the United States.

**Personal:** JD, UCLA, 1982.

## DESMARAIS, John

Kirkland & Ellis LLP, New York
212 446 4800

*Recommended in Intellectual Property*
*Please see New York for profile*

## DETTMER, Scott

Gunderson Dettmer Stough Villeneuve Franklin & Hachigian, Menlo Park
650 321 2400

*Recommended in Corporate/M&A*

## DIAMOND, Susan

Morgan, Lewis & Bockius LLP, San Francisco 415 442 1251
sdiamond@morganlewis.com

*Recommended in Real Estate*

**Practice Areas:** Susan R Diamond is a Partner in the Real Estate Group, specializing in land use and zoning law. She provides strategies for and manages the development and entitlement processes, oversees NEPA and CEQA compliance, secures approvals and negotiates contracts for a wide variety of major developers, corporate users and not-for-profits (eg, downtown and suburban office buildings, gas wells, mixed-use master plans, biotech facilities, alternative energy systems, cemeteries, shopping centers, seniors projects, stadiums).

**Prof. Memberships:** American Bar Association Member, Bar Association of San Francisco Member, Lambda Alpha Real Estate Economic Society Board Member.

## DIBERNARDO, S James

Morgan, Lewis & Bockius LLP, Palo Alto
650 843 7560
jdibernardo@morganlewis.com

*Recommended in Employment*

**Practice Areas:** S James DiBernardo is a Partner in the Employee Benefits/Executive Compensation Practice. Mr DiBernardo specializes in all areas of equity compensation and non-qualified deferred compensation programs for both public and private companies. His breadth of expertise includes the tax, securities, corporate governance and financial accounting implications of such programs. He also provides extensive counseling with respect to section 16 reporting and insider trading matters, parachute tax issues, proxy statement disclosure of executive compensation and preparation of proxy statement proposals covering equity compensation programs and Internal Revenue Code section 162(m) performance-based arrangements.

## DICANIO, Jack P

Skadden, Arps, Slate, Meagher & Flom LLP & Affiliates, Los Angeles
213 687 5430
jdicanio@skadden.com

*Recommended in Litigation*

**Practice Areas:** Represents corporate and individual clients in complex business litigation and criminal and regulatory actions. Areas of specialization include trial practice, internal investigations, federal and state securities litigation, securities regulatory and enforcement proceedings, broker/dealer liability, financial institution fraud, and government procurement fraud.

**Career:** JD, Boston College Law School, 1988; BA, University of Notre Dame, 1985 (magna cum laude). Assistant United States Attorney, Central District of California, Deputy Chief, General Crimes Section (1994-2000). Trained federal prosecutors in trial practice and criminal law/procedure. Recipient of the United States Attorney General's Distinguished Service Award.

## DIEKMANN JR, Gilmore

Seyfarth Shaw LLP, San Francisco
415 397 2823

*Recommended in Employment*

## DINTZER, Jeffrey D

Gibson, Dunn & Crutcher LLP, Los Angeles 213 229 7860
jdintzer@gibsondunn.com

*Recommended in Environment*

**Practice Areas:** Member of the firm's Environment and Natural Resources Practice Group. Focuses on environmental litigation, involving cost recovery, toxic torts, water rights, and land use entitlements. Has served as lead trial counsel in matters involving groundwater contamination, CEQA compliance, landfills, trash transfer/sorting facilities, and environmental crimes. Representative clients include Lockheed Martin Corporation, Goodrich Corporation, Pioneer Electronics Technology, Inc. and the City of Thousand Oaks.

**Publications:** Co-author, 'Cleanup Liability and Cost Recovery', California Environmental Law and Land Use.

**Personal:** JD, Boston University School of Law, 1989, cum laude; former law clerk to Chief Judge Alice-Marie Stotler, Central District of California.

## DIVOLA, Julie

Pillsbury Winthrop Shaw Pittman LLP, San Francisco 415 983 7446
julie.divola@pillsburylaw.com

*Recommended in Tax*

**Practice Areas:** Chair, San Francisco Tax and Benefits, and Political Law Group. Experienced in federal income tax planning for business and financial transactions. Particular emphasis on structuring corporate mergers, acquisitions, divestitures and reorganizations; partnerships and joint ventures; financial products; project finance; and tax controversy matters.

**Prof. Memberships:** ABA Tax Section (Vice-Chair, Corporate Tax Committee); California Bar Association Tax Section

(Former Chair, Corporate Tax Committee; Former Chair, Passthroughs and Real Estate Tax Committee); San Francisco Tax Club (Former President); Fellow, American College of Tax Counsel.

**Personal:** JD, USF Law School, 1986, summa cum laude. BA, UCSB, 1980.

## DODSON, Gerald

Morrison & Foerster LLP, Palo Alto
650 813 5983
gdodson@mofo.com

*Recommended in Intellectual Property*

**Practice Areas:** Over 30-year career, has served as lead trial and appellate counsel in complex technology cases involving hundreds of millions of dollars. Represented electronics, biotechnology and consumer product companies on cases covering pioneering patents in the medical device, biotechnology, optical and electronic hardware, software and mechanical device fields.

**Career:** Admitted to practice in California and before the US Patent & Trademark Office. Served as Chief Counsel, Health and Environmental Subcommittee, US House of Representatives, and Solicitor's Office, US Department of the Interior. Headed congressional investigation of Union Carbide's pesticide plant disaster in Bhopal, India.

**Personal:** BSME, Lafayette College, 1969; JD, University of Maryland Law School, 1972; LLM, George Washington University Law School, 1977.

## DRAGNA, James J

Bingham McCutchen LLP, Los Angeles
213 680 6436
jim.dragna@bingham.com

*Recommended in Environment*

**Practice Areas:** Focuses on counseling and litigation matters in all environmental media, with a particular emphasis in air, waste, wastewater and water-rights matters. Practice also includes the representation of water purveyors in water-rights cases, including litigation involving Native American water rights and representation of clients in more than 50 federal or state Superfund matters nationwide.

**Career:** Served as senior trial counsel at the US Department of Justice, Environmental Enforcement Section. Founding member of Environmental Protection Agency's Hazardous Waste Enforcement Task Force.

**Personal:** Loyola Law School, JD, 1979; University of California, Irvine, BA, cum laude, 1976.

## DRAPKIN, Steven

Law Offices of Steven Drapkin, Los Angeles 310 914 7909

*Recommended in Employment*

## DUFFY, Pamela

Coblentz, Patch, Duffy & Bass LLP, San Francisco 415 391 4800

*Recommended in Real Estate*

## DUNCAN, Helen Lalich

Fulbright & Jaworski L.L.P., Los Angeles
213 892 9209
hduncan@fulbright.com

*Recommended in Litigation*

**Practice Areas:** Complex business litigation including fraud and secondary liability claims, class action litigation, tax-related litigation, securities and insurance insolvency related litigation.

**Prof. Memberships:** Member of the Federal Bar Association, Association of Business Trial Lawyers and George McBurney Los Angeles Complex Litigation Inn, where she served as President in 1996-97.

**Career:** Ms Duncan has tried civil jury cases in both state and federal court in various venues accross the United States, including a three-month long class action jury trial in 2003. She also advocates before the appellate courts. She has been named in The Best Lawyers in America (2005-06), the 'Guide to the Leading US Litigation Lawyers' (2005) and 'Super Lawyers of Southern California' (2003-05). She is admitted to practice in the Northern, Eastern, Southern and Central Districts of California, before the United States Court of Appeals for the Ninth, Fourth and Tenth Circuits, and before the United States Tax Court. Ms Duncan is a Partner in the Los Angeles office of Fulbright & Jaworski, L.L.P. and is the Head of the Litigation Department for the Los Angeles office.

**Personal:** JD. Southwestern University School of Law (1981); BA, Indiana University (1974).

## DURIE, Daralyn J

Keker & Van Nest LLP, San Francisco
415 391 5400
ddurie@kvn.com

*Recommended in Intellectual Property*

**Practice Areas:** Daralyn Durie has tried cases in both the state and federal courts in a wide range of areas including patent, trade secret and unfair competition. Representative clients include Comcast Cable Communications, Inc. and Google, Inc.

**Prof. Memberships:** Lawyer representative to the Ninth Circuit Judicial Conference, Member of the Board of Governors of the Association of Business Trial Lawyers, Member of the faculty of the National Institute for Trial Advocacy, Member of the Board of Directors of Berkeley Montessori School.

**Career:** Law clerk to the Honorable Douglas Ginsberg on the United States Court of Appeals for the District of Columbia Circuit (1992-93). Joined Keker & Van Nest, 1993; became Partner, 1999. Frequent invited speaker on patent litigation, the DMCA, and legal ethics.

**Personal:** Boalt Hall School of Law, University of California (JD 1992); University of California at Berkeley (MA 1989); Stanford University (BA 1988).

## EATMAN, Louis P
Mayer, Brown, Rowe & Maw LLP,
Los Angeles 213 229 5144
leatman@mayerbrownrowe.com
*Recommended in Real Estate*
**Practice Areas:** Advises on real estate
finance, acquisitions and sales, workouts
and restructures, foreclosures and deeds
in lieu of foreclosure. Represents commercial banks, savings banks, life insurance companies, pension funds and their
advisors, investment banks, real estate
investment trusts, portfolio asset managers, other institutional mortgage
lenders and investors, commercial property landlords and tenants.
**Prof. Memberships:** American College
of Real Estate Lawyers. International
Council of Shopping Centers. Pension
Real Estate Association. Board of Directors, Constitutional Rights Foundation
(President and Chair, Executive Commit-
tee, 2003-05). California Mortgage
Bankers Association.
**Career:** Joined Mayer, Brown, Rowe &
Maw LLP as Partner, 1994. Firm Practice
Leader, Global Real Estate Group, 2000-
04. Partner-in-Charge of Los Angeles
Office. Formerly with Loeb & Loeb.
**Publications:** Speaker and panelist on
real estate financing and workout issues.
Faculty Member for the 1995 ALI-ABA
Advanced Course of Study on Real Estate
Defaults, Workouts, and Reorganizations
(1995). Speaker on 'Shopping Center
Financing', 1996 International Council of
Shopping Centers Annual Law Confer-
ence (October 1996).
**Personal:** Stanford Law School, JD, 1974.
Stanford Graduate Business School,
MBA, 1974. Georgetown University
School of Foreign Service, BSFS, cum
laude, 1970; Phi Beta Kappa.

## EDELMAN, Scott
Gibson, Dunn & Crutcher LLP,
Los Angeles 310 557 8061
sedelman@gibsondunn.com
*Recommended in Media &
Entertainment*
**Practice Areas:** Co-Chair of firm's
Media and Entertainment Practice
Group. Represents major entertainment
clients in matters involving antitrust,
intellectual property (copyright, trademark, right of publicity, misappropriation of ideas, and trade secret), profit participation, film distribution, false advertising, royalty disputes. Significant IFTA
(formerly AFMA) experience. Other
commercial litigation experience includes
product liability, employment, sports litigation, breach of contract, professional
negligence, RICO, real estate and construction defects. Representative clients
include Sony Pictures, Fox Broadcasting
Company, Columbia TriStar Home
Entertainment, CBS, Warner Bros
Records and Interainment Licensing
GMBH.
**Personal:** JD, University of California,

Boalt Hall School of Law, 1984. Co-Editor-in-Chief, Ecology Law Quarterly.

## EDWARDS, Steve
O'Melveny & Myers LLP, Newport Beach
949 823 7903
sledwards@omm.com
*Recommended in Real Estate*
**Practice Areas:** Steve Edwards is Co-
Chair of O'Melveny & Myers' Project
Development & Real Estate Practice and
has a broad background in the acquisition, sale, exchange, financing, ground
leasing, leasing and development of
improved and unimproved real estate.
His practice has emphasized the representation of both developers and capital
providers in the formation of joint ventures, limited partnerships and limited
liability companies for the acquisition
and development of housing and commercial properties. Steve's clients have
included pension advisors, universities,
fund sponsors, REITs, investment banking firms, commercial banks, residential
and commercial developers and individual investors.

## EHRHART, Kevin
Allen Matkins Leck Gamble & Mallory LLP,
Los Angeles 213 622 5555
*Recommended in Real Estate*

## EISEN, Rebecca
Morgan, Lewis & Bockius LLP,
San Francisco 415 422 1328
reisen@morganlewis.com
*Recommended in Employment*
**Practice Areas:** Rebecca Eisen is a Partner in the Labor and Employment Law
Practice Group. Ms Eisen represents
employers in all facets of employment
law including wage and hour laws, hiring
practices, leaves of absence, trade secrets,
accommodation of disabled employees,
employee discipline and sensitive terminations. Ms Eisen has litigated class
actions, multiple plaintiff and collective
actions in state and federal court, and
actions before administrative agencies
and appellate courts, including the Ninth
Circuit Court of Appeals and the California Supreme Court.
**Prof. Memberships:** American Arbitration Association; The Employers Group –
Legal Advisory Board; San Francisco
County Bar Association.

## ELACQUA, James J
Dechert LLP, Palo Alto 650 813 4811
james.elacqua@dechert.com
*Recommended in Intellectual Property*
**Practice Areas:** Mr Elacqua is a Partner
in the Intellectual Property Litigation and
Life Sciences Groups. He focuses his
practice on patent litigation and complex
technical cases, and has represented
clients before state and federal courts, as
well as the International Trade Commission. He advises clients on intellectual
property enforcement, litigation and
defense strategies, and settlement negoti-

ations, as well as on appellate matters.
**Career:** Member, Silicon Valley Intellec-
tual Property Law Association, American
Intellectual Property Law Association,
California and Texas Bars.
**Personal:** Clarkson University, BSEE,
1972; Ohio Northern University Pettit
College of Law, JD, 1976.

## ELLISON, Christopher
Ellison Schneider & Harris, Sacramento
916 447 2166
*Recommended in Energy*

## ELLMAN, Howard
Ellman, Burke, Hoffman & Johnson,
San Francisco 415 777 2727
*Recommended in Real Estate*

## ELSON, Vera M
McDermott Will & Emery, Palo Alto
650 813 5112
velson@mwe.com
*Recommended in Intellectual Property*
**Practice Areas:** Trial attorney who has
won numerous IP cases, including Dis-
trict Court jury trials and in the Interna-
tional Trade Commission. Named a
Northern California Super Lawyer. Prior
to legal career, designed high-speed A/D
converters for Hughes Aircraft's
Advanced Circuit Tech. Lab. Masters in
EE from UCLA. Argued and won appeals
at the CAFC. Former intern to late Helen
W Nies, former Chief Judge of the CAFC.
Registered to practice before the USPTO.
Member of Fed Cir Bar Association, ITC
Trial Lawyers Assoc.
**Personal:** USC (JD); UCLA (MSEE, BS).

## EMANUEL, William J
Littler Mendelson, PC, San Francisco
310 553 0308
wemanuel@littler.com
*Recommended in Employment*
**Practice Areas:** Represents management in labor-management relations
matters, including union contract negotiations, labor arbitration, NLRB litigation,
labor injunctions and Section 301 litigation. Advises management in decisions
including mergers and acquisitions,
workforce reductions, plant closings, and
facility sales. Litigates and counsels
employers in wage-hour issues, employee
terminations, employment arbitration,
discrimination and sexual harassment
complaints.
**Prof. Memberships:** Fellow, College of
Labor and Employment Lawyers; member and past Chairman of Employers
Group Legal Committee; member and
past Chairman, Labor Law Section of the
LA County Bar Association; member,
Industrial Relations Research Association.
**Personal:** Georgetown University (JD,
1963); Marquette University (AB, 1960).

## EPSTEIN, Mark
Munger, Tolles & Olson LLP, Los Angeles
213 683 9100
*Recommended in Litigation*

## ERSPAMER, Gordon
Morrison & Foerster LLP, Walnut Creek
925 295 3341
gerspamer@mofo.com
*Recommended in Energy*
**Practice Areas:** Focus on litigation of
complex civil actions in both state and
federal courts. Concentrates on energy
litigation, with emphasis on representation of independent power producers,
large industrial customers and Western
utilities in litigation throughout the
Western US. Extensive experience in matters involving California energy crisis,
power contracts, transmission/intercon-
nection disputes, alternative energy, and
interface between energy and
antitrust/unfair business practice law.
Provides strategic advice to clients on
energy issues.
**Career:** Admitted to practice in California. Co-Chair, firm's Inter-Disciplinary
Energy Group.
**Personal:** BA, Hamline University, 1975;
JD, University of Michigan Law School,
1978.

## ETH, Jordan
Morrison & Foerster LLP, San Francisco
415 268 7126
jeth@mofo.com
*Recommended in Litigation*
**Practice Areas:** Represents public companies and their officers and directors in
securities class actions, SEC investigations
and litigation, internal investigations, and
derivative suits. Representations have led
to significant victories for defendants, as
reflected in several published judicial
decisions.
**Career:** Admitted to practice in California. From 1980 until 1982, worked as an
economist in Washington DC, first for
the US Department of Energy and then
for the Budget Committee of the US
House of Representatives. Currently Co-
Chair of the firm's Securities Litigation,
Enforcement, and White-Collar Crime
Defense Group.
**Personal:** BA, Swarthmore College,
1980; JD, Stanford University Law School,
1985.

## FACKLER, Stephen W
Gibson, Dunn & Crutcher LLP, Palo Alto
650 849 5385
sfackler@gibsondunn.com
*Recommended in Employment*
**Practice Areas:** Advises public and private companies, private equity funds and
boards of directors on compensation and
benefits matters. He also regularly advises
senior executives on their employment
and severance arrangements and directors in connection with compensation
and indemnification arrangements.
**Prof. Memberships:** Chairman, Certification Council for the Certified Equity
Professional Institute. Outside counsel
for Global Equity Organization, the leading international trade association for

stock plan professionals.

**Personal:** JD, Stanford University, 1984; honours BA, St Johns' College, Oxford, 1981; AB, Harvard University, 1979, Phi Beta Kappa.

## FARRAR, Stanley F

Sullivan & Cromwell LLP, Los Angeles
310 712 6600

*Recommended in Banking & Finance, Financial Services*

**Practice Areas:** Extensive experience in representing financial institutions in M&A, securities offerings, corporate governance, commercial transactions and bank regulatory matters.

**Prof. Memberships:** ABA (former Chair, Bank Holding Companies and Letters of Credit subcommittees); CSBA (Member, Opinions Committee; former Chairman, Financial Institutions Committee).

**Career:** Of Counsel since 2005. Partner since 1984.

**Publications:** Frequent lecturer and writer on financial institutions topics.

## FAYNE, Steve

Akin Gump Strauss Hauer & Feld LLP,
Los Angeles 310 229 1069
sfayne@akingump.com

*Recommended in Media & Entertainment*

**Practice Areas:** Media finance. Advises financial institutions regarding international film and television lending. Also counsels borrowers, distributors, completion guarantors, independent producers, equity investors and others in various aspects of financing film and television projects. Advises film and television clients re tax-advantaged financing, subsidies and co-production arrangements worldwide. Lectures frequently on international financing of film and television productions.

**Prof. Memberships:** Adjunct Professor, UCLA School of Film and Television; former Board Member, Los Angeles Copyright Society; Member, Beverly Hills Bar Association (former Chairman, Entertainment Law Committee), Los Angeles County Bar Association, California Bar.

**Personal:** BA, Kent State University; JD, Columbia Law School.

## FEDER, Philip

Paul, Hastings, Janofsky & Walker LLP,
Los Angeles 213 683 6298
philipfeder@paulhastings.com

*Recommended in Real Estate*

**Practice Areas:** Chairman of Paul, Hastings, Janofsky & Walker's Real Estate Department; concentrates practice in real estate transactions, both domestic and international, with emphasis in finance, acquisitions and dispositions, and real estate loan workouts. Regularly represents investors on transactions in Asia and in Europe.

**Prof. Memberships:** American College of Real Estate Lawyers.

**Career:** Frequent speaker to attorneys and other real estate professionals.

**Publications:** 'The State of the North Asian Real Estate Markets', Briefings in Real Estate Finance, September 2002.

**Personal:** AB Degree, Economics, with honors, 1976, Stanford University; JD Degree, 1979, Columbia University Law School. Harlan Fiske Stone Scholar.

## FELDMAN, Boris

Wilson Sonsini Goodrich & Rosati,
Palo Alto 650 493 9300
bfeldman@wsgr.com

*Recommended in Litigation*

**Practice Areas:** Securities litigation and counseling; SEC enforcement; internal investigations; corporate law and governance.

**Prof. Memberships:** Admitted to practice in DC and California.

**Career:** Represented companies and their officers in more than 75 shareholder class actions and derivative suits throughout the US. Advised audit committees and boards of directors in internal investigations into accounting matters. Recently tried and won the case of Walter Hewlett v. Hewlett-Packard Company in the Delaware Court of Chancery, on behalf of HP. Member, WSGR Executive Management Committee and Policy Committee.

**Personal:** JD, Yale University, 1980; BA (summa cum laude), Yale University, 1977. Phi Beta Kappa.

## FELDMAN, Larry

Kaye Scholer LLP, Los Angeles
310 788 1090
larryfeldman@kayescholer.com

*Recommended in Litigation, Media & Entertainment*

**Practice Areas:** Special Counsel, Litigation. Larry Feldman focuses on civil litigation, with primary emphasis in high stakes entertainment, business, insurance, legal malpractice, real estate and personal injury tort litigation. Mr Feldman is one of the outstanding trial lawyers in the United States. He has been honored twice as the Trial Lawyer of the Year, once by the Los Angeles Trial Lawyers Association and once by Loyola Law School. Moreover, he has been elected into the prestigious American College of Trial Lawyers and the International Academy of Trial Lawyers.

**Prof. Memberships:** Member, Bar of California.

**Career:** President, Los Angeles County Bar Association, 1987-88. President Los Angeles Trial Lawyers Association, 1984. Fellow, American College of Trial Lawyers. Fellow, International Academy of Trial Lawyers. Vice President, American Board of Trial Advocates. Board of Directors, Association of Business Trial Lawyers. Board of Governors, California Trial Lawyers Association, 1981. JD (cum laude), Loyola University of Los Angeles,

1969. BS, San Fernando Valley State College, 1966.

## FELDMAN, Lewis G

Pillsbury Winthrop Shaw Pittman LLP,
Los Angeles 310 203 1188
lew.feldman@pillsburylaw.com

*Recommended in Real Estate*

**Practice Areas:** Lewis G Feldman represents participants in commercial, industrial, hotel, multi-family and affordable housing, public infrastructure, single family residential master-planned communities, and tax-exempt bond matters. Clients include: Lennar, LNR, the State of California, Anschutz Entertainment Group, Los Angeles Department of Water & Power, KB Home, FountainGlen Properties, and SunCal. Transactions include: AEG's $4.5 billion mixed-use LA Live! project; Lennar's $1 billion acquisition of Newhall Land & Farming; and the historic $10.9 billion California Economic Recovery Bonds.

**Personal:** JD, University of California at Davis (1982, Executive Editor, Law Review); BA, University of California at Santa Cruz (1978, with highest honors).

## FELDMAN, Robert P

Wilson Sonsini Goodrich & Rosati,
Palo Alto 650 493 9300
rfeldman@wsgr.com

*Recommended in Intellectual Property, Litigation*

**Practice Areas:** His practice has included complex litigation, including trials in all of the substantive areas in which clients litigate, particularly clients in fast-moving, growth industries.

**Prof. Memberships:** Fellow, American College of Trial Lawyers. Admitted to practice in California, as well as several US District Courts, and the US Court of Appeals for the Federal Circuit.

**Career:** Joined WSGR, 1984; became Partner, 1986. Assistant US Attorney and Member, Special Prosecution Unit, Northern District of California, 1979-84.

**Personal:** JD, Columbia University, 1975. Kent Scholar, Stone Scholar; BA (magna cum laude) State University of New York (Buffalo), 1972. Phi Beta Kappa.

## FELDSTEIN, Hydee R

Sullivan & Cromwell LLP, Los Angeles
310 712 6690
feldsteinh@sullcrom.com

*Recommended in Banking & Finance, Bankruptcy*

**Practice Areas:** Strategic, corporate and commercial finance; leveraged lending for acquisitions, mergers, and recapitalizations; senior secured, second lien and subordinated financings and bridge loans, including intercreditor arrangements; debtor in possession and exit facilities; corporate governance and fiduciary issues in insolvency-related restructurings and financings; creditors rights and special purpose and structured financial products.

**Personal:** Swarthmore College (BA, 1979); Columbia Law School (JD, 1982).

## FEO, Edwin

Milbank, Tweed, Hadley & McCloy LLP,
Los Angeles 213 892 4000

*Recommended in Energy, Projects, Transportation*

## FESSLER, Daniel W

Holland & Knight LLP, San Francisco
415 743 6900
daniel.fessler@hklaw.com

*Recommended in Energy*

**Practice Areas:** Of Counsel to the Government Section, practices in the areas of energy, telecommunications law, complex contract issues and alternative dispute resolution. He currently advises government and utility clients in Asia, Africa, Europe, Latin America, and North America on restructuring options, privatization issues, infrastructure development, and project finance. Has extensive experience as both a legal academic and government official. From 1991-96, he was President of the California Public Utilities Commission, which regulates the reliability, safety, and economic terms of service provided to California's population by investor-owned utilities in the fields of energy (gas and electric), telecommunications, water and transportation.

## FIELDS, Bertram

Greenberg Glusker Fields Claman
Machtinger & Kinsella LLP, Los Angeles
310 553 3610

*Recommended in Media & Entertainment*

## FILETI, Thomas

Morrison & Foerster LLP, Los Angeles
213 892 5276
tfileti@mofo.com

*Recommended in Real Estate*

**Practice Areas:** Represents clients in connection with investments in and the financing, operation and disposition of real estate assets. Has expertise in financing of corporate real estate facilities. Practice also emphasizes real estate financings and purchase and sale transactions, including credit leases, lease financings, mezzanine financing, and representation of REITs.

**Prof. Memberships:** Member: American Bar Association; Los Angeles County Bar Association; National Association of Real Estate Investment Trusts.

**Career:** Admitted to practice in California. Head, Real Estate Practice Group, Los Angeles office.

**Personal:** AB Degree, with distinction, Cornell University, 1978; JD, cum laude, University of Pennsylvania Law School, 1981.

## FISCHER, Samuel

Ziffren Brittenham Branca Fischer
Gilbert-Lurie & Stiffelman LLP,
Los Angeles 310 552 3388

*Recommended in Media & Entertainment*

**FLAGEL, Mark**
Latham & Watkins LLP, Los Angeles
213 485 1234
*Recommended in Intellectual Property*

**FLAUM, Keith**
Cooley Godward LLP, Palo Alto
650 843 5000
*Recommended in Corporate/M&A*

**FORBES, Amy R**
Gibson, Dunn & Crutcher LLP,
Los Angeles 213 229 7151
aforbes@gibsondunn.com
*Recommended in Real Estate*
**Practice Areas:** Land use, development,
California Environmental Quality Act
(including litigation), municipal law
(including telecommunications issues),
eminent domain and real estate transac-
tions. Representative clients: Stockbridge
Real Estate Fund; Fashion Institute of
Design and Merchandising, General
Growth Properties, Rockpoint.
**Prof. Memberships:** Member, American
College of Real Estate Lawyers.
**Career:** Luce Scholar, Bangkok, Thailand
1988-89. Named among 50 most powerful women lawyers by Los Angeles Business Journal and a 'best and busiest' real
estate lawyer by California Law Business.
**Personal:** BSE Civil Engineering (Trans-
portation), Princeton University, 1980;
JD, University of Southern California,
1984, Order of the Coif.

**FORST, David**
Fenwick & West, San Francisco
650 335 7254
dforst@fenwick.com
*Recommended in Tax*
**Practice Areas:** International corporate
and partnership taxation.
**Career:** Included in Euromoney's 'Guide
to the World's Leading Tax Advisers';
named one of top tax advisers in the
Western US by International Tax Review.
Editor of and regular contributor to Journal of Taxation. Has published articles on
international joint ventures, international
tax aspects of mergers and acquisitions,
and business purpose and economic substance doctrines. Has chaired and spoken
at numerous tax seminars, including
NYU Tax Institute, TEI Chapter meetings, and San Jose State Tax Institute. Has
taught law school courses on partnership
taxation and section 482 transfer pricing.
**Personal:** Stanford Law School, JD, with
distinction, 1992; Princeton University,
Woodrow Wilson School of Public and
International Affairs, AB, cum laude, Phi
Beta Kappa, 1989.

**FRACKMAN, Russell**
Mitchell, Silberberg & Knupp LLP,
Los Angeles 310 312 2000
*Recommended in Media &
Entertainment*

**FRAM, Robert**
Heller Ehrman LLP, San Francisco
415 772 6160
robert.fram@hellerehrman.com
*Recommended in Intellectual Property*
**Practice Areas:** Intellectual property litigation.
**Prof. Memberships:** State Bar of California; Northern California Chapter,
Association of Business Trial Lawyers;
American Intellectual Property Law
Association.
**Career:** Mr Fram has substantial experience litigating patent, trade secret and
licensing cases. Mr Fram's trial experience
includes proceedings in federal and state
courts, including service as Special Assistant District Attorney, where he tried a
series of criminal cases in front of juries.
**Personal:** Princeton University (AB,
magna cum laude, 1979); Phi Beta
Kappa; Harvard Law School (JD, magna
cum laude, 1985).

**FRANKENHEIMER, John T**
Loeb & Loeb LLP, Los Angeles
310 282 2135
jfrankenheimer@loeb.com
*Recommended in Media &
Entertainment*
**Practice Areas:** Advises on
acquisition/sale, financing and restructuring of companies, including valuation,
securitization and due diligence. Represents record companies and distributors,
music publishing companies as well as
artists and executives in music industry
in connection with talent contracts,
licensing, technology, publishing, touring
and production. Represents technology
and new media companies in intellectual
property and content acquisition/licens-
ing agreements. Represents writers, producers and directors in film/television.
**Prof. Memberships:** Founding Mem-
ber/Advisory Board/past Chair - National
Academy of Recording Arts and Sciences
(Entertainment Law Initiative); advisory
Board/Past Chair Entertainment Law
Symposium – UCLA Law School; Executive Board/Past Chair Music and Entertainment Chapter – City of Hope; Member National Board of Trustees, City of
Hope; Board of Trustees, The Fulfillment
Fund.
**Career:** Partner since 1978. Co-Chair-
man of firm 1998-present; Managing
Partner, Los Angeles office 1997-98; Exec-
utive Committee 1983-92, 1993-97.
**Publications:** Frequent speaker on
entertainment law-related topics at law
schools, California Copyright Society,
NYU State CPA/Entertainment Forum
and industry seminars.
**Personal:** UCLA School of Law (JD,
1973); Claremont McKenna (BS, 1968).

**FREIER, Elliot**
Irell & Manella LLP, Los Angeles
310 277 1010
*Recommended in Tax*

**FRIEDMAN, Alan**
Munger, Tolles & Olson LLP, Los Angeles
213 683 9100
*Recommended in Employment*

**FRIEDMAN, Bruce A**
Alschuler Grossman Stein & Kahan LLP,
Santa Monica 310 907 1000
*Recommended in Insurance*
**Practice Areas:** Regarded as a leading
insurance coverage and professional liability lawyer in California, Bruce represents insurers with respect to coverage
issues and litigation involving D&O,
media, internet, entertainment, professional liability and general liability policies. Bruce also represents the California
Insurance Commissioner with respect to
insolvency and regulatory litigation.
Bruce defends attorneys, directors, and
officers against malpractice, breach of
fiduciary duty and securities claims.
**Prof. Memberships:** Member, Board of
Governors, and past President, Association of Business Trial Lawyers. Member,
Board of Trustees of Public Counsel.
Member, American Bar Association Litigation Section and TIPS Section and
Committees on Insurance Coverage, Professional Liability, Directors and Officers
Liability and Fidelity and Surety law
within those sections.
**Career:** Managing Partner of Alschuler
Grossman Stein & Kahan LLP. In 1996,
obtained one of the top 10 plaintiff's verdicts in California. In 2003, represented
the Los Angeles County Bar Association
as amicus curiae before the California
Supreme Court in Viner v Sweet, which
established the causation requirement in
legal malpractice.
**Publications:** Co-author, 'Insurance
Coverage for Patent Litigation', Patent Litigation, PLI Press, 2001; author, 'Dismissal', Civil Procedure Before Trial, Continuing Education of the Bar, 1990; co-
author, 'Annotated Directors and Officers
Liability Policy', American Bar Association Press, anticipated publication 2006.
**Personal:** Claremont McKenna College
(BA with honors, 1972). George Washington University (JD with honors,
1975). President, Board of Trustees,
Wilshire Boulevard Temple.

**FRIEDRICH, William**
Farella Braun & Martel LLP,
San Francisco 415 954 4400
*Recommended in Insurance*

**FULLER, James**
Fenwick & West LLP, Mountain View
650 335 7205
jpfuller@fenwick.com
*Recommended in Tax*
**Practice Areas:** Chair of firm's Tax
Group. Corporate, domestic and international tax, mergers and acquisitions and
joint ventures.
**Career:** Ranked by Euromoney (2004) as
one of the world's top 25 tax advisors;

ranked by Law and Business Research
(2004) in the top 10 worldwide. Mr Fuller
writes a widely read monthly column in
Tax Notes International and appears in
Woodward White's Best Lawyers in
America. Admitted to and has had cases
in United States Supreme Court, seven
federal circuit courts of appeal, United
States Court of Federal Claims and Unit-
ed States Tax Court.
**Personal:** New York University School of
Law, Graduate School, 1975; New
York University, LLM, in Taxation, 1974;
Fordham University School of Law, JD,
1970; New York University, BS, 1966.

**GALE, Kelley**
Latham & Watkins LLP, San Diego
619 236 1234
*Recommended in Projects*

**GALLO, Greg**
DLA Piper Rudnick Gray Cary US LLP,
Palo Alto 650 833 2020
greg.gallo@dlapiper.com
*Recommended in Corporate/M&A*
**Practice Areas:** Corporate and securities; emerging growth and venture capital; mergers and acquistiions; public
company and corporate governance.
**Career:** He has a wide-ranging venture
capital, corporate and securities, M&A,
and capital markets practice coupled with
extensive experience of acting for clients
in the semiconductor, networking, telecom, enterprise software, internet,
biotechnology, venture capital, and
investment banking sectors. For more
than 30 years, he has represented clients
in a variety of corporate and corporate
finance matters relating to emerging
growth through Fortune 500, Silicon Valley technology and biotechnology companies.
**Personal:** JD, Harvard University; BS,
University of Wisconsin.

**GALLO, Joie**
Christensen, Miller, Fink, Jacobs, Glaser,
Weil & Shapiro, LLP, Los Angeles
310 553 3000
*Recommended in Media &
Entertainment*

**GARTMAN, John**
Fish & Richardson P.C., San Diego
858 678 4313
gartman@fr.com
*Recommended in Intellectual Property*
**Practice Areas:** Principal in Fish &
Richardson's San Diego office. National
trial practice focuses on high technology
litigation. Has deep experience in
telecommunications, semiconductors
and software. Successfully tried jury and
bench cases in federal and state courts
and before the United States International Trade Commission.
**Prof. Memberships:** Invited member of
the Intellectual Property Advisory Committee for the US District Court for the
District of Delaware, and is an approved

mediator for the US District Court for the Northern District of California.
**Personal:** University of Texas BS Electrical Engineering 1983; University of Texas JD 1986.

### GARVIN, Anthony O
Morgan, Lewis & Bockius LLP, San Francisco 415 442 1620
agarvin@morganlewis.com
*Recommended in Environment*
**Practice Areas:** Anthony O Garvin is a Partner in the Litigation Practice, resident in the San Francisco office with broad experience in all aspects of environmental law. He has represented corporate clients in California and the Western United States in litigation and administrative proceedings regarding federal and state environmental laws including Comprehensive Environmental Response Compensation and Liability Act (CERCLA), Resource Conservation and Recovery Act (RCRA), NPDES permits under Clean Water Act and California Porter-Cologne Water Quality Control Act, Clean Air Act, Proposition 65, Endangered Species Act, and underground tank laws.

### GARZA, Oscar
Gibson, Dunn & Crutcher LLP, Irvine 949 451 3849
ogarza@gibsondunn.com
*Recommended in Bankruptcy*
**Practice Areas:** Represents corporate debtors (both publicly traded and privately owned), creditors' committees, secured creditors in Chapter 11 cases, advises buyers and sellers of the assets of financially distressed companies and represents Bankruptcy Trustees in complex cases.
**Publications:** Lecturer on bankruptcy law and practice. Co-authored three articles published in 2005 in the Daily Deal, the California Bankruptcy Journal and the Los Angeles Daily Journal.
**Personal:** JD, University of Arizona College of Law, 1990 (Law Review).

### GIBBS, Kenneth C
Gibbs, Giden, Locher & Turner, Los Angeles 310 552 3400
kgibbs@gglt.com
*Recommended in Construction*
**Practice Areas:** Kenneth C Gibbs is a Senior Partner in the Los Angeles and Las Vegas law firm of Gibbs, Giden, Locher & Turner LLP, which specializes in the representation of owners, contractors, subcontractors, material suppliers, design professionals and insurers in construction industry matters and disputes. He has specialized in construction law, arbitrations and mediations for more than 30 years. Mr Gibbs presently is a full-time mediator and arbitrator and has mediated more than 700 matters. He specializes in the mediation of construction defect, breach of contract and delay, disruption and acceleration claims. He is one of the

leading mediators of complex, multiparty construction defect and breach of contract disputes and has mediated such disputes throughout the nation.
**Prof. Memberships:** Mr Gibbs is a Member of the Large/Complex Case Panel of the American Arbitration Association and an Arbitrator on the California Public Works Arbitration Panel.
**Publications:** Mr Gibbs has authored or co-authored many books and articles on construction industry and mediation-related topics, including 'California Construction Law', now in its 16th edition, and 'Construction Change Order Claims'. He has been a principal speaker at many national conventions and conferences including the annual Construction Law Superconference.

### GILLETTE, Patricia
Heller Ehrman LLP, San Francisco 415 772 6456
patricia.gillette@hellerehrman.com
*Recommended in Employment*
**Practice Areas:** Labor and employment; consumer litigation.
**Prof. Memberships:** American Bar Association; State Bar of California; Bar Association of San Francisco.
**Career:** Ms Gillette's practice at Heller Ehrman has encompassed all aspects of employment law, including wrongful discharge and discrimination litigation in both state and federal court, representation of employers in hearings before administrative agencies and counseling and training employers on preventive personnel practices. Ms Gillette's clients include financial institutions in California, hi-tech firms, hospitals, insurance companies, biotech companies, and telecommunications companies.
**Personal:** Occidental College (AB, 1973); University of San Francisco Law School (JD, cum laude, 1976).

### GIRARD, Robert D
Sonnenschein Nath & Rosenthal LLP, Los Angeles 213 892 5074
rgirard@sonnenschein.com
*Recommended in Healthcare*
**Practice Areas:** Represents institutional and professional providers, including integrated medical groups, faculty practice programs, IPAs, health insurance companies, HMOs, PPOs and other third-party payment and managed care organizations. Experience includes medico-legal and bioethics matters, service contracts, reimbursement, corporate organizational, medical staff and general transactional matters, including handling M&A and related antitrust, tax and corporate securities issues. Has drafted regulatory legislation (including California Hospital Commission Act) and prepared and presented testimony on regulatory initiatives.
**Prof. Memberships:** National Health Lawyers; California Society of Health

Care Attorneys; American Academy of Health Care Attorneys.
**Personal:** Yale Law School LLB; UCLA, AB, Phi Beta Kappa.

### GIUNTA, Joseph J
Skadden, Arps, Slate, Meagher & Flom LLP & Affiliates, Los Angeles 213 687 5040
jgiunta@skadden.com
*Recommended in Corporate/M&A*
**Practice Areas:** Handles all types of merger and acquisition transactions, both friendly and hostile. He is experienced in proxy contests, tender offers, restructurings, recapitalizations and leveraged buyouts. Has represented purchasers, sellers and their financial advisors in a wide variety of merger, acquisition and disposition transactions.
**Career:** JD, American University, Washington College of Law, 1976 (magna cum laude; Associate Editor, American University Law Review); BS, Stanford University, 1972.

### GLAD, Paul E B
Sonnenschein Nath & Rosenthal LLP, San Francisco 415 882 5001
pglad@sonnenschein.com
*Recommended in Insurance*
**Practice Areas:** Managing Partner San Francisco, and firmwide Chair, Insurance Practice Group. Matters range from coverage issues to bad faith claims, class actions to regulatory challenges. Co-author of West's 'California Insurance Laws Annotated' and 'California Insurance Law Handbook'. Editor of and frequent contributor to numerous publications, including 'Insurance Litigation Reporter' and 'California Insurance Law and Regulation'.
**Prof. Memberships:** Volunteer of the Year, Bar Association of San Francisco (BASF) (2005); past Director, BASF; past Chairman, BASF Insurance Law Section; Faculty, Environmental Law Institute, Business Insurance Law Institute.
**Personal:** UCLA Law School JD; Stanford University, with Distinction.

### GLASCOCK, Thomas B
Thelen Reid & Priest LLP, San Francisco 415 369 7004
tbglascock@thelenreid.com
*Recommended in Projects*
**Practice Areas:** Mr Glascock specializes in project development and finance, representing sponsors, lessees, equity investors and lenders in the development, financing, acquisition, lease, operation and restructuring of a variety of energy and infrastructure projects; loan workouts and restructurings, mergers, acquisitions and dispositions of companies and infrastructure projects and general commercial matters including joint venture and partnering arrangements; commercial lending, representing lenders and borrowers in secured and unsecured financings and in subordinated financ-

ings; and equipment leasing, representing lessors, lessees and lenders in leveraged and single investor leases of energy and industrial facilities, aircraft, railroad rolling stock and other equipment. Mr Glascock also represents creditors in structuring and negotiating restructurings.
**Prof. Memberships:** ABA Committees on Commercial Financial Services and Developments in Business Financing and Subcommittees on Project Finance and Aircraft Financing.
**Career:** Partner of Thelen Reid & Priest LLP's San Francisco office. Speaking engagements include: 'Financing Power Plants in North America' Forbes Superconference London, March 2004; 'New Strategies For Financing Energy Power Plants' April 2002, Forbes Convention - Developing, Constructing, Operating and Securing Energy Power Project and 'Structuring and Legal Issues for High Speed Ground Transportation Projects', May 1997, High Speed Ground Transportation Association Annual Convention.
**Personal:** Received his JD from the University of Virginia in 1986 and was the Notes Editor for the Journal of Law and Politics, 1984-86. Received his BS in Business with highest honors from George Mason University in 1983. Listed in: 'Euromoney's Guide to the World's Leading Project Finance Lawyers (2001-04)'; the '2003-04 Guide to the World's Leading Energy and Natural Resources Lawyers'; Chambers, International Financial Review and North American Super Lawyer.

### GLASER, Patricia
Christensen, Miller, Fink, Jacobs, Glaser, Weil & Shapiro, LLP, Los Angeles 310 553 3000
*Recommended in Litigation, Media & Entertainment*

### GODSHALL, Brad
Pachulski, Stang, Ziehl, Young, Jones & Weintraub P.C., Los Angeles 310 277 6910
*Recommended in Bankruptcy*

### GOLDBERG, Phillip
Hassard Bonnington LLP, San Francisco 415 288 9800
*Recommended in Healthcare*

### GOLDBERG, Stephen
Heller Ehrman LLP, Los Angeles 213 689 7585
stephen.goldberg@hellerehrman.com
*Recommended in Insurance*
**Practice Areas:** Insurance recovery, consumer litigation, product liability.
**Career:** Mr Goldberg has engaged in complex commercial litigation in a range of insurance matters including insurance coverage surrounding product liability claims, asbestos liabilities, environmental damage, and first-party property losses.

He represents GMAC Commercial Mortgage Corporation in coverage litigation concerning property damage and business interruption losses from the events of September 11 that is pending in federal district court in New York against almost two dozen insurance companies.
**Personal:** Yale Law School (JD, 1970).

### GOLDMAN, Donald
McDermott Will & Emery, Los Angeles
310 551 9319
dogoldman@mwe.com
*Recommended in Healthcare*
**Practice Areas:** Counsel to healthcare industry clients in a broad range of planning, regulatory, administrative and litigation matters, including hospital physician ventures, Medicare fraud and abuse defense, medical staff relations and bylaws, facilities licensing, hospital-based physician matters and certificate of need. Represents clients in Medicare fraud and abuse investigations and development of corporate compliance programs. Represented professionals in licensing, Medicare and joint venture matters. Advised DaVita Inc., a NYSE-listed company, a leading supplier of renal dialysis services, in its successful appeal of Medicare payment disputes.
**Personal:** University of California-Los Angeles School of Law (JD), University of California-Los Angeles (BA).

### GOLDMAN, Melvin
Morrison & Foerster LLP, San Francisco
415 268 7311
mgoldman@mofo.com
*Recommended in Antitrust, Litigation*
**Practice Areas:** Specializes in defense of antitrust actions and investigations including jury trials of antitrust lawsuits; handling appeals of antitrust judgments; and grand jury and internal investigations of antitrust matters. Has counseled corporations regarding antitrust compliance and lectured on substantive antitrust issues and trial technique in defense of antitrust lawsuits.
**Prof. Memberships:** Member, American College of Trial Lawyers. Past President, Bar Association of San Francisco.
**Career:** Admitted to practice in California and Illinois.
**Personal:** BA, DePaul University, 1958; JD, Northwestern University School of Law, 1961, Order of the Coif; Managing Editor, Law Review; MSL, Stanford University School of Law, 1963.

### GOLDMAN, Robert J
Ropes & Gray LLP, Palo Alto
650 617 4035
robert.goldman@ropesgray.com
*Recommended in Intellectual Property*
**Practice Areas:** IP litigator with 28 years of trial and appellate experience in complex patent, trade secret, copyright, trademark litigation for clients including AstraZeneca Pharmaceuticals LP, Purdue Pharma LP, Tessera, Inc., Hewlett-

Packard/Compaq Computer Corporation, Altera Corporation and Nellcor, Inc. Worked on behalf of Polaroid Corporation in landmark patent infringement action against Eastman Kodak Company relating to instant photography, resulting in $873 million in damages.
**Career:** New York Bar (1978); California Bar (1997); Partner, Fish & Neave (1977); Partner, Ropes & Gray (2005).
**Personal:** JD, Columbia University (1977); BS, Operations, Software Applications, Columbia University (1977).

### GONZALEZ, Josie
Gonzalez & Harris PC, Pasadena
626 229 9806
*Recommended in Immigration*

### GONZÁLEZ, Arturo J
Morrison & Foerster LLP, San Francisco
415 268 7020
agonzalez@mofo.com
*Recommended in Litigation*
**Practice Areas:** Trial lawyer for over 20 years. Has tried cases in state and federal court, for both plaintiffs and defendants, in a wide variety of substantive areas, including fraud, breach of contract, unfair business practices, claims under the Consumer Legal Remedies Act, securities litigation, race and sex discrimination, product liability, medical malpractice, wrongful death and civil rights.
**Career:** Admitted to practice in California. Chair, firm's Trial Practice Group. Named in Top 45 Lawyers Under 45, American Lawyer magazine, 2003; in California's Top 20 Young Lawyers, California Business newspaper, 1998; and among the Top 40 Lawyers Under 40, National Law Journal, 1995.
**Personal:** BA, University of California, Davis, 1982; JD, Harvard Law School, 1985.

### GOODKIND, Jim
Loeb & Loeb LLP, Los Angeles
310 282 2138
jgoodkind@loeb.com
*Recommended in Media & Entertainment*
**Practice Areas:** Partner in Entertainment Practice. Examples of recent matters include advising performing artists, promoters, producers, venues, advertisers and sponsors in connection with major live events, concerts and touring; representing music industry biographical property for documentary and dramatic motion picture projects; counseling casino/resort companies in entertainment transactions; representing recording artists (including estates), producers, personal managers and executives in music and multimedia industries; and working with film/television actors in all aspects (including fashion, music, stage as well as film/television) of their careers.
**Career:** Partner since 1997.
**Personal:** University of California, Hastings Law (JD, 1986); Northwestern University (BSS, 1978).

### GOODMAN, William M
Topel & Goodman PC, San Francisco
415 421 6140
wmg@topelgoodman.com
*Recommended in Litigation*
**Practice Areas:** White-collar criminal defense and related civil and administrative litigation.
**Prof. Memberships:** California Bar Association; American Bar Association; California Attorneys for Criminal Justice; National Association of Criminal Defense Attorneys.
**Career:** BA Northwestern University, 1971; JD University of California, Berkeley (Boalt Hall), 1974; Law Clerk to Chief Justice Donald R Wright, California Supreme Court 1974-75; Assistant Federal Public Defender, Northern District of California 1975-80; Partner, Topel and Goodman 1980-present.

### GOODWIN, David B
Heller Ehrman LLP, San Francisco
415 772 6319
david.goodwin@hellerehrman.com
*Recommended in Insurance*
**Practice Areas:** Appeals and strategy; insurance recovery; consumer litigation; international arbitration and ADR.
**Prof. Memberships:** State Bar of California; Bar Association of San Francisco; Risk and Insurance Management Society (RIMS).
**Career:** Mr Goodwin has represented numerous corporate and individual policyholders in insurance coverage litigation, negotiation and counseling involving both first-party property damage and business interruption losses and third-party liability claims.
**Personal:** University of California, Santa Cruz (AB, 1974); Oxford University (BA, 1976, MA, 1979); Stanford Law School (JD, 1982).

### GORDON, Andrew K
Duane Morris LLP, San Francisco
415 403 8833
akgordon@duanemorris.com
*Recommended in Insurance*
**Practice Areas:** Andrew K Gordon practices in the areas of insurance and commercial litigation, environmental law and labor and employment law with a focus on complex multi-party trials. His commercial litigation experience includes unfair competition claims, unfair lending practices, misappropriation of trade secrets, partnership disputes, obtaining and enforcing judgments against foreign entities, real estate nondisclosures and various other business torts. Mr Gordon counsels employers on employment issues and has litigated cases involving discrimination, disability and harassment issues, wrongful termination, trade secret violations, and wage and hour disputes.
**Prof. Memberships:** Marin County Superior Court - arbitrator, Settlement Judge Pro Tempore; Association of Busi-

ness Trial Lawyers; American Bar Association - Torts and Insurance Practice Section; California Bar Association - Litigation and Employment Section; Bar Association of San Francisco; University of San Francisco Inn of Court.
**Career:** Admitted to practice in California; the United States District Courts for the Northern and Eastern Districts of California; and the United States Court of Appeals for the Ninth Circuit.
**Personal:** University of San Francisco Law School, JD, 1981; Amherst College, BA, 1974.

### GORDON, Eric B
McDermott Will & Emery, Los Angeles
310 551 9315
egordon@mwe.com
*Recommended in Healthcare*
**Practice Areas:** Co-Chair of Academic Medical Center Practice. Represents national hospital systems, medical groups, medical device manufacturers, group purchasing organizations, research institutes. Stark/antikickback, compliance programs, investigations and audits, qui tam defense. Transactional matters include hospital-physician joint ventures, nonprofit affiliations. Focus on academic medical center representation including: organization of faculty practice plans, AMC restructurings, compliance plan development, HIPAA, fraud and abuse policies, Stark audits, residency affiliations, GME/IME planning and appeals.
**Publications:** Author, 'Faculty Practice Plans' (BNA); co-author, 'Guide to Stark Physician Self-Referral Rules' (AIS).
**Personal:** JD (UCLA); MD (Brown University), AB (Brown University).

### GREEN, Josh
Heller Ehrman LLP, Menlo Park
650 233 8409
joshua.green@hellerehrman.com
*Recommended in Corporate/M&A*
**Practice Areas:** Venture law group/emerging companies.
**Prof. Memberships:** State Bar of California; American Bar Association; Federal Regulation of Securities Committee.
**Career:** Mr Green's practice represents emerging growth companies and venture capital firms. He is involved in corporate transactions including private financings, initial public offerings, mergers and acquisitions, corporate partnerships, technology licensing and executive compensation matters. He has been involved with the founding of many life sciences companies, and has architected complex spin-offs and corporate partnerships. He is ranked on Forbes' Midas List.
**Publications:** Member, UCLA Law Review.
**Personal:** University of California, Los Angeles, School of Law (JD 1980).

**GREENBERG, Gordon A**
McDermott Will & Emery, Los Angeles
310 551 9398
ggreenberg@mwe.com
*Recommended in Litigation*
**Practice Areas:** Defends clients in high stakes 'bet the company' matters that often have international components. Recent matters handled include defending a foreign government agency in criminal matter concerning alleged false statements to a US banking regulator; representation of the President of a large telecommunications company in SEC and criminal proceedings; representation of the Chairman of the Board of a public company in a Foreign Corrupt Practices Investigation; and representation of a Big Four accounting firm in a money laundering investigation. Representation of law firms and lawyers.
**Career:** Lecturer, Federal Judicial Center, ABA, and other professional organizations.

**GREENBERG, Jeffrey**
Latham & Watkins LLP, Los Angeles
213 485 1234
*Recommended in Projects*

**GREENFIELD, Robert**
Stutman, Treister & Glatt Professional Corporation, Los Angeles
310 228 5600
*Recommended in Bankruptcy*

**GREENSPAN, Eric**
Myman, Abell, Fineman, Greenspan & Light LLP, Los Angeles
310 820 7717
*Recommended in Media & Entertainment*

**GREENWALD, Steven**
Davis Wright Tremaine LLP, San Francisco 415 276 6500
*Recommended in Energy*

**GRIFFEY, Linda**
O'Melveny & Myers LLP, Los Angeles
213 430 6637
lgriffey@omm.com
*Recommended in Employment*
**Practice Areas:** Linda Griffey co-chairs O'Melveny & Myers' Employee Benefits and Executive Compensation Practice. She advises clients in connection with the design and implementation of equity and cash compensation and incentive plans, qualified and non-qualified pension and profit sharing plans, welfare benefit plans, employment agreements, severance arrangements, change of control agreements and other employee benefit and executive compensation arrangements. Her practice also includes advising clients on benefits and compensation issues in connection with IPOs, mergers, acquisitions and dispositions. She has represented major corporations, compensation committees, management groups and individual executives with respect to executive compensation and benefits matters.

**GROSSMAN, Marshall**
Alschuler Grossman Stein & Kahan LLP, Santa Monica 310 255 9118
*Recommended in Litigation, Media & Entertainment*
**Practice Areas:** He both prosecutes and defends major commercial litigation. Served as lead counsel for the plaintiff classes in the Equity Funding Securities Litigation and represented the owners of Guess? Jeans in their successful litigation against the owners of Jordache. He has represented Apple Computer, Inc. and Packard Bell NEC, Inc. in the defense of patent infringement and Lanham Act litigation, including the highly publicized battle between Compaq and Packard Bell. In 1999, led Arthur Andersen's trial team to a defense jury verdict in a $1 billion securities fraud class action lawsuit. In 2004 settled on the eve of trial for client Suzuki Motor Company against Consumers Union and in 2005 successfully defended Blockbuster, Inc. in action filed by the Walt Disney Co. At this time, represents international public accounting firms in complex federal securities litigation and related federal investigations, Grupo Televisa, S.A. in litigation against Univision, Inc., and Chabad of California against the Russian Federation.
**Prof. Memberships:** American, Beverly Hills (Chair, Civil Practice and Procedure Committee, 1969-70; Member, Board of Governors, 1970-76), Century City, and Los Angeles County Bar Associations; State Bar of California; Beverly Hills Barristers (President, 1972-73); Association of Business Trial Lawyers (Member, Board of Governors, 1973-75).
**Career:** A Partner of Alschuler Grossman Stein & Kahan LLP. Has practiced with the firm since 1964. Lecturer in Law, University of Southern California Law Center, 1966-69. In 1989 and again in 1999, was recognized by a leading US law journal as among 10 of the top trial lawyers in America. Referred to by former Los Angeles Mayor Richard J Riordan as the 'toughest litigator in Los Angeles'. 2003 and 2004 Top 10 SuperLawyer vote recipient in peer survey of Southern California's 65,000 lawyers. Listed in 'The Best Lawyers in America'. Has long been active in community affairs, having served as a Commissioner on the California Coastal Commission and on the boards of Public Counsel, and the United Way. Currently serves as Chair of the State of California Commission on Judicial Performance, on the boards of Bet Tzedek Legal Services, Jewish Big Brothers and on the national board of the American Jewish Committee.
**Personal:** University of California at Los Angeles; University of Southern California (BSL and LLB, 1964). Order of the Coif. Production Editor, Southern California Law Review, 1963-64.

**GROSSMAN, Paul**
Paul, Hastings, Janofsky & Walker LLP, Los Angeles 213 683 6203
paulgrossman@paulhastings.com
*Recommended in Employment*
**Practice Areas:** Represents major private employers in all aspects of employment law, including class actions, wage/hour, wrongful discharge, discrimination, sexual harassment, whistle-blower, and labor-management litigation.
**Prof. Memberships:** American Bar Association Labor and Employment Law Section and its Equal Employment Opportunity Committee.
**Publications:** Co-author of Lindemann & Grossman, 'Employment Discrimination Law' (Bureau of National Affairs, 1996 and 2002), the official book of the American Bar Association in its field.
**Personal:** BA Degree in 1961 from Amherst College; JD Degree in 1964 from Yale Law School; Member of the Board of Editors of the Yale Law Journal.

**GUNDERSON, Bob**
Gunderson Dettmer Stough Villeneuve Franklin & Hachigian, Menlo Park
650 321 2400
*Recommended in Corporate/M&A*

**GUY III, G Hopkins**
Orrick, Herrington & Sutcliffe LLP, Menlo Park 650 614 7452
hopguy@orrick.com
*Recommended in Intellectual Property*
**Practice Areas:** Focuses his practice on patent, trade secret, and commercial contract litigation involving all areas of Web-based telecommunications, electronics, and computer technologies. IP litigation experience includes all phases of discovery, prior art research, pretrial, jury and bench trial work, all phases of trial work, post-trial motions, and appeals before the Federal Circuit. Patent and trade secret litigation experience has involved Web-based technology, telecommunication equipment and semiconductor processing, printed circuit board technologies, and microprocessing, semiconductors and related technology, and ultrasound equipment.
**Prof. Memberships:** State Bars of Virginia and California.
**Personal:** JD, University of Richmond, 1982; BS, University of Virginia, 1979.

**HAAG, Melinda**
Orrick, Herrington & Sutcliffe LLP, San Francisco 415 773 5610
mhaag@orrick.com
*Recommended in Litigation*
**Practice Areas:** Combined 18 years of federal prosecutorial and private sector experience. Handled cases involving allegations of securities fraud, mail and wire fraud, antitrust violations, environmental crimes, civil rights violations, defense contractor fraud, healthcare fraud, bank fraud, money laundering, child exploitation crimes and narcotics violations.

Experience includes more than 16 jury and bench trials, including acting as lead counsel in several complex, multi-defendant cases.
**Career:** Before joining Orrick, Haag was Chief of the White Collar Crime Section of the US Attorney's Office for the Northern District of California.
**Personal:** JD, UC Berkeley, 1987; BA, UC San Diego, 1983.

**HAGEROTT, Edward**
Munger, Tolles & Olson LLP, Los Angeles
213 683 9100
*Recommended in Real Estate*

**HAIGHT, Catherine**
The Law Office of Catherine Haight, Los Angeles 310 242 5554
*Recommended in Immigration*

**HALBREICH, David M**
Morgan, Lewis & Bockius LLP, Los Angeles 213 612 7345
dhalbreich@morganlewis.com
*Recommended in Insurance*
**Practice Areas:** David Halbreich is a Partner in the Litigation Practice. He concentrates his practice on complex litigation and insurance recovery. He has represented clients in a variety of industries including manufacturing, oil and gas, financial services, real estate development, electronics, construction and others.
**Prof. Memberships:** (State Bar of California, Deputy Special Trial Counsel); American Bar Association (Litigation Section, Committee on Insurance Coverage).

**HALL, Michael**
Latham & Watkins LLP, Menlo Park
650 328 4600
*Recommended in Corporate/M&A*

**HALLING, Gary**
Sheppard, Mullin, Richter & Hampton LLP, San Francisco 415 434 9100
*Recommended in Antitrust*

**HANDZLIK, Jan**
Howrey LLP, Los Angeles
213 892 1800
*Recommended in Litigation*

**HANSCHEN, Peter**
Morrison & Foerster LLP, Walnut Creek
925 295 3450
phanschen@mofo.com
*Recommended in Energy*
**Practice Areas:** Advises on all aspects of energy matters, including state and federal regulations, energy-related transactions, energy project financing and arbitrations. Has been in the forefront of electric regulation matters for 25 years.
**Career:** Admitted to practice in California. Began career in Pacific Gas and Electric Company's legal department. During last five years with PG&E, was responsible for all regulatory matters before the California Public Utilities Commission and other state and federal regulatory agen-

cies. Co-Chair, Morrison & Foerster Energy Practice Group.
**Personal:** BA, magna cum laude, San Francisco State University, 1967; JD, University of California, Berkeley, Boalt Hall, 1971.

## HANSEN, John T
Pillsbury Winthrop Shaw Pittman LLP, San Francisco 415 983 1380
john.hansen@pillsburylaw.com
*Recommended in Environment*
**Practice Areas:** Mr Hansen has broad environmental law experience, having practiced in the area since 1976. He handles air quality; defense of enforcement actions under all federal and state environmental laws; federal and state administrative law, including negotiations with regulatory agencies and handling of administrative hearings; judicial challenges to federal and state administrative actions and orders; environmental compliance and audit programs for corporate clients; and environmental aspects of corporate, commercial, real estate and financing transactions.
**Personal:** JD, University of California at Berkeley, Boalt Hall School of Law, 1966; BS, University of California at Berkeley, 1963 (Phi Beta Kappa).

## HANSEN, Tom
Hansen Jacobson Teller Hoberman Newman, Warren, Sloane & Richman, LLP, Beverly Hills 310 271 8777
*Recommended in Media & Entertainment*

## HARRIS, Alan
Farella Braun & Martel LLP, San Francisco 415 954 4400
*Recommended in Construction*

## HARRIS, Marc
Beck, De Corso, Daly, Kreindler & Harris, Los Angeles 213 688 1198
*Recommended in Litigation*

## HART, Gordon
Paul, Hastings, Janofsky & Walker LLP, San Francisco
415 856 6000
*Recommended in Environment*

## HARTIGAN, John F
Morgan, Lewis & Bockius LLP, Los Angeles 213 612 2630
jhartigan@morganlewis.com
*Recommended in Corporate/M&A*
**Practice Areas:** John F Hartigan is a Partner in the Business Transactions and Securities Practice. He advises companies, financial institutions and boards of directors on securities law matters, mergers and acquisitions, corporate governance, broker-dealer matters, Securities and Exchange Commission enforcement and corporate finance. He is also the former Assistant Director of the Securities and Exchange Commission's Division of Enforcement.
**Prof. Memberships:** Vice-Chair, State

Bar of California, Executive Committee of the Business Law Section; former Chair, State Bar of California, Education Committee of the Business Section; Member, Los Angeles County Bar Association, Business and Corporations Section Executive Committee; Chair, Los Angeles County Bar Association, Broker-Dealer Committee; General Counsel of BISA; Member, Board of Georgetown University Law Center.

## HASLAM, Robert
Heller Ehrman LLP, Menlo Park 650 324 7073
robert.haslam@hellerehrman.com
*Recommended in Intellectual Property*
**Practice Areas:** Intellectual property litigation, international arbitration and ADR.
**Career:** Mr Haslam's practice has emphasized a trial practice involving patent and trade secret litigation and other related high technology disputes. He has represented clients in patent and trade secret litigation involving a range of arts and practices, including semiconductor products and processes, cryptography, medical devices and other life science products, electronic circuits, microprocessors and software products. He has tried cases in both federal and state court.
**Personal:** Hastings College of the Law (JD, 1976).

## HAVEL, Richard W
Sidley Austin LLP, Los Angeles 213 896 6017
rhavel@sidley.com
*Recommended in Bankruptcy*
**Practice Areas:** Senior Member of the National Bankruptcy Group located in Los Angeles. He has represented parties in informal workouts and in Chapter 11 proceedings, and has served as counsel to creditors' committees, Chapter 11 trustees, debtors and other parties in interest.
**Prof. Memberships:** Member of the Board of Trustees for the UCLA/Jonsson Cancer Center; the Financial Lawyers Conference, where he served as an officer and Director; the Board of Trustees for the UCLA Law School Alumni Association; the Board of Directors for the Industrial Development Authority for the City of Los Angeles, where he served as Chairman; the Commercial Law and Bankruptcy Section of the Los Angeles County Bar, serving on its Executive Committee; and is a Fellow of the American College of Bankruptcy.
**Publications:** Articles Editor, UCLA Law Review; frequent lecturer on bankruptcy and environmental law at industry and legal programs including ALI-ABA and the Financial Lawyer Conference.
**Personal:** Adjunct Professor at Loyola School of Law. University of California at Los Angeles (UCLA) School of Law, JD, 1971, Order of the Coif; University of

Notre Dame, BA, 1968. Admission: California, 1972; Utah 2006.

## HAYES, David L
Fenwick & West LLP, Mountain View 415 875 2411
dhayes@fenwick.com
*Recommended in Intellectual Property, IT Outsourcing*
**Practice Areas:** Chair of firm's Intellectual Property Group. Focuses on intellectual property counseling, litigation and audits, and technology licensing, distribution and transfer. Counsels a wide range of high technology companies on establishing and maintaining procedures to protect the company's intellectual property through copyrights, patents, trade secrets, mask works and trademarks, and on avoiding infringing the rights of others. Represents numerous clients on high profile, complex technology transactions, including patent license transactions and acquisition strategies for both component technologies and turnkey systems. Nationally recognized expert on copyright issues related to the internet and digital media. He has served as counsel in a number of precedent setting software copyright infringement cases, including Lotus Development Corp v. Borland International, Apple Computer v. Microsoft Corp and A & M Records v. Napster, Inc.
**Prof. Memberships:** Serves on intellectual property advisory committee of Practising Law Institute, Advisory Board of The Berkeley Center for Law & Technology, program committee for USC Intellectual Property Law Institute, as well as Editorial Boards of The Computer and Internet Lawyer, Cyberspace Lawyer, The Intellectual Property Strategist, The Journal of Internet Law, Intellectual Property Counselor and Mealey's Litigation Reports on Intellectual Property.
**Career:** Has testified before Congress and federal agencies concerning intellectual property issues. Law clerk to Hon John Minor Wisdom, US Court of Appeals for the Fifth Circuit.
**Personal:** Harvard Law School, JD, cum laude, Editor of the Harvard Law Review, 1984; Stanford University, MSEE, in Electrical Engineering, 1980; Rice University, BS, in Electrical Engineering, summa cum laude, 1978.

## HEIL, Joseph B
Dechert LLP, San Francisco 415 262 4510
joseph.heil@dechert.com
*Recommended in Real Estate*
**Practice Areas:** Mr Heil focuses on mortgage finance and capital markets and helped develop most of the criteria used in rating CMBS transactions.
**Prof. Memberships:** Member, Commercial Mortgage Securities Association, California Mortgage Bankers Association, Mortgage Bankers Association of Ameri-

ca, American Bar Association.
**Publications:** Frequent author and speaker on issues affecting the commercial mortgage finance and securitization industries.
**Personal:** University of Notre Dame, BA, honors, 1983; University of California, Berkeley, MA, 1985; University of California, Los Angeles School of Law, JD, 1988.

## HEINKE, Rex S
Akin Gump Strauss Hauer & Feld LLP, Los Angeles 310 229 1030
rheinke@akingump.com
*Recommended in Media & Entertainment*
**Practice Areas:** Chair, national Appellate and Litigation Strategy Practice and Head of Los Angeles Litigation Practice. Has handled hundreds of appeals, writs, and substantive motions in state and federal courts throughout the country involving, among other things, antitrust, attorneys' fees, bankruptcy, class actions, complex business disputes, constitutional law, contracts, copyrights, defamation, domestic and international arbitrations, environmental law, false advertising, federal preemption, federal securities, personal jurisdiction, reporters' privilege, sovereign immunity, statutory interpretation, tax, trademarks, unfair competition, wage and hour, and wrongful termination.
**Prof. Memberships:** Member, California Judicial Council (2004 to date); former President, Los Angeles County Bar Association (2000-01).

## HEISSE II, John R
Thelen Reid & Priest LLP, San Francisco 415 369 7225
jrheisse@thelenreid.com
*Recommended in Construction*
**Practice Areas:** Mr Heisse's practice has focused on serving the construction industry, representing builders, owners, developers and engineers in every phase of public and private construction from contract formation through dispute resolution. He is Chair of his firm's Construction Practice and a Managing Partner of Masons Thelen Reid LLP, a strategic partnership with Pinsent Masons of the United Kingdom that serves clients with international infrastructure and building projects from inception through financing, contract negotiation, construction and dispute resolution.
**Prof. Memberships:** Chair, American Bar Association Forum on the Construction Industry (Chair 2003-04, Publications Chair, 2001-02; Governing Committee, 1998-2001; Chair, Division 4: Construction Management, Design/Build and Related Concepts, 1995-97); Public Contract Law Section (Chair, Construction Claims Committee, 1998-99, Vice-Chair, 1995-97); arbitrator, National Panel of Construction Arbitrators, American Arbitration Association;

Member, Legal Advisory Committee, Associated General Contractors of California.

**Career:** Partner of Thelen Reid and Priest LLP. Admitted to practice in California, Maryland, and the District of Columbia. Registered foreign lawyer with the Law Society of England and Wales. Served as a Board Member of the Legal Community Against Violence since 1994 and served as Chair from 1994-97.

**Publications:** Editor, 'The Design/Build Deskbook' (ABA Forum on the Construction Industry, 2000, 3d ed 2004); Editor, 'The Design/Build Process' (ABA Forum on the Construction Industry, 1997); co-author: 'AGCC Handbook of California Construction Law' (Associated General Contractors of California (1991) and 'California Construction Law' (Federal Publications [rev ed 1995]); Pacific States Editor, 'State and Local Construction Contracting Source Book' (ABA Public Contracts Law Section 2002).

**Personal:** Received his JD from the University of California, Hastings College of the Law. Honors include Order of the Coif and Senior Editor, Hastings Constitutional Law Quarterly. Attended Catholic University of America where he received Bachelor of Civil Engineering and was a member of Tau Beta Pi.

---

**HELLOW, John**
Hooper Lundy & Bookman Inc,
Los Angeles 310 551 8111
*Recommended in Healthcare*

---

**HEMMINGER, Pamela L**
Gibson, Dunn & Crutcher LLP,
Los Angeles 213 229 7274
phemminger@gibsondunn.com
*Recommended in Employment*

**Practice Areas:** Counseling and litigation - individual and class cases - involving all aspects of labor/employment law. Expertise in complex, high exposure, high profile matters. Sub-specialties include OSHA, ERISA, wage/hour, privacy, disability/leaves of absence.

**Prof. Memberships:** Fellow, College of Labor and Employment Lawyers. American Arbitration Association arbitrator (Employment Panel - Southern California). Labor and Employment Sections: Los Angeles County Bar Association (past Chair); ABA (past management Co-Chair, Ethics Committee; current management Co-Chair, CLE National Programs subcommittee).

**Publications:** Frequent commentator, including television and radio. Contributing author, 'Employment Discrimination Law', 'California Practice Guide: Employment Litigation'.

**Personal:** JD, Pepperdine University School of Law, magna cum laude, 1976.

---

**HEMMINGER, Steven D**
White & Case LLP, Palo Alto
650 213 0300
SHemminger@whitecase.com

*Recommended in Intellectual Property*

**Practice Areas:** Executive Partner in charge of firm's Palo Alto, California office. Practice focus includes litigating over 35 major intellectual property disputes involving high technology in all forums, nationally and internationally. Substantial expertise in patent, trademark, trade secret litigation in electronics, semiconductor, computer software and hardware fields. Has managed patent and trademark portfolios regarding wireless telephony and LANs, computers, mechanical devices, medical devices in US and foreign patent offices.

**Prof. Memberships:** State Bar of California, 1983; registered to practice before the USPTO.

**Personal:** Southwestern University School of Law (JD, magna cum laude, 1983); Rensselaer Polytechnic Institute (BS, Mechanical Engineering, 1974).

---

**HENDRICKS, Sharon J**
Heller Ehrman LLP, Menlo Park
650 233 8356
sharon.hendricks@hellerehrman.com
*Recommended in Employment*

**Practice Areas:** Compensation and benefits, venture law group/emerging companies, information technology, tax.

**Prof. Memberships:** State Bar of California; Member, Subcommittee on Employee Benefits, Executive Compensation and Section 16, American Bar Association Section of Business Law Federal Regulation of Securities Committee.

**Career:** Ms Hendricks represents emerging growth and public technology companies on executive compensation, employment and benefits matters, equity compensation plans, executive compensation, employment and severance arrangements, insider trading and restricted securities matters, IPOs, mergers and acquisitions and venture financings. Ms Hendricks also represents individual executives in negotiating their employment arrangements.

**Personal:** University of Chicago Law School (JD, cum laude, 1991).

---

**HENNIGAN, Brian**
Irell & Manella LLP, Los Angeles
310 277 1010
*Recommended in Litigation*

---

**HENNIGAN, J Michael**
Hennigan, Bennett & Dorman LLP,
Los Angeles 213 694 1200
*Recommended in Litigation*

---

**HERMLE, Lynne**
Orrick, Herrington & Sutcliffe LLP,
Menlo Park 650 614 7422
lchermle@orrick.com
*Recommended in Employment*

**Practice Areas:** Named one of 50 top female litigators by leading legal publication. Substantial trial experience in employment matters with uniformly good results, including several jury trials

in state and federal court. Special expertise in the area of complex class actions, including wage and hour issues for large employers and technology companies. Counsels and trains employers on all aspects of employment practices. Serves as Early Neutral Evaluator federal court for Northern District of California.

**Publications:** Co-Editor-in-Chief, 'Start-Up & Emerging Companies Strategist Newsletter'; contributor to others.

**Personal:** JD, UC Hastings College of the Law; BA, magna cum laude, UC Santa Barbara.

---

**HERNANDEZ, Gary A**
Sonnenschein Nath & Rosenthal LLP,
San Francisco 415 882 2466
ghernandez@sonnenschein.com
*Recommended in Insurance*

**Practice Areas:** Practices insurance regulatory and administrative law representing insurers and holding companies. Also handles state regulatory compliance. Experienced in insurance insolvency proceedings and insurance and reinsurance matters.

**Prof. Memberships:** Member, International Association of Insurance Receivers, Insurance Regulatory Examiners Society; board member, Latino Community Foundation and Iteris, Inc.; Trustee, University of California, Merced Foundation; appointed board member, California Coastal Conservancy by the Speaker of the California State Assembly; lecturer to private groups and organizations, including American Conference Institute, Defense Research Institute, American Council of Life Insurers and Pacific Claims Executives Association.

**Personal:** University of California-Davis, JD; University of California-Berkeley, BA.

---

**HERNANDEZ, Jennifer L**
Holland & Knight LLP, San Francisco
415 743 6900
jennifer.hernandez@hklaw.com
*Recommended in Environment*

**Practice Areas:** Partner in Government Section, Co-Chair of National Environmental Team. Hernandez represents clients in private, public, and non-profit sectors in land use and environmental permitting, compliance, litigation and public advocacy work. She has taught land use and environmental law for the University of California and Stanford Law School, frequently lectures at professional associations and seminars, and has written two books and more than 30 articles on environmental and land use law, served as a Presidential appointee to the Presidio National Park Trust, and co-founded and served as an officer on the boards of numerous private companies and non-profit organizations.

---

**HERR, Robert**
Pillsbury Winthrop Shaw Pittman LLP,
San Francisco 415 983 1038
robert.herr@pillsburylaw.com

*Recommended in Real Estate*

**Practice Areas:** Mr Herr represents developers, owners, managers and lenders in commercial and residential real estate development, acquisition, operation, leasing, sale and loan transactions. His client list includes Shorenstein Company LLC, Starwood Hotels and Resorts Worldwide, Inc., Stein Kingsley Stein and the San Francisco Giants. Sample transactions handled include the disposition of the two million square foot 555 California office block in San Francisco, California and the related primary and secondary financings; the formation of real estate investment partnerships raising $450 million in capital; and over $6 billion of class A office building acquisition or disposition transactions between 1994 and 2005. As attorney for the San Francisco Giants, Mr Herr handled the financing and other aspects of the acquisition of the team in 1992 and, in 1996-2000, the development of the team's $350 million ballpark located at China Basin in San Francisco.

**Personal:** JD, University of California at Berkeley, Boalt Hall School of Law (Order of the Coif), 1967; AB, University of California at Berkeley (great distinction), 1964; Member, Board of Directors, San Francisco Chamber of Commerce (2006).

---

**HIGGINS, Daniel**
Paul, Hastings, Janofsky & Walker LLP,
San Francisco 415 856 6000
*Recommended in Healthcare*

---

**HILSON, John F**
Paul, Hastings, Janofsky & Walker LLP,
Los Angeles 213 683 6300
johnhilson@paulhastings.com
*Recommended in Banking & Finance*

**Practice Areas:** Complex commercial and corporate finance transactions, including asset-based structured financings, tranche A and tranche B transactions, cash flow and enterprise value financings, and mezzanine debt and equity transactions. His practice also includes specialized secured transactions, Islamic compliant financings, debtor-in-possession financings, acquisition financings, usury, and suretyship law.

**Prof. Memberships:** Board of Regents and Fellow of the American College of Commercial Finance Attorneys.

**Publications:** Author of 'Asset-Based Lending - A Practical Guide to Secured Financing', Practising Law Institute (5th ed 2005).

**Personal:** University of Colorado Law School (JD, Order of the Coif, 1976); Boston University (BA, magna cum laude, 1973).

---

**HINKLEY, Gerry**
Davis Wright Tremaine LLP,
San Francisco 415 276 6500
*Recommended in Healthcare*

## HIRSCH, Barry
Hirsch Wallerstein Hayum Matlof & Fishman,
Los Angeles 310 703 1711
*Recommended in Media &
Entertainment*

## HIRSCH, Reece
Sonnenschein Nath & Rosenthal LLP,
San Francisco 415 882 5040
rhirsch@sonnenschein.com
*Recommended in Healthcare*

**Practice Areas:** Healthcare regulatory
and transactional expert who counsels
and represents health plans, insurers, hospitals, physician organizations, healthcare
IT companies, pharmaceutical and
biotech companies and other healthcare
organizations with Medicare, Medicaid,
fraud and abuse, self-referral, contracting
and privacy issues, including HIPAA and
Gramm-Leach-Bliley Act compliance.
Develops and helps implement policies
and procedures for privacy and security,
fraud and abuse and corporate compliance.
**Prof. Memberships:** California State Bar
Association; ABA's Health Law Section;
California Society for Healthcare Attorneys; American Health Lawyers Association; Healthcare Financial Management
Association.
**Personal:** University of Southern California, JD, Southern California Law
Review; Northwestern University, BS.

## HISERT, George A
Bingham McCutchen LLP, San Francisco
415 393 2577
george.hisert@bingham.com
*Recommended in Banking & Finance*

**Practice Areas:** Serves as Co-Chair of
the firm's Bank, Commercial and Structured Finance Practice Group. Has more
than 32 years of experience representing
major banking and financial institutions
in commercial loan and credit transactions, letters of credit and regulatory matters. Practice also includes substantial
representation of non-financial institutions and borrowers in a broad variety of
credit transactions. Has significant experience in mergers and acquisitions, general corporate matters and international
business transactions.
**Personal:** The University of Chicago
Law School, JD, 1970; Brown University,
ScB and ScM, summa cum laude, 1966.

## HOBEL, Lawrence
Heller Ehrman LLP, San Francisco
415 772 6348
lawrence.hobel@hellerehrman.com
*Recommended in Insurance*

**Practice Areas:** Insurance recovery;
environmental litigation and counseling;
international arbitration and ADR.
**Prof. Memberships:** American Bar
Association; State Bar of California; Bar
Association of San Francisco; Washington, DC Bar.
**Career:** Mr Hobel has extensive experience in litigation and counsel respecting

insurance coverage matters on behalf of
insureds and environmental matters. He
represents policyholders on first-party
and third-party losses. Mr Hobel is
involved in all facets of activity necessary
to realize insurance recoveries.
**Personal:** University of California,
Berkeley (AB, 1973); Phi Beta Kappa;
University of California, Berkeley, Boalt
Hall School of Law (JD, 1976).

## HOCKETT, Christopher
Bingham McCutchen LLP, San Francisco
415 393 2612
chris.hockett@bingham.com
*Recommended in Antitrust*

**Practice Areas:** Serves as Chair of the
firm's Litigation Area and a member of
the firm's management and firm committees. Represents clients in a wide
range of complex commercial matters,
including patent litigation, antitrust and
unfair competition claims, and false
advertising and consumer class actions.
Counsels and represents clients in connection with government investigations
and the antitrust aspects of mergers and
acquisitions.
**Personal:** University of Virginia School
of Law, JD, 1985; College of William &
Mary, BA, 1981.

## HOLDEN JR, Frederick D
Orrick, Herrington & Sutcliffe LLP,
San Francisco 415 773 5985
fholden@orrick.com
*Recommended in Bankruptcy*

**Practice Areas:** Focuses on litigation
and transactions involving insolvent
businesses, with an emphasis on multinational issues. Represents creditors,
debtors, committees, and governmental
interests in chapter 11 cases, corporate
reorganizations, and asset acquisitions.
Served as general counsel to court-
appointed trustees and receivers in some
of the largest international business insolvencies. Named a Fellow of American
College of Bankruptcy.
**Publications:** Frequent author and
speaker for the National Conference of
Bankruptcy Judges, American Bar Association, California Receivers' Forum, California State Bar, and numerous other
organizations. Lectures at UC Berkeley
Graduate Business School.
**Personal:** JD, UC Davis, 1974; BA, UC
Santa Barbara, 1971.

## HOLLIDAY, Thomas E
Gibson, Dunn & Crutcher LLP,
Los Angeles 213 229 7370
tholliday@gibsondunn.com
*Recommended in Litigation*

**Practice Areas:** Co-Chair, Business
Crimes and Investigations Practice.
Focuses on white-collar criminal defense
work and commercial fraud litigation.
Defends individuals and corporate entities against charges of conspiracy to
defraud the US, fraud on federally
insured institutions, false statements,

bribery, money laundering, RICO and
tax fraud.
**Prof. Memberships:** Fellow, American
College of Trial Lawyers. Member,
National Association of Criminal Defense
Lawyers. Vice-Chair, White Collar Crime
Committee, Western Section, ABA.
**Publications:** Editor, 'Antitrust Laws and
Regulations'. Co-author, 'The Effect of
Sentencing Guidelines on Organizational
Defendants'.
**Personal:** JD, University of Southern
California, 1974, Order of the Coif, Exec-
utive Editor, Law Review.

## HOLSCHER, Mark
O'Melveny & Myers LLP, Los Angeles
213 430 6000
mholscher@omm.com
*Recommended in Litigation*

**Practice Areas:** Mark Holscher's practice focuses on white-collar criminal
defense and criminal and civil trials.
Mark is known for the representation of
companies and individuals in federal and
state criminal and regulatory investigations. He has handled a number of state
and federal litigation matters, ranging
from breach of contract disputes, consumer class action defense, alleged bad
faith and insurance fraud cases, as well as
numerous other types of civil actions. In
addition, Mark has conducted a number
of internal investigations for publicly
traded corporations and has developed
corporate compliance programs. USA
Today called Mark a 'prominent legal
lion' in a 2005 news article. Additionally,
Mark was included in the 'International
Who's Who of Business Crime Lawyers
2003'. In 2002, the American Lawyer
named Mark one of the top 45 lawyers in
the country under 45. Mark was selected
for the 2001 California Law Business Top
20 Under 40 rankings, and he was also
named one of California Lawyer's
Lawyers of the Year 2000.

## HOOPER, Patric
Hooper Lundy & Bookman Inc,
Los Angeles 310 551 8111
*Recommended in Healthcare*

## HORTON, Michel Yves
Morgan, Lewis & Bockius LLP,
Los Angeles 213 612 7300
mhorton@morganlewis.com
*Recommended in Insurance*

**Practice Areas:** Michel Y Horton is a
Partner in the Litigation Practice, resident
in the Los Angeles office. He concentrates
his practice on insurance recovery counseling and litigation. Mr Horton has represented numerous Fortune 500 companies in a variety of complex litigation
matters, including coverage disputes
involving toxic torts, environmental
property damage and personal injury,
medical devices, and other financial losses. Mr Horton has also assisted clients in
drafting specialty market insurance policies, particularly in connection with

future environmental and toxic tort
exposures, through domestic insurers
and offshore captives.

## HOWARD, Robert
Latham & Watkins LLP, San Diego
619 236 1234
*Recommended in Environment*

## HOWARD JR, George S
Pillsbury Winthrop Shaw Pittman LLP,
San Diego 619 544 3286
george.howard@pillsburylaw.com
*Recommended in Employment*

**Practice Areas:** Mr Howard has practiced labor and employment law in San
Diego since 1977. He has successfully
tried multi-week bench and jury trials, as
well as numerous shorter trials, arbitrations and administrative proceedings. He
has extensive experience in union/man-
agement relations, as well as all types of
employment litigation.
**Prof. Memberships:** Chair, the Employers Group Legal Committee, a select
group of 16 California lawyers who
appear as amicus curiae in the appeals of
important employment cases in CA. Listed in 'Best Lawyers In America' since
1993.
**Personal:** JD, University of Virginia
(1977); BA, University of Virginia (with
highest distinction, 1974).

## HUGHES, Frank
Miller, Morton, Caillat & Nevis, San Jose
408 292 1765
*Recommended in Construction*

## HUMPHREYS, Ivan H
Wilson Sonsini Goodrich & Rosati,
Palo Alto 650 493 9300
ihumphreys@wsgr.com
*Recommended in Tax*

**Practice Areas:** Specializes in domes-
tic/international tax and related transactions for technology companies and
financial institutions. Represents clients
in transactional matters including
domestic and cross-border mergers and
acquisitions, dispositions, spin-offs,
restructurings, domestic and international debt and equity offerings, taxation of
technology transfers, joint ventures,
establishment of domestic and offshore
investment funds, and structuring offshore sales and manufacturing operations.
**Prof. Memberships:** Admitted to practice in California; Member, ABA (Taxation Section).
**Career:** Joined WSGR as Partner, 1989.
**Personal:** JD (magna cum laude), Harvard University, 1982; BA (with great distinction), University of California (Berkeley), 1979. Phi Beta Kappa. Editor, Harvard Law Review, 1981-82.

## HUNT, James L
Bingham McCutchen LLP, San Francisco
415 393 2212
james.hunt@bingham.com
*Recommended in Antitrust*

**Practice Areas:** Has more than 37 years of experience handling a broad variety of complex litigation matters, including securities, professional negligence, antitrust, contracts, and commercial and business torts. Has handled cases in all of the federal courts in California and other states, and in the state courts of California. Has also been involved in arbitration, mediation and other forms of alternative dispute resolution, both as an attorney, and as an arbitrator/mediator. Formerly served as Chair of the firm's Litigation Area.
**Personal:** Northwestern University School of Law, JD, 1967; DePauw University, BA, magna cum laude, 1964.

## HYMAN, Milt
Irell & Manella LLP, Los Angeles
310 277 1010
*Recommended in Tax*

## IPPOLITO, Peter J
McKenna Long & Aldridge LLP,
San Diego 619 595 5400
pippolito@mckennalong.com
*Recommended in Construction*
**Practice Areas:** International practice in areas of construction law, including architect and engineer malpractice, federal and state construction litigation, federal government and private construction claims and disputes and hearings before state and federal courts, federal, state and local Boards of Contract Appeals, administrative law judges, arbitration panels and mediators. Extensive experience on projects involving public, private, commercial, heavy, highway, industrial, institutional and residential construction, representing owners, developers, public agencies, general contractors, subcontractors and specialty contractors, architects, engineers, designers, suppliers, manufacturers, sureties and insurers.
**Prof. Memberships:** Member of the Judicial Arbitration Panel for the San Diego Superior Court; serves as a State of California Arbitrator for disputes involving state contracts; appointed to the American Arbitration Association's Nationwide Complex Construction Arbitration and Mediation Panels; frequent guest speaker for construction industry groups.
**Publications:** Mr Ippolito serves on the Board of Directors of the Construction Business Review. He has published numerous articles in various construction periodicals and for seminars. Mr Ippolito was selected as one of the top 50 lawyers for San Diego's Magazine Best Lawyers issue April 2006.
**Personal:** Virginia Military Institute, BA, 1963; University of Notre Dame, LLB, 1966; George Washington University, LLM in Taxation, 1975; Officer, US Army.

## IREDALE, Nancy L
Paul, Hastings, Janofsky & Walker LLP,
Los Angeles 213 683 6232
nancyiredale@paulhastings.com
*Recommended in Tax*
**Practice Areas:** Tax controversy; tried/settled international, federal and state civil and criminal tax cases; L.A. Business Journal: 'One of the most powerful women in Los Angeles law'; 'Southern California Super Lawyers/2006, Tax'.
**Prof. Memberships:** First woman elected President, Jonathan Club; Planning Committee, USC Tax Institute; Board, California Taxpayers' Association; Fellow, American College of Tax Counsel.
**Career:** First woman elected Partner, Paul Hastings; legislative assistant to Bill Brock, R-Tenn, on Senate Finance (tax writing) Committee.
**Publications:** 'Avoiding the Pitfalls in U.S. Transfer Pricing', IIR LTD's Forum, London; 'Dealing with IRS Corporate Tax Audits', The Directors' Roundtable; 'International Transfer Pricing: What Every Businessperson Should Know', Asian American Econ Dev Enterprises, Tokyo; 'Recent Developments in Litigation and Administrative Disputes Involving the Franchise Tax Board', UCLA Annual Tax Controversy Institute; 'Section 482 and Section 6662 Regulations: Administration and Litigation', USC Tax Institute; 'The Evolution of a Tax Court Case: From Audit to Trial', Tax Executives Institute; 'Cross-Border Transfer Pricing Issues for U.S. and Canadian Taxpayers', Canada-California Chamber of Commerce.
**Personal:** Graduated first in class from School of Foreign Service, Georgetown University; Phi Beta Kappa; Law Degree from Yale Law School; Member, Yale Legislative Services.

## IVENER, Mark
Ivener & Fullmer LLP, Los Angeles
310 477 3000
*Recommended in Immigration*

## JACKOWAY, James
Jackoway Tyerman Wertheimer Austen Mandelbaum & Morris,
A Professional Corporation, Los Angeles
310 553 0305
*Recommended in Media & Entertainment*

## JACOBS, Michael A
Morrison & Foerster LLP, San Francisco
415 268 7455
mjacobs@mofo.com
*Recommended in Intellectual Property*
**Practice Areas:** Practice concentrates on high technology and intellectual property litigation matters. Has litigated and arbitrated high profile patent, copyright, contract, and trade secret disputes in the information technology and life sciences field. His work on several landmark cases has helped shape emerging technology law.
**Career:** Admitted to practice in California. Co-founder and Co-Chair, Intellectual Property Group, 1990-2002.

Firmwide Managing Partner for Operations, 1995-97.
**Publications:** Co-author, with Prof Donald Chisum, 'World Intellectual Property Guidebook', United States (1992, Matthew Bender & Company, New York).
**Personal:** BA History, Stanford University, 1977, Phi Beta Kappa with honors; United States Foreign Service, assignments in Kingston, Jamaica, and Washington, DC; JD, Yale Law School, 1983.

## JACOBSON, Craig
Hansen Jacobson Teller Hoberman Newman, Warren, Sloane & Richman, LLP, Beverly Hills 310 271 8777
*Recommended in Media & Entertainment*

## JAHN, Paul E
Morrison & Foerster LLP, San Francisco
415 268 6387
pjahn@mofo.com
*Recommended in IT Outsourcing*
**Practice Areas:** Specializes in transactions involving development, licensing, acquisition, and sale of intellectual property and technology. Transactions typically involve strategic alliances and joint ventures; commercialization and distribution arrangements; BPO and IT sourcing, and resolution of related disputes. Frequently represents clients in adversarial patent license negotiations and portfolio acquisition. Clients generally operate in high technology, life sciences, and financial services industries.
**Career:** Former Co-Chair of firm's Technology Transactions Group. Formerly resident in firm's Tokyo and Brussels offices. Admitted to practice in California.
**Personal:** BA, University of California, Berkeley, 1986; JD, Hastings College of the Law, 1993; clerk to Hon Claudia Wilken, Northern District of California, 1995-96.

## JEFFREY, Sheri
Kaye Scholer LLP, Los Angeles
310 788 1270
sjeffrey@kayescholer.com
*Recommended in Media & Entertainment*
**Practice Areas:** Partner, corporate and finance. Practice covers a wide range of entertainment matters. She represents various clients in all types of entertainment industry transactions, including for development, acquisitions, finance and production of motion pictures, television series and new technologies projects (both live action and animation).
**Prof. Memberships:** Member, State Bar of California.
**Career:** LLM, New York University, 1986. JD, Loyola Law School, 1985. BS (cum laude), Loyola Marymount University, 1982.

## JENETT, Bruce
Heller Ehrman LLP, Menlo Park
650 324 7122
bruce.jenett@hellerehrman.com
*Recommended in Corporate/M&A*
**Practice Areas:** Life sciences, venture law group/emerging companies, mergers and acquisitions, international.
**Career:** Mr Jenett's practice is focused on the representation of domestic and international high technology business clients, primarily in the life sciences industry. He is experienced in equity and debt financing, licensing and distribution, strategic alliances, joint ventures, and mergers and acquisitions, as well as general counseling issues, representing both start-ups and large multinational corporations. Mr Jenett is a frequent speaker on corporate and finance issues to both business and attorney audiences.
**Personal:** Princeton University (BA, Sociology, 1969); Georgetown University Law Center (JD, 1976).

## JOHNSON, Edward D
Mayer, Brown, Rowe & Maw, Palo Alto
650 331 2057
wjohnson@mayerbrownrowe.com
*Recommended in Litigation*
**Practice Areas:** Represents clients - often technology, telecommunications and media companies - in a wide variety of proceedings, including antitrust, securities and intellectual property disputes. Successfully handled jury and bench trials and argued appeals ranging from complex commercial matters to libel and criminal cases. Served as antitrust counsel for clients, providing advice in obtaining merger clearance from federal, state and European regulators for major transactions in the mass media, oil, pharmaceutical and retail industries. Acted as lead counsel for a license program holding essential patents for the manufacture of CDs and DVDs.
**Career:** Mayer, Brown, Rowe & Maw LLP, Palo Alto, 2005 to date. Sullivan & Cromwell LLP, Palo Alto, 2000-05. Deputy Solicitor General, Office of the New York State Attorney General Eliot Spitzer, 1999-2000. Simpson Thacher & Bartlett, New York, 1987-99. Law clerk to the Honorable John D Butzner, Jr, United States Court of Appeals for the Fourth Circuit, Richmond, Virginia, 1986-87.
**Personal:** Yale Law School, JD, 1986; Editor, Yale Law & Policy Review. University of Virginia, BA, with highest distinction, 1983; Robert K Gooch Scholar; Phi Beta Kappa.

## JOHNSON JR, Daniel
Morgan, Lewis & Bockius LLP,
San Francisco 415 442 1392
djjohnson@morganlewis.com
*Recommended in Intellectual Property*
**Practice Areas:** Daniel Johnson is a Partner in the Litigation Practice. He specializes in complex commercial litigation

primarily related to technology disputes. He has tried cases in numerous Federal and State courts throughout the US and has handled several matters before the International Trade Commission. He has also handled numerous arbitrations and mediations before the AAA and JAMS. Among the cases Mr Johnson has tried recently include case seeking damages for theft of trade secrets that settled for $400 million after five weeks of trial. In another jury trial he successfully invalidated two patents and recovered damages for theft of trade secrets.

**Prof. Memberships:** Member, American Bar Association; Member, National Bar Association; Member, Inns of Court, Intellectual Property section; Hall of Fame Inductee, Charles Houston Bar Association.

## JOHNSTON, Ronald L
Arnold & Porter LLP, Los Angeles
213 243 4256
Ronald.Johnston@aporter.com
*Recommended in Intellectual Property, Litigation*

**Practice Areas:** Mr Johnston specializes in complex business litigation. He has been a leader in the Information Technology and Intellectual Property Bars for 25 years. Mr Johnston's experience includes jury and non jury trials, appeals, arbitrations, and class actions, as well as strategic counselling for technology and entertainment businesses. He has represented clients in a number of leading cases at the trial and appellate levels. His practice includes copyright, patent, trade secret, trademark, antitrust and unfair competition law.

**Prof. Memberships:** Co-founder and Editor-in-Chief of The Computer & Internet Lawyer (1984 to date, Aspen Publications); founder and Chairperson, University of Southern California Computer & Internet Law Institute (1979-2003); Board of Editors, The Journal of Proprietary Rights; Board of Editors, The Cyberspace Lawyer; Board of Directors, Computer Law Association (1986-2002); Technology and Intellectual Property Panels, American Arbitration Association; Arbitrator, International Chamber of Commerce.

**Career:** Mr Johnston was a Partner in Blanc Williams Johnston & Kronstadt from 1981 through 2000, when the attorneys of that firm joined Arnold & Porter. Prior to 1981, Mr Johnston was a Partner in Irell & Manella.

**Publications:** Frequent published author and speaker on issues of complex litigation and intellectual property and technology law.

**Personal:** Mr Johnston graduated Order of the Coif from the University of Southern California School of Law in 1973, where he served as a note and Article Editor for the University of Southern California Law Review.

## JONES, Robert
Cooley Godward LLP, Palo Alto
650 843 5000
*Recommended in Corporate/M&A*

## JUSTICE, Gary L
Gibson, Dunn & Crutcher LLP,
Los Angeles 213 229 7446
gjustice@gibsondunn.com
*Recommended in Insurance*

**Practice Areas:** Co-Chair of firm's Insurance Practice Group. Litigation and jury trial of all insurance issues, including lack of 'bad faith', primarily for carriers in property and casualty, liability insurance, and health insurance fields. Expertise includes trigger of coverage, number of occurrences, 'lost' policies, ERISA preemption, apportionment among carriers, admissibility of parol evidence, rescission based on material misrepresentation, 'advice of counsel' defense in 'bad faith' litigation, and 'advertising injury' coverages. Representative clients include Travelers, Aetna U.S. Healthcare, Empire Blue Cross Blue Shield and Hartford Steam Boiler.

**Personal:** JD, Duke University, 1979, Order of the Coif, Editorial Board Member Law Review.

## KADUE, David
Seyfarth Shaw LLP, Los Angeles
310 277 7200
*Recommended in Employment*

## KADZIELSKI, Mark A
Fulbright & Jaworski L.L.P., Los Angeles
213 892 9306
mkadzielski@fulbright.com
*Recommended in Healthcare*

**Practice Areas:** Health law.

**Prof. Memberships:** Mr Kadzielski is a Member of the California Bar, the American Health Lawyers Association and the California Society for Healthcare Attorneys.

**Career:** Mark A Kadzielski is the Partner in charge of Fulbright & Jaworski's Los Angeles Health Law Practice. He has been selected numerous times by peers to be included in the Healthcare Law Section of The Best Lawyers in America. Mr Kadzielski is a past Member of the AHLA's Board of Directors and served on the organization's first executive committee. Recently, he was elected to the AHLA's inaugural class of Fellows, whose members are recognized for their extraordinary contributions to health law in the United States. He was selected as a Southern California Super Lawyer in Health Law (2004 and 2005).

**Personal:** AB, magna cum laude, John Carroll University (1968); JD, University of Pennsylvania Law School (1976).

## KAPLAN, Frank
Alschuler Grossman Stein & Kahan LLP,
Santa Monica 310 255 9124
fkaplan@agsk.com
*Recommended in Insurance*

**Practice Areas:** He focuses on class action, securities, insurance coverage, unfair competition, partnership, and professional liability disputes. Represented chip manufacturer Nvidia in Microsoft dispute over Xbox game console; in 2003 argued in the US Supreme Court on behalf of the State of California in litigation over statute requiring insurance companies doing business in the state to disclose information about policies issued during the European holocaust; in 2004, represented California Insurance Commissioner in litigation brought by Anthem to compel approval of merger with WellPoint; represents insurers in major coverage litigation, including environmental coverage cases such as recent Fuller Austin and Lockheed cases.

**Prof. Memberships:** Member, Beverly Hills, Century City, Santa Monica, Los Angeles County and American Bar Associations; State Bar of California; Association of Business Trial Lawyers.

**Career:** A Partner of Alschuler Grossman Stein & Kahan. Has practiced with the firm since 1972. Has served as an arbitrator for the Los Angeles Superior Court and Los Angeles County Bar Association, and as a judge pro tem.

**Personal:** Commissioner, California Law Revision Commission (Chair, 2003-04). Adjunct Professor of securities fraud at University of Southern California.; University of Cincinnati (BA with honors, Phi Beta Kappa, 1968). University of Michigan (JD, 1971).

## KARP, Joseph
White & Case LLP, San Francisco
415 544 1103
jkarp@whitecase.com
*Recommended in Energy*

**Practice Areas:** Energy - regulatory and transactional matters, project development and operations matters for US and international natural gas and electricity concerns. Particular expertise representing end users in retail gas and electricity transactions and generators of electricity in the full range of issues affecting electricity revenues, fuel costs and ongoing operations. Active in administrative litigation, contract negotiation, dispute resolution and regulatory compliance advice and regularly represents, among others, the California Cogeneration Council and the California Wind Energy Association and their members.

**Personal:** JD, cum laude, Harvard Law School, 1989; BA, SUNY Binghamton, 1986 (Foundation Award for Academic Excellence, Phi Beta Kappa).

## KAUFMAN, Christopher
Latham & Watkins LLP, Menlo Park
650 328 4600
*Recommended in Corporate/M&A*

## KEKER, John
Keker & Van Nest LLP, San Francisco
415 391 5400
jkeker@kvn.com
*Recommended in Intellectual Property, Litigation*

**Practice Areas:** John Keker is one of the top trial lawyers in the United States. His trials have included criminal defense, patents, contracts, securities fraud, copyright, and business torts. Cases include: in 2002, winning a jury trial for Genentech in a $300 million patent dispute with Chiron; in 2001, representing Cadence Design Systems, Inc., winning $195 million from Avant! Corporation in restitution for trade secret theft. Other notable cases: chief prosecutor, United States v. Oliver North, 1989, Iran/Contra Independent Counsel's Office, Washington, DC; defense counsel, United States v. Frank Quattrone (SDNY 2003 (hung jury), convicted 2004, on appeal); defense counsel in Ventritex v. Intermedics, listed by the National Law Journal as one of the top 10 defense verdicts of 1992; Plaintiff's counsel in Maglica v. Maglica, listed in the National Law Journal as one of the top 10 plaintiff's verdicts of 1994, and plaintiff's counsel in Xilinx v. Altera (ND Cal), one of the most significant patent trials of 2000.

**Prof. Memberships:** Fellow of the American College of Trial Lawyers, the International Academy of Trial Lawyers, the American Board of Trial Advocates, and the American Bar Foundation.

**Career:** Former law clerk to the Honorable Earl Warren, retired chief justice of the United States (1970-71); staff attorney at the Natural Resources Defense Council, Washington, DC; Assistant Federal Public Defender for the Northern District of California (1971-73); founded Keker & Van Nest in 1978.

**Publications:** Co-author of Effective Direct and Cross Examination, California Continuing Education of the Bar, 1986.

**Personal:** Yale Law School (JD 1970); infantry platoon leader in Vietnam while a lieutenant in the United States Marine Corps (wounded and retired in 1967); Princeton University (BA, 1965).

## KELLER, Don
Orrick, Herrington & Sutcliffe LLP,
Menlo Park 650 614 7609
dkeller@orrick.com
*Recommended in Corporate/M&A*

**Practice Areas:** Focuses on representation of emerging companies, public companies, venture capital firms, and investment banks. Advised clients on more than 60 public offerings, 75 acquisition transactions, and several hundred venture financings. Received many awards, included being named one of the top 100 IPO lawyers during 1998-2003 by IPO Vital Signs, an award based on the number of IPOs completed.

**Career:** Previously a Director and Member of the Executive Committee of the Venture Law Group.

**Personal:** JD, Boston College, 1982; BA, Dartmouth College, 1979.

## KELLER, Kent
Barger & Wolen, Los Angeles
213 680 2800
*Recommended in Insurance*

## KELLY, William
Davis Polk & Wardwell, Menlo Park
650 752 2003
william.kelly@dpw.com
*Recommended in Corporate/M&A*
**Practice Areas:** Focuses on M&A, alliances and capital formation transactions, as well as corporate governance and securities law compliance, largely for technology companies. Represented Oracle in successful unsolicited offer for PeopleSoft and acquisitions of Retek, Siebel and i-Flex. Other prominent M&A transactions: KLA-Tencor (ADE); Affymetrix (Parallele); Silicon Graphics (sale of Alias); Yahoo! (Inktomi); NetIQ (WebTrends); and Francisco Partners and portfolio companies in leveraged acquisitions. Represented Comcast in strategic IP arrangements with Microsoft, TV Guide and TiVo. A founder of Davis Polk's Menlo Park office; formerly general counsel and senior business executive at Silicon Graphics (1994-99) and Partner of Shearman & Sterling (1987-94).

## KENDALL, Richard B
Irell & Manella LLP, Los Angeles
310 277 1010
*Recommended in Media & Entertainment*

## KENNEDY, Mike
O'Melveny & Myers LLP, San Francisco
415 984 8756
mjkennedy@omm.com
*Recommended in Corporate/M&A*
**Practice Areas:** Michael Kennedy concentrates on mergers, acquisitions, divestitures, corporate partnering, joint ventures and corporate governance, with an emphasis in the technology, emerging growth, healthcare, biotechnology and media industries. Mike has extensive experience advising on private equity and leveraged buyout transactions involving a variety of industries (building products, automotive, defense, financial services, media, technology and healthcare). He represents all major investment banks in their merger and acquisitions advisory practices. Mike has significant experience in the debt (bank and high-yield areas) and restructuring areas and is frequently asked by boards to advise on hostile transactions, proxy fights and other governance matters.

## KENT, Ronald D
Sonnenschein Nath & Rosenthal LLP, Los Angeles 213 892 5030
rkent@sonnenschein.com
*Recommended in Insurance*
**Practice Areas:** Insurance Practice Chair; represents insurance companies in coverage and 'bad faith' actions, regulatory matters, underwriting and claims-related class actions, environmental claims, general business disputes. Has appeared in state and federal courts throughout the US, including all California District Courts of Appeal and the Ninth Circuit Court of Appeals. Experienced in alleged discriminatory underwriting practices, retrospective premiums, agents and brokers errors and omissions, surplus lines licensing, and all first and third-party coverage issues.
**Personal:** University of California, Berkeley (Boalt Hall), JD, Order of the Coif, California Law Review; UCLA, BA in English, summa cum laude, Phi Beta Kappa.

## KENYON, Charity
Riegels Campos & Kenyon, Sacramento
916 779 7114
*Recommended in Media & Entertainment*

## KEYES, Judith Droz
Morrison & Foerster LLP, San Francisco
415 268 6638
jkeyes@mofo.com
*Recommended in Employment*
**Practice Areas:** Extensive experience counseling and training clients in all aspects of labor and employment law and representing clients before almost all California and federal labor and employment agencies as well as in negotiations, mediation, arbitration and court. Serves as an evaluator and mediator of employment cases for the US District Court, Northern District, California.
**Prof. Memberships:** Fellow, College of Labor and Employment Lawyers. Named a 'Best Lawyer in America'. Former Chair, Labor and Employment Law Section, Bar Association of San Francisco, 1998-2000; former President, Alameda County Bar Association, 1997.
**Career:** Admitted to practice in California.
**Personal:** BS, Pennsylvania State University, 1966; MA, University of Missouri, 1970; JD, University of California at Berkeley, Boalt Hall School of Law, 1975.

## KILB, Brian D
Gibson, Dunn & Crutcher LLP, Los Angeles 310 551 8871
bkilb@gibsondunn.com
*Recommended in Banking & Finance, Capital Markets*
**Practice Areas:** Partner in the firm's Global Finance Group. Mr Kilb represents private equity groups and other borrowers, and banks and other capital sources, in leveraged acquisition financings and other secured and unsecured senior, mezzanine and subordinated lending transactions, second lien financings, asset securitizations and other financing transactions, and credit and equity derivatives transactions. Mr Kilb also represents issuers and underwriters in debt capital markets transactions. Mr Kilb's finance practice covers many industries, including media and entertainment, gaming, lodging and real estate. Representative clients include Bear Stearns, Hilton Hotels, MGM, Entravision and Wells Fargo.
**Personal:** JD, Harvard Law School, 1983.

## KIMBALL, George
Baker & McKenzie, San Diego
619 235 7781
george.kimball@bakernet.com
*Recommended in Business Process Outsourcing, IT Outsourcing*
**Practice Areas:** His practice emphasizes technology transactions, including negotiation and re-negotiation of IT and business process outsourcing relationships for both customers and suppliers, in such industries as aerospace, broadcasting, chemicals, consumer products, computers, energy, engineering, forest products, healthcare, insurance, pharmaceuticals, and retail, among others.
**Prof. Memberships:** Admitted in California (1978).
**Career:** Regular speaker on outsourcing to trade and professional groups, including PLI, California CEB, and the Sourcing Interests Group.
**Publications:** Has lectured and written extensively on outsourcing and related topics.
**Personal:** University of Michigan (JD cum laude 1978).

## KING, Kenton J
Skadden, Arps, Slate, Meagher & Flom LLP & Affiliates, Palo Alto
650 470 4530
kking@skadden.com
*Recommended in Corporate/M&A*
**Practice Areas:** Head of Skadden's Palo Alto and San Francisco offices and Bay Area Corporate Group. Extensive experience in US and cross-border M&A, capital markets transactions. Recent transactions: Compaq Computer's $25 billion merger with Hewlett-Packard; Ascend Communications's $20 billion acquisition by Lucent Technologies; and Yahoo!'s investment in Alibaba.com (US$4 billion transaction value); its million-dollar unsolicited takeover of HotJobs.com and its $1.6 billion acquisition of Overture Services.
**Career:** JD, Boalt Hall School of Law at the University of California at Berkeley, 1987 (Editor-in-Chief, California Law Review; Order of the Coif); BA, Stanford University, 1977.

## KINSELLA, Dale
Greenberg Glusker Fields Claman Machtinger & Kinsella LLP, Los Angeles
310 553 3610
*Recommended in Media & Entertainment*

## KIRBY, Matthew T
O'Melveny & Myers LLP, Los Angeles
213 430 6553
mkirby@omm.com
*Recommended in Banking & Finance*
**Practice Areas:** Matt Kirby serves as the Co-Chair of O'Melveny & Myers' Finance and Restructuring Group. Matt's focus is in leveraged acquisition financing, restructuring and media finance. He regularly represents Credit Suisse First Boston, BNP Paribas, and Wells Fargo Bank.

## KIRSCHBAUM, Thomas
Irell & Manella LLP, Los Angeles
310 277 1010
*Recommended in Employment*

## KLEE, Kenneth N
Klee, Tuchin, Bogdanoff & Stern LLP, Los Angeles
310 407 4080
kklee@ktbslaw.com
*Recommended in Bankruptcy*
**Practice Areas:** A founding Member of Klee, Tuchin, Bogdanoff & Stern LLP, specializing in corporate reorganization, insolvency, and bankruptcy law. He joined the UCLA Law faculty in July 1997 after teaching bankruptcy and reorganization law as a visiting lecturer since 1979. From 1974-77, was associate counsel to the House Judiciary Committee, where he was one of the principal draftsmen of the 1978 Bankruptcy Code. He currently serves as a Director of the International Insolvency Institute. He also served as an advisor to the American Law Institute's Transnational Insolvency Project. Available as an expert witness, arbitrator, or mediator.

## KLEIN, Anthony
Latham & Watkins LLP, Menlo Park
650 328 4600
*Recommended in IT Outsourcing*

## KLEIN, Deborah
Barnes Morris Klein Mark Yorn Barnes & Levine, Santa Monica
310 319 3900
*Recommended in Media & Entertainment*

## KLEINBERG, Kenneth
Kleinberg, Lopez, Lange, Brisbin & Cuddy, Los Angeles
818 995 5500
*Recommended in Media & Entertainment*

## KLYMAN, Robert
Latham & Watkins LLP, Los Angeles
213 485 1234
*Recommended in Bankruptcy*

## KNAUSS, Robert
Munger, Tolles & Olson LLP, Los Angeles
213 683 9100
*Recommended in Corporate/M&A*

## KORMAN, Martin W
Wilson Sonsini Goodrich & Rosati, Palo Alto 650 493 9300
mkorman@wsgr.com
*Recommended in Corporate/M&A*
**Practice Areas:** Specializes in M&As, strategic transactions, corporate securities and general corporate representation

of public and private technology companies.

**Prof. Memberships:** Admitted to practice in New York and California.

**Career:** Joined WSGR, 1993; became Partner, 1997. Represented Hewlett Packard (HP) in its merger with Compaq, Netscape in its merger with AOL, Sun Microsystems in its acquisition of StorageTek, VMware in its sale to EMC, Overture Services in its sale to Yahoo!, Palm in its merger with Handspring, Healtheon in its merger with WebMD and Infoseek in its merger with Disney.

**Personal:** JD, Yale University, 1989. AB, Stanford University, 1985.

### KOSACZ, Barbara
Cooley Godward LLP, Palo Alto
650 843 5000
*Recommended in Corporate/M&A*

### KRELLER, Thomas
Milbank, Tweed, Hadley & McCloy LLP,
Los Angeles 213 892 4000
*Recommended in Bankruptcy*

### KREVANS, Rachel
Morrison & Foerster LLP, San Francisco
415 268 7178
rkrevans@mofo.com
*Recommended in Intellectual Property*

**Practice Areas:** Focused on both patent litigation and related proceedings, and fiduciary litigation. Patent controversy practice includes district court, International Trade Commission, and appellate experience, prelitigation and licensing strategy analysis, as well as experience in related proceedings, such as re-examination requests, interference proceedings, and interference appeals. Cases have involved a variety of life sciences and electrical engineering technologies. Practiced tax law from 1985-89, focused on ERISA and executive compensation issues and non-profit organizations. Extensive experience counseling fiduciaries in both general and litigation-related matters and has represented fiduciaries in government investigations and court proceedings.

**Career:** Admitted to practice in California. Managing Partner, San Francisco Office.

**Personal:** BA, Dartmouth College, 1979; JD, University of California, Davis, School of Law, 1984.

### KRISCHER, Gordon
O'Melveny & Myers LLP, Los Angeles
213 430 6010
gkrischer@omm.com
*Recommended in Employment*

**Practice Areas:** Gordon Krischer is a trial attorney and counselor with extensive experience representing management in virtually all fields of labor and personnel law in both the private and public sectors. His practice includes individual and complex class action and multiple plaintiff employment discrimina-

tion litigation, ERISA litigation and wrongful discharge litigation including major 'whistle-blower' and toxic tort cases in both state and federal courts. These matters involve bench trials, jury trials, binding arbitration and mediation. His practice under the National Labor Relations Act includes representation elections, opposing nationwide corporate campaigns, collective bargaining negotiations, arbitrations and unfair labor practice proceedings.

### KRUPKA, Robert G
Kirkland & Ellis LLP, Los Angeles
213 680 8456
bkrupka@kirkland.com
*Recommended in Intellectual Property*

**Practice Areas:** Specialist in patent, trade secret, copyright, trademark, advertising, unfair competition, internet and antitrust trials, appeals, and counseling. Extensive experience in contested intellectual property matters, trials involving technologically complex subject matter, obtaining expedited remedies, proceedings before the International Trade Commission, and appeals, especially before the Federal Circuit. Tried over 60 cases to judgment, including 13 jury trials to verdict (all but one victorious). Obtained verdicts totaling over $1 billion; negotiated settlements over $2.5 billion, including the largest patent settlement in history - $1.35 billion. Handled over 30 expedited remedy hearings (TROs, preliminary injunctions, temporary exclusion orders) and 25 Markman (claim interpretation) hearings.

**Personal:** Georgetown University, BS, 1971. University of Chicago Law School, JD, 1974.

### KUPIETZKY, Moshe J
Sidley Austin LLP, Los Angeles
213 896 6020
mkupietzky@sidley.com
*Recommended in Corporate/M&A*

**Practice Areas:** Managing Partner of Sidley's Los Angeles office and Head of the Los Angeles Corporate and Finance Practice Group. He specializes in mergers and acquisitions, private investments and corporate finance transactions. Mr Kupietzky regularly represents companies in various corporate acquisition and merger transactions, either as acquisition or target company counsel. He has also advised Boards of Directors, independent committees and management in various contested and uncontested takeover, acquisition, recapitalizations or divestiture transactions. He regularly represents a number of investment fund sponsors and private equity groups.

**Prof. Memberships:** Vice-Chair of the Opinions Committee of the Business Law Section of the California State Bar.

**Personal:** Harvard Law School, LLB; City College of the City University of New York, BBA, 1965. Admission: Cali-

fornia, 1970.

### LANDSBERG, Barry
Manatt Phelps & Phillips LLP,
Los Angeles 310 312 4000
*Recommended in Healthcare*

### LANGDON, Larry R
Mayer, Brown, Rowe & Maw, Palo Alto
650 331 2075
lrlangdon@mayerbrownrowe.com
*Recommended in Tax*

**Practice Areas:** Tax Controversy and Planning. Head of firm's Global Tax Practice. Former Head of the Large and Midsize Business Division within the US Internal Revenue Service, a unit that serves 150,000 businesses that pay a total of $600 billion in taxes every year.

**Career:** Mayer, Brown, Rowe & Maw, LLP, Palo Alto, 2003 to date; Partner, 2003. Internal Revenue Service, Commissioner, Large & Mid-Size Business Division, 1999-2003. Hewlett-Packard Company, VP, General Transition Manager, 1999; VP, Tax, Licensing and Customs, 1978-99. Vetco, Inc., Director of Taxes and Corporate Secretary, 1976-78. Ford Motor Company, Office of General Counsel, Sr Tax Attorney, 1968-76. Internal Revenue Service, Legislation and Regulations Division, Office of Counsel, 1964-68. CARE, 1962-64. Internal Revenue Service, Joint Committee Division, Office of Chief Counsel, 1961-62.

**Publications:** Speaker at the American Bar Association Section of Taxation, American Institute of CPAs, Manufacturers Alliance [MAPI], Tax Executives Institute and many other professional and industry groups.

Personal: JD, Ohio State University College of Law, 1961. LLM (Taxation), New York University, School of Law, 1963. BS, Ohio State University, 1959. Described by The Daily Deal (Aug 2003) as a "master of the international tax game."

### LANGE, Cynthia
Fragomen, Del Rey, Bernsen & Loewy, LLP,
Santa Clara 408 919 0600
*Recommended in Immigration*

### LARRABEE, Peter
Larrabee & Zimmerman LLP, San Diego
858 642 0420
*Recommended in Immigration*

### LARSON, John
Morgan, Lewis & Bockius LLP,
San Francisco 415 442 1123
jlarson@morganlewis.com
*Recommended in Corporate/M&A*

**Practice Areas:** John W Larson is a Partner in the Business and Finance Practice. Mr Larson's practice involves mergers and acquisitions, corporate governance and securities laws for high technology and other companies. Mr Larson was Assistant Secretary of the US Department of Interior (1971-73) and Counselor to George P Shultz (1973).

**Prof. Memberships:** Member, Board of

Trustees of the California Academy of Sciences.

### LAVELY JR, John
Lavely & Singer PC, Los Angeles
310 556 3501
*Recommended in Media & Entertainment*

### LAWLER, Martin
Lawler & Lawler Law Offices,
San Francisco 415 391 2010
*Recommended in Immigration*

### LAWSON, Michael
Skadden, Arps, Slate, Meagher & Flom LLP & Affiliates, Los Angeles
213 687 5380
mlawson@skadden.com
*Recommended in Employment*

**Practice Areas:** Leader of the Employee Benefits Group in the Los Angeles office. Practice includes all facets of executive compensation and employee benefits matters, including: stock options and other equity-based compensation plans; tax qualified and non-qualified pension plans; fiduciary responsibility/prohibited transactions; single and multi-employer plan liability matters; severance agreements and ERISA-related issues in structured finance transactions; bankruptcy proceedings; and proxy contests.

**Career:** JD, Harvard Law School, 1978; BA, Loyola University of Los Angeles, 1975.

**Personal:** Member, Board of Airport Commissioners - Los Angeles World Airports.

### LAYNE, Jonathan K
Gibson, Dunn & Crutcher LLP,
Los Angeles 310 552 8641
jlayne@gibsondunn.com
*Recommended in Corporate/M&A*

**Practice Areas:** Co-Chair of firm's Corporate Transactions Practice Group. Extensive experience in mergers and acquisitions, public offerings of equity (including IPOs) and debt, corporate finance and securities law, venture capital transactions, and Board of Directors, Special Board Committee and corporate governance representations.

**Career:** Member, firm's Executive Committee. Former Member, firm's Management Committee. Member, Board of Directors, California Chamber of Commerce.

**Publications:** Frequent lecturer on securities law topics.

**Personal:** JD, Emory University School of Law, 1979, Order of the Coif, Managing Editor, Emory Law Journal. MBA, Emory University Graduate School of Business, 1979, beta gamma sigma.

### LAZAROW, Warren T
O'Melveny & Myers LLP, Menlo Park
650 473 2637
wlazarow@omm.com
*Recommended in Corporate/M&A*

**Practice Areas:** Warren Lazarow is a

Partner in O'Melveny & Myers' Silicon Valley office and serves on its Executive Policy Committee and as the Managing Partner of its Silicon Valley Office. He specializes in the general corporate representation of emerging growth corporations, public companies, venture capital and private equity firms and investment banks. His career experience includes approximately 600 public and private offerings and 100 merger and acquisition transactions. He was chosen by Forbes Magazine for its Midas Touch List - The Top 100 Venture Capital Dealmakers in the United States three years in a row.

## LEIDEN, Warren
Berry Appleman & Leiden LLP, San Francisco 415 398 1800
*Recommended in Immigration*

## LEO, Thomas Glen
Sheppard, Mullin, Richter & Hampton LLP, Los Angeles
213 620 1780
*Recommended in Media & Entertainment*

## LERACH, William
Lerach Coughlin Stoia Geller Rudman & Robbins LLP, San Diego
619 231 1058
*Recommended in Litigation*

## LERMAN, Cary
Munger, Tolles & Olson LLP, Los Angeles
213 683 9100
*Recommended in Insurance*

## LESSER, Henry
DLA Piper Rudnick Gray Cary US LLP, Palo Alto 650 833 2425
henry.lesser@dlapiper.com
*Recommended in Corporate/M&A*
**Practice Areas:** Corporate and securities; mergers and acquisitions; private equity; public company and corporate governance.
**Career:** Co-Chair of the firm's Private Equity Practice. He has been involved in corporate securities practice, with a particular focus on corporate acquisitions, corporate governance, and restructuring matters, and all aspects of merger and acquisition work involving public and private companies, including hostile tender offers, proxy contests, friendly mergers, leveraged buyouts, stock acquisitions and asset sales. His clients include a wide variety of bidders, targets, stockholders and financial advisors.
**Personal:** LLM, Harvard University School of Law; MA, Cambridge University; BA, Cambridge University.

## LEVEE, Jeffrey A
Jones Day, Los Angeles
213 243 2572
jlevee@jonesday.com
*Recommended in Antitrust*
**Practice Areas:** Co-ordinator of the Antitrust and Competition Law Practice in Jones Day's California region. His

practice focuses on antitrust litigation, complex business and class action litigation, healthcare litigation, and antitrust counseling. He has successfully litigated matters in numerous state and federal courts on behalf of a wide variety of clients, including healthcare providers, retailers, internet companies, and media companies.
**Prof. Memberships:** Co-Chair of the ABA Antitrust Section 2005 Spring Meeting and previous Council Member.
**Personal:** Northwestern Law School (JD 1984); Duke University (BA 1981).

## LEVIN, Barry S
Heller Ehrman LLP, San Francisco
415 772 6646
barry.levin@hellerehrman.com
*Recommended in Insurance*
**Practice Areas:** Insurance recovery.
**Prof. Memberships:** American Bar Association; State Bar of California; Bar Association of San Francisco.
**Career:** Mr Levin focuses on complex litigation, with a special emphasis on insurance coverage matters. His practice involves representing corporate insureds in coverage matters. He has significant experience covering large environmental and toxic tort claims, and also counsels and litigates in a variety of insurance areas, including patent, copyright and trademark, antitrust, securities, construction, fidelity losses and first-party claims.
**Personal:** Washington University, St Louis (BA, Political Science and Psychology, magna cum laude, 1976); Northwestern University Law School (JD, magna cum laude, 1979).

## LEVINE, Harvey
Levine, Steinberg, Miller & Huver, San Diego 619 231 9449
*Recommended in Insurance*

## LEVINE, Janet
Lightfoot, Vandevelde, Sadowsky, Medvene & Levine, Los Angeles
213 622 4750
*Recommended in Litigation*

## LICHTER, Linda
Lichter Grossman Nicholas Adler & Goodman, Los Angeles
310 205 6999
*Recommended in Media & Entertainment*

## LIEVER, Michael H
Orrick, Herrington & Sutcliffe LLP, San Francisco 415 773 5808
mliever@orrick.com
*Recommended in Real Estate*
**Practice Areas:** Extensive involvement in representing both foreign and domestic investors in the acquisition, disposition, development, leasing, financing, and joint venture of office buildings, shopping centers, hotels, industrial parks, and apartments. Clients include the RREEF Funds, Anheuser-Busch, Black Rock, Morgan Stanley, New York Life Insurance

Company, the City of San Francisco, CalPERS, IowaPERS, Mass PRIM, Merrill Lynch, and Starbucks Corporation.
**Career:** Liever was Managing Partner for Operations for Morrison & Foerster LLP from 1989 through 1994.
**Personal:** JD, Harvard University, 1978; BA, University of Pennsylvania, 1974.

## LIGHTFOOT, Michael
Lightfoot, Vandevelde, Sadowsky, Medvene & Levine, Los Angeles
213 622 4750
*Recommended in Litigation*

## LINCENBERG, Gary
Bird, Marella, Boxer & Wolpert PC, Los Angeles 310 201 2100
*Recommended in Litigation*

## LIPSIG, Ethan
Paul, Hastings, Janofsky & Walker LLP, Los Angeles 213 683 6304
ethanlipsig@paulhastings.com
*Recommended in Employment*
**Practice Areas:** Employee benefits and employment law, including fiduciary matters, litigation, executive compensation, and workforce restructuring and redundancies.
**Prof. Memberships:** Charter member of the American College of Employee Benefits Counsel; member of the American Bar Association and the employee benefits committees of both its Tax Section and its Labor and Employment Section; member of the US Chamber of Commerce's Employee Benefits Committee, Board Member of the European Labour Network.
**Career:** UCLA Law School, JD 1974; Latham & Watkins, 1974-80; Paul Hastings,1980 to present (Partner since 1982).
**Publications:** Downsizing (BNA Books 1995, and annual supplements, second edition to be published in 2006) and numerous other publications.

## LIPTON, Steven
Davis Wright Tremaine LLP, San Francisco 415 276 6500
*Recommended in Healthcare*

## LISET, Robert
Musick Peeler & Garrett, Los Angeles
213 629 7929
*Recommended in Healthcare*

## LITTLE, Jan Nielsen
Keker & Van Nest LLP, San Francisco
415 391 5400
jlittle@kvn.com
*Recommended in Litigation*
**Practice Areas:** Jan Little has a wide-ranging criminal defense practice, representing corporations and individuals in investigations and trials involving business crimes including securities fraud, healthcare fraud, tax fraud, obstruction of justice/perjury, antitrust, intellectual property crimes, and foreign corrupt practices. She also represents corporations and individuals in complex civil liti-

gation in state and federal courts, and in SEC enforcement matters. Her clients include Google, Electronic Arts, McKesson, Safeway, and Johnson & Johnson.
**Prof. Memberships:** Former Co-Chair of the American Bar Association Litigation Section Complex Crimes Committee and the American Bar Association Northern California White Collar Crime Committee; currently active in several federal court committees; serves as a trustee and officer of a non-profit independent school; selected as one of California's Top 75 Women Litigators in 2005 by the Los Angeles Daily Journal.
**Career:** Law clerk to the Honorable William W Schwarzer in the Northern District of California (1981-82); trial attorney in the Public Integrity Section of the United States Department of Justice Criminal Division (1982-86); joined Keker & Van Nest in 1986; Partner since 1988.
**Publications:** 'Opening Statement: Ten Tips', California State Bar Litigation Section (2005); 'What is "Corrupt?" Federal Obstruction of Justice Statutes and The Supreme Court's Grant of Certiorari in United States v. Aguilar' (with Daralyn Durie), 'ABA White Collar Crime National Institute Materials' (1995); 'Parallel Proceedings: The Uncomfortable Intersection of Criminal and Civil Litigation', ABA Litigation Section Complex Crimes Journal (1993); 'The Impact of Criminal Proceedings in Civil Litigation' (with Jerome Matthews), 'California Continuing Education of the Bar' (1991); 'Know Your Investigator: The Basics of How to Handle a Medicare or Medicaid Audit, Review, or Investigation' (with Paul R DeMuro), Homecare Magazine (November 1991); 'Effective Introduction of Evidence in California' (10 chapters), California Continuing Education of the Bar (1st edition, 1990); 'Six Steps: Corporate Counsel's Immediate Response to a Potential Criminal Problem' (with Robert Van Nest), 2 Corporate Criminal Law Reporter 34 (1988).
**Personal:** Yale Law School, (JD, 1981); University of California at Berkeley (BA, summa cum laude, 1978).

## LITVACK, Sanford M
Hogan & Hartson LLP, Los Angeles
213 337 6788
slitvack@hhlaw.com
*Recommended in Media & Entertainment*
**Practice Areas:** Focusing on complex litigation, antitrust, trade regulation, and dispute resolution, he represents both plaintiffs and defendants in jury and non-jury cases. He has tried numerous cases to verdict and has argued before the US Supreme Court and the Courts of Appeals.
**Prof. Memberships:** Fellow, American College of Trial Lawyers; Director, Ameri-

can Arbitration Association; Commissioner, Antitrust Modernization Commission; NY Bar Association.

**Career:** Former Vice-Chairman, Chief of corporate operations, and general counsel of The Walt Disney Company; former assistant attorney general of the Antitrust Division of the US Department of Justice.

**Personal:** Georgetown University (LLB); University of Connecticut (BA).

### LITWIN, Edward
Litwin & Associates, San Francisco
650 588 7100
*Recommended in Immigration*

### LOBEL, William
Irell & Manella LLP, Newport Beach
949 760 0991
*Recommended in Bankruptcy*

### LOGAN III, Ben
O'Melveny & Myers LLP, Los Angeles
213 430 6000
blogan@omm.com
*Recommended in Bankruptcy*

**Practice Areas:** Ben Logan is a Partner in O'Melveny & Myers' Los Angeles office. His practice spans virtually all aspects of Chapter 11 reorganizations and out-of-court restructurings, frequently representing syndicated bank groups, bondholders, fund investors, committees, business debtors, and parties to bankruptcy acquisitions. He has practiced with O'Melveny & Myers since graduating from Stanford Law School in 1976, where he served as a Note Editor on the Law Review. He is a Fellow in the American College of Bankruptcy.

**Personal:** Stanford University, JD, 1976. Note Editor, Law Review. Duke University, BA, 1973, magna cum laude, Phi Beta Kappa.

### LONERGAN, James
Sheppard, Mullin, Richter & Hampton LLP, Los Angeles 213 620 1780
*Recommended in Real Estate*

### LOPES, James
Howard, Rice, Nemerovski, Canady, Falk & Rabkin, San Francisco
415 434 1600
*Recommended in Bankruptcy*

### LORIG, Frederick
Quinn Emanuel Urquhart Oliver & Hedges, LLP, Los Angeles
213 443 3000
fredericklorig@quinnemanuel.com
*Recommended in Intellectual Property*

**Career:** Mr Lorig is Co-Chair of Quinn Emanuel's National Trial Practice and is considered one of the most successful patent trial lawyers in the country. He has not lost a trial. Mr Lorig has been lead trial counsel in efforts to license a number of patent portfolios. Recently Mr Lorig acted as lead trial counsel in actions against 11 defendants involving patents on the smart battery management used in all notebook computers. Eight of these

disputes have been resolved by judgment in his client's favor and three by cross license. At the same time, Mr Lorig has been lead counsel in a similar effort to license a pioneering patent on optical fiber amplifiers which is exclusively licensed to Northrop Grumman. In addition to judgments against Corning, Nortel and Alcatel, Mr Lorig has obtained licenses for his client on advantageous terms. Mr Lorig also obtained the largest verdict for a patent case in history, $1.2 billion in Litton v. Honeywell and one of the largest antitrust judgments, after trebling, for an individual plaintiff, $660 million, in the companion antitrust case. In addition to obtaining verdicts exceeding $2 billion, and settlements of over $1 billion, Mr Lorig has acted as lead defense lawyer in numerous cases for Fortune 100 companies resulting in either dismissals or settlement on terms beneficial to his clients.

**Personal:** University of California, Berkeley, (BA, with distinction, 1969); Harvard Law School (JD, 1973).

### LUCERO, Gene
Latham & Watkins LLP, Los Angeles
213 485 1234
*Recommended in Environment*

### LUNDBERG, G Andrew
Latham & Watkins LLP, Los Angeles
213 485 1234
*Recommended in Insurance*

### LUNDY, Robert
Hooper Lundy & Bookman Inc,
Los Angeles 310 551 8111
*Recommended in Healthcare*

### LUREY, Michael
Latham & Watkins LLP, Los Angeles
213 485 1234
*Recommended in Bankruptcy*

### LYONS, James E
Skadden, Arps, Slate, Meagher & Flom LLP & Affiliates, San Francisco
415 984 6470
jlyons@skadden.com
*Recommended in Litigation*

**Practice Areas:** Co-Head of Skadden's West Coast Litigation Department, his practice emphasizes securities and corporate issues, directors' and officers' liability, international arbitration, and other complex commercial disputes. He has represented corporations in corporate control contests and has defended public corporations and corporate officers and directors in shareholder class action and derivative claims involving disclosure issues and in challenges to directors' business judgment in a wide variety of industries, ranging from aerospace to utilities.

**Career:** JD, New York University, 1976; BA, University of Missouri, 1973 (Phi Beta Kappa).

**Publications:** Editor, 'Winning Strategies and Techniques for Civil Litigators', Practising Law Institute, 1992.

### MACCOBY, Matthew F
Arnold & Porter LLP, Los Angeles
213 243 4213
Matthew.Maccoby@aporter.com
*Recommended in Business Process Outsourcing, IT Outsourcing*

**Practice Areas:** Matthew Maccoby specializes in technology services, outsourcing and other business transactions. He has represented customers and service providers in numerous information technology services and outsourcing transactions relating to computing, software development and maintenance, messaging services, network management, website development and hosting, telecommunications and related services. He has also represented companies outsourcing a wide range of business processes, including finance and accounting, human resource management, check clearing, aircraft maintenance, facility management and entertainment production. Mr Maccoby frequently advises clients regarding mergers, acquisitions, corporate reorganizations and joint ventures.

**Prof. Memberships:** Sourcing Interests Group.

**Career:** Mr Maccoby has spoken to trade and professional groups on a number of topics relating to outsourcing.

**Personal:** JD, Yale Law School, 1988; BA, Yale University, 1982.

### MACK, Joel
Latham & Watkins LLP, San Diego
619 236 1234
*Recommended in Energy*

### MALKIN, Joseph
Orrick, Herrington & Sutcliffe LLP,
San Francisco 415 773 5505
jmalkin@orrick.com
*Recommended in Energy*

**Practice Areas:** Over 30 years experience in high-stakes energy transactions and litigation. His matters have included mergers and acquisitions; utility bankruptcy; multi-billion dollar nuclear power plant prudence reviews; public utility commission investigations; FERC proceedings; purchases and sales of generating plants; and negotiation of power purchase agreements. Has spoken at dozens of conferences and seminars on subjects such as litigating state regulatory proceedings, buying and selling generation assets, the future of nuclear power, key issues facing FERC, and US power workouts and finance.

**Personal:** JD, Yale University, 1972; BA, Claremont McKenna College, 1968.

### MALLORY, Richard
Allen Matkins Leck Gamble & Mallory LLP,
San Francisco 415 837 1515
*Recommended in Real Estate*

### MALLORY, Robert P
McDermott Will & Emery, Los Angeles
310 551 9353

rmallory@mwe.com
*Recommended in Litigation*

**Practice Areas:** Antitrust, unfair competition, contract and professional liability litigation. Complex multi-party, multi-state and class action litigation. Tried many cases to judgment before both state and federal courts, frequently to juries, winning defense verdicts for clients faced with exposure above $250 million and client recoveries ranging to $20 million. Class action experience is extensive and includes both putative consumer classes, as well as quasi-class actions brought under private attorney general and qui tam statutes.

**Prof. Memberships:** Member of California Bar (1971); Fellow of the American College of Trial Lawyers.

**Personal:** University of California-Davis (JD); California State University - Sacramento (BS)

### MANCINO, Douglas M
McDermott Will & Emery, Los Angeles
310 551 9323
dmancino@mwe.com
*Recommended in Healthcare*

**Practice Areas:** Represented nonprofit organizations on tax, business and financial matters. Represents organizations and individuals in connection with the formation of nonprofit organizations such as public charities, private foundations, corporate foundations and trade associations, corporate transactions and restructuring of corporate organizations. Extensive experience in audit, appeals and tax controversy matters, served as lead tax counsel in 12 IRS audits.

**Publications:** Author, 'Taxation of Hospitals and Health Care Organizations' and the co-author of 'Taxation of Exempt Organizations'.

**Personal:** Ohio State University College of Law (JD, summa cum laude); Kent State University BA (cum laude).

### MANSFIELD, Stephen A
Akin Gump Strauss Hauer & Feld LLP,
San Francisco 415 765 9519
smansfield@akingump.com
*Recommended in Litigation*

**Practice Areas:** Heads the San Francisco office and chairs the White Collar Criminal Defense Practice Group in California. Represents corporations and individuals in trials, arbitrations and government enforcement actions before federal and state courts and administrative agencies. Practice focuses on complex fraud litigation, class action defense, corporate and government investigations, and white-collar criminal defense.

**Prof. Memberships:** American Bar Association, White Collar Crime Committee; Board of Directors, San Francisco Legal Aid Society; Member, Pacific Council on International Policy; Chancery Club.

**Personal:** BA (summa cum laude), University of Rhode Island (1977); JD, University of Maine School of Law (1982).

## MARELLA, Vincent
Bird, Marella, Boxer & Wolpert PC,
Los Angeles 310 201 2100
*Recommended in Litigation*

## MARENBERG, Steven
Irell & Manella LLP, Los Angeles
310 277 1010
*Recommended in Media &
Entertainment*

## MARKHAM, Jesse W
Morrison & Foerster LLP, San Francisco
415 268 7448
jmarkham@mofo.com
*Recommended in Antitrust*
**Practice Areas:** Recognized authority on antitrust law, handling complex litigation matters. Represents clients before enforcement agencies on civil and criminal investigations and proceedings. Primarily focused on technology clients. Participated in effort to establish antitrust enforcement mechanisms in Russia and the Ukraine. Represented clients in international cartel investigations.
**Career:** Before private practice, served as Deputy Attorney General (Antitrust) for California and Massachusetts. Authored the California Attorney General's Antitrust Guidelines for the Insurance Industry. Since 1993, Adjunct Professor, antitrust courses, University of San Francisco Law School.
**Personal:** AB, cum laude, Harvard University, 1974; MA, University of Massachusetts, 1976; Boalt Hall School of Law, 1978-79, special status transfer student; JD, Vanderbilt University School of Law, 1979.

## MARKS, Allan
Milbank, Tweed, Hadley & McCloy LLP,
Los Angeles 213 892 4000
*Recommended in Projects,
Transportation*

## MARMARO, Richard
Skadden, Arps, Slate, Meagher & Flom
LLP & Affiliates, Los Angeles
213 687 5480
rmarmaro@skadden.com
*Recommended in Litigation*
**Practice Areas:** Head of Skadden's West Coast SEC Enforcement and White-Collar Defense Practice. He has successfully defended individuals and corporations in all phases of complex civil, criminal and regulatory matters involving allegations of insider trading, accounting and disclosure irregularities, market manipulation, and other financial frauds. He has conducted numerous internal corporate investigations involving insider trading allegations, tax violations, and corporate opportunity issues.
**Career:** JD, New York University School of Law, 1975; BA, George Washington University, 1972 (magna cum laude, Phi Beta Kappa). Law clerk, Federal Judge,

Southern District of New York. Assistant US Attorney, Central District of California, Criminal Division.

## MARMORSTEIN, Vicki
Latham & Watkins LLP, Los Angeles
213 485 1234
*Recommended in Banking & Finance*

## MARTENS, Don
Knobbe Martens Olson & Bear, Irvine
949 760 0404
*Recommended in Intellectual Property*

## MATHIASON, Garry G
Littler Mendelson, PC, San Francisco
415 433 1940
gmathiason@littler.com
*Recommended in Employment*
**Practice Areas:** Defends employers in complex wage and hour and discrimination class action cases. Oversees the firm's Corporate Compliance Practice Group and serves as Chair of OCEG's Employment and Labor Law Domain. Originated several preventive employment law programs, developed employment law training programs and firm's alternative dispute resolution program. Appears on national radio and television regarding violence prevention in the workplace.
**Publications:** Authored over 50 articles on workplace issues. Interviewed and quoted on employment topics in The Wall Street Journal, Business Week, Fortune, Newsweek, Time and scores of other publications.
**Personal:** Stanford (JD, 1971); Northwestern (Bachelor's, 1968).

## MATICHAK, Jill
O'Melveny & Myers LLP, San Francisco
415 984 8774
jmatichak@omm.com
*Recommended in Banking & Finance*
**Practice Areas:** Jill Matichak has significant experience in banking, general corporations, and securities law matters. Jill has acted as lead lender's counsel in a broad range of financial transactions, including secured and unsecured commercial lending arrangements, leveraged acquisitions, project financings, asset based facilities, and restructurings. She also has experience advising lenders in connection with assignments and participations and substantial experience in derivative transactions. In addition, she has represented financial institutions and other clients in foreign and domestic public debt and equity financings, private placements, mergers and acquisitions, and securitization transactions.

## MATKINS, Michael
Allen Matkins Leck Gamble & Mallory
LLP, Los Angeles 213 622 5555
*Recommended in Real Estate*

## MATTHEWS, Philip R
Duane Morris LLP, San Francisco
415 955 2574
prmatthews@duanemorris.com

*Recommended in Insurance*
**Practice Areas:** Philip R Matthews is a Partner in the San Francisco office of Duane Morris. His practice focuses on general civil litigation and insurance counseling and litigation with an emphasis on complex cases. He has been involved in some of the largest trials and appeals in California, including the trial and appeal of Shell Oil Co. vs Accident and Casualty Co of Winterthur (Rocky Mountain Arsenal case) and In Re Coordinated Asbestos Litigation (Manville, Fibreboard, Armstrong and GAF Coverage cases). He also has been liaison and trial counsel in numerous complex cases, and has experience in bankruptcy law, asbestos bankruptcies, and corporate transactions.
**Prof. Memberships:** American Bar Association; Bar Association of San Francisco; Trustee of the Board of the Episcopal Charities of the Diocese of California; active in other non-profit and religious organizations.
**Career:** Admitted to practice in California. Hancock Rothert & Bunshoft LLP - Chairperson, 2004-05; Partner, 1985-2005; Management Committee, 1989-94, 1997-99 and 2004-05; San Francisco Managing Partner, 1991-92 and 1998-99; associate, 1980-84.
**Personal:** George Washington University, BA, 1974; University of California, Hastings College of the Law, JD, 1977.

## MAUTINO, Robert
Mautino & Mautino, San Diego
619 235 9177
*Recommended in Immigration*

## MAYER, Patricia
Mitchell, Silberberg & Knupp LLP,
Los Angeles 310 312 2000
*Recommended in Media &
Entertainment*

## MAYERSON, Michael A
Loeb & Loeb LLP, Los Angeles
310 282 2165
mmayerson@loeb.com
*Recommended in Media &
Entertainment*
**Practice Areas:** Concentrates on film finance including project financing, lines-of-credit, securitizations, co-financing, co-productions and tax-advantaged financings. Represents commercial banks, hedge funds, high-net-worth investors and financial institutions. Advises distributors (domestic and non-US-based), in all forms of licensing/distribution transactions with content owners.
**Career:** Partner since 1989.
**Publications:** Regular speaker at Annual Savannah Film Festival, Paul Kagan's Annual Motion Production and Finance, Annual UCLA Entertainment Symposium.
**Personal:** Columbia University Law School (JD, 1981, Harlan Fiske Stone

Scholar); Wharton School of the University of Pennsylvania (BS, 1978, magna cum laude).

## MCCABE, Patrick
Morrison & Foerster LLP, San Francisco
415 268 6926
pmccabe@mofo.com
*Recommended in Employment*
**Practice Areas:** Practice focuses on the representation of domestic and foreign companies in the areas of executive compensation, stock plans and non-qualified retirement plans. Has extensive experience designing equity-based compensation arrangements, including stock options, restricted stock, phantom stock and stock appreciation rights. Advises clients on all tax issues applicable to compensation arrangements, including 'golden parachute' issues under IRC Section 280 and deferred compensation under IRC Section 409A. Also provides clients with advice regarding the complex accounting and securities law compliance issues that affect compensation arrangements. Provides counsel on change of control matters affecting officers and directors including merger and acquisition compensation planning and negotiation.
**Career:** Bar admission: California.
**Personal:** BA, University of Utah, 1989; JD, Cornell Law School, 1992.

## MCCARTHY, Brian J
Skadden, Arps, Slate, Meagher & Flom
LLP & Affiliates, Los Angeles
213 687 5070
bmccarth@skadden.com
*Recommended in Corporate/M&A*
**Practice Areas:** Concentrates on corporate and securities matters, with particular emphasis on mergers, acquisitions, corporate governance issues and restructurings. Has acted as counsel to numerous companies and investment banking firms in mergers, acquisitions and tender offers, both friendly and hostile, and has also represented special committees of Boards of Directors as well as several investment banking clients, buyers, sellers and management groups in leveraged buyouts and related financings.
**Prof. Memberships:** Member, Executive Committee, Business and Corporations Law Section, Los Angeles County Bar Association.
**Career:** JD, Fordham University School of Law, 1978; BA, Tufts University, 1975 (magna cum laude).

## MCCUTCHEON, Mary
Farella Braun & Martel LLP,
San Francisco 415 954 4400
*Recommended in Insurance*

## MCELHINNY, Harold J
Morrison & Foerster LLP, San Francisco
415 268 7265
hmcelhinny@mofo.com
*Recommended in Intellectual Property*

**Practice Areas:** A trial lawyer with a general federal and state court litigation practice emphasizing intellectual property matters: patent litigation, copyright and trade secret violations, class actions, and enforcement.
**Prof. Memberships:** Member: American Bar Association; Intellectual Property Law section, State Bar of California; American Intellectual Property Law Association; Federal Circuit Bar Association. Former President, Northern California Association of Business Trial Lawyers, 1996-97.
**Career:** Admitted to practice in California. Served as firmwide Chair, Litigation Department, 1996-99. Current Co-Chair, Intellectual Property Group.
**Personal:** BA, University of Santa Clara, 1970; Peace Corps, North Africa; JD, Boalt Hall School of Law, UC Berkeley, 1975, Order of the Coif; law clerk, Honorable Joseph Blumenfeld, US District Court, Connecticut, 1975-76.

### MCGLYNN, Casey
Wilson Sonsini Goodrich & Rosati,
Palo Alto 650 493 9300
cmcglynn@wsgr.com
*Recommended in Corporate/M&A*
**Practice Areas:** Focuses on the organization, funding and corporate representation of companies in the information technology and life sciences industries. Structures and negotiates mergers and acquisitions, licensing arrangements and domestic and international strategic corporate alliances, as well as other innovative financing arrangements.
**Prof. Memberships:** Admitted to practice in California. Member, American Bar Association.
**Career:** Joined WSGR, 1978; became Partner, 1985.
**Personal:** JD, (summa cum laude), 1978 and BS (summa cum laude), 1975, University of Santa Clara.

### MCKNIGHT, Frederick (Rick)
Jones Day, Los Angeles
213 243 2777
fmcknight@jonesday.com
*Recommended in Litigation*
**Practice Areas:** Partner in charge of the Los Angeles office. His practice primarily involves complex business litigation. He has had an active trial docket, including successful bench and jury trials of antitrust, contract, securities, oil and gas, healthcare, fraud, intellectual property, business tort, ERISA, entertainment, product liability, bankruptcy, environmental, and tax cases. He also is active in alternative forms of dispute resolution and has both recovered and defeated the recovery of substantial punitive damages awards. He frequently lectures on trial and pretrial practice and procedures.
**Prof. Memberships:** Fellow of the American College of Trial Lawyers.

### MCMAHON, Terry
McDermott Will & Emery, Palo Alto
650 813 5010
tmcmahon@mwe.com
*Recommended in Intellectual Property*
**Practice Areas:** Trial lawyer, Partner and Head of West Coast IP Practice. Focuses on patent, copyright, trade secret, trade dress, trademark and other high stakes litigation. 30 years of experience representing heavyweights including American Express, Aristocrat, Broadcom, Creative Labs, EMC, Extreme Networks, Fairchild, Fresenius Medical, GE, Logitech, Medtronic, Seagate Technology and Silicon Image.
**Career:** Admitted to practice in California, US Court of Appeals for the Ninth Circuit, Court of Appeals for the Federal Circuit, US District Courts for the Northern and Central Districts of California, and the District of Colorado.
**Personal:** University of Santa Clara, BA and JD cum laude.

### MCMILLAN, Daniel D
Jones Day, Los Angeles
213 243 2582
ddmcmillan@jonesday.com
*Recommended in Construction*
**Practice Areas:** Co-chairs Jones Day's worldwide Construction Practice. Specializes in complex construction litigation, contractual disputes, and claims involving federal and state false claims acts. Substantial trial, law and motion, and appellate experience and extensive experience with all forms of alternative dispute resolution. Served as Adjunct Professor at Loyola Law School and is an instructor for the National Institute of Trial Advocacy. Frequent writer and speaker on issues affecting the construction industry and legal profession.
**Prof. Memberships:** ABA Forum on the Construction Industry/Steering Committee for Dispute Avoidance and Resolution. Los Angeles Economic Development Corporation/Executive Director. Disputes Review Board Foundation.

### MCNAMARA, Mary
Swanson & McNamara LLP,
San Francisco 415 477 3800
*Recommended in Litigation*

### MEISINGER, Louis
Sheppard, Mullin, Richter & Hampton LLP,
Los Angeles 310 228 3700
*Recommended in Media & Entertainment*

### MEMEL, Sherwin
Manatt Phelps & Phillips LLP,
Los Angeles 310 312 4000
*Recommended in Healthcare*

### MENDELSON, Alan
Latham & Watkins LLP, Menlo Park
650 328 4600
*Recommended in Corporate/M&A*

### MENDELSON, Richard C
DLA Piper Rudnick Gray Cary US LLP,
Los Angeles
213 330 7745
richard.mendelson@dlapiper.com
*Recommended in Real Estate*
**Practice Areas:** Real estate.
**Career:** He has particular knowledge in the areas of acquisitions, joint ventures, and financing transactions, as well as in workouts and restructurings. He has extensive experience in representing both domestic and international banks and other financial institutions, insurance companies, pension funds, and major developers in all aspects of commercial residential property.
**Personal:** JD, University of Pennsylvania; AB, Rutgers University.

### MENDEZ, John
Latham & Watkins LLP, Los Angeles
213 485 1234
*Recommended in Banking & Finance*

### MEYER, Michael E
DLA Piper Rudnick Gray Cary US LLP,
Los Angeles 213 330 7777
michael.meyer@dlapiper.com
*Recommended in Real Estate*
**Practice Areas:** Real estate; landlord leasing.
**Career:** With a national reputation as one of the preeminent leasing attorneys in the US, he represents financial institutions, accounting firms and law firms with major lease transactions and is one of the leading authorities on Fair Market Rental Rates, the Assignment and Subleasing Provision, the Tenant Improvement Agreement and the Rent Commencement Date. He has been named to the top rank of influential lawyers in numerous publications.
**Personal:** JD, University of Chicago; BS, University of Wisconsin.

### MIHLSTEN, George
Latham & Watkins LLP, Los Angeles
213 485 1234
*Recommended in Real Estate*

### MILLER, O'Malley
Munger, Tolles & Olson LLP, Los Angeles
213 683 9100
*Recommended in Real Estate*

### MILLER, Robert
Paul, Hastings, Janofsky & Walker LLP,
Los Angeles 213 683 6254
robertmiller@paulhastings.com
*Recommended in Corporate/M&A*
**Practice Areas:** Mr Miller concentrates his practice in corporate finance transactional work, including mergers, acquisitions, public and private placement of securities, venture capital, and investment partnerships. He also represents publicly and privately held companies on general corporate and securities matters.
**Personal:** Mr Miller received his BS Degree in 1976 from the University of North Dakota, and his JD Degree in 1983

from Loyola Law School of Los Angeles, where he was a member of the St Thomas More Law Honor Society. He serves as Chair of the firm's Corporate Department.

### MILLER, Stephen
Law Offices of Stephen D Miller PC,
Beverly Hills 310 247 0080
*Recommended in Litigation*

### MILLET, Craig H
Gibson, Dunn & Crutcher LLP, Irvine
949 451 3986
cmillet@gibsondunn.com
*Recommended in Bankruptcy*
**Practice Areas:** Extensive experience in complex bankruptcy litigation, chapter 11 reorganization cases and international and cross-border bankruptcy matters including appellate, asset acquisition through bankruptcy, representation of both debtors and creditors, out-of-court restructuring and transactional strategic planning. Represented James Hardie Industries' asbestos fund settlement in Australia; the Japanese administrator in In Re Ken International; Callaway Golf in the acquisition of Top Flite, FLAG Telecom in Elliott Group litigation, five major broker/dealers in In Re County of Orange; debtor in In Re Advanced Tissue Sciences and Ingram Micro in BigStore.com litigation.
**Personal:** JD, summa cum laude, Pepperdine University, 1982.

### MINCHELLA, Michael
Monteleone & McCrory, LLP,
Los Angeles 213 612 9900
*Recommended in Construction*

### MONTGOMERY, Cromwell
Gibson, Dunn & Crutcher LLP,
Los Angeles 310 551 8744
cmontgomery@gibsondunn.com
*Recommended in Banking & Finance*
**Practice Areas:** Member of the firm's Global Finance Group. Represents borrowers and various capital providers in a broad variety of secured and unsecured credit transactions, including second lien, mezzanine and subordinated debt transactions. Practice also includes capital markets transactions.
**Personal:** JD, Boalt Hall School of Law, University of California, Berkeley, 1997.

### MOONEY, Ann
Cooley Godward LLP, San Francisco
415 693 2000
*Recommended in Insurance*

### MOORE, Gary
Cooley Godward LLP, Palo Alto
650 843 5000
*Recommended in IT Outsourcing*

### MOORE, Robert
Milbank, Tweed, Hadley & McCloy LLP,
Los Angeles 213 892 4000
*Recommended in Bankruptcy*

**MORROW, Bill**
Cooley Godward LLP, San Francisco
415 693 2000
*Recommended in Tax*

**MULLIKEN, David**
Latham & Watkins LLP, San Diego
619 236 1234
*Recommended in Insurance*

**MUMMERY, Dan**
Latham & Watkins LLP, Menlo Park
650 328 4600
*Recommended in Business Process Outsourcing, IT Outsourcing*

**MURASHIGE, Kate H**
Morrison & Foerster LLP, San Diego
858 720 5112
kmurashige@mofo.com
*Recommended in Intellectual Property*
**Practice Areas:** Focuses on intellectual property and patent issues within the pharmaceutical and healthcare industries.
**Prof. Memberships:** Member, AAAS committee on Scientific Freedom and Responsibility.
**Career:** Admitted to practice in California, and before the US Patent and Trademark Office. Co-Chair of the firm's Patent Group. Invited Speaker, Human Genome Conference (Patent Issues). Has been advisor on gene patenting to the OTA. Spoken before Members of Congress and their staffs regarding the Human Genome Project.
**Personal:** BA, Washington University (St Louis), 1956; PhD, University of California, Los Angeles, 1962; JD, Santa Clara University School of Law, 1977

**MURPHY, Mary**
Farella Braun & Martel LLP,
San Francisco 415 954 4400
*Recommended in Real Estate*

**MURPHY, Michael**
Pillsbury Winthrop Shaw Pittman LLP,
San Francisco 415 983 1303
Michael.Murphy@pillsburylaw.com
*Recommended in Business Process Outsourcing, IT Outsourcing*
**Practice Areas:** Mr Murphy concentrates on complex technology-based transactions and business process outsourcing projects, with a focus on business transformation relationships. His transactional experience spans traditional outsourcing, including IT, human resources, procurement/supply chain and facilities management outsourcing, complex system procurements and mission critical system licensing transactions. Mr Murphy has represented clients in global sourcing transactions involving multi-country delivery solutions.
**Publications:** 'Structuring Outsourcing Technology Relationships: Customer Concerns, Strategies and Processes' (International Journal of Law and Information Technology, Vol 4 No 2); 'Optimizing the Tax Function Through Strate-

gic Sourcing', Journal of Corporate Tax Automation, Spring 2004.

**MURPHY, Patrick A**
Winston & Strawn LLP, San Francisco
415 591 1500
pmurphy@winston.com
*Recommended in Bankruptcy*
**Practice Areas:** Corporate reorganizations and insolvency law.
**Prof. Memberships:** California State Bar; San Francisco Bar Association; American and International Bar Associations; National Bankruptcy Conference; American College of Bankruptcy; International Insolvency Institute.
**Career:** National practice in restructuring and insolvency law; represented Creditors' Committee in Washington Group International.
**Publications:** Creditors' Rights in Bankruptcy (2d Ed, West Group). Participated in more than 50 programs in the fields of bankruptcy, commercial law, and lender liability litigation for organizations such as American Law Institute-American Bar Association and Practising Law Institute.
**Personal:** BA Williams College 1961; JD University of California at Berkeley, Boalt Hall, 1965.

**MURRAY, Christopher**
O'Melveny & Myers LLP, Los Angeles
310 246 6855
cmurray@omm.com
*Recommended in Media & Entertainment*
**Practice Areas:** The legal and business aspects of the production, financing and distribution of motion pictures and television programs, as well as DVDs, digital and wireless media, videogames, the Internet, music, concerts, print publishing and the acquisition of entertainment companies, film libraries and music publishers. Counsels clients in the fields of copyright, trademark and licensing. Represents motion picture studios, television networks, ad agencies, internet and technology businesses and digital content developers and distributors, sports organizations and companies from outside the US in their dealings in Hollywood. Also represents high-profile individual performers, producers and executives.
**Career:** In practice over 30 years.

**MURRAY JR, William G**
Orrick, Herrington & Sutcliffe LLP,
San Francisco 415 773 5807
wgm@orrick.com
*Recommended in Real Estate*
**Practice Areas:** Focuses on negotiating and documenting acquisitions and financing transactions, including substantial work for pension fund advisors, construction and long-term lending, ground leasing, sale-leaseback financing, synthetic leases, and development transactions. Responsible for leasing numerous large retail, office, hotel and resort, and industrial complexes and has been

extensively involved in the workout of troubled financing transactions. Represents buyers, sellers, and developers of real property, including pension funds, individual developers, domestic institutions, and foreign investors. Active in securitization of real estate assets, REITs, private equity fund formation, and pension fund investment.
**Personal:** JD, UC Berkeley, 1975; BA, Utah State University, 1972.

**MUTO, Fred**
Cooley Godward LLP, San Diego
858 550 6000
*Recommended in Corporate/M&A*

**MYERS, Roger**
DLA Piper Rudnick Gray Cary US LLP,
San Francisco
415 615 6048
roger.myers@dlapiper.com
*Recommended in Media & Entertainment*
**Practice Areas:** Media and new media; intellectual property; litigation.
**Career:** His practice focuses on media, cyberspace, intellectual property, and unfair competition law, representing a melding of the old media with the new. He has litigated numerous intellectual property and unfair competition matters and has successfully represented Internet access, service, and content providers in both online defamation and copyright litigation.
**Personal:** JD, Boalt Hall School of Law, University of California at Berkeley; BA, San Jose State University.

**NASH, Glenn**
Latham & Watkins LLP, Menlo Park
650 328 4600
*Recommended in IT Outsourcing*

**NATSIS, Anton**
Allen Matkins Leck Gamble & Mallory LLP,
Los Angeles 310 788 2400
*Recommended in Real Estate*

**NEAL, Stephen**
Cooley Godward LLP, Palo Alto
650 843 5000
*Recommended in Intellectual Property, Litigation*

**NEELY, Sally S**
Sidley Austin LLP, Los Angeles
213 896 6024
sneely@sidley.com
*Recommended in Bankruptcy*
**Practice Areas:** Sally Neely focuses on chapter 11 reorganizations and workouts, representing debtors, committees, creditors, contract parties, purchasers and defendants. She is or has recently been active in representing the Creditors' Committee in the Franchise Pictures chapter 11; Flintkote Co. (chapter 11 debtor); Bombardier and Learjet in litigation in an individual's chapter 11; former shareholders of a chapter 11 debtor who were fraudulent transfer defendants; the purchaser of assets of Canadian subsidiaries of debtor Consolidated Freightways; the Korean parent in the Daewoo Motor America chapter 11; and NewPower Co. (chapter 11 debtor).
**Prof. Memberships:** Member: National Bankruptcy Conference, Co-Chair of Committee on Legislation, Executive Committee, past Chair of Committee on Partnerships; Fellow and Vice President: American College of Bankruptcy, Chair of Educational Programs Committee.
**Publications:** Partnerships and Partners and Limited Liability Companies and Members in Bankruptcy: Proposals for Reform, 71 Amer. Bankr. L.J. 271 (1997); numerous CLE papers.
**Personal:** Assistant professor, Harvard Law School (1975-77); law clerk, Honorable Ozell M Trask, Ninth Circuit Court of Appeals, (1971-72); Stanford University Law School, JD, 1971 (Order of the Coif); Stanford University, BA, 1970 (Phi Beta Kappa). Admissions: Arizona, 1972; California, 1977.

**NELLIS, Noel W**
Orrick, Herrington & Sutcliffe LLP,
San Francisco 415 773 5806
nnellis@orrick.com
*Recommended in Real Estate*
**Practice Areas:** Focuses on negotiating and documenting transactions in the areas of financing (including construction and long-term lending, ground leasing, and sale-leaseback transactions), leasing, development, construction, and operation of real property. Responsible for legal aspects of numerous large-scale land development projects such as high-rise office buildings, shopping centers, hotel and resort properties, and industrial buildings. Represents domestic institutional and pension fund investors and foreign investors in the acquisition and disposition of real estate. Actively involved in the formation and IPOs of REITs and advises a number of public and private REITs.
**Personal:** University of California, Berkeley (JD, 1966; BA 1963).

## NESSIM, Ronald
Bird, Marella, Boxer & Wolpert PC,
Los Angeles 310 201 2100
*Recommended in Litigation*

## NEWCOMBE, George
Simpson Thacher & Bartlett LLP,
Palo Alto 650 251 5050
gnewcombe@stblaw.com
*Recommended in Intellectual Property*
**Practice Areas:** Partner in the firm's Litigation Department and Head of the Palo Alto office. Mr Newcombe's practice is focused on servicing the litigation needs of companies in Silicon Valley, including patent and other intellectual property litigation, commercial arbitration, securities litigation, among other matters. Representative clients include Intel Corporation, Oracle Corporation (Special Litigation Committee), Levi Strauss & Co. (Audit Committee); JDS Uniphase, MCI/World-Com, Inc., Agilent Technologies, Inc., NEC Corporation, Olympus Optical Co. Ltd. and Avistar Communications.
**Prof. Memberships:** Member, the American Law Institute, the American Intellectual Property Lawyers Association, The Association of the Bar of the City of New York, the American Bar Association, the Federal Circuit Bar Association, the Federal Bar Council and the Defense Research Institute.
**Career:** Partner at the firm since 1983.
**Personal:** Received his BS magna cum laude in Chemical Engineering in 1969 from the New Jersey Institute of Technology and his JD from Columbia University School of Law in 1975, where he was a James Kent Scholar and a Founding Editor of the Columbia Journal of Environmental Law.

## NEWMAN, Bradford K
Paul, Hastings, Janofsky & Walker LLP,
Palo Alto 650 320 1827
bradfordnewman@paulhastings.com
*Recommended in Employment*
**Practice Areas:** Chair of the Palo Alto Employment Practice; represents employers in all phases of employment litigation, trade secrets cases, and employee mobility cases.
**Prof. Memberships:** American Bar Association.
**Career:** Graduated cum laude from University of Pennsylvania; JD University of California, Hastings College of The Law. Admitted to practice before the United States Court of Appeals for the District of Columbia, Sixth and Ninth Circuits, and all federal and state courts in California.
**Publications:** Latest Publication: 'Protection for Whistleblowers Under Sarbanes-Oxley', The Practical Lawyer (ALI-ABA).

## NEWMAN, Jeanne
Hansen Jacobson Teller Hoberman Newman, Warren, Sloane & Richman, LLP,
Beverly Hills 310 271 8777
*Recommended in Media & Entertainment*

## NICHOLS, Phillip
Pircher, Nichols & Meeks, Los Angeles
310 201 8900
*Recommended in Real Estate*

## NICHOLSON, Phillip
Cox Castle & Nicholson LLP, Los Angeles
310 277 4222
*Recommended in Real Estate*

## NIEHANS, Daniel
Gunderson Dettmer Stough Villeneuve
Franklin & Hachigian, Menlo Park
650 321 2400
*Recommended in Employment*

## NOCHIMSON, David
Ziffren Brittenham Branca Fischer
Gilbert-Lurie & Stiffelman LLP,
Los Angeles 310 552 3388
*Recommended in Media & Entertainment*

## NOLAN, Thomas J
Skadden, Arps, Slate, Meagher & Flom
LLP & Affiliates, Los Angeles
213 687 5250
tnolan@skadden.com
*Recommended in Antitrust, Litigation*
**Practice Areas:** Co-Head of the firm's West Coast Litigation Practice. Extensive trial experience representing and defending corporations and individuals in significant federal, state, civil and criminal complex litigation in California and in various state and federal courts throughout the United States involving: antitrust, securities, intellectual property and white-collar crime issues, as well as in class action lawsuits and litigation involving a wide variety of contract disputes, unfair business practices, and federal securities issues. He has obtained over $1 billion in jury verdicts for corporate clients.
**Career:** JD, Loyola University, 1975; BBA, Loyola University, 1971.

## NORRIS, Trenton H
Bingham McCutchen LLP, San Francisco
415 393 2062
trent.norris@bingham.com
*Recommended in Environment*
**Practice Areas:** Practice covers complex litigation and problem-solving involving scientific and technical disputes in the areas of environmental, intellectual property and consumer protection law. Substantial portion of practice is devoted to advising and defending companies concerning California's unique toxics and labeling law, Proposition 65, and California's stringent consumer protection laws. Has represented dozens of companies, large and small, in Proposition 65 litigation and compliance counseling matters. Serves as co-chair of the firm's Military Base Reuse and Privatization Group.
**Personal:** Harvard Law School, JD, magna cum laude, 1992; Brown University, BA, magna cum laude, 1986.

## OAKES, Royal
Barger & Wolen, Los Angeles
213 680 2800
*Recommended in Insurance*

## OCKER, Jonathan M
Orrick, Herrington & Sutcliffe LLP,
San Francisco 415 773 5595
jonocker@orrick.com
*Recommended in Employment*
**Practice Areas:** Nationally recognized expertise in the subject of executive compensation. Focuses on related corporate governance, proxy disclosure, employment and retention, merger and acquisition and litigation issues. Advises founders and CEOs, and technology, financial service and communications entities, from start-ups to industry leaders.
**Prof. Memberships:** American College of Employee Benefits Lawyers, Advisory Board of Compensation Standards, State Bars of California and Illinois.
**Publications:** Frequent speaker on executive compensation and has published a number of popular course outlines and articles.
**Personal:** JD, Washington University School of Law, 1978; BA, University of Wisconsin, 1975.

## O'CONNELL, George
Stevens & O'Connell LLP, Sacramento
916 329 9111
*Recommended in Litigation*

## OFFER, Stuart J
Morrison & Foerster LLP, San Francisco
415 268 7052
soffer@mofo.com
*Recommended in Tax*
**Practice Areas:** Concentrates on tax aspects of mergers, acquisitions and divestitures, and general corporate transactions. Handles international tax planning for US-based companies. Advises foreign corporations on the US tax aspects of their operations and investments.
**Prof. Memberships:** Taxation Section, ABA (Chair, Sarbanes-Oxley Task Force); Trustee, American Tax Policy Institute; Regent, American College of Tax Counsel; Advisory Board, NYU Institute on Federal Taxation and 'Mergers and Acquisitions' magazine; Member, International Fiscal Association.
**Career:** Admitted to practice in California and District of Columbia. Chair, Corporate and International Tax Practice Groups.
**Personal:** BA, University of Washington, 1964; LLB, Columbia University School of Law, 1967. Law clerk, Judge Featherston, US Tax Court, 1967-68. Active Duty, US Army Judge Advocate General's Corps, 1968-72.

## OLSEN, Christine
O'Melveny & Myers LLP, Los Angeles
213 430 6073
colsen@omm.com
*Recommended in Banking & Finance*
**Practice Areas:** Christine Olsen has had wide practice experience in general corporate, banking and securities law matters. In particular, she has represented commercial and investment banks, insurance companies and commercial finance lenders in connection with commercial lending, structured financings, private placements, restructurings, subordinated debt, project financings, leveraged buyout financing, letter of credit support for commercial paper and tax-exempt securities, receivables purchase programs and underwriters in connection with the issuance of tax-exempt securities.

## OLSON, Karl
Levy, Ram & Olson, San Francisco
415 433 4949
*Recommended in Media & Entertainment*

## OLSON, Ronald
Munger, Tolles & Olson LLP, Los Angeles
213 683 9100
*Recommended in Litigation, Media & Entertainment*

## ONCIDI, Anthony J
Proskauer Rose LLP, Los Angeles
310 284 5690
aoncidi@proskauer.com
*Recommended in Employment*
**Practice Areas:** A Partner at Proskauer Rose, and the Chair of the Labor and Employment Department in the Los Angeles office. He represents employers in all aspects of labor relations and employment law, including litigation and preventive counseling, wrongful termination, employee discipline, Title VII and the California Fair Employment and Housing Act, wage and hour matters, personnel policies, sexual harassment training and investigations, workplace violence, drug testing and privacy issues, and trade secret protection. He has testified as an expert witness and is an advisor to the executive committee of the Labor and Employment Law Section of the State Bar of California. He has served as an Adjunct Professor of law at the University of Southern California Law School and a guest lecturer at the UCLA School of Law.
**Publications:** Author of the treatise entitled 'Employment Discrimination Depositions' (Juris Pub. 2005; www.jurispub.com) and, since 1990, has been a columnist for the official publication of the State Bar of California, The California Labor and Employment Law Review, and The Los Angeles Daily Journal.
**Personal:** University of Chicago Law School, JD, 1984. Pomona College, BA, cum laude, 1981; Phi Beta Kappa.

## O'NEAL, Stephen V

Thelen Reid & Priest LLP, San Francisco

*Recommended in Construction*

**Practice Areas:** Mr O'Neal is Chair of Thelen Reid & Priest LLP. His practice includes construction, real estate and complex business litigation and ADR. Mr O'Neal is recognized as one of the leading construction attorneys in the United States. His practice includes bench, jury trial and ADR representation of clients in complex civil litigation matters in the technology industry. He has extensive experience as well in real estate litigation matters, including bench and jury trials, ranging from land use and permit issues through commercial landlord-tenant problems, retail center purchase and sale litigation, owner-anchor tenant disputes and judicial foreclosure litigation.

**Prof. Memberships:** American Bar Association, Section of Litigation and the Forum Committee on the Construction Industry; Bar Association of San Francisco; Construction Industry Panel of Arbitrators, American Arbitration Association; Special Master, US District Court Northern District of California; California Bar Association, Real Property Law Section.

**Career:** Admitted to practice in the United States District Courts for the Northern and Eastern Districts of California and pro hac vice in the United States District Courts for the Eastern District of Missouri, Northern District of Georgia, and the District of Guam. Registered Foreign Lawyer in England and Wales.

**Publications:** Co-author: chapter on construction litigation, 'Business and Commercial Litigation in Federal Courts' (2005). Author: 'Use of Mechanic's Liens, Payment Bonds, Miller Act to Protect Rights', Contractor, February (1988); 'Accrual of Statutes of Limitations: California's Discovery Exceptions Swallow the Rule', 68 Cal. L. Rev. 106' (1980).

**Personal:** Received JD in 1980 from the University of California, Berkeley, Boalt Hall School of Law, where he was Associate Editor, 'California Law Review' and received AB in 1975 from the University of California, Los Angeles. Mr O'Neal was recognized as one of the leading construction attorneys in the United States in the 2003-04 Chambers USA Guide to America's Leading Business Lawyers.

## O'NEILL, Brian

Jones Day, Los Angeles

213 243 2856

boneill@jonesday.com

*Recommended in Litigation*

**Practice Areas:** A leading California and nationally recognized trial lawyer with extensive trial experience in civil and criminal cases in federal and state courts. He has substantial appellate experience, arguing cases in federal appeals courts and California appellate courts. Regularly

represents clients in grand jury and administrative investigations.

**Prof. Memberships:** Fellow of the American College of Trial Lawyers and the American Board of Criminal Lawyers. Served as a lawyer representative to the Ninth Circuit Judicial Conference.

**Publications:** Writes and lectures on civil and criminal litigation and related subjects. He has taught trial practice to lawyers and law students.

## O'NEILL, Edward

Davis Wright Tremaine LLP, San Francisco 415 276 6500

*Recommended in Energy*

## OTTENWELLER, Chris R

Orrick, Herrington & Sutcliffe LLP, Menlo Park 650 614 7454

cottenweller@orrick.com

*Recommended in Intellectual Property*

**Practice Areas:** Named one of top IP lawyers in California by leading legal publication. Focuses on patent, copyright, trademark, trade secret, unfair competition and internet litigation. Represents leading technology and Internet companies in trials and complex litigation, often involving multi-million dollar claims and cutting-edge legal issues. Tried many cases to judgment, in all types of forums, including jury trials, bench trials, arbitrations and adverse regulatory proceedings. Serves on Early Neutral Evaluation Panel for US District Court of the Northern District of California.

**Personal:** JD, Georgetown University, 1976; BA, University of Notre Dame, 1971.

## PACHULSKI, Isaac

Stutman, Treister & Glatt Professional Corporation, Los Angeles 310 228 5600

*Recommended in Bankruptcy*

## PACHULSKI, Richard

Pachulski, Stang, Ziehl, Young, Jones & Weintraub P.C., Los Angeles 310 277 6910

*Recommended in Bankruptcy*

## PAGE, Michael

Keker & Van Nest LLP, San Francisco 415 391 5400

mpage@kvn.com

*Recommended in Intellectual Property*

**Practice Areas:** Intellectual property litigation, with extensive experience in copyright, trade secret, trademark, and patent litigation. Recently, he received a CLAY Award (California Lawyer Attorney of the Year) for his success in obtaining a landmark decision in favor of his client Grokster in litigation against all of the major motion picture studios and record companies. That decision (currently on appeal to the United States Supreme Court) established the legality of peer-to-peer file sharing software. Significant intellectual property clients have included Google, Cadence Design Systems,

Nintendo, Electronic Arts, Sega, Intertrust, eBay, Nullsoft, Palm Computing, 3Com, Harris Corporation, Heartport, AOL, E-Loan, and Tegal Corporation.

**Prof. Memberships:** San Francisco Bay Area Intellectual Property Inns of Court; former Co-Chairman of the Litigation Section of the Barrister's Club.

**Career:** Law clerk to the Honorable Samuel Conti, United States District Court, Northern District of California; joined Keker & Van Nest, 1995; became Partner, 1999.

**Publications:** Co-author: 'Copyright Protection of Video Games in the United States: Galoob v. Nintendo', 14 European Intellectual Property Review, January 1992; 'Add-on Infringements: When Computer Add-Ons and Peripherals Should (And Should Not) Be Considered Infringing Derivative Works under Lewis Galoob Toys, Inc. v. Nintendo of America, Inc., and Other Recent Decisions', Vol. 15 No. 3 Hastings Communication and Entertainment Law Journal, 1993.

**Personal:** Boalt Hall School of Law, University of California (JD 1991); University of Pennsylvania (BA 1975).

## PAPARELLI, Angelo

Paparelli & Partners LLP, Irvine 949 955 5555

*Recommended in Immigration*

## PASAHOW, Lynn H

Fenwick & West LLP, Mountain View 650 335 7225

lpasahow@fenwick.com

*Recommended in Intellectual Property*

**Practice Areas:** Chair of firm's Litigation Group. Patent and other intellectual property litigation, counseling, licensing and mediation, principally relating to life sciences, software and Internet technologies. Led teams enforcing Amazon.com's 1-Click patent against Barnesandnoble.com, and winning jury verdict against du Pont enforcing Cetus' patents on Nobel Prize-winning polymerase chain reaction invention. Regularly represents University of California regarding such diverse inventions as FISH DNA detection, prion detection and elimination, transgenic organisms, medical lasers and strawberries.

**Prof. Memberships:** Director of Bay Area Bioscience Center, Alzheimer's Association of Northern California, and Boalt Hall Alumni Association. Member, advisory board of University of California's Berkeley Center for Law and Technology.

**Career:** Law clerk to Honorable AJ Zirpoli, United States District Court, Northern District of California. Co-instructor of 'A Life Scientist's Guide to Intellectual Property' at University of California, San Francisco. Regularly lectures about intellectual property law subjects to groups including Federal Judicial Center, Ameri-

can Association for the Advancement of Science, American Law Institute, Practising Law Institute, and Boalt School of Law. Included among intellectual property lawyers in The Best Lawyers in America.

**Personal:** University of California, Berkeley School of Law (Boalt Hall), JD, Order of the Coif, 1972 Stanford University, BA, Phi Beta Kappa, 1969.

## PASICH, Kirk A

Dickstein Shapiro Morin & Oshinsky LLP, Los Angeles 310 441 8461

PasichK@dsmo.com

*Recommended in Insurance*

**Practice Areas:** Represents insureds in complex coverage matters, including trial and appellate matters. Provides strategic insurance advice in business transactions. Substantial experience in all lines of insurance and industries, including the entertainment industry, and in resolving a wide range of disputes.

**Career:** Partner.

**Publications:** Author of Casualty and Liability Insurance (LexisNexis 2003) and more than 400 articles. Co-author and co-editor of The ABA Manual for Complex Insurance Coverage Litigation. Co-author of 'Directors and Officers: Liabilities and Protections' (Matthew Bender 2003).

## PASS, Brian J

Brown Raysman Millstein Felder & Steiner LLP, Los Angeles 310 712 8303

bpass@brownraysman.com

*Recommended in IT Outsourcing*

**Practice Areas:** Brian Pass focuses on high technology and general corporate law. He represents domestic and international clients in transactions involving new media and internet licensing, development and marketing; licensing, development and distribution of computer software and systems; content distribution; video games and online gaming; intellectual property and trade secret protection; e-commerce; interactive television and VOD. Mr Pass advises companies on internet privacy and new media and e-commerce regulatory issues. He counsels companies in venture capital finance, joint venture formation as well as mergers and acquisitions.

**Personal:** BA, Wesleyan University 1986, with high honors; JD, UCLA School of Law 1991.

## PASSMAN, Donald

Gang Tyre Ramer & Brown, Beverly Hills 310 777 4800

*Recommended in Media & Entertainment*

## PATTERSON, Thomas E

Klee, Tuchin, Bogdanoff & Stern LLP, Los Angeles 310 407 4035

tpatterson@ktbslaw.com

*Recommended in Bankruptcy*

**Practice Areas:** Is a member of Klee, Tuchin, Bogdanoff & Stern LLP. He has represented both debtors and creditors' committees in complex chapter 11 and out-of-court proceedings. He has represented hospital provider groups in most of the recent HMO insolvencies pending in California (including MedPartners Provider Network, Maxicare, Wattshealth, and Lifeguard) and has also been involved in most of the significant insurer insolvencies in California in the past 10 years. Recent debtor cases include All Star Gas, a multi-state propane retailer. Is a frequent speaker on bankruptcy and insolvency related topics.

**PEARL, Julie**
Pearl Law Group, San Francisco
415 771 7500
jpearl@immigrationlaw.com
*Recommended in Immigration*
**Practice Areas:** Business immigration law; global mobility.
**Prof. Memberships:** Academy of Business Immigration Lawyers, ABA, AILA.
**Career:** 1 Woman-Owned Law Firm in the Bay Area (S.F. Business Times, 2003-present). Co-founded by Julie and the former head of the INS (now USCIS), the firm pioneered award-winning technology and management tools for premier customer service. Former Deputy Attorney General for the State of California, Julie is listed as follows: International Who's Who of Business Immigration Attorneys, LawDragon 500 (top 1% of US Attorneys and Judges), Who's Who of American Women, and Who's Who in American Law. Other commendations are at www.immigrationlaw.com.

**PEDLAR, Alan**
Stutman, Treister & Glatt Professional Corporation, Los Angeles
310 228 5600
*Recommended in Bankruptcy*

**PEITZMAN, Lawrence**
Peitzman, Weg & Kempinsky LLP, Los Angeles 310 552 3100
*Recommended in Bankruptcy*

**PETERS, Elliot**
Keker & Van Nest LLP, San Francisco
415 391 5400
epeters@kvn.com
*Recommended in Litigation*
**Practice Areas:** Elliot Peters litigates all manner of complex civil and white-collar criminal cases. He has tried numerous criminal and civil cases in both state and federal courts. In commercial matters, Elliot represents investment companies in securities-related litigation, national law firms in professional liability defense, hig-tech companies in trade secret cases, and businesses and executives in employment and dissolution matters.
**Career:** Former law clerk to United States District Judge Whitman Knapp of the Southern District of New York (1985-

87); Assistant United States Attorney in the Southern District of New York (1987-91); received the Department of Justice Director's Medal For Superior Performance (1991); joined Keker & Van Nest in 1991, Partner since 1993. Named 'Attorney of the Year' in 2004 by California Lawyer Magazine; listed in Best Lawyers in America; named Northern California Super Lawyer by San Francisco Magazine (2004-05).
**Personal:** New York University School of Law (JD, 1985); Yale University (BA, cum laude, 1980).

**PETERS, Gerald**
Latham & Watkins LLP, San Francisco
415 391 0600
*Recommended in Healthcare*

**PETERS, William J**
O'Melveny & Myers LLP, Los Angeles
213 430 7598
wpeters@omm.com
*Recommended in Business Process Outsourcing, IT Outsourcing*
**Practice Areas:** Bill Peters has spent his entire career in the information technology and outsourcing industries, including serving as corporate counsel to a major information technology service provider, general counsel to a leading provider of outsourced human resources services, and as a Partner at O'Melveny & Myers. Bill represents and counsels clients on a wide-range of legal and business issues relating to complex technology and outsourcing transactions (many of them with international dimensions) involving clients in a broad range of industries, including the automotive, financial services, retail, logistics, distribution, aerospace, pharmaceutical, telecommunications, oil and gas, and electric utility industries.

**PETERSON JR, John M**
Baker & McKenzie, Palo Alto
650 856 5538
john.m.peterson@bakernet.com
*Recommended in Tax*
**Practice Areas:** John M Peterson Jr is a Partner in the Palo Alto office of Baker & McKenzie LLP. Mr Peterson joined Baker & McKenzie in 1977. He practices corporate tax law, with heavy emphasis on structuring of international operations, intercompany transfer pricing, international tax planning generally, high technology tax issues, and federal income tax controversies. Mr Peterson is currently the Chair of Baker & McKenzie's Global Tax Practice Group. He received his BBA in Accounting from the University of Notre Dame in 1973 and his JD Degree from Harvard Law School in 1977, graduating cum laude.

**PETRICH, Louis**
Leopold, Petrich & Smith PA, Los Angeles 310 277 3333
*Recommended in Media & Entertainment*

**PETROCELLI, Daniel**
O'Melveny & Myers LLP, Los Angeles
310 246 6850
dpetrocelli@omm.com
*Recommended in Litigation*
**Practice Areas:** Daniel Petrocelli, a Partner in O'Melveny & Myers' Century City office, has a national trial practice representing clients in major litigation in a wide variety of areas, including entertainment, intellectual property, unfair competition, business torts, securities, employment law, and criminal defense. Daniel is Chair of the firm's General Trial & Litigation Practice and is a frequent national commentator on trials and other legal issues, as well as a featured speaker on legal issues at business groups, bar and judges associations, and citizens groups.

**PHILLIPS, Bradley**
Munger, Tolles & Olson LLP, Los Angeles
213 683 9100
*Recommended in Antitrust*

**PHILLIPS, Lee**
Manatt Phelps & Phillips LLP, Los Angeles 310 312 4000
*Recommended in Media & Entertainment*

**PHILPOT, Susan**
Cooley Godward LLP, San Francisco
415 693 2000
*Recommended in Tax*

**PICKETT, Donn P**
Bingham McCutchen LLP, San Francisco
415 393 2082
donn.pickett@bingham.com
*Recommended in Antitrust*
**Practice Areas:** Serves as the firm's Vice Chairman. Has more than 25 years of experience as a corporate litigator, concentrating in antitrust, intellectual property and securities litigation. Developed particular experience in the defense of class actions. Successfully defended numerous major cases either to settlement or through trial. Is an accomplished jury trial attorney and has tried a large number of cases in federal and state courts. Counsels clients on antitrust issues, particularly on intellectual property rights, and represents them in negotiations and proceedings with regulatory agencies.
**Personal:** Yale Law School, JD, 1976; Carleton College, BA, magna cum laude, 1973.

**PIMSTONE, Gregory**
Manatt Phelps & Phillips LLP, Los Angeles 310 312 4000
*Recommended in Healthcare*

**PIRCHER, Leo**
Pircher, Nichols & Meeks, Los Angeles
310 201 8900
*Recommended in Real Estate*

**PITTS, Deborah A**
Duane Morris LLP, Los Angeles
213 689 7427
dapitts@duanemorris.com
*Recommended in Insurance*
**Practice Areas:** Deborah A Pitts practices in the areas of complex litigation, appeals and insurance coverage matters.
**Prof. Memberships:** American Bar Association - Task Force of the Committee on Insurance Coverage Litigation; Association of Business Trial Lawyers; Defense Research Institute; Trial Lawyers Association; Conference of Insurance Counsel - Appellate Advocacy Committee.
**Career:** Admitted to practice in California and New York.
**Publications:** Co-author of the ABA Manual for Complex Insurance Coverage Litigation.
**Personal:** University of California, Los Angeles School of Law, JD, 1979; University of California, Los Angeles, MBA, 1979; University of California, Los Angeles, BA, 1975.

**PLONSKER, Michael**
Alschuler Grossman Stein & Kahan LLP, Santa Monica 310 551 9185
mplonsker@agsk.com
*Recommended in Media & Entertainment*
**Practice Areas:** Co-chairs the firm's Entertainment and Media Department, one of the largest in the country emphasizing talent representation. Focuses on all aspects of the entertainment industry with an emphasis on talent representation, including idea submission, profit participation, trademark and copyright infringement, right of publicity, right of privacy, defamation, guild and labor commission, employment, and internet-related disputes.
**Prof. Memberships:** Member, Century City, Santa Monica, and American Bar Associations; State Bar of California.
**Career:** A Partner of Alschuler Grossman Stein & Kahan LLP. Named 'Entertainment Lawyer of the Year' by the Century City Bar Association in 2005. Recognized as one of 'The Best Lawyers in America'; speaker at various law schools (Harvard, Boalt Hall, USC), organizations, and bar associations; reported cases include Wood Newton v. Harry Thomason, 22 F.3d 1455 (9th Cir. 1994) (obtained summary judgment on behalf of Thomason in right of publicity claim regarding television series 'Evening Shade'); Playboy Enterprises, Inc. v. Terry Welles, 7 F.Supp.2d 1098 (S.D. Cal. 1998) (represented Welles in defeating a preliminary injunction application in one of the first trademark infringement actions

relating to the internet); Charles P Caudle v. Harry Thomason, 992 F.Supp. 1 (D.D.C. 1997) (obtained summary judgment on behalf of Thomason in a case arising from the White House Travel Office matter); Sean Hayes v. Vanguard Management (Labor Commission proceeding; on behalf of Hayes prevailed in a talent agency dispute, later obtaining summary judgment); Rosa Blasi v. Marathon Entertainment (on behalf of Blasi prevailed in a talent agency dispute, later obtaining summary judgment); Sugar Ray Leonard (Labor Commissioner proceeding, prevailed on behalf of Leonard).
**Personal:** Serves on the Board of the Friends of the Los Angeles Free Clinic. University of Michigan (BBA in accounting, 1978); University of Illinois (JD, 1981).

### POMERANTZ, Glenn
Munger, Tolles & Olson LLP, Los Angeles
213 683 9100
*Recommended in Antitrust, Media & Entertainment*

### POOLEY, James
Pooley & Oliver, Palo Alto
650 739 7045
jpooley@pooleyoliver.com
*Recommended in Intellectual Property*
**Practice Areas:** Specializes in the litigation and trial of patent, trade secret, copyright, and technology-related commercial litigation, in state and federal courts, and before the International Trade Commission.
**Prof. Memberships:** Director and Officer: AIPLA, National Inventors Hall of Fame. Also, incoming President (2007), AIPLA. Listed, Guide to the World's Leading Patent Law Experts.
**Career:** Admitted to practice in California. Named a 'Lawyer of the Year', California Lawyer Magazine 2003, for record settlement achieved on behalf of ESS Technology in a software copyright case.
**Personal:** BA, Lafayette College, 1970; JD, Harlan Fiske Stone Scholar, Columbia School of Law, 1973.

### POONJA, Zaitun
Morgan, Lewis & Bockius LLP, Palo Alto
650 843 7540
zpoonja@morganlewis.com
*Recommended in Employment*
**Practice Areas:** Zaitun Poonja is a Partner in the Employee Benefits/Executive Compensation Practice. Ms Poonja specializes in domestic and foreign equity compensation programs for public and private companies. Her expertise includes US tax, securities and financial accounting implications of such programs as well as foreign tax, securities, exchange control, labor law, data privacy and other legal implications related to the use of equity programs in foreign jurisdictions. She also provides counseling with respect to section 16 reporting, corporate gover-

nance, equity compensation issues related to mergers and acquisitions, parachute tax issues and analysis, nonqualified deferred compensation programs, employment agreements and change in control benefit and severance programs.

### POPOFSKY, Laurence
Heller Ehrman LLP, San Francisco
415 772 6310
larry.popofsky@hellerehrman.com
*Recommended in Antitrust, Litigation*
**Practice Areas:** Antitrust and trade regulation; appeals and strategy; securities litigation; corporate governance.
**Prof. Memberships:** American Bar Association; State Bar of California; Bar Association of San Francisco; Fellow, American College of Trial Lawyers; American Bar Foundation; Bureau of National Affairs; California Historical Society.
**Career:** Mr Popofsky has participated in a variety of antitrust, securities fraud and intellectual property matters. He has argued two cases in the US Supreme Court, a half dozen in the California Supreme Court and approximately 70 others in various appellate courts.
**Personal:** Harvard Law School (LLB, cum laude, 1962).

### PORTERFIELD, Curtis
Howrey LLP, Los Angeles
213 892 1800
*Recommended in Insurance*

### POTTER, John
Quinn Emanuel Urquhart Oliver & Hedges, LLP, San Francisco
415 875 6600
johnpotter@quinnemanuel.com
*Recommended in Litigation*
**Practice Areas:** Mr Potter handles complex civil litigation, SEC enforcement proceedings, white-collar criminal defense, and internal investigations. Successfully defends corporations, officers, directors, and employees in state and federal courts against civil and criminal allegations involving securities fraud, healthcare fraud, anitrust violations, False Claims Act, government contract fraud, environmental crimes, money laundering, customs fraud, and public corruption.
**Career:** Assistant United States Attorney in Los Angeles. Received professional commendations from the DOJ, FBI, IRS, Department of Defense, and US Customs Service.
**Personal:** Georgetown University, (JD, 1986, cum laude; BA, 1983)

### POWERS, Matthew D
Weil, Gotshal & Manges LLP, Redwood Shores 650 802 3200
matthew.powers@weil.com
*Recommended in Intellectual Property*
**Practice Areas:** Matthew Powers is the Head of Weil Gotshal's Patent Litigation Practice and specializes in patent and

trade secret cases. He has successfully litigated cases all over the world, and has deep expertise in a range of technologies, including semiconductor devices, manufacturing equipment and processes, DNA sequencing and other biotechnologies, computer hardware and software, telecommunications and the internet. With an unparalleled record for taking bet-the-company cases to trial and winning, his counsel is regularly sought by clients such as Intel, Microsoft, Cisco, Oracle, Applera and Samsung.
**Personal:** Northwestern University, BS, 1979; Harvard Law School, JD, 1982.

### PREOVOLOS, Penelope A
Morrison & Foerster LLP, San Francisco
415 268 7187
ppreovolos@mofo.com
*Recommended in Antitrust*
**Practice Areas:** Has extensive experience in antitrust, consumer class actions, and false advertising/ unfair trade practice litigation and counseling. Has served as lead counsel in numerous antitrust, false advertising and unfair competition cases, as well as in major consumer class action cases.
**Prof. Memberships:** Chair, 1994-95, Secretary, 1993-94, California State Bar Antitrust Section. Member, Litigation and Antitrust Sections, American Bar Association.
**Career:** Admitted to practice in California. Co-Chair, Antitrust, Marketing and Distribution Practice Group 1990-2004.
**Personal:** AB, greatest distinction, University of California, Berkeley, 1976, Phi Beta Kappa, University Medal, English Departmental Citation; JD, cum laude, Harvard Law School, 1979, Executive Editor, Civil Liberties Law Review, 1978-79. Law clerk, Honorable Charles M Merrill, US Court of Appeals, Ninth Circuit (1979-80).

### PRETTY, Laurence
Hogan & Hartson LLP, Los Angeles
213 337 6812
LHPretty@hhlaw.com
*Recommended in Intellectual Property*
**Practice Areas:** Patent litigation and practice.
**Prof. Memberships:** Former Chair, IP Section, California State Bar; Director, AIPLA; Co-Chair, annual patent litigation program, PLI 1988-2004.
**Career:** First Chair in numerous bench and jury trials of patent lawsuits; former law clerk, US Court of Appeals for the Federal Circuit; court-appointed mediator and arbitrator in disputed patent matters; adjunct lecturer in patent law at the UCLA Law School.
**Publications:** Editor/co-author, 'Patent Litigation', PLI; author, 'Going for a Preliminary Injunction', I.P. Litigator, 2006.
**Personal:** Best Lawyers in America, 1993-2006; LA Magazine Southern California 'Super Lawyer', 2005; Southern

California Super Lawyers 'Super Lawyer', 2005.

### PRINGLE, Robert B
Thelen Reid & Priest LLP, San Francisco
415 371 1200
rbpringle@thelenreid.com
*Recommended in Antitrust*
**Practice Areas:** Mr Pringle's practice includes antitrust, unfair competition, securities and complex business litigation before federal and state courts and administrative tribunals. He has been active in criminal grand jury matters, contested mergers, and a variety of civil litigation, including trade secrets and other intellectual property claims, contract disputes, fraud and RICO claims. He has also acted as counsel to corporate boards of directors and as special litigation counsel to corporate boards of directors in shareholder derivative actions. Mr Pringle has been called upon to act as counsel for a number of Fortune 200 and Global 500 companies, both in the United States and abroad. Recent matters have included lead counsel in a worldwide cartel criminal investigation and follow-on class action litigation, lead counsel in a securities class action litigation, special litigation counsel to the Board of Directors of a major software company, lead counsel in the defense of litigation brought by the Attorney General of California against a major utility under Section 7 of the Clayton Act, representation of a major supermarket chain in defense of a litigation brought by the Attorney General of California arising out of the acquisition of generation assets in California, and representation of a party relating to the Enron grand jury matters.
**Prof. Memberships:** State Bar of California, Unfair Competition and Antitrust Section, Executive Committee American Bar Association, Section of Public Utility, Communications and Transportation Law (Vice-Chair, Antitrust Committee); Antitrust Section (Member, Civil Practice and Procedure Committee; Chair, 1992 Annual Meeting); Litigation Section (Member, Federal Practice Taskforce); Board of Visitors (Honorary Lifetime Member), Duke University School of Law; Standing Committee on Professional Conduct, US District Court for the Northern District of California Bar Association of the City of San Francisco.
**Career:** Partner of Thelen Reid & Priest LLP. Currently firm-wide head of the Antitrust and Competition Practice Group and participates in the oversight of the firm's commercial litigation practice.
**Publications:** Co-author of Program Materials and Panelist in the Following Recent Programs: State Bar of California Golden State Antitrust and Trade Regulation Institute, San Francisco, California; State Bar of California Golden State

Antitrust and Trade Regulation Institute, Los Angeles, California, 'Intellectual Property and Antitrust: Litigation of Antitrust Cases Involving Intellectual Property'; Conference Board Annual Antitrust Program, New York City: 'Litigation Complex Antitrust Litigations and the Recent Amendments to the Federal Rules of Civil Procedure'; Price Waterhouse Annual Intellectual Property Conference, Phoenix, Arizona, 'Antitrust and Intellectual Property in the 1990s'; 'High Tech or Low Tech - Presentation of Complex Evidence to a Jury', ABA Annual Meeting (San Francisco); 'Technology and the Business Litigator', State Bar Section Institute (Monterey, CA); Prentice Hall Annual Intellectual Property Conference, San Francisco, CA, 'Cross Examination of a Technical Expert in a Patent Litigation'; 'The 100 Days After Receipt of the Complaint, The 100 Days Before Trial' (ABA Annual Meeting, Atlanta, GA); 'The Use of Experts at Trial in High Technology Cases' (ABA Litigation Section Fall Meeting, San Francisco, CA); 'Technology Licensing and Litigation' (PLI - San Francisco, CA); 'Contesting Computer Disputes' (Harcourt Brace - Washington, DC).
**Personal:** Graduate of Duke University School of Law, JD (1969); Graduate of University of North Carolina at Chapel Hill, BS (1966); Best Lawyers in the United States; Who's Who in America; Who's Who in American Law; Super Lawyer, San Francisco Magazine; Who's Who in American Law; Who's Who in the United States; Previous Employment: law clerk to the Honorable Oliver D Hamlin, Judge, US Court of Appeals for the Ninth Circuit, San Francisco, CA; Assistant Professor, Penn State University, University Park, PA.

### PRUETZ, Adrian
Quinn Emanuel Urquhart Oliver & Hedges, LLP, Los Angeles
213 443 3000
adrianpruetz@quinnemanuel.com
*Recommended in Intellectual Property*
**Practice Areas:** Adrian Pruetz, Co-Chair of Quinn Emanuel's Intellectual Property Litigation Practice. Ms Pruetz concentrates her civil trial practice in the areas of patent, trademark, copyright, trade secret, antitrust and complex commercial matters.
**Career:** Ms Pruetz has tried more than 25 jury cases and argued more than 15 appeals. She has been named one of the top 25 intellectual property lawyers in California and one of the state's most influential trial lawyers by The Daily Journal, a 'Super Lawyer' by the Los Angeles Magazine and one of five 'highly recommended intellectual property practitioners in Los Angeles' by Global Counsel.
**Personal:** Marquette University Law School (JD magna cum laude, 1982);

Loyola Graduate School of Business (1972-73); Loyola University of Chicago (BA, 1972); University of Wisconsin (1966-69).

### QUINN, John
Arnold & Porter LLP, Los Angeles
213 243 4080
John.J.Quinn@aporter.com
*Recommended in Litigation*
**Practice Areas:** Specializes in complex litigation.
**Prof. Memberships:** Mr Quinn is a Member of the American Board of Trial Advocates, and since 1977 has been a Fellow of the American College of Trial Lawyers.
**Career:** He is a former President of the Los Angeles County Bar Association and the recipient of the Association's highest honor, the Shattuck-Price Award, for outstanding achievement in the practice of law. He has also received the Learned Hand Award from the American Jewish Committee, the Distinguished Service Award presented by the United States Courts of the Ninth Circuit and the Legal Hero Award from the Pepperdine University School of Law.
**Personal:** He is a 1959 graduate of the University of Southern California Law Center, where he was a member of the Editorial Board of the Law Review and received the Order of the Coif.

### QUINN, John B
Quinn Emanuel Urquhart Oliver & Hedges, LLP, Los Angeles
213 443 3000
johnquinn@quinnemanuel.com
*Recommended in Intellectual Property, Litigation, Media & Entertainment*
**Practice Areas:** Managing Partner, Quinn Emanuel Urquhart Oliver & Hedges, LLP. Practice areas include general trial practice, intellectual property litigation, antirust and unfair competition litigation, banking and financial institution litigation, real estate litigation, entertainment litigation, securities and class action litigation. Practices in all areas of business litigation.
**Prof. Memberships:** Lecturer, J Reuben Clark School of Law, Brigham Young University, 1977. Lecturer on Federal Practice, California Continuing Education of the Bar. Member, Los Angeles County Bar Association. Member, Federal Courts and Practices Committee. Member, American Bar Association. Member, Forum Committees on: Health Law; Construction Industry. Member, Sections on: Corporations; Public Contract Law; Banking and Business Law; Litigation; Patent, Trademark and Copyright Law. Member, The State Bar of California. Member, Committee on Federal Courts. Member, The State Bar of New York. Member, Million Dollar Advocates Forum. Director, Rose Bowl Operating Company. General Counsel, Academy of

Motion Picture Arts and Sciences, 1987-present.
**Career:** Notable litigation resolutions: won an $295 million verdict against Bertelsmann and its former CEO on breach of contract and other claims arising out of formation of the AOL Europe joint venture. Lead trial lawyer for General Motors in its lawsuit in federal court in Detroit against Volkswagen arising out of the departure of Ignacio Lopez. General Motors received $1.1 billion in settlement. Won an $80 million verdict on behalf of Avery Dennison in breach of trade secrets and RICO case in federal court in Cleveland. Won a defense verdict after a three-month jury trial in action arising out of the sale of a subsidiary of a major defense contractor in which $20 million was at issue. Obtained a defense verdict after a two-month jury trial on behalf of a Fortune 200 company in a trade secret and unfair competition action brought by its major competitor. Obtained a jury verdict for a hospital management company in a race discrimination suit in what was the longest employment trial in California history after plaintiff rejected a $1 million settlement offer. Obtained a defense verdict for an aerospace company in a whistleblower suit after a two-month jury trial. Obtained a defense verdict for an entertainment company in a highly publicized sexual harassment suit. Was successful lead defense trial lawyer for an aerospace company in the retrial of a tortious interference suit in which the plaintiff had won $15 million in the previous trial and had rejected a $1 million settlement offer before the second trial. Obtained summary judgment on behalf of an aerospace company in an action for breach of an alleged joint venture agreement. Obtained dismissal of idea theft against major film and television studio in middle of trial; $54 million verdict subsequently entered against remaining defendants.
**Personal:** Harvard Law School (JD, 1976). Editor, Harvard Law Review, 1974-76. Claremont Men's College (BA, magna cum laude, 1973). Since 1987, Mr Quinn has been General Counsel of the Academy of Motion Picture Arts and Sciences. Finisher, Ironman Triathlon World Championship, Kailua Kona, Hawaii, 1999 and 2004.

### RABINOVITZ, Joel
Irell & Manella LLP, Los Angeles
310 277 1010
*Recommended in Tax*

### RADCLIFFE, Mark F
DLA Piper Rudnick Gray Cary US LLP, Palo Alto 650 833 2266
mark.radcliffe@dlapiper.com
*Recommended in IT Outsourcing*
**Practice Areas:** Banking and finance; outsourcing.
**Career:** He concentrates in strategic

intellectual property advice; private financing; corporate partnering; software licensing; internet licensing; and copyrights and trademark.
**Personal:** JD, Harvard University; BS, University of Michigan.

### RAMER, Bruce
Gang Tyre Ramer & Brown, Beverly Hills
310 777 4800
*Recommended in Media & Entertainment*

### RANDALL, Jeff G
Skadden, Arps, Slate, Meagher & Flom LLP & Affiliates, Palo Alto
650 470 4580
jrandall@skadden.com
*Recommended in Intellectual Property*
**Practice Areas:** Successfully defended numerous companies in multi-billion dollar intellectual property cases and served as lead counsel in significant patent cases throughout the country. He has represented Intel Corporation, Qualcomm, Dell Computer, Genentech, eBay, Applied Materials, Sun Microsystems, Apple Computer Inc., Autodesk, Inc., Cadence Design Systems, Kaufman & Broad Co., Cisco Systems, Genencor, McKesson Corporation, and PayPal. He has argued over 20 Markman hearings, tried more than 30 jury trials, and was recently named one of "California's Top 30 IP Attorneys" by the Daily Journal.
**Career:** JD, University of California, Hastings College of Law, 1987; BS, University of Oregon, 1984.

### RE, Donald
Donald M Re, Los Angeles
*Recommended in Litigation*

### REAMER, David C
Skadden, Arps, Slate, Meagher & Flom LLP & Affiliates, Los Angeles
213 687 5052
dreamer@skadden.com
*Recommended in Banking & Finance*
**Practice Areas:** A member of the firm's Banking and Institutional Investing Group. Has participated in numerous financing transactions, representing lenders, investors, borrowers and equity sponsors in a wide range of transactions encompassing a diversity of industries, including media, telecommunications, real estate, gaming, energy and manufacturing. Such transactions have included secured lending transactions, acquisition financings, high-yield offerings, bridge financings, restructurings and project financings.
**Career:** JD, Columbia University School of Law, 1989 (Harlan Fiske Stone Scholar); BA, Emory University, 1985.

### REDING, John A
Paul, Hastings, Janofsky & Walker LLP, San Francisco 415 856 7004
jackreding@paulhastings.com
*Recommended in Litigation*
**Practice Areas:** Has successfully served

as lead trial and appellate counsel in hundreds of complex litigation matters, across diverse practice areas, including: securities fraud, commercial, constitutional, antitrust, class action, intellectual property, environmental, toxic, products liability, and mass tort claims.

**Prof. Memberships:** Member of the American Bar Association, the State Bar of California, the Bar Association of San Francisco, and serves or has served as the Chair or on the Executive Committee of various national, state and local bar and trial organizations, including the Bar's Federal Courts Committee.

**Career:** 1997 - present, Partner, Paul, Hastings, Janofosky & Walker LLP and immediate past-Chair of the firm-wide Litigation Department; 1975-97, Member, Crosby, Heafey, Roach and May; admitted to practice before all the federal and state courts in California, the United States Claims Court, and the United States Supreme Court.

**Publications:** A frequent lecturer/speaker in his areas of expertise and experience and has published in those areas, for example, 'Securities Law Claims: A Practical Guide', John A Reding, ed, Oceana Publications, 2004.

**Personal:** Received his AB from the University of California at Berkeley and his JD Degree from Boalt Hall School of Law, University of California at Berkeley.

## REIMER, Eric R
McDermott Will & Emery, Los Angeles
310 551 9358
ereimer@mwe.com
*Recommended in Banking & Finance*
**Practice Areas:** Vice-Chair of McDermott's Finance Practice and Head of Project Finance Practice. Practice includes representation of borrowers, issuers and lenders in front end lending transactions, bridge facilities, acquisition facilities, debt issuances and restructurings, including the financing of debtors in bankruptcy, ranging from low middle market asset-based transactions to investment grade syndicated financings to private bank, high net worth individual financings, leveraged leases and project financings, with particular experience in healthcare, retail equipment and transportation.
**Personal:** University of California Hastings College of Law (JD); University of Southern California (BS).

## REINES, Edward R
Weil, Gotshal & Manges LLP,
Redwood Shores 650 802 3022
edward.reines@weil.com
*Recommended in Intellectual Property*
**Practice Areas:** Edward Reines is a Partner in Weil Gotshal's Patent Litigation Practice, and has extensive experience handling complex patent cases involving a range of technologies. Mr Reines is Vice President of the Federal Circuit Bar Association and serves on its Board of Governors, and teaches the patent litigation course at the University of California, Berkeley's Boalt Hall School of Law. Mr Reines is also a frequent speaker at national conferences on intellectual property law and writes on patent law developments.
**Personal:** SUNY Albany, BS, 1985; Columbia University School of Law, JD, 1988.

## REISNER, Jeffrey
Irell & Manella LLP, Newport Beach
949 760 0991
*Recommended in Bankruptcy*

## RESSLER, Alison S
Sullivan & Cromwell LLP, Los Angeles
310 712 6600
resslera@sullcrom.com
*Recommended in Capital Markets, Corporate/M&A*
**Practice Areas:** Broad experience in M&A, private equity, corporate governance and corporate finance in regulated and unregulated industries. Recent M&A transactions: Hilton Hotels Corporation-Hilton Group hotels business; Novartis-Chiron (pending); Occidental Petroleum-Vintage Petroleum; Wachovia-Westcorp (pending); Ares/Ontario Teachers-Serta Bedding; and Cerberus/Talecris Holdings-Bayer worldwide plasma unit. Handles complex transactions involving acquisition financing, high-yield offerings, debt/equity securities offerings for REITS, rights offerings, convertible/exchangeable securities offerings and IPOs.
**Prof. Memberships:** ABA; CSBA; LACBA.
**Career:** Partner since 1991. Member, Management Committee; Co-Head, Private Equity Group.
**Personal:** Columbia Law School (JD, 1983); Brown University (BA, 1980).

## RISHWAIN, James
Pillsbury Winthrop Shaw Pittman LLP,
Los Angeles 310 203 1111
jrishwain@pillsburylaw.com
*Recommended in Real Estate*
**Practice Areas:** Mr Rishwain is co-leader of the firm's national Real Estate Practice. He has extensive real estate transactional experience with emphasis in acquisitions, development, finance, leasing, capital markets and REITs, involving office, retail, hotel, public facilities and infrastructure and single family and multifamily projects. He has been honored in many ways including receiving in 2005 'California Lawyer' Attorneys of the Year Award. He has published several articles including 'When A Lender Becomes An Owner, Builder & Developer' (February 2005).
**Personal:** JD, Pepperdine, 1984, cum laude, Moot Court Honor Board, Note Comment Editor Pepperdine Law Review; BA, UCLA, 1981, honors.

## RIZZI, Robert
O'Melveny & Myers LLP, Washington, DC
202 383 5300
*Recommended in Tax*

## RODRIGUEZ, Denise Rios
Foley & Lardner LLP, Los Angeles
310 975 7798
drodriguez@foley.com
*Recommended in Healthcare*
**Career:** Denise Rios Rodriguez is a Partner in the Los Angeles office of Foley & Lardner LLP. A member of the firm's Health Care Industry Team, Ms Rodriguez focuses her practice on payment issues arising under government programs such as Medicare and Medicaid. She represents public and private healthcare providers in administrative hearings, as well as in state and federal courts. Ms Rodriguez is former Co-Chair of the Payments/Compliance Practice Group. She is a graduate of the University of Michigan Law School.

## ROMÁN, Marissa J
Akin Gump Strauss Hauer & Feld LLP,
Los Angeles 310 552 6408
mroman@akingump.com
*Recommended in Media & Entertainment*
**Practice Areas:** Marissa J Román concentrates on media finance and other entertainment transactions. She represents domestic and foreign financial institutions, borrowers, distributors and others involved in various aspects of the financing, distribution and production of film and television projects, including multinational tax and co-production arrangements.
**Prof. Memberships:** Co-Chair, Entertainment Law Section, Beverly Hills Bar Association.
**Personal:** AB, Art History, Princeton University; JD, Stanford Law School. Named as a Southern California 'Super Lawyer' in arts and entertainment (2004 and 2006) and as a leading US media attorney in Euromoney's 2005 'Guide to the World's Leading Technology, Media & Telecommunications Lawyers'.

## ROOT JR, George L
Foley & Lardner LLP, San Diego
619 685 6412
groot@foley.com
*Recommended in Healthcare*
**Career:** George L Root Jr is the leader of the Regulated Industries Department for Foley & Lardner LLP. He is a member of the firm's Management Committee and former Managing Partner of the firm's San Diego office. He practices in the Health Care Industry Team and the Health Care Finance and Restructuring Group. Mr Root represents healthcare providers, especially in the formation of integrated delivery systems, nonprofit organizations, healthcare districts, medical staff relations, mental health law, provider relationships with third-party payors and implementation of prepaid health plans. He graduated from the University of San Diego School of Law.

## ROSATI, Mario
Wilson Sonsini Goodrich & Rosati,
Palo Alto 650 493 9300
mrosati@wsgr.com
*Recommended in Corporate/M&A*
**Practice Areas:** Corporate law and governance, corporate finance and M&A for high technology and life sciences companies.
**Prof. Memberships:** Admitted to practice in California.
**Career:** Joined WSGR, 1971; became Partner, 1975. Member, WSGR Executive Management Committee and Policy Committee. Adjunct Professor, Haas School of Business, University of California (Berkeley). Serves on Board of Advisors for the Lester Center for Entrepreneurship and Innovation.
**Personal:** JD, Boalt Hall, University of California (Berkeley), 1971. Recipient of Am Jur Award (Corporations). BA, University of California (Los Angeles), 1968.

## ROSE, Stephen
Munger, Tolles & Olson LLP, Los Angeles
213 683 9100
*Recommended in Tax*

## ROSEGAY, Margaret
Pillsbury Winthrop Shaw Pittman LLP,
San Francisco 415 983 1305
Margaret.Rosegay@pillsburylaw.com
*Recommended in Environment*
**Practice Areas:** Ms Rosegay's practice focuses on the regulation of solid and hazardous waste and water quality, including NPDES permitting, TMDLs, industrial discharges, waste discharges to land, and soil and groundwater contamination, with particular expertise in interrelationships between federal, state and local laws. She represents a broad spectrum of companies engaged in petroleum refining, chemical and heavy manufacturing, forest products, scrap metal recycling, electricity generation and other forms of energy production and commercial redevelopment.
**Personal:** JD, University of Colorado School of Law 1980; clerk, Colorado Court of Appeals, 1980-81.

## ROSEN, Peter
Latham & Watkins LLP, Los Angeles
213 485 1234
*Recommended in Insurance*

## ROSENBAUM, Gary B
DLA Piper Rudnick Gray Cary US LLP,
Los Angeles 310 595 3142
gary.rosenbaum@dlapiper.com
*Recommended in Banking & Finance*
**Practice Areas:** Finance, private equity, financial restructuring and bankruptcy
**Career:** Gary Rosenbaum concentrates in commercial and corporate finance, private equity and mezzanine investments, workouts and restructurings, ven-

ture lending and leasing, and other commercial transactions. Extensive experience serving as lead counsel for various financial institutions on leveraged finance tranactions, including senior and subordinated loans, debtor-in-possession financings, acquisition financings, and troubled loan negotiations and workouts, as well as representing borrowers in secured loan transactions, creditors and debtors in chapter 11 cases, and buyers and sellers of distressed companies.
**Personal:** JD, UCLA School of Law; BA, Northwestern University.

### ROSENFELD, Robert
Heller Ehrman LLP, San Francisco
415 772 6609
bob.rosenfeld@hellerehrman.com
*Recommended in Antitrust*

**Practice Areas:** Antitrust and trade regulation; consumer litigation; appeals and strategy; Asia; international arbitration and ADR.
**Prof. Memberships:** American Bar Association; State Bar of California; Fellow, American Bar Foundation; Pacific Council on International Policy; California Pacific Medical Center.
**Career:** Mr Rosenfeld has an antitrust practice. For the last six years, he has led the firm's representation of Microsoft Corporation in numerous cases filed in California and across the United States and abroad.
**Personal:** George Washington University (BA, Public Affairs, highest distinction, 1971); Oxford University (BA, First Class Honours, 1973), Rhodes Scholar; Harvard Law School (JD, cum laude, 1976).

### RUBALCAVA, Sharon
Weston Benshoof Rochefort Rubalcava MacCuish LLP, Los Angeles
213 576 1105
srubalcava@wbcounsel.com
*Recommended in Environment*

**Practice Areas:** Partner, Environmental Strategy and Litigation Department. Ms Rubalcava focuses on air and water quality, toxic emissions, and permitting of major industrial and infrastructure projects. Her practice includes counseling on rulemaking, compliance, permitting, and enforcement actions before a variety of environmental agencies. Ms Rubalcava was appointed by the Mayor of Los Angeles to the No Net Increase Task Force to reduce emissions from the Port of Los Angeles.
**Career:** Past Chair, Air Quality Committee, ABA Section on Natural Resources, Energy and Environmental Law.
**Personal:** JD, University of California, Los Angeles, 1975; AB, University of California, Los Angeles, 1968.

### RUBY, Allen
Ruby & Schofield, San José
408 998 8500
*Recommended in Litigation*

### RUCK, Charles
Latham & Watkins LLP, Costa Mesa
714 540 1235
*Recommended in Corporate/M&A*

### RUST, Neil
White & Case LLP, Los Angeles
213 620 7748
nrust@whitecase.com
*Recommended in Banking & Finance*

**Practice Areas:** Has a broad transactional practice that emphasizes bank finance, corporate finance and M&A. Although he has a broad finance practice, representing agent banks and arrangers in secured and unsecured credit facilities, is best known for expertise in credit and liquidity support facilities for governmental issuers. Heads the LA office Corporate Practice.

### RUTHBERG, Miles
Latham & Watkins LLP, Los Angeles
213 485 1234
*Recommended in Litigation*

### RUTTER, Paul
Gilchrist & Rutter Professional Corporation, Santa Monica
310 393 4000
*Recommended in Real Estate*

### SACKS, Robert A
Sullivan & Cromwell LLP, Los Angeles
310 712 6640
sacksr@sullcrom.com
*Recommended in Litigation*

**Practice Areas:** Extensive experience in a wide range of complex business disputes. Defends and advises clients in securities, M&A, antitrust, intellectual property, and class action litigation; board of director obligations; and SEC and internal corporate investigations. Appears in federal and state courts throughout California and elsewhere, in administrative proceedings before the SEC and other agencies, and in arbitrations and other types of private dispute resolution proceedings.
**Prof. Memberships:** ABA; LACBA; BHBA.
**Career:** Partner since 1990.
**Personal:** University of Texas Law School (JD, 1982); Harvard University (AB, 1979).

### SAGER, Kelli
Davis Wright Tremaine LLP, Los Angeles
213 633 6800
*Recommended in Media & Entertainment*

### SAGGESE, Nicholas P
Skadden, Arps, Slate, Meagher & Flom LLP & Affiliates, Los Angeles
213 687 5550
nsaggese@skadden.com
*Recommended in Capital Markets, Corporate/M&A*

**Practice Areas:** Has been involved with numerous mergers and acquisitions, securities offerings and corporate restructurings. Examples of recent transactions include: the sale of DreamWorks SKG Inc.; the acquisition of MGM; and UnitedGlobalCom, Inc.'s acquisition of the minority shares of UGC Europe.
**Prof. Memberships:** Board member for LA Regional Foodbank and Member, Board of Overseers, Loyola Law School
**Career:** JD, Loyola Law School of Los Angeles, 1980 (cum laude; Member, Loyola Law Review, St Thomas More Law Honor Society); MBA, University of California at Los Angeles, 1973 (Beta Gamma Sigma Honor Society); BA, University of California at Los Angeles, 1969.

### SAMEL, Charles
Latham & Watkins LLP, Los Angeles
213 485 1234
*Recommended in Antitrust*

### SAMUELS, Mark A
O'Melveny & Myers LLP, Los Angeles
213 430 6340
msamuels@omm.com
*Recommended in Intellectual Property*

**Practice Areas:** Mark Samuels serves as Chair of O'Melveny & Myers' 70-lawyer Intellectual Property and Technology Practice and has broad experience in complex patent, trade secret, antitrust, and other technology-based litigation. Mark's recent representations have included electronics, chemical, consumer products, integrated circuit, and software companies in patent infringement litigation in courts nationwide and before the US International Trade Commission. He also specializes in cases at the intersection of antitrust and intellectual property law, having tried antitrust claims involving technology markets on behalf of both plaintiffs and defendants.
**Prof. Memberships:** American Intellectual Property Law Association, Los Angeles Intellectual Property Law Association.

### SANCHEZ, Carl R
Paul, Hastings, Janofsky & Walker LLP, San Diego 858 720 2810
carlsanchez@paulhastings.com
*Recommended in Corporate/M&A*

**Practice Areas:** Mr Carl R Sanchez is a Partner in the firm's Corporate Department and is the Chair of the firm's Global Mergers and Acquisitions Practice Group. Mr Sanchez's practice is focused exclusively in the area of mergers and acquisitions, where he represents public and private companies in a wide variety of strategic transactions. Mr Sanchez has represented numerous companies in the life sciences, biotechnology, medical device, semiconductor, software, computer hardware, information technology, telecommunications and financial services industries. Mr Sanchez is a frequent lecturer and speaker on M&A topics across the country.

### SANCHEZ, Terry
Munger, Tolles & Olson LLP, Los Angeles
213 683 9100
*Recommended in Employment*

### SANDERS, Joel S
Gibson, Dunn & Crutcher LLP, San Francisco
415 393 8268
jsanders@gibsondunn.com
*Recommended in Antitrust*

**Practice Areas:** Antitrust and other complex business litigation. Handles matters involving federal and state antitrust laws and unfair competition in courts and before government agencies. Antitrust work includes mergers, government investigations, and private and class action litigation. Has handled matters in a wide variety of industries, including high technology, retail, telecommunications, consumer services, manufacturing, and professional services.
**Career:** Former law clerk, Honorable Procter Hug Jr of the US Court of Appeals for the Ninth Circuit; former trial attorney in the San Francisco office of the US Department of Justice's Antitrust Division. Member of the Antitrust Sections of various Bar associations.

### SAPER, Jeff
Wilson Sonsini Goodrich & Rosati, Palo Alto 650 493 9300
jsaper@wsgr.com
*Recommended in Capital Markets, Corporate/M&A*

**Practice Areas:** Vice-Chairman of WSGR. Specializes in corporate law and governance, public/private financings of high technology, telecommunications and retail and consumer products companies; corporate partnership transactions; representation of investment banks and corporate issuers in connection with public offerings, mergers and acquisitions.
**Prof. Memberships:** Admitted to practice in New York and California.
**Career:** Joined WSGR as Partner, 1980. Member, WSGR, Executive Management Committee and Policy Committee. Involved in more than 200 public offerings. Company counsel to IPOs of Apple Computer, Infosys, Linear Technology, Micron Technology, and Quantum.
**Personal:** JD, 1974 and BA (summa cum laude), 1968, New York University.

### SAVIKAS, Victor G
Jones Day, Los Angeles
213 243 2451
vgsavikas@jonesday.com
*Recommended in Intellectual Property*

**Practice Areas:** Specializes in handling intellectual property litigation and is co-ordinator for the IP Practice in the Los Angeles Office. He has broad experience in handling and trying complex patent cases. Regularly lectures on trying patent litigation cases to a jury.

**Prof. Memberships:** Fellow of the American College of Trial Lawyers. ABA; Los Angeles County Bar Association; Los Angeles Intellectual Property Law Association.

**Publications:** Contributed articles to the Chicago Bar Record, the Illinois Institute of Continuing Legal Education, and The National Law Journal and was co-editor of the CAFC Newsletter co-sponsored by the ABA and The Federal Circuit Bar Association.

### SAX, Paul
Orrick, Herrington & Sutcliffe LLP, San Francisco 415 773 5949
pjsax@orrick.com
*Recommended in Tax*

**Practice Areas:** Divides practice between tax planning for domestic and multinational corporations and handling IRS disputes and litigation. Principal architect of the tax treatment of mortgage and credit card securitization industries. Represented taxpayers in federal and state audits and appeals, including seminal litigation in the courts. Extensive experience in the issues of large family owned businesses, California state taxation, and charitable and other nonprofit organizations. Recognized as a preeminent authority on matters of ethics and standards of tax practice.

**Personal:** LLM in Taxation, New York University, 1969; JD, UC, Hastings College of the Law, 1968; AB, CSU, Sacramento, 1965.

### SAXE, Deborah
Jones Day, Los Angeles
213 689 0200
*Recommended in Employment*

### SCHARF, Stephen
O'Melveny & Myers LLP, Los Angeles
310 246 6813
sscharf@omm.com
*Recommended in Media & Entertainment*

**Practice Areas:** Steve Scharf specializes in entertainment and media finance, production and distribution of motion pictures and television programs, the purchase and sale of entertainment companies and assets, and formation and capitalization of entertainment companies. A substantial part of his practice involves motion picture, television and multimedia financing transactions including banking transactions, securitizations, tax shelter financings and equity investments.

### SCHINDLER, David
Latham & Watkins LLP, Los Angeles
213 485 1234
*Recommended in Litigation*

### SCHMALL, Deborah
Farella Braun & Martel LLP, San Francisco 415 954 4400
*Recommended in Environment*

### SCHUCHARD, Robert L
Sonnenschein Nath & Rosenthal LLP, Los Angeles 213 892 5075
rschuchard@sonnenschein.com
*Recommended in Healthcare*

**Practice Areas:** Handles general business, M&A, contract, financing matters. Transactional and commercial practice includes private and public companies in various industries, including healthcare, educational institutions, equipment maintenance, other service businesses. General corporate and commercial matters include corporate governance, employment contracts, equipment and real property sales and leases, commercial joint ventures, structuring and negotiating limited partnerships and LLCs.

**Prof. Memberships:** Past Chair, California State Bar Committee on Revision of the Nonprofit Corporation Law; Business Law Section of the State Bar of California; AHLA.

**Personal:** Santa Clara University Law School, JD, Business Editor, Santa Clara Law Review; Stanford University, BA Political Science.

### SCHUCK, Edwin
McDermott Will & Emery, Los Angeles
310 551 9307
eschuck@mwe.com
*Recommended in Tax*

**Practice Areas:** Corporate, finance, partnership, real estate, executive compensation and international taxation and federal, state and local tax controversies. Tax-oriented transactions, including M&A, public offerings, joint ventures, start-ups, leveraged leases, project finance, real estate deals, entertainment projects, cross-border transactions, international structuring, work-outs, minerals, ESOPs and financial products.

**Career:** Admitted, New York and California Bars; former Chair, Los Angeles County Bar Association Tax Section; executive committee, California State Bar Tax Section.

**Publications:** Contributor to Tax Review, USC Tax Institute, NYU Tax Institute and The Tax Lawyer.

**Personal:** Columbia University School of Law (JD, cum laude); Columbia University (MBA; BS, cum laude).

### SCHULMAN, Alan
Bernstein Litowitz Berger & Grossmann LLP, San Diego 858 720 3185
alans@blbglaw.com
*Recommended in Litigation*

**Practice Areas:** Complex litigation; class action.

**Prof. Memberships:** Member, American Law Institute (Elected 2004). Member, Louisiana State, Washington State, Federal and American Bar Associations. Co-Chair, Securities Law Committee, American Bar Association's Litigation Section (1998-2001); President (2001) and Member of Board of Governors, Association of

Business Trial Lawyers of San Diego (1995-2001); Co-Chair, Southern District of California Lawyer Representatives to Ninth Circuit Judicial Conference (2000-01); Ninth Circuit Judicial Conference Committee (2002-05) – Program Co-Chair (2003-04) and Conference Co-Chair (2004-05).

**Career:** Litigation counsel to many public and private institutional investors. Lead counsel in many of largest and most significant US securities cases including BFA Liquidation Trust v. Arthur Andersen LLP which resulted in $217 million recovery for defrauded investors. "Heavy hitter nationally who is on everyone's short list of top securities lawyers" (New York Law Journal, January 2000). In 2005, named one of the 'Top 30 Securities Litigators' in California handling high-stakes litigation by the Daily Journal.

**Publications:** Has written and lectured extensively on securities fraud, shareholder rights and corporate governance trends.

**Personal:** New York University, 1971; Louisiana State University School of Law, 1974; Order of the Coif; associate editor, Louisiana Law Review.

### SCHULMAN, Robert
Fulbright & Jaworski L.L.P., Los Angeles
213 892 9272
rschulman@fulbright.com
*Recommended in Litigation*

**Practice Areas:** Litigation.

**Career:** Trial experience in civil litigation matters involving accounting firms and insurance brokerages. Matters relating to: intellectual property; post LBO bankruptcy; defamation; professional negligence; audit malpractice; tax; standard of care matter; litigation for many of the world's largest insurance brokerages including: bad faith matters and regulatory involving the CA Dept. of Insurance. Admitted to practice in New Jersey in 1967 and in California in 1976. Admitted to the US Supreme Court, Ninth and Third US Courts of Appeal, and all of the federal district courts in California and New Jersey. Member of the Association of Business Trial Lawyers, Los Angeles Bar Association and State Bar of California. JD, cum laude, Rutgers School of Law, BA, Rutgers University.

### SCHWAB, Douglas
Heller Ehrman LLP, San Francisco
415 772 6376
douglas.schwab@hellerehrman.com
*Recommended in Litigation*

**Practice Areas:** Securities litigation; corporate governance.

**Prof. Memberships:** State Bar of California, Bar Association of San Francisco, Fellow, American College of Trial Lawyers.

**Career:** Mr Schwab's practice in securities litigation has included leading the firm's defense of many corporations, out-

side directors, officers, venture investors, and domestic and foreign accounting firms. Recent engagements include the litigation concerning financial frauds at Cendant Corporation and Parmalat.

**Personal:** Stanford University, (AB, 1965); University of California, Berkeley, Boalt Hall School of Law (JD, 1968).

### SCHWARTZ, James R
Manatt Phelps & Phillips LLP, Los Angeles 310 312 4182
jschwartz@manatt.com
*Recommended in Healthcare*

**Practice Areas:** Healthcare law focused on advising non-profit organizations on corporate governance, fiduciary duties and officer-director liability issues; on alliances and conversions in the industry, with emphasis on regulated transactions; and matters pertaining to charitable trust law. Co-Chair of the Firm's Healthcare Industry Practice Group. Former California Deputy Attorney General with over 25 years' experience in charitable trust and nonprofit corporation law.

**Prof. Memberships:** CA Attorney General's Task Force on Charity Care; American Health Lawyers Association; CA Society for Healthcare Attorneys; legal Framework Work Group.

**Career:** Partner.

**Personal:** UC Berkeley, Boalt Hall School of Law, (JD, 1971); UC Berkeley, (AB, 1968).

### SCHWARTZ, Robert
O'Melveny & Myers LLP, Los Angeles
310 246 6835
rschwartz@omm.com
*Recommended in Media & Entertainment*

**Practice Areas:** Robert M Schwartz chairs the O'Melveny & Myers LLP Entertainment and Media Litigation Practice. During his 22 years at the firm, he has represented America's leading motion picture and television studios, broadcast networks, individual producers, and other businesses in all manner of disputes in the entertainment, internet, copyright, and trademark fields, including antitrust, contract, accounting, and performer disputes, as well as content creation, advertising and distribution, First Amendment, and right of privacy and publicity issues. He is named in the Best Lawyers In America, Southern California Super Lawyers, and Chambers guides to leading attorneys.

### SCHWARTZ, William
Morrison & Foerster LLP, San Francisco
415 268 7449
wschwartz@mofo.com
*Recommended in IT Outsourcing*

**Practice Areas:** Represents companies in business transactions and counseling involving intellectual property and technology, including license and development agreements, distribution and commercial activities, and joint ventures. Par-

ticularly active in transactional and counseling matters relating to computers, telecommunications equipment, software, the internet, electronic commerce and other advanced information technology and in a wide variety of patent licensing matters.
**Career:** Admitted to practice in California. Worked in Tokyo and Hong Kong as a reporter and Editor for the Asian edition of The Wall Street Journal from 1977 to 1980.
**Personal:** BA, Amherst College, 1976; JD, University of Chicago Law School, 1983.

### SCOTT IV, William
Sheppard, Mullin, Richter & Hampton LLP, Los Angeles 213 620 1780
*Recommended in Banking & Finance*

### SCZUDLO, Paul
Loeb & Loeb LLP, Los Angeles
310 282 2290
psczudlo@loeb.com
*Recommended in Tax*
**Practice Areas:** Focuses on tax planning and structuring for international business transactions. Advises on taxation in connection to entertainment, international estate administration, gift tax planning, partnership and limited liability companies, corporate and planning for high-net-worth individuals, international wealth transfer planning and taxation of litigation settlements.
**Prof. Memberships:** ABA (Co-Chair, International Private Client Committee); LA Country Bar Association; International Bar Association; International Fiscal Association.
**Career:** Partner since 1991.
**Publications:** Writes and lectures on international and entertainment tax topics for businesses and high net worth individuals.
**Personal:** University of California, Berkeley, Boalt Law (JD 1980); Harvard Law School; Yale University (BA, 1977).

### SEABOLT, Richard L
Duane Morris LLP, San Francisco
415 403 8812
rlseabolt@duanemorris.com
*Recommended in Insurance*
**Practice Areas:** Richard L Seabolt, a Partner in the firm's San Francisco office, has extensive experience in complex trials and appeals arising from commercial disputes. He focuses his practice in the area of litigation involving construction contracts, insurance contracts, trade secrets, noncompete clauses and semiconductor fabrication contracts. During his more than 30 years as a lawyer, he has tried a number of significant jury trials to defense verdicts, including three cases in which the plaintiffs' claimed financial losses were between $20 million and in excess of $500 million.
**Prof. Memberships:** State Bar of California – Litigation Section Executive

Committee (Chair), Technology and the Law Committee (Chair); Association of Business Trial Lawyers – Board of Governors; American Arbitration Association – Large Complex Case Panel.
**Career:** Admitted to practice in California; the Supreme Court of the United States; United States Court of Appeals for the Ninth Circuit; and the United States District Court for the Northern, Eastern, Central and Southern Districts of California.
**Publications:** Author/editorial consultant, LexisNexis Matthew Bender California Pretrial Civil Procedure and Discovery Practice Guide (four volume set, published September 2003).
**Personal:** University of Michigan BGS, with distinction, 1971; University of California, Hastings College of the Law, JD, 1975.

### SEGEL, Alvin
Irell & Manella LLP, Los Angeles
310 277 1010
*Recommended in Corporate/M&A*

### SEIDEN, Richard
Foley & Lardner LLP, Los Angeles
310 975 7722
rseiden@foley.com
*Recommended in Healthcare*
**Career:** Richard Seiden, a Partner in the Los Angeles office of Foley & Lardner LLP, is a member of the firm's Health Care Industry Team and Transactional and Securities Practice Group. His practice focuses on all aspects of healthcare business counseling, including formation of business entities, general business and financing matters, and mergers and acquisitions. He has supervised many of the firm's major Southern California transactions involving mergers and acquisitions, and has participated in a number of venture capital, commercial, and tax-exempt financing transactions. Mr Seiden is a graduate of Boalt Hall School of Law, University of California, Berkeley.

### SEKA, Georg
Townsend and Townsend and Crew LLP, San Francisco 415 576 0200
*Recommended in Intellectual Property*

### SENEKER, Carl (Kim)
Morrison & Foerster LLP, San Francisco
415 268 6619
cseneker@mofo.com
*Recommended in Real Estate*
**Practice Areas:** Focused on, and with extensive experience in, commercial real estate transactions, secured debt restructuring and creditors' rights, environmental law, zoning, and land use regulation. Negotiates and documents a variety of substantial real estate debt and equity transactions, with particular expertise in hotel properties, senior living complexes, property portfolio acquisitions and dispositions, and syndicated financings.

**Prof. Memberships:** Member and past President, American College of Real Estate Lawyers; Member, American College of Mortgage Attorneys, Anglo-American Real Property Institute, Lambda Alpha National Land Economics Society.
**Career:** Admitted to practice in California.
**Personal:** AB, Stanford University, 1964; JD, Boalt Hall School of Law, 1967; Editor-in-Chief, California Law Review. Law clerk, associate Justice William O Douglas, US Supreme Court, (1967-68).

### SETTELMAYER, Daniel
Latham & Watkins LLP, Los Angeles
213 485 1234
*Recommended in Healthcare*

### SFREGOLA, Michael F
Gibson, Dunn & Crutcher LLP, Los Angeles
213 229 7558
msfregola@gibsondunn.com
*Recommended in Real Estate*
**Practice Areas:** Experience includes the structuring of the acquisition and financing of hotel, resort, commercial, industrial and residential properties, including multi-jurisdiction and major portfolio acquisitions from private and public sellers in the United States and Asia. Accomplished tax lawyer, representing domestic and foreign institutional investors, including private equity funds and REITs, in connection with structured finance transactions, mergers, divestitures and workouts, as well as tax planning with respect to real estate joint ventures.
**Publications:** Lectures on real estate joint ventures and tax and legal issues affecting private equity funds.
**Personal:** JD, University of Southern California, Order of the Coif, 1979.

### SHANKS, Patricia L
Bingham McCutchen LLP, Los Angeles
213 680 6414
pat.shanks@bingham.com
*Recommended in Environment*
**Practice Areas:** Counsels on environmental and health and safety issues, represents clients in environmental and health and safety permitting and enforcement proceedings, and provides substantive advice in civil and criminal environmental and health and safety litigation. Practice includes water quality, air quality, CERCLA, RCRA, TSCA, FIFRA and OSHA matters. Supervises corporate compliance audits and advises clients on the formation and improvement of corporate compliance management systems. Manages environmental due diligence and negotiates environmental issues for clients in mergers, acquisitions, and real estate and financing transactions.
**Personal:** University of Colorado School of Law, JD, 1978; Stanford University, BA, with distinction, 1962.

### SHARF, Jesse
Gibson, Dunn & Crutcher LLP,
Los Angeles 310 552 8512
jsharf@gibsondunn.com
*Recommended in Real Estate*
**Practice Areas:** Co-Chair of firm's Real Estate Practice. Experience includes extensive representation of funds and other investors, lenders and developers in all areas related to real estate and real estate finance, including forming ventures, financing, loan restructuring and workouts, commercial development, acquisition and sale of land, residential and commercial properties, and operating companies, commercial leasing, contractor, architect, broker and management agreements, environmental aspects of real estate transactions, and acquisition, sale and financing of loan portfolios.
**Publications:** Frequent lecturer; funds, entity formation (including preferred equity), financing, and leasing issues.
**Personal:** JD, New York University School of Law, 1986, editor, Law Review.

### SHARRON, Stephanie L
Wilson Sonsini Goodrich & Rosati,
Palo Alto 650 493 9300
ssharron@wsgr.com
*Recommended in IT Outsourcing*
**Practice Areas:** Helps clients structure and negotiate commercial arrangements of all kinds with particular expertise with high-level, complex transactions. Acts as senior advisor to clients on technology transactions including strategic collaborations and alliances, mergers and acquisitions, outsourcing transactions, the gamut of licensing arrangements, and all other types of product- and technology-related relationships (eg, manufacturing agreements, including foundry agreements; development agreements; distribution arrangements; software licenses; cooperative marketing arrangements; and in-licenses of core technologies).
**Career:** Joined WSGR, 1992; became Partner, 1999. Admitted to practice in California.
**Personal:** JD, Cornell Law School, 1992; Managing Editor, Cornell Law Review. BS, University of California (Los Angeles), 1987.

### SHERMAN, Steven E
Shearman & Sterling, San Francisco
415 616 1260
sesherman@shearman.com
*Recommended in Banking & Finance*
**Practice Areas:** Partner at Shearman & Sterling specializing in private financing and bankruptcy. He has spent the majority of his career representing financial institutions, as well as corporate clients, in private domestic and offshore debt and equity financing transactions, with a particular emphasis in secured financings, chapter 11 bankruptcies and out-of-court reorganizations.

**Prof. Memberships:** Lecturer on financings, workouts and reorganizations at numerous PLI programs and American Bankers Association and California State Bar Association Workshops.
**Career:** Joined Shearman in 1978 and became Partner in 1984.
**Personal:** BS, University of Pennsylvania, Wharton School of Finance (1972); JD, Georgetown University Law School (1975)

## SHERNOFF, William
Shernoff, Bidart & Darras LLP, Claremont 909 621 4935
*Recommended in Insurance*

## SHOCKRO, Michael
Latham & Watkins LLP, Los Angeles 213 485 1234
*Recommended in Business Process Outsourcing, IT Outsourcing*

## SHORTZ, Richard
Morgan, Lewis & Bockius LLP, Los Angeles 231 612 2526
rshortz@morganlewis.com
*Recommended in Projects*
**Practice Areas:** Richard Shortz is a Partner in the Business and Finance Practice and Co-Chair of the Energy and Infrastructure Finance Group. Mr Shortz practices in the corporate area with an emphasis on energy and project finance; corporate mergers, acquisitions, and other business combinations; corporate finance; and general representation of publicly held companies and corporate securities.
**Prof. Memberships:** American Bar Association (Business Law, Natural Resources, Energy, and Environmental Law Sections); Los Angeles County Bar Association (Corporate and Banking, and Real Property Law Sections).

## SHULMAN, Ron
Wilson Sonsini Goodrich & Rosati, Palo Alto 650 493 9300
rshulman@wsgr.com
*Recommended in Intellectual Property*
**Practice Areas:** IP Litigation, focusing primarily on defending companies against claims of patent infringement.
**Prof. Memberships:** Admitted to practice in New York & California.
**Career:** Joined WSGR as Partner, 1995. Partner, Fish & Neave, 1981-95. Has represented clients in more than 50 patent suits throughout the US, and has tried numerous cases, all of which resulted in victories for his clients. Most recently, tried and won a multi-patent jury case brought by Intel against client, Broadcom Corporation, in the United States District Court for the District of Delaware.
**Personal:** JD, Rutgers Law School, 1981; BA, Amherst College, 1977.

## SHUSTERMAN, Carl
The Law Offices of Carl Shusterman, Los Angeles 213 623 4592
*Recommended in Immigration*

## SIEGEL, Clark
Irell & Manella LLP, Los Angeles 310 277 1010
*Recommended in Media & Entertainment*

## SIEGEL, David
Irell & Manella LLP, Los Angeles 310 277 1010
*Recommended in Litigation*

## SIEGEL, Robert
O'Melveny & Myers LLP, Los Angeles 213 430 6005
rsiegel@omm.com
*Recommended in Employment*
**Practice Areas:** Bob Siegel, Vice-Chair of O'Melveny & Myers, a member of the firm's Office of the Chair, and Co-Chair of the firm's Adversarial Department, is a labor lawyer who has represented United Airlines, US Airways, Alaska Air, Pan Am, America West, Northwest, AMR Eagle, American Airlines, Atlas Air, Flying Tigers, Federal Express, PSA, Polar Air, Astar Air Cargo, Mesa, and StatesWest in employment law litigation and counseling, and in labor negotiations, National Mediation Board matters, arbitrations, and litigation under the Railway Labor Act. Bob has also been labor counsel to several airlines regarding mergers, asset acquisitions, and ESOP transactions. Bob served as Co-Chairman of the American Bar Association's Railway and Airline Labor Law Committee, and is a Senior Editor of The Railway Labor Act. Bob has argued significant labor law cases before the US Second, Third, Seventh, Ninth, Tenth, Eleventh, and District of Columbia Court of Appeals, and the Colorado Supreme Court. During the 2001-02 term, he represented US Airways before the US Supreme Court in US Airways, Inc. v. Barnett, a case involving reasonable accommodation requirements under the Americans with Disabilities Act. He currently serves on the Board of Governors of The College of Labor and Employment Lawyers.

## SILVERMAN, Karen
Latham & Watkins LLP, San Francisco 415 391 0600
*Recommended in Antitrust*

## SIMMONS, Richard
Sheppard, Mullin, Richter & Hampton LLP, Los Angeles 213 620 1780
*Recommended in Employment*

## SIMONS III, Laird H
Fenwick & West LLP, Mountain View 650 335 7233
lsimons@fenwick.com
*Recommended in Corporate/M&A*
**Practice Areas:** Focuses on initial public offerings (for both domestic and foreign corporations) and follow-on offerings, ongoing securities advice and counseling for public companies. Has worked on more than 75 initial public offerings for a wide range of high technology companies and more than 25 follow-on offerings for the same companies. Has represented a number of underwriters in initial public offerings and follow-on offerings. Former Securities Group Chair for Fenwick & West and firm Managing Partner.
**Career:** Recognized by The American Lawyer as one of 12 'Dealmakers of the Year' for the entire United States in 1999; by Chambers USA as one of 'America's Leading Lawyers for Business' for the last three years; by Best Lawyers in America 2006 as one of the top securities attorneys in the United States; and by San Jose Magazine as one of Silicon Valley's top lawyers.
**Personal:** Harvard Law School, JD, 1974; Harvard Business School, MBA, with distinction, 1974; Haverford College, BA, with honors, Phi Beta Kappa, 1970.

## SINGER, Gary
O'Melveny & Myers LLP, Newport Beach 949 823 6915
gsinger@omm.com
*Recommended in Corporate/M&A*
**Practice Areas:** Gary Singer practices corporate and securities law, with a focus on mergers and acquisitions, public offerings and finance matters. Gary's breadth of legal experience enables him to successfully represent a broad range of interests, from family-owned businesses to large, public companies.

## SINGER, Martin
Lavely & Singer PC, Los Angeles 310 556 3501
*Recommended in Media & Entertainment*

## SINISCALCO, Gary
Orrick, Herrington & Sutcliffe LLP, San Francisco 415 773 5833
grsiniscalco@orrick.com
*Recommended in Employment*
**Practice Areas:** Focuses on litigating complex employment cases and client counseling. Extensive expertise in EEO, affirmative action, wrongful discharge, and wage-and-hour matters. Litigated class actions and individual employment cases before federal and state courts and administrative agencies for some of the leading industrial and technology companies in the US. Counseling expertise includes working with clients on reductions in force, complex employment disputes, alternative dispute resolution, and corporate compliance matters.
**Career:** Formerly Regional Counsel and Senior Trial Attorney for the United States Equal Employment Opportunity Commission (EEOC) in San Francisco.
**Personal:** JD, Georgetown University, 1969; BA, LeMoyne College, 1965.

## SINK, Charles
Farella Braun & Martel LLP, San Francisco 415 954 4400
*Recommended in Construction*

## SMITH, Brian D
Heller Ehrman LLP, San Francisco 415 772 6534
brian.smith@hellerehrman.com
*Recommended in Real Estate*
**Practice Areas:** Hospitality; real estate and finance; international.
**Prof. Memberships:** American Bar Association; State Bar of California; San Francisco Bar Association; Lambda Alpha International.
**Career:** Mr Smith's practice extends to most aspects of commercial real estate law, including acquisition and sale, partnership/joint venture, fund formation, operating company investments, financing, land use and development, leasing and the workout of distressed investments.
**Personal:** Brown University (AB, 1972); University of Virginia School of Law (JD, 1977), Order of the Coif; Cambridge University (PhD, 1986).

## SMITH, Douglas D
Gibson, Dunn & Crutcher LLP, San Francisco 415 393 8390
dsmith@gibsondunn.com
*Recommended in Corporate/M&A*
**Practice Areas:** Mergers and acquisitions, securities law compliance for public companies, public debt and equity offerings. In-depth experience in financial services, real estate, semiconductor and software businesses. Has led over 200 public offerings and 50 M&A transactions. Recent representations include PeopleSoft in its $1.8 billion acquisition of JD Edwards; its response to Oracle's unsolicited offer and subsequent $10.3 billion sale; and AskJeeves in its $2.3 billion sale to IAC/InterActiveCorp.
**Publications:** Co-Chair, Glasser Institute on Annual Meetings and Disclosure Documents, 1999-2005.
**Personal:** JD, Vanderbilt University, 1979, Order of the Coif.

## SMITH, Gregory C
Skadden, Arps, Slate, Meagher & Flom LLP & Affiliates, Palo Alto 650 470 4590
grsmith@skadden.com
*Recommended in Corporate/M&A*
**Practice Areas:** Extensive experience in the areas of mergers and acquisitions, corporation finance, licensing and partnering transactions, and corporate restructurings. Represents mature and emerging growth technology and life science companies in all stages of development, including venture financings, initial public offerings, and mergers and acquisitions. Also represents underwriters, financial advisors and venture capitalists, and advises clients involved with international transactions.
**Career:** JD, Columbia Law School, 1988 (Harlan Fiske Stone Scholar); BA, Stanford University, 1985 (with distinction; Phi Beta Kappa).

**Personal:** Board, Friends of Music at Stanford University.

### SMITH, Neil
Sheppard, Mullin, Richter & Hampton LLP, San Francisco 415 434 9100
*Recommended in Intellectual Property*

### SMITH, Paul
Davis Wright Tremaine LLP, San Francisco 415 276 6500
*Recommended in Healthcare*

### SNYDER, David R
Pillsbury Winthrop Shaw Pittman LLP, San Diego 619 544 3369
Dave.Snyder@pillsburylaw.com
*Recommended in Capital Markets, Corporate/M&A*

**Practice Areas:** Chair of firm's Business Department. Mr Snyder specializes in corporate finance and general corporate matters. He has led numerous public offerings of equity and debt securities, represents NASDAQ and NYSE public companies in their on-going SEC reporting obligations and advises on public and private merger and acquisition transactions. Mr Snyder has counseled boards and special committees of directors in contested takeovers and in stockholder litigation in California, Delaware and federal courts.

**Personal:** JD, Cornell Law School (with Distinction; Order of the Coif; Editor, Cornell Law Review), 1974; BA, Michigan State University (high honors, Phi Beta Kappa), 1971.

### SONSINI, Larry W
Wilson Sonsini Goodrich & Rosati, Palo Alto 650 493 9300
lsonsini@wsgr.com
*Recommended in Corporate/M&A*

**Practice Areas:** Corporate law and governance; M&A; corporate finance.
**Prof. Memberships:** Admitted to practice in California.
**Career:** Chairman of Wilson Sonsini Goodrich & Rosati. Served as a Member of the Board of Directors of the New York Stock Exchange from 2001-03. Currently the NYSE's Chairman of the Regulation, Enforcement and Listing Standards Committee and Chairman of the Legal Advisory Committee. Director of the following public companies: Echelon, PIXAR, and Silicon Valley Bancshares.
**Personal:** JD, Boalt Hall School of Law, University of California (Berkeley), 1966. AB, University of California (Berkeley), 1963.

### SPECTOR, Scott
Fenwick & West LLP, Mountain View 650 335 7251
sspector@fenwick.com
*Recommended in Employment*

**Practice Areas:** Chair of the firm's Executive Compensation and Employee Benefits Group. Mr Spector specializes in designing and implementing executive compensation, equity compensation and

other employee benefit arrangements for technology companies. His practice emphasizes the compensation issues that arise in connection with mergers and acquisitions, corporate governance matters involving executive compensation and representation of executives in employment negotiations.
**Career:** Mr Spector is the former Chair of the Subcommittee on Executive Compensation of the Federal Regulation of Securities Committee of the Business Law Section of the American Bar Association; former Chair of the Subcommittee on the Federal Securities Regulation of the Committee on Employee Benefits of the Tax Section of the American Bar Association. Mr Spector is a Member of the Practicing Law Institute Board of Advisors.
**Personal:** Juris Doctor from Tulane University in 1974; Masters in Law (in Taxation) from New York University in 1975.

### SPIEGEL, John
Munger, Tolles & Olson LLP, Los Angeles 213 683 9100
*Recommended in Litigation*

### SPIELBERG, David
Thelen Reid & Priest LLP, San Francisco 415 369 7319
dspielberg@thelenreid.com
*Recommended in Projects*

**Practice Areas:** Mr Spielberg specializes in Business and Project Finance transactions: Project Finance – project financing of power plants, including fossil fuel, cogeneration and renewable energy facilities, natural gas pipelines, infrastructure projects, public facilities and arenas, and large industrial and commercial facilities throughout the United States, as well as in Asia and Latin America. Energy Transactions – development, construction, acquisition and disposition of electric generation facilities and natural gas pipelines, mergers and acquisitions of energy companies, and negotiation of power purchase agreements, interconnection and transmission agreements and gas supply and transportation agreements. Corporate and Commercial Finance – representation of borrowers and lenders in connection with construction and term loan facilities, revolving credit facilities, convertible and participating loans, leveraged leases and issuance of bonds and notes. Real Estate Transactions – acquisition, disposition, development, leasing and financing of major real estate projects, including regional shopping centers, apartment complexes, condominium developments, mixed-use developments, office buildings, industrial facilities and undeveloped land. Land Use and Environmental Law – acquisition of development entitlements and approvals, environmental impact statements and reports, and regulation and development of wetlands and water-

related properties.
**Prof. Memberships:** State Bar of California – Sections on Real Estate, Business Law and Environmental Law; American Bar Association – Sections on Natural Resources, Energy and Environmental Law, Real Property and Business Law; Bar Association of San Francisco. Power Association of Northern California.
**Career:** Partner of Thelen Reid & Priest LLP's San Francisco office.
**Personal:** Graduate of Stanford Law School, JD (1976) and Massachusetts Institute of Technology (BS, Electrical Engineering, 1973); named to The Best Lawyers in America (2006 edition). Northern California Super Lawyer 2004 in corporate finance, San Francisco magazine. Rated one of the five best project finance lawyers in California, 2003-04 and 2004-05, America's Leading Lawyers for Business (Chambers and Partners). Refinancing Deal of the Year (North America) 2004, Project Finance International. Refinancing Deal of the Year (North America) 2003, Project Finance International. Project Finance Deal of the Year (North America) 2000, Project Finance International. Project Finance Deal of the Year (North America) 1999, Project Finance International.

### SPRATLING, Gary R
Gibson, Dunn & Crutcher LLP, San Francisco 415 393 8222
gspratling@gibsondunn.com
*Recommended in Antitrust*

**Practice Areas:** Focuses on international antitrust issues. Global expertise regarding the anti-cartel enforcement practices of all major competition enforcement authorities and development of integrated international strategies in all response thereto. Has guided numerous successful representations of major organizations and high-ranking individuals facing exposure in multiple jurisdictions.
**Career:** Former US Department of Justice prosecutor. Two-time recipient of the Presidential Rank Award, the highest honor conferred on federal government executives. Recipient of the Antitrust Lawyer of the Year Award from the State Bar of California. Chair of the ABA Antitrust Section's International Cartel Task Force.

### STANTON, W Clark
Davis Wright Tremaine LLP, San Francisco 415 276 6500
*Recommended in Healthcare*

### STARRETT, Cindy
Latham & Watkins LLP, Los Angeles 213 485 1234
*Recommended in Real Estate*

### STEEL, Michael J
Pillsbury Winthrop Shaw Pittman LLP, San Francisco 415 983 7320
Michael.Steel@pillsburylaw.com

*Recommended in Environment*
**Practice Areas:** Mr Steel defends clients in enforcement actions brought by governmental agencies and citizens' groups. Clients look to Mr Steel for counseling and litigation relating to air and water pollution, waste management and workplace safety. He is also well-known for his work in actions involving the Unfair Practices Act and Proposition 65. He often works closely with experts in medicine, epidemiology, toxicology, chemical analysis and risk assessment. Mr Steel has appeared in state and federal courts, as well as before the USEPA, state EPAs and state and federal OSHA.

### STEIN, Laurence
Latham & Watkins LLP, Los Angeles 213 485 1234
*Recommended in Tax*

### STEIN, Stanton 'Larry'
Alschuler Grossman Stein & Kahan LLP, Santa Monica lstein@agsk.com
*Recommended in Media & Entertainment*

**Practice Areas:** Heads the firm's Entertainment and Media Litigation Department, one of the largest in the country emphasizing talent representation. Focuses on film, television, and music, including copyright, trademark, and publicity rights. Renowned for pioneering success in 'vertical integration' lawsuits, representing actors, writers and producers shortchanged on profits by media empire self-dealing.
**Prof. Memberships:** Past President, Public Counsel. Past Member, Board of Directors, Bet Tzedek Legal Services. Present Member of the Board of Directors of OPPC (homeless shelter). Present Member of the Board of Directors of the Foundation of the State Bar of California. Member, Beverly Hills, Los Angeles County, and American Bar Associations, Association of Business Trial Lawyers.
**Career:** A Partner of Alschuler Grossman Stein & Kahan LLP. Adjunct Professor at USC School of Law and Distinguished Speaker at Harvard, Yale, Stanford, and Boalt Law Schools. Named 'Entertainment Lawyer of the Year' by the Beverly Hills and Century City Bar Associations. He was ACLU Pro Bono and Civil Liberties Award recipient for 2004. Listed in the Daily Journal (100 Most Influential Lawyers in California). In 2005, he was named among the Law Dragon 500 leading lawyers in America. Has been featured in Forbes Magazine, Variety, and on the covers of Los Angeles Magazine and the National Law Journal.
**Personal:** University of Southern California (current Adjunct Professor of Entertainment Law; BA with honors, 1966; JD, 1969; Captain, USC Debate Team winner of numerous national debate championships; Associate Editor, Southern California Law Review; Moot

Court Champion).

## STEINBERG, Jonathan
Irell & Manella LLP, Los Angeles
310 277 1010
*Recommended in Intellectual Property*

## STEINTHAL, Kenneth
Weil, Gotshal & Manges LLP,
Redwood Shores 650 802 3081
kenneth.steinthal@weil.com
*Recommended in Media & Entertainment*
**Practice Areas:** Kenneth Steinthal Co-Heads Weil Gotshal's Intellectual Property and Media Practice and specializes in trying cases in the music and broader entertainment/content distribution and new media industries. He has extensive trial experience and a track record of success litigating matters in these areas (as well as matters concerning a variety of IP, trade secret and other issues). He also leads Weil's preeminent music rights counseling and licensing practice, concentrating on the representation of online/new media and traditional offline media entities engaged in distribution of audio and audio-visual content.
**Personal:** Williams College, BA, 1974; Fordham University, JD, 1978.

## STERN, Claude M
Quinn Emanuel Urquhart Oliver & Hedges, LLP, Redwood Shores
650 801 5000
claudestern@quinnemanuel.com
*Recommended in Intellectual Property*
**Practice Areas:** Claude M Stern serves as Co-Chair of the firm's National Intellectual Property Litigation Practice, and as Managing Partner of the firm's Silicon Valley Office. In his 25 years of practice, he has developed extensive experience in business litigation, with an emphasis in intellectual property, technology and class action defense litigation, and has been repeatedly recognized as a leading intellectual property trial lawyer in the Silicon Valley.
**Career:** Mr Stern has been lead trial counsel in numerous cases around the United States, with precedent-setting cases in all areas of intellectual property and technology litigation, including patent infringement litigation (E-Data v. CompuServe), copyright infringement litigation (Broderbund v. Unison), trade secret misappropriation litigation (Gemisys v. Phoenix American), false advertising litigation (Kramer v. Intuit) and trademark infringement litigation. Mr Stern routinely represents clients in cases around the United States, including in California, Washington, Delaware, Texas, New York, Illinois and Virginia. Mr Stern has extensive experience in all areas of civil litigation, including trials (jury and non-jury), arbitration, mediation and other forms of alternative dispute resolution. Mr Stern's representative clients have included Shell Oil, Electronic

Arts, Intuit, Macrovision, Palm, Game-Tech International, Symyx Technologies and Corbis Images. Mr Stern serves in 2006 as President of the Association of Business Trial Lawyers, and also routinely lectures around the United States on various issues associated with intellectual property litigation and complex civil business litigation. Mr Stern has also been invited abroad (to China, India, Israel, Morocco and Taiwan), including on US State Department-sponsored trips, to teach judges and lawyers about complex civil litigation, intellectual property litigation and alternative dispute resolution.

## STERN, Roger D
Wilson Sonsini Goodrich & Rosati,
Palo Alto 650 493 9300
rstern@wsgr.com
*Recommended in Employment*
**Practice Areas:** Structures compensation and benefit programs to cover the full range of equity and cash compensation arrangements, including stock options and purchase plans, 401(k) plans, employee stock ownership plans (ESOPs), cafeteria plans, nonqualified deferred compensation plans, and severance and other fringe-benefit arrangements. Special expertise in the tax, securities, and accounting considerations, with a particular emphasis on the unique issues faced by start-up and growth companies.
**Personal:** JD, University of Chicago Law School, 1989; Comment Editor, University of Chicago Legal Forum; Recipient, Bradley Fellowship. BA, (With Distinction), University of California (Berkeley), 1981

## STEUBER, David
Howrey LLP, Los Angeles
213 892 1800
*Recommended in Insurance*

## STEVENS, Charles
Stevens & O'Connell LLP, Sacramento
916 329 9111
*Recommended in Litigation*

## STEVENS, Mark C
Fenwick & West LLP, Mountain View
650 335 7257
mstevens@fenwick.com
*Recommended in Corporate/M&A*
**Practice Areas:** Represents companies, ranging from newly formed start-up teams to mature public companies, venture capitalists and investment banks involved in the information technology industries, with particular focus on complex transactions. Has led teams handling merger, acquisition and divestiture transactions with total announced value in excess of $20 billion. Has directed more than 25 initial public offerings and hundreds of strategic alliance transactions, ranging from technology and distribution partnerships to multinational joint

venture transactions.
**Career:** Former Executive Vice-President of Business and Corporate Development at Excite.
**Personal:** Northwestern University School of Law, JD, cum laude, Order of the Coif and Law Review, 1983; Santa Clara University, BS, in mathematics, magna cum laude, 1979.

## STORK, Anita
Cooley Godward LLP, San Francisco
415 693 2000
*Recommended in Antitrust*

## STREETER, Jon
Keker & Van Nest LLP, San Francisco
415 391 5400
jstreeter@kvn.com
*Recommended in Intellectual Property*
**Practice Areas:** Complex commercial civil litigation cases including intellectual property, antitrust, securities, banking and energy. He recently obtained a $41 million jury verdict in a breach of contract dispute. Representative clients include Fresenius USA, Memorex, Oakland Alameda Coliseum Authority, PG&E, Inc., Schlumberger, and Tegal Corporation.
**Prof. Memberships:** Vice-Chair, California Senate Commission on the Fair Administration of Justice; former President of the San Francisco Bar Association; former President of the Association of Business Trial Lawyers of Northern California; former Chair of the Northern District of California Lawyer Representatives to the Ninth Circuit Court of Appeals; Member of the Executive Committee of the Edward McFetridge Chapter of the American Inns of Court; Member of the American Law Institute; Member of the Ninth Circuit Task Force on Self-Represented Litigants; Chair of Keker & Van Nest's Pro Bono Committee.
**Career:** Partner, Keker & Van Nest (1997-present); Orrick, Herrington & Sutcliffe (Partner, 1989-97) (associate 1981-82, 1983-88); law clerk to the Hon. Harry T Edwards, United States Court of Appeals for the District of Columbia Circuit (1982-83).
**Personal:** Boalt Hall School of Law, University of California (JD 1981); Stanford University (AB 1978).

## STROMBERG, Ross E
Jones Day, San Francisco
415 875 5724
restromberg@jonesday.com
*Recommended in Healthcare*
**Practice Areas:** Extensive national experience representing healthcare industry clients in corporate transactions, mergers and acquisitions, integrated delivery system development, hospital/physician integration, managed care, and healthcare-related technology. Recognized in Who's Who in America and The Best Lawyers in America, among others.

**Prof. Memberships:** State Bar of California; Bar Association of San Francisco; American Health Lawyers Association; California Society for Healthcare Attorneys. Editorial Board Member of Integrated Health Care Report, Medical Staff Strategy Report, and Hospital Strategy Report.
**Publications:** Co-authored 'Joint Ventures for Hospitals and Physicians: Legal Considerations and Acquiring and Enhancing Physician Practices'.

## STURGEON, John A
White & Case LLP, Los Angeles
213 620 7755
jsturgeon@whitecase.com
*Recommended in Litigation*
**Practice Areas:** Has a general Business Trial and Appellate Practice. Practice also includes lender liability and banking litigation, trade secret and unfair competition cases, defense of securities class actions, real property disputes, trust and probate litigation, business torts, energy industry litigation and disputes among partners and shareholders.
**Prof. Memberships:** CalBar; LACBA; ABTL.
**Career:** White & Case since 1991.
**Publications:** Co author of 'California Business Litigation', California Continuing Education of the Bar, 2002.
**Personal:** Stanford Law School (JD, 1962); Stanford University (AB, cum laude) 1957.

## SULLIVAN, Peter
Gibson, Dunn & Crutcher LLP,
Los Angeles 213 229 7165
psullivan@gibsondunn.com
*Recommended in Antitrust*
**Practice Areas:** Co-Chair of firm's Antitrust and Trade Regulation Practice. Represents US/International clients in civil/criminal litigations (including class actions) as well as governmental investigations concerning cartels, mergers, distribution, pricing, exclusive dealing and all other types of vertical and horizontal arrangements. Matters encompass both jury/non-jury trials and hearings (US federal and state courts, the EC and member states) and counseling.
**Publications:** Co-author, 'Antitrust Laws and Trade Regulation, Second Edition'. Author, 'Pricing Practices;' 'Distribution Practices;' 'A Guide to Joint Ventures and Other Cooperative Business Endeavors'.
**Personal:** JD, Fordham University Law School, 1977, cum laude, Articles Editor, Law Review.

## SULLIVAN, William F
Paul, Hastings, Janofsky & Walker LLP,
San Diego 858 720 2525
williamsullivan@paulhastings.com
*Recommended in Litigation*
**Practice Areas:** Securities litigation and enforcement, focusing on the representation of companies and their officers and directors in the defense of federal and

state securities class actions, derivative actions and regulatory proceedings. He is a veteran trial counsel with substantial appellate experience.

**Prof. Memberships:** American Bar Association, State Bar of California.
**Career:** Paul, Hastings, Janofsky & Walker, LLP, Partner, 2003 to present; Chair, Securities Litigation Practice Group; Managing Partner, San Diego office. Brobeck, Phleger & Harrison, 1981-2003.
**Personal:** JD, University of California at Los Angeles School of Law, 1977. AB, with distinction, University of California at Berkeley, 1974.

### SUN, Brian A
Jones Day, Los Angeles
213 243 2858
basun@jonesday.com
*Recommended in Litigation*

**Practice Areas:** He has earned a national reputation as a distinguished trial lawyer specializing in complex business litigation and white-collar criminal defense. He has successfully litigated cases against some of the nation's top trial lawyers. As an assistant US attorney, he distinguished himself by drafting and pioneering the passage of anti-money laundering legislation. Named one of America's 500 leading lawyers in 2005 by Lawdragon magazine. Lectured and written extensively on trial practice, ethics, white-collar crime, and corporate compliance with government regulation.
**Prof. Memberships:** Former President of the Southern California Chinese Lawyers Association and the National Asian Pacific American Bar Association.

### SWANSON, Daniel G
Gibson, Dunn & Crutcher LLP, Los Angeles 213 229 7430
dswanson@gibsondunn.com
*Recommended in Antitrust*

**Practice Areas:** Co-Chair since 1996 of firm's Antitrust Practice Group. Specializes in domestic and international antitrust/competition law, including civil and appellate litigation, class actions, mergers/JVs, counseling and compliance, amnesty/leniency matters and international cartel investigations. Has broad trial and appellate experience throughout the United States, intellectual property expertise (testified in DOJ-FTC IP/Antitrust hearings), and a practice regularly involving international representations and cross-border issues.
**Prof. Memberships:** Co-Chair, ABA Antitrust Section's International Committee.
**Publications:** Author/editor of numerous books and articles on antitrust law.
**Personal:** JD, 1984, magna cum laude; MA, 1984; and PhD (Economics), 1985; Harvard University.

### TALBERT, Cecily
Bingham McCutchen LLP, Walnut Creek
925 975 5339

cecily.talbert@bingham.com
*Recommended in Real Estate*

**Practice Areas:** Serves as Chair of the firm's Land Use Practice Group. Focuses on land use, real estate and local government law. Regularly assists landowners, developers and public agencies throughout California in all aspects of land use processing, including compliance with CEQA, and drafting, negotiating and obtaining the approval of development agreements, general plan amendments, specific plans, planned unit development zoning, and tentative and final subdivision maps.
**Personal:** Harvard Law School, JD, with honors, 1988; University of California, Berkeley, BA, with highest honors, 1983.

### TANOURY, Mark
Cooley Godward LLP, Palo Alto
650 843 5000
*Recommended in Corporate/M&A*

### TAYLOR, Robert
Howrey LLP, Menlo Park
650 463 8100
*Recommended in Antitrust*

### TEPLIN, Lawrence
Cox Castle & Nicholson LLP, Los Angeles
310 277 4222
*Recommended in Real Estate*

### THOMPSON, Jocelyn Niebur
Weston Benshoof Rochefort Rubalcava MacCuish LLP, Los Angeles
213 576 1104
jthompson@wbcounsel.com
*Recommended in Environment*

**Practice Areas:** Partner, Environmental Strategy and Litigation Department. Ms Thompson has extensive experience in environmental permitting, compliance and auditing, including matters related to air and water quality, CEQA, NEPA, coastal zones, endangered and threatened species, and California's Proposition 65.
**Prof. Memberships:** American Bar Association; California Bar Association (Environmental Law Section); California Mining Association (Air Quality Committee); Environmental Justice Advisory Group, South Coast Air Quality Management District.
**Personal:** JD, University of California, Los Angeles, 1982; BA, University of California, Santa Barbara (magna cum laude), 1978

### THOMPSON, Martin
Manatt Phelps & Phillips LLP, Los Angeles 310 312 4000
*Recommended in Healthcare*

### THOMPSON, Robert
Sheppard, Mullin, Richter & Hampton LLP, San Francisco
415 434 9100
*Recommended in Real Estate*

### THOMPSON, Tracy
Morgan, Lewis & Bockius LLP, Philadelphia 215 963 5000

*Recommended in Employment*

### THORNTON, Charles
Paul, Hastings, Janofsky & Walker LLP, San Francisco 415 856 7001
charlesthornton@paulhastings.com
*Recommended in Real Estate*

**Practice Areas:** Practice concentrated in real estate and related matters, including joint ventures, complex structures, development, acquisition, leasing and financing.
**Prof. Memberships:** Authored several articles on corporate and real estate matters. Member, Lambda Alpha; Vice-Chair of the Board, YMCA of San Francisco.
**Career:** Chair of Real Estate Department in San Francisco office; former Chair of San Francisco and Los Angeles offices.
**Personal:** AB Degree Cornell University; JD Degree University of Michigan Law School (1967); Assistant Editor of the Michigan Law Review.

### THUM, Robert B
Thelen Reid & Priest LLP, Los Angeles
213 576 8014
rthum@thelenreid.com
*Recommended in Construction*

**Practice Areas:** Mr Thum has specialized in engineering and construction law since 1974, providing contract advice and dispute resolution services for owners (public and private), engineers, general contractors and major trade subcontractors. He has litigated and arbitrated a wide variety of cases involving major infrastructure projects (dams, highways and bridges, power plants, rail, airports and water treatment plants), as well as refineries, pipelines, industrial plants, hospitals, schools, and high-rise buildings. Mr Thum serves as Construction Arbitrator on the State of California's Public Works Arbitration Program and is a member of the American Arbitration Association's National Panel of Construction Arbitrators. For over 20 years he has participated in Alternative Dispute Resolution of engineering and construction disputes, and has mediated many cases to settlement. Mr Thum has published widely on construction law topics, including contract interpretation, scheduling, productivity and damage calculation. He has been invited to speak to numerous industry groups throughout the nation on subjects related to construction law and ADR.
**Prof. Memberships:** Arbitrator, National Panel of Construction Arbitrators, American Arbitration Association; Arbitrator, Public Construction Arbitration Program; CA Office of Administrative Hearings; Member, American Bar Association's Forum Committee on the Construction Industry, and Public Contract Law and Litigation Sections; Member, California State Bar Association's Sections on Construction, Real Estate and Litigation; Board of Contributing Edi-

tors, California Construction Reporter (West).
**Career:** Partner of Thelen Reid & Priest LLP. Admitted to bar: Ohio, 1970; US Court of Military Appeals, 1971; California, 1974; US Supreme Court, 1975.
**Publications:** 'California Construction Law' (Federal Publications 2001); 'Guide to Construction Contracts and Disputes' (3d ed., California CEB 2000); 'Practical Construction Law' (Federal Publications 1999); 'The Authority to Issue Changes', in 'Changes' (Wiley Law 1994); 'Handbook of California Construction Law' (AGC of California 1993); 'Bid Guarantees', in 'Construction Bidding Law' (Wiley Law 1991); 'Changes', in 'Construction Subcontracting: Legal Guide' (Wiley Law 1990); 'Liability of Designers and Contractors to the End-User' (ABA Forum Committee 1985); 'Claims and Project Schedule' in 'Scheduling and Proof of Claims' (Fed. Publications 1985); 'The Owner's Warranty of Plans and Specifications' 14 Public Contract L.J. 240 (1984); 'Interpretation of Plans and Specifications', in 'Government Construction Contracting' (Federal Publications 1982).
**Personal:** Received his JD from the Cornell Law School, 1970, Editor of the Cornell Law Review (1969-70). Received AB cum laude from Princeton University, 1967.

### THUMANN, Henry
O'Melveny & Myers LLP, Los Angeles
213 430 6130
hthumann@omm.com
*Recommended in Antitrust*

**Practice Areas:** Henry Thumann is a Partner in the O'Melveny & Myers Los Angeles office. His antitrust experience includes the representation of major industrial, IT, transport and entertainment corporations both in government initiated enforcement actions and in the defense of private litigation brought both on an individual and class action basis. He is a Fellow of the American College of Trial Lawyers and is recommended in litigation by a leading legal publication.

### TITLE, Gail
Katten Muchin Rosenman LLP, Los Angeles 310 788 4727
gail.title@kattenlaw.com
*Recommended in Media & Entertainment*

**Practice Areas:** Ms Title's practice includes all aspects of the entertainment industry, from motion picture and television development, finance, and production, to distribution in all media worldwide. Her representation covers a broad range of legal and business issues that arise in the entertainment industry, including copyright, trademark, unfair competition, contract, and business torts. Ms Title has extensive experience in state and federal, trial and appellate courts and in arbitration tribunals. She also frequently provides non-litigation advice and counsel.

**Prof. Memberships:** Top Women Lawyers in Business WLALA Women of Distinction award; 2004-06 'Super Lawyer' in Los Angeles and Orange County; Marquis Who's Who; Century City 2006 Litigator of the Year; 9th Circuit Judicial Conference lawyer representative; Vice-Chair of Magistrate Judge Merit Selection Panel for the Central District of California; Board of Directors of Public Counsel Law Center, Constitutional Rights Foundation, and Pacific Southwest Region of the Anti-Defamation League.

**Career:** Los Angeles Office Managing Partner; member of the firm's national Executive Committee and Board of Directors; Head of the firm's national Entertainment Litigation Practice.

**Personal:** Wellesley College, Massachusetts, BA (with honors) (1967); University of California, Boalt Hall School of Law, JD (1970).

## TOLLES, Stephen L
Gibson, Dunn & Crutcher LLP,
Los Angeles 213 229 7502
stolles@gibsondunn.com
*Recommended in Tax*

**Practice Areas:** Advises clients on a wide variety of corporate tax issues, including taxable stock and asset acquisitions, tax-free reorganizations, leveraged buyouts, liquidations, redemptions, spin-offs, public offerings of stock and debt, publicly traded partnerships, real estate investment trusts, and executive compensation. Substantial experience handling administrative appeals before Internal Revenue Service, California Franchise Tax Board, and the California State Board of Equalization.

**Prof. Memberships:** Member, Planning Committee, USC Tax Institute. Member, Board of Advisors, Graduate Tax Program, Loyola Law School.

**Personal:** JD, University of California Law School at Boalt Hall, 1982, Order of the Coif, Member Law Review.

## TONSFELDT, Steven
Heller Ehrman LLP, Menlo Park
650 233 8475
steven.tonsfeldt@hellerehrman.com
*Recommended in Corporate/M&A*

**Practice Areas:** Mergers and acquisitions, venture law group/emerging companies, private equity and fund formation, corporate governance.

**Prof. Memberships:** State Bar of California; Committee on Negotiated Acquisitions of the Business Law Section of the American Bar Association.

**Career:** Mr Tonfeldt's practice represents publicly traded and privately held companies in domestic and cross-border M&A, leveraged buyouts, significant recapitalizations, corporate partnering

arrangements, joint ventures and strategic alliances and minority equity investments. He has represented investment partnerships in leveraged acquisitions and financial advisors who are advising companies engaged in acquisition transactions.

**Personal:** University of California at Berkeley, Boalt Hall School of Law, (JD, 1987).

## TOSETTI, Paul
Latham & Watkins LLP, Los Angeles
213 485 1234
*Recommended in Corporate/M&A*

## TOULON, Rik
Katten Muchin Rosenman LLP,
Los Angeles 310 788 4480
rik.toulon@kattenlaw.com
*Recommended in Media & Entertainment*

**Practice Areas:** Represents institutions and individuals in various transactions in connection with all aspects of the worldwide development, production, financing, promotion, distribution (all media), sale and acquisition of motion pictures (live action and CGI), television programming (scripted and non-scripted), music videos, video games and other entertainment content, and the exploitation of all related ancillary rights. His broad knowledge of both the legal and business aspects of the entertainment industry allows him to provide clients with specialized services with respect to deal structuring, risk assessments, complex chain-of-title and rights clearance issues, the purchase and sale of literary material/films/other intellectual properties, VOD, wireless, domestic and international television licensing arrangements, co-productions, joint ventures, merchandising campaigns, and advising on entertainment and media assets in significant M&A transactions and financings. Mr Toulon was lead entertainment counsel to NBC in its acquisition of Vivendi Universal Entertainment, to Sony in its acquisition of MGM, and to Intermedia Films in connection with its parent company's German public offering.

**Prof. Memberships:** USC Law School – Beverly Hills Bar Association Institute on Entertainment Law and Business.

**Career:** BA Degree in Economics, University of California, Los Angeles, 1990; JD, University of Southern California, 1994.

## TOWNSEND, Robert S
Morrison & Foerster LLP, San Francisco
415 268 7080
rtownsend@mofo.com
*Recommended in Corporate/M&A*

**Practice Areas:** Extensive transactional experience in the fields of mergers and acquisitions, securities law, technology and intellectual property matters, leveraged buyouts and venture capital. Represented public and private companies in

corporate and finance matters ranging from mergers and acquisitions to seed round financings and initial public offerings. Regularly advises CEOs, Boards of Directors and Special Committees in strategic and corporate governance issues. Has represented clients in more than 100 public and private company acquisitions, strategic alliances and financings, ranging from over several billion dollars to much smaller transactions.

**Career:** Admitted to practice in California. Chair, firm's Global Business Department, 1996-2003. Co-Chair, firm's 200-lawyer Corporate Practice Group, 2004-present.

**Personal:** BS, University of California, Berkeley, 1978; JD, Stanford University Law School, 1984

## TRUAX, Tim
Cox Castle & Nicholson LLP, Los Angeles
310 277 4222
*Recommended in Construction*

## TRUCKER, Lee
Trucker Huss PC, San Francisco
415 788 3111
*Recommended in Employment*

## TUBACH, Michael
O'Melveny & Myers LLP, San Francisco
415 984 8876
mtubach@omm.com
*Recommended in Antitrust, Litigation*

**Practice Areas:** Michael Tubach's practice focuses on civil litigation and white-collar criminal defense. Michael represents individuals as well as large public companies in criminal, securities, intellectual property, and class action disputes. His trial experience includes over 37 trials and 20 appellate arguments.

## TUCHIN, Michael L
Klee, Tuchin, Bogdanoff & Stern LLP,
Los Angeles 310 407 4040
mtuchin@ktbslaw.com
*Recommended in Bankruptcy*

**Practice Areas:** Is a member and Co-Manager of Klee, Tuchin, Bogdanoff & Stern LLP. On the debtor side, he currently represents Crescent Jewelers (the largest retailer of fine jewelry in California, with approximately 125 stores) and, as special counsel, American Restaurant Group (the owner of the Stuart Anderson's Black Angus chain of restaurants). He recently represented Samuels Jewelers, Inc. (retailer of fine jewelry operating more than 130 stores), Fountain View, Inc. (operator of more than 50 skilled care nursing and assisted care living facilities) and Frederick's of Hollywood, Inc (world-renowned retailer of innovative specialty apparel operating more than 150 stores, a catalogue, and an internet business) in connection with their highly successful chapter 11 cases. Out of court, he has led successful restructurings of the Lusk Company (a large California homebuilder with close to $1 billion in debts),

an international giftware manufacturer, an international manufacturer of computer accessories, a national express delivery business, and LA Kings, Ltd. (the then-owner of the Los Angeles Kings hockey franchise). He represents, and has represented, creditors in numerous chapter 11 cases, including American Rice, Ameriserve, Carmike Theatres, Catapult Entertainment, Chevy's, Edwards Theatres, Fresh Choice, Kmart, Sega Gameworks, Tower Records, United Airlines, and Wherehouse Records. In addition, he represented a large equity holder of the Pittsburgh Penguins hockey team in connection with the Penguins' chapter 11 case in Pittsburgh, Pennsylvania. He has also represented numerous purchasers of assets (including Viacom, Paramount Pictures, and The Gap). He is the President of the Los Angeles Bankruptcy Forum and a past President and member of the Board of Governors of the Financial Lawyers Conference of Los Angeles.

## TULLY, W Bradley
Hooper Lundy & Bookman Inc,
Los Angeles 310 551 8111
*Recommended in Healthcare*

## TURNER III, Glenn E
Gibbs, Giden, Locher & Turner,
Los Angeles 310 552 3400
gturner@gglt.com
*Recommended in Construction*

**Practice Areas:** Glenn Turner is a Senior Partner of the Los Angeles and Las Vegas law firm of Gibbs, Giden, Locher & Turner which specializes in the representation of prime contractors, owners, subcontractors, design professionals and all others active in the construction industry. Mr Turner specializes in trials and arbitrations of major construction disputes involving delay, disruption, extra work claims, lost productivity and abandonment of contract. Mr Turner has both prosecuted and defended major construction claims.

**Prof. Memberships:** Mr Turner is a Member of the Los Angeles County Bar Association.

**Career:** Mr Turner has practiced law with his firm for over 25 years.

**Publications:** Mr Turner has authored numerous articles for construction industry trade publications and has conducted numerous seminars for industry and legal professionals on a broad range of construction related topics from contract intrepretation and extra work claims to mechanics liens and statutory remedies.

**Personal:** Mr Turner holds BS and MBA degrees from Arizona State University ('75 and '77) and a Juris Doctorate from Pepperdine University ('80).

## ULMAN, Lawrence J
Gibson, Dunn & Crutcher LLP,
Los Angeles 310 551 8794
lulman@gibsondunn.com

*Recommended in Media & Entertainment*

**Practice Areas:** Co-Chair of firm's Media and Entertainment Practice Group. Specializes in entertainment finance with significant experience representing film studios in their distribution and financial matters, including negotiating and documenting tax advantaged transactions, domestic and foreign film rights acquisitions, credit arrangements, library acquisitions and sales, product placements and negotiating output arrangements for films and television. Representative clients include Universal Pictures, New Line Cinema, Twentieth Century Fox, Volkswagen AG and Constantin Film AG.

**Career:** Adjunct Professor at the University of Southern California School of Cinema and Television.

**Personal:** JD, University of Southern California School of Law, 1975; MBA, UCLA, 1980.

### URQUHART, A William

Quinn Emanuel Urquhart Oliver & Hedges, LLP, Los Angeles
213 443 3000
billurquhart@quinnemanuel.com
*Recommended in Litigation*

**Practice Areas:** Mr Urquhart specializes in complex business litigation. Practice areas include class action litigation, securities litigation, anti-trust and trade regulation litigation, intellectual property litigation, banking and financial institution litigation, entertainment litigation, domestic and international arbitration and mediation and energy litigation.

**Career:** He has repeatedly been named 'One of California's Most Successful Business Lawyers' by California Law Business, named 'One of the Most Influential Attorneys in California' by The Los Angeles Daily Journal and listed as one of the world's leading litigators in the Euromoney Guide to the World's Leading International Law Firms, repeatedly named a 'Super Lawyer' by Los Angeles Magazine. Notable litigation resolutions: obtained a $120+ million award for an aerospace company in a breach of contract/misappropriation of trade secret matter before London Court of International Arbitration. Resolved seven class actions for a major financial institution, with no cost for settlement or judgment. Obtained dismissal of 27 class actions filed against Northrop-Grumman arising out of the failure of Northrop's merger with Lockheed to close. Tried and won two class actions. Obtained an injunction barring the allocation of losses as a result of defaults by major California utilities. Obtained summary judgment in a class action, the appeal of which established the California rule limiting bondholders' rights to those provided by contract. Obtained settlements of several shareholder derivative actions at no cost to

company or directors. Obtained $152 million settlement for a Zurich subsidiary claiming fraud in connection with the sale of an insurance company. Obtained a $25 million settlement for a manufacturing company after court granted judgment based on a finding of literal infringement of two patents. Obtained dismissal of a $40 million breach of warranty lawsuit against IBM and obtained a $25 million judgment on a counterclaim. Obtained dismissal of a $100 million suit against an entertainment company in which plaintiff alleged the company stole trade secrets regarding computerized animation. Obtained a $6.5 million verdict for a manufacturer in a dispute concerning post-closing adjustments following the sale of a business. Obtained a defense verdict for a mortgage lender in a Lanham Act passing off suit. Obtained a $20+ million settlement of a misappropriation of trade secrets case after obtaining a preliminary injunction. Both obtained and resisted temporary restraining orders and preliminary injunctions in numerous cases involving recruitment of employees by competitors. Obtained favorable settlements in a number of multi-million dollar business disputes without resort to litigation or arbitration.

**Personal:** Fordham Law School (JD, cum laude, 1977). Member, Fordham Law Review. Fordham College (BA, 1969).

### VAN NEST, Robert

Keker & Van Nest LLP, San Francisco
415 391 5400
rvannest@kvn.com
*Recommended in Intellectual Property, Litigation*

**Practice Areas:** Practice ranges widely over the field of complex business litigation, and white-collar crime. He has tried cases involving patent infringement, securities fraud, trademarks, commercial contracts, RICO, partnership disputes, real estate, insurance bad faith, mail and wire fraud, and other issues. Representative clients include American Honda Motor Company, Electronic Arts, Inc., Genentech, Inc., Intel Corporation, LSI Logic Corp., Pacific Gas & Electric, Topcon American Corporation, and Xilinx, Inc.

**Prof. Memberships:** Served on the faculties of the Hastings College of Advocacy, the National Institute for Trial Advocacy and the Sedona Conference on Patent Litigation and has been a lecturer in Developments in Tort Practice for the California Continuing Education of the Bar since 1985. He recently served as a Member of the State Bar Commission on Mandatory Continuing Legal Education. Former director of the Association of Business Trial Lawyers (1992-2000) and chairs the Development Committee of Bay Area Legal Aid (1995-present).

**Career:** Law clerk to the Honorable

William H Orrick in the Northern District of California (1978-79); joined Keker & Brockett, 1979; Partner since 1982.

**Personal:** Harvard Law School (JD, magna cum laude, 1978); Stanford University (BA, with honors, 1973). Member Phi Beta Kappa.

### VANDEVELDE, John

Lightfoot, Vandevelde, Sadowsky, Medvene & Levine, Los Angeles
213 622 4750
*Recommended in Litigation*

### VANYO, Bruce G

Katten Muchin Rosenman LLP, Los Angeles 213 680 8365
bvanyo@kirkland.com
*Recommended in Litigation*

**Practice Areas:** Securities litigation.

**Career:** In the last four years, has prevailed in 13 cases, including six appellate victories in five different Courts of Appeal (1st, 2nd, 4th, 8th, and 9th). Asked by technology industry, and by Congress, to provide recommendations on securities litigation reform and draft major portions of the Private Securities Litigation Reform Act of 1995 and the Securities Litigation Uniform Standards Act of 1998. Argued the two appellate cases that have interpreted the Reform Act most favorably to defendants, Silicon Graphics (Ninth Circuit) and FTP Software (First Circuit).

**Personal:** JD, Columbia University, 1972; BS, Miami University, 1967.

### VARNER, Carlton

Sheppard, Mullin, Richter & Hampton LLP, Los Angeles 213 620 1780
*Recommended in Antitrust*

### VERHOEVEN, Charles K

Quinn Emanuel Urquhart Oliver & Hedges, LLP, San Francisco
415 875 6600
charlesverhoeven@quinnemanuel.com
*Recommended in Intellectual Property*

**Practice Areas:** Charles K Verhoeven's practice focuses primarily on intellectual property, antitrust, entertainment and complex commercial litigation.

**Career:** Mr Verhoeven has been recognized by California Law Business as one of the top 20 lawyers in California under 40 years old.

**Personal:** University of Iowa (JD, with high distinction, 1988). Member, 1986-87, Articles Editor, 1987-88, Iowa Law Review. University of Iowa (BBA, with distinction, 1985).

### VETTER, Jeff

Fenwick & West LLP, Mountain View
650 335 7631
jvetter@fenwick.com
*Recommended in Corporate/M&A*

**Practice Areas:** Focuses on public and private offerings of securities, mergers and acquisitions, counseling public and late-stage private companies and other

securities law matters. Has represented underwriters of numerous initial public offerings and other public and private offerings of debt and equity securities.

**Personal:** University of California, Hastings College of the Law, JD, magna cum laude, Order of the Coif, member of the Hastings Law Journal, 1990; University of California, Berkeley, BA, with honors and with distinction, 1987.

### VILLENEUVE, Tom

Gunderson Dettmer Stough Villeneuve Franklin & Hachigian, Menlo Park
650 321 2400
*Recommended in Corporate/M&A, IT Outsourcing*

### VIRJEE, Framroze

O'Melveny & Myers LLP, Los Angeles
213 430 6045
fvirjee@omm.com
*Recommended in Employment*

**Practice Areas:** Fram Virjee's practice includes representing employers in employment-related litigation (especially multi-party and class action litigation), collective bargaining negotiations, arbitrations and before state and federal agencies. He practices before both state and federal courts and provides preventive labor and employment law advice to clients on an ongoing basis through client counseling, policy and procedure review and drafting, and extensive in-house training and education on important labor and employment law issues.

### VISCOUNTY, Perry

Latham & Watkins LLP, Costa Mesa
714 540 1235
*Recommended in Intellectual Property*

### WALDMAN, Ira

Cox Castle & Nicholson LLP, Los Angeles
310 277 4222
*Recommended in Real Estate*

### WALKER, Paul

Sidley Austin LLP, Los Angeles
213 896 6789
pwalker@sidley.com
*Recommended in Real Estate*

**Practice Areas:** Real estate debt and equity investment, workout, capital markets, acquisition, disposition, development and leasing, and creditors' rights, representing domestic and foreign capital sources, real estate funds, liquidating banks, and major real estate developers.

**Personal:** University of Notre Dame, BA, 1966; University of Pennsylvania, LLB, 1969. Admissions: NY, CA.

### WALL, Daniel

Latham & Watkins LLP, San Francisco
415 391 0600
*Recommended in Antitrust*

### WAYTE, Alan

DLA Piper Rudnick Gray Cary US LLP, Los Angeles 213 330 7734
alan.wayte@dlapiper.com
*Recommended in Real Estate*

**Practice Areas:** Real estate.
**Career:** He has experience in all aspects of real estate transactions, including real estate finance, purchases and sales, leasing, sale-leasebacks, joint ventures and other forms of partnership, workouts, and foreclosures. His experience also includes extensive work in the organization of business entities such as limited partnerships, limited liability companies, and corporations. He is a writer and frequent speaker for professional groups.
**Personal:** JD, Stanford University; AB, Stanford University.

## WEG, Howard
Peitzman, Weg & Kempinsky LLP, Los Angeles 310 552 3100
*Recommended in Bankruptcy*

## WEINER, Peter
Paul, Hastings, Janofsky & Walker LLP, San Francisco 415 856 7010
peterweiner@paulhastings.com
*Recommended in Environment*
**Practice Areas:** Heads West Coast Environmental Practice. Represents property owners, developers, manufacturers, retailers, waste companies, energy producers, in federal, state, and local (including water boards and air districts) environmental, energy, land use, and OSHA regulatory matters, legislation, and litigation. Areas include 'brownfields' development, environmental insurance, hazardous waste, Superfund, air and water quality, California Environmental Quality Act, Proposition 65, pesticide registration, OSHA, and California energy law. Registered lobbyist, California State government.
**Personal:** BA, Harvard, 1966 (magna cum laude, phi beta kappa). LLB, Yale, 1970, (member, Yale Law Journal). MScEcon, 1967, London School of Economics. Admissions: California, federal courts, US Supreme Court.

## WEINER, Samuel
Latham & Watkins LLP, Los Angeles 213 485 1234
*Recommended in Tax*

## WEISSBURG, Carl I
Foley & Lardner LLP, Los Angeles 310 975 7750
cweissburg@foley.com
*Recommended in Healthcare*
**Career:** Carl I Weissburg is of counsel in the Los Angeles office of Foley & Lardner LLP and is a member of the Health Care Industry Team. He was one of the founding principals of Weissburg and Aronson, which merged with Foley on February 1, 1996. He has been involved extensively in mergers and acquisitions, as well as the formation and operation of independent practice associations, preferred provider organizations and prepaid health plans. His practice focuses on structuring integrated delivery systems and managed care issues. Mr Weissburg is a graduate of Boalt Hall School of Law, University of California, Berkeley.

## WEISSMANN, Eric
Weissmann, Wolff, Bergman, Coleman, Grodin & Evall, LLP, Beverly Hills 310 858 7888
*Recommended in Media & Entertainment*

## WEISSMANN, Henry
Munger, Tolles & Olson LLP, Los Angeles 213 683 9100
*Recommended in Energy*

## WEITZEL, Mark P
Thelen Reid & Priest LLP, San Francisco 415 369 7007
mweitzel@thelenreid.com
*Recommended in Projects*
**Practice Areas:** Mr Weitzel has broad experience in project and infrastructure development and financing, equipment and project leasing transactions, and mergers and acquisitions. His practice includes federal, state and international tax matters and planning. He has experience in the negotiation of investment, acquisition, and shareholder agreements, as well as in structuring complex equity and debt investments.
**Prof. Memberships:** Member, American Bar Association, Sections on Taxation and Business Law; Member, Committees on Capital Recovery and Leasing, and Partnerships. Member, California Bar Association, Sections on Taxation and Business Law.
**Career:** Admitted to practice in California and is also a registered foreign lawyer with the Law Society of England and Wales. Partner of Masons Thelen Reid LLP, a strategic partnership with Masons of the United Kingdom, which serves clients with international infrastructure and buiding projects from inception through financing, contract negotiation, construction and dispute resolution.
**Publications:** 'Restructuring of Energy Projects, US Power Finance Conference', 2005; 'New Strategies for Financing Power Projects, Forbes Infrastructure Conference', 2002; 'Leasing of Power Projects, Energy Notes', 2001
**Personal:** Received his JD and MBA (Finance Concentration) in 1980 from UCLA. Member of the UCLA Law Review and Order of the Coif at UCLA Law School, and National Business Honor Society at the UCLA Graduate School of Management. Undergraduate Degree in 1976 from Stanford University, with distinction. Named by Euromoney as 'One of World's Leading Project Finance Lawyers' and 'One of World's Leading Energy and Natural Resource Lawyers'. Selected by Chambers as one of America's Leading Energy Lawyers and named in the Best Lawyers in America.

## WEST, David
Gibson, Dunn & Crutcher LLP, Los Angeles 213 229 7654

dwest@gibsondunn.com
*Recommended in Employment*
**Practice Areas:** Member of the firm's Employee Benefits and Executive Compensation Practice Groups. Has handled numerous significant matters involving compliance counseling and planning, transactions and litigation in connection with pension and profit sharing, employee stock ownership plans, health and life insurance, and executive compensation.
**Publications:** Has lectured and written extensively on employee benefits subjects, including the ramifications of Financial Accounting Statement 106, employee stock ownership, deferred and equity compensation and the use of the Internet in benefit plan administration.
**Personal:** JD, Fordham University Law School, 1979, Member, Law Review.

## WHEELER, Raymond
Morrison & Foerster LLP, Palo Alto 650 813 5656
rwheeler@mofo.com
*Recommended in Employment*
**Practice Areas:** Advises on all aspects of labor and employment law, including litigation before federal and state courts and administrative agencies. Experienced in representing corporations in collective bargaining, union organizing and decertification efforts. Has handled employment discrimination and wage/hour class actions, hundreds of arbitrations, injunctive actions, wrongful discharge suits and administrative proceedings.
**Prof. Memberships:** Charter Fellow, College of Labor and Employment Lawyers; Management Co-Chair, Publications Committee of the Labor and Employment Law section, ABA; National Advisory Board, Berkeley Journal of Employment and Labor Law.
**Career:** Admitted to practice in California. Chair, Labor and Employment Department.
**Personal:** BA, University of Texas at Austin, 1967; JD, Harvard Law School, 1970; law clerk, Honorable Irving Goldberg, US Court of Appeals, Fifth Circuit, 1970-71.

## WHITE, Andrew
White O'Connor Curry & Avanzado LLP, Los Angeles 310 712 6100
*Recommended in Media & Entertainment*

## WHITE, Robert J
O'Melveny & Myers LLP, Los Angeles 310 246 8485
rwhite@omm.com
*Recommended in Bankruptcy*
**Practice Areas:** Bob White founded O'Melveny & Myers' Restructuring Practice. He has extensive experience in major business restructurings and reorganizations. Bob has been involved in some of the largest chapter 11 reorganization cases in the retail, telecommunications, manufacturing, financial services, energy,

entertainment, healthcare, grocery and insurance related industries. He has also acted as lead counsel in a number of out of court restructurings and has represented bank groups, bank agents, debtors, individual creditors, official creditors' committees and acquirerors. Bob also serves as Chair of the Chapter 11 Committee of the National Bankruptcy Conference.

## WICKERS IV, Alonzo
Davis Wright Tremaine LLP, Los Angeles 213 633 6800
*Recommended in Media & Entertainment*

## WILCOX, Kirby
Paul, Hastings, Janofsky & Walker LLP, San Francisco 415 856 6000
*Recommended in Employment*

## WOHL, Jeffrey
Paul, Hastings, Janofsky & Walker LLP, San Francisco 415 856 6000
*Recommended in Employment*

## WOLFSDORF, Bernard
Bernard P Wolfsdorf PC, Pacific Palisades 310 573 4242
*Recommended in Immigration*

## WONG, Karen
Milbank, Tweed, Hadley & McCloy LLP, Los Angeles 213 892 4000
*Recommended in Projects*

## WONG, Ray L
Duane Morris LLP, San Francisco 415 955 2549
rlwong@duanemorris.com
*Recommended in Insurance*
**Practice Areas:** Ray L Wong practices in the area of litigation with a focus on a variety of business litigation, including employment and other complex civil litigation. He has practiced for more than 26 years in courts throughout California and the United States, representing individual and corporate clients in all facets of civil litigation. Mr Wong also has served as a mediator and arbitrator, and has testified as an expert consultant and witness in civil litigation.
**Prof. Memberships:** Bar Association of San Francisco – Judiciary Committee (past Chair); American Bar Association – Insurance Litigation Committee; Bay Area Asian American Bar Association; San Francisco Legal Aid Society – Board of Directors.
**Career:** Admitted to practice in California. Hancock Rothert & Bunshoft LLP – Chairman, 2000-04, Partner, 1985-2005, associate, 1981-85.
**Personal:** Harvard Law School, JD, 1978; University of Utah, BA, 1975, Phi Beta Kappa.

## WOOD, Mark
O'Melveny & Myers LLP, Los Angeles 213 430 6220
mwood@omm.com

*Recommended in Insurance*
**Practice Areas:** Mark Wood Co-Chair's O'Melveny & Myers' Adversarial Department and handles major litigation and arbitration, including insurance and reinsurance matters, class action product liability cases, and major aircraft accident litigation. Mark is lead counsel for Logan Airport in connection with claims arising from the 9/11 terrorist attack on the World Trade Center and is counsel for underwriters in several arbitrations involving satellite losses. Mark tried a major aircraft accident case and obtained a jury defense verdict for a major airplane manufacturer and has also represented a large hotel chain with respect to matters relating to its hotel management activities.

**WOODS, Daniel**
White & Case LLP, Los Angeles
213 620 7772
dwoods@whitecase.com
*Recommended in Litigation*
**Practice Areas:** Practices complex business litigation with an emphasis on banking, real estate, energy and employment cases. Practice also includes bankruptcy, healthcare, professional negligence, and unfair competition litigation.
**Prof. Memberships:** CalBar; LACBA; Judge Pro Tem, Los Angeles County Superior Court (1999-present) and Municipal Court (1985-present).
**Career:** White & Case since 1996.
**Publications:** Extensive writings on California law.
**Personal:** University of Southern California (AB, cum laude, 1974); University of Southern California Law Center (JD, 1977).

**WYMAN JR, Robert**
Latham & Watkins LLP, Los Angeles
213 485 1234
*Recommended in Environment*

**WYNNE, Richard**
Kirkland & Ellis LLP, Los Angeles
213 680 8400
richard_wynne@la.kirkland.com
*Recommended in Bankruptcy*
**Practice Areas:** Richard Wynne leads Kirkland's West Coast Restructuring Practice. He is an ABC (American Board of Certification) Certified Business Bank-

ruptcy Attorney, and is listed in The K&A Restructuring Register as one of the top 72 lawyers in the United States who "practice in the restructuring, reorganization, insolvency and bankruptcy arenas."
**Prof. Memberships:** Fellow, American College of Bankruptcy; American Bankruptcy Institute; American Bar Association; Los Angeles Bankruptcy Forum; Financial Lawyers Conference; Los Angeles County Bar Association
**Personal:** Indiana University (BA, 1979); Columbia Law School (JD, 1982); Parker School of Foreign and Comparative Law, Columbia University (1983).

**YAFFE, Joseph**
Latham & Watkins LLP, Menlo Park
650 328 4600
*Recommended in Employment*

**YANNEY, Fred**
Fulbright & Jaworski L.L.P., Los Angeles
213 892 9319
fyanney@fulbright.com
*Recommended in Energy*
**Practice Areas:** Energy and utilities; public finance
**Prof. Memberships:** California Bar Association; Los Angeles Bar Association; American Public Power Association; California Municipal Utilities Association.
**Career:** Fred is a Partner in the firm's Los Angeles office. He focuses on energy related matters, with particular emphasis on the electric industry. His practice also includes public finance, where he has served as bond counsel and underwriters' counsel on complex financings. He has represented utilities before the Federal Energy Regulatory Commission (FERC) and the California Public Utilities Commission (CPUC). He has assisted numerous electric utilities and marketers with respect to California's deregulation of the electric utility industry, having been involved in the process from its earliest stages. He has also negotiated and drafted a wide range of electric utility agreements, including joint ownership agreements, construction management agreements, interconnection agreements and various operating agreements regarding large power plants and high voltage transmission lines.
**Personal:** JD, University of Nebraska

(1977); BS, University of Nebraska (1974).

**YOOD, Kenneth J**
Paul, Hastings, Janofsky & Walker LLP, Los Angeles 213 683 6110
kennethyood@paulhastings.com
*Recommended in Healthcare*
**Practice Areas:** Healthcare regulatory compliance; state and federal fraud and abuse and physician referral law limitations, medicare and medicaid fraud.
**Prof. Memberships:** Member, California, Massachusetts and New York bars. Member, American Health Lawyers Association.
**Career:** 1990-93 Weissburg and Aronson, Inc. 1993-99 McCutchen Doyle Brown & Enerson, LLP 1999-present Paul Hastings Janofsky & Walker, LLP.
**Publications:** 'Fraud and Abuse in the Pharmaceutical Industry', Using Health Care Professionals as Consultants, (2004) Los Angeles County Bar Association, Healthcare Section, 'The Medicare Modernization Act: Medicare Part B'. (2004) Council of Ethical Organizations, 'Managed Care Contracting and Corporate Compliance' (2003).

**YOUNG, Douglas**
Farella Braun & Martel LLP, San Francisco 415 954 4400
*Recommended in Litigation*

**YOUNGBLOOD, Juliette**
Irell & Manella LLP, Los Angeles
310 277 1010
*Recommended in Media & Entertainment*

**ZIFFREN, Kenneth**
Ziffren Brittenham Branca Fischer Gilbert-Lurie & Stiffelman LLP, Los Angeles 310 552 3388
*Recommended in Media & Entertainment*

**ZISCHKE, Michael H**
Morrison & Foerster LLP, San Francisco 415 268 6718
mzischke@mofo.com
*Recommended in Environment, Real Estate*
**Practice Areas:** Specializes in the California Environment Quality Act (CEQA), land use litigation and compliance, covering environmental impact, ballot mea-

sure and land use issues. Represents public agencies, businesses, developers, lenders, and investors.
**Prof. Memberships:** Programs Vice-Chair, Environmental Impact Assessment Committee, ABA Section on Environment, Energy & Resources; Member: Lambda Alpha International, Association of Environmental Professionals, California Building Industry Association, Select Committee on Industry Litigation.
**Career:** Admitted to practice in California. The 'Go-To Lawyer: CEQA', The Recorder newspaper (2003).
**Publications:** Co-author: 'Practice Under the CEQA (California Continuing Education of the Bar, two volumes, 1993, supplemented annually); 'Land Use Initiatives and Referenda in California' (Solano Press, 1990).
**Personal:** BA, magna cum laude, Dartmouth College, 1977; JD, Boalt Hall School of Law, 1982.

**ZOVICKIAN, Stephen**
Bingham McCutchen LLP, San Francisco
415 393 2382
stephen.zovickian@bingham.com
*Recommended in Construction*
**Practice Areas:** Serves as Co-Chair of the Construction and Project Finance Litigation Group. Has nearly 30 years of experience, including representation of owners, public entities, contractors and design-builders in arbitrations, mediations, dispute review boards and litigation in state and federal court. Claims prosecuted or defended against include defective work, extra work, disruption and loss of productivity, delay, cumulative impact, breach of implied warranty, constructive changes, acceleration and other theories of recovery for direct and indirect costs allegedly incurred.
**Personal:** University of California Berkeley School of Law (Boalt Hall), JD, 1977; University of California, Berkeley, BA, summa cum laude, 1974.

# ALLEN MATKINS LECK GAMBLE & MALLORY LLP

## THE FIRM

**Managing Partner:** Brian C Leck

**Number of partners:** 108
**Number of other lawyers:** 113

**FIRM OVERVIEW:** Allen Matkins Leck Gamble & Mallory LLP provides clients with creative, cost-effective solutions to complex legal problems. Its 221 attorneys in six locations across California operate in a wide spectrum of business sectors such as real estate, financial services, healthcare, and hospitality. The firm does more than resolve problems; it helps its clients avert legal difficulty by providing them with responsive advice, preventive counseling, and corporate training. The firm brings unique value to its relationships. In providing the highest level of service and individualized attention, Allen Matkins attorneys develop longstanding relationships with clients, continually seeking innovative ways to manage their clients' legal affairs and advance their business objectives. The efficiency and dedication of its attorneys and staff enables Allen Matkins to consistently exceed client expectations.

**MAIN AREAS OF PRACTICE:** Allen Matkins' main practice areas are real estate, litigation, corporate, labor and employment, bankruptcy, and tax.

**CLIENTS:** The firm's clients include Arden Realty Group, Inc., ProLogis (formerly Catellus Development Corporation), CB Richard Ellis Investors, The Dole Food Company, E-Loan, Inc., Exxon-Mobil Corporation, Fox Entertainment Group, Michael A. Grassmueck, Receiver, The Home Depot, IKEA, Imperial Irrigation District, IndyMac Bank Corporation, JP Morgan, Kilroy Realty, L.P., Lennar Corporation, Marriott International, Inc., New York State Teachers' Retirement System, RAD Management, LLC, Sares-Regis Group, Sunstone Hotel Investors, Inc., Tishman-Speyer Properties, L.P., Visa International Service Association, Washington Mutual, and Wells Fargo Bank.

## OFFICES

### CALIFORNIA

515 South Figueroa Street, 7th Floor, **Los Angeles**, CA 90071
**Tel:** 213 622 5555 **Fax:** 213 620 8816

1901 Avenue of the Stars, Suite 1800, **Los Angeles**, CA 90067
**Tel:** 310 788 2400 **Fax:** 310 788 2410

1900 Main Street, 5th Floor, **Irvine**, CA 92614
**Tel:** 949 553 1313 **Fax:** 949 553 8354

501 West Broadway, 15th Floor, **San Diego**, CA 92101
**Tel:** 619 233 1155 **Fax:** 619 233 1158

12348 High Bluff Drive, Suite 100, **San Diego**, CA 92130
**Tel:** 858 481 5055 **Fax:** 858 481 5028

Three Embarcadero Center, 12th Floor, **San Francisco**, CA 94111
**Tel:** 415 837 1515 **Fax:** 415 837 1516

# Allen Matkins

# ALSCHULER GROSSMAN STEIN & KAHAN LLP

## THE FIRM

**Chief Operating Officer:** Richard Jones

**Number of partners:** 60
**Number of other lawyers:** 35

**FIRM OVERVIEW:** Founded in 1952, Alschuler Grossman Stein & Kahan LLP enjoys a national reputation for vigorous and creative advocacy in complex business and entertainment litigation and business transactions. This select group of diverse professionals is committed to finding practical solutions that produce tangible and cost-effective results for clients. The firm's hands-on commitment to the practice of law sets Alschuler Grossman Stein & Kahan LLP apart from many other leading law firms. The firm's involvement in and knowledge of the business, judicial, political, and cultural characteristics unique to its hometown of Los Angeles is unparalleled. The scope of the firm's practice has led it to establish relationships with leading law firms throughout the world. These relationships give the firm the access necessary to represent clients' interests effectively in out-of-state and foreign jurisdictions.

**CLIENTS:** The firm's clientele includes domestic and multinational Fortune 500 companies, emerging companies, and individuals in diverse areas of business and the entertainment industry.

**INTERNATIONAL WORK:** Alschuler Grossman Stein & Kahan LLP represents domestic and international clients in all aspects of international business, trade, and investment. It advises clients about such matters as litigation (including patent and intellectual property litigation), foreign and domestic regulatory compliance, investigations, product distribution, licensing, franchising, and contractual issues. The firm has particular experience representing US clients throughout the Pacific Rim, and representing Pacific Rim clients in the United States. Several of the firm's lawyers are fluent in various Chinese dialects and in Japanese.

## HEAD OFFICE

**CALIFORNIA**
The Water Garden, 1620 26th Street, Fourth Floor, North Tower,
**Santa Monica,** CA 90404-4060
**Tel:** 310 907 1000   **Fax:** 310 907 2000
**Email:** info@agsk.com
**Website:** www.agsk.com

## CONTACTS

| | |
|---|---|
| Business Litigation | Marshall B Grossman |
| Corporate Transactions | Robert L Kahan |
| Entertainment Litigation | Stanton 'Larry' Stein |
| Financial Institutions | William S Small |
| Franchise | Susan Grueneberg |
| Insolvency | Henry S David |
| Insurance/Reinsurance | Bruce A Friedman |
| Intellectual Property | Jeffrey C Briggs |
| Professional Liability Defense | Bruce A Friedman |
| Real Estate | James D Richman |
| Securities Litigation | Frank Kaplan |
| Taxation | M Katharine Davidson |

ALSCHULER GROSSMAN STEIN & KAHAN LLP

# BECK, DE CORSO, DALY, KREINDLER & HARRIS APLC

## THE FIRM

**Managing Shareholders:** Mark E Beck, Bryan D Daly

**Number of shareholders:** 10
**Number of other lawyers:** 4

**FIRM OVERVIEW:** Beck, De Corso is a leading complex civil litigation and white collar criminal defense firm. It represents Fortune 500 corporations, small companies and individuals in civil and criminal trials and appeals, administrative proceedings and alternative dispute resolution proceedings, exemplifying the 'great things in small packages' paradigm. Before joining Beck, De Corso, some of its attorneys served in supervisory positions in the criminal division of the United States Attorney's office. Its attorneys have been honored with numerous awards, including the Department of Justice Director's Award and Special Achievement Award; and the title of Fellow of the American College of Trial Lawyers.

## MAIN AREAS OF PRACTICE

**White Collar Criminal Defense:** Beck, De Corso has substantial experience in defending federal and state white-collar criminal cases. It represents individuals and businesses from the pre-indictment, investigatory phase (including grand jury and corporate internal investigations) through any sentencing and appeal. The firm is also consulted regularly by other counsel, for expert advice on criminal law issues.

**Civil Litigation:** Beck, De Corso represents clients in a wide array of business litigation in state and federal courts, sometimes parallel to criminal proceedings. The firm is often retained to negotiate the resolution of allegations that threaten the stability or financial integrity of the client company.

**Administrative Proceedings:** The firm has substantial experience representing companies and individuals before administrative tribunals in various types of proceedings, including licensing and permit revocations, forfeitures, security clearance reviews, and debarment and suspension actions.

**Appellate Advocacy:** Beck, De Corso has extensive experience representing companies and individuals before state and federal courts of appeal, on direct appeal, and in writ proceedings.

**CLIENTS:** Representative criminal defense clients include individuals as well as, multinational and Fortune 500 companies, and their officers, directors, shareholders, and employees in allegations involving the following industries and subjects: aerospace (false testing, product substitution, quality assurance fraud, mischarging, defective pricing, and violations of the Foreign Corrupt Practices Act); banking and finance (currency reporting violations, money laundering, fraud, and embezzlement); healthcare (kickbacks, state and federal fraud and abuse violations, and fraudulent insurance claims); securities (violations of various SEC regulations and related federal criminal statutes); public corruption (election campaign contribution violations, bribery, and acts of political corruption); export/import (violations of laws regulating the export and import of technology, munitions, and other items); trademark (trademark misappropriation and counterfeiting); tax (violations of state and federal tax laws and regulations); environmental (violations of state and federal environmental regulations and statutes, including RCRA, CERCLA, and the Clean Air Act); and other crimes (including mail and wire fraud, RICO claims, extortion, embezzlement, and bankruptcy fraud). Representative civil litigation clients include privately and publicly held companies, foreign sovereign interests, community organizations, lending institutions, public officials, and an array of individuals with diverse professional and business interests. Cases have included: business torts such as unfair competition, anti-trust violations, and interference with business relationships; complex RICO claims; major fraud cases; securities violations involving alleged insider trading, SEC reporting violations, and related issues; defamation cases involving public and private figures; employment termination and discrimination claims; defense and prosecution of qui tam fraud actions brought under the False Claims Act; and breach of contract claims, among others.

## HEAD OFFICE

**CALIFORNIA**
601 West 5th Street, 12th Floor, **Los Angeles**, CA 90071-2025
**Tel:** 213 688 1198  **Fax:** 213 489 7532
**Email:** beckdecorso@earthlink.net
**Website:** www.beckdecorso.com

# BLECHER & COLLINS

## THE FIRM

**Managing Partner:** Maxwell M Blecher

**Number of attorneys:** 14

**FIRM OVERVIEW:** Founded in 1971, Blecher & Collins engages in complex litigation with emphasis on antitrust. The firm's exceptional expertise in the antitrust field has resulted in many precedent setting decisions in the US Supreme Court and several courts of appeals. Blecher & Collins has had extensive trial experience in federal and state courts on behalf of both plaintiffs and defendants for a broad spectrum of domestic and international clients. The firm has handled cases against the US Department of Justice and such companies as ARCO, AT&T, the NFL, the NBA, 3M and HBO. Small by design, Blecher & Collins consists of a team of highly skilled attorneys experienced in all aspects of complex commercial litigation. The firm strives to provide a high degree of flexibility and responsiveness to the needs of its clients.

**MAIN AREAS OF PRACTICE:** In addition to antitrust, the firm's litigation practice includes copyright infringement; professional negligence and malicious prosecution; complex commercial litigation; and class actions. Some of the major matters the firm has recently handled include complex commercial cases involving claims of fraud, breach of contract, breach of fiduciary duty, intentional interference with contract or prospective business advantage, as well as cases under the Federal Communications Act and numerous class actions under the California Code. The firm recently won a significant malicious prosecution case which was affirmed by the Ninth Circuit Court of Appeals.

**CLIENTS:** The firm's clients range from Fortune 500 companies to small and medium-sized businesses, as well as individuals across a wide range of industries including telecommunications, oil and gas, entertainment, sports, healthcare, consumer goods, automotive parts, and technological goods and services.

**HEAD OFFICE**

**CALIFORNIA**
515 South Figueroa Street, 17th Floor, **Los Angeles**, CA 90071
**Tel:** 213 622 4222   **Fax:** 213 622 1656
**Website:** www.blechercollins.com
**Email:** info@blechercollins.com

# BLECHER & COLLINS

# FENWICK & WEST LLP

## THE FIRM

**Chairman:** Gordon K Davidson
**Managing Partner:** Kathryn J Fritz
**Number of partners:** 82
**Number of other lawyers:** 162

**FIRM OVERVIEW:** Fenwick & West LLP provides comprehensive legal services to high technology and life sciences companies of national and international prominence. More than 240 attorneys offer corporate, intellectual property, litigation and tax services from the firm's offices in Mountain View and San Francisco, California.

## MAIN AREAS OF PRACTICE:

**CORPORATE GROUP:** Fenwick & West services high technology and life sciences companies, from early start-ups to mature public companies.

**Mergers & Acquisitions:** Fenwick & West's Mergers and Acquisitions Practice is ranked among the top 25 practices in the United States according to the American Lawyer. The firm's lawyers understand the problems that arise in technology company acquisitions and focus their efforts on issues that are of the most value to the client. The Mergers and Acquisitions Group's expertise spans the entire spectrum of high technology, from life sciences to semiconductors, and its lawyers are equally adept at small private company transactions and multi-billion dollar public transactions. For clients involved in larger deals, the firm's antitrust lawyers are experienced in working with the Department of Justice and Federal Trade Commission in the pre-merger clearance process. Fenwick & West attorneys understand the many issues that can mean the difference between a successful transaction and a broken promise.

**Public Offerings & Securities Law Compliance:** Fenwick & West's extensive representation of emerging companies has given it substantial depth of experience in public offerings. In recent years, the firm has represented companies or investment banks in more than 100 initial public offerings, which, combined, have raised over $7 billion dollars. The firm has helped clients raise billions more in follow-on debt and equity offerings. The firm's counseling practice for technology companies regarding ongoing public securities law issues includes extensive Sarbanes-Oxley compliance and board or audit committee counseling.

**Strategic Alliances:** For many high technology companies, the path to financing and commercialization begins with their first collaboration or joint venture with an industry partner. These agreements can often make or break a young technology company. Fenwick & West attorneys help clients think through the business, intellectual property, tax and other legal issues that arise in their corporate partnering transactions and joint ventures.

**Executive Compensation:** As an integral part of the Corporate Practice, Fenwick & West attorneys counsel clients on a wide range of employee benefits and compensation matters.

**Start-Up Companies:** The firm has represented hundreds of growth-oriented companies from inception through maturity. Fenwick & West attorneys understand what it takes to start with only an idea, build a team, found a company, raise venture capital funding and grow a business. They have represented many of the nation's leading venture capital firms and do multiple deals each year with companies financed by these market leaders.

**INTELLECTUAL PROPERTY GROUP:** Fenwick & West delivers comprehensive, integrated advice regarding all aspects of intellectual property protection and exploitation. The firm has been consistently ranked as one of the top five West Coast firms in intellectual property litigation and protection for the past 10 years by Euromoney's Managing Intellectual Property publication. From providing sophisticated legal defense in precedent-setting lawsuits to crafting unique license arrangements and implementing penetrating intellectual property audits, Fenwick & West's intellectual property lawyers have pioneered and remain at the forefront of legal innovation. They are continually in sync with their clients' technological advances in order to protect their positions in this fiercely competitive marketplace. The Intellectual Property Group is comprised of approximately 80

## HEAD OFFICE

**CALIFORNIA**
Silicon Valley Center, 801 California Street, **Mountain View**, CA 94041
**Tel:** 650 988 8500   **Fax:** 650 938 5200
**Website:** www.fenwick.com

## BRANCH OFFICE

**CALIFORNIA**
Embarcadero Center West, 275 Battery Street, **San Francisco**, CA 94111
**Tel:** 415 875 2300   **Fax:** 415 281 1350

## CONTACTS

| | |
|---|---|
| **Corporate Group** | Matthew P Quilter |
| **Intellectual Property Group** | David L Hayes |
| **Litigation Group** | Lynn H Pasahow |
| **Tax Group** | James P Fuller |

lawyers and other professionals, a significant number of whom have technical and advanced degrees, and substantial industry work experience. More than 40 attorneys are licensed to practice before the US Patent and Trademark Office. The technical skills and industry experience of Fenwick & West's lawyers help them render sophisticated advice with respect to novel technologies and related intellectual property rights issues.

**LITIGATION GROUP:** The Fenwick & West Litigation Group has the range of experience and critical mass to protect clients' interests in virtually any type of dispute, large or small. While the firm's attorneys have extensive litigation experience in a wide range of industries, they have exceptional depth and breadth in the areas of the law critical to their high technology clients, including software and programming; Internet and entertainment; computer hardware; semiconductors and life sciences. Fenwick & West is regularly involved in significant cases involving intellectual property (patents, copyright, trademarks and trade secrets), employment disputes, corporate governance, securities, antitrust and general commercial litigation. In addition to civil litigation, the firm's attorneys are experienced in representing clients in civil and criminal government investigations. Using a network of experienced local counsel, they routinely represent clients in cases throughout the United States.

**TAX GROUP:** Fenwick & West has one of the nation's leading domestic and international tax practices. The Tax Group's unusually exciting and sophisticated practice stems from a client base that is represented in every geographic region of the United States, as well as a number of foreign countries, and has included approximately 100 Fortune 500 companies, 38 of which are in the Fortune 100. In recent surveys of 1,500 companies published in International Tax Review, Fenwick & West was selected as the top tax advisor in the Western United States.

**INTERNATIONAL WORK:** Fenwick & West routinely handles corporate transactions, venture capital financing, licensing transactions and litigation, as well as intellectual property, trademark and tax matters in foreign jurisdictions for its US clients. The firm also represents a growing number of foreign technology companies throughout Asia, Europe and the Middle East on US-related transactions.

**FENWICK & WEST LLP**

# GIBBS, GIDEN, LOCHER & TURNER LLP

## THE FIRM

**Managing Partner:** Richard J Wittbrodt
**Senior Partner:** Kenneth C Gibbs

**Number of partners:** 21
**Number of other lawyers:** 19

**FIRM OVERVIEW:** Founded to represent and serve the unique interests of clients involved in the planning and building of construction projects, Gibbs, Giden, Locher & Turner LLP currently has one of the largest teams of attorneys dedicated to dealing with these issues in the western United States. In the process of providing full service to its construction clients, the firm's practice has expanded to include the related areas of business and commercial law, employment and labor law, real property transactions, environmental law, and title insurance, suretyship, and property, casualty and liability insurance. From offices in Los Angeles and Las Vegas, the firm's attorneys counsel clients involved in projects, transactions and litigation throughout the United States.

## MAIN AREAS OF PRACTICE:

**Construction & Public Contracts:** The Construction and Public Contracts Department of the firm provides legal guidance and counseling to clients at every stage of a construction project. The firm's attorneys regularly draft, analyze and review procurement and custom contract documents for all forms of project delivery systems, including the traditional design-bid-build, design-build and multi-prime contracts and is well-versed and routinely works with AIA construction documents. The firm is also extensively involved in all phases of preconstruction, including bid protests and contractor substitution issues. The firm has extensive experience in virtually every type of construction project, including airports, power plants, hospitals, major sports and entertainment venues, office buildings, correctional facilities, retail locations, major residential projects, transportation projects, universities, courthouses, petrochemical plants, dams, pipelines, and wastewater and water treatment facilities. The firm has represented public and private owners, design professionals, general contractors, subcontractors and material suppliers with respect to almost every conceivable circumstance that can arise before, during and after completion of a construction project. The firm has litigated numerous delay and disruption cases, including: the construction of various Metro Rail Transit projects, the Port of Long Beach, Cedars-Sinai Medical Center in Los Angeles, San Francisco International Airport, John Wayne Airport in Orange County, Ritz-Carlton Huntington Hotel in Pasadena, Kaiser Riverside Medical Center, Los Angeles County Central Jail Expansion Project, Southeast Resource Recovery Facility in Long Beach, the Space Shuttle launch facility at Vandenberg Air Force Base, Hyperion Wastewater Treatment Plant in Los Angeles, Coso Geothermal Plant located near China Lake, the Aladdin and Venetian Hotels in Las Vegas, Nevada, and the Disney Concert Hall in Los Angeles, California.

**Business & Commercial Law:** The Business and Commercial Law Department of the firm was formed to assist the firm's construction industry clients in collection matters and the enforcement of statutory mechanic's lien, stop notice, and payment bond rights. The firm also handles all aspects of creditor representation in bankruptcy proceedings, including preference claims, motions for relief from the automatic stay, motions to assume or reject executory contracts, and non-dischargeability actions. Its litigators have substantial experience in bringing and defending business tort actions such as fraud, unfair competition, RICO antitrust, trade secrets, and business interference claims. Clients include contractors, manufacturers, distributors, technology companies and financial institutions.

## HEAD OFFICE

**CALIFORNIA**
2029 Century Park East, 34th Floor, **Los Angeles**, CA 90067
**Tel:** 310 552 3400  **Fax:** 310 552 0805
**Email:** postmaster@gglt.com
**Website:** www.gglt.com

## BRANCH OFFICE

**NEVADA**
3993 Howard Hughes Parkway, Suite 530, **Las Vegas,** NV 89109
**Tel:** 702 836 9800  **Fax:** 702 836 9802

## CONTACTS

**Construction & Public Contracts** Kenneth C Gibbs, Barbara R Gadbois
**Business & Commercial Law** ..James D Lipschultz, Richard J Wittbrodt
**Labor & Employment Law** ...........Gerald A Griffin, Gary E Scalabrini
**Insurance & Suretyship** ...................Theodore L Senet, Anya Stanley
**Real Estate & Environmental Law** .......................William D Locher
**Las Vegas Office** ................................................William H Luttrell

**Labor & Employment Law:** For over two decades, the attorneys of the firm's Labor and Employment Department have provided their expertise to a wide range of private businesses, municipalities and institutions. The firm's attorneys have extensive experience defending against claims of wrongful termination, retaliation, employment discrimination, harassment and are actively involved in collective bargaining, labor arbitrations, and administrative hearings. The firm has defended employers against claims filed with the National Labor Relations Board, the California Labor Commissioner, the Division of Labor Standards Enforcement, the Department of Industrial Relations, the Employment Development Department, and the Federal Department of Labor. The firm represents employers not only in federal and state court, but also before governmental agencies, such as the Equal Employment Opportunity Commission and the Department of Fair Employment and Housing. In addition, the firm frequently prosecutes and defends appeals to state and federal appellate courts.

**Insurance & Suretyship:** The Insurance and Suretyship Department of the firm represents both insureds and insurers in claims and coverage disputes, including first-party property losses, casualty claims, surety claims, reinsurance, excess insurance, and multi-carrier litigation. Within the practice group, the firm has expertise in risk management and the analysis, negotiation and litigation of insurance coverage issues common to the business, real estate, manufacturing and construction industries.

**CLIENTS:** Representative Clients Include: Alameda Corridor Transportation Authority, Arrow Electronics, Brinderson Corporation, Centex Corporation, City of Buena Park, City of Anaheim, City of Burbank,  City of Glendale, City of Huntington Beach, City of Long Beach, City of Pasadena, City of Redondo Beach, City of Reno, Nevada, County of San Bernardino, Crescent Heights of America, EQR/Equity Residential, Ferguson Enterprises, Inc., General Electric Company, Kajima Engineering & Construction, Kiewit Pacific Company, Macsteel Service Centers USA, Inc, Metropolitan Water District of Southern California, Morley Construction Company, M.A. Mortenson Company, Ojai Valley Inn & Spa, Port of Long Beach, Schuff Steel Company, Snap-On Tools, Snyder Langston Builders, State Farm Insurance Co., Swinerton Builders, University of Southern California, and Vulcan Materials Company.

GIBBS, GIDEN, LOCHER & TURNER LLP

# GIBSON, DUNN & CRUTCHER LLP

## THE FIRM

**Managing Partner:** Kenneth M Doran

**FIRM OVERVIEW:** With approximately 800 attorneys in 13 locations worldwide, Gibson, Dunn & Crutcher is distinctively positioned for doing business in today's global marketplace. Consistently ranking among the world's top law firms in industry surveys and major publications, Gibson Dunn represents some of the world's largest multinational corporations in all major industries, leading government entities, commercial and investment banks, start-up ventures, emerging growth businesses, partnerships and individuals.

## MAIN AREAS OF PRACTICE:

**Business Restructuring & Reorganization:** The firm has participated in many of the most complex insolvency-related proceedings and transactions of the last decade. The attorneys regularly represent Chapter 11 debtors in possession, enterprises seeking to restructure their obligations, enterprises and individuals contemplating Chapter 11 protection, creditors' committees and individual creditors, bondholders and often lenders, acquisition candidates, potential acquirers, insurers and trustees.

**Capital Markets & Finance:** Gibson Dunn has a reputation for excellence and creativity as counsel to issuers, underwriters, initial purchasers and placement agents. A well-balanced practice, with an extensive representation of issuers and underwriters, combined with exceptional regulatory strength, gives Gibson Dunn the breadth and insight that few firms can match.

**Commercial Litigation & Arbitration:** Gibson Dunn has represented many Fortune 500 companies in cases involving securities fraud, antitrust, administrative law, accountancy defense, intellectual property, employment discrimination, environmental, entertainment, white collar crime, business torts, among many others. Many of these cases have included class action claims and involved hundreds of millions of dollars in alleged damages.

**Global Finance:** The firm focuses on the representation of lenders, borrowers, underwriters and issuers in a large variety of debt and structured finance transactions, including leveraged loans, high yield bond offerings, mezzanine, project finance, equipment financings, restructurings and securitizations. During 2005, Gibson Dunn attorneys handled finance transactions with an aggregate value in excess of $87 billion.

**Intellectual Property:** Gibson Dunn assists clients with a wide range of IP issues, including litigating critical IP disputes; negotiating licenses and joint ventures; navigating local, national and international regulations governing privacy, trade and the protection of IP; and advocating for change in IP law and policy.

**Labor & Employment:** Recent representations include some of the most prominent labor relations matters in the country, high stakes wage-and-hour class actions, one of the most significant Americans with Disabilities Act cases brought by the EEOC to date, and aggressive advocacy on OSHA issues.

**Mergers & Acquisitions:** Gibson Dunn is one of the top-ranked M&A law firms in the world. The firm has extensive experience in all types of M&A transactions, including: mergers of public and private companies, stock and asset purchases, tender and exchange offers, restructurings and acquisitions out of bankruptcy, divestitures and spin-offs, leveraged buyouts and private equity investments, strategic investments and joint ventures, special committee representations, and cross-border M&A transactions.

**Real Estate:** Gibson Dunn handles a variety of sophisticated matters for clients ranging from privately held entrepreneurial developers to the owners, developers and financiers of the largest real estate projects in the US and Europe. The firm's attorneys are skilled in a broad spectrum of real estate matters including real estate finance, development, sales and acquisitions, land use and environmental, leasing and workout transactions.

## HEAD OFFICE

**CALIFORNIA**
333 S Grand Avenue, **Los Angeles**, CA 90071
**Tel:** 213 229 7000   **Fax:** 213 229 7520
**Website:** www.gibsondunn.com

## BRANCH OFFICES

**CALIFORNIA**
Jamboree Center, 4 Park Plaza, **Irvine**, CA 92614
**Tel:** 949 451 3800   **Fax:** 949 451 4220

2029 Century Park East, Suite 4000, **Los Angeles**, CA 90067
**Tel:** 310 552 8500   **Fax:** 310 551 8741

1881 Page Mill Road, **Palo Alto**, CA 94304
**Tel:** 650 849 5300   **Fax:** 650 849 5333

One Montgomery Street, Suite 3100, **San Francisco**, CA 94104
**Tel:** 415 393 8200   **Fax:** 415 986 5309

**COLORADO**
1801 California Street, Suite 4200, **Denver**, CO 80202
**Tel:** 303 298 5700   **Fax:** 303 296 5310

**DISTRICT OF COLUMBIA**
1050 Connecticut Avenue NW, **Washington**, DC 20036
**Tel:** 202 955 8500   **Fax:** 202 467 0539

**NEW YORK**
200 Park Avenue, **New York**, NY 10166
**Tel:** 212 351 4000   **Fax:** 212 351 4035

**TEXAS**
2100 McKinney Avenue, Suite 1100, **Dallas**, TX 75201
**Tel:** 214 698 3100   **Fax:** 214 571 2900

## INTERNATIONAL OFFICES

The firm also has offices in Brussels, London, Munich and Paris.

**CLIENTS:** The firm represents many of the Fortune 100 companies in the following industries: accounting, banking, biotech/biomedical, energy, gaming, healthcare, industrial and aerospace, insurance, merchant banks/VC funds, media and entertainment, real estate/REITs, retail, sports and transportation.

**INTERNATIONAL WORK:** Gibson Dunn's international team consists of US, UK, French and German qualified lawyers, many of whom are dual qualified. The Paris and London offices have been open since 1967 and 1979, respectively. The firm's Munich office opened in 2002 and the Brussels office opened in 2003. This long-term European presence has given them considerable experience in representing clients with international business interests requiring a coordinated response within and across national borders, throughout Europe and beyond. The firm's international offices handle all types of corporate transactions, corporate financing, tax structuring, real estate and antitrust matters. Gibson Dunn has expanded in a way that preserves firm culture and in particular the high value the firm places on teamwork, top level skills and professional practice.

# HELLER EHRMAN LLP

## THE FIRM

**Chairman:** Matthew L Larrabee
**Executive Director:** Phyllis A Gardner

**FIRM OVERVIEW:** Heller Ehrman LLP has more than 700 attorneys and professionals in 12 offices worldwide (Anchorage, Beijing, Hong Kong, Los Angeles, Madison WI, New York San Diego, San Francisco, Seattle, Silicon Valley, Singapore and Washington DC). As a full-service law firm, Heller Ehrman represents a wide range of industry leaders, from entrepreneurial, technology-driven enterprises to established, global corporations. Heller Ehrman takes a multidisciplinary approach to the practice of law, drawing upon its legal, industrial and technical expertise from across the firm to build the best legal teams for its clients. Through commitment to the core values of excellence, people, teamwork, innovation, community and 'one firm', Heller Ehrman offers clients unparalleled legal service. In 2005, The American Lawyer ranked Heller Ehrman number nine on its 2005 'A-List', recognizing the best law firms in the United States based on scores for revenue per lawyer, pro bono, associate satisfaction and diversity. 16 lateral shareholders joined the firm in 2005, including a former Assistant Director for the Bureau of Competition at the Federal Trade Commission and a former member and Director of the Irish Competition Authority. In 2004, Heller Ehrman implemented an innovative Diversity Fellowship program that provides summer employment and scholarships to four first-year law students who show promise of contributing meaningfully to the diversity of the legal community. In 2005, Heller Ehrman moved to larger offices in New York, Washington, DC, Los Angeles and Beijing. The firm's attorneys are graduates of the country's top academic institutions and include former Rhodes Scholars, US and state Supreme Court clerks, and law review editors. Heller Ehrman attorneys also include former federal prosecutors, seven fellows of the American College of Trial Lawyers, a former Federal Trade Commissioner, a former general counsel to the Department of Commerce, former Patent and Trademark Office examiners, as well as a number of attorneys who hold PhDs in disciplines such as neuroscience, microbiology, chemistry and computer science. For more information, please visit the firm's website: www.hellerehrman.com.

**MAIN AREAS OF PRACTICE:** Clients rely on Heller Ehrman to address their most important business issues and solve their most challenging problems.
**Litigation:** The firm's nationally recognized Litigation Team handles bet-the-company litigation in a range of key arenas, including antitrust, securities, intellectual property, consumer class action, insurance recovery, product liability, employment and environmental law.
**Business Law:** Heller Ehrman's business and transactional attorneys are leaders in corporate securities, M&A, finance, real estate, tax, corporate governance and a range of regulatory issues.
**Intellectual Property:** The firm's Intellectual Property Practice combines a highly reputed Patent Litigation Team with extensive in-house patent and trademark resources.

**CLIENTS:** The firm secured a nine-zero victory in the Supreme Court of the United States for its client Merck KGaA in Merck KGaA v. Integra LifeSciences. The firm currently represents the largest manufacturer of vitamin C in China in the first antitrust proceedings brought against a Chinese company in the United States. The firm represents clients involved in many of the highest profile securities matters in the country, including Enron, Parmalat, Cendant and AOL Time Warner. Heller Ehrman is part of the team defending Visa U.S.A Inc. in a series of putative antitrust class actions filed on behalf of consumers in a number of states. Yahoo! Inc. turned to Heller Ehrman for their patent infringement case with Google; the settlement is estimated at a value in excess of $500 million. The firm continues to be counsel for Microsoft and Philip Morris in some of the largest antitrust matters in the US. Heller Ehrman regularly negotiates investment terms for funds organized by some of the world's leading venture capital and buyout investment firms, including Morgan Stanley, Texas Pacific Group, Blackstone, Thomas H. Lee, Warburg Pincus, Draper Fisher Jurvetson, Silver Lake Partners, Venrock Associates and Whitney & Co. The firm has one of the world's leading hospitality practices and count among its clients Four Seasons Hotels and Resorts, Fairmont Hotels & Resorts and Starwood Hotels & Resorts. The firm has handled multiple transactions involving some of the world's leading companies, including Yahoo!, Cisco, Microsoft, Washington Mutual, IBM, Nokia, Johnson & Johnson and QUALCOMM.

## HEAD OFFICE

**CALIFORNIA**
333 Bush Street, **San Francisco**, CA 94104-2878
**Tel:** 415 772 6000 **Fax:** 415 772 6268
**Email:** info@hellerehrman.com
**Website:** www.hellerehrman.com

## BRANCH OFFICES

**ALASKA**
510 L Street, Suite 500, **Anchorage**, AK 99501-1959
**Tel:** 907 277 1900 **Fax:** 907 277 1920

**CALIFORNIA**
333 South Hope Street, 39th Floor, **Los Angeles**, CA 90071-1406
**Tel:** 213 689 0200 **Fax:** 213 614 1868

275 Middlefield Road, **Menlo Park**, CA 94025-3506
**Tel:** 650 324 7000 **Fax:** 650 324 0638

4350 La Jolla Village Drive, 7th Floor, **San Diego**, CA 92122-1246
**Tel:** 858 450 8400 **Fax:** 858 450 8499

**DISTRICT OF COLUMBIA**
1717 Rhode Island Ave, N.W., **Washington,** DC 20036-3001
**Tel:** 202 912 2000 **Fax:** 202 912 2020

**NEW YORK**
Times Square Tower, 7 Times Square, **New York**, NY 10036-6524
**Tel:** 212 832 8300 **Fax:** 212 763 7600

**WASHINGTON**
701 Fifth Avenue, Suite 6100, **Seattle**, WA 98104-7098
**Tel:** 206 447 0900 **Fax:** 206 447 0849

**WISCONSIN**
One East Main Street, Suite 201, **Madison,** WI 53703-5118
**Tel:** 608 663 7460 **Fax:** 608 663 7499

## INTERNATIONAL OFFICES

The firm also has offices in Hong Kong, Beijing and Singapore.

## CONTACTS

**Firmwide Managing Shareholder** ............................Robert B Hubbell
**Managing Director - Business** .......................................Mark B Weeks
**Managing Director - Litigation** .........................................Marie L Fiala
**Managing Director - People** ............................................Judith C Miles
**Managing Director - International** ...............................Paul D Downs
**Managing Director - Client Relationships** ......................Mark S Parris
**Executive Committee - Practice**...................................George E Greer

HellerEhrman LLP

# HENNIGAN, BENNETT & DORMAN LLP

## THE FIRM

**Managing Partner:** Robert L Palmer
**Senior Partners:** J Michael Hennigan, Bruce S Bennett, Roderick G Dorman

**Number of partners:** 22
**Number of other lawyers:** 26

## HEAD OFFICE

**CALIFORNIA**
865 South Figueroa Street, Suite 2900, **Los Angeles**, CA 90017
**Tel:** 213 694 1200   **Fax:** 213 694 1234
**Website:** www.hbdlawyers.com

**FIRM OVERVIEW:** Hennigan, Bennett & Dorman LLP (HBD) is dedicated to delivering innovative and practical legal solutions to a wide range of commercial disputes of extraordinary size and complexity. The firm consists of forty-eight highly-credentialed, experienced lawyers who effectively resolve difficult business problems by integrating skill in complex commercial litigation, bankruptcy and reorganization matters, and intellectual property disputes. The firm and its principals have achieved unusual success for its clients in these three practices areas. The firm is entrepreneurial and frequently unconventional. It employs innovative strategies to end commercial disputes quickly and advantageously for its clients. From the very beginning of a case the firm employs a collaborative process of thesis development involving its lawyers, forensic accountants, and financial analysts. This allows the firm to penetrate complex interrelated business and legal issues and to develop a winning thesis that will resonate in an effective discovery strategy on through trial or other resolution. HBD is known for its successes in trial. Most of the firm's cases settle well because its opponents know both that the firm likes to try cases and that it wins the vast majority of those tried. All of the firm's lawyers understand that HBD sells results, not hours.

## MAIN AREAS OF PRACTICE:

**Complex Commercial Litigation:** HBD is a trial firm with particular expertise handling individual and class actions involving financial and securities frauds, shareholder derivative claims, directors' and officers' liability claims, antitrust claims, breach of fiduciary duty claims, commercial contract disputes, and the prosecution and defense of professional liability claims. Its practice covers a broad range of industries including banking, finance, securities, high technology and the internet, energy, public accounting, real estate development, aviation, health care, pharmaceutical, and entertainment and media. In the securities law area, the firm has extensive experience representing both plaintiffs and defendants in cases involving alleged violations of the Securities Exchange Act of 1934, and under state 'blue-sky' securities laws, as well as tender offer and takeover litigation and related matters. The firm also has extensive experience representing individuals and companies involved in investigations conducted by the Securities and Exchange Commission, the Justice Department, the California Department of Corporations, and the California Attorney General's Office.

**Business Reorganization & Bankruptcy:** The Business Reorganization and Bankruptcy Group at HBD is a national leader in its field. Its senior members have successfully represented major positions in some of the most complex and difficult reorganization and bankruptcy cases to have been filed in the last two decades. The firm's practice encompasses representation of debtors, secured creditors, unsecured creditors and equity interest holders, and statutory committees and informal or ad hoc committees of bondholders or other creditors. It also represents persons or entities in connection with the acquisition of assets of, equity interests in, or control of troubled businesses, including corporations.

**Patent & Technology:** The firm's Patent and Technology Group is a nationally recognized leader in successfully representing major corporations and entrepreneurs to acquire, maximize and enforce their intellectual property asset portfolio. HBD lawyers have also enjoyed extraordinary success in defending clients in technology and trade secret disputes. The senior attorneys have been and continue to be lead trial counsel in major, high stakes patent, copyright, trademark and trade secret litigation for major corporations and also for well-known inventors and entrepreneurs. The partners of the Patent and Technology Group have been lead trial counsel in over 60 patent, copyright, and trade secret cases. The firm has repeatedly and successfully handled important patent matters before the Federal Circuit Court of Appeals.

**CLIENTS:** Hennigan, Bennett & Dorman LLP represents clients in a wide array of industries, including banking, finance, securities, digital technology and the internet, energy, real estate development, aviation, health care, pharmaceutical, entertainment and media.

# KEKER & VAN NEST LLP

## THE FIRM

**Managing Partner:** Christopher C Kearney
**Number of partners:** 24
**Number of attorneys:** 53

## AREAS OF PRACTICE:
Litigation . . . . . . . . . . . . . . . . . . . . . . . . . . . . . . . . . . . . . . . . . . . . 100%

**FIRM OVERVIEW:** Keker & Van Nest is a trial-practice litigation firm located in San Francisco. For more than 25 years, the firm has devoted its practice exclusively to complex civil and criminal litigation. The firm's practice is national in scope and includes trials of complex, high-stakes civil or criminal litigation cases in state and federal courts throughout California and the nation. In its January 2005 edition, The American Lawyer Magazine named Keker & Van Nest as the 'Litigation Boutique of the Year,' singling out the firm for litigation success in high stakes matters. "Keker & Van Nest lawyers handle cases of national importance...Not only do they win consistently, they do so while working in an environment that is a model for the legal industry in the areas of diversity and pro bono."

## MAIN AREAS OF PRACTICE:
**Intellectual Property:** Keker & Van Nest represents plaintiffs and defendants in patent, trade secret, trademark, and copyright cases. The firm's clients include companies in the fields of semiconductors, medical equipment, biotech, software, networking, the internet, and consumer goods such as wineries, and include four of Wired Magazine's top ten new economy companies. The American Lawyer Magazine, in connection with awarding the firm with Litigation Boutique of the year honor, cited the firm for its "precedent setting copyright cases," and stated "Keker & Van Nest has been in the vanguard of emerging intellectual property precedents, winning key decisions protecting the patent rights of biotech leader Genentech and successfully defending client Grokster when it was sued by virtually the entire entertainment industry."

**Antitrust:** Keker & Van Nest maintains a diverse antitrust practice. On the civil side, the firm defends against and prosecutes antitrust claims. The firm represents individuals and corporations in individual and class-action suits in federal and state court, administrative proceedings and investigations by enforcement authorities. On the criminal side, the firm represents individuals and corporations in investigations by both federal and state prosecutors.

**White Collar Criminal:** Keker & Van Nest is one of the pre-eminent federal criminal defense trial firms in the country. The firm has handled a wide variety of financial fraud cases, including allegations of securities fraud, and bank fraud, tax fraud, as well as medicare fraud, false claims act charges, foreign corrupt practices act and other transnational crimes, and environmental violations. Many of these cases are resolved during the grand jury stage with no charges being brought and thus never become public.

**Contract & Commercial:** Keker & Van Nest represents plaintiffs and defendants in a broad range of commercial disputes, including class actions. The firm has handled class actions relating to discrimination and other unfair business practice claims, employee claims, false advertising claims, and securities related claims.

**Professional Liability:** Keker & Van Nest has been hired by major law firms, particularly those insured by Attorneys Liability Assurance Society (ALAS) and MPC Insurance, Ltd. in professional liability litigation involving claims of malpractice, malicious prosecution, allegations of fraud, conflicts of interest, and breach of fiduciary duty. In addition, the firm has represented two national accounting firms in defending breach of contract, professional negligence and fraud claims.

**CLIENTS:** The firm's corporate clients include American Honda Motor Company, Inc.; AT&T Wireless; Cadence Design Systems; Comcast Cable Communications, Inc.; eBay, Inc.; Electronic Arts, Inc.; The Gap, Inc.; Genentech, Inc.; Google, Inc.; Intel Corporation; Johnson & Johnson; National Semiconductor; Netflix, Inc.; Pacific Gas & Electric; Palm, Inc.; Taiwan Semiconductor Manufacturing Corp.

# KEKER & VAN NEST LLP

# KLEE, TUCHIN, BOGDANOFF & STERN LLP

## THE FIRM

**Co-Managing Partners:** Lee R Bogdanoff, Michael L Tuchin

**Number of partners:** 11
**Number of other lawyers:** 8

**FIRM OVERVIEW:** Klee Tuchin Bogdanoff & Stern is a national, boutique law firm that specializes in business reorganizations, corporate insolvency, commercial litigation, bankruptcy-related asset acquisitions, bankruptcy litigation and appellate advocacy, and expert witness services in the bankruptcy field. KTB&S represents debtors, creditors, equity holders, committees, trustees, landlords, potential acquirers of assets, and other parties with interests in financially distressed businesses. KTB&S also provides expert witness services on matters of bankruptcy law. The members of KTB&S have decades of experience practicing in this unique area of law, and are actively involved in teaching and providing expert witness consultation and testimony in this field. KTB&S lawyers are headquartered in Los Angeles, California, but regularly handle matters and appear in bankruptcy proceedings throughout the United States. KTB&S is widely recognized as a national leader in its field.

**CLIENTS:** Since KTB&S was established in June 1999, the firm has attracted a notable list of clients. The nature and diversity of these representations illustrate the breadth and depth of KTB&S' expertise in all aspects of bankruptcy and insolvency practice. The firm's non-confidential representations include the following, which are listed by client categories:

**DEBTORS:** Anacomp, Inc.: document storage and information retrieval technology company; successfully confirmed prepackaged chapter 11 plan in 57 days. Crescent Jewelers: jewelry retailer; successful out-of-court restructuring. Custom Food Products: Processor of custom and value added meat products; successful confirmation of plan of reorganization financed by Fleet Capital Corporation, junior capital provided by Simon/Triton Partners I, LLC. Fountain View, Inc. and Affiliates: skilled nursing facilities, assisted living facilities, pharmacy and therapy businesses; chapter 11 debtors presently undergoing reorganization. Frederick's of Hollywood and Affiliates: retailers of innovative specialty apparel; chapter 11 debtors presently undergoing reorganization. Guidance Software: s oftware development company; successful chapter 11 restructuring and voluntary dismissal. Incomnet, Inc.: reseller of long distance telephone services; successful development, proposal and confirmation of a chapter 11 plan of reorganization in eight months. Matthews Studio Equipment Group, Hollywood Rental Co. LLC, FourStar Inc., Matthews Studio Sales, Inc. (a/k/a Olesen) and related entities: major sellers, lessors, and outsourcers of production equipment for the entertainment industry, including theatrical, motion picture and television production; currently chapter 11 debtors. Outsource International And Affiliates: temporary employment services; successfully preserved operations for purposes of an orderly chapter 11 sale. Pacific Gateway Exchange, Inc., International Exchange Communications, Inc., Onyx Networks, Inc. and Affiliates: international wholesaler of telecommunications services, retail long distance reseller, and internet/co-location services provider; coordinated sale of assets and negotiation of chapter 11 liquidating plan. Prime Matrix Wireless Communications: retail reseller of cellular communications capacity; successfully coordinated orderly sale of the company.

**BONDHOLDERS & OTHER CREDITORS:** Adelphia Communications Corporation Unsecured Creditors' Committee: KTB&S presently serves as special counsel to the official unsecured creditors' committee in this case, investigating potential claims relating to approximately $13 billion in secured and unsecured debt. Ameriserve: represented one of the largest unsecured creditors in the chapter 11 case of Ameriserve. First Alliance Mortgage Company Official Unsecured Creditors' Committee: represent official committee of unsecured creditors in

**HEAD OFFICE**

**CALIFORNIA**
Fox Plaza 2121 Avenue of the Stars, 33rd Floor,
**Los Angeles,** CA 90067
**Tel:** 310 407 4000  **Fax:** 310 407 9090
**Website:** www.ktbslaw.com

chapter 11 case of major sub-prime residential real estate lender. ICO Global Communications: represented bondholder group in ICO Global Communications chapter 11 case, comprised of Magten Asset Management Corp., Oaktree Capital Management, Cerberus Capital Management, LLC, Aristeia Capital LLC, Mackay Shields Financial Corporation. Iridium Official Unsecured Creditors' Committee: represented official committee of unsecured creditors in chapter 11 cases of the Iridium companies, a failed satellite enterprise involving over $3 billion in debt; KTB&S served as special litigation counsel to investigate and prosecute claims against Iridium's lenders; successfully negotiated a settlement for unsecured creditors in excess of $50 million. Maxicare Official Unsecured Creditors' Committee: represent official committee of unsecured creditors in chapter 11 case of major health maintenance organization. Paramount Studios/Viacom: major creditor in the Kmart, Carmike, Edwards Cinemas, General Cinemas and United Artists Theater bankrupties; creditor and purchaser in Weststar (Mann Theaters) chapter 11 cases. Prandium, Inc.: represent an informal group of bondholders holding a majority of approximately $120 million (principal plus interest) in outstanding bonds in connection with pre-packaged chapter 11 restructuring; company engaged in the operation of restaurants in the full-service and fast-casual industry segments. ZiLOG, Inc.: represent an informal group of secured bondholders holding approximately $157 million of $280 million in outstanding bonds in connection with prepackaged chapter 11 restructuring; company designs, manufactures and markets semiconductor micro devices.

**EQUITY HOLDERS:** 203 North LaSalle Street Limited Partnership and Related Entities: represented investors under chapter 11 reorganization plan on remand from the United States Supreme Court in the case of 203 North LaSalle Street Partnership; subsequent plan successfully confirmed. Einstein/Noah Bagel Corporation: represented Gerald K. Smith, Trustee for the Boston Chicken Plan Trust, in the chapter 11 case filed by Einstein/Noah Bagel Corporation and Einstein/Noah Bagel Partners, L.P. Transpacific Enterprises, Inc.: represent the Joint Administrators of Ansett Holdings, Ltd., the sole shareholder of Transpacific Enterpises, Inc., a full service airline support company. Pittsburgh Penguins: represented a significant shareholder in the Pittsburgh Penguins hockey team, in connection with the chapter 11 case of that team.

**ACQUIRERS & OTHERS:** The Century Trust: purchaser of real estate assets in chapter 11 case of Trancas Town Ltd. Crusader Entertainment: acquirer of intellectual properties out of the Red Fern bankruptcy. GAP / Old Navy: purchaser in the Loehman's, Service Merchandise, Lauriat's, Crowley's, Steinbachs, and Caldor chapter 11 cases. The Lusk Company: landlord in numerous chapter 11 cases. Paramount Pictures and Affiliates: creditor and purchaser of the Mann Theatre chain. Starwood Ceruzzi LLC and Vornado Realty LLC: purchaser in Hechingers chapter 11 case.

Klee,
Tuchin,
Bogdanoff &
Stern
LLP

# LITTLER MENDELSON, P.C.

## THE FIRM

**President & Managing Director:** Marko Mrkonich
**Chairman of the Board:** Wendy Tice-Wallner

**Number of shareholders:** 217
**Number of other attorneys (inc. associates and counsel):** 219

**FIRM OVERVIEW:** Today's litigious environment and constantly changing regulatory landscape raise extraordinary questions and risks for employers. With over 400 attorneys strategically located in major metropolitan areas, and a practice that extends into every area and sub-area of workplace law, Littler Mendelson has the ability to provide rapid, integrated solutions for any labor, employment, or benefits issue. Littler's employment litigation practice is the nation's largest. They routinely defend many of the world's largest employers, and just as routinely derail high-stakes litigation. In the last five years, their Appellate Group has concluded 50 cases that have changed, or reaffirmed, workplace law to the benefit of business. The Class Action, Employee Benefits, Workplace Safety, Trade Secret, and other practice groups concentrate the firm's considerable resources and experience in the areas where employers face the greatest challenges and highest stakes. Preventative programs, such as class action audits, rectify problems before they develop into lawsuits. And every day, in novel ways, large and small, Littler make it easier for their clients to go about their business, without having to worry about the business of workplace law.

## MAIN AREAS OF PRACTICE:

**Class Action Avoidance & Defense:** Regardless of its merits, an employment class action can threaten the reputation, good will, and economic standing of your company. Littler attorneys help business to avoid or withstand class-wide claims by putting in place preventative programs. In court, the firm's aggressive approach and use of statistics has been particularly successful in defeating certification and securing victories on summary judgment.

**Unfair Competition & Trade Secrets:** As the nation's largest firm devoted exclusively to employment and labor law, Littler is in a unique position to counsel and represent employers in disputes involving unfair competition, trade secrets and covenants not to compete. Littler attorneys litigate in federal and state courts across the United States to safeguard the information that is vital to clients. And they provide business of practically every size and industry with step-by-step methods to preserve confidential information, investigate suspected misappropriation, and develop action plans.

**Labor Management Relations:** For more than six decades, Littler has represented management in its dealings with organized employees and their union representatives, serving as counterpoint to the world's most powerful labor organizations. As business partners, Littler attorneys take a strategic approach to every engagement, helping employers: they manage representation elections; negotiate contracts; prepare for and respond to strikes; arbitrate grievances; and minimize the effectiveness of corporate campaigns.

**Employee Benefits:** Because of Littler's experience in the workplace as employment attorneys, they understand the wider implications of each benefits issue. Littler's Employee Benefits Practice Group is one of the nation's largest and most sophisticated. Whether it is a benefits question, problem or opportunity, Littler has the multidisciplinary knowledge and capability to provide a unique and creative solution that best meets the client's business and legal objectives.

**Employment Litigation:** Employment litigation is an unavoidable reality in the business world and is a significant part of Littler's practice. Employers caught up in high stakes employment litigation require the skills and experience of highly specialized and accomplished trial attorneys. Littler has literally defended thousands of employment, benefits and labor law cases. The firm's aggressive approach informed through years of experience in the workplace, and success in the courtroom, has earned Littler a reputation as the go-to firm for complex multi-jurisdictional employment litigation.

## HEAD OFFICE

**CALIFORNIA**
650 California Street, 20th Floor, **San Francisco**, CA 94108
**Tel:** 415 399 1940   **Fax:** 415 399 8490
**Email:** info@littler.com
**Website:** www.littler.com

## BRANCHES

The firm has 30 offices in major metropolitan areas nationwide. Please visit www.littler.com.

## CONTACTS

| | |
|---|---|
| **Appellate Practice** | Henry D Lederman (Walnut Creek) |
| | Phillip L Ross (San Francisco) |
| **Business Restructuring** | Gerald T Hathaway (New York) |
| | Robert C Long (Columbus) |
| **Class Action Avoidance & Defense** | Allan G King (Dallas) |
| | Keith C Hult (Chicago) |
| **Corporate Compliance** | Garry G Mathiason (San Francisco) |
| | Jennifer A Youpa (Dallas) |
| **Employee Benefits** | Steven J Friedman (New York) |
| **Employment Taxes** | GJ MacDonnell (San Francisco) |
| **Labor Management Relations** | John M Skonberg (San Francisco) |
| | James M L Ferber (Colombus) |
| **Unfair Competition & Trade Secrets** | |
| | Marguerite S Walsh (Philadelphia) |
| | Paul J Kennedy |
| **Workers' Compensation** | Please contact the nearest office managing shareholder |
| **Workplace Safety** | Peter Susser (Washington DC) |

**INTERNATIONAL WORK:** Littler Global is a multicultural, transnational, full-service corporate migration law practice providing employment law and international migration solutions for global companies anywhere in the world. Their capacity to deliver sophisticated training on all labor, employment, and migration issues facilitates companies' strategic planning. Littler Global offers state of the art technology and tactical communications to keep the flow of information constant and accurate and benchmark practices worldwide.

**CLIENTS:** Littler Mendelson represents employers interests across the nation. Littler Mendelson's national client base, like its practice, is diverse beyond compare. Many Fortune 250 companies regularly turn to the firm for labor and employment defense, and its clients comprise businesses from every size, and from virtually every industry, including, among others, retail, insurance telecommunications, manufacturing, hospitality, and finance.

# LITTLER MENDELSON, P.C.
### THE NATIONAL EMPLOYMENT & LABOR LAW FIRM®

# LOEB & LOEB LLP

## THE FIRM

**Co-Chairs:** John T Frankenheimer (LA office)
　　　　　　Michael D Beck (NY office)

**Number of partners:** 119
**Number of other lawyers:** 117

**FIRM OVERVIEW:** Loeb & Loeb LLP is a multiservice national law firm with more than 200 attorneys and offices in Los Angeles, New York, Nashville and Chicago. The firm is recognized as a leading law firm in the areas of corporate and securities; litigation; entertainment and media; finance; real estate; intellectual property; private equity; employment; advertising and promotions; and tax and wealth services. Their clients include some of the world's largest financial institutions, major media and entertainment companies, advertising groups, real estate companies and Big Four accounting firms, as well as many high-net-worth individuals. Loeb & Loeb believes that diversity is integral to the culture and success of the firm. The firm places a high value on maintaining a diverse workforce, and are committed to achieving a workplace environment in which all attorneys and staff feel welcome, valued and included. The firm is a signatory of the Diversity Statement and Policies promulgated by the New York City and Los Angeles Bar Associations. Both of these initiatives call upon law firms to hire diverse incoming classes and to maintain this diversity as associates rise in seniority and are considered for partnership. To demonstrate their commitment to diversity, Loeb & Loeb is a member and/or sponsor of several organizations that support and reflect our diverse society, such as the California Minority Counsel Program and Lambda Legal, among others. They also participate in programs that promote diversity in the legal profession, including the Judicial Intern Opportunity Program, a program recently expanded in Los Angeles and in which the ABA Section of Litigation places law students of color or from disadvantaged backgrounds in judicial internships. Loeb & Loeb has a particularly strong commitment to pro bono activities on behalf of children and represents such organizations as the Children's Aid Society, Children's Rights, the Council of Family and Child Caring Agencies (COFCCA), Hope for Youth, Lawyers for Children and JFS. As part of their commitment to the protection of neglected and abused children, the firm has established the Loeb & Loeb Child Advocacy Fellowship at Lawyers For Children, one of the nation's leading providers of free legal and social work services for children.

**MAIN AREAS OF PRACTICE:** Advertising and promotions; bankruptcy, restructuring, creditors' rights; corporate and securities; employment and labor; entertainment and media; financial services; high-net-worth families; intellectual property; litigation; private equity; real estate; tax; trusts and estates.

**INTERNATIONAL WORK:** Loeb & Loeb's International Group continues to build on their extensive experience and strengthen the firm's commitment to their international clients. Loeb & Loeb's goal is to assist non-US companies who wish to do business in the United States and counsel domestic companies looking to expand their business across the globe. The firm's numerous international services include corporate transactions, financial services, intellectual property, tax transactions, trademark services and work in the entertainment industry. Loeb & Loeb is able to provide their international clients the benefit of their legal knowledge and experience and the security of local counsel with their network of affiliates. They have been especially successful with their ties in Asia, particularly with corporate transactions, and have honed their ability to both speak and write Chinese. The firm represents dozens of Chinese and other Asian companies and has taken more than 30 public in the US, including the first Chinese,

Taiwanese and Thai companies to list on the American Stock Exchange. Loeb & Loeb represents both public and private companies in numerous industries ranging from technology to transportation to toys from numerous countries in Asia, as well as the UK, Israel, Greece and Australia.

---

### HEAD OFFICE

**CALIFORNIA**
10100 Santa Monica Boulevard, Suite 2200,
**Los Angeles**, CA 90067-4120
**Tel:** 310 282 2000　**Fax:** 310 282 2200
**Email:** jfrankenheimer@loeb.com
**Website:** www.loeb.com

### BRANCH OFFICES

**NEW YORK**
345 Park Avenue, **New York**, NY 10154
**Tel:** 212 407 4000　**Fax:** 212 407 4990
**Email:** dshaefer@loeb com

**TENNESSEE**
1906 Acklen Avenue, **Nashville**, TN 37212-3700
**Tel:** 615 749 8300　**Fax:** 615 749 8308
**Email:** kkraus@loeb com

**ILLINOIS**
321 North Clark, Suite 2300, **Chicago**, IL 60610-4746
**Tel:** 312 464 3100　**Fax:** 312 464 3111
**Email:** dmasters@loeb com

### CONTACTS

| | |
|---|---|
| **Los Angeles** | Michael A Mayerson |
| **New York** | David S Schaefer |
| **Nashville** | Kenneth L Kraus |
| **Chicago** | Douglas N Masters |

# MORRISON & FOERSTER LLP

## THE FIRM

**Chair of the Firm:** Keith C Wetmore
**Managing Partners for Operations:** Mark W Danis, Larren M Nashelsky, Pamela J Reed

**Number of partners worldwide:** 349
**Number of US partners:** 302
**Number of other lawyers worldwide:** 698
**Number of other US lawyers:** 608

**Email:** info@mofo.com **Website:** www.mofo.com

**FIRM OVERVIEW:** With more than one thousand lawyers in nineteen offices around the world, Morrison & Foerster offers clients comprehensive, global legal services in business and litigation. Founded in 1883, the firm is distinguished by its unsurpassed expertise in finance, life sciences, and technology, its legendary litigation skills, and an unrivaled reach across the Pacific Rim, particularly in Japan and China. The firm has one compelling mission: to deliver success for clients. The firm's employment, litigation and arbitration, and tax practices are widely regarded as amongst the pre-eminent practices in their respective fields.

**MAIN AREAS OF PRACTICE:** Antitrust, bankruptcy and restructuring, capital markets, communications and media, corporate, energy, entertainment, environmental, financial services, financial transactions, government contracts, intellectual property, international, investment management, labor and employment, land use and natural resources, life sciences, litigation, privacy, project finance and development, real estate, tax and technology transactions.
**Corporate:** The firm's Corporate Group represents some of the most dynamic companies in the world and can provide a full range of corporate finance advice, including venture financing, public offerings, strategic alliances, technology transactions, and mergers and acquisitions.
**Litigation:** The firm's Litigation Department includes some of the top trial and appellate lawyers in the United States, as well as leading practitioners in the areas of antitrust, securities, financial services, criminal defense, environmental and patent litigation.
**Intellectual Property:** The firm has one of the largest intellectual property practice of any general practice firm, with more than 280 attorneys and a full-service patent prosecution and trademark practice of over 80 attorneys.
**Labor & Employment:** The firm's Employment Law Group advises and represents companies in all areas of employment-related law, ranging from traditional labor to trade secret/intellectual property matters in virtually every industry.
**Tax:** The firm's Tax Department contains the country's leading state and local tax practice, as well as providing federal and international tax advice.

**INTERNATIONAL WORK:** The firm has offices in key business centers around the world including London, Brussels, Hong Kong, Beijing, Shanghai, Singapore and Tokyo, as well as a strategic alliance with Cabanellas, Etchebarne, Kelly & Dell'Oro Maini in Buenos Aires, Argentina. Representative work includes: serving as the International Counsel to the Beijing Organizing Committee for the XXIX Olympiad 2008 Summer Games (BOCOG); Hurray! Holding Co., Ltd. in the first NASDAQ IPO out of China in 2005, valued at US$70.5 million; Dubai Investment Group and Milestone Group in their joint $1 billion acquisition of 69 apartment buildings from Olympus Real Estate Partners (the largest apartment portfolio in the US since 2001); China HR.com in a 40% stake purchase by Monster Worldwide for $50 million; Joyo.com, the leading PRC Internet online retailer, in a cash acquisition by Amazon.com valued at US$75 million.

## OFFICES

**CALIFORNIA**
425 Market Street, **San Francisco**, CA 94105-2482
**Tel:** 415 268 7000  **Fax:** 415 268 7522

755 Page Mill Road, **Palo Alto**, CA 94304-1018
**Tel:** 650 813 5600  **Fax:** 650 494 0792

101 Ygnacio Valley Road, Suite 450, **Walnut Creek**, CA 94596-4095
**Tel:** 925 295 3300  **Fax:** 925 946 9912

400 Capitol Mall, Suite 2600, **Sacramento**, CA 95814
**Tel:** 916 448 3200  **Fax:** 916 448 3222

555 West Fifth Street, Suite 3500, **Los Angeles**, CA 90013-1024
**Tel:** 213 892 5200  **Fax:** 213 892 5454

19900 MacArthur Boulevard, Twelfth Floor, **Irvine**, CA 92612
**Tel:** 949 251 7500  **Fax:** 949 251 0900

1925 Century Park East, Suite 2200, **Los Angeles**, CA 90067-2701
**Tel:** 310 203 4000  **Fax:**310 203 4040

12531 High Bluff Drive, **San Diego**, CA 92130-2040
**Tel:** 858 720 5100  **Fax:** 858 720 5125

**COLORADO**
5200 Republic Plaza, 370 Seventeenth Street, **Denver**, CO 80202-5638
**Tel:** 303 592 1500  **Fax:** 303 592 1510

**DISTRICT OF COLUMBIA**
2000 Pennsylvania Avenue, NW, Suite 5500,
**Washington,** DC 20006-1888
**Tel:** 202 887 1500  **Fax:** 202 887 0763

**NEW YORK**
1290 Avenue of the Americas, **New York**, NY 10104-0050
**Tel:** 212 468 8000  **Fax:** 212 468 7900

**VIRGINIA**
1650 Tysons Boulevard, Suite 300, **McLean,** VA 22102
**Tel:** 703 760 7700  **Fax:** 703 760 7777

## CONTACTS

| | |
|---|---|
| Business | Nicholas J Spiliotes |
| Labor | Raymond L Wheeler |
| Litigation | Lori A Schechter |
| Tax | Paul H Frankel |
| | Thomas A Humphreys |

**MORRISON | FOERSTER**

# O'MELVENY & MYERS LLP

## THE FIRM

**Chair:** Arthur B Culvahouse, Jr

**Number of partners:** 254
**Number of other lawyers:** 748

**Website:** www.omm.com

**FIRM OVERVIEW:** O'Melveny & Myers is a values-driven law firm guided by the principles of excellence, leadership and citizenship. With the breadth, depth and foresight to serve clients competing in a global economy, their lawyers devise innovative approaches to resolve problems and achieve business goals. Established in 1885, the firm maintains 13 offices around the world, with more than 1,000 lawyers. O'Melveny & Myers' capabilities span virtually every area of legal practice, including antitrust/competition; appellate; aviation; capital markets; class action defense; corporate; entertainment and media; finance and restructuring; global enforcement and criminal defense; healthcare; insurance and mass torts; intellectual property and technology; labor and employment; mergers and acquisitions; private equity; project development and real estate; SEC; securities litigation; strategic counseling; tax; and trial and litigation.

## MAIN AREAS OF PRACTICE

**Adversarial:** Litigation is increasingly a battleground where today's social, economic, technological, and even political conflicts are resolved. Leading corporations, government agencies, and individuals from around the globe turn to O'Melveny & Myers to handle matters that are not only crucial to the litigants, but frequently have wide-ranging global implications. With over 500 lawyers engaged in litigation in 13 offices worldwide, the firm fields exceptional teams of lawyers to prevail in the largest and most demanding cases. Geographically, the firm is involved in matters in courts at all levels of both the state and federal systems, including a very active US Supreme Court practice. Substantively, the firm's cases range from international commercial arbitrations to intellectual property disputes, from state law product liability cases to Federal Trade Commission antitrust challenges, from criminal defense to federal regulatory work and almost everything in between.

**Transactions:** Major corporations, financial institutions, governmental entities, and individuals from around the globe turn to O'Melveny & Myers to handle their most critical transactions. With over 400 transactional attorneys, the firm is uniquely equipped to manage the increasing complexity of transactions and the accelerating globalization of the business and financial communities. The department consists of the following practice areas: mergers and acquisitions; private equity; finance and restructuring; capital markets; business practice; entertainment and media; project development and real estate; and international.

## INTERNATIONAL WORK:

**Asia:** The Asia practice covers the full spectrum of business and commercial matters and controversies from establishing joint ventures, to providing advice on complex acquisition, investment, commercial, financial, and capital markets transactions, to international trade matters and other cross-border disputes.

**London:** The London office is strategically positioned to handle the domestic, cross-border and multi-jurisdictional aspects of our clients' legal and business requirements throughout Europe. The London office has key strengths within private equity, corporate finance, mergers and acquisitions, banking, financing and capital markets. The London office offers full transactional service to its clients with resident experts supporting the fund and deal teams in the following areas of legal practice: taxation (including cross-border structuring), real estate, employment, regulatory, IP/IT and arbitration.

**Brussels:** The Brussels office focus on EU and member country competition and regulatory law, including mergers and acquisitions and joint ventures, anti-competitive agreements and concerted practices, cartel investigations, abuse of monopoly positions and state aid.

## US OFFICES

**CALIFORNIA**
1999 Avenue of the Stars, **Los Angeles**, CA 90067
**Tel:** 310 553 6700    **Fax:** 310 246 6779

400 South Hope Street, **Los Angeles**, CA 90071
**Tel:** 213 430 6000    **Fax:** 213 430 6407

2765 Sand Hill Road, **Menlo Park**, CA 94025
**Tel:** 650 437 2600    **Fax:** 650 473 2601

610 Newport Center Drive, **Newport Beach**, CA 92660
**Tel:** 949 760 9600    **Fax:** 949 823 6994

Embarcadero Center West, 275 Battery Street, **San Francisco**, CA 94111
**Tel:** 415 984 8700    **Fax:** 415 984 8701

**DISTRICT OF COLUMBIA**
1625 Eye Street, NW, **Washington**, DC 20006
**Tel:** 202 383 5300    **Fax:** 202 383 5414

**NEW YORK**
7 Times Square, **New York**, NY 10036
**Tel:** 212 326 2000    **Fax:** 212 326 2061

## INTERNATIONAL OFFICES

The firm also has offices in Beijing, Brussels, Hong Kong, London, Shanghai and Tokyo.

## CONTACTS

**Adversarial** ...................................................Robert Siegel (Los Angeles)
.......................................................................Mark Wood (Los Angeles)
**Transactions** ...........................................David Krinsky (Newport Beach)
.......................................................................John Suydam (New York)
**Intellectual Property & Technology** ..........Mark Samuels (Los Angeles)
**Labor & Employment** ..............................Scott Dunham (Los Angeles)
**Tax** .......................................................Robert Rizzi (Washington, DC)

# ORRICK, HERRINGTON & SUTCLIFFE LLP

## THE FIRM

**Chairman & Chief Executive Officer:** Ralph H Baxter, Jr
**Chief Operating Officer:** Douglas Benson

**Number of partners:** 311
**Number of other lawyers:** 544
**Email:** info@orrick.com

**FIRM OVERVIEW:** Established in 1863, Orrick is a global law firm with 16 offices and approximately 850 lawyers worldwide. The firm provides advice under US, English, French, Italian, German, Russian and Japanese law. Orrick's clients include major commercial and investment banks, industrial and financial corporations, technology companies, developers, universities and other public institutions, and governmental entities.

## MAIN AREAS OF PRACTICE:

**Banking & Finance:** The firm's Banking and Finance Group has broad expertise in virtually every area of commercial finance, including secured and unsecured lending, project and infrastructure finance, leasing and asset-based financing, aircraft finance, institutional private placements, letters of credit, swaps and other hedging mechanisms, asset-backed commercial paper financings, workouts, bankruptcy and bank regulatory issues.

**Capital Markets:** Orrick's capital markets lawyers structure transactions that allow companies to achieve their strategic objectives. Their broad experience includes private placements, initial public offerings, investment grade and high-yield debt offerings.

**Compensation & Benefits:** Orrick's Compensation and Benefits Group advises clients on all aspects of their employee benefits and compensation arrangements, including advice regarding executive compensation, benefit plan investments, mergers and acquisitions, qualified retirement plans and ESOPs, welfare plans and dispute resolution.

**Employment:** Many of Orrick's employment lawyers are recognized as leading lawyers. All of Orrick's lawyers handle a variety of employment litigation, wrongful discharge claims, EEO affirmative action compliance and general employment matters.

**Energy & Project Finance:** Orrick's global energy, communications and infrastructure lawyers work collaboratively on projects throughout the world, including power plants, telecommunication facilities, industrial plants, waste disposal and resource recovery facilities, pipelines, toll roads, renewables and other infrastructure projects.

**Intellectual Property:** Orrick's intellectual property lawyers have extensive experience in virtually every aspect of intellectual property law, including patent, copyright and trademark infringement, unfair competition and trade secret actions. They also advise clients in licensing, litigation avoidance, due diligence and other securities litigation and international arbitration matters across the complete spectrum of intellectual property issues.

**Litigation:** Orrick's Litigation Division comprises more than 300 lawyers world wide and their experience encompasses virtually every business-related issue encountered today, including intellectual property, securities, antitrust, distribution and trade regulation, product liability, environmental, tax, white collar litigation and international arbitration. Their lawyers handle cases in both federal and state courts and matters before administrative agencies and self-regulatory organizations.

**Mergers & Acquisitions:** Orrick's corporate lawyers represent both buyers and sellers in M&A transactions for *Fortune* 500 as well as middle market and emerging companies. Their work includes acquisitions, mergers, leveraged buyouts, purchases and sales of divisions and subsidiaries, going-private transactions, spin-offs, reorganizations and recapitalizations.

**Public Finance:** The firm's Public Finance Group is the largest and most diverse in the United States. The firm routinely ranks first in the country in the volume of financings for which it serves as bond counsel and as underwriters' counsel.

**Real Estate:** Orrick's Real Estate Group represents clients in the United States, Asia and Europe on all phases of real estate investment, development, financing and operations, ranging from purchases and sales, leases and financings to sophisticated joint ventures and large portfolio, multistate and cross-border transactions.

**Structured Finance:** Orrick is a key player in the development of new structures for the asset-securitization market throughout the United States, Asia and Europe, and serves as counsel to issuers, underwriters, credit enhancers, sellers, servicers and institutional purchasers. Orrick advises the world's leading financial institutions in securitization transactions that add real value to companies and institutions around the world.

**Tax:** Orrick's Tax Group advises companies of all sizes on all aspects of US federal, state and international tax planning and litigation. The group also provides tax planning advice to individuals through its private group.

**INTERNATIONAL WORK:** Orrick is one of the world's leading securitization and structured finance firms. Its Securitization Group has been active in Europe and Asia. The firm's extensive project finance and infrastructure experience includes projects throughout Latin America, Asia and Europe. The firm recently strengthened its M&A and litigation platform, among other areas, when the Paris office merged with Rambaud Martel, one of France's preeminent corporate law firms. Orrick also has one of the leading emerging market financial sector reform and corporate debt restructuring practices and is currently increasing its high-profile work in the information technology and telecommunications sectors.

## US OFFICES

### CALIFORNIA
777 South Figueroa Street, Suite 3200, **Los Angeles**, CA 90017-5855
**Tel:** 213 629 2020    **Fax:** 213 612 2499

1000 Marsh Road, **Menlo Park**, CA 94025-1015
**Tel:** 650 614 7400    **Fax:** 650 614 7401

4 Park Plaza, Suite 1600, Irvine, **Orange County**, CA 92614-2558
**Tel:** 949 567 6700    **Fax:** 949 567 6710

400 Capitol Mall, Suite 3000, **Sacramento**, CA 95814-4497
**Tel:** 916 447 9200    **Fax:** 916 329 4900

The Orrick Building, 405 Howard Street, **San Francisco**, CA 94105
**Tel:** 415 773 5700    **Fax:** 415 773 5759

### DISTRICT OF COLUMBIA
Washington Harbour, 3050 K Street, NW, **Washington**, DC 20007-5135
**Tel:** 202 339 8400    **Fax:** 202 339 8500

### NEW YORK
666 Fifth Avenue, **New York**, NY 10103-0001
**Tel:** 212 506 5000    **Fax:** 212 506 5151

### PACIFIC NORTHWEST
719 Second Avenue, Suite 900, **Seattle**, WA 98104-7097
**Tel:** 206 839 4300    **Fax:** 206 839 4301

1125 NW Couch Street, Suite 800, **Portland**, OR 97209
**Tel:** 503 943 4800    **Fax:** 503 943 4801

## INTERNATIONAL OFFICES

The firm also has offices in France, Hong Kong, Italy, Japan, Russia, Taiwan and the United Kingdom.

# PACHULSKI, STANG, ZIEHL, YOUNG, JONES & WEINTRAUB P.C.

## THE FIRM

**Management Committee:** Richard M Pachulski, Dean A Ziehl, Ira D Kharasch, William P Weintraub, Laura Davis Jones, Henry C Kevane

**Number of partners:** 34
**Number of other lawyers:** 26

**FIRM OVERVIEW:** Pachulski, Stang, Ziehl, Young, Jones & Weintraub P.C. was founded in 1983, and has developed into one of the largest insolvency practices in the US. With over 70 attorneys in four offices, the firm's attorneys concentrate on business reorganizations (workouts, restructurings and chapter 11), commercial and real estate transactions, general commercial law and business litigation. Because the core of the firm's practice involves debtor-creditor relations and sophisticated financial restructurings, all of the firm's senior attorneys have broad and deep experience in business reorganization, bankruptcy and insolvency matters.

## MAIN AREAS OF PRACTICE:

**Business Reorganization & Workouts:** The firm has a nationally recognized bankruptcy practice that is one of the largest in the country. The firm represents all of the major constituencies in bankruptcy proceedings and out of court workouts, including debtors, creditors' committees, equity committees, trustees, secured and major unsecured creditors, bondholders, asset purchasers and third-party plan proponents.

**Litigation:** The firm represents both plaintiffs and defendants in general commercial and business litigation, as well as banking, bankruptcy and insurance litigation. The prosecution and defense of litigation in bankruptcy court is a particular strength and the firm's litigators are well versed in bankruptcy jurisdictional disputes. The firm's national insolvency practice frequently requires client representation in fraudulent conveyance, preference and other bankruptcy-related litigation.

**Corporate & Transactional:** The firm's Transactions Practice features expertise over a broad spectrum, including real estate purchase and sales, development and commercial leasing; financing and workouts; sales of companies or their assets. The firm's transactional attorneys are uniquely qualified to handle the problems and issues associated with representing clients in complex bankruptcy transactions.

**High Technology/Telecommunications:** The firm has considerable experience with the special issues facing high technology/telecommunications debtors and sophisticated acquirers of high technology/telecommunications companies, including Covad Communications Group, Inacom Corp., Northpoint Communications, Peregrine Systems Inc., Tie Communications Inc., UniSil Corporation and Yipes Communications.

**Retail & Restaurant Chains:** The firm's combination of insolvency, real estate and commercial financial expertise enables members of the firm to represent a wide range of interests arising from the insolvency of large restaurant chains and retail outlets, including B.U.M. International Inc., C&R Clothiers Inc., Fedco Inc., The Boston Store, Sizzler International Inc. and Specialty Restaurants Corporation.

**Insurance & Reinsurance:** The firm's extensive involvement with restructuring in the insurance industry has given its lawyers recognized expertise in handling insurance and reinsurance disputes. Members of the firm have represented receivers, reinsurers, policyholders and other creditors in some of the largest insurance and reinsurance insolvencies in the world, including First Capital Holdings, Corp., First Executive Corporation (Executive Life Insurance Company), Superior National, Transit, Mission, Fremont and Kwelm.

**Entertainment Insolvency:** The firm has played prominent roles in some of the nation's largest production and distribution company chapter 11 cases, including United Artists, Loews Cinemas, General Cinemas, Mann Theaters, 21st Century Film Group and Quintex Entertainment, and has been involved in the cases of high-profile entertainers/athletes, including Toni Braxton, Ronald Isley, Johnny Gill and Mike Tyson.

**CLIENTS:** The firm acts or has acted as bankruptcy counsel to many large public and private corporations, including AgriBioTech Inc., American Rice Inc., AmeriServe Food Distributors Inc., Breed Technologies Inc., F&C Corp., Federal-Mogul Inc., Gencor Inc., Harnischfeger Industries Inc., HomePlace Stores Inc., Imperial Hotels Corporation, LogoAthletics Inc., MVP.com, PG&E Corporation, RBX Corporation, Sunbelt Nursery Group Inc., Trans World Airlines, TreeSweet Juice Company, Tri Valley Growers, Webvan Group (Homegrocer.com), W.R. Grace & Co. and Zenith Electronics. The firm has also served as counsel to court-appointed committees of creditors or other interest groups in the chapter 11 cases of America West Airlines Inc., Cirrus, DirecTV Latin America LLC, Fruit of the Loom, FundAmerica, Guy F. Atkinson Company, Home Fed Corp., Lynx Golf Inc., Orange County, Pannell Kerr Forster, Pioneer Take-Out Corp., and Sun World International Inc. Other clients represented by the firm in litigation, transactions or as creditors or other parties in interest in bankruptcy cases include Chicago Title, DSL Transportation, Farmers Commonwealth Insurance Co., Fuji Photo Film USA Inc., Gilda Marx Incorporated, Heller Financial Inc., Hilton Hotels, Imperial Hotels Inc., National Broadcasting Company Inc., PaineWebber Funding Inc., Peoplesoft Inc., Safeway Corporation, The Hahn Company and Xerox Corporation.

## HEAD OFFICE

**CALIFORNIA**
10100 Santa Monica Boulevard, 11th Floor, **Los Angeles**, CA 90067
**Tel:** 310 277 6910 **Fax:** 310 201 0760
**Email:** dziehl@pszyj.com
**Website:** www.pszyj.com

## BRANCH OFFICES

**CALIFORNIA**
150 California Street, 15th Floor, **San Francisco**, CA 94111
**Tel:** 415 263 7000 **Fax:** 415 263 7010

**DELAWARE**
919 North Market Street, 17th Floor, **Wilmington**, DE 19801
**Tel:** 302 652 4100 **Fax:** 302 652 4400

**NEW YORK**
780 Third Avenue, 36th Floor, **New York**, NY 10017-2024
**Tel:** 212 561 7700 **Fax:** 212 561 7777

# PAUL, HASTINGS, JANOFSKY & WALKER LLP

## THE FIRM

**Chairman:** Seth Zachary
**Managing Partner:** Greg Nitzkowski
**Number of partners worldwide:** 255
**Number of other lawyers worldwide:** 735

**FIRM OVERVIEW:** Founded in 1951, Paul, Hastings, Janofsky & Walker LLP is a leading international law firm with approximately 1,000 attorneys is 17 offices. Paul Hastings conducts its global law practice through an international network of offices serving a diverse client base including many of the top financial institutions and Fortune 500 companies. The firm's position as a leading international law firm is built on its ability to support clients in all of their legal needs and offers deep capabilities in banking and finance, capital markets, corporate/M&A, litigation and dispute resolution, intellectual property, project finance, investment management, real estate, labor and employment, and tax advisory services.

## MAIN INTERNATIONAL AREAS OF PRACTICE:

**Corporate:** Teams of Paul Hastings' corporate attorneys provide clients with the sophisticated, cross-border legal and business expertise they need to finance and operate companies. Their M&A, Lending, Project Finance, Private Equity, Investment Management and Securitization practices are nationally and internationally ranked. Their attorneys are experienced in every aspect of modern transactional practice in virtually every industry and service sector. Clients include major financial institutions, domestic, international, public and private companies.

**Employment:** Paul Hastings' Labor and Employment Practice is recognized as one of the largest and most accomplished in its field. Their attorneys are widely recognized for their outstanding record in defending class actions for some of the largest international companies. The attorneys counsel clients with respect to traditional labour law, equal employment opportunity laws, wrongful discharge, sexual harassment, employee benefits matters and other employment related issues. Recently ranked as the #1 Employment and Labor Law Firm by Chambers USA and named the 'Labor and Employment Litigation Department of the Year' by The American Lawyer, the firm is frequently called upon by many of the nation's leading attorneys and law firms to represent them in their employment law matters.

**Litigation:** The firm's Litigation Department provides premier litigation services to clients facing complex legal issues in the US, Europe, South America, the Middle East and Asia. With more than 225 lawyers in the Litigation Department, in addition to 150 litigators in the Employment Department, Paul Hastings is well positioned to handle all aspects of a client's litigation needs. Their sophisticated Litigation Practice covers every major practice including securities, intellectual property, class action and employment litigation, international arbitration, and white collar crime. The Litigation Department has an impressive track record of winning large and difficult cases. Many of the cases the firm handles are cross border in nature.

**Real Estate:** Paul Hastings has the largest Real Estate Practice in the US, the strongest practice of any international law firm and is recognised for its excellence both nationally and internationally. The practice covers all areas of real estate finance, sales and acquisitions, private equity, development, hotels and hospitality, leasing, joint ventures, partnerships and limited liability companies, and bankruptcy and restructuring of real estate portfolios. The practice's environmental, planning, construction and real estate litigation expertise is extensive, as is their experience in debt, equity and hybrid investment. Their attorneys represent some of the largest and best-known developers, financial institutions, opportunity funds, real estate operating companies, pension funds and advisors.

**Tax:** The firm's international Tax Practice offers clients the skills of a seasoned team of tax lawyers, who advise and represent companies across the complete spectrum of transactional, business planning and litigation tax issues. The scope of their tax practice is global, reaching across all industries and types of businesses and across both established and emerging economies and markets. The firm's Transactional Practice covers mergers and acquisitions, capital market offerings, investment and joint venture structuring, leasing, structured and project finance, and financial product planning and structuring. They are internationally known as having one of the preeminent tax practices in telecommunications, real estate, executive compensation, and tax-exempt and tax-favored investments.

## HEAD OFFICE

### CALIFORNIA
515 South Flower Street, **Los Angeles**, CA 90071
**Tel:** 213 683 6000   **Fax:** 213 627 0705
**Email:** info@paulhastings.com   **Website:** www.paulhastings.com

## BRANCH OFFICES

### CALIFORNIA
695 Town Center Drive, **Costa Mesa**, CA 92626
**Tel:** 714 668 6200   **Fax:** 714 979 1921

5 Palo Alto Square, **Palo Alto**, CA 94306
**Tel:** 650 320 1800   **Fax:** 650 320 1900

3579 Valley Centre Drive, **San Diego**, CA 92130
**Tel:** 858 720 2500   **Fax:** 858 720 2555

55 Second Street, **San Francisco**, CA 94105
**Tel:** 415 856 7000   **Fax:** 415 856 7100

### CONNECTICUT
1055 Washington Boulevard, **Stamford**, CT 06901
**Tel:** 203 961 7400   **Fax:** 203 359 3031

### DISTRICT OF COLUMBIA
875 15th Street NW, **Washington**, DC 20005
**Tel:** 202 551 1700   **Fax:** 202 551 1705

### GEORGIA
24th Floor, 600 Peachtree Street, NE, **Atlanta**, GA 30308
**Tel:** 404 815 2400   **Fax:** 404 815 2424

### NEW YORK
75 East 55th Street, **New York**, NY 10022
**Tel:** 212 318 6000   **Fax:** 212 319 4090

## INTERNATIONAL OFFICES

The firm also has offices in Beijing, Brussels, Hong Kong, London, Milan, Paris, Shanghai and Tokyo.

# QUINN EMANUEL URQUHART OLIVER & HEDGES, LLP

## THE FIRM

**Managing Partners:** John B Quinn

**Number of partners worldwide:** 73
**Number of other lawyers worldwide:** 189

**THE FIRM:** Quinn Emanuel Urquhart Oliver & Hedges, LLP is a 260+ lawyer business litigation firm – the largest in the United States devoted solely to business litigation. The firm's lawyers have tried 1073 cases and won 92%. When representing defendants, the firm's trial experience allows it to achieve better settlements or defense verdicts. When representing plaintiffs, the firm's lawyers have garnered over $3.3 billion in judgments and settlements in the last several years. The firm has obtained three jury verdicts and two settlements in excess of $100 million in the last four years. The firm will consider taking matters on a contingent fee basis or other alternative billing arrangements in appropriate cases. Over 60% of the firm's revenues are derived from intellectual property litigation. Patent litigation is the fastest growing practice area in the firm. The firm protects and exploits some of the world's most valuable intellectual property for companies such as IBM, Nike, Shell Oil, Seiko-Epson, Johnson & Johnson and many others. As plaintiffs in intellectual property cases the firm has obtained two verdicts in an excess of $100 million in the last three years.

**CLIENTS:** IBM; Mattel Inc.; Shell Oil; Nike; Genentech; General Motors; The Scotts Companies; Seiko Epson Corporation; American West Homes Incorporated; Delphi Automotive Systems; DIRECTV; Electronic Arts; Morgan Stanley; MP3.com, Inc.; Credit Suisse First Boston; TRW Inc.; AIG; Oracle Corporation; Izumi Products Company; DHL Airways, Inc.; The Parsons Corporation; Hughes Electronics Corporation; Jefferies & Company, Inc.; Fox, Inc.; Union Bank of California, N.A.; The Walt Disney Company; Washington Mutual Bank; Invensys Software Systems; Mirage Animation, Inc.; Idealabs; Nike, Inc.; ING Barings, LLC; PharmaSystem Therapeutics, Inc.; Bancorp Services; GMAC Mortgage Corporation; Academy of Motion Picture Arts and Sciences; Callidus Software, Inc.; United Talent Agency; Borland Software, Inc.; Loral Space and Communications; Computer Sciences Corporation; Vishay Siliconix; Trust Company of the West; Lazard Freres & Co. LLC; Marsh & McLellan Companies, Inc.; Time Warner; Tribune Company; Hollywood Entertainment; CBS, Inc.; Home Box Office; Kmart; Avery Dennison Corporation; Leland Stanford University; Newscorp; eBay Inc.; General Motors Corporation; Johnson & Johnson; Lockheed Martin Corporation; The Los Angeles Times; Northrop Grumman Corporation; Sony Electronics; PeopleSoft; Intuit; Hyundai.

**MAIN INTERNATIONAL AREAS OF PRACTICE:** Business litigation in the areas of intellectual property (patent, copyright, trademark and trade secrets litigation); international and domestic arbitration; unfair competition, antitrust and trade regulation litigation; employment and employee movement litigation; securities litigation; entertainment litigation; real estate development and construction litigation; banking and financial institution litigation; government contracts litigation and counseling; insurance coverage; healthcare; internet and new media litigation; white collar criminal litigation; corporate governance and internal investigations.

**INTERNATIONAL WORK:** The firm regularly advises international companies operating within the US and also advises US companies on their overseas activities. In addition, the firm's lawyers have arbitrated cases under rules of the London Court of International Arbitration, the International Chamber of Commerce, and the American Arbitration Association, UNCITRAL, ICSID, and arbitration statutes of various countries, in such diverse locations as New York, Los Angeles, London, Paris, Stockholm, Bermuda, Montreal and Lima involving companies from England, Germany, Greece, Peru, Sweden, the United Kingdom, Russia and Venezuela. Each year the firm sponsors an international arbitration conference attended by advocates and arbitrators from around the world. The firm's lawyers are familiar with, and in some cases helped draft, international and domestic arbitration codes.

## HEAD OFFICE

856 South Figueroa Street, 10th Floor, **Los Angeles,** CA 90017, USA
**Tel:** 213 443 3000  **Fax:** 213 443 3100
**Email:** johnquinn@quinnemanuel.com
**Website:** www.quinnemanuel.com

## BRANCH OFFICES

### CALIFORNIA

555 Twin Dolphin Drive, Suite 560, **Redwood Shores**, CA 94065
**Tel:** 650 620 4500  **Fax:** 650 620 4555
**Email:** claudestern@quinnemanuel.com

50 California Street, 22nd Floor, **San Francisco**, CA 94111
**Tel:** 415 875 6600  **Fax:** 415 875 6700
**Email:** charlesverhoeven@quinnemanuel.com

4445 Eastgate Mall, Suite 200, **San Diego**, CA 92121
**Tel:** 858 812 3107  **Fax:** 858 812 3336
**Email:** michadanzig@quinnemanuel.com

### NEW YORK

335 Madison Ave, 17th Floor, **New York**, NY 10017
**Tel:** 212 702 8100  **Fax:** 212 702 8200
**Email:** petercalamari@quinnemanuel.com

## CONTACTS

| | |
|---|---|
| **Los Angeles** | John B Quinn |
| | A William Urquhart |
| | Fred G Bennett |
| **New York** | Peter E Calamari |
| | Michael Carlinsky |
| **San Francisco** | Charles K Verhoeven |
| **Silicon Valley** | Claude M Stern |
| **San Diego** | Mitch Danzig |

quinn emanuel trial lawyers
quinn emanuel urquhart oliver & hedges, llp

# STUTMAN, TREISTER & GLATT PROFESSIONAL CORPORATION

## THE FIRM

**Chairman of the Executive Committee:** Robert A Greenfield

**Number of partners and senior of counsel:** 21
**Number of counsel:** 5
**Number of associates:** 9

**FIRM OVERVIEW:** Stutman, Treister & Glatt Professional Corporation is a pre-eminent bankruptcy boutique law firm. For more than 50 years, ST&G has been a leader in the field of business reorganization and restructuring. Other firms may have bankruptcy departments, but no other firm in the country has the depth and experience provided by ST&G's bankruptcy professionals. The firm has successfully concluded some of the most complex out-of-court restructurings, chapter 11 plans, chapter 11 reorganizations, and purchases and sales of distressed assets and businesses.

**MAIN AREAS OF PRACTICE:** Since 1948, the law firm has focused particularly on the representation of (i) financially troubled business organizations; (ii) creditors' and equity holders' committees; (iii) sellers and buyers of troubled companies; (iv) bondholders and bondholders committees; (v) significant secured and unsecured creditors; and (vi) parties in bankruptcy and insolvency related litigation.

**Firm Lawyers:** The firm's lawyers are well-known throughout the country for their leadership and contributions to the practice: four lawyers are members of the National Bankruptcy Conference, eight lawyers are members of the American College of Bankruptcy, two lawyers are editors of 'Collier's on Bankruptcy', numerous lawyers are listed on various 'Who's Who' lists, 13 lawyers were listed as California Super Lawyers 2005, and the firm's lawyers routinely publish articles and lecture at professional conferences. Collectively, nine lawyers have more than 30 years' experience, an additional seven lawyers have 20 to 30 years of experience, and an additional eight lawyers have 10 to 20 years of experience.

**CLIENTS:** ST&G's national practice is highlighted by the cases in which the firm has been actively involved. The firm's debtor representations, both in-court and out-of-court, include Applied Magnetics Corporation, Barney's Inc., Barry's Jewelers, Inc., Broadbandsports.com, Bumble Bee Seafoods, Inc., Carter Hawley Hale Stores, Inc., Clark Retail Enterprises, Inc., County of Orange, Daewoo Motor America, Inc., Diva Systems Corporation, Edwards Theatres Circuit, Inc., El Camino Resources, Ltd., Falcon Industries, Graham & James LLP, Hawaiian Holdings, Inc., Home Fed Corporation, Huntsman Corporation, Itel Corporation, Kenetech Windpower, Inc., Krause's Furniture, Inc., Lamonts Apparel, Inc., Leasing Solutions, Inc., Lyon & Lyon LLP, Mariner Health Group, Maxicare, MTP Grand Place Tower, a Maguire Company, NBI, Public Service Co. of New Hampshire, The Regent Las Vegas (The Resort at Summerlin), Restaurant Enterprises Group, Inc., Southern California Edison Company, Sirius Satellite Radio, Standard Brands Paint Co., Storage Technology Corporation, Store of Knowledge, Inc., Thrifty Oil Co., Toy Time.com, Inc., UHP Healthcare, Westmoreland Coal Company, and Wickes Companies, Inc. ST&G's present and former creditor, equity and strategic investor clients include Apollo Advisors, LP, Ares Corporate Opportunities Fund LP, The Baupost Group, BP America, Inc., Catholic Healthcare West, Converse, Inc., Davidson Kempner Partners, DDJ Capital, Elliot Advisors, Fantastic Sams, Fidelity Investments, FINOVA, First American Title Insurance Co., General Cinemas, Home Savings of America, Leonard Green and Partners, Leucadia National Corporation, Litton Industries, Metro-Goldwyn-Mayer Studios, Inc., Paramount Pictures Corporation, Pennzoil Co., Pouschine Cook Capital Management, LLC, RC Aviation LLC, Sony Corporation of America (and its affiliates), Tri-Star Pictures, United Airlines, Inc., U.S. Airways, Inc., and Viacom, Inc. The firm also represents creditors, equity holders and creditor's committees in chapter 11 cases and out-of-court restructurings, including formal and informal committees; such representations have been in connection with the restructuring of Adelphia, Aladdin Gaming LLC, American Restaurant Group, Bally's Grand, Inc., Charter Medical Corporation, Consolidated Freightways, Inc., Enron Corp., Global Crossing, Globalstar, Golden Ocean Group, Limited, House2Home, Inc., JP Stevens, NRG, Orion Pictures Corporation, O'Sullivan Industries, Owens-Corning, Papercraft Corporation, PRIMESTAR, Inc., Resorts International, Inc., Trump Hotels and Casino Resorts, and World-Com.

**INTERNATIONAL WORK:** The firm has represented foreign debtors, or their foreign representatives. These representations have included both chapter 11 cases for a foreign debtor with assets in the United States and ancillary proceeding pursuant to Section 304 and the new chapter 15 of the United States Bankruptcy Code to enjoin the enforcement of remedies against assets located in the United States.

**HEAD OFFICE**

**CALIFORNIA**
1901 Avenue of the Stars, Twelfth Floor, **Los Angeles**, CA 90067
**Tel:** 310 228 5600   **Fax:** 310 228 5788
**Email:** info@stutman.com
**Website:** www.stutman.com

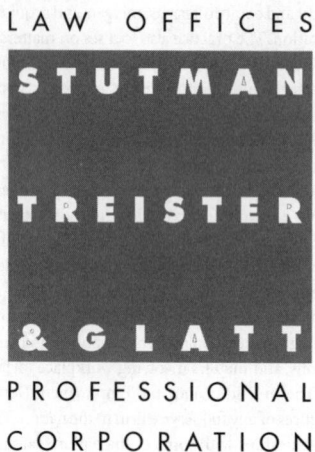

LAW OFFICES
STUTMAN
TREISTER
& GLATT
PROFESSIONAL
CORPORATION

# THELEN REID & PRIEST LLP

## THE FIRM

**Chairman:** Stephen V O'Neal
**Vice Chairman:** Michael S Elkin

**Number of partners:** 190
**Number of other lawyers:** 234

**FIRM OVERVIEW:** Thelen Reid & Priest LLP is a national law firm with more than 400 attorneys and offices in New York, San Francisco, Washington DC, Los Angeles, Silicon Valley and Northern New Jersey. In 2006, the firm plans on opening an office in Shanghai, China, where it has had two partners stationed since mid-2005. Serving *Fortune* 500 companies and their privately held counterparts, the firm provides superior legal services with a focus on complex commercial litigation, corporate and capital markets transactions, project and asset finance, construction and government contracts, labor and employment, intellectual property, domestic and international tax, employee benefits, government affairs, and real estate. Thelen Reid is recognized as a leader in the construction, infrastructure, and energy and utilities industries in the United States.

## MAIN AREAS OF PRACTICE:

**Commercial Litigation:** Thelen Reid's Commercial Litigation Team has earned a national reputation for excellence in areas including antitrust, arbitration, banking, bankruptcy, corporate governance, entertainment, environmental, insurance, intellectual property, product liability, real estate, securities, technology, toxic tort and white collar investigations and criminal defense. Thelen Reid has been at the forefront of international arbitration law and practice and has pioneered efforts to develop faster, more economical mechanisms for resolving commercial disputes outside of traditional litigation.

**Construction & Government Contracts:** Thelen Reid's Construction Practice is the preeminent practice of its kind in the United States. Its lawyers work with clients from the initiation of projects and preparation of contract documents through dispute resolution, including negotiation, mediation, arbitration and trial. The firm's construction attorneys have worked on projects ranging from individual buildings through some of the largest infrastructure projects in the world. In 2003, the firm launched Masons Thelen Reid LLP, a joint venture with Pinsent Masons of the United Kingdom, creating the largest construction, engineering and infrastructure practice in the world. The firm's attorneys have substantial experience in the broad range of issues involved in contracting with the Federal, state, and local governments.

**Corporate & Capital Markets:** The firm's Business and Finance Practice provides legal representation and counseling in a wide range of domestic and international corporate and commercial finance transactions. The practice is involved in capital markets transactions, including underwriting and issuer representation in debt and equity offerings, mergers and acquisitions, and general corporate representation. The practice also focuses on matters involving federal regulation of utilities, securities law compliance, corporate governance, general contract matters, partnerships, creditors' rights, and patent, copyright and trademark prosecution and counseling. The firm has particular expertise in the energy business sector, including public utilities, and the private equity market, including fund formation, capitalization and investment.

**Government Affairs:** The firm's Government Affairs Team represents key players in today's global economy on complex and sophisticated issues before Congress and the Executive Branch. Thelen Reid government affairs attorneys, representing a group of Nevada dairy farmers, won a 2003 decision before the United States Supreme Court.

**Labor & Employment:** With attorneys representing clients on a national basis in connection with high-stakes employment litigation, discrimination and wage and hour class actions, and matters involving workplace torts, ADA and traditional labor issues, Thelen Reid's Labor and Employment Department is one of the largest such practices of any full service firm in the nation. The firm has developed long-term partnerships with some of the nation's largest employers, and

## HEAD OFFICES

**CALIFORNIA**
101 Second Street, Suite 1800, **San Francisco**, CA 94105
**Tel:** 415 371 1200 **Fax:** 415 371 1211

**NEW YORK**
875 Third Avenue, 10th Floor, **New York**, NY 10022
**Tel:** 212 603 2000 **Fax:** 212 603 2001
**Website:** www.thelenreid.com

## CONTACTS

| | |
|---|---|
| **Corporate & Capital Markets** | Douglas E Davidson |
| **Commercial Litigation** | Michael S Elkin |
| **Construction & Government Contracts** | John R Heisse |
| **Government Affairs** | Walter L Raheb |
| **Labor & Employment** | Linda S Husar |
| **Project & Asset Finance** | Mark P Weitzel |
| **Real Estate** | Richard M Sharpiro |
| **Tax & Employee Benefits** | James I Warren |
| **San Francisco Office Managing Partner** | Richard A Lapping |
| **New York Office Managing Partner** | Douglas E Davidson |
| **Washington, DC Office Managing Partner** | Andrew D Ness |
| **Los Angeles Office Managing Partner** | Thomas E Hill |
| **Silicon Valley Office Managing Partner** | Kenneth L Nissly |
| **Northern New Jersey Office Managing Partner** | Marc B Lasky |

has helped to create in-house training and compliance programs and audits that help clients manage and remedy problems before potential litigation can begin.

**Project & Asset Finance:** Thelen Reid's project and asset finance attorneys have represented clients in the development and acquisition of energy, telecommunications and other infrastructure projects throughout the US and in more than 60 foreign countries. The firm has been rated in the top group of US project finance law firms by *The American Lawyer*, *Privatization International* and *Euromoney*, and draws upon the unsurpassed experience of its construction law and dispute resolution groups. The firm also has extensive experience representing investors in the financing of assets through leveraged lease and related structures.

**Tax & Employee Benefits:** The firm provides a full range of federal, state and local tax services to all forms of public and private business organizations including corporations, partnerships and limited liabilitiy companies as well as to individuals, fiduciaries and tax-exempt organizations. The firm is experienced in providing advice in the areas of entity formations, acquisitions or dispositions, financings, restructurings, recapitalizations, joint ventures, asset-based and project-based financings as well as general tax planning and representation in tax controversies. The firm also provides advice in the areas of design, implementation and administration of executive compensation, retirement and other employee benefit plans.

**Real Estate:** Thelen Reid's Real Estate Practice covers the entire spectrum of real estate and real estate financing, representing domestic and foreign individuals and institutional investors, developers, lenders and investment bankers in connection with the acquisition, sale, financing, development, leasing, management, rehabilitation and construction of all types of commercial and industrial properties including hotels, master-planned communities and government buildings.

**INTERNATIONAL WORK:** Thelen Reid represents clients around the world in their international endeavors and in their business activities in the United States. Their attorneys' extensive foreign language capabilities and knowledge of different cultures and legal systems allows them to understand the particular needs of the firm's international clientele, resolve problems and attain critical objectives.

# WESTON BENSHOOF ROCHEFORT RUBALCAVA & MacCUISH LLP

## THE FIRM

**Managing Partner:** Edward J Casey
**Number of partners:** 38
**Number of other lawyers:** 30

**FIRM OVERVIEW:** Weston Benshoof is a California-based law firm focused on business counseling, complex commercial litigation, environmental law, and real estate development. The firm provides a range of integrated legal services, maintaining the highest level of responsiveness to help clients achieve their goals.

## MAIN AREAS OF PRACTICE:

**Business Litigation:** Weston Benshoof's Commercial Litigation Practice is distinguished by the substantial court experience of its attorneys, who have successfully handled complex trials of national significance in diverse industries. The firm's experience includes antitrust, unfair competition, consumer class actions, contract disputes, and a variety of other major claims facing large and small businesses.

**Construction:** The firm provides a full range of construction law services to owners, contractors and construction managers primarily in large public and private infrastructure, industrial and commercial projects. This expertise includes project planning, procurement and contracting; project start-up, counseling and close-out; and litigation of complex construction claims.

**Corporate & Business Transactions:** Weston Benshoof provides counseling to businesses at all stages of their growth, from inception through public offering. This expertise includes mergers and acquisitions, securities offerings, debt and equity financing, restructurings, corporate governance, licensing agreements, joint ventures, and technology transfer agreements.

**Energy:** Weston Benshoof's full-service Energy Group assists in positioning clients in California's unique energy market. The group has years of experience in the power industry, integrating the firm's broad capabilities in business counseling, land development, environmental permitting and compliance, public law, construction and litigation.

**Environmental Compliance & Litigation:** Environmental law has been one of Weston Benshoof's core practice areas since the firm's founding, matching the specific needs of each client for permitting, compliance, counseling, and lobbying. The firm also handles a wide range of environmental litigation matters, including government enforcement, citizen suits, toxic tort, and Proposition 65 actions.

**Franchise:** Weston Benshoof provides franchise and distribution counseling to oil companies, manufacturers, restaurants, and a variety of goods and service franchisors and franchisees alike. The firm's extensive litigation experience includes enforcing franchise agreements, upholding challenged franchise terminations, and defending nationwide franchise and distribution practices in precedent-setting antitrust cases.

**Insurance:** The firm represents commercial policyholders in obtaining settlements and judgments from their insurers when first or third party coverage has initially been disputed. This experience includes a range of general liability, environmental, toxic tort, professional liability, employer's liability, construction bond, intellectual property, workers' compensation, and oil and gas issues.

**Intellectual Property:** Weston Benshoof has extensive experience in intellectual property litigation, with an emphasis in the areas of trade secrets, trademarks, and economic espionage, in addition to patents and copyrights. The firm also guides clients through complex licensing agreements, including joint technology development projects with leading universities and other research institutions.

**Labor & Employment:** The firm has assisted clients with litigation and counseling on all manner of employment-related claims, including wrongful termination, discrimination, harassment, wage and hour issues, OSHA matters, 'whistle blower' cases, union issues, restrictive covenant disputes, and protection of trade secret matters.

## HEAD OFFICE

**CALIFORNIA**
333 South Hope Street, 16th Floor, **Los Angeles,** CA 90071
**Tel:** 213 576 1000   **Fax:** 213 576 1100
**Website:** www.wbcounsel.com

## BRANCH OFFICE

**CALIFORNIA**
2801 Townsgate Road, Suite 215, **Westlake Village,** CA 91361
**Tel:** 805 497 9474   **Fax:** 805 497 8804

## CONTACTS

| | |
|---|---|
| **Business Litigation & Franchise** | John M Rochefort |
| **Construction** | G. Christian Roux |
| **Corporate & Business Transactions** | Thomas J Wingard |
| **Energy** | David S MacCuish |
| **Environmental Compliance** | Sharon Rubalcava |
| **Environmental Litigation** | Ward L Benshoof |
| **Insurance** | Richard Giller |
| **Intellectual Property** | Louis A Karasik |
| **Labor & Employment** | Martha S Doty |
| **Land Use** | Steven W Weston |
| **Real Estate** | Pamela J Privett |
| **Telecommunications** | Jesse M Jauregui |
| **Toxic Torts/Product Liability** | Samuel C Taylor |
| **Water Resources** | Edward J Casey |

**Land Use:** Weston Benshoof's Land Use Practice is one of the largest in the region, and has a range and depth of experience unrivaled by any other California law firm. The firm's attorneys have assisted clients with obtaining and defending land use entitlements for all types of development projects, including residential and master planned communities, commercial and retail centers, industrial operations and infrastructure projects.

**Real Estate:** Weston Benshoof is uniquely situated among California law firms because of its track record of providing premier 'A to Z' counseling and legal services on major commercial real estate projects. The firm has experience in structuring, drafting, negotiating and closing a broad spectrum of real estate deals - including acquisition, disposition, secured finance, and leasehold transactions.

**Telecommunications:** California has emerged as one of the key centers for telecommunications, and Weston Benshoof represents leading companies in the industry, including major providers of wireless service and infrastructure. A team of attorneys provides a wide range of litigation, transactional, counseling, and governmental advocacy services to meet the unique needs of communications and information technology businesses.

**Toxic Torts/Product Liability:** The firm is a recognized leader in resolving complex toxic tort and product liability lawsuits on behalf of aerospace, petroleum, chemical, manufacturing, waste disposal, and other companies. The firm's creative defense strategies and case management techniques reflect its substantial technical and legal experience across the spectrum of environmental law and litigation.

**Water Resources:** Weston Benshoof provides a full range of water-related counseling and legal services to public agencies, private water companies, residential developers, and other clients. This experience includes a broad spectrum of matters involving water rights, water quality, conjunctive use, import and export of water, infrastructure projects, water reclamation and water marketing.

**CLIENTS:** Weston Benshoof's clients range from Fortune 500 corporations to emerging companies to public agencies at all levels of government.

# WILSON SONSINI GOODRICH & ROSATI

## THE FIRM

**Chairman:** Larry W Sonsini
**CEO:** John V Roos

**Number of partners:** 177
**Number of attorneys:** 605

**FIRM OVERVIEW:** Wilson Sonsini Goodrich & Rosati is the premier legal advisor to technology and growth business enterprises worldwide. The firm's legal expertise serves clients at all stages of development, from venture-backed start-up companies to multi-billion dollar global enterprises. Wilson Sonsini Goodrich & Rosati's broad range of services and legal disciplines are focused on serving the principal challenges faced by management and the board of directors of the business enterprise. The firm's clients are in a variety of industries including information technology, software, life sciences and retail. Wilson Sonsini Goodrich & Rosati is nationally recognized as a leader in corporate governance, public and private offerings of equity and debt securities, mergers and acquisitions, securities class action litigation, intellectual property litigation, joint ventures and strategic alliances, and technology licensing and other intellectual property transactions. Over the past four decades, the firm has established its reputation by having a superior knowledge of its clients' industries, as well as deep and long-standing contacts throughout the technology sector.

**MAIN AREAS OF PRACTICE:** Wilson Sonsini Goodrich & Rosati's main areas of practice include corporate law and governance; corporate finance – private equity, public equity, and debt finance; mergers and acquisitions; litigation – securities litigation, intellectual property litigation, commercial litigation, white collar crime and internal investigations, and employment law; intellectual property counseling and transactions – technology transactions, intellectual property counseling and patents, trademarks, copyrights and advertising; antitrust counseling; employee benefits and compensation; fund services; real estate and environmental; tax; and wealth management.

**CLIENTS:** Wilson Sonsini Goodrich & Rosati's client base includes: communications and networking, electronics/computer hardware, financial institutions, information service providers, life sciences, media and entertainment, retail and consumer products and services, semiconductors, software and venture capital.

**INTERNATIONAL WORK:** Headquartered in Silicon Valley, with offices in six technology hubs throughout the US, Wilson Sonsini Goodrich & Rosati has a national presence with a global reach. Over the past four decades, the firm has developed a wide ranging international practice, with particular strength in Asia and Europe. Recently, the firm has applied for a license to open an office in Shanghai, China. Wilson Sonsini Goodrich & Rosati represents both US and foreign clients in a variety of international matters including: cross-boder merger and acquisition transactions, joint ventures, foreign investment, branch operations, and intellectual property.

## HEAD OFFICE

**CALIFORNIA**
650 Page Mill Road, **Palo Alto,** CA 94304-1050
**Tel:** 650 493 9300  **Fax:** 650 493 6811
**Email:** wsgr@wsgr.com
**Website:** www.wsgr.com

## BRANCH OFFICES

**CALIFORNIA**
12235 El Camino Real, Suite 200,
**San Diego,** CA 92130-3002
**Tel:** 838 350 2300  **Fax:** 858 350 2399

One Market, Spear Tower, Suite 3300,
**San Francisco,** CA 94105-1126
**Tel:** 415 947 2000  **Fax:** 415 947 2099

**NEW YORK**
12 East 49th Street, 30th Floor,
**New York,** NY 10017-8203
**Tel:** 212 999 5800  **Fax:** 212 999 5899

**TEXAS**
8911 Capital of Texas Highway North, Westech 360, Suite 3210,
**Austin,** TX 78759-8497
**Tel:** 512 338 5400  **Fax:** 512 338 5499

**UTAH**
2795 East Cottonwood Parkway, Suite 300,
**Salt Lake City,** UT 84121-6928
**Tel:** 801 993 6400  **Fax:** 801 993 6499

**VIRGINIA**
Two Fountain Square, Reston Town Center, 11921 Freedom Drive,
Suite 600, **Reston,** VA 20190-5634
**Tel:** 703 734 3100  **Fax:** 703 734 3199

**WASHINGTON**
701 Fifth Avenue, Suite 5100, **Seattle,** WA 98104-7036
**Tel:** 206 883 2500  **Fax:** 206 883 2699

WSGR  Wilson Sonsini Goodrich & Rosati
PROFESSIONAL CORPORATION

## How lawyers are ranked

Every year we carry out thousands of in-depth interviews with clients and lawyers in order to assess the reputations and expertise of business lawyers across the USA. Chambers rankings and editorial are referred to extensively by General Counsel and other purchasers of legal services who look to our recommendations when choosing their lawyers.

# CONSTRUCTION

| Construction | |
|---|---|
| Leading Firms | |
| 1 | FAEGRE & BENSON LLP *Denver* |
| | HOLLAND & HART LLP *Denver* |
| | SHERMAN & HOWARD LLC *Denver* |

| Leading Individuals | |
|---|---|
| 1 | ARKELL J David *Faegre & Benson LLP* |
| | BENSON Robert *Holland & Hart LLP* |
| | COOK Michael *Sherman & Howard LLC* |
| | FROST Daniel *Holland & Hart LLP* |
| | GUNNELL Bret *Sherman & Howard LLC* |
| 2 | BRIDSTON Kevin *Holland & Hart LLP* |
| | MCDANIEL Janet *Faegre & Benson LLP* |

## Band 1

### Faegre & Benson LLP
See firm details p.1170

**The Firm:** This "*tremendous*" full-service firm is one of the few in Colorado to field a dedicated construction team. The group is devoted to all manner of construction-related litigation and transactions focusing mainly on contracts and disputes. It represents a wide cross-section of industry clients throughout the Rocky Mountains including owners of projects, public and private contractors, lenders and sureties. Recently, the team has represented a general contractor in a dispute with the Colorado Department of Transportation over delays and disruption to a new project. The team is popular with clients who say "*they can bring legal expertise to the table, but they also have a practical legal perspective.*" They also appreciate the team's extensive knowledge of the field, noting "*they know the construction industry inside-out and that kind of knowledge is rare.*"

**The Lawyers:** "*He explains the law in a way that we understand,*" say clients of **David Arkell** (see p.357). His practice features construction planning and disputes through negotiation, mediation, arbitration and litigation. Clients like his approach, saying "*with his experience and his confidence he makes the legal side of our work pleasurable, which is hard.*" With 15 years' experience in the commercial construction industry **Janet McDaniel** (see p.363) stands out in the marketplace. Her practical expertise is highly valued, along with her litigation skills.

**Clients/Work Highlights:** Palace Construction; M.A. Mortenson; Yenter Companies; Intermountain Electric and City of Aspen.

### Holland & Hart LLP
See firm details p.369

**The Firm:** "*One of the best construction firms in the region*" is the view of many commentators. This sizable team handles construction matters across the board for both private and public companies. These include a range of businesses such as contractors, developers, architects, and surety companies. The team provides clients with general business advice related to the construction industry as well as dispute resolution. Major work undertaken by the team has recently included acting as lead counsel in BRW v Dufficy & Sons, a case involving the construction of two bridges across the Platte River by the City and County of Denver.

**The Lawyers:** **Robert Benson** (see p.358) is the patriarch of construction law in Colorado, agree many interviewees. His practice covers many areas of commercial litigation, but it is arguably his construction specialism that is best known. He also has a wealth of experience as an arbitrator and mediator.

With over 20 years' experience in complex construction claims and transactions **Daniel Frost** (see p.360) stands out in the field. He has been appointed as the special assistant attorney general to assist the State of Colorado with construction matters. "*He has always given us great advice*" say clients about **Kevin Bridston** (see p.358), adding that "*he is intelligent and presents information in a constructive way.*" He advises on heavy and commercial construction matters and undertakes some residential work as well.

### Sherman & Howard LLC
See firm details p.373

**The Firm:** This Denver-based firm has established a dedicated construction team. It handles both public and private construction matters for a range of clients including general contractors, owners, designers and engineers. Dispute resolution and claim management are two cornerstones of the firm's practice, which are often resolved through mediation, arbitration and negotiation. This expertise was recently brought to the fore in a series of successful arbitrations including its advice to a general contractor in a dispute over extra work. The team is ever popular with clients who say that "*they are just excellent, they have helped us on a range of issues and have been successful.*"

**The Lawyers:** The "*levelheaded and tenacious*" **Michael Cook** (see p.359) is a leading light in construction law. According to sources "*he has the unique blend of industry experience and legal know-how.*" **Bret Gunnell** (see p.360) has an engineering background and "*has provided us with exceptional service*" say clients. The primary focus of his practice is construction litigation.

# CORPORATE/M&A

| Corporate/M&A |
| --- |
| Leading Firms |
| [1] COOLEY GODWARD LLP *Broomfield* |
| HOGAN & HARTSON LLP *Denver* |
| HOLME ROBERTS & OWEN LLP *Denver* |
| [2] BARTLIT BECK HERMAN PALENCHAR & SCOTT |
| DAVIS GRAHAM & STUBBS LLP *Denver* |
| FAEGRE & BENSON LLP *Denver* |
| [3] BROWNSTEIN HYATT & FARBER PC *Denver* |
| GIBSON, DUNN & CRUTCHER LLP *Denver* |
| HOLLAND & HART LLP *Denver* |
| [4] MORRISON & FOERSTER LLP *Denver* |
| PERKINS COIE LLP *Denver* |
| SHERMAN & HOWARD LLC *Denver* |

| Leading Individuals |
| --- |
| [1] HILTON Paul *Hogan & Hartson LLP* |
| LEVINE Ronald *Davis Graham* |
| LINFIELD James *Cooley Godward LLP* |
| PALENCHAR James *Bartlit Beck* |
| SALTER Dean *Holme Roberts* |
| WHEELER Francis *Cooley Godward LLP* |
| [2] HOLMES Whitney *Morrison & Foerster LLP* |
| JENSEN Garth *Holme Roberts* |
| KRENDL Cathy *Krendl Krendl Sachnoff* |
| LEVY Mark *Holland & Hart LLP* |
| RUPPERT John *Perkins Coie LLP* |
| RUSSO Richard *Gibson, Dunn* |
| STOCKS Bruce *Perkins Coie LLP* |
| WALSH Christopher *Hogan & Hartson LLP* |
| WRIGHT Douglas *Faegre & Benson LLP* |
| [3] ARKELL Betty *Holland & Hart LLP* |
| BLAIR Andrew *Sherman & Howard LLC* |
| CAMPBELL William *Faegre & Benson LLP* |
| CUDNEY Kevin *Brownstein Hyatt* |
| KNETSCH Jeffrey *Brownstein Hyatt* |
| MAGUIRE JR Charles *Holme Roberts* |
| MOYE John *Moye White LLP* |
| PLUMRIDGE Richard *Holme Roberts* |
| STEPHENS Thomas *Bartlit Beck* |
| TALLEY Steven *Gibson, Dunn* |
| TROUPE Warren *Morrison & Foerster LLP* |
| VAN WESTRUM Anthony *Anthony van Westrum LLC* |

## Band 1

### Cooley Godward LLP

**The Firm:** This is *"clearly one of the best firms in the country,"* according to interviewees who praise it for sheer quality. It is headquartered in California but the Colorado office is an established player in the Midwest and serves clients throughout the Rocky Mountains. The corporate team has extensive expertise that includes M&A and securities; it also has unrivaled strength in venture capital. Lawyers recently represented Webroot in a $108 million private finance deal – a transaction that illustrates the

sterling reputation the team has earned advising hi-tech companies.

**The Lawyers:** **James Linfield** is an experienced rainmaker whose clients find comfort in the knowledge that they *"can reach out to him when a deep understanding of an issue is needed."* He represents private and public technology companies and venture capital funds. **Francis Wheeler** is known for advising larger companies across a range of industries including biotechnology, manufacturing and retail. Sources commend his knowledge of corporate restructuring and M&A.

**Clients/Work Highlights:** The substantial client list includes private and public companies with a particular emphasis on the hi-tech and life sciences sector. Venture capital groups also feature.

### Hogan & Hartson LLP
See firm details p.568

**The Firm:** With offices across the globe, including three in Colorado, this firm maintains one of the strongest practice groups in the state. It has garnered a reputation that stretches far afield and attracts clients from as far away as the East Coast. The team advises across the full spectrum of corporate work including M&A, securities and tax. It specializes in large and complex transactions. Lawyers acted for Accellent in its $1.27 billion merger with private equity firm Kohlberg Kravis Roberts. Sources confirm: *"They are consistently responsive and produce high-quality work that helps us achieve the results we want."*

**The Lawyers:** The *"wonderful and capable"* **Paul Hilton** (see p.361) is *"a veteran lawyer who has seen it all."* His broad practice covers a range of industries including software, telecommunications and mining. A source described **Christopher Walsh** (see p.367) as *"one of the best lawyers I've ever known,"* echoing the opinion of many commentators.

**Clients/Work Highlights:** CDM Optics; Ellora Energy; National CineMedia; Royal Gold; Qwest Partners; Regal Entertainment Group and KRG Capital Partners.

### Holme Roberts & Owen LLP
See firm details p.370

**The Firm:** This is one of the most respected teams in the region and commentators extol the depth of its practice and the experience of its lawyers. With offices in Denver, Boulder and Colorado, it advises public and private clients on diverse corporate matters. These include banking and finance, M&A, and securities, for which the group has gained a prodigious reputation. The team recently advised on several major public offerings, fielding lawyers who are *"pragmatic in their advice and technically excellent."*

**The Lawyers:** Clients praise the no-nonsense **Dean Salter** as a *"straight shooter,"* declaring: *"He has immense wisdom and is totally committed to us."* Corporate law and securities are the mainstays of his practice. **Garth Jensen** is recommended for his experience of international M&A and regularly advises

on cross-border transactions. With a practice that spans most areas of corporate work, the *"impeccably knowledgeable"* **Richard Plumridge** is popular with clients. **Charles Maguire**'s practice centers on M&A and securities, and clients single out his ability to manage complex transactions.

**Clients/Work Highlights:** UnitedGlobalCom and Newmont Mining both feature in the list of local and regional clients.

## Band 2

### Bartlit Beck Herman Palenchar & Scott

**The Firm:** This team is smaller than many of its competitors but packs a punch across a full range of corporate matters including securities, compliance, and M&A. It handles some of the largest and most complex transactions in the region, and interviewees report: *"The team is especially bright and talented. They hire and retain the cream of the crop."* Clients admire the firm's straightforward approach, declaring: *"There are no complications with them – they knuckle down and get the job done."*

**The Lawyers:** Clients value **James Palenchar**'s *"deep experience and great bedside manner."* He has a nationally renowned general corporate practice and is commended for his *"keen mind and abilities as a creative problem solver."* **Thomas Stephens** is acknowledged to be *"a careful drafter and a good negotiator."*

**Clients/Work Highlights:** The clientele includes Stratos International and Alpha Natural Resources. The firm also represents a number of private equity businesses.

### Davis Graham & Stubbs LLP

**The Firm:** This Denver-based firm's corporate practice is national in scope and admired for doing *"marvelous work."* The prestigious client base includes Endeavour Capital, which lawyers recently advised on its investment in Grand Canyon University in Phoenix, Arizona. The team is skilled in general M&A and securities, and is sought after for its money management and investment expertise. Clients laud the dedicated lawyers: *"If we have a problem we can count on them to work around the clock to get the job done."*

**The Lawyers:** The verdict is unanimous: **Ronald Levine** is *"just a damn fine lawyer."* His practice focuses on the representation of private and public companies in M&A transactions. According to clients, he is *"smart, practical and creative, and aware of issues you hadn't even thought of."*

**Clients/Work Highlights:** Delta Petroleum; Apex Silver Mines; Endeavour Capital; Coors family trusts and M2P Capital.

## Faegre & Benson LLP

See firm details p.1170

**The Firm:** With offices in both Denver and Boulder, this group enjoys a first-class reputation across the Rocky Mountain region and acts for a significant clientele. It keeps "*on top of all developments in corporate law*," according to interviewees. The team is one of the largest and most experienced in the state, and it is seen on major deals. For example, it represented Time Warner in a $200 million 144a note offering. Lawyers advise across a variety of industries that includes technology, energy and telecommunications. Clients declare them "*incredibly responsive – they jump to answer our needs.*"

**The Lawyers: Douglas Wright** (see p.367) avoids the sort of esoteric discussions that switch clients off, focusing instead on "*practical advice formulated around real needs.*" He recently advised Black Hills on the $103 million sale of subsidiary Black Hills Fiber Systems to PrairieWave. Colleague **William Campbell** (see p.358) enjoys a considerable reputation for advising on diverse matters including corporate governance and public and private securities.

**Clients/Work Highlights:** Time Warner Telecom; Frontier Airlines; Displaytech; StarTek; CROCS; CIBER and CH2M HILL.

---

## Band 3

### Brownstein Hyatt & Farber PC

See firm details p.368

**The Firm:** This group has "*a dynamic New York style that produces excellent results*," according to commentators. It has a broad corporate practice and a national reputation for private equity work. Lawyers advised on HJ Heinz's purchase of Newark-based dessert manufacturer Nancy's Speciality Foods.

**The Lawyers:** Clients say of talented all-rounder **Kevin Cudney** that "*his approach is thorough, his responses timely and his work product excellent.*" **Jeffrey Knetsch** (see p.362) is thought to be "*professional and even-keeled with a wide knowledge base.*" He advises across the board on private equity, public company, M&A and venture capital matters. The team recently lost members of its Colorado team, but it maintains a strong presence in the region.

**Clients/Work Highlights:** Alongside established clients such as Guilford Securities, ITU Ventures and KRG Capital Partners, the firm advises many local and national companies.

## Gibson, Dunn & Crutcher LLP

See firm details p.328

**The Firm:** The Colorado office of this national powerhouse enters the table this year, having made substantial inroads into the local market. Clients aver that it is "*particularly good at completing a transaction efficiently without getting bogged down.*" Though small, the team serves an enviable roster of high-profile national clients. For example, it recently advised Qwest on a number of billion-dollar transactions including a $1.15 billion note offering by a Qwest subsidiary. The lawyers are well liked by clients, who note: "*They take an interest and understand our business.*"

**The Lawyers:** The richly experienced **Richard Russo**'s (see p.365) clients declare him "*a terrific lawyer.*" He advised Transcontinental Gas Pipeline (Transco) on its $75 million offering of floating rate senior notes. **Steve Talley** (see p.367) is described as "*knowledgeable and plain-speaking.*" His practice covers M&A, private and public equity matters and debt offerings.

**Clients/Work Highlights:** The firm serves an array of local, national and international businesses such as CSK Auto; The Williams Companies; Petro Shopping Centers; Qwest and several Fortune 500 companies.

---

## Holland & Hart LLP

See firm details p.369

**The Firm:** Five offices across the state give this outfit a strong local and regional presence. The sizable team offers varied corporate expertise and is adept in M&A, venture capital and securities matters. It operates across a number of industries including technology and energy. Lawyers acted for Shell Wind Energy in a $123.5 million financing transaction.

**The Lawyers: Mark Levy** (see p.362) is "*a superb lawyer who is also easy to work with.*" He specializes in securities law, particularly relating to public companies. **Betty Arkell**'s (see p.357) fans describe her as "*one of the most experienced and dedicated lawyers in town.*" She is expert in venture capital and private equity funds.

**Clients/Work Highlights:** Clients include Exabyte, Centennial Ventures and Navigant International.

---

## Band 4

### Morrison & Foerster LLP

See firm details p.335

**The Firm:** This much-admired firm fields "*a responsive and well-informed team*," according to commentators. The Colorado branch of this international player enters the tables because of its involvement in high-profile complex work and the arrival of Whitney Holmes. The group advised TransMontaigne on the restatement of its $400 million capital credit facility.

**The Lawyers:** "*Brainy yet approachable*" **Whitney Holmes** (see p.361) is "*a terrific lawyer*" who joins

the team from Hogan & Hartson. He is warmly endorsed for his skills in corporate finance, securities and M&A. **Warren Troupe** (see p.367) is noted for his insistent manner and strong client base.

**Clients/Work Highlights:** CH2M Hill; Atrix Laboratories; United Dominion Realty Trust; Collect America; Connetics; Bank of the West and HMS Healthcare.

## Perkins Coie LLP

**The Firm:** The corporate department here is growing healthily thanks to a steady flow of major deals. The team has won itself a first-class reputation and earns its place in the table this year. Satisfied clients observe: "*There is nothing we require that they don't have.*"

**The Lawyers: John Ruppert** joins the team from Brownstein Hyatt & Farber. He is an established bankruptcy and restructuring expert. Clients declare **Bruce Stocks** "*one of the best out there – he really knows what he is talking about and is so focused.*"

**Clients/Work Highlights:** The client list features local and national companies.

## Sherman & Howard LLC

See firm details p.373

**The Firm:** This firm operates two offices in Colorado and three more in the Rocky Mountains region. It has a sterling reputation for telecom work and advises on a range of corporate and real estate transactional matters. M&A and securities form the core of the practice and interviewees avow: "*If you go to them, you know you are going to work with a great lawyer.*"

**The Lawyers: Andrew Blair** (see p.358) is a "*diligent and commonsensical*" lawyer, say commentators. His practice is focused on securities work and he also advises on general corporate matters.

**Clients/Work Highlights:** Clients include Bubba Gump Shrimp, General Communications and Liberty Media.

## Other Notable Practitioners

Summing up the market's view of Krendl Krendl Sachnoff & Way's **Cathy Krendl**, a source comments: "*She is extremely easy to work with and attuned to business needs.*" She has a creditable reputation for working with small and medium-sized companies. **John Moye** of Moye White LLP is "*professional and very involved in the community.*" Clients praise his business nous. Sole practitioner **Anthony van Westrum** is admired for his detailed knowledge of the Colorado market.

# EMPLOYMENT

## Band 1

### Holland & Hart LLP
See firm details p.369

**The Firm:** This firm "*really stands out*" for the scale and quality of its labor and employment services in Colorado. With five offices across the state, the team is one of the largest in Colorado and offers advice across the board. It is particularly admired in the arena of traditional union-related matters. It is also one of the few firms to field a dedicated employee benefits team. Lawyers have worked on a number of high-profile cases including union disputes in the airline industry. Clients "*hold the team in high esteem,*" declaring the practitioners "*skillful and well-informed.*"

**The Lawyers: Gregory Eurich** (see p.359) is a good bet for "*top-notch legal advice,*" according to clients. He is a courtroom operator of high repute and has represented clients in a range of matters including discrimination and wrongful discharge suits. The "*talented and ethical*" **John Husband** (see p.361) has developed a specialty in class action cases under both federal and state law. The "*extremely cordial*" **Brian Mumaugh** (see p.363) manages the group. He strikes interviewees with his combination of knowledge with common sense. **Jane Francis** (see p.360) heads the employee benefits group and is experienced in ERISA, healthcare and executive compensation issues. **Sheldon Smith** (see p.366) is a veteran in the field according to sources, who "*would go to him in a heartbeat.*"

**Clients/Work Highlights:** UPS, AIMCO and United Technologies feature on the firm's substantial client list.

### Sherman & Howard LLC
See firm details p.373

**The Firm:** This is a high-profile group that has earned a sterling reputation throughout the Rocky Mountain region. Clients attribute its "*outstanding*" track record to an "*ability to fit the right person to the case.*" The sizable team represents companies on matters such as union disputes, wage and hour cases and improper discharge cases, as well as employee benefits. The group houses a dedicated ERISA and executive compensation team. Lawyers recently acted in a number of multiparty and class action cases relating to ADA.

**The Lawyers: Raymond Deeny** (see p.359) enjoys a deep rapport with his management clients. His practice focuses on litigation. **Charles Newcom's** (see p.364) "*analytical skills and calm demeanor*" enable him to steer his clients on the right course. He is active in discrimination and wrongful discharge cases and has developed a specialty in health and safety matters. **Theodore Olsen's** (see p.364) opponents freely admit: "*If I am against him I worry about it.*" **Bernie Siebert** (see p.366) is recognized as one of the most accomplished employment lawyers in the state. **Bruce Muir** (see p.363) engages in employee benefits work, including retirement and stock ownership plans. **Kathleen Odle** (see p.364) is a full time ERISA expert with a growing reputation in executive compensation. **Michael Sanchez** (see p.365) stands out for employee benefits planning.

**Clients/Work Highlights:** Ball Corporation; Newmont Mining; Kroeger and Cleveland-Cliffs.

## Band 2

### Brownstein Hyatt & Farber PC
See firm details p.368

**The Firm:** This group offers all the services one would expect from a respected full-service firm. Over and above that, according to sources, "*the team has wonderful morale; everyone is sincere, diligent and caring.*" It represents management on issues ranging from discrimination and wrongful discharge claims to wage and hour and fair labor standards matters. The group also handles the occasional plaintiff case. This expertise was recently illustrated when the firm successfully represented an employee who had been prohibited from working after suffering an aneurysm.

**The Lawyers:** The "*warm, personable and smart*" **David Powell** (see p.364) has a broad and thriving practice. He recently defended a car dealership against claims brought by an ex-employee.

**Clients/Work Highlights:** United Airlines; HealthONE Alliance; Wellbridge; Mercury Companies and TIAA-CREF.

### Hogan & Hartson LLP
See firm details p.568

**The Firm:** This premier firm makes its mark with excellent customer service and a "*breathtaking knowledge of the law.*" The small team advises clients on diverse matters such as discrimination litigation, trade secret issues and a growing number of whistle-blower cases. It also advises on traditional labor issues and recently represented a labor union in a criminal lawsuit.

**The Lawyers:** The hugely experienced **Edwin Aro** (see p.357) "*has a unique way of reaching out to people,*" according to sources: "*He speaks a language people can relate to.*" The "*professional and client-oriented*" **Sean Gallagher** (see p.360) focuses his practice on traditional discrimination matters, although in the last year he represented a national mortgage broker in a wage and hour-related lawsuit.

**Clients/Work Highlights:** Janus Capital Group; Regal CineMedia/National CineMedia; P2 Energy Solutions; Boston Market; Classified School Employees Association and TMG Marketing.

### Holme Roberts & Owen LLP
See firm details p.370

**The Firm:** Those who work with this tight and talented group declare the experience "*a real eye-opener.*" According to commentators, the team fields "*such highly qualified people that it rivals the strength of national firms.*" One of the largest practices in the Rocky Mountain region, it offers employment counseling and litigation services on a broad spread of matters. These include traditional labor law, discrimination cases and employee benefits work.

**The Lawyers: Preston Oade** is praised for his "*strategic business advice*" and trial skills. His courtroom performance causes one client to observe: "*It is his job to make me look good, and he does.*" **David Mitzner** is vastly experienced in employee benefits and ERISA, and also expert in executive compensation matters.

**Clients/Work Highlights:** Both local and national companies stud the client list.

## Band 3

### Davis Graham & Stubbs LLP

**The Firm:** This full-service Denver firm includes a small, dedicated employment team. Appreciative clients agree that the team is effective and keeps them well informed. It advises on all types of employment and labor work; counseling is a significant part of the workload. Lawyers recently defended a national origin discrimination case for one of Colorado's major manufacturers.

**The Lawyers:** **Janet Savage** is *"one of the best strategists out there,"* according to commentators, and has handled virtually every type of employment case. Interviewees observe that she is *"fun to work with and really cares about the client."*

**Clients/Work Highlights:** The firm has a long and varied client list of local and national companies including healthcare organizations and hospitals.

### Faegre & Benson LLP

See firm details p.1170

**The Firm:** This sizable group *"can deal with any problem that comes up,"* which makes it very popular with clients. The team is rich in experienced lawyers, and *"whatever you need there is someone at*

the firm who is an expert.*" It also has an active employee benefits practice. The team recently successfully represented State Farm in a race discrimination lawsuit.

**The Lawyers:** **Elizabeth MacDonald** (see p.362) is an employment and labor expert and has a substantial arbitration and mediation practice. **Charles Weese** (see p.367) is *"the ultimate professional,"* and his thoroughness and timeliness are popular with clients. He represents employers in both state and federal courts. The *"focused and always pertinent"* **Renee O'Rourke** (see p.364) is widely recognized as a premier employee benefits specialist. Significant recent projects include analyzing proposed regulations under the Internal Revenue Code.

**Clients/Work Highlights:** State Farm; Crocs; Black Hawk Gaming & Development; Colorado Rockies; MCPN; United Agri Products; Exempla Healthcare and Enterprise Rent-A-Car.

### Other Notable Practitioners

The *"approachable and personable"* **Jessica Brown** (see p.358) of Gibson, Dunn & Crutcher LLP is recommended for her practical approach. Clients assert: *"She understands the pressures of our business."* She represents employers both locally and nationally

in a range of discrimination matters; she successfully represented Hewlett-Packard against claims of discrimination and retaliation in federal district court. **Raymond Martin** of Wheeler Trigg Kennedy LLP enters the tables on the strength of compelling peer and client praise. This talented trial lawyer handles employment cases across the region and recently settled a class action under the FLSA in Idaho's federal court. The *"helpful and pleasant"* **Kristen Mix** (see p.363) of Snell & Wilmer LLP *"does a great job of expressing complicated issues in a crystal clear way."* She undertakes the occasional plaintiff's case, as exemplified by her recent trial success for an executive director claiming unfair dismissal. **Daniel Satriana** of Clisham, Satriana & Biscan LLC has an excellent courtroom reputation. Ducker, Montgomery, Aronstein & Bess PC's **David Stacy** *"does an amazing job,"* according to his clients: *"He really understands our company and our culture."* He acts for employers across the board on employment issues and recently defended a physician in three separate harassment cases, obtaining the dismissal of all three.

# ENVIRONMENT

## Band 1

### Davis Graham & Stubbs LLP

**The Firm:** This Denver-based firm offers one of the largest environmental teams in the state and is popular with clients, who say: *"They do stellar work, particularly on local issues."* It covers all manner of disciplines including compliance, litigation, permitting and transactional matters. Members of the team apply their expertise to a variety of areas, including air quality and radioactive materials, brownfield sites and hazardous waste. Proficiency in the latter is illustrated by the team's recent work for Colorado's Summit County, where it advised on the cleanup of some newly acquired property containing mine waste.

**The Lawyers:** Head of practice **Robert Lawrence** *"provides excellent customer service,"* according to clients. He specializes in environmental litigation involving such topics as Superfund and brownfield

sites, hazardous waste and clean water compliance. He remains popular with interviewees for his *"first-class judgment and strategic thinking."* The *"bright, thoughtful and experienced"* **Zach Miller** is another key member of the team. He enjoys a strong reputation for his expertise relating to clean water and air and endangered species.

**Clients/Work Highlights:** The firm boasts an enviable client list of local and national clients.

### Faegre & Benson LLP

See firm details p.1170

**The Firm:** Acknowledged as *"a premier firm"* by market sources, its practitioners are lauded for their *"tremendous"* work in the field. The firm has offices in Denver and Boulder, and houses one of the larger environmental teams in the state. It advises clients across the Rocky Mountain region on a variety of environmental matters concerning tribal land and endangered species concerns. Recently the team represented both regional and national clients in numerous Superfund proceedings relating to natural resource damage claims. The firm remains popular with clients, who say: *"It produces brilliant work and has lawyers who are talented in all aspects of the practice area."*

**The Lawyers:** *"Excellent negotiator"* **Linda Rockwood** (see p.365) is credited with *"the ability to find consensus and keep the parties working with rather than against one another."* Her practice spans the broad spectrum of environmental work and includes air quality, Superfund and brownfield redevelopment work. The *"outstanding"* **James**

**Spaanstra** (see p.366) has an established reputation in the field and over 20 years' experience of advising on all manner of concerns. Clients note: *"He understands communities and how legal and political issues impact upon them."*

**Clients/Work Highlights:** BFI Waste Systems; Duke Energy Field Services; Kaiser-Hill; Roche Colorado; US Bank and Western Gas Resources.

### Hogan & Hartson LLP

See firm details p.568

**The Firm:** With its impressive reputation for environmental work, this firm remains at the top of the tables. The team is among the largest in the state and spans the firm's three Colorado offices. It has a genuinely national practice, as is evident in its recent representation of Rexair in a lawsuit with the Michigan Department of Environmental Quality regarding the cleanup of contaminated groundwater in the Cadillac Industrial Park.

**The Lawyers:** **Tom Strickland** (see p.366) represents clients from many industries in a range of litigation matters. However, interviewees agreed that he stands out above all for his environmental work, with an emphasis on ski area and mining-related matters. Clients say of **Dennis Arfmann** (see p.357): *"There is no question about it, he is great in his field."* He is noted for his air quality practice, which covers compliance and permitting matters, and was recently called upon by EnCana to provide specialized advice on the Jonah infill development project. **Scott Reisch** (see p.364) is lauded for his broad knowledge of all matters environmental, but focuses on Superfund

## Environment
### Leading Individuals

[1] DUNN Daniel *Holme Roberts & Owen LLP*
LAWRENCE Robert *Davis Graham & Stubbs LLP*
PHILLIPS Paul *Holland & Hart LLP*
ROCKWOOD Linda *Faegre & Benson LLP*
SPAANSTRA James *Faegre & Benson LLP*
STRICKLAND Tom *Hogan & Hartson LLP*
TEMKIN Elizabeth *Temkin Wielga & Hardt LLP*
[2] ARFMANN Dennis *Hogan & Hartson LLP*
CONNERY Robert *Holland & Hart LLP*
EDDY Ronald *Sherman & Howard LLC*
EID Troy *Greenberg Traurig LLP*
FOGNANI John *Fognani & Faught, PLLC*
IPSEN Henry *Holme Roberts & Owen LLP*
MILLER Zach *Davis Graham & Stubbs LLP*
RAISCH Jerry *Vranesh and Raisch, LLP*
REISCH Scott *Hogan & Hartson LLP*

and brownfield sites as well as voluntary cleanup work.

**Clients/Work Highlights:** Rexair; Smithfield Foods; Kroenke Sports Enterprises; EnCana; Wolf Creek Ski Area; Silverton Mountain Ski Area; Black Hills Energy and PacifiCorp.

## Holland & Hart LLP
See firm details p.369
**The Firm:** This *"superb"* full-service firm is one of the largest in Colorado and is proud of its long-established reputation as a *"go-to"* outfit for all aspects of environmental work. The team here offers a wide knowledge base that covers solid and hazardous waste, Superfund sites and endangered species concerns. Mining and utilities specialists can also be called upon as required. The firm has offices across the Rocky Mountain area, assuring the team a strong regional presence.
**The Lawyers:** Sources say **Paul Phillips** (see p.364) *"knows the law inside-out."* He has over 25 years' experience in the field and is skilled in a variety of areas such as clean water, Superfund and mining-related work. He is admired for his voluminous writings on environmental matters. **Robert Connery** (see p.358) is a *"seasoned professional,"* say commentators, and his niche expertise relating to the NEPA is much in demand.

**Clients/Work Highlights:** The firm maintains a long client list featuring companies such as Bechtel; Valero Energy; Saunders Construction and Duke Energy.

## Holme Roberts & Owen LLP
See firm details p.370
**The Firm:** Described as *"one of the finest firms around,"* it wins promotion in the table this year upon receiving a great deal of positive feedback. Clients say: *"The firm's talented group offers a comprehensive service and is pleasant and easy to work with."* A large, dedicated environmental team represents regional as well as national clients. It offers expertise in most environmental law and toxic tort matters. Recent highlights include representing a well-known chemical company in a radiation toxic tort case pending in the US District Court.
**The Lawyers:** *"A very astute attorney with excellent judgment,"* **Daniel Dunn** climbs the tables as an experienced environmental law practitioner heavily involved in toxic torts. Clients say his ability to *"think of the big picture and always consider the best interests of the client"* is invaluable. Head of the environmental and toxic tort practice group, **Henry Ipsen** debuts in the rankings this year. He is popular with sources, who *"admire his integrity."*
**Clients/Work Highlights:** The firm advises numerous national corporations including some Fortune 500 companies.

## Band 2

## Greenberg Traurig LLP
See firm details p.664
**The Firm:** This international firm has a small, dedicated environment team in Colorado, and lawyers in the Denver office increasingly advise clients across the Rocky Mountain region on environmental matters. The outfit covers all facets of the practice area, including air and water rights and general land use issues. Sources reserved special praise for the consistency of service, saying: *"You could hire any individual there and be sure of receiving the best possible advice."*
**The Lawyers:** The *"bright and hard-working"* **Troy Eid** (see p.359) covers most aspects of environmental law and is particularly knowledgeable when it

comes to federal Indian law and Native American tribal law. Indeed, he recently renegotiated a right of way agreement with the Navajo Indian tribe on behalf of El Paso's Western Pipeline Group.
**Clients/Work Highlights:** Wal-Mart; El Paso; Staubach and ChoicePoint.

## Sherman & Howard LLC
See firm details p.373
**The Firm:** The compact environmental team at this regional firm maintains an active and well-recognized practice. It advises local and national corporations on both regulatory and transactional fronts, and also covers litigation. Wetland issues, Superfund and asbestos concerns are all covered.
**The Lawyers:** Interviewees described **Ronald Eddy** (see p.359) as *"a wonderful lawyer with a fine reputation."* He is a member of the firm's litigation department and specializes in environmental work involving hazardous substances and waste, air and water quality, and issues relating to underground storage tanks.

## Temkin Wielga & Hardt LLP
**The Firm:** Market sources praised this boutique environmental firm for its *"top-quality work product."* Its lawyers specialize in litigation, permitting, compliance and risk management. The group has recently been busy working on a major Superfund case, which is reported to be the largest ever to reach trial.
**The Lawyers:** **Elizabeth Temkin** garnered praise as *"a vastly experienced practitioner"* who covers both contentious and noncontentious matters. She specializes in providing advice relating to the RCRA and CWA.
**Clients/Work Highlights:** Fortune 500 companies, public businesses and private individuals can all be counted as clients.

## Other Notable Practitioners
In terms of environmental litigation, **John Fognani** of Fognani & Faught, PLLC is highly respected for *"taking on the hard cases and getting brilliant results."* **Jerry Raisch** of Vranesh and Raisch, LLP focuses on federal and state water quality requirements. In this respect, commentators rate him as being *"among the top practitioners in the field."*

# INTELLECTUAL PROPERTY

## Band 1

### Faegre & Benson LLP
See firm details p.1170

**The Firm:** Market commentators agree that this *"wonderful full-service firm possesses one of the most active and well-regarded practices in the state."* It also has one of the largest IP groups in Colorado and is consequently employed up and down the West Coast, often in complex and high-profile cases. The team covers all manner of IP work including litigation, patent prosecution, trademark registration and transactions. Recent highlights include acting for several major motion picture studios in Huntsman v Soderbergh, regarding the electronic editing of films.

**The Lawyers:** *"One of the best,"* **Natalie Hanlon-Leh** (see p.361) is well respected by peers and clients alike for her prowess in IP protection and litigation. As one interviewee remarked: *"I adore her, she is helpful, easy to work with and understands our business."* The *"sincere"* **Peter Kinsella** (see p.362) is perhaps best known for his work on transactional matters including trademarks and licensing.

**Clients/Work Highlights:** Quark; Bad Boy Brands; Meredith Corporation; Level 3 Communications and Genetic Technologies.

## Townsend and Townsend and Crew LLP

**The Firm:** The Denver office of this national firm has made considerable inroads into the local market, to the extent that it is now a major player in Colorado. Commentators say the team is *"populated by young and talented people,"* and they advise on the full gamut of IP-related matters. The firm's first-class client list includes established businesses, inventors, entrepreneurs and scientists hailing from a range of industries from biotechnology to manufacturing and telecommunications.

**The Lawyers:** *"I rate him extremely highly,"* said one client, echoing the general consensus on **Darin Gibby** (see p.360). His practice encompasses IP counseling, transactional support and licensing. He is held in particularly high regard for his work with small businesses and startups. *"Solid professional"* **Steve Jewett** *"knows as much as anyone in the field,"* according to clients. He specializes in trademark and copyright work. **David Sipiora** (see p.366) completes the firm's triumvirate of standout lawyers, and he handles both litigation and transactional matters.

**Clients/Work Highlights:** An impressive client list includes Qwest, First Data and CoorsTek.

## Band 2

### Gibson, Dunn & Crutcher LLP
See firm details p.328

**The Firm:** While this *"fantastic"* full-service operation has a strong presence in Colorado, the Denver office has capitalized on the firm's national reach by winning many clients outside the state. For example, the team successfully defended Metabolite Laboratories at Court of Appeals level after it was sued in the Minnesota federal court for infringing two patents. Active international clients include the likes of Aristocrat, one of the largest gaming companies in the world. Patent-related work is the mainstay of the practice, though litigation and trademark matters are also covered.

**The Lawyers:** Clients *"think the world of"* **Glenn Beaton** (see p.357), who cochairs the practice. He is heavily involved in IP litigation and appeals involving patents, trademarks, copyrights and trade secrets. Beaton remains popular with clients, one of whom commented: *"He is extremely smart and writes better than any lawyer I've ever known."*

**Clients/Work Highlights:** Pamlab; Competitive Technologies; Boulder Scientific; Empire BlueCross BlueShield and Vail Resorts.

### Hogan & Hartson LLP
See firm details p.568

**The Firm:** The firm is developing a significant reputation in the state for its IP work. A relatively lean team is able to draw on Hogan & Hartson's extensive national network for support as required. It covers litigation, patent and trademark counseling, licens-

ing and transactions. Indeed, negotiating several technology transactions relating to telecom services and software development on behalf of Regal Entertainment and its affiliate National CineMedia has contributed substantially to the workload of late. Clients commended the group's *"hard-working and diligent practitioners,"* not least for being *"proactive in suggesting a variety of solutions to problems."*

**The Lawyers:** Up-and-comer **Tracy Gray** (see p.360) enters the tables this year upon attracting positive feedback from clients. Characterized as *"professional and proactive,"* she advises clients on a wide range of IP issues.

**Clients/Work Highlights:** Regal Entertainment; National CineMedia; Sun Microsystems; Coldwater Creek; Dex Media; Accenture; Textron and Leanin' Tree.

### Holland & Hart LLP
See firm details p.369

**The Firm:** *"An excellent practice that is particularly talented at handling local IP issues"* was the verdict returned by the market on this full-service firm. Its IP team provides a comprehensive service, covering litigation and patents, trademarks and copyrights. Advising Spyder Active Sports on the seizure of a range of counterfeit merchandise by European authorities was a challenging work highlight of recent times.

**The Lawyers:** **Jane Michaels** (see p.363) has a solid reputation for her general commercial and IP litigation work, with an emphasis on technology and telecom matters. She successfully defended a major software developer against claims of copyright infringement and misappropriation of trade secrets. **Scott Havlick** (see p.361) heads up the firm's trademark practice, an area in which he is highly regarded. His caseload is international in scope.

**Clients/Work Highlights:** The firm acts for the likes of Frontier Airlines and Sears.

## Band 3

### Cooley Godward LLP

**The Firm:** The Broomfield office of this national full-service firm has a thriving IP practice and a caseload that often includes out-of-state matters. For example, the team defended Picolight against claims of patent infringement in the District of Delaware. This lawsuit also highlighted the team's proficiency in hi-tech and communications work, which it has gained a considerable reputation for.

**The Lawyers:** **James Brogan** *"really knows his stuff"* according to sources. He focuses on patent litigation, where he recently represented Outlast Technologies, as well as licensing, counseling and prosecution.

**Clients/Work Highlights:** Advanced Energy; Applied Films; eBay; Picolight; Outlast Technologies and Monolithic Power Systems.

## Lathrop & Gage L.C.

See firm details p.1214

**The Firm:** This Kansas City-based outfit opened its Boulder office in 2001 and has already established itself as a player in the local IP market. The firm has amassed a sizable team including three patent agents and offers expertise in most IP-related disciplines,

including litigation, copyright, licensing and trademarks.

**The Lawyers:** Chair of the firm's IP department William Rudy splits his time between the Boulder and Kansas City offices.

**Clients/Work Highlights:** Hewlett-Packard; Yahoo!; Payless ShoeSource and Pod-Ners.

## Other Notable Practitioners

Entering the tables this year is **George Matava** (see p.363) of Greenberg Traurig LLP. He received many positive comments for his "*tremendous*" work in the field and, with over twenty years of experience under his belt, he advises on a broad spectrum of IP issues.

# LITIGATION

| Litigation: General Commercial |
|---|
| **Leading Firms** |
| [1] BARTLIT BECK *Denver* |
| DAVIS GRAHAM & STUBBS LLP *Denver* |
| HOFFMAN REILLY POZNER & WILLIAMSON *Denver* |
| HOLLAND & HART LLP *Denver* |
| [2] BALLARD SPAHR ANDREWS & INGERSOLL *Denver* |
| HILL & ROBBINS PC *Denver* |
| JACOBS, CHASE, FRICK, KLEINKOPF *Denver* |
| ROTHGERBER JOHNSON & LYONS LLP *Denver* |
| WHEELER TRIGG KENNEDY LLP *Denver* |
| [3] FAEGRE & BENSON LLP *Denver* |
| GIBSON, DUNN & CRUTCHER LLP *Denver* |
| HOLME ROBERTS & OWEN LLP *Denver* |

| Litigation: White-Collar Crime & Government Investigations |
|---|
| **Leading Firms** |
| [1] HADDON, MORGAN, MUELLER, JORDAN *Denver* |
| [2] BALLARD SPAHR ANDREWS & INGERSOLL *Denver* |
| HOGAN & HARTSON LLP *Denver* |
| ISAACSON ROSENBAUM PC *Denver* |
| ROTHGERBER JOHNSON & LYONS LLP *Denver* |

## Band 1

### Bartlit Beck Herman Palenchar & Scott

**The Firm:** Commentators enthused that Bartlit Beck Herman Palenchar & Scott is "*one of the top firms in the country*" for litigation work. With offices in both Denver and Chicago, this firm has built a truly national practice. Certainly, much of the Colorado team's work originates outside of the state. The group has won a formidable reputation for its impeccable courtroom skills and for successfully taking on many high-stakes, complex commercial cases. This talent was recently utilized when the team represented travel product innovators Sabre Holdings in a breach of contract and antitrust lawsuit against Northwest Airlines.

**The Lawyers:** **Fred Bartlit** is universally considered to be "*as good as it gets*" for litigation matters. He has had a long and distinguished career as a trial lawyer. One source notes "*It is hard to find anyone with more varied experience.*" He practices across the country on some extremely high-profile cases. For example, he has recently represented pharmaceutical giant Bayer

in class action antitrust litigation. Renowned litigator **Donald Scott** is a "*tenacious trial lawyer with a keen intelligence.*" He also recently defended Bayer against claims that individuals had suffered strokes after taking Bayer's Alka-Seltzer Plus product.

**Clients/Work Highlights:** Bayer; DuPont; United Technologies; 3M; Ernst & Young and Nicor.

## Davis Graham & Stubbs LLP

**The Firm:** An outstanding firm, this Denver-based group undertakes a variety of litigation matters, ranging from antitrust and securities disputes to white-collar crime and fraud. The broad capabilities of the group have won it many fans, who say: "*They can handle all our needs.*" Recently, the firm has acted for pharmaceutical giant Wyeth in litigation involving a diet pill product. The team has also built an excellent reputation throughout the Rocky Mountain region for its natural resources work. Clients appreciate that the attorneys are "*thorough, detail-oriented and understand how important it is to be cost-effective.*"

**The Lawyers:** **Gale Miller** garners much praise for his antitrust work. According to sources, he is "*articulate, practical and extremely responsive.*" His practice also includes natural resources, securities and environment matters. **Dale Harris** is a well-rounded attorney who has cultivated a broad commercial practice and represents both individuals and companies.

**Clients/Work Highlights:** The firm maintains a long client list of local and national companies.

## Haddon, Morgan, Mueller, Jordan, Mackey & Foreman PC

**The Firm:** This boutique firm of "*terrific, talented lawyers*" has built a formidable reputation for white-collar work. Interviewees continue to be impressed by the team's considerable strength and depth, observing: "*It's hard to single out just one name, they are all extremely good.*" The team has an impressive case list defending companies and individuals. For example, it has garnered national attention for its representation of a woman who refused to show identification to federal police while riding a bus through the Federal Center in Lakewood, Colorado.

**The Lawyers:** **Lee Foreman** is a veteran in the field. Commentators appreciate his ability "*to deal with any problem in a creative and thoughtful way.*" According to sources, **Harold Haddon** is "*the consummate criminal defense lawyer,*" while **Pamela Mackey** is also widely admired for her work in the field, particularly regarding criminal defense.

## Hoffman Reilly Pozner & Williamson

**The Firm:** This boutique litigation firm is called "*one of the best and definitely a leader*" by sources. Based in Denver, the firm has built a sizable team covering both civil and criminal litigation. The team handles all matters, from commercial and PI to white-collar criminal and antitrust matters. Sources commended the team's breadth of experience and courtroom skills, saying: "*They have some of the leading trial lawyers around.*"

**The Lawyers:** **Daniel Hoffman** is one of the most celebrated lawyers in the state. According to commentators, "*he is in a class by himself*" on litigation matters. With over 40 years' experience in the field, he has handled a wide variety of cases including class actions, toxic torts and complex commercial litigation. **Daniel Reilly** is acknowledged to be "*a great trial lawyer.*" He concentrates on civil litigation, acting on behalf of individuals and corporations.

**Clients/Work Highlights:** Coors Brewing Co; Denver Broncos; GE Supply; Touch America; University of Colorado and World Wide Capital Mortgage.

## Holland & Hart LLP

See firm details p.369

**The Firm:** With 12 offices concentrated in the Rocky Mountain region, this team is "*among the strongest litigation firms around.*" The sizable team handles a mixture of defense work and plaintiff cases. Expertise in the latter was utilized recently when the firm represented homeowners in both individual and class actions against Goodyear regarding its hydronic heating hose, Entran II. Product liability is just one strand of experience in this broad-ranging practice. Clients appreciate the depth of expertise, saying: "*They have a remarkable ability to handle queries on almost any topic.*" The group also includes a dedicated antitrust team and a full-time appellate practice.

**The Lawyers:** Acknowledged as "*bright and talented,*" **Scott Barker** (see p.357) is widely commended for his trial skills. He has developed a broad commercial practice with a particular forte in natural resources litigation. **Peter Houtsma** (see p.361) impresses as "*an exceptional strategist,*" who is "*organized and hard-working.*" Head of the firm's antitrust practice, **James Hartley** (see p.361) remains among the top in his field; his practice also encompasses patent litigation.

**Clients/Work Highlights:** Among the firm's clientele are First Data, AT&T and BP US.

## Litigation: General Commercial

### Leading Individuals

#### Senior Statesman

HOFFMAN Daniel *Hoffman Reilly Pozner*

[1] BARTLIT JR Fred *Bartlit Beck*

CERIANI Gary *Davis & Ceriani*

CHASE Jeffrey *Jacobs, Chase, Frick*

HILL Robert *Hill & Robbins PC*

LYONS James *Rothgerber Johnson*

[2] BARKER Scott *Holland & Hart LLP*

BAUMANN Frederick *Rothgerber Johnson*

REILLY Daniel *Hoffman Reilly Pozner*

SCOTT Donald *Bartlit Beck*

THOMASCH Roger *Ballard Spahr*

WHEELER Malcolm *Wheeler Trigg Kennedy LLP*

[3] CURTIS George *Gibson, Dunn*

FRICK Ann *Jacobs, Chase, Frick, Kleinkopf*

GARNSEY JR Walter *Kelly Haglund Garnsey + Kahn*

GOLDBERG Charles *Rothgerber Johnson*

GOTTSCHALK Hugh *Wheeler Trigg Kennedy LLP*

HARRIS Dale *Davis Graham*

HOUTSMA Peter *Holland & Hart LLP*

MCCARTHY Michael *Faegre & Benson LLP*

PECK Neil *Snell & Wilmer LLP*

TREECE Lawrence *Sherman & Howard LLC*

## Litigation: Antitrust

### Leading Individuals

[1] BLACK Bruce *Holme Roberts*

HARRIS Dale *Davis Graham*

HARTLEY James *Holland & Hart LLP*

HILL Robert *Hill & Robbins PC*

KANAN Gregory *Rothgerber Johnson*

MILLER Gale *Davis Graham*

SHIVELY John *Faegre & Benson LLP*

THEIS Lawrence *Musgrave & Theis LLP*

## Litigation: White-Collar Crime & Government Investigations

### Leading Individuals

[1] BAUMANN Frederick *Rothgerber Johnson & Lyons*

EVANS Kevin *Steese & Evans PC*

FOREMAN Lee *Haddon, Morgan, Mueller*

HADDON Harold *Haddon, Morgan, Mueller*

LOZOW Gary *Isaacson Rosenbaum PC*

MACKEY Pamela *Haddon, Morgan, Mueller*

RICHILANO John *Richilano & Ridley PC*

SHEA Daniel *Hogan & Hartson LLP*

SHEA Kevin *Ballard Spahr*

SHOEMAKER Andrew *Hogan & Hartson LLP*

WALSH John *Hill & Robbins PC*

ZISSER David *Isaacson Rosenbaum PC*

## Band 2

### Ballard Spahr Andrews & Ingersoll LLP

See firm details p.1746

**The Firm:** This national firm continues to impress commentators, who say that its *"level of client service is to be applauded."* The team covers both defendant and plaintiff work across a range of areas including white-collar, securities, antitrust and general business litigation. Its expertise in the telecom sector was brought to the fore recently when the team defended Comcast against claims of fraud and racial discrimination. Clients admire the team's approach, noting: *"They are thorough and handle our work in a businesslike fashion."*

**The Lawyers:** The *"effective and incredibly efficient"* **Roger Thomasch** (see p.367) is a favorite of interviewees. *"A smart and strategic trial attorney,"* he remains busy handling ongoing product liability work for Goodyear. **Kevin Shea** (see p.365) is singled out for his white-collar work, although his practice also involves environmental and antitrust litigation.

**Clients/Work Highlights:** Goodyear and Comcast are only two among the firm's long list of local and national clients.

### Hill & Robbins PC

**The Firm:** This firm is one of the smaller groups in Colorado but it continues to have a high profile throughout western USA. Its commercial litigation practice features expertise in water and natural resources law. Plaintiff work, and especially class actions, are also a specialty of the firm, and it remains well equipped to handle defendant cases.

**The Lawyers:** According to interviewees, **Robert Hill** (see p.361) is both *"highly ethical and a commanding presence in court."* Recently, he worked on a large IBM pension-related class action, highlighting his expertise in complex commercial litigation. His practice also includes antitrust and securities matters. The *"impressive"* **John Walsh** (see p.367) is well recognized in the market for his defense of white-collar criminal cases.

**Clients/Work Highlights:** The team has assisted many well-known local and national firms.

### Hogan & Hartson LLP

See firm details p.568

**The Firm:** *"Among the best for white-collar work,"* this is one of the largest firms in the region and has developed a thriving litigation practice with a specialism in white-collar defense matters. The team principally handles violations of securities law, and its proficiency was recently utilized in advice to Vail Resorts when the SEC conducted a lengthy investigation into the company's financial statements.

**The Lawyers:** **Daniel Shea** (see p.365) has a diverse practice covering many aspects of white-collar and civil litigation. He successfully obtained a resolution of an SEC investigation for Fischer Imaging. Formerly with the SEC, **Andrew Shoemaker** (see p.366) won praise for his expert and insightful advice.

**Clients/Work Highlights:** Vail Resorts; Red Robin Gourmet Burgers; Janus Capital; Carrier Access; UBS Financial Services and American-Amicable Life Insurance.

### Jacobs, Chase, Frick, Kleinkopf & Kelley

**The Firm:** According to clients, this is *"one of the smaller groups in the state but the people are more than equal to their counterparts at larger firms."* The commercial litigation practice includes securities, corporate and trade secrets matters. The group is particularly expert in handling complex commercial litigation. This prowess was recently brought to the fore in the firm's work for telecom giant Qwest.

**The Lawyers:** Sources say **Jeffrey Chase** *"is in a league of his own."* He is one of Colorado's leading lights for litigation work, and his practice encompasses a broad spectrum of litigation matters such as securities, legal malpractice and telecom. *"I always choose her, she is tough, thorough and creative"* is how one client described **Ann Frick**, echoing the consensus of many. She is also singled out for her proficiency as an arbitrator and mediator.

**Clients/Work Highlights:** The firm acts for a variety of companies in a range of industries such as telecom, media and natural resources.

### Rothgerber Johnson & Lyons LLP

See firm details p.372

**The Firm:** This firm is one of the oldest in Colorado and has built a sizable team that works throughout the Rocky Mountain region. The team carries out a broad spectrum of litigation including general commercial, securities, white-collar and bankruptcy matters. The firm also has an active practice representing religious institutions. The attorneys here are popular with clients because *"they represent us with real dedication"* and *"they have a universal view of how legal issues impact on business."*

**The Lawyers:** The *"fiercely dedicated"* **James Lyons** (see p.362) *"gets down to the nub of a deal,"* according to commentators. *"He is respected on both sides of the aisle,"* agree peers. With over 30 years' courtroom experience, he has developed an extensive practice covering all types of complex business litigation. Recently, he has acted as lead counsel in pending civil and regulatory matters for Qwest. **Frederick Baumann** (see p.357) is *"an extremely able attorney with a lot of depth to his practice."* Often considered to be Lyons' protégé, he has established a formidable reputation in his own right. His practice includes many aspects of business and corporate litigation, as well as white-collar and regulatory work. **Charles Goldberg** (see p.360) specializes in civil litigation with an emphasis on religious institutions, while **Gregory Kanan**'s (see p.362) practice includes antitrust matters, in particular those relating to the healthcare sector.

**Clients/Work Highlights:** Alpine Partners, Triple Peaks and Qwest feature prominently on the firm's client list.

## Wheeler Trigg Kennedy LLP

**The Firm:** While the firm is particularly strong in product liability matters, it has also built a solid reputation across the range of complex litigation, class action and appellate work. Recently the firm has acted as national counsel for the pharmaceutical giant Pfizer in litigation concerning its antidepressant Zoloft. Interviewees admire the firm, valuing that *"the team is attentive to the clients' needs and steadily delivers good results."*

**The Lawyers:** Sources were quick to extol **Malcolm Wheeler** as *"creative and confident."* He *"has the ability to work through any legal issues,"* say clients. **Hugh Gottschalk** covers a broad base of commercial disputes. He has gained a reputation for his commercial, product liability and toxic tort litigation.

**Clients/Work Highlights:** BDO Seidman; Duke Energy; FMC; Crown Equipment; Honda; Qwest and ConocoPhillips.

## Band 3

## Faegre & Benson LLP

See firm details p.1170

**The Firm:** This firm, with offices in both Denver and Boulder, has a large team focused on a variety of litigation matters. These include general commercial matters, product liability, antitrust and an active First Amendment practice. Major work for the team includes the successful defense of State Farm in a multiple class action regarding allegations of consumer fraud.

**The Lawyers:** Sources praise the *"intelligent and dedicated"* **Michael McCarthy** (see p.363) for his expertise in complex commercial matters. The respected **John Shively** (see p.365) has recently been busy defending DuPont in a class action regarding claims of crop loss.

**Clients/Work Highlights:** sanofi pasteur; Colorado Rockies; DuPont; Frontier Airlines; Novartis; Zateca Foods and CH2M HILL.

## Gibson, Dunn & Crutcher LLP

See firm details p.328

**The Firm:** According to clients, *"the lawyers are thorough and well educated"* at this nationwide firm. The Denver-based team has the ability to draw on the firm's considerable assets. As one interviewee notes: *"They have got the resources you need and they know when to call in the extra troops."* The team has lately defended Lehman Brothers in a trial regarding a fairness opinion given by the investment bank in the sale of a cable system.

**The Lawyers:** **George Curtis** (see p.359) is greatly admired for his expertise in complex litigation, predominantly in the securities and regulatory arena. With over 25 years' experience in the field, he maintains an impressive roster of household name clients.

**Clients/Work Highlights:** Merrill Lynch; Deloitte & Touche; KPMG and UBS.

## Holme Roberts & Owen LLP

See firm details p.370

**The Firm:** The litigation team carries out a range of work encompassing securities, antitrust and general commercial matters. As well as litigation, the group maintains a high profile for its mediation and arbitration work.

**The Lawyers:** Sources agree that **Bruce Black** is *"a fine lawyer and a personable litigator."* He has gained a considerable following for his antitrust practice, although he also specializes in securities and torts.

**Clients/Work Highlights:** The firm has a long list of clients throughout the Rocky Mountain region.

## Isaacson Rosenbaum PC

**The Firm:** Based in Denver, this firm handles a range of litigation matters from environmental law to real estate transactions. However, it is for securities, government and white-collar criminal defense work that the firm has acquired a strong reputation.

**The Lawyers:** **Gary Lozow** has a thriving criminal and white-collar defense practice. Former SEC employee **David Zisser** is characterized as a *"guru in securities work."*

## Other Notable Practitioners

The *"uniquely gifted lawyer"* **Gary Ceriani** of Davis & Ceriani is widely praised as *"a focused, independent thinker who is engaging in the courtroom."* One source believed: *"He often has the jury eating out of his hand."* His practice focuses on securities and business fraud matters. **Walter Garnsey** (see p.360) of Kelly Haglund Garnsey + Kahn LLC carries out a range of commercial litigation covering areas as diverse as employment and real estate. Recently, he successfully represented a former dealer of ADT Security Services in a trial concerning a breach of good faith and fair dealing. **Neil Peck** (see p.364) of Snell & Wilmer LLP has impressed sources with his efficient handling of complex litigation. **Larry Treece** (see p.367) of Sherman & Howard LLC is described as *"a smart attorney with strong trial skills."* His current work includes defending Liberty Media against claims of damages. **Kevin Evans** (see p.359) of Steese & Evans PC is held in high regard for his persistent litigation style. He is well known for his white-collar and regulatory defense work. This expertise was utilized in his recent representation of a former Qwest accountant in a SEC investigation regarding the company's former CEO. The *"terrific"* **John Richilano** of Richilano & Ridley PC continues to impress commentators with the strength of his white-collar practice, while **Lawrence Theis** of Musgrave & Theis LLP focuses on antitrust, as well as trade regulation and other commercial litigation matters.

# REAL ESTATE

| Real Estate | |
| --- | --- |
| Leading Firms | |
| [1] | BROWNSTEIN HYATT & FARBER PC *Denver* |
| | OTTEN, JOHNSON, ROBINSON, NEFF *Denver* |
| [2] | BALLARD SPAHR ANDREWS & INGERSOLL *Denver* |
| | HOLME ROBERTS & OWEN LLP *Denver* |
| | ISAACSON ROSENBAUM PC *Denver* |
| | JACOBS, CHASE, FRICK, KLEINKOPF *Denver* |
| | SHERMAN & HOWARD LLC *Denver* |
| [3] | DAVIS GRAHAM & STUBBS LLP *Denver* |
| | FAEGRE & BENSON LLP *Denver* |
| | HOLLAND & HART LLP *Denver* |
| | LOTTNER RUBIN FISHMAN BROWN *Denver* |

## Band 1

## Brownstein Hyatt & Farber PC

See firm details p.368

**The Firm:** This *"aggressive"* national powerhouse retains a leading position in the real estate arena, and is particularly accomplished at handling development, environmental and waste matters. It also benefits from influential political connections and the presence of *"outstanding lobbyists."* A varied diet of work this year involved advising on retail development, securitized loans, REITs and zoning.

**The Lawyers:** *"Smart and thoughtful"* **Edward Barad** (see p.357) cochairs the real estate practice and shines in real estate finance and development. Commanding respect among peers, *"he knows more about the way lenders work than anyone."* Among many high-profile building sales and large-scale developments, he recently advised CSFB on a $110 million golf course project. **Lynda McNeive** (see p.363) is particularly active in development work, and prides herself on counseling clients on real estate transactions, from the early stages all the way through to closing. Managing partner **Bruce James** (see p.362) has forged a reputation for himself in the hotel industry, where he covers finance and development work as well as acquisitions and disposals. He advised Redwood Capital on a $1 billion mezzanine fund and on closing the $130 million sale of Larkridge shopping center in Denver. **Wayne Forman**'s (see p.360) impressive real estate litigation profile is complemented by niche water law expertise, which he has put to good use in matters such as defending national home builders with regard to federal stormwater enforcement action.

**Clients/Work Highlights:** Landowners, commercial and residential developers, financial institutions, manufacturers and government agencies all feature as clients.

| Real Estate |
| --- |
| Leading Individuals |

**Senior Statesman**

CARPENTER Willis *Carpenter & Klatskin*

[1] BARAD Edward *Brownstein Hyatt & Farber PC*
BROWN Robert *Sherman & Howard LLC*
RAGONETTI Thomas *Otten, Johnson, Robinson, Neff*
ROBINSON Frank *Otten, Johnson, Robinson, Neff*
SENN Mark *Senn Lewis & Visciano*
STERNBERG John *Otten, Johnson, Robinson, Neff*

[2] CULHANE James *Davis Graham & Stubbs LLP*
FIELDS Leslie *Faegre & Benson LLP*
JACOBS Paul *Jacobs, Chase, Frick, Kleinkopf*
PERMUT Barry *Isaacson Rosenbaum PC*
QUAIL Beverly *Ballard Spahr*

[3] BACH Robert *Holme Roberts & Owen LLP*
DONOVAN JR Lawrence *Isaacson Rosenbaum PC*
HOLMES Robert *Holme Roberts & Owen LLP*
LOTTNER Alan *Lottner Rubin Fishman Brown*
MCNEIVE Lynda *Brownstein Hyatt*
SAMUELS JONES Karen *Perkins Coie LLP*
WESTOVER Michael *Otten, Johnson, Robinson, Neff*

| Real Estate: Zoning/Land Use |
| --- |
| Leading Individuals |

[1] FORMAN Wayne *Brownstein Hyatt & Farber PC*
GRIMSHAW Thomas *Grimshaw & Harring PC*
KAPLAN Stephen *Kaplan Kirsch & Rockwell LLP*
MACDONALD Thomas *Otten, Johnson, Robinson*
RAGONETTI Thomas *Otten, Johnson, Robinson*
ROCKWELL Sarah *Kaplan Kirsch & Rockwell LLP*

| Real Estate: Hotels & Leisure |
| --- |
| Leading Individuals |

[1] CLOWDUS Michael *Ballard Spahr*
FISCHER Rebecca *Sherman & Howard LLC*
KLEINKOPF David *Jacobs, Chase, Frick*
STEINER Beat *Holland & Hart LLP*

[2] CALVIN Charles *Faegre & Benson LLP*
JAMES Bruce *Brownstein Hyatt*

## Otten, Johnson, Robinson, Neff & Ragonetti, PC

See firm details p.371

**The Firm:** "*It is the gold standard,*" clients asserted, and peers made similarly flattering comments: "*Every lawyer at this firm has a canny ability to cut to the chase,*" remarked one. This real estate boutique has captured a particularly impressive market share in terms of development work and real estate transactions. Around 45 lawyers cover all aspects of the practice area, and its land use and zoning department is said to be the largest in the region. A recent highlight was handling a range of matters for Archstone-Smith, one of the largest multifamily developers in the USA. Resort developments and transport projects have also featured prominently in the workload.

**The Lawyers:** The "*outstanding*" **Frank Robinson** (see p.365) maintains a stellar reputation in the transactional sphere, while **John Sternberg** (see p.366) was billed as a "*premier leasing lawyer.*" Sternberg is especially admired for his pragmatic, assiduous style: "*He is very bright and focused and, above all, an eminently reasonable practitioner.*" The "*larger than life*" **Thomas Ragonetti** (see p.364) takes center stage as a "*zoning guru,*" and combines skills in government regulation, land use and public-private transactions to great effect. As one client noted: "*He is a master when it comes to understanding the intricacies of zoning, and has a very pragmatic, practical approach.*" **Thomas Macdonald** (see p.363) also has a thriving zoning practice, and regularly advises on land use and constitutional litigation. In addition, he is conversant in representing financial institutions in bankruptcies, workouts and foreclosures involving significant real estate elements. "*Excellent*" **Michael Westover** (see p.367) is active on the real estate finance front, where he is credited with a "*sophisticated practice*" and a "*gentlemanly manner.*"

**Clients/Work Highlights:** The firm regularly advises local and national commercial developers, multifamily and residential developers, international retailers and major ski resorts.

## Band 2

### Ballard Spahr Andrews & Ingersoll LLP

See firm details p.1746

**The Firm:** The "*first-class*" Denver office boasts an impressive standing in the field, with real estate finance and REITs being the mainstay of the practice. Niche expertise in handling mixed-use developments and hotel projects around the country for major clients such as Four Seasons, Marriott International, St Regis and Westin further defines the outfit's profile. Sources commended the group's deftness in the context of complex real estate transactions, where "*it has proven itself time and again.*" Highlights for the 13-lawyer operation include acting for the City and County of Denver in a 16,000-acre property sale and exchange with Aurora, and completing the $30 million sale of the Mile High Center, Denver.

**The Lawyers:** "*Rainmaker*" **Beverly Quail** (see p.364) focuses on transactional and lending matters, earning praise from clients for her winning style: "*She is calm under fire – extremely fair but tough. And if she's on the other side, you'd better pick up your stuff and run!*" She has honed her skills orchestrating numerous apartment sales, a recent highlight being a $120 million sale of apartments in Maryland. Peers enjoy working with **Michael Clowdus** (see p.358), who has an unsurpassed reputation in the resorts sector. He cochairs the firm's hotel and resorts group, and clients perceive him as an invaluable asset when structuring projects and related securities issues.

**Clients/Work Highlights:** Clients include national developers, landlords and tenants, entrepreneurs, banks, pension funds and insurance companies.

### Holme Roberts & Owen LLP

See firm details p.370

**The Firm:** The success of this "*high-caliber*" firm hinges on its hybrid real estate and corporate prowess, and its practice is increasingly biased towards real estate finance. Clients lauded the group's "*professional and practical approach,*" not to mention the willingness of its members to make themselves available for the duration of a project. Large development work is another of its fortes, particularly where hospital, retail and residential developments are concerned. That the team acts on behalf of the likes of Compass Group gives an indication of its stature, while Wells Fargo uses the firm as its main real estate counsel.

**The Lawyers:** While the "*very experienced*" **Robert Bach** devotes a good portion of his time to his managerial duties as chair of the firm's executive committee, he is nonetheless highly regarded in the industry. He is active in lending as well as sale and acquisition matters, and won praise for being "*great at thinking outside the box: he is someone you can bounce an idea off, even if it's something out of the ordinary.*" "*Knowledgeable*" **Robert Holmes** covers real estate development and finance, with an emphasis on loan and foreclosure work. He was credited with an "*efficient negotiating style.*"

**Clients/Work Highlights:** Major lenders, developers, property owners, independent owners and operators of hotels and resorts, and institutional investors feature in the firm's client base.

### Isaacson Rosenbaum PC

**The Firm:** Prized for its generalist real estate practice, the firm performs well in areas such as commercial and residential development, leasing, financing, land use and zoning. It boasts one of the larger retail practices, and shopping center developers feature heavily among the firm's clientele. Other areas of involvement include complex hotel and multiuse condominium developments.

**The Lawyers:** Peers regard the "*seasoned*" **Barry Permut** as an "*excellent, smart and responsive*" player, whose core areas of specialization are real estate development and acquisitions. Clients assert that his drawing card is "*focusing with crystal clarity on the specifics.*" "*Standout*" **Lawrence Donovan** is particularly conversant in commercial real estate leasing and has negotiated major leasing transactions throughout the Rocky Mountain region. His "*attentiveness and swiftness*" is much admired by clients. Acquisition and development work also contributes to his workload.

**Clients/Work Highlights:** The client base spans commercial construction lenders and developers, home builders, buyers and sellers, retail, and hotel and ski resort owners.

### Jacobs, Chase, Frick, Kleinkopf & Kelley

**The Firm:** The well-regarded, compact real estate team at this midsized firm retains a loyal following that enables it to compete with the larger players in the market. General corporate and real estate finance work is the order of the day, with notable depth in resort and sports sector developments as a distinguishing feature.

**The Lawyers:** **Paul Jacobs** is well known for his national sports sector work, which stems from his niche expertise in baseball stadium developments. Additionally, he covers the gamut of real estate issues and acts extensively for the City of San Diego. **David Kleinkopf** has a prestigious hotel and resorts practice, covering an array of acquisitions and developments.

**Clients/Work Highlights:** The firm often advises major lenders, owners and developers of sports facilities and mountain resorts. Notable examples include Intrawest and M&C Hotel Interests.

## Sherman & Howard LLC

See firm details p.373

**The Firm:** Development work in the healthcare and resort sectors has come to the fore at the real estate practice here. Members of the team are also involved in retail and education sector developments, as well as general transactional work. Other areas of specialization include workouts and foreclosures, where the group dovetails nicely with the firm's litigation, bankruptcy and environment practices.

**The Lawyers:** The *"knowledgeable"* **Robert Brown** (see p.358) has carved out a niche practice and a *"great reputation"* for himself in receivership work. He won plaudits for his *"smart and thoughtful"* stance, and he also covers healthcare projects, trophy ranch sales and foreclosures. **Rebecca Fischer** (see p.358) is prominent in the field of commercial leasing and resort development.

**Clients/Work Highlights:** Alongside major lenders and financial institutions, the firm acts for resort and retail corporations.

## Band 3

## Davis Graham & Stubbs LLP

**The Firm:** This full-service team concentrates on a blend of real estate development and transactional work, spanning joint ventures and land acquisitions for major healthcare providers, national home builders, retail sector players and manufacturers. Niche areas of expertise include student housing developments, where the firm recently completed a $70 million project in New Jersey. Its *"practical and strategic"* approach in all matters means that clients

are able to *"place a great deal of trust in the firm's work product."*

**The Lawyers:** Practice head **James Culhane** was described as an *"extremely responsive, knowledgeable and client-oriented"* attorney, who benefits from his team's *"excellent technical support."* Negotiating and structuring transactions, such as multiproperty sale and leasebacks, is considered his true forte.

**Clients/Work Highlights:** Property owners and developers.

## Faegre & Benson LLP

See firm details p.1170

**The Firm:** Billed as *"a dedicated group providing a comprehensive service,"* the focus here is on real estate transactions, leasing and land use. Recent highlights include acting for Xcel Energy in a new $1.3 billion power plant development in Pueblo, Colorado, and representing DR Horton in $100 million worth of projects. The team also handles acquisitions and disposals for United Agri Products nationwide, and can call upon the resources of its three overseas offices for work with an international dimension. Commentators appreciated the personalized touch of the firm's services, which gave one interviewee *"the impression that you are the only client they're working for."*

**The Lawyers:** Prominent in the hotel and resorts sphere, **Charles Calvin** (see p.358) carves his name as a *"very bright and levelheaded"* lawyer with *"great expertise."* **Leslie Fields** (see p.359) is best known for her finesse in condemnation cases; a recent highlight was her involvement on behalf of a client in a condemnation action taken against the Department of Transportation with respect to gaming property in Colorado.

**Clients/Work Highlights:** Xcel Energy; Target; DR Horton, INVESCO; Lincoln Property; United Agri Products; Beaver Creek Lodge Condominium Association and Club Telluride Owners Association.

## Holland & Hart LLP

See firm details p.369

**The Firm:** The arrival of Beat Steiner from Steiner, Darling & Hutchinson LLP is perceived to have considerably boosted the firm's real estate capacity, especially with regard to the resorts and leisure sectors. This national operation prides itself on its broad coverage of real estate issues. It was involved in a lending matter, relating to the development and

leasing of one of the largest office parks in the Denver metropolitan area. It also focuses on residential developments, acquisitions, zoning and condominium projects.

**The Lawyers:** **Beat Steiner**'s (see p.366) practice incorporates real estate development, financing and acquisitions. Interviewees marveled at his mastery of all sorts of resorts work, and Steiner has experience of projects in Colorado, California and further afield, including New Zealand.

**Clients/Work Highlights:** Commercial, resort and housing developers, home building companies, mixed-use project owners, and retail and commercial landlords and tenants all feature in the practice's client list.

## Lottner Rubin Fishman Brown & Saul, PC

**The Firm:** This boutique upholds a fine reputation in the field, impressing clients across the USA. Real estate acquisitions and disposals remain at the hub of the practice, together with associated lending work.

**The Lawyers:** *"Rainmaker"* **Alan Lottner**'s practice is biased towards finance, and commercial lenders greatly value his *"careful"* approach to transactions.

**Clients/Work Highlights:** The firm counsels financial institutions, national and international real estate developers, owners, contractors and builders, title insurance companies and architects.

## Other Notable Practitioners

*"Highly respected"* **Mark Senn** of Senn Lewis & Visciano enjoys unparalleled success on the commercial leasing front. *"Creative problem solver"* **Karen Samuels Jones** at Perkins Coie LLP focuses predominantly on commercial leasing and lending. She is dubbed *"hard-working and service-oriented,"* particularly in the real estate finance area. **Willis Carpenter** of Carpenter & Klatskin is touted by many as *"the dean of real estate law,"* and his wisdom is recognized as *"an invaluable resource."* **Thomas Grimshaw** of Grimshaw & Harring PC attracted his fair share of commendation as a *"sagacious zoning lawyer."* Meanwhile, the boutique firm Kaplan, Kirsch & Rockwell LLP offers considerable talent in the form of **Stephen Kaplan** and **Sarah Rockwell**, who are both highly regarded for their land use expertise.

# Leaders in Colorado

### ARFMANN, Dennis
Hogan & Hartson LLP, Boulder
720 406 5374
darfmann@hhlaw.com
*Recommended in Environment*
**Practice Areas:** Practice focuses on air quality; hazardous waste and water quality, with particular emphasis on resolving notices of violation and citizen suits; legislative and regulatory development issues; environmental litigation; and helping industry negotiate flexible permits. He has tried over 100 cases to the court or to juries.
**Prof. Memberships:** Chairman, Air Regulatory Committee, Colorado Association of Commerce and Industry; Member, Denver Regional Air Quality Council; Member, American Bar Association SONREEL; Member, Colorado Bar Association; Member, Nebraska Bar Association.
**Career:** Career as environmental litigator representing refineries, energy companies and manufacturers in high-profile clean air act permitting, enforcement investigation, BART determinations, NEPA EIS matters, and litigation matters throughout the Intermountain West.
**Publications:** Published author and frequent lecturer on environmental topics. Lectures include: 'Tips for Successful New Energy Facility Permitting' (January 2006), 'An Industry Perspective of the Navajo Nation Clean Air Act Program' (September 2005), 'Regulatory and Air Quality Trends in the Rocky Mountains', Colorado Bar Association (March 2005). Publications include: 'Kyoto Protocol Enters into Force' (16 February 2005); 'Environment and Energy - Climate Change Update', Hogan & Hartson L.L.P. (16 February 2005); 'The Grand Canyon Visibility Transport Commission: Reasonable Progress Toward the National Visibility Goal', Environmental Lawyer (June 1996); 'Logistical Problems of Implementing the Clean Air Act Operating Permit Program at the State Level', Shepard's Clean Air Reporter (1993); 'Air Toxics for 1990's and Beyond', Colorado Bar Journal (1991).
**Personal:** LLM, Environmental Law, with highest honors, The George Washington University Law School (1991); JD, University of Nebraska - Lincoln College of Law (1979); BA, University of Nebraska - Lincoln (1974).

### ARKELL, Betty
Holland & Hart LLP, Denver
303 295 8321
barkell@hollandhart.com
*Recommended in Corporate/M&A*
**Practice Areas:** Head of the firm's Corporate Finance Practice Group with over 30 years of experience as a corporate and securities lawyer. She specializes in venture capital investments, mergers, acquisitions, leveraged buyouts, acquisition finance, corporate restructurings, and general corporate counseling. She also has experience in the formation of private and public venture capital funds. Her clients include established and emerging growth companies as well as venture capital and other private equity funds. She recently completed a $72 million Rule 144A offering and $170 million senior secured financing for Navigant International, Inc.
**Prof. Memberships:** Member of the American Bar Association; Colorado Bar Association; and Denver Bar Association. Appointments: Board of Directors, Colorado Software and Internet Association; Leadership Council, Center for Entrepreneurship, University of Colorado at Denver; Board of Advisors, CTEK; past Chair, Business Law Section, Colorado Bar Association; past President, Colorado Association of Corporate Counsel.
**Career:** Admitted to the Colorado Bar (1975). Partner at Holland & Hart since 1994. Previously a Partner in the Denver office of Kirkland & Ellis.
**Personal:** Received a JD (Order of the Coif) from the University of Colorado (1975), an MA from the University of Colorado (1972) and a BA (with honors) from Northwestern University (1969).

### ARKELL, J David
Faegre & Benson LLP, Denver
303 607 3637
darkell@faegre.com
*Recommended in Construction*
**Practice Areas:** David's primary area of practice is construction law. He represents general contractors, subcontractors, suppliers, owners, and sureties, and provides advice regarding planning and dispute avoidance as well as dispute resolution through negotiation, mediation, arbitration, and litigation.
**Prof. Memberships:** American Arbitration Association, Construction Industry Arbitrator and Mediator; American Bar Association, Forum on the Construction Industry; Colorado Bar Association, Construction Law Forum, past Chairman.

### ARO, Edwin
Hogan & Hartson LLP, Denver
303 899 7389
eparo@hhlaw.com
*Recommended in Employment*
**Practice Areas:** Litigation Partner, Practice Group Director, Labor and Employment Group, Co-Chair, Colorado Litigation Group. A trial lawyer who represents businesses in intellectual property, commercial and employment matters.
**Prof. Memberships:** Colorado Bar Association.

**Career:** Law Clerk to the Hon Richard P Matsch, US District Court, District of Colorado. Joined Hogan & Hartson in 1998, after nine years with Holme Roberts & Owen. Adjunct Law professor at the University of Denver, 1994-2006.
**Personal:** Born 20 July 1964, in Colorado Springs, Colorado. BA Denver University. JD, magna cum laude, Boston University. Member and Editor, Boston University Law Review.

### BACH, Robert
Holme Roberts & Owen LLP, Denver
303 861 7000
*Recommended in Real Estate*

### BARAD, Edward N
Brownstein Hyatt & Farber PC, Denver
303 223 1108
ebarad@bhf-law.com
*Recommended in Real Estate*
**Practice Areas:** Shareholder and co-chair of Brownstein Hyatt & Farber's Real Estate Group. Focuses on commercial development and finance. Extensive experience representing developers and lenders in commercial real estate transactions.
**Prof. Memberships:** Board of Governors, American College of Real Estate Lawyers; Member, Colorado & American Bar Associations; Chairman, Legislative Speaker's Bureau; Supreme Court Grievance Committee; Co-Chairman, Opinion Letter Standards Committee Colorado Bar Real Estate Section; Hearing Examiner Colorado Bar Ethics Committee; Vice-Chairman, Opinion Letter Subcommittee University of Colorado Real Estate Council.
**Personal:** University of Colorado School of Law (JD, 1973); University of Colorado (BS, 1969).

### BARKER, Scott
Holland & Hart LLP, Denver
303 295 8513
sbarker@hollandhart.com
*Recommended in Litigation*
**Practice Areas:** Partner practicing in complex civil litigation, with experience in more than 65 trials, one third of which were to juries. Cases tried in Colorado, Utah, Wyoming, Idaho, New Mexico, California and Washington. Extensive experience in complex litigation, including class actions. Mr Barker was voted Best of the Bar for business litigation in 2003 by his peers, which was sponsored by a leading Colorado business publication.
**Prof. Memberships:** ACTL Fellowship; International Association of Defense Counsel; American Bar Association; Colorado Bar Association; Denver Bar Association; and the American and Colorado Bar Foundations. Appointments: Fellow of the American College of Trial Lawyers;

included in leading American publication's list of top attorneys.
**Career:** Admitted to Colorado Bar (1981). Past Chair of Holland & Hart's Management Committee.
**Personal:** Received a JD from Harvard University (cum laude) 1981, a MPhil from Oxford University (1973) and a BA from the US Air Force Academy (1970). Rhodes Scholar.

### BARTLIT JR, Fred
Bartlit Beck Herman Palenchar & Scott, Denver 303 592 3100
*Recommended in Litigation*

### BAUMANN, Frederick J
Rothgerber Johnson & Lyons LLP, Denver 303 628 9542
fbaumann@rothgerber.com
*Recommended in Litigation*
**Practice Areas:** Complex corporate and business litigation, including class and derivative actions and claims under federal securities laws, and arbitration of business disputes.
**Prof. Memberships:** ABA; CBA; DBA; American College of Trial Lawyers; Master Barrister, William E Doyle American Inn of Court; Member, USDC of Colorado Committee on Conduct; Chair, Legal Aid Foundation of Colorado (2000-01).
**Career:** Admitted Colorado and New York, USDC for Southern and Eastern Districts of New York and District of Colorado, US Court of Appeals Second and Tenth Circuits.
**Personal:** JD, New York University, 1979; BA, Williams College, 1976.

### BEATON, Glenn K
Gibson, Dunn & Crutcher LLP, Denver
303 298 5773
gbeaton@gibsondunn.com
*Recommended in Intellectual Property*
**Practice Areas:** Co-Chair of the firm's Intellectual Property Practice Group. Advises on intellectual property litigation and appeals, including patents, trademarks, copyrights and trade secrets. Experience includes counseling a number of patent infringement, misappropriation of trade secret cases, Patent Office proceedings, prosecuting over 200 patent applications to issuance and numerous re-examination, reissuance and interference proceedings, and successfully leading one Supreme Court and four Federal Circuit appeals.
**Career:** Appointed a Special Master, US District Court of Colorado.
**Publications:** Former adjunct professor and frequent lecturer on intellectual property.
**Personal:** JD, University of Denver, 1982, Order of St Ives, member of DU Law Review.

## BENSON, Robert E
Holland & Hart LLP, Denver
303 295 8234
rbenson@hollandhart.com
*Recommended in Construction*
**Practice Areas:** Mr Benson today practices arbitration, mediation, professional ethics, and legal malpractice, calling upon his 40 years' experience in civil litigation, emphasizing construction and commercial/business disputes. His business litigation has included contract issues, business torts, fraud and deceit, antitrust, professional liability, fiduciary relationships. His construction practice has included breach of contract, wrongful termination, delay, interference and extended performance, changed conditions, extra work, change orders, defective construction, negligent supervision, and defective design.
**Prof. Memberships:** Founding Chair, Colorado Bar Association Construction Law Forum; Denver, Colorado, and American Bar Associations; Rocky Mountain Advisory Council of the American Arbitration Association; American Arbitration Association Panel of Arbitrators for Large Complex Cases and Panel of Mediators; College of Commercial Arbitrators
**Career:** Holland & Hart LLP since 1965, Partner since 1971.
**Publications:** Managing Editor of 'Practitioner's Guide to Colorado Construction Law' (1999, 2003 and 2005); co-author, 'How to Prepare for, Take and Use a Deposition' (6th Ed. 1995); co-author, 'Cornell University Law School Ethics Library' (section on 'Colorado Rules of Professional Conduct'); author, 'Colorado Law of Arbitration' (anticipated publication 2006); frequent speaker at and author for CLE seminars on arbitration, mediation, construction and ethics.
**Personal:** University of Pennsylvania (LLB 1965); University of Iowa (BA 1962)

## BLACK, Bruce
Holme Roberts & Owen LLP, Denver
303 861 7000
*Recommended in Litigation*

## BLAIR, Andrew
Sherman & Howard LLC, Denver
303 299 8138
ablair@sah.com
*Recommended in Corporate/M&A*
**Practice Areas:** Andy Blair is a member of the Business & Real Estate Department. His practice focuses on corporate, securities and commercial law. He has had extensive experience in the formation, acquisition, operation, financing, disposition and reorganization of public and private corporations, partnerships, limited liability companies and other business entities. Mr Blair joined Sherman & Howard in 1972. He has spoken to various industry and professional

groups in the US and other countries on the legal aspects of raising capital in the US, and he has taught Securities Regulation at the University of Denver and the University of Colorado Law School.

## BRIDSTON, Kevin
Holland & Hart LLP, Denver
303 295 8104
kbridston@hollandhart.com
*Recommended in Construction*
**Practice Areas:** Construction, real estate, and commercial cases, including trials, appeals, arbitration and mediation. His experience includes basic and complex construction disputes, commercial disputes, corporate governance disputes, and disputes arising from complex financial transactions. He also has extensive experience, for both plaintiffs and defendants, with complex real estate litigation.
**Prof. Memberships:** Admitted to practice before the state and federal courts in Colorado, the Tenth Circuit Court of Appeals, and the Federal Circuit Court of Appeals.
**Career:** Established Holland & Hart's Construction and Real Estate Litigation Practice Group. Partner since 1997.
**Publications:** He has written and lectured extensively on construction law topics. Contributor to 'The Practitioner's Guide to Colorado Construction Law'.
**Personal:** University of Colorado School of Law (JD 1988, Order of the Coif); University of Colorado (BA 1985, Phi Beta Kappa).

## BROGAN, James
Cooley Godward LLP, Broomfield
720 566 4000
*Recommended in Intellectual Property*

## BROWN, Jessica
Gibson, Dunn & Crutcher LLP, Denver
303 298 5944
jbrown@gibsondunn.com
*Recommended in Employment*
**Practice Areas:** Represents clients in a wide array of labor and employment matters, including nationwide class actions, and employment discrimination, wrongful termination, retaliation, misappropriation of proprietary information, breach of contract, breach of fiduciary duty, unfair competition, and ERISA cases, in state and federal court and before agencies such as the EEOC and the Colorado Civil Rights Division. Has tried employment cases in jury and non-jury settings and argued significant matters in the courts of appeals.
**Career:** Frequent author and speaker on labor and employment issues.
**Personal:** JD, University of Texas, 1993, Executive Editor, Texas Law Review, Order of the Coif.

## BROWN, Robert
Sherman & Howard LLC, Denver
303 299 8350
rbrown@sah.com
*Recommended in Real Estate*
**Practice Areas:** Bob Brown is a Member of the Business and Real Estate Department. He practices principally in the area of commercial real estate, representing lenders, landlords, receivers, purchasers, sellers, and developers. He specializes in representing lenders with respect to defaulted loans, workouts, foreclosures, and receiverships. He has also practiced extensively in the franchise law area, representing both franchisors and franchisees. Mr Brown joined Sherman & Howard in 1976. He is the ex-chair of the Real Estate Section of the Colorado Bar Association. He was a principal drafter of the 1990 recodification of Colorado's foreclosure statutes and the 2001 amendments.

## CALVIN, Charles
Faegre & Benson LLP, Denver
303 607 3677
ccalvin@faegre.com
*Recommended in Real Estate*
**Practice Areas:** Real estate.
**Prof. Memberships:** Colorado, Denver and American Bar Associations.
**Career:** Representations include: owners' association for a 700-member resort condominium; developers of mixed-use condominium projects in Denver; nonprofit healthcare organization in acquiring multiple hospitals, clinics and related facilities across Colorado; construction lender for major Denver office building.
**Publications:** 'Legislative Framework/Common Interest Ownership Act', NBI; 'Owners' Associations: Management and Operations During Declarant Control', NBI; 'Realizing on Multiple Assets Securing the Same Debt: Some Thoughts on Wells Fargo Realty Advisors Funding v. UIOLI', CLE International; 'Participation and Intercreditor Agreements', CLE International.
**Personal:** BA, Pomona College, cum laude; JD, Yale University.

## CAMPBELL, William J
Faegre & Benson LLP, Denver
303 607 3630
wcampbell@faegre.com
*Recommended in Corporate/M&A*
**Practice Areas:** Public and private securities, corporate governance, mergers and acquisitions, and international transactions.
**Prof. Memberships:** Colorado Bar Association, Business and International Law Sections; First Judicial District Bar Association, Past President; Colorado Association of Corporate Counsel; World Trade Center Denver, Board of Directors; Colorado College, Board of Trustees.
**Career:** Over 30 years of general corporate practice, with recent emphasis on

public companies, corporate governance, and international business.
**Personal:** BA in Economics, Colorado College (1967), cum laude, Phi Beta Kappa; JD, University of Colorado, Boulder (1971), Law Review; Rotary Foundation Graduate Fellow in Economics, University of Newcastle, New South Wales, 1969.

## CARPENTER, Willis
Carpenter & Klatskin, Denver
303 534 6315
*Recommended in Real Estate*

## CERIANI, Gary
Davis & Ceriani, Denver
303 534 9000
*Recommended in Litigation*

## CHASE, Jeffrey
Jacobs, Chase, Frick, Kleinkopf & Kelley, Denver 303 685 4800
*Recommended in Litigation*

## CLOWDUS, W Michael
Ballard Spahr Andrews & Ingersoll LLP, Denver 303 299 7351
clowdus@ballardspahr.com
*Recommended in Real Estate*
**Practice Areas:** Focuses on resort development. Represents developers in the design, documentation, registration, financing (both debt and equity), construction and marketing and sales of high end fractional projects at major resorts throughout the Rocky Mountain West and in Mexico.
**Prof. Memberships:** Chair, Federal Issues Committee. Past Chair, State Legislative Committee of the American Resort Development Association (ARDA). Member of the Urban, State and Local Government and Real Property Probate and Trust Law sections of the American Bar Association.
**Career:** Admitted to the Colorado Bar (1975).
**Personal:** JD, University of Denver (1975); AB, cum laude, Duke University (1972).

## CONNERY, Robert T
Holland & Hart LLP, Denver
303 295 8133
rconnery@hollandhart.com
*Recommended in Environment*
**Practice Areas:** Partner practicing environmental law with experience in environmental planning, permitting, and compliance work on major industrial and mining projects and environmental litigation. Represented major natural resource companies in complex litigation over environmental impact statement requirements, EPA regulatory requirements, state regulations and enforcement actions, including cases before US District Courts, Courts of Appeal for the District of Columbia, the Ninth and Tenth Circuits, and the US Supreme Court. Covered regulatory matters such as air and water quality requirements,

solid and hazardous waste requirements, reclamation, historic preservation laws, threatened and endangered species laws, and fish and wildlife coordination.

**Prof. Memberships:** Former Council Member and past Chairman, Air Quality Committee of the American Bar Association's Natural Resources, Energy and Environment Section, and former Trustee of the Rocky Mountain Mineral Law Foundation.

**Career:** Admitted to the Colorado (1966) Bar.

**Personal:** Received a LLB (1966) from Harvard and a BA (1962) from Yale.

### COOK, Michael
Sherman & Howard LLC, Denver
303 299 8200
mcook@sah.com
*Recommended in Construction*

**Practice Areas:** Michael Cook practices in the areas of construction law and litigation in Sherman & Howard's Denver office. He regularly represents general contractors, subcontractors, owners, securities, and design professionals in all phases of construction law. He's litigated and arbitrated all types of construction disputes, including a three month jury trial in which he obtained a $20 million verdict for his client. He is a Member of the American Bar Association Section of Public Contract Law, the American Bar Association's Forum Committee on the Construction Industry and a Member of the American Arbitration Association's construction industry panel of arbitrators.

### CUDNEY, Kevin
Brownstein Hyatt & Farber PC, Denver
303 223 1100
*Recommended in Corporate/M&A*

### CULHANE, James
Davis Graham & Stubbs LLP, Denver
303 892 9400
*Recommended in Real Estate*

### CURTIS, George B
Gibson, Dunn & Crutcher LLP, Denver
303 298 5743
gcurtis@gibsondunn.com
*Recommended in Litigation*

**Practice Areas:** Counsels on complex corporate, securities and accountancy matters, specifically defending allegations of securities law violations, professional negligence and related causes of action. Has tried cases before judges, juries, self-regulatory organizations, and in federal and state administrative tribunals. Represents clients before the SEC, the Department of Justice, the NYSE and the NASD and in settlement proceedings and procedures conducted by federal and state magistrates.

**Publications:** Lectures on accounting matters and Sarbanes-Oxley certification requirements.

**Personal:** JD, University of Chicago, 1976, Russell Sage Foundation Fellowship

in law and social science. PhD, MA, American Legal History, University of Virginia.

### DEENY, Raymond
Sherman & Howard LLC, Colorado Springs 719 448 4016
rdeeny@sah.com
*Recommended in Employment*

**Practice Areas:** Ray Deeny is a Member in the Labor and Employment Department of Sherman & Howard. His practice is devoted exclusively to management representation, and he is involved in handling all types of labor and employment litigation, including matters before the National Labor Relations Board, EEOC and state agencies, and the defense of federal and state court actions involving employment discrimination and common law claims. He has amassed an unrivaled number of successful defense verdicts around the country. One of his clients reported to the firm: "I am one who believes that good trial lawyers are born and that great trial lawyers build upon those innate skills to separate themselves from the pack. Ray is one of those great trial lawyers. He is a born trial lawyer and, through years of hard work and study, has become one of the truly great trial lawyers. His mastery of the courtroom, from opening to closing, strategic decision-making, evidentiary matters and cross examination, is impressive and a delight to observe. And, not only that, he genuinely enjoys what he does." Ray serves on the Executive Committee of the prestigious Denver law firm of Sherman & Howard.

### DONOVAN JR, Lawrence
Isaacson Rosenbaum PC, Denver
303 292 5656
*Recommended in Real Estate*

### DUNN, Daniel
Holme Roberts & Owen LLP, Denver
303 861 7000
*Recommended in Environment*

### EDDY, Ronald M
Sherman & Howard LLC, Denver
303 299 8338
reddy@sah.com
*Recommended in Environment*

**Practice Areas:** Ron Eddy is a Member in the Litigation Department. He advises clients on a variety of environmental issues concerning hazardous substances and wastes, air and water quality, asbestos, and underground storage tanks. He joined Sherman & Howard in 1981. Prior to law school he was a physical scientist with the Denver Regional Office of the EPA from 1972-78. He speaks widely to academic and industry trade groups on various environmental law topics. He's been an Adjunct Professor at the University of Denver Graduate School of Business Administration.

### EID, Troy A
Greenberg Traurig LLP, Denver
303 572 6500
eidt@gtlaw.com
*Recommended in Environment*

**Practice Areas:** Environmental.

**Prof. Memberships:** Advisory Board Member, Natural Resources Law Center, University of Colorado School of Law. Co-Chair, Governor's Commission on Civil Service Reform. Member, Governor's Commission on Science and Technology. Chairman, Colorado Board of Ethics.

**Career:** Listed, Chambers & Partners USA Guide, 2005-06.

**Publications:** 'Strategic Democracy-Building: How States Can Help' (co-authored with Governor Bill Owens), in Alexander TJ Lennon, editor, 'Winning Hearts and Minds: Using Soft Power to Undermine Terrorist Networks' (Massachusetts Institute of Technology Press, 2003).

**Personal:** JD, University of Chicago Law School, 1991; AB, Russian Language and Literature, Stanford University, 1986.

### EURICH, Gregory
Holland & Hart LLP, Denver
303 295 8166
geurich@hollandhart.com
*Recommended in Employment*

**Practice Areas:** Partner practicing in labor law, with particular emphasis on litigation of labor disputes. Work has included defending major clients against claims of race, sex, age, disability and national origin discrimination, actions involving collective bargaining agreements, and wrongful discharge claims in lawsuits before state and federal trial and appellate courts in much of the Western United States. Lead trial counsel in nearly 100 trials, a substantial portion of which have been jury trials.

**Prof. Memberships:** Member of the Colorado Supreme Court Committee on Pattern Jury Instructions; Colorado Trial Lawyers Association; the Association of Trial Lawyers of America; Defense Research Institute; and the Colorado Defense Lawyers Association. Appointments: Co-Chair of the Colorado Pledge to Diversity Law Firm Group.

**Career:** Admitted to the Colorado and US District Court, District of Colorado (1973), US Court of Appeals, Tenth Circuit (1977) and US Supreme Court.

**Personal:** Received JD (magna cum laude, Order of the Coif) from the University of Michigan (1973) and a BA (cum laude, Phi Beta Kappa) from the University of Michigan (1970).

### EVANS, Kevin D
Steese & Evans PC, Denver
720 200 0613
kdevans@s-elaw.com
*Recommended in Litigation*

**Practice Areas:** White-collar and regu-

latory defense; complex civil litigation.

**Career:** Clients have described Evans as 'tough, tenacious and extremely talented.' His peers note that his work ethic and talent translates into a 'terrific trial lawyer'. Evans represents clients in white collar criminal defense, SEC and complex litigation matters, as well as internal investigations. Most recently, he has represented numerous individuals in SEC proceedings, a large French chemical company in a criminal RCRA case, a large French company in antitrust litigation, several clients in qui tam litigation, the United States Olympic Committee, and several Olympic and professional athletes, as well as the owner of various professional sports teams.

**Personal:** Evans is a second degree black belt in Tae Kwon Do, and an avid scuba diver and skier.

### FIELDS, Leslie
Faegre & Benson LLP, Denver
303 607 3622
LFields@faegre.com
*Recommended in Real Estate*

**Practice Areas:** Eminent domain; land use; property tax valuations.

**Career:** Represented governments in major open space acquisitions; private landowners in the condemnation of 15,000 acres of land, mineral and water rights for the new Denver International Airport; private landowners in prosecuting and defending the condemnation of property for private purposes; private landowners in unauthorized urban renewal takings; and a wide assortment of condemnation cases involving waste transfer facilities, churches, athletic facilities, restaurants, high rise office buildings, fast food franchises, gas stations, manufacturing facilities, residential subdivisions, and others.

**Personal:** BA, University of Denver (1978); JD, Denver College of Law (1981).

### FISCHER, Rebecca
Sherman & Howard LLC, Denver
303 299 8324
rfischer@sah.com
*Recommended in Real Estate*

**Practice Areas:** Rebecca Fischer is a Member in the Business & Real Estate Department of Sherman & Howard's Denver office. The primary areas of her commercial real estate practice include common interest community law, commercial leasing and resort planning, and development and marketing. Ms Fischer's experience covers a broader spectrum, including acquisitions of businesses in transactions involving financing, environmental, permitting and title issues in multiple states. Ms Fischer joined Sherman & Howard in 1982. She has participated in a number of continuing legal education programs in her field.

**FOGNANI, John**
Fognani & Faught, PLLC, Denver
303 382 6200
*Recommended in Environment*

**FOREMAN, Lee**
Haddon, Morgan, Mueller, Jordan,
Mackey & Foreman PC, Denver
303 831 7364
*Recommended in Litigation*

**FORMAN, Wayne F**
Brownstein Hyatt & Farber PC, Denver
303 223 1120
wforman@bhf-law.com
*Recommended in Real Estate*

**Practice Areas:** Shareholder in Brownstein Hyatt & Farber's Water Rights, Public Lands, Real Estate, Environmental Law, Administrative Law, and Litigation Groups. A counsel of record in a number of reported appellate decisions involving water rights matters. Represents private landowners and public entities in a variety of land use and condemnation matters. Extensive experience in the water quality area, including NEPA compliance, Section 404 permitting, and Section 401 state certifications.
**Prof. Memberships:** American Bar Association; Colorado Bar Association; Denver Bar Association.
**Personal:** University of Colorado School of Law (JD, 1984); Cornell University (BS, 1980).

**FRANCIS, Jane**
Holland & Hart LLP, Denver
303 295 8599
jfrancis@hollandhart.com
*Recommended in Employment*

**Practice Areas:** ERISA, employee benefits, executive compensation and health and welfare plan issues for corporate and tax-exempt clients. Ms Francis represents clients in IRS and DOL audits and various IRS and DOL correction programs such as the Employee Plans Compliance Resolution System and the Delinquent Filers Voluntary Compliance program. She provides advice to fiduciaries and serves as counsel to the internal benefits and investment committees at several large companies. She drafts and interprets qualified, non-qualified, equity incentive, welfare and fringe benefit plans.
**Prof. Memberships:** Admitted to practice in Colorado and the District of Columbia; Western Pension and Benefits Conference (Steering Committee 1998); American Bar Association; District of Columbia Bar Association; Colorado Bar Association; Denver Bar Association.
**Career:** Chair of the Employee Benefits Practice Group (2000-05).
**Publications:** Ms Francis has spoken on numerous benefits-related topics, including HIPAA, FMLA benefit issues, employee classification, benefits for older workers, and executive compensation following the passage of Code Section 409A.

**Personal:** Duke University (JD 1988); Stanford University (AB 1985, with distinction).

**FRICK, Ann**
Jacobs, Chase, Frick, Kleinkopf & Kelley, Denver 303 685 4800
*Recommended in Litigation*

**FROST, Daniel**
Holland & Hart LLP, Denver
303 295 8323
dfrost@hollandhart.com
*Recommended in Construction*

**Practice Areas:** Construction services in the areas of litigation and claims presentation, claims avoidance and management, construction contracts and documentation, project development, project administration, and public contracting matters.
**Prof. Memberships:** Denver, Colorado and American Bar Associations.
**Career:** Partner/Shareholder, Fairfield and Wood, PC, 1985-99; Partner, Holland & Hart LLP, 1999-present.
**Publications:** Frequent speaker on construction topics and construction trial techniques. Mr Frost has taught trial and advocacy at the University of Colorado and has handled cases across the Intermountain West.
**Personal:** University of New Mexico (JD 1978); Brigham Young University (BA 1974).

**GALLAGHER, Sean**
Hogan & Hartson LLP, Denver
303 454 2415
srgallagher@hhlaw.com
*Recommended in Employment*

**Practice Areas:** Litigation Group Partner. Trial lawyer who represents businesses in employment, commercial and public policy litigation matters. Has tried numerous litigation matters to juries and judges in both state and federal courts.
**Prof. Memberships:** Member, Employment Rights and Responsibilities Sub-Committee, Labor Law Committee, American Bar Association; Member, Colorado Bar Association.
**Publications:** One of two managing editors of 'The Practitioner's Guide to Colorado Employment Law', published by the Colorado Bar Association; 'Privacy Versus Freedom of Speech: Telemarketing and Government's Ability to Limit It', The Colorado Lawyer, Colorado Bar Association (1 October 2004).
**Personal:** JD, University of Denver College of Law (1987); BA, Baylor University (1984).

**GARNSEY JR, Walter W**
Kelly Haglund Garnsey + Kahn LLC, Denver
303 296 9412
wgarnsey@khgk.com
*Recommended in Litigation*

**Practice Areas:** Complex commercial litigation in federal and state courts,

administrative agencies, and arbitration tribunals. Commercial litigation emphasis on law of contracts, business entities, financial institutions, construction, and real estate. Additional emphasis on employment litigation and land use matters under federal Indian law.
**Prof. Memberships:** Fellow, American College of Trial Lawyers; Member, American, Colorado, and Denver Bar Associations.
**Career:** Associate, Holland & Hart (Denver, Colorado): 1971-73; trial attorney, Denver Regional Litigation Center, Equal Employment Opportunity Commission: 1973-74; Member, Kelly Haglund Garnsey + Kahn LLC : 1974-present.
**Personal:** Stanford University Law School, JD 1971; Yale University, BA (cum laude) 1967.

**GIBBY, Darin J**
Townsend and Townsend and Crew LLP, Denver 303 571 4000
djgibby@townsend.com
*Recommended in Intellectual Property*

**Practice Areas:** Darin J Gibby is Partner-in-Charge of the Denver office of Townsend and Townsend and Crew, a 170-attorney firm specializing in intellectual property, antitrust and complex business litigation. Mr Gibby regularly assists clients with intellectual property counseling, transactions and technology licensing matters, and he is experienced in handling the intellectually property aspects of mergers and acquisitions. He counsels start-ups and small businesses on the intellectual property challenges they face. In addition, he manages several patent portfolios for Fortune 500 companies. His practice emphasizes patent prosecution and licensing in business methods, medical devices, telecommunications, software, biotechnology-related devices, ceramics and internet-related technology.
**Personal:** JD, Brigham Young University, magna cum laude, Order of the Coif, 1993; MBA, Brigham Young University, 1993; BS, Brigham Young University, cum laude, 1990.

**GOLDBERG, Charles**
Rothgerber Johnson & Lyons LLP, Denver 303 628 9533
cgoldberg@rothgerber.com
*Recommended in Litigation*

**Practice Areas:** Complex civil litigation, religious liberty issues, condemnations, professional and products liability, personal injury, securities arbitrations, will contests, mediation and arbitration.
**Prof. Memberships:** ABA; CBA; DBA; American College of Trial Lawyers; Executive Committee for the National Diocesan Attorneys Association; Large Complex Case Panel of Arbitrators, American Arbitration Association.
**Career:** Denver District Court Judge (1974-78); Chairman, Board of Trustees,

Colorado Attorneys' Fund for Client Protection; Director, National Client Protection Organization. Admitted Colorado, USDC of Colorado, US Court of Appeals Tenth Circuit and US Supreme Court.
**Personal:** JD, University of Denver College of Law (1964); BA, University of Colorado (1961).

**GOTTSCHALK, Hugh**
Wheeler Trigg Kennedy LLP, Denver
303 292 2525
*Recommended in Litigation*

**GRAY, Tracy**
Hogan & Hartson LLP, Boulder
720 406 5333
TBGray@hhlaw.com
*Recommended in Intellectual Property*

**Practice Areas:** Represents clients ranging from Fortune 100 domestic and international corporations to start-up companies; counsels and advises clients on a wide range of IP issues.
**Prof. Memberships:** IAPP; ABA; Colorado Bar Association, IP and Technology Sections; Boulder County Bar Association; Boulder County Chamber of Commerce, Women's Leadership Council; INTA.
**Publications:** Various Hogan & Hartson publications; bi-monthly Privacy and Security Briefings; articles pertaining to privacy, security, and evolving legislation.
**Personal:** Certified Information Privacy Professional; Advisory Board, Family Learning Center; University of Colorado Athlete Mentor Program; Brown University Alumni Association.

**GRIMSHAW, Thomas**
Grimshaw & Harring PC, Denver
303 839 3800
*Recommended in Real Estate*

**GUNNELL, Bret**
Sherman & Howard LLC, Denver
303 299 8242
bgunnell@sah.com
*Recommended in Construction*

**Practice Areas:** Bret Gunnell is a Member in the Litigation Department of Sherman & Howard's Denver office. His practice focuses exclusively in the area of construction law and litigation. He has extensive experience in mediating, arbitrating and litigating a broad range of construction disputes. He has an engineering background, lectures and publishes frequently on legal issues affecting the construction industry, and teaches a graduate-level construction law course at Colorado State University entitled 'Legal Aspects of the Construction Process' in the Department of Manufacturing Technology and Construction Management.

**HADDON , Harold**
Haddon, Morgan, Mueller, Jordan,
Mackey & Foreman PC, Denver
303 831 7364
*Recommended in Litigation*

## HANLON-LEH, Natalie
Faegre & Benson LLP, Denver
303 607 3639
NHanlon-Leh@faegre.com
*Recommended in Intellectual Property*
**Practice Areas:** Intellectual property litigation (including patents, copyrights, trademarks, unfair competition, false advertising and trade secrets); media and entertainment; advertising; technology and software; trial practice; and trademark and copyright protection and licensing.
**Prof. Memberships:** Chair, Colorado Bar Association Intellectual Property Section; Programs Committee, International Trademark Association; past President, Colorado Women's Bar Association.
**Publications:** Frequent speaker and author on intellectual property and technology law issues. Adjunct professor, University of Colorado School of Law.
**Personal:** JD, Harvard University, cum laude; BS, University of Colorado, Boulder, cum laude; Judicial Clerk, Judge John Portfilio, 10th Circuit (1989-90).

## HARRIS, Dale
Davis Graham & Stubbs LLP, Denver
303 892 9400
*Recommended in Litigation*

## HARTLEY, James E
Holland & Hart LLP, Denver
303 295 8237
jhartley@hollandhart.com
*Recommended in Litigation*
**Practice Areas:** Partner with primary areas of practice in antitrust litigation and counseling, and patent infringement litigation. Chair of firm Litigation Department and mentioned in leading American publications. Extensive trial experience in complex patent infringement, antitrust, trade secrets and unfair competition cases. Represented clients before state and federal criminal grand juries and defended deceptive practice cases brought by the Federal Trade Commission. Advised clients concerning pre-merger notification rules and frequently makes presentations about antitrust compliance procedures.
**Prof. Memberships:** Former adjunct professor at the University of Denver School of Law; Member of the governing Council of the Antitrust Section of the American Bar Association.
**Career:** Admitted to the Colorado Bar (1974).
**Personal:** Received a JD (1974) and a BA (1971) from the University of California at Berkeley.

## HAVLICK, Scott
Holland & Hart LLP, Denver
303 473 2710
shavlick@hollandhart.com
*Recommended in Intellectual Property*
**Practice Areas:** Partner heading the Intellectual Property Practice Group with specialization in US and foreign trademark matters. Assists with all phases of trademark management from the selection, searching, investigation and clearance of new brands to the registration and proper use of trademarks that have been selected. Handled a wide range of trademark litigation matters on behalf of both plaintiffs and defendants involving counterfeit goods, gray market importation, passing off, reverse passing off, dilution, and fair use. Tried numerous trademark cases in state and federal courts, and the US Court of Appeals, as well as before the US Trademark Trial and Appeal Board.
**Prof. Memberships:** Member, International Trademark Association; Member, American Intellectual Property Lawyers Association; Member, Patent, Trademark and Copyright Sections of the American and Colorado Bar Associations; former Co-Chair, Intellectual Property Section, Boulder County Bar Association.
**Career:** Admitted to the Colorado (1986) Bar and the US District Court, District of Colorado; (1987) US Court of Appeals, Ninth Circuit; (1991) US Court of Appeals, Tenth Circuit.
**Personal:** Received a JD (1986) from the University of Utah and a BA (1981) from the University of Colorado.

## HILL, Robert F
Hill & Robbins PC, Denver
303 296 8100
RobertHill@HillandRobbins.com
*Recommended in Litigation*
**Practice Areas:** Complex civil litigation, with an emphasis in the areas of pension benefits, securities, antitrust and intellectual property rights.
**Prof. Memberships:** Fellow, American College of Trial Lawyers, International Academy of Trial Lawyers, American Bar Foundation and Colorado Bar Foundation. Denver, Colorado and American Bar Associations. Colorado and American Trial Lawyers Associations, Colorado Lawyers Committee.
**Career:** University of Colorado Law School (1970); Order of the Coif; Co-Editor in Chief, University of Colorado Law Review; Clerk, Hon Warren J Ferguson, USDC California (1970-71); Associate, Covington & Burling (1971-74); Visiting Associate Professor of Law, University of Colorado Law School (1974-75); First Assistant Attorney General, State of Colorado (1975-78); Hill & Robbins, P.C. (1978-present).
**Personal:** Co-founder of Invest in Kids and Board Member (1996-present); Chairman of the Board of Nurse-Family Partnership (2005-present); Hoagland Award for Public Service (1997), Colorado Bar Association; Individual of the Year Award (1989) and Outstanding Sustained Contribution Award (1999), Colorado Lawyers Committee; National Philanthropy Day's Outstanding Volunteer Award in Colorado (2003).

## HILTON, Paul
Hogan & Hartson LLP, Denver
303 454 2414
philton@hhlaw.com
*Recommended in Corporate/M&A*
**Practice Areas:** A Practice Group Director of firm's Corporate, Securities and Finance Group, as well as a Practice Group Director of Denver office's Business, Finance & Tax Group. His practice focuses on securities, mergers and acquisitions, corporate governance, and general corporate matters. He represents public companies, startups and venture-backed companies, investment banking firms, venture capital and private equity firms, and public and private acquirers and targets in acquisition transactions.
**Prof. Memberships:** Colorado Bar Association.
**Career:** Began career on Wall Street, was a Partner, Corporate Group Leader and Executive Committee Member at a law firm based in Denver, and following that was the Managing Partner of the Colorado office of a San Francisco-based international law firm.
**Publications:** Co-author, 'Director's Guide to Sarbanes-Oxley Compliance', (Gorham Lamont August 2004); 'SEC Issues New Interpretive Guidance Regarding MD&A', SEC Update, Hogan & Hartson LLP (30 January 2004); 'Disclosure Regarding Director Nomination Process and Security Holder Communications With Boards of Directors', SEC Update, Hogan & Hartson LLP (16 December 2003).
**Personal:** JD, Cornell University Law School (1977); MA, University of Colorado (1977); BA, with honors, University of Colorado (1972).

## HOFFMAN, Daniel
Hoffman Reilly Pozner & Williamson, Denver 303 893 6100
*Recommended in Litigation*

## HOLMES, Robert
Holme Roberts & Owen LLP, Denver
303 861 7000
*Recommended in Real Estate*

## HOLMES, Whitney
Morrison & Foerster LLP, Denver
303 592 2205
wholmes@mofo.com
*Recommended in Corporate/M&A*
**Practice Areas:** Specializes in public and private securities and corporate finance, mergers and acquisitions. Expertise in IPOs, secondary offerings, and private placements of equity and debt securities, plus all aspects of friendly and hostile acquisitions, leveraged buyouts, joint ventures, and proxy contests. Has represented companies in financing transactions, including bank credit financing and public and private placements of debt securities, reporting obligations under federal securities laws and general corporate governance matters.

**Prof. Memberships:** American and Colorado Bar Associations. Chairman, Securities Law Subsection, Colorado Bar Association, September 2002-05.
**Career:** Admitted in Colorado and New York.
**Personal:** BA, Pomona College, 1984; JD, magna cum laude, Cornell Law School, 1987.

## HOUTSMA, Peter C
Holland & Hart LLP, Denver
303 295 8259
phoutsma@hollandhart.com
*Recommended in Litigation*
**Practice Areas:** Complex commercial litigation, including contract litigation, construction litigation, insurance litigation, litigation involving financial institutions, royalty and real estate litigation, business tort litigation, products liability, class action matters on both the plaintiff and defense side, intellectual property litigation, Indian law matters, and professional liability matters, including director and officer liability and attorney and accountant liability matters in federal and state courts.
**Prof. Memberships:** Commercial Panel of Arbitrators; American Arbitration Association; Denver Bar Association; Colorado Bar Association; American Bar Association; American Trial Lawyers Association; Colorado Trial Lawyers Association.
**Career:** Partner at Holland & Hart since 1982; youngest Partner to serve on the firm's Management Committee (1982-85); Financial Partner (1990-95), Managing Partner (1995-1997); Chair of the firm's Litigation Department (1998-2001); Chair of the firm's Diversity Committee (2002-05). Over 50 trials and complex arbitrations. Jury verdicts in excess of $100 million. See comments from jurors in resume on firm site.
**Personal:** Cornell Law School (JD 1976, magna cum laude, Order of the Coif, Notes Editor, Cornell Law Review); University of Colorado (BA 1973, magna cum laude, Phi Beta Kappa, outstanding undergraduate in college of Arts and Sciences).

## HUSBAND, John
Holland & Hart LLP, Denver
303 295 8228
jhusband@hollandhart.com
*Recommended in Employment*
**Practice Areas:** Partner practicing in labor and employment law. Mr Husband was voted Best of the Bar by his peers for labor and employment law, which was sponsored by a leading Colorado business publication. He has been involved in hundreds of cases, tried cases in 20 states and been lead trial counsel in over 300 adversarial proceedings, trials, major arbitrations or administrative actions that have been tried to conclusion. He advises on a range of employment mat-

ters, including class action lawsuits, wrongful discharge, equal employment opportunity, trade secrets and covenants not to compete, wage and hour, privacy, disability, occupational safety, affirmative action and the law involving collective action, strikes, unions and collective bargaining.

**Prof. Memberships:** Appointments: Fellow, College of Labor and Employment Lawyers; American Bar Association, co-Chair, Class Action and Complex Litigation Sub-Committee; Column Editor, The Colorado Lawyer; Editor, the Colorado Employment Law Letter; Director and Officer, Colorado Safety Association; and Board of Governors, University of Toledo, College of Law. Management Chair of the National Labor Relations Board, Practices and Procedures Committee Region 27; Leadership Denver Association.

**Career:** Admitted to Colorado Bar (1978).

**Personal:** Received a JD from University of Toledo (1977) and a BS from Ohio State University (1974).

## IPSEN, Henry
Holme Roberts & Owen LLP, Denver
303 861 7000
*Recommended in Environment*

## JACOBS, Paul
Jacobs, Chase, Frick, Kleinkopf & Kelley, Denver 303 685 4800
*Recommended in Real Estate*

## JAMES, Bruce A
Brownstein Hyatt & Farber PC, Denver
303 223 1167
bjames@bhf-law.com
*Recommended in Real Estate*

**Practice Areas:** Managing Partner and CEO of Brownstein Hyatt & Farber. Practice involves real estate, corporate finance and real estate development, dispositions, and acquisitions.

**Prof. Memberships:** Colorado Bar Association; Denver Bar Association; Board Member, Junior Achievement; Littleton Hospital.

**Personal:** University of Denver College of Law (JD, 1985); University of Michigan (BBA, 1982).

## JENSEN, Garth
Holme Roberts & Owen LLP, Denver
303 861 7000
*Recommended in Corporate/M&A*

## JEWETT, Steve
Townsend and Townsend and Crew LLP, Denver 303 571 4000
*Recommended in Intellectual Property*

## KANAN, Gregory B
Rothgerber Johnson & Lyons LLP, Denver 303 628 9530
gkanan@rothgerber.com
*Recommended in Litigation*

**Practice Areas:** Corporate, commercial, securities and antitrust litigation, includ-

ing plaintiff and defense antitrust litigation, criminal antitrust, cases involving price fixing, monopolies, unlawful dealer termination, exclusive dealing and illegal tying arrangements. Advises on healthcare antitrust issues.

**Prof. Memberships:** ABA; CBA; DBA; American Board of Trial Advocates; Past Chairman and Board Member, Colorado Lawyers Committee; National Health Lawyers Association; DBA, Board of Governors.

**Career:** Admitted Colorado, USDC of Colorado, US Court of Appeals Tenth Circuit and US Supreme Court.

**Personal:** JD, University of Colorado School of Law, Order of the Coif (1975); BA, University of Colorado (1972).

## KAPLAN, Stephen
Kaplan Kirsch & Rockwell LLP, Denver
303 825 7000
*Recommended in Real Estate*

## KINSELLA, Peter
Faegre & Benson LLP, Denver
303 607 3645
pkinsella@faegre.com
*Recommended in Intellectual Property*

**Practice Areas:** Intellectual property protection and commercialization; international and domestic licensing and distribution; technology-related corporate and commercial; transactions; intellectual property litigation and counseling; trademark portfolio and brand management; e-business, computer and internet law; software and product development and distribution; open source licenses.

**Career:** Peter is a Partner practicing technology law in Faegre & Benson's Denver office and is the Chair of the firm's Intellectual Property Transaction Practice. He focuses on advising start-up, emerging and large companies on intellectual property and technology related commercial transaction matters.

**Personal:** BS, North Dakota State University, Dean's List; JD, University of Minnesota, Dean's List.

## KLEINKOPF, David
Jacobs, Chase, Frick, Kleinkopf & Kelley, Denver 303 685 4800
*Recommended in Real Estate*

## KNETSCH, Jeffrey
Brownstein Hyatt & Farber PC, Denver
303 223 1160
jknetsch@bhf-law.com
*Recommended in Corporate/M&A*

**Practice Areas:** Shareholder in Brownstein Hyatt & Farber's Corporate & Securities Group. Represents corporations, venture capital firms, and investment banking firms in a wide range of complex corporate transactions, including mergers and acquisitions, public and private securities offerings, corporate restructurings and workouts, exchange offers, tender offers, leveraged buyout transactions, and bank financings.

**Prof. Memberships:** American Bar Association; Colorado Bar Association; New York Bar Association.

**Personal:** University of Southern California (JD, 1982); University of Virginia (BA, 1978).

## KRENDL, Cathy
Krendl Krendl Sachnoff & Way PC, Denver 303 629 2600
*Recommended in Corporate/M&A*

## LAWRENCE, Robert
Davis Graham & Stubbs LLP, Denver
303 892 9400
*Recommended in Environment*

## LEVINE, Ronald
Davis Graham & Stubbs LLP, Denver
303 892 9400
*Recommended in Corporate/M&A*

## LEVY, Mark
Holland & Hart LLP, Denver
303 295 8073
mlevy@hollandhart.com
*Recommended in Corporate/M&A*

**Practice Areas:** Has substantial experience with securities laws. Assists public companies with ongoing compliance with securities laws, including periodic reports, proxy statements, corporate governance, press releases, Section 16 matters, Rule 144 sales, fiduciary duties and other matters. Also works on public and private offerings. Substantial experience in the acquisitions and dispositions of a variety of small and large businesses, bank loans and other private financings, the formation and operation of corporations and general business agreements.

**Prof. Memberships:** Member of the Federal Securities Regulation and Law and Accounting Committees of the Section of Business Law, American Bar Association. Appointments: Chairperson (1999-2000), Colorado Bar Association Convention Committee; Member, Colorado Bar Association, Article 8 (Securities Transactions) of the Uniform Commercial Code Committee (1995-96) (review of Article for Colorado); Chairperson (1994-95), Alumni Board of Directors, University of Colorado Law School; and Co-Chairman (1989-91), Colorado Bar Association, Securities Law Review Committee (prepared the Colorado Securities Act enacted in 1990 and proposed legislation on investment advisers).

**Career:** Admitted to Colorado Bar (1972).

**Personal:** Received a JD (1972, Order of the Coif) and a BA (1968) from the University of Colorado.

## LINFIELD, James
Cooley Godward LLP, Broomfield
720 566 4000
*Recommended in Corporate/M&A*

## LOTTNER, Alan
Lottner Rubin Fishman Brown & Saul, PC, Denver 303 292 1200
*Recommended in Real Estate*

## LOZOW, Gary
Isaacson Rosenbaum PC, Denver
303 292 5656
*Recommended in Litigation*

## LYONS, James M
Rothgerber Johnson & Lyons LLP, Denver 303 628 9546
jlyons@rothgerber.com
*Recommended in Litigation*

**Practice Areas:** Complex business litigation, mediation, commercial arbitration, including high technology, intellectual property, corporate, environmental and securities law. Extensive government relations and international trade and diplomacy experience in Ireland and United Kingdom.

**Prof. Memberships:** CBA; DBA; ISBA; American College of Trial Lawyers; International Academy of Trial Lawyers; Master Barrister, Doyle's Inn Chapter of the American Inns of Court.

**Career:** Special Advisor to President and Secretary of State for Economic Initiatives in Ireland and Northern Ireland (1996-2001); US Observer, International Fund for Ireland (1993-2001); Lecturer, Peace and Economic Development, University of Ulster, Belfast and Derry, Northern Ireland (2004); adjunct professor, International Conflict Resolution and Management Seminar, University of Denver School of Law and Graduate School of International Studies (2004); President, Faculty of Federal Advocates, USDC, Colorado (2003); General Counsel, Office of President-Elect, William Jefferson Clinton (1992-93); Instructor, University of Denver College of Law, University of Colorado School of Law, National Institute of Trial Advocacy. Admitted Colorado, Illinois, USDC of Colorado and Northern District of Illinois, US Court of Appeals Seventh and Tenth Circuits and US Supreme Court.

**Personal:** Honorary LLD, University of Ulster, Belfast, Northern Ireland (2002); JD, DePaul University College of Law (1971); BA, College of the Holy Cross (1968).

## MACDONALD, Elizabeth A
Faegre & Benson LLP, Denver
303 607 3680
EMacDonald@faegre.com
*Recommended in Employment*

**Practice Areas:** Age discrimination, alternative dispute resolution, Americans With Disabilities Act, arbitrations, breach of contract, employer counseling, employment law, employment litigation, Family and Medical Leave Act, internal investigations, mediations, race discrimination, sexual harassment, Title VII, trial practice, wrongful discharge.

**Prof. Memberships:** The American

Employment Law Council.

**Career:** Elizabeth MacDonald, a Partner in the firm's Denver office, has over 20 years' experience defending employers in litigation and administrative law matters.
**Personal:** BA, Middlebury College (1975), magna cum laude, Phi Beta Kappa; JD, University of Colorado, Boulder (1982).

### MACDONALD, J Thomas
Otten, Johnson, Robinson, Neff + Ragonetti, PC, Denver
303 575 7520
mac@ottenjohnson.com
*Recommended in Real Estate*
**Practice Areas:** Real estate, real estate finance, bankruptcy and insolvency, land use, litigation.
**Prof. Memberships:** American Bar Association; Colorado Bar Association; Denver Bar Association.
**Career:** Tom has substantial experience representing commercial lenders, with particular emphasis on loan foreclosures, workouts and bankruptcies. He also represents private sector clients in complex litigation involving land use and governmental regulation.
**Publications:** Frequent lecturer at continuing legal education seminars.
**Personal:** JD (1981) and BA (1977), University of Colorado School of Law; graduated first in his class; Phi Delta Phi; Order of the Coif.

### MACKEY, Pamela
Haddon, Morgan, Mueller, Jordan, Mackey & Foreman PC, Denver
303 831 7364
*Recommended in Litigation*

### MAGUIRE JR, Charles
Holme Roberts & Owen LLP, Denver
303 861 7000
*Recommended in Corporate/M&A*

### MARTIN, Raymond
Wheeler Trigg Kennedy LLP, Denver
303 292 2525
*Recommended in Employment*

### MATAVA, George
Greenberg Traurig LLP, Denver
303 572 6571
matavag@gtlaw.com
*Recommended in Intellectual Property*
**Practice Areas:** Intellectual property; intellectual property litigation.
**Prof. Memberships:** Chairman, Vice Chairman, Secretary of Intellectual Property Section - Colorado Bar Association, 1997-99; Member, Colorado Bar Association; Member, Denver Bar Association.
**Personal:** JD, Wake Forest University School of Law, 1978; BS, Trinity College, 1971.

### MCCARTHY, Michael S
Faegre & Benson LLP, Denver
303 607 3670
mmccarthy@faegre.com
*Recommended in Litigation*

**Practice Areas:** Civil trial practice; class action; corporate; securities; complex commercial; environmental; energy and natural resources; insolvency; sports; and trade regulation and antitrust.
**Prof. Memberships:** Fellow, American College of Trial Lawyers; ABA; CBA; DBA; Fellow, Colorado Bar Foundation.
**Career:** Lead trial counsel for the Colorado Rockies Baseball Club in numerous matters; including successful trial defense of the Club and its owners in a Bankruptcy Court fraudulent transfer claim involving valuation of the Rockies franchise. Lead trial counsel for State Farm Insurance in multiple Colorado class action claims.
**Personal:** BA, University of Michigan; JD, University of Colorado, Boulder, Law Review.

### MCDANIEL, Janet Lawler
Faegre & Benson LLP, Denver
303 607 3659
JLMcDaniel@faegre.com
*Recommended in Construction*
**Practice Areas:** Construction law.
**Career:** Janet's practice focuses on commercial litigation, with an emphasis on construction law. She was the chapter editor and contributing author for the chapter on the contractor that was published in Colorado Construction Law (CLE of Colorado, Inc. 1999). She drafted a bill which was sponsored by AGC of Colorado in the 2000 Legislative Session permitting contractors to substitute a bond for claims on Public Works Projects. She is the past Chair of the Construction Law Forum for the Colorado Bar Association.
**Personal:** BS, Colorado State University (1979), Phi Beta Kappa; JD, University of Denver (1995).

### MCNEIVE, Lynda A
Brownstein Hyatt & Farber PC, Denver
303 223 1129
lmcneive@bhf-law.com
*Recommended in Real Estate*
**Practice Areas:** Shareholder and Co-Chair of Brownstein Hyatt & Farber's Real Estate Group. Focuses on commercial real estate transactions, representing developers of retail, office, industrial, residential, and mixed-use properties. Counsels clients from the initial due diligence stage through site acquisition, entitlement approvals, construction and permanent financing, construction of improvements, leasing, and sale.
**Prof. Memberships:** National Association of Industrial and Office Properties; Title Standards Committee of the Colorado Bar Association; American Bar Association; Colorado Bar Association; Denver Bar Association; Colorado Women's Bar Association.
**Personal:** Stanford Law School (JD, 1980); Marymount College, (BA, 1970).

### MICHAELS, Jane
Holland & Hart LLP, Denver
303 295 8162
jmichaels@hollandhart.com
*Recommended in Intellectual Property*
**Practice Areas:** Partner specializing in intellectual property and complex commercial litigation, with an emphasis on telecommunications and computer industry cases. Extensive experience in complex jury trials, as well as bench trials, in trademark, trade secrets, copyright, patent and technology cases. Certified arbitrator and mediator. Has handled numerous arbitrations and mediations, both as an advocate and as the arbitrator or mediator. Has lectured around the country on intellectual property and trial advocacy issues.
**Prof. Memberships:** Past President, Denver Bar Association; past Chair of the firm's Litigation Department; Honors: Fellow, American College of Trial Lawyers; Fellow, International Society of Barristers; listed as one of Colorado's top 10 trial lawyers and one of the best lawyers in the country in leading American publications.
**Career:** Admitted to the Colorado Bar (1973), US District Court, District of Colorado; US Court of Appeals, Tenth Circuit (1974); US Supreme Court (1985); US Court of Appeals for the Federal Circuit (1999); US Court of Appeals, Sixth Circuit (2002); US Court of Appeals, Fourth Circuit and District of Columbia (2003).
**Personal:** Received JD (1973) from Boston University (cum laude), MAT (1970) from Harvard University (cum laude), and BA (1968) from Wellesley College (with distinction).

### MILLER, Gale
Davis Graham & Stubbs LLP, Denver
303 892 9400
*Recommended in Litigation*

### MILLER, Zach
Davis Graham & Stubbs LLP, Denver
303 892 9400
*Recommended in Environment*

### MITZNER, David
Holme Roberts & Owen LLP, Denver
303 861 7000
*Recommended in Employment*

### MIX, Kristen
Snell & Wilmer LLP, Denver
303 634 2091
kmix@swlaw.com
*Recommended in Employment*
**Practice Areas:** Represent employers regarding agreements, handbooks, wage/hour, hiring, retention, termination, protection of confidential information, investigations, employment litigation, arbitration and mediation.
**Prof. Memberships:** Colorado Bar Association: Co-Chair, Labor and Employment Law Committee (1999-2001),

Member, Board of Governors (April 2004-present); Colorado Lawyers Committee: Executive Committee (Oct 2005-present); Hate Violence Task Force, Co-Chair (2002-present); American Arbitration Association: Employment Law Panel of Neutrals (2002-present).
**Career:** Admitted 1985.
**Publications:** Model Employment Law Jury Instructions, November 2005; A Sexual Harassment Primer, The Colorado Lawyer, October, 2000; The Nuts and Bolts of Unlawful Retaliation, Trial Talk Magazine, June 1998.
**Personal:** Born Buffalo, New York, 1958.

### MOYE, John
Moye White LLP, Denver
303 292 2900
*Recommended in Corporate/M&A*

### MUIR, Bruce
Sherman & Howard LLC, Denver
303 299 8217
bmuir@sah.com
*Recommended in Employment*
**Practice Areas:** Mr Muir's practice involves employee benefits and representation of professional groups, including representation of physician groups and their joint ventures with other healthcare providers. Representations include a broad range of employee benefit matters, including planning and establishment of retirement plans, employee stock ownership plans, deferred compensation plans and non-pension fringe benefits for businesses and professional groups, and other non-profit entities. In the healthcare area, he has represented physician groups in numerous practice mergers, the development of medical campuses, surgery centers and imaging facilities, and negotiation of contracts and structuring of joint ventures between hospitals and physician groups.

### MUMAUGH, Brian
Holland & Hart LLP, Greenwood Village
303 290 1067
bmumaugh@hollandhart.com
*Recommended in Employment*
**Practice Areas:** Partner practicing in labor and employment law. Represents employers in a range of matters including race, sex, age, disability and national origin discrimination, FLSA collective actions, wrongful discharge, breach of contract, public policy discharge, covenants not to compete, theft of trade secrets and management in labor matters. Represents employers as lead counsel in Federal and State courts and Agencies. Significant experience representing management in labor matters under both the NLRA and the RLA, including unfair labor practice proceedings, unit determinations, representation elections, collective bargaining, and major arbitrations.
**Prof. Memberships:** ABA; Colorado Bar Association; Nebraska Bar Association; Colorado Defense Lawyers Association;

Contributor to the Colorado Employment Law Letter.

**Career:** Chair, Holland & Hart Labor Practice Group, 2004 to present; admitted to the Nebraska (1983) and Colorado Bar (1989); US District Courts: District of Colorado, District of Columbia, District of Nebraska, So. District of Florida, District of Florida, District of Idaho. US Court of Appeals, Eighth, Ninth, Tenth and DC Circuits. Private practice, Omaha, NE (1982-83); Washington, DC (1984); UAL, Inc. Chicago (Labor) (1984-89). Member, Board of Directors, Executive Committee, The Children's Museum of Denver; Board Member, Rocky Mountain Children's Cancer Foundation.

**Personal:** JD, Creighton University (1982); BA, University of Nebraska (1979).

### NEWCOM, Charles W
Sherman & Howard LLC, Denver
303 299 8246
cnewcom@sah.com
*Recommended in Employment*

**Practice Areas:** Chuck Newcom is a Member of Sherman & Howard's Labor and Employment Department. He's been involved in all aspects of employment law, representing management only. His experience in the range of legal problems typically facing employers includes employment discrimination and wrongful discharge advice and litigation, employee benefits litigation, various aspects of health and safety law, and wage and overtime pay disputes. He has represented clients in financial, insurance, defense, mining and high tech industries, among others. Mr Newcom joined Sherman & Howard in 1974.

### OADE, K Preston
Holme Roberts & Owen LLP, Denver
303 861 7000
*Recommended in Employment*

### ODLE, Kathleen
Sherman & Howard LLC, Denver
303 299 8116
kodle@sah.com
*Recommended in Employment*

**Practice Areas:** Kathy Odle is a Member of the firm's Tax & Probate Department. She practices primarily in the area of employee benefits and ERISA, including retirement plans, welfare benefit plans (including COBRA and HIPAA compliance), executive compensation, equity arrangements (including stock options, stock appreciation rights and other equity incentive arrangements), severance arrangements, and related taxation and compliance matters. She provides plan document assistance for any type of employee benefit plan or arrangement (including drafting and obtaining IRS approval of qualified plans and prototype and master plans), defense of audits, and day to day advice with respect to all employee benefit matters.

### OLSEN, Theodore
Sherman & Howard LLC, Denver
303 299 8212
tolsen@sah.com
*Recommended in Employment*

**Practice Areas:** Ted Olsen is a Member of the firm's Labor & Employment Department. He represents employers of all sizes, ranging from international corporations with hundreds of thousands of employees to local businesses with only a few workers. His clients are in a wide range of industries, including telecommunications, computer software and systems development, engineering, banking, mining, oil and gas, city and county government, insurance and hospitality. His practice concentrates primarily on wrongful discharge litigation, employment discrimination litigation, sexual harassment litigation, negligent hiring and supervision, assorted tort and contract litigation, wage and hour law, class actions, and appeals.

### O'ROURKE, Renee
Faegre & Benson LLP, Denver
303 607 3673
RORourke@faegre.com
*Recommended in Employment*

**Practice Areas:** Employee benefits; retirement plans; healthcare plans; executive and stock C compensation; defined benefit plans; ESOPs; 401(k) plans; 403(b) plans; 457 plans; and ERISA.

**Career:** Renée W O'Rourke is a Partner in the Employee Benefits Group in Faegre & Benson's Denver office. Renée's experience in employee benefits includes representation of clients before the Internal Revenue Service (at both the audit and appellate levels) and the Department of Labor.

**Personal:** LLM, University of Denver (1985); JD, University of Denver (1984); BS, University of Southern Colorado (1981).

### PALENCHAR, James
Bartlit Beck Herman Palenchar & Scott, Denver 303 592 3100
*Recommended in Corporate/M&A*

### PECK, Neil
Snell & Wilmer LLP, Denver
303 634 2006
npeck@swlaw.com
*Recommended in Litigation*

**Practice Areas:** Practice is concentrated in complex civil and criminal litigation involving issues such as fraud, false advertising, antitrust, environmental, natural resources damages, foreign corrupt practices and international.

**Prof. Memberships:** CPR International Institute for Dispute Prevention and Resolution (Member, Executive Committee); Visiting Professor of Law, Nottingham Law School, Board of Editors, Environmental Liability; Member, Colorado Council on the Arts; Honorary British Consul 1994-2000; admitted Colorado and New York.

### PERMUT, Barry
Isaacson Rosenbaum PC, Denver
303 292 5656
*Recommended in Real Estate*

### PHILLIPS, Paul D
Holland & Hart LLP, Denver
303 295 8131
pphillips@hollandhart.com
*Recommended in Environment*

**Practice Areas:** Partner practicing in environmental law and litigation. Substantial experience defending companies against citizens' suits and EPA actions brought under Clean Water Act, RCRA, Clean Air Act, other environmental statutes; toxic tort litigation; environmental audits; and preparing detailed 'permit letters' outlining all state and federal environmental laws and regulations applicable to new projects.

**Prof. Memberships:** Admitted to the Colorado Bar (1977); US Supreme Court, DC and other Circuit Courts of Appeal and various other courts.

**Career:** Named 'Best of the Bar' in Environmental Law, 2004, Denver Business Journal.

**Publications:** Mr Phillips has published extensively in both legal and technical periodicals. Founding editor of 'Natural Resources and Environment', the ABA's Natural Resources magazine, and issues editor for 'Environmental Permitting: Negotiating the Maze'.

**Personal:** Received a JD (1976) from Yale and a BA (1973) from Harvard. Chairman, Holland & Hart Management Committee.

### PLUMRIDGE, Richard
Holme Roberts & Owen LLP, Denver
303 861 7000
*Recommended in Corporate/M&A*

### POWELL JR, David D
Brownstein Hyatt & Farber PC, Denver
303 223 1157
dpowell@bhf-law.com
*Recommended in Employment*

**Practice Areas:** Shareholder and co-Chair of Brownstein Hyatt & Farber's Employment Group. Specializes in the counsel and defense of employers on a variety of matters arising from the employer-employee relationship, including wrongful discharge, disability and family leave issues, sexual harassment and discrimination based on race, national origin, gender, and age.

**Prof. Memberships:** American Bar Association; Sam Cary Bar Association; Community Advisory Board, Rocky Mountain Public Broadcasting System; Colorado Bar Association; National Bar Association; Faculty of Federal Advocates; editor, Colorado Employment Law Letter.

**Personal:** UCLA Law School (JD, 1983); Univesity of Santa Clara (BA, 1980).

### QUAIL, Beverly J
Ballard Spahr Andrews & Ingersoll LLP, Denver
303 299 7305
quail@ballardspahr.com
*Recommended in Real Estate*

**Practice Areas:** Focuses on all aspects of real estate matters with an emphasis on financing and development.

**Prof. Memberships:** Past Chair, American Bar Association, Section of Real Property, Probate and Trust. Past Governor and Treasurer of the American College of Real Estate Lawyers. Fellow in the American College of Mortgage Attorneys and in the American Bar Foundation and University of Denver College of Law's DU Law Stars Alumni Professionalism Award recipient.

**Career:** Admitted to the Colorado Bar (1974).

**Publications:** Authors 'Colorado Real Estate Forms'.

**Personal:** JD, University of Denver (1974); BA, magna cum laude, University of Southern California (1971).

### RAGONETTI, Thomas J
Otten, Johnson, Robinson, Neff + Ragonetti, PC, Denver
303 575 7509
tjr@ottenjohnson.com
*Recommended in Real Estate*

**Practice Areas:** Real estate; land use.

**Prof. Memberships:** Co-Chair, The Colorado Blue Ribbon Panel on Housing; President, Rocky Mountain Land Use Institute; American, Colorado and Denver Bar Associations.

**Career:** Tom is a recognized specialist in land use planning and regulation, public finance for private developments, annexation, urban development, zoning and historic preservation and real estate.

**Publications:** Tom is a frequent speaker at and chair of local and national continuing legal education programs.

**Personal:** JD (cum laude), Harvard Law School (1977), Masters Degree in City and Regional Planning Cornell University (1973); BA, Cornell University (1971); summa cum laude; Phi Beta Kappa.

### RAISCH, Jerry
Vranesh and Raisch, LLP, Boulder
303 443 6151
*Recommended in Environment*

### REILLY, Daniel
Hoffman Reilly Pozner & Williamson, Denver 303 893 6100
*Recommended in Litigation*

### REISCH, Scott H
Hogan & Hartson LLP, Denver
303 899 7355
shreisch@HHLAW.com
*Recommended in Environment*

**Practice Areas:** Practice includes litigation and counseling on environmental matters with emphasis on Superfund, Brownfields, and voluntary cleanups, as well as environmental issues in commercial transactions, environmental laws affecting the food and agriculture industries, and compliance with state and federal laws relating to hazardous and solid wastes. Also represents clients in audits and in developing environmental management programs.

**Prof. Memberships:** Member, Advisory Council, Environmental Law Section, Colorado Bar Association; Member of Colorado, California and District of Columbia Bars.

**Publications:** 'Dirty Money: EPA Issues Brownfields Grant Guidelines', co-authored with Catherine M van Heuven, The Colorado Lawyer (April 2003); 'The Brownfields Amendments: New Opportunities, New Challenges - Parts I and II', The Colorado Lawyer (June 2002 and September 2002); 'EPA's Final TMDL Rule: A Load of Trouble for Agriculture and Industry', co-authored with Catherine M van Heuven, The Colorado Lawyer (May 2001); 'Colorado's Not-So-Little Pig Farms Meet the Big Bad Wolf', The Colorado Lawyer (June 1999); 'Yielding "Green" Harvests from "Brownfields": Strategies for Protecting Lenders from Liability at Contaminated Sites', The Colorado Lawyer (January and February 1997).

**Personal:** JD, Stanford University (1988); BA, with distinction, Stanford University (1985).

### RICHILANO, John
Richilano & Ridley PC, Denver
303 893 8000
*Recommended in Litigation*

### ROBINSON, Frank L
Otten, Johnson, Robinson, Neff + Ragonetti, PC, Denver
303 575 7501
frobinson@ottenjohnson.com
*Recommended in Real Estate*
**Practice Areas:** Real estate.
**Prof. Memberships:** American College of Real Estate Lawyers; American, Colorado and Denver Bar Associations.
**Career:** Frank's practice in the transactional area has spanned the United States. His experience includes involvement in the acquisition, disposition and financing of virtually every property type, including office, retail, multi-family, industrial, assisted living centers and mobile and modular home communities. Frank and his group have structured and completed numerous multi-property and multi-state transactions.
**Publications:** Frank has lectured extensively on real property issues for Colorado continuing legal education programs.

### ROCKWELL, Sarah
Kaplan Kirsch & Rockwell LLP, Denver
303 825 7000
*Recommended in Real Estate*

### ROCKWOOD, Linda
Faegre & Benson LLP, Denver
303 607 3642
LRockwood@faegre.com
*Recommended in Environment*
**Practice Areas:** Administrative law; air quality; brownfields and voluntary cleanups; environmental audits; environmental law; environmental liability and litigation; environmental aspects of corporate and real estate transactions; environmental permitting, auditing, and compliance; land use/zoning/environmental review; natural resource damages; site remediation; superfund and hazardous waste; toxic substances control act.
**Career:** Linda Rockwood is the administrative partner for the firm's Denver office and heads the firm's Business Environmental Practice Group.
**Personal:** BA, University of Denver, Phi Beta Kappa; JD, University of Texas, Order of the Coif, with honors.

### RUPPERT, John
Perkins Coie LLP, Denver
303 291 2322
*Recommended in Corporate/M&A*

### RUSSO, Richard M
Gibson, Dunn & Crutcher LLP, Denver
303 298 5715
rrusso@gibsondunn.com
*Recommended in Corporate/M&A*
**Practice Areas:** Co-Chair of the firm's Corporate Transactions Practice Group. Advises local, national and international clients on the representation of business entities, with emphasis on securities and disclosure matters, public and private debt and equity offerings, mergers and acquisitions, restructurings and corporate governance matters. Counselor for independent directors in connection with acquisitions, spin-offs and leveraged buyouts. Clients include Qwest Communications, CSK Auto, The Williams Companies, Petro Stopping Centers.
**Career:** Member of the firm's Executive and Management Committees.
**Publications:** Co-author, 'Colorado Limited Liability Company, Forms and Practice Manual'.
**Personal:** JD, Yale Law School, 1974, Director, Yale Moot Court of Appeals.

### SALTER, Dean
Holme Roberts & Owen LLP, Denver
303 861 7000
*Recommended in Corporate/M&A*

### SAMUELS JONES, Karen
Perkins Coie LLP, Denver
303 291 2322
*Recommended in Real Estate*

### SANCHEZ, R Michael
Sherman & Howard LLC, Denver
303 299 8114
rsanchez@sah.com
*Recommended in Employment*
**Practice Areas:** Mike Sanchez is a

Member in the Tax & Probate Department of Sherman & Howard's Denver office. He is involved primarily in handling various aspects of employee benefit planning, his principal area of expertise, including employee benefits, qualified and non-qualified plans, and welfare benefits. Throughout his career, Mr Sanchez has published 28 articles and participated in more than 150 continuing legal education programs on both national and regional levels on subjects related to his principal areas of practice. Mr Sanchez joined Sherman & Howard in 1972 and he currently serves as the firm's Chief Executive.

### SATRIANA, Daniel
Clisham, Satriana & Biscan LLC, Denver
303 468 5400
*Recommended in Employment*

### SAVAGE, Janet
Davis Graham & Stubbs LLP, Denver
303 892 9400
*Recommended in Employment*

### SCOTT, Donald
Bartlit Beck Herman Palenchar & Scott, Denver 303 592 3100
*Recommended in Litigation*

### SENN, Mark
Senn Lewis & Visciano, Denver
303 298 1122
*Recommended in Real Estate*

### SHEA, Daniel
Hogan & Hartson LLP, Denver
303 454 2475
dfshea@hhlaw.com
*Recommended in Litigation*
**Practice Areas:** Practice includes defending white-collar criminal and complex civil litigation as well as Securities and Exchange Commission (SEC), New York Stock Exchange (NYSE), and National Association of Securities Dealers (NASD) enforcement proceedings; conducting internal investigations; and providing advice regarding corporate governance and broker-dealer/investment adviser compliance issues.
**Prof. Memberships:** Member of the Colorado Bar.
**Career:** Prior positions include serving in an in-house capacity with UBS PaineWebber, Inc. as director of compliance for regulatory affairs, policy, products and trading and as deputy general counsel; director of the central region for the SEC, based in Denver, Colorado; trial attorney for the SEC and the US Departments of Justice and Energy; and in private practice in Washington, DC, defending regulatory enforcement actions and handling civil litigation involving federal securities, energy, and antitrust laws.
**Publications:** 'How Juries and Judges Reexamining Directors', Officers' Duties in the Wake of Corporate Scandals', Corporate Counsel Weekly (28 January 2004).

**Personal:** BA, College of the Holy Cross; MA, The Catholic University of America; JD, The Catholic University of America, Columbus School of Law.

### SHEA, Kevin
Ballard Spahr Andrews & Ingersoll LLP, Denver
303 299 7337
shea@ballardspahr.com
*Recommended in Litigation*
**Practice Areas:** Focuses on complex civil and criminal business, environmental, constitutional, legal malpractice and insurance coverage litigation. Tried cases to verdict in federal and state courts throughout the Western United States as well as before regulatory and private arbitration panels. Appearances in state and federal appellate courts. Represents corporations and individuals in federal and state grand jury and regulatory investigations throughout the country.
**Prof. Memberships:** Member, American Bar Association, Colorado Bar Association, and Denver Bar Association, the National Association of Criminal Defense Lawyers, and Colorado Criminal Defense Bar Association. Board of Trustees for the Legal Aid Foundation of Colorado. Past Chairman of Colorado Bar Association Criminal Law Section; Past Vice-Chair of American Bar Association Environmental Crimes Section.
**Career:** Admitted to Colorado Bar (1976); US District Court for the District of Colorado (1976); US Court of Appeals for Tenth Circuit (1976); United States Supreme Court (1983). Deputy District Attorney, Boulder, Colorado 1976-80; Associate/Partner Roath & Brega P.C., Denver, CO 1980-83; Partner Holme, Roberts & Owen LLP Denver, CO 1984-94; Partner Ballard Spahr Andrews & Ingersoll, LLP Denver, CO 1995-Present.
**Personal:** JD, University of Detroit (1976); BS, University of Colorado (1973).

### SHIVELY, John D
Faegre & Benson LLP, Denver
303 607 3616
jshively@faegre.com
*Recommended in Litigation*
**Practice Areas:** Antitrust and trade regulation; franchise law; distribution and franchise litigation; complex contract and business torts litigation; agribusiness litigation; product liability litigation.
**Career:** John's practice focuses on antitrust litigation and counseling, and the litigation of other large, complex commercial actions including contract, distribution and franchise litigation, fraud, and product liability actions. John served as the Managing Partner in Denver from 1994-2005.
**Personal:** AB, Harvard University, cum laude; JD, Harvard University; Judge Advocate and Special Court Martial Judge, US Marine Corps, 1973-77; Staff

Attorney, Federal Trade Commission, 1979-81; 'Who's Who in Law', Denver Business Journal, 2003 and 2004.

### SHOEMAKER, Andrew
Hogan & Hartson LLP, Denver
303 454 2423
arshoemaker@hhlaw.com
*Recommended in Litigation*
**Practice Areas:** Practice includes complex civil litigation and representation in connection with government investigations. He has handled disputes involving securities fraud, corporate governance, shareholder rights, executive compensation and termination, patent infringement, misappropriation of trade secrets, and breach of contract. He regularly represents corporations, board committees, and individual directors and officers in connection with internal and regulatory investigations. He also represents broker-dealers and clearing firms in connection with customer disputes and inquiries by government agencies and self-regulatory organizations.
**Prof. Memberships:** Member of the Colorado, District of Columbia and Virginia Bars.
**Career:** Enforcement attorney with the Central Regional Office of the US Securities Exchange Commission (SEC) and as a special assistant United States attorney for the District of Colorado; law clerk for the Honorable Charles R Richey of the US District Court in Washington, DC Awarded the Federal Bar Association's Manuel F Cohen Award (Outstanding young SEC attorney), 1998.
**Personal:** JD, University of Virginia School of Law, 1992; BA, summa cum laude, Hampden-Sydney College, 1989.

### SIEBERT, W Bernie
Sherman & Howard LLC, Denver
303 299 8222
bsiebert@sah.com
*Recommended in Employment*
**Practice Areas:** Mr Siebert is one of the few lawyers in the Rocky Mountain region who has practiced traditional labor law for over 30 years. His experience includes collective bargaining, arbitration, and administrative proceedings before the NLRB. He has represented employers with respect to wage-hour matters, including class and collective actions, employment at will, veterans re-employment, employment discrimination, sexual harassment, and other matters affecting the employer-employee relationship. Mr Siebert has represented employers before state and federal trial courts, courts of appeal, and the US Supreme Court. He has handled numerous jury trials as well as trials to the court.

### SIPIORA, David E
Townsend and Townsend and Crew LLP, Denver 303 571 4000
desipiora@townsend.com
*Recommended in Intellectual Property*
**Practice Areas:** Mr Sipiora litigates major patent, trademark, copyright, and trade secret cases for large and small clients. He also advises clients on intellectual property matters in the context of transactional, employment, licensing, and pre-litigation law, and helps clients protect their businesses through strategic intellectual property portfolio management and development.
**Prof. Memberships:** American Intellectual Property Law Association; International Trademark Association.
**Personal:** JD, Harvard Law School, cum laude, 1986; BA, Columbia University, summa cum laude, 1982.

### SMITH, Sheldon H
Holland & Hart LLP, Denver
303 295 8540
ssmith@hollandhart.com
*Recommended in Employment*
**Practice Areas:** ERISA, executive compensation, fiduciary duties and qualified retirement plans. Mr Smith designs and assists clients with the implementation and operation of pension plans and equity-based plans, advises clients regarding fiduciary duties, performs fiduciary compliance audits, represents clients before the IRS, DOL/EBSA and PBGC, and defends clients in ERISA and benefits, tax and probate litigation.
**Prof. Memberships:** ABA; Colorado Bar Association; Denver Bar Association; Past President, Western Pension & Benefits Conference; Vice President and Director, American Society of Pension Professionals and Actuaries.
**Career:** Law firm Partner since 1980.
**Publications:** 'In Vogue Compensation Plan' (Trusts & Estates); 'Attracting Employees to Closely Held Companies Without Sacrificing Control of the Business' (Warren, Gorham Lamont, Inc.), 'Understanding Pension and Profit Sharing Plans' (Bisk Publishing Co.), 'Non-qualified Deferred Compensation' (Bisk Publishing Co.) among others; has lectured extensivley to tax and benefits organizations throughout the country; adjunct and visiting professor in the Graduate Tax Program at the University of Denver College of Law and Sturm College at the University of Denver College of Law.
**Personal:** University of Denver (LLM 1980); University of Denver College of Law (JD 1973); Washington University in St Louis (BA 1970).

### SPAANSTRA, James R
Faegre & Benson LLP, Denver
303 607 3629
jspaanstra@faegre.com
*Recommended in Environment*
**Practice Areas:** Environmental law; natural resource and energy; land use/zoning/environmental review.
**Career:** Jim's practice has focused principally on counseling commercial, industrial and governmental clients regarding compliance and enforcement matters involving the federal environmental laws (e.g., RCRA, CERCLA, SMCRA, NEPA, EPCRA, CAA and CWA) and their state counterparts, with a particular emphasis on advising national commercial solid and hazardous waste management companies regarding the siting, permitting, operation and remediation of commercial solid and hazardous waste management facilities throughout the country.
**Personal:** BS, Grand Valley State University, with highest honors; JD, University of Michigan.

### STACY, David
Ducker, Montgomery, Aronstein & Bess PC, Denver 303 861 2828
*Recommended in Employment*

### STEINER, Beat
Holland & Hart LLP, Boulder
303 473 2736
bsteiner@hollandhart.com
*Recommended in Real Estate*
**Practice Areas:** Real estate and corporate law, emphasizing the acquisition, disposition, development and financing of real estate. Extensive Resort Practice, including ski and golf resorts in Colorado, California, Vermont and New Zealand. Presently represents the owner of the Winter Park Resort. He also has extensive corporate law experience and advises clients frequently in choice of entity, corporate, partnership and limited liability company organizational matters and represents clients in joint venture transactions, mergers and acquisitions.
**Prof. Memberships:** Colorado Bar Association (past Chair, Real Estate Law Section; Executive Council, Business Law Section; Title Standards Committee); Colorado Secretary of State Advisory Committee; Co-Chair, ABA Real Property, Probate & Trust Division Committee on Partnerships and LLCs.
**Career:** Partner; admitted in Colorado (1983), New York (1981).
**Publications:** Frequent lecturer on topics related to real estate, real estate finance and choice of entity law, he chairs an annual seminar on Real Estate Development for CLE International. Has published articles in ABA Real Property, Probate and Trust Journal; The Practical Real Estate Lawyer; The Colorado Lawyer; and Colorado Real Estate Journal.
**Personal:** University of Virginia (JD 1980); (BA 1973, with high honors).

### STEPHENS, Thomas
Bartlit Beck Herman Palenchar & Scott, Denver 303 592 3100
*Recommended in Corporate/M&A*

### STERNBERG, John D
Otten, Johnson, Robinson, Neff + Ragonetti, PC, Denver
303 575 7505
john.sternberg@ottenjohnson.com
*Recommended in Real Estate*
**Practice Areas:** Real estate.
**Prof. Memberships:** American Bar Association, Colorado Bar Association, Denver Bar Association.
**Career:** John has been counsel to some of the nation's largest developers on projects ranging from the redevelopment of entire city blocks to development of shopping centers, office buildings and industrial facilities. He also has devoted substantial time to the representation of retail tenants, construction and permanent lenders and real property investors and asset managers.
**Personal:** JD, University of Denver College of Law (1982); graduated first in his class; Order of St Ives; BA, University of Colorado (1978); summa cum laude; Phi Beta Kappa.

### STOCKS, Bruce
Perkins Coie LLP, Denver
303 291 2322
*Recommended in Corporate/M&A*

### STRICKLAND, Tom
Hogan & Hartson LLP, Denver
303 899 7364
tlstrickland@hhlaw.com
*Recommended in Environment*
**Practice Areas:** Managing Partner of Denver office. Represents clients in a wide range of industries and business issues, including environmental, natural resources, public lands, transportation, real estate, government relations, and business finance. He also has a significant practice focused on white collar criminal defense, securities enforcement and internal investigations.
**Prof. Memberships:** Member, Colorado Bar Association.
**Career:** US attorney for the District of Colorado from 1999 through 2001. Prior to his appointment as the top Justice Department official for Colorado, he spent 15 years with another major Denver law firm where he was a Senior Partner in charge of the regulatory, administrative, and public law practice. He also served as director of policy for Colorado Governor Richard D Lamm, chaired the Colorado Transportation Commission, served as legal counsel to the Denver Metro Chamber of Commerce, and was a founder and board member of Great Outdoors Colorado, the lottery-funded endowment for Colorado's public parks system. He served as a law clerk for US District Judge, The Honorable Carl Bue, Jr from 1977-79.

**Personal:** JD, with honors, University of Texas School of Law (1977); BA, with honors, Louisiana State University (1974).

### TALLEY, Steven K
Gibson, Dunn & Crutcher LLP, Denver
303 298 5775
stalley@gibsondunn.com
*Recommended in Corporate/M&A*
**Practice Areas:** Has extensive experience in mergers and acquisitions of public and private companies, including both auctions and privately negotiated sales. Additionally advises clients on public and private equity issuances and debt offerings. Counsels local, national and international clients from a variety of industries. Clients include private equity firms, First Reserve Corporation, Oryx Capital International, as well as their portfolio companies and other corporate clients.
**Career:** Partner-in-Charge of Denver office.
**Personal:** JD, University of California at Berkeley, 1991, articles editor, High Technology Law Journal, Order of the Coif.

### TEMKIN, Elizabeth
Temkin Wielga & Hardt LLP, Denver
303 292 4922
*Recommended in Environment*

### THEIS, Lawrence
Musgrave & Theis LLP, Denver
303 385 4700
*Recommended in Litigation*

### THOMASCH, Roger
Ballard Spahr Andrews & Ingersoll LLP, Denver 303 299 7301
thomasch@ballardspahr.com
*Recommended in Litigation*
**Practice Areas:** Chairman, Litigation Department and Managing Partner, Denver office. Has concentrated in the trial of business cases for over 35 years. He has appeared before courts throughout the country and has tried to verdict virtually every type of business and commercial case.
**Prof. Memberships:** Fellow of the American College of Trial Lawyers, Fellow of the American Bar Foundation and the Fellow of the Colorado Bar Foundation.
**Career:** Trial Attorney, United States Department of Justice (1970-73); visiting professor of Law, Drake University School of Law (1973-74) (Recipient of LeLand Forest Outstanding Professor Award). Lectures at trial lawyer seminars. Admitted to Connecticut Bar (1967); Colorado Bar (1974).
**Personal:** LLB, Duke University (1967); BA, The College of William and Mary (1964).

### TREECE, Lawrence
Sherman & Howard LLC, Denver
303 299 8460
ltreece@sah.com
*Recommended in Litigation*
**Practice Areas:** Larry Treece is a trial lawyer with extensive experience in the litigation, trial and appeal of complex corporate and commercial cases, including securities and other financial fraud litigation. His trial experience includes multi-week jury and bench trials, in both state and federal courts, in cases involving products liability, commercial and financial fraud, toxic torts, contracts, employment discrimination, damages, and the valuation of complex assets, including commercial real estate and oil and gas properties. His substantial appellate experience includes cases in labor, securities, tax, probate, Defamation/First Amendment, and Truth in Lending.

### TROUPE, Warren L
Morrison & Foerster LLP, Denver
303 592 2255
wtroupe@mofo.com
*Recommended in Corporate/M&A*
**Practice Areas:** Focused on transactional and financing matters, as well as corporate, securities, and mergers and acquisitions. Concluded a large number of mergers and acquisitions for both public and private companies, including tender offers, hostile proxy contests, and negotiated acquisitions. Represented companies in a range of financing and restructurings, including public and private equity offerings, traditional loan structures, debt placements, subordinated debt financings, workouts, recapitalizations, and formation and financing of REITs.
**Career:** Admitted to practice in Colorado and Florida. Chair of the firm's Denver Corporate Group.
**Personal:** BA, Colorado State University, 1975; JD, Denver College of the Law, 1978.

### VAN WESTRUM, Anthony
Anthony van Westrum LLC, Denver
303 295 1515
*Recommended in Corporate/M&A*

### WALSH, Christopher J
Hogan & Hartson LLP, Denver
303 454 2480
cjwalsh@hhlaw.com
*Recommended in Corporate/M&A*
**Practice Areas:** Practice focuses on mergers and acquisitions, public offerings and private placements of equity and debt securities, leveraged buyouts, tender offers, proxy contests and joint ventures. He also counsels public and private companies in all aspects of their business, including compliance and reporting obligations under the federal securities

laws and corporate governance matters.
**Prof. Memberships:** Member, Colorado Bar Association.
**Career:** Joined firm after nine years of practice, including as in-house counsel for a Nasdaq listed company and a privately held technology company.
**Personal:** JD, University of Wyoming (1991); BS, University of Wyoming (1988).

### WALSH, John F
Hill & Robbins PC, Denver
303 296 8100
johnwalsh@hillandrobbins.com
*Recommended in Litigation*
**Practice Areas:** Complex commercial litigation; securities litigation; antitrust litigation; class action litigation; white collar criminal defense and internal investigations
**Prof. Memberships:** American Bar Association; ABA White Collar Crime Subcommittee; Colorado Bar Association; Denver Bar Association; US-Mexico Law Institute.
**Career:** Stanford Law School, Order of the Coif, Law Review (1986). Law clerk, Hon J Skelly Wright, US Court of Appeals, DC Circuit (1986-87). Assistant US Attorney, Los Angeles, California (1987-95). Chief, Major Frauds Section (1993-95), Holland & Hart, LLP, Denver, Colorado (1995-99). Partner (1998-99) Hill & Robbins, PC, Denver, Colorado. Member (1999-present).
**Publications:** 'Practical Considerations in Federal Grand Jury Practice' (chapter, in 'Federal Criminal Practice') ABA 1994.
**Personal:** Commissioner, Denver Public Safety Review Commission. Co-Chair of Board, Invest in Kids, Inc. CBS News legal commentator, Oklahoma City Bombing Trials (1996-99). John speaks Spanish.

### WEESE, Charles W
Faegre & Benson LLP, Denver
303 607 3663
CWeese@faegre.com
*Recommended in Employment*
**Practice Areas:** Labor and employment law.
**Career:** Chuck is a member of the firm's Labor and Employment Law Group and, since 1992, has defended national and regional employers on a broad range of employment and labor issues. Chuck has represented employers before virtually every federal and state agency, and has handled trials and appeals in federal and state courts.
**Personal:** BA, Rice University; JD, Boston University, Law Review (Executive Editor), magna cum laude.

### WESTOVER, Michael
Otten, Johnson, Robinson, Neff + Ragonetti, PC, Denver
303 575 7514
mwestover@ottenjohnson.com
*Recommended in Real Estate*
**Practice Areas:** Real estate; real estate finance.
**Prof. Memberships:** American, Colorado, Denver Bar Associations.
**Career:** Mike represents owners, developers and lenders in a variety of transactions throughout the United States. Among other clients, he is counsel to one of the country's largest developers of apartment communities, representing this client in all aspects of its acquisition, development, financing and disposition activities. In addition to his work with owners and developers, Mike has been counsel for numerous real estate lending institutions in complicated commercial real estate financings.
**Personal:** JD, Harvard Law School (1982); cum laude; BS, Brigham Young University (1979); high honors.

### WHEELER, Francis
Cooley Godward LLP, Broomfield
720 566 4000
*Recommended in Corporate/M&A*

### WHEELER, Malcolm
Wheeler Trigg Kennedy LLP, Denver
303 292 2525
*Recommended in Litigation, Products Liability*

### WRIGHT, Douglas R
Faegre & Benson LLP, Denver
303 607 3671
dwright@faegre.com
*Recommended in Corporate/M&A*
**Practice Areas:** Corporate counseling; corporate finance and securities; entrepreneurial and emerging companies; initial public offerings; mergers and acquisitions; private debt and equity financings; venture capital financing; distribution agreements; proxy contests; securities regulation.
**Career:** Representation of several public companies in merger and acquisition and financing transactions, including IPOs and 144A transactions. Negotiation of over $1.5 billion in private equity investments for a state public employees retirement fund. Corporate and securities counseling for a major Denver-based airline.
**Personal:** BA, Hamilton College; JD, Cornell Law School, Law Review (Research Editor).

### ZISSER, David
Isaacson Rosenbaum PC, Denver
303 292 5656
*Recommended in Litigation*

# BROWNSTEIN HYATT & FARBER

## THE FIRM

**Founding Shareholders:** Norman Brownstein
Steven W Farber
Jack A Hyatt (retired)
**Managing Shareholder:** Bruce A James

**Number of shareholders:** 62
**Number of other attorneys:** 61
**Number of policy advisors:** 13

**FIRM OVERVIEW:** Founded in the late 1960s, Brownstein Hyatt & Farber has a national client base, four offices, 136 attorneys and policy advisors, and more than 20 practice and industry groups. The firm is committed to providing top-quality legal counsel that is cost-effective, accessible, and comprehensive. Operating in partnership with their clients, they strive to be a seamless extension of in-house resources, linked by constant interaction and an infrastructure that allows them to bring resources to bear on the full range of business and legal issues.

## MAIN AREAS OF PRACTICE:

**Corporate & Securities:** Brownstein Hyatt & Farber's senior attorneys regularly handle sophisticated finance and securities transactions for companies across the United States. They focus on matters related to mergers and acquisitions, emerging business and technology, corporate finance, public and private transactions, and general corporate representation.

**Real Estate:** With the largest Real Estate Practice in the Rocky Mountain region, the firm handles all aspects of real estate law including leasing, acquisition, development, disposition, water and mineral rights, finance, lending, taxation, public/private partnerships, municipal financing, zoning, and land use.

**Litigation:** Representing clients in virtually every industry, Brownstein Hyatt & Farber employs an integrated and cost-effective approach to each case. If the courtroom is the only alternative, the firm's senior litigators draw upon a wealth of trial experience that includes hundreds of jury trials and other major adversarial proceedings.

**Employment Law:** Focusing on employment-related issues impacting businesses of all sizes, the firm's employment lawyers handle disputes related to age, gender, sexual orientation, religion, race, and national origin.

**Government Relations:** Comprised of lawyers and policy advisors, the group helps companies, associations, and organizations interpret and integrate federal, state, and local government actions, solve challenges and seize opportunities through interaction with legislative and executive branch officials and private institutions.

**Environment & Natural Resources:** The firm works closely with corporate clients to create well planned, carefully executed, and proactive environmental strategies. Firm believers in prevention, Brownstein Hyatt & Farber's team of seasoned attorneys perform environmental due diligence and audits. When problems arise, they have the knowledge, know-how, and relationships to help mitigate environmental risk.

**Banking & Finance:** The firm offers clients comprehensive banking and commercial finance counsel, providing guidance in an array of secured and unsecured loans and credit facilities. Representing leading financial institutions and corporate borrowers, the group has closed more than $4 billion in loans in 40 states in the past five years.

**Public Finance:** The firm has a multi-faceted finance practice encompassing bond transactions for state and local governments and governmental authorities. They are well-equipped to assist any participant in a municipal bond transaction.

## HEAD OFFICE

### COLORADO
410 Seventeenth Street, Twenty-Second Floor, **Denver,** CO 80202-4437
**Tel:** 303 223 1100  **Fax:** 303 223 1111

## BRANCH OFFICES

### DISTRICT OF COLUMBIA
1350 I Street, N.W., Suite 510, **Washington, DC**, 20005-3344
**Tel:** 202 296 7353  **Fax:** 202 296 7009

### NEW MEXICO
201 Third Street N.W., Suite 1700, **Albuquerque**, NM 87102
**Tel:** 505 244 0770  **Fax:** 505 244 9266

### COLORADO
PO Box 357, 888 Colorado Ave., Suite 306, **Glenwood Springs**, CO 81602-0375
**Tel:** 970 945 5302  **Fax:** 970 384 2360

**Additional Practice Areas:** Bankruptcy and restructuring; corporate finance; employee benefits/ERISA; energy law; engineering and construction; family law; housing finance; intellectual property and technology; land use; litigation; mergers and acquisitions; regulatory and administrative law.

**CLIENTS:** AIG SunAmerica, Inc., City of Albuquerque, New Mexico, Comcast Corporation, Credit Suisse First Boston, Idaho Power Company, KeyBank, National Cable Television Association, Qwest, Lennar Homes, Shea Homes, Trammell Crow Company, US Bank.

**Brownstein | Hyatt | Farber**

# HOLLAND & HART LLP

## THE FIRM

**Managing Partner:** Edward H Flitton III
**Senior Partner:** Paul D Phillips (Chair, Management Committee)

**Number of partners:** 152
**Number of other lawyers:** 180

**Email:** info@hollandhart.com
**Website:** www.hollandhart.com

**FIRM OVERVIEW:** Since its inception in 1947, Holland & Hart has grown to more than 300 lawyers in 12 offices in Colorado, Wyoming, Idaho, Montana, New Mexico, Utah, and the District of Columbia. The firm offers a full range of integrated legal solutions to companies of all sizes, from emerging businesses to Fortune 500 corporations located throughout the country and internationally. The firm is focused on the issues facing clients who have business interests in the Mountain West. Holland & Hart is the only law firm based in the Rocky Mountain Region to make a leading American legal publication's list of the top 200 firms in the United States.

**MAIN AREAS OF PRACTICE:** The firm handles appellate; bankruptcy; broadband transactions; business transactions and litigation; construction and real estate transactions and litigation; corporate finance; credit finance and lending; emerging growth and venture capital; employee benefits; energy; environment and resources; intellectual property protection and litigation; international; labor and employment; mining; oil and gas; project development and finance; taxes and estates; technology transfer; torts and insurance; water.

**CLIENTS:** Holland & Hart represents business entities of all sizes, including more than 100 of the Fortune 500 companies. Holland & Hart serves clients in a wide variety of industries, including aerospace, agriculture, airlines, biotechnology, construction, energy, financial, healthcare, hospitality, manufacturing, mining, oil and gas, real estate, resorts and recreation, retail, services, technology, telecommunications and broadband, and water rights and quality, among others.

**INTERNATIONAL WORK:** The firm has been involved in a broad range of transactions in most Latin American, Pacific Rim and European countries. These transactions have included mergers, project finance transactions, venture capital investments, mezzanine financings, telecommunications (including telephony, internet services and cable television), power generation and distribution projects, private placements, license or concession acquisitions, privatizations, environmental matters and capital markets transactions.

## HEAD OFFICE

### COLORADO
Suite 3200, 555 Seventeenth Street, **Denver**, CO 80202
**Tel:** 303 295 8000  **Fax:** 303 295 8261

## BRANCH OFFICES

### COLORADO
Suite 104, 600 East Main Street, **Aspen**, CO 81611
**Tel:** 970 925 3476  **Fax:** 970 925 9367

Suite 300, One Boulder Plaza, 1800 Broadway, **Boulder**, CO 80302
**Tel:** 303 473 2700  **Fax:** 303 473 2720

Suite 1000, 90 South Cascade Avenue, **Colorado Springs**, CO 80903
**Tel:** 719 475 7730  **Fax:** 719 634 2461

Suite 400, 8390 East Crescent Parkway, **Greenwood Village**, CO 80111
**Tel:** 303 290 1600  **Fax:** 303 290 1606

### DISTRICT OF COLUMBIA
Suite 550, 1200 G Street, NW, **Washington**, DC 20005
**Tel:** 202 347 9272  **Fax:** 202 347 1684

### IDAHO
Suite 1400, 101 South Capitol Blvd, **Boise**, ID 83702
**Tel:** 208 342 5000  **Fax:** 208 343 8869

### MONTANA
Suite 1500, 401 North 31st Street, **Billings**, MT 59101
**Tel:** 406 252 2166  **Fax:** 406 252 1669

### NEW MEXICO
Suite 1, 110 North Guadalupe, **Santa Fe**, NM 87504
**Tel:** 505 988 4421  **Fax:** 505 983 6043

### UTAH
Suite 2000, 60 East South Temple, **Salt Lake City**, UT 84111
**Tel:** 801 595 7800  **Fax:** 801 364 9124

### WYOMING
Suite 450, 2515 Warren Avenue, **Cheyenne**, WY 82001
**Tel:** 307 778 4200  **Fax:** 307 778 8175

Suite 200, 25 South Willow Street, Box 68 **Jackson Hole**, WY 83001
**Tel:** 307 739 9741  **Fax:** 307 739 9744

## CONTACTS

| | |
|---|---|
| **Appellate** | Marcy Glenn |
| **Bankruptcy** | Risa Wolf-Smith |
| **Broadband Transactions** | Stephen Villano |
| **Business Transactions** | Brad Wiskirchen |
| **Coal** | Patrick Day |
| **Commercial Litigation** | Christopher Toll |
| **Construction & Real Estate Litigation** | Daniel Frost |
| **Emerging Growth & Venture Capital** | Betty Arkell |
| **Employee Benefits** | Jane Francis |
| **Energy** | Robert Pomeroy |
| **Environment & Resources** | Bradford Berge |
| **Financial** | Robert Faucher |
| **Indian Law** | Jennifer Harvey |
| **Intellectual Property Litigation** | Donald Degnan |
| **Intellectual Property Protection** | Scott Havlick |
| **International** | Kevin Johnson |
| **Labor & Employment** | Brian Mumaugh |
| **Mining** | Michael Feldewert |
| **Oil & Gas** | Donald Schultz |
| **Project Development & Finance** | Mark Safty |
| **Real Estate Transactions** | Rebecca Dow |
| **Securities** | Mark Levy |
| **Taxes & Estates** | John Maxfield |
| **Technology Transfer** | Kevin Crandell |
| **Product Insurance & Tort Defense** | Joe Teig |
| **Water** | Christopher Thorne |

# HOLME ROBERTS & OWEN LLP

## THE FIRM

**Managing Directors:** Kenneth W Lund, Robert H Bach

**Number of Directors:** 108
**Number of other lawyers:** 111

**FIRM OVERVIEW:** Holme Roberts & Owen LLP (HRO) is an international law firm with more than 200 lawyers and eight offices in Denver, Boulder, Colorado Springs, Salt Lake City, San Francisco, Los Angeles, London and Munich with a focus on corporate law and securities and litigation. The firm also has a variety of support practices that include antitrust, banking, constitutional law, employee benefits, intellectual property, international business transactions, emerging growth, employment, environmental, mergers and acquisitions, real estate, products liability, sports and entertainment and tax.

## MAIN AREAS OF PRACTICE:

**Commercial Law & Securities:** Approximately 75 lawyers spend all or a substantial amount of their time on sophisticated corporate deals both nationally and internationally. HRO participates in the general representation of corporations, partnerships and other business entities, large and small. This practice includes general business planning, mergers and acquisitions, tender offers, joint ventures, public and private securities offerings, venture capital and traditional finance, franchising and corporate reorganizations, bankruptcy and liquidation proceedings.

**Litigation:** HRO has more than 75 lawyers in its litigation practice which includes former federal and state prosecutors, former Justice Department attorneys and a former member of the United States Solicitor General's office, who have tried cases and have appeared in all of Colorado's state and federal courts and in numerous other courts and tribunals across the United States, including the United States Supreme Court. These cases have covered virtually all areas of civil and criminal litigation, including antitrust, bankruptcy, business torts, securities fraud, shareholder rights, contracts, insurance coverage, intellectual property, products liability, personal injury, professional malpractice, federal criminal defense and civil and criminal appeals. HRO's general litigators have also represented firm clients in a wide range of arbitrations and administrative proceedings, and they have participated in all forms of formal and informal alternative dispute resolution.

**CLIENTS:** Coors Brewing Company, Johns Manville, Lockheed Martin, Questar, Qwest, Rolex, Skyy Vodka, UnitedGlobalCom, Union Pacific Railroad, Vail Resorts and Wells Fargo.

**INTERNATIONAL WORK:** HRO's international practice serves a substantial number of US-based and foreign clients with multi-national interests. With offices in London and Munich, the firm is involved in substantial international transactions. The group assists clients with international contracts, acquisitions, mergers and financing of foreign companies, international tax, financing and investments, technology transfer issues, export licensing and international dispute resolution.

## HEAD OFFICE

**COLORADO**
1700 Lincoln Street, Suite 4100, **Denver**, CO 80203-4541
**Tel:** 303 861 7000   **Fax:** 303 866 0200
**Email:** information@hro.com
**Website:** www.hro.com

## BRANCH OFFICES

**COLORADO**
1801 13th Street, Third Floor, **Boulder**, CO 80302
**Tel:** 303 444 5955   **Fax:** 303 444 1063

90 South Cascade Avenue, Suite 1300, **Colorado Springs,** CO 80903-1615
**Tel:** 719 473 3800   **Fax:** 719 633 1518

**CALIFORNIA**
560 Mission Street, 25th Floor, **San Fransisco**, 94105-2994
**Tel:** 415 268 2000   **Fax:** 415 268 1999

777 South Figueroa, Suite 2800, **Los Angeles**, CA 90017
**Tel:** 213 892 4925   **Fax:** 213 892 4942

**UTAH**
299 South Main Street, Suite 1800, **Salt Lake City**, UT 84111-2263
**Tel:** 213 572 4300   **Fax:** 213 572 4400

## INTERNATIONAL OFFICES

The firm also has offices in London and Munich.

## CONTACTS

**Corporate Law & Securities**.............................Charles D Maguire Jr
**Litigation** ................................................................David S Steefel

Holme Roberts & Owen LLP
*Attorneys at Law*

# OTTEN JOHNSON

## THE FIRM

**Managing Shareholder:** Michael Westover
**Founding Shareholders:** Frank L Robinson, William R Neff,
Thomas J Ragonetti, Bruce B Johnson (deceased).

**Number of Shareholders:** 30
**Number of Other Lawyers:** 19

**FIRM OVERVIEW:** Otten Johnson's inception in January 1985 was guided by a single, formative principle: effective partnership between client and counsel. Guided by that principle, they've built a firm recognized for its commitment, inventiveness and practicality. The result: a synergy between every client's goals and the firm's commitment to realizing them. The firm's desire to serve the full range of their clients' needs has led them to establish practice specialties in land use, real estate, finance, litigation, corporate, securities and tax, bankruptcy and insolvency, and labor and employment law. Due to a rapidly expanding client base, the firm has grown quickly, yet careful attention has guided their growth in a way that empowers each client while preserving the firm structure and values that have been important to them from the start. Otten Johnson strives to make every client's experience remarkable. For over 20 years, they have done just that. With great optimism and with a continuing commitment to unparalleled client service, they are eager to continue that tradition.

## MAIN AREAS OF PRACTICE:

**Real Estate:** Otten, Johnson, Robinson, Neff & Ragonetti, P.C. provides legal services to the real estate industry at the local, national and international levels. Their clients include developers, builders, investors, operators, managers, brokers and title insurers of single and multi-family residential projects, office buildings, retail shopping centers and other commercial projects, and resort properties. The firm has represented these clients in all phases of their business from acquisition through development approvals, environmental regulation review and compliance, financing, title insurance matters and construction and development to leasing and disposition. They also have served as lessee's counsel in numerous leasing transactions (including leveraged leases) involving commercial real estate facilities. Additionally, the firm advises its real estate clients on a wide variety of sophisticated federal, state and local tax matters, including entity selection and formation, operational tax matters, partnership taxation, nonprofit taxation, property tax assessment protests and appeals and 1031 exchanges.

**Land Use/Government & Condemnation:** The firm provides a full range of services to a variety of clients in routine and complex land use and urban development approvals, transactions, issues and litigation. The firm handles zoning, subdivision, annexation and related approval matters, both on a standalone basis and as part of their ongoing real estate representation. They frequently provide representation in complex and leading-edge land use and urban development matters, such as largescale, long-term planned developments, historic preservation projects, development agreements and vested rights arrangements, complex annexation agreements, initiative and referendum elections, public highway and interchange issues, urban renewal projects, special district and other public financing and subsidy arrangements and public-private partnerships and transactions. They also represent clients in complex litigation in the areas of regulatory takings, governmental authority, unauthorized or excessive fees and taxes and the constitutional rights of private property owners. The firm has a well-developed practice in representing property owners facing condemnation as part of a public project.

**Corporate:** The firm represents numerous large and small corporations, partnerships and other business entities in the areas of general corporate, securities and business law. Their services to these clients include providing counsel and representation in debt and equity financings, mergers and acquisitions, venture capital, private placement securities transactions, syndications, formation and

restructuring, antitrust, employment contracts, employee benefit plans, product distribution arrangements and franchising, technology issues, including computer law and telecommunications regulation, licensing, trademark and copyright registration and licensing, gaming and tax planning. The firm also provides pro bono counsel to various charitable organizations.

**Litigation:** The firm handles a broad range of complex commercial litigation. Their litigation lawyers, who have substantial trial experience in the federal, state and bankruptcy courts, have represented clients in contract disputes, employment, energy, product liability, creditors' rights, lender liability, securities, environmental, environmental insurance coverage, antitrust, trade secrets, copyrights, trademarks and unfair competition, real estate title issues, construction and mechanic's lien claims and commercial landlord/tenant disputes.

**Employment:** The firm represents employers in all labor and employment matters, including those involving issues of wrongful discharge; employment discrimination and harassment, wages and hours; employment contracts (including covenants not to compete, trade secrets, compensation and related issues); hiring and termination procedures; plant closings and reductions in force, traditional labor (including representation in unfair labor practice and representation proceedings before the National Labor Relations Board, responding to union organizational campaigns, collective bargaining negotiations and administration, arbitration, strikes, picketing and boycotts); occupational safety and health; and other employment issues. The group represents clients in litigation in federal and state courts, state and federal administrative agencies, and mediation and arbitration, in all parts of the United States. The group is also heavily involved in helping clients to avoid litigation or if litigation cannot be avoided, to maximize the chances of success, by advising clients in situations which might lead to litigation, in developing employment policies and procedures, and in training client managers and supervisors on labor and employment issues.

**CLIENTS:** The firm represents a diverse clientele of local, national and international entities and individuals operating in a wide array of industries, including banking; construction; financial services; insurance; investment banking; manufacturing; mortgage; private equity and venture capital; real estate; resort development; telecommunications and transportation, among others.

## HEAD OFFICE

950 Seventeenth Street, Suite 1600, **Denver**, Colorado 80202
**Tel:** 303-825-8400  **Fax:** 303-825-6525
**Website:** www.ottenjohnson.com

## BRANCH OFFICES

420 East Main Street, Suite 210, **Aspen**, Colorado 81611
**Tel:** 970-544-4637  **Fax:** 970-544-4632

## CONTACTS

| | |
|---|---|
| **Real Estate** | Mark F Copertino |
| **Land Use/Government & Condemnation** | Thomas J Ragonetti |
| **Corporate** | Douglas J Becker |
| **Litigation** | Brad W Schacht |
| **Labor & Employment** | Darin L Mackender |

# OTTENJOHNSON
## ROBINSON NEFF + RAGONETTI PC

# ROTHGERBER JOHNSON & LYONS LLP

## THE FIRM:

**Managing Partner:** Michael D Nosler

**Number of partners:** 45
**Number of attorneys:** 70

**FIRM OVERVIEW:** Founded in 1903, Rothgerber Johnson & Lyons LLP is Colorado's oldest continuously operating legal partnership and is among the state's ten largest law firms. The firm has a diversified litigation and commercial practice, with expertise in the major areas of the law, and including agricultural, construction, election and campaign finance, intellectual property, natural resources and energy, public law and religious institutions. The firm is uniquely qualified to provide the highest quality professional legal services to a growing roster of corporate clients across the Rocky Mountain region.

## MAIN AREAS OF PRACTICE:

**Litigation:** RJ&L's litigation attorneys are recognized as among the most prominent in the region, with experience in all areas of federal, state and administrative litigation, involving real estate, complex corporate disputes, securities law, labor and employment, tort and products liability, breach of contract, class actions, multi-district litigation, environmental, governmental, bankruptcy, financial institutions, collections and general commercial disputes.

**Transactional:** The firm's transactional lawyers understand the art of the deal and are experienced in business and commercial financing with the primary goal to facilitate the successful completion of transactions. They have substantial experience in the acquisition of a variety of businesses and represent both domestic and international clients in stock and asset purchases, technology and intellectual property transfers, joint ventures, tender offers and statutory mergers.

**Labor & Employment:** RJ&L's labor and employment attorneys counsel businesses on personnel, wage and benefit and union issues. They represent clients before all administrative agencies and courts, defend against claims of discrimination, sexual harassment, wrongful discharge, defamation and breach of contract, and frequently represent management in labor law matters, including union organizing, collective bargaining and arbitrations. The firm has several employee benefits specialists to assist clients in designing benefits programs and executive compensation programs.

**Financial Institutions:** The firm has maintained its national reputation in banking law, which encompasses virtually every legal discipline used by banks, savings and loans and others in the financial arena, including regulatory, financing, acquisitions, securities, taxation, labor and employment, real estate and litigation.

**Insurance:** The firm has built a national insurance practice, serving various states' life and health insurance guaranty associations and practices. The firm has also been involved with the sale of insurance companies and the assumption and reinsurance of blocks of insurance business.

**Religious Institutions:** For more than 20 years, the firm has served as general counsel for the Archdiocese of Denver and has built a unique national practice assisting churches, parachurches and faith-based organizations with everything from organizational structuring to employment matters to First Amendment rights.

**Securities:** RJ&L offers legal services to broker-dealers, investment bankers, investment advisers and investment companies in all aspects of securities business, from operational advice to employment to complex litigation, arbitration and regulatory proceedings.

**Real Estate:** RJ&L has a thriving real estate practice assisting clients with acquisitions, planning, development, operation, leasing, and sales of real property. The firm proudly represents the Colorado Association of REALTORS®, the Wyoming Association of REALTORS® and many of the region's leading developers and builders.

## HEAD OFFICE

### COLORADO
One Tabor Center, Suite 3000, 1200 Seventeenth Street, **Denver**, CO 80202-5855
**Tel:** 303 623 9000   **Fax:** 303 623 9222

## BRANCH OFFICES

### COLORADO
Wells Fargo Bank Tower, 90 South Cascade Avenue, Suite 1100, **Colorado Springs**, CO 80903-1662
**Tel:** 719 386 3000   **Fax:** 719 386 3070

### WYOMING
123 West First Street, Suite 200, **Casper**, WY 82601-2480
**Tel:** 307 232 0222   **Fax:** 307 232 0077

**INTERNATIONAL WORK:** The firm frequently offers legal services to foreign companies and investors dealing in the Rocky Mountain region and US companies conducting business outside of the United States. RJ&L attorneys have tried cases involving international business issues, handled international arbitrations and mediations, structured foreign joint ventures and negotiated numerous international contracts. They also have established valuable international business relationships, representing companies from or engaged in business in Japan, the United Kingdom, Germany, the Netherlands, Switzerland, Australia, China, Taiwan, Canada, Mexico, and other countries in the European Community and South America.

**CLIENTS:** RJ&L's vast roster of corporate clients includes ABM Industries, Alpine Partners, FirstBank Holding Company, Triple Peaks and Qwest.

ROTHGERBER
JOHNSON &
LYONS LLP
ATTORNEYS AT LAW

# SHERMAN & HOWARD L.L.C

## THE FIRM

**Managing Partner:** R Michael Sanchez
**Number of partners:** 112
**Number of lawyers:** 41

**FIRM OVERVIEW:** Sherman & Howard was founded in 1892 by James H Pershing, a young lawyer from Pittsburgh. As Denver's oldest law firm, it has watched the region grow in population and in its economic base. Today, the firm continues a long tradition of providing quality legal services to its clients and a commitment to professional excellence.

## AREAS OF PRACTICE:

| | |
|---|---|
| Business & Real Estate | 25% |
| Labor & Employment | 19% |
| Litigation | 30% |
| Public Finance | 14% |
| Tax & Probate | 12% |

## MAIN AREAS OF PRACTICE:

**Business & Real Estate:** General and specialized counsel in business, commercial and financial transactions. Concentrated experience in banking, commercial transactions, corporations, limited liability companies and partnerships, government contracts, healthcare, immigration, intellectual property, international business, joint ventures and securities. Clients include financial institutions and companies in various industries, including telecommunications, healthcare delivery, manufacturing, financial services, food service, electronics, construction, transportation, agribusiness, publishing, oil, gas and mineral exploration, and institutional and individual investors. Real estate attorneys represent a broad spectrum of clients in every facet of the real estate industry. The firm represents lenders, investors, brokers and others who are involved in every type of real estate from blocks of downtown skyscrapers to mountain resorts, from farms and ranches to shopping centers, from leasing office space to developing special use facilities. Special expertise in foreclosures, workouts, receiverships and refinancings, and work regularly with other Sherman & Howard attorneys in bankruptcy, environmental and litigation areas, providing a full range of services to its clients.

**Labor & Employment:** Providing representation exclusively to employers, the firm's labor and employment attorneys have the specific expertise and practical know-how to plan legal strategies that minimize employment disputes and to respond effectively when such disputes occur. The size and scope of the practice enables the firm to respond quickly and expertly to the clients' personnel issues even when the lawyer with the primary client relationship is in court or a deposition.

**Litigation:** The litigation attorneys at Sherman & Howard defend and prosecute lawsuits in state and federal courts throughout the nation and represent clients in arbitrations, mediations and other forms of alternative dispute resolution. The attorneys are highly experienced in the litigation of highly complex, multi-million dollar disputes involving contract issues of all varieties; securities; real estate; antitrust; unfair trade practices and other business torts; lender liability; products liability; ERISA; corporate governance and shareholder rights; the entire range of issues involving the production, transportation, distribution and marketing of oil and gas products; fraud; intellectual property; personal injury; professional malpractice; insurance coverage; construction; environmental and other matters. The firm has also defended complex class actions in a variety of substantive areas, including securities, antitrust, retail sales, telecommunications, ERISA, wireless services, oil and gas production, distribution and marketing and products liability.

**Public Finance:** Sherman & Howard L.L.C. has been a leader in public finance in the Rocky Mountain West for over a century. Since industry rankings became available in the early 1990's, the firm has consistently been ranked each year as a top bond counsel firm in Colorado and Nevada (ranked by dollar volume, number of transactions, or both), and as one of the top firms in New Mexico. The firm's public finance lawyers practice out of offices in Denver and Colorado Springs, Colorado, and Las Vegas and Reno, Nevada.

## HEAD OFFICE

**COLORADO**
633 Seventeenth Street, Suite 3000, **Denver**, CO 80202-3624
**Tel:** 303 297 2900   **Fax:** 303 298 0940
**Website:** www.shermanhoward.com

## BRANCH OFFICES

**ARIZONA**
1850 North Central Avenue, Suite 500, **Phoenix**, AZ 85004
**Tel:** 602 636 2000   **Fax:** 602 234 7979

**COLORADO**
90 South Cascade Avenue, Ste 1500, **Colorado Springs**, CO 80903-4015
**Tel:** 719 475 2440   **Fax:** 719 635 4576

**NEVADA**
317 South 6th Street, **Las Vegas**, NV 89101
**Tel:** 702 387 6073   **Fax:** 702 382 9370

50 West Liberty Street, Suite 1000, **Reno**, NV 89501
**Tel:** 775 323 1980   **Fax:** 775 323 2339

## CONTACTS

| | |
|---|---|
| Business & Real Estate | Gregory J Ramos |
| Labor & Employment | Theodore A Olsen |
| Litigation | Lawrence W Treece |
| Public Finance | Peter J Whitmore |
| Tax & Probate | Kathleen A Odlee |
| Phoenix, AZ | Raymond M Deeny |
| Colorado Springs | Raymond M Deeny |
| Las Vegas, NV | John O Swendseid |
| Reno, NV | John O Swendseid |

**Tax & Probate:** The firm's tax and probate lawyers have the expertise to assist Sherman & Howard's clients in; simple and complex estate planning; probate and estate administration; trust administration; choice of entity and related advice; corporation; S Corporation; limited liability company and partnership taxation; business planning; qualified plan advice and compliance; executive compensation; employee benefits advice (including HIPAA and COBRA); ESOPs; international taxation; natural resource taxation; tax exempt organizations ; and representation before the Tax Court and Federal, State and Local Taxing Agencies. For more information visit: www.interlaw.org

**INTERNATIONAL WORK:** Sherman & Howard is a member of Interlaw, one of the most well established international associations of law firms in the world. With 60 member firms in over 110 business centers globally, Interlaw provides access to more than 4100 lawyers globally.

**CLIENTS:** Sherman & Howard provides general representation to clients ranging from individuals and small businesses to very large corporations. Sherman & Howard also provides specialized counsel to in-house Legal Departments and to other law firms that have requirements for its special expertise. The firm's clients include: Apotex Corp., Arcadis G&M, Inc., Avaya Inc., Ball Corp., Charter Communications, Inc., CH2M Hill, Inc., Clark County, Nevada, CoBIZ Inc., Colorado Housing & Finance Authority, Deloitte & Touche LLP, East West Partnership, Eastman Kodak Company, Exxon Mobil Corporation, County of Los Alamos, New Mexico, J. R. Engineering , Kaiser-Hill Company, L.L.C., Kennecott Utah Copper Corp., Liberty Global, Inc., Liberty Media Corporation, Lowry Economic Redevelopment Authority, Metro Wastewater Reclamation District, Newmont Mining Corp., Qwest Communications International, Inc., Regional Transportation District, SEATAC Fuel Facilities LLC, State of Nevada, Target Stores, Inc., Ticketmaster Corp, University of Nevada.

## How lawyers are ranked

Every year we carry out thousands of in-depth interviews with clients and lawyers in order to assess the reputations and expertise of business lawyers across the USA. Chambers rankings and editorial are referred to extensively by General Counsel and other purchasers of legal services who look to our recommendations when choosing their lawyers.

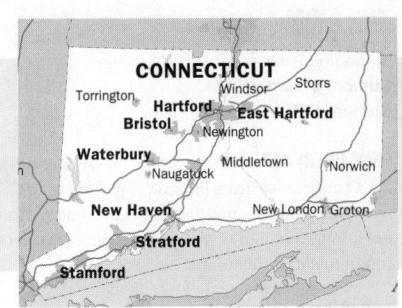

# CORPORATE/M&A

| Corporate/M&A |
|---|
| **Leading Firms** |
| 1 FINN DIXON & HERLING LLP *Stamford* |
| 2 DAY, BERRY & HOWARD LLP *Hartford* |
|   EDWARDS ANGELL PALMER & DODGE *Hartford* |
|   PAUL, HASTINGS, JANOFSKY & WALKER *Stamford* |
|   SHIPMAN & GOODWIN LLP *Hartford* |
|   WIGGIN AND DANA LLP *New Haven* |
| 3 MURTHA CULLINA LLP *Hartford* |
|   ROBINSON & COLE LLP *Hartford* |

| Leading Individuals |
|---|
| 1 FINN III Harold *Finn Dixon & Herling LLP* |
|   LOTSTEIN James *Edwards Angell Palmer & Dodge* |
| 2 ALBIN David *Finn Dixon & Herling LLP* |
|   DIXON Brett *Finn Dixon & Herling LLP* |
|   DOWNEY III Charles *Finn Dixon & Herling LLP* |
|   HAWKINS John *Paul, Hastings, Janofsky & Walker* |
|   HERLING Michael *Finn Dixon & Herling LLP* |
|   MARCO Frank *Wiggin and Dana LLP* |
|   PINNEY JR Willard *Murtha Cullina LLP* |
|   SWERDLOFF David *Day, Berry & Howard LLP* |

## Band 1

### Finn Dixon & Herling LLP

See firm details p.387

**The Firm:** Yet again this *"stellar firm"* monopolizes the top tier of the table. *Chambers'* research indicates that neither clients nor competitors disagree with this assessment; indeed, rivals envy the firm's *"excellent client base which is obviously reflective of their enormous capabilities."* Relatively small in size, this is a corporate boutique practice handling high-value, complex deals with regularity. It has been able to recruit top-notch lawyers and offers clients a winning combination of expertise and experience. The volume of work undertaken means there are few occasions when lawyers are on unfamiliar territory. As ever, the emphasis is on offering clients a highly personalized service rather than the expansion of the firm. In the Connecticut legal market, at least, small still is beautiful.

**The Lawyers:** The number of lawyers who appear in the table speaks volumes. At the top of the tree is *"the best known of the group,"* the *"excellent"* **Harold Finn** (see p.382), who is working on increasing numbers of hedged private equity transactions and related tax work. One of the highlights of the past year was leading a group of FDH attorneys who were selected to serve as corporate and tax counsel for Blyth, Inc in connection with the tax-free spin-off to the Blyth shareholders of Blyth's Wholesale Group. The Wholesale Group has about 3,200 employees and annual revenues of about $700 million. **David Albin**'s (see p.382) name is most often heard in the context of healthcare and specialist medical device manufacturing. He has led on some impressive work lately, including the recapitalization of a private equity-held healthcare service worth around $50 million. He additionally worked on the sale of a telecommunications business for $45 million, where both parties were public companies. **Brett Dixon** (see p.382) specializes in taxation advice and business structuring and was responsible for the tax aspects of the Blyth transaction. He has undertaken numerous hedge fund formations and nontraditional investments for hedge funds. **Charles Downey** (see p.382) was described to researchers as *"a particularly gifted lawyer"* capable of handling the full range of corporate work. **Michael Herling** (see p.383) has felt the benefit of a particularly buoyant market this year, seeing a marked increase in the number of private equity transactions, especially hedge fund and PIPE transactions.

**Clients/Work Highlights:** Clients include major multinationals, smaller midmarket companies and private equity funds. Representative clients include Halyard Capital; Oak Investment Partners; TSG Capital; Peak Medical and Citizens Communications.

## Band 2

### Day, Berry & Howard LLP

See firm details p.386

**The Firm:** Five of DBH's seven offices are in Connecticut, making it the state's largest law firm. Its transactional business law practice is comparatively small, but works side by side with sterling IP/technology, tax planning and litigation limbs. Handling a wide range of corporate work, lawyers are familiar with everything from M&A and securities to private equity and venture capital. Naturally there has been an increase in the provision of compliance advice in the wake of Sarbanes-Oxley. Clients report favorably on *"excellent advice and work product,"* one praising the firm's lawyers for *"their responsiveness, their integrity and their ability to understand my company's needs and objectives."* In the recently opened New Haven office, lawyers are attempting to penetrate the local market, acting for many closely held businesses in the process.

**The Lawyers:** Emerging from *Chambers'* research as a real favorite with clients is *"accomplished, excellent problem solver"* **David Swerdloff** (see p.385), who provides clients with *"sound, practical, sensible solutions."* Working from the Stamford office he chairs the firm's business law group.

**Clients/Work Highlights:** The firm represented management consulting services provider CTA in a variety of matters, the largest of which was its $60 million acquisition by Tejas, a public company that also owns investment banking and securities subsidiaries. In another deal, the firm helped Globix to double its size through a merger with NEON Communications. The holders of NEON stock, valued at some $140 million, received publicly registered shares of Globix stock, and NEON's preferred stockholders also received cash. Globix exchanged some of its outstanding indebtedness for Globix stock, allowing it to qualify for listing its shares.

### Edwards Angell Palmer & Dodge LLP

See firm details p.1112

**The Firm:** This East Coast firm has two offices in Connecticut: Hartford and Stamford. Sources agreed that the firm has *"an excellent reputation"* for providing legal counsel and transactional support, always demonstrating business savvy in its style of working. Lawyers take on everything from M&A to private equity, venture capital and corporate governance advisory work.

**The Lawyers:** *"Leader in the Connecticut corporate Bar,"* **James Lotstein** (see p.384) is *"highly regarded for his legal abilities and common-sense approach to the law."* Much of his time has been spent on middle-market M&A transactions lately, for example representing Truebro, a manufacturer of under-sink protection devices, to Watertite Products. Lotstein also advises larger Connecticut-based companies on corporate governance issues and, among his many professional activities, sits on the ABA's Committee on Corporate Laws.

**Clients/Work Highlights:** The firm represented American Community Newspapers on its $85 million sale to an investor group led by Spire Capital Partners and Wachovia Capital Partners. Other clients include Gerber Scientific; St. Paul Travelers; Brynwood Partners; Ascent Media Network Services; Best Friends Pet Care; Boon Edam Tomsed and Utrecht Art Supplies.

## Paul, Hastings, Janofsky & Walker LLP

See firm details p.339

**The Firm:** A new entrant to the tables this year is the Connecticut practice group of this international law firm with 17 offices worldwide (nine of which are in the USA). This group boasts eight partners who undertake a variety of corporate, securities, finance, projects and corporate governance work. M&A features large and for some lawyers there is a particular focus on asset acquisition in the energy and projects area. Others specialize in the healthcare and biotechnology fields.

**The Lawyers:** One name mentioned often to researchers is that of **John Hawkins** (see p.383), chair of the firm's project finance practice group. He handles a variety of projects matters, primarily involving energy facilities, but also including paper mills, refineries and other industrial facilities. A highlight from the past year was the sale of a 260 MW coal-fired power plant located in New Jersey, in which Hawkins represented the sellers, Delta Power and ArcLight Capital, in the disposal of their 40% interest for over $100 million.

**Clients/Work Highlights:** The firm has started working for AIG Highstar Capital, active private equity funds sponsored by AIG, and also counts among its clients Chrysler Capital; GE Energy; Union Bank of California; Ford Motor Credit and Delta Power.

## Shipman & Goodwin LLP

**The Firm:** The business law department at Shipman & Goodwin is felt to have had a good year. The market's perception of this four-office Connecticut firm is that of *"very solid lawyers with good business insight, who are doing some top-flight national work."* One recent major deal involved representing WellPoint (previously Anthem) in acquisitions in six states. The firm is organized into several specialist practice groups, among them the venture and intellectual property group and the healthcare group, where lawyers have significant experience of M&A and other transactions in the highly regulated sector of health insurance companies.

**The Lawyers:** The mergers, acquisitions and corporate transactions group is chaired by Marcus Wilkinson, and the venture and intellectual property group is chaired by Tom Flynn and Donna Brooks.

**Clients/Work Highlights:** Top deals this year include acting as counsel to Byram Healthcare Centers, a leading provider of in-home healthcare, on its acquisition of Choice Medical Supplies. The combined company will be one of the leading healthcare product suppliers in the USA, generating annual revenues in excess of $100 million. The firm also recently represented the largest dairy cooperative in New England, Agri-Mark, and an eight-year relationship with the Stamford-based IT advisory service provider Gartner ensures a steady supply of transactions.

## Wiggin and Dana LLP

**The Firm:** Sources consider Wiggin & Dana to be *"a fine local firm."* The Connecticut business practice is based in the firm's original New Haven office and is renowned for venture capital, emerging business, biotech and PIPE securities transactions. A vibrant market has increased the number of recapitalizations in which the team has engaged, as companies endeavor to free up capital. More specifically, it is in the fields of information technology, healthcare services, insurance products and telecommunications that it comes into its own. Undoubtedly, the arrival in 2004 of a team of lawyers from Mintz Levin had a major effect on the business practice. Now viewed as a leader in biotech sector transactions, the team has unparalleled ties to the venture capital market, with key partners having been involved in venture capital work from the outset. Also important are connections with key trade organizations that serve the technology industry and other local industries.

**The Lawyers:** **Frank Marco** (see p.384) heads the private equity and emerging companies limb of the business practice. He undertakes work for a healthy spread of businesses from small concerns to Fortune 500 companies. One highlight from the past year was the represention of CyVera (a leading developer of digital microbead technology) in a $17.5 million stock-for-stock merger with Illumina. Marco has a unique perspective, having worked in the venture capital sector for over 30 years, including spending six years as general counsel to GE Venture Capital. Clients described the service he offers as *"ideal"* and commended the subtlety of the support he provides as outside counsel during complex merger negotiations.

**Clients/Work Highlights:** The past year's venture capital and angel financing transactions have an aggregate transaction value in excess of $600 million. This includes representing Healthtrax, a private equity-funded national leader in preventive health-

care, in a leveraged recapitalization. The firm also advised e-Onehundred Group in connection with the sale of substantially all of its assets to Stellent.

Band 3

## Murtha Cullina LLP

**The Firm:** This five-office, full-service Massachusetts and Connecticut firm continues to earn positive feedback from the market. Though primarily a local practice, it does represent a number of out-of-state and international clients, including many from the manufacturing, hi-tech, defense, healthcare and hospitality sectors. As well as M&A and other business acquisitions and disposals, the firm advises securities, corporate governance, taxation and numerous other specialist areas. Murtha Cullina is a member firm of Lex Mundi.

**The Lawyers:** **Willard Pinney** is deemed by peers to be the star of the show. Pinney is the current vice chairman of the corporate department and chairs the department's M&A practice group. He has been working with developing companies, several of them technology-oriented, on issues such as financing and ownership structures.

**Clients/Work Highlights:** Work in the past year includes involvement in the acquisition of a domestic manufacturer of plastic sheeting for specialized applications; the acquisition of assets of two affiliated textile testing laboratories in the UK and Sri Lanka; the acquisition of a music distribution company; and the sale of a specialist insurance company. Among the clients are Kaman, Specialized Technology Resources and ACMAT.

## Robinson & Cole LLP

**The Firm:** Connecticut hosts three of the seven offices of this 160-year-old East Coast firm. Its northeastern corporate and M&A practice spans Boston, Hartford and New York City. The firm as a whole has one of the largest environmental practices in the USA. On the agenda are business acquisitions, joint ventures, and debt and equity financings for public and private companies. Lawyers assist on everything from venture capital for startups in the technology sector to transactions for multinational corporations. They also provide support in the areas of corporate governance, commercial agreements, taxation and environmental law, among other things.

**The Lawyers:** John Lynch and Larry Coassin cochair the firm's M&A practice group, working frequently in the firm's New York office.

**Clients/Work Highlights:** The firm's clientele includes many manufacturers plus companies in the aerospace and pharmaceuticals industries.

# EMPLOYMENT

# MAINLY DEFENDANT

## Band 1

### Day, Berry & Howard LLP

See firm details p.386

**The Firm:** For employment the state has a clear leader in Day, Berry & Howard. *"They are just so damn sharp,"* enthused one competitor. The firm eschews traditional labor law to concentrate its efforts on employment work, and this degree of specialization helps to mark it out from competitors. Its hugely experienced trial attorneys are said to be adept at predicting the likely outcome of a case, thus giving clients confidence that the appropriate method of resolution will be pursued. The employment team comes into its own when handling complex and multiplaintiff claims. Also undertaken are noncompete agreements and trade secrets as well as the standard range of discrimination cases. The overhaul of the FLSA this year has also led to a rise in the demand for advisory services.

**The Lawyers:** *"Tenacious and meticulous"* **Felix Springer** (see p.384) was portrayed as *"very, very thorough: he leaves no stone unturned. If you've got a problem, he will get to the bottom of it; you can be absolutely confident he will do a great job."* Meanwhile, *"masterful trial attorney"* **Albert Zakarian** (see p.385)

was dubbed *"the most prominent employment litigator in Connecticut."* Despite such accolades, one client confirmed they liked his *"low-key"* manner outside the courtroom, adding of this wise counsel: *"He's very smart and very able."* Younger partner **Daniel Schwartz** (see p.384) has *"a great work ethic and is very experienced."* Considered by one interviewee to be *"the number-one choice for discrimination matters,"* Schwartz also tackles complex, multiplaintiff litigation, enforceability of noncompete agreements and trade secrets. According to one client, *"he is like a chess player, knowing what move to make and when – that kind of talent is rare and he was able to win my case very quickly by playing all the right moves."*

**Clients/Work Highlights:** The firm obtained a preliminary injunction on behalf of a medical practice seeking to prevent a practitioner from soliciting employees away from the practice. In another matter the firm is representing an employer trying to recover several thousand dollars from a former employee whom it has accused of embezzlement.

## Band 2

### Murtha Cullina LLP

**The Firm:** *"This outstanding firm mobilizes its resources very quickly to deliver tremendous outcomes."* Such is the clients' verdict on this exclusively New England-based law firm. This practice sees a lot of noncompete and trade secret cases, and the conduct of one such case led a client to tell researchers: *"They couldn't have done any better: we needed an attorney who understood how important the case was to us and wouldn't be wishy-washy. They gave us the pros and cons and were fastidious."* On the employment law side, the firm notes greater reliance on alternative dispute resolution, while on the labor law side there has been an upturn in work, especially in manufacturing and service industries such as restaurants, hotels and healthcare.

**The Lawyers:** **Thomas Cloherty** gives *"a very high level of professional service and presents himself with great confidence and common sense."* He is said to be *"a natural trial attorney."* Clients trust him to be *"objective and dispassionate"* in his advice. *"Outstanding"* **Barry Waters** *"is able to grasp technical issues very quickly and delivers work that is intellectually sophisticated."* As a litigator he is praised for being *"simultaneously aggressive and smooth, with the goal always in sight."* Again, clients trust him to give clients an honest appraisal of their prospects.

**Clients/Work Highlights:** In one case before the NLRB, the firm represented an employer that had replaced half its workforce during the course of a strike. The NLRB issued a declaration that appropriate procedures had been followed, although an appeal has been filed. Clients of the firm include Tyco International; DuPont; Ninety Nine Restaurant and Pub; Comcast and UPS.

### Shipman & Goodwin LLP

**The Firm:** Operating from four offices in Connecticut, Shipman has a 25-strong employment and labor practice working for management in both the public and private sectors. In particular the firm has many clients in public education, municipal employment and state employment. The firm advises on union organizing, collective bargaining, grievance issues and labor arbitrations as well as the standard range of employment issues such as sex, age and race discrimination claims.

**The Lawyers:** **Brian Clemow** cochairs the labor and employee relations practice group. More than 30 years of experience working on a wide range of labor and employment matters have made him a *"very able"* adviser.

**Clients/Work Highlights:** Last year Clemow won a reversal in the Connecticut Supreme Court of a lower court decision setting aside an award issued by the Waterbury Financial Planning Assistance Board. Representing the City of Waterbury, Clemow helped to secure more than $2 million in annual savings under the City's collective bargaining agreement with the International Association of Firefighters, Local 1339.

### Wiggin and Dana LLP

**The Firm:** Founded in New Haven more than 120 years ago, Wiggin & Dana offers a full-service labor and employment practice from its three offices in the state and two beyond. Matters from the past year include advising a large unionized manufacturer on the closure of part of its business, involving labor negotiations, grievance handling and discrimination charges. The firm also counseled a major healthcare client on a union's corporate campaign; advised a biotech company on a significant sex discrimination and sexual harassment investigation and charge; testified before Connecticut's Labor Committee on behalf of an employer association in opposition to pro-union legislation; and was involved in numerous labor negotiations, arbitrations and NLRB proceedings.

**The Lawyers:** **John Zandy** (see p.385) chairs the practice group; he is well known throughout the state and has been working in this field since the 1970's. Long-standing clients value his excellent legal and communication skills, saying: *"He is an excellent listener and so easy to get along with."* Having worked at the NLRB, Zandy can offer clients a good insight into its workings. A popular choice, the *"knowledgeable and communicative"* **Peter Lefeber** (see p.383) continues to be admired by clients and peers. He too has a considerable amount of experience.

**Clients/Work Highlights:** An impressive and diverse client list includes Yale University plus companies in the biotech, financial services and healthcare sectors.

## Band 3

### Brown Raysman Millstein Felder & Steiner LLP

See firm details p.1521

**The Firm:** The Hartford office of this firm has a small employment practice that is led by Beverly Garofalo. Advisory work is conducted in the full range of employment law from sexual harassment to wage and hour law to e-mail and Internet policies. Common-law causes of action are taken by the firm to federal and state courts and administrative agencies.

**The Lawyers: Beverly Garofalo** (see p.383) is a pure employment lawyer. She is *"smart, personable and has a high level of integrity."* Said one former colleague: *"I always had the sense that she was looking out for the best interests of her client."* Garofalo's practice concentrates on advisory work, though she is a skilled employment litigator with a track record of success in complex and time-pressured summary judgment applications.

**Clients/Work Highlights:** In a recent gender discrimination, retaliation and breach of contract case, Lettieri v Equant, Inc., the firm secured a summary judgment in Virginia. An appeal is pending. In Ungerleider v Fleet Mortgage, which involved gender discrimination, hostile environment harassment, disability discrimination/failure to accommodate, religious discrimination, violation of the FMLA and retaliation, it secured another summary judgment. An appeal was dismissed as frivolous. Representative clients include Washington Mutual; Huntleigh Healthcare; Rotech Healthcare; eBenefits Group; Citizens Bank.

### Durant, Nichols, Houston, Hodgson & Cortese-Costa, P.C.

**The Firm:** A 12-lawyer boutique firm operating in Bridgeport in the southwest of the state, Durant Nichols delivers comprehensive labor and employment law services to unionized and nonunionized employers in the public and private sectors. The caseload includes fairly equal measures of employment law, including the usual discrimination cases, and labor relations work.

**The Lawyers: Terry Durant**'s reputation is built on labor relations. His commitment to the field has not wavered since he left law school and spent the first years of his career with the NLRB. He is credited with the prevention of a statewide strike by workers at convalescent homes.

**Clients/Work Highlights:** Employment discrimination work this year has included the successful defense of a reverse discrimination claim concerning a homosexual supervisor alleged to have shown favoritism towards a homosexual subordinate.

### Jackson Lewis

**The Firm:** Another specialist labor and employment firm, Jackson Lewis has a network of 21 offices across the nation, its Connecticut branches being located in Stamford and Hartford. The lawyers are renowned for their tough, uncompromising style, and certain clients rather like this. Said one: *"They do an outstanding job!"* Opinion is split, however, as others in the state find the firm a little too *"hard-hitting."*

**The Lawyers: Rob Fischer** (see p.383) drew warm praise from satisfied clients: *"He bested a very well-prepared attorney on virtually every point, was expert in examining and cross-examining witnesses and adapted quickly to the ebb and flow of the trial. I would definitely not want him litigating against me."* Both he and **Conrad Kee** (see p.383) work in the Stamford office. Kee is said to *"really shine"* in trade secrets cases, an area of work which forms an important part of his practice.

**Clients/Work Highlights:** There are few industries that the team has not advised, but particular emphasis is given to healthcare, insurance, financial services, oil, technology and pharmaceuticals.

### McCarter & English LLP

**The Firm:** Two of McCarter & English's eight East Coast operations are in the state, located in Stamford and Hartford. The Connecticut practice of eight attorneys covers both employment and traditional labor law, providing an across-the-board service to unionized and nonunionized organizations.

**The Lawyers: Gregory Nokes** is a traditional labor lawyer who spends much of his time giving preventive advice. He recently worked on a sexual harassment case involving allegations against a CEO following the acrimonious end of a consensual affair. *"Able, smart and analytical"* **Richard Voigt** has impressed clients with his employment work. He has considerable experience defending all types of claim, and prior to private practice worked as assistant counsel for regional litigation in the OSHA division of the Office of the Solicitor in the DOL in Washington, DC.

**Clients/Work Highlights:** Matters from the past year include a sexual harassment case concerning the behavior of an employee outside office hours. This case tackled the thorny issue of how the courts determine the point at which an environment becomes hostile. Clients include Middlesex Hospital, Fairfield University and Centrix.

### Paul, Hastings, Janofsky & Walker LLP

See firm details p.339

**The Firm:** The Connecticut branch of this New York-based firm has been building up its employment practice over the past few years. Lawyers handle the usual range of employment litigation, noting an increase in class actions and, since the passing of the Sarbanes-Oxley Act, major whistle-blower cases.

**The Lawyers: Carla Walworth** is adept at dealing with whistle-blower allegations and the media interest these can generate. She has recently been defending a class action glass-ceiling sex discrimination complaint brought by a human resources executive, a case with added difficulties as the plaintiff had access to sensitive information. **Ken Gage** has joined from Day, Berry & Howard. He is best known for undertaking EEOC work, discrimination and wage and hour class actions.

**Clients/Work Highlights:** The group represents the management of local, national and international companies.

### Siegel, O'Connor, O'Donnell & Beck PC

**The Firm:** This smaller Hartford labor and employment boutique has been operating for more than 45 years. NLRB matters are a forte and lawyers report an increase in wage and hour disputes this year.

**The Lawyers:** Edward 'Bud' O'Donnell's practice has an emphasis on labor matters.

**Clients/Work Highlights:** Clients include companies in the hospitality industry, education boards, trade associations and governmental departments.

### Tyler Cooper & Alcorn, LLP

**The Firm:** The group provides the full range of labor and employment services, including litigation and administrative proceedings, personnel training, union issues and immigration. Changes in wage and hour regulations have required advice to employers on the reclassification of their employees.

**The Lawyers: George O'Brien** chairs the practice group and takes on traditional labor law matters for both public and private sector clients. One recent case involved him representing a group of towns against a claim by a union. O'Brien also undertakes arbitration.

**Clients/Work Highlights:** Clients include Bridgeport; SBC; the town of Hamden and several hospitals such as St. Vincent's Medical Center.

# LITIGATION

## GENERAL COMMERCIAL

### Litigation: General Commercial
#### Leading Firms

**1** DAY, BERRY & HOWARD LLP *Hartford*

WIGGIN AND DANA LLP *New Haven*

**2** CARMODY & TORRANCE LLP *New Haven*

JACOBS, GRUDBERG, BELT & DOW PC *New Haven*

MURTHA CULLINA LLP *Hartford*

ROBINSON & COLE LLP *Hartford*

SHIPMAN & GOODWIN LLP *Hartford*

**3** BROWN RAYSMAN *Hartford*

HURWITZ & SAGARIN LLC *Milford*

MCCARTER & ENGLISH LLP *Hartford*

#### Leading Individuals

##### Senior Statesmen

GROARK JR Thomas *Day, Berry & Howard LLP*

STAPLETON James *Day, Berry & Howard LLP*

WADE James *Robinson & Cole LLP*

**1** BRADY Francis *Murtha Cullina LLP*

DUNHAM Edward *Wiggin and Dana LLP*

FITZGERALD Anthony *Carmody & Torrance LLP*

SULLIVAN Shaun *Wiggin and Dana LLP*

**2** BELT David *Jacobs, Grudberg, Belt & Dow*

BRIGHT JR William *McCarter & English LLP*

GREENSPAN Steven *Day, Berry & Howard LLP*

MORRISON III Francis *Day, Berry & Howard LLP*

ROBERTSON JR James *Carmody & Torrance LLP*

SAGARIN Daniel *Hurwitz & Sagarin LLC*

SHEARIN James *Pullman & Comley LLC*

SICILIAN James *Day, Berry & Howard LLP*

SILVESTRI JR Frank *Levett Rockwood P.C.*

**3** FITZMAURICE Daniel *Day, Berry & Howard LLP*

FOGARTY James *Fogarty, Cohen, Selby & Nemiroff*

SANSON Paul *Shipman & Goodwin LLP*

TAYLOR Allan *Day, Berry & Howard LLP*

WYLD Robert *Shipman & Goodwin LLP*

#### Up-and-coming individuals

SIMPSON Robert *Shipman & Goodwin LLP*

### Band 1

#### Day, Berry & Howard LLP

See firm details p.386

**The Firm:** *"An outstanding firm"* and the largest in the state, Day Berry's size allows it to handle complicated matters with ease. Some 50% of the firm's lawyers are litigators and a majority of these work from the firm's Stamford and Hartford offices covering all types of business disputes. Said one rival: *"I like to see them most in litigation because it means it will be conducted at a high level and will be professional... of course, I want to see them least because they are very, very good."* From another source researchers learned of *"some tremendous trial lawyers; in terms of depth and breadth of experience they are deserving of the number one spot."* Corporate and securities litigation is increasingly prevalent at this firm. The only

note of caution concerned bench strength at junior level.

**The Lawyers:** Seven attorneys appear in the table, two of them Senior Statesmen. The first of these is **James Stapleton** (see p.385), who has been engaged in much arbitration work this year, mainly large commercial disputes involving M&A transactions, regulatory issues and telecommunications. In the area of securities litigation, Stapleton has been involved with the cases of Xerox and Star Gas Partners. The second legendary figure is **Thomas Groark** (see p.383), who has played a major role in the development of Connecticut class action litigation and dispute resolution over the years. *"Phenomenal lawyer"* **Steven Greenspan** (see p.383) is *"a great strategist with a commanding presence and boundless energy in the courtroom. He is someone who judges and juries trust because he is always honest and straightforward."* Much of Greenspan's work concerns franchise and distribution cases. Well-respected **James Sicilian** (see p.384) is currently managing partner of the firm, though finds time enough to maintain an impressive reputation as a litigator. *"Excellent and pleasant"* **Francis Morrison** (see p.384) has been doing more IP lately: in the past year he has defended a patent claim relating to ratchet wrenches. He also continues to undertake products liability and pharmaceuticals cases. Competitors and clients consider **Daniel FitzMaurice** (see p.383) to be a very fine lawyer; his practice includes a good deal of insurance work. **Allan Taylor** (see p.385) has been working on the $150 million development of Blue Back Square, representing the developers on this heavily opposed project. Taylor has a reputation for appellant work in almost all areas. This year, he filed an amicus brief in the US Supreme Court on the high-profile and controversial case of Kelo v New London.

**Clients/Work Highlights:** The firm boasts a diverse client base. United Technologies has chosen the firm for all of its commercial litigation in the USA. Sensotec has engaged it to represent the company in a patent infringement case with an antitrust counterclaim. Other clients include Xerox; Star Gas Partners; Pratt & Whitney and Excel Capital.

#### Wiggin and Dana LLP

**The Firm:** As one lawyer told researchers: *"If you want your client well taken care of then send them here."* Still flourishing after its merger with Howe & Addington in 2003, the litigation group at New Haven-based Wiggin & Dana has nudged its way into the top tier of the table this year. Taking on the full gamut of business litigation from patents to securities, torts and professional liability, the firm shines in a number of areas, among them medical malpractice. Another area of great strength is franchise and distribution disputes. Two recent examples of this type of work involve Texas client Schlotzsky's Ltd, a franchiser of quickserve restaurants. The company is defending an antitrust case, brought by a supply chain management company that orches-

trates distribution arrangements between manufacturers and customers. Schlotzsky's has already persuaded the court to deny an application for an injunction. In another case for the franchiser – which had been brought by its owners out of bankruptcy – lawyers prevented a group of restaurants in Colorado from breaking away to start a competing chain.

**The Lawyers:** Chairman of the firm **Edward Wood Dunham** (see p.382) is *"one of the best in the franchise area"* and handles many such cases. More recently he has been engaged in increasing amounts of alternative dispute resolution and mediation. *"Strong trial attorney"* **Shaun Sullivan** (see p.385) chairs the litigation department and has experience of everything from securities litigation to energy cases and intellectual property. Rivals say: *"He undoubtedly knows his way around a courtroom."*

**Clients/Work Highlights:** The client list includes many names from the healthcare sector, including Yale-New Haven Hospital and Yale Medical School.

### Band 2

#### Carmody & Torrance LLP

**The Firm:** Located in New Haven, Southbury and Waterbury, this old-line firm has a litigation practice comprising 35 lawyers. It is especially active in the healthcare and energy sectors, as well as in patents and other IP matters, though its caseload is certainly very varied. The market is well aware of the achievements of key individuals within the practice but much less familiar with the junior lawyers.

**The Lawyers:** *"Amazingly effective, insightful and sharp,"* **Anthony Fitzgerald** was described to researchers as *"both an outstanding lawyer and an outstanding human being."* He has been working on energy matters lately, in particular leading a team representing an energy company trying to install power lines across the state. Popular consensus is that *"honorable"* and *"interesting and well-educated"* **James Robertson** is *"a very smart guy and a very fair guy."* According to one client, *"in court he is terrific at getting across his point and he sees right to the heart of the issue."* And the view of one rival was this: *"He is the perfect match for me, we beat the hell out of each other in court!"* This said, Robertson has been engaged more as a mediator and arbitrator lately, although he continues to litigate successfully on everything from employment cases to wholesale energy power contracts.

**Clients/Work Highlights:** This group is best known for its representation of one of the country's largest utilities, Northeast Utilities. The client roster also includes banks, insurers and governmental bodies.

#### Jacobs, Grudberg, Belt & Dow PC

**The Firm:** Showing an improved position in the rankings this year, this 15-lawyer firm is *"an excellent litigation boutique that does the important job of bridging the gap between commercial and criminal practices."* Criminal defense is combined with business disputes, plaintiff PI and family litigation. Peers say they have *"utmost respect for all their members; they are very selective and very good at what they take on."*

**The Lawyers:** Primarily handling business litigation, **David Belt** has been litigating on behalf of the supermarket chain Big Y Foods, defending a class action involving allegations of overcharging of State Sales Tax. Other matters include an arbitration in New York concerning a breach of contract dispute with a major international aerospace manufacturer, and a role as Connecticut counsel to a group of underwriters from Lloyd's on hundreds of millions of dollars' worth of claims damages.

**Clients/Work Highlights:** The firm works for Memry, United Aluminum and Chelsea GCA Realty among others.

## Murtha Cullina LLP

**The Firm:** Murtha Cullina's reputation for the quality of its insurance coverage work goes well beyond the state line. Other areas of work include energy matters, the defense of securities litigation and traditional breach of contract cases. The firm has recently taken on antitrust litigation involving hospitals and nursing homes.

**The Lawyers:** Sources consider that the firm's reputation for litigation is centered on **Fran Brady**, who is *"greatly respected."* He is best known for his insurance work, acting most often on coverage issues for policyholders. This was reflected in comments made by a client who said: *"He is an incredibly ethical and efficient lawyer. He has the ability to try a case that involves complicated matters in a way that makes it accessible to the average person. He can make a jury interested in insurance language – that's quite something!"*

**Clients/Work Highlights:** The group is best known for its representation of DuPont and UPS.

## Robinson & Cole LLP

**The Firm:** *"An excellent firm with a number of great litigators,"* this national player has a healthy corporate litigation practice in the state where it was founded. As well as tackling a full spread of business litigation, personal injury and other types of civil disputes, lawyers uphold a long tradition of representing businesses and individuals in criminal matters and governmental investigations. They defend not only white-collar crime but also cases of violent crime, including murder.

**The Lawyers:** Known for his wisdom, *"fabulous"* **James Wade** recently took an environmental case to the federal court in Connecticut for the largest paper box manufacturer in the USA. Wade spent 20 years as counsel to the Connecticut Democratic Party and is fully versed in constitutional law.

**Clients/Work Highlights:** Lawyers have been representing the city of West Hartford in a very large piece of litigation brought by the owner of a shopping mall which is objecting to a grant of permission

for a new mall. They also successfully resolved a case for insurance carriers in a matter arising out of 9/11.

## Shipman & Goodwin LLP

**The Firm:** This large, well-established Connecticut firm has offices in Hartford, Stamford, Greenwich and Lakeville, and a comprehensive litigation practice that complements its noncontentious areas of expertise. Notable areas of specialization include healthcare, products liability, IP, white-collar civil investigatory work and complex business litigation. There is also a special ombudsmen practice, whereby the firm provides independent legal advice to industry ombudsmen and major national blue-chips and other companies.

**The Lawyers:** Chair of the firm's litigation department **Robert Wyld** is *"undoubtedly one of the best lawyers around on legal arguments."* He focuses on complex business and commercial litigation, including corporate governance, business torts, partnership disputes and allegations of improper dealings. Wyld is currently the president of Oliver Ellsworth Inn of Court. *"Aggressive and effective"* **Paul Sanson** is much admired. His specialty is franchise and distribution litigation across New England, and his main client is Shell for which he is lead New England litigation attorney; the firm has been selected as Shell's Northeastern strategic partner. **Robert Simpson** is a very promising up-and-comer. Said one source: *"He is sound, good on his feet and a pleasure to deal with; most importantly he doesn't roll around in the muck but moves the case along."* Simpson's experience ranges from products liability and toxic torts to complex business litigation, particularly cases including fraud and unfair trade practices.

**Clients/Work Highlights:** Highlights from the past year include defending cases brought against quasi-public organizations following the allegations of improper use of state monies and improper relationships with government contractors that ultimately led to the resignation of former state governor John Rowland. Among the firm's other clients are Shell, for which it conducts major litigation, as well as ExxonMobil, Rockwell Automation and Alderwoods Group.

## Band 3

## Brown Raysman Millstein Felder & Steiner LLP

See firm details p.1521

**The Firm:** This four-state firm has increased the number of commercial litigators working in its Connecticut office to around 17. In particular it is known for commercial and construction litigation; indeed, the Hartford office heads the firm's construction practice and Yale University has just selected it to conduct its construction litigation.

**The Lawyers:** Brian Donnell is best known for contract and construction litigation and is the chair of the firm's construction law group.

**Clients/Work Highlights:** The group worked on the high-profile Ameriquest Mortgage case and the investigation into its practices regarding loan refinancings. The company was neither fined, nor did it lose its license to operate in Connecticut.

## Hurwitz & Sagarin LLC

**The Firm:** This five-attorney firm undertakes a variety of business and other litigation from its Milford office.

**The Lawyers:** The market considers its reputation in the area of business litigation to rest with *"very able"* **Daniel Sagarin**. He is recognized for his adept handling of class actions in the fields of antitrust, securities and fraud.

## McCarter & English LLP

**The Firm:** McCarter & English's Stamford and Hartford offices field a team of litigators that have experience of a variety of civil litigation at all levels.

**The Lawyers:** Sources suggest that the *"outstanding"* **William Bright** (see p.171264) in Hartford is the standout name. He is a committed trial attorney with a focus on IP and patent litigation as well as large contract disputes, often pertaining to distribution agreements. He spent much of the past year working on a $20 million contract dispute between an energy plant and the contractor operating it. Commentators say Bright *"picks up complicated technical matters extremely quickly"* and makes them juror-friendly. As one client reported: *"Bright has both a great understanding of patent law and the technology that surrounds our products. It is because of this that he is able to make our position so clear to the court."*

**Clients/Work Highlights:** CUNO, GE and MetLife are clients.

## Other Notable Practitioners

*"A man of integrity,"* Pullman & Comley LLC litigator **James Shearin** (see p.384) is considered *"a very fine lawyer: highly regarded, very knowledgeable and industrious."* He is currently cochair of the Connecticut Bar Association and has a reputation for being *"very well regarded among judges."* **Frank Silvestri** (see p.384) at Levett Rockwood P.C. in Westport is referred to as *"a cool customer."* A general commercial litigator, Silvestri is the current cochair of the Federal Practice of the Connecticut Bar Association and a familiar name in the area of healthcare litigation. **James Fogarty** at Fogarty, Cohen, Selby & Nemiroff LLC in Greenwich is widely acknowledged to be an *"experienced and intelligent litigator."* Engaged in all types of commercial litigation, work from the past year has included representing a large New York law firm in a series of alleged malpractice cases and a pharmaceutical company on numerous insurance coverage claims.

# REAL ESTATE

## Real Estate
### Leading Firms

| 1 | BINGHAM MCCUTCHEN LLP *Hartford* |
|---|---|
| | BROWN RUDNICK BERLACK ISRAELS *Hartford* |
| | ROBINSON & COLE LLP *Hartford* |
| 2 | BROWN RAYSMAN *Hartford* |
| | DECHERT LLP *Hartford* |
| | SHIPMAN & GOODWIN LLP *Hartford* |
| | WIGGIN AND DANA LLP *New Haven* |
| 3 | DAY, BERRY & HOWARD LLP *Stamford* |
| | KRASOW, GARLICK & HADLEY LLC *Hartford* |
| | NEUBERT, PEPE & MONTEITH PC *New Haven* |

### Leading Individuals

| 1 | ASMAR Mark *Brown Rudnick* |
|---|---|
| | BRYSON Susan *Wiggin and Dana LLP* |
| | HAWKINS Barry *Shipman & Goodwin LLP* |
| | MERRIAM Dwight *Robinson & Cole LLP* |
| 2 | APPICELLI Frank *Bingham McCutchen LLP* |
| | BAKER III Frank *Robinson & Cole LLP* |
| | BERKMAN Jerome *Day, Berry & Howard LLP* |
| | BERMAN Garry *Brown Raysman* |
| | DEROSA Franca *Brown Rudnick* |
| | GILLIES JR John *Dechert LLP* |
| | HOLLISTER Timothy *Shipman & Goodwin LLP* |
| | KRASOW Herbert *Krasow, Garlick & Hadley LLC* |
| | LUBIN Andrew *Neubert, Pepe & Monteith PC* |
| | OLAND Mark *Bingham McCutchen LLP* |
| | ROOS Norman *Brown Raysman* |
| | SVONKIN Mark *The Law Office of Mark J. Svonkin* |

## Band 1

### Bingham McCutchen LLP
See firm details p.1110

**The Firm:** This *"excellent"* branch of the nationwide firm operates with an ethos more akin to a New York outfit; indeed lawyers are closely allied with their colleagues in New York, Boston and beyond. As well as taking on a string of flagship deals in Connecticut (eg Hartford's Civic Center and Hilton Hotel), they represent clients on transactions spanning multiple states. Lawyers split their time between advising lenders on real estate finance, steering investors through acquisitions and disposals of single sites and portfolios, and assisting developers/owners with their projects, including all necessary funding elements of these. Zoning and regulatory advice is also given. The team engenders huge client loyalty – as one said: *"In the course of hundreds of transactions this team has done for me, I have never once felt that the other side was better represented."*

**The Lawyers:** The general opinion is that **Frank Appicelli** (see p.382) is someone that any top real estate practice would be proud to have on their team. A client who rarely uses anyone else for complex real estate matters enthused that Appicelli is *"one of our most trusted legal advisers: he is the consummate busi-*ness lawyer – in addition to being responsive, he is knowledgeable of the issues that are important to us and has excellent business judgment."* Displaying *"wisdom beyond his years,"* **Mark Oland** (see p.384) is an enormous hit with clients, who assured researchers that *"his assistance is a true value-added component to any transaction. He understands the difference between a business decision and a legal decision and which needs to take precedence. He is a first-rate counselor to his clients."*

**Clients/Work Highlights:** Appicelli represented Northland Investment in the Goodwin Square project, a mixed-use facility in downtown Hartford consisting of a 124-room hotel and 331,000 sq ft of Class A office and retail space. Oland's diverse practice has included the development of a large age-restricted condo complex in Southington, and representing Bristol Connecticut concerning the complex closure of a landfill.

### Brown Rudnick Berlack Israels LLP

**The Firm:** The Hartford office of this international law firm fields a group of six real estate specialists who conduct matters both regionally and nationally. Some have an interesting niche practice in the privatization of housing on military bases. These have included Patrick Air Force Base in Florida; Moody AFB in Georgia; Hanscom AFB in Massachusetts; Fort Leonard Wood in Missouri and a project covering 14 naval sites in the Seattle, Washington area. The team also boasts specialist shopping center expertise and it has undertaken a number of deals relating to large home and DIY stores. Peers considered this *"a group comprised of some truly fine attorneys;"* clients meanwhile spoke of how lawyers work with *"honesty and integrity"* and *"always make the effort to truly learn about our assets."*

**The Lawyers:** Talented and experienced **Mark Asmar** earns his place in the top tier of the table. The Hartford office's real estate heavyweight takes on large and complex commercial projects on both the development and financing sides. **Franca DeRosa's** practice is weighted towards environmental and energy law, and in this realm few in the state could be said to match her. As one client reported: *"She is able to assess risk and determine an appropriate course of action; I use her in other states as well."*

**Clients/Work Highlights:** Dutch insurance client ING used the firm in relation to its new North American HQ in Connecticut.

### Robinson & Cole LLP

**The Firm:** Boasting the largest real estate practice, this firm maintains its top-tier status and its reputation for *"intellectual high-flying."* As well as excellent capacity in traditional real estate areas, it also encompasses top-quality environment and land use teams. Though its reach extends well beyond the state line, Robinson & Cole has capitalized on its significant presence in Connecticut (offices in Hartford, Stamford and New London), building a sterling name for itself in the local market. Its lawyers have significant involvement in complex mixed-use projects, and note the continued rise of new urbanism, greater demand for smaller residential units and increased interest from out-of-state investors.

**The Lawyers:** Affable **Dwight Merriam** is the creator of the firm's land use practice group in the Hartford office. His *"top-notch"* reputation in this field cannot be overstated; testament to this is the recent publication by McGraw-Hill of Merriam's 'The Complete Guide to Zoning', a layperson's guide to this thorny area of law. **Frank Baker** practices from the Stamford office, which has close links with the firm's New York practice. Work this year has included representing FactSeT Research Systems on a number of major leases in the USA and overseas.

**Clients/Work Highlights:** This year the firm was appointed as real estate counsel to a large retirement fund that was reviewing its extensive portfolio of investments. It was also involved in seeking initial approval for a 1000-acre residential and golf course project for a subsidiary of Lehman Brothers, and completed a transaction for General Investment & Development Companies relating to two apartment complexes, which were part of a $1 billion, 1351-unit portfolio sale.

## Band 2

### Brown Raysman Millstein Felder & Steiner LLP
See firm details p.1521

**The Firm:** This smaller *"responsive and thorough"* Hartford-based team makes its debut in the tables. Though not as prominent or as large as the team in the firm's New York office, the Connecticut group is really felt to be making its mark, both on sophisticated financings and other types of transaction. The real estate practice works nationally, yet much of the work of this office is now self-generated.

**The Lawyers:** *"Sophisticated"* **Garry Berman** (see p.382) is considered *"a hard-driving lawyer who zealously advocates his client's position."* It is this thoroughness that clients appreciate: *"No one has ever returned a higher quality of work to me than Berman – he always covers the waterfront of all the issues and everything he has done for me has always held up."* One referred to him as *"a breath of fresh air."* **Norman Roos** (see p.384) has been practicing real estate law for some 30 years and boasts *"a deep and impressive knowledge of the area."* With a background in traditional real estate and banking, he now focuses on mortgage banking and brokerage.

**Clients/Work Highlights:** The team represents all the major mortgage lenders in the state and does notable work for Ameriquest Mortgage Company.

### Dechert LLP
See firm details p.1752

**The Firm:** The Hartford office of this *"fabulous national firm"* houses a small but significant real estate group of *"very bright lawyers"* that has earned itself a particular name for securitized financings and related areas. Work generated by this office runs far beyond state lines, with its lawyers being as well known in New York as Connecticut.

**The Lawyers:** Managing partner and member of the executive committee of the firm's finance and real estate group, **John Gillies'** (see p.383) practice is not typical of the Connecticut market, boasting a client base that is very institutional investor-heavy. The focus of his practice is perhaps best illustrated by his membership both of the American College of Real Estate Lawyers and the American College of Investment Counsel. And it is his expertise in real estate financing that has earned him his adamantine reputation. One peer bordered on the profane in his praise of Gillies: *"He is as bright a real estate lawyer as there is in the Hartford market. He engages in large complicated transactions that only he and God understand."*

**Clients/Work Highlights:** The group represents institutional investors, insurance companies and various lending entities. Specific clients include Pacific Life Insurance Company; Wells Fargo; Freddie Mac; GMAC; Starwood Capital Group; Aetna; Criimi Mae; The Hartford and Citigroup.

## Shipman & Goodwin LLP

**The Firm:** This is a true Connecticut law firm with offices in Hartford, Stamford, Greenwich and Lakeville. Its two major offices conduct quite different types of real estate law, with Hartford handling the lion's share of zoning, affordable housing and multifamily occupancies; and most of the commercial and high-end residential deals being undertaken in the Stamford office.

**The Lawyers:** **Barry Hawkins** is the team's brightest star. He is known for not only traditional transactional work, but also real estate litigation and challenged zoning and tax appeals. A member of the litigation department, **Timothy Hollister**'s areas of expertise are environmental, land use, administrative and regulatory law. He provides crucial support to the real estate practice.

**Clients/Work Highlights:** One highlight from the past year was Marriott's development of the first new hotel in downtown Stamford for ten years. Lawyers have also continued working on the headquarters of SAC Capital Advisors.

## Wiggin and Dana LLP

**The Firm:** A stalwart Connecticut firm with offices in New Haven, Hartford and Stamford, Wiggin & Dana's real estate department is split into four smaller practice groups: business and institutions; smart growth and development; real estate finance and acquisitions; and land use approvals and permits. A focus on urban redevelopment, brownfield and contaminated properties is underlined by the close working of the firm's real estate and environment lawyers. Among the three Connecticut offices, Stamford stands out for its work for foreign investors.

**The Lawyers:** Popular New Haven-based **Susan Bryson** (see p.382) received high praise from some of the sector's biggest names. Her sophisticated understanding of urban regeneration puts her ahead of the pack in this area of work.

**Clients/Work Highlights:** The group continues to represent the New London Development Corporation, advises on development and refinancing for a number of affordable housing projects in Stamford, Bridgepoint and New Haven, and buys, sells and leases real estate around the country for Olin.

## Band 3

## Day, Berry & Howard LLP

See firm details p.386

**The Firm:** The real estate department of this large firm covers all bases, from large, high-profile commercial leasings to sales, acquisitions and financing, to multiproperty transactions and low-income housing tax credit. Clients trust the team to provide *"an excellent service that is great value for money."*

**The Lawyers:** In practice for 30 years, **Jerome Berkman** (see p.382) is an established name in Stamford, and peers agree that his fine reputation is well deserved. His practice covers real estate development, sales & acquisitions, commercial leasing – representing landlords and tenants – and real estate finance, commonly acting for borrowers. He has worked on several significant leases this year within Fairfield County; these transactions related to properties between 50,000 and 100,000 sq ft and totaled around three-quarters of a million square feet.

**Clients/Work Highlights:** The team represents developers, borrowers, landlords and tenants. Clients include AvalonBay Communities, Citigroup and Building and Land Technology.

## Krasow, Garlick & Hadley LLC

**The Firm:** A *"small but very capable practice"* that has earned enormous respect for its work on smaller transactions. Despite its size, work is not limited to the immediate region: Krasow lawyers have worked on projects throughout the country and in Canada, Europe and the Caribbean.

**The Lawyers:** *"Thorough and learned"* was one peer's assessment of **Herbert Krasow**, the biggest name in this *"group of very strong lawyers."* His practice encompasses leasing, development, financing and land use.

**Clients/Work Highlights:** The group represents a range of real estate clients from landlords, tenants, lenders and borrowers through to investors and developers.

## Neubert, Pepe & Monteith PC

**The Firm:** This Connecticut firm has offices in New Haven and Southport and runs its small but notable real estate practice from the former. In the past year it has been engaged in high-end, minimum-age residential leasing among other things.

**The Lawyers:** **Andrew Lubin** is respected by peers for being *"a very good technical lawyer."* Well known for his work with banks, they say *"he does an excellent job."* Lubin is experienced in a variety of business and finance fields as well as real estate work.

**Clients/Work Highlights:** Recent work has included advice to a lender on the development of a $30 million, high-end condominium in Fairfield.

## Other Notable Practitioners

**Mark Svonkin** practices from The Law Office of Mark J Svonkin PC and is known as *"an exceptionally bright and gifted lawyer"* who represents small to medium-sized companies. He recently advised a small real estate company on the sale of five office/retail buildings in West Hartford for over $28 million. Svonkin is a member of the Connecticut Bar Association's Real Property Executive Committee.

# Leaders in Conneticut

## ALBIN, David I
Finn Dixon & Herling LLP, Stamford
203 325 5000
dalbin@fdh.com
*Recommended in Corporate/M&A*

**Practice Areas:** Focus on private equity, mergers and acquisitions and securities law matters. Also has broad experience in venture capital transactions, corporate governance matters and the general representation of public and private business entities.
**Prof. Memberships:** Admitted to the Bar of the State of Connecticut. Member of the Negotiated Acquisitions Committee of the Business Law Section of the American Bar Association, and reporter for such committee's Model Asset Purchase Agreement. Vice-Chairman of the Business Law Section of the Connecticut Bar Association.
**Publications:** Publications of numerous articles in the areas of mergers and acquisitions, venture capital and business law. Frequent lecturer in areas of mergers and acquisitions and venture capital, including frequent lecturer in the American Bar Association's National Institute's Annual Program on 'Negotiating Business Acquisitions.'
**Personal:** Received Undergraduate Degree from Trinity College with honors in Political Science in 1981 and received Law Degree from Yale University in 1984.

## APPICELLI, Frank A
Bingham McCutchen LLP, Hartford
860 240 2984
frank.appicelli@bingham.com
*Recommended in Real Estate*

**Practice Areas:** Concentrates on commercial finance and real estate. Represents commercial banks, insurance companies, finance companies and other debt and equity providers in mortgage loan transactions involving acquisition and construction financings, permanent financings, bond-lease and credit tenant loans, and revolving credit facilities. Properties involved in such transactions have included shopping centers; office buildings; industrial and warehouse facilities; hospitals and medical facilities; assisted living projects; hotels and lodging properties; resort facilities; apartment and other multifamily housing complexes; condominium and timeshare projects; restaurants and entertainment facilities.
**Personal:** Georgetown University Law Center, JD, 1989; Fairfield University, BA, 1986.

## ASMAR, Mark
Brown Rudnick Berlack Israels LLP, Hartford 860 509 6524
*Recommended in Real Estate*

## BAKER III, Frank
Robinson & Cole LLP, Stamford
203 462 7500
*Recommended in Real Estate*

## BELT, David
Jacobs, Grudberg, Belt & Dow PC, New Haven 203 772 3100
*Recommended in Litigation*

## BERKMAN, Jerome
Day, Berry & Howard LLP, Stamford
203 977 7369
jberkman@dbh.com
*Recommended in Real Estate*

**Practice Areas:** Real estate development, sales and acquisitions, commercial leasing, real estate finance.
**Prof. Memberships:** The Boys & Girls Club of Stamford, President and Director; Jewish Community Endowment Foundation of Stamford, Vice President and Director.

## BERMAN, Garry C
Brown Raysman Millstein Felder & Steiner LLP, Hartford 860 275 6466
gberman@brownraysman.com
*Recommended in Real Estate*

**Practice Areas:** Garry Berman practices commercial real estate law, concentrating in: office and retail leasing/subleasing for landlords and tenants; purchase/sale of commercial, industrial and retail properties for purchasers and sellers; development of commercial, industrial and retail properties for property owners, landlords and tenants; mortgage and construction lending, and workouts and restructuring loans for lenders and borrowers; brokerage matters for landlords, tenants and brokers; and cable television and telecommunications licenses for landlords and tenants.
**Prof. Memberships:** Admitted in Connecticut and New York.
**Personal:** BA, Tufts University 1986, magna cum laude, Phi Beta Kappa; JD, New York University School of Law 1989.

## BRADY, Francis
Murtha Cullina LLP, Hartford
860 240 6000
*Recommended in Litigation*

## BRIGHT JR, William
McCarter & English LLP, Hartford
860 275 6700
*Recommended in Litigation*

## BRYSON, Susan J
Wiggin and Dana LLP, New Haven
203 498 4337
sbryson@wiggin.com
*Recommended in Real Estate*

**Practice Areas:** Chair of Wiggin and Dana's Real Estate, Environmental and Land Use Department. Concentrates on large-scale urban development projects involving public and private financing,

including tax-exempt and taxable bonds, tax increment financing, low income housing and historic tax credits. Represents business and institutional clients in all aspects of real estate, real estate finance and real estate development. Clients include national and international corporations, hospitals and healthcare facilities, biotech companies, for-profit and non-profit developers, opportunity funds, lending institutions and manufacturers.
**Personal:** Received her Bachelor's Degree in 1970 from Stanford University and her JD, with highest honors, in 1977 from the University of Connecticut School of Law. Clerked for the Honorable Alva P Loiselle.

## CLEMOW, Brian
Shipman & Goodwin LLP, Hartford
860 251 5000
*Recommended in Employment*

## CLOHERTY, Thomas
Murtha Cullina LLP, Hartford
860 240 6000
*Recommended in Employment*

## DEROSA, Franca
Brown Rudnick Berlack Israels LLP, Hartford 860 509 6524
*Recommended in Real Estate*

## DIXON, Brett W
Finn Dixon & Herling LLP, Stamford
203 325 5000
bdixon@fdh.com
*Recommended in Corporate/M&A*

**Practice Areas:** Practices primarily in the law relating to business taxation and the structuring of investment and other business arrangements. Key practice areas include planning for taxable and tax-free acquisitions and dispositions of public and private entities, and representing principals and investors in designing partnerships and other investment or business vehicles.
**Prof. Memberships:** Admitted to the Bars of the State of Connecticut and the United States Tax Court. Member of the Corporate Tax Committee of the Tax Section of the American Bar Association and of the Executive Committee of the Tax Section of the Connecticut Bar Association.
**Personal:** Graduated magna cum laude from Williams College in 1977. Received Law Degree, magna cum laude, from Cornell Law School in 1982 and MBA, with distinction, from Johnson School of Management at Cornell University in 1981.

## DOWNEY III, Charles J
Finn Dixon & Herling LLP, Stamford
203 325 5000
cdowney@fdh.com
*Recommended in Corporate/M&A*

**Practice Areas:** Focus on private equity,

mergers and acquisitions and venture capital. Also has broad experience in securities law matters (including PIPE transactions and advising private equity funds, venture capital funds and hedge funds with respect to securities law matters).
**Prof. Memberships:** Admitted to the Bars of the States of Connecticut and New York. Member of the Business Law Section of the American Bar Association and the Business Law Section of the Connecticut Bar Association. Member of the Board of Directors of the Connecticut Venture Group.
**Publications:** Publications and lectures in the areas of mergers and acquisitions, private equity, venture capital and securities law matters.
**Personal:** Graduated cum laude from Wharton School of the University of Pennsylvania (BS Economics, Major in Finance) in 1986 and received Law Degree from New York University School of Law in 1989. Member, Steering Committee, Greenwich Alliance for Education, Inc.

## DUNHAM, Edward Wood
Wiggin and Dana LLP, New Haven
203 498 4327
edunham@wiggin.com
*Recommended in Litigation*

**Practice Areas:** Trial lawyer. For over a quarter century has represented businesses in complex litigation and arbitration. Handles a broad variety of matters, with special concentration in franchise and distribution disputes. Chair of the firm's Executive Committee.
**Prof. Memberships:** Fellow of the American College of Trial Lawyers; Governing Committee, American Bar Association Forum on Franchising; formerly Editor-in-Chief, ABA Franchise Law Journal.
**Personal:** Law clerk to Judge Robert A Ainsworth, Jr, of the US Court of Appeals for the Fifth Circuit (1978-79); New York University School of Law (1978); Trinity College (Phi Beta Kappa) (1975).

## DURANT, E Terry
Durant, Nichols, Houston, Hodgson & Cortese-Costa, P.C., Bridgeport
203 366 3438
*Recommended in Employment*

## FINN III, Harold B
Finn Dixon & Herling LLP, Stamford
203 325 5000
hfinn@fdh.com
*Recommended in Corporate/M&A*

**Practice Areas:** Concentrates practice in the law relating to business organizations and financial transactions, including corporate governance, mergers and acquisitions, the public and private offering of securities, banking and lending,

and related litigation. Represents both publicly-held corporations and private companies, including pooled investment vehicles in the form of partnerships, limited liability companies and trusts.
**Prof. Memberships:** Admitted to the Bars of the States of Connecticut and New York. Former Member of the Council of the Business Law Section of the American Bar Association and former Chair of such Section's Banking Law Committee. Chairman of the Securities Advisory Committee to the Banking Commissioner of the State of Connecticut. Past Co-Chair of Task Force on the Revision of the Connecticut Business Corporation Act. Former Chair of the Business Law Section of the Connecticut Bar Association. Elected Member of the American Law Institute.
**Personal:** Received Undergraduate Degree from Yale University in 1960 and received law degree, magna cum laude, from Columbia University in 1966, where he was articles editor of the Columbia Law Review. Following law school, he served as a law clerk to the late Chief Justice Earl Warren and the late Associate Justice Stanley F Reed.

### FISCHER, A Robert
Jackson Lewis, Stamford
203 961 0404
FischerA@jacksonlewis.com
*Recommended in Employment*
**Practice Areas:** Co-Chair of Trade Secret, Non-Compete and Workplace Technology Practice Group. Has litigated breach of non-competition agreements, theft of trade secrets and breach of the duty of loyalty claims in 14 states and enforced non-competes with world-wide scope.
**Prof. Memberships:** Past Executive Committee Member, Connecticut Bar Association's Labor and Employment Law Section; past Chair, Stamford-Norwalk Regional Bar Association's Employment Law Committee.
**Career:** Partner since 1995. Special Master, United States District Court for the District of Connecticut. Former adjunct instructor, Hartford Graduate Center.
**Publications:** Has written and lectured extensively on employment law topics.
**Personal:** The University of Texas School of Law (JD, 1983). US Army Security Agency, 1975-78.

### FITZGERALD, Anthony
Carmody & Torrance LLP, New Haven
203 777 5501
*Recommended in Litigation*

### FITZMAURICE, Daniel L
Day, Berry & Howard LLP, Hartford
860 275 0181
dlfitzmaurice@dbh.com
*Recommended in Litigation*
**Practice Areas:** Insurance litigation, commercial litigation, direct liability and casualty, disability insurance, life insur-

ance and annuities, franchise and distributorship litigation, reinsurance, regulatory insurance proceedings and litigation, appellate practice group, alternative dispute resolution.
**Prof. Memberships:** AIDA Reinsurance and Insurance Arbitration Society (ARIAS-US); American Bar Association, ABA Section Member in Torts and Insurance Practice Section and Franchise Law Section; Connecticut Bar Association; Hartford County Bar Association.

### FOGARTY, James
Fogarty, Cohen, Selby & Nemiroff LLC, Greenwich 203 661 1000
*Recommended in Litigation*

### GAROFALO, Beverly W
Brown Raysman Millstein Felder & Steiner LLP, Hartford 860 275 6404
bgarofalo@brownraysman.com
*Recommended in Employment*
**Practice Areas:** Beverly W Garofalo practises employment law on behalf of management. She regularly defends employers in court and before administrative agencies and also counsels companies on a wide range of employment issues, including sex harassment; discrimination; accommodating disabled employees; family and medical leave laws; wage and hour laws; hiring, disciplining and terminating employees; downsizing and reductions-in-force; employee benefits; email and internet policies; employment, non-competition and confidentiality agreements; mergers and acquisitions; and outsourcing.
**Personal:** BA, Colorado College 1985; JD, University of Connecticut School of Law 1991, magna cum laude.

### GILLIES JR, John J
Dechert LLP, Hartford
860 524 3938
john.gillies@dechert.com
*Recommended in Real Estate*
**Practice Areas:** Mr Gillies is a Partner and Member of the Executive Committee of Dechert's Finance and Real Estate Group. He advises institutional investors and investment advisors in the creation, acquisition, and disposition of investments in real estate.
**Prof. Memberships:** Member, New Jersey and Connecticut Bars; Member, American College of Real Estate Lawyers; Member, American College of Investment Counsel.
**Career:** Joined Dechert in 1997. Partner, Hebb & Gitlin, Hartford, Connecticut, 1979-97.
**Personal:** Georgetown University, AB, 1968; Boston College Law School, JD, 1971.

### GREENSPAN, Steven M
Day, Berry & Howard LLP, Hartford
860 275 0346
smgreenspan@dbh.com
*Recommended in Litigation*

**Practice Areas:** Franchise and distributorship litigation, commercial litigation, bankruptcy, workouts and restructuring.
**Prof. Memberships:** President, Hartford County Bar Association; American Bar Association, Section of Natural Resources; Member, Executive Committee, Franchise Law Committee, Connecticut Bar Association; Trustee, University of Connecticut School of Law Foundation, 2000-present; Board of Directors, Hartford County Bar Association, 1997-present; Treasurer, Hartford County Bar Association, 2000-01; Secretary, 2001-02; Co-Chair, ABA Oil Refining and Marketing Subcommittee, 1992-98.

### GROARK JR, Thomas J
Day, Berry & Howard LLP, Hartford
860 275 0216
tjgroark@dbh.com
*Recommended in Litigation*
**Practice Areas:** Securities litigation, direct liability and casualty, life insurance and annuities, commercial litigation, insurance litigation, regulatory insurance proceedings and litigation, alternative dispute resolution.
**Prof. Memberships:** Fellow, American College of Trial Lawyers (1987-present); Diplomat, American Board of Trial Advocates (1986-94); Fellow, American Bar Foundation; Connecticut Bar Association; American Bar Association.

### HAWKINS, Barry
Shipman & Goodwin LLP, Hartford
860 251 5000
*Recommended in Real Estate*

### HAWKINS, John
Paul, Hastings, Janofsky & Walker LLP, Stamford 203 961 7486
johnhawkins@paulhastings.com
*Recommended in Corporate/M&A*
**Practice Areas:** Project finance, acquisition and development. Chair of Paul Hastings Global Project Group.
**Career:** Partner at Paul, Hastings, Janofsky & Walker LLP since 1995. Previously Partner at Mudge Rose Guthrie Alexander & Ferdon in New York. Started at Mudge Rose firm as an associate in 1980.
**Personal:** Law School - University of North Carloina School of Law, JD 1980, with honors; Undergraduate - Lehigh University, BA 1977, cum laude. Married, two children.

### HERLING, Michael J
Finn Dixon & Herling LLP, Stamford
203 325 5000
mherling@fdh.com
*Recommended in Corporate/M&A*
**Practice Areas:** Firm practice leader in private equity and venture capital. Has extensive experience in mergers and acquisitions, securities law, corporate finance, and venture capital and private equity. He represents venture capital and private equity funds, publicly held and private corporations, and entrepreneurs

in connection with acquisition, finance and securities activities, as well as general business matters.
**Prof. Memberships:** Admitted to the Bar of the State of Connecticut. He is a Member of the Business Law Section of the Connecticut Bar Association and the Section of Business Law of the American Bar Association, as well as the Venture Capital and Private Equity Committee of the Section of Business Law. He also served as the co-reporter for the Task Force on the Connecticut Business Corporation Act.
**Personal:** Received Undergraduate Degree from Colgate University in 1979 and received Law Degree from Stanford Law School in 1982.

### HOLLISTER, Timothy
Shipman & Goodwin LLP, Hartford
860 251 5000
*Recommended in Real Estate*

### KEE, Conrad
Jackson Lewis, Stamford
203 961 0404
KeeC@jacksonlewis.com
*Recommended in Employment*
**Practice Areas:** Workplace law, including litigation and advice. Co-Chair of the Trade Secret, Non-Compete and Workplace Technology Practice Group and Member of the International Employment Issues Practice Group. Extensive experience in litigating and arbitrating disputes with senior executives and employee benefits matters. Has represented European companies on a variety of matters. Assists companies with conducting due diligence of workplace law issues in connection with mergers and acquisitions.
**Career:** Partner since 2000.
**Publications:** Has lectured and written extensively on workplace law matters.
**Personal:** Washington University (AB, 1984); Washington University School of Law (JD, 1987); Diploma of Advanced International Legal Studies, Salzburg, Austria (1987).

### KRASOW, Herbert
Krasow, Garlick & Hadley LLC, Hartford
860 549 7100
*Recommended in Real Estate*

### LEFEBER, Peter J
Wiggin and Dana LLP, New Haven
203 498 4329
plefeber@wiggin.com
*Recommended in Employment*
**Practice Areas:** Represents management in all aspects of the employment relationship, including union organizing drives, unfair labor practice cases, arbitrations, labor contract negotiations, strike management, immigration matters, discrimination claims, wage and hour cases, and wrongful discharge suits and related issues. Clients include major healthcare institutions, manufacturing companies,

insurance organizations, utilities, educational institutions, and not-for-profit entities.

**Prof. Memberships:** Member ABA's Labor and Employment Section, and has served on the Executive Committee of the Connecticut Bar Association Section on Labor and Employment Law.

**Personal:** Graduated St. Michael's College (AB, summa cum laude) and the University of Connecticut School of Law (JD cum laude), where he was Administrative Editor of the Connecticut Law Review.

**LOTSTEIN, James I**
Edwards Angell Palmer & Dodge LLP,
Hartford 860 541 7708
JLotstein@eapdlaw.com
*Recommended in Corporate/M&A*

**Practice Areas:** Jim's practice is devoted primarily to the representation of businesses and financial institutions. He regularly assists clients in the areas of mergers and acquisitions, corporate governance, joint ventures, venture capital transactions and general corporate work.

**Prof. Memberships:** American Bar Association, Committee on Corporate Laws; Connecticut Bar Association, Business Law Section Executive Committee; NACD, Steering Committee, CT Chapter; ASCS, Advisory Committee, Hartford Chapter.

**Publications:** Jim is the author of a number of articles on Connecticut Corporate Law. He is also the co-author of the Connecticut Business Corporate Act Sourcebook.

**Personal:** University of Connecticut, JD, 1968; Northwestern University, BS, 1965.

**LUBIN, Andrew**
Neubert, Pepe & Monteith PC, New
Haven 203 821 2000
*Recommended in Real Estate*

**MARCO, Frank J**
Wiggin and Dana LLP, New Haven
203 498 4344
fmarco@wiggin.com
*Recommended in Corporate/M&A*

**Practice Areas:** Chairs the firm's practice in representing venture capital investors and emerging growth companies in capital formation, mergers and acquisitions, public offerings, joint ventures, strategic alliances, licensing, research and development, and related matters. Counsels institutional clients on corporate transactions such as mergers and acquisition, spin-offs and corporate ventures.

**Prof. Memberships:** Executive Committee of The Connecticut Technology Council (and Chair of Corporate Innovation Program); Member of, CURE and Connecticut Venture Group.

**Personal:** Admitted in Connecticut and New York. St Lawrence University JD cum laude, Fordham Law School, editor of the Fordham Law Review.

**MERRIAM, Dwight**
Robinson & Cole LLP, Hartford
860 275 8200
*Recommended in Real Estate*

**MORRISON III, Francis H**
Day, Berry & Howard LLP, Hartford
860 275 0231
fhmorrison@dbh.com
*Recommended in Litigation*

**Practice Areas:** Intellectual property and technology litigation, probate controversies, disability insurance, negligence defense, product liability, commercial litigation, life insurance and annuities, torts litigation.

**Prof. Memberships:** Certified Trial Advocate, National Institute of Trial Advocacy; Member, Defense Research Institute; Former President, Connecticut Defense Lawyers Association.

**NOKES, Gregory**
McCarter & English LLP, Hartford
860 275 6700
*Recommended in Employment*

**O'BRIEN, George**
Tyler Cooper & Alcorn LLP, New Haven
203 784 8200
*Recommended in Employment*

**OLAND, Mark**
Bingham McCutchen LLP, Hartford
860 240 2929
mark.oland@bingham.com
*Recommended in Real Estate*

**Practice Areas:** Concentrates on commercial real estate law and finance, real estate loan workouts and mortgage law. Has served on the Board of Directors of the Real Estate Finance Association, the Developer's Council and the Community Associations Institute. Has also served as an adviser to the Connecticut Law Revision Commission on a variety of real estate legislation. Clients include developers of commercial and residential properties, including both privately and publicly owned entities; real estate investment trusts; pension funds; and banking institutions.

**Personal:** Columbia University School of Law, JD, 1972; University of Vermont, BA, 1969.

**PINNEY JR, Willard**
Murtha Cullina LLP, Hartford
860 240 6000
*Recommended in Corporate/M&A*

**ROBERTSON JR, James**
Carmody & Torrance LLP, Waterbury
203 573 1200
*Recommended in Litigation*

**ROOS, Norman H**
Brown Raysman Millstein Felder &
Steiner LLP, Hartford 860 275 6429
nroos@brownraysman.com
*Recommended in Real Estate*

**Practice Areas:** Norman H Roos is the Managing Partner of the firm's Hartford office and concentrates on transactional

and regulatory matters relating to the real estate and financial services industries. He represents banks, insurance companies, diversified financial service companies and other publicly and privately held companies on a broad range of matters involving mortgage banking, consumer and commercial credit transactions, regulatory compliance and electronic commerce.

**Personal:** BS, University of Pennsylvania (Wharton School of Finance and Commerce) 1969; JD, University of Michigan 1972.

**SAGARIN, Daniel**
Hurwitz & Sagarin LLC, Milford
203 877 8000
*Recommended in Litigation*

**SANSON, Paul**
Shipman & Goodwin LLP, Hartford
860 251 5000
*Recommended in Litigation*

**SCHWARTZ, Daniel**
Day, Berry & Howard LLP, Stamford
203 977 7536
dlschwartz@dbh.com
*Recommended in Employment*

**Practice Areas:** Employment law and litigation, securities litigation.

**Prof. Memberships:** Federal Bar Council, Member.

**SHEARIN, James T**
Pullman & Comley LLC, Bridgeport
203 330 2240
jtshearin@pullcom.com
*Recommended in Litigation*

**Practice Areas:** Chair of Litigation Department. Has wide-ranging experience in state and federal courts (trial and appellate levels) and before arbitration and mediation boards. Represents clients in areas of commercial, intellectual property, banking, securities, antitrust, civil rights, employment and general civil litigation.

**Prof. Memberships:** Connecticut Legal Service Corp. (Director), University of Connecticut Law School Foundation, Inc. (Director), Greater Bridgeport Bar Association (Former President), House of Delegates and Executive Committees of Federal Practice (Co-Chair) and Intellectual Property Sections of Connecticut Bar Association, Raymond E Baldwin Inn of Court, American Red Cross (Director).

**Career:** Joined firm, 1988; became Partner, 1994; Executive Committee Member.

**Publications:** 'National Banks: Where Does Diversity Jurisdiction Lie?' Banking Law Journal, January 2005; 'The Admissibility of Expert Opinions,' Litigation Solutions, Fall 2004; 'Priority Legal Services for the Poor: A Difficult Task,' Connecticut Lawyer, February 2003.

**Personal:** JD, high honors, University of Connecticut School of Law, 1986; BA, summa cum laude, University of Connecticut, 1983.

**SICILIAN, James**
Day, Berry & Howard LLP, Hartford
860 275 0303
jsicilian@dbh.com
*Recommended in Litigation*

**Practice Areas:** Intellectual property and technology litigation, commercial litigation, antitrust.

**Prof. Memberships:** Past Chair, Antitrust and Trade Regulation Section, Connecticut Bar Association; Executive Committee, Intellectual Property Law Section, Connecticut Bar Association; Member, Computer Law Section, Connecticut Bar Association; Member, Antitrust and Intellectual Property Law Sections, American Bar Association; Special Master, US District Court for the District of Connecticut, 2000-present; Member, Grievance Committee, US District Court for the District of Connecticut.

**SILVESTRI JR, Frank J**
Levett Rockwood P.C., Westport
203 222 0885
fsilvestri@levettrockwood.com
*Recommended in Litigation*

**Practice Areas:** Commercial litigation, arbitration.

**Prof. Memberships:** Fellow, American College of Trial Lawyers; ABA (Litigation, Antitrust Sections); Connecticut Bar Assoc. (Co-Chair, Federal Practice Section 2004-present; Member, Task Force on Confidentiality and Courts 2003-present); American Inns of Court; Federal Bar Council; American Health Lawyers Association.

**Career:** Member, Levett Rockwood, P.C., 2004-present; Zeldes, Needle & Cooper, P.C., Bridgeport CT 1975-2004; Law clerk, US Circuit Judge J Joseph Smith, 2d Circuit, 1974-75.

**Publications:** Has spoken on litigation topics for Connecticut Bar Association.

**Personal:** Yale Law School (JD 1974); Georgetown University (AB 1968, summa cum laude, Phi Beta Kappa); US Navy 1968-71.

**SIMPSON, Robert**
Shipman & Goodwin LLP, Hartford
860 251 5000
*Recommended in Litigation*

**SPRINGER, Felix**
Day, Berry & Howard LLP, Hartford
860 275 0184
fjspringer@dbh.com
*Recommended in Employment*

**Practice Areas:** Employment law and litigation, alternative dispute resolution.

**Prof. Memberships:** Chair of ABA Subcommittee on Ethics; Executive Committee, Center for Public Resources; Employment ADR Committee; Special Master for US District Court, District of Connecticut; Fellow, Connecticut Bar Foundation.

## STAPLETON, James F
Day, Berry & Howard LLP, Hartford
203 977 7315
jfstapleton@dbh.com
*Recommended in Litigation*
**Practice Areas:** Commercial litigation, alternative dispute resolution.
**Prof. Memberships:** Connecticut Bar Association, President, 1988-89; Federal Bar Council for the Second Circuit, Trustee, Vice President and Vice-Chair, 1980-92; Federal Bar Council Foundation, Chair, 1992-95, Director, 1996-2002; American Bar Association, House of Delegates, 1987-91; American Arbitration Association, Commercial Arbitrators' Panel and Member, Advisory Committee for the AAA Large Case Management Program; CPR International Institute for Conflict Prevention and Resolution, Panelist; New England Bar Association, Director, 1989-92; Connecticut Bar Foundation, Director, 1987-91; New England Bar Foundation, Director, 1987-91.

## SULLIVAN, Shaun S
Wiggin and Dana LLP, New Haven
203 498 4315
ssullivan@wiggin.com
*Recommended in Litigation*
**Practice Areas:** Chairs the firm's Litigation Department. He has represented clients for 30 years in a variety of major disputes. He has been active on behalf of both plaintiffs and defendants in complex commercial litigation involving Fortune 500 companies. Most recently, in a suit involving a large electric generation plant, he successfully represented a public utility seeking to enforce its rights under a joint ownership agreement. He also recently successfully defended several non-profit healthcare institutions in a series of class actions involving, among other things, novel tax-exempt issues.
**Prof. Memberships:** American College of Trial Lawyers, International Academy of Trial Lawyers. International Bar Association.

## SVONKIN, Mark
The Law Office of Mark J. Svonkin P.C., West Hartford
860 521 2811
*Recommended in Real Estate*

## SWERDLOFF, David A
Day, Berry & Howard LLP, Stamford
203 977 7334
daswerdloff@dbh.com
*Recommended in Corporate/M&A*
**Practice Areas:** Emerging companies, technology and intellectual property - business, strategic joint ventures, mergers and acquisitions, closely held businesses, tax-exempt organizations.
**Prof. Memberships:** Former President, Regional Bar Association (lower Fairfield County); Vice-Chair and Legislative Liaison, Executive Committee, Committee on Business Law, Connecticut Bar Association; Co-Chair, Business Law Program Committee, WESFACCA.

## TAYLOR, Allan B
Day, Berry & Howard LLP, Hartford
860 275 0225
abtaylor@dbh.com
*Recommended in Litigation*
**Practice Areas:** Commercial litigation, appellate practice group, insurance litigation.
**Prof. Memberships:** Chair, City of Hartford Charter Revision Commissions, 1999-2000, 2002; Board of Directors, Hartford Stage Company; Board of Directors, Hartford Action Project on Infant Health; Fellow, American Leadership Forum; Member, State Board of Education, 1994-present; Chair, 2005; Hartford Board of Education, 1989-93; Hartford City Council, 1981-87.

## VOIGT, Richard
McCarter & English LLP, Hartford
860 275 6700
*Recommended in Employment*

## WADE, James
Robinson & Cole LLP, Hartford
860 275 8200
*Recommended in Litigation*

## WATERS, Barry
Murtha Cullina LLP, New Haven
203 772 7700
*Recommended in Employment*

## WYLD, Robert
Shipman & Goodwin LLP, Hartford
860 251 5000
*Recommended in Litigation*

## ZAKARIAN, Albert
Day, Berry & Howard LLP, Hartford
860 275 0290
azakarian@dbh.com
*Recommended in Employment*
**Practice Areas:** Employment law and litigation, commercial litigation.
**Prof. Memberships:** Fellow, American College of Trial Lawyers; Fellow, The College of Labor and Employment Lawyers; past President, Hartford County Bar Association; advocate and past President, American Board of Trial Advocates, Connecticut Chapter; past Chairman, Connecticut Bar Association, Litigation Section; National Board of Trial Advocates; Defense Research Institute; Fellow, American and Connecticut Bar Foundations; Oliver Ellsworth Inns of Court.

## ZANDY, John C
Wiggin and Dana LLP, New Haven
203 498 4330
jzandy@wiggin.com
*Recommended in Employment*
**Practice Areas:** Advises employers in labor relations, including negotiating collective bargaining agreements, handling grievances and arbitrations and proceedings before the National Labor Relations Board, and defending against union organizing campaigns. Also defends employers in cases involving allegations of discrimination, sexual harassment, wrongful discharge, wage and hour, and OSHA violations, and also advises them on human resource issues such as discipline and discharge, family and medical leave, union-free policies, affirmative action requirements, employment and non-competition agreements, and ADA compliance.
**Prof. Memberships:** Labor and Employment Law Sections of the Connecticut and American Bar Associations.
**Personal:** JD, Valparaiso University School of Law with honors, LLM, Labor Law, New York University Graduate School of Law, and a BA, Miami University 1970.

# DAY, BERRY & HOWARD LLP

## THE FIRM

**Chairman of the Executive Committee:** James Sicilian
**Executive Director:** Howard Shafer

**FIRM OVERVIEW:** Day, Berry & Howard LLP is a full-service law firm representing individuals and businesses in a wide variety of sophisticated legal matters. It has one of the most respected trial practices in the Northeast and a diverse business law practice counseling major corporations, small businesses and individuals. The firm has strong regional, national and international practices in a wide range of areas including technology and intellectual property, commercial litigation, employment, energy, finance and insolvency, estate planning and trust administration, environmental law, international tax law and business law.

## MAIN AREAS OF PRACTICE:

**Commercial Litigation:** The firm's commercial litigation attorneys handle a wide variety of commercial litigation matters in federal and state courts throughout the United States. They have worked on large, complex cases, involving teams of attorneys and disputes involving hundreds of millions of dollars. They have also represented individuals and businesses in smaller disputes that were every bit as important to the clients who were involved. In all of its engagements, the firm offers lean staffing; direct client access to the partner in charge; early evaluation of litigation options, alternative dispute resolution and settlement strategies; and the skill and experience to handle everything from preliminary motions to trial to appeal. The firm's goal is not simply to win cases; but to find cost-effective solutions for its clients. The firm's commercial litigation attorneys have worked on almost every type of commercial litigation, including contract disputes; securities and shareholder litigation; antitrust; intellectual property; trade secrets litigation; accountants' liability and other professional liability; real estate disputes; lender liability claims; bankruptcy litigation; creditors' rights litigation; distributor and franchise litigation; and consumer credit litigation.

**Capital Markets:** The firm's capital markets attorneys help institutional lenders and investors structure, negotiate and close financial transactions of many different kinds and virtually all sizes. These deals take place all over the United States, as well as in Europe, South America and the Far East. The reputation of the firm's capital markets attorneys is founded on depth and experience in a number of industry areas, including: bank lending; credit tenant lease finance; equipment leasing/finance; municipal finance; structured finance; bankruptcy; real estate finance; and private equity funds. The capital markets practice is diverse, but ultimately connected by a common approach to transactional work. The firm often staffs matters with attorneys from more than one office, with the goal being to assemble the best possible team to meet the client's needs. Knowing that clients want to get deals closed efficiently and creatively, these lawyers are trained to be practical, to never lose sight of the client's business objectives and to represent clients aggressively but never in an inappropriate manner.

**Energy Law:** The firm's energy attorneys have been at the forefront of energy industry restructuring. They have helped clients navigate critical restructuring issues that define their evolution and identity in the changing world of energy purchase and supply, including issues of: wholesale market design, operation and participation; retail market design, operation and participation; development and finance of new generation; transfers of existing fossil, nuclear and hydroelectric generation; nuclear power in the evolving marketplace; stranded cost securitization; market participant workouts and bankruptcies; siting, environmental and land use; creation of new organizational vehicles to drive electric industry restructuring, such as independent system operators, regional transmission groups, regional transmission organizations, and stakeholder boards; mergers, consolidations, reorganizations and divestitures; financing of energy companies; and alternative dispute resolution of complex energy issues. These attorneys have advised clients on energy project development internationally, and energy restructuring matters throughout the United States.

**Government Investigations:** The firm has a team of attorneys available to

### HEAD OFFICE

**CONNECTICUT**
CityPlace I, 185 Asylum Street, **Hartford**, CT 06103
**Tel:** 860 275 0100   **Fax:** 860 275 0343
**Website:** www.dbh.com

### ADDITIONAL OFFICES

**CONNECTICUT**
One East Putnam Avenue, **Greenwich**, CT 06830
**Tel:** 203 862 7800   **Fax:** 203 862 7801

One Audubon Street, **New Haven**, CT 06511
**Tel:** 203 752 5000   **Fax:** 203 752 5001

One Canterbury Green, **Stamford**, CT 06901
**Tel:** 203 977 7300   **Fax:** 203 977 7301

29 South Main Street, **West Hartford**, CT 06107
**Tel:** 860 313 5700   **Fax:** 860 313 5701

**MASSACHUSETTS**
One International Place, **Boston**, MA 02110
**Tel:** 617 345 4600   **Fax:** 617 345 4745

**NEW YORK**
875 Third Avenue, **New York**, NY 10022
**Tel:** 212 829 3600   **Fax:** 212 829 3601

counsel clients in connection with criminal, civil and regulatory investigations conducted by federal and state agencies and to advise clients how to minimize the risks of being a target of a government probe. This team includes attorneys with extensive experience in government - including the former United States Attorney for Connecticut and former federal prosecutors - as well as attorneys versed in numerous substantive areas of the law that are the subject of government scrutiny. Among these 'hot spots' are healthcare, environmental compliance, tax, securities, banking, antitrust, public corruption, and international trade. Thus, in fashioning a strategy to respond to a government investigation, clients can draw upon the experience of attorneys who have conducted - and now defend against - such investigations. Their collective experience enables the team to provide a prompt and effective response to government probes. This team assists clients in conducting internal investigations to detect possible wrongdoing by rogue employees and work with law enforcement agencies to avoid corporate liability under the laws that impose criminal responsibility for the actions of even low-level employees.

**Diversity Efforts:** Each staff member at Day, Berry & Howard, working individually and together, is committed to the principle that everyone deserves to be treated with dignity and respect. The firm is proud of its tradition of fostering and maintaining an environment in which the diversity of each individual is valued and celebrated. The firm believes that the contributions of each individual are essential to its continued growth and to its ultimate goal of providing the highest quality legal services in a timely manner at a reasonable cost. The firm is committed to, and each staff member is expected to support, its efforts to foster an inclusive atmosphere that actively seeks to employ people of diverse backgrounds at all levels of the firm, and to provide, wherever possible, challenging opportunities, meaningful guidance and positive incentives to assist each person to achieve his or her greatest potential. The firm is committed to taking full advantage of the rich backgrounds and abilities of its colleagues and to promoting greater diversity and inclusiveness whenever and wherever possible. It is committed to encouraging individual initiatives and contributions as well as teamwork and collaboration. The firm believes that it can create advantage from its differences to build richer, broader common values and goals.

# FINN DIXON & HERLING LLP

## THE FIRM

**Founding Partners:** Harold B Finn III
Brett W Dixon (also Managing Partner)
Michael J Herling

**Number of partners:** 12
**Number of other lawyers:** 15

**FIRM OVERVIEW:** Finn Dixon & Herling LLP provides a broad spectrum of legal services to the business and financial community. The firm's clients are located throughout the United States, and many of them have international operations. Since its founding in 1987, Finn Dixon has focused on issues affecting businesses and business transactions. The firm strives to provide the highest level of customer service and practical, solution-oriented advice, grounded on a thorough understanding of each client's business. The firm has developed a litigation capability that supports the firm's core client base and serves other clients involved in commercial litigation matters.

## MAIN AREAS OF PRACTICE

**BUSINESS:** Finn Dixon's business practice is focused on eight key areas:

**Mergers & Acquisitions/Private Equity:** Represents buyers, sellers and investors in various transactions, including mergers and other business combinations, leveraged buy-outs and recapitalizations, growth capital investments, 'add-on' acquisitions, proxy contests, stock swaps and public company mergers.

**Venture Capital/Emerging Companies:** Represents venture capital firms in both early-stage and growth capital investments and in the formation, organization and operation of venture capital funds.

**Investment Management:** Represents domestic and offshore investment partnerships and trusts, common and collective trust funds, investment advisers, commodity trading advisers and commodity pool operators and registered broker-dealers. Investment advisory clients include a number of nationally-renowned firms, as well as smaller state-registered entities. Also represents sources of private equity and money managers in their investments in domestic and offshore funds, including hedge funds and other alternative investment vehicles.

**Securities:** Advises clients regarding federal and state securities laws that affect public offerings and private placements by both publicly-held companies and privately-owned businesses, annual reports and proxy statements and the organization of, and offerings by, private investment companies.

**Banking & Lending:** Advises banks and other financial institutions on all aspects of lending and other credit transactions. Also assists such clients on various regulatory issues, including with respect to general compliance as well as acquisitions and dispositions of banks and bank holding companies and the establishment by out of state banks of branch offices or other operations in Connecticut.

**Public Finance:** Represents issuers, underwriters and trustees in municipal bond issuances, including the state of Connecticut, state agencies and municipalities in general finance or specialized project finance matters.

**Tax:** Finn Dixon offers tax expertise, including structuring and other advice to its transactional clients as well as advice in connection with federal and state taxation of the ongoing activities of its corporate, partnership and limited liability clients.

**General Business Representation:** Finn Dixon helps many clients address a wide variety of operational and strategic issues on a continuous basis, including consultation on choice of entity, protection and coordination of the rights of owners, commercial real estate transactions, employment matters, including executive compensation, severance arrangements, stock options and employee benefits, financings, licensing and strategic alliance and joint venture arrangements and compliance with regulatory requirements.

**LITIGATION:** Finn Dixon's Litigation Practice encompasses civil litigation in state and federal courts, appellate advocacy, arbitration and other forms of alternative dispute resolution and proceedings before administrative agencies. The firm's practice also includes bankruptcy and workouts and employment law.

**CLIENTS:** Finn Dixon's clients include a wide array of commercial entities, from substantial private equity and venture capital groups, middle market public and private corporations, and banks and financial institutions to risk-taking entrepreneurs and start-up ventures.

## HEAD OFFICE

**CONNECTICUT**
One Landmark Square, Suite 1400, **Stamford**, CT 06901 2689
**Tel:** 203 325 5000   **Fax:** 203 348 5777
**Website:** www.fdh.com

## BRANCH OFFICES

**CONNECTICUT**
31 Whitney Avenue, 2nd Floor, **New Haven**, CT 06510
**Tel:** 203 848 6488   **Fax:** 203 348 5777

## How lawyers are ranked

Every year we carry out thousands of in-depth interviews with clients and lawyers in order to assess the reputations and expertise of business lawyers across the USA. Chambers rankings and editorial are referred to extensively by General Counsel and other purchasers of legal services who look to our recommendations when choosing their lawyers.

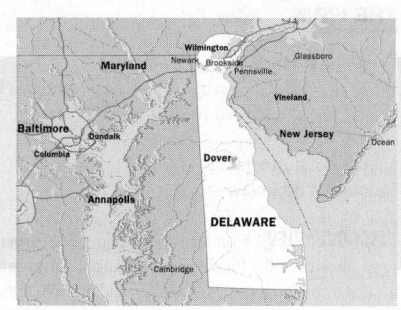

# BANKRUPTCY/RESTRUCTURING

## Bankruptcy/Restructuring
### Leading Firms

1. RICHARDS, LAYTON & FINGER PA *Wilmington*
   SKADDEN, ARPS *Wilmington*
   YOUNG CONAWAY STARGATT *Wilmington*
2. MORRIS, NICHOLS, ARSHT & TUNNELL *Wilmington*
   SAUL EWING LLP *Wilmington*
3. PACHULSKI, STANG, ZIEHL, YOUNG *Wilmington*
   PEPPER HAMILTON LLP *Wilmington*
   POTTER ANDERSON & CORROON LLP *Wilmington*
   THE BAYARD FIRM *Wilmington*
4. ASHBY & GEDDES *Wilmington*
   BLANK ROME LLP *Wilmington*
   COZEN O'CONNOR *Wilmington*
   LANDIS RATH & COBB LLP *Wilmington*
   MORRIS, JAMES, HITCHENS *Wilmington*
   REED SMITH LLP *Wilmington*

## Band 1

### Richards, Layton & Finger PA
See firm details p.423

**The Firm:** Leading clients across the country praise this "*impressive, home-grown firm*" for its "*thorough and professional*" bankruptcy practice. Indeed, the quality of market feedback garnered by the operation won it promotion to the top tier. A 16-strong team has built up "*an unsurpassed knowledge of Delaware bankruptcy court process, and maintains healthy relations with the court,*" according to market commentators. As well as being home to a respected secured creditor practice, the department is recognized for its strength in representing the debtor in Chapter 11 proceedings, typically acting for clients such as JPMorgan Chase and Congress Financial. A full-service firm, it is the largest in the state and is regarded as "*uniformly excellent*" across the board. It is commended for its depth of resources and the high caliber of expertise in complementary practice areas. The firm is revered for simultaneously taking the lead in cases and performing as a "*seamless extension of in-house counsel.*"

**The Lawyers:** Chairman of the bankruptcy department is "*cool customer and even-headed attorney*" **Mark Collins** (see p.403). Routinely going above and beyond the call of duty, Collins is regarded as being "*at the top of his game*" and is well respected for his representation of secured lenders. Clients often referred to his "*creativity, which allows the bankruptcy to proceed while still capturing value for creditors.*" **Daniel DeFranceschi** (see p.403) also impresses clients with his "*understated yet hands-on and proactive approach.*" He is noted for his debtor-oriented and bankruptcy litigation work and is well versed in cases involving telecom, natural resources, healthcare and asbestos issues. **John Knight** (see p.407) rounds off this department of "*committed individuals who would work on Christmas day if required.*" He "*keeps on grinding away until the goals are achieved,*" according to clients, and affirms his position in the tables this year.

**Clients/Work Highlights:** JPMorgan Chase; Congress Financial; Bank of America; GE Capital; Teleglobe; USG; FINOVA Group; Armstrong World Industries; IWO Holdings; Smarte Carte and DecisionOne.

### Skadden, Arps, Slate, Meagher & Flom LLP & Affiliates
See firm details p.1557

**The Firm:** This "*bluest of the blue-chip law firms*" has the "*philosophy and presence in the state to distinguish it as a definite leader.*" A "*world-class player,*" it operates on a national basis with an established office in Wilmington and is well respected for its leading roles in both nationwide and Delaware-specific proceedings. For example, the firm represented Deutsche Bank, agent to pre-petition bank group JA Jones in North Carolina, and acted for KBC, agent to pre-petition bank group Perryville Energy Holdings in Louisiana. The vast majority of the workload is debtor-oriented, although clients also point to the group's strength when it comes to counseling creditors and acquirers of assets from troubled companies.

**The Lawyers:** "*Head and shoulders above the rest,*" **Gregg Galardi** (see p.404) is recognized as one of the preeminent restructuring lawyers in the state. Clients are quick to point to his "*vast knowledge of the law*" and his "*high level of ethics and integrity,*" further stating that "*when he speaks, people listen.*" Displaying "*a sharp understanding of business,*" Galardi represented Ultimate Electronics in Chapter 11 proceedings. **Mark Chehi** (see p.402) is another big hitter who handles high-profile workouts, restructurings and Chapter 11 proceedings. "*One of the best in town,*" Chehi has represented Birch Telecom in a prominent Chapter 11 case. "*A class operator in the courtroom,*" **Anthony Clark** (see p.402) heads this corporate restructuring and bankruptcy litigation practice. Clark combines his bankruptcy work with high-stakes corporate litigation.

**Clients/Work Highlights:** KBC; Ultimate Electronics; Hayes Lemmerz International and Deutsche Bank are just a few examples of this department's impressive client roster.

### Young Conaway Stargatt & Taylor LLP
See firm details p.424

**The Firm:** "*A top-flight Delaware firm,*" clients say this multiservice outfit is at the top of the list for debtor-oriented work. Fielding a 30-strong team, including nine dedicated partners, this is one of the largest departments in the state and clients value the "*depth of talent available at every level.*" It primarily represents debtors but is also commended for its work on behalf of creditors and creditors' committees and its expertise in mass tort bankruptcy proceedings. In line with the national trend, the group has been particularly active in cases emanating out of the automotive industry and acted as special Delaware counsel for Meridian Automotive Systems in its recent reorganization. The department has both built on its established relationships with out-of-state law firms and achieved some high-profile successes as lead counsel during the past year.

**The Lawyers:** Chairman of the firm and "*all-around class act*" **James Patton** (see p.410) is described by clients as "*an even-keeled, unflappable attorney at the top of his game.*" A nationally prominent figure, he is particularly acclaimed for his involvement in large asbestos bankruptcies. An "*outstanding bankruptcy lawyer,*" **Robert Brady** (see p.402) is chair of the bankruptcy and corporate restructuring section. "*A lawyer who cut his teeth on bankruptcy in the 90's and really made an impact,*" he is well versed in all aspects of the Chapter 11 restructuring process. **Brendan Shannon** (see p.411) is renowned for his experience of representing official committees in Chapter 11 cases. He acted as sole counsel to the official committee of unsecured cred-

## Bankruptcy/Restructuring
### Leading Individuals

**[1]**
COLLINS Mark *Richards, Layton & Finger PA*
GALARDI Gregg *Skadden, Arps*
PATTON JR James *Young Conaway Stargatt*
PERNICK Norman *Saul Ewing LLP*

**[2]**
BRADY Robert *Young Conaway Stargatt*
CHEHI Mark *Skadden, Arps*
DAVIS JONES Laura *Pachulski, Stang, Ziehl,*
DEHNEY Robert *Morris, Nichols, Arsht & Tunnell*
FATELL Bonnie *Blank Rome LLP*
SELBER SILVERSTEIN Laurie *Potter Anderson*
SUDELL William *Morris, Nichols, Arsht & Tunnell*

**[3]**
CLARK Anthony *Skadden, Arps*
DEFRANCESCHI Daniel *Richards, Layton & Finger*
FELGER Mark *Cozen O'Connor*
GLASSMAN Neil *The Bayard Firm*
LANDIS Adam *Landis Rath & Cobb LLP*
MINUTI Mark *Saul Ewing LLP*
SHANNON Brendan *Young Conaway Stargatt*
STRATTON David *Pepper Hamilton LLP*

**[4]**
BOWDEN William *Ashby & Geddes*
FOURNIER David *Pepper Hamilton LLP*
GWYNNE Kurt *Reed Smith LLP*
KNIGHT John *Richards, Layton & Finger PA*
MILLER Stephen *Morris, James, Hitchens*
MORGAN Pauline *Young Conaway Stargatt*
PACITTI Domenic *Saul Ewing LLP*
SCHLERF Jeffrey *The Bayard Firm*

### Up-and-coming individuals
ABBOTT Derek *Morris, Nichols, Arsht & Tunnell*
COUNIHAN Victoria *Greenberg Traurig LLP*
NESTOR Michael *Young Conaway Stargatt*
YODER Steven *The Bayard Firm*

itors in connection with the sale of Trenwick America's foreign subsidiaries and related debt restructuring. An equally "*strong attorney*," **Pauline Morgan** (see p.409) was active in the sale of Cone Mills in 2005. She practiced in Philadelphia before moving to Delaware and commentators point to her broad-based skill set as a defining feature. Rounding off this group is **Michael Nestor** (see p.409). "*A terrific strategist and a consensus-building, practical guy*," Nestor is a firm favorite of clients and peers alike.
**Clients/Work Highlights:** Further clients include Touch America Holdings, Meridian Automotive Systems and Garden Ridge.

## Band 2

### Morris, Nichols, Arsht & Tunnell LLP
See firm details p.420
**The Firm:** Both clients and out-of-state referring attorneys credit this "*large, indigenous law firm*" with "*greater depth than most*." The bankruptcy litigation law group comprises 14 attorneys and is recommended by clients for its "*responsiveness and knowledge of local laws, courts and nuances*." The group is noted in particular for its litigation success rate and is

a key port of call for prominent national clients. Clients also praised the firm's capability in handling cases of national significance which bridge practice areas. The firm's involvement in the Court of Chancery action commenced by Calpine against Bank of New York and Wilmington Trust is a case in point. This is a declaratory judgment concerning the interpretation of a bond indenture and Calpine's proposed use of asset sale proceeds, and is a good example of how the firm draws on the "*true bankruptcy specialists*" on offer across departments. Other work of note undertaken during the year includes acting on the subsequent consolidation of all the debtors in the Chapter 11 case of Thaxton Group. The team is recognized for its representation of debtors and unsecured creditors' committees.
**The Lawyers:** Described as "*a dean of the bankruptcy Bar*," **William Sudell** (see p.412) is held in high esteem for his "*vast experience in the field*", and particularly commended for his prowess in terms of bankruptcy litigation. Clients view **Robert Dehney** (see p.403) as "*an exceptionally bright attorney making a real name for himself*," especially where representing debtors is concerned, although he also acts for creditors. "*Part of the next wave of great lawyers*," **Derek Abbott** (see p.401) enters the tables on the back of strong client recommendation.
**Clients/Work Highlights:** Chapter 11 debtor clients include Rouge Industries; The Glass Group; Orion Refining and Oakwood Homes. Official creditors' committee cases include Jillian's and Digital Legal Services. EchoStar Communication, Fortistar and Wilmington Trust are also regular clients.

### Saul Ewing LLP
See firm details p.1763
**The Firm:** This Philadelphia-based firm "*has successfully expanded its footprint in Wilmington*" and is considered a serious player in Delaware. The firm has a diverse bankruptcy and restructuring practice and is among the few operations in the state to offer and utilize offices outside of Delaware. Clients appreciate the team's depth of experience in terms of debtor representation and point to the firm as a good choice for both secured and unsecured creditors. The group has acted in the Owens Corning case during the year, which determined under what circumstances a court exercising bankruptcy powers may substantially consolidate affiliated entities.
**The Lawyers:** Of the many "*excellent, knowledgeable bankruptcy lawyers*" in this department, clients pinpointed the "*top-class*" **Norman Pernick** (see p.410). "*A sure-fire leader*," Pernick has been involved in the Owens Corning case and is respected for his experience of acting as lead counsel to companies in Chapter 11 proceedings. "*Always prepared and meticulous over every detail*," **Mark Minuti** (see p.409) debuts in the tables this year. He often works closely with Pernick and is widely respected as a bankruptcy litigator with experience of Chapter 11 proceedings in Delaware as well as other states. **Domenic Pacitti** (see p.409) also enters the tables this year and is recommended for his "*broad substantive knowledge and experience*."

**Clients/Work Highlights:** This department represents debtors; secured and unsecured creditors; committees; trustees and landlords in a range of sectors.

## Band 3

### Pachulski, Stang, Ziehl, Young, Jones & Weintraub PC
See firm details p.338
**The Firm:** This is one of the largest devoted bankruptcy firms in the country and is noted for its "*substantial Delaware bankruptcy and restructuring practice*." While it differs from the Delaware-based, multiservice firms in the table, competitors agree: "*It is a firm to reckon with*." Interviewees mostly pointed to the team's strength in debtor-oriented work, but clients also value the "*quality representation on offer*" in terms of unsecured creditors' committees.
**The Lawyers:** **Laura Davis Jones** is the managing stockholder of the firm's Delaware office and is widely respected for her representation of debtors and creditors' committees in complex Chapter 11 cases and workout proceedings. "*She gets as much business as anyone in town*" and is admired for her devotion to client service.
**Clients/Work Highlights:** Examples of clients include Chapter 11 debtors in Focal Communications and Superior TeleCom, and creditors' committees in FINOVA Group and Key3Media.

### Pepper Hamilton LLP
See firm details p.1760
**The Firm:** Its lawyers were described as "*tough and to the point*," and they regularly feature in high-end cases. The Delaware office is part of an integrated nationwide network, and clients pointed to the depth of resources and vast experience on offer as major advantages of using the firm. Its department is considered particularly adept at representing debtors in Chapter 11 proceedings but also comes highly recommended for advising creditors' committees. Of the many notable cases undertaken during the past year, one of the most significant engagements was representing Northwestern Corporation in the Netexit Chapter 11 proceedings.
**The Lawyers:** **David Stratton** (see p.412) was recently appointed managing partner of the Wilmington office and is a firm favorite of clients across the country. He is considered "*good at negotiating a complicated deal by getting to the heart of the matter while keeping an eye on the bigger picture*." He represented the PresGar Companies, the major debtors in the DVI Chapter 11 proceedings. "*Bright, clear-thinking attorney*" **David Fournier** (see p.412) is just as well regarded for his involvement in lending transactions as for his bankruptcy litigation skills.
**Clients/Work Highlights:** PresGar Companies; SoundExchange; CSFB; Northwestern Corporation and the creditors' committee in the Metalforming Technologies case.

## Potter Anderson & Corroon LLP

See firm details p.421

**The Firm:** This primarily nondebtor-oriented practice is widely admired by clients for "*keeping its finger on the pulse of the Delaware bankruptcy scene*" and for "*effortlessly coordinating cases that are national in scope.*" The six-strong team represents individual creditors, banks, bondholders, trade creditors and borrowers and has been heavily involved in telecommunications bankruptcies of late. Clients mention the depth of expertise across a range of areas as an added attraction. Of the many noteworthy cases undertaken in the year, the team acted for SBC Telecommunications in resolving several cases across the country.

**The Lawyers:** Of the many "*extremely competent and aggressive lawyers*" in the department, **Laurie Selber Silverstein** (see p.411) is the standout figure and head of the department. "*One of the best creditor lawyers in the state,*" she is described by peers as being "*a bright and able advocate who is really tenacious in court,*" and has been prominent in the telecommunications sector during the year.

**Clients/Work Highlights:** ConAgra Foods; Fleet National Bank; CIBC; Perot Systems and Norfolk Southern.

## The Bayard Firm

See firm details p.417

**The Firm:** The large national companies favor this "*pedigree Delaware law firm*" for the "*nimble and responsive approach adopted by its attorneys.*" Speaking highly of its general efficiency and in-depth knowledge of the Delaware system, clients recommend it as "*a good choice for middle-market cases or acting as co-counsel on the mammoth projects.*" This 13-strong team is well known for its representation of debtors, creditors' committees, purchasers, trustees, lenders and stockholders. Chapter 11 and Chapter 7 matters are the order of the day. Highlights include representing the equity committee in relation to the Chapter 11 bankruptcy petition filed by Trump Hotel & Casino Resorts.

**The Lawyers:** This bankruptcy group is the firm's flagship department and is run by chairman of the firm **Neil Glassman** (see p.404). He is credited with an "*in-depth knowledge of local nuances and of the judges' requirements,*" and impresses clients with "*his skillful use of negotiation and settlement schemes that avoid the time and cost of litigation.*" He led the team representing AmeriKing in relation to its Chapter 11 bankruptcy petition. New to the tables this year, the "*ever-calm and clear-headed*" **Jeffrey Schlerf** (see p.270764) led the prosecution of approximately 1,200 adversary proceedings on behalf of the litigation trust created under the Chapter 11 plan in the IT Groups case. **Steven Yoder** (see p.414) also makes his debut in the tables, with clients remarking upon the benefits of "*his network of contacts in Delaware*" and his "*aggressive and savvy style in court.*" He acted alongside Glassman in the AmeriKing case.

**Clients/Work Highlights:** Mobile Tool International, Executive Sounding Board Associations and Joseph Pardo, Hobart Truesdell and Perry Mandarino (liquidating trustees) are representative clients of the group.

## Band 4

## Ashby & Geddes

See firm details p.416

**The Firm:** This "*solid, diversified*" department is respected for both litigation and transactional work, in which it represents debtors, creditors' committees, bidders and asset purchasers. The group also acts for secured and unsecured creditors, lenders and other interested parties. Clients praise the nine-strong team for "*offering holistic and constructive advice that covers the bankruptcy process from every angle.*" The firm acted as co-counsel to the creditors' committee in the ongoing Meridian Automotive Systems, Kaiser Aluminum and Budget Group bankruptcies. Debtor/trustee representation in cases concerning Napster and Trenwick America also contributed to the workload.

**The Lawyers:** **William Bowden** (see p.402) is a respected member of the bankruptcy Bar, with clients admiring his "*courteous, knowledgeable and respectful style.*" Bowden heads up the team and is mostly praised for his creditor-oriented practice.

**Clients/Work Highlights:** AIG; Lehman Brothers; The Shaw Group; Supervalu; US Bank; JPMorgan Chase; Williams Communications Services and the Minnesota Twins.

## Blank Rome LLP

See firm details p.1747

**The Firm:** This regional firm has an office in Wilmington that is increasingly recognized as a serious competitor in the market. Although smaller than some of the other groups in the state, what it lacks in size it makes up for in quality. Bankruptcy reorganizations, related litigation and out-of-court workouts form the staple diet here. Clients pointed to the advantages of being able to draw on the resources of the firm's other offices and its lawyers' multidisciplinary approach.

**The Lawyers:** **Bonnie Fatell** (see p.403) is universally regarded as a "*top-notch attorney,*" with over 20 years of experience in the field. "*Creative and savvy,*" she is said to understand the business consequences of the law and "*always thinks a couple of steps ahead.*"

**Clients/Work Highlights:** The firm represents the gamut of parties, including creditors' committees; debtors; institutional lenders; trade creditors and asset purchasers.

## Cozen O'Connor

**The Firm:** "*Its lawyers are attentive to the needs of the client, sometimes almost going overboard in terms of effort,*" remarked one client in summing up the ethos of this regional firm. "*Fully geared towards the provision of good value,*" the outfit's professionalism and success rate were also noted by clients. With headquarters in Philadelphia, it has the added attraction of being able to draw on 12 full-time bankruptcy attorneys in the region. The department undertakes Chapter 11 debtor and creditors' committee work and has represented Chapter 7 trustees in two high-profile cases during the year. However, the department does not represent banks or secured creditors.

**The Lawyers:** **Mark Felger** is the managing partner of the Wilmington office and is favored by clients for his "*confident performances before bankruptcy judges.*" "*Professional in every respect,*" he has been actively involved on both contentious and noncontentious fronts with regard to the Glass Group bankruptcy.

**Clients/Work Highlights:** Argenbright Security; Cognisa Security; Lorrilard Tobacco Company and GlassRatner Advisory & Capital Group.

## Landis Rath & Cobb LLP

**The Firm:** This firm is a relatively new entrant in the Delaware market, having opened for business in 2003, but has carved out a solid reputation for itself as a key port of call for larger firms with conflict issues. Highly recommended by clients, this firm "*out-performs expectations*" and offers "*the highest levels of expertise.*" Some examples of the work undertaken this year include being retained as the sole counsel to the official committee of unsecured creditors in the bankruptcy case of AstroPower, and representing ASM Capital, the largest claimholder in the Thaxton Group bankruptcy case.

**The Lawyers:** Clients awarded **Adam Landis** an "*A-plus on all fronts,*" and one went on to describe him as a "*forceful, articulate advocate.*" "*Not one to follow the cookbook style of bankruptcy law,*" Landis utilizes the bankruptcy system to maximum advantage and is "*proactive not reactive.*"

**Clients/Work Highlights:** In addition to debtor representations, the group acts for creditors, lenders and other interested parties. Clients include ASM Capital; LNR Property; Cognistar and C&S Wholesale Grocers.

## Morris, James, Hitchens & Williams LLP

See firm details p.419

**The Firm:** Clients recommend this "*extremely competent, well-structured*" firm as a user-friendly, responsive outfit. A seven-strong bankruptcy and reorganization group primarily acts for creditors. Lenders, secured and unsecured creditors, liquidating agents, bidders and purchasers of assets out of bankruptcy also feature as clients. As well as practicing in Delaware, the firm has been able to forge good working relationships with clients and firms in several other states. The group has been involved in the Fleming and Winn-Dixie bankruptcies lately, representing the reclamation creditors and dairy producers respectively.

**The Lawyers:** **Stephen Miller** (see p.409) chairs the bankruptcy and reorganization group and comes highly recommended by clients for being "*firm and helpful in finding solutions.*" Always calculating his advice in terms of "*what makes sense from a financial point of view,*" Miller is one of the few attorneys who render third-party legal opinions on matters of Delaware state law.

**Clients/Work Highlights:** Afco Credit Corporation; DuPont; Sprint Nextel and Wilmington Trust.

## Reed Smith LLP

See firm details p.1762

**The Firm:** The practitioners at the Wilmington office of this international firm impressed onlookers with the extent to which they have immersed themselves in the market. The outfit has enjoyed a growing profile as a result, particularly where representing creditors' committees and creditors in complex bankruptcy cases is concerned. The team of six full-time bankruptcy attorneys is also adept at representing secured lenders and debtors-in-possession. A proportion of bankruptcy litigation further contributes to the workload. Recent highlights include representing the creditors' committees in cases concerning AAIPharma, Women First Health-Care, Birch Telecom and Rouge Industries.

**The Lawyers:** Research indicated that **Kurt Gwynne** (see p.405) has made waves with clients. Described as "*young, smart and dedicated,*" he is the managing partner of the Wilmington office and head of the bankruptcy practice. Gwynne primarily represents creditors' committees and creditors in complex bankruptcies. He also serves as a court-appointed Chapter 11 trustee.

**Clients/Work Highlights:** Devcon Construction; Qwest and Qwest Communications; Del Monte Foods; HJ Heinz; GE Information Financial Services; IKON Financial Services and IKON Office Solutions.

### Other Notable Practitioners

Following the departure of Scott Cousins, **Victoria Counihan** (see p.403) of Greenberg Traurig LLP enters the spotlight this year. Described as "*young and extremely capable,*" Counihan is widely thought of as one to watch out for in the future.

# CHANCERY

## Band 1

### Morris, Nichols, Arsht & Tunnell LLP

See firm details p.420

**The Firm:** Clients billed this operation as "*the premier firm in the chancery market,*" agreeing: "*It offers everything you would expect of such an established name in the field.*" Sources value the fact that the firm is home to some of the finest practitioners in the state, who "*really know how to gain an advantage in the system.*" The outfit is a favorite of the big New York law firms and also captures a share of the Delaware market that is the envy of its competitors in the state. The corporate litigation group offers a range of expertise including, but by no means limited to, breach of fiduciary, appraisal and special litigation committee cases. As the Delaware Court of Chancery is considered one of the country's leading forums for the resolution of business disputes, the group often represents multi-billion-dollar international corporations in cases of national significance. Clients also praised this large multiservice law firm's cross-departmental approach. A major coup for the team was representing defendants Roy Disney and Stanley Gold, the former directors of The Walt Disney Company, in Re The Walt Disney Company Derivative Litigation, a significant case tried over 37 days in the Court of Chancery.

**The Lawyers:** "*A cut above in the pecking order*" is "*chancery supremo*" **Gilchrist Sparks** (see p.412). Clients find his "*tremendous strategic vision*" and "*encyclopedic knowledge of the law and procedure*" key to his success. He is undoubtedly one of the finest chancery lawyers in the state and is envied as being "*always the first to receive calls about the heavyweight cases.*" **William Lafferty** (see p.407) has assembled quite a client following for his chancery practice as well as his legal acumen, and is much sought after for his "*impressive, civil and courteous performances in court.*" **Kenneth Nachbar** (see p.409) is also well respected for his chancery practice and accumulated a number of recommendations for his "*no-nonsense, yet effective style.*" "*Real star*" **Alan Stone** (see p.412) is described by clients as having many of the same qualities as the other experienced members of the group and is an "*energetic, dependable and personable attorney.*"

**Clients/Work Highlights:** 3M; Cadbury Schweppes; Comcast; Dow Chemical; Motorola; Regal Entertainment Group; Ford; Unocal and Viacom.

### Potter Anderson & Corroon LLP

See firm details p.421

**The Firm:** "*This firm has written a chapter in the book of Chancery Court practice,*" according to clients, who truly value the group's transparent billing structure and depth of expertise across a range of disciplines. Clients are so enamored with the service this firm offers that one commented: "*We rely on the firm in the same way that we rely on our own staff,*" further wishing that the firm had offices elsewhere so that they could handle more work. Cases involving corporate governance, fiduciary matters and M&A issues remain a mainstay of the work undertaken by the group, which is also singled out for its experience of handling hostile takeovers. Various members of this group have recently been involved in representing some of the director-defendants in Re The Walt Disney Company Derivative Litigation, the 37-day trial concluded this year. Further work of note includes representing Maytag in litigation surrounding the proposed acquisition of Whirlpool.

**The Lawyers:** **Robert Payson** (see p.410) was singled out for his "*seasoned judgment*" and "*familiarity with the local judiciary,*" which, in turn, affords clients a good insight into what to expect throughout litigation. He has a real flair for drawing evidence out of witnesses, with clients paying homage to his "*plain-speaking, responsive and congenial style.*" **Michael Goldman** (see p.405) was heavily recommended and divides his time between chancery and corporate M&A work. Clients find him immensely reassuring: "*He is so respected that you feel confident just walking into court with him.*" Indeed, Goldman is so attuned with the local procedures and Delaware statutes that he can "*tell you what the judges had for breakfast that morning.*" **Donald Wolfe** (see p.414) is widely respected for his coauthorship of a leading treatise on Delaware corporation law. Armed with "*a comprehensive knowledge of the law*" and "*a real depth of experience,*" he is a definite leader in the field. Wolfe is head of the 20-strong corporate litigation group and represented Disney during the year. Not one to sugar-coat advice, **Stephen Norman** (see p.409) is thoroughly recommended by clients who admire his ability to "*jump in, roll up his sleeves and get the job done.*" Special praise was reserved for his handling of stockholder class and derivative actions, and clients regularly utilize his experience in major takeover battles. Clients declare **Peter Walsh** (see p.413) is a "*proactive and hard-working*" attorney who is "*cool under fire.*" He was on the trial team representing PeopleSoft and its board of directors in connection with a hostile tender offer by Oracle. "*Communicative, knowledgeable and results-oriented,*" **Kevin Shannon** (see p.411) is very much one to watch out for in the future. A "*great writer and an effective advocate,*" he has a financial background and recently represented PNC Bank in a fiduciary duty appraisal case.

**Clients/Work Highlights:** PeopleSoft; Disney; Nextel; Deutsche Bank; CIBC; Butler Manufacturing Company; Hewlett-Packard; Maytag; El Paso; Johnson & Johnson; LNR Corporation and Brook Group.

### Richards, Layton & Finger PA

See firm details p.423

**The Firm:** It is one of the oldest and largest firms in Delaware and consensus remains strong nationwide that it is "*still the best.*" As such, it is considered something of a landmark, especially for clients keen to tap into its fine tradition and gain an understanding of local procedures and practices. Home to some of the magical practitioners in the state, this corporate department is well versed in advising on issues of corporate governance and fiduciary duties, as well as stockholder agreements and federal securities laws. The department successfully defended the outside directors of Disney in litigation challenging the terms under which Michael Ovitz was employed. By way of an example of the caliber of the clients of this firm, it continues to represent the directors of JPMorgan Chase and Citigroup in stockholder litigations.

**The Lawyers:** The inimitable **Franklin Balotti** (see p.401) is a national figure who is widely respected for his *"years of valuable experience"* and is seen as the *"behind the scenes helmsman"* of the corporate department. He advises corporations and corporate directors on litigation, transactions and corporate governance issues. **Jesse Finkelstein** (see p.404) is best known for his work in the Court of Chancery, though he is also involved in corporate M&A. He is

also president of the firm and considered *"one of the biggest of the big guns in the state."* *"One of the senior and premier members of the Bar,"* Finkelstein is a nationally respected figure and was lead counsel in the Disney litigation. Another attorney held in high esteem by clients is **Gregory Williams** (see p.413). Favored for his *"dedicated and professional approach,"* he also had a role in the Disney case. **Gregory Varallo** (see p.413) amassed the support of leading clients, who recommend his *"classic chancery practice"* and *"great reputation."*

**Clients/Work Highlights:** Goldman Sachs; Citigroup; Boeing; Morgan Stanley; Texas Instruments; JPMorgan Chase; Bristol Myers Squibb; NASDAQ and NASD.

## Band 2

### Ashby & Geddes
See firm details p.416

**The Firm:** Although this is a smaller outfit than some of the other leading firms, it is considered to compete directly with its larger rivals. Its *"transformation from a cute boutique shop into a real player"* wins the firm promotion in the table, and its achievements in some of the major cases in the market continue to impress. Known for its prowess in contentious matters, the group is a popular choice for derivative and class action litigation, takeover battles and appraisal actions.

**The Lawyers:** **Larry Ashby** (see p.401) is widely recognized as *"easily one of the best practitioners in the state."* *"Overflowing with knowledge and experience of chancery litigation,"* he featured in the dream team of numerous leading clients. He and **Stephen Jenkins** (see p.406) were indicated as being at the forefront of a formidable team. Jenkins is respected for his litigious abilities, particularly where cases involving institutional stockholders are concerned.

**Clients/Work Highlights:** The firm is probably best known for its representation of directors, officers and substantial stockholders, although it has experience of representing the full range of corporate clients.

### Skadden, Arps, Slate, Meagher & Flom LLP & Affiliates
See firm details p.1557

**The Firm:** This extremely well-respected international law firm is proof that out-of-state firms can enter the Delaware chancery market and *"become a dominant force."* Clients could not emphasize enough the value they place on the wealth of resources and local knowledge of the attorneys at this firm. Close links with the firm's other offices in the region guarantee its lawyers appearances in some of the most critical cases to hit the market. The Wilmington office is also a prolific generator of Delaware-specific instructions in its own right and is recommended for its work on the full range of corporate, securities and contract litigation. It was deemed to offer a particularly strong suit in creditor-related litigation.

**The Lawyers:** **Thomas Allingham** (see p.401) was

described by an important client as *"one of the brightest lawyers I have ever met."* Noted for *"always having the best interests of the client at heart,"* he possesses *"wonderful litigation skills"* and is certainly at the top of many commentators' lists. Another widely respected attorney at this firm is **Edward Welch** (see p.413). *"One hell of a chancery litigator,"* peers even go as far as to say that he is the advocate they would choose to represent them personally. He is held in high regard for his advice on both contentious and noncontentious matters. *"Among the best in the state,"* **Anthony Clark**'s (see p.402) practice includes corporate restructuring and corporate, securities and general commercial litigation. This eclectic practice affords clients a cross-fertilized skill set, at the heart of which lies a *"class litigator."* **Robert Saunders** (see p.411) is a respected litigator with a growing profile, having recently represented an impressive array of clients.

**Clients/Work Highlights:** HealthSouth; The Williams Companies; Tyson Foods and Compaq.

### Young Conaway Stargatt & Taylor LLP
See firm details p.424

**The Firm:** *"Among the top firms in the Delaware hierarchy,"* this corporate counseling and litigation group is recommended both for its litigation avoidance techniques and for pursuing litigation in the Court of Chancery. An established favorite of clients, it is commended for its profile in stockholders' and derivative litigation and its experience in takeover battles. Rather than pointing to a particular type of case, clients applaud this firm for its experience in every type of corporate dispute. It was notably involved in one of the longest-running cases in the Court of Chancery, In Re The Walt Disney Company Derivative Litigation.

**The Lawyers:** Clients commonly refer to **David McBride** (see p.408) as *"the firm's number-one corporate litigator."* *"The true bedrock of this operation,"* he is well versed in litigation arising out of M&A transactions as well as a popular port of call for corporate counseling. Also toward the top of several commentators' lists is **Bruce Silverstein** (see p.412). Chairman of the firm's corporate litigation and counseling section, he is considered to be among *"the new guard of great chancery litigators"* and both prosecutes and defends corporate and commercial matters.

**Clients/Work Highlights:** The group advises and represents the full range of corporate clients, from corporations, directors, officers and stockholders through to other law firms.

## Band 3

### Abrams & Laster LLP
See firm details p.415

**The Firm:** Two former Richards, Layton & Finger partners formed this corporate litigation and advisory boutique in September 2005. Generally thought of as *"both having sterling reputations,"* onlookers agree that they will continue to represent clients in the same "*extraordinarily able way they did before.*" The firm focuses on high-stakes business litigation and transactions carrying a risk of litigation, and loyal clients consistently refer to the national reputations and experience of its attorneys in these fields. Therefore, when going toe-to-toe against the most prominent firms in the country, clients readily recommend its "*aggressive litigation skills.*" The team was involved in the heavily litigated appraisal Liberty Digital case, successfully proving that the fair value of the company was less than the merger consideration.

The Lawyers: Clients praise name partner **Kevin Abrams** (see p.401) for the "*professional, frank and knowledgeable*" approach he adopts. "*Quick on his feet,*" he is said to have an exhaustive command of Delaware jurisprudence and "*can craft unusually apt responses to fit a particular need.*" Meanwhile, **Travis Laster** (see p.407) was described as a "*good writer and first-rate, aggressive chancery litigator.*" "*Very knowledgeable and experienced,*" clients praised his firm grasp of Delaware law and procedure, which is considered particularly useful by the national law firms supplying the outfit with referrals.

Clients/Work Highlights: AMD; Liberty Media; The Fairchild Corporation; Vail Resorts; Leucadia National; Insight Communications and Welsh, Carson, Anderson & Stowe.

## Bouchard Margules & Friedlander PA

The Firm: This firm impresses market commentators with the range of cases in which its lawyers appear. Commentators summed it up as being "*small but damn effective.*" A "*well-respected outfit,*" it lives up to its reputation for handling hard-fought cases with considerable aplomb. Clients also value the level of partner involvement and the timely responses of all of the firm's attorneys. It is equally renowned for acting on behalf of both plaintiffs and defendants, and its impressive track record on both fronts makes it a popular port of call for referrals.

The Lawyers: Clients praised **Andre Bouchard** for his "*combination of skill and brightness,*" further stating: "*He has an excellent reputation in court as an honest and fair litigator.*" Dubbed a "*formidable opponent*" by peers, Bouchard was also routinely praised by clients for his responsiveness and "*stellar reputation in town.*"

Clients/Work Highlights: McKesson; Disney; Liberty Mutual; Corporation Service Company; Special Committee of the Board of Directors of Union Pacific; CV Starr & Co and Goldman Sachs.

## Grant & Eisenhofer PA

The Firm: "*It is remarkable for a firm to have made a name for itself in such a short period of time,*" according to sources, and this litigation boutique is now an established contender for some of the best work around. It is considered a cut above other plaintiff and securities firms in town, primarily due to its successful track record in large cases. It is experienced in complex civil matters in state and federal courts

across the country, with chancery litigation arising from disputes filed in Delaware accounting for a sizable portion of the overall workload. Its true forte is considered to lie in representing institutional investors in significant securities fraud class actions. Additional resources in New York are deemed to have further contributed to its growing profile.

The Lawyers: Both name partners received impressive market feedback for "*making this niche practice a terrific success.*" As such, a new table was created for them. **Jay Eisenhofer** earns respect for his strong performances in the courtroom and is the founder and managing partner of the firm. He is well known for representing institutional investors in corporate and securities litigation and was lead counsel in the $425 million partial settlement of the Global Crossing case. **Stuart Grant** enters the tables this year in recognition of his representation of institutional investors nationwide in securities and corporate governance litigation.

Clients/Work Highlights: Florida State Board of Administration; Hermes; Ohio Retirement Systems; Franklin Mutual Funds; New York City pension funds; California Public Employees' Retirement System (calPERS); State of Wisconsin Investment Board; OppenheimerFunds; Capital Research and Management; Bastion Capital and ING Pilgrim Investments.

## Morris, James, Hitchens & Williams LLP

See firm details p.419

The Firm: Clients are effusive in their praise of "*the high-quality work product*" and "*efficient and effective methods*" that are the signature of this firm's service. Clients also value its lawyers' "*detailed knowledge of the applicable Delaware corporate law.*" Considered to have struck "*the right balance between efficiency and deliberation,*" this corporate and commercial litigation group is equally at home whether handling corporate governance and fiduciary litigation in the Court of Chancery or before a jury in the Delaware Superior Court or District Court. Highlighting the mix of chancery and non-chancery work, the department deals with matters involving strategic alliances and joint ventures. Highlights include advising Air Products and Chemicals on limiting damages relating to breach of contract in a strategic alliance, where over $100 million is at stake.

The Lawyers: Described by clients as a "*completely clear thinker, active, inventive and hard-working*" **Lewis Lazarus** (see p.408) continues to impress. "*He will find a way through come hell or high water,*" and led the team in representing Air Products and Chemicals. **Clarkson Collins** (see p.403) is "*an effective planner and strategist,*" according to clients. He is described as possessing an understated style: "*Collins always gives realistic advice and is never one to posture.*" Contrasting in style but not in effectiveness is "*tough*" **Edward McNally** (see p.408). Head of the corporate and commercial litigation department, he has represented the McKesson outside directors seek-

ing over $200 million in damages and secured the dismissal of most claims against them.

Clients/Work Highlights: Other clients include DuPont, McMoRan Oil & Gas Co and Siliconix.

## Proctor Heyman LLP

See firm details p.422

The Firm: This boutique opened in January 2006 under the aegis of two attorneys formerly of The Bayard Firm. Although it is early days for the firm, market observers agree: "*With the pedigree of the attorneys involved and the track records they have, it is sure to do well.*" The firm concentrates on high-stakes corporate and commercial litigation, including corporate governance, M&A, stockholder class and derivative actions. It is also involved in litigation surrounding LLCs and limited partnerships. As a smaller operation, it has the advantage of avoiding the conflicts of interest that some of the larger firms may be faced with. There was consensus that it has hit the ground running, and current cases include representing UbiquiTel in a two-week Court of Chancery trial.

The Lawyers: "*The driving force behind many notable cases,*" **Kurt Heyman** (see p.406) rallies support from clients who thoroughly endorse his "*smart, knowledgeable and enthusiastic approach.*" "*An engaging attorney who is familiar with the workings of the Chancery Court,*" he is praised by clients for "*his attention to detail*" and "*timely, smart and accurate responses.*" **Vernon Proctor** (see p.410) also debuts in the tables and won praise from clients for his transactional capabilities, not to mention "*his client-awareness and responsiveness.*"

Clients/Work Highlights: UbiquiTel; Albert Nasser and Kids International; Tyson Foods; AirGate PCS; Plumtree Software; Mobius Management Systems and Audiovox.

## The Bayard Firm

See firm details p.417

The Firm: "*Always players in the chancery ball park,*" this firm is widely thought to have had a good year, despite the departure of some prominent attorneys. Respected more for the variety of work undertaken than in a specific area, its team is experienced in disputes relating to corporate governance, stock appraisal and stockholder class and derivative actions alleging breaches of fiduciary duty. It is also praised for its handling of federal securities litigation. Recent highlights include successfully defending Atlantic Coast in a nationwide consumer fraud class action relating to the advertising and sale of software. The group also acted as Delaware counsel to Eon Labs in connection with its $1.7 billion acquisition by Novartis.

The Lawyers: Following the departure of Kurt Heyman and Vernon Proctor to start their own practice, Ted Johnson is now the key contact at the firm.

Clients/Work Highlights: Further clients include AIG, HealthSouth and McKesson HBOC.

**Other Notable Practitioners**

John Reed (see p.410) recently moved to the Wilmington office of the newly merged Edwards Angell Palmer & Dodge LLP. Focusing solely on chancery work, he brings with him a wealth of experience in bet-the-farm litigation. Clients refer to the fact that *"his jurisdictional expertise affords us much comfort,"* and drew attention to his *"engaging, professional approach and technical acumen, which make him an effective and aggressive litigator."* Cathy Reese (see p.410) of Greenberg Traurig LLP is another respected name in the state. Head of litigation in Delaware, Reese is *"a consistent performer in the Chancery Court,"* and is well known for her business-oriented approach.

# CORPORATE/M&A

## Corporate/M&A
### Leading Firms

[1] MORRIS, NICHOLS, ARSHT & TUNNELL *Wilmington*
POTTER ANDERSON & CORROON LLP *Wilmington*
RICHARDS, LAYTON & FINGER PA *Wilmington*

[2] MORRIS, JAMES, HITCHENS *Wilmington*
SKADDEN, ARPS *Wilmington*

[3] PRICKETT, JONES & ELLIOTT PA *Wilmington*
YOUNG CONAWAY STARGATT *Wilmington*

### Leading Individuals

#### Senior Statesmen

BALOTTI R Franklin *Richards, Layton & Finger*
BLACK JR Lewis *Morris, Nichols, Arsht & Tunnell*
[1] ALEXANDER Frederick *Morris, Nichols, Arsht & Tunnell*
BUSSARD Donald *Richards, Layton & Finger*
[2] FINKELSTEIN Jesse *Richards, Layton & Finger*
GENTILE Mark *Richards, Layton & Finger*
GOLDMAN Michael *Potter Anderson & Corroon*
JOHNSTON John *Morris, Nichols, Arsht & Tunnell*
MCBRIDE David *Young Conaway Stargatt & Taylor*
SPARKS A Gilchrist *Morris, Nichols, Arsht & Tunnell*
SYMONDS JR Robert *Morris, James, Hitchens*
TUMAS Michael *Potter Anderson & Corroon*
[3] BIGLER C Stephen *Richards, Layton & Finger*
BROWN David *Potter Anderson & Corroon*
EASTON Richard *Skadden, Arps*
GROSSBAUER John *Potter Anderson & Corroon*
MORTON Mark *Potter Anderson & Corroon*
MULLEN Thomas *Prickett, Jones & Elliott*
O'TOOLE Matthew *Morris, James, Hitchens*
PINCUS Robert *Skadden, Arps*
SMALL John *Prickett, Jones & Elliott*

#### Up-and-coming individuals

HAUBERT William *Richards, Layton & Finger*

#### Associates to watch

SALOMONE Janine *Potter Anderson & Corroon*

## Band 1

### Morris, Nichols, Arsht & Tunnell LLP

See firm details p.420

**The Firm:** This *"prestigious practice sustains its position at the top of the market"* and impresses clients by *"consistently hitting the mark without wasting a single breath."* With an impressive armory of resources, it is *"responsive and accessible,"* and is a favorite of clients for structurally complex international projects and joint ventures. As well as referring to its deep-rooted expertise in the field of alternative entities, public company M&A work and financings, clients pointed to the user-friendliness of the group as a strength. Private equity, corporate governance, spin-offs and financings are further areas of specialization. Clients value the close cooperation between departments, especially when it comes to the valuable strategic advice provided by the esteemed corporate litigation department. During the year, the group was involved in one of the larger mergers to take place in the telecom sector.

**The Lawyers:** Of the many true specialists in this department, senior statesman Lewis Black (see p.402) remains *"at the very top of the tree."* An exceptional practitioner by all accounts, Black is of counsel to the firm and is considered to *"play at a higher level than most."* *"A fine gentleman and an excellent lawyer,"* Black is one of the best-recognized practitioners in the state and a real *"power player."* Meanwhile, clients consider Frederick Alexander (see p.401) to be *"head and shoulders above the rest."* *"Super bright and hands-on, with a creative and agile mind,"* he has *"a wealth of experience"* and is billed as *"an old-school counselor who always explains things so they are crystal clear."* Leading corporate law counselor John Johnston (see p.406) impressed clients with *"the academic, intellectual line he takes in cases."* He has *"a complete knowledge of the law, knows how it fits into the big picture and understands all the subtleties."* Gilchrist Sparks (see p.412) was routinely referred to as *"probably the best corporate lawyer in the state."* *"He spends so much time in the courtroom and is invaluable in the boardroom,"* according to sources. Indeed, his prolific litigation capabilities mean that he is perceived as being unrivaled when strategic advice is required. In terms of work in the field of alternative entities, especially LLC partnerships and general and statutory trusts, Louis Hering (see p.405) is *"simply the best."* He works closely with the *"absolute authority on Delaware LLCs,"* Walter Tuthill (see p.413). Clients describe Tuthill as *"collaborative, analytical and careful,"* not to mention *"a great draftsman who always ensures a logical division of labor to reduce costs in the long run."*

**Clients/Work Highlights:** Colgate-Palmolive; Viacom; Ford; Coca-Cola; JPMorgan Chase; McDonald's; Comcast; Northrop Grumman; Interactive Corp; Texas Pacific Group; Prudential Insurance and DuPont.

### Potter Anderson & Corroon LLP

See firm details p.421

**The Firm:** *"The quality of this firm is as good as any New York firm in terms of expertise, but with a personal interaction and a reasonable pricing structure that you simply would not find in New York,"* according to clients. The willingness of lawyers to *"tell it like it is"* and provide practical advice is also much valued: *"They will get into the trenches with the client and understand client needs and the way businesses operate."* The group is renowned for defending large stockholder lawsuits, representing special committees and advising clients on Delaware corporate law as it relates to large M&A transactions. The firm is also highly commended for its advice on alternative entities and corporate governance issues.

**The Lawyers:** Chairman of the firm Michael Goldman (see p.405) is *"a respected senior member of the department."* Although probably best known for his work in the Court of Chancery, Goldman is also respected by clients for his corporate practice. He is commended for *"providing quick simple answers to complex questions."* The *"insightful"* Michael Tumas (see p.413) enters the tables for the first time and is referred to by clients as a *"key member of our team; he really explains the legal issues and sets out the commercial consequences."* David Brown (see p.402) won praise for his ability to *"translate his technical knowledge into good clear advice that is focused on results."* Acting as lead M&A counsel in substantial transactions has won him a loyal client following; as a result of which, Brown's practice is often national in scope. John Grossbauer (see p.405) is another debutant to *Chambers'* tables. He is praised by clients for *"his ability to convey complex issues in an easy to understand way"* and for his *"well-organized approach."* With *"the ability to distill advice down to its essence,"* Mark Morton (see p.409) is seen by many clients as *"a go-to guy for transactional and litigious corporate law advice."* Rounding off this team *"packed full of diligent, bright, careful and commercially minded attorneys"* is one to watch, Janine Salomone (see p.411). She has *"substantive transactional experience"* and is *"competent and responsive,"* according to sources. In the field of alternative entities Scott Waxman (see p.413) comes highly recommended. *"There is no question that he could not answer"* and his tax background means he is particularly sought after, according to clients. Up-and-comer Matthew Fischer (see p.404) has carved out a favorable reputation for alternative entities litigation: *"He quickly grasps the situation and forges strong relationships with his clients,"* say sources.

**Clients/Work Highlights:** Examples of corporate/M&A clients include PeopleSoft; DuPont; NRG Energy; Kao Corporation and Sony. Alternative entities clients include Disney; Babcock & Brown;

Barclays Bank; RBS; Groupe DANONE; XM Satellite Radio and Bear Stearns.

## Richards, Layton & Finger PA
See firm details p.423

**The Firm:** Competitors talk of its *"sheer quality"* while clients point to the *"thread of excellence that runs through this well-established, indigenous firm."* It is *"locally well connected"* and clients feel reassured that *"the job will always be done right."* As well as corporate governance advice, transactional work and M&A, this firm is also noted for its proficiency in the field of alternative entities. Complex, high-value cases are the order of the day and the team is highly regarded for acting as special Delaware counsel, although it also frequently acts as lead counsel. Clients value the specialist expertise on offer in the firm's corporate and litigation arms, and like the cross-departmental approach, which enables the deployment of resources as and when the case dictates. For example, its involvement in Re Toys 'R' Us Shareholder Litigation led to a significant Court of Chancery decision, which provided guidance on the use of deal protection measures in negotiated acquisitions.

**The Lawyers:** Billed as a *"peerless M&A lawyer,"* **Don Bussard** (see p.402) is at once *"extraordinarily active in the field"* and *"very down to earth."* He is the senior member of the corporate transactional group. Clients value his complete grasp of local jurisprudence and enjoy the benefits of having such a well-respected lawyer represent them. President of the firm **Jesse Finkelstein** (see p.404) is one of the best-respected Court of Chancery litigators in the state and spends approximately half of his time advising corporations and directors. He provides corporate governance, transactional and control dispute advice to clients. *"One of the most respected names in the corporate arena,"* **Franklin Balotti**'s (see p.401) practice covers both contentious and noncontentious matters. He is a director of the corporate department and is perceived by clients to provide invaluable behind-the-scenes strategic advice that only comes

with *"years of experience at the top."* **Mark Gentile** (see p.404) is *"a personable attorney with a big book of business"* and is a valuable member of the group. *"Lateral thinker"* **Stephen Bigler** (see p.402) debuts in *Chambers'* tables this year. Clients *"like the way he operates"* and he is seen as an increasingly prominent transactional attorney with a fine reputation in the state. Up-and-comer **William Haubert** (see p.405) also enters the rankings. He is *"young, sharp and bright,"* according to clients. In terms of alternative entities advice, **Paul Altman** (see p.401) *"does not miss a thing."* He is chairman of the business department and is nationally recognized as special Delaware counsel in the field of limited partnerships, on which he co-authored a leading treatise, and LLCs. Special praise was reserved for his *"encyclopedic"* knowledge of both areas. The *"fabulously intelligent"* **Bernard Kelley** (see p.407) is another respected attorney in the business department and is valued for his strategic advice on alternative entities. Leading clients *"are more than satisfied"* with **James Leyden** (see p.408). He focuses on a variety of transactional matters involving alternative entities and is a member of the TriBar Opinion Committee. The *"very knowledgeable and approachable"* **Eric Mazie** (see p.408) is also highly regarded by clients and is respected for *"his vast knowledge of statutory trusts."* Up-and-comer **Greg Ladner** (see p.407) garnered plaudits from clients for his knowledge of partnerships and LLCs.

**Clients/Work Highlights:** Toronto-Dominion Bank; Disney; Oracle; Univision Communications; Morgan Stanley and GM.

## Band 2

## Morris, James, Hitchens & Williams LLP
See firm details p.419

**The Firm:** This firm fosters a *"collegial, friendly atmosphere in which good decisions are made,"* and its lawyers *"tend to think beyond the law, utilizing their business awareness to provide innovative ideas that go beyond the legal issue in question."* A sustained theme in the feedback from clients this year is the operational differences between the firm and its competitors. Whereas other outfits adopt a rigid business model, which the client is required to fit into, this firm has a more flexible structure, allowing it to tailor services to fit the business needs of the client. *"The firm is very client-oriented and is able to align itself with the client by acting as a strategic partner not just a legal consultant."* The group offers clients a variety of Delaware-specific services in the corporate M&A sphere, although clients pointed to its expertise in the field of alternative entities as its true strength. In this area alone, the aggregate value of the transactions handled by the group is over $10 billion. Highlights include providing Delaware law advice to a Fortune 100 acquirer in a $1.6 billion cross-border telecom deal, and representing the acquirer in a $132 million cross-border purchase of an industrial tools and machinery business.

**The Lawyers:** Clients described **Matthew O'Toole** (see p.409) as a *"fantastically smart, simply wonderful lawyer."* He is active at the heart of the Delaware corporate market and is *"able to offer tremendous insight, regarding both the black letter of the law and general business matters as well."* *"Creative, knowledgeable and talented,"* he is said to work well with **Robert Symonds** (see p.412), always providing the client with consistent advice. Symonds is chair of the transactions practice and is recommended by clients for *"his creativity, his intimate knowledge of Delaware business and his careful analysis."* He has the ability to *"focus on the details without losing sight of the big picture,"* and understands what the client is trying to achieve as a company, using his knowledge of how to navigate the Delaware system to best effect.

**Clients/Work Highlights:** The firm's clients include corporations, limited and general partnerships, LLCs and statutory trusts.

## Skadden, Arps, Slate, Meagher & Flom LLP & Affiliates
See firm details p.1557

**The Firm:** Clients hire this *"international powerhouse"* on those cases *"where an elephant gun is required."* *"There are cases where you need a firm like this to throw resources at an issue, and they do a great job in this respect."* Clients find that *"its swift provision of armies of lawyers"* means that the firm is suited to the big-money cases, which often utilize the global reach of the firm. Therefore, though the Wilmington office has an attractive client base within the state, *"it is unlikely to be chosen as special Delaware counsel."*

**The Lawyers:** Clients recommend **Richard Easton** (see p.403) as *"an exceptional lawyer for the bigger deals."* He is *"just your classic first-chair lawyer,"* according to commentators, and has a broad practice that encompasses M&A, securities and Delaware corporate law matters. **Robert Pincus** (see p.410) is a *"quick and practical lawyer,"* according to interviewees, who *"has the ability to simultaneously handle multiple issues in a transaction, making the process virtually painless."* He also has the capacity to marshal the *"bottomless"* resources of the firm in order to achieve the results, and always brings *"top-flight negotiation skills"* to the table.

**Clients/Work Highlights:** Some of the biggest international corporations are faithful clients of this firm, including Polaroid and Hayes Lemmerz International.

## Band 3

## Prickett, Jones & Elliott PA
**The Firm:** Leading clients admire the *"collegiate"* ethos here, which makes for *"a real relationship-building firm."* The corporate and business law practice group mostly serves as special Delaware counsel and is often found working with out-of-state law firms on significant corporate and alternative entity transactions. The market increasingly recognizes that the transactional profile of the firm is growing, and the team served as Delaware counsel to the special

committee of the general partner of Buckeye Partners in connection with a change of control transaction during the year.

**The Lawyers:** John Small covers both corporate M&A and alternative entities work. He is described by clients as "*an absolutely impeccable lawyer, easy to get hold of and you just know the matter will be done expeditiously and properly.*" He is a popular choice for referrals and is also in demand nationally as an expert witness on Delaware-specific fiduciary and corporate law matters. Head of corporate and business law **Thomas Mullen** is "*extremely capable.*" He is highly recommended for his corporate governance, M&A and alternative entities expertise. The firm served as Delaware counsel to Danisco during the year, and Mullen advised on its negotiated tender offer for outstanding publicly held shares of Genencor International.

**Clients/Work Highlights:** CSFB and EDS are examples of the most important active clients of the group.

## Young Conaway Stargatt & Taylor LLP

See firm details p.424

**The Firm:** This large, multiservice firm attracts national and international clients and sources agree that it is "*not to be underestimated*" for corporate work. Clients and peers note that the corporate counseling and litigation department is most prominent and experienced in terms of litigation. However, its litigious prowess has led to the department's involvement in a range of transactions, and it is widely recommended for its advice on takeover battles and related stockholder disputes.

**The Lawyers:** "*Clearly among the best corporate attorneys in the state,*" **David McBride** (see p.408) continues to impress clients. He is as well versed in complex litigation as he is in advising on transactional issues and is noted for his "*meticulous representation*" of leading national corporate clients. The corporate profile of the firm has recently been bolstered by the arrival of **Norman Powell** (see p.410), who comes highly recommended for his work in the field of alternative entities. He is particularly noted for his niche statutory trusts expertise.

**Clients/Work Highlights:** The client base includes corporations; directors; officers; stockholders and a wide range of law firms.

### Other Notable Practitioners

**Ellisa Opstbaum Habbart** (see p.405) of the Delaware Counsel Group LLP is "*an impressive individual in terms of style and manner of presentation,*" according to sources. Making her debut in the tables this year, she impresses leading national clients and attorneys for "*properly understanding and managing the expectations of the client, so as to facilitate the best result.*" She focuses her practice on transactions involving corporations, partnerships, business trusts and LLCs and is a key destination for referrals demanding Delaware-specific advice.

# EMPLOYMENT

# MAINLY DEFENDANT

| Employment: Mainly Defendant |
|---|
| **Leading Firms** |
| [1] **YOUNG CONAWAY STARGATT** Wilmington |
| [2] **POTTER ANDERSON & CORROON** Wilmington |
| [3] **MORRIS, JAMES, HITCHENS** Wilmington |

| Leading Individuals |
|---|
| [1] **SANDLER Sheldon** Young Conaway Stargatt |
| [2] **MCDONOUGH Kathleen** Potter Anderson |
| **WILLOUGHBY Barry** Young Conaway Stargatt |
| [3] **BOWSER William** Young Conaway Stargatt |
| **HOLT Scott** Young Conaway Stargatt |
| **WILLIAMS David** Morris, James, Hitchens |

| Up-and-coming individuals |
|---|
| **VOSS Wendy** Potter Anderson |

## Band 1

### Young Conaway Stargatt & Taylor LLP

See firm details p.424

**The Firm:** Universally acknowledged as Delaware's preeminent employment practice, it boasts the largest team in the state. Its lawyers are said to "*always know exactly what they're doing,*" according to admiring clients. Eight full-time attorneys, assisted by an employee benefits specialist, advise a broad range of public and private sector employers across the full spectrum of employment and labor law issues. On the litigious front, the team often defends clients against class actions relating to discrimination in both state and federal courts, or before the EEOC. Its advisory practice is equally developed, and lawyers advise on all aspects of best practice and workplace protocols, as well as offering bespoke training programs. The team also impressed clients in more traditional areas such as strike control and resolution and collective bargaining. It drew praise for its "*collegiate and human*" approach.

**The Lawyers:** Possessing a "*wealth of experience*" derived from over 30 years' practice, the admired **Sheldon Sandler** (see p.411) is described as "*the father of employment law in Delaware.*" Although commentators note that he has been less visible of late, both his breadth and depth of expertise continue to impress. Recent highlights for Sandler include a successful defense of the City of Newark against a police union grievance. Chair of the employment law section **Barry Willoughby** (see p.413) is involved in all manner of discrimination, whistle-blower and racial or sexual harassment cases. Having successfully defended Ursuline Academy against sex discrimination charges, Willoughby won a case for Waste Management, in which the plaintiff claimed to have been the subject of race discrimination. **William Bowser** (see p.402) is a seasoned hand when it comes to sex discrimination cases or representing employers in collective bargaining. "*Emerging talent*" **Scott Holt** (see p.406) merits his ranking this year having received significant praise from sources. His practice includes discrimination and harassment cases, in addition to advising on terminations, trade secrets and wage and hour matters.

**Clients/Work Highlights:** MBNA; Procter & Gamble; Shellhorn & Hill and Ciba Specialty Chemicals.

## Band 2

### Potter Anderson & Corroon LLP

See firm details p.421

**The Firm:** By virtue of its excellent all-around employment expertise and preventive counseling for important multinational, national and regional clients, this team is increasingly perceived as a market leader. Members of the firm offer traditional labor law advice on issues such as union grievances, collective bargaining and working practices, and in the continuing adverse economic conditions, it has developed a distinctive strength in advising clients on the planning and implementation of corporate downsizing. Also respected for their litigation capabilities, the team exclusively acts for management and is often found representing the defendant in significant contentious cases, the majority of which relate to discrimination. Recently lawyers advised a major multinational on an in-state wrongful employment termination claim.

**The Lawyers:** The highly visible head of labor and employment **Kathleen McDonough** (see p.408) is "*on a par with the best,*" according to clients. Equally respected for her advisory, litigation avoidance and trial skills, McDonough's recent work has included successfully acting in a case involving the posting of corporate secrets online. Up-and-comer **Wendy Voss** (see p.413) is a new addition to the rankings, with a practice that spans union contract negotiations and discrimination cases. Sources say that her "*sensible approach and excellent trial record*" fully justify her inclusion in the table.

**Clients/Work Highlights:** The firm advises the Delaware arm of multinationals such as DuPont and Hercules. Regional or state business and government entities also feature in the client base. Further clients include Newcastle County; City of Wilmington; Winterthur Museum; Premier Museum and Delaware Park.

## Band 3

### Morris, James, Hitchens & Williams LLP

See firm details p.419

**The Firm:** Possessing a three-strong team of attorneys, this firm may not have the capacity of the other two operations that feature in the table, but is highly respected for both its broad employment know-how and specialized education sector and governmental expertise. Clients spoke glowingly of an "*unparalleled schools law capacity,*" which involves attorneys advising school districts on substantial procedural and

constitutional matters such as desegregation and separation of church and state. Further areas of expertise include termination, wrongful discharge and discrimination. As such, lawyers successfully settled a class action brought by the DOJ against the State of Delaware concerning police reading and writing tests potentially discriminating against ethnic minority applicants. The firm is also frequently involved in representing employers in collective bargaining negotiations, as well as providing general advisory and training assistance.

**The Lawyers:** "*Damned hard work*" and the ability to "*always look out for the client's best interests*" secure

David Williams (see p.413) a place in the table. As head of the employment team, he has a balanced public-private sector practice and is lauded as the "*leading schools law practitioner in Delaware.*" He boasts "*vast experience in the field*" and recently represented an educational institution in a case regarding the termination of senior employees involving First Amendment rights issues.

**Clients/Work Highlights:** The firm represents a variety of private clients and government entities, including more than 11 school districts and several municipalities.

# INTELLECTUAL PROPERTY

## Intellectual Property
### Leading Firms

1. **CONNOLLY BOVE LODGE & HUTZ LLP** *Wilmington*
   **MORRIS, NICHOLS, ARSHT & TUNNELL** *Wilmington*
2. **FISH & RICHARDSON P.C.** *Wilmington*
   **POTTER ANDERSON & CORROON** *Wilmington*
3. **ASHBY & GEDDES** *Wilmington*
   **RICHARDS, LAYTON & FINGER PA** *Wilmington*
   **THE BAYARD FIRM** *Wilmington*
   **YOUNG CONAWAY STARGATT** *Wilmington*

### Leading Individuals

1. **BLUMENFELD Jack** *Morris, Nichols, Arsht*
   **HUTZ Rudolf** *Connolly Bove Lodge*
2. **HORWITZ Richard** *Potter Anderson*
   **MARSDEN JR William** *Fish & Richardson P.C.*
3. **CONNOLLY JR Arthur** *Connolly Bove Lodge*
   **GEIGER Kathleen** *Potter Anderson*
   **GRAHAM Mary** *Morris, Nichols, Arsht*
   **GRIMM Thomas** *Morris, Nichols, Arsht*
   **NOREIKA Maryellen** *Morris, Nichols, Arsht*
4. **BALICK Steven** *Ashby & Geddes*
   **COTTRELL III Frederick** *Richards, Layton*
   **INGERSOLL Josy** *Young Conaway Stargatt*
   **KIRK Richard** *The Bayard Firm*
   **LOUDEN Karen** *Morris, Nichols, Arsht*
   **ROGOWSKI Patricia** *Connolly Bove Lodge*
   **ROVNER Philip** *Potter Anderson*
   **SHAW John** *Young Conaway Stargatt*

## Band 1

### Connolly Bove Lodge & Hutz LLP

See firm details p.418

**The Firm:** This excellent IP team "*deserves to be up there with the best,*" according to interviewees, and the firm is duly promoted to the top tier. Clients emphasized the breadth of the service on offer: "*From soup to nuts, they can handle all your needs.*" Although the firm boasts an office in Washington, DC close to the PTO, 70 of its 90 attorneys are based in Wilmington. With around 60 lawyers specializing

in IP, this is "*one of the biggest players in the field.*" Commentators cite the Delaware team's capacity to handle both patent prosecution and patent litigation as a distinct asset, although the firm is equally comfortable dealing with trademark applications and copyright or trade secrets litigation. Counseling and due diligence, increasingly important spheres of activity, also contribute heavily to the workload, especially where patent infringements are concerned. Competitors are quick to praise "*this group of excellent lawyers,*" who are comfortable working in the life sciences, pharmaceutical, biotechnology, electrical and mechanical fields.

**The Lawyers:** Clients respect the "*superb*" **Rudolf Hutz** (see p.406) for being "*the main guy actually trying the cases.*" As such, his unparalleled experience led sources to fully endorse his promotion to the top band this year. His practice primarily incorporates pharmaceutical, biotech and life sciences matters, and he is recognized as a leader by many key industry figures. He is currently acting as lead counsel for Pfizer in a trial relating to the piggybacking of its research and development for the cholesterol-lowering drug Lipitor by an Indian generic medicines rival. A "*fine gentleman of a lawyer,*" **Arthur Connolly**'s (see p.403) long experience of IP litigation impressed sources, who remarked upon his continued prominence in the field. New entrant to the rankings **Patricia Smink Rogowski** (see p.411) was commended for her solid work as local counsel to a number of national companies and for her patent prosecution experience.

**Clients/Work Highlights:** Afton Chemical; IBM; Steelcase; Bayer; Altria Group; Henkle Corporation; Helena Chemical Company; Philip Morris; Pfizer and Colgate-Palmolive.

### Morris, Nichols, Arsht & Tunnell LLP

See firm details p.420

**The Firm:** A major Delaware firm with outstanding patent law credentials, Morris, Nichols is universally recognized as possessing "*far and away the best IP litigation practice in the state.*" Indeed, admiring competitors agreed: "*It's simply number one.*" Its high trial success rate is a key attraction, but so too is "*the profound knowledge its lawyers have of judges and*

court procedures." The practitioners here are also credited with "*the ability to find commercial solutions and give straightforward guidance.*" The well-established team regularly represents pharmaceutical and hi-tech electronics or medical device manufacturers, in all manner of patent litigation, trade secrets and trademark matters. It is often hired as Delaware special counsel, though members of the firm also possess substantial first chair experience and can draw upon out-of-state experience to offer "*plenty of bang for the buck.*" The team recently obtained a significant result for Pfizer, affirming the judgment in the Hatch-Waxman Act litigation against Par Pharmaceutical.

**The Lawyers:** The "*exceptional*" **Jack Blumenfeld** (see p.402) heads up the IP group and clients are full of praise for "*his all-around knowledge of patent law and litigation.*" Billed as an "*assured trial lawyer and not just a rainmaker,*" he is admired for the clarity of his approach and his tenacious style. Together with the "*very experienced*" **Mary Graham** (see p.405), whose practical style is popular with clients, Blumenfeld has cultivated strong relationships with top pharmaceutical firms such as Pfizer, Abbott Laboratories and AstraZeneca. The "*personable and knowledgeable*" **Thomas Grimm** (see p.405) is new to the rankings this year. He takes on a proportion of general litigation work, but the majority of his time is spent on contentious IP matters. In 2005, he took the lead role representing Qualtronic in a patent licensing dispute. Clients applaud his ability to offer "*commercial responses*" in complex cases. Praise was also forthcoming for **Maryellen Noreika** (see p.409), a gutsy courtroom performer who continues to "*craft a good practice for herself.*" **Karen Jacobs Louden** (see p.408) was commended for her involvement in pharmaceutical and medical device litigation in the past twelve months and for her "*softly spoken style of persuasion.*"

**Clients/Work Highlights:** Merck; Medtronic; Bausch & Lomb; Qualcomm; Scientific Games; Intermec Technologies; Invista; Advanced Energy and Honeywell.

## Band 2

### Fish & Richardson P.C.
See firm details p.1113

**The Firm:** A national firm commanding an impressive countrywide reputation for its involvement in high-profile IP litigation, Fish & Richardson's "*active and expanding*" Delaware office is increasingly prominent in the local market. Representing clients in patent, trademark, copyright and trade secrets litigation, the team's depth of technical expertise means it also offers sound expertise in patent prosecution. Clients particularly admire the ability of attorneys to explain "*highly technical issues in a straightforward, easy to understand manner*." Prestigious cross-state matters make up a proportion of the practice, with recent highlights including a jury verdict in a patent infringement case for Kyphon, a California-based manufacturer of minimally invasive medical devices. Peers note that on a state level the firm "*mostly acts as local counsel rather than lead*." IP counseling and business advisory services are also offered.

**The Lawyers:** Described as "*a leader and a fine lawyer alright*," office managing principal **William Marsden** (see p.408) is a seasoned trial attorney with a flair for leading in complex patent litigation cases. He recently defended TeleCheck against a patent infringement suit brought by LML Payment Systems concerning point of sale terminals for check processing.

**Clients/Work Highlights:** Ciena; Hewlett-Packard; Chi Mei Optoelectronics and Genzyme.

### Potter Anderson & Corroon LLP
See firm details p.421

**The Firm:** This major Delaware firm is renowned for its prowess in commercial litigation, a reputation to which the IP litigation team contributes significantly. The fact that many attorneys also work on general commercial or chancery matters counts in the firm's favor, according to clients, who were full of praise for "*its lawyers' clear understanding of business goals and how to use the law to achieve them*." This was felt to be especially true in the context of technically complex patent infringement, trademark or copyright disputes. Equally comfortable in local counsel or first chair roles, the team's "*rapport with Delaware judges*" and "*ability to handle a wide variety of matters*" led many out-of-state companies to express a preference for the operation over its larger competitors. While peers compliment an "*impressive, technically expert practice*," Potter Anderson's "*responsiveness*" and "*cost-effectiveness*" were further features that met with the approval of clients.

**The Lawyers:** Sources were impressed by **Richard Horwitz**'s (see p.406) "*calm demeanor and sensitive approach*," and clients drew comfort from the certainty that "*when he says something he is listened to, because he never overreaches in his advice*." A varied practice allows him to "*bring commercial insight to IP litigation*," and he "*communicates ideas clearly and without condescension*." Substantial patent litigation experience includes recent successful action for Advanced Medical Optics in a patent dispute with Alcon. The "*knowledgeable and experienced*"

Kathleen Geiger (see p.404) is admired for the "*detail of her analysis*" and her specialized patent prosecution, patent opinion and IP due diligence practice. Bringing a "*trial lawyer's skill set to technical IP cases*," **Philip Rovner** (see p.411) continues to earn plaudits for his forceful courtroom performances. Representing pharmaceutical and technological companies in significant litigation, sources reported that "*he knows what clients want and how to get there*."

**Clients/Work Highlights:** DuPont; Hercules; Baxter; Genentech and Schwarz Pharma.

## Band 3

### Ashby & Geddes
See firm details p.416

**The Firm:** Its "*fine reputation for litigation*" means this compact and punchy practice is often referred to on complex patent or IP litigation matters. Described as an "*efficient and polished*" team, the majority of its work is as local counsel. Clients praise the outfit's ability "*to stay one step ahead*," while also remarking upon its "*reasonable, practical approach that rests upon building harmonious relations between in-house and outside counsel*." General advisory IP and trademark services round off the practice.

**The Lawyers:** As the firm's most experienced patent litigator, "*straight shooter*" **Steven Balick** (see p.401) "*does a tremendous job*," according to clients. His practice predominantly centers on local counsel patent work for pharmaceutical, electronics and technology companies, and clients appreciate his assured touch. They also stressed the value of his being "*well regarded by judges*."

**Clients/Work Highlights:** A variety of local corporations and national Fortune 500 companies in the pharmaceutical, computing, electronics and hi-tech sectors consult the firm.

### Richards, Layton & Finger PA
See firm details p.423

**The Firm:** Delaware's largest firm possesses a solid IP capability within its broader litigation team and is particularly well regarded for its complex patent litigation work. Around four partners and half a dozen associates dedicate the majority of their time to IP, for the most part defending pharmaceutical, computing, biotech and hi-tech clients in matters such as patent infringement, product disparagement and trade secrets disclosure. Some applicant cases are also taken on, such as Micron Technology's counterclaim against Rambus, following a long-running infringement dispute concerning patents on computer random access memory. General IP business advisory work also features regularly.

**The Lawyers:** Litigator **Frederick Cottrell** (see p.403) principally acts in a local counsel capacity on IP disputes, although he also takes on a small proportion of commercial litigation. Commentators note his impressive track record in pharmaceutical matters, and in 2005 Cottrell successfully acted for Guidant Advanced Cardiovascular System in a trial

concerning patented technology in devices used to prevent occlusion in coronary arteries.

**Clients/Work Highlights:** St Clair Intellectual Property Consultants; Guidant ACS; Cephalon; Micron Technology; Novo Nordisk and Safety 1st.

### The Bayard Firm
See firm details p.417

**The Firm:** This firm enters the tables having been recommended by sources for its "*excellent IP litigation profile*" and the quality of advice its eight IP attorneys offer. Its growing team has experienced an increase in litigious matters over the past twelve months, with cases including a favorable settlement for a generic agrochemical producer on a suit encompassing trademark and unfair competition issues. It also successfully defended a major technology company in a federal court jury trial of a patent infringement case. Clients praise the firm's "*sensitive guidance regarding courts, judges and procedures*," a strength that means the firm is regularly appointed as local counsel by national corporations. Trademark, copyright and domain name matters are also handled, along with corporate support issues relating to mergers, loans and acquisitions.

**The Lawyers:** Clients appreciate the fact that **Richard Kirk** (see p.407) is "*forthright, knows what he's doing and is tough when he needs to be*," while peers describe him as "*easy to deal with and practical.*" He is a director in both business litigation and IP groups, and his practice spans general business and environmental litigation. However, clients particularly recommend him as local counsel in litigious IP cases.

**Clients/Work Highlights:** Clients include JPMorgan Chase, Sipcam Agro USA and Spectrum Pharmaceuticals.

### Young Conaway Stargatt & Taylor LLP
See firm details p.424

**The Firm:** The respected IP team at this firm is best known for its capabilities in representing local, national and international clients in patent and trademark infringement matters in state courts. Nine attorneys and one special counsel draw on their commercial litigation experience as well as the expertise of other departments, and are particularly noted for "*their impressive track record in patent litigation.*" Lawyers have recently represented Syngenta Seeds in a patent infringement suit brought against Monsanto, which also saw the involvement of Young Conaway antitrust attorneys. Trade secrets and unfair competition advice is also offered, as well as general advisory IP assistance.

**The Lawyers:** **Josy Ingersoll** (see p.406) displays "*good, balanced judgment*" and "*knows her way around the courtroom.*" Sources observe that she enjoys a high-volume workload primarily focused on patent litigation. Cochair of the IP litigation section **John Shaw** (see p.412) mixes general commercial lawsuits with IP litigation in the district courts, and is respected for his experience in a variety of IP disputes. "*A strong courtroom performer*," he is currently working as local counsel on a food-packaging patent application for a regional manufacturing company.

Clients/Work Highlights: The firm represents clients in the telecommunications, biotechnology and pharmaceuticals industries, including Lucent Technologies and Syngenta Seeds.

# REAL ESTATE

## Real Estate
### Leading Firms

| | |
|---|---|
| 1 | **RICHARDS, LAYTON & FINGER PA** *Wilmington* |
| | **YOUNG CONAWAY STARGATT** *Wilmington* |
| 2 | **MORRIS, NICHOLS, ARSHT & TUNNELL** *Wilmington* |
| | **SAUL EWING LLP** *Wilmington* |
| | **THE BAYARD FIRM** *Wilmington* |

### Leading Individuals

| | |
|---|---|
| 1 | **ISKEN Donald** *Morris, Nichols, Arsht* |
| | **KRAPF Robert** *Richards, Layton & Finger* |
| 2 | **DIPRINZIO Eugene** *Young Conaway Stargatt* |
| | **GEE William** *Saul Ewing LLP* |
| | **KLEIN Daniel** *Richards, Layton* |
| | **KRAPF Daniel** *Saul Ewing LLP* |
| | **KRISTOL Daniel** *Richards, Layton & Finger* |
| | **LAMB Christopher** *Pepper Hamilton LLP* |
| 3 | **HERSHMAN Douglas** *The Bayard Firm* |

## Band 1

### Richards, Layton & Finger PA
See firm details p.423

**The Firm:** "*Definitely one of the top two in the state,*" clients respect this eminent real estate team both for the depth of its practice and its thorough knowledge of all aspects of commercial real estate transactions. A five-strong team of attorneys advises national and regional developers on a variety of acquisitions, developments, leasings and sales, and are equally comfortable working in industrial, manufacturing or residential sectors. Recent highlights include acting for the developer in the $250 million construction of privatized housing at Dover Air Force Base. The team has a formidable reputation when it comes to advising lenders on loan transactions and refinancings, and also offers some land use capacity.

**The Lawyers:** Such is the esteem in which competitors hold **Robert Krapf** (see p.407), that one even professed: "*He would certainly feature in my real estate dream team.*" Clients describe him as an "*extremely bright, knowledgeable and experienced*" attorney whose technical skills are much in demand. Predominantly focusing on transactional real estate issues, he represents a range of regional and national land developers, and recently advised on a resort development involving the construction of over 1,000 housing units. **Daniel Kristol** (see p.407) is lauded as "*a wonderful guy,*" and although sources suggest he is less visible than in previous years, he continues to excel in a local context, advising landowners on sales, leasings and development. According to clients,

**Daniel Klein** (see p.407) is "*level-headed, very helpful and incredibly thorough,*" with a flexible working style that means "*he always gets his point across.*" Transactional and real estate finance matters make up the bulk of his workload. In 2005, Klein represented The City of Wilmington on the privatization of a wastewater treatment center and acted for AIG on the foreclosure and subsequent redevelopment of a large Wilmington complex.

**Clients/Work Highlights:** Lenders; borrowers; developers; landlords; tenants and insurance companies all instruct the firm. Further notable clients include Wilmington Trust and Wilmington Savings Fund Society.

### Young Conaway Stargatt & Taylor LLP
See firm details p.424

**The Firm:** This firm offers a one-stop shop approach to commercial real estate work and is the largest team in the state, comprising ten attorneys. This means clients are confident in entrusting it with all aspects of complex transactional matters. The outfit is fully equipped to handle acquisitions, leasings, development finance and disposals for major developers, builders and investors. Attorneys recently handled the development, financing, acquisition and condominium creation of the Apex Office Park. The commercial real estate, banking and land use section is also adept at acting for major Delaware lenders. Meanwhile, its prominent position in the new Zoning/Land Use table reflects the firm's highly rated services on the land use front.

**The Lawyers:** **Eugene DiPrinzio** (see p.403) is perceived as being at the heart of the team's commercial real estate practice, working mainly for financial institutions on in-state lending, asset-based loans and development finance. Clients speak highly of his ability to "*simultaneously hit numerous moving targets*" in highly complex matters. In recent months he acted for the banks granting a $16 million construction loan for frozen food warehousing and distribution company Burris Logistics, and was also involved in major Delaware construction projects.

**Clients/Work Highlights:** The Buccini/Pollen Group; Preit Rubin; Handler Corporation; Wal-Mart; Eastern States Development Company; Benchmark Builders; Ryan Homes; Wachovia and Wilmington Trust.

## Band 2

### Morris, Nichols, Arsht & Tunnell LLP
See firm details p.420

**The Firm:** This firm is well regarded for its solid real estate development and transactional practice, which sits comfortably within the larger commercial law counseling group. Several attorneys are dedicated to real estate matters, and cooperate closely with their commercial law colleagues, predominantly on in-state matters for a range of local and national clients. Land use issues are also covered. In a recent deal, the team acted on the real estate components of the purchase of an indigenous bank by a large international financial institution, including the acquisition of a 250,000 sq ft office building and 1,200-space car park. The firm is well placed to advise on financings and this year represented the developer in arranging a $100 million loan pertaining to the construction of one of the state's largest office buildings.

**The Lawyers:** The "*quick-witted*" Donald Isken (see p.406) leads the way on real estate matters for the firm. Clients commented with satisfaction that his "*no-nonsense style and business-oriented approach*" are distinctive features, reflecting a more commercial background than many of his peers. Competitors were quick to compliment the high-quality work of a practitioner they recognize as "*one of the best real estate lawyers in Delaware.*"

**Clients/Work Highlights:** GE; JPMorgan Chase; Shell; Port of Wilmington and Delaware River and Bay Authority.

### Saul Ewing LLP
See firm details p.1763

**The Firm:** Justly renowned for its full-service real estate abilities, this firm wins praise for handling developments and financings for local lenders, as well as acting on large multistate acquisitions, leasings and sales across the East Coast region. Shopping complex portfolio transactions are a focus area in this respect. Members of the firm are also active in construction, and attorneys in the first-class zoning/land use practice are on hand as required. Involvement in developments and financings in industrial and office sectors further define the practice.

**The Lawyers:** "*Professional all the way,*" **William Gee** (see p.404) is a vastly experienced attorney, whose practice encompasses real estate and corporate commercial transactional matters. He acts for both lenders and developers, and is especially skilled in acquisitions, disposals and multijurisdictional financings. Sources noted that his well-rounded knowledge of the procedural machinations and the black letter law is a valuable asset: "*He's just as good*" at the politics as on the legal side." "*Experienced and capable,*" **Daniel Krapf** (see p.271070) enters the rankings this year upon receiving several ringing endorsements. Vice chair of the real estate department, he is also active on the corporate front.

**Clients/Work Highlights:** The firm acts for local lenders, borrowers and developers, as well as in the capacity of local counsel for national corporations. Clients include AT&T Wireless; Conectiv; AstraZeneca; The Welfare Foundation and Wilmington College.

## The Bayard Firm

See firm details p.417

**The Firm:** Possessing "*an impressive level of know-how,*" this compact firm has earned a sound reputation for advising Delaware-based clients in all three counties across a broad spectrum of real estate needs. A team of two full-time attorneys represents residential and commercial buyers and sellers in acquisitions, retail and home building projects. The practice is a firm favorite of developers, and lending institutions favor the firm for its work on secured loans and other real estate financings. Over the past twelve months, lawyers have been involved in a $12.6 million acquisition of a residential apartment as part of a reverse like-kind exchange and the $10.3 million refinancing of an apartment complex. The firm also represents several national title insurance companies

on many aspects of their Delaware business.

**The Lawyers:** The "*thoroughly capable*" **Douglas Hershman** (see p.406) is head of the real estate department and is admired for his "*wide experience in the field,*" the detached focus he brings to both transactional and financial matters and his strong connections in the community.

**Clients/Work Highlights:** Clients include developers, owners, lenders and title insurance companies.

### Other Notable Practitioners

"*Not one to toot his horn,*" **Christopher Lamb** (see p.194467) of Pepper Hamilton LLP is described by clients and contemporaries as a "*quiet and knowledgeable*" real estate lawyer. "*A fabulous attorney,*" he is particularly well known for advising clients on the financing of real estate acquisitions.

# REAL ESTATE

# ZONING/LAND USE

| Real Estate: Zoning/Land Use |
| --- |
| **Leading Firms** |
| 1  SAUL EWING LLP *Wilmington* |
|    YOUNG CONAWAY STARGATT *Wilmington* |
| 2  KLETT ROONEY LIEBER & SCHORLING *Wilmington* |

| Leading Individuals |
| --- |
| 1  GOODMAN Lisa *Young Conaway Stargatt* |
|    SCOTT Pamela *Saul Ewing LLP* |
|    STABLER Wendie *Saul Ewing LLP* |
|    TARABICOS Larry *Young Conaway Stargatt* |
| 2  FORSTEN Richard *Klett Rooney Lieber* |
|    MANNING William *Klett Rooney Lieber* |
|    PARADEE John *Prickett, Jones* |
| 3  DUNKLE Mark *Parkowski Guerke* |
|    FUQUA James *Fuqua & Yori PA* |
|    RHODUNDA JR William *Oberly, Jennings & Rhodunda* |

## Band 1

### Saul Ewing LLP

See firm details p.1763

**The Firm:** This firm's celebrated all-around reputation for real estate work is in no small part due to its land use/zoning practice, which is considered "*among the best in the state.*" Attorneys regularly handle a wide variety of development matters, including rezonings, variances, special exceptions and zoning appeals and compliance, for a broad spread of regional and local developers. Noted for a keen understanding of the public side of the approvals process, the team is renowned for its success rate in obtaining approval for developments. **The Lawyers:** "*A reliable and effective adviser*" and a "*very astute, practical lawyer,*" **Pamela Scott** (see p.411) covers general real estate work, but she is most often recommended for her accomplished handling of land use matters. Vastly experienced in representing local and regional developers and business enti-

ties in approvals processes, clients greatly value her "*deft hand when dealing with the relevant bodies.*" **Wendie Stabler** (see p.412) is a "*well-respected*" attorney and "*one of the best*" for land use work, according to sources. Several peers commented: "*She's the first person I would send a case to in a conflict.*"

**Clients/Work Highlights:** Clients include local or regional industrial and commercial developers in telecom, municipal facilities, home building and leisure sectors. Clients of the group include AT&T Wireless; Conectiv; AstraZeneca; The Welfare Foundation and Wilmington College.

### Young Conaway Stargatt & Taylor LLP

See firm details p.424

**The Firm:** The largest real estate team in the state features a sophisticated land use and zoning contingent renowned for its heavy workload and particular flair for assisting national clients on in-state development projects. "*Undoubtedly one of the top teams in Delaware,*" matters handled include land use approvals for major commercial and residential developers. Clients praise the lawyers' "*personal touch*" and excellent connections in an area that is "*about much more than just book law.*" Rezoning matters also feature prominently and the team is currently advising one of the country's largest brownfield developers, O'Neill Properties Group, in the redevelopment of a 200-year-old fabric finishing plant into around 1,000 residential properties. Attorneys also advise clients on code compliance, site acquisition and variance matters.

**The Lawyers:** Respected as a "*good land use lobbyist,*" head of the real estate, banking and land use department **Lisa Goodman** (see p.405) is a "*sophisticated and competent*" attorney. Her understated style wins her many admirers. Goodman covers all manner of land use issues, and she is experienced in gaining approvals for telecom, construction and mixed-use development projects. Recently, she has

advised WL Gore & Associates, makers of Goretex, on the development of a new 1.3 million sq ft office, manufacturing and research facility. "*First choice for zonings,*" **Larry Tarabicos** (see p.413) is a high-profile attorney with a "*thorough knowledge of codes, people and practices.*" According to clients, he "*excels where you need to think on your feet*" and also takes on commercial real estate cases. In 2005, Tarabicos was involved with the $20 million privately funded redevelopment of a brownfield site in Delaware into a 120,000 sq ft athletics and fitness center.

**Clients/Work Highlights:** The Buccini/Pollen Group; Hercules; O'Neill Properties Group; Wal-Mart; Preit-Rubin; Eastern States Development Company and Chesapeake Property Management.

## Band 2

### Klett Rooney Lieber & Schorling

See firm details p.1757

**The Firm:** The Delaware office of this Pittsburgh-based East Coast firm has a general real estate team that clients rate highly for its advice on regulatory land use matters. Interviewees described the three-attorney team as "*good, tough and unafraid of confrontation.*" It handles zoning and land use approval matters for large developers, contractors and construction companies, and draws praise for its willingness to litigate approval matters when required. Recent highlights include advice to a major national supermarket chain on zoning and land use matters pertaining to the opening of a new Delaware outlet. The team has provided ongoing advice on the rezoning of the Brandywine Town Center project.

**The Lawyers:** Billed as a "*constant and very intelligent thinker,*" **Richard Forsten** (see p.404) balances land use work with some transactional commercial real estate and real estate litigation. Clients are impressed by his "*knowledgeable*" no-nonsense attitude, while peers turn to him when they prefer not to litigate land use matters themselves, remarking:

"*He is not soft, let's put it that way.*" The similarly straightforward **William Manning** (see p.408) "*tells you the truth, not what you want to hear*," and specializes in land use, zoning and utilities regulation. His flair for making presentations before approvals bodies came in for special praise from interviewees. Clients/Work Highlights: Clients include a variety of owners, developers, construction companies and other business entities.

## Other Notable Practitioners

**Mark Dunkle** of Parkowski Guerke & Swayze PA is recognized as a "*very competent, increasingly prominent, downstate Delaware attorney.*" With a practice spanning land use and related litigation matters, he was described as "*well connected*" and praised for "*knowing the law backwards, forwards and inside out.*" The "*go-to guy in Sussex*" for the growing amount of land use work in the county, **James Fuqua** of Fuqua & Yori PA "*has a solid lock on a lot of work*" in southern Delaware, according to sources. Former county

attorney **William Rhodunda** of The Law Offices of Oberly, Jennings & Rhodunda was recommended for his growing land use practice, with clients commenting: "*He is fast becoming one of the land use attorneys of choice.*" **John Paradee** of Prickett, Jones & Elliott PA is held in high regard for both his land use and transactional experience. Dubbed "*the man in Dover for land use,*" he is often found handling both commercial and residential transactions and is a well-versed commercial litigator too.

# Leaders in Delaware

## ABBOTT, Derek C
Morris, Nichols, Arsht & Tunnell LLP, Wilmington 302 351 9357
dabbott@mnat.com
*Recommended in Bankruptcy*
**Practice Areas:** Member of the Bankruptcy Group and Corporate and Business Litigation Groups, focusing his practice principally on corporate restructuring and bankruptcy matters. Mr Abbott represents debtors, official and ad hoc committees of creditors, professionals and other creditor and transactional case constituents in Chapter 11 matters and other litigation.
**Prof. Memberships:** ABA, Delaware State Bar Association (Bankruptcy Section and Chapter 11 Committee), American Bankruptcy Institute, Turnaround Management Association.
**Career:** Partner; Admissions to practice: Delaware; District of Delaware; United States Court of Appeals for the Third Circuit.
**Personal:** United States Military Academy (BS, 1987); Active Duty with the 82nd Airborne Division, United States Army (1987-91, including participation in Operations Desert Shield and Desert Storm); University of North Carolina School of Law (JD, with honors, 1995).

## ABRAMS, Kevin G
Abrams & Laster LLP, Wilmington 302 778 1002
Abrams@AbramsLaster.com
*Recommended in Chancery*
**Practice Areas:** Corporate and business litigation; transactional advice.
**Prof. Memberships:** Admitted to practice in the Delaware Supreme Court, US District Court for the State of Delaware, US Court of Appeals for the Third Circuit; Delaware State Bar Association; American Bar Association.
**Career:** Founding Partner; Director (1991-2005), Associate (1984-91), Richards Layton & Finger, P.A.
**Publications:** Frequent contributor and speaker at numerous law firm meetings, seminars and continuing legal education programs on various issues relating to

Delaware business law and associated litigation, opinion and advisory issues.
**Personal:** JD, 1984, University of Virginia; AB, 1978, University of Pennsylvania.

## ALEXANDER, Frederick H
Morris, Nichols, Arsht & Tunnell LLP, Wilmington 302 351 9228
falexander@mnat.com
*Recommended in Corporate/M&A*
**Practice Areas:** Corporation Law Counseling Group: providing advice on the Delaware General Corporation Law and related matters; counseling boards of directors and board committees; and providing formal legal opinions on Delaware corporate law issues.
**Prof. Memberships:** Member, Delaware State Bar Association; Member, Council of the Corporation Law Section of DSBA; Member, Negotiated Acquisitions Committee of ABA Business Law Section and Acquisitions of Public Companies Task Force. Serves on the ABA Business Law Section's Committee on Federal Regulation of Securities, and its Task Force on Shareholder Proposals.
**Career:** Partner.
**Publications:** Co-author of 'The Delaware Corporation; Legal Aspects of Organization and Operation', 1-4th C.P.S. (BNA 2004); recent articles: 'Analysis of the 2005 Amendments to the Delaware General Corporation Law' (Aspen Law & Business 2005); 'Delaware Supreme Court Decision On Protection Of The Stockholder Franchise', 35 Sec. Law & Regulation 243 (BNA 2003); 'Delaware Supreme Court Addresses Deal Protection, Enjoins Acquisition In Omnicare, Inc. v. NCS Healthcare, Inc.' 6 Mergers & Acquisitions, 101 (BNA 2003).
**Personal:** Georgetown Law Center (JD, magna cum laude, 1988); University of Maryland (BA 1985).

## ALLINGHAM II, Thomas J
Skadden, Arps, Slate, Meagher & Flom LLP & Affiliates, Wilmington 302 651 3070
tallingh@skadden.com
*Recommended in Chancery*

**Practice Areas:** Has experience in a wide range of corporate litigation, including mergers and acquisitions, shareholder and bankruptcy litigation, and statutory appraisal actions. For example, headed the firm's Litigation Team in The Southland Corporation's 1991 Chapter 11 restructuring, represented the chairman of Avondale Industries, Inc. against insurgent efforts to unseat the Chairman, and worked on the successful defenses of Walt Disney Productions against Saul Steinberg and Irwin Jacobs, Pogo Producing Co. against Northwest Industries, and Warner Communications against Rupert Murdoch.
**Career:** JD, University of Pennsylvania, 1977; BA, Williams College, 1974 (cum laude).

## ALTMAN, Paul M
Richards, Layton & Finger PA, Wilmington 302 651 7664
altman@rlf.com
*Recommended in Corporate/M&A*
**Practice Areas:** Paul Altman is the Chairman of the Business Department. Mr Altman's practice involves alternative entities, including limited partnerships and limited liability companies.
**Prof. Memberships:** Mr Altman is active on many subcommittees, and was a past Chairman of the Limited Partnership Subcommittee, of the Committee on Partnerships and Unincorporated Business Organizations of the ABA and is a member of the Committee of the Delaware State Bar Association responsible for updating the Delaware limited partnership, general partnership and limited liability company statutes.
**Publications:** Mr Altman is the co-author of 'Lubaroff & Altman on Delaware Limited Partnerships' and numerous other publications.

## ASHBY, Lawrence C
Ashby & Geddes, Wilmington 302 654 1888
lashby@ashby-geddes.com
*Recommended in Chancery*
**Practice Areas:** Managing Partner. Practice concentrated in counseling cor-

porate boards and committees and in related corporate and commercial litigation.
**Prof. Memberships:** Member, Board of Bar Examiners, 1983-90; Delaware Supreme Court Rules Advisory Committee, 1987-93; Member, Permanent Lawyers Advisory Committee for the United States District Court of Delaware, 1985-88; Member, Delaware State Bar Association and Chairman, Corporate Law Section, 1996-98.
**Personal:** Born Philadelphia, Pennsylvania in 1945; admitted to the Delaware Bar in 1970; Williams College (BA 1967); Vanderbilt University (JD 1970) (Order of the Coif).

## BALICK, Steven J
Ashby & Geddes, Wilmington 302 654 1888
sbalick@ashby-geddes.com
*Recommended in Intellectual Property*
**Practice Areas:** Practice concentrated in the prosecution and defense of patent, trademark, and other intellectual property litigation.
**Prof. Memberships:** Member, Permanent Lawyers Advisory Committee, United States District Court for the District of Delaware, 1992-95; Member, Delaware State Bar Association, Delaware Trial Lawyers Association, and Association of Trial Lawyers of America.
**Career:** Judicial Clerkship, Delaware Superior Court, 1981-82; Deputy Attorney General, State of Delaware, 1982-86; Joined firm as an associate in 1986; Partner since 1990.
**Personal:** Boston University (JD, 1981); University of Delaware (BA, 1978).

## BALOTTI, R Franklin
Richards, Layton & Finger PA, Wilmington 302 651 7710
balotti@rlf.com
*Recommended in Chancery, Corporate/M&A*
**Practice Areas:** R Franklin Balotti is a Director in the Corporate Department. His practice focuses on advising and representing corporations and corporate directors in litigation, transactions and

corporate governance matters.

**Prof. Memberships:** Mr Balotti is a Member of the Business Law, Litigation and International Sections of the American Bar Association, American College of Trial Lawyers and Corporate Law Section of the Delaware State Bar Association. **Publications:** Mr Balotti is the co-author of The Delaware Law of Corporations and Business Organization and Meetings of Stockholders and has authored and co-authored numerous articles on a host of corporate law topics.

### BIGLER, C Stephen
Richards, Layton & Finger PA,
Wilmington 302 651 7724
bigler@rlf.com
*Recommended in Corporate/M&A*

**Practice Areas:** Mergers, acquisitons, venture capital, entity formation, defensive planning, capital raising transactions, stockholder meetings, divestitures, proxy contests.
**Prof. Memberships:** Mr Bigler is a Member of the Business Law Section of the American Bar Association and the Corporate Law Section of the Delaware State Bar Association. He is a member of the Public Companies Task Force of the ABA Business Law Section Negotiated Acquisitions Committee and the Corporate Practice Committee. He also participated in drafting model venture capital financing documents for the NVCA.
**Publications:** Mr Bigler is the author of numerous articles on various aspects of Delaware corporate law.

### BLACK JR, Lewis S
Morris, Nichols, Arsht & Tunnell LLP,
Wilmington 302 351 9201
lblack@mnat.com
*Recommended in Corporate/M&A*

**Practice Areas:** Member of the Corporation Law Counseling Group concentrating in the area of corporation and securities law.
**Career:** DSBA (1964); District of Columbia Bar (1965); New York Bar (1966).
**Publications:** Author: Drexler, Black and Sparks, 'Delaware Corporation Law and Practice', (2004).
**Personal:** Yale Law School (LLB, 1963), Princeton University (AB, 1960).

### BLUMENFELD, Jack B
Morris, Nichols, Arsht & Tunnell LLP,
Wilmington 302 351 9291
JBlumenfeld@MNAT.com
*Recommended in Intellectual Property*

**Practice Areas:** Member of the Intellectual Property Litigation Group, concentrating in patent litigation encompassing many different areas of technology.
**Prof. Memberships:** ABA; DSBA (1979); has served on the Third Circuit Advisory Committee, Advisory Committee to the US District Court for the District of Delaware, the Civil Justice Reform Act Advisory Group and the Intellectual

Property Advisory Committee of that Court; and has chaired the Delaware Minority Job Fair Committee of the Delaware State Bar Association
**Career:** Partner since 1985; Associate, 1979-84; Law Clerk to The Honorable Walter K Stapleton, US District Court for the District of Delaware, 1977-79.
**Publications:** 'Solving the Mystery of Patentees' "Collective Enthusiasm" for Delaware', Del. Law Rev. 7:145-162 (2004) (with D Parsons, M Graham and L Polizoti).
**Personal:** Yale University (JD, 1977); State University of New York at Albany (BA, 1974); has served on the Board of Trustees of the Jewish Federation of Delaware and the Albert Einstein Academy.

### BOUCHARD, Andre
Bouchard Margules & Friedlander PA,
Wilmington 302 573 3500
*Recommended in Chancery*

### BOWDEN, William P
Ashby & Geddes, Wilmington
302 654 1888
wbowden@ashby-geddes.com
*Recommended in Bankruptcy*

**Practice Areas:** Practice concentrated in bankruptcy matters for debtors, creditor committees, secured lenders, and other parties in interest in such proceedings.
**Prof. Memberships:** American Bankruptcy Institute; Bankrutpcy Section of the Delaware State Bar Association; Advisory Board to the Views from the Bench Program.
**Personal:** Born Wilmington, Delaware in 1957; admitted to Delaware Bar in 1989; University of Delaware (BS 1985); Brooklyn Law School (JD 1988).

### BOWSER, William W
Young Conaway Stargatt & Taylor LLP,
Wilmington 302 571 6601
wbowser@ycst.com
*Recommended in Employment*

**Practice Areas:** Advises and represents employers in all areas of labor and employment law, including federal and state employment discrimination claims, collective bargaining, wrongful discharge litigation, and litigation of claims governed by the NLRB.
**Prof. Memberships:** Admitted to practice in Delaware (1983). Past Chair, Delaware State Bar Association Section on Labor and Employment Law.
**Career:** Joined Young Conaway as Partner, 1993. County Attorney, New Castle County, Delaware, 1989-93.
**Publications:** Editor, Delaware Employment Law Letter.
**Personal:** JD (cum laude), Villanova University, 1983; BA, University of Delaware, 1979. Governor-Appointed Chair of the Delaware Advisory Council on Cancer Incidence and Mortality.

### BRADY, Robert S
Young Conaway Stargatt & Taylor LLP,
Wilmington
302 571 6690
rbrady@ycst.com
*Recommended in Bankruptcy*

**Practice Areas:** Partner in the Business Reorganization and Restructuring Department. Bankruptcy clients have included, among others, Continental Airlines, Integrated Health Services, Budget Rent-a-Car, Golden Books, Alterra Healthcare Touch America Corporation, Metalforming Technologies, Inc., Meridian Automotive Systems.
**Prof. Memberships:** Member: Delaware State (Member, Sections on: General Corporation Law; Litigation) and American (Member, Sections on: Business Law; Litigation) Bar Associations; American Bankruptcy Institute; Federal Bar Association; Turnaround Management Association; Rodney Inns of Court.
**Career:** Admitted to Delaware Bar (1990).
**Publications:** Co-author, 'TWA Evens the Score on the Availability of the 502(d) Claim Preclusion Defense in Delaware' (2004); co-author, 'Determining and Preserving the Assets of Dot-Coms' (2003).
**Personal:** Born Salem, New Jersey, November 20, 1964. Education: Virginia Polytechnic Institute and State University (BS, 1987); Dickinson School of Law (JD, cum laude, 1990). Member, Woolsack Honor Society, a law school honorary society limited to graduates in the top 10% of their class. Member, Dickinson Law Review, 1989-90.

### BROWN, David B
Potter Anderson & Corroon LLP,
Wilmington 302 984 6013
dbrown@potteranderson.com
*Recommended in Corporate/M&A*

**Practice Areas:** Mr Brown practices in the area of corporate and commercial transactional law, including mergers and acquisitions, joint ventures, licensing and other business transactions. He served as lead counsel to a multinational company in the recent sale of a hair products business and serves as lead counsel to another multinational company in its attempted acquisition of a major industrial company. Other experience includes purchases and sales of companies in the cosmetics and specialty chemical industries, the negotiation of a number of multinational manufacturing and distribution agreements, and business counseling of companies in a variety of industries.

### BUSSARD, Donald A
Richards, Layton & Finger PA,
Wilmington 302 651 7716
bussard@rlf.com
*Recommended in Corporate/M&A*

**Practice Areas:** Donald A Bussard is a Director in the Corporate Department and is the senior member of the Depart-

ment's Corporate Transactional Group. His practice focuses on advising corporations, boards of directors and board committees in connection with mergers and acquisitions, recapitalizations, stock issuances, and corporate governance matters.
**Prof. Memberships:** Mr Bussard was formerly Chairman of, and since 1986 has been a Member of, the Council of the Corporation Law Section of the Delaware State Bar Association.
**Publications:** Mr Bussard is a contributing author to The Delaware Law of Corporations and Business Organizations, a multi-volume treatise on Delaware corporate law.

### CHEHI, Mark S
Skadden, Arps, Slate, Meagher & Flom LLP & Affiliates, Wilmington
302 651 3160
mchehi@skadden.com
*Recommended in Bankruptcy*

**Practice Areas:** Focuses on negotiated and contested workouts and restructurings, 'prepackaged' bankruptcies and traditional chapter 11 cases. Has represented public company debtors, creditors, shareholders, lenders, acquirors, creditors' committees, committee members and board special committees in a wide variety of matters, including international and cross-border situations and related litigations. Advises officers and directors on corporate governance and fiduciary duty matters, and he has experience representing companies confronting asbestos and other mass tort liabilities.
**Prof. Memberships:** Member, Turnaround Management Association; Member, International Federation of Insolvency Practitioners.
**Career:** JD, The University of Chicago Law School, 1990; BA, Haverford College, 1980.

### CLARK, Anthony W
Skadden, Arps, Slate, Meagher & Flom LLP & Affiliates, Wilmington
302 651 3080
tclark@skadden.com
*Recommended in Bankruptcy, Chancery*

**Practice Areas:** Heads the Corporate Restructuring and Bankruptcy Litigation Practice in Wilmington. Handles complex corporate, securities and general litigation matters. Has extensive experience representing debtors, creditors and acquirors in major corporate reorganization cases. Significant Chapter 11 debtor representations include Refco Inc., Hayes Lemmerz International, Inc., Mid-American Waste Systems, Inc., UDC Homes, Wang Laboratories, Inc., and Cardinal Industries Inc.
**Prof. Memberships:** President (2001-03) and Bencher, Richard S Rodney Chapter, American Inns of Court; Member, Board of Visitors, Temple University

School of Law.

**Career:** Adjunct professor, University of Pennsylvania Law School, 2005; JD, Temple University School of Law, 1979; BA, State University of New York at Cortland, 1973.

## COLLINS, Mark D
Richards, Layton & Finger PA, Wilmington 302 651 7531
Collins@rlf.com
*Recommended in Bankruptcy*
**Practice Areas:** Mark D Collins is a director of Richards, Layton & Finger, where he is Chair of the firm's Restructuring and Bankruptcy Group. Mr Collins has served as counsel to numerous chapter 11 debtors, lenders, formal and informal committees and other significant parties in large bankruptcy cases.
**Prof. Memberships:** Mr Collins is currently Co-Chair of the Finance and Banking Committee of the American Bankruptcy Institute and formerly served as Chair of the Secured Creditors Subcommittee of the Business Reorganization Committee of the ABI. Mr Collins is also Chair of the Legislation Committee of the Bankruptcy Section of the DSBA.

## COLLINS JR, P Clarkson
Morris, James, Hitchens & Williams LLP, Wilmington 302 888 6990
pcollins@morrisjames.com
*Recommended in Chancery*
**Practice Areas:** Member, Business Litigation and Corporate and Fiduciary Litigation Practice Groups. Has extensive experience in representing boards of directors, other corporate and business entity constituencies, financial institutions, businesses and professionals in actions involving governance, control contests and claims for indemnification and advancement, fiduciary and contract actions including lender liability, trade secret, and antitrust and unfair competition.
**Prof. Memberships:** Admitted to Delaware Bar, 1976. Member of American and Delaware Bar Associations.
**Career:** Joined Morris James, 1978; became Partner 1983.
**Personal:** Born in Pittsburgh, PA. JD, Dickinson School of Law, 1975. BA, University of Virginia, 1971.

## CONNOLLY JR, Arthur G
Connolly Bove Lodge & Hutz LLP, Wilmington 302 658 9141
aconnollyjr@cblh.com
*Recommended in Intellectual Property*
**Practice Areas:** Intellectual property, corporate/commercial litigation. Mr Connolly is a former President of the Delaware State Bar Association, a Fellow of the American College of Trial Lawyers, and served on the State Public Integrity Commission from 1991 to 2003, the last two years as Chair.
**Prof. Memberships:** Delaware State Bar Association, American Bar Association,

and the American Bar Foundation.
**Career:** Partner since 1967. Adjunct professor at Widener Law School (1981-86).
**Personal:** Georgetown University Law Center (JD, 1962); Georgetown University (BSS, 1959).

## COTTRELL III, Frederick L
Richards, Layton & Finger PA, Wilmington 302 651 7509
Cottrell@rlf.com
*Recommended in Intellectual Property*
**Practice Areas:** Fred Cottrell is a Director of Richards, Layton & Finger, where he is a member of the firm's Litigation Department. Mr Cottrell has represented a number of parties in significant patent litigation before the United States District Court for the District of Delaware.
**Prof. Memberships:** Mr Cottrell presently serves as Co-Chair of the Delaware District Court's Intellectual Property Law Advisory Committee. He is the former Chair of the Delaware State Bar Association's Intellectual Property Law Section. Mr Cottrell has spoken at seminars in his fields of practice including Delaware District Court practice and intellectual property law in Delaware.

## COUNIHAN, Victoria W
Greenberg Traurig LLP, Wilmington 302 661 7000
counihanv@gtlaw.com
*Recommended in Bankruptcy*
**Practice Areas:** Business reorganization and bankruptcy.
**Prof. Memberships:** President, International Women's Insolvency and Restructuring Confederation (IWIRC), Delaware Network, 2004-06; Vice President, Women and the Law Section, Delaware Bar Association; Member, Commercial Law Section, Delaware Bar Association; Member, Finance Committee for Semi-Annual Biden Seminars Sponsored by Delaware Senator Joseph R Biden Jr.
**Publications:** Contributing author, Wiley Bankruptcy Law Update, 1999-2001.
**Personal:** JD, magna cum laude, Villanova University School of Law, 1996; BA, magna cum laude, St Joseph's University, 1993.

## DAVIS JONES, Laura
Pachulski, Stang, Ziehl, Young, Jones & Weintraub PC, Wilmington
302 652 4100
*Recommended in Bankruptcy*

## DEFRANCESCHI, Daniel J
Richards, Layton & Finger PA, Wilmington 302 651 7816
DeFranceschi@rlf.com
*Recommended in Bankruptcy*
**Practice Areas:** Daniel J DeFranceschi is a Director in the firm's Restructuring and Bankruptcy Group. His practice focuses on representing debtors and creditors in Chapter 11 cases. Mr DeFranceschi has served as counsel to

numerous chapter 11 debtors in several business segments including telecommunications, high tech, retail, manufacturing, natural resources, flexible office solutions, and healthcare. Mr DeFranceschi also has an active creditor practice.
**Prof. Memberships:** Mr DeFranceschi is actively involved in the American Bankruptcy Institute and the Turnaround Management Association, and is the current Chair of the Delaware State Bar Association Bankruptcy Section.

## DEHNEY, Robert J
Morris, Nichols, Arsht & Tunnell LLP, Wilmington 302 351 9353
rdehney@mnat.com
*Recommended in Bankruptcy*
**Practice Areas:** Member of the Bankruptcy Group focusing on corporate restructuring and bankruptcy. Currently represents publicly-held (e.g., Rouge Steel) and privately-held (e.g., Thaxton Group, Inc.) companies in their efforts to restructure; represents official and ad hoc committees (eg, USG, aaiPharma), and acquirors of assets (eg, McDonald's Corporation, IER Corp., EchoStar).
**Prof. Memberships:** ABA; TMA; ABI; INSOL; Admissions to Practice: Connecticut (1990); New York (1995); Delaware (1997); Pennsylvania (1997).
**Career:** Partner; Law Clerk to the Honorable Prudence Beatty, US Bankruptcy Judge, SDNY.
**Personal:** Pace University (JD, 1990); Dickinson College (BA, 1987); Managing Editor Environmental Law Review.

## DIPRINZIO, Eugene A
Young Conaway Stargatt & Taylor LLP, Wilmington 302 571 6664
ediprinzio@ycst.com
*Recommended in Real Estate*
**Practice Areas:** Partner; his practice emphasizes the handling of complex commercial real estate transactions and the representation of financial institutions and other lenders involving commercial mortgage loans and asset-based lending. In addition, he has represented numerous property developers and borrowers in connection with their overall activities and has more than 25 years experience in closing real estate transactions on a primary basis. He has been engaged in many substantial leasing transactions on behalf of landlords and tenants and has successfully represented building owners in prosecuting their property tax assessment appeals. He is counsel to title insurers and assists with the closing of multi-state transactions.
**Prof. Memberships:** He is a member of the American College of Real Estate Lawyers and Fellow and Delaware State Chair of the American College of Mortgage Attorneys and a frequent lecturer on a variety of real estate topics.
**Career:** Admitted to practice law in both Pennsylvania and Delaware.

## DUNKLE, Mark
Parkowski Guerke & Swayze PA, Dover 302 678 3262
*Recommended in Real Estate*

## EASTON, Richard L
Skadden, Arps, Slate, Meagher & Flom LLP & Affiliates, Wilmington
302 651 3040
reaston@skadden.com
*Recommended in Corporate/M&A*
**Practice Areas:** Has a wide-ranging corporate practice, concentrating on mergers and acquisitions, securities and Delaware corporate law matters. Advises other lawyers in the firm and its affiliates on the Delaware law aspects of their transactions and leads the firm's representation in other transactions. Has represented many corporate, investment banking and individual clients in a variety of transactions, including negotiated acquisitions, contested takeovers, proxy contests and going-private, leveraged buyout and restructuring transactions. Also provides general corporate and securities law advice to a number of corporate clients on an ongoing basis and regularly deals with disclosure, fiduciary duty and corporate governance-related matters.
**Career:** JD, Georgetown University Law Center, 1975; BA, Wesleyan University, 1972 (cum laude).

## EISENHOFER, Jay
Grant & Eisenhofer PA, Wilmington 302 622 7000
*Recommended in Chancery*

## FATELL, Bonnie Glantz
Blank Rome LLP, Wilmington 302 425 6423
fatell@blankrome.com
*Recommended in Bankruptcy*
**Practice Areas:** Chair of Blank Rome's Business Restructuring and Bankruptcy Group and member of the firm's Distribution Committee. Ms Fatell has extensive experience in major bankruptcy reorganizations, out-of-court restructurings and other commercial matters in Delaware and nationally, representing secured and unsecured creditors, creditors' committees, debtors, plan of reorganization proponents, asset purchasers, landlords and other parties in interest. Recent representations include representing the debtors in USGen New England Corporation, ANC Rental Corporation and New Global Telecom, creditors' committees in Datatec Systems, InaCom Corporation, and Merry Go Round Enterprises, and creditors in Delphi, Northwest Airlines and FLYi.
**Prof. Memberships:** Fellow in American College of Bankruptcy, Member, American Bankruptcy Institute and International Women's Insolvency and Restructuring Confederation.
**Career:** Admitted to practice: Pennsylvania, 1981; Delaware, 1999; United States

Supreme Court, 2002.

**Publications:** Contributing author, 'Collier Bankruptcy Forms Manual' (2005-present), 'Inside the Minds: Best Practices for Corporate Restructuring' (Aspatore Books, 2006); frequent lecturer and author. Recognized among America's leading bankruptcy lawyers in The Best Lawyers in America (2006).

**Personal:** Temple University School of Law, JD, 1981; Pennsylvania State University, BS, 1973.

## FELGER, Mark
Cozen O'Connor, Wilmington
302 295 2000
*Recommended in Bankruptcy*

## FINKELSTEIN, Jesse A
Richards, Layton & Finger PA, Wilmington 302 651 7754
finkelstein@rlf.com
*Recommended in Chancery, Corporate/M&A*

**Practice Areas:** Jesse A Finkelstein is the firm President and Chairman of the Corporate Department. Mr Finkelstein provides corporate governance, transactional and control dispute advice, and represents both corporate and individual clients in complex or high stakes litigation.

**Prof. Memberships:** Mr Finkelstein is a fellow of the American College of Trial Lawyers, a Member of the Business Law, Litigation and International Sections of the American Bar Association and is a Member of the Council of the Corporate Law Section of the Delaware Bar Association.

**Publications:** The Delaware Law of Corporations and Business Organizations, Meetings of Stockholders and numerous other publications.

## FISCHER, Matthew E
Potter Anderson & Corroon LLP, Wilmington 302 984 6153
mfischer@potteranderson.com
*Recommended in Corporate/M&A*

**Practice Areas:** Mr Fischer practices in the areas of corporate, commercial and alternative entities litigation, and advises directors regarding mergers and acquisitions, tender offers, proxy contests, and shareholder derivative and class action suits. He represented BlueScope Steel in an appraisal suit, represented PeopleSoft in connection with Oracle's hostile offer, represented Hallwood Realty against a hostile bid from Carl Icahn, represented Hewlett-Packard in its dispute with Walter Hewlett over the HP-Compaq merger, and represented Baxter HealthCare in a commercial dispute with Aventis Behring.

**Prof. Memberships:** Mr Fischer was admitted to the Delaware Bar in 1992 and the Pennsylvania Bar in 1993.

## FORSTEN, Richard
Klett Rooney Lieber & Schorling,

Wilmington 302 552 4230
forsten@klettrooney.com
*Recommended in Real Estate*

**Practice Areas:** Real estate and land use.
**Career:** Experienced in the areas of land use and land use litigation, commercial and real estate transactions, financings, litigation, construction and mechanics' liens law, and environmental law and permitting. Has represented owners and developers on some of the most complex and challenging land use matters throughout the state of Delaware. Also has extensive legislative drafting experience, both at the state and local level.

**Personal:** BS, University of Virginia; JD, University of Virginia School of Law.

## FOURNIER, David M
Pepper Hamilton LLP, Wilmington
302 777 6565
fournierd@pepperlaw.com
*Recommended in Bankruptcy*

**Practice Areas:** Partner, Bankruptcy and Reorganization Group, Wilmington, Delaware. Experienced in: secured lending, workout counseling and bankruptcy litigation. Represents secured and unsecured creditors, official creditors' committees and debtors in various industries including retail, food processing, equipment leasing and financing, communications.

**Prof. Memberships:** Member, Caesar Rodney Inn of Court. Delaware Bar Association, Chair, International Law Section.
**Career:** JD, 1989, Villanova University School of Law; BA 1985 Pennsylvania State University.

## FUQUA, James
Fuqua & Yori PA, Georgetown
302 856 7777
*Recommended in Real Estate*

## GALARDI, Gregg M
Skadden, Arps, Slate, Meagher & Flom LLP & Affiliates, Wilmington
302 651 3150
ggalardi@skadden.com
*Recommended in Bankruptcy*

**Practice Areas:** Represents major corporations in business reorganizations, restructurings, acquisitions and divestitures. Clients have included debtors, creditors, creditors' committees, bank groups, investors, acquirors and financial advisors in all stages of complex restructuring transactions, from Chapter 11 reorganizations to out-of-court negotiations and workouts.

**Career:** University of Pennsylvania: JD, 1990 (cum laude; Special Projects Editor, University of Pennsylvania Law Review, 1989-90, Associate Editor 1988-89); PhD, Philosophy, 1990; MA, Economics, 1985; BA, 1979 (cum laude; honors in dual majors).

## GEE, William S
Saul Ewing LLP, Wilmington
302 421 6823

wgee@saul.com
*Recommended in Real Estate*

**Practice Areas:** Partner in firm's Real Estate Department. Focuses on complex commercial transactions, with emphasis on real estate-related matters. Experience in acquisition and disposition of commercial real estate portfolios. Worked extensively as Delaware opinion counsel in connection with corporate, partnership and limited liability company law.

**Prof. Memberships:** Admitted in Delaware, Delaware Supreme Court, US District Court for the District of Delaware. Member, American and Delaware State Bar Associations.
**Career:** Acted as lead counsel in billions of dollars worth of multi-state acquisitions, sales, and financings.
**Personal:** JD (summa cum laude), Washington and Lee University School of Law, BA, Yale University.

## GEIGER, Kathleen W
Potter Anderson & Corroon LLP, Wilmington 302 984 6075
kgeiger@potteranderson.com
*Recommended in Intellectual Property*

**Practice Areas:** Ms Geiger concentrates her practice in intellectual property, primarily patents. Her patent practice encompasses the biotechnology, pharmaceutical and chemical areas, including patent application drafting and prosecution, infringement and validity opinions, licensing and IP due diligence within the context of business transactions and corporate mergers and acquisitions. Ms Geiger oversees the trademark legal services provided by Potter Anderson, and provides support and patent advice to the firm's Intellectual Property Litigation Group, and the E-Commerce Practice Area. Ms Geiger is a frequent presenter on legal aspects of intellectual property law including written description, trade secret law and joint development agreements.

## GENTILE, Mark J
Richards, Layton & Finger PA, Wilmington 302 651 7722
gentile@rlf.com
*Recommended in Corporate/M&A*

**Practice Areas:** Director, Corporate Advisory Group; focuses on the General Corporation Law of the State of Delaware, advising corporations, officers, directors, committees of the board of directors and stockholders in connection with mergers and acquisitions, divestitures, recapitalizations and corporate governance issues.

**Prof. Memberships:** ABA Committee on Corporate Laws of Business Law Section (Member), Committee on Federal Regulation of Securities (Member), Corporate Law Section of the Delaware State Bar Association (Member).

**Publications:** Contributing author to 'The Delaware Law of Corporations and

Business Organizations' and has co-authored numerous articles on various aspects of corporate law.

## GLASSMAN, Neil
The Bayard Firm, Wilmington
302 429 4224
nglassman@bayardfirm.com
*Recommended in Bankruptcy*

**Practice Areas:** Neil focuses his practice on bankruptcy and insolvency law, and regularly represents debtors, official committees of unsecured creditors, insurance companies and creditors in large bankruptcy cases, insurance insolvencies and other insolvency proceedings. An experienced transactional attorney, Neil has also developed an expertise relating to the law of Delaware business entities including corporations, business trusts, general partnerships, limited partnerships, and limited liability companies.

**Prof. Memberships:** American Bankruptcy Institute; Delaware State Bar Association (Chairman, Commercial Law Section, 1987-89; Member: Bankruptcy Section and Corporation Law Section; Uniform Commercial Code Committee; Committee on Business Trusts); and American Bar Association.

**Career:** Neil is the Chairman of The Bayard Firm and leads the firm's Bankruptcy Group. He obtained a Bachelor of Arts degree from Trinity College, and later received a Master of Business Administration degree in Corporate Finance from the University of Connecticut. Neil began practicing law after graduating Order of the Coif with his Juris Doctor degree from Case Western Reserve University School of Law. Neil joined The Bayard Firm in 1986, and is now a Director and shareholder at the firm.

**Publications:** Co-author: 'Equity Committees: A Consequence of the 'Zone of Insolvency', published in American Bankruptcy Institute Journal, December 2005/January 2006. Co-author: 'Equity Committees - Representation of Shareholders in Bankruptcy Cases', appearing in Financier Worldwide's 2005 Restructuring and Insolvency Series. Author: 'US Bankruptcy Roundtable', published in Financier Worldwide, May 2005. Co-author: 'Are You In The Vicinity of Insolvency? Serving More Than One Master', published in The Americas 2004/2005 Restructuring and Insolvency Guide. Co-author: 'Cybergenics: A Corporate Solution to a Bankruptcy Problem', published on the website of Delaware Law Weekly, November 27, 2002. Author: 'Awarding Attorneys' Fees From Class Action Judgments', Case Western Reserve Law Review, Vol. 30, 1979.

**Personal:** Born Philadelphia, Pennsylvania, October 14, 1952. Trinity College (BA, 1974); University of Connecticut (MBA, 1978); Case Western Reserve University (JD, 1981).

## GOLDMAN, Michael
Potter Anderson & Corroon LLP,
Wilmington 302 984 6007
mgoldman@potteranderson.com
*Recommended in Chancery,*
*Corporate/M&A*
**Practice Areas:** Mr Goldman practices in the corporate law and corporate litigation areas and provides advice and formal opinions as to the advisability, propriety and legal consequences of proposed decisions, transactions, and business combinations under Delaware law. His practice focuses primarily on the fiduciary relationship between Delaware business entities and their owners and managers, particularly in connection with tender offers, proxy contests, and other transactions involving changes of corporate control. He is regularly called to provide advice and formal opinions as to the advisability, propriety and legal consequences of proposed decisions, transactions, and business combinations under Delaware law.

## GOODMAN, Lisa
Young Conaway Stargatt & Taylor LLP,
Wilmington 302 571 6683
lgoodman@ycst.com
*Recommended in Real Estate*
**Practice Areas:** Partner practicing land use, zoning, and subdivision law.
**Prof. Memberships:** Member, Delaware State Bar Association and American Bar Association.
**Career:** Joined Young Conaway Stargatt & Taylor in 1994, became Partner in 2002. Wolcott law clerk, Delaware Supreme Court, 1993-94.
**Publications:** 'Preserving Urban Estates: A Case Study', Delaware Lawyer, Fall 2000; 'One Aspect of the Land Use Debate: Cellular Transmission Sites', In Re, September 1996.
**Personal:** JD Widener University School of Law; MA University of Delaware; BA West Chester University.

## GRAHAM, Mary B
Morris, Nichols, Arsht & Tunnell LLP,
Wilmington 302 351 9199
mgraham@mnat.com
*Recommended in Intellectual Property*
**Practice Areas:** Member of Intellectual Property Litigation Group, litigating patent, trade secret and contract disputes involving diverse technologies from pharmaceuticals and chemicals to software and medical devices.
**Prof. Memberships:** ABA; DSBA; AIPLA; District of Delaware Intellectual Property Advisory Committee (Member); Delaware State Board of Education (Member, 1999-present); Delaware Higher Education Commission (Chair, 1993-99); Board on Professional Responsibility (Member, 1999-2005); Preliminary Review Committee of Board on Professional Responsibility (Member 1994-99).
**Career:** Partner; Admission to Practice: Delaware; Third Circuit and Federal Circuit Court of Appeals; Law Clerk to The Honorable Walter K Stapleton, United States District Court for the District of Delaware.
**Publications:** Parsons, Blumenfeld, Graham & Polizoti, 'Solving the Mystery of Patentees' "Collective Enthusiasm" for Delaware,' 7 Del. L. Rev. 145, 145-161 (2004).
**Personal:** Stanford University (BS in mathematics, with distinction, 1974); Massachusetts Institute of Technology (MS in mathematics, 1978); Yale Law School (JD, 1982).

## GRANT, Stuart
Grant & Eisenhofer PA, Wilmington
302 622 7000
*Recommended in Chancery*

## GRIMM, Thomas C
Morris, Nichols, Arsht & Tunnell LLP,
Wilmington 302 351 9595
tgrimm@mnat.com
*Recommended in Intellectual Property*
**Practice Areas:** Member of the Intellectual Property Litigation and the Corporate and Business Groups. Mr Grimm has represented primarily corporate clients, including in recent years Georgia-Pacific, QUALCOMM, Honeywell and Advanced Energy.
**Prof. Memberships:** ABA (1980); Delaware Bar (1980); Pennsylvania Bar (1981); US Court of Appeals for Federal Circuit; US Court of Appeals for 3rd Circuit; Chairman of the Board on the Unauthorized Practice of Law.
**Career:** Morris, Nichols (1981-present); Partner (1989-present); Law Clerk to The Honorable William Duffy, Delaware Supreme Court (1980-81).
**Publications:** Thomas C Grimm and Matt Neiderman, 'Individual Rights', (Delaware Supreme Court Golden Anniversary, Ch. 9, 2001); Thomas C Grimm, Karen Jacob Louden & Julia Heaney, 'Trademarks in Cyberspace', (Delaware Lawyer, Vol. 18, No. 4, Winter 2000-01); Eugene L Grimm Sr and Thomas C Grimm, 'Trademarks: How to Get Them, Keep Them, and Enforce Them', (Delaware Lawyer, Vol. 7, No. 3, March 1989).
**Personal:** Villanova University (JD, cum laude, 1980); Staff Member and Editor, Villanova Law Review; University of Notre Dame (BBA, 1977); Board Member, Special Olympics of Delaware; Trustee, Archmere Academy.

## GROSSBAUER, John
Potter Anderson & Corroon LLP,
Wilmington 302 984 6131
jgrossbauer@potteranderson.com
*Recommended in Corporate/M&A*
**Practice Areas:** Mr Grossbauer practices in the areas of corporation law and commercial transactions, advising public and private corporations and their boards of directors with respect to all aspects of Delaware General Corporation Law, including the fiduciary duties of directors and technical compliance with various provisions of the Delaware General Corporation Law. Mr Grossbauer has also represented purchasers and sellers in negotiated acquisitions of assets and businesses.
**Prof. Memberships:** ABA Business Law Section; Member, Council of Delaware Bar Corporation Law Section.
**Personal:** JD, Duke Law School, 1986.

## GWYNNE, Kurt F
Reed Smith LLP, Wilmington
302 778 7550
kgwynne@reedsmith.com
*Recommended in Bankruptcy*
**Practice Areas:** Head of Corporate Restructuring and Bankruptcy Group in, and Managing Partner of, Wilmington office; represents clients in bankruptcy cases and creditors' rights litigation in many jurisdictions.
**Prof. Memberships:** Business Bankruptcy Committee, American Bar Association; Delaware Bankruptcy Inn of Court; Eastern District of Pennsylvania Bankruptcy Conference.
**Career:** Law clerk, Honorable Bruce Fox, US Bankruptcy Court, Eastern District of Pennsylvania.
**Publications:** Co-authored revisions to Chapter 40, Contempt, 'Collier Bankruptcy Practice Guide,' and numerous bankruptcy articles.
**Personal:** University of Pennsylvania Law School (JD, 1992), Senior Editor, Journal of International Business Law; University of Central Florida (BA, 1988).

## HABBART, Ellisa Opstbaum
Delaware Counsel Group LLP,
Wilmington 302 576 9600
ehabbart@delawarecounselgroup.com
*Recommended in Corporate/M&A*
**Practice Areas:** Ellisa Habbart's practice includes transactions involving Delaware partnerships, corporations, statutory trusts and limited liability companies. She counsels attorneys and in-house counsel nationally and internationally on Delaware law issues that relate to transactions and structures involving these Delaware entities. Ms Habbart advises boards of directors on fiduciary duties and corporate governance issues, mergers and acquisitions and opinions on Delaware legal issues.
**Prof. Memberships:** Ellisa Habbart is the appointed American Bar Association Advisor to the National Conference of Commissioners on Uniform State Laws (NCCUSL) Drafting Committee on Statutory Trust Act. This Committee is responsible for drafting the Uniform Statutory Trust Act. As ABA Advisor, Ms Habbart represents the interests of the Association and reports on the result of each drafting committee meeting. She chairs the ABA Section of Business Law Subcommittee on Business Trusts: REITs, Financing and Operating Vehicles, is an Executive Committee Member of the Partnerships and Unincorporated Business Organizations Committee, and a member of the Negotiated Acquisitions Committee. Ms Habbart is an appointee to the Delaware State Bar Association Committee on Statutory Trusts. This committee is responsible for recommending legislative amendments to the Delaware State Legislature regarding changes to the Delaware Statutory Trust Act. Ms Habbart chairs the Association's Subcommittee on REITs which is in the process of considering new Delaware legislation. Ms Habbart is a Member of the International Bar Association.
**Career:** Partner, Admissions to Practice: Delaware (1988)
**Publications:** Ms Habbart has co-authored 'Delaware Limited Liability Company Forms and Practice Manual' and 'Delaware Limited Partnership Law', a chapter of the New York Law Journal text, 'Partnership & Joint Venture Agreements'.
**Personal:** Villanova University School of Law, (JD, 1986); Drexel University, (MS Taxation, 1983); Temple University, (BBA, 1981).

## HAUBERT, William J
Richards, Layton & Finger PA,
Wilmington 302 651 7559
Haubert@RLF.com
*Recommended in Corporate/M&A*
**Practice Areas:** William Haubert is a Director in the firm's Corporate Department. His practice focuses on advisory, transactional and opinion matters relating to Delaware corporations. He provides corporate governance, transactional and control dispute advice to clients, and represents both corporate and individual clients in complex transactions.
**Prof. Memberships:** Mr Haubert is a Member of the Business Law Section of the ABA and a Member of the Corporate Law Section of the Delaware State Bar Association.
**Career:** Prior to joining RL&F, Mr Haubert was a law clerk to then Vice Chancellor William B Chandler, III, in the Delaware Court of Chancery.

## HERING, Louis G
Morris, Nichols, Arsht & Tunnell LLP,
Wilmington 302 351 9213
lhering@mnat.com
*Recommended in Corporate/M&A*
**Practice Areas:** Commerical law counseling including mergers and acquisitions, organization and structuring of all Delaware alternative entities, secured transactions and opinions on full range of Delaware legal issues.
**Prof. Memberships:** ABA Business Law Section Committee on Partnerships and Unincorporated Business Associations; DSBA Committees responsibile for updating Delaware limited liability com-

pany, partnership and statutory trust acts.
**Career:** Partner; admissions to practice: Delaware; New York; District of Columbia; Law Clerk to Honorable Carolyn Berger, Delaware Court of Chancery.
**Publications:** Frequent lecturer and author on alternative entity matters including co-author of BNA Portfolio on LLCs.
**Personal:** Cornell University (AB 1982); UCLA (JD 1986).

## HERSHMAN, Douglas M
The Bayard Firm, Wilmington
302 429 4207
dhershman@bayardfirm.com
*Recommended in Real Estate*
**Practice Areas:** Doug has a diverse real estate practice, representing clients engaged in all aspects of the real estate industry throughout Delaware and its surrounding states. His practice has included representations of both buyers and sellers of commercial and residential properties, as well as borrowers in financing transactions. He also represents lenders making commercial real estate loans. Doug handles both residential and commercial transactions, including retail centers, office buildings and apartment complexes. He is a licensed issuing agent for Transnation Title Insurance Company, Lawyers Title Insurance Company, Stewart Title Guaranty Company and Ticor Title Insurance Company.
**Prof. Memberships:** Delaware State Bar Association (Chair, Real and Personal Property Section, 1988-2001 and Executive Committee, 2005); American Bar Association (Member, Real Property, Probate and Trust Section); New York State Bar Association (Member, Real Property Law Section); Home Builders Association of Delaware (Secretary, Board of Directors).
**Career:** After graduating from the University of Delaware, Doug attended Syracuse University where he was awarded a Juris Doctor degree, magna cum laude. He was also awarded admission to the Order of the Coif and the Justinian Honor Society. Doug joined The Bayard Firm in 1999 after having practiced law in New York and Delaware for 13 years. He is now a Director and shareholder at The Bayard Firm and serves as Chair of the Executive Committee.
**Publications:** Author: 'Quality of Life in the Homebuilding Industry', published in the Delaware Bar Foundation Journal, date unknown.
**Personal:** Born Queens, New York, September 28, 1961. University of Delaware (BA, 1983); Syracuse University (JD, magna cum laude, 1986). Admitted to practice in New York (1987), Delaware (1988), and Pennsylvania (1995). Secretary, Board of Governors, University & Whist Club of Wilmington, Delaware.

## HEYMAN, Kurt
Proctor Heyman LLP, Wilmington
302 472 7300
kheyman@proctorheyman.com
*Recommended in Chancery*
**Practice Areas:** Corporate and commercial litigation. Please see firm profile for Proctor Heyman LLP.
**Prof. Memberships:** Secretary, Corporation Law Council, Delaware State Bar Association. Vice-Chair, Corporate Counseling and Litigation Subcommittee, Business Law Section, American Bar Association. Editorial Board Member, Delaware Law Review.
**Career:** Law Clerk to Hon Jack B Jacobs, Delaware Court of Chancery, 1991-92. Founded Proctor Heyman LLP with Vernon R Proctor on January 1, 2006.
**Publications:** Frequent author/lecturer on issues of corporate law and practice before the Delaware Court of Chancery.
**Personal:** University of Michigan (AB, With High Distinction, 1988); University of Chicago (JD, 1991). Phi Beta Kappa.

## HOLT, Scott
Young Conaway Stargatt & Taylor LLP, Wilmington 302 571 6623
sholt@ycst.com
*Recommended in Employment*
**Practice Areas:** Partner and member of Young Conaway's Employment and Litigation Departments. Area of practice includes laws concerning FMLA, ADEA, Title VII, ADA, NLRA, FLSA, WARN, trade secrets and restrictive covenants, and defense of class actions.
**Prof. Memberships:** Admitted in Delaware and Third, Fourth and Sixth Circuit Courts of Appeals. Labor & Employment Sections, ABA and DSBA (past Chairman).
**Career:** Delaware Supreme Court clerkship; joined Young Conaway Stargatt & Taylor, LLP in 1995.
**Publications:** Delaware Employment Law Letter, Editor; Navigating the WARN Act, ABA Section of Business Law (Spring 2002).
**Personal:** Temple University (high honors); Widener University, JD (honors).

## HORWITZ, Richard L
Potter Anderson & Corroon LLP, Wilmington 302 984 6027
rhorwitz@potteranderson.com
*Recommended in Intellectual Property*
**Practice Areas:** Mr Horwitz' practice includes intellectual property, commercial and Delaware corporate litigation, representing corporate clients in patent infringement, antitrust and business tort issues, insurance coverage for D&O, product liability and business tort claims, and Delaware fiduciary duty and related corporate and partnership claims.
**Prof. Memberships:** ABA Litigation Section (Co-Chair Pretrial Practice and Discovery Committee); Intellectual Property Section; Business Law Section; Delaware

District Court IP Advisory Committee.
**Career:** Chaired firm's Litigation Group for the past six years.
**Personal:** Amherst College, 1979; Duke University School of Law, 1982; Law Clerk to Hon Robert L Clifford, NJ Supreme Court, 1982-83.

## HUTZ, Rudolf E
Connolly Bove Lodge & Hutz LLP, Wilmington 302 658 9141
rhutz@cblh.com
*Recommended in Intellectual Property*
**Practice Areas:** Intellectual property law, litigation, patents, trademarks, trade secrets, and antitrust law. Mr Hutz has conducted successful IP trials, ADR proceedings, and appeals before various United States Courts, including the United States Supreme Court in Dawson v Rohm and Haas, 448 US 176 (1980). His experience extends to such technologies as pharmaceuticals, herbicides, medical devices, genetically engineered plants and biological chemicals.
**Prof. Memberships:** Delaware State Bar Association, American Intellectual Property Law Association, Philadelphia Intellectual Property Law Association, Federal Bar Association, Federal Circuit Bar Association, American College of Trial Lawyers - Fellow.
**Career:** Partner since 1967.
**Publications:** Mr Hutz has written and lectured extensively on a variety of IP matters, and has acted as an arbitrator/special master in resolving intellectual property disputes.
**Personal:** Georgetown University Law Center (JD, 1963); Princeton University (BA, 1959).

## INGERSOLL, Josy W
Young Conaway Stargatt & Taylor LLP, Wilmington 302 571 6672
jingersoll@ycst.com
*Recommended in Intellectual Property*
**Practice Areas:** Firm Practice Leader intellectual property, commercial, corporate litigation.
**Prof. Memberships:** Admitted Delaware (1980). Member, Delaware Board of Bar Examiners (1991-2002); Delaware Intellectual Property Committee; Delaware Bar Association; Governor's Commission on Major Commercial Litigation Reform; ABA; IBA.
**Career:** Joined firm, 1980; Partner, 1986. Member of firm's Management Committee (main planning and policy group).
**Publications:** 'Marking the Right Time - Pros and Cons on a Timeline for Scheduling the Markman Hearing' (article); Business Strategy Protection a/k/a 'The White Knight Privilege' (outline); 'Shareholder Rights Bylaws' (article), others.
**Personal:** JD, Temple University; AB, Douglass College; Phi Beta Kappa, Cum Laude.

## ISKEN, Donald N
Morris, Nichols, Arsht & Tunnell LLP, Wilmington 302 351 9222
disken@mnat.com
*Recommended in Real Estate*
**Practice Areas:** Member of the Commercial Law Counsel Group with a concentration in real estate law and land use regulation.
**Prof. Memberships:** ABA; DSBA (1978), Real Property Committee (Co-Chairman of subcommittee to Revisions to the Delaware Unit Property Act, 1989-92); Member, American College of Real Estate Lawyers; Board of the Directors of the Association of Retarded Citizens.
**Career:** Partner; Admission to practice: Delaware (1978).
**Personal:** Bucknell University (AB, 1975); University of Miami School of Law (JD, cum laude, 1978).

## JENKINS, Stephen E
Ashby & Geddes, Wilmington
302 654 1888
sjenkins@ashby-geddes.com
*Recommended in Chancery*
**Practice Areas:** Practice concentrated in counseling and litigating on behalf of large stockholders, including hedge funds and other activist stockholders, as well as counseling and litigating on behalf of corporate boards and committees, related corporate and commercial litigation, and corporate valuation issues including Delaware statutory appraisals.
**Prof. Memberships:** Member, Delaware Court of Chancery Rules Advisory Committee; Member, Delaware State Bar Association, formerly Co-Chair, Committee on Professional Ethics; Articles Editor, Delaware Law Review.
**Personal:** Born Wilmington, Delaware 1954; admitted to Delaware Bar in 1982; Georgetown University (AB 1976); JD, magna cum laude, 1982), Executive Editor, Georgetown Law Journal; US Army, 1976-79; US Army Reserve 1979-83.

## JOHNSTON, John F
Morris, Nichols, Arsht & Tunnell LLP, Wilmington 302 351 9203
jjohnston@mnat.com
*Recommended in Corporate/M&A*
**Practice Areas:** Corporation Law Counseling Group: providing advice on the Delaware General Corporation Law and related matters; counseling boards of directors and board committees; and providing formal legal opinions on Delaware corporate law issues.
**Prof. Memberships:** ABA (Member, Federal Regulation of Securities Committee, Business Law Section); Delaware State Bar Association.
**Career:** Partner since 1985.
**Publications:** Has written extensively on corporate governance matters.
**Personal:** Northwestern University (BA 1968); Duke University (PhD 1972); University of Pennsylvania (JD, cum laude, 1977).

## KELLEY, Bernard J
Richards, Layton & Finger PA,
Wilmington 302 651 7674
Kelley@RLF.com
*Recommended in Corporate/M&A*
**Practice Areas:** Bernard J Kelley is a
Director of Richards, Layton & Finger,
where he is a member of the firm's Business Department. His practice focuses on
a wide variety of transactional matters
involving alternative entities such as
Delaware limited liability companies,
limited partnerships, general partnerships and statutory trusts. Mr Kelley's
practice also includes the representation
of banks and trust companies in commercial transactions and regulatory matters, including before Delaware state regulatory authorities.
**Prof. Memberships:** Mr Kelley is the
former Chair of the Delaware Banking
Law Committee of the Delaware State
Bar Association.

## KIRK, Richard D
The Bayard Firm, Wilmington
302 429 4208
rkirk@bayardfirm.com
*Recommended in Intellectual Property*
**Practice Areas:** Dick's practice focuses
on intellectual property litigation, envi-
ronmental litigation and counseling, gen-
eral business litigation and alternative
dispute resolution.
**Prof. Memberships:** Delaware State Bar
Association (President, 1993-94; Founding Chair, Environmental Law Section;
Chair, Committee on Response to Public
Comment; Member, Delaware Supreme
Court's Standing Committee on Professionalism; Former Chair, Delaware
Supreme Court's Commission on Continuing Legal Education); American Bar
Association; and United States District
Court for the District of Delaware (Member, Rules Advisory Committee).
**Career:** Dick received a Bachelor of Arts
degree at Georgetown University and
later a Juris Doctor degree from the University of Virginia School of Law. Subsequently, Dick clerked for Justice William
Duffy of the Delaware Supreme Court,
one of the founding members of what is
now The Bayard Firm. Dick served as a
Deputy Attorney General and full-time
counsel to the Delaware State Board of
Education. Dick joined the firm in 2005
after 20 years at a local law firm in Wilmington, Delaware, of which the last 17
years he was a Partner. Dick is a Director
and shareholder at The Bayard Firm.
**Personal:** Born Washington, District of
Columbia, January 23, 1953. Georgetown
University (BA, 1975); University of Virginia School of Law (JD, 1978).

## KLEIN, Daniel L
Richards, Layton & Finger PA,
Wilmington 302 651 7638
Klein@rlf.com
*Recommended in Real Estate*

**Practice Areas:** Daniel L Klein is Chairman of the Real Estate Group of the firm,
specializing in complex business transactions and in public/private joint ventures.
**Prof. Memberships:** Mr Klein is active
in the Real Property Section of the
Delaware State Bar Association, the
American Bar Association where he is
active in the financing and leasing areas,
the Anglo-American Real Property Institute and the American College of Real
Estate Lawyers (where he served two
terms on its Board of Governors).
**Career:** Mr Klein has also been listed in
the Best Lawyers in America, Best
Lawyers in Delaware and Who's Who
Legal.

## KNIGHT, John H
Richards, Layton & Finger PA,
Wilmington 302 651 7512
knight@RLF.com
*Recommended in Bankruptcy*
**Practice Areas:** John H Knight is a
Director in the firm's Restructuring and
Bankruptcy Group. His practice focuses
on representing debtors, secured credi-
tors and other parties in interest in Chap-
ter 11 cases. Mr Knight has served as
counsel to numerous chapter 11 debtors
in varied business segments.
**Prof. Memberships:** Mr Knight is a
member of the firm's substantive non-
consolidation opinion team. He is also a
member of the State Bars of Delaware,
Maryland and New Jersey; United States
District Court, Districts of Delaware and
New Jersey; Third Circuit Court of
Appeals.

## KRAPF, Daniel H
Saul Ewing LLP, Wilmington
302 421 6841
dkrapf@saul.com
*Recommended in Real Estate*
**Practice Areas:** Mr Krapf is a Partner
and Vice-Chair of Saul Ewing's Real
Estate Department. Mr Krapf concentrates his practice in commercial real
estate and business transactions. He
serves on the firm's Hiring Committee.
**Prof. Memberships:** Member, Delaware
State Bar Association.
**Career:** Prior to joining Saul Ewing, he
was a partner at Green, Ward & Krapf,
Vice President and General Counsel of
Allied Properties Group, a diversified
company engaged in real estate development, management and construction and
a Partner in the Wilmington firm of Morris, James, Hitchens and Williams.
**Personal:** JD, Dickinson School of Law,
BA, University of Delaware.

## KRAPF, Robert J
Richards, Layton & Finger PA,
Wilmington 302 651 7609
krapf@rlf.com
*Recommended in Real Estate*
**Practice Areas:** Robert Krapf is a Direc-
tor in the Real Estate Group of Richards,
Layton & Finger. His practice focuses on

transactional matters generally in the
areas of real estate and land use law.
**Prof. Memberships:** Mr Krapf is a past
Chair of the Real and Personal Property
Section of the Delaware State Bar Association and past Chair of the American Bar
Association Real Property, Probate and
Trust Section Land Use Regulation Committee, among others.
**Career:** Mr Krapf has served as a member and officer of the boards of many
local, national and international business,
charitable and cultural organizations.

## KRISTOL, Daniel M
Richards, Layton & Finger PA,
Wilmington 302 651 7768
kristol@rlf.com
*Recommended in Real Estate*
**Practice Areas:** Daniel M Kristol is a
director in the firm's Business Department. His practice focuses on real estate
transactions, primarily on behalf of
landowners and developers. However,
Mr. Kristol's practice is broad ranged and
he also represents tenants as well as landlords, lenders as well as borrowers and
title insurance companies as well as their
insureds.
**Prof. Memberships:** He is a member of
the American College of Real Estate
Lawyers. He is also a member of the
American Bar Association and the
Delaware State Bar Association where he
serves as Chair of the Senior Lawyers
Committee.

## LADNER, Gregory W
Richards, Layton & Finger PA,
Wilmington 302 651 7547
Ladner@RLF.com
*Recommended in Corporate/M&A*
**Practice Areas:** Gregory Ladner is a
director in the firm's Business Department. As a transactional attorney, his
practice focuses primarily on rendering
advice as to matters of Delaware state law
relating to Delaware partnerships (general, limited and limited liability) and limited liability companies. His work includes
rendering advice with respect to mergers,
conversions and other structural changes
involving partnerships and limited liability companies.
**Prof. Memberships:** Mr Ladner is a
member of the Delaware State Bar Association and the ABA.
**Publications:** Mr Ladner has spoken at
Continuing Legal Education programs
and has published articles concerning
Delaware partnerships and limited liability companies.

## LAFFERTY, William M
Morris, Nichols, Arsht & Tunnell LLP,
Wilmington 302 351 9341
wlafferty@mnat.com
*Recommended in Chancery*
**Practice Areas:** Member of Corporate
Litigation Group involving corporate and
commercial litigation with an emphasis
on cases involving mergers and aquisi-

tions, proxy contests and consent solicita-
tions, and shareholder class and deriva-
tive actions; concentrating in the
Delaware Court of Chancery and
Delaware Supreme Court.
**Prof. Memberships:** ABA (Member
Business Law Section Committee on
Business and Corporate Litigation);
DSBA (1989), Member of Corporation
Law Section and Committee on Profes-
sional Ethics; Appointed by Delaware
Supreme Court to Board of Bar Examin-
ers (2001-); Appointed by the Delaware
Supreme Court as Chair of the Delaware
Commission on Continuing Legal Edu-
cation (2004-); Pennsylvania State Bar
Association (1990).
**Career:** Law Clerk to The Honorable
Maurice A Hartnett, III, Delaware Court
of Chancery (1989-90).
**Publications:** Has written a number of
articles on Delaware law issues and is a
contributing editor of two chapters of
Contemporary Corporation Forms (Dis-
senters' Rights and Inspection of
Records).
**Personal:** University of Delaware (BSBA
(1985)); The Dickinson School of Law
(JD 1989), Articles Editor, Dickinson Law
Review 1988-89.

## LAMB, Christopher J
Pepper Hamilton LLP, Wilmington
302 777 6548
lambc@pepperlaw.com
*Recommended in Real Estate*
**Practice Areas:** Partner, Financial Services Group, Wilmington, Delaware.
Experienced in: Commercial law in
major US corporate venue, including real
estate acquisitions, secured financing,
leasing and public finance. Litigation
experience includes representation of
creditors and debtors in workouts, foreclosures, mechanics' lien actions and state
court proceedings. Represents financial
institutions, developers and investors.
**Prof. Memberships:** Member, Committee of 100; Delaware Homebuilders;
Delaware and American Bar Associations.
**Career:** JD 1988 Temple University
School of Law, BA 1984 La Salle University.

## LANDIS, Adam
Landis Rath & Cobb LLP, Wilmington
302 467 4400
*Recommended in Bankruptcy*

## LASTER, J Travis
Abrams & Laster LLP, Wilmington
302 778 1003
Laster@AbramsLaster.com
*Recommended in Chancery*
**Practice Areas:** Corporate and business
litigation; transactional advice.
**Prof. Memberships:** Delaware State Bar
Association; Virginia State Bar Associa-
tion; American Bar Association; Editorial
Board of the Delaware Law Review.
**Career:** Founding Partner; Director

(2002-05), Associate (1996-2002), Richards Layton & Finger P.A.; Law Clerk to The Honorable Jane R Roth, US Court of Appeals for the Third Circuit.
**Publications:** Frequent speaker and author on stockholder, takeover and director liability issues.
**Personal:** MA 1996 University of Virginia; JD 1995 University of Virginia School of Law; Order of the Coif; AB 1991 Princeton University (summa cum laude).

## LAZARUS, Lewis H
Morris, James, Hitchens & Williams LLP, Wilmington 302 888 6970
llazarus@morrisjames.com
*Recommended in Chancery*
**Practice Areas:** Member, Corporate and Commerical Litigation Practice Group.
**Prof. Memberships:** Admitted to practice in California, Delaware and District of Columbia. Member, Council of Corporation Law Section of the Delaware State Bar Association. Member, American Bar Association Litigation Section's Class Actions and Derivative Suits Committee.
**Career:** Joined Morris James, 1985; Partner, 1989; Member, Executive Committee.
**Publications:** Author, 'Standards of Review of Conflict of Interest Transactions: An Examination of Decisions Rendered on Motions to Dismiss,' 26 Del. J. Corp. L. 911 (2001).
**Personal:** JD, Stanford Law School, 1982; BA (high honors), Swarthmore College, 1978. Member, Phi Beta Kappa. Fluent in Spanish.

## LEYDEN, James G
Richards, Layton & Finger PA, Wilmington 302 651 7620
Leyden@RLF.com
*Recommended in Corporate/M&A*
**Practice Areas:** James G Leyden Jr is a Director in the firm's Limited Liability Company/Partnership Group. His practice focuses on matters involving Delaware limited liability companies, limited partnerships, general partnerships, trusts and corporations.
**Prof. Memberships:** Mr Leyden is a member of the TriBar Opinion Committee. Mr Leyden is a member of the American Bar Association (Business Law Section). Mr Leyden is a Member of the Committee responsible for drafting Delaware's Limited Liability Company Act and partnership statutes.
**Publications:** Mr Leyden is a co-reporter of The TriBar Opinion Committee Report 'Third Party Closing Opinions: Limited Liability Companies', published February 2006.

## LOUDEN, Karen Jacobs
Morris, Nichols, Arsht & Tunnell LLP, Wilmington 302 351 9227
klouden@mnat.com
*Recommended in Intellectual Property*

**Practice Areas:** Member of the Intellectual Property Litigation Group focusing primarily on patent litigation. Ms Louden is also involved in a wide variety of other intellectual property and commercial litigation, including copyright, trademark, trade secret and unfair competition litigation, and contract and licensing disputes.
**Prof. Memberships:** ABA; Delaware State Bar Association (1990); AIPLA; President, Delaware Volunteer Legal Services; Co-Chair, Delaware State Bar Professional Guidance Committee; DSBA Intellectual Property Section (Executive Committee); Women and the Law Section (Former chair); Board of Bar Examiners (prior Associate Member).
**Career:** Partner; Admissions to Practice: Delaware (1990); District of Delaware (1991); US Court of Appeals for the Third Circuit (1991); US Court of Appeals for the Federal Circuit (1998); US Supreme Court (2000).
**Publications:** Louden and Fonseca, 'Does the Federal Trademark Dilution Act Provide A Right Without A Remedy? The Supreme Court's First Foray Into Trademark Dilution; Moseley v. V Secret Catalogue', 7 Del. L. Rev. 31 (2004); Grimm, Louden and Heaney, 'Trademarks in Cyberspace' (Delaware Lawyer, Vol 18, No. 4, Winter 2000-01).
**Personal:** University of Pennsylvania (BA, summa cum laude, 1987); Harvard Law School (JD, cum laude 1990). Past Appointments and Recognitions: Committee for Provision of Legal Services to Low Income People; American Civil Liberties Union of Delaware (Past Legislative Chair & Board Member); Gubernatorial appointment to State of Delaware Council on Early Care and Education (2001-03); Recipient of Delaware State Bar Association Community Service Award 2003.

## MANNING, William E
Klett Rooney Lieber & Schorling, Wilmington 302 552 4210
manning@klettrooney.com
*Recommended in Real Estate*
**Practice Areas:** Land use regulation and litigation; general commercial litigation; utility regulation and transactional services.
**Career:** Represented a variety of owners and developers in some of Delaware's most significant land use approval and litigation matters, including the rezoning of the Brandywine Town Center and much of the development in southern New Castle County. Litigation associated with this land use practice has included civil rights claims brought on behalf of real estate developers as well as the defense of challenges to zoning and subdivision approvals.
**Personal:** BA, University of Delaware; JD (cum laude), University of Louisville Law School.

## MARSDEN JR, William
Fish & Richardson P.C., Wilmington 302 778 8401
marsden@fr.com
*Recommended in Intellectual Property*
**Practice Areas:** Managing principal in Fish & Richardson P.C.'s Delaware office. His practice is focused on complex litigation with particular emphasis on patent trials. He has participated in over 25 patent trials, including more than 15 jury trials. He is a frequent speaker at seminars on complex litigation.
**Prof. Memberships:** Co-Chair (2003) The Sedona Conference on Patent Litigation. Member (2004-) The District Court Advisory Committee for the United States District Court for the District of Delaware. Master (2003-) Richard S. Rodney Inn of Court.
**Personal:** Haverford College BA 1978; University of North Carolina at Chapel Hill JD 1983.

## MAZIE, Eric A
Richards, Layton & Finger PA, Wilmington 302 651 7678
Mazie@RLF.com
*Recommended in Corporate/M&A*
**Practice Areas:** Eric Mazie is a Director of the firm and a member of the firm's Business Department. His practice focuses on a wide variety of transactional matters involving Delaware entities and business law with particular emphasis on the use of common law and statutory trusts.
**Prof. Memberships:** Mr Mazie has authored numerous texts and articles on the use of trusts and the role of trustees in financing transactions, including Chapter 19, Delaware Statutory Trusts in The Delaware Law of Corporations and Business Organizations and Chapter 9, Role of Trustee in Leasing Transactions in Equipment Leasing - Leveraged Leasing.

## MCBRIDE, David
Young Conaway Stargatt & Taylor LLP, Wilmington 302 571 6639
dmcbride@ycst.com
*Recommended in Chancery, Corporate/M&A*
**Practice Areas:** Practice is concentrated in the area of corporate law and corporate and commercial litigation, including involvement in a plethora of Delaware corporate law cases, particularly in the area of mergers and acquisitions, including Paramount Communications Inc. v QVC Network, Inc., Paramount Communications Inc. v Time Inc., Revlon Inc. v MacAndrews & Forbes Holding Inc., In re First Boston Inc. Shareholders Litig., In re Resorts Int'l. Shareholders Litig., Freedman v Restaurant Associates Indus., Inc., Robert M. Bass Group, Inc. v Evans (Macmillan, Inc.), Shamrock Holdings Inc. v Polaroid Corp., In re RJR Nabisco, Inc. Shareholders Litigation, Henley Group v Santa Fe Southern Pacific Corp., Pennzoil Co. v Getty Oil Co., Edelman v

Phillips Petroleum, Omnicare, Inc. v NCS Healthcare, Inc., In re Oracle Corporation Derivative Litigation, In re the Walt Disney Company Derivative Litig., and Hollinger International Inc. v Black.
**Prof. Memberships:** Admitted to practice in Delaware (1975). Member of the American Law Institute, Vice-Chairman and Chairman (2004-06) of the Corporate Council of the Corporate Law Section of the Delaware State Bar Association, the Rules Committee of the Delaware Court of Chancery, the Board of Editors of the Delaware Lawyer, a Director of the Historical Society for the Court of Chancery.
**Career:** Partner, Young Conaway. Serves on firm's Management Committee. Began in private practice in 1975.
**Personal:** JD, Emory University School of Law, 1975; BSFS, Georgetown University.

## MCDONOUGH, Kathleen Furey
Potter Anderson & Corroon LLP, Wilmington 302 984 6032
kmcdonough@potteranderson.com
*Recommended in Employment*
**Practice Areas:** Kathleen Furey McDonough is founder and Head of firm's Labor and Employment Practice, exclusively representing management. Also represents secondary and post-secondary institutions with respect to employment and education law issues. Regularly provides clients with training and advice regarding all aspects of personnel policies and practices. Represents employers before EEOC and numerous state administrative agencies. Has represented both multinational and local companies before the state and federal courts in Delaware and has tried successfully numerous employment-related lawsuits. Martindale-Hubbell AV rating. Chair of the District Court Advisory Committee for the US District Court for the District of Delaware.

## MCNALLY, Edward M
Morris, James, Hitchens & Williams LLP, Wilmington 302 888 6880
emcnally@morrisjames.com
*Recommended in Chancery*
**Practice Areas:** Chair of Litigation Practice Group. Focuses practice on corporate law and business litigation. Has extensive experience in representing stockholders, directors, special committees and corporations in corporate disputes. He has also represented plaintiffs and defendents in jury and bench trials.
**Prof. Memberships:** Admitted to Delaware Bar, 1972. Member of American and Delaware Bar Associations.
**Career:** Joined Morris James, 1972; became Partner, 1976. Past Chairman, Supreme Court Lawyers' Fund for Client Protection.
**Publications:** Author, 'Delaware Voluntary Mediation Act'.

**Personal:** Born in Wilmington, DE. JD, Columbia University, 1972; BA, Boston College, 1969.

## MILLER, Stephen M
Morris, James, Hitchens & Williams LLP, Wilmington 302 888 6853
smiller@morrisjames.com
*Recommended in Bankruptcy*
**Practice Areas:** Represents purchasers, trustees, creditors committees, and secured and unsecured creditors, including financial institutions, equipment lessors, landlords and vendors, in complex Chapter 11 reorganizations. Also represents clients in transactional matters including issuance of legal opinions.
**Prof. Memberships:** American and Delaware Bar Associations; American Bankruptcy Institute; Delaware Chapter of the Federal Bar Association; Delaware Bankruptcy American Inn of Court.
**Career:** Chair, Bankruptcy and Reorganization Group. Joined Morris James, 1999; Partner, 1999. Admitted to Delaware Bar, 1987, and Pennsylvania Bar, 1988.
**Publications:** Co-author, 'Delaware Limited Liability Company Practice Guide'.
**Personal:** JD (honors), George Washington University, 1987; BS, University of Delaware, 1982.

## MINUTI, Mark
Saul Ewing LLP, Wilmington
302 421 6840
mminuti@saul.com
*Recommended in Bankruptcy*
**Practice Areas:** Mark Minuti is a Partner in Saul Ewing's Bankruptcy and Restructuring Department, and Managing Partner of the firm's Wilmington, Delaware office. Mr Minuti's practice includes the representation of debtors, unsecured creditors committees, equity committees, trustees, asset purchasers, landlords, secured and unsecured creditors, both in and out of Delaware.
**Prof. Memberships:** Member, American Bar Association; Member, Delaware State Bar Association; Member, American Bankruptcy Institute.
**Career:** Prior to joining Saul Ewing, Mr Minuti was a law clerk to the Honorable Clarence W Taylor of the Delaware Superior Court.
**Personal:** JD, Widener University School of Law; BS, University of Delaware.

## MORGAN, Pauline
Young Conaway Stargatt & Taylor LLP, Wilmington 302 571 6707
pmorgan@ycst.com
*Recommended in Bankruptcy*
**Practice Areas:** Partner, specializing in the representation of Chapter 11 debtors-in-possession and official committees appointed in Chapter 11 corporate reorganizations.
**Prof. Memberships:** Member: Delaware, Pennsylvania, and New Jersey Bars;

American Bankruptcy Institute; District Court Advisory Committee for the US District Court for the District of Delaware.
**Personal:** Education: University of Pennsylvania Law School (JD, 1987); Duquesne University (BA, cum laude, 1978).

## MORTON, Mark A
Potter Anderson & Corroon LLP, Wilmington 302 984 6078
mmorton@potteranderson.com
*Recommended in Corporate/M&A*
**Practice Areas:** Mr Morton's practice involves corporate counseling, governance and opinion work. Mr Morton advises clients and provides formal legal opinions regarding all aspects of the Delaware General Corporation Law and the governance of Delaware corporations. He represents corporations, directors, and board committees regarding transactions such as mergers, recapitalizations, reorganizations, asset sales, dividends, stock repurchases, charter and bylaw amendments, preferred stock designations, and dissolutions. He is frequently called upon to advise board members concerning their fiduciary obligations, both in the context of daily business affairs and with respect to specific corporate transactions.
**Prof. Memberships:** American Bar Association, Negotiated Acquisitions Committee.

## MULLEN, Thomas
Prickett, Jones & Elliott PA, Wilmington 302 888 6500
*Recommended in Corporate/M&A*

## NACHBAR, Kenneth J
Morris, Nichols, Arsht & Tunnell LLP, Wilmington 302 351 9294
knachbar@mnat.com
*Recommended in Chancery*
**Practice Areas:** Member of Corporate Litigation Group concentrating in litigation arising from mergers and acquisitions and disputes relating to Delaware corporations, and advice to corporate boards of directors and special committees with respect to transational and litigation issues.
**Prof. Memberships:** ABA; DSBA (1981); Member, Rules Committee of US District Court for the Distrct of Delaware; Chairman, Delaware Board on Certified Court Reporters.
**Career:** Partner; Admissions to Practice: Delaware (1981); Member, New York University Review of Law and Social Change (1980-81).
**Publications:** Contributor, Drexler, Black and Sparks, 'Delaware Corporation Law and Practice'; contributor, 'Settlement Agreements in Commercial Disputes' (Ed. Richard Rosen, 2000); author, 'Revlon Inc., v. MacAndrews and Forbes, Inc. The Requirements of a Level Playing Field in Contested Mergers, And Its Effect

on Lock-Ups and Other Bidding Deterrents,' 12 Del.J.Corp. 473 (1987).
**Personal:** Haverford College (BA, 1978); New York University School of Law (JD, 1981).

## NESTOR, Michael R
Young Conaway Stargatt & Taylor LLP, Wilmington 302 571 6699
mnestor@ycst.com
*Recommended in Bankruptcy*
**Practice Areas:** Partner in the Business Reorganization and Restructuring Department and Marketing Partner for the firm. His practice emphasizes the restructuring of corporations ranging in size from large publicly-held companies to mid-market closely-held companies, and also includes extensive experience representing official committees, chapter 11 trustees, lenders, secured and unsecured creditors, shareholders, plan sponsors, and purchasers throughout the chapter 11 process. Representative clients include: Top Flite Golf Company; Lason, Inc.; Biogan International, Inc.; Evolve Software Corporation; Crown Books Corporation; Berkshire Hathaway; Bank of America; and Mondi of America.
**Prof. Memberships:** Turnaround Management Association (Member, Board, Philadelphia Chapter; Member, International Webinar Committee); Delaware State (Member, Sections on Bankruptcy and Litigation) and American Bar Associations (Member, Sections on Business Law, Litigation); American Bankruptcy Institute; Association for Corporate Growth.
**Career:** Admitted to Pennsylvania and New Jersey Bars (1995), Delaware (1996).
**Publications:** 'Avoiding Pitfalls in the Retention Process' (2005); 'State Court Reorganization Proceedings: Statutory Relics or a Viable Alternative to Chapter 11' (2005); 'Bankruptcy Courts Construe New Committee Disclosure Obligations - A First Step in the Right Direction' (2006).

## NOREIKA, Maryellen
Morris, Nichols, Arsht & Tunnell LLP, Wilmington 302 351 9278
mnoreika@mnat.com
*Recommended in Intellectual Property*
**Practice Areas:** Member of the Intellectual Property Litigation Group concentrating on patent cases in a variety of technical areas, including digital technology, consumer products and pharmaceuticals.
**Prof. Memberships:** ABA; DSBA; Delaware District Court Advisory Committee; Delaware District Court Local Rules Subcommittee.
**Career:** Partner (2001-present); associate (1993-2000).
**Personal:** Lehigh University (BS, 1988); Columbia University (MS, 1990); University of Pittsburgh (JD, magna cum laude, 1993).

## NORMAN, Stephen C
Potter Anderson & Corroon LLP, Wilmington 302 984 6038
snorman@potteranderson.com
*Recommended in Chancery*
**Practice Areas:** Mr Norman practices in the areas of corporate and commercial litigation. He has substantial experience in litigating corporate and commercial disputes in the Court of Chancery and the District Court of Delaware, including stockholder class and derivative actions, takeovers and various proceedings under Delaware Law. Mr Norman counsels stockholders, directors, partners, and Delaware corporations regarding Delaware corporate and partnership law.
**Prof. Memberships:** ABA. Co-Chair of Litigation Management Techniques Subcommittee of Corporate Counsel Committee; Co-Chair of Derivative Subcommittee of Class Action and Derivative Suits Committee.
**Personal:** Law Clerk to The Honorable William W Caldwell, Middle District of Pennsylvania.

## O'TOOLE, Matthew J
Morris, James, Hitchens & Williams LLP, Wilmington 302 888 6875
motoole@morrisjames.com
*Recommended in Corporate/M&A*
**Practice Areas:** Focuses on corporate and business transactions, particularly structure and use of Delaware business entities.
**Prof. Memberships:** Admitted to Delaware Bar in 1994.
**Career:** Joined Morris James, 1993; became Partner, 2000. Member, Council of Corporation Law Section of Delaware State Bar Association; Member of Council's Limited Liability Company/Partnership Sub-Committee.
**Publications:** Co-author, 'Delaware Limited Liability Company Practice Guide', State Limited Liability Company & Partnership Laws, published by Aspen Law & Business.
**Personal:** JD, College of William & Mary, 1992; MA, 1988, BA, 1985, Fordham University.

## PACITTI, Domenic E
Saul Ewing LLP, Wilmington
302 421 6864
dpacitti@saul.com
*Recommended in Bankruptcy*
**Practice Areas:** Mr Pacitti is a Partner in Saul Ewing's Bankruptcy and Restructuring Department and serves on the firm's Audit Committee. He concentrates his practice in bankruptcy and workouts representing debtors, creditors' committees, trustees, secured and unsecured creditors, and various other parties involved in bankruptcy, insolvency, and workout cases throughout the country.
**Prof. Memberships:** Member, American Bankruptcy Institute; Member, Eastern District of Pennsylvania Bankruptcy

Conference.

**Career:** Mr Pacitti previously served as a law clerk to the Honorable Rosemary Gambardella, United States Bankruptcy Court for the District of New Jersey.

**Personal:** JD, University of Richmond, BA, Lycoming College

## PARADEE, John
Prickett, Jones & Elliott PA, Dover
302 674 3841
*Recommended in Real Estate*

## PATTON JR, James L
Young Conaway Stargatt & Taylor LLP, Wilmington
302 571 6684
jpatton@ycst.com
*Recommended in Bankruptcy*

**Practice Areas:** Corporate restructurings and mass tort-related insolvencies. Clients have included, among many others, Continental Airlines, Inc., Columbia Gas Systems, Inc., Days Inns of America, Inc., MEI Diversified, Inc., Simmons Upholstered Furniture, Inc., Lomas Financial Corporation, Fuller-Austin Insulation Company; Florida Coast Paper Company, Alterra Healthcare Corporation, the Asbestos Future Claims Representative in connection with The Celotex Corporation, Babcock & Wilcox Company, Owens-Corning, Armstrong World Industries, Inc., Federal-Mogul Global Inc., USG Corporation, Pittsburgh Corning Corporation, Kaiser Group International, Inc., Narco, and Halliburton Company, as well as debtors in over 40 prepackaged bankruptcy cases.

**Prof. Memberships:** Member, Delaware State Bar Association; Chairman, Bankruptcy Law Subcomittee, Commercial Law Section (1986-2005); Chairman, Chapter 11 Committee, Bankruptcy Section (2005-); Member, American Bar Association, Business Law Section, Business Bankruptcy Committee, Claims Trading Subcommittee (Vice-Chair, 2002-); Member, Association of Trial Lawyers of America; Member, American Bankruptcy Institute; Member of Board of Contributors, Fletcher Corporate Bankruptcy, Reorganization and Dissolution, Clark, Boardman, Callaghan (1992); Participant on Judge Scirica's Working Group on Mass Torts in connection with the Report of the Advisory Committee on Civil Rules and the Working Group on Mass Torts to the Chief Justice of the United States and to the Judicial Conference of the United States (1999); Fellow, American College of Bankruptcy.

**Career:** Chairman, Young Conaway Stargatt & Taylor, LLP; joined firm in 1983 and became Partner in 1989.

**Publications:** Co-author, 'Effects of Bankruptcy on Director & Officer Liability' and 'Directors & Officer Liability Insurance Presented at Third Circuit Judicial Conference', 2002; co-author, 'Futures Representative's Informational

Brief', Mealey's 'Asbestos Bankruptcy Conference', 2001; co-author, 'Dancing with Scylla and Charybdis: the Tough Job of Directors of a Troubled Company', presented at the American Bar Association, Section of Business Law, Spring Meeting, 2000.

## PAYSON, Robert
Potter Anderson & Corroon LLP, Wilmington 302 984 6003
rpayson@potteranderson.com
*Recommended in Chancery*

**Practice Areas:** Mr Payson practices primarily in the area of corporate litigation, particularly in the Delaware Court of Chancery and the Delaware Supreme Court. Mr Payson also advises Boards of Directors of Delaware corporations and committees thereof with respect to the Delaware General Corporation Law, mergers and acquisitions, and class and derivative litigation.

**Personal:** Mr Payson was admitted to the Delaware Bar in 1964. He is also a Member of the Bars of the United States Supreme Court, the United States Court of Appeals for the Third Circuit, and the United State District Court for the District of Delaware.

## PERNICK, Norman L
Saul Ewing LLP, Wilmington
302 421 6824
npernick@saul.com
*Recommended in Bankruptcy*

**Practice Areas:** Chair of Saul Ewing's Bankruptcy and Reorganization Department. Practices in bankruptcy and workouts, representing debtors, creditors' committees, secured and unsecured creditors, and trustees.

**Prof. Memberships:** Admitted in Delaware, the US District Court for the District of Delaware, and the Third Circuit Court of Appeals.

**Career:** Currently lead counsel for Owens Corning in its Chapter 11 case. Ranked one of Delaware's Top Business Bankruptcy Lawyers by Delaware Today. Rated 'AV' by Martindale Hubbell.

**Publications:** Author, 'Bankruptcy Deadline Checklist'.

**Personal:** JD, The National Law Center, George Washington University, (with honors); BA, Brandeis University, (magna cum laude, with high honors).

## PINCUS, Robert B
Skadden, Arps, Slate, Meagher & Flom LLP & Affiliates, Wilmington
302 651 3090
bpincus@skadden.com
*Recommended in Corporate/M&A*

**Practice Areas:** Represents and advises clients in a wide variety of corporate matters, including mergers and acquisitions, private equity investments and unsolicited takeovers. Extensive experience in advising clients and other lawyers in the firm on Delaware law aspects of transactions and fiduciary duty and corporate

governance matters.

**Career:** LLM, Securities Regulation, Georgetown University Law Center, 1983; JD, American University, The Washington College of Law, 1980 (magna cum laude); BBA, College of William and Mary, 1977.

## POWELL, Norman M
Young Conaway Stargatt & Taylor LLP, Wilmington 302 571 6629
npowell@ycst.com
*Recommended in Corporate/M&A*

**Practice Areas:** Partner; member of Young Conaway's Business Planning, Transactions and Restructuring Department. Corporate and commercial transaction practice. Structured and real estate finance, secured transactions, third party legal opinions.

**Prof. Memberships:** Commercial Financial Services, Legal Opinions, and Uniform Commercial Code Committees, American Bar Association; Uniform Commercial Code Committee, Delaware State Bar Association.

**Publications:** 'Ongoing Searching and Filing Issues Under Article 9', 37 UCC L.J. 35 (2005); various articles in the Commercial Law Newsletter, the Joint Newsletter of the Uniform Commercial Code and Commercial Financial Services Committees, American Bar Association Section of Business; 'Uniform Commercial Code Issues in Securitisations - Filings Against Trusts, Trustees, and LLCs Under Revised Article 9', Global Securitisation and Structured Finance 2004, at 127 (Adrian Preston & Aileen Booey, eds., 2003); 'Filings Against Trusts and Trustees Under Revised Article 9 - Thirteen Variations', 35 UCC L.J. 91 (2002); Revised UCC Article 9 Takes Effect in DE on July 1, 2001, The Corporate Edge, Newsletter of the Delaware Division of Corporations, Fall 2000, at 1.

**Personal:** JD/MBA, Villanova University (1989); BSBA, Georgetown University (1985; cum laude).

## PROCTOR, Vernon
Proctor Heyman LLP, Wilmington
302 472 7300
vproctor@proctorheyman.com
*Recommended in Chancery*

**Practice Areas:** Corporate and commercial litigation. Please see firm profile for Proctor Heyman LLP.

**Prof. Memberships:** Member, Partnership/Limited Liability Company Subcommittee, Delaware State Bar Association. Former Member, Corporation Law Council, DSBA. Former Chair, Partnership and Alternative Business Entities Litigation Subcommittee, Business Law Section, American Bar Association.

**Career:** Founded Proctor Heyman LLP with Kurt M Heyman on January 1, 2006. Director, The Bayard Firm, 1990-2005.

**Publications:** Frequent author/lecturer on issues of corporate and partnership

law. Author, 'Recent Developments in Delaware Corporate Law', 6 Del. L. Rev. 177 (2003).

**Personal:** Harvard College (AB, 1976); Harvard Law School (JD, 1979). Phi Beta Kappa.

## REED, John L
Edwards Angell Palmer & Dodge LLP, Wilmington 302 425 7114
jreed@eapdlaw.com
*Recommended in Chancery*

**Practice Areas:** John L Reed maintains a national Litigation Practice and a significant 'Delaware Counsel' Practice that covers all facets of business law. He concentrates his practice on high-stakes corporate/commercial litigation and pre-litigation counseling, which includes the representation of corporations, boards, individual directors, special committees, and large investors, with regard to breach of fiduciary duty claims, mergers-and-acquisitions litigation, and all issues involving Delaware corporate law and governance.

**Prof. Memberships:** American Bar Association; Delaware State Bar Association - Nominating Committee, Corporation Law Section, Litigation Section; American Inns of Court - Master; Federal Civil Panel.

**Career:** State of Delaware - Deputy Attorney General, 1991-95.

**Personal:** Widener University School of Law, JD, cum laude 1991; Villanova University, BA, 1986.

## REESE, Cathy L
Greenberg Traurig LLP, Wilmington
302 661 7389
reesec@gtlaw.com
*Recommended in Chancery*

**Practice Areas:** Litigation; corporate and securities; technology, media and telecommunications.

**Prof. Memberships:** Board of Trustees, Delaware Leadership Foundation; Member, Delaware State Bar Association.

**Career:** Listed, Chambers & Partners USA Guide, 2004-06; selected one of Delaware's 'Top Lawyers' in Corporation Law/Litigation, Delaware Today, October 2001.

**Publications:** Co-author, 'Recent Developments in Delaware Corporate Law', Delaware Law Review, Volume 7:2, February 2005; Author, 'Locked and Loaded: Delaware Supreme Court Takes Aim at Deal Certainty', M&A Lawyer, June 2003.

**Personal:** JD, with honors, George Washington University Law School, 1989; BS, magna cum laude, Columbia University, 1982.

## RHODUNDA JR, William
The Law Offices of Oberly, Jennings & Rhodunda, Wilmington
302 576 2000
*Recommended in Real Estate*

## ROGOWSKI, Patricia Smink
Connolly Bove Lodge & Hutz LLP,
Wilmington 302 658 9141
progowski@cblh.com
*Recommended in Intellectual Property*
**Practice Areas:** Intellectual property
law, copyrights, patents, trademarks, science and technology law, trade secrets,
and litigation. Ms Rogowski's experience
includes patent, trademark and copyright
prosecution, litigation in federal district
courts and in appeals to the Court of
Appeals for the Federal Circuit. She has
assisted clients in various technology sectors including medical devices,
polyurethane foams, fibers and textiles,
and industrial equipment.
**Prof. Memberships:** Delaware State Bar
Association, American Bar Association,
Intellectual Property Law Association,
Pennsylvania Bar Association, Philadelphia Intellectual Property Law Association. She has chaired the IP section of the
Delaware State Bar Association and is
President-Elect of the Philadelphia Intellectual Property Law Association.
**Career:** Partner since 1994.
**Personal:** University of Pennsylvania
Law School (JD, 1987); Lehigh University
(BSME, 1984).

## ROVNER, Philip A
Potter Anderson & Corroon LLP,
Wilmington 302 984 6140
provner@potteranderson.com
*Recommended in Intellectual Property*
**Practice Areas:** Mr Rovner practices in
the areas of commercial and corporate
litigation, focusing primarily on intellectual property litigation, and commercial
and licensing disputes. Mr Rovner
appears before all state and federal courts
in the State of Delaware and has significant trial experience in a variety of intellectual property and commercial disputes
in the United States District Court for the
District of Delaware and Delaware's state
courts, including the Court of Chancery
and the Superior Court.
**Personal:** University of Pennsylvania
(BA 1981); Fordham University School of
Law (JD 1987).

## SALOMONE, Janine M
Potter Anderson & Corroon LLP,
Wilmington 302 984 6128
jsalomone@potteranderson.com
*Recommended in Corporate/M&A*
**Practice Areas:** Ms Salomone's practice
involves counseling Delaware corporations on corporate law and governance
issues arising from both routine operations and extraordinary transactions such
as corporate reorganizations, mergers
and acquisitions, recapitalizations, asset
sales, dividends, stock repurchase, charter
and bylaw amendments, stock issuances
and dissolutions. Ms Salomone advises
directors, officers and board committees
with respect to their fiduciary duties
under Delaware law and provides written

legal opinions regarding all aspects of the
Delaware General Corporation Law and
the governance of Delaware corporations.
**Personal:** Ms Salomone was admitted to
the Delaware and Pennsylvania Bars in
1996.

## SANDLER, Sheldon N
Young Conaway Stargatt & Taylor LLP,
Wilmington
302 571 6673
ssandler@ycst.com
*Recommended in Employment*
**Practice Areas:** Partner in the Employment Law Department of Young
Conaway Stargatt & Taylor, LLP. He also
serves on the firm's Management Committee.
**Prof. Memberships:** Only Delaware Fellow of the College of Labor and Employment Lawyers; Founding Chairman of
the Delaware State Bar Association's
Labor and Employment Law Section, has
chaired the Lawyers' Advisory Committee
to the Court of Appeals for the Third Circuit, served as President of the Delaware
Chapter of the Federal Bar Association,
served on the Delaware Court of
Chancery Rules Committee, and has
taught Legal Aspects of Human Resource
Management in Widener University's
MBA program.
**Publications:** Author of the chapter on
employment law in 'The Delaware
Supreme Court: The First Fifty Years', a
book commissioned by the Delaware
Supreme Court in commemoration of its
first half-century as Delaware's highest
court. Listed in The Best Lawyers In
America for 20 years.
**Personal:** He is a graduate of the University of Michigan and the University of
Pennsylvania Law School, and holds a
degree of Master of Laws in Labor Law
from Temple University.

## SAUNDERS, Robert S
Skadden, Arps, Slate, Meagher & Flom
LLP & Affiliates, Wilmington
302 651 3170
rsaunder@skadden.com
*Recommended in Chancery*
**Practice Areas:** Handles litigation in
federal and state courts, concentrating on
cases involving the governance of business organizations, with emphasis on
mergers and acquisitions and limited
partnerships. Provides transactional
advice on Delaware limited partnership
law. Has extensive experience in litigation
arising from mergers and acquisitions
and in litigation involving Delaware limited partnerships and private equity
funds.
**Career:** JD, University of Virginia School
of Law, 1991 (Virginia Law Review); AB,
Dartmouth College, 1987.

## SCHLERF, Jeffrey M
The Bayard Firm, Wilmington
302 429 4218
jschlerf@bayardfirm.com.
*Recommended in Bankruptcy*
**Practice Areas:** Jeffrey maintains a
diverse law practice in the areas of commercial bankruptcy, insolvencies and
restructurings, loan workouts and business law. Jeffrey's Chapter 11 practice
focuses on the representation of debtors,
creditors' committees, trustees, large
secured and unsecured creditors and
purchasers.
**Prof. Memberships:** American Bar
Association; Delaware State Bar Association; Pennsylvania State Bar Association;
Delaware Lawyer (Member, Board of
Editors); and American Bankruptcy
Institute.
**Career:** Jeffrey has over 20 years of professional experience involving the financial markets. He received a Bachelor of
Arts degree in Economics from the University of Pennsylvania and a Master of
Arts degree in Economics from the University of Delaware. His concentration
during graduate school was Federal
Reserve monetary policy. After receiving
his Masters degree and prior to attending
law school, Jeffrey worked as an economist in the public sector at the Federal
Reserve and subsequently for a large
financial institution. He later received a
Juris Doctor degree from the Marshall-
Wythe School of Law at the College of
William and Mary. Jeffrey joined The
Bayard Firm in 1995, and is currently a
director and shareholder at the Firm. He
is also a member of the Firm's Executive
Committee and Chair of the Hiring
Committee.
**Publications:** Co-author: 'Equity Committees: A Consequence of the Zone of
Insolvency' published in American Bankruptcy Institute Journal, December
2005/January 2006. Co-author: 'Equity
Committees - Representation of Shareholders in Bankruptcy Cases', appearing
in Financier Worldwide's 2005 Restructuring and Insolvency Series.
**Personal:** Born Philadelphia, Pennsylvania, February 6, 1959. University of Pennsylvania (BA, 1982); University of
Delaware (MA, 1983); Marshall-Wythe
School of Law, College of William and
Mary (JD, 1991).

## SCOTT, Pamela J
Saul Ewing LLP, Wilmington
302 421 6878
pscott@saul.com
*Recommended in Real Estate*
**Practice Areas:** Ms Scott is a Partner in
Saul Ewing's Real Estate Department. She
handles commercial transactions and
land use approvals for large commercial,
institutional and residential projects, and
site approvals for the telecommunications industry. She works extensively with
State and local government boards and

agencies.
**Prof. Memberships:** Admitted to practice in Delaware, New Jersey, and Pennsylvania.
**Career:** Member, Real Property Section
of the Delaware Bar, the Board of Directors of the Committee of 100, the Small
Business Legislative Committee of the
Delaware State Chamber and TMA
Delaware.
**Personal:** JD, Widener University School
of Law, BS, University of Delaware.

## SELBER SILVERSTEIN, Laurie
Potter Anderson & Corroon LLP,
Wilmington 302 984 6033
lsilverstein@potteranderson.com
*Recommended in Bankruptcy*
**Practice Areas:** Mrs Silverstein leads the
Restructuring and Bankruptcy Group
and is a member of the firm's Executive
Committee. She practices in the areas of
bankruptcy and creditors rights in
national chapter 11 cases. Mrs Silverstein
represents individual secured and unsecured creditors, committees, banks and
bank groups and acquirers in a variety of
industries and market sectors. She has
represented debtors and trustees. Representative clients include SBC Communications Inc., Canadian Imperial Bank of
Commerce, International Lease Finance
Corporation, Norfolk Southern Corporation and the official committee of unsecured creditors in the cases of Aurora
Foods, Inc. and Epic Capital Corporation.

## SHANNON, Brendan Linehan
Young Conaway Stargatt & Taylor LLP,
Wilmington 302 571 6696
bshannon@ycst.com
*Recommended in Bankruptcy*
**Practice Areas:** Partner; specializing in
the representation of Chapter 11 debtors-
in-possession and official committees
appointed in Chapter 11 corporate reorganizations.
**Prof. Memberships:** Member of the
Delaware and Pennsylvania Bars, and a
Member of the Delaware Chapter of the
Federal Bar Association and the American Bankruptcy Institute.
**Personal:** He is a graduate of Princeton
University and Marshall-Wythe School of
Law at the College of William and Mary.

## SHANNON, Kevin
Potter Anderson & Corroon LLP,
Wilmington 302 984 6112
kshannon@potteranderson.com
*Recommended in Chancery*
**Practice Areas:** Mr Shannon practices
primarily in the areas of corporate and
commercial litigation, including stockholder class and derivative actions in the
Delaware Court of Chancery. He litigates
and provides advice regarding various
proceedings under the Delaware General
Corporation Law, including actions for
appraisal, indemnification, and dissolution. Mr Shannon also has extensive

experience litigating disputes involving partnerships, limited partnerships, and limited liability companies. In light of his financial/accounting background, Mr Shannon has been involved in numerous cases involving financial and accounting issues, as well as advising special committees in connection with investigations of alleged wrongdoing (including accounting irregularities).

### SHAW, John
Young Conaway Stargatt & Taylor LLP, Wilmington 302 571 6689
jshaw@ycst.com
*Recommended in Intellectual Property*
**Practice Areas:** Mr Shaw practices in the Intellectual Property, Commercial Litigation, and Trial and Litigation Practice Departments of Young Conaway Stargatt & Taylor, LLP. Mr Shaw appears before all state and federal courts in the State of Delaware, and he has extensive experience in a wide variety of intellectual property and commercial disputes pending before the United States District Court for the District of Delaware. Mr Shaw also devotes a significant portion of his practice to counseling intellectual property owners on trademark, patent, trade secret, and other intellectual property matters.
**Prof. Memberships:** Admitted to practice in Delaware, Pennsylvania, and the United States Courts of Appeals for the Third and Federal Circuits; registered to practice before the United States Patent & Trademark Office; Co-Chair, Intellectual Property Advisory Committee to the United States District Court for the District of Delaware; Member, Patent Jury Instruction Revision Committee of the Delaware Bar Association.
**Career:** Law Clerk for the Honorable Murray M Schwartz, Senior District Judge, United States District of Delaware, 1994-95; joined Young Conaway Stargatt & Taylor, LLP in 1995; became Partner, January, 2002.
**Personal:** JD (magna cum laude), University of Pittsburgh, 1994; BS (with high honors and distinction), Pennsylvania State University, 1989; Recipient of the US District Court for the District of Delaware Caleb R Layton Service Award.

### SILVERSTEIN, Bruce L
Young Conaway Stargatt & Taylor LLP, Wilmington 302 571 6659
bsilverstein@ycst.com
*Recommended in Chancery*
**Practice Areas:** Chairman of firm's Corporate Litigation and Counseling Section. Extensive experience both litigating on behalf of clients and counseling clients in corporate and commercial matters, including significant merger and acquisition transactions. Prosecuted and defended a number of significant corporate and commercial matters before the Delaware Chancery Court and Delaware

Supreme Court. Appointed Master in Chancery Pro Hac Vice and has lectured with members of the Chancery Court on litigation practice and substantive legal issues. Advised clients on a number of significant merger and acquisition transactions.
**Prof. Memberships:** Admitted to practice in Delaware (1986). Member, Corporate Council of Corporate Law Section, Delaware Bar Association; former associate member of the Delaware Board of Bar Examiners; American Bar Association.
**Career:** Joined Young Conaway, 1986; became Partner, 1992. Significant cases include: Alabama By-Products Corp. v Cede & Co., Elliott Assocs, L.P. v Avatex Corp., In re Best Lock Corporation Shareholder Litigation, In re Pure Resources, Inc. Shareholders Litigation, In re RJR Nabisco, Inc. Shareholders Litigation, M.G. Bancorporation v Le Beau, Paramount Communications Inc. v QVC Network, Inc., Paramount Communications, Inc. v Time, Inc., Rapid-American Corp. v. Harris, and Robert M. Bass Group, Inc. v Evans.
**Publications:** Serves on Editorial Board of Judges & Lawyers Business Valuation Update; contributed editorial comment and review for 'The Lawyer's Business Valuation Handbook' and 'Valuing a Business: The Analysis and Appraisal of Closely Held Companies'; various law review articles and seminar materials.
**Personal:** JD, Villanova University (1986; cum laude); BA, Beaver College (1983).

### SMALL, John
Prickett, Jones & Elliott PA, Wilmington 302 888 6500
*Recommended in Corporate/M&A*

### SPARKS III, A Gilchrist
Morris, Nichols, Arsht & Tunnell LLP, Wilmington 302 351 9276
asparks@mnat.com
*Recommended in Chancery, Corporate/M&A*
**Practice Areas:** Member of the Corporate Litigation Group and works closely with the Corporate Counseling Group, concentrates in litigation and counseling arising from mergers, acquisitions and disputes relating to the governance of Delaware corporations.
**Prof. Memberships:** ABA; DSBA (1973); Delaware Supreme Court Advisory Committee on Delaware Uniform Rules of Evidence (Co-Chairman); The American Law Institute (Member); ABA Committee on Corporate Laws of Business Law Section (Member); Board of Advisors, University of Pennsylvania Institute for Law and Economics (Member); American Bar Foundation; Delaware Law Review (Executive Editor); Advisory Board, Weinberg Center for Corporate Governance (Co-Chairman).
**Career:** Partner; admissions to practice: Delaware (1973); Delaware Supreme

Court (1973); US District Court of Delaware (1973); Third Circuit Court of Appeals (1982; United States Supreme Court (1984); Second Circuit Court of Appeals (1991).
**Publications:** Author, Drexler, Black and Sparks, 'Delaware Corporation Law and Practice'; Sparks and Alexander, 'The Delaware Corporation: Legal Aspects of Organization and Operation', 1-4th C.P.S. (BNA).
**Personal:** Yale University (BA, magna cum laude, 1966); University of Pennsylvania (JD, magna cum laude, 1973); University of Pennsylvia Law Review, Associate Editor (1971-72), Editor (1972-73).

### STABLER, Wendie C
Saul Ewing LLP, Wilmington
302 421 6865
wstabler@saul.com
*Recommended in Real Estate*
**Practice Areas:** Ms Stabler is a Partner in the firm's Real Estate Department. In her land use and administrative practice, she has worked with State and local governmental boards and departments. Her zoning and land use work has included successful negotiations and application for rezonings, traffic mitigation agreements, level of service waivers, variances, historic zone overlays and other similar permits/approvals.
**Prof. Memberships:** Admitted in Delaware and Georgia; Co-Chair, New Castle County Economic Development Council.
**Career:** Named one of Delaware's Top 75 'Power Lawyers' in Delaware Today Magazine.
**Personal:** JD, Emory University School of Law, BA (magna cum laude), Tufts University.

### STONE, Alan J
Morris, Nichols, Arsht & Tunnell LLP, Wilmington 302 351 9277
astone@mnat.com
*Recommended in Chancery*
**Practice Areas:** Member of the Corporate Litigation Group, primarily litigating cases arising out of corporate mergers and acquisitions, proxy contests and consent solicitations, complex valuation disputes and interested party transactions, as well as providing advice to corporate boards of directors and special committees with respect to transactional and litigation issues.
**Prof. Memberships:** ABA; DSBA; Delaware (1988); New York (1988).
**Career:** Partner; Law Clerk to The Honorable Andrew GT Moore, II, Delaware Supreme Court.
**Personal:** Tulane University (BSE, cum laude, 1983); Tulane University (JD, magna cum laude, 1987); Senior Notes and Comments Editor, 1987-86, Tulane Law Review.

### STRATTON, David B
Pepper Hamilton LLP, Wilmington
302 777 6566
strattond@pepperlaw.com
*Recommended in Bankruptcy*
**Practice Areas:** Partner; Executive Committee Member, Wilmington, Delaware. Experienced in representing debtors, creditors' committees, secured creditors, individual creditors. Lead counsel and co-counsel in bankruptcy courts in Delaware, Maryland and New York in § 304 and Chapter 11 proceedings involving retailers, high-tech companies, entertainment, transportation companies, manufacturing, energy and others. Handles complex bankruptcy litigation. Advises on bankruptcy and litigation strategy, asset sales, restructurings and dispute resolution.
**Prof. Memberships:** Member, American Bankruptcy Institute; American Bar Association. Board of Directors, Better Business Bureau of Delaware, Inc.
**Career:** JD, 1978, University of Pittsburgh School of Law, AB 1975 Gettysburg College.

### SUDELL, William H
Morris, Nichols, Arsht & Tunnell LLP, Wilmington 302 351 9284
wsudell@mnat.com
*Recommended in Bankruptcy*
**Practice Areas:** Member of the Bankruptcy Litigation and General Business Litigation Groups concentrating in the areas of commercial litigation and bankruptcy and creditors' rights. Has represented or is currently representing debtors, creditors' and bondholders' committees, unsecured creditors, secured creditors, DIP lenders, acquirers and other parties in interest in many of the major Chapter 11 cases that have been filed in the District of Delaware since 1990.
**Prof. Memberships:** ABA; ABI; DSBA; Delaware Community Legal Aid Society (Board Member and past president).
**Career:** Partner; admissions to practice: Delaware (1971); Third Circuit Court of Appeals (1978); Supreme Court of the United States (1990).
**Personal:** Brown University (BA and BS (Aerospace Engineering), 1966); University of Pennsylvania (JD 1971).

### SYMONDS JR, Robert L
Morris, James, Hitchens & Williams LLP, Wilmington 302 888 6803
rsymonds@morrisjames.com
*Recommended in Corporate/M&A*
**Practice Areas:** Chair of Transactions Group. Focuses practice on corporate and business transactions, particularly the structure and use of Delaware business entities.
**Prof. Memberships:** Admitted to practice in Delaware, 1986. Member of Delaware State Bar Association and American Bar Association. Member of

DSBA drafting committees for Delaware Limited Liability Company Act; Delaware Statutory Trust Act; Delaware Revised Uniform Limited Partnership Act; Delaware Revised Uniform Partnership Act.

**Career:** Joined Morris James, 1990; became Partner, 1994.

**Personal:** Born in Danbury, CT. JD, University of Pittsburgh, 1985; BA, Villanova University, 1975.

### TARABICOS, Larry J

Young Conaway Stargatt & Taylor LLP, Wilmington 302 571 6667
ltarabicos@ycst.com
*Recommended in Real Estate*

**Practice Areas:** Firm practice leader in real estate. Has extensive experience in commercial real estate, zoning and land development.

**Prof. Memberships:** Admitted to practice in Delaware (1986). Member, Delaware State Bar Association; American Bar Association.

**Career:** Joined Young Conaway, 1993; became Partner 1993.

**Personal:** JD, Emory University; BAAS, University of Delaware. Finalist, Jessup Cup International Law Southeast Regional Moot Court Competition (1985). Frequent lecturer on commercial real estate and land use topics.

### TUMAS, Michael B

Potter Anderson & Corroon LLP, Wilmington 302 984 6029
mtumas@potteranderson.com
*Recommended in Corporate/M&A*

**Practice Areas:** Mr Tumas concentrates his practice in the area of corporate law and the law governing alternative business entities, with specific emphasis on mergers and acquisitions, issues of internal governance, structured finance and commercial transactions involving Delaware corporations, partnerships, limited liability companies and business trusts. Mr Tumas' practice often involves counseling boards of directors, special committees of boards of directors, general partners, managers and trustees regarding their duties, fiduciary and otherwise. As Chairman of the firm's opinion committee, Mr Tumas regularly reviews and renders opinions on corporate, partnership and other commercial transactions.

### TUTHILL, Walter C

Morris, Nichols, Arsht & Tunnell LLP, Wilmington 302 351 9204
wtuthill@mnat.com
*Recommended in Corporate/M&A*

**Practice Areas:** Member of the Commercial Law Counseling Group, concentrating in the fields of partnership, limited liability company and statutory trust law, as well as bank and insurance regulatory matters, consumer banking law and general merger and aquisition and contract law matters.

**Prof. Memberships:** ABA Business Law Section Committee on Partnerships and Unincorporated Business Associations; Delaware State Bar Association, Chairman, Partnerships/Limited Liability Company Subcommittee of Corporate Law Section of Delaware Bar.

**Career:** Partner; Admissions to Practice: Delaware (1977).

**Publications:** Co-author of Tuthill, Pulsifer, Hering & Lessner, 'Limited Liability Companies: Legal Aspects of Organization, Operation and Dissolution' (The Bureau of National Affairs, Inc., 1996); contributing author of 'The General Partnership, LP and LLP: Formation and Organization; Transactional Lawyer's Desk Book: Advising Business Entities' (West Publishing Co., 2001).

**Personal:** Northwestern University (MM and JD, cum laude, 1977); Denison Unversity (BA, 1973).

### VARALLO, Gregory V

Richards, Layton & Finger PA, Wilmington 302 651 7772
varallo@rlf.com
*Recommended in Chancery*

**Practice Areas:** Gregory Varallo is a director in the Corporate Department. His practice is concentrated in the area of complex corporate and business litigation, corporate governance and corporate transactions.

**Publications:** Mr Varallo is a frequent author and speaker at various seminars and institutes. He is a co-author of 'Fundamentals of Corporate Governance' (ABA, 1996), a contributor to the 'Handbook for the Conduct of Shareholders' Meetings' (ABA, 2000), a member of the Editorial Board of The Business Lawyer and has published in The Securities Regulation Law Journal, M&A Lawyer, The Business Lawyer, Corporate Governance Advisor, Insights and Business Law Today.

### VOSS, Wendy K

Potter Anderson & Corroon LLP, Wilmington 302 984 6076
wvoss@potteranderson.com
*Recommended in Employment*

**Practice Areas:** Ms Voss practices in the areas of labor and employment and commercial law. She represents management in a variety of industries and locations throughout the United States. She provides counsel to management regarding personnel policies and practices, union avoidance and collective bargaining, wage and hours practices, reductions in force, employee supervisions, discipline and discharge, wrongful harassment, and employment discrimination. She represents employers in federal and state courts and before administrative agencies, including the EEOC and the NLRB. She also represents public employers in the State of Delaware before the Public Employee Relations Board, in union negotiations, and arbitrations.

### WALSH JR, Peter J

Potter Anderson & Corroon LLP, Wilmington 302 984 6037
pwalsh@potteranderson.com
*Recommended in Chancery*

**Practice Areas:** Mr Walsh practices in the areas of corporate and commercial litigation, including stockholder class and derivative actions, summary proceedings pursuant to the Delaware General Corporation Law, and dissolution proceedings. He counsels officers and directors, and the Delaware corporations they serve, in matters of Delaware corporate law, primarily as such matters bear upon ongoing or anticipated litigation. Mr Walsh has significant experience in the representation of corporate and governmental policyholders in insurance coverage litigation in state and federal courts in Delaware. He serves as the Co-Chair of the ABA Business Section Task Force on Director and Officer Liability.

### WAXMAN, Scott E

Potter Anderson & Corroon LLP, Wilmington 302 984 6114
swaxman@potteranderson.com
*Recommended in Corporate/M&A*

**Practice Areas:** Chair of Potter Anderson & Corroon's Business Group and a member of the firm's Executive Committee, Mr Waxman practices in the areas of tax, alternative entities and general business. His practice extends into mergers and acquisitions, joint ventures, business and commercial law, focusing on organizational and operational issues related to statutory trusts, partnerships, limited liability companies and special purpose corporations. Mr Waxman serves on Delaware's Partnership Committee, responsible for drafting Delaware's preeminent partnership and limited liability company statutes. Mr Waxman serves on Delaware's Statutory Trust Committee, responsible for drafting Delaware's renowned statutory trust statute.

### WELCH, Edward P

Skadden, Arps, Slate, Meagher & Flom LLP & Affiliates, Wilmington
302 651 3060
ewelch@skadden.com
*Recommended in Chancery*

**Practice Areas:** Concentrates on corporate and securities litigation, including the defense of class and derivative actions, with an emphasis on mergers and acquisitions. Frequently represents clients in administrative proceedings, usually in connection with mergers and acquisitions. Provides Delaware General Corporation Law advice with respect to transactional matters.

**Prof. Memberships:** Chairman of the Board of Directors of the Mary Campbell Center, Inc. (1985-present); Vice-Chair, Delaware Corporation Law Council.

**Career:** JD, Villanova University School of Law, 1976; BS, Georgetown University, 1972.

### WILLIAMS, David H

Morris, James, Hitchens & Williams LLP, Wilmington 302 888 6900
dwilliams@morrisjames.com
*Recommended in Employment*

**Practice Areas:** Member, Government Relations and Employment Law and Education Law Practice Groups. Has extensive experience in preventive counseling concerning employment matters, employment litigation, administrative hearings and collective bargaining negotiations.

**Prof. Memberships:** Admitted Delaware Bar, 1975. Member of Labor and Employment Law Sections of the Delaware State and American Bar Associations; National School Boards Association Council of School Attorneys; President, Delaware Council of School Board Attorneys.

**Career:** Joined Morris James, 1975; became Partner 1980. Member, Morris James' Executive Committee; Managing Partner, effective January 1, 2004.

**Personal:** Born Wilmington, DE. JD, Dickinson School of Law, 1975; BA, Gettysburg College, 1972.

### WILLIAMS, Gregory P

Richards, Layton & Finger PA, Wilmington 302 651 7734
williams@rlf.com
*Recommended in Chancery*

**Practice Areas:** Mr Williams' practice consists primarily of representing corporations and their directors and officers, providing non-litigation advice and counseling to clients, and representing them in litigation in the Delaware courts.

**Prof. Memberships:** He is the Chairman of the Litigation Rules Committee of the Delaware Supreme Court, a member of the Chancery Court Rules Committee and a member of the Board of Bar Examiners of the State of Delaware.

**Publications:** Mr Williams is a co-author of a treatise entitled 'Meetings of Stockholders'. He also has authored numerous articles regarding corporate law and has lectured extensively on various corporate law topics.

### WILLOUGHBY, Barry M

Young Conaway Stargatt & Taylor LLP, Wilmington
302 571 6666
bwilloughby@ycst.com
*Recommended in Employment*

**Practice Areas:** Partner; Chair, Employment Law Department of Young Conaway Stargatt & Taylor, LLP. Mr Willoughby's practice is primarily limited to representation of employers in claims of employment discrimination, retaliation, and 'wrongful discharge' under federal and state law, including defense of charges of racial and sexual harassment. He also defends public employers in First

Amendment 'whistleblower' cases and other constitutional law allegations such as asserted violations of due process or equal protection. He also represents employers in union related conflicts, including representation in organizing campaigns, unfair labor practice proceedings, and grievance/arbitration hearings. Mr Willoughby has achieved an 'A' rating in Martindale-Hubbell and is listed in a leading legal publication for management labor and employment law attorneys.

**Prof. Memberships:** Community and civic activities include pro bono service as Counsel and ex-officio Board Member of the United Way of Delaware, Inc. and General Counsel and Corporate Secretary of Junior Achievement of Delaware, Inc.

**Publications:** In surveys of Delaware lawyers published by Delaware Today magazine, he was named one of Delaware's leading labor lawyers.

**Personal:** Graduated from the University of Delaware in 1976 with high honors and with distinction. In 1979, he graduated cum laude from the Dickinson School of Law where he was a member of the Law Review and Woolsack Society, a law school honor society limited to graduates in the top 10 percent of their class.

## WOLFE JR, Donald J

Potter Anderson & Corroon LLP, Wilmington 302 984 6015
dwolfe@potteranderson.com
*Recommended in Chancery*

**Practice Areas:** Corporate litigation counseling boards and special committees on mergers, acquisitions, fiduciary responsibilities and issues of internal corporate governance.

**Prof. Memberships:** Board of Advisors, University of Pennsylvania Institute for Law and Economics. Previous Chair, Board of Bar Examiners; Trustee, Delaware Bar Foundation; Chair, Delaware Supreme Court Advisory Committee on IOLTA; Assistant to the President DSBA; Chair, PAC Corporate Practice Group; Member, PAC Executive Committee. Recipient New Lawyers' Distinguished Service Award.

**Publications:** Co-author, Corporate and Commercial Practice in the Delaware Court of Chancery (Lexis Law Publishing), an annually updated treatise on litigation practice in the nation's premier corporation law tribunal.

## YODER, Steven M

The Bayard Firm, Wilmington
302 429 4238
syoder@bayardfirm.com
*Recommended in Bankruptcy*

**Practice Areas:** Steve focuses on bankruptcy and insolvency law, and specifically the representation of debtors in large commercial bankruptcies, creditors' rights and commercial litigation. Steve has been involved in several significant bankruptcy cases, the most notable of which has been his representation of the Official Committee of Equity Security Holders in In Re: Trump Hotels and Resorts, Inc.

**Prof. Memberships:** American Bar Association; American Bankruptcy Institute; Delaware Board of Bar Examiners; and Delaware State Bar Association (Member, Bankruptcy Section).

**Career:** After graduating magna cum laude from Millersville University with a Bachelor of Science degree in Business Administration and Finance, Steve received his Juris Doctor degree from Temple University School of Law. Prior to joining The Bayard Firm, Steve served as a judicial law clerk to The Honorable Thomas I Twardowski, United States Bankruptcy Judge for the Eastern District

of Pennsylvania, and worked as an associate attorney at a local law firm in Wilmington, Delaware, practicing bankruptcy law. Steve joined The Bayard Firm in 1999, and is now a Director and shareholder at the firm. Steve currently serves as a member of the firm's Executive Committee and is Chair of the Associates Committee.

**Personal:** Born Reading, Pennsylvania, June 30, 1967. Millersville University (BS, 1994); Temple University School of Law (JD, 1997). President, The Estates at London Brook Homeowner's Association. Commissioner, Wilmington Lawyers' Softball League.

# ABRAMS & LASTER LLP

## THE FIRM

**Founding partners:** Kevin G Abrams, J Travis Laster
**Number of partners:** 2
**Number of other lawyers:** 5

**FIRM OVERVIEW:** Abrams & Laster LLP is a business litigation and advisory boutique that focuses on high stakes controversies and transactions carrying a high risk of litigation. The firm's practice primarily involves litigation in the Delaware Court of Chancery and the Delaware Supreme Court, proceedings in other Delaware courts, and advice on matters of Delaware corporate, partnership and business law.

## MAIN AREAS OF PRACTICE:

**Corporate & Business Litigation:** The firm's Litigation Practice primarily involves actions in the Delaware Court of Chancery, the nation's preeminent corporate and commercial law court, and the Delaware Supreme Court. The founding partners have been involved in over 100 decisions and many more cases. The firm's litigators have extensive experience representing public and private companies, stockholders, directors and executives in a wide range of business, corporate and alternative entity litigation matters at the trial and appellate level. The firm regularly litigates actions involving corporate control disputes, rights of equity holders, major public and private company controversies, complex transactions, and significant valuation and appraisal proceedings. Unlike many other firms, Abrams & Laster represents plaintiffs and defendants, giving their attorneys an added measure of insight on strategic and tactical issues in transactions and litigation. The firm has a proven track record of offensive and defensive litigation, including successfully pursuing and defeating injunction applications, conducting expedited trials, and prosecuting and defending claims for significant monetary, declaratory or equitable relief. In addition to their Delaware practice, Abrams & Laster frequently represents clients in other jurisdictions on matters involving Delaware law, corporate or business organization issues, or other commercial disputes.

**Transactional Advice:** The firm's Transactional Practice primarily involves matters where there is a high risk of litigation or which raise complex or novel issues of Delaware law, such as contests for corporate control, private equity and portfolio company matters, going-private transactions, recapitalizations, refinancings, and stockholder or board level disputes. Abrams & Laster also advises business entities and their constituents on Delaware issues relating to all phases of their life cycle, ranging from formation questions to ongoing issues involving the payment of dividends and asset sales to end-of-life matters such as dissolution and receiverships. The firm regularly provides advice on the preparation and interpretation of certificates of incorporation and bylaws, whether for newly formed entities, initial public offerings, operating companies with internal disputes, reincorporations, or corporations seeking to amend their existing governance documents. Abrams & Laster similarly advises business entities, directors, officers and stockholders on contracts relating to the corporation's governance structure and commercial relationships, including stockholder rights plans, stockholder agreements and indemnification agreements.

**CLIENTS:** Abrams & Laster represents a broad array of clients including national and international corporations, limited partnerships, limited liability companies, joint ventures, stockholders, directors, equity investors and executives.

## HEAD OFFICE

**DELAWARE**
Brandywine Plaza West, 1521 Concord Pike, Suite 303,
**Wilmington**, DE 19803
**Tel:** 302 778 1000   **Fax:** 302 778 1001
**Website:** www.abramslaster.com

## CONTACTS

| All Areas | Kevin G Abrams |
|---|---|
| All Areas | J Travis Laster |

# ASHBY & GEDDES

## THE FIRM

**Managing Partner:** Lawrence C Ashby

**Number of partners:** 12
**Number of other lawyers:** 13

### AREAS OF PRACTICE:

| | |
|---|---|
| Corporate Litigation & Transactions | 39% |
| Bankruptcy | 27% |
| Commercial Litigation & Transactions | 12% |
| Intellectual Property Litigation | 10% |
| Personal Injury/Medical Malpractice | 7% |
| Public Utility Law | 7% |

**FIRM OVERVIEW:** Ashby & Geddes is best known for its litigation expertise. The firm represents clients ranging from Fortune 500 corporations to individuals. In addition to its Litigation Practice, Ashby & Geddes has a substantial Corporate Reorganization Practice and regularly provides transactional and opinion services to local, national and international clients in connection with matters involving Delaware law. The firm remains committed to its founding principle of providing the best possible work product at highly competitive rates.

## MAIN AREAS OF PRACTICE:

**Bankruptcy:** Ashby & Geddes represents a wide variety of nationally based enterprises with diverse interests in most of the larger Chapter 11 reorganization proceedings filed in Delaware. These representations include debtors, creditor committees, secured creditors and lenders, prospective acquirers of assets, and other parties-in-interest. For example, the firm recently achieved confirmation of the plan of reorganization of Trenwick America in its Chapter 11 case. The firm also represents the creditor committees in the Meridian Automotive, Pliant, Kaiser Aluminum, and a number of other bankruptcy proceedings.

**Corporate Litigation & Transactions:** The firm represents corporate clients, directors, officers and substantial stockholders in stockholder derivative and class actions challenging a wide variety of corporate matters, including business combinations, hostile takeovers, going-private transactions, and proxy contests. For example, the firm served as Delaware counsel for Walter Hewlett in connection with his proxy contest and court challenge to the Hewlett-Packard merger with Compaq. The firm also serves as Delaware counsel to Michael Eisner in defense of a derivative suit brought by stockholders of The Walt Disney Company challenging the hiring and termination of Michael Ovitz. In addition, the firm serves as counsel to boards of directors and special committees in connection with proposed transactions, internal investigations, and similar matters requiring Delaware law advice and opinions.

**Intellectual Property Litigation:** The firm's intellectual property lawyers regularly appear in federal court in Delaware where they serve as Delaware counsel to some of the country's largest corporations in prosecuting and defending patent, trademark, and other intellectual property litigation.

**Commercial Litigation & Transactions:** Ashby & Geddes attorneys represent corporate and banking clients in the litigation of a wide variety of matters, including contract disputes, secured transactions, product liability claims, environmental matters, business torts, and insurance coverage issues. In addition, the firm has experience in the formation of various business entities and advises clients with respect to commercial transactions, including the purchase and sale of businesses and assets.

### HEAD OFFICE

**DELAWARE**
222 Delaware Avenue, 17th Floor, PO Box 1150, **Wilmington**, DE 19899
**Tel:** 302 654 1888  **Fax:** 302 654 2067
**Website:** www.ashby-geddes.com
**Email:** lashby@ashby-geddes.com

### CONTACTS

| | |
|---|---|
| Generally | Lawrence C Ashby |
| Bankruptcy | William P Bowden |
| Corporate Litigation & Transactions | Stephen E Jenkins |
| Intellectual Property Litigation | Steven J Balick |
| Commercial Litigation | Philip (Lee) Trainer |
| Commercial Transactions | James McC Geddes |
| Public Utility Law | James McC Geddes |
| Personal Injury/Medical Malpractice | Randall E Robbins |

**Public Utility Law:** The firm has specialized expertise in public utility law and rate regulation matters. In addition to advising clients generally about such matters, the firm acts as special counsel to the Governor and the Attorney General in connection with the Delaware Public Service Commission, an agency with exclusive jurisdiction over matters concerning the regulation of investor-owned gas and electric utilities. Most recently, the firm has provided consulting services to a major industrial client with regard to service reliability and rate issues involving an out-of-state utility.

**Personal Injury/Medical Malpractice Litigation:** The firm has extensive experience in litigating personal injury matters, importantly including the successful representation of plaintiffs in medical malpractice cases.

**CLIENTS:** Ashby & Geddes clients range from large national and multi-national businesses (or their directors and officers) in corporate and commercial litigation to local businesses in a wide array of commercial matters to individual clients in personal injury and medical malpractice cases.

# THE BAYARD FIRM

## THE FIRM

**Chairman:** Neil B Glassman

**Number of partners:** 11
**Number of other attorneys:** 19

**FIRM OVERVIEW:** The Bayard Firm is one of Delaware's premier law firms. The original members of the firm included former Delaware Supreme Court Chief Justice Daniel L Herrmann and Associate Justice William Duffy as well as Alexis I DuPont Bayard. The firm has a national practice in the areas of commercial bankruptcy, corporate litigation, commercial litigation, corporate law and partnership, business trust and limited liability company law, intellectual property, commercial transactions and insurance law. The firm also offers a full service practice in many other areas, including trial and appellate litigation in state and federal courts; real estate and land use; business transactions; federal and state taxation; estate planning; family law; employment law; regulatory and administrative law; personal injury; products liability and white collar crime. The Bayard Firm is the sole Delaware member of Meritas, the largest worldwide association of national and international business law firms. The firm's subsidiary, The Delaware Corporation Agency, Inc., is a registered agent of the Secretary of State of Delaware, enabling the firm to provide a full range of services relating to formation of new Delaware entities and registered agent services for new and existing Delaware entities.

## MAIN AREAS OF PRACTICE:

**Bankruptcy & Creditor's Rights:** The firm provides services to debtors, creditors, official committees of unsecured creditors and equity holders, bank groups, purchasers, trustees and shareholders in bankruptcy and other insolvency proceedings. The firm's insolvency attorneys are experienced in federal bankruptcy cases, in state corporate receiverships and insurance company rehabilitations and liquidations. The firm has served or continues to serve as counsel to debtors, trustees, creditors' committees and bank groups in many Chapter 11 and Chapter 7 cases. The firm represents business entities in cases across the country, but has focused its practice on cases in the District of Delaware and has participated in virtually every significant bankruptcy case in Delaware in the last decade.

**Business Litigation:** The firm's Business Litigation Group has broad experience in all types of business litigation matters in Delaware state and federal courts. The firm has a strong expertise in corporate litigation in the Delaware Court of Chancery, the preeminent state court in the nation for the adjudication of corporate matters. Delaware is the forum of choice for incorporations and the creation of alternative business entities such as limited liability companies, business and statutory trusts, and limited partnerships. The firm's litigators have handled numerous types of corporate governance cases, including contests for the control of boards of directors; corporate election disputes; stock appraisal cases; stockholder class and derivative actions alleging breaches of fiduciary duty; proceedings involving the rights of preferred stockholders and debt holders; expedited proceedings for the inspection of corporate records; limited liability company and partnership governance and dissolution proceedings; and litigation against lenders and accounting firms. The firm also handles commercial disputes in state and federal courts in Delaware and other jurisdictions, in both jury and nonjury trials. The firm's experience includes business contract and tort litigation; consumer fraud defense; construction and mechanic's lien litigation; and environmental cases. The Business Litigation Group shares with the Intellectual Property Group the ability to represent clients in trade secrets, unfair competition and deceptive trade practice litigation.

## HEAD OFFICE

**DELAWARE**
222 Delaware Avenue, Suite 900, PO Box 25130, **Wilmington**, DE 19899
**Tel:** 302 655 5000 **Fax:** 302 658 6395
**Website:** www.bayardfirm.com

**Opinions/Transactions:** The firm renders third party legal opinions regarding corporations and all alternative entities (LLCs, general and limited partnerships and statutory trusts), and transactions in which they engage. Its lawyers regularly advise clients in connection with the formation and operation of Delaware entities, including corporations, limited liability companies, general and limited partnerships and statutory trusts. The firm also advises clients regarding purchase/sale of businesses and assets, asset based financing and securitizations. The firm represents corporate trustees in structured finance and securitization transactions, frequently through the use of Delaware statutory trusts involving institutional investors.

**Intellectual Property:** The firm represents a wide variety of clients on matters concerning intellectual property, both in litigation and in negotiating resolutions prior to litigation (unfair competition, breach of employment or confidentiality agreements, theft or misuse of trade secrets and patent infringement). The firm counsels clients on the selection, protection and enforcement of trademarks as well as securing copyright or trademark protection and drafting technology and software licensing and sales agreements and non-competition arrangements.

**Real Estate:** The firm has a diverse Real Estate Practice, representing clients engaged in all aspects of the real estate industry throughout Delaware and the surrounding states. The firm's clients include residential and commercial buyers and sellers, owners and developers of apartment complexes, office buildings and residential subdivisions, homebuilders, and real estate lenders. The firm handles all aspects of title insurance business.

**Taxation, Estate Planning & Probate:** The firm handles both business and personal tax planning, personal estate planning, wills, trusts, guardianships, probate and trust administration. The firm advises clients in the law of income tax, gift and estate tax and taxation of partnerships, corporations, and other business entities.

**Family Law:** The firm's Family Law Practice includes representation of clients in connection with divorce and separation, child custody and support, and negotiation of prenuptial agreements.

# CONNOLLY BOVE LODGE & HUTZ LLP

## THE FIRM

**Managing Partner:** Jeffrey B Bove

**Number of partners:** 39
**Number of other lawyers:** 56

**FIRM OVERVIEW:** Connolly Bove Lodge & Hutz serves international, national and local clients in a wide range of legal disciplines. Founded in 1944, the firm began in Wilmington, Delaware as an intellectual property firm. Its practice areas include all phases of intellectual property services and all major technologies. From its Delaware home office the firm also offers corporate, commercial and bankruptcy services for which the Delaware courts are renowned, as well as taxation. In 2001, the firm established an office in Washington, DC, which gives it a presence close to the United States Patent and Trademark Office, the United States Court of Appeals, for the Federal Circuit and the International Trade Commission. By 2005, the firm entered Southern California and opened an office in downtown Los Angeles. This office, staffed by intellectual property attorneys previously with first tier national firms, provides the advantage of litigation services in the Central District of California and other courts throughout the State of California. In addition, the firm is now closer to technology centers on the west coast.

## MAIN AREAS OF PRACTICE:

**Intellectual Property:** The firm handles all types of intellectual property matters, many of national and international significance. It has served as lead counsel in trials and appeals in courtrooms throughout the country since the inception of the firm. Its patent work has always concerned important inventions of the time, including miniaturized electronics, pharmaceuticals, industrial chemicals, films, herbicides, and freeze-dried coffee. The firm has continued as a major player over the decades, with significant depth in biotechnology, crop science, computer and Internet technologies. It remains at the forefront not only in patent litigation, but also in patent prosecution and counseling, trademarks, trade secrets, copyrights and all other facets of intellectual property law. The firm has handled numerous patent cases centering on important issues of first impression.

**Corporate, Commercial, & Business Law:** Connolly Bove Lodge & Hutz's services to clients range from litigation in all Delaware courts including the Delaware Court of Chancery, to the selection and formation of business structure. The firm offers a full range of services related to contract and tax law in addition to transactional work. The firm also has a growing practice centering on opinions relating to Delaware business entities.

**Bankruptcy:** Connolly Bove Lodge & Hutz's Bankruptcy Group represents local, regional, and national clients in some of the largest and most complex reorganization and liquidation bankruptcy cases in the country. Its Bankruptcy Group represents trustees, creditors, debtors, and other interest holders including lenders, government agencies, trade vendors, landlords, equipment lessors, contractors, asset purchasers, insurance companies, bondholders and stockholders. The firm also represents clients in all types of bankruptcy related litigation, such as actions to recover preferential transfers and fraudulent conveyances.

**CLIENTS:** Connolly Bove Lodge & Hutz LLP serves international, national, and local clients from multinational, publicly-held corporations to startup enterprises. Representative clients: Altria Group, Inc, BASF, Bayer AG, Bayer Healthcare, Colgate-Palmolive Company, General Electric Company, Helena Chemical Company, Henkel Corporation, Parker-Hannifin, Pfizer Inc, Rohm and Haas Company, Steelcase Inc.

## HEAD OFFICE

**DELAWARE**
1007 North Orange Street, PO Box 2207, **Wilmington**, DE 19899
**Tel:** 302 658 9141 **Fax:** 302 658 5614
**Email:** cblh@cblh.com
**Website:** www.cblh.com

## BRANCH OFFICES

**CALIFORNIA**
355 South Grand Avenue, Suite 3150, **Los Angeles**, CA 90071-1560
**Tel:** 213 787 2500 **Fax:** 213 687 0498

**DISTRICT OF COLUMBIA**
1990 M Street NW, Suite 800, **Washington**, DC 20036-3425
**Tel:** 202 331 7111 **Fax:** 202 293 6229

## CONTACTS

**Intellectual Property** .......................................................Rudolf E Hutz
**Corporate, Commercial & Business Law** ...................Collins J Seitz Jr
.......................................................................................Arthur G Connolly III
**Bankruptcy** ...............................................................Jeffrey C Wisler

CONNOLLY BOVE LODGE & HUTZ LLP
ATTORNEYS AT LAW

# MORRIS, JAMES, HITCHENS & WILLIAMS LLP

## THE FIRM

**Managing Partner:** David H Williams

**Number of partners:** 30
**Number of other lawyers:** 20

**FIRM OVERVIEW:** Morris, James, Hitchens & Williams LLP, one of the largest law firms in the state of Delaware, is organized into two major sections: litigation and transactions. The Morris James Litigation Group represents a wide variety of domestic and international clients in corporate/fiduciary litigation, bankruptcy and business litigation. The Transactions Group represents national and international clients as well as regional clients engaged in corporate and alternative entity transactions, commercial real estate transactions and business tax and estate planning. The firm's innovative legal work, creative use of technology and responsiveness to client needs have led to many significant client representations. For example, the DuPont Company selected Morris, James, Hitchens & Williams LLP as a member of its Primary Law Firm Network. The firm is also an ALFA International member.

## MAIN AREAS OF PRACTICE:

### LITIGATION

**Corporate/Fiduciary Litigation:** The firm devotes a major portion of its litigation practice to corporate disputes and disputes involving limited liability companies, partnerships, trusts and other entities in which fiduciary duty constitutes an integral part of the parties' relationship. Morris James litigators have significant experience in expedited proceedings before the Delaware Court of Chancery. Members of the litigation group have served as counsel for independent board committees to negotiate transactions in which certain board members may not be disinterested.

**Bankruptcy:** The firm represents debtors, creditors, creditors' committees, purchasers, investors and other parties in interest before the United States Bankruptcy Court for the District of Delaware. Morris James bankruptcy attorneys also counsel clients in both reorganization and liquidation cases before the Bankruptcy Court and in out-of-court workouts and debt restructurings.

**Business Litigation:** The firm has a substantial business litigation practice that involves representing clients in contract disputes, tort claims and insurance coverage litigation. This practice includes trials before judges and juries in every trial court in Delaware and appeals to the Delaware Supreme Court. The firm also serves as Delaware counsel in intellectual property litigation.

### TRANSACTIONS

**Delaware Corporations & Alternative Entities; Structured Finance:** The firm provides strategic advice to clients who are establishing, managing, investing in or financing business ventures that take advantage of Delaware's unique corporate, business and tax laws. A substantial portion of the firm's alternative entity practice involves structuring Delaware special purpose entities for use in asset securitizations and other structured finance transactions. Morris James transactions attorneys frequently render legal opinions on matters of Delaware and United States federal law, and regularly participate in the drafting of Delaware's corporate and alternative entity legislation.

**Real Estate:** The firm represents many of the major developers, investors and builders doing business in the Delaware real estate industry. Morris James real estate attorneys advise lenders and borrowers in a full spectrum of financial transactions, from acquisition and construction financing to permanent financing, working capital, receivables, and other asset-based financings ancillary to real estate as well as conveyancing, leasing, zoning, subdivision, variance and other land use matters.

## HEAD OFFICE

**DELAWARE**
222 Delaware Avenue, 10th Floor, **Wilmington**, DE 19801
**Tel:** 302 888 6800  **Fax:** 302 571 1750
**Email:** mjhw@morrisjames.com
**Website:** www.morrisjames.com

## BRANCH OFFICES

**DELAWARE**
29 North State Street, Suite 100, **Dover**, DE 19901-3832
**Tel:** 302 678 8815  **Fax:** 302 678 9063
**Email:** mjhw@morrisjames.com
**Website:** www.morrisjames.com

16 Polly Drummond Hill Road, **Newark**, DE 19711-5703
**Tel:** 302 368 4200  **Fax:** 302 368 6259
**Email:** mjhw@morrisjames.com
**Website:** www.morrisjames.com

803 North Broom Street, **Wilmington**, DE 19806-4624
**Tel:** 302 655 2599  **Fax:** 302 655 8831
**Email:** mjhw@morrisjames.com
**Website:** www.morrisjames.com

## CONTACTS

**Corporate/Fiduciary Litigation** ................................Lewis H Lazarus
**Bankruptcy** ................................................................Stephen M Miller
**Business Litigation** ...............................................Edward M McNally
**Corporations & Alternative Entities; Structured Finance**..................
................................................................................Robert L Symonds Jr
**Real Estate** .................................................................Richard P Beck
**Business Tax & Estate Planning** ...........................Daniel P McCollom

**Business Tax & Estate Planning:** The firm assists clients with complex business transactions, including purchase and sale agreements, joint ventures, mergers, consolidations, spin-offs, split-ups, acquisitions and divestitures. Morris James tax attorneys have substantial experience in the formation of tax-exempt organizations and obtaining determination letters for such entities. The firm's estate and trust practice provides advice as to the tax advantages of family giving and charitable gift planning, including the use of various types of trusts to accomplish the tax and non-tax objectives of the firm's clients.

**CLIENTS:** Morris, James, Hitchens & Williams LLP regularly represents large multi-national corporations, major financial institutions and other law firms, both within and outside of Delaware. The firm's attorneys are frequently consulted on matters of Delaware and United States federal law.

# MORRIS, NICHOLS, ARSHT & TUNNELL LLP

## THE FIRM

**Managing Partner:** Walter C Tuthill
**Number of partners:** 38
**Number of other lawyers:** 53

**FIRM OVERVIEW:** Morris, Nichols, Arsht & Tunnell LLP was founded in 1930 by former United States District Judge Hugh M Morris. The firm combines a broad national practice of corporate, intellectual property, business reorganization and restructuring, commercial law, litigation with a general business, tax, estate planning and real estate practice within the State of Delaware. The firm is regularly involved as lead counsel or co-counsel in matters of national and international significance, as well as those affecting its immediate community.

## MAIN AREAS OF PRACTICE:

**Corporate Litigation:** The firm has long focused much of its litigation practice on matters related to the law governing corporations and alternative entities, areas where Delaware has developed a national preeeminence. This litigation practice is focused in the Delaware courts, principally the Court of Chancery and the Delaware Supreme Court, and often involves derivative suits or class actions brought in connection with M&A transactions, takeover battles and proxy contests. Members of the corporate litigation group regularly provide guidance on corporate governance and fiduciary duty issues, including representation of boards and board committees.

**Corporate Counseling:** The firm's Corporate Counseling Practice often involves advice on complex corporate transactions such as mergers, spin-offs and financings and on corporate governance issues. Members of this practice are also often called upon to represent boards or board committees, particularly in transactions that may create director or stockholder conflicts. The firm is also often asked to provide formal legal opinions. Members of the corporate counseling group also play an important role in drafting and updating the Delaware General Corporation Law.

**Business Reorganization & Restructuring:** The firm appears in jurisdictions throughout the US representing debtors and creditors in reorganization proceedings under the Bankruptcy Code. The firm regularly advises national and international clients concerning creditors' and debtors' rights issues and assists clients in negotiating workouts, restructurings and other solutions outside of formal insolvency proceedings. The firm has represented debtors-in-possession, secured and unsecured creditors, official committees of unsecured creditors, bondholders' committees, pre and post-petition lenders, purchasers of assets and other parties in interest, both as lead and local counsel.

**Banking & Financial Services:** The firm represents lenders, borrowers, issuers, and investors in all forms of financing transactions. The firm provides bank and insurance regulatory counseling and represents clients before Delaware's Office of the State Bank Commissioner and Department of Insurance.

**Commercial Transactional/Alternative Entities:** The firm provides a complete range of commercial law services to local, national and international clients. Delaware has the most advanced statutes governing the formation and operation of limited liability companies, general and limited partnerships, and statutory business trusts. The firm provides specialized advice on all types of alternative entity transactions and handles a variety of complex transactions. In addition, because Delaware law is often selected as the governing law for major national and international transactions, the firm works with both in-house and regular outside counsel in the structuring and documenting of such transactions.

**General Business/Environmental Litigation:** The firm provides a full range of litigation services, including commercial, contract, environmental and employment cases, to national, international and local clients. The firm regularly appears before all Delaware trial and appellate courts, state and federal, local boards and administrative agencies, and before trial and appellate courts nationwide. The firm defends its clients in connection with governmental investigations including negotiations of consent orders or other types of settlements.

**Trust, Estate & Tax:** The firm provides federal income, estate, gift and generation skipping transfer tax advice to individuals, trusts, estates, business enter-

### OFFICE

**DELAWARE**
1201 North Market Street, PO Box 1347, **Wilmington**, DE 19899
**Tel:** 302 658 9200   **Fax:** 302 658 3989
**Website:** www.mnat.com

### CONTACTS

| | |
|---|---|
| Corporate Litigation | A Gilchrist Sparks III |
| | Kenneth J Nachbar |
| Corporate Counseling | Frederick H Alexander |
| Banking & Financial Services | David A Harris |
| Business Reorganization & Restructuring | William H Sudell |
| | Robert J Dehney |
| Commercial Transactional/Alternative Entity | Walter C Tuthill |
| General Business/Environmental Litigation | Donald E Reid |
| | R Judson Scaggs Jr |
| Trust, Estate & Tax | Thomas R Pulsifer |
| Intellectual Property | Jack B Blumenfeld |
| Real Estate | Donald N Isken |
| Regulation/Governmental Affairs | Michael Houghton |

prises and their owners, and charitable organizations nationwide. The firm also advises on employee benefit matters including ERISA compliance. The firm advises individuals and businesses concerning all aspects o Delaware income tax law including the use of Delaware holding companies designed to minimize state income taxation incurred with respect to intangible assets such as trademarks, patents and investment properties. The firm acts as trust counsel to wealthy families with trusts in Delaware. The firm also represents numerous Delaware trust companies and national banks conducting trust business in Delaware as well as large institutional and individual trustees and beneficiaries of trusts in Delaware and other jurisdictions.

**Intellectual Property:** The firm is at the forefront of the development of IP law and has the reputation as the premier patent litigation firm in Delaware. As a result, the firm has achieved pre-eminence in IP litigation in Delaware and nationwide serving as lead counsel in many cases and assisting as co-counsel in other cases brought to Delaware by patent litigators nationwide. In one role or the other, the firm is counsel in nearly half of the intellectual property cases pending in the District of Delaware.

**Real Estate:** The firm provides legal advice with respect to planning, zoning, subdivision and development of real property, environmental matters and contracts for purchase and sale of residential and commercial property. The firm also represents lenders and borrowers in the financing, acquisition and development of residential, commercial and industrial property, and landlords and tenants in property leasing.

**Regulation/Governmental Affairs:** The firm represents various public entities and agencies, as well as private sector clients, before legislative bodies and city, county, state and federal regulatory agencies including unclaimed property matters. The firm is involved in drafting, advocating and monitoring legislation and regulations that affect clients.

**REPRESENTATIVE CLIENTS:** Abbott Laboratories, Advanced Energy, AstraZeneca, Bausch & Lomb, BP Amoco, Citicorp, Coca-Cola Company, Ford Motor Company, Georgia-Pacific Corporation, Honeywell, Intermec Technologies, Invista, JPMorgan Chase, Lucite International, Inc., Marsh & McLennan, McDonald's Corporation, Medtronic, Merck, Merrill Lynch, New York Life Insurance & Annuity Corporation, Oracle Corporation, Pfizer, Qualcomm, Rambus Inc., Sabre/Travelocity, Scientific Games, Viacom Inc. Sample representation of debtors in Chapter 11 cases include Fruehauf Trailer Corporation, The Loewen Group, Net2000 Communications, eToys, CyberCash, Valley Media, Oakwood Homes, Orbcomm Global, L.P., G-Mark, Inc. and USN Communications, Inc.; representative unsecured creditors' committees in bankruptcy cases include Montgomery Ward, Planet Hollywood, Safety-Kleen and United Artists.

# POTTER ANDERSON & CORROON LLP

## THE FIRM

**Chairman:** David B Brown

**Number of partners:** 37
**Number of other lawyers:** 31

**FIRM OVERVIEW:** Founded in 1826, Potter Anderson & Corroon has a broad practice designed to meet the needs of its clients of all sizes and has developed a national reputation and practice in the areas of corporate litigation and counseling, bankruptcy, intellectual property, commercial transactions and litigation.

## MAIN AREAS OF PRACTICE:

**Bankruptcy:** Potter Anderson's practice focuses on representations in 'mega' Chapter 11 cases of creditors' committees, individual creditors (including banks and other financial institutions, landlords, equipment lessors, and trade creditors), debtor-in-possession financiers, acquirers and shareholders, with occasional work for debtors and/or trustees and plan administrators. The firm also practices in other creditors' rights areas including out-of-court restructuring/workouts, state law receiverships, and secured transactions. Due to the complexity of the bankruptcy practice, the bankruptcy group lawyers often interact with other areas of the firm when special litigation and business transactional expertise are required.

**Business & Commercial Law:** Potter Anderson provides advice to clients with regard to a full range of legal issues arising in connection with the formation and day-to-day operation of business organizations. Its clients include both privately-held and public companies with local, regional, national and international operations. The firm provides clients with sophisticated corporate structuring and tax advice in connection with a broad range of transactions, including business formations and choice of entity, mergers and acquisitions, and financings. The firm regularly acts as 'special' Delaware counsel in nationally prominent mergers, acquisitions, tender offers, divestitures, spin-offs and other types of business transactions.

**Commercial Litigation:** Potter Anderson attorneys represent clients with litigation needs in a wide array of business and commercial litigation matters. For example, in insurance coverage litigation the firm represents corporate policyholders in actions against their insurers for CGL, D&O, E&O, product hazard and other coverages. The firm's labor and employment attorneys represent employers around the country in actions involving employment discrimination claims, reverse discrimination claims, non-competition and trade secret controversies and breach of employment contract claims. Additionally, the firm has represented clients in litigation involving the Uniform Commercial Code, federal and state securities statutes, antitrust laws, franchise law, and commercial lending.

**Delaware Corporate Litigation & Counseling:** Potter Anderson's Corporate Litigation Practice centers upon litigation seeking injunctive and other equitable and compensatory relief, often on an expedited basis, in connection with disputed questions of internal corporate governance. Those suits most frequently focus on the fiduciary obligations of care, loyalty, good faith and disclosure owed by directors, and officers in the context of a wide variety of corporate acts and business combinations, including mergers, tender offers, sales of assets, and proxy fights. The firm's Litigation Practice also embraces the many statutory summary proceedings authorized by the Delaware General Corporation Law and committed to the subject matter jurisdiction of the Delaware Court of Chancery, viewed by many as the single most influential state tribunal in the nation. The firm's Corporate Counseling Team consists of a number of transaction specialists who are routinely retained to advise corporations and their directors with respect to a multitude of corporate questions and interpretations - ranging from matters of day-to-day management to the interpretation of the DGCL in matters involving bylaw and charter amendments, annual meetings, indemnification obligations, stock sales and issuances, and dissolutions.

## OFFICE

**DELAWARE**
1313 North Market Street, PO Box 951, **Wilmington**, DE 19899-0951
**Tel:** 302 984 6000   **Fax:** 302 658 1192
**Website:** www.potteranderson.com

## CONTACTS

| | |
|---|---|
| Bankruptcy | Laurie Selber Silverstein |
| Corporate & Alternative Equity Litigation | Donald J Wolfe, Jr |
| | Peter J Walsh, Jr |
| Corporate Counseling | Michael B Tumas |
| | Mark A Morton |
| Intellectual Property Litigation | Richard L Horwitz, |
| | Philip A Rovner |
| Mergers & Acquisitions | David B Brown |
| | Michael B Tumas |
| Structured Finance & Alternative Entity | Scott E Waxman |
| Commercial Transactions | David B Brown |
| | Harold I Salmons, III |
| Commercial Litigation | Richard L Horwitz |
| | Philip A Rovner |
| Insurance Coverage | John E James |
| | Richard L Horwitz |
| Patent Prosecution & Transactions | Kathleen W Geiger |
| Labor & Employment | Kathleen Furey McDonough |
| | Wendy K Voss |

**Intellectual Property Practice & Litigation:** Potter Anderson's intellectual property practitioners render a variety of services relating to patents, trademarks and copyrights, including preparation and prosecution of patent and trademark applications in the United States Patent and Trademark Office and preparation of legal opinions regarding intellectual property rights. Potter Anderson has long represented national and local clients in disputes regarding patents, trademarks, copyrights and trade secrets, particularly in the Delaware federal court that has experienced unprecedented growth in filings of patent and trademark cases.

**Structured Finance & Alternative Entity Practice:** The Structured Finance and Alternative Entities Practice Group focuses primarily on the use of alternative and special purpose business entities in a wide array of financings, including secured and unsecured financings, acquisition financings, asset-backed and structured financings, project financings, and other bankruptcy-remote structures. The attorneys specialize in representing lenders, borrowers, and other parties in the formation, utilization, termination, and dissolution of all forms of alternative entities. In addition to rendering advice to alternative business entities on a myriad of legal issues, the Structured Finance and Alternative Entity practice frequently renders third-party legal opinions, which are relied upon by other parties to the transaction, by rating agencies, such as Standard & Poor's and Moody's, and by governmental authorities, such as the SEC.

**CLIENTS:** Representative clients include: AT&T Inc., Bank of America, CareFirst, Inc., Citicorp, City of Wilmington, Delaware, Daimler Chrysler Corp., E.I. duPont de Nemours and Company, El Paso Corporation, Exxon Corp., General Motors Corp., Hercules Incorporated, Hewlett-Packard Company, KAO Corp., Monsanto Co., Norfolk Southern Corporation, PeopleSoft, Inc., Philips Electronics Corporation of North America, Wal-Mart Stores, Inc., The Walt Disney Company.

# PROCTOR HEYMAN LLP

## THE FIRM

**Founding Partners:** Vernon R Proctor, Kurt M Heyman

**Number of partners:** 2
**Number of other attorneys:** 1

**FIRM OVERVIEW:** Founded on January 1, 2006, by two partners and an associate from a larger firm, Proctor Heyman LLP is Delaware's newest corporate litigation and counseling boutique. While the firm is new, its lawyers have a rich tradition in the Delaware legal community. The firm's attorneys boast nearly 50 years combined of practice in Delaware, principally in corporate and commercial litigation matters before the Delaware Court of Chancery. Two of its attorneys clerked for the Court of Chancery prior to entering private practice. The firm acts as both lead counsel and local counsel in matters before Delaware state and federal courts. In its local counsel practice, the firm has worked with some of the leading firms in the country. Proctor Heyman LLP is the smallest firm in Delaware to have representation on the Corporation Law Council and the Partnership/Limited Liability Company Committee of the Delaware State Bar Association - the bodies charged with recommending changes to Delaware's corporate and alternative entity statutes. The firm's attorneys are also frequent authors and lecturers on issues of corporate and alternative entity law and practice before the Court of Chancery. Proctor Heyman LLP is also the newest and smallest firm in Delaware to have its attorneys (including both of its name partners) recognized as Leaders in their Field for Chancery and Commercial Litigation by Chambers USA 2006.

**MAIN AREAS OF PRACTICE:** Proctor Heyman LLP handles a full array of corporate and commercial litigation matters, including corporate governance, mergers and acquisitions, stockholder class and derivative actions, fiduciary duties, stockholder appraisal actions, and litigation involving limited liability companies and limited partnerships. The firm also advises special committees and audit committees of corporate boards of directors in connection with their reviews or investigations of transactions. The firm also has considerable experience in litigation involving claims of business torts, consumer fraud, deceptive trade practices and trade secret misappropriation.
Representative reported cases involving Proctor Heyman LLP attorneys include: *Beck v Atlantic Coast PLC*, 868 A.2d 840 (Del. Ch. 2005); *Production Resources Group, L.L.C. v NCT Group, Inc.*, 863 A.2d 772 (Del. Ch. 2004); *Comrie v Enterasys Networks, Inc.*, 837 A.2d 1 (Del. Ch. 2003); *Anglo American Sec. Fund, L.P. v S.R. Global Intern. Fund, L.P.*, 829 A.2d 143 (Del. Ch. 2003); *Grimes v Alteon, Inc.*, 804 A.2d 256 (Del. 2002); *State ex rel. Brady v Preferred Florist Network, Inc.*, 791 A.2d 8 (Del. Ch. 2001); *Emerald Partners v Berlin*, 726 A.2d 1215 (Del. 1999).

**CLIENTS:** Proctor Heyman LLP attorneys have recently represented the following clients: UbiquiTel, Inc.; Tyson Foods, Inc.; Eon Labs, Inc.; Alamosa Holdings, Inc.; AirGate PCS, Inc.; Plumtree Software, Inc.; Intraware, Inc.; Mobius Management Systems, Inc.; CERBCO, Inc.; Kids International Corp.; Mobility Electronics, Inc.; Louisville Bedding Co.; Delta Star, Inc.

## HEAD OFFICE

**DELAWARE**
1116 West Street, **Wilmington**, DE 19801
**Tel:** 302 472 7300   **Fax:** 302 472 7320
**Website:** www.proctorheyman.com

# RICHARDS, LAYTON & FINGER, P.A.

## THE FIRM

**President:** Jesse A Finkelstein
**Vice President:** Gregory P Williams
**Number of Directors:** 56
**Number of other lawyers:** 76

**FIRM OVERVIEW:** Richards, Layton & Finger, a professional association, is Delaware's largest law firm and one of its oldest. With approximately half the country's Fortune 500 corporations incorporated in Delaware, the firm's practice has a national and international focus as well as a local and regional base.

## MAIN AREAS OF PRACTICE:

**Alternative Entities:** The firm's Alternative Entity Group provides advice and legal opinions to businesses throughout the world with respect to Delaware limited liability companies, partnerships and other non-corporate entities, including advice concerning the formation, merger, acquisition, dissolution or restructuring of, and other transactions involving, these entities.

**Banking:** The firm represents banks, trust companies and other financial institutions located in Delaware and elsewhere. The Banking Group's experience includes counseling on financial institution structuring and formation, federal and state regulatory issues, lending and leveraged leasing transactions, corporate and personal trust matters, and consumer lending activities.

**Business/Commercial Transactions:** The firm is actively involved in regional, national and international business transactions. Areas of the business/commercial transactions practice include Insurance and Uniform Commercial Code.

**Corporate (Litigation & Advisory):** Throughout its history, Richards, Layton & Finger's corporate lawyers have played leading roles in the corporate bar, both within the State and nationally. The firm's corporate lawyers counsel clients, provide opinions and negotiate transactions with respect to matters of Delaware corporate law and fiduciary duties of corporate directors. Richards, Layton & Finger's corporate litigators have argued many of the landmark cases arising under Delaware's General Corporation Law, fiduciary duties of directors and corporate governance issues. This group also litigates fiduciary and other issues relating to alternative entities, such as limited partnerships and limited liability companies.

**Environmental:** The firm regularly represents individuals and corporations in all types of enforcement actions brought by environmental agencies and has defended nuisance, personal injury and property damage toxic tort cases brought by private litigants. Firm lawyers litigate environmental claims involving all media, including air, water and soil, and represent landowners, haulers and generators as potentially responsible parties in Superfund and RCRA litigation.

**Labor & Employment:** The firm provides employers with both advice and litigation support in all aspects of labor and employment law, including providing transactional advice, drafting employment and severance contracts, reviewing personnel manuals, and providing compliance training to management and employees regarding state and federal employment laws

**Litigation (General):** Richards, Layton & Finger represents local, regional and national clients in a wide variety of litigation matters in state and federal courts and agencies, and in arbitrations and mediations. Some of the areas of their litigation practice include administrative, commercial and civil litigation, and media and communications law.

**Litigation (Intellectual Property):** Richards, Layton & Finger has extensive expertise in intellectual property litigation and has prosecuted and defended a substantial number of actions for patent, trademark and copyright infringement. The firm also has considerable experience in litigating related actions for product disparagement, misappropriation of trade secrets, and inappropriate disclosure of confidential and/or proprietary information.

**Real Estate:** The firm's Real Estate Group specializes in complex regional and local commercial transactions, including lending, development and public/private joint ventures.

## OFFICE

**DELAWARE**
One Rodney Square, 920 North King Street, **Wilmington** DE 19801
**Tel:** 302 651 7700  **Fax:** 302 651 7701
**Website:** www.rlf.com

**Restructuring & Bankruptcy:** As one of the largest and most active bankruptcy practices in Delaware, the firm has been involved in virtually every major Chapter 11 case in Delaware and many major cases in the US outside of Delaware. The group represents debtors, creditors, committees, acquirers, investors and others in these cases.

**Tax/Trusts & Estates:** The firm's Tax Group assists clients in many different areas, including estate planning and counseling, audits and refunds, trust litigation, regulation and rulemaking.

**Trust & Agency Services:** The firm's Trust and Agency Services Group advises all types of financial institutions in connection with their acting as trustee or agent in transactions such as structured finance transactions, leveraged lease financings, creditor trusts and other complex transactions. This group also provides advice and legal opinions with respect to the use of common law and statutory trusts in a variety of financing and other transactions and in connection with the formation of investment funds and real estate investment trusts.

**CLIENTS:** Richards, Layton & Finger's clients include some of the largest public companies in the world, innovative technology companies, national, regional and international financial and credit institutions, insurance companies, chemical and other manufacturers, agricultural producers and processors, healthcare providers, real estate developers, defense contractors, consulting professionals, governments and governmental agencies, professional sports teams, utility companies, telecommunications companies, retailers, investment bankers, prominent individuals and entrepreneurs of all types.

# YOUNG CONAWAY STARGATT & TAYLOR, LLP

## THE FIRM

**Chairman:** James L Patton, Jr
**Administrative Partner:** Richard A Levine
**Number of partners:** 52
**Number of other lawyers:** 52

## AREAS OF PRACTICE:

| | |
|---|---|
| Bankruptcy & Corporate Restructuring | 33% |
| Corporate Counseling & Litigation | 21% |
| Personal Injury & Workers' Compensation | 10% |
| Employment Law | 8% |
| Commercial Real Estate, Banking & Land Use | 8% |
| Tax/Trusts & Estate & Benefits | 6% |
| Litigation & Trial Practice | 5% |
| Business Planning, Transactions & Restructuring | 4% |
| Intellectual Property Litigation | 3% |
| Environmental Law | 2% |

**FIRM OVERVIEW:** Founded in 1959, Young Conaway Stargatt & Taylor, LLP has grown into Delaware's second-largest law firm, with more than 100 attorneys experienced in a wide range of practice areas important for business clientele throughout the state and around the world. Young Conaway attorneys appear frequently before state and federal agencies and actively participate in vital issues pending before its state legislature.

## MAIN AREAS OF PRACTICE:

**Bankruptcy & Corporate Restructuring:** The largest in Delaware, playing a major role in virtually every significant bankruptcy in this district. The group routinely represents debtors, creditor committees, and shareholder groups in this jurisdiction and around the country. It provides a full array of services including out-of-court workouts, debt restructurings and pre-planned bankruptcies. This group is often referred to as Delaware's leading bankruptcy experts by the media.

**Corporate Counseling & Litigation:** One of the most experienced teams in the country, providing advice to corporations, stockholders and other law firms throughout the world. The practice ranges from structuring corporation transactions to litigating takeover battles and shareholder suits. The team includes members of the Council of the Corporation Law Section of the Delaware State Bar Association, which drafts amendments to the Delaware General Corporation Law.

**Personal Injury & Workers' Compensation:** The firm's personal injury litigators are recognized as some of the most experienced and skilled trial attorneys in the state. The litigators handle an array of personal injury matters including automobile and construction accident litigation, medical negligence, product liability and premises liability actions, complex tort litigation and workers' compensation, and consistently obtain substantial verdicts and settlements.

**Employment Law:** The Employment Law Group is the largest in Delaware, providing services to private and public employers in every area of employment law, including discrimination and sexual harassment claims, wrongful discharge lawsuits, union issues, workforce reductions, immigration and restrictive covenant issues.

**Commercial Real Estate, Banking & Land Use:** The firm offers a full range of services required for commercial development and financing for interstate and intrastate projects, including acquisitions, sales, financing for banks or businesses, leasing, zoning and land use projects such as shopping centers, office buildings, residential developments, and communications towers.

**Tax/Trusts & Estate & Benefits:** The firm's Taxation Group is engaged in federal and state tax planning for businesses and individuals. The group advises large and small businesses and their owners on matters of equity formations, shareholder, partnership and LLC agreements, business organization, sales and acquisitions, employee benefits, pension plans and more. The estate planning attorneys represent individuals in the creation of trusts and wills for intergenerational asset management and tax and charitable giving planning.

**Litigation & Trial Practice:** The continued success and growth of the firm's litigation experience, coupled with client needs, led to the formation of one of Delaware's largest litigation teams. The group combines the strongest litigators and trial practitioners from every practice section within the firm, coordinating the depth and experience in all traditional practice areas with extensive litigation and trial experience in both bench and jury trials throughout Delaware and the United States. Representative matters include the handling of complex commercial disputes, contract and fraud claims, and applications for expedited injunctive relief.

**Business Planning, Transactions & Restructuring:** The section handles matters arising at every stage in the formation, growth and development of corporations, limited liability companies, limited partnerships and other types of entities. The attorneys combine expertise in Delaware corporate law, alternative-entity law, tax, commercial transactions and bankruptcy reorganizations.

**Intellectual Property Litigation:** The firm's intellectual property attorneys represent national corporate clients and local businesses in the litigation of intellectual property disputes, including issues of trade secrets, trademarks, copyrights, patent infringement and unfair competition.

**Environmental Law:** The firm provides counsel on regulatory compliance matters and representation in administrative agency proceedings and in public and private party litigation, as well as matters ranging from compliance law to permits to environmental audits.

**CLIENTS:** Ranging from national and international corporations (some doing business as Delaware business entities), to businesses throughout the Delaware Valley (including state and local governments, school districts, banks, developers, professional practices) and individuals.

## HEAD OFFICE

**DELAWARE**
1000 West Street, The Brandywine Building, 17th Floor
**Wilmington**, DE 19801
**Tel:** 302 571 6600  **Fax:** 302 571 1253
**Website:** www.YoungConaway.com

## BRANCH OFFICES

**DELAWARE**
110 West Pine Street, **Georgetown**, DE 19947
**Tel:** 302 856 3571  **Fax:** 302 856 9338

## CONTACTS

| | |
|---|---|
| Bankruptcy & Corporate Restructuring | Robert S Brady |
| Corporate Counseling & Litigation | Bruce L Silverstein |
| Personal Injury & Workers' Compensation | Neilli Mullen Walsh |
| Employment Law | Barry M Willoughby |
| Commercial Real Estate, Banking & Land Use | Lisa B Goodman |
| Tax/Trusts & Estate & Benefits | Jerome K Grossman |
| Litigation & Trial Practice | Richard H Morse |
| Business Planning, Transactions & Restructuring | Craig D Grear |
| Intellectual Property Litigation | John W Shaw |
| Environmental Law | Anthony G Flynn |

YOUNG CONAWAY STARGATT & TAYLOR, LLP

## How lawyers are ranked

Every year we carry out thousands of in-depth interviews with clients and lawyers in order to assess the reputations and expertise of business lawyers across the USA. Chambers rankings and editorial are referred to extensively by General Counsel and other purchasers of legal services who look to our recommendations when choosing their lawyers.

# ANTITRUST

| Antitrust |
| --- |
| Leading Firms |
| 1   ARNOLD & PORTER LLP *Washington, DC* |
| 2   CLEARY GOTTLIEB *Washington, DC* |
|     JONES DAY *Washington, DC* |
| 3   GIBSON, DUNN & CRUTCHER LLP *Washington, DC* |
|     HOGAN & HARTSON LLP *Washington, DC* |
|     HOWREY LLP *Washington, DC* |
|     O'MELVENY & MYERS LLP *Washington, DC* |
|     WEIL, GOTSHAL & MANGES LLP *Washington, DC* |
|     WILMERHALE *Washington, DC* |
| 4   BOIES, SCHILLER & FLEXNER *Washington, DC* |
|     FRIED, FRANK *Washington, DC* |
|     KING & SPALDING LLP *Washington, DC* |
|     MORGAN, LEWIS & BOCKIUS LLP *Washington, DC* |
|     SKADDEN, ARPS *Washington, DC* |
|     WHITE & CASE LLP *Washington, DC* |
| 5   CROWELL & MORING LLP *Washington, DC* |
|     FRESHFIELDS *Washington, DC* |
|     HELLER EHRMAN LLP *Washington, DC* |
|     KIRKLAND & ELLIS LLP *Washington, DC* |
|     LATHAM & WATKINS LLP *Washington, DC* |
|     MAYER, BROWN *Washington, DC* |
|     MCDERMOTT WILL & EMERY *Washington, DC* |
|     PAUL, WEISS *Washington, DC* |

## Band 1

### Arnold & Porter LLP

See firm details p.560

**The Firm:** Arnold & Porter's antitrust crown shows no sign of slipping. Boasting more than 45 attorneys in the DC office, much of the praise showered on the practice centers on its "*broad collection of talent and experience.*" The firm offers a formidable range of expertise, defending some of the biggest players in the pharmaceutical and hi-tech industries against monopolization claims, cartel investigations and distribution challenges. For example, attorneys representing Wyeth won summary judgment in a difficult class action brought by direct purchasers of the manufacturer's estrogen therapy product, Premarin. The purchasers alleged that Wyeth had violated the Sherman Act by entering into restrictive contracts with pharmacy benefit managers. The area

in which the group receives most acclaim, however, is M&A. To this end, sources draw attention to its "*excellent working relationships*" with both the FTC and DOJ. These ties are consolidated by the large percentage of high-ranking former officials who now work at the firm. Currently, the group is acting for Adobe Systems in its $4 billion acquisition of Macromedia, the company responsible for the Flash web animation standard. It has also made its mark in the entertainment industry, overseeing the merger between AMC Entertainment and Loews Cineplex. Offering "*absolutely spectacular*" service in these and a raft of other matters, Arnold & Porter continues to raise the bar for the rest of the market.

**The Lawyers:** Former director of the FTC's competition bureau, **William Baer** (see p.498) brings an "*intuitive, bone-deep understanding*" of antitrust law to a vast practice that encompasses M&A, cartel investigations and grand jury appearances. Peers envy the pianist's touch he displays in sensitive matters ("*he can deliver good or bad news without upsetting anyone*") and clients value a "*thoughtful and methodical*" approach that never leaves them in the dark. Chairman of the firm **Michael Sohn** (see p.547) is another FTC alumnus with his finger securely on the pulse of regulatory change. His management position has not prevented him from being involved in some of the firm's most substantial matters of late, including the representation of Adobe Systems on the Macromedia acquisition. Interviewees unanimously relish the presence of this "*smart, creative and thoughtful guy*" in the DC antitrust environment. "*Hard-working, reliable and experienced,*" **Deborah Feinstein** (see p.511) has traced Baer's steps as a former senior official in the FTC's bureau of competition. She applies the skills cultivated in this capacity to merger work. **Donna Patterson** (see p.537) earns recognition for her successful tenure as deputy assistant attorney general; "*pragmatic and credible,*" she is involved in advising NASDAQ in a transaction. Prior to joining the firm, **Richard Rosen** (see p.542) served as chief of the communications and finance section at the DOJ. He specializes in assisting in merger clients drawn from the computer software, telecom, network equipment and broadcasting industries. Noted for his "*great presence*" before the agencies, he is also a "*delight to work with,*" according to clients. Observers attest to

**Douglas Wald**'s (see p.553) "*encyclopedic knowledge of antitrust laws.*" He is "*an exceptional analyst of proposed initiatives because he shapes them to minimize potential business risks.*" He conjoins knowledge of marketing, pricing, and distribution restrictions with a thorough grounding in joint venture and acquisition issues. In keeping with his colleagues, **Kenneth Letzler** (see p.526) is regarded as "*analytically sound, and effective before the agencies.*" Companies such as GlaxoSmithKline and AstraZeneca regularly turn to him for consultation, taking advantage of his insight into the regulatory framework underlying the pharmaceutical industry. "*Bright and aggressive,*" **Jonathan Gleklen**'s (see p.515) recent success and market visibility belie his years. His considerable talent in IP has attracted an impressive clientele of which Adobe, Expedia and Xerox are eminent examples.

**Clients/Work Highlights:** The firm succeeded in obtaining a defense verdict on behalf of Philip Morris USA in a trial arising from allegations that the manufacturer's merchandising and promotional programs violated the Robinson-Patman Act. The team also acts for GE; Pfizer; Guardian Industries; Microsoft; Roche Molecular Systems and State Farm.

## Band 2

### Cleary Gottlieb Steen & Hamilton LLP

See firm details p.1525

**The Firm:** The attorneys at this firm "*sweat the deals, do the work and know the facts.*" The lion's share of its antitrust caseload is conducted out of DC, where transactions are the main order of the day. For example, the team advised UCB on the sale of its surface specialties business to Cytec Industries, and oversaw a merger between Premcor and Valero Energy – a union that has created the largest oil refinery in the USA. As well as strength in the chemical, energy and pharmaceutical markets, a prestigious corporate practice bolsters the team's prominence in the investment bank arena. The firm's litigation arm also enjoys clear lines of communication with the FTC. As a result of the group's intervention, AspenTech and attorneys for the FTC settled a dispute stemming from the company's acquisition of Hyprotech in 2003. The firm also scores

## Antitrust
### Leading Individuals

| | |
|---|---|
| [1] **BAER William** *Arnold & Porter LLP* | **LEDDY Mark** *Cleary Gottlieb* |
| **MELAMED A Douglas** *WilmerHale* | **SIMS Joe** *Jones Day* |
| [2] **CARY George** *Cleary Gottlieb* | **KLAWITER Donald** *Morgan, Lewis* |
| **KOLASKY William** *WilmerHale* | **MCDAVID Janet** *Hogan & Hartson LLP* |
| **NEWBORN Steven** *Weil, Gotshal & Manges LLP* | **PARKER Richard** *O'Melveny & Myers LLP* |
| **PROGER Phillip** *Jones Day* | **RILL James** *Howrey LLP* |
| **RULE Charles** *Fried, Frank* | **SOHN Michael** *Arnold & Porter LLP* |
| [3] **DENGER Michael** *Gibson, Dunn & Crutcher* | **FLEXNER Donald** *Boies, Schiller & Flexner* |
| **KATTAN Joseph** *Gibson, Dunn & Crutcher* | **LOFTIS III James** *Gibson, Dunn & Crutcher* |
| **MALESTER Ann** *Weil, Gotshal & Manges LLP* | **MURIS Timothy** *O'Melveny & Myers LLP* |
| **NANNES John** *Skadden, Arps* | **SCHECHTER Mark** *Howrey LLP* |
| **SCHILDKRAUT Marc** *Heller Ehrman LLP* | **ZWISLER Margaret** *Latham & Watkins LLP* |
| [4] **ANTALICS Michael** *O'Melveny & Myers LLP* | **CRISMAN JR C Benjamin** *Skadden, Arps* |
| **FAVRETTO Richard** *Mayer, Brown, Rowe & Maw* | **FEINSTEIN Deborah** *Arnold & Porter LLP* |
| **GELFAND David** *Cleary Gottlieb* | **GIDLEY J Mark** *White & Case LLP* |
| **PATTERSON Donna** *Arnold & Porter LLP* | **ROSEN Richard** *Arnold & Porter LLP* |
| **SMITH Tefft** *Kirkland & Ellis LLP* | **SMITH Wm Randolph** *Crowell & Moring LLP* |
| **SULLIVAN Kevin** *King & Spalding LLP* | **SUNSHINE Steven** *Cadwalader, Wickersham & Taft* |
| **VARNEY Christine** *Hogan & Hartson LLP* | **WALD Douglas** *Arnold & Porter LLP* |
| **WINTERSCHEID Joseph** *McDermott Will & Emery* | **YDE Paul** *Freshfields Bruckhaus Deringer* |
| [5] **BELL Robert** *WilmerHale* | **BLOCH Robert** *Mayer, Brown, Rowe & Maw* |
| **DENIS Paul** *Dechert LLP* | **EGAN JR James** *Weil, Gotshal & Manges LLP* |
| **FENTON Kathryn** *Jones Day* | **GALLO Kenneth** *Paul, Weiss* |
| **GARZA Deborah** *Fried, Frank* | **HENRY Roxann** *Howrey LLP* |
| **IMUS Neil** *Vinson & Elkins LLP* | **JACOBSEN JR Raymond** *McDermott Will & Emery* |
| **KRAUSS Joseph** *Hogan & Hartson LLP* | **LETZLER Kenneth** *Arnold & Porter LLP* |
| **LIPSKY Abbott** *Latham & Watkins LLP* | **MACAVOY Christopher** *Howrey LLP* |
| **MOLTENBREY MJ** *Freshfields Bruckhaus Deringer* | **SCHLOSSBERG Bob** *Freshfields Bruckhaus Deringer* |
| **SIMONS Joseph** *Paul, Weiss* | **TALADAY John** *Howrey LLP* |
| **TOM Willard** *Morgan, Lewis* | |

### Up-and-coming individuals

| | |
|---|---|
| **ARP D Jarrett** *Gibson, Dunn & Crutcher LLP* | **GLEKLEN Jonathan** *Arnold & Porter LLP* |
| **MCFALLS Michael** *Jones Day* | **NELSON Mark** *Cleary Gottlieb* |
| **POPOFSKY Mark** *Kaye Scholer LLP* | |

highly for its consummate international practice, with the Brussels office singled out for particular praise, while partners from both sides of the Atlantic assist European clients with US interests. The group was involved in GlaxoSmithKline's acquisition of ID Biomedicals, which produces flu vaccines, and the attainment of Roche's vitamins business for DSM. Clients relish the "*creative thinking*" endemic to this firm, while peers give a sigh of relief at its presence on the other side of a deal, observing that professionalism and efficiency are both adjectives synonymous with Cleary's antitrust practice.

**The Lawyers:** According to peers, **Mark Leddy** (see p.525) has done a great job of leveraging Cleary's expertise in the international arena. Specializing in antitrust law with both US and European dimensions and utilizing his DOJ background and time spent in Brussels, Leddy is uniquely positioned to handle multijurisdictional issues. He is a familiar face before the courts and regulatory agencies in relation to merger and cartel matters: "*He understands and listens to the government, works with the client to try and figure out whether there are immediate answers to*

*a problem, and if there aren't he'll think creatively – with great success.*" Before joining the firm, **George Cary** (see p.505) was deputy director of the FTC's bureau of competition in charge of merger enforcement. As such "*he has a superb understanding of the commission*" that proves an immense attraction to clients. As well as defending companies such as GlaxoSmithKline with trademark tenacity and unswerving dedication, his practice includes advising major corporates on mergers. If Leddy and Cary "*form the nucleus of a very strong group,*" **David Gelfand** (see p.514) contributes greatly to its cohesion. Recently returned from the Brussels office, where he was based for three years, he played an important role in the GlaxoSmithKline and ID Biomedicals merger and has undertaken cartel litigation on behalf of Dow Chemical against marine shippers of chemical products. Observers report that in the area of competition law he is "*extremely effective.*" Colleague **Mark Nelson** (see p.534) is a "*straight shooter who has credibility with the agencies, and demonstrates sophisticated analytical skills.*" He counsels clients on mergers in the USA and at EU

member state level and has experience of civil and criminal litigation.

**Clients/Work Highlights:** The group is currently representing Broadcom in major monopolization litigation. Other clients on the firm's roster include ConocoPhillips; United Technologies; Alcoa; American Express; T-Mobile; Fred Meyer and Siemens.

## Jones Day
See firm details p.570

**The Firm:** Attorneys at this legal behemoth prioritize nationwide office integration to provide clients with geographically seamless advice and advocacy. Peers see the team on an extensive array of transactions and identify merger clearance as an unequivocal strength of the firm's 95-strong antitrust and competition law practice, with about 50 lawyers focusing on this area. The "*strategically sound*" team acted as domestic and international counsel to Procter & Gamble in connection with its acquisition of Gillette, valued at $57 billion. Peers also point to the firm's clout in criminal and governmental circles as evidence of the breadth and depth of its bench. Team members are defending Apple in class action litigation alleging that the company has monopolized the online music market by tying the iTunes Music Store to its iPod products.

**The Lawyers:** For many, **Joe Sims** (see p.546) is the quintessential antitrust lawyer: demonstrating the ability to "*reduce a difficult point to a simple, powerful thought,*" he is ideally suited to explaining complex areas of law to clients. Sims has recently added the Apple litigation and the Gillette merger to his extensive experience and enjoys the reputation of one who "*conforms to the highest standards of candor and good faith.*" If, as interviewees assert, his presence determines the character and focus of the practice, it is in the safest of hands. Head of the group **Phillip Proger** (see p.539) is similarly accomplished when it comes to people skills, combining "*intellectual savvy with street smart.*" A former chair of the antitrust section, he has enormous credibility with the government and is recognized by his peers for first-rate work in the healthcare sector. **Kathryn Fenton** (see p.511) is an "*understated and extremely able individual who works exceptionally hard for her clients.*" Noted for the quality of her counseling, she has also handled a number of transactions for clients such as American Tower and Ameren, one of the largest public utilities in the USA. Sat at "*Joe's right arm,*" **Michael McFalls** (see p.530) impresses as a "*bright and effective*" partner who combines antitrust expertise with IP experience. He represents many of the firm's pharmaceutical clients, including Abbott Laboratories.

**Clients/Work Highlights:** Proger led the team representing Federated Department Stores in relation to its $17 billion acquisition of The May Department Stores Company. The group's diverse range of clients also encompasses Chevron; AOL; Eastman Chemical; Inventus BioTec; Bayer; Koch Industries; ICANN; GM and Cabot.

## Band 3

### Gibson, Dunn & Crutcher LLP

See firm details p.328

**The Firm:** "*Held in high esteem*" by peers, Gibson Dunn's antitrust practice has made considerable progress since its West Coast inception. It now boasts a substantial domestic and international footprint, with additional offices in Brussels, London and Munich. In DC, the 15-attorney antitrust and trade regulation group has refined its litigation expertise to become a standout presence in cartel investigations. Sources point to the work of Gary Spratling, a former US government official who worked on global policy and enforcement, as one of the main reasons for this. Although based in San Francisco, his role as practice cochair, alongside the firm's multioffice team mentality, ensures that his influence pervades the DC group's caseload. Lawyers are, for example, representing Daiichi Pharmaceutical, one of the vitamins defendants in the Empagram case involving worldwide cartels that allegedly fixed prices of vitamins for more than ten years, before the Supreme Court and DC Circuit. Attorneys are also "*extremely well versed*" in the technology issues that inform allegations directed at the firm's entertainment and electronic media clients. Currently, the group is defending Sony in multidistrict litigation relating to putative class actions challenging the formation and management of a patent pool by the holders of patents used in the manufacturing of DVD players.

**The Lawyers:** Clients report approvingly that **Michael Denger** (see p.508) is "*a lovely man who is a terrier in court.*" As well as being co-lead in the Daiichi litigation, Denger represented Hollywood Video in its acquisition by Movie Gallery. "*Intellectually as good as anybody you're likely to meet,*" **Joseph Kattan** (see p.522) applies his "*exceptional knowledge of hi-tech law*" to a caseload that includes acting for Intel in a diverse range of matters. For example, he obtained an FTC denial of AMD's application to discover Intel documents for use before the EC. Observers find **James Loftis** (see p.527) to be a "*refreshingly commonsensical adviser to clients and great at dealing with the agencies.*" His current docket ranges from involvement in a Fortune 500 company's internal investigation to the defense of class actions centering on the high-pressure laminates industry. "*Dedicated, available and very knowledgeable,*" **Jarrett Arp**'s (see p.498) practice, although containing a merger component, is weighted more toward cartel investigations and civil litigation. He and Spratling recently brought to a halt a long-standing government investigation against a major industry client. Arp also obtained summary judgment for McDonald's in a suit pending in Seattle.

**Clients/Work Highlights:** American Airlines; Delta Air Lines; Jostens; Callaway Golf; Sempra Energy; Nissan; Akzo Nobel and International Paper.

### Hogan & Hartson LLP

See firm details p.568

**The Firm:** Parlaying a reputation for "*history and depth*" in this area, the firm represents companies undergoing government investigation and provides comprehensive assistance with merger clearance. A team of 50 attorneys, split between DC and New York, "*satisfies within tight timeframes the needs of clients*" in healthcare, hi-tech, defense, heavy manufacturing and media litigation. As antitrust counsel to major producer of EDA software and services Synopsys, the firm settled an IP dispute with Nassda arising from the company's most recent acquisition. The group's work within the computer arena also included representing IBM in an $850 million transaction with Microsoft. It has likewise made its presence felt in the areas of health insurance and entertainment. This includes overseeing WellPoint's attainment of Empire BlueCross BlueShield and obtaining a consent order from the FTC that will permit Penn National Gaming's $2.2 billion acquisition of Argosy Gaming.

**The Lawyers:** **Janet McDavid**'s (see p.530) stock continues to rise following her virtuoso performances in the Penn National Gaming acquisition and the Mandalay-MGM Mirage deal, which has established the largest casino operation in the USA. In light of these successes, one peer's observation that she is "*the cream of the crop*" reflects current market sentiment toward her abilities and connections. Held in high regard by the FTC, McDavid "*understands how business people operate.*" **Christine Varney** (see p.551) adopts an innovative and original approach to her practice, combining her antitrust caseload with expertise in data security and Internet privacy issues. She was deeply involved in the Synopsys merger and subsequent litigation. "*Impressive guy*" **Joseph Krauss** (see p.524) applies his competition skills to merger work, representing Wal-Mart during its involvement in the contentious Blockbuster-Hollywood Video transaction.

**Clients/Work Highlights:** A team co-led by Joseph Krauss received a favorable decision in its defense of AEP against claims alleging price-fixing, fraud and breach of fiduciary duty. Other clients range from American Express; Amgen; Association of American Medical Colleges; Carnival Cruise Lines and eBay to EMI Group; General Dynamics; IBM; PacifiCare and Twentieth Century Fox.

### Howrey LLP

**The Firm:** Historically "*one of the premier antitrust firms in town,*" it has been a year of transition for Howrey. Observers are curious to see what shape the practice will take following the departure of Peggy Zwisler and Marc Shildkraut for pastures new. The sheer size and quality of the team, however, should ensure that any deleterious effects are negligible. It maintains a "*wonderfully healthy*" reputation for dispute work, having won an action on behalf of Arch Coal against the FTC's attempt to block a merger with Triton Coal. The firm continues to attract work in this area as a consequence of its vigorous and resourceful approach to potentially contentious acquisitions. Subsequent to involvement in the ScanSoft-Nuance union, group members are representing Whirlpool in the review arising from the company's headline-grabbing acquisition of Maytag.

**The Lawyers:** One of the "*undisputed deans of the Bar,*" **James Rill** is highly active in the realm of merger negotiation and defense. His reputation for being "*worldly wise*" in these matters manifests itself in the awe expressed at his "*incredible connections*" on both sides of the Atlantic. He offers clients a level of strategic skill and courtroom panache that peers find hard to match. Colleague **Mark Schechter** – "*talented, pleasant and great to work with*" – is currently representing Whirlpool in the Maytag review. He counseled Samsung during its DRAM price-fixing investigation and is acting for American Airlines in its opposition to a proposal by SkyTeam for antitrust immunity. For interviewees, the sheer volume of **Roxann Henry**'s caseload assures her prominence in this market. Responsible for advising on the Arch Coal litigation, other work includes representing Nestlé in virtually all of its acquisitions. Henry also specializes in consumer credit-related matters. Set against a background of expertise in the retail arena, **Christopher MacAvoy** brings "*finely tuned economic skills*" to mergers, government investigations and litigation involving suppliers, distributors and producers of grocery products, as well as trade associations. Peers would not hesitate to refer clients to **John Taladay**, admiring his "*excellent work and established presence.*" In addition to a quarter-back role in Oracle's investigation by the DOJ as a result of its attempted takeover of PeopleSoft, he is currently advising Inco on its pending acquisition of Falconbridge, valued at $11 billion. He is equally adept in media-related matters, having undertaken a large amount of work for Univision Communications in recent years.

**Clients/Work Highlights:** Verizon; Intel; Xerox; Rockwell Collins and Checkpoint Systems.

### O'Melveny & Myers LLP

See firm details p.336

**The Firm:** In the antitrust cosmos, "*the signs are great*" for this ambitious and progressive firm. Boasting a stellar reputation for matters with a litigation bent, the practice frequently presents "*an extremely strong front*" before grand juries in class actions and government investigations. It represented Triton Coal throughout the FTC's attempted block of its acquisition by Arch Coal, winning in a case that marked the first time in nearly 15 years that the government organization had lost an injunction outside the healthcare industry. Clients, ranging from domestic companies to large multinationals, are "*profoundly impressed*" by the expertise currently on display. This praise is in large part the consequence of Timothy Muris' appointment to the firm. His experience as chairman of the FTC has had a galvanizing effect on the practice, increasing its visibility and compass while bolstering its government connections. Although the group's aptitude for litigation tends to overshadow its merger and transaction profile, this has not prevented it from maintaining a steady stream of work in this department. Sources await with interest the eventual destination of this rapidly evolving practice.

**The Lawyers:** Former director of the FTC's bureau of competition, practice cochair **Richard Parker** (see p.537) has *"rolled up his sleeves and delved into his work"* since his return to private practice. Finely attuned to the calibrations of government, he is referred to by clients such as Triton Coal for his insight into the issues at stake when obtaining merger approval. A *"gregarious guy with solid litigation instincts,"* Parker is a formidable presence during investigations. *"One of the bright lights in terms of thinking about policy issues,"* **Timothy Muris'** (see p.533) *"top-level analytical skills"* and illustrious career in the areas of consumer protection, regulation and counseling has changed the face of the team. Another FTC alumnus, **Michael Antalics'** (see p.498) *"practical mind"* is well suited to a practice that, in continuation of his public sector heritage, focuses on price-fixing and cartel investigations.

**Clients/Work Highlights:** The group obtained clearance for Honeywell in its proposed merger with the UK-listed company, Novar – a move previously challenged by the EC. The firm's extensive antitrust client roster also includes Marriott; Fannie Mae; Degussa and Crompton.

## Weil, Gotshal & Manges LLP

See firm details p.1565

**The Firm:** This *"aggressive and distinctive"* group is capitalizing on its national reputation for antitrust to become a *"force with which to be reckoned"* in the DC merger market. Bolstered by the recent addition of Steven Newborn from Clifford Chance, all the signs indicate that Weil Gotshal is investing in this practice area as a major franchise for the firm, beefing up an already impressive array of services with specialist expertise. In addition to counseling and representing regulated and unregulated industries before the FTC and DOJ, the team is adept at handling litigation arising from government investigations. Its clientele spans every conceivable business sector, with attorneys advising pharmaceutical, computer, automobile and electronics companies and manufacturers. The firm's combination of *"impressive communication skills,"* experience and dedication bodes well for the future.

**The Lawyers:** Co-head of the global antitrust/competition practice, *"clever and savvy"* **Steven Newborn** (see p.535) cuts an impressive figure in the market. Noted by peers for his superlative merger review skills and steadfast temperament before the agencies, his practice also includes guiding clients through all forms of transaction-related litigation. All who encountered the *"smart and personable"* **Ann Malester** (see p.529) in her former position as deputy director of the FTC's bureau of competition hold her in extremely high esteem. Malester enjoys a reputation for making *"great decisions without dragging things out"* and tackling enforcement issues with a directness and assuredness born of experience. Observers are eager to see what she accomplishes in

private practice. *"Tenacious, with a nice courtroom presence,"* **James Egan** (see p.509) specializes in representing corporate clients in federal, state and administrative litigation arising from price-fixing allegations, boycotts and other restraints.

**Clients/Work Highlights:** Citibank; Hoffman-La Roche; Johnson & Johnson; Sherwin-Williams; The Sports Authority and Sun Chemical.

## WilmerHale

See firm details p.580

**The Firm:** This pragmatic and extremely competent team is small but perfectly formed, *"attracting a steady flow of highly visible work."* As evidence of this, peers draw attention to its impressive performance on behalf of telecom giant Verizon in obtaining merger clearance for its acquisition of MCI. In addition to its successful efforts in the media arena, which recently included acting as Sony's lead US counsel during its takeover of MGM, the firm also offers substantial hi-tech expertise. Team members are currently defending Philips in a class action filed on behalf of Chinese DVD manufacturers alleging that Philips, Sony and Pioneer Electronic's 3C patent pool contravenes US antitrust laws. The group has also embarked on major Section 2 litigation for Intel, which is currently involved in a lawsuit with AMD. Elsewhere, time-honored cartel and enforcement experience guarantees the practice a groundswell of tax and insurance-related work.

**The Lawyers:** *"One of the finest antitrust lawyers of his generation,"* **Douglas Melamed** (see p.532) led the team that acted for Verizon in obtaining clearance for its MCI acquisition. Involvement in such centerpiece merger work is typical of a practice with its roots in the DOJ, where – as deputy assistant attorney general in charge of the antitrust division – Melamed was responsible for merger investigations. Clients praise his continuing aptitude in this area while peers recognize his *"analytical supremacy."* A former deputy assistant attorney general for international enforcement in the DOJ's antitrust division, **William Kolasky's** (see p.524) time since leaving the government has been devoted to litigation arising from major acquisitions. Combining *"incredible knowledge"* with courtroom élan, he is applauded by sources for the judgment he displays before the agencies. He secured clearance for BAE Systems' $4.2 billion acquisition of United Defense Industries and played a pivotal role in the defense of Philips. Market veteran **Robert Bell** (see p.500) undertakes a wide variety of merger work, with a particular specialty in the defense arena. In the past year he has represented Akamai Technologies in its acquisition of Speedera.

**Clients/Work Highlights:** Regal Cinemas; Danaher; Powerwave Technologies; Skyworks Solutions; Thermo Electron and Fisher Scientific International.

## Boies, Schiller & Flexner

See firm details p.1520

**The Firm:** An authoritative presence in DC, this litigation boutique bears the distinctive stamp of its legendary progenitor, David Boies. As such, it offers expertise molded by far-reaching counseling and prosecution to clients drawn from the aviation and electronic industries, among others. While some interviewees express doubts concerning the extent of the practice, a group containing a former deputy assistant attorney general of the antitrust division is never going to be short of work. Correspondingly, partners at the firm have battled as lead or co-lead trial counsel in important matters including United States v Microsoft and United States v Northwest Airlines and Continental Airlines.

**The Lawyers:** Commentators agree that **Donald Flexner** (see p.512) is *"a force to be reckoned with."* His market reputation rests on his skill in the cartel and government investigation arena although he also handles merger reviews. *"Strategic and competent,"* his recent caseload includes defending a major domestic airline in a suit brought by the US administration.

**Clients/Work Highlights:** Additional clients range from EchoStar and DuPont to Del Monte Foods.

## Fried, Frank, Harris, Shriver & Jacobson LLP

See firm details p.1532

**The Firm:** This firm continues to deploy a range of some of the most well-established and respected attorneys in the market. Day-to-day engagement with the agencies guarantees the team a steady stream of high-profile work acting for major corporations and companies in connection with merger investigations. Undoubtedly the most prominent example from the past twelve months is the firm's representation of MGM Mirage in its acquisition of Mandalay Resort Group. Approved by the FTC in February 2005, this deal ensures that MGM Mirage now owns almost half of the casino resorts in Las Vegas. The group also advises Microsoft, most recently in connection with its acquisition of ContentGuard. Cross-jurisdictional matters are dealt with by lawyers in DC liaising with colleagues in London, Paris and Frankfurt. Closer to home, comprehensive support is in evidence from colleagues in the litigation department who assist with complex processes such as grand jury investigations.

**The Lawyers:** **Rick Rule's** (see p.543) rich and varied career at the DOJ has translated into a *"free-standing reputation"* for technical excellence and business perspicacity. His most recent matters include acting as lead counsel to MGM Mirage during its Mandalay acquisition. Colleague **Deborah Garza** (see p.514) once deputized for Rule at the DOJ, and was appointed in 2004 by President Bush to the prized role of chair to a 12-member antitrust modernization commission.

**Clients/Work Highlights:** The group represented Goldman Sachs in its acquisition of Euramax International, including notification of the transaction to the German antitrust authority. The firm's clientele in this arena also includes Canadian Automobile Dealers Association; Bacardi-Martini; Peabody Coal; IPC; Merck and US Airways.

## King & Spalding LLP
See firm details p.1933

**The Firm:** King & Spalding's reputation in the antitrust market is founded on widely acknowledged excellence in the telecom and pharmaceutical industries. Eight partners based in DC represent companies from these sectors in class actions and multidistrict litigation involving monopolization allegations, price-fixing and trade restraints. For example, the group acted for major client Sprint in a spree of multimillion-dollar acquisitions, including Nextel, US Unwired, Gulf Coast Wireless and IWO Holdings. It has also turned its hand to prosecutions connected with the insurance business, defending RLI and its subsidiaries in a lawsuit filed in New Jersey alleging antitrust, and RICO violations as a consequence of artificially inflated coverage premiums. Interviewees anticipate that the hiring of Jim Griffin, former deputy assistant attorney general responsible for the antitrust division's criminal investigations, will push the firm into new areas of expertise and raise its profile considerably.

**The Lawyers:** The "*impressively experienced*" **Kevin Sullivan** (see p.549) divides his time between the firm's DC and London offices. As well as spearheading the RLI matter alongside Grace Rodriquez, he defended Mylan Laboratories in a three-week jury trial in DC arising from the alleged violation of an exclusive supply agreement. Sullivan also offers advice on telecom issues.

**Clients/Work Highlights:** The firm is engaged in a number of civil cartel actions, including representing UCB in federal and state actions relating to the sale of vitamins. Other clients include Acuity Brands; Beazer Homes; Coca-Cola; Federal Home Loan Mortgage; ING Clarion; Miller Brewing and Roper Industries.

## Morgan, Lewis & Bockius LLP
See firm details p.1758

**The Firm:** Peers have considerable respect for this firm's litigious muscle, drawing researchers' attention to the sophistication of its cartel and merger enforcement work. The team acts for companies facing government investigations, large damage actions and mergers implicating regulatory systems across the globe. In the past year, attorneys have represented a major corporation in a price-fixing and bid-rigging grand jury investigation touching on the transportation, food products and chemical industries. The group's easy conversance with such sensitive situations was highlighted once more by its involvement in an inquiry into boycott and bid-rigging allegations connected with US government contracts.

**The Lawyers:** "*One of the best there is*" for cartel investigations and prosecutions, **Donald Klawiter** (see p.523) has served as international coordinating counsel in multijurisdictional proceedings stemming

from pharmaceutical, automotive, food and chemical issues. His recent appointment as chair of the ABA's section of antitrust law consolidates his market prominence. Few match **Willard Tom** (see p.551) for his "*crisp, succinct and illuminating*" writing, and his ability to "*get to the heart of the matter.*" A former editorial chair of the ABA's antitrust reference work, Tom's FTC background is a further bonus for clients.

**Clients/Work Highlights:** As well as a variety of US and non-US senior executives caught up in government investigations, the firm's clientele includes Jungbunzlauer and Degussa.

## Skadden, Arps, Slate, Meagher & Flom LLP & Affiliates
See firm details p.1557

**The Firm:** A firm that has always benefited from "*a fantastic corporate platform*" continues to impress market observers with the quality of its merger and acquisition antitrust work: it displays an enviable knack of assigning to deals "*well-blooded individuals who are highly attuned to the company dynamics of their clients.*" The 45-strong practice, operating primarily out of DC and New York, is involved in eye-catching matters, ranging from overseeing the America West Airlines/US Airways merger to advising on the planned acquisition by Exelon of Public Service Enterprise Group – a move that would create the largest electric utility in the USA. Although the team's stellar presentation in this arena tends to overshadow its endeavors in litigation defense, of late it has represented a substantial number of companies embroiled in cartel investigations and enforcement actions. Clear lines of communication with the firm's Brussels office provide a valuable European dimension to this well-established and highly competent group.

**The Lawyers:** **John Nannes** (see p.534) adopts a meticulous and conscientious approach to antitrust matters that grants him "*a good command of the area.*" In the past twelve months, he has turned his attention toward complex cartel investigation work. He advised on the application for antitrust immunity filed by members of the SkyTeam alliance in the wake of the KLM-Air France merger. Sources concur that **Benjamin Crisman** (see p.507) is "*yin to Nannes' yang – together they provide the perfect blend of expertise.*" He provides BHP Billiton with regulatory advice and risk assessment and was successful recently in ending an investigation initiated by the EU and US administrations. Crisman "*is the first person to put on his hard hat and go into the mine,*" interviewees report.

**Clients/Work Highlights:** The firm's vast clientele includes JPMorgan Chase, News Corporation and Entergy.

## White & Case LLP
See firm details p.1566

**The Firm:** This group draws praise for its "*insight into the mindset of the DOJ.*" As befits a firm with universally acknowledged global clout, the team typically represents European companies with US interests. For instance, it acted for Stolt-Nielsen in a

matter that culminated in the Eastern District Court of Pennsylvania, enjoining the antitrust division from indicting or prosecuting Stolt-Nielsen for any violations of the Sherman Act. As this demonstrates, White & Case is no stranger to trying cases against the government and its caseload during the past twelve months provides further testimony. In 2001, the FTC alleged that the Upsher-Smith/Schering settlement violated US antitrust laws, arguing that a $60 million payment from Schering was intended to persuade Upsher-Smith Laboratories to delay the launch of its generic equivalent to Schering's brand-name drug. This past year, attorneys representing Upsher-Smith obtained a judgment from the Eleventh Circuit that there was no evidentiary basis for this complaint. As the firm continues to advance into the hotly contested branded products arena, it seems set for ever-increasing prominence in the febrile antitrust market.

**The Lawyers:** Global head of antitrust **Mark Gidley** (see p.515) received particular acclaim for being "*in tune with enforcement trends for merger activity. He knows where the landmines are.*" He co-lead on both the Stolt-Nielsen and Upsher-Smith cases.

**Clients/Work Highlights:** Comcast; Gap; Houghton Mifflin; KPN; Kos Pharmaceuticals; OSRAM SYLVANIA and Watts Water Technologies.

## Band 5

## Crowell & Moring LLP
See firm details p.564

**The Firm:** This team regularly defends corporations against domestic and international cartel allegations. The DC group in particular offers "*top-notch*" counsel, demonstrating a "*real-world focus*" and business pragmatism that wins acolytes throughout the market. It acted for a Fortune 100 company in two related investigations into allegations of worldwide collusion connected with a joint venture enterprise, and negotiated settlements with the DOJ and civil plaintiffs to bring the second matter to a swift conclusion. The team also undertakes significant merger work characterized by its visibility in the telecom industry, such as acting as lead counsel to SBC throughout the review of its $16 billion acquisition of AT&T. The team has also made an impressive showing in the healthcare sector.

**The Lawyers:** One of "*the pillars of the firm,*" **Randolph Smith** (see p.547) adopts an "*analytically rigorous*" approach to business counseling, carving a sizable niche in the chemical and hi-tech arenas.

**Clients/Work Highlights:** Reed Elsevier; United Technologies; Yamaha Corporation of America; Humana; Aetna; Sagamore Health Network; Bluefield Regional Medical Center; Health Net and Harvard Pilgrim healthcare.

## Freshfields Bruckhaus Deringer LLP

**The Firm:** A relatively recent entrant to the formidable US antitrust market. Although small, it has bolstered its brand name by adding ex-agency heavyweights to its ranks and offering clients invaluable insight into the mechanism of the EC as it affects global competition law. Attorneys handle a score of second request proceedings, including assisting Alcan in its bid for Pechiney.

**The Lawyers:** **Paul Yde** brings to the table merger and enforcement expertise accumulated during his tenure as counsel to two FTC commissioners and, latterly, as cochair of Vinson & Elkin's antitrust practice. **MJ Moltenbrey**'s origins in the DOJ, where she served as the director of civil nonmerger enforcement, stand her in good stead with clients. **Bob Schlossberg** advises clients drawn from the chemical, medical device, pharmaceutical and transportation industries.

**Clients/Work Highlights:** Alcan; Anheuser-Busch; ArcLight Capital Partners; Continental AG; Duke Energy Fields Services; Lufthansa Cargo; Monsanto and The Thompson Corporation.

## Heller Ehrman LLP

See firm details p.329

**The Firm:** Deemed by its competitors to "*have had a great year,*" this firm has made its mark nationally as well as in DC. With highly robust sister offices in New York and San Francisco, it is able to provide an integrated service to its roster of high-flying clients. The likes of Microsoft, Visa and 3M have all entrusted some of their largest and most complex matters to a team "*capable of handling anything thrown at it.*" Its service is a comprehensive one encompassing all matters relating to mergers, government investigations and private litigation.

**The Lawyers:** **Marc Schildkraut** (see p.545) is credited by many with putting the firm "*on the map*" in 2005. Cochair of the antitrust and trade regulation practice group, he focuses on mergers, civil investigations and litigation. Following a "*deeply successful*" period at Howrey, sources are certain that he will be a great business generator for his new firm.

**Clients/Work Highlights:** Visa; Microsoft; Philip Morris and Mylan Pharmaceuticals.

## Kirkland & Ellis LLP

See firm details p.875

**The Firm:** A firm operating an "*active and well-organized practice*" in DC, Kirkland may not have achieved a level of market penetration commensurate with its profile elsewhere. Despite this, representation of numerous public companies and private equity firms ensures that the group regularly oversees some of the most complex mergers in the market. It has handled hundreds of Hart-Scott-Rodino filings and represented Concord EFS before the FTC during its $7.1 billion acquisition by First Data. Kirkland's true forte, however, is "*intelligent aggressiveness*" in litigious circumstances. Recently, the team has battled numerous cartel allegations while continuing to play a pivotal role in the ongoing Infineon Technologies DRAM litigation. It

extends the skills it has cultivated in this capacity to the developing of industry-specific compliance programs intended to offset or minimize the potential prosecution of its clientele.

**The Lawyers:** In charge of the antitrust competitive law group, and exemplifying the best qualities of his firm, the "*tough and highly focused*" **Tefft Smith** (see p.547) "*spends time absorbing the facts of the case and deploying them to devastating effect*" in criminal, civil, pricing and distribution litigation. He represented Dow Chemical in a prosecution arising from its joint venture with DuPont, which had entered into a unit facing prosecution for price-fixing. DuPont agreed to accept full responsibility for all antitrust liabilities arising from this prior arrangement.

**Clients/Work Highlights:** BP; Allstate; SC Johnson; Bayer; Chiquita Brands International and Coors Brewing Co.

## Latham & Watkins LLP

**The Firm:** Observers agree that the addition of Margaret 'Peggy' Zwisler has put Latham & Watkins firmly on the map where DC antitrust matters are concerned. Making the most of a substantial global footprint and an "*utterly superb*" white-collar practice, the newly expanded team offers a combination of merger review counseling and class action defense to a rich vein of domestic and international clients. The team is representing Ford in more than 80 federal and state court lawsuits alleging that a raft of US automotive companies colluded with dealer associations to restrict the import of vehicles from Canada. So far, the group has been successful in winning a motion to dismiss national class federal claims. Members also draw on the firm's supraregional experience to provide major corporations and companies such as Oracle with comprehensive advice on antitrust-related competition issues.

**The Lawyers:** Howrey's loss is Latham's gain with **Margaret Zwisler** attracting accolades praising her "*level of talent,*" with one interviewee expressing the belief that "*there is nothing she can't do.*" Zwisler has represented companies before state and federal courts in antitrust actions relating to motor vehicles, chemicals, pharmaceuticals and tobacco. By way of example, she is representing UST, the manufacturer of Skoal and Copenhagen snuff, in a series of class actions stemming from its loss of more than $1 billion to a competitor in a case involving allegations that UST had monopolized the market for smokeless tobacco. **Tad Lipsky** is a "*quirky and extremely smart guy*" who receives universal recognition and commendation for his efforts to restructure and synchronize global antitrust enforcement.

**Clients/Work Highlights:** The firm is representing home-building products conglomerate Masco in class actions arising from the allegation that it arranged a conspiracy with its supplier of insulation materials to fix the price leveled at independent contractors for the same products.

## Mayer, Brown, Rowe & Maw LLP

See firm details p.876

**The Firm:** Mayer, Brown has a long heritage in this arena. While some question the longevity of the practice beyond its current generation of high-profile antitrust attorneys, it is clear that this is not a debate for the near future. The team's size and level of expertise equips it for mergers and investigations of considerable magnitude. It was lead counsel to Fresenius Medical Care in its $4 billion acquisition of the Renal Care Group and represented Dow in the $7 billion sale of Marion Merrill Dow to Hoechst. Its success rate in these and similar matters is greatly aided by a firm ethos that stresses the importance of interdepartmental collaboration. Group members regularly solicit the advice of colleagues in IP, trade access, healthcare regulation, M&A and insurance coverage. Clients assert that in IT-related antitrust matters, the firm is "*head of the class*" when it comes to electronic discovery.

**The Lawyers:** The market abounds with praise for **Richard Favretto** (see p.511). A veteran of the DOJ's antitrust division, he combines years of experience of antitrust and trade regulation issues, including grand jury investigations and criminal litigation, with an equanimity and intelligence that make him a "*pleasure to deal with.*" Head of the practice **Robert Bloch** (see p.502) is a respected presence in antitrust circles. In addition to taking the lead in the Fresenius Medical Care and Marion Merrill Dow cases, he counseled Aetna in its acquisitions of US Healthcare and Prudential.

**Clients/Work Highlights:** Other clients include Bertelsmann, ETI (Explosives Technology International) and Cargill.

## McDermott Will & Emery

See firm details p.878

**The Firm:** "*Responsive and competent,*" the team at McDermott receives applause for an enviable ability to translate the more esoteric aspects of antitrust law into "*real world advice.*" Centered in Washington, the practice comprises partners who have held senior positions in the DOJ, FTC and state attorney general's offices. Peers note the firm's long-standing relationship with major technology company Lockheed Martin and concede that it attracts a high volume of merger and litigation work. As well as overseeing Blackboard's merger with WebCT, the group is involved in a suit brought by Johnson & Johnson connected with the lawfulness of bundled discounts. According to one interviewee "*quality pervades the practice.*"

**The Lawyers:** **Joseph Winterscheid** (see p.556) is a "*master at applying legal concepts to everyday activities.*" While observers heartily commend him for the "*depth of knowledge*" he demonstrates in matters relating to pricing and distribution practices, they reserve special praise for his performance on the international stage: global merger policy has changed a lot in the past year, and his work for the International Competition Network (ICN) makes him an important person in this process. He specializes in advising clients on US and EU pre-merger notification requirements. Head of the regulation and government affairs department and antitrust and competition practice group, **Raymond Jacobsen** (see p.520) is "*excellent at shepherding mergers through the system.*" Transactional work is his specialty, sources report; however, his practice has also recently included preparing the US Supreme Court brief for the Chamber of Commerce in Dagher v Texaco and Shell.

**Clients/Work Highlights:** Alliant Techsystems; Morton Salt; Foundation Coal; Orica and Health Management Associates.

## Paul, Weiss, Rifkind, Wharton & Garrison

See firm details p.1548

**The Firm:** The DC antitrust group's brisk expansion in recent years ensures greater market profile for the team, with observers confident that the firm will be a significant presence in the very near future. The practice, which now boasts three antitrust specialists with FTC and economics backgrounds, offers "*extremely thorough, detailed and conscientious work*" to many of the world's largest companies. As well as conducting high-profile transactions for clients such as Time Warner, the team continues to represent MasterCard in a variety of matters. For example, it has obtained dismissals in 15 states of indirect purchaser suits alleging that stores required to accept MasterCard and Visa debit as well as credit cards carried higher transaction costs in the form of greater product prices. The team was also involved in

the FTC's investigation of the American Tower/SpectraSite union.

**The Lawyers:** One year in and **Kenneth Gallo**'s (see p.514) appointment as managing partner of the DC office is paying dividends for the firm. Highly respected by his peers, his recent caseload included defending MasterCard in a class action brought by more than four million retailers arising from illegal tying arrangement allegations. Following the cessation of his FTC recusal, cochair of the practice **Joseph Simons** (see p.546) is free to spread his wings in the antitrust environment. His former role as director of the bureau of competition has led to eminent roles in transactions such as the AT&T Wireless merger, where he was selected as management trustee for the deal. Peers observe that he is thriving in his role.

**Clients/Work Highlights:** ACNielsen; Dun & Bradstreet; IMS Health; Siemens and Becton Dickinson.

## Other Notable Practitioners

The mid-2005 migration of **Steven Sunshine** (see p.549) and his team from Shearman & Sterling LLP to Cadwalader, Wickersham & Taft LLP is expected to raise the latter's game considerably by virtue of the "*stellar legal talent*" it has acquired. Clients rhapsodize about Sunshine's ability to "*provide creative solutions to difficult problems*" and assert that he is, invariably, "*right on the money.*" **Paul Denis** (see p.508) joined Dechert LLP from Swidler Berlin Shereff Friedman LLP. Principal draftsman of the DOJ and FTC's horizontal merger guidelines, he brings

with him a "*really strong government practice*" that, sources assert, will add texture and depth to a firm already known for its general litigation skills. Interviewees agree that for pre-clearance work Vinson & Elkin LLP's **Neil Imus** (see p.520) demonstrates a "*good sense of how to deal with the regulators.*" He tailors his practice to reflect the firm's superlative M&A department and boasts expertise in the energy market. **Mark Popofsky** (see p.539) at Kaye Scholer LLP is a widely recognized figure from the DOJ's antitrust division, where he served as senior counsel to the assistant attorney general. As well as representing parties in mergers, he assists clients with Internet privacy policy issues and resolves technology-related antitrust issues.

# BANKRUPTCY/RESTRUCTURING

| Bankruptcy/Restructuring Leading Firms | |
|---|---|
| **1** | ARNOLD & PORTER LLP *Washington, DC* |
| | ORRICK *Washington, DC* |
| | WILMERHALE *Washington, DC* |
| **2** | AKIN GUMP *Washington, DC* |
| | COVINGTON & BURLING *Washington, DC* |
| | DICKSTEIN SHAPIRO *Washington, DC* |
| **3** | ARENT FOX PLLC *Washington, DC* |
| | HOGAN & HARTSON LLP *Washington, DC* |
| | WHITE & CASE LLP *Washington, DC* |
| | ZUCKERMAN SPAEDER LLP *Washington, DC* |

## Band 1

## Arnold & Porter LLP

See firm details p.560

**The Firm:** A real force in the DC bankruptcy and restructuring market, this weighty practice represents debtors, unsecured creditors' committees and asset purchasers. Following on from its "*excellent job*" in the second US Airways Chapter 11 filing, it has developed a particular expertise in airline-related cases and has picked up some enviable clients such as Northwest Airlines and Gate Gourmet. It also

continues to represent the Office of the People's Counsel in the Mirant case. Clients praised the practice for its "*substance, client responsiveness and great strategic skills.*"

**The Lawyers:** Splitting his time between DC and Denver, head of the group **Brian Leitch** (see p.525) is "*good at coming up with creative, cost-effective solutions.*" He has spent much of his year on the US Airways case but generally has a varied practice attending to clients who value his "*low ego, cooperative approach.*" The "*totally brilliant*" **Daniel Lewis** (see p.526) combines a valuable consultancy role with his fee-earning work and is part of a team that includes **Michael Bernstein** (see p.501). Bernstein continues to build on an already established reputation and is praised by clients for his "*ability to assess risks in a meaningful way and address the tribunal in a strong and tenacious manner.*"

**Clients/Work Highlights:** Northwest Airlines; Perseus Group; Gate Gourmet; Major League Baseball; Office of the People's Counsel; American Capital and Texas Pacific Group.

## Orrick, Herrington & Sutcliffe LLP

See firm details p.337

**The Firm:** With the move of Roger Frankel and his entire bankruptcy team from Swidler Berlin in early

2006, this firm has now become a force in the DC market. The group, recognized as the "*deans of the bankruptcy arena,*" has substantial expertise in asbestos-related cases, an area in which it has enjoyed marked growth in the past year. It has also been carving a niche for itself representing nondebtor parties in Chapter 11 proceedings. For example, it has involved itself in the second US Airways reorganization where it has represented a major creditor. Other notable highlights include acting for claimants in the Combustion Engineering, WR Grace and Congoleum cases. The firm has also had several notable victories in representing Pepco in the Mirant case.

**The Lawyers:** Heading the group is the "*smart, effective and creative*" **Roger Frankel** (see p.513), "*a man you'd call if you had a major problem.*" He is bolstered by a "*strong supporting cast*" that includes "*talented right-hand man*" **Richard Wyron** (see p.556). An experienced partner, Wyron spends much of his time on asbestos-related matters.

**Clients/Work Highlights:** Pepco and Cooper Industries rank among a clientele that includes debtors, indenture trustees, secured and unsecured creditors, and banks and other financial institutions.

| Bankruptcy/Restructuring |
| --- |
| Leading Individuals |

**Senior Statesman**

LEWIS Daniel *Arnold & Porter LLP*

[1] FRANKEL Roger *Orrick, Herrington & Sutcliffe*

PERLSTEIN William *WilmerHale*

[2] BAXTER Michael *Covington & Burling*

KUNEY David *Sidley Austin LLP*

LEITCH Brian *Arnold & Porter LLP*

LITT Daniel *Dickstein Shapiro*

SAMORAJCZYK Stanley *Akin Gump*

WYRON Richard *Orrick, Herrington & Sutcliffe*

[3] ALBERTS Sam *White & Case LLP*

BERNSTEIN Michael *Arnold & Porter LLP*

BRAN Paul *Dickstein Shapiro*

DOLAN Edward *Hogan & Hartson LLP*

DOWD Mary *Arent Fox PLLC*

GOLDBLATT Craig *WilmerHale*

GOLDSTEIN Bruce *Zuckerman Spaeder LLP*

PLEVIN Mark *Crowell & Moring LLP*

**Up-and-coming individuals**

AUERBACH Dennis *Covington & Burling*

## WilmerHale

See firm details p.580

**The Firm:** The firm boasts a diverse practice that benefits from a strong New York presence. It covers the whole bankruptcy spectrum, representing clients ranging from large commercial lenders and bondholders to companies seeking restructuring assistance. It continues to advise Kmart in post-confirmation bankruptcy matters and acted as debtors' counsel in the KB Toys case. In common with many of the other firms in this area, it is handling a large amount of mass tort asbestos work. For instance, it is acting as national bankruptcy counsel for The Hartford in connection with its mass tort-related liabilities.

**The Lawyers:** Joint managing partner **Bill Perlstein** (see p.538) has "*built a prominent practice*" and, although no longer as involved in day-to-day bankruptcy cases as he was, remains a respected and totemic figure. Able to handle the most complex of cases, he "*interfaces with the court and any other parties in a case extraordinarily effectively.*" Partner **Craig Goldblatt** (see p.515) is "*skillful, creative and able to advise on unique and difficult issues.*" He is currently involved in representing the Pension Benefit Guaranty Corporation in the Northwest Airlines bankruptcy.

**Clients/Work Highlights:** Citibank; The Hartford; Kmart; KB Toys; Lucent Technologies and Verizon.

## Band 2

### Akin Gump Strauss Hauer & Feld LLP

See firm details p.559

**The Firm:** Part of "*an excellent firm with a nationwide practice,*" the team here capitalizes on its relationship with a strong New York office. It is known particularly for its representation of formal and informal creditors' committees; for example, it is representing the committee in the Delta Air Lines Chapter 11 filing. The firm has been involved in many of the major recent bankruptcy cases including Federal-Mogul, Owens Corning and Armstrong World Industries, and this year has focused particularly on the retail and healthcare sectors. It is also noted for its international expertise.

**The Lawyers:** "*There's not a more respected attorney in town*" than head of the group **Stanley Samorajczyk** (see p.544). Recognized by the market as an experienced strategist with a facilitative approach, clients praised his business judgment and "*ability to find solutions that are not readily evident.*"

**Clients/Work Highlights:** The NFL, Allstate and Starbucks form just part of a client list that includes major insurance companies, debtors and purchasers of debt or assets of financially distressed companies, and official and unofficial committees of creditors.

### Covington & Burling

See firm details p.563

**The Firm:** This "*highly ethical and sophisticated*" practice continues to be occupied with high-profile creditor work such as the WorldCom and Armstrong World Industries cases. It has also acted in the second US Airways Chapter 11 filing where it represented one of the major creditors. Asbestos-related matters form a large part of the team's workload and it recently represented the debtor in the Owens Corning case, appearing as special insurance counsel. This involved obtaining insurance coverage for asbestos, personal injury and property damage claims. Increasingly, the team is advising on IP matters, including the structuring of license agreements in order to protect clients in case of bankruptcy.

**The Lawyers:** "*Straight shooter*" **Michael Baxter** (see p.500) is a "*deal-oriented lawyer,*" admired by clients for his "*reasonable style.*" Recognized for raising the firm's profile and developing the practice into a truly national one, he is respected as "*a man of his word who is a pleasure to deal with.*" **Dennis Auerbach** (see p.498) is viewed as an "*in the trenches litigator*" who adds value to the practice with his "*forceful and smart*" manner.

**Clients/Work Highlights:** The firm's clientele includes debtors, creditors and official committees in bankruptcy cases.

### Dickstein Shapiro Morin & Oshinsky LLP

See firm details p.565

**The Firm:** Primarily a creditors' practice, the firm has gained particular recognition for its "*aggressive litigation skills in bankruptcy-related issues.*" Work includes representing lenders' interests in bankruptcy proceedings, asset purchases from distressed companies and some debtor work. Recent highlights include representing the Maryland Public Service Commission in the Mirant case. The practice has a particular focus on IP and energy.

**The Lawyers:** Chair of the group **Daniel Litt** (see p.527) impressed clients with his "*mind-boggling*" command of what he does." A strong litigator with a particular skill for presenting cases to the judiciary, clients particularly liked "*his ability to take the Bankruptcy Code and apply it to the business issues in a case.*" Also making a name for himself as a litigator, "*rising star*" **Paul Bran** (see p.503) is an "*energetic attorney who has great mental horsepower.*"

**Clients/Work Highlights:** AT&T and Pepco are just two examples of a client base rich in lenders, creditors' committees and debtors.

## Band 3

### Arent Fox PLLC

**The Firm:** This excellent practice draws on manpower from both the firm's DC and New York offices. The team's diverse clientele includes committees, liquidating trustees and defendants in massive preference litigation. It is currently representing bondholders in the Delta Air Lines, United Airlines and ATA Airlines cases and has acted for a number of entities in the Enron case. The firm has niche expertise in the construction industry and has recently undertaken two large cases in this field in DC and Florida respectively.

**The Lawyers:** **Mary Jo Dowd** (see p.509) is a "*wonderful person and a talented, assertive bankruptcy litigator.*" Credited with raising the firm's profile in DC, she is seen to have particular expertise in the real estate, construction and retail sectors.

**Clients/Work Highlights:** The firm acts on behalf of creditors' committees, debtors, indenture trustees, bondholders and noteholders in large bankruptcy cases.

### Hogan & Hartson LLP

See firm details p.568

**The Firm:** This solid practice concentrates on representing secured and unsecured creditors and asset purchasers. Especially experienced in the airline, Internet and telecom sectors, it has been involved in most of the major bankruptcy filings in these areas including the Delta Air Lines, United Airlines, US Airways and WorldCom cases. The team handles a lot of international work, a notable example being its representation of the Commission of the EU in defending the pre-petition antitrust award levied against the Carbide/Graphite Group. It has also been active in a number of cross-border IP-related cases.

**The Lawyers:** "*A real benefit to the Bar,*" partner **Edward Dolan** (see p.508) was praised by clients for being "*easy to work with and able to speak in layman's terms.*" He is currently involved with the representation of AEP with regards to Enron issues.

**Clients/Work Highlights:** Airlines Clearing House; LCC International; Umicore and WilTel Communications.

### White & Case LLP

See firm details p.1566

**The Firm:** This "*excellent group*" continues to grow both its national and international practice and has expanded its core bankruptcy team accordingly. It focuses on representation of creditors' committees and is counsel to that for MCSi Inc and several domestic affiliates. It has also been representing Comcast in a series of lawsuits alleging Bankruptcy Code violations, and has acted as primary bankruptcy counsel for Mirant in Chapter 11 cases pending in northern Texas. Close relationships with other offices allow it to "*really come across as an international firm.*"

**The Lawyers:** Practice head **Sam Alberts** (see p.497) is "*thorough and tenacious with a capacity for adapting to unusual circumstances.*" Interviewees appreciated the fact that he "*takes every opportunity to improve his clients' position and never takes on an engagement half-heartedly.*" Alberts is particularly known for his expertise in the healthcare industry. **Clients/Work Highlights:** ANZ; Bank of New York; Comcast; Commerzbank; DCHC Liquidating Trust; Deutsche Bank, IFC; Grupo IMSA; JPMorgan Chase; Mirant; Royal Bank of Canada and Sallie Mae.

## Zuckerman Spaeder LLP

**The Firm:** This "*terrific*" small practice has more of a DC than a national focus, but nevertheless enjoys a strong reputation among its rivals. It primarily does debtor business work, although it does also handle some creditor work. Lately, it has trended toward representing liquidating trusts in the larger bankruptcy cases.

**The Lawyers:** **Bruce Goldstein** is an "*excellent lawyer*" with a long-standing reputation for his expertise in transactional work.

### Other Notable Practitioners

"*One of the leading bankruptcy litigators in DC,*" the "*intellectual*" **David Kuney** (see p.524) at Sidley Austin LLP continues to be heavily involved in the Enron litigation. Other clients include the American Red Cross and St. Paul Travelers. Praised by market observers for his expertise in insurance and bankruptcy, the "*articulate and knowledgeable*" **Mark Plevin** (see p.539) at Crowell & Moring LLP is best known for his asbestos-related and other mass tort work. Clients were particularly impressed by his "*creative approach to litigation.*" New additions to his firm's client roster include Liberty Mutual.

# CONSTRUCTION

## Band 1

### Thelen Reid & Priest LLP
See firm details p.342

**The Firm:** Thelen Reid & Priest LLP preserves its position as outright leader, along with its renowned vigor on both national and international fronts in the construction, infrastructure and engineering arenas. After two years of being affiliated with the UK-based firm Pinsent Masons, the operation is turning its sights to South-East Asia with a view to consolidating its already formidable profile in the USA. Boasting a strong team of 24 lawyers in DC, the "*impressive*" practice covers a plethora of construction issues. Its litigation prowess is perceived as the mainstay – "*it has the best construction lawyers in the country and they like to fight*" – and members of the firm have acted on behalf of contractors in claims relating to baseball stadiums, power plants and residential projects. However, the team advises on a range of matters, from insurance coverage issues to international arbitration proceedings.

**The Lawyers:** The "*extremely knowledgeable and talented*" **Andrew Ness** (see p.534) commands much respect among contemporaries. Alongside fulfilling his duties as managing partner, he has sustained a strong reputation in major national and international infrastructure projects, as well as environmental remediation matters. He is lauded for "*his adroitness in getting cases resolved and his excellent style.*" **Michael Jaffe** (see p.520) has established a reputation for himself as a "*brilliant litigator who takes no prisoners.*" He was instrumental in a recent wetlands remediation case in which the firm was involved, and also represented the suppliers, Metso Panelboard, at the ICC in Singapore in a case centering on rescission and contractual damage claims. A "*tremendous practitioner who can aggressively protect her clients' interests when required,*" **Barbara Werther**'s (see p.554) recent performances have propelled her up the rankings. She is best known for representing general contractors in sophisticated commercial litigation and US government claims. A highlight for Werther was reaching an $8 million settlement during a mediation pertaining to the construction of an office complex.

**Clients/Work Highlights:** Clark Construction Group; Centex Construction; Hunt Construction Group; Structure Tone and Foster Wheeler Environmental.

**Band 2**

### Holland & Knight LLP
See firm details p.1534

**The Firm:** Infrastructure, maritime and power plant construction matters are where the firm is considered to excel. Sources agreed that advising on associated government contracts is a particular forte for the outfit. The breadth and depth of its practice was further bolstered by the recent expansion of its ranks following new arrivals. Clients were impressed not only by the "*responsive and time-conscious*" approach of the firm's lawyers, but also noted their cost-effective delivery. As one source remarked: "*They sail through the issues.*"

**The Lawyers:** Practice head **Andrew Stephenson** (see p.548) delivers excellent advice to an array of clients, and is admired for his persistence. As one client remarked: "*I respect him. Rather than using a scorched earth approach, he tries hard to find ways of working in the best interest of the client.*" While he is experienced at both national and international levels, Stephenson is particularly adept in the contract administration and dispute resolution fields. His recent highlights include advising on the construction of the $100 million IMF headquarters in Washington, DC. **Stephen Shapiro** (see p.545) is newly ranked this year. Interviewees attribute his enhanced profile to important appearances in the litigation arena and praise his assiduous style: "*He goes above and beyond the call of duty,*" said one client.

**Clients/Work Highlights:** The firm's clientele also spans research institutes, industrial architects, engineers and power organizations.

### Peckar, Abramson, Bastianelli & Kelley
See firm details p.1549

**The Firm:** There is strong consensus that, since the two firms involved have already established outstanding niche practices in their respective states, the merger between Bastianelli, Brown & Kelley and the New York-based Peckar & Abrahamson in July

2005 has created a "*high caliber*" construction outfit. A team of ten "*trustworthy and responsive*" lawyers handles a blend of government contract and construction matters in areas such as the power and highway sectors, with construction litigation having come to the fore of late. That a high proportion of the firm's lawyers have government experience is considered a major boon, as it means the firm can provide unique strategic insight when representing contractors in government contract claims. Clients appreciate the group's "*efficiency; its members understand the issues at play in a given case instantly.*"

**The Lawyers:** **Adrian Bastianelli** (see p.499) possesses a "*stellar*" reputation in terms of dispute resolution, whether it be arbitration, other forms of alternative dispute resolution or traditional litigation. While clients credited him with a "*wonderfully persuasive*" demeanor, he came in for praise among peers for his masterful performances in mediation. Recent highlights include his involvement in settling a large arbitration relating to a power plant, where over $50 million was at stake.

**Clients/Work Highlights:** The firm regularly advises contractors, subcontractors, engineers, architects, developers and financial institutions and sureties.

## Seyfarth Shaw LLP
See firm details p.882

**The Firm:** The firm's "*significant*" DC team operates at the hub of this nationwide operation and covers a variety of issues, ranging from the litigious to the contractual. Dispute resolution remains a forte, and members of the firm recently represented an engineer in a dispute concerning the construction of water purification facilities. Besides handling major projects such as the Pentagon renovations, the firm has proved especially popular with stadium contractors, having worked on the construction of the Gillette Stadium outside Boston, Pittsburgh's PNC Park, Chicago's Soldier Field, Lane Stadium in Virginia, and FedEx Field outside Washington, DC. Both peers and clients alike commended the "*first-rate practice*" for its "*depth and capability.*"

**The Lawyers:** Managing partner **Richard Preston** is highly regarded in international construction dispute circles. He thrives in the arbitration arena, where he wins plaudits for his winning style: "*There is real substance to his arguments. There's not the posturing that you see in a lot of people; no screaming or yelling. He has finesse and simply exudes credibility.*" Indeed, he proved indispensable in a large commercial arbitration against the Singapore government by a US entity, relating to the building of a waste treatment plant. A "*good supporting cast*" includes **Bennett Greenberg**, a newcomer to the table, whose advocacy skills have also been remarked upon: "*He is extremely skilled at weaving through the legalities.*"

**Clients/Work Highlights:** Major contractors, engineers, architects and owners form the base of the team's clientele.

## Band 3

### DLA Piper Rudnick Gray Cary US LLP
See firm details p.870

**The Firm:** Interviewees especially rate the DC construction group for its expertise on government contracts and litigation. Its practice dovetails nicely with the firm's market-leading real estate practice. Local and national issues are the mainstay for the practice but the operation's UK arm provides a springboard for the firm when it comes to capturing deals with an international dimension. While a healthy diet of stadium and infrastructure-linked projects in the USA has sustained the outfit's profile, the team also recently advised on construction projects in Iraq.

**The Lawyers:** The "*focused*" **Larry Harris** (see p.518) was identified as the driving force behind the practice, and is considered to have earned the firm considerable kudos in the field. He is held in particularly high regard for his transactional expertise, and recently advised on an $80 million utility plant deal. However, since it is "*his people skills that set him apart,*" Harris is just as well suited to litigation and arbitration settings, and he recently defended a telecom company against several multimillion-dollar claims.

**Clients/Work Highlights:** Clients include domestic and international owners, contractors, subcontractors and lenders.

### Gibson, Dunn & Crutcher LLP
See firm details p.328

**The Firm:** Its comparatively small DC construction practice benefits from a blue-chip client base that befits the firm's national status in the construction field. Indeed, the "*quality*" team here retains a loyal following among contractors and owners. Government contract matters feature prominently in the firm's diet of work, along with an expansive alternative dispute resolution caseload.

**The Lawyers:** **Joseph West** (see p.554) sustains his top-tier status and is considered to be at the zenith of his career. Among peers, he is highly respected as an established government contracts man, but this "*polished and remarkable*" attorney also wins praise for his handling of disputes. As such, he is dubbed a "*careful, meticulous and savvy litigator, with excellent presentation skills, which means many claims are resolved without ending in litigation.*" Projects handled by West of late include acting on remediation contracts relating to waste facilities, along with an array of major construction assignments.

**Clients/Work Highlights:** The firm often advises government agencies, construction companies, manufacturers, architects, engineers and financial institutions.

## McManus Schor Asmar & Darden, L.L.P.

**The Firm:** The 17-lawyer team here sustains its presence on the domestic scene, and is one of the larger operations in town. It came in for praise for its depth of expertise in arbitration and complex government contract matters, and the firm also offers support in real estate, development and defects issues. The deliberate cultivation of its construction litigation practice, combined with international expansion, is expected to enhance its grip on the market. It has a special focus on construction matters relating to the Caribbean Basin.

**The Lawyers:** **Geoffrey Keating** is exceptionally conversant in matters relating to international infrastructure and public works, whether involving US embassies or USAID projects. He is also experienced advising on facilities in the power, hotel, retail and defense sectors. Eponymous partner **Joseph McManus** leads the contract drafting and special projects groups. A "*rainmaker par excellence,*" he shines in arbitration and is particularly skilled in contracts. Indeed, the Granada Supreme Court recently accepted his expert testimony on American Institute of Architects (AIA) contract documents in the case of Liberty Club Limited and New India Assurance Company (Trinidad & Tobago) Limited. Up-and-comer **Charles Asmar** was praised for his "*great common sense and parking his ego on the curb.*" He is perceived to be building a solid reputation in government contracts and alternative dispute resolution.

**Clients/Work Highlights:** The firm represents owners, contractors, subcontractors, trade associations and home builders.

## Band 4

### Arent Fox PLLC

**The Firm:** Though best known for its top-tier real estate practice, the firm exhibits significant depth in public contract and litigation work relating to residential and professional complexes, condominiums, waste plants, factories and major sports stadiums. Its sophisticated approach proves advantageous in dealing with multiple-party transactions with complex legal structures.

**The Lawyers:** Interviewees agreed that **Kathy Taub** (see p.550) is an effective anchor for the practice. With over 20 years of experience, she is billed as a construction sector deal-doer who engages with the practical realities of the case in hand. According to one client, she retains "*a nice sense of balance: she's very logical and sensible, and never fails to gain the respect of the opposition during negotiations.*"

**Clients/Work Highlights:** Architects, owners, designers, developers and contractors feature among the firm's clientele.

## Bell, Boyd & Lloyd LLC

**The Firm:** Interviewees identified the firm's links with construction sector trade associations and its deft handling of claims resolutions as distinguishing features. Insurance coverage issues also feature prominently in the workload. Further expertise offered by this Chicago firm's satellite office relates to mechanical liens, bidding processes and compliance.
**The Lawyers:** Head of construction law and government contracts **Joel Rubinstein** is considered "*a very smart and very fine attorney indeed.*" Market sources pointed in particular to his flair as a mediator and arbitrator: "*He never stops looking for a creative way to settle things.*" Complex bid protests are another of his fortes.

**Clients/Work Highlights:** Engineers, sureties, suppliers, architects, owners, contractors and subcontractors provide the bulk of the work.

## Bradley Arant Rose & White LLP

See firm details p.162
**The Firm:** The defection of Spriggs & Hollingsworth's construction team to Bradley Arant in August 2005 provides a significant boost to its profile and lends further credibility to the group's expansion plans, which currently focus on the Southeast USA. A ten-strong team of "*talented*" lawyers marshals clients through the full gamut of issues, ranging from contract negotiation and privatizations to construction dispute resolution. A recent

high note was settling one of the largest claims on the Big Dig, Boston's Central Artery project.
**The Lawyers:** Managing partner **Douglas Patin** (see p.537) won respect as an "*effective litigator.*" His prominence in the insurance industry is considered crucial to his success in the field. Recent highlights for Patin include representing Limbach Company LLC against Zurich American Insurance Company in a dispute pertaining to the interpretation of liability insurance.
**Clients/Work Highlights:** Tompkins Builders; John J Kirlin; Limbach LLC and Indyme can all be counted as clients.

# CORPORATE/COMMERCIAL

| Corporate/Commercial |
|---|
| **Leading Firms** |
| [1] GIBSON, DUNN & CRUTCHER LLP *Washington, DC* |
|      HOGAN & HARTSON LLP *Washington, DC* |
| [2] LATHAM & WATKINS LLP *Washington, DC* |
| [3] ARNOLD & PORTER LLP *Washington, DC* |
|      COVINGTON & BURLING *Washington, DC* |
|      KIRKLAND & ELLIS LLP *Washington, DC* |
|      PILLSBURY WINTHROP *Washington, DC* |
|      SKADDEN, ARPS *Washington, DC* |
| [4] DICKSTEIN SHAPIRO *Washington, DC* |
|      WILMERHALE *Washington, DC* |

| Leading Individuals |
|---|
| [1] ADLER Howard *Gibson, Dunn & Crutcher* |
|      GLOVER Stephen *Gibson, Dunn & Crutcher* |
|      GORRELL JR J Warren *Hogan & Hartson LLP* |
| [2] LENNON Daniel *Latham & Watkins LLP* |
|      STAMAS George *Kirkland & Ellis LLP* |
| [3] JACK Andrew *Covington & Burling* |
|      KAPLAN Steven *Arnold & Porter LLP* |
|      MAZO Mark *Hogan & Hartson LLP* |
|      MUTRYN William *Holland & Knight LLP* |
|      POLON Ira *Dickstein Shapiro* |
|      ROBBINS Robert *Pillsbury Winthrop* |
|      ROGAN Michael *Skadden, Arps* |
|      SINHA Pankaj *Skadden, Arps* |

## Band 1

### Gibson, Dunn & Crutcher LLP

See firm details p.328
**The Firm:** This robust practice has won an impressive national and regional reputation. Fêted for its breadth of experience, it offers expertise in M&A, IPOs, venture capital financings and securities compliance. Highlights of recent work include representing Arlington Capital Partners as the acquirer of SECOR International, a California environmental firm, and representing MCI in its acqui-

sition of the telecom security firm NetSec. The team also continues to act for Capital One in a number of matters.
**The Lawyers:** **Howard Adler** (see p.497) is the relationship partner for Friedman Billings Ramsey, whom he advises on a wide range of transactional matters. Respected for his corporate expertise, Adler also undertakes an increasing amount of REIT-related work. Clients liked his "*deep understanding*" of corporate, securities and bank regulatory matters, and appreciated that he is "*conscientious and careful about protecting client interests.*" His partner **Stephen Glover** (see p.515) "*stands out as a trusted man and a fine lawyer.*" A busy year has seen him acting for NeuStar in its IPO and representing United Defense in its merger with BAE Systems.
**Clients/Work Highlights:** Friedman Billings Ramsey; United Defense; Marriott International; Capital One; Sallie Mae; Del Monte Foods; GE and Atlantic Coast Airlines.

### Hogan & Hartson LLP

See firm details p.568
**The Firm:** Considered "*one of the Washington elite,*" this firm has a broad corporate practice that includes M&A, private equity and capital markets issues. Recent highlights in these areas include representing both XM Satellite Radio and WellCare Health Plans in common stock offerings. The team also advised U-Store-It in its $460 million IPO. The firm is also widely respected by both peers and clients for having "*built an incredible REIT practice.*" It represented Lehman Brothers in a private equity joint venture to purchase Gables Residential, a US-based REIT.
**The Lawyers:** Head of the team **Warren Gorrell** (see p.516) is "*the REIT expert of the world.*" Clients also praised him as a "*real business lawyer,*" who possesses the "*ability to translate the law and the application of the law in a constructive manner.*" **Mark Mazo** (see p.530) concentrates on the international side of the practice. He has a particular focus on cross-border M&A with European countries. Mazo continues to act for EADS North America on M&A and related matters.

**Clients/Work Highlights:** News Corporation; Lehman Brothers; CapitalSource; XM Satellite Radio; Regal Entertainment Group and GE Commercial Finance.

### Band 2

### Latham & Watkins LLP

**The Firm:** An "*outstanding*" traditional transactional practice and "*a very deep bench in terms of subject matter expertise*" form the foundations of this respected corporate practice. Working closely with the New York office, the team has an impressive M&A and private equity caseload, attracting clients such as LBO sponsors, private equity funds and venture capital firms. The firm's respected profile in the DC market owes much to its work for The Carlyle Group, which it recently represented as an investor in the $8 billion LBO of Hertz. Other major Carlyle-related transactions include the acquisitions of AxleTech International and SS&C Technologies. The team is also well equipped to provide securities regulatory advice.
**The Lawyers:** **Daniel Lennon** "*approaches every M&A transaction with an entrepreneurial attitude and full knowledge of the applicable laws.*" As client partner for The Carlyle Group, he is a well-established figure in the corporate arena. He won praise for his skills as a negotiator and for the excellent client service standards he instills into the team: "*He would lie in front of a train for his clients,*" enthused clients.
**Clients/Work Highlights:** Other clients include Halifax Group, Standard Aero Holdings and Piedmont Hawthorne Holdings.

### Band 3

### Arnold & Porter LLP

See firm details p.560
**The Firm:** This well-regarded practice encompasses regulatory, M&A, sovereign finance and securities matters. The group has advised on an increasing

number of M&A transactions, including acting as lead counsel to US Airways throughout its Chapter 11 reorganization and merger with America West and the related equity capital-raising transactions. On the sovereign finance side, the team also continues to be busy, having represented clients from countries including Venezuela and Brazil. Sector focuses include transportation, real estate and government contracts.

**The Lawyers:** Head of the corporate and securities practice, **Steve Kaplan** (see p.522) *"is a first-rate attorney and a real deal-doer,"* reported sources.

**Clients/Work Highlights:** Perseus LLC; AOL; Branch Banking and Trust; US Airways; CSX; BAE Systems North America; Arlington Capital Partners and American Capital Strategies.

## Covington & Burling
See firm details p.563

**The Firm:** This group fields *"attorneys of a very high standard across the board."* With an established reputation as a regulatory firm, it continues to build a respected profile for corporate deals. Areas of particular focus include sport, life sciences, media and communications, energy and technology. Recent highlights include advising the National Football League in its deal to secure Sprint as the official wireless telecommunications service sponsor of the NFL and representing MediaSentry in its acquisition by SafeNet. The firm also advised the DC Sports and Entertainment Commission in agreements with Major League Baseball and related matters to relocate the Montreal Expos franchise to DC. Clients commented on the team's *"very talented people and good ethical sense."*

**The Lawyers: Andrew Jack** (see p.520) *"thinks through all the issues carefully and is great at protecting his client."* He won client praise for his *"excellent judgment, good business skills and meticulous attention to detail."* Jack continues to act as outside counsel for JLG Industries and the DC Sports and Entertainment Commission.

**Clients/Work Highlights:** Adelphia Communications; American Biophysics Corp; Bacardi-Martini; Bank of America; Freddie Mac; ImClone Systems; JLG Industries; NFL and Procter & Gamble.

## Kirkland & Ellis LLP
See firm details p.875

**The Firm:** Known for its national private equity practice, this firm continues to see an upswing in all areas of its corporate work in both the national and international markets. The DC-based group continues to be an active venture capital counselor for NEA (New Enterprise Associates) as well as acting as primary outside counsel for Constellation Energy Group. The team fields expertise across the sports, technology and healthcare industries. One notable highlight in this area was representing Allion Healthcare in its recent IPO.

**The Lawyers:** The *"tireless"* **George Stamas** (see p.548) *"is willing to work around the clock and knows how to get difficult deals done."* He is widely credited with raising the group's profile in the corporate arena

and wins the respect of the market for his ability to establish strong client relationships. *"Clients really love him,"* said one peer. For their part, clients praised his *"creative, business-oriented thinking."* He recently advised Constellation Energy in its merger with FPL Group, creating a company with a market capitalization of $28 billion.

**Clients/Work Highlights:** MidOcean Partners; Constellation Energy Group; NEA; Friedman Billings Ramsey; Arlington Capital Partners; Fountainhead Title Group and Legg Mason Wood Walker.

## Pillsbury Winthrop Shaw Pittman LLP
See firm details p.1550

**The Firm:** Traditionally associated with the technology market, the team continues to increase its broader corporate profile in the DC arena. The merger of Shaw Pittman and Pillsbury Winthrop has boosted the resources of the practice, providing a particular advantage in the REIT sector. The firm has developed a significant corporate securities practice, and is respected for its work on private equity funds and corporate finance. A notable illustration of this is its work for Schroders, much of which is international in its scope.

**The Lawyers:** Clients endorsed **Bob Robbins** (see p.541) because he is *"scarily smart and incredibly experienced."* Chair of the corporate practice, he has a *"practical approach and the ability to cut through technicalities."* He recently represented Crescent Real Estate Equities Company in a reorganization and joint venture financing of health and wellness company Canyon Ranch and in other corporate finance transactions.

**Clients/Work Highlights:** Crescent Real Estate; Schroders; SVG Capital; Legg Mason Wood Walker; Friedman Billings Ramsey; Chevy Chase Bank; GenCorp; Trustreet Properties; Capital Automotive REIT and Federal Realty Investment Trust.

## Skadden, Arps, Slate, Meagher & Flom LLP & Affiliates
See firm details p.1557

**The Firm:** The DC office of this major international law firm was praised by clients for its *"outstanding lawyers"* and the *"exceptional quality and understanding of their associates."* It handles a wide range of complex M&A work as well as advising on all aspects of corporate governance, including the Sarbanes-Oxley Act and related matters. The practice has particular expertise in cross-border transactional work especially in the energy and IT sectors. Recent highlights include representing Cinergy in the $100 million purchase of the Wheatland facility from Allegheny Energy and representing Refco in the auction to sell the company out of bankruptcy. The team also handles securities counseling and enforcement.

**The Lawyers:** Head of the group **Michael Rogan** (see p.542) is *"strong both in the boardroom and in face-to-face negotiations."* Clients praised his breadth of knowledge and experience and the fact that he *"gives a practical answer that a company can use, not a law school response."* He was also popular for his

problem-solving ability: *"He looks for solutions rather than putting up roadblocks,"* said one client, echoing the sentiments of others. **Pankaj Sinha** (see p.546) is a *"thorough and practical attorney who is a pleasure to work with."* Sources also appreciate that he is a *"a magnificent communicator who is always unruffled in negotiations."*

**Clients/Work Highlights:** Macquarie Securities; Cinergy; PPL Corporation/PPL Global; AES and Helmerich & Payne.

## Band 4

### Dickstein Shapiro Morin & Oshinsky LLP
See firm details p.565

**The Firm:** This firm is praised for having a *"great core of well-respected lawyers."* Attorneys here work closely with the New York office on M&A for a wide range of clients, although the practice has a particular focus on the energy and telecom industries. It is also involved in the government contracts sector. The group has a strong international track record and recently acted for Emergent Telecom Ventures in its acquisition, with consortium partners First National Holding, of a 71% interest in Russian telecom company PeterStar.

**The Lawyers: Ira Polon** (see p.539) *"knows how to preempt trouble and ensure a smooth transaction."* He is a *"personable lawyer who can be as pleasant or as firm as the circumstances demand."* He has a long-standing relationship with the Harbour Group.

**Clients/Work Highlights:** Loews Corporation; Harbour Group; Wachovia; Branch Banking and Trust; KeySpan Corporation; Gladstone Commercial; Duke Energy; Stanley Associates; Allied Capital and Owens Corning.

### WilmerHale
See firm details p.580

**The Firm:** This dedicated corporate transactional practice works closely with the firm's renowned securities enforcement and litigation team. Its broad remit includes M&A deals, IPOs, securities compliance and venture fund formation and management. One particular area of growth has been representing venture-backed companies, especially in the technology sector. The team recently assisted Distributed Energy Systems in its acquisition of Northern Power Systems.

**clients/work Highlights:** The firm's clientele includes Distributed Energy Systems, GEF Management and Legend Ventures.

### Other Notable Practitioners
At Holland & Knight LLP, **William Mutryn** (see p.533) focuses his practice on midmarket M&A for a clientele of federal contractors in the IT and energy sectors. Employing a *"fair, even-handed manner that is well received by opposing counsel,"* he is a respected negotiator who *"seeks a win-win resolution."*

# EMPLOYEE BENEFITS & EXECUTIVE COMPENSATION

## Band 1

### Groom Law Group

**The Firm:** "*Nationally recognized as a premier benefits boutique,*" this firm is known for its depth of experience in ERISA. A team of over 50 dedicated lawyers covers the full spectrum of employee benefits, fielding experts in tax, litigation, fiduciary responsibility, legislation and the transactional elements of ERISA. Among the group's recent caseload is the representation of a national trade association and a major bank lobbying Congress and the Treasury on executive compensation regulations. The group also represented a major health insurance company before the Supreme Court on whether health plans can enforce their reimbursement and subrogation provisions under ERISA. The group has been involved with restructuring the pension and welfare plans of numerous Fortune 500 companies to reduce the exposure of boards and other senior company officers to ERISA fiduciary liability. The team is also seeing an increasing amount of stock drop litigation.

**The Lawyers:** Renowned for his ERISA skill and experience, **Robert Gallagher** "*really understands what drives government issues and is realistic and savvy about government policy.*" **Gary Ford** was general counsel at the Pension Benefit Guaranty Corporation and is "*clearly a leader in the field.*" He has particular expertise in advising companies facing bankruptcy or restructuring on the ramifications this has on their employee benefits policies. **Jon Breyfogle** focuses his practice on the health aspects of employee benefit law. He is seen as "*a problem solver with a clear, concise style of communication.*" **Lou Mazawey** is a "*terrific lawyer*" specializing in the tax aspects of employee benefits.

**Clients/Work Highlights:** Blue Cross and Blue Shield Association, Central States Health, Welfare and Pension Funds and the American Benefits Council are examples of the firm's clientele, which also includes large plan sponsors, trade associations, financial services firms and a number of Fortune 100 companies.

### Kilpatrick Stockton LLP
See firm details p.735

**The Firm:** The employee benefits group of this full-service firm offers a range of specialist expertise in areas such as ERISA litigation, executive compensation and health and welfare plans. The group also continues to focus on fiduciary responsibility, advising a number of major clients on 401(k) plans and the impact of the new 409A rules on their executive compensation plans. On the litigation side, the team is currently involved in the defense of Xerox, RJ Reynolds, and Delta Air Lines in connection with 401(k) plan company stock litigation.

**The Lawyers:** A "*tremendous attorney,*" **Steve Sacher** (see p.543) is "*extraordinarily knowledgeable*" on employee benefit plans and ERISA. He is widely respected for his legislative expertise and experience of dealing successfully with agencies. Partner **Mark Wincek** (see p.556) is a "*standout quality guy*" with expertise in executive compensation and tax.

**Clients/Work Highlights:** The firm represents financial institutions, investment advisers, third-party administrators, corporations and ERISA fiduciary committees. A large part of the group's client base consists of plan sponsors.

### O'Melveny & Myers LLP
See firm details p.336

**The Firm:** This respected group has secured a following among clients and peers for its renowned Title 1 practice. While the DC team works closely with its West Coast offices, operating as one national practice, its attorneys focus more on the contentious side. Recent triumphs include the affirmation by the Court of Appeals for the Seventh Circuit of a judgment after a trial dismissing all claims against US Trust in Keach v US Trust, and affirmation by the Second Circuit Court of Appeals in Nechis v Oxford Health Plans of the grant of a motion to dismiss all claims against Oxford. The team also undertakes regulatory work and fiduciary advice.

**The Lawyers:** The "*fabulous*" **Bob Eccles** (see p.509), head of the practice, is "*the premier ERISA litigator in the country,*" claimed sources. With experience gained at both the DOJ and DOL, he "*really understands policy issues and can make proposals that are likely to be accepted.*" Younger partner **Gary Tell** is well versed in fiduciary counseling and regulatory advice, although he is also "*an up-and-coming star in ERISA litigation.*" Another lawyer building an impressive profile is **Karen Wahle** (see p.553). "*One of the top young practitioners in the area,*" her practice focuses on litigation.

**Clients/Work Highlights:** The firm's clientele ranges from employers to financial institutions and comes from a wide range of industry sectors. Examples include US Trust and Humana.

### Steptoe & Johnson LLP
See firm details p.576

**The Firm:** This highly regarded practice covers litigation, tax, Titles I and IV of ERISA, transactions and legislation for plan sponsors, fiduciaries and consultants. Other clients include banks, insurers, investment managers and various employee benefits service providers. The team recently represented the independent fiduciary of the pension plan in the United Airlines bankruptcy and is currently performing the same role in a number of other airline bankruptcies. It also has experience in SEC investigations on behalf of financial institutions and the representation of clients who are being investigated by the DOL. The group enjoys a particularly impressive reputation for ERISA litigation, and continues to have major defense roles for clients in high-profile stock drop cases, including those involving Enron, Dynergy and Qwest.

**The Lawyers:** A regulatory specialist, **Melanie Nussdorf** (see p.535) is "*fast on her feet and very insightful and effective.*" Respected for her breadth of knowledge, experience and excellent relations with the DOL, she is also "*gracious and a pleasure to work with,*" said sources. The "*exceptional*" head of the practice **Paul Ondrasik** (see p.536) leads the litigation group. He is seen as "*among the very best for benefits work*" and this year has seen an increasing amount of work in 401(k) plan-related cases.

**Clients/Work Highlights:** The Masters, Mates and Pilots Pension Plan, Individual Retirement Account Plan, and Health and Welfare Plan; Trustees of the United States Army Nonappropriated Fund Employee Retirement Trust and 401k Plan; Deutsche Bank; UBS and Goldman Sachs.

## Band 2

### Gibson, Dunn & Crutcher LLP
See firm details p.328

**The Firm:** This practice encompasses the whole range of employee benefits expertise. It is regularly involved in high-profile ERISA litigation, such as pre-emption, class action and multiemployer cases. Notable examples of this include representing Merrill Lynch in the WorldCom ERISA litigation and in actions filed in the wake of the bankruptcy of the RCN Corporation regarding RCN's 401(k) plan. Attorneys also provide transactional, design and compliance advice for all types of plans.

**The Lawyers: William Kilberg** (see p.523) is a "*tremendous litigator*" whose practice features both labor and employment and employee benefits. He was recently lead negotiator for Hawaiian Airlines in negotiations with its pilots' union regarding the pilots' pension plan.

**Clients/Work Highlights:** Merrill Lynch; Aetna; Boeing; Hawaiian Airlines; Cincinnati Bell; Enterprise Rent-A-Car and Hewlett-Packard.

## Hogan & Hartson LLP
See firm details p.568

**The Firm:** This group is recognized for its expertise in the health benefits sector, representing health insurance companies and large employers in developing defined health benefit programs. The group also acts on ERISA counseling and litigation. It is currently national ERISA monitoring counsel to Federal Insurance Company in connection with a number of class action cases, and special ERISA counsel to Home Box Office with various matters involving the American Federation of Radio and Television Artists' pension plan.

**The Lawyers: Evan Miller** (see p.532) is a "*smart, thoughtful lawyer*" with a strong reputation as an ERISA litigator. Clients appreciated his insurance-related expertise and his "*innovative solutions to complicated issues.*" He is also "*a very strong negotiator in mediations and settlement conferences.*"

**Clients/Work Highlights:** Blue Cross and Blue Shield of Massachusetts; Home Box Office; International Truck and Engine; WellPoint; Federal Insurance Company; EADS North America; Winn-Dixie; Vanderbilt University and Georgetown University.

### Band 3

## Covington & Burling
See firm details p.563

**The Firm:** This group is well equipped to advise on a range of employee benefits and executive compensation matters. As well as designing and implementing benefits plans, the group also deals with the employee benefits aspects of corporate transactions such as M&A and debt financing. It also undertakes litigation, including class actions. The firm is counsel to the ERISA Industry Committee.

**The Lawyers:** Partner **John Vine** (see p.552) is a "*first-rate*" lawyer whose practice covers a wide scope of employee benefits, but he is particularly known for his tax-related work. Respected by both peers and clients, he was praised for being "*careful, candid and very bright.*" Clients appreciated the fact that "*he has an encyclopedic knowledge of employee benefits law and can make it easily understandable.*"

**Clients/Work Highlights:** The practice's clients include companies from sectors such as construction, manufacturing, transportation, financial services, technology and sports. Examples include Verizon, Honeywell and the National Geographic Society.

## Kirkpatrick & Lockhart Nicholson Graham LLP

**The Firm:** This prominent practice is particularly known for its financial services and products expertise. Integrated with national focus groups that deal with employee stock ownership and executive compensation, the team also works closely across offices with the firm's investment management lawyers. Attorneys have taken on an increasing amount of ERISA litigation, although the team is still better known for its noncontentious practice. One area of focus this year has been working with large plan sponsors on risk control, particularly with regard to 401(k) plans.

**The Lawyers: William Schmidt** is "*Mr ERISA when it comes to transactional work and setting up ERISA funds.*" Enjoying an impressive reputation among peers and clients alike, this "*really superb lawyer*" is particularly renowned for his expertise and experience on fiduciary and DOL issues.

**Clients/Work Highlights:** This group's clientele consists of investment managers, advisers and plan sponsors.

## McDermott Will & Emery
See firm details p.878

**The Firm:** This strong local practice concentrates on representing large corporate clients and third-party service providers. The team covers the full spectrum of employee benefits and executive compensation, including tax, ERISA, COBRA and the provision of benefits in bankruptcy. Health benefits are also a particular area of focus. Recent highlights include developing a series of defenses for a major corporation in its bankruptcy reorganization to avoid assumption of COBRA liability. The team also acted as deal counsel and employee benefits counsel for a Fortune 100 brokerage firm in a $50 million acquisition involving an employee benefit plan record-keeping business.

**The Lawyers: Paul Hamburger** (see p.517) "*has encyclopedic knowledge of ERISA.*" Clients appreciate that he is "*available, responsive, patient and articulate as well as a master at managing relationships.*" Hamburger advises employers on tax-qualified retirement plans, executive compensation and welfare benefit plans.

**Clients/Work Highlights:** Examples of clients are Merrill Lynch, Automated Data Processing and DaimlerChrysler.

### Other Notable Practitioners

The "*terrific*" **Robert Davis** (see p.507) of Mayer, Brown, Rowe & Maw LLP splits his practice between employee benefits and employment. He is "*a very incisive thinker, who sees and analyzes issues with great clarity and rigor.*" His areas of focus include fiduciary responsibility and ERISA litigation class actions. He is particularly respected for his DOL knowledge and experience and the practice often represents large employers and investment fiduciaries in ERISA investigations conducted by the DOL. **Donald Myers** (see p.533) of Reed Smith LLP focuses much of his practice on counseling financial institutions on ERISA matters. "*A fiduciary guru,*" he is highly regarded for his regulatory expertise and his "*imaginative, accessible and literate*" counsel. This year has seen him working with a number of clients regarding DOL investigations and advising on pension funding regulations. **Tess Ferrera** (see p.512) has moved her practice over to Tighe Patton Armstrong Teasdale PLLC where she will continue to concentrate on Title I defense litigation and compliance advice. She is "*thorough, practical and knowledgeable*" and clients found her "*a smart, dedicated lawyer who is a pleasure to work with.*" One client summed up: "*I feel she puts everything into our projects and is always thinking up new angles and alternative approaches.*"

# EMPLOYMENT

## MAINLY DEFENDANT

## Band 1

### Gibson, Dunn & Crutcher LLP

See firm details p.328

**The Firm:** This team of "*exceptionally talented lawyers*" has cultivated a national reputation, particularly for its "*valuable government expertise.*" A successful track record in high-level litigation and specialist niches adds depth to the practice. As well as being experienced in age, race and disability discrimination cases, the group also specializes in OSHA work. Recently, it successfully resolved a number of OSHA-related cases involving employee fatalities.

**The Lawyers:** With a long-standing reputation for excellence, **William Kilberg** (see p.523) practices both labor and employment law and advises on employee benefits. "*One of the deans of employment law,*" he is appreciated by both peers and clients for his experience, expertise and practicality. He has argued a number of significant matters before the Supreme Court and the Courts of Appeals. Former

Solicitor of Labor, **Eugene Scalia** (see p.544) is "*terrifically smart and provides wonderful advice.*" He has recently been concentrating on the increasing number of whistle-blower actions under Sarbanes-Oxley. OSHA specialist **Baruch Fellner** (see p.511) inspires tremendous respect in clients, who value his expertise and ability to be "*an aggressive advocate when he needs to be.*" This year has seen him represent both Coca-Cola Enterprises and Pepsi Bottling Group in groundbreaking ergonomics cases.

**Clients/Work Highlights:** Coca-Cola Enterprises; Pepsi Bottling Group; Boeing; Hewlett-Packard; FLYi; Parsons; Wal-Mart; Sprint Nextel and UPS.

### Jones Day

See firm details p.570

**The Firm:** This robust group is the "*team that major corporations routinely go to,*" sources agreed. With its "*impressive and wide-ranging practice,*" this group is well equipped to advise on all aspects of labor and employment law. The team is particularly known for litigation, where it has continued to deal with an increasing number of wage and hour discrimination class actions. One notable example of this is Murray v Ohio Casualty Corporation, where the group secured a denial of class certification in a nationwide wage and hour collective action. Attorneys are also routinely involved in high-profile labor negotiations for a number of major clients. For example, it recently negotiated a major labor contract for Timken involving the United Steelworkers of America.

**The Lawyers:** **Willis Goldsmith** (see p.515) has an impressive reputation among both clients and peers. He is an "*exceptionally capable oral advocate*" and clients praised him as a "*true gentleman who is very easy to work with.*" From early 2006 he will be primarily based in New York, but he maintains a high presence in the DC market. **Andrew Kramer** (see p.524) is one of the country's leading traditional labor lawyers. He is known for his collective bargaining work and was involved in the Timken case. Clients said he is "*a smart, practical and tenacious litigator, who is very personable and works well with business people.*" **Alison Marshall** (see p.529) is an "*extremely strong*" litigator who continues to raise her profile in discrimination class actions. She was involved in achieving the settlement of the McReynolds v Sodexho case.

**Clients/Work Highlights:** Albertson's; The Washington Post; GM; Century Aluminum; Crown Cork & Seal; Knight Ridder; Verizon Communications and Verizon Wireless.

### Paul, Hastings, Janofsky & Walker LLP

See firm details p.339

**The Firm:** "*One of the powerhouses for employment,*" the DC office of this national firm is recognized for its prowess across the range of employment and labor issues. The team is especially known for its class action defense work. Notable examples include

securing a number of victories for Boeing in class actions across several states and defending Ford in a nationwide class action challenging their apprenticeship testing admission procedure. Wage and hour cases continue to feature heavily in the caseload. The group is also engaged in disputes arising out of the railroad and airline industries, such as the Continental Airlines age discrimination class action. Other key areas include trade secrets and noncompetition agreements, particularly for clients in the technology sector.

**The Lawyers:** **Barbara Brown** (see p.504) is "*smart, unflappable*" and clients liked the way she is "*proactive and responsive with the ability to consistently come up with practical, easy-to-follow strategy responses.*" "*I adore her!*" raved one peer, while others praised her "*generous and self-effacing*" manner. Appellate lawyer **Neal Mollen** (see p.533) possesses a "*great intellect.*" Clients particularly appreciated his cooperative approach, praising his "*incredible availability and drive to make a partnership with in-house counsel work.*" He recently represented the Chamber of Commerce in litigation brought by the AARP against the EEOC.

**Clients/Work Highlights:** Fannie Mae; Wal-Mart; Boeing; Ford; Motorola; Orbital Sciences and Continental Airlines.

## Band 2

### Akin Gump Strauss Hauer & Feld LLP

See firm details p.559

**The Firm:** The arrival of former EEOC general counsel Eric Dreiband has "*beefed up an already respected EEOC practice,*" sources agreed. This firm, which competes at both local and national levels, adopts a "*focus that clients respect and reward.*" The team works on discrimination litigation, labor disputes and an increasing volume of wage and hour class actions, where it has represented a number of large companies in California and nationally. The practice acts for a number of household names; for example, it is external labor counsel for Starbucks.

**The Lawyers:** A former general counsel of the EEOC, **Donald Livingston** (see p.527) "*understands that world and understands the law.*" Clients are attracted by his expertise, experience and "*strong business sense,*" appreciating his ability to "*get resolutions that are not just legally sound but in the best business interest.*" Litigator **Joel Cohn** (see p.506) specialises in wage and hour work. Clients recognize that he is a "*real asset with a smart, methodical and careful manner.*"

**Clients/Work Highlights:** The group's clientele comes from a variety of industry sectors. Examples include Albertson's; Google; Tyson Foods; Food Lion; CSX; Starbucks; Allstate and the NFL.

### Morgan, Lewis & Bockius LLP

See firm details p.1758

**The Firm:** A "*top-shelf practice with a strong bench,*" this firm is historically a major player in the DC market. For many sources, these are the "*go-to guys for traditional labor*" and especially matters arising out of the transportation and manufacturing sectors. Recent work in this area includes counseling Rolls-Royce through a lengthy strike in Ohio and achieving a landmark NLRB decision in the ABX Air case, which extended coverage of the secondary boycott laws to a dispute where the employer is an airline. This "*truly collaborative group*" works closely with the teams specializing in employee benefits and health and welfare plans.

**The Lawyers:** Traditional labor specialist **Charles Cohen** (see p.506) is an "*outstanding lawyer with a very sophisticated practice.*" A former NLRB member, he brings to the table "*a tremendous insight into NLRB cases.*" Cohen focuses on high-level government negotiations and cutting-edge labor matters. **James Kelley** (see p.522) is an "*effective and practical*" lawyer, whose practice covers both labor and employment. He is "*incredibly effective at dealing with labor unions and good at selling difficult deals.*"

**Clients/Work Highlights:** BellSouth; ABX Air; Lockheed Martin; Pacific Maritime Association; American Airlines and United Space Alliance.

## Band 3

### Arent Fox PLLC

**The Firm:** Its "*high quality throughout*" ensures this team its prominence in the market. Attorneys here handle issues across the board of labor and employment law. The practice has a strong litigation focus, and enjoys an enviable reputation for its OSHA work. Examples over the past year include negotiating the first collective bargaining agreement for an acute care psychiatric hospital and successfully defending a luxury hotel against a breach of contract claim filed by its former general manager.

**The Lawyers:** Co-manager of the firm's litigation department, **Michael Stevens** (see p.548) is "*friendly, personable and a pleasure to deal with.*" Clients valued his "*outstanding legal skills and his personal integrity,*" as well as his practicality and sound business judgment. OSHA specialist **Steve Yohay** (see p.556) was recognized in the market for his expertise and experience in this sector. Clients liked the fact that he is "*highly respected both in the industry and with the federal agencies.*"

**Clients/Work Highlights:** Choice Hotels International; National Journal; The Atlantic Monthly; The Advisory Board Company; VSE Corporation; Washington Real Estate Investment Trust; Mattress Discounters; George Washington University; Corporate Executive Board and Pioneer Behavioral Health.

### Dickstein Shapiro Morin & Oshinsky LLP

See firm details p.565

**The Firm:** This well-regarded employment team has developed a full-service practice covering both noncontentious and litigation matters. Advice on compliance issues and class actions, particularly in the wage and hour arena, has occupied the group of late. One recent example of this was representing the home builder association NVR in a New York wage and hour class action case. The firm has also established a Web-based PolicyPartner service, which helps companies negotiate the intricacies of federal and state laws.

**The Lawyers:** Head of the practice **Deborah Kelly** (see p.522) "*knows the employment area backwards.*" A talented litigator who is "*willing to get her hands dirty,*" she won plaudits for her "*lively and engaging manner and ability to defuse difficult or emotional situations.*" Clients also appreciated that "*she can take a case from the first phone call to the courtroom.*" **Tammy McCutchen** (see p.530) is a former administrator of the Wage and Hour Division of the DOL. A "*bright and knowledgeable attorney,*" and the author of the new overtime regulations, her expertise is helping the practice expand into this area.

**Clients/Work Highlights:** Fannie Mae; MCI; AT&T; Greenwich Capital Markets; National Association of Chain Drug Stores and Sears.

### Hogan & Hartson LLP

See firm details p.568

**The Firm:** This team works closely with offices in North Virginia and Baltimore on a wide and varied range of matters. It regularly advises Fortune 100 clients on litigation, counseling and labor issues and is undertaking an increasing amount of work on discrimination cases brought under the FLSA. Among recent highlights is achieving a ruling in favor of DARO Realty on the application of the FLSA to property managers. The group also continues to advise George Washington University on a number of labor relations matters.

**The Lawyers:** Head of the group **Paul Skelly** (see p.546) has a broad practice that covers counseling and labor issues. He is the attorney that clients turn to when facing "*really hairy employment cases that are too complex to handle in-house.*"

**Clients/Work Highlights:** George Washington University; Virginia Hospital Center; BT Americas; Georgetown University; National Geographic; Pepco Holdings and EADS North America.

### Ogletree, Deakins, Nash, Smoak & Stewart, PC

See firm details p.738

**The Firm:** A respected player in the traditional labor market, this labor and employment group fields "*wonderful specialists.*" Well known for its union-related work, it has taken an increased involvement on the international stage as unions seek to become established in global corporations. As well as representing a number of trade associations, the group also involves itself in government lobbying. Other

areas of specialization include OSHA and mine safety. Recent highlights include obtaining a summary judgment in the District of Maryland on behalf of 91 companies in a Coal Industry Retiree Health Benefit Act case and a number of summary judgment victories in age and race discrimination cases.

**Clients/Work Highlights:** The client base includes a number of Fortune 100 companies and trade associations; including Associated Builders and Contractors; Associated General Contractors of America; Fluor and Peabody Energy.

### Seyfarth Shaw LLP

See firm details p.882

**The Firm:** A national employment and labor specialist, this firm is "*a tremendous asset to any organization,*" agree clients. It continues to build on an impressive reputation in the DC market, especially in the hospitality industry. Attorneys recently secured labor agreements in negotiations on behalf of the Hotel Association of Washington DC. In addition, the firm was involved in labor negotiations with a number of the city's unions including AFSCME and the police and fire unions. The firm also advises on discrimination issues, wage and hour, employee benefits and international labor law.

**The Lawyers:** Renowned for his experience and expertise in the hospitality sector, the "*wonderful*" **Peter Chatilovicz** is a tough negotiator capable of handling difficult labor situations. Clients also praised his availability: "*If you call him at one in the morning, Peter will be there for you.*"

**Clients/Work Highlights:** Hilton Hotels; Marriott International; Howard University; United Way of America; Goodwill Industries and Hotel Association of Washington DC.

### Other Notable Practitioners

**David Fortney** of Fortney & Scott, LLC has a "*terrific substantive knowledge of DOL issues.*" He runs a boutique practice that focuses on compliance issues and is known particularly for his wage and hour expertise. The majority of his clients come from such diverse sectors as aerospace, national defense, newspapers and trade associations. The practice recently developed a national compliance program for the National Association of Mortgage Brokers. At Mayer, Brown, Rowe & Maw LLP, the "*impressive*" **Bob Davis** (see p.507) splits his practice between employment and employee benefits matters. A former solicitor for the DOL and an "*outstanding practitioner,*" he primarily concentrates on wage and hour compliance and litigation. At Steptoe & Johnson LLP, **Ron Cooper** (see p.507) impressed clients with his "*top-notch communication skills and pragmatic business advice.*" Known for his expertise in international matters, Cooper has this year counseled a major overseas client with US operations on discrimination matters, and represents several international NGOs.

# ENERGY

# OIL & GAS

## Band 1

### Skadden, Arps, Slate, Meagher & Flom LLP & Affiliates

See firm details p.1557

**The Firm:** *"Absolutely the best for gas,"* according to the market. There is no denying this firm's strength in the sector, which it has cultivated from its depth and breadth of talent, historical grounding in the electricity arena and formidable finance and regulatory expertise. LNG features heavily in the deals the team has completed in the past year, including the construction of LNG terminals across the northeast. One also cannot ignore the substantial FERC expertise of the group, which complements the firm's undisputed strength in M&A and the integrated projects practice.

**The Lawyers:** Ex-FERC commissioner and recognized don of the DC market, **Clifford Naeve** (see p.534), applies his regulatory expertise to the gas sector. His reputation is endorsed by clients who describe him as *"extremely responsive and an amazing advocate."* FERC alumnus **William Scherman** (see p.544) *"consistently delivers timely and astute advice"* to clients in the gas and electricity sectors.

**Clients/Work Highlights:** The team advised the City of Philadelphia in the construction of an oil terminal. Other clients include Sempra Energy and Atlantic LNG.

### Steptoe & Johnson LLP

See firm details p.576

**The Firm:** This firm applies its undisputed federal and state regulatory expertise effortlessly to oil pipeline work, with clients nominating the group as a *"go-to team for oil issues, without question."* Although boasting a reputation grounded in its regulatory ability, the team is also increasing its transactional work, advising on joint ventures, leases and throughput agreements. The Trans-Alaska Pipeline System is a key client for the firm, and the energy group has defended its owners at both the FERC and the Regulatory Commission of Alaska. Internationally, the team has a strong reputation for assisting foreign pipeline companies with US regulatory and cross-border issues. The breadth of the practice is matched by its depth. Researchers were told: *"It's not a one-man show – you know there's a strong team behind the partners."*

**The Lawyers:** Retained by a swath of pipeline companies, **Steven Brose** (see p.504) attracts strong praise for his *"truly innovative approach"* to regulatory matters. He is credited with founding and developing the firm's relationship with the Trans-Alaska Pipeline System. Colleague **Steven Reed** (see p.540) is *"really sharp and responsive"* and the primary partner for Enbridge, the operator of Canada's largest pipeline.

**Clients/Work Highlights:** Frontier Pipeline; Santa Fe Pacific Pipeline Partners; TEPCO; Sunoco; Rocky Mountain Pipeline; ConocoPhillips; ExxonMobil; Colonial Pipeline and Enterprise Products Partners.

## Band 2

### Baker Botts LLP

See firm details p.1922

**The Firm:** This *"first-class"* Houston-based firm is one of the key players in the market, leveraging its international oil and gas experience to take advantage of the domestic upswing in LNG projects. The Washington, DC office forms a key link in the firm's global projects nexus spanning Houston, London and Moscow. Clients enjoy the fact that the team *"really offers the full package of services,"* injecting regulatory, transactional and finance capability into its lauded projects expertise. Standout work this year includes obtaining FERC regulatory approval for the Weaver's Cove LNG receiving terminal project in Massachusetts and representing Marathon in the structuring of an LNG facility in Equatorial Guinea. Flexing its transactional muscle, the team also represented Hunt Oil in its securing a long-term sale and purchase agreement with Repsol YPF.

**The Lawyers:** **Thomas Eastment** (see p.509) offers deep regulatory and litigation experience at FERC, the California Public Utilities Commission, federal district courts and courts of appeal. Researchers were told he is *"well organized and knows the industry."* Head of the global LNG group **Bruce Kiely** (see p.523) is *"so experienced in that field – if he doesn't know the answer, no one does."* Meanwhile, colleague **Randolph McManus** (see p.531) is a *"fine attorney"* who has attracted a reputation for developing client relationships and subsequently bringing business to the firm. **Mark Lewis** (see p.526) was recommended by clients for his FERC expertise: *"He's the one you want on your team because he is genuinely interested in your business."*

**Clients/Work Highlights:** BP; Shell; ExxonMobil; ConocoPhillips; Chevron; Hess LNG; Wisconsin Distributor Group; Guardian Pipeline; BTC Pipeline; Fort Chicago Energy Partners; BASF and Weaver's Cove Energy.

### Sidley Austin LLP

See firm details p.883

**The Firm:** Rated by peers for its regulatory expertise in natural gas and oil pipeline matters, the group represents operators, investors and independents. In the oil sector, the group is strong on rate reasonableness and competition advice, and in natural gas it has developed a solid reputation for advising joint ventures and partnerships investing in the sector. The firm boasts an impressive array of clients ranging from a number of owners of the Trans-Alaska Pipeline System to crude oil and petroleum products pipelines in the lower 48 states.

**The Lawyers:** *"A recognized name in the market,"* **Eugene Elrod** (see p.510) provides regulatory and transactional advice across the natural gas, crude oil and electricity sectors; peers praised him as an attorney who *"has truly earned his great reputation."* **Frederic Berner** (see p.501) has cultivated a practice which focuses on litigating at FERC and state commissions. He has a particular flair for competitive and antitrust issues. **Lawrence Miller** (see p.532) provides "*a safe pair of hands*" as a regulatory expert across a range of sectors. Within energy, he is lauded for his antitrust and competition work in the crude oil and petroleum pipelines sector.

**Clients/Work Highlights:** Barrett Resources; Colonial Pipeline; Explorer Pipeline; ExxonMobil; Marathon Ashland Pipe Line; BP; Shell; Sierra Pacific Power and Nevada Power.

## Vinson & Elkins LLP

See firm details p.1938

**The Firm:** This is a Houston firm whose global footprint encompasses the DC market, serving the regulatory requirements of its traditional oil and gas clients. The group's regulatory ability is as highly regarded by the market as its deep and historical transactional strength. According to one client, "*the team has such depth that I know I can throw anything at its attorneys and they'll respond quickly.*" The group's regulatory expertise is highlighted by its work for the Trans-Alaska Pipeline System, which it represents at a variety of proceedings at the FERC and the Alaska superior court. Unsurprisingly, LNG is a key area of focus for the group and is appreciated by clients such as Total, who retained the team to negotiate an import terminal use agreement. Transactional work remains a mainstay of the firm. As an illustration, the group represented Energy Transfer Partners in its acquisition of the controlling interests in the companies which own the Houston Pipeline system and related storage facilities.

**The Lawyers:** **David Andril** (see p.498) is a force to be reckoned with, and clients report that he is "*scary smart.*" His regulatory knowledge is sought after by clients, who remark: "*We like him because he has an ability to interpret rulings quickly and effectively as well as to portray the meaning and impact they will have on your project.*" **David Cohen** (see p.506) is lauded for his transactional capability and his "*sharp and savvy*" approach. **Anita Wilson** (see p.555) "*does an amazing job,*" according to her clients, who note her strength in natural gas regulation. Her negotiation skills also garnered strong praise from clients who report: "*She has a constructive approach to negotiations; she represents us aggressively but is never antagonistic.*"

**Clients/Work Highlights:** The team negotiated a long-term natural gas transportation agreement for BG LNG Services and has undertaken extensive gas regulation work for Duke Energy. Other clients include AIG; Enbridge; Shell; Sierra Pacific and Repsol YPF.

## Band 3

## Fulbright & Jaworski L.L.P.

See firm details p.1928

**The Firm:** This Texas energy giant has built a significant profile in energy-related litigation and appellate work, with the DC office adding significant FERC and regulatory strength. Perhaps unsurprisingly, oil and gas dominate the team's work at the FERC and state regulatory proceedings. Interstate pipelines are a recognized specialty of the team; for example, it represented TransCanada Corporation in connection with its proposed $1.7 billion Keystone project. The market also applauded the firm's extensive knowledge and experience in administrative litigation relating to Native American land.

**The Lawyers:** **Bill Williams** (see p.555) spearheads the firm's FERC work in relation to interstate pipelines, while colleague **Poe Leggette** (see p.525) is gaining a reputation as the "*go-to*" person for disputes and approvals for use of Native American land. Clients seek his policy know-how on a range of projects, and he is currently advising on projects in Wyoming and Utah.

**Clients/Work Highlights:** Alliance Pipeline; National Fuel Gas Company; El Paso Pipelines; Texas Gas Transmission; Independent Petroleum Association of America; Domestic Petrol Council; Oklahoma Independent Petroleum Association; Shell Exploration and Production; Total USA; Exxon Mobil; EOG Resources; Kerr-McGee; Bill Barrett Corporation and Anadarko Petroleum.

## Hogan & Hartson LLP

See firm details p.568

**The Firm:** A reputed name in the market, this firm has spent the past year building on its solid credentials to offer an expanded team of experts to its impressive client base. The team has recently showcased its regulatory knowledge in natural gas by representing Nicor, one of the largest local distribution companies in the USA, to challenge the applicability of a Texas county property tax on natural gas held in storage in Texas. The group has also secured a key role advising Dominion Resources as an interested party on the competitive consequences for the energy market of the pending merger of Exelon and Public Service Electric and Gas Company.

**The Lawyers:** A popular attorney, **Kevin Lipson** (see p.527) offers FERC regulatory knowledge to gas and electricity clients, who praise his ability to "*always get the best result – in terms of representation and negotiation skills, there's no one better.*" Offering the benefit of his extensive pipeline experience, **Lee Alexander** (see p.497) was praised by clients as "*extremely service-oriented.*" He recently joined the team, having moved from Dickstein Shapiro Morin & Oshinsky. **Pat Nevins** (see p.535) was nominated by market sources as "*a real performer and one to keep watching.*" He represents Dominion Cove Point, the largest LNG terminal in the USA.

## LeBoeuf, Lamb, Greene & MacRae LLP

See firm details p.1540

**The Firm:** This firm has a deep history in the energy industry and has recently developed a greater profile for its LNG work; this is in addition to a full range of services to oil and gas companies at every stage of the production process. Given its M&A pedigree, it is no surprise that the group has also advised on some of the largest M&A work in the gas sector. The DC office is highly integrated with its New York counterpart, offering regulatory advice on deals as well as appearing at the FERC on market issues.

**The Lawyers:** "*A true leader in the field,*" **Lawrence Acker** (see p.497) has a broad practice and his natural gas work attracted especial praise. Head of the DC energy practice of the firm, **Brian O'Neill** (see p.536) is "*a great guy and a great attorney – he's built some very strong client relationships,*" say sources.

**Clients/Work Highlights:** Anadarko; Idaho Power; Tractebel Calypso; Occidental Petroleum; Sempra Energy Global Enterprises; TransCanada; Conoco-Phillips; Transwestern Pipeline and Colonial Pipeline.

## Band 4

## Andrews Kurth LLP

See firm details p.1921

**The Firm:** "*A team of lawyers finely in tune with the industry,*" Andrews Kurth has a well-established presence in the energy sector. The backbone of the practice is historically gas, and its pipeline work garnered strong praise from peers. The firm has also developed its FERC experience over the past 25 years, and looks set to remain a solid presence in the market. For example, it recently filed a gas rate case for Southern Natural Gas which settled favorably.

**The Lawyers:** **Mark Sundback** is highly respected by peers, while clents say that he "*does a nice job and has built strong relationships that are useful to us as clients.*" Colleague **Michael Fremuth** has worked on LNG projects in the Caribbean and is developing a strong antitrust practice in the energy arena.

**Clients/Work Highlights:** Southern Natural Gas Pipeline; Northern Border Pipeline Company; Tennessee Gas Pipeline and MidWestern Gas Transmission.

## Bracewell & Giuliani LLP

See firm details p.1924

**The Firm:** This firm is "*a trusted name for oil and gas,*" according to clients. The energy practice has steadily built up over the years and now provides 20 full-time lawyers. It is in the gas sector where the firm's reputation as a key energy player is rooted. Providing expertise in regulatory and transactional matters, the team has proved well positioned to take advantage of the increase in activity in the LNG market, representing importers in connection with pipeline infrastructure, gas interchangeability, rates, and terms of service. The team is also strong on the transaction side and is currently advising on the acquisition of an interstate gas pipeline.

**The Lawyers:** **Charles Shoneman** (see p.545) has developed a solid reputation for his dispute prowess, but clients also turn to him for transactional matters, informing researchers that he is "*quite simply a terrific attorney and always a pleasure to work with.*"

**Clients/Work Highlights:** The firm represents a number of international oil majors and is a designated strategic partner of Shell. Other clients include Peoples Gas System; Citigroup; Société Générale and JPMorgan Chase.

## Jones Day

See firm details p.570

**The Firm:** This team is recognized by clients and peers alike as "*a high-quality firm that produces good all-around work.*" Natural gas regulation is the focus of the practice, and its solid FERC experience sees it providing a one-stop regulatory shop for clients. For example, CenterPoint Energy Gas Transmission is a key client and the team continues to advise it on all significant regulatory matters, in addition to achieving a favorable settlement regarding its compliance to FERC regulations.

**The Lawyers:** **Richard Avil** (see p.498) is "*a top-notch litigator who is thorough, experienced and well respected,*" according to clients. Colleague **Carolyn Thompson** (see p.550) is highly recommended by the market for her rate and rulemaking expertise.

**Clients/Work Highlights:** SCANA has sought the firm's counsel in connection with the merger of its interstate pipeline, SCG, with its intrastate pipeline. Other clients include Ameren, Dominion East Ohio and Xcel Energy.

## Morgan, Lewis & Bockius LLP

See firm details p.1758

**The Firm:** Clients report that this team's "*advice is invaluable, its knowledge of FERC is the best bar none – it is simply head and shoulders above the rest.*" This firm has made a concerted effort in recent years to build up its oil and gas practice, highlighted by recent key lateral hirers. The effort is clearly paying off – clients and peers told researchers that this is "*a solid practice and a key contender, particularly in the gas sector.*" Regulatory expertise spans both transactional and litigation matters, with the team providing deep FERC experience. Recent work includes negotiating and drafting long-term natural gas transportation agreements litigating complex FERC rate case proceedings and litigating a FERC complaint proceeding involving long-term negotiated rate agreements. The team's commercial acumen is also appreciated by clients, who increasingly retain the firm to work on project developments.

**The Lawyers:** Sources comment that the key attorneys here are "*outstanding.*" **Mark Haskell** (see p.518) is "*knowledgeable and thorough,*" impressing clients with his FERC litigation expertise. **Karol Lyn Newman** (see p.535) was singled out for her understanding of LNG issues; clients say: "*She's so easy to work with, and her knowledge is so broad – we'd follow her anywhere.*" Newman advised Anadarko in a rulemaking proceeding relating to access to capacity on Alaska Natural Gas Pipeline projects.

**Clients/Work Highlights:** Anadarko Petroleum; BP Energy; FP&L; Allegheny Energy; Occidental Petroleum; Marathon Oil Company; PPL and Ameron are among the firm's key clients.

## Troutman Sanders LLP

**The Firm:** The natural gas group at this firm offers a full service to clients across all FERC, transaction and legislative matters. Lately it has advised an interstate pipeline company in its project development, obtaining certificate applications on its behalf before FERC.

The team also supports clients in rate and tariff matters, principally shippers in tariff change proceedings before FERC. Market sources report that one of the key strengths this team offers is a high profile in the energy industry and deep government experience and contacts.

**The Lawyers:** A "*strong attorney on top of the industry issues,*" **Lisanne Crowley** leads the natural gas team.

**Clients/Work Highlights:** Puget Energy; Iroquois Transmission System; Saltville Gas Storage and New Jersey Natural Gas.

## Van Ness Feldman PC

**The Firm:** This energy and environment boutique fields an extremely strong team of professionals with deep industry and government experience, making it first choice among clients who seek its "*dedicated and thorough advice, as well as its friendly approach.*" Natural gas and oil pipeline advice are strengths of the team, although its LNG work attracts most attention. Offering an integrated service across all practice areas, the team has transactional, litigation and regulatory expertise. It is currently representing six US LNG terminals.

**The Lawyers:** **Julia Richardson** coordinates the natural gas and LNG practice and is lauded as "*a dynamic and creative attorney*" by her peers.

**Clients/Work Highlights:** Natural gas pipelines and LNG project developers number among the firm's clients. As an illustration, the team is advising on the development of the Bradwood Landing LNG facility in Oregon.

## Wright & Talisman PC

**The Firm:** This local boutique has established itself firmly in the energy sector, with its natural gas pipeline practice now attracting the same level of attention previously reserved for its electricity group. The team concentrates on providing day-to-day counseling to clients, who are predominantly gas companies. Sources report the team is a key player in the market.

**The Lawyers:** **Joseph Khoury** enters the table this year on the strength of the market's recognition of his natural gas practice. Clients report: "*He never disappoints – he's a solid, hard-working attorney.*" Colleague **Michael Thompson** is "*a classy operator*" boasting significant FERC expertise.

**Clients/Work Highlights:** The firm's significant gas pipeline practice represents Williams Pipelines as well as Southern and Star.

## Band 5

## Crowell & Moring LLP

See firm details p.564

**The Firm:** With deep roots in oil and gas, this team continues to serve clients on FERC and other regulatory issues. Interviewees noted that the team is not as prominent as in recent years, but assured researchers that there is "*a depth of experience that will allow the group to prosper.*" Representing clients

at the FERC on tariff and rate cases is a significant part of the practice, and the firm recently represented the East Tennessee Customer Group on rate and certificate proceedings relating to pipeline supplier services. The group also recently demonstrated its strong policy capabilities by representing a consortium of LNG developers in connection with the development of coast guard regulations for LNG facilities.

**The Lawyers:** **Jennifer Waters** (see p.553) concentrates on domestic electric and gas issues, and the market recognizes her particularly for expertise in handling FERC gas matters.

**Clients/Work Highlights:** Memphis Light, Gas and Water is another client of the firm, as are a number of international oil and gas development companies.

## Dewey Ballantine LLP

See firm details p.1530

**The Firm:** This firm fields a "*deep bench of talent*" across the energy sector and is considered an especial expert in oil and gas, with a focus on natural gas-related transactions. The team provides the full gamut of project development financing and regulatory advice on natural gas storage facilities and natural gas pipelines. Recent highlights include advising Sempra Energy Trading in the development and subsequent disposition of the Pine Prairie Gas Storage project in Louisiana. The group's expertise also extends to the financial markets, advising hedge funds and trading companies on long and short-term gas arrangements. Oil pipeline clients seek out the firm's heralded M&A capabilities for structuring the sale and purchase of pipeline facilities and producing properties.

**The Lawyers:** A man who "*understands how deals work – when he gives regulatory advice, it is within a commercial context,*" **James Bowe** (see p.503) is a highly regarded practitioner whose expertise extends to electricity as well as oil and gas. Clients report that "*regulatory lawyers are rare enough as it is, and lawyers that have the depth of knowledge that he does are a truly valuable find.*"

**Clients/Work Highlights:** The team has recently advised investment banks and startups on their potential participation in the energy sector. Other clients include hedge funds and gas storage projects.

## Kirkland & Ellis LLP

See firm details p.875

**The Firm:** Boasting a "*consistent and solid*" practice, this firm maintains a steady profile in the market thanks to its transaction, litigation and regulatory offering. Representing primarily unregulated players, the team acts for some of the industry's key figures. BP is a prestigious client that keeps the firm in steady work on a plethora of divestitures, as well as retaining the firm as lead counsel for the Destin Pipeline, BP's sole regulated interstate pipeline. The team also offers regulatory knowledge, advising Lion Oil in connection with market-based rates. The firm's corporate restructuring pedigree is also called upon by gas industry clients.

**The Lawyers:** Mitch Hertz and Neil Levy head a team that is *extremely knowledgeable, well respected and has fantastic commercial acumen,"* according to clients.

**Clients/Work Highlights:** Other clients include CornerStone Propane and DP&L.

### Other Notable Practitioners

**Robert Loeffler** (see p.527) of Morrison & Foerster LLP joins the table due to his high-profile work representing the State of Alaska on the development of the Alaska Natural Gas Pipeline. He is said to be "*a person of integrity and assiduous in his representation of clients."* **Barbara Heffernan** (see p.518) of Schiff Hardin LLP is recognized for her ability in handling complaint proceedings involving interstate natural gas pipelines, of which she dealt with two high-profile proceedings recently. Her clients include Columbia Gas Transmission and Columbia Gulf Transmission.

# ENERGY

# ELECTRICITY

| Energy: Electricity |
|---|
| Leading Firms |
| [1] SKADDEN, ARPS *Washington, DC* |
| [2] DEWEY BALLANTINE LLP *Washington, DC* |
| STEPTOE & JOHNSON LLP *Washington, DC* |
| [3] ALSTON & BIRD LLP *Washington, DC* |
| DICKSTEIN SHAPIRO *Washington, DC* |
| LATHAM & WATKINS LLP *Washington, DC* |
| LEBOEUF, LAMB *Washington, DC* |
| WRIGHT & TALISMAN PC *Washington, DC* |
| [4] BAKER BOTTS LLP *Washington, DC* |
| CHADBOURNE & PARKE LLP *Washington, DC* |
| CROWELL & MORING LLP *Washington, DC* |
| HUNTON & WILLIAMS LLP *Washington, DC* |
| JONES DAY *Washington, DC* |
| KIRKLAND & ELLIS LLP *Washington, DC* |
| MILLER, BALIS & O'NEIL, PC *Washington, DC* |
| MORGAN, LEWIS & BOCKIUS LLP *Washington, DC* |
| TROUTMAN SANDERS LLP *Washington, DC* |
| VAN NESS FELDMAN PC *Washington, DC* |
| [5] BRACEWELL & GIULIANI LLP *Washington, DC* |
| BRUDER GENTILE & MARCOUX LLP *Washington, DC* |
| DAVIS WRIGHT TREMAINE LLP *Washington, DC* |
| HOGAN & HARTSON LLP *Washington, DC* |
| MCDERMOTT WILL & EMERY *Washington, DC* |
| VINSON & ELKINS LLP *Washington, DC* |
| WINSTON & STRAWN LLP *Washington, DC* |

## Band 1

### Skadden, Arps, Slate, Meagher & Flom LLP & Affiliates

See firm details p.1557

**The Firm:** "*The premier firm for electricity – you just can't get any better,"* was the resounding consensus of clients. Covering the waterfront on electricity matters, there appears to be no stopping this New York giant. The team represents independent power producers, marketers and regulated utilities on corporate, finance and regulatory issues. Bolstered by the firm's "*jaw-dropping"* M&A practice, the energy team has won roles on some of the market's most recent headline deals. For example, it is representing Exelon in its acquisition of Public Service Electricity and Gas, acting for Duke in its merger with Cinergy and advising FPL Group on the regulatory aspects of its acquisition of Constellation Energy. The repeal of

the Public Utility Holding Company Act (PUHCA) further led market sources to note that this team is well positioned to harness the predicted increase in corporate activity. On regulatory matters, Neptune Regional Transmission System has engaged the firm to obtain regulatory approval and financing advice for its underground project serving Long Island. The team is also representing a large coalition of generators in FERC proceedings to establish compensation capacity in New England.

**The Lawyers:** The team boasts a number of lawyers with significant in-house FERC experience. The hugely respected **Clifford Naeve** (see p.534) offers expertise which spans several practice areas and is viewed by the market as spearheading the practice. "*A first-class person and attorney,"* Naeve's calm manner is appreciated as much as his technical ability, with clients observing: "*Life's too short to deal with jerks; he gets the job done and isn't self-important."* FERC litigation specialist **John Estes** (see p.510) is an "*excellent attorney who gets the work done effectively."* Estes is leading a coalition of generators, including Mirant, FPL Group and Entergy in litigation at FERC. "*Extremely talented and highly capable,"* **William Scherman** (see p.544) is another lawyer with significant previous experience at FERC, while colleague **Lynn Coleman** (see p.506) is viewed as a stalwart of the group with deep energy experience. He is often called on for his policy expertise. John Moot recently left the firm to take up the general counsel role at FERC.

**Clients/Work Highlights:** The team is working in conjunction with the Houston office to represent NRG Energy in its acquisition of Texas Genco, a deal worth approximately $5.8 billion. The group's enviable client roster also includes Portland General Electric; FPL Energy; Allegheny Energy and PG&E.

## Band 2

### Dewey Ballantine LLP

See firm details p.1530

**The Firm:** This is a "*well-integrated and industry-focused"* practice which continues to impress market commentators with its "*soup-to-nuts"* coverage of the electricity market. The group complements its regulatory and FERC expertise by drawing on the firm's finance, litigation and transaction capabilities. The team has subsequently developed a reputation for focusing on high-stakes litigation and market-shap-

ing advice to a diverse client base. The team's breadth of knowledge is now such that it represents buyers, for example, PG&E in its request for offers (RFO) for long-term power purchase agreements, while it can also represent generators in multiple proceedings before the FERC in their push for the development of capacity markets.

**The Lawyers:** "*An extremely significant player in this market,"* **Earle O'Donnell** (see p.535) is an attorney whose regulatory knowledge and ability to develop strong client relationships is admired by peers. Clients report that he is "*a one-stop shop"* for all their requirements and boasts "*a deft style which plays well to our commercial needs."* Colleague **Donna Attanasio** (see p.498) was highly recommended by clients as a "*font of knowledge"* who is "*easy to work with."* She is credited with leading the way on the firm's work for PG&E.

**Clients/Work Highlights:** Clients include Lake Road Generating, Edison Mission Energy and Midwest Generation.

### Steptoe & Johnson LLP

See firm details p.576

**The Firm:** This firm fields "*a really sharp bunch"* for electricity work, with a reputation for excellent service grounded in regulatory expertise, and a particular flair for utility work. The team's reputation is traditionally based in its FERC and litigation experience, although it is increasingly making a splash with its bulk power and transmission transactional work. Headline instructions this year include serving as regulatory counsel to PSEG in its merger with Exelon and representing the company at FERC proceedings, before the DOJ and in state regulatory hearings in Pennsylvania and New Jersey. The team also lends its considerable regulatory and policy prowess to Duke Energy, piloting it through FERC to obtain regulatory approval for its merger with Cinergy. The group has also earned a solid reputation for obtaining approvals for the formation of Regional Transmission Organizations (RTOs) and Independent System Operators (ISOs), and clients such as Northeast Utilities have tapped into this expertise, retaining the firm to help establish an RTO for New England.

**The Lawyers:** The departure to Edison International of heavyweight Lon Bouknight, often credited with building up the practice, has not gone unnoticed by commentators; however, clients and competitors were united in their opinion that he "*has*

## Energy: Electricity
### Leading Individuals

★ **NAEVE Clifford** *Skadden, Arps*

[1] **ACKER Lawrence** *LeBoeuf, Lamb*
    **DOWNS Clark** *Jones Day*
    **ESTES III John** *Skadden, Arps*
    **O'DONNELL Earle** *Dewey Ballantine LLP*
    **SCHERMAN William** *Skadden, Arps*

[2] **EISENSTAT Larry** *Dickstein Shapiro*
    **GREEN Douglas** *Steptoe & Johnson LLP*
    **JAFFE Kenneth** *Alston & Bird LLP*
    **MCMANUS Randolph** *Baker Botts LLP*
    **RASKIN David** *Steptoe & Johnson LLP*
    **ROBERTS Richard** *Steptoe & Johnson LLP*
    **SCHWARTZ David** *Latham & Watkins LLP*

[3] **ANGLE Stephen** *Vinson & Elkins LLP*
    **BALIS Stanley** *Miller, Balis & O'Neil, PC*
    **COLEMAN Lynn** *Skadden, Arps*
    **MCGRANE John** *Morgan, Lewis*
    **NORDHAUS Robert** *Van Ness Feldman PC*
    **NORTON IV Floyd** *Morgan, Lewis*
    **SHAPIRO Howard** *Van Ness Feldman PC*
    **SMALL Michael** *Wright & Talisman PC*
    **SMITH Roger** *Troutman Sanders LLP*

[4] **ATTANASIO Donna** *Dewey Ballantine LLP*
    **BACHMAN Gary** *Van Ness Feldman PC*
    **BEHRENDS IV Samuel** *LeBoeuf, Lamb*
    **BELL Joseph** *Hogan & Hartson LLP*
    **CONTRATTO Dana** *Crowell & Moring LLP*
    **GENTILE Carmen** *Bruder Gentile & Marcoux LLP*
    **GERGEN Michael** *Latham & Watkins LLP*
    **HERTZ Mitch** *Kirkland & Ellis LLP*
    **LEVY Neil** *Kirkland & Ellis LLP*
    **MOORE Margaret** *Van Ness Feldman PC*
    **O'SULLIVAN John** *Chadbourne & Parke LLP*
    **PERLIS Mark** *Dickstein Shapiro*
    **QUINT Arnold** *Hunton & Williams LLP*
    **SHAPIRO Robert** *Chadbourne & Parke LLP*
    **SIKORA Clifford** *Troutman Sanders LLP*
    **SPECTOR Barry** *Wright & Talisman PC*
    **WENNER Adam** *Chadbourne & Parke LLP*

[5] **AGRESTA Steven** *Alston & Bird LLP*
    **BLACKBURN Thomas** *Bruder Gentile & Marcoux LLP*
    **CANNON JR George** *Latham & Watkins LLP*
    **CLARKE Donald** *Law Offices of GKRSE*
    **DANKNER Donald** *Winston & Strawn LLP*
    **KRAMER Merrill** *Chadbourne & Parke LLP*
    **MADDEN William** *Winston & Strawn LLP*
    **MCCREA Keith** *Sutherland Asbill & Brennan LLP*
    **PANTANO Paul** *McDermott Will & Emery*
    **REED Wendy** *Wright & Talisman PC*
    **RUTKOWSKI Joanne** *Baker Botts LLP*
    **SMITH Douglas** *Van Ness Feldman PC*
    **SULLIVAN Mary Anne** *Hogan & Hartson LLP*
    **VASILE James** *Davis Wright Tremaine LLP*
    **WALSH Linda** *Hunton & Williams LLP*
    **YUFFEE Michael** *McDermott Will & Emery*

left, as a legacy, a team of highly trained lawyers, dedicated to deep industry knowledge and astute analysis." Among these, vice chairman of the firm **Douglas Green** (see p.516) was lauded as "*superb*" by market sources, who pointed to his electricity industry knowledge and ability to tackle complex competition matters. Green is leading the team for PSEG. "*Strong performer*" **David Raskin** (see p.540) is highly respected by commentators for his utilities work. **Richard Roberts** (see p.542) is lead partner in the firm's work for Southern California Edison and led the coalition in obtaining interests from sellers arising from the California energy crisis.

**Clients/Work Highlights:** American Electric Power Service; Edison International; Idaho Power; MidAmerican Energy; Orange & Rockland Utilities; Dominion Resources and Primary Energy.

## Band 3

### Alston & Bird LLP
See firm details p.728

**The Firm:** The firm enters the tables following the acquisition of the highly respected energy team from Swidler Berlin. The grouping now has a strong platform of national capabilities, from which it can drive its practice forward while looking set to offer clients a continuance of the "*innate competence*" for which it is famed. With recognized strength in all FERC and regulatory matters, the team has developed a formidable reputation for its work in structured markets and ISOs in particular. This year it has acted on FERC proceedings in connection with mechanisms for generation adequacy in New England, and has been heavily involved in establishing the New England ISO.

**The Lawyers:** **Kenneth Jaffe** (see p.520) is a respected name in the market and "*a smart guy with a lot of common sense who understands the industry well,*" say clients. His colleague **Steven Agresta** (see p.497) enters the tables on the strength of his "*truly excellent*" capabilities and specialized knowledge of the economic regulation of electricity markets.

**Clients/Work Highlights:** The California ISO and PJM number among the team's clients.

### Dickstein Shapiro Morin & Oshinsky LLP
See firm details p.565

**The Firm:** This "*incredibly responsive*" group was described by clients as "*a team of exceptional strategists,*" and it has built a reputation for offering creative solutions for independently owned power plants. This profile is complemented by a broad practice, which serves developers, utilities and private equity groups. The team handles trading emissions, compliance, corporate finance, FERC and state commission litigation. Highlight deals this year include advising CPV Wind Ventures in its funding and development agreement with ArcLight. Duke Energy is also a significant client, which the group advised in the sale of its control area services division.

**The Lawyers:** **Larry Eisenstat** (see p.510) heads up the electric power practice and has a forthright approach that appeals to clients, who say he is "*the one you want in your corner when things get sticky.*" "*Lawyers' lawyer*" **Mark Perlis** (see p.538) is "*cerebral*" in his approach and highly regarded by market sources. He advised client Duke Energy in its resolution of refund issues and regulatory matters stemming from the California energy crisis.

**Clients/Work Highlights:** KeySpan Energy and InterGen are also clients of the team.

### Latham & Watkins LLP

**The Firm:** "*Young and talented,*" according to industry insiders, the energy team at this highly regarded firm has chosen to focus its attention on the electricity sector. The group's dedication to this industry has paid off, and it has as broad base advising on regulatory issues, transactions and litigation. The team has also shrewdly anticipated the upswing in energy trading to capture a significant share of that market. It has done this by building on the firm's strong relationship with financial houses such as Goldman Sachs, which the firm advised on its restructuring of a number of power purchase agreements. Clients report that they are "*completely blown away*" by the efficiency and knowledge of this group. It has applied its skill to representing upstream lenders on distressed asset transactions for clients such as MACH Gen and Entegra. Reliability must-run (RMR) contracts are also a subject of this team's expertise. Mirant is one of a number of clients to have sought the firm's counsel in this area, charging the team with obtaining an RMR agreement with the ISO in New England for its Kendall facility in Massachusetts.

**The Lawyers:** Clients are attracted to the "*can-do attitude and excellent manner*" of **David Schwartz**. Although his practice tends to focus on the transactional side of deals, he can also turn his hand to litigation and has drafted federal and state energy legislation. Schwartz is especially recognized for his flair for interconnection and tolling agreements. Colleague **Michael Gergen** has developed experience in energy litigation, including involvement in the Mirant bankruptcy proceedings, in which it acted as the company's primary FERC counsel. **George Cannon**'s practice centers on energy regulatory and market matters. He represents a broad remit of clients before FERC, federal courts and state agencies.

**Clients/Work Highlights:** The team has continued to assist Sempra in resolving residual California energy crisis issues. Additional clients include Citibank and Société Générale.

### LeBoeuf, Lamb, Greene & MacRae LLP
See firm details p.1540

**The Firm:** A stalwart of the legal power market, LeBoeuf maintains a constant presence in the sector. Market sources commended the firm's "*well-developed and diversified practice,*" which encompasses the FERC, state proceedings and regulatory matters. The firm's stellar M&A reputation also ensures that transactional work features strongly in the team's repertoire. For example, the team represented MidAmerican Energy Holdings in connection with its acquisition of PacifiCorp. The team also advised Cinergy on the regulatory aspects of its Duke Energy merger.

**The Lawyers:** Focusing his practice on FERC matters, **Lawrence Acker** (see p.497) won plaudits as "*a true expert with deep experience in the power sector.*" Clients praised **Samuel Behrends** (see p.500) as "*a wonderful, strategic thinker.*" He offers clients the benefit of his 25 years' experience in electric utility representation, assisting utilities and nonutility generators in a variety of regulatory matters.

**Clients/Work Highlights:** Recognized for its work for traditional utilities, the practice also counts power marketers and finance houses among its clients. Other clients include Berkshire Hathaway; Central Maine Power and other regulatory affiliates of Energy East; Interstate Power & Light and Enron.

## Wright & Talisman PC

**The Firm:** This true specialist law firm is tailored for the counseling and representation of the modern energy industry. Researchers were told that this team is skilled in providing regulatory knowledge in a commercial context, with clients reporting that its attorneys are "*so knowledgeable, they give the pros and cons of each possible course of action and provide alternatives to help us move forward.*" The firm has deep roots in the energy regulatory market, with attorneys offering the benefit of years of industry expertise and clients who appreciate the team's "*great connections in Washington.*" In addition, the firm's reputation for representing RTOs and ISOs is formidable, and it can count PJM and SouthWest Power Pools as key clients.

**The Lawyers:** **Michael Small** attracted strong market commendation for his "*almost unrivaled*" knowledge and understanding of FERC issues, with observers pointing to his particular expertise in ratemaking and rulemaking matters. Managing shareholder of the firm **Barry Spector** "*knows all there is to know*" about ISOs and RTOs, according to clients, who equally appreciate his "*considered and efficient*" approach. Colleague **Wendy Reed** attracted significant praise from interviewees for her dedication and relentless efforts to secure optimal results for her clients. Peers observed: "*Representing a group of entities isn't easy, and she is so good she appears to do it effortlessly.*"

**Clients/Work Highlights:** Other clients include Ameron and Western Farmers Electric.

## Band 4

## Baker Botts LLP

See firm details p.1922

**The Firm:** An undisputed player in the oil and gas market, the electricity practice here more than holds its own. The firm's excellent finance and corporate reputation is naturally a big draw ticket to clients, but

this team also "*has real FERC experience and depth,*" say sources. Rate, tariffs and disputes are all handled by the group, which also has experience representing clients at state public utility commissions and on the federal circuit. The firm recently represented key client CenterPoint at the Texas Public Utility Commission, in addition to representing the company in its sale of Texas Genco.

**The Lawyers:** **Randolph McManus** (see p.531) has developed a reputation as a dean of the energy Bar, handling both regulatory and transactional matters. Peers remark: "*He's a great lawyer who draws in business and keeps clients happy.*" **Joanne Rutkowski** (see p.543) is highly regarded for her corporate skills in the electricity sector.

**Clients/Work Highlights:** The firm recently had three complaints stemming from the California crisis dismissed on behalf of key client Reliant. Other clients include Zilkha Renewable Energy; Exelon; Madison Gas & Electric; Mirant; Texas Pacific Group and AES.

## Chadbourne & Parke LLP

See firm details p.1524

**The Firm:** "*A slick outfit,*" which "*brings a real understanding of the commercial market as well as regulatory requirements to the table,*" say clients. The firm leverages off its mammoth projects expertise and reputation to provide both regulatory and finance advice to clients. Counseling independent power producers is a particular niche strength of the firm, especially on interconnection and transmission issues.

**The Lawyers:** Market commentators note that **John O'Sullivan** (see p.536) "*has an extremely strategic mind and articulate manner.*" Concentrating on advising IPPs, O'Sullivan recently represented the owner of a transmission line in a contested interconnection proceeding at FERC. Project finance and energy attorney **Robert Shapiro** (see p.545) is rated for his regulatory and finance expertise. He has defended several cogeneration projects and power marketers with long-term power contracts against challenges by utilities at both state and federal agencies and courts. Boasting more than 25 years of energy industry experience, **Adam Wenner** (see p.554) also combines a finance and regulatory practice, and is noted for his fine work for RTOs. **Merrill Kramer** (see p.524) represents energy industry and financial clients in the USA and internationally, and was praised by peers as "*a sharp transactional operator.*"

**Clients/Work Highlights:** CEMEX; AES; GE Structured Finance; Ormat; El Paso; GE Energy and Exelon. Generators, traditional utilities and RTOs also feature on the client list.

## Crowell & Moring LLP

See firm details p.564

**The Firm:** "*A sound outfit,*" according to sources, this broad practice is anchored in gas and electricity and its lawyers are equally expert in both. The practice advises on domestic FERC issues, while internationally, the team is developing a profile for electricity and hydro plants. Large legislative representations for

Knoxville Utilities and Memphis Light, Gas and Water have highlighted the team's ability to coordinate large cases and apply its regulatory knowledge. The group also represented Carrier Corporation in administrative proceedings at the DOE on energy efficiency standards for air conditioning and refrigeration products.

**The Lawyers:** **Dana Contratto** (see p.506) chairs the energy group and is recognized for his significant international practice.

**Clients/Work Highlights:** The group defended the Republic of Bolivia in international arbitration proceedings in connection with terminated water and electric concessions.

## Hunton & Williams LLP

See firm details p.1989

**The Firm:** This expanded team offers clients a "*one-stop shop,*" with capabilities across the regulatory, finance, antitrust and policy practice areas. Over the past year, five new senior members have joined the team, a number of which have significant Capitol Hill experience to boost the firm's legislative policy power. Clients report that attorneys here are "*tenacious, experienced and give considered answers.*" The firm advises electric utilities in all FERC regulatory and complaints issues, while the market also recognizes its expertise in advising ISOs.

**The Lawyers:** **Arnold Quint** (see p.540) provides "*efficient advice that covers all contingencies,*" say clients; he is the key contact for the New York ISO. Focusing on regulatory issues, **Linda Walsh** (see p.553) is noted for her RTO experience and the calm intelligence which she brings to matters.

**Clients/Work Highlights:** Clients include Superior Renewable Energy and Madison Gas & Electric.

## Jones Day

See firm details p.570

**The Firm:** According to market sources, this firm enjoys "*a reputation for quality work.*" While the focus of this team is on the regulatory side, it works hand in hand with the transactional team. This synergy was demonstrated by the firm's advice to AEP in its $325 million sale of its stake in the South Texas Project nuclear plant. Rate reasonableness issues are also a forte of the group, which has been called upon by OGE Energy to assist it in a recent hearing.

**The Lawyers:** **Clark Downs** (see p.509) enjoys a high profile in the industry thanks to his "*technical expertise, regulatory knowledge and excellent bedside manner.*" His practice is concentrated on state and federal regulation rate and competition issues.

**Clients/Work Highlights:** The team is representing Xcel Energy subsidiaries Southwestern Public Service Company and Public Service Company of Colorado in a transmission rate case. Other clients include AEP, OGE Energy and Dominion East Ohio.

## Kirkland & Ellis LLP

See firm details p.875

**The Firm:** This firm has made a concerted push into the electricity sector, and its key role in advising on some of the most significant deals of the year underlines the success of its strategy. Viewed as the "*go-to*"

firm for IPPs, the team advises on all corporate, commercial and regulatory matters, with the market noting its excellent work with transmission credits and reactive power tariffs matters. The firm also offers a mature energy trading practice, dealing with commodities, swaps and fuel agreements. Headline deals include serving Constellation Energy as corporate and regulatory counsel in its merger with FPL Group. The team also advised Calpine Energy, for which it filed the eighth largest bankruptcy case ever filed in the USA, and 295 affiliated entities seeking bankruptcy protection.

**The Lawyers:** **Mitch Hertz** (see p.519) received warm praise from clients who recommended him for his user-friendly service: "*He has a good depth of knowledge of the area, is timely and responsive.*" **Neil Levy** (see p.526) was also praised by clients: "*He tries to resolve rather than create problems and looks for the most workable solution for us.*"

**Clients/Work Highlights:** Madison Dearborn is a key client, and the team is advising it on its purchase of three New York City power plants from Reliant Energy. Dynegy and NRG Energy also instruct the team on a range of corporate and regulatory issues. Other clients include Tenaska; Integra; SUEZ Energy North America; Mustang Energy; InterGen Services; Bain Capital; The Dayton Power and Light Company and Reliant Resources.

## Miller, Balis & O'Neil, PC

**The Firm:** This local boutique enjoys a great reputation within the market for its tailored and expert advice to clients, who are usually owners of generating capacity or wholesale customers of utilities. The full range of FERC issues are handled, as are technical matters relating to the generation, transmission and distribution of power.

**The Lawyers:** **Stanley Balis** is a distinguished practitioner and is particularly recommended for his strength in representing municipal interests. A standout name in the sector, Balis handles a mix of electricity and gas work.

**Clients/Work Highlights:** Clients include public agencies and associations; consumer-owned electric distribution systems; the owners of electricity generating facilities; wholesale customers of utilities and natural gas distribution systems

## Morgan, Lewis & Bockius LLP

See firm details p.1758

**The Firm:** The electricity team at this firm forms part of a terrifically integrated energy department providing clients with "*efficient, fast and friendly*" advice. In addition to advising clients on FERC matters in both transactions and proceedings, the team has a strong policy bent, utilizing its extensive expertise to explore alternative regional transmission structures on behalf of clients. In addition to transmission issues, the bulk of the team's work is in internal compliance, where, for example, it has represented Arizona Public Service Company in audit proceedings and compliance work. One client reported: "*It is such a solid team, and is particularly great on interconnection agreements.*"

**The Lawyers:** "*Outstanding in every way,*" according to clients, **John McGrane** (see p.531) is noted for his work representing clients during investigations and audits. **Floyd Norton** (see p.535) is "*knowledgeable and creative.*" Clients told researchers: "*I have a conversation with him and get exactly the right information I need – as an in-house counsel I find that extremely useful.*"

**Clients/Work Highlights:** Pinnacle West; Reliant Energy; UGI; Arizona Public Service Company; Midwest Reliability Organization; Minnesota Power; Entergy; Exelon; Alliant Energy; Black Hills; Cargill Power Markets and Northeast Utilities.

## Troutman Sanders LLP

**The Firm:** Researchers heard that this firm is "*one to look out for, it's really making its mark.*" The electricity practice concentrates on advising utilities on corporate restructurings, negotiating power purchase agreements and FERC matters, including rate proceedings.

**The Lawyers:** **Roger Smith** accrued extensive FERC experience prior to joining the firm and is highly regarded by the market. Head of the energy team **Clifford Sikora** was recommended particularly for his drafting skills. He is "*extremely diligent and articulate,*" concluded clients.

**Clients/Work Highlights:** Traditional utilities constitute the bulk of the team's clients, of which Southern California Edison is a key client.

## Van Ness Feldman PC

**The Firm:** This highly respected firm fields a deep team of electricity industry experts with significant in-house FERC experience. Indeed, clients report that this "*slick outfit*" provides "*excellent value for money.*" Electric utilities form the core of the client base, and the team advises on the full range of legal services, with its work on appellate matters warranting special mention. In addition to traditional electricity work, the team takes great interest in clean air, climate change and energy technology issues.

**The Lawyers:** Peers agree that **Robert Nordhaus** is "*impressive in terms of experience and political and legal skills.*" With prior FERC and DOJ experience, he advises on all regulatory and transactional matters. Another ex-FERC alumnus, **Howard Shapiro** is an experienced appellate litigator who attracts high praise from clients. Colleague **Gary Bachman** is "*extremely effective, I'd certainly rate him up there,*" say clients. He is noted for his work in hydroelectricity sector. **Margaret Moore** concentrates on energy project work, advising traders and merchant generators. Clients report that "*she has the ability to take complicated regulations and apply them in a commercial context – it's a gift.*" **Douglas Smith** brings his prior experience as FERC general counsel to advise on gas and electricity issues.

**Clients/Work Highlights:** Clients are predominantly major investor-owned utilities; smaller utilities; trade associations; independent generators and power marketers.

## Bracewell & Giuliani LLP

See firm details p.1924

**The Firm:** Entering the electricity table this year, the firm has made a play for work in this sector and it is paying off. Power purchase, tolling and profit sharing as well as transactional work are all undertaken by the team for a range of industry players. Energy trading is where the firm is really making a splash, advising clients such as Shell subsidiary Coral Energy on a range of matters.

**The Lawyers:** Dan Watkiss is the key contact for power matters.

**Clients/Work Highlights:** Diamond Generating; PSEG Power; Dynergy; Hydro-Quebec TransEnergie and SCANA Corporation are among the firm's clients.

## Bruder Gentile & Marcoux LLP

**The Firm:** "*A solid and respected player in the industry,*" according to peers, this boutique outfit tailors its advice to electric and gas utilities. It is particularly noted for its work in restructuring the electricity industry and on counseling on transmission, tariffs and interconnection agreements. While not bankruptcy lawyers, the firm has been heavily involved in assisting the California Power Exchange through its bankruptcy.

**The Lawyers:** **Carmen Gentile** is a standout name at the firm and has extensive experience appearing before the FERC and the federal appeals court. "*Skilled operator*" **Thomas Blackburn** generates praise for his work in developing standards and codes of conduct.

**Clients/Work Highlights:** Nstar Electric & Gas; Progress Energy; Pepco Holdings; El Paso Electric and Dominion.

## Davis Wright Tremaine LLP

**The Firm:** The firm joins the energy table this year due to strong praise by the market for the entire team. Clients report that the firm's attorneys "*have a great understanding of the industry and bridge the regulatory and finance worlds in an exceptional way.*" Energy-related projects are a specialty of the team.

**The Lawyers:** **James Vasile** heads up the Washington, DC team and focuses on FERC-related issues. He is recognized for his expertise in the hydroelectricity sector.

**Clients/Work Highlights:** Idaho Power is an important client, and it has instructed the firm on the Hell's Canyon project. Calpine is another key client which the firm advises largely on regulatory matters.

## Hogan & Hartson LLP

See firm details p.568

**The Firm:** "*A great team covering a complex and broad-based field,*" say clients who are increasingly drawn to this accomplished group. The firm displays a real dedication and understanding of the industry, advising a raft of clients on regulatory and transactional matters. Work such as advising Dominion

Resources in the transfer of control of its entire multistate electric transmission system to PJM Interconnection has been a definite highlight this year. Clients also report that the group is *great at handling investigations,* a skill which clients such as the Public Service Company of New Mexico have made use of.
**The Lawyers:** *"One of the smartest people on earth,"* according to clients, **Joseph Bell** (see p.500) is widely respected for his work in the area, which has recently concentrated on advising governments and civic organizations on both electricity and oil matters. Well regarded by both clients and peers, **Mary Anne Sullivan** (see p.549) is *"incredibly sharp in terms of following through and final review."*
**Clients/Work Highlights:** The firm represents AEP in a series of investigations before the FERC. California Independent System Operator is a key client, and the team has represented them in connection with multiple RMR unit rate proceedings. Other clients include Aquila; Bonneville Power Administration; Cleco; Midwest Generation EME and Western Electricity Coordinating Council.

## McDermott Will & Emery
See firm details p.878
**The Firm:** This team continues to attract attention for its specialized energy offering, which originally grew out of the firm's commodities trading practice. In addition to FERC regulatory expertise, it is one of the key players for energy trading. Sources report that the firm is *"building a good, diverse practice and has developed a core of great people."* Clients were quick to praise this team, commenting: *"It does strike the right balance of partners and associates, and provides an appropriate level of contact with us as clients. It understands that cost is a concern and staff deal accordingly."*

**The Lawyers:** **Paul Pantano** (see p.537) heads the group and is well liked within the trading industry. Researchers were told that *"he's a great client guy."* **Michael Yuffee** (see p.556) works on the regulatory side of transactions, and clients appreciate his aggressive advocacy skills, describing him as *"a pitbull – we know that when he goes in to negotiate, we'll get what we want."*
**Clients/Work Highlights:** Key clients include Morgan Stanley Capital; Merrill Lynch Commodities; Mirant; Constellation Energy; Lehman Brothers; Independent Energy Producers Association and J. Aron.

## Vinson & Elkins LLP
See firm details p.1938
**The Firm:** The firm offers strong regulatory capability in the electricity and power sector, complementing its renowned oil and gas practice. Utilities, IPPs and RTOs seek the team's counsel for not only regulatory but transactional and finance matters. For example, Complete Energy holdings engaged the firm to assist in its acquisition of all the equity interests in La Paloma Generating Company for $561 million. The group also enjoys an impressive FERC strike rate, and successfully applied on behalf of TransAlta for compensation for reactive power services that TransAlta was required to provide to Bonneville Power Administration under an interconnection agreement.
**The Lawyers:** **Stephen Angle** (see p.498) *"is a solid performer"* whose practice is strong on regulation in the electricity sector. He is the key contact for Calpine.
**Clients/Work Highlights:** Allegheny; TransAlta Energy; Calpine; New Brunswick Power; TXU; AIG and Sigma.

## Winston & Strawn LLP
See firm details p.886
**The Firm:** A major player in the nuclear legal market, the electricity team more than holds its own. It has advised on a number of bankruptcy divestitures in recent years and is utilizing its FERC regulatory knowledge in the RTO and ISO sector. It also has a strong conduct compliance practice, advising Westar Energy throughout a FERC audit. Clients report: *"The team is of the strength and ability of any other top firm, but without the ego."*
**The Lawyers:** **Donald Dankner** (see p.507) *"has a great reputation"* and advises clients on all aspects of negotiating and litigating on FERC issues, on both electricity and gas matters. **William Madden** has spearheaded the firm's lauded hydroelectricity practice and is *"a prominent presence in the market."*
**Clients/Work Highlights:** The firm has a wide range of clients in the electricity sector.

## Other Notable Practitioners
**Donald Clarke** of the Law Offices of GKRSE is a hydroelectric specialist whose clients include the National Hydropower Association. **Keith McCrea** (see p.530) of Sutherland Asbill & Brennan LLP is *"a seasoned attorney"* who works across electricity, oil and gas. Clients remark that *"he has a great ability to work in multiparty matters."*

# ENERGY

# NUCLEAR

| Energy: Nuclear |
| --- |
| Leading Firms |
| [1] MORGAN, LEWIS & BOCKIUS LLP *Washington, DC* |
| PILLSBURY WINTHROP *Washington, DC* |
| WINSTON & STRAWN LLP *Washington, DC* |

## Band 1

## Morgan, Lewis & Bockius LLP
See firm details p.1758
**The Firm:** Boasting the largest nuclear team in Washington, DC, clients assured researchers that the breadth and depth of expertise in this team matched its size. The firm represents approximately 40% of the installed nuclear capacity in the USA. Work includes obtaining licensing approval for new plants and counseling clients with regulatory difficulties, as well as transactional matters and whistle-blower

complaints. Clients observed that this recently expanded team *"is a tight ship – the level of coordination and integration between attorneys results in us obtaining thorough advice efficiently."* Recent work includes representing Exelon in its application for renewal of its Oyster Creek nuclear power plant, and assisting AREVA in obtaining a nuclear design certification. The team also assisted key client Southern Nuclear in its application for an early site permit.
**The Lawyers:** A key name in the marketplace, **George Edgar** (see p.509) deftly melds technical expertise gained during his studies of nuclear engineering with more than 30 years of legal experience. He was praised by clients for being *"technically brilliant, diligent and incredibly thorough."* Colleague **Jay Gutierrez** (see p.517) has *"great depth of knowledge and experience in the area,"* according to sources, who also praised his ability to *"identify the issues and create a forum for clients to discuss them."* The *"excellent and efficient"* **Steven Frantz** (see p.513) is noted for his

expertise in obtaining approvals for new plants, while **Kathryn Sutton** (see p.549) is new to the tables and new to the team. Sutton moved from Winston & Strawn during the year and attracted praise from market sources for her knowledge of the sector, where she focuses on nuclear plant licensing issues and renewal.
**Clients/Work Highlights:** The firm represents NuStart Energy Development, a consortium of electric utilities that operates more than half of the nuclear power reactors in the USA. It also represented USEC before the Nuclear Regulatory Commission (NRC) to obtain a license for the American Centrifuge Plant. Other clients include Duke Cogema Stone & Webster, US Department of Energy and FirstEnergy.

## Pillsbury Winthrop Shaw Pittman LLP
See firm details p.1550
**The Firm:** *"A go-to firm for nuclear,"* according to

clients, Pillsbury created the first nuclear energy practice in the USA more than 40 years ago and now represents over 40 electric utilities, providing a soup-to-nuts service in the nuclear sector. The group's work on contentious matters at the NRC and state level attracted especial praise from market sources. For example, the team obtained approval for the Private Fuel Storage Facility, and advised Florida Power & Light on the acquisition of the Duane Arnold plant.

**The Lawyers:** Clients benefit from the team's prac-tical and legal knowledge of the industry. Chair of the firm's energy practice **Jay Silberg** (see p.545) served as a lawyer in the US Atomic Energy Commission and enjoys a strong reputation within the industry. Invariably described as a fine and exp-erienced attorney, clients report: "*He can get to matters quicker and with more insight than others in the field.*" **David Lewis** (see p.526) is noted for his "*encyclope-dic knowledge of nuclear licensing,*" while colleague **John O'Neill** (see p.536) boasts a "*strong background and thorough knowledge*" of the area, bolstered by having served in the US Navy and being licensed by the Atomic Energy Commission to supervise the operation and maintenance of naval nuclear propul-sion power plants. MBA qualified **Charles Peterson** (see p.538) is recommended for his fantastic business sense and for adding strong commercial under-standing to the team.

**Clients/Work Highlights:** AEP; Entergy; Xcel Energy; Duke Energy; Indiana Michigan Power; Omaha Public Power District and Detroit Edison.

## Winston & Strawn LLP

See firm details p.886

**The Firm:** Respected for its NRC administrative licensing and litigation capability, this firm has a long history in the nuclear industry. Covering the full range of services to the sector, the team's workload has been dominated this year by providing advice on the NRC aspects of mergers for clients such as Duke Energy and Exelon. Other highlights include advis-ing Yankee Atomic Energy on the decommissioning of its Yankee Row nuclear plant. Louisiana Energy Services has instructed the firm in connection with its proposal to build a national enrichment facility in New Mexico.

**The Lawyers:** "*Well respected in the industry and forthright in his advice,*" **Nicholas Reynolds** (see p.541) oversees the practice and is managing partner of the firm. Focusing on energy policy and nuclear regulatory law, **James Curtiss** (see p.507) enjoys a significant reputation in the sector, with clients reporting that he "*is excellent at questioning witnesses*" and is "*extremely well connected.*" His colleague **David Repka** (see p.541) "*is an outstand-ing lawyer with a solid grasp of technical as well as legal aspects,*" say clients. Repka is particularly noted for his strength in NRC issues, with clients observing: "*He has good working relationships with regulators and is able to get things done without annoying people.*"

**Clients/Work Highlights:** Other clients include ARRIVA, Connecticut Yankee and Chemico.

# ENVIRONMENT

## Band 1

### Hunton & Williams LLP

See firm details p.1989

**The Firm:** This "*long-standing force*" in the DC market deals with the full range of environmental issues on both a national and international level. Peers particularly commend its excellent clean air practice. Environmental permitting is a growth area, especially with regard to new energy facilities, includ-ing coal and LNG, and commercial and residential developments. During the past year, the team also dealt with several water resource issues, with an emphasis on those pertaining to the west of the country. A large group of environmental lawyers liaise with colleagues in the government relations, energy and litigation departments as required. More-over, Hunton & Williams has staffed its offices, not only in the USA but also in Europe and Asia, to handle whatever international environmental matters are thrown up. For example, the Brussels office can handle a wide range of regulatory matters under both EU and national laws. Given the recent trend toward the internationalization of environ-mental regulation, clients said they found the firm's global strategy to be particularly beneficial.

**The Lawyers:** "*A key player in DC,*" **William Brownell** (see p.504) has been involved in several high-profile new source review (NSR) cases. He defended several electric utilities in district courts against CAA enforcement actions, where the most publicized case was US v Duke Energy. Peers note that he and **Andrea Bear Field** (see p.512) "*are a class act.*" Field's "*no-nonsense*" approach goes down well with commentators and she is acknowledged as a real expert in the clean air and regulatory arena. **Henry Nickel** (see p.535) is another of the firm's "*top clean air lawyers,*" and he "*brings to the table a tremendous knowledge of all the case law involving the CAA.*" He also offers expertise in the CWA and NEPA. **Virginia Albrecht** (see p.497) is "*one of the leading wetland lawyers in the country,*" according to market observers. She was involved in the $1.2 billion Mills-Mack/Cali project that is under construction at the Meadowlands Sports Complex in New Jersey. **Turner Smith** (see p.547) heads the firm's interna-tional environmental practice and focuses on inter-national environmental and energy law. He has represented clients on major Superfund matters and has been involved in shaping Superfund regulations before the EPA.

**Clients/Work Highlights:** In addition to an impressive raft of clients from the utility industries, the firm acts for a range of national and international companies.

### Latham & Watkins LLP

**The Firm:** "*A big, robust environment practice,*" Latham has 20 lawyers in DC and more than 100 lawyers nationwide focusing on environmental work. It is one of the busiest groups in the firm. Clients marvel at the coordination between offices, including those as far afield as London, Moscow and Shanghai. The DC office won special praise for its breadth of expertise. Practice areas covered include chemical and pesticides regulations, litigation, mass torts, Superfund sites and project work, all of which is complemented by a global climate change practice group. Meanwhile, its air and regulatory practice is held in particularly high regard among peers. Members of the firm were repeatedly commended for their "*sound judgment,*" and in the past year they represented 3M on regulatory and litigation matters relating to fluorochemicals, acted for Kuhlman Elec-tric and The Carlyle Group in a toxic torts case concerning the discovery of PCB contamination at a site in Crystal Springs, Mississippi, and assisted Syngenta with one of the largest pesticide data compensation cases ever brought.

**The Lawyers:** "*Top-notch*" **David Hayes** is Latham's global chair of the environment, land and resources department. A former deputy secretary of the Department of the Interior under the Clinton administration, he is admired for his regulatory and natural resources work. He has developed more of an international focus of late, not least by contributing to the firm's climate change initiative. Clients note that he "*exudes confidence and trust and is a strategic thinker.*" A former deputy administrator of the EPA, **Robert Sussman** is lauded as "*smart and extremely successful at preventing big problems occurring.*" He chairs the firm's DC environmental practice. His focus includes emerging trends in air quality issues, toxic substances regulation and environmental management reform. **Julia Hatcher** is "*extremely hard-working*" and is noted for her chemicals sector

## Environment
### Leading Firms

1. **HUNTON & WILLIAMS LLP** *Washington, DC*
   **LATHAM & WATKINS LLP** *Washington, DC*
   **SIDLEY AUSTIN LLP** *Washington, DC*
2. **ARNOLD & PORTER LLP** *Washington, DC*
   **BEVERIDGE & DIAMOND PC** *Washington, DC*
   **COVINGTON & BURLING** *Washington, DC*
   **HOGAN & HARTSON LLP** *Washington, DC*
   **MORGAN, LEWIS & BOCKIUS LLP** *Washington, DC*
3. **BAKER BOTTS LLP** *Washington, DC*
   **BINGHAM MCCUTCHEN LLP** *Washington, DC*
   **GIBSON, DUNN & CRUTCHER LLP** *Washington, DC*
   **KING & SPALDING LLP** *Washington, DC*
   **KIRKLAND & ELLIS LLP** *Washington, DC*
   **SKADDEN, ARPS** *Washington, DC*
   **VENABLE LLP** *Washington, DC*
   **VINSON & ELKINS LLP** *Washington, DC*
4. **CROWELL & MORING LLP** *Washington, DC*
   **DLA PIPER RUDNICK GRAY CARY US** *Washington, DC*
   **FOLEY & LARDNER LLP** *Washington, DC*
   **JONES DAY** *Washington, DC*
   **MCKENNA LONG & ALDRIDGE LLP** *Washington, DC*
   **PILLSBURY WINTHROP** *Washington, DC*
   **VAN NESS FELDMAN PC** *Washington, DC*
   **WEIL, GOTSHAL & MANGES LLP** *Washington, DC*
   **WILLKIE FARR & GALLAGHER LLP** *Washington, DC*
   **WILMERHALE** *Washington, DC*

## Environment: Mainly Transactional
### Leading Individuals

1. **BERLIN Kenneth** *Skadden, Arps*
2. **BERZ David** *Weil, Gotshal*
   **CONNOLLY Annemargaret** *Weil, Gotshal*
   **FROST JR Don** *Skadden, Arps*
   **LOHMANN Walter** *Kirkland & Ellis LLP*

expertise, particularly where perfluorooctanoic acid or PFOA is concerned, a substance on which she is a recognized authority. Her broad practice includes CAA matters and advising clients on strategies for managing short and long-term regulatory, public policy, communications and litigation issues. **Ken Weinstein** maintains a sound reputation among his peers and is an acknowledged expert on pesticide issues. His areas of expertise include chemical regulation, the Federal Insecticide, Fungicide and Rodenticide Act (FIFRA) and enforcement actions.

**Clients/Work Highlights:** Kuhlman Electric; PG&E Company; 3M; Cinergy; Syngenta; Ford and CropLife America.

## Sidley Austin LLP
See firm details p.883

**The Firm:** This thriving environmental practice has "*great depth*" and market commentators acknowledge it as a leader in the field. Approximately 40 attorneys practice environmental law full-time in the Chicago, DC, New York and Los Angeles offices. They assist the firm's other offices, including those in Tokyo, Shanghai and Geneva, as required. The practice is credited with "*exceptionally fine lawyers who have excellent experience. They give solid, practical advice and are good at strategic development and implementation.*" The environmental group boasts expertise in numerous areas including Superfund sites, enforcement defense, clean air and toxic tort cases. It also has a distinguished environmental litigation practice.

**The Lawyers:** Peers agree that **David Buente** (see p.504) is "*at the top of his game and a first-rate professional.*" Formerly of the DOJ, he is "*brilliant, pragmatic and resourceful with a tremendous breadth of knowledge.*" He is noted for his expertise in Superfund, CAA and criminal environmental matters. His colleague **Angus Macbeth** (see p.528) "*has done some top-notch and creative work. He is a lawyer of remarkable stature and one of the top DC litigators.*" His extensive experience, both at the DOJ and in private practice, has elevated him to senior statesman.

**Clients/Work Highlights:** The practice has an impressive client base that includes GE, Cinergy and ExxonMobil.

## Band 2

### Arnold & Porter LLP
See firm details p.560

**The Firm:** This national environmental practice spans offices in Northern Virginia, New York, Denver and Los Angeles, as well as in London and Brussels. It is the preferred choice for several clients when it comes to handling litigation matters. The DC operation offers just under 20 environmental lawyers. They have also made a name for themselves in litigation, hazardous materials, toxic torts and clean air matters. Clients spoke appreciatively of their breadth of experience and responsiveness.

**The Lawyers:** Interviewees agreed **Blake Biles** (see p.502) is a "*big hitter*" at the firm who is blessed with an "*easygoing Midwestern charm.*" Billed as a "*real deal-maker*" by peers and clients alike, he is lauded for his expertise in chemical regulation matters. Clients also value his "*realistic assessments of risk.*" **Thomas Milch** (see p.532) won praise for his expertise in contamination and environmental compliance issues. One interviewee went so far as to say that he is "*one of the brightest, most capable and innovative lawyers I've worked with.*"

**Clients/Work Highlights:** Clariant; American Capital Strategies; Occidental Petroleum and Honeywell.

### Beveridge & Diamond PC
See firm details p.562

**The Firm:** With "*one of the largest environmental practices in the country*" and more than 75 lawyers to boot, this boutique is a "*truly specialized operation.*" As one satisfied client put it: "*There is a specialist available for virtually every environmental issue that could possibly arise, whether it's toxic substances, a Superfund matter or something wholly esoteric that defies categorization, there is someone on hand to help.*" The firm is proud of the range of expertise and strength in depth it offers to clients, both on domestic and international fronts. Practice areas include hazardous waste, regulatory and recovery work, environmental management, noise regulation and biotechnology. It also has a considerable pesticide practice.

**The Lawyers:** **Paul Hagen** (see p.517) is much in demand for his "*in-depth knowledge of international law,*" and chairs the firm's international environmental practice section. Praised as "*extremely focused on client needs,*" Hagen has worked with numerous clients on international chemical regulations and continues to contribute to projects where the American Chemistry Council is involved. These include the negotiation and implementation of the Stockholm Persistent Organic Pollutants Convention, the Rotterdam PIC Convention and the Strategic Approach to International Chemicals Management. **Karl Bourdeau** (see p.503) is another member of the team credited with "*a real fierce devotion to client service.*" Hailed for his hazardous waste expertise, one client remarked that he is "*creative with strategy in a way I haven't really seen in hazardous waste issues before.*" He is currently representing clients in Salt Institute v Leavitt. This is the first appellate case to determine whether affected parties have a right to judicial review of a federal agency's failure to correct information allegedly disseminated in derogation of information quality standards established under the Information Quality Act.

**Clients/Work Highlights:** BASF; Unisys; Kimberly-Clark; US Steel; GE; WR Grace; Electronic Industries Alliance and American Chemistry Council.

### Covington & Burling
See firm details p.563

**The Firm:** "*A first-rate firm with first-rate lawyers,*" Covington & Burling move up the tables this year due to strong market feedback. The team takes a multidisciplinary approach, working together seamlessly with other practice groups as necessary. The firm set up a new carbon markets industry group in 2005 to assist clients with climate change matters and related transactional, regulatory and compliance issues. Other areas covered include defending claims for natural resource damages by federal, state and tribal trustees under CERCLA, and representing clients in legislative, rulemaking, permitting and licensing proceedings.

**The Lawyers:** The "*fabulous*" **Ted Garrett** (see p.514) is "*extraordinarily knowledgeable across the board.*" He cochairs the firm's environmental practice group. His typical workload includes advising on the environmental aspects of selling divisions of major corporations and on permitting procedures relating to new energy plants.

**Clients/Work Highlights:** Boeing; Procter & Gamble; Del Monte Foods; Alcan/Pechiney; Vulcan Materials Company; ITOCHU; Northrop Grumman; Kerr-McGee; Kansas City Power & Light; Holly Corporation and Microsoft.

## Environment
### Leading Individuals

#### Senior Statesmen

GARRETT Theodore *Covington & Burling*

MACBETH Angus *Sidley Austin LLP*

QUARLES John *Morgan, Lewis*

WARREN Edward *Kirkland & Ellis LLP*

[1] BUENTE David *Sidley Austin LLP*

HAYES David *Latham & Watkins LLP*

[2] BILES Blake *Arnold & Porter LLP*

BROWNELL William *Hunton & Williams LLP*

BUCKLEY JR Christopher *Gibson, Dunn*

DINKINS Carol *Vinson & Elkins LLP*

FIELD Andrea Bear *Hunton & Williams LLP*

GAYNOR Kevin *Vinson & Elkins LLP*

HAGEN Paul *Beveridge & Diamond PC*

KNAUSS Charles *Bingham McCutchen LLP*

LEWIS William *Morgan, Lewis*

MENOTTI David *Pillsbury Winthrop*

MILCH Thomas *Arnold & Porter LLP*

NICKEL Henry *Hunton & Williams*

STARR Judson *Venable LLP*

STEINBERG Michael *Morgan, Lewis*

SUSSMAN Robert *Latham & Watkins LLP*

[3] ALBRECHT Virginia *Hunton & Williams LLP*

BERGESON Lynn *Bergeson & Campbell PC*

BOURDEAU Karl *Beveridge & Diamond PC*

ELLIOTT E Donald *Willkie Farr & Gallagher LLP*

HATCHER Julia *Latham & Watkins LLP*

LUDWISZEWSKI Raymond *Gibson, Dunn*

LUXTON Jane *King & Spalding LLP*

RAHER Patrick *Hogan & Hartson LLP*

RHYNE Katherine *King & Spalding LLP*

RITTS Leslie Sue *Hogan & Hartson LLP*

SMITH JR Turner *Hunton & Williams LLP*

WEINSTEIN Ken *Latham & Watkins LLP*

[4] BANKS Jim *Hogan & Hartson LLP*

BIEKE James *Goodwin Procter LLP*

BLOCK Joseph *Venable LLP*

BUMPERS Heidi *Jones Day*

BUMPERS William *Baker Botts LLP*

CARR Don *Pillsbury Winthrop*

DRAKE Stuart *Kirkland & Ellis LLP*

FROST JR Don *Skadden, Arps*

HALL JR Ridgway *Crowell & Moring LLP*

HOLEWINSKI Kevin *Jones Day*

JACKSON Thomas *Baker Botts LLP*

KASTNER Ken *Hogan & Hartson LLP*

LOHMANN Walter *Kirkland & Ellis LLP*

PENNA Richard *Van Ness Feldman PC*

STOLL Richard *Foley & Lardner LLP*

STRAND Margaret *Venable LLP*

#### Up-and-coming individuals

JENKS Carrie *Willkie Farr & Gallagher LLP*

### Hogan & Hartson LLP
See firm details p.568

**The Firm:** This firm has a strong national and international presence with 23 offices in the USA, Europe and Asia. Its "*extremely able*" environment lawyers in DC wowed clients with their "*outstanding professionalism and breadth of expertise.*" DaimlerChrysler is one of many impressive clients, and the team advised the corporation on environmental and safety compliance for its automotive assembly and fleet sales operations in the USA. Other important mandates include representing the National Environmental Development Association in its Clean Air Project, a CAA regulatory coalition in Washington, DC.

**The Lawyers: Patrick Raher** (see p.540) is director of the firm's environmental group and has been a member of the EPA's CAA Advisory Committee since 1992. Recent case highlights include representing communities adjacent to Chicago's O'Hare Airport in contesting the FAA and City of Chicago's proposed $20 billion O'Hare Airport expansion. **Leslie Sue Ritts** (see p.541) "*really knows the air field and is really something.*" Highly respected by peers and clients alike, she has a straightforward style and gives precise advice. **Jim Banks** (see p.499) is an "*excellent litigator.*" His contentious highlights include representing the State of Florida in a matter concerning water flows in the Chattahoochee, Flint and Apalachicola rivers. He also advised Tyson Foods on water and air pollution issues. **Ken Kastner** (see p.522) was praised for his regulatory work, especially where chemicals and hazardous waste transportation are concerned. He is also national RCRA counsel to several manufacturers of chemicals and allied products.

**Clients/Work Highlights:** Mercedes-Benz; Mitsubishi Motors North America; Freightliner; Procter & Gamble; Verizon; National Chicken Council; Cargill; Diesel Technology Forum; International Wood Products Association and GATX.

### Morgan, Lewis & Bockius LLP
See firm details p.1758

**The Firm:** Morgan Lewis was one of the first major law firms to establish an environmental practice. Currently, market commentators point to the group's excellent handling of Superfund and clean air matters as distinguishing it from competitors. Its national practice comprises more than 100 environment lawyers who can utilize resources in the firm's international network, which extends as far afield as Paris, Brussels and Tokyo, as required. A multidisciplinary approach hinges on an integrated team of environmental regulatory experts, litigators, and insurance recovery, toxic tort and real estate lawyers, who cooperate according to the needs of the client.

**The Lawyers:** Senior litigator **William Lewis** (see p.526) is "*good at seeing and delivering creative solutions.*" His reputation in the CAA arena precedes him. The "*extremely talented*" **Michael Steinberg** (see p.548) is held in particularly high esteem for his Superfund work. He focuses exclusively on environmental law matters, particularly hazardous waste and environmental justice issues under federal and state civil rights laws. "*One of the real stalwarts in the environmental law area in Washington, DC*" and a "*top name in Superfund work,*" **John Quarles** (see p.540) is acknowledged as a senior statesman this year. Clients applaud his ability to grasp the significance of all the latest developments in the field, and find "*his understanding of the political as well as the legal arena*" to be of great benefit.

**Clients/Work Highlights:** The firm represents a broad range of clients including multinationals and national bodies.

### Band 3

### Baker Botts LLP
See firm details p.1922

**The Firm:** Market commentators agree that the firm boasts a "*serious air practice.*" However, its sizable department covers the full gamut of environmental matters, from spill response and release reporting through endangered species to environmental considerations in bankruptcy. The team in DC benefits from the firm's national and international reach – it has several offices across the country as well as in Asia and Europe.

**The Lawyers: Bill Bumpers** (see p.505) "*is huge in the CAA area,*" where he is busy on both noncontentious regulatory and litigation fronts. He counts petroleum refiners, electric generators and pharmaceutical manufacturers as clients. Special counsel **Tom Jackson** (see p.520) sustains a varied practice, incorporating Superfund, wetlands, endangered species and Marine Mammal Protection Act compliance work. He recently assisted a landowner in California with a case concerning designation of critical habitat.

**Clients/Work Highlights:** The firm acts for a variety of landowners, resort developers and trade associations. Further clients hail from the industrial and consumer products arenas.

### Bingham McCutchen LLP
See firm details p.1110

**The Firm:** At the time of going to press, Swidler Berlin had announced its intention to merge with Bingham McCutchen. Swidler Berlin's environment group has built up a name for itself in CAA-related matters and legislative challenges. Indeed, a multidisciplinary approach means it often works in tandem with the firm's government affairs group, as well as bankruptcy and litigation groups. Meanwhile, the clean air group has been heavily involved in providing guidance on the CAA and NSR. Part of a broad national practice with extensive resources, the merger also provides the team with a greater international reach. This bodes well as the Swidler team had already witnessed an increase in telecom work with an international twist.

**The Lawyers:** A "*terrific lawyer,*" **Chuck Knauss** (see p.524) is renowned for his expertise in CAA matters. He has a broad client base with an emphasis on the manufacturing and energy sectors.

**Clients/Work Highlights:** Clients include multinational companies.

## Gibson, Dunn & Crutcher LLP

See firm details p.328

**The Firm:** What sets the firm apart in DC is its heavy involvement in the natural resources sector and its toxic torts practice. The environment practice is one of the operation's largest and most profitable groups, and continues to go from strength to strength. It has attracted a dedicated client following full of praise for its *"high-caliber attorneys."* As for costs, clients say they get *"value for money from a firm that does not just run the meter."*

**The Lawyers: Chris Buckley** (see p.504) founded the firm's environmental and natural resources practice group. Clients and peers alike point to his sound understanding of the issues as well as the scientific aspects of the cases he handles. Buckley is also credited with *"excellent litigation skills,"* and his wealth of experience covers natural resources and toxic tort matters. **Raymond Ludwiszewski** (see p.528) has *"tremendous legal acumen and an ability to see the bigger picture."* He is also *"extremely dedicated"* to his clients. His broad-based practice has led to Ludwiszewski defending, for example, corporations against major enforcement actions and toxic tort cases. He represented the Association of International Automakers in a challenge to a state regulation concerning the emission of greenhouse and global warming gases.

**Clients/Work Highlights:** California Farm Bureau Federation; American Farm Bureau Federation; Goodyear; Solutia; Tyco Industries; Unisys and AIG.

## King & Spalding LLP

See firm details p.1933

**The Firm:** Notable for its outstanding expertise in metals and its chemicals risk assessments, this firm has advised Chevron USA and Texaco regarding the regulation of naturally occurring radioactive materials associated with oilfield and pipeyard activities. It has also represented the Coalition for Mercury Management in matters before the EPA and the United Nations Environment Programme. Clients appreciate the firm's ability to understand and draw together scientific, legal and policy strands. One contented client remarked that the lawyers here *"know what they are doing and give us what we need."* While the DC office houses 14, the firm boasts almost 50 environment lawyers firmwide, with offices in Atlanta, Houston and New York further contributing to the firm's nationwide profile in the field.

**The Lawyers: Jane Luxton** (see p.528) focuses on environmental issues arising in the metals sector, although she also advises on those associated with chemicals and on national environmental regulations in general. She is well known for representing the North American Metals Council and the Coalition of Mercury Management. Clients are impressed by her contacts in DC as well as her efficiency. One claimed: *"I've never met a practitioner who could turn around something quicker. It's amazing how efficient she is."* Head of practice **Kathy Rhyne** (see p.541) is *"tough when she needs to be but has a personality that encourages compromise where necessary."* Her practice

encompasses regulatory work, toxic torts litigation and chemical risk assessment issues. She recently advised The Houston Exploration Company on complex wastewater permitting issues.

**Clients/Work Highlights:** ChevronTexaco; North American Metals Council; The Chlorine Institute; Bridgestone/Firestone; Post Properties; Dow Chemical; Freeport LNG Development; GlaxoSmithKline and Union Carbide.

## Kirkland & Ellis LLP

See firm details p.875

**The Firm:** The practice offers a broad range of environmental services to its clients and *"high-quality attorneys"* to boot. Peers point to its air, toxic torts and transactional work as distinguishing features. Growth on the transactional front has shaped the workload of late, whereby the firm is felt to have capitalized on its deep roots in DC. The firm's representation of automobile industry clients and its work in mobile source and other air enforcement matters also drew the attention of market commentators.

**The Lawyers: Edward Warren** (see p.553) is highly regarded by peers for his enviable breadth of experience. Although an adjunct professor at the University of Chicago, he sustains an active private practice at the firm. It focuses on appellate litigation, administrative law, environmental law and toxic torts litigation. The *"extremely bright"* **Stuart Drake** (see p.509) is noted for his mobile source CAA knowledge and his motor vehicle work. His impressive automobile sector clientele includes Toyota and GM. Other features of Drake's practice include defending enforcement actions and counseling clients in agency rulemaking process. **Walt Lohmann** (see p.527) heads the environmental transactional group and is *"one of the leaders in that sector."* Clients extol his *"great business and legal sense."* He also provides general environmental counseling.

**Clients/Work Highlights:** First Atlantic Capital; JPMorgan Partners; Bear Stearns Merchant Banking; Bain Capital; Madison Dearborn Partners; Sun Capital; Solutia; Sara Lee; Berry Plastics and Material Sciences.

## Skadden, Arps, Slate, Meagher & Flom LLP & Affiliates

See firm details p.1557

**The Firm:** Consistently positive market feedback and a truly *"exceptional"* corporate support environmental practice combine to elevate the firm in the tables this year. Its department may not be as large as those of some of its competitors in DC but, as one market analyst observed: *"Don't hold that against it – the firm's environmental lawyers win demanding work."* Renowned for its sophisticated transactional work, the environmental practice also attracts a proportion of standalone work. The firm is also building up its international environmental and environmental litigation capacities.

**The Lawyers: Don Frost**'s (see p.513) mix of transactional ability, regulatory knowledge and litigation experience means he continues to be held in high regard in the marketplace. His recent highlights

include representing Alcoa in several cases associated with a Superfund site in Louisiana. One such case involved defending a $43 million cost recovery claim. **Kenneth Berlin** (see p.501) heads the firm's East Coast and international practice. He is lauded for his *"transactional know-how, excellent judgment and creativity."* Berlin advised Caesars Entertainment on the environmental aspects of its $6 billion casino sale to Harrah's Entertainment. He has also represented United Airlines in numerous bankruptcy issues, as well as representing them in major litigation with American Airlines over the cleanup at JFK Airport.

**Clients/Work Highlights:** First Reserve; Kelso & Company; Caesars Entertainment; United Airlines; CF Industries; Interstate Brands Corporation; Owens Corning; Severstal Group and Alcoa.

## Venable LLP

**The Firm:** Time and again, market commentators highlight the firm's track record in environmental criminal defense work, an area in which more than 13 lawyers specialize. While this accounts for the majority of the DC practice group, the practice offers the full range of environmental services, including compliance and government lobbying. Niche wetlands expertise is also on offer and, in addition, the firm is credited with *"one of the finest enforcement practices in town."*

**The Lawyers:** *"Effective, experienced and knowledgeable, with an extremely commanding presence,"* is how interviewees summed up head of environment **Jud Starr**. One peer went so far as to say that he is *"the only person I would refer clients to for criminal environmental issues."* He cochairs the environmental crimes section with **Joseph Block**. A former chief of the DOJ's Environmental Crimes Section, Block's practice focuses on environmental criminal defense, environmental compliance and internal investigations. Finally, **Margaret Strand** is marked out for her expertise in wetlands and natural resources matters. Clients admire her for the passion she invests in her work and her strong work ethic.

**Clients/Work Highlights:** The firm represents companies and boards of directors in real estate, shipping, transportation and construction sectors.

## Vinson & Elkins LLP

See firm details p.1938

**The Firm:** This practice continues to punch above its weight in DC despite being smaller than its sister office in Houston and other environmental practices in DC. Its success in the field wins it promotion in the rankings this year. The firm is best known for its energy practice, with which a good portion of the DC environmental practice is associated, especially when it comes to energy-related transactions. Elsewhere, the firm has a strong reputation in civil and criminal environmental defense work. Clients are also impressed by the quality of its environmental litigation.

**The Lawyers:** *"A true force in the field,"* **Carol Dinkins** (see p.506) makes the upper echelons of the table due to the vast amount of positive feedback received about her practice. Special praise was reserved for her experience and government contacts: "*She knows how the system works, knows who to speak to and how to deal with them.*" Although resident in Houston, she spends a third of her time in DC. Her practice includes compliance work, civil and white-collar criminal defense of enforcement cases, natural resources and air and waste matters. Dinkins and **Kevin Gaynor** (see p.514) are co-section heads of the environmental practice and were described in research as "*two of the best problem solvers in the business.*" Gaynor came in for particular praise with regard to his creativity and client care. As one interviewee remarked, he tells clients "*what they need to hear rather than what they might want to hear.*" Well respected for his regulatory work, he also deals with enforcement matters, environmental litigation and mediation. He also advises utility clients on NSR issues.

**Clients/Work Highlights:** Clients include utilities such as Vectren and the Virgin Island Water & Power Authority. Duke Energy, Tierra Solutions and BP America are also clients.

## Band 4

### Crowell & Moring LLP
See firm details p.564

**The Firm:** This firm has approximately 15 lawyers working in DC in its natural resources and environment practice. Clients sing the firm's praises and identify as a key strength the ability of its lawyers to "*develop a way of working with the client and use the culture of the company to solve its problems.*" In addition to core natural resource-related matters, CWA and endangered species issues are important areas of work for the group. Recent highlights include representing Glamis Gold, a mining company, in a NAFTA case where approximately $50 million was at stake. Crowell & Moring also successfully represented BedRoc in a mineral rights case involving the sand and gravel industry before the US Supreme Court. The case reversed a decade-long position of the Department of the Interior.

**The Lawyers:** **Ridge Hall** (see p.517) is a founding partner of the firm. Clients observe that he has a wealth of experience, most notably from his time at EPA. Hall focuses on regulatory work, toxic and hazardous waste issues, Superfund matters and toxic tort cases. He was the court-appointed monitor for BP Amoco regarding the design and implementation of a nationwide environmental management program.

**Clients/Work Highlights:** National Association of Home Builders; National Mining Association; Wisconsin Builders Association; National Pork Producers Council; BedRoc; Glamis Gold and KB Home.

### DLA Piper Rudnick Gray Cary US LLP
See firm details p.870

**The Firm:** Being part of an international network of law firms with 54 offices in 20 countries can have its advantages. One of them is that DLA Piper's DC environment practice can provide a full service to clients all around the world. Indeed, the environmental practice is part of the global legislative and regulatory group. Regulatory and enforcement litigation matters, CWA and chemical and pesticide issues are just a few of the areas covered. Recent work includes assisting a major domestic chemical company with Toxic Substances Control Act (TOSCA) compliance issues. The DC office recently added Steven Shimberg to its ranks as of counsel in 2005. This move, some market commentators opine, will "*probably revitalize the practice*" as Shimberg's former DOJ and EPA experience speaks for itself.

**The Lawyers:** Contacts include Doug Green and Bill Weissman, who both concentrate on administrative law matters with a heavy environmental content.

**Clients/Work Highlights:** Manufacturers, power utilities and trade associations all feature as clients, as does the Utility Solid Waste Activities Group, an association of 80 utilities and four trade associations.

### Foley & Lardner LLP
See firm details p.2007

**The Firm:** The environmental regulation practice group at Foley & Lardner has 21 lawyers spread across its Chicago, Milwaukee, Madison, Orlando, San Diego and DC offices. It is known for its expertise in environmental counseling, legislative and administrative law, and enforcement defense work. Clients particularly appreciate its "*outstanding, personalized style of service,*" which they discerned as an important distinguishing feature of the practice, along with the responsive and collegial approach of its lawyers.

**The Lawyers:** **Dick Stoll** (see p.549) is the standout lawyer at the firm. Clients say: "*He listens and has a sharp legal mind that can get through the technical chaff. He considers the issues and brings a broad perspective to his work.*" Essentially an administrative lawyer, he devotes the majority of his time to environmental matters, with healthcare and pharmaceutical sector matters making up the balance. CAA, hazardous waste, Superfund, TOSCA and Emergency Planning and Community Right to Know Act matters all contribute to his environmental practice.

**Clients/Work Highlights:** Clients include Tyco International, Lafarge North America and GE Capital.

### Jones Day
See firm details p.570

**The Firm:** Although a small team of environmental lawyers works in the DC office, the firm can bring to bear the full weight of its considerable resources as required, whether from other departments or from its 30 offices around the world. A full range of services is offered, covering toxic torts, corporate support and compliance counseling. Clients extol the firm's "*extremely hard-working and cooperative*" lawyers. Institutional clients of the firm are one source of work for the environmental team, in respect of which Bridgestone Americas Holding is an important client. Jones Day represents it on all facets of environmental counseling, transactional support, permitting, remedial projects management and litigation.

**The Lawyers:** **Kevin Holewinski** (see p.519) coordinates the DC environmental practice. His work highlights include defending Eramet Marietta against claims for alleged natural resource damages and CWA violations. He also defended Xcel Energy against private and public nuisance claims brought by the attorney generals of eight states and New York City, and two private citizen groups. The claims center on allegations that carbon dioxide emissions from coal-fired electric power plants contribute to global warming. The "*wonderful*" **Heidi Bumpers** (see p.505) primarily focuses on Superfund matters, but she is also involved in hazardous waste enforcement defense, counseling on compliance issues and environmental audits. Clients appreciate her responsiveness and accuracy in dealing with issues.

**Clients/Work Highlights:** Bridgestone Americas Holding; Brush Wellman; Eastman Chemical Company; Eramet Marietta; IBM; PCS Nitrogen; Textron; The Dole Food Company; The Riverside Company; The Sherwin-Williams Company; Xcel Energy and Yellow Roadway.

### McKenna Long & Aldridge LLP
See firm details p.737

**The Firm:** Its impressive chemicals and pesticide practice makes this DC environmental group stand out, according to sources. Representing several pesticide task forces, such as the 2,4-D Task Force, accounts for a good portion of the workload. The team also represented CropLife America as amicus curiae before the US Supreme Court in Bates v Dow AgroScience, an important case concerning the regulation of labeling and packaging under FIFRA. Specialized chemical regulation practitioners are also located in the firm's San Francisco and Brussels offices. The firm can offer further technical support to clients via its technical consulting subsidiary, Technology Sciences Group, comprising 17 regulatory scientists who assist on chemical and pesticide issues in the USA and Canada. In addition, the practice covers a range of environmental litigation, regulatory issues and corporate support matters, and offers expertise in areas as diverse as wetlands and brownfield development.

**The Lawyers:** Charles O'Connor chairs the firm's environmental and regulatory department.

**Clients/Work Highlights:** 3M; Bayer CropScience; Chemtura; Consumer Specialty Products Association; Dow AgroSciences; DuPont; Goldschmidt Chemical Company; Hewlett-Packard; McLaughlin Gormley King Company, SC Johnson & Son; The Hartz Mountain Corporation and Sumitomo Chemical Co.

## Pillsbury Winthrop Shaw Pittman LLP

See firm details p.1550

**The Firm:** Market commentators agree that the merger of Pillsbury Winthrop and Shaw Pittman in 2005 has created an operation with the potential to become a colossus in the environmental field. Though the jury is out as to the success with which the cultures of the two firms might blend, geographical bases covered now include New York, Houston, San Francisco, London and Sydney. The counseling practice has expanded to include Homeland Security issues, particularly with respect to the transportation of hazardous materials. Further growth areas include toxic torts and air work. Advising on the environmental law aspects of the retirement of 27 major oil and gas drilling platforms off California was one major highlight. Another was representing Great Dismal Swamp Restoration Bank in negotiations with an interagency task force. This concerned new uses of wetlands mitigation banking credits and the potential sale of credits worth $25-50 million to a major phosphate mining expansion project.

**The Lawyers: David Menotti** (see p.532) stands out for the way in which "*he just cuts through the minutiae of the detail to what really needs to be done and keeps things moving.*" His scope of expertise includes dealing with matters under the CAA, TOSCA, FIFRA and the Federal Food, Drug and Cosmetic Act. The "*eloquent*" **Don Carr** (see p.505) advises on cutting-edge market trading mechanisms for emissions as well as white-collar environmental defense. He also has a strong background in endangered species and wetlands.

**Clients/Work Highlights:** American Coke and Coal Chemicals Institute; American Iron and Steel Institute; Asahi Glass Co; ChevronTexaco; Clark Enterprises; Emerson Electric; GE; National Oilseed Processors Association; Scottish Widows Pension Fund and Sharp Electronics.

## Van Ness Feldman PC

**The Firm:** A player in the energy field, Van Ness also has a solid environmental practice. The electric utilities and automotive sectors are the two key industries on which the operation focuses. For example, it represented the trade association for vehicle manufacturers during a five-year process in which regulations to control hazardous air pollutant emissions from paint shops at vehicle assembly facilities were developed. Natural resources issues contribute further to the practice.

**The Lawyers: Dick Penna** is the go-to lawyer for mobile source emissions expertise. He has represented clients in the motor vehicle, chemical and transportation industries.

**Clients/Work Highlights:** The Alliance of Automobile Manufacturers; Engine Manufacturers Association; National Marine Manufacturers Association; Tecumseh Power Company; Toyota Motor Sales, USA; Toyota Motor North America and Toyota Motor Manufacturing North America.

## Weil, Gotshal & Manges LLP

See firm details p.1565

**The Firm:** This firm boasts a leading transactional practice in DC as well as some environmental litigation capability. Market commentators also noted the firm's track record in toxic torts and regulatory matters. As part of a national and international network with more than 1,200 lawyers across the USA, Europe and Asia, the DC office has to hand a much-envied pool of resources.

**The Lawyers:** The "*excellent*" **David Berz** (see p.501) is managing partner of the DC office and heads the firm's environmental practice. An experienced litigator, he also counsels multinational corporations and boards of directors in compliance matters. He was environmental counsel to Canada in relation to the NAFTA negotiations. **Annemargaret Connolly**'s (see p.506) predominantly transactional practice also came in for much praise. One market commentator went so far as to say that she is "*a real star. She is super and her clients love her.*"

**Clients/Work Highlights:** Elementis America; Crow Holdings; CBS Corporation; SEACOR Holdings; Citigroup (GCIB); Leucadia; GECC; Enron; Thomas H Lee Partners and Oneida Indian Nation of New York.

## Willkie Farr & Gallagher LLP

See firm details p.1567

**The Firm:** This burgeoning practice is marginally better known for its transactional rather than its regulatory work. It provides the full range of environmental services and represents clients in both the USA and the EU. Indeed, the firm boasts six European offices, including one in Brussels. A recent highlight includes representing an oil refinery in litigation with the EPA where $60 million dollars was at stake.

**The Lawyers: Donald Elliott** (see p.510) chairs the firm's global environmental department. A "*strategic thinker and a real heavyweight,*" his colorful professional life has included serving as a professor at Yale Law School and as a US EPA general counsel. He has strong expertise in the CAA, toxic substances and toxic tort litigation. Elliott was the lead negotiator on the $1.1 billion settlement of an NSR dispute between Ohio Edison and the EPA, along with three states. This was one of the largest CAA settlements of 2005. Meanwhile, **Carrie Jenks** (see p.521) was billed by clients as "*capable beyond her years,*" and joins the table accordingly as an up-and-comer.

**Clients/Work Highlights:** Federal-Mogul; Commonwealth of Puerto Rico; FirstEnergy; NRG Energy and Bristol-Myers Squibb.

## WilmerHale

See firm details p.580

**The Firm:** This "*superb*" full-service firm has a commendable environmental practice. Clients note: "*The team does exceptionally good work and provides a comprehensive service on all matters environmental.*" Issues relating to TOSCA, enforcement, environmental litigation including toxic torts, permitting and environmental due diligence are all covered. The team in DC is "*extremely responsive to clients*" and is praised for its consistently high service.

**The Lawyers:** The highly respected Boyden Gray left the firm following his appointment by President George W Bush as Ambassador to the European Union. Jeffrey Davidson is a senior partner in the environmental department in Washington, DC.

**Clients/Work Highlights:** Clients include trade organizations and Fortune 100 companies.

## Other Notable Practitioners

**Lynn Bergeson** (see p.501) of Bergeson & Campbell PC is prominent in the chemicals and pesticide spheres. One client effused that she is "*a delightful person, honest and upfront. When providing legal advice, she is right on the money.*" **James Bieke**'s (see p.502) strength in Superfund and cleanup work is reflected in his long-running representation of GE in the Hudson River PCB Superfund site and Pittsfield-Housatonic river site matters. He practices at Goodwin Procter LLP.

# HEALTHCARE

## Epstein Becker & Green PC

**The Firm:** Heavily engaged with managed care companies and hospitals in particular, this large and well-resourced practice is also said to be "*one of the first names that comes to mind in town*" for healthcare work. Its expertise includes corporate and antitrust work, Medicare/Medicaid regulatory issues, and fraud and abuse matters. Clients believe its lawyers to be "*responsive and knowledgeable on a wide range of subject matters.*"

**The Lawyers:** Chair of the health and life sciences team, the well-known **Doug Hastings** is also a past president of the American Health Lawyers Association. Rated for his transactional work in particular, clients believe he has "*a personable style and is pretty easy to get in touch with,*" while competitors commented: "*He's a decent guy who travels about the country and works on a variety of transactions.*" His recent work includes advising on the restructuring of the entire financial and contractual relationship between the hospital component and university faculty component of a major academic medical center. He also advised in relation to a joint venture

between a community hospital system and a large cardiology group that resulted in a brand new heart hospital. Peers praised both **Lynn Shapiro Snyder** and **David Matyas** for their "*strong presence in the regulatory arena.*"

**Clients/Work Highlights:** Carilion Health System; Beverly Enterprises; Palmetto Health; Shands HealthCare and University of Maryland Medical System.

## Hogan & Hartson LLP
See firm details p.568

**The Firm:** This "*homegrown*" DC practice is seen to have "*made a sizable and long-standing commitment*" to the general healthcare field and is rated by interviewees for its FDA work, especially on behalf of drug companies. Peers commented: "*It's hard to find fault with the depth on offer,*" citing the ranks of former senior level government officials and litigators on offer within the team.

**The Lawyers:** **Ann Vickery** (see p.552) is managing partner of the firm's DC office and director of the firm's health practice. Her expertise includes counseling clients as to the impact of payment policies on their businesses, particularly in respect of federal government regulation. **Helen Trilling** (see p.551) won plaudits from interviewees for her "*exceptional*" representation of hospices and home health agencies in regulatory work, while **Jonathan Kahan** (see p.521) is seen to be "*very knowledgeable about devices*" and **Bob Leibenluft** (see p.525) is especially noted for his antitrust work in the healthcare arena. "*Smart, congenial and well respected at the FDA,*" **Bob Brady** (see p.503) is head of the firm's drug/biotech practice group and is described by peers as having "*good insight into what's going on in the biologics industry and where it's moving.*" **Tom Bulleit** (see p.505) is noted by peers for his fraud and abuse work, with clients commenting: "*If you deal with Bulleit, he's thoughtful, he's backed up by years of experience, he's a good strategist and he won't bluster his way through cases.*"

**Clients/Work Highlights:** Recent highlights for the practice include acting for Amgen in the dismissal by a New Jersey state court of four products liability cases on the grounds of forum non conveniens. The practice also represented MedImmune in its successful acquisition by merger of Cellective Therapeutics for an aggregate purchase price of up to $160 million. In addition, lawyers have been advising in five internal investigations involving the intersection of FDA laws, healthcare laws and criminal statutes. Further clients include Adventist Health System; American Hospital Association; Cornell University; HRA Pharma; LabCorp; NDCHealth; The Scripps Research Institute; UnitedHealth Group and VITAS Healthcare.

## Reed Smith LLP
See firm details p.1762

**The Firm:** A strong full-service player in the field, with "*a deep regulatory capability and a long-term commitment to DC,*" this practice is particularly rated by competitors for its work in relation to the long-term care industry and is active for a range of hospitals and other providers as well as pharmaceuticals and device companies. Its recent work has included fraud and abuse defense work, in addition to advising on issues involving coding, coverage, reimbursement, and investigations and enforcements.

**The Lawyers:** A "*smart lawyer with good judgment,*" **Elizabeth Carder-Thompson** (see p.505) was especially praised by peers for her work in relation to drugs and devices. **Gene Tillman** (see p.551) is a past president of the American Health Lawyers Association and has a practice that includes Medicare and Medicaid payment and coverage issues, healthcare acquisitions and regulatory matters. **Gordon Schatz** (see p.544) is noted by peers for being "*one of the best around*" in relation to healthcare reimbursement, pricing and compliance issues. Described by peers as the practice's most senior healthcare expert, **Tom Fox** (see p.513) is also said to be "*a top-notch lawyer*" in the long-term care field and "*a wonderful human being.*"

**Clients/Work Highlights:** Clients include hospitals; academic medical centers; physicians' practice groups; long-term care facilities; pharmaceuticals; medical device companies and biotech companies.

## Fulbright & Jaworski L.L.P.
See firm details p.1928

**The Firm:** Interviewees praise this practice for its expertise in antikickback and False Claims Act work in particular, in addition to general compliance work. One client noted that its lawyers "*add value because they know the substantive areas they deal in extremely well, such that they can take on different facts and circumstances and provide quick responses that are practical and correct.*" Researchers were further told: "*They take a lot of time to understand a client's business, so can make decisions in context.*" Its clients include hospitals, academic medical centers, managed care organizations, clinical laboratories and physicians. In recent times it has become increasingly active for medical device companies.

**The Lawyers:** Partner-in-charge of the DC office's health law practice, the "*smart and thoughtful*" **Rick Robinson** (see p.542) was noted by clients for his litigation expertise, especially in relation to fraud and abuse, investigations and compliance work. He recently represented a number of academic medical centers in 'PATH' (Physicians at Teaching Hospitals) investigations by the DOJ, and helped to establish case law immunizing state universities from whistleblower lawsuits under the False Claims Act. He also represented a number of hospitals and health centers in federal and state investigations regarding the 72-hour rule, pneumonia DRG coding, unbundling of lab charges, and implantation of non-FDA-approved

## Healthcare
### Leading Individuals

[1] **BARRY Dennis** *Vinson & Elkins LLP*
**BRENNAN JR John** *Crowell & Moring LLP*
**CARDER-THOMPSON Elizabeth** *Reed Smith LLP*
**HASTINGS Douglas** *Epstein Becker & Green PC*
**LUCE Gregory** *Jones Day*
**MICHAELS Joel** *McDermott Will & Emery*
**ROBINSON Frederick** *Fulbright & Jaworski L.L.P.*
**SULLIVAN TJ** *Gardner Carton & Douglas LLP*
**TILLMAN Eugene** *Reed Smith LLP*
**VICKERY Ann** *Hogan & Hartson LLP*

[2] **BULLEIT JR Thomas** *Hogan & Hartson LLP*
**FITZGERALD Mark** *Powers Pyles Sutter & Verville*
**FOX Thomas** *Reed Smith LLP*
**FRIED Bruce** *Sonnenschein*
**GOLDMAN Roger** *Latham & Watkins LLP*
**LEIBENLUFT Robert** *Hogan & Hartson LLP*
**LERNER Arthur** *Crowell & Moring LLP*
**MATYAS David** *Epstein Becker & Green PC*
**MILES John** *Ober Kaler Grimes & Shriver*
**PHILP Mary** *Powers Pyles Sutter & Verville*
**REIDER Alan** *Arent Fox PLLC*
**SALCIDO Robert** *Akin Gump*
**SANER Robert** *Powers Pyles Sutter & Verville*
**SCHATZ Gordon** *Reed Smith LLP*
**SNYDER Lynn** *Epstein Becker & Green PC*
**STEWART David** *Ropes & Gray LLP*
**THORNTON D McCarty** *Sonnenschein*
**TRILLING Helen** *Hogan & Hartson LLP*
**YAMPOLSKY Harvey** *Arent Fox PLLC*
**YOUNG Howard** *Sonnenschein*
**ZIMMERMAN Eric** *McDermott Will & Emery*

## Healthcare: Pharmaceutical/ Medical Products Regulatory
### Leading Individuals

[1] **HUTT Peter** *Covington & Burling*
**VODRA William** *Arnold & Porter LLP*

[2] **BASILE Edward** *King & Spalding LLP*
**BENNETT Alan** *Ropes & Gray LLP*
**BRADY Robert** *Hogan & Hartson LLP*
**COOPER Richard** *Williams & Connolly LLP*
**GLEASON Kathryn** *Morgan, Lewis*
**HELLER Mark** *WilmerHale*
**HYMAN Paul** *Hyman Phelps & McNamara*
**KAHAN Jonathan** *Hogan & Hartson LLP*
**KALB Paul** *Sidley Austin LLP*
**KINGHAM Richard** *Covington & Burling*
**LEVINE Arthur** *Arnold & Porter LLP*
**SAFIR Peter** *Covington & Burling*
**YINGLING Gary** *Kirkpatrick & Lockhart*

medical devices. In addition, he represented a national home healthcare company in several False Claims Act cases, including whistle-blower lawsuits regarding Medicaid and Medicare cost reports.
**Clients/Work Highlights:** Duke University Health System; Baptist Health System; Zimmer; Trinity

Mother Frances Health System and Universal Health Services.

### Gardner Carton & Douglas LLP
See firm details p.872
**The Firm:** Bolstered by a wave of recruitments in recent times, the long-standing DC healthcare practice of this Chicago-based firm is particularly noted by peers for its general tax advice and representation of various healthcare organizations before the IRS. Its expertise also includes antitrust and transactional advice, compliance counseling and defense, long-term and managed care and Medicare/Medicaid reimbursement.
**The Lawyers:** TJ Sullivan (see p.549) won praise from interviewees for his tax-related work for nonprofit health organizations such as hospitals and HMOs. Recently, he has advised a number of these in relation to various hearings on Capitol Hill concerning their tax-exempt status.
**Clients/Work Highlights:** Clients include traditional hospitals; multiprovider healthcare systems; integrated delivery systems; academic medical centers; managed care organizations; nursing homes; home health agencies and clinics.

### McDermott Will & Emery
See firm details p.878
**The Firm:** This Chicago-based firm has a fairly sizable DC office that offers the full spectrum of healthcare services. A long-term fixture on the scene, it was described by one rival as "*a tough competitor that has the resources to cover five or six different investigation spots on the same day.*"
**The Lawyers:** Partner-in-charge of the firm's health department, the long-standing **Joel Michaels**' (see p.532) expertise includes healthcare insurance and delivery system organization, financing and regulation. **Eric Zimmerman** (see p.557) won praise from clients for being "*thorough, an excellent communicator and good on his feet at meetings.*" Particular mention was made of his expertise in relation to lobbying for funding and his expertise in relation to Medicare reimbursement issues.
**Clients/Work Highlights:** Foote Health System; Gateway Health System; St Vincent's Medical Center; Apex Foot Health Industries; Inova Health System; William Beaumont Hospital; Prince William Health System and The Reading Hospital and Medical Center.

### Powers Pyles Sutter & Verville PC
**The Firm:** One of the last boutiques left in the field in DC, this practice maintains a "*significant presence*" with its "*technically strong lawyers*" who are especially rated by competitors for their regulatory counseling and Medicare reimbursement expertise. Its work also includes advising in relation to healthcare transactions, fraud and abuse matters, corporate compliance work and antitrust issues.
**The Lawyers:** The "*down-to-earth*" **Mark Fitzgerald** (see p.512) is especially rated by interviewees for his transactional expertise, with particular mention being made of his work in relation to physician

compensation, Stark and antikickback issues. One client noted: "*He's a generous guy – not a guy who would regularly run the clock on me for a 15-minute call.*" **Mary Susan Philp** (see p.538) was lauded by clients for her work in relation to Medicare regulatory, reimbursement and hospital cost reports. **Bob Saner** (see p.544) was described by peers as having "*great experience and judgment.*" His practice focuses largely on physician organizations.
**Clients/Work Highlights:** Clients include integrated delivery systems; multihospital systems; hospitals; medical group practices; nursing homes and medical equipment providers.

### Sonnenschein Nath & Rosenthal LLP
See firm details p.884
**The Firm:** This Chicago-based firm's DC office is seen by peers to have built up a substantial presence in the healthcare field in recent times. It has accrued a deep stable of attorneys who are particularly rated for their fraud and abuse expertise and representations of hospitals. Clients commented: "*There are no better lawyers to use in defense of government enforcement actions.*" The practice's expertise also includes antikickback, self-referral, M&A and affiliations, corporate compliance programs, Medicare/Medicaid reimbursement and antitrust matters.
**The Lawyers:** The "*stellar*" **Mac Thornton** (see p.550) is another former chief counsel to the Department of Health and Human Services (HHS) Office of Inspector General (OIG), and is especially rated by competitors for his expertise in relation to government enforcement actions. Clients commented: "*He's very to the point and makes you feel comfortable by always giving the impression he's your biggest supporter. He tries to help you figure out the best way to follow the law but also explains the practical realities of the situation.*" A former director of both the Health Care Financing Administration (HCFA)'s Center for Health Plans and Providers and the HCFA's Office of Managed Care, **Bruce Fried**'s (see p.513) expertise includes advising in relation to Medicare, Medicaid and the Health Insurance Portability Accountability Act (HIPAA). He also advises on privacy and technology applications in the healthcare sector. With a practice encompassing fraud and abuse work and a background as government prosecutor for the HHS-OIG in healthcare matters, the "*practical*" **Howard Young** (see p.556) was rated by clients for the fact that "*he knows the law and, more importantly, has real experience negotiating with government.*" His work in recent times has included representing both healthcare organizations and individual providers in False Claims Act investigations.
**Clients/Work Highlights:** Recent work for the practice includes advising the American Association for Homecare on rate-setting issues, as a result of which the association saved $300 million over five years. Further clients include Tenet Healthcare; Ochsner Clinic Foundation; Mayo Clinic; University of North Carolina; University of Arizona; Northwestern University and University of Chicago.

## Akin Gump Strauss Hauer & Feld LLP
See firm details p.559

**The Firm:** Viewed by peers as "*well connected politically,*" this practice is also said to be "*a small but solid group*" of healthcare litigators and reimbursement attorneys. Its expertise turns on health industry M&A, the formation of managed care networks, private placements and other securities offerings, as well as Medicare and Medicaid reimbursement litigation and counseling, and fraud and abuse matters.
**The Lawyers:** Robert Salcido's (see p.544) expertise includes responding to governmental investigations, conducting internal investigations, defending lawsuits filed under the False Claims Act and defending wrongful retaliation lawsuits brought by alleged whistle-blowers.
**Clients/Work Highlights:** Clients include hospital networks and healthcare systems; major academic medical centers; community and specialty hospitals; home care companies and physician groups.

## Arent Fox PLLC

**The Firm:** "*A local firm with a good amount of national work,*" it is especially rated by peers for its fraud and abuse work and is active in a variety of criminal and civil investigations, acting for clients ranging from individual physicians to large national and international healthcare corporations. Its work also includes internal review, compliance, reimbursement and coverage advice. Other clients include physician and nursing groups, and a trade association for ambulatory surgery centers.
**The Lawyers:** Practice chair Alan Reider's (see p.541) expertise includes advising on regulatory issues relating to reimbursement, coverage and certification, in addition to antikickback and Stark issues. Harvey Yampolsky (see p.556) is a former chief counsel to the HHS-OIG. His practice encompasses advising with regard to compliance with Medicare and Medicaid statutes and regulations relating to billing, coding and reimbursement.
**Clients/Work Highlights:** Clients include physicians and physician practice management companies; hospitals; ambulatory surgery centers; nursing homes; dialysis facilities; clinical laboratories; diagnostic centers; home health agencies; health maintenance organizations and medical device and drug manufacturers.

## Crowell & Moring LLP
See firm details p.564

**The Firm:** A practice that has been "*aggressive in acquiring attorneys and building itself up*" has, according to clients, lawyers who are "*professional and knowledgeable in just about every area of nuts and bolts, substantive healthcare.*" One interviewee noted: "*They're people who give you answers quickly, concisely and in layman's terms, as opposed to a lot of lawyers who are afraid to stick their necks out.*" The firm's expertise includes advising in relation to legislative and health policy issues, managed care, corporate and transactional matters, regulatory/licensing issues, fraud and abuse, litigation and antitrust.
**The Lawyers:** Practice head John Brennan (see

p.503) is particularly noted by interviewees for his representation of hospitals, physicians and other healthcare providers in the fraud and abuse arena. He won praise from clients for being "*a nice guy to work with, confident and smart,*" with one competitor noting: "*I'd be comfortable giving a case to John if I was conflicted out because I know the client would thank me for it.*" His recent work has included representing Tenet Healthcare in an investigation by a US House of Representatives subcommittee into the manner in which hospitals nationwide deal with the 40 million patients in the USA who have no insurance and are not eligible for Medicaid. Art Lerner (see p.525) won praise from competitors for his healthcare antitrust expertise. He is chair of the antitrust practice group of the American Health Lawyers Association and has recently been advising Kaiser Foundation Health Plan in relation to offering an innovative, high deductible health benefit plan for participants in the federal employees health benefit program. He also represented HealthAmerica Pennsylvania in a dispute that arose from audits that questioned $31.1 million of subscription charges under the federal employees health benefits program.
**Clients/Work Highlights:** Bon Secours Health System; Tenet Healthcare; Centene; Health Net; Aetna; Humana; Kaiser Foundation Health Plan and Medco Health Solutions.

## Jones Day
See firm details p.570

**The Firm:** This Cleveland-based firm's DC office is especially noted by interviewees for its healthcare transactional work and "*hard-nosed litigation expertise,*" particularly in the fraud and abuse arena. Its expertise also includes compliance counseling and defense and healthcare antitrust work, mainly for healthcare providers but also for some health insurers.
**The Lawyers:** Cohead of the healthcare practice Greg Luce (see p.527) is particularly rated by competitors for his litigation expertise. Clients feel that "*he's not aggressive for the sake of it, but if he feels you've got a good case he's very forceful in representing you.*" Especially active in False Claims Act defense and counseling, he also represents hospitals in various class actions and claims against the federal government, commercial insurers or private payers. His recent work includes representing eight nonprofit multihospital health systems in litigation brought by a consortium of plaintiffs' attorneys. In this matter, the plaintiffs are challenging the tax-exempt status of hospitals.
**Clients/Work Highlights:** Other recent highlights for the practice include defending Abbott Laboratories in actions brought by state attorneys general, insurance companies and putative classes of Medicare beneficiaries. Another highlight has involved representing MedStar Health and University Hospitals of Cleveland in the Jung v AAMC litigation, a class action suit that challenges the national residency match program and alleges a conspiracy to unlawfully suppress the salaries of medical residents. Further clients include Ascension Health; Banner

Health; Bon Secours Health System; Catholic Health Initiatives; Catholic Healthcare Partners; Capital BlueCross; Cedars-Sinai Medical Center; Cleveland Clinic Health System; Ohio State University Medical Center; ProMedica Health System and Sutter Health.

## Latham & Watkins LLP

**The Firm:** This "*small but effective*" healthcare presence in DC is particularly rated for its litigation expertise in the fraud and abuse arena. It is also active on a range of corporate transactions and does well on regulatory and reimbursement work.
**The Lawyers:** Cochair of the DC healthcare and life sciences practice, Roger Goldman's expertise encompasses False Claims Act and white-collar criminal litigation, particularly healthcare fraud defense. His recent work has included representing Tenet Healthcare in a series of court actions and investigations being conducted by the DOJ.
**Clients/Work Highlights:** Other highlights for the practice include the representation of New York Presbyterian Hospital in US Congressional investigations and various healthcare-related issues. The practice has also been representing McKesson in a number of healthcare regulatory and litigation matters. Further clients include University Hospitals Health System of Cleveland; Beverly Enterprises; Biogen Idec; Schering-Plough; KCI and dj Orthopedics.

## Ober Kaler Grimes & Shriver

**The Firm:** Peers believe that one certainly cannot ignore this Baltimore-based firm's DC office, which is said to be "*pretty much devoted to healthcare*" and has "*a number of prominent regulatory lawyers.*" Its areas of interest include reimbursement, allegations of Medicare/Medicaid fraud and abuse, major policy issues, white-collar criminal actions, and disputes arising out of the relationships between hospitals and their medical staff.
**The Lawyers:** Noted by peers for his healthcare antitrust enforcement background in the DOJ, Jeff Miles is described as having written the leading treatise on healthcare antitrust law, namely the 'Antitrust Health Care Handbook'.
**Clients/Work Highlights:** Clients include academic and community hospitals; health systems; long-term care organizations; physicians and physician organizations.

## Ropes & Gray LLP
See firm details p.1117

**The Firm:** This "*multidimensional*" healthcare practice, "*full of smart, hands-on lawyers,*" has "*a clear eye on expansion,*" according to interviewees. It is especially noted for its regulatory compliance, reimbursement and government investigation work.
**The Lawyers:** Alan Bennett (see p.501) is managing partner of the firm's DC office and cochair of the life sciences group. He is particularly noted by competitors for his medical device work, where he "*handles potentially problematic situations with aplomb.*" Peers especially rate David Stewart (see p.548) for his litigation work in the healthcare field,

with one commenting: "*Anyone represented by him has a very intelligent guy on their team.*"

**Clients/Work Highlights:** Clients include academic medical centers; community hospitals; pharmaceutical companies; managed care organizations; physician practice groups and healthcare technology and biomedical companies.

## Vinson & Elkins LLP
See firm details p.1938

**The Firm:** Although seen by peers as a relatively small shop in the healthcare area, this practice nevertheless wins plaudits for its regulatory expertise. In particular, it can lay claim to an "*expert knowledge of the insides and outsides of Medicare matters,*" an area in which it has few peers.

**The Lawyers:** An "*engaging personality*" and intelligent speaker, DC practice head **Dennis Barry** (see p.499) won praise from peers for having long been a fixture in the reimbursement arena. One client commented: "*He's one of the few people we can pick up the phone to and ask a detailed Medicare billing question, confident that he will know the answer without recourse to the texts on the subject.*"

**Clients/Work Highlights:** The practice recently acted for Abbott Northwestern Hospital in connection with a decision by the District Court of DC that will allow the hospital to receive payments from the Medicare program wrongly denied it for the years 1983 to 1988. Further clients include Montefiore Medical Center; Henry Ford Health System; Adventist Health Systems/Sunbelt; Aon; Pfizer; Johnson & Johnson and University of Virginia Medical Center.

## Arnold & Porter LLP
See firm details p.560

**The Firm:** "*Still one of the best FDA firms in the city,*" this practice is particularly lauded by interviewees for its work for pharmaceutical manufacturers, university and research clients and device manufacturers. Its work includes traditional manufacturing issues, FDA compliance and regulatory investigations and counseling in relation to approvals, clinical investigations, adverse events, risk management and regulatory strategy. In recent times, it has been expanding into areas such as fraud and abuse, and reimbursement.

**The Lawyers:** **Bill Vodra** (see p.552) is "*among the best FDA lawyers in the country*" and was particularly praised for his representation of pioneer companies in the pharmaceutical field. His practice involves advising on regulatory issues relating to the safety, effectiveness and marketing of medical products. He also handles crisis management, products liability, white-collar criminal matters and civil actions. **Art Levine** (see p.526) was described as "*a lion of the FDA Bar.*" A former FDA deputy general counsel for litigation, he has a practice that encompasses advising pharmaceutical and medical device companies on compliance and regulatory issues.

**Clients/Work Highlights:** Abbott Laboratories; AstraZeneca; Hoffmann-La Roche; Boehringer-Ingelheim; GlaxoSmithKline; Wyeth and Pfizer.

## Covington & Burling
See firm details p.563

**The Firm:** "*One of the usual suspects playing in the biggest FDA sandpit,*" according to interviewees, this robust practice is seen to attract a large amount of work due to being "*huge and historically well known*" in the area: "*They've got the resources and backup to handle just about anything.*" It is especially rated by competitors for its pharmaceutical work but is also active in a range of medical device matters.

**The Lawyers:** "*A legend in FDA land*" and "*on anybody's shortlist in the field,*" the "*enormously respected*" **Peter Hutt** (see p.520) is described by clients as "*responsive and accessible – when I call him, I invariably hear from him within the day.*" Further comment was that "*he's efficient and economical – he knows the answers to your questions or else he can give you some options or alternatives without sending a brigade of young lawyers in.*" Cochair of the firm's life sciences practice, **Dick Kingham** (see p.523) is "*an extraordinarily versatile and astute lawyer*" in the food and drug field, whose work includes administrative and court proceedings involving the FDA and other federal regulatory agencies. He also acts in the defense of pharmaceutical companies and individuals in criminal cases, as well as other enforcement actions brought by the FDA. A "*first-class FDA regulatory lawyer,*" **Peter Safir** (see p.544) is seen by clients as having "*a strong pragmatic side on top of a knowledge base of pretty much everything that's going on in the pharmaceutical industry.*" He recently advised PhRMA on the drafting of its code and represented Johnson & Johnson in successfully obtaining exclusivity for Duragesic at the FDA.

**Clients/Work Highlights:** A further highlight for the practice involved the defense of Pfizer on several investigations into Bextra and Celebrex by the DOJ, multiple state attorneys general, Congress, and the SEC. Clients include Astellas; sanofi-aventis; Pfizer; PhRMA; Johnson & Johnson; Schering-Plough; Purdue Pharma; GlaxoSmithKline; TriPath Imaging and Lifecore Biomedical.

## Hyman Phelps & McNamara

**The Firm:** Praised by competitors for its "*wonderful food and drug client base,*" this practice was also described as the "*best of the FDA boutiques.*" Its expertise includes regulatory and litigation work in relation to pharmaceutical and Drug Enforcement Administration (DEA) matters. It also handles issues concerning medical devices and food additives, international drug scheduling and, increasingly, fraud and abuse work.

**The Lawyers:** The "*experienced and mature*" **Paul Hyman** won plaudits from peers for being "*good at making sure his clients succeed at the FDA*" due to his "*ability to master both the science and the regulatory philosophy.*" He has been especially active of late in relation to Dietary Supplement Health & Education Act (DSHEA) claims.

**Clients/Work Highlights:** Clients include Johnson & Johnson; Pfizer; Purdue Pharma; Affinergy and Bausch & Lomb.

## Morgan, Lewis & Bockius LLP
See firm details p.1758

**The Firm:** Well known by peers for its medical device work, this FDA/product regulation practice is also active in relation to a range of food, drug and biotech matters. Its work includes joint venturing and licensing, the marketing and promotion of products, healthcare reimbursement and product pricing, inspections, recalls, and compliance and enforcement matters.

**The Lawyers:** Competitors especially rate "*outstanding*" practice head **Kathryn Gleason** (see p.515) for her work in the device field. Recently she has been working with the FDA in rewriting the law as to hybrid products, where she has been representing AdvaMed, the principal trade association for the medical device industry.

**Clients/Work Highlights:** Other recent highlights for the practice include working on a patent extension matter relating to a new vaccine. The practice also assisted Pfizer in preparing a citizen petition and related filings with the FDA. This requested deferral of clearance of an application by Sandoz for approval of the first proposed generic biologic. Clients include Playtex Products; Biotechnology Industry Organization; ViroPharma; Takeda Pharmaceutical; American Red Cross; bioMérieux and MedImmune.

## King & Spalding LLP
See firm details p.1933

**The Firm:** This practice's expertise includes regulatory counseling and litigation work for pharmaceutical manufacturers and medical device companies. Its clients include a range of biotech and genomics companies.

**The Lawyers:** **Ed Basile** (see p.499) is a "*go-to guy for medical device work in the regulatory field.*" He is especially noted for his work in relation to clinical trials, FDA inspections, and compliance. His recent work includes advising two major device manufacturers in relation to product recalls by the FDA.

**Clients/Work Highlights:** American Association of Homes and Services for the Aging; WellCare Health Plans; Guidant; McKesson; Schering-Plough; Central Georgia Health Systems; Serono; Piedmont Healthcare; Memorial Health and Kaiser Permanente.

## Kirkpatrick & Lockhart Nicholson Graham LLP

**The Firm:** The firm advises a range of clients from the food, pharmaceutical, medical device and cosmetics sectors. Its work includes regulatory counseling and product development, as well as representation before the FDA and other state and federal agencies. In addition, it also handles business transactions, government contracts and enforcement proceedings.

**The Lawyers:** The "*super-bright*" **Gary Yingling** is especially rated by interviewees for his representation of generic applicants in the pharmaceutical industry. One interviewee noted: "*He gets right to the scientific core of the argument and takes a reasoned and* *balanced approach to dialogue with the FDA better than anyone in town."*

Clients/Work Highlights: Clients include manufacturers and distributors within the biotech, cosmetics and food industries, as well as those involved with personal care, medical device and dietary supplement products.

### Sidley Austin LLP

See firm details p.883

The Firm: This Chicago-based firm has a substantial DC office that has benefited in recent times from a number of lateral hires. It is particularly rated by interviewees for its FDA regulatory expertise, as well as its reimbursement and policy development work.

The Lawyers: Head of the firm's national healthcare practice group, **Paul Kalb** (see p.521) is praised by peers for his FDA regulatory and life sciences expertise. His work includes representing drug manufacturers and institutional healthcare providers in criminal, civil and administrative enforcement actions.

Clients/Work Highlights: Apria Healthcare; Bayer; Charter Behavioral Health Systems; Eli Lilly; Magellan Health Services; Schering-Plough; Sun Healthcare Group and Vencor.

### Williams & Connolly LLP

The Firm: This *"cost-effective"* practice scores highly for its litigation expertise, including medical malpractice, products liability defense relating to medical devices, and civil and criminal fraud investigations in the healthcare sector. One client commented: *"For high risk litigation in the government sector, they've got a phenomenal profile – they're the only reason I sleep at night."*

The Lawyers: A former FDA chief counsel, **Rich Cooper** attracted comment from competitors that *"if you want an FDA litigation lawyer, he's an obvious choice."* His clients include pharmaceutical companies and medical device manufacturers.

Clients/Work Highlights: Recent work for the practice includes representing Medco Health Solutions in a federal False Claims Act and antikickback action brought by healthcare fraud prosecutors in the Eastern District of Pennsylvania. The practice also successfully represented a major university and its medical center in obtaining the dismissal of claims of intentional and negligent infliction of emotional distress arising out of a radiology technician's alleged substitution of contaminated syringes for sterile syringes and the deprivation of patients' pain medication. In addition, the practice successfully represented a healthcare attorney in an extended,

seven-defendant trial in the federal court in Kansas City, Kansas. This related to Medicare fraud and conspiracy charges in connection with an alleged patient referral scheme. Clients include hospitals, healthcare systems, clinics and doctors, as well as pharmaceutical and medical device companies.

### WilmerHale

See firm details p.580

The Firm: Effective in the medical device arena, this practice also undertakes a range of drug and biological regulatory matters. Its work includes advising in proceedings before the FDA and cases in the federal courts, in addition to corporate and IP services for FDA-regulated companies.

The Lawyers: FDA department chair **Mark Heller** (see p.518) is noted by competitors for his experience as former associate chief counsel for medical devices at the FDA. His expertise includes representing device manufacturers and pharmaceutical companies in FDA product approval processes. He also advises on compliance matters ranging from administrative notices of violation to enforcement actions in court.

Clients/Work Highlights: Clients include medical device, drug and biological companies.

# IMMIGRATION

## Band 1

### Duane Morris LLP

See firm details p.1753

The Firm: This full-service firm has developed a specialist group that advises on complex corporate immigration issues and litigation. Its attorneys are well versed in obtaining both immigrant and nonimmigrant visas, and have established a number of training and compliance programs for corporate clients. The group has also introduced a specialist management database program to ensure clients can be kept up to date on relevant issues. While the bulk of the practice is focused on business clients, the team does handle family-based immigration and litigation matters. The group interacts regularly with the Departments of State, Labor and Homeland Security on legislative issues and government affairs.

The Lawyers: Head of the immigration practice group, **Denyse Sabagh** (see p.543) is a *"good fighter who always has the best interests of her clients at heart."* Sources also described her as *"proactive and well connected."* Sabagh enjoys a particularly strong reputation in litigation and has a niche focus on Arab-American issues. Another respected partner is **Roberta Freedman** (see p.513). *"She really knows what she's talking about and does a great job,"* enthused clients.

Clients/Work Highlights: The firm's clientele includes companies from the manufacturing, technology, healthcare and pharmaceutical sectors.

### Fragomen, Del Rey, Bernsen & Loewy, LLP

The Firm: This dedicated immigration giant employs its *"huge resources"* to assist corporate clients with both outbound and inbound immigration. Working as part of an impressive national practice, the team is able to utilize the firm's size and scope to handle clients' visa requirements quickly and cost-effectively. It also offers strategic planning advice, policy guidance and compliance counseling. In recognition of the global scope of its practice, the firm has established Fragomen Global Immigration Services to assist clients with the relocation of employees between countries worldwide. *"They offer a truly global service that is seamless for the client,"* agreed interviewees.

The Lawyers: **Andrew Greenfield** is a *"wonderful, thoughtful attorney,"* whose move to the DC office brought many positive comments from the market. He is former vice chair of the DC chapter of the American Immigration Lawyers Association (AILA).

Clients/Work Highlights: The firm serves domestic and foreign clients ranging from major corporations to smaller firms.

### Greenberg Traurig LLP

See firm details p.664

The Firm: *"What sets them apart is their customer focus,"* said one client of this large national practice. Split across the firm's DC and McLean offices, the team has a strong compliance focus and has been kept busy assisting companies with government audits of I-9 and H-1B programs, as well as helping clients conduct internal audits. This full-service practice encompasses labor certification, temporary and permanent international transfer of personnel and litigation, working closely with Greenberg partners overseas to ensure an international reach. The team is also involved in legislative work and lobbying.

**The Lawyers:** The "*knowledgeable and creative*" **Laura Reiff** (see p.541) inspires client confidence with her ability to deal with complex compliance issues. Cochair of the business immigration group, she is well regarded in the immigration policy arena, and her practice has a strong legislative component. **Elissa McGovern** (see p.530) focuses on citizenship issues and counseling employers on international transfers. An experienced lobbyist, she is active in directing legislative and agency advocacy efforts on immigration issues. McGovern is particularly experienced in the healthcare sector, working with medical professionals.

**Clients/Work Highlights:** The firm's clientele includes companies from a wide range of sectors including telecom, entertainment, healthcare, education and energy. Examples include Primaris Airlines; CEMEX; Southwest Research Institute; CSG Systems; Ingersoll-Rand Company and CVS Pharmacy.

## Hogan & Hartson LLP
See firm details p.568

**The Firm:** This full-service national practice covers the full scope of immigration work including involvement in government lobbying. An impressive national and international client roster includes a number of household names. Examples include the National Geographic Society, whom the group represented in connection with the transfer to the US of journalists, photographers and other professionals. The team assisted Cadbury Schweppes in obtaining blanket authorization to transfer key personnel from hundreds of overseas locations and helped Wal-Mart obtain a favorable settlement in a grand jury investigation regarding Wal-Mart's contractors' employment of undocumented floor cleaners. The group also handles a significant level of sports-related and higher education work.

**The Lawyers:** Head of the department **Paul Virtue** (see p.552) is "*totally straightforward, honest and reliable,*" sources said. A former general counsel of the Immigration and Naturalization Service (INS), he is respected in the market for his government experience. Clients liked that he "*is totally responsive and gets results.*" **Beth Peters**' (see p.538) practice focuses on both immigration and international trade. Clients praised her as "*knowledgeable, likeable and very responsive.*"

**Clients/Work Highlights:** American University; Cadbury Schweppes Americas Beverages; National Geographic Society; United States Olympic Committee; EADS; Fox International Channels; Janus and Wal-Mart.

## Maggio & Kattar PC

**The Firm:** This "*highly prestigious*" immigration boutique wins praise for the high quality of its representation across the board. "*Everyone there is a fine lawyer,*" said sources. The practice encompasses the whole range of immigration services including work, permanent resident and business visas, relocation services, citizenship and waivers. Alongside its caseload for corporate clients, the firm also assists individuals in matters relating to deportation, asylum, residency and criminal issues.

**The Lawyers:** The firm's chairman **Michael Maggio** is a nationally respected figure in the immigration field. Seen as "*a terrific go-getter and a creative practitioner,*" he is also an expert litigator. "*The thing I love about him is he's a real fighter,*" claimed one peer. A former president of AILA and lobbyist on Capitol Hill, he is highly regarded for his expertise in complex immigration matters. A younger attorney who is building a profile is **Andres Benach**. He has a particular focus on complicated deportation and naturalization cases and has also been involved in a number of high-profile waiver cases.

**Clients/Work Highlights:** A broad-based clientele includes national and multinational companies from a wide range of sectors including manufacturing, industrial, biomedical, hospitality, IT, engineering and education.

## Band 2

## Baker & McKenzie
See firm details p.866

**The Firm:** This impressive business immigration practice offers "*a boutique-firm service with big-firm resources.*" Clients liked this "*responsive, efficient team whose service delivery is everything you could want and more.*" The group represents domestic and international corporate clients in a range of cross-border matters, and works closely with other practice areas and offices to ensure an integrated approach. The group also has a strong global network of contacts with embassies, consulates and immigration and labor ministries.

**The Lawyers: Elizabeth Stern** (see p.548) "*understands all the complexities of modern immigration law.*" Clients spoke of her "*good grasp of what's going on in Congress; she is well connected to the people who can get things done.*" According to one client: "*She's a godsend.*" Stern has testified before Congress on immigration reforms and works closely with the Congressional committees and federal agencies involved in developing immigration laws.

**Clients/Work Highlights:** The firm's client roster includes large companies from a variety of industry sectors including financial services, manufacturing, multimedia, IT and telecom. Examples include Airbus North America Holdings; Ameriprise Financial; National Railroad Passenger Corporation; Blackboard; RSM McGladrey and Toyota Tsusho America.

## Morgan, Lewis & Bockius LLP
See firm details p.1758

**The Firm:** This practice serves clients on a nationwide basis, handling both their inbound and outbound immigration needs. Alongside its visa and employment eligibility verification workload, the firm has a strong training and advisory focus. It offers I-9 compliance training programs and management training on the immigration aspects of hiring foreign nationals. Advice on how to structure international employee transfer programs and related compliance issues is a further string to this group's bow. It has also carried out I-9 audits for a number of major clients.

**The Lawyers:** Managing director of Morgan Lewis Resources **Eleanor Pelta** (see p.537) coordinates the immigration practice nationally. Clients appreciate that she "*remembers every individual and knows their story.*" According to one client: "*Her biggest strength is that she really cares,*" while another praised her as "*a tremendous resource, whose level of service is outstanding.*"

**Clients/Work Highlights:** Clients include major travel, technology, healthcare, logistics and hospitality companies, as well as a number of financial and scientific institutions.

## Paul, Hastings, Janofsky & Walker LLP
See firm details p.339

**The Firm:** The DC offshoot of this impressive national practice concentrates primarily on government relations. While its respected Atlanta office handles the bulk of the firm's immigration work, the DC team works with the Departments of Homeland Security, State and Labor on legislative matters. The office also increasingly advises clients on immigration compliance issues.

**The Lawyers:** Former general counsel of the INS, **Bo Cooper** (see p.506) "*knows as much about immigration law as anyone in the world.*" He is highly regarded for his government expertise and experience and interacts regularly with government agencies on visa-related and other immigration matters.

**Clients/Work Highlights:** The firm has attracted a roster of national and international clients.

## Other Notable Practitioners

**Jan Pederson** of Pederson Immigration Law Group PC is "*an aggressive and gutsy lawyer.*" She is known particularly for her expertise in handling consular processing issues and representing medical personnel. At Hunton & Williams LLP, **Ian Band** (see p.499) focuses exclusively on business immigration. "*A wonderful person with a great practice,*" he has experience in counseling corporate and individual clients in all aspects of business immigration law.

# INSURANCE

# INSURER FIRMS

## Band 1

### Hogan & Hartson LLP

See firm details p.568

**The Firm:** This firm has sustained its reputation as "*a provider of quality and expert advice*" with a consistently impressive workload. This year the 24-attorney team represented two large insurers undergoing investigations by the US Attorney General and SEC and advised two other insurers on company stock cases. It also secured a recent victory on behalf of Federal Insurance Company in litigation brought by Campbell's in the appellate division of New Jersey. This was a high-value case typical of the matters taken on by the firm. Elsewhere, it acted as lead counsel for long-standing client The Hartford on several asbestos-related coverage matters and represented a major insurer in relation to an asbestos bankruptcy. Indeed, asbestos-related work continues to occupy the firm heavily and seems set to do so for a number of years. It is not, however, the firm's sole concern. Increased representation of insurers in Roman Catholic Church sexual molestation cases has been evident, as has litigation emanating from lead paint and pollution coverage. The firm has also been retained to represent The Chubb Corporation, Federal Insurance Company, Executive Risk Indemnity and Vigilant Insurance Company in a multidistrict litigation action pending in the US District Court in New Jersey. The sheer size of the firm's insurance department is one of its key assets, say clients, while peers regard it as a powerhouse of insurance defense work whose profile has been strengthened by its work on the Silverstein Properties litigation. It regularly represents insurance carriers on coverage issues relating to the full spectrum of insurance matters in litigation, arbitration or alternative dispute resolution, and taps into expertise housed elsewhere within the firm as and when required.

**The Lawyers:** Widely perceived as the driving force behind the firm's recent successes, **William Bowman**'s (see p.503) aptitude for "*skillful negotiation and deal-making*" is juxtaposed with "*an affable and articulate demeanor.*" Clients welcome the fact that in negotiations he comes across as "*a straight shooter*" who "*exerts a lot of behind-the-scenes expertise.*" Others in the marketplace have picked up on his newsworthy successes and share the view that "*he is a tremendous courtroom lawyer.*" **David Hensler**'s (see p.519) reputation hinges around the wealth of his experience, particularly in errors and omissions (E&O), D&O and fiduciary claims work. Interviewees stated that he is "*great at whatever he turns his hand to.*" **James Ruggeri** (see p.543) is well known for his litigation work and handles extensive work on behalf of The Hartford.

**Clients/Work Highlights:** The Hartford; Federal Insurance Company; XL Capital; St. Paul Travelers; Pacificare; Chubb Atlantic Indemnity; Horizon Management Group and Genesis Professional Liability Managers.

### Steptoe & Johnson LLP

See firm details p.576

**The Firm:** With insurance work one of its hallmarks, Steptoe & Johnson can count some of the world's largest carriers as clients. This year, it represented Zurich in products liability insurance litigation with pharmaceutical giant Merck over products such as Vioxx, Paxil and hormone replacement drugs. Currently, it is involved in a high-value London-based arbitration between Merck and its insurers, in which James Rocap is lead counsel. It further represents AIG on matters across the country pertaining to first-party property insurance, and is also developing its D&O defense work: it recently represented the CEO of tiremakers Bridgestone/Firestone in defending allegations of securities fraud. Other big-name clients include St. Paul Travelers, whom it advises particularly on the issues of asbestos and environmental matters. The practice is growing, both from within and by making lateral hires, and is broadening its area of insurance-related specialization so that it now encompasses reinsurance, professional liability, E&O, corporate insurance, insurance tax matters and long-tail coverage claims. Its clients are based in major insurance hubs across the USA and Europe and consistently hail the service they receive as "*superb.*"

**The Lawyers:** Sources agreed that the team has a reputation for "*advocating on a more elevated plain than others at the insurance Bar,*" while maintaining a "*very trustworthy*" reputation. **James Rocap** (see p.542) is head of the firm's worldwide insurance practice. He and his team are perceived as being "*great lawyers with a whole range of talents.*" Rocap, in particular, can be counted upon to "*give a strong performance for his clients,*" thanks to his wealth of experience. Acknowledged as "*a great advocate for insurers,*" he is also described as "*very bright and reliable.*" Litigator **Roger Warin** (see p.553) also enjoys widespread acclaim as "*an extremely affable man and practical lawyer.*"

**Clients/Work Highlights:** AIG; Swiss Re; Zurich; St. Paul Travelers; Liberty Mutual and The Hartford.

### Wiley Rein & Fielding LLP

See firm details p.579

**The Firm:** Building on its core foundations of traditional insurance work, this broad-based firm has undergone a period of evolution. While maintaining its strong general practice, it has increasingly moved into other areas leading to a growth in activity in the regulatory, international and legislative areas. The increasingly rigorous nature of insurance regulation, in particular, has ensured that the firm has been busy on compliance work at both a federal and national level. In this work, it has been aided by the fact that a close nexus exists between the firm's government and insurance departments, allowing lawyers from each to feed off one another's knowledge. In the wake of recent corporate scandals, professional liability has also become a more important area of focus, although commentators were keen to stress that the firm's "*top-notch*" coverage work is still its main area of dominance. Work highlights from the past year include acting as US counsel for Winterthur Group in a dispute with XL Capital. Clients say the firm has been "*phenomenal*" in assessing coverage issues, drafting opinions and acting as litigation counsel in coverage disputes.

**The Lawyers:** Practice founder and department head **Thomas Brunner** (see p.504) is acknowledged to be something of a pioneer in insurance law and the development of the firm's product. A "*zealous advocate of his clients' position,*" he is said to have "*more experience than just about anyone*" in the area of insurance coverage and is always able to come up with *"fresh and creative solutions."* Commentators spoke highly of **Laura Foggan** (see p.512), whose profile has been bolstered by her presence on trade associations and through speaking engagements on the lecture circuit. She is universally *"trusted to get superb results for her clients"* and has become increasingly active in directing commercial litigation across the country in matters as diverse as technology, environmental, employment, products liability, mass tort and pharmaceutical claims. **Daniel Standish**'s (see p.548) reputation as *"one of the key people in the industry"* has been sealed through his prowess in D&O and professional liability. Clients appreciate his level of expertise, while peers acknowledge that he is a visible presence at industry functions and has been instrumental in some recent key decisions, particularly concerning rescission. **Theodore Howard** (see p.519) has experience in representing clients in disputes involving asbestos, dioxin, hazardous waste and noise, chemical exposure, pharmaceuticals, repetitive stress injuries, artificial breast implants, HIV-contaminated blood, defective building products, reinsurance and agent-broker disputes. He is commended for his *"all-around professional and businesslike demeanor."* Similarly, **John Yang** (see p.556) was felt to be *"reliable and knowledgeable"* by clients, who also believe that his skill sets opportunely complement those of other members of the team.

**Clients/Work Highlights:** Winterthur Group; Chubb Group; Genesis Professional Liability Managers; Gulf Insurance Associates and CNA Insurance Companies.

## Band 2

### Baach Robinson & Lewis PLLC

**The Firm:** A *"fine and respected"* authority on all matters relating to the London and Lloyd's insurance markets, this firm was felt to offer niche expertise in *"understanding the culture of the London market and translating it for the American legal system."* Underwriters and insurers on both sides of the Atlantic are represented by the firm in matters concerning asbestos, pollution, health hazards, pharmaceutical claims, workers' compensation, antitrust, reinsurance, professional liability, political risk and intellectual property claims. It also regularly undertakes alternative dispute resolution proceedings as a supplement to its regular diet of coverage disputes and policy drafting.

**The Lawyers: Martin Baach** is *"a master"* in providing a conduit of knowledge that links the US and London markets. He has experience in civil, commercial and white-collar criminal litigation and his insurance and reinsurance experience spans coverage matters, products liability, professional liability disputes and international and domestic arbitration. He has also been pivotal in leading state and federal government relations projects and is widely regarded as *"one of the smartest and most talented lawyers in town."*

**Clients/Work Highlights:** The firm represents Lloyd's and London market underwriters and domestic insurers.

### Crowell & Moring LLP
See firm details p.564

**The Firm:** A pool of *"excellent resources in all aspects of coverage law"* is on offer at a firm that takes on work from across the country and provides an *"extremely accommodating and understanding"* service. Its litigation heritage has stood it in good stead for tackling the increasing amount of alternative dispute resolution its clients seek and it has been active in a growing number of complex insurance resolutions in recent times. Its regular workload comprises coverage litigation and client counseling plus negotiation across lines such as property and casualty, E&O, D&O and healthcare. It is now being more frequently retained by multiple insurers for single complex cases. In this regard it is thriving to the extent that commentators speak of its *"exceptional work output"* and *"creative, thoughtful attorneys."* Clients appreciate that these lawyers are consistently *"loyal, up front and frank with us."*

**The Lawyers:** Cochair of the practice **Paul Kalish** (see p.521) is a *"rising star"* who serves as national counsel for property and casualty companies in coverage matters while also representing defendants and insurers in asbestos, silica and other mass torts. Clients value the fact that he is *"responsive, intelligent and resourceful."* **Clifford Hendler** (see p.519) also scored well in clients' esteem. He was thought to have *"a deep breadth of knowledge of insurance coverage matters"* while being *"very hard-working and reachable day or night."* A renowned mediator, he is being asked with increasing frequency to put his alternative dispute resolution skills to the test on his clients' behalf, and recently acted in a mediation capacity in a case against an oil and gas services company. Entering the tables for the first time this year, **Mark Plevin** (see p.539) is rated by clients as *"thorough and aggressive in a positive way."* Devoting his time to insurance coverage litigation and bankruptcy cases, his *"deep understanding of complex issues"* and ability to *"approach matters in a creative and independent way"* are an enormous help for clients. Also making his debut is trial and appellate advocate **Clifton Elgarten** (see p.510), whose *"impressive courtroom manner"* has won him a number of admirers. His background in commercial disputes has provided him with a platform for his highly respected trial practice.

**Clients/Work Highlights:** The firm represents over 20 large insurance carriers and firms such as Resolute Management and Mt. McKinley Insurance.

### Ross Dixon & Bell LLP

**The Firm:** This firm's *"spectacular"* insurance practice spans four offices but has a concentration of expertise in Washington, DC. Its *"impeccably professional"* team represents clients from major insurance carriers to those covering specialty lines. Subdivisions at the group include a well-established and highly respected D&O practice and also professional liability and employment practice liability teams. A recent

spate of activity has focused on Enron-type corporate scandals with the firm being involved in representing insurers in high-profile cases such as WorldCom, HealthSouth, REFCO and Vioxx. Security actions and class actions such as the one it conducted on behalf of Wal-Mart have also occupied the practice this year, and it has been involved in litigation over rescission matters. It is currently representing CNA Insurance Companies in a general liability trial involving Congoleum. Interviewees believe that the firm offers the kind of top-level service that is usually the centerpiece of far larger – and more expensive – firms, and appreciate the fact that the firm's high degree of internal organization and consistent client focus are key assets.

**The Lawyers:** Founding partner, and *"one of the best attorneys in his field,"* **Gary Dixon** continues to receive abundant praise for his *"tireless and unbelievably responsive"* manner. A recognized authority on D&O liability litigation, he has acted on behalf of insurers and insureds in some of the most significant cases across the country. Clients believe his *"wealth of experience"* is complemented by his *"attention to detail, level of knowledge, and practical business sense."* One commented: *"He makes us feel like we're his only client."* New entrants to *Chambers'* tables this year include managing partner **David Gische**, who debuts on the strength of testimonies to his *"exceptional talent."* His D&O work has won him the accolade of being *"a wonderful legal negotiator."* **Leslie Ahari** has represented insurers in a variety of D&O cases and has also defended accountants in professional malpractice claims, while **Wallace Christensen** is included this year in recognition of his long-standing experience in handling commercial litigation across the country. He is retained by several large insurers to represent them on a variety of matters and also serves as an arbitrator. He advises insurers on D&O and E&O coverage and is widely thought of as *"a superb trial lawyer who wins the cases you don't expect him to win."* **John Duchelle** has also litigated insurance coverage cases in courts nationwide and regularly represents D&O liability carriers in prosecuting rescission litigation in the wake of recent corporate accountancy scandals. With his verve for *"great legal analysis,"* clients believe he merits a place in this year's tables. Likewise, **Cathy Simon**'s appearance was prompted by support for her *"high-caliber"* practice. She represents professional liability insurers in a variety of matters before the district courts and the court of appeals.

**Clients/Work Highlights:** The firm acts on behalf of large domestic and international insurers engaged with a cross section of industries.

## Band 3

### Chadbourne & Parke LLP
See firm details p.1524

**The Firm:** With a heavy focus on both reinsurance and primary insurance, this firm has carved out a niche for itself in environmental liabilities; asbestos, pollution and health hazards; issues emanating from the New York terrorist attacks; contract wordings; fraud and rescission claims; pools; and finite reinsurance matters. The team regularly counsels its clients on run-off and commutations issues too, and has strong links with its London base at the heart of the growing run-off community. In the finite reinsurance arena it represented a venture capital firm in the formation of a new reinsurance facility, and as part of its run-off work represented Rosemont Re in an arbitration over bail bond insurance. The 25-strong Washington team receives acclaim for the depth of experience and specialist knowledge that is the firm's hallmark.

**The Lawyers:** As cochair of the group, **David Raim**'s (see p.540) reputation in the reinsurance community as *"one of the most experienced lawyers around"* has been strengthened this year by his increasing involvement in national and international arbitrations and litigations. Acting on behalf of cedents and reinsurers, he is viewed by client sources as a *"widely respected figure"* in the marketplace.

**Clients/Work Highlights:** Zurich; RenaissanceRe Holdings; The Guardian Life Insurance Company of America; AIG; CIGNA; United National Group; Atlantic Mutual; ACE and Nationwide Insurance Company.

### Hunton & Williams LLP
See firm details p.1989

**The Firm:** Although based in Virginia, this broad-based practice scored highly with interviewees due to its activity in the DC market. Its biggest area of focus at the moment is first-party property and business interruption cases arising out of the New York terrorist attacks, many of which are still being litigated. It is also dealing with issues pursuant to recent natural disasters, the knock-on effects of which will emerge over the coming year. The firm has further witnessed growth in demand for its services in reinsurance disputes as clients strive to resolve issues such as the asbestos problem. At the same time, it continues to marshal a regular diet of D&O, E&O and risk management work on behalf of insurance carriers. National in scope, it has acted across the country on reinsurance arbitrations while financial fraud, construction defect and mold claims are all well to the fore. On the general liability side, it acts in cases relating to welding rods and Superfund site claims.

**The Lawyers:** *"One of the most sophisticated, experienced and practical lawyers in his field,"* **Walter Andrews** (see p.498) has great visibility and has built up a well-respected practice since his arrival at the firm.

**Clients/Work Highlights:** Clients include St. Paul Travelers, The PMA Insurance Group and ULLICO.

### Band 4

### Drinker Biddle & Reath LLP

**The Firm:** This Philadelphia firm is expanding into the Washington market with its property/casualty and professional liability practices. A name that is gaining increasing prominence, the ten-lawyer DC team collaborates with its counterparts in offices across the country on national and international work. It represents insurers and reinsurers, agents and brokers in a variety of work, and is well versed in defending class actions and bad-faith claims and in resolving regulatory issues.

**The Lawyers:** Alan Joaquin and Douglas Mangel are key contacts in the DC office.

### Thompson, Loss & Judge LLP

**The Firm:** Formed in 2003, and making its debut in the *Chambers* tables this year, this nine-lawyer boutique firm is active across a number of insurance and reinsurance matters. It undertakes insurance coverage litigation and bad-faith counseling in addition to representing reinsurers in disputes nationwide. Its conscious effort to remain a small firm that houses a concentration of insurance expertise has not gone unnoticed by interviewees, who further commented that it is a firm with a growing reputation for quality work.

**The Lawyers:** *"Highly analytical and sophisticated,"* **Lewis Loss** is another new addition to this year's rankings. The reputation he gained at his former firm Ross Dixon & Bell has followed him to his current firm, with interviewees keen to praise the fact that *"he can always get a good result for his client."* He represents liability insurers with respect to coverage issues affecting many different insurance products and has litigated in the federal and state courts. Observers describe him as a *"terrific lawyer."*

### WilmerHale
See firm details p.580

**The Firm:** Another firm making its first appearance in these tables is WilmerHale, whose insurance practice has been the subject of peer and client admiration. With offices worldwide, the DC arm of its insurance practice is fast becoming a discernible player, with particularly strong links to the bankruptcy practice, and the team regularly represents debtors, creditors, secured lenders and asset purchasers in all stages of bankruptcy proceedings. It also undertakes bankruptcy planning, out-of-court negotiations and bankruptcy-related trial litigation and appellate proceedings in the courts of appeals and the US Supreme Court. It recently represented The Hartford in several bankruptcy cases filed by debtors with asbestos and other long-tail liabilities.

**The Lawyers:** Craig Goldblatt is the contact partner, and also a bankruptcy specialist.

**Clients/Work Highlights:** The firm's clients in insurance and financial services include The Hartford; John Hancock; JPMorgan Chase; Lehman Brothers and Morgan Stanley.

### Zuckerman Spaeder LLP

**The Firm:** This firm's insurance practice was given a boost by the arrival of James Sottile, whose experience in the Lloyd's and London insurance markets has added an extra dimension to its traditionally domestic focus. It can now boast a wealth of experience in helping settle long-tail asbestos, pollution and health hazard claims, particularly those handled by the Lloyd's run-off vehicle Equitas, and is acting with more frequency for European insurers and reinsurers in an advisory role. This addition to the firm's renowned litigation basis prompted commentators to say: *"You can't pull a fast one on them – if you make a less than well-crafted argument they'll find holes in it."* It is also a firm whose *"high ethical standards"* inspire admiration among clients and peers.

**The Lawyers:** **James Sottile** has a *"well-deserved excellent reputation"* for his specialist knowledge of the Lloyd's market. Contemporaries say he is *"one of the best there is"* in this arena and his workload has brought him growing recognition and accolades.

**Clients/Work Highlights:** The firm represents Equitas and Lloyd's underwriters.

# INSURANCE

# POLICYHOLDER

## Band 1

### Covington & Burling
See firm details p.563

**The Firm:** The toast of DC's policyholder Bar, Covington has once again scooped many plaudits. Described as "*an excellent policyholder practice from top to bottom,*" this multitalented team represents insureds across a varied milieu and it acts in many of the most complex, high-value and high-profile cases around. Its place in the history of the DC market is firmly established, as it was where many of the luminaries on the scene began their careers. According to clients, the firm possesses the vital ingredients for success, namely "*financial nous, access to sophisticated and important deals, great preparation and a savvy and experienced outlook.*" The practice comprises a strong litigation arm, helping clients across many industries in resolving coverage disputes with their insurers. It recently brokered a complex deal of over $25 million for Mittal Steel in a bankruptcy proceeding between it and LTV that involved government and state entities attempting to resolve its environmental liabilities. Asbestos work continues to form a substantial portion of the firm's caseload: it is involved with engineering firm Foster Wheeler, a company being sued over its manufacture of boilers containing asbestos, and has recently concluded the settlement of a large asbestos non-products coverage matter in Ohio. Other mass tort work has involved pharmaceuticals, medical devices, property, D&O and professional liability. In addition to trying cases in state and federal courts across the country, it is developing its national and international arbitration capability, having conducted several recent arbitrations taking place in Bermuda and London.

**The Lawyers:** **Robert Sayler** (see p.544) takes up a place in this year's senior statesman category. He has put his experience in trying insurance coverage cases toward his new position as lecturer in advocacy and insurance coverage law at the University of Virginia. Despite this permanent move, he arbitrated a coverage case this year and will continue to act in a similar capacity over the coming years. "*A terrific and bright lawyer,*" **Mitchell Dolin** (see p.508) is "*first choice*" for many clients. His practice area is mainly focused on high-value coverage disputes. Although asbestos issues still constitute a major part of this, he has also been involved in disputes over pharmaceutical and medical devices, as well as property disputes resulting from the 2001 New York terrorist attacks and more recent natural disasters. According to clients, it is his "*intellectual firepower*" which is the force behind recent successes, coupled with the fact he "*brings the right balance*" of litigation expertise, settlement ability and insurance experience. **William Greaney** (see p.516) moves up to the top ranking in this year's *Chambers* tables in acknowledgement of his "*pragmatic and focused*" approach to achieving settlements. He represents public and private entities in coverage disputes and alternative dispute resolution proceedings, often serving as a party-appointed arbitrator. In his role as negotiator and adviser, **John Buchanan**'s (see p.504) practice strives to resolve problems between insureds and their insurers at a fundamental level. He is thought of as "*a very creative and aggressive lawyer,*" who is an essential component of the mechanics of the practice group. Commentators say **William Skinner**'s (see p.546) "*cool and reliable*" demeanor helps him provide "*excellent counsel,*" making him indispensable to clients. "*Busy and prolific,*" he displays "*creativity and intelligence*" in negotiating, arbitrating and litigating complex insurance coverage disputes. He is currently representing two pharmaceutical companies in London arbitrations on excess general liability policies and advising two financial institutions in claims arising from the New York terrorist attacks. **Anna Engh** (see p.510) has handled coverage litigation over matters such as asbestos, breast implants, lead and other mass torts, environmental claims, political risks, D&O and E&O, and has also represented clients in bankruptcy proceedings. She is currently special insurance counsel for Owens Corning in its Chapter 11 proceeding. In addition to being practice coordinator, **Saul Goodman** (see p.516) undertakes the role of full-time negotiator in insurance disputes and this year handled complex bankruptcy-related work for clients in the steel industry.

**Clients/Work Highlights:** Cardinal Health; Owens Corning; Mittal Steel; Foster Wheeler; Textron; Cytec Industries; Merck; Nestlé; Société Générale; Dow Chemical and Eli Lilly.

## Band 2

### Dickstein Shapiro Morin & Oshinsky LLP
See firm details p.565

**The Firm:** Operating under the firm's litigation umbrella, this insurance practice represents large US and international policyholders in a variety of coverage disputes. It regularly acts for Fortune 500 companies in the federal and state courts and is well known for its securities work involving SEC issues and D&O liabilities for the likes of WorldCom, Enron and Tyco International. The past year has seen it settle a number of cases involving matters such as mold exposure, asbestos and other pollution liabilities. It also obtained representation of a defunct company whose insurers refused to provide coverage due to the alleged actions of the company directors. This resulted in a multimillion-dollar settlement against the insurance company. A number of claims resulting from Hurricane Katrina have also kept the firm busy.

**The Lawyers:** **Leon Kellner** (see p.522), a "*highly accomplished and experienced*" practitioner, has the rare ability to "*see opportunities for compromise and pursue them.*" He is part of a team that includes **Divonne Smoyer** (see p.547), an attorney rapidly attracting a growing band of followers. Interviewees were astonished at the "*sheer amount of information she can carry around in her head – on paper it would be like a Manhattan skyscraper.*" She represents clients in multiparty disputes over asbestos, breast implants, pharmaceuticals and insurance coverage and handles the negotiations and background work. Commentators report that she is "*very client-responsive and able to see all the consequences of intended actions so that the client can be counseled appropriately for whatever may lie ahead.*" **Jerry Oshinsky** (see p.536), head of the group, divides his time between DC and work on the West Coast. His "*good instincts for which arguments will fly*" make him an effective trial lawyer.

**Clients/Work Highlights:** The firm represents large industrial policyholders, small companies, municipalities, state governments and charities.

### Gilbert Heintz & Randolph LLP
**The Firm:** This firm is synonymous with the "*innovative and creative*" approach it takes to its work. It

handles manifold work on behalf of clients across a range of sectors, a substantial amount of which is cutting-edge asbestos work for corporate policyholders and claimant committees. It also handles matters on claimants' behalf against defunct insurance companies. It represents a significant number of property owners, hotels and REITs in dealing with their insurers, with some of the work it undertakes in this area being pro bono or public service. The team is increasingly called upon to act in consumer fraud issues as they relate to insurance, and envisages an uptake in asbestos disputes registered between policyholders and insurance companies.

**The Lawyers:** *"Brilliant and bright,"* **Scott Gilbert** was singled out by the whole market for being *"able to understand even the most complex negotiations at a glance."* His field of expertise lies in asbestos and bankruptcy work, areas in which he is widely held to be the master, but he is also a pioneer in alternative dispute resolution. Possessed of the dexterity to administer *"the appropriate injection of mediation skills to get the best results for his client,"* he has a national reputation for obtaining asbestos recoveries for his clients. **John Heintz**'s expertise in multiparty insurance litigation has highlighted his aptitude for *"handling complex and high-profile cases with aplomb."* He has acted in significant pieces of litigation for over 20 years and in that time has built up a reputation for a *"prolific and distinguished"* output of work. **Gary Thompson** is responsible for coordinating the firm's pro bono efforts. In this capacity he recently secured insurance payouts for cancer patients and victims of the terrorist attacks on the Pentagon and the World Trade Center. He represents policyholders in many forms of insurance disputes including political risk, D&O, fidelity bonds and commercial general liability. Interviewees focused on his *"tireless and thorough"* representation of his clients and talked of his *"experienced demeanor that belies his relative youth."*

**Clients/Work Highlights:** AOL; Dow Chemical; Equal Rights Center; Host Marriott; Millennium Chemicals; Pfizer; Schlumberger; SEPCO and Verizon.

### Howrey LLP

**The Firm:** Custodians of a fine policyholder practice, the *"truly tenacious"* team at Howrey has attracted the attention of many market commentators with its string of coverage cases. It continues to act as lead counsel for two paper manufacturing companies in actions seeking recoveries for liabilities arising from the manufacture of allegedly defective siding products. In the wake of the Spitzer investigations into broking practices, it is also acting in an advisory role for parties concerned about the implications of increased market scrutiny. The DC team forms a large part of the 75-attorney national practice and can offer specialist expertise in D&O and E&O claims, appellate work and alternative dispute resolution in pre- or mid-insurance litigation.

**The Lawyers:** **Robert Shulman** is cochair of the insurance recovery practice and is widely thought of as a *"quality lawyer"* whose recent successes in

*"impressively high-stakes cases"* have assured him an entrenched position at the forefront of leading market practitioners.

**Clients/Work Highlights:** The firm represents policyholders from a broad spectrum of industries including aerospace, banking, building products, chemicals, construction, consumer products, electric utilities, fashion, food and beverage, financial services, healthcare, motion picture, paper and wood products, petroleum, pharmaceutical, railroad, real estate development, retail, securities, telecom, television and transportation.

### Band 3

### Heller Ehrman LLP
See firm details p.329

**The Firm:** At the time of going to press, Swidler Berlin's entire insurance group has joined Heller Ehrman's DC office, bolstering its policyholder-side insurance recovery practice. The new arrivals include Mark Plumer, the former chair of Swidler's insurance group, and fellow director David Klein, with the move itself motivated by the desire to avoid client conflicts arising from the recent merger of Swidler and Bingham McCutchen. Recent and ongoing work for the practice includes advising in relation to claims arising out of the collapse of the World Trade Center and Hurricane Katrina.

**The Lawyers:** **Mark Plumer** (see p.539) is credited for his *"prescience in negotiations."* His recent work includes acting as lead counsel for Fortune 500 companies in litigation and he is consistently perceived as *"a bright and talented attorney"* by his clients and fellow practitioners. **David Klein** (see p.523) is celebrated for his victories in obtaining multimillion-dollar payouts from large companies in the petrochemicals and mining sectors. He recently represented a major regional utility in complex litigation and negotiations involving general and environmental impairment liability coverage for multiple sites. He also acted for a cable television provider in a case involving catastrophic direct losses and business interruption. In addition to negotiation work, associate **Alex Lathrop** (see p.525) has represented clients in all aspects of insurance coverage and other commercial litigation before federal and state courts. His recent work has included advising companies regarding the Foreign Corrupt Practices Act, and he assists in the development of corporate compliance and ethics programs.

**Clients/Work Highlights:** The firm has recently been representing corporate policyholders such as Kaiser Aluminum, Sony Electronics, Hewlett-Packard and GMAC.

### McDermott Will & Emery
See firm details p.878

**The Firm:** This multifaceted practice makes its debut in *Chambers* this year following enthusiastic praise for its 50-lawyer DC insurance team. Its area of focus spans insurance and reinsurance work and it is involved in a number of ongoing 9/11 claims as well

as other general disputes involving large insurers. It acts for Allianz in matters pursuant to alleged sexual abuse by Roman Catholic priests in California and also has a regular diet of environmental, asbestos, breast implants, mass torts and long-tail liabilities. A strong strategic counseling service is another service offered.

**The Lawyers:** **Margaret Warner** (see p.553) is head of the trial department in Washington and is cochair of the firm's interdisciplinary insurance markets practice group. The bulk of her role lies in acting as strategic adviser to clients, and she is outside general counsel for a company that was formed to handle insurance claims arising from the 9/11 rescue effort and debris removal. She also undertook a major arbitration emanating from the Silverstein Properties case and serves as national coordinator for a major property and casualty company in trials. Her work has impressed many others in the market, who say of her: *"She has earned great kudos."* She and her team are considered *"extremely capable of negotiating a deal and litigating."*

### Morgan, Lewis & Bockius LLP
See firm details p.1758

**The Firm:** The muscle behind this practice lies in its national presence and A-list clients. Previously unranked in this section, it appears in *Chambers'* tables by dint of the work it has taken on recently. For example, it has acted for Kraft in a successful environmental liability recovery case in Indiana and represented Sunoco in a successful insurance recovery claim relating to environmental coverage issues. Interviewees spoke of a six-strong DC team of *"fine strategic vision"* that works alongside its counterparts nationally to provide a *"good, tight service to the client."*

**The Lawyers:** Regarded not only as *"a terrific lawyer but also a great businessman,"* **Paul Zevnik** (see p.557) undertakes all aspects of insurance litigation, transactions, environmental recoveries, coverage counseling and toxic torts. His *"brilliantly creative"* approach has wowed clients, who also appreciate the capped monthly fee system arranged by the firm. Many clients perceive Zevnik to be *"one of the best lawyers we've ever worked with."*

**Clients/Work Highlights:** Kraft; Sara Lee; Sunoco and Tyco International.

### Spriggs & Hollingsworth

**The Firm:** A well-known name in local dispute resolution circles, this firm is active across a number of industries. Its insurance department accommodates multistate coverage claims concerning the environmental, asbestos, pharmaceutical and medical device arenas to name but a few. It also has sturdy ties with the London market, where it works on run-off matters, particularly alongside Equitas, in addition to other company insolvencies. In-house pharmaceuticals, products liability and white-collar defense expertise can be tapped into when required, and on the advisory side the firm is experienced in constructing insurance programs for clients and advising them on risk management and alternative risk transfer mechanisms.

**The Lawyers:** Practice leader **Marc Mayerson** was singled out by his peers as an insurance luminary whose "*small but powerful*" policyholder practice continues to attract admirers. Described as "*a very bright guy,*" he also writes for the blog Insurance Scrawl, an insurance news and discussion forum that has caught the eye of The Wall Street Journal. His technical skill is manifest and interviewees felt that his accomplishments reveal a "*reliable, effective and talented*" litigator.

## Other Notable Practitioners

Competitors endorsed **Lori Masters** (see p.529) at Jenner & Block LLP for her adroitness in long-tail environmental and asbestos liability issues, areas in which she works closely with Equitas and the London market. She also advises on property claims and business interruption policies and has been seen an upswing in this work in the aftermath of Hurricane Katrina. **Philip Hecht** and **Matthew Jacobs** (see p.520) at Kirkpatrick & Lockhart Nicholson Graham LLP were also the subject of market acclaim, thanks

to their "*top-tier, unfussy and client-focused*" service. Clients were in agreement that these two lawyers "*take time to get to know our idiosyncrasies so that they are as aligned as possible with our overall corporate philosophy.*" Environmental liability forms a large tranche of their workload and they recently represented Waste Management in a coverage case. On the D&O and E&O side, they have worked closely with clients in response to the Spitzer investigation and recently represented Strong Financial Corporation in the sale of mutual funds to Wells Fargo.

# INTELLECTUAL PROPERTY

## Intellectual Property
### Leading Firms

| 1 | **FINNEGAN HENDERSON** *Washington, DC* |
| 2 | **FISH & RICHARDSON P.C.** *Washington, DC* |
| | **HOWREY LLP** *Washington, DC* |
| 3 | **ARNOLD & PORTER LLP** *Washington, DC* |
| | **BANNER & WITCOFF, LTD** *Washington, DC* |
| | **KIRKLAND & ELLIS LLP** *Washington, DC* |
| | **MCDERMOTT WILL & EMERY** *Washington, DC* |
| | **STERNE, KESSLER, GOLDSTEIN** *Washington, DC* |
| 4 | **MAYER, BROWN, ROWE & MAW LLP** *Washington, DC* |
| | **PILLSBURY WINTHROP SHAW** *Washington, DC* |
| | **PROSKAUER ROSE LLP** *Washington, DC* |
| | **SIDLEY AUSTIN LLP** *Washington, DC* |
| | **SKADDEN, ARPS, SLATE, MEAGHER** *Washington, DC* |
| | **WEIL, GOTSHAL & MANGES LLP** *Washington, DC* |

### Leading Individuals

| ★ | **DUNNER** Donald *Finnegan Henderson* |
| 1 | **FARABOW** Ford *Finnegan Henderson* |
| | **FREED** Joel *McDermott Will & Emery* |
| | **LUPO** Raphael *McDermott Will & Emery* |
| 2 | **GOTTS** Lawrence *Pillsbury Winthrop* |
| | **LIPSEY** Charles *Finnegan Henderson* |
| | **PAPPAS** George *Covington & Burling* |
| | **POTENZA** Joseph *Banner & Witcoff, Ltd* |
| | **SIRILLA** George *Pillsbury Winthrop* |
| | **WEST JR** William *Howrey LLP* |
| 3 | **BAUMGARTEN** Jon *Proskauer Rose LLP* |
| | **CORDELL** Ruffin *Fish & Richardson P.C.* |
| | **GONZALEZ** Cecilia *Howrey LLP* |
| | **HADJIS** Alexander *Weil, Gotshal* |
| | **KAUFMAN** Kenneth *Skadden, Arps* |
| | **SHARER** Paul *Mayer, Brown, Rowe & Maw* |
| | **STERNE** Robert *Sterne, Kessler, Goldstein & Fox* |
| 4 | **ATTRIDGE** Daniel *Kirkland & Ellis LLP* |
| | **DOYLE** Scott *Steptoe & Johnson LLP* |
| | **GONZALEZ** Jorge *Sterne, Kessler, Goldstein & Fox* |
| | **HUNTINGTON** Danny *Bingham McCutchen LLP* |
| | **MCELWAIN** William *WilmerHale* |

## Band 1

### Finnegan Henderson Farabow Garrett & Dunner LLP

See firm details p.567

**The Firm:** One of America's "*marquee names*" in IP, this impressive 200-attorney team continues to command great respect in the field. It covers the full spectrum of IP issues, and with its track record stretching back over four decades, clients say they "*cannot praise the firm highly enough.*" The practice covers a range of sectors, from consumer goods, electronics and manufacturing to pharmaceutical and nanotechnology. The firm recently acted for Guidant in its $800 million dispute over the validity of a stent technology patent. IP-related matters pertaining to international trade, unfair competition, e-commerce, portfolio management, antitrust and government contracts further contribute to the workload.

**The Lawyers:** Sources unanimously agreed that there is clear blue water between **Donald Dunner** (see p.509) and the rest of the field. Indeed, peers consider him deserving of a lifetime achievement award for his contribution to the practice. His profile is perceived to stem in no small part from his "*unbelievable*" track record as an appellate lawyer on the Federal Circuit. One recent highlight for Dunner was representing SanDisk against Memorex Products in its appeal to the Federal Circuit. **Ford Farabow** (see p.511) is a trial lawyer with a "*razor-sharp mind,*" who is possessed of a "*Southern charm that judges and juries find really attractive.*" He focuses on chemical and pharmaceutical arenas, and peers describe him as an "*honorable and persuasive*" adversary with an "*outstanding courtroom presence.*" **Charles Lipsey** (see p.527) is a name "*you hear around town a lot.*" This "*extraordinarily hard worker*" is a patent infringement litigator who is quick on his feet. Admired by peers, he is currently representing Eli Lilly in its Zyprexa drug appeal – a case in which an estimated $3 billion is at stake.

**Clients/Work Highlights:** Eli Lilly; GlaxoSmithKline; sanofi-aventis; Gateway; Nikon and Telcordia Technologies.

## Band 2

### Fish & Richardson P.C.

See firm details p.1113

**The Firm:** This large, well-established firm specializes first and foremost in IP. Special praise was reserved for its sophisticated litigation practice, which has an enviable track record in Section 337 cases before the ITC. Overall, clients billed it as a "*terrific operation*" with a "*solid team and a lot of depth.*"

**The Lawyers:** The "*talented*" **Ruffin Cordell** (see p.507) was described as a "*tough and articulate*" trial lawyer. He has an impressive list of clients and has been heavily involved in Section 337 proceedings. "*Creative and highly skilled,*" he has provided ongoing advice to Intel in American Video Graphics v Intel Corporation et al, a dispute over graphics parts.

**Clients/Work Highlights:** 3M Innovative Properties; Atari; Bose; Harvard University; Intel; Microsoft; Nokia; Ocean Spray Cranberries; Porsche Cars North America and Yahoo!

### Howrey LLP

**The Firm:** The "*substantial*" IP practice here benefits greatly from the reputations of its "*renowned patent litigators,*" according to sources. With the recent addition of four copyright attorneys from Pillsbury Winthrop, the team goes from strength to strength, and representing Research in Motion in its high-profile appeal over its BlackBerry system was a major recent highlight. The clientele of the practice hails from industries ranging from telecom to biotechnology and pharmaceutical.

**The Lawyers:** The experienced **William West** is a "*smooth*" attorney who is "*high up*" on everyone's list of recommendations. When asked why, one peer responded: "*He's just such a superb and articulate trial attorney.*" Patents are considered his true forte, and he defended QUALCOMM against an allegation of CDMA wireless technology patent infringement by Broadcom. The "*go-to*" name for ITC work, **Cecilia Gonzalez** is an "*agile*" attorney who peers admit is "*tough to litigate against.*" She is described as a "*positive, capable lawyer who is always in control.*" Liaising with their New York team, she is co-counsel to a major flooring manufacturer asserting its patent against foreign competitors.

Clients/Work Highlights: Caterpillar; QUAL-COMM; American Stock Exchange; Ingram Industries and Research in Motion.

## Band 3

### Arnold & Porter LLP
See firm details p.560

The Firm: Arnold & Porter has been able to establish itself as a "*prominent player*" within a short space of time. A team of 80 IP lawyers deals with the full range of matters, and is particular strong in licensing. It recently won a directed verdict on behalf of Confluence Kayaks in a dispute with Old Town Canoe. The case concerned alleged patent infringement by Confluence of Old Town's canoes. The firm is particularly well regarded in hi-tech and pharmaceutical sectors, where it services a wide range of clients.

The Lawyers: Charles Ossola is a senior partner in Arnold & Porter's intellectual property and technology practice group.

Clients/Work Highlights: Dell; Microsoft; Verizon; AOL; Gilead; Tiffany and Random House.

### Banner & Witcoff, Ltd

The Firm: These "*great*" IP experts are said to excel when it comes to patents, an area in which the firm is perceived to have contributed heavily to the development of the law. The 45-attorney team has an impressive workload, generated by prominent clients in the computer and electronics sectors. In addition, it is involved in biotechnology casework for several leading universities. Its "*quality litigation*" group successfully defended Nike in a dispute with Triple Tee Golf. The case concerned Nike's alleged infringement of trade secrets relating to the design of golf clubs.

The Lawyers: An "*able adversary,*" **Joseph Potenza** is renowned above all as a patent litigation lawyer, but performs some copyright work. This "*focused*" attorney has substantial experience of Section 337 investigations and recently represented Scientific-Atlanta in an ITC proceeding against Gemstar-TV Guide International. The case concerned Scientific-Atlanta's alleged infringement of a Gemstar patent relating to set top boxes. His client service skills make him a popular choice of practitioner, and one happy customer said: "*He's among the best I've worked with.*"

Clients/Work Highlights: AOL; Microsoft; Harvard University; The Johns Hopkins University; Nike; Scientific-Atlanta; Nokia; Colgate-Palmolive and AT&T.

### Kirkland & Ellis LLP
See firm details p.875

The Firm: The "*depth of legal talent*" offered by Kirkland & Ellis' 25-attorney IP team was what impressed

clients most, and the outfit has won a respectable market profile for itself. Both litigation and transactional work is covered, with commentators generally agreeing that the firm is at its best when handling contentious matters, to which it can bring the full force of "*its stellar bench of litigators.*" Clients also appreciate the flexibility of these "*go-getters*" when it comes to accommodating their needs. The team is particularly strong on the patents front, where it has successfully represented a number of medical device and generic and branded pharmaceutical firms. It also performs a large amount of work for the likes of Siemens.

The Lawyers: Combining "*business acumen with a strong legal background,*" **Daniel Attridge** (see p.498) won praise from clients for doing an "*exceptional job.*" His "*strong understanding*" of the federal court system has been put to good use in Ferring BV v Barr Laboratories Inc. The case began in 2002 and since then he has been representing Barr Laboratories in its Abbreviated New Drug Application (ANDA).

Clients/Work Highlights: Barr Laboratories; B. Braun Medical; Teva Pharmaceuticals USA; Honeywell; ACTV Inc; Siemens; BASF; Hershey Foods and Samsung.

### McDermott Will & Emery
See firm details p.878

The Firm: "*This excellent firm attracts excellent lawyers,*" say sources, and plentiful resources are available to deal with the largest cases. Litigious matters are considered its true forte. The team successfully represented Trend Micro before the ITC in a case concerning alleged patent infringement of software by FortuNet.

The Lawyers: The "*much sought-after*" **Ray Lupo** (see p.528) is an attorney who has "*had a significant presence in the field since the beginning.*" An experienced and articulate trial attorney, peers say he can "*connect with the jury and elegantly distill the simple facts of the most complicated cases.*" With his "*confident, calm and steady*" manner, he has developed a well-respected practice during the last 35 years. He has continued to act for Medtronic against Cordis in a case concerning alleged patent infringement relating to Medtronic's stent technology. "*Superstar*" **Joel Freed** (see p.513) has recently joined the firm from Arnold & Porter and is widely acclaimed among peers as an "*excellent*" litigator. "*Tenacious, yet honorable,*" one interviewee commented, "*he has met with considerable success.*"

Clients/Work Highlights: Medtronic; Research Corporation; Trend Micro; Hitachi; Panasonic and Linear Technologies.

### Sterne, Kessler, Goldstein & Fox P.L.L.C.
See firm details p.577

The Firm: This specialist IP firm has met with great success in the biotech sector. It focuses on representing startups, more often than not in medium-sized cases. Members of the firm are renowned for their patent procurement work, and regularly represent generic clients such as Barr Laboratories in ANDAs.

The Lawyers: A founding director of the firm, **Rob Sterne** (see p.516) is described as a "*first-class*" lawyer by clients and peers alike. Although not heavily involved in litigation, he provides strategic advice on patents and licenses. He recently advised several patent-holding companies on electronics and business methods. **Jorge Goldstein** (see p.516) has a PhD in chemistry from Harvard, and is "*highly respected*" for his patent procurement and interference work in the biotech arena.

Clients/Work Highlights: Broadcom; QUAL-COMM; Nanosys; Reebok; Human Genome Sciences; Intellectual Ventures; ParkerVision; Biogen Idec; Hasbro; University of Pennsylvania and Locus Pharmaceuticals.

## Band 4

### Mayer, Brown, Rowe & Maw LLP
See firm details p.876

The Firm: "*Always up to the task,*" this firm is admired by clients for its ability to select the right partners and associates to suit their needs. Several international matters have occupied the 12-attorney team recently, which is praised for "*efficiently handling every case that comes its way.*" In this regard, market observers highlighted the "*flexible*" manner of the firm's attorneys as being integral to its success. The outfit recently commenced an ITC case on behalf of Fabio Perini, alleging a breach of patent by Chan Li Machinery.

The Lawyers: Clients say that what sets **Paul Sharer** (see p.545) apart from others is his combination of technical expertise and "*excellent*" client skills. Offering "*comprehensive legal advice,*" he marries legal expertise with strategy to good effect. Described by clients as a "*fine lawyer who thinks outside the box,*" he continues to advise a large pharmaceutical company in its patent litigation.

Clients/Work Highlights: Polaroid; Solvay; IVAX; DSM Desotech; Uniqema and Johnson Matthey.

### Pillsbury Winthrop Shaw Pittman LLP
See firm details p.1550

The Firm: Litigating a number of big-ticket Section 337 ITC cases against foreign companies has come to the fore in the firm's workload of late. The firm's ability to strike the "*right balance*" between senior and junior practitioners impressed market observers. A "*top-drawer*" group, its "*professional and attentive*" approach has secured the confidence of clients. A particularly successful trademark team further defines the firm's profile.

The Lawyers: The "*ever-diligent*" **Larry Gotts** (see p.516) is an outstanding litigator who will "*know his case backwards*" before setting foot in the courtroom. He is cochair of the firm's national IP group and commentators identify him as the driving force behind its success in the field. A "*top dog with tremendous personality,*" clients say he is "*relentless*" in trying to achieve the best possible results. He litigates and counsels on the full scope of IP issues and recently filed a case for trial against the US government and

Lockheed Martin alleging infringement of Honeywell's night vision patent. Respected patent litigator **George Sirilla** (see p.546) was billed as a "*hugely effective*" lawyer who offers excellent client representation.

**Clients/Work Highlights:** STX; Armor Holdings; VTech Communications; Cingular Wireless; Waters Corporation and Honeywell.

## Proskauer Rose LLP

See firm details p.1551

**The Firm:** Sophisticated expertise in areas such as copyright and digital content protection distinguishes the firm's practice, according to clients for whom it is the "*first choice.*" Representing groups from the recording industry and individual recording artists in the Grokster case, in which the US Supreme Court found peer-to-peer software to infringe copyrights, was a recent highlight. Licensing and counseling work also featured heavily in the past year.

**The Lawyers:** Former general counsel at the US Copyright Office, **Jon Baumgarten** (see p.500) is a "*true standout*" copyright attorney, who is regularly identified as being "*among the best copyright lawyers in town.*" He acted for Sony in Silvers v Sony Pictures Entertainment, a case concerning the right to sue for copyright infringement.

**Clients/Work Highlights:** The firm's clientele originates in the publishing, motion picture, music, communications, arts and Internet sectors.

## Sidley Austin LLP

See firm details p.883

**The Firm:** With the support of a prominent network of offices, this firm's DC arm continues to represent a number of clients in the research industry. A dozen IP lawyers focus on patent litigation and licensing, partic-

ularly in the biotech and pharmaceutical industries.

**The Lawyers:** Jeffrey Kushan is a key contact for IP matters in the firm's DC office.

**Clients/Work Highlights:** GlaxoSmithKline; Anheuser-Busch; Eli Lilly; Bill & Melinda Gates Foundation and LG Electronics.

## Skadden, Arps, Slate, Meagher & Flom LLP & Affiliates

See firm details p.1557

**The Firm:** The ten-attorney team at Skadden Arps performs a high volume of work for media and entertainment sector clients, which has done much to strengthen its copyright practice. In addition, the group advises and counsels hi-tech sector clients on product distribution and joint venture agreements. Recent highlights include representing Intel in a patent infringement case against an Australian government entity.

**The Lawyers:** Copyright lawyer **Ken Kaufman** (see p.522) won plaudits for his "*thorough*" approach, which "*leaves no stone unturned.*" Described as a "*lawyer's lawyer,*" he is heavily involved in the entertainment and media industry, where he represented Virgin Mobile USA in relation to music licensing and copyright issues. Kaufman is also outside counsel for Apple's iTunes music store.

**Clients/Work Highlights:** Apple; Intel; News Corporation; Virgin Mobile USA; Starz Entertainment Group; Vulcan; Goldman Sachs and eBay.

## Weil, Gotshal & Manges LLP

See firm details p.1565

**The Firm:** A relatively new arrival in the market, the firm's group focuses primarily on patent litigation and particularly ITC casework, for the purposes of

which it recently established a discrete litigation group. However, with "*all the resources of a first-class firm*" at its disposal, the overall operation is able to tackle a host of cases.

**The Lawyers:** An "*excellent litigator,*" clients deem **Alex Hadjis** (see p.517) to have "*everything you look for in outside counsel.*" This "*articulate and levelheaded*" lawyer has litigated several cases before the ITC and recently tried a billion dollar patent infringement case for MediaTek relating to disk drive chip technology.

**Clients/Work Highlights:** Intel; Lexar Media; MediaTek; Samsung; Atmel; Genesis Microchip and Cypress Semiconductor.

## Other Notable Practitioners

Clients describe the "*formidable*" **George Pappas** (see p.537) of Covington & Burling as a "*well-respected*" pharmaceuticals patent litigator. He successfully argued an ANDA case for Ortho-McNeil, establishing the enforceability of its patent against a generic company. **Danny Huntington** (see p.519) at Bingham McCutchen LLP enters the table as a highly recommended litigator. This "*smart and imaginative*" attorney was praised for his excellent track record in the biotech sector. At Wilmer Hale, the "*sharp*" **William McElwain** (see p.530) is an "*accomplished, strategic litigator,*" with whom clients say they enjoy working. **Scott Doyle** has recently relocated from the McLean office of Morrison & Foerster to Steptoe & Johnson LLP. His engineering background and spells in-house have made Doyle a popular choice among clients, who appreciate his "*ability to understand the business ramifications of patent portfolio – he's analytical but combines this with a pragmatic business sense.*"

# INVESTMENT MANAGEMENT

## Investment Management
### Leading Firms

1. **DECHERT LLP** *Washington, DC*
   **KIRKPATRICK & LOCKHART** *Washington, DC*
   **MORGAN, LEWIS & BOCKIUS LLP** *Washington, DC*
   **WILLKIE FARR & GALLAGHER LLP** *Washington, DC*
   **WILMERHALE** *Washington, DC*
2. **MAYER, BROWN, ROWE & MAW** *Washington, DC*
   **MORRISON & FOERSTER LLP** *Washington, DC*
   **SUTHERLAND ASBILL & BRENNAN** *Washington, DC*

## Band 1

### Dechert LLP

See firm details p.1752

**The Firm:** "*This formidable practice has a depth that makes it stand out.*" Possessing a roster of former regulators, this respected firm has attracted commendation from across the board for its national presence and diversity of practice. The team covers

the full gamut of investment management work, with expertise in registered and nonregistered products, broker-dealers and insurance commodities, as well as in handling litigation. It provides advice and representation for clients in SEC inquiries and has witnessed an upswing in new product development. One recent highlight was representing Legg Mason in its acquisition of the Permal Group.

**The Lawyers:** **Robert Helm** (see p.518) is a "*knowledgeable and capable lawyer who is on everybody's shortlist.*" His practice covers both domestic and international investment management. Clients like him because he is "*practical, helpful and responsive.*" With experience at the SEC Division of Investment Management, **Jack Murphy** (see p.533) is "*a brilliant lawyer who knows where the Commission is coming from and where they are going.*" Clients praised him as "*a great fellow who's extremely knowledgeable.*" The "*terrific*" **Jeff Puretz** (see p.539) is a "*very client-friendly*" attorney who has particular expertise in insurance products. This year saw him handle a successful closed-end fund offering for a significant

financial client, as well as advising on the mutual fund investments of a number of major insurance companies. Another respected partner is the "*exceptional*" **Jane Kanter** (see p.522). With experience at both the DOL's Office of the Solicitor and the Division of Investment Management, she also enjoys a particularly strong reputation for insurance products.

**Clients/Work Highlights:** An enviable client list covers major insurance companies and complexes; financial institutions; mutual funds and their directors, and asset management companies. Examples include UBS Global Asset Management, American Express and PIMCO and its funds.

### Kirkpatrick & Lockhart Nicholson Graham LLP

**The Firm:** Market sources endorsed "*a very strong group of lawyers and one of the strongest investment practices in the country.*" The group continues to be busy counseling mutual funds, their boards and directors, but has also expanded its hedge fund and broker-dealer practice. With the investment management arena remaining under government scrutiny, compliance, governance and enforcement continue to be strong areas of focus. This year has seen the firm assist a number of mutual fund clients develop compliance infrastructures and programs. On the regulatory side, the firm has been dealing with both the NASD and SEC in connection with broker-dealer sales activities related to mutual funds. Clients were impressed by the group's *"accurate advice and good exercise of judgment."*

**The Lawyers: Diane Ambler** is *"extremely impressive and knowledgeable and connected to the people you need to get your problems solved."* She has recently spent a large amount of time developing compliance infrastructures for the advisers of mutual funds and other investment companies. Clients like her because she is *"responsive and easy to deal with."* The *"superb"* **Arthur Brown** has experience at both the SEC and the Division of Investment Management and is respected for his regulatory compliance expertise. His practice has recently focused on dealing with the increasing levels of consolidation in the sector, advising on mergers and mutual fund reorganizations. Another respected partner is **Robert Zutz**. He is a talented attorney, whose *"star is in the ascendance."* He specializes in representing investment companies, their directors and trustees, broker-dealers and investment advisers.

**Clients/Work Highlights:** An impressive client list includes banks; mutual funds; insurance companies; broker-dealers; investment advisers and their companies.

## Morgan, Lewis & Bockius LLP
See firm details p.1758

**The Firm:** Home to *"one of a handful of premier '40 Act practices in America,"* this national group has *"a strong body of expertise and a strong network of senior lawyers backed up by associates,"* sources said. As well as handling the standard mutual fund work, the firm has particular strengths on the brokerage, securities and enforcement side. It regularly fields large, multi-disciplinary teams to handle litigation, SEC enforcement matters and regulatory inquiries. Mutual fund compliance also remains an area of focus. The firm has enjoyed a successful year on the product development side, with particular expertise in exchange-traded funds. It has also seen an increase in the hedge fund arena, advising clients on changing regulations and representing hedge funds in both national and international transactions.

**The Lawyers: Thomas Harman** (see p.518) is *"a very talented lawyer who does an awesome job in terms of investment company regulatory issues."* Respected for his *"wealth of experience with the SEC,"* he now primarily works with fund groups. This year, he has advised a major client on written compliance procedures reviews. Head of the practice group, **Steve Stone** (see p.549) has a client list that is the envy of many peers. Possessing *"a sharp mind and good judgment,"* he has particular expertise in advising broker-dealer firms. *"His strength is his broad client base, because he's seen everything,"* enthused one client. **John Ford** (see p.513) splits his practice between Philadelphia and Washington, DC. He is *"well spoken and articulate, with a mastery of the '40 Act and the investment management business as a whole."* Ford specializes in new product development. Another SEC alumnus is partner **John McGuire** (see p.531). Clients appreciate the fact that *"he is able to see things from a business as well as legal perspective."* He is also very active in the development of new investment products.

**Clients/Work Highlights:** Goldman Sachs; Rydex; Alliance Capital; Fidelity Investments; The Vanguard Group; Merrill Lynch; Barclays and a number of industry associations.

## Willkie Farr & Gallagher LLP
See firm details p.1567

**The Firm:** This firm enters the rankings this year with the arrival of Barry Barbash and Karrie McMillan from Shearman & Sterling. Many interviewees recognized that Barbash has *"done an outstanding job in building an excellent practice and bringing a formidable competition to the market."* The team is praised by clients for its expertise and judgment and areas of experience include brokerage, revenue sharing and market timing matters. The practice also covers all aspects of asset management from registered to nonregistered funds, and the team has spent much of the past year advising hedge fund and private equity managers on the changes to the hedge fund registration rules. Enforcement and compliance issues continue to be important, with the team having represented a number of clients in various actions before government agencies.

**The Lawyers:** A former director of the SEC Division of Investment Management, **Barry Barbash** (see p.499) *"is a star."* His broad base of experience ensures *"he has good relationships with the regulators and understands how they think."* Clients appreciate that he *"gives good technical advice but has an excellent ability to see the big picture."* *"He's always thinking about the ten other things that might affect you and helps you think through the issues on multiple levels."* Another alumnus of the Division of Investment Management is partner **Karrie McMillan** (see p.531). She is a *"terrific"* attorney who has been doing an increasing amount of M&A in the asset management area, as well as conducting a number of internal reviews for clients.

**Clients/Work Highlights:** Clients include private equity funds; hedge funds; venture capital funds; mutual fund complexes and managers; directors and other institutional investors.

## WilmerHale
See firm details p.580

**The Firm:** Aligned closely with its *"first-rate"* securities group, this practice boasts *"a strong set of practitioners"* with considerable SEC experience and an impressive reputation for regulatory work. *"They have insight into the SEC and how to navigate the regulations,"* said interviewees. With the industry still feeling the fallout from the scandals of recent years, compliance and enforcement continue to be an unsurprisingly strong area of focus. As well as assisting clients with compliance reviews, the team has been kept busy this year defending a number of clients in SEC enforcement actions. The 2004 merger has also reaped rewards, with the group being involved in an increasing amount of traditional fund work and fund formation. The firm also has a *"very high-quality"* broker-dealer practice.

**The Lawyers:** *"Superstar"* **Marianne Smythe** (see p.547) is the *"godmother of mutual funds."* Seen in the market as *"a legend in her own time,"* clients like her practical, solution-oriented style. She is *"hard-nosed and smart and takes no nonsense,"* as well as being *"responsive and pleasant to deal with."* A former director of the SEC Division of Investment Management, her practice has a particular focus on SEC enforcement. **Martin Lybecker** (see p.528) has *"a first-class intellect and an unbelievably broad knowledge of money management and broker-dealer work."* He has particular expertise in the insurance arena. Clients appreciate his ability to deal with the more complex aspects of investment management. *"He's the first one I would go to on difficult investment issues,"* said one. **Brandon Becker** (see p.500) specializes in broker-dealer work. Clients see him as an *"extremely bright"* attorney and value his *"informed and well thought-out"* judgment. **James Anderson** (see p.497) is a *"well-rounded"* lawyer with particular expertise in the hedge fund arena. This year has seen him advising a number of hedge fund managers on SEC registration. The *"top-notch"* **Robert Bagnall** (see p.499) is another respected partner. His practice focuses on investment management regulation.

**Clients/Work Highlights:** Citigroup; PIMCO; GM Investment Management; Merrill Lynch; National Planning Holding; Barclays Group and Lord Abbett Funds.

## Band 2

### Mayer, Brown, Rowe & Maw LLP
See firm details p.876

**The Firm:** With the arrival of Kathryn McGrath and her team from Crowell & Moring LLP, this firm "*now has a serious impact on the market.*" The resources of the firm are seen as offering the group "*a more substantial platform from which to work,*" with strong support particularly on tax and ERISA issues and a close relationship with the firm's New York office. The practice continues to focus on compliance work, carrying out compliance reviews for its fund clients. The group has expertise in regulatory and disclosure matters under the '40 Act and ERISA and also handles securities enforcement matters.

**The Lawyers:** Former director of the SEC Division of Investment Management, the "*superb*" **Kathryn McGrath** (see p.531) enjoys an impressive reputation with both clients and peers. She is "*extremely intelligent, proactive and committed*" and clients appreciate her expertise and "*high integrity.*" Partner **Stephanie Monaco** (see p.533) possesses an extensive knowledge of the Advisers Act, "*has a keen understanding of industry issues*" and "*knows when to step back and when an issue has to be forced,*" reported clients.

**Clients/Work Highlights:** The client roster includes insurance and investment management companies; banks; broker-dealers, and domestic and offshore hedge funds.

### Morrison & Foerster LLP
See firm details p.335

**The Firm:** This firm has a comprehensive mutual fund practice with an emphasis on representing banks and other financial institutions on mutual fund and investment adviser issues. The firm houses a successful transactional practice as well as regulatory and compliance expertise, and has seen an increasing amount of disclosure compliance work in response to the new regulatory burdens facing clients. The past year has seen the team continue to be busy advising Wells Fargo on its acquisition of assets from Strong Capital Management, resulting in the merger of the Strong Funds into the Wells Fargo Advantage Funds.

**The Lawyers:** **Marco Adelfio** (see p.497) is a "*thoughtful, diligent and conscientious*" attorney who is "*attentive to client needs and the needs of the boards.*" He won praise for being "*committed and accommodating and willing to roll up his sleeves and work hard.*"

**Clients/Work Highlights:** The practice acts for financial institutions, venture capital managers and investment companies and advisers. Examples include Wells Fargo and Bank of America.

### Sutherland Asbill & Brennan LLP
See firm details p.578

**The Firm:** This firm enjoys a high-market profile for its variable insurance product practice. A broad remit sees this team providing development and compliance advice regarding all types of insurance matters, with a particular focus of late on closed-end fund and broker-dealer work. One notable highlight in this area was the firm serving as issuer's counsel for an IPO of around $345 million of the common shares of ING Global Advantage and Premium Opportunity Fund, a closed-end management investment company managed by ING.

**The Lawyers:** Chair of the business practices group, **Steve Roth** (see p.543) is "*a leader in the industry on variable annuity products,*" agree sources. Respected for his expertise in the insurance arena, he is "*extremely smart, with the ability to comprehend complicated issues.*" He is also "*a real people person who clients look to a lot.*"

**Clients/Work Highlights:** AIG; TIAA-CREE: MetLife; Merrill Lynch; ING; AEGON USA; Lincoln Financial Group and State Farm.

## Other Notable Practitioners
**Kenneth Berman** of Debevoise & Plimpton LLP "*has a real depth of both SEC and practical experience.*" He is seen by interviewees as "*a very knowledgeable transaction lawyer with deep experience in the investment area.*" Clients appreciate his "*pragmatic, measured and straightforward approach*" and the fact that "*he knows how regulators think.*" His practice focuses on compliance issues.

# LITIGATION

| Litigation |
|---|
| Leading Firms |
| [1] WILLIAMS & CONNOLLY LLP *Washington, DC* |
| [2] ARNOLD & PORTER LLP *Washington, DC* |
| BAKER BOTTS LLP *Washington, DC* |
| COVINGTON & BURLING *Washington, DC* |
| HOGAN & HARTSON LLP *Washington, DC* |
| JONES DAY *Washington, DC* |
| KIRKLAND & ELLIS LLP *Washington, DC* |
| SKADDEN, ARPS *Washington, DC* |
| WILMERHALE *Washington, DC* |
| [3] DICKSTEIN SHAPIRO MORIN *Washington, DC* |
| FRIED, FRANK *Washington, DC* |
| GOODWIN PROCTER LLP *Washington, DC* |
| HOWREY LLP *Washington, DC* |
| SIDLEY AUSTIN LLP *Washington, DC* |
| STEPTOE & JOHNSON LLP *Washington, DC* |
| VINSON & ELKINS LLP *Washington, DC* |

### Williams & Connolly LLP
**The Firm:** The lawyers at this specialist firm are "*completely committed to litigation, it is their focus and their meat.*" From the single DC office, 200 litigators coordinate trial and appellate appearances in state and federal courts across the USA. The team is not broken down into practice areas but instead offers overlapping expertise as comprehensive as its geographical reach. It is probably best known for its high-profile, white-collar criminal practice, but market feedback also rates the group as "*superb*" at both IP and general commercial disputes. The amount of trial work the group undertakes means it is often in the public eye and the lawyers have gained a reputation as "*street-fighters who do whatever it takes for their clients.*" Such clients respect both the quality of work and the responsiveness of the team, praising the lawyers as incredibly quick on the uptake: "*From the very beginning they hit the ground running.*"

**The Lawyers:** "*Unquestionably one of the best civil trial lawyers in Washington,*" **Brendan Sullivan** is characterized as a hard litigator who surrounds himself with an equally tough team. Commentators remarked on the quality of his government investigation and criminal skills, saying his depth of experience means that he is "*a great attorney to turn to in a sticky situation.*" Also touted as a specialist in complex cases, **William McDaniels** has covered medical malpractice, business torts and money-laundering cases throughout his 35 years of practice. For the past decade, **John Vardaman** has been known primarily for his representation of corporations facing mass torts and disaster claims. He usually takes the position of national counsel, planning and implementing litigation strategies across a range of jurisdictions. Described as "*scholarly and hard-working,*" **David Kendall**'s "*first-rate intellect and commitment to excellence*" stand him in good stead with both colleagues and clients. He is perhaps best known for acting for former President Bill Clinton during his impeachment proceedings, but also has a long record of civil rights and media cases to his credit. Concentrating on the intersection of corporate, financial and securities litigation, **John Villa** has a robust practice representing troubled banking clients. Interviewees identified him as a lawyer who "*can do pretty much anything he turns his hand to.*"

**Clients/Work Highlights:** The firm represents both companies and individuals in securities and associated white-collar litigation, although its scope extends to all commercial and criminal matters. Representative clients include American Airlines; GE; Waste Management and Time Warner.

## Litigation: General Commercial
### Leading Individuals

1. JEFFRESS William *Baker Botts LLP*
   SULLIVAN Brendan *Williams & Connolly LLP*
2. ALDOCK John *Goodwin Procter LLP*
   BURCHFIELD Bobby *McDermott Will & Emery*
   HENSLER David *Hogan & Hartson LLP*
   HOLDER Eric *Covington & Burling*
   MCDANIELS William *Williams & Connolly LLP*
   SAYLER Robert *Covington & Burling*
   VARDAMAN John *Williams & Connolly LLP*
   YANNUCCI Thomas *Kirkland & Ellis LLP*
3. BOWMAN William *Hogan & Hartson LLP*
   BROGAN Stephen *Jones Day*
   GERSCH David *Arnold & Porter LLP*
   KENDALL David *Williams & Connolly LLP*
   KLEIN Michael *WilmerHale*
   NIELDS John *Howrey LLP*
   SACKS Stephen *Arnold & Porter LLP*
   VILLA John *Williams & Connolly LLP*
   WEGENER Mark *Howrey LLP*

## Litigation: Specialist Firms in White-Collar Crime & Government Investigations
### Leading Firms

1. JANIS SCHUELKE & WECHSLER *Washington, DC*
   SCHERTLER & ONORATO LLP *Washington, DC*
   TROUT CACHERIS PLLC *Washington, DC*
   ZUCKERMAN SPAEDER LLP *Washington, DC*

## Litigation: White-Collar Crime & Government Investigations
### Leading Individuals

1. BENNETT Robert *Skadden, Arps*
   EGGLESTON W Neil *Debevoise & Plimpton LLP*
   JEFFRESS William *Baker Botts LLP*
   SILBERT Earl *DLA Piper*
   SULLIVAN Brendan *Williams & Connolly LLP*
   WEINGARTEN Reid *Steptoe & Johnson LLP*
2. BRAY John *King & Spalding LLP*
   CACHERIS Plato *Trout Cacheris PLLC*
   GORELICK Jamie *WilmerHale*
   GREEN Thomas *Sidley Austin LLP*
   NATHAN Irvin *Arnold & Porter LLP*
   RAUH Carl *Skadden, Arps*
   ROBBINS Lawrence *Robbins, Russell*
   ROBERTS Michele *Akin Gump*
   SHAPIRO Howard *WilmerHale*
   TUOHEY Mark *Vinson & Elkins LLP*
3. BARCELLA JR E Lawrence *Paul, Hastings*
   BREUER Lanny *Covington & Burling*
   KRAKOFF David *Mayer, Brown, Rowe & Maw*
   SCHERTLER David *Schertler & Onorato LLP*
   SCHUELKE III Henry *Janis Schuelke & Wechsler*
   TAYLOR III William *Zuckerman Spaeder LLP*
   ZUCKERMAN Roger *Zuckerman Spaeder LLP*

## Arnold & Porter LLP
See firm details p.560

**The Firm:** Part of a native Washington firm that boasts a network of national and international offices, the litigation team here primarily caters to the needs of big businesses, covering their interactions with both government agencies and other companies. To this end, the team has respected antitrust, securities, products liability and general commercial practices, with the added attraction of top-flight criminal expertise. As the SEC and DOJ begin to work more closely together, the rise in parallel proceedings means the firm's composite securities, fraud, criminal and mass tort expertise is increasingly important to clients. Recently, the group brought all these skills to bear representing Motorola in securities fraud cases surrounding the bankrupt Adelphia Communications. The firm also has a long and distinguished record representing tobacco and drug companies in products liability cases and is currently handling a series of antitrust cases for Visa.

**The Lawyers:** Respected white-collar lawyer **Irvin Nathan** (see p.534) takes an "*intellectual and measured approach*" to cases. He represents both companies and individuals in securities fraud and RICO matters. His most significant case of late was representing the former CFO of WorldCom, Scott Sullivan, in his indictment for accounting fraud. **David Gersch** (see p.514) divides his time between products liability and general commercial cases and is currently acting for Visa in its series of antitrust cases. He is well versed in class action and multijurisdictional cases and wins praise for his "*incredibly good judgment on large complex matters.*" SEC lawyer and general commercial litigator **Stephen Sacks** (see p.544) "*always instills confidence in clients*" through successfully comprehending the complexities of their problems. Observers remarked that he "*judges well when to fight and when to settle.*" Clients also commented on the quality of the midtier lawyers in the group, hailing them as forceful and organized advocates who will produce "*the next generation of stars.*"

**Clients/Work Highlights:** A cross-section of the group's clients includes Motorola; Visa; Adelphia Communications; Hoffmann-La Roche; Wyeth; Monsanto; Intel; American Red Cross and Philip Morris.

## Baker Botts LLP
See firm details p.1922

**The Firm:** Founded in Texas and with international offices in Europe, Asia and the Middle East, the firm has far-reaching litigation and arbitration capabilities. The DC office is home to the firm's white-collar defense practice and undertakes a full range of criminal and government investigations work. Its band of 25 litigators is, however, wide enough to accommodate a range of work and commentators were quick to praise it for its commercial work too. In addition to landing the incredibly high-profile criminal representation of the vice president's adviser Lewis 'Scooter' Libby, the team currently acts for Drummond Coal in an alien tort claim arising out of the murder of three employees in Colombia. The firm also has considerable appellate strength and boasts a number of litigators who specialize in US Supreme Court cases.

**The Lawyers:** "*Sensational litigator*" **William Jeffress** (see p.521) is judged one of the top whitecollar lawyers in the country. Together with Paul Weiss' Ted Wells, he is representing Scooter Libby in his indictment for perjury over the Valerie Plame affair – accusations that Ms Plame's identity as a CIA operative was deliberately leaked by government officials. "*An extraordinarily tenacious advocate,*" Jeffress' "*combination of experience, insight and strategy*" is just formidable in commercial trials. As one commentator stated: "*I would pay the firm just for that guy's judgment.*"

**Clients/Work Highlights:** The team recently represented Reliant Energy regarding allegations of manipulating prices during the energy crisis and negotiated AIG's settlement with the DOJ and SEC over alleged securities fraud. It has also represented pharmaceutical companies such as Merck in the Vioxx litigation.

## Covington & Burling
See firm details p.563

**The Firm:** This DC firm has a long-established pedigree and a broad practice that encompasses traditional trial work, arbitration and proceedings against the government. Described as a team with "*a multiple speed approach*" on criminal defense and SEC matters, much of what the firm does is under the radar as it utilizes its vast regulatory knowledge to craft effective pretrial strategies. On the commercial side, the team has strong antitrust, IP and products liability practices and also covers securities fraud class actions. It recently represented Freddie Mac in the Federal Home Loan litigation. The presence of this talented group of insurance litigators is further recognized as "*a draw for a client in any commercial case,*" and adds yet more luster to a team whose "*work is routinely of the highest level.*"

**The Lawyers:** "*A lawyer who epitomizes the creative, smart and adaptable approach to litigation,*" **Eric Holder** (see p.519) is described as someone who has the right touch for each different circumstance and client. His commercial practice includes class actions, and Foreign Corrupt Practices Act (FCPA) and securities work, as well as associated criminal DOJ proceedings. As a senior member of the team, **Robert Sayler** (see p.544) has extensive experience in all manner of complex commercial cases. "*A lawyer who has seen it all,*" he has served as trial counsel to industry giants such as Boeing, Monsanto and ExxonMobil. "*Young hotshot*" **Lanny Breuer** (see p.503) is an emerging name in the white-collar field. He recently hit the headlines through his representation of ex National Security Adviser Samuel 'Sandy' Berger, regarding charges of unauthorized removal and retention of classified material from the National Archives.

**Clients/Work Highlights:** Microsoft; Coca-Cola; Morgan Chase; Freddie Mac; Yahoo! and pharmaceutical companies Pfizer and Merck.

**The Firm:** "*A solid performer across the board,*" the team in this firm's flagship office has cultivated both domestic and international litigation expertise. Its classic strength lies in the healthcare arena where it handles both civil and criminal litigation surrounding medical device, pharmaceutical, FDA and environmental matters. The group is particularly experienced in defending class action lawsuits and most recently acted for the American Hospital Association (AHA) over challenges to their billing practices in 20 states. It also represents foreign governments in US courts, often in connection with one or more of the firm's international offices. For example, the team represented the Government of Japan in the DC Court of Appeals, successfully arguing for the dismissal of private suits for compensation for alleged war crimes. The group's white-collar practice encompasses SEC, DOJ and Congressional proceedings and has been strengthened by the addition of practice head Ty Cobb who recently moved from the Denver office.

**The Lawyers:** Primarily a commercial litigator, **David Hensler** (see p.519) has a practice with an international reach. He has just concluded a $50 million reinsurance arbitration in Bermuda, and is heavily involved for insurance companies in a range of general and class action suits. Also with an insurance bent, **William Bowman** (see p.503) principally represents major insurers in toxic torts and asbestos-related litigation.

**Clients/Work Highlights:** WellPoint; The Hartford; Chubb Group; Amgen; American Hospital Association; Medtronic and the Government of Japan.

## Jones Day

See firm details p.570

**The Firm:** According to commentators, the litigation group at this national powerhouse "*has bridged the gap between civil and criminal work extremely well.*" The team has particular strengths in employment, antitrust and products liability and, being connected to a network of national offices, has the capacity to handle the largest class action suits. In a recent example, the group successfully defended pharmaceutical giant Bayer against 30 antitrust class actions brought by purchasers of the antibiotic Cipro. The group also benefits from its close relationship with a team of dedicated appellate and Supreme Court litigators in the DC office.

**The Lawyers:** One of the team's biggest assets is a generation of "*sensational younger lawyers,*" who clients say are developing into a promising resource for the future. Very much a star of the present, **Stephen Brogan** (see p.504) is "*a lawyer who commands respect in the litigation world.*" He has significant commercial and criminal experience and has a fine trial record acting for large corporates such as JC Penney Company, Gillette and GE. Tim Cullen now heads the DC litigation practice and oversees the firm's nationwide trial practice.

**Clients/Work Highlights:** IBM; Ernst & Young; Dell; Bayer; Chevron; Nextel Communications and RJ Reynolds.

## Kirkland & Ellis LLP

See firm details p.875

**The Firm:** This international firm is famous for its litigation culture. "*Excellent for top-range cases,*" the DC group is particularly noted for its strengths in antitrust, defamation, IP and products liability. The huge scope of the practice, however, means that the team can muster support in any area of law. Recent matters of note include representing Barr Laboratories in patent challenges and antitrust claims surrounding the manufacturing and distribution of oral contraceptives, as well as other antibiotic drugs. On the securities and white-collar side, the group represents Fannie Mae in its ongoing SEC investigation.

**The Lawyers:** Foremost among this "*tough group of seasoned litigators*" is **Thomas Yannucci** (see p.556). He divides his time between management and litigation, but commentators report that he is still very busy with his caseload and "*gets a lot of play in high-profile areas.*" He represented Honeywell in connection with its role in the over-budget Big Dig tunnel system in Boston and has been described as "*a hard-nosed advocate who is not afraid to aggressively state his case.*"

**Clients/Work Highlights:** Siemens; Honeywell; Barr Laboratories; Bear Stearns and ConocoPhillips.

## Skadden, Arps, Slate, Meagher & Flom LLP & Affiliates

See firm details p.1557

**The Firm:** "*Naturally one of the biggest competitors in the area,*" the DC group caters to the commercial litigation needs of the firm's huge corporate client base but is best known for its white-collar practice. Commentators single it out because the team can coordinate the entire range of SEC, DOJ and civil class actions. This they do for the biggest names in the business. For example, the team recently negotiated a deferred prosecution agreement with the government for KPMG and represented BNP Paribas in investigations and Congressional hearings into the Oil For Food program. The firm's size and geographic reach is an advantage as it can assemble a team of lawyers with various specialties to suit each client's circumstance.

**The Lawyers:** The team's biggest weapon lies in the combined force of **Robert Bennett** (see p.501) and **Carl Rauh** (see p.540), whose complementary approach is known to bring remarkable results for clients. Bennett is one of the most prominent white-collar litigators in DC and, according to one commentator, "*one of the greatest lawyers of all time.*" He represented New York Times reporter Judith Miller who was jailed for contempt of court when she refused to testify in front of a grand jury investigation into the Valerie Plame affair. Rauh is more of a "*quiet strategist,*" but he is a definite force to be reckoned with in relation to Congressional investigation work.

**Clients/Work Highlights:** Recent litigation cases include those for healthcare providers, pharmaceutical companies and auto manufacturers. The firm also represents KPMG and BNP Paribas.

## WilmerHale

See firm details p.580

**The Firm:** This group has a sophisticated litigation practice and particularly excels in regulatory and government litigation. It also has a heavyweight securities team, with the litigators being renowned for their adept coordination of SEC and DOJ proceedings. In this regard, they were most recently enlisted by accounting giant PwC. In the white-collar area, the group has represented The Washington Post in the grand jury investigation of the Valerie Plame CIA leak, and acted for Congressman William Jefferson over criminal investigations into his business dealings. The healthy commercial practice is especially strong in IP litigation and spans a wide range of areas. The team has acted for a host of Internet companies in defamation, copyright, trademark and free speech cases.

**The Lawyers:** With a practice that encompasses litigation, public policy and securities, **Jamie Gorelick** (see p.516) is highly valued for her strategic litigation advice to multinational corporations. She works with GM and Time Warner on FCPA issues and is also outside litigation counsel for Lucent Technologies. "*Savvy trial lawyer*" **Howard Shapiro** (see p.545) is well liked by commentators who report: "*He has a fantastic intellect and a personality to match.*" He is best known as a white-collar litigator but also draws praise for his commercial flair. His recent matters include working with PwC in its multiagency investigation and assisting it with four current civil trials. **Michael Klein** is best known in the securities area but also undertakes corporate litigation and complex intra-company disputes.

**Clients/Work Highlights:** Boeing; BP; Shell; GM; Time Warner; Lucent Technologies; CBS; Reuters; The Washington Post; eBay; Amazon.com; Google and Yahoo!

## Dickstein Shapiro Morin & Oshinsky LLP

See firm details p.565

**The Firm:** With close to 300 lawyers in its DC headquarters, half of them litigators, commentators see this firm as an emerging force in commercial litigation. The firm's growth was powered by efforts in this sphere and it now covers the full range of practice areas. It probably draws most praise, however, in the antitrust and securities fields. The team regularly represents both companies and individuals in SEC and DOJ proceedings, and has a cadre of litigators dedicated to attorney general investigations in various states.

**The Lawyers:** Robert Higgins in the DC office is the firm's chief of litigation.

**Clients/Work Highlights:** Duke Energy is one of the firm's biggest clients and the group has recently represented the company in SEC, FTC and various civil class actions. Other securities litigation matters include acting for Tyson Foods and a major Chicago trading firm. Attorneys have represented both DuPont and Pfizer in relation to attorney general investigations.

## Fried, Frank, Harris, Shriver & Jacobson LLP

See firm details p.1532

**The Firm:** Nationally, this firm's litigation group typically grew as an adjunct to its successful M&A practice, but the evolution of the DC office is slightly different. Instead, it concentrated on developing strengths in Native Indian law and government contracts, although today is best known for securities litigation. Working in concert with a powerful corporate and advisory group, the litigators handle the civil and criminal aspects of securities investigations for large companies such as defense contractor Northrop Grumman. Praise was also forthcoming for its representation of Time magazine's Matthew Cooper in the special prosecutor's investigation into the Valerie Plame leak.

**The Lawyers:** Richard Sauber is cochair of the litigation practice and is responsible for leading the DC office.

**Clients/Work Highlights:** NYSE; City of Houston; University of Alabama; Merrill Lynch; Northrop Grumman and Newport News Shipbuilding.

## Goodwin Procter LLP

See firm details p.1114

**The Firm:** The 80-strong DC team at this Boston-based firm has a solid grounding in complex commercial cases. Although a relatively large group, the lawyers pride themselves on their personal approach to cases and foster close relationships with clients. As one reported, "*the firm excels in customer services. Someone always returns my calls and that is important.*" The group is comfortable litigating in any area of the law and is particularly recognized for its products liability skills and involvement in nationwide class actions. Extremely versatile, the team represents Lafarge both as national counsel in asbestos and silica litigation and in a suit brought against the firm following a levee breach in New Orleans during Hurricane Katrina. In the white-collar area, the group is primarily known for representing government officials but also represents officers in major companies like Arthur Andersen.

**The Lawyers:** "*A terrific litigator with great instincts,*" **John Aldock**'s (see p.497) gift for strategy lends itself well to coordinating class action litigation. He is acting for Lafarge in the Hurricane Katrina litigation.

**Clients/Work Highlights:** The group represents Teva, one of the largest manufacturers of generic drugs; Countrywide Home Loans; GE; CNA Insurance Companies and Prudential Insurance Company of America.

## Howrey LLP

**The Firm:** Commentators recommend this group for its high-profile civil litigation practice and appreciate its ability to "*bring complex cases down to the most understandable level.*" As members of the wider global litigation group, the DC litigators are experienced in state, federal and international proceedings, with clients being struck by their "*fundamental trial skills and technical acuity.*" In antitrust litigation, the

team has acted for clients such as PepsiCo, Nestlé and Texaco both in relation to major mergers as well as class actions brought by retailers and consumers. However, commentators see its biggest strength as IP as well as associated trademark, copyright and trade secrets litigation.

**The Lawyers:** While some regard the departure of Neil Eggleston as a blow to the team's white-collar practice, others underline the "*spectacular*" criminal talents of **John Nields**. "*A brilliant guy and a marvelous lawyer,*" Nields' practice covers both criminal and civil litigation and he is also recommended as an adept appellate lawyer. Chairman of the global litigation practice, **Mark Wegener** comes highly recommended as "*one of those superior attorneys whose attention to detail, loyalty and dedication to clients is unparalleled.*" He is an experienced antitrust and trade secrets litigator with particular skills in coordinating multijurisdictional class actions.

**Clients/Work Highlights:** PepsiCo; Nestlé; Texaco; Procter & Gamble; Cable & Wireless and GE.

## Sidley Austin LLP

See firm details p.883

**The Firm:** The appellate group at this firm continues to garner the lion's share of the market's approbation. Nevertheless, commentators also highlight the solid general commercial practice on offer. The prodigious size and spread of the firm means clients can expect comprehensive litigation coverage including civil class action and white-collar criminal defense expertise.

**The Lawyers:** "*Smart, able and experienced,*" **Thomas Green** (see p.516) manages the firm's government investigations and white-collar defense practice group from the DC office. A "*remarkable*" criminal defense lawyer, peers report: "*Green is a fighter who will take a case all the way; he's always in court.*"

**Clients/Work Highlights:** Sidley's status as an international player means the firm has a stable of large corporate and financial clients. These regularly turn to the DC office, especially for regulation and government litigation advice.

## Steptoe & Johnson LLP

See firm details p.576

**The Firm:** With six offices and 400 lawyers internationally, this firm has an incredibly deep well of litigation expertise to draw on. The DC team primarily attracts those clients in search of top-notch criminal defense through its white-collar practice group. This team conducts internal investigations and handles criminal trials relating to antitrust, FCPA, securities and RICO violations. On the commercial side, the group also wins acclaim for its insurance litigation strength, which is part of "*an increasingly impressive general commercial practice.*"

**The Lawyers:** The "*extraordinarily talented*" **Reid Weingarten** (see p.554) is touted as one of the main drivers behind the success of the firm's white-collar practice. A fine trial lawyer with "*backbone and guts,*" he has represented both corporate executives and national and foreign government officials.

## Vinson & Elkins LLP

See firm details p.1938

**The Firm:** While DC is home to the firm's white-collar, government contracts and regulatory practices, the group has maintained an excellent balance of commercial and criminal litigation services. On top of a broad-based securities practice, the group of 40 lawyers also regularly tackles antitrust and multi-district class action cases. It is currently assisting the Long Island Catholic diocese in mediating claims of sexual abuse and representing senior Congress member Robert Ney who is under federal investigation over dealings with lobbyist Jack Abramoff.

**The Lawyers:** **Mark Tuohey** (see p.551) is the standout in a group of lawyers with strong individual practices. He is a well-respected white-collar defender and is also chair of the DC Sports and Entertainment Commission.

## Janis Schuelke & Wechsler

**The Firm:** This "*first-rate white-collar boutique*" of five partners represents some of the top corporate officers in the country. While its size may preclude it from undertaking huge company representations, it regularly defends such companies in collaboration with other leading firms. The group is best known for its defense of individuals in the Enron and KPMG prosecutions.

**The Lawyers:** "*Smooth, steady and savvy,*" **Henry Schuelke** represented Time reporter Viveca Novak in connection with her grand jury appearance in the Valerie Plame leak. He has also been hired by Greenberg Traurig to investigate the $11 million in lobbying fees Jack Abramoff received from the Mississippi Band of Choctaw Indians. Commentators praise his skillful touch with both clients and judges, describing him as "*someone you always want in your corner.*"

## Schertler & Onorato LLP

**The Firm:** Previously known as Coburn & Schertler, the current incarnation of this firm was established by two former DOJ prosecutors in 1996, and focuses solely on litigation. The group of ten attorneys handles civil litigation and administrative proceedings but grabs most of its headlines representing officials and executives in criminal fraud and malpractice cases.

**The Lawyers:** "*A truly gifted trial lawyer,*" **David Schertler** has carved out a niche representing individuals in FCPA and other government investigations. He has been involved in the Teamster corruption investigation in New York City, as well as those regarding Senator Robert Torricelli's campaign finances.

## Trout Cacheris PLLC

**The Firm:** Established in 1996, this boutique firm is a collection of seven accomplished litigators. Its remit is a little broader than some of the other comparable boutiques and includes real estate, IP, employment and insurance litigation, as well as the higher-profile securities and white-collar criminal defense areas.

**The Lawyers:** Criminal defense attorney **Plato Cacheris** has a long and distinguished career stretching back to Watergate, where he was co-counsel for former attorney general John Mitchell. He also represented Monica Lewinsky in the investigation of former President Bill Clinton and commentators still rate him as a force to be reckoned with in criminal trials.

## Zuckerman Spaeder LLP

**The Firm:** This firm began in 1976 as an outward-looking DC litigation firm, quickly expanding to include more than 90 lawyers in five other US centers. It has formidable antitrust and complex commercial experience and, in the criminal defense area, has the resources to defend companies as well as individuals. Its *"phenomenal"* white-collar practice also stretches to internal investigations for large corporations.

**The Lawyers:** *"One of the best litigation lawyers in the city,"* **William Taylor** represented various Democratic National Committee officials in the Whitewater and DNC fundraising investigations and, most recently, secured a dismissal of federal charges against the former president of the Salt Lake City Olympics Committee. **Roger Zuckerman** has a broad practice that encompasses both civil and criminal litigation. Commentators rate his experience and determination, appreciating that he is *"never afraid to go to trial."*

## Other Notable Practitioners

**Neil Eggleston** has made the move to Debevoise & Plimpton LLP. Commentators expect that, together with Mary Jo White in New York, the pair will be a formidable white-collar combination. Described as *"a brilliant lawyer and a likable human being,"* peers observe that he enjoys a good rapport with government agencies but is still able to challenge them on behalf of his clients. With SEC, FCPA and insider trading expertise, Eggleston *"has the energy to jump in on the white-collar side and literally save companies."* Admiringly referred to as *"the godfather"* of the DC litigation Bar, **Earl Silbert** (see p.546) of DLA Piper Rudnick Gray Cary US LLP is *"a legend, and anyone with any sense trusts his judgment."* He has been in the spotlight since his role as the first Watergate prosecutor in the 1970's and currently represents Ken Lay in his defense of federal criminal charges stemming from Enron's collapse. Head of the complex litigation practice at McDermott Will & Emery, **Bobby Burchfield** (see p.505) is a general commercial litigator with significant government investigations experience. He recently defended several antitrust prosecutions for pharmaceutical companies and represented the Majority Leader of the House of Representatives, Tom DeLay, over allegations of House ethics violations. A prominent senior member of the Washington Bar, **John Bray** (see p.503) of King & Spalding LLP has tried cases across a broad range of civil and criminal areas but is best known for his skills in criminal tax investigations. With many accounting and auditing firms currently facing inquiries, Bray is increasingly involved in advising boards on risk management and also in civil trials for RICO claims. **Lawrence Robbins** of Robbins Russell Englert Orseck &

Untereiner LLP divides his time between appellate and criminal trial work, which effectively means he has the additional talent and reputation to take cases directly to the appeals court himself. In the Merrill Lynch Nigerian barge case he represented Daniel Bayly, former head of investment banking for the firm, in both his trial and subsequent appeal against sentence. *"Intense and articulate,"* **Michele Roberts** (see p.542) spent eight years in the Office for the Public Defender before joining Akin Gump Strauss Hauer Feld LLP. She is *"a terrific courtroom lawyer"* cultivating a practice in both white-collar and civil litigation. New to the rankings this year is the *"very able and well-respected criminal defense lawyer"* **Lawrence Barcella** of Paul, Hastings, Janofsky & Walker LLP. Barcella is currently representing a number of high-profile individuals, including a former KPMG partner in federal indictments relating to accounting and securities fraud. Another new addition to the white-collar list is **David Krakoff** (see p.524) of Mayer, Brown, Rowe & Maw LLP. He joined the firm in 2004 from Beveridge & Diamond and is recommended as an *"active and forceful white-collar litigator."*

# LITIGATION

# APPELLATE

| Litigation: Appellate |
|---|
| Leading Firms |
| [1] **FARR & TARANTO** *Washington, DC* |
| **GIBSON, DUNN & CRUTCHER LLP** *Washington, DC* |
| **JENNER & BLOCK LLP** *Washington, DC* |
| **JONES DAY** *Washington, DC* |
| **MAYER, BROWN, ROWE & MAW LLP** *Washington, DC* |
| **ROBBINS, RUSSELL** *Washington, DC* |
| **SIDLEY AUSTIN LLP** *Washington, DC* |
| **WILMERHALE** *Washington, DC* |

## Band 1

### Farr & Taranto

**The Firm:** While not voluminous, the quality of work at this two-partner firm is *"absolutely outstanding in every possible way."* Dedicated to appellate litigation, the two powerhouses here are most often enlisted by clients to appear before the Supreme Court. This they do with aplomb, covering a wide range of work that takes in even the most hi-tech subject areas. As a recent example, the firm appeared in a Supreme Court argument over file-sharing software in MGM Studios v Grokster.

**The Lawyers:** *"A fantastic appellate lawyer and a*

*gifted brief writer,"* **Bartow Farr** has argued numerous Supreme Court cases in his career. His practice is wide ranging and his more recent appearances have covered determining the scope of federal arbitration laws to how disabilities rights law affects pro sports. A *"spellbinding advocate,"* he creates arguments that sources say *"are magnetic, they draw you in and you simply have to listen."* His partner and other half of the firm, **Richard Taranto**, is a former clerk for Justice Sandra Day O'Connor and has over 18 Supreme Court appearances to his name. He is known for the *"elegance of his arguments and his effectiveness at the podium."* This was most recently on display when he argued on behalf of Grokster and StreamCast Networks in the Supreme Court.

### Gibson, Dunn & Crutcher LLP

See firm details p.328

**The Firm:** This team's appellate practice is both wide and deep. In addition to its Supreme Court experience, litigators regularly appear in both federal and state appellate courts and can draw on the resources of offices in California, Texas, New York and Colorado. The subject matter of the practice is as broad as its jurisdictional reach, encompassing constitutional, statutory, regulatory and common law issues. All this is backed up by a general litigation

strength which allows it to provide a continuum of litigation advice; many of the appellate lawyers will often brief and argue issues in the trial courts with an eye to higher appellate proceedings.

**The Lawyers:** The firmwide appellate and constitutional law practice has around 100 litigators to draw upon, with two of the four cochairs being based in Washington, DC. One of these is **Miguel Estrada** (see p.510), *"a lawyer of exceptional brilliance who argues with great force."* In addition to his Supreme Court appearances, he was lead counsel for PwC in a number of international arbitrations. He is appearing for radio giant Clear Channel on a challenge to the FCC's media ownership rules. Peers respect his *"mastery of the law and ability to think his way through the thorniest problem."* Former US solicitor general **Ted Olson** (see p.536) has argued a staggering 42 cases in the Supreme Court and, together with Estrada, is viewed as *"a powerful presence in the marketplace."* He enjoys a general practice with a media and commercial flavor to it, although clients *"will enlist his help when anything appellate even looks like it is heading toward the Supreme Court."*

| Litigation: Appellate |
| --- |
| **Leading Individuals** |

**Senior Statesman**

STARR Kenneth *Kirkland & Ellis LLP*

★ WAXMAN Seth *WilmerHale*

[1] DELLINGER Walter *O'Melveny & Myers LLP*

ENGLERT JR Roy *Robbins, Russell*

ESTRADA Miguel *Gibson, Dunn & Crutcher LLP*

FARR Bartow *Farr & Taranto*

GELLER Kenneth *Mayer, Brown, Rowe & Maw*

MAHONEY Maureen *Latham & Watkins LLP*

NAGER Glen *Jones Day*

OLSON Theodore *Gibson, Dunn & Crutcher LLP*

PHILLIPS Carter *Sidley Austin LLP*

ROBBINS Lawrence *Robbins, Russell*

SMITH Paul *Jenner & Block LLP*

TARANTO Richard *Farr & Taranto*

VERRILLI Donald *Jenner & Block LLP*

[2] BRINKMANN Beth *Morrison & Foerster LLP*

CARVIN Michael *Jones Day*

FRANKLIN Jonathan *Hogan & Hartson LLP*

GOLDSTEIN Thomas *Akin Gump*

LAMKEN Jeffrey *Baker Botts LLP*

LONG JR Robert *Covington & Burling*

PINCUS Andrew *Mayer, Brown, Rowe & Maw*

TAGER Evan *Mayer, Brown, Rowe & Maw*

UNTEREINER Alan *Robbins, Russell*

## Jenner & Block LLP

See firm details p.873

**The Firm:** The appellate and supreme court practice group at this national firm has over 30 lawyers with more than half of them headquartered in Washington, DC. The experienced team has particular strengths in media and telecom and, most recently, represented the entertainment industry in its successful appeal to the Supreme Court in MGM v Grokster. In addition to its impressive record of 14 Supreme Court cases in the past five terms, it also has an extensive federal and state appellate practice in areas ranging from fraud to Native American law. The group is also widely applauded for its pro bono work, especially on behalf of those facing the death penalty.

**The Lawyers:** In addition to cochairing both the appellate and media practices, **Paul Smith** (see p.546) is also managing partner of the Washington, DC office. In what will be his 12th Supreme Court appearance, he is representing the Jackson appellants in their part of a consolidated appeal against the 2003 Texas Congressional redistricting plan. Known for his deft handling of complicated cases, **Donald Verrilli** (see p.552) *"knows the technical nuances of a case and often the minds of the judges as well."* It was he who successfully argued the Grokster case for the entertainment industry, persuading the Court to hold file-sharing software manufacturers liable for copyright infringement.

## Jones Day

See firm details p.570

**The Firm:** This team has been particularly prolific of late, something commentators put down to the *"huge stable of talent"* available not only in DC but throughout the country. Five lawyers argued six Supreme Court cases in the past term and while most of those were conducted out of the Washington office, one of the draws for clients is that the firm spreads its appeals expertise between all its offices. The group is perceived as having particular strengths in employment and labor law but the sheer volume of cases it handles means it has expertise in almost all industry areas.

**The Lawyers:** Head of the issues and appeals practice, **Glen Nager** (see p.534) is *"without peer"* in his specialist area of employment, labor and discrimination. Most recently, he successfully represented the City of Jackson in the Supreme Court in a matter where allegations of age discrimination in police pay schemes were rejected. **Michael Carvin** (see p.505) concentrates on constitutional and civil rights law, as well as statutory challenges to federal government actions. His highest profile case this year was in the DC Court of Appeal where, on behalf of RJ Reynolds Tobacco, he successfully argued that billion-dollar disgorgement penalties were not allowed under RICO legislation.

## Mayer, Brown, Rowe & Maw LLP

See firm details p.876

**The Firm:** With a large group of experienced appellate lawyers to hand, one commentator remarked: *"Mayer Brown never ceases to amaze me with the quality and quantity of work they do."* Others also commented that with such a big team *"they are always in the Supreme Court,"* and a string of recent cases including Ballard v IRS and Wachovia Bank v Schmidt proves this to be no idle boast. The group also regularly files numerous amicus briefs in all the appellate courts, appears before federal administrative agencies and testifies before Congress in support of various legislative reforms. Considering the firm's substantial business clientele, a strong commercial vein runs through the appellate practice though does not define it. For example, the most recent case to have gained certification to the Supreme Court is an immigration case, Fernandez v Gonzales.

**The Lawyers:** One of the practice's leading lights, **Kenneth Geller** (see p.514) is *"a standout lawyer in a very talented group."* He has argued extensively before the Supreme Court and is described as *"extremely experienced and seasoned, with superb judgment."* A new addition to the tables this year, **Andy Pincus** (see p.538) is recommended as a *"wonderful all-around appellate lawyer"* who is *"an exceptional writer as well as very good on his feet."* He returned to the firm in 2003 after periods as general counsel to both the US Department of Commerce and Anderson Worldwide. Cochair of the practice **Evan Tager** (see p.550) is a talented and prolific brief writer. He is particularly skilled in the areas of punitive damages, dormant commerce clauses, classification issues and the enforceability of arbitration provisions.

## Robbins, Russell, Englert, Orseck & Untereiner LLP

**The Firm:** This *"high-octane boutique"* has a workload that belies its size, as commentators appreciate: *"They do a lot and do it well."* The group has a varied practice that includes white-collar crime, civil litigation and products liability, although its biggest strength is in antitrust. The group has argued eight Supreme Court cases since its inception six years ago and is currently representing a high-profile anti-abortionist in Schneider v National Organization for Women, a 20-year lawsuit concerning holding anti-abortion protestors liable under RICO laws.

**The Lawyers:** The three stars of this practice work closely together, making it more than the sum of its parts. Already very well respected, interviewees are of the opinion that **Roy Englert** is possessed of *"so much talent and sheer capability"* that he is *"destined for great things."* He has particular skills in antitrust and is currently representing Volvo in the Supreme Court case Volvo Trucks NA v Reeder Simco GMC. His written work is praised as *"so persuasive that any person with an ounce of common sense should choose his brief."* Unusually for most in the appellate area, **Lawrence Robbins** is also a devoted trial lawyer. He divides his time between appellate and criminal SEC work and is involved *"from soup to nuts: appellate, trial, brief writing, you name it, he does it."* A *"clear and deft brief writer,"* **Alan Untereiner** is representing Schneider in the Supreme Court. He is described as a polished advocate who *"always has a concise, clear answer to any question the court throws at him."*

## Sidley Austin LLP

See firm details p.883

**The Firm:** The skilled team at this national firm has the resources to handle appellate litigation in any court in the USA. While particularly known for its constitutional challenges to state and federal laws, commentators respect that the lawyers *"truly are across the board and can handle any case that is pitched at them."* As testament to that, at the time of publishing, the group had six Supreme Court cases scheduled for argument. These cover an array of matters from employment and RICO to patent law. The attorneys here are talented writers who *"produce powerful briefs."* They are experienced at arguing in front of the DOJ, the SEC and other administrative agencies.

**The Lawyers:** The firm is fortunate in having *"a polestar litigator at the top of his game"* in the form of **Carter Phillips** (see p.538). He is *"a highly skilled oral advocate,"* who acts as managing partner for the DC office and enjoys the backup of a talented and extensive team of appellate lawyers. Currently, he is involved in an antitrust case in the DC Court of Appeal, although he generally focuses on the Supreme Court, an arena in which he comes across as *"incredibly comfortable"* and where *"he is conversational, yet speaks with complete authority."*

## WilmerHale

See firm details p.580

**The Firm:** This practice is one of ten overlapping areas of specialization within the firm's litigation practice. A dozen partners in DC alone tend to the work and boast extensive Supreme Court experience. Neither the offices nor practice areas here are hermetically sealed, allowing appellate lawyers to reach into all levels of federal and state courts. The team has areas of particular strength in government and public policy litigation but offers general advice and is "*universally well thought of.*" Called upon to handle the toughest issues across the board, it was involved in one of the weightier Supreme Court cases of recent times, Simmons v Roper, a landmark case that ultimately ruled that the execution of juvenile offenders was unconstitutional.

**The Lawyers:** The DC group is praised as a "*wonderful collection of talented litigators,*" many of whom have previous experience in the solicitor general's office. Leading the group is "*superstar*" **Seth Waxman** (see p.553) who is admired for his ability to "*digest the hardest issues and present them with flair and humor.*" Peers are in awe of his abilities, with one recounting: "*I thought I was good until I watched Seth, he is on a whole other level.*" He successfully argued the unconstitutionality of executing juvenile offenders in the Roper case and also represented Canada in its unanimous win over the USA in the NAFTA softwood lumber appeal, one of the biggest trade disputes of recent times.

## Other Notable Practitioners

**Walter Dellinger** (see p.508) is head of the appellate practice at O'Melveny & Myers LLP. He not only has an impressive list of Supreme Court cases to his name but has also served as both solicitor general and assistant attorney general. In the Supreme Court, he represented the successful party in Jackson v Birmingham School District, while in the Courts of Appeal he represented Martha Stewart in her recent appeal against conviction. "*Possessed of an incredible presence,*" **Maureen Mahoney** of Latham & Watkins LLP is described as immediately persuasive in her interactions with both judges and other lawyers. Head of the firm's appellate practice, she is known as an extraordinarily clear oralist and "*a person of tremendous poise.*" An attorney of "*terrific analytic abilities,*" her successful challenge of Arthur Anderson's criminal conviction for obstructing the SEC's investigation of Enron was widely applauded by peers. Chair of Morrison & Foerster LLP's appellate practice, **Beth Brinkmann** (see p.504) has cultivated a practice with "*real gravitas and backbone.*" A former solicitor general, she has 20 Supreme Court cases to her credit, the most recent of which was the trademark case KP Makeup v Lasting Impression. Brinkmann has also filed innumerable amicus briefs and has a well-respected pro bono practice. **Jonathan Franklin** (see p.513) has emerged as Hogan & Hartson LLP's leading appellate practitioner following Gregory Garre's return to the solicitor general's office. He is currently focusing on the up-and-coming Supreme Court case Laboratory Corporation of America v Metabolite, but also routinely argues in the circuit appeal courts. Another new addition to the tables is Supreme Court specialist **Thomas Goldstein** (see p.516), who has just left the three-partner firm Goldstein & Howe to join Akin Gump Strauss Hauer & Feld LLP. "*Not a man to let much get in his way,*" he has carved out a practice with great purpose and commentators agree that "*the sheer volume of Supreme Court cases he has handled is impressive.*" He has amassed 14 arguments in the last six years and, at the time of going to press, was lining up his 15th, 16th and 17th in the next session. The "*deeply talented*" **Jeffrey Lamken** (see p.525) is credited with building up a healthy appellate practice for Baker Botts LLP. He is possessed of "*tremendous credibility and subtle persuasiveness,*" qualities that served him well in successfully arguing for the City of Rancho Palos Verdes in the Supreme Court. The experience of Covington & Burling's **Robert Long** (see p.527) has earned him a "*well-deserved reputation as a fine appellate lawyer.*" He has an impressive roster of high-profile representations that includes the Supreme Court medicinal marijuana case Raich v Ashcroft, Ortega v Starkist Foods and amicus briefs in the recent MGM v Grokster. Author of 'The Starr Report' into President Clinton's affair with Monica Lewinsky, **Kenneth Starr** (see p.546) is of counsel with Kirkland & Ellis. A former appeals circuit judge and solicitor general, he is now dean of Pepperdine University Law School in California. He continues to lend his significant experience to the firm's appellate matters and, most recently, weighed in on the question of Robin Lovitt's death penalty. Lovitt, scheduled to be the 1000th person executed in the USA since the reinstatement of the death penalty in 1976, was granted clemency at the 11th hour.

# MEDIA & ENTERTAINMENT

| Media & Entertainment |
|---|
| Leading Firms |
| [1] **LEVINE SULLIVAN KOCH & SCHULZ** Washington, DC |
| **WILLIAMS & CONNOLLY LLP** Washington, DC |
| [2] **DAVIS WRIGHT TREMAINE LLP** Washington, DC |
| **JENNER & BLOCK LLP** Washington, DC |
| [3] **BAKER & HOSTETLER LLP** Washington, DC |
| **COVINGTON & BURLING** Washington, DC |
| **HOLLAND & KNIGHT LLP** Washington, DC |
| **NIXON PEABODY LLP** Washington, DC |
| [4] **WILEY REIN & FIELDING LLP** Washington, DC |
| **WILMERHALE** Washington, DC |

## Band 1

### Levine Sullivan Koch & Schulz LLP

**The Firm:** This 20-lawyer firm is widely admired for its great client roster and for having a media team "*brimming with highly specialized First Amendment experts.*" Its "*terrific team*" enjoys an established reputation as "*one of the nation's leading media practices*" and has "*considerably greater depth and breadth than its competitors,*" clients say. Its attorneys are involved in every major case of national significance concerning the news media and recently appeared in Wen Ho Lee v Department of Justice. In this, one of the most talked-about cases of the year, it represented two journalists from the Los Angeles Times and the Associated Press, held in contempt for refusing to reveal confidential sources to a litigant suing agencies of the US government. The group has further advised high-profile clients in Hatfill v New York Times and Hatfill v Foster et al., acting for The New York Times, its columnist Nicholas Kristof and Vanity Fair in two of the year's most significant defamation cases. In other matters, it successfully defended the Associated Press and its reporter against invasion of privacy and copyright infringement claims arising from the publication of photographs depicting US Navy SEALs detaining Iraqi prisoners.

**The Lawyers:** "*Prince of a guy*" **Lee Levine** is a prominent attorney who "*exudes integrity and thoughtfulness.*" According to sources, he is feared but respected by rivals because he "*offers impeccable judgment, understands the needs of the press like no other and knows how it relates to the courts.*" "*Exceptionally bright*" **Michael Sullivan** has 25 years of expertise under his belt and "*always delivers top-quality work.*" He recently obtained judgment for King World Productions in Pitts Sales v King World Productions, an important test of the legal protections afforded to investigative, hidden-camera journalism. Also on board are the "*amazingly intelligent*" **Jay Ward Brown**, a lawyer who delivers "*continuously high-quality service,*" and the "*fantastically focused*" **Nathan Siegel**, former in-house counsel at ABC, who impresses with his copyright and defamation expertise.

**Clients/Work Highlights:** ABC; American Lawyer Media; The Baltimore Sun; CBS Broadcasting; Chicago Tribune; Paramount Pictures; Reuters; The Washington Post; MTV Networks; Simon & Schuster; Tribune Company; Disney; NBC; NPR and Discovery Communications.

### Williams & Connolly LLP

**The Firm:** This "*great team pulls out all the stops for its clients*" and is consistently hailed as a "*top-notch firm for traditional media issues,*" which "*has*

| Media & Entertainment |
|---|
| Leading Individuals |

**1** BAINE Kevin *Williams & Connolly LLP*
CORN-REVERE Robert *Davis Wright Tremaine LLP*
HANDMAN Laura *Davis Wright Tremaine LLP*
LEVINE Lee *Levine Sullivan Koch & Schulz*
SMITH Paul *Jenner & Block LLP*
YANNUCCI Thomas *Kirkland & Ellis LLP*

**2** BARNETT Robert *Williams & Connolly LLP*
BERNIUS Robert *Nixon Peabody LLP*
KENDALL David *Williams & Connolly LLP*
SANFORD Bruce *Baker & Hostetler LLP*
SULLIVAN Michael *Levine Sullivan Koch & Schulz*
TOBIN Charles *Holland & Knight LLP*
WILEY Richard *Wiley Rein & Fielding LLP*
ZWEIFACH Gerson *Williams & Connolly LLP*

**3** BROWN Jay Ward *Levine Sullivan Koch & Schulz*
CAROME Patrick *WilmerHale*
KAUFMAN Kenneth *Skadden, Arps*
SIEGEL Nathan *Levine Sullivan Koch & Schulz*
WEISWASSER Stephen *Covington & Burling*
WIMMER Kurt *Covington & Burling*

| Up-and-coming individuals |
|---|
| LYSTAD Robert *Baker & Hostetler LLP* |

effectively conquered the world in the new media arena." With litigation as its principal focus, the firm is consistently involved in the defense of claims for high-profile defamation, invasion of privacy and related torts. Clients feel it provides "*a bunch of exceedingly responsive, extremely results-focused and intellectually strong media attorneys.*" Acting on behalf of a high-profile clientele, the group has recently resisted subpoenas to journalists, fought orders denying access to courtrooms and court records and pursued claims under the Freedom of Information Act. It is rightly celebrated as "*first-rate counsel*" and an effective representative of individual journalists, authors, broadcast anchors and producers in contract negotiations and related matters.

**The Lawyers:** According to commentators, the media lawyers here "*get results by thinking strategically and by doing tactically brilliant things.*" Clients particularly value "*strategic thinker*" **Kevin Baine** as someone who "*has mastered the substance of law.*" One client went so far as to say: "*His creativity in handling legal problems and his understanding of newspapers' interests is simply astonishing.*" Entertainment aficionado and "*deal-maker*" **Robert Barnett** attracts a lot of media attention and is, according to sources, "*highly effective in negotiating deals for his clients.*" He sits in a team that also includes **David Kendall**, a nationally recognized attorney "*blessed with a huge brain,*" and **Gerson Zweifach**, a performer admired for his "*outstanding commitment*" when advising tabloids, movie studios, book publishers and television networks.

**Clients/Work Highlights:** The Washington Post; Newsweek; ABC; NBC; CBS Broadcasting; News Corporation; Fox Television Stations; Twentieth Century Fox; CNN; Time; Disney; Universal Studios;

Paramount Pictures; MGM; Sony Pictures Entertainment; Tribune Company; The National Enquirer; Simon & Schuster; Playboy Enterprises; Woman's World; Beacon Communications; Motion Picture Association of America and Recording Industry Association of America.

## Band 2

### Davis Wright Tremaine LLP

**The Firm:** This formidable group is known as a "*truly national player*" and wins market recognition for "*providing first-rate advice*" to its clients. Sources unanimously praise it as "*outstanding*" and "*very responsive.*" Clients value its "*constructive, practical and useful*" advice on traditional as well as new media issues and point to a raft of excellent lawyers in the firm. One client found the attorneys here "*extremely proactive with a deep understanding of the client's needs.*" Others felt the firm "*digs deeper and goes way beyond the necessary to bring information to the table that would not have been discovered otherwise.*" The group's sophisticated clientele includes media organizations, publishers, broadcasters and producers. Recently, it defended various clients in response to FCC investigations involving allegedly indecent broadcasts, and represented ICM Registry in its bid to create a top-level .xxx domain for adult material on the Internet. It has also counseled various media trade associations in FCC proceedings including one inquiry on the regulation of televised violence.

**The Lawyers:** The "*innovative and creative*" **Robert Corn-Revere** has expertise in First Amendment law, Internet-associated matters and FCC regulatory issues. His recent work has touched on matters relating to the Child Online Protection Act and the Communications Decency Act. He has further advised on Internet content filtering in public libraries and on public broadcasting regulations. The "*legendary*" **Laura Handman** is focused almost entirely on media law and has a stable of clients that includes national and international broadcasters and book, magazine, newspaper and electronic publishers. Advising on aspects relating to First Amendment, libel, copyright and privacy, she is a "*highly energetic media leader*" who is "*more than ready to share her brilliant and inexhaustible mind,*" clients said.

**Clients/Work Highlights:** Viacom; ICM Registry; CNN; CBS Broadcasting; Association of National Advertisers; American Association of Advertising Agencies; Discovery Communications; National Association of Broadcasters and Playboy Enterprises.

### Jenner & Block LLP

See firm details p.873

**The Firm:** "*Outstanding, attentive, committed, sensible and intelligent lawyers*" are to be found in this admired media and entertainment group. The firm is notable among its top-tier rivals for its success in maintaining a strong traditional media law practice while also concentrating resources on new media

issues. Its cases include Judith Miller v USA, a high-profile matter involving reporter's privilege, in which the firm filed amicus briefs representing 18 press companies and media organizations. Amicus briefs for 21 press companies and media organizations were filed in Wen Ho Lee v Department of Justice, another case concerning reporter's privilege. In other matters, the team represented the appellant in Broadcast Innovation v Charter Communications, a significant patent appeal involving television technology.

**The Lawyers:** "*The best-known media lawyer in the state*" is how commentators described **Paul Smith** (see p.546). He "*has extraordinary judgment and deep knowledge*" and is "*a hugely influential figure*" in the media field.

**Clients/Work Highlights:** The firm advises a wide range of clients including publishers, broadcasters and related industry organizations. It also advises non-media companies on issues such as Internet copyright, video games access and confidentiality.

## Band 3

### Baker & Hostetler LLP

**The Firm:** The market was quick to bestow praise on the "*dynamic*" media practice of this major full-service firm. Work continues to flow freely in its direction due to its "*passion for its clients and will to succeed.*" Possessed of an "*outstanding dispute resolution expertise,*" it involves itself in sophisticated defamation, copyright, privacy and trademark infringement cases. It is also prominent in challenging the government on First Amendment rights. As a result of its "*efficiency and legal proficiency,*" it has effortlessly expanded into the new media arena where its work crosses over onto the government policy side and issues such as the Internet.

**The Lawyers:** "*First Amendment genius*" **Bruce Sanford** is "*one of the best-known appellate lawyers in the country.*" He is, according to clients, "*erudite, professional and a leading name*" on all issues concerning the media. Interviewees favored up-and-coming new entry **Robert Lystad** for his "*excellent demeanor and tremendous work*" and noted his strength on First Amendment matters.

**Clients/Work Highlights:** ABC; Bertelsmann; Chicago Sun-Times; Rocky Mountain News; The E.W. Scripps Company; El Dia; Fox Television Stations; The New York Times and The Washington Times.

### Covington & Burling

See firm details p.563

**The Firm:** This team has beefed up its resources and has worked on some high-profile matters in recent times. "*An admirable outfit with a fine reputation,*" it is said to offer clients a "*hands-on approach.*" Its many areas of interest include First Amendment, news gathering and access issues, television programming and content agreements, broadcasting matters and FCC indecency and content regulation. It has lately advised the NFL in its negotiations with concerns such as ABC, CBS and ESPN regarding a multifaceted series of content licensing transactions for the distribution of NFL football and NFL Sunday Ticket. The team has also been successful in several libel matters such as Bangoura v The Washington Post in Canada, where it represented the defendant and a coalition of 50 media companies and organizations, and Clawson v St. Louis Post-Dispatch. Recently, it negotiated a favorable settlement in Raycom National v City of Cleveland, a First Amendment challenge to a mayor's refusal to provide access to its client Raycom.

**The Lawyers:** "*Thorough and approachable,*" the "*incredibly helpful*" **Stephen Weiswasser** (see p.554) offers "*a superb understanding of all aspects of the media business.*" One client commented: "*He knows how things interact with each other so we don't ever get any vacuum answers.*" He primarily provides legal and tactical support to companies in the media, telecommunications and new media industries. Cochair of the technology, media and communications practice, **Kurt Wimmer** (see p.555) offers specific expertise regarding international media issues. Commentators praised this attorney for his "*fantastic expertise*" in communications and new media, while clients thought him "*an excellent writer who is very careful and smart.*" One of his strong suits appears to be that he offers an "*analytical approach to problems.*"

**Clients/Work Highlights:** Electronic Arts; Equestrian Entertainment Partners; Lifetime Entertainment Services; LIN TV; Microsoft; National Geographic Society; Newsweek; National Press Photographers Association; Radio Free Europe/Radio Liberty; NBA; The New York Times; Yahoo!; Newspaper Association of America and the National Hockey League.

## Holland & Knight LLP

See firm details p.1534

**The Firm:** The First Amendment attorneys at this firm "*get to the heart of matters quickly in order to represent clients with gusto.*" Its sophisticated experts are engaged in the representation of a number of the industry's leading broadcasters and publishers, including newspaper, television, radio, motion picture, satellite and Internet concerns. In Baltimore Sun Co v Ehrlich, the firm brought a civil rights suit on behalf of the Baltimore Sun newspaper and two journalists against the governor of Maryland. This was in response to the governor's decision to prohibit the executive branch from communicating in any way with journalists whom he regarded as unobjective in their reporting. The team also secured a

pretrial dismissal of an invasion of privacy lawsuit against the local Fox television affiliate, WTTG, in Ross v Fox Television Stations. It further had a role in Wen Ho Lee v Department of Justice where it represented a former CNN journalist who had been subpoenaed as a witness in a civil lawsuit and asked to reveal a confidential source.

**The Lawyers:** **Charles Tobin** (see p.551) is "*able to persuade a judge even if a case seems impossible from the start.*" A "*street-smart*" operator who "*has all the tools to make things happen,*" he has worked in-house at a media company and is "*good at keeping clients in the loop.*"

**Clients/Work Highlights:** CNN; Fox Entertainment Group; The E.W. Scripps Company and Gannett.

## Nixon Peabody LLP

See firm details p.1546

**The Firm:** Armed with the expertise of numerous "*intelligent and sophisticated*" First Amendment attorneys, this team advises a range of media clients, including newspapers, publishing companies and television stations. It acts on matters including privacy, defamation and access. Its strength in the area of copyright does not go unnoticed and increases the firm's media and entertainment profile within the region.

**The Lawyers:** Market sources queued up to praise the extensive knowledge and experience of **Robert Bernius** (see p.501), former assistant district attorney in Brooklyn, New York. Counseling corporate clients on a wide range of issues including discrimination, libel and Internet matters, "*he shows a deep and highly impressive analysis of arising issues and offers an absolute understanding of the media field.*"

**Clients/Work Highlights:** The firm is renowned for its high-profile advice to established client Gannett and its subsidiaries as well as many others.

## Band 4

## Wiley Rein & Fielding LLP

See firm details p.579

**The Firm:** This growing practice enters the tables for the first time following a number of strong recommendations. It is particularly lauded for its representation of broadcasters before the FCC and for its communications expertise. Clients include single station licensees; market group owners; financial institutions; television networks; program producers and distributors. "*It offers one of the largest FCC regulatory practices in town,*" according to sources.

**The Lawyers:** A former chairman of the FCC, **Richard Wiley** (see p.555) is said to be "*one of the hardest-working men around.*" Others know this "*extremely hands-on*" attorney as "*the dean of the communications Bar.*"

## WilmerHale

See firm details p.580

**The Firm:** This large, full-service firm enters the tables following positive market feedback. Clients feel that the team is "*gifted in bringing the right resources to issues exactly when needed.*" Composed of a widely respected cluster of media and entertainment lawyers, it has recently represented The Washington Post and two of its reporters in connection with proceedings before the grand jury in the Valerie Plame leak inquiry. Commentators deem it a leading expert in defending Internet service providers and Web site operators from liability for tortious or illegal speech of third parties. It is a regular adviser to AOL and Yahoo! and has represented Salt Lake Tribune Publishing in litigation in various courts over rights to ownership of the Salt Lake Tribune newspaper.

**The Lawyers:** A favorite with clients, **Patrick Carome** (see p.505) is a "*brilliant attorney who achieves outstanding results.*"

**Clients/Work Highlights:** AOL; Yahoo!; Google; Time Warner; Washingtonpost.Newsweek Interactive; The New York Times; the Los Angeles Times; ABC; NBC; CNN; ESPN and Newspaper Association of America.

## Other Notable Practitioners

Plaintiff defamation and libel virtuoso **Thomas Yannucci** (see p.556) of Kirkland & Ellis LLP "*can take on the world and its mother-in-law,*" according to sources. He was recently involved in GM's successful defamation lawsuit against Dateline NBC, which exposed NBC's use of hidden detonating devices on fuel tanks of GM C/K pickup trucks during a simulated crash test. The case resulted in the first nationally broadcast retraction by a major television network and the payment of substantial damages to GM. "*Competent and energetic*" **Kenneth Kaufman** (see p.522) of Skadden, Arps, Slate, Meagher & Flom LLP & Affiliates impresses in music and general copyright issues and is perceived to be a "*practical, thorough and approachable*" entertainment lawyer. He focuses on areas including Internet and e-commerce law, entertainment law, content licensing and the evolving new technologies in the computer and entertainment fields.

# PROJECTS

## Band 1

### Chadbourne & Parke LLP

See firm details p.1524

**The Firm:** This is a strong practice in the DC market; clients report that they can rely on its *"great team of people who work very well together – it's a highly coordinated group."* Sources also praised the team's ability to consistently attract new clients, while building on relationships with existing clients. The firm is the last word on advising multilateral and bilateral agencies, with emerging markets providing a platform for the group to demonstrate its expertise in complex projects. Power infrastructure has long been a mainstay of the practice although its LNG capabilities are increasingly attracting attention. A recent highlight includes the closing of a Columbian

power project for the Inter-American Development Bank.

**The Lawyers:** *"Someone who makes difficult projects almost a pleasure,"* say clients of **Peter Fitzgerald** (see p.512). He splits his time between Washington, DC and London and is applauded for his expertise in emerging markets. Colleague **Keith Martin** (see p.529) is highly regarded by the market and provides specialist tax knowledge to clients. **Kenneth Hansen** (see p.518) is noted for his work with multilaterals. He recently represented OPIC in the restructuring of the Dhabol power project and in related political risk insurance claims.

**Clients/Work Highlights:** Inter-American Development Bank; Sovereign Risk Insurance; Greka Energy; RBS and OPIC.

### Latham & Watkins LLP

**The Firm:** A *"dynamic office staffed by quality attorneys from the top down,"* was the conclusion of clients of this projects powerhouse. Indeed, the firm is a leader in global project finance and in 2005 provided counsel on 27 leading projects worldwide, such as the $8.1 billion RasGas II/3 LNG expansion in Qatar. The team used offices in New York and London to act on the deal and it is the enmeshed integration between offices on both sides of the Atlantic that helps keep this firm in big-ticket work: *"The coordination between the attorneys makes our life much easier, and gives us access to a formidable team,"* say clients. Latham is also particularly noted for its work for sponsors, as well as bilateral and multilateral agencies, while the increasingly acquisitive private equity houses are also proving a fertile source of work for the team. These houses are showing a particular interest in investing in early-stage projects in South and Central America. A recent standout deal includes advising the Inter-American Development Bank on the financing of a Brazilian electricity line; the team also negotiated documents for several of the other lenders.

**The Lawyers:** *"A real star,"* **John Sachs** was lauded for his work in the power sector. His deal list encompasses all relevant industry sectors, while his expertise in serving multilateral agencies attracted especial praise. **Paul Hunt** is an established figure in the DC market and is particularly noted for his banking and lender work. Meanwhile, *"quality operator"* **Kenneth Schuhmacher** played a key role on the RasGas II/3 deal.

**Clients/Work Highlights:** Globeleq; Nord/LB; Dynegy; PPL Global; United Technologies; BTU Power; Marubeni America and Catamount Energy.

### Skadden, Arps, Slate, Meagher & Flom LLP & Affiliates

See firm details p.1557

**The Firm:** This *"highly responsive"* group maintains a strong presence in the DC market, complementing teams in New York and Houston. It uses its broad geographic reach and extensive skill base to advise clients who are lenders, sponsors and multilaterals.

The firm is also noted for combining deep industry knowledge and expertise with an innovative approach to transactions and finance. For example, the team advised Lehman Brothers as underwriters of the IPO of ITC Holdings. Clients also pointed to a soup-to-nuts practice, observing that *"the energy regulatory knowledge is so deep, we don't need to look anywhere else."*

**The Lawyers:** *"Probably the best projects lawyer in the world,"* **Martin Klepper** (see p.524) enjoys a great reputation among peers and clients alike; he is *"extremely diplomatic and a pleasure to work opposite."* **Erica Ward** (see p.553) is heralded for her work on power projects. Clients claim that *"she is dedicated, responsive and smart – what more could we want?"* Colleague **Lance Brasher** (see p.503) is recommended by the market for his expertise in the LNG sector.

**Clients/Work Highlights:** The group represented Wisconsin Energy in the construction of a coal-fired plant, and NRG Energy is a significant client of the group.

### White & Case LLP

See firm details p.1566

**The Firm:** This team has established itself as one of the preeminent advisers to multilateral lenders and commercial banks in the projects sphere. The DC office displays a flare for both domestic and international undertakings. As an illustration, the team advised the export credit agencies, multilateral lenders and commercial bank lenders to the Sakhalin II project. South America is a key market for the group, and it has recently ramped up its Asian capabilities, advising the project and developers on the financing of the Tangguh LNG project in Indonesia. Domestically, the Chicago Skyway project provided the team with a platform to display its finance skills, advising Skyway Concession Company as issuer of $1.4 billion in senior secured floating rate bonds. Clients remarked that the team is *"really a great bunch of people who are easy to work with and can make gruesome deals less painful."*

**The Lawyers:** The *"responsive, proactive, resourceful"* **Victor DeSantis** (see p.508) is noted for his sound advice to both sponsors and lenders. **Edward Neaher** (see p.534) was said to be *"practical and easy to work with."* He brings his considerable experience to bear on international transactions, having worked in Hong Kong and London.

**Clients/Work Highlights:** The firm advised Société Générale and a syndicate of banks in connection with a senior secured refinancing for the Brazilian electricity distribution company Coelba (Companhia de Eletricidade do Estado da Bahia). Other clients include Ambac Assurance; Deutsche Bank; US Ex-Im Bank; Inter-American Development Bank; IFC; OPIC; BNP Paribas and Unocal.

## Band 2

### Hogan & Hartson LLP

See firm details p.568

**The Firm:** A respected player in the marketplace, the DC office is very much the driver of the firm's project practice, with a clear penchant for international work. For example, the team is advising Framatome ANP on its development of over 6,000 MW of nuclear generating facilities in the USA. The group is also counseling key client AES Paraná on the restructuring of a large power-generating portfolio. Domestically the firm has advised EnCana on the Rockies Express natural gas pipeline project.

**The Lawyers:** **Bob Pender** (see p.538) spearheads the firm's project and international finance practice and drew market praise as a "*well-liked and capable*" attorney offering clients the benefit of his "*great business sense.*"

**Clients/Work Highlights:** FPL Energy; Sithe Global Power; PDVSA and Petrobras are among the team's clients.

### Mayer, Brown, Rowe & Maw LLP

See firm details p.876

**The Firm:** Market sources were unanimous in their praise for this firm, applauding its work in the domestic and international markets. The projects group is streamlined in its approach, leading clients to observe that "*the more manageable size of this group ensures tighter quality control.*" The firm's reputation is traditionally grounded in its work for multilateral agencies. For example, US Ex-Im Bank provides the team with a steady stream of work such as instructing the group in connection with the Egypt Basic Industries (EBIC) gas-to-ammonia facility in Egypt. Latterly, the firm has also made a concerted effort to attract more commercial lenders and sponsors to its client base. This strategy is clearly paying dividends, with the firm increasing the amount of work it carries out for sponsors in notoriously difficult international markets. Domestic work is also important to the group; it recently advised the City of Chicago on the Chicago Skyway project.

**The Lawyers:** Cochair of the firm's global project finance practice group, **Barry Machlin** (see p.528) is "*reasonable and commercially practicable,*" according to clients, who also praise his "*great attention to detail and super customer service; he's always trying to think ahead, makes legally sound decisions and minimizes surprises.*" John Taylor (see p.550) is "*patient and methodical,*" according to clients. Although both Machlin and Taylor are based in the Chicago office, their multilateral client base ensures that they are a constant presence in the DC marketplace.

**Clients/Work Highlights:** Commercial lender clients include WestLB, Nord/LB and BNP Paribas.

### Paul, Hastings, Janofsky & Walker LLP

See firm details p.339

**The Firm:** This firm has industry sources watching with interest as it makes a concerted push into the local and national projects market. Key lateral hires and subsequent client feedback confirm that this strategic move is paying off. The team leans to the sponsor side of work, with a healthy growth in the number of multilateral lenders joining the client roster. The team has also established a reputation for its expertise in IPPs; a highlight deal was advising InterGen on its $1.75 billion sale of its IPP development and operations business. Internationally, Latin America is an important market for the group. For example, it represents a consortium on the project financing of a merchant hydroelectric project in Guatemala.

**The Lawyers:** **Jeffrey Schroeder** (see p.545) handles both domestic and international projects and is liked by clients for his "*deal-oriented*" approach and "*personable manner.*" Boasting finance experience and electricity regulatory knowledge, **William DeGrandis** (see p.507) is new to the table and was lauded by market sources as "*a one-stop shop for IPP clients.*" Another new entrant to the tables is the "*technically excellent*" **Peter Saba** (see p.543), who clients report has "*superb strategic and tactical skills.*" Clients are also drawn to his ability to offer "*creative solutions to complex problems*" in an efficient and straightforward manner.

**Clients/Work Highlights:** InterGen; DTE Energy Company; DTE Energy Services; Cogentrix; IDC; OPIC and Foster Wheeler.

## Band 3

### Clifford Chance US LLP

See firm details p.1526

**The Firm:** Clifford Chance is synonymous with top-tier global projects. The DC office maintains its position as a significant player in the market, providing the quality of advice expected of the firm. Citigroup is a key client; the team advised it and other lenders in connection with a $2 billion alumina mining and refining project in Guinea. The team has also secured work in the relatively quiet telecom sector, advising the lenders on a $1.3 billion financing in Turkey.

**The Lawyers:** **Chris McIsaac** (see p. 531) is the key contact at the firm having joined in 2006 from Winston & Strawn. He attracts strong praise from industry insiders: "*He's a good lawyer, risk-averse, fair and gets the job done.*"

**Clients/Work Highlights:** EDF Energy; IFC; Inter-American Development Bank; Corporación Andina de Fomento; John Hancock; Scudder Latin America Fund and Siemens.

### Fulbright & Jaworski L.L.P.

See firm details p.1928

**The Firm:** This firm enters *Chambers'* table this year, underlining the success of its push into the projects market in recent years. Clients report that the team is "*outstanding, thorough, sophisticated and knows what it's doing.*" The bulk of the work is international and weighs heavily on the lender side. The IFC is a significant client and sought the group's advice on the project financing of a 65 MW power plant in Senegal, one of the few IPP financings in sub-Saharan Africa. Domestically, the firm advised the owners of a power project in Maryland on the restructuring of a leveraged lease. The manageable size of the group is a big draw for clients, who told researchers that they "*get personalized service; we never get lost in the comings and goings as can happen sometimes with larger firms.*"

**The Lawyers:** **Gregg Harris** (see p.518) chairs the firm's project finance group and enjoys a strong reputation among peers and clients, with one client commenting: "*He's a good, careful lawyer, I love him big time.*"

**Clients/Work Highlights:** Darby Overseas Investments; JPMorgan Chase; Verizon and Union Bank of California.

### Hunton & Williams LLP

See firm details p.1989

**The Firm:** This respected team continues to advise both sponsors and lenders on international and domestic projects. With its particular niche in the energy sector, clients report that the team is "*excellent*" on regulatory matters. The group has also developed a reputation for its market-leading equipment lease financing practice, and acquisition of distressed projects. A recent highlight includes advising a GE subsidiary in the refinancing of its leveraged lease debt. This was secured by the Colver facility, a 110 MW waste coal-fired power plant in Pennsylvania.

**The Lawyers:** **Andrew Murphy** (see p.533) heads the energy and project finance team and is said to possess "*great business acumen.*"

**Clients/Work Highlights:** Other clients include DTE Energy, John Hancock and MetLife.

### Vinson & Elkins LLP

See firm details p.1938

**The Firm:** This Texas energy stalwart brings its stellar reputation to bear on traditional energy and renewable projects for both developers and lenders. For example, the team represented WestLB in the construction financing of the 750 MW El Cajón hydroelectric power project. This is the largest financing to date in the Mexican power sector. Another key deal involved advising Complete Energy Holdings on its acquisition of the equity interests in La Paloma Generating Company. Clients report that the team "*offers extremely thorough advice – taking business, not just legal issues, into consideration.*"

**The Lawyers:** **Mark Spivak** (see p.547) is respected for his work with both developers and financial institutions. He has recently advised AES and Public Service Enterprise Group on a series of transactions.

**Clients/Work Highlights:** Other clients include The Shaw Group, NRGenerating International and Bank Austria Creditanstalt.

### Winston & Strawn LLP

See firm details p.886

**The Firm:** Clients report that this is a team which is "*strong across the board and great at building relationships with clients and other players.*" The global projects team has developed a solid reputation for its work representing multilateral lenders in both domestic and international developments. A highlight for the team this year was representing Energy Transfer Partners in a $1.45 billion refinancing.

**The Lawyers:** Following the departure of Chris McIsaac to Clifford Chance, Vincent Salvatore and Raul Herrera are the go-to partners at the firm for project finance.

**Clients/Work Highlights:** AES; Central Hudson Gas & Electric; CIT Group; Constellation Energy Group; Crédit Lyonnais; Entergy; Exelon; US Ex-Im Bank; Florida Power & Light; Société Générale; Merrill Lynch; Prudential Financial; RBS and WestLB.

### Other Notable Practitioners

**Jonathan Maizel** of Milbank, Tweed, Hadley & McCloy advises multilateral agencies, in addition to representing commercial lenders and sponsors. He recently advised KGen Partners on the refinancing of the senior credit facility originally provided to finance its acquisition of gas-fired facilities owned by Duke Energy. **Steven Miles** (see p.532) of Baker Botts LLP enjoys an enviable reputation for his work across the energy sector, with his LNG expertise attracting especial praise from market sources. Highlights this year include closing the Camisea LNG deal in Peru on behalf of Hunt Oil.

# REAL ESTATE

| Real Estate |
| --- |
| Leading Firms |

| 1 | ARENT FOX PLLC *Washington, DC* |
| --- | --- |
| | ARNOLD & PORTER LLP *Washington, DC* |
| | DLA PIPER RUDNICK GRAY CARY US *Washington, DC* |
| | HOLLAND & KNIGHT LLP *Washington, DC* |
| | PILLSBURY WINTHROP SHAW *Washington, DC* |
| 2 | BINGHAM MCCUTCHEN LLP *Washington, DC* |
| | MAYER, BROWN, ROWE & MAW *Washington, DC* |
| 3 | GREENSTEIN DELORME & LUCHS *Washington, DC* |
| | GROSSBERG YOCHELSON FOX *Washington, DC* |
| | HOGAN & HARTSON LLP *Washington, DC* |
| 4 | COVINGTON & BURLING *Washington, DC* |
| | GOULSTON & STORRS *Washington, DC* |
| | NIXON PEABODY LLP *Washington, DC* |
| | VENABLE LLP *Washington, DC* |

## Band 1

### Arent Fox PLLC

**The Firm:** This firm has a long and prestigious history of doing real estate work in DC. Clients point to its impressive local knowledge and ties to the business community as a key asset: "*The firm's lawyers really know the people and the lie of the land here. They are also familiar with the peculiarities of the municipal laws.*" Real estate finance is a key part of the practice, where practitioners assist various banks and financial institutions. The outfit also represents a wide variety of clients in acquisitions, dispositions, leasing, development and construction. Renowned assisted living and hospitality practices further define its profile in the field. Multifamily housing is another area in which it has made a name for itself representing clients in all phases of such developments. Indeed, the firm is lead counsel to Fannie Mae, the largest credit enhancer of tax-exempt multifamily revenue bonds in the country.

**The Lawyers:** The "*creative*" **Richard Newman** (see p.535) has carved a niche for himself in bond financing, and advising on the real estate issues associated with nonprofit organizations and municipal finance in particular. He also covers conventional real estate work. The old guard at the firm is particularly well regarded in DC. **Joe Fries** (see p.513) was described as a "*tremendous lawyer,*" and he moves into the senior statesman category this year. Planning, structuring and negotiating complex real estate transactions are his fortes. The "*spectacular*" **David Osnos** (see p.536) joins him in the senior statesman category, and industry analysts believe "*there is no one who combines real estate and business acumen like he can.*" His "*expertise goes beyond real estate*" and he can "*combine a superior intellect with the ability to grasp clients' problems.*"

**Clients/Work Highlights:** Representative transactions include representing Lowe Enterprises on a development and construction scheme relating to the Wax Museum site in DC. The team was involved in the financing and development side of the new headquarters of the Society for Neuroscience. It also acted for The Buccini/Pollin Group in the acquisition, construction, development and financing of a two-hotel conference center near Dulles Airport and a full-service hotel in Anne Arundel County. Several Fortune 100 companies help to make up the balance of the operation's clientele.

### Arnold & Porter LLP

See firm details p.560

**The Firm:** Arnold & Porter's "*high-quality group*" received glowing feedback from interviewees this year and is duly promoted to the top tier. Boasting "*terrific clients, some extremely talented lawyers and involvement in the best transactions in DC,*" this sizable operation has gone from strength to strength. Major mixed-use projects in Washington's downtown have come to the fore of late, where lawyers represented George Washington University in redeveloping the former GWU Hospital site on Washington Circle. That Wilmer Hale chose to instruct Arnold & Porter in connection with its relocation into three separate buildings on Pennsylvania Avenue reflects the fact that peers hold the firm in high regard. Indeed, this deal was one of the largest private sector lease transactions in DC history. The firm prides itself on its multidisciplinary approach to real estate law, and its real estate practitioners work alongside experienced tax, securities and bankruptcy lawyers, as well as litigators, according to a client's needs. It has a particularly strong profile in the hospitality industry but can adapt its expertise in financing, zoning and land use, build-to-suits and development as required.

**The Lawyers:** **Michael Goodwin** (see p.516) has a "*stellar reputation*" and moves up the tables this year: "*He's unbelievably smart and slick,*" say sources. Goodwin focuses on development, and debt and equity finance transactions, with a bias towards the hospitality sector. In the public-private partnership arena, he drafted DC's tax increment financing (TIF) law. He also represented the District of Columbia in the disposition and redevelopment of the downtown 10.2-acre Old Convention Center site. **Gary Humes** (see p.519) heads the real estate group and covers build-to-suit transactions, large-scale office leases, PPPs, development and financing. He assisted JBG with the development and financing of the 1.35 million sq ft Department of Transportation headquarters on the Southeast Waterfront. **Stephen Porter** (see p.539) is known for his work on complex real estate transactions, real estate financing and leasing.

**Clients/Work Highlights:** The group represented The Kaempfer Company in multiple projects, including redeveloping Waterside Mall in Southwest Washington into 2.1 million sq ft of upscale office space, retail units and housing. Host Marriott was also represented by the practice in connection with the acquisition of the Fairmont Kea Lani Resort in Maui for $355 million and the Hyatt Regency Maui Resort for $321 million. Other clients include The Hillman Company; Gould Property; John Akridge Company and The Shakespeare Theatre.

### DLA Piper Rudnick Gray Cary US LLP

See firm details p.870

**The Firm:** "*Clearly one of the go-to firms*" for real estate work, DLA's real estate practice continues to develop apace. This is a "*sophisticated*" national operation that continues to make its presence felt both on a local and a national level. The ever-expanding Washington team has recruited two more lawyers since 2005 and is increasingly representing out-of-town investors in DC, as well as DC-based investors initiating transactions in other states. The office also has a strong reputation in leasing and development and offers comprehensive expertise in acquisitions, dispositions and financing.

**The Lawyers:** Praised for being "*one of the greatest thinkers and strategists in the field,*" **Jay Epstien** (see p.510) is highly regarded for his leasing work. He is national chair of the firm's real estate group and focuses principally on acquisitions, dispositions and leasing. He represented the Bureau of National

Affairs on the evaluation of its corporate headquarters. The *"terrific"* **Frederick Klein** (see p.523) is considered to excel in sale and purchase transactions as well as real estate finance, where he acts for both lenders and borrowers. He represented a German open-end fund on major acquisitions involving over 2.8 million sq ft of office space in DC, Virginia and New York City. He also acts for Boston Properties in connection with the development of a major mixed-

use project in Chevy Chase, Maryland.

**Clients/Work Highlights:** The team represented Equity Office Properties Trust in its purchase of 36 buildings from Basin Street Properties for $263 million. Further highlights include acting for Hilton Hotels on its sale of the Palmer House Hotel in Chicago for $230 million. The firm can also count Wachovia; Wells Fargo; AXA Equitable; ASB Capital Management and The Carlyle Group among its client list.

## Holland & Knight LLP
See firm details p.1534

**The Firm:** Replete with *"top-drawer lawyers,"* this firm continues to impress market commentators. It has one of the largest real estate groups in DC, and clients draw attention to the *"extraordinary"* land use and zoning practice and the *"top-notch"* retail leasing group in particular. With a huge army of lawyers at its disposal, the firm is able to capitalize on its *"high level of expertise."* As one client stated: *"It makes the best use of its resources and a matter can be referred within the organization so that if you have a specific question that one attorney cannot answer, there is always one that can."* International reach in the finance and hospitality sectors is a further benefit, and the firm has also represented several foreign investors in American real estate matters.

**The Lawyers: Alan Vollmann** (see p.552) is *"one of the brightest attorneys anywhere and has the ability to handle extremely complicated transactions."* More of a real estate development lawyer, he is also known for his leasing work, and sustains a degree of involvement in lending matters. He was involved in the Government of Sweden's development and acquisition of a new embassy building on the Potomac River in Washington, a project valued at $54 million. He also represented Johns Hopkins University in the development of a research campus on 35 acres in Montgomery County, Maryland. A recurring theme whenever **David Kahn**'s (see p.521) name is mentioned is his *"extraordinary"* advocacy and negotiation skills. Clients observe that he is *"hands-on, tough and responsive,"* not to mention a *"ceaseless worker."* Renowned as lenders' counsel, Kahn also represents developers and institutional owner entities. However, clients note that his breadth of experience spans all aspects of real estate. **Janis Schiff** (see p.544) enters the tables this year on the sheer strength of her retail leasing and development practice. She has a loyal following and an *"enormous stable of good clients."* She represented Roadside Development and Madison Marquette on the development and leasing of a high-profile retail and residential renovation and construction project on top of the Tenleytown Metro station in Washington, DC. She also advised CVS on new sites in DC, Maryland and Virginia. Clients rate her as an *"outstanding negotiator"* and praise her swift turnaround times. Another new entry to the tables is national chair of real estate **Chad Tiedemann** (see p.550). He practices primarily in commercial real estate finance, development and leasing. Described as a *"super dealmaker,"* Tiedemann has the necessary stature to

*"humble the opposition"* during negotiations. **Whayne Quin** (see p.540) is a *"legend"* in zoning and land use matters and is *"unbelievably talented"* to boot. His clients have included educational institutions, nonprofit organizations, builders, developers, financial institutions, international and national agencies and property owners. Recent highlights include representing The World Bank in obtaining federal and local approvals for a property improvement plan involving public space. **Chip Glasgow** (see p.515) is another *"extraordinarily good"* zoning lawyer at the firm. He represented Tauber Estate in a disposition of $1 billion worth of real estate assets in DC and New York. He also worked on a Zoning Commission case concerning the conversion of the Watergate Hotel into a cooperative.

**Clients/Work Highlights:** Highlights include counseling Akridge Companies on the development of 1.4 million sq ft in the air rights above Union Station. It also advised Soave Enterprises in the leasing of the retail portion of the Brambleton development project in Loudoun County, Virginia. The project includes 600,000 sq ft of retail space. Other clients include MetLife; The World Bank; Monument Realty; Thrivent Financial; Cellular Telecommunications & Internet Association; Protestant Episcopal Cathedral Foundation; Divaris Real Estate and Compson Development.

## Pillsbury Winthrop Shaw Pittman LLP
See firm details p.1550

**The Firm:** The merger of Pillsbury Winthrop LLP and Shaw Pittman LLP in April 2005 created a law firm with more than 900 lawyers in 16 locations. In DC, more than 35 lawyers are involved in real estate, zoning and land use. While it is too early to gauge the true effects of the merger, it is generally agreed that the new firm has an enhanced platform on which to handle local and national transactions. Indeed, the real estate practice covers both East and West Coasts as well as the Gulf Coast, and can also service clients internationally. In terms of traditional niche strengths, the Shaw Pittman contingent is particularly renowned for its REIT expertise, while the Pillsbury Winthrop side boasts in-depth knowledge of complex public sector financings and large-scale PPPs. In addition, the firm attracts a diverse mix of matters including acquisitions, development, financing, leasing, military housing and affordable housing. It is counsel to the development team at Lowe Enterprises that is redeveloping the former Wax Museum site in DC, and also advised the US General Services Administration on its plan to redevelop the 44-acre Southeast Federal Center along the DC waterfront.

**The Lawyers: John Engel** (see p.510) cochairs the global real estate practice and is described as a *"smart, low-key, even-tempered and thoughtful fellow, who does an excellent job representing his clients."* His practice is mainly transactional, and he primarily represents developers, as well as lenders and sellers. Engel has provided ongoing advice to the Mark Winkler Company on a portfolio sale of 5,000 apartment units and over 30 office buildings in the DC metropolitan area. **Anne Planning**'s (see p.539) focus is on commercial lease transactions and various agreements, such as exclusive listing, commission and management agreements. The "*smart and thoughtful*" **Debbie Spartin** (see p.547) is also rated for her leasing experience. **Lee Carter** (see p.505) joins the tables as an up-and-comer who built a name for herself in military housing privatization. In the land use and zoning field, where the firm boasts a national practice, **Maureen Dwyer** (see p.509) features as "*someone you'd want on your side of the table.*" She has strong links to the Washington community, and is noted for her representation of universities, nonprofit groups and private schools. Her colleague, **Phil Feola**, also came in for praise for his "*terrific*" zoning and land use work, while **Allison Prince** (see p.539) is an acknowledged zoning specialist. She acted for the Washington Convention Center Authority in connection with the proposed Convention Center Hotel. She also represented the Catholic University of America in its application to secure zoning for a recently acquired 49-acre site.

**Clients/Work Highlights:** Boston Properties; Clark Enterprises; Commercial Net Lease Realty; Corporate Office Properties Trust; Crescent Real Estate Equities; Fannie Mae; Federal Realty Investment Trust; George Washington University; International Union of Bricklayers and Allied Craftworkers; JBG; Lehman Brothers; Lincoln Property; Penzance Properties; Saul Centers; Scottish Widows; T-Rex Capital and Vornado Realty Trust.

## Band 2

### Bingham McCutchen LLP

See firm details p.1110

**The Firm:** A relatively lean team focuses on highly visible and complicated transactions and sustains a broad practice that covers acquisitions, dispositions and financing. Though its DC lawyers do not advise on land use, practitioners in some of the other eight offices around the country are at hand should such issues arise. The team represents lenders, owners and developers, and counts financial institutions and pension fund advisers as clients. Bingham McCutchen is perceived as growing nationally and also has offices in London and Tokyo.

**The Lawyers:** Billed as "*one of the best in town,*" **Barry Rosenthal** (see p.543) cochairs the real estate group. He has "*excellent judgment and is good on business issues.*" These qualities undoubtedly aid his finance, acquisitions and joint ventures practice. Rosenthal was involved in the $300 million acquisition by JBG of the Marriott Wardman Park Hotel in DC. Clients are extremely satisfied with **Erica Weiss** (see p.554); one said enthusiastically: "*She makes a great counsel and does a brilliant job representing us.*" She focuses on representing financial institutions, pension fund advisers and developers in real estate finance transactions. However, she also covers acquisitions, sales and leasing. Weiss represented Wells Fargo in closing a $70 million first lien and mezzanine debt loan relating to three apartment projects

in suburban Maryland.

**Clients/Work Highlights:** JBG; Paradigm Development; TA Associates Realty; First Washington Realty; Perseus Realty; the Bernstein Companies; Wells Fargo and US Bank.

### Mayer, Brown, Rowe & Maw LLP

See firm details p.876

**The Firm:** Rising to the second tier this year, this firm has a great national reputation for real estate. The array of "*A-plus real estate lawyers*" now includes Frank Henneburg, who was scooped from Akin Gump in 2005. This arrival has helped to boost the reputation and profile of an already solid DC real estate group. Interviewees singled out REITs, financing and development as impressive features in the practice. Cross-border transactions can also be handled here, as the practice makes full use of the firm's international network of offices, including those located in London, Frankfurt and Paris, to name a few.

**The Lawyers:** **Keith Willner** (see p.555) stands out as the firm's foremost real estate practitioner in DC. He represented Archstone-Smith in a $1.6 billion acquisition of a portfolio of 37 multifamily residential properties across the USA. His broad-based practice includes acquisitions, dispositions, acting for lenders and buyers in real estate finance transactions, and joint ventures. He is also experienced in advising hotel-owner clients, pension fund advisers and publicly traded REITs. **Frank Henneburg**'s (see p.519) signature is real estate finance. However, he spends an equal amount of time representing public and private companies and institutional investors in acquisitions and sales. Work highlights include assisting GE Capital with a $215 million revolving credit loan to Winston Hotels, and acting for ING Clarion Partners in the $214 million purchase of Chevy Chase Pavilion, a mixed-use project in DC.

**Clients/Work Highlights:** The team represented a large state pension fund in a $125 million joint venture for the acquisition of self-storage facilities and portfolios across the USA. It also acted for Athena Group in the $79.5 million acquisition and mortgage financing of Summit Reston, a condominium conversion project in Virginia. Further examples of its clientele include Archstone-Smith; Berwind Property; Carlyle Realty Partners; CarrAmerica Realty; CTF Hotels & Resorts; Fremont Investment & Loan; IKEA Property; L&B Real Estate Counsel; MetLife; New York Life and Florida State Board of Administration.

## Band 3

### Greenstein Delorme & Luchs

**The Firm:** Based in DC, this specialist real estate firm sustains a greatly respected practice with a local focus. It has a loyal client following and comes highly recommended as "*the go-to firm for landlord and tenant*" issues. Other strengths include land use, leasing and real estate transactions.

**The Lawyers:** Clients and competitors alike hail

**Abe Greenstein** as "*a major and long-standing force in DC real estate.*" One client enthused that he is a "*smart, savvy lawyer who knows almost all there is to know about the field.*" Not one for time wasting, Greenstein's excellent negotiation skills also make him a favorite with clients. His practice focuses mainly on commercial leasing, acquisition, development, financing and rental housing. **Richard Luchs** is much sought-after for his landlord and tenant prowess, while **Jacques DePuy** is identified as a "*terrific land use lawyer.*" His land use and assessment appeal practice means he represents clients before various DC agencies. These include the Zoning Commission, the Board of Zoning Adjustment, the DC Council, the Board of Real Property Assessments and Appeals, and the Historic Preservation Review Board.

**Clients/Work Highlights:** Commercial and residential real estate developers; construction contractors; real estate brokers and property managers.

### Grossberg Yochelson Fox & Beyda

**The Firm:** One of the oldest firms in DC, Grossberg Yochelson is another boutique with a strong local presence. Smaller than some of the other players in the table, it offers a wide range of real estate services, covering acquisitions, development, leasing and real estate finance. Niche areas of expertise include Section 1031 tax-deferred exchanges.

**The Lawyers:** The "*spectacular*" **Richard Beyda** is seen as a central figure at the practice, who knows "*exactly how to make a transaction work with a minimum amount of effort.*" His practical ability and knowledge of DC ("*he knows every block in downtown Washington*") are put to good use in his representation of developers. **Lawrence Miller** also won plaudits as a leader in the field.

**Clients/Work Highlights:** The practice has advised developers; building owners; landlords; tenants; borrowers and lenders.

### Hogan & Hartson LLP

See firm details p.568

**The Firm:** This full-service firm has an excellent overall reputation. The DC office continues to provide the gamut of services to clients in the real estate field, and its practice is national and international in scope. A huge REIT practice further defines the firm's profile, while its growing presence in the hotels and hospitality market has not gone unnoticed. That it acts for the likes of Exclusive Resorts, Highland Hospitality and Host Marriott gives some indication as to the stature of the outfit in this respect.

**The Lawyers:** "*Talented*" **Bruce Parmley** (see p.537) is co-director of the firm's real estate practice. His areas of expertise include real estate transactions, including those in the hotel and hospitality industry. **Carol Weld King** (see p.523) focuses on financing, acquisitions and development. She has represented a variety of owners, developers, lenders and investors in office, multifamily, hotel and hospitality, mixed-use and light industrial projects.

**Clients/Work Highlights:** Centurion Capital; GE

Capital; the Mohegan Tribe of Indians of Connecticut; the Mohegan Tribal Gaming Authority; MONY Life Insurance; Patriot Group; Thayer Lodging and Trizec Properties.

## Band 4

### Covington & Burling

See firm details p.563

**The Firm:** Viewed as being equally strong in both contentious and noncontentious contexts, Covington & Burling boasts an impressive real estate capability, centering on DC. "*The technical knowledge the lawyers bring to the table is excellent,*" say satisfied clients. Competitors discern a particularly strong leasing capacity, with the overall workload being, for the most part, local in scope. However, this is a national practice, and the firm's offices can pool resources as necessary.

**The Lawyers:** **Bob Gage** (see p.514) impresses clients with his creative flair and dedication to his work. One client went as far as to say: "*I don't think he sleeps. He lives and breathes his work. He has vast legal knowledge and an ability to give advice that ensures we're covered.*" His work encompasses acquisitions, finance and leasing, as well as the representation of nonprofit organizations. Gage is principal outside counsel to the Brookings Institution and real estate counsel to the Union Station Redevelopment Corporation.

**Clients/Work Highlights:** The practice represented the DC Sports & Entertainment Commission in negotiations with Major League Baseball and Baseball Expos that resulted in the relocation of the Montréal Expos to Washington. It is currently negotiating the new stadium lease for the Washington Nationals with Major League Baseball. Further highlights include representing RLA Revitalization in the proposed mixed-use redevelopment of its 3.2-acre former Wax Museum site in DC. Other clients include American Trucking Associations; GOJO Industries; the Association of American Railroads; Goodyear; National Capital Revitalization; DC Sports & Entertainment Commission; Lockheed Martin and Potomac Electric Power.

### Goulston & Storrs

**The Firm:** This Boston-based firm is perceived as beginning to really make a mark on the Washington, DC scene. Competitors observed that "*Goulston has raised its profile and is doing a good job hiring people.*" Four real estate lawyers have been recruited in less than a year, bringing the total number of specialist practitioners to nine. The practice focuses on commercial real estate transactions and devotes a proportion of time to affordable housing matters. Recent highlights include representing Boston Properties in the development of a large piece of prime

urban property in DC owned by George Washington University.

**The Lawyers:** **Sheldon Weisel** is acclaimed for his leasing work and for his analytical skills. He also handles matters involving real estate financing, acquisitions and joint ventures. Weisel acted for developer Ellis Enterprises in a multiuse project that is being planned for a neighborhood in DC near the new Convention Center. It would house the corporate headquarters of Radio One and include retail units and several hundred condominiums. **Dennis Moyer** focuses primarily on commercial real estate work, with financings making up the bulk of his practice. He has the "*right combination of intelligence, expertise and temperament and is extremely effective.*" Moyer has represented Seaton Benkowski & Partners in various matters, including acquisitions, joint ventures and financing.

**Clients/Work Highlights:** New England Development; RCP Development; Boston Properties; Mack-Cali Realty; AvalonBay Communities; Lehman Brothers; Volunteers of America; MONY Life Insurance and Hart Advisers.

### Nixon Peabody LLP

See firm details p.1546

**The Firm:** Nixon Peabody has developed a respected niche practice in low-income housing work. The 50-lawyer strong real estate practice in DC can "*handle some pretty sophisticated stuff.*" It is essentially divided into three groups: affordable housing, syndication and development. The affordable housing practice advises multifamily housing developers, management companies, financiers and housing authorities, among others. The syndication arm is highly specialized when it comes to advising clients on tax credit transactions and equity investment in real estate. Other areas covered include real estate workouts and bankruptcy matters, where the department collaborates with the firm's bankruptcy and litigation groups.

**The Lawyers:** The "*dynamic*" **Ed Rogers** (see p.542) advises on a range of real estate development and commercial finance work. However, he focuses on the development of large-scale, mixed-use projects. Rogers represented the District of Columbia in relation to the development of DC's Convention Center Hotel. **Debra Yogodzinski** (see p.556) is a new addition to the tables. An "*excellent*" lawyer, market commentators note that she is particularly visible working with trade associations, retail developments and low-income housing projects.

**Clients/Work Highlights:** The practice represents Freedom Forum in various matters, including the relocation of its Newseum to DC. Members of the firm also act for the likes of Forest City Enterprises.

### Venable LLP

**The Firm:** This broad-based real estate group represents local, regional and national clients. The development side of the practice sees the firm advising on various matters such as stock purchase agreements, joint ventures, shopping centers, and golf course and resort developments. Acquisitions and dispositions of offices, warehouses and hotels further contribute to the workload. On the leasing front, members of the firm benefit from their experience of advising on build-to-suit transactions, telecom facility leasing and general commercial leasing. Other specialist areas include low-income housing, land use and finance and securitization. The practice also advises on real estate-related tax issues.

**The Lawyers:** President of ACREL, **Philip Horowitz** is promoted in the table this year. He represents owners, developers and institutions in complex real estate transactions. Recent work highlights include acting for Westfield Realty in the $1.05 billion sale of 12 buildings in Northern Virginia. Horowitz also represented Louis Dreyfus Property in its development of both 1101 New York Avenue NW and the new headquarters for the SEC adjacent to Union Station. The real estate-related tax expertise of "*creative thinker*" **Stef Tucker** is much in demand. One interviewee opined that Tucker is "*the best real estate tax lawyer in DC.*" Another said: "*His advice goes beyond the usual chapter and verse. He also has an excellent grasp of a company's business objectives.*"

**Clients/Work Highlights:** Clients include developers; syndicators; lenders; life insurance companies; pension funds; retailers; utility companies; brokers and property managers.

### Other Notable Practitioners

"*A venerable name in DC real estate,*" **Jeffry Dwyer** (see p.509) of Greenberg Traurig's practice neatly marries his corporate and real estate expertise to good effect. He stands out for his REIT experience, and clients point out that he "*quickly gets to the heart of a matter.*" He advised Sentinel on setting up a complex global REIT. "*Extremely capable and experienced,*" WilmerHale's **Allen Fox** (see p.513) is a new entry to the table. He focuses on acquisitions, development, financing, sales and leasing. Finally, **Leonard Zax** of Latham & Watkins is notable in real estate development and finance matters. He represents REITs, private investment funds, lenders, developers, corporations and investment bankers locally and nationally. Zax heads up the firm's DC real estate practice and acted for Gaylord Entertainment in the acquisition and development of a $625 million hotel and convention center at National Harbor, Maryland.

# SECURITIES

## Band 1

### WilmerHale
See firm details p.580

**The Firm:** Home to "*the finest securities practice in the city by far,*" this firm has over 200 lawyers whose collective expertise ranges from pure advisory work, all the way through enforcement, to civil and criminal litigation. A "*regulatory powerhouse,*" the group routinely advises major investment banks and broker-dealers on compliance and best practice issues in complex trading matters. It also advises on cutting-edge enforcement issues and has the resources to coordinate the complex parallel SEC, DOJ and civil proceedings that can arise out of government investigations. A significant number of the lawyers formerly held senior positions in the SEC, and clients benefit from the team's intimate knowledge of government procedure and policy.
**The Lawyers:** Cochair of the securities department, **William McLucas** (see p.531) is regarded as "*the preeminent SEC enforcement lawyer in the country.*"

A former SEC Director of Enforcement, his practice focuses on internal investigations and SEC enforcement proceedings. A highly skilled litigator, he has advised special committees in a number of high-profile investigations, including the committees in the Enron and WorldCom cases. **Harry Weiss** (see p.554) is also on the enforcement side and another alumnus of the SEC Division of Enforcement. Sources spoke of his "*extraordinary judgment and enormously effective style.*" He has developed an excellent rapport with the regulators and brings a calming influence to troubled situations. Corporate cochair **Meredith Cross** (see p.507) focuses on securities advice. A former deputy director of the SEC Division of Corporate Finance, her practice covers the full spectrum of issues securities disclosure and the impact of the Sarbanes-Oxley Act. Clients praised her for being "*accessible, thoughtful and incredibly responsive.*" Well versed in the intersection of law and policy, **Jamie Gorelick** (see p.516) cochairs both the securities and the public policy and government practices. She assists multinational companies on strategic planning and litigation issues relating to securities and the Foreign Corrupt Practices Act. In addition to the high caliber of partners on call, clients are also impressed with the quality of its midlevel associates who contribute to the firm's "*very experienced and practical securities team.*"
**Clients/Work Highlights:** A broad-based clientele includes Fortune 100 companies, major financial services firms and their senior managers. The group also regularly advises international companies on best practice securities compliance, and represents them in front of the SEC and DOJ.

## Band 2

### Arnold & Porter LLP
See firm details p.560

**The Firm:** This full-service securities enforcement and litigation group works closely with attorneys in the firm's corporate, financial institutions, public policy and white-collar criminal defense practices to offer clients a truly multidisciplinary approach. The team regularly defends clients in SEC and congressional investigations. It also assists clients in internal investigations and advises on a wide range of matters, including Sarbanes-Oxley and compliance issues and other regulatory counseling.
**The Lawyers:** Head of the firm's securities enforcement practice, **Michael Trager** (see p.551) focuses on defending governmental investigations and counseling corporations on crisis management, disclosure and governance. With experience of working in the SEC's Division of Enforcement, he has a broad understanding of the sector. "*If I personally got in trouble, he'd be my first call,*" said one client, echoing the sentiment of others. Recognized by the market as an exceptionally talented practitioner, he won client praise for being "*thorough, measured and hard working.*"
**Clients/Work Highlights:** The practice has a broad

client base including public companies; broker-dealers; hedge funds; accounting firms and financial institutions and their directors, officers, partners, principals and employees.

### Covington & Burling
See firm details p.563

**The Firm:** This impressive corporate and securities practice focuses on regulatory advice, with much of the work centering on '34 Act compliance and disclosure issues. The team acts as outside securities counsel for Procter & Gamble, which it advised on aspects of its acquisition of Gillette. It also advises Adelphia Communications on its securities compliance matters. Clients praised the team for its "*impeccable work and great drive to solve problems and bring about solutions.*"
**The Lawyers:** Head of the firm's securities practice, **David Martin** (see p.529) is a former director of the SEC Division of Corporate Finance. He is "*articulate and analytical with excellent communication skills,*" and clients also appreciate his "*outstanding judgment and ability to see the broader picture.*" Martin is also cochair of the firm's corporate practice group.
**Clients/Work Highlights:** The firm advises clients from a wide range of sectors including sport; life sciences; media and communications; energy and technology. Examples include Procter & Gamble, Adelphia Communications and Kerr-McGee.

### Gibson, Dunn & Crutcher LLP
See firm details p.328

**The Firm:** This securities team is respected as being "*on the cutting edge*" of the market. The practice covers all aspects of the sector, including Internet-related securities law, financial reporting and SEC regulatory and enforcement issues. The regulatory practice counsels three of America's big four audit firms as well as companies across the USA on issues including Sarbanes-Oxley compliance, corporate governance and other regulatory obligations. On the enforcement side, a notable recent example is the team's advice to the audit committee of MCI in a SEC investigation and federal criminal investigation. The group also represented the audit committee of hospital chain Bon Secours in matters relating to alleged financial misrepresentations.
**The Lawyers:** Former director of the Division of Corporate Finance at the SEC, **Brian Lane** (see p.525) counsels companies on all aspects of corporate governance and securities regulatory issues. A "*strong, practical lawyer,*" he also handles enforcement matters. The group's founder, **John Olson** (see p.536), specializes in regulatory work. He is widely respected for his experience and expertise in this sector and regularly handles audit committee investigations for high-profile clients.
**Clients/Work Highlights:** An extensive client list includes Amazon.com; Capital One; Del Monte Foods; Kodak; GE; Hewlett-Packard; HJ Heinz; Intel; Marriott International; Mirant; Union Pacific and Wells Fargo.

## Hogan & Hartson LLP

See firm details p.568

**The Firm:** This practice focuses on providing advice on the establishment and monitoring of securities compliance programs, as well as representing issuers and underwriters in securities offerings. The group also counsels on corporate governance issues such as NYSE listing standards, SEC disclosure requirements and insider trading policies.

**The Lawyers:** Securities counsel **Alan Dye** (see p.509) *"wrote the book on Section 16."* An alumnus of the SEC Division of Corporate Finance, he is a *"wonderful guy with a substantive knowledge of the law and the ability to apply it in a practical way,"* said clients. As well as advising on securities issuance, he is well versed in all aspects of securities compliance.

**Clients/Work Highlights:** The firm's clientele includes issuers and underwriters, and public companies and their boards of directors. Examples include McDonald's and McCormick & Company.

## Latham & Watkins LLP

**The Firm:** Respected for its securities regulatory advice practice, this team works out of the firm's corporate department. It handles compliance issues for companies and audit committees, including advice on Sarbanes-Oxley Act-related matters. The group has particular expertise in public offerings and private placements of securities. On the enforcement side, it has represented major clients in SEC proceedings, including on matters involving financial statement issues. The firm is also well regarded for its securities litigation practice.

**The Lawyers:** Securities specialist **John Huber** has both litigation and transactional experience. A former director of the SEC's Division of Corporate Finance, he is respected for his substantive knowledge of securities law and SEC practices. Clients regard him as *"an incredible lawyer who brings a strong set of skills to the table."*

**Clients/Work Highlights:** The firm's client roster includes a number of major public companies.

## Skadden, Arps, Slate, Meagher & Flom LLP & Affiliates

See firm details p.1557

**The Firm:** This firm's comprehensive practice has one foot firmly in the corporate governance team and the other in securities enforcement and litigation. Its securities advice has its foundations in corporate compliance programs that the team tailors to each individual company it counsels. This is often combined with auditing and FCPA advice. Further along the line, the enforcement team represents clients in SEC investigations and congressional hearings, and assists in negotiating deferred settlement agreements with the government. The support of a top-flight, white-collar criminal litigation team

ensures that any parallel criminal proceedings can be coordinated.

**The Lawyers:** **Colleen Mahoney** (see p.529) is head of the securities and enforcement practice. She is an outstanding lawyer with valuable SEC experience. Her practice focuses on representing clients in SEC investigations and in federal court litigations. In addition, she counsels on security-related issues and consumer financial regulation.

**Clients/Work Highlights:** A premier transactional firm, the team caters to an enormous corporate client base, representing companies and their boards, as well as individual CEOs and board members. It regularly advises on reporting issues for international manufacturing clients and accounting firms.

## Band 3

## Dechert LLP

See firm details p.1752

**The Firm:** This impressive securities enforcement group works closely with the firm's white-collar practice to represent companies and individuals in investigations or litigation involving the SEC, NASD and state and federal prosecutors. In tandem with its corporate and financial services departments, attorneys here also deal with regulatory matters. It recently represented a public company in an SEC investigation that arose from a $1 billion restatement, and the former head of investments of a substantial mutual fund complex in SEC and state investigations of market timing.

**The Lawyers:** Cochair of the financial services and securities litigation group, **Paul Huey-Burns** (see p.519) has a *"strong understanding of federal securities law and in-depth knowledge of the SEC."* A former assistant director in the SEC Division of Enforcement, he represents clients in investigations by the SEC, NASD and state prosecutors.

**Clients/Work Highlights:** The client base includes broker-dealers; financial advisers; public companies and their senior officers and directors.

## Dickstein Shapiro Morin & Oshinsky LLP

See firm details p.565

**The Firm:** This firm's expertise in the insurance arena is key to its market prominence. The practice covers regulatory advice, enforcement and litigation. Among the wide range of services it offers, the firm prepares and negotiates disclosure, securities purchase agreements and SEC and NASD applications. It also represents clients in SEC enforcement proceedings and investigations, as well as in civil litigation and criminal investigations by federal and state attorneys.

**Clients/Work Highlights:** The firm represents a wide range of clients including company executives; brokerage firms; investment companies; insurance companies; issuers; underwriters; institutional investors and finance and leasing companies.

## Fried, Frank, Harris, Shriver & Jacobson LLP

See firm details p.1532

**The Firm:** This firm is particularly known for its strong enforcement practice, which covers SEC enforcement actions, civil and criminal insider trading investigations and corporate counseling. For example, the team represented eFunds in an SEC enquiry into a 2002 financial restatement, resulting in a settlement agreement that required no penalty be paid by the company.

**The Lawyers:** **Dixie Johnson** (see p.521) co-heads the firm's securities regulation and enforcement practice group. A *"superior, well-regarded lawyer,"* she focuses on enforcement and litigation. **Karl Groskaufmanis** (see p.517) is *"intelligent, analytical and knows how to balance business and legal considerations."* He is well respected for his SEC enforcement and defense counseling and has particular expertise in insider trading and corporate internal investigations. Clients liked his *"diligent and attentive"* manner.

**Clients/Work Highlights:** The firm's clientele includes public companies and their senior executives; board committees; broker-dealers; investment advisers and legal and accounting professionals.

## Other Notable Practitioners

**Ralph Ferrara** (see p.512) of LeBoeuf, Lamb, Greene & McRae LLP is widely respected for his work in securities enforcement and litigation. Prior to joining the firm, he was managing partner of Debevoise & Plimpton's DC office, and also held the position of general counsel to the SEC. He is known for his involvement in *"blockbuster financial deals,"* particularly in the energy and insurance industries, and recently advised Royal Dutch Shell regarding investigation by the SEC and the UK's Financial Services Authority. Chair of Foley & Lardner LLP's securities litigation, enforcement and regulation practice, **Greg Bruch** (see p.504) has 12 years' experience at the SEC's Division of Enforcement under his belt. His practice encompasses enforcement, compliance and litigation matters, and he is also a member of the firm's white-collar practice. *"Terrific SEC lawyer"* **Richard Morvillo** (see p.533) chairs Mayer Brown Rowe & Maw LLP's securities enforcement practice. He has over 30 years' experience in securities and related white-collar proceedings, and also represents companies and individuals in both insider trading and shareholder class action suits.

# TAX

## Band 1

### Skadden, Arps, Slate, Meagher & Flom LLP & Affiliates

See firm details p.1557

**The Firm:** With a team of around 40 tax attorneys, *"the undisputed champion"* has firmly established its position as a premier tax practice in DC. The firm's vast corporate clientele and the broad expertise possessed by its attorneys is clearly a good fit. The group has the resources to efficiently undertake planning and transactional matters across a range of sectors, displaying *"profound expertise on all levels, from its associates through to its partners."* It represented Quiksilver in its $318 million acquisition of Skis Rossignol. Clients also pointed to international tax as a key element of the practice as its *"super lawyers know how the market functions. The firm dominates in terms of its enormity and excellence when measured against its opponents."* An extensive tax controversy practice and IRS expertise is illustrated by advice to KPMG on investigations by the DOJ, the US Attorney for the Southern District of New York and the IRS concerning allegations of tax shelters. In 2005, the firm won a key case for FedEx in the US Court of Appeals, in which the court upheld that the company's aircraft engine maintenance costs were deductible, not capital, items.

**The Lawyers:** A *"magician in the tax arena,"* **Fred Goldberg** (see p.515) impresses clients who describe him as a *"savvy and politically connected attorney – he is so smart, he can work an issue in such a way that everybody ends up happily agreeing with him."* He combines his terrific judgment with a problem-solving approach. **Paul Oosterhuis** (see p.536) *"brings a unique level of sophistication and an unmatched, refined understanding"* to his international tax law cases. Clients feel that the key to his success in nego-

tiations is his broad ranging experience; *"his strongest point is his balanced and objective perspective on what the right solution to a problem may be."* **Kenneth Gideon** (see p.515) offers clients an outstanding breadth of experience and is considered *"the finished article"* for those seeking counsel on tax controversy matters. *"Down-to-earth"* **Pamela Olson** (see p.536) is principally known for her expertise in domestic and international taxation. Clients spoke of her *"practical and balanced"* approach and her understanding of government policy. She is the first woman to chair the ABA Section of Taxation and has served as assistant secretary for tax policy at the Treasury Department.

**Clients/Work Highlights:** Alcoa; American Council of Life Insurers (ACLI); Bank of New York; Dell; Deloitte & Touche; Eli Lilly; Ernst & Young; FMR; IBM; Intel; GlaxoSmithKline; International Paper Company; Merck; Shell and Schering-Plough.

## Band 2

### Baker & McKenzie

See firm details p.866

**The Firm:** This global tax player with its *"eminent stars"* has carved out an outstanding reputation in the international tax market. While Mary Bennett's departure to the OECD in Paris is a loss to firm, it does illustrate the enormous amount of respect and credibility held by team members. The 25-strong team is famed for its aptitude in dealing with a range of highly sophisticated matters, including transfer pricing, tax dispute resolution and litigation, and international tax planning. The group advised Boeing in its recent acquisition of Jeppessen Sandersen and offered counsel in the successful tax litigation for Time Warner. Clients praised *"the sheer brain power"* that underpins the controversy practice and its *"ever growing insight"* in tax treaty work.

**The Lawyers:** While interviewees emphasized that the entire team is *"impressive in its depth of talent,"* many pointed to *"genius"* **Len Terr** (see p.550) and his *"balanced and thoughtful approach."* He is an *"incredibly astute international wiz"* for his involvement in controversies, lobbying and tax planning.

**Clients/Work Highlights:** Boeing; Time Warner; MetLife; Nissan-Renault; The Clorox Company and Aegon/Transamerica.

### Caplin & Drysdale

**The Firm:** *"The Rolls-Royce of tax boutiques,"* according to clients, who agree that *"the quality runs throughout the team, with an increase in younger stars coming to the fore."* The group is well equipped to handle complex tax litigation, as well as counseling clients on a range of multiyear controversies concerning, among others, transfer pricing, foreign tax credits and foreign exchange issues. Its fine status in the DC market is credited to *"a high knowledge base, fine clientele and excellent intellectual capability."*

**The Lawyers:** **David Rosenbloom**'s *"long-estab-*

lished and stellar" international tax practice is where much of the firm's profile rests. His practice is predominantly concerned with cross-border tax issues for high-profile companies and increasingly providing counsel to individuals. *"One of the brightest minds on the planet,"* his stance may sometimes be provocative: *"He likes to stir things up at times, but it's always in our best interests,"* said clients.

**Clients/Work Highlights:** The group advises financial institutions and a wide range of companies on a national and international level.

### McDermott Will & Emery

See firm details p.878

**The Firm:** The caliber of advice provided by this team of *"superior tax attorneys"* has earned it a strong, national reputation. Its capabilities span the full range of transactional, litigation and controversy work. High on the agenda are matters involving international tax for major multinational corporations, M&A and partnership tax. Its role as special tax counsel to Chevron in its acquisition of Unocal is evidence of its transactional skills, and the team has also advised on the tax-free spin-off of Hospira by Abbott Laboratories. Attorneys here are familiar sights in proceedings before the IRS, and clients value their *"capacity and talent to deal with the most intricate matters."*

**The Lawyers:** The *"thoughtful"* **James Riedy** (see p.541) advises on the tax aspects of structuring and financing acquisitions. This *"questioning and bright"* attorney is an expert on tax transfer price matters and day-to-day technical international tax matters. **Stephen Wells** (see p.554) produces *"thorough, investigative work"* and is said to be *"a super nice guy and a pleasure to deal with."* He concentrates on M&A, joint ventures and restructurings for some of the most prominent public and private multinational corporations.

**Clients/Work Highlights:** Chevron, Eli Lilly and Prudential Financial are all clients.

### McKee Nelson LLP

See firm details p.574

**The Firm:** This is a team capable of finding *"the best legal solutions to business problems,"* according to clients, who are impressed with its *"proficiency in legal issues and clued-up business approach."* Its reputation is foremost in the tax controversy sphere, with both litigation and international tax planning as its forte. However, these intelligent attorneys *"can deal with anything put before them,"* clients said.

**The Lawyers:** **John Magee** (see p.528) displays a *"strong analytical and strategic sense"* and necessary skills to articulate his advice to a range of specialists and laymen. He has been the lead lawyer in the representation of Dow Chemical and GlaxoSmithKline. **William McKee** (see p.531) is *"extremely bright and unsurpassed in the area of partnership tax."* Clients also found this *"exceptionally engaging"* attorney *"the go-to guy"* for a broad range of tax issues and his caseload features partnership tax provisions and the international and corporate requirements of the Internal Revenue Code (IRC). *"Marvelous,"* *"supreme"* and *"brilliant"* are only a few of the superlatives that flooded in for **William Nelson** (see p.534). Former chief counsel for the IRS, he is a familiar sight on the largest pieces of litigation and enforcement matters. *"Detail-oriented"* **Scott Farmer** (see p.511) is a *"fantastic technician who digs into things and analyses everything,"* while **Raj Madan** (see p.528) wins his fair share of plaudits as a client-focused attorney who *"can relate to just about every-*

*body."* The *"thoughtful and hard-working"* **Sheri Dillon** (see p.508) typifies the next generation of attorneys coming through the ranks at McKee Nelson.

**Clients/Work Highlights:** Dow Chemical, Glaxo-SmithKline and GE Capital are among the firm's prestigious clients.

## Miller & Chevalier Chartered
See firm details p.575

**The Firm:** According to clients, this premier tax boutique has secured its international reputation for its success in producing *"remarkably high-quality attorneys."* Their expertise and integrity is widely commended by clients who said, *"when you seek their help you know you will get the best advice possible."* The team handles every aspect of international tax, corporate tax, policy, accounting and financial products. However, its work in the field of tax controversy takes much of the limelight.

**The Lawyers:** Former commissioner of the IRS, **Lawrence Gibbs** (see p.514) is a *"seasoned and versatile"* adviser. Clients point to years of experience and praise his integrity and effective handling of complex matters. *"He stays calm at the helm without ever being ruffled."* The *"unbelievably business-savvy"* **Phillip Mann** (see p.529) is predominantly involved with regulation and administrative tax law issues as well as appeals and controversy work. He represents a broad range of large multinational clients, who agree, *"there is not a person with better judgment in the country."* **Herbert Odell** (see p.535) is a *"tough contender"* who successfully advised Black & Decker in a case of whether a taxpayer is entitled to capital loss from the sale of stock in a contingent liability healthcare subsidiary. **Steven Rosenthal** (see p.543) and **Alex Zakupowsky** are *"polished and exceptionally bright"* attorneys.

**Clients/Work Highlights:** American Petroleum Institute; Blue Cross and Blue Shield Association; FPL Energy and Federal National Mortgage Association.

## Band 3

## Fried, Frank, Harris, Shriver & Jacobson LLP
See firm details p.1532

**The Firm:** This *"first-rate and thoroughly trusted group"* has fostered a *"hard work will get you results"* type of culture, clients said. Services offered include counsel on the tax aspects of M&A, financings, real estate and controversy matters. The team recently advised BellSouth in Cingular's $41 billion purchase of AT&T Wireless. It also counseled LabOne in its agreement to be acquired by Quest Diagnostics for approximately $934 million in cash. The legendary Martin Ginsburg, professor of law at Georgetown University, remains of counsel to the tax department.

**The Lawyers:** **Alan Kaden** (see p.521), chairman of the DC tax department, has developed a practice that is rooted in transactional work; he is *"the cross-border mergers ace,"* said clients. He is also on hand to

provide effective litigation counseling. **Kevin Keyes** (see p.521) concentrates on federal income taxation, especially in the taxation of financial products and transactional tax planning.

**Clients/Work Highlights:** BellSouth; Permira; Sinclair Broadcast Group; El Paso; The Rouse Company; MCG Capital and Cargill.

## Ivins, Phillips & Barker

**The Firm:** Market sources spoke of a *"superb tax boutique full of handpicked experts."* The firm's characteristic attribute is that it dedicates as much time to tax planning and consulting as it does to its *"successful and highly valuable"* controversy work. Its expertise encompasses corporate transactions, employee benefits, international, accounting methods and inventories. The group recently represented HJ Heinz in a case before the US Court of Federal Claims concerning a stock redemption made by Heinz in 1995. It also provides arbitration and expert witness services in tax-related commercial issues.

**The Lawyers:** A *"mastermind of the tax field,"* **Leslie Schneider** is an authority on inventory taxation and devotes a significant portion of his practice to accounting method changes. Formerly with PwC, **Alan Granwell** *"delivers high standards"* to clients and is an expert in the international tax arena. Meanwhile **Robert Wellen** impresses as an *"incredibly bright and thoughtful attorney."*

**Clients/Work Highlights:** Northrop Grumman; Milliken; Bayer; Xerox; Heinz; Boeing and GE. The firm also provides consulting advice to a number of public accounting firms and law firms.

## King & Spalding LLP
See firm details p.1933

**The Firm:** Clients appreciate that this practice has been *"truly dedicated to tax for years and knows how to deliver a first-class service."* It works closely with clients' own in-house tax advisers to deal with multi-faceted international tax issues. Attorneys advise both US and non-US industrial companies and financial institutions on an extensive range of issues such as M&A, audits and tax planning. Much of the work is cross-border in nature and there is *"a considerable number of top professionals at hand."* Equally well regarded is the group's proficiency in tax controversy and the US foreign tax credit and antideferral rules. The team dealt recently with a major IRS audit concerning foreign tax credits for a Fortune 50 industrial client and worked with four major international banks in the structuring and execution of tax-efficient cross-border financing transactions.

**The Lawyers:** According to clients, the firm is *"full of marvelous lawyers."* **Robert Culbertson** (see p.507) is a *"great negotiator, who exudes confidence and knows how to make transactions happen."* Clients applauded his *"thorough, effective yet easygoing approach."* He specializes in international tax planning and controversy resolution in both the public and private sectors. Up-and-comer **Michael Caballero** (see p.505) impressed clients as a rising star in international tax planning.

**Clients/Work Highlights:** The team offers counsel

to international and domestic clients, Fortune 500 companies and financial institutions.

## Latham & Watkins LLP

**The Firm:** According to clients, this international player *"stunned everybody with how rapidly it has built a respected and sought after practice in DC."* The team represented Ernst & Young before the IRS and other investigative bodies concerning alleged tax shelter promotional activities. The firm has become *"even more treasured"* in the area of tax controversies. It recently counseled DaimlerChrysler and Cardinal Health before the IRS concerning federal income tax controversies. A fantastic addition to the group is the former deputy chief counsel at the IRS, Nicholas DeNovio.

**The Lawyers:** Rivals praised the *"exceptionally smart"* **Rita Cavanagh** for her great judgment, while clients deemed her *"unflappable."*

**Clients/Work Highlights:** CIGNA; Citibank; HCA; The Carlyle Group and Amgen.

## Band 4

### Morgan, Lewis & Bockius LLP

See firm details p.1758

**The Firm:** This respected national firm fields a *"vibrant and dynamic practice, packed with talented people."* Clients point particularly to its profound *"depth and vigor"* in the tax-exempt area but also praise its ability to handle a broad range of tax issues including corporate and partnerships matters. For example, it recently counseled Smiths Group in its $925 million acquisition of medical device manufacturer Medex, and represented InKine Pharmaceutical in its $205 million tax-free merger with Salix Pharmaceuticals. The group has also built on its experience in tax controversy matters, including the provision of advice to PacifiCorp and Cadbury Schweppes.

**The Lawyers:** Versatile **Gary Wilcox** (see p.555) is a *"brilliant problem solver – he can identify the real problems efficiently and effectively,"* clients said. He is *"extremely business-oriented"* and offers a broad based understanding of tax issues relating to M&A, spin-offs, partnerships and joint ventures. **Celia Roady** (see p.541) attracted widespread recommendation as an *"affable and engaging"* attorney, who is particularly skilled in the representation of tax-exempt organizations.

**Clients/Work Highlights:** The team has advised long-standing client GE in the sale of its IT Solutions Business Unit to Platinum Equity. Other clients include GMH Communities Trust; FirstEnergy; Cadbury Schweppes; Barrick Gold; Commercial Office Properties Trust and PacifiCorp and Subsidiaries.

### Shearman & Sterling

See firm details p.1554

**The Firm:** The group generates *"intelligent and persuasive lawyers"* whose broad knowledge sees them active on a range of tax issues. It handles an array of tax matters including cross-border M&A and spin-offs, as well as restructurings, and debt and equity financings. Sources spoke of the group's outstanding controversy capabilities and its increasing caseload of tax structuring and planning for startup companies, principally in the area of e-commerce.

**The Lawyers:** Financial products guru **Robert Rudnick** (see p.543) is *"innovative and highly devoted to clients."* According to one source: *"If one was to check the term 'common sense' in the dictionary, his photo would be found right next to it."* The greater part of his practice focuses on the structuring of financial transactions, including securitized funding and acquisition finance.

**Clients/Work Highlights:** Attorneys represent high-profile domestic and international clients, as well as major investment banks and financial institutions.

### Steptoe & Johnson LLP

See firm details p.576

**The Firm:** Interviewees were keen to stress the *"intellectual acumen"* on offer at *"a firm populated with some great legal minds."* Its attorneys tender an impressive diversity of skills, approaching their cases with a *"hard-driven and unfaltering style,"* clients said. Recently, the group has represented industrial companies, financial institutions and high net worth individuals in order to attain case-specific and interpretive competent authority agreements. Its *"calculated and efficient"* advice has been seen in matters before the IRS and the Treasury Department, as well as issues related to recent tax legislation. International tax, consumer products and tax-efficient structures for foreign investment in US real estate are all key strands to this practice.

**The Lawyers:** A *"high-flyer"* among a stable of respected legal advisers is **Mark Silverman** (see p.546), who offers a *"wealth of tremendous practical experience."* He chiefly concentrates in the areas of planning, audit and controversy and transactional tax matters. *"Showing some real intellectual leadership"* is the *"dogged and diligent"* **Philip West** (see p.555). A former Treasury Department international tax counsel, he advises clients on international tax issues, controversy and transactional matters. Clients also appreciated the responsive service provided by *"sensible and practical"* **Suzanne McDowell** (see p.530).

**Clients/Work Highlights:** Gillette; LVMH; EMC Corporation and Bear Stearns.

### Sutherland Asbill & Brennan LLP

See firm details p.578

**The Firm:** Clients appreciated that this talented group *"has all areas well covered."* Its *"marvelous"* attorneys are principally celebrated for their tax litigation and controversy advice, but they are also commended for work on corporate, international and partnership taxation. The group is also well equipped to advise on legislation, accounting and state and local tax.

**The Lawyers:** *"No-nonsense lawyer"* **Jerome Libin**

(see p.526) is an intelligent and thoughtful attorney: he has *"deep experience and knows the law like the back of his hand."* **Herbert Beller** (see p.501), a former chair of the ABA Tax Section, is *"amazingly smart and delivers an outstanding level of service to his clientele."* One client referred to him as a *"reality check kind of guy – he knows what is required for each type of matter."*

**Clients/Work Highlights:** GM; Philip Morris; Procter & Gamble and Honeywell.

## Band 5

### Dewey Ballantine LLP

See firm details p.1530

**The Firm:** Clients hold the group's deeply experienced lawyers in high regard and endorse their enviable status in transactional and planning matters as well as tax controversy. Its tax *"proficiency and breadth"* is illustrated in its representation of Automatic Data Processing before the Treasury Department, the IRS and Congress, on issues relating to income and employment tax collection as well as the regulation of the payroll processing industry.

**The Lawyers:** **Joseph Pari** (see p.537) is a *"mature and sophisticated lawyer who knows what to focus on,"* agreed sources. He forges strong relationships with clients and tackles a range of transactional and controversy issues on their behalf. According to one source: *"He is incredibly smart and so thorough he grinds issues to dust."*

**Clients/Work Highlights:** The team has represented The Clorox Company on IRS audit matters and Archer Daniels Midland on federal and state tax issues.

### Freshfields Bruckhaus Deringer LLP

**The Firm:** Clients described this as a gifted team that displays good quality depth. It is particularly commended for its expertise in financial products.

**The Lawyers:** The *"star of the show"* continues to be **Gregory May**. He is *"a tremendously skilled and trusted attorney,"* reported clients.

**Clients/Work Highlights:** Clients the firm advised in the past include SAIC, The Carlyle Group and Carlyle Europe Venture Partners.

### Jones Day

See firm details p.570

**The Firm:** This capable team has secured a track record for *"responsiveness and sound judgment,"* according to market sources. Clients praised its *"experience in all tax, legal and business issues."* Particular strengths include international and cross-border planning and transactions, bankruptcy, M&A and private equity-related tax.

**The Lawyers:** International tax expert **Kenneth Krupsky** (see p.524) *"questions, analyzes and looks at issues profoundly,"* clients said. The level of Krupsky's tax proficiency is matched by the *"thoughtful and detail-oriented"* **Raymond Wiacek** (see p.555), who has secured a loyal client base.

**Clients/Work Highlights:** Citibank; Ambac; Alfa

Finance; The Riverside Company; Tesoro; Converse; Mattel; WorldSpace; Bank of America; Pfizer; Bridgestone/Firestone and Isuzu Motors.

## WilmerHale

See firm details p.580

**The Firm:** "*Attentive and committed to clients,*" was the market consensus on this group. The full spectrum of tax work is covered here, though there are particular specializations in bankruptcy and structuring of multinational groups in connection with M&A and spin-offs, and cross-border investments. Recent work includes the advice to Educational Testing Service on transactions involving the sale of subsidiaries and revision of contract for computer-based testing services.

**The Lawyers:** "*Unflappable*" **Terrill Hyde** (see p.520) is the former deputy tax legislative counsel for regulatory affairs at the Treasury Department. Clients appreciated her "*wonderful judgment and versatility.*" She is an expert in the areas of consolidated returns, exempt organizations and partnerships. **William Wilkens** (see p.555) has made "*enormous contributions over the years in the area of tax.*" He is skilled in tax compliance, investment structures and federal tax legislation and regulation. **Clients/Work Highlights:** BAE Systems; Braintree Laboratories; Idenix Pharmaceuticals; Keane; Netegrity; Predix Pharmaceuticals and Bottomline Technologies.

### Other Notable Practitioners

"*Tremendously perceptive*" **Peter Baumbusch** (see p.500) at Gibson, Dunn & Crutcher LLP focuses on international and domestic corporate taxation, M&A, restructurings and foreign investment in the USA. "*Detail-oriented*" **Kenneth Klein** (see p.523) of Mayer, Brown, Rowe & Maw LLP received accolades for his skill in international taxation. He recently advised on the restructuring of healthcare services company McKesson. The "*outstanding and incredibly smart*" **William Paul** (see p.537) of Covington & Burling regularly represents clients before the IRS, the Treasury Department and Congress.

# TECHNOLOGY & IT OUTSOURCING

## Technology & IT Outsourcing

### Leading Firms

1. **MAYER, BROWN, ROWE & MAW** *Washington, DC*
   **PILLSBURY WINTHROP** *Washington, DC*
2. **LATHAM & WATKINS LLP** *Washington, DC*
   **MILBANK** *Washington, DC*

### Leading Individuals

1. **MASUR Daniel** *Mayer, Brown, Rowe & Maw*
   **ZAHLER Robert** *Pillsbury Winthrop*
2. **KLEIN Allen** *Latham & Watkins LLP*
3. **ALBERG James** *Pillsbury Winthrop*
   **GLASSPIEGEL Harry** *Pillsbury Winthrop*
   **OSER Aaron** *Pillsbury Winthrop*

### Up-and-coming individuals

**WHITE Debra** *Milbank*

### Associates to watch

**BALDIA Sonia** *Mayer, Brown, Rowe & Maw*
**MILLER Van** *Mayer, Brown, Rowe & Maw*

## Band 1

### Mayer, Brown, Rowe & Maw LLP

See firm details p.876

**The Firm:** Clients believe this DC office's attorneys are "*resourceful, committed, continually on point*" and "*adept at understanding what issues will surface and what compromise positions are potentially available.*" Its expertise includes the outsourcing of IT services and support, application development and maintenance, telecommunications services, network management and support, and e-commerce processing and support.

**The Lawyers:** Peers believe **Dan Masur** (see p.529) "*brings a tremendous knowledge of the outsourcing environment and the reasonableness of issues, having acted for both customers and vendors.*" Clients were equally effusive in their praise: "*Meet him, and you just know he's the man to run your job for you.*" His recent work includes representing Archstone-Smith

in connection with the development, maintenance, support and commercialization of systems performing lease-rent optimization functions. He also represented United Technologies in connection with the outsourcing to Affiliated Computer Services of payroll, finance, accounting and other business process functions. **Sonia Baldia** (see p.499) is "*bright, supportive and hard-working,*" in the view of clients, and has a practice that encompasses outsourcing, IT and IP. Associate **Van Miller** (see p.532) has "*great timing*" and "*does good work at all times within budget.*" His practice takes in a variety of ITO and BPO work.

**Clients/Work Highlights:** Wachovia; Kodak; United Technologies and US Airways.

### Pillsbury Winthrop Shaw Pittman LLP

See firm details p.1550

**The Firm:** Clients believe this DC office's "*professional attorneys focus on the right issues and seek to obtain the right outcome for both parties.*" They also praise its unique business model combining both legal and consulting services in the outsourcing space.

**The Lawyers:** A talented cadre of lawyers includes **Bob Zahler** (see p.557), an attorney who "*thinks about what's going on and tries to create the paradigm.*" He works alongside "*well-organized*" **Aaron Oser** (see p.536), who recently led the team assisting Educational Testing Service (ETS) in negotiating and closing a cutting-edge, $142 million, five-year supply chain BPO with Accenture. **Jim Alberg** (see p.497) is "*reasonable to deal with*" and has "*earned his spurs*" in the sector, **Harry Glasspiegel** (see p.515) has recently rejoined the practice after eight years as a business leader, adviser and investor in the sourcing and technology markets.

**Clients/Work Highlights:** Dun & Bradstreet; Capital One; GE Consumer Finance; Stop & Shop Supermarket Companies; ETS and PG&E Co.

## Band 2

### Latham & Watkins LLP

**The Firm:** This DC office's lawyers were commended by clients for being "*practical and strategic business attorneys.*" As one interviewee stated: "*They understand you don't have to win every battle, and they know what is a reasonable market position.*"

**The Lawyers:** The "*client-attentive*" **Allen Klein** has recently been representing a major business software company in a customer care and call center transaction. He has also been acting for a major healthcare payor in a series of five BPO transactions to support a substantial new line of business.

**Clients/Work Highlights:** CGI Group; Charles Schwab; Fidelity and Guaranty Life Insurance; Hawaiian Telcom; Valeant Pharmaceuticals International; WellCare and WellPoint.

### Milbank, Tweed, Hadley & McCloy LLP

**The Firm:** This firm's DC office works closely with its New York office on a variety of BPO and ITO matters. Although it lacks the depth in outsourcing personnel that the New York epicenter possesses, it nevertheless benefits from the firm's "*marquee reputation*" in the field.

**The Lawyers:** Client opinion as to newly made partner and now DC-based **Debra White** was summed up in one comment: "*She's outstanding – you can let her loose and she'll do her magic.*"

**Clients/Work Highlights:** General Atlantic; Prudential Financial; Home Depot; AT&T; DuPont; Cendant; Pepsi Bottling Group; MasterCard and Tyco International.

## TELECOM, BROADCAST & SATELLITE

## REGULATORY

### Band 1

### Covington & Burling

See firm details p.563

**The Firm:** *"Famous in the media area,"* the group's ascent in this year's rankings reflects expansive market endorsement for its *"consistent involvement at the very highest level of broadcast work."* The communications and media practice group undertakes a wide range of telecom and broadcast work, including litigation, regulatory work and lobbying activity. It is said to be *"on top of minute-by-minute changes in the industry,"* a trait borne out by its attorneys' ability to *"marry current law and policy issues in their counsel."* An example of this skill came with the team's recent focus on spectrum issues. This work involved abstract debate as to the virtues of a licensed spectrum as well as work on specific disputes concerning spectrum rights. At the heart of the team's standing in this area is an impressive reputation for representing TV stations across the country, in front of Congress and the FCC. It was intimately involved in the digital transition in the broadcast industry, handling legislation, litigation and rulemaking for the 450 television stations in the Associ-

ation of Maximum Service Television, as well as many other major station groups. In other areas, significant highlights have included representing BT in its acquisition of Infonet and involvement in broadband issues and the concept of 'net neutrality'.

**The Lawyers:** *"One of the leading lawyers in the field,"* **Jonathan Blake** (see p.502) spearheads the group. A particularly active client of his is The New York Times, whose broadcast stations have sought representation in relation to FCC compliance, retransmission consent arrangements and network affiliation agreements. He has also represented it on the acquisition of KAUT-TV. Clients and peers unanimously agreed that he is *"an outstanding broadcast lawyer."* The team also benefits from the assistance of special counsel **William Fitz** (see p.512), described by commentators as *"a phenomenal FCC attorney."* **Eric Greenberg** (see p.517) is a corporate lawyer with a particular focus on regulatory and financial issues as they relate to the broadcast communications area. *"He thinks outside the box to come up with creative deal structures"* and is noted for his commitment to a client's cause. *"To say he was diligent would be an understatement; he is always prepared to go the extra mile."* **Kurt Wimmer** (see p.555) is heavily focused on working with television broadcasters. His recent highlights include representing CBS and NBC in relation to the Satellite Home Viewer Act. He is also particularly active in relation to indecency claims.

**Clients/Work Highlights:** Amazon.com; Barrington Broadcasting Company; Cook Inlet; Dispatch Broadcast Group; Microsoft; National Geographic; NBA; NBC Weather Plus; Newsweek; NFL; NHL; QUALCOMM; Raycom Media; TDS Telecom; Terrestar and USDTV.

### Kellogg, Huber, Hansen, Todd, Evans & Figel, PLLC

**The Firm:** The market consensus for this communications boutique is that it's *"the go-to firm for appellate work in the telecom arena."* Especially rated by competitors for its litigation, antitrust and regulatory expertise, it is also said to be *"by far the best practice for local telephone companies."* It is particularly noted for its representation of SBC and other Bell companies. Clients noted that its lawyers have distinguished themselves in terms of longevity and high intelligence – *"they're the smartest people that practice in the area, so you get a stronger product from them."*

**The Lawyers:** The *"special and hugely talented"* **Michael Kellogg** is a premier appellate lawyer who handles many matters for wireline telephone companies. His recent work includes representing North-Point in NorthPoint v FCC, in which the client challenged the FCC's rules allowing terrestrial multichannel video distribution and data service (MVDDS) to share the 12.2-12.7 GHz band with direct broadcast satellite services. Colleague **Mark Evans** is said to be *"the best in town for agency order appeals."*

**Clients/Work Highlights:** Other recent work includes helping to advise Verizon on its $8.5 billion merger with MCI. Clients include the Bell companies.

### Latham & Watkins LLP

**The Firm:** *"Accomplished at marrying transactional and regulatory expertise,"* this group is not only regarded as one of the premier local outfits but also one of the strongest telecom groups in the whole country. It boasts a strong international footprint and *"impressive breadth of knowledge and work product."* In terms of regulatory expertise, clients commented: *"There are few teams as well connected and regarded at the commission."* The team was further praised for its commitment to a client's cause. *"Latham people always get into the bowels of an organization,"* one interviewee commented. In the broadcast space, the team has been involved in a lot of work relating to the transition to digital television as it applies to television stations and program distribution. Commentators also highlighted the group's towering status in the satellite realm, with Inmarsat included among a strong client roster.

**The Lawyers:** *"The leading communications lawyer for two or three decades,"* **Gary Epstein** spearheads the team. A highlight of the past twelve months involved representing a leading industry group, including SBC, AT&T, MCI and Sprint, in attempting to resolve an FCC telecom proceeding. For clients, *"he is an obvious choice due to his thoughtfulness, skill set and ability to leverage many years of experience in the area."* **Jim Barker** is also a popular choice among clients: *"He provides regulatory and transactional expertise across a number of areas, including media, telecom, broadcast and wireless industries, and is a pleasure to deal with."* He recently worked alongside Epstein in providing global regulatory advice to Yahoo! in connection with its launch of VoIP service offerings. *"Top satellite guy"* **John Janka** is active in many different aspects of telecom work, including commercial and M&A, spectrum issues, television and programming. *"Not only is he brilliant and creative but he is also one of the most hard-working attorneys I have ever come across."* Bilingual **Teresa Baer** is renowned for her predominantly international focus. One of her key clients is South American telecommunications giant América Móvil, which she represents on regulatory, litigation and transactional matters. A former commissioner and *"one of the best policymakers,"* **Karen Brinkmann** is now devoted to regulatory and transactional work on behalf of incumbent local exchange carriers and new entrants. Clients noted that *"her relationships and understanding of the FCC allow her to navigate through proceedings quicker than anyone else."*

**Clients/Work Highlights:** Alaska Communications Systems Group; The Carlyle Group; CenturyTel; Leap Wireless and Verizon.

## Wiley Rein & Fielding LLP

See firm details p.579

**The Firm:** This practice is one of the primary communications firms in the city and *"still holds a lot of sway at the FCC and in Congress."* Peers particularly praised this practice's regulatory and litigation expertise in the telecom arena, with additional mention made of its broadcast expertise, particularly for ClearChannel. Clients praised it on several counts: *"It obviously has the franchise, has a huge stable of good attorneys across the board, and no one could ever hold a candle to Dick Wiley for lobbying and salesmanship."* The practice's recent work has included advising on FCC aspects in relation to the ComCast/Adelphia/Time Warner merger, the Verizon/MCI merger and the Intelsat/PanAmSat merger. **The Lawyers:** Competitors lauded *"king of the DC communications Bar"* **Dick Wiley** (see p.555) for being a *"lion in the field"* and *"worth any accolade you give him – Dick is just Dick."* Further comment was that *"he's still very connected and he's managed to preserve his standing with the commission even through changes of administration and commission staff."* Clients agreed: *"If you want somebody who can give you terrific FCC access and a 60,000 ft view of where the commission's head is at, he's a very good person to consult with."* Communications litigation group chair **Andrew McBride** (see p.530) won praise from peers for his telecom litigation expertise in particular, while communications media group chair **Larry Secrest**'s (see p.545) practice includes advising clients on regulations governing broadcasters, cable television, satellite television and other electronic media.

**Clients/Work Highlights:** BellSouth; Belo; Emmis Communications; Gannett; GM; Gray Television; Motorola; Newspaper Association of America; SBC; Viacom/CBS; Verizon and Zenith.

## Band 2

## Harris, Wiltshire & Grannis LLP

**The Firm:** A *"small but strong DC boutique with some big clients,"* this practice has become one of the premier firms for telecom regulatory work in a very short period. *"Young, aggressive and cutting edge,"* it employs a host of former FCC staff and is noted for its expertise in relation to spectrum and satellite work.

**The Lawyers:** A former head of the FCC's international bureau, **Scott Blake Harris** won praise from peers for his international telecom work and spectrum work in particular. Clients commented that *"if you're looking for strategic counsel, call Scott. He's someone you can send into the FCC when you have an important agenda to work through – he knows everybody, he's well respected and he has a real political feel."* **John Nakahata** is especially rated for his enforcement expertise. Clients commented that *"he can read the underlying law, analyze it and present his case in a compelling way."* **Bill Wiltshire** won praise from clients for being *"hard-working and bright."* As one interviewee said: *"He doesn't make himself the center*

*of attention, he just gets the work done and does a good job of managing information flow and projects."*

**Clients/Work Highlights:** 3G Americas; Cisco Systems; Cingular Wireless; DIRECTV; Microsoft; North American Submarine Cable Association; New Skies Satellites; News Corporation; Nextel Communications; Tyco Telecommunications and Wi-Fi Alliance.

## Hogan & Hartson LLP

See firm details p.568

**The Firm:** The domestic practice at this large multinational firm houses the majority of the attorneys in the firm's esteemed worldwide telecommunications, media and entertainment practice. The team advises a number of high-profile, blue-chip clients from the USA and beyond, benefiting from strong links with the firm's highly regarded commercial and litigation practices. It boasts a very broad approach with expertise covering IP and the media industry, as well as regulatory expertise that has been refined over a long history in the telecom space. In many clients' opinions, *"you can't get much better in DC than Hogan & Hartson."* The group has advised Qwest on a number of issues, recently representing the company in front of the FCC and the DOJ concerning the potential impacts of the SBC/AT&T and Verizon/MCI mergers on its national operations. The international potential of the team was displayed in its handling of several multimillion dollar transactions for BT.

**The Lawyers:** *"First-rate"* **Peter Rohrbach** (see p.542) is renowned in the market for possessing *"excellent strategic intelligence."* Commentators see him as the go-to attorney at the firm and further praised his *"impressive writing skills."* A recent highlight involved representing WilTel Communications before the FCC on VoIP and access charges. **Michele Farquhar** (see p.511) impressed interviewees with her solid background and contacts in the area, having served previously as chief of the Wireless Bureau at the FCC. She has led the team in representing many wireless clients including Nextel and SunCom.

**Clients/Work Highlights:** AirCell; Bahamas Telecommunications; Bell Canada; Cable & Wireless; Callnet; Crown Castle International; Lehman Brothers; Morgan Stanley; Polaris Wireless; Sprint; SES Americom; US Cellular; Toshiba America and Western Wireless.

## Lawler, Metzger, Milkman & Keeney, LLC

**The Firm:** Noted by interviewees for its traditional representation of players on the competitive side, this boutique continues to represent wireless and wireline firms and other industry participants in matters before the FCC. Clients commented that *"if you're focusing on regulatory work at the FCC level, you really want to use Lawler Metzger. They're very highly skilled and specialized, with people who've worked at the FCC and have done this work their whole career."* Further comment was that *"they have people who are focused on telecom, broadcast, media, wireless, all the subspecialties in the area."* The practice's recent work includes representing Nextel in the FCC proceedings concerning its proposed merger with Sprint. It also represented MCI in FCC proceedings relating to its proposed merger with Verizon and has advised various wireline and satellite-based clients in relation to the ramifications of the FCC's e911 rules.

**The Lawyers:** A "*quite splendid*" attorney, **Richard Metzger** heads the firm's telecom practice and advises clients on a range of regulatory, antitrust and other issues. Drawing on his background as a former FCC common carrier bureau chief, he has also served as an expert witness in relation to common carrier regulation. **Gina Keeney** is particularly praised by peers and clients alike for her expert witness testimony in relation to FCC wireless laws. She also has an FCC background, having been a former international bureau chief. One interviewee commented: "*If I need an expert witness she's the first person I call: she's bright, practical and less likely to be conflicted out because of the firm she works for.*" Continuing the FCC theme, **Ruth Milkman** is a former deputy international bureau chief who has a practice encompassing common carrier, wireless, satellite, and international telecommunications matters.

**Clients/Work Highlights:** Sprint Nextel; MCI; Comcast; Epok; The Blackstone Group; New Skies Satellites and XO Communications.

## Levine, Blaszak, Block & Boothby LLP

See firm details p.573

**The Firm:** This DC telecom boutique is particularly rated by interviewees for its expertise in relation to large telecom user arrangements. With a number of former FCC personnel on board, its expertise encompasses negotiating custom network service agreements, network outsourcings and related transactions on behalf of large users and IT companies. It also advises enterprise customers in relation to disputes over agreements with carriers and in proceedings before the FCC.

**The Lawyers:** A "*colorful character,*" **Hank Levine** (see p.526) is "*the absolute leader in his niche,*" namely negotiating contracts for telecom services. "*A real trailblazer,*" he specializes in representing business customers in commercial telecom arrangements with carriers. **Jim Blaszak** (see p.502) is a former FCC chief of the domestic facilities and international satellite branch. His practice focuses on representing large users in regulatory and public policy matters and in relation to contracts for telecommunications services. **Colleen Boothby**'s (see p.502) distinguished tenure at the FCC included serving as legal adviser to the common carrier bureau chief and to the deputy bureau chief for policy. Her practice focuses on advising enterprise customers and providers of communications and IT services and products in relation to a range of regulatory, business and litigation matters. **Mark Johnston** (see p.521) is especially noted for his work representing companies and trade associations in FCC proceedings concerning the implementation of the Telecommunications Act of 1996.

**Clients/Work Highlights:** Ad Hoc Telecommunications Users Committee; Bank of America; Chevron; Dow Jones; First Data; IBM; Merrill Lynch; Oracle; The Washington Post and Xerox.

## Morrison & Foerster LLP

See firm details p.335

**The Firm:** This practice's forte is the representation of competitors seeking to challenge established incumbents in the telephone industry. Its recent work includes representing clients such as T-Mobile and the Cellular Telecommunications & Internet Association (CTIA) before the FCC in relation to spectrum issues and intercarrier compensation. Recent notable developments for the practice include the arrival of Bill Maher, the former head of the wireline competition bureau at the FCC. Highlight transactions from the past year include advising ICO Communications on a $650 million debt financing, and Clearwire on a $250 million debt financing. It also advised NewStar on regulatory aspects of an IPO, counseled ALLTEL on its merger with Western Wireless and handled a number of transactions for T-Mobile.

**The Lawyers:** **Cheryl Tritt** (see p.551) has international telecom expertise but also advises on wireless, satellite and multimedia issues. Colleague **Margaret Tobey** (see p.551) is a broadcast expert who wins plaudits for her "*first-rate regulatory expertise.*" Her clients include radio and television stations and direct broadcast satellite operators.

**Clients/Work Highlights:** ALLTEL; GE Capital; ICO Global Communications; LIN TV; National Exchange Carrier Association; NBC Universal; Satellite Broadcasting and Communications Association; Telephone Systems International; CTIA; Clearwire and Space Data.

## Sidley Austin LLP

See firm details p.883

**The Firm:** This practice has represented AT&T for a number of years, tackling a range of antitrust, litigation and regulatory matters. It is also rated for its broadcast expertise and continues to advise a variety of clients, including radio and television stations, broadcast network affiliate associations, satellite carriers and cable programming networks. It has recently offered counsel on the strategic implications of the FCC ruling that new equipment capable of receiving digital television broadcasts has to include approved copy protection technologies.

**The Lawyers:** **Clark Wadlow** (see p.553) won praise from clients for being a "*top-notch broadcast attorney*" who has "*put together a first-rate team, many of whom are former government people.*" He undertakes a significant amount of work for Tribune, which he recently represented, along with NBC, CBS and Fox, in an effort to get the Supreme Court to review the FCC's ownership rules. His work has also included advising clients such as Tribune and Fox Affiliates Association in relation to indecency issues. "*A bright guy,*" **David Lawson** (see p.525) is rated by peers for his work for long-distance companies in the telecom industry, in particular

AT&T. He assisted in advising the telecom giant in relation to its $16 billion acquisition by SBC Communications.

**Clients/Work Highlights:** AT&T; Tribune; Allbritton Communications; Dispatch Broadcast Group; Pegasus Communications and Fox Affiliates Association.

## Willkie Farr & Gallagher LLP

See firm details p.1567

**The Firm:** "*Always strong in broadcast*" and "*highly thought of at the FCC,*" this practice is famed for its work as principal federal regulatory representative of cable company Comcast. Clients were effusive in their praise of lawyers who "*are able to craft an argument, either orally or in writing, that is well researched and persuasive.*" The team advised satellite company Loral in its attempts to emerge from bankruptcy and acted for Adelphia on the antitrust and regulatory clearances relating to the sale of virtually all its assets to Time Warner and Comcast.

**The Lawyers:** A dean of the communications Bar who is especially rated for his broadcast expertise, **Phil Verveer** (see p.552) has "*credibility at the FCC*" and is "*an extremely astute observer of the inner workings of government agencies.*" His highlight transaction from the past year involved advising Sprint on the federal regulatory aspects of its merger with Nextel. He has also been advising Nielsen Media Research in relation to its introduction of local people meters, a maneuver that News Corporation has been lobbying against. A "*spectacular advocate*" who "*knows how to draft and present winning policy arguments,*" **Jim Casserly** (see p.506) is also a "*gentleman of the first order who can be counted on for a well-reasoned analysis of the legal points underpinning a case.*" His practice includes advising on high-speed cable Internet service, interactive television, digital television, competition policies and ownership issues.

**Clients/Work Highlights:** Home Box Office; YES Network; Bloomberg Television; iNDEMAND; QVC; Motorola and National Cable & Telecommunications Association.

## WilmerHale

See firm details p.580

**The Firm:** "*Highly respected by the FCC for its telecom work,*" this team has been recently bolstered by a number of new arrivals. These parvenus have added strength to a group already celebrated for its work on behalf of the Bell companies. Over the past twelve months, lawyers have represented SBC and Verizon in their recent mergers and handled multiple VoIP and broadband issues. A host of clients from the satellite, e-commerce, broadcasting and wireless industries queued up to extol the virtues of the team to researchers. One client eloquently summed up the prevailing market view: "*These lawyers are extremely effective as not only are they well connected in the area, but they are excellent at coming up with novel legal arguments that can move matters forward.*"

**The Lawyers:** The "*absolutely first-rate*" **Bill Lake** (see p.525) was commended by clients for being "*completely attuned to the business objectives of regulated companies.*" He recently acted for a number of satellite operators in connection with a variety of spectrum-related matters, and represented the CTIA in an amicus filing to the US Supreme Court concerning wireless phone health issues. "*Creative*" **Jon Nuechterlein** (see p.535) is an appellate lawyer with a focus on telecom litigation who regularly represents regional Bell companies in front of the FCC. "*He is absolutely fabulous; when you need to find your way from A to B at the FCC he is invaluable.*" **John Rogovin** (see p.542) recently joined the team following a long career in private practice and with the federal government where he was general counsel of the FCC. Clients see him as "*an excellent addition to the firm who brings the whole portfolio to the table.*"

**Clients/Work Highlights:** Clients include Bell-South, Qwest and Yahoo!

## Band 3

### Arnold & Porter LLP
See firm details p.560

**The Firm:** This practice's lawyers are especially noted by peers for receiving the vast bulk of their work from SBC, in their capacity as the company's primary FCC regulatory and transactional representatives. One of the highlights for the practice over the past year involved advising SBC in obtaining antitrust approvals for the company's $16 billion acquisition of AT&T. It also acted for SBC, along with Cingular Wireless, in obtaining antitrust and telecommunications approval for Cingular's $41 billion acquisition of AT&T Wireless Services. The practice's other recent matters include advising Comcast on local franchising matters, the Recording Industry Association of America (RIAA) on FCC regulations such as payola and copyright work and Crowley Enterprises on telecommunications work.

**The Lawyers:** Practice head **Norman Sinel** (see p.546) offers counsel on legislative issues, project development and implementation matters, franchising and licensing needs, and transactional requirements.

**Clients/Work Highlights:** SBC; ComCast; Crowley Enterprises; RIAA and National Captioning Institute.

### Bingham McCutchen LLP
See firm details p.1110

**The Firm:** At the time of going to press, Bingham McCutchen was set to benefit from the expertise of the Swidler Berlin team following the merger of these two firms. Competitive local exchange carriers have flocked to this practice in the past for the corporate/M&A, tax and regulatory expertise on offer. In recent times, it has been active in relation to various FCC proceedings including unbundling, universal service and intercarrier compensation. Other areas of activity include VoIP, net neutrality and advising foreign carriers operating in the USA.

**The Lawyers:** Vice chair of the firm's telecommunications, media and technology group, **Andy Lipman** (see p.527) was described by competitors as "*a dominant figure in the field.*" His TMT expertise includes advising on regulatory, transactional, litigation, legislative and land use issues.

**Clients/Work Highlights:** Clients include competitive local exchange carriers (CLECs), VoIP providers and foreign telecom carriers.

### Dow, Lohnes & Albertson, PLLC
See firm details p.566

**The Firm:** Competitors especially praised this "*blue-chip broadcast practice*" for its work for key client Cox Communications: "*They grew up together as Cox started in newspapers then branched out into radio and TV.*" Clients noted that its lawyers have "*an understanding of how the FCC works, especially when it comes to the law relating to TV stations.*" The practice's expertise also includes tax work for media companies and broadcast-related finance work for a number of investment and commercial banks. The team has recently been advising clients such as Nextel, Intel, Gannett Co and TiVo on issues including federal policy and IP law.

**The Lawyers:** Head of the communications law practice group **Kevin Reed** (see p.540) was praised by clients for being a "*terrific FCC guy.*" His recent work includes advising in relation to regulatory matters and business transactions for various companies of Cox Enterprises. **John Feore** (see p.512) won praise from peers for his long-term representation of Paxson Communications, in particular. His practice encompasses the representation of television and radio station clients (particularly group owners) and emerging broadcast networks before the FCC, Congress and other Washington agencies. **Anne Swanson**'s (see p.549) practice includes defending clients against FCC enforcement actions and advising on complex spectrum and broadcast regulatory issues.

**Clients/Work Highlights:** Cox Enterprises and its affiliates Cox Television, Cox Communications and Cox Radio; Advance/Newhouse Cable; Comcast; Media General; McGraw-Hill; Meredith Corporation; Paxson Communications and Allbritton Communications.

### Mintz Levin Cohn Ferris Glovsky and Popeo PC
**The Firm:** Competitors commend this firm for its cable and broadcast work, areas in which it handles a range of regulatory and legislative matters. It advises on ownership limits as they impact upon broadband and VoIP services and the appropriate response of cable competitors such as direct broadcast satellite concerns, telephone companies, and Internet-based video providers. The practice's work also includes satellite procurement transactions and regulatory work for clients including domestic and international satellite operators. In addition, it advises new entrants in the VoIP service provider industry.

**The Lawyers:** The "*knowledgeable*" **Howard Symons** (see p.549) and former FCC chair **Charlie Ferris** are both rated by interviewees for their cable

expertise in particular.

**Clients/Work Highlights:** Clients include multiple-system and program networks in the cable industry, stations and networks in the broadcast industry, and wireline and wireless telecommunications carriers and equipment manufacturers.

### Paul, Weiss, Rifkind, Wharton & Garrison
See firm details p.1548

**The Firm:** This practice has historically been rated for its satellite work for leading clients such as SES Americom and the now merged Intelsat and PanAmSat. While the recent departure of star satellite expert and former practice head Phil Spector to join Intelsat as executive vice president and general counsel is a setback to the practice, that said, it continues to undertake transactional and regulatory work for a number of satellite companies, in addition to advising investment banks and hedge funds in relation to the wireless industry. Other work that the practice is noted for includes litigation on the cable side, especially for key client Time Warner. The highlight transaction for the practice over the past year was representing Intelsat in its acquisition of PanAmSat. It also advised Nextel in relation to regulatory aspects of its merger with Sprint.

**The Lawyers:** **Henk Brands** (see p.503) is especially rated for his litigation expertise in relation to the cable industry. He is particularly active in appealing FCC orders to the Court of Appeals. His recent work includes advising in the case of National Cable & Telecommunications Association v Brand X Internet Services. In this case, the Supreme Court upheld cable companies' rights to restrict rival Internet service providers from their networks. He has also been advising in relation to the Vonage appeal concerning an FCC decision prohibiting states from regulating VoIP services.

**Clients/Work Highlights:** Time Warner; Intelsat/PanAmSat; SES Americom; NEC Electronics; NTT Communications; News Corporation; Fox Entertainment Group and Lehman Brothers.

### Skadden, Arps, Slate, Meagher & Flom LLP & Affiliates
See firm details p.1557

**The Firm:** The close relationship with leading client News Corporation and its associated companies ensures that this practice has a busy caseload. News Corporation aside, the practice's work includes advising investment banks on FCC regulation and representing clients on pending legislative proposals in relation to the regulation of broadband Internet and VoIP. It also advises on matters relating to the relaxation of the franchising process for cable television. The practice continues to act for the Independent Communications Authority Of South Africa in relation to telecom regulation and has recently counseled the South African government in the production of the convergence bill, the new legal framework for regulation of telecom in South Africa. Another recent highlight involved filing petitions on behalf of Fox, NBS, Universal and Viacom opposing various

FCC regulations in relation to children's television programming.

**The Lawyers:** Peers believe **John Quale** (see p.540) "*does terrific work*" on the transactional and regulatory side for a number of broadcast, satellite and wireless companies. His recent work has included representing Fox television stations in filing an opposition to a $1.2 million FCC fine alleging indecent broadcasting in an episode of the reality series 'Married by America'. **Toni Cook Bush** (see p.506) continues to represent Border Media, one of the largest Hispanic radio networks, on a number of transactions and regulatory matters. She has also been representing Virgin Mobile in relation to its entry into the prepaid cellular phone service market.

**Clients/Work Highlights:** News Corporation; Gemstar-TV; Virgin Mobile USA and Gray Television.

## Band 4

### Cole, Raywid, Braverman LLP

**The Firm:** This relatively small DC communications boutique has "*been around a long time and has a good stable of experienced attorneys.*" "*Nuts-and-bolts FCC work*" is a specialty with the lawyers, offering expertise on licensing and the interpretation of regulations. It is particularly well regarded by competitors for its cable work, an area in which clients feel its attorneys have "*encyclopedic knowledge*" and have been active since the beginning of the industry. The practice's cable work includes advising leading US providers of broadband networks and cable television services on federal and state regulatory, franchising, content-related and competition issues. Other areas of expertise include handling litigation for clients in the communications industry and advising in relation to e-commerce, IP, media content, music licensing and general Internet issues.

**The Lawyers:** Jack Cole is the founder of the firm, while Burt Braverman is one of its senior members. Wes Heppler and Bob Scott are also key members of the practice.

**Clients/Work Highlights:** Clients include cable television operators; telecommunications providers; broadcasters; programming networks and Internet companies.

### Goldberg Godles Weiner & Wright

**The Firm:** Historically heavily involved in the satellite field, especially for long-standing client PanAmSat, this DC communications boutique was described by peers as a "*training ground for satellite lawyers.*" Its expertise also encompasses traditional FCC work in both the broadcast and common carrier fields, in addition to cutting-edge wireless issues.

**The Lawyers:** Described by clients as "*a satellite expert par excellence,*" **Henry Goldberg** is well known for having represented PanAmSat "*forever*" in a range of regulatory work. He is cochair of the engineering and technical committee of the Federal Communications Bar Association.

**Clients/Work Highlights:** Clients include domestic and international satellite companies; mobile communications companies; telephone resale carriers; providers of enhanced data services and commercial and public broadcasters.

### Jenner & Block LLP
See firm details p.873

**The Firm:** The practice at Jenner & Block has a regulatory public policy focus with a strong reputation for litigating the lawfulness of FCC and state commission rulings. In this vein, it has represented CTIA in challenging FCC rules that the wireless industry is in disagreement with. The team's flagship client has traditionally been MCI. It recently represented the company regarding its merger with Verizon, securing the approval of both the DOJ and the FCC. Commentators were also quick to note the strength of the firm in representing new entrants in the wireline and wireless telecom fields.

**The Lawyers:** Telecommunications Act specialist **Michael DeSanctis** (see p.508) frequently appears before the FCC for a range of telecom clients. Over a number of years, he has acted for MCI as outside counsel in Section 252 litigation. **Don Verrilli** (see p.552), "*a senior appellate lawyer with a wonderful mind,*" chairs the telecommunications practice. Interviews unearthed admiration for his work among both clients and peers.

**Clients/Work Highlights:** Covad Communications Group; MGM Studios; National Association of Broadcasters; Netwave and the Recording Industry Association of America.

### Kelley Drye Collier Shannon

**The Firm:** This practice is a great favorite of the local exchange carrier industry. In this respect, clients rate its lawyers' "*skill at representing CLECs in their dealings with the incumbents.*" The other engine room of the practice is its representation of overseas telephone companies such as Deutsche Telekom, BT and Cable & Wireless. It also tackles traditional work for service providers and clients in the wireless industry and is handling an increasing amount of VoIP matters. Recent work for the practice includes advising VSNL on its $130 million acquisition of Tyco Global Network and its $239 million acquisition of Teleglobe. At the time of going to press, the office was scheduled to move into Collier Shannon Scott's premises, with whom the firm has merged.

**The Lawyers:** Bob Aamoth chairs the firm's telecommunications practice group.

**Clients/Work Highlights:** Deutsche Telekom; BT; Cable & Wireless; SingTel; VSNL; Telstra; KDDI and various CLECs.

### Leventhal Senter & Lerman PLLC

**The Firm:** Praised by interviewees for its work in the broadcast field in particular, this DC communication boutique's expertise encompasses advising clients in the traditional broadcast, satellite, and common carrier fields on a range of regulatory and business matters.

**The Lawyers:** **Steve Lerman** excels at advising in

relation to the acquisition and sale of radio and television properties. He also advises broadcast stations in relation to FCC regulation and has particular expertise in cases involving governmental intrusion into content and other First Amendment-related issues.

**Clients/Work Highlights:** American Society for Information Science & Technology; CBS; Davis Television; Great Scott Broadcasting; Infinity Broadcasting; Lockheed Martin; Maritime Telecommunications Network; Playboy Entertainment Group; Sesame Workshop and Viacom.

### Pillsbury Winthrop Shaw Pittman LLP
See firm details p.1550

**The Firm:** The "*thorough, professional and paternalistic*" communications practice at this large full-service law firm is highly regarded in the market. Boasting impressive bench strength, commentators complimented the firm on the quality of its practitioners. "*The group is made up of extremely talented lawyers who are very competent regarding technology.*" One of its most active clients is MSV, for which the team undertakes a range of licensing and rulemaking work. By way of example, the team secured FCC authorization to reuse its satellite spectrum for a national terrestrial wireless network. The firm also has a good track record for representing startup companies such as XM Satellite Radio, which the team has acted for since its inception with regard to satellite, radio broadcast and digital copyright matters.

**The Lawyers:** The "*extremely smart and technically savvy*" **Bruce Jacobs** (see p.520) is said to "*live, eat and breathe for the client.*" His practice is centered around new technology with a focus on attempting to minimize FCC regulation. Alongside him, **Richard Zaragoza** (see p.557) undertakes regulatory, transactional and litigation work in the electronic media space. For a number of years, he has provided regulatory advice to Millennium Radio Group in relation to acquisitions and ongoing operations.

**Clients/Work Highlights:** National Alliance of State Broadcasters Associations, VON Coalition and Wells Fargo Foothill are among the clients.

### Preston Gates Ellis & Rouvelas Meeds LLP

**The Firm:** This practice's clients include a variety of telecom, broadband and media companies. Its expertise encompasses advising in relation to regulatory and facilities deployment, M&A and bankruptcy work, litigation and local competition matters. In recent times, it has increasingly been advising on issues concerning new media and gaming, VoIP, Telecommunications Act reform and competitive video in the cable industry. Recent work includes advising US/Japanese undersea telecom cable company Pacific Crossing in relation to complex regulatory issues arising from its reorganization and emergence from bankruptcy.

**The Lawyers:** Martin Stern chairs the firm's global telecom and media group.

**Clients/Work Highlights:** Verizon; AT&T; T-Mobile; Pacific Crossing and Broadband Service Providers Association.

## Steptoe & Johnson LLP
See firm details p.576

**The Firm:** Newcomers to this year's rankings, this largely regulatory practice is highly regarded for its long-standing presence in the satellite area. For more than a decade, the firm has been advising Motorola on regulatory and licensing aspects surrounding its Project Iridium, the first global mobile satellite system. The practice has also been advising EchoStar, another very active client, on legislative and regulatory matters following the Satellite Home Viewer Improvement Act 1999 and its extension in 2004. Elsewhere, the team has been kept busy by its involvement in the MCI/Verizon merger where it has acted as lead antitrust counsel to MCI.

**The Lawyers:** *"Top-notch"* **Pantelis Michalopoulos** (see p.532) is the attorney commentators particularly favored in this group, describing him as *"smart and incredibly hard-working."* He was recently involved in representing library, public interest and consumer groups in successfully overturning the broadcast flag rule adopted by the FCC.

**Clients/Work Highlights:** Boeing; The Carlyle Group; Providence Equity Partners; Public Knowledge; Stratos Global and VeriSign.

## Vinson & Elkins LLP
See firm details p.1938

**The Firm:** Entering the rankings this year for the first time, this four-attorney team focuses on representing television and radio stations. In particular, it has represented a range of broadcasters in the relocation of FM radio stations to communities in order to increase their value. In another representation that received considerable press attention, the firm acted for Continental Airlines in a dispute with the landlords of Boston Logan International Airport. This matter concerned the use of wireless broadband devices in airports.

**The Lawyers:** Formerly an FCC commissioner and now head of the department, **Henry Rivera** (see p.541) was praised by clients for the extra dimension he brings to the table. Recently, a lot of his work has come from TMI Communications for whom he has been acting as regulatory counsel.

**Clients/Work Highlights:** American Media Services; Clear Channel Communications; Cox Communications; Cumulus Broadcasting; iBiquity Digital; Motient; MultiCultural Radio Broadcasting; Open Park; SkyTerra Communications; Susquehanna Radio and VarTec Telecom.

## White & Case LLP
See firm details p.1566

**The Firm:** This small domestic group enters the rankings in recognition of the regulatory and finance work it has done in the telecom realm. The team is certainly well equipped to handle international projects, with clients commending the enormous depth and resources of the firm well beyond the state lines. *"They do a great job of coordinating resources and personnel from many different offices."* Highlights for the Washington, DC office include its involvement as satellite industry and FCC expert counsel to Deutsche Bank Securities, the joint legal arranger of credit facilities in connection with the private equity acquisitions of New Skies Satellites by The Blackstone Group, and Intelsat by Apax, Permira, Apollo and Madison Dearborn. These transactions were valued at $535 million and $650 million respectively.

**The Lawyers:** **Maury Mechanick**'s (see p.531) workload covers the regulatory and transactional areas. A long business history in the satellite area has given him an additional perspective for which multiple clients showed their appreciation. *"He has a great mix of business and legal skills and also a great deal of personal integrity."*

**Clients/Work Highlights:** US Ex-Im Bank; Global Internetworking; International Launch Services; International Telecommunications Satellite Organization; Lockheed Martin Commercial Space Systems; Swe-Dish Satellite Systems; Telenor Satellite Services and Teletronics International.

## Wilkinson Barker Knauer LLP

**The Firm:** The lawyers of this DC communications and technology boutique were lauded by clients for *"having their pulse on what's going on at the FCC."* This is due in no small way to the fact that *"they're extremely committed to a high-quality relationship with the FCC"* and are *"well versed in policy and advocacy and all the arcane stuff that you learn appearing in front of the FCC."* Peers especially praise its wireless expertise and its work for the Bell companies in particular, in relation to matters on the *"routine regulatory"* or transactional side, such as *"seeking FCC consent for a merger."*

**The Lawyers:** *"Constantly in the know"* as to the FCC environment, the *"really smart"* **Kathy Zachem** is *"one of the best around"* when it comes to wireless issues, according to interviewees.

**Clients/Work Highlights:** Clients include regional Bell operating companies; independent providers of telecommunications and media services; communications equipment manufacturers; educational institutions; trade associations; utilities; municipalities and foundations.

---

# TELECOM, BROADCAST & SATELLITE                    FINANCE

| Telecom, Broadcast & Satellite: Finance |
|---|
| Leading Firms |
| 1 MILBANK *Washington, DC* |
| 2 COVINGTON & BURLING *Washington, DC* |

| Leading Individuals |
|---|
| 1 GERSTELL Glenn *Milbank* |
| 2 VOLTMER Ralph *Covington & Burling* |

## Band 1

## Milbank, Tweed, Hadley & McCloy LLP

**The Firm:** Continually rated by interviewees for its strength in emerging markets throughout Latin America and Asia, this global practice undertakes a variety of telecom work. Handling both financings and M&A matters, it acts for telecom operators, banks and vendors around the world. In ProtoStar's new satellite television project, which will involve one-way DTV to serve a wide portion of south and east Asia, the practice is advising the project company regarding all of its development work.

**The Lawyers:** *"Knowledgeable and creative"* global communications practice head **Glenn Gerstell** *"gets straight to the point."* *"An attorney who always adds credibility to any discussion,"* he is *"a good negotiator who doesn't get hung up on issues."*

**Clients/Work Highlights:** Hughes Network Systems; US Ex-Im Bank; Canada Economic Development; ABN AMRO; Citibank; Telemar; Huawei Technologies; Standard Bank; Alestra; Inter-American Development Bank and ProtoStar.

## Band 2

## Covington & Burling
See firm details p.3826

**The Firm:** Increasingly active in financings for a range of clients in the communications sector, this practice's lawyers won praise from clients for being *"good at stepping back and seeing the totality of the deal."*

**The Lawyers:** The *"incredibly sharp"* **Ralph Voltmer** (see p.553) was praised by clients for his *"persuasiveness in negotiations"* and his *"ability to conceptualize all the angles, no matter how complicated the deal."* His recent work includes representing Reliance Infocomm in connection with its $750 million financing by the US Ex-Im Bank and Export Development Canada. He also represented Telemobil, a Romanian wireless telecommunications service provider, in arranging $40 million in senior loans and $54 million in sponsored subordinated loans. In addition, he has been representing MediaFLO USA in connection with the acquisition and clearing of the portion of the 700 MHz spectrum to be used by MediaFLO in connection with its nationwide multimedia network.

**Clients/Work Highlights:** Reliance Industries; Telemobil; Inquam and QUALCOMM.

# Leaders in District of Columbia

### ACKER, Lawrence G
LeBoeuf, Lamb, Greene & MacRae LLP,
Washington, DC 202 986 8016
lacker@llgm.com
*Recommended in Energy*

**Practice Areas:** Litigates major, complex cases before administrative agencies and secures regulatory authorizations for substantial energy projects, including contested applications. Advises senior company officials respecting strategic planning, contract negotiation and corporate compliance with regulatory and enforcement requirements. Assists clients in every phase of the administrative process from case and project planning to document preparation and witness examination through appeals.
**Prof. Memberships:** Energy Bar Association.
**Career:** Joined LeBoeuf Lamb in 1984; Bracewell & Patterson (1981-84); Federal Energy Regulatory Commission (1978-81); Acker & Mansfield, Arlington, Virginia (1976-78); Arlington Legal Aid Society (1974-76).
**Personal:** Georgetown University (JD) 1974; Syracuse University (BA) 1971.

### ADELFIO, Marco
Morrison & Foerster LLP, Washington,
DC 202 887 1530
madelfio@mofo.com
*Recommended in Investment Management*

**Practice Areas:** Focuses on investment companies and investment advisors. Clients include open- and closed-end funds, multi-class funds and master-feeder funds. Advises on ongoing SEC regulatory and registration activities. Handles complex acquisition and reorganization transactions for fund companies and consolidations following mergers of advisers. Serves as independent counsel to independent directors of fund companies. Counsels registered investment advisers on regulatory and transactional matters. Advises on fiduciary responsibilities, the provision of investment management services, and compliance matters.
**Career:** Admitted to practice in District of Columbia and Massachusetts.
**Personal:** BA, Bucknell University, 1978; JD, magna cum laude, Order of the Coif, Boston College Law School, 1982.

### ADLER, Howard B
Gibson, Dunn & Crutcher LLP,
Washington, DC 202 955 8589
hadler@gibsondunn.com
*Recommended in Corporate/Commercial*

**Practice Areas:** Represents corporations, investment and merchant banks and financial institutions in securities offerings, M&A, joint ventures and venture capital investments. M&A: Arlington Capital (NLX, LLC; Secor); Arguss Communications, Inc. in sale to Dycom Industries, Inc., after staving off proxy challenge for Arguss; Capital One Financial Corp (various acquisitions). Finance: IPO- Friedman, Billings, Ramsey & Co., Inc.; American Capital Strategies; Corporate Executive Board; American Home Mortgage; Saxon Capital; Franklin Bank; KMG America; Taberna Realty Finance Trust; significant follow-on offerings and major 144A transactions; recapitalization Matrix Bancorp.
**Personal:** JD, New York University; note and comment editor, Law Review.

### AGRESTA, Steven J
Alston & Bird LLP, Washington, DC
202 756 3074
steven.agresta@alston.com
*Recommended in Energy*

**Practice Areas:** Economic regulation of electricity markets, representing US electric utilities in financial consequences of nuclear construction and operation, deregulation of electric markets, litigation against contractors and vendors, restructuring purchased power agreements, purchases and sales of generation, rate making, and mergers and acquisitions. Representing foreign electric utilities seeking to enter the US market in target identification, assesement of the regulatory environment, valuation, due diligence and regulatory approvals. Representing energy traders in federal regulatory matters and internal investigations of trading practices.
**Career:** Leader of the firm's Energy Group.
**Personal:** AB, University of North Carolina (1970); SM, Massachusetts Institute of Technology (1972); JD Harvard University (1975), senior editor, Harvard Law Review.

### AHARI, Leslie
Ross Dixon & Bell LLP, Washington, DC
202 662 2000
*Recommended in Insurance*

### ALBERG, James L
Pillsbury Winthrop Shaw Pittman LLP,
Washington, DC 202 663 9123
James.Alberg@pillsburylaw.com
*Recommended in Technology*

**Practice Areas:** Mr Alberg is firm-wide leader of Pillsbury's global sourcing practice, focusing on multinational outsourcings, services agreements, software licensing and distribution, and related corporate transactions. He has over 25 years of experience in technology-related transactions. Mr Alberg's practice consists of representing purchasers in structuring large-scale multinational commercial information technology and other business process outsourcing transactions, with particular emphasis in the financial services market.
**Prof. Memberships:** District of Columbia, New York, and Massachusetts Bars; Registered Foreign Lawyer in England.
**Personal:** JD, Boston University School of Law, 1977; BA, Political Science and Computer Science, Union College, 1974 (cum laude).

### ALBERTS, Sam J
White & Case LLP, Washington, DC
202 626 3600
salberts@whitecase.com
*Recommended in Bankruptcy*

**Practice Areas:** Concentrates on financial restructuring, Chapter 11 bankruptcies, healthcare restructurings, cross-border issues and creditor committees. Frequent speaker on insolvency issues.
**Prof. Memberships:** American Bankruptcy Institute; INSOL; Walter Chandler Inns of Court; Maryland and Virgina Bankruptcy Bars.
**Career:** Admitted: District of Columbia, Virginia and Washington (all courts); Maryland (federal only); Courts of Appeal for Fourth and Ninth Circuits.
**Personal:** JD, George Washington University (1992); BA, New York University (1987).

### ALBRECHT, Virginia S
Hunton & Williams, Washington, DC
202 955 1943
valbrecht@hunton.com
*Recommended in Environment*

**Practice Areas:** Virginia Albrecht's practice focuses exclusively on environmental law and administrative law – in particular, the Clean Water Act (CWA) wetlands program, the Endangered Species Act (ESA), the National Environmental Policy Act (NEPA) and other federal regulatory programs that affect the use of land. Experience in permit negotiation, litigation of policy issues, lobbying Congress and the Administration, enforcement defense, and compliance counseling. Representative clients include development companies, agricultural and mining companies, state and local agencies, and trade associations. Extensive experience with federal environmental agencies both in Washington and in district and regional offices.

### ALDOCK, John D
Goodwin Procter LLP, Washington, DC
202 346 4000
jaldock@goodwinprocter.com
*Recommended in Litigation*

**Practice Areas:** Mr Aldock specializes in complex litigation, class actions and mass torts. Representative clients for which Mr Aldock has been lead counsel include Prudential Insurance Company of America in numerous state and federal class actions including MDL and other national class actions brought by physicians and healthcare subscribers under RICO, ERISA and state law; Arthur Andersen LLP in class actions brought under the US securities laws; and Rockwell Automation in multiple toxic tort class actions at the Rocky Flats nuclear weapons plant in Colorado and the Hanford Reservation in Washington State.
**Prof. Memberships:** CPR Institute; Panel of Distinguished Neutrals: Member; Commercial Arbitration Panel of the American Arbitration Association: Member; US District Court for the District of Columbia: Mediator; Washington Legal Clinic for the Homeless: Member of the Board of Directors; American Bar Foundation: Fellow; American College of Trial Lawyers: Fellow.
**Personal:** JD, University of Pennsylvania Law School, 1967 (cum laude); BS, Northwestern University, 1964.

### ALEXANDER, Lee
Hogan & Hartson LLP, Washington, DC
202 637 5526
laalexander@hhlaw.com
*Recommended in Energy*

**Practice Areas:** Practices energy, regulatory, environmental and appellate law. Focuses on federal regulatory and transactional energy issues, including natural gas and oil pipelines, LNG and storage facilities, and natural gas producers, as well as marketers and electric generators.
**Prof. Memberships:** Energy Bar Association.
**Career:** Partner, Dickstein Shapiro Morin & Oshinsky LLP; prior experience in a variety of positions at the Federal Energy Regulatory Commission, including Deputy Chief of Staff to the Chairman, and Interstate Commerce Commission.
**Publications:** Lectured and written extensively on energy issues.
**Personal:** University of Pittsburgh Law School (JD, 1976); Pennsylvania State University (BS, with Distinction, 1973).

### AMBLER, Diane
Kirkpatrick & Lockhart Nicholson
Graham LLP, Washington, DC
202 778 9000
*Recommended in Investment Management*

### ANDERSON, James E
WilmerHale, Washington, DC
202 663 6180
james.anderson@wilmerhale.com
*Recommended in Investment Management*

**Practice Areas:** Advises and represents investment advisors, broker-dealers, banks, mutual funds and other investment companies on investment advisor, investment company and broker-dealer regulatory and compliance issues; on

related issues pertaining to pension plans and other types of retirement accounts; in investigations and proceedings brought by the Securities and Exchange Commission; and in civil litigation.
**Publications:** Co-author, 'Investment Advisers: Law & Compliance', a leading treatise on investment advisor regulation; contributing author, 'Mutual Fund Regulation', a treatise on investment company regulation.
**Personal:** Brigham Young University, J Reuben Clark Law School (JD 1992); University of Utah (BA 1988).

## ANDREWS, Walter J
Hunton & Williams, McLean
703 714 7400
*Recommended in Insurance*
**Practice Areas:** Contract and insurance coverage litigation and counseling. Represent insurers in coverage and bad faith disputes involving business interruption, construction defect, reinsurance, e-commerce issues, and other emerging claims. Matters involve a variety of insurance contracts, including professional liability, first party property, and general liability insurance policies. Represent clients in contract matters, particularly those involving technology disputes. Extensive experience in trial and appellate courts nationwide as well as reinsurance arbitrations.
**Prof. Memberships:** ABA, Section of Litigation, Division Director; FDCC; DRI; IADC; admitted to practice in Virginia and the District of Columbia and pro hac vice in 39 states.

## ANDRIL, David T
Vinson & Elkins LLP, Washington, DC
202 639 6542
dandril@velaw.com
*Recommended in Energy*
**Practice Areas:** Practice concentrates on natural gas and liquefied natural gas sales and transportation contracting, and regulation of the natural gas industry in the United States and overseas.
**Prof. Memberships:** Federal Energy Bar Association.
**Career:** Admitted to District of Columbia Bar in 1980. Came to the firm in 1980 and was admitted to the partnership in January 1989.

## ANGLE, Stephen
Vinson & Elkins LLP, Washington, DC
202 639 6565
sangle@velaw.com
*Recommended in Energy*
**Practice Areas:** Electric utility ratemaking, restructuring, power markets, regional transmission organizations.
**Prof. Memberships:** Energy Bar Association; American Bar Association, Section of Public Utilities, Transportation and Communication.
**Career:** Former Assistant General Counsel for Electric Lititgation, Federal Energy Regulatory Commission.

**Publications:** 'Implications of the Energy Policy Act of 2005', Oil & Gas Journal, September 2005; Public Utilities Fortnightly, August 2005; 'Independent Transmission Companies: The For-Profit ISO Alternative in the Quest for Competitive Markets', Energy Law Journal, 19 (2) (1998).
**Personal:** University of Texas Law School (JD, 1974); Texas Christian University (BA, 1971).

## ANTALICS, Michael
O'Melveny & Myers LLP, Washington, DC
202 383 5300
mantalics@omm.com
*Recommended in Antitrust*
**Practice Areas:** Mike Antalics has been a Partner in O'Melveny & Myers' Washington, DC office since leaving the Federal Trade Commission, where he served as Deputy Director in the Bureau of Competition from 2000-01, as Assistant Director for Mergers from 1997-99, and as Assistant Director for Non-Merger Litigation from 1991-97. He was twice named the FTC's outstanding litigator and received the Distinguished Service Award, the agency's highest honor. Since joining O'Melveny, he has represented corporations facing criminal investigations by the DOJ, merging firms before the FTC and DOJ, and has litigated antitrust class actions in federal and state courts.

## ARP, D Jarrett
Gibson, Dunn & Crutcher LLP, Washington, DC 202 955 8678
jarp@gibsondunn.com
*Recommended in Antitrust*
**Practice Areas:** Specializes in antitrust counseling and complex litigation defending domestic and international clients before US courts. Significant experience with respect to civil and criminal government antitrust investigations and a wide range of industries.
**Career:** Partner since 2002; Adjunct Professor of Law, Washington & Lee Law School, 2002-05; Captain, US Army's 101st Airborne Division, 1992-94.
**Publications:** Author/editor of numerous books, chapters, articles and papers on domestic and international antitrust law.
**Personal:** JD, College of William & Mary, 1991; BA, Wheaton College, 1988.

## ASMAR, Charles
McManus Schor Asmar & Darden, L.L.P., Washington, DC 202 296 9260
*Recommended in Construction*

## ATTANASIO, Donna
Dewey Ballantine LLP, Washington, DC
202 429 2372
dattanasio@deweyballantine.com
*Recommended in Energy*
**Practice Areas:** Ms Attanasio practices in the Energy Group, working closely with the project finance, bankruptcy and

litigation groups with respect to energy matters. Ms Attanasio's practice consists of counseling and representing electric utilities; developers of independent generation and their lenders and investors; energy marketers; transmission providers; and other integrated and disaggregated utility service providers with respect to matters arising under the Federal Power Act, the Public Utility Regulatory Policies Act, and the Public Utility Holding Company Act.
**Career:** Partner, Dewey Ballantine LLP.
**Personal:** Born February 22, 1959. AB, Smith College, 1981. JD, Harvard Law School, 1988.

## ATTRIDGE, Daniel F
Kirkland & Ellis LLP, Washington, DC
202 879 5012
dattridge@kirkland.com
*Recommended in Intellectual Property*
**Practice Areas:** Mr Attridge has practiced in Kirkland's Washington office since 1980 and chaired the office's operations committee since 1998. He is an experienced trial and appellate lawyer who has litigated cases before federal and state courts, administrative agencies, and arbitration panels throughout the United States. His cases have involved a wide range of industries and practice areas, including intellectual property (patents, trade secrets, trademarks, false advertising), antitrust, contracts, insurance, and corporate/securities.
**Personal:** University of Pennsylvania (BA, 1976); Georgetown University Law Center (JD, 1979).

## AUERBACH, Dennis B
Covington & Burling, Washington, DC
202 662 5226
dauerbach@cov.com
*Recommended in Bankruptcy*
**Practice Areas:** Dennis Auerbach is Of Counsel to the firm, specializing in commercial, bankruptcy, and white-collar litigation. Major matters handled in recent years include representation of clients on breach of fiduciary duty claims arising out of corporate bankruptcies; charges of financial fraud; preference/fraudulent transfer claims; and complex contract disputes. In addition to this broad litigation practice, he represents clients in a variety of corporate bankruptcy matters.
**Personal:** BA (1984) from Princeton University, and JD (1989) from Harvard Law School.

## AVIL, Richard
Jones Day, Washington, DC
202 879 5401
rdavil@jonesday.com
*Recommended in Energy*
**Practice Areas:** His practice is focused on regulatory counseling of energy delivery and power companies, other energy companies, and service companies on matters including rates, new services, competition, and regulatory compliance.

He is experienced in the regulatory components of mergers, acquisitions, and other transactions in the energy industry. His practice also concentrates on administrative and appellate litigation at the state and federal level. Listed in 'Who's Who' in America and 'Who's Who' in the World.
**Prof. Memberships:** Energy Bar Association.

## BAACH, Martin
Baach Robinson & Lewis PLLC, Washington, DC 202 833 8900
*Recommended in Insurance*

## BACHMAN, Gary
Van Ness Feldman PC, Washington, DC
202 298 1800
*Recommended in Energy*

## BAER, Teresa
Latham & Watkins LLP, Washington, DC
202 637 2200
*Recommended in Telecom, Broadcast & Satellite*

## BAER, William
Arnold & Porter LLP, Washington, DC
202 942 5936
William.Baer@aporter.com
*Recommended in Antitrust*
**Practice Areas:** Heads Arnold & Porter LLP's highly regarded Antitrust Practice. Splits his time between Arnold & Porter's DC and Brussels offices.
**Career:** Represents clients on a wide range of high stakes issues, including mergers and joint ventures, antitrust and intellectual property litigation and cartel investigations by DOJ's Antitrust Division and other competition authorities. From 1995-99, he served as Director of the Federal Trade Commission's Bureau of Competition. Among other matters he oversaw the Commission's successful court challenges to the Staples/Office Depot and drug wholesaler mergers, review of Time Warner's acquisition of Turner Broadcasting System and the Ciba-Geigy/Sandoz merger, as well as challenges to exclusionary tactics of Toys R Us, Intel and Mylan Laboratories. Practiced law at Arnold & Porter from 1980-95, where he helped secure the 1994 acquittal of the General Electric Company on criminal price fixing charges. He also served at the Federal Trade Commission from 1975-80, where he held a number of positions, including attorney advisor to the Chairman, and Assistant General Counsel and Director of Congressional Relations.
**Publications:** 'Taking Stock: Recent Trends in U.S. Merger Enforcement'; 'Transatlantic Tension'; 'Competition Leniency'; 'Solving Competition Problems in Merger Control: The Requirements for an Effective Divestiture Remedy'; 'Item 4(c): The Next Step in HSR Reform Education'.
**Personal:** Mr Baer holds a JD from Stan-

ford Law School (1975) and a BA from Lawrence University (1972). Mr Baer is repeatedly recognized by Chambers & Partners and other organizations as one of the leading competition lawyers in the US.

### BAGNALL, Robert G
WilmerHale, Washington, DC
202 663 6974
robert.bagnall@wilmerhale.com
*Recommended in Investment Management*
**Practice Areas:** Practice focuses on investment management regulation, concentrating on investment company and investment advisor matters.
**Career:** Served as Senior Special Counsel in the Office of Chief Counsel of the SEC's Division of Investment Management from 1995 through 1996, supervising no-action letters and special projects and serving as liaison for interpretive questions arising in disclosure review and in inspections of investment companies and investment advisers. Served as Assistant Chief of the Office of Regulatory Policy, which is responsible for rulemaking under the Investment Company Act and other federal securities laws.
**Personal:** Harvard Law School (JD 1985); Yale College (BA 1977).

### BAINE, Kevin
Williams & Connolly LLP, Washington, DC 202 434 5000
*Recommended in Media & Entertainment*

### BALDIA, Sonia
Mayer, Brown, Rowe & Maw LLP, Washington, DC 202 263 3395
sbaldia@mayerbrownrowe.com
*Recommended in Business Process Outsourcing, Technology*
**Practice Areas:** Partner in Information Technology and Outsourcing Practices. Represents national and international clients in intellectual property procurement and management as well as information technology and business process outsourcing transactions, particularly involving India.
**Career:** Joined Mayer, Brown, Rowe & Maw LLP in 2001. Prior to that, served as a consultant to the US Agency for International Development and the US Department of Commerce advising foreign governments on IT, telecommunications, e-commerce, and IP-related development projects and as adjunct faculty in IP law at George Washington University. She is the author of a number of published articles as well as a contributor to IP-related books published by Kluwer Law International.
**Personal:** George Washington University, SJD, 1998. University of Georgia, LLM, 1992. University of Delhi (India), LLB, 1991. Punjabi University (India), BS, 1987.

### BALIS, Stanley
Miller, Balis & O'Neil, PC, Washington, DC 202 296 2960
*Recommended in Energy*

### BAND, Ian P
Hunton & Williams, Washington, DC
202 955 1913
iband@hunton.com
*Recommended in Immigration*
**Practice Areas:** Mr Band's practice focuses exclusively on business immigration law. He has in-depth experience providing legal services and counseling in all aspects of business immigration law to corporate and individual clients. Mr Band represents businesses and individuals before the US Citizenship and Immigration Services, the Department of Labor, the State Department, Department of Homeland Security and US consular offices. He counsels corporations on compliance with the Immigration Reform and Control Act of 1986 and represents corporations before the Office of Special Counsel and the Office of the Chief Administrative Hearing Officer.

### BANKS, Jim
Hogan & Hartson LLP, Washington, DC
202 637 5802
jtbanks@hhlaw.com
*Recommended in Environment*
**Practice Areas:** Environmental, including audits and compliance programs, Clean Water Act issues (also wetlands), water resources, NEPA, enforcement and debarment defense, hazardous waste, solid waste and superfund issues.
**Career:** 1996-present, Hogan & Hartson, Partner; prior to joining Hogan, served for 10 years in the private sector after a decade as a public-interest environmental lawyer; positions included General Counsel of Chemical Waste Management, Inc.; senior attorney/Director of Clean Water Project, Natural Resources Defense Council; staff attorney, US Marine Mammal Commission.
**Personal:** University of Michigan Law School (JD, 1975); University of Kansas (BS, CE, 1972).

### BARBASH, Barry
Willkie Farr & Gallagher LLP, Washington, DC 202 303 1201
bbarbash@willkie.com
*Recommended in Investment Management*
**Practice Areas:** Partner in the Corporate and Financial Services Department and Head of the firm's Asset Management Practice Group. A former Director of the Securities and Exchange Commission's Division of Investment Management, he has built a diverse asset management practice covering all aspects of the business. He regularly advises mutual fund and hedge fund clients on a variety of transactional, compliance and regulatory matters. His areas of expertise include mutual fund operations and reg-

ulation, hedge fund formation, operations and regulation, private equity fund structuring and financing, venture capital fund operations and offerings, and independent reviews and investigations. He also regularly represents buyers and sellers in asset management merger and acquisition transactions. He has particular expertise in the area of investment management business operations. He is often sought to conduct detailed reviews of clients' investment management, administrative and marketing operations and to assist in the development of policies and procedures intended to enable them to meet their fiduciary and other legal obligations. He is also frequently called upon to assist clients in responding to actions of regulators, such as examinations, inspections and enforcement proceedings. Recent significant matters include representing Legg Mason, Inc. in its $3.7 billion acquisition of the significant portion of the asset management business of Citigroup, and Marsh & McLennan in its independent review of the compliance operations of its subsidiary, Putnam Investments.
**Prof. Memberships:** Admitted to the Bars of the District of Columbia, New York and Massachusetts. Member of the New York, Massachusetts and American Bar Associations. He is also a Member of the Program Committee of the Investment Company Institute's Mutual Funds and Investment Management Conference, and a Member of the Advisory Board of Board IQ. Serves as Co-Chairman of the Practising Law Institute and the Investment Management Institute. He was awarded the Presidential Distinguished Rank Award for exceptional achievement during his SEC tenure while a member of the Senior Executive Service of the United States.
**Career:** Previously served as the Director of the SEC's Division of Investment Management, where he was among the most senior financial services regulators in the United States, with principal oversight for the multi-trillion dollar mutual fund industry. During his tenure as Division Director, he played a central role in a number of well-publicized SEC initiatives and completed a number of substantial rulemaking and interpretive projects.
**Personal:** Received a JD from Cornell University Law School in 1978, and an AB (summa cum laude) from Bowdoin College in 1975.

### BARCELLA, E Lawrence
Paul, Hastings, Janofsky & Walker LLP, Washington, DC 202 551 4700
*Recommended in Litigation*

### BARKER, James
Latham & Watkins LLP, Washington, DC
202 637 2200
*Recommended in Telecom, Broadcast & Satellite*

### BARNETT, Robert
Williams & Connolly LLP, Washington, DC 202 434 5000
*Recommended in Media & Entertainment*

### BARRY, Dennis M
Vinson & Elkins LLP, Washington, DC
202 639 6791
dbarry@velaw.com
*Recommended in Healthcare*
**Practice Areas:** Healthcare, medicare and medicaid, compliance.
**Prof. Memberships:** Healthcare Financial Management Association (HFMA), past President Washington Metro chapter; American Health Lawyers Association (AHLA), Chair, Medicare and Medicaid Institute, member, Board of Directors.
**Career:** Ohio Wesleyan University, BA economics, 1972 (Phi Beta Kappa); University of Virginia School of Law, JD, 1975 (co-editor, Virginia Journal of International Law).
**Publications:** Dennis Barry's Reimbursement Advisor, monthly newsletter published by Aspen Publishers; Cost Reimbursement (AHLA Health Law Practice Guide), Chpt 15 (West 2004); Legal Issues Surrounding Hospital and Physician Relationships, Health Care Fraud and Abuse: Practical Perspectives (ABA & BNA 2003).

### BASILE, Edward
King & Spalding LLP, Washington, DC
202 626 2903
EBasile@KSLAW.com
*Recommended in Healthcare*
**Practice Areas:** FDA/healthcare with over 25 years of experience interpreting the laws and regulations of the Food and Drug Administration.
**Prof. Memberships:** The District of Columbia Bar.
**Personal:** BSME, Lafayette College, 1969; JD, George Washington University, 1972.

### BASTIANELLI, Adrian
Peckar, Abramson, Bastianelli & Kelley, Washington, DC 202 293 8815
bastianelli@govconlaw.com
*Recommended in Construction*
**Practice Areas:** Mr Bastianelli has practiced law almost exclusively on construction related matters for over 33 years. He has extensive experience with Federal Government construction contracts. He also has an active ADR practice and regularly serves as a mediator, arbitrator, and DRB member.
**Prof. Memberships:** Mr Bastianelli has held leadership positions in professional organizations including: Fellow, Board of Governors, and Co-Chair of the ADR Committee of the American College of Construction Lawyers; Governing Committee for the ABA Forum on the Construction Industry; President of the Washington Building Congress; editor of

The Construction Lawyer, Construction Advisory Council for Thomson/West; and regional representative for the DRB Foundation. He is also a member of the Government Contracts, Dispute Resolution, Tort and Insurance Practice (Fidelity and Surety Law), and Litigation Sections of the ABA.

**Career:** Mr Bastianelli is a member of Peckar, Abramson, Bastianelli & Kelley, LLP in Washington, DC. He has been a name Partner in a law firm for 27 years. He began his career as a civil engineer with the Corps of Engineers. He served as a law clerk with the US Court of Claims.

**Publications:** Mr Bastianelli was the editor and associate editor of The Construction Lawyer for seven years and has been selected as Editor-in-Chief for the new law journal for the American College of Construction Lawyers. He was the editor and a chapter author for Federal Government Construction Contracts, a book published by the ABA Forum on the Construction Industry. He wrote chapters for State by State Guide to Construction Contracts, New York Construction Law, and Construction Claims Deskbook. He has published numerous articles on construction law, Government contracts, and ADR topics for the ABA, Federal Publications, and the DRB Foundation.

**Personal:** Mr Bastianelli received his BSCE from Purdue University and his JD from the University of Louisville. He obtained his professional engineers license in Kentucky (inactive).

## BAUMBUSCH, Peter L
Gibson, Dunn & Crutcher LLP, Washington, DC 202 955 8530
pbaumbusch@gibsondunn.com
*Recommended in Tax*

**Practice Areas:** Provided tax advice relating to the acquisition of over $10 billion in US and foreign corporate and real estate transactions. Provides advice to hedge funds and with respect to multi-jurisdictional option and compensation programs.

**Prof. Memberships:** Former Chair of the ABA Tax Section Committee on Foreign Activities of US Taxpayers.

**Publications:** Has lectured on international taxation, tax shelters, transfer pricing and cost sharing. Primary draftsperson of ABA 'White Paper on Section 482 Intercompany Pricing', and assisted Senator Bill Bradley in developing tax reform proposals.

**Personal:** JD, Harvard Law School, 1972, Harvard Law Review and Board of Student Advisors.

## BAUMGARTEN, Jon
Proskauer Rose LLP, Washington, DC
202 416 6810
jabaumgarten@proskauer.com
*Recommended in Intellectual Property*

**Practice Areas:** He is widely recognized

as one of the United States' leading domestic and international intellectual property lawyers, with particular emphasis in copyright matters. Emphasis on domestic and international copyright, licensing, contract, litigation and related matters pertaining to the publishing, computer, motion picture, music and recording, communications, arts and Internet communities. He anchored the firm's trial and appellate teams in precedent setting cases under the US Copyright Act and Digital millennium Copyright Amendments (DMCA), and regularly counsels teams of business persons and technologists in the development and formulation of cross-industry technical standards and DRM solutions for content protection. He served as General Counsel of the United States Copyright Office.

**Prof. Memberships:** Serves on several bar association committees on copyright and is past Chair of the Committee on International Copyright of the Section of Patent, Trademark and Copyright Law of the American Bar Association. He has served on the Editorial Boards of the Journal of the Copyright Society of the USA; the Advisory Boards of the Patent, Trademark and Copyright Journal, World Intellectual Property Report, Computer Lawyer and Journal of Proprietary Rights, and was a founding director of the American Copyright Council, the Computer Law Association, the DC Computer Law Forum and Washington Area Lawyers for the Arts.

**Career:** From his admission to the Bar in 1968 until January 1976, and since June 1979, from January 1976 through May 1979, Jon served as General Counsel of the United States Copyright Office. During this period, he was a leading participant in the formulation of the new Copyright Act, was responsible for the preparation of Copyright Office regulations and practices under the new law, represented the Copyright Office before courts and Congressional committees and represented the United States Government in international copyright fora.

**Publications:** Author of numerous articles and a book entitled 'US-USSR Copyright Relations Under the Universal Copyright Convention'.

**Personal:** City College of the City University of New York, BA, 1964. New York University School of Law, LLB, 1967; research editor, New York University Law Review, 1966-67.

## BAXTER, Michael St Patrick
Covington & Burling, Washington, DC
202 662 5164
mbaxter@cov.com
*Recommended in Bankruptcy*

**Practice Areas:** Practice includes advising creditors, debtors and official committees in bankruptcy reorganization, workouts and restructurings. He has been

involved in many notable bankruptcy cases, including US Airways, Congoleum, Worldcom, and Mirant.

**Prof. Memberships:** American Law Institute; American College of Bankruptcy; International Insolvency Institute; Vice-Chair, ABA Business Bankruptcy Committee.

**Career:** Covington, 1983 to present. Adjunct Professor, George Washington University Law School.

**Publications:** Contributing editor, 'Norton Bankruptcy Law and Practice 2d'. He has published extensively in the insolvency area and is a frequent speaker at professional programs.

**Personal:** LLM, Harvard Law School, 1983; LLB, University of Western Ontario, 1979.

## BECKER, Brandon
WilmerHale, Washington, DC
202 663 6979
brandon.becker@wilmerhale.com
*Recommended in Investment Management*

**Practice Areas:** Co-Chair, Securities Department; advises broker-dealers and financial market participants regarding transactional and compliance matters, development of financial products and trading systems.

**Prof. Memberships:** Chair, Subcommittee on Market Regulation, Federal Regulation of Securities Committee, American Bar Association; Board of Advisers, Center for the Study of Securities Markets.

**Career:** Lawyer at SEC; Director, SEC's Division of Market Regulation; President's Working Group on Financial Markets; Financial Products Advisory Committee of the Commodity Futures Trading Commission; SEC's representative to Secondary Markets Working Party of International Organization of Securities Commissions.

**Personal:** LLM Columbia University; JD University of San Diego; BA University of Minnesota.

## BEHRENDS IV, Samuel
LeBoeuf, Lamb, Greene & MacRae LLP, Washington, DC 202 986 8018
sbehrend@llgm.com
*Recommended in Energy*

**Practice Areas:** Has represented utilities before the Federal Energy Regulatory Commission, the Nuclear Regulatory Commission, and state commissions in various matters involving traditional rate cases, mergers and acquisitions, transmission both before and after open access, power marketing and code of conduct issues, qualified facilities and independent power producers. His present clients include, among others, power marketers and independent energy producers.

**Prof. Memberships:** American Bar Association; Energy Bar Association; District of Columbia Bar.

**Career:** Joined LeBoeuf Lamb in 1982;

Reid & Priest, Washington, DC (1979-82).

**Personal:** Wake Forest University (JD) 1979; Harvard University (BA) 1974.

## BELL, Joseph C
Hogan & Hartson LLP, Washington, DC
202 637 5780
jcbell@hhlaw.com
*Recommended in Energy*

**Practice Areas:** Oil and economic development; energy regulation and policy; project and international finance; international transactions (energy and non-energy); special expertise with respect to Poland.

**Prof. Memberships:** Council on Foreign Relations; Polish American Freedom Foundation (Founding Director); International Senior Lawyers Project (Director); Revenue Watch (Advisory Board); International Bar Association; Energy Bar Association; ABA (International, Administrative and Business Sections).

**Career:** 1969-70 Cabinet Task Force on Oil Import Control, attorney; 1970-72 US Department of Justice, attorney advisor, Antitrust Division; 1972-74 Duke University Law School and Institute for Public Policy, assistant professor; 1974-77 Federal Energy Administration, Assistant General Counsel, International and Special Programs; 1979-89, Citizens Energy Corporation, Outside General Counsel; 1989-90, Special Counsel to Ministry of Finance, Poland; 1977-present Hogan & Hartson, Partner; 2003-05, pro bono adviser to Sao Tome and Principe regarding Oil Revenue Management law.

**Publications:** 'Sao Tome and Principe Enacts Oil Revenue Law, Sets New Governance, Transparency, and Accountability Standards for Industry'. OGEL, Vol. 3 Issue 1 (March 2005); 'Systematic Risk Factors in Russian and Eurasia', Russian-Eurasian Renaissance? (2003); 'Legal Issues in Resource Management Laws. Escaping the Resource Curse' (Columbia Univ, forthcoming 2006).

**Personal:** Yale Law School (JD, 1968, Yale Law Journal); Harvard University (MA, Economics, 1965); University of Colorado (BA, summa cum laude, 1962).

## BELL, Robert B
WilmerHale, Washington, DC
202 663 6533
robert.bell@wilmerhale.com
*Recommended in Antitrust*

**Practice Areas:** Has extensive experience in securing antitrust clearance for mergers and acquisitions from both the Department of Justice and the Federal Trade Commission. Practice includes antitrust litigation, both criminal and civil; merger clearance; and antitrust counseling on issues ranging from competitor collaborations to vertical distribution arrangements. Has represented clients from a wide variety of sectors, including imaging, communications,

defense, entertainment, manufacturing, mining, chemicals and transportation.
**Publications:** Articles have appeared in Antitrust, Global Competition Review (March 2003, p 9), Legal Times, and National Law Journal.
**Personal:** Stanford Law School (JD 1980); Cambridge University (MA 1977); Dartmouth College (BA 1975).

### BELLER, Herbert N
Sutherland Asbill & Brennan LLP, Washington, DC 202 383 0120
herb.beller@sablaw.com
*Recommended in Tax*
**Practice Areas:** Transactional tax planning, including acquisitions, dispositions, spin-offs and other restructurings involving domestic and foreign entities. IRS National Office and Treasury matters. Tax controversy matters at administrative and judicial levels. Representation of private foundations, public charities and other non-profit entities.
**Prof. Memberships:** Chair, American Bar Association Section of Taxation (2002-03). Editor-in-Chief, The Tax Lawyer, (1993-96). Co-Chair, National Conference of Lawyers and CPAs (2000-06). Regent, American College of Tax Counsel (2003-06). Trustee, American Tax Policy Institute (2003-05). Fellow, American Bar Foundation.
**Personal:** JD, cum laude, Northwestern University School of Law, 1967. BSBA, Northwestern University, 1964. Law clerk to US Tax Court Judge Theodore Tannenwald, Jr (1967-68). Certified Public Accountant. Listed in 'Best Lawyers in America', 'International Who's Who of Corporate Tax Advisers', and 'International Tax Review's Guide to the World's Leading Tax Advisers'.

### BENACH, Andres
Maggio & Kattar PC, Washington, DC 202 483 0053
*Recommended in Immigration*

### BENNETT, Alan
Ropes & Gray LLP, Washington, DC 202 508 4604
alan.bennett@ropesgray.com
*Recommended in Healthcare*
**Practice Areas:** Serves as outside counsel to pharmaceutical and biotechnology firms, with particular emphasis on issues within the jurisdiction of the Food and Drug Administration (FDA). Regularly lectures and publishes extensively on FDA-related issues. Represents clients before Congress and the FDA on issues including pharmaceutical promotion and compliance, exclusivity and lifecycle management, follow-on biologics, procedures to switch drugs from prescription to non-prescription status and food additive approvals.
**Career:** District of Columbia Bar; New York State Bar; Partner, Bennett, Turner & Coleman; Partner, Ropes & Gray.
**Personal:** JD, Columbia Law School,

Harlan Fiske Stone Scholar; BA, University of Connecticut.

### BENNETT, Robert S
Skadden, Arps, Slate, Meagher & Flom LLP & Affiliates, Washington, DC 202 371 7180
rbennett@skadden.com
*Recommended in Litigation*
**Practice Areas:** Heads Skadden's International Government Enforcement Group. Leads Civil and Criminal Litigation Practice in the Washington, DC office. Has tried several high profile cases. Represents corporations, directors and officers in criminal, civil and SEC enforcement matters. Advises management and boards on preventive and remedial measures. Assists boards and audit committees in conducting internal investigations. Represents corporations and officers and directors in complex civil and criminal matters and qui tam actions. Has extensive experience representing clients before Congressional committees.
**Career:** LLM, Harvard Law School, 1965; LLB, Georgetown Law Center, 1964; University of Virginia Law School, 1961-62; BA, Georgetown University, 1961.

### BERGESON, Lynn
Bergeson & Campbell PC, Washington, DC 202 557 3801
lbergeson@lawbc.com
*Recommended in Environment*
**Practice Areas:** Regulatory, litigation, and science policy issues associated with chemicals and emerging transformative technologies, including TSCA, FIFRA, and the nanobio interface.
**Prof. Memberships:** Chair, ABA Section of Environment, Energy, and Resources (2005-06); Member, Board of Directors, Environmental Law Institute; ANSI Nanotechnology Standards Panel Steering Committee; Editorial Board, The Environmental Forum, Pesticide & Toxic Chemical News, Environmental Quality Management, EPA Administrative Law Reporter, and Pollution Prevention Review, among others. Member of the District of Columbia Bar; Bar Association of the District of Columbia; Women's Bar Association of the District of Columbia; The Cosmos Club.
**Career:** Has practiced chemicals regulation and occupational safety and health law since 1980.
**Publications:** Selected publications include 'Selected Challenges in Applying Toxicogenomic Data in Federal Regulatory Settings' (2005); 'The TSCA Basic Practice Book,' ABA (2000); 'The FIFRA Basic Practice Book', ABA (2000); 'Pesticides Law Handbook', Government Institutes (1999); Avoiding Liability for Hazardous Waste: RCRA, CERCLA and Related Corporate Law Issues, BNA, Corporate Practice Series (1999).
**Personal:** Columbus School of Law,

Catholic University of America (Member, Law Review); Michigan State University (BA, magna cum laude).

### BERLIN, Kenneth
Skadden, Arps, Slate, Meagher & Flom LLP & Affiliates, Washington, DC 202 371 7350
kberlin@skadden.com
*Recommended in Environment*
**Practice Areas:** Heads the firm's Environmental Practice. Has extensive background in representing clients analyzing environmental issues in business transactions and in environmental litigation, including representing parties in environmental cleanup, bankruptcy, criminal and civil penalty cases, and arguing cases in federal appeals court. Has significant experience in representing clients in connection with environmental issues at controversial facilities, dealing with environmental and community groups, trading and developing emission credits, including greenhouse gas credits, and preparing complex environmental impact assessments.
**Prof. Memberships:** Former Chairman of the Board of the Environmental Law Institute (2003-05); Chairman of the Board of the American Bird Conservancy; Member of the Board, Center for International Environmental Law.
**Career:** JD, Columbia Law School, 1973; BA, University of Pennsylvania, 1969.

### BERMAN, Kenneth
Debevoise & Plimpton LLP, Washington, DC 202 383 8000
*Recommended in Investment Management*

### BERNER, Frederic
Sidley Austin LLP, Washington, DC 202 736 8232
fberner@sidley.com
*Recommended in Energy*
**Practice Areas:** Partner in Washington, DC. Has served as lead counsel for many partnerships and joint ventures of energy companies in the development of major energy projects such as the Millennium Pipeline Project and the Great Plains Coal Gasification Project. He has represented a broad spectrum of clients in the litigation of energy issues before federal and state commissions and courts. Mr Berner has prepared and negotiated hundreds of construction, supply and transportation agreements.
**Personal:** The George Washington University Law School (JD, 1973); American University (MBA, 1970); Middlebury College (BA, 1965). Admission: District of Columbia, 1973.

### BERNIUS, Robert
Nixon Peabody LLP, Washington, DC 202 585 8312
rbernius@nixonpeabody.com
*Recommended in Media & Entertainment*

**Practice Areas:** Litigation for corporate clients in libel, discrimination, general commercial, and internet-related cases.
**Prof. Memberships:** Admitted to practice in New York, Maryland, DC, US Supreme Court, US Courts of Appeals (Second, Third, Fourth, Sixth, Ninth, Tenth, Eleventh, DC Circuits), US District Courts (Eastern, Northern, Southern, Western Districts of NY; DC; MD, Colo.). Chair, Professional Standards Committee. Advisory Board, Media Law Reporter. Formerly Managing Partner, Washington, DC, office. Former assistant DA, Brooklyn, New York. Fellow, American College of Trial Lawyers.
**Publications:** Lectures on First Amendment issues throughout US.
**Personal:** Yale Law School, JD; Brown University, ScBEE, magna cum laude.

### BERNSTEIN, Michael
Arnold & Porter LLP, Washington, DC 202 942 5577
Michael.Bernstein@aporter.com
*Recommended in Bankruptcy*
**Practice Areas:** Michael Bernstein represents parties in bankruptcy and workout matters, and in related litigation throughout the United States.
**Prof. Memberships:** American Bankruptcy Institute; ABA Business Bankruptcy Committee; Walter Chandler American Inn of Court.
**Career:** Mr Bernstein has been involved in bankruptcy and insolvency matters in many industries, including telecommunications, energy, real estate, finance, manufacturing, technology, retail, airline, healthcare, and pharmaceuticals. His clients have included America Online, American Capital Strategies, American Red Cross, Ardent Communications Creditors' Committee, BB&T, Bear Stearns, Boehringer Ingelheim, Cingular Wireless, CRIIMI Mae Creditors' Committee, Dynex Bondholders Committee, Gate Gourmet, Guinness Import Company, Health Care REIT, Lennar Partners, Major League Baseball, Perseus LLC, Sodexho, Texas Pacific Group and The George Washington University, among others.
**Publications:** Mr Bernstein is co-author of 'Bankruptcy in Practice', published by the American Bankruptcy Institute. He is a member of the ABI Journal's editorial board and co-authors a monthly column on chapter 11 issues. He has also written articles, lectured on bankruptcy law topics, and been interviewed by major newspapers and on television and radio.
**Personal:** JD, Northwestern University School of Law, 1989; BA, Brandeis University, 1986.

### BERZ, David
Weil, Gotshal & Manges LLP, Washington, DC 202 682 7190
david.berz@weil.com
*Recommended in Environment*

**Practice Areas:** David Berz heads Weil Gotshal's Environmental Practice. He serves as lead counsel in civil and criminal environmental matters involving federal and state water, air, and hazardous waste and substance statutes. He routinely counsels clients regarding environmental issues that arise in mergers, acquisitions and bankruptcies. Mr Berz also has experience handling declaratory judgment cases brought to resolve insurance coverage disputes in a variety of contexts. He regularly advises multinational corporations, their senior management and boards of directors in developing environmental compliance programs, and serves as environmental counsel to several financial institutions.
**Personal:** George Washington University, BA, 1970; JD, 1973.

### BEYDA, Richard
Grossberg Yochelson Fox & Beyda, Washington, DC
202 296 9696
*Recommended in Real Estate*

### BIEKE, James R
Goodwin Procter LLP, Washington, DC
202 346 4000
jbieke@goodwinprocter.com
*Recommended in Environment*
**Practice Areas:** Mr Bieke specializes in environmental and natural resources law and policy, with a particular emphasis on complex scientific, technical, economic and legal issues. For the past 25 years, Mr Bieke has handled cases in federal and state courts and before federal and state administrative agencies. He provides advice to clients on numerous legal, technical, scientific and policy issues under the Comprehensive Environmental Response, Compensation and Liability Act (CERCLA), the Resource Conservation and Recovery Act (RCRA), the Toxic Substances Control Act (TSCA), the Clean Air Act, the Clean Water Act, and other federal and state environmental statutes and regulations.
**Personal:** LLM, New York University Law School, 1971; JD, University of Michigan Law School, 1970 (Order of the Coif); MA, University of Michigan, 1970; BA, Sacred Heart Seminary, 1967.

### BILES, Blake A
Arnold & Porter LLP, Washington, DC
202 942 5836
Blake.Biles@aporter.com
*Recommended in Environment*
**Practice Areas:** Blake Biles has provided services to business interests concerning the full range of substantive environmental requirements and virtually all types of legal matters - counseling, transactions, rulemakings, compliance audits, and enforcement and appellate litigation. He has particular expertise in the regulation of commercial chemicals and products, including toxic substances legislation, hazard communication and right-to-

know standards, biotechnology and life sciences legal frameworks, consumer product safety laws, and related product liability matters. Mr Biles also advises concerning international environmental treaties and laws.
**Prof. Memberships:** Mr Biles began his career at the US EPA, and served as the first Director of the Agency's new-chemicals notification program. In addition to his work for business interests, Mr Biles has been active in a number of American Bar Association committees and programs, and he regularly represents clients in Arnold & Porter LLP pro bono matters.
**Career:** Mr Biles served the Environmental Protection Agency, first in the Agency's Office of Water Enforcement, and then in the Office of the General Counsel. Thereafter, he was the first Director of the Premanufacture Review Division in the Office of Toxic Substances.
**Personal:** JD, University of Kansas School of Law, 1975; BA, University of Kansas, 1968.

### BLACKBURN, Thomas
Bruder Gentile & Marcoux LLP, Washington, DC 202 296 1500
*Recommended in Energy*

### BLAKE, Jonathan D
Covington & Burling, Washington, DC
202 662 5506
jblake@cov.com
*Recommended in Telecom, Broadcast & Satellite*
**Practice Areas:** Communications/media (television, broadband, cable, programmers and new media, wireless, satellite, new technologies): mergers and other transactions, legislation, litigation, and strategic counseling; international and domestic. Highlights: advises NFL and other sports leagues on media issues; advises television industry on digital transition issues; assists coalition of internet service providers on net neutrality issues; counsel on innovative satellite licensing projects; advises on various new media projects.
**Prof. Memberships:** Federal Communications Bar - President, 1984-85; ABA - Chair, 1993-99, International Telecommunications Committee.
**Career:** Former Chair of Covington's Management Committee, 1996-2001, Senior Communications Partner, Co-Head of Technology, Media and Communications Group. Clients include National Association of Broadcasters, the CBS and NBC Television Affiliate associations, the trade association for television industry on spectrum and technology issues, Public Broadcasting Service, 150 television stations, programmers, equipment manufacturers, satellite companies, internet companies, and wireless providers.

**Publications:** Numerous publications.
**Personal:** Yale University (LLB, 1964; BA 1960 Phi Beta Kappa); Oxford University (MA in Law; Rhodes Scholar); editor of Yale Law Journal (1963-64).

### BLASZAK, James S
Levine, Blaszak, Block & Boothby LLP, Washington, DC 202 857 2541
jblaszak@lb3law.com
*Recommended in Telecom, Broadcast & Satellite*
**Practice Areas:** Specialization is evaluating, negotiating and documenting telecommunications service contracts for buyers of such services. He has advised purchasers in connection with scores of those agreements, as well as customized agreements for cellular, frame relay, and satellite services. Among the clients he has assisted are numerous Fortune 100 companies. Also has participated in complex rate and regulatory cases, and has prosecuted applications for radio licenses and operating authority and satellite system authorizations. He has counseled clients on a wide range of matters implicating federal and state telecommunications laws. He is counsel to the Ad Hoc Telecommunications Users Committee, whose members are among the largest purchasers of communications services.
**Prof. Memberships:** Member of the District of Columbia Bar and the Federal Communications Bar Association.
**Career:** Partner at Gardner, Carton and Douglas before joining Levine, Blaszak, Block & Boothby as a Partner. Before entering private practice, he served in a variety of positions at the Federal Communications Commission, including Chief of the Domestic Facilities and Satellite Branch and legal advisor to the Chief, Common Carrier Bureau. Graduated from the University of Texas School of Law.

### BLOCH, Robert E
Mayer, Brown, Rowe & Maw LLP, Washington, DC 202 263 3203
rbloch@mayerbrownrowe.com
*Recommended in Antitrust*
**Practice Areas:** Represents major corporations and officials in criminal and civil investigations before Antitrust Division and FTC for price fixing, bid rigging, boycotts and mergers; defense of private class action litigation in federal and state courts. Antitrust counsel in major mergers/acquisitions and joint ventures. Recent antitrust class action defenses: Bertelsmann, Inc. (In Re Compact Disc Antitrust Litigation and Compact Disc Minimum-Advertised Price Antitrust Litigation); ETI Explosives Technologies International, Inc.; in In Re Commercial Explosives Antitrust Litigation and defense of Cargill, Inc. in In Re Citric Acid Antitrust Litigation and In Re High Fructose Corn Syrup Antitrust Litigation. Antitrust counsel to major healthcare

companies and leading academic medical centers.
**Career:** Mayer, Brown, Rowe & Maw LLP, Washington, DC, 1993-date; Partner. Antitrust Division, US Department of Justice: Chief Professions and Intellectual Property Section, 1988-93; Assistant Chief, Litigation I, 1985-88; Assistant Chief, Trial Section, 1981-85; trial attorney, 1975-81. Assistant Attorney General, Office of the Attorney General of Ohio, Antitrust Section, 1973-75.
**Publications:** Writes and speaks extensively on antitrust issues.
**Personal:** JD (honors) George Washington University, 1973. BA, Franklin and Marshall College, 1969. John Marshall Award, 1992. US Department of Justice: The Harold M Stevens Award for Outstanding Service, 1993.

### BLOCK, Joseph
Venable LLP, Washington, DC
202 962 4800
*Recommended in Environment*

### BOOTHBY, Colleen
Levine, Blaszak, Block & Boothby LLP, Washington, DC 202 857 2550
cboothby@lb3law.com
*Recommended in Telecom, Broadcast & Satellite*
**Practice Areas:** Represents enterprise customers, IT companies, and associations (including IBM, Microsoft, First Data, the Ad Hoc Telecommunications Users Committee, and the High Tech Broadband Coalition) before the US Federal Communications Commission and courts. Provides strategic counsel on a broad range of subjects, including the regulation of telecommunications, information services, IT products, the internet and public/private intranets; privacy, wiretapping, telemarketing, and proprietary network information; inside wire and building access; and the pricing of local exchange and interexchange services. Frequent speaker before enterprise customer groups.
**Prof. Memberships:** Federal Communications Bar Association (Co-Chair, Common Carrier Practice Committee, 1998-99). District of Columbia Bar Association (Steering Committee, Administrative Law and Agency Practice Committee, 2000-04).
**Career:** Admitted to District of Columbia Bar in 1980. Federal Communications Commission (Deputy and Associate Chief, Tariff Division; legal assistant to the Bureau Chief, Common Carrier Bureau; Senior Supervising Attorney, International and Tariff Divisions), 1983-93.
**Personal:** AB, Pomona College, 1977. JD, Boalt Hall School of Law (associate editor, California Law Review), 1980.

## BOURDEAU, Karl S
Beveridge & Diamond PC, Washington, DC 202 789 6019
kbourdeau@bdlaw.com
*Recommended in Environment*
**Practice Areas:** Practices principally in a wide range of litigation, regulatory, transactional and legislative matters involving hazardous substance and hazardous waste issues under the federal Resource Conservation and Recovery Act (RCRA), the Comprehensive Environmental Response, Compensation and Liability Act (CERCLA), and analogous state laws. Also has been active in representing clients on a variety of international environmental and federal Information Quality Act issues.
**Prof. Memberships:** American Bar Association; District of Columbia Bar Association; Federal Bar Association.
**Career:** Admitted to District of Columbia Bar (1978). Director of Beveridge & Diamond, P.C. Frequent lecturer and author on hazardous substance liability issues, and presently serves as a Co-Chairman of the Board of Advisors of the National Brownfields Association.
**Publications:** Author: 'Energy Conservation in the 94th Congress: A Solution to the Problem or Problems with the Solution?', 1 Harv Envtl L Rev 225 (1977); 'Corrective Action Requirements Under the Resource Conservation and Recovery Act', 'Environmental Risk Management – A Desk Reference', RTM Communications, Inc. (1991); co-author: 'Investing in the USA: Environmental Compliance and Liability', Law Business Research, The American Legal Yearbook (1998); co-author: 'Corrective Action Requirements', Chapter 13, The RCRA Practice Manual; author: 'Summary of Small Business Liability Relief of Brownfields Revitalization Act of 2001', Beveridge & Diamond, P.C. (2002); author: 'New Brownfields Law Will Affect Transactions of Potentially Contaminated Property', Real Estate Finance Journal (2002); author: 'Information Quality Act Challenges to Flawed Use of Science', ABA Natural Resources & Environment (2005); co-author: '25 Years of Superfund Liability: Progress Made, Progress Needed', BNA Environmental Reporter (2006).
**Personal:** JD from Harvard University (1978) and BS (summa cum laude) from Muhlenberg College (1975).

## BOWE JR, James F
Dewey Ballantine LLP, Washington, DC 202 429 1444
jbowe@deweyballantine.com
*Recommended in Energy*
**Practice Areas:** Energy (including energy project development, energy regulatory matters, energy company M&A). Project finance (US, North America, Latin America). Oil and gas law.
**Prof. Memberships:** Energy Bar Association. American Bar Association. Mem-

ber of the Bar of the District of Columbia and the bars of several federal courts.
**Career:** Admitted to practice 1982, District of Columbia. Private practice since 1982. Partner, Dewey Ballantine LLP, July 1994-present. Adjunct Professor, oil and gas law, Georgetown University Law Center, 1990-95.
**Personal:** Born May 17, 1955. BA, Williams College, 1977. JD, Northwestern University School of Law, 1982.

## BOWMAN, William
Hogan & Hartson LLP, Washington, DC 202 637 6434
wjbowman@hhlaw.com
*Recommended in Insurance, Litigation*
**Practice Areas:** Focuses principally in the area of litigation, including trial and appellate matters involving commercial, insurance coverage, environmental, contract, and product liability litigation. He has practiced actively in federal and state courts throughout the country.
**Prof. Memberships:** Member, ABA; Member, District of Columbia Bar Association.
**Career:** Former assistant US attorney for the District of Columbia; former Chief Counsel to the US Senate Judiciary Committee Subcommittee on Juvenile Justice; former law clerk for Judge Thomas A Flannery of the US District Court of the District of Columbia.
**Personal:** Georgetown University Law Center (JD).

## BRADY, Robert P
Hogan & Hartson LLP, Washington, DC 202 637 6969
rpbrady@hhlaw.com
*Recommended in Healthcare*
**Practice Areas:** Pharmaceutical and biotech product development and clinical investigation; product approvals involving New Drug Applications and Biologics License Applications; product promotion and post-approval requirements, including compliance with Good Manufacturing Practices and safety reporting; conducts regulatory due diligence in a wide array of corporate transactions.
**Career:** Former Executive Vice President, Vice President, and general counsel of the Cosmetic, Toiletry and Fragrance Association; 1981-83 served as the executive assistant to the commissioner of the FDA; 1975-81 FDA's Office of Chief Counsel served as associate chief counsel for biologics, associate chief counsel for foods, and associate chief counsel for enforcement.
**Publications:** 'Making Medicine Out of Us: Harmonizing US and EU Rules on Human-tissue Products May Help Spark New Therapies', Legal Times (6/20/2005).
**Personal:** The George Washington University Law School (JD, with honors, 1972); University of Rochester (BA, 1969).

## BRAN, Paul Bennett
Dickstein Shapiro Morin & Oshinsky LLP, Washington, DC 202 861 9144
BranP@dsmo.com
*Recommended in Bankruptcy*
**Practice Areas:** Business bankruptcy, restructurings, and out-of-court workouts, as well as state court receiverships, related proceedings, and commercial litigation in various jurisdictions across the United States.
**Prof. Memberships:** Member of the Maryland, District of Columbia, and Virginia State Bars, as well as the Bankruptcy Bar Association of the District of Maryland, American Bar Association, American Bankruptcy Institute, and Walter Chandler American Inn of Court.
**Career:** Partner since 1994.
**Personal:** Georgetown University Law Center (JD, 1985); University of Maryland (BA, 1982).

## BRANDS, Henk
Paul, Weiss, Rifkind, Wharton & Garrison LLP, Washington, DC
hbrands 202 223 7373
*Recommended in Telecom, Broadcast & Satellite*
**Practice Areas:** Henk Brands is a Partner in the Communications and Technology Department and focuses on a broad range of appellate litigation and communications issues. Mr Brands has handled matters before the Federal Communications Commission (FCC) and in federal courts across the United States. He is an Adjunct Professor of Telecommunications Law at the George Washington University Law School.

## BRASHER, Lance
Skadden, Arps, Slate, Meagher & Flom LLP & Affiliates, Washington, DC
202 371 7402
lbrasher@skadden.com
*Recommended in Projects*
**Practice Areas:** Concentrates in the development, financing, and acquisition of power, LNG and gas pipeline assets, sports facilities and other large energy and infrastructure projects. Handles major transactions involving restructurings and privatizations. Advises clients on power procurement and renewable energy matters. Represents sponsors, financial institutions, utilities, contractors and fuel suppliers in transactions in the US, Europe, Asia, Australia, South America and the Caribbean. Lecturer at project financing and energy conferences and author.
**Career:** JD, Harvard Law School, 1990 (cum laude); BS, United States Naval Academy, 1982 (with distinction).

## BRAY, John
King & Spalding LLP, Washington, DC 202 626 5618
jbray@kslaw.com
*Recommended in Litigation*
**Practice Areas:** Over 35 years' experi-

ence in civil and criminal litigation in federal district courts including: asbestos liability, federal tax, environmental, defense procurement, insurance coverage, antitrust cases, and cases presenting a host of business, financial and government regulatory issues. Has also been involved in numerous historic criminal conspiracy cases and trials throughout the US dealing with complex issues in tax, antitrust claims, international investigations, fraudulent conveyances, environmental issues and insurance coverage.
**Prof. Memberships:** Fellow of the American College of Trial Lawyers.
**Personal:** Undergraduate Degree from St Louis University and JD Degree from St Louis University School of Law.

## BRENNAN JR, John T
Crowell & Moring LLP, Washington, DC 202 624 2760
jbrennan@crowell.com
*Recommended in Healthcare*
**Practice Areas:** Chair of Crowell & Moring's Health Care Group. Focuses on healthcare fraud and abuse matters, especially relating to federal false claims, anti-kickback, and Stark Law issues. Advises on compliance matters and conducts internal investigations related to potential fraud and abuse issues.
**Prof. Memberships:** American Health Lawyers Association and American Bar Association's White Collar Crime Health Law Subcommittee; former Chair of the AHLA's Substantive Law Committee on Fraud and Abuse, Self-Referrals and False Claims.
**Career:** Voted one of the nation's top healthcare provider attorneys by Nightingales in 2004; former hospital administrator.

## BREUER, Lanny A
Covington & Burling, Washington, DC 202 662 5538
lbreuer@cov.com
*Recommended in Litigation*
**Practice Areas:** Partner and Co-Chair of Covington's White Collar Practice Group. Handles high-stakes criminal and civil litigation, including cases involving alleged fraud of all types, alleged bribery, and other cases involving political or national security issues. Widely recognized for his role representing President Clinton at the impeachment trial and in other matters and for representing other high profile individuals and corporations. Also specializes in internal corporate and congressional investigations, and matters before government agencies. Extensive experience managing complex criminal and associated civil investigations, including high profile investigations that may contain legal, political, and public relations risks.
**Career:** Returned to Covington in 1999 after two years as Special Counsel to President Clinton. Assistant District Attorney,

NY (1985-89).

**Personal:** Columbia University's School of Law (JD, 1985) and Columbia University (Bachelor's, 1980).

## BREYFOGLE, Jon

Groom Law Group, Washington, DC
202 857 0620
*Recommended in Employee Benefits*

## BRINKMANN, Beth

Morrison & Foerster LLP, Washington, DC 202 887 1544
bbrinkmann@mofo.com
*Recommended in Litigation*

**Practice Areas:** US Supreme Court and other appellate matters. Consults on complex litigation and regulatory matters. Has argued 20 cases before the Supreme Court, more than any other women currently in private practice.
**Career:** Admitted in California and District of Columbia. Assistant to Solicitor General of the United States, 1993-2001. Assistant Federal Public Defender, 1991-93. Law clerk, Justice Harry A Blackmun, US Supreme Court, 1986-87; Judge Phyllis Kravitch, Eleventh Circuit Court of Appeals, 1985-86. Named one of 12 Leading Appellate Lawyers in Washington, DC by the Legal Times.
**Personal:** AB, University of California, Berkeley; JD, Yale Law School.

## BRINKMANN, Karen

Latham & Watkins LLP, Washington, DC
202 637 2200
*Recommended in Telecom, Broadcast & Satellite*

## BROGAN, Stephen J

Jones Day, Washington, DC
202 879 3939
sjbrogan@jonesday.com
*Recommended in Litigation*

**Practice Areas:** Jones Day's Managing Partner. Extensive litigation practice, including securities, banking, contests for corporate control, corporate criminal investigations, product liability, independent counsel investigations, and qui tam actions. Matters include representing: JC Penney in a grand jury investigation; General Motors in the GM-Toyota joint venture, air bag safety, and Cadillac V8-6-4 litigation; Gillette in a takeover contest; General Electric in a grand jury defense; Bridgestone/Firestone in product liability litigation; the directors of Northrop in a grand jury investigation; Dart Group in a corporate governance dispute; and First American and First American Bankshares in investigations arising from the collapse of BCCI.

## BROSE, Steven

Steptoe & Johnson LLP, Washington, DC
202 429 6250
sbrose@steptoe.com
*Recommended in Energy*

**Practice Areas:** Head of the Regulatory and Industry Affairs Department at Steptoe & Johnson LLP and resident in the Washington office. Has more than 30 years of experience in a broad range of administrative and judicial matters, principally involving the oil and natural gas industries. Counsels numerous pipeline companies with respect to their rates, regulated practices, and business opportunities. Has also represented entities in a variety of sectors on the natural gas industry in matters involving rates, certificates, royalties and abandonments.
**Personal:** JD, Columbia University, 1972; BA, Pennsylvania State University, 1969.

## BROWN, Arthur

Kirkpatrick & Lockhart Nicholson Graham LLP, Washington, DC
202 778 9000
*Recommended in Investment Management*

## BROWN, Barbara B

Paul, Hastings, Janofsky & Walker LLP, Washington, DC 202 551 1717
barbarabrown@paulhastings.com
*Recommended in Employment*

**Practice Areas:** Represents employers in entire range of employment law matters, particularly discrimination class actions, executive and law firm personnel matters, harassment investigations, OFCCP advice and audit defense, and selection criteria and compensation self-audits and litigation defense.
**Prof. Memberships:** Management Vice-Chair and Council member, American Bar Association Labor and Employment Law Section; Fellow, College of Labor and Employment Lawyers.
**Publications:** Co-author: 'Equal Employment Law Update' (BNA 7th ed, Fall 1999), and 'The Legal Guide to Human Resources' (West/Thomson, 3d rev ed 1996, Supp 2005).
**Personal:** BA - Harvard University (magna cum laude, Phi Beta Kappa); JD - Yale Law School.

## BROWN, Jay Ward

Levine Sullivan Koch & Schulz LLP, Washington, DC 202 508 1100
*Recommended in Media & Entertainment*

## BROWNELL, William

Hunton & Williams, Washington, DC
202 955 1555
bbrownell@hunton.com
*Recommended in Environment*

**Practice Areas:** William Brownell's practice focuses on environmental and administrative litigation, regulation and counseling. He represents clients in both the United States and internationally. In the United States, his practice involves proceedings before courts, federal and state agencies, and Congress; in Europe and Asia, it involves advice on the developing environmental law of the European Community and under the Kyoto protocol, and under other international treaties and agreements. Representative

matters: environmental appellate litigation, defense of environmental citizen suits and enforcement actions, defense of environmental public nuisance claims, environmental permit proceedings, advice on carbon regulation and trading, and environmental management issues.

## BRUCH, Gregory S

Foley & Lardner LLP, Washington, DC
202 672 5460
gbruch@foley.com
*Recommended in Securities*

**Career:** Gregory S Bruch is a Partner in the Washington, DC office of Foley & Lardner LLP and is the leader of the Securities Litigation, Enforcement and Regulation Practice Group. Mr Bruch also practices with the White Collar Defense and Corporate Compliance Practice Group and the Entertainment and Media Industry Team. He represents public companies, broker-dealers, officers and directors, and other institutions and individuals in connection with securities law enforcement, compliance and litigation matters. He received his JD Degree with high distinction in 1985 from the University of Iowa College of Law.

## BRUNNER, Thomas W

Wiley Rein & Fielding LLP, Washington, DC 202 719 7225
tbrunner@wrf.com
*Recommended in Insurance*

**Practice Areas:** Chairs firm's 40-attorney insurance practice (among the largest and most prominent in the US). Counsels insurance industry clients in major trial and appellate cases; active in coverage litigation for insurers for more than 20 years. Named by Corporate Counsel as one of the 'Best Lawyers in America' for excellence in business litigation.
**Prof. Memberships:** Member, Mealey Publications, Insurance Advisory Council (2003-present).
**Career:** Member, Center for Public Resources Distinguished Panel of Insurance Neutrals; Counsel, Complex Insurance Claims Litigation Association; Counsel, National Health Care Anti-Fraud Association; Counsel, National Insurance Crime Bureau.
**Personal:** Yale Law School (JD); Columbia University (AB).

## BUCHANAN, John

Covington & Burling, Washington, DC
202 662 5366
JBuchanan@cov.com
*Recommended in Insurance*

**Practice Areas:** Represents policyholders in complex insurance coverage disputes and transactions. Experience includes environmental, asbestos and other GL claims; media liability, IP- and competition-related claims; D&O, Software E&O, and fidelity claims; product tampering, time-element, marine, satellite in-orbit, and other first-party claims.
**Career:** Partner since 1986. Firm's first

Insurance Practice Group Co-ordinator, 1987-97. Admitted DC Bar, 1979. Law clerk, 3d Circuit USCA, 1978-79.
**Publications:** Frequent speaker and writer on insurance topics, including recent panels and articles on 'Other People's Insurance' and 'Other People's Reinsurance'.
**Personal:** JD, Harvard, 1978; honors BA (1st Class), Oxford, 1974; AB (Phi Beta Kappa), Princeton, 1972.

## BUCKLEY JR, Christopher

Gibson, Dunn & Crutcher LLP, Washington, DC 202 887 3621
cbuckley@gibsondunn.com
*Recommended in Environment*

**Practice Areas:** Extensive experience in environmental, natural resource, and toxic tort litigation. He has led the defense of some of the largest and most significant toxic tort cases ever filed. His focus includes complex cases involving design and construction of water and wastewater treatment plants, design and manufacture of fossil fuel and nuclear power plants, operation of nuclear weapons manufacturing facilities, allocation of natural resources such as Western water and endangered species.
**Publications:** Frequent lecturer and author on environmental regulatory programs and environmental litigation.
**Personal:** JD, Harvard Law School.

## BUENTE, David

Sidley Austin LLP, Washington, DC
202 736 8000
dbuente@sidley.com
*Recommended in Environment*

**Practice Areas:** Head of firm's Environmental Practice Group. Represents clients in environmental litigation, legislative and rulemaking matters.
**Prof. Memberships:** Vice-Chair, American Bar Association's Environmental Litigation Committee and the National Association of Criminal Defense Lawyers' Environmental Crimes Committee.
**Career:** Chief of the Environmental Enforcement Section, Environment and Natural Resources Division with the Department of Justice, directing federal, civil and criminal environmental enforcement litigation. Handled federal environmental trial and appellate litigation for the EPA and other federal agencies as a Department of Justice trial attorney. Has extensive experience in agency rulemakings from prior service with the Interior Department and the Pennsylvania Attorney General's Office.
**Personal:** University of Pennsylvania Law School, JD, 1975; Lehigh University, BS, 1968. Admissions: District of Columbia; US Court of Appeals, 3rd Circuit; US Court of Appeals, 4th Circuit; US Court of Appeals, 5th Circuit; US Court of Appeals, 7th Circuit; US Court of Appeals, 8th Circuit; US Court of Appeals, 9th Circuit; US Court of

Appeals, 10th Circuit; US Court of Appeals, 11th Circuit; US Court of Appeals, DC Circuit; US District Court, WD of Pennsylvania, 1975; US District Court, District of Utah; District of Columbia, 1991.

### BULLEIT JR, Thomas N
Hogan & Hartson LLP, Washington, DC
202 637 8276
tnbulleit@hhlaw.com
*Recommended in Healthcare*
**Practice Areas:** Healthcare regulatory and transactional law including advice on compliance with Medicare, Medicaid, and state requirements, antikickback and self-referral laws, false claims act matters, technology transfer, clinical trials, and other biomedical research regulation. Clients include major pharmaceutical and medical device manufacturers, smaller biotech companies, managed care organizations, academic medical centers, and hospitals.
**Prof. Memberships:** ABA; MSBA; DC Bar (former three-time Chair, Health Law Section); American Health Lawyers Association (Master's Program in Healthcare Fraud and Abuse).
**Career:** Partner, Hogan & Hartson since 1994.
**Publications:** 'Proposed Health Information Technology Protections Under New Antikickback Statute Safe Harbors and New Stark Exceptions', Health Update, Hogan & Hartson, L.L.P. (10/28/2005); 'New Industry Guidance on Interactions With Healthcare Professionals'. Health Update, Hogan & Hartson L.L.P. (03/21/2005); 'New California Law May Affect Medical Device Manufacturer Compliance Plans and Reporting Obligations', Health Update, Hogan & Hartson L.L.P. (02/24/2005).
**Personal:** University of Michigan Law School (JD, 1985. Louis Honigman Award); Yale University (AB, cum laude, 1979).

### BUMPERS, Heidi
Jones Day, Washington, DC
202 879 7616
hhbumpers@jonesday.com
*Recommended in Environment*
**Practice Areas:** Former Section Chief in EPA's Office of Enforcement. Litigated RCRA enforcement cases, Superfund and natural resource damage cases, EPCRA, OSHA, and asbestos enforcement actions. Negotiated voluntary cleanup agreements and private cost recovery settlements. Client counseling matters include establishing a comprehensive environmental management system for a hi-tech manufacturer, coordinating environmental matters and legislative strategy for a tire manufacturer, and advising on international regulations, compliance audits, records retention, multimedia inspections, and release reporting. Regularly lectures and has published numerous articles on environ-

mental law issues.
**Prof. Memberships:** Oregon and Washington, DC Bar associations.

### BUMPERS, William
Baker Botts LLP, Washington, DC
202 639 7718
william.bumpers@bakerbotts.com
*Recommended in Environment*
**Practice Areas:** Focuses practice on environmental compliance and litigation. Clients represented include petroleum refiners, electric generators, and pharmaceutical and chemical manufacturers. Regarded as a national authority on new source review issues affecting the electric generation and petroleum refinery industries.
**Prof. Memberships:** Member, District of Columbia Bar; Member, American Bar Association.
**Career:** Admitted to DC Bar in 1984. Joined Baker Botts in 1996.
**Personal:** Hendrix College, BA, 1977; Antioch College, MA, 1979; University of Virginia, JD, 1984.

### BURCHFIELD, Bobby R
McDermott Will & Emery, Washington, DC 202 756 8003
bburchfield@mwe.com
*Recommended in Government: Political Law, Litigation*
**Practice Areas:** Co-Chair, firm's Washington, DC office; Head of firm's Complex Litigation Group. Corporate litigation, including jury and bench trials, appeals, and arbitrations for such clients as Dow Corning Corporation, The Washington Post Company's subsidiary LegiSlate, Inc., the American Automobile Association, the Republican National Committee, Northrop Grumman Corporation, and CNH America. Constitutional litigation, including arguing McConnell v FEC, 540 US (10 December 2003).
**Prof. Memberships:** Federalist Society; American Bar Association; George Washington Law School Dean's Advisory Board (2002-present); Board of Trustees, Wake Forest University (2004-present).
**Personal:** George Washington Law School (JD, high honors); Wake Forest University (BA, cum laude).

### CABALLERO, Michael J
King & Spalding LLP, Washington, DC
202 661 7942
mcaballero@kslaw.com
*Recommended in Tax*
**Practice Areas:** Tax specializing in international tax planning.
**Prof. Memberships:** New York State Bar, District of Columbia Bar.
**Personal:** BS, Notre Dame, 1991; JD, cum laude, Georgetown University, 1994; LLM, New York University, 2000.

### CACHERIS, Plato
Trout Cacheris PLLC, Washington, DC
202 464 3300
*Recommended in Litigation*

### CANNON JR, George
Latham & Watkins LLP, Washington, DC
202 637 2200
*Recommended in Energy*

### CARDER-THOMPSON, Elizabeth
Reed Smith LLP, Washington, DC
202 414 9213
ecarder@reedsmith.com
*Recommended in Healthcare*
**Practice Areas:** Represents associations and individual providers and suppliers of health services, including hospitals, physicians, hospices, pharmaceutical manufacturers, suppliers and manufacturers of medical equipment, and nursing homes. Specific responsibility includes reimbursement, fraud and abuse, and regulatory, legislative, and enforcement issues.
**Prof. Memberships:** Board of Directors of American Health Lawyers Association, Co-Chair of its annual Healthcare Fraud and Compliance Forum; DC Bar; past Chair, Health Law Forum, Women's Bar Association.
**Personal:** College of William & Mary (JD, 1978), notes and comments editor of William & Mary Law Review; Brown University (AB, 1975), Phi Beta Kappa.

### CAROME, Patrick J
WilmerHale, Washington, DC
202 247 3489
patrick.carome@wilmerhale.com
*Recommended in Media & Entertainment*
**Practice Areas:** Partner, Litigation and Communications Departments. Focus: defamation, privacy, intellectual property, Freedom of Information Act, press access, reporters' privilege and other First Amendment matters. Has represented broad range of media clients: America Online, Time Warner, Netscape, eBay, Google, Yahoo!, Washington Post, New York Times, Los Angeles Times, ABC, Cable News Network. Practice recently focused on litigation and counseling for on-line and other internet companies.
**Career:** Staff attorney for Washington Post; staff counsel to US House of Representatives Select Committee to Investigate Covert Arms Transactions with Iran.
**Personal:** JD, Harvard Law School; Member, Harvard Legal Aid Bureau; BA, Boston College.

### CARR, Don
Pillsbury Winthrop Shaw Pittman LLP, Washington, DC 202 663 9277
donald.carr@pillsburylaw.com
*Recommended in Environment*
**Practice Areas:** Advice on clean air issues for utility and industrial facilities, wetlands and protected species matters for real estate, forestry and mining, remediation and natural resource damages analysis for responsible parties in hazardous waste problems, and coastal zone, outer continental shelf and oceans law for marine and vessel-related activities. Spe-

cial areas of concentration include emissions trading, conservation banking and complex assignments in American Indian law. Mr Carr is an experienced litigator in the environmental and natural resources field, including the defense of environmental criminal cases.
**Personal:** JD, George Washington University, 1974; BA, Cornell University of Washington at Seattle, 1970.

### CARTER, Lee C
Pillsbury Winthrop Shaw Pittman LLP, Washington, DC
202 663 8135
lee.carter@pillsburylaw.com
*Recommended in Real Estate*
**Practice Areas:** Ms Carter concentrates in the areas of military housing privatization and real estate development. She represented developers, underwriters and credit enhancers in more than $2 billion of US Navy and Marine Corps military housing privatizations, including the privatization of more than 26,000 housing units in California, Arizona, Maryland, Virginia, West Virginia, Hawaii, New York, Missouri, North Carolina and South Carolina. In addition to her military housing expertise, Ms Carter represents developers in the acquisition, disposition, and development of real estate.
**Personal:** JD, University of Chicago Law School (1993, cum laude); BA, Denison University (1989, magna cum laude)

### CARVIN, Michael A
Jones Day, Washington, DC
202 879 7643
macarvin@jonesday.com
*Recommended in Litigation*
**Practice Areas:** Specializes in constitutional, appellate, civil rights, and civil litigation against the federal government. He has argued numerous cases in the US Supreme Court and in virtually every federal appeals court. These cases include the decisions overturning the federal government's plan to statistically adjust the census, limiting the Justice Department's ability to create 'majority-minority' districts, and preventing the Justice Department from seeking monetary relief against the tobacco industry under RICO. He was one of the lead lawyers, and argued before the Florida Supreme Court, on behalf of now-President George W Bush in the 2000 election Florida recount controversy.

### CARY, George S
Cleary Gottlieb Steen & Hamilton LLP, Washington, DC 202 974 1920
gcary@cgsh.com
*Recommended in Antitrust*
**Practice Areas:** Antitrust counseling and litigation, focusing on mergers and acquisitions, FTC and DoJ investigations, antitrust issues in high technology markets, and antitrust and intellectual property issues. Representative clients and transactions: Dow Chemical (Union Car-

bide), Time Warner (AOL and EMI), SmithKline Beecham (GlaxoWelcome), Cable & Wireless (MCI Internet), Northern Telecom (Bay Networks), Conoco (Phillips Petroleum), AspenTech (Hyprotech), Lafarge (Blue Circle), Broadcom, Toyota.

**Prof. Memberships:** California and DC Bars. ABA Antitrust Section, (Past Chair, Government Antitrust Litigation Committee). California Judicial Nominees Evaluation Commission (Commissioner).

**Career:** Joined firm as a Partner, 1998. Deputy Director, Bureau of Competition, Federal Trade Commission (1995-98) (responsible for merger enforcement), Partner, Irell & Manella (1984-95). Trial attorney, FTC Bureau of Competition (1976-84). JD, Boalt Hall School of Law, UC Berkeley (1976), BA, (Economics) UC Santa Cruz (1973).

**Publications:** 'Mergers in Media Industries'; 'Government Enforcement Priorities for High Technology Industries'; 'Software Mergers: The Enforcement Record'; 'US View on Refusal to License IP and Antitrust'; 'Patent Settlements and Antitrust'; 'Antitrust Implications of Patent Settlements'; 'Hoechst/Andrx - Anatomy of a Restraint of Trade'.

## CASSERLY, James L
Willkie Farr & Gallagher LLP, Washington, DC 202 303 1119
jcasserly@willkie.com
*Recommended in Telecom, Broadcast & Satellite*

**Practice Areas:** Partner in the Telecommunications Department, specializing in communications, policy and transactional matters, including high-speed cable internet service, interactive television, digital television, competition policies, and ownership issues. He represents cable, programming, and wireline telecommunications companies. Has produced outcome-changing advocacy in multiple Federal Communications Commission (FCC) rulemaking and authorization proceedings. He regularly represents clients before the FCC, district and appellate courts, and Congress.
**Prof. Memberships:** Admitted to the Bar of the District of Columbia. Member of the Federal Communications Bar Association, where he has been a Co-Chair of the Annual Seminar Committee (2004-05), Law Journal Committee (2000-04), and the Committee on Legislation (1984-87).
**Career:** From 1994 to 1999, he served as senior legal advisor to FCC Commissioner Susan Ness, in which capacity he was active in deliberations concerning the full scope of matters arising before the FCC, ranging from competitive safeguards and intercarrier compensation to spectrum auctions and children's television programming. He was also integrally involved in all aspects of the agency's

implementation of the Telecommunications Act of 1996, with particular attention to local telephone competition, universal service, and federal-state jurisdictional relationships.
**Personal:** Received a JD from Columbia University School of Law in 1976, where he was a Harlan Fiske Stone Scholar and a Teaching Fellow in Civil Procedure, and an AB (magna cum laude) from Tufts University in 1973, where he was a reporter for the Tufts Observer.

## CAVANAGH, Rita
Latham & Watkins LLP, Washington, DC 202 637 2200
*Recommended in Tax*

## CHATILOVICZ, Peter
Seyfarth Shaw LLP, Washington, DC 202 463 2400
*Recommended in Employment*

## CHRISTENSEN, Wallace
Ross Dixon & Bell LLP, Washington, DC 202 662 2000
*Recommended in Insurance*

## CLARKE, Donald
Law Offices of GKRSE, Washington, DC 202 408 5400
*Recommended in Energy*

## COHEN, Charles
Morgan, Lewis & Bockius LLP, Washington, DC 202 739 5710
ccohen@morganlewis.com
*Recommended in Employment*

**Practice Areas:** Charles I Cohen is a Partner in the Labor and Employment Law Practice. Mr Cohen represents management in complex labor and employment law matters in the private and federal sectors. Mr Cohen has a comprehensive background in collective bargaining issues and all facets of labor and employee relations and litigation. Mr Cohen was appointed by the President and confirmed by the Senate and served as a Member of the National Labor Relations Board (NLRB) from 1994-96.
**Prof. Memberships:** American Bar Association; US Chamber of Commerce - NLRB Subcommittee; Chair - Fellow, College of Labor and Employment Lawyers; Committee on Practice and Procedure Under the National Labor Relations Act.

## COHEN, David
Vinson & Elkins LLP, Washington, DC 202 639 6566
dcohen@velaw.com
*Recommended in Energy*
**Practice Areas:** Practice concentrates on mergers and acquisitions, joint ventures and project development.
**Career:** Admitted to District of Columbia Bar in 1989 and was admitted to the partnership in 1991.

## COHN, Joel M
Akin Gump Strauss Hauer & Feld LLP, Washington, DC 202 887 4065
jcohn@akingump.com
*Recommended in Employment*
**Practice Areas:** Labor and employment law. Mr Cohn represents management in federal and state court complex litigation, with emphasis on wage and hour and employment discrimination class litigation. He has represented a broad range of employers in the financial services, retail, food processing and telecommunications industries.
**Prof. Memberships:** District of Columbia Bar Association; American Bar Association and its Section of Labor and Employment Law.
**Career:** Appellate Litigation Division, Equal Employment Opportunity Commission; Office of Representation Appeals, National Labor Relations Board.
**Personal:** BA, University of Wisconsin (1971); JD, Catholic University of America (1976).

## COLEMAN, Lynn R
Skadden, Arps, Slate, Meagher & Flom LLP & Affiliates, Washington, DC 202 371 7600
lcoleman@skadden.com
*Recommended in Energy*
**Practice Areas:** Started and led Domestic and International Energy Practice and coordinates the Legislative and Public Policy Practice. Handles energy transactions, regulatory proceedings and complex litigation; deals with oil, gas, electric, coal and nuclear energy issues. Represents clients on issues of government policy including legislation in Congress and executive branch initiatives, and has worked extensively on government regulation of energy projects and transactions as well as privatizations; also represents international energy companies on US and multilateral trade sanctions.
**Career:** LLB, University of Texas, 1964 (editor, Texas Law Review; Order of the Coif; Chancellor); BA, Abilene Christian College, 1961.

## CONNOLLY, Annemargaret
Weil, Gotshal & Manges LLP, Washington, DC 202 682 7037
annemargaret.connolly@weil.com
*Recommended in Environment*
**Practice Areas:** Annemargaret Connolly practices environmental, health and safety law. She advises clients on a range of environmental concerns, notably in the context of M&A, real estate transfers and financing transactions. Ms Connolly works with consultants and engineers to quantify potential liabilities, and drafts and negotiates contract language to allocate the risk of environmental liabilities between the parties. She also counsels clients on a variety of other environmental topics, including compliance with hazardous waste laws, occupational safety

issues, asbestos, and corporate and successor liability.
**Personal:** Syracuse University, BA, 1984; Syracuse University, BS, 1984; George Washington University Law School, JD, 1988.

## CONTRATTO, Dana
Crowell & Moring LLP, Washington, DC 202 624 2600
dcontratto@crowell.com
*Recommended in Energy*
**Practice Areas:** Chair of Crowell & Moring's Energy Group. Represents clients in environmental, natural resources, and energy litigation, regulatory, legislative, business development, commercial negotiation, and general corporate matters. Handles projects involving oil and gas concessions, electric power generation and transmission, natural gas pipeline and distribution systems, liquid petroleum gas fuels procurement, oil and natural gas purchases and sales, and complex commercial and corporate arrangements. Representations include Memphis Light, Gas and Water Division, Knoxville Utilities Board, and Petroleos Mexicanos.
**Personal:** Undergraduate Degree in Marketing from Southern Illinois University; JD from Washington University.

## COOK BUSH, Antoinette
Skadden, Arps, Slate, Meagher & Flom LLP & Affiliates, Washington, DC 202 371 7230
abush@skadden.com
*Recommended in Telecom, Broadcast & Satellite*
**Practice Areas:** Represents companies in administrative, legislative, and transactional matters involving communications issues as well as other legislative matters. A significant portion of practice is devoted to representing clients before the Federal Communications Commission. Specifically, clients include entities involved in the broadcast, cable, satellite, telephone and mobile communication business. Also represents a number of not-for-profit communications companies.
**Career:** JD, Northwestern University School of Law, 1981; BA, Wellesley College, 1978.

## COOPER, Bo
Paul, Hastings, Janofsky & Walker LLP, Washington, DC 202 551 1750
bocooper@paulhastings.com
*Recommended in Immigration*
**Practice Areas:** Bo served as General Counsel of the Immigration and Naturalization Service (INS) from 1999 until 2003, functioning as the most senior immigration advisor to two administrations, and was responsible for the transition of immigration services to Homeland Security. Twice recipient of INS' Exceptional Service award. Heads Paul Hastings' Washington, DC Immigration

Practice. Focuses on strategic counseling, corporate compliance, immigration-related legislation and government relations primarily for globally active companies. Co-chairs the Immigration Group's Federal Enforcement and Corporate Compliance Team. Has testified frequently before Congress. Teaches immigration at the University of Michigan. Director and Washington Representative of Global Personnel Alliance.

## COOPER, Richard
Williams & Connolly LLP, Washington, DC 202 434 5000
*Recommended in Healthcare*

## COOPER, Ronald
Steptoe & Johnson LLP, Washington, DC 202 429 8075
rcooper@steptoe.com
*Recommended in Employment*
**Practice Areas:** Partner, Steptoe & Johnson LLP, Washington, DC. Defended employers in employment discrimination cases under federal and state law. Represented employers in administrative proceedings including 'glass ceiling' investigations concerning utilization of women in senior management. Defended and prosecuted cases involving restrictions on post-employment competition. Defended and prosecuted executive compensation cases; successfully represented the employer in Oracle Corp. v Falotti, 319 F.3d 1106 (9th Cir 2003). Employer Co-Chair of ABA Labor and Employment Section International Labor Law Committee. Managed force reduction involving selection and management of counsel in 20 foreign jurisdictions.
**Personal:** JD, University of Georgia, 1969; AB, 1966.

## CORDELL, Ruffin
Fish & Richardson P.C., Washington, DC 202 626 6449
cordell@fr.com
*Recommended in Intellectual Property*
**Practice Areas:** Principal of Fish & Richardson in the firm's Washington, DC office. Practice emphasizes all aspects of intellectual property litigation, including patent, copyright, and trade secret law. Appears regularly as lead counsel before federal district courts in Virginia, Texas, California, and throughout the country, and has extensive experience before the ITC in Section 337 proceedings. Has handled patent and trade secret cases involving microprocessors, graphics controllers, cellular camera phones, Ethernet network systems, DSL devices, hybrid video/graphics processors, and digital memory structures, and storage devices.
**Personal:** Louisiana State University BS Electrical Engineering 1985; Georgetown University Law Center JD 1989.

## CORN-REVERE, Robert
Davis Wright Tremaine LLP, Washington, DC 202 508 6600
*Recommended in Media & Entertainment*

## CRISMAN JR, C Benjamin
Skadden, Arps, Slate, Meagher & Flom LLP & Affiliates, Washington, DC 202 371 7330
bcrisman@skadden.com
*Recommended in Antitrust*
**Practice Areas:** Focuses on antitrust, trade regulation and white-collar crime matters. Has obtained Department of Justice and Federal Trade Commission approval for a number of high profile and complex US and international mergers and acquisitions. Specializes in technology, defense sector and natural resources. Regularly counsels clients on sophisticated, cross-border joint ventures and compliance progams. Represents clients in international cartel and antitrust grand jury investigations.
**Career:** JD, Creighton University, 1975 (senior editor, Creighton Law Review); BA, Syracuse University, 1970.

## CROSS, Meredith B
WilmerHale, Washington, DC 202 663 6644
meredith.cross@wilmerhale.com
*Recommended in Securities*
**Practice Areas:** Co-Chair, Corporate Department. Focus: advising public companies and underwriters on corporate finance securities law matters. Serves as issuer's counsel and underwriters' counsel in public and private offerings of debt and equity securities. Handles matters for companies with the SEC, including requests for no-action or interpretive positions and disclosure and financial statement reviews by staff of Division of Corporation Finance at SEC.
**Career:** Former Deputy Director and Chief Counsel of the Division of Corporation Finance of the US Securities and Exchange Commission.
**Personal:** BA, Duke University; JD, Vanderbilt University School of Law.

## CROWLEY, Lisanne
Troutman Sanders LLP, Washington, DC 202 274 2950
*Recommended in Energy*

## CULBERTSON, Robert E
King & Spalding LLP, Washington, DC 202 626 2642
rculbertson@kslaw.com
*Recommended in Tax*
**Practice Areas:** Over 20 years experience in international taxation, both the public and private sectors, specializing in international tax planning/controversy resolution.
**Career:** Prior to joining King & Spalding, he was leader of the Washington international tax services office of PricewaterhouseCoopers. Began his career with the

IRS drafting regulations. Joined staff of the Joint Committee on Taxation working on international provisions of the Tax Reform Act of 1986. Rejoined IRS in 1986, then served as Associate Chief Counsel International 1991-95, responsible for international tax regulations, rulings, and litigation policy.
**Personal:** BA, Yale College and graduate of Harvard Law School.

## CURTISS, James
Winston & Strawn LLP, Washington, DC 202 282 5751
jcurtiss@winston.com
*Recommended in Energy*
**Practice Areas:** Jim Curtiss, who chairs the firm's Energy Group, specializes in strategic advice and counsel for utilities, nuclear fuel cycle companies, government contractors, and trade associations on regulatory and legislative matters, including corporate governance, industry restructuring, legislative and regulatory policy issues, and new nuclear plant licensing. He has appeared before the NRC's Atomic Safety and Licensing Board. Mr Curtiss is a frequent speaker at nuclear industry conferences and has spoken on topics that include licensing and regulatory reform, advanced reactors, fuel cycle issues, and performance-based regulation. While serving as Senate Staff Counsel, he was involved in the formulation of the Nuclear Waste Policy Act of 1982, the Price-Anderson Reauthorization, and the Low-Level Radioactive Waste Policy Act.
**Prof. Memberships:** Admitted, District of Columbia Court of Appeals and US Supreme Court; Member, Nuclear Energy Institute Lawyers Committee; Director, Constellation Energy Group and Cameco Corporation, Member, Nuclear Oversight Board, Southern California Edison; prior member, INPO Advisory Council.
**Career:** Partner, Winston & Strawn, since 1993; Commissioner, US Nuclear Regulatory Commission, 1988-93 (appointed by President Reagan); Counsel and Staff Director, Senate Environment and Public Works, Committee Subcommittee on Nuclear Regulation, 1981-88.
**Personal:** University of Nebraska, BA, 1976, JD, 1979.

## DANKNER, Donald
Winston & Strawn LLP, Washington, DC 202 282 5778
ddankner@winston.com
*Recommended in Energy*
**Practice Areas:** Representation of electric and gas companies before the Federal Energy Regulatory Commission, other agencies, and the courts. This includes industry restructuring, mergers and acquisitions, market-based rates, purchase power agreements, generator interconnections, bankruptcy reorganizations and claims, transmission rates, transmis-

sion expansions, independent transmission company development, securities issuances, compliance with standards of conduct and market manipulation rules, litigation of contract disputes, pipeline rates, and pipeline expansions, including LNG development.
**Prof. Memberships:** Energy Bar Association.
**Personal:** BA from the University of Wisconsin, 1969; JD, with honors, from the George Washington University Law School, 1973 (member of Law Review).

## DAVIS, Robert P
Mayer, Brown, Rowe & Maw LLP, Washington, DC 202 263 3207
rdavis@mayerbrownrowe.com
*Recommended in Employee Benefits, Employment*
**Practice Areas:** Represents employers in trial and appellate employment litigation in federal and state courts. Extensive experience in Fair Labor Standards Act and state wage and hour litigation. Trial and appellate ERISA litigation. Advises on Fair Labor Standards Act and state counterpart statutes. ERISA advice on fiduciary issues, prohibited transactions, and other matters under Title I Advisory opinions and prohibited transaction exemptions. Substantial experience in OSHA regulatory and enforcement matters. Former solicitor of the US Department of Labor under the senior President Bush (1989-91).
**Career:** Mayer, Brown, Rowe & Maw LLP, Washington, 1991 to date; Partner, 1991. Solicitor of Labor, US Department of Labor, Washington, DC, 1989-91. Chief of Staff to the Secretary of Transportation, US Department of Transportation, Washington, DC, 1983-85. US Department of Justice, Washington, DC: Special assistant to the Deputy Attorney General, 1978-80; Senior Staff Member, Office of the Attorney General, 1974-78. Senior Staff to the Majority Leader, New York State Senate, 1973-74.
**Personal:** JD (magna cum laude), Georgetown University,1980; editor, Georgetown Law Journal. MPA, Syracuse, 1973. MA, Boston University, 1972. AB, Brown University, 1971. Chairman, Tripartite Advisory Panel on International Labor Standards, 1989-91. Outstanding performance awards from three US Attorneys General.

## DEGRANDIS, William D
Paul, Hastings, Janofsky & Walker LLP, Washington, DC
202 551 1720
billdegrandis@paulhastings.com
*Recommended in Projects*
**Practice Areas:** Energy/infrastructure regulatory and transactional matters; including Federal Energy Regulatory Commission practice.
**Prof. Memberships:** Energy Bar Association (Vice-Chair, Electric Utility Regula-

tion Committee); American Bar Association (Public Utility Section); District of Columbia Bar Association (Energy Section); Electric Cooperative Bar Association.

**Career:** Paul Hastings Janofsky & Walker LLP (1986-present). Elected Partner in 1999. Prior to 1986, associated with Sidley & Austin and Ely, Ritts, Pietrouski and Brickfield.

**Publications:** Published recent articles on the Energy Policy Act of 2005 in Project Finance International, Electric Power & Light, and New Power Executive. Other articles have appeared in: United States-Mexico Law Journal, Independent Energy, The Electricity Journal, Energy Law Journal, and CFC Power Review.

**Personal:** Pennsylvania State University, BA, 1977 (with highest distinction) (Political Science Major/Economics Minor); University of California at Los Angeles School of Law, JD, 1980 (UCLA Law Review - member and comments editor).

## DELLINGER, Walter

O'Melveny & Myers LLP, Washington, DC
202 383 5300
wdellinger@omm.com
*Recommended in Litigation*

**Practice Areas:** Walter Dellinger is Head of the Appellate Practice at O'Melveny & Myers and is the Douglas B Maggs Professor of Law at Duke University. He served as acting Solicitor General for the 1996-97 Term of the Supreme Court. During that time, Walter argued nine cases before the Court, the most by any Solicitor General in more than 20 years. His arguments included cases dealing with physician-assisted suicide, the line item veto, the cable television act, the Brady Act, the Religious Freedom Restoration Act, and the constitutionality of remedial services for parochial school children. His most recent successful arguments before the US Supreme Court include Jackson v Birmingham School District, Brown v Legal Foundation of Washington, US Airways v Barnett, Utah v Evans, Hunt v Cromartie, and Hunt v Easley. His recent Court of Appeals arguments include Martha Stewart v United States; Whiteside v United States, Exxon v Alabama and LCI v Phillips.

## DENGER, Michael L

Gibson, Dunn & Crutcher LLP,
Washington, DC 202 955 8526
mdenger@gibsondunn.com
*Recommended in Antitrust*

**Practice Areas:** Extensive experience in civil and criminal antitrust investigations (domestic and international) and litigation, including substantial experience in trade regulation law, false advertising law, government enforcement actions, private antitrust litigation, class actions, and corporate takeover litigation.

**Prof. Memberships:** Served as Chair of

the American Bar Association Section of Antitrust Law in 1992-93 and as a member of the Antitrust Section Task Force which prepared a report to the Bush administration on 'Federal Antitrust Enforcement'. A member of the US Chamber of Commerce Antitrust Council.

**Publications:** Frequent speaker on antitrust and trade regulation subjects.

**Personal:** JD, Harvard Law School, 1970.

## DENIS, Paul T

Dechert LLP, Washington, DC
202 261 3430
paul.denis@dechert.com
*Recommended in Antitrust*

**Practice Areas:** Mr Denis is a Partner in Dechert's Antitrust Group. He advises clients on mergers and acquisitions, joint ventures, and other business combinations to help clients avoid antitrust problems. He also handles non-merger investigations, litigation, and counseling.

**Prof. Memberships:** Member, New York and District of Columbia Bars.

**Career:** Counselor to the Assistant Attorney General, Acting Deputy Assistant Attorney General for Regulation of the Antitrust Division of the US Department of Justice.

**Personal:** Villanova University (BA, summa cum laude, 1980); University of Michigan (MA, 1983; JD, cum laude, 1984).

## DEPUY, Jacques

Greenstein Delorme & Luchs,
Washington, DC 202 452 1400
*Recommended in Real Estate*

## DESANCTIS, Michael

Jenner & Block LLP, Washington, DC
202 637 6323
mdesanctis@jenner.com
*Recommended in Telecom, Broadcast & Satellite*

**Practice Areas:** Michael B DeSanctis is a Partner in Jenner & Block's Washington, DC office. He is a Member of the firm's Appellate and Supreme Court, Litigation and Dispute Resolution, Products Liability and Mass Tort Defense, Entertainment and New Media, and Telecommunications Practices. Mr DeSanctis represents leading telecommunications companies in the federal courts and before the Federal Communications Commission in all range of matters, and he has extensive experience in matters arising under the Telecommunications Act of 1996. Pursuant to the firm's role as national coordinating counsel for MCI Inc.'s litigation under Section 252 of the 1996 Act, he has primary responsibility for outside counsel's role in the management of those cases nationwide. His Telecommunications Practice has extended to the US Supreme Court, the US Courts of Appeals for the District of Columbia, Third, Fourth, Sixth, Eight, Ninth and Eleventh Circuits, and federal

district and state courts across the country. Mr DeSanctis regularly appears as lead counsel for national communications companies in enforcement matters before the Investigations and Hearings Division and the Market Disputes Resolution Division of the FCC's Enforcement Bureau. Mr DeSanctis has an active Complex Civil Litigation and Mass Tort Practice. His appellate and trial litigation work in these areas has focused on a diverse range of substantive fields including product liability, commercial contract disputes, aviation, banking and copyright. He regularly represents Fortune 500 companies in complex civil litigation in federal and state courts and in arbitrations.

**Personal:** New York University School of Law, JD, 1995, cum laude.

## DESANTIS, Victor J

White & Case LLP, Washington, DC
202 626 3607
vdesantis@whitecase.com
*Recommended in Projects*

**Practice Areas:** Partner in the Corporate Department concentrating on international, multi-lender project finance, and other cross-border financing and investment transactions. Extensive experience representing sponsors, multilateral and commercial lenders and export credit agencies on enterprises financed on a project basis. Has been involved in financings involving a wide range of sectors, including power, mining, oil and gas, transportation, telecommunications and other industrial projects.

**Prof. Memberships:** New York State Bar, 1986; District of Columbia Bar, 1987.

**Personal:** BA Yale University, 1982; JD Harvard Law School, 1985.

## DILLON, Sheri A

McKee Nelson LLP, Washington, DC
202 775 8657
sdillon@mckeenelson.com
*Recommended in Tax*

**Practice Areas:** Tax controversy; taxation. Particular emphasis on IRS administrative proceedings and tax litigation. Experience includes: partnership issues, economic substance, financial products, life insurance, and foreign tax credits, as well as procedural issues relating to TEFRA partnerships, corporations, and individuals.

**Prof. Memberships:** Active Member of the ABA Section of Taxation, currently chair of the Large and Midsize Business Subcommittee of the Administrative Practice Committee.

**Career:** Joined McKee Nelson in 1999. Has taught partnership taxation at Columbus School of Law (Catholic University). Regularly provides pro bono representation for low income taxpayers, most recently prevailing in Steve Harvey v Commissioner.

**Personal:** Received a JD, cum laude,

from the Georgetown University Law Center in 1999, where she served as notes editor of the American Criminal Law Review.

## DINKINS, Carol

Vinson & Elkins LLP, Houston
713 758 2222
*Recommended in Environment*
*Please see Texas for profile.*

## DIXON, Gary

Ross Dixon & Bell LLP, Washington, DC
202 662 2000
*Recommended in Insurance*

## DOLAN, Edward

Hogan & Hartson LLP, Washington, DC
202 637 5677
ecdolan@hhlaw.com
*Recommended in Bankruptcy*

**Practice Areas:** Represents secured and unsecured, domestic and foreign creditors, vendors and investors in matters involving bankruptcy, creditors' rights, complex commercial financing and asset dispositions and acquisitions. Has extensive experience in litigating commercial claims and enforcing creditors' rights in state and federal courts throughout the United States.

**Prof. Memberships:** ABA; American Bankruptcy Institute; Director, past President, Maryland Bankruptcy Bar Association; Master, Chandler Bankruptcy Inn of Court Member; Member, past-Chair, Maryland Bankruptcy Court's Local Rules Committee; former Member, Bankruptcy Advisory Group, US State Department Task Force on Cross-Border Insolvencies.

**Career:** Partner. Has lectured extensively on US bankruptcy and insolvency matters, most recently on the 2005 amendments to the federal Bankruptcy Code.

**Personal:** Columbia University (BA, 1975); Georgetown University Law Center (JD, 1978).

## DOLIN, Mitchell F

Covington & Burling, Washington, DC
202 662 5210
mdolin@cov.com
*Recommended in Insurance, International Arbitration*

**Practice Areas:** Practice concentrated on the arbitration, litigation, and mediation of complex commercial cases, with particular emphasis on representing corporate policyholders in insurance disputes concerning asbestos and mass torts, directors and officers, and other large loss situations.

**Prof. Memberships:** American Law Institute (Member); CPR Institute for Dispute Resolution (Regional Panel of Neutrals).

**Career:** With Covington & Burling since 1982, as a Partner since 1989. Served as law clerk to Chief Judge Charles Clark, US Court of Appeals for the 5th Circuit, from 1981-82.

**Personal:** Tufts University, BA, 1978; New York University School of Law, JD, 1981.

## DOWD, Mary Joanne
Arent Fox PLLC, Washington, DC
202 857 6059
dowd.mary@arentfox.com
*Recommended in Bankruptcy*
**Practice Areas:** Concentrates in business bankruptcy and financial restructuring. Her practice includes representation of debtors, creditors, trustees, committees and purchasers of assets in bankruptcy court cases, as well as borrowers and lenders in out of court debt restructures and structured finance transactions. She has particular expertise in bankruptcy cases involving real estate, intellectual property, construction, manufacturing, airline and retail. She is admitted to practice before the bankruptcy courts in the District of Columbia, Maryland, and New York.
**Personal:** State University of New York at Buffalo, Faculty of Law and Jurisprudence, JD 1980; State University of New York College at Buffalo, BA (summa cum laude) 1976.

## DOWNS, Clark Evans
Jones Day, Washington, DC
202 879 3883
cedowns@jonesday.com
*Recommended in Energy*
**Practice Areas:** His practice is concentrated on North American electricity markets and related areas of state and federal regulation of rates and competition and includes administrative and appellate litigation and counseling. He has especially broad experience in dealing with the federal regulation of mergers and acquisitions and with the full range of traditional utility rate and other regulatory issues. He is listed in numerous publications that recognize the world's leading energy lawyers. He regularly appears before the FERC and state public service commissions.
**Prof. Memberships:** ABA; Energy Bar Association; Fellow of the American Bar Foundation.

## DRAKE, Stuart AC
Kirkland & Ellis LLP, Washington, DC
202 879 5094
sdrake@kirkland.com
*Recommended in Environment*
**Practice Areas:** Mr Drake has represented companies whose products are subject to air pollution control regulation by the US Environmental Protection Agency and various State government agencies. His work includes the defense of enforcement actions in federal and State courts and before the agencies, other litigation involving regulations, and the representation of clients in agency rulemaking processes and in Congressional matters.
**Personal:** Yale University, BA, 1977.

Cambridge University, MLitt, 1981. Yale University, JD, 1981.

## DUCHELLE, John
Ross Dixon & Bell LLP, Washington, DC
202 662 2000
*Recommended in Insurance*

## DUNNER, Donald
Finnegan Henderson Farabow Garrett & Dunner LLP, Washington, DC
202 408 4062
don.dunner@finnegan.com
*Recommended in Intellectual Property*
**Practice Areas:** Works in all phases of patent law including prosecution, licensing, litigation, validity and infringement studies, and counseling. Has technical expertise in the areas of chemical engineering, chemistry, biotechnology, and pharmaceuticals. Has litigated numerous cases in the federal district courts, but is best known for appellate practice before the US Court of Appeals for the Federal Circuit. Has argued more Federal Circuit cases than any other lawyer in the US.
**Prof. Memberships:** District of Columbia Bar (Chair, Steering Committee, Division 14, 1976-77); Bar Association of the District of Columbia (Section on Patent, Trademark and Copyright Law, Chair, 1964-65; Board of Directors, 1965-66); American Bar Association (Section on Intellectual Property Law, Chair, 1995-96); American Intellectual Property Law Association (President, 1979-80); National Council of Patent Law Associations (Secretary, 1963-66); American College of Trial Lawyers (1995-); American Academy of Appellate Lawyers (2004-); ABA House of Delegates (2002-).
**Personal:** Purdue University (BS, Chemical Engineering, 1953); Georgetown University Law Center (JD, 1958).

## DWYER, Jeffry
Greenberg Traurig LLP, Washington, DC
202 331 3100
dwyerj@gtlaw.com
*Recommended in Real Estate*
**Practice Areas:** Real estate; corporate and securities; REITs.
**Prof. Memberships:** Member, District of Columbia Bar Association; Member, New York State Bar Association; Member, American College of Real Estate Lawyers; Corporate Secretary and General Counsel, Association of Foreign Investors in US Real Estate, 1988-96.
**Career:** Listed, Chambers & Partners USA Guide, 2003-06; listed, 'Best Lawyers in America'.
**Publications:** Co-authored a major law treatise on real estate financing.
**Personal:** JD, Georgetown University Law Center, 1970; BS, Foreign Service, Georgetown University, 1967.

## DWYER, Maureen
Pillsbury Winthrop Shaw Pittman LLP, Washington, DC
202 663 8834

maureen.dwyer@pillsburylaw.com
*Recommended in Real Estate*
**Practice Areas:** Ms Dwyer's practice concentrates on zoning/municipal law. She represents clients developing new, retail, institutional, office and residential properties. Her knowledge includes land use, historic preservation, environmental, and building code approvals, including litigation and appellate work. Her clients include real estate developers and investors, corporate owners, institutions, foundations and individuals. She has a special emphasis on representing private universities.
**Prof. Memberships:** American College of Real Estate Lawyers, Greater Washington Board of Trade, Urban Land Institute, Federal City Council and DC Chamber of Commerce.
**Personal:** JD, Catholic University of America, Columbus School of Law, 1978; BA, Smith College, 1973.

## DYE, Alan L
Hogan & Hartson LLP, Washington, DC
202 637 5737
aldye@hhlaw.com
*Recommended in Securities*
**Practice Areas:** Alan Dye concentrates his practice on advising public companies and their directors and officers regarding their obligations under the federal securities laws and stock exchange listing requirements.
**Prof. Memberships:** Chairman, Securities, Commodities and Exchanges Committee, Administrative Law and Regulatory Practice Section, American Bar Association; Member, Securities Law Committee and Listing Standards Committee, Society of Corporate Secretaries and Governance Professionals.
**Career:** SEC, 1982-86; Adjunct Professor, Georgetown University Law Center, 1991-96; co-author of numerous books and articles on federal securities laws.
**Personal:** Emory University (BA, with high honors, 1975); University of Georgia (JD, salutatorian and Order of the Coif).

## EASTMENT, Thomas
Baker Botts LLP, Washington, DC
202 639 7717
tom.eastment@bakerbotts.com
*Recommended in Energy*
**Practice Areas:** Represents producers, refiners and other shippers in oil and gas pipeline transportation and enforcement matters before FERC and federal trial and appellate courts; represents producers regarding royalty matters before the Department of the Interior and in state and federal courts; represents project owners regarding FERC certificate applications for pipeline projects; and represents electric generation and other clients on gas supply and transportation contract matters.
**Prof. Memberships:** District of Columbia Bar; New York Bar; Energy Bar Asso-

ciation.
**Personal:** JD from the University of Michigan Law School, 1975; BChE from Manhattan College, 1972.

## ECCLES, Bob
O'Melveny & Myers LLP, Washington, DC
202 383 5363
beccles@omm.com
*Recommended in Employee Benefits, ERISA Litigation*
**Practice Areas:** Bob Eccles' practice focuses on ERISA litigation and in providing advice pertaining to Title I of ERISA and other statutes affecting employee benefit plans. Bob joined the firm in 1988 after 15 years as an attorney for the federal government, including five years as a trial attorney for the Department of Justice and 10 years as an ERISA attorney at the Department of Labor (DOL). From 1982-88, he was Associate Solicitor of Labor in charge of DOL attorneys who conducted litigation and provided legal advice under ERISA.

## EDGAR, George
Morgan, Lewis & Bockius LLP, Washington, DC 202 739 5459
gedgar@morganlewis.com
*Recommended in Energy*
**Practice Areas:** George L Edgar is a Partner in the Energy Practice and the firm's Client Service Partner. Mr Edgar represents nuclear industry clients before the Nuclear Regulatory Commission (NRC) and in related litigation in the federal courts.
**Prof. Memberships:** Member, Nuclear Energy Institute Lawyers' Committee; Vice-Chairman, American Bar Association, Section of Public Utility, Communications and Transportation Law, Atomic Energy Law Committee.

## EGAN JR, James C
Weil, Gotshal & Manges LLP, Washington, DC 202 682 7036
jim.egan@weil.com
*Recommended in Antitrust*
**Practice Areas:** James Egan specializes in antitrust counseling and litigation. He represents corporate clients in a range of industrial sectors, and has acted as lead counsel in federal, state and administrative litigation involving price fixing, mergers, joint ventures, boycotts, and other horizontal and vertical restraints. He served as Director of Litigation for the FTC's Bureau of Competition. Prior to being named Director of Litigation, Mr Egan held various FTC positions including Assistant Director for Mergers and Joint Ventures and Assistant Director for General Litigation.
**Personal:** University of South Florida, BA, 1966; St John's University, JD, 1971.

## EGGLESTON, W Neil
Debevoise & Plimpton LLP, Washington, DC 202 383 8000
*Recommended in Litigation*

## EISENSTAT, Larry

Dickstein Shapiro Morin & Oshinsky LLP, Washington, DC
202 828 2224
EisenstatL@dsmo.com
*Recommended in Energy*

**Practice Areas:** Energy, antitrust, eminent domain, and commercial litigation; focus on energy-related lawsuits, administrative proceedings, and rulemakings pertaining to virtually all aspects of energy project development, operations, and regulation, most commonly on behalf of competitive generation suppliers, energy marketers, financial institutions, and merchant transmission companies; extensive experience with utility solicitations, contract disputes, transmission interconnection and open access matters, power marketing and pricing issues, market rules, and system operations and planning.
**Career:** Partner and Head of Dickstein Shapiro's Electric Power Practice.
**Publications:** Lectured and written extensively on a variety of energy issues.
**Personal:** University of Chicago (BA, 1982; JD, 1985).

## ELGARTEN, Clifton S

Crowell & Moring LLP, Washington, DC
202 624 2523
celgarten@crowell.com
*Recommended in Insurance*

**Practice Areas:** Primary concentration is commercial disputes, arising in a variety of contexts. Active trial practice, before arbitrators, judges, and juries. Often called upon to analyze commercial and contractual disputes and to guide clients to a successful non-litigation outcome.
**Career:** Law clerk to the Honorable Louis H Pollak, US District Judge for the Eastern District of Pennsylvania, and to the Honorable William J Brennan, Associate Justice, US Supreme Court.
**Personal:** BA (magna cum laude), in 1975 from the City College of New York; JD (summa cum laude), from the Benjamin N Cardozo School of Law, Yeshiva University, in 1979.

## ELLIOTT, E Donald

Willkie Farr & Gallagher LLP, Washington, DC 202 303 1120
delliott@willkie.com
*Recommended in Environment*

**Practice Areas:** Partner and Chair of the firm's worldwide Environment Department. Advises companies in the US and European Union on environmental aspects of complex corporate and real estate sales and acquisitions. He has been lead negotiator on three environmental consent decrees involving over $1 billion each. He also represents companies and trade associations on major regulatory policy issues, class action litigation, product liability and legislative matters. Practice includes crisis management

involving product and site contamination issues, as well as environmental advocacy and legislative work for companies, trade associations and governments. Also has significant experience in environmental enforcement cases involving air, water and waste, class actions and complex product liability and toxic tort litigations, and food and drug law.
**Prof. Memberships:** Serves as a Member of the National Academy of Sciences Board on Environmental Studies and Toxicology, the top group that advises the federal government on environmental issues. Formerly served on the Regulation Committee of the Administrative Conference of the United States, the OTA Committee on Innovative Regulatory Techniques, the Federal Courts Study Committee, the Carnegie Commission on Science, Technology and Government, and Yale's 'Next Generation Project' to reform environmental laws. Also previously served as Sector Chair for the National Environmental Policy Institute, and Chair and Vice-Chair of the American Bar Association's Administrative Law and SONREEL Committees. A Member of the advisory boards of the Center for Clean Air Policy, the Environment Reporter, the Journal of Industrial Ecology and the Carnegie Mellon University Center for the Study and Improvement of Regulation.
**Career:** Has over 25 years of experience in all aspects of environmental and product liability law, including serving as general counsel of the US Environmental Protection Agency (1989-91), where he was the primary legal advisor to EPA administrator William Reilly. At the EPA, he was responsible for managing 125 attorneys, a $15 million legal budget and a litigation docket of more than 450 cases.
**Publications:** Author of more than 60 articles in professional journals, and a treatise on environmental regulation of the chemical industry.
**Personal:** From 1981-93, served as a tenured professor at the Yale Law School, teaching complex litigation, torts, environmental law, toxic torts, administrative law and constitutional law. Continues as an Adjunct Professor of environmental and administrative law and complex civil litigation at Yale and Georgetown Law Schools. Has lectured to international audiences on international and comparative environmental law and risk management topics in Germany, Italy, Belgium, Spain, Brazil and the United States. Received a JD (1st in class) from Yale Law School in 1974 and a BA from Yale College (Phi Beta Kappa, summa cum laude) in 1970.

## ELROD, Eugene R

Sidley Austin LLP, Washington, DC
202 736 8206
eelrod@sidley.com

*Recommended in Energy*

**Practice Areas:** Focuses on federal and state regulation of the production, transmission and distribution of natural gas, crude oil, petroleum products, and electric energy. He has represented a range of clients, including oil and gas producers, pipelines, local distribution and gas storage companies; electric utilities; and end-users of natural gas and electric power. He has tried cases at the Federal Energy Regulatory Commission, in state courts and before state regulatory commissions, and has briefed and argued cases in both federal and state appellate courts.
**Prof. Memberships:** He currently serves on the Board of Directors of the Charitable Foundation of the Energy Bar Association, and on the Advisory Board of the Institute for Energy Law of The Center for American and International Law. He previously served as a Director of the Energy Bar Association, and as the Association's liaison with FERC's Administrative Law Judges.
**Personal:** Mr Elrod was a trial attorney for gas pipeline and electric utility rate matters (1974-76) at the Federal Power Commission and also worked at the Federal Energy Administration (1977), predecessor of DOE, on crude oil pricing and allocation matters. Emory University School of Law, JD, 1974; Dartmouth College, AB, 1971. Admissions: District of Columbia and Georgia.

## ENGEL, John

Pillsbury Winthrop Shaw Pittman LLP, Washington, DC
202 663 8863
john.engel@pillsburylaw.com
*Recommended in Real Estate*

**Practice Areas:** Mr Engel's practice includes counseling institutional lenders; local, regional, and national developers; international organizations and non-profit institutional clients. As Co-Leader of the firm's national Real Estate Section, he works with more than 100 lawyers from offices in Washington, DC, Northern Virginia, Houston, New York City, San Francisco, Century City and other key California locations. His practice encompasses traditional purchase and sale transactions, as well as working with investment advisors to structure and consummate the sale of property portfolios and privatization of military housing.
**Personal:** JD, Georgetown University Law Center, 1971; BA, Yale University, 1965.

## ENGH, Anna

Covington & Burling, Washington, DC
202 662 5221
aengh@cov.com
*Recommended in Insurance*

**Practice Areas:** Represent policyholders in insurance coverage litigation and in insurance settlement contexts for a variety of claims, including asbestos, breast

implants, lead, and other mass torts; environmental liability; political risks; property damage including hurricane claims; and D&O and errors and omissions claims.
**Personal:** William and Mary Law School, (JD, 1989); Davidson College (BA, 1981).

## ENGLERT JR, Roy

Robbins, Russell, Englert, Orseck & Untereiner LLP, Washington, DC
202 775 4500
*Recommended in Litigation*

## EPSTEIN, Gary

Latham & Watkins LLP, Washington, DC
202 637 2200
*Recommended in Telecom, Broadcast & Satellite*

## EPSTIEN, Jay

DLA Piper Rudnick Gray Cary US LLP, Washington, DC 202 861 3850
jay.epstien@dlapiper.com
*Recommended in Real Estate*

**Practice Areas:** Real estate.
**Career:** Represents owners, developers, and users in all aspects of real estate transactions involving urban office buildings, shopping centers, and multifamily residential projects. The lead lawyer on many of the largest downtown office leases in Washington, DC, he was named the Top Real Estate Lawyer in DC by the Washington Business Journal and is listed in 'The Best Lawyers in America', 'An International Who's Who of Real Estate Lawyers', PLC's 'Global Counsel Handbook of Corporate Real Estate', and LMG's 'Guide to the World's Leading Real Estate Lawyers'.
**Personal:** JD, Cornell University; BS, Case Western Reserve University.

## ESTES III, John N

Skadden, Arps, Slate, Meagher & Flom LLP & Affiliates, Washington, DC
202 371 7950
jestes@skadden.com
*Recommended in Energy*

**Practice Areas:** Focuses on complex FERC litigation and enforcement matters, often involving restructured electric markets. Played a lead role in obtaining a favorable decision in 2005 from the FERC trial judge in the New England LICAP case, representing a large coalition of generators. Other key trials include the California Refund Case, the California Long-Term Contract Case and the AEP into PJM Case. Also has an active FERC enforcement and compliance practice. Spent five years at the FERC briefing and arguing cases before the various United States courts of appeals.
**Career:** JD, Louisiana State University, 1983; BA, Tulane University, 1979.

## ESTRADA, Miguel A

Gibson, Dunn & Crutcher LLP, Washington, DC 202 955 8257
mestrada@gibsondunn.com

*Recommended in Litigation*

**Practice Areas:** Represented clients in federal - state courts and in international arbitrations. Has handled numerous matters before United States Supreme Court, under False Claims Act, bankruptcy law, RICO, and ERISA. Extensive Supreme Court experience includes lead counsel (Prometheus Radio Project v FCC, Aetna v Davila) and part of team (Bush v Gore).

**Career:** Former Supreme Court Law Clerk; former assistant, solicitor general of US; former assistant, US attorney and Deputy Chief of Appellate Section, US Attorney's Office, Southern District of New York.

**Personal:** JD, Harvard Law School, 1986, editor Harvard Law Review.

## EVANS, Mark
Kellogg, Huber, Hansen, Todd, Evans & Figel, PLLC, Washington, DC
202 326 7900
*Recommended in Telecom, Broadcast & Satellite*

## FARABOW, Ford F
Finnegan Henderson Farabow Garrett & Dunner LLP, Washington, DC
202 408 4044
ford.farabow@finnegan.com
*Recommended in Intellectual Property*

**Practice Areas:** Practice includes trials in federal district and state courts throughout the country, domestic and foreign arbitrations, as well as mini-trials and other alternative dispute resolution processes. Has successfully tried jury and non-jury patent infringement cases for both patentees and for companies accused of infringement. Litigates jury and non-jury patent infringement cases. His work as lead counsel in patent, trade secret, and licensing disputes has focused on the technical fields of chemistry, pharmaceuticals, chemical engineering, and materials science. At the appellate level, has handled and won numerous cases in the federal circuit and other circuits.

**Prof. Memberships:** District of Columbia Bar, South Carolina Bar, Federal Circuit Bar Association, American Intellectual Property Law Association, Giles S Rich American Inn of Court.

**Personal:** Clemson University (BS, Chemical Engineering, 1959), George Washington University National Law Center (JD, 1963).

## FARMER, Scott
McKee Nelson LLP, Washington, DC
202 775 8672
sfarmer@mckeenelson.com
*Recommended in Tax*

**Practice Areas:** Taxation, tax controversy, international taxation. Advises clients on all aspects of international tax planning and controversy with the Internal Revenue Service. Clients include US firms engaged in foreign business activities, as well as foreign-based firms operating

within the United States.

**Career:** Prior to joining McKee Nelson in January 2000, was Head of the International Tax Practice at Miller & Chevalier, Chartered, Washington, DC. He is Vice-Chair of the US Council for International Business and a frequent lecturer at the World Trade Institute and the Tax Executives Institute.

**Publications:** Has written frequently on international tax topics, including 'Section 1248 and Partnerships' (2006) and 'Branching Out - Reexamining Branch Rules in the Context of Check-the-Box', 15 Tax Notes International 1951 (December 15, 1997).

**Personal:** Received LLM in Taxation, with highest honors, from the George Washington University Law School in 1983, and JD from the University of North Carolina at Chapel Hill Law School in 1982.

## FARQUHAR, Michele C
Hogan & Hartson LLP, Washington, DC
202 637 5663
mcfarquhar@hhlaw.com
*Recommended in Telecom, Broadcast & Satellite*

**Practice Areas:** Michele Farquhar serves as Co-Director of the firm's Communications Group and is the current President of the Federal Communications Bar Association. Her practice focuses on commercial and private wireless and mass media regulation, strategic planning on complex spectrum allocation and auction-related transactional issues, regulation and licensing of new domestic and foreign technologies, and global telecommunications convergence and competition issues.

**Career:** Prior to joining the firm, Michele has served in many important roles, including chief of the Wireless Telecommunications Bureau at the Federal Communications Commission, assistant secretary and chief of staff for the National Telecommunications and Information Administration at the US Department of Commerce, Vice President for law and regulatory policy at the Cellular Telecommunication Industry Association, and senior advisor/mass media legal advisor for an FCC commissioner.

**Personal:** University of Virginia School of Law (JD); Duke University (BA, magna cum laude).

## FARR, Bartow
Farr & Taranto, Washington, DC
202 775 0184
*Recommended in Litigation*

## FAVRETTO, Richard J
Mayer, Brown, Rowe & Maw LLP, Washington, DC 202 263 3250
rfavretto@mayerbrown.com
*Recommended in Antitrust*

**Practice Areas:** 15 years' service in the Antitrust Division of the US Department

of Justice, culminating as Deputy Assistant Attorney General and Acting Assistant Attorney General. Two+ decades of private practice focusing on antitrust law. Experience in government and private practice covers the entire range of US and international antitrust substance and procedure involving mergers and acquisitions, joint ventures, criminal and civil trial litigation, and appellate arguments in the US Supreme Court and various state and federal courts of appeal. Rose to highest career position in DOJ Antitrust Division and served successively as a trial attorney, Assistant to the Director of Operations, Assistant Trial Section Chief, Deputy Director of Operations, Deputy Assistant Attorney General, and Acting Assistant Attorney General in charge of the Antitrust Division.

**Career:** Mayer, Brown, Rowe & Maw LLP, Washington, DC, 1981 to date; Partner, 1981. Antitrust Division, US Department of Justice: Deputy Assistant Attorney General, 1979-81; Deputy Director of Operations, 1976-79; Assistant Chief, Trial Section, 1973-76; Assistant to the Director of Operations, 1970-73; trial attorney, New York Field Office, 1966-70.

**Personal:** LLB, Catholic University of America, 1966; student material editor, Law Review. BA (cum laude), Iona College, 1963.

## FEINSTEIN, Deborah
Arnold & Porter LLP, Washington, DC
202 942 5015
Deborah.Feinstein@aporter.com
*Recommended in Antitrust*

**Practice Areas:** Ms Feinstein is a leading antitrust lawyer, principally focusing on merger and acquisition matters before the Federal Tarde Commission and the Department of Justice. Ms Feinstein has advised clients on hundreds of transactions, involving virtually all sectors of the economy. She has special expertise in the following areas: retail, food, consumer products, healthcare, chemicals, and automotive parts. She represented The Kroger Co. in its acquisition of Fred Meyer, the largest grocery store transaction ever completed. She represented Philip Morris and Kraft in connection with their acquisition of Nabisco. She also represents General Electric in transactions involving a variety of its business units, most recently its transactions with Instrumentarium, a competing medical equipment provider, and Vivendi.

**Career:** From 1989-91, she served as a special assistant to the Director of the Bureau of Competition of the Federal Trade Commission and attorney advisor to Commissioner Dennis Yao.

**Publications:** 'Merger Enforcement in Innovation Markets: The Latest Chapter - Genzyme/Novazyme'; The Antitrust Source, July 2004. 'Taking Stock: Recent Trends in U.S. Merger Enforcement'; Antitrust Volume 18, No 2, Spring 2004.

Item 4(c): The Next Step in HSR Reform; Clayton Act Newsletter, Vol I, No 2, Spring 2001.

**Personal:** In July 2004, Ms Feinstein was named in Global Competition Review's international list of Top 100 Women in Antitrust, which profiles 100 women who are at the top of their field from around the world. In addition, she has been named by Chambers & Partners Global's survey of The World's Leading Lawyers as one of the 'top' antitrust attorneys in Washington, DC in each year from 2001-05.

## FELLNER, Baruch A
Gibson, Dunn & Crutcher LLP, Washington, DC 202 955 8591
bfellner@gibsondunn.com
*Recommended in Employment*

**Practice Areas:** Practice focuses on employment law with special emphasis on occupational safety and health. Extensive experience in litigation, including labor and pension issues. Has argued numerous cases in all the courts of appeals throughout the nation and two major constitutional cases in the Supreme Court of the United States.

**Career:** Served as NLRB Supervisory Apellate Counsel, Department of Labor OSHA Counsel for Appellate and Regional Litigation and as Pension Benefit Guaranty Corporation Associate General Counsel for Litigation.

**Publications:** Frequent speaker on OSHA matters; author of 'Occupational Safety and Health Law and Practice'.

**Personal:** JD, Harvard Law School, 1968.

## FENTON, Kathryn M
Jones Day, Washington, DC
202 879 3746
kmfenton@jonesday.com
*Recommended in Antitrust*

**Practice Areas:** Represents clients in mergers and acquisitions and on competitive issues before the Department of Justice, the Federal Trade Commission, the Department of Transportation, and the Federal Communications Commission. Advises on antitrust issues of joint ventures, distribution, information exchanges, and dealings with competitors. She has written and lectured on issues of professional responsibility, conflicts of interest, and legal ethics. Listed in 'The Best Lawyers in America' and 'Who's Who in American Law'.

**Prof. Memberships:** Vice-Chair of the ABA Section of Antitrust Law and will become Chair of the Section in August 2007.

## FEOLA, Phil
Pillsbury Winthrop Shaw Pittman LLP, Washington, DC 202 663 8000
*Recommended in Real Estate*

## FEORE, John R

Dow, Lohnes & Albertson, PLLC,
Washington, DC 202 776 2786
jfeore@dowlohnes.com
*Recommended in Telecom, Broadcast & Satellite*

**Practice Areas:** Mr Feore represents television and radio station clients (particularly group owners) and emerging broadcast networks before the Federal Communications Commission, Congress and other agencies in Washington. He has represented buyers, sellers and financiers of broadcast stations, assisted in structuring media investments and the construction of new facilities and has advised lenders/investment funds on federal regulatory issues.

**Prof. Memberships:** Federal Communications Bar Association; District of Columbia Bar Association; American Bar Association.

**Career:** Partner since 1980.

**Personal:** Georgetown University (JD, 1974); University of Wisconsin-Madison (MA, 1969); Boston College (BA, 1968).

## FERRARA, Ralph C

LeBoeuf, Lamb, Greene & McRae LLP,
Washington, DC 202 986 8020
rferrara@llgm.com
*Recommended in Securities*

**Practice Areas:** Managing Partner of LeBoeuf's Washington office. Represents corporations and individuals in complex securities class and shareholder derivative actions; advises corporate clients on SEC reporting and disclosure requirements; represents corporations and individuals in government investigations and enforcement proceedings; conducts corporate internal investigations; and counsels corporate officers and boards. Former general counsel at the SEC.

**Career:** Joined LeBoeuf in 2005; Debevoise & Plimpton (1981-2004).

**Publications:** Co-author, 'Practicing At Your Peril: Attorneys Increasingly Face SEC Enforcement Actions and Criminal Prosecutions', Bloomberg Law Reports (2005).

**Personal:** George Washington National Law Center (LLM) 1972; University of Cincinnati (JD) 1970; Georgetown University (BS/BA) 1967.

## FERRERA, Tess

Tighe Patton Armstrong Teasdale PLLC,
Washington, DC 202 545 2860
tferrera@tighepatton.com
*Recommended in Employee Benefits*

**Practice Areas:** Partner in the Washington office of Tighe Patton Armstrong Teasdale, LLP. Ms Ferrera provides advice and handles litigation under ERISA for a broad range of clients, including financial institutions, investment advisors, third party administrators, plan sponsors and MEWAs in actions alleging breach of fiduciary duty, prohibited transactions and other matters under Title I. Ms Ferrera routinely defends clients under investigation by the United States Department of Labor (DOL). Before entering private practice, Ms Ferrera was an ERISA attorney at the DOL where she litigated numerous cases raising issues of first impression in the context of Multiple Employer Welfare Arrangements (MEWAs).

**Prof. Memberships:** ABA, Women's Bar Association of the District of Columbia.

**Publications:** Author of Aspen Publishers ERISA Fiduciary Answer Book, fifth edition as well as the third and fourth edition and all annual supplements of the book since 1997. Senior editor for the Journal of Pension Benefits and quarterly columnist on fiduciary issues under ERISA. Ms Ferrera is also a frequent author for periodicals published by the National Association of Professional Employer Organizations and a frequent speaker on ERISA's fiduciary standards of care and prohibited transactions.

**Personal:** JD, Georgetown University Law Center, 1990, with honors; BA, George Washington University, 1980.

## FERRIS, Charles

Mintz Levin Cohn Ferris Glovsky and Popeo PC, Washington, DC
202 434 7300
*Recommended in Telecom, Broadcast & Satellite*

## FIELD, Andrea Bear

Hunton & Williams, Washington, DC
202 955 1500
afield@hunton.com
*Recommended in Environment*

**Practice Areas:** Andrea Bear Field focuses on environmental and administrative law, representing clients in federal rulemakings and litigation arising under the Clean Air Act and other environmental statutes, with recent emphasis on enforcement actions brought under the Clean Air Act's new source review provisions. She also counsels clients on a range of environmental permitting issues. Representative clients: electric utility, paper, coal, oil, and chemical companies. She has been named among The Best Lawyers in America for Environmental Law, one of Washingtonian magazine's 'Top Lawyers' for environmental law and a 2005 'Star of the Bar' by the DC Women's Bar Association.

## FITZ, William A

Covington & Burling, Washington, DC
202 662 5120
wfitz@cov.com
*Recommended in Telecom, Broadcast & Satellite*

**Practice Areas:** Federal licensing, legal compliance, rulemaking and strategic planning, including technical facility developments (eg, conversion to and use of digital spectrum); programming, advertising and noncommercial fundraising; foreign ownership, EEO and antitrust compliance; and business arrangements with programmers and other media outlets. Strategic planning, due diligence and evaluations for financing.

**Career:** Recent highlights: FCC approval including special ownership waivers for 15-station merger; FCC approval of client's station acquisition, spin-off of second station to third party with client's ability to program second station which it could not own.

## FITZGERALD, Mark R

Powers Pyles Sutter & Verville PC,
Washington, DC 202 466 6550
mark.fitzgerald@ppsv.com
*Recommended in Healthcare*

**Practice Areas:** Healthcare fraud and abuse and healthcare transactional work. Mr Fitzgerald advises clients on issues involving the federal anti-kickback statute, the Stark law, and rules governing Medicare reimbursement in connection with government investigations, voluntary disclosures, and business transactions.

**Prof. Memberships:** DC Bar; Maryland Bar; American Health Lawyers Association.

**Career:** PPSV, 1984-present.

**Publications:** 'Manufacturer Patient Assistance Programs - Inside or Outside Part D?' BNA's Medicare Report, Vol 17, No 03 (January 20, 2006); 'Stark II, Phase II: What it Means for AMC Financial Support Arrangements', American Health Lawyers Association Health Lawyers News, Vol 8, No 5, May 2004.

**Personal:** JD, Catholic University, 1982; BA, Fairfield University, 1979. Recognized as one of 12 'Outstanding Hospital Lawyers - 2003' by Nightingale's Healthcare News, 2003.

## FITZGERALD, Peter

Chadbourne & Parke, London
+44 207 337 8000
pfitzgerald@chadbourne.com
*Recommended in Projects*

**Practice Areas:** Represents multilateral agencies, lenders and developers in international project financings. Involved in power, telecom, oil and gas, transportation, petrochemical and other projects in emerging markets. Negotiates project financings involving multilateral and/or bilateral agency support. Represents foreign investors, lenders and political risk insurers in investment disputes and political risk matters, including political risk insurance and contract claims.

**Prof. Memberships:** New York State Bar Association; District of Columbia Bar Association; American Bar Association; International Bar Association.

**Career:** Previously served as chief counsel for project finance and political risk insurance matters at the Overseas Private Investment Corporation.

## FLEXNER, Donald L

Boies, Schiller & Flexner, Washington,
DC 202 237 2727
dflexner@bsfllp.com
*Recommended in Antitrust*

**Practice Areas:** Don Flexner's work includes all aspects of antitrust litigation in civil and criminal matters, as well as antitrust counseling involving mergers, acquisitions, joint ventures and a broad variety of compliance issues and merger reviews. He appears regularly in federal and state courts and before the US Department of Justice, Federal Trade Commission, and other federal agencies and state enforcement authorities. He currently serves as co-lead counsel for American Express in pursuing multi-billion dollar monopolization claims against Visa, Mastercard and member banks; he helped SBC Communications secure government approval of its merger with AT&T and successfully defended a major international airline in a recent government antitrust suit. Other clients include pharmaceutical and chemical manufacturers, telecommunications firms, entertainment companies and railroads.

**Career:** Antitrust Division, US Department of Justice (1967-80), serving as a trial attorney, Section Chief, and as Deputy Assistant Attorney General. Partner, Crowell & Moring (1980-99). Managing Partner, Boies, Schiller & Flexner LLP (1999-present).

**Personal:** BA (1964) and LLB (1967), New York University. Former Chair, Industry Regulation Committee of ABA Section on Antitrust Law.

## FOGGAN, Laura

Wiley Rein & Fielding LLP, Washington,
DC 202 719 3382
lfoggan@wrf.com
*Recommended in Insurance*

**Practice Areas:** More than 20 years of experience representing insurers in coverage disputes and critical appeals. Named one of the '100 Leading Women' in insurance by Business Insurance magazine.

**Prof. Memberships:** Counsel, Complex Insurance Claims Litigation Association; Member, Center for Public Resources Distinguished Panel of Neutrals for the Inter-Insurer Program; Member, Defense Research Institute, Appellate Advocacy and Insurance Coverage Committees; Elected Member, Federation of Defense and Corporate Counsel; Co-Chair, Steering Committee, District of Columbia Bar, Courts, Lawyers and the Administration of Justice Section.

**Personal:** The George Washington University Law School (JD); University of Pennsylvania (MS Ed); University of Pennsylvania (BA).

## FORD, Gary

Groom Law Group, Washington, DC
202 857 0620
*Recommended in Employee Benefits*

## FORD, John M

Morgan, Lewis & Bockius LLP,

Washington, DC 202 739 5856
jmford@morganlewis.com
*Recommended in Investment Management*

**Practice Areas:** John M Ford is a Partner in the Investment Management/Securities Industry Practice at Morgan Lewis. His practice focuses on investment company and investment advisor regulation, and counseling clients on the complex legal and operational issues affecting major financial institutions operating in today's challenging climate. He serves as fund counsel to a broad array of mutual fund complexes, and is experienced in the diverse issues impacting both large-scale fund operations and smaller complexes operating as niche players. Mr Ford routinely counsels fund and advisor clients in mergers, acquisitions and fund reorganizations and adoptions.

**FORTNEY, David**
Fortney & Scott, LLC, Washington, DC
202 689 1200
*Recommended in Employment*

**FOX, Allen H**
WilmerHale, Washington, DC
202 663 6087
allen.fox@wilmerhale.com
*Recommended in Real Estate*

**Practice Areas:** Partner, Real Estate Department. Practice involves all aspects of real estate investment, development, finance, leasing, and sale and focuses on transactions involving acquisition, development, financing, sale and lease of office, industrial, multifamily residential, mixed-use, shopping center, and hotel properties. Served as counsel to broad range of clients engaged in real estate related transactions, including: New York Life Insurance Company, John Hancock Life Insurance Company; Spaulding and Slye, West*Group Properties, Aviation Facilities Company, Inc.; General Electric Capital Investment Advisors; Boston Consulting Group, Bookham Technology, Inc.
**Personal:** JD, with honors, George Washington University Law School; BA, cum laude, Washington University.

**FOX, Thomas**
Reed Smith LLP, Washington, DC
202 414 9222
tfox@reedsmith.com
*Recommended in Healthcare*

**Practice Areas:** Litigation and counseling healthcare clients on business relationships, corporate restructuring, bankruptcy reorganizations and government investigations. Has handled or supervised the presentation of numerous health law-related cases before the US Supreme Court, various Circuit Courts of Appeal, District Courts, and other courts and agencies.
**Publications:** Contributing author and editor of healthcare law publications, including the 'Health Care Financial

Transactions Manual'.
**Personal:** George Washington University (LLB, 1966); Muskingum College (BA, 1963); listed in Corporate Counsel's 'Best Lawyers: Healthcare', National Law Journal's 'Who's Who in Health Care Law', 'Best Lawyers in America', Washingtonian's 'Best Lawyers in Washington'.

**FRANKEL, Roger**
Orrick, Herrington & Sutcliffe LLP,
Washington, DC 202 339 8513
rfrankel@orrick.com
*Recommended in Bankruptcy*

**Practice Areas:** Practice ranges from multi-bank out-of-court workouts to proceedings under state insolvency statutes and Federal Bankruptcy Code. Counsels clients in a variety of industries including healthcare, energy and asbestos.
**Prof. Memberships:** Admitted to practice in Washington, DC (1971); Maryland (1972). Member, Maryland Merit Selection Panels.
**Career:** Co-Chair, Orrick's Bankruptcy and Debt Restructuring Practice. Formerly, Partner, Swidler Berlin (1992-2005), Managing Partner (1998-2000).
**Publications:** Co-author, 'Inside the Minds: The Art and Science of Bankruptcy Law', 2003.
**Personal:** JD (with honors), George Washington Law School, 1971; BA, Brandeis University, 1968.

**FRANKLIN, Jonathan S**
Hogan & Hartson LLP, Washington, DC
202 637 5766
jsfranklin@hhlaw.com
*Recommended in Litigation*

**Practice Areas:** Focuses on Supreme Court and appellate litigation, with extensive experience in both judicial and administrative proceedings. Has argued five cases before the US Supreme Court; has litigated numerous other cases before the Court at the certiorari and merits stages; and has argued and briefed many other cases in federal and state courts at trial and appellate levels. His cases have involved constitutional law, administrative law and procedure, and intellectual property, contract, tort, insurance, civil rights, antitrust, labor, telecommunications and international law.
**Prof. Memberships:** Barrister, Edward Coke Appellate Inn of Court.
**Personal:** Yale Law School (JD); Harvard College (AB).

**FRANTZ, Steven**
Morgan, Lewis & Bockius LLP,
Washington, DC 202 739 5460
sfrantz@morganlewis.com
*Recommended in Energy*

**Practice Areas:** Steven P Frantz is a Partner in the Energy Practice. Mr Frantz represents and counsels electric utilities, manufacturers of reactors and materials licensees on the regulation and licensing of nuclear power plants, as well as other

facilities regulated by the Nuclear Regulatory Commission (NRC) and the Department of Energy (DOE). Mr Frantz has devoted a substantial part of his practice to the licensing and certification of new nuclear power plants and assisting utilities in developing strategies for helping nuclear plants obtain permission to resume construction or operation following NRC enforcement action.

**FREED, Joel**
McDermott Will & Emery, Washington,
DC 202 756 8080
jfreed@mwe.com
*Recommended in Intellectual Property*

**Practice Areas:** Practice covers nearly every aspect of intellectual property law and its interface with antitrust, including jury and bench trials, appellate advocacy, licensing, proceedings before the United States Patent and Trademark Office, and International Trade Commission actions.
**Career:** Former Patent Examiner; Patent and Trademark Prosecution; Lead Counsel in Patent, Trademark and Trade Secret cases (including patent interferences, Section 337 actions, and trademark oppositions and cancellations) spanning electrical, mechanical, pharmaceutical, and biotechnology fields; Adjunct Law Professor (intellectual property).
**Personal:** Georgetown University Law Center (JD); Lehigh University (BA, BS).

**FREEDMAN, Roberta**
Duane Morris LLP, Washington, DC
202 776 7804
rfreedman@duanemorris.com
*Recommended in Immigration*

**Practice Areas:** Roberta Freedman practices in the area of immigration and nationality law. Ms Freedman has more than 20 years of experience in representing clients, including healthcare providers, business professionals, outstanding professors and researchers, and Fortune 500 corporations. She has been selected by the US Citizenship and Immigration Services (CIS) to lead high profile joint CIS-private sector projects.
**Prof. Memberships:** American Immigration Lawyers Association; American Bar Association.
**Career:** Admitted to practice in the District of Columbia; the Supreme Court of the United States; United States District Court of Appeals for the Fourth Circuit; Court of Appeals of Maryland; and the District of Columbia Court of Appeals.
**Publications:** Contributing author, 'Professionals: A Matter of Degree', 4th ed, 2003; contributing author, 'The Visa Processing Guide', 1994, 1995, 1996, 1997, 1998, 1999, 2000, 2002-03; co-author, 'A Survey of J-1 Physicians Interested Government Agency Waiver Programs Available Following the Completion of the Exchange Visitor Program', Immigration Law Committee Update, 1998.
**Personal:** University of Baltimore School

of Law, JD, 1983; Syracuse University, BA, 1980.

**FREMUTH, Michael**
Andrews Kurth LLP, Washington, DC
202 662 2700
*Recommended in Energy*

**FRIED, Bruce Merlin**
Sonnenschein Nath & Rosenthal LLP,
Washington, DC
202 408 9159
bfried@sonnenschein.com
*Recommended in Healthcare*

**Practice Areas:** Counsels and represents health plans, physician organizations, hospital groups, healthcare information technology and data companies, pharmaceutical and biotech companies with regard to Medicare, Medicaid, HIPAA and other federal healthcare programs and policies, and privacy and technology applications in the healthcare sector.
**Prof. Memberships:** Member, American Health Lawyers Association; Board of Trustees, United Cerebral Palsy; Member, National Advisory Committee of the Berman Bioethics Institute of Johns Hopkins University; Chair, Advisory Committee for the Department of Health Policy at George Washington University.
**Personal:** University of Florida College of Law, JD; University of Florida, BA.

**FRIES, Joseph**
Arent Fox PLLC, Washington, DC
202 857 6156
fries.joseph@arentfox.com
*Recommended in Real Estate*

**Practice Areas:** Principal area of expertise is in the planning, structuring, negotiation and documentation of complex real estate transactions. Joe represents individuals and firms that are active in the real estate industry (such as developers, architects, lenders and real estate investors), in addition to institutions that are not engaged in the real estate business, but that have real estate needs.
**Prof. Memberships:** Member and former governor of American College of Real Estate Lawyers.
**Career:** Served several years as a contributing editor of the Legal Times.
**Personal:** Harvard Law School, LLB (cum laude) 1961; Cornell University, AB (high honors in Government) 1958.

**FROST JR, Don J**
Skadden, Arps, Slate, Meagher & Flom
LLP & Affiliates, Washington, DC
202 371 7422
dfrost@skadden.com
*Recommended in Environment*

**Practice Areas:** Focuses on environmental litigation, including civil and criminal enforcement matters, government cost recovery actions, administrative cleanup and permitting proceedings, private cost recovery and contribution actions, bankruptcy matters, and alterna-

tive dispute resolution proceedings. Has substantial experience in environmental transactional matters and compliance counseling.
**Career:** JD, Duke University School of Law, 1988 (with honors; articles editor, Alaska Law Review); MA, Duke University Graduate School, 1988 (Resource Economics and Policy); BA, Carleton College, 1983 (cum laude).

## GAGE, Robert J
Covington & Burling, Washington, DC
202 662 5636
rgage@cov.com
*Recommended in Real Estate*
**Practice Areas:** Chair of Real Estate Group, his practice focuses on commercial real estate, including acquisitions, joint ventures, financings, development, construction, leasing and sales. He also has a significant practice representing not-for-profit organizations, including quasi-governmental entities. Representative clients include: Brookings Institution, GOJO Industries, NHP Foundation, Ourisman Automotive Group, RREEF, and Union Station Redevelopment Corporation.
**Prof. Memberships:** Member, DC Bar Association, Urban Land Institute and Building Industry Association.
**Career:** Joined Covington, 1977; Partner, 1985.
**Personal:** JD (cum laude), Harvard Law School, 1977; MPP, Harvard University John F Kennedy School of Government, 1977; BA (summa cum laude), Kent State University, 1973.

## GALLAGHER, Robert
Groom Law Group, Washington, DC
202 857 0620
*Recommended in Employee Benefits*

## GALLO, Kenneth A
Paul, Weiss, Rifkind, Wharton & Garrison LLP, Washington, DC
202 223 7356
kgallo@paulweiss.com
*Recommended in Antitrust*
**Practice Areas:** Represents clients in private and government antitrust disputes including claims related to monopolization, tying, mergers and acquisitions, civil and criminal price fixing, Kodak theories, product distribution and the interplay between the antitrust and intellectual property laws. Litigation Partner with substantial trial experience in antitrust, patent and major commercial disputes. Has trial experience involving the banking and payments industries, computer hardware and software products, medical and telecommunications equipment, commercial real estate, and biotechnology products. Managing Partner of the Washington, DC office.

## GARRETT, Theodore
Covington & Burling, Washington, DC
202 662 5398

tgarrett@cov.com
*Recommended in Environment*
**Practice Areas:** Extensive experience in environmental compliance, transaction and enforcement issues, including air and water regulatory matters and Superfund sites.
**Career:** Law clerk to Chief Justice Warren Burger, US Supreme Court. Special assistant to Assistant Attorney General William Rehnquist, USDOJ. Co-Chair, Covington's Environmental Practice.
**Publications:** Editor and principal author, 'Environmental Guide for Corporate Counsel'; editor, 'RCRA Compliance Manual'; co-author, 'Clean Air Deskbook' (1992); authored chapters of 'Environmental Litigation' and 'The Clean Water Act Handbook'.
**Personal:** Past Chair, ABA Section of Environment, Energy and Resources. Member, DC, NY, and US Supreme Court Bars. BA, Yale University; JD, Columbia Law School.

## GARZA, Deborah
Fried, Frank, Harris, Shriver & Jacobson LLP, Washington, DC
202 639 7270
Deborah.Garza@FriedFrank.com
*Recommended in Antitrust*
**Practice Areas:** Antitrust Partner.
**Career:** Currently also Chairperson of US Antitrust Modernization Commission (by appointment of President George W Bush), which will submit a report and recommendations on US antitrust law to the US President and Congress by April 2007. Also member of US Chamber of Commerce Antitrust Council and non-governmental advisor to International Competition Network. Formerly Chief of Staff and Counselor and special assistant to Assistant Attorney General for Antitrust, US Department of Justice.
**Personal:** JD (1981), University of Chicago.

## GAYNOR, Kevin
Vinson & Elkins LLP, Washington, DC
202 639 6688
kgaynor@velaw.com
*Recommended in Environment*
**Practice Areas:** Co-chairs the firm's Environmental Practice.
**Prof. Memberships:** Member: Environment, Energy, and Natural Resources Steering Committee, DC Bar; Environment and Litigation Sections, American Bar Association.
**Career:** Admitted to Connecticut Bar in 1973, District of Columbia Bar in 1978, and Maryland Bar in 1991. Joined the firm as a Partner in 1993.
**Publications:** Environmental Enforcement Developments in 2003, 'The Environmental Law Reporter', News & Analysis, January 2004. 'TVA Decision Calls EPA's Unilateral Enforcement Authorities Into Question', Environment Reporter,

Analysis & Perspective, August 2003.

## GELFAND, David I
Cleary Gottlieb Steen & Hamilton LLP, Washington, DC 202 974 1690
dgelfand@cgsh.com
*Recommended in Antitrust*
**Practice Areas:** Antitrust and litigation. Represents clients in M&A before DOJ and FTC. Litigates cases in state and federal courts. Spent three years (2001-04) in Brussels and represented clients before European Commission. Significant matters in recent years include: Alcoa/ Reynolds merger; Glaxo/SmithKline merger; Conoco/Phillips merger; Siemens' acquisition of Alstom's turbine business; IBM's sale of hard drive business to Hitachi; DSM's acquisition of Roche's vitamins business; Alcoa's acquisition of Russian aluminum rolling mills; UCB's sale of its chemicals business to Cytec; Premcor/Valero merger; GlaxoSmithKline acquisition of ID Biomedical; and treble damage actions in various courts. Counsels clients on antitrust aspects of proposed business arrangements including IP licenses, joint ventures, and business practices.
**Career:** Joined firm, 1991, became Partner, 1997. JD, summa cum laude, Georgetown University Law Center (1987); BS, magna cum laude, University of Pennsylvania (1981).

## GELLER, Kenneth S
Mayer, Brown, Rowe & Maw LLP, Washington, DC 202 263 3225
kgeller@mayerbrownrowe.com
*Recommended in Litigation*
**Practice Areas:** Appellate litigation, specializing in Supreme Court and appellate practice. Wrote or edited some 300 briefs and certiorari petitions in the Supreme Court. Argued some 40 cases in the Supreme Court.
**Career:** Joined Mayer, Brown, Rowe & Maw LLP as Partner, 1986. Partner in Charge of Washington, DC, office and Member of firm Management Committee. Former Deputy Solicitor General, US Department of Justice, 1979-86; assistant to the Solicitor General, United States Department of Justice, 1975-79; Assistant Special Prosecutor, Watergate Special Prosecution Force, 1973-75; Nickerson, Kramer, Lowenstein, Nessen and Kamin, New York, 1972-73; law clerk to The Honorable Walter R Mansfield, US Court of Appeals for the Second Circuit, 1971-72.
**Publications:** Co-author: 'Supreme Court Practice', 8th ed, 2002; 7th ed, BNA (1993). Contributing author: 'Business and Commercial Litigation in Federal Courts' (2d edn 2005).
**Personal:** Harvard University, JD magna cum laude, 1971; editor, Law Review. City College of New York, BA magna cum laude, 1968. Presidential Award for Distinguished Service, 1983.

## GENTILE, Carmen
Bruder Gentile & Marcoux LLP, Washington, DC 202 296 1500
*Recommended in Energy*

## GERGEN, Michael
Latham & Watkins LLP, Washington, DC 202 637 2200
*Recommended in Energy*

## GERSCH, David P
Arnold & Porter LLP, Washington, DC
202 942 5125
David.Gersch@aporter.com
*Recommended in Litigation*
**Practice Areas:** David Gersch, a Senior Partner of Arnold & Porter LLP, is an experienced trial and appellate lawyer who has appeared as lead counsel in numerous complex antitrust, commercial and tort actions.
**Career:** Mr Gersch has a broad litigation practice. In recent years, he has successfully tried jury cases involving diet drugs and transfusion-AIDS. He has also tried significant commercial disputes. He has argued appeals in the United States Courts of Appeal and the state appellate courts. He represents clients in significant antitrust matters and is national counsel for a major insurer. Other actions handled by Mr Gersch include defense of intellectual property, pension, and toxic tort suits.
**Personal:** JD, New York University School of Law, 1982; AB, Oberlin College, 1978.

## GERSTELL, Glenn
Milbank, Tweed, Hadley & McCloy LLP, Washington, DC 202 835 7500
*Recommended in Telecom, Broadcast & Satellite*

## GIBBS, Lawrence
Miller & Chevalier Chartered, Washington, DC 202 626 5800
lgibbs@milchev.com
*Recommended in Tax*
**Practice Areas:** Tax audits and administrative appeals; tax litigation and judicial appeals; alternative dispute resolution procedures; exempt organizations; research and experimentation credit; tax legislation; tax regulation.
**Prof. Memberships:** Tax Management - Advisory Board; American Bar Association - Committees on Government Relations, Formulation of Tax Policy, Administrative Practice, and Corporate Tax of the Taxation Section; American Tax Policy Institute Board; American College of Tax Counsel; American College of Trust and Estate Counsel; American Law Institute; Bar Association of DC; Federal Bar Association; Southern Federal Tax Institute; Tax Council Policy Institute; Tax Foundation Policy Committee.
**Career:** Member - Miller & Chevalier Chartered (1994-present); Commissioner - Internal Revenue Service (1986-89); Partner - Johnson & Gibbs, P.C. (former-

ly Johnson & Swanson) (1976--86); Assistant Commissioner - Internal Revenue Service (1973-75); Deputy Chief Counsel/Acting Chief Counsel - Internal Revenue Service (1972-73).
**Publications:** The Tax Executive - Reflections on Practicing Tax in Today's World (Winter 2005). Legal Times - Leading Lawyers: Ten Top Tax Attorneys (July 2005).
**Personal:** LLB, University of Texas School of Law, 1963; BA, Yale University, 1960.

### GIDEON, Kenneth W
Skadden, Arps, Slate, Meagher & Flom LLP & Affiliates, Washington, DC
202 371 7540
kgideon@skadden.com
*Recommended in Tax, Tax Litigation*
**Practice Areas:** Focuses on representation of clients before the US Department of the Treasury and the Internal Revenue Service; clients seeking guidance on novel transactions; and issues of federal tax law, tax controversy and tax planning. Advises clients on a wide variety of guidance, controversy (including tax litigation) and planning matters. Advises clients in connection with corporate mergers, acquisitions and restructurings, particularly in situations in which the transaction may require a ruling or informal discussion with the IRS.
**Prof. Memberships:** Chair, ABA Section of Taxation (2004-05).
**Career:** JD, Yale University Law School, 1971; BA, Harvard University, 1968.

### GIDLEY, J Mark
White & Case LLP, Washington, DC
202 626 3609
mgidley@whitecase.com
*Recommended in Antitrust*
**Practice Areas:** Chair of White & Case Global Antitrust Group. Extensive experience representing parties before global competition agencies and in court. Active Merger and Joint Venture Practice. Represents defendants in global cartel and class action cases. Strong transnational focus in practice.
**Prof. Memberships:** ABA (Antitrust Section).
**Career:** Acting Assistant Attorney General, US Department of Justice (DOJ) Antitrust Division, 1992-93; Deputy Assistant Attorney General, Antitrust Division, 1991-92.
**Personal:** JD, Columbia Law School, 1986; notes and comments editor, Columbia Law Review, 1985-86.

### GILBERT, Scott
Gilbert Heintz & Randolph LLP, Washington, DC 202 772 2225
*Recommended in Insurance*

### GISCHE, David
Ross Dixon & Bell LLP, Washington, DC
202 662 2000
*Recommended in Insurance*

### GLASGOW, JR, Norman
Holland & Knight LLP, Washington, DC
202 955 3000
norman.glasgowjr@hklaw.com
*Recommended in Real Estate*
**Practice Areas:** Partner in the firm's Real Estate Section, representing real estate developers in zoning, building code and historic preservation law matters before the Board of Zoning Adjustment, Zoning Commission, State Historic Review Board and Commission of Fine Arts. He has handled numerous cases before the Board of Zoning Adjustment and has participated in many major Zoning Commission cases. He also represents clients in street and alley closings. He is active in civic affairs; addressing the area's affordable housing crisis by working extensively with a number of non-profit affordable housing providers and community development corporations.

### GLASSPIEGEL, Harry
Pillsbury Winthrop Shaw Pittman LLP, Washington, DC 202 663 8170
harry.glasspiegel@pillsburylaw.com
*Recommended in Technology*
**Practice Areas:** Mr Glasspiegel, co-founder of the firm's Sourcing Customer Advisory Practice, is a well-known innovator and thought leader in the sourcing field. He has advised numerous companies and governmental entities in complex BPO, HRO and ITO sourcing arrangements inside and outside the US, and has worked closely on all phases of outsourcing transactions with customers, service providers, governmental entities, advisors and investors in diverse geographies and industry sectors.
**Prof. Memberships:** Admitted to practice: District of Columbia; founding advisor, Sourcing Interests Group (SIG).
**Personal:** JD, Wisconsin Law School, 1976; BA, Wesleyan University, 1972 (magna cum laude).

### GLEASON, Kathryn L
Morgan, Lewis & Bockius LLP, Washington, DC 202 739 5207
kgleason@morganlewis.com
*Recommended in Healthcare*
**Practice Areas:** Kathryn L Gleason is a Partner and Manager of the FDA/Healthcare Regulation Practice, resident in the Washington, DC, office. Her practice involves counseling and litigation for a broad range of institutional clients, both domestic and international, on regulatory science and legal issues involving premarket development, manufacturing, marketing and other areas of regulation compliance relating to medical devices, pharmaceuticals, biologicals, foods and food additives, nutritional supplements, functional foods, medical foods, cosmetics and radiological products.
**Prof. Memberships:** Member, AdvaMed Committee on Combination Products and Jurisdiction (2000-05).

### GLEKLEN, Jonathan
Arnold & Porter LLP, Washington, DC
202 942 5454
Jonathan.Gleklen@aporter.com
*Recommended in Antitrust*
**Practice Areas:** Jonathan Gleklen is a Partner in Arnold & Porter's Antitrust Practice Group. He is involved in a wide variety of civil litigation, government investigation, counseling, and transactional matters, with a focus on antitrust and intellectual property issues affecting clients in high technology industries.
**Publications:** He served as the Editorial Chair of the ABA's 2003 Annual Review of Antitrust Law Developmentsand was a principal author of 'The Federal Antitrust Guidelines for the Licensing of Intellectual Property: Origins and Applications' (2nd ed 2002). He currently serves on the Editorial Board of Antitrust Law Developments (sixth), the leading two-volume antitrust law treatise, and as a senior editor of the ABA's Antitrust Law Journal. His articles have appeared in publications including Antitrust Law Journal, Antitrust & Intellectual Property, and the Antitrust Source.
**Personal:** Mr Gleklen was one of four US antitrust lawyers identified by Global Competition Review as among the 'world's 40 brightest young antitrust lawyers and economists' in its February 2004 '40 Under 40' issue.

### GLOVER, Stephen I
Gibson, Dunn & Crutcher LLP, Washington, DC 202 955 8593
siglover@gibsondunn.com
*Recommended in Corporate/Commercial*
**Practice Areas:** Represents public and private companies in M&A, joint ventures, equity and debt offerings and corporate governance matters.
**Prof. Memberships:** Advisory Board of BNA's M&A Law Report; Editorial Board, The M&A Lawyer. Member, Securities Regulation, Negotiated Acquisitions and Venture Capital Committees, ABA's Business Law Section. Served as Adjunct Professor, Georgetown University Law Center. Chair, DC Bar Community Economic Development Committee. Former Co-Chair, DC Bar Corporations, Securities/Finance Committee. DC Bar representative, Tribar Opinion Committee.
**Publications:** Author/co-author of books, articles on corporate and securities law issues.
**Personal:** JD, Harvard Law School, 1980. Law clerk, US Supreme Court Justice Marshall.

### GOLDBERG, Henry
Goldberg Godles Weiner & Wright, Washington, DC 202 429 4900
*Recommended in Telecom, Broadcast & Satellite*

### GOLDBERG JR, Fred T
Skadden, Arps, Slate, Meagher & Flom LLP & Affiliates, Washington, DC
202 371 7110
fgoldber@skadden.com
*Recommended in Tax, Tax Litigation*
**Practice Areas:** Focuses on advising clients as special tax counsel on sensitive matters and representing clients on tax controversies, IRS administrative and regulatory proceedings, and tax legislation. Has directed compliance and management reviews on behalf of senior executives and boards of directors of various companies. Represents business, tax-exempt and individual clients during all phases of civil audit, administrative appeals and litigation. Also represents clients involved in IRS collection matters, clients subject to third-party IRS discovery proceedings and clients involved in IRS criminal investigations.
**Career:** Former IRS Chief Counsel (1984-86); former IRS Commissioner (1989-91); former Assistant Secretary for Tax Policy (1992); JD, Yale University, 1973; BA, Yale University, 1969.

### GOLDBLATT, Craig
WilmerHale, Washington, DC
202 663 6483
craig.goldblatt@wilmerhale.com
*Recommended in Bankruptcy*
**Practice Areas:** Practice focuses on complex civil litigation, with an emphasis on bankruptcy-related litigation and other restructuring matters. Has represented parties in many of the highest stakes and most complex bankruptcy disputes over the past several years, including trial and appellate matters arising out of the Enron collapse, the telecom 'bubble', and the nation's asbestos crisis.
**Prof. Memberships:** Advisory Committee of the United States District Court for the District of Columbia on Electronic Filing and Electronic Case Management.
**Personal:** University of Chicago Law School (JD 1993); Georgetown University (BA 1990).

### GOLDMAN, Roger
Latham & Watkins LLP, Washington, DC
202 637 2200
*Recommended in Healthcare*

### GOLDSMITH, Willis J
Jones Day, Washington, DC
202 879 3920
wgoldsmith@jonesday.com
*Recommended in Employment*
**Practice Areas:** Heads the firm's Labor and Employment Practice. Represents management in all phases of labor and employment law, including state and federal trials and appeals. Actively involved in collective bargaining and labor contract administration. Identified as one of the top 36 labor and employment lawyers in the US by The National Law Journal.
**Prof. Memberships:** Fellow of the College of Labor and Employment Lawyers.

Adviser, American Law Institute (Restatement Third, Employment Law). Advisory Board NYU School of Law Center for Labor and Employment Law. Admitted, District of Columbia and New York.
**Career:** Partner since 1983.

## GOLDSTEIN, Bruce
Zuckerman Spaeder LLP, Washington, DC 202 778 1800
*Recommended in Bankruptcy*

## GOLDSTEIN, Jorge A
Sterne, Kessler, Goldstein & Fox P.L.L.C., Washington, DC 202 371 2600
jgold@skgf.com
*Recommended in Intellectual Property*
**Practice Areas:** Dr Goldstein founded the Biotechnology Practice at Sterne, Kessler, Goldstein & Fox over 20 years ago. Recognized as a leader in his field, Dr Goldstein is often called in as an intellectual property strategist to look at the larger landscape and give advice.
**Career:** Dr Goldstein serves as Managing Director of Sterne, Kessler, Goldstein & Fox P.L.L.C.

## GOLDSTEIN, Thomas C
Akin Gump Strauss Hauer & Feld LLP, Washington, DC 202 887 4000
tgoldstein@akingump.com
*Recommended in Litigation*
**Practice Areas:** Mr Goldstein has argued 16 cases before the US Supreme Court. His practice focuses on briefing and arguing cases spanning a broad array of federal law questions, including both constitutional and statutory issues, for corporate, governmental and individual clients.
**Career:** Lecturer, Harvard Law School (2005-present); lecturer, Stanford Law School (2004-present); Goldstein & Howe, PC (1999-2006); Boies & Schiller (1997-99).
**Publications:** Founder and editor, www.scotusblog.com.
**Personal:** BA, University of North Carolina; JD, American University; former clerk, US Court of Appeals for the District of Columbia Circuit.

## GONZALEZ, Cecilia
Howrey LLP, Washington, DC 202 783 0800
*Recommended in Intellectual Property*

## GOODMAN, Saul
Covington & Burling, Washington, DC 202 662 5472
sgoodman@cov.com
*Recommended in Insurance*
**Practice Areas:** Represents policyholders in complex insurance coverage disputes, transactions and advice. Experience includes coverage for wide range of losses, including asbestos and other mass torts, environmental, D&O, first party property, IP and other major losses. Practice group coordinator for Covington's 70-member Policyholder Practice Group since 1997.

**Career:** Joined Covington in 1987; became Partner in 1989. Law Clerk to Judge Carl McGowan, US Court of Appeals for the District of Columbia Circuit (1978-79) and Justice Potter Stewart, US Supreme Court (1979-80).
**Publications:** Insurance publications include: 'Settlement of Insurance Coverage Disputes', in 'Law and Practice of Insurance Coverage Litigation' (West 2000).
**Personal:** BA, cum laude, Yale, 1975; JD, Virginia, 1978; executive editor, Virginia Law Review (1977-78).

## GOODWIN, Michael
Arnold & Porter LLP, Washington, DC 202 942 5558
Michael.Goodwin@aporter.com
*Recommended in Real Estate*
**Practice Areas:** His practice encompasses all facets of commercial real estate, with special focus on development, hospitality, financing and public/private partnership transactions. He represents developers in assemblages, debt and equity financing, and sales, and is heavily involved in structuring and negotiating public incentives for real estate development such as TIFs, PILOTs and tax abatement. He also represents hotel owners and operators in the acquisition, development, operation and sale of hospitality properties nationwide, including full service, convention center and resort hotels.
**Prof. Memberships:** He is a Member of the American College of Real Estate Lawyers.
**Career:** Dunnells, Duvall, Bennett & Porter, 1984-93; Arnold & Porter LLP 1993-present.
**Personal:** He is a 1984 graduate cum laude of Harvard Law School. Mr Goodwin is ranked in 'Who's Who Legal: USA' - Real Estate 2006. Based on peer and client reviews, Mr Goodwin was selected as one of America's leading real estate lawyers by Chambers & Partners, a respected English research firm, and by the first edition of the 'Global Counsel Corporate Real Estate Handbook'.

## GORELICK, Jamie
WilmerHale, Washington, DC 202 663 6500
jamie.gorelick@wilmerhale.com
*Recommended in Litigation, Securities*
**Practice Areas:** Represents corporations and individuals on a wide array of problems, particularly in the regulatory and enforcement arenas. Particular experience in corporate governance and compliance, as well as internal corporate investigations.
**Career:** Deputy Attorney General, US Department of Justice; General Counsel, US Department of Defense. Member of 9/11 Commission. Vice-Chair of Fannie Mae.
**Publications:** Co-author of leading treatise on the maintenance of corporate

documents, 'Destruction of Evidence' (Wiley 1983). Recent articles on anti-terrorism regulations and on the Committee on Foreign Investment in the US.
**Personal:** Harvard School of Law (JD 1975); Harvard University (BA 1972).

## GORRELL JR, J Warren
Hogan & Hartson LLP, Washington, DC 202 637 8618
jwgorrell@hhlaw.com
*Recommended in Corporate/Commercial*
**Practice Areas:** Warren Gorrell is Chairman of Hogan & Hartson and a Co-Director of the Corporate, Securities and Finance Practice Group. His practice, which is primarily transactional, covers several different areas and involves a diverse array of industries. He represents publicly and privately held companies and real estate investment trusts (REITs), and their controlling shareholders in all aspects of their businesses, including mergers and acquisitions, public offerings and private placements of equity and debt securities, senior and subordinated debt financings, tender offers and exchange offers, going private transactions, restructurings and recapitalizations, joint ventures, and general business matters. Warren also represents a number of major investment banking firms in connection with domestic and international mergers and acquisitions, offerings of both equity and debt securities, including initial public offerings, primary and secondary offerings (including 144A placements), and corporate restructurings and reorganizations.
**Career:** He joined Hogan & Hartson LLP as an associate in 1979, became a Partner in 1986 and became Chairman of the firm in 2001. He was recognized in 1999 as a 'Dealmaker of the Year' by The American Lawyer.
**Personal:** Princeton University (AB, magna cum laude, 1976); University of Virginia School of Law (JD, 1979).

## GOTTS, Lawrence J
Pillsbury Winthrop Shaw Pittman LLP, Washington, DC 703 770 7604
lawrence.gotts@pillsburylaw.com
*Recommended in Intellectual Property*
**Practice Areas:** National leader, Pillsbury's 200 attorney IP Section. Advises on all facets of intellectual property, with a primary focus on litigation and trial of patent disputes and strategic IP counseling. Clients include Fortune 100 to emerging companies. Has successfully litigated 75+ cases in Federal District Courts, the ITC and the Court of Appeals for the Federal Circuit, including multiple trials through successful verdict and judgment. Top Washington IP Lawyer, Washington Business Journal (2004).
**Career:** Patent examiner, US Patent and Trademark Office.
**Personal:** BS, University of Maryland

(1980, summa cum laude); JD, George Washington University Law School, (1985, high honors).

## GRANWELL, Alan
Ivins, Phillips & Barker, Washington, DC 202 393 7600
*Recommended in Tax*

## GREANEY, William
Covington & Burling, Washington, DC 202 662 5486
wgreaney@cov.com
*Recommended in Insurance*
**Practice Areas:** Represents corporate policyholders in insurance coverage disputes before federal and state courts throughout the country, including disputes over coverage for underlying asbestos, environmental, toxic tort, intellectual property, construction defects, directors and officers, securities and broker-dealer claims. Extensive experience representing policyholders in arbitrations and court disputes arising under first-party property policies, including coverage for business interruption, contingent business interruption losses under 'all-risk' property policies, and disputes arising under crime/fraud and fidelity policies. Has an active counseling practice negotiating structured settlements of complex insurance disputes.
**Personal:** Harvard University (JD 1981, cum laude); University of Maryland (BA 1977, summa cum laude).

## GREEN, Douglas G
Steptoe & Johnson LLP, Washington, DC 202 429 6212
dgreen@steptoe.com
*Recommended in Energy*
**Practice Areas:** Partner in Steptoe & Johnson LLP's Washington office. Vice-Chairman 2004-05. Practice encompasses electric power, antitrust, and litigation. Represents domestic and international companies in the electric power sector in matters involving competition, mergers and acquisitions, restructuring, commercial transactions, and FERC and SEC regulation. Litigation practice includes commercial disputes, including breach of contract, fraud and money laundering, torts, toxic torts, class actions, and major arbitration and mediation matters.
**Personal:** JD, Georgetown University Law Center, 1973; MA, University of Virginia 1969; BA, Bowdoin College, 1968.

## GREEN, Thomas C
Sidley Austin LLP, Washington, DC 202 736 8069
tcgreen@sidley.com
*Recommended in Litigation*
**Practice Areas:** Tom Green is a nationally known and highly regarded trial lawyer who has tried countless complex criminal and civil cases. He counsels corporate officials in connection with state and federal criminal investigations and conducts internal investigations of

alleged corporate wrongdoings and advises on implementation of compliance and anti-fraud programs. Representative matters include: Pickett v Tyson Fresh Meats (MD Alabama) in which as lead trial counsel for the class action in which plaintiffs claimed $2 billion in damages, he obtained a successful verdict for Tyson Foods; Coronet Industries (Florida Cir Ct) in which he is lead counsel for Coronet in both a class action and a putative joinder involving over 900 plaintiffs; and United States v Cinergy (SD Indiana) in which he represents Cinergy in 'bet the company' litigation involving the Clean Air Act. His victory for Tyson Foods in a jury trial was named National Law Journal's top defense verdict of the year for 2003 and he was named as one of the top five white-collar criminal defense lawyers in 2003 by Corporate Crime Reporter. Mr Green has represented Members of Congress, public officials and individuals in connection with state, federal and Congressional investigations and advised the World Bank on compliance and anti-fraud programs.
**Prof. Memberships:** Mr Green is a Fellow of the American College of Trial Lawyers, a past President of the Assistant United States Attorneys Association of Washington, DC as well as a Member of the National Association of Criminal Defense Lawyers where he served as the initial Chairman of the Committee on Environmental Crime.
**Personal:** Mr Green is a former Assistant US Attorney for the District of Columbia. Yale Law School, LLB, 1965; Dartmouth College, BA, 1962. Admissions: US Supreme Court; DC; Minnesota.

### GREENBERG, Bennett D
Seyfarth Shaw LLP, Washington, DC
202 463 2400
*Recommended in Construction*

### GREENBERG, Eric Dodson
Covington & Burling, Washington, DC
202 662 5193
egreenberg@cov.com
*Recommended in Telecom, Broadcast & Satellite*
**Practice Areas:** Corporate law focusing on telecommunications, broadcasting and new media. Emphasis on M&A involving television stations; start-ups and equity financings, including telecom, broadcast and digital ventures; programming agreements (traditional/new media); IP licensing; media transactions ranging from LMAs to digital spectrum leases; advice on corporate structure and FCC issues. Illustrative matters: LIN TV station acquisitions; NBC Weather Plus joint venture; equity financing and spectrum leasing for US Digital Television; formation of Washington Post Radio for The Washington Post.
**Career:** DOJ, Office of Legal Counsel;

clerk to Hon. Harold Greene.
**Personal:** GWU (JD, HH, 1991); Tufts (BA, cl, 1986)

### GREENFIELD, Andrew
Fragomen, Del Rey, Bernsen & Loewy, LLP, Washington, DC
202 223 5515
*Recommended in Immigration*

### GREENSTEIN, Abraham
Greenstein Delorme & Luchs, Washington, DC 202 452 1400
*Recommended in Real Estate*

### GROSKAUFMANIS, Karl
Fried, Frank, Harris, Shriver & Jacobson LLP, Washington, DC
202 639 7314
Karl.Groskaufmanis@FriedFrank.com
*Recommended in Securities*
**Practice Areas:** Corporate, Securities and Enforcement Partner. Practice includes United States Securities and Exchange Commission enforcement actions, civil, criminal insider trading investigations, corporate internal investigations, securities litigation and corporate counseling.
**Career:** Joined Fried Frank in 1988. Became a Partner in 1995. Co-Chair of Practising Law Institute's Advanced Securities Workshop.
**Personal:** JD (1988), University of Pennsylvania. LLB (1987), University of Toronto Law School. BS (1984), with honors, Cornell University.

### GUTIERREZ, Jay
Morgan, Lewis & Bockius LLP, Washington, DC 202 739 5466
jgutierrez@morganlewis.com
*Recommended in Energy*
**Practice Areas:** Jay M Gutierrez is the Energy Practice Group Leader, a group that represents approximately half the utilities in the US. Mr Gutierrez represents companies in a variety of matters before the US Nuclear Regulatory Commission (NRC), including licensing, inspection, investigation, and enforcement issues.
**Prof. Memberships:** Member, American Bar Association, editor, Rutgers Law Journal.

### HADJIS, Alexander J
Weil, Gotshal & Manges LLP, Washington, DC 202 682 7506
alex.hadjis@weil.com
*Recommended in Intellectual Property*
**Practice Areas:** Alex Hadjis is a patent trial attorney and leads the Washington, DC office's Patent Litigation Practice. He is known for possessing both outstanding trial skills and the ability to fully and quickly understand complex technical issues. In addition to complex patent cases, he focuses on cases involving the interface between IP and antitrust and cases involving technology standards. He has served as lead trial counsel before several federal district courts and the US

International Trade Commission on cases involving patent, antitrust, and breach of contract issues in the semiconductor, optical storage media, liquid crystal display, telecommunications, computer network, software, xerography, chemical, and automotive component technologies.
**Personal:** Ohio State University, BS, 1990; University of Pittsburgh, JD, 1993; George Washington University Law School, LLM, 1996.

### HAGEN, Paul
Beveridge & Diamond PC, Washington, DC 202 789 6022
phagen@bdlaw.com
*Recommended in Environment*
**Practice Areas:** As Chair of the firm's International Environmental Practice Section, he counsels multinational corporations, trade associations and leading non-profit organizations on the negotiation and implementation of regional and global environmental agreements. Works extensively with clients in the chemicals, electronics and pharmaceuticals sectors. His work includes representing clients on a wide range of product stewardship legislation and on issues arising under numerous international agreements, including the Basel Convention, the Biosafety Protocol, the Kyoto Protocol, the Rotterdam Prior Informed Consent Convention, and the Stockholm Convention on Persistent Organic Pollutants. Advises clients on the environmental and social guidelines of the World Bank and IFC and on the environmental aspects of trade and investment agreements, including matters arising under the NAFTA and WTO. His domestic practice includes counseling on environmental compliance and enforcement matters. He has recently assisted non-profits on efforts to protect whales and albatross and rainforests in Asia.
**Prof. Memberships:** Currently serves as Chairman of the Board of Directors of the Environmental Law Institute (ELI). He is also a Member of the Board of Directors for the American Bird Conservancy. Appointed to the ABA Standing Committee on Environmental Law (2001-04). Member of the IUCN Commission on Environmental Law.
**Career:** Admitted to Maryland (1990) and District of Columbia (1992) Bars. Director of Beveridge & Diamond, P.C. Adjunct Professor of law, Washington College of Law at American University. He has advised governments in Asia, Africa and the Middle East on the development of environmental and natural resources legislation.
**Publications:** Author: 'Product-Based Environmental Regulations: Europe Sets the Pace,' ABA Trends (2006); co-author: 'The Stockholm Convention on Persistent Organic Pollutants', ABA Natural Resources & Environment (2005); author: 'The Green Diplomacy Gap', The

Environmental Forum (August 2000); co-author: 'The Cartagena Protocol on Biosafety: New Rules for International Trade in Living Modified Organisms', Georgetown International Environmental Law Review (2000); co-author: 'The Convergence of Trade and Environmental Law', 8 Natural Resources and Envir. 2 (ABA 1993); co-author: 'Courts Examine US Environmental Law's Extraterritorial Reach', National Law Journal (September 1993); co-author: 'The Application of the United States Hazardous Waste Cleanup Laws in the Canada-U.S. Context', 18 Can.-US LJ 137 (1992); co-author, 'Wetlands' in Environmental Law and Practice Guide (Mathew Bender 1992); author: 'The International Community Confronts Plastics Pollution from Ships: MARPOL Annex V and the Problem that Won't Go Away', 5 Am. U.J. Int'l L. & Pol'y 425 (1990).
**Personal:** Received BA, Providence College (1986) and JD, Washington College of Law at American University (1990).

### HALL JR, Ridgway M
Crowell & Moring LLP, Washington, DC
202 624 2620
rhall@crowell.com
*Recommended in Environment*
**Practice Areas:** Partner in Crowell & Moring's Natural Resource and Environmental Group. Practice includes all areas of environmental law and litigation. Works with clients in administrative and judicial proceedings, enforcement and appellate litigation, rulemaking proceedings, permitting, and toxic tort litigation. Practice includes all of the federal environmental statutes and corresponding state laws and regulatory programs. Handled numerous Superfund/hazardous waste/toxic tort cases for large and small companies in the manufacturing/mining/consumer products and construction industries, among others.
**Career:** Former associate general counsel for water at US Environmental Protection Agency.
**Personal:** Yale University magna cum laude; Harvard Law School in 1966.

### HAMBURGER, Paul M
McDermott Will & Emery, Washington, DC 202 756 8306
phamburger@mwe.com
*Recommended in Employee Benefits*
**Practice Areas:** Advises employers, plan trustees and service providers on federal tax and ERISA issues and employee benefit programs, including tax-qualified retirement plans, executive compensation plans, and health and welfare benefit plans. Represents clients before the Internal Revenue Service, the Department of Labor and the Pension Benefit Guaranty Corporation.
**Career:** American College of Employee Benefits Counsel; Adjunct Professor, Georgetown University Law Center; Rec-

ognized for superior level of client service in BTI Consulting Group's Law Firm Client Service All-Star Team survey of Fortune 1000 clients.

**Personal:** University of Michigan Law School (JD, cum laude 1983); University of Michigan (BA 1979).

## HANDMAN, Laura
Davis Wright Tremaine LLP, Washington, DC 202 508 6600
*Recommended in Media & Entertainment*

## HANSEN, Kenneth W
Chadbourne & Parke LLP, Washington, DC 202 974 5656
khansen@chadbourne.com
*Recommended in Projects*
**Practice Areas:** Represents project sponsors, banks, bilateral and multilateral agencies, and political risk insurers in international infrastructure financings, trade financings, and the settlement of political risk insurance claims and investment disputes. Advised both agencies and commercial insurers on the design and implementation of novel financial guaranty products. Sectoral experience includes power generation, transmission and distribution, oil and gas, transport, telecoms, and tourism. Representative agency clients include OPIC, US Ex-Im Bank, MCC, ADB, EBRD and IDB.
**Prof. Memberships:** Admitted: District of Columbia and Massachusetts; Washington Foreign Law Society (President, 2004-05).
**Career:** Formerly General Counsel, US Ex-Im Bank; Associate General Counsel, OPIC.

## HARMAN, Thomas
Morgan, Lewis & Bockius LLP, Washington, DC 202 739 5662
tharman@morganlewis.com
*Recommended in Investment Management*
**Practice Areas:** Thomas Harman is a Partner in the Investment Management Practice. Mr Harman's practice focuses on investment management matters involving mutual funds, closed-end funds, private investment companies, ETFs and investment advisers. He also serves as counsel to the board of directors of several fund families.
**Career:** Mr Harman served as Chief Counsel, subsequently Associate Director (Chief Counsel), of the Securities and Exchange Commission's Division of Investment Management from 1988-94. From 1987-88, he directed the Division's Office of Disclosure and Adviser Regulation. Mr Harman was an Adjunct Professor in the securities law program at Georgetown University Law Center from 1991-2002.

## HARRIS, Gregg
Fulbright & Jaworski L.L.P., Washington, DC 202 662 4694

gharris@fulbright.com.
*Recommended in Projects*
**Practice Areas:** Structured and project finance, energy projects, debt restructurings/workouts.
**Prof. Memberships:** International Bar Association; Member, Strathmore's 'Who's Who'; former Co-Chair, American Bar Association Subcommittee on International Independent Power Projects.
**Career:** Gregg Harris is Chair of the firm's Structured and Project Finance Group. He has significant experience representing clients in domestic and international transactions in a variety of sectors, including numerous projects in the power sector throughout the world. Mr Harris has worked on independent power project financings in India, Pakistan, Nepal, Bangladesh, Africa, and Latin America, as well as financings in other sectors, including mining, manufacturing (such as paper and pulp, cement, and carbon black), telecommunications, and toll roads. A substantial part of Mr Harris' practice focuses on debt restructurings, including a wide range of domestic and international restructurings.
**Personal:** 1984 - JD, Northwestern University; 1981 - BA, cum laude, Williams College; Admitted: Illinois, 1984; District of Columbia, 1985.

## HARRIS, Larry D
DLA Piper Rudnick Gray Cary US LLP, Washington, DC 202 861 6423
larry.harris@dlapiper.com
*Recommended in Construction*
**Practice Areas:** Construction; government contracts.
**Prof. Memberships:** Fellow, American College of Construction Lawyers, Board of Governors.
**Career:** Experience in government contracts and construction matters including litigation before boards of contract appeals and arbitration tribunals in cases involving changes, cost reimbursement, acceleration, delay, disruption, defective work, and termination. Counseled domestic and international contractors, subcontractors, and owners regarding claims and changes under supply, service, aerospace, healthcare, and construction contracts. He has also served as a mediator, arbitrator, and dispute review board member in construction matters.
**Personal:** JD, George Washington University; BS, University of Dayton.

## HARRIS, Scott
Harris, Wiltshire & Grannis LLP, Washington, DC 202 730 1300
*Recommended in Telecom, Broadcast & Satellite*

## HASKELL, Mark
Morgan, Lewis & Bockius LLP, Washington, DC 202 739 5766
mhaskell@morganlewis.com
*Recommended in Energy*

**Practice Areas:** Mark R Haskell is a Partner in the Energy Practice. His practice focuses on natural gas, oil and electric matters, encompassing both litigation before the Federal Energy Regulatory Commission (FERC) and transactions subject to FERC jurisdiction.
**Prof. Memberships:** Member, American Bar Association; Member, Energy Bar Association.

## HASTINGS, Douglas
Epstein Becker & Green PC, Washington, DC 202 861 0900
dhastings@ebglaw.com
*Recommended in Healthcare*
**Practice Areas:** Provides a wide range of healthcare organizations with strategic and transactional legal guidance in responding to the legal challenges and opportunities of the rapidly changing American healthcare system. Represents organizations in mergers, acquisitions, joint ventures, governance issues, complex contractual arrangements and other affiliations and collaborative efforts.
**Prof. Memberships:** American Bar Association, Healthcare Section; American Health Lawyers Association, President, 2001; American Society of Law, Medicine & Ethics; Institute of Medicine, Board on Health Care Services; National Committee for Quality Health Care, Board of Directors.
**Publications:** Mr Hastings speaks and publishes regularly on topics related to healthcare law, complex healthcare transactions, collaborative healthcare ventures, legal issues related to quality improvement and the legal trends influencing the US healthcare system.
**Personal:** BA, Duke University, Phi Beta Kappa. JD, University of Virginia, Order of the Coif.

## HATCHER, Julia
Latham & Watkins LLP, Washington, DC 202 637 2200
*Recommended in Environment*

## HAYES, David
Latham & Watkins LLP, Washington, DC 202 637 2200
*Recommended in Environment*

## HECHT, Philip
Kirkpatrick & Lockhart Nicholson Graham LLP, Washington, DC 202 778 9000
*Recommended in Insurance*

## HEFFERNAN, Barbara
Schiff Hardin LLP, Washington, DC 202 778 6440
bheffernan@schiffhardin.com
*Recommended in Energy*
**Practice Areas:** Energy, telecommunications, and public utilities.
**Prof. Memberships:** American Bar Association, Energy Bar Association (past President).
**Career:** Co-leader of Schiff Hardin's Energy Group. Concentrates in energy

regulation, litigation, and transactions. Has represented numerous clients before the Federal Energy Regulatory Commission and the federal courts for more than 25 years on a variety of matters concerning the regulation of natural gas and electricity.
**Personal:** University of Maryland (BA, 1975), Catholic University Law School (JD, 1978).

## HEINTZ, John
Gilbert Heintz & Randolph LLP, Washington, DC 202 772 2225
*Recommended in Insurance*

## HELLER, Mark A
WilmerHale, Washington, DC 202 663 6005
mark.heller@wilmerhale.com
*Recommended in Healthcare*
**Practice Areas:** Chair, FDA Department; concentrates on Food and Drug Administration and Federal Trade Commission law and enforcement counseling and litigation. Represents clients in FDA's product approval processes and in compliance matters ranging from administrative notices of violation to enforcement actions in court.
**Career:** Spent almost 10 years in FDA's General Counsel's office, majority of which as associate chief counsel for medical devices. Involved in development of Safe Medical Devices Act of 1990 while in Senator Edward Kennedy's office, Chairman of Senate Committee on Labor and Human Resources
**Personal:** JD, University of Wisconsin - Madison; BA, University of Wisconsin - Madison.

## HELM, Robert W
Dechert LLP, Washington, DC 202 261 3356
robert.helm@dechert.com
*Recommended in Investment Management*
**Practice Areas:** Mr Helm advises investment companies and funds, alternative investments; investment advisors, insurance companies; broker-dealers and other financial institutions in regulatory and corporate matters.
**Prof. Memberships:** Chair, Investment Companies and Mutual Funds Committee, International Bar Association; organizing committee, International Bar Association/Investment Company Institute Globalisation of Investment Funds conference; advisory board, Mutual Fund Directors Forum; securities and commodities law committees of American Bar Association and District of Columbia Bar Association.
**Publications:** Authored articles for Review of Securities and Commodities Regulation, The Investment Lawyer, Journal of International Banking Law.
**Personal:** Stanford University (AB, with distinction, 1979); Stanford Law School (JD, 1982).

## HENDLER, Clifford B
Crowell & Moring LLP, Washington, DC
202 624 2928
chendler@crowell.com
*Recommended in Insurance*

**Practice Areas:** Chair of Crowell & Moring's Complex Insurance Coverage Litigation Group. Serves as national counsel for ACE USA Insurance Companies (formerly CIGNA Property & Casualty Companies). Has orchestrated the successful negotiation of global resolutions of disputes involving dozens of insurance companies and underlying case policyholder liabilities.
**Career:** Appointed by the US District Court for the District of Columbia to mediate to resolution a 20-year dispute regarding taped conversations recorded by former President Richard Nixon.
**Personal:** Undergraduate Degree from Yale University with honors, 1975; JD from Stanford Law School, 1978, Order of the Coif Member.

## HENNEBURG, Frank H
Mayer, Brown, Rowe & Maw LLP, Washington, DC 202 263 3231
fhenneburg@mayerbrownrowe.com
*Recommended in Real Estate*

**Practice Areas:** Advises institutional owners and lenders in the acquisition, construction, leasing, financing and disposition of large commercial projects throughout the United States. Has significant experience in single-property construction and permanent loans involving all property types, and has served as lead counsel in cross-collateralized portfolio financings involving as many as 50 properties in 20 states. Has managed numerous consensual restructurings of troubled real estate loans and has considerable experience with foreclosure and bankruptcy proceedings. Also has significant hotel experience, including the representation of institutional owners in acquiring hotels and negotiating management agreements with major operators and the representation of lenders making secured loans to hotel operating companies.
**Prof. Memberships:** Illinois and District of Columbia Bars.
**Personal:** AB, Georgetown University; JD, University of Chicago.

## HENRY, Roxann
Howrey LLP, Washington, DC
202 783 0800
*Recommended in Antitrust*

## HENSLER, David
Hogan & Hartson LLP, Washington, DC
202 637 5630
djhensler@hhlaw.com
*Recommended in Insurance, Litigation*

**Practice Areas:** A director of the firm's Litigation Practice Group. Handles complex civil litigation with focus on securities fraud, internal investigations, insurance coverage disputes, aviation and noise impact litigation, government con-

tracts, and other general commercial litigation.
**Prof. Memberships:** Fellow, American College of Trial Lawyers (ACTL) and Chair of the State Committee for the ACTL, District of Columbia; District of Columbia Bar Association; Litigation Section, ABA; Federal Bar Association.
**Career:** Formerly served in General Counsel's Office of SEC.
**Publications:** Co-author of several articles on asset valuation in context of corporate takeovers and divestitures.
**Personal:** St Louis University (JD cum laude).

## HERTZ, Mitch
Kirkland & Ellis LLP, Washington, DC
202 879 5270
mhertz@kirkland.com
*Recommended in Energy*

**Practice Areas:** Mr Hertz is Co-Chair of Kirkland's Energy Practice Group. He represents oil and gas companies, interstate pipelines, independent power producers, electric and gas utitlies and private equity funds on mergers and acquisitions, leveraged buy-outs, commercial transactions and restructuring matters. Mr Hertz also represents clients before federal and state agencies on transactional and regulatory matters, including policy issues arising in the evolving energy industry. Among the highlights over the past year, Mr Hertz was the lead attorney for Madison Dearborn Partner's $975 million acqusition of Reliant Energy's New York City power plants and is Constellation Energy Group's lead energy attorney on its $28 billion merger with FPL Group.
**Personal:** American University (BA, 1986); Columbia Law School (JD, 1989).

## HOLDER, Eric
Covington & Burling, Washington, DC
202 662 5372
eholder@cov.com
*Recommended in Litigation*

**Practice Areas:** Handles complex civil and criminal cases, domestic and international advisory matters, and internal corporate investigations.
**Career:** Deputy Attorney General of the US (1997-2001); US Attorney for the District of Columbia (1993-97); Associate Judge of the Superior Court of the District of Columbia (1988-93); Department of Justice Public Integrity Section (1976-83). As Deputy Attorney General, supervised all of the DOJ's litigating, enforcement, and administrative components in both civil and criminal matters. Under his guidance, the DOJ developed and issued its guidelines on the criminal prosecution of corporations (the so-called 'Holder Memorandum').
**Personal:** Columbia University (JD, 1976; BS, 1973).

## HOLEWINSKI, Kevin
Jones Day, Washington, DC

202 879 3797
kpholewinski@jonesday.com
*Recommended in Environment*

**Practice Areas:** Oversees the Environmental, Health and Safety Practice in the Washington office. Substantial complex civil, environmental, toxic tort, and criminal litigation experience. Represents clients in civil enforcement actions, criminal investigations, insurance coverage litigation, toxic tort litigation, and cost recovery litigation, among others. Has developed extensive experience in air and groundwater contamination issues, human and ecological risk assessment, and in the pursuit of claims in the US Court of Federal Claims.
**Career:** At the DOJ, he was lead trial counsel in several of the most significant enforcement matters and received a number of awards for his trial work.

## HOROWITZ, Philip
Venable LLP, Washington, DC
202 962 4800
*Recommended in Real Estate*

## HOWARD, Theodore A
Wiley Rein & Fielding LLP, Washington, DC 202 719 7120
thoward@wrf.com
*Recommended in Insurance*

**Practice Areas:** Counsels and represents national and international insurers in a broad range of insurance coverage disputes and related matters, with significant experience in asbestos-related coverage disputes. Litigates in the areas of eminent domain and natural resource valuation and represents the Federal Deposit Insurance Corporation in failed bank litigation.
**Prof. Memberships:** American Bar Association, Co-Chair, Section of Litigation, Insurance Coverage Committee, ADR Subcommittee; President and Chairman, Board of Directors, District of Columbia Prisoners' Legal Services Project.
**Career:** Adjunct Professor, Insurance Theory and Regulation, George Mason School of Law.
**Personal:** Harvard Law School (JD); University of Notre Dame (BA).

## HUBER, John
Latham & Watkins LLP, Washington, DC
202 637 2200
*Recommended in Securities*

## HUEY-BURNS, Paul
Dechert LLP, Washington, DC
202 261 3433
paul.huey-burns@dechert.com
*Recommended in Securities*

**Practice Areas:** Mr Huey-Burns Co-Chairs the Financial Services and Securities Litigation Group. He defends broker-dealers, investment advisors, public companies, and individuals in SEC and regulatory investigations, and against charges of accounting fraud, misrepresentations,

omissions, and insider trading. He conducts internal investigations and counsels public companies on structuring compliance programs.
**Prof. Memberships:** Member, securities and corporate law committees of American Bar Association and District of Columbia Bar Association.
**Career:** 1986-1998: SEC; 1991-98: Assistant Director, SEC Division of Enforcement.
**Personal:** Johns Hopkins University, BA, 1978; University of Pennsylvania Law School, JD, 1982, associate editor of the University of Pennsylvania Law Review.

## HUMES, Gary
Arnold & Porter LLP, Washington, DC
202 942 5001
Gary.Humes@aporter.com
*Recommended in Real Estate*

**Practice Areas:** Build-to-suit transactions and large-scale office leases, public-private partnerships and other complex transactions involving the Federal Government, and real estate development and financing. Clients include Fortune 500 companies, non-profit organizations, large law firms, hotel owners and operators, and real estate developers. Structures and negotiates ground and space leases, joint ventures, purchase agreements, design and construction contracts, brokerage and development management agreements, and tax-exempt and taxable financings.
**Personal:** Education: JD from Cornell Law School (1981), SM from the University of Chicago (1974), PhD candidate in Theoretical Physics (1974-76), BA from Wesleyan University (1972).

## HUNT, Paul
Latham & Watkins LLP, Washington, DC
202 637 2200
*Recommended in Projects*

## HUNTINGTON, Danny
Bingham McCutchen LLP, Washington, DC 202 778 3167
danny.huntington@bingham.com
*Recommended in Intellectual Property*

**Practice Areas:** Involved in all phases of intellectual property law, including US and foreign patent prosecution, litigation in the federal and state courts, licensing and general client counseling. Has extensive patent interference experience, with emphasis on biotechnology and pharmaceuticals.
**Career:** Former chemist for The Gillette Research Institute.
**Personal:** The George Washington University Law School, JD, 1976; Indiana University, BS in Chemistry, 1972.

## HUTT, Peter Barton
Covington & Burling, Washington, DC
202 662 5522
phutt@cov.com
*Recommended in Healthcare*

**Practice Areas:** Specializes in food and

drug regulation, biotechnology, and trade association law.

**Prof. Memberships:** Member of the Institute of Medicine of the National Academy of Sciences; served on the IOM Executive Committee, and other NAS and IOM committees; currently serves on the Panel on the Administrative Restructuring of the National Institutes of Health.

**Career:** Served as chief counsel for the Food and Drug Administration (1971-75). Teaches a full course on Food and Drug Law during Winter term at Harvard Law School (1994-present). Noted by The Washingtonian magazine as one of Washington's 50 best lawyers (out of more than 40,000) and as one of Washington's 100 most influential people; by the National Law Journal as one of the 40 best healthcare lawyers in the United States; by European Counsel as the best FDA regulatory specialist in Washington, DC; by Business Week and Legal Times as the unofficial dean of Washington Food and Drug lawyers.

**Publications:** Co-author (with Professor Richard A Merrill of the University of Virginia Law School) of 'Food and Drug Law: Cases and Materials' (Foundation Press, 1st edition 1980, 2nd edition 1991).

**Personal:** Harvard University (LLB, 1959); New York University (LLM, in Food/Drug Law, 1960); Yale University (BA, 1956, magna cum laude).

## HYDE, Terrill

WilmerHale, Washington, DC
202 663 6238
terrill.hyde@wilmerhale.com
*Recommended in Tax*

**Practice Areas:** Provides advice on structuring and restructuring of multinational groups in connection with acquisitions; domestic mergers, acquisitions and spin-offs; bankruptcy and insolvency restructurings; and structuring cross-border investments. Advises exempt organizations on issues relating to formation and ongoing activities, including IRS ruling requests, structuring innovative programs and transactions, intermediate sanctions and private foundation provisions.

**Prof. Memberships:** Former member of the Council of the ABA Section of Taxation; former Council Director for the Corporate Tax and Affiliated and Related Corporations Committees.

**Personal:** University of Nebraska College of Law (JD 1979); South Dakota State University (MA 1976); Dakota State College (BS 1973).

## HYMAN, Paul

Hyman Phelps & McNamara, Washington, DC  202 737 5600
*Recommended in Healthcare*

## IMUS, Neil W

Vinson & Elkins LLP, Washington, DC
202 639 6675

nimus@velaw.com
*Recommended in Antitrust*

**Practice Areas:** US antitrust including practice before the DOJ and FTC in HSR, merger and acquisitions and other agency investigations and in antitrust litigation.

**Prof. Memberships:** ABA Antitrust Section - Book & Treatises Co-Chair.

**Career:** Partner.

**Publications:** Editor: Premerger Notification Practice Manual, Third Ed.

**Personal:** Georgetown University Law Center (JD, 1985); George Washington University (MBA, 1981); Davidson College (BS, 1975).

## JACK, Andrew

Covington & Burling, Washington, DC
202 662 5232
ajack@cov.com
*Recommended in Corporate/Commercial*

**Practice Areas:** Diverse corporate and securities practice with clients principally in the manufacturing, real estate and sports and entertainment industries. Experience includes M&A, financing activities, strategic alliances, securities law compliance, and corporate governance counseling.

**Prof. Memberships:** Society of Corporate Secretaries and Governance Professionals.

**Career:** 19 years with Covington highlighted by serving as lead transactional counsel in: successful effort to return Major League Baseball to Washington DC (2002-05), Cleveland Browns relocation and expansion (1996-99), JLG Industries' global alliance with Caterpillar (2005) and acquisitions of Gradall Industries (1999) and OmniQuip (2003).

**Personal:** George Washington University, (JD, 1986, with highest honors; BA, 1983).

## JACKSON, Thomas C

Baker Botts LLP, Washington, DC
202 639 7710
thomas.jackson@bakerbotts.com
*Recommended in Environment*

**Practice Areas:** Tom Jackson handles all aspects of environmental law, including client counseling, permitting, trial court and appellate litigation, administrative hearings and arbitrations, and legislative matters. He also helps clients assess proposed rules and other public documents such as Environmental Impact Statements.

**Prof. Memberships:** District of Columbia Bar, US Court of Federal Claims, US Courts of Appeals (for the Third, Fifth, Ninth, Eleventh, Federal, and District of Columbia Circuits), US District Court for the District of Columbia, US Supreme Court.

**Personal:** JD (with honors), Harvard Law School (1984), BA (summa cum laude), Political Science, Amherst College (1981).

## JACOBS, Bruce D

Pillsbury Winthrop Shaw Pittman LLP, Washington, DC 202 663 8077
bruce.jacobs@pillsburylaw.com
*Recommended in Telecom, Broadcast & Satellite*

**Practice Areas:** Mr Jacobs counsels companies whose technologies are regulated by the Federal Communications Commission. Since their founding, he has represented Mobile Satellite Ventures, which launched the first domestic mobile satellite service system and is a leading proponent of reusing satellite spectrum to operate terrestrial radio facilities; XM Satellite Radio Corporation, a satellite radio pioneer and the largest satellite radio service provider; and the Voice on the Net Coalition, a trade association of companies active in the development of internet voice applications and services.

**Personal:** JD, Harvard Law School, 1980; BA, New College of the University of South Florida, 1976.

## JACOBS, Matthew L

Kirkpatrick & Lockhart Nicholson Graham LLP, Washington, DC
202 778 9393
mjacobs@klng.com
*Recommended in Insurance*

**Practice Areas:** Concentrates on insurance coverage counseling and litigation, arbitration and strategic issues; represents policyholders in connection with disputes related to liabilities arising from directors and officers' exposures, products liability, environmental liability, professional liability, business interruption and first-party property matters. He has extensive experience in the placement of Directors and Officers/Errors and Omissions insurance programs for mutual fund and investment companies, and has litigated claims arising from market timing and late trading liabilities for several mutual fund complexes.

**Prof. Memberships:** Admitted to practice in the District of Columbia, the US Courts of Appeal for the DC and Second Circuits.

**Career:** Joined Kirkpatrick & Lockhart Nicholson Graham LLP in 1989, when he started the Insurance Practice Group in the firm's Washington, DC office. Clerked for the Honorable John W Kern, III on the District of Columbia Court of Appeals from 1981 to 1982, then joined Baker & Hostetler in Washington, DC. Worked as an associate at Covington & Burling from January 1984 to July 1989.

**Publications:** Has published numerous articles in the field of insurance coverage regarding coverage for regulatory investigations, environmental exposures, products liabilities, tobacco exposures and EMF matters.

**Personal:** JD, University of Virginia School of Law, 1981; BA, Woodrow Wilson School of Public and International Affairs, Princeton University, 1977.

## JACOBSEN JR, Raymond A

McDermott Will & Emery, Washington, DC 202 756 8028
rayjacobsen@mwe.com
*Recommended in Antitrust*

**Practice Areas:** Head of Regulation and Government Affairs Department and Antitrust and Competition Practice. Focuses on mergers, acquisitions and other antitrust work, with significant experience in defense, high-tech, consumer product, energy and healthcare industries.

**Prof. Memberships:** Chairman of two American Bar Association Committees.

**Career:** Successfully defended over 200 complex mergers, acquisitions and joint ventures in US, Europe and Far East. One of the first to obtain amnesty for client under Justice Department's expanded amnesty program.

**Personal:** Georgetown University Law Center (JD); University of Delaware (BA, cum laude).

## JAFFE, Kenneth G

Alston & Bird LLP, Washington, DC
202 756 3154
kenneth.jaffe@alston.com
*Recommended in Energy*

**Practice Areas:** Specializes in regulatory matters affecting participants in competitive energy markets. Represents electric u utilities and other market participants in wide range of transactions and regulatory proceedings. Particular concentration on matters connected with restructuring of the electiric utility industry and operations of independent systems operators and regional transmission organizations.

**Personal:** JD, cum laude, Harvard University; BA, with honors, State University of New York at Binghamton, 1978.

## JAFFE, Michael E

Thelen Reid & Priest LLP, Washington, DC 202 508 4215
mjaffe@thelenreid.com
*Recommended in Construction*

**Practice Areas:** During his more than 30 years as a trial lawyer, Mr Jaffe has participated, and has been lead counsel, in a wide array of commercial litigation matters. He has appeared in state and federal trial and appellate courts in more than 20 states and the District of Columbia. Mr Jaffe also has been counsel in commercial arbitrations and mediations across the United States and in international cases. The matters have involved a broad range of subjects - eg, antitrust, securities litigation, partnership disputes, financing transactions, insurance law, trusts and estates, construction litigation, bankruptcy adversary proceedings, and government contracts, as well as a variety of business issues covering a spectrum of contract, warranty and tort claims. In addition, Mr Jaffe has served as an arbitrator in proceedings both in the United States and internationally. Mr Jaffe's practice has also focused on counseling and representing foreign businesses in litigation proceedings in the United States and in international arbitrations. A significant portion of his practice focuses on construction litigation. He has represented contractors, owners and designers in a host of construction litigation disputes throughout the United States.

**Career:** Partner of Thelen Reid & Priest. Court admissions include US Supreme Court, US Courts of Appeals for the District of Columbia, Third, Fourth, Fifth, Sixth, Seventh, Eighth, Ninth, Tenth, Eleventh Federal Circuits. Admitted to practice in Maryland, District of Columbia and Texas.

**Personal:** Received his LLB from Columbia University Law School and received his BA from Rice University.

### JANKA, John
Latham & Watkins LLP, Washington, DC
202 637 2200
*Recommended in Telecom, Broadcast & Satellite*

### JEFFRESS, William
Baker Botts LLP, Washington, DC
202 639 7751
william.jeffress@bakerbotts.com
*Recommended in Litigation*

**Practice Areas:** Has tried 30 complex criminal and civil cases to juries in nine states and Washington, DC, plus dozens of nonjury trials before judges and administrative tribunals. Matters include fraud, securities, antitrust, federal procurement, international transactions, newsgathering, public corruption, tax, money laundering, professional liability and others. Deals regularly with Justice Department, Treasury Department, State Department, SEC and other agencies.

**Career:** Serves on firm's Executive Committee. Former Editor-in-Chief of Yale Law Journal, law clerk to Supreme Court Justice Potter Stewart, fellow of American College of Trial Lawyers, Former Member of ABA Ethics Committee and Chair of Criminal Justice Standards Committee.

### JENKS, Carrie F
Willkie Farr & Gallagher LLP, Washington, DC 202 303 1160
cjenks@willkie.com
*Recommended in Environment*

**Practice Areas:** Carrie Jenks focuses on advising clients on emerging issues relating to greenhouse gas management, climate change, and emissions trading. She has worked on Clean Water Act and Clean Air Act enforcement cases and has been involved in corporate and real estate transactions as well as private cleanups of contaminated sites.

**Prof. Memberships:** Member of the American Bar Association and the Women's Bar Association of the District of Columbia.

**Career:** Admission to the District of Columbia Bar and Massachusetts Bar.

**Personal:** Received a JD from Georgetown University Law Center in 2003, where she was an Executive Editor for the Georgetown International Environmental Law Review, and a BA (cum laude) from Harvard University in 1999.

### JOHNSON, Dixie
Fried, Frank, Harris, Shriver & Jacobson LLP, Washington, DC 202 639 7269
Dixie.Johnson@FriedFrank.com
*Recommended in Securities*

**Practice Areas:** Co-heads Fried Frank's Securities Regulation and Enforcement Practice Group. Practice includes United States Securities and Exchange Commission enforcement actions, civil, criminal insider trading investigations, corporate internal investigations, securities litigation and corporate counseling.

**Career:** Joined Fried Frank in 1986. Became a Partner in 1993. Chair of ABA Committee on Federal Regulation of Securities. Legal Advisory Committee of New York Stock Exchange.

**Personal:** JD(1986), University of New Mexico School of Law, MBA (1983) New Mexico Highlands University, BA(1977), Oklahoma Baptist University.

### JOHNSTON, Mark G
Levine, Blaszak, Block & Boothby LLP, Washington, DC 202 857 2548
mjohnston@lb3law.com
*Recommended in Telecom, Broadcast & Satellite*

**Practice Areas:** Specializes in advising on and negotiating communications, network outsourcing, and IT sourcing arrangements for commercial enterprises purchasing products and services. Represents clients in contract disputes with carriers and network services providers. Represents clients in transactions involving the development, licensing, maintenance, and hosting of software applications. Advises clients on carriers' regulatory obligations and the regulatory status of service offerings incorporating communications services. Represents commercial telecommunications customers and IT companies in FCC proceedings.

**Prof. Memberships:** Member of the New York State and the District of Columbia Bar Associations, American Bar Association, and Federal Communications Bar Association.

**Career:** Admitted to the Bars of New York and the District of Columbia. Associate and Partner with Levine, Blaszak, Block & Boothby, LLP, since 1997. Prior to joining LB3, practiced EC competition law with Van Bael & Bellis, in Brussels, Belgium, and practiced with the firm of Shiomi & Yamamoto in Osaka, Japan, specializing in the negotiation of international sales, distribution, and licensing transactions.

**Personal:** BA, magna cum laude and University Honors, University of Illinois, Urbana-Champaign, 1987. JD, cum laude, University of Michigan, 1991.

### KADEN, Alan
Fried, Frank, Harris, Shriver & Jacobson LLP, Washington, DC 202 639 7073
Alan.Kaden@FriedFrank.com
*Recommended in Tax*

**Practice Areas:** Chairman of the DC Tax Department. Practices in all the principal areas of tax law, emphasis on the structuring and negotiation of taxable and tax-free corporate acquisitions, reorganizations, spin-off transactions and dispositions of ongoing business enterprises, the structuring of investment funds, the development of partnership and other joint-venture arrangements for various business ventures and tax planning for financings and other capital formation transactions.

**Career:** Joined Fried Frank in 1981. Became a Partner in 1987.

**Personal:** JD (1981), Columbia University. BS (1978), University of Pennsylvania.

### KAHAN, Jonathan S
Hogan & Hartson LLP, Washington, DC 202 637 5794
jskahan@hhlaw.com
*Recommended in Healthcare*

**Practice Areas:** Medical device premarket clearance and approval; FDA enforcement actions criminal/injunction/seizure; investigational device regulation and device clinical study design; import and export of FDA-regulated products.

**Prof. Memberships:** ABA; general counsel, Association of Medical Diagnostics Manufacturers; contributing editor, Medical Device & Diagnostic Industry magazine(MD&DI); Editorial Advisory Board, MD&DI; Phi Beta Kappa; Order of the Coif.

**Career:** Dean's Advisory Board of the George Washington University Law School; former Chairman of the Federal Bar Association Section on Health and Human Services, which includes the Food, Drug and Cosmetic Law Committee.

**Publications:** Publisher of numerous law review and other articles concerning FDA regulatory issues; Medical Device Development: A Regulatory Overview (Parexel 2000) and Medical Devices: Obtaining FDA Market Clearance (Parexel 1995).

**Personal:** The George Washington University Law School (JD, with honors, Order of the Coif, 1973); The George Washington University (BA, with honors, 1970).

### KAHN, David S
Holland & Knight LLP, Washington, DC 202 955 3000
david.kahn@hklaw.com
*Recommended in Real Estate*

**Practice Areas:** Head of the firm's Real Estate Practice Group in Washington, DC. Practices in the areas of commercial real estate development and finance, and commercial leasing. He represents numerous real estate developers, as well as institutional owners, investors and lenders, including domestic and foreign insurance companies, pension funds and national banks in connection with their real estate development/investment activities nationwide. This representation includes the negotiation and documentation of purchase and sale agreements, development agreements, construction and permanent loan agreements, deeds of trust, ground leases, loan and equity participations, joint venture agreements, construction contracts, and office and retail leases.

### KALB, Paul E
Sidley Austin LLP, Washington, DC
202 736 8050
pkalb@sidley.com
*Recommended in Healthcare*

**Practice Areas:** Partner in the firm's Washington, DC, office and heads the firm's National Health Care Practice Group. He principally represents drug manufacturers and institutional healthcare providers in criminal, civil, and administrative enforcement actions and related civil litigation involving healthcare fraud and abuse and off-label promotion. In that capacity, he has negotiated a number of ground-breaking settlement agreements and corporate integrity agreements.

**Prof. Memberships:** Member of the Board of the Spina Bifida Foundation, Member of the American Health Lawyers' Association.

**Publications:** He is a co-author of 'Health Care Fraud: Enforcement and Compliance' and the author (or co-author) of numerous articles in legal, medical, and industry publications.

**Personal:** Yale Law School, JD, 1990; Boston University School of Medicine, MD, 1983; Boston University, BA, 1979. Admissions: US Supreme Court; US Court of Appeals, 5th Circuit; US Court of Appeals, 8th Circuit; US Court of Appeals, DC Circuit; US Court of Appeals, Federal Circuit; District of Columbia, 1991.

### KALISH, Paul W
Crowell & Moring LLP, Washington, DC
202 624 2644
pkalish@crowell.com
*Recommended in Insurance*

**Practice Areas:** Co-Chair of Crowell & Moring's Insurance Group. Serves as national counsel for property and casualty companies regarding toxic tort, environmental and other types of coverage issues. Serves as counsel for the Coalition for Litigation Justice, a group formed by property and casualty insurers to address abuses in the mass tort litigation environment.

**Prof. Memberships:** Served as Co-Chair

for the American Bar Association Section of Litigation's 2002 Annual Meeting, a member of ABA's Task Force on the State of the Civil Justice System, and a Co-Chair of the Section of Litigation's Pretrial Practice and Discovery Committee.

## KANTER, Jane A
Dechert LLP, Washington, DC
202 261 3302
jane.kanter@dechert.com
*Recommended in Investment Management*

**Practice Areas:** Ms Kanter concentrates her practice in the regulation and counseling of investment advisors, mutual funds, closed-end funds, fund directors, and private investment funds. She also handles insurance companies and investment and insurance product matters.
**Career:** Attorney, Office of the Solicitor, Plan Benefits Security Division, US Department of Labor (1979-80). Special counsel, US Securities and Exchange Commission's Division of Investment Management (1981-84). Vice President and legal counsel, T. Rowe Price Associates, Inc. (1984-87).
**Personal:** Queens College (BA, honors, 1970); Brooklyn Law School (JD, 1973); Washington University School of Law (LLM in Taxation, 1978).

## KAPLAN, Steven
Arnold & Porter LLP, Washington, DC
202 942 5998
Steven.Kaplan@aporter.com
*Recommended in Corporate/Commercial*

**Practice Areas:** Steven Kaplan is the Responsible Partner for Arnold & Porter LLP's Corporate and Securities Practice Group. He serves as corporate and securities counsel to a wide range of corporations, including those in financial services, life sciences, transportation, and a variety of other industries, with emphasis on mergers and acquisitions, public and private securities offerings, corporate governance and Securities and Exchange Commission compliance matters.
**Prof. Memberships:** In October 2004, Mr Kaplan began a three-year term as a member of the Municipal Securities Rulemaking Board. He also is a Member of the Board of Washington Trustees of the Federal City Council, the Economic Club of Washington and the Japan Commerce Association of Washington. He has addressed Bar, trade, and professional education conferences on corporate and securities law matters, including programs sponsored by the Securities Industry Association, the American Institute of Certified Public Accountants, the Bank Administration Institute, the District of Columbia Bar, the North Carolina Banking Institute, Strategic Research Institute, Executive Enterprises Inc. and the Israel Securities Authority.
**Career:** Mr Kaplan has represented

clients in scores of business combination and divestiture transactions valued in the tens of billions of dollars. Recent representations include CSX Corporation in the $1.15 billion sale of its global port assets to Dubai Ports International, Provident Financial Group in its $2.1 billion merger with National City Corporation and M&T Bank Corp. in its $3 billion acquisition of Allfirst Financial from Allied Irish Bank plc. Other representative clients currently include Bank of Hawaii Corporation, CIVC Partners and GenVec, Inc.
**Publications:** He has published articles on legal topics in Legal Times of Washington, The National Law Journal and Banking Expansion Reporter.

## KASTNER, Ken
Hogan & Hartson LLP, Washington, DC
202 637 5653
kmkastner@hhlaw.com
*Recommended in Environment*

**Practice Areas:** Nationally recognized authority on hazardous waste and hazardous materials transportation. Represents clients in all EPA regions and states on complex compliance and enforcement matters, remediation, litigation, permitting, and regulatory and legislative advocacy.
**Career:** Private practice, including Partner 2002-present at Hogan & Hartson; 1982-88, assistant general counsel for waste and transportation matters at the Chemical Manufacturers Association (currently American Chemistry Council).
**Publications:** Editorial Board of Hazardous Waste Consultant; frequent author for American Bar Association, Bureau of National Affairs, and American Corporate Counsel Association publications.
**Personal:** University of Virginia (JD, 1978); University of Virginia (BA, 1974); London School of Economics, visiting student (1973).

## KATTAN, Joseph
Gibson, Dunn & Crutcher LLP, Washington, DC 202 955 8239
jkattan@gibsondunn.com
*Recommended in Antitrust*

**Practice Areas:** Competition practice focused on litigation, counseling, and enforcement agency work. Mr Kattan has shepherded numerous mergers and acquisitions through the competition review process. Recent transactions include Seagate/Maxtor, Conexant/GlobespanVirata, and Sony/BMG. Mr Kattan has broad experience in technology and IP antitrust. Recent representations include the defense of Intel, Sony, and Unocal in IP antitrust litigations. Mr Kattan also represents Intel in various antitrust actions brought by AMD. He represents many other leading technology companies.

**Publications:** Mr Kattan has published numerous articles on competition law. He has presented by invitation at many government hearings and frequently speaks at leading conferences.

## KAUFMAN, Kenneth M
Skadden, Arps, Slate, Meagher & Flom LLP & Affiliates, Washington, DC
202 371 7170
kaufman@skadden.com
*Recommended in Intellectual Property, Media & Entertainment*

**Practice Areas:** Focuses on intellectual property, internet, e-commerce law, entertainment law, content and music licensing and evolving new technologies in the computer and entertainment fields. Represents a wide range of clients in online, entertainment and communications industries, including television networks, e-commerce companies, media businesses and computer and internet technology companies.
**Prof. Memberships:** Chair, Copyright Society of the USA, Washington, DC Chapter (2003-present); Washington Area Lawyers for the Arts, Board of Directors (1996-present); Washington Area Music Association, Advisory Board (1996-present).
**Career:** JD, Yale Law School, 1972 (editor, Yale Law Journal; AB, Harvard College, 1969 (magna cum laude).

## KEATING, Geoffrey T
McManus Schor Asmar & Darden, L.L.P., Washington, DC 202 296 9260
*Recommended in Construction*

## KEENEY, Regina
Lawler, Metzger, Milkman & Keeney, LLC, Washington, DC 202 777 7700
*Recommended in Telecom, Broadcast & Satellite*

## KELLEY, James J
Morgan, Lewis & Bockius LLP, Washington, DC 202 739 5095
jkelley@morganlewis.com
*Recommended in Employment*

**Practice Areas:** James J Kelley, II is a Partner in the Labor and Employment Law Practice Group. Mr Kelley is engaged in the full range of labor and employment law practice areas, including employment litigation, collective bargaining, grievance administration and arbitration, Department of Labor regulatory compliance, trade secrets and wage and hour laws. Mr Kelley also counsels clients on developing Employee Assistance Programs in the workplace. Mr Kelley concentrates in manufacturing, defense, aerospace, construction, downstream oil industries and government contractors and service companies.
**Prof. Memberships:** American Bar Association - Employment Law Section, College of Labor and Employment Lawyers.

## KELLNER, Leon B
Dickstein Shapiro Morin & Oshinsky LLP, Washington, DC 202 828 2283
KellnerL@dsmo.com
*Recommended in Insurance*

**Practice Areas:** General, civil, and insurance coverage litigation in federal and state courts. Represents policyholders in complex insurance coverage matters including asbestos, environmental, first-party losses, directors and officers insurance, and errors and omissions policies. Successfully represented clients in fraud- and employment discrimination-related litigation matters.
**Prof. Memberships:** ABA.
**Career:** Partner, Dickstein Shapiro's Insurance Coverage Practice. Partner, Anderson Kill Olick & Oshinsky, LLP. US Attorney for the Southern District of Florida, 1985-88; Civil Division Chief, 1982-84.
**Personal:** Harvard Law School (JD, 1971); State University of New York at Buffalo (BA, 1967).

## KELLOGG, Michael
Kellogg, Huber, Hansen, Todd, Evans & Figel, PLLC, Washington, DC
202 326 7900
*Recommended in Telecom, Broadcast & Satellite*

## KELLY, Deborah
Dickstein Shapiro Morin & Oshinsky LLP, Washington, DC
202 775 4772
KellyD@dsmo.com
*Recommended in Employment*

**Practice Areas:** Employment litigation and compliance. Defends companies against all types of employment claims, including litigation, wage and hour class/collective action suits, and enforcing covenants not to compete. Counsels; provides EEO training.
**Prof. Memberships:** ABA; Executive Committee Member; Council for Court Excellence; Board Member Kyle's Treehouse.
**Career:** Head of Employment Practice; Deputy General Counsel; Member of firm's Executive Committee; Professor, American University, 1983-1988; Adjunct Law Professor, 1992-93.
**Publications:** Regular television appearances, including CNN and MSNBC, discussing controversial employment decisions.
**Personal:** Washington College of Law (America University) (JD, 1988); Johns Hopkins University (MA, 1977; PhD, 1982); University of Vermont (BS, 1974).

## KENDALL, David
Williams & Connolly LLP, Washington, DC 202 434 5000
*Recommended in Litigation, Media & Entertainment*

## KEYES, Kevin M
Fried, Frank, Harris, Shriver & Jacobson

LLP, Washington, DC 202 639 7022
Kevin.Keyes@FriedFrank.com
*Recommended in Tax*

**Practice Areas:** Tax Partner. Concentrates practice in federal income taxation, including taxation of financial products, capital formation, private equity, cross-border financing and investment, and acquisition and disposition transactions. Adjunct Professor of Law, Georgetown University. Author: Federal Taxation of Financial Instruments and Transactions. Chair, American Bar Association, Section on Taxation, Financial Transactions Committee. Corporate Editor, Journal of Taxation. Board of Advisors, Journal of Taxation of Investments.
**Career:** Joined Fried Frank as a Partner in 1998.
**Personal:** JD (1983), Case Western Reserve University. Order of the Coif.

### KHOURY, Joseph
Wright & Talisman PC, Washington, DC
202 393 1200
*Recommended in Energy*

### KIELY, Bruce
Baker Botts LLP, Washington, DC
202 639 7711
bruce.kiely@bakerbotts.com
*Recommended in Energy*

**Practice Areas:** Practice involves regulatory, transactional litigation, project development work for project sponsors, gas pipelines, local distribution companies, LNG sellers, buyers and terminal operators. Experience includes LNG sales and purchase agreements, project development including permitting of pipelines and LNG terminals, fuel supply agreements, administrative and appellate litigation, and advice on changing regulatory policy.
**Prof. Memberships:** District of Columbia Bar; Virginia Bar; Federal Energy Bar Association.
**Career:** Head of firm-wide LNG practice and Global Projects Department in Washington office.
**Personal:** JD from The University of Texas School of Law, 1970; BS from the University of Colorado, 1967.

### KILBERG, William J
Gibson, Dunn & Crutcher LLP, Washington, DC 202 955 8573
wkilberg@gibsondunn.com
*Recommended in Employee Benefits, Employment, ERISA Litigation*

**Practice Areas:** Counsels and represents clients in employee relations, labor relations, and employee compensation - benefits. Argued significant matters before US Supreme Court and US Court of Appeals, involving ERISA, age, gender, race discrimination and the Americans with Disabilities Act. Appeared often in federal/bankruptcy/state courts.
**Career:** Solicitor, US Department of Labor; associate solicitor, Labor for Labor Relations/Civil Rights; General Counsel,

Federal Mediation – Conciliation Service; and White House Fellow/Special Assistant, Secretary of Labor George Shultz.
**Publications:** Co-author, 'Saga of Reform: Regulation of Worker Overtime.' Frequent speaker on employment - employee benefits issues.
**Personal:** JD, Harvard Law School, 1969.

### KING, Carol Weld
Hogan & Hartson LLP, Washington, DC
202 637 5634
cwking@hhlaw.com
*Recommended in Native Law, Real Estate*

**Practice Areas:** For nearly 20 years, Carol Weld King has practiced in commercial real estate in the hospitality and lodging industries. Her focuses include transaction structuring, financing, acquisition, and development.
**Prof. Memberships:** DC and Virginia Bar Member.
**Career:** Carol has represented owners, investors, developers, and lenders in varying transactions for hospitality, gaming, office, multi-family, and mixed-use projects. She currently serves as principal counsel to several hotel equity funds, and public and private corporations in a series of hotel acquisitions, financings, and ground up developments. Carol also represents a leading Native American tribe with casino and gaming developments in Connecticut and other states, assisting in public and private financing facilities and general business counseling.
**Personal:** University of Virginia School of Law (JD, 1986); University of Virginia (BA, with distinction, 1983).

### KINGHAM, Richard F
Covington & Burling, Washington, DC
202 662 5268
rkingham@cov.com
*Recommended in Healthcare*

**Practice Areas:** Food and drug law, European Community law, and product safety.
**Prof. Memberships:** District of Columbia Bar, registered foreign lawyer in England and Wales.
**Career:** General counsel to National Pharmaceutical Council since 1974, legal advisor to Pharmaceutical Research and Manufacturers of America and Consumer Healthcare Products Association, Member of National Advisory Allergy and Infectious Diseases Council (NIH), committees of the Institute of Medicine of the National Academy of Sciences and the World Health Organization. Adjunct Professor, Georgetown University Law Center and lecturer at University of Virginia School of Law and Cardiff University.
**Publications:** Co-author, 'FDLI Practical Handbook of Food and Drug Law and Regulation'; numerous articles in professional journals.
**Personal:** BA 1968, George Washington University; JD 1973, University of Vir-

ginia.

### KIRKWOOD, Martin
Jones Day, Washington, DC
202 879 3939
*Recommended in Energy*

### KLAWITER, Donald
Morgan, Lewis & Bockius LLP, Washington, DC 202 739 5222
dklawiter@morganlewis.com
*Recommended in Antitrust*

**Practice Areas:** Donald C Klawiter is a Partner in the Antitrust Practice Group at Morgan Lewis and is the Chair of the ABA Section of Antitrust Law for 2005-06. His practice focuses on antitrust civil and criminal investigations and litigation, corporate internal antitrust investigations, and compliance and corporate governance issues. He has defended corporations from many countries in major civil treble damage litigation and he has defended corporations and their senior executives in government enforcement matters, civil and criminal. He has regularly served as international coordinating counsel in multijurisdictional antitrust cases. Mr Klawiter previously held senior positions at the Antitrust Division, US Department of Justice.
**Prof. Memberships:** Professional Membership: Chair, Section of Antitrust Law, American Bar Association (2005-06); previously, Chair-Elect (2004-05); Vice-Chair (2003-04); Program Officer (2001-03); Secretary (2000-01); Chair, Criminal Practice and Procedure Committee (1995-97).

### KLEIN, Allen
Latham & Watkins LLP, Washington, DC
202 637 2200
*Recommended in Business Process Outsourcing, Technology*

### KLEIN, David F
Heller Ehrman LLP, Washington, DC
202 912 2023
david.klein@hellerehrman.com
*Recommended in Insurance*

**Practice Areas:** Insurance recovery.
**Prof. Memberships:** District of Columbia Bar Association; New York State Bar; Law Society of British Columbia; American Civil Liberties Union.
**Career:** Mr Klein's practice focuses on resolving disputes with insurance carriers, often without resort to litigation, through the development and presentation to insurers of a persuasive description of their coverage risks that combines legal argument with scientific, technical and economic analysis. Mr Klein also has experience litigating cases involving insurance coverage, public and administrative law.
**Personal:** Boston University (BA, summa cum laude, 1985); Yale Law School (JD, 1988); Phi Beta Kappa.

### KLEIN, Frederick
DLA Piper Rudnick Gray Cary US LLP,

Washington, DC 202 861 6668
frederick.klein@dlapiper.com
*Recommended in Real Estate*

**Practice Areas:** Real estate; real estate finance.
**Career:** He practices in all areas of commercial real estate law, representing construction and permanent lenders, domestic and foreign banks, life insurance companies, local and national developers, and owners and developers of office buildings, multifamily projects, shopping centers, and urban and suburban office buildings. Has handled the acquisition, disposition, and financing of commercial projects in the mid-Atlantic region and elsewhere throughout the United States.
**Publications:** Co-author, 'American Bar Association's Real Property Tax Deskbook', chapter on District of Columbia real property taxation.
**Personal:** JD, University of Miami; AB, Duke University.

### KLEIN, Kenneth
Mayer, Brown, Rowe & Maw LLP, Washington, DC 202 263 3377
kklein@mayerbrownrowe.com
*Recommended in Tax*

**Practice Areas:** International taxation of multinational corporations, including planning, transactions, controversies, and public policy work in numerous industries. Advises on outbound/inbound investments, structuring/restructuring, controlled foreign corporations, US property investments, offshore intangibles, manufacturing, transportation, cross-border financings, withholding tax, tax treaties, investment funds, swaps, and other derivatives. International individual tax planning.
**Career:** Partner, Mayer, Brown, Rowe & Maw LLP, Washington, DC, July 2002 to date. Cadwalader, Wickersham & Taft, 1990-2002. Internal Revenue Service, associate chief counsel (Technical), 1988-90. Cadwalader, Wickersham & Taft, 1981-88. Internal Revenue Service, assistant branch chief and attorney, Legislation & Regulations Division and General Litigation Division, 1977-81. Fellow, American Society of International Law, 1976-77.
**Publications:** Speaks on international tax issues at numerous tax seminars and writes extensively on international tax issues in numerous publications.
**Personal:** JD (cum laude), University of Georgia School of Law, 1976; Articles Editor, Georgia Journal of International & Comparative Law. MLT, Georgetown University Law Center, 1980. BA (magna cum laude) University of Delaware, 1973. National Law Alumni Board, Georgetown University Law Center, 2005-; past Member, Board of Visitors, University of Georgia School of Law.

### KLEIN, Michael
WilmerHale, Washington, DC

202 663 6000
*Recommended in Litigation*

## KLEPPER, Martin
Skadden, Arps, Slate, Meagher & Flom LLP & Affiliates, Washington, DC
202 371 7120
mklepper@skadden.com
*Recommended in Projects, Sport*
**Practice Areas:** Specializes in the development, financing, acquisition, privitization and restructuring of energy facilities, sports stadiums and other large infrastructure projects throughout the world. He has been the lead lawyer representing owners, lenders, investors, fuel suppliers and contractors in the electric power, gas and LNG industries involving transactions exceeding $10 billion.
**Prof. Memberships:** Board of Trustees, Legal Aid Society of the District of Columbia.
**Career:** Adjunct Professor, Georgetown Law School, 2002 - present; JD, Rutgers Law School, 1973 (articles editor, Rutgers Law Review); BS, University of Pennsylvania, Wharton School, 1969.

## KNAUSS, Charles
Bingham McCutchen LLP, Washington, DC 202 373 6644
chuck.knauss@bingham.com
*Recommended in Environment*
**Practice Areas:** Nationally recognized as an authority on the Clean Air Act. Has 25 years of experience addressing all aspects of this federal statute, including several years as counsel to the US House of Representatives Committee on Energy and Commerce where he figured prominently in the development of the comprehensive 1990 Clean Air Act Amendments. Represents clients in the manufacturing and energy sectors, including automotive, aerospace, pharmaceutical, chemical, paper, refinery, power generation and utilities.
**Personal:** University of Michigan Law School, JD, 1981; Brown University, AB, 1977.

## KOLASKY, William J
WilmerHale, Washington, DC
202 663 6357
william.kolasky@wilmerhale.com
*Recommended in Antitrust*
**Practice Areas:** Co-Chair, Antitrust and Competition Department. Practice includes full range of antitrust representation and counseling. Secured antitrust clearance from Federal Trade Commission and Department of Justice for more than 100 mergers and acquisitions, including Second Request investigations; coordinates merger reviews in multiple other jurisdictions worldwide, including European Commission. Represents companies and individuals in criminal and civil antitrust investigations; represents clients in broad range of private litigation.
**Career:** Deputy Assistant Attorney Gen-

eral for International Enforcement, Antitrust Division, US Department of Justice. Taught antitrust law at the Washington College of Law of American University.
**Personal:** AB, Dartmouth College; JD, Harvard University.

## KRAKOFF, David S
Mayer, Brown, Rowe & Maw LLP, Washington, DC 202 263 3370
dkrakoff@mayerbrownrowe.com
*Recommended in Litigation*
**Practice Areas:** Represents corporations and corporate executives in all aspects of criminal and related civil and administrative matters. Federal and state trials, primary trial responsibility in over 50 cases. Internal investigations. Grand jury investigations. SEC enforcement proceedings. Shareholder actions. Appeals. Debarment proceedings. Audit committee counseling. Client matters include accounting fraud, securities, tax, foreign corrupt practices, public corruption, antitrust, healthcare, export control, trade secrets, environmental.
**Career:** Mayer, Brown, Rowe & Maw LLP, Washington, DC, 2004 to date. Beveridge & Diamond, P.C., 1993-2004. Skadden, Arps, Slate, Meagher & Flom, 1990-93. Dunnells, Duvall, Bennett & Porter, 1987-90. United States Attorney's Office for the District of Columbia, Assistant US Attorney, 1976-86.
**Publications:** Recent writing: 'For Client's Sake: Under Assault From Government And The ABA, The Privilege Needs Defenders', Legal Times, October 1, 2001. 'Environmental Crimes Case - From Pretrial Proceedings to Sentencing Guidelines', American Bar Association, July 1999. 'Environmental Crimes: Recent Trends', 1999 Wiley Environmental Law Update, June 1999. 'The Hidden Cost to Corporate Settlements of Environmental Prosecutions - Is It Worth the Price?', The Environmental Corporate Counsel Report, January 10, 1999.
**Personal:** Antioch School of Law, JD Dartmouth College.

## KRAMER, Andrew
Jones Day, Washington, DC
202 879 4660
akramer@jonesday.com
*Recommended in Employment*
**Practice Areas:** He has represented employers in state and federal courts and before administrative agencies; negotiated collective bargaining agreements; and provided counseling and advice on the development of employment and labor relations strategies to a variety of industries. He has lectured on labor and employment law matters at numerous conferences throughout the US. Identified as one of the country's best employment/labor lawyers by The National Law Journal, Legal Times, and other leading business and legal publications.

**Prof. Memberships:** The College of Labor and Employment Lawyers; ABA.

## KRAMER, Merrill
Chadbourne & Parke LLP, Washington, DC 202 974 5660
mkramer@chadbourne.com
*Recommended in Energy*
**Practice Areas:** Represents energy, institutional banking and private equity clients globally, including public utilities, energy project developers, investment banks, private equity investors, commercial lenders and commodity energy traders. Experienced with transactions, M&A, trading and derivatives, and regulatory matters before the SEC and FERC. Chairs Trading and Derivatives Practice. Represents many active and innovative players in the deregulating energy industry.
**Prof. Memberships:** Energy Bar Association, former Board of Director and Vice-Chair of its International Energy Committee; International Swaps and Derivatives Association, Member, New Products Committee
**Career:** Former Head of Cogeneration and Independent Power Task Force; former Senior Trial Attorney, FERC

## KRAUSS, Joseph G
Hogan & Hartson LLP, Washington, DC 202 637 5832
jgkrauss@hhlaw.com
*Recommended in Antitrust*
**Practice Areas:** Joseph Krauss' practice is devoted to antitrust and economic regulation, merger and acquisition counseling, regulatory review, and litigation.
**Prof. Memberships:** Member, Antitrust Law Section, ABA (Council Member; Co-Chair, Merger Review Process Task Force; Chair, Mergers and Acquisitions Committee (2001-05); Vice-Chair, Clayton Act Committee (1999-2001)); nongovernmental advisor to the Mergers Working Group of the International Competition Network, 2004 to present.
**Career:** Joe joined Hogan & Hartson in 1999 after serving 11 years at the FTC. During his tenure at the FTC, he served in a variety of capacities, including Assistant Director of the Premerger Notification Office. Joe also was Acting Assistant Director and Deputy Assistant Director of the Mergers II Division where he was responsible for investigations of proposed mergers in a number of industries.
**Publications:** 'Antitrust Investigations 501: Successfully Managing Your Relationship with Agency Staff and Increasing Your Chances for Approval', ACC Docket, Association of Corporate Counsel (1 September 2004); 'Coordinated Effects Analysis in Mergers', Global Competition Review (1 September 2003); 'Antitrust Review of New Economy Acquisitions', Antitrust Magazine (Fall 2000).
**Personal:** Delaware Law School of Widener University (JD); Member,

Delaware and District of Columbia Bars.

## KRUPSKY, Kenneth J
Jones Day, Washington, DC
202 879 3664
kjkrupsky@jonesday.com
*Recommended in Tax*
**Practice Areas:** US and international tax law; planning, negotiation and documentation of global business transactions; tax administrative proceedings and litigation; tax policy matters. Deputy Assistant Secretary of the Treasury for Tax Policy under President Clinton; Chair, International Tax Committee, District of Columbia Bar Association; Adjunct Professor of Law, Georgetown University Law Center. Named by Euromoney's International Tax Review as one of the world's leading tax and transfer pricing advisors. Member, Tax Management International Journal's 'Panel of Leading Practitioners'.
**Personal:** Columbia College (National Merit Scholar); Columbia Law School (Harlan Fiske Stone Scholar, Columbia Law Review, Columbia Journal of Transnational Law).

## KUNEY, David
Sidley Austin LLP, Washington, DC
202 736 8650
dkuney@sidley.com
*Recommended in Bankruptcy*
**Practice Areas:** Represents both debtors and creditors in complex Chapter 11 cases, including complex partnership cases, retail bankruptcies, real estate bankruptcies and corporate cases. He has extensive litigation experience and served as lead counsel in both jury and non-jury civil matters throughout the United States.
**Prof. Memberships:** Chairs the American College of Real Estate Lawyers Bankruptcy Committee.
**Publications:** Published numerous articles, and is the author of 'Commercial Real Estate Leases in Bankruptcy'.
**Personal:** Mr Kuney is an Adjunct Professor of Bankruptcy at Georgetown University Law Center and chairs the annual 'Views from the Bench' symposium. University of Virginia School of Law, JD, 1973; University of Virginia, BA, 1967. Admissions: US Supreme Court; DC, 1976; MD, 1973.

## LAKE, William T

WilmerHale, Washington, DC
202 663 6725
william.lake@wilmerhale.com
*Recommended in Telecom, Broadcast & Satellite*

**Practice Areas:** Partner and senior member of Communications Department. Advises companies in the US and international communications industries on regulatory, competition, intellectual property, and trade issues.
**Prof. Memberships:** Federal Communications Bar Association, the American Bar Association, the US Council for International Business, and the District of Columbia and California Bars.
**Career:** Law clerk to Justice John M Harlan, US Supreme Court, and to Judge Henry J Friendly, US Court of Appeals for the Second Circuit. Served as Principal Deputy Legal Adviser at the US Department of State, 1980-81.
**Personal:** Yale University (BA 1965); Stanford University (LLB 1968).

## LAMKEN, Jeffrey A

Baker Botts LLP, Washington, DC
202 639 7978
jeff.lamken@bakerbotts.com
*Recommended in Litigation*

**Practice Areas:** Head of Supreme Court and Appellate Practice in firm's Washington office. Argued 16 cases before US Supreme Court on matters such as administrative law, bankruptcy, civil rights, criminal law and procedure, intellectual property, and telecommunications law.
**Prof. Memberships:** District of Columbia Bar; California Bar.
**Career:** Assistant to the Solicitor General, US Department of Justice; law clerk to Associate Justice Sandra Day O'Connor and to Judge Alex Kozinski, US Court of Appeals for the Ninth Circuit.
**Personal:** JD, Stanford Law School, 1990 (Order of the Coif, Nathan Abbott Scholar); BA (magna cum laude), political science, Haverford College, 1986.

## LANE, Brian

Gibson, Dunn & Crutcher LLP, Washington, DC 202 887 3646
blane@gibsondunn.com
*Recommended in Securities*

**Practice Areas:** Experienced in range of SEC issues. Counsels top domestic and international companies on corporate governance, capital raising, and regulatory issues under the federal securities laws. Focuses on resolving difficult disclosure, regulatory and accounting issues with the SEC.
**Career:** Counsels companies on issues relating to details of federal securities law, including: helping public companies resolve accounting issues with auditors and SEC, developing securities products and transactions, resolving disclosure and accounting issues and assisting in

response to SEC inquiries from Divisions of Corporation Finance and Enforcement.
**Publications:** Nationally recognized as expert in field as author, media commentator, conference speaker.

## LATHROP, Alex

Heller Ehrman LLP, Washington, DC
202 912 2034
alexander.lathrop@hellerehrman.com
*Recommended in Insurance*

**Practice Areas:** Insurance recovery.
**Career:** Mr Lathrop has participated in omnibus settlements of environmental claims for mining and utility companies and has taken part in all phases of complex coverage litigation. He also has practiced general commercial litigation, advised companies regarding the Foreign Corrupt Practices Act and developed corporate compliance and ethics programs.
**Personal:** University of California at Berkeley (BA, 1991); University of Virginia Law (JD, 1999).

## LAWSON, David L

Sidley Austin LLP, Washington, DC
202 736 8088
dlawson@sidley.com
*Recommended in Telecom, Broadcast & Satellite*

**Practice Areas:** David L Lawson, Co-Chair of the firm's Washington DC Communications Group, represents AT&T Inc. and other communications clients on competition-related matters involving state and federal regulation, mergers and acquisitions, constitutional and appellate litigation and federal district court litigation. Mr Lawson also handles a wide range of matters before the Federal Communications Commission, including rulemaking and complaint proceedings relating to video, internet and other broadband services, intercarrier compensation, universal service, VoIP, E911, privacy, network interconnection and preemption.
**Career:** Mr Lawson clerked for the Honorable Stephen F Williams, United States Court of Appeals for the District of Columbia Circuit (1990-91).
**Personal:** The University of Chicago Law School, JD, 1990; Southern Methodist University, MBA, 1984; University of Oklahoma, BS Engineering, 1983. Admission: DC.

## LEDDY, Mark

Cleary Gottlieb Steen & Hamilton LLP, Washington, DC 202 974 1570
mleddy@cgsh.com
*Recommended in Antitrust*

**Practice Areas:** US and European antitrust law, including civil and criminal litigation, analysis of competitive issues in mergers and acquisitions, and appearances before antitrust regulatory agencies and courts.
**Prof. Memberships:** Bars in Massachusetts and the District of Columbia.

Admitted to practice before US Supreme Court and US Courts of Appeal.
**Career:** Joined firm as Partner, 1986. Resident in firm's Brussels office from 1991-94. US Department of Justice (1972-86); named Deputy Assistant Attorney General (1984). Adjunct Professor at Georgetown Law School (1996). JD, Boston College Law School (1971); BA, Boston College (1968).

## LEGGETTE, Poe

Fulbright & Jaworski L.L.P., Washington, DC 202 662 4646
pleggette@fulbright.com
*Recommended in Energy*

**Practice Areas:** Litigation; administrative law.
**Prof. Memberships:** Mr Leggette is a trustee of the Rocky Mountain Mineral Law Foundation.
**Career:** Poe Leggette joined the Washington DC office of Fulbright & Jaworski LLP as a Partner in 1998. His practice focuses on judicial and administrative litigation concerning natural resources development on federal and Native American lands. In private practice, Mr Leggette has successfully handled cases at all levels of the federal court system. Prior to private practice, Mr Leggette served as assistant solicitor for the US Department of Interior. While with the Department of Interior, he authored or co-authored virtually all briefs filed in the federal courts on outer continental shelf issues, obtaining, among other things, two Supreme Court reversals of unfavorable Ninth Circuit decisions. A Co-Chairman of the firm's Energy Practice Group, Mr Leggette is a frequent speaker and writer on issues of national energy policy involving energy efficiency, alternative energy sources, and traditional energy sources.
**Personal:** BA, magna cum laude, Tufts University (1974); JD, University of Virginia (1977).

## LEIBENLUFT, Robert F

Hogan & Hartson LLP, Washington, DC
202 637 5789
rfleibenluft@hhlaw.com
*Recommended in Healthcare*

**Practice Areas:** Health and antitrust matters, including counseling and litigation regarding antitrust issues in the health, medical device, and pharmaceutical industries.
**Prof. Memberships:** Fellow, American Health Lawyers Association; Health Care Committee Chair, Antitrust Section, ABA.
**Career:** Hogan & Hartson LLP, 1981-95; 1998-present; Assistant Director for Healthcare in the FTC's Bureau of Competition, 1996-98; advisor in the FTC's Office of Policy Planning, 1980-81.
**Publications:** Writes and lectures extensively on health law topics, appearing in Health Affairs, The New England Journal

of Medicine, Vanderbilt Law Review, The American Journal of Psychiatry, Business and Health, Pharmaceutical Executive, Medical Device & Diagnostic Industry, and other books and journals.
**Personal:** University of California, Berkeley Boalt Hall School of Law (JD, 1980); Yale University (BA, 1973).

## LEITCH, Brian P

Arnold & Porter LLP, Denver
303 863 1000
*Recommended in Bankruptcy*

**Practice Areas:** Resident in the firm's Denver office, Mr Leitch heads Arnold & Porter's Bankruptcy Practice Group. He represents parties in large, complex reorganizations. He has particular expertise in airline bankruptcies. He has represented private equity funds, public corporations, and other investors in acquiring or bidding to acquire numerous debtors, including airlines, beverage companies, clothing companies, and high-tech companies. He has also represented companies in transactions to avoid Chapter 11, through debt for equity swaps, or by attracting new investors.
**Prof. Memberships:** American Bankruptcy Institute.
**Personal:** JD, University of Iowa College of Law, 1982 BA, University of Iowa, 1980 Iowa Society of CPAs, 1980.

## LENNON, Daniel

Latham & Watkins LLP, Washington, DC
202 637 2200
*Recommended in Corporate/Commercial*

## LERMAN, Steven

Leventhal Senter & Lerman PLLC, Washington, DC 202 429 8970
*Recommended in Telecom, Broadcast & Satellite*

## LERNER, Arthur N

Crowell & Moring LLP, Washington, DC
202 624 2820
alerner@crowell.com
*Recommended in Healthcare*

**Practice Areas:** Partner in Crowell & Moring LLP's Healthcare Group. Focuses practice on antitrust/transactions/fraud and abuse issues for managed care organizations/healthcare providers/other healthcare entities. Advises and represents HMOs and other managed care organizations/hospitals/pharmaceutical/medical device/supply companies/professional and trade associations/prescription benefit management firms/medical group practices/group purchasing organizations/charitable groups/other health organizations. Handles mergers and acquisitions/joint ventures/Federal Employees Health Benefit Program compliance and disputes/Medicare Advantage and ERISA matters/antitrust proceedings with DOJ and FTC.
**Prof. Memberships:** Chair of American

Health Lawyers Association Antitrust Group; Chair-elect for 2004-05 of American Bar Association Antitrust Section's Federal Trade Commission Committee.
**Career:** Directed FTC's healthcare antitrust program; attorney advisor to FTC Chairman; assistant to Director of the Bureau of Competition.

## LETZLER, Kenneth
Arnold & Porter LLP, Washington, DC
202 942 5921
Kenneth.Letzler@aporter.com
*Recommended in Antitrust*
**Practice Areas:** Specializes in antitrust and trade regulation with an emphasis on the pharmaceutical business, biotechnology, and similar high-tech fields. Served as counsel in private antitrust litigation and in merger matters before the Federal Trade Commission and the Department of Justice, including cases where the principal assets were patent, know-how, and other intellectual property. He clerked for the US Court of Appeals, District of Columbia Circuit. Admitted to the District of Columbia Bar and to practice before the US Supreme Court.
**Personal:** JD from Harvard Law School, 1968; BA from Columbia University, 1965.

## LEVINE, Arthur N
Arnold & Porter LLP, Washington, DC
202 942 5740
Arthur.Levine@aporter.com
*Recommended in Healthcare*
**Practice Areas:** Arthur Levine counsels pharmaceutical and medical device companies on a wide variety of compliance and regulatory issues. Mr Levine's work with pharmaceutical and device companies includes FDA advertising and promotional issues, GMP compliance, FDA inspections, and handling FDA regulatory and compliance initiatives. He works with new and existing companies to assess potential FDA regulatory jurisdiction over new products. Mr Levine's practice includes counseling clients on legislative and product liability issues associated with their business.
**Career:** Prior to joining Arnold & Porter LLP, he was the deputy general counsel for Litigation at the Food and Drug Administration. In this capacity, he served as FDA's principal legal advisor on compliance and enforcement matters and processes, supervised all litigation involving the FDA and represented the agency on enforcement and litigation issues with the Justice Department. Before becoming the Deputy Chief Counsel, Mr Levine prosecuted cases on behalf of FDA, including several precedent-setting cases involving medical devices and blood-banks.
**Publications:** Mr Levine is the author of the 'FDA Enforcement Manual' (Thompson Publishing Group, 1992), and taught for several years as an Adjunct Professor

at The George Washington University National Law Center.

## LEVINE, Henry D
Levine, Blaszak, Block & Boothby LLP, Washington, DC 202 857 2550
hlevine@lb3law.com
*Recommended in Telecom, Broadcast & Satellite*
**Practice Areas:** Specializing in the representation of large telecommunications users in transactions and disputes with carriers, he has negotiated contracts and resolved disputes on behalf of such Fortune 100 Companies as Merrill Lynch, General Motors, IBM, Marriott, Lockheed Martin, DuPont, the Securities Industry Association, Honeywell and Visa. In the government sector, he has advised the United States and the City of New York, among others, in connection with their procurement of telecommunications and related network services.
**Prof. Memberships:** The District of Columbia Bar, the ABA Forum Committee on Communications Law, and the Federal Communications Bar Association.
**Career:** Admitted to the Bars of New York, the District of Columbia, and Federal courts including the United States Supreme Court. From 1983 through 1992, he was a Partner in the Washington, DC office of Morrison & Foerster, where he founded and chaired the firm's Communications Group. He has been a Partner in Levine, Blaszak, Block & Boothby, LLP since the firm was founded in 1993. In 1996, Network World named him one of the 25 most powerful people in networking, citing his 'unique experience, knowledge and savvy' in 'dealing with the pricing, terms and conditions that shape custom network contracts'.
**Personal:** BA (magna cum laude) from Yale in 1972; JD (magna cum laude) from Harvard Law School in 1976; Master's Degree in Public Policy from Harvard's Kennedy School of Government in 1976.

## LEVINE, Lee
Levine Sullivan Koch & Schulz LLP, Washington, DC 202 508 1100
*Recommended in Media & Entertainment*

## LEVY, Neil L
Kirkland & Ellis LLP, Washington, DC
202 879 5116
nlevy@kirkland.com
*Recommended in Energy*
**Practice Areas:** Mr Levy serves as Co-Chair of Kirkland's Energy Practice Group. He represents independent power producers, electric power and natural gas marketers, natural gas and oil pipelines, and local distribution companies before the Federal Energy Regulatory Commission, state public utility commissions, and the federal courts with respect to regulatory, litigation, and transactional issues arising under the Federal Power

Act, the Natural Gas Act, the Public Utility Holding Company Act of 1935, the Public Utility Holding Company Act of 2005, and the Public Utility Regulatory Policies Act of 1978. Additionally, Mr Levy represents private equity clients in energy sector M&A transactions.
**Personal:** The George Washington University (BA, 1987, with special honors); Ohio Northern University (JD, 1990).

## LEWIS, Daniel
Arnold & Porter LLP, Washington, DC
202 942 5661
Daniel.Lewis@aporter.com
*Recommended in Bankruptcy*
**Practice Areas:** As Head of the firm's Bankruptcy Practice Group, Mr Lewis has extensive experience in all aspects of Chapter 11 practice. He has particular experience in representing parties in large, complex Chapter 11 reorganizations and has played a significant role in many of the country's most notable Chapter 11 cases. For example, he is representing U.S. Airways, Inc. in its most recent Chapter 11 filing, and has represented Braniff Airways, Inc., Baker Hughes Inc., Owens Corning, Allied Chemical, New York Life, Texas Pacific Group, Fannie Mae, Boehringer Ingelheim, Glaxo Wellcome, Coopers & Lybrand, the Official Committee of Unsecured Creditors of CRIIMI MAE Inc., the Official Committee of Unsecured Creditors of Covanta Energy Corp., Honeywell, the Official Equity Securities Holders Committee in the Global Marine reorganization, the State of Maryland and other parties in major Chapter 11 bankruptcy proceedings throughout the United States.
**Career:** Mr Lewis, who has served as a panelist and lecturer, has testified before Congress as an independent expert on amendments to the Bankruptcy Code and has authored numerous articles on issues and trends in bankruptcy law.
**Personal:** Mr Lewis was named by Washington Business Journal as a 'Top Washington Lawyer' for Bankruptcy in 2005.

## LEWIS, David
Pillsbury Winthrop Shaw Pittman LLP, Washington, DC 202 663 8474
david.lewis@pillsburylaw.com
*Recommended in Energy*
**Practice Areas:** Involved in all aspects of nuclear plant regulation, including siting, initial licensing, license renewal, decommissioning, investigations and enforcement, and whistleblower proceedings. Involved in reactor design certifications, early site permitting and proposals for combined construction permit and operating licenses. Advises on nuclear business and organizational transactions, including nuclear plant acquisitions, the formation of operating companies, and approvals related to electric utility deregulation.

**Prof. Memberships:** Nuclear Energy Institute's License Renewal Working Group; NEI's COL Task Force and Financial Issues Task Force; American Nuclear Society.
**Personal:** JD, George Washington University Law School, 1982; BS, Massachusetts Institute of Technology, 1979.

## LEWIS, Mark
Baker Botts LLP, Washington, DC
202 639 7732
mark.lewis@bakerbotts.com
*Recommended in Energy*
**Practice Areas:** Energy regulatory, energy transactions (oil and gas sales and transportation agreements), project development; advise and counsel clients in oil and gas transactions and projects, with a focus on midstream (pipeline-related) transactions and projects, both US and international.
**Prof. Memberships:** Association of International Petroleum Negotiators, Energy Bar Association, State Bar of Maryland, District of Columbia Bar
**Career:** Deputy Chair of firmwide Global Projects Department.
**Personal:** JD from Georgetown University Law Center (magna cum laude), 1990; BS from the University of Maryland (magna cum laude), 1987.

## LEWIS, William
Morgan, Lewis & Bockius LLP, Washington, DC 202 739 5145
wlewis@morganlewis.com
*Recommended in Environment*
**Practice Areas:** William Lewis is senior counsel in the Litigation Practice. His practice focuses almost exclusively on issues related to implementation of the 1990 Clean Air Act Amendments. He regularly represents corporate clients on clean air issues in district court and appellate litigation, rulemaking proceedings, enforcement actions, new source review and other permitting matters, and compliance counseling.
**Prof. Memberships:** American Bar Association; District of Columbia Bar Association; State Bar California; EPA's National Clean Air Act Advisory Committee; EPA's Subcommittee for air toxics and permits (Co-Chair).

## LIBIN, Jerome
Sutherland Asbill & Brennan LLP, Washington, DC 202 383 0145
jerome.libin@sablaw.com
*Recommended in Tax*
**Practice Areas:** Principal areas of concentration are tax controversy and litigation, tax planning, corporate acquisitions, dispositions and restructurings and financial transactions involving domestic and/or international tax considerations. Extensive experience in Treasury Department matters, including revision of proposed regulations and negotiation of tax treaty provisions. Handled legislative matters involving presentations to the

Congressional tax-writing committees and the Joint Committee on Taxation. Successfully litigated a number of important federal tax cases. Also handles constitutional challenges to state tax statutes. **Prof. Memberships:** President, International Fiscal Association (2001-05); Vice President, USA Branch, IFA (1992-); American Bar Association, Section of Taxation (Chair: Special Committee on Standing to Sue, 1973-75; Special Committee on Integration, 1983-86; Special Projects Committee, 1998-2000; Globalization Task Force, 1998-2000; Member of Council, 1992-95); DC Bar Taxation Division (Chair: 1975-77); American Law Institute. **Career:** Chair of firm's 80-lawyer Tax Group; law clerk, Associate Justice Charles E Whittaker of the United States Supreme Court, 1959-1960; Master of the Bench, J Edgar Murdock American Inn of Court; Fellow: American College of Tax Counsel and American Bar Foundation. **Personal:** JD, University of Michigan Law School, 1959 (Editor-in-Chief, Michigan Law Review); BS, Northwestern University, 1956.

### LIPMAN, Andrew D
Bingham McCutchen LLP, Washington, DC 202 373 6033
andrew.lipman@bingham.com
*Recommended in Telecom, Broadcast & Satellite*
**Practice Areas:** Serves as Chair of the firm's Telecommunications, Media and Technology Group. Practices in virtually every aspect of communications law and related fields, including regulatory, transactional, litigation, legislative and land use. Represents clients in both the private and public sectors, including those in the areas of local, long distance and international telephone common carriage; internet services and technologies; conventional and emerging wireless services; satellite services; broadcasting; competitive video services; telecommunications equipment manufacturing; and other high technology applications. **Personal:** Stanford Law School, JD, 1977; University of Rochester, BA, summa cum laude, 1974.

### LIPSEY, Charles
Finnegan Henderson Farabow Garrett & Dunner LLP, Reston 571 203 2700
*Recommended in Intellectual Property*
**Practice Areas:** Concentrates on intellectual property litigation, particularly patent infringement litigation, in the district courts, the US Court of Appeals for the Federal Circuit, and the US Supreme Court. Has handled cases involving mechanical, chemical, and electrical technologies, with emphasis on biotechnology and pharmaceutical chemistry. Also has handled numerous patent arbitration proceedings and patent interferences. **Prof. Memberships:** District of Colum-

bia Bar, Virginia State Bar, American Intellectual Property Law Association. **Personal:** Georgia Institute of Technology (BS, Chemical Engineering, 1972); George Washington University National Law Center (JD, 1977; LLM, Patent and Trademark Regulation Law, 1981).

### LIPSKY, Abbott
Latham & Watkins LLP, Washington, DC 202 637 2200
*Recommended in Antitrust*

### LIPSON, Kevin J
Hogan & Hartson LLP, Washington, DC 202 637 5614
kjlipson@hhlaw.com
*Recommended in Energy*
**Practice Areas:** Energy, including natural gas pipeline, local distribution company, regulatory, and commercial issues, generation fuel management, electric generation procurement, and energy commercial and contracting issues; antitrust, competition and consumer protection; infrastructure; environmental; legislative; litigation. **Prof. Memberships:** ABA; Energy Bar Association; Woodbine House Publishing Company (Board of Directors); Port Clyde Properties, Inc. (Board of Directors); Anti-Defamation League, B'nai B'rith (Lay Board); Jewish Advocacy Center (President and Co-Founder). **Career:** Partner with Hogan & Hartson since 1994; has been in private practice since 1980. **Personal:** Washington University (JD, 1980); The George Washington University (BA, 1977).

### LITT, Daniel
Dickstein Shapiro Morin & Oshinsky LLP, Washington, DC 202 775 4747
LittD@dsmo.com
*Recommended in Bankruptcy*
**Practice Areas:** Chairs Bankruptcy and Creditors' Rights Practice; represents diverse clients (creditors, debtors, trustees, creditors' committees, equity interest holders) in bankruptcy courts throughout US. Over the last 28 years, participated in hundreds of bankruptcy cases involving manufacturing and retail businesses; commercial real estate; airlines; government contracting firms; radio, television, telecommunications, healthcare and numerous other businesses. **Prof. Memberships:** American Bankruptcy Institute; served on Rules Committee for the US Bankruptcy Court for the District of Maryland. **Career:** Bankruptcy practitioner since 1979. **Publications:** Quoted in The Washington Post and Washington Business Journal. **Personal:** Syracuse University (BS, cum laude, 1974); Georgetown University (JD, 1978).

### LIVINGSTON, Donald R
Akin Gump Strauss Hauer & Feld LLP, Washington, DC 202 887 4242
dlivingston@akingump.com
*Recommended in Employment*
**Practice Areas:** Represents large employers in all aspects of civil rights and employment discrimination law, with emphasis on employment litigation. Has served as defense litigation counsel in numerous fair employment class actions. **Prof. Memberships:** Elected Member, College of Labor and Employment Lawyers; Member, American Bar Association, Labor and Employment Law Section and Equal Employment Opportunity Committee; Member, Georgia and District of Columbia Bars. **Career:** Former General Counsel, US Equal Employment Opportunity Commission. **Publications:** 'EEOC Litigation and Charge Resolution' (BNA 2005), the only comprehensive book on EEOC litigation. **Personal:** AB and JD, University of Georgia.

### LOEFFLER, Robert H
Morrison & Foerster LLP, Washington, DC 202 887 1506
rloeffler@mofo.com
*Recommended in Energy*
**Practice Areas:** Energy law representing private and public parties for over 30 years on a variety of novel federal and state electric, oil, gas and pipeline issues, involving some of the largest regulatory proceedings. For three decades, has been the State of Alaska's lead counsel on federal energy regulatory issues. Has litigated cases from Alaska to New Hampshire. Intellectual property is a second specialty, particularly defending against broad licensing campaigns. **Career:** Admitted to practice in New York and Washington, DC. **Personal:** AB, Harvard University, mcl 1965; JD, Columbia Law School, cl 1968. Editor, Columbia Law Review; law clerk H Medina (2nd Circuit).

### LOFTIS III, James R
Gibson, Dunn & Crutcher LLP, Washington, DC 202 955 8581
jloftis@gibsondunn.com
*Recommended in Antitrust*
**Practice Areas:** Over 30 years experience in antitrust, and consumer protection matters, both civil and criminal, including M&A counseling, joint ventures, teaming, strategic alliances, vertical distribution restraints, and IP. **Career:** Trial counsel, United States v NL Industries (criminal); involved in defense industry mergers, including Northrop Grumman/TRW, Lockheed Martin/Northrop Grumman, Raytheon/TI, Northrop Grumman/Westinghouse, Alliant/Olin, and others; and counsel in numerous civil antitrust class actions.

**Publications:** Frequent lecturer and author on antitrust and microeconomics. **Personal:** JD, George Washington University Law School, 1968; Order of the Coif and Editor-in-Chief of The George Washington Law Review.

### LOHMANN, Walter H
Kirkland & Ellis LLP, Washington, DC 202 879 5923
wlohmann@kirkland.com
*Recommended in Environment*
**Practice Areas:** Walter Lohmann leads the firm's Environmental Transactional Practice Group. His practice has focused on managing environmental compliance and liability issues as they arise in the context of corporate and real estate transactions, both in the US and around the world including conducting or coordinating environmental due diligence assessments, retaining and supervising technical experts, counseling clients on deal-related liability and risk allocation issues, drafting and negotiating contract language and pursuing post-closing resolution of issues identified in the course of due diligence. **Personal:** Cornell University, AB, 1980; George Washington University Law School, JD, 1983.

### LONG JR, Robert A
Covington & Burling, Washington, DC 202 662 5612
rlong@cov.com
*Recommended in Litigation*
**Practice Areas:** Chair of Covington's Appellate and Supreme Court Groups. Twelve oral arguments before the US Supreme Court and substantial role in over 100 appellate cases. Focus on administrative, antitrust, banking, communications, constitutional, ERISA, and intellectual property law. **Career:** Law clerk to Justice Lewis F Powell, Jr US Supreme Court, and Judge John Minor Wisdom, US Court of Appeals for the Fifth Circuit. Assistant to the Solicitor general of the United States, 1990-93. Associate and Partner (since 1995), Covington & Burling. **Personal:** Yale Law School (JD, 1985); Oxford University (BA/MA 1982); University of North Carolina at Chapel Hill (BA 1980).

### LOSS, Lewis
Thompson, Loss & Judge LLP, Washington, DC 202 772 5170
*Recommended in Insurance*

### LUCE, Gregory
Jones Day, Washington, DC 202 879 4278
gmluce@jonesday.com
*Recommended in Healthcare*
**Practice Areas:** Co-Head of the firm's Healthcare Practice, his experience includes litigation and regulatory matters for the healthcare industry. He has represented healthcare institutions in litigation

involving state and federal fraud and abuse laws and the False Claims Act, Medicare reimbursement, and the design and implementation of compliance programs. He has also written and lectured on healthcare-related issues.

**Prof. Memberships:** American Health Lawyers Association (Board of Directors, 1995-2001; Fellow, elected 2005); ABA Health Law Section; Virginia State Bar Health Law Section (Chair, 1990-91); 'Who's Who in American Law'; Best Lawyers in America.

## LUCHS, Richard

Greenstein Delorme & Luchs, Washington, DC 202 452 1400
*Recommended in Real Estate*

## LUDWISZEWSKI, Raymond B

Gibson, Dunn & Crutcher LLP, Washington, DC 202 955 8665
rludwiszewski@gibsondunn.com
*Recommended in Environment*

**Practice Areas:** Has handled numerous significant environmental and natural resources litigation matters, including constitutional issues before the Supreme Court.

**Career:** Served as general counsel and assistant administrator for enforcement at United States Environmental Protection Agency; was special counsel to Assistant Attorney General for Environment and Natural Resources Division at the Justice Department. Environmental enforcement cases: United States v Westvaco, United States v Lockheed Martin, United States v Tyco, United States v Bethlehem Steel, United States v General Motors and United States v Raymark.

**Publications:** Frequent speaker/writer on environmental issues.

**Personal:** JD, Harvard Law School, 1984, Articles Editor, Harvard Law Review.

## LUPO, Raphael

McDermott Will & Emery, Washington, DC 202 756 8366
rlupo@mwe.com
*Recommended in Intellectual Property*

**Practice Areas:** Focuses on patent, trademark, copyright and trade secrets litigation and counseling. Extensive patent trial experience as lead counsel in federal district courts and before International Trade Commission. Presented and argued over 100 appeals before Court of Appeals for Federal Circuit and its predecessor (CCPA). Has represented clients in complex technology involving medical devices, computers and computer-related technologies, including integrated circuit cases, flash memories, microprocessors and other semiconductor configurations.

**Career:** Has been accepted by 11 federal district courts as a recognized patent law expert and expert on Patent Office matters.

**Personal:** George Washington University (BSEE, JD).

## LUXTON, Jane

King & Spalding LLP, Washington, DC 202 626 2627
jluxton@kslaw.com
*Recommended in Environment*

**Practice Areas:** Environmental practice with a focus on environmental regulation of toxic substances, particularly metals, under the full range of federal and state environmental laws, as well as international environmental regulation. Extensive experience in international trade matters and litigation.

**Prof. Memberships:** American Bar Association; District Court for the District of Columbia; District of Columbia Circuit, 4th, 11th and Federal Circuit; District of Columbia Bar; US Supreme Court.

**Personal:** AB, cum laude, Harvard University, 1973; JD, Cornell University, 1976.

## LYBECKER, Martin E

WilmerHale, Washington, DC 202 663 6240
martin.lybecker@wilmerhale.com
*Recommended in Investment Management*

**Practice Areas:** Serves as counsel to investment companies and independent directors, investment advisors, broker-dealers, depository institutions and holding companies, insurance companies, several financial services trade associations.

**Prof. Memberships:** Former Chair, American Bar Association, Section of Business Law's Committee on Banking Law; American Law Institute; Editorial Advisory Board of The Investment Lawyer (Aspen Law & Business).

**Career:** Associate Director of Division of Investment Management at SEC; served as lawyer in Division's Office of Chief Counsel.

**Personal:** University of Pennsylvania Law School (LLM 1973); New York University School of Law (LLM 1971); University of Washington (JD 1970); University of Washington (BA 1967).

## LYSTAD, Robert

Baker & Hostetler LLP, Washington, DC 202 861 1621
*Recommended in Media & Entertainment*

## MACAVOY, Christopher

Howrey LLP, Washington, DC 202 783 0800
*Recommended in Antitrust*

## MACBETH, Angus

Sidley Austin LLP, Washington, DC 202 736 8000
amacbeth@sidley.com
*Recommended in Environment*

**Practice Areas:** Angus Macbeth's practice emphasizes matters including contaminated sediments cases under remedial and natural resource damage provisions of Superfund, global warming issues and

corporate environmental management programs. He has experience with multi-facility enforcement cases under the Clean Air and Clean Water Acts and with regulatory advocacy and challenges under those statutes. He has dealt repeatedly with State-federal issues under RCRA and the hazardous waste management statutes and those controlling the discharge of pollutants to the environment. He is a member of the firm's Executive Committee and a Member of the Board of the Environmental Law Institute.

**Career:** Mr Macbeth clerked for Judge Harold R Tyler, Jr in the Southern District of New York and was an assistant US attorney in the Criminal Division of the Southern District of New York. He served as Deputy Assistant Attorney General in what is now the Environment and Natural Resources Division of the Justice Department. Mr Macbeth has written and spoken extensively on topics in environmental law.

**Personal:** Yale Law School, LLB, 1969; Yale University, BA, 1964. Admissions: DC and New York.

## MACHLIN, Barry N

Mayer, Brown, Rowe & Maw LLP, Chicago 312 782 0600
*Recommended in Projects*

**Practice Areas:** Partner and Co-Chair of Global Project Finance Practice. Represents international banks and financial institutions and multilateral and bilateral official lending agencies. Transactions include the $226 million San Fernando gas pipeline project (Mexico), the $440 million Baijio power project (Mexico), the $800 million Quezon power project (Philippines), a CDMA telecom upgrade financing (Mexico), the $2.5 billion Paiton I project (Indonesia), and the Khalda and Qarun oil concession developments (Egypt). Also represents banks and financial institutions in syndicated lending and Eurodollar transactions, sovereigns, state-owned enterprises and investors in privatisation and restructuring matters, and parties in cross-border investment and financial transactions. Widely experienced in representing clients in connection with transactions throughout Europe, Asia and the Middle East.

**Career:** Joined Mayer, Brown, Rowe & Maw LLP as a Partner, 1997, serving first in Washington, DC, and currently in Chicago. Partner (first associate) with White & Case, Washington, DC, and London, 1985-97.

**Publications:** Speaking engagements: 'Building Infrastructure Projects in Developing Markets', Practising Law Institute; 'Project Finance', International Bar Association; 'Venture Capital and Private Equity Investments in Emerging Markets', Harvard International Develop-

ment Conference.

**Personal:** JD, Harvard Law School, 1985; BA, summa cum laude, Brandeis University, 1982; Phi Beta Kappa.

## MADAN, Raj

McKee Nelson LLP, Washington, DC 202 775 8681
rmadan@mckeenelson.com
*Recommended in Tax*

**Practice Areas:** Tax controversy and litigation. Has represented numerous clients in all stages of IRS administrative practice, Federal District Court litigation, and Tax Court litigation. Substantive experience includes a wide range of complex tax issues in the following areas: foreign tax credits, transfer pricing, business purpose/economic substance, life insurance and investment tax credits.

**Career:** Prior to joining McKee Nelson in January 2000, was a senior associate at the Washington, DC law firm of Miller & Chevalier where he focused on large case tax controversy matters. From 1992-97, served as a trial attorney for the Internal Revenue Service, Manhattan District Counsel, where he was a member of two significant trial teams, Nestle and Riggs.

**Personal:** Received a JD, with honors, from the George Washington University Law School in 1992 and a BA (Economics) from New York University in 1990.

## MADDEN, William

Winston & Strawn LLP, Washington, DC 202 282 5000
*Recommended in Energy*

## MAGEE, John B

McKee Nelson LLP, Washington, DC 202 775 8671
jmagee@mckeenelson.com
*Recommended in Tax, Tax Litigation*

**Practice Areas:** Taxation, tax controversy, international tax, transfer pricing. Has extensive experience in all aspects of income tax planning, IRS administrative proceedings and tax litigation.

**Career:** Joined McKee Nelson in January 2000, where he heads the Tax Litigation Group and serves on the Executive Committee of the firm. Previously, he spent 23 years at the Washington, DC law firm of Miller & Chevalier as Chair of its Tax Practice Department, and as a member of the firm's Executive Committee. He is an Adjunct Professor in the Graduate Tax Program of the Georgetown Law Center, teaching 'International Transfer Pricing: Theory vs. Practice'.

**Personal:** Received an LLM in Taxation from Georgetown University Law Center in 1977 and a JD in 1972 from the University of Washington School of Law, where he served on the Law Review and received the Order of the Coif distinction.

## MAGGIO, Michael
Maggio & Kattar PC, Washington, DC
202 483 0053
*Recommended in Immigration*

## MAHONEY, Colleen P
Skadden, Arps, Slate, Meagher & Flom
LLP & Affiliates, Washington, DC
202 371 7900
cmahoney@skadden.com
*Recommended in Securities*

**Practice Areas:** Heads the firm's Securities Enforcement and Compliance Practice in the Washington, DC office. Represents corporations and their officers, directors and employees in SEC and other law enforcement investigations, as well as in federal court securities litigation. Assists management and boards of directors performing internal investigations. Advises public companies, financial services firms and financial institutions on preventive and remedial measures before and after securities-related issues arise. Counsels clients on issues in the emerging field of consumer financial regulation.
**Career:** JD, American University, 1981 (summa cum laude); BA, American University School of Government and Public Administration, 1978 (magna cum laude).

## MAHONEY, Maureen
Latham & Watkins LLP, Washington, DC
202 637 2200
*Recommended in Litigation*

## MAIZEL, Jonathan
Milbank, Tweed, Hadley & McCloy LLP,
Washington, DC
202 835 7500
*Recommended in Projects*

## MALESTER, Ann
Weil, Gotshal & Manges LLP,
Washington, DC 202 682 7500
ann.malester@weil.com
*Recommended in Antitrust*

**Practice Areas:** Ann Malester focuses her practice on antitrust counseling and litigation. Prior to joining Weil Gotshal, Ms Malester was Deputy Director of the FTC's Bureau of Competition, where she supervised antitrust enforcement activities throughout the agency. During her 12 previous years as an Assistant Director, she headed FTC merger enforcement in several market sectors, including the defense, pharmaceutical, biotech and medical device and equipment industries, and led the Mergers I Division in investigating, litigating or obtaining consent agreements in hundreds of significant mergers, acquisitions and joint ventures.
**Personal:** Bryn Mawr College, BA; George Washington University Law School, JD.

## MANN, Phillip L
Miller & Chevalier Chartered,
Washington, DC 202 626 5890
pmann@milchev.com
*Recommended in Tax*

**Practice Areas:** Tax; tax litigation and judicial appeals; tax policy and administration; tax audits and administrative appeals; alternative dispute resolution procedures; corporate, partnership, and joint venture tax planning/international tax planning; taxation of natural resources; transfer pricing; tax legislation; tax regulation; financial products, transactions, and institutions.
**Prof. Memberships:** American Bar Association; American College of Tax Counsel; American Law Institute; Bar Association of District of Columbia; Internal Revenue Service Commissioner's Advisory Group (1987-88; 1994-96); National Tax Association.
**Career:** Member - Miller & Chevalier Chartered (1982-present); Tax Legislative Counsel - US Department of Treasury (1974-75); Deputy Tax Legislative Counsel - US Department of Treasury (197 - 74).
**Publications:** Has written and spoken widely on oil and gas taxation, tax shelters, and selected corporate taxation issues and has taught in the graduate tax program at Georgetown University Law Center.
**Personal:** LLB, The University of Texas School of Law, 1962; BBA, University of Oklahoma and University of Texas at Austin, 1962.

## MARSHALL, Alison
Jones Day, Washington, DC
202 879 7611
abmarshall@jonesday.com
*Recommended in Employment*

**Practice Areas:** An active litigator with extensive experience handling complex employment litigation matters including employment discrimination class actions and FLSA collective and state wage and hour class actions. Routinely counsels employers on sexual and racial harassment policies, ADA compliance, workplace violence, wage and hour law developments, early retirement programs, and reductions in force. She also represents universities on employment matters, with particular emphasis on gender discrimination issues in intercollegiate athletics.
**Prof. Memberships:** ABA (Equal Employment Opportunity and the Employee Rights and Responsibilities Committees of the Labor and Employment Law Section). National Association of College and University Attorneys.

## MARTIN, David B H
Covington & Burling, Washington, DC
202 662 5128
dmartin@cov.com
*Recommended in Securities*
**Practice Areas:** As Head of the firm's

Securities Practice Group, he advises clients in corporate, corporate governance, securities regulation and transactional matters, including corporate finance and business combination transactions. His practice also includes internal investigations and corporate compliance issues.
**Career:** His career includes seven years of service with the SEC, including as Director of the Division of Corporation Finance and special counsel to the Chairman.
**Personal:** He served four years in the US Navy and received his JD from the University of Virginia Law School, where he was managing editor of the law review, and his BA from Yale University.

## MARTIN, Keith
Chadbourne & Parke LLP, Washington,
DC 202 974 5600
kmartin@chadbourne.com
*Recommended in Projects*

**Practice Areas:** Provided tax advice last year to 143 companies and worked on transactions in the United States and 11 foreign countries. Frequent speaker at conferences on project and structured finance, particularly in the energy sector. Author of more than 125 articles on tax subjects. Editor of Chadbourne's Project Finance NewsWire and a contributing editor of International Tax Report, Practical US/International Tax Strategies and Natural Gas & Electricity. Also lobbies the US government on policy issues.
**Career:** Former counsel to Senator Daniel Patrick Moynihan (D-NY) and a legislative assistant to Senator Henry M Jackson (D-Wash). Partner at Chadbourne since 1983.

## MASTERS, Lori
Jenner & Block LLP, Washington, DC
202 639 6076
lmasters@jenner.com
*Recommended in Insurance*

**Practice Areas:** Lorelie S Masters is a Partner in Jenner & Block's Washington, DC office. She is a member of the firm's Insurance Litigation and Counseling, Arbitration: Domestic and International, and Litigation & Dispute Resolution Practices. Since 1983, Ms Masters has advised and represented companies and individuals seeking to enforce their insurance coverage under general liability, directors & officers, first-party property, health, and other types of insurance. She has written two legal treatises: Insurance Coverage Litigation, and Liability Insurance in International Arbitration: The Bermuda Form. Ms Masters has handled, tried, and settled cases in state and federal trial and appellate courts across the country and, more recently, in arbitrations in the United States and abroad. At issue in these cases typically have been millions of dollars of insurance coverage for products liability and directors and officers

claims. Ms Masters served as lead trial counsel for policyholder Hoechst Celanese Corporation in its action enforcing general liability insurance coverage for hundreds of thousands of product-liability claims against the policyholder in what the press called the largest property damage class action settlement ever. The National Law Journal called the jury's verdict in Hoechst Celanese's coverage case one of the 'most significant jury verdicts of 1997'. More recently, Ms Masters obtained an award of more than $92 million to cover product-liability claims against a major pharmaceutical and chemical manufacturer in an arbitration conducted in London under the English Arbitration Act, 1996.
**Personal:** Notre Dame Law School, JD, 1981.

## MASUR, Daniel A
Mayer, Brown, Rowe & Maw LLP, Washington, DC 202 263 3226
dmasur@mayerbrownrowe.com
*Recommended in Business Process Outsourcing, Technology*

**Practice Areas:** Partner in the Corporate, Information Technology, and Outsourcing Practices. Former Vice-President and general counsel of I-NET, a provider of information technology and outsourcing services. Represents national and international firms in range of onshore, nearshore, and offshore information technology and outsourcing transactions. Representative business process outsourcing transactions include the outsourcing of employee services, finance and accounting functions, customer relations management, recruiting, collections, procurement, e-commerce processing and support, financial services operations and other business processes and functions. Representative information technology transactions include the outsourcing of IT infrastructure services and support, application development and maintenance, telecommunications services, network management and support, and help desk/call center services. Representative clients include established and emerging companies in aerospace, defense contracting, electronic commerce, financial services, pharmaceuticals, insurance, healthcare, banking, life sciences, chemicals, consumer products, manufacturing, oil/gas, real estate, forestry products, telecommunications, information technology and utilities/electrical power.
**Prof. Memberships:** Admitted to practice in the District of Columbia (1977).
**Career:** Mayer, Brown, Rowe & Maw LLP as Partner, 1997. Partner, Reed, Smith, Shaw & McClay, 1977-94. Vice-President and General Counsel for I-NET, Inc., 1994-97.
**Personal:** JD, Georgetown University, 1977; editor, Georgetown Law Journal. BA, Marquette University, 1974.

## MATYAS, David E

Epstein Becker & Green PC,
Washington, DC 202 861 0900
dmatyas@ebglaw.com
*Recommended in Healthcare*
**Practice Areas:** Legal and regulatory
matters arising under Medicare, Medicaid, and other third-party payment programs. Represents healthcare entities in
connection with Medicare/Medicaid
fraud issues including anti-kickback, false
claims, secondary payor issues, and false
billings.
**Prof. Memberships:** American Bar
Association, American Health Lawyers
Association.
**Publications:** Served as an Adjunct Professor of Law at American University's
Washington School of Law. Has spoken
and published numerous articles on the
subjects of healthcare fraud, corporate
compliance programs, the Stark Law,
mergers and acquisitions in the healthcare
industry, and other health-related topics.
Co-authored a book sponsored by the
American Health Lawyers Association
entitled 'Legal Issues in Health Care Fraud
and Abuse: Navigating the Uncertainties'.
**Personal:** JD, University of Texas School
of Law, 1992. BA, University of Pennsylvania, 1990.

## MAY, Gregory

Freshfields Bruckhaus Deringer LLP,
Washington, DC 202 777 4500
*Recommended in Tax*

## MAYERSON, Marc S

Spriggs & Hollingsworth, Washington,
DC 202 898 5881
*Recommended in Insurance*

## MAZAWEY, Louis

Groom Law Group, Washington, DC
202 857 0620
*Recommended in Employee Benefits*

## MAZO, Mark

Hogan & Hartson LLP, Washington, DC
202 637 5673
memazo@hhlaw.com
*Recommended in*
*Corporate/Commercial*
**Practice Areas:** Mark Mazo's practice
focuses on cross-border transactions with
particular emphasis on strategic and financial investments, joint ventures, and acquisitions for major international investors
and European and US companies.
**Career:** Mark represents major international investors and European and US
companies in mergers and acquisitions
and strategic investments and alliances in
Western Europe and the United States.
He also handles equity and debt financings. Mark works out of the Paris office as
well as the Washington office.
**Personal:** Harvard Law School (JD, cum
laude, 1974); Princeton University (AB,
magna cum laude, Phi Beta Kappa, US
Army Distinguished Military Graduate,
1971).

## MCBRIDE, Andrew G

Wiley Rein & Fielding LLP, Washington,
DC 202 719 7135
amcbride@wrf.com
*Recommended in Telecom, Broadcast*
*& Satellite*
**Practice Areas:** Chairs firm's Communication Litigation Group; co-chairs its
Appellate Practice. Significant trial,
appellate and Supreme Court experience
in the areas of telecommunications,
internet services, administrative law, con-
stitutional law and general commercial
litigation involving copyright, commer-
cial speech, utility deregulation and pri-
vacy law.
**Prof. Memberships:** Member, Federal
Communications Bar Association.
**Career:** Special Assistant, US Depart-
ment of Justice, Office of Legal Counsel;
Associate Deputy Attorney General,
Office of the Deputy Attorney General;
Assistant US Attorney, US Attorney's
Office for the Eastern District of Virginia
and Chief of Appeals for the District.
**Personal:** Stanford Law School (JD);
College of the Holy Cross (BA).

## MCCREA, Keith R

Sutherland Asbill & Brennan LLP,
Washington, DC 202 383 0705
keith.mccrea@sablaw.com
*Recommended in Energy*
**Practice Areas:** Practiced before FERC,
DOE, and other federal agencies and the
courts in a wide variety of natural gas,
electric power, and oil pipeline matters.
Spent the past 15 years, at the forefront of
efforts to restructure the natural gas and
electric power industries consistent with
FERC policies promoting open access
and competitive markets. Assisted a
diverse group of clients in their efforts to
cope with a rapidly changing regulatory
environment. Actively involved in legislative efforts dealing with industry restructuring issues at both the national and
state levels.
**Personal:** JD, Georgetown University
Law Center, 1973; BSChE, Lehigh University, 1969.

## MCCUTCHEN, Tammy D

Dickstein Shapiro Morin & Oshinsky LLP,
Washington, DC 202 828 6998
McCutchenT@dsmo.com
*Recommended in Employment*
**Practice Areas:** FLSA, FMLA,
OFCCP/Government Contracting, Title
VII, ADA, ADEA, and similar state laws.
Leads the firm's PolicyPartner compli-
ance services.
**Career:** Partner. Previously administra-
tor of the Wage and Hour Division of the
US Department of Labor and a primary
author of the revised Part 541 white-col-
lar exemption overtime regulations. Prior
to joining the USDOL, Senior counsel for
Hershey Foods Corporation.
**Personal:** Northwestern University
School of Law (JD); Western Illinois Uni-

versity (BA).

## MCDANIELS, William

Williams & Connolly LLP, Washington,
DC 202 434 5000
*Recommended in Litigation*

## MCDAVID, Janet L

Hogan & Hartson LLP, Washington, DC
202 637 8780
jlmcdavid@hhlaw.com
*Recommended in Antitrust*
**Practice Areas:** Focuses on antitrust
and competition, with a particular
emphasis on government investigations,
mergers and acquisitions, litigation, and
antitrust policy issues.
**Prof. Memberships:** Former Chair, Section of Antitrust Law, ABA (1999-2000);
Member, Antitrust Council of the US
Chamber of Commerce and the US
Council for International Business.
**Career:** Advisor to the Transition Team
for the Federal Trade Commission (FTC)
for the Bush Administration in 2000 and
a member of the FTC Transition Team
for the Clinton Administration in 1992.
Served on two US Department of
Defense (DoD) Antitrust Task Forces
(1993-94 and 1996-97) appointed by the
Secretary and General Counsel of the
DoD to advise on antitrust issues
involved in defence industry mergers and
joint ventures, and on vertical integration
among defence contractors.
**Publications:** Author/co-author of
many books and articles involving
antitrust law, including: 'Mergers &
Acquisitions', 'The Antitrust Evidence
Handbook', 'Antitrust and Health Care',
and 'Antitrust & Trade Associations Prac-
tice Guide' (all published by the ABA
Antitrust Section). She is a frequent
speaker on antitrust issues.
**Personal:** Georgetown University Law
Center (JD, editor of the Georgetown
Law Journal); Northwestern University
(BA, with honors).

## MCDOWELL, Suzanne Ross

Steptoe & Johnson LLP, Washington, DC
202 429 3000
*Recommended in Tax*
**Practice Areas:** Partner in Steptoe &
Johnson LLP's Washington office. Practice
focuses on tax-exempt organizations,
emphasizing tax and corporate governance
issues. Experience with tax planning, structuring transactions, and representing
clients before the IRS, Treasury, Congress
and courts. Clients include educational,
healthcare, medical research, religious and
advocacy organizations; private foundations; professional and trade associations;
and government agencies and instrumentalities. Serves on IRS Advisory Committee
for Tax-Exempt and Government Entities;
as Vice-Chair of the ABA Co-ordinating
Committee on Nonprofit Governance; and
Chair of DC Bar Tax Section.
**Personal:** JD, with high honors, George
Washington University, 1977; BA, Smith

College, 1971.

## MCELWAIN, William G

WilmerHale, Washington, DC
202 942 8406
william.mcelwain@wilmerhale.com
*Recommended in Intellectual Property*
**Practice Areas:** Focuses practice on
intellectual property litigation. Has tried
cases in courts nationwide and before the
US International Trade Commission. In
patent litigation, represents clients in
matters involving wide variety of technologies, ranging from genetic engineering to integrated circuit manufacturing to
textile finishing. Also maintains a general
commercial litigation practice.
**Prof. Memberships:** Admitted to practice in the Commonwealth of Virginia,
the District of Columbia and the Commonwealth of Massachusetts.
**Personal:** JD, Harvard Law School; BA,
Yale College.

## MCFALLS, Michael

Jones Day, Washington, DC
202 879 3864
msmcfalls@jonesday.com
*Recommended in Antitrust*
**Practice Areas:** Antitrust matters,
including government investigations and
counseling on joint ventures and
antitrust issues involving intellectual
property. He has spoken, written, and testified about antitrust issues involving
intellectual property and joint ventures in
the US and abroad.
**Prof. Memberships:** Chair of the Computer and Internet Committee and a former Co-Chair of the Intellectual Property
Committee of the ABA's Section of
Antitrust Law.
**Career:** Federal Trade Commission
(1997-2000). He was attorney advisor to
Chairman Pitofsky from 1998 to 2000.
He also assisted the policy planning office
in the development and drafting of the
Antitrust Guidelines for Collaborations
among Competitors.

## MCGOVERN, Elissa M

Greenberg Traurig LLP, McLean
703 749 1300
*Recommended in Immigration*
**Practice Areas:** Immigration.
**Prof. Memberships:** Member, Steering
Committee, American Business for Legal
Immigration; Member, Essential Worker
Immigration Coalition; Chair, Greater
DC Chapter of the American Immigra-
tion Lawyers Association, Board of Gov-
ernors, 2003-04; Member, DOL-ESA
Liaison Committee, American Immigra-
tion Lawyers Association; Member, The
District of Columbia Bar; Member Steer-
ing Committee, Compete America Coali-
tion.
**Publications:** Immigration Issues, Rep-
resenting the Restaurant Industry, ALI-
ABA (May 2002) Immigration Legislative
Roundup, American Hotel & Lodging
Association (May 2001).

**Personal:** JD, New York University School of Law, 1989; BA, English and American Literature and History, Manhattanville College, 1984.

### MCGRANE, John
Morgan, Lewis & Bockius LLP, Washington, DC 202 739 5621
jmcgrane@morganlewis.com
*Recommended in Energy*
**Practice Areas:** John D McGrane is a Partner in the Energy Practice and has more than 25 years of experience representing electric utilities, power marketers and other participants in the electric power industry. Mr McGrane advises clients on market investigations; restructuring; mergers, acquisitions and asset transactions; affiliate issues; power purchase sales and agreements; antitrust; and reliability issues. He has particular experience in transmission-related issues and representing clients in investigations and audits by the Federal Energy Regulatory Commission's Office of Market Oversight and Investigations.
**Prof. Memberships:** Edison Electric Institute (Legal Committee); American Bar Association; Energy Bar Association.

### MCGRATH, Kathryn B
Mayer, Brown, Rowe & Maw LLP, Washington, DC 202 263 3374
kmcgrath@mayerbrownrowe.com
*Recommended in Investment Management*
**Practice Areas:** Corporate and securities law, concentrating on the representation of mutual funds, investment managers, broker-dealers and other financial services providers.
**Prof. Memberships:** Member of the Advisory Board, Mutual Fund Directors Forum; Executive Council, Securities Law Committee, Federal Bar Association; NASD Legal Advisory Board; American Bar Association; District of Columbia Bar.
**Career:** Mayer, Brown, Rowe & Maw LLP, Washington, DC, 2005 to date. Trustee of the Hansberger Institutional Series, 1997 to date. Engaged in the private practice of law in Washington, DC from 1990-2005. Director, Division of Investment Management, US Securities and Exchange Commission, 1983-90. Associate Director of the SEC's Division of Market Regulation, assistant and then Associate General Counsel to the SEC; Assistant Director of the Division of Corporate Finance; Special Counsel and then Executive Assistant to SEC Chairman Ray Garrett, Jr and Roderick M Hills; Legal Assistant to Commissioner Philip Loomis; and Staff Attorney in the Office of the General Counsel, 1970-79.
**Personal:** Georgetown University Law Center, JD, 1969. Mount Holyoke College, AB, 1966.

### MCGUIRE, W John
Morgan, Lewis & Bockius LLP, Washington, DC 202 739 5654
wjmcguire@morganlewis.com
*Recommended in Investment Management*
**Practice Areas:** John McGuire is a Partner in the Investment Management/ Securities Practice at Morgan Lewis. His practice focuses on investment company and investment advisor regulation. He counsels clients on a wide variety of regulatory and transactional matters, including development of new products and services. He has extensive experience in the establishment and representation of exchange traded funds, popularly known as ETFs, their advisors and listing markets.
**Prof. Memberships:** ABA; DC Bar (former Chair, Investment Management Committee; former Steering Committee Member, Corporation, Finance and Securities Law Section).
**Career:** Securities and Exchange Commission, Division of Investment Management, 1986-90.

### MCISAAC, Christopher
Clifford Chance US LLP, Washington, DC 202 912 5000
*Recommended in Projects*
**Practice Areas:** Joint Head of the Americas Energy and Projects Group, which is focused on the development and financing of complex infrastructure projects. Broad-based finance experience including lender and sponsor representation across a range of industry sectors, particularly oil and gas, power generation and other energy projects.
**Career:** Joined firm as Partner in 2006.
**Publications:** 'Leveraged Leasing of Power Facilities', 'Equipment Leasing - Leveraged Leasing, Practising Law Institute', 1999.
**Personal:** University of North Carolina, BA, with highest honors, Phi Beta Kappa, 1982, Morehead Scholar; University of Virginia School of Law, JD, 1985, Dillard Fellow.

### MCKEE, William S
McKee Nelson LLP, Washington, DC 202 775 8580
*Recommended in Tax*
**Practice Areas:** Taxation. Practice encompasses all areas of federal taxation, with a special emphasis on partnership taxation.
**Career:** Prior to founding the firm in November 1999, was a Tax Partner in the DC office of King & Spalding. Joined King & Spalding in 1983. Served as Tax Legislative Counsel at the US Treasury Department from 1981-83. Is a Member of the American Law Institute, the American College of Tax Counsel, and the National Institute for Tax Professionals. Was a law Professor at the University of Virginia School of Law from 1969-81.

Also a visiting Professor in the Graduate Tax Programme at the New York University School of Law from 1975-77. Frequent speaker at seminars around the country on the subject of partnership taxation.
**Publications:** Co-author of the treatise 'Federal Taxation of Partnerships and Partners' (Warren, Gorham & Lamont, 3rd edition, 1997), and also co-authored 'Federal Taxation of Partnerships and Partners: Structuring and Drafting Agreements' (Warren, Gorham & Lamont, 2nd edition, 1993).
**Personal:** A 1966 cum laude graduate of Yale University, received a JD, magna cum laude, in 1969 from the Harvard Law School, and was an editor of the Harvard Law Review.

### MCLUCAS, William
WilmerHale, Washington, DC 202 663 6622
william.mclucas@wilmerhale.com
*Recommended in Financial Services, Securities*
**Practice Areas:** Co-Chair, Securities Department; practice focuses on securities enforcement, regulation and litigation matters.
**Career:** Director of Enforcement, US Securities and Exchange Commission's Division of Enforcement for eight years. While at the SEC, received the National Public Service Award, the Tom C Clark Outstanding Lawyer Award, and the President's Award for Distinguished Executive Service.
**Personal:** Pennsylvania State University (BA 1972); Temple University (JD 1975).

### MCMANUS, Randolph
Baker Botts LLP, Washington, DC 202 639 7725
rmcmanus@bakerbotts.com
*Recommended in Energy*
**Practice Areas:** Practice focuses on energy-related regulatory, litigation and transactional work on behalf of project sponsors, merchant energy companies, utilities, and LNG importers and terminal operators. Experience includes mergers and acquisitions, power and gas sales agreements, transmission issues, interconnection agreements, fuel supply arrangements, permitting of major energy projects and administrative and appellate litigation before federal agencies and courts.
**Prof. Memberships:** District of Columbia Bar; State Bar of Texas; Energy Bar Association.
**Career:** Head of firm-wide Energy Regulatory Practice.
**Personal:** JD from the University of Houston Law School, 1975 (Order of the Barristers); BA from Williams College, 1972.

### MCMANUS JR, Joseph A
McManus Schor Asmar & Darden, L.L.P., Washington, DC 202 296 9260
*Recommended in Construction*

### MCMILLAN, Karen
Willkie Farr & Gallagher LLP, Washington, DC 202 303 1202
kmcmillan@willkie.com
*Recommended in Investment Management*
**Practice Areas:** Partner in the Asset Management Group. Part of her diverse practice involves directing on-site examinations of major fund complexes and their advisors and other service providers, and counseling clients on corporate governance matters. She regularly serves as counsel to registered investment companies and their advisors, and to alternative investment products managers. She has also counseled clients in connection with a number of SEC and state regulatory investigations and enforcement matters. Additionally, she has advised on a number of mergers and acquisitions of fund managers located both inside and outside of the United States.
**Prof. Memberships:** Member of the District of Columbia and Texas Bars. Also a Member of the Texas and District of Columbia Bar Associations. She previously served as an Adjunct Professor at Georgetown University Law Center (LLM program), where she co-taught Regulation of Investment Companies and Advisers.
**Career:** Has served in positions of increasing responsibility on the staff of the US Securities and Exchange Commission's Division of Investment Management, which has principal oversight over the mutual fund industry. While Assistant Chief Counsel of the Division's Office of Chief Counsel, she oversaw the development of a number of key interpretive positions on matters involving the investment management industry.
**Personal:** Received a JD from the University of Virginia School of Law in 1987, where she was a Member of the Journal of Law and Politics, and a BA from the College of William and Mary in 1983, where she was elected to Phi Beta Kappa.

### MECHANICK, Maury J
White & Case LLP, Washington, DC 202 626 3596
mmechanick@whitecase.com
*Recommended in Telecom, Broadcast & Satellite*
**Practice Areas:** Represents public and private sector clients in the telecommunications, satellite and high-tech sectors, in a broad range of transactional and regulatory matters in the United States and abroad. Having previously spent nearly 20 years as a senior executive in the satellite industry, possesses an in-depth understanding of the business, opera-

tional and financial, as well as legal, aspects of the telecommunications industry. Led US efforts to privatize the INTELSAT and Inmarsat intergovernmental organizations, serving as Chairman of the Intelsat Board of Governors during the pivotal year leading up to that organization's privatization.

## MELAMED, A Douglas
WilmerHale, Washington, DC
202 663 6090
doug.melamed@wilmerhale.com
*Recommended in Antitrust*
**Practice Areas:** Co-Chair, Antitrust and Competition Department. Secures clearance for major acquisitions in merger clearance process, argues cases in United States Supreme Court and other appellate courts, litigates in federal and state trial courts and before Federal Trade Commission, and counsels numerous firms on wide range of antitrust matters.
**Career:** Acting Assistant Attorney General, Antitrust Division, US Department of Justice (2000-01) and Principal Deputy Assistant Attorney General, Antitrust Division, US Department of Justice (1996-2000). Distinguished Visitor from Practice (1992-93) and Adjunct Professor (1993-94) at Georgetown University Law Center.
**Personal:** Harvard Law School (JD 1970); Yale College (BA 1967).

## MENOTTI, David E
Pillsbury Winthrop Shaw Pittman LLP, Washington, DC 202 663 8675
david.menotti@pillsburylaw.com
*Recommended in Environment*
**Practice Areas:** Mr Menotti's practice emphasizes the regulation of hazardous substances under laws such as the Federal Insecticide, Fungicide, and Rodenticide Act; the Toxic Substances Control Act; the Federal Food, Drug, and Cosmetic Act; and the Clean Air Act. He also represents clients with matters arising under related state laws and regulations.
**Prof. Memberships:** Environmental sections of the American and District of Columbia Bar Associations.
**Personal:** JD, University of Pennsylvania Law School, 1967 (magna cum laude; rditor, University of Pennsylvania Law Review, 1966-67; Order of the Coif); AB, Syracuse University, 1964.

## METZGER JR, Richard
Lawler, Metzger, Milkman & Keeney, LLC, Washington, DC
202 777 7700
*Recommended in Telecom, Broadcast & Satellite*

## MICHAELS, Joel
McDermott Will & Emery, Washington, DC 202 756 8375
jmichaels@mwe.com
*Recommended in Healthcare*
**Practice Areas:** Partner-in-charge of Washington Health Practice. Experience

in healthcare insurance and delivery system organization, financing and regulation. Assists in obtaining state and federal licenses, contracts and approvals and developing viable organizational and contractual arrangements. Counsels on federal law issues, including Medicare and Medicaid regulation, False Claims Act, Federal Anti-Kickback Statute, ERISA, and Health Insurance Portability and Accountability Act. Works on complex litigation matters in health insurance industry, including payment and claims processing disputes involving health plans and providers, and assistance to insurers on state insurance examinations and investigations.
**Personal:** American University-Washington College of Law (JD); George Washington University (BA).

## MICHALOPOULOS, Pantelis
Steptoe & Johnson LLP, Washington, DC
202 429 6494
pmichalopoulos@steptoe.com
*Recommended in Telecom, Broadcast & Satellite*
**Practice Areas:** Partner in the Washington office of Steptoe & Johnson LLP. Communications (spectrum issues, satellite television, broadband, media, program access, telephone regulation, internet regulation); practices before Federal Communications Commission (FCC) and US Courts of Appeals. Highlights: on behalf of consumers and libraries, presented oral argument in the DC Circuit in successful challenge of FCC rule restricting internet distribution of television shows - the so-called 'broadcast flag' rule.
**Prof. Memberships:** Washington, New York Bar.
**Publications:** Numerous publications.
**Personal:** LLM, University of Pennsylvania, 1989; Law Diploma, Law School of the National University of Athens, 1988; BA, American College of Greece, 1987.

## MILCH, Thomas
Arnold & Porter LLP, Washington, DC
202 942 5030
Thomas.Milch@aporter.com
*Recommended in Environment*
**Practice Areas:** A Partner in Washington, DC, Mr Milch directs the firm's national Environmental Group. His practice principally includes federal enforcement and private party litigation, counseling multinational companies on environmental compliance, and addressing environmental issues that arise in complex corporate transactions. He has served as lead counsel on major Superfund cleanups and in contaminated property litigation for Fortune 100 companies. He has particular expertise in complex environmental disputes involving toxic tort claims, natural resources damages, sediment cleanups and corporate environmental liability, such as par-

ent/subsidiary and successor liability.
**Prof. Memberships:** He served as a Member of the ABA's Standing Committee on Environmental Law (1996-98), and was Chairman of the ABA's Special Committee on Environmental Litigation Techniques (SONREEL) (1991-94). From 1992-98, he served on the Board of Directors and Executive Committee of the Environmental Law Institute. From 1999 until 2003, he also served on the Board of Wildlife Trust International, an international conservation group. He has served for many years on the Board of RESOLVE, Inc., a nonprofit organization committed to environmental alternative dispute resolution.
**Personal:** He graduated from Yale College summa cum laude and from Yale Law School, where he served as an officer of the Yale Law Journal.

## MILES, John J
Ober Kaler Grimes & Shriver, Washington, DC 202 408 8400
*Recommended in Healthcare*

## MILES, Steven
Baker Botts LLP, Washington, DC
202 639 7951
steven.miles@bakerbotts.com
*Recommended in Projects*
**Practice Areas:** Project development and finance, with emphasis on liquefied natural gas (LNG), natural gas, and electric power industries, both in the United States and internationally.
**Prof. Memberships:** Association of International Petroleum Negotiators (AIPN) LNG Committee, Co-Chair, 2005-; American Bar Association, Committee on International Energy and Resources, Vice-Chair, 2001; Saudi Arabia Country Co-ordinator, 1996; National US-Arab Chamber of Commerce, General Counsel, 1995-2004.
**Career:** Manages the Middle East Practice at Baker Botts.
**Personal:** JD from the Cornell Law School in 1984 (editor, Cornell Law Review); MBA from Cornell University in 1984; BA (summa cum laude) from Union College in 1980.

## MILKMAN, Ruth
Lawler, Metzger, Milkman & Keeney, LLC, Washington, DC 202 777 7700
*Recommended in Telecom, Broadcast & Satellite*

## MILLER, Evan
Hogan & Hartson LLP, Washington, DC
202 637 5776
emiller@hhlaw.com
*Recommended in Employee Benefits*
**Practice Areas:** Focuses on ERISA litigation, COBRA, HIPAA, and ERISA legislation. Represents companies in private-party fiduciary benefit plan design litigation, and audit and other benefit-related investigations conducted at the regional and national level by the US Department

of Labor, and in excise tax matters before the Internal Revenue Service (IRS).
**Prof. Memberships:** ABA: 2003-2005, Co-Chair, Employee Benefits Committee, Labor and Employment Section; Employee Benefits Committee, Tax Section.
**Career:** Partner since 1994.
**Publications:** Co-Chair, Board of Senior Editors, 'Employee Benefits Law' (BNA Books); 'COBRA Primer', ABA/JCEB National Institute on ERISA Basics (5/1/2004); 'Update on Class Action Litigation Involving Employer Securities', Continuing Legal Education Institute (1/1/2004).
**Personal:** Georgetown University Law Center (JD); Columbia University (BA).

## MILLER, Lawrence
Sidley Austin LLP, Washington, DC
202 736 8209
lmiller@sidley.com
*Recommended in Energy*
**Practice Areas:** Focuses on regulatory, antitrust and other matters pertaining to telecommunication, railroad and pipeline common carriers. He has practiced before the ICC, FERC, state and federal courts. For the last 15 years, Mr Miller's practice has focused primarily on crude oil and petroleum product pipelines with respect to rate, competitive access and discrimination issues.
**Personal:** Yale Law School, JD, 1976; Northwestern University, BA, 1969; Oxford Rhodes Scholar, 1969-73. Admissions: Illinois, 1976; District of Columbia, 1992.

## MILLER, Lawrence
Grossberg Yochelson Fox & Beyda, Washington, DC 202 296 9696
*Recommended in Real Estate*

## MILLER, Van A
Mayer, Brown, Rowe & Maw LLP, Washington, DC 202 263 3349
camiller@mayerbrownrowe.com
*Recommended in Technology*
**Practice Areas:** Represents national and international firms in structuring, negotiating and drafting complex information technology and business process outsourcing agreements. Represents both customers and providers of outsourcing services, effectively collaborating with sourcing advisory firms such as TPI and Everest Group. Assists clients in developing and negotiating a wide range of other technology agreements such as licensing, marketing and consulting service agreements. Representative Transactions: representation of leading apparel company VF Corporation in outsourcing of its global IT infrastructure; representation of Wachovia Corporation in HR BPO transaction involving contact center, payroll, learning and benefits services to more than 90,000 Wachovia employees; representation of Triad Hospitals, Inc. in outsourcing and transforming its IT infra-

structure functions, including applications support, network management and help desk activities, as well as server and desktop computing with a estimated contract value exceeding $1.2 billion; representation of Eastman Kodak Company in outsourcing key business processes, including payroll, credit and collections management, and benefits administration.
**Career:** Mayer, Brown, Rowe & Maw LLP, Washington, DC, 2004 to present.
**Personal:** Tulane School of Law, JD, cum laude, 2002. University of Mississippi, BA, cum laude, 1993.

### MOLLEN, Neal D
Paul, Hastings, Janofsky & Walker LLP, Washington, DC 202 551 1738
nealmollen@paulhastings.com
*Recommended in Employment*
**Practice Areas:** Chair of Washington Office Employment Law Department; Co-Chair, firm Appellate Practice Group. Represents employers in employment litigation, with emphasis on class actions and appellate matters; advises employers in bargaining disputes under the NLRA and RLA, and represents management in labor arbitrations and labor-management litigation; particular expertise in the use of experts in employment litigation.
**Publications:** Chapter co-editor, 'Employment Discrimination Law' (ABA-BNA) (2000, 2002, and 2005 editions); contributing author, 'Equal Employment Law Update' (ABA-BNA) (through Fall 1999); contributing author, 'Employee Benefits Law' (ABA-BNA 1991).
**Personal:** JD - University of Richmond, 1985, with honors; notes and comments editor, Law Review.

### MOLTENBREY, MJ
Freshfields Bruckhaus Deringer LLP, Washington, DC 202 777 4500
*Recommended in Antitrust*

### MONACO, Stephanie
Mayer, Brown, Rowe & Maw LLP, Washington, DC 202 263 3379
smonaco@mayerbrownrowe.com
*Recommended in Investment Management*
**Practice Areas:** Securities, regulation and enforcement law, focusing on investment company and investment advisor regulation and compliance. Advises registered investment companies; hedge funds; private equity funds; investment advisors; and other entities seeking either to become registered or to structure their business affairs to avoid registration and regulation. Advises concerning the interrelationship of these practice areas and other related practices, such as broker-dealer regulation, state advisor issues, and ERISA matters. Currently, she has been assisting clients in connection with SEC examinations (routine and non-routine) and enforcement inquiries, investiga-

tions, and actions.
**Career:** Mayer, Brown, Rowe & Maw LLP, Washington, DC, 2005 to date. Crowell & Moring LLP, Washington, DC, 2001-05. Morgan, Lewis & Bockius, 1991-2001. Securities and Exchange Commission, Division of Investment Management, Office of Investment Company Regulation, 1988-91. Rosenman & Colin, 1986-88. Securities and Exchange Commission, Division of Investment Management, Chief Counsel's Office, 1983-86.
**Publications:** Co-author: 'Operating a Hedge Fund in a Regulated Environment, The Review of Securities & Commodities Regulation - An Analysis of Current Laws and Regulations Affecting the Securities and Futures Industries'.
**Personal:** University of Baltimore, JD, 1982. University of Maryland, BA, 1979.

### MOORE, Margaret
Van Ness Feldman PC, Washington, DC 202 298 1800
*Recommended in Energy*

### MORVILLO, Richard J
Mayer, Brown, Rowe & Maw LLP, Washington, DC 202 263 3290
rmorvillo@mayerbrownrowe.com
*Recommended in Securities*
**Practice Areas:** Chair of firm's Securities Enforcement Group. 30 years in SEC enforcement and related white-collar criminal matters as well as private securities litigation. Numerous SEC, NYSE, NASD and grand jury investigations on behalf of corporations, corporate executives, brokerage firms, investment advisors, accountants, lawyers, hedge funds and individual investors. Successfully litigated several SEC enforcement cases to judgment. Litigated numerous complex securities cases, including class actions and shareholder derivative suits, in federal courts throughout the country. Extensive experience conducting internal investigations for corporations. Advised members of special committees of directors concerning obligations and rights in corporate transactions, internal investigations and shareholder litigation.
**Career:** Mayer, Brown, Rowe & Maw LLP, Washington, DC, 2005 to date. Crowell & Moring LLP, former Chair, Securities Regulation and Enforcement Group, Washington, DC, Partner, 2001-05; Chair, Business Crimes Group, 1994-2000. Kirkpatrick & Lockhart LLP, Washington, DC, Partner, 2000-01. Richardson, Berlin & Morvillo, Washington, DC, Partner, 1987-94. Verner, Liipfert, Bernhard, McPherson, and Hand, Chartered, Washington, DC, Partner/Shareholder, 1978-87. Branch Chief, Division of Enforcement, Securities and Exchange Commission, Washington, DC, 1977-78; Trial Attorney, Division of Enforcement, 1974-77.
**Personal:** Fordham University Law

School, JD, 1974. Colgate University, AB, 1970.

### MOYER, Dennis
Goulston & Storrs, Washington, DC 202 721 0011
*Recommended in Real Estate*

### MURIS, Timothy J
O'Melveny & Myers LLP, Washington, DC 202 383 5350
tmuris@omm.com
*Recommended in Antitrust*
**Practice Areas:** Timothy Muris joined O'Melveny & Myers' Washington, DC office in September 2004 and is Co-Chair of the firm's Antitrust/Competition Practice. Tim has a long and distinguished career in public and private service and has a broad background, including substantial experience in the areas of antitrust, consumer protection, privacy regulation, and strategic counseling. He was Chairman of the Federal Trade Commission from 2001-04. Earlier, Tim was the Assistant to the Director of the Planning Office from 1974-76, the Director of the Bureau of Consumer Protection from 1981-83, and the Director of the Bureau of Competition from 1983-85. Tim is the only person ever to head both enforcement bureaus at the FTC. After leaving the FTC in 1985, Tim served with the Executive Office of the President, Office of Management and Budget, for three years.

### MURPHY, J Andrew
Hunton & Williams, Washington, DC 202 955 1543
dmurphy@hunton.com
*Recommended in Projects*
**Practice Areas:** Drew Murphy is the Head of the firm's Project and Energy Finance Team. His practice focuses on the development, acquistion and financing of energy and infrastructure assets. He has extensive experience in representing developers, investors and lenders in a variety of US and international project and structured financings, including private equity financings, syndicated bank loans, and private placements. He also has significant experience in renewable energy transactions, including biomass and landfill gas projects.
**Prof. Memberships:** ABA; American Council on Renewable Energy; AWEA.
**Career:** Partner - 1995.
**Personal:** George Washington University (JD, 1987); Harvard (BA, 1983).

### MURPHY, Jack W
Dechert LLP, Washington, DC 202 261 3303
jack.murphy@dechert.com
*Recommended in Investment Management*
**Practice Areas:** Mr Murphy is a Partner who focuses his practice on investment management matters for mutual funds, fund directors, and fund managers.

**Prof. Memberships:** Member, District of Columbia and New York Bars.
**Career:** Securities and Exchange Commission, Division of Investment Management (1985); private practitioner (1988); associate general counsel of PaineWebber/Mitchell Hutchins Asset Management, Inc. (1991-94); Associate Director and chief counsel of the division of investment management, (1994-97).
**Personal:** State University of New York at Albany (BA, 1980); Boston College Law School (JD, 1983).

### MUTRYN, William J
Holland & Knight LLP, Washington, DC 202 955 3000
william.mutryn@hklaw.com
*Recommended in Corporate/Commercial*
**Practice Areas:** Co-leader of the Corporate and M&A Practice Group, his practice emphasizes M&A, securities, corporate governance and corporate finance. Served as lead counsel for middle market M&A transactions in buy-side and sell-side engagements. Mutryn serves as principal outside counsel to regional and national businesses in fields including government IT services, healthcare, defense and aerospace, computer software, telecommunications and satellites, environmental, energy, manufacturing, finance, and staffing. He represents companies in M&A, debt and equity financing, stock transactions, joint ventures and complex agreements; and parties in securities offerings, private equity and venture capital transactions and acquisitions of subsidiaries or divisions.

### MYERS, Donald J
Reed Smith LLP, Washington, DC 202 414 9231
dmyers@reedsmith.com
*Recommended in Employee Benefits*
**Practice Areas:** Represents corporations and financial institutions on a variety of benefits issues, specializing in the fiduciary responsibility provisions of ERISA.
**Prof. Memberships:** Chairman, Prohibited Transactions Subcommittee, ABA Taxation Section Committee on Employee Benefits; Charter Fellow of the American College of Employee Benefits Counsel.
**Career:** Counsel for ERISA Regulation and Interpretation, Department of Labor; Assistant Chief of the Office of Disclosure Policy, SEC.
**Publications:** Author of numerous books, chapters, and other publications.
**Personal:** Cornell Law School (JD); Georgetown University Law Center (LLM); College of the City of New York (BA); Adjunct Professor, Georgetown University Law Center.

## NAEVE, Clifford M
Skadden, Arps, Slate, Meagher & Flom LLP & Affiliates, Washington, DC
202 371 7070
mnaeve@skadden.com
*Recommended in Energy*

**Practice Areas:** Partner, Washington, DC. Involved in energy policy and regulatory matters, including the restructuring of the electric power industry, having represented clients in a variety of federal and state regulatory proceedings and restructuring transactions. Represented utilities before FERC in merger proceedings and involved in friendly and unsolicited merger transactions. Worked with utilities on innovative electric transmission cases, wholesale rate proceedings and retail access experiments. Represented major oil and gas producers, natural gas pipelines, electric co-operatives and financial institutions in commercial and regulatory matters. Represents clients before Congress on issues ranging from energy and environmental matters to taxes and tender offer reforms.
**Prof. Memberships:** Member, Electricity Advisory Board to the Secretary of Energy (2002 - Present).
**Career:** Commissioner, Federal Energy Regulatory Commission (1985-88); Legislative Director, Office of US Senator Lloyd Bentsen (1978-80); JD, George Washington University, 1984 (highest honours; Order of the Coif); MPA, LBJ School of Public Affairs, The University of Texas at Austin, 1972; BS, Mechanical Engineering, The University of Texas at Austin, 1970.

## NAGER, Glen
Jones Day, Washington, DC
202 879 5464
gdnager@jonesday.com
*Recommended in Litigation*

**Practice Areas:** Chairs the firm's Issues and Appeals Practice. He has argued 11 cases before the US Supreme Court. He has argued appeals in the areas of IP, government contracts, and environmental cases. His substantive specialty is employment law, doing jury trials, class action litigation, and counseling, with particular emphasis on discrimination and employee benefits law. Named one of the top 12 employment lawyers in Washington, DC. Adjunct Professor at Georgetown University Law Center teaching administrative law.
**Prof. Memberships:** Member of the Edward Coke Appellate American Inn of Court. ABA. District of Columbia Bar.

## NAKAHATA, John
Harris, Wiltshire & Grannis LLP, Washington, DC 202 730 1300
*Recommended in Telecom, Broadcast & Satellite*

## NANNES, John M
Skadden, Arps, Slate, Meagher & Flom LLP & Affiliates, Washington, DC
202 371 7500
jnannes@skadden.com
*Recommended in Antitrust*

**Practice Areas:** Broad Antitrust Practice includes mergers and acquisitions reviewed by US and foreign antitrust agencies, civil non-merger governmental investigations, US and foreign cartel investigations, and private treble-damage actions. Substantial experience in network industries such as airlines, securities, shipping, and energy.
**Prof. Memberships:** Trustee of the Legal Aid Society of Washington, DC and of the Supreme Court Historical Society.
**Career:** Acting Assistant Attorney General (2001) and Deputy Assistant Attorney General, Antitrust Division, US Department of Justice (1998-2001); law clerk to Justice William Rehnquist (1974-75); JD (1973) and BBA (1970), University of Michigan.

## NATHAN, Irvin B
Arnold & Porter LLP, Washington, DC
202 942 5070
Irvin.Nathan@aporter.com
*Recommended in Litigation*

**Practice Areas:** A senior litigation Partner who represents corporations, and their officers, directors, and employees, in criminal and complex civil litigations, including antitrust, securities fraud, civil RICO, and corporate compliance matters. He has tried many jury and bench trials and emergency injunctive hearings in federal and state courts. He has also successfully represented corporate and individual targets of federal grand jury investigations.
**Prof. Memberships:** He is a Member of American College of Trial Lawyers, American Law Institute, and American Bar Foundation.
**Career:** In addition to his practice at Arnold & Porter, he has served as Principal Associate Deputy Attorney General at the US Department of Justice (1993-94); Deputy Assistant Attorney General for Enforcement in the Criminal Division (1979-81); Special Minority Counsel to the United States Senate Intelligence Committee (1981); Chairman of the White Collar Crime Committee of the Criminal Justice Section of the American Bar Association (ABA) (1982-84); and has served as a liaison for the ABA's Criminal Justice Section to the ABA's Antitrust Section. He is currently a court-appointed member of the DC Board on Professional Responsibility and is a past Chair of the DC Bar Legal Ethics Committee.
**Personal:** He received a LLB at Columbia Law School in 1967 and a BA at Johns Hopkins University in 1964.

## NEAHER JR, Edward R
White & Case LLP, Washington, DC
202 626 3622
eneaher@whitecase.com
*Recommended in Projects*

**Practice Areas:** Corporate transactional lawyer, specializing in domestic and international project finance and international private equity. Represents lenders, developers and other participants in infrastructure projects in a wide variety of sectors, including power, oil and gas, airports, toll roads, telecommunications and other industrial projects. Also represents international private equity investors. Extensive experience in complex project financings involving commercial banks, multilateral and bilateral institutions, bond offerings and monoline insurers. Broad international experience, having been previously based in Hong Kong and London and extensive experience in Latin America, Asia and the Middle East.
**Personal:** Williams College (BA,1980), Cornell University (JD, 1983).

## NELSON, Mark W
Cleary Gottlieb Steen & Hamilton LLP, Washington, DC
202 974 1622
mnelson@cgsh.com
*Recommended in Antitrust*

**Practice Areas:** US practice includes extensive merger work and antitrust counseling, as well as civil litigation and FTC administrative proceedings. European practice involves merger cases at both EU and Member State levels, and representing clients in Article 81 and 82 actions. Represents clients in a wide range of industries, including airlines, aluminum, cement, computer networking, consumer products, industrial equipment, fiber optic systems, financial information services, oil and gas, petrochemicals, pharmaceuticals, securities and foreign exchange trading, software, travel services, and wireless telephony.
**Prof. Memberships:** Member of DC and New York Bars.
**Career:** Joined firm, 1993; Partner, 2002. JD, magna cum laude, Harvard Law School (1992); BS, Cornell University (1989). Law clerk to Judge Andrew Kleinfeld, US Court of Appeals, Ninth Circuit (1992-93).

## NELSON, William F
McKee Nelson LLP, Washington, DC
202 775 8582
wnelson@mckeenelson.com
*Recommended in Tax, Tax Litigation*

**Practice Areas:** Taxation, tax controversy. Practice encompasses all areas of federal taxation, with a special emphasis on partnership taxation and controversy matters.
**Career:** Prior to founding the firm in November 1999, was a Tax Partner in King & Spalding's Atlanta office, joining the firm in 1972. From 1986-88, served as chief counsel for the Internal Revenue Service, returning to King & Spalding at the end of his appointment. Frequent lecturer at various tax institutes.
**Publications:** Co-author of the treatise 'Federal Taxation of Partnerships and Partners' (Warren, Gorham & Lamont, 3rd edition, 1997), and also co-authored 'Federal Taxation of Partnerships and Partners: Structuring and Drafting Agreements' (Warren, Gorham & Lamont, 2nd edition, 1993). Has written articles on tax law for numerous journals, including The Tax Law Review, Taxes, and the Virginia Law Review.
**Personal:** Received a JD from the University of Virginia School of Law in 1972, where he was Editor-in-Chief of the Virginia Law Review and was named to the Order of the Coif.

## NESS, Andrew D
Thelen Reid & Priest LLP, Washington, DC 202 508 4368
adness@thelenreid.com
*Recommended in Construction*

**Practice Areas:** Mr Ness' practice focuses on dispute resolution and counseling with respect to construction and design-related matters representing primarily owners/developers, engineers, and prime contractors. Mr Ness has been lead counsel on a wide variety of major construction disputes in federal and state courts, and in both domestic and international arbitrations. He also has extensive experience in the use of mediation and other alternative dispute resolution techniques to resolve construction disputes. In addition, he has worked extensively in drafting and negotiating design and construction contracts, and in resolving problems short of litigation. Mr Ness is a registered foreign lawyer with the Law Society of England and Wales and a Partner of Masons Thelen Reid LLP, a strategic partnership that serves clients involved in international infrastructure and building projects from inception through financing, contract negotiation, construction and dispute resolution.
**Prof. Memberships:** American Bar Association Forum on the Construction Industry (past Chair of Division 10). American Bar Association Public Contract Law Section (Vice-Chair, Construction Division). Member of the Advisory Board for bi-weekly publications of the West Group.
**Career:** Managing Partner of Thelen Reid & Priest LLP's Washington, DC office and Member of the firm's Executive Committee and Partnership Council. Admitted to practice in the District of Columbia, Virginia and California, the US Court of Federal Claims, and five US District Courts.
**Publications:** Author of numerous articles on construction law topics and frequent speaker on a wide range of con-

struction law issues. Review Panel member, ASCE Journal of Construction Engineering and Management, published by the American Society of Civil Engineers, Construction Division.
**Personal:** Graduate of Harvard Law School, JD (1977), magna cum laude, served as articles editor of the Harvard Journal on Legislation. BS (1974) from Stanford University, with distinction, majoring in Electrical Engineering. Served as law clerk to the Hon Robert F Peckham, Chief Judge, US District Court for Northern District of California.

### NEVINS, Patrick
Hogan & Hartson LLP, Washington, DC
202 637 6441
jpnevins@hhlaw.com
*Recommended in Energy*
**Practice Areas:** Energy, including regulatory, litigation and commercial matters in gas, LNG and oil industries; clients include gas and oil pipelines, an LNG import terminal, storage providers, major customers on pipelines, and new entrants acquiring energy assets; practice also focuses on FERC proceedings, project development and FERC-influenced commercial transactions; experience in State regulatory proceedings and judicial appeals of agency decisions.
**Prof. Memberships:** ABA; Energy Bar Association.
**Career:** Hogan & Hartson, 1994-present and Partner since January 2001; in private practice since 1992.
**Personal:** Georgetown University Law Center (JD, magna cum laude, Order of the Coif, 1992); University of Virginia (BA, with distinction, 1989).

### NEWBORN, Steven A
Weil, Gotshal & Manges LLP, Washington, DC 202 682 7005
steven.newborn@weil.com
*Recommended in Antitrust*
**Practice Areas:** Steven Newborn is global Co-Head of Weil Gotshal's Antitrust/Competition Practice and specializes in high stakes antitrust litigation and 'bet the company' mergers for Fortune 100 companies. He has experience in a wide array of industries and international venues. Previously, he was Director of Litigation at the FTC's Bureau of Competition in charge of its Merger Enforcement Program, and was a major contributor to the 1992 Federal Merger Guidelines. Mr Newborn received the Brandeis Award presented to the Commission's finest litigator. He has been cited by every publication that ranks antitrust lawyers as a leader in the field.

### NEWMAN, Karol Lyn
Morgan, Lewis & Bockius LLP, Washington, DC 202 739 5786
klnewman@morganlewis.com
*Recommended in Energy*
**Practice Areas:** Ms Newman is a Partner in the firm's Energy Practice. She rep-

resents major energy companies in a wide variety of matters including business transactions focused on liquefied natural gas (LNG), natural gas storage and transportation and their related regulatory approvals.
**Prof. Memberships:** Member, American Bar Association; Member, District of Columbia Bar Association; Member, Maryland Bar Association; Member, Federal Energy Bar Association, Chair, Legislation and Regulatory Reform Committee.

### NEWMAN, Richard
Arent Fox PLLC, Washington, DC
202 857 6170
newman.richard@arentfox.com
*Recommended in Real Estate*
**Practice Areas:** Represents clients in the areas of real estate and finance, with special emphasis on municipal finance, low-income housing finance and the representation of non-profit organizations. As Co-Chair of Arent Fox's Public Finance Group, Richard provides services as borrower's counsel, underwriter's counsel, credit enhancement counsel, trustee's counsel, servicer/originator counsel and bond counsel to clients nationally. Richard has extensive experience in both real estate and municipal and public finance.
**Personal:** Case Western Reserve University School of Law, JD 1980; New York University, BA (cum laude) 1977.

### NICKEL, Henry
Hunton & Williams, Washington, DC
202 955 1561
hnickel@hunton.com
*Recommended in Environment*
**Practice Areas:** Henry Nickel's practice focuses on administrative and judicial proceedings arising under the National Environmental Policy Act, the Clean Air Act and the Clean Water Act. He has represented companies in virtually every major Clean Air Act rulemaking and related judicial review proceedings. He has briefed and argued cases in federal Circuit Courts and District Courts throughout the country and defended clients in major Clean Air Act enforcement actions and citizen suits. Over the years he has lobbied Congress on Clean Air Act and regulatory reform legislation. He is Head of the firm's Administrative Law Group.

### NIELDS, John
Howrey LLP, Washington, DC
202 783 0800
*Recommended in Litigation*

### NORDHAUS, Robert
Van Ness Feldman PC, Washington, DC
202 298 1800
*Recommended in Energy*

### NORTON IV, Floyd L
Morgan, Lewis & Bockius LLP, Washington, DC 202 739 5620
fnorton@morganlewis.com
*Recommended in Energy*
**Practice Areas:** Floyd Norton is a Partner in the Energy Practice. His practice focuses on electric utility issues, with an emphasis on utility responses to competition. Mr Norton has broad and comprehensive experience in electric utility market power issues, utility mergers and acquisitions, the negotiation of power contracts, and wholesale and transmission rates and services. Mr Norton has represented a number of electric utility clients in the areas of market pricing, mergers and industry restructuring, and investigations of electric trading practices.
**Prof. Memberships:** American Bar Association (Chair, Public Utility Law Section Antitrust Committee).

### NUECHTERLEIN, Jonathan
WilmerHale, Washington, DC
202 663 6850
jonathan.nuechterlein@wilmerhale.com
*Recommended in Telecom, Broadcast & Satellite*
**Practice Areas:** Practice focuses on appellate litigation and competition issues, particularly those arising under federal telecommunications law. Has represented major telecommunications clients before the federal courts and the FCC in connection with the IP services market, federalism issues, broadband deployment, and antitrust. Previously served as FCC Deputy General Counsel and as Assistant to the Solicitor General.
**Publications:** Author (with Phil Weiser) of 'Digital Crossroads: American Telecommunications Policy in the Internet Age' (MIT Press 2005).
**Personal:** Yale University (JD 1990, BA 1986). Law clerk to Justice David Souter (Supreme Court, 1991-92) and Judge Stephen Williams (DC Circuit, 1990-91).

### NUSSDORF, Melanie
Steptoe & Johnson LLP, Washington, DC
202 429 3009
mnussdorf@steptoe.com
*Recommended in Employee Benefits*
**Practice Areas:** Partner in the Washington office of Steptoe & Johnson LLP. Practice spans the entire range of employee benefits, from tax-based rules for qualified pension plans to fiduciary issues, welfare benefits, and plan termination. Represents numerous financial institutions including banks, brokerage houses, and insurance companies. Has substantial experience with ERISA issues relating to hedge funds and private equity vehicles, the exemption and advisory opinion process, and related legislation. Significant legislative background with the laws that affect employee benefit plans.
**Personal:** JD, New York University, 1973; BA, University of Pennsylvania, 1970.

### ODELL, Herbert
Miller & Chevalier Chartered, West Conshohocken 610 729 7800
*Recommended in Tax*
**Practice Areas:** Tax; tax audits and administrative appeals; tax litigation and judicial appeals; corporate, partnership, and joint venture tax planning; international tax planning; tax accounting; transfer pricing; tax reduction transactions; research and experimentation credit.
**Prof. Memberships:** American Bar Association; Bar Association of DC; Philadelphia Bar Association; Pennsylvania Bar Association; Florida Bar Association.
**Career:** Member - Miller & Chevalier Chartered (2000-present); Partner - Odell & Partners LL.P. [formerly Zapruder & Odell] (1989-99); Partner - Morgan, Lewis & Bockius (1967-89); associate, Walton, Lantaff, Schroeder, Carson & Wahl (1965-67); Trial Attorney, Tax Division - US Department of Justice (1963-65).
**Publications:** 'The Role of Economic Substance in Tax Shelter Controversies - Corporate Counselor' (January 2005).
**Personal:** LLM, Harvard Law School,1963; JD, University of Miami Law School, 1962 (Editor-in Chief, Law Review); BS in Economics, Wharton School of the University of Pennsylvania, 1959. Member, Harvard Club of New York, Beta Alpha Psi, Omicron Delta Kappa, Phi Kappa Phi, Adjunct Professor, University of Miami and Villanova University.

### O'DONNELL, Earle
Dewey Ballantine LLP, Washington, DC
202 429 2327
eodonnell@deweyballantine.com
*Recommended in Energy*
**Practice Areas:** Energy (including trial and appellate litigation, energy project development, energy company M&A, and compliance).
**Prof. Memberships:** Member of the United States Supreme Court Bar; President Foundation of the Energy Law Journal; Member, Board of Directors, Charitable Foundation of the Energy Bar Association (2002-04).
**Career:** Chair of Energy Markets and Regulatory Practice, Dewey Ballantine LLP; private practice since 1975.
**Publications:** Consulting editor and co-author of 'Global Overview' and US Chapters, Electricity Regulation, published by Global Competition Review (2003-2006).
**Personal:** Born February 2, 1949. JD with honors, George Washington University National Law Center (Law Review, Order of the Coif), 1975.

## OLSON, John F
Gibson, Dunn & Crutcher LLP,
Washington, DC 202 955 8522
jolson@gibsondunn.com
*Recommended in Securities*
**Practice Areas:** Identified in surveys as
one of the nation's foremost authorities
on securities law, corporate governance
and M&A. Advises boards and committees of leading companies including General Electric, Coca Cola, CIGNA, Marriott, Textron, ConEd and Del Monte.
Leads teams conducting independent
internal investigations.
**Prof. Memberships:** Executive Council,
Securities Committee, Federal Bar Association; Former Chair, ABA Committees
on Corporate Governance and Federal
Regulation of Securities.
**Career:** Adjunct Professor, Northwestern
Law; Former Distinguished Visiting Practitioner, Cornell Law.
**Publications:** Over 100 articles and sev-
eral books. Frequent lecturer.
**Personal:** JD, Harvard Law School, 1964.

## OLSON, Pamela F
Skadden, Arps, Slate, Meagher & Flom
LLP & Affiliates, Washington, DC
202 371 7240
polson@skadden.com
*Recommended in Tax*
**Practice Areas:** Tax policy and tax controversy. Former assistant secretary for
tax policy at the US Department of the
Treasury, where she had supervisory
responsibility for providing policy analysis, advice and recommendations relating
to issues of federal taxation, including all
legislative proposals, regulatory guidance
and tax treaties. Was responsible for official estimates of all government receipts
for the President's budget, fiscal policy
decisions and Treasury cash management
decisions. First woman to chair the ABA
Section of Taxation.
**Prof. Memberships:** Board of Directors,
Tax Analysts (2004-present).
**Career:** University of Minnesota: MBA,
1984; JD, 1980; BA, 1976 (magna cum
laude).

## OLSON, Theodore B
Gibson, Dunn & Crutcher LLP,
Washington, DC 202 955 8668
tolson@gibsondunn.com
*Recommended in Litigation*
**Practice Areas:** One of the nation's premier appellate and US Supreme Court
advocates, argued 43 cases in the
Supreme Court (including Bush v Gore
cases). Practice encompasses constitutional law, appellate, federal legislation,
media, commercial disputes and crisis
management. Handled cases at all levels
of state/federal court systems; US/inter-
national tribunals.
**Prof. Memberships:** American College
of Trial Lawyers; American Academy of
Appellate Lawyers.
**Career:** Served as Solicitor General of

US; served as Assistant US Attorney Gen-
eral Office of Legal Counsel; served as
private counsel for Presidents Ronald
Reagan and George W Bush.
**Personal:** JD, University of California -
Berkeley, 1965.

## ONDRASIK, Paul
Steptoe & Johnson LLP, Washington, DC
202 429 8088
pondrasik@steptoe.com
*Recommended in Employee Benefits,
ERISA Litigation*
**Practice Areas:** Heads Steptoe's ERISA
and Employment Group. National
ERISA Practice, emphasizing litigation
(including appellate), fiduciary, and government matters. 25 plus years of experience. Lead counsel in numerous ERISA
class and other actions, including prominent 'employer stock drop' cases. Has
handled matters involving preemption,
investments, Taft-Hartley Plans, ESOPs,
contingent workers, benefit changes,
provider fees, retiree medical benefits,
and complex corporate transactions. Key
role in Supreme Court decisions on
ERISA remedies and preemption.
Clerked for Chief Justice Burger. Charter
Fellow - American College of Employee
Benefit Counsel, frequent author and
speaker.
**Personal:** JD, University of Virginia,
1975; AB, Princeton University, 1972.

## O'NEILL, Brian D
LeBoeuf, Lamb, Greene & MacRae LLP,
Washington, DC 202 986 8012
boneill@llgm.com
*Recommended in Energy*
**Practice Areas:** Advises clients on energy projects, privatizations and regulatory
matters. Clients include electric utilities,
major natural gas and oil pipelines and
several LNG companies. An experienced
litigator in regulatory proceedings involving complex ratemaking issues, multi-
million dollar construction projects,
transportation and supply contract matters. An author and lecturer on energy
matters.
**Prof. Memberships:** ABA; Energy Bar
Association; Florida Bar; DC Bar.
**Career:** Joined LeBoeuf Lamb in 1980;
Farmer, Shibley, McGuinn & Flood
(1975-80); Federal Power Commission,
Trial Attorney (1972-75); Military Service: US Air Force (1971-72).
**Publications:** Contributing author,
Energy Law and Transactions.
**Personal:** Florida State University (JD)
1971, (BA) 1968.

## O'NEILL JR, John H
Pillsbury Winthrop Shaw Pittman LLP,
Washington, DC 202 663 8148
john.o'neill@pillsburylaw.com
*Recommended in Energy*
**Practice Areas:** Concentrates on energy,
environmental, public utility and public
policy law. Represents electric utilities
and companies in the nuclear industry in

major commercial transactions, regulatory proceedings, and dispute resolution
matters. Extensive expertise in domestic
and international transactions involving
the acquisition and sale of nuclear power
plants, major plant components, nuclear
fuel, and services; 30 years experience in
the licensing of new nuclear plants.
**Prof. Memberships:** International Bar
Association; International Nuclear Law
Association; US Naval Academy Foundation, Trustee.
**Personal:** JD, Yale Law School, 1976; US
Navy Nuclear Power School, 1969; BS, US
Naval Academy, 1968 with Distinction.

## OOSTERHUIS, Paul W
Skadden, Arps, Slate, Meagher & Flom
LLP & Affiliates, Washington, DC
202 371 7130
poosterh@skadden.com
*Recommended in Tax*
**Practice Areas:** Represents clients on a
wide range of international and domestic
tax matters with experience in international M&A, dispositions and joint venture transactions. Represents US and
non-US multinational companies in
cross-border financing arrangements and
non-transactional international tax planning, and acquisitions. Has represented
various clients with respect to the international aspects of public spin-off transactions. Regularly represents clients on
international tax planning matters generally, including transfer pricing matters.
Represents clients before the US Department of Treasury and the Congress on
tax policy matters and technical issues.
**Career:** JD, Harvard University, 1973
(cum laude); BA, Brown University, 1969
(magna cum laude).

## OSER, Aaron M
Pillsbury Winthrop Shaw Pittman LLP,
Washington, DC 202 663 8031
Aaron.Oser@pillsburylaw.com
*Recommended in Technology*
**Practice Areas:** Mr Oser counsels
clients on large-scale, complex strategic
information technology and business
process outsourcing, transformational
outsourcing, development, integration,
facilities management and telecommunications transactions. He has negotiated
and documented a wide variety of technology-related transactions including
information technology, business process
and transformational outsourcing
arrangements; turn-key system acquisition and systems integration agreements;
software licensing, development, maintenance and distribution contracts; multimedia agreements; professional services
arrangements; and hardware acquisition
and maintenance agreements.
**Personal:** JD, St. John's University School
of Law, 1989; MPA, New York University,
1985; BA, State University of New York,
University at Albany, 1983.

## OSHINSKY, Jerold
Dickstein Shapiro Morin & Oshinsky LLP,
Washington, DC 202 828 2251
OshinskyJ@dsmo.com
*Recommended in Insurance*
**Practice Areas:** Specializes in representing policyholders in insurance coverage
cases. Has adjudicated many cutting-edge
insurance coverage issues - asbestos, construction defects, directors and officers,
employment issues, environmental liability, errors and omissions, fidelity bonds,
professional indemnity, intellectual property, products liability, and first-party
property policies.
**Career:** Became a name Partner in 1996,
after 24 years at his prior firm, and leads
the Insurance Coverage Practice.
Publications: Principal author/editor of
'Practitioner's Guide to Litigating Insurance Coverage Actions' (Aspen Law &
Business, second edition 2002) updated
annually.
**Personal:** Columbia Law School, cum
laude (JD) 1967); Brooklyn College (BA)
1964).

## OSNOS, David
Arent Fox PLLC, Washington, DC
202 857 6150
osnos.david@arentfox.com
*Recommended in Real Estate*
**Practice Areas:** Principal areas of activity include real estate, tax, securities, corporate, estate planning and sports law. He
served for 20 years as Chairman of Arent
Fox's Executive Committee. David has
performed work for office buildings,
shopping centers, industrial properties,
multifamily and single-family developments, as well as hotels. He guided Clark
Construction Group in converting from
a C corporation to an LLC. In his Sports
Law Practice, David represents teams
such as the Wizards (NBA) and the Capitals (NHL) as well as sports arenas on a
myriad of issues.
**Personal:** Harvard Law School, JD (cum
laude) 1956; Harvard College, AB
(summa cum laude) 1953.

## O'SULLIVAN, John
Chadbourne & Parke LLP, Washington,
DC 202 974 5600
josullivan@chadbourne.com
*Recommended in Energy*
**Practice Areas:** Represents independent
power producers, off-takers, and lenders,
including in FERC and state regulatory
proceedings, in negotiations for interconnection, power purchase, and transmission contracts, and in project financing;
active in facility or corporate acquisitions
(including participation in and conducting RFPs) and in bankruptcy matters;
substantial international experience in
project development, privatization, and
political risk insurance claims.
**Prof. Memberships:** New York, District
of Columbia, US Court of Appeals for the
Second, Third and District of Columbia

Circuits.

**Career:** Previously New York City Assistant Corporation Counsel, and FERC Chief Advisory Counsel and Assistant General Counsel for Electric Rates and Corporate Regulation.

### PANTANO, Paul
McDermott Will & Emery, Washington, DC 202 756 8026
ppantano@mwe.com
*Recommended in Energy*

**Practice Areas:** Heads the firm's Energy and Derivatives Markets Practice Group. Represents energy companies, commodity dealers, investment and commercial banks, trade associations and financial industry professionals in a wide variety of transactional, regulatory and litigation matters. Experience negotiating and drafting structured commodity and derivative transactions. Represents clients before the Commodity Futures Trading Commission, Federal Energy Regulatory Commission, and other governmental agencies.

**Prof. Memberships:** Chair, American Bar Association Committee on Regulation of Futures & Derivative Instruments; Member, Futures Industry Association, Inc. Law & Compliance Division and Energy Bar Association.

**Personal:** Duke University School of Law (JD) 1980; Trinity College (BA) 1977.

### PAPPAS, George F
Covington & Burling, Washington, DC 202 662 5594
gpappas@cov.com
*Recommended in Intellectual Property*

**Practice Areas:** Intellectual Property Litigation. Emphasis on pharmaceutical, biotech, medical device and software. Has served as lead counsel in more than 200 cases throughout USA. Since 1990, has been lead counsel in over 80 patent cases for US and foreign companies. Recent highlight: Successfully asserted patent on J&J subsidiary, Ortho-McNeil's LEVAQUIN product that sells over $1 billion annually.

**Prof. Memberships:** American Law Institute (ALI), ABA, US District Court of Delaware Judges' Intellectual Property Advisory Committee, & Court's Electronic Discovery Committee

**Career:** Fellow and Vice-Chair of the Complex Litigation Committee of the American College of Trial Lawyers. Lectured on patent law at Federal Judicial Center (FJC) workshops for District Judges of the Fourth (twice), Fifth (twice), Sixth (twice), Seventh and Ninth Circuits and at 22 FJC National Workshops for federal District and Magistrate Judges. Member of the District Judge Education Advisory Committee for the Federal Judicial Center. Co-Chairman of a national program, Trial of a Patent Case, sponsored by the ALI-ABA Com-

mittee on Continuing Professional Education which has become a permanent annual course offering.

### PARI, Joseph
Dewey Ballantine LLP, Washington, DC 202 862 4516
jpari@deweyballantine.com
*Recommended in Tax*

**Practice Areas:** Tax.

**Prof. Memberships:** Former Council Director for American Bar Association Tax Section's Corporate Tax Committee, Committee on Affiliated and Related Corporations and Bankruptcy Committee; adjunct faculty Georgetown University Law Center; Advisory Boards of New York University Institute on Federal Taxation, Federal Bar Association, National Foreign Trade Council, Inc.; Journal of Corporate Taxation and Corporate Business Taxation Monthly.

**Career:** Partner, Dewey Ballantine since 1996; adjunct faculty member at the Georgetown University Law Center.

**Personal:** LLM, 1988, Taxation, New York University School of Law; JD, 1987, Boston College Law School (magna cum laude); BS, 1984, Providence College (cum laude).

### PARKER, Richard G
O'Melveny & Myers LLP, Washington, DC 202 383 5380
rparker@omm.com
*Recommended in Antitrust*

**Practice Areas:** Rich Parker Co-Chair's O'Melveny & Myers' Antitrust/Competition Practice. He has extensive experience in antitrust and other litigation matters both before the enforcement agencies and in the courts. Rich returned to the firm after three years at the Federal Trade Commission (FTC) as the Director of the Bureau of Competition. Both before entering government and after his return to O'Melveny & Myers, Rich has been involved in many major antitrust representations, both civil and criminal. He has particular expertise in representing clients in proceedings involving the FTC, the Department of Justice and the state attorneys general.

### PARMLEY, Bruce
Hogan & Hartson LLP, Washington, DC 202 637 5644
BEParmley@HHLAW.com
*Recommended in Real Estate*

**Practice Areas:** For almost 30 years, Bruce Parmley has served as principal counsel in hundreds of transactions involving acquisition, development, investment, financing, leasing, management, portfolio consolidation and securitization of commercial properties, with a major focus on hotels and resorts.

**Prof. Memberships:** Former Co-Chair, Real Estate Division, DC Bar Member, Real Property Section, ABA.

**Career:** Bruce's practice is international. He is Co-Director of the firm's Real

Estate Practice and its Hospitality Group, and has been elected twice by Hogan & Hartson's partners to the firm's five-member Executive Committee.

**Personal:** The Catholic University of America (JD, 1976); Ohio University (BSC, 1970).

### PATIN, Douglas L
Bradley Arant Rose & White LLP, Washington, DC 202 719 8241
dpatin@bradleyarant.com
*Recommended in Construction*

**Practice Areas:** Practice leader: construction/government contracts

**Prof. Memberships:** Virginia, Maryland, DC.

**Publications:** '2003 Government Contract Decisions of the Federal Circuit', American University Law Review (2004); 'USA, Dispute Resolution and Conflict Management in Construction', An International Review (E&FN Spon 1998). Co-editor: 'State Public Construction Law Sourcebook', CCH Incorporated (2002); 'Construction Insurance', Chapter 45, Law and Practice of Insurance Coverage Litigation (West 2000); co-author: 'Construction Insurance: Coverages and Disputes' (Michie 1994); 'Construction Contracting', GWU National Law Center (1991); Construction Briefings: 'Surety's Role in Default Terminations', 90-4, 'Liability Insurance 89-9, Federal Publications.

**Personal:** 8/8/54. University of Wisconsin-River Falls (1976). GWU Law Center (1979).

### PATTERSON, Donna
Arnold & Porter LLP, Washington, DC 202 942 5006
Donna.Patterson@aporter.com
*Recommended in Antitrust*

**Practice Areas:** A Partner in the Antitrust and Litigation Practice Groups. She joined the firm in 1988 and has represented numerous clients in FTC and Antitrust Division investigations of proposed mergers and acquisitions, in state and federal court antitrust and complex commercial litigation, and as an antitrust counselor.

**Career:** She was lead US antitrust counsel for General Electric in its proposed acquisition of Honeywell in 2001 and successfully represented Nucor Corp. in its acquisition of Birmingham Steel in 2002. In 2004, she represented NBC in its acquisition of Vivendi Universal Entertainment. In 2005, she represented Kraft in the sale of its candy business to Wrigley, and represented Nasdaq in its acquisition of Instinet. From 1997 until August 2000, she was Deputy Assistant Attorney General in the Antitrust Division of the United States Department of Justice with primary responsibility for merger investigations.

**Personal:** Was named by Chambers & Partners 'Chambers Global' in 2003,

2002-03 and 2001-02 as one of the top 25 antitrust attorneys in Washington, DC.

### PAUL, William M
Covington & Burling, Washington, DC 202 662 5300
wpaul@cov.com
*Recommended in Tax*

**Practice Areas:** Advises clients on federal income tax matters, with focus on representing clients before the Treasury Department, the Internal Revenue Service and Congress. Specialties also include advising on the taxation of financial products and financial transactions.

**Prof. Memberships:** Vice-Chair (Government Relations), ABA Tax Section (2005-07); Fellow, American College of Tax Counsel; Member, American Law Institute.

**Career:** Deputy Tax Legislative Counsel, US Treasury Dept. (1988-89); BA Johns Hopkins University (1973); JD magna cum laude, University of Michigan (1973).

### PEDERSON, Jan
Pederson Immigration Law Group PC, Washington, DC 202 785 1960
*Recommended in Immigration*

### PELTA, Eleanor
Morgan, Lewis & Bockius LLP, Washington, DC 202 739 5050
epelta@morganlewis.com
*Recommended in Immigration*

**Practice Areas:** Immigration and nationality law.

**Prof. Memberships:** Elected Member of the Board of Governors, American Immigration Lawyers Association (AILA), Chair, Citizenship and Immigration Services Liaison Committee, AILA, Trustee, American Immigration Law Foundation (AILF), Chair, Immigration Curriculum Project, AILF.

**Career:** Eleanor Pelta is Managing Director of Morgan Lewis Resources and a Partner in the Labor and Employment Law Practice. Ms Peltar's practice focuses on immigration and nationality law assisting corporate clients in various industries with the international transfer of key personnel. Her specialties include managing high-volume employee transfers and assisting employers with temporary and permanent visas for all types of business, scientific and executive personnel. Ms Pelta advises clients on strategic issues involving movement of staff internationally, including the use of blanket visa programs and qualification of companies as 'treaty investor' or 'treaty trader' entities. She counsels on the immigration implications of corporate changes, including mergers and acquisitions, downsizing, reductions in force and salary level changes.

**Publications:** 'Brave New World: Minimum Requirements, Business Necessity, and Alternative Minimum Requirements under PERM', published in The David

Stanton Manual on Labor Certification: Successful Strategies for Practice Under PERM, 2d ed. (AILA 2005) at 63. 'Immigration and Tax - At The Crossroads: Immigration Issues for Tax and Payroll Professionals' Eleanor Pelta and Donna Kepley/ Arctic International LLC, 2004.
**Personal:** Born 25 July 1960, Graduated Princeton University, AB cum laude 1982, University of Bonn, Germany, 1982 to 1983, Harvard Law School, JD cum laude 1986.

## PENDER, Bob
Hogan & Hartson LLP, Washington, DC
202 637 6814
rbpender@hhlaw.com
*Recommended in Projects*
**Practice Areas:** Partner, Practice Group Director, Project & International Finance Group. Focus on infrastructure project finance with a concentration in power, transportation and energy, including LNG. Represents independent power companies, utilities, and investors in the development, financing, restructuring, and purchase and sale of energy facilities. Represented AES restructure of multiple projects in South America and US Represented AREVA regarding the Unistar nuclear projects with Constellation Energy.
**Career:** Worked on over $15 billion in projects throughout the US, South America, Central America, and South Asia.
**Personal:** Georgetown University Law Center (JD, 1982); Middlebury College (BA, 1976). White House Staff 1978-80.

## PENNA, Richard A
Van Ness Feldman PC, Washington, DC
202 298 1800
*Recommended in Environment*

## PERLIS, Mark
Dickstein Shapiro Morin & Oshinsky LLP, Washington, DC 202 775 4703
PerlisM@dsmo.com
*Recommended in Energy*
**Practice Areas:** Focuses broad federal regulatory and litigation practice on energy and environmental matters, with emphasis on electric utility and industry restructuring. Represents clients before Federal Energy Regulatory Commission. Counsels on energy trading and compliance, contract disputes, and tradable environmental emission allowances.
**Prof. Memberships:** Environmental Markets Association (past Board of Directors Member and Vice President); ABA.
**Career:** Partner, Dickstein Shapiro's Energy Practice; Tax Legislative Counsel's Office, US Treasury Department; editor, Harvard Law Review.
**Publications:** Writes extensively on energy, emissions trading, and global warming.
**Personal:** Harvard Law School (JD, 1977); Yale College (BA, 1974).

## PERLSTEIN, William J
WilmerHale, Washington, DC
202 663 6274
william.perlstein@wilmerhale.com
*Recommended in Bankruptcy*
**Practice Areas:** Co-Chair of the firm's Management Committee and former Head of the firm's Bankruptcy and Commercial Department. Represents creditors' committees, bank groups, debtors, trustees and claims acquirers in bankruptcy and workout cases around the country.
**Prof. Memberships:** Fellow and Counsel to the American College of Bankruptcy; American Law Institute, American Bar Association Business Bankruptcy Committee
**Publications:** 'At the Intersection of Regulation and Bankruptcy'; 'Minimizing Risks When Acquiring Assets From A Financially Troubled Company'.
**Personal:** Yale Law School (JD 1974); Union College (BA 1971); London School of Economics, 1970.

## PETERS, M Beth
Hogan & Hartson LLP, Washington, DC
202 637 5837
mepeters@hhlaw.com
*Recommended in Immigration*
**Practice Areas:** Beth Peters' practice centers on international trade and immigration law matters. She provides advice and representation to clients before the US Departments of State, Treasury, Commerce, Labor, and Homeland Security, and US embassies and consulates abroad. Beth assists US and foreign corporations, sports teams, universities, and nonprofit organizations in sponsoring individuals for immigrant and nonimmigrant status in the United States. She counsels telecommunications, satellite, engineering, chemical, medical, and other companies on complicated export and other compliance matters related to their foreign national employees under the USA Patriot Act and the US export controls and sanctions laws.
**Prof. Memberships:** Chairman, International Trade Committee, DC Bar; Member, ABA; Member, American Immigration Lawyers Association; Member, National Association of College and University Attorneys.
**Publications:** Monthly contributor to Hogan & Hartson's Immigration Update. 'Complying with Immigration, Export Control and Industrial Security Requirements When Working Collaboratively with Foreign nationals: A Case Study', The International Lawyer, Vol. 35, No. 1 (21 May 2001). 'Foreign Nationals in U.S. Technology Programs: Complying with Immigration, Export Control, Industrial Security, and Other Requirements', Immigration Briefings, West Group (1 October 2000).
**Personal:** Columbia University (JD); Duke University (BA).

## PETERSON, Charles
Pillsbury Winthrop Shaw Pittman LLP, Washington, DC 202 663 8083
Charles.Peterson@pillsburylaw.com
*Recommended in Energy*
**Practice Areas:** Practice concentrates on nuclear fuel procurement, international energy transactions and new nuclear reactors. Represents companies in the international energy industry in major commercial transactions. Experienced in commercial transactions in Russia, Kazakhstan and Ukraine. Advises major US companies concerning key DOE contracts, and represents teams that bid for the Maintenance and Operation contracts with the DOE.
**Prof. Memberships:** American Bar Association; American Arbitration Association, National Energy Panel; International Nuclear Lawyers Association; California Bar Association; District of Columbia Bar Association; American Nuclear Society.
**Personal:** JD, Stanford Law School, 1973; MBA, Stanford Business School, 1971; BS, US Naval Academy, 1960.

## PHILLIPS, Carter
Sidley Austin LLP, Washington, DC
202 736 8270
cphillips@sidley.com
*Recommended in Litigation*
**Practice Areas:** Heads the firm's Appellate Practice, routinely representing clients before the United States Supreme Court, state supreme courts, federal courts of appeals and other appellate forums. Managing Partner of the DC office, and Member of the firm's Management and Executive Committees. Served as assistant to the Solicitor General for three years, during which time he argued nine cases on behalf of the federal government in the US Supreme Court. To date, he has argued 51 cases before the Supreme Court. In 2004, he argued six Supreme Court cases including: Intel Corp. v Advanced Micro Devices, where he represented the European Commission in its first appearance before the Court (as an amicus); Norfolk Southern Railway v Kirby, in which the Court ruled unanimously in favor of Sidley client Norfolk Southern in a case involving contracts of carriage in international trade; and Sosa v Alvarez-Machain, in which the Court issued a unanimous ruling in favor of Sidley client Sosa, limiting the scope of the Alien Tort Statute. In the October 2005 Term, he again argued six cases for clients, including Tyson Foods, eBay, Inc. and the State of Arkansas.
**Prof. Memberships:** Member of the American Law Institute, American Academy of Appellate Lawyers, and Fellow in the American College of Trial Lawyers. Member of Federal Circuit Advisory Committee and Chairman of the Dean's Advisory Committee of Northwestern University's School of Law. On the Board

of Trustees and the Publications Committee of the Supreme Court Historical Society, the Amicus Curiae Committee of the Federal Bar Association, and the Board of Directors of the Institute of Judicial Administration at NYU School of Law. Serves on Advisory Committee of Georgetown University Law Center's Supreme Court Institute and Editorial Board of the National Law Journal.
**Publications:** A Year at the Supreme Court: Was Affirmative Action Saved By Its Friends? (2004); Petitioning The Supreme Court For Certiorari, For The Defense; The Supreme Court and State Taxation: 2001-2002, Silent Acceptance, The State and Local Tax Lawyer (2003).
**Personal:** Served as a law clerk to both Judge Robert Sprecher on the United States Court of Appeals for the Seventh Circuit and Chief Justice Warren E Burger on the United States Supreme Court. Northwestern University School of Law, JD, 1977; Northwestern University, MA, 1975; The Ohio State University, BA, 1973. Admissions: US Supreme Court; all US Courts of Appeals; District of Columbia, 1979; Illinois, 1977.

## PHILP, Mary Susan
Powers Pyles Sutter & Verville PC, Washington, DC 202 466 6550
susan.philp@ppsv.com
*Recommended in Healthcare*
**Practice Areas:** Focuses on the federal and state regulatory requirements applicable to hospitals, physicians, clinical laboratories, and other healthcare providers and suppliers. Ms Philp has substantial experience in Medicare and Medicaid reimbursement, corporate compliance, managed care contracting, and the fraud and abuse implications of various practices and business arrangements.
**Prof. Memberships:** DC Bar; CA Bar; American Health Lawyers Association; Healthcare Financial Management Association.
**Career:** O'Connor & Hannan, 1979-83; Hassard, Bonnington, Rogers & Huber, 1984-85; Powers Pyles Sutter & Verville, P.C., 1985-present.
**Publications:** AHLA Health Law Practice Guide (contributing author).
**Personal:** JD, Duke. 1979; BS, MacMurray College, 1976; Member, Arlington Commission on Aging.

## PINCUS, Andrew J
Mayer, Brown, Rowe & Maw LLP, Washington, DC 202 263 3220
apincus@mayerbrownrowe.com
*Recommended in Litigation*
**Practice Areas:** Briefing and argues cases in US Supreme Court, federal, and state appellate courts. Argued 14 cases before the Supreme Court; filed briefs in 100+ cases in that Court. Advises on legislative and regulatory matters. As general counsel of the United States Department of Commerce, formulated and imple-

mented policy concerning intellectual property, electronic authentication, privacy, domain name management, taxation of electronic commerce, telecommunications matters, export controls, international trade, and consumer protection. Advocated these policies in negotiations with foreign governments and testimony before Congress; principal responsibility for Digital Millennium Copyright Act and Electronic Signatures in Global and National Commerce Act. Successfully represented clients in passage of Securities Litigation Reform Act of 1995. **Career:** Mayer, Brown, Rowe & Maw LLP, Washington, DC 1988-97; 2003-present. General counsel, Andersen Worldwide S.C., 2001-03. General counsel, US Department of Commerce, 1997-2000. Assistant to the solicitor general, US Department of Justice, 1984-88. Hughes, Hubbard & Reed, Washington, DC, 1982-84. Law clerk to The Honorable Harold H Greene, US District Court for the District of Columbia, 1981-82. **Personal:** Columbia University School of Law, JD, 1981; James Kent Scholar; Harlan Fiske Stone Scholar; notes & comments editor, Columbia Law Review. Yale College, BA cum laude, 1977.

### PLANNING, Anne K
Pillsbury Winthrop Shaw Pittman LLP, Washington, DC 202 663 9164
anne.planning@pillsburylaw.com
*Recommended in Real Estate*
**Practice Areas:** Ms Planning focuses primarily on commercial lease transactions and related agreements, such as exclusive listing agreements, commission agreements and management agreements. Her practice includes representing both landlords and tenants in connection with office, retail and warehouse leases. **Prof. Memberships:** National Association of Industrial and Office Parks, International Conference of Shopping Centers, American Bar Association, Virginia Bar Association. **Career:** Served on the staffs of former US Senator David F Durenberger and the Senate Subcommittee on Intergovernmental Relations. **Personal:** JD, George Washington University Law School (1988, Order of the Coif); BA, Iowa State University, 1982.

### PLEVIN, Mark
Crowell & Moring LLP, Washington, DC
202 624 2801
mplevin@crowell.com
*Recommended in Bankruptcy, Insurance*
**Practice Areas:** Partner in Crowell & Moring's Litigation Group, and litigates in the bankruptcy and insurance coverage areas. Assumed lead counsel role on behalf of insurers in key asbestos bankruptcy cases including Mid-Valley, Quigley, Combustion Engineering, Congoleum, Federal-Mogul, Harbison-Walk-

er, JT Thorpe, and Owens Corning. Serves as bankruptcy counsel to both the American Insurance Association and the Coalition for Litigation Justice, a group formed by property and casualty insurers to advance awareness about asbestos issues. In insurance coverage, served as lead counsel representing insurers in cases involving environmental, asbestos, and products liability underlying claims.

### PLUMER, Mark J
Heller Ehrman LLP, Washington, DC
202 912 2021
mark.plumer@hellerehrman.com
*Recommended in Insurance*
**Practice Areas:** Insurance recovery. **Prof. Memberships:** American Bar Association. **Career:** Mr Plumer specializes in resolving insurance coverage disputes of all kinds on behalf of insured companies. He has resolved coverage disputes with insurance companies involving broad array of losses, including products (including asbestos and pharmaceutical devices), environmental (including utility, oil and gas, pharmaceutical, mining and other large-scale claims), and business-related claims, including errors and omissions, first party property damage, fidelity and directors and officers claims. **Personal:** Franklin & Marshall College (BA, cum laude, 1983); George Washington Law School (JD, cum laude, 1986).

### POLON, Ira H
Dickstein Shapiro Morin & Oshinsky LLP, Washington, DC 202 828 2238
PolonI@dsmo.com
*Recommended in Corporate/Commercial*
**Practice Areas:** Corporate law practice with substantial experience in mergers, acquisitions, and financing. Personally directed the representation of buyers and sellers in over 160 transactions, involving a wide variety of industrial businesses and government contractors. Has acted in a general counsel capacity for numerous significant companies. **Career:** Partner; heads the firm's M&A Section. **Publications:** Frequently serves as a panelist and lectures and writes extensively on mergers and acquisitions, securities laws, and venture capital issues; co-authored 'Asset Sales - Were Causes of Action Transferred?' The M&A Lawyer (April 2002). **Personal:** Columbia University School of Law (LLB, 1968); Lehigh University (BA, 1965).

### POPOFSKY, Mark
Kaye Scholer LLP, Washington, DC
202 682 3530
mpopofsky@kayescholer.com
*Recommended in Antitrust*
**Practice Areas:** Partner and Chair, Technology and Competition Practice Group. Represents clients in antitrust,

intellectual property, and commercial litigation, counsels clients concerning a variety of competition-related matters, and represents parties in mergers and other transactions before the US Department of Justice and Federal Trade Commission. **Prof. Memberships:** Chair, Intellectual Property Committee, American Bar Association, Antitrust Section; past Chair of Section 2 Committee; Member, US Council for International Business; California Bar Association Antitrust and Trade Regulation Section; District of Columbia Antitrust Trade Regulation and Consumer Affairs Section; Adjunct Professor, Georgetown Law Center. **Career:** Senior Counsel, Antitrust Division, US Dept of Justice, 1994-99; law clerk to Judge Dorothy W Nelson, US Court of Appeals for the Ninth Circuit; JD (magna cum laude), Harvard Law School, executive editor, Harvard Law Review; AB (magna cum laude), Brown University, Phi Beta Kappa. **Publications:** 'Defining Exclusionary Conduct', 73 Antitrust LJ (2006) (forthcomong); 'Charting Antitrust's New Frontier', 9 Geo. Mason L Rev 656 (2001); 'The New Competition Law Paradigm', Symposium, UWLA L Rev (2001); 'Vertical Restraints in the 1990s', 62 Antitrust LJ 729 (1994).

### PORTER, Stephen
Arnold & Porter LLP, Washington, DC
202 942 5004
Stephen.Porter@aporter.com
*Recommended in Real Estate*
**Practice Areas:** His practice principally involves large-scale, complex real estate transactions, corporate and real estate financing, leasing, and general business counseling. He has counseled a number of major corporations, non-profit organizations, and professional firms seeking to relocate their offices, as well as developers of hotels, marinas, and office buildings. **Prof. Memberships:** He has also served as a Member of the Advisory Board of the Center for Strategic & International Studies; Chairman of the Board of the Washington Performing Arts Society; Chairman of the Board of the Forum for Psychiatry and the Humanities; and as a Member of the Board of Directors of the Washington School of Psychiatry. He is currently a Member of the Board of Trustees of the Federal City Council and a Member of the Boards of both the Greater Washington Board of Trade and the District of Columbia Chamber of Commerce and is Chair of the Board of Trade's Public Affairs Committee in addition to Chairman of the District of Columbia Chamber of Commerce. He also serves on the District of Columbia Comprehensive Planning Task Force by appointment of Mayor Williams. **Career:** Has practiced in the real estate, tax, and corporate areas for more than 35 years. In 1974, he was a founding Partner of Dunnells, Duvall & Porter. He has also

lectured on business subjects at the Georgetown University Law Center and American University Washington College of Law.

### POTENZA, Joseph
Banner & Witcoff, Ltd, Washington, DC
202 508 9100
*Recommended in Intellectual Property*

### PRESTON, Richard
Seyfarth Shaw LLP, Washington, DC
202 463 2400
*Recommended in Construction*

### PRINCE, Allison
Pillsbury Winthrop Shaw Pittman LLP, Washington, DC 202 663 8853
allison.prince@pillsburylaw.com
*Recommended in Real Estate*
**Practice Areas:** Ms Prince practices zoning and land development law with a focus on the multi-family housing, education and nonprofit practice areas. Her practice involves appearances before the DC Board of Zoning Adjustment, the DC Zoning Commission and the District of Columbia Council. She represents several large commercial and residential developers, colleges, universities, schools and retirement communities. She also is the land use counsel for the Washington Convention Center Authority. Prior to joining Pillsbury, Ms Prince was affiliated with Wilkes Artis in Washington, DC. **Personal:** JD, Catholic University, Columbus School of Law, 1983; BA, Bucknell University, 1980.

### PROGER, Phillip A
Jones Day, Washington, DC
202 879 4668
paproger@jonesday.com
*Recommended in Antitrust*
**Practice Areas:** Oversees the firm's Antitrust and Competition Law Practice. Antitrust practice with an emphasis on matters before US and international enforcement agencies, including mergers and cartel investigations, as well as antitrust litigation. Testified before Congress, the Federal Trade Commission, and the International Competition Policy Advisory Committee. Frequent speaker at seminars sponsored by the International Bar Association, The American Law Institute, and The Conference Board. **Prof. Memberships:** Member of the Board of Governors of the ABA. The American Law Institute. Fellow of the American Bar Foundation. Advisory board member of BNA Antitrust & Trade Regulation Report and The M&A Lawyer.

### PURETZ, Jeffrey S
Dechert LLP, Washington, DC
202 261 3358
jeffrey.puretz@dechert.com
*Recommended in Investment Management*
**Practice Areas:** Mr Puretz co-ordinates the Financial Services Group's services for insurance companies. He also advises on

investment management matters for mutual funds, fund directors, and fund managers.

**Prof. Memberships:** Member, ABA Federal Regulation of Securities Committee; ABA Securities Activities of Insurance Companies Subcommittee; Investment Management Committee of the District of Columbia Bar.

**Career:** Founder and Co-Chair, Practising Law Institute conference on 'Understanding Securities Products of Insurance Companies.' Former staff attorney, SEC's Division of Investment Management.

**Personal:** University of Maryland (BA, 1976); The Catholic University of America School of Law (JD, 1981); Georgetown University Law Center.

## QUALE, John C

Skadden, Arps, Slate, Meagher & Flom LLP & Affiliates, Washington, DC
202 371 7200
jquale@skadden.com
*Recommended in Telecom, Broadcast & Satellite*

**Practice Areas:** Represents companies on a broad range of communications law issues arising in regulatory, legislative and transactional matters. Clients include broadcast, satellite and wireless companies, venture capital and investment firms and commercial banks. Counsels on structuring transactions and assists in negotiating and documenting purchases and sales of media properties. Advises clients concerning FCC multiple and alien ownership regulations and assists in rule waivers to permit market entry. In connection with these transactions, obtained FCC approval of license transfers in large numbers of contested cases.

**Career:** JD, Harvard Law School, 1971 (cum laude); AB, Harvard College, 1968 (cum laude).

## QUARLES, John

Morgan, Lewis & Bockius LLP, Washington, DC 202 739 5150
jquarles@morganlewis.com
*Recommended in Environment*

**Practice Areas:** John Quarles is a Partner in the Litigation Practice. Mr Quarles's practice focuses on a variety of environmental law issues, providing counseling and litigation assistance on Superfund, hazardous waste, and air and water pollution matters. He heads several groups working on Superfund and RCRA implementation and reauthorization issues. Mr Quarles served as the Environmental Protection Agency's first general counsel from 1970 through 1973, and then served four years as deputy administrator, also serving two periods as acting administrator.

**Prof. Memberships:** American Bar Association (Environment, Energy & Resources Section); District of Columbia Bar Association; Environmental Law Institute.

## QUIN, Whayne

Holland & Knight LLP, Washington, DC
202 955 3000
whayne.quin@hklaw.com
*Recommended in Real Estate*

**Practice Areas:** Partner and Practice Group Leader in the Real Estate Section, practicing in the area of municipal law focusing on land use, zoning, urban planning, building and housing codes, historic preservation, environmental, transportation and urban real estate matters. His clients have included builders, developers, educational institutions, nonprofit organizations, financial institutions, chanceries, international and national agencies, and property owners. Nationally, he has been a consultant to the private sector in the fields of land use, historic preservation, housing and building-related matters. As an urban strategist, he has advised clients on the procedures necessary to accomplish residential, commercial and industrial development.

## QUINT, Arnold

Hunton & Williams, Washington, DC
202 955 1542
aquint@hunton.com
*Recommended in Energy*

**Practice Areas:** Arnold Quint's practice focuses on all aspects of regulation, deregulation and restructuring of the electric utility industry, including electric rates and corporate regulation, long-term power sales agreements, transmission access and pricing, the licensing of hydroelectric projects and competition issues arising in the public utility industry. He represents utility companies, independent system operators and transcos in connection with matters arising under the Federal Power Act especially in matters pending before the Federal Energy Regulatory Commission (FERC).

## RAHER, Patrick M

Hogan & Hartson LLP, Washington, DC
202 637 5682
pmraher@hhlaw.com
*Recommended in Environment, Transportation*

**Practice Areas:** Environmental, including Clean Air Act Permitting of Stationary Sources, defense of companies in Clean Air Act Enforcement Actions; transportation, including safety regulation of mobile sources and railroad equipment; legislative.

**Prof. Memberships:** EPA Clean Air Act Advisory Committee; EPA Mobile Source Advisory Committee; EPA New Source Review Subcommittee (Co-Chairperson); ABA (Co-Chairman, Ad Hoc Committee on Government Attorneys-EPA); District of Columbia Judicial Tenure Commission.

**Career:** 1973-present, Hogan & Hartson, current Environmental Practice Director; 1992-present, appointed member, Environmental Protection Agency Clean Air

Act Advisory Committee.

**Publications:** 'Lead in Office Building Drinking Water: A Key Environmental Analysis Issue for the 1990's', Environmental Liability in Commercial Transactions Reporter, February 1991; 'Hidden Pitfalls in Groundwater Cleanup Rules', Prentiss Hall Environmental Hazards Reporter, May 1990; "Gualtney' and its Progeny: The Current Status of Citizen's Suits Under the Clean Water Act', The Environmental Counselor, October 1989; 'Being Aware of 18 USC 1001 and the EPA Regulatory Thicket', Corporate Counsel's Guide to Environmental Law, 1989; 'What Might the Supreme Court Say on Officer and Director Liability if US v Park Applies to Environmental Statutes?' Corporate Counsel, 1989; 'How to Get Things Done At the EPA' The Brief, Winter 1986; 'Economic Internationalism vs National Parochialism: Barcelona Traction: Journal of Law and Policy in International Business', Fall 1971.

**Personal:** Georgetown University Law Center (JD, 1972); University of Notre Dame (BBA, with honors, 1969).

## RAIM, David

Chadbourne & Parke LLP, Washington, DC 202 974 5625
draim@chadbourne.com
*Recommended in Insurance*

**Practice Areas:** Co-Chair, Reinsurance and Insurance Group. Has represented parties in hundreds of reinsurance arbitrations and litigations on wide range of issues, including property/casualty and life/health reinsurance, finite reinsurance, London Market matters, MGAs, allocation issues, rescission claims, 'fronting' issues, surety, clash and catastrophe covers. Additionally, provides advice to clients in the reinsurance and insurance industry on wide range of subject matters, including commutations, contract wordings, inspections and insolvencies.

**Prof. Memberships:** ARIAS-US; District of Columbia Bar - Chairman, Members Benefits Committee (1988-94).

## RASKIN, David

Steptoe & Johnson LLP, Washington, DC
202 429 6254
draskin@steptoe.com
*Recommended in Energy*

**Practice Areas:** Partner, Steptoe & Johnson LLP, Washington, DC. Represents electric power industry clients in cases involving electric industry restructuring, mergers and acquisitions, antitrust, wholesale electric and transmission service pricing, transmission access, market design, and contract disputes. Structured and negotiated complex bulk power and transmission service transactions and agreements to construct and operate transmission lines and generating facilities. Participated in negotiations and related regulatory proceedings

to establish several Regional Transmission Organizations. Experienced with cases before the Nuclear Regulatory Commission concerning the licensing and operation of nuclear power plants.

**Personal:** Georgetown University Law Center, JD, 1979; BA, University of Pennsylvania, 1976.

## RAUH, Carl S

Skadden, Arps, Slate, Meagher & Flom LLP & Affiliates, Washington, DC
202 371 7190
crauh@skadden.com
*Recommended in Litigation*

**Practice Areas:** A Leader of the firm's Government Enforcement Litigation Department. Represents corporations, directors, officers and employees in complex litigation, particularly matters involving simultaneous criminal, civil and administrative proceedings. Has defended corporations and their officers in cases involving allegations of procurement fraud, securities and tax violations, environmental crimes, healthcare fraud, bank and insurance fraud, antitrust offenses, food and drug adulteration, bribery and conflicts of interest.

**Career:** LLM, Georgetown University Law Center, 1968; LLB, University of Pennsylvania Law School, 1965; AB, Columbia University, 1962.

## REED, Kevin F

Dow, Lohnes & Albertson, PLLC, Washington, DC 202 776 2693
kreed@dowlohnes.com
*Recommended in Telecom, Broadcast & Satellite*

**Practice Areas:** Kevin Reed represents diversified media companies, television and radio stations, newspapers, cable television systems and new technology businesses. In addition to a regulatory practice before the Federal Communications Commission, much of his work involves broadcast network/affiliated station relations and the acquisition and sale of broadcast stations and other regulated communications companies.

**Prof. Memberships:** DC Bar; Federal Communications Bar Association.

**Career:** Law Clerk to Hon. Charles Fahy, United States Court of Appeals for the DC Circuit, 1973-74. Partner at Dow Lohnes since 1981.

**Publications:** Law journal articles and communications trade press op-ed pieces.

**Personal:** Georgetown Law Center (JD, 1973); Case and Note Editor of the Georgetown Law Journal; Holy Cross College (BA, 1970).

## REED, Steven

Steptoe & Johnson LLP, Washington, DC
202 429 6232
sreed@steptoe.com
*Recommended in Energy*

**Practice Areas:** Partner in Steptoe & Johnson LLP's Washington office. Focus-

es on federal and state energy regulation, particularly for oil and gas pipelines. Represents numerous US oil pipeline companies before the FERC, state regulatory agencies, arbitrators, and US Courts of Appeals covering various pipeline issues, such as tariff rates, development of the cost-of-service approach, and pipeline market power. Gas pipeline regulatory experience includes royalty issues, abandonments, and gas pipeline certificates. Frequently assists pipeline clients in structuring proposed transactions to meet regulations and in securing regulatory approvals for innovative rate approaches.
**Personal:** JD, Harvard Law School, 1979; BA, Harvard College, 1974.

### REED, Wendy
Wright & Talisman PC, Washington, DC
202 393 1200
*Recommended in Energy*

### REIDER, Alan E
Arent Fox PLLC, Washington, DC
202 857 6462
reider.alan@arentfox.com
*Recommended in Healthcare*
**Practice Areas:** Alan has been Chair of Arent Fox's Healthcare Practice and serves on the firm's Executive Committee. He represents national healthcare corporations, as well as institutional providers and individual practitioners and suppliers. His representation focuses on regulatory, compliance, and enforcement issues involving federal programs, including fraud and abuse, reimbursement, and coverage. Alan has been lead counsel on several major enforcement cases and appears before federal agencies, including CMS, the OIG, the Department of Justice, and US Attorneys Offices throughout the country.
**Personal:** Boston University School of Law, JD 1975; University of Texas School of Public Health, MPH 1972; Brown University, AB 1971.

### REIFF, Laura F
Greenberg Traurig LLP, Washington, DC
202 331 3100
reiff@gtlaw.com
*Recommended in Immigration*
**Practice Areas:** Immigration; labor and employment; technology, media and telecommunications.
**Prof. Memberships:** Co-Chair, Essential Workers Immigration Coalition; Co-Chair, Workforce Committee, Northern Virginia Technology Council; Board of Trustees, American Immigration Law Foundation (AILF) and Chair of AILF Immigration Policy Committee; Member, US Chamber of Commerce, Labor and Employment Subcommittee on Immigration.
**Career:** 'Who's Who of International Corporate Immigration Lawyers', 1996 to present; Presidential Award for legislative advocacy in the field of immigration law,

1996, 1997, 1998.
**Personal:** JD, with honors, George Washington University Law School, 1989; BA, magna cum laude, American University, 1986.

### REPKA, David A
Winston & Strawn LLP, Washington, DC
202 371 5726
drepka@winston.com
*Recommended in Energy*
**Practice Areas:** Regulation of nuclear power and radiological materials. Extensive experience in administrative hearings; licensing, compliance and enforcement matters; investigations; and federal court appeals.
**Prof. Memberships:** District of Columbia Bar.
**Career:** Partner since 1991.
**Publications:** Co-author 'The Revival of Nuclear Power Plant Licensing', Natural Resources & Environment, ABA Section of Environment, Energy, and Resources, Vol 19, No 3, Winter 2005; Speaker, 'NRC Licensing Hearings - Uncertainty and Reform', NEI International Uranium Fuel Seminar, San Diego, California, October 2003.
**Personal:** Northwestern University, BA, 1978; Georgetown University Law Center, JD, 1981.

### REYNOLDS, Nicholas S
Winston & Strawn LLP, Washington, DC
202 282 5717
nreynolds@winston.com
*Recommended in Energy*
**Practice Areas:** Electric utilities in connection with industry restructuring, deregulation, and Sarbanes-Oxley, as well as mergers and acquisitions; nuclear power reactor and materials licensees before the US Nuclear Regulatory Commission, the Department of Labor, and the courts.
**Personal:** Wilkes College, BS, 1968; College of William and Mary School of Law, 1968-70; The George Washington University Law School, JD, with honors, 1971.

### RHYNE, Katherine L
King & Spalding LLP, Washington, DC
202 626 3743
krhyne@kslaw.com
*Recommended in Environment*
**Practice Areas:** Focuses on chemical risk assessment issues in the context of environmental regulation or tort litigation. Experience includes environmental tort litigation, environmental litigation, scientific programs, environmental regulation, and site-specific risk assessment.
**Prof. Memberships:** American Bar Association (Member, Environmental and Natural Resources, Toxic Tort Sections); District of Columbia Bar; Virginia State Bar; Women's Bar Association of the District of Columbia.
**Personal:** University of Virginia, Phi Beta Kappa; University of Virginia Law School, 1980.

### RICHARDSON, Julia
Van Ness Feldman PC, Washington, DC
202 298 1800
*Recommended in Energy*

### RIEDY, James
McDermott Will & Emery, Washington, DC 202 756 8314
jriedy@mwe.com
*Recommended in Tax*
**Practice Areas:** Partner in Tax Department. Main area of work includes US federal income tax law applicable to cross-border transactions and investments. Practice encompasses both US multinational investments outside the US and non-US, multinational investments in the US. Practice includes consulting on technical tax matters, advising on major corporate acquisitions, corporate internal restructuring and transfer pricing.
**Prof. Memberships:** Past Co-Chair of International Tax Committee of District of Columbia Bar.
**Publications:** Frequent commentator and lecturer on US international tax issues.
**Personal:** University of Kansas College of Law (JD); Georgetown University Law Center (LLM); Kansas State University (BS).

### RILL, James
Howrey LLP, Washington, DC
202 783 0800
*Recommended in Antitrust*

### RITTS, Leslie Sue
Hogan & Hartson LLP, Washington, DC
202 637 6573
lsritts@hhlaw.com
*Recommended in Environment*
**Practice Areas:** Clean Air Act enforcement, compliance and permitting; EU chemical regulation; toxic tort/general environmental litigation; environmental due diligence; and energy.
**Prof. Memberships:** Federal Clean Air Act Advisory Committee (New Source Review Simplification and Operating Permit Subcommittees); ABA (Section on Environmental Law); Virginia Bar Association (Section on Environmental Law); District of Columbia Bar Association (Section on Environmental Law).
**Career:** Hogan & Hartson, Partner; 1993-96, Chair, Air & Waste Management Association's Government Affairs Committee.
**Publications:** 'Clear Skies Legislation and NSR Reform: The Policitcs of Clean Air', 61 PUBL Power 22 (Jan. 2003); 'Protecting Wastewater Assets After 9/11... Legal Issues At A Time Of Crisis Checklist', AMSA (2001); 'The Shields Are Failing: An Analysis of the Clean Air Act Permit Shield', 3 J. Envt'l Permitting 315 (Summer 1992).
**Personal:** William and Mary School of Law (JD, 1980); Princeton University (AB, cum laude, 1977).

### RIVERA, Henry M
Vinson & Elkins LLP, Washington, DC
202 639 6770
hrivera@velaw.com
*Recommended in Telecom, Broadcast & Satellite*
**Practice Areas:** US and international communications regulatory matters.
**Prof. Memberships:** American Bar Association; District of Columbia Bar; New Mexico Bar; Federal Communications Bar Association (former President).
**Publications:** Lectured and written extensively on communications regulatory matters.

### ROADY, Celia
Morgan, Lewis & Bockius LLP, Washington, DC 202 739 5279
croady@morganlewis.com
*Recommended in Tax*
**Practice Areas:** Ms Roady is a Partner in the Tax Practice. Ms Roady focuses her practice on the representation of tax-exempt organizations, including charities, foundations, colleges and universities, museums, associations and other non-profit coalitions. She advises clients on a wide range of tax and non-profit governance issues, including representation of tax-exempt organizations in audits and controversies with the Internal Revenue Service.
**Prof. Memberships:** Immediate Past Vice-Chair - Communications, American Bar Association Taxation Section; Fellow, American College of Tax Counsel.

### ROBBINS, Lawrence
Robbins, Russell, Englert, Orseck & Untereiner LLP, Washington, DC
202 775 4500
*Recommended in Litigation*

### ROBBINS, Robert B
Pillsbury Winthrop Shaw Pittman LLP, Washington, DC 202 663 8136
Robert.Robbins@pillsburylaw.com
*Recommended in Corporate/Commercial*
**Practice Areas:** Leader of Pillsbury's Corporate and Securities Practice Section and also the leader of the firm's REITs and Real Estate Capital Markets Group. His practice involves the legal aspects of securities offerings, mergers, acquisitions and restructurings, and institutional private equity funds. Transactions involving REITs, investment management firms and institutional private equity funds are a particular focus. In the last year he has assisted in institutional private offerings totaling over €1 billion.
**Prof. Memberships:** American Bar Association, National Association of Real Estate Investment Trusts.
**Personal:** JD, Harvard Law School, 1975 (cum laude); AB, Cornell University, 1972 (magna cum laude).

## ROBERTS, Michele

Akin Gump Strauss Hauer & Feld LLP, Washington, DC
202 887 4306
mroberts@akingump.com
*Recommended in Litigation*

**Practice Areas:** Michele Roberts is regarded as one of the 'finest pure trial lawyers in Washington – magic with juries, loved by judges, feared by opposing counsel'. She began her career as a DC Public Defender, where she cut her teeth in more than 40 jury trials, and has built a fearsome reputation as a talented, determined and very persuasive advocate for her clients in complex civil and criminal litigation.
**Personal:** BA, Wesleyan University; JD, University of California at Berkeley (Boalt Hall).

## ROBERTS, Richard

Steptoe & Johnson LLP, Washington, DC
202 429 6756
rroberts@steptoe.com
*Recommended in Energy*

**Practice Areas:** Energy, antitrust, litigation.
**Prof. Memberships:** Energy Bar Association.
**Career:** Richard L Roberts is a Partner at Steptoe & Johnson LLP. His practice focuses on the areas of energy law, antitrust, and litigation. He is a leader in issues concerning the restructuring of the electric power industry, including market power litigation, the formation of ISOs and other power pools, the sale and purchase of power plants, and the establishment and enforcement of electricity trading rules.
**Personal:** JD, with honors, University of Maryland School of Law, 1988; BS, Towson State University, 1984.

## ROBINSON, Frederick

Fulbright & Jaworski L.L.P., Washington, DC 202 662 4534
frobinson@fulbright.com
*Recommended in Healthcare*

**Practice Areas:** Health law, criminal law, and litigation.
**Prof. Memberships:** American Bar Association's Health Law and Criminal Justice Section, White Collar Crime Committee, Health Care Fraud Subcommittee; American Health Lawyers Association; District of Columbia Bar Association; National Association of College and University Attorneys; District of Columbia Bar and the Maryland State Bar Association.
**Career:** Rick Robinson began his legal career in Fulbright's Litigation Group, where, beginning in 1982, he represented a wide variety of corporations and their officers in government investigations and white-collar criminal cases. Mr Robinson is now the Partner-in-charge of the Health Law Practice in Fulbright & Jaworski's Washington, DC office. His

cases cover all phases of trial and appellate practice in both criminal and civil cases, including qui tam and 'whistle-blower' lawsuits under the federal False Claims Act. He also advises clients on internal investigations and voluntary disclosure matters.
**Personal:** BA Duke University (1979); JD Duke University (1982).

## ROCAP III, James

Steptoe & Johnson LLP, Washington, DC
202 429 8152
jrocap@steptoe.com
*Recommended in Insurance*

**Practice Areas:** Complex civil litigation with current emphasis on large insurance coverage disputes. Experience in a wide range of large-scale civil and white-collar criminal matters. Represented numerous companies and individuals in complex business litigation, including claims involving antitrust violations, fraud, tortious interference with contract, and breach of contract. Represents two death row inmates, one for 20+ years, and provides legal services to the homeless.
**Career:** Serves as Chairman of the firm's Public Service Committee and member of the Hiring Committee.
**Personal:** JD, Georgetown University Law Center, 1975; Articles/Notes Editor, 'Georgetown Law Journal'; BA, University of Notre Dame, 1971.

## ROGAN, Michael P

Skadden, Arps, Slate, Meagher & Flom LLP & Affiliates, Washington, DC
202 371 7550
mrogan@skadden.com
*Recommended in Corporate/Commercial*

**Practice Areas:** Joined Skadden in 1980, has headed the Washington, DC office Corporate Group since 1994, and has been the leader of the firm's Washington, DC office since 1998. Practices in the areas of mergers and acquisitions, securities regulation, corporate finance and corporate governance. Experienced in SEC matters and provides corporate and securities law advice to a number of public companies on an ongoing basis. Has represented bidders, targets and investment bankers in domestic and cross-border M&A deals, as well as friendly and hostile situations. Experienced in asset acquisitions and dispositions (including electric utility restructurings), proxy contests, white squire investment and the adoption of shareholder rights plans. Has an active corporate governance practice and regularly advises boards on Sarbanes-Oxley Act-related matters, and board committees on compliance and internal investigation matters. In the corporate finance area, has represented public and private companies in debt and equity financings, including venture capital investments and Rule 144A financings.

**Career:** JD, University of Connecticut, 1974; BA, Oberlin College, 1970. Admitted in the District of Columbia, New York and Connecticut.

## ROGERS, Ed

Nixon Peabody LLP, Washington, DC
202 585 8726
erogers@nixonpeabody.com
*Recommended in Real Estate*

**Practice Areas:** Real estate development, commercial finance and related matters. Large-scale, mixed-use projects including shopping centers, office buildings, museums, theaters, hotels, resorts, residential and telecommunications facilities. Currently representing: Freedom Forum/Newseum, Inc. (mixed-use project comprised of a world-class museum, organization headquarters, a conference center, residential units, retail and parking); Waterfront Associates (mixed-use project near the southwest DC waterfront); Forest City Washington (several major, mixed-use projects in the DC metropolitan area); and Anacostia Waterfront Corporation (ground leases for a new baseball stadium for the Washington Nationals).
**Prof. Memberships:** Admitted to practice in DC and NY.
**Personal:** University of Virginia, JD, BA.

## ROGOVIN, John

WilmerHale, Washington, DC
202 663 6270
john.rogovin@wilmerhale.com
*Recommended in Telecom, Broadcast & Satellite*

**Practice Areas:** Partner, Communications and E-commerce, Litigation, Public Policy and Strategy Departments. Represents broadcasting, wireless, satellite and telecommunications clients in wide variety of matters, including litigation, proceedings before regulatory agencies, and transactions. Represents other clients on a variety of employment and transactional matters.
**Career:** General Counsel, Federal Communications Commission. Deputy Assistant Attorney General in the Civil Division, Department of Justice, supervising the Federal Programs Branch, which defends US in lawsuits challenging constitutionality or legality of governmental policies, programs and actions. Deputy Transition Counsel during the 1992-93 Presidential Transition.
**Personal:** JD, University of Virginia School of Law; AB, Columbia University.

## ROHRBACH, Peter

Hogan & Hartson LLP, Washington, DC
202 637 8631
parohrbach@hhlaw.com
*Recommended in Telecom, Broadcast & Satellite*

**Practice Areas:** Co-Director of the Hogan & Hartson Communications Group and member of the firm's Executive Committee. 25-year practice focusing

on representation of major telecommunications, satellite and media companies in regulatory matters, antitrust proceedings, mergers and acquisitions. His clients have included national and international carriers, as well as newer companies that have grown in response to opportunities created by the Internet, liberalized opportunities for competition, and related developments. Appears regularly before the Federal Communications Commission, Justice Department Antitrust Division, and state public utility commissions. Recent major matters have included representation of SES Global in its acquisition of New Skies Satellites, and Qwest in its proposed acquisition of MCI.
**Prof. Memberships:** Member, Federal Communications Bar Association.
**Career:** Joined Hogan & Hartson in 1979. Has taught a law school seminar in communications law, speaks regularly on telecommunications policy matters, and participates in various industry organizations.
**Personal:** Stanford University Law School (JD 1979, Senior Note Editor, Stanford Law Review); Yale University (BA 1975, magna cum laude).

## ROSEN, Richard L

Arnold & Porter LLP, Washington, DC
202 942 5499
Richard.Rosen@aporter.com
*Recommended in Antitrust*

**Practice Areas:** Richard Rosen handles a wide range of antitrust matters, with a focus on clients in the telecommunications, information technology and media industries. His practice includes representation of clients in mergers and acquisitions and civil and criminal enforcement matters before federal antitrust agencies, as well as antitrust counseling and litigation. He has represented SBC Communications and Cingular Wireless in Cingular's acquisition of AT&T Wireless and SBC's acquisition of AT&T; Computer Associates in its acquisitions of Legent Corporation, Platinum Technology International and Sterling Software; and Cisco Systems in its acquisitions of the Linksys Group and Airespace Corporation. Mr Rosen has been recognized as a leading competition lawyer by 'Chambers Global - The World's Leading Lawyers'; as 'highly recommended' by Global Counsel's 'Competition Law Handbook'; and in 'Who's Who Legal - The International Who's Who of Business Lawyers'.
**Career:** Prior to joining Arnold & Porter LLP, Mr Rosen served as Chief of the Communications and Finance Section of the US Department of Justice Antitrust Division, Assistant Director of the Federal Trade Commission's Bureau of Competition, and as Attorney Advisor to the Chairman of the Federal Trade Commission.

## ROSENBLOOM, David
Caplin & Drysdale, Washington, DC
202 862 5000
*Recommended in Tax*

## ROSENTHAL, Barry P
Bingham McCutchen LLP,
Washington, DC 202 778 3178
barry.rosenthal@bingham.com
*Recommended in Real Estate*

**Practice Areas:** Serves as Co-Chair of the firm's Real Estate Practice Group. Has represented clients in sophisticated real estate and finance-related matters for more than 25 years. Regularly involved in all aspects of a transactional real estate practice – acquisitions, sales, financing, joint ventures, partnerships, leasing and real estate development. Clients include banks, insurance companies and other financial institutions; pension fund advisors; institutional investors; and owners, operators and developers of real estate.
**Personal:** University of Pennsylvania Law School, JD, 1974; University of Rochester, BA, cum laude, 1970.

## ROSENTHAL, Steven M
Miller & Chevalier Chartered,
Washington, DC 202 626 5962
srosenthal@milchev.com
*Recommended in Tax*

**Practice Areas:** Financial products, transactions, and institutions, tax, tax audits and administrative appeals, tax legislation.
**Prof. Memberships:** American Bar Association; Bar Association of DC; Federal Bar Association; Journal of Taxation of Financial Institutions; Investment Company Institute.
**Career:** Member - Miller & Chevalier Chartered (2001-present); National Director, Financial Products Taxation - KPMG LLP (1995-2001); Legislation Counsel, Joint Committee on Taxation - US Congress (1990-95); Associate - Wilmer, Cutler & Pickering (1985-90).
**Publications:** International Tax Review's World Tax 2006 (November 2005). Journal of Taxation of Financial Institutions - Bank One, A Mark-to-Market Roadmap (July/August 2003). Taxation of Financial Products - New Options to Resolve Financial Product Tax Controversies (Spring 2003). Tax and Accounting for Derivatives: Time for Reconciliation.
**Personal:** JD, University of California at Berkeley, 1985; MPP, Harvard University, 1982; BA, University of California at Berkeley, 1979. Former Chair, Taxation Section of DC Bar.

## ROTH, Stephen E
Sutherland Asbill & Brennan LLP,
Washington, DC 202 383 0158
steve.roth@sablaw.com
*Recommended in Investment Management*

**Practice Areas:** Chairs the firm's Business Practices Group and Financial Services Team. Leading authority in the

development of new insurance products, including registration of variable life, fixed life and annuity contracts with the Securities and Exchange Commission. Advises in the development, regulation and compliance of mutual funds and other regulated investment companies, as well as securities compliance and regulatory issues affecting broker/dealers and investment advisors. Counsels financial service clients on insurance regulatory and licensing matters as well as on merger, acquisition and reinsurance transactions.
**Prof. Memberships:** Member, American Bar Association. Member, ABA's Committee on Federal Regulation of Securities. Member, ABA's Subcommittee on Securities Activities of Insurance Companies. Member, Association of Life Insurance Counsel.
**Personal:** JD, Yale Law School, 1976, editor, Yale Law Journal; AB, summa cum laude, University of Notre Dame, 1973, Phi Beta Kappa.

## RUBINSTEIN, Joel
Bell, Boyd & Lloyd LLC, Washington, DC
202 466 6300
*Recommended in Construction*

## RUDNICK, Robert
Shearman & Sterling, Washington, DC
202 508 8020
rrudnick@shearman.com
*Recommended in Tax*

**Practice Areas:** Partner in Shearman & Sterling's Tax Group. Represents clients in federal income tax matters, including corporate tax, partnership tax, the taxation of financial products and tax controversy work. Participated in the creation of many novel financial products with tax significance, including the first CMO, the first foreign-targeted CMO, the REMIC legislation, credit card securitization and stripped mortgages.
**Career:** Joined Shearman as Partner in 1997; Previously a Partner at Cadwalader, Wickersham & Taft (1981-97).
**Personal:** BA, Colby College (1969); JD, Cornell University (1972).

## RUGGERI, James
Hogan & Hartson LLP, Washington, DC
202 637 5875
jpruggeri@hhlaw.com
*Recommended in Insurance*

**Practice Areas:** Focuses principally in the areas of litigation, including trial and appellate involving insurance coverage, general commercial and bankruptcy litigation. He practices actively in federal and state courts around the country.
**Prof. Memberships:** Member, American Bar Association; Member, New York Bar Association.
**Career:** Prior to joining Hogan & Hartson, James served as law clerk to the Honorable Rebecca Beach Smith, US District Judge for the US District Court for the Eastern District of Virginia.
**Personal:** Vanderbilt University (JD).

## RULE, Charles F (Rick)
Fried, Frank, Harris, Shriver & Jacobson LLP, Washington, DC
202 639 7300
Rick.Rule@FriedFrank.com
*Recommended in Antitrust*

**Practice Areas:** Chairman of Antitrust Department. Practice focuses on all aspects of US and international antitrust, including mergers, joint ventures, IP licensing, civil and criminal investigations by national antitrust authorities, and trial and appellate antitrust litigation. Represents major international corporations, including Microsoft before the US Justice Department and Exxon in its merger with Mobil.
**Career:** Joined Fried Frank as a Partner in 2001. Assistant Attorney General, in charge of the Antitrust Division of the US Justice Department (1986-89), Deputy Assistant Attorney General (1984-86).
**Personal:** JD (1981), University of Chicago Law School. BA (1978), Vanderbilt University.

## RUTKOWSKI, Joanne
Baker Botts LLP, Washington, DC
202 639 7785
joanne.rutkowski@bakerbotts.com
*Recommended in Energy*

**Practice Areas:** Partner in the Washington office. Has extensive experience in the area of regulatory matters under the federal securities laws. She regularly advises clients regarding governmental and regulatory procedures, both federal and state.
**Career:** Earlier in her career, Associate Director at the Securities and Exchange Commission and Trial Attorney at the US Department of Justice.
**Personal:** JD, Harvard Law School, 1983; BS (magna cum laude), Mathematics, Albright College, 1979.

## SABA, Peter B
Paul, Hastings, Janofsky & Walker LLP,
Washington, DC 202 551 1794
petersaba@paulhastings.com
*Recommended in Projects*

**Practice Areas:** Development and financing of energy and other infrastructure projects, both domestically and internationally. Concentrates on US government and multilateral guarantee, lending and risk insurance programs. International trade and investment matters.
**Career:** General Counsel (2001-05) and Chief Operating Officer (2003-05), US Export-Import Bank; Principal Deputy Assistant Secretary for Domestic and International Energy Policy (1991-93) and Counselor to the Deputy Secretary (1989-91), US Department of Energy; Adjunct Professor, Georgetown University Law Center (2004-06).
**Personal:** Harvard Law School (JD, 1985); University of Virginia (BA, 1982).

## SABAGH, Denyse
Duane Morris LLP, Washington, DC
202 776 7817
dsabagh@duanemorris.com
*Recommended in Immigration*

**Practice Areas:** Denyse Sabagh is the Head of Duane Morris' Immigration Practice Group. She practices in the areas of immigration and nationality law and litigation. Ms Sabagh has more than 25 years of experience in representing a diverse client base, helping corporate clients manage both inbound and outbound employment immigration. She also develops strategic business immigration programs and policies.
**Prof. Memberships:** American Bar Association; The District of Columbia Bar; The Virginia State Bar; Arlington County Bar Association; Fairfax County Bar Association; American Immigration Lawyers Association - Board of Governors, Legislative Advocacy Committee (Chair).
**Career:** Admitted to practice in the District of Columbia and Virginia; the United States District Court for the District of Columbia; United States District Court for the Eastern District of Virginia; United States District Court for the District of Maryland; Supreme Court of Virginia; and the Supreme Court of Maryland.
**Publications:** 'U.S. Immigration Requirements and Procedures for the Permanent Hire of Foreign Nurses', Medicom International, Long Term Care Interface, Volume 5 (12), pages 50-52, December 2004.
**Personal:** George Mason University Law School, JD, 1977; University of Maryland, BA, 1970.

## SACHER, Steven
Kilpatrick Stockton LLP, Washington, DC
202 508 5800
SSacher@KilpatrickStockton.com
*Recommended in Employee Benefits, ERISA Litigation*

**Practice Areas:** Mr Sacher is a Partner in the law firm of Kilpatrick Stockton LLP in Washington, DC. He counsels corporate clients on ERISA/employee benefits matters and represents them in the federal courts and before relevant federal agencies and congressional committees. Before entering private practice in 1981, was intimately involved in the development and drafting of ERISA during 1972-74, in its administration and enforcement during 1975-77, and in the legislative consideration and enactment of the Age Discrimination in Employment Act Amendments of 1978, and the Multiemployer Pension Plan Amendments Act of 1980.
**Prof. Memberships:** A charter Fellow of the American College of Employee Benefits Counsel and a Fellow of the College of Labor and Employment Lawyers, Mr Sacher lectures and publishes frequently on ERISA/employee benefits matters. He

co-chaired the Senior Editors of 'Employee Benefits Law' (Bureau of National Affairs, 1991, 2000), an annually-supplemented ERISA case law treatise, from its inception in 1991 until 2000.
**Career:** Mr Sacher is listed in 'The Best Lawyers in America' for Employee Benefits and Labor Law (continuously since 1988); The Top Benefits Lawyers, National Law Journal (1998); The Best Employee Benefits Lawyers, Corporate Counsel magazine (2003); 'Who's Who' (US, the East, Law (continuously since 1983)); and is ranked by 'Chambers USA' in 2005. BS, University of Wisconsin, with senior honors, 1964; JD, University of Chicago, 1967.

### SACHS, John
Latham & Watkins LLP, Washington, DC
202 637 2200
*Recommended in Projects*

### SACKS, Stephen
Arnold & Porter LLP, Washington, DC
202 942 5681
Stephen.Sacks@aporter.com
*Recommended in Litigation*
**Practice Areas:** Specializes in litigation, with particular emphasis on securities fraud and commercial disputes. He has also represented a number of corporate and accounting firm clients in investigations conducted by the SEC and in class actions alleging securities law violations. Representative clients include Fannie Mae, Motorola, Rhodia, PricewaterhouseCoopers, Deloitte & Touche, the PGA and Bear Stearns.
**Career:** Prior to joining Arnold & Porter LLP, Mr Sacks was Assistant to the General Counsel, Department of the Army.
**Personal:** LLB, Harvard Law School, 1966; BS, Cornell University, 1963.

### SAFIR, Peter
Covington & Burling, Washington, DC
202 662 5162
psafir@cov.com
*Recommended in Healthcare*
**Practice Areas:** Food and drug law.
**Career:** Mr Safir represented numerous research-based pharmaceutical and device companies on all aspects of US regulation, including drug/device approval and marketing, manufacturing and compliance issues. He advised PhRMA in drafting the new PhRMA Code and has advised many companies on complying with the Code as well as with Federal and State Anti-Kickback statutes. He has been a Professorial Lecturer in Food and Drug Law at George Washington University Law School since 1991.
**Personal:** BA Princeton University 1967; JD Yale Law School 1972.

### SALCIDO, Robert S
Akin Gump Strauss Hauer & Feld LLP, Washington, DC 202 887 4095
rsalcido@akingump.com

**Practice Areas:** Represents companies and individuals in responding to governmental investigations, in conducting internal investigations, and in defending False Claims Act and wrongful retaliation lawsuits brought by alleged whistleblowers, and provides counseling regarding the application of healthcare fraud and abuse laws. He has authored a treatise on the False Claims Act and lectured extensively on defenses to False Claims Act actions, healthcare coding compliance and fraud and abuse laws and voluntary disclosures.
**Personal:** BA, Claremont McKenna College; JD, Harvard Law School.

### SAMORAJCZYK, Stanley J
Akin Gump Strauss Hauer & Feld LLP, Washington, DC 202 887 4002
ssamorajczyk@akingump.com
*Recommended in Bankruptcy*
**Practice Areas:** Mr Samorajczyk represents debtors, creditors and other parties in complex national and cross-border restructuring, reorganization, insolvency and creditors' rights cases, often leading multidisciplinary teams of professionals in addressing clients' needs. He has lectured nationally and internationally on business reorganization and restructuring and has served as an expert witness on creditors' rights and reorganization.
**Prof. Memberships:** Fellow and Fourth Circuit Regent, American College of Bankruptcy; Co-Chairman, Mid-Atlantic Institute on Bankruptcy and Reorganization; Member, District of Columbia and Virginia Bars.
**Personal:** AB, Georgetown University; JD, Catholic University.

### SANER, Robert J
Powers Pyles Sutter & Verville PC, Washington, DC 202 466 6550
robert.saner@ppsv.com
*Recommended in Healthcare*
**Practice Areas:** Focuses on legislative and regulatory work for healthcare provider organizations, including professional societies, associations, hospitals, medical groups, academic practices and integrated systems. Mr Saner's environmental and public health practice focuses on the regulation of municipal water utilities under the federal Safe Drinking Water Act and includes emerging issues in public infrastructure protection and homeland security.
**Prof. Memberships:** DC Bar; American Health Lawyers Association.
**Career:** Currently President and Executive Committee Chairman, Powers Pyles Sutter & Verville, PC; General Counsel, National Organization on Disability; and Washington Counsel, Medical Group Management Association. Prior to joining PPSV, Mr Saner was a Partner in White, Verville, Fulton and Saner in Washington, DC. From 1972 to 1974, he

served in the United States Department of Health, Education and Welfare and the Executive Office of the President.
**Personal:** JD, Harvard, 1972; AB, Princeton, 1969.

### SANFORD, Bruce
Baker & Hostetler LLP, Washington, DC
202 861 1621
*Recommended in Media & Entertainment*

### SAYLER, Robert
Covington & Burling, Washington, DC
202 662 6000
RSayler@cov.com
*Recommended in Insurance, Litigation*
**Practice Areas:** A Partner who has been lead counsel for successful insurance policyholders in billion dollar-plus insurance coverage disputes for asbestos, DES, environmental clean-up, and breast implant liabilities; acting for Armstrong World Industries, Boeing, Pittston, Dow Corning, 3M, Monsanto, Exxon, Procter & Gamble, ITT, National Medical Enterprises and the National Football League.
**Prof. Memberships:** Fellow of the American College of Trial Lawyers and the American Bar Foundation; CPR DC Panel of Distinguished Arbitration Neutrals; and the CPR Commission on the Future of Arbitration.
**Career:** 1965-present, Covington & Burling.
**Personal:** LLB from Harvard University and an AB from Stanford University.

### SCALIA, Eugene
Gibson, Dunn & Crutcher LLP, Washington, DC 202 955 8500
escalia@gibsondunn.com
*Recommended in Employment*
**Practice Areas:** Co-Chair of the firm's Labor and Employment Practice Group and Chair of the Administrative Law and Regulatory Practice Group. Experienced in a broad range of labor and employment matters (including discrimination law, labor relations, and ERISA) and regulatory matters involving SEC, FCC, Department of Transportation, and other agencies.
**Career:** 2002-03, Solicitor of Labor: principal legal officer, Department of Labor, responsible for government litigation involving ERISA, OSHA, Family/Medical Leave Act, wage-hour requirements, and Sarbanes-Oxley. 1992-93, Special Assistant, Attorney General of US.
**Publications:** More than 30 articles and papers.
**Personal:** JD, University of Chicago: Editor-in-Chief, Law Review.

### SCHATZ, Gordon B
Reed Smith LLP, Washington, DC
202 414 9259
gschatz@reedsmith.com
*Recommended in Healthcare*
**Practice Areas:** Represents device, drug

and diagnostic manufacturers on technology reimbursement issues. Helps firms obtain coverage, codes and payment to advance product development and to link reimbursement with strategic planning and marketing.
**Prof. Memberships:** American Health Lawyers Association, Health Law Sections of the District of Columbia and Maryland Bar Associations.
**Career:** Associate General Counsel and Assistant Secretary for the Health Industry Manufacturers Association, now AdvaMed.
**Publications:** Author of numerous articles and chapters in various publications and books.
**Personal:** Temple University School of Law (JD, 1980), Barristers Award for Excellence in Trial Advocacy; Haverford College (BA, 1974).

### SCHECHTER, Mark
Howrey LLP, Washington, DC
202 783 0800
*Recommended in Antitrust*

### SCHERMAN, William S
Skadden, Arps, Slate, Meagher & Flom LLP & Affiliates, Washington, DC
202 371 7060
wscherma@skadden.com
*Recommended in Energy*
**Practice Areas:** Provides strategic, commercial, regulatory, legislative and litigation advice to clients regarding US and international energy markets. At FERC, played a key role in a number of major pro-competitive policy initiatives. For example, helped guide FERC's efforts to foster greater competition in the electric utility industry, contributed to the development of the Energy Policy Act of 1992 and testified before Congress on numerous occasions with regard to legislation and other energy policy-related matters.
**Career:** JD, University of Louisville School of Law, 1984 (articles editor, Law Review); BA, George Washington University, 1980.

### SCHERTLER, David
Schertler & Onorato LLP, Washington, DC 202 628 4199
*Recommended in Litigation*

### SCHIFF, Janis
Holland & Knight LLP, Washington, DC
202 955 3000
janis.schiff@hklaw.com
*Recommended in Real Estate*
**Practice Areas:** Marketing Partner and member of Real Estate Section, focusing her practice in retail and office development and leasing. She founded and continues to oversee the firm's Rising Stars program, a year-long professional development program that provides hands-on leadership, marketing and management training, and professional mentoring for women attorneys who have practiced for seven or more years. Schiff is an active

member of the DC and Suburban Maryland Chapters of Commercial Real Estate Women (CREW), Women in Retail Real Estate (WIRRE), and an Adjunct Professor in the Allan L Berman Real Estate Institute Program at The Johns Hopkins University.

**SCHILDKRAUT, Marc**
Heller Ehrman LLP, Washington, DC
202 912 2140
marc.schildkraut@hellerehrman.com
*Recommended in Antitrust*
**Practice Areas:** Antitrust and trade regulation.
**Prof. Memberships:** District of Columbia Bar; New York State Bar; American Bar Association.
**Career:** Mr Schildkraut practices antitrust law before US and international enforcement agencies and the courts, focusing on mergers, civil investigations and antitrust litigation. In the merger area, he has obtained agency clearance in every case in which he was lead attorney. Previously, he served at the Federal Trade Commission for 17 years in various positions, including Assistant Director for the Bureau of Competition.
**Personal:** Columbia College (BS, magna cum laude, 1973); Columbia University School of Law (JD, 1976).

**SCHLOSSBERG, Bob**
Freshfields Bruckhaus Deringer LLP, Washington, DC 202 777 4500
*Recommended in Antitrust*

**SCHMIDT, William**
Kirkpatrick & Lockhart Nicholson Graham LLP, Washington, DC
202 778 9000
*Recommended in Employee Benefits*

**SCHNEIDER, Leslie**
Ivins, Phillips & Barker, Washington, DC
202 393 7600
*Recommended in Tax*

**SCHROEDER, Jeffrey P**
Paul, Hastings, Janofsky & Walker LLP, Washington, DC 202 551 1789
jeffschroeder@paulhastings.com
*Recommended in Projects*
**Practice Areas:** Practice focuses on project development and finance (both domestic and international), restructuring of financing and commercial arrangements for projects and stock and asset acquisitions and dispositions.
**Prof. Memberships:** Member, District of Columbia Bar.
**Publications:** Co-author: 'Regulatory Considerations for Cross-Border Power Plant Development' (Project Finance, September 2001).
**Personal:** BA, University of Virginia; JD, Washington and Lee (cum laude).

**SCHUELKE III, Henry**
Janis Schuelke & Wechsler, Washington, DC 202 861 0600
*Recommended in Litigation*

**SCHUHMACHER, Kenneth**
Latham & Watkins LLP, Washington, DC
202 637 2200
*Recommended in Projects*

**SCHWARTZ, David**
Latham & Watkins LLP, Washington, DC
202 637 2200
*Recommended in Energy*

**SECREST III, Lawrence W**
Wiley Rein & Fielding LLP, Washington, DC 202 719 7074
lsecrest@wrf.com
*Recommended in Telecom, Broadcast & Satellite*
**Practice Areas:** Chairs the firm's nationally renowned Media Group. Counsels and represents clients on regulations governing broadcasters, cable television, satellite television and other electronic media, as well as international telecommunications matters.
**Prof. Memberships:** Member, Federal Communications Bar Association.
**Career:** Deputy General Counsel, Federal Communications Commission; Chief of Staff to Chairman Richard E Wiley, Federal Communications Commission.
**Personal:** The George Washington University Law School (JD); American University (BA).

**SHAPIRO, Howard**
Van Ness Feldman PC, Washington, DC
202 298 1800
*Recommended in Energy*

**SHAPIRO, Howard**
WilmerHale, Washington, DC
202 663 6606
howard.shapiro@wilmerhale.com
*Recommended in Litigation*
**Practice Areas:** Co-Chair, Litigation Department; member Executive Committee. Focus: white-collar criminal defense, complex civil litigation, internal investigations. Conducts sensitive internal investigations for major banking and corporate clients in connection with franchise-threatening regulatory and criminal probes in US, England, and Asia.
**Career:** General Counsel, Federal Bureau of Investigation; Assistant United States Attorney, Southern District of New York; Associate Professor of Law, Cornell Law School. Awarded the National Intelligence Distinguished Service Medal by the Director of Central Intelligence for his efforts to improve relations between that agency and the FBI.
**Personal:** JD, Yale Law School; AB, Williams College.

**SHAPIRO, Robert**
Chadbourne & Parke LLP, Washington, DC 202 974 5670
rshapiro@chadbourne.com
*Recommended in Energy*
**Practice Areas:** Project finance, utility and energy law, representing firms and developers that build, finance, own, operate, sell and use energy output from

renewable resource, cogeneration, waste to energy, and conventional power facilities in the US and abroad. Also representation of investors and lenders to these facilities. Extensive experience in negotiating power purchase agreements, tolling agreements, other standard hedging agreements, fuel and operating and maintenance agreements, and the defense of long-term power contracts before federal and state regulatory agencies and courts. Worked on numerous power project developments, financings and privatizations in Latin America.
**Career:** FERC, 1977-84.

**SHAPIRO, Stephen Brett**
Holland & Knight LLP, Washington, DC
202 955 3000
stephen.shapiro@hklaw.com
*Recommended in Construction*
**Practice Areas:** Partner in the Litigation Section, focuses his practice on construction law, public contracts and commercial litigation. Building on his experience representing contractors, public and private owners, architects, engineers and construction managers, he has developed extensive legal experience in all aspects of construction procurement, administration, claims, government contract and construction litigation, proposal preparation, bid protests, contract management, regulatory compliance and subcontractor, supplier and surety relations. Shapiro also has significant experience with legal issues arising from building defects and mold and is a frequent speaker on topics relevant to the construction industry.

**SHARER, Paul L**
Mayer, Brown, Rowe & Maw LLP, Washington, DC 202 263 3340
psharer@mayerbrownrowe.com
*Recommended in Intellectual Property*
**Practice Areas:** Extensive intellectual property counseling expertise in handling a broad range of intellectual property issues in the biotech/pharma/medical device industry. In particular, Mr Sharer's expertise includes Hatch-Waxman issues and product life cycle management expertise. Mr Sharer's extensive experience includes counseling clients through transactions, for example acquisitions and divestitures and financings for intellectual property intensive businesses as well as patent litigation and interferences, patent licenses and joint development agreements. Mr Sharer has assisted many clients in developing and strategically managing large patent estates and is frequently called upon to render patentability, validity, non-willfulness, and clearance opinions.
**Career:** Mayer, Brown, Rowe & Maw LLP, Washington, DC, 2004 to date. Pillsbury Winthrop LLP, Washington, DC, 1997-2004; Member of the Office Management Committee, 2001-04; Managing Partner, DC Office, 2000-01. Dickinson,

Wright, Moon, Van Dusen & Freeman, Washington, DC, 1995-97. ICI Americas, Inc., Wilmington, DE, 1991-95.
**Personal:** JD, Widener University School of Law, 1991. BSc Ch Eng, Drexel University, 1985. Mr Sharer is a frequent lecturer at national/international forums such as the PharmalQ - Patent Litigation & Protection Conference, GCTBIO International Conference on Vaccines and was recently featured in the Business Section of the Washington Post.

**SHONEMAN, Charles H**
Bracewell & Giuliani LLP, Washington, DC 202 828 5860
charles.shoneman@bracewellgiuliani.com
*Recommended in Energy*
**Practice Areas:** Expertise includes federal and state energy regulatory matters before the Federal Energy Regulatory Commission, Department of Energy, Department of Interior, various state public utility commissions, and appellate courts. Practice includes project authorization, ratemaking, compliance, regulatory litigation and enforcement matters. Advises clients with respect to the regulatory aspects of project development, commercial transactions, mergers and acquisitions, financings and litigation; federal royalty matters; natural gas and electric import and export matters; liquefied natural gas matters; and the restructuring of the gas and electric industries.
**Personal:** JD, with honors, The George Washington University Law School, 1972; BA, Duke University, 1969.

**SHULMAN, Robert**
Howrey LLP, Washington, DC
202 783 0800
*Recommended in Insurance*

**SIEGEL, Nathan**
Levine Sullivan Koch & Schulz LLP, Washington, DC
202 508 1100
*Recommended in Media & Entertainment*

**SIKORA, Clifford**
Troutman Sanders LLP, Washington, DC
202 274 2950
*Recommended in Energy*

**SILBERG, Jay**
Pillsbury Winthrop Shaw Pittman LLP, Washington, DC
202 663 8063
Jay.Silberg@pillsburylaw.com
*Recommended in Energy*
**Practice Areas:** Chair of firm's Energy Section. Represents electric utilities, nuclear suppliers, utility groups, nuclear waste facilities, government entities, and others on the regulatory, litigation, transactional and other aspects of their nuclear-related projects and enterprises. Has appeared on behalf of these clients before the Nuclear Regulatory Commission, the Department of Energy, state regulatory agencies, the courts, and Con-

gress in all phases of nuclear licensing, regulation, enforcement, and litigation. Advises US and international clients on nuclear-related transactions. Has led industry-wide litigation on key nuclear issues.

**Personal:** JD, Harvard Law School, 1966; BA, Amherst College, 1963 (cum laude).

## SILBERT, Earl
DLA Piper Rudnick Gray Cary US LLP, Washington, DC 202 861 6250
earl.silbert@dlapiper.com
*Recommended in Litigation*

**Practice Areas:** Litigation; professional liability and ethics; white-collar.

**Prof. Memberships:** President, American College of Trial Lawyers, 2000-01; Master of Bench, American Inn of Court.

**Career:** He had a distinguished career in public service before entering private practice, including five years in the US Department of Justice, service as the first Watergate prosecutor, and five years as the US Attorney for the District of Columbia. He has lectured and authored numerous articles on evidence, the attorney-client and work product privileges, RICO, and representations in grand jury investigations.

**Personal:** LLB, Harvard Law School; BA, Harvard University.

## SILVERMAN, Mark
Steptoe & Johnson LLP, Washington, DC
202 429 6450
msilverman@steptoe.com
*Recommended in Tax*

**Practice Areas:** Head of the Tax Practice and Partner in the Washington office of Steptoe & Johnson LLP. Practice focuses on corporate tax transaction and planning matters. Has extensive experience in structuring acquisitions, mergers, and spin-off transactions for large public corporations as well as closely held businesses. Focuses on the resolution of tax policy and administrative issues before Congress and the Treasury Department. Handles significant audit and controversy matters with the IRS, including resolution of tax shelter matters on behalf of promoters and investors.

**Personal:** LLM, New York University School of Law, 1971; JD, Suffolk University Law School, 1970.

## SIMON, Cathy
Ross Dixon & Bell LLP, Washington, DC
202 662 2000
*Recommended in Insurance*

## SIMONS, Joseph J
Paul, Weiss, Rifkind, Wharton & Garrison LLP, Washington, DC
202 223 7370
jsimons@paulweiss.com
*Recommended in Antitrust*

**Practice Areas:** Co-Chair of Antitrust Group. Former Director of Bureau of Competition at the Federal Trade Commission (FTC). Has extensive experience

representing clients before the FTC, Department of Justice (DOJ), Department of Defense, and Congress in a wide range of antitrust and regulatory matters. Appointed by DOJ and Federal Communications Commission as trustee for wireless telephone businesses relating to the GTE/ Bell Atlantic/ Vodafone and Cingular/ AT&T Wireless transactions. Co-developer of 'Critical Cost Analysis', technique for market definition that has been adopted and used by DOJ, FTC, and the US Court of Appeals. Has published a wide range of articles on antitrust-related topics.

## SIMS, Joe
Jones Day, Washington, DC
202 879 3863
jsims@jonesday.com
*Recommended in Antitrust*

**Practice Areas:** Concentrates in antitrust and related areas of government regulation, including litigation, counseling, and agency practice before state and federal courts, antitrust enforcement agencies, and various specialized agencies. He has especially broad experience in mergers and acquisitions and with the antitrust issues involving the technology, telecommunications, and electronic media industries. Regularly recognized as a leading antitrust lawyer worldwide.

**Prof. Memberships:** Fellow of the American Bar Foundation. ABA. The American Law Institute. Serves on the Executive Committee of the Institute for Law and Technology of The Center for American and International Law.

## SINEL, Norman
Arnold & Porter LLP, Washington, DC
202 942 5222
Norman.Sinel@aporter.com
*Recommended in Telecom, Broadcast & Satellite*

**Practice Areas:** Norman Sinel has practiced communications law since 1971. Experienced in development and regulation of new technologies, he has counseled communications companies, governmental agencies, and local governments on legislative issues, project development and implementation matters, franchising and licensing needs, and transactional requirements. Mr Sinel has also represented clients on administrative matters before the Federal Communications Commission.

**Career:** Prior to joining Arnold & Porter LLP, he served as Senior Vice President and General Counsel of the Public Broadcasting Service.

**Publications:** PLI Cable Law (annually).

**Personal:** LLB, Stanford Law School, 1966; BA, Yale University, 1963.

## SINHA, Pankaj K
Skadden, Arps, Slate, Meagher & Flom LLP & Affiliates, Washington, DC
202 371 7307
psinha@skadden.com

*Recommended in Corporate/Commercial*

**Practice Areas:** Concentrates his practice in the areas of mergers and acquisitions, corporate finance, and general corporate and securities matters and has represented purchasers, sellers and their financial advisors in transactions, including public and private acquisitions and divestitures, negotiated and contested public acquisitions, auctions, going private transactions, proxy fights, initial public offerings and other financings, and joint ventures and other strategic alliances. Also advises clients on general corporate and securities matters, including securities law compliance, disclosure issues, stock repurchase programs, joint ventures, shareholder agreements, corporate governance matters, annual meetings and proxy contests.

**Prof. Memberships:** Vice-Chairman, Corporate Finance Committee, The Bar Association of the District of Columbia (1997-2000), Director, Maryland India Business Roundtable.

**Career:** JD, Georgetown University Law Center, 1990, MBA, Georgetown University, 1990, AB, Columbia College, Columbia University, 1986.

## SIRILLA, George M
Pillsbury Winthrop Shaw Pittman LLP, McLean 703 905 2000
*Recommended in Intellectual Property*

**Practice Areas:** Mr Sirilla has led teams that successfully upheld as well as invalidated patents in numerous cases, both in the federal courts and before the US International Trade Commission. He has considerable experience in technology licensing, patents and trade secrets, and in litigating disputes over such licenses.

**Personal:** JD, Georgetown University Law Center; BS, Rensselaer Polytechnic Institute (Mechanical Engineering, Tau Beta Pi and Pi Tau Sigma national engineering honor societies).

## SKELLY, Paul
Hogan & Hartson LLP, Washington, DC
202 637 8614
pcskelly@hhlaw.com
*Recommended in Employment*

**Practice Areas:** Counsels on employment practices and compliance with employment law requirements; employment litigation; class action defense; labor union-management relations; noncompetition/trade secrets litigation; union organizing campaigns, collective bargaining, and administrative proceedings before the NLRB; executive compensation and employment agreements.

**Prof. Memberships:** ABA; VABA.

**Career:** Partner since 1988.

**Publications:** 'Update on the New FLSA's New Regulatory Regime'. Hogan & Hartson L.L.P. Employment Law & Strategies for a Global Economy, Hogan & Hartson L.L.P. (5/9/2005).

**Personal:** University of Virginia School of Law (JD, 1979); University of Virginia (BA, 1976).

## SKINNER, William P
Covington & Burling, Washington, DC
202 662 5470
wskinner@cov.com
*Recommended in Insurance*

**Practice Areas:** Areas include insurance coverage litigation, insurance advice, group captive insurers and general litigation. Extensive experience with general liability, errors and omissions, D&O and first party-property policies written on a variety of insurance forms, including US forms, Bermuda forms and London forms. Clients include manufacturers of industrial products, utilities, pharmaceutical companies, banks, mutual funds and other financial services companies. Insurance litigation experience includes the: Armstrong Non-Products ADR; 3M Breast Implant Litigation; Dow Corning Breast Implant Litigation; PSE&G environmental coverage case; and Coordinated California Asbestos Coverage Cases.

**Personal:** JD, Harvard Law School, 1975, magna cum laude; BA, Harvard College, 1972.

## SMALL, Michael
Wright & Talisman PC, Washington, DC
202 393 1200
*Recommended in Energy*

## SMITH, Douglas
Van Ness Feldman PC, Washington, DC
202 298 1800
*Recommended in Energy*

## SMITH, Paul
Jenner & Block LLP, Washington, DC
202 639 6060
psmith@jenner.com
*Recommended in Litigation, Media & Entertainment*

**Practice Areas:** Paul M Smith is a Partner in Jenner & Block's Washington, DC office and Member of the firm's Management Committee. He is Co-Chair of the Appellate and Supreme Court, and Media and First Amendment Practices and is a Member of the Litigation & Dispute Resolution Practice. Mr Smith has had an active Supreme Court Practice for two decades, including oral arguments in twelve Supreme Court cases. These arguments have included two recent congressional redistricting cases (Vieth v Jubelirer and LULAC v Perry), Lawrence v Texas, involving the constitutionality of the Texas sodomy statute, United States v American Library Ass'n, involving a First Amendment challenge to the Children's Internet Protection Act and Mathias v WorldCom (2001), dealing with the Eleventh Amendment immunity of state commissions. His first argument was in Celotox Corp. v Catrett in 1986. He also worked extensively on other First Amendment cases in the Supreme Court,

including Rubin v Coors (1995), dealing with restrictions on beer labeling, Reno v ACLU (1997), involving a challenge to content restrictions for the internet in the Communications Decency Act, and Masson v New Yorker Magazine, Inc. (1991), a significant defamation case. Mr Smith also represents clients in trial and appellate cases involving commercial and telecommunications issues, the First Amendment, intellectual property, antitrust, and redistricting and voting rights, among other areas. His recent trial work has included several cases involving congressional redistricting as well as challenges to State video game restrictions under the First Amendment.
**Personal:** Yale Law School, JD, 1979.

### SMITH, Roger
Troutman Sanders LLP, Washington, DC
202 274 2950
*Recommended in Energy*

### SMITH, Tefft W
Kirkland & Ellis LLP, Washington, DC
202 879 5212
tsmith@kirkland.com
*Recommended in Antitrust*
**Practice Areas:** Tefft heads Kirkland & Ellis' 125+ person Antitrust Practice, an integrated team of lawyers with offices in Washington DC, Chicago, London, Los Angeles, New York, Munich and San Francisco. He has 35 years of trial experience and has managed high profile government criminal and civil antitrust cases for many major US and international companies. He has managed scores of sensitive multinational transactions through the merger clearance process, requiring coordination of US, EU, member-state, and other national filings. Tefft has tried more than 25 cases to verdict and argued cases before judges and juries throughout the US, including before the US Supreme Court.
**Personal:** Brown University, BA, 1968. University of Chicago, JD, 1971.

### SMITH, Wm Randolph
Crowell & Moring LLP, Washington, DC
202 624 2700
wrsmith@crowell.com
*Recommended in Antitrust*
**Practice Areas:** Senior Partner at Crowell & Moring, a Member of the executive and Management Board, and Chair of the firm's Antitrust Group. Practice involves mergers/ acquisitions/ joint ventures/ trade association law/ cartel enforcement and the intersection of antitrust laws and intellectual property. Recent matters include advising SBC in its acquisition of AT&T Corp. and SBC/Cingular Wireless in its acquisition of AT&T Wireless. Served as antitrust counsel for United Technologies Corp. and its Pratt & Whitney division in the proposed acquisition of Boeing Co.'s Rocketdyne liquid space propulsion and power unit. Other principal clients

include Alcoa/CSX Transportation/DuPont/Georgia-Pacific/United Technologies Corporation.
**Career:** Prior to joining the firm in 1981, completed six years of service with the FTC, where positions included serving as executive assistant to the Chairman.

### SMITH JR, Turner T
Hunton & Williams, Washington, DC
202 955 1692
tsmith@hunton.com
*Recommended in Environment*
**Practice Areas:** Turner Smith's international Environmental Law Practice focuses on international environmental and energy law, and involves policy, transactional and litigation work, as well as regulatory reform and US regulatory work. He is the Head of Hunton & Williams' International Environmental Practice and the former resident Managing Partner of the firm's Brussels office, and has specialized in energy and environmental law for over 25 years.

### SMOYER, Divonne
Dickstein Shapiro Morin & Oshinsky LLP, Washington, DC  202 572 2665
SmoyerD@dsmo.com
*Recommended in Insurance*
**Practice Areas:** Negotiation and litigation involving complex, multiparty disputes pertaining to asbestos, silicone implants, pharmaceutical products, insurance coverage disputes, and other mass torts. Successfully represented policyholders in insurance disputes for directors and officers, and errors and omissions liabilities.
**Career:** Counsel; previously, an attorney with Kaye Scholer, LLP and Gilbert Heintz & Randolph, LLP, and a mediator with the Bickerman Dispute Resolution Group, PLLC. Taught courses on negotiation and alternative dispute resolution at the Georgetown University Law Center and The George Washington University Law School.
**Personal:** Harvard Law School (JD, 1995); Smith College (BA, 1992).

### SMYTHE, Marianne
WilmerHale, Washington, DC
202 663 6711
marianne.smythe@wilmerhale.com
*Recommended in Investment Management*
**Practice Areas:** Advises and represents banks, investment banking firms, mutual funds and other investment companies, investment advisors, pension fund administrators and insurance companies on investment company, investment advisor, and broker-dealer regulatory issues, related issues affecting banks and pension funds and other matters involving investment and financial products.
**Career:** Director, Division of Investment Management, US Securities and Exchange Commission. Professor and Assistant Provost, University of North

Carolina at Chapel Hill School of Law.
**Personal:** JD, University of North Carolina at Chapel Hill; BS, Bucknell University.

### SNYDER, Lynn Shapiro
Epstein Becker & Green PC, Washington, DC 202 861 0900
lsnyder@ebglaw.com
*Recommended in Healthcare*
**Practice Areas:** Assists clients in navigating federal, state and international health regulatory issues, such as healthcare providers, payors, pharmaceutical/device manufacturers and those companies and financial services firms that support the healthcare industry. Specializes in legal and regulatory matters arising under third-party payment programs such as Medicare, Medicaid and TRI-CARE. Also focuses on federal and state fraud issues, including anti-kickback, self-referral, false claims, secondary payor issues, and false billings.
**Prof. Memberships:** American Health Lawyers Association; Founding Member, Health on Wednesday - A group of Women Health Policy Makers; American Bar Association, Health Care White Collar Crime Committee; National Association of Criminal Defense Lawyers; Food and Drug Law Institute; Founder and Board Member of the Women Business Leaders of the US Health Care Industry Foundation.
**Publications:** Is a frequent speaker and publishes extensively on Medicare, Medicaid, managed care and a variety of health law issues. Has been quoted in The New York Times and other leading publications.
**Personal:** JD, George Washington University Law School, 1979. AB, Franklin & Marshall College, Phi Beta Kappa, Economics with Health Economics concentration, magna cum laude, 1976.

### SOHN, Michael N
Arnold & Porter LLP, Washington, DC
202 942 5000
Michael.Sohn@aporter.com
*Recommended in Antitrust*
**Practice Areas:** Mike Sohn, Chairman of Arnold & Porter LLP, maintains a substantial antitrust practice of international scope. A former general counsel of the Federal Trade Commission, his practice encompasses a broad range of antitrust and consumer protection matters, with particular focus on the antitrust aspects of mergers and acquisitions and treble damage class actions. He has represented such clients as Adobe Systems Incorporated, Boston Scientific Corporation, Brunswick Corporation, General Electric Company, Hoffmann-La Roche Inc., Homestore.com, Intel Corporation, Merck & Company, Inc., NASDAQ, Nucor, Occidental Petroleum Corporation, PepsiCo, Inc., Sanofi-Synthelabo and Wyeth (formerly American Home

Products Corporation) in merger investigations and litigations before the FTC and the Justice Department.
**Career:** During his tenure as General Counsel of the FTC, he was designated a Council Member of the Administrative Conference of the United States and a Member of the Executive Committee of the Regulatory Council of the United States.
**Publications:** Mr Sohn is a contributing author to 'The Ernst & Young Management Guide to Mergers and Acquisitions'. He has written a variety of articles of interest in the antitrust field including an overview of the Department of Justice's high profile monopolization suit entitled 'The Microsoft Case' and an article on merger remedies entitled 'Crown Jewel Provisions in Merger Consent Decrees'.
**Personal:** Successive editions of Chambers & Partners' USA and Global surveys of 'The World's Leading Lawyers' have named Mr Sohn as one of the five top-ranked antitrust attorneys in Washington, DC. Euromoney's 2004 and 2005 'Best of the Best' named Mr Sohn one of the world's leading lawyers in competition and antitrust. Most recently, the Legal Times recognized him as a 'Leading Antitrust Lawyer in Washington, DC' for 2005.

### SOTTILE, James
Zuckerman Spaeder LLP, Washington, DC 202 778 1800
*Recommended in Insurance*

### SPARTIN, Debbie B
Pillsbury Winthrop Shaw Pittman LLP, Washington, DC
202 663 8526
debbie.spartin@pillsburylaw.com
*Recommended in Real Estate*
**Practice Areas:** Ms Spartin regularly represents a wide variety of clients with respect to all phases of commercial real estate, including the purchase and sale of office buildings, shopping centers, industrial and flex space, as well as raw land for development, the leasing of office and retail space, including build-to-suit leasing transactions, and construction and permanent financing secured by real estate assets.
**Prof. Memberships:** American Bar Association, District of Columbia Building Industry Association, The Real Estate Group of Washington, DC.
**Personal:** JD, Harvard Law School, 1987; BA, University of Virginia, 1984.

### SPECTOR, Barry S
Wright & Talisman PC, Washington, DC
202 393 1200
*Recommended in Energy*

### SPIVAK, Mark
Vinson & Elkins LLP, Washington, DC
202 639 6664
mspivak@velaw.com
*Recommended in Projects*
**Practice Areas:** Development, financ-

ing and restructuring of US and overseas infrastructure projects, including energy, telecommunications and other infrastructure and industrial projects. Mergers, acquisitions and dispositions of infrastructure assets, and companies owning infrastructure assets. Advise clients in connection with obtaining political risk insurance from multilateral institutions and private insurers.

**Prof. Memberships:** District of Columbia Bar.

**Career:** Partner at V&E since 1994.

**Personal:** Georgetown University Law Center (JD, 1983); Muhlenberg College (BA, 1980).

## STAMAS, George
Kirkland & Ellis LLP, Washington, DC
202 879 5090
gstamas@kirkland.com
*Recommended in Corporate/Commercial*

**Practice Areas:** Mr Stamas is a Senior Partner of Kirkland & Ellis LLP, dividing his time between the Washington, DC and New York offices. For the past two decades, Mr Stamas has been the lead legal advisor on numerous public and private corporate transactions, including most recently the $2.8 billion merger between Constellation Energy and FPL Group, the $1.6 billion management buyout of DB Capital Partners, the largest private equity secondary, as well as corporate transactions for numerous leading companies and financial institutions such as MidOcean and NEA, and leading sports franchise acquisitions.

**Personal:** University of Pennsylvania, BS, 1973; University of Maryland School of Law, JD, 1976.

## STANDISH, Daniel J
Wiley Rein & Fielding LLP, Washington, DC 202 719 7130
dstandish@wrf.com
*Recommended in Insurance*

**Practice Areas:** Leads the firm's Professional Liability Practice. Nationally recognized as a leading attorney in professional liability insurance coverage matters and disputes, he has more than 20 years of experience counseling insurance clients on issues relating to directors and officers liability and other professional liability lines of coverage and representing professional liability insurers in coverage litigation before federal and state courts across the country.

**Prof. Memberships:** Professional Liability Underwriting Society: Member, Board of Trustees; Chairperson, Editorial Board; Chairperson, Communications Committee.

**Career:** Assistant US Attorney for the District of Columbia.

**Personal:** The University of Chicago Law School (JD); Bowdoin College (BA).

## STARR, Judson
Venable LLP, Washington, DC
202 962 4800

*Recommended in Environment*

## STARR, Kenneth W
Kirkland & Ellis LLP, Los Angeles
213 680 8400
*Recommended in Litigation*

**Practice Areas:** Appointed Dean of Pepperdine University Law School in the summer of 2004. Remains of counsel to Kirkland & Ellis which he joined in February 1993. In August 1994, he was appointed Independent Counsel on the Whitewater matter and served until October 1999. From May 27, 1989 to January 20, 1993, he served as Solicitor General of the United States, where he argued 25 cases before the Supreme Court involving a wide range of governmental regulatory and constitutional issues of commercial importance. Prior to that, he served as a United States Circuit Judge appointed on October 11, 1983.

**Personal:** Brown University, AM, 1969. George Washington University, AB, 1968. Duke Law School, JD, 1973.

## STEINBERG, Michael W
Morgan, Lewis & Bockius LLP, Washington, DC 202 739 5141
msteinberg@morganlewis.com
*Recommended in Environment*

**Practice Areas:** Michael Steinberg is Senior Counsel in the Litigation Practice. His practice focuses exclusively on environmental law matters, with special emphasis on litigation and counseling involving (1) hazardous waste issues under the Resource Conservation and Recovery Act, (2) liability, cleanup, and enforcement issues under the federal Superfund program, and (3) environmental justice issues under federal and state civil rights laws. Mr Steinberg rejoined Morgan Lewis after serving as Assistant Chief of the Environmental Defense Section at the US Department of Justice, where he supervised and handled litigation against EPA under all of the federal environmental statutes. Among his better-known cases are Missouri v Westinghouse, No. 4:03CV1318 (ED Mo March 11, 2004) (obtained complete dismissal of complaint seeking Natural Resource Damages); Hercules Inc. v US Army Corps of Engineers (DDC 2002) (successful contribution action against Army Corps of Engineers for disposal of contaminated dredge spoil); and United States v Olin Corp., 927 F Supp 1502 (SD Ala 1996) (holding CERCLA unconstitutional as applied to purely intrastate contamination), rev'd, 107 F3d 1506 (11th Cir 1997); Mr Steinberg is counsel to the Superfund Settlements Project, and has testified before Congress on such issues as liability and remedy selection.

**Prof. Memberships:** American Bar Association; District of Columbia Bar Association.

## STEPHENSON, Andrew W
Holland & Knight LLP, Washington, DC
202 955 3000
andrew.stephenson@hklaw.com
*Recommended in Construction*

**Practice Areas:** Partner-in-Charge of the Construction Industry Practice Group, practices in the areas of construction and labor law, representing owners, architect-engineers, general contractors, and construction managers in virtually all phases of the private and public sectors of the industry. Stephenson's construction experience covers the drafting and negotiation of construction contract documents, counsel during project administration, and dispute resolution on a wide-range of both medium size and large, complex building and infrastructure projects including billion dollar design-build projects. He also has been involved in the construction of numerous power generation facilities, including both nuclear and fossil fuel power plants.

## STERN, Elizabeth E
Baker & McKenzie, Washington, DC
202 452 7055
elizabeth.e.stern@bakernet.com
*Recommended in Immigration*

**Practice Areas:** Works in a wide range of cross-border global disciplines, including immigration, tax, employment, benefits, corporate formation, and policy, that are essential to the movement of employees across borders in a variety of industry sectors, including financial services, information technology and telecommunications, multimedia, and manufacturing.

**Prof. Memberships:** ABA; District of Columbia and Virginia Bar Associations; US Chamber of Commerce; American Immigration Lawyers Association; and Society for Human Resources Management.

**Career:** Principal Shareholder, Baker McKenzie, LLP, Global Migration & Executive Transfers Section, Washington, DC (2005 to present); Partner and Leader of Business Immigration Practice, Pillsbury Winthrop Shaw Pittman (1986-2005).

**Publications:** Authored, 'Keep Us Competitive: Businesses Require More Visa Slots To Fill Need For Foreign Professionals', ALM Legal Times, October 24, 2005; ALI-ABA Immigration Law: Basics and More, Treaty Traders/Treaty Investors (E Visas) and Intracompany Tranferees (L-1 Visas), May 24, 2005; Security Delays Hurt US Business, Legal Times, August 23, 2004 vol XXVII, no 34, August 23, 2004; How to Navigate in the US Visa System, WorkIndex.com, May 3, 2004; Immigration Laws May Hurt Offshore Outsourcing, New York Law Journal, Volume 7, no 5, October 27, 2003.

**Personal:** JD, University of Virginia School of Law, 1986; BA, University of Virginia, magna cum laude, 1983.

## STERNE, Robert
Sterne, Kessler, Goldstein & Fox P.L.L.C., Washington, DC 202 772 8555
rsterne@skgf.com
*Recommended in Intellectual Property*

**Practice Areas:** Mr Sterne is recognized as a thought leader on board of director responsibility and best practices concerning intellectual property. He specializes in the area of intellectual property for cutting edge technologies in the electronics and computer arenas, the monetization of patents and patent licensing.

**Career:** Founding Partner, Director of Sterne, Kessler, Goldstein & Fox P.L.L.C. and its predecessor firms. Internationally recognized as a thought leader and an expert on software and business method patents having been lead attorney for IBM in the Federal Circuit case that led to the USPTO Software Patent Guidelines.

## STEVENS, Michael L
Arent Fox PLLC, Washington, DC
202 857 6382
stevens.michael@arentfox.com
*Recommended in Employment*

**Practice Areas:** Represents management clients throughout the United States in diverse and complex matters arising out of the employment relationship. He litigates employment-related cases; advises and trains clients on complying with employment laws, such as discrimination, harassment, family and medical leave and wage and hour laws; and negotiates a variety of agreements, including employment, confidentiality, noncompetition and collective bargaining agreements. He co-manages Arent Fox's Litigation Department and sits on its Executive Committee.

**Personal:** University of Pennsylvania Law School, JD 1984; Colgate University, BA (magna cum laude) 1981.

## STEWART, David O
Ropes & Gray LLP, Washington, DC
202 508 4610
david.stewart@ropesgray.com
*Recommended in Healthcare*

**Practice Areas:** Experience in complex litigation includes appellate and Supreme Court litigation, antitrust and commercial disputes, white-collar criminal defense work, healthcare law, and a variety of challenges to government regulation and enforcement. Served as principal counsel in federal jury trials, state court trials, administrative proceedings, numerous appeals, and the impeachment trial of Judge Walter L Nixon, Jr before the US Senate. Established Ropes & Gray's Litigation Group Washington, DC.

**Career:** District of Columbia Bar (1980); Maryland Bar (1986); Partner, Ropes & Gray (1989).

**Personal:** JD, Yale Law School, (1978); BA, summa cum laude, Yale University (1973).

## STOLL, Richard G
Foley & Lardner LLP, Washington, DC
202 295 4021
rstoll@foley.com
*Recommended in Environment*
**Career:** Richard G Stoll is a Partner in the Washington, DC office of Foley & Lardner LLP. He is a member of the Environmental and Chemical & Pharmaceutical Practice Groups, as well as the firm's Nanotechnology Industry Team. Mr Stoll concentrates his practice on federal administrative and environmental law matters. He counsels corporations and trade associations on environmental issues before the US Environmental Protection Agency (EPA) and state environmental agencies. He also handles a variety of administrative, rulemaking, and judicial review matters in the fields of intellectual property, healthcare, and environmental law. Mr Stoll graduated from Georgetown University Law School.

## STONE, Steven W
Morgan, Lewis & Bockius LLP, Washington, DC 202 739 5453
sstone@morganlewis.com
*Recommended in Investment Management*
**Practice Areas:** Steven W Stone leads the Investment Management/Securities Practice at Morgan Lewis and serves as Managing Partner of the Washington office. His practice focuses on broker-dealer and investment manager regulation and enforcement defense and securities markets regulation. He has extensive experience in all aspects of broker-dealer and investment management regulation, representing major investment banks, broker-dealers and investment managers in a broad range of matters. Mr Stone serves as counsel to the private wealth management businesses of several Wall Street firms, and the trading desks of major broker-dealers and investment managers on complex trading issues.

## STRAND, Margaret
Venable LLP, Washington, DC
202 962 4800
*Recommended in Environment*

## SULLIVAN, Brendan
Williams & Connolly LLP, Washington, DC 202 434 5000
*Recommended in Litigation*

## SULLIVAN, Kevin
King & Spalding LLP, Washington, DC
202 626 2624
krsullivan@kslaw.com
*Recommended in Antitrust*
**Practice Areas:** Defends and prosecutes antitrust civil cases from initiation through trial and appeal, and provides counseling services to clients on antitrust and telecommunications issues. Extensive experience in international antitrust matters and has co-ordinated merger approvals and responses to foreign gov-

ernment antitrust investigations.
**Prof. Memberships:** District of Columbia Bar; Pennsylvania Bar; Bar of the United States Supreme Court.
**Personal:** BA, Gannon University, 1971; JD, Catholic University, 1975.

## SULLIVAN, Mary Anne
Hogan & Hartson LLP, Washington, DC
202 637 3695
masullivan@hhlaw.com
*Recommended in Energy*
**Practice Areas:** Electricity, nuclear, alternative energy technologies and climate change, Department of Energy contracts/grants, and energy class action defense.
**Prof. Memberships:** District of Columbia Bar Association (Energy and Environment Section); Department of Energy Contractor Attorneys Association (Board of Directors); Energy Bar Association.
**Career:** 1984-93 and since 2001, Partner, Hogan & Hartson; 1998-2001, general counsel, US Department of Energy; 1994-98, deputy general counsel for Environment & Nuclear Programs, DOE; 2004, Senior Lecturer in Law at Duke University Law School; 2006, Professorial Lecturer in Law at George Washington University Law School, teaching energy law.
**Publications:** 'Voluntary Plans Will Not Cut Greenhouse Gas Emissions in the Electricity Sector', Sustainable Development Law & Policy (2/2006), 'Kyoto Protocol Enters into Force February 16, 2005', Climate Change Update, Hogan & Hartson (2/16/2005); 'The Hard Realities of Energy Policy in an Election Year', Electric Light & Power (9/1/2004); 'Standard Market Design: What Went Wrong? What Next?', The Electricity Journal (7/1/2003).
**Personal:** Yale Law School (JD, 1976); Fordham University (BA, summa cum laude, 1973).

## SULLIVAN, Michael
Levine Sullivan Koch & Schulz LLP, Washington, DC 202 508 1100
*Recommended in Media & Entertainment*

## SULLIVAN, T J
Gardner Carton & Douglas LLP, Washington, DC 202 230 5157
tsullivan@gcd.com
*Recommended in Healthcare*
**Practice Areas:** Healthcare, tax Partner; represents clients in corporate, tax, regulatory matters; formerly Special Assistant (Healthcare) to the Internal Revenue Service Assistant Commissioner (Employee Plans and Exempt Organizations), where he concentrated in matters involving tax treatment of hospitals, HMOs, other tax-exempt organizations; co-ordinated development of Service positions on healthcare matters, advised field agents during examinations, co-chaired Exempt Organizations Health Care/College and University Industry Specialization Program (ISP) team; served on White House

Task Force on Health Reform (1993); Founding Director, General Counsel, Coalition for Nonprofit Health Care.
**Prof. Memberships:** Board of Directors, American Health Lawyers Association (1995-2001); Chair, Tax Issues Program Committee, American Health Lawyers Association; Co-Chair, Health Care Subcommittee, Committee on Exempt Organizations, American Bar Association Tax Section; Editorial Advisory Board, BNA's Health Law Reporter; Editorial Advisory Board, The Exempt Organization Tax Review.
**Career:** Prior to joining IRS, private practitioner in health law; evaluated federal health policies with US General Accounting Office.
**Publications:** Frequent author, lecturer on tax, healthcare issues.
**Personal:** George Washington University, JD, 1985, graduated with honors; Georgetown University Law Center, LLM, 1991, graduated with distinction; West Virginia University, 1979, Masters of Public Administration; Salem College, BA, 1977.

## SUNDBACK, Mark
Andrews Kurth LLP, Washington, DC
202 662 2700
*Recommended in Energy*

## SUNSHINE, Steven C
Cadwalader, Wickersham & Taft LLP, Washington, DC 202 862 2329
steve.sunshine@cwt.com
*Recommended in Antitrust*
**Practice Areas:** Head, Antitrust Practice Group. Concentrates in antitrust aspects of litigation, mergers and acquisitions, counseling and grand jury investigations. Regularly appears before the federal courts in connection with antitrust civil and criminal matters and before the European Commission. Litigation experience includes defending clients in the resolution of antitrust indictments, class actions relating to antitrust allegations in the pharmaceuticals, mining and securities industries, Department of Justice criminal investigations, and formulating key antitrust in the areas of biotechnology and US treasury futures. M&A transactions include StorageTek/Sun Microsystems; Gambro/Davita; Rhone Poulenc/Hoechst (Aventis); SmithKline/GlaxoWellcome; Bell Atlantic/Nynex; and Fiat-New Holland/Case.
**Prof. Memberships:** New York and District of Columbia Bars.
**Personal:** JD, Boston College Law School, magna cum laude (Law Review, Order of the Coif); AB, Brown University. Former Deputy Assistant Attorney General, Merger Enforcement, US Department of Justice, Antitrust Division.

## SUSSMAN, Robert
Latham & Watkins LLP, Washington, DC
202 637 2200
*Recommended in Environment*

## SUTTON, Kathryn M
Morgan, Lewis & Bockius LLP, Washington, DC 202 739 5738
ksutton@morganlewis.com
*Recommended in Energy*
**Practice Areas:** Ms Sutton is a Partner in the Energy Practice Group. She represents nuclear utility clients in licensing, regulatory and adjudicatory matters. Ms Sutton has advised numerous utilities regarding the content and implementation of the Nuclear Regulatory Commission (NRC) license renewal regulations, including attendant NEPA requirements. In particular, she has represented utilities that have successfully renewed the operating licenses of nearly 20 nuclear units. She also represents several utilities in their efforts to license, construct, and operate new reactors.
**Prof. Memberships:** Member, Energy Bar Association; Member, Women in Nuclear; Member, International Nuclear Law Association; Member, Women's Bar Association of the District of Columbia; Member, Women's Council on Energy and the Environment.

## SWANSON, M Anne
Dow, Lohnes & Albertson, PLLC, Washington, DC 202 776 2000
aswanson@dowlohnes.com
*Recommended in Telecom, Broadcast & Satellite*
**Practice Areas:** Federal communications regulatory matters, including complex rulemakings, transactions, and enforcement matters.
**Prof. Memberships:** ABA (Forum on Communications, former Governing Committee member); Federal Communications Bar Association (former President, Treasurer, and ABA Delegate); DC Bar; Cosmos Club, Washington, DC.
**Career:** Editor, President's Daily News Summary, The White House, Washington, DC, 1974-75; Law Clerk to Hon. CB Renfrew, United States District Court for the ND of California, 1979-80, and Hon RD Cudahy, United States Court of Appeals for Seventh Circuit, 1980. Joined Dow Lohnes as Partner in 1997.
**Publications:** Lectured and written extensively on communications regulatory issues.
**Personal:** Georgetown University (LLM, 1997); Yale Law School (JD, 1979); Princeton University (MPA, 1979); West Virginia University (BSJ, 1974).

## SYMONS, Howard
Mintz Levin Cohn Ferris Glovsky and Popeo PC, Washington, DC
202 434 7305
hsymons@mintz.com
*Recommended in Telecom, Broadcast & Satellite*
**Career:** Howard Symons has more than 25 years of experience in communications law and policy. A Member in the firm's Washington office, Mr Symons

549

represents cable, wireless, and telecommunications companies and their trade associations on a wide range of federal and state regulatory and legislative matters. Before joining the firm, Mr Symons served as Senior Counsel to the Subcommittee on Telecommunications in the US House of Representatives, where he was responsible for the development of legislation on matters ranging from domestic telephone policy to cable franchising and international telecommunications. For 10 years, he was an Adjunct Professor at the National Law Center of George Washington University, where he taught a course in telecommunications law and regulation. Mr Symons is admitted to practice in the District of Columbia. He received his BA, summa cum laude, from Yale University (1975), and his JD from Harvard Law School (1978).

## TAGER, Evan M
Mayer, Brown, Rowe & Maw LLP, Washington, DC 202 263 3240
etager@mayerbrown.com
*Recommended in Litigation*
**Practice Areas:** Appellate litigation. Areas of expertise include punitive damages, constitutional and procedural limitations on class actions, limiting expert testimony, enforcement of arbitration provisions, and the dormant Commerce Clause.
**Career:** Mayer, Brown, Rowe & Maw LLP, Washington, DC, 1988 to present; Partner, 1994. Weil, Gotshal & Manges, Washington, DC, 1986-88. Law Clerk to The Honorable Mary M Schroeder, US Court of Appeals for the Ninth Circuit, Phoenix, Arizona, 1985-86.
**Publications:** Recent publications: Co-author of Chapter 42, 'Punitive Damages', in Business and Commercial Litigation in Federal Courts (2d ed 2005). 'The Implications of State Farm v Campbell for the Future of Punitive Damages in Bad Faith Litigation', Mealey's Litigation Report: Insurance Bad Faith, Apr 22, 2003, at 28. 'The Constitutional Limitations on Class Actions', Mealey's Litigation Report: Class Actions, Jan 2001, at 34. 'Punitive Damages Claims in Environmental Tort Cases: Lessons from Johansen v Combustion Engineering, Inc.', 29 Environmental Law Reports 10196 (Mar 2000). 'Tips on Preserving Arguments for Appeal', Mealey's Insurance Law Weekly, December 1, 1998, at 18.
**Personal:** JD, Stanford Law School, 1985; articles editor, Law Review. BA (magna cum laude), Princeton University, 1982.

## TALADAY, John
Howrey LLP, Washington, DC
202 783 0800
*Recommended in Antitrust*

## TARANTO, Richard
Farr & Taranto, Washington, DC
202 775 0184
*Recommended in Litigation*

## TAUB, Kathy S
Arent Fox PLLC, Washington, DC
202 857 6234
taub.kathy@arentfox.com
*Recommended in Construction*
**Practice Areas:** Concentrates in structuring and negotiating contracts for owners, developers, architects and contractors involved in development, design and construction matters. With over 20 years of experience in construction law, Kathy has negotiated contracts for numerous major projects nationwide. Before joining Arent Fox, Kathy served as Vice President and General Counsel of Clark Enterprises, Inc where she advised senior management on all business and legal aspects of its significant real estate portfolio, $1.2 billion of construction activities, and other business enterprises.
**Personal:** University of Maryland School of Law, JD (with honors) 1980; Duke University, BA (cum laude) 1977.

## TAYLOR, John D
Mayer, Brown, Rowe & Maw LLP, Chicago 312 782 0600
*Recommended in Projects*
**Practice Areas:** Represents a variety of financial institutions, including export credit agencies, multilateral institutions and commercial lenders in project finance transactions.
**Prof. Memberships:** Illinois, 1994. District of Columbia, 1996.
**Career:** 3 Mayer, Brown, Rowe & Maw LLP, Chicago, 1998 to date; Partner, 2004. International Finance Corporation, Washington, DC, 1997-98.
**Personal:** University of Virginia, School of Law, JD, 1994; Articles Review Board, Virginia Journal of International Law. Georgetown University, School of Foreign Service, BSFS cum laude, 1989.

## TAYLOR III, William
Zuckerman Spaeder LLP, Washington, DC 202 778 1800
*Recommended in Litigation*

## TELL, Gary
O'Melveny & Myers LLP, Washington, DC 202 383 5300
*Recommended in Employee Benefits*

## TERR, Leonard
Baker & McKenzie, Washington, DC
202 452 7087
leonard.b.terr@bakernet.com
*Recommended in Tax*
**Practice Areas:** Mr Terr has over 25 years' experience representing US and foreign-based multinationals, foreign governments, international organizations and trade associations in all phases of international tax practice. Mr Terr's practice includes tax planning for multi-country restructurings, mergers and acquisitions, divestitures and tax minimization strategies involving companies in the automotive, aerospace, consumer products, electronics, insurance, natural

resources, pharmaceutical, services, telecommunications and other industries; securing Advance Pricing Agreements; providing comments and testimony on pending tax treaties and proposed regulations; and obtaining favorable settlements in Exam, Appeals or Competent Authority of tax controversies involving most European, Asia-Pacific and North American treaty jurisdictions.
**Prof. Memberships:** Mr Terr is a member of the International Fiscal Association and was US National Reporter. He is a Member of the IFA-USA Council. Mr Terr sits on the American Bar Association Tax Section's Foreign Activities of US Taxpayers Committee and has served as Chairman of the Section 367 Subcommittee and chaired the Source Subcommittee. Mr Terr serves on the Tax Sections Task Force on Global Tax Policy. He has served as a Consultant to the American Law Institute Project on Tax Treaties. Mr Terr has served on the editorial boards of Tax Notes International, Tax Management International Journal and The Journal of Corporate Taxation. He is a Member of the firm's North American Tax Group Management Committee. Mr Terr has chaired the Washington International Tax Study Group since 1990.
**Career:** Mr Terr served as International Tax Counsel of the US Treasury Department from 1987-89. He headed the US delegation in the negotiation of the current US-Germany tax treaty, in addition to over a dozen other US tax treaties and protocols. He directed Treasury's work on international tax legislation and regulations, the transfer pricing White Paper and other US and OECD international tax policy initiatives. He served as Law Clerk to Chief Judge Wilson Cowen of the US Court of Appeals for the Federal Circuit. He is an Adjunct Professor of International Tax Law at the Georgetown University Law Center. He has lectured and published widely on international tax matters.
**Personal:** Mr Terr holds an AB from LaSalle College, an AM and PhD from Brown University and a JD from Cornell University.

## THOMPSON, Carolyn
Jones Day, Washington, DC
202 879 5426
carolynthompson@jonesday.com
*Recommended in Energy*
**Practice Areas:** Represents electric utilities, gas pipelines and local distribution companies before the Federal Energy Regulatory Commission. She has participated in numerous ratemaking and rulemaking proceedings on behalf of gas pipelines, local distribution companies, investor-owned electric utilities, and cogenerators. She has assisted clients with drafting tariffs, precedent agreements, and contracts. She has represented clients in enforcement matters at the FERC and

has represented electric utilities at the Department of Energy in securing presidential permits and export authorizations for the export of electricity across international borders.
**Prof. Memberships:** District of Columbia Bar; Energy Bar Association (Member of the Board of Directors).

## THOMPSON, Gary
Gilbert Heintz & Randolph LLP, Washington, DC 202 772 2225
*Recommended in Insurance*

## THOMPSON, Michael
Wright & Talisman PC, Washington, DC
202 393 1200
*Recommended in Energy*

## THORNTON, D McCarty
Sonnenschein Nath & Rosenthal LLP, Washington, DC
202 408 6432
mthornton@sonnenschein.com
*Recommended in Healthcare*
**Practice Areas:** Healthcare fraud and abuse counseling and defense, including anti-kickback, False Claims Act, civil monetary penalty, and exclusion actions. He also handles the negotiation and implementation of corporate integrity agreements.
**Prof. Memberships:** Member, American Health Lawyers Association; Member; Health Care Compliance Association
**Career:** Former Chief Counsel to the Inspector General of the US Department of Health & Human Services (HHS) for 12 years. Former white-collar crime prosecutor, US Department of Justice.
**Personal:** Stanford Law School, JD, with high honors; Stanford University, BA.

## TIEDEMANN, Charles Welch (Chad)
Holland & Knight LLP, Washington, DC
202 955 3000
chad.tiedemann@hklaw.com
*Recommended in Real Estate*
**Practice Areas:** Partner and Head of the firm's Nationwide Real Estate Section, he has practiced in the areas of commercial real estate finance, development, and leasing for 25 years. He represents institutional clients including investment advisors, pension funds, insurance companies, banks and foreign investors, as well as developers, tenants and syndicators. The complex commercial transactions he has been responsible for include acquisitions, sales, recapitalizations, joint venture formations, construction and permanent loans, ground leases, sale-leasebacks, syndications and commercial leases. He has experience with retail, office, multifamily housing, hotels, residential subdivisions, industrial properties, real estate workouts, foreclosures, and bankruptcies.

## TILLMAN, Eugene
Reed Smith LLP, Washington, DC
202 414 9244
etillman@reedsmith.com
*Recommended in Healthcare*
**Practice Areas:** Counsels hospitals and other institutional and alternate site providers, manufacturers of pharmaceuticals and medical devices, pharmacy benefits, managers, retail drug chains, mail order and other specialty pharmacies, and healthcare professional and trade associations. Concentrates on Medicare and Medicaid payment and coverage issues, acquisitions and provider integration issues, and licensing and regulatory matters. Member of Executive Committee.
**Prof. Memberships:** Past President, American Health Lawyers Association; member, California and DC Bar Associations.
**Career:** Four years, Department of Health and Human Services.
**Personal:** University of California at Los Angeles School of Law (JD, 1976); UCLA (1973).

## TOBEY, Margaret
Morrison & Foerster LLP, Washington, DC 202 887 6935
mtobey@mofo.com
*Recommended in Telecom, Broadcast & Satellite*
**Practice Areas:** Focuses on communications regulatory and transactional matters, including licensing, regulatory compliance, transactions and litigation involving radio and television stations, direct broadcast satellite operators, providers of new technology services, equipment manufacturers and lenders to the communications industry.
**Prof. Memberships:** Former President (2001-02), President-Elect (2000-01), and Secretary (1999-2000), Federal Communications Bar Association (FCBA); Chair, FCBA Foundation (1993-94).
**Career:** Admitted to practice in District of Columbia.
**Personal:** BA (1974), MA (1980), University of Iowa; JD, with high distinction, University of Iowa College of Law (1980), Editor-in-Chief, Iowa Law Review (1979-80).

## TOBIN, Charles D
Holland & Knight LLP, Washington, DC
202 955 3000
charles.tobin@hklaw.com
*Recommended in Media & Entertainment*
**Practice Areas:** Chair of the firm's National Media Practice Team. A former journalist, Tobin appears for media clients in state and federal courts around the country. He also conducts pre-publication review for newsrooms; provides journalists with advice on subpoenas, access, and freedom of information matters; and advises commercial clients on

unfair competition claims. Tobin spent eight years as in-house counsel at Gannett Co., Inc., which publishes 'USA TODAY' and owns newspapers and television stations throughout the country. He is Editor-in-Chief of the ABA publication 'LITIGATION' and chairs the DC Bar Media Law Committee.

## TOM, Willard K
Morgan, Lewis & Bockius LLP, Washington, DC 202 739 5389
wtom@morganlewis.com
*Recommended in Antitrust*
**Practice Areas:** Willard K Tom is a Partner at Morgan, Lewis & Bockius, LLP, resident in our Washington, DC office. Will has had more than 25 years of experience in the antitrust field, both in private practice and in government. He served as Deputy Director at the FTC and as Counselor to the Head of the Antitrust Division at DOJ, and was a principal drafter of the DOJ and FTC Antitrust Guidelines for the Licensing of Intellectual Property.
**Prof. Memberships:** Co-Chair, Merger Process Reform Task Force, American Bar Association Antitrust Section; Member of Council, American Bar Association Section of Business Law.

## TRAGER, Michael D
Arnold & Porter LLP, Washington, DC
202 942 6976
Michael.Trager@aporter.com
*Recommended in Securities*
**Practice Areas:** Michael Trager is a Partner in the Washington, DC office of Arnold & Porter LLP, where he heads the firm's Securities Enforcement Practice and co-heads the firm's Securities Enforcement and Litigation Practice Group. Mr Trager defends investigations conducted by the Securities and Exchange Commission, Department of Justice, other federal agencies, Congress, NASD, NYSE, and state regulators. He also conducts internal investigations, defends securities litigation, and counsels on compliance, crisis management, corporate governance, and disclosure matters. Mr Trager's practice is international in scope and involves high profile matters. His clients include public companies, broker-dealers, financial institutions, investment advisers, hedge funds, accounting firms, officers, directors, and other individuals.
**Prof. Memberships:** Mr Trager is a Member of several Bar associations and committees and has served on Task Forces established by the American Bar Association and District of Columbia Bar.
**Career:** Mr Trager has two decades of private practice experience devoted exclusively to securities enforcement matters. Prior to entering private practice, he served in the SEC's Division of Enforcement in Washington, DC, where he conducted investigations and repre-

sented the government in litigation.
**Publications:** Mr Trager has authored numerous publications and spoken frequently on SEC enforcement issues.
**Personal:** Mr Trager's outside activities include serving as a Member of the Board of Directors of The Washington Ballet.

## TRILLING, Helen R
Hogan & Hartson LLP, Washington, DC
202 637 8653
hrtrilling@hhlaw.com
*Recommended in Healthcare*
**Practice Areas:** Expertise includes healthcare fraud and abuse (eg, anti-kickback/false claims) compliance, investigations and enforcement; coverage and reimbursement of new medical services and technologies; strategic advice on development of medical technologies, business models, sales and marketing initiatives. Clients include pharmaceutical, medical device and healthcare information technology companies, academic medical centers, clinical laboratories, and trade associations.
**Prof. Memberships:** AHLA; President's Council, National Partnership for Women & Families.
**Career:** Partner, Hogan & Hartson since 1987; special assistant to three general counsels in two different administrations at HHS; assistant general counsel at Blue Cross and Blue Shield of Massachusetts.
**Publications:** Lectured extensively on healthcare fraud and abuse compliance and investigations.
**Personal:** Harvard Law School (JD, 1976); Radcliffe College (AB, magna cum laude, 1973).

## TRITT, Cheryl
Morrison & Foerster LLP, Washington, DC 202 887 1510
ctritt@mofo.com
*Recommended in Telecom, Broadcast & Satellite*
**Practice Areas:** Partner advising on a range of telecommunications issues, including wireless, satellite, local competition and broadband technologies. Focuses on regulatory implications of emerging technologies and transactional matters: mergers, acquisitions, stock spin-offs and new business ventures.
**Prof. Memberships:** American Bar Association, Federal Communications Bar Association.
**Career:** Admitted to practice in the District of Columbia and Illinois. Joined firm in 1993, after being Chief of the Common Carrier Bureau, Federal Communications Commission (FCC). Co-Head of firm's Communications Practice.
**Personal:** BS, cum laude, Phi Beta Kappa, University of Nebraska; MS, Journalism, Northwestern University; JD, cum laude, Northwestern University School of Law, 1976.

## TUCKER, Stefan
Venable LLP, Washington, DC
202 962 4800
*Recommended in Real Estate*

## TUOHEY, Mark H
Vinson & Elkins LLP, Washington, DC
202 639 6660
mtuohey@velaw.com
*Recommended in Litigation*
**Practice Areas:** Complex civil and white-collar litigation; internal investigations; representation of corporate corporations and their officers and directors in regulatory investigations and litigation.
**Prof. Memberships:** DC Bar (President 1993-94); American Bar Association; Fellow, American College of Trial Lawyers.
**Career:** Admitted to DC Bar, 1973; New York, 1981; former Assistant US Attorney, DC 1973-77; Special Counsel to Attorney General, 1978-79; Principal Deputy Independent Counsel, 1994-95.
**Publications:** Frequent author and lecturer on trial advocacy, legal ethics and white-collar litigation.
**Personal:** Chair, DC Sports & Entertainment Commission 2003-. Mark and his wife Marty live in Washington, DC.

## UNTEREINER, Alan
Robbins, Russell, Englert, Orseck & Untereiner LLP, Washington, DC
202 775 4500
*Recommended in Litigation*

## VARDAMAN, John
Williams & Connolly LLP, Washington, DC 202 434 5000
*Recommended in Litigation*

## VARNEY, Christine
Hogan & Hartson LLP, Washington, DC
202 637 6823
cvarney@hhlaw.com
*Recommended in Antitrust*
**Practice Areas:** Practice provides full-service assistance to companies doing business globally, including providing advice on antitrust, privacy, business planning and corporate governance, intellectual property, and general liability issues.
**Prof. Memberships:** Chair, Committee on Election Law, ABA (1998-2000); ABA, Antitrust Section (1986-present); District of Columbia Bar Association (1986-present); Secretary/Treasurer, Vice-President's Residence Foundation (1997-2000); National Lawyers' Council (1985-present).
**Career:** Federal Trade Commissioner (1994-97). Prior to becoming a commissioner, Christine was an assistant to the President and secretary to the Cabinet. She also served as chief counsel to the Clinton/Gore Campaign, general counsel to the 1992 Presidential Inaugural Committee, and general counsel to the Democratic National Committee from 1989-92.
**Publications:** She regularly contributes

to a variety of publications, including Newsweek, Antitrust Magazine and Wired.

**Personal:** Georgetown University Law Center (JD); Syracuse University (MPA); State University of New York at Albany (BS).

## VASILE, James
Davis Wright Tremaine LLP, Washington, DC 202 508 6600
*Recommended in Energy*

## VERRILLI, Donald B
Jenner & Block LLP, Washington, DC 202 639 6095
dverrilli@jenner.com
*Recommended in Litigation, Telecom, Broadcast & Satellite*

**Practice Areas:** Donald B Verrilli, Jr is Chair of the firm's Telecommunications Practice, and Co-Chair of Appellate and Supreme Court Practice. He is a member of the Litigation & Dispute Resolution Practice and the firm's Policy Committee. Mr Verrilli has argued frequently before the US Supreme Court. Recently, he argued successfully on behalf of the entertainment industry in Metro-Goldwyn-Mayer Studios Inc. v Grokster, Ltd., in which the Court held software companies that build businesses on the illegal distribution of copyrighted material liable for copyright infringement. He also successfully argued General Dynamics Land Systems v Cline, in which the Court ruled that the Age Discrimination in Employment Act does not authorize 'reverse discrimination' suits, FCC v NextWave Personal Communications, in which the Court returned to NextWave billions of dollars worth of wireless spectrum licenses the FCC had sought to repossess from NextWave while it was in bankruptcy and Verizon Communications v FCC, the most important case arising out of the Telecommunications Act of 1996. On a pro bono basis, he successfully defended the right to effective counsel in Wiggins v Smith. Mr Verrilli also has an active practice in the trial courts and courts of appeals representing clients on matters involving the First Amendment, the Takings Clause, copyright, telecommunications and administrative law.

**Personal:** Columbia University School of Law, JD, 1983. Law Clerk to the Honorable William J Brennan, Jr, Supreme Court of the United States and to the Honorable J Skelly Wright, United States Court of Appeals for the DC Circuit.

## VERVEER, Philip L
Willkie Farr & Gallagher LLP, Washington, DC 202 303 1117
pverveer@willkie.com
*Recommended in Telecom, Broadcast & Satellite*

**Practice Areas:** Partner in the Telecommunications Department, specializing in communications, antitrust, and adminis-

trative law. Provides counseling and administrative agency representation to a variety of communications clients. An internationally recognized authority in antitrust and communications law. Recent significant matters include serving as regulatory counsel to Sprint Corp. in its $35 billion merger with Nextel Communications Inc.; regulatory and antitrust counsel to New Skies Satellite in its acquisition by SES Global; and antitrust counsel to Adelphia Communications in its acquisition by Comcast and Time Warner.

**Prof. Memberships:** Admitted to the Bar of the District of Columbia. Member of the Federal Communications Bar Association and the American Bar Association.

**Career:** From 1969-77, served as a trial attorney in the Department of Justice's Antitrust Division, where he was the first lead counsel in the investigation and prosecution that led to the Bell System divestiture. Also served as a supervisory attorney in the Federal Trade Commission's Bureau of Competition from 1977-78. Between 1978 and 1981, was Chief of the Federal Communication Commission's Cable Television Bureau, Broadcast Bureau, and Common Carrier Bureau. Served as Chairman of the Federal Public Safety Wireless Advisory Committee and as US Representative to the INTELSAT Panel of Legal Experts. Was a charter Member of the US Government Senior Executive Service. In 1980, received the Distinguished Presidential Rank Award, one of the highest awards given to federal government employees. In 1996, received the Cellular Telecommunications Industry Association President's Award.

**Personal:** Received a JD from the University of Chicago in 1969 and a BSFS from Georgetown University in 1966.

## VICKERY, Ann Morgan
Hogan & Hartson LLP, Washington, DC 202 637 8605
amvickery@hhlaw.com
*Recommended in Healthcare*

**Practice Areas:** Represents manufacturers, associations, and providers of various healthcare products and services; counsels clients regarding the impact of payment policies on their businesses, with particular emphasis on federal government regulation.

**Prof. Memberships:** ABA; American Health Lawyers Association; National Hospice Foundation (Trustee).

**Career:** 1978-present, Hogan & Hartson, currently Managing Partner of the Washington, DC office and Health Practice Director; 1975-78, US Secretary of the Treasury staff; 1969-74, White House researcher and staff assistant.

**Publications:** Speaks and writes on Medicare and Medicaid reimbursement, legislative developments, and trends in healthcare. Publications and presenta-

tions include: 'A Washington Lawyer's View of National Health Policy', Health Policy Institute Lecture Series, University of Pittsburgh (September 17, 2003); 'Reimbursement and Coverage for New Technology', seminar at Stanford University sponsored by Hogan & Hartson and the California Healthcare Institute (December 8, 1997); 'When Staff Object to Participating in Care' (with Anne M Dellinger), 28 Journal of Health and Hospital Law 269 (1995).

**Personal:** Georgetown University Law Center (JD, 1978); Mary Baldwin College (AB, 1965); Woman of the Year, National Hospice and Palliative Care Organization, 1986.

## VILLA, John
Williams & Connolly LLP, Washington, DC 202 434 5000
*Recommended in Financial Services, Litigation*

## VINE, John M
Covington & Burling, Washington, DC 202 662 5392
jvine@cov.com
*Recommended in Employee Benefits*

**Practice Areas:** Practice focuses on the ERISA, tax, and equal employment aspects of pension, profit-sharing, 401(k), and health plans, as well as stock incentive, stock option, executive compensation, deferred compensation, and fringe benefit programs. He serves as counsel to the ERISA Industry Committee.

**Publications:** He wrote 'Cash or Deferred Arrangements: What's the Beef? What's at Stake?', 5 Va. Tax Rev. 855 (1986).

**Personal:** He received his AB, magna cum laude, from Amherst College (1966), and his JD, magna cum laude, from Harvard Law School (1969). He was a member of the Board of Editors of The Harvard Law Review.

## VIRTUE, Paul
Hogan & Hartson LLP, Washington, DC 202 637 5649
pwvirtue@hhlaw.com
*Recommended in Immigration*

**Practice Areas:** Paul Virtue has more than six years of experience representing individual, business, and institutional clients in immigration law and related policy, regulatory, and legislative areas, and more than 22 years of experience in the immigration field.

**Prof. Memberships:** Member, American Immigration Lawyers Association Customs and Border Protection Committee; Vice-Chairman, Board of Trustees, American Immigration Law Foundation; Board of Directors, National Immigration Forum.

**Career:** Prior to joining the firm, Paul served as general counsel of the US Immigration and Naturalization Service (INS), where he provided legal and policy

advice to the INS commissioner and the attorney general, directed the regulatory implementation of the Illegal Immigration Reform and Immigrant Responsibility Act of 1996, represented the INS on the White House Interagency Working Group on Human Rights, and supervised a nationwide litigation staff of more than 600 attorneys.

**Publications:** Paul is a frequent author and participant at legal and business conferences and seminars. He is responsible for Hogan & Hartson's monthly Immigration Update, and has authored 'An Immigration Law Primer for the Corporate Executive', National Legal Center for the Public Interest (January 2006).

**Personal:** West Virginia University College of Law (JD); West Virginia University (BS).

## VODRA, William
Arnold & Porter LLP, Washington, DC 202 942 5088
William.Vodra@aporter.com
*Recommended in Healthcare*

**Practice Areas:** Bill Vodra specializes in regulatory issues and crisis management involving the safety, effectiveness, and marketing of medical products. He has led teams defending embattled products and companies in criminal, civil and regulatory proceedings.

**Career:** Bill served as FDA Associate Counsel for Drugs (1974-79) and as DEA Assistant Counsel (1971-74). He drafted many agency regulations still in use, including those implementing the Controlled Substances Act and FDA's rules for Good Manufacturing Practices, Good Laboratory Practices, Good Clinical Practices, bioequivalency and the Orange Book.

**Publications:** 'Building Successful Relationships with Clients' in Inside the Minds: Best Practices for Food and Drug Law (2005); 'Past Evolution and Future Prospects of the Pharma Industry and Its Regulation in the USA' in Textbook of Pharmaceutical Medicine (2005); 'Parallel Trade in the EU and US Pharmaceutical Markets', Global Counsel Life Sciences Handbook 2005/206; 'Do Users Fees Compromise the Integrity of the FDA?', Regulatory Affairs J (Pharma) (2004); 'Anchors Away: FDA's Use of Disgorgement Abandons Legal Moorings', Food & Drug L. J. (2004).

**Personal:** 'Chambers USA' Leading Healthcare Lawyer (2003-06); Legal Times Leading Lawyer in Food and Drug Law (September 2005); Practical Law Company Global Counsel Leading Lawyer in Life Sciences: Regulatory (2003-05).

## VOLLMANN, Alan P
Holland & Knight LLP, Washington, DC 202 955 3000
alan.vollmann@hklaw.com
*Recommended in Real Estate*

**Practice Areas:** Partner in Real Estate Section, representing institutional owners and investors in all aspects of finance, development, and leasing, most recently the Kingdom of Sweden in connection with its new embassy, the developer of air rights over Union Station, Johns Hopkins University in the development of its Montgomery County campus, the bond underwriter for the US Patent and Trademark Office, and the National Music Center and Museum Foundation. Vollmann is an Adjunct Professor of the Berman Real Estate Institute, Johns Hopkins University, and a 1980 graduate of Catholic University Law School, where he was Editor-in-Chief of the Law Review.

### VOLTMER, Ralph C
Covington & Burling, Washington, DC
202 662 5479
rvoltmer@cov.com
*Recommended in Telecom, Broadcast & Satellite*

**Practice Areas:** Corporate law focusing on telecommunications, media, and technology. Advises US and foreign multinational companies, start-up ventures, and investors in cross-border transactions and US-based transactions, including M&A, joint ventures, strategic alliances, financings (debt and equity), and transfer of intellectual property. Clients include Qualcomm, Reliance Industries, Telemobil S.A., National Geographic.
**Prof. Memberships:** NY, TN, DC Bar Associations.
**Career:** Serves as Co-Chair of Covington's Media and Communications Industry Group; judicial clerk US District Court for the District of Delaware (1987-88); English teacher (1982-84).
**Personal:** Georgetown (JD, mcl, Order of the Coif, 1987); UC (MA, 1984), Wheaton College (BA, 1982).

### WADLOW, R Clark
Sidley Austin LLP, Washington, DC
202 736 8215
rwadlow@sidley.com
*Recommended in Telecom, Broadcast & Satellite*

**Practice Areas:** Clark Wadlow heads the firm's Communications Group and represents a broad range of communications clients in connection with their corporate, regulatory and industry issues.
**Prof. Memberships:** He has served on numerous committees of the American Bar Association, including the Governing Committee of the Forum on Communications Law, which he chaired from 1987-89, and the Standing Committee on the Continuing Education of the Bar, which he has chaired from 1993-98. He was a Member-at-Large on the Association's Board of Governors. Mr Wadlow served as President of the Federal Communications Bar Association in 1997-98.
**Publications:** He is a frequent lecturer

and author, focusing on current developments in communications regulation and policy.
**Personal:** Mr Wadlow served as law clerk to the Honorable George F Boney, Chief Justice of the Supreme Court of Alaska. Harvard Law School, JD, 1971; Dartmouth College, AB, 1968. Admissions: US Supreme Court, 1974; DC and Alaska District Courts, 1971; DC Bar, 1972.

### WAHLE, Karen
O'Melveny & Myers LLP, Washington, DC
202 383 5366
kwahle@omm.com
*Recommended in Employee Benefits*

**Practice Areas:** Karen Wahle's practice focuses on litigation involving Title I of ERISA, including class actions, and is a member of the firm's Employee Benefits Group. Karen has a broad range of experience in all aspects of ERISA litigation, including defending clients against claims of breach of fiduciary duty, reporting and disclosure violations, vesting and funding violations, as well as against claims for benefits under employee welfare and pension plans. She also counsels clients on compliance issues involving Title I and Title IV of ERISA.

### WALD, Douglas
Arnold & Porter LLP, Washington, DC
202 942 5112
Douglas.Wald@aporter.com
*Recommended in Antitrust*

**Practice Areas:** Specializes in antitrust and trade regulation, and general litigation. Since joining the firm, his experience has involved a broad range of antitrust matters, including counseling, private litigation (including federal class actions), and representation before governmental agencies. He has advised clients on matters involving marketing, pricing, and distribution restrictions (Sherman Act 1), price discrimination (Robinson-Patman Act), monopolization (Sherman Act 2), and joint ventures and acquisitions (Clayton Act 7). He has also represented clients on appellate matters such as 3M Company v Browner, 17 F.3d 1453 (DC Cir. 1994) (applicability of federal statute of limitations to agency civil penalty proceedings).
**Career:** Prior to joining Arnold & Porter LLP in 1980, he clerked for Judge William H Timbers on the US Court of Appeals for the Second Circuit.
**Personal:** He graduated in 1979 from Harvard Law School (JD), and was an editor of the Harvard Law Review. He received an AB from Harvard College in 1975.

### WALSH, Linda
Hunton & Williams, Washington, DC
202 955 1526
lwalsh@hunton.com
*Recommended in Energy*

**Practice Areas:** Linda Walsh's practice focuses on regulatory matters affecting

electric utilities, particularly in industry restructuring, rates and administrative litigation. She serves as FERC counsel to a stand-alone transmission company, investor-owned utilities and independent power producers. She provides ongoing representation in transmission rate proceedings, negotiating generator interconnection agreements, obtaining regulatory approvals for the acquisition of jurisdictional facilities and providing general regulatory advice on generation, transmission and RTO formation and operational issues.

### WARD, Erica A
Skadden, Arps, Slate, Meagher & Flom LLP & Affiliates, Washington, DC
202 371 7050
eward@skadden.com
*Recommended in Projects*

**Practice Areas:** Advises on development, construction and financing, as well as acquisition and sale, of major industrial facilities throughout the world, with emphasis on electric power projects. Represents utility companies and their unregulated subsidiaries, independent power companies, commercial lenders, investment banks, and equity investors in project finance and utility transactions. Experience includes transactions involving construction and long-term debt instruments, equity/debt syndications, leveraged leases, public and private securities offerings, guarantees, support obligations, municipal bond financings, international agency financings and interest rate swaps.
**Career:** JD, University of Michigan Law School, 1975 (Managing Editor, Michigan Law Review); BA, Stanford University, 1972.

### WARIN, Roger
Steptoe & Johnson LLP, Washington, DC
202 429 6280
rwarin@steptoe.com
*Recommended in Insurance*

**Practice Areas:** Managing Partner in the Washington office of Steptoe & Johnson LLP. Lead counsel in numerous major nationwide insurance and reinsurance coverage disputes involving pharmaceuticals, products liability, asbestos, financial services and environmental claims. Recognized as one of the leading legal malpractice defense lawyers. Successfully handled a wide range of complex commercial litigation cases involving securities fraud, the Racketeer Influenced and Corrupt Organizations Act, libel, trademark, products liability, directors' and officers' liability, employment discrimination, attorneys' fees, First Amendment, legal malpractice and other professional liability, negligence, real estate, surety, construction, environmental, toxic tort, and insurance coverage claims. Also a successful appellate advocate, having argued more than 20 cases in various

Federal Circuit Courts of Appeals and State Supreme Courts.
**Personal:** JD, Georgetown University, 1970; AB, Creighton University, 1967.

### WARNER, Margaret H
McDermott Will & Emery, Washington, DC 202 756 8228
mwarner@mwe.com
*Recommended in Insurance*

**Practice Areas:** Partner-in-charge of Washington Trial Department. Complex litigation and arbitration practice specializing in disputes in the international insurance/reinsurance markets. Experience covers a wide range of disputes including virtually all lines of insurance. Recent cases involve the 9/11 terrorist attack, clergy sexual abuse scandals and asbestos/environmental issues. Clients include a mix of major domestic and foreign insurers, as well as specialty carriers and captive entities.
**Personal:** University of Notre Dame (JD); St. Lawrence University (BA).

### WARREN, Edward W
Kirkland & Ellis LLP, Washington, DC
202 879 5018
ewarren@kirkland.com
*Recommended in Environment*

**Practice Areas:** Mr Warren has extensive litigation experience before federal agencies and courts under a broad range of federal statutes. He also has appellate litigation experience including approximately 50 significant arguments before the US Courts of Appeals, state Supreme Courts and the US Supreme Court.
**Personal:** Yale College, BA, 1966. University of Chicago Law School, JD, 1969.

### WATERS, Jennifer N
Crowell & Moring LLP, Washington, DC
202 624 2715
jwaters@crowell.com
*Recommended in Energy*

**Practice Areas:** Partner in Crowell & Moring's Energy Group and a Member of the firm's Management Board. Focuses on energy law, having participated in the restructurings and transformations of the natural gas and electric industries that have occurred in the last two decades. Represents the Los Angeles Department of Water & Power in developing strategic natural gas and electric projects. Represents the cities of Knoxville, Memphis, and Nashville, which turn to her to manage their relationships with the Tennessee Valley Authority. Also represents a major international oil company and LNG producer.

### WAXMAN, Seth
WilmerHale, Washington, DC
202 663 6800
seth.waxman@wilmerhale.com
*Recommended in Litigation*

**Practice Areas:** Partner, Litigation Department. Focus: Supreme Court, appellate, and complex civil and criminal trial litigation; corporate advice on complex litigation and public policy challenges. Has argued over 40 cases in Supreme Court.

**Prof. Memberships:** Fellow, American College of Trial Lawyers, American Academy of Appellate Lawyers, American Law Institute, American Bar Foundation. Director, Legal Affairs magazine, Supreme Court Institute, Supreme Court Historical Society.

**Career:** Solicitor General of the United States (1997-2001). Law faculty, Georgetown University; previously taught at Harvard University's Kennedy School of Government.

**Personal:** JD, Yale Law School; AB, Harvard College.

## WEGENER, Mark
Howrey LLP, Washington, DC
202 783 0800
*Recommended in Litigation*

## WEINGARTEN, Reid
Steptoe & Johnson LLP, Washington, DC
202 429 6238
rweingarten@steptoe.com
*Recommended in Litigation*

**Practice Areas:** Partner in Steptoe and Johnson LLP's Washington office. Practice focuses mainly on complex criminal matters in state and federal courts at the pretrial, trial, and post-trial stages, including cases involving public corruption, the Racketeer Influenced and Corrupt Organizations Act, bank fraud, accounting fraud, bribery, government procurement fraud, antitrust, healthcare fraud, and tax and securities fraud. Nationally recognized for his representation of many high profile individuals including former senior executives of major US corporations, as well as the president of a national labor union and former cabinet-level government officials.

**Personal:** JD, Dickinson Law School, 1975; BS, Cornell University, 1971.

## WEINSTEIN, Ken
Latham & Watkins LLP, Washington, DC
202 637 2200
*Recommended in Environment*

## WEISEL, Sheldon
Goulston & Storrs, Washington, DC
202 721 0011
*Recommended in Real Estate*

## WEISS, Erica H
Bingham McCutchen LLP, Washington, DC 202 778 3160
erica.weiss@bingham.com
*Recommended in Real Estate*

**Practice Areas:** Represents financial institutions, pension fund advisors and developers in a variety of real estate finance transactions, including conventional asset-based lending transactions, syndicated financings, multi-state transactions and other commercial finance matters. Practice also involves all other aspects of a transactional real estate prac-

tice – acquisitions, sales, joint ventures, partnerships and leasing. Represents financial institutions in transactions involving construction lending, acquisition financing, merchant banking and bridge facilities. Also represents pension funds, national real estate investment trusts and local developers in developing innovative finance structures.

**Personal:** University of Pennsylvania Law School, JD, 1989; University of Pennsylvania, BS, cum laude, 1986.

## WEISS, Harry J
WilmerHale, Washington, DC
202 663 6993
harry.weiss@wilmerhale.com
*Recommended in Financial Services, Securities*

**Practice Areas:** Represents clients in SEC enforcement matters and counsels corporations and their officers regarding disclosure and corporate compliance issues.

**Prof. Memberships:** Former Co-Chair of the Securities Enforcement Subcommittee of the ABA Litigation Section; former director, National Society of Compliance Professionals; current director, Regulatory Data Corporation.

**Career:** Served on the staff of the Securities and Exchange Commission for 11 years, ultimately as Associate Director of the Division of Enforcement, leading investigations involving insider trading, financial reporting, accounting and disclosure problems and broker-dealer and investment advisor violations.

**Personal:** Boston University School of Law (JD 1976); Johns Hopkins University (AB 1973).

## WEISWASSER, Stephen A
Covington & Burling, Washington, DC
202 662 5508
SWeiswasser@cov.com
*Recommended in Media & Entertainment*

**Practice Areas:** Media, new media, content, telecommunications, and technology industries. Work includes strategic consulting, M&A, joint ventures and other transactions, international, litigation and corporate governance.

**Prof. Memberships:** ABA, FCBA, International Radio & Television Society Foundation (past President).

**Career:** EVP and GC Gemstar - TV Guide International 1999-2000; President & CEO Americast 1995-98; SVP Capital Cities/ABC, Inc. 1986-95 (President Capital Cities/ABC Multimedia Group 1993-95; EVP ABC News 1991-93; EVP ABC Television Network Group 1991; GC 1986-91).

**Personal:** Harvard (JD, mcl, 1966); Johns Hopkins 1962-63 (Woodrow Wilson Fellowship); Wayne State (BA, distinction, 1962).

## WELLEN, Robert
Ivins, Phillips & Barker, Washington, DC

202 393 7600
*Recommended in Tax*

## WELLS, Stephen E
McDermott Will & Emery, Washington, DC 202 756 8316
swells@mwe.com
*Recommended in Tax*

**Practice Areas:** Partner-in-charge of Washington Tax Practice. Focuses on taxation of transactions involving US and foreign corporations, including formation of corporate ventures, reorganizations and restructurings, corporate distributions and liquidations, and corporate acquisitions and dispositions, including spin-offs. Instrumental in structuring and implementing many of the largest corporate M&As, joint ventures and spin-offs undertaken by various prominent public and private multinational corporations. Developed and implemented numerous innovative tax strategies of major corporate transactions, and in pursuing or defending against hostile tender offers.

**Personal:** Georgetown University Law Center (JD, LLM); University of Maryland (BS).

## WENNER, Adam
Chadbourne & Parke LLP, Washington, DC 202 974 5600
awenner@chadbourne.com
*Recommended in Energy*

**Practice Areas:** More than 25 years. experience in the electric power industry, representing generators, electric utilities, RTOs, independent transmission projects, and lenders and financial institutions in transactions, regulatory hearings and litigation. Represents energy companies before the Federal Energy Regulatory Commission and state commissions, as well as project developers and financial institutions in the development and sale of power and transmission projects. Mr Wenner has recently focused on the development of wind energy projects, and he represents leading participants in the renewable energy industry.

**Prof. Memberships:** DC Bar Association; Florida Bar; Energy Bar Association.

**Career:** Deputy Assistant General Counsel, FERC.

## WERTHER, Barbara G
Thelen Reid & Priest LLP, Washington, DC 202 508 4279
bwerther@thelenreid.com
*Recommended in Construction*

**Practice Areas:** Ms Werther is a Member of Thelen Reid's Construction and Government Contracts Department where she focuses on construction litigation. Prior to joining Thelen Reid, she was a Senior Partner with Arent Fox and also with a government contract and construction litigation boutique firm in the Washington area. For more than 23 years, Ms Werther has represented both owners and contractors in disputes

regarding substantial claims for delays, acceleration, inefficiencies and default terminations, locally as well as nationally. She has also represented both general contractors and sureties in performance and payment bond disputes. In the government contracts arena, Ms Werther has litigated numerous claims for equitable adjustment, as well as bid protests at the Boards of Contract Appeals and the Court of Federal Claims. In 1997, Ms Werther was responsible for the only victory ever by a contractor in federal court in the District of Columbia where the Court overturned the contracting officer's non-responsibility determination and directed award to the contractor. Among other recent successes, Ms Werther obtained the largest jury verdict ever in a commercial case in Jackson County, Mississippi, on behalf of a subcontractor on a complex project involving the dismantling of a fertilizer manufacturing facility. The Mississippi Supreme Court affirmed this ruling in 1999. In 2001, in the United States District Court for the Eastern District of Virginia, Ms Werther won summary judgment in a default termination case on behalf of a prime contractor against a subcontractor.

**Prof. Memberships:** Member of the American Bar Association.

**Career:** Partner of Thelen Reid & Priest. Admitted to practice in the District of Columbia and Virginia.

**Publications:** Terminations chapter in 'Construction Law Handbook', 1999; updated annually.

**Personal:** Received her JD from George Washington University, and her BA, magna cum laude, from the University of Pennsylvania.

## WEST, Joseph D
Gibson, Dunn & Crutcher LLP, Washington, DC 202 955 8658
jwest@gibsondunn.com
*Recommended in Construction, Government Contracts*

**Practice Areas:** Extensive experience with government and construction contracts. Represents contractors, subcontractors and government agencies. Areas of expertise include contract counseling, dispute avoidance/resolution, claims analysis, suspension/debarment, and ADR. Has engaged in cases before various United States Courts of Appeals and District Courts, the United States Court of Federal Claims, and Boards of Contract Appeals.

**Prof. Memberships:** Fellow, American College of Construction Lawyers.

**Career:** Registered Professional Engineer and former officer of the United States Navy Civil Engineer Corps.

**Personal:** JD, George Washington University, 1977, editor of The George Washington Law Review, Order of the Coif.

## WEST, Philip
Steptoe & Johnson LLP, Washington, DC
202 429 6247
pwest@steptoe.com
*Recommended in Tax*

**Practice Areas:** Partner in Steptoe & Johnson LLP's Washington office. 20 years legal tax experience. Focuses on complex international tax matters. Extensive experience with transactions, tax controversies, tax minimization planning, and advocacy before IRS, Treasury, Congress, courts, and attest auditors. Expertise with deferral, foreign tax credit, transfer pricing, and treaty matters. Served as the Treasury Department's International Tax Counsel and led US work at OECD. Practical experience with foreign tax systems and good relationships with foreign tax officials and private practitioners. Frequent speaker and author.
**Personal:** LLM, Georgetown University Law Center, 1987; JD, New York Law School, 1984.

## WEST JR, William
Howrey LLP, Washington, DC
202 783 0800
*Recommended in Intellectual Property*

## WHITE, Debra
Milbank, Tweed, Hadley & McCloy LLP, Washington, DC 202 835 7500
*Recommended in Business Process Outsourcing, Technology*

## WIACEK, Raymond
Jones Day, Washington, DC
202 879 3908
rjwiacek@jonesday.com
*Recommended in Tax*

**Practice Areas:** Oversees the firm's Tax Practice. His practice involves the tax and business aspects of corporate and international transactions, including structured and cross-border financings, mergers and acquisitions, restructurings, transfer pricing, and international licensing for intellectual property, as well as disputes with the IRS and foreign governments related to such transactions. Testified on international tax matters and proposed regulations before the House Ways and Means Committee, the Senate Finance Committee, the Senate Foreign Relations Committee, and the IRS. Named a top lawyer in 'The World's Leading Lawyers, America's Leading Lawyers for Business', Euromoney's International Tax Review, and other publications.

## WILCOX, Gary B
Morgan, Lewis & Bockius LLP, Washington, DC 202 739 5509
gwilcox@morganlewis.com
*Recommended in Tax*

**Practice Areas:** Mr Wilcox is a Partner in the Tax Practice. Mr Wilcox advises US and international clients on a range of tax matters, including tax aspects of mergers and acquisitions, spin-offs, formations of

joint ventures and partnerships, post-acquisition integration planning in cross-border transactions, and structuring REIT offerings and transactions. He also represents clients in US federal tax controversies and appears before the US Treasury and Internal Revenue Service (IRS) to seek published guidance and rulings on behalf of clients.
**Career:** Former Deputy Chief Counsel for the IRS.
**Personal:** LLM, New York University, 1986; JD, University of Oklahoma (with highest honors), 1984.

## WILEY, Richard E
Wiley Rein & Fielding LLP, Washington, DC 202 719 7010
rwiley@wrf.com
*Recommended in Media & Entertainment, Telecom, Broadcast & Satellite*

**Practice Areas:** Head of largest communications practice in United States. Former FCC Chairman and widely recognized as the leading communications attorney in the United States. Profiled in The New York Times ('Telecommunications' Ubiquitous Man of Influence'), The Los Angeles Times ('The Sixth Commissioner'), The Globe and Mail ('Father of High-Definition Television'), The American Lawyer ('Brand Name of Communications Bar') and the National Law Journal ('An Enduring Influence and one of the nation's 100 Most Influential Lawyers').
**Prof. Memberships:** Chair, American Bar Association Section on Administrative Law and Regulatory Practice; Past President, Federal Bar Association and Federal Communications Bar Association; Chairman, FCC's Advisory Committee on Digital Television (1987-96).
**Career:** FCC Chairman, Commissioner and General Counsel; firm's Managing Partner.
**Personal:** Northwestern University (JD and BS with honors); Georgetown University (LLM).

## WILKINS, William J
WilmerHale, Washington, DC
202 663 6204
William.Wilkins@wilmerhale.com
*Recommended in Tax*

**Practice Areas:** Partner, Tax Department. Advises clients on tax and business matters, including tax compliance, exempt organization issues, corporate and partnership transactions, investment structures and federal tax legislation and regulation.
**Prof. Memberships:** Former Vice-Chair, ABA Section of Taxation; Regent, American College of Taxation; Trustee, American Tax Policy Institute.
**Career:** United States Senate Committee on Finance, 1981-88; Staff Director and Chief Counsel of Committee staff, 1987-88.
**Personal:** JD, Harvard Law School; BA, Yale College.

## WILLIAMS, William
Fulbright & Jaworski L.L.P., Washington, DC 202 662 4673
wwilliams@fulbright.com
*Recommended in Energy*

**Practice Areas:** He was an attorney for the Federal Energy Regulatory Commission from 1977-80. The majority of his practice deals with the representation of interstate pipelines and other clients before the Federal Energy Regulatory Commission and in related appellate matters. He has also represented clients in state regulatory proceedings. In addition to his regulatory practice, he advises clients involved in litigation or commercial transactions with regulated companies.
**Prof. Memberships:** Virginia Bar, District of Columbia Bar, Federal Energy Bar Association.
**Personal:** Lives in Falls Church, Virginia; two children, William and Erin; leisure activities involve spending time with his children.

## WILLNER, Keith J
Mayer, Brown, Rowe & Maw LLP, Washington, DC 202 263 3215
kwillner@mayerbrownrowe.com
*Recommended in Real Estate*

**Practice Areas:** Represents institutions in major real estate financing, acquisition, sale, venture, and leasing transactions. Counsels major REITs, pension funds, banks, insurance companies, credit companies, and other investors on their real estate needs. Structures and executes acquisitions and dispositions of major commercial property types. Organizes investment and ownership vehicles to purchase and operate real estate projects. Assists clients in permanent, construction, mezzanine, securitized, and syndicated loans on all types of commercial real estate. Handles complex portfolio and multistate transactions. Serves as national leasing counsel for leading companies across US including major headquarters leases.
**Career:** Joined Mayer, Brown, Rowe & Maw LLP as Partner, 1996. Formerly with Morrison & Foerster; Lane and Edson, P.C.; Bronson, Bronson & McKinnon. Served on Steering Committee of Real Estate Section of DC Bar Association and as Chair of Commercial Transactions Committee and Commercial Leasing Committee.
**Publications:** Articles in numerous publications, including Mortgage and Real Estate Executives Report, CREI Interactive, The Corridor Real Estate Journal, and Real Estate Rescues. Frequent speaker and author on real estate topics.
**Personal:** University of Virginia School of Law, JD, 1984; Virginia Tax Review. University of Virginia, BA, magna cum laude, 1981; Phi Beta Kappa.

## WILSON, Anita
Vinson & Elkins LLP, Washington, DC
202 639 6776
awilson@velaw.com
*Recommended in Energy*

**Practice Areas:** Federal and state energy regulation and energy transactions. Represents natural gas pipelines, storage facility operators and shippers in proceedings before the Federal Energy Regulatory Commission. Advises clients in certificate, rate, compliance, restructuring and rule-making proceedings, as well as complaint and enforcement matters, related appellate litigation, and due diligence review of pipeline and LNG terminal assets.
**Prof. Memberships:** American Bar Association; Energy Bar Association.
**Career:** Partner since 1999.
**Personal:** University of Virginia (JD 1990) (President of Law School Class); College of William and Mary (BS 1986) (Phi Beta Kappa).

## WILTSHIRE, William
Harris, Wiltshire & Grannis LLP, Washington, DC 202 730 1300
*Recommended in Telecom, Broadcast & Satellite*

## WIMMER, Kurt A
Covington & Burling, Washington, DC
202 662 5278
kwimmer@cov.com
*Recommended in Media & Entertainment, Telecom, Broadcast & Satellite*

**Practice Areas:** Media law and intellectual property – content liability, representation of television, satellite and new media companies before the FCC and Congress; newsgathering advice and litigation, international jurisdiction and regulation, privacy, defamation. Clients include Washington Post, Raycom, TerreStar, Newspaper Association of America, Yahoo!, CBS/NBC Affiliate Associations.
**Prof. Memberships:** ABA Forum on Communications Law, International Bar Association, Federal Communications Bar Association.
**Career:** President, Media Law Resource Center's Defense Counsel Section; Chair, First Amendment Advisory Council of Media Institute; Chair, Board of Directors, IREX. Managing Partner of Covington's London office 2000-03. Named by UN to Advisory Group on Defamation & Freedom of Information legislation for Bosnia and Herzegovina. First lawyer to receive highest accolade of National Press Photographers Ass'n, 2002.
**Publications:** 'International Libel & Privacy Handbook' (Bloomberg 2006), 'Who Rules the Net?' (Cato Institute 2004), numerous journal and law review articles.
**Personal:** Syracuse University (JD 1985, MA Communications Policy 1985); University of Missouri-Columbia (BJ, 1982).

## WINCEK, Mark D

Kilpatrick Stockton LLP, Washington, DC
202 508 5800
MWincek@KilpatrickStockton.com
*Recommended in Employee Benefits*
**Practice Areas:** Employee benefits, with an emphasis on qualified retirement plans, welfare benefits and flexible and executive compensation.
**Prof. Memberships:** American College of Employee Benefits Counsel; ECFC Flex Advisory Council; American Bar Association, Tax Section (Chairman of the Statutory Welfare Benefits Subcommittee, 1986-90).
**Career:** Staff of US House Ways and Means Committee (1976-81); former Adjunct Professor of law at Georgetown University Law Center; Head of the firm's Employee Benefits Group.
**Publications:** Frequently lectures and writes on employee benefits matters; Editorial Advisory Board, Benefits Law Journal (1988-present).
**Personal:** BA and JD degrees, cum laude, from Boston College in 1972 and 1976.

## WINTERSCHEID, Joseph F

McDermott Will & Emery, Washington, DC 202 756 8061
jwinterscheid@mwe.com
*Recommended in Antitrust*
**Practice Areas:** US and international antitrust law, with emphasis on EU competition law. Advises clients on US and multi-jurisdictional mergers, acquisitions and joint ventures, including premerger notification requirements. Also advises antitrust aspects of US and international distribution practices and intellectual property licensing arrangements.
**Career:** Joined McDermott after 24 years of practice with another leading international law firm, and headed their Brussels office from 1989-94. Former Chair of ABA Antitrust Section International Antitrust Committee and Vice-Chair of Corporate Counseling Committee. Private Sector Advisor to International Competition Network.
**Personal:** University of Notre Dame (JD, magna cum laude and BA, summa cum laude).

## WYRON, Richard H

Orrick, Herrington & Sutcliffe LLP, Washington, DC 202 339 8514
rwyron@orrick.com
*Recommended in Bankruptcy*
**Practice Areas:** Represents debtors, creditors, equity holders, contracting parties and others in non-judicial restructurings and proceedings under the US Bankruptcy Code. Extensive experience representing debtors, future claimants representatives and other key parties in major asbestos-related bankruptcy cases. Counsels clients in bankruptcy and restructuring matters across a range of industries including energy, real estate, retail and financial services.

**Prof. Memberships:** Admitted to practice Washington, DC (1981); Maryland (1987); Member, American Bankruptcy Institute.
**Career:** Previously, Partner, Swidler Berlin (1992-2005); Law Clerk, Honorable Albert V Bryan, Jr, Eastern District of Virginia (1979-80).
**Personal:** JD, University of Virginia, 1979; BA, University of Virginia, 1976.

## YAMPOLSKY, Harvey A

Arent Fox PLLC, Washington, DC
202 857 6149
yampolsky.harvey@arentfox.com
*Recommended in Healthcare*
**Practice Areas:** Practice involves compliance with the many Medicare and Medicaid statutes and regulations relating to billing, coding and reimbursement issues or to marketing, innovative delivery systems and business relationships among healthcare providers. He has defended several of the country's most prominent healthcare companies that have been investigated under healthcare laws and has assisted numerous companies in the operation of their compliance programs.
**Career:** Joined Arent Fox in 1990, after 11 years as Chief Counsel to the Inspector General at the Department of Health and Human Services (HHS).
**Personal:** New York University, LLM 1971; University of Chicago, JD 1969; University of Rochester, AB 1966.

## YANG, John C

Wiley Rein & Fielding LLP, Washington, DC 202 719 4483
jyang@wrf.com
*Recommended in Insurance*
**Practice Areas:** Represents insurers in coverage cases, including general liability and professional liability coverage issues. Counsels clients on litigation, transactional and regulatory issues affecting the business of insurance, and represents industry trade associations, including the Complex Insurance Claims Litigation Association.
**Prof. Memberships:** President and Board of Governors, National Asian Pacific American Bar Association; Chair and Board of Directors, National Asian Pacific American Legal Consortium; Co-Founder and Board of Directors, Asian Pacific American Legal Resource Center.
**Career:** General Counsel and Secretary, District of Columbia Bar; General Counsel, Organization of Chinese Americans.
**Personal:** George Washington University Law School (JD); Washington University (AB).

## YANNUCCI, Thomas D

Kirkland & Ellis LLP, Washington, DC
202 879 5056
tyannucci@kirkland.com
*Recommended in Litigation, Media & Entertainment*
**Practice Areas:** Acted as trial and appel-

late counsel in individual and class action suits involving claims in the following areas: defamation, antitrust, intellectual property, securities, government enforcement and regulatory matters (DOJ, FDA, EPA, FTC, SEC, ITC, FEC, CIA, NLRB), RICO, insurance coverage, ERISA, international trade and white-collar crime. Has handled jury and bench trials, and appeared in state and federal courts and arbitrations. Has also served as an arbitrator for complex commercial cases for the American Arbitration Association.
**Personal:** University of Notre Dame, AB, 1972. University of Notre Dame Law School, JD, 1976; Editor-in-Chief, Notre Dame Law Review.

## YDE, Paul

Freshfields Bruckhaus Deringer LLP, Washington, DC 202 777 4500
*Recommended in Antitrust*

## YINGLING, Gary

Kirkpatrick & Lockhart Nicholson Graham LLP, Washington, DC
202 778 9000
*Recommended in Healthcare*

## YOGODZINSKI, Debra D

Nixon Peabody LLP, Washington, DC
202 585 8746
dyogodzinski@nixonpeabody.com
*Recommended in Real Estate*
**Practice Areas:** Development, acquisition, financing of commercial real estate; real estate securities matters; acquisition and disposition of mortgage loans. Current and recent representations include Forest City Washington in connection with various mixed-use developments; redevelopment of the Maison Blanche department store into a mixed-use development, including Ritz-Carlton, New Orleans and other hotels, spa and retail; and underwriters in connection with military housing transactions.
**Prof. Memberships:** DC Building Industry Association (Member, Board of Directors); Washington DC Economic Partnership (Member, Board of Directors).
**Personal:** Pennsylvania State University, BA, 1975; Catholic University of America, JD, 1978.

## YOHAY, Stephen

Arent Fox PLLC, Washington, DC
202 857 6410
yohay.stephen@arentfox.com
*Recommended in Employment*
**Practice Areas:** Steve devotes his practice to occupational safety and health law, and also has extensive experience in employment matters. Steve represents major employers nationwide in OSHA inspections and citation contests, as well as industry associations in OSHA rulemaking proceedings. He has significant experience in defending OSHA and related criminal investigations and litigation following major industrial accidents, and

advises clients on accident contingency plans, including preparing for OSHA inspections. He also advises on 'whistleblower' claims, including under Sarbanes-Oxley.
**Personal:** George Washington University, LLM (Labor Law) 1974; Georgetown University Law Center, JD 1970 (honors: Law Journal); Union College (NY), BA 1967.

## YOUNG, Howard J

Sonnenschein Nath & Rosenthal LLP, Washington, DC 202 408 9210
hyoung@sonnenschein.com
*Recommended in Healthcare*
**Practice Areas:** Advises a broad range of healthcare businesses, including hospital, medical supply, medical device, pharmaceutical, diagnostic imaging, hospice, physician, GPO, and dialysis sectors. Expertise in fraud and abuse, regulatory, reimbursement and compliance program matters and defends companies and providers involved in False Claims Act, Anti-Kickback Law litigation matters.
**Prof. Memberships:** Member, American Bar Association, Health Law Section; Member, American Health Lawyers Association; Member, Health Care Compliance Association.
**Career:** Served with the Office of Counsel to the HHS Inspector General (OIG).
**Personal:** Duke University School of Law, JD; Tufts University, BA, magna cum laude.

## YUFFEE, Michael

McDermott Will & Emery, Washington, DC 202 756 8066
myuffee@mwe.com
*Recommended in Energy*
**Practice Areas:** Member of Energy and Derivatives Markets Group. Represents energy clients on various regulatory, litigation and transactional matters. Represents and advises on all facets of the wholesale power market, including various Independent System Operator (ISO) and Regional Transmission Organization (RTO) proceedings, rate and market design proceedings, merger proceedings, and investigation and litigation matters before Federal Energy Regulatory Commission (FERC), state public utilities commissions, and federal courts. Has advised on structured physical energy transactions and wholesale power transactions. Participated in many FERC proceedings concerning development of ISO and RTO markets.
**Personal:** Washington University School of Law (JD); Boston University (BA).

## ZACHEM, Kathryn

Wilkinson Barker Knauer LLP, Washington, DC 202 783 4141
*Recommended in Telecom, Broadcast & Satellite*

## ZAHLER, Robert

Pillsbury Winthrop Shaw Pittman LLP,
Washington, DC 202 663 8130
Robert.Zahler@pillsburylaw.com
*Recommended in Business Process
Outsourcing, Technology*

**Practice Areas:** Mr Zahler participates
in a wide range of legal work at Pillsbury
and its consulting entity (Pillsbury Global Sourcing), with special emphasis on
sourcing, both information technology
outsourcing and business process outsourcing. His work includes counseling
and negotiating large-scale facilities management; information technology outsourcing and business process outsourcing arrangements (both onshore and offshore); the structuring of telecommunications and managed network services
transactions; the development of systems
integration and custom system contracts;
the protection of intellectual property
rights; and the licensing of computer
software.

**Personal:** JD, Harvard Law School, 1975,
cum laude; SB, Physics, Massachusetts
Institute of Technology, 1972.

## ZAKUPOWSKY, Alex

Miller & Chevalier Chartered,
Washington, DC 202 626 5800
*Recommended in Tax*

## ZARAGOZA, Richard R

Pillsbury Winthrop Shaw Pittman LLP,
Washington, DC 202 663 8266
richard.zaragoza@pillsburylaw.com
*Recommended in Telecom, Broadcast
& Satellite*

**Practice Areas:** Mr Zaragoza counsels a
broad range of communications clients,
focusing on regulatory, transactional and
litigation matters. Among his clients, he
represents the National Alliance of State
Broadcasters Associations, comprised of
the State Broadcasters Associations
throughout the United States. Mr
Zaragoza is past President of the Federal
Communications Bar Association
(FCBA); former FCBA delegate to the
American Bar Association; and recipient
of FCBA's 1995 Distinguished Service
Award. It was his vision to establish the
FCBA Foundation for community service.

**Career:** Former appellate attorney, Federal Communications Commission.

**Personal:** JD, Boston College Law
School, 1969; AB, Georgetown University,
1966.

## ZAX, Leonard

Latham & Watkins LLP, Washington, DC
202 637 2200
*Recommended in Real Estate*

## ZEVNIK, Paul

Morgan, Lewis & Bockius LLP,
Washington, DC 202 739 5755
pzevnik@morganlewis.com
*Recommended in Insurance*

**Practice Areas:** Paul A Zevnik's principal area of practice is insurance coverage
advice and litigation, with an emphasis
on environmental, asbestos, toxic tort
and product liability coverage disputes.
Mr Zevnik is also broadly experienced in
transactions in the insurance, broadcasting and media businesses, including tax-
driven transactions involving IRC §468B
trusts and insurance captives, as well as
corporate-owned life insurance (COLI).

**Prof. Memberships:** Member, The District of Columbia Bar; Member, State Bar
of California; Member, Pennsylvania Bar
Associations.

## ZIMMERMAN, Eric

McDermott Will & Emery,
Washington, DC 202 756 8148
ezimmerman@mwe.com
*Recommended in Healthcare*

**Practice Areas:** Recognized Medicare
law and policy authority. Represents
clients before Congress and federal agencies, helping clients to navigate legislative
and regulatory processes and advance
changes, improve reimbursement, maintain compliance and evaluate transactions. Clients include healthcare service
providers, device and equipment manufacturers and suppliers, medical trade
associations and professional societies.
Advises financial community on federal
legislative and regulatory developments.

**Prof. Memberships:** Chair, American
Health Lawyers Association's Regulation,
Accreditation and Payment Practice
Group. Advisory Board, Bureau of
National Affairs' Medicare Report. Editorial Board, Outpatient Surgery Magazine.

**Personal:** George Mason University
School of Law (JD); George Washington
University (MBA); Emory University,
(BA).

## ZUCKERMAN, Roger

Zuckerman Spaeder LLP,
Washington, DC 202 778 1800
*Recommended in Litigation*

## ZUTZ, Robert

Kirkpatrick & Lockhart Nicholson Graham LLP, Washington, DC
202 778 9000
*Recommended in Investment
Management*

## ZWEIFACH, Gerson

Williams & Connolly LLP, Washington,
DC 202 434 5000
*Recommended in Media &
Entertainment*

## ZWISLER, Margaret

Latham & Watkins LLP, Washington, DC
202 637 2200
*Recommended in Antitrust*

# ADDUCI, MASTRIANI & SCHAUMBERG, L.L.P.

## THE FIRM

**Managing Partner:** V James Adduci, II

**Number of partners:** 10
**Number of other lawyers:** 13

**HEAD OFFICE**

**DISTRICT OF COLUMBIA**
1200 Seventeenth Street, NW, **Washington, DC** 20036
**Tel:** 202 467 6300   **Fax:** 202 466 2006
**Website:** www.adduci.com

**FIRM OVERVIEW:** For 25 years, Adduci, Mastriani & Schaumberg, L.L.P. has provided thorough, expert counsel to meet clients' unique legal needs in international trade, intellectual property litigation and customs transactions. The firm specializes in pursuing clients' legal actions effectively and quickly before federal regulatory agencies and tribunals including: US International Trade Commission, US Department of Commerce, Federal Courts, Office of the US Trade Representative, US Customs and Border Protection, and US Patent and Trademark Office. Many of the firm's attorneys have worked as legal counsel, examiners or advisors to one or more of these government agencies. The firm maintains good working relations with these offices. The attorneys' extensive experience in litigating import-related intellectual property, antidumping, countervailing duty and customs cases enables Adduci, Mastriani & Schaumberg, L.L.P. to handle clients' international trade concerns rapidly and accurately.

## MAIN AREAS OF PRACTICE:

**Section 337 Investigations:** The firm's most recognized expertise is in handling Section 337 investigations. In fact, it has been involved in nearly 25% of the over 500 Section 337 investigations that have been filed before the US International Trade Commission (ITC). The firm's attorneys have served as legal counsel to the ITC and have helped revise its statutes, rules and procedures. The firm has represented both complainants and respondents, thus clients receive the benefit of highly effective legal strategies and guidance regardless of their role in a case. The firm has been involved with a wide range of products including, semiconductors, back supports, set top boxes, warehouse sorting equipment and disposable cameras.

**Antidumping & Countervailing Duty Investigations:** The firm has been active in antidumping cases since the early 1980s. It has represented both domestic and foreign clients in antidumping and countervailing duty investigations before the US Department of Commerce (DOC), the ITC and in appeals before the US Court of International Trade in cases involving, for instance, outboard motors, crawfish, flat panel displays, pistachios and aramid fiber.

**Customs Transactions:** Effectively guiding importers through the maze of US Customs and Border Protection regulations at the US Department of Homeland Security is an integral part of the firm's international trade practice. The firm's Washington, DC location allows attorneys to act quickly and effectively at the headquarters level to resolve the varied types of difficulties clients may face. The attorneys at the firm offer nearly 60 years of combined experience in working for Customs.

**Related International Trade Investigations:** US and foreign companies seek the firm's broad expertise in investigations designed to control access by foreign competitors to the US market. On the other hand, the firm has also successfully obtained export licenses for goods, such as computer hardware and software, telecommunications equipment and various electronic products and components.

**Intellectual Property Litigation:** The firm has extensive experience in Federal Court litigation, appellate practice and arbitration. In addition to litigating intellectual property and unfair competition cases, Adduci, Mastriani & Schaumberg, L.L.P. also represents clients in general commercial and business regulation disputes.

**CLIENTS:** The firm represents both domestic and international clients, including companies in the industrial, pharmaceutical and automotive industries. Adduci, Mastriani & Schaumberg, L.L.P. is committed to providing excellence by listening to clients, offering realistic legal evaluations, developing strategies and implementing those strategies cost effectively. The firm's practice continues to grow through referrals from existing clients.

**INTERNATIONAL WORK:** International trade law is one of the core areas of the firm's practice and one for which Adduci, Mastriani & Schaumberg, L.L.P. has become best known.

**ADDUCI, MASTRIANI & SCHAUMBERG, L.L.P.**
ATTORNEYS AT LAW

# AKIN GUMP STRAUSS HAUER & FELD LLP

## THE FIRM

**Chairman:** R Bruce McLean

**Number of lawyers:** 950
**Website:** www.akingump.com

**FIRM OVERVIEW:** Recognized for its sophisticated clients and capabilities as well as its outstanding team of professionals, Akin Gump Strauss Hauer & Feld is one of the world's largest law firms, with 15 offices and over 900 lawyers in more than 50 practice disciplines. Akin Gump's steadfast dedication to providing exemplary client service and its visionary leadership are key factors in this first-generation law firm's swift rise to the top of the profession. A 2005 survey of corporate directors ranked Akin Gump among corporate America's 20 most-admired law firms.

## MAIN AREAS OF PRACTICE:

**Corporate & Securities:** Akin Gump advises on mergers and acquisitions, corporate finance and securities, international transactions, investment fund management, private equity and corporate restructuring, providing counsel on US and international tax and governance issues.

**Energy:** The firm is well-known for its diverse and full-service practice, encompassing project finance and development, transactional and regulatory matters. The firm's lawyers have represented virtually every major segment of the energy industry on issues ranging from energy policy to tax questions to environmental and land use challenges.

**Financial Restructuring:** Akin Gump has represented committees of bondholders, noteholders, institutional investors and trade creditors in more than 120 major restructurings since 1999. Among its most significant recent engagements are the representations of the official creditors' committees in the Delta Airlines and Calpine Energy bankruptcy cases, as well as the official creditor's committee in the WorldCom reorganization, the largest corporate bankruptcy in US history.

**Intellectual Property:** The firm provides counsel on patent prosecution and litigation, trademark, copyright, trade secret and unfair competition matters to Fortune 500 companies, multinational corporations and entertainment conglomerates, as well as small businesses, universities, research foundations, government agencies and individual inventors.

**Labor & Employment:** The firm advises management in both traditional matters, such as collective bargaining and discrimination lawsuits, and emerging issues, including class action wage-hour and EEO litigation.

**Litigation:** Akin Gump represents many of the country's largest Fortune 500 companies, as well as numerous smaller business entities and individuals, in civil and criminal matters in state and federal trial and appellate courts.

**Project & Infrastructure Development:** The firm provides fully integrated project development counsel in the fields of environment and land use, development, energy, transportation, construction and project finance.

**Public Law & Policy:** Akin Gump has one of the world's most sophisticated and diverse US and international public law and policy practices, representing corporations, individuals, nonprofits, foreign governments, and coalitions and trade associations.

**INTERNATIONAL WORK:** The firm is recognized for its Russia/CIS Practice, which is comprised of two former ambassadors to the Russian Federation and top-ranking former US government officials with significant experience in the region. The firm also numbers among its members former ambassadors to South Korea, Japan and the United Nations.

## OFFICES

**CALIFORNIA**
1950 University Avenue, Suite 505, **East Palo Alto**, CA 94303
**Tel:** 415 765 9500 **Fax:** 415 765 9501

2029 Century Park East, Suite 2400, **Los Angeles**, CA 90067
**Tel:** 310 229 1000 **Fax:** 310 229 1001

580 California Street, Suite 1500, **San Francisco**, CA 94104
**Tel:** 415 765 9500 **Fax:** 415 765 9501

**DISTRICT OF COLUMBIA**
Robert S Strauss Building, 1333 New Hampshire Avenue, NW,
**Washington,** DC 20036
**Tel:** 202 887 4000 **Fax:** 202 887 4288

**NEW YORK**
590 Madison Avenue, **New York**, NY 10022
**Tel:** 212 872 1000 **Fax:** 212 872 1002

**PENNSYLVANIA**
One Commerce Square, 2005 Market Street, Suite 2200,
**Philadelphia**, PA 19103
**Tel:** 215 965 1200 **Fax:** 215 965 1210

**TEXAS**
300 West 6th Street, Suite 2100, **Austin**, TX 78701
**Tel:** 512 499 6200 **Fax:** 512 499 6290

1700 Pacific Avenue, Suite 4100, **Dallas**, TX 75201
**Tel:** 214 969 2800 **Fax:** 214 969 4343

1111 Louisiana Street, 44th Floor, **Houston**, TX 77002
**Tel:** 713 220 5800 **Fax:** 713 236 0822

300 Convent Street, Suite 1500, **San Antonio**, TX 78205
**Tel:** 210 281 7000 Fax: 210 224 2035

## INTERNATIONAL OFFICES:

The firm has offices in Brussels, Dubai, London, Moscow and Taipei.

AKIN GUMP
STRAUSS HAUER & FELD LLP

# ARNOLD & PORTER LLP

## THE FIRM

**Chairman:** Michael N Sohn
**Managing Partner:** Richard M Alexander

**Number of partners worldwide:** 259
**Number of other lawyers worldwide:** 366

**FIRM OVERVIEW:** Arnold & Porter LLP is an international firm responsive to the needs of clients in a highly competitive and litigious marketplace. With offices in Washington, DC, New York, London, Brussels, Los Angeles, San Francisco, Northern Virginia, and Denver, and over 600 lawyers worldwide, Arnold & Porter has a distinct perspective on the pivotal relationship between government and business. The firm offers clients a unique window on the legal, policy, and political processes affecting almost every aspect of the international economy. Arnold & Porter maintains substantial litigation, transactional, and regulatory practices, as well as those involving many contemporary areas of law.

**EXPERIENCE:** The firm represents clients in a full range of legal and policy processes affecting both the national and international economy and business. The firm conducts business with companies in many jurisdictions around the globe including North America, Europe, Latin America, and Asia.

## MAIN AREAS OF PRACTICE:

**Antitrust/Competition & Trade Regulation:** The firm has a strong tradition in antitrust/competition policy and trade regulation policy. Lawyers work with clients from a broad range of industries and represent them in matters under federal, state, and European laws governing competition, pricing, distribution, advertising, and intellectual property.

**Bankruptcy:** The firm's National Bankruptcy, Creditors' Rights, and Workout Practice represents a diverse client base including secured and unsecured creditors, bondholders, landlords, parties dealing with financially distressed businesses, investors and asset purchasers, committees, debtors, equity holders and other interested parties in bankruptcy proceedings, and related counseling and litigation. Cases range from single-asset debtors to large complex reorganizations.

**Commercial, Corporate & Securities:** The firm's Corporate Practice has particular experience in mergers and acquisitions and corporate control matters involving banks, savings associations, and other financial institutions. The firm also represents issuers, underwriters, security holders, and indenture trustees in a full range of public and private offerings of debt and equity securities.

**Employment Benefits:** The firm represents employers and employees, pension plans, unions, corporations, and nonprofit organizations in matters ranging from tax qualification requirements to the use of employee stock ownership plans (ESOPs) in buyouts and other takeovers.

**Environmental:** Arnold & Porter represents corporations, developers, utilities, and public agencies in a wide range of environmental regulatory matters. Litigation is a prominent aspect of the firm's work in this area.

**Financial Services:** The firm's practice covers every aspect of the legal, business, and regulatory issues encountered by financial institutions, including growth and expansion, regulatory matters, financial products and services, capital markets, and corporate governance.

**Government Contracts:** The firm advises companies and institutions doing substantial business with federal, state and local agencies. The Government Contracts Group, which includes several nationally recognized partners, advises clients on the full range of government contracts issues, including contract negotiation and formation, dispute resolution and litigation, internal investigations and enforcement actions, compliance programs, corporate transactions and mergers and acquisitions, construction, intellectual property, international procurement and cooperative projects, foreign corrupt practice act compliance, privatization, outsourcing, acquisition policy issues, and legislation.

**Healthcare:** Arnold & Porter attorneys combine insight into the healthcare fraud and abuse enforcement processes, substantive knowledge of the full range of federal and state healthcare laws and regulations, and a clear understanding of the healthcare and pharmaceutical industries.

**Hedge Funds:** The firm's Hedge Fund Practice Group possesses deep legal expertise and a broad client base. It is expert in the structuring and syndication of US and non-US alternative investment funds. Representation includes advice regarding selection of jurisdiction, structuring and distribution issues, exchange listings and memberships, allocations of assets to outside advisors and funds and the establishment of prime broker, ISDA and other over-the counter counterparty trading relationships.

**Intellectual Property & Technology:** This group has wide experience in the acquisition, protection, exploitation, and enforcement of intellectual property rights. It is particularly knowledgeable in the areas of computer and information technology, the i1nternet, pharmaceuticals, and biotechnology.

**International Trade:** The firm represents domestic and foreign corporations, governments, government agencies, international organizations, trade associations, labor unions, nongovernmental organizations, investors, banks, financial institutions, and individuals in virtually all aspects of international activity.

**Life Sciences/Biotech:** Arnold & Porter offers an innovative, integrated Life Sciences/Biotech Practice with a global perspective. The depth of the firm's involvement in life sciences places it squarely in the forefront of the development and evolution of the new life science technology drivers or 'toolbox.' The firm is closely attuned to the current state of play and future of genomics, proteomics, bioinformatics, biochips, pharmacogenetics, and the other technological developments of the day.

**Litigation:** This is a major area of the firm's work, with almost half of its domestic lawyers involved. Product liability, antitrust, and securities have been traditional areas of strength. The firm's work is diverse and includes civil and criminal, regulatory and commercial, and national and international matters.

**National Security Law & Policy:** The firm is uniquely able to advise clients on national security and homeland security issues. Among the firm's partners are a former General Counsel of the Central Intelligence Agency, a former General Counsel of the National Security Agency and a former Member of Congress who was the ranking Member of the House Homeland Security Committee. National

## HEAD OFFICE

**DISTRICT OF COLUMBIA**
555 Twelfth Street, NW, **Washington**, DC 20004-1206
**Tel:** 202 942 5000   **Fax:** 202 942 5999
**Website:** www.arnoldporter.com

## BRANCH OFFICES

**CALIFORNIA**
777 South Figueroa Street, 44th Floor, **Los Angeles**, CA 90017-5844
**Tel:** 213 243 4000   **Fax:** 213 243 4199

90 New Montgomery Street, Suite 600, **San Francisco**, CA 94105
**Tel:** 415 356 3000   **Fax:** 415 356 3099

**COLORADO**
370 Seventeenth Street, Suite 4500, **Denver**, CO 80202-1370
**Tel:** 303 863 1000   **Fax:** 303 832 0428

**NEW YORK**
399 Park Avenue, **New York**, NY 10022-4690
**Tel:** 212 715 1000   **Fax:** 212 715 1399

**VIRGINIA**
1600 Tysons Boulevard, Suite 900, **McLean**, VA 22102-4865
**Tel:** 703 720 7000   **Fax:** 703 720 7399

## INTERNATIONAL OFFICES

The firm also has offices in London and Brussels.

# ARNOLD & PORTER LLP CONT'D

security law and policy issues are increasingly important to clients and the National Security Group provides a wide range of services, including risk analysis and mitigation, data security and privacy, corporate governance issues and mergers & acquisitions involving the defense and intelligence communities, foreign ownership and control of US companies performing classified or sensitive work, unauthorized disclosures of classified information and First Amendment issues, and export control and trade sanctions.

**Pharmaceutical & Medical Devices:** When it comes to the pharmaceutical and medical devices industries, Arnold & Porter covers the field in transatlantic litigation, regulatory, and transactional matters. The largest global pharmaceutical companies, as well as the smaller ones, frequently turn to the Arnold & Porter team for product liability and European regulatory counsel.

**Privacy:** The growing patchwork of privacy laws and regulations presents companies with serious legal and compliance challenges. Companies failing to abide by privacy laws face civil and criminal prosecution, administrative enforcement actions, and private and class action lawsuits by plaintiffs' lawyers. Equally important, reports of privacy violations splashed across the front page of newspapers can result in serious harm to a business's reputation. Arnold & Porter's Privacy Team provides legal and strategic counsel through its command of key laws and regulations, understanding of emerging technology platforms, and deep experience with key industry sectors to help companies meet their privacy obligations in a demanding and competitive marketplace.

**Product Liability:** Managing complex product liability litigation requires a coordinated legal strategy that is sensitive not only to demands of the litigation, but also to the regulatory, congressional, and public relations concerns that often arise during a product liability crisis. With more than 100 of its attorneys actively engaged in product liability matters, Arnold & Porter is one of the most experienced firms in defending large and complex mass tort matters, acting both as national counsel and as trial counsel in cases asserting personal injury and property damage claims. The European Product Liability Group has wide experience in handling the defence of all types of product liability claims, from individual cases to major multi-claimant 'group actions', and is a recognized leader in the field in both the UK and Europe. The combined expertise of the US and European product liability groups means that Arnold & Porter is eminently placed to offer clients an integrated product liability service on a transatlantic basis.

**Real Estate:** The firm's Real Estate Practice mirrors the increasing complexity, sophistication, and international integration of the global economy in the twenty-first century. The firm's attorneys structure and negotiate real estate deals for owners and developers in connection with acquisition, development, construction, federal transactions, financing, leasing, management and sale of office buildings, shopping centers, industrial sites, multifamily projects, single family home developments, condominiums, hotels, resorts, and recreational developments. The firm handles all aspects of inbound investments by foreign funds and individuals who invest in US real estate and provides counsel to its US-based developers when they undertake projects in the UK and Europe, working closely with its tax department to maximize the after-tax returns.

**Securities Enforcement & Litigation:** The firm's Securities Enforcement and Litigation Practice Group defends investigations conducted by the SEC, DOJ, other federal agencies, Congress, NASD, NYSE, state regulators, and other regulatory bodies. The practice group also defends securities litigation, including class action and derivative litigation, conducts internal investigations, and provides counseling on compliance, disclosure, corporate governance, and crisis management matters. Clients of the group include major financial services companies (such as broker-dealers, investment banks, and financial institutions), public companies, accounting firms, law firms, investment advisers, hedge funds, and mutual funds, as well as directors, officers, and other individuals.

**Tax:** With approximately 30 attorneys in the firm's Washington and New York offices, the Tax Practice provides representation in all major areas of corporate, partnership, employment, individual, trusts and estates, and gift tax law.

**Telecommunications:** The firm provides regulatory, administrative, litigation, and legislative advice to corporations, government entities, institutions, and individuals. Governments and enterprises from other countries also seek the firm's advice on the domestic and international implications of existing and emerging technologies and on new regulatory and marketplace structures.

## INTERNATIONAL
### LONDON OFFICE
Tower 42, 25 Old Broad Street, London EC2N 1HQ, United Kingdom
**Lawyers:** 26
**Office Profile:** Arnold & Porter's London office advises on a full range of regulatory, transactional, and litigation matters, and focuses especially on competition, corporate transactions, intellectual property and technology, life sciences, litigation, product liability litigation and regulation, and telecommunications. The firm is committed to strategic growth in London in these and other areas with the same emphasis on quality of service and in-depth expertise as it provides in the United States. Arnold & Porter's London office has grown rapidly to include: the leading team of attorneys for the pharmaceutical and medical technology industries in product liability litigation and regulatory matters; one of the largest groups of intellectual property and technology lawyers of any US firm operating in the UK, including the UK's leading Life Sciences Transactions Group; a leading IP/IT Transaction Group and a major IP litigation capability; one of the leading european regulatory and commercial telecommunications groups; a powerful Competition Practice combined with its leading US antitrust practice; and a growing corporate and commercial transactional capability.

### BRUSSELS OFFICE
11, Rue des Colonies-Koloniënstraat 11, B-1000 Brussels, Belgium
**Lawyers:** 7
**Office Profile:** Arnold & Porter opened its Brussels office in 2003 to serve the firm's multinational client base by complementing their top-ranked US Antitrust Practice, most recently designated the number one antitrust law firm in the US (2004) and in North America (2003) by Chambers & Partners. Arnold & Porter's Brussels team represents clients before the European Commission in regard to a range of competition concerns under EU laws - including allegations of abuse of dominant position or anti-competitive practices. The firm's lawyers also have experience in dealing with major antitrust inquiries, price-fixing issues, distribution and licensing agreements, strategic alliances, and joint ventures. Members of the team undertake and coordinate the work necessary to obtain competition clearances for mergers, acquisitions, and joint ventures from the European Commission and from national authorities in the EU, Central/Eastern Europe and beyond, as well as advising on other aspects of EU law, particularly those relating to the free movement of goods, advertising, and other regulatory laws within the EU.

ARNOLD & PORTER LLP

# BEVERIDGE & DIAMOND, P.C.

## THE FIRM

**Managing Director:** Robert Brager
**Number of Directors:** 36
**Number of other lawyers:** 39

**FIRM OVERVIEW:** Since opening in 1974, Beveridge & Diamond, P.C. has focused on environmental and land use law and litigation. In court, in negotiations, and before government agencies, Beveridge & Diamond resolves complex problems and disputes, particularly in the environmental area, keeping in mind its clients' business goals.

## MAIN AREAS OF PRACTICE:

**Environmental:** Beveridge & Diamond's practice encompasses all areas of environmental law, and the firm's long history and experience allow it to successfully handle the most significant and complicated environmental matters. Beveridge & Diamond represents domestic and international clients on environmental issues related to air, surface water and groundwater, solid and hazardous wastes, product use, stewardship and recycling, environmental reporting and disclosure, and compliance with the wide array of federal and state environmental laws and regulations. The firm also represents clients across the country with regard to environmentally contaminated properties, including 'brownfields' projects, and in negotiations with buyers, sellers, developers, and insurers of these properties. In addition, Beveridge & Diamond provides strategic advice to clients with regard to their environmental management systems, and has assisted clients with their environmental due diligence efforts in the United States and across the world.

**Environmental Litigation & ADR:** The firm's Environmental Litigation and Alternative Dispute Resolution Practice challenges agency actions in administrative, trial and appellate proceedings, defends against government enforcement actions and citizen suits, and represents clients in cases brought under the federal 'Superfund' law, other federal or state statutes, or common law with regard to the extent of remediation necessary to protect the environment and who should pay for the rememdiation. The firm litigates numerous other environmental cases in state and federal courts across the country, including takings and related land use matters.

**Civil & White Collar Litigation:** Beveridge & Diamond's Civil Litigation Practice is accomplished in defending against toxic tort, product liability, and mass tort claims, and includes a strong commercial litigation component. The firm's appellate practice safeguards clients' rights after trial, and its litigators have pursued or defended against countless appeals in the United States Supreme Court, every federal circuit court of appeals, and state appellate courts around the country. In the white collar criminal area, the firm has extensive experience in assisting its clients in responding to ever increasing criminal enforcement efforts aimed at corporate entities and individual officers, directors, and employees. Its white collar attorneys have a unique environmental criminal practice, combining their experience on criminal matters with the firm's renowned reputation in environmental law to provide comprehensive and effective defenses.

**Project Development:** Major private project developments in the United States generally require one or more federal, state, or local permits or approvals under statutes protecting endangered species, wetlands, and other environmentally sensitive areas. The firm assists its clients with successful development strategies that are comprehensive, timely, and responsive to project needs and environmental regulatory requirements.

**CLIENTS:** Beveridge & Diamond represents domestic and international resource and energy companies, manufacturers, chemical companies, makers of pesticides, biotechnology companies, producers of raw materials, transportation companies, high-tech component makers, food and consumer products companies, financial institutions, trade associations, and real estate developers.

## HEAD OFFICE

**DISTRICT OF COLUMBIA**
Suite 700, 1350 I Street, NW, **Washington**, DC 20005-3311
**Tel:** 202 789 6000   **Fax:** 202 789 6190
**Email:** contact.bd@bdlaw.com
**Website:** www.bdlaw.com

## BRANCH OFFICES

**CALIFORNIA**
Suite 1800, 456 Montgomery Street, **San Francisco**, CA 94104-1251
**Tel:** 415 262 4000   **Fax:** 415 262 4040

**MARYLAND**
Suite 2210, 201 North Charles Street, **Baltimore**, MD 21201-4150
**Tel:** 410 230 3850   **Fax:** 410 230 3868

**MASSACHUSETTS**
45 William Street, Suite 120, **Wellesley**, MA 02481-4004
**Tel:** 781 416 5700   **Fax:** 781 416 5799

**NEW JERSEY**
Beveridge & Diamond, 26 Franklin Street, **Tenafly**, NJ 07670-2515
**Tel:** 201 568 2797   **Fax:** 201 568 9570

**NEW YORK**
15th Floor, 477 Madison Avenue, **New York**, NY 10022-5802
**Tel:** 212 702 5400   **Fax:** 212 702 5450

**TEXAS**
98 San Jacinto Boulevard, Suite 1420, **Austin**, TX 78701-4039
**Tel:** 512 391 8000   **Fax:** 512 391 8099

## CONTACTS

**Environmental/Environmental Litigation** ........Donald J Patterson, Jr
**Litigation** .......................................................John N Hanson
**Project Development** ....................................Fred R Wagner

**INTERNATIONAL WORK:** As clients pursue international trade and investment opportunities, the firm has continued to expand its International Environmental Practice in order to help companies identify, understand, and comply with the expanding body of international, national, and subnational environmental law in countries and regions throughout the world. The firm regularly advises clients on a wide range of matters arising under multilateral environmental agreements, international mergers and acquisitions, the environmental aspects of multilateral trade and investment agreements, and significant environmental regulatory and policy developments across the globe.

# COVINGTON & BURLING

## THE FIRM

**Chair of Management Committee:** Stuart C Stock

**Number of partners worldwide:** 166
**Number of other lawyers worldwide:** 402

**FIRM OVERVIEW:** Covington & Burling is one of the world's preeminent law firms, representing leading multinationals on many of their most significant transactional, litigation, regulatory, and public policy matters. Founded in Washington, DC in 1919, the firm has long emphasized the strength of its Corporate and Litigation Practices derived from the firm's industry expertise acquired through its broad regulatory expertise. The firm's New York office was established in 1983, and has strong ties to the corporate and financial communities. The New York office is known for its experience with mergers and acquisitions, securities, corporate finance and for white collar, securities and general commercial litigation. Covington & Burling's offices in London and Brussels, formed respectively in 1988 and 1990, now include about 60 lawyers. The major practice areas in Europe include the top-ranking Global Life Sciences and Pharmaceutical Regulatory Practice, corporate and securities law, intellectual property, communications and technology issues, taxation, employment, litigation and arbitration, competition and trade. The firm's San Francisco office, opened in 1999, focuses on meeting clients' litigation, corporate and regulatory needs in a broad range of subject areas with special emphasis on software, technology, life sciences, financial services and insurance.

## MAIN AREAS OF PRACTICE:

**Litigation:** Covington & Burling's Litigation Practice in the United States covers virtually every important area of civil and criminal law. Covington prosecutes and defends cases before juries and judges in state and federal courts nationwide, before arbitration panels convened by US and international arbitral organizations, before all major federal agencies, and in the courts of selected foreign jurisdictions. The subject matters of the firm's Civil Litigation and Arbitration Practice cover the range of high-stakes commercial disputes, but focus heavily on antitrust, employment and ERISA, insurance coverage, intellectual property, product liability, and securities litigation. The firm's Criminal Practice covers all areas of white-collar criminal representation, on behalf of both corporate and individual clients, and the related areas of regulatory enforcement, internal investigations, and ethics inquiries.

**Corporate, Tax & Benefits:** With more than 140 lawyers actively practicing in the corporate, securities, finance, bankruptcy, real estate, tax, and employee benefits areas, Covington provides a full range of transactional and advisory services. The firm's corporate and securities lawyers draw on the firm's deep regulatory expertise in areas such as communications, food and drug law, transportation, energy, financial institutions, environmental regulation, antitrust, and international trade. The firm's substantial Intellectual Property and Information Technology Practices provide an important additional resource in handling the firm's clients' multidisciplinary needs efficiently and comprehensively.

**International Trade & Antitrust:** The firm's practices in antitrust and international trade involve a wide range of transactional, litigation, and regulatory matters. The firm has handled complex civil and criminal antitrust and consumer protection matters, including major treble-damage actions, nationwide class actions, investigations, and short fuse preliminary injunction proceedings. The firm's International Trade and Finance Practice ranges from trade policy and regulatory advice to trade disputes and international arbitration and draws on the resources of all of the firm's offices. The firm appears on behalf of companies and national governments in antidumping, countervailing duty, and other proceedings brought pursuant to the US and European trade laws. To complement and strengthen its international trade and other capabilities, the firm recently formalized a strategic alliance with the international advisory firm, Kissinger McLarty Associates. The firm successfully represented IBM in securing national security approvals from the Committee on Foreign Investment in

### HEAD OFFICE

**DISTRICT OF COLUMBIA**
1201 Pennsylvania Avenue NW, **Washington**, DC 20004-2401
**Tel:** 202 662 6000  **Fax:** 202 662 6291
**Email:** sstock@cov.com
**Website:** www.cov.com

### OTHER OFFICES

**CALIFORNIA**
One Front Street, **San Francisco**, CA 94111
**Tel:** 415 591 6000  **Fax:** 415 591 6091

**NEW YORK**
1330 Avenue Of The Americas, **New York**, NY 10019
**Tel:** 212 841 1000  **Fax:** 212 841 1010

### INTERNATIONAL OFFICES

The firm also has offices in London and Brussels.

### CONTACTS

| | |
|---|---|
| **Antitrust & International Trade** | Jim Atwood |
| | Ted Voorhees |
| | Stuart Eizenstat |
| **Corporate, Tax & Benefits** | Scott Smith |
| **Life Sciences** | Richard Kingham |
| **Litigation** | Gregg Levy |
| | Will Phillips |
| | Sonya Winner |
| **Technology, Media & Communications** | Jonathan Blake |

the United States (CFIUS) in connection with the sale of its personal computing division to the PRC-based Lenovo Group. The firm's antitrust work in the merger arena includes the ExxonMobil transaction. In the antitrust litigation field, the firm's recent successes include the outright dismissal of a high profile action challenging the National Football League's eligibility rules and a class action lawsuit against leading medical schools and teaching hospitals.

**Technology, Media & Communications:** Covington & Burling's Technology Practice covers the full range of issues confronting companies engaged in technology, supported by lawyers who are authorities on such subjects as internet intellectual property, electronic payment systems, encryption and data privacy. The firm advises clients on all aspects of the technology and software industry, combining experience in Internet intellectual property, telecommunications, and other cutting-edge fields with traditional strength in such important areas as antitrust, securities and finance, and tax. Covington assists companies around the world in the creation, acquisition, protection and exploitation of intellectual property rights. In representing clients such as Microsoft and the Business Software Alliance, the firm has been at the forefront of international efforts to strengthen software copyright protection. The firm's Communications Practice is one of the most comprehensive in Washington. Covington is well known for its experience in broadcasting, mass media, telecommunications, multichannel video distribution, satellite, PCS/cellular, international, programming, newsgathering and the first amendment.

# COVINGTON & BURLING

# CROWELL & MORING LLP

## THE FIRM

**Chairman:** John A Macleod

**Number of attorneys:** 303

**FIRM OVERVIEW:** Crowell & Moring LLP is a full-service law firm with more than 300 attorneys practicing in litigation, antitrust, government contracts, corporate, intellectual property and more than 40 other practice areas. More than two-thirds of the firm's attorneys regularly litigate disputes on behalf of domestic and international corporations, start-up businesses, and individuals. Crowell & Moring's extensive client work ranges from advising on one of the world's largest telecommunications mergers to representing governments and corporations on international arbitration matters. The firm's range of practice areas also includes two consulting subsidiaries, C&M Capitolink and C&M International, which provide government relations and international trade services.

**Diversity Efforts:** The firm appreciates that its success as a law firm and its well-being as a community are greatly enhanced by creating and maintaining a diverse team of talented professionals. In June 2005, the Minority Corporate Counsel Association named Crowell & Moring one of four finalists among all Mid-Atlantic states firms for the MCCA's "Sager Award" recognizing law firm diversity efforts. Multicultural Law Magazine named Crowell & Moring 38th nationally for diversity. Two other recent awards recognize efforts to enhance quality of life: Bar Association of the District of Columbia's 'Quality of Life Award' and Washington Business Journal's 'Best 50 Places to Work Award'.

**Pro Bono:** Recently ranked 18th in American Lawyer's 'Pro Bono Report', Crowell & Moring has committed itself - as a firm and as a community of professionals - to assure that all citizens have access to the legal system. Crowell & Moring's promotion of broad participation in pro bono work by the firm's attorneys and staff has enabled the firm to serve a range of community needs.

## MAIN AREAS OF PRACTICE:

**Antitrust:** The firm's Antitrust Group represents a range of clients from established Fortune 50 corporations to start-up companies in emerging industries. The Group's practice includes the full complement of antitrust and trade regulation matters: civil litigation and investigations; mergers and acquisitions; grand jury investigations and trials; and counseling on ways to manage antitrust risks in all manner of business transactions. Recent matters include lead antitrust counsel for SBC Communications Inc. in its acquisition of AT&T Corp., and lead antitrust counsel for United Technologies Corporation's Pratt & Whitney Division in the acquisition of Boeing's rocket engine unit, Rocketdyne Propulsion. In 2004, the firm advised SBC/Cingular Wireless in the $41 billion acquisition of AT&T Wireless. Other firm antitrust clients include Alcoa, DuPont and Reed Elsevier.

**Corporate:** The firm's Corporate Group is transaction oriented, focusing on mergers and acquisitions, corporate finance and securities offerings. It also assists clients with all manner of business arrangements, including joint ventures, commercial contracts and intellectual property licensing transactions. The group regularly advises directors and senior executives on disclosure, governance and compliance issues. Clients include large public corporations, emerging companies and privately held firms in a wide range of industries, including major defense contractors, aerospace and telecommunications companies, and financial institutions.

**Government Contracts:** The firm's Government Contracts Group has a 40-year history and lawyers who are bar and industry leaders. Both private contractors and government agencies - domestic and foreign – turn to Crowell & Moring for expertise in procurement law and litigation. Whatever the issue, the Group's almost 50 government contracts lawyers have 'been there' and 'done that' - from contract formation issues and strategies, through bid protests, to contract interpretation and performance disputes, to post-performance audits, investigations,

## HEAD OFFICE

### DISTRICT OF COLUMBIA
1001 Pennsylvania Ave, NW, **Washington**, DC 20004
**Tel:** 202 624 2500   **Fax:** 202 628 5116
**Website:** www.crowell.com

## OTHER OFFICES

### CALIFORNIA
3 Park Plaza, 20th Floor, **Irvine**, CA 92614-8505
**Tel:** 949 263 8400   **Fax:** 949 263 8414

## INTERNATIONAL OFFICES

The firm also has offices in London and Brussels.

and allegations of fraud.

**Intellectual Property:** The firm's Intellectual Property Group offers the full array of intellectual property legal services, from patent to trademark, to unfair competition and litigation, to copyright and trade secret matters, in a variety of technological and commercial fields. The Group offers a range of services in patent prosecution and procurement that puts them among the top 20 United States firms, measured by volume of patents procured.

**Complex Litigation:** A core strength of Crowell & Moring and a principal foundation of the firm's success, the firm's Complex Litigation Group brings and defends lawsuits for clients in courts and tribunals nationwide, and globally, on matters spanning all practice and industry competencies. The Group's litigators practice in federal and state trial and appellate courts, administrative tribunals, and before arbitration panels throughout the United States. The Group also handles matters in Canada, Europe, and Central and South America.

**White Collar & Securities Litigation:** For more than twenty years, the firm's White Collar and Securities Litigation Group has defended clients from across the country and around the world with interests affected by investigations in federal judicial districts throughout the United States. The practice spans investigations by grand juries, congressional committees, independent and special counsels, federal agency inspectors general, and other investigative officials and bodies.

**INTERNATIONAL WORK:** The firm's European offices provide a range of transactional, counseling, regulatory, and litigation capabilities. International work ranges from high-profile antitrust concerns for Fortune 500 companies to strategic counsel through C&M International. The firm's international arbitration work includes assisting clients with informal negotiations, mediations, and arbitrations in the US, Canada, India, Europe, Africa, and the Middle East.

# DICKSTEIN SHAPIRO MORIN & OSHINSKY LLP

## THE FIRM

**Managing Partner:** Michael E Nannes
**Managing Partner, New York:** Robin L Cohen
**Managing Partner, Los Angeles:** Linda D Kornfeld
**Managing Partner Emeritus:** Angelo V Arcadipane

**Number of attorneys:** more than 375

**FIRM OVERVIEW:** Dickstein Shapiro Morin & Oshinsky LLP, founded in 1953, is a multiservice law firm with more than 375 attorneys in offices in Washington, DC, New York City, and Los Angeles, representing clients in diverse industries with a wide variety of requirements. While Dickstein Shapiro's work generally originates from a client's need for legal representation, the firm is mindful that legal service is but one ingredient in achieving a client's strategic business goals. The firm prides itself on learning and understanding client objectives and partnering with clients to generate genuine business value. Dickstein Shapiro is proud that the diversity of its clients coincides with the diversity of its practice. Clients include more than 100 of the *Fortune* 500 companies, as well as start-up ventures and entrepreneurs, multinational corporations and leading financial institutions, charitable organizations, and government officials in high profile investigations. Dickstein Shapiro's five core practice groups involve the firm in virtually every major form of counseling, litigation, and advocacy. Dickstein Shapiro provides comprehensive representation to clients through the multiple resources available in its five core groups listed below. Detailed descriptions of each practice and biographies of individual attorneys are available upon request.

## MAIN AREAS OF PRACTICE:

**Corporate & Finance Group:** Dickstein Shapiro is a leader in providing sophisticated legal services to business entities of all types, including financial institutions and individuals. The firm's Corporate and Finance Group is international in scope and involves representation of some of the world's largest corporations, commercial banks, investment banks, and venture capital firms. The group's practice ranges from small, traditional transactions to large, highly complex transactions, and provides a full range of corporate, finance, and transactional legal services to its clients. To best meet all the needs and objectives of its clients, the Corporate and Finance Group offers the complete resources of the firm for problem solving and transaction implementation. Regardless of the transaction or the client, Dickstein Shapiro brings to the table its reputation as an innovative, effective, and efficient law firm.

**Energy Group:** Dickstein Shapiro offers a multiservice, domestic and international Energy and Natural Resources Practice, with particular strengths in federal and state energy regulation, and international and domestic energy transactions. The firm's clients are engaged in all aspects of electricity, natural gas, transmission, and distribution. They include utilities, natural gas and petroleum pipelines, independent power producers, natural gas storage providers, energy marketers, trade groups, financial institutions, energy customers, governmental entities, and others. The firm's work ranges from the acquisition, sale, financing, and structuring of US and international energy companies and energy assets, to the development, construction, operation, and restructuring of generating facilities, natural gas and crude oil pipelines, and gas storage facilities. The firm also represents suppliers and purchasers of water, water treatment services, and desalinized water in connection with the financing, construction of, and permitting of facilities, as well as with respect to contract negotiations and ongoing operational issues. In addition, Dickstein Shapiro is at the forefront of the burgeoning wind power sector, and this sector's efforts to develop, construct, finance, and/or sell wind energy. The firm advises an ever-increasing number of clients with an active or emerging presence in wind development.

**Intellectual Property Group:** Dickstein Shapiro works with companies to develop strategies which capitalize on their intellectual property assets so as to achieve clients' business objectives. The firm has the experience, skill, and knowledge to solve these and other intellectual property problems successfully for clients striving to succeed in this ever-changing, highly competitive arena. The firm is

### HEAD OFFICE

**DISTRICT OF COLUMBIA**
2101 L Street, NW, **Washington**, DC 20037-1526
**Tel:** 202 785 9700  **Fax:** 202 887 0689
**Email:** info@dsmo.com
**Website:** dicksteinshapiro.com

### BRANCH OFFICES

**NEW YORK**
1177 Avenue of the Americas, **New York**, NY 10036-2714
**Tel:** 212 835 1400  **Fax:** 212 997 9880

**CALIFORNIA**
10866 Wilshire Boulevard, Suite 300, **Los Angeles**, CA 90024-4350
**Tel:** 310 441 8460  **Fax:** 310 441 8470

### CONTACTS

**Corporate & Finance Group** ...............................Frederick M Lowther
**Energy Group** ................................Kenneth M Simon, Larry F Eisenstat
**Intellectual Property Group** .....................................Gary M Hoffman
**Legislative & Regulatory Affairs Group** ................ L Andrew Zausner
**Litigation & Dispute Resolution Group** ...............Richard J Leveridge

engaged in all phases of pursuing, licensing, acquiring, and litigating intellectual property rights and rights in all areas of technology, including electronics, telecommunications equipment, pharmaceuticals, biotechnology, polymers and other specialty chemicals, and computer hardware and software. Such litigation includes representation before the US courts, the International Trade Commission, various state courts, and coordination of litigation in foreign countries.

**Legislative & Regulatory Affairs Group:** The Legislative and Regulatory Affairs Group seeks to advance clients' interests before the legislative and executive branches of government – a practice unique to Washington, DC. Increasingly, this demands a sophisticated combination of political and substantive resources, as well as a close coordination of skills drawn from traditionally separate disciplines, including government representation, regulatory and administrative counseling, and even litigation. A wealth of experience and knowledge exists among the attorneys within the Legislative and Regulatory Affairs Group who advise clients in a variety of practice areas including, government affairs, communications, and immigration.

**Litigation & Dispute Resolution Group:** Dickstein Shapiro provides clients with creative and sophisticated strategies to resolve some of the most complex, multifaceted disputes in the United States and abroad. The firm is widely known for its settlement and litigation capabilities. The Dickstein Shapiro team of approximately 200 litigators and negotiators, which includes 17 former federal prosecutors, has a track record of recovering billions of dollars for clients and saving comparable amounts by keeping them out of court. The firm is prepared to – and often does – try cases to conclusion, but only after exploration of alternative solutions that may better serve clients' needs. The firm's premier Insurance Coverage Practice expanded its services in 2005 with the addition of the attorneys and staff from the Los Angeles, California-based law firm of Pasich & Kornfeld, LLP.

**CLIENTS:** The firm is proud of the breadth and depth of its client roster. Dickstein Shapiro represents *Fortune* 500 companies, Global 1000 companies, and small, regionally-based concerns across a variety of industries. It also represents nonprofit and government entities. For more information on the firm's representative clients, please visit dicksteinshapiro.com.

# DOW, LOHNES & ALBERTSON, PLLC

## THE FIRM

**Chairman:** Leonard Baxt
**Chair, Management Committee:** John Byrnes

**FIRM OVERVIEW:** Since 1918, Dow Lohnes has served as a strategic partner with its clients in a number of growing and dynamic industries including communications and traditional media, new media and information technology, education, healthcare and more. Dow Lohnes' service offerings have grown as its clients' businesses have become more complex and demanding. With offices in Washington, DC and Atlanta, the firm has over 150 lawyers supported by extensive resources and a considerable depth of experience. The firm's quality of service is unique to the legal profession: Dow Lohnes possesses the strength of a large Washington-based regulatory practice as well as a sophisticated business and transactional law practice. Together with litigation, taxation and human resource practices, the firm offers a comprehensive array of legal services.

## MAIN AREAS OF PRACTICE:

**Communications & Telecommunications:** Dow Lohnes' Communications and Telecommunications Groups encompass one of the largest and most diverse communications law practices in the United States. For decades, they have represented all segments of the communications and media industries including commercial and non-commercial broadcast stations, cable television operators, cellular, PCS, paging and other wireless communications companies, local and long distance landline service providers, commercial satellite operators and broadband service providers. Dow Lohnes attorneys are well-versed in assisting other entities who need to know how changes in the industry affect their non-telecommunications businesses.

**Compensation, Employee Relations & Benefits:** Dow Lohnes' Compensation, Employee Relations and Benefits Group offers an integrated approach to human resource matters. Its compensation and benefits lawyers address issues including the creation, administration and termination of a wide range of employee benefits such as qualified and non-qualified retirement plans, health care programs, incentive compensation plans and equity-based plans. Its labor and employee relations lawyers counsel clients on executive employment and talent employment contracts, collective bargaining negotiations, discrimination, affirmative action plans and more. The group has a distinct expertise for ensuring smooth transitions for employees affected by major corporate acquisitions, dispositions and joint ventures.

**Corporate (Mergers & Acquisitions, Securities & Transactions):** Dow Lohnes' corporate lawyers specialize in mergers and acquisitions, private and public securities offerings, loan and financing transactions, joint ventures and venture capital investments. The firm enjoys a diverse clientele comprised of communications, entertainment and information technology companies, leading investment banks, underwriters, venture capital firms and lending institutions whom they guide through complex negotiations, multi-level financings and all other phases of major transactions from inception to closing. Dow Lohnes is a leader in the area of high-yield debt financings for media and communications companies and has ranked among the top ten firms in *The American Lawyer*'s annual listing of public debt issuer's counsel.

**Education:** Dow Lohnes provides specialized legal services to clients in the higher education community. The firm's attorneys are experienced in leveraging human and capital resources to promote new ways of delivering educational services such as e-learning, navigating the complicated regulatory environment that surrounds instruction across state and national borders, and protecting and capitalizing on the value created by such activities. Dow Lohnes offers its education clients a unique blend of expertise in finance, intellectual property, technology and corporate law.

**Intellectual Property:** Dow Lohnes has developed a distinguished intellectual property practice and represents a broad cross-section of businesses ranging from health care to real estate development to media to education. The firm's specific areas of expertise include domestic and international trademark and copyright law, unfair competition, merchandising, and licensing. Clients include national media firms with interests in broadcasting, entertainment, telecommunications, cable television, satellite communications, newspapers and book publishing, as well as a wide range of colleges, universities and public broadcasting stations. Dow Lohnes attorneys are experienced in drafting and negotiating agreements involving intellectual property rights including licenses, acquisition, distribution, development and confidentiality agreements for content, software and technology.

**Litigation:** Dow Lohnes' experienced litigators represent clients from large, publicly held companies to small, closely held businesses, as well as individuals and estates. The firm's litigators regularly practice before federal and state trial and appellate courts throughout the country, as well as a number of federal and state administrative agencies. The firm has specific expertise in areas such as antitrust, intellectual property and high technology issues, commercial law, federal and state taxation, communications and telecommunications, Constitutional and First Amendment issues, environmental law and higher education matters.

**Media & Information Technologies:** Dow Lohnes' Media and Information Technologies Practice Group represents clients in traditional and new media, information technology, telecommunications and other industries. Its attorneys are experts on matters ranging from the protection, acquisition, licensing and use of intellectual property to negotiating matters affecting virtually every kind of Internet business. Dow Lohnes represents some of the largest information technology companies on transactions, intellectual property and public policy issues. For example, it has represented the country's largest computer companies in negotiations with Hollywood studios and major consumer electronics manufacturers relating to security and copy protection for DVDs and digital broadcast television.

**Taxation:** Dow Lohnes' tax lawyers have developed a diverse national practice in federal, state and local tax matters, reflecting the varied nature of the firm's domestic and foreign clients and their activities. Engagements involve all areas of corporate, partnership, trust, and individual federal and state income taxation, as well as estate and gift taxation, sales and use taxation, employment taxation, and the taxation of foreign and nonprofit entities. Dow Lohnes affiliate DL&A Price Tax Consulting Group, LLC has specific experience in state and local tax requirements, transfer issues, tax planning, audits and appeals and transactions.

## OFFICES

**DISTRICT OF COLUMBIA**
1200 New Hampshire Avenue, NW, Suite 800, **Washington**, DC 20036
**Tel:** 202 776 2000   **Fax:** 202 776 2222
**Website:** www.dowlohnes.com

**GEORGIA**
6 Concourse Parkway, Suite 1800, **Atlanta**, GA 30328
**Tel:** 770 901 8800   **Fax:** 770 901 8874

## CONTACTS

| | |
|---|---|
| Atlanta | Peter Canfield |
| Communications | Kevin Reed |
| Compensation, Employee Relations & Benefits | Richard McHugh |
| Corporate (Mergers & Acquisitions, Securities & Transactions) | Stuart Sheldon |
| Education | Michael Goldstein |
| Intellectual Property | David Wittenstein |
| Litigation | Michael Hays |
| Media & Information Technologies | Jonathan Hart |
| Taxation | J Michael Hines |
| Telecommunications | To-Quyen Truong |

# FINNEGAN, HENDERSON, FARABOW, GARRETT & DUNNER, LLP

## THE FIRM

**Managing Partner:** Richard B Racine
**Chairman:** Thomas H Jenkins

**Number of partners:** 113
**Number of other lawyers:** 193

**FIRM OVERVIEW:** Finnegan Henderson is the largest law firm in the world focusing solely on intellectual property law. With 300 lawyers and offices in the US, Europe, and Asia, Finnegan Henderson practices all aspects of patent, trademark, copyright, and trade secret law. Surveys conducted by legal and business publications consistently rank Finnegan Henderson as one of the leading intellectual property law practices in the world. In 2006 *The American Lawyer* and *IP Law & Business* named Finnegan Henderson as the top IP litigation law firm of the year. The publications cited the firm's winning record, technical expertise, and deep bench of talent in all aspects of IP litigation, including trials, appeals, interferences at the PTO, and ITC proceedings. For the past five years, American Lawyer Media has also ranked the firm as one of the top two firms that America's largest corporations rely on for IP counseling and litigation. In *Managing Intellectual Property*'s 2002, 2003-04, 2005, and 2006 World IP surveys of 4,000 global practitioners, the firm was ranked as the number one US law firm for patent litigation and non-contentious patent work. During the same time period, the publication also ranked Finnegan Henderson as the first- or second-place US firm for trademark litigation. In another recent listing, *The 2006 Vault Guide to the Top 100 Law Firms* ranked Finnegan Henderson number one for best intellectual property practice and number one for quality of life.

**MAIN AREAS OF PRACTICE:** Finnegan Henderson practices all aspects of patent, trademark, copyright, and trade secret law, including counseling, prosecution, licensing, and litigation. It also represents clients on IP issues related to international trade, portfolio management, the internet, e-commerce, government contracts, antitrust, and unfair competition.

The firm's reputation for resolving some of the most complicated IP issues lies with its ability to match the needs of each unique case with the right combination of legal and technical capabilities. Nearly 100 of the firm's legal professionals hold PhDs or other advanced degrees in cutting-edge scientific disciplines. They bring a wealth of intellectual property law experience to the firm from their past positions as law clerks for federal judges (including many from the US Court of Appeals for the Federal Circuit, the US Court of Federal Claims, and various US District Courts); as lawyers for the International Trade Commission and the Justice Department; as corporate patent, trademark, and copyright counsel; and as patent examiners or trademark lawyers for the US Patent and Trademark Office.

The firm represents its clients' litigation interests in courts throughout the US, including US district courts, a variety of state courts, and the US Supreme Court. Over the years, it has developed a particular expertise arguing before the US Court of Appeals for the Federal Circuit and has argued more patent cases before it than any other law firm. The firm represents clients in actions against the US Government in the US Court of Federal Claims, in actions before the International Trade Commission, and in actions before the US Customs Service. Finnegan Henderson lawyers also coordinate with firms in other countries regarding international litigation matters.

Finnegan Henderson's services extend beyond litigation. Much of the firm's work centers on efforts to avoid litigation. Its lawyers serve as both advocates and arbitrators in domestic and international arbitration, and frequently provide advice and opinions on the infringement and validity of all forms of intellectual property. Other work includes assisting clients in achieving the greatest value from their intellectual property law assets. The firm conducts intellectual property audits and due diligence analysis, provides patent and trademark watch services, formulates strategies for using intellectual property assets, formulates and carries out IP licensing programs, and negotiates and drafts domestic and international licensing agreements. It obtains appropriate licenses under the US export control laws and nego-

tiates as well as litigates US government contract disputes, especially in the area of data rights issues.

In addition, Finnegan Henderson has an extensive Patent Prosecution Practice. More than 220 of the firm's lawyers are registered to practice before the US Patent and Trademark Office. Annually, a staff of over 800, including lawyers, technical assistants, legal assistants, and other support personnel, handle more than 3,000 patent applications, file several thousand new trademark applications, and render legal opinions for numerous national and international clients. In the firm's Washington, DC office, an entire department is dedicated to coordinating, filing, and managing applications for patents and trademarks in the US, Europe, Asia, and other parts of the world.

**CLIENTS:** Finnegan Henderson represents clients in virtually every business sector, including biotechnology, pharmaceuticals, chemicals, electronics, computers, telecommunications, consumer products, financial services, the internet, manufacturing, and publishing. The firm's clients range from Fortune 500 and Global 100 companies to emerging companies involved in a wide range of cutting-edge technologies, such as gene therapy, multimedia content delivery systems, cardio-care products, and internet operating systems.

## HEAD OFFICE

**DISTRICT OF COLUMBIA**
901 New York Avenue, NW, **Washington**, DC 20001-4413
**Tel:** 202 408 4000   **Fax:** 202 408 4400
**Website:** www.finnegan.com
**Email:** info@finnegan.com

## OTHER US OFFICES

**CALIFORNIA**
Standard Research Park, 3300 Hillview Avenue, **Palo Alto**, CA 94304-1203
**Tel:** 650 849 6600   **Fax:** 650 849 6666

**GEORGIA**
3500 SunTrust Plaza, 303 Peachtree Street, NE **Atlanta**, GA 30308-3263
**Tel:** 404 653 6400   **Fax:** 404 653 6444

**MASSACHUSETTS**
55 Cambridge Parkway, **Cambridge**, MA 02142-1292
**Tel:** 617 452 1600   **Fax:** 617 452 1666

**VIRGINIA**
Two Freedom Square, 11955 Freedom Drive, **Reston**, VA 20190-5675
**Tel:** 571 203 2700   **Fax:** 202 408 4400

## INTERNATIONAL OFFICES

The firm also has offices in Brussels, Taipei and Tokyo.

FINNEGAN HENDERSON FARABOW GARRETT & DUNNER LLP

# HOGAN & HARTSON LLP

## THE FIRM

**Chairman:** J Warren Gorrell, Jr
**Number of partners in US offices:** 405
**Number of other lawyers in US offices:** 483

**FIRM OVERVIEW:** Founded in 1904, Hogan & Hartson is the oldest major law firm based in Washington, DC, with more than 1,000 attorneys in 23 offices on four continents. From its beginnings as a single lawyer operation to the current status as one of the top international law firms, Hogan & Hartson carries on a tradition of excellence established by its founder, Frank J Hogan. As the economy and clients' businesses have globalized, so, too, has Hogan & Hartson. What remains constant, however, are the transcending professional and cultural values that distinguish Hogan & Hartson from other major law firms: their unwavering commitment to client service, excellence, integrity, community service, and diversity, and their recognized industry focus and team-oriented approach.

## MAIN AREAS OF PRACTICE:

**Business, Finance & Tax:** Hogan & Hartson's Business, Finance and Tax Practice represents in transactions throughout the United States, Europe, Asia, Latin America, the Middle East, and Africa. Nearly 500 attorneys in this practice group assist a wide range of clients, including leading public and private companies, private investors, investment banking firms, financial institutions, and governmental entities. The firm has been consistently ranked in the top five legal counsel for real estate investment trust offerings and ranked among the law firms recognized for initial public offering representations. In the past year, the firm's corporate finance attorneys have advised on more than 250 transactions, with a total value of exceeding $152 billion. The firm's attorneys regularly advise multinational corporations and international investors on cross-border business transactions. Hogan & Hartson also represents private equity funds in leveraged buyouts, recapitalizations and other types of investment transactions.

**Litigation:** With more than 325 skilled trial and appellate attorneys in offices worldwide, the firm's diverse Litigation Practice boasts a century of achievement in the courtroom. The firm's practice is built around 'hands-on' trial lawyers who have an intimate knowledge of the bench and bar in major jurisdictions throughout the United States and in numerous international courts and tribunals. The *American Lawyer* has recognized the firm's Litigation Department's excellence in each of its last two biennial surveys of the best litigation departments among the top 200 US law firms.

**Intellectual Property:** With more than 125 IP lawyers, including more than 45 registered patent lawyers and patent agents, Hogan & Hartson boasts a full service IP practice with core patent and trademark groups. The firm's IP lawyers help companies solve their most difficult IP challenges and maximize the value of their IP assets. The firm handle matters involving some of the most cutting-edge technologies and some of the most famous brands and characters, providing sophisticated analysis and opinions, patent and trademark prosecution and counseling, and representation in patent, trademark, copyright, and trade secret litigation.

**Antitrust, Competition & Consumer Protection:** Hogan & Hartson is involved in every major area of antitrust, competition, and consumer protection law, including the most significant multinational mergers and joint ventures, 'bet the company' government investigations and litigation, intellectual property and high tech issues, policy issues and legislation, and compliance programs and ongoing advice to help clients avoid pitfalls.

**Aviation & Surface Transportation:** Lawyers and regulatory specialists who comprise the Aviation and Surface Transportation Group represent clients from broad segments of the aviation, automotive, motor carrier, rail, and commercial space industries, including air carriers, airport operators, aerospace manufacturers and repair facilities, business aviation operators and providers, vehicle manufacturers, engine, tire, and component makers, passenger and cargo railroads, rail car owners and lessors, and investors and participants in space tourism activities.

**Education:** Hogan & Hartson's Education Group represents public school districts, independent schools, public and independent colleges and universities,

## HEAD OFFICE

### DISTRICT OF COLUMBIA
555 Thirteenth Street, NW, **Washington**, DC 20004-1109
**Tel:** 202 637 5600　**Fax:** 202 637 5910
**Website:** www.hhlaw.com

## OTHER US OFFICES

### CALIFORNIA
1999 Avenue of the Stars, Suite 1400, **Los Angeles**, CA 90067
**Tel:** 310 785 4600　**Fax:** 310 785 4601

Biltmore Tower, Ste 1900, 500 South Grand Ave, **Los Angeles**, CA 90071
**Tel:** 213 337 6700　**Fax:** 213 337 6701

### COLORADO
1470 Walnut Street, Suite 200, **Boulder**, CO 80302
**Tel:** 720 406 5300　**Fax:** 720 406 5301

Two North Cascade Avenue, Suite 1300, **Colorado Springs**, CO 80903
**Tel:** 719 448 5900　**Fax:** 719 448 5922

One Tabor Center, 1200 Seventeenth Street,
Suite 1500, **Denver**,CO 80202
**Tel:** 303 899 7300　**Fax:** 303 899 7333

### FLORIDA
Mellon Financial Center, 1111 Brickell Avenue,
Suite 1900, **Miami**, FL 33131
**Tel:** 305 459 6500　**Fax:** 305 459 6550

### MARYLAND
111 South Calvert Street, **Baltimore**, MD 21202
**Tel:** 410 659 2700　**Fax:** 410 539 6981

### NEW YORK
875 Third Avenue, **New York**, NY 10022
**Tel:** 212 918 3000　**Fax:** 212 918 3100

### VIRGINIA
8300 Greensboro Drive, Suite 1100, **McLean**, VA 22102
**Tel:** 703 610 6100　**Fax:** 703 610 6200

## INTERNATIONAL OFFICES

The firm also has offices in Beijing, Berlin, Brussels, Budapest, Caracas, Geneva, Hong Kong, London, Moscow, Munich, Paris, Shanghai, Tokyo, and Warsaw.

## CONTACTS

| | |
|---|---|
| **Business, Finance & Tax** | James Rosenhauer |
| **Litigation** | Robert Duncan |
| **Intellectual Property** | Ray Kurz |
| **Antitrust, Competition & Consumer Protection** | Philip Larson |
| **Aviation & Surface Transportation** | George Carneal |
| **Education** | Elizabeth Meers |
| **Energy** | Kevin Lipson |
| **Environmental** | Patrick Raher |
| **Food, Drug, Medical Device & Agriculture** | Gary Kushner |
| **Government Contracts** | Robert Kenney |
| **Health** | Ann Morgan Vickery |
| **Immigration** | Paul Virtue |
| **International Trade** | Jeanne Archibald |
| **Labor & Employment** | Stanley Brown |
| **Latin America** | Claudette Christian |
| **Legislative** | Michael House |
| **Privacy** | Tracy Gray |
| **Pro Bono** | Patricia Brannan |
| **Real Estate & Hospitality** | Bruce Parmley |
| **Telecommunications, Media & Entertainment** | Peter Rorhbach |

# HOGAN & HARTSON LLP CONT'D

education associations, education-focused businesses and investment groups, educational institutions formed and operating in other countries, foundations and institutes in the education field, and other organizations involved with the teaching, research, and public service missions of education.

**Energy:** Hogan & Hartson's energy attorneys practice in every area of the energy business, whether corporate, finance, or regulatory. The firm works in all sectors of the industry – upstream oil and gas, oil and natural gas pipelines, local distribution companies, liquefied natural gas (LNGs), coal, and regulated utilities – and in all parts of the electric industry, including IOUs, IPPs, wind, renewables, and traditional generation.

**Environmental:** Proactive anticipation and resolution of compliance matters is the goal of Hogan & Hartson's Environmental Practice Group. The Group provides regulatory compliance counseling, legislative and regulatory advocacy, enforcement defense, permit negotiation and appeals, remediation, commercial transaction advice, and litigation representation worldwide.

**Food, Drug, Medical Device & Agriculture:** Hogan & Hartson's Food, Drug, Medical Device, and Agriculture Practice is one of the most unique, dynamic, and comprehensive in the country. Worldwide, the firm helps clients chart a course through complex government regulations – such as FDA and USDA requirements, European Union (EU) directives, member state laws, and comparable regulations in Asia and South America – so that they can launch products and have a voice in policy formulation in Washington, Brussels, Tokyo, Beijing, and other major capitals.

**Government Contracts:** Combining the deep experience of recognized leaders in government contracts and grants law with the broad resources of a full-service global law firm, Hogan & Hartson offers comprehensive solutions to the increasingly complex problems that arise from doing business with the government. The firm's attorneys are experienced in dealing with the complete range of legal issues inherent in government contracting and grants, including responses to audits/investigations, cost accounting and allowability issues, protests, claims and suspension/debarment matters.

**Health:** Hogan & Hartson's Health Practice is grounded in an in-depth understanding of the industry and its relationship with government. Most of the firm's health attorneys have had experience in government, industry, or both. Ranging from start-ups to multinational enterprises, Hogan & Hartson's clients come from every part of the economy's health sector.

**Immigration:** Hogan & Hartson's immigration attorneys represent clients around the world in the full range of matters arising out of US and foreign immigration laws. The firm handles a wide variety of matters, from advising clients on the best options for non-US nationals to obtain authorization to live and work in the United States, to legislative advocacy, to regulatory compliance and enforcement issues.

**International Trade:** With offices in Washington, Brussels, Geneva, Beijing and numerous capitals around the world and partners with years of experience in the private sector and in senior government positions, the firm's international trade group is well-positioned to offer clients a full array of services relating to international trade, including trade remedy proceedings, WTO and FTA dispute settlement, compliance and enforcement in export control, anti-bribery, economic sanctions, and Exon-Florio matters, trade negotiations and complex trade litigation.

**Labor & Employment:** Hogan & Hartson's labor and employment lawyers assist employers throughout the world in meeting the challenges of an increasingly regulated global workplace. Their clients benefit from the counsel of employment lawyers working in eleven offices in the United States and Europe. The firm's labor and employment lawyers acts as litigators, advisors, and negotiators.

**Latin America:** Hogan & Hartson's 35-member Latin America Practice Group possesses a wide range of experience. Located principally in the firm's Caracas, Miami, New York, and Washington, DC offices, members of this group help Fortune 500 corporations successfully complete mergers and acquisitions as well as assist Latin American state-owned entities to form public-private partnerships and develop infrastructure projects.

**Legislative:** Hogan & Hartson is consistently ranked as one of the top lobbying practices in Washington, DC. Clients rely on the firm for its broad-based experience in the legislative and political arenas, combined with significant industry and regulatory knowledge. The core strength of Hogan & Hartson's Legislative Practice is the experience of their attorneys and professionals, many of whom have been honored for their government service.

**Privacy:** Hogan & Hartson is a leader in the privacy, security and data protection arena, and has assisted in creating best practices in a number of online industries, including the Online Privacy Alliance, the Network Advertising Initiative, and the Health Internet Ethics coalitions. As a fully integrated international law firm, they produce seamless client solutions with a maximum degree of flexibility across the globe.

**Pro Bono:** Over 35 years ago, Hogan & Hartson became the first major firm in the United States to establish a separate practice group devoted exclusively to providing pro bono legal services. Since 1970, the firm's Community Services Department (CSD) has been charged with attracting and staffing both high impact matters raising issues of public importance, and smaller cases addressing individual problems.

**Real Estate & Hospitality:** Hogan & Hartson's Real Estate Practice encompasses commercial real estate acquisitions, joint ventures, development, financing, leasing, land use, brokerage, and lending. The firm's attorneys have experience in working with virtually every aspect and type of real estate project, including office buildings, hotels and resorts, sports facilities, shopping centers, mixed-use developments, energy plants, industrial and research complexes, warehouses, senior housing facilities, planned communities, and multi-family residential projects.

**Telecommunications, Media & Entertainment:** With the firm's strategic positioning in 23 offices worldwide, the telecommunications, media, and entertainment practice is among the most interconnected in the world. This global reach, combined with Hogan & Hartson's extensive experience, allows the firm to serve clients in industries that are ever more complex, increasingly reliant on cross-border transactions, and frequently subject to regulations at multiple jurisdictional levels.

## INTERNATIONAL WORK:

**Asia:** Hogan & Hartson has offices in Beijing, Hong Kong, Shanghai, and Tokyo, and has a long history of representing both clients throughout the Pacific Rim and Western clients doing business in the region.

**Europe:** Hogan & Hartson is a significant force in Europe, with nine offices and more than 150 attorneys dedicated to meeting the diverse needs of international businesses investing and operating in the region. The firm is ideally positioned to help clients capitalize on opportunities in the European Union.

**Latin America:** Located principally in the firm's Caracas, Miami, New York, and Washington, DC offices, Hogan & Hartson's Latin America attorneys and advisors possess a wide range of experience. The firm's attorneys conduct due diligence investigations, draft project and financing documents, negotiate contracts, arbitrate, litigate, work in civil law jurisdictions, and handle all other aspects of major transactions.

**Middle East:** Hogan & Hartson's current activities in the Middle East and North Africa are wide-ranging, from oil and gas, power and water, port and other infrastructure initiatives, to strategic policy advice to governments. In December 2004, Hogan & Hartson entered into a strategic alliance with The Law Firm of Salah Al-Hejailan, the oldest and largest law firm in Saudi Arabia.

# JONES DAY

## THE FIRM

**Managing Partner:** Stephen J Brogan
**Number of partners worldwide:** 643
**Number of other lawyers worldwide:** 1565
**Website:** www.jonesday.com

**FIRM OVERVIEW:** Since 1893, Jones Day has evolved and grown, staying in step with rapidly changing business and legal environments both in the US and around the world. Their dedication to delivering the best of the firm in every client engagement has not gone unnoticed, and it has earned Jones Day industry awards and recognition year after year. Today, they are one of the largest law firms, with more than 2,200 lawyers in 30 offices around the world. Their clients are numbered among the Fortune Global 500. Jones Day continues to earn recognition for its high quality service to clients across the nation and around the world. In 2005, Jones Day was ranked number one for client service by BTI Consulting Group, Inc., in a survey of Fortune 1000 corporate counsel; was named International Law Firm of the Year at the 2005 Asian Legal Business China Law Awards; captured first place as the 'most mentioned' firm across all categories in Corporate Counsel's 2005 'Who Counsels Who'; garnered top mentions for IP counsel in IP Law & Business's 'Who Protects IP America' survey of the Fortune 250; and ranked in the top 5 of Corporate Board Member magazine's annual survey of top corporate law firms.

**MAIN AREAS OF PRACTICE:** Jones Day's global legal services encompass the following practices and industries: antitrust and competition law; business restructuring and reorganization; capital markets; corporate criminal investigations; employee benefits and executive compensation; energy delivery and power; government regulation; healthcare; intellectual property; international litigation and arbitration; issues and appeals; labor and employment; lending/structured finance and derivatives; life sciences; mergers and acquisitions; oil and gas; private equity; product liability and tort litigation; real estate; securities and shareholder litigation and SEC enforcement; tax; and trial practice.

## US OFFICES

### IRVINE

3 Park Plaza, Suite 1100, Irvine, CA 92614-8505

**Office Profile:** Jones Day's Irvine office is located in the center of Southern California's Technology Coast. The office provides legal services to both emerging and established companies responding to today's accelerated business environment. These services involve focused legal teams active in the litigation and intellectual property arenas.

### LOS ANGELES

555 South Flower Street, Fiftieth Floor, Los Angeles, CA 90071

**Office Profile:** Jones Day's Los Angeles office represents major corporations, institutions, and emerging companies located throughout the western United States and the Pacific Rim. The office has a dominating litigation practice and is home to the firm's strong healthcare practice and a burgeoning technology and intellectual property practice.

## US OFFICE CONTACTS

### CALIFORNIA
3 Park Plaza, Suite 1100, **Irvine**, CA 92614-8505
**Tel:** 949 851 3939   **Fax:** 949 553 7539
**Email:** counsel@jonesday.com

555 South Flower Street, Fiftieth Floor, **Los Angeles**, CA 90017
**Tel:** 213 489 3939   **Fax:** 213 243 2539
**Email:** counsel@jonesday.com

2882 Sand Hill Road, Suite 240, **Menlo Park**, CA 94025
**Tel:** 650 739 3939   **Fax:** 650 739 3900
**Email:** counsel@jonesday.com

12750 High Bluff Drive, Suite 300, **San Diego**, CA 92103-2083
**Tel:** 858 314 1200   **Fax:** 858 314 1150
**Email:** counsel@jonesday.com

555 California Street, 26th Floor, **San Francisco**, CA 94104
**Tel:** 415 626 3939   **Fax:** 415 875 5700
**Email:** counsel@jonesday.com

### DISTRICT OF COLUMBIA
51 Louisiana Avenue, NW, **Washington**, DC 20001-2113
**Tel:** 202 879 3939   **Fax:** 202 626 1700
**Email:** counsel@jonesday.com

### GEORGIA
1420 Peachtree Street, NE, Suite 800, **Atlanta**, GA 30309-3053
**Tel:** 404 521 3939   **Fax:** 404 581 8330
**Email:** counsel@jonesday.com

### ILLINOIS
77 West Wacker, **Chicago**, IL 60601-1692
**Tel:** 312 782 3939   **Fax:** 312 782 8585
**Email:** counsel@jonesday.com

### OHIO
North Point, 901 Lakeside Avenue, **Cleveland**, OH 44114-1190
**Tel:** 216 586 3939   **Fax:** 216 579 0212
**Email:** counsel@jonesday.com

325 John H McConnell Boulevard, Suite 600, **Columbus**, OH 43215
**Tel:** 614 469 3939   **Fax:** 614 461 4198
**Email:** counsel@jonesday.com

### NEW YORK
222 East 41st Street, **New York**, NY 10017-6702
**Tel:** 212 326 3939   **Fax:** 212 755 7306
**Email:** counsel@jonesday.com

### PENNSYLVANIA
One Mellon Bank Center, 31st Floor, 500 Grant Street, **Pittsburgh**, PA 15219-2502
**Tel:** 412 391 3939   **Fax:** 412 394 7959
**Email:** counsel@jonesday.com

### TEXAS
2727 North Harwood Street, **Dallas**, TX 75201-1515
**Tel:** 214 220 3939   **Fax:** 214 969 5100
**Email:** counsel@jonesday.com

717 Texas, Suite 3300, **Houston**, TX 77002-2712
**Tel:** 832 239 3939   **Fax:** 832 239 3600
**Email:** counsel@jonesday.com

# JONES DAY CONT'D

## MENLO PARK

2882 Sand Hill Road, Suite 240, Menlo Park, CA 94025

**Office Profile:** The Menlo Park office enables the firm's technology practice to provide high quality legal services for Silicon Valley entrepreneurial and venture capital clients and also provides localized capacity for new and existing public companies focused on emerging technology.

## SAN DIEGO

12750 High Bluff Drive, Suite 300, San Diego, CA 92130-2083

**Office Profile:** Jones Day's San Diego office is located in the center of San Diego's biotechnology industry. The office provides legal services to both emerging and established companies responsible for the significant growth of San Diego's life sciences community. These services are provided by lawyers with advanced technical degrees and experience in the full spectrum of intellectual property issues facing Southern California's technology-driven companies.

## SAN FRANCISCO

555 California Street, 26th Floor, San Francisco, CA 94104

**Office Profile:** The San Francisco office extends Jones Day's presence into a region where clients face significant litigation and other legal problems. The 52 lawyers in San Francisco focus primarily on complex civil litigation, including antitrust, employment law, product liability, and securities.

## WASHINGTON, DC

51 Louisiana Avenue, N.W., Washington, D.C. 20001-2113

**Office Profile:** The Jones Day lawyers in the nation's capital are ideally positioned to serve national and international clients locally and globally. The office provides a complete range of legal services, from its award-winning litigation practice to government regulatory and antitrust advice. In addition, the Washington office has extensive capabilities in corporate, intellectual property, and tax law. These are complemented by industry-specific knowledge of manufacturing, technology, banking, financial services, real estate, healthcare, energy, consumer products, retail, and telecommunications.

## ATLANTA

1420 Peachtree Street, N.E., Suite 800, Atlanta, GA 30309-3053

**Office Profile:** Lawyers in Jones Day's Atlanta office advise on the full range of issues relevant to leading corporations doing business in the southeastern United States and worldwide. With approximately 140 attorneys, Jones Day's Atlanta office draws upon a highly qualified and diverse team, including lawyers admitted to practice in a number of states in the US and internationally, and provides its clients immediate access to the firm's global resources, coupled with its commitment to service excellence.

## CHICAGO

77 West Wacker, Chicago, IL 60601-1692

**Office Profile:** With more than 160 lawyers, the Chicago office provides a full range of legal services for clients ranging from Fortune 500 companies to privately held and emerging companies and international concerns. Chicago lawyers handle a wide variety of US and international business transactions as well as litigation.

## CLEVELAND

North Point, 901 Lakeside Avenue, Cleveland, OH 44114-1190

**Office Profile:** The Cleveland office encompasses more than 270 lawyers who provide legal services to clients in diverse businesses in all facets of activity at the local, national, and international levels. A highly qualified staff and state-of-the-art technology provide extensive support for the firm's attorneys.

## COLUMBUS

325 John H. McConnell Boulevard, Suite 600, Columbus, OH 43215

**Office Profile:** Jones Day Columbus today has approximately 86 lawyers and provides a full range of legal services to public and private businesses and individuals located or having legal needs in Central Ohio and around the country.

## NEW YORK

222 East 41st Street, New York, NY 10017-6702

**Office Profile:** The New York office has more than 270 lawyers, ranking it among the largest New York offices of any non-New-York-based national firm. Jones Day New York plays a leading role in the firm's capital markets and international activities.

## PITTSBURGH

One Mellon Bank Center, 31st Floor, 500 Grant Street, Pittsburgh, PA 15219-2502

**Office Profile:** Jones Day Pittsburgh has approximately 58 lawyers who provide diverse legal services in southwestern Pennsylvania, nationally, and internationally.

## DALLAS

2727 North Harwood Street, Dallas, TX 75201-1515

**Office Profile:** Jones Day's Dallas office consists of approximately 200 lawyers who provide a full range of legal services to clients ranging from Fortune 500 companies to privately held and emerging companies engaged in diverse business locally, nationally and internationally. The office has substantial capability in litigation, corporate and real estate transactions, and federal and state taxation.

## HOUSTON

717 Texas, Suite 3300, Houston, TX 77002-2712

**Office Profile:** The Houston office lawyers provide legal services in three principal areas of practice: business transactions, litigation, and energy regulation. The Houston office offers clients substantial national and international resources, experience, and talent to resolve sophisticated legal issues.

# KING & SPALDING LLP

## THE FIRM

**Chairman:** Robert D Hays
**Managing Partner, Atlanta:** Mason W Stephenson
**Managing Partner, Houston:** Robert E Meadows
**Managing Partner, London:** John L Keffer
**Managing Partner, New York:** Michael J O'Brien
**Managing Partner, Washington:** J Sedwick Sollers

**Number of partners:** 240
**Number of other lawyers:** 560

**FIRM OVERVIEW:** King & Spalding LLP is an international law firm with more than 800 lawyers in Atlanta, Houston, London, New York, and Washington, DC. The firm represents more than 250 public companies, including over half of the Fortune 100.

## MAIN AREAS OF PRACTICE:

**Antitrust:** King & Spalding's antitrust lawyers are trial lawyers who know how to litigate in 'bet the company' situations. The firm has been counsel for clients in numerous antitrust litigation settings, ranging from class actions and multidistrict litigation to disputes between particular suppliers and their customers or competitors.

**Financial Transactions:** The practice group provides legal services for domestic and non-US banks and other financial institutions. It handles all aspects of credit-facilities and financial products.

**Construction:** Today, the Construction and Procurement Practice Group represents some of the world's largest organizations involved in global construction projects. King & Spalding was one of the first large, general practice firms in the nation to establish a practice devoted to construction and procurement law.

**Corporate/M&A:** Consistently ranks among the leading M&A practices in the United States in terms of aggregate deal value and total number of transactions handled.

**Corporate Finance:** The firm represents issuers, underwriters, investors, and other corporate finance participants, and provides corporate advice to public and private companies.

**Employment & Labor Law:** The firm defends Fortune 500 corporate defendants against complex claims of unlawful employment policies and conduct involving allegations of discrimination under federal and state non-discrimination statutes.

**Energy:** The firm's energy attorneys have been involved in transactions throughout the world related to energy and natural resources. King & Spalding's experience includes developing project structures as well as the drafting and negotiating of project agreements, contracts and documentation. Additionally, King & Spalding lawyers have been active advisors to the Liquefied Natural Gas (LNG) marketplace for the last 30 years. As pioneers on this legal scene, the internationally recognized group of lawyers have been key participants in LNG export, transport, and import projects . Today, King & Spalding's team is sought after by LNG players worldwide owing to depth of experience, knowledge, skill, and determination.

**Environment:** King & Spalding is recognized as one of the leading environmental firms and combines substantive expertise, technical knowledge and litigation experience on numerous environmental issues.

**Insolvency/Corporate Recovery:** The Financial Restructuring Group at King & Spalding provides valuable knowledge and experience in the areas of corporate reorganizations, commercial debt restructuring, workouts, bankruptcy, and insolvency litigation.

**Intellectual Property:** The firm's IP lawyers concentrate on acquiring, creating, licensing, protecting, and litigating intellectual property rights, both domestically and internationally.

## HEAD OFFICE

### GEORGIA
1180 Peachtree Street, **Atlanta**, GA 30309-3521
**Tel:** 404 572 4600   **Fax:** 404 572 5100
**Email:** kingspalding@kslaw.com
**Website:** www.kslaw.com

## BRANCH OFFICES

### NEW YORK
1185 Avenue of the Americas, **New York**, NY 10036-4003
**Tel:** 212 556 2100   **Fax:** 212 556 2222
**Email:** kingspalding@kslaw.com

### TEXAS
1100 Louisiana, Suite 4000, **Houston**, TX 77002-5213
**Tel:** 713 751 3200   **Fax:** 713 751 3290
**Email:** kingspalding@kslaw.com

### DISTRICT OF COLUMBIA
1700 Pennsylvania Avenue, N.W., **Washington,** DC 200006-4706
**Tel:** 202 737 0500   **Fax:** 202 626 3737
**Email:** kingspalding@kslaw.com

## INTERNATIONAL OFFICES

King & Spalding International LLP, London.

**Litigation & Arbitration:** The firm provides litigation services in the areas of antitrust, appellate, class action, commercial disputes, product liability, shareholder and securities litigation, trade and customs, and toxic tort. The firm also has a substantial international arbitration practice.

**Real Estate:** The firm's Real Estate Practice includes acquisition, development, financing and leasing of commercial real estate primarily for nationally recognized developers, and non-US institutional and private investors.

**Tax:** The firm works with clients on the planning and execution of business transactions of all sizes and types arising in domestic and cross border settings, including acquisitions, disposition, joint ventures, and financing transactions.

**CLIENTS:** 3M, Brown & Williamson Tobacco Corporation, Chevron Corporation, The Coca-Cola Company, Credit Suisse First Boston LLC, The Dow Chemical Company, Ernst & Young LLP, ExxonMobil Corporation, General Electric Company, General Motors Corporation, Georgia-Pacific Corporation, GlaxoSmithKline, Goldman Sachs & Company, The Home Depot, Inc., Honeywell International Inc., KPMG LLP, Lehman Brothers Inc., Lockheed Martin Corporation, Merrill Lynch & Co., Inc., Morgan Stanley Capital Group, Inc., Purdue Pharma L.P., Scientific-Atlanta, Inc., Shell Oil Company, Sprint Nextel Corporation, SunTrust Banks Inc., Turner Broadcasting System, Inc., UCB Inc., UPS.

## KING & SPALDING

# LEVINE, BLASZAK, BLOCK & BOOTHBY, LLP

## THE FIRM

**Senior Partner:** Henry D Levine

**Number of partners:** 14
**Number of other lawyers:** 3

### AREAS OF PRACTICE:
Telecom/IT Procurement ................................... 60%
Telecom/IT Workouts & Dispute Resolution ................. 20%
Telecom/IT Regulation ................................... 20%

**FIRM OVERVIEW:** Founded in 1993, Levine, Blaszak, Block & Boothby, LLP (LB3) specializes in communications and technology law, with particular emphasis on the representation of large users (including approximately 50% of the Fortune 100), information technology companies, and companies built on new technologies. LB3 has unparalleled experience in negotiating custom network service agreements, network outsourcings, and related transactions on behalf of large users. In partnership with its consulting affiliate, TechCaliber, LLP, the firm provides its clients with the legal and financial expertise they need to secure leading edge telecom contracts. The firm is also the principal representative of large end users and IT companies before the FCC and other regulators, and before courts and arbitrators when their relationships with communications providers break down. And LB3 advises clients in connection with e-business and software development, implementation and maintenance agreements, and telecom related acquisitions and securities offerings.

## MAIN AREAS OF PRACTICE:

**Custom Network Service Agreements:** LB3 specializes in the negotiation of custom network service agreements and other complex telecommunications transactions. Such agreements typically involve an array of voice and data services, and often include MPLS, satellite, internet and network management services as well. The purchase/lease of complex equipment and wireless services may be folded in or negotiated separately. LB3 lawyers pioneered these agreements, and today assist clients in the development of telecom procurement strategies; assist in vendor selection; and negotiate the required contracts.

**Network Outsourcing/Managed Network Services:** Over the past decade, network service arrangements have evolved to encompass sophisticated management services and the purchase of customer equipment, software licenses and the hiring of customer personnel as part of an agreement under which the customer outsources telecommunications operations and/or management to a third party. LB3 has represented the purchaser in many of the largest and most sophisticated telecom outsourcings.

**Internet & E-Business:** The firm develops creative and durable frameworks that minimize risk and scale to meet clients' evolving workforces, network topologies, and application platforms. LB3 lawyers have negotiated agreements for internet access, internet protocol multicasting, Virtual Private Networks (VPNs), and voice-over-internet services to support client business requirements. LB3 attorneys have also structured e-business transactions ranging from web hosting to application hosting, content management, remote application maintenance, streaming media, co-branding and global portal development. In connection with web services, the firm negotiates software agreements covering applicatons development, implementation and maintenance.

**Carrier Purchasers & New Entrants:** Carriers have turned to the firm for advice on carrier-to-carrier transport and dark fiber agreements. The firm also represents new carriers in negotiating (and arbitrating) interconnection agreements.

**Corporate & IPO Support:** The firm frequently works with securities counsel on the telecommunications regulatory or industry-specific portions of SEC filings and prospectuses.

**HEAD OFFICE**

**DISTRICT OF COLUMBIA**
2001 L Street NW, Suite 900, **Washington**, DC 20036
**Tel:** 202 857 2550   **Fax:** 202 223 0833
**Website:** www.lb3law.com

**Communications Policy & Regulation:** LB3 keeps large users informed of regulatory and legal developments that affect their service acquisition strategies, and represents them in policy proceedings before regulatory and legislative bodies. The firm is known for its ability to penetrate the complex issues spawned by changes in the telecom law and regulations; the growth of competition; the emergence of new technologies; the convergence of IT and communications; and the rise of the internet. The policy debates confronting the information technology industry often raise issues for which there is no precedent. In these areas, the firm has helped to write, not just interpret, the law. The issues in which LB3 has been involved include usage-based charges for internet services; efforts to regulate the internet; competitive deployment of broadband services, cable equipment, and wireless internet services; and US digital television standards.

**Contract Workouts:** Disputes are inevitable, and the firm is a leader in the representation of purchasers in disputes arising out of the terms or termination of their telecom agreements. The firm has been involved in the amicable (or not so amicable) resolution of scores of disputes involving service levels; shortfall penalties; and billing.

**FCC Complaints & Litigation:** The firm's lawyers have broad and deep expertise with telecom-related claims and complaint proceedings before courts, state regulators and the FCC. The firm's lawyers have also assisted parties and counsel when communications issues arise in areas such as the interpretation of contracts and tariffs; service cost and reliability; and billing disputes, and have served as expert witnesses on such issues in a variety of settings.

**CLIENTS:** The firm's international clients include General Motors, IBM, DuPont, Merrill Lynch, Pearson, Inc., WPP, Nestlé, and Hyatt International.

**INTERNATIONAL WORK:** The firm has helped a number of the world's largest multinational corporations negotiate contracts to purchase telecommunications and related services on a regional or global basis with reasonable uniformity of terms, appropriate accountability for performance, and due regard for the special regulatory, technical and business challenges posed by these transactions.

# MCKEE NELSON LLP

## THE FIRM

**Senior Partners:** William S McKee, William F Nelson

**Number of partners:** 51
**Number of other lawyers:** 105

**FIRM OVERVIEW:** McKee Nelson LLP is an independent, entrepreneurial law firm specializing in structured finance, tax litigation and planning, corporate finance and M&A, securities, and white collar/investigations and enforcement, founded with the common vision to engage only in those practices in which it could be truly excellent. Built by experienced lawyers who were leaders of their former practices and firms, McKee Nelson serves the tax litigation, tax planning, transactional structuring, capital markets, and white collar/investigations needs of multinational companies. Established in 1999, the firm has grown rapidly to include more than 150 lawyers, solidifying its broad experience in its chosen areas and positioning itself to help companies conduct business throughout the world.

## MAIN AREAS OF PRACTICE:

**Structured Finance & Securitization:** Recognized as one of the biggest players nationwide in mortgages, auto loans and collateralized debt obligations (CDOs), McKee Nelson is experienced in all asset classes, including domestic and cross-border offerings and private placements of mortgage backed and asset-backed securities through US and offshore issuing vehicles. The firm has structured a broad range of transactions, fixed and revolving, including REMICs, FASITs, owner trusts, grantor trusts, master trusts and commercial paper vehicles, using virtually every cash flow structure and form of credit enhancement, as well as a wide array of complex structured products. The firm's structured finance and securitization attorneys have represented every major Wall Street investment bank, most major federal agency guarantors and sponsors, and numerous other parties in domestic and international structured finance transactions, including CDO offerings.

**Tax Litigation:** Attorneys in McKee Nelson's Tax Litigation Practice represent US and foreign taxpayers in some of the largest and most legally significant federal tax cases. McKee Nelson offers clients the combination of technical tax expertise and tax litigation experience to respond effectively to any federal tax challenge – from IRS audits, appeals and competent authority matters, to the most complex trial and appellate litigation. Attorneys in this practice area are tax lawyers as well as veteran trial and appellate lawyers with considerable insight into government behavior. The group includes a former IRS Chief Counsel, former IRS and US Treasury Department officials, and former IRS and Justice Department tax litigators. They have appeared before the US Tax Court, US Court of Federal Claims, US District Courts and numerous US Courts of Appeals.

**Tax Planning:** The firm's founding partners, Bill McKee and Will Nelson, co-authored the leading treatises on partnership taxation and the structuring and drafting of partnership agreements. Mr Nelson was Chief Counsel of the IRS, and Mr McKee was the Tax Legislative Counsel at the US Treasury Department. Their practice helps businesses strategize and structure complex transactions in ways that minimize their tax burden. Transactions often involve multinationals doing business in multiple jurisdictions, regions and countries, where tax implications can be significant. The key areas of focus include partnerships, joint ventures, asset securitizations, complex financings, mergers, acquisitions and dispositions. Because most deals are economically complex and require signifi-

cant structuring, the practice makes cross-disciplinary solutions a top priority.

**White Collar/Investigations & Enforcement:** McKee Nelson's White Collar/Investigations and Enforcement Group specializes in white collar defense, investigations and representation of companies and individuals in connection with government enforcement initiatives and parallel civil proceedings. Clients are primarily Fortune 500 companies, high-ranking public officials, civic leaders and prominent corporate executives throughout the country who are involved in major criminal cases, congressional and other governmental investigations involving alleged violations of fraud, environmental, securities, tax, antitrust, Foreign Corrupt Practices Act, obstruction of justice, bribery, wiretapping, and other statutes. The group also conducts corporate internal investigations and assists clients in developing and maintaining effective corporate compliance programs.

**Corporate/Securities, Finance & Mergers & Acquisitions:** This practice handles a diverse range of the most sophisticated public and private transactions. The firm provides sector-specific expertise to corporations from various industries doing business in multiple jurisdictions, regions and countries, and its lawyers are experienced in closing deals that are complex and require significant structuring. They also make cross-disciplinary solutions a top priority by working closely with McKee Nelson's premier structured finance and tax planning practices to structure and execute innovative transactions.

**CLIENTS:** McKee Nelson represents some of the world's largest corporations. The firm's clients are generally Fortune 500 companies, including nine of the Fortune 16, from a diverse range of business sectors. Clients include US firms engaged in foreign business activities, as well as foreign-based firms operating within the United States.

## HEAD OFFICE

**DISTRICT OF COLUMBIA**
1919 M Street NW, Suite 800, **Washington**, DC 20036
**Tel:** 202 775 1880   **Fax:** 202 775 8586
**Email:** info@mckeenelson.com
**Website:** www.mckeenelson.com

## BRANCH OFFICES

**NEW YORK**
One Battery Park Plaza, 34th Floor, **New York**, NY 10004
**Tel:** 917 777 4200   **Fax:** 917 777 4299
**Email:** info@mckeenelson.com

*McKee Nelson* LLP

# MILLER & CHEVALIER

## THE FIRM

**Chairman:** Samuel M Maruca

**FIRM OVERVIEW:** Since Miller & Chevalier was founded in 1920, it has been based in Washington, DC, the natural location for each of the firm's disciplines. From Washington – close to administrative and policy developments, as well as the specialized litigation fora vital to its clients' interests – the firm serves clients dispersed across the United States and around the world. Because of its specialized experience, the firm's clients trust Miller & Chevalier to provide solutions to their most difficult problems arising from government regulation or taxation of business. The firm typically finds solutions for issues, in the US and abroad, that are novel or ground breaking. Clients rely on the firm's intimate knowledge of the areas in which it practices to help manage the risks it confronts. For issues that cannot practically be resolved otherwise, the firm is prepared to litigate in US and international courts and arbitral bodies.

## MAIN AREAS OF PRACTICE:

**Taxation:** Miller & Chevalier was founded as the first tax practice in the United States. Since its founding, the firm has stayed at the forefront of the evolution of tax law and policy, through the breadth of its practice, the experience of its lawyers, the positions its lawyers have held in government and the tax bar, and the results they have achieved for their clients. Now providing its fourth generation of leaders in the US tax bar, the firm continues its close involvement with the emergence and development of issues of tax law and policy through the federal, legislative, and regulatory processes. Focused on corporate tax issues, the firm's Tax Practice spans business transactions and reorganizations, employee benefits, international tax, tax accounting, financial products, and tax policy. Resolving controversies with the IRS through numerous alternative dispute resolution programs, as well as through major litigation, has become a particular focus for the practice. Although most of the firm's docketed cases are filed in the US Tax Court, where its cases represent a substantial part of all dollars at issue, the firm also litigates cases in federal district courts and the US Court of Federal Claims.

**International:** Miller & Chevalier's International Practice spans the entire range of international trade regulations, policies, and dispute resolution. With over 40 professionals working full-time in the international field, Miller & Chevalier has one of the largest Trade Groups in the nation. The firm's international lawyers are recognized in the specialized areas of antidumping and countervailing duty proceedings, section 337 (intellectual property) litigation, import relief cases, customs, trade policy and legislation, civilian and military export controls, economic sanctions, the FCPA and international anti-bribery laws US anti-boycott regimes, international arbitration and litigation, global regulatory compliance, and bilateral and multilateral trade agreements. Drawing on extensive networks of proven foreign trade professionals in key markets around the world, the firm's lawyers also have years of experience solving client problems that reach beyond its shores. Clients have involved the firm centrally in a series of seminal cases, including the largest countervailing duty, antidumping, WTO dispute settlement, and section 337 cases that have ever been litigated, and landmark cases before NAFTA binational panels and NAFTA 'Extraordinary Challenges'. In recognition of the depth and breadth of its international trade disciplines, the firm is regularly called upon by some of the world's largest multinational corporations to design and implement international regulatory compliance programs, perform internal audits and investigations, and defend against enforcement actions.

**Government Contracts:** Miller & Chevalier is a recognized leader in the government contracts bar. It represents many of the nation's largest aerospace and defense companies, insurers, managed healthcare entities, information technology firms, and service providers in their business dealings with the US Government. The firm advises and represents clients in the areas of international procurement, including technology transfer and export controls; requests for equitable adjustment, claims, and terminations; Medicare, Medicaid, Federal Employment Health Benefits Program (FEHBP), and TRICARE issues and investigations; compliance counseling and training; cost allowability and allocation, including Cost Accounting Standards; defective pricing; intellectual property protection, including software, data, and patent rights; teaming agreements; suspension and debarment; and procurement integrity and conflicts of interest. The firm's lawyers provide experienced representation in bid protests, contract and subcontract disputes, civil and criminal fraud investigations, qui tam litigation, and internal investigations.

**Government Affairs:** Miller & Chevalier's Government Affairs Practice focuses on legislation, regulations, and policies in the areas of tax, international trade, homeland security, and government contracts. The team brings together a unique mix of government experience and technical expertise. It provides clients with more than access to key decision-makers; the firm offers the ability to draft complex bills, regulations and treaty provisions, and a strategic vision for securing adoption of its proposals. Miller & Chevalier's government affairs professionals have served in the White House, Congress, the Department of Treasury, the Internal Revenue Service, the US Customs Service, the Department of Commerce, the US International Trade Commission, the Office of Management and Budget, the Department of Defense, and the Office of the US Trade Representative.

**Litigation:** Two-thirds of the firm's engagements involve actual or threatened litigation. It works cooperatively with clients to devise strategies that may prevent litigation or provide the best resolution possible for the client through negotiation, arbitration and mediation, or litigation. The firm's ability to communicate with its clients, opponents, judges, and juries is a distinctive feature of the firm and a direct result of insight gained from years of practical experience in litigation. The firm's experience extends to jury and bench trials in courts and tribunals across the US and internationally. Its teams are composed of lawyers with expertise focused on the substantive areas of the firm's practice as well as general litigation skills, and include lawyers with successful records in a wide array of regulatory and commercial disputes. The firm's litigators include former Assistant United States Attorneys, Justice Department attorneys, public defenders and judicial clerks.

### HEAD OFFICE

**DISTRICT OF COLUMBIA**
655 Fifteenth Street, NW, Suite 900, **Washington**, DC 20005-5701
**Tel:** 202 626 5800   **Fax:** 202 626 5801
**Website:** www.millerchevalier.com

### BRANCH OFFICES

**PENNSYLVANIA**
300 Conshohocken State Rd, Suite 570, **Philadelphia**, PA 19428
**Tel:** 610 729 7800   **Fax:** 610 729 7805

MILLER & CHEVALIER
CHARTERED

# STEPTOE & JOHNSON LLP

## THE FIRM

**Managing Partner:** Roger Warin
**Vice Chair:** Phil Malet

**Number of partners:** 134
**Number of other lawyers:** 302

**FIRM OVERVIEW:** With more than 425 attorneys, Steptoe & Johnson LLP provides counsel and representation in a wide range of legal matters. In over 60 years of practice, the firm has gained a national and international reputation for vigorous representation of clients before governmental agencies, successful advocacy in litigation and arbitration, and creative and practical advice in guiding business transactions. The firm has offices in Washington, New York, Phoenix, Los Angeles, London, and Brussels.

## MAIN AREAS OF PRACTICE:

**Business Solutions:** Whether routine or complex, national or global, this practice group of over 100 attorneys capably advances clients' business interests. Steptoe attorneys have extensive experience in corporate legal services and offer clients general business counseling and transactional services, along with specific support in the areas of tax; corporate, securities and finance; cross-border transactions; and real estate.

**Industry & Regulatory Affairs:** Many clients turn to Steptoe attorneys to provide a critical edge in developing and implementing regulatory and legislative strategies. The firm's electric power lawyers represent a number of major electric utility companies in a wide range of subject areas, and also assist the owners and financiers of non-utility generators of electricity. Steptoe also represents many of the largest crude oil and refined petroleum products pipeline systems in the United States and Canada in regulatory and transactional matters. The backbone of the firm's transportation practice is the representation of rail carriers before the Surface Transportation Board and in federal courts. The Aviation Practice advises clients on regulatory compliance, hazardous materials transportation, relationships with travel intermediaries, aviator safety and security, US economic sanctions, and international trade regulations. The firm's National Environmental and Natural Resources Group has experience dealing with mining, mineral leasing, forestry, grazing, land exchanges, water rights, and wildlife law. The firm's lawyers have handled a number of complex antitrust litigation and class actions and frequently counsel on the antitrust aspects of major transactions. Layered across its expertise with these various industries and regulatory regimes, the firm has the experience to guide clients through legislative strategies and solutions.

**International:** For more than four decades, Steptoe has been consistently involved in complex and high-profile international trade cases. The lawyers in the firm are top-ranked by Chambers USA International Group and have in-depth knowledge and experience in a wide range of areas, including international trade litigation, international trade policy and strategy, World Trade Organization, EU law, international arbitration, export controls and international regulatory compliance, customs, immigration, international business transactions, international aviation, and public international law.

**Litigation:** When the future of a company hangs in the balance, many of the nation's high-profile executives and corporations choose Steptoe. According to a recent National Law Journal survey, Steptoe is among the most often used litigation outside counsel for a number of Fortune 500 companies. The firm's experience includes litigation in such areas as appellate, ERISA, labor and employment, government contracts, insurance, intellectual property, toxic torts, and mass torts. The firm also has substantial experience in complex commercial litigation, cross-border and multi-jurisdictional litigation, white-collar criminal defense, and securities litigation. Additionally, Steptoe attorneys, representing both complainants and respondents, have litigated a wide variety of unfair import cases under Section 337, including complex matters that include every possible act the ITC considers unfair.

## HEAD OFFICE

**DISTRICT OF COLUMBIA**
1330 Connecticut Ave, NW, **Washington**, DC 20036
**Tel:** 202 429 3000  **Fax:** 202 429 3902
**Email:** jneidecker@steptoe.com
**Website:** www.steptoe.com

## BRANCH OFFICES

**ARIZONA**
Collier Center, 201 East Washington St, 16th Floor, **Phoenix**, AZ 85004
**Tel:** 602 257 5200  **Fax:** 602 257 5299

**CALIFORNIA**
633 West 5th Street, Suite 700, **Los Angeles**, CA 90071
**Tel:** 213 439 9400  **Fax:** 213 439 9599

**NEW YORK**
750 Seventh Avenue, Suite 1900, **New York**, NY 10019
**Tel:** 212 506 3900  **Fax:** 212 506 3950

## INTERNATIONAL OFFICES

The firm also has offices in London and Brussels.

## CONTACTS

| | |
|---|---|
| **Antitrust & Competition** | Ken Ewing |
| **Corporate, Securities & Finance** | Scott Katzman |
| **Electric Power** | David Raskin |
| **Environment & Natural Resources** | Seth Goldberg |
| **ERISA/Labor & Employment** | Paul Ondrasik |
| **Insurance** | Toni Ianniello |
| **International** | Sue Esserman |
| **Intellectual Property** | Alfred Mamlet |
| **Litigation** | Steve Fennell |
| **Mass Tort** | Steve Fennell |
| **Pipeline** | Steve Reed |
| **Tax** | Mark Silverman |
| **Telecom, Media & E-Commerce** | Phil Malet |
| **White-Collar Crime** | Mark Hulkower |

**Technology:** This leading international practice represents information technology, financial services, intellectual property, telecommunications, and other technology-intensive companies on cutting-edge legal issues. The firm's attorneys are experienced in all phases of intellectual property representations, including the evaluation, acquisition, licensing, and transfer of patent, copyright, database, trademark, and trade secret rights. Steptoe's Telecommunications Practice represents a number of the world's leading and most innovative international companies in the wireline, wireless, satellite, cable, media, and Internet sectors. They are globally recognized for their work before US, European, and international (ITU, CEPT and WTO) regulators.

# STERNE, KESSLER, GOLDSTEIN & FOX P.L.L.C.

## THE FIRM

**Managing Director:** Jorge A Goldstein, PhD

**Number of directors:** 25
**Number of other lawyers:** 47

**FIRM OVERVIEW**: Sterne, Kessler, Goldstein & Fox P.L.L.C. specializes in the protection, transfer and enforcement of intellectual property rights. Founded in 1978 and based in Washington, DC, the law firm has over 100 patent attorneys, agents and technical specialists who have a unique combination of legal and technical skills.

## MAIN AREAS OF PRACTICE:

**Abbreviated New Drug Application Filings:** The firm counsels clients in matters arising at the interface between patent law and the FDA approval process. The practice includes patent validity and infringement analyses, exclusivity strategies, preparation of patent certifications for ANDA's, ANDA-related litigation and appeals before the Court of Appeals for the Federal Circuit.

**Clean Technology:** The firm provides intellectual property counsel to clients innovating in the CleanTech industry. Technologies in this sector include bioplastics, fuel cells, photovoltaics, biomass and green building materials. One of the advantages enjoyed by those innovating in clean technologies is the possibility of being accorded 'special' status by the United States Patent and Trademark Office.

**Interferences:** The firm's experience runs the gamut from pre-declaration activities to successful appeals to the Federal Circuit. It is experienced in all phases of the practice, including the copying of claims, motions, count formation, testimony period, depositions, corroborated proofs, etc, as well as final hearings before the Board and appeals to the court. The firm has represented US and foreign clients in two-party and multiparty interferences and has acted on behalf of either junior or senior parties and has successfully represented patentees in defending against post issuance interferences and has also successfully represented applicants against both patentees and other applicants.

**Inventorship Dispute Resolution:** The firm serves as a neutral third party in inventorship disputes that have reached the point of impasse, often leading to costly litigation or interferences to resolve the dispute. The firm provides intervention as a disinterested third party who is deeply knowledgeable in the technology involved, who is an experienced patent attorney, and who is sensitive to personal issues in contests between scientists, to lead to quick out-of-court resolutions.

**Litigation, Trial & Appellate:** The firm's attorneys have experience in all phases of litigation practice. They handle patent enforcement and defensive actions, including complex litigation. Their experience extends to disputes involving a variety of technologies including biotechnology, communications, consumer products, electronics, mechanical equipment, pharmaceuticals, robotics, semiconductors and wireless communications. The firm has extensive litigation experience in the fields of trade secret law, contracts, trademarks, and design patents. The firm practices before numerous Federal District Courts and its attorneys have successfully appeared before the Court of Appeals for the Federal Circuit and other regional Circuit Courts of Appeal.

**Nanotechnology:** The firm began serving nanotechnology clients in 1994 and has steadily seen interest grow in this area of its practice since that time. It represents nanotechnology clients in areas including semiconductors, nanoelectronics, nanocomputing, quantum dots, biosensors and microfluidics.

**Patent Preparation & Prosecution:** The firm has extensive experience in preparing and prosecuting patent applications. It prosecutes and enforces utility and design patents for a variety of clients ranging from those with extensive, active patent portfolios, to small, start-up companies that rely on the patent system to obtain funding and head off competition. Its professionals have expertise in a range of technologies including: biotechnology, bioinformatics, computer hardware and software, communications, consumer products, medical equipment, mechanical devices, microfluidics, nanotechnology, pharmaceuticals

and business methods.

**Technology Transfer:** The firm is committed to working closely with its clients' business, legal and scientific personnel to develop contractual relationships that advance their business objectives through agreements intended to govern alliances instead of adversarial relationships. The firm works with its clients to develop strategies for exploiting their technologies and for navigating the myriad legal and technological issues that arise in drafting and negotiating agreements involving technology transfer. The firm has experience in drafting and negotiating all types of technology and tangible asset transfer agreements. Its attorneys are well versed in both intellectual property law and transactional law.

**Trademark:** The firm counsels trademark clients in industries that range from consumer products to cutting-edge technologies such as bio-pharmaceutical products. Among the services it provides are federal, state and foreign trademark clearance, registration, licensing, enforcement and defense, domain name registration and dispute resolution, oppositions and cancellations, protection of non-traditional marks, review of product literature and corporation communications, website audit and trademark valuation.

**CLIENTS:** Legal pioneers in fields such as intellectual property protection of biotechnology, software, bioinformatics, genomics, e-commerce, generic pharmaceuticals, nanotechnology and business methods, the firm represents a broad range of clients, including emerging and established companies, venture capital firms, universities and select individuals.

## HEAD OFFICE

**DISTRICT OF COLUMBIA**
1100 New York Avenue, NW, **Washington**, DC 20005
**Tel:** 202 371 2600  **Fax:** 202 371 2540
**Website:** www.skgf.com

## CONTACTS

| | |
|---|---|
| **ANDA** | Robert C Millonig, Jr, PhD |
| **Appellate** | Kenneth C Bass, III |
| **Biotechnology** | Jorge A Goldstein, PhD |
| **Clean Technology** | David KS Cornwell |
| **Interferences** | Jorge A Goldstein, PhD |
| **Inventorship Disputes** | Jorge A Goldstein, PhD |
| **Litigation** | David KS Cornwell |
| **Nanotechnology** | Donald J Featherstone |
| **Negotiation, Electronics** | Robert Greene Sterne |
| **Pharmaceuticals** | John M Covert |
| **Technology Transfer** | Timothy J Shea, Jr |
| **Trademark** | Tracy-Gene G Durkin |

**Sterne Kessler Goldstein Fox**
ATTORNEYS AT LAW

# SUTHERLAND ASBILL & BRENNAN LLP

## THE FIRM

**Managing Partner:** Mark D Wasserman (Atlanta, GA)
**Administrative Partner:** W Mark Smith (Washington, DC)

**Number of partners:** 168
**Number of associates:** 255
**Total number of attorneys:** 423

**FIRM OVERVIEW:** Sutherland is a national law firm known for solving challenging business problems and resolving unique legal issues for many of the nation's largest corporations. Founded in 1924, the firm has grown to more than 425 lawyers handling matters in every part of the world. The firm consistently attracts lawyers who have the skills and perspective to address issues of significance in virtually every area of practice. Seven major practice areas – corporate, financial services, energy, intellectual property, litigation, real estate and tax – provide the framework that contains an extensive range of specialty areas, allowing its lawyers to serve a diverse client base that includes a number of Fortune 500 companies.

## MAIN AREAS OF WORK:

**Corporate:** Sutherland's lawyers advise clients on mergers and acquisitions, capital formations, governance, and business and financial transactions of all types. The firm's Corporate Practice includes more than 130 lawyers with vast knowledge of the legal, regulatory and commercial environment in which businesses operate. They have the resources to manage complex, global transactions and the experience required to deliver solutions efficiently. The practice includes representation of: public and private buyers and sellers in acquisitions and dispositions of businesses; lenders and borrowers in corporate finance transactions; derivatives and hedge fund and fund formations; securities law including initial and secondary public offerings of debt and equity securities, IPOs, private equity, and venture funding; LBOs; all corporate governance-related matters; and public and private companies in their general commercial affairs.

**Financial Services:** Sutherland's comprehensive, nationally recognized Financial Services Practice offers highly developed expertise across the entire financial marketplace and is home to some of the most highly regarded attorneys in the country. Many of Sutherland's financial services attorneys also have practical experience from prior careers with the federal government and regulatory agencies such as the SEC, the NASD and the Department of Justice. Key areas of counsel include insurance products, broker-dealer, mutual funds, investment advisors, and securities enforcement and litigation. Sutherland also has one of the nation's most prominent practices for taking private equity funds, and similar structures, public (including business development companies, SPACs, and holding company trusts).

**Energy:** Sutherland has a highly active Energy Regulatory, Transactional, Finance and Litigation Practice at the state, federal and international levels. Matters handled by the group embrace virtually all aspects of the natural gas, LNG, electric power and petroleum industries. The firm's lawyers have been at the forefront of the developing regulatory issues surrounding the energy industries, both at the policy stage and in the implementation phases. The firm has also developed extensive experience analyzing and assisting clients in taking advantage of business opportunities involving natural gas, electricity, cogeneration and petroleum products.

**Intellectual Property:** Sutherland has an extensive Intellectual Property Practice. The firm represents a broad mix of clients – emerging technology start-ups, small and mid-sized companies, Fortune 500 and other public companies – in all areas including patents, trademarks, service marks, copyrights, trade secrets and unfair competition. The firm handles intellectual property matters in a number of technical fields including biotechnology, pharmaceuticals, computers, chemical technology, telecommunications, software and minerals. A significant number of Sutherland's intellectual property lawyers hold specialized or advanced degrees in biology, chemical engineering, computer engineering, mechanical engineering, microbiology, immunology, molecular genetics and other scientific disciplines, with many registered to practice before the United States Patent and Trademark Office.

**Litigation:** Litigation is a major part of the firm's practice. Approximately one-third of its 425 lawyers practice in this area and have tried and/or argued cases in the US Supreme Court, all 13 circuits of the US Court of Appeals, the Court of Federal Claims, the Tax Court and many other federal district and state trial and appellate courts. The firm also has extensive experience in arbitrations and mediations as well as in administrative proceedings and hearings before various federal and state agencies. The areas of concentration within the firm's Litigation Group include: general commercial and civil litigation; antitrust, trade regulation and consumer protection; construction and procurement litigation; criminal investigations and litigation; education; employment and ERISA; environmental; healthcare; insurance; intellectual property; international trade disputes; motor vehicle franchise law; professional liability litigation; securities litigation; tax litigation; telecommunications; and timber.

**Real Estate:** The Real Estate Practice is national in scope, handling real estate matters in virtually every state and in all major real estate markets. The broad range of experience of the firm's real estate lawyers enables it to provide this continuity. The lawyers in the Real Estate Group have the ability to manage dispute resolutions, to provide creditors' rights and bankruptcy advice and representation, to advise on regulatory issues, and to identify and resolve tax questions, thus saving the expense and inefficiency of engaging different legal counsel for each of a client's separate business and legal problems. The areas of focus for the firm's Real Estate Practice include acquisition and development; real estate finance and equity formation; pension fund investments; commercial leasing; hospitality industry; international transactions; natural resources; foreclosure; bankruptcy and workouts; mergers and acquisitions; partnerships and partnership taxation; and environmental issues.

**Tax:** The firm serves as tax counsel to a number of Fortune 500 corporations and medium-sized and small corporations and their shareholders, as well as cooperatives, partnerships, joint ventures, tax-exempt organizations, trusts, estates and individuals. By virtue of the size of the Tax Practice and its varied client base, the firm has an active practice in almost every area of taxation, including corporate taxation, employee benefits and executive compensation, taxation of financial products, timber taxation, international taxation, partnership taxation, state and local tax, tax accounting, tax legislation, federal tax litigation, business and estate planning, and tax-exempt organizations.

## HEAD OFFICES

### GEORGIA
999 Peachtree Street, NE, **Atlanta**, GA 30309-3996
**Tel:** 404 853 8000   **Fax:** 404 853 8806
**Email:** info@sablaw.com   **Website:** www.sablaw.com

### DISTRICT OF COLUMBIA
1275 Pennsylvania Avenue, NW, **Washington**, DC 20004-2415
**Tel:** 202 383 0100   **Fax:** 202 637 3593

Sutherland also has offices in Austin, Houston, New York and Tallahassee. For more details visit the website.

# WILEY REIN & FIELDING LLP

## THE FIRM

**Managing Partner:** Richard E Wiley

**Number of partners:** 123
**Number of other lawyers:** 144

**FIRM OVERVIEW:** Wiley Rein & Fielding LLP attorneys counsel leaders in numerous industries nationwide, conduct business in over fifty countries throughout the world, and practice in more than twenty federal departments and agencies in Washington, DC, as well as in federal and state courts across the country. With offices in Washington, DC and Northern Virginia, the firm has more than 250 attorneys practicing in more than two dozen specialties of law. Clients range from Fortune 500 corporations and start-up ventures to trade associations and individuals with substantial business interests. The firm is led by Richard E Wiley, former Chairman of the Federal Communications Commission; Bert W Rein, former Deputy Assistant Secretary of State for Economic and Business Affairs; Fred F Fielding, former Counsel to the President of the United States; and Thomas W Brunner, head of the firm's Insurance Law Practice. Many partners have held high federal government posts in the legislative and executive branches and come to the firm with distinguished careers in private law practice as counselors, litigators, negotiators and strategic advisors.

## MAIN AREAS OF PRACTICE:

**Communications:** Wiley Rein & Fielding has the most comprehensive team of communications law specialists in the United States. Led by Richard E Wiley, former Chairman, Commissioner and General Counsel of the Federal Communications Commission (FCC), the group includes more than 75 attorneys, engineers and specialists. WRF represents clients in virtually all aspects of the federal, state and international laws governing the media and telecommunications industry, with particular experience in international and satellite, litigation, media, telephony and wireless services. The group handles the full scope of media transactions, from headline-setting, billion-dollar mergers to the sale of a single radio station, in addition to business disputes and regulatory initiatives.

**Government Contracts:** WRF's Government Contracts Practice, led by leading lawyer Rand L Allen, is comprised of more than 25 attorneys and consultants handling every aspect of government contracting, including bid protests, disputes, commercial litigation, terminations, mergers and acquisitions and regulatory issues. Clients rely on WRF for advice and representation on local and international procurement-related matters and the firm's attorneys regularly appear in every legal forum that addresses government contract issues, including the US Government Accountability Office, US district courts and courts of appeals, the US Court of Federal Claims (COFC), the US Court of Appeals for the Federal Circuit and the numerous agency Board of Contract Appeals.

**Insurance:** WRF's Insurance Practice is among the largest and most prominent in the United States. Led by Thomas W Brunner, a nationally recognized authority in this field and outside counsel to several insurance industry associations, the practice includes more than 40 attorneys, whose work encompasses counseling and litigation concerning general liability coverage, directors and officers, and errors and omissions coverage, cutting edge property insurance and other first and third party coverage, reinsurance disputes, construction, privacy and other regulatory issues, health insurance and insurance fraud. Many clients seek the firm's expertise in interpreting policies, developing new types of coverage, negotiating innovative settlements and evaluating large claims exposures.

**Intellectual Property:** WRF offers comprehensive intellectual property services for owners and users of patents, trade secrets and copyrights. The firm is well known for its infringement litigation capabilities, public policy advocacy, licensing expertise, dealings with relevant government agencies and experience in dealing with music licensing and rights management technology. The firm's patent attorneys handle matters involving the internet, satellite communications, semiconductors, biotechnology, pharmaceuticals, computer software and hardware and medical devices. The firm's trademark attorneys are engaged in the selection

and clearance of marks, domestic, foreign and international registration, maintenance of registrations, licensing, franchising, and proceedings before the US Patent and Trademark Office. The firm is experienced in the management of complex cross-border cases in the areas of unfair competition, counterfeiting and seizures. The firm's Copyright Practice has been at the forefront of legislative development in response to the digital environment, playing a central role in recent policy debates.

**International Trade:** WRF's 20-member International Trade Group, led by internationally recognized attorney Charles O Verrill, Jr, represents clients in domestic and international trade regulation and dispute resolution, including antidumping and countervailing duty investigations, safeguards proceedings, Section 337 actions to protect intellectual property rights, export enforcement proceedings and investor/state arbitration. The firm regularly provides advice on market access issues, the negotiation of trade agreements, customs regulation and privacy requirements of US and European law. Additionally, the firm's attorneys represent foreign and domestic clients in corporate structuring, overseas financial transactions, Treasury Department sanctions and embargoes, licensing and distributorship arrangements, government export financing, export trade certificates of review and the Foreign Corrupt Practices Act.

**Litigation:** Wiley Rein & Fielding provides clients with unparalleled advocacy in federal and state courts across the country. More than half of the firm's attorneys are seasoned litigators whose combined experience encompasses a wide range of trial, appellate, alternative dispute and agency tribunal matters. Members of the firm's Litigation Team include six former clerks to the Supreme Court of the United States and more than 40 former clerks to courts of appeals and district courts; others have served as federal prosecutors, general counsels of federal agencies and senior government officials. The breadth of the firm's experience is matched by a substantive depth of knowledge in numerous specialized areas of law, including communications, criminal/congressional investigations, election law, employment, First Amendment, franchise, government contracts, health care, insurance, internet and intellectual property. The firm's specialized litigation expertise, in tandem with the innovative and creative approaches to complicated legal issues, has resulted in a proven record of success in the courtroom. Recent landmark decisions obtained by WRF include verdicts that have appeared on the *The National Law Journal's* annual list of 'Top 100 Verdicts'. Many of the cases the firm handles are high profile matters that garner widespread media attention.

### HEAD OFFICE

**DISTRICT OF COLUMBIA**
1776 K Street NW, **Washington**, DC 20006
**Tel:** 202 719 7000   **Fax:** 202 719 7049
**Website:** www.wrf.com

### BRANCH OFFICE

**VIRGINIA**
7925 Jones Branch Drive, Suite 6200, **McLean**, VA 22102
**Tel:** 703 905 2800   **Fax:** 703 905 2820

# WILMER CUTLER PICKERING HALE AND DORR LLP

## THE FIRM

**Co-Managing Partners:** William F Lee, William J Perlstein
**Email:** law@wilmerhale.com
**Website:** www.wilmerhale.com

**FIRM OVERVIEW:** WilmerHale offers unparalleled legal representation across a comprehensive range of practice areas that are critical to the success of its clients. The firm has over a thousand lawyers operating in five countries and practices at the very top of the legal profession. With a practice unsurpassed in depth and scope, it has the ability to anticipate obstacles, seize opportunities and get the case resolved or the deal done – and the experience and know-how to prevent it from being undone. WilmerHale was formed in May 2004 through the merger of two of the nation's leading law firms, Hale and Dorr LLP and Wilmer Cutler Pickering LLP. The formation of the new firm fused two storied pro bono and public service traditions. This commitment continues to be an integral part of the cultural fabric of the firm.

## MAIN AREAS OF PRACTICE:

**Antitrust & Competition:** With more than 50 years' experience and over 75 competition lawyers in the US and Europe, the firm has secured antitrust clearance for hundreds of complex mergers and joint ventures, helped clients avoid fines and prison terms in many cartel investigations, and won numerous victories for clients in private and government litigation.

**Aviation:** Regarded as one of the world's premier commercial aviation practices, the firm advises airlines, airports, associations and governments on aviation-specific legal and policy issues, from certification to licensing to enforcement.

**Bankruptcy & Commercial:** Named by *Business Week* as one of the 'top bankruptcy shops' in the United States, the firm has broad experience representing debtors, creditors and creditors' committees in bankruptcy, insolvency and debt restructuring matters, and in related litigation and commercial transactions.

**Communications & E-commerce:** WilmerHale has played a major role in shaping the rules governing the wireline and wireless telecommunications, e-commerce and mass media industries. When important issues and transactions arise, companies turn to them for the highest quality representation and effective problem solving.

**Corporate:** The firm is widely recognized for its preeminence in the representation of technology and life sciences companies in the US and Europe. Its corporate lawyers are renowned for their work in initial public offerings, venture capital and private equity, mergers and acquisitions, strategic alliances, corporate governance matters and the representation of start-up companies.

**Defense, National Security & Government Contracts:** With extensive experience serving in senior national security posts in the US government, the firm's lawyers provide regulatory, legislative, transactional and enforcement advice to clients supplying products and services to military, governmental and commercial customers worldwide.

**Environmental:** Clients rely on the firm to address complex environmental liabilities, permit key operations and understand evolving environmental laws.

**FDA:** The firm's FDA Practice includes considerable experience before the FDA and other administrative agencies, Congress and the federal courts.

**Financial Institutions:** Over the past 30 years, the firm has built a practice of extensive breadth and depth in regulatory, transactional and litigation matters for banks and other financial institutions.

**Intellectual Property:** The Intellectual Property Practice serves as a one-stop solution for clients' IP prosecution, litigation and licensing needs in the US and Europe. *The American Lawyer* recently recognized WilmerHale as having one of the top IP litigation departments in the US.

**International Trade, Investment & Market Access:** Recognized as one of the world's leading trade law firms, WilmerHale represents clients from the US, EU, China, Canada, and more than 30 other countries before administrative, judicial and legislative bodies across the globe, as well as in proceedings under the WTO, NAFTA and the World Customs Organization.

## OFFICES

**CALIFORNIA**
1117 California Ave., **Palo Alto**, CA 94304
**Tel:** 650 858 6000  **Fax:** 650 858 6100

**DISTRICT OF COLUMBIA**
1875 Pennsylvania Avenue, NW, **Washington**, DC 20006
**Tel:** 202 663 6000  **Fax:** 202 663 6363

**MARYLAND**
100 Light Street, **Baltimore**, MD 21202
**Tel:** 410 986 2800  **Fax:** 410 986 2828

**MASSACHUSETTS**
60 State Street, **Boston**, MA 02109
**Tel:** 617 526 6000  **Fax:** 617 526 5000

WilmerHale Venture Group, Bay Colony Corporate Center,
1100 Winter Street, **Waltham**, MA 02451
**Tel:** 781 966 2000  **Fax:** 781 966 2100

**NEW YORK**
399 Park Avenue, **New York**, NY 10022
**Tel:** 212 230 8800  **Fax:** 212 230 8888

**NORTHERN VIRGINIA**
1600 Tysons Boulevard, Suite 1000, **McLean**, VA 22102
**Tel:** 703 251 9700  **Fax:** 703 251 9797

## INTERNATIONAL OFFICES

The firm has offices in Beijing, Berlin, Brussels, London, Munich and Oxford.

**Labor & Employment:** With capabilities including comprehensive labor and employment law counseling, employment litigation and custom-designed training programs, the firm offers clients in the US and Europe practical solutions for effectively dealing with employment issues and achieving their business objectives.

**Litigation & Arbitration:** The firm's preeminent Litigation Practice is widely recognized for its excellence in civil and criminal trial and appellate litigation, as well as in intellectual property and securities litigation. In addition, it has one of the world's leading international arbitration practices. Many of its litigators formerly held senior government positions and have particular expertise in litigation strategies designed to advance clients' objectives in regulatory and political arenas.

**Private Client:** Attorneys in the Private Client Group advise clients on gift, estate and income taxation, sophisticated gifting and diversification strategies, private philanthropy, trusts and fiduciary investments, and the administration of estates.

**Public Policy & Strategy:** This practice consolidates the extensive work that the firm's lawyers do across the public policy landscape, from providing broad-gauged advice to companies or industries on how to manage public policy risk, to crafting legislative or regulatory solutions to problems, to strategic support for proposed business transactions or initiatives, to crisis management, the response to congressional investigations and advice on multi-state challenges and opportunities.

**Real Estate:** The firm has extensive expertise in real estate capital management, institutional and pension fund equity and debt investment, development and permitting, leasing and foreign investment.

**Securities:** The firm's lawyers have successfully resolved some of the most significant and complex securities investigations and litigation over the last two decades and have established the firm as a leading defender of companies charged with violations of the securities laws and market misconduct.

**Tax:** The firm's top-ranked Tax Practice includes lawyers recognized by 'Who's Who Legal' as among 'the world's leading tax practitioners.' It handles all aspects of domestic and international tax advice for public and private companies, non-profit organizations and individuals.

**CONTENTS:**

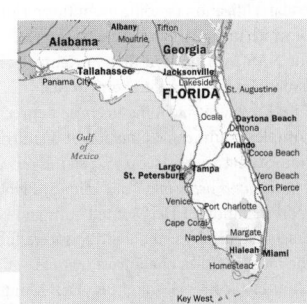

## How lawyers are ranked

Every year we carry out thousands of in-depth interviews with clients and lawyers in order to assess the reputations and expertise of business lawyers across the USA. Chambers rankings and editorial are referred to extensively by General Counsel and other purchasers of legal services who look to our recommendations when choosing their lawyers.

# ANTITRUST

### Antitrust
#### Leading Firms

**1** AKERMAN SENTERFITT *Orlando*
KENNY NACHWALTER PA *Miami*

**2** BOIES, SCHILLER & FLEXNER LLP *Miami*
CARLTON FIELDS *Tampa*
HOLLAND & KNIGHT LLP *Miami*
HUNTON & WILLIAMS LLP *Miami*

**3** BERMAN DEVALERIO PEASE *West Palm Beach*
FOLEY & LARDNER LLP *Tallahassee*
GREENBERG TRAURIG LLP *Miami*
NAGIN GALLOP FIGUEREDO PA *Coconut Grove*
ZUCKERMAN SPAEDER LLP *Miami*

#### Leading Individuals

**1** ARNOLD Richard *Kenny Nachwalter PA*
BLECHMAN Bill *Kenny Nachwalter PA*
COUTROULIS Chris *Carlton Fields*
PERWIN Scott *Kenny Nachwalter PA*
ROUNSAVILLE Keith *Akerman Senterfitt*
SILVERMAN Lawrence *Akerman Senterfitt*

**2** HOFFMAN D Bruce *Hunton & Williams LLP*
HOFFMAN Jerome *Holland & Knight LLP*
LITCHFORD Hal *Litchford & Christopher*
NACHWALTER Michael *Kenny Nachwalter PA*
NAGIN Stephen *Nagin Gallop Figueredo PA*
PALMER Scott *Berman DeValerio Pease*
SINGER Stuart *Boies, Schiller*

**3** DAVIDSON Barry *Hunton & Williams LLP*
LANDIS James *Foley & Lardner LLP*
RAVIKOFF Ronald *Zuckerman Spaeder LLP*
ROSS David *Greenberg Traurig LLP*
STEINBERG Marty *Hunton & Williams LLP*

## Band 1

### Akerman Senterfitt

See firm details p.657

**The Firm:** With eight offices and over 400 attorneys, this is one of the largest firms in the state. It fields a seven-strong team of *"real leaders in the antitrust field,"* who successfully assert and defend a wide variety of claims. In particular, clients value *"its ability to coordinate a statewide response to any situation."* These include price-fixing, bid-rigging, group boycotts and covenants not to compete. The firm has been involved in some of the largest and most significant cases in the market. Indicative of this was its success in obtaining summary judgment on the eve of trial for a large tour company in the defense of a $45 million monopolization lawsuit in Key West, Florida. Attorneys also argued the appeal of summary judgment for Gulfstream Park racetrack in the Florida Supreme Court, a case of national significance for the horseracing industry.

**The Lawyers:** Head of the antitrust and trade regulation department **Keith Rounsaville** (see p.649) impresses clients with his *"academic prowess and practicality as a lawyer."* He provides on-point procedural and substantive advice, and recently assisted a major oil company in its response to the Florida attorney general's civil investigative demands concerning the retail prices of gasoline. **Lawrence Silverman** (see p.651), head of the litigation department, is favored by clients for his *"outstanding business mind – he understands the economic landscape."* Among his other clients, Silverman is primary outside counsel to Samsung Electronics America.

**Clients/Work Highlights:** Allied Universal; Gulfstream Park Racing Association; Historic Tours of America; Marathon Petroleum; Nielsen Media Research; Transitions Optical; Del Monte Foods and The GEO Group.

### Kenny Nachwalter PA

See firm details p.666

**The Firm:** Clients believe this firm has *"one of the finest reputations in the field on a national basis,"* due to its commitment of resources and the dedication of its attorneys. Some clients commented: *"You can't get better than this firm anywhere."* The firm concentrates on complex business litigation, of which antitrust litigation plays a prominent part, and is well versed in plaintiff cases of national importance: *"It is always seen on the critical cases,"* said sources. For example, the team is involved in the large civil antitrust case against Visa and MasterCard, a case concerning alleged monopolization and conspiracy to fix prices. Another recent highlight is its successful representation of the plaintiff-appellant in Spirit Airlines v Northwest Airlines, a case involving issues of predatory pricing. This significant victory provides an important decision in an uncertain area of jurisprudence.

**The Lawyers:** *"Every bit the key lawyer in the state,"* **Richard Arnold** (see p.626) attracts clients with his wealth of experience: *"He has long been fully entrenched in the area."* Skilled in his representation of plaintiffs, Arnold divides his time between offices in Tennessee, Florida and Washington, DC. **Bill Blechman** (see p.629) is *"one of the impressive young guns at this firm"* and a key figure in the Visa/MasterCard case. He was involved in reversing summary judgment by the US District Court for the Eastern District of Michigan in the Spirit Airlines v Northwest Airlines appeal. This reinstates Spirit Airline's illegal-monopoly suit filed under Section 2 of the Sherman Act. A class act, **Scott Perwin** (see p.647) is *"omnipresent in the field"* and impresses clients as being *"supremely smart and a vociferous advocate."* He obtained a large verdict against the City of Key West in an appeal involving a large tour company and a monopolization lawsuit, and has advised on antitrust cases against pharmaceutical manufacturers. Although **Michael Nachwalter** (see p.646) is better known for his involvement in complex commercial litigation, he is also a force in antitrust matters. He is *"senior, experienced and a fantastic trial lawyer."*

**Clients/Work Highlights:** While best known for its representation of plaintiffs in cases of national significance, the firm is also found representing defendants. Retailers, drugstores, manufacturers and government bodies are examples of the types of client this firm represents.

## Band 2

### Boies, Schiller & Flexner LLP

See firm details p.1520

**The Firm:** This firm has four offices in Florida, twelve offices across the country and is home to 200 attorneys. Clients view the firm as a *"key port of call for high-stakes antitrust litigation"* and are impressed by the *"efficiency with which matters are handled"* by this 14-strong Florida antitrust team. The firm represents both plaintiffs and defendants, although sources pointed to its *"ardent plaintiff representation"* as a real strength. Recently, the firm acted for Del Monte Foods in the pineapple antitrust litigation filed in the Southern District of New York and the banana litigation pending in southern Florida, both of which involve monopolization claims. It also acted for NASCAR in a suit filed in Kentucky involving issues pertaining to the Sherman Act.

**The Lawyers:** Dividing his time between general complex commercial litigation and antitrust litigation, **Stuart Singer** (see p.652) stands out as "*bright, creative and accessible,*" said clients. Pivotal in the representation of Del Monte Foods and NASCAR, Singer has displayed the ability to successfully handle the most complex of antitrust matters.

**Clients/Work Highlights:** Del Monte Foods, NASCAR and The SCO Group are representative clients of the antitrust group.

## Carlton Fields

See firm details p.661

**The Firm:** This multidisciplinary firm has six offices in Florida and impresses clients not only with the depth of resources available, but also with its experience in antitrust cases: "*They can provide valuable strategic advice through their deep involvement in the field.*" The antitrust team mostly operates out of the Tampa office, but clients highlighted the cohesive approach of the firm and its willingness to draw in specialists from other offices. The tactical knowledge of the team on issues surrounding class certification is first class, and the antitrust and trade regulation team has a strong track record in defending indirect purchaser litigation. Recent highlights include successfully representing Visa in two cases involving claims of conspiracy, alleging that merchants who accepted Visa and MasterCard credit cards were also forced to accept the debit cards, which in turn artificially inflated the fees. The team is also representing Toyota in an action alleging antitrust violations concerning the sale and leasing of automobiles.

**The Lawyers:** The "*engaging and enlightening*" **Chris Coutroulis** (see p.632) is head of the antitrust and trade regulation department. According to clients, he possesses "*not only an encyclopedic knowledge of the law, but also a great business sense.*" A respected author on antitrust issues, Coutroulis is also skilled in defending indirect purchaser litigation.

**Clients/Work Highlights:** AIG; AstraZeneca; Bill Heard Chevrolet; Brinker International; Clear Channel Outdoor; HCA; Infineon Technologies North America; Pfizer; Restaurant Services (RSI); State Farm; Stauffer Management and Zenith Insurance Management.

## Holland & Knight LLP

See firm details p.1534

**The Firm:** Above all, clients point to the "*knowledge, experience and resources*" of this antitrust, trade regulation and competition team as its distinguishing factors. A hugely respected national firm, it can handle the large antitrust cases that cross many disciplines. The firm has recently consolidated its smaller offices in St. Petersburg, Lakeland and Bradenton into the firm's base in Tampa, and onlookers agree that this will "*streamline the firm and allow it to focus on its strongholds.*" The Tallahassee office stands out

as the antitrust hub, yet clients were quick to highlight the "*protection a multinational firm like this can afford one's interests.*" The 30-strong department (approximately 15 of which are based in Florida) provides industry-specific advice and training, auditing and compliance programs.

**The Lawyers:** "*There is not an area of antitrust law that* **Jerome Hoffman** (see p.640) *does not have experience in,*" according to sources. He is well versed in healthcare law, especially in the representation of hospitals in antitrust cases. His prior appointment as chief of the antitrust section of the Florida attorney general's office has provided him with an astute insight into many areas of antitrust law.

**Clients/Work Highlights:** Clients of this antitrust department are drawn from a variety of industries, from computer and consumer electronics to financial institutions and the pharmaceutical and biotechnology sectors.

## Hunton & Williams LLP

See firm details p.1989

**The Firm:** The commercial trial prowess of this firm combines well with the experience of its antitrust specialists. The competition and antitrust group is a subdivision of the litigation practice group and clients value the fact that this is a large multidisciplinary firm: "*It brings its wide expertise to bear*" on those cases that cut across many areas of law. The firm has been involved in the representation of Dole Food in the pineapple and banana antitrust litigation.

**The Lawyers:** Onlookers describe **Barry Davidson** (see p.633) as a seasoned practitioner and "*a thoughtful business litigator.*" He focuses on civil litigation and is heavily engaged in antitrust disputes. **Marty Steinberg** (see p.653), managing partner of the Miami office, has a national reputation for being "*tenacious, thorough and very smart.*" Clients are endeared to his "*meticulous preparation*" and thoroughly recommend "*his bulldog-like qualities; he really won't let go until he feels he has conquered the issue.*" Making his return to practice having served at the FTC since 2001, **Bruce Hoffman** (see p.639) is a welcome addition to the team, not least for the practical experience he brings with him.

**Clients/Work Highlights:** Dole Food Company; BellSouth; Boeing and Honeywell.

## Band 3

## Berman DeValerio Pease Tabacco Burt & Pucillo

**The Firm:** "*One heck of a class action plaintiff antitrust firm,*" this outfit is increasingly making its presence felt in the market. This West Palm Beach firm has a high success rate on behalf of plaintiffs and is regarded as "*a real contender*" in major matters. In a recent case, the team filed a suit against seven major carmakers, accusing them of conspiring to eliminate imports of new cars from Canada in an effort to illegally stifle competition.

**The Lawyers:** **Scott Palmer** impresses clients with

his broad experience in class action litigation and "*the tight grip he has on the law.*" "*He's just a pleasure to deal with,*" according to onlookers. A team of four partners and four associates is dedicated to antitrust matters.

**Clients/Work Highlights:** The team predominantly represents plaintiffs in multiparty lawsuits.

## Foley & Lardner LLP

See firm details p.2037

**The Firm:** The firm has the resources to handle large multijurisdictional cases with its 19 offices worldwide (five of which are in Florida), and clients appreciate the "*seamless interplay between offices.*" The group displays a confident handling of the full range of antitrust issues, from compliance and criminal antitrust to high-stakes litigation. The antitrust litigation team is also well versed in handling cases involving price-fixing, monopolization and predatory pricing.

**The Lawyers:** **James Landis** (see p.642) in the Tampa office is "*a high-quality lawyer who has a wealth of antitrust experience.*" A skilled counselor and trial lawyer, he is a former attorney with the DOJ's Antitrust Division.

**Clients/Work Highlights:** Clients are drawn from a range of sectors. For example, in terms of healthcare, this firm represents healthcare plans, hospitals, medical groups and preferred provider organizations.

## Greenberg Traurig LLP

See firm details p.664

**The Firm:** This "*giant of a firm*" is revered for its prowess in all forms of litigation and is also a force in terms of antitrust. Fielding the wealth of resources and endless reach a firm of this size can offer, it also has specific knowledge of antitrust issues in relation to M&A and joint ventures. Litigation is an obvious strength of this team, yet clients also commended its trade regulation advice and preventive antitrust counseling.

**The Lawyers:** A hugely respected commercial litigator, **David Ross** (see p.649) is also highlighted for his work in the antitrust field. He has been heavily involved in tobacco litigation and has successfully represented State Farm in a six-week antitrust jury trial.

**Clients/Work Highlights:** National and international companies in a range of industries retain this firm, including the tobacco, insurance and healthcare industries among others.

## Nagin Gallop Figueredo PA

**The Firm:** This compact Miami-based boutique "*routinely punches above its weight,*" reported sources. Although the firm represents business clients on the full range of antitrust issues, it is unfair competition and patent and trademark infringement cases that ensure the group its prominence. The high caliber of its attorneys guarantees the firm's involvement in some of the state's most important cases.

**The Lawyers:** The analytical **Stephen Nagin** possesses a diverse practice. Combining patent and trademark law with antitrust, he not only has "*an interesting practice, but he is also a great adviser – one of the best.*"

**Clients/Work Highlights:** The firm is often found representing regional and local businesses in antitrust cases.

## Zuckerman Spaeder LLP

**The Firm:** This litigation outfit is first choice for many seeking advice on criminal antitrust issues. A leader in white-collar litigation and government investigations, clients value the fact that the group can draw on "*the experience of a number of respected criminal practitioners.*" The firm excels in the areas of

antitrust counseling, distribution law and unfair trade practice litigation. Over the past year, the firm has advised on the provision of antitrust counseling for a large client in the photography sector.

**The Lawyers: Ronald Ravikoff**, managing partner of the firm's Miami office, divides his practice between general commercial litigation and antitrust matters. A respected trial lawyer, he has "*an eye for the details.*"

**Clients/Work Highlights:** The firm represents both plaintiffs and defendants in antitrust litigation, and regularly counsels clients in antitrust compliance. The representation of healthcare industry clients who are engaged in joint ventures is another

emerging area of strength for the team.

## Other Notable Practitioners

**Hal Litchford** of Litchford & Christopher in Orlando has won a following among clients and attorneys across the state: "*If I had a matter in Orlando, it would be Hal, hands down.*" He was involved in the antitrust appeal concerning a large tour company and a monopolization lawsuit in Key West.

# BANKING & FINANCE

| Banking & Finance |
| --- |
| **Leading Firms** |

| | |
| --- | --- |
| [1] | **AKERMAN SENTERFITT** *Orlando* |
| | **GREENBERG TRAURIG LLP** *Miami* |
| | **HOLLAND & KNIGHT LLP** *Miami* |
| | **SHUTTS & BOWEN LLP** *Miami* |
| [2] | **HUNTON & WILLIAMS LLP** *Miami* |
| | **STROOCK & STROOCK & LAVAN LLP** *Miami* |
| | **WHITE & CASE LLP** *Miami* |
| [3] | **GUNSTER, YOAKLEY & STEWART, PA** *Miami* |
| | **SMITH MACKINNON PA** *Orlando* |
| | **STEARNS WEAVER MILLER WEISSLER** *Miami* |

| Leading Individuals |
| --- |

| | |
| --- | --- |
| [1] | **ALVAREZ** Victor *White & Case LLP* |
| | **AVILA** Alcides *Holland & Knight LLP* |
| | **BROWN** Bowman *Shutts & Bowen LLP* |
| | **CARDWELL** J Thomas *Akerman Senterfitt* |
| | **LOUMIET** Carlos *Hunton & Williams LLP* |
| | **VÁZQUEZ-BELLO** Clemente *Gunster, Yoakley* |
| [2] | **ALVAREZ** Pedro *White & Case LLP* |
| | **AMES** Stuart *Stearns Weaver Miller Weissler* |
| | **BASILE** Michael *Stroock & Stroock & Lavan LLP* |
| | **BLOOM** Warren *Greenberg Traurig LLP* |
| | **FORNARIS** Carl *Greenberg Traurig LLP* |
| | **GREELEY** Jack *Smith Mackinnon PA* |
| | **JONES** Rod *Shutts & Bowen LLP* |
| | **STUTTS** Charles *Holland & Knight LLP* |
| | **VOGEL III** Edward *Holland & Knight LLP* |

## Band 1

### Akerman Senterfitt

See firm details p.657

**The Firm:** Strong market endorsement, a year full of successful finance and banking deals and a boosted visibility with new offices in both Washington, DC and New York has ensured this firm its prominence in the banking community. With 45 lawyers across its eight Florida offices, the team is heavily engaged in three core areas: regulatory advice, lender's repre-

sentation in transactions and finance-related litigation. Observers lavished praise on this "*zesty and energetic player*" for its ongoing representation of the Florida Bankers Association, a relationship that spans over 50 years of "*mutual success and growth.*" In a recent development, the team assisted this client in a rewrite of the Florida Trust Code. In another highlight, attorneys here acted for SunTrust Banks in the modification, renewal and increase of a $1.8 billion syndicated revolving line of credit. This marquee client also instructed the team as counsel in the defense and settlement of a $7 million breach of fiduciary duty claim.

**The Lawyers: Thomas Cardwell** (see p.630) is hailed as "*one of Florida's biggest and most excellent names*" in the regulatory and legislative sides of the field. He is the firm's key link to the Florida Bankers Association and juggles a busy caseload with his role as Akerman Senterfitt's CEO and duties at the helm of the banking group.

**Clients/Work Highlights:** Recent mandates included the representation of Colonial Bank in a $350 million syndicated warehouse facility to a national mortgage company, and advice to Wachovia in a $42 million acquisition, development and construction loan for a retail center in Newport News, Virginia. Marquee client Bank of America retained the firm as counsel in a unique loan-purchase structure of a $550 million facility to provide financing for existing and future residential projects. In another development, the team acted for FINOVA Capital in three coordinated foreclosures of a total of nine restaurants.

### Greenberg Traurig LLP

See firm details p.664

**The Firm:** This Florida heavyweight "*truly belongs up there*" in the top echelon of the banking and finance market. Clients flock to the firm thanks to its excellence in cross-border regulatory, public and general finance and securitization. Inbound and outbound Latin American lending and finance-related litigation are also on the menu from this "*talent-pool of lawyers who are available 24/7 and offer New York-style service with Miami rates.*" The firm

recently hit the headlines as US counsel for the Republic of Chile in tracking financial assets of former Chilean dictator Augusto Pinochet.

**The Lawyers:** Among the 175-strong Miami group, sources "*think the world of incredibly efficient attorney*" **Carl Fornaris** (see p.636). Cochair of the national financial institutions practice group, he has a mixed caseload that spans regulatory matters and antimoney laundering to cross-border lending transactions. He advised Barclays on the establishment of bank and broker-dealer subsidiaries in Mexico. Orlando-based partner **Warren Bloom** (see p.629) impresses with his public finance work. His workload spans the nation, and includes the representation of Lennar in the purchase and development of prime real estate in San Francisco Bay. He also acted for the buyers of $9 million worth of City of Atlanta tax allocation bonds.

**Clients/Work Highlights:** Allstate Corporation; American Express; Atlas One Financial Group; Banco Colpatria; Banco Industrial de Venezuela; Citibank; First Magnus Financial; SunTrust Banks; Wachovia and the Republic of Chile.

### Holland & Knight LLP

See firm details p.1534

**The Firm:** This national giant retains its position at the zenith of the banking and finance sector. The highly skilled team scores well with "*its depth of experience, agility and highly competent capabilities,*" particularly in intricate financial operations with a Latin American component. Other key strengths are banking M&A, municipal finance, finance-related litigation and compliance counsel arising from the Patriot Act and Banking Secrecy Act.

**The Lawyers: Alcides Avila** (see p.627) combines a busy compliance and banking caseload with heading the firm's banking and finance group and a role as general counsel of the Florida International Bankers Association. Sources credited him with being "*the heart and engine*" of the Florida team's cross-border financial services prowess. **Charles Stutts** (see p.653) remains a favorite of broker dealers and money services clients operating in and out of Tampa. He wins plaudits for his "*shining and capable demeanor,*" which he puts to good use in tough negotiations. Public finance star **Edward Vogel** (see p.655) "*takes a lot of pride in his work product and provides timely high-quality service.*" Vogel recently assisted Polk County in two separate multimillion-dollar bond financings.

**Clients/Work Highlights:** Amscot Financial; Financial Service Centers of Florida; AmSouth Bank; Sarasota County; SunTrust Capital Markets; City of Gainesville, Caja Madrid; Banco de Crédito del Perú; Wachovia; Bank of America; NetBank; SouthTrust Bank and Prudential.

## Shutts & Bowen LLP

See firm details p.673

**The Firm:** According to sources, this 17-strong team successfully steams ahead in an increasingly sophisticated financial market, drawing its inspiration from the complex transactions handled by counterparts in New York. A Latin American-flavored bi-directional deal flow dominated this year's workloa; however, the firm's domestic proficiency was shown by its work restructuring the US banking and brokerage operations of a large global financial services conglomerate. On the regulatory side, lawyers here drafted and lobbied into legislation landmark facilities for insurers to sell policies to non-US residents, effectively opening up the market.

**The Lawyers:** "*Father of banking law*" **Bowman Brown** (see p.629) is chair of Shutts & Bowen's executive committee and its financial services practice group. He displays a "*big-picture sense and highly effective creativeness*" in both domestic and cross-border transactions. Brown was recently in the spotlight when he counseled legislators drafting the new international insurance bill. "*He masters the arts of the possible,*" said sources in regards to the practical problem-solving skills of partner **Rod Jones** (see p.640). He excels in the niche market of community banks.

**Clients/Work Highlights:** Other key mandates of late include assisting a major Mexican lender in substantial credit extensions to borrowers, and representing several US financial services providers in the sale of their Latin American units.

## Band 2

## Hunton & Williams LLP

See firm details p.1989

**The Firm:** The Richmond-headquartered player maintains its preeminent profile in Florida with a stronghold in securities, cross-border project financing, regulatory and compliance work. The firm has also enhanced its outreach and muscle with the opening of offices in Beijing and Houston.

**The Lawyers:** **Carlos Loumiet** (see p.643) "*is the*

experienced leader of this highly dynamic team,*" reported sources. He splits his time between Miami and New York, with a hefty assignment roster recently dominated by committee group work, Sarbanes-Oxley-related issues and funds counsel. Loumiet cochairs the firm's international practice group and "*tops everyone's list*" for cross-border banking work and cradle-to-grave counsel of financial startups.

**Clients/Work Highlights:** Among the team's recent successes are the brokering of several separate telecom and power plant projects across Latin America. Also, Carlos Loumiet headlined a team that drafted anti-money-laundering legislation for Panama and for Antigua and Barbuda.

## Stroock & Stroock & Lavan LLP

**The Firm:** With roots in the financial world as far back as 1876, this New York-based firm is already a "*force to reckon with*" in Florida, according to rivals. The Miami office houses 18 lawyers out of a national headcount of 350.

**The Lawyers:** **Michael Basile** is the firm's main claim to fame in Florida. Sources describe him as "*a standout character capable of making a difference for the client and not for the fee.*" Basile draws on his experience as general counsel to the Florida Department of Banking and Finance to advise clients on compliance and regulatory matters arising from M&A and securitizations. Of late, Basile has advised the organizers of a Coral Gables-based community bank, and acted for a major national investment bank in the development of an international real property fund and a domestic real property fund.

## White & Case LLP

See firm details p.1566

**The Firm:** "*The White & Case difference lies firstly in its unparalleled expertise in multijurisdictional and cross-border transactional and lending work, secondly in its Latin American focus, and thirdly in its consistency and availability across both partner and associate levels,*" remarked one source, reflecting much of what was said about this global giant's Florida team. The day-to-day caseload of the 20-strong Miami group covers the full range of asset finance, bank lending, capital markets and project finance-related transactions. Particularly of note was the firm's work on the landmark financial restructuring of Durango and its advice to Sol Meliá in a $100 million securitization.

**The Lawyers:** **Pedro Alvarez** (see p.626) enjoys "*a well-deserved reputation for all things Latin American*" and scooped plaudits for leading the Sol Meliá operation. He is also heavily involved in domestic M&A and financings, and recently brokered a $47.5 million financing for an energy client in the Dominican Republic to build a wind farm. **Victor Alvarez**

(see p.626) heads the practice and is considered "*one of the most preeminent names in the Florida Bar.*" His recent workload includes acting for BBVA Securities as administrative agent in a $100 million senior credit facility for an Aruba-based wholly-owned subsidiary of Chilean specialty fertilizer maker SQM. ING Capital retained Victor Alvarez's team as counsel in a $100 million senior unsecured loan facility for Banco Security of Chile.

**Clients/Work Highlights:** BSCH; BellSouth; Corporación Durango; Instituto Costarricense de Electricidad; ING Barings; JPMorgan Securities and Wachovia.

## Band 3

## Gunster, Yoakley & Stewart, PA

**The Firm:** A leader in the south Florida market, this firm is home to 130 lawyers in six offices across the region. It enjoys a reputation among peers for its "*no-nonsense approach to business strategy*" in securities, international banking and regulatory compliance.

**The Lawyers:** **Clemente Vázquez-Bello** "*is a star in anti-money-laundering matters*" and remains a favorite among domestic and Latin American banking clients.

## Smith Mackinnon PA

**The Firm:** This compact team in Orlando was singled out to researchers as one of the most active Florida teams in banking regulatory issues.

**The Lawyers:** Among the firm's six attorneys, the market underlined the brilliant reputation of **Jack Greeley** for his work in new bank formations and community and smaller banks. Sources concurred that Greeley "*is the equal of the big boys at the best national firms.*"

## Stearns Weaver Miller Weissler Alhadeff & Sitterson, PA

**The Firm:** Though better known for its expertise in litigation and restructuring, this high-octane operation has made its mark in the finance sector. Housing 100 lawyers in three key Florida cities, the firm is engaged in the full panoply of finance-related services, from regulatory compliance matters to investment and brokerage activities.

**The Lawyers:** A "*world-class negotiator and gentleman extraordinaire,*" **Stuart Ames** heads the firm's commercial and asset-based finance practice. His practice concentrates on the representation of lenders in large secured and unsecured loans. Ames was recently retained by a major bank in a $700 million syndicated financing to a national homebuilder.

# BANKRUPTCY/RESTRUCTURING

## Band 1

### Akerman Senterfitt

See firm details p.657

**The Firm:** In what the market saw as a profile-boosting coup, veteran bankruptcy lawyer Francis Carter joined Akerman Senterfitt this year. With one of the largest head counts in the state and a *"fantastic lineup"* at all levels in the bankruptcy department, the firm has cemented its profile as a leader in the state and beyond. Its increased visibility in high-profile cases is exemplified in work such as the Tropical Sportswear assets disposition.

**The Lawyers:** *"He brings prestige, experience and depth of knowledge and rolls it into the firm's existing prowess,"* summarized observers on the arrival of **Francis Carter** (see p.630). He continues to advise on Chapter 11 cases and has a broad understanding of related transactional matters. *"Deal-maker"* Carter heads the Miami bankruptcy team. **Jules Cohen** (see p.631) is the *"real dean of the Florida Bar"* and remains a *"driving force and an icon in Orlando."* He has a varied practice that often sees him acting for secured creditors. *"Effective and smart are the words for"* **Michael Goldberg** (see p.637), said commentators. He is admitted in the New York Bar, which supports his East Coast-weighted practice. Among other successes, Goldberg recently represented HIG Capital in its purchase of Supra Telecom out of bankruptcy. He currently acts for AutoNation in its defense of a $600 million claim in connection with its pre-petition spin-off of a rental company.

**Clients/Work Highlights:** SunTrust Banks; Criimi Mae; Banco Popular; CHEP International; Choice Hotels; Magna Entertainment; AutoNation and GE Healthcare Financial Services, a division of GE Capital.

### Berger Singerman

**The Firm:** It is *"the level of personal service, client focus"* and *"depth of talent"* that clients point to as particular drawing cards for this business reorganization team. The debtor-oriented practice with its *"creative solutions to complex issues"* is widely recognized, and with 11 dedicated attorneys spread across the Fort Lauderdale and Miami offices, it is one of the largest dedicated teams in southeast Florida. The firm combines cost-effectiveness with a high-quality client service and is equally adept at handling midmarket cases as it is at handling complex billion-dollar cases. Clients also recommend the interaction between the different teams at this firm and note how beneficial its interdisciplinary approach can be. Instructions in 2005 included representing Banco Espirito Santo, the third largest bank in Portugal, in one of the largest bank fraud cases in south Florida to date. The team also represented Aloha Airlines in its Chapter 11 reorganization cases pending in the bankruptcy court in Hawaii, the result of which was its recapitalization with $100 million of debt and its successful emergence from bankruptcy.

**The Lawyers:** *"The star of the bankruptcy market,"* **Paul Singerman** is both the energy behind the firm and *"one of the best attorneys in the country; he's that good."* He is a practical attorney who is responsive and hard working. He was recently involved in the Banco Espirito Santo and Aloha Airlines cases. Combining with Singerman to make a formidable team, **Jordi Guso** is *"more personal than your average lawyer"* while also being *"responsive and effective,"* said clients. **Arthur Spector** is a former bankruptcy judge who brings a *"tremendous amount of experience and insight from his time on the bench."* He has made the transition from being a member of the federal judiciary into a brilliant commercial lawyer and business reorganization specialist. Residing in the Fort Lauderdale office, Spector manages the firm's business reorganization team.

**Clients/Work Highlights:** This firm represents debtors, creditors' committees, trustees and private equity firms in a range of industries from telecom to transportation and restaurants. Clients include Prime Succession, Gulf Atlantic Capital and Piccadilly Cafeterias.

### Genovese Joblove & Battista, PA

See firm details p.663

**The Firm:** This large, Florida-based specialty practice is a *"cutting-edge player"* deserving the highest praise. With 12 of the firm's 25 lawyers devoted to bankruptcy, this insolvency, bankruptcy and creditors' rights practice is one of the largest in the state. Workwise, the team excels in creditor litigation, insolvency and out-of-court workouts, although it is also highly praised for its involvement in a number of cross-border bankruptcy cases.

**The Lawyers:** A talented attorney, **Paul Battista** (see p.628) is acknowledged as being *"good on his feet"* and *"a very practical, insightful and meticulous adviser."* An aggressive litigator and a tireless worker,

Battista specializes in all areas of complex commercial bankruptcy, particularly restructuring and related litigation. Clients appreciate that he *"brings an infallible expertise in reorganizations that works brilliantly in tandem with the litigious expertise of* **John Genovese** (see p.636)." Genovese impresses clients with his *"superior intellect"* and *"aggressive, results-driven litigious skills."* He is head of the firm's reorganization and insolvency practice and is considered proficient in handling troubled loan workouts and insurance insolvencies, with a particular emphasis on litigation in the bankruptcy court.

**Clients/Work Highlights:** This team is often found representing Chapter 11 and Chapter 7 trustees, debtors in possession, creditors' committees and receivers.

### Greenberg Traurig LLP

See firm details p.664

**The Firm:** This national giant has secured its place on some of the most significant cases in the sector. It is *"very agile for its size"* and fields interdisciplinary capabilities and a depth of talent and resources that few firms can match. Commentators also noted its growing national practice: *"They are just making inroads everywhere."* Nationally, the firm is home to 65 lawyers, 14 of whom are housed in the Florida offices.

**The Lawyers:** Many think that *"there is no need to look any further than* **Mark Bloom** (see p.629) *if you are looking for a brilliant strategic thinker and an astounding oral advocate."* His *"warm and genuine approach,"* his involvement in the most complex cases and his leadership qualities make him *"the go-to guy."* Bloom is cochair of the national business reorganization and bankruptcy practice and has expertise in all areas of acquisitions and bankruptcy, particularly for troubled companies seeking restructuring. The *"business-oriented"* **Brian Gart** (see p.636) is a *"zealous advocate"* and vastly experienced in Chapter 11 business reorganizations and loan restructurings. He has also developed a focus on distressed M&A transactions, and can often be found representing private equity groups acquiring distressed assets. In Miami, **John Hutton** (see p.640) is respected both for his bankruptcy litigation practice and his representation of creditors' committees in a number of significant cases.

**Clients/Work Highlights:** Debtors, secured and unsecured creditors, investors and purchasers of assets, directors and trustees comprise the client base of this firm.

### Kozyak Tropin & Throckmorton

See firm details p.668

**The Firm:** This *"lean and aggressive outfit is a sure-fire leader"* in the Florida market. It is noted for its preeminence in litigation as well as bankruptcy-related matters, with clients pointing to the proficiency and talent of attorneys across the board. The group *"gets the desired results and gets them quickly and efficiently,"* according to clients, who go on to acknowledge the responsiveness of the attorneys and "*the good relationships they have with judges.*" The firm currently represents the trustee of the bankrupt Commercial Financial Services in litigation in Tulsa against its former lawyers, accountants and investment bankers for contributing to the company's $1 billion losses.

**The Lawyers:** Clients feel that **John Kozyak** (see p.642) "*puts his heart and soul into working on his client's behalf.*" A strategic thinker, he is solutions-driven and gets right to the point with "*his methodi-*

cal, deliberate and awe-inspiring performances." Kozyak represented the largest unsecured creditor in the Bentley Bay condominium reorganization in the past year, one of the largest real estate bankruptcies in South Florida. **Charles Throckmorton** (see p.654) is "*a star in his own right*" and a respected bankruptcy litigation specialist. He is sought after by various high net worth individuals for advice on bankruptcy-related litigation and workouts. He recently served as special litigation counsel to the bankruptcy trustee in the Bankest Capital case. **Corali Lopez-Castro** (see p.643) is making a name for herself through her "*energy and dedication*" to her clients. In addition to playing a role in the Commercial Financial Services litigation, she has guided several local businesses through successful out-of-court workouts. Last year saw the appointment of Laurel Isicoff to the bench, a development that indicates the high level of prestige achieved by this team.

## Stichter, Riedel, Blain & Prosser PA
See firm details p.674

**The Firm:** This is "*an excellent firm which delivers excellent results,*" and it is particularly famed for its debtor-oriented work. A high-caliber boutique, it is "*packed full of skillful, creative lawyers, who are well regarded by the Tampa bench.*" This group is also a key port of call for complex referrals and garnered respect for its "*sheer level of dedication to the client.*" A feather in the firm's cap this year includes acting for the official committee of unsecured creditors of Anchor Glass, a manufacturer of glass products. The firm also served as lead counsel for Lykes Bros Steamship in its successful reorganization efforts this past year.

**The Lawyers:** The "*extraordinarily academic*" **Harley Riedel** (see p.648) is one of the most highly prized bankruptcy attorneys in Florida. "*A true gentleman and a star in court,*" he not only knows the code inside-out, but also "*makes every case he works on a joyful and intellectually challenging experience.*" Riedel is well versed in Chapter 11 debtor cases and the representation of creditors' committees; he was chosen as co-counsel for the official committee of unsecured creditors of Anchor Glass in 2005. **Russell Blain** (see p.628) impresses with his "*imaginative, knowledgeable and diligent*" handling of Chapter 11 reorganizations. **Don Stichter** (see p.653) is a long-standing member of the firm and a valuable source of advice on all areas of the bankruptcy market. He is a highly effective adviser and is hugely respected in the market.

**Clients/Work Highlights:** Outback Steakhouse, Espirito Santo Bank and JAM Cruises are representative clients of the group.

## White & Case LLP
See firm details p.1566

**The Firm:** The Florida team of this national giant stole the headlines with the successful completion of the landmark $1 billion restructuring of Corporación Durango under both US and Mexican law. Market consensus has it that while the team of "*highly sophisticated and resourceful lawyers*" some-

times slips under the Florida radar, this is due to its broader reach: "*Its national and international prowess and its unparalleled ability to attract big-ticket work*" guarantee the group a place at the forefront of the market.

**The Lawyers:** **Thomas Lauria** (see p.642) co-heads the global bankruptcy practice team and scoops admiration for a busy caseload full of high-profile restructurings. He "*pushes right to the end for what is best and holds his ground till he gets the right answer and everything gets done.*" Among a string of successes, Lauria acted for Mirant in its $19 billion insolvency settlement and restructuring case, in which he settled the matter and achieved agreements with all parties involved. **Emilio Alvarez-Farré's** (see p.626) profile is currently riding high because of the Corporación Durango matter. He is "*one of the few selected stars that can really make everything positive no matter what,*" and is a good port of call for advice on Latin America.

**Clients/Work Highlights:** White & Case represents the Ad Hoc Committee of Arahova Noteholders in the Chapter 11 of cable operator Adelphia Communications.

### Band 2

## Bilzin Sumberg Baena Price & Axelrod LLP
See firm details p.660

**The Firm:** This firm has "*a real depth of experience from top to bottom*" and houses 11 full-time bankruptcy lawyers as well as five other bankruptcy-oriented litigators. The group inspires loyalty from clients due to its responsive and efficient service across the range of bankruptcy litigation, Chapter 11s and asbestos-related bankruptcies. It is well equipped to advise building owners in asbestos-related bankruptcy cases. The team was involved in some heavy-duty cases this year, including one in which Scott Baena was appointed by the Delaware Bankruptcy Court to be the litigation trustee and plan administrator for Lernout & Hauspie Speech Products upon confirmation of its plan of liquidation.

**The Lawyers:** "*Seasoned, skilled and diligent bankruptcy practitioner*" **Scott Baena** (see p.627) is credited as the driving force behind the group. Clients spoke of "*his limitless talent and star qualities.*" He was central in adversary proceedings arising out of the bankruptcy of PhyAmerica Physician Group, and a number of subsidiaries and related companies. **Mindy Mora** (see p.645) works in tandem with Baena and complements his style with her "*capable, tenacious and hard-working manner.*" Mora is advising a major international law firm in various matters related to its representation of an official committee in the FiberMark bankruptcy pending in the US Bankruptcy Court for the District of Vermont.

**Clients/Work Highlights:** The firm was involved in many of the largest asbestos-related Chapter 11 cases pending around the country, including WR Grace, US Gypsum and Armstrong World Industries. Specific clients of the group include Dr Steven

M Scott, the ad hoc committee of bondholders of Southeast Banking and the unsecured creditors' trust in the Viasource Communications proceedings.

## Hunton & Williams LLP

See firm details p.1989

**The Firm:** This international bankruptcy group wins plaudits for its depth and "*its ability to draw on the resources and expertise a full-service firm such as this offers.*" This firm divides its practice into bankruptcy and creditors' rights, debt restructurings and workouts, and troubled and defaulted bond issues. It is home to 30 dedicated lawyers, ten of whom are housed in Florida.

**The Lawyers: Craig Rasile** (see p.648) is the cochair of the bankruptcy and creditor-debtor rights law practice group, and is endorsed by clients for his "*effective running of a tight ship.*" He is central to the success of the department and adopts a hard-working and meticulous approach to his cases.

**Clients/Work Highlights:** This versatile group undertakes bankruptcy restructuring and insolvency for debtors; trustees; creditors' committees; equity committees and financial institutions. Specific examples include Bank of New York and HSBC.

## Kluger, Peretz, Kaplan & Berlin P.L.

See firm details p.667

**The Firm:** Fielding 13 lawyers who spend the majority of their time in bankruptcy matters, this department offers its clients the full range of bankruptcy services. As such, the group is also a key port of call for referrals. Last year, mandates included guiding the debtor through a court-imposed reconstitution of the Pan American Hospital Corporation's entire management structure. To illustrate the versatility of the group, it also represented the official committee of unsecured creditors in the case of Supra Telecom. After negotiations with the incumbent carrier, the result, on a percentage basis, was one of the most successful dividends delivered to creditors in a telecom case in recent years.

**The Lawyers:** Cochair of the department **Howard Berlin** is a "*savvy, experienced litigator and a brilliant negotiator,*" who has put this firm on the map. He was pivotal in the Pan American Hospital Corporation case. His partner **Robert Charbonneau** is "*a brilliant individual and a wonderful technician,*" and he has a strong focus on the high quality of his client service. He led representation of the creditors' committee in the Supra Telecom matter.

**Clients/Work Highlights:** Other significant representations in 2005 included acting for Epixtar in a Chapter 11 issue.

## Smith Hulsey & Busey

**The Firm:** Clients extol this full-service Florida business firm as the "*go-to bankruptcy address in Jacksonville.*" It is equally proficient in restructuring and bankruptcy litigation, and recent high-profile mandates are widely perceived to have increased its exposure in the market. This high-octane group of eight lawyers focuses on bankruptcy litigation and Chapter 11 reorganizations, and it impresses onlook-

ers with its "*slick efficiency*" and big-ticket cases. A major coup for the firm was acting as the debtors' Florida co-counsel in the Winn-Dixie Chapter 11.

**The Lawyers: Stephen Busey** is chairman of the firm and its litigation department. He is "*top-notch in everything he does,*" especially in reference to his courtroom performances. Complex, high-stakes bankruptcy litigation and Chapter 11 reorganizations of publicly held companies all fall into his remit.

**Clients/Work Highlights:** Clients include debtors; creditors' committees; secured and unsecured lenders and trustees.

## Trenam, Kemker, Scharf, Barkin, Frye, O'Neill & Mullis PA

**The Firm:** This full-service Florida-based law firm has more than 60 attorneys across offices in Tampa and St. Petersburg and over 35 years of heritage in the state. Clients refer to its strength in creditors' rights issues as a real drawing card. The firm adopts an interdisciplinary approach, often drawing on the resources and experience of other departments for its broad range of commercial bankruptcy cases. Its caseload of late has included Chapter 11s, workouts, foreclosures, and preference and fraudulent transfer litigation.

**The Lawyers:** Clients have "*only wonderful things to say about* **Roberta Colton.**" She is at the top of her game and is in high demand for her experience of creditor, creditor's committee and bankruptcy trustee representation. **William Zewadski** has a long history with the firm and a practice that encompasses commercial litigation as well as most aspects of bankruptcy law. "*An admired and experienced attorney,*" he is skilled in workouts, lender liability and banking litigation.

**Clients/Work Highlights:** Clients include state and national financial institutions; Chapter 7 and 11 trustees and examiners; creditors' committees; landlords and equipment lessors.

## Band 3

## Carlton Fields

See firm details p.661

**The Firm:** This firm has been a fixture on the Florida legal landscape for many years and is recommended for its "*experienced and talented lawyers.*" The bankruptcy and creditors' rights department is experienced in all forms of bankruptcy litigation, including defending truth-in-lending and fair debt collection practices. The group is also fluent in representing debtors-in-possession in Chapter 11 cases. Among its recent caseload, the firm has acted as counsel for the debtor-in-possession Anchor Glass, a corporation with about $500 million in debts.

**The Lawyers: Robert Soriano** (see p.652) is head of department and "*an effective strategist.*" According to clients, "*he knows when and when not to litigate,*" and is often found in Chapter 11 cases, normally representing secured creditors. He played a fundamental role in the Anchor Glass case. Experienced

**Robert Gilbert** (see p.637) "*is a technical lawyer, not one to let go of an issue lightly.*" He is well known for his creditors' rights work.

**Clients/Work Highlights:** The firm represents commercial lenders; creditors' committees; Chapter 11 and 7 trustees; equity holders and purchasers of assets of bankruptcy estates.

## Foley & Lardner LLP

See firm details p.2037

**The Firm:** With five offices across the state and 19 offices worldwide, this large, national firm has the resources behind it to handle the most sophisticated work in the bankruptcy market. Clients welcome the interdisciplinary approach adopted here and value the "*insightful advice provided on a range of bankruptcy topics.*" It is the firm's expertise in the representation of secured creditors and creditors' committees that is most highly prized by clients, although debtor work is also undertaken.

**The Lawyers: Mark Wolfson** (see p.656) is chair of the litigation department in Tampa and leader of the firm's business reorganizations practice group for the southeast region. The key bankruptcy contact at the firm, Wolfson wins approval for his "*intuitive brightness and creativity.*" He is the current chair of the Florida Bar's Business Law Section and advised a large insurance company on lenders' liability issues during the year.

**Clients/Work Highlights:** Bank of America and Apache Products are examples of the clients of this firm.

## Glenn Rasmussen Fogarty & Hooker

**The Firm:** This Tampa-based firm is home to 17 "*experienced and dedicated*" lawyers and fields a four-strong banking and bankruptcy practice group. Clients value the level of personal attention afforded to them due to the compact nature of the group. They also appreciate the "*unified approach of the group*" and point out the representation of creditors and committees as its core strength.

**The Lawyers: Robert Glenn** is "*very persuasive in his arguments,*" according to commentators. "*He has the confidence of the bench*" and enjoys an excellent statewide and national reputation. Glenn is fully conversant in loan enforcement litigation and is considered vastly experienced in the representation of lenders.

**Clients/Work Highlights:** Lenders; lessors; trustees; committees and debtors in Chapter 11 cases are representative of the types of clients serviced by this group.

## Gronek & Latham

**The Firm:** This Orlando-based firm is heavily involved in all strands of bankruptcy, but is most thoroughly recommended for its work on debtor matters. Following a marked increase in real estate-related bankruptcies during the past year, the firm demonstrated a flexibility larger firms would find hard to emulate by siphoning off expertise from other practice groups to meet the demand. Clients believe this "*personal attention and flexibility*" to the case in hand is attractive. The firm has developed its reputation in Ponzi scheme cases and continues to act for the Chapter 11 trustee in the Evergreen Security $200 million case.

**The Lawyers:** The *"absolutely top-flight"* **Scott Shuker** is a diligent practitioner often found on the largest Chapter 11s filed in Orlando.

**Clients/Work Highlights:** Midsized Orlando-based corporations form the staple diet of this group, an example being Evergreen Security.

## Holland & Knight LLP

See firm details p.1534

**The Firm:** According to clients, the strength of this firm lies in its *"balance of good lawyers across the whole state."* As such, the national and statewide coverage of this international firm is a significant drawing card for clients, who also place value in the attorneys' *"extensive connections in both legal and business circles and their formidable advocacy skills."* As is expected with a firm of this size, it fields experience in all areas of bankruptcy law, noted for both creditor and debtor representation in cross-border and international workouts.

**The Lawyers:** As the *"business savvy"* chair of the firm's creditors' rights group, **Leonard Gilbert** (see p.637) has an impeccable reputation throughout the state and is the first choice for many leading clients. He is one of the more senior attorneys at Holland & Knight and, as such, is often found providing strategic insolvency advice to attorneys throughout the firm, as well as counseling businesses on how to avoid bankruptcy. Gilbert has recently been involved in the firm's representation as Florida and Georgia counsel for the debtor in the Chapter 11 proceedings of Friedman's, a large national chain of jewelry stores.

**Clients/Work Highlights:** The firm has experience representing debtors; creditor and bondholder committees; financial institutions; secured creditors and claims traders.

## Meland Russin Hellinger & Budwick

**The Firm:** Small by design, this ten-strong firm is recommended by clients *"without qualification."* It is endorsed for its representation of corporate debtors in the real estate and telecom sector, and for its representation of secured creditors, lending institutions and trustees. Providing clients with a personal, tailor-made service while not losing sight of the big picture, this firm has had some real successes of late. For example, in a recent real estate-related case, the firm successfully enabled the creditors to be paid in full

and managed to keep the entity running. The firm is also defending O2HR in bankruptcy litigation brought by the trustee in bankruptcy.

**The Lawyers:** **Michael Budwick** *"has gone head-to-head and proved his mettle with some of the best in the business."* He is steadily increasing his presence throughout the state through his involvement in top-quality work. *"Brilliant"* **Peter Russin** concentrates his practice in the areas of business reorganization and creditors' rights. He is cofounder of the firm and is widely respected for *"the excellent job he does for his clients."*

**Clients/Work Highlights:** Corporate debtors; secured creditors; lending institutions and trustees in bankruptcy are typical clients of this group.

## Rice Pugatch Robinson & Schiller

**The Firm:** This eight-partner business restructuring boutique based in Miami and Fort Lauderdale is a *"smart and aggressive unit – great when it is on your team and really tough when it is up against you."* Clients also singled out the *"specialty service and advice"* and the efficiency of the group as some of the key attractions. Workouts, Chapter 11 and 7 bankruptcies, and bankruptcy litigation are well-documented areas of strength for this firm. The group successfully represented the former directors of Renaissance Cruise Lines in litigation brought by the liquidating trustee for Renaissance, and it has continued to provide bankruptcy-related advice to Regions Bank.

**The Lawyers:** **Arthur Halsey Rice** is a *"real character and great attorney,"* according to sources. He is both experienced and respected for his trial skills and bankruptcy code knowledge. **Lisa Schiller** is a *"brilliant deal-doer."* She focuses her practice on Chapter 11 work and has nurtured her expertise in various aspects of reorganization, as well as bankruptcy litigation.

**Clients/Work Highlights:** Creditors; debtors; trustees; assignees; receivers and institutional lenders comprise this firm's client base. Examples include the Commodore companies; Gateway Inn; Union Planters Bank; Regions Bank and Morande Enterprises.

## Stearns Weaver Miller Weissler Alhadeff & Sitterson, PA

**The Firm:** This full-service, Florida-based law firm houses more than 100 lawyers, seven of whom are dedicated to bankruptcy law. With offices in Miami, Fort Lauderdale and Tampa, the group impresses clients with its geographical coverage of the state and

the amount of varied expertise and resources on offer. The firm's representation of secured creditors in foreclosure proceedings is a much sought-after commodity, as is its experience of air transportation-related cases.

**The Lawyers:** *"Wonderful guy and talented attorney"* **Harold Moorefield** is chairman of the firm's bankruptcy department and has a broad practice encompassing creditor, debtor and trustee representation. Clients are impressed with his creditor representation, his litigious know-how and the tight ship he runs. *"Plainly amazing"* **Patricia Redmond** is *"a wonderful strategist and a top-notch negotiator,"* according to sources. She is in demand for her creditors' rights and insolvency counseling practice, as well as her experience representing secured creditors. Senior figure John Olson has gone to the bench.

**Clients/Work Highlights:** Debtors and creditors, particularly secured creditors in foreclosure proceedings, feature in the client roster, with clients in the airlines and manufacturing fields appearing heavily.

## Other Notable Practitioners

**John Emmanuel** of Fowler White Boggs Banker has cultivated a respected Chapter 11 practice that includes the representation of creditors' committees. He is acting for the liquidation trustee in the Tropical Sportswear Chapter 11 case, providing assistance in bringing avoidance actions, objecting to claims and making distributions to creditors. **Roy Kobert** is chairman of Broad and Cassel's bankruptcy and creditors' rights practice group and cochairs the special assets practice group. He is commended by clients for the *"water-tight job he does,"* and for his *"safe pair of hands."* Kobert represents secured creditors, commercial debtors and creditor committees throughout the country. **Jeffrey Warren** of Bush Ross Gardner Warren & Rudy, PA is *"a very effective lawyer with a national reputation."* A skilled trial lawyer, he is president of the firm and has a long track record of Chapter 11 reorganizations. **Thomas Messana** of Ruden McClosky SC is *"not flashy but seriously effective,"* according to sources. *"A brilliant consensus builder,"* he focuses his practice on bankruptcy, insolvency and financial restructuring, bankruptcy-related litigation and creditors' rights. **Karen Specie** of Scruggs & Carmichael PA in Gainesville is *"one of the most effective bankruptcy lawyers in the northern district,"* reported interviewees.

# CONSTRUCTION

## Band 1

### Becker & Poliakoff PA

**The Firm:** From its offices in Orlando and Miami, this "*sophisticated and skillful*" team has secured an enviable reputation for its national construction practice. Its representation of homeowner and condominium associations is a real forte and the trial skills of its attorneys have led some to conclude: "*They are a real force to be reckoned with in regard to the claims and defect area.*" Condominium defect litigation and insurance work have also featured highly of late due to the repercussions of Florida's hurricanes. The recent number of lateral hires ensures that the team has the capacity to deal with the transactional elements that sit alongside construction matters, thus equipping it with "*all-around capability and strength.*"

**The Lawyers:** **Steven Lesser**'s wide-ranging knowledge of the area coupled with his skills as a litigator makes him an "*excellent choice for complex matters,*" agreed clients. He has represented Broward County School Board in all its delay and defect claims involving schools in Florida. He is also a certified arbitrator dealing with construction issues for the AAA. **Lee Weintraub** "*gets to the point without beating around the bush.*" His recent caseload includes acting for Masvidal Partners, the largest developer in Miami, in the building of a performing arts center. Clients appreciated his "*ambitious and diligent nature*" and were impressed with his handling of all their matters in "*a very timely and efficient manner.*"

Clients/Work Highlights: The team has been retained by Masvidal Partners in dealing with the construction issues arising from the building of a metro rail system. A further highlight is its advice to the owners SETAI on matters concerning an ultra-luxury hotel.

### Carlton Fields

See firm details p.661

**The Firm:** A "*well-seasoned team deriving from good stock,*" these attorneys display "*a magnitude of experience and sophistication,*" say clients. They also bring a broad business perspective to construction law issues. This 28-strong team of specialists advises on matters in Florida and nationwide. Contentious work remains a focus for the team, with much work undertaken in the claims sphere, yet the team also offers a transactional practice viewed by many to be "*top of the pile.*" One client summed up the consensus of many: "*What keeps me returning is the focus on key issues and the favorable end results – all without wasting my time or money.*"

**The Lawyers:** Construction law veteran **Mike Nuechterlein** (see p.646) has been "*instrumental in creating the towering standard to which others abide.*" His wisdom and experience in the field makes him a highly sought-after attorney. While his practice has taken on a mediation slant of late, he has also acted as special counsel to Panama City Beach in advising and assisting the city in all their construction law matters. **Bruce King** (see p.641) excels in the area of surety law and clients spoke of his effective advice in attaining their goals. Accomplished **Charles Cacciabeve** (see p.630) is a solution-driven litigator – it is his "*savvy industry knowledge that gives him that edge.*" **Patricia Thompson** (see p.654) is "*always sensitive and responsive to our needs.*" She recently defended a third-party claim brought by the developers of a luxury condominium against a general contractor and its surety concerning alleged widespread construction defects. "*A real icon in the industry,*" **George Meyer** (see p.645) has carved out a strong profile on the transactional side of the construction practice. He "*nails things with his precise analysis,*" and displays "*wonderful negotiation skills, which makes him an excellent problem solver.*" **Luis Prats** (see p.647) has shown a real ability to communicate the strengths and weaknesses of a case to the client. Managing partner of the Tampa practice, his "*thorough approach to matters gets you where you need to go.*" He recently represented a condominium association in a complex construction defects case against the developer, and also advised the developer, Fairfield Resorts, in a dispute concerning a high-rise timeshare project in Destin.

Clients/Work Highlights: The team recently represented the Hunt/Clark/Construct Two joint venture in claims arising from the $520 million Orange County convention center phase V project. The matter involved claims for design defects; delays and storm damage were brought by multiparty trade contractors. It also acted for Pinellas County in the design and construction of a healthcare facility. Other clients include City of Panama City Beach, Lennar Homes and Caribbean Resorts Owners Association.

### Greenberg Traurig LLP

See firm details p.664

**The Firm:** The arrival of Leslie O'Neal-Coble in 2005 has given the group a boost: "*This team has raised its game.*" Geographic diversity is a key drawing card for clients, and attorneys turn their hands to many of the largest construction projects throughout the state and beyond. The fielding of a "*deep and erudite team that, more importantly, is available*" proved to be a positive lure for clients who also appreciated team members for their individual political and legislative connections. The team is currently handling a number of high-profile construction projects with dollar values ranging from $450 million to $4.3 billion.

**The Lawyers:** **Leslie O'Neal-Coble** (see p.646) is an excellent source of advice on mold and water intrusion issues that affect construction projects; indeed, in this niche area "*you would be hard pressed to find anyone better.*" She recently represented a development partnership in its dispute with a construction manager on a $100 million part-historic and part new construction building in Baltimore. Her "*calming resolve*" also ensures she is a popular choice as mediator and she demonstrates "*unmatched expertise in contract documentation.*" **Michael Hornreich** (see p.640) can be a "*nemesis across the table*" acknowledge peers, calling him "*a tough, smart and always well-prepared litigator.*" He has recently handled a number of claims relating to water intrusion.

Clients/Work Highlights: Brasfield & Gorrie Construction; 3D/International Program Managers; Capital Hotel Management; Kolter Construction; Marriott International; Hensel Phelps Construction; Florida Department of Transportation; Tri-Rail Transit Authority; Centex Group and Orlando Performing Arts Center.

### Holland & Knight LLP

See firm details p.1534

**The Firm:** The sizable firm has the depth of resources and talent to ensure it "*simply cruises through complex construction issues.*" The 12-strong team is spread across the Orlando and Tampa offices and advises on the spectrum of construction work, from general business advice to issues surrounding the power and plant industry. Sources also pointed to its handling of water penetration claims resulting from hurricane damage as an area of expertise. The diversity of experience and approachability of its attorneys was highlighted as an attractive attribute. The team has recently been working on a $42 million desalination plant claim, defending a reverse osmosis membrane manufacturer.

**The Lawyers:** **Christopher Weiss** (see p.655) is "*always pushing toward a resolution.*" His wealth of experience is a real advantage and clients, also highlighted his ability to "*understand the nature of the problem in almost any matter he chooses to tackle.*" He has represented a national apartment owner in several water intrusion cases involving 18 different

affecting a desalination facility in Tampa Bay, the largest such facility in northern Florida.

**Clients/Work Highlights:** On the firm's client list are Turner Construction, Northwestern Mutual and Trammell Crow. The firm also represents a host of contractors and power-generating companies.

## Moye, O'Brien, O'Rourke, Pickert & Martin, LLP

See firm details p.669

**The Firm:** Based in Maitland, this construction and commercial litigation group has developed a stronghold in the civil engineering sector. Its lawyers tend to be dual-qualified as engineers or have building expertise, leading to *"a real understanding of of our concerns,"* said clients. Contentious work forms a sizable portion of the caseload, such as contract disputes, delay, acceleration, defect and disruption claims. Attorneys have successfully negotiated the south and north terminal airport expansion project contracts for Miami International Airport and continue to represent the joint venture as issues and claims arise. Its broad geographical scope has seen matters conducted in the USA, the Caribbean basin, Central America and Canada. The 15-member team was singled out for the high levels of support it provides for clients: its attorneys are *"professional and always true to their words."*

**The Lawyers:** *"People-oriented"* **James Moye** (see p.645), is a name associated with many of the highest-profile civil engineering projects throughout the country. He recently completed a $600 million contract negotiation for Parsons/Oderbrack Construction in its work for Miami Airport. Sources appreciate his *"textbook knowledge"* of the subject and his strategic insight, which *"always achieves the desired result!"* A skilled trial lawyer, **Stephen Pickert**'s (see p.647) *"novel and creative approach to matters"* ensures his involvement in the most complex construction litigation. Defect cases are an area of specialty and he has been involved in a litigation arising out of bridge and road construction projects across the country. **Gregory Martin** (see p.644) is *"an aggressive litigator – he is always on the ball and keeps things moving."* He has acted in a number of large litigation defect and damage claims in the past year. A *"future star,"* **Sean Dillon** (see p.634) represents building contractors in the heavy civil and rail sector and has recently represented Balfour Beatty in the $450 million high-speed rail project spanning New Haven to Boston.

**Clients/Work Highlights:** AMEC Civil Archer Western Contractors; Balfour Beatty; Centex Homes; Hazen & Sawyer; PCL Civil Construction; PCL Construction Services; Peter Kiewit Sons; Traylor Bros; Universal City Development Partners; Universal Studios and Zom Companies.

## Peckar & Abramson

See firm details p.1549

**The Firm:** Renowned specialists in the field, this national construction law firm houses a number of *"true connoisseurs"* in its Florida offices. Its 2005 merger with Washington, DC law firm Bastianelli,

Brown & Kelley gives the team an enlarged national reach and depth, while its strong Miami presence continues to make it a prime choice for Latin American, Caribbean and European construction investors. *"One would find the dedication and loyalty evidenced by this team hard pressed to match,"* state clients who further regarded the *"innate capabilities and integrity"* of its members as reasons to keep coming back. Construction matters facing leading national construction contractors and construction managers are on the agenda here. Attorneys frequently advise on disputes arising out of high-profile projects such as the development of the north terminal of Miami Airport.

**The Lawyers:** **Stephen Reisman** (see p.648) combines his robust construction law practice with duties as managing partner of the firm's Florida offices. His *"excellent judgment and reasoning"* and effective negotiation, mediation and litigation skills have attracted a broad set of clients. **Melinda Gentile** (see p.637) is *"certainly making her mark in the field,"* pronounce sources. Among a broad skill set, her *"impressive trial skills"* stand out, as does her thorough preparation and attention to detail.

**Clients/Work Highlights:** The team represents many of the country's largest construction management firms including the nation's largest building contractor, in addition to general contractors.

## Band 2

## Akerman Senterfitt

See firm details p.657

**The Firm:** These attorneys are *"willing to go that extra mile – they provide a high quality and attentive service – all at incredible value,"* said clients. The department's geographic scope is broad as there are specialist construction attorneys in most of its Florida offices. While the team caters to both the litigation and transactional elements of the construction industry, the past year has seen an increased workload within construction defect litigation as a result of hurricane damage. On the transactional side, the team has been busy drafting construction contracts for a host of developers, contractors, and condominium and homeowner associations. Lender representation is also a key facet. *"Never ones to disappoint,"* this group's dedication to its lawyer-client relationships was also highly prized.

**The Lawyers:** Department chair **Kimberly Ashby** (see p.627) is valued for her *"experience and integrity."* Her recent work includes the construction contract drafting and oversight of Veranda Park, a $80 million state-of-the-art executive commercial condominium and mixed-use development.

**Clients/Work Highlights:** Recent highlights include obtaining a favorable settlement for a national financial institution in a complex contract, construction defect, delay and lien dispute against a general contractor handling renovations and improvements to seven branch offices in Miami-Dade and Broward. Other key clients include Shoma Development; GE Financial; Delta Air Lines; Wash-

parties with claims of over $15 million. Cochair of the group **Ben Subin** (see p.653) always *"rolls up his sleeves and dives into his cases."* A skilled technician, he understands the engineering aspects to each case. He recently advised on a construction law issue

ington Mutual; Doubletree Hotel (Coconut Grove); St. Paul Fire and Marine Insurance; USF&G; The Bomasada Group; Helix Electric; Starwood Urban Retail; Taubco, Fisher Island; Marriott International; T&G Constructors and Town Center Properties.

## Boose Casey Ciklin Lubitz Martens McBane & O'Connell

**The Firm:** Located in the West Palm Beach area, this law firm "*puts many in the shade*" when it comes to construction law, assert sources. General contractor and subcontractor clients benefit from the contract drafting and litigation skills of this group. The team's recent caseload has featured a high number of delay and defect claims, particularly in relation to high-rise buildings. This has been mainly for large commercial contractors, who rated the team for its "*awareness of our strengths and weaknesses throughout.*" Construction-related insurance matters arising from hurricane damage have also been high on the agenda.

**The Lawyers:** A "*tenacious and intelligent adversary,*" **Bruce Alexander**'s litigation practice is underpinned by a broad knowledge and appreciation of construction law. Many clients felt "*you can trust what he says is right – he is a true student of the law*" and emphasized the "*star-like*" quality he exudes. He has recently advised on construction contracts, particularly in relation to condominiums. **Linda Dickhaus Agnant** has forged a statewide reputation representing large commercial contractors and brings a business perspective to legal matters. She possesses expertise in the environmental factors affecting construction projects.

**Clients/Work Highlights:** The team advises an assorted selection of private developers and public sector bodies.

## Daniels, Kashtan, Downs, Robertson & Magathan

**The Firm:** The core of this group's practice involves representing design professionals, particularly architects and engineers in design, defect and insurance-related litigation. The group of 23 lawyers are "*engaging, intelligent and diligent*" and as such, this firm is often a popular place for referrals from peers. A smaller element to the practice is its work for contractors and owners and also the preparation of complex construction documents.

**The Lawyers:** **Joe Downs** has a superb understanding of the problems facing the design profession as illustrated by the "*innovative thought process*" he applies to all his cases. He advised a major architectural firm on a $500 million project involving the high-rise, beach-front Diplomat Hotel in Halandale. **Michael Kashtan** is a "*tough, highly ethical and undeniably fair attorney.*" A commercial litigator, he works principally on matters involving construction and insurance coverage litigation and has recently represented a design team in claims arising from a performing arts center project in downtown Miami.

**Clients/Work Highlights:** The team represents design professionals, architects and engineers.

## Ferencik, Libanoff, Brandt, Bustamante & Williams

**The Firm:** This construction law boutique based in Fort Lauderdale is staffed with "*accommodating and professional lawyers,*" all of whom are "*bright, experienced and available,*" say clients. The hallmark of the practice is its expertise in construction litigation including liability issues. It caters to a variety of construction industry clientele, including municipalities such as Munroe County in all their construction law requirements.

**The Lawyers:** **Peter Brandt** received accolades for his work in the surety area and was also praised for the depth of his knowledge. One client described him as "*awesome – you can bounce bullets off him.*" The preparation and review of contracts, litigation and arbitration are components of his practice. According to sources, **Robert Ferencik** is "*very good on his feet and dominates the courtroom.*" His practice over the past year has seen a greater focus on public entities, such that he was retained by the Florida Department of Transportation. **Ira Libanoff** has "*a memory like you have never seen.*" A "*capable and effective*" practitioner, he is well versed in all aspects of construction law.

**Clients/Work Highlights:** Aneco; ANF Group; Astaldi Construction; Ballast-Nedam Construction; Casino Drywall; Charter Builders; Concreform; Current Builders of Florida; Florida Department of Transportation; GLF Construction; Jennings Construction; Lanzo Construction and Pavarini Construction.

## Leiby Stearns and Roberts, P.A.

**The Firm:** "*Always a pleasure to deal with,*" this boutique has carved out a strong profile in the commercial construction domain. Construction litigation, contract drafting and negotiations, as well as dispute resolution via mediation and arbitration, are core areas in which this team shines. Contractors, sureties, subcontractors, construction owners, material suppliers and design professionals all benefit from this firm's experience.

**The Lawyers:** "**Larry Leiby** *has set the standard for others to follow.*" A dean of the construction Bar, he recently acted in the Beyer v Turtle Beach case, a dispute concerning the defect claims related to a luxury home. He displays the "*highest levels of ethics and professionalism*" and is a respected mediator and arbitrator in the field.

**Clients/Work Highlights:** Opus; Colter Property Group; GT Macdonald Enterprises; DiPompeo Construction; Arellano Construction and Pomeroy Electric.

## Siegfried, Rivera, Lerner, De La Torre & Sobel, PA

**The Firm:** A force in the contentious construction sphere, this smaller boutique firm enjoys a solid market reputation throughout the state as an "*excellent place to solve your litigation disputes.*" Litigation is by no means the only service provided by the group, with contract drafting and negotiations also a prominent feature of the workload.

**The Lawyers:** "*Always a challenge to be up against,*" **Steven Siegfried** stands out as one of the principal litigators in the state. His "*finely tuned*" way of dealing with delay and defect claims sets him apart from the rest, said interviewees.

**Clients/Work Highlights:** The team caters to the requirements of a broad client base including lenders, developers, suppliers and contractors.

## Vezina Lawrence & Piscitelli

**The Firm:** This vibrant group advises on the range of construction law issues; however, many sources feel that its work in the heavy civil industry is where it exhibits "*real power.*" Such experience is bolstered by the impressive relationships the firm has formulated and maintained with leading construction agencies and companies. "*Side-stepping the periphery and jumping straight to the heart of the issues,*" this team "*attains the requisite goals at incredible value.*" With operations in Fort Lauderdale and Tallahassee, it has recently been involved in a number of high-profile roadways, bridges and major infrastructure projects. Advisory work also forms a sizable portion of the practice and clients were delighted with the talented younger attorneys climbing the ladder.

**The Lawyers:** **Rob Vezina** adopts a "*smooth and nonconfrontational style,*" which clients believe helps him to effectively present his cases to a jury. His "*adroit manner and quick-thinking abilities*" are often put to the test in litigious issues, such as a recent case involving a construction delay matter against the Federal Court of Engineers. He also continues to advise contractors on large public procurements for infrastructure projects. **Michael Piscitelli** is "*incredibly bright and thoughtful,*" and excels in construction litigation with an emphasis on surety and fidelity bond law.

## Band 3

## Baker & Hostetler LLP

**The Firm:** This "*vastly experienced group*" is focused on dispute resolution for its client base of general contractors, subcontractors and owners. The group works closely with other offices and departments of this full-service firm, especially in the hospitality, timeshare and condo-hotel sectors. The correction of damage caused by hurricanes has formed a sizable element of the practice over the past year.

**The Lawyers:** Described as an "*expert of the highest order,*" **Denis Durkin**'s practice is predominantly litigious in nature, and he has a niche specialty advising clients on compliance matters in accordance with federal regulatory agencies. Durkin recently concluded a multimillion-dollar settlement against the Department of Veteran Affairs.

**Clients/Work Highlights:** The team has also been involved in handling the construction issues arising from the construction of a power plant adjacent to the veteran's administrative hospital in Tampa, and a host of litigation matters across the country. It can also count Disney among its clients.

## Bilzin Sumberg Baena Price & Axelrod LLP

See firm details p.660

**The Firm:** A close alignment with its own outstanding real estate practice underpins this firm's respected construction practice. Construction litigation forms the bedrock, with commentators highlighting the *"wonderful selection of trial lawyers"* available to deal with delay and defect claims as they arise. The representation of developers on the drafting, reviewing and negotiating of contracts related to development projects are also important facets of this practice.

**The Lawyers:** Michael Kreitzer and Scott Kravetz are key members of the construction team.

**Clients/Work Highlights:** The team recently represented Sea Oak Investments in the construction-related litigation arising from the large-scale residential project in Vero Beach. The ocean-front project included over 600 units of condominiums, single-family homes and townhouses.

## Broad and Cassel

**The Firm:** This full-service Florida firm is home to a small but *"highly skilled"* team of experts, who are respected for *"attaining the business goals of clients."* It represents a desirable mix of construction clients such as managers, engineers, architects and material suppliers. In supporting the strength of the firm's real estate team, the representation of owner-developer clients remains a focus for this group.

**The Lawyers:** Practice chair **Michael Wilson** exudes a *"thoughtful, analytical and persuasive aura,"* said sources. A skilled litigator, he represents developer clients in construction delay impact and defects claims and sureties. His *"creativity in advocacy"* was a particularly identified trait of his practice: *"He doesn't litigate for the sake of it – he wants to get a result."*

## Foley & Lardner LLP

See firm details p.2037

**The Firm:** A national heavyweight, the team's contractor and owner representation is widely commended. Dispute resolution, procurement and construction contract negotiation and drafting form the foundations of the practice. Sources highlighted the professional approach of these attorneys and the availability of resources of the firm's national network are drawing cards for clients.

**The Lawyers:** **Edmund Baxa** (see p.628) is a leading light of this construction team. He combines his workload with a role as managing partner of the Orlando and West Palm Beach offices. A *"prince of a guy,"* his professionalism, high-quality advice and impressive work ethic stand out.

**Clients/Work Highlights:** The team acts predominantly for contractor and owner clients in a number of industries including commercial, industrial and healthcare sectors.

## Forizs and Dogali PL

**The Firm:** This midsized firm based in Tampa has the capacity to handle a multitude of projects for parties including those in the hospital, retail, leisure, highways and office-building sectors. An *"effective legal counsel"* in avoidance, defect and delay claims, the group's broad practice also includes advice on performance and payment bond disputes.

**The Lawyers:** Managing partner of the firm, **Andy Dogali** is an all-around construction specialist. Clients appreciated his *"conscientious and sincere approach and his reliable judgment calls."*

**Clients/Work Highlights:** The team works closely with architectural and engineering firms, contractors, finance companies and developers across the state.

## Gray Robinson PA

**The Firm:** Amid this broad-ranging construction practice lies a specialty in dispute resolution with six of the 11 members as dedicated trial lawyers. *"They always match the right skill set to the case,"* say impressed clients. The defense of design professionals and architects features highly, especially in relation to hurricane damage. The responsiveness and high-quality advice is also a key ingredient in the mix.

**The Lawyers:** According to sources, construction litigator **Jeffrey Keiner** exhibits *"a hard-ball approach to litigation,"* which in turn leads to results *"that never disappoint."* He is well versed in issues faced by architects and engineers and was recently involved in the construction of a sea wall along the Atlantic Ocean, requiring consideration of both construction and environmental issues.

## Kirwin Norris PA

**The Firm:** This construction boutique represents all parties in the construction process but wields a strong grip on a general contractor client base within the Florida market. This specialist ten-member team was hailed for having *"players who are courteous and play within the rules,"* who regularly negotiate, litigate, mediate or arbitrate to resolution in commercial and construction-related disputes. Clients were quick to praise this team's understanding of their issues, owing to many of its members' previous experience in the construction industry.

**The Lawyers:** **Brian Kirwin** *"always looks for a solution rather than a fight,"* agree market sources. Recent accomplishments include successfully representing long-standing client Seminole County Board of County Commissioners in a water intrusion and microbial growth dispute. Clients were impressed with his all-around capabilities: *"Whether counseling or litigating, he can do it all!"* **Bruce Norris** has a *"charming personality"* that makes him a user-friendly adviser, well versed in construction disputes. *"You'd better be prepared when facing him in battle,"* reported clients.

**Clients/Work Highlights:** South of Florida Water Management District; Skanska USA; Wharton-Smith; Clancy RJ Griffin and Edwards Construction Services.

## Welbaum, Guernsey, Hingston, Greenleaf & Gregory LLP

**The Firm:** This boutique firm is a force in the surety representation field, and has attracted a loyal base of general contractor and subcontractor clients. Its attorneys advise on the drafting of construction documents and take a solution-focused approach to the management of disputes.

**The Lawyers:** Sources spoke of **Earl Welbaum**'s long track record in the field and described him as a dean of the construction Bar. Famed for work in the surety law area, his *"sheer experience and wealth of knowledge in the area"* are widely recognized.

**Clients/Work Highlights:** Andrade Gutierrez Construction; Atlantic Interiors; Bovis Lend Lease; CIGNA; Coastal Construction; Copeland Steel Erectors; JJW Construction; Rovel Construction; Western Surety and Wesley Construction.

## Other Notable Practitioners

**Fred Lyon** from The Lyon Firm PA has a comprehensive understanding of the energy construction market. According to clients, he is adept at handling *"complicated and sophisticated disputes – often bringing the parties together effectively,"* and keeps clients fully up-to-date with developments in their cases. He recently represented a large utility contractor in its dispute involving a power plant in New York, and counts AEP, Progress Energy and Tampa Electric among his clientele. Construction litigator **John Dannecker** (see p.633) of Shutts & Bowen LLP is able to perfectly *"balance force and diplomacy in working toward a resolution."* A litigator, his expertise in construction defect and delay litigation, including mold and mildew-related disputes is widely commended. Residing at boutique firm Carey, O'Malley, Whitaker & Manson PA, **Michael Carey** has developed a thriving construction litigation practice. He is a *"dogged litigator, who does an excellent job for his clients."* **Malcolm Cunningham** belongs to three-member boutique construction firm The Cunningham Law Firm. The lion's share of his work includes representing public and private owners in their claims arising from construction projects, predominantly against contractors and surety companies. Sarasota-based attorney **Thomas Icard** from Icard, Merrill, Cullis, Timm, Furen & Ginsburg PA is an *"experienced and highly respected individual throughout the construction community – and beyond,"* said sources. He has recently been acting for a developer in a significant delay claim arising out of a substantial condominium development. *"Terrific"* **Joe Lane** from Lowndes Drosdick Doster Kantor & Reed PA is a *"steadfast litigator – he certainly knows his way around the major construction litigation issues."* Surety and bond work form facets to his well respected practice. Sole practitioner **Steve Rakusin**'s expertise and understanding of Florida lien law is illustrated by his first-class caseload and his prominence as a published author on the subject. It is within the area of surety law that **David Gurley** from Sarasota-based Gurley Dramis received most praise. Described as a top-drawer attorney, he has the ability to *"synthesize issues and pull parties together."*

Mateer & Harbert PA's chief construction attorney is **Lawrence Phalin**. A highly regarded construction litigator, he *"has a wonderful temperament in addition to a wealth of knowledge,"* which he displays most

often in the subcontractor market. **Jorge Diaz-Silveira** (see p.634) from Hogan & Hartson LLP concentrates on the transactional side of construction law. In the past year, he acted for AES in

the development of its LNG project in the Bahamas. Representative clients include Florida Power and Light and the Scripps Research Institute. *"He brings a hard-working and creative ethos to each matter."*

# CORPORATE/M&A

| Corporate/M&A |
|---|
| Leading Firms |
| [1] AKERMAN SENTERFITT *Miami* |
| GREENBERG TRAURIG LLP *Miami* |
| HOLLAND & KNIGHT LLP *Jacksonville* |
| [2] CARLTON FIELDS *Tampa* |
| FOLEY & LARDNER LLP *Jacksonville* |
| SQUIRE, SANDERS & DEMPSEY L.L.P. *Miami* |
| TRENAM, KEMKER, SCHARF, BARKIN, FRYE *Tampa* |
| [3] GLENN RASMUSSEN FOGARTY & HOOKER *Tampa* |
| HILL, WARD & HENDERSON, PA *Tampa* |
| KIRSCHNER & LEGLER *Jacksonville* |
| SHUMAKER LOOP & KENDRICK LLP *Tampa* |
| SHUTTS & BOWEN LLP *Miami* |
| STEARNS WEAVER MILLER WEISSLER *Miami* |

## Band 1

### Akerman Senterfitt
See firm details p.657

**The Firm:** This high-octane Orlando-headquartered player has cemented its position as *"way up there among the top three"* in the Florida market. In fact, this robust firm has seen its profile bolstered by the opening of two new offices in New York and Washington, DC, lateral hires from rivals and an enviable deal flow. With more than 100 *"formidable, impressive and highly responsive"* attorneys, this is one of the largest corporate law practices in Florida. It represents domestic and foreign public companies, including over 30% of the largest public companies headquartered in Florida, and leading private equity funds in corporate, securities, M&A and other transactional matters.

**The Lawyers:** **Jonathan Awner** (see p.627) is *"a very seasoned corporate star, who knows how to get things done quickly and remains at the top of the game."* Among his recent highlights, he represented Republic Services in its $276 million exchange note offering. Miami-based Awner is a popular choice for big-league M&A. **Stephen Roddenberry** (see p.649) wins plaudits as the driving force that took Akerman to its current positioning, with clients stating: *"He runs a five-star team."* Roddenberry recently brokered the $1.5 billion sale of long-running client Boca Resorts to The Blackstone Group. A prominent and trusted attorney, **Teddy Klinghoffer** (see p.642) steers the private equity department. He recently sealed the $408 million sale of CarePlus Health Plans. Klinghoffer has also advised on an environmentally sensitive real estate development project in Southwest Florida. Miami-based **Bradley Houser**

(see p.640) is one of the firm's resident IPO gurus, said clients. He acted for online retailer BabyUniverse in its $21.9 million offering. The *"first lady of securities law"* **Kara MacCullough** (see p.643) and *"exceptional deal-maker"* **Carl Roston** (see p.649) are also widely commended. MacCullough draws on her experience as a former Wall Street investment banker to better help clients in negotiations with the investment community. She has under her belt an enviable number of multimillion-dollar issuances for luminaries such as SBA Communications and Technical Olympic USA. MacCullough was also retained by Aphton in its $52 million public offering and its $81 million stock-for-stock acquisition of Igeneon. Carl Roston acted for NASDAQ-listed Answerthink in its acquisition of Active Interest. Among other recent successes, he represented Sweet Paper Sales in its $130 million sale to United Stationers.

**Clients/Work Highlights:** Akerman Senterfitt lawyers acted for Entertainment Resource in its $74 million sale to Glencoe Capital, and counseled Palm Beach County Bank in its $100 million merger with Commerce Bancorp. The firm also acts for Auto-Nation, Jacuzzi Brands and GEO Group (formerly Wackenhut Corrections), among others.

### Greenberg Traurig LLP
See firm details p.664

**The Firm:** *"Year in, year out, Greenberg Traurig remains ahead of the pack as the undisputed market leader,"* summarized sources. Many highlighted the firm's work on the IVAX deal, the $7.6 billion sale of the publicly traded drug maker, as an example of its efficient handling of headline deals. With offices across Florida (including a stronghold in Miami), this full-service national heavyweight scores highly in M&A, bankruptcy, private equity and venture capital, for the benefit of clients across the country and from overseas.

**The Lawyers:** From a team of *"strong and preeminent operators,"* **Gary Epstein** (see p.635) stands out as *"numero-uno deal maker and one of the market's most respected attorneys."* Head of the corporate and securities department firmwide, he caused a stir this year with his lead role acting for IVAX. Commentators lavished praise on **Daniel Aronson** (see p.626) for his *"commanding presence"* in deals related to national venture capital and startup operations. Aronson brokered the $2.35 billion sale of San Francisco-based education loan provider Chela Education Financing. He co-heads the firm's private equity and venture capital practice. **Paul Berkowitz** (see p.628) impresses as *"a low-key but decidedly smart and efficient corporate practitioner."* He completed a $900 million acquisition of real estate assets for Tech-

nical Olympic USA. **Robert Grossman** (see p.638) is an *"unpretentious attorney and remarkably professional – he adopts a business approach to his legal counsel."* He was Epstein's right hand in the blockbuster IVAX deal.

**Clients/Work Highlights:** Among other mandates, attorneys here acted for Florida East Coast Industries in its $270 million acquisition of real estate developer Codina.

### Holland & Knight LLP
See firm details p.1534

**The Firm:** Clearly a leading force across Florida, this firm's hub for transactions is Tampa, marking the difference between this national player and more Miami-centered rivals. Clients prize the *"one-firm national platform and quality at both partner and associate levels."* The 30-lawyer team was busy this year with headline deals, such as its continued representation of Kos Pharmaceuticals in a string of acquisitions, product licensing and corporate governance matters.

**The Lawyers:** *"Clients adore him and that is the ultimate telltale on the quality of a lawyer!"* asserted sources about **Robert Grammig** (see p.638). Among other highlights, he counseled Kforce on its purchase of VistaRMS, and assisted IT business services provider CGI in a number of acquisitions of hi-tech businesses. **Steven Sonberg** (see p.652) heads the firm's business section and continues to impress with his first-class securities practice. He acts for Kos Pharmaceuticals. **Rodney Bell** (see p.628) *"is now a star among stars,"* said interviewees, alluding to his rising profile. He joins Sonberg in the work for Kos and recently represented ClientSoft in its $15 million sale to NEON Systems. Bell also advises clients on disclosure, compliance and governance matters. **Chester Bacheller** (see p.627) is a *"tough, sophisticated and effective negotiator."* His current workload includes ongoing representation of semiconductor maker Jabil Circuit in multiple transactions inside and outside the country. **Scott Macleod** (see p.643) brings *"a brilliant sense of the business issues"* to his work, advising hedge fund managers and investment advisers. Macleod's recent representations include acting for Trusco Capital Management, the investment advisory arm of SunTrust, and giving counsel to BPI Global Asset Management in the reorganization of a joint venture. *"Legendary figure"* **Kinder Cannon** (see p.630) serves as general counsel and wins admiration for his work as mentor to lawyers across the firm.

## Band 2

### Carlton Fields

See firm details p.661

**The Firm:** While the firm's corporate prowess is sometimes overshadowed by its reputation on the litigation front, it forges ahead as *"a superb force across the board and a challenger to bigger corporate rivals."* A new office in Atlanta opened its doors this year, in a bid to further expand the firm's national platform. One client summarized the market consensus: *"The Carlton Fields difference rests in the fact that everyone in the team is particular about providing the exact answers you need, or putting you directly to the right lawyer, without over-expanding in scope or any kind of fuzz."* Advice on compliance and corporate governance issues, and on securities and M&A is on the agenda.

**The Lawyers:** Sources singled out the Tampa head office as *"the greatest jewel of the firm's crown"* as it houses **Nathaniel Doliner** (see p.634), chair of the corporate, securities, taxation and asset-based financing practice group. He is *"a sharp-minded, star deal maker who knows everything there is to know*

*about the work,"* and is currently taking on a more M&A-flavored caseload. Among recent highlights, Doliner acted for the buyer in the acquisition of a manufacturer of insulation products, and in a separate case, brokered the sale of stock of a lumber and building materials entity. **Richard Denmon** (see p.634) is winning a profile as a talented securities lawyer. He advised Coast Bank on its public offering of stock, acted for Allen Systems in a string of M&A operations, and represented Eagle Supply in a tender offer/merger transaction.

### Foley & Lardner LLP

See firm details p.2037

**The Firm:** This midsized national player is focusing on its established core operating centers, leading sources to describe it as *"strongly rooted to the local business community."* The practice is not limited to work generated in the Jacksonville market, but is *"undoubtedly on the ball as one of the leading forces"* for transactions across the USA and beyond. Its *"practical and highly efficient lawyers"* are well versed in M&A and securities transactions across a range of industries.

**The Lawyers:** **Gardner Davis** (see p.633) scores highly among commentators for a *"robust and respectable"* practice that in 2005 was punctuated by landmark real estate M&A transactions. He is also heavily engaged in transactions arising out of the food industry. Davis and *"extraordinarily talented"* partner **Linda Kelso** (see p.641) acted for NYSE-listed Regency Centers, in its $2.7 billion sale to First Washington Realty. Kelso was recently appointed head of the firm's national securities practice.

### Squire, Sanders & Dempsey L.L.P.

See firm details p.1650

**The Firm:** In one of the most talked about mergers of 2005, Steel Hector & Davis LLP joined forces with Cleveland-based Squire, Sanders & Dempsey LLP. While the market waits for the dust to settle on how this affects the firm's positioning, branding and staff turnover, there is a general consensus that the merger provides a strong platform on which to grow. Both firms come with *"strong muscle, reputation, complementary areas of influence and years of experience in both the domestic and international arenas. "*

**The Lawyers:** The most visible corporate lawyer of the group comes from the Steel Hector side of the marriage: **Thomas McGuigan** (see p.644). He is a *"highly reputed operator with tons of knowledge under his belt"* and a broad caseload with a distinct capital markets flavor. McGuigan recently gave counsel to the issuer of $1.5 billion mandatory convertible financing and, in a separate deal, acted for the issuer of a $500 million debenture financing. His SEC-related counsel is also highly sought after.

### Trenam, Kemker, Scharf, Barkin, Frye, O'Neill & Mullis PA

**The Firm:** This traditional full-service firm, fielding more than 60 highly respected corporate attorneys, has built up a strong profile across Florida and beyond. Operating out of two offices in central

Florida, the team provides general corporate counsel *"of the finest caliber,"* particularly in venture capital matters.

**The Lawyers:** **Gary Teblum** and **Richard Leisner** are among the key figures for transactional advice. Teblum cochairs the corporate and business transactions practice groups, and wins plaudits for a busy caseload that includes a range of transactional and tax advice. Leisner *"leads the way"* in securities work.

## Band 3

### Glenn Rasmussen Fogarty & Hooker

**The Firm:** Although this firm may be smaller than some of its direct competitors, it has the transactional prowess to *"take on a much bigger firm's work,"* agreed sources. This Tampa stalwart continues to attract admiration for its breadth of expertise and its sensible approach to deal negotiations.

**The Lawyers:** *"One of the smartest attorneys around,"* **Robert Rasmussen** runs a terrific group that is a magnet for private financing transactions.

### Hill, Ward & Henderson, PA

**The Firm:** This smaller firm is the preferred address for venture capitalists, who seek *"an agile, can-do team that does not put on the intimidating show of bigger rivals, but can turn around a successful deal in the blink of an eye."* The group now numbers nine lawyers, following the arrival of former Carlton Fields lawyer Mark Danzi.

**The Lawyers:** *"My overall opinion of lawyers is not very favorable, but in terms of honesty and integrity there is no better lawyer on this planet. I would call him for advice on personal matters even if he wasn't a lawyer; he is simply superb,"* was the verdict offered by one source on **David Felman**, echoing market consensus. His practice spans securities offerings, venture capital investments, corporate governance matters and M&A.

**Clients/Work Highlights:** Highlights of the year included assisting Solicore in a $15 million investment and, separately, Ballast Point Ventures in a series of deals that totaled over $32 million. Banyan Mezzanine Fund retained David Felman's team for a number of deals, while Lovett Miller; Inflexion Partners; Asbury Automotive and Paradyne are other key clients.

### Kirschner & Legler

**The Firm:** This two-lawyer boutique impresses clients as a credible alternative to building an in-house legal department and mandating other firms when required. Core to the practice is its experience in real estate, insurance and retail-related transactional work. The team is currently acting in the $600 million debt restructuring of a food distribution client, and represents a major Dutch pension fund in connection with its real estate investments in the USA.

**The Lawyers:** *"Top-flight attorneys"* **Kenneth Kirschner** and **Mitchell Legler** are the key contacts here. Kirschner is currently busy acting for a provider of malpractice liability coverage in an insurance-related case, while a portion of Legler's time is dedicated to providing counsel for client Stein Mart.

## Shumaker Loop & Kendrick LLP

The Firm: This midmarket Ohio-based player is "*growing steadily and becoming more of a competitor in Florida.*" Its full-service Tampa base offers the panoply of corporate services, with an emphasis on public company transactions.

The Lawyers: A "*brilliant and trusted attorney,*" **Gregory Yadley** is the driving force behind the growing profile of the team. His principal areas of practice are securities and M&A. Yadley recently handled a going private reverse stock split transaction for a NASDAQ-listed client that involved SEC litigation, Sarbanes-Oxley issues, and related legal and accounting costs.

Clients/Work Highlights: Among other highlights this year, the team brokered a $40 million acquisition of two national financial services businesses, which included the structuring of an investment partnership, the mergers of different business entities, and the negotiation of related financing, mezzanine debt and business credit facilities. In a separate development, another NASDAQ client retained the firm as counsel in a $60 million-plus refinancing and capital restructuring.

## Shutts & Bowen LLP

See firm details p.673

The Firm: "*This firm did international work before it was 'cool' to go international,*" said sources referring to Shutts & Bowen's long-standing capabilities in cross-border transactions. The group houses 170 lawyers in five offices in Florida and two in Europe, and advises clients on the gamut of corporate services, with an emphasis on financial work.

The Lawyers: **Luis de Armas** (see p.633) "*has the wonderful capability of not allowing details to slip away from him.*" He is experienced in cross-border capital markets and M&A work, both outbound and inbound.

## Stearns Weaver Miller Weissler Alhadeff & Sitterson, PA

The Firm: With more than 100 lawyers in offices in three key Florida cities, this firm is well placed to advise clients on transactions arising out of the state. The firm combines a strong reputation for litigation and finance work with its corporate prowess, and is described as a "*solid port of call*" for securities and M&A proceedings.

The Lawyers: Alison Miller heads the corporate department and is the main contact for the practice.

Clients/Work Highlights: The team has recently represented a number of commercial banks in

aircraft acquisition-financing transactions worth over $200 million.

## Other Notable Practitioners

**Luis Perez** (see p.647) has joined Hogan & Hartson LLP from Akerman Senterfitt. Among his recent leading mandates, he advised a US developer in the acquisition and development of a large waterfront commercial and residential real restate project in the Caribbean. Following commendation for his successful handling of the Lennar $1 billion credit facility, **Alan Axelrod** (see p.627) of Bilzin Sumberg Baena Price & Axelrod LLP joins the corporate table. He chairs the corporate and securities group at the firm, and has a mixed practice that includes M&A, dispositions and corporate restructurings. While the White & Case LLP Florida team wins extensive applause for its Latin American expertise (see Latin American Investment table), **Jorge Freeland** (see p.636) has a leading market share in the domestic private equity and M&A world. He heads the domestic side of the practice and recently acted for National Product Services in its $55 million leveraged recapitalization and its acquisition of substantially all the assets of Covington Sales & Service. Freeland also acted for Securus Technologies in its $120 million acquisition of Evercom Holdings.

# CORPORATE/M&A

# LATIN AMERICAN INVESTMENT

| Corporate/M&A: Latin American Investment |
|---|
| **Leading Firms** |
| [1] HOGAN & HARTSON LLP *Miami* |
| WHITE & CASE LLP *Miami* |
| [2] GREENBERG TRAURIG LLP *Miami* |
| HOLLAND & KNIGHT LLP *Miami* |
| HUNTON & WILLIAMS LLP *Miami* |

| Leading Individuals |
|---|
| [1] ALVAREZ Victor *White & Case LLP* |
| ALVAREZ-FARRÉ Emilio *White & Case LLP* |
| AVILA Alcides *Holland & Knight LLP* |
| LOUMIET Carlos *Hunton & Williams LLP* |
| ZALDIVAR Miguel *Hogan & Hartson LLP* |
| [2] ALONSO Fernando *Hunton & Williams LLP* |
| ALVAREZ Pedro *White & Case LLP* |
| DE ARMAS Luis *Shutts & Bowen LLP* |
| MENCIO JR George *Holland & Knight LLP* |
| MENENDEZ CAMBO Patricia *Greenberg Traurig LLP* |
| VALDIVIA III José *Hogan & Hartson LLP* |

## Band 1

## Hogan & Hartson LLP

See firm details p.568

The Firm: "*If you want a team to handle your day-to-day operation with the real feeling of the Latin American region, you have to call Hogan & Hartson in Florida,*" said one source echoing the conclusions of many on this firm's current dynamics in the region. A string of big-ticket deals including Wal-Mart's expansion into Central America and a nine-figure dollar development project for Pemex have helped bolster the already strong positioning of this firm. Add into this mix a new office in Caracas and lateral hires from Florida rivals and the firm's prominence is assured. On offer here is expert advice in cross-border acquisitions and lending, corporate compliance, private placements and public finance. This "*unrivaled, savvy and sharp-witted*" team of bilingual and bicultural lawyers is also well equipped to advise on litigious matters such as antitrust, as well as trading regulations and alternative dispute resolutions.

The Lawyers: "*At the top of everyone's wish list*" sits **Miguel Zaldivar** (see p.656), who co-chairs the firm's Latin America practice. He is famed for "*knowing all the sensitivities, the ins and outs of doing business in the region and getting all the corners covered.*" Clients extolled the virtues of both Zaldivar and partner **José Valdivia** (see p.654) as a "*highly impressive team to have on your side for their unique skill set of practical knowledge and cultural closeness to the region.*" Besides the mandates for Pemex and Wal-Mart, both partners have been retained by Pequiven in the negotiations of a $3.5 billion olefins industrial complex in the east of Venezuela.

Clients/Work Highlights: Other highlights include

acting for Central America beverage producer CabCorp in a $50 million high-yield bond issuance, and in joint venture negotiations for the production of Brava beer in Guatemala. In a separate development, independent power producer AES engaged the team in the development of a $200 million coal generation facility in El Salvador.

## White & Case LLP

See firm details p.1566

The Firm: "*Not many giant US firms have the strong Latin American reach of White & Case, not only in ground presence but also in understanding the local culture of the countries where they have been operating longer than everyone else,*" asserted interviewees about this legal powerhouse south of the River Bravo. Key mandates of recent times include advising the Instituto Costarricense de Electricidad in a multimillion-dollar lending transaction, and representing a consortium in connection with a $600 million airport concession in Quito. Lawyers here also completed the landmark $1 billion restructuring of Corporación Durango.

The Lawyers: According to sources, **Victor Alvarez** (see p.626) is "*the first one that comes to mind for Latin American work.*" His practice covers the representation of financial institutions in corporate and structured finance transactions, including equity and debt securities. **Emilio Alvarez-Farré** (see p.626) "*makes sure all the 'i's are dotted and the 't's crossed.*" He chairs the international side of the corporate team and was key counsel in the Durango restructuring. Another of his highlights was representing Empresa Eléctrica de Guatemala and Comercializadora Eléctrica de Guatemala in a $200 million structured finance transaction. Alvarez-Farré also continues to act in financial restructurings of several entities in the aftermath of the Argentine crisis. "*Securities guru*" **Pedro Alvarez** (see p.626) comes highly recommended, completing "*the trio of White & Case stars for all things Latin America.*" His highlights of the year include advising hotelier Sol Meliá on the US aspects of its expanding securitization program, and counseling IFC in the proposed redevelopment of the former Howard Air Force Base in the Panama Canal.

**Clients/Work Highlights:** Royal Ahold; Cisco Systems; Copa Airlines; ING; the Republic of Costa Rica; Deutsche Bank; JPMorgan Chase; UBS; France Télécom and Aeroméxico.

## Band 2

### Greenberg Traurig LLP

See firm details p.664

**The Firm:** The Miami-headquartered heavyweight is perceived as "*well placed among rivals for its muscle and depth across the board.*" The team has cultivated an impressive track record in lending and M&A in the telecom, real estate development, aviation and energy sectors, with emphasis in Central America and Mexico.

**The Lawyers:** **Patricia Menendez Cambo** (see p.645) is credited for the firm's current high visibility in the region. She draws on experience as former US in-house counsel for Telefónica to assist clients in cross-border privatizations, regulatory issues, projects and structured finance transactions. Menendez Cambo is at the helm of the international practice group. Among other highlights, she assisted regional airline TACA in securing finance for aircraft and the setting up of a low-cost carrier joint venture in Mexico. She also counseled Citibank in several transactions across the region.

### Holland & Knight LLP

See firm details p.1534

**The Firm:** This national powerhouse warrants its entry in the Latin American table on the basis that it "*cuts a wide swath in the financial investment front.*" Investors and brokerage houses alike flock to its "*unsurpassed advice*" on issues related to the region.

**The Lawyers:** Observers single out **Alcides Avila** (see p.627) and **George Mencio** (see p.645) when it comes to cross-border financings and M&A with a Latin American component. Avila adopts an approach that is "*minimalist but highly effective and thorough.*" A skilled finance lawyer, he also advises clients in Patriot Act-related compliance issues. Mencio heads the international practice and is a seasoned deal negotiator.

### Hunton & Williams LLP

See firm details p.1989

**The Firm:** This long-standing national player thrives in the Latin American-oriented Miami environs. Clients looking for a broader scope of representation benefit from multicultural and multilingual lawyers operating out of multiple offices. The day-to-day caseload of the 40-strong team includes joint ventures, acquisitions, privatizations, structured products and international tax advice.

**The Lawyers:** One of the founders of the firm's international practice, **Carlos Loumiet** (see p.643) impresses interviewees "*with his superior business judgment – he knows the Latin American market inside-out,*" particularly in project financing and regulatory matters. Loumiet splits his time between New York and Miami. **Fernando Alonso** (see p.626) juggles a role as the Latin American practice group chairman with a busy inbound and outbound M&A workload. He continues to act for BSCH and Telecom Italia in matters both in the USA and the region.

**Clients/Work Highlights:** Panamanian bank Banistmo retained the team in its purchase of over 50% of the shares of Salvadoran financial services company Inversiones Financieras BancoSal.

### Other Notable Practitioners

The market endorsed **Luis de Armas** (see p.633), chairman of the corporate practice at Shutts & Bowen LLP, as a Florida stalwart. He scores highly among clients in the region as "*he gives the securities practice its good name because of his deep understanding of the law.*"

# EMPLOYMENT

## MAINLY DEFENDANT

| Employment: Mainly Defendant Leading Firms |
| --- |
| [1] **FORD & HARRISON LLP** *Tampa* |
| **MORGAN, LEWIS & BOCKIUS LLP** *Miami* |
| **ZINOBER & MCCREA, P.A.** *Tampa* |
| [2] **AKERMAN SENTERFITT** *Orlando* |
| **COFFMAN, COLEMAN, ANDREWS** *Jacksonville* |
| **FISHER & PHILLIPS LLP** *Fort Lauderdale* |
| **JACKSON LEWIS** *Miami* |
| **STEARNS WEAVER MILLER WEISSLER** *Miami* |
| **THOMPSON, SIZEMORE & GONZALEZ** *Tampa* |
| [3] **BAKER & HOSTETLER LLP** *Orlando* |
| **CARLTON FIELDS** *Tampa* |
| **CONSTANGY, BROOKS & SMITH, LLC** *Jacksonville* |
| **EPSTEIN BECKER & GREEN PC** *Miami* |
| **FOLEY & LARDNER LLP** *Jacksonville* |
| **FOWLER WHITE BOGGS BANKER** *Tampa* |
| **GREENBERG TRAURIG LLP** *Miami* |
| **HOLLAND & KNIGHT LLP** *Tampa* |
| **MACFARLANE FERGUSON & MCMULLEN PA** *Tampa* |

## Band 1

### Ford & Harrison LLP

See firm details p.733

**The Firm:** This national labor and employment firm is experiencing growth at a steady rate of knots across the USA. The quality and breadth of work, undertaken by a team of more than 40 "*talented and capable*" lawyers out of four Florida offices, is outstanding. The firm handles all manner of labor and employment issues for corporate management, owners and employers. The bankruptcy of airline and heavy industry clients has caused an influx of cases seeking to control union activity in the workplace. Additionally, recent surges of activity have been witnessed in FLSA cases, as well as discrimination, arbitration and mediation on a range of issues including age, race and sex.

**The Lawyers:** "*A highly talented labor lawyer,*" **Thomas Garwood** (see p.636) is involved in many cases relating to increased union activity in the healthcare and service industries. Typical work in this sphere includes counseling, contract negotiation and arbitration. Additionally, Garwood advises on employment discrimination, wage and hour claims and mediation. **John-Edward Alley** (see p.626) spends much of his time providing employment law advice and strategic planning to large corporate clients, as well as traditional labor matters and wage and hour claims. Alley is a "*valuable resource*" to employers seeking counseling during union elections and strikes. Certified mediator **James Brown** (see p.630) "*knows everything about labor and employment law – it's all at the tip of his fingers.*" He has recently successfully negotiated labor relations and fair employment matters on behalf of a major aircraft manufacturer, and his mediation portfolio is expanding significantly.

**Clients/Work Highlights:** BellSouth; Darden Restaurants; Delta Air Lines; Comair; Jacobs Engineering Group; Life Care Centers of America; Lockheed Martin; Northlake Foods; Orlando Utilities Commission; Orange County School Board; Science Applications International; Siemens Power Generation and State Farm.

### Morgan, Lewis & Bockius LLP

See firm details p.1758

**The Firm:** This firm's lawyers have "*a plethora of experience working for some very impressive clients.*"

The team's recent case portfolio includes defending wage and hour collective actions, employment discrimination, noncompete covenants and trade secrets work. Its particular strength lies in employment litigation matters, although attorneys also demonstrate considerable expertise in mediation and arbitration. Furthermore, the team provides counseling and training regarding FLSA and OSHA compliance. Clients across the USA value the firm's network of support and expertise.

**The Lawyers:** A "*consummate professional,*" **Terence Connor**'s (see p.631) expertise is built on a host of discrimination and employment cases in state and federal courts. He has acted on sex discrimination cases in Florida and other states, including defending large pharmaceutical companies in a positive discrimination case. He also recently defended a national airline in a jury trial involving a discrimination claim stemming from an employee discipline matter. "*At the top of the tree thanks to his vast experience,*" **Russell Hamilton** (see p.639) is characterized by clients as "*knowledgeable, responsive, personable and reliable.*" Clients appreciate his ability to understand their specific business needs. Key focuses of his caseload include mediating, arbitrating and litigating wage and hour, discrimination and retaliation matters and noncompete covenants. Hamilton is also regarded as a top ERISA and employee benefits litigator. **Mark Zelek** (see p.656) is "*well steeped in labor law.*" He regularly uses his fluency in Spanish to the benefit of clients, advising Latin American clients on US labor law and vice versa. Further experience is garnered in wage and hour, discrimination and trade litigation. **Anne Marie Estevez** (see p.635) is rapidly establishing a reputation as a "*superb up-and-coming lawyer.*" Her portfolio focuses on employment litigation, particularly wage and hour cases. She recently successfully defeated a motion for conditional class certification in a nationwide action brought against a large household name chain, whose store managers claimed that they had been wrongly classified as exempt from the FLSA and were owed substantial overtime.

**Clients/Work Highlights:** An impressive array of corporate entities, such as Northrop Grumman, turn to the firm for employment and labor advice and litigation.

## Zinober & McCrea, P.A.

**The Firm:** This labor and employment boutique massively impresses both clients and peers, who agree that "*this first-rate firm has outstandingly talented attorneys.*" Its lawyers are among the highest praised in the state and despite its relatively compact size, the firm is credited with substantial depth in employment and labor cases. Its attorneys have carved out a reputation for their effective handling of litigation and alternative methods of resolving disputes. They also provide clients with highly valued counseling on policies and litigation avoidance.

**The Lawyers:** "*The best – incredibly broadly experienced,*" **Peter Zinober** attracts high praise. He is credited with providing practical solutions "*which work in the real world rather than purely theoretically.*" A recent highlight has included defending a major theme park in arbitrations and NLRB charges. "*Hard-working and efficient,*" **Richard McCrea** represents clients in all manner of employment cases.

His litigation skills are highly acclaimed by clients who value his "*aggressive but not offensive*" courtroom demeanor. Up-and-comer **Scott Silverman** has worked on sophisticated cases for large companies and has established a reputation as a smart, emerging attorney "*with a passionate desire to win cases.*"

**Clients/Work Highlights:** The firm represents a host of household name corporate entities, Florida private companies, universities and other public sector clients.

## Band 2

### Akerman Senterfitt
See firm details p.657

**The Firm:** Many commentators believe that since the Muller Mintz merger in 2003, Akerman is becoming one of the strongest contenders in the employment law market. Indeed, as one noted: "*This is one of the best all-around practices with some big-name clients.*" A team of nearly 40 lawyers provides a variety of services, including discrimination and wage and hour counseling, and litigation and advice on preemptive methods to deal with unionization. The group is seasoned in handling the implications of M&A and provides companion services in ERISA and immigration to clients.

**The Lawyers:** Clients appreciate the "*proactive stance*" adopted by **Jim Bramnick** (see p.629) to preempt potentially problematic issues, and "*he is extremely clear and personable and makes cases seem simple.*" Recent work has included a large wage and hour collective action that settled successfully for the client, and assisting companies to design human resource processes to ensure compliance with state and federal law. **Susan Eisenberg** (see p.635) is a skilled litigator credited with "*a superior command of the law*" and the ability to "*develop practical, reasoned responses quickly.*" Wage and hour collective actions, statutory discrimination, whistle-blower and retaliation claims all contribute to her portfolio. "*Excellent, seasoned attorney*" **David Kornreich** (see p.642) brings over 40 years of experience to the group. His workload usually consists of large, sophisticated cases, such as the labor implications following M&A and defending a disability discrimination claim brought against a public body. Clients praise **Carmen Johnson** (see p.640) for her "*intelligent and pragmatic approach*" in dealing with a vast range of both labor and employment matters as a respected litigator and negotiator. Further experience includes preemptive counseling of human resources departments, defending Sarbanes-Oxley claims, and drafting and enforcing noncompete covenants. "*First choice for public sector issues,*" **Jeffrey Mandel** (see p.644) is regarded as highly experienced in labor law and the Florida Public Employees Relations Act. Indeed, he recently successfully represented the City of Winter Springs in the Florida First District Court of Appeal, reversing an earlier decision that the city had committed unfair labor practices. The case also resulted in a reversal of the Public Employees

Relations Commission prohibition on employers freezing employees' salaries prior to negotiation of a new agreement. Clients regard *"fantastic problem solver"* **Jennifer Taylor** (see p.654) as a promising associate to watch out for in the future. Her drafting and litigation skills are particularly noteworthy.

Clients/Work Highlights: Iberia Airlines; Nintendo; Florida Panthers; Steiner Leisure; Holy Cross Hospital; JM Family Enterprises; US Sugar; City Furniture; Memorial Healthcare System; Sunbelt Rentals; AOL; Carnival Cruise Lines; Miami Dolphins; Scripps Research Institute and Pharmed Group.

## Coffman, Coleman, Andrews & Grogan

**The Firm:** Sources regard this Jacksonville employment, labor and immigration boutique as *"a top-notch group of trusted attorneys."* The firm's deep bench of lawyers represents a range of private and public sector management clients both within the state and nationally.

**The Lawyers:** **Michael Grogan** has carved out a reputation as a *"big-name player,"* particularly in public law issues. **William Andrews**'s skill in handling traditional labor issues is widely recognized, while **Eric Holshouser** is a skilled litigator active in both discrimination and wage and hour cases. **Patrick Coleman** wins plaudits for his *"fantastic contribution to labor and employment work in the state over a sustained period."*

## Fisher & Phillips LLP

See firm details p.732

**The Firm:** Commentators pointed to the *"incredible depth and resources"* possessed by this national employment and labor specialist firm as its distinguishing features. The firm's coveted lawyers have witnessed exponential growth in litigation of late, including multiparty wage and hour, discrimination and traditional labor claims. The firm is also developing niches in several industries including hospitality and automobile dealerships.

**The Lawyers:** Highly experienced **Theresa Gallion** (see p.636) is at the top of many referral lists when recommending a trial lawyer. She is a hugely talented attorney who establishes a strong rapport with clients, whether litigating or counseling management on employment issues. Gallion is especially well versed in legislation such as the ADA, the FLSA and the Equal Pay Act. **Charles Caulkins** (see p.631) combines his first-rate labor practice with his insightful approach to employment matters. He has been assisting management in developing preventive steps to avoid unionization and in enforcing noncompete covenants. **Carlos Burruezo** (see p.630) has carved a successful niche handling multiparty litigation, especially in the wage and hour sector. He continues to act on a race discrimination claim brought by seven plaintiffs against his restaurant client, and has witnessed a general increase in religious and national origin discrimination claims. Clients/Work Highlights: Clients include both national and Florida-based employers.

## Jackson Lewis

**The Firm:** The sheer size of this labor and employment law firm ensures its prominence in the Florida market and across the USA. It is able to draw additional muscle from its 21 offices nationwide. The firm has developed outstanding breadth not only in the current hotbeds of OSHA, wage and hour, and discrimination claims, but also in diverse areas from immigration and ERISA to workplace violence, substance abuse and drug testing. The firm is also active in labor cases, particularly on behalf of healthcare industry clients.

**The Lawyers:** **Susan McKenna** (see p.645) is *"an outstanding lawyer with a fantastic calmness about her – she doesn't get her way by being an 800-pound gorilla."* McKenna divides her time between preemptive counseling, training management and defending employment-related disputes. She has recently settled a large class action race discrimination case for a national retailer brought by the EEOC. **David Block** (see p.629) has worked on an increasing number of collective action wage and hour claims recently. He counsels clients on protecting themselves from claims by taking preemptive measures, and has been involved in numerous litigation and alternative dispute resolution cases.

Clients/Work Highlights: Tupperware; Hilton Hotels; Scholastic; Orlando Regional Healthcare System; Regis and CNL.

## Stearns Weaver Miller Weissler Alhadeff & Sitterson, PA

**The Firm:** Commentators agree that this full-service commercial law firm has established *"a splendid group of high-quality employment and labor lawyers."* The team has attracted a host of household-name clients in healthcare, hospitality, national and international banking, real estate and other key industries. Across its three offices in Miami, Fort Lauderdale and Tampa, the team covers a range of cases, from discrimination and wage and hour defense to union avoidance and NLRB proceedings.

**The Lawyers:** The *"sophisticated, bright and pragmatic"* **Bob Kofman** is a respected litigator, whose caseload is mainly litigation, with a smaller degree of counseling. He has defended employers on cases ranging from pregnancy and religious discrimination to wage and hour claims. He also assists clients in planning appropriate management policies to avoid unionization. **Bob Turk** provides clients with *"legal advice infused with business considerations."* His workload divides fairly evenly between counseling and litigation, including sexual harassment, wage and hour, and age discrimination claims. Recent labor experience has included representing an employer when one union wanted to be substituted for another, resulting in the issuing of an NLRB opinion that this was inappropriate. *"Creative, courageous and truly ethical,"* **Joan Canny** displays thorough preparation skills and courtroom presence in her trial work and proceedings before the NLRB. Clients also appreciate her ability to *"think outside the box."* **Jon Stage** is a *"highly effective, resourceful attorney."* His recent work has included litigating cases

defending race discrimination claims, such as those facing restaurants.

Clients/Work Highlights: The firm acts for local and national employers including AutoNation; CompUSA; Hilton Hotels; Publix Supermarkets; Bank of America; ANC Rental and Denny's.

## Thompson, Sizemore & Gonzalez

**The Firm:** This labor and employment group is endorsed for its deep litigation skills in representing business owners, managers and government entity clients. Its esteemed attorneys are credited with having *"superb energy in the courtroom."* The firm has a particularly strong reputation in public sector work, representing healthcare, education and nonprofit organizations, as well as a range of private companies. It also provides counseling and training to clients in order to avoid legal issues.

**The Lawyers:** The *"energetic, compassionate and highly effective advocate"* **Thomas Gonzalez** has an enviable portfolio of management clients on both the employment and labor side. One of the best trial lawyers in Florida, his courtroom skills are frequently highlighted. *"Cut from the same cloth as Gonzalez,"* **Gregory Hearing** is the firm's managing partner and has also established a sterling reputation in the courtroom.

Clients/Work Highlights: Citrus Memorial Hospital; City of Clearwater; Associated Builders & Contractors; Shriners Hospitals for Children; News-Journal; South Florida Baptist Hospital; School Board of Volusia County; Winter Haven Hospital and Wuesthoff Memorial Hospital.

## Band 3

## Baker & Hostetler LLP

**The Firm:** Increased resources have allowed this firm to rapidly establish a name for itself as one of Florida's key players in labor and employment law. Its *"fine team of lawyers"* recently achieved a significant victory in defeating a sizable application for class certification of wage and hour claims. Its attorneys are seasoned in providing counseling and advice, as well as trial representation, to its primarily private sector management clients. Current areas of activity include race and disability discrimination, where it is representing a range of clients such as major financial institutions, Fortune 100 companies and growing businesses and industries.

**The Lawyers:** The *"highly professional and ethical"* **Kevin Shaughnessy** impresses clients with his *"excellent understanding of business objectives in employment counseling and litigation."* His recent caseload has included half a dozen race and religion discrimination cases before the federal court, large wage and hour collective actions, and union negotiations for nursing home and hospital organizations. An *"outstanding lawyer,"* **Joyce Ackerbaum Cox** is skilled in discrimination and sexual harassment litigation. She also undertakes audits for private and public sector clients to assess compliance with the ADA.

Clients/Work Highlights: Irby Construction; Yellow Roadway; Sprint; Wachovia; Ocean Spray; CHEP USA; Darden Restaurants; Wuesthoff Hospital; Novartis; Oak Street Mortgage; Winn-Dixie and Bernard Egan.

## Carlton Fields

See firm details p.661

**The Firm:** This full-service law firm represents a host of large corporate clients from its six offices in Florida. Its "*strong presence and efficiency*" attract high praise. The team's expertise spans litigation, class and collective actions, counseling and advising on issues such as discrimination, EEOC claims, wage and hour claims, and compliance with state and federal legislation. The firm also provides employment and labor advice on the implications of M&A for management, and niche areas such as immigration services.

**The Lawyers:** Certified mediator **George Barford** (see p.627) is respected for his "*wisdom and seniority,*" especially in labor matters. He is a former NLRB attorney and specializes in advising employers on union-related issues and OSHA fatality cases. Recent successes include assisting a company to become union-free. **Patricia Thompson** (see p.654) "*has a tremendous ability to balance business objectives with legal realities.*" She has undertaken employment litigation defending discrimination, wage and hour, and sexual harassment cases before juries in the federal court. For example, she recently defeated class action notices filed against limousine and restaurant company clients.

Clients/Work Highlights: CF industries; AIG; Brinker International; HCA; Progressive Casualty Insurance; RT Tampa Franchise and Mahaffey Apartment.

## Constangy, Brooks & Smith, LLC

**The Firm:** This nationwide labor and employment specialist has offices in Jacksonville, Lakeland and Tampa. Its attorneys cover the full range of employment and labor matters spanning OSHA, union negotiation and avoidance, benefits and discrimination defense. Growth has been witnessed in defending wage and hour collective actions and assisting employers to avoid workplace violence.

**The Lawyers:** **John Dickinson** is "*an ethical attorney and an excellent communicator*" who pays "*fastidious attention to detail.*" Recently, he has defended the employer in a high-profile OSHA case and also argued a civil rights case before the Eleventh Circuit Court of Appeals in Atlanta. **Damon Kitchen** has established a strong profile for his employment discrimination defense work and is current chair of the Labor and Employment Section of the Florida Bar.

Clients/Work Highlights: NASCAR; International Speedway; BellSouth; Boeing; Duke Energy; FedEx; HCA; Kmart; RadioShack and University of South Florida.

## Epstein Becker & Green PC

**The Firm:** This national firm boasts around 200 labor and employment attorneys in 11 cities. The Miami team provides advice and guidance to clients regarding employee discipline issues and compliance with statutes in order to reduce clients' exposure to litigation. It has strong mediation, arbitration and litigation expertise and is a specialist in Title III of the ADA regarding architectural access to newly constructed buildings.

**The Lawyers:** The "*fantastically talented*" **Michael Casey** (see p.631) has worked on a number of Sarbanes-Oxley whistle-blower cases and regularly advises clients on union avoidance. He is a respected litigator and his recent portfolio incorporates discrimination, trade secrets and noncompete covenant cases.

Clients/Work Highlights: Clients include Stiefel Laboratories and large financial service institutions such as UBS PaineWebber, Deutsche Bank and CSFB. Further clients are drawn from the manufacturing and healthcare industries.

## Foley & Lardner LLP

See firm details p.2037

**The Firm:** This national firm has a strong presence in Florida. Its team of 15 lawyers represents management on employment matters, including discrimination, retaliation, OSHA and wage and hour collective action litigation. Its traditional labor law workload is increasing of late, and the firm is regularly called upon to counsel service industry clients on methods of preempting unionization. The firm is also actively involved in noncompetes and safeguarding the IP rights of businesses.

**The Lawyers:** **Kevin Hyde** (see p.640) is skilled in both labor and employment matters. His present portfolio comprises day-to-day employment counseling and Sarbanes-Oxley class actions. He is also well versed in union, compensation and discrimination matters.

Clients/Work Highlights: The firm represents one of the nation's largest consumer packaged goods marketers, a very large retail store and a community college system.

## Fowler White Boggs Banker

**The Firm:** This growing employment team now houses 17 lawyers across nine offices in Florida. The firm provides a full range of services to clients drawn from industries such as construction, hospitality, technology and retail. It has recently defended several access cases where claims have been filed alleging that many of a street's buildings violate disability access legislation. The group's recent litigation successes include an IP and noncompete case for a restaurant chain, and winning a multimillion-dollar sexual harassment case brought by the EEOC.

**The Lawyers:** Highly acclaimed **John Robinson** has successfully contested unionization efforts on behalf of household-name clients. He recently obtained two summary judgments on discrimination cases and the dismissal of an unfair labor practice charge against a large construction industry

client. **Cathy Beveridge** is an "*ethical, competent and articulate attorney.*" She specializes in employment issues in the defense and transportation industries, and her litigation skills won high praise from clients.

Clients/Work Highlights: General Dynamics; Omnicare; WCI Communities; New York Yankees; FedEx; Taylor Woodrow; John Hancock and Raymond James.

## Greenberg Traurig LLP

See firm details p.664

**The Firm:** Clients value the national and international resources available to them when working with Greenberg Traurig. Such reach and resources mean the firm remains up to date with the latest employment law developments and can draw expertise from multiple disciplines, such as IP, to complement its well-established practice.

**The Lawyers:** "*Conscientious, thorough and professional,*" **Joseph Fleming** (see p.635) has developed strong links with the airline industry, undertaking work such as negotiating outsourcing with unions and performing due diligence checks. Further experience is to be found in ERISA, whistle-blower cases, and drafting and litigating noncompete covenants.

Clients/Work Highlights: The firm serves a range of clients including those from the airline, manufacturing, hotel, restaurant and entertainment industries.

## Holland & Knight LLP

See firm details p.1534

**The Firm:** This national employment practice comprises 65 lawyers, with 16 based in Florida. The group takes a proactive stance to potential employment law problems through counseling and training clients, writing employee handbooks and, where necessary, arbitrating, mediating and litigating claims. Clients value the firm's network of highly competent lawyers across the USA and its ability to draw expertise from complementary practice areas.

**The Lawyers:** Clients described head of employment law section, **Bill deMeza** (see p.633), as "*a truly valuable asset in my arsenal.*" He provides sound and sensible advice covering the spectrum of employment law. Collective actions on wage and hour claims have occupied his attention for much of the past year, as has a 15-plaintiff Equal Pay Act case. The "*professional, knowledgeable and personable*" **Guy Farmer** (see p.635) has been involved of late in a major OFCCP case that settled successfully, and a significant sexual harassment case under Title VII of the 1964 Civil Rights Act. Employers commend his "*dependable and effective*" representation on employment matters, from wrongful termination to ERISA and whistle-blower cases. **Marilyn Holifield**'s (see p.640) employment litigation is respected, particularly her work regarding noncompete covenants.

Clients/Work Highlights: McDonald's; Boston Market; Pacer International; Harris; Media General; Jabil Circuit and Cardinal Health.

## Macfarlane Ferguson & McMullen PA

**The Firm:** The employment and labor team at this full-service firm has been boosted by the arrival of Frank Brown from Zinober & McCrea PA in September 2005. With offices in Tampa, Clearwater and Lakeland, the group works on a broad mix of employment and labor matters, from noncompete covenants to discrimination and wage and hour litigation. The firm also counsels employers on the implications of business moves, such as M&A.

**The Lawyers:** A "*superb lawyer,*" **Frank Brown** is currently working on two labor pool cases and a workers' compensation coverage issue. His recent portfolio comprises numerous discrimination cases that have settled before litigation and several cases of employee benefits litigation.

**Clients/Work Highlights:** Clients include a household-name fast-food restaurant, employee leasing and staffing companies, and public sector clients such as a major Florida hospital and a pension board.

### Other Notable Practitioners

**Ralph Peterson** of Beggs & Lane in Pensacola is a popular figure in the employment and labor law market, particularly for his trial skills. **Allan Weitzman** (see p.655) of Proskauer Rose LLP is, according to his clients, an "*excellent advocate with strong ethics and an unrivalled understanding of business.*" He represents national and local clients from the firm's Boca Raton office on matters including discrimination, wage and hour and executive compensation, and noncompetes. Labor work advising employers on union organization drives also constitutes part of his caseload. **Daniel Kunkel**, of the labor and employment boutique Kunkel Miller & Hament in Tampa, provides services including counseling and litigation to a range of corporate clients.

# ENVIRONMENT

| | Environment |
|---|---|
| | Leading Firms |
| [1] | HOPPING GREEN & SAMS, PA *Tallahassee* |
| [2] | CARLTON FIELDS *Tampa* |
| | GREENBERG TRAURIG LLP *Miami* |
| | HOLLAND & KNIGHT LLP *Orlando* |
| | LANDERS & PARSONS *Tallahassee* |
| | LEWIS, LONGMAN & WALKER PA *West Palm Beach* |
| | RUDEN MCCLOSKY SC *Tallahassee* |
| | WHITE & CASE LLP *Miami* |
| [3] | BALES WEINSTEIN *Tampa* |
| | BILZIN SUMBERG BAENA PRICE & AXELROD *Miami* |
| | GUNSTER, YOAKLEY & STEWART *West Palm Beach* |
| | OERTEL, FERNANDEZ, COLE & BRYANT *Tallahassee* |
| | SHOOK, HARDY & BACON LLP *Miami* |

## Band 1

### Hopping Green & Sams, PA

See firm details p.665

**The Firm:** Based in Tallahassee, this multifaceted environmental and land use team is "*undeniably top of the field,*" agree market sources. The provision of an all-encompassing service, described as "*every client's dream,*" successfully combined with high lawyer availability throughout the department, makes this an attractive choice for many clients. The group is "*bursting with talent,*" but as one client commented: "*More importantly they have integrity – you know they are not just there to make money.*" In the past year, the environmental team has been active in the legislative lobbying arena and in its work with the Florida Department of Environmental Protection, aiding clients through complex permitting requirements such as wetlands, water and air issues. The firm's work relating to the Everglades is also widely commended. Of late, the team has advised on the successful licensing of a phosphate mine and assisted clients on complex licensing issues associated with power plants.

**The Lawyers:** The Everglades restoration projects have formed a key strand to **William Green**'s (see p.638) practice. He possesses a doctorate in physical chemistry and an MBA in business, which one client claimed ensures "*a unique blend of scientific, legal and business analysis to any matter.*" He is acting as special master for the Loxahatchee National Wildlife Refuge in a trial concerning alleged failing to meet air quality standards. **Frank Matthews** (see p.644) has a niche in handling land use and permitting matters with a wetlands and water focus. In this field, he is the "*crème de la crème – he never lets the window of opportunity pass by.*" Matthews asserts the appropriate level of aggressiveness in negotiation and is respected by both clients and the regulatory agencies within Tallahassee. The legendary **Wade Hopping** (see p.640) is a formidable force in the legislative lobbying arena: his experience and connections in the field ensure he wields clout. A key rainmaker at the firm, Hopping recently advised on the environmental issues related to the sale of a 91,000-acre ranch. **Gary Sams** (see p.650) sees the bigger picture when it comes to large permitting matters. Clients value his "*invaluable strategic advice*" as a major plus in guiding them through the regulations of the permitting process. Impeccable legal credentials combined with experience within the business community also explain his popularity across the board. Sams has recently been involved in the permitting aspects concerning the construction of a major power plant. **Peter Cunningham** (see p.632) is a specialist in air quality regulation. With "*technical finesse*" he represents utility clients, including Florida Power & Light, on large projects in the permitting and development of power plant facilities. Commended for his solid and hazardous waste practice, **Ralph DeMeo** (see p.633) is a skilled toxic torts litigator. His recent caseload has included toxic mold and construction defects disputes. Often working with state agencies, DeMeo's connections in the field were seen as an advantage: "*He knows everyone and can always give you the inside perspective,*" one client remarked.

**Clients/Work Highlights:** The firm has attracted some of the market's largest industrial clients such as Air Products and Chemicals; CF Industries; EBSCO Industries; DuPont; Exxon Mobil Corporation; Fina Oil & Chemical; Florida Manufacturing and Chemical Council; Progress Energy Florida; Seminole Electric Cooperative; Sugar Cane Growers Cooperative of Florida and The Williams Company.

## Band 2

### Carlton Fields

See firm details p.661

**The Firm:** This full-service firm continues to earn plaudits for the strength of its environmental team. The selection of "*experienced, personable and skillful individuals*" available makes dealing with this firm "*not only successful but enjoyable as well.*" Displaying proven might in areas such as brownfield development and Superfund matters, the team has negotiated a number of specialty environmental pollution legal liability policies with insurance carriers on behalf of clients. Its attorneys are also well versed in the issues arising out of groundwater contamination sites, mold and toxic tort. Clients emphasized the team's creative advice and declared: "*Their provision of service is almost impossible to fault.*"

**The Lawyers:** Possessing over 30 years' experience, **Rodger Schwenke** (see p.651) has developed a practice that cuts across both the environmental and real estate fields. "*One of the veterans,*" he was extolled for his ethical approach and for his expertise in the environmental remediation and permitting arena. Schwenke has recently advised on the redevelopment of contaminated properties and has acted as a mediator in private CERCLA proceedings. **Laurel Lockett** (see p.643) is a great all-rounder whose workload encompasses industrial and domestic wastewater permitting, Florida brownfield designation and related real estate transactions. She recently acted for Martin County, Florida in a number of groundwater contamination issues, and often uses her "*finely tuned skills*" to deal with matters cropping up within the toxic tort and mold sphere.

**Clients/Work Highlights:** The team has represented Honeywell before the US EPA in the remediation of groundwater contamination emanating from a former semiconductor manufacturing facility. Other clients include Siemens and National Gypsum.

## Greenberg Traurig LLP

See firm details p.664

**The Firm:** This sizable national firm has the capacity to handle a range of environmental matters. In line with the heavy real estate focus of the Florida market, this environmental team works hand in hand with the firm's land use practitioners. "*It caters to every client's needs and demands.*" The team's caseload of late includes the due diligence aspects of major sales and acquisitions, brownfield redevelopment and land contamination issues. Clients highlighted the previous governmental experience of its attorneys as "*a major plus.*" The group successfully negotiated a $7.9 million remediation cleanup contract with a municipality for the cleanup of a former city coal gasification plant.

**The Lawyers:** "*Always impressive in dealing with even the most complex of matters,*" **Alfred Malefatto** (see p.644) wins respect from all corners of the market. He evenly divides his practice between land use and environmental law, and has advised some of Florida's largest homebuilders on their water law concerns. The due diligence aspects of major real estate transactions is a key strand of Malefatto's practice; he assisted a major corporate client in the acqui-

sition of manufacturing facilities in North Carolina, Indiana, Nevada and further afield in Germany.

**Clients/Work Highlights:** Environmental team members secured approval of a vertical expansion of a landfill in southern Dade County on behalf of JR Capital and Waste Management. Other clients include Terra Group; The Ginn Company; The Related Group of Florida; Swerdlow Group; Technical Olympic USA; Lennar; Rinker Materials; AIG Baker Development; Centex Homes; Fisher Island Holdings; Flagstone Property Group; GL Homes; Kolter Property; LandMar Group and Turnberry Associates.

## Holland & Knight LLP

See firm details p.1534

**The Firm:** This "*mature and focused*" group is a popular choice for national clients with operations in Florida. The phosphate industry has historically provided an anchor to the practice, and the team has also developed its expertise in air and water issues. Well-established relationships with many of the states regulatory bodies enable the team to resolve matters "*promptly and with ease,*" explain sources. While an "*amazing variety of lawyers*" cater to the index of environmental concerns firmwide, it was the Orlando and Tallahassee offices that were distinguished for the depth of resources and dedicated expertise offered.

**The Lawyers:** **Lawrence Seller**'s (see p.651) practice sees him more engaged with enforcement-oriented work. He is currently representing Environmental Risk Solutions in a significant enforcement matter involving alleged violations of hazardous waste permit and regulations in Polk County. A "*real star of the field,*" peers unabashedly stated, "*We would love to have him on our team.*" Seller's heavy involvement in the environmental legislative arena impacted clients, who felt assured he remains on the cutting edge of an ever-changing area of law. **Lawrence Curtin** (see p.632) impresses with his activity lobbying at the state legislature level. Perhaps best known for his expertise in the phosphate industry sector, he has assumed the role of counsel to the Florida Phosphate Council. A seasoned lawyer, Curtin understands the heavy industry sector and regularly advises clients on the permitting and expansion of power generating facilities. **Roger Sims** (see p.651) is a water expert and leads the firm's specialty water resources group. He regularly deals with matters concerning the supply and allocation of water and additionally advises on issues relating to the phosphate industry. In 2005, Sims resolved a water supply permitting issue for major client Mosaic Phosphates. He also represented Sarasota Manatee Airport Authority with regard to plume emitting solvents.

**Clients/Work Highlights:** An impressive roster of clients includes Rinker Materials, National Association of Home Builders and National Stone, Sand & Gravel Association.

## Landers & Parsons

**The Firm:** This is a smaller boutique concentrating on environmental and land use issues. This team is "*as good as it gets*" and has attracted clients who value that they "*are really able to develop relationships with these lawyers – you can trust them.*" This firm's cost-effective advice is underpinned by a "*true understanding*" of the regulatory climate in which its clients work.

**The Lawyers:** **Philip Parsons** is a specialist in Everglades matters. His "*practical and intelligent approach*" is valued by his clients, who further depict him as a man of great integrity. Parson's practice spans environmental and administrative law, and he regularly advises on regulatory issues concerning the agricultural sector for surety companies and water management companies. Although many say **David Dee** is a "*name we would call on first*" in the handling of permitting issues surrounding solid waste, his practice spans a far wider remit. Involved in some of the state's largest projects, he recently acted in the successful permitting of a new regional landfill in central Florida. A "*talented attorney,*" Dee also regularly develops contracts and procurement documents for local government, indicating his versatility in the area.

**Clients/Work Highlights:** Representative clients of this group include local municipalities and the Florida sugar cane industry. It also advises agricultural interests, utilities that operate water and wastewater systems, and the developers of cogeneration facilities and power plants.

## Lewis, Longman & Walker PA

**The Firm:** Although smaller than some in the Florida market, this environmental and land use boutique firm is "*one of the heavy hitters.*" Housing a raft of attorneys with prior DEP experience, the firm is well equipped to advise on the environmental concerns of a project as "*they can see both sides of the coin.*" Endorsed for its work in the Everglades and wetlands area, this "*highly sophisticated*" team has also carved out a niche in water management, Superfund and hazardous and solid waste areas. Attorneys frequently carry out work for the public sector and local municipalities in areas such as the CWA, the National Pollutant Discharge Elimination System (NPDES) and the Endangered Species Act.

**The Lawyers:** **Terry Lewis** is "*one of the top names in the state,*" declare sources. Long-time veteran in the field, he represents national and regional developer clients in matters involving Everglades restoration, the CWA and environmental resource permits. Commentators aligned Lewis's negotiations skills to the "*calm, collected and thoughtful demeanor*" he exhibits. **Steve Walker** "*really understands clients' needs and gets good results.*" He undertakes high-end Everglades litigation and water-related issues. Walker acts as environmental counsel to the Seminole Tribe of Florida and can count various water utilities, such as Florida Water Services and Florida's Water Management Districts, among his clientele. **Steve Lewis** has spent much of the last year negotiating the issuance of federal permits for large-scale developments impacting wetlands, endangered species and water quality. Clients perceive his prior experience as deputy director of environmental permitting in the Department of Environmental Regulation as a "*compelling reason to turn to him for advice.*"

**Clients/Work Highlights:** Public and private sector clients make up the core of this group's client base, with names such as South Florida Water Management District, Sugar Cane Growers Cooperative of Florida and Palm Beach County.

## Ruden McClosky SC

**The Firm:** Equipped with ten offices statewide, this full-service firm fields an environmental law team that continues to go "*from strength to strength.*" The group is particularly strong in the regulatory field and handles matters associated with environmentally sensitive lands and land acquisitions, hazardous and solid waste, air and water pollution and wetlands protection. On the contentious side, the team regularly advises clients on potential environmental liability arising from ownership or transfer of contaminated property, in addition to representing clients in the complex litigation and enforcement matters.

**The Lawyers:** **Mary Smallwood** practices "*in the highest echelons*" of the field, reported sources. Spearheading the group, her previous experience in the Florida Department of Environmental Regulation and "*string of exhaustive connections with the right people*" make her a popular choice for advice in the environmental regulatory arena. **Lee Worsham** focuses on water law, including issues such as drainage and wetlands. The permitting aspects associated with urban and agricultural development also fall within "*this talented young lawyer's*" remit.

**Clients/Work Highlights:** This team regularly handles matters for a host of national real estate developers; financial institutions; corporations; insurance companies and governmental agencies.

## White & Case LLP

See firm details p.1566

**The Firm:** Miami is home to this international firm's environmental team, which for many south Florida industry clients is the "*first choice for dealing with complex litigation.*" This "*small but highly experienced*" team has been busy representing the nation's largest solid waste company in its litigious and regulatory work. The group also regularly represents the limestone mining industry in federal court cases. Toxic tort litigation has been a mainstay of the practice and has produced "*an enviable track record of success*" thanks to the firm's "*comprehensive understanding of the issues.*"

**The Lawyers:** The environmental team continues to flourish under the leadership of "*five-star attorney*" **Doug Halsey** (see p.639). A skilled trial lawyer, he is equally adept at handling complex matters on the noncontentious side of the practice. His "*sharp intellect and bright mind*" ensures practical solutions, and he has "*captured the respect of the entire environmental community.*" Halsey represented a waste management company in a lawsuit brought by a municipality seeking to limit the operation of a

major municipal landfill.

**Clients/Work Highlights:** The firm recently acted for the developer in the redevelopment of a mobile home park into a waterfront condominium development in the Florida Keys. Manual Diaz Farms; MorningSide Development; St. Joe Towns & Resorts and Sandler at Greater Marathon Bay are all within its stable of clients.

## Band 3

### Bales Weinstein

**The Firm:** This compact, cohesive group handles a wide-ranging number of environmental litigation cases "*with a wonderful marshaling of resources.*" Clients also praised the team's "*efficient responses*" to their needs.

**The Lawyers:** **David Weinstein** is one of the market's finest environmental trial lawyers. His practice includes toxic tort and class actions, which alongside his "*facilitative thought process*" and "*excellent command of the English language*" make him an ideal choice before regulatory agencies and courts. He recently represented The Mosaic Company in a class action by commercial fishermen alleging damages purportedly resulting from a release of processed water caused by hurricane damage.

**Clients/Work Highlights:** SYSCO Corporation; ExxonMobil; Ashland; Sunoco; AIG Environmental; Coronet Industries; Orion Marine Group; Misener Marine Construction; Mercedes Homes; Syngenta and MacDill Federal Credit Union.

### Bilzin Sumberg Baena Price & Axelrod LLP

See firm details p.660

**The Firm:** A small team successfully advises clients on a range of environmental law issues, but it was discerned most heavily for work carried out in the wetlands permitting and litigation area. This growing practice also acts in the defense of regulatory and enforcement actions by local, state and federal agencies. Matters relating to Superfund, brownfield sites and landfills also form sizable portions of this team's work.

**The Lawyers:** Environmental litigator **Matthew Coglianese** (see p.631) recently represented Legend Properties in the defense of three construction defect and mold claims in high-profile litigation. "*His intelligence and prior scientific background sees him through the most complex of matters,*" and clients appreciate how he "*keeps his eye on his clients' interests at all times.*" Another hallmark of his practice is handling large multiparty matters within the Superfund area.

**Clients/Work Highlights:** The team recently represented a developer client in the $20 million Cutler Cay project, a 300-acre, 500-unit residential development adjoining Biscayne National Park and sensitive wetlands coastal region. This involved the obtaining of environmental permitting and close coordination with the Comprehensive Everglades Restoration Plan.

## Gunster, Yoakley & Stewart PA

**The Firm:** Five attorneys operate as a combined environmental and land use group from this firm's Fort Lauderdale office. The team has experience in Everglades protection and permitting, as well as Superfund and brownfield site development. The provision of specialist due diligence support to M&A transactions forms a facet of this practice.

**The Lawyers:** **Rick Burgess** is "*a force to be reckoned with*" in Everglades matters, often representing local developers and clients within the agricultural sphere. He is equally familiar with land use law and advises clients on a range of zoning and permitting matters.

**Clients/Work Highlights:** Clients include Republic Services and AutoNation.

## Oertel, Fernandez, Cole & Bryant, PA

**The Firm:** This small Tallahassee firm has ten attorneys practising chiefly within the area of environmental law and land use. It represents a variety of public and private developers in wetlands, hazardous waste, water, air quality and condemnation issues. Clients were quick to praise the impressive work product produced by these attorneys: "*Not only do they get you good results, they do with it without burning a hole in your pocket!*" The team also figures in an abundance of regulatory matters affecting the healthcare industry.

**The Lawyers:** Group head **Terry Cole** draws on his experience at the Florida Department of Environmental Regulation to advise on air and water issues. He is also an authority on concerns facing the forestry industry and has successfully represented a number of landowners in litigation concerning wetlands.

**Clients/Work Highlights:** The team counts Florida Fruit & Vegetable Association International Paper and Georgia-Pacific among its clients.

## Shook, Hardy & Bacon LLP

See firm details p.1218

**The Firm:** This national firm is widely commended for its work in the environmental litigation area, which is conducted by trial lawyers who really know their way around the courtroom. The team carries out work for a mixed set of clients, including some in the food and agricultural industry.

**The Lawyers:** **John Barkett** (see p.627) "*is the best environmental law alternative dispute resolution attorney in the state, bar none,*" proclaim sources. He has been appointed as special master in the Everglades remediation program, where he displays his "*never-ending knowledge*" and technical skills. Clients admire how he "*regularly blows the opposition away with his expertise and gets the mission accomplished.*" His workload crosses state borders and Barkett wins national acclaim for his roles as a Superfund mediator and an authority on hazardous waste.

**Clients/Work Highlights:** Clients of this team include Motorola; Wal-Mart; Morton Salt; Aquila; ConocoPhilips and DuPont.

## Other Notable Practitioners

Sole practitioner **William Preston** (see p.647) "*is without a doubt, a veteran of the field.*" Offering "*unique perspectives,*" he is famed for his advice on the regulatory aspects of environmental law. His client base mainly comprises national corporate clients with operations in Florida, and he also represents a number of public entities. Preston recently undertook the assessment and remediation of a number of Florida sites for a major Florida electricity utility and was also involved in the permitting efforts of a major water management company seeking to expand its landfills. **Parker Thomson** (see p.654), a widely respected member of Hogan & Hartson LLP's litigation team, has played an important role in a number of high-profile environmental

litigation cases. Based in the Miami office, he was asked by Governor Bush to represent the state in litigation concerning the ecological integrity of Everglades National Park and the Loxahatchee National Wildlife Refuge and an inflow of nutrients, including phosphorus. Rodgers Towers PA is home to environmental law specialist **Richard McGuire**. A "*provider of practical solutions,*" he is well versed in every aspect of the field but is most recognised for his work in the Superfund and contaminated land area. He also assists clients in obtaining permits for marina developments. Esteemed Floridian firm Fowler White Boggs Banker fields **Ron Noble**, a lawyer whose broad environmental and land use practice features advice on petroleum contamination and cleanup programs, as well as wastewater treat-

ment and a range of regulatory and enforcement matters. Broad and Cassel attorney **Douglas Rillstone** has carved out a niche regulatory practice concerning endangered species and wetlands issues. His influential lobbying of such wildlife matters, at both state and legislature level, makes him a popular choice among landowners and developers seeking to use land inhabited by protected species. **Tim Sleeth**, from Jacksonville-based firm Smith Hulsey & Busey, "*will always approach problems in a novel fashion,*" claim sources. The core of his practice focuses on handling private dispute resolution in the areas of hazardous and contaminated waste. He has also recently undertaken a substantial amount of work in the toxic tort and Superfund arena.

# HEALTHCARE

| Healthcare Leading Firms | |
|---|---|
| 1 | **MCDERMOTT WILL & EMERY** *Miami* |
| 2 | **AKERMAN SENTERFITT** *Tampa* |
| | **BROAD AND CASSEL** *Miami* |
| | **CARLTON FIELDS** *Tampa* |
| | **FOWLER WHITE BOGGS BANKER** *Tampa* |
| | **HOLLAND & KNIGHT LLP** *Miami* |
| 3 | **BUCHANAN INGERSOLL PC** *Tampa* |
| | **DUANE MORRIS LLP** *Miami* |
| | **GREENBERG TRAURIG LLP** *Miami* |
| | **HOGAN & HARTSON LLP** *Miami* |
| | **RUDEN MCCLOSKY SC** *Miami* |

## Band 1

### McDermott Will & Emery

See firm details p.878

**The Firm:** The Miami office of this international firm certainly lives up to the "*impeccable national reputation for excellence in the healthcare field*" that so many interviewees have spoken about. Clients find the firm's expertise in healthcare to be beneficial on a wide range of transactions and business issues, and see the firm as "*a trusted counsel, legal adviser and partner to make business objectives happen.*" Unlike other competitors, this firm has 12 dedicated and "*exceedingly responsive*" healthcare attorneys who are able to "*deliver on the sort of cases that would overwhelm others.*" The department's one-stop shop approach and its ability to handle the full range of regulatory, commercial and contentious cases is impressive. Clients also rate the team for "*really understanding the operations of healthcare facilities*" and for the benefits it offers to their business objectives, particularly in the areas of managed care and business divestiture transactions.

**The Lawyers: Ira Coleman** (see p.631) understands not only the law but the business too: "*He will really try to figure out how to make things work for his*

client." He advises private equity firms on investment in healthcare companies and represents public healthcare companies, providers, insurers and HMOs. Coleman is the partner-in-charge of the Miami office and head of the Miami health department, and during the past year, he worked on the first special purpose acquisition corporation for NationsHealth. **Gary Davis** (see p.633) "*is not only a fantastic attorney with a wealth of knowledge of healthcare law, he is also a great strategist and a man of integrity.*" He is a prime candidate for advice on the managed care sector and is revered for his work with hospitals and for restructuring contractual or economic relationships with physicians. The "*skillful and well-regarded young star*" **Jerry Sokol** (see p.652) impresses with his representation of ambulatory surgery and diagnostic imaging centers, especially regarding their transactional and regulatory needs and the private equity firms that invest in them.

**Clients/Work Highlights:** Pediatrix Medical Group; Symbion Healthcare; University Community Health; Mayo Clinic; NationsHealth; Baptist Health Systems; HIG Capital; Palm Beach Capital and JM Family Enterprises.

## Band 2

### Akerman Senterfitt

See firm details p.657

**The Firm:** This healthcare practice group is comprised of 25 lawyers structured as five teams: hospital/institutional; pharmacy and regulatory; physicians; corporate compliance and fraud. Clients point to the proficiency of the group in healthcare litigation, peer review and the representation of institutional providers. The group is also highly recommended for its work on M&A and joint ventures of healthcare facilities. The team's recent successes include advising Ion Beam Applications on the negotiation, transaction and finance of the Florida Proton Therapy Institute project in Jacksonville, a $100 million transaction that will provide the third proton

beam therapy center of its kind in the country.
**The Lawyers:** Peers are keen to work with "*a man of the caliber of* **Kirk Davis** (see p.633), *as you invariably learn something new,*" while clients praise his "*exemplary litigious and technical abilities.*" He is the chair of the group and concentrates on all forms of healthcare litigation, representing hospitals and other healthcare providers in civil and administrative trials. He is also particularly noted for his peer review work. The "*quite exceptional*" **Joseph Rugg** (see p.649) is the managing partner of the Tampa office and practices on the corporate side of healthcare law. Working mostly on private transactions, Rugg has provided assistance to clients who are growing or setting up ambulatory surgery or diagnostic centers. He is well equipped to advise institutional providers and health systems on the corporate and tax aspects of M&A. Clients appreciate **Martin Dix**'s (see p.634) user-friendly mode of practice: "*He is always helpful and flexible and if you are in a pinch, he is there for you.*" "*He has made it his business to be an expert in pharmacy and healthcare law*" and is skilled in all aspects of the drug delivery system. **Valerie Larcombe** (see p.642) has lots of practical experience from her time as general counsel of a hospital and is recommended for her broad practice, which encompasses advice on transactional, regulatory and operational issues. Clients describe **John Schwartz** (see p.650) as "*a low-key character and a supreme technician.*" He focuses on the corporate elements to transactional healthcare and is often found representing institutional providers in the M&A and joint ventures of healthcare institutions.

**Clients/Work Highlights:** Boca Raton Community Hospital; Ion Beam Applications; Jacksonville Orthopaedic Institute; St. Francis Health Services and South Beach Community Hospital.

### Broad and Cassel

**The Firm:** This "*well-rounded,*" full-service firm is a key contender in terms of healthcare work. Perennially involved in some of the best work in the market, its representation of healthcare systems and physician groups is widely recognized. Clients recommended the "*all-around caliber of the group,*" particularly its advice on contentious, compliance and transactional issues. Medicare and Medicaid fraud and abuse criminal, civil and administrative matters are also handled.

**The Lawyers:** "*Clients always get the best representation from*" **Edward Hopkins**. With a stellar reputation and a broad set of skills, he is a popular port of call for healthcare providers and companies seeking advice on issues such as corporate and financial transactions and compliance plan development, including advice on Health Insurance Portability and Accountability Act (HIPAA) compliance. "*As well as being technically brilliant, he is a gentleman too.*" **Gabriel Imperato** is head of the white-collar criminal and civil fraud defense practice group and a key member of the health law practice group. He is experienced in healthcare fraud and abuse and is "*spectacularly good at healthcare litigation, particularly in the problematic cases.*" **Mike Segal** is chair of the health law practice group and utilises his tax and transactional experience to best effect in healthcare cases. He is experienced in both the structuring of joint venture transactions and fraud and abuse cases. "*Skillful operator*" **Lester Perling** is also sought out for his experience in fraud and abuse cases. He is noted for his experience in Medicare and Medicaid

reimbursement issues and corporate compliance programs.

**Clients/Work Highlights:** This group represents hospitals; managed care organizations; health maintenance organizations; nursing homes; pharmaceutical companies and individual physicians. Caremark and Adventist Health are two examples of the caliber of clients this firm has attracted.

## Carlton Fields
See firm details p.661

**The Firm:** This healthcare department is home to 24 attorneys who excel in compliance, regulatory work and litigation. Fraud and abuse is another area of strength. By way of example of the work undertaken this year, the group represented a hospital in a case involving claims by a physician that disciplinary action was motivated by improper reasons. This case involved important issues relating to Florida's statutory immunity for conducting physician peer reviews. Another case of note involved claims by a physician that the non-renewal of a contract was discriminatory. This case involved issues relating to whether medical staff physicians are considered employees of hospitals.

**The Lawyers:** **Don Schmidt** (see p.650) is an attorney who is "*driven to serve the best needs of his clients.*" He is skilled in complex business litigation and is often found counseling healthcare institutions on healthcare matters. His experience in the relations between hospitals and medical staff has made him a sought-after adviser on peer review hearings for many a large healthcare institution. Schmidt also advises hospitals on antitrust issues and is the chair of the firm's healthcare practice group.

**Clients/Work Highlights:** HCA; Health First; Baptist Health System; PharMerica; Indian River Memorial Hospital; Hospice of North Central Florida; Bert Fish Medical Center; Omnicare; North Florida Retirement Village and Lifeline Health Group.

## Fowler White Boggs Banker

**The Firm:** This is one of the largest and oldest firms in the state and it has developed an esteemed healthcare department. Particularly fêted for healthcare litigation and advice on operational issues, this group not only has specialist healthcare attorneys but also draws in attorneys from other practice groups when necessary. Healthcare corporate compliance, nursing home litigation and managed care are at the top of the bill for this group. A distinguishing feature of this firm is its immigration department, which affords clients advice on specific healthcare immigration issues. The group has been involved in a series of class actions brought by uninsured patients during the year.

**The Lawyers:** **Edward Waller** is head of the healthcare group and, according to leading national clients, has "*good judgment, an impressive intellect and is responsive and accessible.*" Waller overlaps his healthcare practice with class action litigation and is a respected and long-standing member of the firm. **Francis Geary** provides "*invaluable counsel and*

*strategic guidance.*" Respected for his prowess in the healthcare litigation field, Geary also handles regulatory compliance and malpractice defense on behalf of physicians.

**Clients/Work Highlights:** Caremark; HCA; IASIS Healthcare; Kindred Healthcare; Omnicare and Tandem healthcare.

## Holland & Knight LLP
See firm details p.1534

**The Firm:** In the healthcare sector, this multinational outfit is "*increasing its presence through involvement in some serious work.*" Clients value the firm's flair on cases that cross-pollinate numerous practice areas, and praise the fact that the firm only hires "*super smart attorneys.*" Work in the healthcare field mostly has a corporate or financial bent to it, such as M&A, refinancings or loan transactions. The team recently acted for SHP Senior Housing Fund in a $130 million refinancing of its Florida independent living facilities. It is also acting as counsel to SantaFe HealthCare in its acquisition and development of senior living communities as part of an expansion into the senior living market.

**The Lawyers:** Clients describe **Morris Miller** (see p.645) as "*bright, knowledgeable and very down to earth.*" As well as being a member of the healthcare transactions and health law practice groups, Miller is also a member of the firm's corporate and M&A department. He is well versed in cases with a real estate finance element to them. A former doctor, **Augustine Weekley** (see p.655) impresses clients with his practical experience in health and hospital law. His knowledge of nursing home law and medical malpractice defense is outstanding. Up-and-comer **Shannon Hartsfield** (see p.639) is favored by clients for her regulatory know-how. She is "*accessible, responsible and knowledgeable.*"

**Clients/Work Highlights:** SHP Senior Housing Fund; SantaFe HealthCare; Sunrise Senior Living and American Retirement Corporation.

## Band 3

## Buchanan Ingersoll PC
See firm details p.1749

**The Firm:** Commentators paid tribute to this healthcare practice, pointing to the knowledge and experience of its attorneys in the group. This Pittsburgh-headquartered firm has offices in eight states and provides clients with an integrated network of offices and nearly 400 lawyers firmwide. The full range is covered, and there are separate groups handling healthcare litigation, the senior care industry, fraud and abuse, and academic medical centers. Work of note includes acting for Tampa General Hospital on the development of a $100 million expansion, the biggest component of which was a new vascular institute.

**The Lawyers:** Peers refer operational or regulatory issues to **James Kennedy** (see p.641) safe in the knowledge "*that he will handle it with his usual excellence.*" Kennedy specialises in healthcare law but is also well versed in general business law and is a member of the firm's executive committee. The "*very bright and very sharp*" **Andrew Rock** (see p.649) impresses with his work on hospital regulatory and operational matters. He is cochair of the firm's HIPAA practice group and is particularly noted for his experience in fraud and abuse and healthcare joint ventures.

**Clients/Work Highlights:** The Tampa General Hospital is a prominent client of the group. Academic medical centers, long-term care nursing homes and physician groups are also on the roster.

## Duane Morris LLP
See firm details p.1753

**The Firm:** This firm has a "*huge national presence in terms of healthcare*" and is growing in stature in the Florida market. Clients appreciate the international reach of its 18 offices and, in terms of healthcare, the sector coverage of the overall healthcare group is a big selling feature. Advice on healthcare fraud and abuse, regulatory and operational issues are key features of the practice, although the negotiation of Medicare and Medicaid reimbursement issues is considered the true forte of the group.

**The Lawyers:** Clients agree that **Joanne Erde** (see p.635) is "*clear-cut, responsive and not one to beat around the bush.*" A leader in the specialty area of healthcare reimbursement, clients find it "*unusual to find an attorney like her who understands the accounting issues as well as the jurisdictional and legal.*" **Nanette O'Donnell** (see p.646) mainly focuses on fraud and abuse, compliance and operational matters and is described as "*one for us all to watch out for.*"

**Clients/Work Highlights:** Hospitals; nonprofit organizations; diagnostic imaging centers and other healthcare providers are the generic staple clients of this group.

## Greenberg Traurig LLP
See firm details p.664

**The Firm:** The overall theme of the market feedback for this Florida giant is its responsiveness and "*ability to manage the expectations of both sides; never one to over-lawyer a situation.*" According to clients, attorneys at this firm are also prepared "*to attack a problem from a business perspective and work through the legal ramifications.*" This health business group provides clients all the added advantages that a multidisciplinary, multinational law firm can offer.

In Florida, the healthcare business department operates mainly out of the Fort Lauderdale office, but the Tallahassee office is also recognized for its regulatory and legislative advice.

**The Lawyers:** **Joel Stocker** (see p.653) is of counsel to the health business group and impresses onlookers with his strong healthcare regulatory practice and the "*client relationships he forges.*" Stocker is the founder of this firm's health law practice and represents clients across a range of corporate and healthcare regulatory compliance matters.

**Clients/Work Highlights:** Hospitals; physicians; home health agencies; medical device companies and managed care organizations are typical clients of this group.

## Hogan & Hartson LLP
See firm details p.568

**The Firm:** Clients rely on this firm for its "*national expertise in health law*" and further find its work product to be "*timely, fee-sensitive and of outstanding quality.*" The healthcare group has four dedicated healthcare partners in the state, but it is the ability and willingness of the group to work with, and draw on, specialist attorneys in other offices that sets it apart. According to one client, "*they just have the depth and expertise to basically provide the full service; on any problem, we consistently get high-quality advice.*" Notably, the firm has represented The Scripps Research Institute in establishing Scripps Florida, a new biomedical research institute that is expected to boost the state's economic development in biotechnology. The group had previously worked with this client on the passage of state legislation and the negotiation of agreements to provide over $500 million in funding for the project.

**The Lawyers:** Clients rate **Mark Sterling** (see p.653) for "*his understanding of the many facets of health law*" and his technical abilities: "*It is rare for an attorney to have such a good grasp of the overall picture yet still have a keen eye on the minutiae.*" Sterling's practice focuses on the intersection between regulatory and transactional work, and he is sought out for his expertise in cases involving the elderly and terminally ill. His corporate and regulatory representation of VITAS Healthcare, the largest provider of hospice and end-of-life services in the country, is a good example of this.

**Clients/Work Highlights:** Adventis Health System; American Hospital Association; Baptist Health South Florida; Beth Abraham Family of Health

Services; Kinderhook Industries; Lifeline Biotechnologies; The Scripps Research Institute; United-Health Group; University of Miami; Vista Healthplan; VITAS Healthcare and WellCare Health Plans.

## Ruden McClosky SC

**The Firm:** This firm has almost 50 years' heritage under its belt and has carved out a name for itself as one of the major players for healthcare litigation. With ten offices across the state and seven attorneys dedicated to healthcare, the firm lives up to its reputation as having a "*real depth to its bench strength.*" Medicare, Medicaid, practice acquisitions and hospital joint ventures are the daily workload for this group, which is also regularly found counseling on fraud and abuse issues and administrative and regulatory healthcare law.

**The Lawyers:** "*Senior figure and astute tactician*" **Chet Barclay** combines healthcare regulatory advice with HIPAA advice and a respected corporate and governmental practice. A key port of call for "*technically knotty issues,*" Barclay concentrates on representing healthcare providers and statewide healthcare associations. Clients rate **Stephen Siegal**'s "*approachability and common sense.*" He is noted particularly for his representation of physicians, and is also thoroughly recommended for his advice on joint ventures and M&A.

**Clients/Work Highlights:** The group represents physicians; physician group practices; pharmaceutical companies; hospitals; nursing homes and integrated service networks.

## Other Notable Practitioners

**Ronald Christaldi** of de la Parte & Gilbert PA in Tampa is recommended for litigious and transactional advice. A key port of call for referrals, Christaldi is a "*hard worker who knows the ins and outs of the market.*" The "*incredibly talented*" **Maria Currier** (see p.632) of Hunton & Williams LLP is a prominent fixture on the managed care scene and is endorsed for her corporate and regulatory advice. **William Spratt** (see p.653) of Kirkpatrick & Lockhart Nicholson Graham LLP provides outstanding advice on a range of healthcare issues. As a former healthcare administrator, he possesses valuable practical experience in the field and is respected for his "*high-quality representation of some high-quality clients.*"

# IMMIGRATION

## Band 1

### Akerman Senterfitt

See firm details p.657

**The Firm:** The outstanding immigration practice group of this national firm undertakes cases for businesses and business people. International personnel transfers to and from the USA are its particular forte. Clients describe **Brian Garcia** (see p.636) as one of the best immigration lawyers in southern Florida. He is *"knowledgeable, professional and reliable"* and a go-to guy for the most complex issues. His recent caseload includes advising a major foreign commercial aircraft manufacturer on the repercussions of its restructuring of its nonimmigrant visas and applications for permanent residency connected with its US operations.

### Fowler White Boggs Banker

**The Firm:** Fowler White's immigration practice represents clients before the Departments of Labor, Homeland Security and State. It represents foreign nationals and corporations employing foreign nationals. Sources credited **William Flynn** as a key member of the group and one who possesses a broad immigration expertise in all manner of business law matters.

### Fragomen, Del Rey, Bernsen & Loewy, LLP

**The Firm:** This national firm has a substantial presence in Florida and a reputation for providing extensive immigration services. The practice has the resources to assist clients on a vast array of issues such as the preparation of immigrant and nonimmigrant visa applications, as well as counseling and training on strategies, policies and staffing solutions. **Enrique Gonzalez** in Coral Gables is widely recognized for high-quality work and his dedication to his cases.

### Greenberg Traurig LLP

See firm details p.664

**The Firm:** Greenberg Traurig has developed one of the most extensive business immigration practices in Florida. Attorneys here benefit from the national and global reach enjoyed by the firm and its capabilities to handle a range of services. The group frequently advises on obtaining US work authorization for foreign nationals and the necessary foreign visas for US clients. It also advises businesses on immigration strategies and policies. Its clients include those drawn from the entertainment, tourist and education sectors. Based in Miami, **Oscar Levin** (see p.643) has extensive federal court trial experience and is skilled in *"the full brushstroke of immigration work."*

### Holland & Knight LLP

See firm details p.1534

**The Firm:** This firm uses its Miami office as a hub for its national immigration practice. It represents companies of various sizes on immigration issues such as transferring executives. Its particular skills lie in complex immigration-related litigation such as defending businesses against charges that they have breached immigration laws and defending individuals in deportation proceedings. It also assists investors and household-name artists and entertainers with their visa requirements. Experienced **Luis Cordero** (see p.632) works on high-level cases such as reviewing and correcting visa irregularities to avoid business interruption and fines for his clients. **Eugenio Hernandez** (see p.639), head of the national immigration practice, is widely respected for his work with businesses and professionals on a range of issues.

### Rifkin and Fox-Isicoff PA

**The Firm:** This Miami-based immigration and nationality law boutique is a great name both in Florida and nationwide. It represents multinational and foreign enterprises and businesses of all sizes as well as individuals. Visas, exclusion, deportation and naturalization are among its vast experience. **Tammy Fox-Isicoff** is an experienced former DOJ attorney with a *"deservedly strong national profile,"* agreed sources. She undertakes federal court work both in business and enforcement and is a highly sophisticated litigator.

### Other Notable Practitioners

Nationally renowned, **Ira Kurzban** of Kurzban, Kurzban, Weinger & Tetzeli PA is *"the grandfather of immigration law,"* said sources. His highly sought-after immigration litigation skills have been honed during numerous federal court cases regarding the rights of aliens. His experience has also been bolstered through his roles as past national president and former general counsel of the American Immigration Lawyers Association. *"Great lawyer and personable too,"* **Anis Saleh** of Saleh & Associates acts on all manner of immigration and nationality law issues as part of his wider employment and family law practice. He is the immediate past chairman of the Florida Bar's Immigration & Nationality Law Certification Committee.

# INSURANCE

## Band 1

### Akerman Senterfitt

See firm details p.657

**The Firm:** This firm is one of the largest in the state and has nearly 40 members in the insurance practice group. In terms of location, the Miami office is the hub of insurance litigation, while the Tallahassee office remains home to a large contingent of specialist regulatory and administrative attorneys. Following the merger with Katz, Kutter, Haigler, Alderman, Bryant & Yon in 2004, onlookers enthuse that this firm has developed its insurance practice and is now one of the few that has *"the all-around package of insurance regulatory and litigation skills."* As well as providing litigious and regulatory advice, this group is also home to attorneys who are dedicated to class action and bad faith litigation and insurance appellate work. The consultative services of the group are also singled out, with the risk avoidance and best practice advice *"often proving to be invaluable in avoiding costly litigation."* The group was successful in getting numerous class action lawsuits against automobile insurers dismissed during the year.

**The Lawyers:** **Marcy Levine Aldrich** (see p.626) impresses with the *"strategic advice"* she provides throughout the course of litigation, and her expertise in handling class actions. She is cochair of the insurance practice group and has been pivotal in getting many class actions against automobile insurers dismissed both at trial and appeals level. **Bruce Culpepper** (see p.632) is famed for his work in the regulatory field, and does *"a wonderful job handling the clientele that moved with the Katz Kutter firm."* He has successfully integrated the litigious and regulatory sides of the insurance group and helped raise the profile of the Tallahassee office. **Allan Katz** (see p.641) is the managing shareholder of the Tallahassee office and is the chair of the firm's policy practice group. Katz is an influential figure in the insurance market and overlaps his regulatory practice with the legislative and governmental affairs practice group. He is a former general counsel of the Florida Department of Insurance and is currently serving as Mayor Pro-Tem and City Commissioner for the City of Tallahassee.

Clients/Work Highlights: The group has been active in the representation of automobile insurers during the year, and is found representing insurance trade associations, health entities, brokers, agents, claims adjusters and self-insured clients.

## Carlton Fields
See firm details p.661

The Firm: This 20-strong insurance litigation and regulation group is distinguished by national clients for *"its ability to expertly handle cases from start to finish."* The full range of high-stakes litigation, regulatory and class action advice is on offer, with clients also pinpointing the efficacy of its specialist government consultants. During the year, the group has defended large insurance class actions, generally on behalf of property insurers, as well as prosecuting a significant rate case involving issues pertaining to the Terrorism Risk Insurance Act of 2002.

The Lawyers: **Daniel Brown** (see p.630) is cochair of this insurance and regulation practice group, and many clients dub him *"the go-to person"* in northern Florida for insurance. *"Professional, responsive and always delivering what he promises,"* his hallmark is his *"thorough preparation, conceptual understanding of the case and firm grasp of the nuances."* Aggressive when needs be, Brown is the attorney of choice *"if you have a war on your hands."* **Kelly Cruz-Brown** (see p.632) *"really understands the true nature of the laws"* in part due to her time at the Florida Department of Insurance. She primarily practices in the areas of insurance regulation and administrative law. **Robert Pass** (see p.646) embodies all the qualities of the firm through *"his technical knowledge and real flair for cross-examination."*

Clients/Work Highlights: AIG; Prudential Financial; State Farm; Golden Rule Insurance and TIG Insurance.

## Fowler White Boggs Banker

The Firm: One of the cornerstones of the insurance law market in Florida, this firm is heartily recommended by clients for its litigation prowess: *"If you need a firm skilled in class action defense, you need look no further."* Its work in the regulatory field and its advice to clients concerning the rights and obligations of parties to an insurance contract are also formidable.

The Lawyers: **Donald Cox** is head of the litigation department and is hugely experienced in insurance regulatory litigation. Acclaimed for *"effortlessly doing a superb job,"* Cox has been defending national clients in large class actions during the year. **Charles Wachter** is another regular face on the insurance scene and garners support from clients for his *"vast experience of litigation in the insurance market."* Wachter is particularly skilled in consumer cases and big-ticket class actions.

Clients/Work Highlights: John Hancock, AIG and MetLife are representative of the firm's major insurance clients.

## Band 2
### Foley & Lardner LLP
See firm details p.2037

The Firm: The insurance practice of this large national outfit spans the litigation and regulatory spheres and is further divided into distinct areas such as insurance taxation, reinsurance and transactional matters. The firm's insurance M&A practice is widely commended, with clients appreciating the fact that the group can easily draw on other groups to *"get the best possible person on the case."* Its insurance taxation practice is a further distinguishing feature, and attorneys often advise on tax planning and tax controversy matters. As the insurance group is based in Tallahassee, it comes as no surprise that it is also respected in terms of regulatory representation.

The Lawyers: **Thomas Maida** (see p.643) is the managing partner of the Tallahassee office and stands out for his understanding of workers'

compensation and regulatory issues, a statement illustrated by his service as general counsel to the Florida Workers' Compensation Joint Underwriting Association. His litigious capabilities do not go unnoticed either: *"He's great on his feet and on paper."* Up-and-comer **Austin Neal** (see p.646) has played an important role in some of the market's significant cases. A *"young, smart attorney,"* he is one to watch.

Clients/Work Highlights: The group has a varied client base, including insurance companies, broker-dealers and mutual funds.

## Holland & Knight LLP
See firm details p.1534

The Firm: Commentators agreed on *"the proficiency of the firm in all forms of regulatory work,"* and were equally as complimentary in terms of its trial capabilities. Following the recent streamlining of its offices throughout Florida, this firm has taken a renewed focus both in the state and nationwide. Its ability to draw on specialists in New York and other states, and in Washington, DC is a real drawing card for clients.

The Lawyers: **Thomas Jones** (see p.641) is a commercial litigator whose practice focuses on insurance regulatory issues. A problem solver, Jones is widely seen as *"thorough, business-oriented and a consummate professional."* Also, peers are happy to refer work to him *"safe in the knowledge it is in good hands."* He is often found before the regulatory agencies and is particularly skilled in the field of care facilities.

Clients/Work Highlights: The firm advises a range of insurers, brokers, agents and adjusters.

## Pennington, Moore, Wilkinson, Bell & Dunbar, PA

The Firm: This firm is one of the largest firms in Tallahassee and its flagship governmental affairs department has garnered support from all corners of the market. *"The first choice for regulatory work"* for many a client, this firm is well placed at the seat of Florida government to make valuable representations. The insurance regulatory practice is closely aligned to the governmental affairs practice and clients find this an effective and useful alliance in the provision of regulatory advice. Clients seek out this firm for advice on lobbying on state issues, but moreover it is the *"practical knowledge"* of the seven-strong group that is most admired. They point to the usefulness of the special consultants at the firm, many of whom have previously held positions in public office. The firm is also home to an insurance defense, medical malpractice defense and workers' compensation law group, a full service that provides *"great value for money"* according to clients.

The Lawyers: **Mark Delegal** is one of the hardest-working attorneys in the capital. An *"engaging and thorough attorney,"* he has a low-key approach, *"until that is, you get him on an issue he's passionate about, then he really gets his teeth into it."* Delegal is head of the governmental and legislative affairs practice group and also a key member of the insurance groups.

**Clients/Work Highlights:** State Farm; New York Life; First Professionals Insurance and ProAssurance.

## Radey, Thomas, Yon & Clark

**The Firm:** This firm has "*a significant amount of insurance law talent*" and is reported to have several "*good people coming up through the ranks*". It is for this reason, and the fact that the group is seen as "*exponentially developing*," that many described the firm as a hot tip for the future. Focusing predominantly on insurance, including regulatory and litigious representation, it is experienced in rate and form filings and property and casualty matters. The firm is also recommended for its transactional work arising out of the insurance sector.

**The Lawyers:** **David Yon** is much sought after for his regulatory know-how and his expertise in property and casualty matters, especially rate and form disputes on the property side. Clients also commended **Harry Thomas**'s trial skills in the insurance arena: "*When he litigates, he does it properly.*" Thomas focuses his practice on litigation and appellate advocacy and is also experienced in class action defense.

**Clients/Work Highlights:** Allstate is a key client of the group.

## Band 3

### Broad and Cassel

**The Firm:** Although not historically known for its work in the insurance field, the arrival of Ken Levine as chairman of the insurance and financial services practice has significantly raised the profile of this group. Regulatory and litigious insurance advice is on offer, and clients were quick to point to the strength of the insurance group in terms of warranty and service contract compliance programs, licensing issues, expansion applications and insurance contractual work.

**The Lawyers:** **Ken Levine** has a distinguished track record in the insurance market. "*A real details man,*" he has represented several trade associations on such matters as bid protests and rule challenges, and he also serves as national warranty counsel to numerous computer, electronic and appliance manufacturers.

**Clients/Work Highlights:** Levine serves as retained counsel for, inter alia, Philips Magnavox, Frigidaire and IBM, and also acts as general counsel to the American Manufacturers Warranty Association. He has recently been appointed to serve on the insurance advisory board of LexisNexis/Matthew Bender and a national workers' compensation insurer.

### Butler Pappas Weihmuller Katz Craig LLP

**The Firm:** This general civil practice law firm is home to over 90 attorneys and is much sought after for its powerful insurance defense and insurance

contracts practice. It is "*full of real smart attorneys providing good rates for clients.*" This firm may not have the regulatory prowess of some of the other firms in the state, but is seen as "*a perennial contender for the high-profile work.*" This group defends a plethora of clients in all types of coverage, liability, fire and theft, subrogation and extracontractual claims. The firm also has respected appellate and class action departments.

**The Lawyers:** John Pappas is a key contact in the firm.

**Clients/Work Highlights:** Many of the best-known names in the insurance world have instructed this firm to defend them: these include Allianz; Chubb Group; First State Insurance; John Hancock; Zurich American Insurance Company; Liberty Mutual and Royal & SunAlliance.

### Other Notable Practitioners

**Michael Colodny** of Colodny, Fass, Talenfeld, Karlinsky & Abate PA is a regular face on the insurance scene. He is the general counsel for Citizens Property Insurance and is a well-connected figure in the state. **Timothy Meenan** of Blank, Meenan & Smith PA is swiftly becoming "*one of the go-to guys in the state,*" and has amassed an impressive level of support for his insurance regulatory practice. He is general counsel for several insurer trade associations and is frequently called in to assist specialty insurers on such matters as obtaining licensure.

# LITIGATION

| Litigation: General Commercial |
| --- |
| Leading Firms |

| | |
| --- | --- |
| **1** | GREENBERG TRAURIG LLP *Miami* |
| | KENNY NACHWALTER PA *Miami* |
| | PODHURST ORSECK P.A. *Miami* |
| **2** | AKERMAN SENTERFITT *Orlando* |
| | COLSON HICKS EIDSON *Coral Gables* |
| | HILL, WARD & HENDERSON, PA *Tampa* |
| | HUNTON & WILLIAMS LLP *Miami* |
| | KOZYAK TROPIN & THROCKMORTON *Coral Gables* |
| **3** | BEDELL, DITTMAR, DEVAULT, PILLANS *Jacksonville* |
| | CARLTON FIELDS *Miami* |
| | HOGAN & HARTSON LLP *Miami* |
| | HOLLAND & KNIGHT LLP *Tallahassee* |
| | KING, BLACKWELL & DOWNS PA *Orlando* |
| | RICHMAN GREER WEIL BRUMBAUGH *Miami* |
| | SHOOK, HARDY & BACON LLP *Miami* |
| | STEARNS WEAVER MILLER WEISSLER *Miami* |
| | ZUCKERMAN SPAEDER LLP *Miami* |
| **4** | BERGER SINGERMAN *Fort Lauderdale* |
| | BILZIN SUMBERG BAENA PRICE & AXELROD *Miami* |
| | DEAN, MEAD, EGERTON, BLOODWORTH *Orlando* |
| | JONES, FOSTER, JOHNSTON *West Palm Beach* |
| | KLUGER, PERETZ, KAPLAN & BERLIN PL *Miami* |
| | SQUIRE, SANDERS & DEMPSEY LLP *Miami* |

### Greenberg Traurig LLP

See firm details p.664

**The Firm:** This Florida behemoth is not only one of the biggest firms in Florida, but one of the fastest growing nationally. According to some of the most sophisticated international purchasers of legal services, it certainly lives up to its illustrious reputation for first-class client service and for the depth of talented attorneys on offer. The firm is skilled in the full range of litigation, from complex general commercial litigation to white-collar crime and appeals. It has an emphasis on the defense of large class actions and during the year has been involved in some of the largest civil judgments ever entered. Examples include successfully representing Lorillard Tobacco in the appeal from the $145 billion judgment against the five major American tobacco companies, and further arguing the case on discretionary review before the Florida Supreme Court. The firm was also approached by the Attorney General of Chile to help locate funds allegedly hidden by General Augusto Pinochet, a case that attracted much media attention in the year.

**The Lawyers:** Clients point to the "*extensive mass tort experience*" and "*infinite international resources*" of this trial team as overriding factors for the success it enjoys. **Barry Richard** (see p.648) has developed a

strong appellate and civil litigation practice, and he is also respected for his constitutional and election law experience, having argued before the Florida Supreme Court in the 2000 Bush-Gore litigation. Richard has been successfully involved in a $3.5 billion, seven-week jury trial on behalf of Alliance Capital Management over the past year. **David Ross** (see p.649) "*has many feathers in his cap.*" A talented trial lawyer, with a forte in antitrust law, he has been heavily engaged in tobacco litigation this year. He also successfully acted as counsel to the Sugar Cane Growers Cooperative in the appeal of a long-running multimillion-dollar class action alleging breach of contract. **Hilarie Bass** (see p.628) is chair of the national litigation practice group and has represented Microsoft in the resolution of a national class action in 2005. In the white-collar crime and government investigations field, **Mark Schnapp** (see p.650) is praised for his "*wonderful reputation for representing corporations under scrutiny.*" According to sources, "*he can master a million facts and effortlessly synthesize them all together,*" and is widely respected for his "*virtual wizardry*" in SEC investigations and healthcare fraud and abuse cases. **Holly Skolnick** (see p.652) is "*another of the spectacularly talented attorneys at this firm.*" She represented an international financial institution and research analyst in

## Litigation: General Commercial
### Leading Individuals

**1** DEVAULT John *Bedell, Dittmar, DeVault, Pillans*
HILL III Benjamin *Hill, Ward & Henderson, PA*
NACHWALTER Michael *Kenny Nachwalter PA*
RICHARD Barry *Greenberg Traurig LLP*

GREER Alan *Richman Greer Weil Brumbaugh Mirabito*
JOSEFSBERG Robert *Podhurst Orseck P.A.*
PODHURST Aaron *Podhurst Orseck P.A.*
TROPIN Harley *Kozyak Tropin & Throckmorton*

**2** COLSON Dean *Colson Hicks Eidson*
DAVIS Alvin *Squire, Sanders & Dempsey LLP*
KING David *King, Blackwell & Downs PA*
MARTINEZ Roberto *Colson Hicks Eidson*
MOSS Edward *Shook, Hardy & Bacon LLP*
ROSS David *Greenberg Traurig LLP*
STEINBERG Marty *Hunton & Williams LLP*
WAKSHLAG Stanley *Kenny Nachwalter PA*

CRITCHLOW Richard *Kenny Nachwalter PA*
GONZALEZ Ervin *Colson Hicks Eidson*
LILES Rutledge *Liles, Gavin, Costantino & Murphy*
MATTHEWS Joseph *Colson Hicks Eidson*
REID Benjamine *Carlton Fields*
STEARNS Eugene *Stearns Weaver Miller Weissler Alhadeff*
STUBBS Sidney *Jones, Foster, Johnston & Stubbs, PA*

**3** BASS Hilarie *Greenberg Traurig LLP*
BRUMBAUGH John *Richman Greer Weil Brumbaugh*
DIAZ JR Victor *Podhurst Orseck P.A.*
HELLER William *Akerman Senterfitt*
LICKO Carol *Hogan & Hartson LLP*
NICHOLS Tracy *Holland & Knight LLP*
REILLY Kenneth *Shook, Hardy & Bacon LLP*
SASSO Gary *Carlton Fields*
THOMSON Parker *Hogan & Hartson LLP*
YOUNG Terry *Lowndes Drosdick Doster Kantor*

BLOODWORTH Darryl *Dean, Mead, Egerton, Bloodworth*
DAVIDSON Barry *Hunton & Williams LLP*
FROST II John *Frost Tamayo Sessums & Aranda PA*
HILL William *Bilzin Sumberg*
MEEKS Thomas *Zuckerman Spaeder LLP*
PILLANS III Charles *Bedell, Dittmar, DeVault, Pillans*
RICHMAN Gerald *Richman Greer Weil Brumbaugh*
SOTO Edward *Weil, Gotshal & Manges LLP*
SPECTOR Brian *Kenny Nachwalter PA*

**4** BECERRA Jacqueline *Greenberg Traurig LLP*
BLOOMBERG Mitchell *Adorno & Yoss LLP*
CARRIUOLO Anthony *Berger Singerman*
FOSTER Joseph *Akerman Senterfitt*
HAMILTON William *Holland & Knight LLP*
LOWRY Patricia *Squire, Sanders & Dempsey LLP*
RONZETTI Tucker *Kozyak Tropin & Throckmorton*
SINGER Stuart *Boies, Schiller & Flexner LLP*

BIANCHI Jaime *White & Case LLP*
BROWN Christopher *Shook, Hardy & Bacon LLP*
DANON Samuel *Hunton & Williams LLP*
GONZÁLEZ Daniel *Hogan & Hartson LLP*
KREITZER Michael *Bilzin Sumberg*
RAVIKOFF Ronald *Zuckerman Spaeder LLP*
SILVERMAN Steve *Kluger, Peretz, Kaplan*
TEW Thomas *Tew Cardenas LLP*

### Up-and-coming individuals
GERAGHTY William *Shook, Hardy & Bacon LLP*

### Associates to watch
GONZALEZ Eduardo *Hunton & Williams LLP*
ROSENTHAL Stephen *Podhurst Orseck P.A.*

hundreds of securities arbitrations alleging fraud and conflict of interest. She also has a broad experience of investigations and enforcement actions brought by the SEC. "*Superstar in the making*" **Jacqueline Becerra** (see p.628) is "*wonderfully smart*" and "*aggressive and tough.*"

**Clients/Work Highlights:** Lorillard Tobacco; Alliance Capital Management; Anheuser-Busch; Regents Bank; Morgan Stanley and Hilton Hotels.

### Kenny Nachwalter PA
See firm details p.666
**The Firm:** This 21-attorney business litigation boutique "*sits proudly at the top of the tree*" through "*its countless experienced attorneys*" and its "*reputation for success,*" agree sources. "*Quality through and through,*" it benefits from a range of litigious expertise that includes securities, IP, employment and white-collar crime, as well as prowess in antitrust litigation. This firm concentrates on a small number of large, complex cases and even though it is recognized more for its work on the plaintiff side, it also has a great track record in defense. Indicative of this, the firm is

currently representing one of the four major defendant insurance companies in complex HMO litigation.
**The Lawyers:** According to peers, **Michael Nachwalter**'s (see p.646) name "*echoes greatness.*" He enjoys a national reputation and has a practice that encompasses antitrust and trade regulation as well as all forms of complex federal and state litigation. Clients are full of admiration for the "*absolutely top-notch*" **Richard Critchlow** (see p.632). "*Terrific both on his feet and on paper,*" he has the full range of business-related litigation in his arsenal, and is noted for his corporate, securities and professional liability know-how. Gifted trial lawyer **Brian Spector** (see p.652) overlaps his practice with teaching at the University of Miami School of Law. He is "*an extremely hard-working and technically proficient litigator; he knows all the laws and rules inside out.*" His caseload has seen an increasing number of mediations and arbitrations, alongside his trial work in securities and legal malpractice disputes. A coup for the firm this year was the arrival of **Stanley Wakshlag** (see p.655) from Akerman Senterfitt. His wealth of knowledge and high-quality advice ensures he

meets even the most demanding client's expectations. "*Thorough, experienced and client-driven,*" he is a good project manager and "*hands-on and tough when needs be.*"

**Clients/Work Highlights:** The firm mostly represents major corporations, but law firms, accountants, directors and officers also feature on the client roster. Its clients are drawn from a range of industries, from real estate to pharmaceutical and telecom.

### Podhurst Orseck P.A.
See firm details p.670
**The Firm:** This 15-strong firm is an alliance of "*some seriously talented individuals,*" who "*are stronger overall than most others in the market.*" The talents of its effective litigators span general commercial litigation, white-collar crime and appeals, and the firm attracts clients to its general tort and aviation litigation practice. Mass torts and plaintiff representation are the hallmarks of the firm, with commercial disputes comprising over half its practice. This firm is a favored port of call for clients and entrepreneurs who do not want to adhere to the big-firm culture, but instead prefer to work with a business and fee model more in harmony with their own enterprise. The firm has been involved in some headline-grabbing cases this year, including suing the PLO on behalf of two people who were killed by terrorists in Israel and acting in a civil case for damages against the baseball player Jose Canseco. The firm serves as litigation counsel for Perry Ellis and is representing over 750,000 doctors across the country in a large class action against most of the major US medical insurance carriers.

**The Lawyers:** "*Phenomenal*" **Robert Josefsberg** (see p.641) "*has been one of the finest lawyers in Florida for many years now.*" He "*not only talks a good fight, but also fights a good fight.*" He is often found on the most newsworthy cases, and is brought in to represent other law firms in litigation such as malpractice suits. He has such a broad-based skill set that he is also respected for his work in the field of white-collar crime and government investigations. **Aaron Podhurst** (see p.647) impresses with his understanding of the nuances of a trial; he is first choice to pick a jury, said commentators who pointed to his "*versatility and courtroom skills.*" He is heavily involved in plaintiff aviation litigation and is also liaison counsel in one of the largest class actions to date, the representation of over 750,000 doctors against most of the major US medical insurance carriers. **Victor Diaz** (see p.634) is "*one of the keys to the firm's future success.*" A "*real mover and shaker,*" Diaz serves as principal litigation counsel to both Codina Group and Alienware. The firm is also home to some of the state's most talented young attorneys, of which the "*extremely intelligent*" associate **Stephen Rosenthal** (see p.649) is one. "*He can only get better through the experience he will gain from his involvement in the high-profile cases a firm like this undertakes,*" said clients.

**Clients/Work Highlights:** Ryder System; Mellon United National Bank; Lennar Corporation and Florida East Coast Industries.

## Litigation: White-Collar Crime & Government Investigations

### Leading Firms

**1** **BLACK, SREBNICK, KORNSPAN & STUMPF** *Miami*
**GREENBERG TRAURIG LLP** *Miami*
**MOSCOWITZ, MOSCOWITZ & MAGOLNICK** *Miami*
**RASKIN & RASKIN PA** *Miami*
**ZUCKERMAN SPAEDER LLP** *Miami*

**2** **BEDELL, DITTMAR, DEVAULT, PILLANS** *Jacksonville*
**COLSON HICKS EIDSON** *Coral Gables*
**GEORGE & TITUS PA** *Tampa*
**HOLLAND & KNIGHT LLP** *Miami*
**LEVENTHAL & SLAUGHTER PA** *Orlando*
**PODHURST ORSECK** *Miami*
**RUDEN MCCLOSKY, S.C.** *Fort Lauderdale*
**SALE & KUEHNE PA** *Miami*

### Leading Individuals

**1** **AARON William** *William Aaron*
**BLACK Roy** *Black, Srebnick, Kornspan*
**BRONIS Stephen** *Zuckerman Spaeder LLP*
**CHAYKIN Steven** *Zuckerman Spaeder LLP*
**HOGAN John** *Holland & Knight LLP*
**JOSEFSBERG Robert** *Podhurst Orseck P.A.*
**MARTINEZ Roberto** *Colson Hicks Eidson*
**MOSCOWITZ Jane** *Moscowitz, Moscowitz & Magolnick*
**MOSCOWITZ Norman** *Moscowitz, Moscowitz*
**PASANO Michael** *Zuckerman Spaeder LLP*
**RASKIN Jane** *Raskin & Raskin PA*
**RASKIN Martin** *Raskin & Raskin PA*
**SCHNAPP Mark** *Greenberg Traurig LLP*
**ZIMET Bruce** *Bruce A Zimet PA*

**2** **CACCIATORE Ronald** *Ronald K Cacciatore PA*
**COXE Henry** *Bedell, Dittmar, DeVault*
**GEORGE Peter** *George & Titus PA*
**JUNG William** *Jung & Sisco*
**KUEHNE Benedict** *Sale & Kuehne PA*
**LEVENTHAL Robert** *Leventhal & Slaughter PA*
**MANDEL David** *Mandel & Mandel LLP*
**MASON J Cheney** *J Cheney Mason PA*
**NORTMAN William** *Akerman Senterfitt*
**NURIK Marc** *Ruden McClosky, S.C.*
**PRIETO Peter** *Holland & Knight LLP*
**QUIÑON Jose** *Sole Practitioner*
**SALE Jon** *Sale & Kuehne PA*
**SHOHAT Edward** *Bierman, Shohat, Loewy*
**SKOLNICK Holly** *Greenberg Traurig LLP*
**SLAUGHTER JR Harrison** *Leventhal & Slaughter PA*
**SONNETT Neal** *Neal Sonnett PA*
**SREBNICK Howard** *Black, Srebnick, Kornspan*
**STEINBERG Marty** *Hunton & Williams LLP*
**TARBE Susan** *Colson Hicks Eidson*
**TROMBLEY Gary** *Trombley & Hanes*
**UDOLF Bruce** *Berger Singerman*
**WEINBERG JR Morris** *Zuckerman Spaeder LLP*

## Akerman Senterfitt

See firm details p.657

**The Firm:** Clients point to the *"very deep bench strength and excellence across the board"* as the drawing cards for this expanding full-service law firm. With three former judges, 21 commercial litigators and a presence in New York and DC, this is one of the largest commercial litigation departments in the state and is fully equipped to handle the most complex, high-level cases. Securities litigation is a recognized forte of the group, although the full range, including class actions, white-collar criminal defense and patent infringement is covered. Work of note in the past year includes representing Rolls-Royce in an action brought by Royal Caribbean Cruises alleging that Rolls-Royce sold defective propulsion systems on four cruise ships with prices totaling $1.3 billion. The firm is also building up a portfolio of national clients; it is currently acting as national coordinating counsel for Samsung North America.

**The Lawyers:** *"Absolute gentleman with a good sense for litigation strategy,"* **William Heller**'s (see p.639) *"intricate knowledge"* of mortgage foreclosures, class actions and consumer protection does not go unnoticed by clients. He is *"ahead of most lawyers when tracking the trends in the law,"* and has recently acted in Laslo v Countrywide Home Loans, a case involving claims for unlawful auto-debiting. **Joseph Foster** (see p.636) impresses with his *"ability to cut through the minutiae to solve a problem; he doesn't just follow the rabbit trail of discovery."* Judged to *"always look at the equitable solution and give the best way forward for both parties,"* he is particularly experienced in financial institution litigation and has recently represented National Health Investors as lead counsel in the $16 million foreclosure of three nursing homes.

**Clients/Work Highlights:** International Speedway Corporation; SunTrust Banks; FINOVA Capital; GE Transportation/GE Infrastructure; Samsung of North America; National Health Investors; Qantum Communications; Rolls-Royce; Countrywide Home Loans; Asset Acceptance; Aurora Loan Services and Collect America.

## Colson Hicks Eidson

See firm details p.662

**The Firm:** Clients were quick to distinguish this firm from others in the market for its proficiency in every facet of litigation, including commercial litigation, white-collar crime and appellate law: *"It covers the whole caboodle."* Home to 15 of the *"best and most widely respected attorneys in the state,"* its experience in products liability, wrongful death liability, professional malpractice and business litigation is where the firm shines. Clients also value the spectrum of expertise housed under one roof: *"There is no need to go anywhere else: they handle cases from start to finish."*

**The Lawyers:** **Dean Colson** (see p.631) is a *"huge presence in the community"* and *"a behind the scenes power player – extremely talented and effective."* He focuses on personal injury and commercial cases. According to market authorities, *"no one can connect*

*better to a jury"* than **Ervin Gonzalez** (see p.638); *"he has a real gift for it."* *"Preparation is 90% of the game and he is always 100% prepared"* and hones his practice on civil trial law and business litigation. **Roberto Martinez** (see p.644) is the epitome of a successful trial lawyer; respected by all, a great counselor and *"a real fighter when he needs to be."* Martinez is a former US attorney with a combined white-collar criminal defense and civil law practice. According to clients, **Joseph Matthews** (see p.644) is *"great in the courtroom; he instills a sense of security in his client."* He is a respected arbitrator and focuses his practice on business, fraud and professional liability litigation. The *"tenacious and extraordinarily well-prepared,"* **Susan Tarbe** (see p.654) has a comprehensive white-collar crime practice. Drawing on her experience as a former assistant US attorney, Tarbe focuses on civil and criminal healthcare fraud, SEC enforcement and internal corporate investigations.

## Hill, Ward & Henderson, PA

**The Firm:** Clients favor this 30-strong litigation group for its service to broad-reaching operations, depth of talent and extensive repertoire of experience. *"Ethical, client-focused and talented"* is a typical comment from clients. It is currently defending Honeywell in litigation involving allegations of general fraud. There is also a respected healthcare litigation practice group.

**The Lawyers:** Head of the firm's litigation group, **Ben Hill** is *"not only a gentleman but also one of the premier trial lawyers in Florida"* according to sources. He is *"disciplined, organized and articulate"* and has a diverse practice that includes professional liability, products liability and general commercial matters. A large law firm has also retained Hill to represent it in a legal malpractice case.

**Clients/Work Highlights:** DaimlerChrysler; Honeywell; Asbury Automotive Group; Pulte Homes; All Children's Hospital and some of the largest law firms in the country are clients.

## Hunton & Williams LLP

See firm details p.1989

**The Firm:** According to clients, this firm has a good bench strength and can be relied upon to do *"a comprehensively high-quality job."* An international law firm with 850 attorneys and 17 offices, it certainly has the resources to handle even the most complex commercial litigation, and the depth of experience in the Miami office is no exception. The group is well versed in commercial disputes, antitrust, business and IP litigation. It recently represented Diageo North America in a breach of contract, tort and RICO action brought by one of its distributors. The potential damages were in excess of $1 billion and the plaintiff voluntarily dismissed the case after witnesses were discredited on cross-examination.

**The Lawyers:** **Marty Steinberg** (see p.653) is the Miami office managing partner and *"has brilliantly built up the Miami office to have a great presence and reputation in the community."* A *"pure technician,"* he earns the support of clients for *"working harder than* *most – he is always meticulously prepared in the courtroom."* His practice combines antitrust, commercial litigation and white-collar disputes. Senior litigator **Barry Davidson** (see p.633) adopts a *"thoughtful and skillful approach"* when handling complex commercial cases. He has had a busy year and was co-lead counsel in the defense of the Government of Belize in a nonjury trial involving investment for the modernization of the telephone system. **Samuel Danon** (see p.633) wins clients with his *"approachable demeanor, excellent courtroom presence and strong cross-examination."* Danon focuses on commercial litigation and has particular experience in franchise litigation and government relations. Associate **Eduardo Gonzalez** (see p.637) *"has got a great future ahead of him"* according to clients, particularly in the field of domestic and international arbitration.

Clients/Work Highlights: Pfizer; Diageo; BellSouth; Bacardi; Bausch & Lomb; Carnival Corporation; CIGNA; ExxonMobil and Ryder Systems.

## Kozyak Tropin & Throckmorton
See firm details p.668
The Firm: This firm commands client approval for its experience of securities fraud and bankruptcy litigation: *"When I think of great Florida litigation firms, I think of this one first."* This is not the extent of this firm's practice however, as clients also heartily recommend its mastery of professional malpractice, class actions and IP litigation. The firm is co-lead counsel in one of the largest class actions in history against the healthcare industry. The firm represents a nationwide class of over 750,000 physicians who are challenging the historic billing and payment practices of some of the nation's largest HMOs. So far, seven settlements totaling more than $4 billion have been reached.
The Lawyers: **Harley Tropin** (see p.654) *"is successful in getting the desired results for his clients"* and is one of the most preeminent plaintiff lawyers for complex class actions in the state. He is respected by the courts as *"an ethical and smart attorney who is a pleasure to deal with."* He also *"takes the reckoning of issues to a different level through his tenacity and insight."* Although Tropin is seen as being the star of the firm, **Tucker Ronzetti** (see p.649) also features high in clients' affections.
Clients/Work Highlights: Trustees, receivers, large medical societies or significant institutions facing 'bet the company' litigation utilize the services of this firm.

## Bedell, Dittmar, DeVault, Pillans & Coxe
The Firm: This is the oldest law firm in Florida and comes thoroughly recommended by clients for both commercial litigation and white-collar crime. The firm handles all kinds of state and federal trial and appellate work, including professional malpractice defense, products liability and construction litigation. Its 15 attorneys are adept at handling virtually any form of litigation and are classed as *"among the best in Florida."* A recent highlight includes successfully defending a large law firm in a legal malpractice case involving a substantial claim for damages.
The Lawyers: *"The doyen of trial lawyers,"* **John DeVault** wins praise for his performances in court: *"He comes across as the sincerest, most down-to-earth, personable human being you can imagine – you just trust everything he says,"* according to clients. **Charles Pillans** impresses with his accounting malpractice and securities litigation acumen. In terms of white-collar work, **Henry Coxe** is *"the go-to guy"* at this establishment. He is the current president elect of the Florida Bar and widely sought after for his experience in the criminal sphere.
Clients/Work Highlights: A significant portion of the client base is acquired through referrals from other law firms, and is predominantly Florida-based companies or individuals such as legal professionals.

## Carlton Fields
See firm details p.661
The Firm: Clients familiar with the Florida litigation Bar endorsed this long-established firm's *"experience in the trenches"* and *"ethos of practicing law with an unwavering commitment to the client."* They also appreciate the *"responsive, professional, experienced, well-trained and effective unit,"* which is experienced in a range of business disputes. Class action defense, securities, products liability and real estate litigation are particular strengths of the group. A significant recent appointment includes work on a sizable national class action for State Farm involving thousands of flood insurance policies, and representing Bell Sports in Jones v Bell Sports. The latter case involved a claim for damages that asserted the design of a bicycle helmet was defective, a claim that was defeated following a five-week trial.
The Lawyers: **Benjamine Reid** (see p.648) is *"an admired trial lawyer who can turn his hand to any form of litigation"* and has a fair share of class action litigation and appellate cases under his belt. **Gary Sasso** (see p.650) is head of the litigation department and *"exhibits a high degree of competence and professionalism."* Clients find him *"responsible, and respectful"* and fondly relived *"the many scrapes he has pulled us through by his efficient marshaling of resources and winning oral arguments."*
Clients/Work Highlights: AT&T; Altria Corporate Services (Philip Morris); Bell Sports; Ford; PwC; Progress Energy Service Company; RJ Reynolds; Pfizer; Wachovia; WCI Communities; Wyeth and Cendant Timeshare Resort Group.

## Hogan & Hartson LLP
See firm details p.568
The Firm: This international player remains a fixture on the litigation scene in Florida and with over 300 international litigators, it is no surprise that clients appreciate *"its experience in complex, high-stakes cases"* and *"its reach and resources."* The complete scope of complex commercial litigation is covered by this 22-strong team, although constitutional law cases, consumer protection, antitrust and litigation in the healthcare field are particular areas of note. The group is involved in ongoing water rights litiga-

tion, representing the State of Florida in three cases in the federal district courts in Alabama, Georgia and the District of Columbia; these cases involve water rights to the river waters flowing through the Apalachicola-Chattahoochee-Flint Basin. The firm is also representing News Corporation in a stockholder's dispute filed by Darlene Investments alleging damages in excess of $1 billion.
The Lawyers: Senior statesman and *"civic leader"* **Parker Thomson** (see p.654) is the Miami office managing partner and represents Florida in the water rights litigation. According to clients, *"the wisdom he has gained through his illustrious practice is hard to duplicate"* and he has a courtroom style that *"is convincing and compelling without being forceful."* **Carol Licko** (see p.643) is a talented complex commercial litigator, who draws on her background in constitutional law and has an eclectic practice including appellate work, healthcare and business litigation. Licko has successfully settled a federal court action filed against Medical Savings Insurance Company in a case that established a favorable ruling on the confidentiality of the client's agreements with other insurance companies. **Dan González** (see p.638) *"adopts astute techniques, is a very polished performer and regularly utilizes his experience to best effect."* González is the director of the firm's international litigation and arbitration practice. He has a useful accounting background, and is someone clients *"regularly turn to for international litigation advice."*
Clients/Work Highlights: Florida Hospital; State of Florida; Florida Department of Environmental Protection; The Scripps Research Institute and Miami-Dade College.

## Holland & Knight LLP
See firm details p.1534
The Firm: Clients feel that when they retain this *"prestigious firm,"* they are *"working with attorneys at the top of their field."* As well as the diverse range of litigation covered and the resources on offer, distinguishing factors for this firm include the industry-specific knowledge of the attorneys and their *"fee sensitivity."* The firm excels in all forms of complex commercial litigation, specifically its securities and white-collar litigation expertise.
The Lawyers: Clients feel that **Tracy Nichols** (see p.646) is *"worthy of special mention"* because of her *"control of difficult situations."* She is *"incredibly confident and smart in her approach to cases."* Nichols' practice emphasizes securities shockholder litigation and class actions and she is the national practice group leader for the securities litigation group. **William Hamilton** (see p.639) is *"a very intelligent man; he can grasp the complexities of a case and then strategically lay down a path on how to approach the dispute."* IP class action defense and the telecom and general technology fields form a significant portion of his caseload. In terms of white-collar crime, *"you cannot get better than"* chair of the litigation practice **John Hogan** (see p.640). He is well connected, *"a pillar of sensitivity"* and understands the pressures his clients face during investigations or criminal proceedings, often utilizing his previous experience

at the DOJ to best effect. Seasoned professional **Peter Prieto** (see p.647) is also a skilled white-collar litigator. He is thorough in his advice and pays great attention to his clients. As a former federal prosecutor, he is respected for his "*trial experience and plain-speaking good judgment*" in the criminal sphere.
**Clients/Work Highlights:** This firm's diverse client base ranges from Fortune 500 companies to small business and nonprofit organizations.

## King, Blackwell & Downs PA

**The Firm:** This compact litigation boutique has secured its membership of the Florida litigation elite through its practical advice, "*trusted personal service*" and the broad skill sets of its six attorneys. It has represented Boeing in the resolution of a billion-dollar trade secrets case, and successfully acted for a large Houston law firm in a malpractice case arising from a claim for misrepresentation and a $51 million verdict during the year.
**The Lawyers: David King** "*is everything you expect in a lawyer*" according to clients: "*the perfect gentleman and an excellent trial lawyer*." He is a real force in Orlando.
**Clients/Work Highlights:** A range of clients feature on the roster at this firm, including Boeing.

## Richman Greer Weil Brumbaugh Mirabito & Christensen

See firm details p.671
**The Firm:** This 24-strong firm is fixed in the affections of clients and has marshaled a loyal following from some of the state's most respected clients for both the assertion and defense of their rights. The firm is high up on the referral lists of fellow Florida law firms and has offices in Miami and West Palm Beach. A flair for handling high-end real estate, antitrust, professional malpractice, corporate and political litigation makes these attorneys "*a wise choice on complicated or technically challenging cases*." Recent representations include codefending DIRECTV in a suit brought by the Cisneros Group of Venezuela, a case seeking over a billion dollars in damages arising out of the break-up of DIRECTV Latin America. The firm also continues to provide litigious advice to its impressive list of loyal clients, including Janet Reno.
**The Lawyers:** "*Top-flight*" **Alan Greer** is an expert in legal malpractice suits, cases involving political issues and general high-stakes business or civil litigation. He is representing officers and directors of Banco Espírito Santo as third party defendants in a $175 million accounting malpractice suit. **John Brumbaugh** is "*one of the main players in the state*" and manages the firm's representation of Merrill Lynch and 3M. **Gerald Richman** (see p.648) is president of the firm and has had a successful year in court. He has worked in some major litigation and appeals relating to Premier Aviation's fixed-base operation at Boca Raton Airport.
**Clients/Work Highlights:** Equifax; 3M; Precision Response; Merrill Lynch; Banco Espírito Santo and DIRECTV.

## Shook, Hardy & Bacon LLP

See firm details p.1218
**The Firm:** This respected international firm, through its ten offices worldwide, remains a "*contender for the best work*." In litigation, the practice brings with it a "*degree of gravitas*" and has the ability and resources to handle virtually all forms of general commercial litigation. Its recent work in aviation litigation, products liability, and employment disputes have caught the limelight. The group has acted as lead counsel for Philip Morris and Lorillard Tobacco and defended a subsidiary of Boeing.
**The Lawyers:** Seasoned litigator **Edward Moss** (see p.645) is a tremendously well-respected trial lawyer who brings to the table his "*wise judgment and ability to never lose focus on the big picture*." Similarly, **Kenneth Reilly** (see p.648), managing partner of the Miami office, is "*a respected big-league player*." He is often found representing public companies in large products liability suits. **Christopher Brown** (see p.629) impresses clients with his "*concise, persuasive paperwork*" and effective arguments. His aviation litigation stands out, and he also undertakes tort and employment litigation. Younger lawyer **William Geraghty** (see p.637) has made a splash with clients and is reported to "*always get excellent results*."
**Clients/Work Highlights:** Clients include many Fortune 500 companies such as Philip Morris and Lorillard Tobacco.

## Stearns Weaver Miller Weissler Alhadeff & Sitterson, PA

**The Firm:** The 35-strong litigation group continues to enhance its reputation for commitment and responsiveness. The competency of this group has been consistently illustrated this past year through its representation of large companies and banks as well as its plaintiff representation. The group's ability to handle complex cases is underscored in one of the largest compensatory damages verdicts in the state to date, the $1 billion verdict against Exxon on behalf of direct-service dealers. This firm also offers a seamless appellate practice and has a fast-growing labor and employment group.
**The Lawyers:** Chairman of the litigation department and president of the firm **Eugene Stearns** is a long-admired member of the Florida legal profession. "*Tough, aggressive and with some major victories under his belt*," he is a great advocate, who brings to the courtroom over 33 years of experience in the field.
**Clients/Work Highlights:** BankAtlantic; Bank of America; IVAX; Wachovia; Regions Bank; Knight Ridder; Publix and Miami HEAT.

## Zuckerman Spaeder LLP

**The Firm:** This firm "*demonstrates spectacular depth on a regular basis*," especially through its preeminence in white-collar crime and government investigations. Clients also endorsed the civil litigation and institutional capacity of the firm. Criminal cases often have a civil component to them and clients are quick to point out that the firm is "*well equipped to handle all elements*." The litigation group is spread

between the Tampa and Miami offices and has been involved in some high-profile cases over the past year. These include representing large law firms in legal malpractice suits with a criminal bent to them and representing HCA on a variety of issues.
**The Lawyers: Thomas Meeks** calls upon his broad litigation expertise for a caseload that has featured trade secrets and IP litigation. His management skills in large complex cases of national significance are widely commended. **Ronald Ravikoff**'s practice covers antitrust, securities and commercial litigation: "*He knows both sides of the coin*." He successfully represented Turnberry Country Club in a claim for $90 million in the past year. **Stephen Bronis** routinely sets the mark as "*accessible, attentive and a master of the details*." He is skilled in white-collar crime and complex civil litigation, particularly in the securities and healthcare fraud arenas. "*If I was in trouble I would go to* **Steven Chaykin**" is the frequent response of clients. He is "*150% dedicated and very aggressive, although he never crosses the line*." His background as a federal prosecutor provides him with an added edge and ensures he is a regular face on complex high-stakes criminal and fraud litigation. **Michael Pasano** is "*very comfortable with sophisticated, paper-heavy cases and good both pre and post-indictment*." An efficient and effective trial lawyer, he defended the owner of a viaticals company at the trial and appeal stage. White-collar specialist **Morris Weinberg** is another of the former federal prosecutors at this firm. He has handled some heavyweight legal malpractice cases and has represented Kindred Healthcare.
**Clients/Work Highlights:** Lifetime Capital; Life Extension Foundation; Turnberry Country Club; Gutierrez & Gutierrez; Kindred Healthcare; LabCORE and HCA.

## Berger Singerman

**The Firm:** Clients described this 49-strong business-oriented firm as "*responsive, capable – it provides excellent results*." A Florida-based firm, it has four offices across the state, and a Broward County dispute resolution team housing 14 "*client-driven*" attorneys. Bankruptcy, securities fraud, employment, real estate and complex business litigation are areas of strength. Clients also noted the "*seamless interplay*" with the business reorganization team. The group acted as special litigation counsel to Chapter 11 debtors in possession of a nationally known paper products company. The arrival of Bruce Udolf early in 2006 will increase this firm's litigious capabilities, especially in the white-collar criminal sphere.
**The Lawyers:** "*Personable, thorough and good in front of a jury*," **Anthony Carriuolo** manages the dispute resolution team and is experienced in bankruptcy, construction and employment disputes. Clients extolled his "*steady head in a crisis situation*." **Bruce Udolf** is a new arrival to the team from Ruden McClosky. He has developed a superb trial practice, representing corporate entities and individuals and has been elected president of the Broward County chapter of the Federal Bar Association.
**Clients/Work Highlights:** Banco Espírito Santo;

American Tissue; Waste Management; US Sugar; Aloha Airlines; Transeastern Properties; CHS Electronics and Fidelity National Financial.

## Bilzin Sumberg Baena Price & Axelrod LLP

See firm details p.660

**The Firm:** Clients thoroughly recommend the bankruptcy litigation plank of the group, but also note the firm's proficiency in civil matters and the "*industry-specific knowledge and trial experience of its attorneys.*" Work for this 24-strong group includes representing The International Bank of Miami in litigation arising out of the collapse of the second largest bank in the Dominican Republic, Banco Intercontinental. It also advised Eller & Company in the defense of a hostile takeover bid by a minority shareholder.

**The Lawyers:** Clients find **William Hill** (see p.639) "*thorough, professional, efficient and knowledgeable,*" further highlighting his "*ability to listen to what the client wants, make valuable suggestions and ultimately deliver the results.*" Hill is experienced in representing companies in IP, bankruptcy and class action cases and is often found in cases concerning the aviation or construction industries. **Michael Kreitzer** (see p.642) is chair of the litigation department and has a loyal following of clients who admire his "*eloquence in court*" and his tenacious, yet careful and scholarly approach: "*The reason he wins is due to his studied care.*" Like Hill, Kreitzer focuses on complex commercial disputes and is in demand for his experience of construction litigation and shareholder and partnership disputes.

**Clients/Work Highlights:** The International Bank of Miami; Regency Properties of Boca Raton; HT Hackney; Degussa and Continental Stevedoring.

## Dean, Mead, Egerton, Bloodworth, Capouano & Bozarth PA

**The Firm:** This 12-strong litigation department is experienced in commercial litigation, with strength in eminent domain, ERISA, probate litigation and "*effective mediation services.*" The firm is also experienced in representing professionals, from lawyers and law firms to accountants, physicians and architects. Indeed, this firm is a favored choice for professionals facing malpractice suits, and represents some major local law firms in such matters.

**The Lawyers:** The "*serious and effective*" **Darryl Bloodworth** (see p.629) is the standout attorney in this group and successfully represented the Mayor of Orlando in a civil action during the past year. He practices in the areas of business and commercial litigation, probate litigation and eminent domain.

**Clients/Work Highlights:** Clients include the Mayor of Orlando and A Duda & Sons and this group is a key port of call for referrals.

## Jones, Foster, Johnston & Stubbs, P.A.

**The Firm:** This high-octane Palm Beach County law firm has a long history in the state and has developed an impressive local and national client base. Although it is not as big as some of the other leading firms in the state, clients find value in the "*compact unit of ethical, responsive and experienced*" attorneys on offer. Legal malpractice cases and issues of eminent domain are just two strands to this broad litigation practice.

**The Lawyers:** "*Real star*" **Sidney Stubbs** is president of the firm and "*the person you first think of for litigation in West Palm Beach.*" He has an intricate knowledge of the local laws and procedures and "*often utilizes dispute resolution methods to best serve his clients.*"

**Clients/Work Highlights:** Abbott Laboratories and Dow Chemical are examples of the caliber of clients using this firm.

## Kluger, Peretz, Kaplan & Berlin P.L.

See firm details p.667

**The Firm:** Clients voiced their approval of the firm's accessibility and responsiveness, strong courtroom performances and transparent fee structure. This litigation and dispute resolution department houses 23 lawyers and has a reputation for its aggressive approach and for nurturing the talents of its junior lawyers. It is well equipped to handle class actions, securities fraud and products liability matters, and cases involving corporate governance and professional liability are further areas of strength. Recent highlights include the filing of a national class action against DuPont, alleging deceptive and unfair trade practices regarding the safety of its Teflon product. This is one of the first actions filed under the Class Action Fairness Act of 2005 and could influence the way the law develops in this area.

**The Lawyers:** The "*creative, smart and accessible*" head of the department **Steve Silverman** "*is good at holding the client's hand through the whole process*" and producing innovative solutions. Silverman's practice encompasses directors and officers liability, the assertion or defense of class actions and real estate litigation.

**Clients/Work Highlights:** Racing Properties and Mastech are among the broad client base of this firm.

## Squire, Sanders & Dempsey L.L.P.

See firm details p.1650

**The Firm:** This firm cuts a swath across the litigation front. The merger with Steel Hector & Davis has cause some changes in personnel however most sources agreed: "*Once it gets through the transitional period, the firm will be a true contender.*" Loyal clients appreciate the international reach the firm now offers and the wealth of resources and experience that enables it to handle even the most complex commercial litigation. The provision of advice on white-collar, appellate work and class actions is also an advantage.

**The Lawyers:** Managing partner of the Miami office **Alvin Davis** (see p.633) is the driving force

behind this group's prominence. He is "*quick-witted and incisive,*" but also "*cerebral and a respected strategist.*" Davis is regularly found representing major international companies on complex products liability, securities class actions and environmental claims. **Patricia Lowry** (see p.643) "*emanates quality.*" Her portfolio has this year focused primarily on products liability cases and she has represented pharmaceutical companies as Florida counsel in high-profile litigation involving products such as VIOXX, Baycol and phenylpropanolamine. In the latter two cases she has also acted as a member of the national trial team. In 2005 she was involved in employment litigation following whistle-blower allegations made by a former employee of a pharmaceutical company client.

**Clients/Work Highlights:** Bayer; Merck; Purdue Pharma and Delta Air Lines.

## Black, Srebnick, Kornspan & Stumpf PA

**The Firm:** This 13-strong firm has secured a part in some of the most newsworthy, high-profile cases to reach the courts and "*allays the fears of the client in what is a very difficult time through devastatingly thorough advocacy and good tactics.*" In the past year, the firm has represented Rosenthal Jewelers Supply, its owner and sales manager in a federal grand jury indictment alleging that more than $8 million in cash was taken from drug dealers as payment for gold bullion. A Miami jury returned not guilty verdicts on all eight counts of money laundering. The firm is also defending BioMed and its principal against an indictment that it was engaged in a scheme to defraud the Medicaid and Medicare programs.

**The Lawyers:** "*No one is as well prepared or has the presence in court of* **Roy Black**." According to sources nationwide, he is "*uniquely gifted in front of juries;*" Black is "*so good he is famous for it.*" His creativity, resourcefulness and fine cross-examination skills stand out: "*Its' like poetry in motion: each person gets unique treatment.*" His colleague **Howard Srebnick** is also a "*great tactician and masterful trial attorney.*" Clients agree: "*He's thorough and creative, preempts everything and leaves no stone unturned.*"

## Moscowitz, Moscowitz & Magolnick PA

**The Firm:** Clients commended this four-partner criminal boutique, expressing admiration for its "*damned fine, A-plus, first-tier lawyers.*" Instilling confidence in the client at an early stage in the proceedings, this husband-and-wife duo are widely sought after for their white-collar expertise. The firm is high up on the referrals list for all forms of white-collar work, and also offers civil representation.

**The Lawyers:** **Jane Moscowitz** is well known for her experience in federal cases and her "*wonderful presence in the courtroom.*" According to clients, **Norman Moscowitz** "*routinely does a great job on complicated cases and has a real knack of distilling issues down for a jury to understand.*" He is a "*talented tactician, a terrific trial attorney and good on paper too.*"

## Raskin & Raskin PA

**The Firm:** *"Credible with the courts, creative and easy to work with,"* this *"professional and responsive firm"* is widely considered expert in the field of federal criminal defense. Clients note the *"confidentiality ethic"* of the attorneys who *"get the desired results through understanding the specifics of the client's business as well as the law."* High-profile mandates in the past year include representing a nationally prominent physician in a six-week trial, the charges of which concern a counterfeit Botox product, and representing a real estate company accused of laundering millions of dollars.

**The Lawyers:** The *"incontrovertibly brilliant"* **Jane Raskin** is often found involved in grand jury investigations in the healthcare fraud arena and is in much demand for her expertise in Internet pharmacy fraud cases. **Martin Raskin** is *"an experienced practitioner who forges good relationships"* and advises on issues arising from the banking and finance, securities and aviation sectors. Raskin has represented a major liquor distributor, a large construction firm and a judge in 2005.

## George & Titus PA

**The Firm:** This Tampa-based firm is a popular choice for many clients and referring attorneys on white-collar crime, government investigations and related litigation. Commentators note the *"dexterity"* of the firm's three attorneys, further praising their *"determination and drive."* A range of criminal matters is covered, with cases involving environmental, tax and healthcare law featuring prominently.

**The Lawyers:** *"Vociferous advocate"* **Peter George** enjoys a wonderful reputation in the state and comes highly recommended for his slick handling of white-collar cases and impressive courtroom performances.

## Leventhal & Slaughter PA

**The Firm:** A long history of successful white-collar representation has ensured this firm its prominence. Clients point to the one-stop shop approach adopted here, with experienced specialists on offer from the investigation stage to the ultimate completion of the case. Four attorneys are on hand to provide a service for the complete spectrum of criminal matters, from computer fraud to racketeering and even appeals.

**The Lawyers:** **Robert Leventhal** and **Harrison Slaughter** are both highly acclaimed litigators. *"Respected members of the small group of white-collar specialists, they are well regarded by the courts and the legal community."*

## Ruden McClosky, S.C.

**The Firm:** This full-service firm has almost 50 years of experience under its belt and houses seven dedicated white-collar and criminal defense attorneys. It is noted for its ethos of *"preventive counsel"* and impresses with its often successful involvement at early stages of the process. That said, attorneys are on hand to assist clients through the whole process, offering *"smart and useful tactical suggestions"* throughout. The firm fields attorneys experienced in money laundering, securities and healthcare fraud, embezzlement, price-fixing and tax offences.

**The Lawyers:** Client favorite **Marc Nurik** is a key port of call for white-collar referrals from leading law firms throughout the state and overlaps his civil litigation practice with governmental work.

## Sale & Kuehne PA

**The Firm:** This *"compact and punchy"* three-attorney unit is *"a tried and tested winner"* according to interviewees. Covering corporate criminal defense such as securities fraud and procurement, it has a successful track record in internal investigations and money laundering disputes, but also offers experience in the full range of white-collar crime and government investigations work.

**The Lawyers:** Both **Ben Kuehne** and **Jon Sale** are respected members of the Florida Bar and are *"extraordinarily well regarded – smart and well connected."* Their wealth of expertise enables them to handle the complex, paper-heavy cases.

## Other Notable Practitioners

Clients *"think the world of"* **Rutledge Liles** of four-partner firm Liles, Gavin, Costantino & Murphy. Retained for his *"aggressive, assertive, professional and ethical approach to cases"* he is able to convey the most complex areas of law to clients and has the *"ability to cut straight to the bottom line."* Managing partner of the firm, Liles handles legal malpractice and IP cases, among others. **John Frost** of Frost Tamayo Sessums & Aranda PA in Bartow has a steadfast client following because his advice is *"quality through and through."* **Edward Soto** (see p.652) of Weil, Gotshal & Manges LLP picks up plaudits for his flourishing defense practice and *"effective litigation management skills."* He is the senior trial partner and head of the litigation department in the Miami office and well versed in class actions, professional liability and securities litigation. **Terry Young** of Lowndes Drosdick Doster Kantor & Reed, PA, possesses *"finely honed litigation techniques"* and is frequently found on highly complex disputes. He has recently represented Lockheed Martin. **Mitchell Bloomberg** of Adorno & Yoss LLP impresses the legal community by *"making the case his own with his sharp, astute methods."* Bloomberg is partner-in-charge of the Miami office and a regular face in business disputes. **Stuart Singer** (see p.652) of Boies, Schiller & Flexner LLP is highly recommended by clients for both antitrust and commercial litigation and stands out with his national practice. Singer is currently representing The SCO Group in IP litigation against IBM in Utah. Clients also extol **Thomas Tew** of Tew Cardenas LLP as *"a senior, respected attorney, who is very driven by the right result."* He is experienced in securities, legal malpractice and bankruptcy litigation. At White & Case LLP **Jaime Bianchi** (see p.628) has found favor with clients for his *"intelligence and articulation"* and for his *"dogged determination."* *"Good at finding the underpinning of the argument,"* he adopts a thorough and thoughtful approach to his cases. Faith Gay has recently left the firm to join the New York office of Quinn Emanuel. Sole practitioner **William Aaron** is adept at *"amassing the right team for the case"* and in the past year has represented a major international construction company that was involved in an investigation concerning alleged corruption with contracts at a major international airport. **Bruce Zimet** *"is so talented that he has to be the go-to-guy in Fort Lauderdale for white-collar crime,"* reported sources. He utilizes his experience gained from being a prosecutor and is a true leader in the field. **Ronald Cacciatore** is a key figure in the Tampa market, providing clients with advice on both criminal trial and appellate law. **William Jung** of Tampa-based Jung & Sisco has a practice that encompasses crime, appeals, healthcare fraud and professional malpractice. He is *"a considerate lawyer with a great practice"* and is a former law clerk to Chief Justice Rehnquist. **David Mandel** (see p.644) is managing partner of Mandel & Mandel LLP and has a practice that encompasses general commercial litigation as well as white-collar criminal work. *"So good, he deserves all the success he gets,"* Mandel has represented the former CEO of Qwest in a civil matter in Florida recently. **Cheney Mason**'s practice includes family and entertainment law, but comes to the fore with his criminal defense caseload, where he shines as *"a gifted trial attorney."* **William Nortman** (see p.646) of Akerman Senterfitt makes his debut in *Chambers* and is classed as being *"among the best white-collar and SEC defense lawyers around."* Miami-based **Jose Quiñon** is a well-respected attorney who is *"devastating in cross-examination"* and *"a superb trial lawyer,"* according to interviewees. **Edward Shohat** of Miami law firm Bierman, Shohat, Loewy & Klein PA has a track record of highly publicized successes in terms of white-collar criminal defense, and is *"a quick-thinking and vociferous lawyer for his clients."* *"Anyone in Miami who is in trouble should think of"* **Neal Sonnett** of Neal Sonnett PA. *"He does a tremendous job and is high up on the list for referrals,"* according to market sources. Former federal prosecutor **Marty Steinberg** (see p.653) of Hunton & Williams features in the antitrust and general commercial litigation tables yet is also praised for *"his efficient handling of a great deal of delicate white-collar crime."* Former prosecutor **Gary Trombley** of Trombley & Hanes in Tampa *"has built up quite a reputation for white-collar work through his many years in the field"* and is also respected for his trial techniques.

# LITIGATION

# APPELLATE

## Notable Practitioners

Greenberg Traurig LLP is home to a number of the nation's most prominent appellate attorneys. Peers, competitors, satisfied clients and jurists unite to praise "*the best appellate lawyer in the country,*" **Elliot Scherker** (see p.650). Clients refer to the "*absolute confidence we have that we are getting the best representation possible*" when appellate specialist and "*classic business lawyer*" Scherker is retained. Scherker demonstrated his skill on his feet in representing Lorillard Tobacco on appeal from a $145 billion judgment against the five largest tobacco companies in the country, resulting in the judgment being reversed and the smokers' class action being decertified. The case was also argued on discretionary review before the Florida Supreme Court. **Charles Auslander** (see p.627) wins plaudits for the "*very clear, concise and measured*" approach he adopts, and is often drawn in at an early stage in the proceedings to utilize his appellate experience in establishing a strategy for the effective resolution of a case. **Barry Richard** (see p.648) garners as many plaudits for his commercial litigation practice as he does for his "*thriving appellate practice,*" and his experience in electoral and consti-

tutional issues. "*Appellate guru*" **Arthur England** (see p.635), chairman of the appellate department at Greenberg Traurig LLP, is a former chief justice of the Florida Supreme Court and devotes his practice to appellate work and trial counseling. He enjoys a "*legendary status*" in the state and is affectionately referred to as "*one of the big bears in the neighborhood.*" **John Beranek** of Ausley & McMullen, is a former judge in the Fourth District Court of Appeals and "*a true gentleman who always keeps it on the high plain.*" Peers agree that it is "*as much of a delight to be against this superb advocate as it is to be on the same side.*" **Joel Eaton** (see p.635) of Podhurst Orseck P.A. has "*a unique, laconic style.*" He undertakes appellate work for several plaintiff firms across the state and "*is one of the most meticulous appellate lawyers around; a beautiful writer and an excellent oral advocate.*" Eaton won a case in the Florida Supreme Court in 2005, representing the parents of a 12-year-old girl killed in an intersection collision and reversing the Court of Appeal decision in favor of Florida Power & Light. **Jane Kreusler-Walsh** of Jane Kreusler-Walsh PA "*is certainly a leader in the West Palm Beach area,*" according to those in the know. "*One of the best appellate lawyers in the state; particularly in the Fourth District Court of Appeals,*" she is said by clients to be both a "*good writer and good on her feet.*" **Joel Perwin**, a leading civil appellate lawyer, represented the Government of Belize in an appeal concerning the services of a telephone company. Fort Lauderdale-based **Bruce Rogow** of Bruce S Rogow, P.A. is widely respected for his "*academic career and experience of arguing in the Supreme Court.*" "*A specialist in delicate cases,*" he is skilled on his feet. Similarly, **Rodolfo Sorondo** (see p.652) of Holland & Knight LLP impresses with his "*stellar career and his time in the Florida judiciary*" and focuses his practice on appeals and trial support. "*Always doing the best job possible for his client,*" Sorondo is the leader of the appellate practice group in the Miami office. **Richard Strafer** "*is among the best of the best and is the first choice when a criminal appeal crops up.*" A talented all-rounder, he mainly undertakes federal and state criminal appeals, and is respected for his input at the trial stage. He has been heavily involved in Medicaid fraud cases recently. **Sylvia Walbolt** (see p.655), chair of the appellate practice at Carlton Fields, has "*a sterling reputation*" across the USA. She handles federal and state appeals in all areas of law and is currently acting

as co-counsel to Morgan Stanley in an appeal from a final judgment awarding $1.5 billion in compensatory and punitive damages. **Marc Cooper** (see p.632) of Colson Hicks Eidson in Coral Gables is "*intellectually gifted, an excellent writer and well recognized in the community as a fine appellate lawyer.*" He established the firm's appellate group and is pivotal to the overall success of the firm as his appellate expertise is often utilized in trial motions. An example of this was his provision of tactical advice in the firm's successful representation of the parents of a 12-year-old boy who was electrocuted at a bus shelter, a case that returned a $65.1 million verdict against one of the nation's largest outdoor advertisers. Sole practitioner **Robert Glazier** (see p.637) impresses clients through his "*ability to read, listen and then apply deductive, cognitive and imaginative reasoning.*" Glazier has successfully represented Costa Cruises in seven consolidated appeals involving forum non conveniens and admiralty issues, the substance of which is whether foreign crew members could sue in Florida. **Adam Lawrence** of Lawrence & Daniels may not be as high-profile as some of the other leading individuals, "*but in any case, he is top-flight*" and a popular port of call for appellate referrals. "*Appellate veteran* **Jay Levy** *has vast experience in state and federal court*" and routinely impresses members of the legal fraternity for his dedication to the sector. In the past year, he has worked on an appeal regarding Florida's statewide school voucher system. **Lauri Ross** of two-partner firm Lauri Waldman Ross PA in Miami is "*a superb young appellate lawyer who is exceedingly well respected.*" Ross has been involved in two cases in the Florida Supreme Court in the past year, one of which changed the law in respect of earth-moving exclusions for all-risk property insurance. **Hala Sandridge** of Fowler White Boggs Banker impresses clients with her "*unmatched knowledge of appellate procedure at both state and federal levels,*" and her "*ability to master complex facts and apply them in a persuasive fashion to opposing counsel and the courts.*" Her presentation "*reflects careful preparation and persuasive argument of the highest level,*" according to clients. **Scott Srebnick**, recommended for his work on criminal appeals, is indicative of the "*younger generation of talented appellate lawyers coming through the ranks.*"

# REAL ESTATE

## Bilzin Sumberg Baena Price & Axelrod LLP

See firm details p.660

**The Firm:** One of "*Florida's finest,*" this firm houses a real estate group that is "*always visible in the major transactions,*" reported sources. A combination of 28 real estate and 13 land use attorneys make up this robust practice, which is able to handle "*any project every step of the way.*" The past year has seen the team undertake substantial development projects in the revitalization of downtown Miami, Miami Beach and North Beach, providing commercial real estate counsel and zoning advice for a number of hotels, condominiums, mixed-use and retail properties, office buildings and marinas. Clients applauded the lack of ego displayed by Bilzin attorneys: "*Our concerns always receive the highest levels of attention from whoever is dealing with us.*" The team is also said to possess the "*ability to achieve the best results.*" Florida land use law and governmental relations are also specialties of the group.

**The Lawyers:** **Brian Bilzin** (see p.628) is nationally renowned for his work in real estate transactions and the financing arena. He is a deal-maker who owes his success to his ability to "*always see the wood for the trees.*" Recent highlights include representing Stephen Muss and Hotelrama in the sale of the flagship Miami hotel, Fountainebleau, to Turnberry Associates. **John Sumberg** (see p.653) brings to transactions "*tremendous legal expertise and common sense.*" He represented Fortune International in the development of Sonesta Beach Hotel on Key Biscayne. This $1 billion project encompasses over

900,000 sq ft. An excellent strategist, he knows how to "*easily structure complicated arguments.*" Chairing the real estate group, **James Shindell**'s (see p.651) practice involves the representation of developers, investors and lenders in a broad array of real estate matters, including leasings, sales and financings. "*A careful and diligent practitioner,*" his practical judgment earned him applause from clients. **Stanley Price** (see p.647) practices "*in the highest echelons of the field, without a doubt.*" Leading the land use team, he possesses over 30 years' experience in the area. His "*professional, yet affable style*" is utilized in "*a most attractive manner,*" and he has well-established relationships with local government and agencies. He is currently representing Shoma Homes in the mixed-use urban development of the new town center in Doral, a project encompassing retail, office and residential units, in addition to an amphitheater. **Carter McDowell**'s (see p.644) prior experience as director of building, zoning and community development makes him a popular choice among clients for handling regulatory approval procedures associated with the development of regional malls, hotels, industrial complexes and marinas. "*He really understands our issues,*" explain sources.

**Clients/Work Highlights:** The team represented subsidiaries of Lennar in two recent acquisitions of real estate from Roseland Partners, and has represented Merrill Lynch Capital in the provision of a $40 million financing for the purchase of 400 North Ashley Plaza, an office building in downtown Tampa.

## Greenberg Traurig LLP

See firm details p.664

**The Firm:** The real estate and land use team of this Florida heavyweight undertakes high-profile work reflecting the most significant trends in the real estate market. For example, its work in the condominium and timeshare development sphere attracted plaudits, while its core service provision, catering to every aspect of real estate and land use, was equally distinguished. Clients celebrated the "*number of resources and variety of bright folks to draw from,*" and were further impressed by the team members' willingness to "*jump on matters – in the state and beyond.*" The firm's land use attorneys have established strong political connections and they impress with "*the speed at which they can get matters resolved.*"

**The Lawyers:** **Gary Saul** (see p.650) has been labeled the "*condo king*" for his success in advising on this substantial area of activity. Project developers benefit from his "*formidable understanding and experience of the area,*" and he is instrumental in projects converting old apartment buildings into new condominiums. National head of the firm's real estate group, **Matthew Gorson**'s (see p.638) availability "*at the flick of a switch*" makes him a popular choice for real estate transactions and "*he never lets ego get in the way of making a deal.*" He represented Related Group in approximately 50 high-rise development acquisitions with an average value of $200-400 million. **Burt Bruton** (see p.630) is relied on implicitly for his

expert guidance, agreed clients. At all times helpful, he is "*great to bounce ideas off – he just knows it all.*" He advises on a range of real estate sales, acquisitions and financings. **Brian Sherr** (see p.651) heads the firm's Fort Lauderdale office in tandem with a flourishing practice in the condominium conversions area. Clients appreciated his "*ability to deal with matters with a commercial slant.*" Senior figure **Robert Traurig** (see p.654) remains a pivotal figure in the land use arena with many pronouncing him "*a real icon of the industry.*" Head of the land use department, **Clifford Schulman** (see p.650) is "*someone you would want on your team any day of the week.*" A "*creative solution-provider,*" he displays intimate knowledge of the area and brandishes connections with all the relevant people in the state. **Debbie Orshefsky** (see p.646) is particularly noted for her skill in handling large-scale projects, while **Lucia Dougherty** (see p.634) possesses expertise within the DRI arena. **Julie Kendig-Schrader** (see p.641) combines a land use practice with an environmental law specialism. Her excellent preparation and fine presentation skills are widely recognized.

**Clients/Work Highlights:** The team has acted for Capital Partners in several real estate transactions totaling more than $600 million. In the lending sphere, it recently structured a $650 million master loan facility for GL Homes. Other clients include Related Group; Swire Pacific Holdings; Midtown Equities; Burger King; CNL Retirement Properties; Archon; INVESCO; Bayview Financial; Crescent Heights; Flag Luxury Properties; Millennium Partners; Regents Bank and TA Realty Advisors.

## Lowndes Drosdick Doster Kantor & Reed, PA

**The Firm:** Clearly focused on the real estate sector, this firm is a real force and its remit extends across the catalog of real estate matters and clients. However, the group has a particular niche directed at those in the hospitality, leisure and recreation, and retirement industries. The land use group dominates the central Florida market, as "*no one is able to contend with its experience, expertise or connections,*" reported sources. Clients were impressed with the professional relationships they were able to foster with this group: "*They really get to know us and our business aims.*" The team has been central in handling the land acquisitions and development projects for major residential homebuilder client Greater Homes.

**The Lawyers:** "*Thorough, fair and bright,*" **Michael Ryan** is "*always up to date on the latest laws and how they may apply to our situation.*" Dominant in the real estate financings sphere, including bond financings, his experience places him at the forefront of the market. "*Bright as a bulb,*" **Nicholas Pope** has played a key role in much of the firm's DRI and hotel and resort development work. He also displays niche strength in the infrastructure finance arena. **Richard Fildes** continues to cause a stir with his work in the hospitality industry, where his practice is "*simply one* of the best." **Hal Kantor**'s *"great client manner, combined with tremendous technical skill and terrific instinct"* stand him in good stead, while **Miranda Fitzgerald**'s *"extraordinary knowledge of her subject is coupled with a great intuition about how to handle situations,"* enthused sources. DRIs remain a sizable aspect of the practice and she was recently lead counsel in creating a 25,000-acre village in West Lake County.

**Clients/Work Highlights:** CNL; Wachovia; Greater Construction; Meritage; Wal-Mart; Apollo Real Estate Investors; The Simon Companies; Darden Restaurants and KUD International.

## Akerman Senterfitt

See firm details p.657

**The Firm:** Clients celebrated this team's impressive service-oriented approach, saying: *"They are willing to work the hours required to get things done."* Its offices across the USA ensure a depth of resources for assistance on any matter. The integrated land use team provides a seamless service *"from the conceptual stage all the way to closing."* The group is experienced in land acquisitions, sales and developments in the condominium sector. Real estate financing is also on the agenda, and attorneys have advised on the creation of funds for investment groups.

**The Lawyers: Andrew Smulian** (see p.652) recently represented the owner of Fisher Island Holdings, Miami's premier privately held residential island on Biscayne Bay, in the sale of the company. Head of the group, he adopts a *"smart and thoughtful stance on matters, which in turn leads to successful results."* He regularly advises his out-of-state clients in their Florida operations. **Janice Russell** (see p.649) represents investors and developers and brings to the negotiating table a *"cool head under pressure."* She recently represented the owner and developer in the redevelopment of Rybovich Marina, the largest commercial marina in West Palm Beach. **Dwight Saathoff** (see p.650) impresses with his direct manner; *"thanks to him, we know where we stand from start to finish in the transaction,"* clients said. He represented the developer of a large, multiuse DRI in negotiations with Orange County Public Schools to privately fund and build a number of schools. Exhibiting a *"great local touch"* and wonderful rapport, **Cecelia Bonifay** (see p.629) is a skilled land use lawyer. Her caseload of late has been heavily focused on Lake and Polk counties, where her *"awareness of the political ups and downs"* places her in the position to *"achieve the best results."* **Ted Brown**'s (see p.630) practice spans the areas of real estate, land use and environmental law. However, it is his extensive knowledge of environmental permitting, endangered species and wetlands that makes him a primary choice for developers requiring advice on proposed mixed-use developments.

**Clients/Work Highlights:** America's Capital Partners; Scripps Research Institute; Fisher Island Holdings; Shoma Development; Bank of America; Lennar Homes; Wal-Mart; St Joe; Wachovia and Centex Homes.

## Carlton Fields

See firm details p.661

**The Firm:** This Florida powerhouse fields a *"great selection of highly seasoned lawyers."* So good is the firm's anticipation of client needs, *"they answer problems even before we know we have them!"* The full range of real estate matters is handled here, including commercial leasing, acquisition, development and financing. Clients liked the fact that the team presented *"just enough of the big names, with a good sprinkling of younger lawyers on the bench,"* to cater to any matter. Its excellent relationships with governmental bodies ensure that regulatory approval matters are handled *"with the minimum of fuss."* The team was also highlighted for its strength in representing large financial institutions.

**The Lawyers: Ruth Barnes Kinsolving** (see p.641) provides high-quality advice in the sale, acquisition, leasing and development of commercial and resort property. Another attractive facet of her practice is her representation of foreign investors in the Tampa real estate market. **Robert Freedman** (see p.636) focuses on real property law, including condominium, subdivision and timeshare development. *"A real client-pleaser and terrific problem solver,"* he is also head of the firm's condominium group. Statewide chair of the real estate group, **Edgel Lester** (see p.643) represents clients in acquiring property for residential development and acts for lenders in complex loan workouts. Sources perceived him to be an *"excellent rainmaker"* for this nationwide group.

**Clients/Work Highlights:** The team has acted for CityPlace in the development of a $600 million mixed-use streetfront retail, residential and entertainment project in downtown West Palm Beach. Other clients include CF Industries; Cendant Timeshare Resorts; John Hancock; Wachovia; Walter Industries and WCI Communities.

## Holland & Knight LLP

See firm details p.1534

**The Firm:** Fielding one of the largest real estate teams in Florida, this group has *"the requisite expertise needed to guide us through to resolution,"* reported clients. Active across the board in real estate and land use matters, it has secured a national presence in the hotel and resort development sector. The firm has also cultivated a first-rate lender practice, providing clients with *"expert advice and counsel"* in real estate financings.

**The Lawyers: James Seay** (see p.651) wins high marks all around for his professional demeanor and expert negotiation skills. Commercial investors and developer clients were quick to point to his *"wonderful temperament"* and reliability. His caseload of late has included acting for client VisaHomes in its land acquisition and joint venture work. **John Halula** (see p.639) possesses *"great knowledge and familiarity"* of the key elements involved in real estate financings. Popular land use attorney **Juan Mayol**'s (see p.644) workload chiefly consists of representing builders and developers in large-scale residential and retail projects. A personable and client-friendly attorney, he advised on the development of a mixed-use retail and office site in the City of Coral. **Joseph Goldstein**'s (see p.637) government and planning background helps him retain a *"level head in guiding clients through complex issues."* Featuring regularly in some of the state's largest DRI projects, he continues to represent the Scripps Research Institute in the zoning aspects of the new Palm Beach County Research Park.

**Clients/Work Highlights:** The team works for a host of developer clients including Pizzuti, Pier Point Developers and Lennar Homes.

## Real Estate: Zoning/Land Use
### Leading Firms

**1** AKERMAN SENTERFITT *Orlando*

BILZIN SUMBERG BAENA PRICE & AXELROD *Miami*

GREENBERG TRAURIG LLP *Miami*

HOPPING GREEN & SAMS, PA *Tallahassee*

LOWNDES DROSDICK DOSTER KANTOR *Orlando*

PAPPAS METCALF JENKS AND MILLER *Jacksonville*

**2** BERCOW & RADELL PA *Miami*

FOWLER WHITE BOGGS BANKER *Tampa*

GUNSTER, YOAKLEY & STEWART *Fort Lauderdale*

HOLLAND & KNIGHT LLP *Miami*

RUDEN MCCLOSKY, S.C. *Fort Lauderdale*

SHUTTS & BOWEN LLP *Miami*

STEARNS WEAVER MILLER WEISSLER *Miami*

**3** BRICKLEMYER SMOLKER & BOLVES PA *Miami*

FOLEY & LARDNER LLP *Tampa*

GRAY ROBINSON PA *Orlando*

ROGERS TOWERS PA *Jacksonville*

SHUBIN & BASS *Miami*

### Leading Individuals

#### Senior Statesmen

HOPPING Wade *Hopping Green*

MCCLOSKY Donald *Ruden McClosky, S.C.*

SIEMON Charles *Sole Practitioner*

TRAURIG Robert *Greenberg Traurig LLP*

**1** FITZGERALD Miranda *Lowndes Drosdick Doster Kantor*

KANTOR Hal *Lowndes Drosdick Doster Kantor*

PAPPAS Lynn *Pappas Metcalf Jenks and Miller*

PRICE Stanley *Bilzin Sumberg Baena Price*

SCHULMAN Clifford *Greenberg Traurig LLP*

WEAVER Ronald *Stearns Weaver Miller Weissler*

**2** BERCOW Jeffrey *Bercow & Radell PA*

BONIFAY Cecelia *Akerman Senterfitt*

DELEGAL Susan *Billing Cochran Heath Lyles & Mauro*

GOLDSTEIN Joseph *Holland & Knight LLP*

GRINDSTAFF Michael *Shutts & Bowen LLP*

HALL Donald *Gunster, Yoakley*

LAW Rhea *Fowler White Boggs Banker*

MCDOWELL Carter *Bilzin Sumberg Baena Price*

MELE Dennis *Ruden McClosky, S.C.*

ORSHEFSKY Debbie *Greenberg Traurig LLP*

PELHAM Thomas *Fowler White Boggs Banker*

SAATHOFF Dwight *Akerman Senterfitt*

**3** BRICKLEMYER Keith *Bricklemyer Smolker*

BRINDELL James *Gunster, Yoakley*

BROWN Ted *Akerman Senterfitt*

CARDENAS Alberto *Tew Cardenas LLP*

DOUGHERTY Lucia *Greenberg Traurig LLP*

GOREN Samuel *Goren Cherof Doody*

HAINLINE JR Theodore *Rogers Towers PA*

KENDIG-SCHRADER Julie *Greenberg Traurig LLP*

LEONHARDT Frederick *Gray Robinson PA*

MAYOL Juan *Holland & Knight LLP*

SHUBIN John *Shubin & Bass*

WOODSON R Duke *Foley & Lardner LLP*

## Ruden McClosky, S.C.

**The Firm:** The team has carved out a considerable profile in south Florida, particularly West Palm Beach, and it also fields specialist attorneys from its Tampa and Tallahassee offices. Distinguished for its diversity in the area, the land use group undertakes a range of work, such as municipal special exceptions, rezoning and land use plan amendments. Large projects have featured heavily in its caseload of late, including some of Florida's largest DRIs, particularly in the eastern Palm Beach communities. The group is adept at dealing with the environmental concerns facing developers, including approvals for solid waste facilities, properties containing sensitive lands or those located on coastal construction lands. According to clients; "*you name it, they can do it.*"

**The Lawyers:** "*A transactional attorney of the highest order,*" **Barry Somerstein** has a national practice, with much of the work he undertakes occurring out of the state. He is presently acting for a number of national home builders in their acquisition, finance and workout agreements. A highly intelligent attorney, peers agreed: "*You'd better be prepared facing him across the table – if not, he will tear you to pieces.*" **Donald McClosky**'s years of experience, understanding and political connections within the industry enable him to "*bring a creative approach to the table,*" and he is a "*wonderful sounding-board.*" **Dennis Mele** is "*one of the best in the business*" on land use matters. Often prime choice for those seeking counsel in Fort Lauderdale, his knack for finding solutions earns him respect across the board.

**Clients/Work Highlights:** Clients include property owners, real estate developers, financial institutions, national corporations, insurance companies and pension funds.

## Stearns Weaver Miller Weissler Alhadeff & Sitterson, PA

**The Firm:** Sources agreed that this team has secured an "*undeniable presence*" through its all-encompassing real estate practice. The Tampa and Miami offices comprise "*an experienced assortment of intelligent attorneys,*" carrying out work "*to the highest standards.*" A particular niche of this team is its work in the affordable housing sector. The land use group's six members were all praised for "*handling matters with a touch of finesse.*" A large portion of the past year's work has included involvement in litigation regarding approvals for new community and retail developments. Securing federal and state assistance for multifamily housing and Federal Housing Association-insured lending is another widely recognized element of this practice.

**The Lawyers:** Commentators look to real estate group centerpiece **Richard Alhadeff** as someone "*that understands how to make a deal work.*" Clients agree: "*He is truly a wonder when it comes to negotiations.*" Skilled in the lending arena, he carries out high-profile loan work for Bank of America. **Chava Genet** has been involved in advising foreign investors buying property in the USA, and was distinguished for "*her thorough understanding of the most complex of issues.*" Meanwhile, **Ronald Weaver** "*impresses with everything he does,*" say sources about his land use practice.

**Clients/Work Highlights:** This team's practice includes the representation of developers, lenders, contractors, architects and engineers.

## Broad and Cassel

**The Firm:** Strong political connections ensure this group retains its status as one of the leading real estate and land use groups in Florida. Lenders and developers are more than satisfied beneficiaries of this service, with much of the workload carried out in the condominium and office building arena.

**The Lawyers:** Sources point to chairman **David Brown** as the group's most prominent figure. A major drawing card for clients, his substantial connections in the political arena "*make him a number-one choice*" within the state. **James Slater** "*is always able to get the deal done,*" said sources. He represents developers at all stages of the process, "*smoothly taking the transaction from start to finish.*" He displays equal strength handling the acquisition and sale aspects of transactions as he does fulfilling the permitting requirements.

**Clients/Work Highlights:** The team represents private sector lenders and developers and a number of local authorities and government agencies.

## Dean, Mead, Egerton, Bloodworth, Capouano & Bozarth PA

**The Firm:** This compact real estate group received praise for the "*splendid individuals*" it houses. Team members are well versed in all aspects of real estate and are seen as "*generalists – they are able to see through any matter.*" The team has been involved in sales and acquisitions of land parcels in Orange, Osceola, Lake, Polk, Brevard, and St. Lucie counties for development as single-family residential sites. Another well-regarded element of this team was its extensive experience in real estate finance, and it regularly represents financial institutions and borrowers throughout the state.

**The Lawyers:** **Stephen Bozarth** (see p.629) has "*combined remarkable technical knowledge and skills*" to become one of the leading real estate lawyers in central Florida. A generalist, his practice encompasses development, sale and purchase, leasing, and secured and unsecured lending.

**Clients/Work Highlights:** The team regularly represents owners, developers, investors, lenders, landlords, tenants and other real estate professionals.

## Hill, Ward & Henderson, PA

**The Firm:** Clients were especially appreciative of the diligence and flexibility offered by members of this team, claiming it to be "*the first port of call for real estate advice.*" Although based in Tampa, the workload taken on by the group is by no means restricted to the region, with its geographic reach extending across the entire state and beyond. Work within the commercial and residential arena forms the core of this practice and clients attributed team members with an understanding of the issues. They "*really put themselves in our shoes.*"

**The Lawyers: Thomas Henderson** *"really cares about the client and the work."* Much of his practice falls within the transactional side of real estate, advising leading developers. Clients applaud him for his evaluation of problems *"with precision and accuracy,"* and his *"kind and generous nature"* ensures he is never without client loyalty. He is currently being retained by Pulte Homes as general counsel throughout Florida.

**Clients/Work Highlights:** The group represents local and national developers of office buildings, suburban office parks, residential subdivisions, condominium projects, apartment complexes and shopping centers.

### Rogers Towers PA

**The Firm:** A sizable force in Jacksonville, the real estate and land use team *"caters to the region's most complex projects."* Its caseload shows a bias in favor of residential developers, banks and financial institutions, and the team has recently seen an increased involvement in matters concerning the retail development sphere. Attorneys handle matters, including land use and zoning, with *"confidence and skill."*

**The Lawyers:** A *"capable and active member of the community,"* **William Scheu**'s real estate practice is skewed towards issues affecting shopping center and office building developments. To this end, he excels in acquisitions and leasing. He regularly represents national retailers throughout Florida. **Theodore Hainline** is the group's leading land use practitioner. His *"personable and friendly nature"* is employed in zoning and related permitting matters for developments in northeast Florida.

**Clients/Work Highlights:** The clientele includes Fortune 500 companies, large publicly traded REITs, financial institutions, national home builders, developers and other real estate professionals.

### Tew Cardenas LLP

**The Firm:** The Miami office of this firm works in tandem with the Tallahassee office in order to provide real estate advice across the state and further afield. The 11-strong group advises on acquisitions, disposals and finance projects and is respected for its expert handling of land use matters, due in part to its strong political connections.

**The Lawyers: Brian Tague** has secured a strong developer-led practice. *"He's always protective of his clients' interests, but by no means an obstructionist – if there is a deal to be made, he will make it,"* say clients, keen to emphasize his expert judgment. Demonstrating *"unfaltering focus,"* he recently advised Skyline, a Chicago-based developer, on its project in Miami. Clients appreciate that **Al Cardenas** is *"always aware of our concerns and issues."* A skilled land use attorney, he is an *"approachable visionary."*

**Clients/Work Highlights:** This team represents foreign and domestic institutions, lenders, developers, investors, brokers and asset managers.

### Trenam, Kemker, Scharf, Barkin, Frye, O'Neill & Mullis PA

**The Firm:** A flourishing practice in the Tampa region has seen this team's profile increase over the past twelve months. This *"proactive group"* impresses clients by *"knowing how to get deals done."* The past year has seen greater developer representation in retail, residential and condominium projects, but the team also caters to a range of local lender clients such as life insurance companies, banks and agribusinesses. Its *"dedicated and bright"* individuals, who provide a *"service even ahead of time,"* are a popular choice in the area.

**The Lawyers:** Practice chair **Richard Sollner** shows an *"innate ability to construct detailed and creative arguments."* Clients are reassured by his presence in negotiations and competitors stated: *"He is an incredibly bright man to have across the table."* Much of his caseload features lenders' representation. A *"standout name,"* **David Brittain** works on the developer side, often undertaking work in the shopping center and condominium arena.

### White & Case LLP

See firm details p.1566

**The Firm:** This international heavyweight fields a compact team in Miami that is hailed for its representation of developers in south Florida. Transactional matters remain the team's strongest suit, and hotel development has formed a sizable portion of the workload of late. *"Experienced individuals are always at hand,"* said clients, who also praised the team's *"undeniable prowess in handling the related tax matters."*

**The Lawyers:** Senior figure **William Walker** (see p.655) is *"always a pleasure to deal with,"* according to sources. His intelligence and high motivation to get the deal done are further reasons for his popularity. He recently represented WCI Communities in the sale of land in Jupiter, Palm Beach County, to luxury home builder Toll Brothers for the formation of a 483-acre golf course community.

**Clients/Work Highlights:** The team represented Starwood Capital Group in the acquisition of the Sheraton Yankee Clipper, the Sheraton Yankee Trader and the Nina Lee Imperial House hotels located in Fort Lauderdale. The team also counts Arvida; JMB Realty; Crocker & Company; Disney; AMFAC Property Development; Codina Development and Temple Development Company among its clients.

### Foley & Lardner LLP

**The Firm:** This heavyweight firm has offices spanning the state, which ensures a depth of resources for advice on a range of transactional matters. Particular praise was attributed to the Tampa office, where the land use practice stands out with its high standards and proficiency.

**The Lawyers: Fred Ridley** (see p.648) is a *"highly facilitative person"* who attracts clients with his personable approach to case management. Head of the Tampa real estate group, he has been involved in the financing and development of golf courses and resorts. Also heavily involved with the firm's golf and

resort services industry team, **Charles Commander** (see p.631) employs his sharp strategic skills and a *"real ability to be creative in dealing with transactions."* **Duke Woodson** (see p.656), head of the firm's Florida environmental law practice, is respected for his advice on land use and the impact of water law on real estate transactions.

**Clients/Work Highlights:** The team continues to serve resort developers and lenders including Meadowbrook Golf Club; Pacific Life Insurance; Oak Ridge Investments and Textron Financial.

### Gray Robinson PA

**The Firm:** This Florida firm is going *"from strength to strength."* Highly praised for its internal structure, the real estate and land use team works closely with environmental and administrative law attorneys, creating a *"seamless service"* that clients noted *"takes you from start to finish without a glitch."*

**The Lawyers:** Rainmaker **Frederick Leonhardt** has a wealth of expertise and strong political connections in the field. His practice consists chiefly of advice to developer clients on permits for brownfield or infill developments in urban areas.

**Clients/Work Highlights:** The team represents landowners and developers, in addition to acting as counsel to counties, cities and special districts throughout Florida in their real estate permitting processes.

### Gunster, Yoakley & Stewart, P.A.

**The Firm:** This firm's full-service capacity in dealing with real estate matters gains it a profile in the market, but its work in the condominium development arena stands out. The team has *"more than enough experience to ensure that matters run a smooth course."* The land use practice was also admired for its *"substantial political connections,"* making it a premier choice in the south Florida developer market.

**The Lawyers:** Respected figure **Donald Hall** has considerable experience in the field and is distinguished by his political connections. *"Always effective in getting a result,"* he is often found representing developers. Clients viewed **James Brindell**'s background in environmental law as attractive, noting that for any real estate matter with an environmental slant, *"he is the man for the job."* The hospitality industry is where **Andrew Robins** generates most acclaim. He is a dab hand at dealing with the development of hotels and resorts around the state.

**Clients/Work Highlights:** The team has been representing the City of Miami in the negotiations and drafting of lease and development agreements for Watson Island near downtown Miami. This includes the creation of a village that will contain a mega-yacht facility, an entertainment complex and public space for gardens and areas of cultural interest.

### LeBoeuf, Lamb, Greene & MacRae LLP

See firm details p.1540

**The Firm:** Complementing the New York office, this Jacksonville team is geared toward developer and lender representation in large commercial real estate loans. It houses a team *"that always works in the best interests of the client,"* and can draw upon the skills of other departments to ensure a rounded service. The team carries out much work within Florida, but of late has seen its caseload include matters from the Caribbean islands.

**The Lawyers:** The core of **Karl Hanson**'s (see p.639) practice focuses on representing individuals acquiring and developing land, although recently he has also represented some Florida banks. In the past year he represented a client in a 6,000-unit residential development in the Dominican Republic. Clients were quick to say: *"It is difficult to find any faults in his practice,"* and appreciated his *"cool head and technical abilities."*

**Clients/Work Highlights:** The team has been involved in raising the capital for a client developing 85,000 acres of land in Montana for a planned residential community. It also acts as statewide general counsel for Fidelity Investments.

## Shutts & Bowen LLP

See firm details p.673

**The Firm:** Home to more than 30 attorneys statewide, this real estate group was highlighted for its expertise in finance, zoning and environmental issues surrounding the acquisition and development of real estate projects. The past year has seen the team handle a variety of projects, including apartment complexes, office buildings, regional malls and nursing homes. The group has provided advice and representation in projects such as the American Airlines Arena, the Key Biscayne Ritz-Carlton resort and the Seminole Towne Center mall.

**The Lawyers:** According to clients, **Kevin Cowan** (see p.632) is *"always a good choice as he always gets good results."* Practice chair, he continues to be involved in all aspects of corporate and commercial real estate, including development, financing and leasing. **Michael Grindstaff** (see p.638) is a *"favored choice"* because of his previous experience as chairman of the Orange County Planning and Zoning Commission. He *"gives us that in-depth experience and knowledge we want,"* explain clients.

**Clients/Work Highlights:** The team represents a broad range of foreign and domestic entrepreneurs, developers, investors and lenders, including life insurance companies, banks and other institutional clients.

## Smith Hulsey & Busey

**The Firm:** This seven-member team based in Jacksonville was noted for its inclusive coverage of the areas traditionally associated with real estate. A *"significant presence"* in the regional market, clients pointed to the team's strength in the transactional and finance arenas as key reasons for selection.

**The Lawyers:** **Harry Wilson** acts for major client Wachovia on various workout loans, as well as advising property owners and banking industry clients. He recently acted for a Californian developer in a project in northeast Florida.

**Clients/Work Highlights:** The team has carried out a wealth of work in the financings arena for

clients both within the state and across the USA. The group also represents developers, investors, lenders and business users.

## Smith, Gambrell & Russell, LLP

**The Firm:** The profile of this national, full-service firm does not go unnoticed in Florida where a compact group operates from its Jacksonville office. Although it represents a diverse group of clients, ranging from corporate users, public and private companies, landlords and tenants, it is most recognized for a robust practice representing clients in the banking, institutional investor and retail sectors. The team advised a client in the financing of its 500 stores across the state. Clients appreciated the attorneys here for their *"facilitative nature and strong sense of teamwork."*

**The Lawyers:** **Douglas Stanford** *"ensures all the angles of a problem are considered."* The past year has seen him act chiefly for client Winn-Dixie, handling the real estate assets of 1,000 grocery stores across the state. Clients particularly cherished his deal mentality: *"He thinks as if he is part of our business."* Another strand to his practice is the real estate aspect of complex, multiproperty, multistate office construction.

**Clients/Work Highlights:** The team also acts for Haverty Furniture; Sawgrass Country Club; Fresh Market and St Joe.

## Squire, Sanders & Dempsey LLP

See firm details p.1650

**The Firm:** The merger with Steel Hector & Davis LLP will, according to sources, *"strengthen an already mighty firm."* The Tampa office now benefits from twelve real estate attorneys who cater to clients seeking *"extensive legal insight from start to finish."* Its recent transactional activity has included developments in the hospitality industry. Another area of strength is public finance, where the team regularly advises state government and public bodies on municipal bond issues.

**The Lawyers:** *"A steel fist in a velvet glove"* in negotiations, **Stephen Mitchell**'s (see p.645) approach may be aggressive, but he never loses his cool. A large part of his practice involves representing developer and investor clients throughout the state in their DRI matters. He is currently working on a mixed-use residential project in Costa Rica.

**Clients/Work Highlights:** The team has been involved in a major inner-city project in Tampa, comprising a mixed-use development. This includes affordable housing and luxury homes, and the team was instrumental in the DRI elements and tax increments associated with the project.

## Hopping Green & Sams, PA

See firm details p.665

**The Firm:** This firm is known throughout Florida as *"the top administrative and environmental law firm – if not the best in the state!"* Its strength in these areas makes it a popular choice for land use and environmental representation, with sources agreeing that the firm's standing with the government agencies is

second to none. Specialist land use attorneys counsel clients on community development districts, DRIs and compliance with local government plans, as well as negotiating water and utility agreements. Eminent domain and condemnation proceedings are also on the agenda here.

**The Lawyers:** **Wade Hopping** (see p.640) was hailed as a *"legendary name in the field."* Recognized and respected for being one of the senior figures at the Florida Bar, sources were keen to emphasize his unfailing involvement and active practice in the field. *"Always first choice,"* he has been particularly active in the lobbying arena of late.

**Clients/Work Highlights:** The team continues to advise private landowners and developers as well as local governments, regional planning councils and other public entities.

## Pappas Metcalf Jenks and Miller

**The Firm:** Sources showed no hesitation in agreeing that this growing real estate boutique is a force to be reckoned with in the Jacksonville area. Frequently noted for its successful track record in land use and zoning matters, its recent projects include the acquisition and redevelopment of 11 East Forsyth, a historic property in downtown Jacksonville. Home to a *"hard-working and intelligent"* team, the firm has also worked on the DRI for the Palencia mixed-use development.

**The Lawyers:** **Lynn Pappas** is a *"tenacious, bright and imaginative"* attorney, who is able to pull large projects together. One of the best land use attorneys in the state, she is further distinguished by her strength in transactional work.

**Clients/Work Highlights:** This team represent and provide advice to Florida landowners and developers in a variety of industries and sectors.

## Bercow & Radell PA

See firm details p.659

**The Firm:** This six-lawyer boutique focuses exclusively on land use, zoning and environmental law. Frequently appearing in high-profile redevelopment projects for major clients, it represents the interests of landowners and developers seeking approvals from governmental boards and agencies.

**The Lawyers:** **Jeffrey Bercow**'s caseload has been dominated by the redevelopment and conversion of existing property in central Miami. An *"incredibly intelligent man,"* his *"take no prisoners"* approach earned him much endorsement from the market. He frequently advises shopping center and residential developers on the zoning aspects of major projects throughout South Florida.

## Fowler White Boggs Banker

**The Firm:** This respected old-line Florida firm houses *"a really strong cast"* of land use attorneys. Although the firm has offices across the state, sources point to the Tampa office as *"setting the standard for the rest to follow."* A 27-member team handles the full range of transactions, entitlements and permitting, and stands out for its work in DRI and the environmental and land use issues surrounding major redevelopment on brownfield and infill sites. Urban development is another respected facet of this team's work.

**The Lawyers:** President of the firm **Rhea Law** is instrumental in handling some of the biggest DIR projects in the state and beyond. She recently acted in the Becksley ranch project, a 6,000-acre mixed-use project in California. **Thomas Pelham** is a certified planner, who advises both public and private sector clients on the permitting, zoning and planning aspects of major projects. "*He is thoughtful, extremely bright and just outstanding in the field,*" reported sources.

**Clients/Work Highlights:** The department represents major developers and businesses, including residential, commercial and industrial entities, electronic-manufacturing firms, chemical plants, phosphate operations, petroleum storage facilities, and commercial and industrial plant operators.

## Bricklemyer Smolker & Bolves PA

**The Firm:** A Tampa-based boutique, this firm has successfully positioned itself at the crossroads of environmental and real estate law. The land use practice encompasses the full spectrum of advice, from small-scale local permitting to major DRIs. It also possesses expertise in more specialist areas such as dredge and fill permits, wetland and upland habitat mitigation agreements, stormwater management permits and water use permits.

**The Lawyers:** Sources point to name partner **Keith Bricklemyer** as this group's leading light. He employs his "*finely tuned legal skills*" in dealing with zoning and planning matters, often requiring careful consideration of environmental matters. In addition, he is frequently involved in DRIs.

**Clients/Work Highlights:** The team regularly represents property owners, businesses and local governments.

## Shubin & Bass

See firm details p.672

**The Firm:** In contrast with most of the other firms in the market, this team has built up a fine reputation and flourishing practice representing objectors in development disputes. The team is composed of a number of trial lawyers, who specialize in litigation with elements of public law. The team typically represents local governments and other public sector bodies opposing development and contesting the actions of developers.

**The Lawyers:** **John Shubin** is an experienced litigator, who is "*effective and articulate in public hearings and successfully promotes his client's opinion by bringing matters to court,*" said sources. Frequently representing local authorities and Florida cities, he is a popular choice among clients for his handling of eminent domain issues and development-related litigation.

**Clients/Work Highlights:** Representative clients include the University of Miami; State of Florida; City of North Miami; Fairfield Residential; Montenay Power and Rouse.

## Other Notable Practitioners

**PK Fletcher** (see p.636) from Hogan & Hartson LLP is among the "*crème de la crème*" of real estate lawyers. Currently acting as statewide counsel for Lennar, she displays "*all-around impressive skills*" within the real estate arena. Sources also endorsed **Samuel Goren** of Fort Lauderdale firm Goren, Cherof, Doody & Ezrol PA as "*a truly excellent local government lawyer – everyone respects him to the highest degree.*" **Charles Siemon** is "*certainly one of the preeminent land use lawyers.*" Although based in Boca Raton, his trial activities and notable "*academic credence*" ensure he is well known across the USA. Former Holland & Knight LLP attorney **Susan Delegal** (see p.633) now resides at Fort Lauderdale firm Billing, Cochran Heath Lyles & Mauro PA. She represents a wealth of developer clients in their zoning matters and is "*a splendid adviser*" in the field.

# TAX

## Band 1

## Greenberg Traurig LLP

See firm details p.664

**The Firm:** Sophisticated clients agree that it is the sheer depth of this tax department that sets it out as a clear leader: "*Not many firms can lay claim to having international, federal, state and local tax covered, but this firm nails them all.*" Clients value the obvious advantages that an international powerhouse of a firm such as this can offer, that is its bottomless resources and wealth of technical expertise across a national network of offices, but there are more subtle reasons too. The attorneys have the "*industry-specific knowledge*" and tailor their advice accordingly; they are "*book-smart and user-friendly, a unique combination in the area.*" International tax is a recognised forte of the group, although clients also noted the proficiency of the firm in negotiating and structuring real estate joint ventures.

**The Lawyers:** Transactional tax attorney **Joel Maser** (see p.644) is "*well recognized at the Bar as a terrific and popular tax lawyer,*" according to clients. "*A very talented guy,*" Maser is often found negotiating and structuring real estate joint ventures and has recently been busy representing The Related Group of Florida in this regard. He also has niche experience representing auto dealerships on pure tax matters. **Ozzie Schindler** (see p.650) is a recent arrival to this

team and is growing an enviable international tax practice for himself. "*A fixture in the tax community,*" Schindler's practice encompasses all aspects of international tax planning, including corporate and private client tax planning. **Charles Stiver** (see p.653) has a great reputation as a transactional tax attorney and is a "*real tax professional.*" He is best known for his corporate and M&A tax practice, and is also involved in major international tax projects and the taxation of capital markets transactions. **Steve Lapidus** (see p.642) is chair of both the executive compensation and employee benefits practice and the Miami tax, trusts and estates group. He is one of the most respected attorneys in the field: "*He's been the leader in the area for many years now.*" Lapidus is in great demand from compensation committees and boards of directors regarding their obligations to shockholders, and he has a practice that encompasses negotiating and drafting executive employment agreements, equity compensation plans and pension plans. Up-and-comer **Russel Hintze** (see p.639) impresses clients with his transactional and controversy practice; they "*admire the quality of his work product.*" Hintze is knowledgeable on federal and state tax litigation and controversy and is classed as one to watch out for in the future.

**Clients/Work Highlights:** INVESCO; Hilton Hotels; The Related Group of Florida and Swire Properties.

## Holland & Knight LLP

See firm details p.1534

**The Firm:** Clients respect this firm "*for its high-quality advice, knowledge and efficiency. It is of course one of the best firms in the market.*" Running themes of the client feedback on this practice include the "*personal touch of the impressive attorneys*" and the thorough understanding they have of the business deal in hand: "*They regularly apply their practical knowledge of our industry to best effect.*" Workwise, the firm has the full range of tax covered, proving itself adept at handling international, federal, state and local, tax controversies and employee benefits. There are over 70 lawyers involved in tax across the firm. Clients were quick to point to the team's handling of tax controversies and specialist knowledge of the tax laws that apply to tax-exempt organizations.

**The Lawyers:** Clients were keen to emphasize that "*the reason the firm is held in such high regard is primarily due to its superb attorneys.*" The "*true standout*" **Bernie Barton** (see p.627) is key to their affections. "*A man of integrity,*" Barton routinely impresses clients with his in-depth understanding of technically challenging tax issues and their practical application to business. A well-known figure at the Florida Department of Revenue, Barton's "*opinion on matters carries a substantial amount of weight.*" Senior partner in the private wealth services group

**Andrew Weinstein** (see p.655) evokes the highest regard for his domestic and international tax, trust and estate planning practice. Weinstein is sought after for his experience in tax disputes and maintains an impressive international private client practice, often found advising clients in the shipping industry. The "*academically exceptional*" Mark Holcomb (see p.640) adopts a "*details-oriented approach.*" According to clients, he "*gets straight to the point while still giving you all the different perspectives; he follows his client's instructions and routinely delivers.*" He is the go-to person for state and local tax issues. Peers do not hesitate to refer work to **James Ervin** (see p.635), being safe in the knowledge that "*clients would just get the best service possible.*" He is experienced in the tax controversy, litigation and legislative arenas. **Robert Friedman** (see p.636) is well versed in employee benefits, pension and tax planning issues. He excels in the design and drafting of 401(k) plans and corporate M&A with a focus on public finance tax issues.

Clients/Work Highlights: This taxation group's clients range from the largest international and domestic companies to individuals protecting their personal and business assets. Regulated and unregulated common carriers, national and international charities and other tax-exempt or nonprofit organizations are the types of clients this department represents.

## Band 2

### Akerman Senterfitt
See firm details p.657

The Firm: Brimming with "*experience and practicality,*" this large Florida outfit is a key player in the tax market. Clients particularly value the statewide reach of the firm and highlight the experience of its tax lawyers in structuring business entities. The tax department overlaps with the corporate team to a client's advantage. International tax planning, executive compensation, state and local tax and work for tax-exempt entities form the backbone of the department, but it is in M&A and reorganizations that the group is most highly praised. Work of note during the past year includes acting in several tax disputes and handling nationwide litigation for auto finance companies regarding bad debt sales tax refunds.

The Lawyers: Attorneys in this group "*really know what their individual strengths are and play on them to best effect for the client,*" according to sources. "*Cut above the rest*" **Henry Raattama** (see p.648) is revered for his representation of tax-exempt organizations and has been pivotal in developing a nonprofit governance project for south Florida this year. "*Just a damned good attorney and a solid citizen to boot,*" **Don Duffy** (see p.634) impresses with his transactional and controversy practice. Meanwhile, **Russell Hale** (see p.638) is gaining profile for his "*flourishing state and local practice*" and has built up valuable experience in the banking and financial institutions sectors. **Frank Cordero** (see p.632) is a younger member of the team and is acknowledged by leading clients for "*his highly intelligent drafting skills, often on very complex matters.*" Cordero has an international and transactional tax practice and is one to watch in the coming years. Rounding off the veritable bazaar of experienced practitioners on offer here is **Alan Lederman** (see p.642), who joined from Broad and Cassel in December 2005. Lederman is the "*smartest tax lawyer in Florida,*" according to some sources, with one commenting: "*If you go to him with an issue, he can cite you every relevant case and even open the book at the right page, he really is super-brilliant.*" His encyclopedic mind and eye for the minutiae will add obvious weight to the department, as will his vast experience in the real estate sector.

Clients/Work Highlights: Darden Restaurants; Mears Transportation Group; Florida Bankers Association; DaimlerChrysler and the University of Miami.

### Baker & McKenzie
See firm details p.866

The Firm: It is partially due to the daunting size and stature of this "*huge international powerhouse*" that its Miami office has an impressive litany of tax clients, but it is also because the "*brilliance*" of the attorneys. The full range is undertaken here, including transactional, state and local taxation, but it is in the field of international tax that this firm excels. It has the ability to seamlessly draw on a wealth of resources and true specialists in other offices and

clients find particular value in the fact that a one-stop shop approach can be adopted: "*For any eventuality, you need look no further than this firm.*" Transactional tax advice and tax controversy and litigation are other noted strengths.

The Lawyers: **Robert Hudson** (see p.640) is pivotal to the standing of the firm in the Florida tax market. "*One hell of a smart cookie who is just in a different league to most,*" Hudson is not only sought out by referring attorneys, but is pinpointed by some of the leading international clients for his expertise. He is frequently found undertaking restructuring and global tax planning for foreign-controlled business with US interests, and also advises a few non-US nationals seeking to invest in Florida. Up-and-comer **Stewart Kasner** (see p.641) is a new arrival to the team from Karp & Genauer PA and is an "*energetic young lawyer who is hard working and doing a great job.*"

Clients/Work Highlights: As well as representing the major corporations a firm of this size attracts, it is also found advising private banks, trustees and wealth management professionals through its respected international private banking group.

### Bilzin Sumberg Baena Price & Axelrod LLP
See firm details p.660

The Firm: The start of 2005 heralded the arrival of some of the market's biggest hitters to this firm's tax department, and throughout the year the firm has grown in acclaim and defined its position at the top end of the marketplace. This tax department covers all areas, from local property tax to advising on the acquisition of multinational companies. Traditional tax planning, tax litigation and state and local tax issues form the daily caseload of the group; however the arrival of such esteemed practitioners from the former Steel Hector Davis law firm brings with it a broad-based skill set and experience in the full range of tax issues. A coup for the team this year was providing tax advice to tax-exempt organization North Broward Hospital District.

The Lawyers: Enthusiastic comments such as "*he is just the best of the best*" earn **Samuel Ullman** (see p.654) the sobriquet "*the professor of Florida tax.*" Ullman concentrates his practice on federal tax issues and has built up an enviable reputation for his transactional and tax controversy work. He has also developed an expertise serving as tax counsel in fraud matters. Cochair of the tax department **Richard Goldstein** (see p.637) wins the loyalty of clients through "*his ability to put together a solution to work for both sides*" and his "*bright and creative thinking.*" He advises on complex tax planning and structuring involving M&A. Goldstein has handled tax planning advice in connection with the $4 billion privatisation of LNR Property.

Clients/Work Highlights: Altadis; Alachua County Sheriff's Office; Catalina Marketing; Haas Publishing; Interstate Hotel & Resorts; Leon Medical Centers; North Broward Hospital District; Naples Community Hospital; NBC; TradeStation Securities; Tropicana and Vivendi Universal.

## Carlton Fields

See firm details p.661

**The Firm:** This firm is a favorite for referrals from large national law firms and the clients' choice for international tax planning and real estate tax issues. The taxation group is comprised of 12 attorneys, mostly centered in the Tampa and Miami offices, and undertakes international, federal and state, and local work for corporate clients across the country. As well as tax planning and controversy work, the firm has represented clients on property tax issues in every major metropolitan area of Florida.

**The Lawyers:** **David Burke** (see p.630) is head of the taxation practice group and is referred to by clients as a "*real tax superstar.*" Burke has a broad tax practice that encompasses state and federal tax controversies, international tax consulting and transactional M&A tax issues. He has designed and implemented significant tax deferral techniques and represented clients in substantial tax controversy matters before state and federal authorities. **Cristin Conley** (see p.631) has been involved in some of the best quality work in the tax sector. "*Young, smart and bright,*" she helped to design plans that developed and restructured the foreign operations of US individuals and entities across the world.

Clients/Work Highlights: Citigroup; Hunt Construction Group; Amalie Oil Company; Healthcare Parking Systems; Progress Telecom; Taylor Woodrow; WCI Communities; Barnes & Noble and Brinker International.

## Dean, Mead, Egerton, Bloodworth, Capouano & Bozarth PA

**The Firm:** This well-rounded, medium-sized player is home to 41 lawyers, 16 of whom concentrate on tax matters. It is no surprise that clients point to the proficiency of the group in transactional tax matters, such as providing tax advice in the sale and purchase of businesses, as the tax lawyers at this firm are also corporate transactional attorneys. This tax team also provides advice on a full range of issues, including real estate tax expertise, tax controversy work and the representation of tax-exempt organizations. A coup for the team last year was the engineering of a complex tax-free split-up of Ben Hill Griffin Inc.

**The Lawyers:** **Charles Egerton** (see p.635) is an expert in partnership taxation and clients value his user-friendliness and "*experience in the trenches.*" Like other attorneys in the department, Egerton overlaps his tax practice with corporate and transactional work. However, real estate clients thoroughly recommend his tax planning know-how, and he is also considered a dab hand at handling federal tax controversies. Based in the Fort Pierce office, **Michael Minton** (see p.645) is "*just a great attorney to work with, reliable and responsive,*" said clients. He is one of the preeminent agricultural tax attorneys in the state and has a respected federal income, estate and gift tax practice. **Lauren Detzel** (see p.634) is head of the firm's wealth transfer and estate planning department: "*You will find it hard to find a better estate planning attorney in Florida.*" Her inventive techniques to reduce or avoid paying estate tax and

her expertise in contested tax matters in the transfer tax arena are widely sought after.

Clients/Work Highlights: As well as representing ALICO, Atlantic Blue Trust and A Duda & Sons, the firm is also tax counsel for the Jacksonville Jaguars.

## Tescher Gutter Chaves Josepher Rubin Ruffin & Forman PA

**The Firm:** This midsized tax boutique represents companies and high net worth individuals in "*some heavy-duty sophisticated cases.*" Its skills in estate planning, international and tax controversy work stand out: "*It may not have as many lawyers as other firms, but it is focused on tax and home to quality attorneys.*" The firm is also recommended for its work in the transactional field and its representation of tax-exempt organizations.

**The Lawyers:** Popular attorney **Marvin Gutter** is "*personable, articulate and respected.*" He practices in the areas of federal tax dispute resolution, business combinations, estate planning and probate. He formerly served as a trial counsel with the IRS and has practical knowledge of its workings. A true leader in estate planning, **Donald Tescher** has a loyal following of clients. "*He has the integrity and knowledge that you would expect of a lawyer of his standing,*" according to clients. **Richard Josepher** is a knowledgeable and highly respected attorney, particularly noted for his partnership tax expertise. Peers would "*not hesitate to refer leading clients to **Robert Chaves** as he always does a great job,*" especially on matters related to international tax and estate planning.

## White & Case LLP

See firm details p.1566

**The Firm:** The tax expertise of this "*huge international player*" certainly does not go unnoticed by leading international clients and fellow tax practitioners. Its Miami-based tax team has a glowing reputation for work in the fields of state, local, federal and international tax, and it is one of the few firms to have the global reach to properly serve major clients with multijurisdictional problems. Representations during the year include acting for Babcock Florida Company stockholders in the agreed sale of land to a joint venture, a sale that would not have closed had the firm not resolved an issue involving potential liability for $181 million in corporate income taxes. It also represented Copa Airlines in connection with an IRS audit last year.

**The Lawyers:** **Lawrence Gragg** (see p.638) is commonly thought to have "*an unsurpassed practice.*" He is "*absolutely first rate; bright, creative and hard working,*" and has a broad practice that encompasses federal and state tax work. He has a particular forte representing large Florida real estate developers and is often found structuring real estate ventures. Clients also note the "*numerous qualities*" of **Ed Sawyer** (see p.650): "*He's responsive and intelligent, with a good legal and business mind.*" Described as a "*hands-on partner and well worth the fees,*" Sawyer is experienced in the tax and non-tax aspects of joint ventures and other entities. He is also experienced in issues arising out of the healthcare and real estate spheres.

**Clients/Work Highlights:** Berkley Group; Codina Group; Crocker & Company; CRT Properties; Gulf Bay Group; JDC America; Kelly Tractor; PhyAmerica Physician Group; Stiles Corporation and Westgate Resorts.

## Band 3

### Fowler White Boggs Banker

**The Firm:** This sizable outfit is one of the largest and oldest firms in the state, with nine offices across the state and over 60 years of heritage. Its profile in the tax market is steadily growing in stature throughout the state, although it is the Tampa office which is mostly highly commended. The full range is covered, including international, federal, state and local tax. Clients pointed to the group's expertise in tax controversy work and its appearances before the IRS and the Florida Department of Revenue as particular drawing cards.

**The Lawyers:** Chairman of the firm **Jack Boggs** is a senior tax lawyer and is widely revered for his "*invaluable experience.*" Overlapping trusts and estates and straight tax advice, Boggs wins the loyalty of clients because he is "*a very sharp lawyer, making you feel at ease and throwing out suggestions in a very low-key, yet effective way.*" Clients appreciate how **Mitchell Horowitz**, the corporate practice group leader, utilizes the experience he gained from his time at the IRS to best effect in tax controversy work. He "*truly excels at tax litigation*" and is often found representing corporations and individuals in matters against the IRS and the Florida Department of Revenue. **Steven Barber** is the employee benefits practice group leader. Clients value his "*keen eye for the details*" and for his experience of Section 401(k) plans. At the time of going to press, **Bill Townsend** and **Rex Ware** announced that they would shortly be joining the firm's Tallahassee office from Bilzin Sumberg. One of the most knowledgeable authorities on Florida tax matters, Bill Townsend is "*a gregarious, well-connected guy who sure knows his way around the Florida Department of Revenue*" from his time as general counsel there. At his former firm he represented a multinational corporation in a case

involving issues of corporate income tax and provided consultation and advice to multinational audit firms regarding various Florida tax matters this past year. "*Fabulous technician*" Rex Ware is seen by clients as a behind-the-scenes tactician and a valuable resource on state and local tax issues. He has represented a distribution subsidiary of a major publication company regarding Florida sales tax compliance issues during the year.

**Clients/Work Highlights:** This firm is often found representing closely held corporations and affluent families that may or may not have a business.

### Fox Rothschild LLP

See firm details p.1755

**The Firm:** This full-service firm entered into a merger with the nationally recognized tax boutique August, Kulunas & Dawson, PA at the start of 2005. Although the tax and estates department of this firm is home to over 40 tax attorneys already, the addition of such a well-recognized Florida-based boutique undoubtedly raises its profile in the state. Reported to have made "*a strong tax group even stronger,*" this firm is certainly the one to watch in the market. It undertakes the full range of tax counseling, estate planning and litigation, and the group now has the advantage of offering specialist advice on the taxation of S Corporation. Existing clients are happy that they now have the opportunity of procuring tax advice in Florida, and the combination of service provided will not only ensure a broader service but also expand the firm's national client base.

**The Lawyers:** One of the foremost experts on the provisions of S corporations and flow-through entities, **Jerald August** has more than earned the moniker of "*Mr S Corporation.*" August is the cochair of the tax and estates department, managing partner of the firm's West Palm Beach office and also practices out of the Philadelphia office. A preeminent lawyer, he is skilled in tax planning for closely held businesses and an authority on federal tax matters.

### Hopping Green & Sams, PA

See firm details p.665

**The Firm:** Based in Tallahassee, this midsized, 40-lawyer firm is a perennial contender for the most sophisticated domestic work in the market. It has carved out a national reputation in the areas of administrative and governmental law, yet the presence of tax specialist Victoria Weber ensures that it is also widely sought after for state and local tax matters. The department worked on a number of cases that went to the Florida Supreme Court during the past year, representing major trade associations challenging proposed constitutional amendments that would impose tax on goods and services.

**The Lawyers:** **Victoria Weber** (see p.655) is a former general counsel for the Florida Department of Revenue. As well as her state and local tax expertise, she has experience of the legislative process and ad valorem tax expertise.

**Clients/Work Highlights:** Disney; GM; Florida Power & Light; ExxonMobil and Florida Chamber of Commerce.

### Packman, Neuwahl & Rosenberg

**The Firm:** This impressive tax boutique has garnered quite a reputation for its armory of "*highly experienced tax practitioners*" and the array of tax matters it covers. Although the full range is covered, its work in international asset protection, tax controversy and estate planning is most highly commended by clients. Indeed, nine of the 15 attorneys at the firm are dedicated to international tax planning. High net worth clients also value the immigration expertise provided by the firm.

**The Lawyers:** **Michael Rosenberg** has a flourishing international tax practice. Clients value his accounting background and refer to "*the wealth of talent he possesses, his thoroughness and his managerial skills.*" **Dennis Ginsburg** is similarly recognized for "*the exceptionally good job he does for his clients.*" Ginsburg concentrates on international and domestic estate planning, and he is well versed in structuring pre-immigration tax plans for a mostly wealthy Latin American client base seeking to relocate to the USA. He also frequently advises US-based clients on tax efficient outbound investments.

**Clients/Work Highlights:** The firm is often found representing a high net worth Latin American client base and is a key port of call for referrals from domestic and overseas sources.

### Vickers Madsen & Goldman

**The Firm:** Home to some smart state and local tax attorneys, this three-partner tax boutique "*may be small but it certainly packs a punch.*" The firm is also experienced in administrative and governmental law.

**The Lawyers:** **Robert Goldman** has "*a great command of state and local tax issues,*" say clients. His knowledge of ad valorem and sales taxes is coupled with a niche expertise in the tax treatment of e-commerce. **Cass Vickers** is also skilled in state and local taxation issues and has helped to shape and develop many state tax policies.

**Clients/Work Highlights:** This firm represents a raft of notable clients, such as Lennar, Florida Telecommunications Industry Association and United Technologies.

## Band 4

### Ausley & McMullen

**The Firm:** This firm is home to over 30 attorneys and fields a compact, two-partner tax team. Clients place a high value on the level of partner attention and experience they get here. State and local tax advice are areas in which the firm excels. Recommendations were also forthcoming for the group's work in tax planning and structuring for limited partnerships and joint ventures.

**The Lawyers:** **Robert Pierce** is described as "*a real force in Tallahassee,*" and is often found impressing clients with "*the ingenious ideas he always comes up with.*" A former general counsel with the Florida Department of Revenue, Pierce has developed a respected state and local tax, estate planning and lobbying practice.

Clients/Work Highlights: The firm is general counsel to Capital City Bank Group, the Tallahassee Democrat and the Florida Institute of Certified Public Accountants.

### Barnett, Bolt, Kirkwood, Long & McBride

The Firm: Tax law is a key strength of this full-service firm, with seven of its 20 lawyers dedicated to tax and three devoted to estate planning. Even though the firm has grown from its tax boutique beginnings into a full-service law firm, its specialist knowledge in this sector has become its trademark. However, clients now have the added advantage of being able to draw on specialists in other practice areas. "*An exceptionally well thought of firm in Tampa,*" it has a reputation with its clients for consistency and "*has been and will remain a prominent fixture at the Florida tax Bar.*"

The Lawyers: **Leslie Barnett** has been "*a key figure in the tax community for many years now.*" He advises clients on estate planning and excise, state and local tax, and is also well versed in real estate transactions. **Peter Kirkwood** possesses "*all the admirable qualities you would expect in a lawyer,*" which clients went on to suggest is a trait found in the majority of the attorneys at the firm. Kirkwood advises clients on estate planning and represents closely held businesses.

Clients/Work Highlights: The firm maintains a client roster of closely held companies and high net worth individuals.

### Bronstein, Carlson, Gleim & Smith, PA

The Firm: This St. Petersburg-based firm is home to attorneys who are experienced in handling tax planning as well as representing all kinds of healthcare providers. Clients select this firm for the level of dedicated partner attention on offer and thoroughly recommend the quality of advice provided, particularly the firm's expertise in complex estate planning. The firm enjoys a loyal following among local high net worth individuals and is praised for its "*client-driven ethos.*"

The Lawyers: **Joel Bronstein** is the main contact at this firm for taxation matters and represents some of the state's most affluent private clients. His workload includes complex estate planning and corporate and business law.

### Comiter, Singer & Baseman, LLP

The Firm: This Palm Beach-based tax boutique has eight specialist tax attorneys who are well versed in all forms of tax law. From estate planning to all facets of corporate and partnership law, clients report that this firm "*has it covered.*" Business succession planning and asset and estate planning are the recognized fortes of the firm, with clients pointing to the user-friendliness of the attorneys as a key strength. A coup for the team this past year was representing the Rendina Companies in the tax planning and structuring of a sale of $400 million worth of medical office buildings.

The Lawyers: Tax specialist **Richard Comiter** is one of the top partnership attorneys in the state. However, this is not the extent of his practice, with

business succession, wealth transfer planning and real estate transactions also featuring heavily.

Clients/Work Highlights: The firm undertakes a lot of wealth succession planning for entrepreneurs and high net worth individuals. The team also provides tax advice to the Florida Panthers, Abrika Pharmaceuticals and Rendina Companies.

### Gunster, Yoakley & Stewart, PA

The Firm: This well-respected, full-service law firm has six offices across the state, 120 lawyers and a long lineage in the state. International tax advice is a true forte of this practice, which also advises companies, partnerships and high net worth families on domestic tax issues and tax controversies. Corporate tax planning is another area recognized by clients, who describe the firm as possessing "*business awareness as well as legal awareness.*" During the past year, it has represented a large international family in the resolution of certain domestic and international tax matters.

The Lawyers: **Martin Press** comes very highly recommended by clients for his "*technical acumen and effective estate planning.*" He represents private clients in both the USA and Europe and wins plaudits for his international and tax controversy work. **James Davis** is a member of the firm's corporate department and instills in clients the feeling of there being "*a positive solution to each case.*" He is experienced in employee benefits and tax and estate planning.

Clients/Work Highlights: Domestic and international high net worth families and individuals comprise the backbone of the client base of this taxation department, however large conglomerates also feature in the client roster.

### Johnson, Pope, Bokor, Ruppel & Burns, PA

The Firm: This respected full-service law firm operates out of Clearwater and Tampa and has built on its "*tradition for tax excellence*" by developing into an excellent and rounded business firm.

The Lawyers: Much of the profile of the tax planning and controversies department rests on the shoulders of **Bruce Bokor**. Clients spoke of him as "*a very smart attorney – he brings years of experience with him to the table.*" His practice encompasses planning advice for the sale and purchase of businesses and estate planning, and he has developed a niche in advising on tax planning for charitable organizations.

Clients/Work Highlights: Businesspersons; professionals; closely held businesses and charitable groups make up the client base of this firm.

### Karp & Genauer PA

The Firm: This Miami-based tax boutique fields four tax specialists who have developed an admired reputation for international tax advice. Although clients note that this firm may not have the resources some of the other leading firms in the state have, it is the dedicated partner attention and high level of service that clients admire.

The Lawyers: **Joel Karp** is a senior figure in the tax community and widely esteemed for being "*not only an international tax supremo but also a prince of a man.*"

### Squire, Sanders & Dempsey L.L.P.
See firm details p.1650

The Firm: Following its merger with Steel Hector & Davis LLP and a number of departures, this firm is currently going through a period of transition and growth. The merger has facilitated a shift from representing local or regional clients to now operating as an international firm with a Miami office and a more national client base. Offering all the advantages and resources of a global firm, this tax department has over 30 dedicated attorneys in total. Clients appreciate the fact that they "*tend to think less like lawyers and more like businesspeople, which is invaluable.*" International and transactional tax matters are where the firm excels, and during the past year, it has provided corporate, international and cross-border tax advice to many a Fortune 500 company.

The Lawyers: The "*thorough, diligent and creative*" **Richard Winston** (see p.656) impresses clients with his "*sharp, up-to-the minute corporate and international tax advice.*" Considered "*good at pulling together the right team for the case,*" Winston is also frequently sought after for his advice on domestic and cross-border transactions. He has provided international tax advice to Warner Channel/Time Warner with respect to media operations conducted in various Latin American countries.

Clients/Work Highlights: Research in Motion; Mailboxes Etc. Latin America; Oxbow Carbon & Minerals; Florida Power & Light; Florida Crystals and the University of Miami.

### Other Notable Practitioners

**Robert Panoff** of Robert E Panoff PA is regularly sought out for his criminal tax and litigious expertise: "*For criminal tax work, it has to be Bob.*" He also handles a slew of civil and pre-detection criminal cleanup cases, and is a favored port of call for referrals because of his "*extreme confidentiality*" and "*direct, no-nonsense approach.*" **Albert O'Neill** of Trenam, Kemker, Scharf, Barkin, Frye, O'Neill & Mullis PA in Tampa impresses with his "*all-around tax know-how*" and federal and state tax practice. O'Neill is particularly skilled in partnership planning, executive compensation and estate planning. **Jonathan Warner** of the Law Offices of Jonathan H. (Jason) Warner, PA, continues to be singled out by clients for "*the great relationships he forges,*" and he is the first choice for referrals for many a law firm. **Sherwin Simmons** (see p.651) of Buchanan Ingersoll PC is a popular and senior attorney on the tax circuit and "*has been president and chairman of everything over the years.*" "*Far from slowing up, he is still an absolute engine*" and is well equipped to handle the full range of tax issues. During the past year, Simmons worked on the high-profile estate of Frazier Jelke III. **Sharon Quinn Dixon** of Stearns Weaver Miller Weissler Alhadeff & Sitterson, PA is "*one of the few great employee benefits specialists in the* *state*," and is mostly found representing corporate clients on qualified retirement plans, M&A due diligence reviews, tax and ERISA compliance and related litigious matters. **Michael Canan** of Gray Robinson PA in Orlando provides a "*wonderful and responsive service.*" His employee benefits practice includes retirement planning, and work on ESOPs and Section 401(k) plans.

# Leaders in Florida

## AARON, William
William Aaron, Miami
305 371 5800
*Recommended in Litigation*

## ACKERBAUM COX, Joyce
Baker & Hostetler LLP, Orlando
407 649 4000
*Recommended in Employment*

## ALDRICH, Marcy Levine
Akerman Senterfitt, Miami
305 374 5600
marcy.aldrich@akerman.com
*Recommended in Insurance*
**Career:** Marcy Levine Aldrich, a shareholder who focuses her practice on class actions and complex insurance litigation, has represented automobile, property and life insurance companies in the defense of over 100 class actions in both state and federal courts. She has handled other complex insurance litigation, including bad faith litigation and appeals in state and federal courts and has been involved in the defense of securities and products liability class actions. She is a Member of the American Bar Association and has written for the Defense Research Institute and American Bar Association publications on the subject of class action litigation.

## ALEXANDER, Bruce
Boose Casey Ciklin Lubitz Martens McBane & O'Connell, West Palm Beach
561 832 5900
*Recommended in Construction*

## ALHADEFF, Richard
Stearns Weaver Miller Weissler Alhadeff & Sitterson, PA, Miami
305 789 3200
*Recommended in Real Estate*

## ALLEY, John-Edward
Ford & Harrison LLP, Tampa
813 261 7801
jalley@fordharrison.com
*Recommended in Employment*
**Practice Areas:** Having practiced in traditional labor and employment law for more than 30 years, John-Edward Alley has represented employers in hundreds of union election cases, including the decertification of incumbent unions. He has negotiated union contracts and handled trials of representation cases and unfair labor practice charges. In addition, he has successfully represented employers in hundreds of discrimination charges and lawsuits, including employment class actions. He earned his Undergraduate and Law Degrees (with honors) from the University of Florida and his LLM (Labor Law) from New York University.

## ALONSO, Fernando C
Hunton & Williams, Miami
305 810 2570
falonso@hunton.com
*Recommended in Corporate/M&A*
**Practice Areas:** Mr Alonso's clients include a broad range of publicly owned and privately held US and foreign companies and financial institutions. Mr Alonso has led numerous significant acquisitions, mergers, joint ventures and other business transactions, including those involving cross-border complexities. His practice involves representation of companies in connection with their equity and debt financings. Mr Alonso regularly represents foreign clients in connection with US acquisitions, as well as domestic companies in connection with their international expansion. He has particular experience in representing multinational telecommunications carriers and service providers, as well as energy companies.
**Prof. Memberships:** Florida State Bar; American, Cuban-American, and Miami-Dade County Bar Associations; Executive Committee, Yale Law School.
**Career:** Partner and Chairman of the firm's Latin American Practice Group.
**Publications:** Lectures regularly at conferences and seminars on international corporate and finance matters.
**Personal:** Mr Alonso received his BA with distinction in History in 1980 from Yale College, having graduated summa cum laude and as a member of Phi Beta Kappa. He received his JD in 1983 from the Yale Law School. Before commencing his practice, Mr Alonso served as a judicial clerk for the United States District Court for the Southern District of New York.

## ALVAREZ, Pedro A
White & Case LLP, Miami
305 995 5246
palvarez@whitecase.com
*Recommended in Banking & Finance, Corporate/M&A*
**Practice Areas:** Practice involves a broad range of corporate and corporate finance matters with an emphasis on transactions related to Latin America. Regularly counsels private and public companies in all aspects of general corporate matters including mergers and acquisitions. Practice also involves the representation of issuers, underwriters and lenders in a wide variety of corporate finance transactions. Has also participated extensively in the formation and restructuring of significant transnational joint ventures in the financial, telecommunications, mining and other sectors.
**Prof. Memberships:** Florida Bar Association.

## ALVAREZ, Victor M
White & Case LLP, Miami
305 995 5223
valvarez@whitecase.com
*Recommended in Banking & Finance, Corporate/M&A*
**Practice Areas:** Engaged primarily in the representation of financial institutions in corporate and structured finance transactions, particularly in Latin America. Has extensive experience in the representation of issuers, underwriters and other financial intermediaries in all aspects of international and Latin American capital markets transactions.
**Prof. Memberships:** American Bar Association; Florida Bar Association.

## ALVAREZ-FARRÉ, Emilio J
White & Case LLP, Miami
305 995 5219
ealvarez@whitecase.com
*Recommended in Bankruptcy, Corporate/M&A*
**Practice Areas:** Concentrates on cross-border mergers and acquisitions, including privatizations, and international financial transactions. Has represented major corporations and banks in Latin America on numerous acquisitions, dispositions and financings. Has also represented the governments of Argentina, Chile, Venezuela and Panama in numerous privatizations.
**Prof. Memberships:** The Florida Bar.

## AMES, Stuart
Stearns Weaver Miller Weissler Alhadeff & Sitterson, PA, Miami
305 789 3200
*Recommended in Banking & Finance*

## ANDREWS, William
Coffman, Coleman, Andrews & Grogan, Jacksonville 904 389 5161
*Recommended in Employment*

## ARNOLD, Richard
Kenny Nachwalter PA, Miami
305 373 1000
rarnold@kennynachwalter.com
*Recommended in Antitrust*
**Practice Areas:** Antitrust and trade regulation, complex commercial litigation.
**Prof. Memberships:** The Florida Bar, American Bar Association, The American Law Institute, Advisory Committee, US District Court, Southern District of Florida, Special Assistant Attorney General, Antitrust, State of Florida, 1982-85, 1987-89.
**Personal:** University of Illinois, LLM 1975, University of South Carolina, JD, 1973, East Tennessee State University, BS 1969.

## ARONSON, Daniel H
Greenberg Traurig LLP, Fort Lauderdale
954 768 8201
aronsond@gtlaw.com
*Recommended in Corporate/M&A*
**Practice Areas:** Corporate and securities, M&A.
**Prof. Memberships:** State of Florida, Capital Development Board and Capital Development Advisory Committee

(appointed by governor) (1997-present).
**Career:** Recognized, South Florida's Top Dealmakers of the Year in Mergers & Acquisitions, Daily Business Review, 2005; listed, Top Lawyer, South Florida Legal Guide, 2005; listed, Best Lawyers, 2006; listed, 'Chambers & Partners USA Guide', 2003, 2004, 2005, 2006 editions; listed, 2004 Legal Elite, Florida Trend Magazine.
**Publications:** Author, 'Raising Capital for the Emerging Business: A Primer for Entrepreneurs', Donnelley (4th edition - 2001).
**Personal:** JD, New York University School of Law, 1983; BA, summa cum laude, Vanderbilt University, 1979.

### ASHBY, Kimberly
Akerman Senterfitt, Orlando
407 843 7860
kim.ashby@akerman.com
*Recommended in Construction*
**Career:** Kimberly Ashby, a shareholder Board Certified in Construction and Appellate Law, focuses her practice on construction law, appellate law and commercial litigation. She is listed in Best Lawyers in America, was named one of the 'Best Lawyers of Orlando' by Orlando Magazine, one of the Top 5 Women in Construction Litigation and a Top 40 under 40 by the Orlando Business Journal, and as an Appellate Specialist in Florida Trend's Legal Elite. She is Chair of The Florida Bar Construction Certification Committee and Co-Chair of the ABA Construction Litigation Committee. She is General Counsel for Central Florida Builders Exchange.

### AUGUST, Jerald
Fox Rothschild LLP, West Palm Beach
561 835 9600
*Recommended in Tax*

### AUSLANDER, Charles
Greenberg Traurig LLP, Miami
305 579 0500
auslanderc@gtlaw.com
*Recommended in Litigation*
**Practice Areas:** Appellate; litigation.
**Career:** Listed, 'Best Lawyers in America', 2006; listed, 'Chambers & Partners USA Guide', 2004-06; 2002 Champions for Children, Chairman's Recognition Award, Children's Services Council; 2002 Child Professional of the Year Award, Department of Children and Families, State of Florida; Alliance for Human Services of Miami-Dade County, Recognition Award for commitment to Children, Youth and Families, November 2002; Kathleen Wright Award, 10/21/2000, presented by Family Central, Inc.; 'Put Something Back, Child Advocacy' pro bono award, Dade County Bar Association, 4/94.
**Personal:** JD, George Washington University Law School, 1982; BA, with high honors, University of Virginia, 1979.

### AVILA, Alcides
Holland & Knight LLP, Miami
305 374 8500
alcides.avila@hklaw.com
*Recommended in Banking & Finance, Corporate/M&A*
**Practice Areas:** Partner in the firm's Business Law Section, focusing on international and domestic banking law and commercial transactions. A significant portion of his practice involves the representation of state and national banks, bank holding companies, Edge Act corporations, international bank agencies and representative offices. Specific areas of experience include counseling foreign banks, bank holding companies, and foreign investors on establishing banking operations in the United States; licensing, de novo charters, and regulatory compliance matters; complex bank holding company formations; bank acquisitions; and the general representation of banking clients before all state and federal regulatory agencies.

### AWNER, Jonathan L
Akerman Senterfitt, Miami
305 374 5600
jonathan.awner@akerman.com
*Recommended in Corporate/M&A*
**Career:** Jonathan Awner, National Chair of the firm's Corporate Practice Group, has broad experience in public and private securities transactions, mergers and acquisitions, and private equity investments. He has served as lead issuer's Counsel in underwritten equity and debt offerings that have raised over $4 billion, including several IPO transactions. He has represented buyers, sellers, boards of directors and other stakeholders in over 300 mergers and acquisitions. Corporate governance, compliance and advisory services, including internal investigations, are also a focus of his work. His clients include AutoNation Inc., Jacuzzi Brands, Republic Services, Spherion Corporation, and several private equity funds.

### AXELROD, Alan D
Bilzin Sumberg Baena Price & Axelrod LLP, Miami 305 350 2369
aaxelrod@bilzin.com
*Recommended in Corporate/M&A*
**Career:** Mr Axelrod represents public companies in all aspects of their business, including 1934 Act reporting, and public and private companies in M&A transactions. He also handles public and private offerings for a varied group of commercial concerns. His representation encompasses a wide range of businesses and assets, several with aggregate market values in excess of a billion dollars. Specific matters include M&A, private placements of equity and debt (including real estate funds), venture capital financings, secured and unsecured credit facilities, master repurchase and warehouse facility arrangements, joint venture and partner-

ship agreements, and structure and negotiation of diverse business ventures.

### BACHELLER, Chester E
Holland & Knight LLP, Tampa
813 227 8500
chet.bacheller@hklaw.com
*Recommended in Corporate/M&A*
**Practice Areas:** Partner in the Business Section, practicing in the areas of M&A, securities, and finance, including venture capital financing. He has substantial experience in a wide range of mergers, acquisitions and dispositions; public offerings of securities registered under the federal securities laws; and SEC reporting and compliance matters. Mr Bacheller's merger and acquisition practice focuses on representing significant companies on domestic and cross-border transactions. In addition to providing routine securities law advice, Mr Bacheller has been the lead lawyer on dozens of public securities offerings, including IPO's, preferred stocks, junk bonds and investment grade debt, including overnight public offerings.

### BAENA, Scott L
Bilzin Sumberg Baena Price & Axelrod LLP, Miami 305 350 2403
sbaena@bilzin.com
*Recommended in Bankruptcy*
**Career:** Chair of firm's Restructuring and Bankruptcy Department with a personal focus on bankruptcy, restructurings and commercial loan transactions. Active in the development of Florida's commercial laws, having co-sponsored the 1980 revisions to Article 9 of Florida's Uniform Commercial Code. Frequent lecturer and author on subjects within his specialty areas. Has counseled high-visibility clients in many major bankruptcy proceedings, nationally, as well as in Florida. Listed as one of America's Top 100 in the K&A Restructuring Register since 2003 and in Best Lawyers in America since 1988.

### BARBER, Steven
Fowler White Boggs Banker, Tampa
813 228 7411
*Recommended in Tax*

### BARCLAY, James
Ruden McClosky SC, Tallahassee
850 412 2000
*Recommended in Healthcare*

### BARFORD, George
Carlton Fields, St Petersburg
727 821 7000
gbarford@carltonfields.com
*Recommended in Employment*
**Practice Areas:** Employment litigation, discrimination law, wage-hour issues, occupational safety and health law, NLRB matters, non-compete agreements, employment contracts. He represents management exclusively. Board Certified in Labor and Employment Law by The Florida Bar; Florida Supreme Court Cer-

tified mediator.
**Prof. Memberships:** Admitted to practice in Florida and the US Supreme Court. Member, American Bar Association, Labor and Employment Law Section; Fellow, College of Labor and Employment Lawyers; Charter Member, Academy of Florida Management Attorneys.
**Career:** Attorney, Region 12, NLRB; State of Florida, 13th Circuit, Felony Prosecutor.
**Personal:** JD, University of Florida College of Law; BA, University of Illinois.

### BARKETT, John
Shook, Hardy & Bacon LLP, Miami
305 358 5171
jbarkett@shb.com
*Recommended in Environment*
**Practice Areas:** Environmental law, commercial litigation, labor law, and antitrust litigation. Over the years, has been a commercial litigator, independent investigator, environmental litigator, environmental counselor, and, for the past several years, a peacemaker and problem solver, serving as an arbitrator, mediator, facilitator, or allocator in a variety of substantive contexts.
**Prof. Memberships:** Admitted to practice in Florida and before the US Court of Appeals for the Eleventh Circuit. Member of American Bar Association and The Florida Bar. Serves on the CPR Institute for Dispute Resolution's Panel of Distinguished Neutrals. Is a Member of the Chartered Institute of Arbitrators and was a guest lecturer in the International Commercial Arbitration class at Yale Law School.
**Career:** Joined Shook, Hardy & Bacon, 2000 (as Partner).
**Publications:** Is the author of numerous publications and speeches.
**Personal:** JD, Yale University School of Law, 1975; BA, summa cum laude, University of Notre Dame, 1972.

### BARNETT, Leslie
Barnett, Bolt, Kirkwood, Long & McBride, Tampa 813 253 2020
*Recommended in Tax*

### BARTON, Bernard
Holland & Knight LLP, Tampa
813 227 8500
bernie.barton@hklaw.com
*Recommended in Tax*
**Practice Areas:** Partner in the Business Law Section, practices federal, state and local taxation, emphasizing tax planning relating to entity and business transaction structuring. Has substantial experience in administrative and litigated tax disputes. Primary client focus is the representation of entrepreneurs, but also represents public companies and regulated industries in tax-related matters. Barton has supervised and handled financing-related matters, including leveraged leases, sale/leasebacks, synthetic leases and tax

aspects of tax-exempt financing. Substantive areas of his state tax experience include sales and use taxes, corporate income tax, documentary stamp tax, intangible tax, ad valorem tax and various excise tax.

## BASILE, Michael
Stroock & Stroock & Lavan LLP, Miami
305 358 9900
*Recommended in Banking & Finance*

## BASS, Hilarie
Greenberg Traurig LLP, Miami
305 579 0745
bassh@gtlaw.com
*Recommended in Litigation*
**Practice Areas:** Litigation.
**Prof. Memberships:** American Bar Association, Chair, Legal Opportunity Scholarship Committee (2005-present); Member, Task Force on Attorney Client Privilege (2004-present); President, The Florida Bar Foundation; The Florida Bar; United Way of Dad County.
**Career:** Listed, 'Chambers & Partners USA Guide', 2005-06; listed, 2004 Legal Elite, Florida Trend Magazine, listing of Florida's top attorneys as selected by their peers; listed as one of South Florida's Top Lawyers by the South Florida Legal Guide, 2001-05.
**Personal:** JD, summa cum laude, University of Miami School of Law, 1981; BA, magna cum laude, George Washington University, 1975.

## BATTISTA, Paul J
Genovese Joblove & Battista, PA, Miami
305 349 2300
pbattista@gjb-law.com
*Recommended in Bankruptcy*
**Practice Areas:** Has developed expertise and significant experience in representing debtors, creditors' committees, trustees and franchisors in Florida and throughout the US in complex commercial reorganizations, as well as in cross-borders insolvency matters. Recent matters include the debtors' representation in the Chapter 11 of Mars Music in Florida, Possible Dreams, Ltd. in Massachusetts and Systech Retail Systems Corp. in North Carolina as well as its concurrent CCAA proceeding in Toronto. Mr Battista also represented the creditors' committee in the Chapter 11 of Abraham Gosman and regularly represents Burger King Corporation in franchisee bankruptcies throughout the country.

## BAXA JR, Edmund T
Foley & Lardner LLP, Orlando
407 244 3268
ebaxa@foley.com
*Recommended in Construction*
**Career:** Edmund T Baxa Jr is the Managing Partner of the Orlando office of Foley & Lardner LLP and is a member of the firm's Management Committee. He is also a member of both the Construction and the White Collar and Corporate Compliance Practices. Mr Baxa maintains a complex commercial litigation practice focusing on construction law. This specialty includes representation of owners, general contractors, design professionals, subcontractors, and suppliers in contract drafting and negotiation, bid protests, workouts, claims litigation, and arbitration proceedings. Mr Baxa received his JD from the University of Virginia.

## BECERRA, Jacqueline
Greenberg Traurig LLP, Miami
305 579 0534
becerraj@gtlaw.com
*Recommended in Litigation*
**Practice Areas:** Litigation.
**Prof. Memberships:** President Elect, Federal Bar Association, South Florida Chapter.
**Career:** Listed, 'Chambers & Partners USA Guide, 2005-06'; Federal Bar Association's Young Federal Lawyers Award, 2000; Director's Award for Superior Performance, Executive Office for the United States Attorneys, 2001; Tim Evans Memorial Award for Outstanding Performance as an Assistant United States Attorney, 2001.
**Personal:** JD, Yale Law School, 1994. BA, cum laude, University of Miami, 1991.

## BELL, Rodney H
Holland & Knight LLP, Miami
305 374 8500
rodney.bell@hklaw.com
*Recommended in Corporate/M&A*
**Practice Areas:** Partner in the Business Law Section, practicing in the areas of securities, mergers and acquisitions, venture capital and corporate governance. He regularly represents public and private companies in financing and acquisition transactions. Bell assists pharmaceutical, software and other technology companies with licensing, development, product acquisition and other arrangements. In addition, he advises public companies, boards of directors and their audit committees on disclosure and compliance matters arising out of Securities and Exchange Commission rules. Bell is a frequent speaker and writer on topics involving securities regulations, corporate governance and venture capital.

## BERANEK, John
Ausley & McMullen, Tallahassee
850 224 9115
*Recommended in Litigation*

## BERCOW, Jeffrey
Bercow & Radell PA, Miami
305 374 5300
*Recommended in Real Estate*

## BERKOWITZ, Paul
Greenberg Traurig LLP, Miami
305 579 0500
berkowitzp@gtlaw.com
*Recommended in Corporate/M&A*
**Practice Areas:** Corporate; M&A; global trade.
**Prof. Memberships:** Former Vice President, member of Executive Committee and Chairman of Planning and Allocations Committee and Community Relations Committee, current member of the Financial Management Committee, Planning and Allocation Committee and Board of Directors, Greater Miami Jewish Federation; Director, University of Pennsylvania Wharton School of Business Dade Alumni Club.
**Career:** Listed in 'Best of the Bar' by the South Florida Business Journal, April 2003.
**Publications:** Author, 'Board Links With Outside Counsel', The Corporate Board, September/October 2004.
Personal: JD, cum laude, University of Pennsylvania Law School, 1973; BS, cum laude, University of Pennsylvania, 1970.

## BERLIN, Howard J
Kluger, Peretz, Kaplan & Berlin P.L., Miami
305 379 9000
hberlin@kpkb.com
*Recommended in Bankruptcy*
**Practice Areas:** Co-Chair of the Bankruptcy and Creditors' Rights Group. Over 25 years' experience representing corporate debtors, secured lenders, creditors' committees and individual creditors in federal, bankruptcy and state court insolvency proceedings, out-of-court workouts, debt restructuring negotiations, and business reorganization proceedings. Reorganized a variety of business enterprises and serves as the Trustee for Piper Aircraft Corporation Irrevocable Trust, a large, lengthy and complex trusteeship which has generated payment of 100% of eligble claims.
**Prof. Memberships:** Member of the American Bar Association, Dade County Bar Association, previously served as Chairman of the Florida Bar Business Law Section and the Bankruptcy UCC Committee. Completed the American Arbitration Association's 40-hour Circuit Court Mediation Training Program.
**Career:** Admitted to the Florida Bar (1979), the US District Court, Southern and Middle Districts of Florida (1979), and to the US Court of Appeals, Eleventh Circuit (1981). Mr Berlin is a founder and managing member of Kluger, Peretz, Kaplan & Berlin PL.
**Publications:** Co-author of the 1987 revisions to Chapter 727 of the Florida Statutes' Assignments for the Benefit of Creditors.
**Personal:** Earned a JD from the University of Miami School of Law (1979) and a BA from George Washington University in Washington DC (1976). Served as Mayor of the City of Bal Harbour, Florida and currently serves as Assistant Mayor and Councilman.

## BEVERIDGE, Cathy
Fowler White Boggs Banker, Tampa
813 228 7411
*Recommended in Employment*

## BIANCHI, Jaime A
White & Case LLP, Miami
305 371 2700
jbianchi@whitecase.com
*Recommended in Litigation*
**Practice Areas:** Focuses on complex commercial litigation, primarily in the defense of class actions, as well as other suits arising in the cable television and real estate industries. Has been involved in defending clients in more than 40 different class actions filed throughout the country-focused on internet piracy, service disruptions, customer billing disputes, construction defects and securities fraud claims.

## BILZIN, Brian L
Bilzin Sumberg Baena Price & Axelrod LLP, Miami 305 350 2363
bbilzin@bilzin.com
*Recommended in Real Estate*
**Career:** Founding Partner of firm and serves as Counsel to several of South Florida's foremost public and private companies. Leads the firm in its commitment to provide able and expert representation in a broad spectrum of legal areas including the full range of complex commercial real estate and corporate transactions. His own practice includes all major real estate matters, from sales, purchases, and leases to financing, workouts, and reorganizations. In the area of general corporate law, handles mergers and acquisitions, joint ventures, and lending matters, including structured financings.

## BLACK, Roy
Black, Srebnick, Kornspan & Stumpf PA, Miami 305 371 6421
*Recommended in Litigation*

## BLAIN, Russell
Stichter, Riedel, Blain & Prosser PA, Tampa 813 229 0144
rblain@srbp.com
*Recommended in Bankruptcy*
**Practice Areas:** Chapter 11 business reorganizations; workouts and out-of-court loan and debt restructurings; asset acquisitions and sales in bankruptcy cases.
**Prof. Memberships:** Business Law Section of The Florida Bar (Member, Executive Council, and past Chair, Bankruptcy/Uniform Commercial Code Committee). Past President, The Tampa Bay Bankruptcy Bar Association. Member, The Florida Bar, American Bar Association, Hillsborough County Bar Association, Commercial Law League, American Bankruptcy Institute, Ferguson-White American Inn of Court, Board of Fellows of University of Tampa.
**Career:** Speaker and writer on bankrupt-

cy law topics on seminars sponsored by the Florida Bar and other groups.

### BLECHMAN, Bill
Kenny Nachwalter PA, Miami
305 373 1000
wjb@kennynachwalter.com
*Recommended in Antitrust*
**Practice Areas:** Antitrust and trade regulation, complex commercial litigation, multidistrict litigation, false claims act litigation.
**Prof. Memberships:** Dade County and American Bar Associations, The Florida Bar.
**Personal:** Harvard College, BA with honors 1990, University of Miami, JD, with honors, 1983.

### BLOCK, David
Jackson Lewis, Miami
305 577 7600
BlockD@jacksonlewis.com
*Recommended in Employment*
**Practice Areas:** Managing Partner of the Jackson Lewis Miami office. Specializes in the practice of labor and employment law.
**Prof. Memberships:** Executive Council of Labor and Employment Section of the Florida Bar.
**Career:** Attorney at Jackson Lewis for the past 19 years. Managing Partner of the Miami office since 1997.
**Publications:** Former editor of FMLA-Business and Legal Reports.
**Personal:** University of Pennsylvania, JD; Cornell University School of Industrial and Labor Relations, BS. DOB 8 January 1945. Married with two children.

### BLOODWORTH, Darryl
Dean, Mead, Egerton, Bloodworth, Capouano & Bozarth PA, Orlando
407 428 5131
dbloodworth@deanmead.com
*Recommended in Litigation*
**Practice Areas:** Mr Bloodworth has tried commercial and business lawsuits in state and federal courts throughout Florida in matters involving complex commercial litigation, corporate control litigation, legal malpractice defense, breach of contract and business torts, probate and fiduciary litigation, and eminent domain.
**Prof. Memberships:** Member, American College of Trial Lawyers; Member and Past President, Central Florida Chapter of the American Board of Trial Advocates.
**Career:** Board Certified in Civil Trial Law by The Florida Bar; listed in 'The Best Lawyers in America'; Martindale-Hubbell Rating: AV.
**Personal:** University of Florida (JD, 1971); United States Air Force Academy (BS, 1964).

### BLOOM, Mark D
Greenberg Traurig LLP, Miami
305 579 0537
bloomm@gtlaw.com
*Recommended in Bankruptcy*
**Practice Areas:** Reorganization, bankruptcy and restructuring.
**Prof. Memberships:** Past President, Bankruptcy Bar Association of Southern District of Florida; Section of Litigation Leadership, ABA; United Way of Miami-Dade County; Founding Chair and Master of Ceremonies, Leukemia Society of America Annual Barristers' Bash.
**Career:** Listed, 'Best Lawyers in America, 1993-94"; 2002-06; The K&A Restructuring Register, America's Top 100; listed, 'Chambers & Partners USA Guide' 2003-06; listed, 2004 and 2005 Legal Elite, Florida Trend Magazine, South Florida Legal Guide, 'South Florida's Top Lawyers'.
**Personal:** JD, with honors, University of Maryland School of Law; BA, Political Science, Yale University.

### BLOOM, Warren S
Greenberg Traurig LLP, Orlando
407 420 1000
bloomw@gtlaw.com
*Recommended in Banking & Finance*
**Practice Areas:** Public finance.
**Prof. Memberships:** Member, National Association of Bond Lawyers; Member, Florida Bar Association; Member, New York State Bar Association.
**Career:** Rated 'AV' in Martindale-Hubbell's Peer Review.
**Publications:** Frequent speaker for the National Association of Local Housing Finance Authorities, National Federation of Municipal Analysts, American Banking Association, Florida Association of Local Housing Finance Authorities.
**Personal:** JD, with honors, University of Miami School of Law, 1986; BA, with honors, Chemistry, Duke University, 1981.

### BLOOMBERG, Mitchell
Adorno & Yoss LLP, Miami
305 460 1000
*Recommended in Litigation*

### BOGGS, Jack
Fowler White Boggs Banker, Tampa
813 228 7411
*Recommended in Tax*

### BOKOR, Bruce
Johnson, Pope, Bokor, Ruppel & Burns, PA, Clearwater 727 461 1818
*Recommended in Tax*

### BONIFAY, Cecelia
Akerman Senterfitt, Orlando
407 843 7860
cecelia.bonifay@akerman.com
*Recommended in Real Estate*
**Career:** Cecelia Bonifay is a shareholder focusing her practice on land use, zoning, environmental permitting, real property and administrative law. She has held positions with the Tallahassee Department of Community Affairs as assistant to the secretary and as the agency's lobbyist; and the Department of Administration, as

liaison to the state's 11 regional planning councils. She has represented the City of Mount Dora, the Lake County School Board and large Central Florida land owners and developers. She is featured as one of the 'Top 5 Rainmakers in the State' by a local publication and is listed in Florida Trend's Legal Elite.

### BOZARTH, Stephen J
Dean, Mead, Egerton, Bloodworth, Capouano & Bozarth PA, Orlando
407 428 5133
sbozarth@deanmead.com
*Recommended in Real Estate*
**Practice Areas:** Real estate development, real estate sales and purchases, real estate leasing (landlord and tenant), secured and unsecured lending, zoning, and land use law.
**Prof. Memberships:** American Bar Association, Real Property, Probate and Trust Law Section.
**Career:** Board Certified in Real Estate Law by The Florida Bar; listed in 'The Best Lawyers in America', 'Chambers USA - America's Leading Business Lawyers', Florida Trend Magazine Legal Elite, Orlando Business Journal Best of the Bar, and Orlando Magazine Top Central Florida Attorneys.
**Personal:** University of Florida (JD, 1968); Wake Forest University (BBA, 1965).

### BRAMNICK, James
Akerman Senterfitt, Miami
305 374 5600
james.bramnick@akerman.com
*Recommended in Employment*
**Career:** James Bramnick is a shareholder, Chair of the Akerman Senterfitt Labor and Employment Law Practice Group, and Board Certified by the Florida Bar in labor and employment law. He has more than 30 years of experience in exclusively representing employers in labor and employment law matters including labor relations, human resources advice, and employment litigation. Mr Bramnick represents clients from various industries including automotive, banking and financial institutions, public utilities, healthcare, and leisure and hospitality. He is a former Chairman of the Labor and Employment Law Section of the Florida Bar.

### BRANDT, A Peter
Ferencik, Libanoff, Brandt, Bustamante & Williams, Fort Lauderdale
954 474 8080
*Recommended in Construction*

### BRICKLEMYER, Keith
Bricklemyer Smolker & Bolves PA, Miami
813 223 3888
*Recommended in Real Estate*

### BRINDELL, James
Gunster, Yoakley & Stewart PA, West Palm Beach
561 655 1980
*Recommended in Real Estate*

### BRITTAIN, David
Trenam, Kemker, Scharf, Barkin, Frye, O'Neill & Mullis PA, Tampa
813 223 7474
*Recommended in Real Estate*

### BRONIS, Stephen
Zuckerman Spaeder LLP, Miami
305 358 5000
*Recommended in Litigation*

### BRONSTEIN, Joel
Bronstein, Carlson, Gleim & Smith, PA, St Petersburg 727 898 6688
*Recommended in Tax*

### BROWN, Bowman
Shutts & Bowen LLP, Miami
305 379 9107
bbrown@shutts-law.com
*Recommended in Banking & Finance*
**Practice Areas:** Chairman Executive Committee, Financial Services Industry Practice Group.
**Prof. Memberships:** Florida, New York, District of Columbia.
**Career:** Member of Executive Committee and Chairman of Regulatory and Legislative Affairs Committee of Florida International Bankers Association; formerly University of Miami Adjunct Professor of Banking Law, Chairman of Florida Bar Banking Law and Credit Regulation Committee, Trustee of Pan American Development Foundation.
**Publications:** Editor, 'International Banking Centres' published by Euromoney, London, 1982; 'Private Banking and the Law' published by Latin-Finance, 1992; Member of Editorial Advisory Board of Banking and Financial Services Policy Report.
**Personal:** MBA, JD Cornell University.

### BROWN, Christopher
Shook, Hardy & Bacon LLP, Miami
305 358 5171
cdbrown@shb.com
*Recommended in Litigation*
**Practice Areas:** Tort, aviation, employment, and commercial litigation. Is a former Adjunct Professor of International Law at Florida International University and speaks French, Russian and Spanish. Has tried numerous cases in both state and federal courts and has argued before the Supreme Court of Florida.
**Prof. Memberships:** Licensed to practice in the Florida and District of Columbia Bars, and all US federal district courts in the state of Florida. Member of the American Bar Association and the Cuban-American Bar Association and is President of the League of Prosecutors.
**Career:** Joined Shook, Hardy & Bacon, 2002; became Partner, 2005.
**Publications:** Co-author, 'Some Suggestions on Admitting Computer Graphics into Evidence at Trial', 65 Defense Counsel Journal 526 (October 1998).
**Personal:** JD, University of Miami School of Law, 1994; MALD, Fletcher

School of Law and Diplomacy, 1995; Diplóme d'Études Superieures, University of Geneva, 1994; BA, Dartmouth College (Russian Language), 1986.

## BROWN, Daniel
Carlton Fields, Tallahassee
850 224 1585
dbrown@carltonfields.com
*Recommended in Insurance*
**Practice Areas:** Practices insurance litigation, insurance regulation, commercial litigation, class action defense, regulatory and administrative law, state and local tax, and constitutional litigation. Co-Chair, firm's Insurance Practice Group.
**Prof. Memberships:** Admitted to practice in Florida and the US Supreme Court. Member, American Bar Association, Litigation, Tort and Insurance, and Employment Law Sections; Member, Federation of Regulatory Counsel.
**Career:** General Counsel, Florida Department of Administration; Deputy General Counsel, Florida Department of Business Regulation; Ad Valorem Tax Counsel, Florida Department of Revenue.
**Personal:** JD (with high honors), Florida State College of Law, 1974; BA (with honors), University of South Florida, 1971.

## BROWN, Frank
Macfarlane Ferguson & McMullen PA, Tampa 813 273 4200
*Recommended in Employment*

## BROWN, James
Ford & Harrison LLP, Orlando
407 418 4342
jbrown@fordharrison.com
*Recommended in Employment*
**Practice Areas:** Jim Brown concentrates his practice on labor and employment law, representing employers before the National Labor Relations Board and the State of Florida Public Employees Relations Commission, and the Department of Labor. He also defends employers in federal and state courts in civil rights litigation involving race, sex, national origin, discrimination, sexual harassment, disability and age discrimination. Jim is also a certified mediator who has mediated over 300 labor and employment law cases. He earned his JD from the University of North Carolina at Chapel Hill where he was on the Holderness Moot Court.

## BROWN, Ted
Akerman Senterfitt, Orlando
407 843 7860
ted.brown@akerman.com
*Recommended in Real Estate*
**Career:** Ted Brown is a shareholder representing developers and owners active in land acquisition and development. He has been involved in the acquisition of over one billion dollars worth of real estate and has extensive experience in land use and development activities with

special emphasis in wetlands and habitat conservation planning in the context of land development. He is a full Member of the Urban land Institute and was a gubernatorial appointee to the Private Property Rights Study Commission II. Prior to joining the firm he served as VP/General Counsel to Arvida Company.

## BROWN II, C David
Broad and Cassel, Orlando
407 839 4200
*Recommended in Real Estate*

## BRUMBAUGH, John
Richman Greer Weil Brumbaugh Mirabito & Christensen, Miami
305 373 4000
*Recommended in Litigation*

## BRUTON, Burt
Greenberg Traurig LLP, Miami
305 579 0500
brutonb!gtlaw.com
*Recommended in Real Estate*
**Practice Areas:** Real estate.
**Prof. Memberships:** Real Property, Probate and Trust Law Section of The Florida Bar: Real Estate Coordinator, Legislative Review Committee; Member, Committees on Mortgage Law, Tax Aspect of Real Property Law, and Legal Opinions.
**Career:** Listed, 'Best Lawyers in America', 2005-06; listed, 2004 and 2005 Legal Elite, Florida Trend Magazine.
**Publications:** Author of a chapter on Florida documentary stamp taxes appearing in the recently published Florida Bar practice manual on Florida Real Property Complex Transactions.
**Personal:** JD, University of Miami School of Law, 1981; BA, University of North Carolina at Chapel Hill, 1973.

## BUDWICK, Michael
Meland Russin Hellinger & Budwick, Miami 305 358 6363
*Recommended in Bankruptcy*

## BURGESS, Rick
Gunster, Yoakley & Stewart, P.A., Fort Lauderdale 954 462 2000
*Recommended in Environment*

## BURKE, David
Carlton Fields, Tampa
813 223 7000
dburke@carltonfields.com
*Recommended in Tax*
**Practice Areas:** Practices in the areas of state and federal tax controversies, federal, state, and international taxation planning, business planning, mergers and acquisitions. Board Certified in Taxation by The Florida Bar. Co-Chair, Corporate, Tax and Asset-Based Financing Practice Group.
**Prof. Memberships:** Admitted to practice in Florida, Ohio, US Tax Court, Court of Federal Claims. Member, American Bar Association, Taxation Section.
**Publications:** Co-author, 'Kuro and Muben-Lamar - In the Eye of the Behold-

er?' (Florida Bar Journal 2002).
**Personal:** LLM, New York University School of Law, 1982; JD (with honors), Cleveland-Marshall College of Law, 1971; BA (with honors), Cleveland State University, 1977.

## BURRUEZO, Carlos
Fisher & Phillips LLP, Orlando
407 541 0888
cburruezo@laborlawyers.com
*Recommended in Employment*
**Practice Areas:** Carlos Burruezo is Managing Partner of the Orlando office of the national law firm of Fisher & Phillips LLP, practicing exclusively in labor and employment law representing management. An experienced trial lawyer, his practice includes proceedings before federal and state administrative agencies and federal and state trial and appellate courts. He also conducts management and other preventive training on workplace issues. Burruezo is the Chairman of the firm's Hispanic Business Practice Group, which provides Spanish-language labor and litigation support services to clients with Spanish-speaking employees. He received his JD from Cornell Law School in New York in 1989.

## BUSEY, Stephen
Smith Hulsey & Busey, Jacksonville
904 359 7700
*Recommended in Bankruptcy*

## CACCIABEVE, Charles
Carlton Fields, Orlando
407 849 0300
ccacciabeve@carltonfields.com
*Recommended in Construction*
**Practice Areas:** Practices in areas of construction litigation, intellectual property litigation, and general commercial litigation. Represents owners, general contractors, subcontractors, suppliers, architects, and engineers. Extensive experience in drafting and negotiating construction contract documents. Orlando office Managing Shareholder.
**Prof. Memberships:** Admitted to practice in Florida. Member, American Bar Association, Forum on the Construction Industry; former Chairman of the Construction Law Committee, Orange County Bar Association; instrumental in setting up the Orange County Bar Arbitration Services; American Arbitration Association Panel Arbitrator.
**Personal:** JD (with honors), University of Florida College of Law, 1981; BA, Rollins College, 1978.

## CACCIATORE, Ronald
Ronald K Cacciatore PA, Tampa
813 223 4831
*Recommended in Litigation*

## CANAN, Michael
Gray Robinson PA, Orlando
407 843 8880
*Recommended in Tax*

## CANNON III, L Kinder
Holland & Knight LLP, Jacksonville
904 353 2000
kinder.cannon@hklaw.com
*Recommended in Corporate/M&A*
**Practice Areas:** Partner in the firm's Jacksonville office, serves as Holland & Knight's General Counsel. He is a business lawyer and has concentrated his practice in the areas of corporate finance, securities, mergers and acquisitions, venture capital, and franchising law, including corporate finance services to technology start-up and emerging companies. He has extensive experience in venture capital financings, corporate credit facilities, leveraged buyouts, joint ventures and other capital transactions. He has represented a broad range of businesses in public and private offerings of equity and debt securities, in business acquisitions and in the development, marketing and expansion of franchise programs.

## CANNY, Joan
Stearns Weaver Miller Weissler Alhadeff & Sitterson, PA, Miami
305 789 3200
*Recommended in Employment*

## CARDENAS, Alberto
Tew Cardenas LLP, Miami
305 536 1112
*Recommended in Real Estate*

## CARDWELL, J Thomas
Akerman Senterfitt, Orlando
407 843 7860
tom.cardwell@akerman.com
*Recommended in Banking & Finance*
**Career:** J Thomas Cardwell is a Fellow of the American College of Trial Lawyers. He has extensive experience representing clients in litigation, administrative, and regulatory matters. Mr Cardwell has served as General Counsel for the Florida Bankers Association since 1982. He is currently Chairman and CEO of the firm.

## CAREY, Michael
Carey, O'Malley, Whitaker & Manson PA, Tampa 813 250 0577
*Recommended in Construction*

## CARRIUOLO, Anthony
Berger Singerman, Fort Lauderdale
954 525 9900
*Recommended in Litigation*

## CARTER, Francis L
Akerman Senterfitt, Miami
305 374 5600
francis.carter@akerman.com
*Recommended in Bankruptcy*
**Career:** Francis L Carter, who heads the Miami Bankruptcy Practice Group, focuses his practice on restructuring, financial reorganization and commercial bankruptcy. He has represented institutional creditors, debtors, landlords, equipment lessors, distressed asset purchasers, committees and other clients in

Chapter 11 reorganizations. He is a Fellow of the American College of Bankruptcy, has been listed in 'Best Lawyers in America' since 1991, and is a former Chairman of the Florida Bar Bankruptcy/UCC Committee.

## CASEY, Michael
Epstein Becker & Green PC, Miami
305 982 1534
mcasey@ebglaw.com
*Recommended in Employment*
**Practice Areas:** Michael W Casey, III is the Managing Partner of EBG's Miami office, and a member of the Labor and Employment Group's National Steering Committee. He has more than 30 years of experience representing management in a broad spectrum of labor and employment law matters. Mr Casey's extensive experience includes defending employment discrimination claims and class-action employment cases, advising and counseling management in Union election campaigns, resolving disputes short of litigation through pretrial motion practice and negotiation of favorable settlements, and advising clients on compliance with federal, state and local labor and employment laws, as well as risk management.

## CAULKINS, Charles
Fisher & Phillips LLP, Fort Lauderdale
954 525 4800
ccaulkins@laborlawyers.com
*Recommended in Employment*
**Practice Areas:** Charles Caulkins is Managing Partner of the Fisher & Phillips LLP Fort Lauderdale office. He advises employers on the development and implementation of preventive labor relations programs to avoid charges and lawsuits, protection of trade secrets, and resolution of disputes. Caulkins counsels employers during union representation elections, decertifications, corporate campaigns, collective bargaining negotiations, strikes, and lockouts. He handles employment-related litigation and arbitrations before state and federal courts and administrative agencies involving claims of discrimination, wrongful discharge, contract breach, OSHA and other statutory claims. Caulkins currently serves as Chairman of the Greater Fort Lauderdale Chamber of Commerce.

## CHARBONNEAU, Robert P
Kluger, Peretz, Kaplan & Berlin P.L., Miami 305 379 9000
rcharbonneau@kpkb.com
*Recommended in Bankruptcy*
**Practice Areas:** Co-Chair of the Bankruptcy and Creditors' Group. Represents corporate debtors, secured lenders, creditors' committees, and individual creditors in Federal Court, Bankruptcy Court, and state court insolvency proceedings, out-of-court workouts, and debt restructuring negotiations.

**Prof. Memberships:** Former President of the Bankruptcy Bar Association of the Southern District of Florida; member of the Dade County Bar Association; member and former Chair of the Commerical Law Section of the Broward County Bar Association; Vice-Chair of the Florida Bar Grievance Committee.
**Career:** Admitted to the Florida Bar and the US District Court, Southern District of Florida in 1992. Admitted to the US District Court, Middle District of Florida and the United States Court of Appeals, Eleventh Circuit. Board certified in business bankruptcy by the American Board of Certification.
**Personal:** Received a JD from Boston College, Boston, Massachusetts and a BA from the University of Florida, Gainsville. Recognized by peers as one of the 'Best of the Bar' in the area of Bankruptcy and Creditors' Rights by the South Florida Business Journal. Honored by the Florida legal community for the past three years as one of Florida's 'Legal Elite' in a survey conducted by Florida Trend magazine.

## CHAVES, Robert
Tescher Gutter Chaves Josepher Rubin Ruffin & Forman PA, Boca Ratón
561 998 7847
*Recommended in Tax*

## CHAYKIN, Steven
Zuckerman Spaeder LLP, Miami
305 358 5000
*Recommended in Litigation*

## CHRISTALDI, Ronald
de la Parte & Gilbert PA, Tampa
813 229 2775
*Recommended in Healthcare*

## COGLIANESE, Matthew
Bilzin Sumberg Baena Price & Axelrod LLP, Miami 305 350 2404
mcoglianese@bilzin.com
*Recommended in Environment*
**Career:** Practices in the area of litigation and environmental law, emphasizing toxic torts, construction defect and mold litigation, CERCLA, RCRA, brownfields redevelopment, and state and local environmental matters. Practice also includes environmental and corporate counseling, permitting and corporate due diligence. Has authored articles and presented numerous courses relating to environmental law. Previously served as Assistant Regional Counsel with the United States EPA in Atlanta, Georgia, where he handled enforcement of federal water and air pollution laws. Also served as senior attorney with a major petroleum company based in Los Angeles.

## COHEN, Jules
Akerman Senterfitt, Orlando
407 843 7860
jules.cohen@akeman.com
*Recommended in Bankruptcy*
**Career:** Jules Cohen is a shareholder with extensive experience in bankruptcy,

representing secured creditors, landlords, lessors and buyers of businesses from bankruptcies and defending preference suits. He is certified in business bankruptcy law by the American Board of Bankruptcy Certification. He is past Chair of the Business Law Section and Bankruptcy Committee of The Florida Bar, Board Member Emeritus, Southeastern Bankruptcy Law Institute and Fellow of the American College of Bankruptcy. He is a frequent author and lecturer on bankruptcy for The Florida Bar, the National Business Institute, Attorneys Title Insurance Fund and many other organizations.

## COLE, Terry
Oertel, Fernandez, Cole & Bryant, PA, Tallahassee 850 521 0700
*Recommended in Environment*

## COLEMAN, Ira
McDermott Will & Emery, Miami
305 347 6556
icoleman@mwe.com
*Recommended in Healthcare*
**Practice Areas:** Partner-in-charge of Florida office and Head of Florida Health Practice. Concentrates on significant healthcare M&As and private equity deals. Counsel in connection with the development and operation of numerous corporate compliance and governance programs for major clients.
**Prof. Memberships:** Board member of Nova Southeastern Law School: Board Member of South Florida Hospital and Healthcare Association: Served as Vice Chairman of American Health Lawyers Association Merger and Acquisition Institute. Elected to Florida Bar Health Law Section Executive Council.
**Personal:** Nova Southeastern University, Law School (JD); University of Miami School of Law (LLM); State University of New York-Albany (BA).

## COLEMAN, Patrick
Coffman, Coleman, Andrews & Grogan, Jacksonville 904 389 5161
*Recommended in Employment*

## COLODNY, Michael
Colodny, Fass, Talenfeld, Karlinsky & Abate PA, Ford Lauderdale
954 492 4010
*Recommended in Insurance*

## COLSON, Dean
Colson Hicks Eidson, Coral Gables
305 476 7400
dean@colson.com
*Recommended in Litigation*
**Practice Areas:** Personal injury; medical malpractice; aviation; products liability; class actions.
**Career:** Mr Colson graduated magna cum laude from the University of Miami School of Law in 1977; he served as a law clerk for Justice William H Rehnquist; he joined Colson Hicks Eidson in 1981. Mr Colson's practice has varied from the

handling of many multi-million dollar malpractice, aviation and products liability cases for injured plaintiffs to being trial counsel for the class of investors defrauded in the Premium Sales case which settled after the start of trial for $170,000,000.

## COLTON, Roberta
Trenam, Kemker, Scharf, Barkin, Frye, O'Neill & Mullis PA, Tampa
813 223 7474
*Recommended in Bankruptcy*

## COMITER, Richard
Comiter, Singer & Baseman, LLP, Palm Beach Gardens
561 626 4742
*Recommended in Tax*

## COMMANDER III, Charles E
Foley & Lardner LLP, Jacksonville
904 359 8702
ccommander@foley.com
*Recommended in Real Estate*
**Career:** Charles E Commander III is a Partner in the Jacksonville office of Foley & Lardner LLP. He is a member of the firm's Finance and Financial Institutions and Real Estate Practice Groups, and the firm's Golf and Resort Services Industry Team. He advises and counsels corporate, financial institution and real estate clients in all aspects of their business and is recognized for practice excellence in real estate law by a leading legal publication. Mr Commander received his Law Degree from the University of Florida.

## CONLEY, Cristin A
Carlton Fields, Tampa
813 223 7000
cconley@carltonfields.com
*Recommended in Tax*
**Practice Areas:** Practices in the areas of state and federal tax planning, including federal taxation of foreign entities and US foreign investments, tax controversies, and laws governing profit and not-for-profit business entities. Board Certified in Taxation by The Florida Bar.
**Prof. Memberships:** Admitted to practice in Florida and US Tax Court. Member, American Bar Association; Hillsborough County Bar Association; The Florida Bar, Vice Chair, New Tax Lawyers Committee; Co-Assistant Chair, C Corporations Committee, Federal Tax Division.
**Personal:** LLM, University of Florida, 1998; JD, University of Florida College of Law, 1997; BA, Duke University, 1994.

## CONNOR, Terence
Morgan, Lewis & Bockius LLP, Miami
305 415 3316
tconnor@morganlewis.com
*Recommended in Employment*
**Practice Areas:** Terence Connor is a Partner in the Labor and Employment Law Practice Group. Mr Connor focuses on federal and state employment and employment discrimination litigation,

and state and federal employment law compliance counseling. He has extensive experience in several industries with specialties in the airline, transportation, biotechnology and pharmaceutical industries. Before joining Morgan Lewis, Mr Connor was a trial attorney with the US Department of Justice Civil Rights/Employment Group and served as Labor Counsel to National Airlines in Florida.
**Prof. Memberships:** Florida Bar; College of Labor and Employment Lawyers; Academy of Florida Management Attorneys.

### COOPER, Marc
Colson Hicks Eidson, Coral Gables
305 476 7400
marc@colson.com
*Recommended in Litigation*
**Practice Areas:** Appellate.
**Career:** After graduating from Yale University, Mr Cooper attended the University of Miami School of Law as a Reid Scholar and graduated magna cum laude. Following graduation, he served as a law clerk for the Honorable David W Dyer, United States Court of Appeals, Fifth Circuit. For almost 25 years, Mr Cooper has handled appeals of all types in all the appellate courts of Florida, as well as in the Fifth Circuit, Eleventh Circuit and other federal circuits. Hundreds of appellate decisions, both reported and unreported, bear his name.

### CORDERO, Frank
Akerman Senterfitt, Miami
305 374 5600
frank.cordero@akerman.com
*Recommended in Tax*
**Career:** Frank Cordero is a shareholder and focuses his practice in the area of tax law. He advises clients with respect to complex domestic and international tax planning issues, including issues relating to the structuring of domestic and international business operations, investments and transactions, public and private offerings of equity and debt securities, domestic and international mergers, acquisitions and reorganizations involving public and private companies, domestic and international partnerships and joint ventures, the formation and operation of limited liability companies and other business entities, and executive compensation. Mr Cordero is a Certified Public Accountant and is fluent in Spanish.

### CORDERO, Luis
Holland & Knight LLP, Miami
305 374 8500
luis.cordero@hklaw.com
*Recommended in Immigration*
**Practice Areas:** Partner in the Business Section, practices in the areas of immigration, nationality and consular law, principally relating to all business aspects of immigration, with an emphasis on corporate transfers, professionals, entrepreneurs, investors, entertainers and artists. He also has litigation experience in deportation, exclusion and removal hearings as well as in employer sanctions cases, representing clients before the Immigration Courts and Administrative Law Judges and has extensive experience in all other aspects of immigration law, including criminal and family matters, and has represented clients from large multinationals to detained asylum seekers.

### COUTROULIS, Chris
Carlton Fields, Tampa
813 223 7000
ccoutroulis@carltonfields.com
*Recommended in Antitrust*
**Practice Areas:** Practices in business and complex litigation covering class action and antitrust, including through trial and binding arbitration, and governmental antitrust investigations. Board Certified by The Florida Bar in Antitrust and Trade Regulation Law. Chair, Business Litigation and Trade Regulation Practice Group.
**Prof. Memberships:** Admitted to practice in Florida and the US Supreme Court. Member, American Bar Association; The Florida Bar, Antitrust and Trade Regulation Certification Committee; American Law Institute.
**Publications:** Co-author: 'Checkmate in Class Actions: Defensive Strategy in Initial Mover' (Litigation Magazine 2002).
**Personal:** JD, Columbia University School of Law, 1979; BA (magna cum laude), Wesleyan University, 1975.

### COWAN, Kevin
Shutts & Bowen LLP, Miami
305 379 9110
kcowan@shutts-law.com
*Recommended in Real Estate*
**Practice Areas:** Co-Chairman of Miami Real Estate Department; involved in corporate and commercial real estate practice, including development, financing, sale and acquisition, foreclosure and work-outs, and leases. Real estate practice focuses on representing developers and institutions in purchase and sale of properties, financing, development, land use, work-outs, and negotiating leases. Corporate practice focuses on individuals and medium-sized practices in corporate, partnership and joint venture arrangements.
**Prof. Memberships:** Florida.
**Career:** Began career with Paul, Hastings, Janofsky & Walker in California; joined Shutts & Bowen in 1983, elected Partner in 1987.
**Personal:** BA Ohio State University 1977; JD Emory Law School.

### COX, Donald
Fowler White Boggs Banker, Tampa
813 228 7411
*Recommended in Insurance*

### COXE, Henry
Bedell, Dittmar, DeVault, Pillans & Coxe, Jacksonville 904 353 0211
*Recommended in Litigation*

### CRITCHLOW, Richard H
Kenny Nachwalter PA, Miami
305 373 1000
rhc@kennynachwalter.com
*Recommended in Litigation*
**Practice Areas:** Business-related litigation, commercial litigation, complex commercial litigation, complex and multi-district litigation, corporate litigation.
**Prof. Memberships:** International Society of Barristers Miami Dade County and American Bar Associations.
**Career:** Partner since 1991.
**Personal:** Union College, BA (1969); University of Miami, JD cum laude (1973).

### CRUZ-BROWN, Kelly A
Carlton Fields, Tallahassee
850 224 1585
kcruz@carltonfields.com
*Recommended in Insurance*
**Practice Areas:** Practices in the areas of insurance regulation and administrative law, representing individuals, insurers, and other entities regulated under Florida's Insurance Code before the Florida Department of Financial Services, Office of Insurance Regulation and Department of Health, Agency for Healthcare Administration and other state agencies.
**Prof. Memberships:** Member, The Florida Bar; American Bar Association.
**Career:** Senior attorney, Florida Department of Insurance (1995-98); senior attorney, Department of Professional Regulations (1994-95); staff attorney, Capital Collateral Representative (1993-94); clerkship, Second Judicial Circuit (Fall 1991).
**Personal:** JD, Florida State University College of Law, 1992; BS (with honors), Florida State University, 1989.

### CULPEPPER, Bruce
Akerman Senterfitt, Tallahassee
850 224 9634
bruce.culpepper@akerman.com
*Recommended in Insurance*
**Career:** Bruce Culpepper is a shareholder and former Managing Partner of the firm's Tallahassee office. He has over 40 years of experience representing clients in civil litigation and appellate matters in state, federal and administrative forums. He focuses his practice in the areas of insurance, healthcare, complex commercial litigation and administrative law. Mr Culpepper is a former city commissioner of the City of Tallahassee, serves on The Florida Bar Foundation board of directors, and is a frequent lecturer on business litigation and procedure.

### CUNNINGHAM, Malcolm
Cunningham Law Firm,
West Palm Beach 561 833 6400
*Recommended in Construction*

### CUNNINGHAM, Peter C
Hopping Green & Sams, PA, Tallahassee
850 222 7500
peterc@hgslaw.com
*Recommended in Environment*
**Practice Areas:** Environmental law; emphasis on air quality, power plant licensing and energy policy.
**Prof. Memberships:** Admitted: Florida, US District Court for Northern Florida and Eleventh US Circuit Court of Appeals. Member National and Florida Small Business Compliance Advisory Panels.
**Career:** Has represented clients on air quality regulatory issues including legislation, rulemaking, permitting and enforcement for 25 years. Lead Counsel in successful licensing of more than 6,000 megawatts of new electric generating capacity. Represented Florida's electric utilities before Governor's Energy 2020 Study Commission.
**Personal:** Born March 22, 1952; BA Harvard College, 1975; JD University of Michigan Law School, 1979.

### CURRIER, Maria
Hunton & Williams, Miami
305 810 2568
mcurrier@hunton.com
*Recommended in Healthcare*
**Practice Areas:** Maria Currier is a Florida Bar Board Certified healthcare law specialist. She has served as Counsel to hospitals, nursing homes, home health agencies, HMOs, provider-sponsored plans, physician groups, preferred provider organizations, physician-hospital organizations, physician management companies, employer self-insured plans and prepaid health plans. Her practice focuses on state and federal fraud and abuse laws, privacy, Medicare health plan regulation, physician self referral laws, and formation of complex integrated healthcare systems.

### CURTIN, Lawrence
Holland & Knight LLP, Tallahassee
850 224 7000
larry.curtin@hklaw.com
*Recommended in Environment*
**Practice Areas:** Executive Partner, Tallahassee office. Partner in Public Policy and Regulation Practice Group in the Government Law Section, practicing administrative and governmental law, focusing on environmental matters. Regularly provides advice on permitting and enforcement matters involving federal, state, and local administrative agencies. Has substantial experience in administrative law, including adjudicatory hearings and rule-making activities. Has extensive experience in permitting major industrial facilities in Florida, including siting of electrical power plants, transmission lines, and natural gas pipelines. He has represented clients before the Florida Legislature for

more than 20 years, primarily involving environmental, land use, and administrative law matters.

## DANNECKER, John H
Shutts & Bowen LLP, Miami
407 835 6727
jdannecker@shutts-law.com
*Recommended in Construction*
**Practice Areas:** Chairman, Construction Law Practice Group in Orlando; practices in the field of commercial litigation, with particular emphasis in the areas of construction litigation, contract negotiation and defect and delay litigation, including mold and mildew-related disputes.
**Prof. Memberships:** Florida.
**Career:** Member of Association of Trial Lawyers of America, Associated General Contractors, Associated Builders & Contractors; lectures extensively on construction law-related topics.
**Personal:** JD Stetson University; BS University of Florida.

## DANON, Samuel A
Hunton & Williams, Miami
305 810 2510
sdanon@hunton.com
*Recommended in Litigation*
**Practice Areas:** Sam Danon's practice focuses on general litigation with an emphasis on franchise litigation, including petroleum marketing, financial institution litigation, class actions, corporate compliance, business torts, contract disputes, products liability and copyright and trademark litigation. Trial experience in both federal and state courts and experience in government regulatory issues and conducting internal investigations. Represented multinational companies in connection with issues related to operations in South and Central America, including internal investigations, corporate compliance and litigation.
**Prof. Memberships:** Member, Florida Bar; American Bar Association; Cuban American Bar Association; Hispanic National Bar Association; Dade County Bar Association.

## DAVIDSON, Barry
Hunton & Williams, Miami
305 810 2539
bdavidson@hunton.com
*Recommended in Antitrust, Litigation*
**Practice Areas:** Barry Davidson's practice focuses in the area of civil litigation throughout the State of Florida, with an emphasis on complex and class action business litigation, intellectual property, antitrust and products litigation. Mr Davidson also represents airlines and hotel companies and does eminent domain work. Has represented every major US air carrier either separately or in industry litigation and represents International Air Transport Association and several foreign carriers.
**Prof. Memberships:** Member, Florida

Bar; ABA, Antitrust Section; American Bar Foundation (Life Fellow).

## DAVIS, Alvin B
Squire, Sanders & Dempsey L.L.P., Miami 305 577 2835
adavis@ssd.com
*Recommended in Litigation*
**Practice Areas:** Managing Partner of firm's Miami office. Practice focuses on litigation and arbitration in products liability, securities class actions, environmental claims, regulatory proceedings and contractual disputes. Litigates at trial and appellate levels for major national and international companies including utilities, manufacturers, insurers, law firms and airlines. Listed in 'The Best Lawyers in America' and recognized among South Florida's Legal Elite by Florida Trend magazine in 2004 and 2005. Lectures regularly to The Florida Bar Association.
**Prof. Memberships:** Dade County Bar Association; Bar Association of the District of Columbia; American Bar Association.

## DAVIS, Gardner F
Foley & Lardner LLP, Jacksonville
904 359 8726
gdavis@foley.com
*Recommended in Corporate/M&A*
**Career:** Gardner Davis is a Partner with the Jacksonville office of Foley & Lardner LLP, where he is a member of the Transactional and Securities; Finance and Financial Institutions; Business Reorganizations; Private Equity and Venture Capital Practice Groups; and Automotive Industry Team. He is particularly knowledgeable in regard to buying, selling, and recapitalizing companies, restructuring financially distressed enterprises, and counseling officers and directors in corporate governance and control situations. Mr Davis frequently represents buyers and sellers in mergers and acquisition transactions, from management buyouts to combinations of large public companies. Mr Davis received his JD Degree from Duke University.

## DAVIS, Gary Scott
McDermott Will & Emery, Miami
305 347 6520
gsdavis@mwe.com
*Recommended in Healthcare*
**Practice Areas:** Concentrates on managed care, emerging health benefit plans, strategic acquisitions, divestitures, restructurings and reorganizations, hospital-physician joint ventures and related transactional, regulatory and reimbursement issues. Has presented more than 130 seminars sponsored by healthcare and legal trade, educational and professional organizations.
**Career:** Florida Bar Board Certified in Health Law; Awarded the prestigious David J Greenburg Service Award (AHLA, 2000), Member inaugural class

of Fellows (AHLA, 2005); recipient of the Follmer Bronze Merit Award for Outstanding Service (HFMA, 1993).
**Personal:** The George Washington University Law School (JD, honors); Binghamton University (BA, honors, Phi Beta Kappa).

## DAVIS, James
Gunster, Yoakley & Stewart, P.A., Fort Lauderdale 954 462 2000
*Recommended in Tax*

## DAVIS, Kirk S
Akerman Senterfitt, Tampa
813 223 7333
kirk.davis@akerman.com
*Recommended in Healthcare*
**Career:** Kirk Davis, shareholder and Board Certified Health Law attorney, focuses his practice in the areas of healthcare and civil litigation. His practice includes representation of hospitals and other healthcare providers in general healthcare matters, primarily civil and administrative trial matters. He has extensive experience in the medical-legal aspects of the healthcare practice and in all aspects of medical staff matters from both the physician and hospital perspectives, including hospital-based physician contracting. He is on the Board of Directors of the Florida Academy of Healthcare Attorneys and was an inaugural member of The Florida Bar Health Law Certification Committee.

## DE ARMAS, Luis
Shutts & Bowen LLP, Miami
305 379 9114
ldearmas@shutts-law.com
*Recommended in Corporate/M&A*
**Practice Areas:** Chairman of Corporate Transactions Practice Group; focus is banking, corporate and securities, real estate finance and transactions; structuring and negotiating mergers and acquisitions, including acquisitions of financial institutions, leveraged and international transactions; securities offerings and transactions, such as partnership offerings, public offerings and offshore offerings; represents foreign institutions in their US investments and operations.
**Prof. Memberships:** Florida.
**Career:** With Shutts & Bowen since 1977; Partner since 1983; served on the firm's Executive Committee from 1988-2000 and as Managing Partner from 1989-94.
**Personal:** JD Duke University 1977; BS Economics University of Pennsylvania Wharton School of Business; Spanish fluency.

## DEE, David
Landers & Parsons, Tallahassee
850 681 0311
*Recommended in Environment*

## DELEGAL, Mark
Pennington, Moore, Wilkinson, Bell & Dunbar, PA, Tallahassee

850 222 3533
*Recommended in Insurance*

## DELEGAL, Susan F
Billing Cochran Heath Lyles Mauro & Anderson, Fort Lauderdale
954 764 7150
sdelegal@bchlm.com
*Recommended in Real Estate*
**Practice Areas:** Partner in the firm's Real Estate Land Use and Government Section, represents clients before agencies of local and state government, administrative agencies, and the federal and state courts. Delegal's practice focuses on zoning and land use approval and permitting, litigation involving governmental entities, telecommunications issues, and representation of community redevelopment agencies. Prior to joining Billing, Cochran, Heath, Lyles, Mauro & Anderson, P.A., she served as the County Attorney for Broward County for five years, representing the Board of County Commissioners, County Administrator, and all other Departments, Divisions and Boards of County government in the legal matters affecting the county.

## DEMEO, Ralph
Hopping Green & Sams, PA, Tallahassee
850 222 7500
ralphd@hgslaw.com
*Recommended in Environment*
**Practice Areas:** Environmental and land use law; toxic torts litigation; local government law; general civil and administrative law and litigation.
**Prof. Memberships:** The Florida Bar.
**Career:** BA, MA, English, Stetson University; JD, FSU; former College English Professor; current Professor of Legal Studies; over 20 years representing private individuals, corporations, and local governments.
**Publications:** Over 25 articles in publications such as Florida Bar Journal, FSU Journal of Land Use and Environmental Law; Stetson Law Review; the Florida Bar Treatise on Environmental and Land Use Law, and others.
**Personal:** Frequent lecturer on environmental, land use, governmental law, and civil and administrative litigation.

## DEMEZA JR, William B
Holland & Knight LLP, Tampa
813 227 8500
bill.demeza@hklaw.com
*Recommended in Employment*
**Practice Areas:** Partner in the firm's Litigation Section, his practice consists of counseling employers about employment issues and defending them in lawsuits brought by employees or governments; a significant segment of his practice focuses on employee safety and health issues. Clients have included restaurants, manufacturers, financial institutions, department stores, pharmaceutical companies, hospitals, government contractors, insurance companies, and mining companies.

DeMeza has served as employers' counsel in race, sex, sexual harassment, age, religion, national origin, and handicap (disability) employment discrimination charges and litigation.

### DENMON, Richard A
Carlton Fields, Tampa 813 223 7000
rdenmon@carltonfields.com
*Recommended in Corporate/M&A*
**Practice Areas:** Practices in the areas of securities, regulation, corporation finance, mergers, acquisitions, and general corporate law, has extensive experience in public and private offerings representing both issuers and underwriters, venture capital transactions, and mergers and acquisitions. Assists public companies in satisfying disclosure obligations and has extensive experience in representing community banks and bank holding companies. Co-Chair, firm's Securities Practice Group.
**Career:** Former Special Counsel with the Securities and Exchange Commission, Division of Corporation Finance, Washington, DC, (1984-89).
**Personal:** JD, State University of New York at Buffalo, 1982; BS, State University of New York at Binghamton, 1979.

### DETZEL, Lauren
Dean, Mead, Egerton, Bloodworth, Capouano & Bozarth PA, Orlando
407 428 5114
ldetzel@deanmead.com
*Recommended in Tax, Wealth Management*
**Practice Areas:** Wealth preservation and estate planning, trust and estate administration, transfer tax controversies, business succession planning.
**Prof. Memberships:** Fellow, American College of Trust and Estate Counsel; Chair, Tax Section, The Florida Bar, 1997-98.
**Career:** Board Certified in Wills, Trusts, and Estates by The Florida Bar; Adjunct Professor of Law, University of Florida College of Law Graduate Tax Program; recipient, Gerald T Hart Award as the Outstanding Tax Attorney in the State of Florida by The Florida Bar Tax Section, 2005.
**Personal:** University of Florida (JD, magna cum laude, 1977); University of Louisville (BA, magna cum laude, 1973).

### DEVAULT, John
Bedell, Dittmar, DeVault, Pillans & Coxe, Jacksonville 904 353 0211
*Recommended in Litigation*

### DIAZ JR, Victor
Podhurst Orseck P.A., Miami
305 358 2800
vdiaz@podhurst.com
*Recommended in Litigation*
**Practice Areas:** Partner focusing on a broad range of civil litigation, including complex commercial and securities litigation, aviation and mass tort litigation.

Practice extends to all federal and state courts. Experienced in multi-district litigation, including being named lead counsel in national MDL proceedings. Special emphasis on trial practice.
**Prof. Memberships:** ABA; ATLA (Vice-President Section on Aviation Litigation); AFTL (sections on Commercial and Aviation Litigation); Florida Bar; Dade County Trial Lawyers (Board of Directors); Cuban American Bar Association (President); American Bar Foundation Fellow.
**Career:** Experienced trial lawyer, recognized by numerous national and regional publications for excellence in the fields of commercial and general civil litigation. A frequent lecturer at a state and national level on complex civil and mass tort litigation topics, also invited to address several international law conferences as an expert on comparative law and US federal court jurisdiction. In 2000, awarded the Tobias Simon Award by the Florida Supreme Court, the state's highest recognition for public and pro bono service.
**Publications:** Has lectured and wriitten extensively on civil procedure and comparative law issues.
**Personal:** Yale Law School (JD, 1985) (Editor-in-Chief, Yale Law and Policy Review); Duke University (BA, 1982) (Valedictorian). Fluent in written and spoken Spanish.

### DIAZ-SILVEIRA, Jorge
Hogan & Hartson LLP, Miami
305 459 6645
jdiaz-silveira@hhlaw.com
*Recommended in Construction*
**Practice Areas:** Partner in Business and Finance Group whose practice focuses on the development, financing and construction of projects throughout the United States and abroad.
**Prof. Memberships:** Construction Law Committee, Florida Bar; Real Property, Probate and Trust Law Section, American Bar Association; American Bar Association; Miami-Dade County Bar Association; Chair, Duke University Alumni Admissions Advisory Committee.
**Career:** After more than 18 years in practice, Jorge is widely recognized as one of the leading international lawyers in the area of engineering, procurement and construction (EPC) contracts.
**Personal:** JD, cum laude, University of Miami School of Law, 1988; AB, Duke University, 1985.

### DICKHAUS AGNANT, Linda
Boose Casey Ciklin Lubitz Martens McBane & O'Connell, West Palm Beach
561 832 5900
*Recommended in Construction*

### DICKINSON, John
Constangy, Brooks & Smith, LLC, Jacksonville 904 356 8900
*Recommended in Employment*

### DILLON, Sean M
Moye, O'Brien, O'Rourke, Pickert & Martin, LLP, Maitland 407 622 5250
*Recommended in Construction*
**Practice Areas:** Construction law and litigation, commercial litigation, management labor and employment law. Has extensive experience representing US and international contractors and engineering firms in the USA in multi-million dollar contracts and claims.
**Prof. Memberships:** The Florida Bar; The State Bar of Georgia; American Bar Association (Member, Forum Committee on the Construction Industry and Public Contract Law, Litigation, Business Law and Labor and Employment Law Sections).
**Career:** Partner of Moye, O'Brien, O'Rourke, Pickert & Martin, LLP (with affilate office in Chicago, Illinois); admitted to Florida Bar and Georgia Bar; US District Court, Southern, Middle and Northern Districts of Florida; US Court of Appeals, Federal and Eleventh Circuits.
**Personal:** Received Bachelor of Science in Building Construction Technologies (with high honors) from the University of Florida and JD (with honors) from the University of Florida. Member of Florida Blue Key.

### DIX, Martin R
Akerman Senterfitt, Tallahassee
850 224 9634
marty.dix@akerman.com
*Recommended in Healthcare*
**Career:** Martin Dix, a shareholder in the Healthcare Practice Group, focuses his practice in the areas of pharmacy/healthcare law dealing with nearly all aspects of the drug delivery system: pharmacies, including chain, independent, institutional, specialty, compounding, etc; pharmacists; physicians, home health, drug wholesalers; DME. His pharmacy practice involves licensing, regulatory, reimbursement, corporate, business, and antitrust issues in the pharmacy healthcare area.

### DIXON, Sharon Quinn
Stearns Weaver Miller Weissler Alhadeff & Sitterson, PA, Miami
305 789 3200
*Recommended in Tax*

### DOGALI, Andy
Forizs and Dogali PL, Tampa
813 289 0700
*Recommended in Construction*

### DOLINER, Nathaniel
Carlton Fields, Tampa
813 223 7000
ndoliner@carltonfields.com
*Recommended in Corporate/M&A*
**Practice Areas:** Corporate law, mergers, and taxation. Transactions involving joint ventures, partnerships, and acquisitions of financially troubled businesses. Extensive experience in public finance and transactions between governmental bod-

ies and private companies. Advises boards of directors of public companies and board committees as to Sarbanes-Oxley, corporate governance, and fiduciary duties. Tampa office managing shareholder.
**Prof. Memberships:** Admitted to practice in Florida. Member, American Bar Association, Council of Business Law Section; American Law Institute; American College of Tax Counsel; Fellow, American Bar Foundation.
**Personal:** LLM, University of Florida College of Law, 1977; JD, Vanderbilt Law School, 1973; BA, George Washington University, 1970.

### DOUGHERTY, Lucia
Greenberg Traurig LLP, Miami
305 579 0603
doughertyl@gtlaw.com
*Recommended in Real Estate*
**Practice Areas:** Environmental, land use.
**Prof. Memberships:** Chairperson, Archbishop's Charities and Development Drive for Miami-Dade County. Chairperson, Miami Beach Chamber of Commerce. Vice-Chairperson, Eminent Domain Committee of The Florida Bar, Member, International Women's Forum, Member, Greater Miami and Beaches Hotel Association, Legal Counsel, Greater Miami Convention and Visitors Bureau.
**Career:** Featured, 'The Power Women of Real Estate', Miami Sun Post, 2005; listed, Best Lawyers in America, 2006.
**Personal:** LLM, Ocean and Coastal Law, University of Miami School of Law, 1980; JD, Oklahoma City University School of Law, 1975; MLS, Library Science, University of Oklahoma, 1972; BS, Syracuse University, 1971.

### DOWNS, Joe
Daniels, Kashtan, Downs, Robertson & Magathan, Miami 305 448 7988
*Recommended in Construction*

### DUFFY, Don
Akerman Senterfitt, Miami
305 374 5600
don.duffy@akerman.com
*Recommended in Tax*
**Career:** Donald Duffy is a shareholder and focuses his practice in the area of tax law advising business entities and individuals with respect to transactions relating to international, corporate and partnership tax law. He also represents clients who have tax controversies with the IRS. He served as an attorney in the former Legislation and Regulations Division of the IRS Office of Chief Counsel drafting regulations on international and corporate tax matters and worked with the Treasury Department in the development and enactment of tax legislation. He also served as an Adjunct Professor of tax law at Georgetown University Law Center.

### DURKIN, Denis
Baker & Hostetler LLP, Orlando

407 649 4000
*Recommended in Construction*

**EATON, Joel**
Podhurst Orseck P.A., Miami
305 358 2800
jeaton@podhurst.com
*Recommended in Litigation*
**Practice Areas:** Appellate.
**Career:** Has handled civil appeals in state and federal courts for 30 years, and is a former Chairman of the Florida Supreme Court's Appellate Rules Committee. He also served two terms as a member of the Supreme Court's Committee on Standard Jury Instructions in Civil Cases. He is a co-founder of the American Academy of Appellate Lawyers, is listed in 'Best Lawyers of America', and currently serves as an advisor to the American Law Institute's 'Restatement of the Law (Third) Torts: Liability for Physical Harm'.
**Personal:** Harvard University (JD cum laude, 1975); Yale University (BA 1965).

**EGERTON, Charles**
Dean, Mead, Egerton, Bloodworth, Capouano & Bozarth PA, Orlando
408 428 5112
cegerton@deanmead.com
*Recommended in Tax*
**Practice Areas:** Tax planning for real estate transactions including tax free exchanges, planning to preserve longterm capital gains in dispositions of real estate, and tax structuring of joint ventures for the acquisition and development of real properties; negotiating and drafting partnership and limited liability company agreements; mergers and acquisitions of businesses; and federal tax controversies at the audit, trial and appeals levels.
**Prof. Memberships:** Vice-Chair (Committee Operations), ABA Tax Section; Fellow and Member, Board of Regents, American College of Tax Counsel; Member, Board of Trustees, Southern Federal Tax Institute; Fellow, American Bar Foundation; Member and former Chairman, Florida Bar Tax Section.
**Career:** Recipient, Gerald T Hart Award as the Outstanding Tax Attorney in the State of Florida by The Florida Bar Tax Section, 1998; listed in 'The Best Lawyers in America'.
**Personal:** New York University (LLM, 1971); University of Florida (JD, 1969); Emory University (BBA, 1966).

**EISENBERG, Susan Nadler**
Akerman Senterfitt, Miami
305 982 5637
susan.eisenberg@akerman.com
*Recommended in Employment*
**Career:** Susan Eisenberg is a shareholder and Board Certified by The Florida Bar in labor and employment law. She has extensive experience representing local, national and international companies in civil actions involving employment discrimination, labor relations, and wage and hour issues. She has extensive litiga-

tion experience, including jury trials and appeals in state and federal courts. She is a certified mediator and an arbitrator with the American Arbitration Association. She is the Associate Editor of the book The Fair Labor Standards Act, and a frequent lecturer for The Florida Bar and American Bar Association on employment issues.

**EMMANUEL, John**
Fowler White Boggs Banker, Tampa
813 228 7411
*Recommended in Bankruptcy*

**ENGLAND, Arthur J**
Greenberg Traurig LLP, Miami
305 579 0605
englanda@gtlaw.com
*Recommended in Litigation*
**Practice Areas:** Appellate and litigation.
**Career:** Listed, 'Chambers & Partners USA Guide', 2004-06; Recognized, Top Lawyers in South Florida, South Florida Legal Guide, 2004-05; listed, 'Best Lawyers in America'.
**Publications:** Author, 'Florida Corporate Income Tax Law' (1971), 'Deceptive and Unfair Trade Practices Act' (1973), and 'Florida Administrative Procedures Act' (1974); lead author, 'Florida Appellate Practice Manual and Florida Administrative Practice Manual'; lead author, 'Quality Discounts in Appellate Justice', 60 Judicature 442, 1977.
**Personal:** LLM, University of Miami School of Law,1972; LLB, magna cum laude, University of Pennsylvania Law School,1961; BS, Wharton School of Finance and Commerce, University of Pennsylvania,1955.

**EPSTEIN, Gary M**
Greenberg Traurig LLP, Miami
305 579 0894
epsteing@gtlaw.com
*Recommended in Corporate/M&A*
**Practice Areas:** Corporate and securities; M&A.
**Prof. Memberships:** Chairman of the Board, American Israel Chamber of Commerce, Florida; President, Miami Beach Jewish Community Center.
**Career:** Recognized, South Florida's Top Dealmakers of the Year in Mergers & Acquisitions, Daily Business Review, 2005; listed, Top Lawyer, South Florida Legal Guide, 2005; listed, 'Chambers & Partners USA Guide', 2003-06; listed, 2004 and 2005 Legal Elite, Florida Trend Magazine, listing of Florida's top attorneys as selected by their peers; listed, 'The Best Lawyers in America' each year since 1985.
**Personal:** JD, Harvard University Law School,1980; MA, New York University, 1970; BA, Yeshiva University, 1969.

**ERDE, Joanne B**
Duane Morris LLP, Miami
305 960 2218
jerde@duanemorris.com

*Recommended in Healthcare*
**Practice Areas:** Joanne B Erde practices in the area of healthcare law, concentrating on Medicare and Medicaid law and regulations, corporate compliance issues, Medicare payment and billing rules, Medicare reimbursement controversies and appeals and healthcare fraud and abuse provisions. In recent years she has represented private nonprofit hospitals, for-profit hospital groups and public hospitals across the country in disputes before the Provider Reimbursement Review Board, the Centers for Medicare and Medicaid Services, Medicare fiscal intermediaries and federal courts. She has handled numerous settlement negotiations and administrative and judicial litigation regarding a wide variety of third-party reimbursement and payment issues.
**Prof. Memberships:** The Florida Bar – Health Law Section; American Health Lawyers Association; Healthcare Financial Management Association.
**Career:** Admitted to practice in Florida and New York.
**Personal:** Hofstra University School of Law, JD, 1977; University of California at Los Angeles, Master of Public Health; State University of New York at Buffalo, magna cum laude.

**ERVIN, James M**
Holland & Knight LLP, Tallahassee
850 224 7000
jim.ervin@hklaw.com
*Recommended in Tax*
**Practice Areas:** Partner in the Business Law Section, has a multi-forum state tax practice that covers the legislative, administrative and judicial areas. Handles assessment negotiations with auditors and the preparing, filing and resolving of protests against assessments. Through his longstanding relationships with the Department of Revenue, he assists clients in tax inquiries to facilitate tax planning and to resolve any questions concerning potential tax liability. His practice also involves a wide array of state taxes, particularly sales tax, corporate income tax, communications services tax, insurance premiums tax, gross receipts tax, documentary stamp tax, intangibles tax, pollutants taxes, and severance tax.

**ESTEVEZ, Anne M**
Morgan, Lewis & Bockius LLP, Miami
305 415 3330
aestevez@morganlewis.com
*Recommended in Employment*
**Practice Areas:** Anne Marie Estevez is a Partner in the Labor and Employment Practice. Ms Estevez's practice focuses on the defense and trial of complex employment and accessibility (ADA) cases in federal and state courts, and advising, training, and counseling companies on state and federal employment and accessibility laws. Ms Estevez is a board certi-

fied labor and employment lawyer, and she is fluent in Spanish.
**Prof. Memberships:** Member, American Bar Association; Member, United Way Leadership Circle.

**FARMER III, Guy O**
Holland & Knight LLP, Jacksonville
904 353 2000
guy.farmer@hklaw.com
*Recommended in Employment*
**Practice Areas:** Partner in the Labor and Employment Group, represents employers locally, regionally and nationally in the full range of employment-related issues. Has defended employers in more than 1,000 cases nationwide involving allegations of employment discrimination and other employment and labor-related matters. His litigation and appellate practice has included the defense of employers in cases involving individual claims, claims by federal and state governments and significant class actions. He also counsels and represents employers in connection with labor union issues, including resisting union organizing efforts, defending against unfair labor practice charges, appearing in labor arbitrations and negotiating collective bargaining agreements.

**FELMAN, David**
Hill, Ward & Henderson, PA, Tampa
813 221 3900
*Recommended in Corporate/M&A*

**FERENCIK, Robert**
Ferencik, Libanoff, Brandt, Bustamante & Williams, Fort Lauderdale
954 474 8080
*Recommended in Construction*

**FILDES, Richard**
Lowndes Drosdick Doster Kantor & Reed, PA, Orlando 407 843 4600
*Recommended in Real Estate*

**FITZGERALD, Miranda**
Lowndes Drosdick Doster Kantor & Reed, PA, Orlando 407 843 4600
*Recommended in Real Estate*

**FLEMING, Joseph**
Greenberg Traurig LLP, Miami
305 579 0517
flemingj@gtlaw.com
*Recommended in Employment*
**Practice Areas:** Labor and employment; litigation; environmental; land development; ADA, Accessibility, Building and Life Safety Codes; technology, media and telecommunications.
**Prof. Memberships:** American Law Institute American Bar Association (ALI-ABA); member, Advisory Group on Labor Law for the Committee on Continuing Professional Education; Chair, ALI-ABA's Course, 'Airline and Railroad Labor and Employment Law'; Co-Chair, Historic Preservation on Historic Preservation Law program.
**Career:** Recognized, Top Lawyers in

South Florida, South Florida Legal Guide, 2004-05; listed, 'Chambers & Partners USA Guide', 2003-06.

**Personal:** New York University (LLM, 1966); University of Virginia School of Law (LLB, 1965); University of Florida (BA, 1962).

## FLETCHER, PK
Duane Morris LLP, Miami
305 960 2255
pkfletcher@duanemorris.com
*Recommended in Real Estate*
**Practice Areas:** Patricia Kimball Fletcher practices in the areas of real estate development, zoning and land use, active adult communities and the Fair Housing Act. She also has extensive experience in matters of transaction, corporate trust and telecommunications law. She has represented clients in the development of condominiums, Planned Unit Developments, and commercial properties involving complex title and zoning issues.
**Prof. Memberships:** The Florida Bar; Builders Association of South Florida; Bankers Club – Board of Governors; Greater Miami Chamber of Commerce; Urban Land Institute – Senior Housing Council.
**Career:** Admitted to practice in Florida.
**Publications:** 'Big v. Small', The Florida Lawyer, September 2001; Title and the Successor Developer, Manual for the 13th Annual Condominium Seminar, 1986.
**Personal:** University of Miami School of Law, JD, summa cum laude, 1983; University of Miami, BA, summa cum laude, 1980.

## FLYNN III, William
Fowler White Boggs Banker, Tampa
813 228 7411
*Recommended in Immigration*

## FORNARIS, Carl A
Greenberg Traurig LLP, Miami
305 579 0626
fornarisc@gtlaw.com
*Recommended in Banking & Finance*
**Practice Areas:** Financial institutions; international; corporate and securities.
**Prof. Memberships:** Member, Planning Committee, 2004 Financial Markets Association Securities Compliance Seminar.
**Career:** Listed, 'Chambers & Partners USA Guide', 2005-06; Pro Bono Service Award, Dade County Bar Association, 2005.
**Publications:** Lectured, 'Financial Institution Business Continuity/Disaster Recovery: Legal And Compliance Primer', Terremark Worldwide, Inc. Conference and 'The New U.S. Bank Secrecy Act Anti-Money Laundering Examination Manual: What You Need To Know Now', Offshore Alert Annual Due Diligence Conference, November 2005.
**Personal:** JD, The Catholic University of America Columbus School of Law, 1993; BS, University of Miami, 1990.

## FOSTER, Joseph E
Akerman Senterfitt, Orlando
407 843 7860
ed.foster@akerman.com
*Recommended in Litigation*
**Career:** Joseph Foster, shareholder and Co-Chair of the firm's Financial Institutions Practice Group, primarily handles commercial and financial institutions litigation, lender liability defense, class action defense, foreclosure, and replevin matters. He also consults regularly with the Florida Bankers Association on proposed legislation affecting the banking industry, particularly as it relates to mortgage foreclosures, proceedings supplementary, and judgment enforcement. He has written and lectured extensively on all aspects of Florida foreclosure law and frequently writes and lectures on Florida judgment collection law.

## FOX-ISICOFF, Tammy
Rifkin and Fox-Isicoff PA, Miami
305 371 2777
*Recommended in Immigration*

## FREEDMAN, Robert S
Carlton Fields, Tampa
813 223 7000
rfreedman@carltonfields.com
*Recommended in Real Estate*
**Practice Areas:** Practices real property law and related issues with emphasis on resort, condominium, subdivision and timeshare development, and also on general real estate transactions.
**Prof. Memberships:** Member, The Florida Bar, Vice-Chair of Condominium and Planned Development Committee, Real Property Probate and Trust Law Section; American Bar Association, Chair of Timeshare and Interval Uses Committee; Hillsborough County Bar Association; American Resort Development Association, Member of State Legislative Committee.
**Publications:** Editor, 'Compendium on State Timeshare Laws', (joint project of ABA and American Resort Development Association).
**Personal:** JD, Stetson University College of Law, 1990; BA, Duke University, 1987.

## FREELAND, Jorge
White & Case LLP, Miami
305 371 2700
jfreeland@whitecase.com
*Recommended in Corporate/M&A*
**Practice Areas:** Head of the Domestic Corporate and Securities Department in the Miami office. Has worked extensively in the corporate and securities area and represented numerous issuers and underwriters in public and private offerings of equity and debt securities. Has also worked with institutional investors and other financing sources in negotiating and documenting debt and equity placements. His experience with clients in a variety of industries and with diverse financial requirements enables him to offer practical and creative advice on securities law issues.

## FRIEDMAN, Robert J
Holland & Knight LLP, Miami
305 374 8500
robert.friedman@hklaw.com
*Recommended in Tax*
**Practice Areas:** Partner in the Business Section and Head of the firm's national Employee Benefits, Executive Compensation and ERISA Practice Group. He has over 20 years of experience with all aspects of benefits work, including the drafting, qualification and compliance of pension, 401(k), and profit sharing plans, corporate mergers, acquisitions and bankruptcies, plan transfers, mergers and terminations, fiduciary matters, investment and hedge funds, executive compensation, non-qualified deferred compensation arrangements, and ERISA-related litigation. Friedman also has been actively involved with welfare benefit plans, particularly with respect to compliance issues. He also has represented companies, trustees and lenders in ESOP transactions.

## FROST II, John
Frost Tamayo Sessums & Aranda PA, Bartow 863 533 0314
*Recommended in Litigation*

## GALLION, Theresa M
Fisher & Phillips LLP, Tampa
813 769 7500
tgallion@laborlawyers.com
*Recommended in Employment*
**Practice Areas:** Theresa Gallion is the Managing Partner in the Tampa office of the national law firm of Fisher & Phillips LLP, practicing exclusively in labor and employment law representing management. She represents clients in a variety of industries and has extensive bench and jury trial experience in employment matters. She has special expertise in defending matters arising under Title VII of the Civil Rights Act of 1964, the Age Discrimination in Employment Act, the Americans with Disabilities Act, the Family and Medical Leave Act, and the Equal Pay Act. Gallion received her BA and JD from Louisiana State University.

## GARCIA, Brian
Akerman Senterfitt, Miami
305 982 5699
brian.garcia@akerman.com
*Recommended in Immigration*
**Career:** Brian Garcia, a shareholder in the Corporate Group also focuses his practice on business immigration. Mr Garcia assists US and multinational companies, hospitals and universities in obtaining employment-based visas and permanent residence, provides strategic planning for recruitment and hiring, acts as immigration counsel for M&As and reorganizations for the preservation of visas and permanent residence applications, establishes training programs to effectuate the transfer of foreign employees and advises clients on employment verification and anti-discrimination procedures and enforcement actions. Mr Garcia is a frequent speaker on business immigration and is a member of the American Immigration Lawyers Association.

## GART, Brian
Greenberg Traurig LLP, Fort Lauderdale
954 768 8212
gartb@gtlaw.com
*Recommended in Bankruptcy*
**Practice Areas:** Reorganization, bankruptcy and restructuring.
**Prof. Memberships:** Member, Local Rules Advisory Committee for the United States Bankruptcy Court for the Southern District of Florida, 2001-06; Member, Business Law Section of the Florida Bar; Director, University of Miami School of Law Alumni Association, 2005-08.
**Career:** Listed, 'Best Lawyers in America, 2003-04', 2006; listed, 'Chambers & Partners USA Guide', 2003-06; listed as one of South Florida's Top Lawyers by South Florida Legal Guide, 2002-06.
**Publications:** Contributing author, 2001-02 'Bankruptcy Law Update', Aspen Publishers.
**Personal:** JD, cum laude, University of Miami School of Law, 1983; BA, cum laude, University of Miami, 1980.

## GARWOOD, Thomas
Ford & Harrison LLP, Orlando
407 418 2315
tgarwood@fordharrison.com
*Recommended in Employment*
**Practice Areas:** Tom Garwood concentrates his practice in the area of advising, counseling and representing management and business enterprises in all facets of labor/employment law. He is board certified as a specialist in labor and employment law by the Florida Bar and is admitted to practice before the US Supreme Court, various circuit courts of appeals and all courts in the State of Florida. Tom graduated from Florida State University (BA, with honors, 1965), and from Stetson University School of Law (JD, 1971). In 1997, Tom was elected as a Fellow to the College of Labor and Employment Lawyers.

## GEARY JR, Francis
Fowler White Boggs Banker,
West Palm Beach 561 655 1100
*Recommended in Healthcare*

## GENET, Chava
Stearns Weaver Miller Weissler Alhadeff & Sitterson, PA, Miami
305 789 3200
*Recommended in Real Estate*

## GENOVESE, John H
Genovese Joblove & Battista, PA, Miami
305 349 2300
jgenovese@gjb-law.com

*Recommended in Bankruptcy*

**Practice Areas:** Heads the firm's Insolvency and Reorganization Practice. His expertise includes troubled loan workouts, bankruptcy, insurance insolvencies with an emphasis on insolvency litigation. Onlookers describe him as 'a dean of the bar – smart and aggressive'. He represents, along with Partner Craig P Rieders, the securities class action plaintiffs in the Enron Chapter 11 case and has acted as special litigation counsel for the Unsecured Creditors' Committee in the Delaware Chapter 11 of the Safety-Kleen litigating avoidance claims related to its LBO. He also represented the outside directors of Flagship, a Florida medical services and equipment firm, in a D&O litigation brought by Flagship's Chapter 7 Trustee.

**GENTILE, Melinda S**
Peckar & Abramson, PC, Fort Lauderdale
954 764 5222
mgentile@pecklaw.com
*Recommended in Construction*
**Practice Areas:** Ms Gentile's primary area of practice is construction law. She has developed a particular expertise in all aspects of construction law and construction dispute resolution and has demonstrated success in preparing and handling construction matters ranging from bid protests to contract disputes and from contractor's liens to defect claims. Her construction law practice also includes project administration assistance toward project success and for early identification and resolution of potential disputes.
**Prof. Memberships:** Ms Gentile is certified as a specialist in Construction Law by the Florida Bar and has served as a Broward County Magistrate. She is a Member of the Florida Bar, the Broward County Bar (Member of the Construction Law Committee), the National Association of Women in Construction, the Construction Association of South Florida, the Associated Builders and Contractors, Inc., and the Stephen R Booher American Inns of Court.
**Career:** She is the Managing Partner of Peckar & Abramson's Fort Lauderdale office and is admitted to practice law before the United States District Court for the Middle and Southern Districts of Florida as well as all courts of the State of Florida.
**Publications:** She has authored several articles and is a frequent lecturer on various construction law topics for the Florida Bar, Construction Association of South Florida, Construction specifications Institute, Lorman Educational Services, National Underground Contractors Association, National Association of Women In Construction, American Society of Professional Estimaors, Florida Real Estate Journal, Southeast Construction, American Bar Association, Associated General Contractors of America and

Stetson University.
**Personal:** She is a graduate of Avila University, Florida International University, and Nova University Shephard Broad Law Center.

**GEORGE, Peter**
George & Titus PA, Tampa
813 273 0355
*Recommended in Litigation*

**GERAGHTY, William P**
Shook, Hardy & Bacon LLP, Miami
305 358 5171
wgeraghty@shb.com
*Recommended in Litigation*
**Practice Areas:** Concentrates on the defense of products liability, tort and personal injury cases. Has significant trial experience with class actions, products liability, insurance coverage, commercial disputes, and attorney malpractice.
**Prof. Memberships:** Admitted before the state courts of Florida, the District of Columbia and Maryland and before US District Courts for the Southern and Middle Districts of Florida and the District of Maryland. Member of The Florida Bar and American Bar Association.
**Career:** Joined Shook, Hardy & Bacon, 1998; became Partner, 2002.
**Personal:** JD, cum laude, Georgetown University Law Center, 1993; BA, cum laude, Duke University, 1989.

**GILBERT, Leonard H**
Holland & Knight LLP, Tampa
813 227 8500
leonard.gilbert@hklaw.com
*Recommended in Bankruptcy*
**Practice Areas:** Partner in the Business Law Section, practicing commercial finance, insolvency, and commercial litigation and maintaining an active transactional practice. His emphasis has been in the representation of financial institutions and other institutional lenders. In his bankruptcy practice, he has represented numerous state, national and international banks, and other financial institutions and public bodies, secured and unsecured creditors' committees and equity and has been involved in various restructurings. He is past President of The Florida Bar and is active in the Business Law Section of the American Bar Association, the International Insolvency Institute, and the International Bar Association.

**GILBERT, Robert**
Carlton Fields, West Palm Beach
561 659 7070
rgilbert@carltonfields.com
*Recommended in Bankruptcy*
**Practice Areas:** Practices in the area of bankruptcy and creditors' rights. Represents creditors, landlords, franchisors, creditors' committees, trustees, debtors; handles out-of-court workouts, litigation involving commerical paper, secured lending and letters of credit.

**Prof. Memberships:** Admitted to practice in Florida. Member, American Bankruptcy Institute; Past President of Bankruptcy Bar Association for Southern District of Florida.
**Publications:** Author, 'A Comparative Analysis of Reorganizations Under the United States Bankruptcy Code and Administrations Under the English Insolvency Act' (Caribbean Law and Business 1997).
**Personal:** JD (cum laude), University of Miami School of Law, 1980; BA (magna cum laude), Alma College, 1977.

**GINSBURG, Dennis**
Packman, Neuwahl & Rosenberg, Coral Gables 305 665 3311
*Recommended in Tax*

**GLAZIER, Robert**
Robert Glazier – Sole Practitioner, Miami 305 372 5900
glazier@fla-law.com
*Recommended in Litigation*
**Practice Areas:** Appeals and trial consultation. Important recent decisions include Tananta v Cruise Ships Catering and Services, 909 So.2d 874 (Fla. 3d DCA 2004)(en banc); Chuck . City of Homestead, 888 So.2d 736 (Fla. 3d DCA 2004)(en banc); Membreno v Costa Crociere SpA, 425 F.3d 932 (11th Cir 2005); In re Martinez, 416 F.3d 1286 (11th Cir 2005).
**Publications:** Co-author of 'Handbook of Florida Evidence' (2d ed, with Michael H Graham). Articles published in the Florida Bar Journal, Nova Law Review, and Trial Magazine. Former Adjunct Professor, University of Miami School of Law.
**Personal:** Law clerk to Honorable Gerald B Cope and Honorable Daniel S Pearson, Third District Court of Appeal of Florida. Nova Law School (JD, 1987); New College of Florida (BA, 1981). Executive editor, Nova Law Review. President, Temple Israel of Greater Miami, 2005-06.

**GLENN, Robert**
Glenn Rasmussen Fogarty & Hooker, Tampa 813 229 3333
*Recommended in Bankruptcy*

**GOLDBERG, Michael**
Akerman Senterfitt, Fort Lauderdale
954 463 2700
michael.goldberg@akerman.com
*Recommended in Bankruptcy*
**Career:** Michael Goldberg is a shareholder and concentrates his practice on bankruptcy and creditors' rights. He regularly represents creditors, debtors and trustees in bankruptcy proceedings and pre-bankruptcy workouts. He has a masters in business administration in finance and is routinely appointed to serve as receiver of distressed corporations. He has been appointed receiver in numerous high profile cases including the Cyprus Fund, a $90 million Ponzi Scheme; AB

Financing and Investments, Inc., a $50 million Ponzi Scheme; the Discovery Capital Group, a defunct broker-dealer; and Loans4Military, a corporation with debts exceeding $30 million.

**GOLDMAN, Robert**
Vickers Madsen & Goldman, Tallahassee
850 523 0400
*Recommended in Tax*

**GOLDSTEIN, Joseph**
Holland & Knight LLP, Miami
305 374 8500
joseph.goldstein@hklaw.com
*Recommended in Real Estate*
**Practice Areas:** Partner in Holland & Knight's Real Estate Section, practices land use and environmental law. Goldstein has significant experience representing developers, major corporations, hospitals and universities to protect their property rights and entitlements and in seeking complex development or other governmental approvals and permits. Goldstein has represented dozens of the most significant and recognizable development projects in South Florida from conception to completion during 20 years of practicing land use and environmental law. Goldstein is active in the Builders' Association of South Florida where he is currently serving as a Life Director and as Chair of its Legislative Committee.

**GOLDSTEIN, Richard M**
Bilzin Sumberg Baena Price & Axelrod LLP, Miami 305 350 2371
rgoldstein@bilzin.com
*Recommended in Tax*
**Career:** Richard Goldstein co-chairs a diverse tax and trusts and estate practice. He represents numerous family businesses, US residents and non-resident aliens, multi-national entities and both publicly and privately held companies. He frequently handles complex tax planning and structuring involving corporate M&A, as well as matters involving partnerships and limited liability companies. Mr Goldstein has lectured frequently throughout Florida on tax and estate planning with respect to closely held businesses. Recently, he has handled the restructuring of a multi-tiered partnership involving extensive real estate holdings of a prominent developer and the complex reorganization of several multinational entities.

**GONZALEZ, Eduardo W**
Hunton & Williams, Miami
305 810 2552
egonzalez@hunton.com
*Recommended in Litigation*
**Practice Areas:** Eduardo Gonzalez's practice focuses on complex commercial litigation including contract disputes, class actions, business torts, franchise litigation, antitrust litigation, appellate advocacy, insurance coverage litigation

and products liability. Experience in international litigation and domestic and international arbitrations. Represented numerous corporations in complex nation-wide class actions. Represented numerous corporations in contractual disputes in international and domestic arbitrations.

**Personal:** JD, University of Miami, magna cum laude, 1997; BA, University of Miami, cum laude, 1994.

### GONZALEZ, Enrique
Fragomen, Del Rey, Bernsen & Loewy, LLP, Coral Gables 305 774 5800
*Recommended in Immigration*

### GONZALEZ, Ervin
Colson Hicks Eidson, Coral Gables
305 476 7400
Ervin@colson.com
*Recommended in Litigation*

**Practice Areas:** products liability; medical malpractice; aviation; class actions; personal injury; toxic torts.

**Career:** Mr Gonzalez is board certified as a specialist in civil trial law by the Florida Bar and the National Board of Trial Advocacy; board certified in business litigation law by the Florida Bar; graduated from the University of Miami School of Law, cum laude in 1985. He has over 20 years' experience practicing products liability, class action, business litigation, medical malpractice and personal injury litigation; has 21 jury trial verdicts and numerous settlements that meet or exceed one million dollars.

### GONZALEZ, Thomas
Thompson, Sizemore & Gonzalez, Tampa 813 273 0050
*Recommended in Employment*

### GONZÁLEZ, Daniel E
Hogan & Hartson LLP, Miami
305 459 6649
degonzalez@hhlaw.com
*Recommended in Litigation*

**Practice Areas:** Director of the firm's International Litigation and Arbitration Practice. Practices principally in international complex commercial litigation and arbitration, having tried and arbitrated cases in English and Spanish throughout the United States, Latin America and Europe.

**Prof. Memberships:** Member, American Bar Association; International Bar Association; International Chamber of Commerce; American Arbitration Association.

**Career:** With his common and civil law experience and financial background, he represents multinational clients involved in all aspects of commercial disputes, including securities, project finance, infrastructure construction, product defects, insurance coverage, distributorships and environmental liability.

**Personal:** University of Miami School of Law (JD, summa cum laude).

### GOREN, Samuel
Goren Cherof Doody & Ezrol PA, Fort Lauderdale 954 771 4500
*Recommended in Real Estate*

### GORSON, Matthew
Greenberg Traurig LLP, Miami
305 579 0777
gorsonm@gtlaw.com
*Recommended in Real Estate*

**Practice Areas:** Real estate, land use and zoning, and governmental negotiations.

**Prof. Memberships:** Chairman, Downtown Miami Charter School; Board Member, City of Miami Downtown Development Authority; Board Member, Tulane University President's Council; Board Member, Mt Sinai Hospital.

**Career:** Listed, 'The Best Lawyers in America', every edition; listed, 2004 and 2005 'Legal Elite', Florida Trend Magazine, listing of Florida's top attorneys as selected by their peers; 'Chambers & Partners USA Guide", 2003-06; named among South Florida's 'Heavy Hitters in Real Estate' by the Business Journal, 2004.

**Personal:** University of Chicago (JD, 1973); Tulane University (BS, 1970).

### GRAGG, K Lawrence
White & Case LLP, Miami
305 995 5209
lgragg@whitecase.com
*Recommended in Tax*

**Practice Areas:** A Board Certified tax lawyer. Has a transactional domestic and international practice, a significant portion of which is devoted to general business counseling, including business formations, acquisitions and dispositions. He also has an active federal and state tax practice. Extensive experience in structuring and negotiating complex joint venture business arrangements, with a particular focus in the real estate area.

**Prof. Memberships:** Florida Bar; United States Tax Court; United States District Court for the Southern District of Florida; United States Courts of Appeals for the Fifth and Eleventh Circuits.

### GRAMMIG, Robert
Holland & Knight LLP, Tampa
813 227 8500
robert.grammig@hklaw.com
*Recommended in Corporate/M&A*

**Practice Areas:** Head of the Public Companies and Securities Practice Group, practices corporate finance, securities law, general corporate law and international business transactions. His practice currently includes a wide range of corporate, securities and commercial law matters, including: both public offerings and private placements registered under the federal and state securities laws; mergers and acquisitions; periodic reporting and compliance matters under the Securities Exchange Act of 1934; corporate governance matters; contests for corporate control; and other commercial law matters. He has devoted a significant

part of his practice to international business transactions, representing both United States and foreign entities.

### GREELEY, Jack
Smith Mackinnon PA, Orlando
407 843 7300
*Recommended in Banking & Finance*

### GREEN, William
Hopping Green & Sams, PA, Tallahassee
850 222 7500
billg@hgslaw.com
*Recommended in Environment*

**Practice Areas:** Environmental law: special emphasis on scientific issues.

**Prof. Memberships:** Florida State and Federal courts, Federal 11th Circuit Court of Appeals, US Supreme Court, American Bar Association, and Florida Bar; Fellow, Royal Astronomical Society.

**Career:** 1967-74: research in spectroscopy and lasers, US Naval Research Laboratory; 1974-79: associate/Partner, Mahoney, Hadlow, Chambers & Adams, P.A.; 1979 to date: shareholder, Hopping Green & Sams, P.A.

**Publications:** 25 publications in Physical Chemistry and Astrophysics; two law review articles.

**Personal:** BS/PhD (Chemistry), University of South Carolina, 1963/67; JD, Georgetown University, 1973; Visiting Scholar, University of Cambridge, 1987; Visiting Scientist, Lawrence Berkeley National Laboratory, 1998.

### GREER, Alan
Richman Greer Weil Brumbaugh Mirabito & Christensen, Miami
305 373 4000
*Recommended in Litigation*

### GRINDSTAFF, Michael J
Shutts & Bowen LLP, Orlando
407 835 6927
mgrindstaff@shutts-law.com
*Recommended in Real Estate*

**Practice Areas:** Chairman, Orlando Real Estate Practice Group; handles transactions involving acquisition, zoning, permitting, development and sale of retail shopping centers, mixed-use developments, multi-family apartment complexes and office buildings; single family residential communities and condominium projects, real estate-related litigation, ad valorem taxation disputes, zoning and land use litigation.

**Prof. Memberships:** Florida, Georgia.

**Career:** Past Chairman Orange County Planning and Zoning Commission; Director/Chairman of Real Estate Committee and Member of Executive Committee of Univeristy of Central Florida Foundation.

**Personal:** JD, cum laude, Mercer University 1982; BSBA University of Central Florida.

### GROGAN, Michael
Coffman, Coleman, Andrews & Grogan, Jacksonville 904 389 5161
*Recommended in Employment*

### GROSSMAN, Robert L
Greenberg Traurig LLP, Miami
305 579 0756
grossmanr@gtlaw.com
*Recommended in Corporate/M&A*

**Practice Areas:** Corporate and securities; M&A; retail; technology, media and telecommunications.

**Prof. Memberships:** Board of Directors, Project Interchange; Board of Directors, Jewish National Fund; Board of Directors, Children's Bereavement Center.

**Career:** Recognized as one of 'South Florida's Top Dealmakers of the Year in Mergers & Acquisitions', Daily Business Review, 2005; Recognized as one of the 'Most Effective Lawyers', South Florida Business Review.

**Personal:** JD, with honors, The Ohio State University College of Law, 1978; MA, The Ohio State University, 1979; BA, The Ohio State University, 1975.

### GURLEY, David
Gurley Dramis, Sarasota
941 365 4501
*Recommended in Construction*

### GUSO, Jordi
Berger Singerman, Miami
305 755 9500
*Recommended in Bankruptcy*

### GUTTER, Marvin
Tescher Gutter Chaves Josepher Rubin Ruffin & Forman PA, Boca Ratón
561 998 7847
*Recommended in Tax*

### HAINLINE JR, Theodore
Rogers Towers PA, Jacksonville
904 398 3911
*Recommended in Real Estate*

### HALE, Russell
Akerman Senterfitt, Orlando
407 419 8556
russell.hale@akerman.com
*Recommended in Tax*

**Career:** Russell Hale is a shareholder and Section Administrator of the Orlando office's Corporate Department. He is Board Certified in Taxation Law by the Florida Bar and practices primarily in the fields of business planning, taxation and transactions. He has extensive experience in issues of Florida state and local taxation including controversy resolution, administrative compliance and legislative support. He is a registered lobbyist with the legislative and executive branches of the Florida State Government and works on policy issues relating to state taxation, trusts and estates. He is a former Municipal Court Judge and is admitted to Florida and Oregon.

### HALL, Donald
Gunster, Yoakley & Stewart, P.A., Fort Lauderdale 954 462 2000
*Recommended in Real Estate*

## HALSEY, Douglas
White & Case LLP, Miami
305 995 5268
dhalsey@whitecase.com
*Recommended in Environment*
**Practice Areas:** Covers all aspects of environmental law, litigation, transactional advice, and regulatory matters before governmental agencies. During the last 25 years, has tried numerous environmental cases in state and federal court with emphasis on cost recovery claims and land use disputes. Has represented manufacturers, developers, and property owners in complex litigation and defended enforcement actions brought by the EPA, Florida Department of Environmental Protection and local government agencies.
**Prof. Memberships:** The Florida Bar; United States District Court for the Southern District of Florida; United States Courts of Appeals for the Fifth and Eleventh Circuits.

## HALULA, John F
Holland & Knight LLP, Miami
305 374 8500
john.halula@hklaw.com
*Recommended in Real Estate*
**Practice Areas:** Partner maintaining his practice in the areas of real estate with a concentration on institutional finance. He represents various domestic and international lenders providing construction and permanent financing for multi-family residential, retail, office and industrial projects. He has substantial experience analyzing land use, zoning, building and water law issues, and development agreements and construction contracts. Halula assists conduit lenders in the origination of mortgage loans to be pooled in connection with the issuance of mortgage pass-through certificates. He also represents clients in real estate transactions involving sales, acquisitions, sale-leasebacks, ground leases, building and space leases, and like-kind exchanges.

## HAMILTON, Russell
Morgan, Lewis & Bockius LLP, Miami
305 415 3440
rhamilton@morganlewis.com
*Recommended in Employment*
**Practice Areas:** W Russell Hamilton III is a Partner in the Labor and Employment Practice. Mr Hamilton's practice focuses on labor, employment and employee benefits matters, representing exclusively employers, employer associations, and employee benefit plans and fiduciaries. Mr Hamilton has represented clients in equal employment opportunity and affirmative action advice and litigation; employee benefits and fiduciary litigation; and arbitration of all types of employment issues.
**Prof. Memberships:** American Bar Association (Labor and Employment Law Section); Florida Bar Association (Labor and Employment Law Section); Georgia Bar Association (Labor and Employment Law Section); North Carolina Bar Association; Dade County Bar Association.

## HAMILTON, William F
Holland & Knight LLP, Tampa
813 227 6480
william.hamilton@hklaw.com
*Recommended in Litigation*
**Practice Areas:** Partner in the Litigation Section, practices complex commercial litigation in the areas of intellectual property, class action defense, telecommunications, antitrust and trade regulation and unfair trade practices. He has significant arbitration experience and is a certified arbitrator with the American Arbitration Association, the International Trademark Association and The Florida Bar Fee Arbitration Program. Hamilton is a member of the Commercial Litigation, and the Patent, Trademark and Copyright Committees of The Florida Bar's Corporation, Banking and Business Law Section and a member of the Intellectual Property, Litigation, and Antitrust Sections of the American Bar Association.

## HANSON JR, Karl B
LeBoeuf, Lamb, Greene & MacRae LLP, Jacksonville 904 630 5330
kbhanson@llgm.com
*Recommended in Real Estate*
**Practice Areas:** An experienced commercial real estate attorney concentrating in acquisitions, dispositions, development, financing, leasing and management of real property. He represents clients in all facets of ownership in the real estate area. He has served as counsel to mortgage banking companies in regard to their operations and financing. He is also an experienced real property title insurance attorney, representing several major national title insurance companies in insuring large real estate transactions.
**Prof. Memberships:** Florida Bar; American Bar Association; Jacksonville Bar Association.
**Career:** Joined LeBoeuf Lamb in 1988.
**Personal:** University of North Carolina (BA) 1968; University of Florida (JD) 1971.

## HARTSFIELD, Shannon
Holland & Knight LLP, Tallahassee
850 224 7000
shannon.hartsfield@hklaw.com
*Recommended in Healthcare*
**Practice Areas:** Partner in the Litigation Section, practices in the area of health law, advising clients on state and federal healthcare regulatory matters including compliance, data privacy, licensure, telemedicine and reimbursement. Her clients include assisted living facilities, health plans, medical technology companies, disease management companies, nursing homes, pharmaceutical manufacturers and distributors, blood and tissue banks, clinical laboratories, medical management companies, and other members of the healthcare industry. Hartsfield is a member of the American Bar Association's Health Law Section, the American Health Lawyers Association, the Tallahassee Bar Association and the Tallahassee Women Lawyers.

## HEARING, Gregory
Thompson, Sizemore & Gonzalez, Tampa 813 273 0050
*Recommended in Employment*

## HELLER, William P
Akerman Senterfitt, Fort Lauderdale
954 759 8945
william.heller@akerman.com
*Recommended in Litigation*
**Career:** William Heller, a shareholder who leads the firm's Consumer Finance Litigation Team, represents mortgage loan originators, servicers and investors, in addition to buyers and collectors of consumer debt, in individual and class actions. He concentrates his practice on defending claims under the Truth in Lending Act, Real Estate Settlement Procedures Act, Fair Credit Reporting Act, Equal Credit Opportunity Act, Fair Debt Collection Practices Act, and state law versions of these statutes. He also has extensive experience investigating and prosecuting origination fraud, enforcing consumer arbitration agreements, and handling the foreclosure and collection aspects of litigation arising from consumer disputes.

## HENDERSON, Thomas
Hill, Ward & Henderson, PA, Tampa
813 221 3900
*Recommended in Real Estate*

## HERNANDEZ, Eugenio
Holland & Knight LLP, Miami
305 374 8500
eugenio.hernandez@hklaw.com
*Recommended in Immigration*
**Practice Areas:** Partner in the Business Section and head of the firm's National Immigration Practice Group. He practices exclusively in the field of immigration, nationality and consular law, principally in business-related matters with an emphasis on corporate transfers, professionals, entrepreneurs and investors. He has served for a number of years as Program Co-Chair and Co-ordinator of the Annual Immigration Law Update, sponsored by the Florida Bar CLE Committee, the International Law Section and the American Immigration Lawyers Association. Hernandez is the author of various published articles in the International Law Quarterly and lectures frequently on the topic of immigration law.

## HILL, William K
Bilzin Sumberg Baena Price & Axelrod LLP, Miami 305 350 7202
whill@bilzin.com
*Recommended in Litigation*
**Career:** William Hill focuses his practice on complex litigation and arbitration in state and federal trial and appellate courts, including bankruptcy courts. He represents companies in disputes involving intellectual property, employment, non-compete, non-disclosure and trade secrets issues, and bankruptcy and class action cases. He has extensive experience in a variety of industries, including aviation, technology, healthcare, retail and banking, among others. Prior to joining Bilzin Sumberg, William spent 16 years with the Miami office of a large, international firm. He also served as law clerk to the Honorable William M Hoeveler, US District Court, Southern District of Florida (1987-88).

## HILL III, Benjamin
Hill, Ward & Henderson, PA, Tampa
813 221 3900
*Recommended in Litigation*

## HINTZE, Russell P
Greenberg Traurig LLP, Orlando
407 420 1000
hintzer@gtlaw.com
*Recommended in Tax*
**Practice Areas:** Tax; corporate and securities; real estate.
**Prof. Memberships:** Member, Orange County Bar Association; former Treasurer and Board Member, Lake Brantley Youth Football Association, Inc.
**Career:** Listed, 2004 Legal Elite, Florida Trend Magazine, listing of Florida's top attorneys as selected by their peers; Board Certified Tax Lawyer, Florida Bar Board of Legal Specialization and Education.
**Personal:** LLM, University of Florida Levin College of Law, 1988; JD, cum laude, Stetson University College of Law, 1987; BS, with honors, Chemistry, University of Florida, 1984.

## HOFFMAN, D Bruce
Hunton & Williams, Miami
305 810 2540
bhoffman@hunton.com
*Recommended in Antitrust*
**Practice Areas:** Bruce Hoffman co-offices in Hunton's Miami and Washington, DC offices. His practice focuses on antitrust and unfair competition, including merger review, government investigations, antitrust counseling, and antitrust litigation. Hoffman was a senior official at the Federal Trade Commission in Washington from 2001 through 2004, serving as Deputy Director and Associate Director of the FTC's Bureau of Competition. At the FTC he supervised merger and conduct investigations, FTC antitrust litigation, and policy development, including heavy involvement in the Government's briefs to the US Supreme Court in

major antitrust cases. Hoffman handles mergers and litigation across the US.

## HOFFMAN, Jerome
Holland & Knight LLP, Tallahassee
850 224 7000
jerome.hoffman@hklaw.com
*Recommended in Antitrust*
**Practice Areas:** Partner in Litigation Section, practicing primarily in antitrust, consumer fraud, RICO, and Medicaid and Medicare fraud, qui tam and other healthcare regulatory matters. Served as chief of the Antitrust Section of the Florida Attorney General's Office, handling cases involving bid rigging, price fixing, monopolization and other restraints of trade, and merger reviews. He also served as General Counsel for the Florida Agency for Healthcare Administration, where he supervised 40 attorneys responsible for prosecuting Medicaid overpayments; regulating hospitals, nursing homes, assisted living facilities and home health agencies and prosecuting disciplinary cases before the Board of Medicine.

## HOGAN, John M
Holland & Knight LLP, Miami
305 374 8500
john.hogan@hklaw.com
*Recommended in Litigation*
**Practice Areas:** Partner and Head of the Litigation Section for South Florida. His experience includes civil and criminal litigation in the areas of securities fraud, healthcare including pharmaceuticals, bank fraud, and foreign Corrupt Practice Act issues. He has extensive experience assisting corporations with internal investigations and compliance issues as well as grand jury matters. Hogan is the former Chief of Staff to the Attorney General of the United States and served as Chief Assistant State Attorney for Miami-Dade County, Florida, where he successfully tried a number of nationally significant cases. He also was the first Statewide Prosecutor of Florida.

## HOLCOMB, Mark E
Holland & Knight LLP, Tallahassee
850 224 7000
mark.holcomb@hklaw.com
*Recommended in Tax*
**Practice Areas:** Partner in the firm's Business Law Section, practices in the area of state and local taxation law. He is experienced in representing clients before the Florida Department of Revenue and in litigating state tax cases at the trial and appellate levels. Holcomb represents and advises taxpayers in a broad range of state and local taxes. His experience includes representing manufacturers, retailers, financial institutions, service companies, utilities, equipment leasing companies, alcoholic beverage distributors, insurance companies, trade associations and hotel management companies in tax controversy work and planning opportunities.

## HOLIFIELD, Marilyn
Holland & Knight LLP, Miami
305 374 8500
marilyn.holifield@hklaw.com
*Recommended in Employment*
**Practice Areas:** Partner in the Litigation Section, represents management and corporate clients in employment matters. Her practice includes business litigation, trade secrets, covenants-not-to-compete and class action litigation. She regularly defends employers in litigation involving wrongful termination cases brought as intentional torts, breach of contract, whistleblower and civil rights discrimination actions. She also counsels and represents employers before local, state and federal agencies in cases involving the Age Discrimination in Employment Act, Americans with Disabilities Act, Title VII and other local, state and federal employment statutes. She was recently named by Black Enterprise Magazine as one of America's top employment lawyers.

## HOLSHOUSER, Eric
Coffman, Coleman, Andrews & Grogan, Jacksonville 904 389 5161
*Recommended in Employment*

## HOPKINS, Edward
Broad and Cassel, West Palm Beach
561 832 3300
*Recommended in Healthcare*

## HOPPING, Wade
Hopping Green & Sams, PA, Tallahassee
850 222 7500
whopping@hgslaw.com
*Recommended in Environment, Real Estate*
**Practice Areas:** Lobbying business issues; land use.
**Prof. Memberships:** The Florida Bar; The Tallahassee Bar; Board of Trustees Pacific Legal Foundation; Board of Govenors Florida Chamber of Commerence.
**Career:** 1968-69: Justice of Florida Supreme Court; President Florida Chamber of Commerence; member 1979 to date: Senior member, Hopping Green & Sams, P.A.

## HORNREICH, Michael
Greenberg Traurig LLP, Orlando
407 418 2397
hornreichm@gtlaw.com
*Recommended in Construction*
**Practice Areas:** Litigation; construction law.
**Prof. Memberships:** Active Member, Associated General Contractors of America (AGC); Board of Directors, Central Florida Chapter of the AGC; Member, AGC's Legislative, Membership, and Safety Committees.
**Career:** Listed, 'Chambers & Partners USA Guide', 2003-06; listed, 2004 and 2005 Legal Elite, Florida Trend Magazine, listing of Florida's top attorneys as selected by their peers; listed, 'Best Lawyers in America'.
**Personal:** JD, University of Florida Levin College of Law, 1983; BS, University of Florida, 1978.

## HOROWITZ, Mitchell
Fowler White Boggs Banker, Tampa
813 228 7411
*Recommended in Tax*

## HOUSER, Bradley D
Akerman Senterfitt, Miami
305 982 5658
Bradley.Houser@akerman.com
*Recommended in Corporate/M&A*
**Career:** Bradley Houser, Shareholder and Co-Chair of the firm's Corporate Practice Group, focuses his practice on corporate, securities, mergers and acquisitions and corporate governance matters for companies in a variety of industries, including banking, technology, healthcare, real estate and retail. In addition, he advises senior management and the board of directors of both public and private companies on corporate compliance matters. Prior to joining the firm, he worked in the Divisions of Enforcement and Corporation Finance for the Securities and Exchange Commission. He is also a Certified Public Accountant.

## HUDSON, Robert
Baker & McKenzie, Miami
305 789 8906
bob.hudson@bakernet.com
*Recommended in Tax*
**Practice Areas:** Tax planning and tax controversy work, particularly for international private banks and high net worth clients, foreign client structuring into US real estate and businesses, and preimmigration tax planning.
**Prof. Memberships:** ABA, IFA, ITPA, ACTC, STEP, Florida Bar and New York Bar.
**Career:** Principal, Baker & McKenzie, Miami (1986 to date).
**Publications:** 'Federal Tax Considerations of Foreign Investment in the US Real Estate' BNA Portfolio and over 50 articles published to date on a wide range of international tax topics.
**Personal:** Vice Chairmain of the Performing Arts Center Foundation and Chairman of the Concert Association of Florida.

## HUTTON III, John B
Greenberg Traurig LLP, Miami
305 579 0500
huttonj@gtlaw.com
*Recommended in Bankruptcy*
**Practice Areas:** Business reorganization and bankruptcy.
**Prof. Memberships:** President, Bankruptcy Bar Association for the Southern District of Florida; Board Member, Family Resource Center of Dade County, Inc; Volunteer Mentor, Big Brothers/Big Sisters of Greater Miami, Inc.; Member, American Bankruptcy Institute; Member, Bankruptcy Bar Association; Member, Dade County Bar Association.
**Career:** Listed, 2005 Legal Elite, Florida Trend Magazine, listing of Florida's top attorneys as selected by their peers; listed as one of the Top Bankruptcy Lawyers, The Deal, June 2004.
**Personal:** JD, Columbia University School of Law, 1991; BA, with honors, Johns Hopkins University, 1988.

## HYDE, Kevin E
Foley & Lardner LLP, Jacksonville
904 359 8786
khyde@foley.com
*Recommended in Employment*
**Career:** Kevin E Hyde is a Partner in the Jacksonville office of Foley & Lardner LLP. He is a member of the firm's Labor and Employment Practice Group and Automotive Industry Team. Mr Hyde represents employers in a variety of human resources matters. His practice focuses on day to day employment counseling, and he regularly advises employers on creating appropriate compensation systems. He has represented employers in numerous charges of discrimination, employment-discrimination cases, wage-hour and management-union matters. Mr Hyde is a graduate of the University of Florida College of Law (JD, with honors, 1988).

## ICARD, Thomas
Icard, Merrill, Cullis, Timm, Furen & Ginsburg PA, Sarasota
941 366 8100
*Recommended in Construction*

## IMPERATO, Gabriel
Broad and Cassel, Fort Lauderdale
954 764 7060
*Recommended in Healthcare*

## JOHNSON, Carmen
Akerman Senterfitt, Miami
305 374 5600
carmen.johnson@akerman.com
*Recommended in Employment*
**Career:** Carmen S Johnson is a shareholder. She is Board Certified in Labor and Employment Law by The Florida Bar. She has 19 years of experience exclusively representing employers in employment law matters including human resources advice, FMLA and ADA issues, employment agreements and all types of employment litigation. She is a former member of the Executive Council of the Labor and Employment Law Section of The Florida Bar, Chair of the Equal Employment Opportunity Committee and Co-Chair of the Individual Employment Rights Committee. She frequently lectures professional associations on all areas of labor and employment law.

## JONES, Rod
Shutts & Bowen LLP, Orlando
407 835 6909
rjones@shutts-law.com
*Recommended in Banking & Finance*

**Practice Areas:** Partner, Financial Services Industry Practice Group; formerly Director of Division of Banking of Florida Department of Banking and Finance, responsibilities included licensing and supervising 500+ state chartered financial institutions.
**Prof. Memberships:** Florida.
**Career:** Was staff counsel, banking analyst for Florida House of Representatives Committee on Commerce; drafted major revisions to Florida Financial Institutions Codes, including legislation authorizing cross-industry mergers, conversions and acquisitions of Florida financial institutions and Regional Reciprocal Banking Act of 1984; taught at Florida School of Banking and Florida Bank Law Institute.
**Personal:** JD, with honors, Florida State University; Florida School of Banking, University of Florida.

### JONES, Thomas J
Holland & Knight LLP, Tallahassee
850 224 7000
tom.jones@hklaw.com
*Recommended in Insurance*
**Practice Areas:** Partner in the firm's Government Section, practices in the area of insurance regulatory law and commercial litigation. His practice routinely brings him into contact with insurance regulators who have authority over insurance companies and their operations and over specialty insurers such as health maintenance organizations, life care retirement communities and prepaid benefit plans. He represents clients' interests on a broad spectrum of issues before regulatory agencies, in proceedings before administrative law judges, and in state and federal courts.

### JOSEFSBERG, Robert
Podhurst Orseck P.A., Miami
305 358 2800
info@podhurst.com
*Recommended in Litigation*
**Practice Areas:** A broad range of civil and criminal litigation in all federal and state courts.
**Career:** One of Miami-Dade County's premier trial lawyers, listed annually since 1987 in the Best Lawyers in America in two categories – Business Litigation and Criminal Law. Past President and Dean of the International Academy of Trial Lawyers, a Fellow of the American College of Trial Lawyers and a Member of the American Board of Trial Advocates. He has served on the American Bar Association Standing Committee on the Judiciary, as Chairman of the Southern District of Florida Judicial Evaluation Committee, and the Florida State University Law School Board of Visitors. In addition to commercial practice, he also handles the firm's white-collar criminal defense work – an outgrowth of his background as an assistant US attorney for the Southern District of Florida, as Special Counsel to

the Dade County Grand Jury, and member of numerous commissions and task forces in the area of criminal law, including the US Supreme Court Advisory Committee on Criminal Rules and Chairmanship of the Florida Bar's Criminal Law Certification Committee.
**Personal:** BA Dartmouth College, 1959; JD Yale Law School, 1962.

### JOSEPHER, Richard
Tescher Gutter Chaves Josepher Rubin Ruffin & Forman PA, Boca Ratón
561 998 7847
*Recommended in Tax*

### JUNG, William
Jung & Sisco, Tampa
813 225 1988
*Recommended in Litigation*

### KANTOR, Hal
Lowndes Drosdick Doster Kantor & Reed, PA, Orlando 407 843 4600
*Recommended in Real Estate*

### KARP, Joel
Karp & Genauer PA, Coral Gables
305 445 3545
*Recommended in Tax*

### KASHTAN, Michael
Daniels, Kashtan, Downs, Robertson & Magathan, Miami 305 448 7988
*Recommended in Construction*

### KASNER, Stewart L
Baker & McKenzie, Miami
305 789 8940
stewart.kasner@bakernet.com
*Recommended in Tax*
**Practice Areas:** Mr Kasner is an international tax attorney and Member of Baker & McKenzie's International Private Banking Group, which for 2006 was included in the top tier of Chambers' International Private Client practice category. He provides US tax advice to foreign clients with respect to their US investments, including US real estate and other US business activities, and advises US clients with respect to their US and foreign investments and business activities. Mr Kasner also develops and provides advice regarding the acquisition of offshore private placement life insurance and annuity contracts. Mr Kasner is board certified in tax law.

### KATZ, Allan J
Akerman Senterfitt, Tallahassee
850 224 9634
allan.katz@akerman.com
*Recommended in Insurance*
**Career:** Allan Katz, Managing Shareholder of the Tallahassee office, concentrates his practice on legislative and governmental affairs, local government, public finance and banking, administrative, healthcare and insurance law. He has been a Member of the City of Tallahassee City Commission since May of 2002. Prior to entering private practice, he was Assistant Insurance Commissioner and

General Counsel for the State of Florida Department of Insurance, General Counsel for the US House of Representatives Commission on Administrative Review, Legislative Director for Congressman David Obey and Legislative Assistant to Congressman Bill Gunter.

### KEINER, Jeffrey
Gray Robinson PA, Orlando
407 843 8880
*Recommended in Construction*

### KELSO, Linda Y
Foley & Lardner LLP, Jacksonville
904 359 8713
lkelso@foley.com
*Recommended in Corporate/M&A*
**Career:** Linda Y Kelso is a Partner in the Jacksonville office of Foley & Lardner LLP. She is the leader of the Securities Practice and a member of the Transactional and Securities Practice Group. She counsels business clients in corporate and partnership organization, finance, and securities. Ms Kelso has worked on numerous public and private offerings, represented public companies in connection with their periodic reporting to the Securities and Exchange Commission, formed hedge funds that invest in securities, and handled business combinations for public and private entities. Ms Kelso received her JD from the University of Florida College of Law.

### KENDIG-SCHRADER, Julie
Greenberg Traurig LLP, Orlando
407 418 2417
kendig@gtlaw.com
*Recommended in Real Estate*
**Practice Areas:** Real estate; environmental; land development.
**Prof. Memberships:** Member, Osceola/Kissimmee Chamber of Commerce Board of Directors, 2004-present; Member, Land Use and Environmental Law Section of the Florida Bar.
**Career:** Listed, 'Chambers & Partners USA Guide', 2004-06; listed, 40 Under 40, Orlando Business Journal, 2005.
**Publications:** Special editor, 'Florida Environmental and Land Use Law Treatise - Environmental and Land Use Section of Florida Bar and Regulation' files; authored, 'Florida's Private Property Rights Act', Environmental and Land Use Law Section Reporter.
**Personal:** JD, University of Florida Levin College of Law, 1992; MA, University of Florida, 1991; BA, University of Florida, 1989.

### KENNEDY III, James J
Buchanan Ingersoll PC, Tampa
813 222 8185
kennedyjj@bipc.com
*Recommended in Healthcare*
**Practice Areas:** Practice is devoted primarily to the representation of hospitals and other healthcare providers. Jim is board certified as a Health Law Specialist

by the Florida Bar, a distinction earned by fewer than one percent of lawyers in the state. Jim regularly counsels clients on subjects related to healthcare business transactions, integrated delivery networks, physician-hospital organizations, managed care contracting, risk management issues, and fraud and abuse prevention.
**Prof. Memberships:** American Academy of Hospital Attorneys; National Health Lawyers Association; Florida Academy of Hospital Lawyers; Trial Lawyers Section, Florida Bar.
**Personal:** JD DePaul University, 1982; BS Florida State University, 1979.

### KING, Bruce
Carlton Fields, Miami
305 530 0050
bking@carltonfields.com
*Recommended in Construction*
**Practice Areas:** Practices commercial litigation and appeals, focusing on construction and surety cases. Board Certified in Construction Law by the Florida Bar.
**Prof. Memberships:** Admitted to practice in Florida, Pennsylvania, the United States Court of Federal Claims. Member, American Bar Association, Litigation and Tort and Insurance Practice Sections; American Arbitration Association; International Association of Defense Counsel.
**Publications:** Presenter, 'Florida Construction Defect and Mold Litigation' (National Business Institute 2003).
**Personal:** JD, University of Pittsburgh, 1978; BA (cum laude), Allegheny College, 1975.

### KING, David
King, Blackwell & Downs PA, Orlando
407 422 2472
*Recommended in Litigation*

### KINSOLVING, Ruth Barnes
Carlton Fields, Tampa
813 223 7000
rkinsolving@carltonfields.com
*Recommended in Real Estate*
**Practice Areas:** Practices general commercial real estate law, concentrating on complex real property. Transactions include sales, purchases and leases of commercial property, shopping center development, leasing and conveyancing of oil, gas, and minerals, and title examination. Represents owners, buyers, and tenants of office buildings, shopping centers, and residential apartments.
**Prof. Memberships:** Admitted to practice in Florida. Member, The Florida Bar, Real Property, Probate and Trust Law Section; American Bar Association; American College of Real Estate Lawyers; American Resort Development Association; International Council of Shopping Centers.
**Personal:** JD, University of Florida College of Law, 1971; AB, (cum laude), Randolph-Macon Woman's College, 1968.

**KIRKWOOD, Peter**
Barnett, Bolt, Kirkwood, Long & McBride,
Tampa 813 253 2020
*Recommended in Tax*

**KIRSCHNER, Kenneth**
Kirschner & Legler, Jacksonville
904 346 3200
*Recommended in Corporate/M&A*

**KIRWIN, Brian**
Kirwin Norris PA, Winter Park
407 740 6600
*Recommended in Construction*

**KITCHEN, Damon**
Constangy, Brooks & Smith, LLC,
Jacksonville 904 356 8900
*Recommended in Employment*

**KLINGHOFFER, Teddy D**
Akerman Senterfitt, Miami
305 374 5600
teddy.klinghoffer@akerman.com
*Recommended in Corporate/M&A*
**Career:** Teddy Klinghoffer is a shareholder in the Corporate Practice Group
and is a Member of the firm's Board of
Directors. He focuses his practice in the
areas of corporate law, mergers and
acquisitions, private equity and venture
capital. His principal clients include a
number of significant private equity
funds, privately-held and public companies and high net worth individuals and
entrepreneurs. Mr Klinghoffer's representative clients include Brockway Moran
& Partners, CitiGroup Private Bank,
MapleWood Partners, MBF Capital Partners and Kitson & Partners.

**KOBERT, Roy**
Broad and Cassel, Orlando
407 839 4200
*Recommended in Bankruptcy*

**KOFMAN, Robert**
Stearns Weaver Miller Weissler Alhadeff
& Sitterson, PA, Miami
305 789 3200
*Recommended in Employment*

**KORNREICH, David**
Akerman Senterfitt, Orlando
407 843 7860
david.kornreich@akerman.com
*Recommended in Employment*
**Career:** David V Kornreich is a shareholder and is board certified by The
Florida Bar in labor and employment
law. He has extensive experience representing employers in all types of labor
and employment matters, including
administrative proceedings, jury and
non-jury trials, and appeals. Prior to
entering private practice, Mr Kornreich
served with the United States Department of Labor and the National Labor
Relations Board. Mr Kornreich is a Fellow
of the College of Labor and Employment
Lawyers.

**KOZYAK, John W**
Kozyak Tropin & Throckmorton, Miami
305 377 0654
jk@kttlaw.com
*Recommended in Bankruptcy*
**Practice Areas:** Senior Bankruptcy
Partner.
**Prof. Memberships:** Fellow, American
College of Bankruptcy (1992-); Fellow,
American Academy of Trial Lawyers
(2005-); ABA Business Bankruptcy Committee (CLE Chair; Vice-Chair 1994-
2003); President, Bankruptcy Bar, Southern District Florida (1986).
**Career:** Former Managing Partner,
Chair, Litigation Department of major
firm. Co-founder, Kozyak Tropin &
Throckmorton (1982). Represents
secured/unsecured creditors, equity,
management, committees, trustees in
major bankruptcies. National counsel for
nation's largest special servicer of securitized commercial mortgages. Listed in
'Best Lawyers in America' (1987-present).
Recipient of Florida Bar President's Pro
Bono Service Award (2006) and Washington University School of Law Distinguished Alumni Award (2003). Listed in
Florida Super Lawyers 2006. Recognized
advocate for diversity.
**Personal:** Born Champaign, Illinois,
1948. University of Illinois (BS Marketing
cum laude, 1970); Washington University
School of Law (JD, 1975).

**KREITZER, Michael N**
Bilzin Sumberg Baena Price & Axelrod LLP,
Miami 305 350 2384
mkreitzer@bilzin.com
*Recommended in Litigation*
**Career:** Michael Kreitzer has been a
Florida Bar Board Certified Attorney in
Business Litigation since 1997. He has a
broad commercial trial practice, with
extensive experience in both jury and
non-jury cases in state and federal trial
courts, as well as appellate courts. His
practice focuses on complex commercial
disputes, construction litigation and
shareholder and partnership disputes. He
also represents clients in eminent domain
concerns, trusts and probate matters,
common carrier law and products liability disputes, as well as intellectual property
claims, professional malpractice and
commercial landlord/tenant disputes.
Michael has substantial experience in all
aspects of construction matters and litigation.

**KREUSLER-WALSH, Jane**
Jane Kreusler-Walsh PA,
West Palm Beach 561 659 5455
*Recommended in Litigation*

**KUEHNE, Benedict**
Sale & Kuehne PA, Miami
305 789 5989
*Recommended in Litigation*

**KUNKEL, Daniel**
Kunkel Miller & Hament, Tampa
813 969 3639
*Recommended in Employment*

**KURZBAN, Ira**
Kurzban, Kurzban, Weinger & Tetzeli PA,
Miami 305 444 0060
*Recommended in Immigration*

**LANDIS, James M**
Foley & Lardner LLP, Tampa
813 225 4115
jlandis@foley.com
*Recommended in Antitrust*
**Career:** James M Landis is a Partner in
the Tampa office of Foley & Lardner LLP.
A member of the Litigation Department
and the Antitrust Practice Group, he represents business clients in several states in
all forms of commercial litigation, including litigation arising from claims of
antitrust and securities violations and
unfair competition, as well as copyright,
trademark, service mark, franchising, and
trade secret challenges and protection. He
has counseled and litigated antitrust cases,
including price discrimination cases
under the Robinson-Patman Act, securities cases, straight breach of contract
claims, UCC cases, fraud claims, franchise
cases, and lender liability claims.

**LANE, Joe**
Lowndes Drosdick Doster Kantor &
Reed, PA, Orlando 407 843 4600
*Recommended in Construction*

**LAPIDUS, Steve**
Greenberg Traurig LLP, Miami
305 579 0509
lapiduss@gtlaw.com
*Recommended in Tax*
**Practice Areas:** Tax, trusts and estates;
executive compensation and employee
benefits.
**Career:** Listed, 'Top Lawyer', South Flori-
da Legal Guide, 2005; listed, The Best
Lawyers in America; listed, 'Chambers &
Partners USA Guide', 2004-06.
**Personal:** LLM, New York University
School of Law, 1977; JD, cum laude, New
York University School of Law, 1973; BS,
Wharton School of the University of
Pennsylvania, 1969.

**LARCOMBE, Valerie G**
Akerman Senterfitt, West Palm Beach
561 671 3605
*Recommended in Healthcare*
**Career:** Valerie Larcombe, a shareholder
and Board Certified Health Law attorney,
practices exclusively in the healthcare area
representing health systems, hospitals,
ambulatory surgical centers, community
mental health centers and home health
agencies in a broad range of transactional
(acquisitions/joint ventures), regulatory
compliance, exempt organizational, governance, medical staff, risk management
and operational matters. She is a frequent
speaker on healthcare topics and is former
Vice President and General Counsel of a

significant healthcare system. She received
her Masters in Healthcare Administration
from St Louis University.

**LAURIA, Thomas**
White & Case LLP, Miami
305 995 5282
tlauria@whitecase.com
*Recommended in Bankruptcy*
**Practice Areas:** Serves as Co-Chairman
of the firm's Financial Restructuring and
Insolvency Department. Regularly represents bondholders, bank groups, strategic
and financial investors, miscellaneous
creditor constituencies, soverigns and
debtors in connection with bankruptcy
and restructuring matters in a variety of
industry and market sectors.
**Prof. Memberships:** The Florida Bar;
Texas State Bar; US District Courts for
the Southern, Middle and Northern Districts of Florida; US District Courts for
the Northern and Southern Districts of
Texas; US Court of Appeals for the Fifth
and Eleventh Circuits.

**LAW, Rhea**
Fowler White Boggs Banker, Tampa
813 228 7411
*Recommended in Real Estate*

**LAWRENCE, Adam**
Lawrence & Daniels, Miami
305 358 3371
*Recommended in Litigation*

**LEDERMAN, Alan**
Akerman Senterfitt, Miami
305 349 4528
alan.lederman@akerman.com
*Recommended in Tax*
**Publications:** Alan Lederman, Of Counsel with the firm's Tax Practice Group,
focuses his practice on international taxation, corporate acquisition and finance,
real estate syndication, and international
law. He has extensive experience in international tax, real estate income tax and
corporate reorganizations. He is a frequent lecturer for tax conferences and has
authored and published numerous articles in academic journals including the
Journal of Taxation.

**LEGLER, Mitchell**
Kirschner & Legler, Jacksonville
904 346 3200
*Recommended in Corporate/M&A*

**LEIBY, Larry**
Leiby Stearns and Roberts, P.A.,
Fort Lauderdale 954 382 9199
*Recommended in Construction*

**LEISNER, Richard**
Trenam, Kemker, Scharf, Barkin, Frye,
O'Neill & Mullis PA, Tampa
813 223 7474
*Recommended in Corporate/M&A*

**LEONHARDT, Frederick**
Gray Robinson PA, Orlando
407 843 8880
*Recommended in Real Estate*

**LESSER, Steven**
Becker & Poliakoff PA, Fort Lauderdale
954 987 7550
*Recommended in Construction*

**LESTER JR, Edgel**
Carlton Fields, Tampa
813 223 7000
elester@carltonfields.com
*Recommended in Real Estate*
**Practice Areas:** Practices real estate and
commercial law, representing clients in
loan transactions, workouts, settlement
agreements, sales and leases of real and
personal property and transfers of equity
interests. Chair, firm's Real Estate and
Mortgage Financing Practice Group. He
is a title agent for seven title insurance
companies.
**Prof. Memberships:** Member, The Florida Bar; American Bar Association; Hillsborough County Bar Association; Association of Commercial Finance Attorneys;
Real Estate Investment Council; Hillsborough County, Florida, Industrial Development Authority.
**Personal:** JD, University of Kentucky,
1982; MA, Middle Tennessee State University, 1975; BA, Vanderbilt University,
1972.

**LEVENTHAL, Robert**
Leventhal & Slaughter PA, Orlando
407 849 6161
*Recommended in Litigation*

**LEVIN, Oscar**
Greenberg Traurig LLP, Miami
305 579 0500
levino@gtlaw.com
*Recommended in Immigration*
**Practice Areas:** Immigration.
**Prof. Memberships:** Member, The Flori-
da Bar; Member, American Immigration
Lawyers Association (AILA); Member,
Dade County Bar Association.
**Career:** Nominated as leading practi-
tioner in the field by 'The International
Who's Who of Corporate Immigration
Lawyers', 2005.
**Publications:** Published and lectured in
the United States, Europe and Asia on
immigration and nationality subjects to
numerous business groups.
**Personal:** JD, University of Florida Levin
College of Law, 1978; BA, University of
Florida, 1975.

**LEVINE, Kenneth**
Broad and Cassel, Tallahassee
850 681 6810
*Recommended in Insurance*

**LEVY, Jay**
Jay M Levy PA, Miami
305 670 8100
*Recommended in Litigation*

**LEWIS, Steve**
Lewis, Longman & Walker PA, West
Palm Beach 561 640 0820
*Recommended in Environment*

**LEWIS, Terry**
Lewis, Longman & Walker PA,
West Palm Beach 561 640 0820
*Recommended in Environment*

**LIBANOFF, Ira**
Ferencik, Libanoff, Brandt, Bustamante
& Williams, Fort Lauderdale
954 474 8080
*Recommended in Construction*

**LICKO, Carol A**
Hogan & Hartson LLP, Miami
305 459 6612
calicko@hhlaw.com
*Recommended in Litigation*
**Practice Areas:** Practice focuses primarily on complex corporate and commercial litigation at all levels from trials
through appeals, with extensive experience in class action litigation, business,
securities and contract litigation. Emphasis on complex problem solving, with
experience in corporate law, health and
educational law, and constitutional law.
Represents state and local governments,
municipalities, universities and community colleges, hospitals, television stations
and a major science research institute.
**Prof. Memberships:** Commissioner,
Florida State Ethics Commission (2000-
04); Chair, Judicial Nominating Procedures Committee, Florida Bar (2003);
Member, ABA.
**Career:** Former General Counsel to
Governor Jeb Bush.
**Personal:** University of Miami School of
Law (JD).

**LILES, Rutledge**
Liles, Gavin, Costantino & Murphy,
Jacksonville 904 634 1100
*Recommended in Litigation*

**LITCHFORD, Hal**
Litchford & Christopher, Orlando
407 841 0325
*Recommended in Antitrust*

**LOCKETT, Laurel**
Carlton Fields, Tampa 813 223 7000
llockett@carltonfields.com
*Recommended in Environment*
**Practice Areas:** Environmental permitting and enforcement issues in diverse
areas including industrial and municipal
domestic wastewater treatment, water
reuse systems, storage tanks, landfills,
used oil processing facilities, and hazardous waste permitting and regulation.
Negotiation of settlements, consent
orders and remediation plans associated
with the cleanup of hazardous waste and
other contaminants. Environmental
aspects of real estate transactions.
**Prof. Memberships:** Admitted to practice in Florida. Member: American Bar
Association, Chair of the Real Property,
Probate and Trust Law Section's Environmental Subcommittee.
**Personal:** JD, Boston University College
of Law, 1984; BA (with honors), Smith
College, 1977.

**LOPEZ-CASTRO, Corali**
Kozyak Tropin & Throckmorton, Miami
305 372 1800
clc@kttlaw.com
*Recommended in Bankruptcy*
**Practice Areas:** Bankruptcy; debtors'
and creditors' rights; commercial litigation.
**Prof. Memberships:** President, Cuban
American Bar Association (2006); Presi-
dent-Elect, Cuban American Bar Association (2005) Director, Cuban American
Bar Association (2003-04; 1998-2001);
Panel of Federal Bankruptcy Trustees,
Southern District of Florida (1998-2002);
Vice-Chair, Bankruptcy Litigation Sub-
committee (ABA Business Law Section)
(2005-present), Bankruptcy Bar, South-
ern District of Florida.
**Career:** Specializes in representing credi-
tors and debtors in Chapter 11 bankrupt-
cy cases, Chapter 11 committees, and
Trustees in Chapter 7. Kozyak Tropin &
Throckmorton (1990-95 and 1997-pre-
sent); Hahn Loeser & Parks (Cleveland,
Ohio, 1995-97).
**Personal:** Born San Juan, Puerto Rico.
Brown University (AB, 1987); University
of Miami School of Law (JD, 1990, cum
laude).

**LOUMIET, Carlos**
Hunton & Williams, Miami
305 810 2575
cloumiet@hunton.com
*Recommended in Banking & Finance,
Corporate/M&A*
**Practice Areas:** Carlos Loumiet has
advised clients in the international business and banking fields in the United
States and overseas for more than 28
years. He has been involved in numerous
mergers and acquisitions, securities offerings, venture capital deals, financings,
infrastructure projects and other commercial transactions, often across borders. He has dealt with regulators and
other governmental authorities in many
different countries and in a wide variety
of contexts. Mr Loumiet is also very
active with emerging US Latino companies.
**Personal:** Yale Law School (JD, 1978);
Oxford University (MA, 1981; BA, Marshall Scholar, 1977); Yale University (BA,
1973).

**LOWRY, Patricia E**
Squire, Sanders & Dempsey L.L.P.,
West Palm Beach 561 650 7214
plowry@ssd.com
*Recommended in Litigation*
**Practice Areas:** Focuses on products
liability and employment litigation. Has
more than 20 years experience defending
products cases, including prescription
medications, over-the-counter products
and medical devices. Represents US and
international companies in discrimination, harassment, whistleblower and wage
and hour claims. Listed in 'Who's Who

Legal USA – Management Labor and
Employment 2006', The Best Lawyers in
America and named a 'Florida Legal Elite'
by Florida Trend.
**Prof. Memberships:** President, Federal
Bar Association, Palm Beach County
2004-05; International Association of
Defense Counsel; Defense Research Insti-
tute; Academy of Florida Management
Attorneys; Human Resource Association
of Palm Beach County; The Florida Bar.

**LYON, Fred**
The Lyon Firm PA, Winter Park
407 647 8900
*Recommended in Construction*

**MACCULLOUGH, Kara L**
Akerman Senterfitt, Miami
305 982 5592
kara.maccullough@akerman.com
*Recommended in Corporate/M&A*
**Career:** Kara L MacCullough is a shareholder who represents corporations
engaged in capital markets transactions
involving the public offering and private
placement of debt and equity securities
and in their mergers and acquisitions
transactions in the US and abroad. She
has served as issuer's counsel in connection with over $2 billion in securities and
debt offerings by public companies in the
past five years and has extensive experience with international business transactions, including cross-border tender
offers. Ms MacCullough advises companies with respect to periodic SEC filings,
executive compensation disclosure, corporate governance, director responsibilities and other regulatory and corporate
matters.

**MACLEOD, Scott R**
Holland & Knight LLP, Orlando
407 425 8500
scott.macleod@hklaw.com
*Recommended in Corporate/M&A*
**Practice Areas:** Partner in the Business
Section, represents investment funds and
investment advisors. MacLeod has
formed and advised many onshore and
offshore hedge funds, private equity
funds, real estate funds and other private
investment funds (including master feeder funds and funds of funds), as well as
mutual funds registered under the Investment Company Act of 1940, group trusts
and bank collective trust funds. He also
has formed and advised numerous private and SEC and state registered investment advisors in all aspects of fiduciary,
contractual, compliance and other regulatory issues under the Investment Advisers Act of 1940.

**MAIDA, Thomas J**
Foley & Lardner LLP, Tallahassee
850 513 3377
tmaida@foley.com
*Recommended in Insurance*
**Career:** Tom Maida is the managing
Partner in the Tallahassee office of Foley

& Lardner LLP. A member of the firm's Insurance Industry Team and the Public Affairs Practice Group, Mr Maida's clients include some of the world's largest insurance companies, as well as many leading regional insurers. He has developed legal strategies for a number of complex business transactions, including the formation of insurance companies, group funds, and health maintenance organizations; mergers and acquisitions of insurance companies; and the demutualization of insurers. Mr Maida is a graduate of the Florida State University College of Law.

## MALEFATTO, Alfred J
Greenberg Traurig LLP,
West Palm Beach 561 650 7908
malefattoa@gtlaw.com
*Recommended in Environment*
**Practice Areas:** Environmental; land development; energy and natural resources; governmental affairs.
**Prof. Memberships:** Board Member and Vice President, Friends of the Academy of Environmental Science and Technology, Inc.; Vice President, Legal Affairs, Grassy Waters Preserve, West Palm Beach.
**Career:** Listed, 'Best Lawyers in America, 2006'; listed, 'Chambers & Partners USA Guide', 2003-06.
**Publications:** Lectures extensively on environmental law issues at programs sponsored by The Florida Bar, the Florida Chamber of Commerce and other organizations.
**Personal:** JD, University of Florida Levin College of Law, 1979; BA, New York University, 1975.

## MANDEL, David S
Mandel & Mandel LLP, Miami
305 374 7771
dmandel@mandel-law.com
*Recommended in Litigation*
**Practice Areas:** Currently handles an array of complex commercial disputes and white-collar criminal defense matters.
**Prof. Memberships:** Member of the Bars of Florida, New York, Illinois and Washington, DC. Member of the Federal Bar Association, the American Bar Association and former Chair of the Federal Court Committee of the Dade County Bar Association. Member of the Wilson Council at the Woodrow Wilson International Center for Scholars, Washington, DC. Also formerly served as the President of Foster Care Review, an organization devoted to assisting the judicial administration of foster children.
**Career:** Former Assistant United States Attorney for the Southern District of Florida, 1989-95.
**Personal:** Born 23 January 1959. JD Cornell Law School, 1986; AB (magna cum laude) Brown University, 1982.

## MANDEL, Jeffrey E
Akerman Senterfitt, Orlando
407 843 7860
jeff.mandel@akerman.com
*Recommended in Employment*
**Career:** Jeffrey Mandel, a shareholder board certified in labor and employment law, represents private and public-sector employers in all aspects of employment and labor law. He counsels clients on employment issues, including: employment discrimination and retaliation, civil rights, ADA accommodations, FMLA compliance, wage and hour, military leave, employment policies, employment agreements, and non-competition/non-solicitation and trade secret agreements. He litigates employment discrimination and retaliation cases before state and federal courts and administrative agencies. His practice also includes representation of employers before the National Labor Relations Board and the Florida Public Employees Relations Commission, as well as representing management in labor arbitrations.

## MARTIN, Gregory S
Moye, O'Brien, O'Rourke, Pickert & Martin, LLP, Maitland
407 622 5250
gmartin@moopm.com
*Recommended in Construction*
**Practice Areas:** Construction and commercial litigation. Has extensive experience representing US and international owners, contractors and engineering firms in the USA and the Caribbean basin in multi-million dollar contracts and claims.
**Prof. Memberships:** The Florida Bar; American Bar Association (Member, Litigation Section and Forum on the Construction Industry); Court of Federal Claims Bar Association.
**Career:** Admitted to Florida Bar (1990); Partner of Moye, O'Brien, O'Rourke, Pickert & Martin, LLP (with affiliated offices in Chicago, Illinois); admitted to the US District Court, Middle and Southern Districts of Florida; US Court of Appeals, Eleventh Circuit; US Court of Federal Claims.
**Personal:** Received Bachelor of Building Construction from the University of Florida (1987) and a JD from the University of Florida (1990); past President of Sigma Lambda Chi (School of Building Construction Honor Society); contractor (residential/inactive).

## MARTINEZ, Roberto
Colson Hicks Eidson, Coral Gables
305 476 7400
bob@colson.com
*Recommended in Litigation*
**Practice Areas:** Commercial litigation; white-collar criminal defense.
**Career:** Mr Martinez was United States Attorney for the Southern District of Florida, as such he was responsible for

representing the United States in all criminal and civil matters in the district; served on the Attorney General's Advisory Committee of United States Attorneys; received his JD Degree from the Georgetown University Law Center where he was on the Dean's List; holds a MS in Accounting and a BS in Economics from the University of Pennsylvania, Wharton School of Business.

## MASER, Joel
Greenberg Traurig LLP, Orlando
407 418 2389
maserj@gtlaw.com
*Recommended in Tax*
**Practice Areas:** Tax.
**Prof. Memberships:** Active Member, Executive Council, The Florida Bar Tax Section and has served as Chairperson of several committees within the Tax Section, Member, Tax Section's Long Range Planning Committee and is serving as the Tax Section's Workshop Director.
**Career:** Listed, 'Best Lawyers in America', 2005 and 2006; listed, 'Chambers & Partners USA Guide', 2003-06.
**Personal:** JD, magna cum laude, University of Miami School of Law, 1984; BS, with honors, University of Florida, 1981.

## MASON, Cheney
J Cheney Mason PA, Orlando
407 843 5785
*Recommended in Litigation*

## MATTHEWS, Frank
Hopping Green & Sams, PA, Tallahassee
850 222 7500
frankm@hgslaw.com
*Recommended in Environment*
**Practice Areas:** Extensive federal and state environmental practice specializing in wetland and water use permitting; lobbying with the Florida legislature on behalf of a variety of utility, mining and development issues and has been engaged in the passage of all significant environmental legislation in Florida for the last 20 years.

## MATTHEWS, Joseph M
Colson Hicks Eidson, Coral Gables
305 476 7400
joseph@colson.com
*Recommended in Litigation*
**Practice Areas:** Commercial law; arbitration; alternative dispute resolution.
**Career:** In 1989, Mr Matthews served as Special Counsel to United States Senator Bob Graham, joining Colson Hicks Eidson later that year; specializes in commercial, intellectual property, fraud, defamation and other business torts, insurance, construction and professional liability litigation; is a member of the American Arbitration Association and the London Court of International Arbitration, as well as the AAA's panel of arbitrators for Large and Complex Cases.

## MAYOL JR, Juan J
Holland & Knight LLP, Miami
305 374 8500
juan.mayol@hklaw.com
*Recommended in Real Estate*
**Practice Areas:** Mr Mayol is a Partner in Holland & Knight's Real Estate Section practicing in the areas of land use and zoning. He represents builders and developers in all aspects of land use law through the entire development process, from zoning approvals to subdivision and building permit issues. In addition, Mayol handles environmental matters as they relate to the development process. Mayol is a member of The Florida Bar and is fluent in Spanish.

## MCCLOSKY, Donald
Ruden McClosky, S.C., Fort Lauderdale
954 764 6660
*Recommended in Real Estate*

## MCCREA, Richard
Zinober & McCrea, P.A., Tampa
813 224 9004
*Recommended in Employment*

## MCDOWELL, Carter N
Bilzin Sumberg Baena Price & Axelrod LLP, Miami 305 350 2355
cmcdowell@bilzin.com
*Recommended in Real Estate*
**Career:** Carter McDowell handles matters involving land use, growth management, environmental and administrative law. He has represented numerous clients through regulatory approval procedures for regional malls, hotels, industrial complexes, professional buildings and marinas, including Developments of Regional Impact. He advises clients on environmental and permitting issues relating to business and real estate transactions, as well as in obtaining and negotiating government contracts. He has defended owners and developers against enforcement actions filed under federal, state and local environmental law. Carter is a former Director of Building, Zoning, and Community Development and Acting City Manager for the City of South Miami.

## MCGUIGAN, Thomas R
Squire, Sanders & Dempsey L.L.P., West Palm Beach 561 650 7278
tmcguigan@ssd.com
*Recommended in Corporate/M&A*
**Practice Areas:** Partner with more than 30 years experience in corporate, securities and financial matters for public and privately held organizations. Represents clients in public and private debt and equity financings. M&A experience includes representation of purchasers and sellers involving privately and publicly held companies and individuals in US and international transactions, and regulated industries. Listed in 'The Best Lawyers in America'.
**Prof. Memberships:** American Bar

Association's Business Law Section and Committee on Negotiated Acquisitions; The Florida Bar, Business Law Section and Corporate Law Revision Committee.

## MCGUIRE, Richard
Rogers Towers PA, Jacksonville
904 398 3911
*Recommended in Environment*

## MCKENNA, Susan
Jackson Lewis, Orlando
407 246 8429
McKennaS@jacksonlewis.com
*Recommended in Employment*
**Practice Areas:** Co-Chair of the Employment Litigation Practice Group. Litigation experience includes Title VII, Age Discrimination in Employment Act, Equal Pay Act, Americans with Disabilities Act, and Family and Medical Leave Act. Conducts management training on workplace law issues.
**Prof. Memberships:** American Bar Association, Federal Bar Association, The Florida Bar, Central Florida Association for Women Lawyers, Hotel Human Resources Association, Central Florida Hotel and Lodging Association.
**Career:** Partner since 2004.
**Publications:** Has written extensively on employment law issues.
**Personal:** Indiana University, BA, summa cum laude, 1978; Duke University School of Law, JD, 1982. Serves on numerous community and charitable boards.

## MEEKS, Thomas
Zuckerman Spaeder LLP, Miami
305 358 5000
*Recommended in Litigation*

## MEENAN, Timothy
Blank, Meenan & Smith PA, Tallahassee
850 681 6710
*Recommended in Insurance*

## MELE, Dennis
Ruden McClosky, S.C., Fort Lauderdale
954 764 6660
*Recommended in Real Estate*

## MENCIO JR, George
Holland & Knight LLP, Miami
305 374 8500
george.mencio@hklaw.com
*Recommended in Corporate/M&A*
**Practice Areas:** Partner in Business Section, practices principally in corporate and international law, with emphasis on cross-border M&A and joint venture transactions, dispute resolution, and administrative matters relating to international trade and commerce and the transportation industry. Mencio has extensive experience in the analysis of foreign countries' competition; licensing and franchise laws; foreign investment restrictions affecting mergers and acquisitions; currency restrictions; and laws affecting international franchising, licensing and joint venture agreements. His

clients include multinational concerns in the transportation, tourism, mining and agricultural sectors, major airlines, software and technology companies, and providers of goods and services in the international arena.

## MENENDEZ CAMBO, Patricia
Greenberg Traurig LLP, Miami
305 579 0766
menendezp@gtlaw.com
*Recommended in Corporate/M&A*
**Practice Areas:** International; corporate and securities; M&A.
**Prof. Memberships:** Board Member, Council of the Americas; Trustee, National Alliance for Autism Research (NAAR).
**Career:** Listed, 'Best Lawyers in America', 2006; Recognized as one of the '40 under 40' attorneys, The National Law Journal, 2005; recognized as one of the 'Top Up-and-Comers in South Florida', South Florida Legal Guide, 2004-05.
**Personal:** JD, University of Pennsylvania Law School; BBA, University of Miami.

## MESSANA, Thomas
Ruden McClosky, S.C., Fort Lauderdale
954 764 6660
*Recommended in Bankruptcy*

## MEYER, George
Carlton Fields, Tampa
813 223 7000
gmeyer@carltonfields.com
*Recommended in Construction*
**Practice Areas:** Practices real property and construction law; preparation, negotiation, administration of design and construction contracts; Florida construction lien law; construction contract administration and claims analysis. Board Certified in Construction Law.
**Prof. Memberships:** Admitted to practice in Florida. Member, The Florida Bar; American Bar Association; Florida Engineering Society; Fellow, American College of Real Estate Lawyers.
**Career:** Construction engineer.
**Publications:** Editor, 'Standard Construction Law Jury Instructions Section of the Florida Construction Law and Practice Manual' (The Florida Bar 2001).
**Personal:** JD (with honors), University of Tulsa College of Law, 1985; BA, BS, State University of New York, Stony Brook, 1974, 1978.

## MILLER, Morris H
Holland & Knight LLP, Tallahassee
850 224 7000
morris.miller@hklaw.com
*Recommended in Healthcare*
**Practice Areas:** Mr Miller, Partner in the Business Law Section, is experienced in transactional and regulatory matters within the healthcare and senior living industries. Represents owners, developers, and operators of healthcare and senior living facilities and has structured, negotiated and documented numerous acquisitions, dispositions, financings, and

other business arrangements involving such facilities. He also represents healthcare entities in matters involving federal and state anti-kickback and patient self-referral laws; Medicare and Medicaid reimbursement issues; health facility licensure and other healthcare regulatory issues; and various kinds of contracts for healthcare facilities, senior living facilities, and medical practices.

## MINTON, Michael D
Dean, Mead, Minton & Zwemer, Fort Pierce 772 464 7700
mminton@deanmead.com
*Recommended in Tax*
**Practice Areas:** Federal income, estate, and gift tax law; family business succession planning; agricultural and resource management law (including legal implications of the citrus canker program).
**Prof. Memberships:** Directors Committee and Chair of Specialty Tax Areas Committee, The Florida Bar Tax Section.
**Career:** President-Elect of Dean Mead; listed in 'Florida Trend Legal Elite', 2005-present.
**Personal:** Chairman, Board of Trustees, Indian River Community College Foundation, Inc.; Board of Trustees, University of Florida Fredric G Levin College of Law; University of Florida (LLM, 1982; JD, 1981; BS, 1979).

## MITCHELL, Stephen J
Squire, Sanders & Dempsey L.L.P., Tampa 813 202 1302
smitchell@ssd.com
*Recommended in Real Estate*
**Practice Areas:** Partner focusing on real estate development, commercial real estate, banking and finance, hotel/conference center development, international law and administrative law. He is listed in 'The Best Lawyers in America'.
**Prof. Memberships:** Hillsborough County Aviation Authority, Chairman of the Board of Directors; ACI-NA, Vice-Chair, commissioners; Florida 2020 Energy Study Commission; Central Florida Technology Transit Corridor Consortium, Chair; International Real Estate Institute; The Florida Bar, International and Real Property Law Sections; US delegation to the Union International des Avocats, Board of Governors; International Committee of the Tampa Chamber of Commerce, Chair.

## MOOREFIELD JR, Harold
Stearns Weaver Miller Weissler Alhadeff & Sitterson, PA, Miami
305 789 3200
*Recommended in Bankruptcy*

## MORA, Mindy A
Bilzin Sumberg Baena Price & Axelrod LLP, Miami 305 350 2414
mmora@bilzin.com
*Recommended in Bankruptcy*
**Prof. Memberships:** Association of Commercial Finance Attorneys, Execu-

tive Board (1993-present); The Florida Bar, Bankruptcy and UCC Committee; International Women's Insolvency and Restructuring Confederation, South Florida Chapter, Vice-President (2003-04).
**Career:** Partner whose practice focuses on insolvency and workouts, corporate restructuring, commercial finance and asset-based lending. Has counseled high-visibility clients in many major bankruptcy proceedings, both nationally and in Florida. Active in the development of Florida's commercial laws, having co-sponsored the 1997 revisions to Article 8 and 1999 revisions to Article 9 Uniform Commercial Code (chapters 678 and 679, Florida Statutes). Frequent lecturer and author on insolvency and restructuring topics.

## MOSCOWITZ, Jane
Moscowitz, Moscowitz & Magolnick PA, Miami 305 379 8300
*Recommended in Litigation*

## MOSCOWITZ, Norman
Moscowitz, Moscowitz & Magolnick PA, Miami 305 379 8300
*Recommended in Litigation*

## MOSS, Edward
Shook, Hardy & Bacon LLP, Miami
305 358 5171
emoss@shb.com
*Recommended in Litigation*
**Practice Areas:** Focuses on the handling and trial of products liability matters, as well as complex commercial cases and securities litigation and defense of class actions. Listed in 'The Best Lawyers in America' and has been selected as one of the top 10 litigators in Florida.
**Prof. Memberships:** Admitted before state and federal courts of Florida; US Court of Appeals for the First, Fifth and Eleventh Circuits; and US Supreme Court.
**Career:** Joined Shook, Hardy & Bacon, 1998 (as Partner).
**Personal:** JD, cum laude, University of Miami School of Law, 1961; BA, cum laude, University of Florida, 1958.

## MOYE, James E
Moye, O'Brien, O'Rourke, Pickert & Martin, LLP, Maitland 407 622 5250
jmoye@moopm.com
*Recommended in Construction*
**Practice Areas:** Construction, commercial litigation, management labor relations law, employment relations law. Has extensive experience representing US and international contractors and engineering firms in the USA, the Caribbean basin, Central America and Canada in multi-million dollar claims.
**Prof. Memberships:** State Bar of Georgia; The Florida Bar; American Bar Association (Member, Sections on Labor and Employment Law, Forum on the Construction Industry); Court of Federal

Claims Bar Association.

**Career:** Admitted to Georgia Bar (1982), Florida (1989); Senior Partner of Moye, O'Brien, O'Rourke, Pickert & Martin, LLP (with affiliate offices in Chicago, Illinois); admitted to US District Court, Middle and Southern Districts of Florida; US Court of Appeals, Fifth, Eleventh and DC Circuits; US Supreme Court.

**Personal:** Received a BSE (cum laude) from University of Central Florida in 1978 and a JD from University of Florida in 1981; inducted into Eta Kappa Nu (Electrical Engineering National Honor Society), Tau Beta Pi (Engineering National Honor Society) and Omicron Delta Kappa; Member of the President's Leadership Council and the University of Florida Law Review from 1980-81.

### NACHWALTER, Michael
Kenny Nachwalter PA, Miami
305 373 1000
mn@kennynachwalter.com
*Recommended in Antitrust, Litigation*

**Practice Areas:** Antitrust and trade regulation, alternative dispute resolution (arbitrator and mediator), business law, business torts, commercial litigation, securities litigation, corporate litigation, legal malpractice, complex and multi-district litigation, federal and state litigation.

**Prof. Memberships:** Dade County Bar Association, Federal Bar Association, American Bar Association.

**Personal:** Yale University, LLM, 1968, University of Miami, JD, cum laude, 1967, Long Island University, MS, 1967, Bucknell University, BS, 1962.

### NAGIN, Stephen
Nagin Gallop Figueredo PA, Coconut Grove 305 854 5353
*Recommended in Antitrust*

### NEAL, Austin
Foley & Lardner LLP, Tallahassee
850 513 3363
aneal@foley.com
*Recommended in Insurance*

**Career:** Austin Neal is a Partner in the Tallahassee office of Foley & Lardner LLP. A member of the firm's Insurance Industry Team, Mr Neal's practice is focused primarily upon corporate and transactional representation of insurance companies and other corporate clients. His experience includes representing members of the insurance industry and other corporate clients in regulatory, administrative, legislative and transactional matters. Mr Neal's practice also includes corporate litigation in federal and state trial and appellate courts. Mr Neal is a graduate of Florida State University College of Law (JD, with high honors, 1994).

### NICHOLS, Tracy A
Holland & Knight LLP, Miami
305 374 8500
tracy.nichols@hklaw.com
*Recommended in Litigation*

**Practice Areas:** Ms Nichols is the firm's National Practice Group Leader for the Securities Litigation Group. She has served as the lead lawyer representing issuers, directors, officers and underwriters in over two dozen securities class actions. She obtained one of the largest Rule 11 sanctions against plaintiffs and their counsel for filing a frivolous securities fraud case. She is a frequent lecturer at the state and national level on securities topics. She was a founding member of the Volunteer Lawyers' Project for the Southern District of Florida, providing pro bono assistance to indigent clients.

### NOBLE, Ron
Fowler White Boggs Banker, Tampa
813 228 7411
*Recommended in Environment*

### NORRIS, Bruce
Kirwin Norris PA, Winter Park
407 740 6600
*Recommended in Construction*

### NORTMAN, William
Akerman Senterfitt, Fort Lauderdale
954 463 2700
william.nortman@akerman.com
*Recommended in Litigation*

**Career:** William Nortman, shareholder in the Corporate Practice Group, represents individuals and corporations involved in investigations and civil and criminal proceedings relating to securities law issues. His work on behalf of clients covers actions initiated by both regulatory and self-regulatory organizations such as the SEC, NYSE, NASD and state securities regulatory offices. His practice involves guiding individuals and businesses through the regulatory and investigatory processes of the government, preparing Wells Submissions, and counseling clients with respect to the resolution of investigations and enforcement proceedings. Before entering private practice, he spent 12 years with the Securities and Exchange Commission.

### NUECHTERLEIN, Mike
Carlton Fields, Tampa
813 223 7000
mnuechterlein@carltonfields.com
*Recommended in Construction*

**Practice Areas:** Practices construction law, including litigation, arbitration, mediation, consulting and advising on construction-related matters including contracts, claims, mechanic liens, design professional malpractice, delay damages, and differing site conditions.

**Prof. Memberships:** Admitted to practice in Florida. Member, International Bar Association; Chair, Governing Committee, ABA Forum on the Construction Industry; Fellow, American College of Construction Lawyers; AAA Construction Master Arbitrator.

**Publications:** Editor, Florida Construction Law: 'What Do You Do When...?'

(National Business Institute); author, 'Recent Developments in Construction Law' (Florida Constructor).

**Personal:** JD (cum laude), University of Michigan Law School, 1973; BA, University of Michigan, 1965.

### NURIK, Marc
Ruden McClosky, S.C., Fort Lauderdale
954 764 6660
*Recommended in Litigation*

### O'DONNELL, Nanette
Duane Morris LLP, Miami
305 960 2264
nodonnell@duanemorris.com
*Recommended in Healthcare*

**Practice Areas:** Nanette O'Donnell practices in the area of healthcare law, with a focus on fraud and abuse matters, self-referral, corporate compliance, licensure and managed care contracting. Her practice also involves institutional operational matters and HIPAA. She represents community hospitals, physician groups, diagnostic imaging centers and other healthcare providers. She is also fluent in Spanish.

**Prof. Memberships:** Florida Bar Board of Legal Specialization and Education – Certified Health Law Attorney; University of Miami Graduate School of Business Administration and Nova Southeastern University – Adjunct Lecturer of Healthcare Law.

**Career:** Admitted to practice in Florida.

**Personal:** University of Miami School of Law, JD, cum laude, 1989; University of Miami (FL), BA, magna cum laude, 1986, Phi Beta Kappa.

### O'NEAL-COBLE, Leslie
Greenberg Traurig LLP, Orlando
407 425 8500
coblel@gtlaw.com
*Recommended in Construction*

**Practice Areas:** Litigation; construction litigation.

**Prof. Memberships:** Member, West Publishing Construction Group Advisory Board; Member, American Board of Trial Advocates.

**Career:** Listed, 'Best Lawyers in America', 2005 and 2006; listed, 'Chambers and Partners USA Guide', 2004 and 2006; listed, 2004 and 2005 Legal Elite, Florida Trend Magazine; Orange County Bar Legal Aid Society Award of Excellence, 2004.

**Publications:** Author, 'An Overview of "Toxic" Mold Litigation in Florida', (chapter in 50 State Survey of Mold Litigation), 2004.

**Personal:** JD, University of Florida Levin College of Law, 1977; BA, with honors, University of Florida, 1974.

### O'NEILL, Albert
Trenam, Kemker, Scharf, Barkin, Frye, O'Neill & Mullis PA, Tampa
813 223 7474
*Recommended in Tax*

### ORSHEFSKY, Debbie
Greenberg Traurig LLP, Fort Lauderdale
954 768 8234
orshefskyd@gtlaw.com
*Recommended in Real Estate*

**Practice Areas:** Environmental, land use.

**Prof. Memberships:** Member, Urban Land Institute and serves on the Executive Committee of the ULI Southeast/Caribbean Council (2002-present); Co-Chair, Broward General Medical Center, Community Advisory Board of the Comprehensive Cancer Center (2002-present).

**Career:** Listed, 'Top Lawyer', South Florida Legal Guide, 2005; listed, Best Lawyers, 2006; listed, 'Chambers & Partners USA Guide', 2004-06; recognized by Broward County 1000+ Club of the American Cancer Society as one of 15 Women of the Year 2005.

**Personal:** JD, George Washington University Law School, 1979; BA, summa cum laude, Urban Studies, Washington University, 1975.

### PALMER, Scott
Berman DeValerio Pease Tabacco Burt & Pucillo, West Palm Beach
561 835 9400
*Recommended in Antitrust*

### PANOFF, Robert
Robert E Panoff PA, Miami
305 670 6547
*Recommended in Tax*

### PAPPAS, Lynn
Pappas Metcalf Jenks and Miller, Jacksonville 904 353 1980
*Recommended in Real Estate*

### PARSONS, Philip
Landers & Parsons, Tallahassee
850 681 0311
*Recommended in Environment*

### PASANO, Michael
Zuckerman Spaeder LLP, Miami
305 358 5000
*Recommended in Litigation*

### PASS, Robert W
Carlton Fields, Tallahassee
850 513 3608
rpass@carltonfields.com
*Recommended in Insurance*

**Practice Areas:** Practices in the areas of commercial litigation, class actions, administrative law and state and federal appeals, including business disputes, insurance disputes, constitution law challenges to state laws, class actions, banking, public utility and local government litigation. Chair, firm's Energy Practice Group.

**Prof. Memberships:** Admitted to practice in Florida and US Supreme Court. Member, The Florida Bar, Business Litigation and Local Government Law Sections; The Florida Bar Foundation; American Bar Foundation; American Law Institute.

**Personal:** JD (with high honors), Florida State University, 1974; BA, Florida State University, 1971.

**PELHAM, Thomas**
Fowler White Boggs Banker, Tallahassee
850 681 0411
*Recommended in Real Estate*

**PEREZ, Luis**
Hogan & Hartson LLP, Miami
305 459 6643
ljperez@hhlaw.com
*Recommended in Corporate/M&A*
**Practice Areas:** Partner in the Business and Finance and International Practice Groups with an emphasis on mergers and acquisitions, corporate, banking and international law. He has served as principal counsel in hundreds of acquisitions throughout the United States and Latin America.
**Prof. Memberships:** President, US-Spain Council; Member, Florida Bar; Member, American Bar Association; Member, Cuban American Bar Association.
**Career:** Over 20 years experience in domestic and international corporate and financing transactions. Clients include US, Latin American and European multinationals.
**Personal:** JD, The Catholic University of America, Columbus School of Law, 1983; BA, Rollins College, 1978. Fluent in Spanish and French.

**PERLING, Lester**
Broad and Cassel, Fort Lauderdale
954 764 7060
*Recommended in Healthcare*

**PERWIN, Joel**
Joel S. Perwin, P.A., Miami
305 779 6090
*Recommended in Litigation*

**PERWIN, Scott**
Kenny Nachwalter PA, Miami
305 373 1000
sep@kennynachwalter.com
*Recommended in Antitrust*
**Practice Areas:** Antitrust and trade regulation, complex commercial litigation, appellate practice.
**Prof. Memberships:** Dade County Bar Association, American Bar Association, The Florida Bar, Academy of Trial Lawyers.
**Publications:** Author: 'Use of Depositions in Federal Trial: Evidence or Procedure?' 16 Litigation 37 (Fall 1989). Co-author: 'Standing of Indirect Purchasers Under the Florida Deceptive and Unfair Trade Practices Act', 71 Florida Bar Journal 81, March 1997.
**Personal:** Stanford University, JD, with distinction, 1987. Princeton University, MA, 1981. Harvard College, BA, magna cum laude, 1977.

**PETERSON, Ralph**
Beggs & Lane, Pensacola
850 432 2451
*Recommended in Employment*

**PHALIN, Lawrence**
Mateer & Harbert P.A., Orlando
407 425 9044
*Recommended in Construction*

**PICKERT, Stephen W**
Moye, O'Brien, O'Rourke, Pickert & Martin, LLP, Maitland 407 622 5250
spickert@moopm.com
*Recommended in Construction*
**Practice Areas:** Construction litigation in state and federal courts and ADR, involving contracts, construction defects, bonds, liens, delay claims, business torts and statutory claims for public, private, commercial and residential projects and representing owners, developers, general contractors, subcontractors, material suppliers and design professionals.
**Career:** Admitted to The Florida Bar in 1981; Senior Partner with the law firm of Moye, O'Brien, O'Rourke, Pickert & Martin, LLP since 1990; admitted in the United States District Court for the Southern and Middle Districts of Florida and the United States Court of Appeals for the Fifth, Ninth and Eleventh Circuits, as well as the United States Supreme Court
**Publications:** Author: 'Civil Theft A Reemerging Weapon in Everyday Commercial Disputes', The Florida Bar Journal; lectured primarily with The Associated General Contractors of America to provide continuing education units for those in the construction industry
**Personal:** Received Bachelor of Science in Banking and Finance in 1978 from The University of Florida with high honors and graduated in 1981 from The University of Florida Law School with honors and as a member of The Law Review.

**PIERCE, Robert**
Ausley & McMullen, Tallahassee
850 224 9115
*Recommended in Tax*

**PILLANS III, Charles P**
Bedell, Dittmar, DeVault, Pillans & Coxe, Jacksonville 904 353 0211
*Recommended in Litigation*

**PISCITELLI, Michael A**
Vezina Lawrence & Piscitelli, Fort Lauderdale
954 728 1270
*Recommended in Construction*

**PODHURST, Aaron S**
Podhurst Orseck P.A., Miami
305 358 2800
info@podhurst.com
*Recommended in Litigation*
**Practice Areas:** A broad range of civil litigation, including complex commercial litigation, aviation and mass tort litigation in all federal and state courts.
**Career:** His distinguished career has brought him honors and offices from virtually every major legal organization, including the presidencies of the International Academy of Trial Lawyers and

Academy of Florida Trial Lawyers, fellowship in the American College of Trial Lawyers, Member of Board of Governors of Association of Trial Lawyers of America, membership in the International Society of Barristers and the Inner Circle of Advocates, and chairmanship of important aviation committees of the American Bar Association, Association of Trial Lawyers of America and the Academy of Florida Trial Lawyers. Although he made his reputation as one of the nation's premiere plaintiff's aviation lawyers and continues to hold that status, he has guided the firm in recent years to its status as one of the major commercial litigation firms in South Florida.
**Personal:** BA from the University of Michigan in 1957, and Harland Fiske Stone Scholar and JD Degree from Columbia University.

**POPE, Nicholas**
Lowndes Drosdick Doster Kantor & Reed, PA, Orlando 407 843 4600
*Recommended in Real Estate*

**PRATS, Luis**
Carlton Fields, Tampa
813 223 7000
lprats@carltonfields.com
*Recommended in Construction*
**Practice Areas:** Practice involves complex commercial disputes, including all types of construction litigation and insurance coverage disputes related to losses in construction projects. Board Certified in Construction Law by The Florida Bar. Chair, firm's Construction Practice Group; Member, firm's Board of Directors.
**Prof. Memberships:** The Florida Bar, Trial Lawyers Section; Hillsborough County Bar Association; American Bar Association, Litigation Section, The Forum on the Construction Industry, Division 8 Steering Committee; Sixth Judicial Circuit Unauthorized Practice of Law Committee.
**Career:** General Counsel for Greater Tampa Chamber of Commerce.
**Personal:** JD, Stetson University College of Law, 1981; BA, Stetson University, 1978.

**PRESS, Martin**
Gunster, Yoakley & Stewart, P.A., Fort Lauderdale 954 462 2000
*Recommended in Tax*

**PRESTON, William D**
William D Preston PA, Tallahassee
850 668 4986
bill@wprestonpa.com
*Recommended in Environment*
**Practice Areas:** 25+ years experience in Florida environmental law.
**Prof. Memberships:** Admitted to practice in Florida (1976). Member of Environmental and Land Use Law Section; Best Lawyers of America; Leadership Florida, Florida Trend Legal Elite.

**Career:** Staff Director, Florida Senate Natural Resources Committee, 1978-79; joined Hopping Boyd Green & Sams, 1979; shareholder 1983-2001; founded William D. Preston, P.A., 2001.
**Publications:** Co-author, 'The Water Quality Assurance Act of 1983- Florida's Great Leap Forward into Groundwater Protection and Hazardous Waste Management', Florida State University Law Review, 1983; 'The 1993 Amendments to Florida's Solid Waste Management Act: The Continuing Search for Solutions', Florida State University Law Review, 1993.
**Personal:** Born 7 August 1947. JD, Florida State University, 1975; BS (Biological Sciences), Rochester Institute of Technology, 1969.

**PRICE, Stanley B**
Bilzin Sumberg Baena Price & Axelrod LLP, Miami 305 350 2374
sprice@bilzin.com
*Recommended in Real Estate*
**Career:** Has worked in the forefront of Florida land use law and has been the principal draftsman of important land use legislation, as well as a frequently consulted expert on the subjects of owners' and developers' rights and complex zoning and permitting issues. Served as special land use counsel to several Florida municipalities and as the special magistrate in land use litigation for Dade and Orange County Circuit Courts. Selected to lecture on the appellate review of land use cases to Dade County Circuit Court, Appellate Division. Adjunct Professor of Land Use Law at University of Miami School of Law.

**PRIETO, Peter**
Holland & Knight LLP, Miami
305 374 8500
peter.prieto@hklaw.com
*Recommended in Litigation*
**Practice Areas:** Partner in the Litigation Section and former federal prosecutor with significant trial experience. Prieto practices in the areas of complex civil litigation and white-collar criminal defense, representing clients, including Fortune 500 companies, in civil litigation, including commercial, securities, antitrust, products liability and class action litigation. He also represents individual and corporate clients in criminal investigations and prosecutions involving public corruption, banking and healthcare fraud, aviation, environmental violations, and money laundering, and clients in a variety of industries, including the healthcare, telecommunications, petroleum, aviation, entertainment, securities and banking industries. Prieto has extensive experience in defending RICO claims.

**QUIÑON, Jose**
Jose M Quiñon - Sole Practitioner, Miami
305 858 5700
*Recommended in Litigation*

## RAATTAMA, Henry
Akerman Senterfitt, Miami
305 374 5600
henry.raattama@akerman.com
*Recommended in Tax*

**Career:** Henry Raattama is a shareholder whose practice areas include charitable and tax-exempt organizations, estate planning and business planning. He is a recipient of the Gerald T Hart Outstanding Tax Attorney for 1998-99, and has chaired the Tax Section of The Florida Bar and The Florida Bar Tax Certification Committee. He is also the recipient of the Outstanding Professional Advisor for 2002. Mr Raattama is a Member of the American College of Tax Counsel and frequently lectures and writes on tax matters and has taught in the University of Miami Graduate Tax Program.

## RAKUSIN, Steve
Stephen Rakusin PA, Fort Lauderdale
954 356 0496
*Recommended in Construction*

## RASILE, Craig
Hunton & Williams, Miami
305 810 2579
crasile@hunton.com
*Recommended in Bankruptcy*

**Practice Areas:** Mr Rasile's practice focuses in the insolvency area, emphasizing bankruptcy, corporate restructuring, creditors' rights, workouts, and commercial litigation in several industries, including retail, healthcare, transportation, franchising, travel and financial institutions. He typically represents corporate and partnership debtors, trustees, committees and financial institutions in bankruptcy cases and workouts. Recent engagements include: receiver for the Lancer Group of hedge funds in their insolvency proceedings; a group of 747 aircraft lessors in Atlas Air; CIT as the exit lender to Friedman's Jewelers; and the Official Committee in Far & Wide Travel Corp. Mr Rasile is Co-Chair of the firm's Bankruptcy Department.

## RASKIN, Jane
Raskin & Raskin PA, Miami
305 444 3400
*Recommended in Litigation*

## RASKIN, Martin
Raskin & Raskin PA, Miami
305 444 3400
*Recommended in Litigation*

## RASMUSSEN, Robert
Glenn Rasmussen Fogarty & Hooker, Tampa 813 229 3333
*Recommended in Corporate/M&A*

## RAVIKOFF, Ronald
Zuckerman Spaeder LLP, Miami
305 358 5000
*Recommended in Antitrust, Litigation*

## REDMOND, Patricia
Stearns Weaver Miller Weissler Alhadeff & Sitterson, PA, Miami 305 789 3200

*Recommended in Bankruptcy*

## REID, Benjamine
Carlton Fields, Miami 305 530 0050
breid@carltonfields.com
*Recommended in Litigation*

**Practice Areas:** Trial and appellate practice representing a diverse corporate clientele. He handles commercial disputes, environmental matters, products liability claims, and class action litigation.
**Prof. Memberships:** Admitted to practice in Florida and the US Supreme Court. Member, American Bar Association, Section of Litigation; American Bar Foundation; products liability Advisory Council.
**Publications:** Author, 'The Trial Lawyer as Story Teller: Reviving a Lost Art' (Litigation Magazine); Co-author, 'Checkmate in Class Actions: Defensive Strategy in the Initial Move' (Litigation Magazine 2002).
**Personal:** JD (cum laude), University of Georgia School of Law, 1974; AB, University of North Carolina at Chapel Hill, 1971.

## REILLY, Kenneth J
Shook, Hardy & Bacon LLP, Miami
305 358 5171
kreilly@shb.com
*Recommended in Litigation*

**Practice Areas:** Is nationally known for serving as lead litigation counsel for Fortune 500 corporations. His defense verdicts for high profile cases have been noted within 'The National Law Journal's Top 10 Verdicts' three years in a row.
**Prof. Memberships:** Admitted to practice in Colorado, Florida, Kansas and Missouri. Frequent lecturer to Bar associations on trial techniques and civil procedure.
**Career:** Joined Shook, Hardy & Bacon, 1995; became Partner, 1997. Managing Partner, Shook Hardy & Bacon's Miami, Florida, office. Member, Shook, Hardy & Bacon Executive Committee.
**Personal:** JD, University of Texas School of Law, 1973; BA, Trinity University, 1970.

## REISMAN, Stephen H
Peckar & Abramson, Miami
305 358 2600
sreisman@pecklaw.com
*Recommended in Construction*

**Practice Areas:** Mr Reisman's primary area of practice is construction law and includes the representation of construction managers, general contractors, subcontractors and owners in the negotiation and preparation of construction documents, and the negotiation, mediation, arbitration and litigation of construction contract claims, construction and design defect claims, insurance claims, and related matters. His construction law practice also includes project administration assistance for the early identification and resolution of potential

conflicts and disputes.
**Prof. Memberships:** He is a Florida Bar Board Specialist in Construction law. He serves on the Construction Advisory Council and Panel of Arbitrators for the American Arbitration Association. He is a Member of the American Bar Association (Construction Industry Forum and Litigation Section), the Academy of Florida Trial Lawyers, the Florida Bar (Litigation and Business Law Sections) and the Construction Association of South Florida.
**Career:** He is the Managing Partner of Peckar & Abramson's Florida offices and formerly a Partner of Rosenberg, Reisman & Stein, which merged with Peckar & Abramson in 2000. He is admitted to practice law before the United States Supreme Court, the United States Court of Appeals for the Fifth and Eleventh Circuits, the United States District Court for the Southern and Middle Districts of Florida, the United States Bankruptcy Court for the Southern District of Florida as well as all courts of the State of Florida.
**Publications:** He has authored several articles and conducted seminars on various construction law topics for The Florida Bar, National Business Institute, Construction Specifications Institute, Construction Association of South Florida, 'Southeast Construction', and Lorman Educational Services.
**Personal:** He is a graduate of Emory University (1973) and the University of Miami School of Law (1976).

## RICE, Arthur Halsey
Rice Pugatch Robinson & Schiller, Miami 305 379 3121
*Recommended in Bankruptcy*

## RICHARD, Barry
Greenberg Traurig LLP, Tallahassee
850 222 6891
richardb@gtlaw.com
*Recommended in Litigation*

**Practice Areas:** Litigation; appellate.
**Prof. Memberships:** Charter member, American Academy of Appellate Lawyers; former Deputy Attorney General, State of Florida.
**Career:** Listed, 'Best Lawyers in America', 2006; listed, 'Chambers & Partners USA Guide', 2003-06; recipient, Florida Bar, Traditions of Excellence Award, 2005; listed, 2004 and 2005 Legal Elite, Florida Trend Magazine, National Law Journal Lawyer of the Year, 2001.
**Publications:** Author, 'Arbitration Clause Risks', The National Law Journal, June 14, 2004; author, 'Mock Jury Exercises', The National Law Journal, March 1, 2004.
**Personal:** JD, University of Miami School of Law, 1967; BA, University of Miami, 1964.

## RICHMAN, Gerald
Richman Greer Weil Brumbaugh
Mirabito & Christensen,
West Palm Beach 561 803 3500
grichman@richmangreer.com

*Recommended in Litigation*

**Practice Areas:** Gerald F Richman is Board Certified by the Florida Bar as both a civil trial lawyer and business litigation lawyer concentrating in trial and appellate practice, and complex commercial litigation with emphasis on antitrust, securities, contract, construction, federal agency, corporate, banking, civil RICO, professional liability, consumer, employment, civil rights and probate litigation and class action issues, representing both plaintiffs and defendants. He also has extensive experience in real estate litigation, including mortgage foreclosures, condominiums, zoning and land use, brokerage disputes and governmental matters.
**Prof. Memberships:** Fellow of the American College of Trial Lawyers; former Member of the Board of Governors of the International Society of Barristers. Charter Member of the Miami Chapter of the American Board of Trial Advocates and the National Association of Consumer Advocates. He is a former President of the Florida Bar, former President of the Dade County Bar Association, and past Chair of the Florida Commission on Human Relations. He is currently a Member of the Board of Directors of the Economic Council of Palm Beach County.
**Career:** After service in the Army's Judge Advocate General Corps, where he earned the Presidential Service Badge for honorable service at the White House, he joined the firm in 1969 and became a Shareholder in 1971.
**Personal:** Mr Richman earned a Degree in Building Construction, with honors, at the University of Florida, his JD at the University of Florida College of Law and studied at Georgetown University Graduate Law School.

## RIDLEY, Fred S
Foley & Lardner LLP, Tampa
813 225 4183
fridley@foley.com
*Recommended in Real Estate*

**Career:** Fred S Ridley is a Partner in the Tampa office of Foley & Lardner LLP and the leader of the firm's Golf & Resort Services Industry Team. He is also a member of the Real Estate Practice Group and the Food and Sports Industry Teams. His practice is focused in the areas of commercial and residential real estate development and finance, golf and recreational amenity and resort development, and multifamily/condominium developments. Mr Ridley has extensive experience in representing developers of high-end, single-family and multi-family real estate projects. He received his JD Degree from Stetson University College of Law.

## RIEDEL, Harley E
Stichter, Riedel, Blain & Prosser PA,
Tampa 813 229 0144
hriedel@srbp.com
*Recommended in Bankruptcy*

**Practice Areas:** Chapter 11 business reorganizations; workouts and out-of-court loan and debt restructurings; asset acquisitions and sales in bankruptcy cases.
**Prof. Memberships:** Founder and past President, The Tampa Bay Bankruptcy Bar Association. Officer and Director, Tampa Bay Federal Bar Association. Fellow, American College of Bankruptcy. Past Member, Local Rules Committee, Bankruptcy Court for Middle District of Florida (1985-98). Member, The Florida Bar, Federal Bar Association, Hillsborough County Bar Association, and Amercian Bankruptcy Institute.
**Career:** Co-founder in 1974 (with Don M Stichter) of Stichter, Riedel Blain & Prosser, P.A.
**Publications:** Speaker and writer on bankruptcy-related topics for American Bar Association, American Bankruptcy Institute, The Florida Bar, and numerous other legal and business groups. Principal author, Chapter 11 practice section, 'Norton Handbook for Bankruptcy Trustees, Debtors-in-Possession, and Committees' (West Publishing Company). Co-authored publications on bankruptcy law for The Florida Bar. Guest lecturer, Advanced Bankruptcy Class, University of Florida College of Law.
**Personal:** BA, Baylor University, 1971. JD, University of Florida, 1974 (with high honors; Order of the Coif). Editor-in-Chief, University of Florida Law Review.

## RILLSTONE, Douglas
Broad and Cassel, Tallahassee
850 681 6810
*Recommended in Environment*

## ROBINS, Andrew S
Gunster, Yoakley & Stewart, P.A.,
Fort Lauderdale 954 462 2000
*Recommended in Real Estate*

## ROBINSON, John
Fowler White Boggs Banker, Tampa
813 228 7411
*Recommended in Employment*

## ROCK, Andrew
Buchanan Ingersoll PC, Tampa
813 222 8186
rockra@bipc.com
*Recommended in Healthcare*
**Practice Areas:** Practice focuses on hospital regulatory and operational matters, physician contracts, the creation and merger of physician group practices, fraud and abuse and other regulatory matters, managed care contracting and the purchase and sale of healthcare facilities. Andrew also handles healthcare joint ventures, Medicare reimbursement issues and issues regarding alternative/complementary medicine.
**Personal:** JD Florida State University, 1983; BA, 1969 (with honors); BA, 1967 (cum laude) University of the Itwatersrand.

## RODDENBERRY, Stephen
Akerman Senterfitt, Miami
305 374 5600
stephen.roddenberry@akerman.com
*Recommended in Corporate/M&A*
**Career:** Stephen K Roddenberry is a shareholder in the Corporate Practice Group where he focuses his practice in the areas of securities, mergers and acquisitions, private equity and venture capital, international and public finance. He has additional industry experience as counsel in aviation, entertainment and sports, and banking and financial institutions. He is a Member of the American Bar Association, Sports Lawyers Association and the Florida Bar Foundation. Mr Roddenberry's representative clients include The Geo Group, Miami Dolphins, Huizenga Holdings, Inc. and Embraer Aircraft Holding, Inc.

## ROGOW, Bruce
Bruce S. Rogow, P.A., Fort Lauderdale
954 767 8909
*Recommended in Litigation*

## RONZETTI, Tucker
Kozyak Tropin & Throckmorton, Miami
305 372 1800
TR@kttlaw.com
*Recommended in Litigation*
**Practice Areas:** Partner, civil and commercial litigation.
**Prof. Memberships:** Florida Bar, Washington, DC Bar.
**Career:** Specializes in civil and complex commercial litigation and class actions. Assistant county attorney, Miami-Dade County, Florida (1994-2001); Valdes-Fauli, Cobb, Bischoff, Kriss & Mandler (1993-94); law clerk for Judge Edward B Davis, Southern District of Florida (1992-93); Instructor, Adjunct Professor, University of Miami School of Law (1992-present); Iron Arrow (1992, highest honor attainable at University of Miami).
**Publications:** 'When Bankers Look The Other Way', ABA Business Law Today, May/June 2005; 'Avoiding Common Pitfalls in Closing Arguments', co-authored by Janet L Humphreys, Florida Bar Journal, December 2003; 'Dodging the Extra Arrow', co-authored by Lee A Kraftchick, Florida Bar Journal, October 2001; 'Levying the Ultimate Sanctions: Punishment by Dismissal or Default in Florida', Florida Bar Journal, July/August 1995; 'Constituting Family and Death through the Struggle with State Power: Curzan v. Director, Missouri Department of Health', University of Miami Law Review, September 1991.
**Personal:** Born Ft Meade, Maryland, 1964. Duke University (BA Economics, 1987); University of Miami (JD, 1992, magna cum laude).

## ROSENBERG, Michael
Packman, Neuwahl & Rosenberg,
Coral Gables 305 665 3311
*Recommended in Tax*

## ROSENTHAL, Stephen F
Podhurst Orseck P.A., Miami
305 358 2800
*Recommended in Litigation*
**Practice Areas:** Partner handling appeals and complex civil litigation, focusing on tort and commercial cases as well as employment, election and First Amendment law.
**Prof. Memberships:** US Supreme Court; US Court of Appeals for the Eleventh Circuit; US District Court, SD Florida; Florida Bar; District of Columbia Bar; Chairman of Board, American Constitution Society, South Florida Chapter; Academy of Florida Trial Lawyers.
**Career:** Trial lawyer, US Department of Justice; law clerk to US Circuit Judge Rosemary Barkett and to US District Judge Mark Wolf.
**Personal:** JD, Harvard Law School, cum laude, 1996, BA Harvard College, magna cum laude, 1992.

## ROSS, David L
Greenberg Traurig LLP, Miami
305 579 0523
rossd@gtlaw.com
*Recommended in Antitrust, Litigation*
**Practice Areas:** Litigation; antitrust; products liability.
**Prof. Memberships:** Member, American Bar Association's Litigation Section.
**Career:** Listed, 'Best Lawyers in America', every edition since 1989; listed, 'Chambers & Partners USA Guide', 2003-06; listed, 2004 and 2005 Legal Elite, Florida Trend Magazine, listing of Florida's top attorneys as selected by their peers.
**Publications:** Frequent lecturer for The Florida Bar's Continuing Legal Education Program, on such topics as Trial Techniques, Antitrust Law and Restrictive Covenants; co-author, 'The Florida Antitrust Act of 1980', The Florida Bar Journal.
**Personal:** JD, with honors, University of Chicago Law School, 1973; BS, with highest distinction, Northwestern University, 1970.

## ROSS, Lauri Waldman
Lauri Waldman Ross PA, Miami
305 670 8010
*Recommended in Litigation*

## ROSTON, Carl D
Akerman Senterfitt, Miami
305 982 5628
carl.roston@akerman.com
*Recommended in Corporate/M&A*
**Career:** Carl Roston, Co-Chair of the firm's Private Equity and Venture Capital Practice Group and member of the Corporate Practice Group, has extensive experience representing public companies, large privately-held and emerging growth companies, and venture capital and private equity firms, on a variety of matters, including M&As, debt and equity financings and investments, securities, joint ventures, and strategic alliances. He

is Chair of the Private Equity/Commercialization Committee for the University of Florida Foundation, a Member (and former Chairman) of the Board of the Florida Venture Forum, and a former General Counsel to and Member of the Executive Committee of BioFlorida.

## ROUNSAVILLE, Keith
Akerman Senterfitt, Orlando
407 843 7860
keith.rounsaville@akerman.com
*Recommended in Antitrust*
**Career:** Keith Rounsaville, shareholder and Chair of the firm's Antitrust and Trade Regulation Practice, is Board Certified by the Florida Bar in Antitrust and Trade Regulation. He has served as lead trial counsel and appellate counsel in civil and criminal antitrust actions throughout the United States, including Alabama, Florida, Georgia, Colorado, Indiana, Texas, Maryland and Virginia. His industry experience in antitrust matters includes pharmaceuticals, consumer electronics, optical lenses, building products, petroleum products, industrial chemicals, automotive products, agricultural products and thoroughbred horseracing. His practice also includes RICO, environmental and intellectual property litigation. He is a Member of the American Law Institute.

## RUGG, Joseph W
Akerman Senterfitt, Tampa
813 223 7333
joseph.rugg@akerman.com
*Recommended in Healthcare*
**Career:** Joseph Rugg is the Office Managing Shareholder of Akerman Senterfitt's Tampa office. His practice focuses on healthcare and business law, including the purchase and sale agreements with physicians and other healthcare providers, ambulatory surgery centers, employment agreements, provider networks, managed care contracting, and Stark and Fraud and Abuse. Previously, he served as the Director, Center for Quality in Healthcare Law, Stetson College of Law. He writes and lectures on healthcare law topics and is a Member of the American Health Lawyers Association and the Sections of Health Law of the American Bar Association and The Florida Bar.

## RUSSELL, Janice L
Akerman Senterfitt, Miami
305 982 5611
janice.russell@akerman.com
*Recommended in Real Estate*
**Career:** Janice Russell, a shareholder with the Real Estate Practice Group, focuses her practice on the acquisition, development and financing of resort hotel properties, golf courses, marinas, sports arenas and privately developed detention and correctional facilities. She has extensive experience with agri-business lending, retail, multi-family and office building development and leasing, and represent-

ing financial institutions in connection with mortgage and construction lending.

## RUSSIN, Peter
Meland Russin Hellinger & Budwick, Miami 305 358 6363
*Recommended in Bankruptcy*

## RYAN, Michael
Lowndes Drosdick Doster Kantor & Reed, PA, Orlando 407 843 4600
*Recommended in Real Estate*

## SAATHOFF, Dwight
Akerman Senterfitt, Orlando
407 843 7860
dwight.saathoff@akerman.com
*Recommended in Real Estate*
**Career:** Dwight Saathoff is a shareholder and focuses his practice on land use, zoning and real property law. He represents many of the largest development companies doing business in Florida. As part of his work in winning development entitlements for new projects, Mr Saathoff has structured numerous public/private joint ventures formed for the purpose of financing the construction of major public works projects such as schools, parking garages and regional road networks. He is a frequent lecturer on current development topics, particularly solving the problem of school overcrowding in high growth areas.

## SALE, Jon
Sale & Kuehne PA, Miami
305 789 5989
*Recommended in Litigation*

## SALEH, Anis
Saleh & Associates, Miami
305 379 2661
*Recommended in Immigration*

## SAMS, Gary
Hopping Green & Sams, PA, Tallahassee
850 222 7500
gsams@hgslaw.com
*Recommended in Environment*
**Practice Areas:** Environmental and land use strategic counseling and litigation with emphasis on cases before Florida Division of Administrative Hearings.
**Prof. Memberships:** Admitted to practice in Florida and before all US District Courts in Florida, 11th US Circuit Court of Appeals, and US Supreme Court.
**Career:** For over three decades has represented throughout Florida: investor-owned, municipal, and independent electric power producers in licensing electrical power plants; land owners and developers; water and wastewater utilities; pipeline and petroleum products companies; mining companies; agricultural interests and natural resource users; and governmental entities in both regulatory and proprietary activities.

## SANDRIDGE, Hala
Fowler White Boggs Banker, Tampa
813 228 7411
*Recommended in Litigation*

## SASSO, Gary L
Carlton Fields, Tampa
813 223 7000
gsasso@carltonfields.com
*Recommended in Litigation*
**Practice Areas:** Securities fraud and consumer fraud class actions and complex litigation at the trial and appellate levels. President/CEO.
**Prof. Memberships:** Council, ABA Section of Litigation and Task Force on Vision Implementation; Fellow, International Academy of Trial Lawyers; Fellow, American Academy of Appellate Lawyers; Fellow, American Bar Foundation; Fellow, International Academy of Trial Lawyers; Fellow, American Academy of Appellate Lawyers; American Law Institute.
**Career:** Law clerk, US Supreme Court; law clerk, US Court of Appeals, District of Columbia Circuit.
**Personal:** JD (magna cum laude), University of Pennsylvania Law School, 1977; BS (magna cum laude), Wharton School, University of Pennsylvania, 1974.

## SAUL, Gary
Greenberg Traurig LLP, Miami
305 579 0846
saulg@gtlaw.com
*Recommended in Real Estate*
**Practice Areas:** Real estate.
**Prof. Memberships:** Member, The Florida Bar's Condominium and Planned Development Committee; former board member of, and lecturer for, the Dade County Chapter of the Community Association Institute.
**Career:** Listed, Best Lawyers in America, 2006; listed, 'Top Lawyer', South Florida Legal Guide, 2005; listed, Chambers & Partners USA Guide, 2003-06; listed, 2004 and 2005 Legal Elite, Florida Trend Magazine, listing of Florida's top attorneys as selected by their peers.
**Personal:** JD, University of Pennsylvania Law School, 1984; BA, Pennsylvania State University, 1981.

## SAWYER, Ed
White & Case LLP, Miami
305 995 5213
esawyer@whitecase.com
*Recommended in Tax*
**Practice Areas:** Represents a broad range of clients, including institutional healthcare providers, real estate development companies, sales and marketing companies, health insurance providers and managed care companies in merger and acquisition, financing, regulatory, general corporate and tax matters. Practice also includes representation of clients engaged in software development, medical device manufacturing and shipping and transportation. Has substantial experience with both the tax and non-tax aspects of joint ventures, limited partnerships, limited liability partnerships, limited liability companies, corporations,

trusts and estates.
**Prof. Memberships:** The Florida Bar; United States Tax Court.

## SCHERKER, Elliot
Greenberg Traurig LLP, Miami
305 579 0500
scherkere@gtlaw.com
*Recommended in Litigation*
**Practice Areas:** Appellate; litigation.
**Prof. Memberships:** Member, American Academy of Appellate Lawyers.
**Career:** Listed, 'Best Lawyers in America', 2001-06; listed, 'Chambers & Partners USA Guide', 2003-06; listed, 2004 and 2005 Legal Elite, Florida Trend Magazine, listing of Florida's top attorneys as selected by their peers; Recognized as one of the Top Lawyers in South Florida, South Florida Legal Guide, 2004-05.
**Publications:** Co-author, 'Florida Bar's Florida Appellate Practice', 1977-2000 and 2006.
**Personal:** JD, University of Miami School of Law, 1975; BA, University of Miami, 1972.

## SCHEU, William
Rogers Towers PA, Jacksonville
904 398 3911
*Recommended in Real Estate*

## SCHILLER, Lisa
Rice Pugatch Robinson & Schiller, Miami 305 379 3121
*Recommended in Bankruptcy*

## SCHINDLER, Ozzie
Greenberg Traurig LLP, Miami
305 579 0762
schindlero@gtlaw.com
*Recommended in Tax*
**Practice Areas:** International tax.
**Prof. Memberships:** Assistant Director, Florida Bar Tax Section, International. Chair of International Fiscal Association, Taxation of Multinationals Group, Palm Beach Chapter. Co-Chair, Florida Bar/FICPA International Tax Conference.
**Career:** Listed, 'Best Lawyers in America', 2006 edition. Listed, 'Chambers & Partners USA Guide', 2004-06. Recipient, American Jurisprudence Awards for International Business Transactions and Family Law.
**Publications:** Co-author, 'US Corporations Doing Business Abroad', editions 2003-05. Co-author, 'BNA Portfolio: Passive Foreign Investment Companies', 2005.
**Personal:** LLM, New York University School of Law, 1995. JD, with honors, University of Florida, 1993. BS, with high honors, University of Florida, 1990.

## SCHMIDT, Don
Carlton Fields, Tampa
813 223 7000
dschmidt@carltonfields.com
*Recommended in Healthcare*
**Practice Areas:** Practices in the areas of major business litigation, antitrust law, and healthcare for national and regional

companies. Has significant experience defending class action cases and clients in investigations by enforcement agencies, handles a variety of hospital medical staff counseling and litigation matters. Chair of the firm's Healthcare Practice Group.
**Prof. Memberships:** Member, The Florida Bar; Hillsborough County Bar Association; American Bar Association, Antitrust Law Section, Health Law Section; Federal Bar Association former Vice-Chair, Healthcare Industry Committee.
**Personal:** JD (with honors), University of Notre Dame Law School, 1979; BA (with honors), University of Notre Dame, 1970.

## SCHNAPP, Mark
Greenberg Traurig LLP, Miami
305 579 0541
schnappm@gtlaw.com
*Recommended in Litigation*
**Practice Areas:** Litigation; international.
**Prof. Memberships:** Former President, Assistant United States Attorneys Association; Chairman, Security and Fraud Prevention Committee, Florida International Bankers Association; Member, Eugene Spellman Inn of Court; Member, Appointed by Chief Judge Zloch to Ad Hoc Committee on Attorney Admissions, Peer Review and Attorney Grievance, SD Fla.
**Career:** Listed, 'Best Lawyers in America', 2006 edition; listed, 'Chambers & Partners USA Guide', 2004-06; recognized, Top Lawyers in South Florida, South Florida Legal Guide, 2004-05.
**Personal:** JD, Hofstra University School of Law, 1976; BS, Electrical Engineering, New York University, 1972.

## SCHULMAN, Clifford
Greenberg Traurig LLP, Miami
305 579 0613
schulmanc@gtlaw.com
*Recommended in Real Estate*
**Practice Areas:** Environmental; real estate, land development.
**Prof. Memberships:** Adjunct Professor, University of Miami Law School, Masters Program; Executive Council and Chairman, Environmental and Land Use Law Section of The Florida Bar; Chairman of the Board, Executive Committee, Aventura Marketing Council.
**Career:** Recognized, Top Lawyers in South Florida, South Florida Legal Guide, 2004-05; listed, 'Chambers & Partners USA Guide', 2003-06; listed, 2004 and 2005 Legal Elite, Florida Trend Magazine; listed, The Best Lawyers in America since 1989.
**Personal:** JD, University of Florida Levin College of Law, 1972; BS, University of Florida, 1969.

## SCHWARTZ, John S
Akerman Senterfitt, Miami
305 374 5600
john.schwartz@akerman.com
*Recommended in Healthcare*
**Career:** John Schwartz, a shareholder with the Healthcare Practice Group, has over 25 years experience handling healthcare merger and acquisitions, hospital-physicians joint ventures, fraud and abuse, compliance and regulatory issues, financings, exempt organization issues and physician contracting. His clients consist primarily of institutional healthcare providers and have included public and privately held companies, community and religiously sponsored not-for-profits, governmental entities and university medical centers. He is the former Senior Vice President-General Counsel of a publicly-traded healthcare company than owned and operated 36 hospitals and 13 nursing homes in 12 states.

## SCHWENKE, Roger D
Carlton Fields, Tampa
813 223 7000
rschwenke@carltonfields.com
*Recommended in Environment*
**Practice Areas:** Practices in the areas of environmental, land use, real estate, and secured financing law. He represents developers, lenders, and companies in a wide range of environmental regulatory, permitting and development projects, ranging from crude oil splitters to recreational theme parks, and from defense of clients in CERCLA/Superfund negotiations and cases to permitting for cable transmission systems.
**Prof. Memberships:** Member, American Bar Association; The Florida Bar; Hillsborough County Bar Association; Fellow, American Bar Foundation; Fellow, American College of Real Estate Lawyers.
**Personal:** JD (with honors), University of Florida College of Law, 1969; BA, The Ohio State University, 1966.

## SEAY, James E L
Holland & Knight LLP, Orlando
407 425 8500
james.seay@hklaw.com
*Recommended in Real Estate*
**Practice Areas:** Partner in the firm's Real Estate Section, practices in the area of commercial real estate law, with an emphasis on the representation of developers of commercial, mixed-use and residential projects, and acquisition and disposition of income-producing properties. He is experienced in multistate financings of real estate projects, tax deferred exchanges, sale and purchase of agricultural property, acquisition, financings, and sale of restaurants; and acquisition, financings, and sale of office and industrial properties, residential subdivisions, apartment complexes, and shopping centers. He is a graduate of Leadership Orlando and a member of the National Association of Office and Industrial Parks.

## SEGAL, Mike
Broad and Cassel, Miami
305 373 9400
*Recommended in Healthcare*

## SELLERS, Lawrence
Holland & Knight LLP, Tallahassee
850 224 7000
larry.sellers@hklaw.com
*Recommended in Environment*
**Practice Areas:** Partner in the firm's Government Section, practicing administrative and governmental law focusing on environmental matters. He regularly provides advice on permitting and enforcement matters involving a variety of federal, state, regional and local administrative agencies. He has substantial experience in administrative law, including adjudicatory hearings and rulemaking. For more than 20 years, he has represented clients before the Florida Legislature, primarily on various environmental, land use and administrative law issues. He is a Member of the Florida Bar's Board of Governors and a Past-Chair of the Environmental and Land Use Law Section of The Florida Bar.

## SHAUGHNESSY, Kevin
Baker & Hostetler LLP, Orlando
407 649 4000
*Recommended in Employment*

## SHERR, Brian J
Greenberg Traurig LLP, Fort Lauderdale
954 765 0500
sherrb@gtlaw.com
*Recommended in Real Estate*
**Practice Areas:** Real estate.
**Prof. Memberships:** Member, Executive Council, Real Property, Probate and Trust Law Section of Florida Bar, for 15 years; Co-Chairman, Condominium and Planned Development Committee of Florida Bar for 15 years.
**Career:** Named among 'South Florida's Heavy Hitters in Real Estate', Business Journal, 2004. Honored at the American Friends of Ariel 8th Annual Peace With Security Dinner, March 7, 2002.
**Publications:** Author, 'The Planning and Structuring of Real Estate Developments Incorporating Associations and Protective Covenants', Florida Condominium Law and Practice, The Florida Bar Continuing Education.
**Personal:** JD, Boston University School of Law, 1970; BA, Rutgers University, 1967.

## SHINDELL, James W
Bilzin Sumberg Baena Price & Axelrod LLP, Miami 305 375 6141
jshindell@bilzin.com
*Recommended in Real Estate*
**Career:** Jim Shindell's practice involves the representation of developers, investors (institutional and private) and lenders in a broad range of real estate matters, including acquisitions, sales, leasing, joint ventures and financings. Such matters have involved office, retail, hotel, warehouse, industrial, residential, mixed-use developments and telecommunications properties. Mr Shindell acts as counsel to both borrowers and lenders in a wide variety of mortgage and secured lending transactions. He represents developers/owners, opportunity funds and private equity firms in connection with joint venture transactions. Jim's practice also includes the representation of both landlords and tenants in commercial leasing transactions.

## SHOHAT, Edward
Bierman, Shohat, Loewy & Klein PA, Miami 305 358 7000
*Recommended in Litigation*

## SHUBIN, John
Shubin & Bass, Miami
305 381 6060
*Recommended in Real Estate*

## SHUKER, R Scott
Gronek & Latham, Orlando
407 481 5800
*Recommended in Bankruptcy*

## SIEGEL, Stephen
Ruden McClosky SC, Miami
305 789 2700
*Recommended in Healthcare*

## SIEGFRIED, Steven
Siegfried, Rivera, Lerner, De La Torre & Sobel, PA, Miami 305 442 3334
*Recommended in Construction*

## SIEMON, Charles
Charles L Siemon - Sole Practitioner, Boca Ratón 561 368 3808
*Recommended in Real Estate*

## SILVERMAN, Lawrence
Akerman Senterfitt, Miami
305 374 5600
lawrence.silverman@akerman.com
*Recommended in Antitrust*
**Career:** Lawrence D Silverman is a shareholder who is Board Certified in antitrust and trade regulation. He has significant litigation, trial and counseling experience in antitrust and trade regulation, commercial litigation, sports law and class actions. Mr Silverman heads the 75 lawyer litigation section of Akerman Senterfitt's Miami office. He is a former Member of the Council of the ABA Antitrust Section, and a multiple winner of the Miami-Dade County Bar Association's 'Put Something Back' pro bono award.

## SILVERMAN, Scott
Zinober & McCrea, P.A., Tampa
813 224 9004
*Recommended in Employment*

## SILVERMAN, Steve I
Kluger, Peretz, Kaplan & Berlin P.L., Miami 305 379 9000
ssilverman@kpkb.com
*Recommended in Litigation*
**Practice Areas:** Litigation and dispute resolution involving business torts and real estate transactions, complex fiancial fraud, director and officer liability, securities fraud, and class action litigation.
**Prof. Memberships:** The Florida Bar, the Dade County Bar Association and the American Bar Association.
**Career:** Graduated State University of New York at Albany, BA, cum laude, 1982 and University of Miami School of Law, JD, 1985. Admitted to the Florida Bar, 1985, the US District Court, Southern District of Florida, 1986, the US Bankruptcy Court, Southern District of Florida, 1986, and the US Court of Appeals, Third, Ninth and Eleventh Circuits, 1986.
**Personal:** Recognized by peers as a 'Legal Elite' by Florida Trends Magazine and 'The Best of the Bar' by South Florida Business Journal. Recieved the American Jurisprudence Book Award in contract law, the Award of Distinction, Society of Wig and Robe and Best Brief Award, Robert Orseck Memorial Moot Court Competition. Former President of IMPACT, Diabetes Research Institute Foundation.

## SIMMONS, Sherwin
Buchanan Ingersoll PC, Miami
305 347 4060
spstax@bipc.com
*Recommended in Tax*
**Practice Areas:** Chair, Florida Tax Practice. Experienced in business transactions including: mergers, acquisitions, reorganizations and partnerships; exempt organizations; healthcare tax issues; international taxation; pension and welfare benefit plans; executive and deferred compensation and fringe benefits; estate planning; civil and criminal tax controversies; tax trials; pension controversies; and legislative and regulatory developments. Expert witness in tax and ERISA matters.
**Prof. Memberships:** Board Certified in tax law, Florida Bar Board of Legal Specialization and Education. Admitted in Florida, Tennessee and before the US Supreme Court, US Tax Court, Court of Federal Claims.
**Personal:** Columbia University AB and JD, Harlan Fiske Scholar.

## SIMS, Roger
Holland & Knight LLP, Orlando
407 425 8500
roger.sims@hklaw.com
*Recommended in Environment*
**Practice Areas:** Partner in the firm's Government Law Section, practicing in the areas of water law and environmental and land use law. He is experienced in groundwater, surface water, wetlands, solid waste and hazardous waste issues.

He deals with many agencies on a regular basis, including Florida's Water Management Districts, the Florida Department of Environmental Protection, and the Department of Community Affairs. He has particular experience in the permitting of large projects, including developments of regional impact. He served on the American Bar Association Standing Committee on Environmental Law from 2000-03.

## SINGER, Stuart
Boies, Schiller & Flexner LLP, Miami
305 539 8400
ssinger@bsfllp.com
*Recommended in Antitrust, Litigation*
**Practice Areas:** Mr Singer's nationwide practice in complex litigation includes antitrust, intellectual property, insurance, securites and constitutional law. His clients have included Carnival Corp., Citibank, Computer Associates, Diebold, Fidelity National Financial, Pacific Enterprises (now Sempra Energy), State Farm Insurance and Vons. Currently, Mr Singer is defending antitrust monopolization claims against Fresh Del Monte Produce and NASCAR; is co-ordinating ADT Security Services' defense of class actions and other litigation; and is prosecuting one of the most closely-followed intellectual property cases in the country – The SCO Group v. IBM. In recent years, Mr Singer obtained dismissal of unfair competition suits against Philip Morris, directed litigation strategy for nationwide consolidated insurance subrogation actions, and successfully defended fraud claims in a two-month arbitration trial.
**Prof. Memberships:** Former Chair, Civil Rules Committee of Florida Bar; Federal Bar Association; American Law Institute.
**Career:** In private practice since 1983 and a Partner at Boies, Schiller & Flexner since 2000, Mr Singer served as law clerk to Justice Byron R White of the US Supreme Court (1981-83).
**Publications:** Lectured and written on litigation, antitrust and constitutional law, including in the Harvard Law Review and a regular newspaper column on law and technology.
**Personal:** Mr Singer received his BS and MA from Northwestern University (1978), where he won the national collegiate debate championship. He graduated magna cum laude from Harvard Law School (1981), and was President of the Harvard Law Review. His community and philanthropic services includes the board of governors of the National Association of Urban Debate Leagues and the Leadership Council of the Harvard School of Public Health.

## SINGERMAN, Paul
Berger Singerman, Fort Lauderdale
954 525 9900
*Recommended in Bankruptcy*

## SKOLNICK, Holly
Greenberg Traurig LLP, Miami
305 579 0860
skolnickh@gtlaw.com
*Recommended in Litigation*
**Practice Areas:** Litigation.
**Prof. Memberships:** President and Founder, Greenberg Traurig Fellowship Foundation; Board of Directors, Florida Immigrant Advocacy Center; Board of Advisors, University of Miami Law School, Center for Ethics and Public Service; Board of Directors, Equal Justice Works; Chair, Greenberg Traurig Pro Bono Program.
**Career:** Listed, 'Best Lawyers in America', 2005 and 2006; listed, 'Chambers & Partners USA Guide', 2004-06; listed, '2005 Legal Elite', Florida Trend Magazine; Recognized as one of the 'Top Lawyers in South Florida', South Florida Legal Guide, 2004-05.
**Personal:** JD, Harvard Law School, 1980; BA, University of Wisconsin-Madison, 1976.

## SLATER, James
Broad and Cassel, Orlando
407 839 4200
*Recommended in Real Estate*

## SLAUGHTER JR, Harrison
Leventhal & Slaughter PA, Orlando
407 849 6161
*Recommended in Litigation*

## SLEETH, Tim
Smith Hulsey & Busey, Jacksonville
904 359 7700
*Recommended in Environment*

## SMALLWOOD, Mary
Ruden McClosky SC, Tallahassee
850 412 2000
*Recommended in Environment*

## SMULIAN, Andrew
Akerman Senterfitt, Miami
305 374 5600
andrew.smulian@akerman.com
*Recommended in Real Estate*
**Career:** Andrew Smulian is a shareholder and the Chair of the firm's Real Estate Practice Group. His extensive practice includes the counseling of major developers, lenders and investors in complex real estate and financing transactions. His clients include financial institutions, foreign investors, real estate investment trusts, pension funds and investment advisors. Mr Smulian has structured and negotiated the purchase, sale and ground leasing of industrial, commercial and multi-family residential properties, complex construction and development contracts, joint ventures, financing facilities and loan restructurings.

## SOKOL, Jerry J
McDermott Will & Emery, Miami
305 347 6514
jsokol@mwe.com
*Recommended in Healthcare*

**Practice Areas:** National practice concentrated on transactional aspects of healthcare law with an emphasis on mergers and acquisitions, joint ventures and various contractual arrangements in healthcare industry. Developed a niche in healthcare private equity transactions and Co-Chairs firm's Healthcare Transactions Group. Experience includes numerous sales, acquisitions and mergers of variety of healthcare entities with a practice focus on ambulatory surgery centers, diagnostic imaging, national and regional large physician practices, and other outpatient providers.
**Personal:** University of Florida College of Law (JD); University of Texas at Austin (MPA); University of Texas at Austin (BBA, with honors).

## SOLLNER, Richard
Trenam, Kemker, Scharf, Barkin, Frye, O'Neill & Mullis PA, Tampa
813 223 7474
*Recommended in Real Estate*

## SOMERSTEIN, Barry
Ruden McClosky, S.C., Fort Lauderdale
954 764 6660
*Recommended in Real Estate*

## SONBERG, Steven
Holland & Knight LLP, Miami
305 374 8500
steven.sonberg@hklaw.com
*Recommended in Corporate/M&A*
**Practice Areas:** Chair of the Business Law Section, practicing in the areas of M&A, securities and corporate law. His broad transactional securities practice involves public and private debt and equity securities offerings, recapitalizations and restructurings of public and closely-held business enterprise, and public company reporting matters. His M&A experience includes the representation of public and private domestic and international businesses in purchases, sales, divestitures and tender offers in a wide range of industries, including life sciences, real estate, healthcare, finance, transportation and communications. He advises senior corporate management and boards of directors in corporate governance, compliance and operational matters.

## SONNETT, Neal
Neal Sonnett PA, Miami
305 358 2000
*Recommended in Litigation*

## SORIANO, Robert
Carlton Fields, Tampa
813 223 7000
rsoriano@carltonfields.com
*Recommended in Bankruptcy*
**Practice Areas:** Practices in the areas of bankruptcy, creditors' rights, and workouts. Chair, firm's Bankruptcy and Creditors' Rights Practice Group.
**Prof. Memberships:** Admitted to practice in Florida and New York. Fellow,

American College of Bankruptcy; American Bankruptcy Institute; American Law Institute; American Bar Association; Hillsborough County Bar Association; Founding Director, The Tampa Bay Bankruptcy Bar Association.
**Career:** Law clerk, Honorable Mark A Costantino, Eastern District of New York.
**Publications:** Contributing Editor, 'Collier Bankruptcy Practice Guide', and the treatise, 'Chapter 11 Theory and Practice' (LRP Publications).
**Personal:** JD (cum laude), Syracuse Law School, 1977; AB (with high distinction), Rutgers College, 1973.

## SORONDO JR, Rodolfo
Holland & Knight LLP, Miami
305 374 8500
rodolfo.sorondo@hklaw.com
*Recommended in Litigation*
**Practice Areas:** Mr Sorondo is a Partner and Leader of South Florida's Appellate Practice Group. He was a trial lawyer from 1979 through 1992. From 1992-2002, he served with distinction as both a trial judge (1992-97), and then as an Appellate Judge (1997-2002) on Florida's Third District Court of Appeal. In 1998, he was awarded the Justice Gerald Kogan Judicial Distinction Award and in 2004, the Justice Award. Mr Sorondo is an Adjunct Professor at the University of Miami's Law School, and lectures extensively on the subjects of jury selection, and appellate advocacy.

## SOTO, Edward
Weil, Gotshal & Manges LLP, Miami
305 577 3177
edward.soto@weil.com
*Recommended in Litigation*
**Practice Areas:** Edward Soto's practice focuses on complex commercial civil litigation and has a consistent record of winning major complex cases in state and federal courts and before arbitration panels. He has had substantial civil litigation experience in cases involving antitrust, business torts, class actions, construction, employment, fraud, insurance coverage, lender liability, products liability and securities litigation, and has handled numerous internal investigations in these areas. Mr Soto has achieved successful outcomes for his clients at every phase of the litigation process.
**Personal:** Florida State University, BA, 1974; Columbia University School of Law, JD, 1978.

## SPECIE, Karen
Scruggs & Carmichael PA, Gainesville
352 376 5242
*Recommended in Bankruptcy*

## SPECTOR, Arthur
Berger Singerman, Fort Lauderdale
954 525 9900
*Recommended in Bankruptcy*

**SPECTOR, Brian F**
Kenny Nachwalter PA, Miami
305 381 7475
bfs@kennynachwalter.com
*Recommended in Litigation*
**Practice Areas:** Complex buisness litigation, intellectual property litigation, legal ethics and professional liability responsibility, professional liability, accountants liability, legal malpractice, securities litigation, securities arbitration, Florida Bar Board certification, business litigation law.
**Prof. Memberships:** The Florida Bar, American Bar Association, American Law Institute, The Florida Bar, Dade County Bar Association.
**Personal:** University of Miami School of Law, Juris Doctor (magna cum laude) 1978 Syracuse University, BA (cum laude) 1974.

**SPRATT, William**
Kirkpatrick & Lockhart Nicholson Graham LLP, Miami
305 539 3320
wspratt@klng.com
*Recommended in Healthcare*
**Practice Areas:** Has significant experience in the areas of acquisitions, sales, mergers, and reorganizations of healthcare businesses (including physician groups, hospitals, skilled nursing facilities, home health agencies), fraud and abuse counseling, federal and state regulatory compliance, antitrust issues, structuring and implementing managed care arrangements, and representation of clients in Medicare, Medicaid, and other third party reimbursement issues. Mr Spratt is a Florida Bar Board Certified Health Lawyer and has been named Best Healthcare Lawyer by South Florida Medical Business and among the Leading Florida Attorneys by Florida Trend magazine.
**Prof. Memberships:** Admitted to practice in Florida. Arbitrator, AHLA Alternative Dispute Resolution Service, American Health Lawyers Association, Florida Association of Hospital Attorneys, Past Chair and Vice-Chair, Florida Bar Health Law Certification Committee.
**Career:** Joined Kirkpatrick & Lockhart Nicholson Graham LLP in 1999. Previously served as the long-term care administrator for Miami-Dade County, Florida.
**Personal:** JD, University of Miami Law School, 1986 (cum laude), MS, Florida International University, 1974, BA, University of South Florida, 1968.

**SREBNICK, Howard**
Black, Srebnick, Kornspan & Stumpf PA, Miami 305 371 6421
*Recommended in Litigation*

**SREBNICK, Scott**
Law Offices of Scott A Srebnick, Miami
305 285 9019
*Recommended in Litigation*

**STAGE, Jon**
Stearns Weaver Miller Weissler Alhadeff & Sitterson, P.A., Fort Lauderdale
954-462-9500
*Recommended in Employment*

**STANFORD, Douglas**
Smith, Gambrell & Russell, LLP, Jacksonville 904 598 6100
*Recommended in Real Estate*

**STEARNS, Eugene**
Stearns Weaver Miller Weissler Alhadeff & Sitterson, PA, Miami
305 789 3200
*Recommended in Litigation*

**STEINBERG, Marty**
Hunton & Williams, Miami
305 810 2505
msteinberg@hunton.com
*Recommended in Antitrust, Litigation*
**Practice Areas:** Mr Steinberg's practice focuses on class actions and complex commercial litigation, including contract disputes, business torts, securities litigation, intellectual property, antitrust and products liability. He is a former US Senate Chief Counsel and federal prosecutor with substantial trial experience in a variety of matters. Has substantial experience representing companies in Grand Jury and Senate inquiries. Mr Steinberg is the Miami Office Managing Partner and Fellow of the American College of Trial Lawyers.
**Prof. Memberships:** Fellow, American College of Trial Lawyers; the Florida Bar; the Ohio Bar; ABA; American Bar Foundation, American Pharmaceutical Association, American Association Corporate Counsel.

**STERLING, Mark**
Hogan & Hartson LLP, Miami
305 459 6611
masterling@hhlaw.com
*Recommended in Healthcare*
**Practice Areas:** Practice focuses on strategic and compliance advice and transactions involving federal and state health regulatory issues. Represents hospital systems, long-term care providers, home care programs, medical research institutes, managed care organizations and other healthcare clients.
**Career:** Over 25 years healthcare experience. Helped establish firm's Miami office and leads its Florida Healthcare Practice. Previously served as General Counsel and in executive management role for leading national healthcare services provider; also practiced 14 years in Washington, DC. Has served as Board Chairman and Board Member of non-profit healthcare organizations.
**Personal:** University of Michigan (JD, MPP); Managing Editor, Michigan Law Review.

**STICHTER, Don M**
Stichter, Riedel, Blain & Prosser PA, Tampa 813 229 0144
dstichter@srbp.com
*Recommended in Bankruptcy*
**Practice Areas:** Chapter 11 business reorganizations; workouts and out-of-court loan and debt restructurings; asset acquisitions and sales in bankruptcy cases.
**Prof. Memberships:** Founder and past President, The Tampa Bay Bankruptcy Bar Association. Past President, Hillsborough County Bar Association; honored by The Florida Bar as outstanding local Bar President. One of first three Florida lawyers selected as a Fellow of the American College of Bankruptcy. Named in 2001 by Hillsborough County Bar as Most Outstanding Lawyer. First recipient of the highest award of the Tampa Bay Bankruptcy Bar Association (the Douglas P McClurg Award) for outstanding lifetime contribution to the Bankruptcy Bar; Member, The Florida Bar, American Bar Association, Hillsborough County Bar Association, American Bankruptcy Institute.
**Career:** Attorney, Antitrust Division, US Department of Justice, Washington, DC. Assistant United States Attorney, Tampa. Private practice since 1962. Co-founded Stichter, Riedel, Blain & Prosser, P.A. in 1974.
**Publications:** Co-authored publications on bankruptcy law for The Florida Bar. Speaker on bankruptcy law topics on seminars sponsored by The Florida Bar and other groups.
**Personal:** BA, Colgate University, 1951. LLB, University of Wisconsin, 1957 (Order of the Coif). Member, Editorial Board, University of Wisconsin Law Review.

**STIVER, Charles**
Greenberg Traurig LLP, Miami
305 579 0760
stiverc@gtlaw.com
*Recommended in Tax*
**Practice Areas:** Tax; structured finance and derivatives; real estate investment trusts (REITS).
**Career:** Listed, 'Best Lawyers in America', 2005 and 2006; listed, 'Chambers & Partners USA Guide', 2005-06.
**Personal:** LLM, New York University School of Law, 1975; JD, Stanford Law School, 1974; BA, Stanford University, 1971.

**STOCKER, Joel L**
Greenberg Traurig LLP, Fort Lauderdale
954 768 8217
stockerj@gtlaw.com
*Recommended in Healthcare*
**Practice Areas:** Health business.
**Prof. Memberships:** Member, American Health Lawyers Association.
**Career:** Listed, 'Best Lawyers in America', 2003, 2004 and 2005 editions.
**Personal:** JD, University of Michigan Law School, 1972; BA, University of Michigan, 1969.

**STRAFER, Richard**
G Richard Strafer PA, Miami
305 857 9090
*Recommended in Litigation*

**STUBBS, Sidney**
Jones, Foster, Johnston & Stubbs, P.A., West Palm Beach 561 659 3000
*Recommended in Litigation*

**STUTTS, Charles**
Holland & Knight LLP, Tampa
813 227 8500
charles.stutts@hklaw.com
*Recommended in Banking & Finance*
**Practice Areas:** Partner in Business Law Department, focusing on securities and banking law. Former General Counsel to the Florida Comptroller's Office and the Department of Banking and Finance, he helped develop the agency's policies on banking, mortgage lending and securities regulation, directed their securities enforcement efforts and co-ordinated prosecutions under Florida's antifraud provisions with the SEC. Devotes a substantial portion of his practice to federal and state supervision and regulation of banks, trust companies, securities broker-dealers and investment advisors. Serves as Equity Receiver in securities and financial fraud matters brought by the SEC and other regulatory and law enforcement agencies.

**SUBIN, Ben**
Holland & Knight LLP, Orlando
407 425 8500
ben.subin@hklaw.com
*Recommended in Construction*
**Practice Areas:** Ben W Subin is a Partner in Holland & Knight's Construction Practice Group. He is a Florida Bar Board Certified Construction Lawyer. Mr Subin has handled matters involving complex construction litigation regarding defects, delay damages, acceleration claims, changed conditions, default terminations and bid protests. Mr Subin also has extensive experience representing clients concerning power generation and water treatment projects. He assists clients in construction contract preparation and review as well as surety claims and defense. Mr Subin is a frequent lecturer on a variety of construction law topics.

**SUMBERG, John C**
Bilzin Sumberg Baena Price & Axelrod LLP, Miami 305 350 2364
jsumberg@bilzin.com
*Recommended in Real Estate*
**Practice Areas:** Mr Sumberg has extensive experience in all aspects of real estate acquisition and disposition, development, financing, joint ventures, workouts and restructurings. He represents owners, investors and lenders in connection with commercial, retail, mixed-use and resi-

dential real estate projects, including condominiums, condo/hotels, apartments and planned community projects. Also serves as Managing Partner of the firm. **Career:** Author of various articles on real estate matters, including urban infill revitalization, sale leasebacks and commercial leasing. Listed in 'Best Lawyers of America' and Florida Trend's Legal Elite. **Personal:** JD Yale Law School, editor, Yale Law Journal; BA magna cum laude, Yale College.

## TAGUE, Brian
Tew Cardenas LLP, Miami
305 536 1112
*Recommended in Real Estate*

## TARBE, Susan J
Colson Hicks Eidson, Coral Gables
305 476 7400
susan@colson.com
*Recommended in Litigation*
**Practice Areas:** Commercial law; white-collar criminal defense
**Career:** Ms Tarbe has over 15 years of experience in commercial litigation and white-collar criminal defense, specializing in civil and criminal healthcare fraud, SEC enforcement and internal corporate investigations; has more than 11 years of federal trial and grand jury practice as an Assistant United States Attorney with the United States Attorney's Office where she was Chief of the Economic Crimes Division; graduated cum laude from the University of Miami School of Law; clerked for the Honorable William M Hoeveler, United States District Court for the Southern District of Florida.

## TAYLOR, Jennifer M
Akerman Senterfitt, Miami
305 374 5600
jennifer.taylor@akerman.com
*Recommended in Employment*
**Career:** Jennifer M Taylor, an associate with the Labor and Employment Practice Group, provides advice, counseling, and representation to private sector employers regarding labor and employment issues. Representation includes litigation in federal and state courts arising under Title VII of the Civil Rights Act, ADA, ADEA, ERISA, FMLA, FLSA, the Florida Civil Rights Act, the Florida Whistleblower Act, and federal and state constitutional claims. In addition, she advises employers on human resources issues, including personnel policies and procedures, discipline and discharge matters, drug and alcohol testing, employee privacy rights, and conducts education and training programs for managers and supervisors.

## TEBLUM, Gary
Trenam, Kemker, Scharf, Barkin, Frye, O'Neill & Mullis PA, Tampa
813 223 7474
*Recommended in Corporate/M&A*

## TESCHER, Donald
Tescher Gutter Chaves Josepher Rubin Ruffin & Forman PA, Boca Ratón
561 998 7847
*Recommended in Tax, Wealth Management*

## TEW, Thomas
Tew Cardenas LLP, Miami
305 536 1112
*Recommended in Litigation*

## THOMAS, Harry
Radey, Thomas, Yon & Clark, Tallahassee 850 425 6654
*Recommended in Insurance*

## THOMSON, Parker
Hogan & Hartson LLP, Miami
305 459 6613
pdthomson@hhlaw.com
*Recommended in Environment, Litigation*
**Practice Areas:** Managing Partner of Florida offices. Currently or recently engaged in intensive federal and state court litigation relating to water rights and endangered species litigation in Apalachicola, Chattahoochee, Flint River basin; Everglades: oil and gas interests in Gulf of Mexico; and sovereignty submerged lands. His commitment to public service has earned him numerous awards for significant pro bono contributions, for volunteer legal assistance to impoverished persons and persons with disabilities and other civic efforts.
**Prof. Memberships:** Chairman or President, Miami-Dade Performing Arts Center Trust, 1988-present.
**Personal:** Harvard Law School (JD, magna cum laude).

## THOMPSON, Patricia H
Carlton Fields, Miami
305 539 7239
pthompson@carltonfields.com
*Recommended in Construction, Employment*
**Practice Areas:** Practices in the areas of construction, surety, fidelity and other commercial insurance coverage, employment, and commercial litigation.
**Prof. Memberships:** Member, American College of Construction Lawyers; The Florida Bar, former Chair of The Florida Bar Eleventh Circuit Unauthorized Practice of Law Committee 'A'; Florida Bar Grievance Committee; American Bar Association, Tort Trial and Insurance Practice Section, Labor and Employment Section; Fellow, American Bar Foundation; The Defense Research Institute; American Arbitration Association. International Who's Who of Construction Lawyers.
**Personal:** JD, Vanderbilt University, 1976; BA (magna cum laude), Saint Olaf College, 1973.

## THROCKMORTON, Charles W
Kozyak Tropin & Throckmorton, Miami
305 377 0655
cwt@kttlaw.com
*Recommended in Bankruptcy*
**Practice Areas:** Bankruptcy; debtors' and creditors' rights; workouts; commercial litigation.
**Prof. Memberships:** American Bar Association; American Bankruptcy Institute; Bankruptcy Bar Association for the Southern District of Florida; Association of Commercial Finance Attorneys.
**Career:** Represents high net worth individuals, debtors, secured/unsecured creditors, equity, management, committees, trustees in major Florida bankruptcies. Also specializes in commercial/business litigation trial practice. Co-founder and Shareholder, Kozyak Tropin & Throckmorton, P.A., 1983-present. Associate, Mahoney Hadlow & Adams, 1979-83. Listed in Best Lawyers in America. Listed in Florida Super Lawyers 2006.
**Personal:** Born Norfolk, Virginia, 1955. University of Virginia School of Law, JD 1979; Duke University, BA (magna cum laude), 1976.

## TOWNSEND, William
Fowler White Boggs Banker, Tampa
813 228 7411
*Recommended in Tax*

## TRAURIG, Robert
Greenberg Traurig LLP, Miami
305 579 0500
traurigr@gtlaw.com
*Recommended in Real Estate*
**Practice Areas:** Environmental; real estate; land development.
**Prof. Memberships:** Member, Citizen's Board of the University of Miami; Director, Greater Miami Jewish Federation; Member, Board of Trustees, Beth David Congregation; past Chairman, Greater Miami Chamber of Commerce; immediate past Chairman, Miami Region of the National Conference.
**Career:** Listed, 'The Best Lawyers in America', all editions; recognized as one of 'Florida's Influential', Florida Trend Magazine, 2004; listed, 'Chambers & Partners USA Guide', 2004-06; listed, South Florida's Top Lawyers by the 'South Florida Legal Guide', 2002 and 2005.
**Personal:** JD, University of Miami School of Law, 1950; BBA, University of Miami, 1947.

## TROMBLEY, Gary
Trombley & Hanes, Tampa
813 229 7918
*Recommended in Litigation*

## TROPIN, Harley S
Kozyak Tropin & Throckmorton, Miami
305 372 1800
hst@kttlaw.com
*Recommended in Litigation*
**Practice Areas:** Senior Litigation Practice Partner.

**Prof. Memberships:** Florida Bar (former Chair, Federal Courts Committee); Eleventh Circuit Judicial Nominating Commission (Member, 1986-90; Chair 1989); Eleventh Circuit Judicial Conference (Southern District Delegate, 1994-97); Professor of Trial Advocacy, University of Miami School of Law; Iron Arrow (2003, highest honor attainable at University of Miami).
**Career:** Specializes in complex commercial litigation and class actions. Co-founder, Kozyak Tropin & Throckmorton (1982) and leads the firm's Litigation Team. Co-lead counsel in the largest class-action lawsuit of its kind on record against managed-care companies. Co-ordinated all litigation resulting from the largest Ponzi scheme in Florida's history. Recognized in 'Best Lawyers in America' (1996-) and named in top-tier litigation category, 'Bet-The-Company' Litigation. Selected a 'Most Effective Lawyer' by Daily Business Review, published by ALM (American Lawyer Media). Listed in Florida Super Lawyers 2006.
**Publications:** Wrote the injunction chapter for 'Florida Civil Practice Before Trial', a standard Florida litigation text.
**Personal:** Born Bayside, New York. The George Washington University (BA, 1974); University of Miami School of Law (JD, 1977, cum laude).

## TURK, Robert
Stearns Weaver Miller Weissler Alhadeff & Sitterson, PA, Miami
305 789 3200
*Recommended in Employment*

## UDOLF, Bruce
Berger Singerman, Fort Lauderdale
954 525 9900
*Recommended in Litigation*

## ULLMAN, Samuel C
Bilzin Sumberg Baena Price & Axelrod LLP, Miami 305 350 7300
sullman@bilzin.com
*Recommended in Tax*
**Prof. Memberships:** The Florida Bar: former Chairman, Tax Section; former Chairman, Tax Law Certification Committee. Fellow, American College of Tax Counsel; Fellow, American Law Institute.
**Career:** Florida Bar Board Certified Tax Attorney since 1983. Business and transactional tax matters, federal tax controversies, state and local tax, tax-exempt organizations. Counsels clients on federal and state tax matters, mergers, acquisitions, business combinations, business law, and taxation of healthcare-related matters. Represents clients in matters before the IRS and state tax authorities. Served as Special Counsel to the Florida Department of Revenue. Recipient Florida Bar Tax Section Outstanding Attorney Award, 1993-94.

## VALDIVIA III, José
Hogan & Hartson LLP, Miami
305 459 6646
jfvaldivia@hhlaw.com
*Recommended in Corporate/M&A*
**Practice Areas:** Practice focuses on development and financing of infrastructure projects, mergers and acquisitions, and other commercial transactions, particularly in Latin America.
**Prof. Memberships:** Board of Directors, Amigos of the Cuban Heritage Collection, University of Miami; International Law Sections, American and Florida Bar Associations; New York Bar Association.
**Career:** Honorary member of the Caracas (Federal District) Bar Association; Adjunct Professor University of Miami School of Law (Project Development and Finance); Certified Public Accountant.
**Personal:** LLM, New York University School of Law, 1985; JD, magna cum laude, Georgetown University Law Center, 1984; BBA, cum laude, University of Notre Dame, 1980.

## VÁZQUEZ-BELLO, Clemente
Gunster, Yoakley & Stewart, PA, Miami
305 376 6000
*Recommended in Banking & Finance*

## VEZINA, Rob
Vezina Lawrence & Piscitelli PA, Tallahassee 850 224 6205
*Recommended in Construction*

## VICKERS, Cass
Vickers Madsen & Goldman, Tallahassee 850 523 0400
*Recommended in Tax*

## VOGEL III, Edward W
Holland & Knight LLP, Lakeland
813 227 8500
ed.vogel@hklaw.com
*Recommended in Banking & Finance*
**Practice Areas:** Partner in the firm's Business Section, he practices in the areas of tax-exempt bond financing, corporate financing and corporate leveraged leasing. He has been responsible for numerous industrial development, city, county, and special district bond issues, and played a key role as bond counsel for the first tax increment bonds issued in Florida and for the first bonds in the US issued to fund post-employment benefit liabilities of a municipality. He is a Member of the American Bar Association, The Florida Bar and the National Association of Bond Lawyers.

## WACHTER, Charles
Fowler White Boggs Banker, Tampa
813 228 7411
*Recommended in Insurance*

## WAKSHLAG, Stanley
Kenny Nachwalter PA, Miami
305 373 1000
sw@kennynachwalter.com
*Recommended in Litigation*
**Prof. Memberships:** American Inns of Court, The Florida Bar, American Bar Association, Dade County Bar Association.
**Career:** Stanley H Wakshlag, is a shareholder who focuses his practice in the areas of securities litigation and regulatory proceedings, complex commercial litigation, antitrust and class actions. Mr Wakshlag's litigation experience includes the representation of major institutional clients in the area of complex commercial litigation including securities, lender liability, banking, foreclosure, antitrust, ERISA, trademark, entertainment, partnership and corporate litigation. He also specializes in internal corporate, audit and special committee investigations. His experience has resulted in numerous favorable published judicial opinions.
**Personal:** 1978, JD New York University School of Law. 1974, BA, Brandeis University, magna cum laude, Phi Beta Kappa.

## WALBOLT, Sylvia
Carlton Fields, Tampa
813 223 7000
swalbolt@carltonfields.com
*Recommended in Litigation*
**Practice Areas:** Practices appellate law in federal and state court, in all areas of the law, including tort, products liability, commercial, constitutional and employment discrimination. She has appeared as counsel in more than 250 published opinions. Board Certified in Appellate Law by The Florida Bar.
**Prof. Memberships:** Admitted to practice in Florida and US Supreme Court. Fellow, American Academy of Appellate Lawyers; Fellow, American College of Trial Lawyers; Member, American Law Institute.
**Publications:** Co-author, 'Amicus Briefs: Friend or Foe of Florida Courts?' (Stetson Law Review 2003).
**Personal:** JD, University of Florida College of Law, 1963; BA, University of Florida, 1961.

## WALKER, Steve
Lewis, Longman & Walker PA, West Palm Beach
561 640 0820
*Recommended in Environment*

## WALKER, JR, H William
White & Case LLP, Miami
305 995 5205
wwalker@whitecase.com
*Recommended in Real Estate*
**Practice Areas:** Areas of practice include all aspects of real estate acquisition and disposition, ownership, use, development and finance, and general corporate matters. Has participated in and represented owners of, investors in and lenders to numerous complex commercial, residential, retail, industrial, hospitality and mixed-use real estate projects, including those of major domestic and international developers. Also participated in the planning, development, financing and sale of a variety of planned communities, including primary housing, resort housing, hospitality and mixed-use properties.
**Prof. Memberships:** The Florida Bar.

## WALLER JR, Edward
Fowler White Boggs Banker, Tampa
813 228 7411
*Recommended in Healthcare*

## WARE, Rex
Fowler White Boggs Banker, Tampa
813 228 7411
*Recommended in Tax*

## WARNER, Jonathan
Law Offices of Jonathan H. (Jason) Warner, PA, Miami
305 670 0007 *Recommended in Tax*

## WARREN, Jeffrey
Bush Ross Gardner Warren & Rudy, PA, Tampa 813 224 9255
*Recommended in Bankruptcy*

## WEAVER, Ronald
Stearns Weaver Miller Weissler Alhadeff & Sitterson, P.A., Tampa 813 223 4800
*Recommended in Real Estate*

## WEBER, Victoria
Hopping Green & Sams, PA, Tallahassee
850 222 7500
vweber@hgslaw.com
*Recommended in Tax*
**Practice Areas:** State and local tax planning and controversy work; economic development incentives; and legislative relations.
**Prof. Memberships:** The Florida Bar, past Chair, State Tax Division; ABA State and Local Tax Committee; Florida Chamber of Commerce, past Chair of both Tax Committee and Legislative Affairs Committee.
**Career:** 26 years in state and local tax, including service as General Counsel to Florida Department of Revenue, Tax Counsel to Florida House of Representatives, and 15 years in private practice representing Florida, national and international businesses, and Florida trade associations.
**Personal:** JD with honors, and BS, Florida State University.

## WEEKLEY, Augustine S
Holland & Knight LLP, Tampa
813 227 8500
gus.weekley@hklaw.com
*Recommended in Healthcare*
**Practice Areas:** Senior counsel in the Business Section, he is experienced in the areas of health and hospital law, medical staff issues, nursing home law, administrative law, Medicare, healthcare provider licensing law and medical malpractice defense. He maintained a private surgical practice prior to practicing law. Dr Weekley is a member of the American Medical Association, National Health Lawyers Association, American Society of Law and Medicine, American Bar Association, The Florida Bar, the District of Columbia Bar and the Association of Trial Lawyers of America.

## WEINBERG JR, Morris
Zuckerman Spaeder LLP, Tampa
813 221 1010
*Recommended in Litigation*

## WEINSTEIN, Andrew
Holland & Knight LLP, Miami
305 374 8500
andrew.weinstein@hklaw.com
*Recommended in Tax*
**Practice Areas:** Partner in the firm's Business Section. His practice involves domestic and international tax, trust and estate planning for high net worth clients. Served as lead counsel for multi-billion dollar estates and trusts. Extensive experience in federal tax disputes, including tax evasion, especially involving tax shelter compliance. Member of ABA Tax Section of Administrative Practice, Fellow of American College of Tax Counsel and American College of Trusts and Estates Counsel.

## WEINSTEIN, David
Bales Weinstein, Tampa
813 224 9100
*Recommended in Environment*

## WEINTRAUB, Lee
Becker & Poliakoff PA, Fort Lauderdale
954 987 7550
*Recommended in Construction*

## WEISS, Christopher
Holland & Knight LLP, Orlando
407 425 8500
christopher.weiss@hklaw.com
*Recommended in Construction*
**Practice Areas:** Partner in the Litigation Section, practices in the area of commercial litigation with particular emphasis on construction law, defects in construction, design claims, delay, disruption and acceleration claims, lien foreclosures, and arbitration on behalf of contractors, subcontractors, materialmen, developers and public bodies. He is a board certified construction lawyer, frequent lecturer and author of articles pertaining to commercial litigation and construction law for Bar and trade associations. He is an active Member and panelist of the American Arbitration Association, Associated Builders and Contractors, the Construction Financial Management Association, Associated General Contractors of America and the American Subcontractors Association.

## WEITZMAN, Allan H
Proskauer Rose LLP, Boca Ratón
561 995 4760
aweitzman@proskauer.com
*Recommended in Employment*
**Practice Areas:** Labor and employment law.
**Prof. Memberships:** College of Labor and Employment Lawyers, Academy of Florida Management Attorneys, New

York State Management Attorneys Conference, Society for Human Resource Management, Human Resouce Association of Palm Beach County, Human Resource Association of Broward County.
**Career:** Proskauer Rose LLP (1973-present).
**Publications:** Numerous articles published in the National Law Journal, HR Advisor and other employment law publications.
**Personal:** Cornell University, BS 1970, Cornell Law School, JD 1973, with distinction. Married: Regina A Weitzman.

**WELBAUM, Earl**
Welbaum, Guernsey, Hingston, Greenleaf & Gregory LLP, Miami
305 441 8900
*Recommended in Construction*

**WILSON, Michael**
Broad and Cassel, Orlando
407 839 4200
*Recommended in Construction*

**WILSON III, Harry**
Smith Hulsey & Busey, Jacksonville
904 359 7700
*Recommended in Real Estate*

**WINSTON, Richard L**
Squire, Sanders & Dempsey L.L.P., Miami 305 577 7025
rwinston@ssd.com
*Recommended in Tax*
**Practice Areas:** Focuses on structuring and analyzing US and cross-border transactions for US and non-US multinationals. Specializes in planning for acquisitions, dispositions, reorganizations, joint ventures and finance company arrangements. Assists clients with foreign tax credit planning, tax deferral techniques, choice of entity decisions, repatriation planning, transfer pricing issues, intellectual property development and Subpart F issues.
**Prof. Memberships:** Lexis-Nexis Butterworths Tolly (UK) International Tax and Investment Service, US Chapter.
**Personal:** JD, University of Virginia,

1994 (Editor, Virginia Law Review and Virginia Tax Review); BA (high distinction), University of Virginia, 1990; LLM (taxation), New York University, 1995.

**WOLFSON, Mark J**
Foley & Lardner LLP, Tampa
813 225 4119
mwolfson@foley.com
*Recommended in Bankruptcy*
**Career:** Mark J Wolfson is Chair of the Litigation Department in the Tampa office of Foley & Lardner LLP, and the Leader of the firm's Business Reorganizations Practice Group for the Southeast region. Mr Wolfson has extensive experience in bankruptcy cases, primarily representing secured creditors, creditors' committees, buyers of assets in Chapter 11, shareholders and parties to contracts. He has experience in both state and US bankruptcy courts litigating fraudulent transfer and preference actions and has been involved in state assignment for the benefit of creditor proceedings. Mr Wolfson received his Law Degree from the University of Florida.

**WOODSON, R Duke**
Foley & Lardner LLP, Orlando
407 244 3247
dwoodson@foley.com
*Recommended in Real Estate*
**Career:** R Duke Woodson, Partner in the Orlando office of Foley & Lardner LLP, heads the firm's Environmental Law Practice in Florida. He also is a member of the Real Estate Practice Group and Golf and Resort Services Industry Team. He represents business and governmental clients throughout the state in environmental compliance and permitting matters. Mr Woodson's extensive experience is in environmental law with emphasis on real estate development. Mr Woodson received his JD from the University of Florida in 1975. He holds Undergraduate and Master's Degrees in civil engineering from Auburn University.

**WORSHAM, Lee**
Ruden McClosky SC, West Palm Beach
561 838 4500
*Recommended in Environment*

**YADLEY, Gregory**
Shumaker Loop & Kendrick LLP, Tampa
813 229 7600
*Recommended in Corporate/M&A*

**YON, David**
Radey, Thomas, Yon & Clark, Tallahasse
850 425 6654
*Recommended in Insurance*

**YOUNG, Terry**
Lowndes Drosdick Doster Kantor & Reed, PA, Orlando
407 843 4600
*Recommended in Litigation*

**ZALDIVAR, Miguel A**
Hogan & Hartson LLP, Miami
305 459 6636
mazaldivar@hhlaw.com
*Recommended in Corporate/M&A*
**Practice Areas:** Focuses on project finance, M&A, privatizations, and cross-border corporate matters in Latin America. Assists US and European corporations in the development and operation of business activities in Latin America as well as Latin American companies in the expansion of their business activities throughout the Americas. Also, advises Latin American state-owned companies in a wide variety of international matters.
**Prof. Memberships:** Member of the Fulbright Association.
**Career:** Adjunct Professor, University of Miami School of Law: Project Finance and Development.
**Personal:** JD, University of Miami, 1995; LLM, University of Illinois College of Law, 1988; LLB, Universidad Católica Andrés Bello, 1986.

**ZELEK, Mark E**
Morgan, Lewis & Bockius LLP, Miami
305 415 3303
mzelek@morganlewis.com
*Recommended in Employment*
**Practice Areas:** Mark E Zelek is a Partner in the Labor and Employment Practice. He currently serves as the Miami office's Managing Partner. Mr Zelek's practice focuses on representing companies in employment law trials and arbitrations, including overtime, discrimination, and non-compete cases and class actions. Mr Zelek also handles international labor law matters, advising foreign companies on US labor law and domestic companies on Latin American labor law. He was recently named 'The Achiever' by Miami Today and is a graduate of Yale and Columbia Law School.
**Prof. Memberships:** Former Chair, American Bar Association, International Section's Subcommittee on Latin American Employment Law; Co-Chair, Greater Miami Chamber of Commerce, Human Resource Committee.

**ZEWADSKI, William Knight**
Trenam, Kemker, Scharf, Barkin, Frye, O'Neill & Mullis PA, Tampa
813 223 7474
*Recommended in Bankruptcy*

**ZIMET, Bruce**
Bruce A Zimet PA, Fort Lauderdale
954 764 7081
*Recommended in Litigation*

**ZINOBER, Peter**
Zinober & McCrea, P.A., Tampa
813 224 9004
*Recommended in Employment*

# AKERMAN SENTERFITT

## THE FIRM

**Chairman & CEO:** J Thomas Cardwell

**FIRM OVERVIEW:** Akerman Senterfitt, one of Florida's leading law firms, has more than 425 attorneys and consultants servicing the needs of local, regional, national and international clients. Founded in 1920, the firm now has offices in Florida's major business centers and in Washington, DC and New York.

## MAIN AREAS OF PRACTICE:

**Corporate:** Akerman Senterfitt has the largest Corporate Practice in Florida with more than 100 attorneys. The firm represents domestic and foreign public companies, including half of the largest public companies in Florida. Akerman Senterfitt also represents financial institutions, private equity and venture capital funds, and the companies in which they invest, and individual entrepreneurs. Primary areas of focus include mergers and acquisitions, securities, taxation, public finance, banking and lending and employee benefits.

**Environmental:** Representing both the private and public sectors, Akerman Senterfitt's environmental attorneys have substantial experience working with a wide variety of businesses, governmental entities, and other organizations. The firm handles federal, state, and local regulatory compliance and permitting, managing environmental risks and conducting due diligence investigations, managing the assessment and remediation of contaminated property, defending enforcement actions, and prosecuting or defending civil actions to recover cleanup costs or environmental damages to property.

**Government Relations:** Akerman Senterfitt has built a large and effective Government Practice with points of entry into almost every governmental or quasi-governmental body of Florida, and into many agencies in Washington. Firm attorneys are experts in effectively lobbying and dialoging with these agencies and when the situation warrants, they also have extensive experience in conduction administrative proceedings or litigation against them.

**Insurance:** Employing a team approach, Akerman Senterfitt attorneys have been providing legal and regulatory services to the insurance industry for more than 30 years. Its group of more than 45 attorneys and consultants represents every major US company and many foreign insurance companies, as well as regional carriers and start-ups. The group includes former regulators, insurance executives and arbitrators, who collectively have knowledge about every aspect of the insurance industry.

**Intellectual Property:** Akerman Senterfitt's Intellectual Property Practice is the largest and most broadly experienced in Florida. The firm's IP lawyers are engineers and scientists from many rapidly developing fields of industry such as fuel cells, biomedical devices, semiconductor materials and software. This knowledge base helps the firm's lawyers to create broader patents, draft better contracts, develop more profitable licenses, and litigate more effectively. The firm represents clients across the globe including many *Fortune* 500 firms and major research universities.

**International:** As Florida's role in international trade and finance expands, Akerman Senterfitt has developed a multilingual, multicultural, cross-disciplinary international practice. The firm's goal is to assist both US clients expand their international business activities and foreign clients in establishing businesses and flourishing in the United States. The International Practice Group includes attorneys from all the firm's offices and from every major practice group.

**Labor and Employment:** Akerman Senterfitt's Labor and Employment Law Practice Group is one of the largest and most comprehensive in the state, with more attorneys Board-Certified by The Florida Bar in employment law than any other law firm in Florida. The firm provides representation to public and private employers in all aspects of human resources, employment discrimination litigation, OSHA compliance and labor relations issues, and has extensive experience in NLRA, FLSA, Older Workers Benefit Protection Act, EPA, OSHA, ERISA, FMLA and ADA issues.

**Litigation:** Akerman Senterfitt's Commercial Litigation Practice Group is the largest in Florida, with more than 200 litigators representing leading public and private companies doing business in Florida and throughout the US. Litigators

## US OFFICES

**DISTRICT OF COLUMBIA**
801 Pennsylvania Avenue NW, Suite 750, **Washington**, DC 20004
**Tel:** 202 393 6222　**Fax:** 202 393 5959

**FLORIDA**
Las Olas Centre II, 350 East Las Olas Boulevard, Suite 1600,
**Fort Lauderdale**, FL 33301-2229
**Tel:** 954 463 2700　**Fax:** 954 463 2224

50 North Laura Street, Suite 2500 **Jacksonville**, FL 32202-3646
**Tel:** 904 798 3700　**Fax:** 904 798 3730

One Southeast Third Avenue, 28th Floor, **Miami**, FL 33131-1714
**Tel:** 305 374 5600　**Fax:** 305 374 5095

CNL Tower II, 12th Floor, 420 South Orange Avenue,
**Orlando**, FL 32801-4904
**Tel:** 407 843 7860　**Fax:** 407 843 6610

106 East College Avenue, Suite 1200, **Tallahassee**, FL 32301
**Tel:** 850 224 9634　**Fax:** 850 222 0103

Suntrust Financial Centre, Suite 1700, 401 East Jackson Street,
**Tampa**, FL 33602-5803
**Tel:** 813 223 7333　**Fax:** 813 223 2837

Esperante Building, 222 Lakeview Avenue, Fourth Floor,
**West Palm Beach**, FL 33401-6183
**Tel:** 561 653 5000　**Fax:** 561 659 6313

**NEW YORK**
335 Madison Avenue, Suite 2600, **New York**, NY 10017-4636
**Tel:** 212 880 3800　**Fax:** 212 880 8965

routinely handle cases encompassing legal claims such as antitrust, patent infringement, construction and property damages, fraud, civil theft and misappropriation, and the violation of banking laws. The firm also has both an Alternative Dispute Resolution Litigation Group and an Appellate Practice Group, both of which benefit from the guidance of two former federal judges.

**Private Client Services:** Akerman Senterfitt has built a broadly experienced and highly respected Trusts, Estates, and Family Law Practice. Not only does the firm administer and litigate personal legal matters, it has crafted some of the laws that govern these affairs. The firm's statewide presence allows it to manage the legal issues of families and their businesses regardless of venue. And the attorneys understand the types of litigation that arise in this area and can design agreements that minimize the possibility of future legal actions.

**Real Estate:** Akerman Senterfitt has more than 80 lawyers who focus on the needs of clients in the real estate industry. This represents one of the largest full-service real estate practices in Florida. The firm manages the legal aspects of large land deals and construction projects, assists developers in meeting tough environmental regulations, and advises on all aspects of transactional work, including workouts and restructurings. The firm's focus areas include land use and entitlements, debt and equity finance, income property, and the acquisition and development of projects within all real estate asset classes.

**CLIENTS:** Akerman Senterfitt represents a high percentage of the largest public companies in Florida, as well as private companies, government entities, educational establishments and high net worth individuals.

# ASTIGARRAGA DAVIS

## THE FIRM

**Contact:** José I Astigarraga

### AREAS OF PRACTICE:
Litigation & Arbitration . . . . . . . . . . . . . . . . . . . . . . . . . . . . . . . . .100%

**FIRM OVERVIEW:** Astigarraga Davis is a litigation and arbitration firm. With a broad range of experience, its lawyers prosecute and defend a wide variety of commercial litigation and business tort cases. Serving primarily multinational corporate clients, the firm's principal areas of practice are international litigation and arbitration; financial services litigation including bankruptcy; prosecution of commercial fraud including asset recovery; defense of consumer class actions; and intellectual property litigation.

## MAIN AREAS OF PRACTICE:

**Litigation & Arbitration:** Representing primarily North American and European multinational companies, Astigarraga Davis both prosecutes and defends cases in federal and state courts involving international business disputes. Using its extensive international experience, multilingual capabilities, multicultural background, and broad network of contacts in the region, the firm also oversees and directs substantial business litigation pending in Latin American courts. The firm has a leading International Arbitration Practice handling cases before the major international arbitral institutions. The firm's lawyers are active in arbitration and litigation initiatives. José Astigarraga, for example, was one of eight delegates appointed by the United States Government to advise the NAFTA Commission on international arbitration and dispute resolution. He is a member of the American Arbitration Association's International Rules Advisory Committee, serves as Vice President of the London Court of International Arbitration, and has lectured extensively on international litigation and arbitration including to the negotiators of the Free Trade Agreement of the Americas. Astigarraga Davis represents companies in investment disputes with foreign states, including before the International Centre for Investment Disputes (ICSID).

**Financial Services Litigation, including Bankruptcy:** Astigarraga Davis has extensive litigation experience representing lenders, creditors, banks and other financial institutions in disputes in the United States and abroad. The firm represents financial institutions in state and federal court litigation in investor disputes, securities issues, and loan enforcement. The firm's lawyers handle much creditors' rights litigation including such pre-judgment creditors' remedies as replevin, garnishment, attachment and injunctions.

As well, the firm represents lenders and creditors domestically in bankruptcy courts in Florida and other states, and internationally in Latin America, including in multijurisdictional insolvencies. Founding shareholder Greg Grossman has extensive bankruptcy experience, having handled cases in a number of domestic bankruptcy courts in a diverse array of cases and has lectured on a variety of insolvency related topics. José Astigarraga has served as consultant to the World Bank on Latin American insolvency law issues and has handled international insolvency cases for both bank and non-bank clients.

**Commercial Fraud & Asset Recovery:** The firm's work includes a strong practice in fraud prosecution and asset recovery. Working with its network of lawyers and contacts, the firm has pursued fraudsters in a variety of jurisdictions to recover fraudulently obtained assets. The firm also devises fraud prevention and contingency response plans for corporate clients and advises audit committees on such issues. Name partner Edward H Davis, Jr. is a Certified Fraud Examiners and has lectured extensively on fraud prosecution and international asset recovery.

### HEAD OFFICE

**FLORIDA**
701 Brickell Avenue, 16th Floor, **Miami** FL 33131
**Tel:** 305 372 8282   **Fax:** 305 372 8202
**Email:** jia@astidavis.com
**Website:** www.astidavis.com

**Defense of Consumer Class Actions:** Astigarraga Davis has experienced class action litigators, including founding shareholder Edward Mullins who has defended numerous class actions in state and federal courts. He has defended financial institutions and insurance companies in claims involving the Truth-in-Lending Act, the Florida Unfair Trade Practices Act, Telephone Protection Act, Florida's usury statute, and claims derived from various consumer insurance statutes. The firm's expertise in arbitration has benefited the class action defense practice, including in litigation over whether arbitration clauses in consumer contracts are unconscionable and unenforceable.

**Intellectual Property:** The firm has extensive experience in intellectual property, with capabilities including trademark, trade secret, internet, e-commerce, and media law disputes. Founding shareholder Edward Mullins, a former chair of the Florida Bar Media and Communications Law Committee, has represented newspapers, magazines, radio and television stations, and television networks in numerous lawsuits involving libel, slander, invasion of privacy, outrage, tortious interference with advantageous relationships, trademark infringement, copyright infringement and other publication disputes. The firm's deep knowledge allows it to represent its corporate clients in domain name disputes, intellectual property infringement claims based on the internet, and similar publication claims.

**CLIENTS:** Astigarraga Davis' clients include multinational companies, global banks, Fortune 500 corporations and government entities.

# ASTIGARRAGA DAVIS

# BERCOW & RADELL, PA

## THE FIRM

**Managing Partner:** Michael Radell
**Senior Partner:** Jeffrey Bercow

**Number of partners:** 4
**Number of other lawyers:** 4

### AREAS OF PRACTICE:

| | |
|---|---|
| Land Use | 25% |
| Zoning | 25% |
| Growth Management | 25% |
| Environmental | 25% |

**FIRM OVERVIEW:** Bercow & Radell, PA commenced its law practice in 1996. The firm's attorneys include Jeffrey Bercow and Michael Radell, its co-founding shareholders, as well as partners Ben Fernandez and Michael Larkin, and Graham Penn, Melissa Tapanes Llahues, Michael Marrero and Matthew Amster, who are associates with the firm. The firm specializes in land use, zoning, growth management and environmental matters. It represents the interests of landowners and developers seeking approvals from governmental boards and agencies at the local, state and federal levels. The firm handles a range of matters that concern the use of real estate including zoning approvals, amendments of local government comprehensive plans, developments of regional impact (DRIs), due diligence reviews, growth management, impact fees, concurrency issues and environmental matters. The attorneys of Bercow & Radell, PA have represented clients before such local governments as: Miami-Dade County, Miami, Coral Gables, Miami Springs, Aventura, Pinecrest, Miami Beach, Doral, Miami Lakes, Miami Gardens, Medley, North Miami Beach, North Miami, Key Biscayne, Opa-Locka, South Miami, Hialeah, Pembroke Pines, Greenacres, Plantation, Homestead, Collier County, Orange County, Marion County and the City of Ocala. Members of the firm appear frequently before the South Florida Regional Planning Council, Miami-Dade County's Board of County Commissioners, Community Councils/Zoning Appeals Boards, Planning Advisory Board, and the Environmental Quality Control Board; the City of Miami Beach City Commission, Zoning Board of Adjustment, Design Review Board/Historic Preservation Board, and Planning Board; City of Miami City Commission, Zoning Board, and Planning Advisory Board; the South Florida Water Management District; the St. John's Water Management District, and other local governmental bodies, and also frequently lobby staff of the Florida Department of Community Affairs. In addition, the firm often represents its clients in appellate litigation involving the administrative matters it has handled.

## HEAD OFFICE

**FLORIDA**
200 South Biscayne Boulevard, Suite 850, **Miami**, FL 33131
**Tel:** 305 374 5300  **Fax:** 305 377 6222
**Email:** Jbercow@brzoninglaw.com

**CLIENTS:** The firm represents developers, landowners, lenders and others with property interests affected by the laws and regulations that govern the use of real estate in various counties and cities within South Florida. Clients include, Florida Rock Industries, Home Depot USA, Turnberry Associates, Woolbright Development, Maefield Development, Adrian Development Group, EB Developers, Crosswinds Communities, The Congress Group, Mt. Sinai Medical Center, Walgreen Company, Lennar Homes, Gulfside-Dadeland, BMS Management Company, Target Stores, Johnson & Wales University, United Homes, Weitzer Development, City Furniture, R.L. Homes, Pinnacle Housing, Lucky Start, Cornerstone Group, General Real Estate Corporation, Sterling Centrecorp, Century Five, International Place Associates, Marriott International, Miami Beach Vacation Resorts, Peebles Development Corporation, Aventura Marina, Trafalgar Associates, Williamson Cadillac Company, Terranova, BP Amoco, Landstar Homes, Pelican Bay Development, Ocwen Federal Bank, and Lowell Dunn Company.

**BERCOW & RADELL**
ZONING, LAND USE AND ENVIRONMENTAL LAW

# BILZIN SUMBERG BAENA PRICE & AXELROD LLP

## THE FIRM

**Managing Partner:** John C Sumberg
**Number of partners:** 46
**Number of other lawyers:** 54

### HEAD OFFICE

**FLORIDA**
200 South Biscayne Boulevard, Suite 2500, **Miami**, Florida, 33131
**Tel:** 305 374 7580  **Fax:** 305 374 7593
**Email:** info@bilzin.com  **Website:** www.bilzin.com

**FIRM OVERVIEW:** Bilzin Sumberg is a full-service, commercial law firm. The firm's attorneys work as a cohesive team, combining legal expertise with business insight and innovative solutions to assist clients in achieving their objectives. The firm views each of its clients and the matters in which they represent them as unique and of paramount importance. Whether in the courtroom or in the boardroom, the firm shoulders every client's problem as if it were its own.

## MAIN AREAS OF PRACTICE:

**Capital Markets:** Bilzin Sumberg represents the country's largest special servicer of commercial mortgage-backed loans, currently servicing in excess of 140 securitized loan pools totaling more than $100 billion in principal and encumbering real property in all 50 states. The firm also handles the acquisition of certificated interests in securitized loan pools, B participations and whole and participated mezzanine interests, and also represents borrowers in significant debt transactions.

**Corporate & Securities:** The attorneys in the Corporate and Securities Group assist and advise domestic and foreign, public and private companies and entrepreneurs in every phase of business, from start up through growth from operations acquisitions and strategic relationships to the ultimate disposition. The group regularly represents clients in complex transactions involving mergers and acquisitions (including with respect to regulatory compliance), the structuring of joint ventures and other strategic relationships, public and private offerings, complex restructurings of entity groups, corporate governance matters, employment and non-competition arrangements, executive compensation and licensing. The group also has substantial venture capital and debt financing experience, including lines of credit, asset-based and cash-flow financing, subordinate and mezzanine financing, securitizations, repurchase, swap and hedging arrangements, and banking and equipment lease financing.

**Environmental:** Bilzin Sumberg represents and counsels clients in a wide range of environmental issues, including all aspects of regulatory and natural resource permitting; business transactions and due diligence; compliance counseling; defense of regulatory enforcement actions at all governmental levels; environmental, mold, takings and insurance coverage litigation; Superfund common counsel work and litigation; brownfields redevelopment; landfill permitting and regulation; toxic tort counseling and defense; and administrative rule development and challenges. Their attorneys were substantially involved in the revision and adoption of the State Uniform Wetland Mitigation Methodology and have lectured extensively on numerous environmental topics.

**Insolvency:** The Restructuring and Bankruptcy Group has extensive experience with complex in-court and out-of-court restructurings, workouts, assignments for the benefit of creditors and bankruptcy litigation. The firm represents all constituencies in chapter 7 and 11 cases. They currently serve as counsel to Heilig-Meyers; the property damage asbestos committees of W.R. Grace and U.S. Gypsum; the liquidating trustees of Lernout & Hauspie Speech Products, Crown Vantage, ContiFinancial, Southern Pacific Financial and Viasource Communications; the Celotex Asbestos Property Damage Claims Facility; subordinate noteholders in Southeast Banking Corp.; the secured lender of and plan agent for SunCruz Casinos; and the largest unsecured creditor in each of Romacorp and CHS Electronics.

**Land Use & Government Relations:** Bilzin Sumberg represents both public and private clients on matters involving Florida land use law and government relations. Its lawyers have extensive experience in all aspects of land use and environmental law, from planning through permitting. The firm's government relations experience encompasses state and local taxation, public procurement (including governmental tax incentives), public-private partnerships for the development of real property, transportation, finance, telecommunications and aviation. Its attorneys have represented public and private clients in administrative proceedings, trial and appellate litigation and general advisory capacities, including service as special counsel to numerous Florida governmental entities.

**Litigation:** The Litigation Group enjoys both a state and national reputation and has vast experience trying complex commercial cases in federal and state trial and appellate courts, as well as before many federal and state administrative bodies. The group's experience includes business torts, construction, real estate disputes, bankruptcy, intellectual property, eminent domain, securities, probate, employment, insurance defense, reinsurance, class actions and products liability litigation. Recent representations include: the prosecution and settlement of a fraudulent conveyance action in the W.R. Grace bankruptcy for $1 billion; the defeat of class certification on behalf of a major developer in a large homeowner class action; and a $20 million settlement of an inverse condemnation claim against the South Florida Water Management District.

**Real Estate:** The Real Estate Group provides legal counsel in every facet of commercial real estate transactions for all types of property, including hotels, hotel/condos and mixed use properties, as well as marinas, retail, office, industrial, residential, entertainment facilities and undeveloped land. Representation spans development and redevelopment of real estate projects, the purchase and sale of commercial real estate assets, financing (including mortgage and mezzanine), leasing, condominium law, and related governmental and regulatory issues. The firm's attorneys work closely with the Land Use Group and other departments in the firm to provide full service counsel to real estate developers in every step of their projects, from site selection through development, financing, leasing, stabilization and the ultimate disposition of the property.

**Tax & Estate Planning:** The Tax Group provides both domestic and foreign clients with sophisticated, solution-oriented tax counseling and representation, including planning to minimize individual and corporate income taxes, as well as taxes related to inbound and outbound investments. The attorneys also represent clients in tax controversy; estate planning; and state and local tax issues, such as internet and electronic commerce taxes. Bilzin Sumberg provides tax analysis and advice in the structuring of corporate, real estate and other commercial transactions, as well as in bankruptcy cases, litigation matters and settlements.

**Technology & Telecommunications:** Bilzin Sumberg has a sophisticated practice representing public and private technology, telecommunications and cable television companies; real estate developers; enterprise users of technology and telecommunications; and local governments in all aspects of technology; telecommunications; and voice, video and data law. By combining corporate, tax, real estate and technology disciplines, the firm maximizes the opportunities for success that are available to its clients.

**CLIENTS:** The firm's clients span a broad array of industries, including aviation, construction, development and home building, financial services, entertainment and hospitality, retail, not-for-profit, manufacturing, distribution and sales, software and e-commerce, real estate, luxury hotels and resorts, and teleservicing and telecommunications.

# CARLTON FIELDS, P.A.

## THE FIRM

**President & CEO:** Gary L Sasso
**Number of shareholders:** 138
**Number of other attorneys:** 85

**FIRM OVERVIEW:** Located in major business centers in Florida and the Southeast, Carlton Fields offers a full range of legal services in more than 30 areas of law. The firm serves a broad variety of national and local corporations, state and local public entities, and individuals and has represented two-thirds of the nation's Fortune 100 companies.

## MAIN AREAS OF PRACTICE:

**Appellate Practice & Trial Support:** In addition to a full appellate practice in state and federal appellate courts, Carlton Fields' appellate lawyers provide comprehensive trial support. They handle appeals on a broad range of issues, including commercial, products liability, insurance, healthcare, and constitutional and statutory claims.

**Bankruptcy & Creditors' Rights:** Carlton Fields has extensive creditors' rights, insolvency, reorganization, and workout experience. The firm represents commercial lenders, creditors' committees, Chapter 11 and Chapter 7 trustees, equity holders, indenture trustees, and corporate debtors, among others.

**Business Litigation & Trade Regulation:** Carlton Fields defends corporations in state and national litigation, including class actions involving consumer fraud, antitrust, securities, and environmental claims, and litigates business disputes. They represent clients on a variety of antitrust issues, including advertising, prospective mergers and acquisitions, government filings, pricing and marketing practices, and franchising and licensing agreements.

**Construction:** Carlton Fields provides legal services concerning all aspects of construction law, including pre-bid considerations, contract drafting and letting, construction administration, liens, bonds, insurance, and mediation, arbitration and trial, in all types of projects such as office buildings, condominiums, power plants, airports, highways, stadiums, and convention centers.

**Corporate, Tax & Asset-Based Financing:** Carlton Fields handles a wide array of corporate transactions including initial and secondary public offerings, corporate governance and compliance advice, mergers and acquisitions, and asset based financing. They provide federal, state and local tax planning advice and handle tax controversy cases with the IRS and state and local taxing authorities.

**Government Law & Consulting:** Carlton Fields provides strategic planning and counseling in all regulated areas, including business and professional regulation, land use and zoning, health and insurance regulation, environmental law, education law, bid processes and public procurement, and governmental affairs and lobbying, rulemaking and challenges and other administrative proceedings.

**Healthcare:** Carlton Fields' attorneys assist clients with their compliance, regulatory, transaction, and litigation needs. Clients include hospitals, DME and pharmaceutical companies, nursing homes, physician practice groups, medical associations, health insurance companies, and universities.

**Insurance:** The firm's insurance representation includes insurance coverage matters, property damage claims, bad faith, class action defense, representation of insurance carriers before the insurance regulator, regulatory litigation, and business litigation.

**Intellectual Property:** Carlton Fields represents clients in acquiring, perfecting and transferring rights to intellectual property and represents clients in claims involving infringement and unfair competition. They are experienced in technology issues relating to commerce on the internet, computer law, licensing, software publishing and copyright protection.

**Labor & Employment:** Carlton Fields represents employers in litigation and agency matters, including discrimination and harassment claims. They defend employers in wage-hour lawsuits, and counsel management regarding discharge decisions and other job actions, OSHA, WARN, IRCA, executive contracts, and union issues.

**Products & Toxic Tort Liability:** The firm's defense experience in products liability covers a variety of products, including pharmaceuticals and medical devices, chemical products, tobacco, automobiles and auto parts, sporting goods and recre-

ational products, electrical equipment, power equipment, and security systems.

**Real Estate & Mortgage Financing:** The firm represents clients in all aspects of real property acquisition, development, investment, regulation, title insurance, financing, leasing, ownership, and use and transfer.

**Securities:** Carlton Fields has a full service securities practice including representation in mergers and acquisitions, business organizations, corporate finance matters, and compliance with federal and state regulatory bodies. They also handle securities litigation arising from class action and individual claims.

**CLIENTS:** Firm clients represent a diverse group of industries, including banking and finance, transportation, government, insurance, energy, healthcare, manufacturing, pharmaceutical, technology, telecommunications, environmental, construction, real estate, tax and securities.

**INTERNATIONAL WORK:** Carlton Fields represents US and non-US clients establishing subsidiaries, acquiring companies, participating in joint ventures and contracting abroad, and assists foreign companies in establishing a presence in the US. The firm supports foreign and domestic clients in trans-national business matters including sales, construction, manufacturing, telecommunications and financing.

## HEAD OFFICE

**FLORIDA**
4221 West Boy Scout Boulevard, Suite 1000, **Tampa**, FL 33607-5736
**Tel:** 813 223 7000   **Fax:** 813 229 4133
**Email:** info@carltonfields.com   **Website:** www.carltonfields.com

## BRANCH OFFICES

**FLORIDA**
4000 International Place, 100 SE Second St, **Miami**, FL 33131-9101
**Tel:** 305 530 0050   **Fax:** 305 530 0055

CNL Center at City Commons, 450 S Orange Ave, Suite 500,
**Orlando**, FL 32801-3336
**Tel:** 407 849 0300   **Fax:** 407 648 9099

One Progress Plaza, 200 Central Ave, Ste 2300,
**St Petersburg**, FL 33701-4352
**Tel:** 727 821 7000   **Fax:** 727 822 3768

215 S Monroe Street, Suite 500, **Tallahassee,** FL 32301-1866
**Tel:** 850 224 1585   **Fax:** 850 222 0398

Esperante, 222 Lakeview Ave, Suite 1400, **West Palm Beach,** FL 33401-6149
**Tel:** 561 659 7070   **Fax:** 561 659 7368

**GEORGIA**
One Atlantic Center, 1201 W Peachtree St, Ste 3000, **Atlanta**, GA 30309
**Tel:** 404 815 3400   **Fax:** 404 815 3415

## CONTACTS

| | |
|---|---|
| **Appellate Practice & Trial Support** | Wendy Lumish (Miami) |
| **Bankruptcy & Creditors Rights** | Rob Soriano (Tampa) |
| **Business Litigation & Trade Regulation** | Chris Coutroulis (Tampa) |
| **Construction** | Luis Prats (Tampa) |
| **Corporate, Tax & Asset-Based Financing** | Bill Rohrer (Miami) |
| | David Burke (Miami) |
| **Energy** | Bob Pass (Tallahassee) |
| **Government Law & Consulting** | Nancy Linnan (Tallahassee) |
| **Healthcare** | Don Schmidt (Tampa) |
| **Insurance** | Dan Brown (Tallahassee), Anthony Pelle (Miami) |
| **Intellectual Property** | Doug McDonald (Tampa) |
| **Labor & Employment** | Jim Wiley (Tampa) |
| **Products & Toxic Tort Liability** | Greg Cesarano (Miami) |
| **Real Estate & Mortgage Financing** | Ed Lester (Tampa) |
| **Real Property Litigation** | Mark Brown (Tampa) |
| **Securities** | Rick Denmon (Tampa), Sam Salario (Tampa) |
| **White Collar Representation** | Kevin Napper (Tampa) |

# COLSON HICKS EIDSON

## THE FIRM

**Managing Director:** Dean Colson
**Number of partners:** 12

**FIRM OVERVIEW:** Colson Hicks Eidson, one of Miami's oldest and most accomplished law firms, is considered among the top, full-service trial firms in the United States, having won hundreds of multi-million dollar verdicts and settlements for its clients. With decades of experience in personal injury, commercial, securities, business torts, insurance, professional liability litigation and white collar criminal defense, as well as domestic and international arbitration, the firm enjoys a long history of landmark decisions that have resulted in national and international recognition.

## MAIN AREAS OF PRACTICE:

**Product Liability:** Colson Hicks Eidson has litigated cases involving the design and manufacture of airplanes, motor vehicles, boats, tires, medical devices, and children's toys. Long considered one of the innovators in the field of product liability law, Mike Eidson, a founding partner of the firm, serves as the national co-lead counsel in the multi-district Fort/Firestone litigation for all personal injury claims.

**Commercial & Business Litigation:** Colson Hicks Eidson handles cases involving complex insurance, construction, intellectual property, and other commercial matters as well as fraud and other business torts. The firm members litigate business lawsuits to judges, juries and arbitration panels. The firm has prosecuted and defended bad faith claims involving major insurance companies. A member of the firm has served as a receiver appointed by the United States District Court in actions brought by the Federal Trade Commission, and the firm's partners have served on plaintiffs' committees in some of the most complex, multi-party class action securities fraud and RICO cases in South Florida. Members of the firm have represented owners, contractors, developers, design professional, lenders, and insurers in construction disputes. The firm has obtained numerous multi-million dollar verdicts, judgments, arbitration awards and settlements on behalf of small and large business enterprises, individual entrepreneurs, and in class action cases involving real estate, lender liability, professional malpractice and other business disputes.

**White Collar Criminal Defense:** With the addition of the former United States Attorney for the Southern District of Florida, Roberto Martínez, former Chief of the Economics Crime Section for that office, Susan Tarbe, and former Assistant United States Attorney Curtis Miner, the firm now offers extensive experience and expertise in federal criminal litigation. These experienced federal litigators have represented businesses and their officers in connection with investigations and trails in matters including securities, money laundering, foreign corrupt practices, asset foreiture, tax; healthcare, bank fraud, environmental, antitrust, obstruction of justice, export, RICO and extortion. In addition to representing business clients in investigations and trials, Colson Hicks Eidson attorneys have provided legal counseling to banks and other financial institutions to ensure compliance with the federal money laundering and currency reporting laws.

**Personal Injury & Wrongful Death:** Colson Hicks Eidson has decades of experience in prosecuting personal injury actions on behalf of its clients. The firm has handled hundreds of multi-million dollar cases arising from wrongful death, traumatic brain injuries, spinal cord injuries and burn cases.

**Professional Malpractice:** Colson Hicks Eidson has handled dozens of medical malpractice cases that have resulted in verdicts and settlements in excess of one million dollars since the firm won the first million-dollar medical malpractice verdict in the United States. The firm has also handled significant legal malpractice cases for both plaintiffs and defendants. Colson Hicks Eidson has been selected to defend several national and regional law firms when they have been accused of professional negligence. In the personal injury and construction fields, the firm has successfully prosecuted and defended claims for professional negligence involving architects, engineers, and other design professionals. The firm

**HEAD OFFICE**

**FLORIDA**
255 Aragon Avenue, Second Floor, **Coral Gables** FL 33134
**Tel:** 305 476 7400   **Fax:** 305 476 7444
**Website:** www.colson.com

was involved in evaluating and prosecuting over $100 million of claims involving engineering, architectural and construction negligence arising out of the destruction caused during Hurricane Andrew.

**Aviation:** Colson Hicks Eidson has represented many clients in litigation arising out of the crashes of commercial and private aircraft over the past two decades. The firm often works in conjunction with local counsel in other states and countries. In several mass death cases, the firm has represented a majority of the passengers in the plane. The firm also has handled individual claims in private aviation crashes relating to failed component parts, faulty design and manufacture and inadequate warnings.

**Recent Cases of Note:** In 2005, the firm obtained a $60.9 million award, the largest amount ever awarded in a Federal Tort Claims Act case in the country. In 2005, a Miami jury awarded a $65.1 million verdict on behalf of our client against Eller Media Company for the electrocution death of our client's 12-year-old son. In 2003, the firm announced a settlement of $100 million in a grave desecration case against Service Corporation International, the world's largest cemetery and funeral company, to settle the individual and class action claims of victims with loved ones buried at Menorah Gardens funeral homes in Florida. In 2002 the firm obtained a $19 million judgment in federal court in Miami against the Government of Aruba on behalf of racecar promoter Ralph Sanchez in connection with the failed efforts to build a racetrack in Aruba. In 2002 the firm obtained a $10 million settlement for the wrongful death caused by the faulty design and installation of a security gate system at a condominium. In 2001 the firm obtained a federal court judgment in the amount of $16 million confirming an arbitration award against the Miccosukee Tribe of Indians arising out of a breach of contract regarding the management of the Indian's gambling operations. A member of the firm was co-lead counsel in the litigation against the Cuban Air Force and the Cuban Government over the murders of their clients who were shot down by the Cuban Air Force while flying a humanitarian mission for Brothers to the Rescue, resulting in a judgment of $188,000,000.00 against the Cuban Air Force and Cuban government. Two of the firm's partners served as co-lead trial counsel on behalf of the Plaintiff class in The Premium Sales case, the largest mass fraud case in South Florida history. The case was settled after the start of trial for $170,000,000. The firm served as co-counsel for nearly two-thirds of the family members of the passengers aboard AeroPeru flight 603, which originated in Miami and crashed off the coast of Peru on October 2nd, 1996. The firm helped the families receive one of the largest cash awards stemming from an airplane crash outside the United States aboard a non-US carrier. The firm represented a Canadian telecommunications company in a complex commercial litigation case involving breach of contract, fraud and intentional interference of a business relationship. Firm members won a jury verdict of $31.2 million for their client, SIRIT Technologies Inc., against Able Telcom-whose largest shareholder is MCI WorldCom, Inc. Two of the firm's partners obtained a $30.7 million jury verdict against the Ford Motor Company for the improper installation of the air valve on the right-rear tire of a 1999 Ford Econoline 15-passenger van that caused the van to crash and roll over on top of a nine-year-old girl.

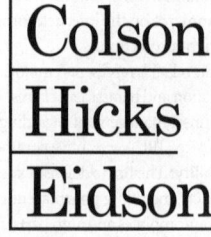

# GENOVESE JOBLOVE & BATTISTA, P.A.

## THE FIRM

**Managing Partners:** Paul J Battista, John H Genovese, Michael D Joblove
**Number of partners:** 14
**Number of other lawyers:** 10

**FIRM OVERVIEW:** Genovese Joblove & Battista P.A. (GJB), with one of the largest insolvency practices in Florida, is a 24-lawyer litigation and bankruptcy boutique. Its lawyers are heavily involved in complex reorganizations and insolvency litigations in Florida and throughout the US. The firm has a nationally recognized Franchise Practice and represents franchisors nationally, in workouts, litigation and Chapter 11s of multiple unit franchises. The firm is also recognized for its expertise and experience in litigation involving directors and officers' liability and in complex cross-border business litigation and insolvency matters given its South Florida location.

## MAIN AREAS OF PRACTICE:

**Insolvency, Bankruptcy & Creditors' Rights:** GJB's Insolvency, Bankruptcy and Creditors' Rights Practice is one of the largest in Florida and the firm's lawyers regularly appear in both federal and state courts throughout the country representing major players in creditor litigation, out of court workouts, restructures and insolvency proceedings, bankruptcy or non-bankruptcy, and all related litigation. In addition to roles in Florida Chapter 11 matters such as AT&T Latin America and Far & Wide Travel, GJB has played a significant role in the Enron Chapter 11 in New York and the Delaware Chapter 11s of Ameriservice and Safety-Kleen. The Insolvency Practice includes litigation representations in insurance and banking receiverships.

**Commercial Litigation:** GJB handles sophisticated business litigation matters, at the trial and appellate levels in all federal and state courts, as well as in arbitration and other alternative dispute resolution forums. The firm represents businesses and individuals, as plaintiffs and defendants, in all types of commercial litigation matters.

**Franchise Representation:** The firm has Florida's premier Franchise Litigation and Bankruptcy Practice. GJB represents Miami-based Burger King Corporation throughout the country, and has handled matters in South Florida for a variety of franchise systems including BP Amoco, Brinker International (franchisor of the Chili's and Romano's Macaroni Grill concepts), Carlsons Restaurants Worldwide (for its TGI Friday's concept), Jamba Juice, Metromedia, Inc. (for its Bennigans and Steak & Ale concepts), Pearle Vision, Inc., Schlotzky's, Inc. and Taco Bell Corp.

**Real Estate Litigation:** GJB has one of Florida's leading real estate litigation practices. The firm's attorneys have represented developers, general contractors, subcontractors and professionals for over 20 years, including Minto Communities, Inc., one of South Florida's largest developers. Other prominent real estate clients have included KB Home, Bendersen Development, Capital Realty Services, and Affiniti Architects.

**Securities Litigation:** The firm represents numerous small and large investors in individual and class action suits and arbitration proceedings before the NASD, NYSE, and other exchanges. Members of the firm include a former assistant general counsel to a major securities brokerage firm. Firm attorneys have experience with various securities law issues, including issues arising under the Private Securities Litigation Reform Act of 1995, the Securities and Exchange Acts of 1933 and 1934, state securities law and common law. GJB has been successful in aiding investors recoup millions of dollars lost to unscrupulous brokers and corporate officers as a result of their financial wrongdoing.

**Director & Officer Litigation:** The firm regularly represents all parties in complex litigation involving potential liability of corporate directors and officers and their insurers.

## HEAD OFFICE

**FLORIDA**
Bank of America Tower at International Place,
100 Southeast Second Street, 44th Floor, **Miami**, FL 33131
**Tel:** 305 349 2300   **Fax:** 305 349 2310
**Email:** plawson@gjb-law.com
**Website:** www.gjb-law.com

## CONTACTS

| | |
|---|---|
| **Commercial Litigation** | Michael D Joblove |
| **Insolvency, Bankruptcy & Creditors' Rights** | John H Genovese |
| | Paul J Battista |
| **Franchise Litigation** | Michael D Joblove |
| | Jonathan E Perlman |
| **Real Estate Litigation** | Michael D Joblove |
| **Governmental Affairs Consulting** | Al Maloof |
| | John H Genovese |
| **Securities Litigation** | Jonathan E Perlman |
| | Melanie S Cherdack |
| **Employment Litigation** | Michael D Joblove |
| | Jonathan E Perlman |
| **Class Action Litigation** | Jonathan E Perlman |

**Employment Litigation:** GJB maintains an active practice in the growing area of employment law. The firm counsels its clients on various types of employment policies and prepares and updates manuals containing policies that protect the rights of both employer and employee in compliance with all applicable laws.

**Class Action Litigation:** The firm enjoys a reputation for successful litigation of significant, complex class action cases. Opposing counsel are generally among the largest and most powerful law firms in the country. GJB has won settlements or judgments for class members of millions of dollars.

**Governmental Affairs Consulting:** GJB provides consulting and lobbying services for clients seeking strategic representation before various local, state and federal departments and agencies.

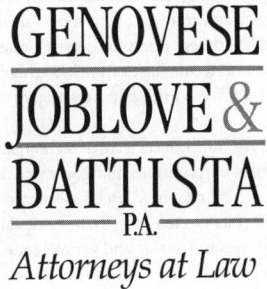

GENOVESE
JOBLOVE &
BATTISTA
P.A.
*Attorneys at Law*

# GREENBERG TRAURIG, LLP

## THE FIRM

**Chief Executive Officer:** Cesar L Alvarez
**Number of partners:** 553
**Number of other lawyers:** 706

**FIRM OVERVIEW:** Greenberg Traurig, LLP is an international business law firm with more than 1500 attorneys and governmental professionals working in 28 offices across the United States and Europe. Greenberg Traurig is the only major law firm in the United States with a Latin CEO and a team of senior lawyers that includes the former Chief Justice of the Appellate body of the World Trade Organization. As a full-service business law firm, Greenberg Traurig is uniquely able to work with its clients towards integrated, multi-disciplinary cross-border solutions.

## MAIN AREAS OF PRACTICE:

**Corporate & Securities:** Greenberg Traurig helps its clients with the legal and business aspects of organizing, operating, financing and expanding their businesses. The firm routinely handles complex mergers, acquisitions and business combinations, divestitures, corporate restructurings and bankruptcy reorganizations, private equity and venture capital financings, leveraged buyouts, IPOs and underwritten securities offerings, project financings, securitizations, going-private transactions, credit enhancement transactions, broker-dealer and investment company advisory matters, derivatives transactions and syndicated lending transactions.

**Litigation:** Greenberg Traurig has been at the center of some of the most pivotal cases of recent times. With more than 400 seasoned trial lawyers, the firm has extensive experience in cases involving antitrust, appellate practice, business disputes, class actions, construction, eDiscovery and eRetention™, financial services, healthcare, intellectual property litigation, international dispute resolution, labor and employment, media and entertainment, probate trusts and estates, products liability, real estate litigation, securities and shareholder litigation, technology, and white collar criminal defense.

**Real Estate:** Greenberg Traurig's representation and counsel spans the entire range of local, national and international real estate transactions affecting commercial, residential, retail and industrial properties, including: acquisitions; traditional and securitized financing; planning and development; hotels; condominium and cooperative offerings; leasing; sale/leaseback transactions; tax free exchanges; and foreclosures, litigation and restructurings.

**Tax, Trusts & Estates:** Greenberg Traurig's tax attorneys help clients develop and implement tax strategies to maximize returns and minimize taxes anywhere in the world. The firm's wealth preservation attorneys assist high net worth individuals, families and closely held businesses grow family assets through planning. It has developed tax saving techniques and designed innovative wealth preservation programs to facilitate the transfer of family wealth to future generations at significant tax savings.

**Intellectual Property:** Multinational companies know that patents, trademarks, copyrights and trade secrets are among their most valuable assets. The firm's Intellectual Property Department offers full-service protection for the intellectual property of clients in all technologies, from biotechnology, pharmaceuticals, medical devices and chemistry to mechanical, electronics and computer software and e-commerce.

**Government:** Greenberg Traurig has a team of highly qualified and experienced strategists who represent corporations and governmental entities before the legislative and executive branches in federal, state and local governments. The firm's team includes former elected officials, top aides and policy officials for members of the US House and Senate and various state legislatures and local government bodies.

**Global Trade:** The team is headed by the former Chief Justice of the Appellate body of the World Trade Organization. The firm advises clients on international trade agreements, trade legislation and lobbying, anti-trust and Foreign Corrupt Practices Act counseling, US Foreign Military Sales Program, US anti-boycott and embargo regulations, identification of complex export control for high tech, defense and aerospace companies, defense of corporations in export-related

## US OFFICES

The firm has offices in Albany, Atlanta, Boca Raton, Boston, Chicago, Dallas, Denver, Fort Lauderdale, Houston, Las Vegas, Los Angeles, Miami, New Jersey, New York, Orange County, Orlando, Philadelphia, Phoenix, Sacramento, Silicon Valley, Tallahassee, Tysons Corner, Washington, DC, West Palm Beach, and Wilmington, Delaware.

## INTERNATIONAL OFFICES

The firm also has offices in Zurich in Switzerland, Amsterdam in The Netherlands and Tokyo, Japan. For further details of all offices please see firm's website: www.gtlaw.com

criminal investigations and unfair trade cases.

**Business Reorganization & Bankruptcy:** Greenberg Traurig's practice is one of the largest and most active in the nation. As part of an integrated national network of professionals who focus their practice on all aspects of reorganizations, bankruptcies, restructurings, workouts and buyouts, the firm's attorneys are able to respond quickly to complex troubled situations arising anywhere and in any industry.

**Employment:** The firm is aware that companies today require labor and employment attorneys who will provide advice and counseling on all aspects of the employment relationship; handle matters involving union avoidance and organizational work; formulate strategies to anticipate problems; keep them informed of new developments in the law; assist in drafting policies and procedures; and defend the company against discrimination charges at the agency level and in court. Greenberg Traurig delivers these services at all levels of the administrative and litigation process.

**Entertainment:** With offices in the center of the entertainment industry, Greenberg Traurig has a preeminent, full-service entertainment practice. The team focuses on the music, motion picture, television, live stage and cable industries, including the convergence of new technologies, digital delivery systems and the role of advertising and sponsor-driven financing models. The firm has access to key players in the entertainment industry and provide clients with the pragmatic counsel needed in today's multi-disciplined, multimedia entertainment marketplace.

**International Practice Group:** Greenberg Traurig's multi-disciplinary team includes senior lawyers who have been the chief legal officers at major multinational companies and have been involved in some of the largest transactions in recent times in markets as diverse as Latin America and Israel, and in a wide range of industries incuding telecommunications, media, technology, real estate, aviation, entertainment, life sciences and financial services. The firm's International Corporate and Securities Team is complemented by market leading International Tax and Intellectual Property Practices and a multilingual International Dispute Resolution Team that is accustomed to coordinating with counsel in multiple jurisdictions and addressing novel issues posed by complex international transactions.

**Business Immigration:** Members of the US Immigration Law Department are experienced in all aspects of corporate immigration law, particularly multinational non-immigrant visa and permanent residency work. The attorneys understand the immigration process in all its complexity. They represent clients in such industries as finance, tourism, insurance, electronics, healthcare, shipping and pharmaceuticals with their immigration needs.

**Public Finance:** Members of Greenberg Traurig's Public Finance Department have extensive experience in serving the needs of state and local issuers and underwriters in all areas of public finance. The firm has broad experience in all forms of tax-exempt financing. For the past several years, the firm has been among the top bond counsel firms in the US, according to the ranking criteria developed by Securities Data Co. and The Bond Buyer, a municipal finance publication.

**CLIENTS:** The firm represents a diverse client base, including public/private companies, financial institutions, governmental entities and entrepreneurs.

# HOPPING GREEN & SAMS

## THE FIRM

**Chairman, Management Committee:** Peter C Cunningham

**Number of shareholders:** 23
**Number of other lawyers:** 19

**FIRM OVERVIEW:** Hopping Green & Sams, P.A., has a specialty practice in administrative and governmental law, legislative representation, litigation, and appellate practice. Within these areas there is emphasis on environmental and land use law, public lands, state and local government taxation, special districts, utility regulation and governmental contracts. The firm represents both private and public sector clients with interests affected by government.

## MAIN AREAS OF PRACTICE:

### ENVIRONMENTAL LAW

**Air Quality:** Firm lawyers have been continuously involved on behalf of industrial clients in Florida's implementation of the federal Clean Air Act and related state statutes, in legislation and rulemaking at the state level, and in federal and state air facility permitting and enforcement.

**Coastal Permitting:** The firm counsels coastal developers on coastal zone management and regulatory issues, and guides coastal developments through the complex state and federal coastal regulatory process.

**Endangered & Threatened Species Protection:** The firm evaluates federal and state endangered and threatened species laws and regulations and assists clients when related issues arise that might affect their projects.

**Everglades Restoration:** Federal and state authorities are refocusing on the remaining Everglades ecosystem to improve its ecological health in a litigious and costly process. The firm has been at the forefront of these matters through representation of growers adjacent to the Everglades.

**Groundwater Regulation/Real Property Contamination:** The firm represents clients in all types of matters pertaining to groundwater regulation and real property contamination, including 'due diligence' for real property acquisition. Solid & Hazardous Waste: The firm handles solid and hazardous waste and pollutant permitting, regulation, enforcement and litigation, under federal, state and local laws.

**Water Resources:** Firm lawyers practice in all areas of water resource regulation, from standard-setting to the permitting of consumptive uses. Wetlands Regulation: The firm has been extensively involved in federal, state, and local wetlands regulation for over 20 years, representing developers, utilities, agricultural interests and local governments. The firm has extensive experience in authorizing mitigation banks.

### LAND USE LAW

**Planning & Entitlements:** Firm lawyers represent landowners and developers in seeking changes to local government land use plans and in obtaining entitlements for residential, commercial, industrial, resort and mixed-use projects. The representation includes appearing before state, regional and local agencies throughout the state.

**Submerged Lands:** Firm lawyers have experience in determining when proprietary consent for use of state lands submerged beneath navigable waters is required, and in negotiating needed approvals for public and private users.

**Oil & Gas:** The firm has extensive experience in licensing on-shore and off-shore oil and gas projects, including exploration, production, storage and transportation.

### LEGISLATIVE LOBBYING

Firm legislative attorneys have been involved in the drafting and passage of most of Florida's landmark environmental and land use legislation for 25 years. As a large lobbying organization, the firm has the experience and relationships to effectively represent clients before the Florida Legislature.

### SPECIAL DISTRICTS

Florida government requires new development to provide infrastructure to accommodate growth, putting pressure on developers to finance, provide and maintain various types of facilities. Firm lawyers have established and serve as counsel to more than 80 community development districts which levy taxes and assessment and issue bonds to provide infrastructure for new communities.

### STATE & LOCAL TAXATION

The firm represents Florida, national and international businesses with state and local tax issues. Areas covered include: State and local tax planning and advice; legislative representation on tax and fee bills; participation in Department of Revenue rulemaking and policy development; representation before the Department, administrative tribunals and the courts in tax controversy matters of all types; and assistance securing economic development incentives.

### UTILITY REGULATION

**Energy Facilities Licensing:** The firm provides assistance in all types of matters concerning new and expanded electrical power plants, electric transmission lines, and fuel pipelines to public and private electric utilities, natural gas companies, and oil companies.

**Telecommunications Regulation:** The firm represents telecommunications clients before the Florida Public Service Commission, the Florida Legislature, and the courts.

**Water & Wastewater Utility Regulation:** Providing water to meet rapidly growing needs continues to consume the attention of state regulators and utilities. The firm represents water utilities before the Public Service Commission and local economic regulators in this area.

### LITIGATION

**Administrative & Civil Litigation:** Firm lawyers represent Florida's development, industrial, and commercial communities as well as public entities in litigation on many highly technical disputes. The firm's lawyers are experienced in using expert witnesses to develop clear, cogent testimony on complex scientific and technical subjects.

**Bid Protests:** Firm lawyers have extensive experience representing contractors in matters involving government contracts, reviewing bid specifications for a contractor to determine whether to challenge the fairness of the bid process, and representing contractors in challenging or defending a bid award by an agency.

### APPELLATE PRACTICE

The firm represents clients on issues at the cutting edge of law and public policy. That representation occasionally requires appeals of administrative agency or lower court decisions to federal or state appellate courts. The firm includes attorneys with special skills and qualifications to handle appellate issues.

## HEAD OFFICE

**FLORIDA**
123 South Calhoun Street, Tallahassee, FL 32301
**Tel:** 850 222 7500   **Fax:** 850 224 8551
**Website:** www.hgslaw.com

Hopping Green & Sams
Attorneys and Counselors

# KENNY NACHWALTER P.A.

## THE FIRM

**HEAD OFFICE**

**FLORIDA**
1100 Miami Center, 201 South Biscayne Blvd., **Miami**, FL 33131
**Tel:** 305 373 1000   **Fax:** 305 372 1861
**Email:** admin@kennynachwalter.com
**Website:** www.kennynachwalter.com

**FIRM OVERVIEW:** Kenny Nachwalter, P.A., was founded in 1978 and has since grown from three to 23 attorneys. The firm's practice is devoted to complex business litigation, including antitrust, securities, professional liability and intellectual property litigation, common law business torts and defending white collar criminal prosecutions, concentrating its efforts on a small number of relatively large cases. The firm is frequently retained in cases involving complicated economic and factual issues, multiple counsel, multiple parties, multiple interrelated cases, competing claims to limited resources, intense discovery and discovery problems, and substantive issues requiring superior legal scholarship and forensic skills. It devotes most of its time to dispute resolution, and as such regularly litigates in federal and state courts, and in various arbitration tribunals. They represent clients before federal administrative bodies and in white collar criminal investigations. Many of the firm's cases originate through referrals from other law firms in the South Florida area and throughout the United States. The firm has a team-oriented approach to staffing cases. Typically, two or more attorneys will work together on a complex case to increase attorney availability, to provide a basis for consultation, and to furnish legal services in a cost efficient and professional manner through allocation of assignments. In situations involving particularly complicated or difficult issues, however, firm lawyers not generally involved in the representation may contribute their particular experience.

## MAIN AREAS OF PRACTICE:

**Antitrust:** Over two hundred years ago Adam Smith wrote: "People of the same trade seldom meet together, even for merriment and diversion, but the conversation ends in a conspiracy against the public, or in some contrivance to raise prices." It is still true today. And, the line separating permissible contact from impermissible conspiracy is a line that they have litigated in scores of cases involving industries from airlines to pharmaceuticals. The firm's Antitrust Practice includes both plaintiff and defense work in cases in federal and state courts nationwide, in which they've represented large public and private corporations, privately held companies, individual entrepreneurs, and government entities. On behalf of plaintiffs - where they often represent individual claimants and groups of claimants who opt out of nationwide class actions and pursue their antitrust claims independent of the class - these have included conspiracy cases involving domestic and international cartels, and monopolization cases. The firm also represents antitrust defendants in proceedings-including both civil and criminal investigations-arising under the Sherman Act and related federal and state statutes. To help business avoid such problems in the first place the firm provides antitrust counseling on issues ranging from the formation of joint ventures to the structuring of distribution networks. In the process, they have represented clients in the airline, automobile, dairy, grocery, insurance, real estate, rental car, pharmaceutical, publishing, telecommunications, transportation and shipping industries. Because of their expertise in this area, the firm's attorneys have taught antitrust law and have served as special assistant attorneys general in several States prosecuting or providing counsel in antitrust cases in a variety of industries.

**Complex Business Litigation:** These disputes, litigated in state and federal courts as well as argued before administrative bodies and arbitration tribunals, cover the gamut of business and legal matters-trade secrets, RICO, class and derivative actions, director and officer liability, lender liability, False Claims Act and qui tam, construction, commercial lease disputes and other real estate related matters, trade libel, tortious interference, franchise and business opportunities, employment and discrimination matters, contracts, fraud and other common law and statutory business torts.

**Intellectual Property Litigation:** The firm's Intellectual Property Practice area helps clients protect their rights. The firm has done so for the makers of computer software, clothing, automobiles, handbags, jewelry and accessories, and the satellite broadcaster of network television signals. Often the firm investigates and prosecute civil injunctive and damage actions against individuals and companies infringing upon, counterfeiting, or diluting the trademarks and copy-rights of the legitimate owners of those trademarks and copyrights.

**Professional Liability:** The issue of the responsibilities of professionals has increasingly become a focus of regulatory bodies and agencies. Because of the expertise this firm has acquired in the area of professional liability, they are often called upon to counsel lawyers and other professionals about issues of ethical behavior and professional responsibilities. They also represent licensees before their state disciplinary bodies, and have represented professionals sued by the FDIC and RTC, as well as architects sued for professional malpractice. In doing so, the firm has defended claims covering malpractice, breach of fiduciary duty, RICO and securities law violations, and fraudulent conveyances under state law and the Bankruptcy Code.

**Securities:** The firm's Securities Practice involves arbitrations against, and the defense of, brokerage firms and registered representatives before the New York Stock Exchange and the National Association of Securities Dealers. These arbitrations have included allegations of churning, selling away, fraud, breach of fiduciary duty, suitability, breach of contract, negligence, civil theft, conversion, and other violations of state and federal securities laws. The firm also represents brokerage firms and their employees, securities issuers and their managements and directors, and accountants in SEC, NYSE and NASD investigations, as well as brokers in federal criminal prosecutions. The firm is not, however, involved in private offerings or public registrations of securities.

**White Collar Criminal Practice:** Corporations, executives and professionals are increasingly the target of aggressive criminal prosecution and regulatory enforcement. For them, the firm offers the services and expertise of its white-collar criminal defense and internal corporate investigations practice group. The firm's work includes the representation of clients in the United States and abroad involved in government investigations, civil enforcement matters, and parallel litigation in criminal, civil and administrative proceedings. They have represented, during investigation and post-indictment, public and privately held corporations, business executives, accountants, lawyers, judges, bankers, physicians, securities brokers and others who are targets or subjects of criminal investigation or prosecution. The practice includes representing clients in investigations by such government agencies as the Department of Justice, various State Attorneys General, the SEC, the IRS and Congress. Their work also includes discreetly conducting internal corporate investigations either incident to or to preempt a government criminal or civil prosecution. They have investigated sensitive matters in diverse areas, including antitrust, environmental issues, health care, insurance and accounting. The experience of our attorneys allows for consultation and advice on corrective actions, compliance plans and the advisability of voluntary disclosure. The practice group draws on years of front-line prosecutorial and criminal defense experience of firm lawyers, including the former United States Attorney for the Southern District of Florida (2002-2005) who, in that capacity, led one of the busiest US Attorney's Offices in the nation and worked closely with both the highest levels of the Department of Justice and the US Attorneys in other major metropolitan areas.

# KLUGER, PERETZ, KAPLAN & BERLIN P.L.

## THE FIRM

**Managing Director:** Howard Berlin
**Administrative Director:** Stuart R Silver

**Number of lawyers:** 50

**FIRM OVERVIEW**: Kluger, Peretz, Kaplan & Berlin, P.L. is in the business of adding value to the identification and accomplishment of its clients' goals. The firm aspires to provide its clients with advice that looks beyond their immediate problem by becoming familiar with their industries and operations in order to help them anticipate additional legal problems before they develop. The firm's services embody leadership, scholarship, teamwork, experience, and ethical responsibility. The firm is continually recognized as one of the top law firms in South Florida and was first to be named "Firm of the Year" by the 'South Florida Business Journal' in 2003. The firm's Miami office is located in The Miami Center, adjacent to the Intercontinental Hotel, and convenient to Miami International Airport. In 2005, the firm opened an office in Boca Raton, Florida, to answer the growing demand for sophisticated legal services in Palm Beach and Broward Counties.

**MAIN AREAS OF PRACTICE:** The firm is committed to being the best choice in Florida for each of the areas in which it practices. Striving for excellence rather than breadth, the firm purposely focuses its practice in four select areas: litigation and dispute resolution, bankruptcy and creditors' rights, business and real estate transactions, and intellectual property and commercialization. Within these four areas, the firm has developed expertise, for example, working with the special issues related to private equity firms, sports and entertainment personalities, and real estate developers. The firm knows first-hand the particular legal issues pertaining to international trade, probate litigation, financial fraud, and creditors' committees.

**Litigation & Dispute Resolution:** A broad-based practice suitable for disputes requiring complex analysis, courtroom experience, creativity, and vision; the firm comprises primarily trial lawyers who litigate, arbitrate, or mediate legal disputes for businesses and individuals both domestically and internationally. Many of the firm's cases involve claims of director and officer liability issues of corporate governance, mergers and acquisitions, real estate, bankruptcy, probate, catastrophic personal injury, class actions, and sports management disputes. The firm mediates or litigates matrimonial disputes involving significant assets and business valuation matters including cross-border and multi-state facts and parties. The firm defends clients involved in product liability claims, and has nationally recognized expertise with claims involving mold, mildew, or other fungal growth. The firm also litigates contract, employment, trade secret, non-competition, and shareholder disputes for individuals, corporations, and private-equity and venture-capital firms, with special experience working with fraudulent transfer and piercing the corporate veil issues.

**Bankruptcy & Creditors' Rights:** Scope of experience, bench strength, and a passion for finding workable solutions are just a few reasons why the firm's Bankruptcy Practice has been so successful in client matters. The firm's lawyers bring to insolvency cases the ability to synthesize a large amount of data and recommend the right strategic decisions. The firm is experienced in business growth issues and has successfully reorganized a variety of business enterprises. The firm's practice encompasses every aspect of companies or high profile individuals experiencing financial distress; from workouts to bankruptcy proceedings both domestically and internationally. The firm works collaboratively to rescue venerable companies from the brink of dissolution, sleuth out assets, and work in state, federal, and international courts to protect businesses and creditors. The firm represents debtors in both out-of-court workouts and bankruptcy proceedings; creditor committees in Chapter 11 proceedings; acquirers of distressed or bankrupt companies (or assets of such companies); trustees in Chapter 11 cases and broker-dealer cases pursuant to SIPA; and, agencies of the US government in various regulatory liquidations.

## HEAD OFFICE

**FLORIDA**
Miami Center, 201 South Biscayne Blvd.,17th Floor, **Miami**, FL 33131
**Tel:** 305 379 9000  **Fax:** 305 379 3428
**Website:** www.kpkb.com

2385 NW Executive Center Drive, Suite 300, **Boca Raton,** FL 33431
**Tel:** 561 961 1830  **Fax:** 561 961 1831
**Website:** www.kpkb.com

## CONTACTS

| | |
|---|---|
| **Litigation & Dispute Resolution** | Steve Silverman |
| **Bankruptcy & Creditors' Rights** | Howard Berlin |
| | Robert Charbonneau |
| **Business & Real Estate Transactions** | Eliot Abbott |
| **Intellectual Property** | Steve Peretz |

**Business & Real Estate Transactions:** The firm works with clients who are buying or selling businesses, commercial real estate, or other assets both domestically and internationally. The firm brings the ability to handle challenging facts and circumstances with creativity and drives to get the transaction successfully completed. The firm helps clients form corporations, partnerships, and joint ventures domestically and internationally and advise those who are developing franchising networks. The firm offers a combination of legal expertise and business insight which seems to inspire clients to involve the firm's lawyers in every stage of their transactions, including: clarifying the business purpose(s) to be accomplished by the transaction; proposing transaction structure alternatives to best achieve the business purpose; evaluating the impact of tax issues on the various structural alternatives; creating legal entities designed to bring about the optimal alternative; sourcing capital to facilitate the transaction; and documenting the respective rights and obligations of the parties to the transaction. As several of the firm's transactional attorneys have served as general or associate counsel for large companies, the firm brings knowledgeable support for in-house legal departments needing outside counsel for their larger deals or disputes.

**Intellectual Property & Commercialization:** The firm advises regarding the protection and/or commercialization of intellectual property both domestically and internationally. Some common representations include: copyright counseling and protection; global trademark portfolio management and brand development; trade secret counseling; anti-counterfeiting programs; patent prosecutions; infringement litigation; management and sale of IP assets in bankruptcy proceedings; IP audits for businesses; and all issues pertaining to licensing and IP protection for sports and entertainment personalities, entities, and brands. Working side by side with corporate and transactional attorneys, the firm prepares non-compete agreements and non-disclosure and trade secret agreements in connection with corporate acquisitions, joint-venture relationships, and employment contracts.

**INTERNATIONAL WORK:** Bilingual and culturally-sensitive legal staff offer services to clients from Asia to Latin America and the Caribbean, as well as to firms that focus on providing goods and services to the Hispanic community in the US. The firm has established a network of preeminent law firms throughout South America and the Caribbean to assist the firm in its representation of US companies that do business in the Southern Hemisphere. For more information visit the firm's the firm's website at www.kpkb.com.

Kluger Peretz
Kaplan & Berlin

# KOZYAK TROPIN & THROCKMORTON, P.A.

## THE FIRM

**Founding Shareholders:** John W Kozyak
Charles W Throckmorton
Harley S Tropin
**Managing Shareholder:** Gail A McQuilkin

**Number of shareholders:** 12
**Number of other attorneys:** 8

**FIRM OVERVIEW:** For more than two decades, Kozyak Tropin & Throckmorton has focused on two specific areas of the law – complex litigation and bankruptcy matters. The firm is nationally recognized and respected for its expertise in and out of the courtroom, zealous client representation, and the highest standards of professionalism and ethical conduct. Kozyak Tropin & Throckmorton has earned its reputation through its attorneys' consistent high caliber work, which is recognized by judges, opponents and clients. In every engagement, the firm's focus is on the client's objectives: to develop a strategy and approach that realizes the client's goals, efficiently and effectively.

## MAIN AREAS OF PRACTICE:

**Complex Commercial Litigation:** Kozyak Tropin & Throckmorton's Litigation Practice concentrates on complex commercial contract, tort and securities fraud litigation. The firm's attorneys serve as litigation counsel for a number of corporations, banks, and prominent individuals, and represent clients in matters involving professional malpractice, lender liability, foreclosure, and intellectual property/unfair competition. The firm's trial lawyers have a reputation for tenacity and efficiency.

**Class Actions:** Kozyak Tropin & Throckmorton represents classes of individuals and businesses in multi-million dollar class actions involving fraud, breach of contract, misrepresentation, and other causes of action. The firm has served as lead or co-lead counsel in many major high-profile class action cases including *In re: Humana, Inc.*, and *In re: US Oil & Gas*. Led by partner Harley Tropin, the firm has gained widespread recognition for its successful role representing plaintiffs in the largest class-action lawsuit on record against managed-care companies.

**Commercial Bankruptcy:** Kozyak Tropin & Throckmorton and its bankruptcy attorneys are widely respected for their expertise, experience and effectiveness in business bankruptcies and high-net-worth individual cases. The firm represents a comprehensive range of client constituencies, including debtors, creditors, statutory and liquidating trustees, creditors' committees, equity holders, and asset purchasers, and represents some of the nation's largest companies and lending institutions when they are involved in bankruptcy matters and workouts in Florida and elsewhere. The firm has particular expertise in prosecuting and defending litigation arising out of corporate insolvencies. John Kozyak, who leads the firm's Bankruptcy Practice, has the unique distinction of being a Fellow of both the prestigious American College of Bankruptcy and American College of Trial Lawyers.

**INTERNATIONAL WORK:** With its office located in Miami, Florida, the gateway to Latin America, Kozyak Tropin & Throckmorton represents a number of Central and South American clients. The firm also serves as co-lead counsel in several class action lawsuits brought in the US on behalf of Latin American citizens. Additionally, Kozyak Tropin & Throckmorton attorneys have handled intellectual property matters for multinational corporations such as Dole, Novartis, and Swiss Watch International.

## HEAD OFFICE

**FLORIDA**
2525 Ponce de Leon, 9th Floor, **Miami**, FL 33134
**Tel:** 305 372 1800    **Fax:** 305 372 3508
**Website:** www.kttlaw.com

## CONTACTS

| | |
|---|---|
| Litigation | Harley S Tropin |
| Bankruptcy | John W Kozyak |

**CLIENTS:** Kozyak Tropin & Throckmorton's clients include public and private companies of all sizes including many Fortune 500 companies, as well as governmental entities, not-for-profit organizations, and individuals. Examples include: American Cyanamid Company; Canadian Imperial Bank of Commerce; The CIT Group/Industrial Financing; Credit Suisse First Boston; Dole Food Company; Dole Fresh Flowers; Ecolab; Fidelity Management Trust Company; Florida International University; General Growth Properties; Greenwich Capital Markets; Harch Capital Management; Interval International; LNR Partners (Lennar); Marriott International; Mellon United National Bank; Miami-Dade County (Florida); Miami Dolphins, Ltd.; Novartis Animal Health, US; The Ritz-Carlton Hotel Company; the Seminole Tribe of Florida; Siemens Dematic Corporation; Swiss Watch International; TotalBank; and University of Miami.

KOZYAK · TROPIN
THROCKMORTON
ATTORNEYS AT LAW

# MOYE, O'BRIEN, O'ROURKE, PICKERT & MARTIN, LLP

## THE FIRM

**Managing Partner:** James E Moye
**Senior Partners:** James E Moye
               Stephen W Pickert
               Gregory S Martin

**Number of partners:** 5
**Number of other lawyers:** 11

## AREAS OF PRACTICE:
Construction Litigation ................................. 85%
Labor & Employment .................................. 10%
Commercial Litigation ................................ 5%

**FIRM OVERVIEW:** Established in 1989, Moye, O'Brien, O'Rourke, Pickert & Martin, LLP dedicates its practice to the representation of national and international clients within the construction industry. The firm has dedicated itself to the prompt, efficient, and economic delivery of such legal services. The firm's philosophy is to provide aggressive, high quality legal services at a fair rate, while always striving to extricate its clients from unavoidable controversies at the earliest practicable, most economical and beneficial juncture.

## MAIN AREAS OF PRACTICE
**Construction Litigation:** The firm represents clients, including national and multinational general contractors, owners, design professionals and other construction-related entities, from contract preparation, review and negotiation through ultimate dispute resolution including litigation, arbitration and other alternative resolution procedures.
**Labor & Employment:** The firm has a wide range of experience in representing clients in all phases of labor and employment law, including union and trade dealings and employment practices and disputes.
**Commercial Litigation:** The firm represents clients in a variety of contract and tort disputes between corporate entities.

**CLIENTS:** The firm has represented clients throughout the United States of America, the Caribbean basin, Central America, and Canada. A representative listing of clients includes: AMEC Civil LLC, Archer-Western Contractors, Ltd.; Arden Villas University, Ltd.; Balfour Beatty, Inc.; Balfour Beatty Construction, Inc.; Balfour Beatty Rail Systems, Inc.; Centex Homes; Hazen and Sawyer, P.C.; Peter Kiewit Sons', Inc.; Leggett & Platt, Inc.; Loews Corporation; MACTEC Engineering & Consulting, Inc.; Marta Track Constructors; Metroplex Corporation; Odebrecht Construction, Inc.; PCL Civil Constructors, Inc.; PCL Construction Services, Inc.; Parsons Transportation Group; Professional Services Industries, Inc.; QORE Property Sciences; Traylor Bros, Inc., Universal City Development Partners, Ltd; Universal Studios Florida; Universal Technical Institute; Walsh Group, Inc.; ZOM Companies.

**INTERNATIONAL WORK:** The firm advises international companies operating within the US. The firm also advises US companies on their foreign activities.

## HEAD OFFICE

**FLORIDA**
800 South Orlando Avenue, **Maitland**, FL 32751
**Tel:** 407 622 5250   **Fax:** 407 622 5440
**Email:** moopm@earthlink.net

## AFFILIATE OFFICE

**ILLINOIS**
O'Rourke, Hogan, Fowler & Dwyer
10 South LaSalle Street, Suite 2900, **Chicago**, IL 60603
**Tel:** 312 739 3500   **Fax:** 312 739 3535

# PODHURST ORSECK, P.A.

## THE FIRM

**Founding & Managing Partner:** Aaron S Podhurst

**Number of partners:** 8
**Number of other lawyers:** 4
**Number of other lawyers (of Counsel):** 2

### OFFICES

**FLORIDA**
City National Bank Building, 25 West Flagler Street, Suite 800,
**Miami**, FL 33130
**Tel:** 305 358 2800   **Fax:** 305 358 2382
**Website:** www.podhurst.com

**FIRM OVERVIEW:** Podhurst Orseck continues a legal practice, established nearly four decades ago, concentrating exclusively in trial and appellate litigation. The firm is dedicated to offering the highest caliber legal representation in both federal and state trial and appellate courts not just in Florida, but throughout the country. The firm's commercial practice focuses on complex civil litigation of all types. The firm serves as general litigation counsel to several major corporations as well as representing companies and individuals in substantial matters of commercial litigation. The firm's General Tort Practice places major emphasis upon representing claimants in aviation, automobile, products liability and medical malpractice litigation. From its inception, the firm has also cultivated an Appellate Practice, handling appeals of not only the firm's own trial lawyers, but of other lawyers throughout the nation, in the various state and federal appellate courts, including the United States Supreme Court. The firm's practice serves clients and corporations throughout the United States, and in several foreign countries.

## MAIN AREAS OF PRACTICE:

**Commercial Litigation:** Nearly fifty percent of the firm's trial and appellate litigation involves the resolution of corporate and commercial disputes. The practice varies from the most complex commercial cases to simple contract litigation. The firm's commercial clientele includes Fortune 500 companies, small and middle-sized companies, and private individuals. Regular litigation clients include: Alienware Corp., Codina Construction Corp., Mellon United National Bank; Lennar Corporation and Florida East Coast Properties, Inc.

**General Tort Practice Concentrating in Automobile Negligence, Product Liability & Medical Malpractice Litigation:** Since its inception, a significant portion of the firm's trial practice has been general tort law. The firm's experience runs the gamut of such cases, from automobile liability to complex products liability, to business-related torts. Literally thousands of general negligence and product liability cases of all sorts have been prepared, negotiated, and either settled or tried by the members of the firm. An abbreviated listing of the types of cases handled would include all types of general negligence cases (from automobile and slip and fall accidents to boating and diving accidents), product liability cases (involving cranes, automobiles, rollover and tire tread separation, trenchers, food processing equipment, marine engines, pharmaceuticals, hand tools and ladders, to name a few) and complex medical, legal, accounting, architectural and engineering malpractice claims.

**Class Actions:** The firm has played a prominent role in class action and multi-district litigation proceedings. Several partners have been court appointed lead or liaison counsel in numerous major class actions, ranging from securities litigation, investor fraud cases, pharmaceutical, health care and insurance litigation. In addition, firm lawyers have chaired and served on the steering committee of many national multi-district litigation proceedings involving products defects, major commercial aviation crashes and other mass tort cases. Significant firm resources and a sizeable support staff have been devoted to this practice area.

**Aviation Litigation:** A major emphasis within the firm's General Tort Practice is aviation litigation. The firm is recognized as one of the premier plaintiffs' aviation law firms in the nation. The firm believes that it has handled more plaintiffs' aviation cases than any other firm in the southeastern United States and more foreign air crashes than almost any other firm in the country. The firm has represented multiple victims of over 40 major air disasters in the past twenty years. In addition, it has handled in excess of 100 small or light plane crashes involving private, non-commercial airplanes.

**Appellate Practice:** Two of the firm's attorneys devote their practice exclusively to appellate litigation and complex trial-level motions, handling all in-house matters and referrals from attorneys and clients all over the United States. They practice primarily in the United States Court of Appeals for the Eleventh Circuit, the Florida Supreme Court, and the intermediate Florida District Courts of Appeal. The head of the Appellate Litigation Division, Joel Eaton, also has handled appellate litigation elsewhere in the United States, has argued several cases in the United States Supreme Court and is recognized as one of the premier appellate practitioners in the state of Florida. The firm's Appellate Practice mirrors the substantive diversity of the firm as a whole, and includes plaintiffs' personal-injury, medical malpractice, and wrongful-death cases, including aviation-related matters and commercial matters of all types.

**Probate & Matrimonial Litigation:** For many years, the firm has represented clients in the field of probate and matrimonial litigation. It has engaged in the preparation of pre-nuptial agreements, and in litigation involving marital dissolution, child custody and property settlement agreements. The firm also has represented clients in claims challenging pre-nuptial agreements. Further, it has had substantial experience in litigation involving post-dissolution of marriage proceedings pertaining to modifications, as well as will contests and complex probate litigation.

**Criminal Litigation:** The firm has a special interest and concentration in the areas of white-collar crime and commercial fraud. The focus of these practices is the representation of individuals, corporate executives and corporations, in both Florida and federal proceedings, ranging from grand jury investigations to criminal prosecutions and appeals. The firm has handled litigation involving environmental matters, bank fraud, tax fraud, mail and wire fraud, RICO violations, securities fraud, anti-trust price fixing, bar grievances, official corruption, and various other economic crimes. The firm has also handled quasi-criminal forfeitures and seizures of assets.

**Recognition:** Firm members are annually recognized by their peers in regional rankings of top trial and appellate lawyers, including 'Florida's Legal Elite' by Florida Trend Magazine and 'Top Lawyers in South Florida' and by numerous publications both nationally and internationally. Five of the firm's eight partners have been selected by their peers for inclusion in the 'Best Lawyers in America'. Three of the firm's partners were also selected to be included in the 'Best Lawyers in America - Commercial Litigation' by Litigation 2005, a supplement to American Lawyer and Corporate Counsel. The firm has also been recognized for overall excellence by 'The Miami Herald', 'The National Law Journal', 'South Florida CEO' and the 'South Florida Business Journal'.

# RICHMAN GREER WEIL BRUMBAUGH MIRABITO & CHRISTENSEN, P.A.

## THE FIRM

**Managing Shareholder:** John M Brumbaugh

**Number of partners:** 15
**Number of other lawyers:** 9

**FIRM OVERVIEW:** Richman Greer Weil Brumbaugh Mirabito & Christensen, P.A., has developed an international reputation for successfully handling complex business litigation in state and federal courts. The firm, founded in 1961, is best known for its tenacious and effective courtroom presence. This trial capability allows the firm to negotiate favorable results for clients not involved in litigation, in areas ranging from corporate transactions and real estate to estate planning, family law and employment matters. The firm industry expertise reflects the New Economy (i.e. telecommunications, media and entertainment) highly regulated businesses (i.e. financial services, energy and manufacturing) and the traditional economy of South Florida: real estate and construction, agriculture, tourism and transportation. The firm also represents high profile individuals, units of state and local government and non-profits.

## MAIN AREAS OF PRACTICE

**Complex Commercial Litigation:** The firm has a long history in all types of business litigation, including commercial class action lawsuits, First Amendment cases and securities fraud matters. Richman Greer acts as counsel to Fortune 500 corporations facing litigation in Florida and is regularly retained on litigation steering committees by the world's largest law firms. Richman Greer lawyers have served on American Arbitration Association panels and have been appointed to serve as mediators for federal and state litigation. Many firm attorneys are board certified by the Florida Bar in civil trial law, and/or business litigation. In addition, members of the firm have been named as fellows of the American College of Trial Lawyers, the International Society of Barristers, the American Board of Trial Advocacy and the International Academy of Trial Lawyers. The firm's alumni include a senior United States Court of Appeals judge, a United States District judge and several state court trial judges.

**Condominium Litigation:** The firm had a major role in the first Florida Supreme Court decision regarding condominium law and has successfully defended a critical case brought by the Federal Trade Commission in its investigation of condominium sales practices. The firm remains a leader in condominium law development, representing both developers, and condominium associations.

**Corporate/Business Services:** Richman Greer provides general business representation, such as assisting in corporate formations or other transactions, and representing parties in business sales and acquisitions.

**Employment Litigation:** Richman Greer represents employers in matters of racial, ethnic, sexual, age and disability discrimination, as well as sexual harassment and fair employment practices. The firm also represents employers in Equal Employment Opportunity Commission proceedings at the administrative level.

**Environmental Law:** The firm handles disputes regarding land use, environmental compliance, water quality, contamination and has litigated environmental contamination cases.

**Estate Planning, Probate & Trusts:** Richman Greer represents clients in probate court litigation, including will contests and estate administration disputes, and provides estate planning services and trust administration. The partner heading this area of practice is board certified by the Florida Bar in wills, trusts and estates.

**Family Law:** Richman Greer has a substantial practice in family law including dissolution of marriage and child custody matters, with particular expertise in representing business executives, sports and entertainments figures and spouses of such individuals. The partner heading this area of practice is board certified by the Florida Bar in marital and family law.

**Insurance Defense:** The firm represents insurance carriers, claims administrators and self-insured entities in the defense of tort claims.

**Intellectual Property, Communications & Technology:** The firm has litigated major trademark, copyright and patent litigation cases in federal court, successfully defending the rights of international corporate clients.

**Manufacturer/Product Liability:** The firm represents numerous manufacturers, distributors and self-insured entities in the defense of product liability claims.

**Officer/Director Representation:** The firm has defended officers and directors of several public companies, including failed financial institutions.

**Real Estate/Construction:** The firm represents major institutional lenders, developers, buyers, sellers and managers of commercial and residential property in real estate development, financing and litigation. This includes significant construction litigation matters, such as failure to fulfill contractual obligations, allegations of defects, and disagreements over financial responsibility.

**Securities Litigation:** The firm has been actively involved in significant antitrust and securities litigation, including shareholder's lawsuits and alleged violations of securities law.

**CLIENTS:** Representative clients of the firm include 3M Company F/K/A Minnesota Mining and Manufacturing Co.; the Republic of Panama; Arthur Anderson (World Wide); Hallmark; DIRECTV; Solutia, Merrill Lynch; Precision Response Corporation; City National Bank of Miami; First International Bank; Landmark Education Corporation; Best Buy; Banque Artesia, S.A.; Goldman Sachs & Co.; Hughes Electronic Corporation; Mt. Sinai Medical Center; Purity Wholesale Grocers; Blood Diagnostics, Inc. and Genstar.

**INTERNATIONAL WORK:** With language capabilities in English, Spanish and Gaelic and membership in Meritas, a leading worldwide association of business law firms, Richman Greer regularly serves overseas clients, having represented foreign governments, banks, airlines, television stations, investment and insurance interests and individuals.

RICHMAN GREER WEIL BRUMBAUGH MIRABITO & CHRISTENSEN
PROFESSIONAL ASSOCIATION

# SHUBIN & BASS, P.A.

## THE FIRM

**Contact:** John K Shubin

### AREAS OF PRACTICE:

Land Use, Administrative & Municipal Litigation . . . . . . . . . . . . . .35%
Business Litigation & Dispute Resolution . . . . . . . . . . . . . . . . . . .35%
Strategic Regulatory Analysis & Governmental Affairs . . . . . . . .15%
Appellate Practice . . . . . . . . . . . . . . . . . . . . . . . . . . . . . . . . . . . . . .15%

**FIRM OVERVIEW:** Established in 1992, Shubin & Bass continues to define itself as a small law firm which handles mission critical matters for a select number of public and private institutional clients, local governments, and large law firms who place a premium on our ability to handle the most complex litigation and administrative matters. They are not a large law firm, and do not aspire to be a large law firm, and they do not measure their success by the number of lawyers they employ or the number of new files open. The firm instead measures its success purely by the results obtained for its clients and the level of trust they place in their abilities.

### MAIN AREAS OF PRACTICE:

**Land Use, Administrative, & Municipal Litigation:** Throughout the State of Florida, the firm has represented the interests of property owners, governmental bodies, and affected individuals and advocacy groups in all types of litigation and administrative proceedings addressing the proposed development of land and government's regulation of land  This representation includes matters relating to eminent domain and the prosecution and defense of claims for inverse condemnation.

**Business Litigation & Dispute Resolution:** The firm has extensive experience in the litigation of complex business and real estate disputes throughout the State of Florida. The firm is highly selective with respect to the litigation it undertakes on behalf of clients, and limits its caseload to those cases which present unique issues of law or which would benefit from the firm's experience in having litigated and tried many complex cases involving its core practice areas. The firm is also regularly called upon to serve as local counsel to numerous national law firms with respect to litigation in the state and federal courts in Florida, and prides itself in its ability to identify, negotiate, and consummate the settlement of extremely contentious matters.

**Strategic Regulatory Analysis & Governmental Affairs:** The firm possesses lawyers with an academic background in economics and public policy analysis, particularly in the context of regulated industries, and combines this academic perspective with years of litigation and public advocacy experience at all levels of municipal, state, and federal government. This balance of theoretical and practical experience enables the firm to offer counsel to clients whose businesses or investments are directly affected by governmental regulation policies. Although most of this representation involves analysis of the regulation of land, it has also offered counsel with respect to water rights, timber rights, and the regulation of various extractive industries, particularly limerock mining.

**Appellate Practice:** The firm has considerable experience in representing its clients before state and federal appellate courts, particularly with respect to complex or novel legal issues presented in the land use, municipal law, and commercial litigation contexts.  Many of the published opinions arising out of the firm's representation of its clients before these appellate tribunals are well recognized as definitive caselaw in these respective practice areas.

### HEAD OFFICE

**FLORIDA**
46 S.W. First Street Third Floor **Miami**, FL 33130
**Tel:** 305 381 6060   **Fax:** 305 381 9457
**Email:** jshubin@shubinbass.com
**Website:** www.shubinbass.com

**CLIENTS:** The firm's clients include: American Financial Realty Trust; Atlantic Civil Engineering, Inc.; Brickell Equities Corporation; Citadel Investment Group; City of Aventura; City of Coral Gables; City of North Miami; City of Vero Beach; Codina Group, Inc.; The Congress Group, Inc.; Core Communities; Crescent Real Estate Equities, L.L.C.; Cuban American Bar Association; Fairfield Residential, L.L.C.; Finger Companies; Flagstone Property Group; Florida Association for Women Lawyers Miami-Dade Chapter; Florida Rock & Sand Company; Gator Investments; GB/JT Hotel Partners; GFS Corporation; Grovenor House; Hellmann Worldwide Logistics; Hispanic National Bar Association; Indian River County; Intervest Properties; The Mills Corporation; Montenay Power Corporation; 9000 Centre Associates; Performing Arts Center Foundation; Premier Developers; Properties of Hamilton; Related Group of Florida; Residential Funding Corporation; Rouse Companies; Stranahan House; Sunny Development, LLC; Swerdlow Development Group; State of Florida, Florida Department of State; TA Associates Realty; Town of Golden Beach, University of Miami; Village of Key Biscayne; and White Rock Quarries.

# SHUTTS & BOWEN LLP

## THE FIRM

**FIRM OVERVIEW:** Shutts & Bowen is a leading Florida law firm, with more than 170 attorneys in offices located in Miami, Fort Lauderdale, West Palm Beach, Orlando, Tallahassee, Amsterdam and London.

## MAIN AREAS OF PRACTICE

**Financial Services:** The Financial Services Practice Group represents foreign banks with a Florida presence, out-of-state banks which have a presence in the state or are attempting to establish one, and local banks and savings and loan associations, and local and national investment banking firms and investment advisors. Unlike other law firms which primarily represent local banks, the firm's practice is largely centered on the representation of foreign and out-of-state banks.

**Corporate:** The Corporate Group provides a wide range of corporate and business services, including structuring and negotiating new business ventures, mergers and acquisitions and advising on traditional corporate, partnership and commercial law issues. In the securities area, they counsel clients in private and public securities offerings in the United States and abroad, as well as assist in preparing corporate and insider filings required by the Securities and Exchange Commission and the stock exchanges.

**Real Estate:** The Real Estate Department represents a broad range of domestic and foreign entrepreneurs, developers, investors and lenders, with emphasis on institutional clients such as national and multi-national corporations, insurance companies and banks. The firm advises its clients in all aspects of their real estate transactions, including acquisitions, sales, development, land use, zoning, environmental, financing, leasing and construction. It also assists the corporate and international departments in structuring the real estate aspects of large corporate and international transactions.

**Litigation:** The Commercial Litigation Department has vigorously represented clients at all levels of federal and state court systems and before numerous state and federal agencies, commissions, boards, and other regulatory and administrative authorities. The firm handles all aspects of the litigation process, from counseling and alternative-dispute-resolution mechanisms, through the prosecution or defense of discovery, pretrial, and trial proceedings in lawsuits, to post trial remedies and review in appellate courts. The Litigation Department's practice includes a wide variety of administrative, trial, and appellate cases.

**International/Tax:** The International/Tax Department advises US clients, multinational corporations, investors in foreign countries and foreign clients investing in the US. The firm counsels its clients in a broad range of tax problems, including foreign tax, partnerships, corporate and individual tax, tax exempt organizations, qualified plans and local taxation, particularly as it relates to banks and private placement tax opinions. The department handles appeals before the IRS and tax court litigation.

**Estate Planning:** The Estate Planning Group assists clients in distributing their assets, while minimizing the payment of estate taxes, through estate planning and estate administration. The firm's services include counseling clients to assure the orderly and efficient transfer of property to their beneficiaries with a minimum of estate, gift, generation-skipping and income tax costs.

## OFFICES

**FLORIDA**
1500 Miami Center, 201 South Biscayne Boulevard, **Miami,** FL 33131
**Tel:** 305 358 6300   **Fax:** 305 381 9982
**Website:** www.shutts-law.com

200 East Broward Boulevard, Suite 2100, **Fort Lauderdale,** FL 33301
**Tel:** 954 524 5505   **Fax:** 954 524 5506

One Clearlake Centre, 250 Australian Avenue South, Suite 500,
**West Palm Beach,** FL 33401
**Tel:** 561 835 8500   **Fax:** 561 650 8530

300 South Orange Avenue, Suite 1000, **Orlando,** FL 32801
**Tel:** 407 423 3200   **Fax:** 407 425 8316

215 South Monroe Street, Suite 804, **Tallahassee,** FL 32301
**Tel:** 850 521 0600   **Fax:** 850 521 0604

## CONTACTS

| Office | Contact |
| --- | --- |
| **Miami** | Bowman Brown |
| **Fort Lauderdale** | Allan Rubin, George Platt |
| **West Palm Beach** | Arthur J Menor |
| **Orlando** | James G Willard |
| **Tallahassee** | Eric Thorn |

**CLIENTS:** Shutts & Bowen offers its clients, whether local, state, national or international, a diverse and complete range of high quality and responsive legal services. The firm represents major industrial corporations and life insurance companies, utilities companies, securities brokerage firms, transportation concerns, national and international financial institutions, local banking firms, major foreign companies, healthcare organizations, local municipalities, local corporations, and individuals and smaller enterprises of every nature.

# STICHTER, RIEDEL, BLAIN & PROSSER, PA

## THE FIRM

**Founding Partners:** Don M Stichter, Harley E Riedel

**Number of partners:** 9
**Number of other lawyers:** 5

**HEAD OFFICE**

**FLORIDA**
110 E. Madison Street, Suite 200, **Tampa**, FL 33602
**Tel:** 813 229 0144  **Fax:** 813 229 1811
**Website:** www.srbp.com

**FIRM OVERVIEW:** Stichter, Riedel, Blain & Prosser, PA is a 14-lawyer firm specializing in the representation of parties in bankruptcy cases, insolvency matters, out-of-court workout arrangements, and related civil litigation. The firm's nine partners have more than 200 years of cumulative experience in the practice of bankruptcy law and can bring this experience and expertise to bear in all types of bankruptcy and insolvency situations, including out-of-court workouts and state court insolvency proceedings. Since its inception in 1974, the firm has been rated AV by Martindale-Hubbell. All of the name partners have served as presidents and chairs of the Tampa Bay Bankruptcy Bar Association. Don M Stichter and Harley E Riedel are Fellows of the American College of Bankruptcy. Mr Stichter was named the Outstanding Lawyer in Hillsborough Country, Florida in 2003 and was the first recipient of the Lifetime Achievement Award by the Tampa Bay Bankruptcy Bar Association in 2004.

**MAIN AREAS OF PRACTICE:** Stichter, Riedel, Blain & Prosser, PA, advises clients faced with insolvency or bankruptcy issues. It regularly represents parties in cases pending in all of the bankruptcy courts in Florida, as well as in other states. As a 'boutique' insolvency firm, Stichter Riedel begins many of its engagements as a result of referrals from other professionals who have a long-standing attorney-client or accountant-client relationship with the client.

**CLIENTS:** The firm has represented numerous debtors in Chapter 11 cases as well as substantial creditors, purchasers, defendants, committees, trustees, or other parties in interest in a number of significant Chapter 11 and Chapter 7 cases. The largest segment of its practice consists of the representation of corporate debtors in Chapter 11 cases. Clients range from small companies to large publicly-owned corporations. Most cases involve companies with assets, liabilities, or annual revenues in excess of $5 million, ranging in size to companies with assets and liabilities of more than $3 billion. Among the more significant debtor representations are: Hillsborough Holdings Corp., formerly known as The Jim Walter Corporation, and its 32 subsidiaries, with assets and liabilities of more than $3 billion; Koger Properties, Inc., a New York Stock Exchange company at the time of filing with assets and liabilities of more than $500 million; The Koger Partnership, Ltd., a publicly traded limited partnership with assets and liabilities of more than $200 million; Bicoastal Corporation, formerly known as The Singer Company, with assets in excess of $500 million and over $2 billion in asserted claims; Lykes Bros. Steamship Co., Inc., the third largest US Flag international shipping company with assetts and liabilities in excess of $300 million; Jumbosports Inc., a major national retailer of sporting goods with 59 stores in more than 20 states and assets and liabilities of more than $300 million; and Moltech Power Services, Inc., a Gainsville-based manufacturer of rechargeable batteries with annual revenues of $140 million and assets and liabilities of

approximately $80 million. Among numerous substantial creditor and purchaser representations are: the Official Creditors' Committee in Anchor Glass, the third largest US glass manufacturer with liabilities of more than $600 million; Outback Steakhouse, Inc., the successful purchaser of the designation rights to 76 restaurants in the Delaware Chapter 11 case of Chi-Chi's, Inc.; and a class of consumer creditors in the New Jersey case of American Family Publishers (a Time, Inc. subsidiary). An extensive list of other representations is set forth on the firm's website. Lawyers with Stichter, Riedel, Blain & Prosser, PA have been involved in more than 300 reported decisions including matters in the Circuit Courts of Appeals, the US District Courts, and the US Bankruptcy Courts.

## How lawyers are ranked

Every year we carry out thousands of in-depth interviews with clients and lawyers in order to assess the reputations and expertise of business lawyers across the USA. Chambers rankings and editorial are referred to extensively by General Counsel and other purchasers of legal services who look to our recommendations when choosing their lawyers.

# ANTITRUST

<table>
<tr><td colspan="2">Antitrust<br>Leading Firms</td></tr>
<tr><td>1</td><td>ALSTON & BIRD LLP Atlanta</td></tr>
<tr><td></td><td>BONDURANT, MIXSON & ELMORE, LLP Atlanta</td></tr>
<tr><td></td><td>KING & SPALDING LLP Atlanta</td></tr>
<tr><td>2</td><td>ROGERS & HARDIN Atlanta</td></tr>
<tr><td></td><td>TROUTMAN SANDERS LLP Atlanta</td></tr>
<tr><td></td><td>VAUGHAN & MURPHY Atlanta</td></tr>
<tr><td>3</td><td>JONES DAY Atlanta</td></tr>
<tr><td></td><td>KILPATRICK STOCKTON LLP Atlanta</td></tr>
<tr><td></td><td>PAUL, HASTINGS, JANOFSKY & WALKER Atlanta</td></tr>
<tr><td></td><td>POWELL GOLDSTEIN LLP Atlanta</td></tr>
<tr><td></td><td>SMITH GAMBRELL & RUSSELL LLP Atlanta</td></tr>
</table>

<table>
<tr><td colspan="2">Leading Individuals</td></tr>
<tr><td colspan="2">Senior Statesman</td></tr>
<tr><td></td><td>BONDURANT Emmet Bondurant, Mixson & Elmore</td></tr>
<tr><td>1</td><td>ALLEN Randall Alston & Bird</td></tr>
<tr><td></td><td>CASHDAN Jeffrey King & Spalding</td></tr>
<tr><td></td><td>GRADY Kevin Alston & Bird</td></tr>
<tr><td>2</td><td>HARRIS JR H Stephen Alston & Bird</td></tr>
<tr><td></td><td>MURPHY JR Charles Vaughan & Murphy</td></tr>
<tr><td></td><td>POWERS Tony Rogers & Hardin</td></tr>
<tr><td></td><td>RHODES Thomas Smith Gambrell & Russell</td></tr>
<tr><td></td><td>SAUNTRY June Troutman Sanders</td></tr>
<tr><td>3</td><td>ASBILL Rick Paul, Hastings</td></tr>
<tr><td></td><td>MARSHALL John Powell Goldstein</td></tr>
<tr><td></td><td>MULLIS Carl Paul, Hastings</td></tr>
<tr><td></td><td>NEWTON Trammell Jones Day</td></tr>
<tr><td></td><td>RUSS Michael King & Spalding</td></tr>
<tr><td></td><td>VAUGHAN C David Vaughan & Murphy</td></tr>
</table>

## Band 1

### Alston & Bird LLP
See firm details p.728

**The Firm:** This "*top-class firm*" is felt to offer "*excellent coverage on antitrust matters and a superb bench strength.*" It is best known for its litigation expertise, which is applied to alleged price-fixing and consumer class actions, as well as more complex multidistrict and federal disputes. The group also picked up plaudits for its merger and transactional

skills and is felt to be "*excellent at spotting problems far in advance of them happening.*"

**The Lawyers:** Kevin Grady (see p.714) is "*a top-notch adviser who gives opinions which are clear, considered and incredibly insightful.*" Although he is active across the automobile, chemical and insurance industries, he is best known for his expertise in healthcare. Commentators say: "*There is no one to beat him on healthcare antitrust matters.*" The "*astute*" Randall Allen (see p.705) is endorsed as "*a sharp and hard-working lawyer who is more than capable of keeping a dozen plates spinning at once.*" Clients say he is particularly adept at merger review, as illustrated by his recent representation of Movie Gallery on its acquisition of Hollywood Entertainment. These are two of the leading players in the video rental market. Stephen Harris (see p.714) is rated by clients for his trenchant advice: "*You can give him a complex matter and he'll have a simple answer in five minutes.*" His practice focuses on federal and transnational matters and he is said to be extremely strong on international arbitrations. One client commented: "*He travels the world and wherever he is, he calls – he's a tremendous resource.*"

**Clients/Work Highlights:** Nokia; Mohawk Industries; T-Mobile; Genuine Parts Company; LaRoche Industries; NASCAR; UPS and Verizon Wireless.

### Bondurant, Mixson & Elmore, LLP
See firm details p.731

**The Firm:** Although the group is perceived to have had a quieter year, it is still regarded as "*the best antitrust litigation practice in town – there is nobody who can really touch it when it comes to the dispute side.*" Clients rhapsodize over these lawyers, citing them as "*undoubted masters of the courtroom who represent a superb marriage of talent and knowledge.*" Although small in size, the team impresses with its versatility and has handled matters in the healthcare, aviation and motor sports industries.

**The Lawyers:** Emmet Bondurant (see p.707) was said by peers to be "*the best antitrust litigator in Georgia – and anyone who tells you different is lying.*" Commentators say: "*He has his hand in every big matter that's come along.*" Although he has not been as active in courtroom antitrust matters recently, he has been advising a number of clients in advance of cases.

**Clients/Work Highlights:** The group has handled matters for Delta Air Lines, Michelin and International Dairy Queen.

### King & Spalding LLP
See firm details p.1933

**The Firm:** Recommended to researchers as "*a good national practice with a strong Southeastern core,*" this team is "*both versatile and practical.*" The range of its skills is wide indeed and it is viewed as being especially adept in large litigations, class actions and government investigations. Clients also praise its transactional abilities, particularly in regard to joint ventures.

**The Lawyers:** Jeffrey Cashdan (see p.708) is the best-known member of the Atlanta team and is extolled as "*an excellent attorney and someone of substance.*" He is rated for his litigation and counseling skills, both at state and national level. One peer commented: "*He's a lawyer I'm most impressed with, I think he's better than nearly all of us.*" He recently represented Home Depot in a billion-dollar case against Visa and MasterCard in federal court in New York. Although better known as a litigator, Michael Russ (see p.723) wins praise as "*a superb advocate with a laser-sharp eye for the key issues.*"

**Clients/Work Highlights:** The group represented UCB in the vitamins antitrust litigation, one of the largest criminal antitrust investigations ever undertaken by the DOJ. This involved 55 separate multiparty lawsuits from 32 different federal courts. Other clients include Coca-Cola; GE; Miliken & Company; Miller Brewing; Scientific Atlantic and UPS.

## Band 2

### Rogers & Hardin

**The Firm:** This litigation-focused firm is regarded as "*a prominent, top-class group that offers a pragmatic and user-friendly service.*" Its small team is known for its skill in textile and construction matters and further enjoys success in the insurance and healthcare sectors. Of its many attributes, however, it is probably most celebrated for its work in relation to government investigations.

**The Lawyers:** Tony Powers was described to researchers as "*an astute lawyer who quickly comes to*" considered and commercial opinions." "A truly experienced practitioner whom it's difficult to surprise," he continues to represent Covad Communications in its ongoing monopolization litigation against BellSouth. The highly recommended and experienced litigator **CB Rogers** also lends his expertise to antitrust matters.

**Clients/Work Highlights:** The group's client base includes members of the textile, transport, healthcare and construction industries.

## Troutman Sanders LLP

**The Firm:** This is a modest team but one endorsed as "a first-class outfit which really speaks the language of business." The group's litigation skills are well known, as evidenced by its recent participation in a large dispute over fiberglass and a number of patent matters. It does, however, have capabilities in a number of areas and is applauded generally for its counseling skills. Over the past year, for example, the attorneys have advised on a large healthcare antitrust matter. Although based in Atlanta, the group continues to attract energy work from Washington, DC.

**The Lawyers:** Much of the team's strength is derived from the "superb" **June Ann Sauntry**. Hailed by clients as "an absolutely fantastic resource," she "understands antitrust in a way many people can only aspire to." "A lawyer who builds a superb client rapport," she has been seen in a number of high-profile matters and recently represented a medical device company alleging that there had been a group boycott of one of its newly developed treatments. She has also acted in a number of cases concerning theater chains being sued in relation to block booking.

**Clients/Work Highlights:** YKK; the Southeastern Electric Exchange; AGCO; B.L. Harbert International; Southern Company; Impact Medical Consulting and Southern Association of Orthodontists.

## Vaughan & Murphy

**The Firm:** This tight-knit unit is "more than capable of locking horns with the larger teams on the most complex issues." Lawyers represent defendants and plaintiffs in a range of cases – some of which carry an international element – and earn particular praise for their work in criminal investigations.

**The Lawyers:** "Gentlemanly" **Charles Murphy** is rated as "a quick on the uptake, no loopholes lawyer." He is particularly known for his representation of individuals in antitrust matters. His partner **David Vaughan** is praised as "absolutely dynamite on criminal antitrust matters."

**Clients/Work Highlights:** The group's clients include entities in the real estate, construction, soft drink, chemical and computer industries.

## Jones Day

See firm details p.570

**The Firm:** The team is not built on a grand scale but enjoys the estimable benefit of being plugged into the firm's national network while also being "more than capable of handling meaty matters on its own." It is endorsed for its litigation skills – particularly in price-fixing, monopolization and dealer protection – and also for its joint venture and merger advice. The group proves particularly effective in the healthcare and textile industries.

**The Lawyers:** Head of the team **Trammell Newton** (see p.720) is regarded as "a dedicated lawyer, who talks a lot of sense." Recommended to researchers for his advocacy skills, he has acted on two high-profile cases for Finnish paper manufacturer UPM. Both these cases involved allegations of horizontal price fixing and had substantial European aspects to them.

**Clients/Work Highlights:** The firm acts for international corporates and regional bodies.

## Kilpatrick Stockton LLP

See firm details p.735

**The Firm:** Although the group enjoys a higher profile in commercial litigation, it continues to be regarded as "a solid antitrust team that one really wouldn't want to mess with." The group's courtroom skills are "exemplary" and clients say the lawyers "never fail to grab hold of the pertinent points." It recently acted for restaurant chain Huddle House in dismissing antitrust claims brought by a number of franchises.

**The Lawyers:** Stephens Clay is the best-known member of the team.

**Clients/Work Highlights:** The group represents international and national corporates on both litigation and merger advice.

## Paul, Hastings, Janofsky & Walker LLP

See firm details p.339

**The Firm:** Clients were enthusiastic about this "small, but razor-sharp" team, picking out its "approachability and good commercial attitude" for special mention. The firm is regarded as equally strong in litigation and commercial matters and is further seen as particularly skilled in franchising and distribution. It has acted on a number of cutting-edge matters in recent times including looking at merger issues in EU deals.

**The Lawyers:** The "business-savvy" **Rick Asbill** (see p.705) is praised as an expert on mergers and corporate deals. He is currently handling the antitrust

aspects of the sale of an internationally based franchise system to a private equity fund. **Carl Mullis** (see p.720) is "a direct and forthright opponent." Recommended as sharp in both securities and antitrust litigation, he has been involved in a large healthcare litigation for a Southeastern company.

**Clients/Work Highlights:** The firm represents regional and international companies and has particular experience of dealing with healthcare, education and hospitality concerns.

## Powell Goldstein LLP

**The Firm:** The firm continues to boast a good reputation in the antitrust arena and is described by clients as "a totally focused and versatile team." Working closely with its partners in Washington, DC, the group represents a range of companies on large litigations, merger advice and franchising and distribution matters.

**The Lawyers:** Although he has not been as active in trial work recently, **John Marshall** remains "a definite presence" in the antitrust market and "one of the most astute lawyers you could find." He has been active in arbitrations in recent times.

**Clients/Work Highlights:** The group represents large corporations and public companies. These include entities in the beverage, media and carpet industries.

## Smith Gambrell & Russell LLP

**The Firm:** "The depth and breadth of this firm's practice never fail to impress," said clients. "It's a good professional outfit you can always rely on." Working cheek by jowl with its Washington, DC office, the group wins plaudits for its litigation skills and handles a range of trade regulation cases across a number of industries. A busy outfit, its experience extends well beyond its Southeastern base.

**The Lawyers:** **Thomas Rhodes** is described by clients as "not only a top litigator, but an excellent counselor who has a full understanding of every aspect of a case." He has been active in matters across a number of states. Recent cases include litigation relating to the artificial raising of alcohol prices in Maryland and a large airline travel agent dispute in North Carolina.

**Clients/Work Highlights:** Although the group is known for its traditional strength in the aviation industry, it represents parties in a number of sectors including the construction, manufacturing and automobile industries.

# BANKING & FINANCE

## Banking & Finance
### Leading Firms

1. **ALSTON & BIRD LLP** *Atlanta*
   **KING & SPALDING LLP** *Atlanta*
   **PAUL, HASTINGS, JANOFSKY & WALKER** *Atlanta*
2. **JONES DAY** *Atlanta*
   **KILPATRICK STOCKTON LLP** *Atlanta*
   **PARKER, HUDSON, RAINER & DOBBS** *Atlanta*
3. **HUNTON & WILLIAMS LLP** *Atlanta*
   **POWELL GOLDSTEIN LLP** *Atlanta*
   **TROUTMAN SANDERS LLP** *Atlanta*

### Leading Individuals

1. **CARSON Christopher** *Jones Day*
   **CONRAD Albert** *King & Spalding*
   **CUSHING Paul** *Alston & Bird*
   **DOBBS C Edward** *Parker, Hudson, Rainer*
   **MOLEN Chris** *Paul, Hastings*
2. **ALFORD Carolyn** *King & Spalding*
   **GRICE Richard** *Alston & Bird*
   **JORDAN Hilary** *Kilpatrick Stockton*
3. **ACORD Bobbi** *Parker, Hudson, Rainer*
   **AUSTIN Jesse** *Paul, Hastings*
   **BLUMEN Rick** *Alston & Bird*
   **DEMPSTER Hazen** *Troutman Sanders*
   **LLORENS JR Hector** *King & Spalding*
   **MOORHEAD Bruce** *Hunton & Williams LLP*

### Up-and-coming individuals

**LAFIANDRA Aldo** *Alston & Bird*
**LEVEILLE Michael** *Parker, Hudson, Rainer*

## Banking & Finance: Mainly Regulatory
### Leading Firms

1. **ALSTON & BIRD LLP** *Atlanta*
   **POWELL GOLDSTEIN LLP** *Atlanta*
2. **KILPATRICK STOCKTON LLP** *Atlanta*
   **SMITH GAMBRELL & RUSSELL LLP** *Atlanta*
   **TROUTMAN SANDERS LLP** *Atlanta*
   **WOMBLE CARLYLE SANDRIDGE & RICE** *Atlanta*

### Leading Individuals

1. **DOUGLAS John** *Alston & Bird*
   **MOELING Walter** *Powell Goldstein*
2. **CHEATHAM Richard** *Kilpatrick Stockton*
   **KNUDSON Kathryn** *Powell Goldstein*
   **POWELL Thomas** *Troutman Sanders*
   **SCHWARTZ Robert** *Smith Gambrell & Russell*
3. **DUNLEVIE Steven** *Womble Carlyle Sandridge*
   **MACDONALD III Ralph** *Alston & Bird*

## Alston & Bird LLP

See firm details p.728

**The Firm:** Sailing into the top band this year is the "A-Team of debtor work," Alston & Bird. The firm's finance group is kept busy with a variety of matters for SunTrust Banks and Wachovia; however its mainstay is large-scale corporate debt financing. Interviewees were lavish in their praise for a "consistently terrific" team of lawyers who are "invaluable in transactions because of the depth of expertise they bring to scenarios." Transactional beacons for the crew this year include completing the acquisition of a large finance company for Wachovia, which involved Wachovia in considerations in the region of $3.9 billion.

**The Lawyers:** One client summed up the opinion of the market when he described **Paul Cushing** (see p.710) as "one of the best attorneys I have ever used." Cushing, who rises into the top band this year following growing applause for his nationally recognized REIT practice, was recommended to researchers as "incredibly knowledgeable with a communication style that is firm but not extreme." He recently represented Wachovia in connection with the $1.7 billion financing of a portfolio of real estate properties. On the regulatory side, "practical, efficient and diplomatic" **John Douglas** (see p.711) is the guiding star of the team, and is thought by some to be "unique in Atlanta." He has been negotiating an $880 million dispute between Bank of New York and the FDIC. **Richard Grice** (see p.714) is a first port of call for clients involved in complex transactions. He chairs the firm's leveraged capital group and recently represented Movie Gallery in connection with the $1.2 billion debt financing for its acquisition of Hollywood Entertainment. Also held in high regard is **Rick Blumen** (see p.706), who is said to be "quick to address issues while never taking his eye off the ball." He regularly acts for private equity firms and their portfolio companies, and has a wealth of experience in transactions in the food services sector. This year, for example, he acted for SunTrust Banks in its acquisition of Churche's Chicken, which involved ensuring that the transaction complied with Islamic law. **Chip MacDonald** (see p.719) was enthusiastically praised for his regulatory expertise, while rising star **Aldo Lafiandra** (see p.718) also garnered plaudits from clients.

**Clients/Work Highlights:** Other clients include Bank of America; BNP Paribas and Regions and Union Planters.

## King & Spalding LLP

See firm details p.1933

**The Firm:** King & Spalding is a hit with clients because it fields a team of "talented lawyers who get great results." It is traditionally renowned for its borrower-side work; however it also enjoys a long-established relationship with SunTrust Banks and has recently won mandates from a clutch of impressive new institutional clients. As well as boasting a high-class national practice with a strong presence across the USA, the team is developing its profile on the global stage by increasing its work for international bank clients.

**The Lawyers:** "Excellent banking attorney" **Albert Conrad** (see p.709) remains one of the highest profile names in the Atlanta finance market. He concentrates on larger transactions, typically involving investment grade syndicated credit facilities, and offers particular experience in the energy sector. In recent months he has completed several multimillion-dollar transactions for Carmike Cinemas. **Carolyn Alford** (see p.704) is "knowledgeable, effective and a pleasure to work with," according to the market. She regularly represents the media group of GE Capital and acted for SunTrust Banks in connection with a $100 million revolving credit facility for AAI. **Hector Llorens** (see p.718) is an "outstanding and really bright" attorney whose areas of expertise include acquisition finance and structured products. He has been busy representing Roper Industries in negotiating a $1.5 billion credit facility to acquire TransCore.

**Clients/Work Highlights:** Highlights from the year include representing SunTrust Banks as administrative agent in the negotiations surrounding a $750 million revolving credit facility for AGL Capital. Other clients include UPS Capital; GE Capital; Coca-Cola Financial; Prudential Financial and Wachovia, while the team has recently added Commerce Bank and JPMorgan to its client roster.

## Paul, Hastings, Janofsky & Walker LLP

See firm details p.339

**The Firm:** "They get the first call and they have always delivered," remarked one satisfied client of this top-class international giant. Its Atlanta-based finance team offers extensive experience in acting for administrative agents in asset-based lending, and has developed a particular specialty in second lien loan concepts. The telecom sector has been a strong source of work over the years, and the firm's growing international footprint is helping it to cope with increased demand from clients for advice on cross-border transactions. Also in response to an increasing workload, the firm has been busy recruiting of late, bolstering its finance practice with a slew of lateral hires. The team's pragmatic approach to deal-making and the thorough integration of its global offices were additionally highlighted by clients.

**The Lawyers:** **Chris Molen** (see p.720) was recommended to researchers as an "excellent attorney with a great practice and the drive to make sure the client gets the right result." He regularly acts for banks and finance companies in DIP financings and is counsel to 15 institutions. **Jesse Austin** (see p.705) is "without question a first-rate attorney." A star in the bankruptcy field, his straight finance practice is focused on structuring senior credit facilities among other things, and he is visible assisting a host of large corporations.

## Jones Day

See firm details p.570

**The Firm:** Clients particularly turn to this huge, multinational firm because of its ability "*to reach out to other offices across the world.*" Its global footprint naturally makes it a first choice for any complex cross-border transactions, and clients appreciate the services of a team of "*scholars of the law with good business sense.*" In recent months, the group has represented both domestic and multinational financial institutions on a wide variety of transactional and advisory services, ranging from syndicated lending and structured finance to regulatory advice.

**The Lawyers:** **Christopher Carson** (see p.708) was warmly praised as "*an excellent lending attorney.*" Hugely respected for his skill, knowledge and integrity, he chairs the firm's financial institutions practice committee. He splits his practice between traditional finance work and bankruptcy, and has also recently represented a number of companies in connection with the sale of assets.

**Clients/Work Highlights:** Citigroup; Wachovia; Société Générale; CIT Group; James River Coal Company and other commercial lenders.

## Kilpatrick Stockton LLP

See firm details p.735

**The Firm:** "*Well versed in the area of finance,*" Kilpatrick Stockton is admired for both its brute transactional strength and its academic finesse. The lawyers' much-valued seminars "*show the quality of their expertise,*" and clients expressed themselves "*extremely pleased – they have always led us down the right path and given us excellent advice.*" The group boasts considerable experience in the healthcare and communications sectors. In the regulatory arena, meanwhile, the team is skilled in securities law and M&A, and regularly represents United Bank.

**The Lawyers:** Noted for his "*wealth of experience in the lending arena,*" **Hilary Jordan** (see p.716) was recommended to researchers as "*an effective lawyer who knows what he's doing.*" He chairs the firm's finance practice group, and has particular expertise in asset-based lending and asset securitizations. **Richard Cheatham** (see p.708) "*has an excellent understanding of the law and always gives solid advice,*" say clients. His practice encompasses a spectrum of bank regulatory matters, and he acts as general counsel to a number of companies.

**Clients/Work Highlights:** Clients include Wachovia, SunTrust Banks, BNP Paribas and a range of independent and community banks.

## Parker, Hudson, Rainer & Dobbs LLP

**The Firm:** Commentators were especially enthusiastic about this "*thriving finance practice with an incredible amount of focus.*" Especially praised were the team's "*always professional*" demeanor and its "*excellent motions in court; you can almost tell when it's one of their documents.*" The boutique firm is particularly admired for its work in asset-based lending, and has recently completed a complex syndicated loan facility for Bank of America.

**The Lawyers:** **Edward Dobbs** is an acknowledged

---

"*master of the lending arena,*" and is celebrated throughout the market as "*a lawyer of the first order with a tremendous presence when it comes to representing financial institutions.*" **Bobbi Acord** spends her time on commercial loan transactions, including syndicated loans. She is a "*great young lawyer,*" according to interviewees, and was widely noted for her experience in representing lenders. **Michael Leveille** exhibits "*good quality in large syndicated deals*" as well as being "*a pleasant fella to work with,*" according to peers. He concentrates on asset-based loans and DIP financings.

**Clients/Work Highlights:** Bank of America; Congress Financial; P&C Bank; Regions Bank; SunTrust Banks; Wachovia and Wells Fargo.

## Hunton & Williams LLP

See firm details p.1959

**The Firm:** This well-established team represents borrowers and financial entities in all types of private financing work. Over the past year, it has seen a substantial increase in its work for agents in syndicated deals in New York. A growing international network adds another string to the team's bow.

**The Lawyers:** **Bruce Moorhead** (see p.720) splits his time between the firm's Atlanta and New York offices. His practice includes representing agent banks in larger syndicated transactions, and he focuses on leveraged finance cross-border work.

**Clients/Work Highlights:** Bank of America; GE Capital; CIT Business Credit and Wachovia.

## Powell Goldstein LLP

**The Firm:** In the banking sphere, Powell Goldstein is best known for its "*strong regulatory practice.*" The geographical reach of the group has grown considerably of late, and it has been busy working with banks in Ohio, Alaska and New Jersey. The core banking group has also expanded, and now numbers 17 lawyers. On the transactional side, the team has a thriving practice advising de novo banks and assisting with capital raising; however its particular forte is in advising community banks on going private. The group has also completed several deregistrations in the past year.

**The Lawyers:** A "*superb lawyer and tremendous rainmaker,*" **Walt Moeling** enjoys a strong profile as strategic adviser to a number of publicly registered banks, which he counsels on corporate governance among other matters. **Kathryn Knudson** is also well known and respected. Her practice is focused on securities law and the regulation and structuring of financial institutions. Clients appreciate the close working relationship between the duo, noting that one can always step in with advice if the other is unavailable.

**Clients/Work Highlights:** The team has been busy this year with the sale of Riverside Bancshares to Synovus Financial. Other clients include Habersham Bank, Gwinnett Commercial Group and Flag Financial.

---

## Troutman Sanders LLP

**The Firm:** The Atlanta office of this major regional player boasts considerable expertise in bank mergers and formations, and the team is currently representing several de novo banks in various stages of growth. Other recent highlights have included acting as counsel to SouthBank, as the target of a $34 million acquisition by Security Bank Corporation. The firm has also assisted Sandler O'Neill & Partners in connection with a series of capital raises.

**The Lawyers:** **Hazen Dempster**'s finance practice is focused on straight and syndicated lending. He is currently negotiating a $120 million credit facility on behalf of an energy company, as well as several credit facilities for technology companies. The regulatory side of the practice revolves largely around **Thomas Powell**. He acts as outside general counsel to Cotton States Insurance Group, representing the client in its sale to Country Mutual Insurance. This transaction involved a number of corporate elements, and totaled $200 million.

**Clients/Work Highlights:** The firm's client list includes Cotton States Insurance Group, SouthBank and Sandler O'Neill & Partners, along with a range of financial institutions and energy and technology companies.

## Smith Gambrell & Russell LLP

**The Firm:** This smaller team was singled out by interviewees for being "*first-rate in every respect.*" Despite its size, it has shown that it has the capacity to handle larger deals, which recently included advising First National Bankshares of Florida on its merger with Fifth Third Ohio, a transaction valued at $1.5 billion. A growing force in all types of financial regulatory work, the team is valued by clients because it is "*extremely skilled and highly knowledgeable about the legality and functioning of publicly traded companies.*"

**The Lawyers:** **Robert Schwartz**'s "*advice is exceptionally impressive and he is always available and responsive,*" said clients. He splits his time between the firm's Atlanta and Florida offices, and recently represented Omni Financial Services in its strategic acquisition of First Georgia Community Bank.

**Clients/Work Highlights:** First National Bankshares of Georgia; Fifth Third Bank; Omni Financial Services and other financial institutions.

## Womble Carlyle Sandridge & Rice PLLC

See firm details p.1589

**The Firm:** According to one of this firm's many fans in the financial services sector, it is "*caring, less bureaucratic, and it has significant bench strength in terms of specialists.*" Although many clients singled it out for its "*ability to relate to smaller companies,*" sources from larger institutions also praised the team. The group represents both established and emerging banks in connection with securities law and capital raises, and recently completed a $100 million shelf offering for Main Street Banks. Other recent highlights include the formation of several de novo banks and holding companies.

**The Lawyers:** "*Captain of the team*" **Steven Dunlevie** (see p.711) "*has great experience and a tremendous handle on the law*," according to interviewees. He advises the CEOs of banks and holding companies, as well as senior officials at regulatory agencies.

**Clients/Work Highlights:** BPP Corporation; Main Street Banks; United Community Bank and MidCountry Financial Corporation.

# BANKRUPTCY/RESTRUCTURING

| Bankruptcy/Restructuring Leading Firms | |
|---|---|
| 1 | **ALSTON & BIRD LLP** *Atlanta* |
| | **KILPATRICK STOCKTON LLP** *Atlanta* |
| | **KING & SPALDING LLP** *Atlanta* |
| 2 | **MCKENNA LONG & ALDRIDGE LLP** *Atlanta* |
| | **PARKER, HUDSON, RAINER & DOBBS** *Atlanta* |
| 3 | **LAMBERTH, CIFELLI, STOKES & STOUT** *Atlanta* |
| | **PAUL, HASTINGS, JANOFSKY & WALKER** *Atlanta* |
| | **POWELL GOLDSTEIN LLP** *Atlanta* |
| | **TROUTMAN SANDERS LLP** *Atlanta* |
| 4 | **GREENBERG TRAURIG LLP** *Atlanta* |
| | **MORRIS, MANNING & MARTIN, LLP** *Atlanta* |
| | **SCROGGINS & WILLIAMSON** *Atlanta* |

| Leading Individuals | |
|---|---|
| **Senior Statesman** | |
| | **BATSON R Neal** *Alston & Bird LLP* |
| 1 | **AUSTIN Jesse** *Paul, Hastings* |
| | **CAMPBELL Charles** *McKenna Long* |
| | **CONNOLLY Dennis** *Alston & Bird* |
| | **DOBBS C Edward** *Parker, Hudson, Rainer* |
| | **PARDO James** *King & Spalding* |
| | **STEIN Grant** *Alston & Bird* |
| 2 | **BORDERS Sarah** *King & Spalding* |
| | **CIFELLI James** *Lamberth, Cifelli, Stokes* |
| | **COHEN Ezra** *Troutman Sanders* |
| | **DORSEY Rufus** *Parker, Hudson, Rainer* |
| | **FERDINANDS Paul** *King & Spalding* |
| | **KAUFMAN Mark** *McKenna Long* |
| | **LUREY Alfred** *Kilpatrick Stockton* |
| | **MEIR Dennis** *Kilpatrick Stockton* |
| | **MEYERS Todd** *Kilpatrick Stockton* |
| 3 | **CRANSHAW David** *Morris, Manning & Martin* |
| | **ELLMAN Jeffrey** *Jones Day* |
| | **KELLEY Jeffrey** *Troutman Sanders* |
| | **KURZWEIL David** *Greenberg Traurig* |
| | **LEVIN Matthew** *Alston & Bird* |
| | **MARSH Gary** *McKenna Long & Aldridge* |
| | **NICHOLSON Penn** *Powell Goldstein* |
| | **ROSENBLATT Paul** *Kilpatrick Stockton* |
| | **WILLIAMSON Robert** *Scroggins & Williamson* |
| **Up-and-coming individuals** | |
| | **DUEDALL Mark** *Alston & Bird LLP* |
| | **WINSBERG Harris** *Troutman Sanders LLP* |

## Band 1

### Alston & Bird LLP
See firm details p.728

**The Firm:** "*The finest bankruptcy department in the Southeast*" was the verdict of at least one client on this "*super firm*." Reputed to be the first choice for debtor work, the team also guides clients through planning for bankruptcy, and offers expertise in a barrage of related financing techniques. Equally strong is the group's representation of creditors and creditors' committees. The team is conspicuous in the market for its size and depth of specialized lawyers; however, the favorite feature of in-house counsel was the "*excellent client service*" provided by "*bright people who are able to play with their good shoes on and be effective.*" Acting as special pension and employee benefits counsel to Delta Air Lines has been keeping the team busy this year, and it also represented Aflac in connection with $250 million of claims against Parmalat.

**The Lawyers:** **Neal Batson** (see p.706) towers over the market as "*the biggest name in Atlanta.*" Still noted for his "*plum position*" in the Enron bankruptcy, he is celebrated for his "*agile and critical mind, unbelievable memory and compelling style.*" The "*magnificent*" **Dennis Connolly** (see p.709) is said by clients to be "*just marvelous in court.*" He is acting as special counsel to Delta Air Lines in connection with its Chapter 11 filing. The third in a trio of outstanding names is **Grant Stein** (see p.725). A versatile practitioner, he concentrates on out-of-court restructurings, and has been acting as pro bono counsel to the Butler Street YMCA. He was described as "*extremely bright, tenacious, and frank about what he knows.*" **Matthew Levin** (see p.718) focuses on representing debtors and has substantial expertise in fraudulent conveyance litigation. He acted as lead partner in the Chapter 11 filing of Southwest Recreational Industries. Warm recommendations from "*highly impressed*" clients added the "*incredibly hard-working and dedicated*" **Mark Duedall** (see p.711) to this year's rankings. Leading the charge among the firm's younger bankruptcy specialists, he boasts experience in cases involving the manufacturing, food service and retail sectors, among others.

**Clients/Work Highlights:** Butler Street YMCA; Delta Air Lines; Southwest Recreational Industries; Aflac and Wachovia.

### Kilpatrick Stockton LLP
See firm details p.735
**The Firm:** Clients were full of admiration for this

"*professional and responsive firm.*" The team's "*willingness to work with in-house counsel*" and sensitive approach to costs made it "*a go-to firm for bankruptcy issues*" for many commentators. The stand-alone financial restructuring group boasts a substantial coast-to-coast practice and considerable experience of sophisticated transactions, representing debtors, creditors and creditors' committees.

**The Lawyers:** **Alfred Lurey** (see p.719) is praised as "*an excellent speaker and impressively knowledgeable.*" According to impressed interviewees, "*he remembers cases and facts that others would have to look up.*" Another of the firm's bankruptcy stalwarts, **Dennis Meir** (see p.719) is "*bright, tenacious and savvy with an impressive grasp of courtroom dynamics.*" He practices nationally, representing debtors, secured and unsecured creditors and trustees. "*Creative*" **Todd Meyers** (see p.720) is, in the words of one commentator, "*smart, skilled and always thinking.*" He focuses on workouts with troubled companies, and has been increasingly active of late representing creditor committees. Recent highlights include acting as co-counsel to the secured lender in the Friedman's Jewelers filings, and representing the creditor committee in a hospital bankruptcy. **Paul Rosenblatt** (see p.723) represents individual creditors in transactional and litigious matters. He also acts as counsel to BellSouth and has amassed considerable expertise in the telecom sector. Recently he represented BI-LO in the purchase of stores during the Chapter 11 filing of Winn-Dixie, a transaction valued at $20 million.

**Clients/Work Highlights:** The team regularly represents BellSouth in telecom-related bankruptcies across the country. Other clients include BI-LO, GE Capital and a host of Fortune 100 companies.

### King & Spalding LLP
See firm details p.1933
**The Firm:** Historically known for representing creditors, this "*outstanding firm*" has also proved that it has the experience and ability to be "*a great team for debtor cases.*" Midmarket companies are the team's main targets; however the opening of a New York office is effectively boosting the practice of a group that already has genuine big-deal experience and international credentials. Recent examples include a role in the headline Delta Air Lines bankruptcy, on behalf of the City of Atlanta. Interviewees were quick to praise "*the public service spirit and attitude*" of the team, which is said to boast a number of talented younger partners in its ranks.

**The Lawyers:** **James Pardo** (see p.721) is "*a fabulous lawyer and a prince of a guy who doesn't go around rabble-rousing,*" according to interviewees. He is representing Imperial Tobacco Canada in connection with the Chapter 11 filing of its former subsidiary, Flintkote. This case includes litigation aimed at recovering $525 million in dividends from Imperial Tobacco. **Sarah Borders** (see p.707) is a "*decisive*" expert in DIP financing. She has been advising the City of Atlanta in relation to the Delta Air Lines bankruptcy, which involved a year of preparation for a filing by Delta. **Paul Ferdinands** (see p.712) typically represents debtors and specializes in distressed M&A out of bankruptcy. He handled the asset dispositions connected to the Chapter 11 filing of Dan River, and is also representing Rhodes Inc.

**Clients/Work Highlights:** The team is representing Dan River and its affiliates in post-confirmation matters, including the sale of its engineered products division. Other clients include Arcapita; GE Capital; Imperial Tobacco Canada; Rhodes Inc; Sprint Nextel; SunTrust Banks and Winn-Dixie.

## Band 2

### McKenna Long & Aldridge LLP

See firm details p.737

**The Firm:** Clients agreed that this team stands out in the market for its "*great commercial sense,*" and its talent for "*thinking outside the box.*" Not only was the group felt to produce a "*first-class product,*" but also to field a number of lawyers who are "*great people to work with on a personal level.*" A creditor-oriented firm, McKenna Long & Aldridge concentrates on mid-market companies. The bankruptcy team boasts a number of lawyers who are devoted solely to cases resulting in court proceedings, and another group that focuses on workouts not resulting in court proceedings.

**The Lawyers:** "*If it was your money at stake, you would call Charlie,*" remarked one interviewee of **Charles Campbell** (see p.707). "*A bankruptcy expert and a true professional,*" he recently secured a $475 million judgment for a diaper manufacturer. He represents trustees, debtors and creditors, all of whom value his talents as a "*stellar litigator.*" **Mark Kaufman** (see p.716) is admired for his "*great grasp of the law and how it affects commercial transactions.*" His practice includes commercial litigation, troubled asset dispositions and out-of-court reorganizations. According to market sources, **Gary Marsh** (see p.719) "*is an excellent attorney who handles difficult situations with ease.*" He concentrates on secured creditors and franchise bankruptcies and is currently representing the trustee of six companies involved in sport and Astroturf. He also acts as counsel for GMAC Commercial Mortgage as servicer of several defaulted franchise loans.

**Clients/Work Highlights:** The team is currently representing a plan investor in its attempts to become the new owner of a large jewelry chain. It is also counseling the creditors of Allied Holdings. Other clients, including a number of Fortune 500 firms, are drawn from the financial services and energy sectors.

### Parker, Hudson, Rainer & Dobbs LLP

**The Firm:** "*Excellent at what they do and outstanding in their field*" was a typical comment by clients on this high-class Atlanta boutique. 'Their field' tends to be representing banks, insurance companies and leasing companies in Chapter 11 cases; however the group also acts for credit committees and was highly praised for its work on behalf of asset-based lenders. Highlights from the year include representing Bank of America as agent for the bank group in the Chapter 11 filing of Friedman's Jewelers. Interviewees applauded the team's "*impeccable integrity, superior intelligence and exceptional service.*"

**The Lawyers:** Commentators agree that **Edward Dobbs** remains "*one of the outstanding practitioners in Atlanta.*" "*A problem solver and a gifted verbal communicator,*" he is hailed as the firm's primary asset. He has been busy this year representing Bank of America as agent for the bank group in the bankruptcy of Allied Holdings. Following closely behind him is the "*superb*" **Rufus Dorsey**, who is not only "*excellent in the courtroom*" but also "*creative with compromises and prepared to make recommendations.*" He continues his role as court-appointed examiner for cases relating to the Enron bankruptcy, and has also been representing Bank of America.

**Clients/Work Highlights:** The firm acted for Fleet Capital in relation to the bankruptcy of Tom's Foods. Other clients include Bank of America; GE Capital; PNC Bank; Regions Financial; Textron Financial; Wachovia and Wells Fargo.

## Band 3

### Lamberth, Cifelli, Stokes & Stout, P.A.

**The Firm:** This Atlanta boutique was singled out by market commentators as "*a go-to for small to medium cases.*" The team here specializes in Chapter 11 filings, restructuring and workouts, as well as litigation and creditors' rights issues. Among its clients are medical service providers, hi-tech manufacturers and retail companies.

**The Lawyers:** **James Cifelli** is regarded as the foremost member of the team. He devotes much of his time to bankruptcy-related litigation, Chapter 11 reorganizations and creditors' rights matters.

### Paul, Hastings, Janofsky & Walker LLP

See firm details p.339

**The Firm:** This international firm is most recognized in Atlanta's bankruptcy law circles for its work on behalf of secured and unsecured creditors. The team is kept especially busy representing banks and other financial institutions in workouts and general bankruptcy matters. DIP financing is recognized as a particular niche.

**The Lawyers:** According to clients, the "*outstanding*" **Jesse Austin** (see p.705) is "*extremely responsive and an excellent negotiator.*" He is regarded by interviewees as the leading light of the firm and one of the outstanding names in the market. An expert on DIP

financing, he was recently lead counsel in connection with a DIP financing loan to Allied Holdings.

**Clients/Work Highlights:** Lawyers recently acted as lead counsel to NorthWestern Energy, which involved taking the company through bankruptcy in 13 months. The team also acts as counsel to GE Capital, as well as other major companies from the financial services, healthcare, insurance, manufacturing and retail sectors.

### Powell Goldstein LLP

**The Firm:** In recent years, the bankruptcy and restructuring team of this solid and respected firm has found itself concentrating on counseling debtors and conducting litigation. However, the group also represents creditors and companies in financial distress.

**The Lawyers:** **Penn Nicholson** was praised for his talents in both the transactional and litigation arenas. Among a number of highlights, he has been busy representing the world's largest manufacturer of floor coverings and carpets. He also acts as counsel to Wells Fargo.

**Clients/Work Highlights:** The team was retained to handle the Chapter 11 filing of Wellington Leisure Products, and is acting as co-counsel in a $600 million fraudulent conveyance case involving Onyx Corporation. Other clients are drawn from a host of industries, including manufacturing, telecom and real estate.

### Troutman Sanders LLP

**The Firm:** The impression left on clients by Troutman Sanders' bankruptcy team is of an "*extremely capable group that does a good job.*" Its strong litigation background is felt to give it an edge in bankruptcy disputes, while the firm's niche energy practice is a considerable attraction for clients in that sector. A high-profile mandate to act as debtor's counsel in the Allied Holdings reorganization is evidence that the group is bouncing back from the loss of Mary Grace Diehl. Also this year, the team has defended the trustee of a cable company in a large fraudulent conveyance case, and provided advice to the largest utility in the Southeast.

**The Lawyers:** "*Great academician*" **Ezra Cohen** is noted for his skill and experience in insolvency and Chapter 11 proceedings. His highlights from the year include representing Wachovia in an appeal against a judgment in a bankruptcy case. He was also recently presented with the Pollard Award for ethics. "*Top-drawer lawyer*" **Jeffrey Kelley** is leading the team in the Allied Holdings reorganization. He focuses on representing secured creditors. **Harris Winsberg** is an up-and-comer who is already "*showing star quality*" according to clients. A newcomer to this year's rankings, he was dubbed a "*talented young lawyer who is not afraid to stand his ground.*"

**Clients/Work Highlights:** Bank of America; CNN; Synovus; Turner Broadcasting System and Wachovia.

## Band 4

### Greenberg Traurig LLP

See firm details p.664

**The Firm:** The Atlanta outpost of this international firm is best known for its work on behalf of creditor committees. The ability to call on resources from across the network is an advantage for the team, which has a solid and growing practice, mainly representing lenders. It offers experience in restructuring and Chapter 11 in a range of sectors, including healthcare, retail, real estate, manufacturing and textiles.

**The Lawyers:** **David Kurzweil** (see p.717) has a wealth of experience in commercial litigation, representing creditors and debtors. Admired not just for his legal expertise but his talents as a rainmaker, he has acted as counsel to the creditors' committees of several large retail chains.

### Morris, Manning & Martin, LLP

**The Firm:** The firm makes its entry into the rankings this year, as peers are increasingly sitting up and taking notice of the "*significant inroads*" it is making into work for creditors' committees. The team of "*effective litigators*" practices at both state and federal level. It can also draw upon the expertise of the firm's other practice groups to assist a client base that ranges from privately held local firms to Fortune 50 companies.

**The Lawyers:** A "*great resolver of issues,*" **David Cranshaw** won particular praise for his "*subtle understanding of the strengths and weaknesses of a case.*" He practices in the area of creditors' rights and bankruptcy, and is especially well known for representing creditors' committees.

### Scroggins & Williamson

**The Firm:** "*A great firm for smaller cases,*" Scroggins & Williamson focuses on business reorganizations and workouts for small to medium-sized private companies. Although it comprises only three active lawyers, this clearly hasn't held it back and it is the first choice referral firm of a number of larger outfits. This year the team has been busy representing debtors in Chapter 11 filings and acting as counsel to several large firms in the construction industry.

**The Lawyers:** **Robert Williamson** is highly thought of by market sources. He recently confirmed a plan of reorganization for a client in the mining and trucking industry after a contested confirmation battle.

### Other Notable Practitioners

**Jeffrey Ellman** of Jones Day recently represented International Paper Company as the largest unsecured creditor in the Androscoggin Energy Chapter 11 case.

# CONSTRUCTION

| Construction<br>Leading Firms | |
|---|---|
| 1 | GRIFFIN COCHRANE & MARSHALL *Atlanta* |
| | KILPATRICK STOCKTON LLP *Atlanta* |
| | SMITH, CURRIE & HANCOCK LLP *Atlanta* |
| 2 | ALSTON & BIRD LLP *Atlanta* |
| | HENDRICK, PHILLIPS, SALZMAN & FLATT *Atlanta* |
| | KING & SPALDING LLP *Atlanta* |
| | SHAPIRO FUSSELL *Atlanta* |
| | SMITH GAMBRELL & RUSSELL LLP *Atlanta* |
| 3 | WEINBERG, WHEELER, HUDGINS, GUNN *Atlanta* |

## Band 1

### Griffin Cochrane & Marshall

See firm details p.734

**The Firm:** This specialist firm had its 25th anniversary in 2005, and interviewees agree the team continues to go from strength to strength. It represents general contractors, construction managers and owners in all aspects of construction work, although litigation remains the primary focus of the group. Clients spoke of "*heavy-hitting lawyers who are well educated, up to date and superior in terms of support.*" The team was also praised for its "*excellent judgment and high responsiveness to tight deadlines.*" One of the team's highlights of the year was representing the City of Atlanta in connection with a $3.5 billion expansion of a water management system.

**The Lawyers:** Clients praised this group for its "*confident and capable individuals who get results.*" **Jennifer Fletcher**'s (see p.713) extensive litigation experience makes her a popular choice among interviewees, who regard her as "*a bright personality who is always exceptionally well prepared.*" She typically represents owners and is advising Ave Maria University on a new development in South Florida. Clients

choose **Lee Davis** (see p.710) because "*he's aggressive when he needs to be, diplomatic when the situation requires it, and willing to explain things.*" He has niche expertise in power plants but has also recently represented a steel erection contractor in Chicago in a $35 million dispute. His other work includes advising on claims relating to a sludge-drying facility in Boston. "*Strong litigator*" **Barry McCabe** (see p.719) recently defended Bovis Lend Lease against claims of $25 million brought by a contractor on The Venetian hotel/casino. Clients described him as "*an impressive communicator who is able to earn respect and get results.*"

**Clients/Work Highlights:** The group has a broad catalog of construction expertise including power plants, sludge-processing facilities, hotels, shopping centers, roads and highways. Some of the group's key clients include BE&K; Bovis Lend Lease; City of Atlanta; Highlands Properties and EMCOR Group.

### Kilpatrick Stockton LLP

See firm details p.735

**The Firm:** Interviewees warmly endorsed this group as "*an excellent choice for construction work.*" It is one of the largest practices in Georgia and is also a regular player on the international stage. The team includes not only lawyers but also several engineers, who give the firm an edge in advising clients on technical issues. In one of its headline cases, the group helped to resolve claims brought by contractors against Massachusetts Turnpike Authority in relation to the 'Big Dig' Central Artery/Tunnel Project. The team is also representing the City of Atlanta in connection with the $5 billion Hartsfield Airport project involving the renovation of the airport and the addition of new terminals and runways.

**The Lawyers:** **William Dorris** (see p.711) specializes in construction contracts and disputes and was recommended to researchers as "*a knowledgeable guy*

who is at the top of his profession.*" Mediation and alternative dispute resolution are further areas of focus for him and he has worked on major cases across the USA. Also noted for his talents in alternative dispute resolution is "*top-notch*" **Brian Corgan** (see p.709). "*He did a masterful job in representing his client in arbitration,*" according to one source. He has worked on a variety of commercial and industrial matters, including disputes involving nuclear and coal-fired power plants. Heading the firm's construction practice is **Randy Hafer** (see p.714) who consistently "*secures exceptional results*" for his clients. He has a strong following among public owners and has niche expertise in underground construction projects. He represents Siemens Transportation Systems in Puerto Rico and is lead counsel to the City of Atlanta in relation to the 'Big Dig' project. Interviewees said that **Neal Sweeney** (see p.725) is "*one of the most effective government contracts lawyers in the country.*" Much of his time is devoted to public construction and large infrastructure schemes, including ongoing projects associated with the rebuilding of Iraq. He is also currently working on disputes relating to the design and construction of a multibillion-dollar mass transit system in Puerto Rico. Interviewees described him as "*focused, smart and great at coming up with creative solutions.*" **Tony Smith** (see p.724) is famed as "*an excellent trial lawyer.*" Arbitration, litigation and contract negotiation at an international level all form part of his workload and he has obtained several multimillion-dollar jury verdicts and arbitral awards for his clients.

**Clients/Work Highlights:** City of Atlanta; Massachusetts Turnpike Authority; Siemens Transportation Systems and Siemens Building Technologies.

### Smith, Currie & Hancock LLP

**The Firm:** This is one of the most established teams in the market and continues to be "*the first name that* springs to mind" for many commentators. The firm has a superb track record in the area of government contracts and has experience in embassy projects in jurisdictions such as Nepal and Ghana. Clients declare the group invaluable for its experience in several types of construction projects, ranging from dams and highways to casinos and country clubs. The firm has traditional strength in litigation and has an enviable practice in alternative dispute resolution. However, it is the team's *"wise counsel, coupled with its outstanding educational programs"* that sets it apart from other firms, according to clients.

**The Lawyers:** Interviewees believe this firm *"has built up one of the finest groups of construction attorneys in the world."* Sources praised **Philip Beck**, saying *"he's excellent at dealing with people, pays attention to detail and has a pleasant demeanor."* Beck splits his time evenly between litigation and transactional work. He has negotiated and drafted several contracts for major casino and hotel resorts in Las Vegas, and recently obtained a favorable verdict for a grading and earthwork contractor. Clients rate **Thomas Kelleher** as *"invaluable for his wealth of knowledge and experience."* His strengths lie in government and construction contracts and he is also adept at arbitration and mediation. **Thomas Abernathy** is an accomplished lawyer whose clients include owners, general contractors and subcontractors. They call on him for assistance on a range of

construction contractual issues including award protests and performance problems. **James Butler's** practice is predominantly international in nature and encompasses engineer construction, design-build projects and engineering, procurement and construction (EPC) contracting. This year he has worked on the construction of methanol plants in Trinidad and Chile and manufacturing facilities in China. **Robert Chambers'** engineering background lends him an advantage over some of his competitors. He has litigated construction cases involving environmental issues, including disputes concerning wastewater treatment plants and sewer line installations. **Aubrey Coleman** is a popular choice of counsel among clients, who confide: *"His knowledge and experience inspire great confidence."* He is well versed in embassy construction projects and recently settled a lawsuit involving embassy projects in Cameroon and Guinea. He is also advising the same client on an embassy scheme in Nepal. **George Wenick** is another of the firm's talented litigators. He successfully acted in a recent large telecom dispute and has been busy representing the developer of a new airport in Atlanta. Sources were quick to praise *"ambitious and talented"* **Reginald Jones** (see p.275123). He is *"hard-working and ethical, and does an excellent job of representing clients."*

**Clients/Work Highlights:** Turner Construction; Caddell Construction; Birmingham Steel; Williams Group International; Chapman Corporation; The Saxon Group and Whitehead Electric.

## Band 2

### Alston & Bird LLP

See firm details p.728

**The Firm:** According to clients, this is a group of *"highly regarded experts who make it their business to stay on the cutting edge of industry developments."* It provides a full-service practice to large general contractors and national development firms and is also busy on behalf of colleges and universities. One of its niche areas of practice includes working with PPPs on large infrastructure projects such as highways. Its dedicated team also handles construction transactions, litigation, arbitration and mediation. In one of its highlights, it acted as construction counsel to a large project in Miami Beach, with construction costs of $500 million.

**The Lawyers: John Spangler** (see p.725) is *"exceptional – he's as good as they come,"* according to clients. He handles joint ventures, negotiates design build and construction contracts, and arbitrates the full spectrum of construction-related disputes. Spangler is currently acting for a design professional in a large dispute relating to an international terminal at an Atlanta airport. The *"flexible and creative"* **Bob Crewdson** (see p.710) concentrates on owner representation. He is advising on the contracts for the mixed-use Santana Row development, a project involving $300 million of construction costs over four years. Litigation for national developers is another aspect of his practice. Researchers heard he

has *"a practical approach to solving problems and is attuned to risks and pitfalls."* **Bill Hughes** (see p.715) is *"an exceptionally straight-up guy"* with a strong energy law theme to his practice. He negotiated contracts for the development of manufacturing plants in Shanghai and Beijing and was involved in litigation in Boston regarding $14 million in claims by a contractor of an electric power plant.

**Clients/Work Highlights:** Beazer Homes; Industrial Developments International; Brasfield & Gorrie; Archstone-Smith and Regions Bank.

### Hendrick, Phillips, Salzman & Flatt P.C.

**The Firm:** Market sources praised this boutique firm for its *"excellent group of aggressive lawyers who excel in representing subcontractors."* It offers a cradle to grave construction service encompassing contracting, project performance and litigation. This year the team has prosecuted and defended claims arising from a number of public works projects and school constructions. It also acted for a surety in its pursuit of an architect and engineer over problems resulting in the termination of a project.

**The Lawyers: David Hendrick** is widely regarded as *"a dean of the construction Bar."* He was fêted for his experience in arbitration and dispute resolution and is an active member of the AAA. Roofing industry expert **Stephen Phillips** is well known for acting as counsel to the National Roofing Contractors Association and the National Roofing Legal Resource Center. He handles litigation and has extensive experience advising on government contracts and environmental issues.

**Clients/Work Highlights:** The group is best known for its representation of contractions and subcontractors. Some of its leading clients include Centex Construction; Siemens Energy & Automation; Keene Construction; ARCADIS Geraghty & Miller International and John W Rooker & Associates.

### King & Spalding LLP

See firm details p.1933

**The Firm:** The construction group of this large Atlanta-based firm is housed within its global transactions practice group, giving the team's workload a distinct international flavor. Sources described it as *"a distinguished team with great experience on international projects."* The mainstay of the practice is representing owners on large infrastructure projects but energy-related work also features prominently. The group has niche expertise in LNG projects and has represented owners in the construction of two LNG terminals. It has also acted for the owners of large oil and gas facilities in the Gulf of Mexico. Other features of the practice include advising owners on the construction of apartments, offices and hotels.

**The Lawyers:** Premier construction lawyer **John Hinchey** (see p.241943) is widely regarded by peers as *"the cream of the crop."* He successfully secured a $30 million jury verdict for an international developer in construction disputes relating to a project in the Cayman Islands. He also serves as a mediator and arbitrator.

**Clients/Work Highlights:** Cheniere Energy; American Arbitration Association; CEMEX; Coca-Cola; El Paso/Southern Natural Gas; Freeport LNG Development; GE Real Estate and UPS.

## Shapiro Fussell

**The Firm:** Clients call on this group for its *"solid array of experienced attorneys who are skilled and aggressive."* It is best known for representing subcontractors, but also acts as counsel to public and private companies, developers, architects and engineers. The team offers a comprehensive construction practice and is experienced in both small projects and major national litigation.

**The Lawyers:** Interviewees praised **Ben Shapiro** as a straightforward operator who *"doesn't beat about the bush."* He represents a range of clients, from owners and general contractors to design professionals, in construction disputes, including arbitration and mediation. The *"gifted"* **Herman Fussell** enters the tables this year following positive market feedback. He is an alumnus of the DOJ and specializes in complex construction disputes.

**Clients/Work Highlights:** The group acts for a variety of clients from the construction industry including developers, general contractors, trade organizations, architects, engineers and surety companies.

## Smith Gambrell & Russell LLP

**The Firm:** This is *"a talented crew of sharp and knowledgeable young attorneys,"* said interviewees. It is involved in a spectrum of construction projects including hotels, nuclear power plants, water treatment plants and hospitals. The group typically represents owners and contractors, but has also acted for subcontractors and government bodies. It has experience litigating on an international level, but also counsels clients on the avoidance of disputes. The group has been busy drafting the AOD (Associated Owners and Developers) Agreement, the first in a series of innovative standard form construction documents soon to be used throughout the industry.

**The Lawyers:** Although **Thomas Asselin** has a forte in mediation, interviewees also said: *"If you want a fight, go to Tom.* He has a breadth of experience ranging from condominiums to highway construction and is currently representing the owner of a hotel with major defects. The damages sought to cover the costs of repair are in excess of 50% of the value of the project. Researchers were inundated with praise for the *"brilliant"* **Ira Genberg.** *"He's won all of our cases and I don't have to worry about being overbilled,"* remarked one happy client. He is currently involved in litigation valued at $100 million involving a major resort facility. Other activities include advising on issues surrounding a series of chemical plants in Argentina, the Netherlands, Spain and the USA.

**Clients/Work Highlights:** Foster Wheeler; Kerzner International; Tyco International; Winn-Dixie; Home Depot; Shimizu; Sierra Aluminum; HKL Cladding Systems and BHN Corporation.

## Band 3

### Weinberg, Wheeler, Hudgins, Gunn & Dial, LLC

**The Firm:** Though not historically a construction firm, the team has proven its ability in this area thanks to its *"attentive, tenacious and broad-based"* service and its knack of providing clients with *"exactly what we need."* Litigation is the core strength of the group, and includes a niche in catastrophic construction claims. The team is well known for its work relating to the Venetian hotel/casino project, and sources applauded the group's proficiency in large-scale construction schemes.

**The Lawyers:** Interviewees declared **David Dial** *"one of the best in the industry."* He is not only *"a persuasive advocate, but has cultivated relationships with the best expert witnesses and arbitrators."* He is noted for his strengths in both litigation and alternative dispute resolution.

**Clients/Work Highlights:** Cirque du Soleil; The Venetian; Bagwell Construction Services; EllisDon; KMI Contracting and Walton Construction.

### Other Notable Practitioners

**Kent Stair** of Carlock Copeland Semler & Stair, LLP divides his practice between Atlanta and South Carolina and specializes in representing design professionals. Stair's practice centers on mediation rather than litigation, and he has handled proceedings relating to owner and contractor disputes, construction disputes, PI and wrongful death.

# CORPORATE/M&A

| Corporate/M&A |
|---|
| Leading Firms |
| 1 **ALSTON & BIRD LLP** *Atlanta* |
| **KING & SPALDING LLP** *Atlanta* |
| 2 **KILPATRICK STOCKTON LLP** *Atlanta* |
| **ROGERS & HARDIN** *Atlanta* |
| **SUTHERLAND ASBILL & BRENNAN LLP** *Atlanta* |
| **TROUTMAN SANDERS LLP** *Atlanta* |
| 3 **MCKENNA LONG & ALDRIDGE LLP** *Atlanta* |
| **PARKER, HUDSON, RAINER & DOBBS LLP** *Atlanta* |
| **PAUL, HASTINGS, JANOFSKY & WALKER** *Atlanta* |
| **POWELL GOLDSTEIN LLP** *Atlanta* |
| 4 **ARNALL GOLDEN GREGORY LLP** *Atlanta* |
| **JONES DAY** *Atlanta* |

## Band 1

### Alston & Bird LLP

See firm details p.728

**The Firm:** Historically known for its financing and securities work, this *"polished and subtle"* firm made a huge splash in the corporate healthcare pond this year with the $1.8 billion sale of Province Healthcare to LifePoint Hospitals. This was just one of a list of major transactions, which also included the Wachovia/WestCo megadeal. Clients appreciate the effort invested by the firm in learning about their companies, and value its attorneys' *"smart and candid but not egotistical"* approach to business. Another attraction was *"the southern charm emanating out of the Atlanta office,"* which, combined with the team's *"refined and cultured presentations,"* make a winning formula.

**The Lawyers:** **Sidney Nurkin** (see p.721) is held in high esteem by clients and peers as the *"dean of the corporate Bar"* and an *"eminent figure"* in Atlanta's legal circles. The counsel to the largest private equity group in the Southeast, he recently acted for NDC Health in its acquisition by Per-Se Technologies for around $1 billion. The *"absolutely outstanding"* **Vaughan Curtis** (see p.710) is especially well regarded in the field of corporate healthcare. Clients value his *"combination of legal experience and good common sense."* **Hill Jeffries** (see p.715) counsels public companies on corporate governance and business strategies. Another of his strengths is funds

work, and he is currently representing Morgan Keegan in a $250 million offering by a closed investment fund. Joining them in the table is *"excellent negotiator"* **Teri Lynn McMahon** (see p.719), who was applauded by the market for her *"considerable expertise and command of the law."*

**Clients/Work Highlights:** One of the firm's transactional highlights of the year was undoubtedly heading the advice for Wachovia on its $4 billion acquisition of WestCo. Other representative clients of the group include AGCO; Beecher Carlson Holdings; CTI Molecular Imaging; Sabre Holdings and NDC Health.

### King & Spalding LLP

See firm details p.1933

**The Firm:** For clients, King & Spalding is not merely *"a premier firm in Atlanta,"* but *"a top-notch business firm to go to in any bet-your-company issue."* Huge transactions for Fortune 500 companies remain its bread and butter, with recent examples including advice to Per-Se Technologies on its pending $1 billion plus merger with NDC Health. Commentators appreciate the team's *"geographic reach and* *ability to handle large volumes of work,*" as well as its reserves of sector-specific expertise, which include considerable experience in the healthcare and energy fields. The creation of a corporate governance task force within the firm has allowed it to offer an even wider range of services and is a popular move with clients.

**The Lawyers:** The market reserved considerable praise for this group of "*fantastic transactional lawyers.*" Foremost among them is **Michael Egan** (see p.712), who was described by clients as "*an excellent lawyer who is able to keep his wits about him when things get chaotic.*" He represented UPS in the $1.3 billion acquisition of Overnite. "*Rocket scientist*" **William Baxley** (see p.706) is also noted for his sure handling of massive M&A, as evidenced by his work for Sprint on its $1.3 billion acquisition of US Unwired. **Russell Richards** (see p.722) is regarded as "*one of the premier corporate lawyers in the Southeast,*" and is felt to particularly excel in midmarket M&A. He recently represented Roper Industries in connection with the acquisition of TransCore Holdings, a deal valued at $600 million. For at least one intervie-

wee, **John Capers** (see p.708) is "*the most efficient transaction lawyer I have ever worked with.*" A highlight of his year was assisting Belk with its $622 million purchase of a chain of department stores. Head of the firm's corporate finance practice group, **John Kelley** (see p.717) is regarded by clients as "*one of the leading securities lawyers,*" and is valued for his "*smart and practical advice.*" His expertise lies particularly in public offerings and Rule 144A offerings. The "*terrific*" **Alan Prince** (see p.722) is noted for his strong practice in securities and corporate governance. He has extensive experience in representing issuers, underwriters and financial companies. Also well known for his work in corporate governance and public offerings is "*superb technical lawyer*" **Jeffrey Stein** (see p.725). He has recently conducted public offerings of debt securities for SunTrust Banks and Synovus, among others. "*Young superstar*" **Ray Baltz** (see p.705) is particularly noted for his work with professional sports franchises. A new addition to this year's rankings, he also represents large corporations in M&A. William Spalding has now left the firm.

**Clients/Work Highlights:** The firm recently advised on the $34 billion merger of Sprint and Nextel Communications, to form Sprint Nextel. Its blue-chip client roster also includes Arcapita Bank BSC; Belk; Roper Industries; Home Depot and UPS.

## Band 2

### Kilpatrick Stockton LLP

See firm details p.735

**The Firm:** This "*sensational*" team rises up the ranks this year following considerable admiration for its "*unparalleled client service*" and strength in M&A. Clients appreciate "*a cohesive, energetic group that is dedicated to getting the best results,*" and highlighted both its "*amazingly responsive*" service and its rare ability to be "*refreshingly mindful of how much it all costs.*" The group is particularly visible in midmarket transactions, where it handles a steady stream of securities issues, public offerings and private fund raising. Top transactions include representing Zodiac in its acquisition of assets of C&D Aerospace Group for $600 million.

**The Lawyers:** "*The chemistry with Rey was really what the doctor ordered,*" remarked one client of **Rey Pascual** (see p.721). He focuses on M&A, recently conducting the $115 million sale of DVT to Cognex. Other highlights include negotiating a $100 million supply agreement between Turbochef Technologies and Subway restaurants. **David Stockton** (see p.725) has recently closed a $130 million public offering of debt and equity for James River Coal. Clients agree that he is "*an excellent lawyer,*" and were "*impressed with his depth of knowledge.*" Striding into the table this year is the "*smart and creative*" **Stanley Blackburn** (see p.706). Renowned for his large cap M&A work, he acted as lead counsel to Certegy in a stock-for-stock merger with Fidelity National Financial. The combined entity is valued at $7.6 billion. Rising star **Daniel Falstad** (see p.712) acted for Smart Corporation in the sale of 90% of the

company to First Islamic Bank of Bahrain, which involved making the transaction compliant with Islamic law. Interviewees describe him as "*articulate and positive-minded.*"

**Clients/Work Highlights:** The team acted for Georgia-Pacific in its sale of pulp manufacturing assets to a subsidiary of Koch Industries, a deal valued at $610 million. Other clients include Bell-South; Certegy; James River Coal Company; National Vision; Turbochef Technologies and Zodiac.

### Rogers & Hardin

**The Firm:** Rogers & Hardin is a winner with clients for its impressive combination of pragmatism and cost-effectiveness. "*A terrific firm providing powerful advice and effective communication,*" it specializes in corporate governance and M&A for a roster of top-class corporates, including one of the largest assisted living companies in the USA. The smaller size of the firm is actually seen as an advantage by many clients, who appreciate the "*hands-on service and quick turnaround*" the team provides.

**The Lawyers:** "*World-class attorney*" **Jack Hardin** is lauded by clients and peers alike for his constructive approach, sure handling of deals and "*tremendous corporate ability.*" He represents many special committees and boards of directors, and recently finished a special investigation for a manufacturer of prostate treatments. **Steve Fox** is "*an excellent negotiator and a learned lawyer.*" He has been busy this year negotiating and structuring broadcasting arrangements for the Olympic Broadcasting Service in relation to the 2008 and 2010 Olympic Games, and also acts as counsel to the Atlanta Hawks. **Alan Leet**, meanwhile, is known as "*a talented draftsman and thinker, who is able to reach and resolve issues well.*" He recently completed the recapitalization of Alterra Healthcare.

**Clients/Work Highlights:** Highlights of the team's year include selling the travel insurance component of Citigroup to MetLife, and advising on the asset acquisition and financing for Rock-Tenn's $500 million purchase of the pulp and paper division of Gulf States. Other clients include Alterra Healthcare; Atlanta Hawks; Olympic Broadcasting Services and Theragenics.

### Sutherland Asbill & Brennan LLP

See firm details p.578

**The Firm:** Interviewees praised this team for its "*excellent client service.*" Indeed, one enthusiastic source went so far as to say "*they give us better than our money's worth.*" The team does a range of corporate work for a range of large, Georgia-based clients, but its strength lies in M&A, where it represents buyers, sellers and special committees in acquiring publicly owned companies. Acting for IMG in the recent sale of Life Insurance Company of Georgia for $250 million was a major transaction for the group this year.

**The Lawyers:** **Mark Kaufman** (see p.716) is known as "*someone you can count on for knowledge and integrity,*" and is highly regarded for his thriving

M&A practice. This year he has acted for Spectrum Brands in acquiring a number of companies, including United Industries for $475 million and Tetra GmbH for $500 million.

**Clients/Work Highlights:** Spectrum Brands and IMG are among the firm's most active clients. It recently acted for the latter company in connection with the $325 million sale of RTM Restaurant Group.

## Troutman Sanders LLP

**The Firm:** Troutman Sanders is an *"exceptional firm,"* according to market sources, with a high-quality corporate and M&A practice. Clients were particularly impressed by the team's *"ability to participate in the decision-making process at a business level,"* and its commitment and dedication. One interviewee even went so far as to say: *"I would give them the Michelin stars."* The group is highly regarded for its work with large utility companies, and has also completed a number of acquisitions for Compu-Credit.

**The Lawyers:** **Robert Grout** offers *"wise counsel,"* according to his clients, and was also praised for being *"unbelievably ethical and practical."* He recently acted for AGCO in a $300 million securitization. **James Smith** is *"a prince of a guy and a great technical lawyer."* He represents issuers in public offerings and is well known for his securities work. New to the rankings is **Brinkley Dickerson**, who was commended as *"a standout lawyer who knows everything about his clients and the ins and outs of their operations."* He concentrates on securities law in relation to public companies, and also advises startups on venture capital financing.

**Clients/Work Highlights:** The firm acts as general counsel to Mizuno USA, as well as representing AGCO, CompuCredit and Georgia Power among others.

## Band 3

## McKenna Long & Aldridge LLP

See firm details p.737

**The Firm:** The Atlanta office of this sizable regional firm provides a broad range of services including M&A, assistance in contested transactions and corporate governance advice. It has extensive experience of purchasing and selling international operations, in which field it represents companies across the world.

**The Lawyers:** The *"superb"* **Clay Long** (see p.718) was recommended to researchers as *"an excellent lawyer who is extremely knowledgeable and always available."* He has been representing the State of Georgia in connection with the 'Tri-State Water Wars,' and is also acting as counsel to a private supplier of airport services.

**Clients/Work Highlights:** Lawyers have worked for a variety of Fortune 500 companies, private corporations, government agencies and nonprofit organizations, of which the State of Georgia is only one example.

## Parker, Hudson, Rainer & Dobbs LLP

**The Firm:** This Atlanta boutique offers extensive experience in M&A, joint ventures and a range of financing techniques, and is particularly noted for its work in the healthcare sector. Here it has been busy of late working with various institutions to develop strategic alliances with a view to creating new healthcare programs and services, including new blood and cardiology centers at a hospital.

**The Lawyers:** **Paul Hudson** acted as local counsel for a UK company in a complex acquisition in Georgia. Corporate healthcare work is a particular focus for him, and here he recently represented a nonprofit organization in developing a medical clinic specializing in the treatment of multiple sclerosis.

## Paul, Hastings, Janofsky & Walker LLP

See firm details p.339

**The Firm:** The international footprint of this large firm makes it part of an exclusive group in Georgia. Naturally this is a major attraction to clients, who also went out of their way to praise the *"extraordinary quality of the people and their high ethical standards."* The corporate team in the Atlanta office handles the full spectrum of transactions, from IPOs to high-yield work, SEC filings and M&A, at both the high-end and midmarket levels. It has recently enhanced its expertise by recruiting a number of new attorneys from Hunton & Williams. The telecom and healthcare sectors are particular areas of strength.

**The Lawyers:** **Walter Jospin** (see p.716) is known as *"a real business guy who comes up with real business solutions."* Traditionally noted for his M&A work, he has recently focused on defending public companies in investigations by the FCC and SEC, which have recently included work for a Southeastern supermarket chain. The *"outstanding"* **Frank Layson** (see p.718) *"does deal after deal after deal."* Notable examples from the past year include acting as lead partner for South Korean Telecom in a $400 million joint venture with EarthLink. Also doing international work this year is **Wayne Bradley** (see p.707). He has been representing a Japanese corporate in its purchase of a US publicly traded entity, as well as completing financings for aviation companies. Rising star **Elizabeth Noe** (see p.721) is an expert in advising special committees on Sarbanes-Oxley. An *"extremely knowledgeable"* adviser, she also represents issuers in high-yield transactions.

**Clients/Work Highlights:** Transactional highlights of the year include a series of acquisitions for Reed Elsevier and high yield issuances for Beazer Homes USA. South Korean Telecom and Superior Essex also feature in the client roster.

## Powell Goldstein LLP

**The Firm:** Powell Goldstein was applauded by the market for its *"impeccable"* client service, and valued by clients for fielding *"a strong group of corporate lawyers who are a pleasure to work with."* A busy year has seen the team maintaining its good run of M&A deals while also increasing its work advising boards of directors on internal investigations. To cope with

this extra caseload, the firm has recruited energetically in recent months, adding considerably to its ranks through lateral hiring.

**The Lawyers:** **Rick Miller** is *"one of those guys who sees the big picture and doesn't get bogged down in the detail."* He is an expert in M&A and corporate governance issues, and often lectures on the roles, responsibilities and expectations of directors. The *"scholarly and effective"* **Thomas McNeill** practices corporate governance and corporate finance. He boasts an international workload, which includes acting as counsel to German and French businesses.

**Clients/Work Highlights:** Miller's team recently represented Mariner Healthcare in its merger with another public company.

## Band 4

## Arnall Golden Gregory LLP

See firm details p.729

**The Firm:** Arnall Golden Gregory is respected in the market as being *"great for business and commercial transactions,"* and impresses its clients by *"consistently performing above expectations."* The Atlanta office offers niche expertise in medical products manufacturing, and boasts a large amount of M&A work for a large cryopreservation company. It also won plaudits for its work in the technology sector.

**The Lawyers:** **Jonathan Golden** (see p.713) was described by his clients as *"a creative legal thinker who is a real asset for structuring sales and acquisitions of businesses."* He has been involved in multimillion-dollar transactions for a broad range of clients, and is especially noted for his work for SYSCO.

**Clients/Work Highlights:** Cryolife; Costco; Georgia Baptist Healthcare System; Profit Recovery Group and SYSCO.

## Jones Day

See firm details p.570

**The Firm:** This global firm serves major corporate entities with a variety of legal advice. Its international presence is thought to be a major draw for clients, providing as it does the resources and coverage for handling any type of deal worldwide. The Atlanta-based corporate group has particular strength in negotiated acquisitions, private equity and venture capital transactions, and corporate governance, as well as expertise in the chemicals, broadcasting and technology sectors.

**The Lawyers:** A *"fantastic problem solver,"* **Lizanne Thomas** (see p.726) has particular experience in corporate governance matters, advising boards of directors and special committees on disclosure, strategic planning and fiduciary issues. She recently assisted the major shareholder of a publicly traded biotechnology company with its decision to monetize investment in the company.

**Clients/Work Highlights:** A major highlight from the year was acting for Eastman Chemical in the sale of its common and preferred stock of Genencor International to Danisco A/S for $487 million. Other clients include Cumulus Media; Elekta AB; Flower Foods; Georgia Gulf; Hagemeyer North America; Integrity Media; Jameson Inns; JM Huber and Merial.

# EMPLOYMENT

# MAINLY DEFENDANT

## Band 1

### Alston & Bird LLP

See firm details p.728

**The Firm:** This full-service firm was applauded for its "*superior depth of expertise and welcoming, southern approach to client care.*" Commentators observed that the team's renowned strength and experience in litigation places it ahead of many of its rivals when handling novel and complex disputes. The past year has seen the firm handling a busy workload of OSHA, class action discrimination and employment contract disputes, alongside an increasing volume of whistle-blower claims. In 2005, the firm represented Wachovia in a 23-day mediation to resolve an age discrimination class action following 11 years of litigation.

**The Lawyers:** Respected by peers as the "*ultimate nice guy who is passionate and truly driven to succeed,*" **Steve Ensor** (see p.712) is also popular among clients who report: "*He really takes the time to truly understand our business culture and policies.*" He has devoted significant time to advising UPS and has successfully defended the company in a four-day jury trial concerning allegations of disability discrimination. He also obtained a defense verdict on behalf of Aflac in an employment arbitration. One peer admitted: "*I would definitely hire him if I could.*" "*Outstandingly effective*" **Thomas Kilpatrick** (see p.717) garnered enthusiastic praise from clients for his ability to "*articulate clear, practical advice that he really believes in and will stand by.*" He is renowned for his expertise in complex class actions and recently secured a victory on behalf of Imerys Carbonates concerning 27 unfair labor practice charges filed by the United Steelworkers. Market sources conferred praise upon **Forrest Hunter** (see p.715) for his skill in a spectrum of labor and employment cases. According to clients: "*Fantastic litigator*" **Glenn**

Patton (see p.721) "*can be counted upon for his diligence and initiative.*"

**Clients/Work Highlights:** UPS; Kmart; Wachovia; Aflac; SunTrust Banks; Alcoa and Fortis Bank.

### Kilpatrick Stockton LLP

See firm details p.735

**The Firm:** This national practice drew hearty praise for its "*holistic approach*" to fulfilling the employment needs of clients, and for the "*universally superb*" quality of service provided by the team. It maintains its widely recognized strength in labor law matters, while still providing quality advice on the full gamut of employment matters. This includes handling discrimination, wage and hour and employee benefits litigation. It also counsels its wide client base on their employment practices and, where possible, on the avoidance of litigation.

**The Lawyers:** **Richard Boisseau** (see p.707) is "*as knowledgeable a labor attorney as you can find,*" enthused clients. This they attributed to his "*off-the-chart level of client service – I can reach him 24 hours of the day,*" and his candid advice that he couples with "*a true business perspective.*" He devotes much of his practice to counseling clients on preventing union-organizing drives and also advises on wage and hour issues, unfair labor practice charges and collective bargaining. Highly skilled practitioner **William Boice** (see p.706) has a busy workload comprising both commercial and employment litigation. His recent highlights include advising Lockheed Martin on a series of lawsuits concerning allegations of a racially hostile working environment. **James Coil** (see p.709) is "*a terrifically creative problem solver*" who was applauded by clients as a "*real business partner who communicates well and is not afraid to take calculated risks.*" He defends clients against employment discrimination and wage and hour claims and has been especially active representing parties in class action litigation. He is currently advising Nestlé Waters North America in a class action brought by 1,500 sales staff concerning overtime pay.

**Clients/Work Highlights:** Nestlé Waters North America; The Pepsi Bottling Group; Sara Lee; INVESCO; Krispy Kreme; Boeing; Delta Air Lines and Georgia-Pacific.

### King & Spalding LLP

See firm details p.1933

**The Firm:** This firm boasts a long-standing reputation in labor and employment law and benefits from a team that is brimming with "*talented attorneys who work well together.*" It has a strong track record advising prominent clients such as Coca-Cola and McDonald's, and has the necessary depth of expertise to handle the most complex cases and to provide clients with its hallmark commercial and practical advice.

**The Lawyers:** **John Wymer** (see p.727) "*has been on top of his game for a long time,*" acknowledged market sources. They praised his "*terrific speaking and teaching skills, and seasoned expertise in both traditional*

labor and employment matters." 2005 has seen him successfully handling arbitrations and litigations for clients such as Home Depot and Weyerhaeuser. Clients applauded Wymer's "*quick thinking, intelligence and ability to understand the business implications and the legal requirements.*" **Mike Johnston** (see p.716) won the admiration of peers and clients alike for his expertise in employment discrimination, restrictive covenants and executive contract matters. He is well known for his role as external counsel to Coca-Cola in various cases that were wrapped up in 2005. Other highlights of the past year include successfully dismissing race discrimination claims against Zales in a nationwide class action brought against the company and several other entities by a class of current and former African American employees. Many peers recommended **Sam Matchett** (see p.719) for his excellent courtroom presentation skills and tipped him as one of the future stars of the group.

**Clients/Work Highlights:** Weyerhaeuser; Coca-Cola; GlaxoSmithKline; Emory University; Zales; City of Atlanta; Home Depot; Winn-Dixie; Lodgian; Oracle and GE.

### Paul, Hastings, Janofsky & Walker LLP

See firm details p.339

**The Firm:** Market commentators applauded the firm's "*deep bench strength and access to top legal talent across the country*" and continue to rate it as "*a leading player in class actions.*" In one of its headline cases, the group successfully secured a favorable settlement for a national timeshare operator in a nationwide class action suit alleging sex discrimination and sexual harassment. The team is also a popular choice among clients looking for advice on the modification of training programs, company procedures and reporting practices.

**The Lawyers:** **Weyman Johnson** (see p.716) is an attorney who is "*comfortable in almost any environment*" and who handles a broad labor and employment workload. Recent highlights have included advising on numerous wage and hour class actions and acting for clients in a steady stream of age discrimination cases. "*Team player*" **Geoff Weirich** (see p.726) is "*so smart I can't believe it,*" enthused one client; while others spoke of his "*great competitive spirit and ability to anticipate what a judge will say, even when there is no precedent.*" His workload is dominated by class actions, with recent examples including acting as nationwide coordinating counsel on five class actions against Boeing alleging sex discrimination. Employment law expert **Leslie Dent** (see p.711) was praised for her "*understanding of clients' goals*" and for being able to "*get in and out of a courtroom quickly and effectively.*" Her recent work includes successfully defending UPS Logistics in an age, gender and disability claim brought by a former supply chain solutions manager, after his employment was terminated following a violation of the company's electronic communications policy.

**Clients/Work Highlights:** UPS; Cracker Barrel Old

Country Store; Publix Super Markets; CNN; American Airlines; Boeing and Turner Broadcasting System.

## Band 2

### Ashe, Rafuse & Hill, LLP

See firm details p.730

**The Firm:** This group was hailed as a "*top-notch*" employment litigation practice, sought out by clients for its "*pertinent and up-to-date advice.*" The 25-lawyer boutique continues to grow at a healthy rate and has captured high-profile clients such as Johnson & Johnson and Waffle House. Areas of expertise include OSHA, wage and hour, FLSA and Title VII matters.

**The Lawyers:** "*Gregarious and aggressive*" **Lawrence Ashe** (see p.705) was heartily applauded by clients for his "*tremendous personality and dominance in the employment litigation market.*" He is particularly renowned for his "*track record of success and his creative thinking when faced with high-profile litigation that threatens the value of a brand.*" **Nancy Rafuse** was singled out for her "*tenacious and detail-oriented*" approach. She is renowned for her wide-ranging employment expertise, which includes having served as lead trial counsel for hospitality clients in the defense of several multifaceted employment cases.

**Clients/Work Highlights:** Lockheed Martin; Cracker Barrel Old Country Store; Educational Testing Service and Home Depot.

### Elarbee, Thompson, Sapp & Wilson, LLP

**The Firm:** Inspiring the full confidence of clients with its "*strategic and tailor-made advice,*" this 37-lawyer team was applauded for its "*client-oriented approach and amazing results in court.*" The considerable size and depth of experience of the group allows it to provide truly specialized expertise across the spectrum of labor and employment law. This includes advice on union campaigns and contract negotiations as well as providing dedicated specialists for immigration and OSHA matters.

**The Lawyers:** **Brent Wilson** is a "*groundbreaker*" in the employment field according to peers, who revere him for his work concerning reverse race discrimination claims. His busy workload also includes wider employment and labor litigation, as well as counseling management on day-to-day employment matters and the avoidance of litigation. His colleague, **Stanford Wilson**, garnered warm praise for his expertise in a range of employment matters and for "*advising clients with a pragmatic understanding of their business.*" He has recently worked with unionized companies on the modification of collective bargaining agreements regarding rising healthcare costs. According to clients, **Alisa Pittman** possesses "*exactly the kind of qualities you look for in an employment practitioner – she's smart, aggressive and takes each case to heart.*" She advises a broad client base but boasts particular experience in the hospitality and service industries, where she is frequently seen acting for clients in litigation and arbitration. Early 2005 saw Pittman secure a defense verdict on behalf of Aegis Communications in a four-day jury trial in Texas, involving allegations of sexual harassment and retaliation. "*Distinguished*" **Lewis Sapp** was lauded for his expertise in employment law and has celebrated many successes in sex, age and race discrimination cases.

**Clients/Work Highlights:** Florida Power & Light; Citibank; Engelhard; Degussa; Lockheed Martin and Beazer Homes.

### Fisher & Phillips LLP

See firm details p.732

**The Firm:** With a 75-lawyer dedicated labor and employment team in Atlanta alone, the firm was acknowledged by rivals to be among the "*biggest and most prominent competitors.*" In the past year, the firm has grown exponentially with the opening of new offices in Kansas City, Dallas and New Jersey. Its team advises on the full spectrum of labor and employment law, spanning areas such as sex, race and age discrimination, union compliance, immigration and noncompete covenants.

**The Lawyers:** Tex McIver is a key contact in the Atlanta office.

**Clients/Work Highlights:** Hyatt Hotels; Textron; Pratt Industries and Wellborn Cabinet.

### Ford & Harrison LLP

See firm details p.733

**The Firm:** This national employment boutique was applauded by market sources for its "*high-quality and competitively priced advice.*" The firm has long been recognized as dominating the airline sector, but also acts for a broader array of clients who call on the group for advice on the full gamut of labor and employment law, including union avoidance, preventative counseling and litigation.

**The Lawyers:** **Thomas Kassin** (see p.716) is renowned for his expertise in airline-related labor and employment law. His practice also encompasses advice on all types of personnel and labor relations matters arising under the Railway Labor Act.

### Ogletree, Deakins, Nash, Smoak & Stewart, PC

See firm details p.738

**The Firm:** This employment and immigration boutique won rave reviews from clients who were quick to note the firm's "*trademark cordiality and extreme responsiveness,*" and its "*engaging and personable approach*" to client care. The Atlanta team works closely with other offices from the firm's national network to provide clients with specialized expertise in traditional labor, OSHA and ERISA law advice. Sarbanes-Oxley-related whistle-blower litigation has featured significantly in the firm's 2005 workload and the team has successfully defended Duke Energy in one such case. Class and collective actions also featured on the workload, with recent successes including obtaining a favorable decision on behalf of Gold Kist.

**The Lawyers:** The "*fabulous*" **Homer Deakins** (see p.710) was recommended by clients as a "*masterful trial lawyer with superb presentation skills.*" One client enthused: "*He is in a league of his own; he possesses tremendous common sense and a great, comforting demeanor – when I am facing a stressful situation he is able to navigate a course around the problem and immediately makes me feel much better.*" Deakins advises on both traditional labor and employment matters. His recent highlights include successfully concluding a two-year collective bargaining contract negotiation for a large helicopter operator in the Gulf of Mexico. "*Smart and versatile*" **Margaret Campbell** (see p.708) is a "*results-focused, wonderful writer who provides effective solutions.*" She handles a busy workload of class and collective actions in the federal courts and also acts for clients in whistle-blower retaliation claims, FLSA litigation and restrictive covenant disputes. Market commentators heartily endorsed "*trustworthy and popular*" **Craig Cleland** (see p.709) as a "*smart guy with a wonderful courtroom manner.*" Recently, he has successfully represented Dillard's in three arbitration cases concerning alleged discrimination and has represented clients such as GE Industrial, Home Depot, WellPoint and Centex in various class action suits. Clients believe **Gregory Hare** (see p.714) "*is really making a name for himself; he is extremely thorough and skilled in handling cases.*"

**Clients/Work Highlights:** In January 2005, the firm was selected as national employment counsel for Tyco. It also acts for WellPoint; Centex; Dillard's; GE Energy; Duke Energy; ArvinMeritor; Ratner Companies and Federal Reserve Bank.

## Rogers & Hardin

**The Firm:** Boasting significant depth and expertise across the employment law spectrum, this quality outfit commands the respect of the market. Interviewees commended its talented litigators who are well placed to advise on discrimination claims, restrictive covenants, wrongful discharge and preventative counseling.

**The Lawyers:** Although increasingly visible as a high-profile mediator, **Hunter Hughes** continues to be regarded by many as a "*beacon for employment law – he commands respect at a national level.*" Peers endorsed him as a "*classic lawyer's lawyer – he's incredibly effective, he knows the law and which buttons to push.*"

## Troutman Sanders LLP

**The Firm:** Market sources hailed this full-service outfit as a "*progressive employment department that inspires confidence.*" In Atlanta, around 25 labor and employment lawyers advise employers on a range of matters, including Title VII discrimination claims, retaliation claims, the FLSA and restrictive covenants. The group acts for a loyal and diverse client base, and enjoys particularly close relationships with Georgia-Pacific and Georgia Power.

**The Lawyers:** According to interviewees, **Robert Buckler** will "*pull out all stops and fight like hell to protect his clients and secure a victory.*" Interviewees warmly recommended employment law expert **Richard Gerakitis** for his skill in litigation. This they attributed to his "*popularity with juries and his superior presentation skills,*" and for always knowing his cases "*inside out.*" "*Exceedingly professional*" **Stephen Riddell** was praised for his "*sensitivity to clients' needs.*" He focuses on class actions, involving matters such as wage and hour and discrimination claims for high-profile clients such as Southern Company. "*Trusted adviser*" **Ashley Hager** enters the table for the first time following enthusiastic praise from the market. Clients described her as "*incredibly helpful; she is quick to sift through the facts and emotions of a case and extract the core issues.*"

**Clients/Work Highlights:** Georgia Power; Southern Company; Chick-fil-A; Mohawk Industries; ChoicePoint; Carmike Cinemas; Scientific-Atlanta; Gray Television; Turner Broadcasting System; Waffle House; Unisource Worldwide and Rayonier.

## Band 3

## Constangy, Brooks & Smith, LLC

**The Firm:** As one of the longest established employment practices in Atlanta, the group was praised for its expertise across the spectrum of labor and employment matters. Particular mention was made of this growing firm's "*excellent local connections*" and its loyal client base. Areas of expertise include labor law, such as workers' compensation matters. The group also advises clients on OSHA, a variety of discrimination litigation and noncompete covenants.

**The Lawyers:** Ed Katze is a key contact for the Atlanta labor and employment group.

**Clients/Work Highlights:** Hertz, Sara Lee and Watkins Motor Lines feature on the list of clients.

## Holland & Knight LLP

See firm details p.1534

**The Firm:** This national player provides a quality litigation service to clients involved in a range of employment disputes. It is able to draw upon the deep resources of its nationwide network of offices to fulfill the needs of a range of clients in the Southeast. One client spoke enthusiastically of the firm's "*commitment to diversity and its open culture.*"

**The Lawyers:** "*Superb*" **Mary Ann Oakley** (see p.721) is the cornerstone of the Atlanta office's employment practice. She handles a mixture of employment counseling and litigation. Her recent areas of focus include handling FLSA claims and retaliation claims, and acting for clients in national origin and religion discrimination cases.

**Clients/Work Highlights:** The client base includes Marriott International and Cardinal Health.

## Hunton & Williams LLP

See firm details p.1959

**The Firm:** Clients hailed this 23-lawyer employment practice as a "*bright group that is well tuned in to our needs.*" The Atlanta office services clients from a broad spectrum of industries, in particular those in the financial, life sciences and healthcare sectors. The team's areas of expertise include advising on Title VII and age discrimination, ADA, FLSA and ERISA litigation. Its lawyers also have experience in handling traditional labor matters.

**The Lawyers:** Interviewees singled out **Traywick Duffie** (see p.711) as a highly experienced employment law practitioner who handles litigation and union negotiations. He has devoted much of his practice in recent months to advising trucking, healthcare and broadcasting clients. The "*sharp*" **Kurt Powell** (see p.722) was applauded by sources as a "*skillful writer and trial lawyer.*" He boasts significant experience in handling class actions – some of his recent highlights include obtaining several victories in Sarbanes-Oxley whistle-blower litigation on behalf of clients in the financial and pharmaceutical industries.

**Clients/Work Highlights:** ING; AEGON USA; World Financial Group; Solvay; UCB; Serologicals; Hitachi Power Tools and Beaulieu Group.

## Jackson Lewis

**The Firm:** This group is widely respected for the depth of its resources, and it won particular praise from clients for its "*excellent level of partner attention.*" It is particularly renowned for its capabilities in advising on traditional labor law but also has acknowledged strengths acting for clients in employment discrimination cases.

**The Lawyers:** **David Gordon** (see p.714) has earned the respect of the market for "*really going the distance*" when handling complex employment litigation. Peers noted that aside from his "*great presentation skills,*" his strength also lies in his ability to be "*comfortable in all environments and able to work closely with people from all walks of life.*"

## Jones Day

See firm details p.570

**The Firm:** The Atlanta office of this international powerhouse impressed clients with its "*great work ethic and considerable bench strength.*" The employment team comprises 15 labor and employment experts who clients praised for their "*seamless interaction*" with lawyers from the firm's network of offices: "*They are able to pool resources from across the USA when it is needed.*"

**The Lawyers:** Clients appreciate the team's "*accommodating approach,*" with one noting: "*I have called them at 1am and they have never hesitated to respond to my questions immediately.*" In particular, sources recommended "*exceptionally balanced and thoughtful*" **Dan Carter** (see p.708) for his ability to "*accurately analyze a situation and provide an objective, business-minded alternative.*" Carter devotes the majority of his practice to traditional labor law matters and handles a steady stream of wage and hour cases. The "*succinct*" **Deborah Sudbury** (see p.725) received hearty praise for her "*unbelievable perspective on the law.*" She also stood out for her business acumen and is famed for her ability to provide "*outstandingly creative solutions.*" She handles a busy caseload covering the full spectrum of labor and employment matters, but has a particular focus on the defense of class actions in areas such as Title VII, ERISA and the FLSA.

**Clients/Work Highlights:** Timken; Bank of America; Farley's and Sathers Candy; DEUTZ; Tomkins Industries; Verizon; CITGO Petroleum and Electronic Warfare Associates.

## Munger & Stone

**The Firm:** This firm earns widespread respect from the market for its employment law expertise and, according to peers, is home to "*two of the brightest lawyers you will ever find.*" It attracts a diverse client base ranging from large companies, such as Delta Air Lines, to smaller local entities including individual professionals. Highlights of 2005 include continuing to act as primary defense counsel to Delta Air Lines. The group obtained a summary dismissal in alleged whistle-blowing action against Delta that was the subject of much media attention. The team also secured successful outcomes on behalf of Beecher Carlson in ongoing restrictive covenant and business tort litigation and arbitration.

**The Lawyers:** Both **Tom Munger** and **Benjamin Stone** garnered warm praise from the market for the depth of their experience and quality of their advice. **Clients/Work Highlights:** Delta Air Lines; Beecher Carlson; MCIC Vermont; Houston Wire & Cable; Navigator Systems; First Tennessee Bank; Merrill Gardens; Golf Club of Georgia; Abaco Mobile and LAD Custom Publishing.

# ENERGY & NATURAL RESOURCES

| Energy & Natural Resources | |
|---|---|
| Leading Firms | |
| [1] SUTHERLAND ASBILL & BRENNAN LLP *Atlanta* | |
| TROUTMAN SANDERS LLP *Atlanta* | |
| [2] ALSTON & BIRD LLP *Atlanta* | |
| MCKENNA LONG & ALDRIDGE LLP *Atlanta* | |
| [3] DUANE MORRIS LLP *Atlanta* | |
| KING & SPALDING LLP *Atlanta* | |

| Leading Individuals | |
|---|---|
| [1] FORRY Robert *Troutman Sanders LLP* | |
| GREENE Kevin *Troutman Sanders LLP* | |
| KILGORE III Cada *Sutherland Asbill* | |
| [2] DEGNAN Peter *Alston & Bird LLP* | |
| DOWDY L Craig *McKenna Long* | |
| MERCER John *Troutman Sanders LLP* | |
| SHORT JR Herbert *Sutherland Asbill* | |
| SWENSON Erik *King & Spalding LLP* | |
| WELLS Della Wager *Alston & Bird LLP* | |
| WHITNEY Charles *Duane Morris LLP* | |

| Up-and-coming individuals | |
|---|---|
| CAEN Melissa *Troutman Sanders LLP* | |

## Band 1

### Sutherland Asbill & Brennan LLP
See firm details p.578

**The Firm:** "*Highly respected*" for its depth of expertise across the energy sector, this group attracted enthusiastic praise from a loyal client base of financial institutions and utilities. The firm competes on a national level to provide clients with the full gamut of energy advice, encompassing regulatory guidance and expertise on LNG, electricity, and oil and gas matters. Recent features of the group's workload include advising on financings, M&A deals, power projects and power supply matters. Its highlights include advising Kansas Electric Power Cooperative on new nuclear and coal generation projects. Lawyers also advised Oglethorpe Power on the issuance of more than $15 million of pollution control revenue bonds.

**The Lawyers:** Clients praised the lawyers here for their "*thorough, team-working approach.*" One of its leading lights is **Cada Kilgore** (see p.717), dubbed by interviewees as a "*great problem solver who sees the bigger picture.*" He boasts vast experience in advising electric cooperatives on corporate restructurings, loan arrangements, M&A deals and government-guaranteed financings. **Herbert Short** (see p.724) was described by market sources as a "*probing,*

*forward-looking and detail-oriented*" energy attorney. His clients marveled at his "*openness and team-playing skills.*" "*His friendliness means he can interact with all the staff in our organization and truly understand our business,*" remarked one. In 2005, Short was elected to serve as general counsel to Oglethorpe Power, a role he combines with his position as a partner in Sutherland's energy group, specializing in energy sector public offerings.

**Clients/Work Highlights:** Old Dominion Electric Cooperative; Basin Electric Power Cooperative; Wolverine Power Supply Cooperative; Goldman Sachs; Great River Energy; JPMorgan Chase and CoBank.

### Troutman Sanders LLP

**The Firm:** Endorsed by market sources as a mainstay of the Georgia energy market, this firm attracted hearty praise for the depth and breadth of its expertise in the sector. The group is famed for its long-standing relationship with Georgia Power and has developed a practice that is in high demand for its advice on a plethora of regulatory matters, contract negotiations and lease financings.

**The Lawyers:** **Robert Forry** is a leading light for regulatory matters and wins recommendations for his "*in-depth understanding of the energy industry.*" Interviewees also highlighted **Kevin Greene** as someone who "*certainly knows his way around the system.*" He is also best known for his energy regulatory expertise. **John Mercer** comes warmly recommended for the depth of his experience in the energy sector. His colleague **Melissa Caen** is fast gaining an impressive reputation for her expert handling of projects, regulatory matters and security offerings for clients such as the Southern Company.

**Clients/Work Highlights:** Kansas City Southern and Georgia Power are among the firm's most prominent clients.

## Band 2

### Alston & Bird LLP
See firm details p.728

**The Firm:** This public energy and finance group comes highly recommended for its quality advice on energy matters and has clinched starring roles acting as general counsel to the Municipal Electric Authority of Georgia and the Municipal Gas Authority of Georgia. It is well versed in corporate, contractual, environmental and bond financing matters in the energy sector. Over the past year, the group has been heavily involved in the development of Public Gas

Partners. This is an entity formed on behalf of seven Southeastern joint action agencies for the acquisition, financing, ownership, management and transportation of natural gas reserves.

**The Lawyers:** The group was boosted in August 2005 by the arrival of a 14-member regulatory energy team from Swidler Berlin, which significantly enhanced the group's capabilities before the FERC. **Peter Degnan** (see p.711) is popular among clients for his "*efficiency and excellence*" in energy litigation. Researchers heard that **Della Wager Wells** (see p.726) is "*always a dependable source of professional and knowledgeable advice.*" Her practice includes tax-exempt financings for power, water and sewerage projects on behalf of governmental entities.

**Clients/Work Highlights:** Municipal Electric Authority of Georgia; Southeast Alabama Gas District; Florida Municipal Power Agency and Municipal Gas Authority of Georgia.

### McKenna Long & Aldridge LLP
See firm details p.737

**The Firm:** This practice is national in scope and is recognized as a key player in the Georgia energy market. It serves a broad client base from the electrical and natural gas industries, and provides them with quality counseling, dispute resolution and regulatory law advice.

**The Lawyers:** **Craig Dowdy** (see p.711) is as "*good as they come for state and federal energy regulatory litigation,*" enthused market sources. He has represented utilities in several high-profile cases concerning their acquisitions.

**Clients/Work Highlights:** Atlanta Gas Light; Chattanooga Gas; Virginia Natural Gas; Cleco and Public Service Company of New Mexico.

## Band 3

### Duane Morris LLP
See firm details p.1753

**The Firm:** The Atlanta office of this national outfit is a new addition to the rankings following enthusiastic praise from both clients and peers for its "*extremely high-quality service*" in handling energy regulatory and projects matters. One satisfied customer claimed: "*The lawyers do a fantastic job of relationship building; they always make me feel like I am their most important client.*" Recent highlights include creating and representing a joint venture involving a greenfield gas-fired power generation project in Michigan and acting for the contractor on a power plant environmental upgrade project in Georgia.

The Lawyers: **Charles Whitney** (see p.727) commands "*the utmost respect*" from interviewees and was declared the bedrock of the firm's Atlanta energy practice. Clients spoke of his "*immense breadth of knowledge – not only is he a fantastic lawyer, but he has worked in the industry, understands the power business and how it feels to be a client.*" His recent work includes representing Mirant, PEPCO and Reliant Energy in a variety of fuel procurement matters.

Clients/Work Highlights: Mirant; PEPCO; Reliant Energy and Orion Power.

## King & Spalding LLP
See firm details p.1933

The Firm: The Atlanta office forms part of the firm's national energy transactions practice and was praised for its "*excellent understanding of the energy sector*" and the close relationships it has built up with the regulatory bodies. One client marveled: "*I went from minor league to major league when I started working with them!*" Recent highlights for the team include assisting the developer of a 1,200+ MW coal-fired generating plant in Georgia and defending the position of Georgia Power before the Georgia Public Service Commission.

The Lawyers: "*Conscientious and responsive*" **Erik Swenson** (see p.725) attracts a large Southeastern client base. His recent workload has included advising the developer of a 30 MW waste-to-electricity generating facility to be located in Georgia. Clients said: "*He puts us first and is always one step ahead of us, offering suggestions to address any issues that might arise.*"

Clients/Work Highlights: The group acts for regional energy project developers and energy users. Some of its key clients include Gulf LNG Energy; Kemira; Blue Ridge Energy; Union Carbide and LongLeaf Energy.

# ENVIRONMENT

| Environment |
|---|
| Leading Firms |
| **1** ALSTON & BIRD LLP *Atlanta* |
| KING & SPALDING LLP *Atlanta* |
| TROUTMAN SANDERS LLP *Atlanta* |
| **2** HUNTON & WILLIAMS LLP *Atlanta* |
| KILPATRICK STOCKTON LLP *Atlanta* |
| MCKENNA LONG & ALDRIDGE LLP *Atlanta* |
| **3** EPSTEIN BECKER & GREEN PC *Atlanta* |
| HUNTER, MACLEAN *Savannah* |
| MORRIS, MANNING & MARTIN, LLP *Atlanta* |
| SMITH GAMBRELL & RUSSELL LLP *Atlanta* |

## Band 1

### Alston & Bird LLP
See firm details p.728

The Firm: Market commentators cite this as "*a phenomenal group at the top of the industry.*" The team includes former government officials and has strong historical connections with the EPA, giving it the upper hand when advising clients on intricate federal issues. The arrival of former environment prosecutor Bruce Pasfield will further enhance the group's abilities in the regulatory arena. The team has unrivaled expertise in hazardous waste transportation and also won plaudits for its defense of wastewater permit challenges. The City of Atlanta recently retained the team to handle important litigation regarding the city's ability to manage residential waste. The group is also acting as lead counsel to US Pipe and its parent, Walter Industries, in controversial litigation and administrative matters associated with alleged PCB contamination throughout Anniston, Alabama. The case includes negotiating a groundbreaking agreement with EPA for lead and PCB cleanup throughout Anniston.

The Lawyers: Master of water cases **Lee DeHihns** (see p.711) has continued his work in the water supply and wastewater areas for cities and countries across the Southeast. One of his highlights includes successfully persuading the Board of Natural

Resources to amend one of the state rules in relation to Gwinnett County's wastewater treatment facility. He also assisted a large brewery in Georgia on the modification of an air permit and frequently acts on behalf of Carnival Corporation. **Robert Mowrey** (see p.720) stood out for his extensive experience in hazardous waste matters. He took a leading role in negotiating an agreement with the EPA in relation to one of the largest investigations into and cleanup of lead in residential areas in US history. He also defended the City of Atlanta in litigation involving a state statute restricting the transportation of waste across county boundaries. The statute was declared unconstitutional in the lower courts and is currently on appeal to the Georgia Supreme Court. **Doug Cloud** (see p.709) enters the tables following strong market feedback. Clients praised him as an "*honest, down-to-earth guy who has a phenomenal ability to put things in perspective and come up with practical solutions.*" His areas of expertise include CAA matters and brownfield redevelopment. He defended a client in a groundbreaking case involving air permitting for the mining industry and is working on brownfield sites in Canada and a number of US states. **Nill Toulme** (see p.726) advises clients on the environmental issues surrounding M&A, real estate and financial transactions. He is also on hand to assist clients in a variety of environmental and toxic tort litigation. James Stokes has left the firm.

Clients/Work Highlights: Dalton Utilities; Dow Chemical; Union Carbide; Printpack; Genuine Parts Company; Electrolux North America; Home Depot; Weyerhaeuser; Wal-Mart; Bank of America and UPS.

## King & Spalding LLP
See firm details p.1933

The Firm: This is "*a well-connected team with sound integrity and a wonderful reputation.*" Interviewees praised the group for its dynamic litigation practice and its "*knowledgeable and pragmatic approach to problem solving.*" Lengthy experience in the sector gives the team enviable grounding in a spectrum of court proceedings, from defending permit challenges to toxic tort cases. On the regulatory side, the team advises on the applicability of statutes and helps

clients on the development and implementation of environmental compliance programs. Transactional matters include advising on issues regarding the purchase and sale of contaminated properties. The workload also includes environmental audits, brownfield redevelopment and Superfund work. Interviewees highlighted the depth of the team as another asset for clients. The dedicated environment group comprises several former environment regulators who offer clients expert technical assistance and invaluable insights into the workings of the regulatory authorities.

The Lawyers: Praise flooded in for "*exemplary litigator*" **Patricia Barmeyer** (see p.705). "*A first-rate lawyer who commands respect in the courtroom,*" she is representing the local government of Metropolitan Atlanta in the high-profile, tri-state water wars against the States of Florida and Alabama. Clients choose her because "*she's an excellent trial advocate, a scholar and has outstanding judgment – she is unflappable.*" Litigation involving permits for marinas in relation to coastal development is another flourishing part of her practice. The firm's resident Superfund expert is **Charles Tisdale** (see p.726) who sources recommended as "*probably one of the most knowledgeable environment lawyers in the state.*" He recently obtained a favorable settlement for 600 parties in relation to the Aqua Tec waste site. Another highlight involved defending 25 corporations against a contamination claim involving Elmore Site in South Carolina. **Leslie Oakes**' (see p.721) engineering background gives him the edge in regulatory work. He has been advising a client on obtaining air and water permits for the first commercial plant that will use plasma gasification to turn tires into a gaseous form. Researchers heard that the "*absolutely brilliant*" **Lewis Jones** (see p.716) has "*wonderful academic credentials and has a flair for creating convincing arguments.*" The addition of former chief of staff to the administrator of US EPA region 4, Allen Barnes, to the practice will enhance the group's expertise even further.

Clients/Work Highlights: Honeywell; Coca-Cola; Eaton; GE; Gillette; Dow Chemical and Brown & Williamson Tobacco.

## Environment
### Leading Individuals

★ **BARMEYER Patricia** *King & Spalding LLP*

[1] **DEHIHNS III Lee** *Alston & Bird LLP*
**HOGFOSS Robert** *Hunton & Williams LLP*
**HORDER Richard** *Kilpatrick Stockton LLP*
**JOHNSON JR John** *Troutman Sanders LLP*

[2] **CAMPBELL Margaret** *Troutman Sanders LLP*
**ERNST Andrew** *Hunter, Maclean*
**GALLO Barbara** *Epstein Becker*
**KAZMAREK Edward** *McKenna Long*
**MOWREY Robert** *Alston & Bird LLP*
**O'DAY Stephen** *Smith Gambrell*
**POUNCEY Gerald** *Morris, Manning*
**TISDALE JR Charles** *King & Spalding LLP*

[3] **CLOUD Douglas** *Alston & Bird LLP*
**DOMBY Arthur** *Troutman Sanders LLP*
**HENDERSON Douglas** *Troutman Sanders LLP*
**HOLDEN G Graham** *Jones Day*
**LASETER Scott** *McKenna Long*
**LITTLE Catherine** *Hunton & Williams LLP*
**OAKES Leslie** *King & Spalding LLP*
**PERRY Charles** *Jones Day*
**POPE David** *Carr, Tabb & Pope LLP*
**SCHULZE Melvin** *Hunton & Williams LLP*
**SILLIMAN Todd** *McKenna Long*
**TOULME Nill V** *Alston & Bird LLP*

### Up-and-coming individuals

**JONES Lewis** *King & Spalding LLP*
**MOORE David** *Troutman Sanders LLP*
**RICHARDSON Susan** *Kilpatrick Stockton LLP*

## Troutman Sanders LLP

**The Firm:** The firm's environmental department is widely regarded as "*a great team that provides a superior legal service.*" Interviewees agreed its strengths include "*really getting to know clients, taking the lead on resolving issues and adopting a proactive approach.*" The team specializes in representing utilities and boasts particular expertise in defending them in litigation. It successfully acted for Southern Company in a lawsuit filed against it and four other utilities by the City of New York, eight states and several environmental groups alleging that carbon dioxide emissions from the utilities were creating a public nuisance by contributing to global warming. The firm's track record in regulatory compliance matters gives it a distinct advantage in litigation and its army of environment lawyers includes a number of specialists, with four lawyers devoted solely to air quality work.

**The Lawyers:** Sources report that **John Johnson** is "*a great, seasoned lawyer and we are always impressed with his experience and insights.*" He specializes in hazardous waste issues but is also rated as a go-to lawyer for air-related work. A significant percentage of his recent workload involved representing a major air carrier in consent order negotiations with the EPA. **Margaret Campbell** is "*one of the best in the state on air matters*" and represents companies in rulemaking and clean air policy matters at federal

and state level. Recently she successfully defended Alabama Power against a lawsuit filed by the EPA alleging that maintenance projects undertaken by the company violated the New Source Review provisions of the CAA. Interviewees agree that **Art Domby** "*does a terrific job*" for clients. He possesses not just "*great interpersonal skills, but he knows how to walk the fence and treat everyone properly.*" He has specialist expertise in nuclear power plants, including radiological waste work and disposal issues at regulated facilities. His recent work includes advising a client on the possible licensing of a cogeneration nuclear power plant. Environment litigator **Doug Henderson** combines "*technical knowledge, legal expertise and business acumen*" to great effect. He recently acted as counsel to a large electric utility in a case involving endangered species. Clients praise his "*pragmatic approach to allocating risk and skill in assessing what the real exposure is.*" The "*intelligent and energetic*" **David Moore** handles civil and administrative litigation and permitting, and counsels clients on a range of waste, water and air issues.

**Clients/Work Highlights:** Alabama Power; Wal-Mart; Omaha Public Power District; Kerr-McGee; Southern Company and the Georgia Department of Transportation.

## Band 2

## Hunton & Williams LLP
See firm details p.1959

**The Firm:** The Atlanta office of this national powerhouse is renowned for its strong track record in energy and environmental regulatory issues. Historically the practice has been involved in several industries, but recently the team has witnessed an upturn in oil and gas transportation work. It has advised on numerous pipeline matters involving the Office of Pipeline Safety, the National Transportation Board, the EPA and the DOJ. The team is also frequently involved in high-profile national matters and maintains active CWA and natural resources components to its practice, including natural resources damages, wetlands and Endangered Species Act issues. Clients were impressed by the "*caliber and creativity of the firm; the lawyers look at the big picture and devise impressive tactical plans.*"

**The Lawyers:** Clients applaud **Robert Hogfoss** (see p.715) as "*a centered and sound attorney who has that rare gift of seeing the big picture and not getting sidetracked by irrelevancies.*" His unassuming personality was also a hit with interviewees, who praised him as a "*low-key yet extremely effective*" operator. Hogfoss has defended some of the largest oil pipelines in the country against enforcement actions brought by government agencies. Sources also celebrated his talent as "*an outstanding writer – once you've read one of his reports you essentially have no questions.*" **Catherine Little**'s (see p.718) strengths lie in her tactical prowess and her ability to formulate successful strategies. She has worked on issues relating to the protection of leatherback and hawksbill turtles in Puerto Rico under the Endangered Species Act. One

source declared **Melvin Schulze** (see p.723) "*the best air attorney I've ever met – he's always the first guy I call.*" This "*smart and diligent*" attorney handles CAA litigation and regulation on behalf of clients such as utilities, chemical plants and pulp and paper companies.

**Clients/Work Highlights:** The group's clients include Colonial Pipeline, Kinder Morgan Energy Partners and a range of oil pipeline companies, energy utilities and national corporations.

## Kilpatrick Stockton LLP
See firm details p.735

**The Firm:** "*A wonderful group that is always cooperative and punctual*" was the assessment of satisfied clients. The environment team is housed within the litigation department, enabling it to focus on any courtroom issues that may arise. However, the group covers all areas of environmental law including wetlands, endangered species, contamination, general environment compliance and transactional issues. Significant cases for the team this year include representing the City of Atlanta in litigation with the EPA over water and sewer compliance issues. It also acted as counsel to developers involved in major litigation in Alabama, concerning the protection of the beach mouse in relation to the Endangered Species Act.

**The Lawyers:** In the eyes of commentators, **Richard Horder** (see p.715) is "*just dynamite – he's an amazingly smart and savvy lawyer.*" He possesses the knowledge and ability to resolve key questions quickly and is in demand for his expertise in water, endangered species, wetlands and waste-related work. He has recently handled several large contamination cases and is respected for his pro bono work. **Susan Richardson** (see p.723) "*can grasp the big picture and still take care of detail,*" and she also won praise for her "*fabulous*" written skills. She has experience in wastewater permitting and enforcement matters, particularly in relation to municipal governments.

**Clients/Work Highlights:** Sun Chemical; City of Atlanta; Georgia-Pacific; BellSouth and Aronov Realty.

## McKenna Long & Aldridge LLP
See firm details p.737

**The Firm:** The group's expertise in niche areas of environmental law sets it apart from many of its competitors in Georgia. It maintains a healthy profile in areas such as pesticide regulation, Toxic Substances Control Act (TSCA) and hazardous waste issues. Brownfield redevelopment accounts for an increasing portion of the team's work and it has unique expertise in manufactured gas plant issues. The close interaction between the firm's environmental and government contracts group means that local government entities, particularly municipalities and counties, remain prominent on the firm's client roster. Clients described the firm as "*first-rate in responding to initial problems and working through to the resolution.*"

**The Lawyers:** Interviewees characterized **Skip Kazmarek** (see p.717) as a "*formidable opponent*" who covers the full spectrum of environment law.

His recent emphasis has been on environment litigation but several major corporations continue to take advantage of his bounteous knowledge in relation to the environmental issues of corporate transactions. According to one source, **Todd Silliman** (see p.724) "*stays on top of his cases and is a force in negotiations.*" He focuses on water law, including state and federal water supply regulations, interstate water rights and disputes. He represents the State of Georgia in the tri-state water wars and has assisted developers and landowners in several large brownfield and coastal development projects. Clients repeatedly praised **Scott Laseter** (see p.718) for his "*imaginative ideas and great strategic sense.*" Litigation involving manufactured gas plants is his specialty. One example includes acting for a city in Maine in litigation against the former owner-operator of a gas plant in relation to the cleanup of ten acres of tar contamination in a river. He also has an established brownfield practice, and recently assisted the owner of a property on the Hazardous Site Inventory on a sale, which involved relieving the prospective purchaser of liability under state brownfield law.

**Clients/Work Highlights:** The group's client base includes chemical companies, oil and gas producers and defense contractors.

## Band 3

### Epstein Becker & Green PC

**The Firm:** This growing group offers a broad range of environment services. It counsels clients on an array of state and federal environmental regulatory issues and has been busy advising the City of Rincon on disputes concerning state water rights. Clients are impressed with the quality of the group's work: "*Frankly, the service is extraordinarily good. They can resolve issues without hassle and will analyze a problem in an efficient and cost-effective manner.*"

**The Lawyers:** Much of the environment group's success is attributed to **Barbara Gallo** (see p.713). She won rave reviews from market commentators who characterized her as "*a smart and professional attorney who has a way of coming up with practical solutions to complex problems.*" She is currently defending Michelin against claims that it contributed to property contamination at a property in Georgia, and is representing a scrap metal recycler in a similar dispute.

**Clients/Work Highlights:** The firm represents clients from a variety of industry sectors, including chemicals and pesticides; agriculture; oil and gas; metal smelting; mining; pulp and paper; tire and rubber manufacturing and transportation.

### Hunter, Maclean, Exley & Dunn, PC

**The Firm:** Although this is a smaller offering than some of its competitors, this group is considered by many to be "*the preeminent practice in Savannah.*" It is best known for its coastal and wetlands practice, where it is renowned for counseling clients on wetlands permits and assessments. The team also handles environmental due diligence in relation to business transactions and has a strong track record in a spectrum of liability litigation.

**The Lawyers:** Coastal development expert **Andrew Ernst** leads the practice. He has particular expertise in issues arising under Georgia's Coastal Zone Management Act. He also represents clients in permitting matters relating to the CAA, CWA and the Solid Waste Management Act.

**Clients/Work Highlights:** Savannah Economic Development Authority, WET Inc and various developers, waste sites and manufacturers feature on the client list.

### Morris, Manning & Martin, LLP

**The Firm:** This smaller team remains in the limelight thanks largely to its role as sole environment counsel in the $2 billion Atlantic Station redevelopment. Recently the team has also helped to draft legislation relating to brownfields and has acted as special counsel on environmental issues on more than 50 major redevelopment projects, ranging from $20 million to $100 million in value. Members of the team are also well known in academic circles and frequently publish articles on environment law.

**The Lawyers:** According to interviewees, the "*sharp and bright*" **Gerald Pouncey** is "*the person to go to with transactional problems.*" He has a background in redevelopment work and is heavily involved in the Atlantic Station project. He has handled a number of brownfield projects and recently completed the representation and sale of a brownfield portfolio worth $400 million.

**Clients/Work Highlights:** The group typically acts for financial institutions and real estate companies.

### Smith Gambrell & Russell LLP

**The Firm:** This long-standing group handles regulation and litigation for a range of clients, including homeowners' associations, in relation to permitting or the enforcement of environmental law. The team is currently representing homeowners and businesses around Lake Lanier in litigation aimed at resisting efforts to pour 40 million tons of waste per day into the lake. The group's caseload includes acting for clients in toxic tort litigation and hazardous waste cleanups. Lawyers also advise on an array of permitting and compliance issues including land and water use.

**The Lawyers:** Heading the environmental team is the "*extremely bright*" **Stephen O'Day**. Recently, he successfully acted for a client in litigation involving $11 million of cleanup costs claimed against a shipper of hazardous materials for a cleanup at a rail yard. He also advises on the full range of environmental law and on business and real estate transactions.

**Clients/Work Highlights:** Arch Chemicals; Arch Wood Protection; Plantation Pipe Line and MACTEC Engineering and Consulting.

### Other Notable Practitioners

**Graham Holden** (see p.715) is a relatively new addition to Jones Day but has already built a reputation in Atlanta as "*an excellent litigator.*" He counsels clients on obtaining and enforcing air permits under the CAA. He is currently working on a challenge to a Title 5 air operating permit for a power facility. Also noted at Jones Day is **Charles Perry** (see p.721), who is frequently retained for his expertise in environmental litigation. Recently, Perry acted as lead defense counsel to a major waste management company in the attempted closure of one of the largest municipal landfills in Georgia. The "*smart and effective*" **David Pope** of Carr, Tabb & Pope LLP stands out to commentators for his work in representing plaintiffs in environmental and toxic tort litigation. He has handled a number of mass-plaintiff environmental cases, including consumer class actions.

# HEALTHCARE

## Band 1

### Alston & Bird LLP
See firm details p.728

**The Firm:** Clients rate this group as "*thorough and responsive – the lawyers have a comprehensive knowledge of healthcare and can always be trusted.*" The team wins plaudits for its corporate and litigation strengths and, most particularly, for its regulatory expertise. It works closely with colleagues in Washington, DC on legislative and policy changes to the Medicare system.

**The Lawyers:** **Jack Schroder** (see p.723) is "*one of the most experienced guys in town,*" hailed by clients as "*a definite go-to guy.*" He is highly respected for his work for the Georgia Hospital Association and is a recognized expert on corporate restructuring and government enforcement. **Donna Bergeson** (see p.706) chairs the group's healthcare regulatory practice group. Clients say: "*She is amazingly smart – a lawyer with her finger constantly on the pulse.*" A regular choice of both academic and nonacademic healthcare organizations, she is "*a superb compliance lawyer.*"

**Clients/Work Highlights:** The group recently acted for Accredo Health in its purchase by Medco, a deal valued at $2.2 billion. It also represents Emory University.

### King & Spalding LLP
See firm details p.1933

**The Firm:** This highly rated and substantial team is "*right at the forefront of transactional work and truly excellent at litigation.*" Gradually, but with great effect, the group has extended beyond its Southeastern base and has now secured a national reach. Its work includes acting for healthcare providers, research bodies, device manufacturers, pharmaceutical distributors and insurance companies. Strong regulatory advice is also on offer.

**The Lawyers:** The "*tenacious*" **Richard Shackelford** (see p.724) is highly praised for his skills in the litigation and regulatory arena. He represents hospital and Medicare clients in a range of commercial litigations and consumer class actions. He is currently defending nonprofit hospitals against claims that they discriminate against the uninsured. **Glen Reed** (see p.722) is "*a healthcare expert with a keen commercial mind.*" He is recommended for his skills in mergers and high-level transactions, particularly in regulatory issues arising there from. He has just acted on a $1.2 billion deal. **Robert Keenan** (see p.717) is also praised for his commercial nous.

**Clients/Work Highlights:** Piedmont Medical Center; Central Georgia Health Systems; Memorial Health, Savannah; St Mary's Hospital, Athens; Humana and WellCare HMO.

## Band 2

### Kilpatrick Stockton LLP
See firm details p.735

**The Firm:** This group wins plaudits for its versatility. Whether it concerns corporate, litigation, IP, licensing or medical device matters, it consistently produces the goods for its clients. Many of these are healthcare providers but, as well as representing traditional hospital clients, it also acts for academic and nonacademic research bodies among others. Biotech is a particular sphere of expertise and the firm has also made something of a name for itself regarding the development of new drugs.

**The Lawyers:** The "*intelligent*" **Phillip Street** (see p.725) was described as "*a man who combines a wealth of knowledge with unbeatable practical experience.*" He is hailed for his skills in both healthcare and life sciences matters and is particularly skilled in M&A issues.

**Clients/Work Highlights:** The group represents healthcare services, research companies and academic bodies.

### Nelson Mullins Riley & Scarborough LLP
See firm details p.1758

**The Firm:** This strong broad-based practice draws client approval for a "*direct approach combined with a multitude of skills: the team can offer clear and practical advice on any aspect.*" It is particularly endorsed for its regulatory advice regarding federal and state investigations. The group's expertise in transactions is also manifest, as is its aptitude for finance work.

**The Lawyers:** **Jeffrey Baxter** is "*a legal expert who combines knowledge with a sharp business acumen.*" A strong litigator, he further handles a rich mix of work that includes compliance, transactional and antitrust matters. "*Straight-talking and approachable*" **Stanley Jones** is rated for his skills in healthcare and government relations.

**Clients/Work Highlights:** The firm represents a range of healthcare providers and also advises financiers looking to invest in the healthcare sector.

### Parker, Hudson, Rainer & Dobbs LLP

**The Firm:** "*Excellent, and with a dedicated focus on healthcare,*" this team draws equal praise for both its regulatory and corporate skills. It is recommended for displaying "*versatility and quality through and through.*"

**The Lawyers:** **John Parker** is rated as "*a smart and quick-thinking lawyer who is great to just ring up and get an opinion from – he never gives you a bum steer.*" He is admired for his corporate and regulatory expertise. Although best known for his skills in pure corporate matters, **Paul Hudson** is endorsed as having "*a fine healthcare knowledge and an intuitive sense of what will work and what won't.*"

**Clients/Work Highlights:** The group acts on state, regional and national matters for a range of healthcare providers.

### Powell Goldstein LLP

**The Firm:** This team is endorsed across the market for its skills in regulatory, enforcement and litigation issues. "*A vibrant team of practitioners*" has recently acted on various matters for physician-owned specialty hospitals, and defended a class action against doctors in Miami. Lawyers work closely with their Washington, DC counterparts.

**The Lawyers:** Veteran **Randall Hughes** was described by peers as "*one of the most experienced practitioners in the market – there is nothing he hasn't done before.*" In the past year, he has acted in a number of investigations and enforcements of substantial magnitude. **Kim Roeder** is "*a genuine healthcare expert who one always feels safe with.*" She is recommended both for her regulatory and transactional skills and for her skill in applying sound business principles to the healthcare model.

**Clients/Work Highlights:** The group has acted on financing issues for a number of nonprofit hospitals. It also acts for public and private healthcare providers, physician practice groups and managed care organizations.

# IMMIGRATION

## Band 1

## Paul, Hastings, Janofsky & Walker LLP

See firm details p.339

**The Firm:** Market sources hailed this group as "*a clear leader in Atlanta*," and believe its immigration team operates like "*a finely tuned watch*." Interviewees attributed the department's leading position to its unrivaled resources, its large team comprising 12 lawyers and its proactive shaping of government immigration policies. Competing on a national level, the firm attracts a stellar client base including Ford and Nestlé, and often works on a cross-departmental basis to provide a comprehensive service. While traditionally strong at inbound work, the firm is also cultivating an impressive outbound workload.

**The Lawyers:** Clients noted that the "*wonderfully engaging*" **Daryl Buffenstein** (see p.707) is "*in a league of his own; his involvement in drafting legislation and vast experience means he is clearly a leader in the field.*" He formerly served as national president of

the American Immigration Lawyers Association. He chairs the firm's national immigration practice and has been involved in drafting a range of business immigration legislation. "*Hands-on*" **Deborah Marlowe** (see p.719) has earned a stellar reputation for the breadth of her business immigration expertise. Her practice involves representing international companies before the DOL and the United States Citizenship and Immigration Services. The "*extremely up-to-date and helpful*" **Kyle Sherman** (see p.724) has a bright future ahead of him. Clients praised him for being "*available to advise us at any time of day – an essential attribute when you are working across borders.*"

**Clients/Work Highlights:** Ford; Nestlé USA; Delta Air Lines; Gulfstream Aerospace; Diageo North America; Turner Broadcasting System; Coca-Cola; E & J Gallo Winery; Microsoft and AOL.

## Band 2

## Alston & Bird LLP

See firm details p.728

**The Firm:** This full-service firm commands the respect of the market for its expert handling of a broad spectrum of business immigration matters. In 2005, this included advising on the immigration aspects of numerous M&A transactions as well as successfully arranging for the immigration of a professional baseball player to the USA. The firm is also skilled in advising individuals facing complex or unique immigration hurdles. Recent highlights include advising a wealthy family in obtaining a visa to allow their personal chef to work in the USA. The department's four immigration attorneys are ably supported by a team of ten paralegals, and advise clients across the technology, financial, manufacturing and service industries.

**The Lawyers:** "*Remarkable*" **Eileen Scofield** (see p.723) is seen by market sources as the cornerstone of the firm's immigration practice. She handles both inbound and outbound visa petitions and regularly works with governmental bodies such as the Department of Homeland Security and the DOJ.

**Clients/Work Highlights:** Mohawk Industries; UPS; EarthLink; The Ritz-Carlton Hotel Company; Duke Energy; The New York Mets; Bertelsmann; Anheuser-Busch; Hitachi Zosen; Fuji Bank; UBE Machinery and Genuine Parts.

## Arnall Golden Gregory LLP

See firm details p.729

**The Firm:** This three-lawyer team is renowned for its proficient handling of business and family immigration matters and for its representations before the immigration law judge. Its lawyers have wide-ranging language abilities and speak English, Spanish and Mandarin and Cantonese Chinese. The group has significant experience working with international companies, particularly German and Indian-owned entities.

**The Lawyers:** Head of the department **Teri Simmons** (see p.724) brings a "*good deal of experience and perspective*" to any case, acknowledged interviewees. She has recently been elected president of the Georgia Indo-American Chamber of Commerce. Simmons handles a busy immigration caseload for both local and international corporations and individuals, and serves as general counsel to a number of German companies.

**Clients/Work Highlights:** Porsche; NIIT (National Institute Information Technology); Intec Telecom Systems; Knology; Gildemeister/DMG and Fundtech.

## Fisher & Phillips LLP

See firm details p.732

**The Firm:** Closely connected to the firm's stellar labor and employment practice, this immigration department was praised for the quality of its advice on a range of business immigration matters. It advises a diverse client base, including an increasing volume of academic institutions on both consultative and litigious immigration matters.

**The Lawyers:** "*Extremely professional and responsive*" **David Whitlock** (see p.726) leads a "*well-coordinated*" team of immigration specialists. Clients enthused: "*He is as good as any lawyer in the country – he has a very thorough understanding of immigration law and is always on top of the constantly changing legislation.*"

## Ford & Harrison LLP

See firm details p.733

**The Firm:** This two-lawyer immigration practice has earned the respect of the market for its quality advice to companies on a range of issues. Clients typically call on it for advice on issues such as the immigration implications of M&A transactions and one-time hiring requirements and on obtaining work visas. Its client base comprises a large volume of healthcare entities, but it also acts for a broad spectrum of commercial corporations from the cement, construction and chemical industries.

**The Lawyers:** Satisfied clients reported that **Joycelyn Fleming** (see p.712) "*knows the immigration minefields*" and applauded her for her "*effective case management and amazing responsiveness.*" She has lengthy experience representing multinational companies and is particularly skilled in working with British and French-owned entities.

**Clients/Work Highlights:** Balfour Beatty; Heery International; Statoil; HCA Healthcare and Renal Care Group.

## Kuck, Casablanca & Howard, LLC

**The Firm:** This six-lawyer immigration boutique advises a national client base of employers on immigration matters, while also handling an active caseload of family sponsorships, asylum claims and deportation cases. It draws clients from the construction, hospitality and public sectors.

**The Lawyers:** "*Bright, able and engaging*" **Charles**

Kuck (see p.717) was applauded as an "*aggressive litigator, well schooled in the nuts and bolts of immigration law.*"

Clients/Work Highlights: ZF, Yum! and Computer Task Group feature on the client roster.

## Ogletree, Deakins, Nash, Smoak & Stewart, PC
See firm details p.738

The Firm: This labor and employment boutique was a popular choice among clients for immigration law advice. Its loyal international client base includes energy companies, healthcare entities and financial institutions, alongside a number of academic establishments, including the Savannah College of Art and Design. The firm has embraced the growing trend in outbound immigration; for example, it has advised numerous US companies on outsourcing projects to India, China and South America. With a 25-lawyer immigration team, the group offers high levels of partner attention and a broad range of language capabilities.

The Lawyers: **Robert Johnson** (see p.716) provides business visa counseling services and often advises multinational companies on the hiring and transfer of foreign executives and specialists. He speaks Japanese and has built up an impressive portfolio of Japanese manufacturing clients. Rising star **Jay Ruby** (see p.723) was praised as "*full of substance and always results-oriented.*" He has developed particular expertise in helping hospitality and construction clients to obtain visas for temporary workers.

## Powell Goldstein LLP

The Firm: The firm provides immigration advice to domestic and foreign, and public and private companies, as well as individual business personnel and investors. Areas of expertise include securing temporary working visas and permanent residency for professionals seeking employment in the USA.

The Lawyers: "*Thoughtful, quiet and effective*" **Rebecca Sigmund** heads the firm's immigration practice. She advises companies on matters relating to the employment eligibility of workers, as well as on immigration alternatives for prospective employees.

## Troutman Sanders LLP

The Firm: This quality immigration practice is staffed by three lawyers and a number of paralegals. It is renowned for its broad-based expertise in corporate immigration and attracts a loyal client base of both domestic and foreign companies.

The Lawyers: Clients hailed "*highly ethical*" **Mark Newman** as the "*benchmark of a wonderful immigration lawyer.*" Interviewees enthused: "*With his broad-based experience and professionalism, he can be counted on to do the best for his clients.*" He handles a mixed caseload of business and family immigration law.

## Band 3

## Banta Immigration Law Ltd

The Firm: This five-lawyer immigration boutique has gone from strength to strength since its inception three years ago. It primarily represents an employer-client base on the full spectrum of business immigration matters, and picks up plaudits for its transparent and cost-effective billing. Its workload encompasses advice on obtaining US visas and green cards, immigration training and compliance, and advice on the immigration components of corporate M&A activity.

The Lawyers: According to market sources, **Robert Banta** has "*the depth of experience one needs to be truly specialized in the immigration field.*" He handles complex and sensitive immigration issues, particularly those involving government intervention.

## Dale M Schwartz & Associates LLP
See firm details p.116586

The Firm: This compact practice attracted recommendations for its proficient handling of a broad spectrum of immigration matters. The lawyers here have lengthy experience in the area and act for both multinational corporations and individuals.

The Lawyers: **Dale Schwartz** is held in high esteem by his peers who regard him as "*the dean of the Atlanta immigration Bar.*" He formerly served as national president of the American Immigration Lawyers Association.

## Elarbee, Thompson, Sapp & Wilson, LLP

The Firm: Market commentators agree that this burgeoning immigration department has become an indispensable component to the firm's prominent labor and employment practice. The team works closely with both employers and employees from a diverse range of industries and advises them on obtaining work visas and permanent residency. Immigration litigation has been a recent addition to the firm's workload.

The Lawyers: Sanford Posner is a key contact for immigration matters.

## Kapoor & Associates

The Firm: This Atlanta-based immigration boutique and its Orlando branch office were applauded for their expert handling of the full gamut of US immigration and nationality issues.

The Lawyers: The "*highly reputable*" **Romy Kapoor** was praised as an excellent immigration expert and has won the widespread respect of his peers.

## Other Notable Practitioners

Sole practitioner **Myron Kramer** has a "*good head on his shoulders,*" according to market sources, who also praise his "*highly ethical, calm and well-rounded*" approach. He boasts long-standing expertise representing businesses and individuals on a broad spectrum of immigration matters. **Jay Solomon** of The Law Offices of Jay I Solomon has garnered the respect of his peers for his "*intelligence, creative thinking and technological know-how*" when handling both business and family immigration matters. He has attracted a diverse client base spanning the technology, manufacturing and service industries.

# INTELLECTUAL PROPERTY

## Band 1

## Kilpatrick Stockton LLP
See firm details p.735

The Firm: Clients and peers place this "*wonderful, rounded team at the pinnacle of the Georgia IP market.*" It is recommended for its range of skills but has a particular understanding of healthcare, biotech and scientific matters. Clients say the team has "*a great business empathy – sometimes I think they know our business better than we do.*" It is also highly regarded for its national coverage and its handling of matters on a global scale. A full-service IP firm, it is as skilled on patent prosecutions as it is on the trademark aspects of multijurisdictional transactions.

The Lawyers: "*On a lawyer-by-lawyer basis this is the best team in town,*" according to commentators. It is led by the "*effortlessly superb*" **Miles Alexander** (see p.704) who is rated as a quality practitioner at both nationwide and international level. His litigation practice, these days, is more focused towards high-level cross-examinations and mediation. For example, he recently handled a major mediation between Coca-Cola and Monsanto. **Anthony Askew** (see p.705) is praised for the range and quality of his experience and is "*undoubtedly one of the most effective courtroom performers in town.*" **Joseph Beck** (see p.706) is rated as "*a top-dollar copyright expert,*" with clients picking him out for his "*sharp business sense.*" He is involved in a high-profile case concerning the publication of materials online. Peers rate **Jim Ewing** (see p.712) as "*an expert's expert on patent – if I want to debate something he's the guy I'd call.*" He is especially recommended for cases with an international flavor. **Jerre Swann** (see p.725) is hailed by clients as "*a strong litigator with a great knowledge of the law,*" while **John Pratt** (see p.722) is said to do "*some brilliant patent work – he's down to earth and really understands our industry.*" **William Brewster** (see p.707) and **James Johnson** (see p.715) are also recommended for their patent abilities.

Clients/Work Highlights: adidas; Citigroup; DaimlerChrysler; Delta Air Lines; Disney; Emory University; Georgia-Pacific; Google; Sony; Vanderbilt University and Wachovia.

## Intellectual Property

### Leading Firms

1. **KILPATRICK STOCKTON LLP** *Atlanta*
   **NEEDLE & ROSENBERG, P.C** *Atlanta*
2. **ALSTON & BIRD LLP** *Atlanta*
   **KING & SPALDING LLP** *Atlanta*
3. **FINNEGAN HENDERSON** *Atlanta*
   **HUNTON & WILLIAMS LLP** *Atlanta*
   **SMITH GAMBRELL & RUSSELL LLP** *Atlanta*
   **SUTHERLAND ASBILL & BRENNAN LLP** *Atlanta*
   **THOMAS KAYDEN HORSTEMEYER & RISLEY** *Atlanta*
   **TROUTMAN SANDERS LLP** *Atlanta*

### Leading Individuals

1. **ALEXANDER Miles** *Kilpatrick Stockton LLP*
   **ASKEW Anthony** *Kilpatrick Stockton LLP*
   **FLINN Patrick** *Alston & Bird LLP*
   **NEEDLE William** *Needle & Rosenberg*
2. **BABER Bruce** *King & Spalding LLP*
   **BANKOFF Joseph** *King & Spalding LLP*
   **BECK Joseph** *Kilpatrick Stockton*
   **BLACKSTOCK Jerry** *Hunton & Williams LLP*
   **ELGISON Martin** *Alston & Bird LLP*
   **EWING Jim** *Kilpatrick Stockton*
   **NODINE Larry** *Needle & Rosenberg*
   **SWANN Jerre** *Kilpatrick Stockton LLP*
3. **HAWKINS Holmes** *King & Spalding LLP*
   **LUNSFORD III Rodgers** *Smith Gambrell*
   **PRATT John** *Kilpatrick Stockton*
   **RAGLAND JR William** *Hunton & Williams LLP*
   **SETTY Nagendra** *Fish & Richardson*
4. **BREWSTER William** *Kilpatrick Stockton LLP*
   **HOBBS JR Michael** *Troutman Sanders LLP*
   **JOHNSON James** *Kilpatrick Stockton LLP*
   **LISCHER Dale** *Smith Gambrell*
   **MCGRATH Robin** *Alston & Bird LLP*
   **NORTH John** *Sutherland Asbill*
   **ROSENBERG Sumner** *Needle & Rosenberg*
   **ROSENBLOUM Robert** *Greenberg Traurig LLP*
   **SALYERS Douglas** *Troutman Sanders LLP*
   **SMITH III Frank** *Alston & Bird LLP*
   **TAYLOR Roger** *Finnegan Henderson*

## Needle & Rosenberg, P.C

**The Firm:** Although a smaller team than Kilpatrick Stockton, the group retains its top-band position thanks to its *"incredible focus, knowledge, dedication and enthusiasm."* Clients say that *"if you cut this team, they will bleed IP."* Endorsed as *"a great team of technicians with a proper business approach,"* it remains best known for patent prosecution and is active in the biotech, chemistry and computer industries. It also enjoys success representing a number of universities. The practice is highly regarded across the region and is a growing presence in national matters.
**The Lawyers:** **William Needle** is *"an outstanding, first-class patent lawyer."* Peers regard him as *"astute and knowledgeable; it's always worthwhile getting his point of view."* He has acted in a number of high-scale patent cases in the past year. **Larry Nodine** wins

client approval as *"an excellent advocate who can easily switch from commonplace disputes to the most complex case imaginable."* He is increasingly active in domain name matters and recently acted for a major broadcaster in a copyright dispute relating to computers. Computer expert **Sumner Rosenberg** continues to receive strong support from the market.
**Clients/Work Highlights:** The group represents clients in the biotech, pharmaceutical, chemical, electrical and mechanical areas and also represents a number of universities and academic bodies.

## Band 2

### Alston & Bird LLP

See firm details p.728
**The Firm:** *"A definite competitor,"* according to peers, *"this group has a great deal of depth in litigation and brings a ferocious style to the courtroom."* Working in tandem with its well-regarded North Carolina lawyers, the team has enjoyed a busy year in both litigation and transactional matters. It has been active on IP rights in a number of corporate deals and has worked on securing patents in the e-business and e-commerce sectors. Technology remains a major area of expertise with the group active in both biotechnology and nanotechnology.
**The Lawyers:** **Patrick Flinn** (see p.713) *"has a complete body of knowledge and superb ability on his feet – he really is a lawyer at his peak."* He wins plaudits for his litigation skills and has been particularly active in technological disputes. **Martin Elgison** (see p.712) is praised for his skills in both transactional and litigation matters and was described as *"a great business-minded lawyer who gets things done without fuss."* He has recently been active in media matters. **Frank Smith** (see p.725) is *"a good, solid lawyer – with an excellent demeanor in court,"* while **Robin McGrath** (see p.719) is *"an excellent litigator with a great client touch."*
**Clients/Work Highlights:** The group's clients include international companies in the Fortune 250. Many of these are major banks, manufacturers, biotechs and universities.

### King & Spalding LLP

See firm details p.1933
**The Firm:** This litigation-focused team is enthusiastically hailed by clients as *"an outfit of extraordinary quality"* that has a great range of knowledge and an identifiable skill in forming strong working relationships. The depth of its litigation skills was an aspect that competitors repeatedly commented upon with the group winning praise for its excellence in patent, trademark and copyright disputes. It is rated as having a fine practice in new technologies and is felt to have created a strong niche for itself in the financial services market.
**The Lawyers:** The *"magnificent"* **Joseph Bankoff** (see p.705) is *"an excellent litigator with a national reputation. His performances on his feet are something that others should emulate."* He is recommended for his skills on patent and trademark cases and recently

won a case for Coca-Cola relating to the use of certain fountain technology by Pepsi and its vendor Rapak. **Bruce Baber** (see p.705) is recognized as *"a superb litigator whose knowledge of IP would rival any encyclopedia."* His skills in patent protection are particularly apparent. *"Shrewd competitor"* **Holmes Hawkins** (see p.714) wins plaudits for his skills in handling cases with computer-related issues. He recently acted for a software company in a patent litigation involving 12 different patents.
**Clients/Work Highlights:** GLOCK; Bank of America; Visa; Software AG; LendingTree and Scientific-Atlanta.

## Band 3

### Finnegan Henderson Farabow Garrett & Dunner LLP

See firm details p.567
**The Firm:** A long-established IP boutique, Finnegan Henderson is *"a great one-stop shop with experience and knowledge stretching into every corner of IP."* Lawyer versatility was felt to be the defining factor of the practice with the group being skilled in computer technologies, electrical engineering, biotech, mechanics, pharmaceuticals and chemical and metallurgical sciences. The group's transactional abilities are facilitated by close office-to-office relations with colleagues in DC, Boston and California. Litigation is regarded as a jewel in the crown with the marketplace recognizing the firm's skill in copyright, trade secrets and patent issues.
**The Lawyers:** **Roger Taylor** (see p.726) is *"a smart, responsive lawyer who works wonders in the courtroom."* He boasts *"an international stature married to a Southern charm,"* according to commentators. An expert patents practitioner, he displays great knowledge, skill and experience particularly when it comes to international matters. He is managing partner of the Atlanta office and has handled a number of high-profile matters including many in the manufacturing and computer industries.
**Clients/Work Highlights:** The group's varied client base includes computer and electronic companies, as well as manufacturers.

### Hunton & Williams LLP

See firm details p.1959
**The Firm:** Clients say the firm offers *"top-class litigators who know their stuff, a great bench strength and superb international contacts."* The group draws particular plaudits for its patent practice, displaying skills in prosecutions – both domestic and foreign – as well as in licensing and transactional work. Trial work remains a key area of excellence for the group and it recently successfully overturned a large counterclaim award in the Georgia Court of Appeals.
**The Lawyers:** *"One of the best litigators in the state,"* **Jerry Blackstock** (see p.706) is, as one interviewee put it, *"as adept at IP litigation as he is at commercial litigation. Frankly there is no one who is as experienced in complex patent matters."* He is currently advising Unimed Pharmaceuticals in patent cases relating to

Androgel male hormone products, and also active in trade secret and trademark work. **William Ragland** (see p.722) is "*a shrewd litigator and a safe pair of hands.*" He recently acted for AudioFAX against Avaya in a sizable patent infringement case.

Clients/Work Highlights: ExxonMobil; EarthLink; Henkel; Chicago Title Insurance and First Horizon Pharmaceutical.

## Smith Gambrell & Russell LLP

The Firm: This well-regarded team remains best known for its IP litigation expertise, particularly in the trademark, patent litigation and prosecution fields. The group draws on a wide range of experience and has a strong history of trademark disputes within the entertainment industry. It also impresses with its work on brand names within the food industry. Although best known for its litigation work, the group is certainly no slouch when it comes to general commercial advice relating to the IP issues of large commercial transactions.

The Lawyers: Market sources declare that **Rodgers Lunsford** is "*on the A-list of trademark litigators. When he's there he just owns the courtroom.*" In the past year, he has been involved in a large matter concerning the trademarks of rock bands. He is also known for his mediation expertise and has settled a number of disputes for Tabasco. **Dale Lischer** is regarded as "*a patent prosecutor of the highest order.*" He does his best work in the fields of energy, construction and new technologies.

Clients/Work Highlights: The group's broad client base includes local, national and international bodies.

## Sutherland Asbill & Brennan LLP

See firm details p.578

The Firm: Patent litigation continues to be a major strength for this highly regarded practice. The group handles complex matters for a range of technologies, pharmaceuticals and electronic companies and is enjoying a marked increase in the amount of work it undertakes in the electrical engineering industry. Biotech is also a strong area for the firm and the team acts in IP and patent matters both nationally and internationally. The practice boasts a sizable team and is able to draw upon further manpower in Washington, DC.

The Lawyers: Chair of the IP group **John North** (see p.721) is "*definitely a strong presence in patent prosecution.*" He is currently representing Minerals Technology in a large patent case with antitrust issues. The matter is a multimillion-dollar dispute with a European company.

Clients/Work Highlights: BASF; BresaGen; Coca-Cola; Gemstar-TV Guide; GE; GMP Companies; Jordan Outdoor Enterprises; Lanier Worldwide; Rinker Materials and Western Union.

## Thomas Kayden Horstemeyer & Risley LLP

The Firm: This niche player is recommended for its skills in patent prosecution work and is, according to interviewees, "*a strong second to Needle & Rosenberg for that type of IP transactional work.*" Technologically astute, the group represents a varied selection of local companies in computer technology, electrical engineering, biosciences and aerospace matters. The group handles all aspects of trademark work – both domestic and foreign – including litigious and transactional matters.

The Lawyers: Scott Horstemeyer is the firm's managing partner.

Clients/Work Highlights: BellSouth; Georgia Tech Research; Hewlett-Packard; Materials International and Scientific-Atlanta.

## Troutman Sanders LLP

The Firm: This diverse practice is felt to have had a strong year in hi-tech IP matters and is a growing force in patent prosecution and protection work. The team is well regarded for its computer hardware and software practice and has expertise in the biotech, electronic and mechanical spheres. Although its heart remains in Atlanta, it has a growing national and international presence.

The Lawyers: **Doug Salyers** heads up the IP litigation group and comes across as "*a sharp litigator who makes IP cases look easy.*" He successfully represented SurgiLance in an appeal in the federal court concerning a medical device. He has also been involved in an arbitration concerning the copyright of exercise routines. Head of the trademark practice **Mike Hobbs** is hailed as "*a young guy with a super amount of expertise.*" He is seen as particularly good on international work.

Clients/Work Highlights: The group represents a good mix of midsize companies and brand names. These include computer companies; fast food concerns; hi-tech businesses and universities.

## Other Notable Practitioners

The "*superb*" **Robert Rosenbloum** (see p.723) at Greenberg Traurig LLP continues to enjoy a niche Atlanta practice, representing recording artists, songwriters and producers – as well as large corporates – in IP and media matters. Highly rated **Nick Setty** (see p.723) has recently moved from Jones Day to IP specialists Fish & Richardson PC. Clients rate him as "*one of the finest IP lawyers we've come across – the expertise he brings to the table is just phenomenal.*" He is noted not just for his skills in patent litigation but also for "*the practical and businesslike advice he offers – he's much more than just a lawyer.*"

# LITIGATION

## Band 1

### Alston & Bird LLP

See firm details p.728

The Firm: This "*mega-firm*" is, according to clients, "*virtually unbeatable in terms of the depth, range and scope of the skills it offers.*" Its expertise stretches across appellate work, antitrust, class actions, real estate, technology and white collar. Interviewees further enthusiastically praised its securities work and noted its growing involvement in the telecom and insurance sectors. In the past year, it has handled a number of class actions for Nokia and has acted on insurance disputes arising out of Hurricane Katrina. The firm is known for its national practice and is felt to be increasingly active on the international stage.

The Lawyers: Possessed of "*fantastic bench strength,*" the team is made up of lawyers who represent the "*cream of the cream.*" **Jud Graves** (see p.714) is "*the spiritual leader of the team – an excellent litigator who rules the courtroom.*" He continues to be extremely active in the medical malpractice field and has recently been involved in a large orthopedic malpractice case. He also represents lawyers in distress. The "*experienced and expert*" **Oscar Persons** (see p.721) is part of the strong securities litigation practice and was described as "*a true gentleman and a quality attorney.*" Other key figures in that group include derivatives and securities class actions expert **Peter Bassett** (see p.706). Recommended as "*a sensible attorney aware of both business and litigation concerns,*" he has been working for a large Atlanta company on a sizable securities case. The "*thorough and conscientious*" **Todd David** (see p.710) also impresses with his securities work while **Michael Kenny** (see p.717) is said to have "*a broad swathe of*

## Litigation: General Commercial
### Leading Individuals

#### Senior Statesmen

BONDURANT Emmet *Bondurant, Mixson*
ROGERS CB *Rogers & Hardin*

[1] CHANDLER John *Sutherland Asbill*
DALTON John *Troutman Sanders LLP*
GRAVES Judson *Alston & Bird LLP*
SINKFIELD Richard *Rogers & Hardin*
VARNER Chilton *King & Spalding LLP*

[2] BASSETT Peter *Alston & Bird LLP*
BLACKSTOCK Jerry *Hunton & Williams LLP*
BOICE William *Kilpatrick Stockton LLP*
CAHOON Susan *Kilpatrick Stockton LLP*
CLAY A Stephens *Kilpatrick Stockton LLP*
FLEMING John *Sutherland Asbill*
MARSHALL John *Powell Goldstein LLP*
MIXSON H Lamar *Bondurant, Mixson*
PERSONS Oscar *Alston & Bird LLP*
RUSS Michael *King & Spalding LLP*

[3] BRAMLETT Jeffrey *Bondurant, Mixson*
DANIEL Harold *Holland & Knight LLP*
DANIEL Laurie *Holland & Knight LLP*
DAVID Todd *Alston & Bird LLP*
FLOYD John *Bondurant, Mixson*
FORTE Stephen *Smith Gambrell*
GARRETT G Lee *Jones Day*
HAYNES Joseph *King & Spalding LLP*
HAYS Robert *King & Spalding LLP*
KENNY Michael *Alston & Bird LLP*
LOVELAND Joseph *King & Spalding LLP*
MURPHY Paul *King & Spalding LLP*
PERSONS Ray *King & Spalding LLP*
REINHARDT Daniel *Troutman Sanders LLP*
REMAR Robert *Rogers & Hardin*
SMITH Gordon *King & Spalding LLP*
THORNTON M Robert *King & Spalding LLP*
ZACKS David *Kilpatrick Stockton LLP*

## Litigation: White-Collar Crime & Government Investigations
### Leading Individuals

[1] COWEN Stephen *King & Spalding LLP*
DEANE JR Richard *Jones Day*
GILLEN Craig *Gillen Parker*
MALOY Bruce *Maloy & Jenkins*
MITCHELSON JR William *Alston & Bird LLP*

*experience*" particularly in class actions and business litigation. **Mitch Mitchelson** (see p.720) continues to enjoy a reputation as "*one of the best white-collar attorneys in town.*"

**Clients/Work Highlights:** Georgia-Pacific; Genuine Parts Company; Delta Air Lines; HealthSouth; Nokia; UPS; Verizon; Vulcan Minerals and Wachovia.

## King & Spalding LLP
See firm details p.1933

**The Firm:** This "*phenomenal outfit*" is said to have "*the strength in depth, the national contacts and sheer depth of skill and experience to be more than a match for anyone in the Atlanta market.*" Composed of a large number of lawyers with "*God-given courtroom talent,*" the team acts in a variety of areas for a client base made up of a mix of domestic corporates and multinationals. Devotees champion it for its expertise in international disputes.

**The Lawyers:** Products liability remains an area of strong focus for the firm. **Chilton Varner** (see p.726) leads the way here and is described by clients as "*the Queen of Atlanta products liability work.*" Peers recommend her as "*the expert's expert – she is never fazed by anything, as she has seen it all before.*" She successfully defended Kia Motors America in a substantial case involving the potentially defective condition of thousands of vehicles. Strong support comes in the form of **Robert Hays** (see p.715) who is "*one of the strongest and most experienced products liability guys in the market*" and a lawyer praised for his skills in defending tort litigation. Also present are **Gordon Smith** (see p.724), "*an excellent and forthright courtroom attorney,*" and "*top-quality commercial litigator*" **Michael Russ** (see p.723), hailed by sources as "*someone who would be an asset to any law firm.*" He is particularly revered for his expertise in SEC investigations. **Joseph Haynes** (see p.715) was described by one interviewee as "*an opponent I've dealt with many, many times and never been less than impressed with.*" An experienced litigator, he is said to be excellent on securities and tax-related litigation. Clients regard **Joseph Loveland** (see p.718) as "*an incredibly bright guy who's comfortable in the courtroom. An excellent strategist, he is superb at client relations.*" A highlight of his past year was the representation of Coca-Cola in a whistle-blower suit filed against the company that led to investigations by the SEC and the DOJ. The "*shrewd-thinking*" **Paul Murphy** (see p.720) is recommended for his skills in pharmaceutical and chemical disputes while "*superb trial lawyer*" **Ray Persons** (see p.722) is known for his excellence in toxic tort matters. New to this year's guide, **Robert Thornton** (see p.726) is endorsed for his skills in SEC and securities matters and is recommended as "*a sharp lawyer, magnificent on his feet.*" **Stephen Cowen** (see p.710) continues to enjoy a strong reputation for white-collar and government investigations work.

**Clients/Work Highlights:** Home Depot; GlaxoSmithKline; GM; GE and Coca-Cola.

## Band 2

## Bondurant, Mixson & Elmore, LLP
See firm details p.731

**The Firm:** "*The top boutique in town,*" according to commentators, this firm "*punches far above its weight and offers stiff competition to all.*" A genuinely diverse practice, it handles complex commercial litigation and boasts expertise in antitrust, employment, IP,

securities, environmental and white-collar law. Although its client base is predominantly made up of corporates, it accepts a range of interesting matters and is currently representing a detainee in Guantanamo Bay.

**The Lawyers:** Commentators agree that **Emmet Bondurant** (see p.707) is "*the name to mention in litigation – absolutely one of the best in the state.*" He is "*superb on complex commercial litigations*" and provides "*an amazing courtroom presence.*" He has a mixed practice and has handled patent and antitrust matters over the past year. **Mickey Mixson** (see p.720) also earns enthusiastic endorsements for his commercial litigation expertise. He is particularly good on securities work and has "*a superb touch with juries.*" **Jeffrey Bramlett** (see p.707) is "*an excellent lawyer with an admirable range of skills*" while **John Floyd** (see p.713) is recommended as "*a magnificent RICO lawyer.*"

**Clients/Work Highlights:** The group represents a range of corporates and other parties.

## Kilpatrick Stockton LLP
See firm details p.735

**The Firm:** This sharp and versatile team impressed commentators due to the quality, range and diversity of its practice. It has a strong band of lawyers and can field expert practitioners in toxic tort, products liability, trademark and white-collar matters. The group's worldwide reach is felt to give it an advantage over many competitors and it is a regular participant in international arbitrations. "*An epic firm,*" according to competitors, "*it's one of the busiest in the marketplace and always provides the highest quality work.*"

**The Lawyers:** Clients describe **William Boice** (see p.706) as "*an incredibly fine lawyer, who gives top-dollar advice.*" His innovation and invention earn him especial praise, with one observer remarking: "*He will think of great ideas that would never occur to anyone else.*" Recommended as a strong trial lawyer, he continues to have a broad commercial litigation practice. The "*phenomenal*" **Susan Cahoon** (see p.707) is "*a lawyer to really trust on complex matters. She is committed, energetic and her advice is gold.*" She is currently involved on a large patent dispute for Smith & Nephew with regards to a device in the orthopedic market. **Stephens Clay** (see p.708) is highly regarded by market sources and recommended as "*an outstanding courtroom lawyer. He really knows how to draw the best from any argument.*" He also wins praise for his international arbitration skills and has been involved in a high-value matter for BellSouth concerning a joint venture in Latin America. One client recommended **David Zacks** (see p.727) as "*a superb lawyer with an excellent record of success – he hasn't lost for us yet.*" He is hailed for both his litigation and mediation expertise.

**Clients/Work Highlights:** The group's client base is primarily Fortune 500 companies and includes such luminaries as Lockheed Martin; Delta Air Lines; Equifax; RJ Reynolds; Krispy Kreme and Sara Lee.

## Rogers & Hardin

**The Firm:** "*Undoubtedly one of the strongest firms in the market,*" this boutique firm receives fulsome praise for the quality and versatility of its work. Its class action and securities work continues to draw the lion's share of comment but the group is recommended as having "*the smarts to take on anything that is thrown at it.*" Although a midsize group, it is felt to be a match for the larger practices in the Atlanta market and to have a genuinely national reach.

**The Lawyers: CB Rogers** is "*a superb presence in the Atlanta litigation market. Highly experienced and highly skilled, he has seen it all and done it all and so it's always worth getting his advice if you can.*" He is experienced across corporate and commercial litigation. The "*truly excellent*" **Richard Sinkfield** is "*a top trial lawyer and a superb choice for all complex commercial disputes.*" He tackles mediation and arbitration within the context of a general litigation practice and is felt to be strong in government representation. **Robert Remar** is, similarly, recommended in this last area and is acting on a major civil rights and discrimination case involving governmental employees. He is "*a polished operator who brings just the right amount of tenacity to a case.*"

**Clients/Work Highlights:** The group's client base includes entities in the banking, computing, entertainment, healthcare, insurance, real estate, technology and textiles sectors.

## Sutherland Asbill & Brennan LLP

See firm details p.578

**The Firm:** Interviewees were quick to extol the virtues of this "*top-quality, highly efficient practice.*" Said to "*keep a constant eye on the client's business needs,*" it impresses particularly in securities work but also comes up trumps in franchise, insurance, professional negligence and products liability disputes. The group, now a growing national presence, tends to an excellent commercial client base and is seen as being strong right along the East Coast.

**The Lawyers:** The "*thorough, meticulous and highly intellectual*" **John Chandler** (see p.708) is recommended as "*probably the best lawyer for financial disputes in Georgia.*" Head of the litigation group, he has acted for a Big Four accountancy firm in a case in Florida involving a merger. Recently, he also represented a client in a major issue in front of the SEC and the DOJ. Clients deem **John Fleming** (see p.712) "*a superb strategic and technical practitioner. He is incredibly sensitive as to what a business needs and creative in thinking of the best result.*" He is skilled in franchise and class action matters and has been involved in a complex dispute for Ford. He has also been active in securities litigations and arbitrations.

**Clients/Work Highlights:** Ford; Merrill Lynch; State of Missouri; Procter & Gamble; Rinker Materials; KPMG; Ernst & Young and City of Atlanta.

## Band 3

### Holland & Knight LLP

See firm details p.1534

**The Firm:** This national firm is felt to be a growing presence in the Georgia litigation market. Although it is not felt to have the numbers on the ground of some of its immediate competitors, it is praised for its expertise across the range of business litigation and possesses a key strength in appellate matters. The group looks after an impressive national client roster and receives increasing referrals from overseas.

**The Lawyers:** The "*excellent*" **Harold Daniel** (see p.710) continues to win praise for his skills in business litigation, particularly in RICO and securities matters. He has recently acted in a dispute between two NYSE-listed companies. This matter involved an alleged breach of warranties in an acquisition. **Laurie Webb Daniel** (see p.710) is a "*smart, finger on the pulse lawyer*" who is particularly recommended for her appellate work. She is currently representing a Fortune 500 company in a commercial and environmental dispute with a German corporation.

**Clients/Work Highlights:** Arrow Electronics; Ingersoll-Rand; Pfizer; Gard and Bridgestone Americas Holding.

### Jones Day

See firm details p.570

**The Firm:** This sizable team continues to draw strong support in the Atlanta market and is recognized as "*a group of very good attorneys with great depth both locally and nationally.*" Its versatility is demonstrated by the fact that it handles large matters in the IP, construction and products liability arenas among others. Although best known for its skills in business litigation, it is also rated in governmental matters and is acting for the City of Atlanta in impeachment proceedings against one of its counsel members.

**The Lawyers: Lee Garrett** (see p.713) is at the helm of the Atlanta litigation team. A lawyer of "*particularly good judgment*" who is "*balanced, sensible and above all commercial,*" he is currently acting for Southern Company in a billion-dollar litigation with Mirant. Although best known for complex business litigation, he is also skilled in First Amendment, construction and environmental work. White-collar specialist **Richard Deane** (see p.710) is further recommended as "*a sharp and tenacious advocate who always battles for his clients.*"

**Clients/Work Highlights:** The group's client base includes large corporates whether it be in the Southeast, nationally or internationally.

### Powell Goldstein LLP

**The Firm:** This strong commercial team fortifies a fine reputation through its work on government relations and securities matters. It has been active in the past year in matters arising from the Sarbanes-Oxley Act, particularly in cases relating to class actions and suits against trustees. The lawyers have also seen a growth of work in bankruptcy matters.

**The Lawyers: John Marshall** remains the best-known member of the team. He is described as "*hugely experienced and one of the top lawyers in the field. He is a superb legal strategist and has an excellent sense of the commercial issues.*" He is increasingly active in alternative dispute resolution and has been handling a number of banking and toxic tort cases.

**Clients/Work Highlights:** The group represents corporations and public companies. It also handles matters for CEOs and former CEOs.

### Troutman Sanders LLP

**The Firm:** This "*undoubtedly impressive*" firm commands attention due to the breadth of its litigation expertise. It is busy at the coalface of commercial litigation, impressing most readily through its media, products liability and toxic tort work. Clients champion it as "*accessible, responsive and detail-oriented. The team has great strategic instincts.*" Although based in Atlanta, the group's international presence brings it a host of referrals.

**The Lawyers:** "*Litigation guru*" **Jack Dalton** is "*a superb lawyer and as good a commercial litigator as there is in the city.*" He is said to be "*incredibly smart on his feet and possessed of the ability to know what judges want.*" His representation of CNN and Turner companies represents a signal feather in his cap. **Daniel Reinhardt** is "*an absolutely excellent products liability attorney. He is fast-thinking and versatile.*" He is part of a vital team that impresses commentators. One commented: "*I bet you anything they'd be on most people's short lists for a grand jury appeal.*"

**Clients/Work Highlights:** The group's clients include national and international corporates in a range of industries.

## Band 4

### Doffermyre, Shields, Canfield, Knowles & Devine

**The Firm:** This small niche practice catches the eye due to its expertise in litigation and arbitration. The quality and variety of its work is noteworthy and it is felt to be "*a place for innovative and interesting matters.*" By way of example, it recently represented all the doctors in the state in a software dispute with insurance companies.

**The Lawyers: Everette Doffermyre** is a highly respected lawyer.

**Clients/Work Highlights:** The group tends to represent midsize and small businesses in disputes with larger entities. In recent times it has drawn a lot of work from bankruptcies.

### Hunton & Williams LLP

See firm details p.1959

**The Firm:** Although the group doesn't have the prominence of other international firms in the Atlanta marketplace, it is said to be "*a team that will be there on the larger matters.*" Particularly celebrated for its endeavors in the IP, employment and environment spheres, it is said to have "*sharp and innovative business dispute lawyers.*" The global aspect of the firm provides both a strong client base and support and it busies itself with the occasional matter of some magnitude. Last year it represented Quest International against Coca-Cola.

**The Lawyers:** The "*fantastic*" **Jerry Blackstock** (see p.706) chairs the Atlanta litigation group. He is regarded as "*one of the most experienced litigators in the state – he has tried what seems like a zillion cases.*" He has a highly regarded courtroom presence and his practice encompasses complex business litigation, as well as IP and PI. He recently represented ExxonMobil in a dispute involving motor racing sponsorship agreements.

**Clients/Work Highlights:** The group's client base includes both multinationals and sizable local companies.

## Paul, Hastings, Janofsky & Walker LLP
See firm details p.339

**The Firm:** Securities work continues to be the best-known area of expertise for a small but well-respected firm that also enjoys a growing profile in real estate, franchise and environmental disputes. Its recent highlights include representing the former officers of a software company who are being sued by shareholders. Other matters include the defense of a major Southeast property developer against a claim that a development had ruined neighboring property. The group has also been defending lenders against a number of class actions.

**The Lawyers:** John Parker heads up the Atlanta litigation team.

**Clients/Work Highlights:** GE; GE Capital; AIG; Delta Air Lines and State Street Bank.

## Smith Gambrell & Russell LLP

**The Firm:** This highly regarded practice has antitrust work at its core but is also a noted player in construction and corporate disputes generally. It has represented a large commercial real estate developer in defense of a class action by property owners, as well as acting for a bank in a dispute with a software company. A substantial part of the midsize team's work comes from banks and lending institutions.

**The Lawyers:** Market sources describe **Stephen Forte** as a "*switched-on lawyer with a great client touch.*"

**Clients/Work Highlights:** The firm represents Wachovia and AirTran Airways among others.

### Other Notable Practitioners

**Bruce Maloy** of Maloy & Jenkins is "*an incredibly fine lawyer. One of the best in the state for representing individuals.*" **Craig Gillen** of Gillen Parker Withers LLC is praised as "*always good to lock horns with.*" He does a lot of work for corporate executives.

# REAL ESTATE

| Real Estate |
|---|
| **Leading Firms** |
| [1] KING & SPALDING LLP *Atlanta* |
| [2] ALSTON & BIRD LLP *Atlanta* |
| KILPATRICK STOCKTON LLP *Atlanta* |
| SUTHERLAND ASBILL & BRENNAN LLP *Atlanta* |
| TROUTMAN SANDERS LLP *Atlanta* |
| [3] MCKENNA LONG & ALDRIDGE LLP *Atlanta* |
| MORRIS, MANNING & MARTIN, LLP *Atlanta* |
| PAUL, HASTINGS, JANOFSKY & WALKER *Atlanta* |
| POWELL GOLDSTEIN LLP *Atlanta* |

| **Leading Individuals** |
|---|
| [1] ADAMS JR Alfred *Sutherland Asbill* |
| GRIFFIN John *Troutman Sanders LLP* |
| JORDAN James *Sutherland Asbill* |
| RUSCHE Mark *Alston & Bird LLP* |
| STEPHENSON Mason *King & Spalding LLP* |
| [2] ARNOLD Scott *King & Spalding LLP* |
| CARSSOW Tim *Kilpatrick Stockton LLP* |
| FRYER William *King & Spalding LLP* |
| LEVIN Jay *Powell Goldstein LLP* |
| PAKENHAM Timothy *Alston & Bird LLP* |
| SHARBAUGH Charles *Paul, Hastings* |
| [3] ALDRIDGE SR John *McKenna Long* |
| BENDER JR Albert *Alston & Bird LLP* |
| BRANNON Jeanna *Morris, Manning* |
| FARRIS JR James *Alston & Bird LLP* |
| PARKS John *Powell Goldstein LLP* |
| SHELEY Raymond *Sheley & Hall* |
| WALKER Homer *Alston & Bird LLP* |

| **Up-and-coming individuals** |
|---|
| GOODWIN Timothy *King & Spalding LLP* |
| RYAN Allison *Alston & Bird LLP* |

## Band 1

### King & Spalding LLP
See firm details p.1933

**The Firm:** This team was widely tipped as an "*exceptional real estate group with terrific lawyers.*" The robust practice comprises around 22 lawyers who advise on multistate portfolio acquisitions and disposals, financings and the formation of public and private REITs and tax-efficient ventures. The team also represents domestic and offshore investors in real estate capital markets transactions and on the acquisition of large commercial real estate assets in the USA and abroad. Macquarie Global Property Advisors called on the firm for its capital markets and fund formation expertise when it created its MGP Fund II, which raised $1.3 billion for investment in Asia and Europe. The team has developed a niche in representing German-based investment funds on the acquisition of commercial real estate in the USA. It also has a burgeoning practice representing developers and owners of commercial properties in the Southeast in projects ranging from shopping centers to office buildings. Examples include representing Post Apartment Homes on the sale of nine apartment communities, valued at an aggregate sale price of $230 million. Lawyers also acted for GE Real Estate on the acquisition of $228 million worth of office properties across the Southeast region.

**The Lawyers:** The "*absolutely wonderful*" **Mason Stephenson** (see p.725) has a flourishing practice representing clients such as GE Real Estate and other investors on the acquisition and financing of real estate portfolios. This past year he has worked on a number of major matters for InterPark and GE and advised a long-standing client on the sale of its Atlanta real estate holdings to a local management group. Practice group leader **Scott Arnold** (see p.705) is an invaluable source for investors and is well versed in REITs and the hospitality industry. Described as "*a businessman's lawyer of the highest order,*" Arnold recently acted for The Brookdale Group in connection with the $550 million sale of a 22-building office portfolio to a European buyer. Paladin Realty Partners also chose him to assist on the reorganization of a $130 million investment fund. The highlight of **Bill Fryer**'s (see p.713) year was handling the massive $2.8 billion acquisition of Gables Residential Trust for ING Clarion Partners. His M&A and funds formation expertise also benefited Morgan Stanley's Prime Property Trust, which retained him as primary fund counsel on its $2.1 billion acquisition of AMLI Residential. Clients praised the "*talented*" **Tim Goodwin** (see p.713) for "*recognizing what is important in a transaction and doing what it takes to close the deal.*" His strengths lie in investment fund work, and most notably tax-exempt pension funds. Goodwin is the lawyer primarily responsible for the firm's relationship with Morgan Stanley and represented it on its recent $400 million acquisition of Safeguard Storage Properties.

**Clients/Work Highlights:** The team acts for several of the largest companies in the Southeast, including Carter Real Estate Fund I; Edens & Avant; GE Real Estate; ING Clarion; Kuwait Finance House; Morgan Stanley; Paladin Realty Partners; The Brookdale Group and WestWind Capital Partners.

## Band 2

### Alston & Bird LLP
See firm details p.728

**The Firm:** Clients endorsed the team as "*wonderful for any kind of real estate.*" The friendliness of this "*likeable group of people*" was a standout feature for commentators, who consistently remarked on its ability to "*interact with the other side and keep everyone happy.*" The Atlanta office is the hub of the firm's real estate practice, and REITs account for a significant portion of the group's work. However, sources also praised its "*comprehensive and deep real estate services*" that include acquisitions, disposals, commercial lending and leasing, joint ventures and land use. Following a national trend, mixed-use development is currently a boom area for the team where clients appreciate its "*contemporary approach to business and law.*" In one of its headline deals, the team is representing International Paper on the sale of Timberland Holdings in the USA.

**The Lawyers: Mark Rusche** (see p.723) is "*a direct business-oriented lawyer who consistently develops innovative solutions to problems.*" He leads the firm's real estate group and is recognized by the market for his extensive experience in joint ventures and commercial leasing. Rusche has handled several major office leases for clients such as KPMG, and has advised Prudential on a number of deals totaling $900 million. He also advises landlords and acts as primary leasing counsel throughout the Southeast for Parthenon. **Tim Pakenham** (see p.721) is counsel to the developer of one of the world's largest and most technologically advanced aquariums, based in Atlanta. He advised it on a joint venture agreement with a major company and on various merchandising agreements. Another major client is InterContinental Hotels, which he advised on the $1 billion sale of several hotels. Clients described him as "*not only a great technical lawyer, but one who is good at maintaining client relationships.*" **Bert Bender** (see p.706) is active on a national scale for a variety of major, multistate institutions. This "*highly skilled and extraordinarily productive*" lawyer has recently assisted a city authority engaged in a tax-incentive development program in undeveloped areas. Bender has also been involved in residential joint ventures relating to condominium and townhouse conversions. **Jay Farris** (see p.712) frequently acts for Duke Realty and also has a following among investors and developers, including pension funds and pension fund advisers. One pension fund retained him to advise on the $500 million sale of a portfolio of industrial distribution facilities located across the country. Joint ventures, especially the formation of investment vehicles, and mixed-use development are the forte of **Lee Walker** (see p.726). He continues to represent the owner of the Tower Place mixed-use development project. The project comprises 28 floors of luxury condominium, retail, office and hotel components. It will be one of the tallest buildings in Buckhead once completed and is valued at $220 million. Walker has handled all of the development, finance and joint venture aspects. **Allison Ryan** (see p.723) is renowned for her enviable client following and was touted as "*an outstanding attorney: capable, efficient and to the point.*" Her practice covers office leasing and mixed-use development. The group has also been boosted by the arrival of Rosemarie Thurston as the practice leader of the real estate securities team.

**Clients/Work Highlights:** The firm's clients include institutional investors; REITs; insurance companies and private developers. Among them are Prudential; Industrial Developments International; InterContinental Hotels; Duke Realty; Parthenon; Regent Partners; Morgan Stanley and Wachovia.

## Kilpatrick Stockton LLP
See firm details p.735

**The Firm:** Kilpatrick Stockton has specialist expertise advising on government acquisitions of real estate for major federal headquarters and facilities. The Atlanta office offers a comprehensive real estate service covering acquisitions, development, leasing, zoning and entitlement issues. It also has wide-ranging experience in representing clients in negotiations with the General Services Administration. The team recently acted for Avanti Properties on the organization of its investment partnerships.

**The Lawyers:** Interviewees recommended **Tim Carssow** (see p.708) as "*astute, pragmatic and easy to work with.*" He has built up an impressive reputation in commercial real estate and has particular experience in development and land use issues and troubled real estate projects.

**Clients/Work Highlights:** The group's key clients include Avanti Properties and ING. It also acts for a range of federal agencies; real estate brokers; national banking associations and investment banks.

## Sutherland Asbill & Brennan LLP
See firm details p.578

**The Firm:** This firm stood out to interviewees for its "*sheer quality and professionalism,*" and its lawyers are widely viewed as "*the people to go to for complex and challenging projects.*" The group excels in real estate finance where it has advised on a glut of securitized financings for GMAC, Bank of America and Wachovia; but it also acts for a number of developers of shopping centers and pension funds. It has a niche representing investors in timber and natural resources and maintains a thriving roster of clients in the hospitality industry. Atlanta is the heart of the firm's real estate section, where the majority of its expertise is housed. Researchers were told of "*a strong group of bright legal technicians who will expend every ounce of effort to thoroughly understand what we are trying to do.*"

**The Lawyers:** Interviewees were full of praise for **Al Adams** (see p.704). He has "*a terrific reputation*" for representing real estate developers and entrepreneurs across the Southeast. He advised a major client on the $150 million acquisition of Wildwood office park and organized $140 million of construction financing and equity financing for Ronus Properties. He is popular among clients because "*he is highly experienced and intelligent, and has the ability to make a deal happen.*" Equally prominent at the firm is "*superstar*" **Jim Jordan** (see p.716) whom interviewees rate as "*a consummate professional who puts his clients first.*" His expertise lies in retail development, and he has advised Sembler on several multimillion-dollar transactions. He has also represented a major retailer in the development, acquisition and roll-out

of stores in Mexico. Office development is another area of strength for Jordan. Recently, he assisted a high-profile Southeast developer on the development of call centers across the country.

**Clients/Work Highlights:** GMAC; Bank of America; Wachovia; Sembler; Simon Property; Ronus Properties and Home Depot.

## Troutman Sanders LLP

**The Firm:** The firm offers a vast array of real estate services and is celebrated for its "*collegial and pleasant atmosphere.*" The firm counsels landlords and tenants on commercial leasing and has extensive experience in representing domestic and foreign investors on the acquisition, development, operation and sale of various real estate assets. On the financial side, the group advises lenders and borrowers on real estate lending transactions and other credit arrangements and is well known for its work on behalf of clients such as Cousins Properties and Wells Real Estate.

**The Lawyers: John Griffin** was identified as "*without doubt the leading guy*" of this firm's real estate group. This "*outstanding lawyer*" won acclaim from interviewees who described him as "*a true professional – he's extremely thorough and bright.*" Griffin represents developers, investors and users of commercial real estate in a variety of transactions, and has also acted for landlords and tenants in relation to office and retail leases. He is experienced in office and retail development, financings and joint ventures.

**Clients/Work Highlights:** Domestic and foreign banks, life insurance companies, and a range of private and publicly held corporations feature in the client list.

## Band 3

## McKenna Long & Aldridge LLP
See firm details p.737

**The Firm:** One of the primary components of this firm's real estate group is representing lenders in real estate financings. It acts for a stable of major financial institutions, life insurance companies and pension funds on the structuring and documentation of credit facilities. Another active tranche of the practice is representing traditional developers in all aspects of development. In response to client demand, the group has built up expertise in issues regarding independent power plants and has niche expertise advising on the privatization of government services. Work here includes advising on the development and financing of privatized housing for military personnel. The firm also secured plaudits for the international aspect of the real estate group and for the "*broader outlook*" it provides clients.

**The Lawyers: John Aldridge** (see p.704) focuses on advising clients on buying distressed properties or debt. He develops strategic planning programs for financial institutions in relation to distressed debt portfolios and high-yield debt transactions. International work dominates his practice and in one of his most significant recent transactions he has been advising on the complex restructuring of a large industrial project in Eastern Europe.

**Clients/Work Highlights:** Column Financial; GMAC; JPMorgan; KSL Recreation; Bank of America; KeyBank; Lehman Brothers and Morgan Stanley Real Estate Funds.

## Morris, Manning & Martin, LLP

**The Firm:** This firm is best known for representing real estate developers in the Atlanta area. It handles a full spectrum of real estate transactions from hospitality and apartment developments to industrial and retail projects. The firm's real estate capital markets group also advises public and private REITs on joint ventures and bond financings. It continues to be held in high regard for its work on the Atlantic Station project, and is regarded by the market as a *"quintessential high-end practice."*

**The Lawyers:** **Jeanna Brannon** has spent much of her recent time advising a major client on the acquisition of large tracts of land in Florida, the Bahamas and the US Virgin Islands. Mixed-use development and retail projects also contribute to her workload and she remains well known for her role as outside general counsel to the Atlantic Station project.

**Clients/Work Highlights:** The team represents some of the most active developers and investors in the Southeast.

## Paul, Hastings, Janofsky & Walker LLP

See firm details p.339

**The Firm:** This team benefits from the firm's overseas network and has completed national and international real estate transactions for a number of clients, including Portman Holdings and SunTrust. Its lawyers advise on acquisitions and disposals, joint ventures, REITs, litigation and real estate restructurings. Every sector of the industry is covered by the practice, including office, retail, residential and industrial real estate. Interviewees particularly highlighted the team's expertise in syndicated lending transactions.

**The Lawyers:** *"Superb lawyer"* **Charlie Sharbaugh** (see p.724) won applause from clients who praised him for his financing skills and his success in complex real estate transactions. He recently advised on several syndicated loans relating to a 27,000-acre community in Colorado, and completed a complex sale-leaseback transaction of a care hospital.

**Clients/Work Highlights:** Prominent clients include GE; Morgan Stanley; Lehman Brothers; Bank of America; Merrill Lynch; KeyBank and Wachovia. New clients for the firm are SunTrust and Portman Holdings.

## Powell Goldstein LLP

**The Firm:** Clients flock to this firm because of its *"in-depth knowledge of the law and the prevailing trends in the industry."* The group in Atlanta has recently been boosted by the arrival of four new lawyers, which in turn has attracted new clients on the lender and developer side. Representing state and local municipalities is a specialty of the team, along-

side its niche expertise in the timber industry. The group has been busy advising on commercial real estate lending transactions as well as zoning and land use issues. It represents developers on a full array of real estate products, from hotels to shopping centers, and is particularly active advising on the acquisition and financing of affordable multifamily rental projects.

**The Lawyers:** **Jay Levin** is a real hit with clients thanks to his *"ability to identify all the issues and his knack of marshaling the firm's resources to deal with them."* He has more than 30 years' experience in the real estate field and has spent the past few years focusing on mixed-use development projects. Representing government entities is a particular area of expertise for Levin, and he is currently representing the City of Atlanta on the rehabilitation of historical buildings. He also works with private sector multi-family developers and is well known for his representation of MARTA. **John Parks** focuses on construction and financing, although he has additional experience in retail leasing, including landlord and tenant representation. He also acts for financial institutions on lending transactions and restructurings.

**Clients/Work Highlights:** Pulte Homes; ING; Bank of America; Compass Bank; Bank of North Georgia; AIMCO and Trammell Crow Residential.

## Other Notable Practitioners

**Raymond Sheley** of Sheley & Hall has an excellent reputation in the commercial office leasing arena. Interviewees repeatedly endorsed him as *"a smart and positive practitioner."*

# TAX

| Tax Leading Firms | |
|---|---|
| **1** | ALSTON & BIRD LLP *Atlanta* |
| | KING & SPALDING LLP *Atlanta* |
| | SUTHERLAND ASBILL & BRENNAN LLP *Atlanta* |
| **2** | CHAMBERLAIN HRDLICKA WHITE *Atlanta* |
| | KILPATRICK STOCKTON LLP *Atlanta* |
| | MORRIS, MANNING & MARTIN, LLP *Atlanta* |
| | PAUL, HASTINGS, JANOFSKY & WALKER *Atlanta* |
| | POWELL GOLDSTEIN LLP *Atlanta* |

## Band 1

## Alston & Bird LLP

See firm details p.728

**The Firm:** Clients warmly recommended this full-service firm for its *"positive, can-do and thoughtful"* attorneys. One client went as far as to say: *"In the quality of their tax advice, they are unrivaled."* With a team comprising 70 lawyers, the group boasts both depth and breadth of expertise and advises on a spectrum of issues including state, local and federal

income tax, wealth planning, exempt organizations, international tax and ERISA. The Atlanta team works closely with the firm's Washington, DC, New York and North Carolina practices to provide *"seamless"* multistate tax advice to a stable of high-profile clients. Recent highlights include advising Delta Air Lines on bankruptcy-related issues and, in particular, pensions matters.

**The Lawyers:** *"Responsive and reliable"* **Pinney Allen** (see p.704) cochairs the tax department and was applauded for her *"broad range of expertise"* in the structuring of M&A and joint venture transactions. She is a leading light in the tax arena and has had a busy year advising clients such as Cingular Wireless and UPS. She has also been involved in structuring a number of complex real estate transactions. Interviewees recommended **John Coalson** (see p.709) as *"top of the ladder"* for state and local tax advice. According to market sources, his colleague **Philip Cook** (see p.709) is a *"pillar of the tax community."* He won praise for his tax litigation expertise, particularly in the areas of federal tax and ERISA. He advises clients from both the Atlanta and Washington, DC offices, and has recently been

involved in tax litigation in the telecom industry. *"Thorough and helpful"* **Sam Kaywood** (see p.717) has *"developed excellent expertise in international tax matters,"* observed market sources. *"Excellent listener"* **Michael Petrik** (see p.722) is renowned for his successes in complex state income tax disputes. His clients described him as *"smart, creative and considerate"* in his advice. He has handled a busy workload in 2005, advising on tax efficiency in dozens of corporate disposals and acquisitions. He has also been involved in the restructuring of a number of public companies. *"Brilliant"* **Benjamin White** (see p.726) has an *"innovative, refreshing and positive approach to transactions,"* said clients. Others claimed that as a public speaker he *"mesmerizes his audience with his fantastic depth of expertise and measured, thoughtful responses."* He chairs the firm's exempt organizations group and is coleader of the wealth planning team. Accordingly, he divides his time evenly between advising nonprofit organizations and individuals and their families.

**Clients/Work Highlights:** UPS; Cingular Wireless; Panasonic USA; Wachovia; Turner Broadcasting System; Roper Industries; Beaulieu Group; American Honda; Delta Air Lines; Home Depot; Katherine John Murphy Foundation; InterContinental Hotels Group and Coca-Cola.

## King & Spalding LLP
See firm details p.1933
**The Firm:** Clients concurred that this is "*a black-belt firm*" for tax law advice. Sources were also quick to point to the group's impressive breadth and superior technical expertise. It enjoys a stellar reputation for advice on corporate, partnership, international and Georgia state tax issues. Clients noted that the tax department houses "*uniformly outstanding senior lawyers*" and praised it for the team's "*excellent coverage across the country.*" Highlights of 2005 include representing Sprint in connection with the recapitalization of Virgin Mobile USA.
**The Lawyers:** This "*well-rounded,*" sophisticated group is home to some of the leading names in the market. Interviewees described **Herschel Bloom** (see p.706) as a "*great lawyer and fabulous person.*" He was singled out for his remarkable depth of expertise in corporate, partnership and real estate transactions. Clients praised **Robert Woodward** (see p.727) for his "*positive, helpful and receptive outlook.*" He possesses broad corporate experience, but is particularly renowned for his tax expertise in relation to M&A transactions, restructurings and financings. **Peter Genz** (see p.713) impressed interviewees with his "*excellent analytical and communication skills*" and superior skills in areas such as structuring

inbound foreign investments, REITs and troubled company workouts. **Suzanne Feese** (see p.712) received high marks for her proficiency in tax controversy work. She is also well versed in transaction planning, particularly concerning the structuring of partnerships, joint ventures and Islamic financings. Clients applauded "*diligent*" **Donald Hensel** (see p.715) as "*exactly what we look for in a lawyer – he has superb technical knowledge of the legislation and tax code as well as a keen business sense. He understands how the tax aspects relate to the rest of a transaction.*" His recent highlights include advising Roark Capital Group on the formation of a private equity fund and the acquisition of a number of companies. Market sources warmly endorsed **James Lokey** (see p.718) remarking: "*He understands the business end of things; he never lets the tax tail wag the business dog.*"
**Clients/Work Highlights:** Sprint; AMB Property; Croft & Bender; Total System Services; GE Capital Real Estate and SunTrust Banks.

## Sutherland Asbill & Brennan LLP
See firm details p.578
**The Firm:** This "*stellar*" tax group was applauded as a long-standing leader in the tax arena and has a national reputation for its federal, international, state and local tax expertise. The group advises a diverse client base consisting of corporations, partnerships, tax-exempt organizations, trusts, estates and individuals. Satisfied clients singled the firm out for its "*strong work ethic and culture.*" One client even remarked: "*The lawyers seem to really care about their clients as people.*" The team represents clients both in the planning of complex transactions and in tax litigation before the IRS.
**The Lawyers:** Described by rivals as "*one of the most distinguished tax lawyers in the country,*" **Jerold Cohen** (see p.709) was hailed as a "*fantastic lawyer's lawyer – his connections in government and tremendous experience mean he can quickly get clients before the right people.*" He formerly served as chief counsel for the IRS and has a wealth of experience representing domestic and foreign clients in a broad range of tax planning and controversy matters. Clients applauded **James Hasson** (see p.714) for his "*sophisticated style, and quiet, unassuming nature.*" He is a renowned expert in planning and controversy tax advice for exempt-organizations and high net worth individuals, and has particularly deep experience in the healthcare and academic sectors. Clients rated him for the "*tremendous thoroughness of his research*" and also acknowledged that his "*great grasp of the nonprofit sector*" lends him the edge over some of his competitors. His headline cases include supervising the unprecedented administration of 12 estates following the deaths of three generations of one family in an aircraft accident. Interviewees also nominated "*sharp*" **Reginald Clark** (see p.708) for his expertise in corporation transaction tax planning and restructurings.
**Clients/Work Highlights:** Duke University; Dartmouth-Hitchcock Medical Center; Emory University; Nortel Networks; Coca-Cola; Procter & Gamble; Philip Morris and Forest Capital Partners.

## Chamberlain Hrdlicka White Williams & Martin
**The Firm:** Interviewees complimented this 12-lawyer practice for its quality tax advice in both the transactional and litigation arenas. Indeed, market sources acknowledged this group as "*first choice*" for complex tax controversies and it is especially busy advising on a series of civil tax fraud cases. It attracts a broad client base, encompassing public and private companies, individuals and tax-exempt organizations.
**The Lawyers:** **David Aughtry** was widely admired as a leading light for complex civil and criminal tax disputes. Interviewees warmly recommended him for his depth of experience and "*high visibility*" in headline cases. "*Talented*" **Charles Hodges** was frequently referred to as a "*bright, rising star*" in the area. Interviewees recommended him for his expertise in transaction planning and litigation.

## Kilpatrick Stockton LLP
See firm details p.735
**The Firm:** This 45-lawyer team consistently provides quality advice on the tax aspects of corporate transactions, estate planning and tax controversies. It is also highly regarded for its representation of exempt organizations in obtaining tax-exempt status and in the planning of appropriate business transactions and joint ventures. Its other niche areas of expertise include advising on the tax aspects of the ownership and employment of IP rights, where it works closely with the firm's 130-strong IP department.
**The Lawyers:** **Lynn Fowler** (see p.713) was singled out as a "*highly talented tax expert who is becoming increasingly visible.*" Her colleague **Jerry Smith** (see p.724) is renowned for his national tax practice that encompasses advice on federal controversies, and transactional, state, local and international tax matters. In 2005, he handled several significant controversy matters for Fortune 100 companies from the banking and aerospace industries.
**Clients/Work Highlights:** Goodrich; Branch Banking and Trust; Southern Company; InterContinental Hotels Group and Equifax.

## Morris, Manning & Martin, LLP
**The Firm:** This "*entrepreneurial*" outfit is admired by market sources as a prominent source of quality tax law advice. Thanks to the buoyancy of the real estate market, the firm has seen a greater volume of real estate and capital markets work over the past year. This has included advising on a host of REITs and real estate partnerships. The team has attracted an expanding client base of emerging and midmarket clients, from industries such as insurance, finance and technology.
**The Lawyers:** "*Brilliant and eclectic*" **Charles Beaudrot** was praised for his ability to "*put up a fight. He has a great bedside manner and will go out of his way to help you,*" reported clients. Market sources singled him out as the cornerstone of the tax practice and praised him for his "*top-notch*" expertise in corporate and partnership tax, transaction planning

and state tax controversy matters.

**Clients/Work Highlights:** Education Realty Trust; Cole Capital; Behringer; Ginn Company and The Reynolds Company.

## Paul, Hastings, Janofsky & Walker LLP

See firm details p.339

**The Firm:** This international firm attracted the enthusiastic praise of clients for its *"hands-on and attentive"* tax advice. They also recommended the group for its *"uniform delivery of excellent service – whether you're dealing with a partner or an associate, this group has a superior skills set."* The six-lawyer Atlanta tax team is adept at handling sophisticated, international and local transactions and can call on the deep resources of its national bench when necessary. Areas of expertise include structuring corporate transactions and advising on joint ventures and partnerships.

**The Lawyers:** Clients lauded **Phil Marzetti** (see p.719) as a *"technically capable and also approachable*

*attorney."* They noted: *"He can absorb highly complex issues and then make them easy for us to understand."* He is renowned for the range of his tax expertise, which, aside from covering corporate and partnership matters, includes advising investors in affordable housing on tax credits. According to clients, new entrant **Mark Lange** (see p.718) *"excels at leading a team on complex transactions that are made up of many components"*. Others described him as *"the most tenacious and hard-working lawyer you can find. He is incredibly responsive and will do whatever it takes to get a transaction done."* He handles a diverse tax workload and has built up significant experience in the healthcare industry.

**Clients/Work Highlights:** UPS; EarthLink; Superior Essex; Bank of America and GE Capital.

## Powell Goldstein LLP

**The Firm:** Market sources regard this four-lawyer tax group as a key player in the Atlanta market and rate it especially highly for its income tax and corporate transaction advice. It has attracted a stable of

clients, including heavy-hitting entities such as Shaw Industries, and also represents a large contingent of tax-exempt organizations.

**The Lawyers:** **Frank Crisafi** is a renowned expert in international tax planning and is frequently called on to advise on the tax aspects of M&A transactions. Interviewees admired him as a *"bulldog – he will work away at a problem until it's solved."*

### Other Notable Practitioners

**Michael Wasserman** of Holt Ney Zatcoff & Wasserman LLP received hearty praise from his peers for his *"mental firepower and creativity"* when handling federal, state and local taxation matters. Market sources enthused: *"Not only is he an experienced, patient and technically skilled tax attorney, but he is also a good guy to boot."* **Morton Harris** of Hatcher, Stubbs, Land, Hollis & Rothschild LLP is based in Columbus and won applause for his long-standing tax expertise. Market commentators admire *"gifted"* tax expert **Robert Hishon** of The Hishon Firm LLC for his savvy advice on criminal and civil tax lawsuits.

# Leaders in Georgia

### ABERNATHY, Thomas
Smith, Currie & Hancock LLP, Atlanta
404 521 3800
*Recommended in Construction*

### ACORD, Bobbi
Parker, Hudson, Rainer & Dobbs LLP, Atlanta 404 523 5300
*Recommended in Banking & Finance*

### ADAMS JR, Alfred G
Sutherland Asbill & Brennan LLP, Atlanta 404 853 8014
al.adams@sablaw.com
*Recommended in Real Estate*
**Practice Areas:** Chairs Real Estate Group. Focuses primarily on real estate and creditors' rights, representing foreign and US investors, lenders and developers on varying projects. Works in the acquisition and development area and on mortgage and joint venture financing of commercial projects. Experienced in real estate workouts, foreclosures and bankruptcy reorganizations. Speaks often at CLE seminars. Serves on the Editorial Advisory Board of the 'Retail Law Strategist'. Adjunct Professor, Duke Law School, teaches course in Real Estate Finance.
**Prof. Memberships:** Former Chair, Real Property Section, State Bar of Georgia; Co-Chaired, State Bar of Georgia's Committee on Legal Opinions in Real Estate Transactions; Fellow, American College of Mortgage Attorneys; Member, State Bar of Georgia; Member, International Council of Shopping Centers; Member, National Association of Industrial and Office Parks; and Member, Board of Visitors of Duke Law School.

**Publications:** 'Springing Exclusive - Another Technique to Resolve Exclusive Use Issues', Retail Law Strategist, (2002); 'Developing a Shopping Center on a Ground Lease', Retail Law Strategist, (2001); 'The Mortgagee's Guide to Single Asset Bankruptcy Reorganizations', 98 Commercial Law Journal 351(1993).
**Personal:** JD with distinction, Duke University School of Law, 1974, Order of the Coif, administrative law editor, 'Duke Law Journal'; AB, Duke University, 1970.

### ALDRIDGE SR, John G
McKenna Long & Aldridge LLP, Atlanta
404 527 4030
jaldridge@mckennalong.com
*Recommended in Real Estate*
**Practice Areas:** Restructuring advisor and legal counsel for US investment banks, financial institutions and investors. Assisted in purchase, restructure and liquidation of more than $25 billion in performing and non-performing commercial loans and assets in the United States, Europe and South America. Develops strategic planning programs for senior management and special loan divisions of US financial institutions to address distressed debt portfolios and high risk, high-yield lending. Trains loan officers and asset managers in analyzing, managing and resolving under- and non-performing loans. Co-founder of Long Aldridge & Norman, predecessor firm of McKenna Long & Aldridge.
**Prof. Memberships:** American Bar Association; Atlanta Bar Association; District of Columbia Bar Association; Georgia Bar

Association; American College of Real Estate Lawyers; Central Atlanta Progress, Board of Directors (Past); Columbia Theological Seminary, Board of Trustees; Commerce Club, Board of Directors, President; Leadership Atlanta; Leadership Georgia; Presbyterian PLSE, Chair of the Board; Samaritan Center, Chairman of the Board of Directors (Past); Georgia Council on Child Abuse, Inc., Board of Directors (Past); Presbyterian College, Board of Visitors (Past); Homeward, Inc., Board of Directors (Past).
**Personal:** JD, University of North Carolina School of Law, with honors, 1968. BA, Duke University, 1965.

### ALEXANDER, Miles
Kilpatrick Stockton LLP, Atlanta
404 815 6410
MAlexander@KilpatrickStockton.com
*Recommended in Intellectual Property*
**Practice Areas:** Nationally known intellectual property and ADR lawyer who has served as lead counsel for numerous Fortune 500 companies in major trademark disputes.
**Prof. Memberships:** ABA; DC/Georgia Bar; International Trademark Association (past legal counsel, Board of Directors member, Editor-in-Chief, 'The Trademark Reporter'); American College of Trial Lawyers.
**Career:** Taught at Harvard Law School; served two years as a USAF Judge Advocate; Partner since 1963; Chair/Co-Chair of firm since 1996.
**Publications:** Written a number of articles in the trademark and unfair competi-

tion fields.
**Personal:** BA, Emory University, Phi Beta Kappa, 1952; JD, Harvard Law School, cum laude, 1955.

### ALFORD, Carolyn Zander
King & Spalding LLP, Atlanta
404 572 3551
czalford@kslaw.com
*Recommended in Banking & Finance*
**Practice Areas:** Represents lenders and borrowers in debt financings, including syndicated and single lender senior credit facilities (for both leveraged and investment grade credits), asset-based loans, mezzanine financing and third-party sponsored loan programs.
**Prof. Memberships:** Atlanta Bar Association; Women's Finance Exchange; State Bar of Georgia, Chair of the Legal Opinion Committee of the Business Law Section; Fellow of the American College of Investment Counsel.
**Personal:** BA, Duke University, magna cum laude, 1989, Phi Beta Kappa; JD Harvard Law School, cum laude, editor of 'Harvard Journal on Legislation'.

### ALLEN, Pinney L
Alston & Bird LLP, Atlanta
404 881 7485
pallen@alston.com
*Recommended in Tax*
**Practice Areas:** Concentrates on the structuring and effecting of complex business transactions, including partnership and corporate tax planning and litigation.
**Prof. Memberships:** Former Trustee and former Chair, Atlanta Tax Forum; past chair, Tax Sections of the State Bar of

Georgia and Atlanta Bar Association; Member of the American Bar Association Tax Section.
**Career:** Former member of the firm's Partners' Committee and chaired the committee in 2002. Co-Chair of the firm's Tax Groups.
**Publications:** Frequent author and speaker on corporate, partnership and real estate income tax problems.
**Personal:** AB (1976), JD (1979) - Harvard University.

### ALLEN, Randall L
Alston & Bird LLP, Atlanta
404 881 7196
rallen@alston.com
*Recommended in Antitrust*
**Practice Areas:** Concentrates on complex commercial litigation with a focus on antitrust litigation and counseling.
**Prof. Memberships:** Former Vice-Chair of the Section 1 Committee of the Antitrust Section of the ABA and Chairman of the Antitrust Section of the Georgia State Bar; member of Georgia State University, College of Law; Board of Visitors and Vice Chairman and general counsel for Ronald McDonald Children's Charities.
**Career:** Leads the firm's antitrust merger counseling effort and frequently appears before the Department of Justice and Federal Trade Commission on behalf of large public clients.
**Personal:** BA (1982), JD (1986) - Georgia State University.

### ARNOLD, Scott
King & Spalding LLP, Atlanta
404 572 4908
sarnold@kslaw.com
*Recommended in Real Estate*
**Practice Areas:** Represents investors (both foreign and domestic) in large commercial properties throughout the US in commercial real estate transactions. Represents real estate investment funds and developers in consolidating within the commercial real estate industry. Assists domestic investors in acquiring and divesting properties.
**Prof. Memberships:** American College of Real Estate Lawyers; American Bar Association; Atlanta Bar Association; State Bar of Georgia.
**Personal:** BA, Economics, University of Missouri, Phi Beta Kappa, 1972; JD, magna cum laude, University of Michigan Law School, 1975.

### ASBILL, Rick
Paul, Hastings, Janofsky & Walker LLP, Atlanta 404 815 2236
rickasbill@paulhastings.com
*Recommended in Antitrust*
**Practice Areas:** Business and commercial law, domestic and international franchising, licensing, intellectual property, antitrust counseling, mergers and acquisitions.
**Prof. Memberships:** American and

International Bar Associations, past Chair IBA International Franchising Committee and ABA Forum on Franchising.
**Career:** Partner, Atlanta office; Co-Chair of firm's Franchise and Distribution Group; Chair, Atlanta Office Corporate Department.
**Publications:** Co-author and editor, Fundamentals of International Franchising (ABA Press, 2001); co-author, 'Franchising Law: Practice and Forms' (Specialty Technical Publishers, Inc., ed 2006); frequently writes and lectures on franchising and distribution at legal and business seminars.
**Personal:** AB Politics, Princeton University, 1965; JD, University of North Carolina, 1968.

### ASHE, JR, R Lawrence
Ashe, Rafuse & Hill, LLP, Atlanta
404 253 6001
lawrenceashe@asherafuse.com
*Recommended in Employment*
**Practice Areas:** Concentrates practice in employment law, civil rights and litigation matters. Is nationally recognized for his class-action experience and employee selection expertise, and is the second career employment law attorney inducted as a Fellow of the American College of Trial Lawyers. Recognized by the National Law Journal as 'the dean of the management class action bar'.
**Prof. Memberships:** Member, State Bar of Georgia; Member, Bar of District of Columbia; Fellow, The College of Labor and Employment Lawyers; past Chair - AELC; past Management Chair - ABA EEO Committee of Labor and Employment Law Section; representative for Northern District of Georgia, Eleventh Circuit Court of Appeals' Committee on Lawyer Qualifications and Conduct (2001-06).
**Career:** Founding Partner of Ashe, Rafuse & Hill, LLP. Founder of Atlanta office of 800 attorney international law firm where he served for 10 years as the Chair of Atlanta office and then as Chair of the firm's East Coast Employment Law and Labor Practices.
**Personal:** AB Degree, high honors - Princeton University (1962); LLB Degree, Honors - Harvard Law School (1967).

### ASKEW, Anthony
Kilpatrick Stockton LLP, Atlanta
404 745 2401
TAskew@KilpatrickStockton.com
*Recommended in Intellectual Property*
**Practice Areas:** Patent, trademark and copyright law and litigation.
**Prof. Memberships:** State Bar of Georgia (Board of Governors and Disciplinary Board); US District Court Bar Council (Chair of the Disciplinary Committee); UGA Law School's Advisory Board for the 'Journal of Intellectual Property Law'.
**Career:** Former patent attorney for Eastman Kodak Company; special assistant

attorney general for the State of Georgia for intellectual property matters since 1983; adjunct faculty member at Emory Law School.
**Publications:** US Trademark Association's 'The Trademark Reporter' (former Editorial Board); 'Wiley Intellectual Property Law Update' (former co-editor).
**Personal:** BA Chemistry, Vanderbilt University, 1962; JD, Emory University, 1965.

### ASSELIN, Thomas
Smith Gambrell & Russell LLP, Atlanta
404 815 3500
*Recommended in Construction*

### AUGHTRY, David
Chamberlain Hrdlicka White Williams & Martin, Atlanta 404 659 1410
*Recommended in Tax*

### AUSTIN, Jesse
Paul, Hastings, Janofsky & Walker LLP, Atlanta 404 815 2208
jessaustin@paulhastings.com
*Recommended in Banking & Finance, Bankruptcy*
**Practice Areas:** Concentrates practice in bankruptcy law, particularly Chapter 11 reorganization cases and large commercial workouts. A principal focus of his workout and insolvency practice is the representation of institutional senior secured lenders in syndicated credit facilities, with particular experience in debtor-in-possession lending and in the healthcare, communications, energy and retail. Also closes senior credit facilities and assists other financial services lawyers in structuring senior credit facilities and negotiating subordination provisions of subordinated debt issues.
**Personal:** BS, Business Administration, Phi Beta Kappa, University of North Carolina (1976). JD, with distinction and MBA from Emory University (1980).

### BABER, Bruce
King & Spalding LLP, Atlanta
404 572 4826
bbaber@kslaw.com
*Recommended in Intellectual Property*
**Practice Areas:** Intellectual property and technology law with focus in patent, trademark, trademark counterfeiting, false advertising and copyright infringement cases before the International Trade Commission and the United States Patent and Trademark Office. Substantial experience in the protection of trademarks, copyrights and other forms of intellectual property, including registration applications prosecution and implementation of worldwide protection strategies.
**Prof. Memberships:** American Bar Association; Atlanta Bar Association; State Bar of Georgia.
**Personal:** BA, with distinction, Princeton University, 1976; JD, cum laude, Duke University, Order of the Coif, 1979.

### BALTZ, Raymond E
King & Spalding LLP, Atlanta
404 572 4715
rbaltz@kslaw.com
*Recommended in Corporate/M&A*
**Practice Areas:** Corporate with focus on strategic corporate transactions. Particular experience in mergers and acquisitions, joint ventures and strategic alliances, LBO and private equity transactions, and general corporate and securities matters.
**Prof. Memberships:** State Bar of Georgia.
**Personal:** BS, Eastern Nazarene College, 1986; JD summa cum laude, Boston University 1995.

### BANKOFF, Joseph R
King & Spalding LLP, Atlanta
404 572 4796
jbankoff@kslaw.com
*Recommended in Intellectual Property*
**Practice Areas:** Technology, communication disputes and contracts relating to software, copyrights, trade secrets, distribution channels and traditional/new media organizations. Experienced trial lawyer in patent, copyright, trade secret, media and technology-related matters.
**Prof. Memberships:** American Bar Association; American Law Institute; Atlanta Bar Association; Georgia Center for Advanced Telecommunications Technology (Board); Illinois State Bar; National Institute for Trial Advocacy (Board of Trustees); State Bar of Georgia.
**Personal:** BS, Purdue University, 1967; JD, University of Illinois, Omicron Delta Kappa, Order of the Coif, 1971.

### BANTA, Robert
Banta Immigration Law Ltd, Atlanta
404 249 9300
*Recommended in Immigration*

### BARMEYER, Patricia
King & Spalding LLP, Atlanta
404 572 3563
pbarmeyer@kslaw.com
*Recommended in Environment*
**Practice Areas:** Regulatory compliance and environmental litigation in the areas of water, waste, air and environmental tort issues. Former assistant attorney general for the State of Georgia. Expertise combines detailed knowledge of environmental law with courtroom experience in environmental cases.
**Prof. Memberships:** American Bar Association (member, Section on Natural Resources, Energy and Environmental Law); American Bar Foundation; Atlanta Bar Association; Fellow, Atlanta Volunteer Lawyers Foundation (past President); State Bar of Georgia.
**Personal:** BA, Hollins College, 1968; JD, cum laude, Harvard University, 1971.

## BASSETT, Peter Q
Alston & Bird LLP, Atlanta
404 881 7343
pbassett@alston.com
*Recommended in Litigation*
**Practice Areas:** Focuses on litigation and trial work covering a broad spectrum of securities class actions, claims and investigations.
**Prof. Memberships:** Member of the AIG/National Union Nation Panel counsel for the defense of securities class actions and D&O claims, Member of the State Bar of Georgia and the Atlanta Bar Association.
**Career:** Listed in two leading US legal publications for business litigation. Frequent author and speaker on topics relating to securities claims, class actions and D&O insurance.
**Personal:** AB, Princeton University (1971); JD, George Washington University (1975).

## BATSON, R Neal
Alston & Bird LLP, Atlanta
404 881 7267
nbatson@alston.com
*Recommended in Bankruptcy*
**Practice Areas:** Concentrates practice in Chapter 11 corporate reorganizations and out-of-court debt restructurings, as well as commercial litigation, corporate investigations, arbitration and mediation.
**Prof. Memberships:** Former Chair of the American College of Bankruptcy (2001-03), member of the American College of Trial Lawyers, former President of the Atlanta Bar Association, conferee of the National Bankruptcy Conference, former member of the Advisory Committee on Bankruptcy Rules by appointment of Chief Justice Rehnquist.
**Career:** Former court appointed examiner for Southmark Corporation and Enron Corp. Listed in several leading US legal publications.
**Personal:** BA (1963), JD (1966) - Vanderbilt University.

## BAXLEY, C William
King & Spalding LLP, Atlanta
404 572 3580
bbaxley@kslaw.com
*Recommended in Corporate/M&A*
**Practice Areas:** Domestic and international mergers and acquisitions and joint ventures in the consumer products, telecom, banking, insurance, transportation, retail and restaurants industries, involving public company mergers, private company acquisitions and dispositions, joint ventures, strategic investments, going private transactions, special committee representations, tender offers and proxy contests.
**Prof. Memberships:** American Bar Association; State Bar of Georgia.
**Personal:** BS, summa cum laude, University of Alabama, 1986; JD, magna cum laude, Harvard University, 1989. Named

one of the top 15 young Atlanta lawyers by 'The Fulton County Daily Report' in 2002.

## BAXTER, Jeffrey
Nelson Mullins Riley & Scarborough LLP, Atlanta 404 817 6000
*Recommended in Healthcare*

## BEAUDROT JR, Charles
Morris, Manning & Martin, LLP, Atlanta
404 233 7000
*Recommended in Tax*

## BECK, Joseph
Kilpatrick Stockton LLP, Atlanta
404 815 6406
JBeck@KilpatrickStockton.com
*Recommended in Intellectual Property*
**Practice Areas:** Copyright, First Amendment, entertainment law. Lead Counsel in SunTrust Bank v Houghton Mifflin; Estate of Martin Luther King, Jr, Inc. v CBS, Inc.; Rosa Parks v LaFace Records; Cooper v Sony Music Entertainment; Fantasy v LaFace Records; D.C. Comics, Inc. v Unlimited Monkey Business, Inc. and numerous other intellectual property cases.
**Prof. Memberships:** Copyright Society of the USA (former trustee); Georgia First Amendment Foundation (Board of Directors).
**Career:** Adjunct Professor (IP and First Amendment) at Emory University; frequent lecturer at law schools across the United States and abroad.
**Personal:** BA Emory University; JD Harvard University.

## BECK, Philip
Smith, Currie & Hancock LLP, Atlanta
404 521 3800
*Recommended in Construction*

## BENDER JR, Albert E
Alston & Bird LLP, Atlanta
404 881 7385
bbender@alston.com
*Recommended in Real Estate*
**Practice Areas:** Commercial real estate investment, development and financing, especially complex, multi-state and portfolio joint ventures, financings, purchases, sales and workouts.
**Prof. Memberships:** ICSC, MBA, NAIOP, ABA.
**Career:** Alston & Bird Real Estate Practice Quality Coordinator; Counsel Coordinator; New Business Acceptance Committee; Legal Education Task Force.
**Publications:** Seminar presentations include mezzanine loan enforcement issues, 'mixing bowl' joint venture transactions, equity participation mortgages, construction loans and workouts, alternative legal fee systems.
**Personal:** AB (Urban Affairs), St. Louis University (1980), Phi Beta Kappa; JD, Northwestern University School of Law (1983).

## BERGESON, Donna
Alston & Bird LLP, Atlanta
404 881 7278
dbergeson@alston.com
*Recommended in Healthcare*
**Practice Areas:** Academic medical center legal issues, healthcare contracting, regulatory compliance.
**Prof. Memberships:** Member, State Bar of Georgia; Georgia Academy of Health Care Attorneys; American Health Lawyers.
**Career:** Former Chair, Alston & Bird Health Care Regulatory Group. Past General Counsel of the Emory Clinic. Frequent author and speaker on compliance and life sciences-related legal issues. Certified as a professional coder by the American Academy of Professional Coders.
**Personal:** BA, University of South Carolina (1981); JD, University of South Carolina (1984).

## BLACKBURN, W Stanley
Kilpatrick Stockton LLP, Atlanta
404 815 6400
sblackburn@kilpatrickStockton.com
*Recommended in Corporate/M&A*
**Practice Areas:** Corporate, corporate finance and international law. Advises on US and international mergers and acquisitions, joint ventures, strategic alliances, and debt and equity issuances. Also advises on corporate governance, legal compliance, shareholder rights and other non-transactional matters.
**Prof. Memberships:** State Bar of Georgia (past Chair, Business Law Section); ABA; IBA; IPBA; American College of Investment Counsel.
**Career:** Partner since 1982. Co-Chair, Institutional Client Team.
**Personal:** BS Economics, high honors, Auburn University, 1973; JD University of Virginia, 1976 (Virginia Law Review; Order of the Coif). Director, executive committee member and secretary, Boys and Girls Clubs of Metro Atlanta; Leadership Atlanta.

## BLACKSTOCK, Jerry
Hunton & Williams, Atlanta
404 888 4298
jblackstock@hunton.com
*Recommended in Intellectual Property, Litigation*
**Practice Areas:** Jerry Blackstock's areas of trial experience after over 35 years of practice and over 200 trials include intellectual property rights involving patents, trademarks and copyrights, trade dress and trade secret issues, diverse business problems such as financing, false advertising, tax disputes, unfair competition claims, contract and lease disputes, corporation-shareholder problems, partnership disputes and employer-employee relationships including employment agreement litigation. He is also experienced in litigation involving real estate

issues and insurance coverage issues. He has tried cases in state and federal courts in Georgia, and other states, and he has handled arbitration trials all over the country.

## BLOOM, Herschel
King & Spalding LLP, Atlanta
404 572 4929
hbloom@kslaw.com
*Recommended in Tax*
**Practice Areas:** Corporate, partnership and real estate tax matters, particularly real estate investment trusts, life insurance companies and state tax issues and controversies.
**Prof. Memberships:** American Bar Association; American College of Tax Counsel; American Law Institute; State Bar of Georgia (former Chairman, Tax Section).
**Personal:** AB, magna cum laude, Vanderbilt University, 1965; JD, cum laude, Harvard University Law School, Phi Beta Kappa; Omicron Delta Kappa, 1968. Former Associate Professor of Law at University of Mississippi Law School. Frequent speaker on corporate and partnership tax subjects.

## BLUMEN, Rick D
Alston & Bird LLP, Atlanta
404 881 7895
rblumen@alston.com
*Recommended in Banking & Finance*
**Practice Areas:** Debt finance, secured and unsecured syndicated credit facilities, structured finance, private placements, high-yield debt offerings, trust preferred securities offerings, mezzanine finance, acquisition finance.
**Prof. Memberships:** Member, State Bar of Georgia.
**Career:** Served as counsel to several of the largest US commercial banks and insurance companies. Former judicial intern with The Honorable Lawrence S Margolis, US Court of Federal Claims. Former intern with President Jimmy Carter.
**Publications:** Published in 'Georgia State University Law Review.'
**Personal:** BA, Emory University (1986); JD, George Washington University (1990).

## BOICE, William
Kilpatrick Stockton LLP, Atlanta
404 815 6464
BBoice@KilpatrickStockton.com
*Recommended in Employment, Litigation*
**Practice Areas:** Has substantial trial experience representing significant corporate clients in a wide variety of cases. Trial practice focused on complex litigation including patent and trade secret litigation, class actions, business torts, securities and other business litigation.
**Prof. Memberships:** Litigation Section of the Atlanta Bar Association and the State Bar of Georgia; Bleckley Inn of

Court; Lawyers Club of Atlanta.
**Career:** United States Navy officer (1968-70); Partner since 1980; Litigation Practice Group Chairman (1997-2001).
**Personal:** BA Economics, Emory University, 1968; JD, University of Virginia School of Law, 1974.

## BOISSEAU, Richard
Kilpatrick Stockton LLP, Atlanta
404 815 6317
RBoisseau@KilpatrickStockton.com
*Recommended in Employment*
**Practice Areas:** Employment relations law with a primary focus in traditional labor relations matters under the National Labor Relations Act.
**Prof. Memberships:** Board of Directors of the Visiting Nurse Health System of Metropolitan Atlanta, Inc. (past President); ABA's Committee on Labor Arbitration and the Law of Collective Bargaining Agreements.
**Career:** Has lectured and written on employment-related topics; contributing author to the sixth edition of 'How Arbitration Works', Elkouri & Elkouri, the most widely used manual on labor arbitration.
**Personal:** Undergraduate Degree, Drexel University, cum laude, 1968; JD, Temple University, cum laude, 1974.

## BONDURANT, Emmet J
Bondurant, Mixson & Elmore, LLP, Atlanta 404 881 4126
bondurant@bmelaw.com
*Recommended in Antitrust, Litigation*
**Practice Areas:** Trial and appellate litigation, antitrust and unfair competition, business torts, constitutional, dispute resolution, franchise, professional liability, securities, and white-collar criminal defense litigation.
**Prof. Memberships:** American College of Trial Lawyers; American Academy of Appellate Lawyers; Trustee, American Inns of Court Foundation; American Law Institute; Chair, Georgia Public Defender Standards Council; Chair, Georgia Resource Center; Chair, Fulton County Justice Commission; former Chair, Common Cause/Georgia; past President, Atlanta Legal Aid Society; former Chair, Atlanta Charter Commission; past President, University of Georgia Law School Association; Member, University of Georgia Board of Visitors; Member, Atlanta Bar Association, State Bar of Georgia, American Bar Association and the American Judicature Society; Fellow, American Bar Foundation.
**Career:** Has represented clients in nearly every forum available for a legal dispute, from rural trial courts through the United States Supreme Court (Hishon v King & Spalding, 467 US 69 (1984), Fortson v Morris, 385 US 231 (1966), Westberry v Sanders, 376 US 1 (1964)). In 2006, he led Atlanta Magazine's poll of Super Lawyers in Georgia for the third year in a row, was

recognized as one of the leading lawyers in Georgia by Georgia Trend Magazine in December 2003, and was recognized by National Law Journal as one of top 10 trial lawyers in the United States in 2001. Selected by ABOTA as Georgia Trial Lawyer of the Year in 1991; recipient of Georgia Indigent Defense Council's Harold G Clarke Equal Justice Award and the Anti-Defamation League's Elbert P Tuttle Award. During the course of his career he has earned a reputation as an independent and implacable adversary who does not shy away from controversial cases, and combines innovative legal theories with sheer determination.
**Personal:** University of Georgia (AB, cum laude, 1958; LLB, magna cum laude, 1960); Harvard University (LLM, 1962); Law Clerk to the late Honorable Judge Clement F Haynsworth Jr, United States Court of Appeals for the Fourth Circuit, 1960-61.

## BORDERS, Sarah
King & Spalding LLP, Atlanta
404 572 3596
sborders@kslaw.com
*Recommended in Bankruptcy*
**Practice Areas:** Insolvency law issues, extensive experience representing creditors and debtors in large workouts, restructurings and bankruptcy cases in the retail, textile, real estate and healthcare industries.
**Prof. Memberships:** American Bar Association; American Bankruptcy Institute; American Law Institute (former President); Atlanta Bar Association; State Bar of Georgia.
**Personal:** BS, Louisiana State University, 1984; JD, University of Virginia, 1988. Frequent speaker on restructuring issues.

## BRADLEY, Wayne N
Paul, Hastings, Janofsky & Walker LLP, Atlanta 404 815 2202
waynebradley@paulhastings.com
*Recommended in Corporate/M&A*
**Practice Areas:** Strategic matters including mergers, acquisitions and joint ventures; private equity and venture capital; internal investigations; representation of non-US companies in connection with US matters. Chief outside counsel for a number of firm clients.
**Prof. Memberships:** Corporate Code Committee (State Bar of Georgia); Board Member, Atlanta Bar Association Business and Finance Section; Association for Corporate Growth; Board Member, Thione International, Inc.
**Career:** Russ Berrie & Co. (NYSE:RUS) (1983-87); clerk, Hon Emmett Cox, US Court of Appeals for Eleventh Circuit (1990-91); McKenna Long & Aldridge (1991-2004; Chair, Corporate Department 2001-04).
**Personal:** Emory Law School (Editor-in-Chief, Emory Law Journal); Rutgers College.

## BRAMLETT, Jeffrey
Bondurant, Mixson & Elmore, LLP, Atlanta 404 881 4192
bramlett@bmelaw.com
*Recommended in Litigation*
**Practice Areas:** Trial lawyer with extensive experience representing both plaintiffs and defendants in business disputes, especially class actions. Repeatedly certified by courts as lead counsel in class actions. Frequently called upon to represent lawyers and their law firms. Experienced in appellate advocacy, arbitration, mediation, and the resolution of cross-border disputes.
**Prof. Memberships:** Served as President of the Atlanta Bar Association and chaired its Section on Litigation. Represents Atlanta on the State Bar of Georgia's Board of Governors. Master Bencher, Lamar American Inn of Court.
**Personal:** JD, University of Texas School of Law; Editor, Texas Law Review; law clerk to Hon Jerre S Williams, United States Court of Appeals for the Fifth Circuit; Legislative Aide to Hon Bob Eckhardt, Member of Congress (Texas); BA, University or Maryland.

## BRANNON, Jeanna
Morris, Manning & Martin, LLP, Atlanta 404 233 7000
*Recommended in Real Estate*

## BREWSTER, William H
Kilpatrick Stockton LLP, Atlanta
404 815 6549
BBrewster@KilpatrickStockton.com
*Recommended in Intellectual Property*
**Practice Areas:** Client counseling and litigation in trademark, copyright, false advertising, unfair competition, trade secrets, and restrictive covenants.
**Prof. Memberships:** INTA (Brand Names Education Foundation Committee; former Publications and US Legislation Committees); AIPLA (Chair of the Trademark Litigation Committee); ACLA; NCLA; State Bar of Georgia (Antitrust, Intellectual Property and Sports and Entertainment Sections).
**Career:** Managing Partner; Adjunct Professor at the Emory University School of Law; lectures on trademark dilution, trade dress, trade secret, and restrictive covenant issues.
**Personal:** BA, Political Science and Economics, Emory University, with honors, 1984; MA Political Science, Emory University; JD, University of Virginia, 1987.

## BUCKLER, Robert
Troutman Sanders LLP, Atlanta
404 885 3000
*Recommended in Employment*

## BUFFENSTEIN, Daryl
Paul, Hastings, Janofsky & Walker LLP, Atlanta 404 815 2232
darylbuffenstein@paulhastings.com
*Recommended in Immigration*
**Practice Areas:** Daryl has extensive

experience representing major US and foreign companies on business immigration issues. Testified on numerous occasions before Congress on immigration issues. Wrote key business provisions in every major piece of immigration legislation enacted by Congress in past 15 years. Focus on strategic counseling, immigration-related government relations and legislative practice. Chaired numerous professional and business conferences. Past national President, former General Counsel, current Director, American Immigration Lawyers Association (AILA); founder, Director and General Counsel, Global Personnel Alliance. Listed in 'Best Lawyers in America', 'Who's Who in American Law' and the 'International Who's Who in Business Law'.

## BUTLER, James
Smith, Currie & Hancock LLP, Atlanta
404 521 3800
*Recommended in Construction*

## CAEN, Melissa
Troutman Sanders LLP, Atlanta
404 885 3000
*Recommended in Energy*

## CAHOON, Susan
Kilpatrick Stockton LLP, Atlanta
404 815 6325
SCahoon@KilpatrickStockton.com
*Recommended in Litigation*
**Practice Areas:** Patent infringement and trade secrets litigation and complex commercial litigation. Trained as a mediator and an arbitrator.
**Prof. Memberships:** Fellow, American College of Trial Lawyers; ABA (former Chair of committees in the TIPS and Litigation Sections and associate editor, 'Litigation'; CPR Institute for Dispute Resolution (Panelist); American Law Institute; Lumpkin Inn of Court.
**Career:** Former Chair of the firm's Litigation Department and member of its Executive Committee; currently firm General Counsel and ex officio member of Executive Committee. Partner since 1977.
**Personal:** BA History and Economics, Emory University, summa cum laude, 1968; JD, Harvard University, cum laude, 1971.

## CAMPBELL, Charles E
McKenna Long & Aldridge LLP, Atlanta
404 527 4590
ccampbell@mckennalong.com
*Recommended in Bankruptcy*
**Practice Areas:** Concentrates in bankruptcy, business litigation and public utilities law. Represents trustees, debtors and creditors and has served as a court-appointed trustee in bankruptcy reorganization proceedings. Served as lead counsel in the Pinegate bankruptcy litigation. Handles jury and non-jury cases involving securities, contracts, fraud, lender liability, trade secrets, computer

software, professional malpractice and defamation. Founding member and managing director of Hicks, Maloof & Campbell, which merged with Long Aldridge & Norman, a predecessor firm to McKenna Long & Aldridge.

**Prof. Memberships:** American College of Bankruptcy; American College of Trial Lawyers; Richard B Russell Foundation, Chairman.

**Publications:** Co-editor, 'Bankruptcy Forms and Faculty' for seminars on bankruptcy law and rules for 'Norton Institutes on Bankruptcy Law'.

**Personal:** JD, Georgetown University Law Center, 1971. MA and BA, University of Georgia, 1964.

### CAMPBELL, Margaret
Troutman Sanders LLP, Atlanta
404 885 3000
*Recommended in Environment*

### CAMPBELL, Margaret H
Ogletree, Deakins, Nash, Smoak & Stewart, PC, Atlanta 404 881 1300
meg.campbell@ogletreedeakins.com
*Recommended in Employment*

**Practice Areas:** Employment, class and collective action, whistleblower, and employment contract litigation, employment and labor law.

**Prof. Memberships:** American, Georgia, and Atlanta Bar Associations, Virginia State Bar, Georgia Association of Women Lawyers.

**Career:** Admitted: Georgia, Virginia, US Supreme Court, US Courts of Appeals (Fourth, Sixth, and Eleventh Circuits). Fellow, College of Labor and Employment Lawyers. Member, Ogletree Deakins' Board of Directors.

**Publications:** 17 Georgia Jurisprudence, 'Liability for Intentional Acts Committed in the Employment Setting', Lawyers Cooperative Publishing 1995.

**Personal:** Goucher College (AB, with Honors in Economics, 1978), Washington & Lee University School of Law (JD, 1981).

### CAPERS, John
King & Spalding LLP, Atlanta
404 572 4658
jcapers@kslaw.com
*Recommended in Corporate/M&A*

**Practice Areas:** Corporate transactions, including domestic and international mergers, acquisitions, securities offerings, joint ventures and governmental and quasi-governmental borrowings. Extensive experience in public offerings of corporate finance and merger, acquisition and joint venture transactions involving different industry groups, including telecommunications, technology, and retail companies. M&A experience includes representing public and private companies, boards of directors and special committees, and financial advisors to companies involved in M&A transactions.

**Prof. Memberships:** American Bar Association; Atlanta Bar Association; State Bar of Georgia.

**Personal:** Vanderbilt University, high honors, 1975; JD, high honors, University of Georgia School of Law, Order of Coif, 1978.

### CARSON, Christopher L
Jones Day, Atlanta
404 581 8035
clcarson@jonesday.com
*Recommended in Banking & Finance*

**Practice Areas:** Chairs the firm's Financial Institutions Practice Committee. Has extensive experience in all types of lending transactions, including secured and unsecured commercial loans, commercial finance, real estate loans, leasing transactions (including leveraged and synthetic leases), and letters of credit, as well as in chapter 11 cases and workouts, primarily representing creditors, especially commercial banks and commercial finance companies. Recognized as a leading lawyer in various publications.

**Prof. Memberships:** American College of Commercial Finance Lawyers; State Bar of Georgia; Atlanta Bar Association; Southeastern Bankruptcy Law Institute; Georgia Financial Lawyers Conference.

**Publications:** Lecturer/writer on banking, bank lending, and bankruptcy matters.

### CARSSOW, Tim
Kilpatrick Stockton LLP, Atlanta
404 815 6610
TCarssow@KilpatrickStockton.com
*Recommended in Real Estate*

**Practice Areas:** Commercial real estate including development and land use issues, limited liability companies and partnerships, and troubled real estate projects.

**Prof. Memberships:** American College of Real Estate Lawyers; Fernbank Museum and Freedom Park Conservancy (trustee); Midtown Alliance (Board of Directors); Paideia School (trustee); NAIOP; American Bar Association; Atlanta Bar Association; Georgia State Bar (former Chairman of the Real Property Law Section).

**Career:** Partner since 1976; Managing Partner of the firm (1996-2001).

**Personal:** BA, Trinity University, 1967; JD, University of Texas School of Law, 1970.

### CARTER, Dan T
Jones Day, Atlanta
404 581 8019
dcarter@jonesday.com
*Recommended in Employment*

**Practice Areas:** Has extensive experience counseling employers and handling matters arising under the National Labor Relations Act, the Occupational Safety and Health Act, the Fair Labor Standards Act, the Workers Adjustment and Retraining Notification Act, the Family and Medical Leave Act, and other state

and federal labor statutes. Has also litigated and tried numerous bench and jury employment cases.

**Prof. Memberships:** ABA; Atlanta Bar Association; State Bar of Georgia; Ohio State Bar Association; Lawyers Club of Atlanta; Georgia Labor - Management Conference.

**Publications:** Author of articles on labor and employment law issues and a regular speaker at employment and management law programs.

### CASHDAN, Jeffrey
King & Spalding LLP, Atlanta
404 572 4818
jcashdan@kslaw.com
*Recommended in Antitrust*

**Practice Areas:** Antitrust, merger and acquisition and complex business litigation counseling, including securities, purported class actions and appellate matters.

**Prof. Memberships:** American Bar Association (Vice-Chair, Sherman Act Section 2, Antitrust and Litigation Sections); Editorial Board for the 2000 Annual Review of Antitrust Law Developments; Antitrust Law Journal (former editor); Atlanta Bar Association; Illinois State Bar; State Bar of Georgia (Chair, Antitrust Section).

**Personal:** BA, cum laude, Claremont McKenna College, 1987; London School of Economics and Political Science; JD, University of Chicago, 1990.

### CHAMBERS, Robert
Smith, Currie & Hancock LLP, Atlanta
404 521 3800
*Recommended in Construction*

### CHANDLER, John A
Sutherland Asbill & Brennan LLP, Atlanta 404 853 8029
john.chandler@sablaw.com
*Recommended in Litigation*

**Practice Areas:** Tries business cases. Has represented clients in numerous complex professional liability, securities, insurance and RICO cases. Has represented all of the 'big four' accounting firms, several local accounting firms, several law firms, insurance companies, individuals and partnerships.

**Prof. Memberships:** Served as President of the Atlanta Bar Association, the Atlanta Council of Younger Lawyers, the Atlanta Legal Aid Society, the Atlanta Volunteer Lawyers Foundation, Travelers Aid of Metropolitan Atlanta. Chair of the Fulton County Ethics Board and Chair of the City of Atlanta Board of Ethics. Member of the Board of Governors of the State Bar of Georgia. Member of the International Association of Defense Counsel, past President of the Bleckley American Inn of Court, a Master of the Lumpkin American Inn of Court, member of the Board of Visitors of the University of Tennessee College of Arts and Sciences, a Fellow of the American Bar Foundation and a Fellow of the American

College of Trial Lawyers.

**Personal:** JD, Vanderbilt University School of Law, 1972, Order of Coif, Managing Editor, 'Vanderbilt Law Review'; BS, University of Tennessee, 1966.

### CHEATHAM Richard R
Kilpatrick Stockton LLP, Atlanta
404 815 6570
RCheatham@KilpatrickStockton.com
*Recommended in Banking & Finance*

**Practice Areas:** Financial institution representation, including bank regulatory matters and corporate and securities law applicable to financial institutions and their holding companies and other affiliates.

**Prof. Memberships:** American Bar Association; State Bar of Georgia.

**Career:** Partner since 1975.

**Publications:** Regularly speaks at seminars on the financial institutions industry.

**Personal:** BS, Commerce, University of Virginia, with Distinction, 1965; LLB, Harvard University, cum laude, 1968.

### CIFELLI, James
Lamberth, Cifelli, Stokes & Stout, P.A., Atlanta 404 262 7373
*Recommended in Bankruptcy*

### CLARK, Reginald J
Sutherland Asbill & Brennan LLP, Atlanta 404 853 8032
reggie.clark@sablaw.com
*Recommended in Tax*

**Practice Areas:** A tax practitioner with particular experience in corporate taxation and in planning corporate acquisitions, restructurings and other transactions. Practice includes advising a number of cooperative organizations, both tax-exempt and taxable. Also experienced in handling tax controversies and representing clients before the National Office of the Internal Revenue Service in connection with requests for rulings or technical advice.

**Prof. Memberships:** Former Adjunct Professor of Law in the Emory University School of Law's Graduate Tax Program. Presently Chair of the Corporate Tax Committee of the American Bar Association's Tax Section, and has spoken at a number of tax seminars and bar programs. Member of the Board of Trustees of the Southern Federal Tax Institute and the Georgia Federal Tax Conference, and member of the American Law Institute.

**Personal:** JD, with distinction, Duke University School of Law, 1978, notes and comments editor, Duke Law Journal; AB, Duke University, 1975 Phi Beta Kappa.

### CLAY, A Stephens
Kilpatrick Stockton LLP, Atlanta
404 815 6514
SClay@KilpatrickStockton.com
*Recommended in International Arbitration, Litigation*

**Practice Areas:** Broad trial and appellate experience in business litigation, including contracts, products liability and business torts, antitrust and intellectual property. Extensive experience in international arbitration as an advocate and arbitrator.

**Prof. Memberships:** American Bar Association, Antitrust Section; International Bar Association; Georgia, Pennsylvania and District of Columbia Bar Associations; Chartered Institute of Arbitrators.

**Personal:** BA, Yale University, 1964; JD, University of Virginia School of Law, 1967. Honors: 'The Best Lawyers in America'; 'Georgia Super Lawyer'; CPR International Institute (various panels); AAA/ICDR International Arbitration panel; ICC Commission on Arbitration; ICC Task Force on Arbitrating Competition Disputes.

## CLELAND, A Craig
Ogletree, Deakins, Nash, Smoak & Stewart, PC, Atlanta 404 881 1300
craig.cleland@ogletreedeakins.com
*Recommended in Employment*

**Practice Areas:** Representing and advising employers in employment law matters, including litigation and class/collective actions.

**Prof. Memberships:** ABA; Atlanta/Georgia Bar Associations.

**Career:** Partner since 2003.

**Publications:** Contributor, Weirich, Employment Discrimination Law (forthcoming 4th ed). Contributor, Lindemann/Grossman, Employment Discrimination Law (3d ed).

**Personal:** Georgia State University (JD cum laude, 1992). Yale University (STM honors, 1983). Vanderbilt University (MDiv honors, 1981). Valdosta State University (BA cum laude, 1978). Law clerk, The Hon Marvin H Shoob, US District Court, Northern District of Georgia. Editor-in-Chief, Georgia State University Law Review. Georgia Trend Magazine 'Legal Elite' (2003-05). Atlanta Magazine 'Super Lawyers' (2006).

## CLOUD, Douglas
Alston & Bird LLP, Atlanta
404 881 7894
dcloud@alston.com
*Recommended in Environment*

**Practice Areas:** Environmental regulatory and transactional matters with special emphasis on brownfields redevelopment, state and federal Superfund cleanups, Clean Air Act enforcement. Advises on environmental risks and liabilities related to mergers, stock and asset deals and real estate transactions.

**Prof. Memberships:** Environmental Committee, Urban Land Institute, Atlanta Chapter; Environmental & Toxic Tort Section, Atlanta Bar Association (past Chair).

**Publications:** Published in 'Mealey's Pollution Liability Report' and 'Legal Times.'

**Personal:** BA, with honors, Grinnell College (1973); MFA, Florida State University (1976); JD, Cornell Law School (1988).

## COALSON JR, John L
Alston & Bird LLP, Atlanta
404 881 7482
jcoalson@alston.com
*Recommended in Tax*

**Practice Areas:** Focuses on counseling/planning as well as dispute and litigation work in the state and local tax area, and unclaimed property.

**Prof. Memberships:** Trustee and member of the Advisory Board of the Paul Hartman Memorial Institute on State and Local Taxation and Editorial Board of the Journal of Multistate Taxation.

**Publications:** Authored over a dozen law review articles that have appeared in the Tax Lawyer, Journal of State Taxation, Georgia Law Review, Mercer Law Review, and The Georgia Bar Journal, as well as the BNA Portfolio on Unclaimed Property.

**Personal:** BBA, Emory University (1974); JD, University of Georgia (1977).

## COHEN, Ezra
Troutman Sanders LLP, Atlanta
404 885 3000
*Recommended in Bankruptcy*

## COHEN, Jerold
Sutherland Asbill & Brennan LLP, Atlanta 404 853 8038
jerry.cohen@sablaw.com
*Recommended in Tax*

**Practice Areas:** Represents clients in domestic and international tax planning and controversy matters. Has planned and structured corporate acquisitions and dispositions, successfully litigated federal tax cases, handled matters before the IRS and Treasury Department, and handled legislative matters for clients. Has testified before Congressional tax writing committees and worked with the Joint Committee on Taxation.

**Prof. Memberships:** Former Chair, IRS Advisory Council; former Chair, American College of Tax Counsel; past Chair, Tax Section of the ABA; Member, Board of Advisors, Virginia Tax Review; past Member, Little Brown and Commerce Clearing House Tax Advisory Boards; Vice Chair, American College of Tax Counsel; former Member, Board of Advisors, IRS's Continuing Professional Education Program; former Member, Advisory Group to the Staff of the Senate Finance Committee on its Subchapter C Revision Act; Member, American Law Institute and its Tax Advisory Board; Member, Board of Regents of ACTC; Member, Board of Trustees of The American Tax Policy Institute.

**Publications:** Published in The Journal of Taxation, The Tax Lawyer, Practicing Law Institute publications, The Journal of the American Bar Association publications and the NYU Tax Institutes, and has spoken at numerous tax institutes. Adjunct Professor of Law, Emory University (1967-76).

**Personal:** LLB, magna cum laude, Harvard Law School, 1961, Book Review editor, 'Harvard Law Review'; BBA, Tulane University, 1957, Beta Gamma Sigma.

## COIL, James
Kilpatrick Stockton LLP, Atlanta
404 815 6348
JCoil@KilpatrickStockton.com
*Recommended in Employment*

**Practice Areas:** Represents management in all phases of employment matters. Numerous successful jury verdicts and summary judgments, and favorable settlements in many other cases. Successfully defended multi-plaintiff and class action claims alleging wage/hour; race, sex, and age discrimination; and ERISA violations.

**Prof. Memberships:** Atlanta Bar Association.

**Career:** Captain, Judge Advocate, US Marine Corps.

**Publications:** Frequent speaker and author or co-author of more than 50 articles, including 'The New Supervisor's EEO Handbook', a guide to help frontline managers become familiar with federal anti-discrimination laws.

**Personal:** BA, Duke University, 1967; JD, Harvard Law School, 1970; Atlanta Symphony Orchestra (Board of Directors).

## COLEMAN, Aubrey
Smith, Currie & Hancock LLP, Atlanta
404 521 3800
*Recommended in Construction*

## CONNOLLY, Dennis J
Alston & Bird LLP, Atlanta
404 881 7269
dconnolly@alston.com
*Recommended in Bankruptcy*

**Practice Areas:** Commercial bankruptcy.

**Prof. Memberships:** Past Chair, Bankruptcy Section of the Atlanta Bar Association and member of State Bar of Georgia and American Bankruptcy Institute; Fellow, American College of Bankruptcy.

**Career:** Recent engagements include representing Chapter 11 debtors, LaRoche Industries and Galey & Lord, and creditors' committees for Einstein Noah Bagel and Dan River. Represented the Enron Corp. examiner in the Enron Corp. bankruptcy.

**Publications:** Published widely in 'Legal Times', the 'Bankruptcy Strategist', and the 'Norton Annual Survey of Bankruptcy Law'.

**Personal:** BA, University of Michigan (1982); JD, cum laude, University of South Carolina (1986).

## CONRAD, Albert H
King & Spalding LLP, Atlanta
404 572 4807
cconrad@kslaw.com
*Recommended in Banking & Finance*

**Practice Areas:** Representing banks and lending institutions in private debt financings and major financing transactions. Serves as the principal outside lawyer for a number of the firm's corporate and REIT clients.

**Prof. Memberships:** American Bar Association (Banking Law Section); American College of Commercial Finance Lawyers (former Chair, Uniform Commercial Code Committee); Atlanta Bar Association; State Bar of Georgia (Chair, Corporate and Banking Law Section).

**Personal:** BS, with highest honors, University of Tennessee, 1972; JD, University of Virginia, Omicron Delta Kappa; Phi Kappa Phi; Order of the Coif, 1975. Frequent speaker on lending-related topics.

## COOK, Philip C
Alston & Bird LLP, Atlanta
404 881 7491
pcook@alston.com
*Recommended in Tax*

**Practice Areas:** Concentrates practice on federal tax and ERISA controversies.

**Prof. Memberships:** Member of the Board of Editors of the Journal of Taxation of Financial Institutions (formerly the Journal of Bank Taxation). Has also served as Chair of the Committee on Banks and Savings Institutions of the ABA Tax Section.

**Career:** Deputy Managing Partner of the firm. Frequent speaker at national Bank Tax Conferences and other seminars and institutes. Listed in two leading legal publications.

**Personal:** BS, with honors, Georgia Institute of Technology (1968); JD, cum laude, Harvard University (1971).

## CORGAN, Brian
Kilpatrick Stockton LLP, Atlanta
404 815 6217
BCorgan@KilpatrickStockton.com
*Recommended in Construction*

**Practice Areas:** Construction contracts, litigation, and alternative disputes resolution. Has handled construction disputes involving nuclear and coal-fired power plants, international airport runway construction, cogeneration (power, cement and lime) plants, wastewater treatment plants, steel mills, oil refineries, hospitals, and other projects.

**Prof. Memberships:** Georgia and Louisiana Bar Associations; American Arbitration Association's National Panel of Arbitrators.

**Publications:** Writes and lectures extensively throughout the US on the subjects of avoiding litigation on large and complex construction projects, alternative disputes resolution procedures and processes, and effective construction litigation.

**Personal:** BA, Tulane University, 1976; JD, Tulane University, summa cum laude, 1979.

**COWEN Stephen**
King & Spalding LLP, Atlanta
404 572 4688
scowen@kslaw.com
*Recommended in Litigation*
**Practice Areas:** Special matters focusing on white-collar criminal defense of corporations, individuals, and civil fraud matters, including healthcare, government procurement, securities, tax, antitrust, foreign payments and campaign finance investigations. Representations have included defense of government and Congressional inquiries and litigation of civil fraud and misrepresentation actions. Extensive government experience as a prosecutor and civil litigator. Frequent lecturer on corporate investigations.
**Prof. Memberships:** State Bar of Georgia, Florida and the District of Columbia.
**Personal:** Emory University, 1969; JD, Harvard Law School, 1972.

**CRANSHAW, David**
Morris, Manning & Martin, LLP, Atlanta
404 233 7000
*Recommended in Bankruptcy*

**CREWDSON, Robert**
Alston & Bird LLP, Atlanta
404 881 7291
rcrewdson@alston.com
*Recommended in Construction*
**Practice Areas:** Construction contracts; mediation and arbitration of construction claims.
**Prof. Memberships:** Member, International Council of Shopping Centers, American College of Healthcare Executives, American Health Lawyers Association, State Bar of Georgia, Atlanta Bar Association (former Chair, Construction Law section).
**Career:** National transactional and litigation practice. Listed in leading US legal publication.
**Publications:** Lectures and publishes frequently regarding a broad range of construction matters. Current guest lecturer, Georgia Institute of Technology.
**Personal:** BA, magna cum laude, University of the South (1983); MA, College of William & Mary (1987); JD, University of Virginia (1987).

**CRISAFI, Frank**
Powell Goldstein LLP, Atlanta
404 572 6600
*Recommended in Tax*

**CURTIS, J Vaughan**
Alston & Bird LLP, Atlanta
404 881 7397
vcurtis@alston.com
*Recommended in Corporate/M&A*
**Practice Areas:** Represents both public and private companies in merger and acquisition transactions, including advising boards and outside board members on matters of corporate governance, change of control issues, and anti-

takeover strategies. Also represents issuers and underwriters in securities offerings.
**Career:** Former Co-Head of the firm's transactional practices. Former member of firm's executive committee. Listed in two leading legal publications in both corporate finance and healthcare. Prior to joining Alston & Bird in 1978, worked at The White House during the Ford Administration.
**Personal:** BA (1973), MA (1975), JD (1978) - University of Kentucky.

**CUSHING, Paul M**
Alston & Bird LLP, Atlanta
404 881 7578
pcushing@alston.com
*Recommended in Banking & Finance*
**Practice Areas:** Representing both financial institutions and companies in corporate finance transactions, including syndicated financings, secured financings, acquisition financings, asset-based loans, securitizations, structured financings, leveraged and synthetic leases and private placements. Extensive representation of financial institutions and their capital markets groups in the financing of real estate companies.
**Prof. Memberships:** Member of the Business Law Section of the American Bar Association and former chairman of UCC Subcommittee of the Business Law Section of the Georgia State Bar.
**Career:** Member of the firm's Leveraged Capital Group.
**Personal:** BA, magna cum laude, (1984), JD (1987) - Vanderbilt University School of Law.

**DALTON, John**
Troutman Sanders LLP, Atlanta
404 885 3000
*Recommended in Litigation*

**DANIEL, Laurie Webb**
Holland & Knight LLP, Atlanta
404 817 8500
laurie.daniel@hklaw.com
*Recommended in Litigation, Products Liability*
**Practice Areas:** Partner in the firm's Litigation Section, she chairs the Appellate Practice Team at Holland & Knight LLP. Her appellate work frequently addresses business, competition, and medical liability issues, among others. Daniel's active motions practice includes class action and other types of complex litigation. She has substantial experience in the trial courts and has argued before the United States Supreme Court. Daniel has served as a commentator for CNN on Supreme Court arguments and on the faculty of many continuing legal education programs.

**DANIEL JR, Harold T**
Holland & Knight LLP, Atlanta
404 817 8500
harold.daniel@hklaw.com
*Recommended in Litigation*

**Practice Areas:** Partner in the firm's Litigation Section, maintains a firm-wide commercial litigation practice. He has handled many lengthy jury trials and routinely deals with complex factual and legal issues involving antitrust, securities, business torts and commercial law. Daniel represented the Eleventh Circuit on the Standing Committee of the Federal Judiciary of the American Bar Association from 2000-03. He is a Fellow of the American College of Trial Lawyers, a former president of the State Bar of Georgia, and received the Distinguished Service Award of the State Bar of Georgia in 2001.

**DAVID, Todd R**
Alston & Bird LLP, Atlanta
404 881 7357
tdavid@alston.com
*Recommended in Litigation*
**Practice Areas:** D&O litigation, securities litigation, internal investigations and corporate governance, professional liability litigation, complex commercial litigation.
**Prof. Memberships:** State Bar of Georgia.
**Career:** Co-Chair, Alston & Bird Litigation Groups; former member, Firm Management Committee; former Chair, Alston & Bird Securities Litigation Group. Lead counsel in numerous class actions, trials, arbitrations and mediations; law clerk for US District Judge Marvin H Shoob.
**Publications:** Published by Securities Regulation Law Journal, The National Law Journal, The Journal of Investment Compliance, Directors Monthly, The Trial Lawyer, National Association of Corporate Directors, and Legal Times.
**Personal:** BA, Queens College (1982); JD, Northeastern University (1985).

**DAVIS, Lee**
Griffin Cochrane & Marshall, Atlanta
404 523 2000
lcdavis@gcm-atty.com
*Recommended in Construction*
**Practice Areas:** Construction law.
**Prof. Memberships:** American (Litigation and Public Contracts Sections, Forum on Construction Industry) and Atlanta (Alternative Dispute Resolution, Construction, and Litigation Sections) Bar Associations; State Bar of Georgia.
**Career:** President and Shareholder, Griffin Cochrane & Marshall; Martindale-Hubbell AV-rated; listed in 'The Best Lawyers in America' (2005-06); selected by peers as 'Georgia Superlawyer' in construction (2004-06 by Atlanta Magazine). Lead counsel in complex cases in court (trials before both judges and juries), arbitration, negotiation, and mediation, throughout the nation and internationally in disputes relating to power plants, industrial facilities, wastewater treatment plants, hotels, resorts, condominiums, shopping centers, hospitals, office build-

ings, and apartments.
**Publications:** Co-author: Construction Law for Builders, Owners and Designers' (1999); 'Design-Build Strategies' (1999); 'Environmental Problems of the Georgia Jobsite' (1992). Lecturer: 'Practical Construction Law', Federal Publications (1989-91; 2000-06); 'Masters Institute in Construction Contracting', Federal Publications (2000-06); 'Design-Build Construction', Centers for Disease Control and Prevention, Atlanta, GA (2004); 'Fundamentals of Construction Law', Sterling Education Services (2004); 'Construction Contracts Year in Review Conference', Thomson-West (2003); 'Construction Management', American Institute for Professional Training and Development (2000); 'Design-Build Strategies', American Institute for Professional Training (1999-2000); 'Construction Claims', American Institute for Professional Training (1997-99); 'Environmental Problems on the Georgia Jobsite', Federal Publications (1992); 'Construction Law', The American Law Center in Moscow, Russia (1992); 'Architect/Engineer Liability under Georgia Law' (1988); 'Construction Law', Colorado State University (1983).
**Personal:** Emory University (JD, 1982; Order of Barristers); Williams College (BA, magna cum laude, 1978; Phi Beta Kappa). Commercial pilot and flight instructor.

**DEAKINS JR, Homer L**
Ogletree, Deakins, Nash, Smoak & Stewart, PC, Atlanta 404 881 1300
homer.deakins@ogletreedeakins.com
*Recommended in Employment*
**Practice Areas:** Labor and employment law, employment litigation.
**Prof. Memberships:** Bar Associations of: GA, DC, NY, SC, TN, TX, American Bar Association.
**Career:** Admitted Georgia, South Carolina, Tennessee, Texas, DC, New York, US Supreme Court, US Court of Appeals (Second, Fourth, Fifth, Sixth, Eleventh Circuits, DC), US District Courts (South Carolina; Northern, Middle, Southern Georgia; Eastern and Middle Tennessee; DC; Southern and Eastern Texas; Southern Alabama). Listed in 'The Best Lawyers in America'; Fellow, College of Labor and Employment Lawyers.
**Personal:** Southern Methodist University (BA, 1957), University of Texas School of Law (LLB, cum laude, 1960).

**DEANE JR, Richard H**
Jones Day, Atlanta
404 581 8502
rhdeane@jonesday.com
*Recommended in Litigation*
**Practice Areas:** Corporate criminal investigations and general litigation practice. Served as Chief of the Criminal Division of the US Attorneys' Office and as a US magistrate judge. Experienced in all

aspects of grand jury operations and investigations. Appointed by President Clinton as US attorney for the Northern District of Georgia, where the office successfully prosecuted numerous cases and defended the government in civil suits. Served on the Attorney General's Advisory Committee to offer advice on policy matters and substantive issues.
**Publications:** Lectured extensively on grand jury practice and procedures. Adjunct Professor, Georgia State University College of Law.

### DEGNAN, Peter
Alston & Bird LLP, Atlanta
404 881 7743
pdegnan@alston.com
*Recommended in Energy*
**Practice Areas:** Focuses practice on energy law, legal issues impacting secondary educational institutions and environmental litigation.
**Prof. Memberships:** Member of the State Bar of Georgia, Atlanta Bar Association.
**Personal:** BS, US Naval Academy (1968); JD, Syracuse University (1976).

### DEHIHNS III, Lee A
Alston & Bird LLP, Atlanta
404 881 7151
ldehihns@alston.com
*Recommended in Environment*
**Practice Areas:** Concentrates on regulatory, environmental and environment defense litigation matters, including corporate audits, compliance program development, debarment, white-collar criminal defense, hazardous waste, air quality, water quality and wetlands matters.
**Prof. Memberships:** Member of the Council of the American Bar Association's Section of Environment, Energy and Resources, Chair of Strategic Planning Committee, previous Chair of Water Quality and Wetlands Committee.
**Career:** Frequent speaker and author on water quality and quantity, corporate environmental responsibility, and citizen suits. Listed in a leading US legal publication.
**Personal:** BS, University of Scranton (1967); JD, Catholic University of America (1974).

### DEMPSTER, Hazen
Troutman Sanders LLP, Atlanta
404 885 3000
*Recommended in Banking & Finance*

### DENT, Leslie
Paul, Hastings, Janofsky & Walker LLP, Atlanta 404 815 2233
lesliedent@paulhastings.com
*Recommended in Employment*
**Practice Areas:** Practice involves all aspects of employment litigation and counseling for private employers. Has tried nearly 25 cases, most of which were individual employment discrimination cases. Also represents employers in class action litigation and multiple plaintiff

cases.
**Prof. Memberships:** American Bar Association Labor and Employment Law Section, State Bar of Georgia, Atlanta Bar Association.
**Career:** Partner at Paul, Hastings, Janofsky & Walker LLP.
**Personal:** Received her BA Degree, magna cum laude with honors, in 1980 from Vanderbilt University, and JD Degree in 1983 from Northwestern University School of Law.

### DIAL, David
Weinberg, Wheeler, Hudgins, Gunn & Dial, LLC, Atlanta 404 876 2700
*Recommended in Construction*

### DICKERSON JR, W Brinkley
Troutman Sanders LLP, Atlanta
404 885 3000
*Recommended in Corporate/M&A*

### DOBBS, C Edward
Parker, Hudson, Rainer & Dobbs LLP, Atlanta 404 523 5300
*Recommended in Banking & Finance, Bankruptcy*

### DOMBY, Arthur
Troutman Sanders LLP, Atlanta
404 885 3000
*Recommended in Environment*

### DORRIS, William
Kilpatrick Stockton LLP, Atlanta
404 815 6104
BDorris@KilpatrickStockton.com
*Recommended in Construction*
**Practice Areas:** Though much of his practice is focused on assisting clients in avoiding construction disputes or resolving them through mediation or other alternative dispute resolution methods, he has been extensively involved in trials, arbitrations, and administrative proceedings.
**Prof. Memberships:** State Bar of Georgia; Kentucky Bar Association; American Bar Association.
**Publications:** Has written a number of articles on construction law, and co-authored the two volume book, 'Construction Disputes: Practice Guide with Forms'.
**Personal:** BA, University of Kentucky, high Distinction, Phi Beta Kappa, 1976; JD, University of Kentucky, High Distinction, Order of the Coif, 1979.

### DORSEY, Rufus
Parker, Hudson, Rainer & Dobbs LLP, Atlanta 404 523 5300
*Recommended in Bankruptcy*

### DOUGLAS, John L
Alston & Bird LLP, Atlanta
404 881 7880
jdouglas@alston.com
*Recommended in Banking & Finance, Financial Services*
**Practice Areas:** Regulation of financial institutions, mergers, acquisitions and other transactions.
**Prof. Memberships:** Steering Commit-

tee, Financial Services Volunteer Corps.; member, State Bar of Georgia and Bar of Washington DC; member, Executive Committee, Banking Law Section, Federal Bar Association.
**Career:** General Counsel, Federal Deposit Insurance Corporation (1987-89); Listed in four leading legal publications with regard to banking law.
**Publications:** Chairman, Editorial Board, Electronic Banking Law and Commerce Report.
**Personal:** BA, cum laude, Davidson College (1972); JD, magna cum laude, University of Georgia (1977).

### DOWDY, L Craig
McKenna Long & Aldridge LLP, Atlanta
404 527 4180
cdowdy@mckennalong.com
*Recommended in Energy*
**Practice Areas:** Heads the firm's Energy Practice, focuses on state and federal public utility law, energy, telecommunications and campaign and election law. Work includes strategic counseling and commercial and regulatory litigation for corporate clients. Practice also includes commercial litigation and public policy representation. Previously served as manager of business and product planning responsible for strategic planning, product development and marketing communications when he left Westinghouse Power Systems to practice law.
**Prof. Memberships:** 2000 George W Bush for President Campaign, Cobb County Co-Chairman, Georgia Steering Committee, and Finance Committee; 2000 George W Bush Recount Team - West Palm Beach, Florida; Barr for Congress Campaign Chairman, Treasurer, and Counsel; Saxby Chambliss for Senate Leadership Council; Governor-Elect Sonny Perdue Inaugural Committee; Cobb County Republican Party, General Counsel; Coverdell Leadership Institute; Georgia Republican Foundation; Georgia Republican Lawyers Foundation; Georgia Republican Party, State Committee; Georgia State Bar; National Moot Court Committee (Past Chairman); Federalist Society, American Bar Association, Atlanta Bar Association, Georgia State Bar-Young Lawyers Section, Georgia Chamber Government Affairs Council.
**Personal:** JD, Georgia State University College of Law, 1988. BS, Electrical Engineering, Auburn University, 1979. Has been listed as one of the Best Lawyers in Atlanta in Atlanta Magazine. He is the Endowment Board Chairman and a member of the Vestry of St Peter St Paul Episcopal Church.

### DUEDALL, Mark I
Alston & Bird LLP, Atlanta
404 881 7887
mduedall@alston.com
*Recommended in Bankruptcy*
**Practice Areas:** Concentrates on bank-

ruptcy and related litigation; debtor's and creditors' commitee counsel. Represented court appointed Examiner in the Enron Corp. case, focusing on bankruptcy aspects of structured finance and derivatives.
**Publications:** Editor, Norton's 'Bankruptcy Law and Practice'.
**Personal:** BS, Florida State University (1991); JD, Emory University (1994), Executive Managing Editor, Bankruptcy Developments Journal.

### DUFFIE, L Traywick
Hunton & Williams, Atlanta
404 888 4004
tduffie@hunton.com
*Recommended in Employment*
**Practice Areas:** Mr Duffie advises, represents and defends management and corporate clients on all employment issues including affirmative action/OFCCP, union organizing, discrimination, OSHA, trade secret and employment noncompetition issues. He defends management and corporate clients in employment litigation (discrimination, harassment, wage-hour, safety related and ERISA). He designs and implements compliance and preventive programs on avoiding discrimination and other employment litigation, staying union-free, building employee morale. He has been recognized by his peers as a Georgia Legal Elite, a Top 100 Super Lawyer, and among the Best Lawyers in America.
**Prof. Memberships:** State Bars of Georgia and Florida; American Bar Association.

### DUNLEVIE Steven S
Womble Carlyle Sandridge & Rice, PLLC, Atlanta 404 888 7401
sdunlevie@wcsr.com
*Recommended in Banking & Finance*
**Practice Areas:** Mr Dunlevie has advised 250+ financial services companies as special counsel on regulatory compliance, corporate governance, capital formation, mergers/acquisitions, 'de novo' bank organization and problem asset resolution.
**Prof. Memberships:** State Bar of Georgia; Atlanta and American Bar Associations; Board of Directors, Georgia and Metro Atlanta Chambers of Commerce; Board of Visitors, University of North Carolina.
**Career:** Leader, Bank Regulatory Team of Capital Markets Practice Group; Managing Member, Atlanta; Member, Firm Management Committee. Founding Partner, Parker, Johnson, Cook & Dunlevie, which merged with Womble Carlyle in 1996.
**Personal:** JD, 1973, Emory University; AB, 1970, University of North Carolina.

## EGAN, Michael
King & Spalding LLP, Atlanta
404 572 4753
megan@kslaw.com
*Recommended in Corporate/M&A*
**Practice Areas:** Mergers and acquisitions, joint ventures and strategic alliances. Substantial experience representing international companies in cross-border transactions. Serves as counsel for the Atlanta Falcons NFL franchise. Served as European Transactions Counsel to The Coca-Cola Company.
**Prof. Memberships:** American Bar Association; International Bar Association; State Bar of Georgia.
**Personal:** BA, University of North Carolina, 1978; JD, cum laude, Harvard University, Phi Beta Kappa, 1982; Morehead Scholar, University of North Carolina.

## ELGISON, Martin J
Alston & Bird LLP, Atlanta
404 881 7167
melgison@alston.com
*Recommended in Intellectual Property*
**Practice Areas:** Founder and Co-Coordinator of the firm's Intellectual Property Practice Groups and leader of the Intellectual Property-Transactional Group. Practices in all facets of intellectual property law with a focus on sports, media, technology and electronic commerce.
**Career:** Listed in a leading US legal publication since 1991-92.
**Publications:** Spoken and written frequently on intellectual property matters, including copyright protection for computer screen displays, the use of metatags and hyperlinks, the Digital Millenium Copyright Act, and intellectual property litigation.
**Personal:** BA, University of South Florida (1972); JD, cum laude, University of Miami, (1981).

## ELLMAN, Jeffrey B
Jones Day, Atlanta
404 581 8309
jbellman@jonesday.com
*Recommended in Bankruptcy*
**Practice Areas:** Oversees the Business Restructuring and Reorganization Practice in the Atlanta Office, focusing primarily on corporate bankruptcy, restructuring, bankruptcy litigation, and other insolvency-related matters. He has provided insolvency-related advice to clients in litigation and transactional contexts and has participated in out-of-court restructurings. In addition, he counsels clients on fraudulent conveyance, illegal dividend, preferential transfer, fiduciary duty, and corporate formalities issues and has represented entities in the related structuring and consummation of spin-offs, recapitalizations, and other corporate transactions. Recognized as a leading bankruptcy attorney in various publications.
**Prof. Memberships:** American Bank-

ruptcy Institute; Turnaround Management Association; Atlanta Bar Association.

## ENSOR, R Steve
Alston & Bird LLP, Atlanta
404 881 7448
sensor@alston.com
*Recommended in Employment*
**Practice Areas:** Representing management for over 19 years in all areas of labor and employment law, including employment litigation, traditional labor union relations and affirmative action planning.
**Prof. Memberships:** Member of the State Bar of Georgia, the Georgia Bar Association and the American Bar Association.
**Publications:** Lectured and written extensively in all areas of labor and employment law. Frequent speaker and panelist for the American Management Association and the Institute for Applied Management and Law.
**Personal:** BA, Duke University (1982); JD, Wake Forest University (1985).

## ERNST, Andrew
Hunter, Maclean, Exley & Dunn, PC, Savannah 912 236 0261
*Recommended in Environment*

## EWING, Jim
Kilpatrick Stockton LLP, Atlanta
404 815 6494
JEwing@KilpatrickStockton.com
*Recommended in Intellectual Property*
**Practice Areas:** Intellectual property strategy, patent litigation and patent portfolio prosecution and management.
**Prof. Memberships:** Patent Bar of the United States; American Intellectual Property Law Association; American Bar Association; State Bar of Georgia; Atlanta Bar Association; Practicing Law Institute Annual Program on Patent Litigation (Co-Chair); Federalist Society's IP Committee (Chair).
**Career:** Partner since 1989.
**Publications:** Writing and speaking credits include Co-Chair, Practicing Law Institute Program on Patent Litigation (1996- 2001, 2005), Chair, PLI How to Prepare and Conduct Markman Hearings (2004).
**Personal:** BS, Aerospace Engineering, United States Naval Academy, 1973; JD, University of Virginia Law School, 1981.

## FALSTAD, Daniel T
Kilpatrick Stockton LLP, Atlanta
404 815 6565
DFalstad@KilpatrickStockton.com
*Recommended in Corporate/M&A*
**Practice Areas:** Corporate finance and securities transactions, focusing on representation of issuers in public offerings, including initial public offerings, and private placements; public and private company mergers and acquisitions; advice regarding compliance with the disclosure, reporting and corporate governance

requirements applicable to public companies.
**Prof. Memberships:** Past Chair and Member of Board of Directors of Business & Finance Section of Atlanta Bar Association; American Bar Association (Business Law Section); State Bar of Georgia.
**Personal:** Yale Law School (JD, 1985); Duke University (BA, summa cum laude, 1982).

## FARRIS JR, James G
Alston & Bird LLP, Atlanta
404 881 7896
jfarris@alston.com
*Recommended in Real Estate*
**Practice Areas:** Real estate; commercial real estate investment; development and leasing
**Prof. Memberships:** Pension Real Estate Association (PREA); Association of Foreign Investors in US Real Estate (AFIRE); State Bar of Georgia; Atlanta Bar Association.
**Career:** Extensive experience representing and counseling pension funds and their advisors, other institutional investors, as well as developers, in various aspects of real estate law. 'Cradle to grave' practice including land acquisition, development, joint ventures, redevelopment, protective covenants, financing, acquisitions, leasing and sales.
**Publications:** Frequent speaker and writer on commercial real estate issues.
**Personal:** BA, Wesleyan University (1984); JD, University of North Carolina (1989).

## FEESE, Suzanne
King & Spalding LLP, Atlanta
404 572 4600
sfeese@kslaw.com
*Recommended in Tax*
**Practice Areas:** Represents clients in all stages of the IRS administrative process and in tax litigation. Extensive experience in a wide range of business/transactional tax areas, with particular emphasis on the taxation of partnerships, taxation of foreign persons with US activities, and the representation of clients in complex partnership and structured financing transactions.
**Prof. Memberships:** State Bar of Georgia; American Bar Association (Member, Tax Section).
**Personal:** BA, Agnes Scott College, 1984, valedictorian; JD Yale University, 1987.

## FERDINANDS, Paul
King & Spalding LLP, Atlanta
404 572 3450
pferdinands@kslaw.com
*Recommended in Bankruptcy*
**Practice Areas:** Bankruptcy and commercial matters, focusing on representing parties in connection with transactions occurring in Chapter 11 cases, debtors in connection with business bankruptcy cases and with the bankruptcy aspects of

structured finance transactions. Represents Chapter 11 debtors in a variety of industries, creditors' committees, parties in connection with the purchase and sale of secured and unsecured claims, institutional lenders extending debtor-in-possession financings, and companies in out-of-court debt restructurings.
**Prof. Memberships:** American Bar Association; Atlanta Bar Association (Member, Section on Banking and Bankruptcy); State Bar of Georgia.
**Personal:** BA, magna cum laude, University of Virginia,1983; JD, Stanford University, 1986.

## FLEMING, John H
Sutherland Asbill & Brennan LLP, Atlanta 404 853 8065
john.fleming@sablaw.com
*Recommended in Litigation*
**Practice Areas:** Chaired Sutherland's Litigation Group (1999-2004). Experienced in complex business litigation, including franchise, professional liability, intellectual property, tax and securities. Experienced as an attorney and arbitrator in alternative dispute resolution mechanisms. Serves as Eastern Regional Counsel for dealer and general litigation for an automobile manufacturer. Trial counsel in successful nine-figure claim against United States, respondent's counsel in successful defense of $90,000,000 arbitration claim against brokerage firm, favorable jury verdicts in state and federal court in Georgia and elsewhere, and an arbitration award for an insurance company in excess of $55,000,000. Handled an appointed death penalty case, from 1980 through 1992, in which he had the death penalty reversed once by the United States Supreme Court and twice by the Georgia Supreme Court, and finally won before a jury. Served as an Adjunct Professor at Emory Law School.
**Career:** Clerked in Dallas with Judge Irving Goldberg of the US Court of Appeals for the Fifth Circuit.
**Personal:** JD, magna cum laude, Harvard Law School, 1975, senior editor, 'Harvard Law Review'; MA, Florida State University, 1972; BA, Emory University, 1970, Phi Beta Kappa.

## FLEMING, Joycelyn L
Ford & Harrison LLP, Atlanta
404 888 3888
jfleming@fordharrison.com
*Recommended in Immigration*
**Practice Areas:** Joyce Fleming has practiced immigration law exclusively for almost 20 years. She handles visa work for businesses relocating entire offices to the United States and other clients with high volume immigration needs, as well as clients with one-time hiring requirements. She frequently consults with corporate lawyers regarding the immigration implications of mergers and acquisitions and handles the necessary visa work for

any individuals affected. Joyce received her Law Degree from Georgia State University.

### FLETCHER, Jennifer
Griffin Cochrane & Marshall, Atlanta
404 523 2000
jwfletcher@gcm-atty.com
*Recommended in Construction*
**Practice Areas:** Construction industry issues exclusively.
**Prof. Memberships:** American College of Construction Lawyers (Fellow); Lumpkin Inn of Court (Master); American Arbitration Association (Construction Arbitrator); ABA (Forum on the Construction Industry; Public Contracts, Litigation Sections); Atlanta Bar Association (Construction, Litigation Sections); State Bar of Georgia; The Florida Bar.
**Career:** Shareholder since 1988.
**Publications:** Managing Complex Construction Cases (ABA); Discovery Deskbook for Construction Disputes (ABA, contributor); Construction Defects: Water Intrusion & Other Calamities; Construction Contracts Year in Review; Practical Construction Law; Design-Build Strategies.
**Personal:** University of Georgia School of Law (JD cum laude, 1981); University of Florida (BA high honors, 1978).

### FLINN, Patrick J
Alston & Bird LLP, Atlanta
404 881 7920
pflinn@alston.com
*Recommended in Intellectual Property*
**Practice Areas:** Focuses practice on the resolution of technology-based disputes, particularly patent, trade secret and copyright litigation.
**Prof. Memberships:** Chair of National Law Alumni Board of Georgetown University Law Center.
**Career:** Listed in a leading US legal publication.
**Publications:** Writer and lecturer on subjects of law and technology. Author of the 'Handbook of Intellectual Property Claims and Remedies'. Speaks regularly at national CLE presentations on patent law, computer law and other technology subjects.
**Personal:** AB, Stanford University (1978); JD, Georgetown University (1982).

### FLOYD, John
Bondurant, Mixson & Elmore, LLP, Atlanta 404 881 4159
floyd@bmelaw.com
*Recommended in Litigation*
**Practice Areas:** Extensive experience in business torts litigation, particularly civil litigation under federal and state Racketeer Influenced and Corrupt Organizations (RICO) statutes. Has also worked as a special prosecutor in two of the state of Georgia's largest RICO prosecutions. Also experienced in litigation under the Federal False Claims Act and the conduct of

corporate internal investigations.
**Prof. Memberships:** Member: American Bar Association (Chair: Antitrust Section Civil RICO Committee, 1997-2001); State Bar of Georgia; Atlanta Bar Association; Special Assistant Attorney General, State of Georgia, 1997-2000; Special Assistant District Attorney, Augusta, 1997-2000, and Stone Mountain Judicial Districts; Member: Fulton County Board of Ethics, 1998-2004; Faculty Member: National College of District Attorneys, White Collar Crime Course, 2002-05.
**Publications:** 'RICO State by State: A Guide to Litigation Under the State Racketeering Statutes' (American Bar Association, Section of Antitrust Law, 1998); 'The Right Against Self-Incrimination in Civil Litigation' (American Bar Association, Section of Antitrust Law, 2001)(editor and chapter author).
**Personal:** AB Degree, with honors, Brown University, 1980; JD Degree, Emory University, 1983.

### FORRY, Robert
Troutman Sanders LLP, Atlanta
404 885 3000
*Recommended in Energy*

### FORTE, Stephen
Smith Gambrell & Russell LLP, Atlanta
404 815 3500
*Recommended in Litigation*

### FOWLER, Lynn E
Kilpatrick Stockton LLP, Atlanta
404 815 6500
lfowler@kilpatrickstockton.com
*Recommended in Tax*
**Practice Areas:** Develops and implements tax-efficient strategies for varied business formation, financing, operation, acquisition, and disposition transactions.
**Prof. Memberships:** American Bar Association (Taxation Section; Committee on Partnership Taxation), State Bar of Georgia (Taxation Section), International Fiscal Association, and Atlanta Tax Forum.
**Career:** Partner since 1995.
**Publications:** Has lectured and written extensively about a variety of tax matters.
**Personal:** BS Accounting, University of Alabama, 1982; JD, University of Alabama, 1986; LLM Taxation, New York University School of Law, 1987.

### FOX, Steven
Rogers & Hardin, Atlanta
404 522 4700
*Recommended in Corporate/M&A*

### FRYER, William
King & Spalding LLP, Atlanta
404 572 4911
bfryer@kslaw.com
*Recommended in Real Estate*
**Practice Areas:** Mergers, acquisitions, funds formation and project developments with emphasis on real estate securitizations.
**Prof. Memberships:** American Bar

Association; Atlanta Bar Association; State Bar of Georgia; University of Virginia School of Law (Alumni Council).
**Personal:** BA, University of Virginia, 1971; JD, University of Virginia, Phi Beta Kappa, Omicron Delta Kappa, Order of the Coif, 1974.

### FUSSELL, Herman
Shapiro Fussell, Atlanta
404 870 2200
*Recommended in Construction*

### GALLO, Barbara
Epstein Becker & Green PC, Atlanta
404 923 9048
bgallo@ebglaw.com
*Recommended in Environment*
**Practice Areas:** Barbara H Gallo is a member of the firm in EBG's Atlanta office, practicing in Environmental Litigation. She handles permitting and compliance issues for new and existing facilities in all areas of environmental law, represents potentially responsible parties at State and Federal Superfund sites, handles civil and administrative litigation, negotiates civil enforcement matters, advises and counsels on rulemaking issues, and assists in corporate and real estate transactions.
**Prof. Memberships:** American Bar Association, Environment, Energy & Resources Section; State Bar of Georgia, Environmental Law Section (Chair 1995); Atlanta Bar Association, Environmental and Toxic Tort Section (Member of Board of Directors, 1998-2001, Chair 2002); Georgia State University Alumni Association Board of Directors (Member of the Executive Committee, 2000-01).

### GARRETT, G Lee
Jones Day, Atlanta
404 581 8013
ggarrett@jonesday.com
*Recommended in Litigation*
**Practice Areas:** Oversees the Litigation Practice in the Atlanta Office. His practice emphasizes complex litigation and has involved First Amendment, product liability, construction, contract, and environmental-related issues; and First Amendment litigation, libel, slander, defamation, and causes of action arising under the Fair Credit Reporting Act. Has argued cases before US District Courts, US Courts of Appeal, the US Supreme Court, the US Government Board of Contract Appeals, the EPA, and various state and local courts.
**Prof. Memberships:** American Board of Trial Advocates.
**Publications:** Written and lectured extensively, including seminars sponsored by The National Law Journal and the Practising Law Institute.

### GENBERG, Ira
Smith Gambrell & Russell LLP, Atlanta
404 815 3500
*Recommended in Construction*

### GENZ, Peter
King & Spalding LLP, Atlanta
404 572 4935
pgenz@kslaw.com
*Recommended in Tax*
**Practice Areas:** Tax lawyer concentrating on corporate, partnership, and real estate tax matters, and also tax controversies. Particularly qualified in matters relating to structuring inbound foreign investment, real estate investment trusts and troubled company workouts.
**Prof. Memberships:** American Bar Association; State Bar of Georgia; The Florida Bar.
**Personal:** MLT, Georgetown University, 1982; JD, University of Florida, 1980; BSBA, University of Florida, 1975.

### GERAKITIS, Richard
Troutman Sanders LLP, Atlanta
404 885 3000
*Recommended in Employment*

### GILLEN, Craig
Gillen Parker & Withers LLC, Atlanta
404 842 9700
*Recommended in Litigation*

### GOLDEN, Jonathan
Arnall Golden Gregory LLP, Atlanta
404 873 8700
jonathan.golden@agg.com
*Recommended in Corporate/M&A*
**Practice Areas:** Mr Golden practices primarily in the areas of corporate and mergers and acquisitions. He is listed in the 'Best Lawyers in America' and is Chairman of the firm.
**Prof. Memberships:** Adjunct Professor, Emory Law School (Securities and Corporate Finance, 1974-79; Mergers and Acquisitions, 1988-89); American Bar Association; State Bar of Georgia.
**Career:** Director, The Profit Recovery Group International, Inc. (NASDAQ), 1996-2005; Director, Sysco Corporation (NYSE) 1983-present; Director, Intermedics, Inc. (NYSE) 1983-88*; Director, Automatic Service Company (AMEX) 1970-76*; Director, Butler Shoe Corp. (NYSE) 1965-68*; Director, Rich Products Corporation; Chairman, The Livingston Foundation; Trustee, The Southern Center for International Studies; Member, Board of Counselors, The Carter Center. (*Company acquired at last date).
**Personal:** Harvard Law School (LLB, 1962); Princeton University (AB, 1959).

### GOODWIN, Timothy J
King & Spalding LLP, Atlanta
404 572 3588
tgoodwin@kslaw.com
*Recommended in Real Estate*
**Practice Areas:** Real estate lawyer experienced in structuring and formation of investment funds, sales and acquisitions, financing, development, construction and leasing. Also experienced in dealing with REITs and tax-exempt pension fund

investors, often requiring complex tax and ERISA structuring.

**Prof. Memberships:** American Bar Association; Atlanta Bar Association; New York State Bar Association; State Bar of Georgia (Real Property Law Section).

**Personal:** BA, summa cum laude, Boston College 1987; JD, with distinction, Emory University,1990.

## GORDON, David L
Jackson Lewis, Atlanta
404 525 8200
GordonD@jacksonlewis.com
*Recommended in Employment*

**Practice Areas:** Employment counseling and litigation.

**Prof. Memberships:** American Bar Association.

**Career:** Joined Jackson Lewis in 1983. Elevated to Partner in 1990.

**Publications:** 'Sexual Harassment Claims After Vinson: Will the Floodgates Swing Open?' and 'The Americans with Disabilities Act of 1990: Questions, Answers and Compliance Strategies', both published in The Atlanta Lawyer, the publication of the Atlanta Bar Association.

**Personal:** University of North Carolina at Chapel Hill, JD, 1983 and BS, 1978; George Washington University, MA, Legislative Affairs, 1980. DOB 7 August 1956. Married with three daughters. Enjoys spending time with his family and playing golf.

## GRADY, Kevin E
Alston & Bird LLP, Atlanta
404 881 7164
kgrady@alston.com
*Recommended in Antitrust*

**Practice Areas:** Competition and trade regulation matters; litigation and counseling.

**Prof. Memberships:** Past Chair of the ABA Section of Antitrust Law, 2004-05; Elected Member of American Law Institute.

**Career:** Member of US Delegation to International Competition Network, Merida, Mexico, 2003. Listed in three leading legal publications.

**Publications:** Co-Editor, 'Georgia Hospital Law Manual' (4th ed 1997); author of Georgia Chapter in 'State Antitrust Practice and Statutes' (3rd ed 2004); author of 'A Framework for Antitrust Analysis of Health Care Joint Ventures', 61 Antitrust Law Journal 765.

**Personal:** AB, Vanderbilt University (1969); JD, Harvard Law School (1974).

## GRAVES, Judson
Alston & Bird LLP, Atlanta
404 881 7279
jgraves@alston.com
*Recommended in Litigation*

**Practice Areas:** Concentrates practice in jury trial work with emphasis on products liability, medical malpractice and intellectual property.

**Prof. Memberships:** Member of State Bar of Georgia, Florida Bar, Atlanta Bar Association, American Bar Association, and Lawyers Club of Atlanta.

**Career:** Fellow of the American College of Trial Lawyers.

**Publications:** Published in Journal of the Medical Association of Georgia, Journal of College and University Law and Georgia State Bar Journal.

**Personal:** BA, Dartmouth College (1969); JD, with distinction, Emory University School of Law (1975).

## GREENE, Kevin
Troutman Sanders LLP, Atlanta
404 885 3000
*Recommended in Energy*

## GRICE, Richard
Alston & Bird LLP, Atlanta
404 881 7576
rgrice@alston.com
*Recommended in Banking & Finance*

**Practice Areas:** Emphasizes representation of domestic and foreign commercial banks, underwriters and debt issuers in financings including recapitalizations, leveraged buyouts and other acquisition financings, public debt issues, private placements, cross-border financings and various asset-based financings. He also represents creditors and debtors in pre-bankruptcy restructurings and Chapter 11 proceedings.

**Career:** Listed in a leading US legal publication for the years 1998-2006. Named as a 'Super Lawyer' in the State of Georgia.

**Publications:** Written and lectured on numerous topics of interest to commercial lenders and borrowers.

**Personal:** BA, University of Wisconsin (1981); JD, Cornell University (1984).

## GRIFFIN, John
Troutman Sanders LLP, Atlanta
404 885 3000
*Recommended in Real Estate*

## GROUT, Robert
Troutman Sanders LLP, Atlanta
404 885 3000
*Recommended in Corporate/M&A*

## HAFER, Randall F
Kilpatrick Stockton LLP, Atlanta
404 815 6289
RHafer@KilpatrickStockton.com
*Recommended in Construction*

**Practice Areas:** Focuses primarily on the representation of owners on a wide variety of construction projects, including mass transit systems, power plants, waste water treatment plants, bridges and highways, hospitals, office buildings, sports arenas, schools, resorts, manufacturing and processing plants and tunnels.

**Prof. Memberships:** American Underground Construction Association.

**Career:** Head of the firm's Construction and Public Contracts Group; member of firm's Executive Committee.

**Publications:** Has lectured and written extensively on a variety of construction industry topics.

**Personal:** BS, Georgia State University, cum laude, 1975; JD, with high honors, University of Tennessee, 1983.

## HAGER, Ashley
Troutman Sanders LLP, Atlanta
404 885 3000
*Recommended in Employment*

## HARDIN, Edward
Rogers & Hardin, Atlanta
404 522 4700
*Recommended in Corporate/M&A*

## HARE, Gregory J
Ogletree, Deakins, Nash, Smoak & Stewart, PC, Atlanta 404 881 1300
greg.hare@ogletreedeakins.com
*Recommended in Employment*

**Practice Areas:** All aspects of labor and employment law, including discrimination and harassment claims, union avoidance, labor litigation, restrictive covenants, franchise disputes.

**Prof. Memberships:** American, Georgia and Atlanta Bar Associations, Lawyers Club of Atlanta, Society for Human Resource Management.

**Career:** Shareholder since 1998. Admitted to US Supreme Court, 11th, 8th & 6th Circuits, all courts in Georgia. Recognized as Rising Star by Georgia Super Lawyers publication.

**Publications:** Frequent publisher and speaker on human resources and employment issues.

**Personal:** LeMoyne College, Industrial and Labor Relations (BS Cum Laude, 1988); University of North Carolina (JD With Honors, 1991).

## HARRIS, Morton
Hatcher, Stubbs, Land, Hollis & Rothschild, LLP, Columbus 706 324 0201
*Recommended in Tax*

## HARRIS JR, H Stephen
Alston & Bird LLP, Atlanta
404 881 7197
sharris@alston.com
*Recommended in Antitrust*

**Practice Areas:** Concentrates practice on US and transnational antitrust litigation, as well as other complex commercial litigation and arbitration.

**Prof. Memberships:** Member of the Council of the ABA Antitrust Section.

**Career:** Listed in a leading legal publication. Selected as a leading competition lawyer by another leading legal publication.

**Publications:** Editor-in-Chief and author of the Overview chapter of the two-volume ABA treatise, 'Competition Laws Outside the United States'.

**Personal:** AB, magna cum laude, Cornell University (1977); JD, Columbia University School of Law (1982). Certified with Honors by the Parker Program in International and Foreign Law, Columbia University (1982).

## HASSON JR, James K
Sutherland Asbill & Brennan LLP, Atlanta 404 853 8083
jim.hasson@sablaw.com
*Recommended in Tax*

**Practice Areas:** Practices in the areas of tax, healthcare and finance. Regularly represents closely-held businesses, family offices, universities, private foundations, hospitals and other organizations. Advises clients and resolves conflicts with the IRS and other federal and state governmental agencies. Focuses on the design and negotiation of acquisition or affiliation contracts, financing arrangements, organizational structures and tax planning for business continuity. Has published numerous articles and speaks at various conferences nationwide. Served as a member of the Exempt Organization Advisory Group to the Commissioner of the IRS, and as an Adjunct Professor of Law at Emory University School of Law.

**Prof. Memberships:** Member of the American and Atlanta Bar Associations; former Division Coordinator, ABA's Tax Section to the Tax Exempt and Governmental Entities Division of the IRS; former Chair, the Exempt Organizations Committee of the Tax Section of the ABA; Fellow, the American College of Tax Counsel; member of the National Association of College and University Attorneys and the American Health Lawyers Association.

**Personal:** JD, Duke University School of Law, 1970, Order of the Coif, comment and project editor, Duke Law Journal; BA, Duke University, 1967.

## HAWKINS, Holmes
King & Spalding LLP, Atlanta
404 572 2443
hhawkins@kslaw.com
*Recommended in Intellectual Property*

**Practice Areas:** Intellectual property law, focusing on patent litigation, including patent infringement lawsuits involving computer systems and software, internet-related technologies, telecommunications and electronics systems, financial service models, consumer products, medical devices, patents, trademarks, copyrights and licensing matters.

**Prof. Memberships:** American Bar Association; Atlanta Bar Association; American Intellectual Property Law Association; Georgia Institute of Technology, Atlanta (Visiting Professor); State Bar of Georgia (Intellectual Property Section).

**Personal:** BEE, high honors, Georgia Institute of Technology, 1990; JD, cum laude, University of Georgia, 1993. National Institute of Trial Advocacy, National Trial Skills program, Colorado.

### HAYNES, Joseph B
King & Spalding LLP, Atlanta
404 572 4792
bhaynes@kslaw.com
*Recommended in Litigation*

**Practice Areas:** Civil and commercial litigation, representing accounting firms in malpractice, securities litigation and professional liability matters, including antitrust, commercial contract litigation, franchisor franchisee relationships, internal corporate investigations, class action lawsuits, derivative shareholder suits, civil RICO claims, banking litigation, construction contract suits, corporate espionage and competitive intelligence.
**Prof. Memberships:** American Bar Association; American College of Trial Lawyers; Atlanta Cancer Society; State Bar of Georgia; State Bar of New York; Atlanta Chamber of Commerce (Public Affairs Committee).
**Personal:** BA, University of the South, 1962; LLB, New York University, Phi Beta Kappa, Omicron Delta Kappa, 1965.

### HAYS, Robert D
King & Spalding LLP, Atlanta
404 572 4674
rhays@kslaw.com
*Recommended in Litigation*

**Practice Areas:** Tort litigation lawyer with extensive experience as lead trial counsel in high exposure product liability and other mass tort litigation, and over 20 years of courtroom experience in state and federal courts.
**Prof. Memberships:** American Bar Association (Member, Product Liability Section); Atlanta Bar Association (Member, Product Liability Section); Defense Research Institute; Georgia Defense Lawyers Association; Georgia Product Liability Committee; State Bar of Georgia (Member, General Practice Section).
**Personal:** BA, summa cum laude, University of North Carolina, 1980; JD, Vanderbilt University, 1983.

### HENDERSON, Douglas
Troutman Sanders LLP, Atlanta
404 885 3000
*Recommended in Environment*

### HENDRICK, David
Hendrick, Phillips, Salzman & Flatt P.C., Atlanta 404 522 1410
*Recommended in Construction*

### HENSEL, Donald
King & Spalding LLP, Atlanta
404 572 4644
dhensel@kslaw.com
*Recommended in Tax*

**Practice Areas:** Corporate, partnership, real estate, and international tax matters, with a particular emphasis on corporate mergers, acquisitions and restructuring transactions.
**Prof. Memberships:** Corporate Tax Committee of the Tax Section of the American Bar Association; State Bar of

Georgia.
**Personal:** BA, Rollins College, summa cum laude, 1992; JD, magna cum laude, Harvard Law School, 1995, editor of the 'Harvard Law Review'.

### HINCHEY, John
King & Spalding LLP, Atlanta
404 572 4922
jhinchey@kslaw.com
*Recommended in Construction*

**Practice Areas:** Construction and commercial contracting matters, including large capital companies; consulting firms; private and public schools and universities; state, city and county governments; public authorities; medical institutions; public utilities; private developers and owners; and design professionals.
**Prof. Memberships:** American Arbitration Association; American Bar Association; American College of Construction Lawyers; Atlanta Bar Association; Chartered Institute of Arbitrators; International Bar Association; London Court of International Arbitration; State Bar of Georgia.
**Personal:** AB, Emory University, 1964; LLB, Emory University, 1965; MLitt, Oxford University, 1980; LLM, Harvard University, 1966.

### HISHON, Robert
The Hishon Firm, LLC, Atlanta
404 817 7791
*Recommended in Tax*

### HOBBS JR, Michael
Troutman Sanders LLP, Atlanta
404 885 3000
*Recommended in Intellectual Property*

### HODGES, Charles
Chamberlain Hrdlicka White Williams & Martin, Atlanta 404 659 1410
*Recommended in Tax*

### HOGFOSS, Robert
Hunton & Williams, Atlanta
404 888 4042
rhogfoss@hunton.com
*Recommended in Environment*

**Practice Areas:** Robert Hogfoss' practice focuses exclusively on energy, environmental and administrative law, with emphasis on Pipeline Safety Act, Clean Water Act, Oil Pollution Act, RCRA, CERCLA and TSCA issues. Experience in compliance advice, enforcement defense, administrative adjudication and environmental litigation. Representative clients: oil and natural gas pipelines, chemical manufacturers and the pulp and paper industry. Recognized by Chambers 'Clients' Guide to Leading US Business Lawyers' as a leading lawyer in the Environmental Practice, and as one of the top Georgia Environmental/Land Use lawyers, selected by Georgia attorneys and published in Atlanta Magazine and Georgia Super Lawyers Magazine, March 2005.

### HOLDEN, G Graham
Jones Day, Atlanta
404 581 8220
ggholden@jonesday.com
*Recommended in Environment*

**Practice Areas:** Advises electric utilities, petro-chemical companies, and cement manufacturers in the interpretation, administration, and enforcement of environmental regulatory laws. His practice concentrates on the Clean Air Act and related state air quality laws, where he assists clients in the application, negotiation, and adjudication of air operating permits. He also advises clients on the creation of new air quality laws and related regulations.
**Prof. Memberships:** State Bar of Georgia, The Florida Bar, ABA, Air and Waste Management Association, Environmental Law Institute.

### HORDER, Richard
Kilpatrick Stockton LLP, Atlanta
404 815 6538
RHorder@KilpatrickStockton.com
*Recommended in Environment*

**Practice Areas:** Experienced in all areas of environmental law, from negotiating permits through litigating environmental cases, particularly water, wetlands, waste, and endangered species matters.
**Prof. Memberships:** State Bar of Georgia; The Florida Bar; American Bar Association.
**Career:** Assistant United States Attorney, Northern District of Georgia (Civil Division) (1974-77); Associate General Counsel, Georgia-Pacific Corporation (1978-89).
**Publications:** Authored numerous papers on environmental law, toxic tort litigation, and litigation management, and a frequent seminar lecturer on these subjects.
**Personal:** BA, University of Florida, 1968; JD, University of Florida, 1971; LLM, London School of Economics and Political Science, 1974; MBA, Georgia State University, 1977.

### HUDSON, Paul
Parker, Hudson, Rainer & Dobbs LLP, Atlanta 404 523 5300
*Recommended in Corporate/M&A, Healthcare*

### HUGHES, Randall
Powell Goldstein LLP, Atlanta
404 572 6600
*Recommended in Healthcare*

### HUGHES III, Hunter
Rogers & Hardin, Atlanta
404 522 4700
*Recommended in Employment*

### HUGHES JR, William H
Alston & Bird LLP, Atlanta
404 881 7273
bhughes@alston.com
*Recommended in Construction*

**Practice Areas:** 'Birth to earth' con-

struction law practice includes drafting and negotiating design, construction and joint venture contracts, for large energy, infrastructure, commercial, hospitality, healthcare, and multi-family housing projects; counseling project participants during construction; and mediating, arbitrating and litigating disputes after project completion.
**Career:** Practice is national in scope, including projects in 38 states and Mexico. Over the past eight years, has negotiated contracts for over $1.8 billion in construction work, and litigated or arbitrated over $100 million in claims.
**Personal:** BA, University of North Carolina (1980); JD, University of Virginia (1983).

### HUNTER, Forrest
Alston & Bird LLP, Atlanta
404 881 7190
fhunter@alston.com
*Recommended in Employment*

**Practice Areas:** Concentrates his practice in representing management in labor and employment matters inlcuding litigation including sex, race, age, disability, national origin and contracts. Counsels companies on terminations, work force reductions and union avoidance.
**Career:** Former senior attorney, Office of Regional Counsel, Department of the Treasury. Listed in three US legal publications.
**Personal:** BA, University of Virginia (1972); JD, Emory University (1975).

### JEFFRIES, M Hill
Alston & Bird LLP, Atlanta
404 881 7823
hjeffries@alston.com
*Recommended in Corporate/M&A*

**Practice Areas:** Practice focuses on securities and corporate finance, including public offerings and ongoing securities and corporate representation of public companies; mergers, acquisitions and dispositions of both public and private companies.
**Prof. Memberships:** A Founding Director of the Business and Finance Law Section of the Atlanta Bar Association; member of the Securities Committee, Business Law Section of the State Bar of Georgia.
**Career:** Heads the firm's Transactional Groups. Listed in two leading US legal publications.
**Publications:** Authored numerous articles on securities and M&A topics.
**Personal:** BA, with high distinction (1977), JD (1980) - University of Virginia.

### JOHNSON, James
Kilpatrick Stockton LLP, Atlanta
404 745 2455
JJohnson@KilpatrickStockton.com
*Recommended in Intellectual Property*

**Practice Areas:** Chemical and biotechnology patent prosecution and licensing of chemical technology and biotechnology, legislative relations.

**Career:** Former Professor at Emory University School of Medicine in the Departments of Biochemistry and Medicine; former adjunct member in the Biology Department at Georgia State University; former senior research scientist at the Veterans Administration Hospital Research Laboratories.

**Personal:** BA Chemistry, University of the South; PhD Biochemistry, Emory University School of Medicine; Post Doctoral Fellowship, Scripps Institute of Oceanography; JD, Emory University School of Law, with honors, 1984.

### JOHNSON, Robert N
Ogletree, Deakins, Nash, Smoak & Stewart, PC, Atlanta 404 881 1300
robert.johnson@ogletreedeakins.com
*Recommended in Immigration*

**Practice Areas:** US and Global Business Immigration. Represents Multinational corporations regarding US Immigration regulations - hiring and transfer of foreign executives, managers and specialists.

**Prof. Memberships:** American Immigration Lawyers Association; Georgia Bar; Japan-America Society.

**Career:** Global employment/immigration and general corporate counseling services. Conversational Japanese.

**Publications:** Has published numerous articles on a variety of business immigration topics. Author, Note, Board of Directors of Rotary International v Rotary Club of Duarte: Redefining Associational Rights, 1988 BYU L Rev 141 (1988).

**Personal:** Brigham Young University (BA), BYU's J Reuben Clark Law School (JD). Editor, BYU Law Review (1987-88); editor, BYU International Law Annual (1986-87).

### JOHNSON, Weyman
Paul, Hastings, Janofsky & Walker LLP, Atlanta 404 815 2209
weymanjohnson@paulhastings.com
*Recommended in Employment*

**Practice Areas:** Practices exclusively in labor and employment law, representing management.

**Prof. Memberships:** Past Chair, Labor and Employment Law Section, State Bar of Georgia; Fellow, College of Labor and Employment Lawyers; Adjunct Professor, University of Georgia School of Law.

**Career:** Frequent speaker on legal, and community affairs, and a contributing editor to various publications.

**Publications:** Co-editor, 'Negligence in Employment Law', BNA (2001); co-author, WARN Act Handbook, BNA (1989).

**Personal:** AB Degree, Mercer University, cum laude, (1973); JD Degree, University of Georgia School of Law (1979). Decisions Editor, 'Georgia Law Review'. Present Chair of board of directors of National Multiple Sclerosis Society.

### JOHNSON JR, John
Troutman Sanders LLP, Atlanta
404 885 3000
*Recommended in Environment*

### JOHNSTON, Mike
King & Spalding LLP, Atlanta
404 572 3581
mjohnston@kslaw.com
*Recommended in Employment*

**Practice Areas:** Labor, ERISA and employment law matters, representing clients in pharmaceutical, grocery, food service and distribution, soft drinks, manufacturing, technology, entertainment and healthcare industries.

**Prof. Memberships:** American Bar Association; Atlanta Bar Association; the Florida Bar; State Bar of Georgia.

**Personal:** BS, with academic distinction, US Air Force Academy, 1975; LLM, Georgetown University, 1986; JD, with high honors, University of Florida, Order of the Coif, 1980.

### JONES, Lewis B
King & Spalding LLP, Atlanta
404 572 2742
lbjones@kslaw.com
*Recommended in Environment*

**Practice Areas:** Tort and environmental litigation focusing on general environmental litigation and environmental aspects of project development, with a particular emphasis on water rights and water resources.

**Prof. Memberships:** State Bar of Georgia.

**Personal:** BS, summa cum laude, University of the South, 1989; MS, University of Wisconsin, 1995; JD, cum laude, Harvard, 1998.

### JONES, Reginald
Smith, Currie & Hancock LLP, Atlanta
404 521 3800
*Recommended in Construction*

### JONES JR, Stanley
Nelson Mullins Riley & Scarborough LLP, Atlanta 404 817 6000
*Recommended in Healthcare*

### JORDAN, Hilary P
Kilpatrick Stockton LLP, Atlanta
404 815 6362
HJordan@KilpatrickStockton.com
*Recommended in Banking & Finance*

**Practice Areas:** Syndicated lending, asset-based lending, and asset securitizations.

**Prof. Memberships:** State Bar of Georgia's Business Section (Chair, 1998-99; Member of Executive Committee, 1996-2000); State Bar of Georgia's Uniform Commercial Code Committee (Chair, 1996-97); American Bar Association.

**Career:** Partner since 1984; Chair of the firm's Finance, Real Estate and Restructuring Department.

**Publications:** Co-author of 'Georgia Jurisprudence: Uniform Commercial Code' (Lawyers Cooperative, 1995); lectures on

various commercial lending topics.

**Personal:** BA Political Science, University of Arizona, high distinction, 1974; JD, Harvard University, cum laude, 1977.

### JORDAN, James B
Sutherland Asbill & Brennan LLP, Atlanta 404 853 8101
jim.jordan@sablaw.com
*Recommended in Real Estate*

**Practice Areas:** Co-Chairs the firm's Retail Practice. Devotes substantial time to retail development and leasing matters. Represents developers and retailers regarding all retail product types, from freestanding facilities, to neighborhood and power center developments, to enclosed regional malls. Represents landlords and tenants in office and industrial development matters and leasing transactions. Clients include one of the largest, most prominent retailers in the United States, as well as other national and regional retail and office developers. Regularly contributes to local and national CLE seminars.

**Prof. Memberships:** Member, American College of Real Estate Lawyers; Member, International Council of Shopping Centers; past Chair, Real Property Law Section of the State Bar of Georgia and past Chair of the Legislative and Legal Opinion Committees of this section; co-author of the Report on Legal Opinions to Third Parties in Georgia Real Estate Secured Transactions (October 15, 1997), establishing a model opinion for Georgia secured loan transactions.

**Personal:** JD, magna cum laude, University of Michigan, 1980, Order of the Coif, Phi Beta Kappa; BBA, with highest honors, University of Michigan, 1977.

### JOSPIN, Walter
Paul, Hastings, Janofsky & Walker LLP, Atlanta 404 815 2203
walterjospin@paulhastings.com
*Recommended in Corporate/M&A*

**Practice Areas:** Mergers and acquisitions, corporate governance, securities, private equity and general corporate practice; SEC and SRO enforcement matters; internal investigations.

**Prof. Memberships:** Georgia Bar (Vice-Chair, Business Law Section); American Bar Association; International Bar Association (former officer, Securities Committee).

**Career:** Prosecutor, Division of Enforcement, US Securities & Exchange Commission (1980-83).

**Publications:** 'Georgia Corporations, Other Business Organizations & Securities Regulation', Lawyers Cooperative Publishing, 1995; 'Representing a Witness in an SEC Investigation', 22 Georgia Bar Journal 122 (1985).

**Personal:** BS Economics, University of Pennsylvania, 1974; JD Emory Law School, 1979.

### KAPOOR, Romy
Kapoor & Associates, Atlanta
404 685 9940
*Recommended in Immigration*

### KASSIN, Thomas
Ford & Harrison LLP, Atlanta
404 888 3839
tkassin@fordharrison.com
*Recommended in Employment*

**Practice Areas:** Tom Kassin focuses his practice on airline labor and employment. He counsels clients on all types of personnel and labor relations matters that arise under the Railway Labor Act. Tom has extensive experience in handling a wide range of airline arbitration cases, having successfully represented clients in more than 300 cases. He spends a substantial portion of his practice in collective bargaining and Railway Labor Act litigation. Prior to joining Ford & Harrison, Tom was a Senior Attorney with Delta Air Lines. He graduated from University of Virginia School of Law.

### KAUFMAN, Mark D
Sutherland Asbill & Brennan LLP, Atlanta 404 853 8107
mark.kaufman@sablaw.com
*Recommended in Corporate/M&A*

**Practice Areas:** Co-chairs the firm's Corporate Teams. Practices in the areas of corporate and securities law. Practice focuses on the general representation of corporations. Has extensive experience in the representation of public corporations, including all aspects of SEC reporting, and in acquisitions and sales of businesses, having worked on more than 50 in the last several years. In addition, has been significantly involved in public and private offerings of securities and has represented underwriters in public offerings of securities. Has extensive experience with fast-growth companies, including their start-up, financing and public offering and sale. In addition, represents companies in a wide variety of businesses, including consumer products, finance, fulfillment, healthcare, hospitality, insurance, internet banking, manufacturing, quick service restaurants and textiles, among many others. Experienced in acquiring businesses in Europe and Latin America.

**Prof. Memberships:** Served for 20 years as Legal Counsel to the Atlanta Bar Association and the Atlanta Bar Foundation.

**Personal:** JD, with distinction, Duke University School of Law, 1974, Order of the Coif, note and comment editor, 'Duke Law Journal'; BA, Northwestern University, 1971.

### KAUFMAN, Mark S
McKenna Long & Aldridge LLP, Atlanta
404 527 4120
mkaufman@mckennalong.com
*Recommended in Bankruptcy*

**Practice Areas:** Senior Partner in the firm's Restructuring and Bankruptcy

Department. Practice devoted to Chapter 11 and out-of-court financial restructurings. Has extensive litigation background and a substantial focus of his practice utilizes those skills and his understanding of financial and accounting principles. Practice includes the representation of secured creditors and creditors committees, though he has also handled significant debtor Chapter 11 cases. Has appeared in bankruptcy and district courts through the country and argued before four courts of appeal.
**Prof. Memberships:** Past President Atlanta Bar Association Bankruptcy Section; Chairperson Georgia Bench and Bar Bankruptcy Conference; Director, Southeastern Bankruptcy Law Institute.
**Personal:** BS Cornell University, 1969, with High Distinction; Phi Kappa Phi, Alpern Memorial Scholar; JD Harvard University, 1973, cum laude; frequent lecturer on bankruptcy and related litigation.

### KAYWOOD, Sam K
Alston & Bird LLP, Atlanta
404 881 7481
skaywood@alston.com
*Recommended in Tax*
**Practice Areas:** Federal income tax, international tax, cross border M&A, joint ventures.
**Prof. Memberships:** Former Chair, ABA Tax Section Committee on US Affairs of Foreigners and Tax Treaties; Member, International Fiscal Association; Member, State Bar of Georgia.
**Career:** Chair, Alston & Bird Federal Income Tax Group. Experience with most forms of cross-border investment, particularly in Canada, Europe and Latin America.
**Publications:** Frequent author and lecturer on a variety of international tax topics. Has presented to such organizations as the International Bar Association, the American Bar Association, and Tax Executives Institute.
**Personal:** BS, Babson College (1979); JD, Emory University (1986).

### KAZMAREK, Edward 'Skip'
McKenna Long & Aldridge LLP, Atlanta
404 527 4160
skazmarek@mckennalong.com
*Recommended in Environment*
**Practice Areas:** Partner in the firm's Environmental Practice. His practice spans the full breadth of environmental law, including regulatory, transactional and litigation. Concentrates practice in environmental litigation, including toxic tort defense, cost recovery actions and the defense and prosecution of statutory claims.
**Prof. Memberships:** American Bar Association, State Bar of Georgia, American Chemical Society.
**Personal:** JD, University of Southern California, 1983. AB, University of Cali-

fornia, Los Angeles, 1977. While in graduate school, Skip performed research in air pollution control and was involved in the testing of the first automobile in the US powered by liquid hydrogen. He was also a teaching assistant and taught undergraduate-level courses in systems engineering principles. After graduate school in Environmental Engineering Systems, he worked in the environmental engineering section of a large, national forestry corporation where he was responsible for the company's compliance with laws regulating chemical substances.

### KEENAN, Robert
King & Spalding LLP, Atlanta
404 572 3591
RKeenan@kslaw.com
*Recommended in Healthcare*
**Practice Areas:** Mergers and acquisitions focusing on health systems, hospitals, pharmaceutical and medical device companies, pharmacy benefit management companies, physicians and physician organizations, and managed care organizations on a wide variety of federal and state regulatory matters, including health information privacy, fraud and abuse, certificate of need, reimbursement, licensure and managed care/insurance issues.
**Prof. Memberships:** Georgia Academy of Healthcare Attorneys; American Health Lawyers Association; Health Law Section of the American Bar Association; State Bar of Georgia.
**Personal:** BS, University of Illinois, 1985; JD, University of Georgia, 1988.

### KELLEHER, Thomas
Smith, Currie & Hancock LLP, Atlanta
404 521 3800
*Recommended in Construction*

### KELLEY, Jeffrey
Troutman Sanders LLP, Atlanta
404 885 3000
*Recommended in Bankruptcy*

### KELLEY, John
King & Spalding LLP, Atlanta
404 572 3401
jkelley@kslaw.com
*Recommended in Corporate/M&A*
**Practice Areas:** Corporate finance transactions and securities matters in Rule 144 and Regulation S public offerings and private placements in the technology, real estate, healthcare and manufacturing industries. Advises corporations regarding SEC reporting and disclosure requirements, securities transactions and compliance matters. Merger and acquisition transactions, including tender offers, leveraged buyouts, going private transactions, stock and asset sales and partnership and joint venture transactions.
**Prof. Memberships:** American Bar Association; Atlanta Bar Association; the Florida Bar; State Bar of Georgia.

**Personal:** AB, cum laude, Hamilton College, 1982; JD University of Virginia, Phi Beta Kappa, 1985.

### KENNY, Michael
Alston & Bird LLP, Atlanta
404 881 7179
mkenny@alston.com
*Recommended in Litigation*
**Practice Areas:** Complex commercial litigation, especially antitrust, telecommunications, business and class action involving patent and copyright infringement, securities, insurance, RICO, accountant's liability, corporate governance, products liability, environmental pollution, state fraud and deceptive trade practices. Lead trial counsel in cases in California, New York, Illinois, Florida, Kansas, Ohio, Maryland, Washington, Nevada, Oregon, Missouri, North Carolina, Colorado, Alabama and Georgia.
**Career:** Recognized in three key US legal publications.
**Publications:** Chapter in 'Antitrust Adviser' on antitrust laws.
**Personal:** BA, Oakland University (1978); MA, Northwestern University (1980); JD, Emory University (1984).

### KILGORE III, Cada T
Sutherland Asbill & Brennan LLP, Atlanta  404 853 8196
cada.kilgore@sablaw.com
*Recommended in Energy*
**Practice Areas:** Practice includes the representation of lenders, underwriters, utilities and other electric industry participants in financings, mergers and acquisitions, power project and corporate transactions and power supply matters. Experience includes publicly-issued and privately-placed bond financings, a variety of secured and unsecured loan arrangements, leasing transactions, corporate restructurings, mergers and acquisitions and government-guaranteed financings. Practice has included construction and permanent financings for electric power plants, mortgage bond financings for electric generation, transmission and distribution systems, power supply arrangements, retail competition, stranded cost recovery and other aspects of industry restructuring.
**Prof. Memberships:** Member of the Business Law Section, the Section of Public Utility, Communications and Transportation and the Section of Environment, Energy and Resource Law of the American Bar Association; Director, Electric Cooperative Bar Association; Member, G&T Lawyers' Association and the G&T TAC Subcommittee.
**Personal:** MBA, University of Georgia, 1979; JD, magna cum laude, University of Georgia School of Law, 1979, Order of the Coif, notes editor, 'Georgia Law Review'; BBA, magna cum laude, Georgia College, 1975, Phi Kappa Phi.

### KILPATRICK, J Thomas
Alston & Bird LLP, Atlanta
404 881 7819
tkilpatrick@alston.com
*Recommended in Employment*
**Practice Areas:** Practice focuses on complex and class action employment litigation and traditional labor law.
**Prof. Memberships:** Member of the Board of Directors of the Georgia Chamber of Commerce and serves as Counsel to the Chamber for labor and employment matters.
**Career:** Senior member of the firm's Labor and Employment Law Group. Member of the Bars of Georgia and Tennessee, the United States Supreme Court and various federal trial and appellate courts nationwide.
**Publications:** Lectures frequently throughout the country on labor management matters.
**Personal:** BS (1965), JD (1968) - University of Tennessee.

### KNUDSON Kathryn
Powell Goldstein LLP, Atlanta
404 572 6600
*Recommended in Banking & Finance*

### KRAMER, Myron
Myron Kramer - Sole Practitioner
Decatur 404 371 9031
*Recommended in Immigration*

### KUCK, Charles H
Kuck, Casablanca & Howard, LLC, Atlanta 404 949 8154
ckuck@immigration.net
*Recommended in Immigration*
**Practice Areas:** Immigration and nationality law, including business immigration, PERM Labor Certifications, investor, extraordinary ability and H-1B, L-1 and E-2 nonimmigrant visas.
**Prof. Memberships:** National Vice President, American Immigration Lawyers Association Georgia, Arizona, and Washington, DC Bar Associations.
**Publications:** 2005, Study on Expedited Removal, Represenation Alternatives, U.S Commission on International Religious Freedom, Congressionally Authorized Study; 2004, Testimony Before Senate Judiciary Committee, Subcommittee on Immigration, The History and Future of the U.S. Refugee Program; 200, The Litigation Toolbox, AILA, Editor-in-Chief; 2000-present, Business Immigration Law Strategies for Employing Foreign Nationals, 'Other Short Terms Needs, B, H-3's, O's, and J's', chapter author.
**Personal:** Fluent in Spanish.

### KURZWEIL, David
Greenberg Traurig LLP, Atlanta
678 553 2680
kurzweild@gtlaw.com
*Recommended in Bankruptcy*
**Practice Areas:** Reorganization, bankruptcy and restructuring and financial institutions.

**Prof. Memberships:** Member, State Bar of Georgia, Bankruptcy Law and Creditors' Rights Sections; Member, Atlanta Bar Association, Bankruptcy Law Section; Member, Turn-Around Management Association; Member, American Bankruptcy Institute.
**Career:** Listed, Chambers & Partners USA Guide, 2004-2005; 2005-2006 editions Listed as one of the 'Top Bankruptcy Lawyers', The Deal, June 2004.
**Publications:** Speaker, Transactions with Financial Troubled Companies', Law Seminars International Conference, Atlanta, Georgia, February 2001; speaker, 'Deals with Financial Troubled Technology', Law Seminars International Conference, Atlanta, Georgia, March 2001.
**Personal:** JD, Emory University School of Law, 1987, BS, Cornell University, 1984.

## LAFIANDRA, Aldo L
Alston & Bird LLP, Atlanta
404 881 7890
alafiandra@alston.com
*Recommended in Banking & Finance*
**Practice Areas:** Represents borrowers and lenders in various types of secured and unsecured credit arrangements, typically in syndicated loan transactions. Advises creditors and publicly and privately held companies and their boards of directors in connection with complex out-of-court workouts, debt restructurings and Chapter 11 bankruptcy cases.
**Prof. Memberships:** Director and President, Turnaround Management Association (Atlanta Chapter); Director, National Association of Certified Turnaround Directors (ACTD).
**Career:** Member of the firm's Leveraged Capital and Bankruptcy Reorganization and Workout Groups.
**Publications:** Written and lectured on numerous topics of interest.
**Personal:** BA, St. John's University (1986); JD, University of Virginia (1989).

## LANGE, Mark S
Paul, Hastings, Janofsky & Walker LLP, Atlanta 404 815 2207
marklange@paulhastings.com
*Recommended in Tax*
**Practice Areas:** US federal and state transactional tax matters, including advice regarding mergers, acquisitions and joint ventures, including joint ventures between taxable and tax-exempt organizations. He regularly advises on the tax aspects of healthcare transactions. He has represented domestic and foreign corporations before the IRS and in tax litigation.
**Prof. Memberships:** American Bar Association, Section of Taxation; American Health Lawyers Association; Atlanta Bar Association.
**Career:** Partner since March 2004; Tax Partner at McKenna Long & Aldridge LLP from October 1990 - February 2004.

**Publications:** 'An Open Transaction Analysis of Promissory Note Transactions Among Partners, Their Partnerships and Third Persons' 8 Va Tax Rev 1 (1988)
**Personal:** Indiana University School of Law (JD cum laude, 1980); DePaul University (MS, 1981); Purdue University (BS, 1977).

## LASETER, Scott
McKenna Long & Aldridge LLP, Atlanta
404 527 4370
slaseter@mckennalong.com
*Recommended in Environment*
**Practice Areas:** Practice includes litigation, regulatory and transactional aspects of environmental law. For the last dozen years, has devoted a substantial portion of his practice to manufactured gas plant issues ranging from investigation and remediation oversight to lost recovery, insurance coverage and common law litigation. Scott also has significant experiences representing publicly traded real estate companies, parties to CMBS transactions, financial institutions, REITs, developers and private investors in connection with environmental problems arising out of buying, selling, owning and financing real estate.
**Prof. Memberships:** American Bar Association, State Bar of Georgia, Past Chair of Environmental and Toxic Tort Section of Atlanta Bar Association. Chairman of Georgia Justice Project.
**Personal:** Mercer University (JD, 1990); University of the South (BA, 1984).

## LAYSON, Frank
Paul, Hastings, Janofsky & Walker LLP, Atlanta 404 815 2206
franklayson@paulhastings.com
*Recommended in Corporate/M&A*
**Practice Areas:** Concentrates in domestic and international mergers, acquisitions and joint ventures for both public and private companies.
**Prof. Memberships:** American Bar Association (Committee on Negotiated Acquisitions); State Bar of Georgia (Corporate Code Revision Committee); Atlanta Bar Association (M&A Forum).
**Personal:** BA, Emory University, 1988, Phi Beta Kappa; JD, magna cum laude, University of Georgia, 1991, Order of the Coif, Woodruff Scholar.

## LEET, Alan
Rogers & Hardin, Atlanta
404 522 4700
*Recommended in Corporate/M&A*

## LEVEILLE, Michael
Parker, Hudson, Rainer & Dobbs LLP, Atlanta 404 523 5300
*Recommended in Banking & Finance*

## LEVIN, Jay
Powell Goldstein LLP, Atlanta
404 572 6600
*Recommended in Real Estate*

## LEVIN Matthew W
Alston & Bird LLP, Atlanta
404 881 7940
mlevin@alston.com
*Recommended in Bankruptcy*
**Practice Areas:** Concentrates his practice on corporate restructurings, bankruptcy litigation and commercial litigation.
**Prof. Memberships:** Member of the Bankruptcy Sections of both the Atlanta Bar Association and the State Bar of Georgia.
**Career:** Member of the firm's Bankruptcy Group.
**Publications:** Spoken and written on bankruptcy issues both in Georgia and nationally.
**Personal:** BA (1988), JD (1991) - University of Virginia.

## LISCHER, Dale
Smith Gambrell & Russell LLP, Atlanta
404 815 3500
*Recommended in Intellectual Property*

## LITTLE, Catherine
Hunton & Williams, Atlanta
404 888 4047
clittle@hunton.com
*Recommended in Environment*
**Practice Areas:** Practice focuses exclusively on energy, environmental and administrative law at the federal, state and local levels. Emphasis on regulatory compliance, enforcement defense and administrative adjudication under the Pipeline Safety Act, Clean Water Act, including wetlands, the Oil Pollution Act and CERCLA. Experience also includes natural resource damage assessment claims, endangered species issues, hazardous waste issues and issues arising under TSCA. Representative clients include oil and natural gas pipelines and chemical manufacturers.

## LLORENS JR, Hector E
King & Spalding LLP, Atlanta
404 572 3523
hllorens@kslaw.com
*Recommended in Banking & Finance*
**Practice Areas:** Financial transactions focusing on debt financings, including secured and unsecured credit facilities, inventory and receivables financing, leveraged buyouts, recapitalizations and acquisition financings, mezzanine financing, structured finance, securitizations and debtor-in-possession financing. His practice includes the representation of foreign and domestic lenders, as well as borrowers.
**Prof. Memberships:** American Bar Association; Atlanta Bar Association (Member, Section on Banking and Bankruptcy); State Bar of Georgia.
**Personal:** B Arch, Auburn University,1983; JD, Columbia University, 1986.

## LOKEY JR, James
King & Spalding LLP, Atlanta
404 572 4927
jlokey@kslaw.com
*Recommended in Tax*
**Practice Areas:** Real estate and private equity investment fund formation, private equity investment structures, real estate transactions (representing both developers and financial institutions in connection with new investments as well as 'workouts'), corporate joint ventures, acquisitions and reorganizations, investments by non-US persons (including foreign governments) in the United States, and tax problems of tax-exempt organizations.
**Prof. Memberships:** American Bar Association (Member, Taxation Section); Atlanta Bar Association; State Bar of Georgia.
**Personal:** BS, David Lipscomb University, magna cum laude, 1974; JD, Vanderbilt University, Founder's Medal for First Honors, Order of the Coif.

## LONG, Clay C
McKenna Long & Aldridge LLP, Atlanta
404 527 4050
clong@mckennalong.com
*Recommended in Corporate/M&A*
**Practice Areas:** Focuses on general business and corporate matters with a concentration on corporate counseling and on the purchase and sale of businesses. Represents such companies as food and beverage, communications, agribusiness, merchant banks and venture capital firms. Prior to the merger with McKenna & Cuneo, was a Founding Partner and Chairman of Long Aldridge & Norman. Has been listed for several years as one of the Most Influential Georgians and was selected as one of Georgia's Legal Elite in 2003 and 2004 in a survey of lawyers conducted by Georgia Trend magazine.
**Prof. Memberships:** Atlanta Bar Association; State Bar of Georgia; American Bar Association; Georgia Bar Foundation; American Law Institute.
**Personal:** LLB, Harvard Law School, magna cum laude, 1962. AB, Birmingham-Southern College, summa cum laude, 1958.

## LOVELAND, Joseph
King & Spalding LLP, Atlanta
404 572 4783
jloveland@kslaw.com
*Recommended in Litigation*
**Practice Areas:** Focuses on complex business litigation and class actions. Extensive trial experience in toxic tort, trademark infringement, breach of contract, fraud, misappropriation of trade secrets, corporate alter ego and fraudulent conveyance claims, antitrust violations, and RICO.
**Prof. Memberships:** American Bar Association; Atlanta Bar Association; International Association of Defense

Counsel; State Bar of Georgia; Texas State Bar.
**Personal:** BA, University of North Carolina, 1973; JD, Harvard, 1976.

### LUNSFORD III, Rodgers
Smith Gambrell & Russell LLP, Atlanta
404 815 3500
*Recommended in Intellectual Property*

### LUREY, Alfred
Kilpatrick Stockton LLP, Atlanta
404 815 6360
ALurey@KilpatrickStockton.com
*Recommended in Bankruptcy*
**Practice Areas:** Bankruptcy and insolvency matters.
**Prof. Memberships:** The Southeastern Bankruptcy Law Institute, Inc. (former President and Chairman of the Board of Directors); State Bar of Georgia, UCC Committee of the Corporate and Banking Law Section (former Chairman); American College of Bankruptcy; American Bar Association.
**Career:** Former Adjunct Professor at Emory Law School.
**Publications:** Wrote the chapters on Insider Litigation and Preferences in the 'Prentice Hall Law & Business Bankruptcy Litigation Manual' (Michael L Cook ed); lectures at seminars on bankruptcy, creditors' rights, and secured lending.
**Personal:** AB, Duke University, summa cum laude, 1964; LLB, Harvard University, cum laude, 1967.

### MACDONALD III, Ralph F
Alston & Bird LLP, Atlanta
404 881 7582
cmacdonald@alston.com
*Recommended in Banking & Finance*
**Practice Areas:** Practice emphasizes securities, mergers and acquisitions, financial institutions, Bank Holding Company Act and corporate governance matters.
**Prof. Memberships:** The American Bar Association; Alabama State Bar (Chairman, Banking, Business, and Corporation Law Section, 1986-87); Financial Markets Association; associate member, ESOP Association; and American Bar Association Subcommittee on Corporate Governance and Banking Law.
**Career:** Named in two leading legal publications. Frequent speaker and author on various matters related to financial institutions.
**Personal:** BS, Washington And Lee University (1975); MBA, JD, University of Virginia (1979).

### MALOY, Bruce
Maloy & Jenkins, Atlanta
404 875 2700
*Recommended in Litigation*

### MARLOWE, Deborah
Paul, Hastings, Janofsky & Walker LLP, Atlanta 404 815 2234
deborahmarlowe@paulhastings.com
*Recommended in Immigration*

**Practice Areas:** Deborah co-chairs Paul Hastings' global Immigration Practice Group. She has over 20 years of experience focusing on strategic counseling and corporate compliance relating to business immigration issues. She represents a large variety of multinational companies with respect to all immigration-related issues, including labor certification and temporary and permanent visa petitions. She also directs outbound immigration services. Deborah develops immigration compliance and training programs for corporate human resources and legal professionals. She was the inaugural recipient of the firm's prestigious Barbra Davis Award for teamwork, dedication and innovation. She is a founder and Director of the Global Personnel Alliance.

### MARSH, Gary W
McKenna Long & Aldridge LLP, Atlanta
404 527 4150
gmarsh@mckennalong.com
*Recommended in Bankruptcy*
**Practice Areas:** Represents creditors and debtors in Chapter 11 reorganization proceedings, out of court restructurings and debtor/creditor litigation. He has extensive experience representing creditors in and out of bankruptcy court. Analyzes and defends against preference and fraudulent conveyance actions, represents buyers of assets out of bankruptcy and represents landlords and other parties who have leases or contracts with debtors.
**Prof. Memberships:** American Bar Association; Georgia Bar Association; Atlanta Bar Association; American Bankruptcy Institute; Emory University, Lamar Inn of Court.
**Career:** Fellow in the American College of Bankruptcy; Board Certified Business Bankruptcy and Creditors' Rights attorney; named by 'Georgia Trend' as one of Georgia's 2003 Legal Elite and by 'Atlanta Magazine' as one of Georgia's Super Lawyers for 2004.
**Personal:** JD, Emory University School of Law, 1985. BA, American University, cum laude, 1982.

### MARSHALL, John
Powell Goldstein LLP, Atlanta
404 572 6600
*Recommended in Antitrust, Litigation*

### MARZETTI, Phil
Paul, Hastings, Janofsky & Walker LLP, Atlanta 404 815 2258
philmarzetti@paulhastings.com
*Recommended in Tax*
**Practice Areas:** US federal and state tax matters encompassing most areas of corporate, partnership and individual income taxation, including the tax aspects of mergers and acquisitions, the structuring of partnerships and joint ventures, and international taxation.
**Prof. Memberships:** ABA, Georgia Federal Tax Conference (Trustee), Atlanta

Tax Forum, International Fiscal Association.
**Career:** Partner at Paul Hastings since 1992. Associate and Partner at Atlanta-based firm from 1975-92.
**Publications:** Pre-Sale Tailoring - Charitable Giving and Charitable Remainder Trusts (USC Tax Inst); co-author of prior Tax Management Portfolios regarding S Corporations.
**Personal:** Harvard Law School (JD, 1975); Boston College (BA, 1972).

### MATCHETT, Sam
King & Spalding LLP, Atlanta
404 572 2414
smatchett@kslaw.com
*Recommended in Employment*
**Practice Areas:** Employment relationship matters, emphasis in labor and employment litigation in state and federal courts, governmental agencies and arbitration tribunals, including employment discrimination matters. Advice on avoidance of employee-related problems, presenting seminars concerning all aspects of employment law. Litigation involving Civil Rights Acts of 1866 and 1964, Age Discrimination in Employment Act and Americans with Disabilities Act.
**Prof. Memberships:** Appeals Court of Georgia; Georgia State Bar; Institute of Applied Management and Law (IAML) (faculty member).
**Personal:** BA, magna cum laude, Morehouse College, 1981; JD, University of Georgia, 1984.

### MCCABE, F Barry
Griffin Cochrane & Marshall, Atlanta
404 523 2000
fbmccabe@gcm-atty.com
*Recommended in Construction*
**Practice Areas:** Construction law; commercial litigation.
**Prof. Memberships:** State Bar of Georgia (Litigation section); State Bar of New Mexico.
**Career:** Shareholder since 2002; Martindale-Hubbell AV-rated; selected by peers as one of best business litigation attorneys in Georgia ('Legal Elite,' 2004, by Georgia Trend magazine); selected by peers as 'Georgia Superlawyer' in construction (2004-06 by Atlanta Magazine).
**Personal:** Emory University School of Law (JD with distinction, 1994); New Mexico State University (BS, 1991); London School of Economics and Political Science (General Course Diploma, 1990).

### MCGRATH, Robin L
Alston & Bird LLP, Atlanta
404 881 7923
rmcgrath@alson.com
*Recommended in Intellectual Property*
**Practice Areas:** Focuses her practice on patent, internet, trademark and copyright litigation and counseling.
**Career:** Has extensive experience with all facets of patent litigation and domain

name and internet dispute issues, representing numerous companies in domain name disputes and action under the Federal Anticybersquatting Consumer Protection Act and ICANN's Uniform Domain Name Dispute Resolution Policy.
**Publications:** Has authored a number of articles in the trademark and internet area.
**Personal:** BBA, magna cum laude, University of Texas (1989); JD, with high honors, University of Florida College of Law (1995).

### MCMAHON, Teri Lynn
Alston & Bird LLP, Atlanta
404 881 7266
tmcmahon@alston.com
*Recommended in Corporate/M&A*
**Practice Areas:** Mergers and acquisitions, prviate corporate finance, leveraged buyouts and general corporate law. Extensive experience in acquisitions, divestitures, public and private company mergers and general corporate management. Negotiates and drafts purchase and sale agreements, shareholders and employment agreements, and documents typical in management-led buyouts.
**Prof. Memberships:** American Bar Association; State Bar of Georgia; Atlanta Bar Association (Board memeber, Business and Finance Section).
**Personal:** BA, Duke University (1984); JD, University of Michigan (1987).

### MCNEILL, Thomas
Powell Goldstein LLP, Atlanta
404 572 6600
*Recommended in Corporate/M&A*

### MEIR, Dennis
Kilpatrick Stockton LLP, Atlanta
404 815 6364
DMeir@KilpatrickStockton.com
*Recommended in Bankruptcy*
**Practice Areas:** Bankruptcy and insolvency matters, with significant involvement in representation of debtors, secured and unsecured creditors, creditors' committees, and trustees.
**Prof. Memberships:** Georgia State Bar, Bankruptcy section, (former chairman); American Bar Association, Business Law section; Atlanta Bar Association, Bankruptcy section.
**Career:** Partner since 1978; formerly firm Managing Partner; currently Chairman, Financial Restructuring Group.
**Publications:** Has lectured and written extensively on bankruptcy issues.
**Personal:** Undergraduate Degree, Amherst College, cum laude, 1967; JD, Harvard University, cum laude, 1972.

### MERCER, John
Troutman Sanders LLP, Atlanta
404 885 3000
*Recommended in Energy*

**MEYERS, Todd**
Kilpatrick Stockton LLP, Atlanta
404 815 6482
TMeyers@KilpatrickStockton.com
*Recommended in Bankruptcy*
**Practice Areas:** Bankruptcy and insolvency matters, including representation of committees, individual creditors, secured lenders and debtors in both workouts and bankruptcy proceedings. Significant experience in healthcare and telecommunications bankruptcy proceedings.
**Prof. Memberships:** State Bar of Georgia, Bankruptcy Section; American Bankruptcy Institute; Atlanta Bar Association, Bankruptcy Section.
**Publications:** Co-authored the chapter on secured transactions under Article 9 of the Georgia Uniform Commercial Code for the treatise Georgia Jurisprudence.
**Personal:** BS Accounting, Indiana University, 1988; JD, Emory University, with honors, 1991.

**MILLER, Rick**
Powell Goldstein LLP, Atlanta
404 572 6600
*Recommended in Corporate/M&A*

**MITCHELSON JR, William (Mitch) R**
Alston & Bird LLP, Atlanta
404 881 7661
mmitchelson@alston.com
*Recommended in Litigation*
**Practice Areas:** Concentrates on defense of government investigations, internal corporate investigations, and corporate legal compliance.
**Career:** Leader of firm's Government Investigations and Compliance Team and chair of False Claims Act Working Group. Designated Georgia Legal Contact for the Health Care Compliance Association. Former Assistant US Attorney for the Middle District of Florida, Criminal Division.
**Publications:** Authored articles on voluntary disclosures to the government, conducting plea negotiations with government prosecutors, development of corporate compliance plans, and incorporating sentencing guidelines considerations into criminal trial strategies.
**Personal:** AB, Duke University (1982); JD, University of Chicago (1985).

**MIXSON, H Lamar**
Bondurant, Mixson & Elmore, LLP, Atlanta 404 881 4171
mixson@bmelaw.com
*Recommended in Litigation*
**Practice Areas:** Business torts, corporate governance, partnership and fiduciary disputes, insurance coverage and bad faith litigation, attorney and accountant liability, RICO, tender offer, proxy and securities litigation.
**Career:** A Fellow of the American College of Trial Lawyers. Has represented individuals and corporations involved in a wide variety of business disputes for more than 25 years. Has successfully presented complex commercial disputes to juries, arbitration panels, and judges. Was co-counsel for the plaintiffs in a breach of fiduciary duty case which resulted in a $454,000,000 jury verdict, the largest verdict ever awarded in Georgia (a verdict which was affirmed on appeal and paid in full). Represented the plaintiff class in Abdallah v Coca-Cola Co., which settled for $192.5 million, the largest class action racial discrimination settlement in history. Selected as a finalist for the Trial Lawyer of the Year Award by the Trial Lawyers for Public Justice for the Abdallah case. Also has an excellent record on the defense side, having obtained summary judgments, dismissals, and defense verdicts of major claims.
**Personal:** BA Degree, magna cum laude, honors with exceptional distinction in English, Washington & Lee University, 1970; JD Degree, cum laude, Harvard University, 1974. Editor, Harvard Law Review, 1972-73.

**MOELING Walter**
Powell Goldstein LLP, Atlanta
404 572 6600
*Recommended in Banking & Finance*

**MOLEN, Chris D**
Paul, Hastings, Janofsky & Walker LLP, Atlanta 404 815 2210
chrismolen@paulhastings.com
*Recommended in Banking & Finance*
**Practice Areas:** Complex commercial and banking transactions, debt restructurings and workouts, asset-based and cash flow financings, and healthcare and communications industry lending practices.
**Prof. Memberships:** Georgia Bar Association, Atlanta Bar Association, Association for Corporate Growth (Director and past President of Atlanta Chapter), and Georgia Finance Lawyers.
**Career:** Over 25 years of experience representing banks and finance companies in loan transactions ranging from $5 million to $3 billion.
**Personal:** Graduated first in class from Indiana University School of Business in 1974 with BS Degree in Accounting, and from Indiana University School of Law in 1977 with a JD degree, cum laude.

**MOORE, David**
Troutman Sanders LLP, Atlanta
404 885 3000
*Recommended in Environment*

**MOORHEAD, Bruce W**
Hunton & Williams, Atlanta
404 888 4090
bmoorhead@hunton.com
*Recommended in Banking & Finance*
**Practice Areas:** Co-Head of Lending Services Team. Practice is concentrated in corporate and commercial finance on behalf of banks and other financial institutions, with a primary focus on syndicated and leveraged lending. Extensive experience representing financial institutions and intermediaries in connection with the resolution of problem loans, as well as DIP and exit financing.
**Prof. Memberships:** Member, State Bar of Georgia; Founding Member and Director, Georgia Financial Lawyers Conference; Member, Standards Committee, Association for the Certification of Turnaround Professionals; Member, Turnaround Management Association; Chairman Emeritus of the Board, The Bridge.

**MOWREY, Robert**
Alston & Bird LLP, Atlanta
404 881 7242
bmowrey@alston.com
*Recommended in Environment*
**Practice Areas:** Environmental law, toxic tort litigation, hazardous waste, Clean Water Act, corporate compliance.
**Prof. Memberships:** State Bar of Georgia (former Chair, Environmental Section).
**Career:** Extensive nationwide experience handling hazardous waste and clean water enforcement and litigation matters. Experienced in the defense of citizens' suits, cost recovery actions, and enforcement actions. Adjunct Professor, Emory University School of Law.
**Publications:** Publishes regularly on environmental issues, most recently in the ABA Section on Environment, Energy and Resources Journal.
**Personal:** BA, summa cum laude, Wittenberg University (1985); JD, cum laude, University of Chicago (1988).

**MULLIS, Carl W**
Paul, Hastings, Janofsky & Walker LLP, Atlanta 404 815 2225
carlmullis@paulhastings.com
*Recommended in Antitrust*
**Practice Areas:** Antitrust litigation and counseling. Complex business and securities litigation.
**Prof. Memberships:** Chairman of Antitrust Section of State Bar of Georgia, 1992-94; Board of Trustees of Georgia ICLE, 1993-94.
**Career:** Of Counsel, Paul Hastings, 2001-present. Partner and Head of Antitrust Team at Long & Aldridge, 1986-2001. Senior trial attorney, Antitrust Division, United States Department of Justice, 1975-86.
**Publications:** Authored numerous articles and contributed to several ABA antitrust treatises.
**Personal:** Emory Law School Council; Board of Directors, Georgia Museum of Art; BA in Economics, Yale University, 1975; JD with Distinction, Emory Law School, 1975; Law Review; Best Brief Award.

**MUNGER, Tom**
Munger & Stone, Atlanta
404 815 1884
*Recommended in Employment*

**MURPHY, Paul J**
King & Spalding LLP, Atlanta
404 572 2720
pmurphy@kslaw.com
*Recommended in Litigation*
**Practice Areas:** Business litigation representing both US and European based corporations in a variety of complex commercial and tort disputes. Recently, his practice has focused on representing companies in business disputes and class actions in the commercial arena and defending corporations in class actions and mass tort litigation in the chemical and pharmaceutical industries.
**Prof. Memberships:** American Bar Association; State Bar of Georgia.
**Personal:** BS, with honors, United States Merchant Marine Academy, 1980; JD, Emory University, 1986.

**MURPHY JR, Charles**
Vaughan & Murphy, Atlanta
404 577 6550
*Recommended in Antitrust*

**NEEDLE, William**
Needle & Rosenberg, P.C., Atlanta
678 420 9300
*Recommended in Intellectual Property*

**NEWMAN, Mark**
Troutman Sanders LLP, Atlanta
404 885 3000
*Recommended in Immigration*

**NEWTON, Trammell**
Jones Day, Atlanta
404 581 8308
tnewton@jonesday.com
*Recommended in Antitrust*
**Practice Areas:** Over 30 years' antitrust and trade regulation experience, including representation of clients before federal and state agencies on merger and other regulatory issues, and in class actions and other civil and criminal antitrust litigation.
**Prof. Memberships:** ABA, the State Bar of Georgia, and the bars of the US District Court for the Northern District of Georgia, the US Court of Appeals for the Eleventh Circuit, and the US Supreme Court.
**Personal:** University of North Carolina (AB, 1970; Morehead Scholar); Columbia University (JD 1973).

**NICHOLSON, Penn**
Powell Goldstein LLP, Atlanta
404 572 6600
*Recommended in Bankruptcy*

**NODINE, Larry**
Needle & Rosenberg, P.C., Atlanta
678 420 9300
*Recommended in Intellectual Property*

### NOE, Elizabeth H
Paul, Hastings, Janofsky & Walker LLP,
Atlanta 404 815 2287
elizabethnoe@paulhastings.com
*Recommended in Corporate/M&A*
**Practice Areas:** Securities, corporate
govenance, mergers and acquisitions and
general corporate practice. Represents
companies in the issuance of high-yield
debt and equity and in compliance with
SEC disclosure requirements. Recent
transactions: representations of Ashton
Woods USA L.L.C. and Beazer Homes
USA, Inc. in issuances of debt securities
under Rule 144A.
**Prof. Memberships:** Georgia Bar (Chair,
Publications Committee, Business Law
Section); ABA.
**Career:** Partner since 2001.Vice-Chair of
Corporate Department and Co-Chair of
Attorney Development.
**Personal:** BA English/Political Science,
(Phi Beta Kappa) Agnes Scott College,
1986, JD (Order of the Coif) University
of Virginia, 1989; President, Board of
Directors Network, Inc.

### NORTH, John L
Sutherland Asbill & Brennan LLP,
Atlanta 404 853 8358
john.north@sablaw.com
*Recommended in Intellectual Property*
**Practice Areas:** Extensive experience in
controversies involving patent infringement, trade secret misappropriation and
related unfair competition and antitrust
controversies. Has tried cases, including
jury trials, in state and federal court, and
has arbitrated and mediated a number of
disputes.
**Prof. Memberships:** Member of the
American Intellectual Property Law
Association, and Intellectual Property
Law, Science & Technology and Litigation
Sections of the American Bar Association. Currently Editor-in-Chief of the
SciTech Lawyer. Served as council member of the Science & Technology Section,
Vice-Chair of the Standing Committee
on Scientific Evidence, Section Liaison of
the ABA's Standing Committee of Publishing Oversight, and editor of the Scientific Evidence Review. Past President of
the Atlanta Chapter of the Federal Bar
Association.
**Personal:** JD, cum laude, Emory University School of Law, 1987, notes and comments editor, Emory Law Journal; BA,
magna cum laude, Duke University, 1984.
Recognized in Chambers USA as one of
America's Leading Business Lawyers,
2004-05. Named 2005 Georgia Super
Lawyer by Atlanta Magazine.

### NURKIN, Sidney J
Alston & Bird LLP, Atlanta
404 881 7260
snurkin@alston.com
*Recommended in Corporate/M&A*
**Practice Areas:** Concentrates practice
on mergers and acquisitions, leveraged

buyouts, corporate finance and corporate
governance matters.
**Prof. Memberships:** Atlanta and American Bar Associations; State Bar of Georgia. Co-Chair, Committee of the Corporate and Banking Law Section (developed
Report on Legal Opinion to Third Parties
in Corporate Transactions and accompanying Interpretive Standards). Member,
Corporate Code Revision Committee of
the Corporate and Banking Law Section,
State Bar of Georgia.
**Career:** Frequent author and speaker on
topics of corporate governance, director
and officer liability, negotiated acquisitions and legal opinions. Listed in three
leading legal publications.
**Personal:** BS (1963), LLB (1966) - Duke
University.

### OAKES, Leslie
King & Spalding LLP, Atlanta
404 572 3314
loakes@kslaw.com
*Recommended in Environment*
**Practice Areas:** Experienced in permit-
ting and enforcement actions, air and
water pollution and hazardous waste.
Environmental due diligence in a number of complex transactions involving
industrial facilities and properties. Over
11 years as environmental engineer with
the Environmental Protection Division,
Georgia Department of Natural
Resources.
**Prof. Memberships:** American Bar
Association; State Bar of Georgia.
**Personal:** BME, Georgia Institute of
Technology, 1974; MS, Georgia State University, 1981; JD, Georgia State University,
1986.

### OAKLEY, Mary Ann
Holland & Knight LLP, Atlanta
404 817 8500
maryann.oakley@hklaw.com
*Recommended in Employment*
**Practice Areas:** Partner in the firm's Litigation Section, practicing for more than
30 years in the areas of labor and employment law, appeals and alternative dispute
resolution. She has substantial experience
in administrative proceedings, trials, and
appellate practice in all aspects of labor
and employment law and is a trained
mediator and arbitrator. She has advised
numerous clients about personnel,
human resources, and employment practices including drafting contracts, policies
and procedures. She has experience training employers in a wide variety of
employment matters including discrimination, harassment, retaliation, Fair
Labor Standards Act and Americans with
Disabilities Act Title III issues.

### O'DAY, Stephen
Smith Gambrell & Russell LLP, Atlanta
404 815 3500
*Recommended in Environment*

### PAKENHAM, Timothy J
Alston & Bird LLP, Atlanta
404 881 7755
tpakenham@alston.com
*Recommended in Real Estate*
**Practice Areas:** Concentrates on the
development and financing of commercial real estate. Extensive experience in
large multiparty credit facilities and
acquisition, development and financing
of hotel properties.
**Prof. Memberships:** American College
of Real Estate Lawyers; Urban Land Institute; Pension Real Estate Association;
Real Property Section of the State Bar of
Georgia; Atlanta Bar Association.
**Career:** Member of the firm's Partners'
Committee. Listed for commercial real
estate in a leading US legal publication.
**Publications:** Written or spoken on real
estate matters, particularly on real estate
finance.
**Personal:** BA, University of Notre Dame
(1978); JD (1983), MBA (1983) - Duke
University.

### PARDO JR, James
King & Spalding LLP, Atlanta
404 572 4794
jpardo@kslaw.com
*Recommended in Bankruptcy*
**Practice Areas:** Financial restructuring
transactions, focusing on representation
of secured and unsecured creditors in
both bankruptcy cases and out of court
debt restructurings.
**Prof. Memberships:** American Bankruptcy Institute; fellow, American College
of Bankruptcy; State Bar of Georgia (past
Chairman, Bankruptcy Section); 'Collier
on Bankruptcy' and 'Collier Bankruptcy
Manual' (former contributing Editor);
Southeastern Bankruptcy Law Institute
(Director).
**Personal:** BA, with honors, University of
Virginia, Phi Beta Kappa, 1979; JD, University of Virginia, Order of the Coif,
1979. Frequent lecturer on bankruptcy
and commercial litigation.

### PARKER, John
Parker, Hudson, Rainer & Dobbs LLP,
Atlanta 404 523 5300
*Recommended in Healthcare*

### PARKS, John
Powell Goldstein LLP, Atlanta
404 572 6600
*Recommended in Real Estate*

### PASCUAL, Rey
Kilpatrick Stockton LLP, Atlanta
404 815 6132
RPascual@KilpatrickStockton.com
*Recommended in Corporate/M&A*
**Practice Areas:** Securities offerings,
mergers and acquisitions, private equity,
investment management, general securities and corporate law. Regularly represents middle market companies in transactional and other strategic matters.
Recent transactions: $102 million Tur-

boChef Technologies Public Offering;
$115 million sale of DVT Corporation
(an Arcapita portfolio company) to
Cognex Corporation; $150 million pri-
vate placement for Wells Real Estate
Funds; sale of Surgical Information Sys-
tems, LLC to Vista Equity Partners; and
$500 million sale of PracticeWorks to
Kodak.
**Career:** Member of firm's Executive
Committee. Founder/Director, United
Americas Bank, N.A.
**Personal:** AB, Syracuse University; JD,
Creighton University, both with honors.
Fluent in Spanish.

### PATTON, Glenn G
Alston & Bird LLP, Atlanta
404 881 7785
gpatton@alston.com
*Recommended in Employment*
**Practice Areas:** Represents management in employment-related litigation,
including discrimination claims, restrictive convenant suits and wage and hour
matters. Advises on ADA and FMLA
compliance, complex wage and hour
audits, employee handbooks, employment agreements, employee discipline,
and the impact of mergers and acquisitions.
**Prof. Memberships:** American Bar
Association; State Bar of Georgia; Atlanta
Bar Association.
**Personal:** AB, Duke University (1991);
JD, University of Virginia (1996), Editorial Board Member, Virginia Journal of
Social Policy and the Law.

### PERRY, Charles
Jones Day, Atlanta
404 581 8236
caperry@jonesday.com
*Recommended in Environment*
**Practice Areas:** Environmental matters,
including defense of administrative
enforcement actions, litigation (including
toxic tort cases), and advisory services
related to business transactions. Involved
in numerous actions under the RCRA
and CERCLA, where he served as common counsel for one of the largest Superfund sites in the Southeast. Involved in
water quality standards issues under the
Clean Water Act.
**Career:** Former Assistant US Attorney
representing the US EPA and the Army
Corps of Engineers. Served as regional
counsel for the US EPA Region IV.
**Publications:** Lectures regularly before
various organizations, including the State
Bar of Georgia Environmental Section.

### PERSONS, Oscar N
Alston & Bird LLP, Atlanta
404 881 7249
opersons@alston.com
*Recommended in Litigation*
**Practice Areas:** Extensive trial and
appellate experience. Concentrates practice on complex litigation, with emphasis
on securities class action and mergers and

acquisitions matters. eg Bryant v Avado Brands, 187 F3d 1271.

**Prof. Memberships:** Member of the State Bar of Georgia and the Atlanta Bar Association.

**Career:** Has been a lecturer in numerous seminars on trial practice, appellate advocacy, securities litigation, restrictive covenants/trade secrets, corporate litigation and discovery.

**Publications:** 'Forward-Looking Statements under the Reform Act,' Alston & Bird, LLP, Securities Litigation Forms and Analysis (West Publishing Co. 2003).

## PERSONS, Ray
King & Spalding LLP, Atlanta
404 572 2494
rpersons@kslaw.com
*Recommended in Litigation*

**Practice Areas:** Focuses on complex litigation, including class actions and mass torts. Regularly appears before the state and federal courts and has been lead counsel in more than 50 jury trials. Has written numerous articles and conducted lectures across the country on strategies for defending complex cases.

**Prof. Memberships:** American Board of Trial Advocates; American College of Trial Lawyers; Atlanta Bar Association; Federation of Insurance and Corporate Counsel; International Society of Barristers; State Bar of Georgia.

**Personal:** BS, Armstrong State University, 1975; JD, Ohio State University, 1978.

## PETRIK, Michael T
Alston & Bird LLP, Atlanta
404 881 7479
mpetrik@alston.com
*Recommended in Tax*

**Practice Areas:** Concentrates his practice on multistate tax planning for businesses, including income tax, franchise tax, sales/use tax, and other state and local taxes.

**Prof. Memberships:** Serves on the boards of the United Way of Metropolitan Atlanta, Leadership Atlanta, Lawyers Committee for Civil Rights Under Law, and the Vasser Woolley Foundation.

**Career:** Chair of the firm's State and Local Tax Group.

**Publications:** Frequent author and speaker on state tax topics, including constitutional questions involving the due process and commerce clauses.

**Personal:** BS (1979), BA (1979) - Eastern Illinois University; JD, Duke University (1983).

## PHILLIPS, Stephen
Hendrick, Phillips, Salzman & Flatt P.C., Atlanta 404 522 1410
*Recommended in Construction*

## PITTMAN, Alisa
Elarbee, Thompson, Sapp & Wilson, LLP, Atlanta 404 659 6700
*Recommended in Employment*

## POPE, David
Carr, Tabb & Pope LLP, Atlanta
404 442 9000
*Recommended in Environment*

## POUNCEY, Gerald
Morris, Manning & Martin, LLP, Atlanta
404 233 7000
*Recommended in Environment*

## POWELL, Kurt
Hunton & Williams, Atlanta
404 888 4015
kpowell@hunton.com
*Recommended in Employment*

**Practice Areas:** Mr Powell's practice focuses on representing management in labor and employment law matters, including employment litigation, trade secret and non-compete litigation, union avoidance, collective bargaining, and preventive employee relations counseling. He has extensive experience in defending class actions and 'mass' actions involving employment discrimination, and ERISA claims. He is a member of Leadership Atlanta and has received recognition in 'Who's Who in Law and Accounting,' as published in Atlanta Business Chronicle, as an Employment Litigation Super Lawyer, as published in Atlanta Magazine and as a Georgia Legal Elite.

**Prof. Memberships:** State Bar of Georgia and American Bar Association.

## POWELL, Thomas
Troutman Sanders LLP, Atlanta
404 885 3000
*Recommended in Banking & Finance*

## POWERS, Tony
Rogers & Hardin, Atlanta
404 522 4700
*Recommended in Antitrust*

## PRATT John
Kilpatrick Stockton LLP, Atlanta
404 815 6367
JPratt@KilpatrickStockton.com
*Recommended in Intellectual Property*

**Practice Areas:** Patent portfolio development and management, litigation and licensing.

**Prof. Memberships:** AIPLA, LES.

**Career:** Founded and led the firm's Atlanta Patent Prosecution Practice; chairs the firm's Intellectual Property Practice; appointed by the Federal court as a special master to handle patent infringement cases. Served from 1999 through 2001 as general counsel to the internet consulting firm Enterpulse.

**Publications:** Was involved in drafting the Georgia Trade Secrets Act of 1990; regularly lecturers at continuing education seminars, particularly on patent law, licensing, trade secret protection and restrictive covenants.

**Personal:** BS Electrical Engineering, Clemson University, 1974; JD, Harvard University, 1977; woodworking; boat-building.

## PRINCE, Alan
King & Spalding LLP, Atlanta
404 572 3595
aprince@kslaw.com
*Recommended in Corporate/M&A*

**Practice Areas:** Corporate finance transactions and securities matters, representing issuers and underwriters in connection with initial and secondary public offerings, 'shelf' offerings, Rule 144A offerings and other private placement transactions. Extensive experience in public offerings of equity securities, including initial public offerings, SEC reporting and disclosure requirements and corporate governance issues. Private merger and acquisition transactions, including mergers, tender offers and stock and asset transactions.

**Prof. Memberships:** American Bar Association; Atlanta Bar Association; State Bar of Georgia.

**Personal:** BA, cum laude, Wake Forest University, 1986; JD, cum laude, University of Georgia, 1989.

## RAFUSE, Nancy
Ashe, Rafuse & Hill, LLP, Atlanta
404 253 6002
nancyrafuse@asherafuse.com
*Recommended in Employment*

**Practice Areas:** Concentrates practice in employment law, litigation, civil rights matters and defense of class actions. Named by the National Law Journal to the '40 Under 40' (May 2005), as one of the top employment lawyers in Georgia by 'Georgia Trend Magazine' and as one of Georgia's top employment lawyers and top women lawyers by 'Law & Politics Magazine' and 'Atlanta Magazine'.

**Prof. Memberships:** Member, Northern District of Georigia's Bar Council and Disciplinary Committee; Board of Directors, Atlanta Urban League; Board of Directors, Atlanta Zoo; Member, ABA and Georgia Bar.

**Career:** Founding and Managing Partner of Ashe, Rafuse & Hill, LLP, largest employment firm in Georgia with a female name Partner. Former Partner of 800 attorney international law firm where she served as Chair of the Employment Law Department of the Atlanta office.

**Personal:** BBA, cum laude, University of Georgia (1988); JD, magna cum laude, University of Georgia (1991), Order of the Coif, notes editor of the Georgia Law Review.

## RAGLAND JR, William M
Hunton & Williams, Atlanta
404 888 4182
wragland@hunton.com
*Recommended in Intellectual Property*

**Practice Areas:** Bill Ragland's practice focuses on intellectual property litigation and licensing. He has extensive experience in litigating disputes involving patents, copyrights, trademarks, trade secrets and non-competition agreements.

A leading technology lawyer, Ragland also provides strategic advice on the structure, negotiation and implementation of IP enforcement and licensing programs. His clients include computer, software, telecommunications, chemical, paper products and manufacturing companies. He has been featured in Corporate Counsel magazine and IP Law & Business magazine, regarding leaders in innovative intellectual property enforcement and licensing programs.

## REED, Glen
King & Spalding LLP, Atlanta
404 572 3393
gareed@gslaw.com
*Recommended in Healthcare*

**Practice Areas:** Focuses on general representation of healthcare systems; specialized regulatory support to healthcare technology, pharmaceutical and device companies; and specialized projects involving compliance planning, healthcare industry restructuring, reimbursement, fraud and abuse, antitrust, managed care, healthcare policy and new service development.

**Prof. Memberships:** American Bar Association; American Health Lawyers Association Fellow; Georgia Academy of Hospital Attorneys; State Bar of Georgia.

**Personal:** BA, University of Tennessee, 1972; JD, Yale, 1976.

## REINHARDT, Daniel
Troutman Sanders LLP, Atlanta
404 885 3000
*Recommended in Litigation*

## REMAR, Robert
Rogers & Hardin, Atlanta
404 522 4700
*Recommended in Litigation*

## RHODES, Thomas
Smith Gambrell & Russell LLP, Atlanta
404 815 3500
*Recommended in Antitrust*

## RICHARDS, Russell
King & Spalding LLP, Atlanta
404 572 4695
rrichards@kslaw.com
*Recommended in Corporate/M&A*

**Practice Areas:** Representing clients in connection with the acquisition and sale of publicly-held and privately-owned companies and establishing domestic and international joint ventures in the United States and in Canada, Mexico, South America, the United Kingdom and Continental Europe.

**Prof. Memberships:** American Bar Association; Atlanta Bar Association; BTI Consulting Group, Inc.'s 2002 Client Service All-Star Team; State Bar of Georgia.

**Personal:** BS, high honors, University of Tennessee, 1971; JD, high honors, Duke University, 1974.

**RICHARDSON, Susan**
Kilpatrick Stockton LLP, Atlanta
404 815 6330
SuRichardson@KilpatrickStockton.com
*Recommended in Environment*
**Practice Areas:** Environmental law,
including regulatory and compliance
counseling, due diligence for real estate
and corporate transactions, permitting,
enforcement and hazardous site remediation. Represents municipal governments
with regard to wastewater collection and
treatment issues, including permitting
and enforcement issues.
**Prof. Memberships:** Georgia Bar Association, Environmental Law Section (Past
Chair).
**Career:** Partner since 1998.
**Publications:** Lectures frequently on
environmental regulation, particularly
with respect to water and wastewater
issues.
**Personal:** BS Biology, University of
Tulsa, cum laude, 1988; JD, Tulane University, magna cum laude, 1991.

**RIDDELL, Stephen**
Troutman Sanders LLP, Atlanta
404 885 3000
*Recommended in Employment*

**ROEDER, Kim**
Powell Goldstein LLP, Atlanta
404 572 6600
*Recommended in Healthcare*

**ROGERS, CB**
Rogers & Hardin, Atlanta
404 522 4700
*Recommended in Litigation*

**ROSENBERG, Sumner**
Needle & Rosenberg, P.C., Atlanta
678 420 9300
*Recommended in Intellectual Property*

**ROSENBLATT, Paul M**
Kilpatrick Stockton LLP, Atlanta
404 815 6321
PRosenblatt@KilpatrickStockton.com
*Recommended in Bankruptcy*
**Practice Areas:** General bankruptcy
with a focus on bankruptcy and related
litigation including fraud, fraudulent
conveyances, preferences and telecom
issues. Bankruptcy transactional issues
including asset sales and auctions. Has
represented Fortune 100 companies as
creditors and purchasers in major bankruptcy cases.
**Prof. Memberships:** American Bankruptcy Institute.
**Career:** Partner since 2003.
**Publications:** Has lectured on the interplay of bankruptcy and telecom issues.
**Personal:** BBA Accounting, Emory University, 1991; JD, Emory University, 1994.

**ROSENBLOUM, Robert**
Greenberg Traurig LLP, Atlanta
678 553 2250
rosenbloumb@gtlaw.com
*Recommended in Intellectual Property*

**Practice Areas:** Entertainment, intellec-
tual property, technology.
**Prof. Memberships:** Chairman, South-
eastern Chapter - Copyright Society of
the USA, Governing Committee Member, ABA Forum on Entertainment &
Sports Industries, Member, Georgia State
Bar Entertainment & Sports Law Section,
Associate Member, NARAS.
**Publications:** 'The Publishing Problem
and The Call for a New Compulsory
License', ABA 10/02; 'The Collision of
Music, Television and the Net - An Analysis of the DMCA Section 104 Report as it
Pertains to the Music Industry', ABA,
10/01; 'Sorting Through the Confusion -
Interpreting Standard Recording Agree-
ment Provisions in the Digital Era', Talent
in the New Millennium, MIDEM 2001.

**RUBY, Jay C**
Ogletree, Deakins, Nash, Smoak &
Stewart, PC, Atlanta 404 881 1300
jay.ruby@ogletreedeakins.com
*Recommended in Immigration*
**Practice Areas:** Immigration, including
advice to corporations regarding Form I-
9 compliance and the procurement of
temporary (H-1B, L-1, E-2, TN, O-1, H-
2B, H-3, J-1, Q-1 and B-1) and perma-
nent employment-based visas.
**Prof. Memberships:** American Immi-
gration Lawyers Association, Louisiana
State Bar Association, Georgia State Bar
Association.
**Career:** Admitted to practice in Georgia,
Louisiana, the US Supreme Court and
the US District Court (Eastern District-
Louisiana).
**Publications:** 'Indiana Guide To Hiring
& Managing Foreign Employees', Indiana
Chamber of Commerce. Has lectured
and written extensively on US immigra-
tion law matters.
**Personal:** Indiana University (BA, 1989),
Louisiana State University (JD, 1992).

**RUSCHE, Mark C**
Alston & Bird LLP, Atlanta
404 881 7281
mrusche@alston.com
*Recommended in Real Estate*
**Practice Areas:** Practice focuses on
commercial office leasing, acquisitions
and dispositions, joint venture work and
senior housing transactions.
**Career:** Leader of the firm's Real Estate
Finance and Investment Group. Represents landlords and tenants across the
country in major office leasing transactions. On the Board of Editors of Commercial Leasing Law & Strategy, a nationally circulated monthly newsletter. Handled over $600 million in senior housing
transactions in the past five years. Frequent writer and speaker on commercial
leasing and other real estate topics.
**Personal:** BA, Furman University
(1981); JD, cum laude, Order of the Coif,
University of South Carolina (1985).

**RUSS, Michael**
King & Spalding LLP, Atlanta
404 572 4774
mruss@kslaw.com
*Recommended in Antitrust, Litigation*
**Practice Areas:** Corporate and securi-
ties litigation, SEC and tax investigations,
as well as general commercial disputes.
Specializes in representation of corporate
clients in securities and antitrust class
actions and internal corporate investiga-
tions.
**Prof. Memberships:** American Bar
Association; American College of Trial
Lawyers; The District of Columbia Bar;
State Bar of Georgia.
**Personal:** AB, Duke University, 1966; JD,
Duke University, Order of the Coif, 1969.

**RYAN, Allison M**
Alston & Bird LLP, Atlanta
404 881 7439
aryan@alston.com
*Recommended in Real Estate*
**Practice Areas:** Represents institutional
real estate investors in commerical office
leasing, joint ventures, acquisitions and
dispositions and senior housing transactions. Represents borrowers and lenders
in traditional and conduit financing.
Focuses on urban, mixed-use developments including retail/condo projects.
**Prof. Memberships:** State Bar of Georgia; Atlanta Bar Association; Commercial
Real Estate Women.
**Personal:** BBA (1993), JD (1996) - University of Michigan.

**SALYERS, Douglas**
Troutman Sanders LLP, Atlanta
404 885 3000
*Recommended in Intellectual Property*

**SAPP, J Lewis**
Elarbee, Thompson, Sapp & Wilson, LLP,
Atlanta 404 659 6700
*Recommended in Employment*

**SAUNTRY, June**
Troutman Sanders LLP, Atlanta
404 885 3000
*Recommended in Antitrust*

**SCHRODER, Jack**
Alston & Bird LLP, Atlanta
404 881 7685
jschroder@alston.com
*Recommended in Healthcare*
**Practice Areas:** Healthcare, regulatory
compliance, peer review, certificate of
need, legislative advocacy.
**Prof. Memberships:** State Bar of Geor-
gia; Georgia Academy of Healthcare
Attorneys (former President); Atlanta Bar
Association (former President); Atlanta
Bar Foundation (former President);
American Health Lawyers Association
(former Member, Board of Directors).
**Career:** Frequent lecturer on programs
sponsored by the American Health
Lawyers Association, the American Bar
Association, and the Georgia Hospital
Association. Listed in three leading legal

publications for healthcare expertise.
**Publications:** Author, 'Credentialing
Strategies for a Changing Environment',
BNA's Health Law & Business Series.
**Personal:** AB, Emory University (1970);
JD, University of Georgia (1973).

**SCHULZE, Melvin S**
Hunton & Williams, Atlanta
404 888 4021
mschulze@hunton.com
*Recommended in Environment*
**Practice Areas:** Mel Schulze's practice
focuses on assisting clients in rulemakings, permitting proceedings, enforcement actions, and litigation under the
Clean Air Act, both in Washington and at
the local and regional level. Representative clients include electric utilities, chemical plants, and pulp and paper facilities.

**SCHWARTZ, Dale**
Dale M Schwartz & Associates LLP,
Atlanta 770 9511100
*Recommended in Immigration*

**SCHWARTZ Robert**
Smith Gambrell & Russell LLP, Atlanta
404 815 3500
*Recommended in Banking & Finance*

**SCOFIELD, Eileen MG**
Alston & Bird LLP, Atlanta
404 881 7375
eileen.scofield@alston.com
*Recommended in Immigration*
**Practice Areas:** Immigration practice
includes incoming and outgoing visa
processing; US citizenship; employment
authorization; Social Security Administration audits; Department of Homeland
Security (Bureau of BICE) audits. Assists
in establishing corporate policies and
procedures related to hiring, I-9, employment of foreign nationals and national
origin issues.
**Prof. Memberships:** State Bar of Georgia; Atlanta Bar Association; American
Immigration Lawyers Association.
**Personal:** BA, University of Hawaii
(1981); JD, University of Georgia (1985),
Recent Developments editor, Georgia
Journal of International and Comparative Law.

**SETTY, Nagendra**
Fish & Richardson P.C., Atlanta
404 942 2751
nsetty@fr.com
*Recommended in Intellectual Property*
**Practice Areas:** Managing principal of
Fish & Richardson's Atlanta office. Practice emphasizes all aspects of intellectual
property litigation and counseling,
including patent, trademark, trade
secrets, and copyright cases, with a special
focus on patent litigation.
**Prof. Memberships:** ABA Intellectual
Property Law Section, Asian Patent Attorneys Association, Atlanta Bar Association,
State Bar of Georgia, International Trademark Association (INTA).
**Publications:** Spoken at numerous IP

and patent law conferences, including the ABA Annual Meeting (2005-06), LSI Biotechnology Conference (2005) and National South Asian Bar Association Annual Meetings (2004 and 2005).
**Personal:** Emory University BS Biology 1987; Emory University School of Law JD 1992.

## SHACKELFORD, Richard L
King & Spalding LLP, Atlanta
404 572 4995
rshackelford@kslaw.com
*Recommended in Healthcare*
**Practice Areas:** Healthcare practice and business litigation focusing on health systems, hospitals, home health agencies, long term care facilities, physician organizations, pharmaceutical and medical device companies, and managed care organizations in a wide variety of litigation and regulatory matters.
**Prof. Memberships:** American Bar Association; American Health Lawyers Association; Atlanta Bar Association; State Bar of Georgia.
**Personal:** BA, University of Georgia, 1976; JD, University of Georgia, 1979.

## SHAPIRO, J Ben
Shapiro Fussell, Atlanta
404 870 2200
*Recommended in Construction*

## SHARBAUGH, Charles
Paul, Hastings, Janofsky & Walker LLP, Atlanta 404 815 2213
charliesharbaugh@paulhastings.com
*Recommended in Real Estate*
**Practice Areas:** Real estate.
**Prof. Memberships:** American Bar Association, Georgia Bar Association, Atlanta Bar Association.
**Career:** Partner, Paul, Hastings, Janofsky & Walker LLP.
**Personal:** Member of the Board of Directors of Zoo Atlanta, Chair of the Finance Committee and of the Property Committee of Zoo Atlanta, Member of the Executive Committee of Zoo Atlanta, Member of the Board of Directors of Druid Hills Golf Club, Graduate of The Pennsylvania State University, BS Economics, Graduate of Duke University, JD.

## SHELEY, Raymond
Sheley & Hall, Atlanta
404 880 1350
*Recommended in Real Estate*

## SHERMAN, Kyle
Paul, Hastings, Janofsky & Walker LLP, Atlanta 404 815 2297
kylesherman@paulhastings.com
*Recommended in Immigration*
**Practice Areas:** Kyle is rapidly attaining national recognition as a seasoned immigration advisor. He represents employers before US Citizenship and Immigration Services (USCIS), the Department of Labor and the Department of State in connection with immigration-related matters. He has particular expertise

regarding I-9 compliance and immigration-related wage and hour issues concerning the hiring of foreign national employees, and he co-chairs the immigration group's Federal Enforcement and Corporate Compliance team. Kyle chairs the American Immigration Lawyer's Association's Atlanta Chapter and has chaired the national association's USCIS Texas Service Center Liaison Committee. He has lectured widely on immigration topics.

## SHORT JR, Herbert J
Sutherland Asbill & Brennan LLP, Atlanta 404 853 8491
herbert.short@sablaw.com
*Recommended in Energy*
**Practice Areas:** Serves as advisor to executives and boards of energy-related companies on a broad range of corporate matters, securities and Sarbanes-Oxley matters. In 2005, began serving as General Counsel for Oglethorpe Power Corporation. Represents Basin Electric Power Cooperative, Goldman, Sachs & Co., Old Dominion Electric Cooperative, Merrill Lynch, JPMorgan, Oglethorpe Power Corporation and Tri-State G&T Association, Inc. in taxable and tax-exempt bond financings.
**Prof. Memberships:** Chairman, Business Law Section of the State Bar of Georgia (1996-97); Member, Corporation, Banking and Business Law Section; Member, Board of Directors of the Georgia Chamber of Commerce; Chair of Red Carpet Tour for Georgia Chamber, 2006; Chair of Economic Development for the Georgia Chamber; Named as one of Georgia's Super Lawyers during 2004, 2005 and 2006 in the Atlanta Magazine; Member, Public Utility Law Section; Member, Electric Cooperative Bar Association of the American Bar Association, Member, Business and Finance Section of the Atlanta Bar Association; Member, Corporate Counsel Section of the Georgia State Bar.
**Personal:** JD, magna cum laude, University of Georgia School of Law, 1985, Phi Kappa Phi, Order of the Coif; BBA, summa cum laude, University of Georgia, 1982 First Honor Graduate.

## SIGMUND, Rebecca
Powell Goldstein LLP, Atlanta
404 572 6600
*Recommended in Immigration*

## SILLIMAN, Todd
McKenna Long & Aldridge LLP, Atlanta 404 527 4914
tsilliman@mckennalong.com
*Recommended in Environment*
**Practice Areas:** Concentrates on advising and representing clients in regulatory matters, environmental litigation, and transactions involving commercial real estate. Assists clients in obtaining water supply, industrial wastewater discharge, wetlands dredge and fill, air pollution

control, and coastal development permits and defends clients in regulatory enforcement actions. Is a member of the legal team representing the State of Georgia in interstate water allocation negotiations with the States of Alabama and Florida and in related litigation in Atlanta, Alabama, and Washington, DC against the US Army Corps of Engineers concerning operation of federal reservoirs in Georgia. Advises clients on issues related to development and permitting of private water supply and wastewater systems.
**Prof. Memberships:** State Bar of Georgia, Environmental Section (Chair 2001); American Bar Association, Section of Environment, Energy, and Resources; Institute for Georgia Environmental Leadership (Member of the Board of Directors).
**Personal:** University of Virginia School of Law (JD, 1993); University of North Carolina (BA, with honors and highest distinction, 1990).

## SIMMONS, Teri A
Arnall Golden Gregory LLP, Atlanta
404 873 8612
teri.simmons@agg.com
*Recommended in Immigration*
**Practice Areas:** Chair, International/Immigration Practice.
**Prof. Memberships:** American Immigration Lawyers Association (former Chapter Chair); Georgia Indo-American Chamber of Commerce (President); Atlanta Sister Cities Commission (Chair); Lawyers Club of Atlanta (member).
**Career:** Arnall Golden Gregory LLP, 1991-present; Cofer & Beauchamp 1989-91.
**Publications:** American Immigration Lawyers Association, articles on mergers and acquisitions, tax issues in an immigration practice, change of status and others, Florida Bar Association. Article on visas for extraordinary foreign nationals, 'Aufenthalt und Einwanderung in die USA fuer auslaendische Staatsbuerger' (Haufe Verlag).
**Personal:** JD, University of Georgia, 1989; University of Tübingen, 1985-86, (Post-Graduate Studies); MA, University of Virginia, 1985 (German Studies); BA, Furman University, 1983 (Mathematics and German).

## SINKFIELD, Richard
Rogers & Hardin, Atlanta
404 522 4700
*Recommended in Litigation*

## SMITH, George Anthony
Kilpatrick Stockton LLP, Atlanta
404 815 6070
TSmith@KilpatrickStockton.com
*Recommended in Construction*
**Practice Areas:** Construction contract negotiation, arbitration, litigation, and international dispute resolution, focusing on power, water and wastewater, transportation and other major infrastructure

projects.
**Prof. Memberships:** International, American, Georgia, and Kentucky Bar Associations; American College of Construction Lawyers; Centre for International Legal Studies; Chartered Institute of Arbitrators; London Court of International Arbitration; Construction Panel Advisory Committee of the CPR Institute for Dispute Resolution (Chair).
**Publications:** Has lectured and written extensively on many topics of interest to the construction industry and the international arbitration community.
**Personal:** BA, with distinction, University of Kentucky, 1970; JD, with high distinction, University of Kentucky, 1973.

## SMITH, Gordon
King & Spalding LLP, Atlanta
404 572 4777
gsmith@kslaw.com
*Recommended in Litigation*
**Practice Areas:** Defense of high profile products liability cases across the US. Served as lead trial and appellate counsel for a number of the country's largest tobacco, automotive, pharmaceutical and heavy equipment manufacturers. Successfully coordinated defense of hundreds of product liability cases on behalf of several manufacturers as regional and national counsel.
**Prof. Memberships:** American Bar Association; American College of Trial Lawyers; Atlanta Bar Association; State Bar of Georgia.
**Personal:** ABJ, magna cum laude, University of Georgia, 1975; JD, University of Georgia, 1978, Order of the Barrister, Chairman of the Moot Court Board.

## SMITH, James
Troutman Sanders LLP, Atlanta
404 885 3000
*Recommended in Corporate/M&A*

## SMITH, Jerry
Kilpatrick Stockton LLP, Atlanta
404 815 6529
JnSmith@KilpatrickStockton.com
*Recommended in Tax*
**Practice Areas:** US federal and state tax matters, including advice regarding merger, acquisition structuring; federal and state tax credits; and optimal ownership of intellectual property. Has advised corporations regarding inbound and outbound investments. Has represented corporations and partnerships related to controversy matters before the IRS and state departments of revenue.
**Prof. Memberships:** American Institute of Certified Public Accountants; American Bar Association.
**Career:** Spent 20 years with KPMG as a tax Partner. Tax Partner at Kilpatrick Stockton since 2004.
**Personal:** BS Accounting, University of North Carolina, Chapel Hill, 1979; JD, Vanderbilt Law School, 1985, associate editor, Vanderbilt Law Review.

## SMITH III, Frank G
Alston & Bird LLP, Atlanta
404 881 7240
fsmith@alston.com
*Recommended in Intellectual Property*
**Practice Areas:** Intellectual property litigation, including patents and copyrights; antitrust; white-collar crime.
**Prof. Memberships:** State Bar of Georgia.
**Career:** Co-Chair, Alston & Bird IP-Litigation Group. Former member of firm's Partners' Committee. Litigated complex matters in federal courts in Alabama, California, Florida, Georgia, Louisiana, Mississippi, North Carolina, South Carolina, Massachusetts, Michigan and Virginia.
**Publications:** Authored numerous articles on intellectual property issues and litigation generally.
**Personal:** BA, Davidson College (1974); JD, Stanford University (1977).

## SOLOMON, Jay
The Law Offices of Jay I. Solomon
Atlanta 770 955 1055
*Recommended in Immigration*

## SPANGLER III, John I
Alston & Bird LLP, Atlanta
404 881 7146
jspangler@alston.com
*Recommended in Construction*
**Practice Areas:** Extensive experience with construction disputes and transactions, including design-build, construction management, general construction, design, program management. Project finance transactions; prosecuting and defending delay, interference, acceleration, extended overhead and defective construction and design claims.
**Prof. Memberships:** Atlanta Bar Association Construction Law Section (Chair 1994-95); American Bar Association (Construction Industry Forum and Litigation Sections); Forum Governing Committee (2004-07); State Bar of Georgia (Litigation Section).
**Career:** Chairs the firm's Construction and Government Contracts Group.
**Publications:** Authored numerous articles on construction law issues; co-editor of 'The Construction Contracts Book' (ABA 2004).
**Personal:** AB, University of Illinois (1977); JD, Washington University (1980).

## STAIR, Kent
Carlock Copeland Semler & Stair, LLP, Atlanta 404 522 8220
*Recommended in Construction*

## STEIN, Grant T
Alston & Bird LLP, Atlanta
404 881 7285
gstein@alston.com
*Recommended in Bankruptcy*
**Practice Areas:** Practice includes regular representation of debtors, secured and unsecured creditors, creditors' committees, and fiduciaries in complex out-of-court workouts, debt restructurings and bankruptcy cases, and in bankruptcy related litigation.
**Prof. Memberships:** Fellow, American College of Bankruptcy; Director, Southeastern Bankruptcy Law Institute, Director and Vice President, Association of Insolvency and Restructuring Advisors (AIRA).
**Career:** Listed in leading legal publications.
**Publications:** Written numerous articles on bankruptcy and workout issues, and regularly lectures around the country.
**Personal:** BBA, cum laude, Emory University (1978); JD, cum laude, University of Georgia (1981).

## STEIN, Jeffrey
King & Spalding LLP, Atlanta
404 572 4729
jstein@kslaw.com
*Recommended in Corporate/M&A*
**Practice Areas:** Corporate finance transactions and securities matters, focusing on public offerings, representing corporate issuers and underwriters in shelf registrations of investment-grade debt securities, medium-term note programs, high-yield securities offerings and initial public offerings of common stock. Advice regarding SEC reporting and disclosure requirements, securities transactions and corporate governance and compliance matters.
**Prof. Memberships:** American Bar Association (Legal Opinions Committees); New York State Bar Association; New York City, County and State Bar Associations (Tri-Bar Legal Opinion Committee); State Bar of Georgia.
**Personal:** BA, summa cum laude, Yeshiva University, 1977; JD, Harvard University, 1980.

## STEPHENSON, Mason W
King & Spalding LLP, Atlanta
404 572 4945
mstephenson@kslaw.com
*Recommended in Real Estate*
**Practice Areas:** Commercial real estate law, representing banks, credit companies, life insurance companies, pension funds and institutional investors in secured financings and equity investments in income properties, including office buildings, hotels, apartments and industrial properties. Extensive experience in workout, restructure and foreclosure of real estate investments.
**Prof. Memberships:** American College of Real Estate Lawyers; Atlanta Bar Association (former Chairman, Real Estate Section); State Bar of Georgia (former member, Executive Committee, Real Estate Section).
**Personal:** AB, cum laude, Phi Beta Kappa, Davidson College, 1968; JD, University of Chicago, 1971. Frequent lecturer on commercial real estate and ethics topics.

## STOCKTON, David
Kilpatrick Stockton LLP, Atlanta
404 815 6444
DStockton@KilpatrickStockton.com
*Recommended in Corporate/M&A*
**Practice Areas:** Advises businesses in all aspects of corporate finance, including initial, secondary and follow-on public offerings, private placements, securities regulations, and mergers and acquisitions. Advises special committees, management groups and issuers in structuring, negotiating and documenting going private transactions.
**Prof. Memberships:** State Bar of Georgia (Chair of the Business Law Section, former chairman of its Securities Committee); Atlanta Bar Association (past Chair – Business Practice Section).
**Publications:** 'Going Private: The Best Option?' National Law Journal (June 2003).
**Personal:** BA, Emory University; JD, University of North Carolina at Chapel Hill School of Law (Order of the Coif).

## STONE, Benjamin
Munger & Stone, Atlanta
404 815 1884
*Recommended in Employment*

## STREET, Phillip
Kilpatrick Stockton LLP, Atlanta
404 815 6455
PStreet@KilpatrickStockton.com
*Recommended in Healthcare*
**Practice Areas:** Healthcare and life sciences transactions, including business mergers, acquisitions and joint ventures and the commercialization of life sciences research. Serves as legal advisor to life sciences companies, medical research organizations, medical device and pharmaceutical companies, hospitals and other healthcare and life sciences related companies.
**Prof. Memberships:** Grady Health System Board of Visitors; State Bar of Alabama; State Bar of Georgia; American Health Lawyers Association; Atlanta Tax Forum.
**Career:** Chairs the firm's Healthcare and Life Sciences Groups.
**Personal:** BA, Economics, Vanderbilt University, 1982; JD, Vanderbilt University School of Law, 1986; LLM, in Taxation, New York University, 1989.

## SUDBURY, Deborah A
Jones Day, Atlanta 404 581 8443
dsudbury@jonesday.com
*Recommended in Employment*
**Practice Areas:** Leads the Labor and Employment Practice in the Atlanta Office, specializing in defense of class and collective actions, having successfully represented many large companies in defeating class certification. Represented employers before state and federal trial and appellate courts and in a variety of state law wrongful discharge, contract, and tort claims. Her extensive trial experience includes successfully defending clients in bench and jury trials.
**Prof. Memberships:** ABA and the state bar associations of California, Illinois, and Georgia.
**Publications:** Frequent national speaker on employment law and class action defense topics and author of a book on plant closing laws.

## SWANN, Jerre
Kilpatrick Stockton LLP, Atlanta
404 815 6540
JSwann@KilpatrickStockton.com
*Recommended in Intellectual Property*
**Practice Areas:** Trademark/unfair competition litigation, survey/expert witness issues.
**Prof. Memberships:** INTA (Director, member of the Special Committee with respect to the FTDA).
**Career:** Partner since 1972; recipient 2000 Ladas Memorial Award and 2002 INTA Volunteer Service Award for the Advancement of Trademark Law.
**Publications:** Has authored more than 25 law review articles in the trademark field; has spoken at more than 25 national or regional seminars; former Editor-in-Chief of 'The Trademark Reporter'.
**Personal:** BA, Williams College, Phi Beta Kappa, National Merit Scholar, 1961; University of St. Andrews, Scotland, Rotary Foundation Fellow, 1962; JD, Harvard Law School, 1965.

## SWEENEY, Neal
Kilpatrick Stockton LLP, Atlanta
404 815 6616
NSweeney@KilpatrickStockton.com
*Recommended in Construction*
**Practice Areas:** Construction law and dispute resolution on major public works and federal projects, including dams, highways, hotels, hospitals, airports, schools, and waste water treatment facilities.
**Prof. Memberships:** State Bar of Georgia; American Bar Association (Forum Committee on the Construction Industry and the Public Contract Law Section); American Arbitration Association's National Panel of Arbitrators; Design - Build Institute of America (lecturer and President, Southeast Chapter).
**Publications:** Has written and lectured extensively on construction law and design-build, including editing or co-authoring more than 20 books.
**Personal:** Rutgers University, with high honors, 1979; JD, George Washington University, with honors, 1982.

## SWENSON, Erik
King & Spalding LLP, Atlanta
404 572 3540
eswenson@kslaw.com
*Recommended in Energy*
**Practice Areas:** Nationwide representation of energy project participants, including developers, equity investors and lenders and industrial companies in

energy matters, including the purchase and sale of electricity and energy regulation matters.

**Prof. Memberships:** District of Columbia Bar; New York State Bar.

**Personal:** BA, cum laude, Columbia College; JD, Columbia University School of Law, 1982. Lectures before energy industry leaders on project development and energy regulation. Regular contributor to energy industry publications.

**TAYLOR, Roger**
Finnegan Henderson Farabow Garrett & Dunner LLP, Atlanta
404 653 6480
roger.taylor@finnegan.com
*Recommended in Intellectual Property*

**Practice Areas:** Serves as Managing Partner of the firm's Atlanta office. Has extensive experience in protecting intellectual property rights and defending against charges of infringement in both state and federal courts. He has successfully represented numerous computer, electronic, and manufacturing companies in patent infringement litigation in various US District Courts. Has also achieved success in a series of trademark and copyright cases which stopped counterfeiting of computer components in several states. In addition to litigation practice, assists domestic and foreign corporations in obtaining patent protection for their inventions.

**Prof. Memberships:** State Bar of Georgia, District of Columbia Bar, Federal Circuit Bar Association, American Intellectual Property Law Association, Licensing Executives Society.

**Personal:** University of Arkansas (BS, Electrical Engineering, 1973); George Washington University Law Center (JD, 1980).

**THOMAS, Lizanne**
Jones Day, Atlanta
404 581 8411
lthomas@jonesday.com
*Recommended in Corporate/M&A*

**Practice Areas:** Firmwide Administrative Partner responsible for overseeing various administrative functions throughout Jones Day. She also heads the Corporate Practice in the Atlanta Office. Experienced in public and private mergers and acquisitions, corporate finance, and defensive planning. She is actively involved in corporate counseling, including advising boards of directors and committees with corporate governance, disclosure, strategic planning, and fiduciary issues. She is a recurring panelist for the Directors' Institute, sponsored by The Conference Board, and lectures at seminars sponsored by the Practising Law Institute, the ABA, and the State Bar of Georgia.

**Prof. Memberships:** State Bar of Georgia.

**THORNTON, M Robert**
King & Spalding LLP, Atlanta
404 572 4778
bthornton@kslaw.com
*Recommended in Litigation*

**Practice Areas:** Litigation focusing primarily on the areas of shareholder claims, director and officer liability and insurance, securities, SEC and NASD investigations, audit committee and other internal investigations, consumer fraud class actions, professional liability and legal ethics.

**Prof. Memberships:** American Bar Association; Atlanta Bar Association; State Bar of Georgia.

**Personal:** BA, cum laude, Princeton University, 1973; JD, cum laude, Harvard, 1976.

**TISDALE JR, Charles H**
King & Spalding LLP, Atlanta
404 572 4820
ctisdale@kslaw.com
*Recommended in Environment*

**Practice Areas:** 30 years' experience in environmental law, representing clients on air, water, and superfund and hazardous waste issues before state and federal agencies and in litigation.

**Prof. Memberships:** American Bar Association; Chemical Waste Litigation Reporter (Board); State Bar of Georgia (former Chairman, Environmental Law Section).

**Personal:** BA, cum laude, Vanderbilt University, 1969; JD, with distinction, Emory University, Order of the Coif; Omicron Delta Kappa, 1972.

**TOULME, Nill V**
Alston & Bird LLP, Atlanta
404 881 7143
ntoulme@alston.com
*Recommended in Environment*

**Practice Areas:** Focuses on litigation and counseling regarding environmental, science and toxic tort issues and environmental aspects of mergers and acquisitions and real estate, financial and fiduciary transactions.

**Prof. Memberships:** Chairs the Technology Committee of international law firm consortium, Lex Mundi. Founder and past Chairman, Environmental & Toxic Tort Section of the Atlanta Bar Association; past Chairman, State Bar of Georgia Environmental Law Section.

**Personal:** BA, magna cum laude, Duke University (1974); JD, University of Virginia School of Law (1978).

**VARNER, Chilton**
King & Spalding LLP, Atlanta
404 572 4789
cvarner@kslaw.com
*Recommended in Litigation, Products Liability*

**Practice Areas:** 25 years of courtroom experience defending corporations in product liability, commercial and civil disputes. Trial and appellate counsel for

large automotive, pharmaceutical and medical device manufacturers in mass tort litigation, class actions and MDL litigation, including attorney-client privilege and Daubert issues.

**Prof. Memberships:** American Bar Association; American College of Trial Lawyers; Atlanta Bar Association; Emory University (Trustee); Product Liability Advisory Council (Member); State Bar of Georgia.

**Personal:** AB, with distinction, Phi Beta Kappa, Smith College, 1965; JD, with distinction, Emory University, Order of the Coif, 1976. Distinguished Alumni Award, Emory University Law School.

**VAUGHAN, C David**
Vaughan & Murphy, Atlanta
404 577 6550
*Recommended in Antitrust*

**WALKER, Homer Lee**
Alston & Bird LLP, Atlanta
404 881 7338
lwalker@alston.com
*Recommended in Real Estate*

**Practice Areas:** Mixed-use and multi-use, retail, hotel, residential and office projects from a developer's perspective. Experienced in joint venture and project finance transactions, as well as complex easement and restrictive covenant agreements related to these types of development projects.

**Prof. Memberships:** Member, Real Estate Section of the State Bar of Georgia, International Council of Shopping Centers, Urban Land Institute, and Real Estate Group of Atlanta.

**Career:** Partner in the firm's Real Estate Finance and Investment Group. Frequent speaker on developer oriented topics related to commercial real estate assets.

**Personal:** BA, University of Georgia (1983); JD, Emory University (1986).

**WASSERMAN, Michael**
Holt Ney Zatcoff & Wasserman, LLP, Atlanta 770 956 9600
*Recommended in Tax*

**WEIRICH, Geoff**
Paul, Hastings, Janofsky & Walker LLP, Atlanta 404 815 2221
geoffweirich@paulhastings.com
*Recommended in Employment*

**Practice Areas:** Exclusively advises and represents employers regarding a wide range of employment law issues. Particularly known for defending complex employment discrimination claims. Has handled over three dozen employment class actions.

**Prof. Memberships:** ABA Labor and Employment Law Section (Publications Chair, Equal Employment Opportunity Committee).

**Publications:** Editor-in-Chief (Fourth Edition (in progress) and 2002 Third Cumulative Supplement to Third Edition) of the B Lindemann & P Grossman

treatise, 'Employment Discrimination Law'.

**Personal:** MA, Labor and Industrial Relations and BA, Economics (Michigan State University). JD (Duke University School of Law)(Order of the Coif, Executive Editor of 'Duke Law Journal').

**WELLS, Della Wager**
Alston & Bird LLP, Atlanta
404 881 7891
dwells@alston.com
*Recommended in Energy*

**Practice Areas:** Concentrates on municipal bond law and authority representation and related corporate, tax and securities matters involving taxable and tax-exempt financings for electric and gas facilities and commodities, water and sewerage facilities and other public projects on behalf of governmental entities.

**Prof. Memberships:** Member of the National Association of Bond Lawyers and has served two terms on the Executive Committee of the Atlanta Contemporary Art Center.

**Personal:** BA, magna cum laude, University of Georgia (1980); MA, University of Virginia (1983); JD, with distinction, Emory University (1986).

**WENICK, George**
Smith, Currie & Hancock LLP, Atlanta
404 521 3800
*Recommended in Construction*

**WHITE, Benjamin T**
Alston & Bird LLP, Atlanta
404 881 7488
bwhite@alston.com
*Recommended in Tax*

**Practice Areas:** Exempt organizations, estate and tax planning.

**Prof. Memberships:** Fellow, American College of Trust and Estate Counsel; founding faculty member, American Institute for Philanthropic Studies; former president, Harvard Law School Association of Georgia; Member, American Bar Assocciation Section of Real Property, Probate and Trust Law and Exempt Organizations Committee, Tax Section.

**Career:** Chairs the firm's Exempt Organizations Group and co-chairs the Wealth Planning Group.

**Publications:** Co-author, 'Georgia Estate Planning, Will Drafting and Estate Administration Forms – Practice'. Author, 'Foundation Desk Reference: A Compendium of Private Foundation Rules'.

**Personal:** AB, University of North Carolina (1969); JD, Harvard University (1973).

**WHITLOCK, David C**
Fisher & Phillips LLP, Atlanta
404 240 4210
dwhitlock@laborlawyers.com
*Recommended in Immigration*

**Practice Areas:** David C Whitlock is a Partner in the Atlanta office of the national law firm of Fisher & Phillips LLP and the Chief Information Officer of Prevention Point, a human resources consulting affiliate company of Fisher & Phillips LLP. His practice is focused on immigration and nationality law, including both temporary and permanent visa cases, as well as compliance with the I-9, discrimination, and document abuse provisions of the Immigration Reform and Control Act of 1986. Whitlock received a JD with honors from the University of Iowa College of Law and his Undergraduate Degree from Hamilton College.

**WHITNEY, Charles W**
Duane Morris LLP, Atlanta
404 253 6940
cwwhitney@duanemorris.com
*Recommended in Energy*
**Practice Areas:** Charles W Whitney focuses his practice on energy, regulatory, construction and labor law. He has legal experience that spans a broad range of activities in both private practice and as chief counsel to a nuclear generating plant project. He has represented independent power producers and engineering, procurement and construction (EPC) contractors in the development, construction and operation of power projects in Georgia, New York, Pennsylvania, Ohio, Michigan and Wisconsin. His nuclear work has included negotiating and documenting all commercial activities; construction claim litigation;

applying for and prosecuting a license to operate the facility from the Nuclear Regulatory Commission (NRC); negotiating and documenting the resolution of warranty and contract claims against suppliers, vendors, and professional service providers; and 'whistleblower' defense.
**Prof. Memberships:** American Bar Association; State Bar of Georgia; Atlanta Bar Association.
**Career:** Admitted to practice in Georgia; Supreme Court of the United States; United States Courts of Appeals for the Fifth and Eleventh Circuits; United States District Courts for the Northern, Middle and Southern Districts of Georgia; State Courts of Georgia.
**Personal:** Case Western Reserve University School of Law, JD, Order of the Coif and Order of Barristers, 1977.

**WILLIAMSON, Robert**
Scroggins & Williamson, Atlanta
404 893 3880
*Recommended in Bankruptcy*

**WILSON, Brent**
Elarbee, Thompson, Sapp & Wilson, LLP, Atlanta 404 659 6700
*Recommended in Employment*

**WILSON, Stanford**
Elarbee, Thompson, Sapp & Wilson, LLP, Atlanta 404 659 6700
*Recommended in Employment*

**WINSBERG, Harris**
Troutman Sanders LLP, Atlanta
404 885 3000
*Recommended in Bankruptcy*

**WOODWARD, Robert**
King & Spalding LLP, Atlanta
404 572 3353
bwoodward@kslaw.com
*Recommended in Tax*
**Practice Areas:** Business tax issues, focusing on corporate mergers, acquisitions, restructurings and financings. Experience in tax, business and estate planning issues relating to corporate executives and closely held businesses and owners in tax controversies.
**Prof. Memberships:** American Bar Association (Chair, Subcommittee on Tax-Free Acquisitions); Atlanta Tax Forum (Former President and Trustee); Georgia Federal Tax Conference (Trustee); State Bar of Georgia.
**Personal:** BA, magna cum laude, Washington & Lee University, 1971; JD, Yale University, 1975.

**WYMER, John**
King & Spalding LLP, Atlanta
404 572 2413
jwymer@kslaw.com
*Recommended in Employment*
**Practice Areas:** Representing employers (private and public) in labor and employment-related disputes, class action litigation, employment discrimination cases,

sexual harassment claims, National Labor Relations Board matters, arbitrations, wage/hour disputes and labor negotiations.
**Prof. Memberships:** Alabama State Bar; The College of Labor and Employment Lawyers Fellow; Management Labor and Employment Law Roundtable.
**Personal:** BA, University of Alabama, 1971; JD, University of Virginia, 1974.

**ZACKS, David M**
Kilpatrick Stockton LLP, Atlanta
404 815 6100
DZacks@KilpatrickStockton.com
*Recommended in Litigation*
**Practice Areas:** Representing and defending major healthcare institutions, serving as counsel for Plaintiffs in catastrophic injury cases, and serving as arbitrator and mediator for Alternative Dispute Resolution matters.
**Prof. Memberships:** Georgia and North Carolina Bar Associations (former Chairman Antitrust Section, Georgia State Bar); Leadership Georgia (former Trustee).
**Career:** Partner since 1976.
**Personal:** Wake Forest University, JD, 1967; Wake Forest University BA, 1964; Judge Advocate General Army JAGC; certified Military Judge. Served as National Chair, American Cancer Society.

# ALSTON & BIRD LLP

## THE FIRM

**Managing Partner:** Ben F Johnson III
**Deputy Managing Partner:** Philip C Cook
**Number of partners:** 300
**Number of other lawyers:** 400

**FIRM OVERVIEW:** Alston & Bird is a major US law firm with 700 attorneys located in offices in Atlanta, Charlotte, New York, the Research Triangle and Washington, DC, offering services in virtually every practice area from antitrust to wealth planning. An important factor that differentiates Alston & Bird is its culture. For the seventh consecutive year, Alston & Bird is ranked on the 'FORTUNE 100 Best Companies To Work For' list.

## MAIN AREAS OF PRACTICE:

**Capital Markets/Mergers & Acquisitions:** The firm's attorneys have extensive experience with complex mergers and acquisitions, spin-offs, going private transactions, joint ventures and similar transactions for clients in a broad range of industries. Alston & Bird attorneys work on deals ranging from high-profile public transactions to acquisitions for closely-held businesses. The firm represents bidders, target companies, stockholders, boards of directors and financial advisors. Alston & Bird lawyers have been involved in all aspects of leveraged buyouts and distressed sales and can handle the acquisition and financing of public and non-public companies of any size.

**Energy:** The Energy Group has a wide-ranging practice before the Federal Energy Regulatory Commission (FERC), federal and state courts, and state public utility commissions. The subjects of their federal and state representations include energy-related transactions, the development and operation of energy markets, and the ongoing regulation of the production, transportation, distribution and trading of electric energy products. Other members of the group focus exclusively on energy finance.

**Financial Services:** The financial services and products lawyers provide a wide range of corporate governance, merger and acquisition, regulatory, securities and structured finance and products services to the firm's banking, insurance, investment management, broker-dealer, mutual fund, payments system and alternative investment vehicle clients.

**Healthcare:** Alston & Bird has a national healthcare practice with more than 60 attorneys dedicated to the healthcare industry and one of the largest practices in the US. The signature strength of this practice is Alston & Bird's ability to master complex representations that draw on the coordinated expertise of the firm's regulatory, transactional, biotechnology, and litigation groups. The healthcare group includes DOJ lawyers and former federal prosecutors who were involved in healthcare matters, former FDA officials, a former OIG lawyer, two former US Senate Majority Leaders (Senators Bob Dole and Tom Daschle) who championed healthcare legislation, Tom Scully (former Administrator of the Centers for Medicare & Medicaid Services (CMS)), and several Congressional staffers who conceived, drafted and saw through passsage of the most significant healthcare legislation in decades - the Medicare Prescription Drug, Improvement and Modernization Act of 2003.

**Intellectual Property:** Numbering more than 130 lawyers, including 90 legal professionals registered to practice before the US Patent and Trademark office, Alston & Bird's Intellectual Property Group is one of the largest in any general practice firm in the country. The group provides a full range of intellectual property services including: patentability and prosecution; appeals; oppositions; patent maintenance; counseling regarding infringement avoidance; and validity and infringement studies and opinions. In 2005, Alston & Bird tied for 3rd among top US law firms protecting the IP rights of the Fortune 250 as ranked by *IP Law and Business*.

**Legislative & Public Policy:** Alston & Bird's Legislative & Public Policy Group has unique experience with how policy is made with the people who make it. The firm represents clients before Congress, the executive branch, and regulatory agencies. It prepares and delivers testimony before congressional commit-

## OFFICES

### GEORGIA
One Atlantic Center, 1201 West Peachtree Street, **Atlanta**, GA 30309-3424
**Tel:** 404 881 7000  **Fax:** 404 881 7777
**Email:** info@alston.com  **Website:** www.alston.com

### DISTRICT OF COLUMBIA
The Atlantic Building, 950 F Street, NW, **Washington,** DC 20004
**Tel:** 202 756 3300  **Fax:** 202 756 3333

### NEW YORK
90 Park Avenue, **New York,** NY 10016-1387
**Tel:** 212 210 9400  **Fax:** 212 210 9444

### NORTH CAROLINA
Bank of America Plaza, 101 South Tryon Street, Suite 4000
**Charlotte,** NC 28280-4000
**Tel:** 704 444 1000  **Fax:** 704 444 1111

3201 Beechleaf Court, Suite 600, **Raleigh,** NC 27604-1062
**Tel:** 919 862 2200  **Fax:** 919 862 2260

tees on behalf of clients, and works directly with staff and members to help craft legislative and regulatory language. The firm's clients get the unique perspective of two highly respected former Senate Majority Leaders (Senators Bob Dole and Tom Daschle), the former tax counsel for the US Senate Finance Committee, the former general counsel of the INS, the former general counsel of the Department of Homeland Security and former senior officials from the FDA and Departments of Justice, State, and Treasury.

**Litigation:** Alston & Bird's more than 280 litigators have litigated in every state in the country and in international disputes in virtually every major industrialized jurisdiction, including Latin America, Europe and Asia. The firm's litigation practice groups include antitrust, bankruptcy, construction, environmental and land use, ERISA, international, international trade and regulatory, labor and employment, products liability and securities.

**Tax:** With nearly 70 tax lawyers, Alston & Bird has one of the largest law firm tax practices in the United States. Divided into six main practice groups – Federal, International, State & Local, Employee Benefits and Executive Compensation, Wealth Planning and Exempt Organizations – Alston & Bird is broadly experienced in serving the tax planning, dispute resolution, and tax legislative and regulatory needs of both US and foreign businesses and their owners.

**CLIENTS:** AFLAC, Assurant Inc., BellSouth Corporation, The Boeing Company, Delta Air Lines, Inc., The Dow Chemical Company, Genuine Parts Company, IMERYS, Mohawk Industries, Inc., NASCAR, Nokia, The Prudential Insurance Company of America, Regions Financial Corporation, Sabre, Skanska USA Building Inc., UnumProvident Corporation, UPS, Verizon Communications Corporation, and Wachovia.

**INTERNATIONAL WORK:** Alston & Bird's International Group is a multidisciplinary team of business investment, intellectual property, tax, finance, regulatory, immigration, customs, and litigation experts. The group has structured deals and handled disputes around the globe - from Latin America and Europe to Asia and the Middle East. Alston & Bird's international practice has extensive experience in planning, structuring and implementing business deals in virtually every major commercial jurisdiction in the world. The firm can find and help you select the best local counsel, as well as help you determine the optimal structure for your business transaction abroad, whether it involves an acquisition, joint venture, licensing arrangement, technology transfer, manufacturing contract, distribution agreement or other arrangement.

# ALSTON+BIRD LLP

# ARNALL GOLDEN GREGORY LLP

## THE FIRM

**Chairman:** Jonathan Golden
**Managing Partner:** William H Kitchens
**Total number of attorneys:** 128

**FIRM OVERVIEW:** Arnall Golden Gregory LLP is an Atlanta firm that serves the business transaction needs of growing public and private companies. Through mergers and acquisitions, capital markets financing, strategic alliances, joint ventures, litigation and other business-related guidance, the firm helps clients across a broad range of industries turn legal challenges into business opportunities.

## MAIN AREAS OF PRACTICE:

**Mergers & Acquisitions:** AGG's Mergers and Acquisitions Practice covers a range of acquisition-related legal services, including tax, securities, technology and intellectual property, environmental, healthcare, employee benefits, and food and drug law. The firm's clients include companies from a variety of industries and business types, with transaction size typically ranging from $10m to $1b. The firm represents both purchasers and sellers, many of which are public companies and non-US companies engaged in US and non-US transactions.

**Real Estate:** Attorneys in the Real Estate Practice help domestic and international real estate owners, developers, and investors navigate the diverse business and legal issues that impact commercial real estate transactions. They also have a great deal of experience with foreign investors in US real estate. AGG represents companies in affordable housing, retail, office leasing and mixed-use development, regional/super regional malls, real estate-based lending, and portfolio investment.

**Litigation/Bankruptcy:** The firm's Litigation Practice handles matters at the trial and appellate court levels and before administrative agencies. General business, intellectual property, and employment law litigation are key areas of focus. AGG's Bankruptcy Practice concentrates on commercial debt restructuring, settlements, bankruptcy trusteeships, and creditors' rights litigation.

**Securities & Corporate Governance:** AGG counsels public and private companies, as well as officers, directors, investors, and underwriters, in matters regarding securities transactions, compliance and corporate governance. Clients include entrepreneurial private companies, as well as large companies listed on the NYSE, NASDAQ, AMEX and OTC Bulletin Board.

**Healthcare:** AGG has a nationally-recognized Healthcare Practice that serves a range of healthcare providers, including hospitals, nursing homes, assisted living facilities, outpatient clinics, home health agencies, and clinical laboratories. Acquisition, financing and reorganization of healthcare facilities, Medicare/Medicaid reimbursement advice and litigation, fraud and abuse compliance, investigations and defense, and HIPAA compliance are all areas in which the firm's healthcare attorneys provide counsel.

**Life Sciences:** The firm's Life Sciences attorneys help emerging and established medical device, biologics and pharmaceutical companies turn scientific innovation into commercial viability. The firm's attorneys address legal problems and offer counseling at every stage of product development and organizational growth, including FDA compliance and product approval, clinical investigations and bioresearch, acquisitions and strategic alliances, intellectual property protection, and licensing.

### HEAD OFFICE

**GEORGIA**
171 17th Street, Suite 2100, **Atlanta** GA 30363
**Tel:** 404 873 8500   **Fax:** 404 873 8501
**Email:** info@agg.com
**Website:** www.agg.com

### CONTACTS

| | |
|---|---|
| **Mergers & Acquisitions** | Jonathan Golden |
| **Real Estate** | Steven A Pepper |
| **Litigation/Bankruptcy** | Stephen M Dorvee, Darryl S Laddin |
| **Securities & Corporate Governance** | T Clark Fitzgerald III |
| **Healthcare** | Glenn P Hendrix |
| **Life Sciences** | Thomas O Duvall, Jr |
| **Growth Companies/Private Equities** | Clinton D Richardson |
| **Private Wealth Planning** | Bertram L Levy |

**Growth Companies/Private Equities:** The Growth Companies/Private Equities Practice works with growing public and private companies and the financial institutions, venture capital firms, private equity providers, investment banks and individuals that fund their growth. Clients include businesses in the technology, life sciences, information, distribution, manufacturing and service industries. The firm helped found the Southeast's oldest venture capital trade association and plays an active role in the regional venture and entrepreneurial communities.

**Private Wealth Planning:** The firm's Private Wealth Planning Practice focuses on representing high net worth families in sophisticated wealth transfer matters, as well as fiduciaries in multi-faceted issues occurring during the estate administration process.

**INTERNATIONAL WORK:** AGG's foreign clients include businesses from over 40 countries whose activities in the United States range from a two person sales office, to a 1,000 employee manufacturing plant, to the Atlanta and New York offices of the world's largest banks. The firm's international attorneys conduct business in the Chinese, German, Spanish and French languages.

# ASHE, RAFUSE & HILL, LLP

## THE FIRM

**Managing Partner:** Nancy E Rafuse
**Chair:** R Lawrence Ashe, Jr

**Number of Partners:** 7
**Number of other lawyers:** 17

### HEAD OFFICE

**GEORGIA**
1355 Peachtree Street, N.E., Suite 500,
**Atlanta**, GA 30309-3232
**Tel:** 404 253 6000  **Fax:** 404 253 6060
**Email:** nancyrafuse@asherafuse.com
**Website:** www.asherafuse.com

**FIRM OVERVIEW:** Ashe, Rafuse & Hill, LLP, has as its three name partners, Lawrence Ashe, Nancy Rafuse and William Hill who are each recognized as some of the 'Leading Lawyers' in Georgia, *Georgia Trend Magazine* and some of "the Best Attorneys in Atlanta" in *Law & Politics*, as published by *Atlanta Magazine*. Additionally, Partner Dan Turner and associate Cynthia Burnside were recently recognized as two of Georgia's 'Rising Stars' as published by *Atlanta Magazine* (October 2005).

Ashe, Rafuse & Hill, LLP is a law firm based in Atlanta, Georgia, and has an active national trial practice with a focus on employment, civil rights, and commercial litigation. The partners collectively, successfully tried or arbitrated seven cases in 2005 alone, with vericts favourable to their clients in every case tried in 2005. The firm is fast establishing its reputation for recruiting and developing outstanding courtroom attorneys with significant jury trial experience. Ashe, Rafuse & Hill, LLP also prides itself on providing outstanding legal services more efficiently and at more reasonable rates than are typically associated with national firms. Indeed, the seven partners of Ashe, Rafuse & Hill, LLP and many of its 17 other attorneys left a large international law firm of approximately 800 attorneys fueled by the desire to practice law in an environment where the focus is on quality client service at a reasonable price.

## MAIN AREAS OF PRACTICE:

**Employment & Civil Rights:** Ashe, Rafuse & Hill, LLP represents and advises clients on virtually every aspect of employment law, including by way of illustration, representation of employers in response to claims asserted under every non-discrimination statute (e.g., Title VII, ADEA, ADA), traditional labor laws, as well as other employment-related statutes (e.g., WARN, FMLA, OSHA, FLSA) and related state statutes and causes of action. The breadth of Ashe, Rafuse & Hill, LLP's employment practice has resulted in the expansion of its expertise into other areas of civil rights litigation, including Title II, Section 1981, and ADA customer accommodation claims. Recently, Nancy Rafuse and William Hill successfully tried public accomodation cases to complete defense verdicts on behalf of a national restaurant chain.

**Class & Collective Actions:** The partners at Ashe, Rafuse & Hill, LLP have tried to a conclusion more discrimination class actions than any other management employment firm in the country and have defeated class certification in numerous cases. Lawrence Ashe has been recognized by the National Law Journal as the "dean of the management class action bar" and is one of only two career employment lawyers selected for membership into the American College of Trial Lawyers. Lawrence Ashe and Nancy Rafuse represented the State of California against a challenge to the use of the State's teacher licensing examination, which is believed to be the largest employment class action ever to be tried to a successful defense result. Ashe, Rafuse & Hill, LLP is frequently retained as co-counsel to many companies' regular outside counsel because of its lawyers' unique experience and expertise in employment and civil rights class and collective actions. The firm also represents employers in FLSA 'opt-in' matters, recently defeating certification of an alleged nationwide challenge to use of the exemption for store managers of a national retail chain.

**Commercial Litigation:** Ashe, Rafuse & Hill, LLP's Litigation Department is composed of trial lawyers who prosecute and defend multifaceted, sophisticated commercial matters for their clients. Ashe, Rafuse & Hill, LLP's litigators have significant experience litigating various types of matters including those involving business transactions, financial services, real estate, products liability, insurance coverage, professional negligence, unfair competition, false advertising, intellectual properties and securities. They have substantial trial and appellate experience in federal and state courts in Georgia and throughout the country as well as multi-district litigation experience. They also regularly represent clients in alternative dispute resolution proceedings including arbitrations and mediations, as well as provide arbitration and mediation services as the neutral. William B Hill, a former trial court judge, is the Chair of the Litigation Section and has an outstanding trial record, including representing a defendant in a products liability case which was recognized by the National Law Journal as one of the top 20 defense verdicts in 2000.

**Reported Cases:** AMAE, et al. v. The State of California, et al., 937 F. Supp. 1397 (N.D. Cal. 1996), affirmed en banc, 231 F.3d 572 (9th Cir. 2000); Reid, et al. v. Lockheed Martin Aeronautics Company, 205 F.R.D. 655 (N.D. Ga. 2001); Yarbrough, et al. v. Lockheed Martin Aeronautics Company, 205 F.R.D. 655 (N.D. Ga. 2001); Rhodes, et al. v. Cracker Barrel Old Country Store, Inc., 213 F.R.D. 619 (N.D. Ga. March 7, 2003). Yaali, Ltd., et al. v. Barns & Noble, Inc., et al., 269 Ga. 695, 506 S.E.2d 116 (1998).

# BONDURANT, MIXSON & ELMORE, LLP

## THE FIRM

**Managing Partner:** H Lamar Mixson
**Senior Partner:** Emmet J Bondurant

**Number of partners:** 12
**Number of other lawyers:** 15

**FIRM OVERVIEW:** The law firm of Bondurant, Mixson & Elmore represents plaintiffs and defendants in a wide variety of disputes, including complex business lawsuits, class actions, multi-party and multi-district cases.

## MAIN AREAS OF PRACTICE:

**Antitrust:** Since the firm's inception, antitrust has been an integral part of its practice. During the last 25 years, it has handled complex civil and criminal antitrust matters arising in a variety of different industries and commercial contexts, including the airline industry, hospital and healthcare, carpet products, dredging, dairy products, poultry products, motorsports, cement and aggregate products, key manufacturing, electrical generation, franchising and distributorship agreements, and others.

**Appellate:** The firm has extensive experience representing clients in the state and federal appellate courts. Its appellate practice is in part an extension of its trial practice, devoted to representing clients that the firm also represented at the trial level. A significant portion of the firm's Appellate Practice, however, consists of handling appeals where it was not counsel of record in the trial court. In those cases, the firm typically works closely with trial counsel to ensure the effective representation of its clients in the appellate court.

**Business Torts:** The firm routinely prosecutes and defends suits arising out of business torts. Over the last several years, the firm has seen substantial growth in the number of such suits as plaintiffs have come to realize that significant verdicts, including punitive damages, may be available to the successful claimant. Recently, the firm was co-counsel to the plaintiffs in the Six Flags v Time Warner case, which resulted in a verdict of $454,000,000, which was affirmed entirely on appeal and which was the largest jury verdict in the history of the State of Georgia.

**Contracts:** The firm has prosecuted and defended a wide variety of cases involving contract disputes. A complete list of the types of contract disputes Bondurant, Mixson & Elmore has handled would be too lengthy for this publication. However, the following partial list gives an indication of the types of contract disputes the firm has handled: construction disputes, employee/employer relationships, partnership disputes, indemnification disputes, insurance coverage disputes, franchisor/franchisee relationships, shareholder agreements, and covenants not to compete.

**Corporate Governance:** Bondurant, Mixson & Elmore is one of the preeminent practitioners of corporate governance litigation in the Southeastern region. The firm has represented parties involved in all sides of corporate governance disputes, including minority and majority shareholders, limited and general partners, receivers, and corporate and partnership officers, directors and managers. The firm has also participated in corporate control disputes including hostile tender offers and proxy litigation involving public companies.

**Employment & Civil Rights:** The firm's attorneys have extensive experience in handling employment and civil rights litigation. This tradition began in 1964, when Emmet Bondurant successfully argued Wesberry v Sanders in front of the

## HEAD OFFICE

**GEORGIA**
1201 W Peachtree Street, NW, One Atlantic Center, Suite 3900,
**Atlanta,** GA 30309
**Tel:** 404 881 4100  **Fax:** 404 881 4111

**Website:** www.bmelaw.com

United States Supreme Court, affirming the one-person, one-vote principle. 376 US 1 (1964). In 1984, Bondurant again prevailed in the United States Supreme Court, successfully representing a female attorney who had been denied partnership in a major Atlanta law firm. Hishon v King & Spalding, 467 US 69 (1984). In 2000, the firm served as lead plaintiffs' counsel in the class action race discrimination case against The Coca-Cola Company, Abdallah v The Coca-Cola Company, 133 F.Supp.2d 1364 (ND Ga. 2001). In that case, the firm obtained a $192.5 million settlement - the largest settlement ever achieved in a private race discrimination class action.

**Environmental Litigation:** Bondurant, Mixson & Elmore has handled cases under CERCLA, RCRA, FIFRA, HSRA and other environmental statutes and regulatory schemes. It has extensive experience handling environmental cases asserting claims under state common law theories (trespass, nuisance, negligence, negligence per se). The firm's environmental cases have included toxic tort (personal injury) claims as well as claims for property damage, response costs and injunctive relief. Bondurant, Mixson & Elmore also has experience handling insurance coverage litigation in the environmental field.

**RICO:** Bondurant, Mixson & Elmore has extensive experience with the difficult issues presented by litigation under the federal Racketeer Influenced and Corrupt Organizations Act and its numerous state law counterparts. It has represented both plaintiffs and defendants at the trial and appellate levels in federal and state RICO cases.

**Professional Liability:** The firm has broad and deep experience representing both plaintiffs and defendants in the resolution of high-stakes professional liability disputes. The firm's experience extends to disputes in the fields of accounting, architecture and engineering, but its professional liability practice focuses on the professional duties and liabilities of attorneys, corporate directors and officers, and public officials.

**Intellectual Property & Trade Secrets:** Bondurant, Mixson & Elmore is dedicated to excellence in litigation on the cutting edge of the law involving the protection of intellectual property. The firm's attorneys have a wealth of experience in the full spectrum of intellectual property litigation including patents, trademarks and unfair competition, copyrights, and trade secrets.

**White Collar Crime:** The firm has wide experience in the business crimes field particularly in the area of antitrust.

**CLIENTS:** Avon Products, Inc.; Brinks Home Security Systems, Inc.; Delta Air Lines, Inc.; Fina Oil and Chemical Company; Lincare, Inc.; Michelin North America, Inc.; Primerica Financial Services, Inc.

# FISHER & PHILLIPS LLP

## THE FIRM

**Chairman:** Roger K Quillen
**Number of partners:** 96
**Number of senior counsel :** 8
**Number of counsel:** 24
**Number of associates:** 73

**FIRM OVERVIEW:** Fisher & Phillips LLP is one of the oldest and largest firms in the United States which represents management in the areas of labor, employment, civil rights, employee benefits and immigration law. The firm's expertise and continuing focus on employment-related matters provides clients with reduced start-up times, greater cost efficiencies, and better outcomes. The firm's businesslike approach to workplace issues enables it to bring an efficient and practical perspective to today's labor and employment law problems.

## MAIN AREAS OF PRACTICE:

**Affirmative Action Plans:** Fisher & Phillips drafts affirmative action plans and policies and represents clients in enforcement proceedings before the OFCCP.

**Business Immigration Services:** Fisher & Phillips assists businesses in obtaining visas for alien employees, advises employers on compliance with federal employment verification requirements, represents clients in verification audits and defends immigration discrimination claims.

**Employee Benefits:** The firm handles pension and benefit matters under ERISA, continuation of insurance coverage issues under COBRA, and compliance issues under HIPAA. Attorneys prepare qualified employee benefit plans, executive compensation programs and health and welfare benefit plans.

**Employment Discrimination & Harassment:** The firm handles EEOC and state human rights commission charges, as well as federal and state lawsuits alleging discrimination and harassment on the basis of race, sex, age, national origin, religion and disability. The firm also assists employers in developing effective policies against discrimination and harassment, and in investigating complaints of discrimination and harassment.

**Labor Relations:** The firm assists its non-union clients in remaining union free and represents its unionized clients in collective bargaining, arbitration and unfair labor practice cases.

**Mergers, Acquisitions & Divestitures:** Fisher & Phillips advises clients on the labor, employment and benefits aspects of buying or selling a business, including union representation issues, benefit plan mergers and terminations, severance plans, executive employment agreements, and withdrawal liability issues.

**Occupational Safety & Health:** The firm works with clients to prevent health and safety problems and to achieve practical compliance with applicable requirements. Attorneys also represent employers during safety and health inspections and enforcement proceedings by federal OSHA and state agencies.

**Trade Secrets & Unfair Competition:** The firm prepares non-competition, non-solicitation, non-disclosure, non-recruitment and confidentiality agreements (where permitted by law) to protect clients' business interests and counsels clients on strategies designed to prevent misappropriation of trade secrets and proprietary information.

**Wage & Hour Laws:** Fisher & Phillips performs audits of compliance status, preparation for and representation of clients during government wage-hour investigations, defense of wage-hour lawsuits, review and design of pay plans, and advice on exempt/non-exempt classifications.

**CLIENTS**: The firm has a broad and diverse client base, representing a wide range of public and private employers. Some clients are large multinational corporations with thousands of employees; others are smaller entrepreneurial businesses. Clients include employers in a variety of industries: agriculture, automobile dealerships, banking, broadcasting, casinos and gaming, construction, education, financial services, healthcare, hospitality, insurance, legal and professional services, manufacturing, mining, real estate, retail, state and local government entities, technology, transportation, and wholesale and distribution industries.

## HEAD OFFICE

### GEORGIA
1500 Resurgens Plaza, 945 East Paces Ferry Road, **Atlanta**, GA 30326
**Tel:** 404 231 1400   **Fax:** 404 240 4249
**Email:** fp@laborlawyers.com
**Website:** www.laborlawyers.com

## BRANCH OFFICES

### CALIFORNIA
Suite 400, 18400 Von Karman Avenue, **Irvine**, CA 92612
**Tel:** 949 851 2424   **Fax:** 949 851 0152

Suite 950, 4225 Executive Square, **La Jolla**, CA 92037
**Tel:** 858 597 9600   **Fax:** 858 597 9601

Suite 200, City Center, 501 Fourteenth Street, **Oakland**, CA 94612
**Tel:** 510 763 4411   **Fax:** 510 763 4418

### FLORIDA
Suite 800, 450 East Las Olas Boulevard, **Fort Lauderdale**, FL 33301
**Tel:** 954 525 4800   **Fax:** 954 525 8739

1250 Lincoln Plaza, 300 South Orange Avenue, **Orlando**, FL 32801
**Tel:** 407 541 0888   **Fax:** 407 541 0887

2525 SunTrust Financial Centre, 401 E Jackson Street, **Tampa**, FL 33602
**Tel:** 813 769 7500   **Fax:** 813 769 7501

### ILLINOIS
1000 Marquette Building, 140 South Dearborn Street, **Chicago**, IL 60603
**Tel:** 312 346 8061   **Fax:** 312 346 3179

### LOUISIANA
Suite 3710, 201 St Charles Avenue, **New Orleans**, LA 70170
**Tel:** 504 522 3303   **Fax:** 504 529 3850

### MISSOURI
Suite 400, 104 West 9th Street, **Kansas City**, MO 64105
**Tel:** 816 842 8770   **Fax:** 816 842 8767

### NEVADA
Suite 650, 3993 Howard Hughes Parkway, **Las Vegas**, NV 89109
**Tel:** 702 252 3131   **Fax:** 702 252 7411

### NEW JERSEY
Corporate Park III, 580 Howard Avenue, **Somerset**, NJ 08873
**Tel:** 732 560 7100   **Fax:** 732 560 0788

### NORTH CAROLINA
Suite 2020, 227 West Trade Street, **Charlotte**, NC 28202
**Tel:** 704 334 4565   **Fax:** 704 334 9774

### OREGON
Suite 1250, 111 SW Fifth Avenue, **Portland**, OR 97204
**Tel:** 503 242 4262   **Fax:** 503 242 4263

### SOUTH CAROLINA
Suite 1400, 1901 Main Street, **Columbia**, SC 29201
**Tel:** 803 255 0000   **Fax:** 803 255 0202

### TEXAS
Suite 4343, Thanksgiving Tower, 1601 Elm Street, **Dallas**, TX
**Tel:** 214 220 9100   **Fax:** 214 220 9122

FISHER & PHILLIPS LLP
ATTORNEYS AT LAW

*Solutions at Work*®

# FORD & HARRISON LLP

## THE FIRM

**Managing Partner:** C Lash Harrison

**Number of partners:** 83
**Number of other lawyers:** 74

**FIRM OVERVIEW:** Founded in 1978, Ford & Harrison has evolved into one of the premier national labor and employment law firms with 16 offices in key US markets. The firm provides labor and employment legal advice and services to employers, in areas including employment litigation, discrimination, harassment, class action litigation, affirmative action, wrongful termination, wage and hour law, ADA/FMLA, airline labor law, labor union organizing, collective bargaining, arbitration, layoffs and plant closings, mergers and acquisitions, employment contracts, alternative dispute resolution, business immigration, employee benefits, workplace safety and environmental law.

## MAIN AREAS OF PRACTICE:

**Employment:** Ford & Harrison advises clients on all matters affecting the employment relationship, from recruiting and retention to termination issues. The firm's attorneys design policies and practices that minimize the risk of successful claims of discrimination, equal pay violations, breaches of employment contract and wrongful or retaliatory discharges. Ford & Harrison attorneys counsel clients on the changes in federal and state wage and hour laws, Family Medical Leave Act (FMLA), the Americans With Disabilities Act (ADA) and Health Insurance Portability and Accountability Act (HIPAA). The firm's attorneys and consultants evaluate employment vulnerabilities through personnel audits, reviews of personnel policies or handbooks, and management training. In addition, Ford & Harrison attorneys develop and assist in implementing affirmative action plans. The firm advises clients on health and safety issues, including the establishment of workable safety programs, compliance with the Occupational Safety and Health Act (OSHA) and compliance with employee 'right to know' statutes.

**Labor Law:** Collective bargaining and union organizing drives can be handled successfully if management teams are given the knowledge and insight necessary to deal with these issues. Ford & Harrison attorneys represent and advise employers in all phases of labor relations matters as they arise under the NLRA and RLA.

**Litigation:** The proliferation of state and federal laws creating employee rights has prompted an increasing number of lawsuits that make their way into court. Ford & Harrison recognizes that clients expect and deserve quality litigation services, which are delivered efficiently and cost effectively. In addition to representation of management in employment disputes, the firm also represent clients in all types of business litigation. Ford & Harrison attorneys litigate such matters as employment contracts, trade secrets, unfair competition and covenants not to compete and also have significant experience in class action litigation. The firm has successfully opposed class certification in all cases where it has been lead counsel. This experience has given the firm special knowledge about the process in defending class action lawsuits that translates into cost savings for employer clients. Preventing protracted litigation is always a key goal and Ford & Harrison attorneys are leaders in achieving results through preventative strategies.

**Employee Benefits:** Ford & Harrison's Employee Benefits Group has experience in assisting numerous public and private employers with their compensation and benefit plans. Some of the issues that the firm advises employers on are related to pension plans, profit sharing plans, trusts, welfare benefit plans, leave policies and Department of Labor investigations.

**Immigration:** The firm's attorneys provide immigration advice to clients who hire or transfer foreign employees. In compliance with the Immigration Reform and Control Act, Ford & Harrison assists clients in obtaining temporary visas and permanent resident status ('Green Cards') in the United States, obtain necessary labor certification and temporary work permits, and counsel employers on hiring and transferring foreign employees.

## HEAD OFFICE

### GEORGIA
1275 Peachtree Street, NE, Suite 600, **Atlanta** GA 30309
**Tel:** 404 888 3800  **Fax:** 404 888 3863
**Website:** www.fordharrison.com

## BRANCH OFFICES

### ALABAMA
2100 Third Avenue North, Suite 400, **Birmingham** AL 35203
**Tel:** 205 244 5900  **Fax:** 205 244 5901

### CALIFORNIA
350 South Grand Avenue, Suite 2300, **Los Angeles** CA 90071
**Tel:** 213 237 2400  **Fax:** 213 237 2401

### COLORADO
1675 Broadway, Suite 2150, **Denver** CO 80202
**Tel:** 303 592 8860  **Fax:** 303 592 8861

### DISTRICT OF COLUMBIA
1300 19th Street NW, Suite 700, **Washington** DC 20036
**Tel:** 202 719 2000  **Fax:** 202 719 2077

### FLORIDA
225 Water Street, Suite 710, **Jacksonville** FL 32202
**Tel:** 904 357 2000  **Fax:** 904 357 2001

100 SE 2nd Street, Suite 4500, **Miami** FL 33131
**Tel:** 305 808 2100  **Fax:** 305 808 2101

300 South Orange Avenue, Suite 1300, **Orlando** FL 32801
**Tel:** 407 418 2300  **Fax:** 407 418 2327

101 East Kennedy Boulevard, Suite 900, **Tampa** FL 33602-5133
**Tel:** 813 261 7800  **Fax:** 813 261 7899

### MINNESOTA
223 South Sixth Street, Suite 3150, **Minneapolis**, MN 55402
**Tel:** 612 486 1700  **Fax:** 612 486 1701

### MISSISSIPPI
1128 N Lamar, **Oxford**, MS 38655
**Tel:** 662 238 7785  **Fax:** 662 234 4270

### NEW YORK
100 Park Avenue, Suite 2500, **New York** NY 10017
**Tel:** 212 453 5900  **Fax:** 212 453 5959

### NORTH CAROLINA
One Town Square, Suite 341, **Asheville**, NC 28803
**Tel:** 828 687 4071  **Fax:** 828 687 4471

### SOUTH CAROLINA
101 North Pine Street, Suite 400, **Spartanburg** SC 29302-5398
**Tel:** 864 699 1100  **Fax:** 864 699 1101

### TENNESSEE
795 Ridge Lake Boulevard, Suite 300, **Memphis** TN 38120
**Tel:** 901 291 1500  **Fax:** 901 291 1501

### TEXAS
1601 Elm Street, Suite 4450, **Dallas**, TX 75201
**Tel:** 214 256 4700  **Fax:** 214 256 4701

FORD & HARRISON LLP
THE RIGHT RESPONSE AT THE RIGHT TIME

# GRIFFIN COCHRANE & MARSHALL
**A PROFESSIONAL CORPORATION**

## THE FIRM

**Shareholders:** Lee C Davis, Jennifer W Fletcher, W Henry Parkman
J Dean Marshall, Jr, F Barry McCabe

**Number of other lawyers:** 7

**FIRM OVERVIEW:** Since its founding in 1980, Griffin Cochrane & Marshall has devoted its practice to providing legal services to the construction industry nationwide. GCM enjoys the reputation of a specialty practice firm offering equal sophistication and quality to the multi-national mega firms. GCM and its lawyers have achieved the first-tier rating for 'Leading Firms in Georgia (Construction)' by Chambers & Partners; the AV rating by Martindale-Hubbell; and recognition of its partners as 'Georgia SuperLawyers' by Law & Politics. GCM's five shareholders each bring unique talents to the firm's client service, and have resolved successfully many multi-million dollar disputes for construction contractors, owners, suppliers, and specialty contractors. The four older shareholders have practiced together at Griffin Cochrane & Marshall for more than 20 years, and uphold the tradition of service and quality established by firm founder, Harry 'Buck' Griffin, who maintains an office notwithstanding his retirement several years ago. The firm offers state-of-the-art construction counsel, including project planning, dispute avoidance, and dispute resolution. GCM has long been a leader in using mediation and alternative methods to resolve construction disputes. In addition, its lawyers have litigated many large cases to successful resolution, including lead roles in some of the largest and most complex jury trials involving construction issues. GCM's attorneys are uniquely qualified to draft contracts, provide advice, conduct negotiations, handle bid protests, and to present claims or defenses in arbitration or in court. The firm is committed to achieving excellent results for clients. Whether prosecuting or defending claims, or guiding a client through day-to-day decisions, the firm's goal is to add value to the business efforts of construction industry clients.

## MAIN AREAS OF PRACTICE: Construction industry dispute resolution and avoidance nationwide.

**CLIENTS:** GCM represents some of the nation's largest contractors, public entities, and private owners, including several Fortune 100 corporations, and numerous privately-held construction industry participants. The projects GCM has been involved with include every variety of construction work, including infrastructure, commercial, industrial, process, retail, hotel and resort, residential, and public works facilities. The diversity of client base and the types of construction matters handled by the firm enables GCM to approach problem-solving from a broad base of knowledge and experience. GCM is committed to understanding its clients and their objectives. The firm prides itself on high level commitment and personal attention to each client's needs. GCM maintains its focus on achieving the client's objectives through the most cost-effective and innovative legal and business solutions.

## REPORTED CASES:

**Federal Appellate Decisions:** Venetian Casino Resort, L.L.C. v Lehrer McGovern Bovis, Inc., 92 Fed. Appx. 402, 2004 WL 42384 (9th Cir. Jan. 7, 2004); Eng. Contractors Assoc. of South Florida, Inc. v Metropolitan Dade County, 122 F.3d 895 (11th Cir. 1997), cert. denied, 118 S.Ct. 1186 (1998); Davidson & Jones Dev. Co. v Elmore Dev. Co., 921 F.2d 1343 (6th Cir. 1991); S.J. Groves & Sons Co. v Fulton County, 920 F.2d 752 (11th Cir.), cert. denied, 500 US 959 (1991); Pinnacle Port Community Assn., Inc. v Orenstein, 872 F.2d 1536 (11th Cir. 1989); Weyher/Livsey Constructors, Inc. v International Chem. Co., 864 F.2d 130 (11th Cir. 1989); Pathman Constr. Co. v United States, 817 F.2d 1573 (Fed. Cir. 1987); T.S.I., Inc. v Metric Constructors, Inc., 817 F.2d 94 (11th Cir. 1987).

## HEAD OFFICE

**GEORGIA**
127 Peachtree Street, 14th Floor **Atlanta**, GA 30303-1810
**Tel:** 404 523 2000   **Fax:** 404 523 9655
**Website:** www.gcm-atty.com

**Federal District Decisions:** Pitt-Des Moines, Inc. v Metropolitan Pier & Exposition Authority, 1999 WL 162786 (N.D. Ill. Mar. 16, 1999); JWP/Hyre Electric Co. v Mentor Village School District, 968 F. Supp. 356 (N.D. Ohio 1996); L.K. Comstock & Co. v Becon Constr. Co., 932 F. Supp. 948 (E.D. Ky 1994), aff'd, 73 F.3d 362 (6th Cir. 1995); USF&G v Ernest Constr. Co., 854 F. Supp. 1545 (M.D. Fla. 1994); Robert Lamb Hart Planners and Architects v Evergreen, Ltd., 787 F. Supp. 753 (S.D. Ohio 1992); Blue Circle Atlantic, Inc. v Falcon Maerials, Inc., 760 F. Supp. 516 (D. Md. 1991), aff'd, 960 F.2d 145 (4th Cir. 1992); W.L. Jorden & Co. v Blythe Indus. Inc., 702 F. Supp. 282 (N.D. Ga. 1988); Pinkerton and Laws Co. v Roadway Express, Inc., 650 F. Supp. 1138 (N.D. Ga. 1986); G.D. Searle & Co. v Metric Constructors, Inc., 572 F. Supp. 836 (N.D. Ga. 1983); Robert E. McKee, Inc. v City of Atlanta, 431 F. Supp. 1198 (N.D. Ga. 1977).

**State Appellate Decisions:** Amprite Elec. Co. v Tenn. Stadium Group, LLP., No. M2002-00892-COA-R3-CV, 2003 WL 22171556 (Tenn. Ct. App. Sept. 22, 2003); J. Kinson Cook, Inc. v Weaver, 252 Ga. App. 868, 556 S.E.2d 831 (2001); Republic Contracting Corp. v S.C. Dept. of Transp., 332 S.C. 197, 503 S.E.2d 761 (1998); R.J. Griffin & Co. v Continental Ins. Co., 230 Ga. App. 822, 497 S.E.2d 586 (1998); Ga. Dept. of Transp. v Dalton Paving & Constr. Inc., 227 Ga. App. 207, 489 S.E.2d 329 (1997); Collins v Lunda Constr. Co., 214 Ga. App. 512, 448 S.E.2d 236 (1994); J. Lee Gregory, Inc. v Scandinavian House, L.P., 209 Ga. App. 285, 433 S.E.2d 687 (1993); C.B.I. Na-Con Inc. v Macon Bibb County Water & Sewerage Auth., 205 Ga. App. 82, 421 S.E.2d 111 (1992); Lunda Constr. Co. v Clayton County, 201 Ga. App. 106, 410 S.E. 2d 446 (1991); Robert & Co. Assocs. v Rhodes-Haverty Partnership, 250 Ga. 680, 300 S.E.2d 503 (1983); Hilton Constr. Co. v Martin Mechanical Contractors, Inc., 251 Ga. 701, 308 S.E.2d 830 (1983); Space Leasing Assoc. v Atlantic Bldg. Sys. Inc., 144 Ga. App. 320, 241 S.E.2d 438 (1977).

**Decisions from Federal Claims Court & Board of Contract Appeals:** Appeal of J. Slotnik Co., VABCA No. 3254, 94-3 BCA ¶27,012 (1994) (14 consolidated cases); Appeal of Murray Walter, Inc., VABCA No. 1848, 87-2 BCA ¶19,947 (1987); Hoel-Steffen Constr. Co. v United States, 684 F.2d 843 (Ct. Cl. 1982).

**Griffin Cochrane & Marshall**
A Professional Corporation

# KILPATRICK STOCKTON LLP

## THE FIRM

**Managing Partner:** William H Brewster
**Firm Co-Chairs:** Miles Alexander, A Stephens Clay, J Robert Elster

**Number of partners:** 235
**Number of other lawyers:** 241

**Email:** webmaster@kilpatrickstockton.com
**Website:** www.kilpatrickstockton.com

**FIRM OVERVIEW:** Kilpatrick Stockton LLP is a full-service law firm with more than 470 attorneys in nine offices across the eastern US and in Europe. To support the increasing significance of international markets and global business transactions to their clients, Kilpatrick Stockton maintains offices in London and Stockholm. As a result, the firm serves international and multinational clients including those in Europe, Latin Amercia, Asia and Australia. It is one of the world's 100 largest and most successful law firms, and the firm delivers innovative business solutions and results-oriented counsel for corporations at all stages of the growth cycle. Kilpatrick Stockton's core value of community service resulted in the dedication of more than 27,500 hours of pro bono work, an $8.2 million value, in 2005.

## MAIN AREAS OF PRACTICE:

**Corporate:** Kilpatrick Stockton's more than 100 corporate attorneys offer valuable counsel through a wide range of general corporate, corporate finance, securities, cross-border transactions, technology licensing and outsourcing, tax, mergers, acquisitions, and transactional services to clients at every end of the business spectrum, from *Fortune* 500 companies to promising start-ups. On nearly every continent, the firm advises companies in market sectors as diverse as communications, financial, manufacturing, retail, technology, food and beverage, and health and life science. In the US, the firm counseled clients on more than 300 venture capital transactions since the start of the new century.

**Intellectual Property:** With a force of more than 95 dedicated intellectual property attorneys practicing in patent, trademark, copyright and entertainment law and litigation, Kilpatrick Stockton is unique among general practice firms. In the area of patent law, 50 attorneys registered to practice before the United States Patent and Trademark Office offer experience in more than 100 areas. In copyright, the firm's attorneys operate registration programs for clients across a range of industries from carpet to computer software, and in trademark law their past and present prosecution has consistently placed them on the top 10 lists for global trademark counsel.

**Litigation:** More than 100 lawyers in the Litigation Practice have the depth to effectively handle the most complex commercial cases and the flexibility to represent clients in the routine business disputes that require efficient resolution. The firm appears on behalf of clients in state and federal trial and appellate courts throughout the US and before arbitration tribunals and mediators around the world. Kilpatrick Stockton's lawyers have received recognition in numerous national and trade publications for being some of the most results-oriented litigation attorneys in the world.

**Financial Transactions:** Kilpatrick Stockton's Financial Transactions Practice provides counsel to both large financial institutions and corporate borrowers in a wide variety of corporate and commercial financial transactions, financial restructuring, commercial mortgage-backed securities transactions, and public finance transactions for the health care, technology and communications industries.

**Labor, Employment & Employee Benefits:** Kilpatrick Stockton's attorneys represent employers during union organizational and de-certification attempts, arbitrations, collective bargaining negotiations, unfair labor practice proceedings, and ERISA litigation. They represent employers in discrimination employment and restrictive covenant litigation, and provide counseling. They advise employers on employee discipline and termination decisions, defend EEOC and other administrative charges, and defend all types of wrongful discharge and discrimi-

nation litigation. The firm also helps clients with affirmative action requirements, occupational safety and health law, benefit plan design, and fiduciary responsibility, as well as reporting and disclosure obligations and executive compensation law.

**Real Estate:** Kilpatrick Stockton's real estate attorneys represent large commercial developers, leading lenders, *Fortune* 500 corporations and the federal government in the acquisition of real estate, development, zoning and entitlement, ownership, management, leasing and capital formation for real estate investment.

**Environmental:** Kilpatrick Stockton has one of the largest and most diverse environmental regulatory and litigation practices in the US. The firm's attorneys assist public- and private-sector clients in avoiding environmental liability and regulatory conflicts through preventive counseling and management of environmental permit processes.

**Construction:** With more than 35 professionals, Kilpatrick Stockton has one of the largest, most experienced construction and public contracts practices of any general practice firm in the world. The Construction Practice's attorneys have assisted clients with construction matters in all 50 states and more than 25 countries and regularly handle a wide varierty of high-profile, complex matters on global projects with scopes as substantial as $15 billion. The firm represents clients from project inception through project completion and beyond.

**Government Relations:** Kilpatrick Stockton's Government Relations attorneys represent clients before Congress and federal agencies on a broad range of issues including healthcare, employee benefits, energy, tax, trade, telecommunications and intellectual property matters. The group is made up of accomplished professionals with extensive Capitol Hill, federal agency and political experience.

**CLIENTS:** Aaron Rents, Inc., BellSouth Corporation, Certegy Inc., DaimlerChrysler Corporation, Delta Air Lines, Inc., Equifax Inc., Google Inc., Harbert Management Corporation, IMAX Corporation, Interface, Inc., Krispy Kreme Doughnut Corporation, Miller Industries, Inc., National Vision, Inc., Nestle Waters of North America, Office Depot, PepsiCo, Inc., Science Applications International Corporation, Turbochef Technologies, Inc., Wachovia Corporation.

## US OFFICES

**GEORGIA**
Suite 2800, 1100 Peachtree Street, **Atlanta**, GA 30309-4530
**Tel:** 404 815 6500   **Fax:** 404 815 6555

Suite 1400, Wachovia Bank Building, 699 Broad Street,
**Augusta**, GA 30901-1453
**Tel:** 706 724 2622   **Fax:** 706 722 0219

**DISTRICT OF COLUMBIA**
Suite 900, 607 14th Street NW, **Washington**, DC 20005-2018
**Tel:** 202 508 5800   **Fax:** 202 508 5858

**NORTH CAROLINA**
Suite 2500, 214 North Tryon Street, **Charlotte**, NC 28202-2381
**Tel:** 704 338 5000   **Fax:** 704 338 5125

Suite 400, 3737 Glenwood Avenue, **Raleigh**, NC 27612
**Tel:** 919 420 1700   **Fax:** 919 420 1800

1001 West Fourth Street, **Winston-Salem**, NC 27101-2400
**Tel:** 336 607 7300   **Fax:** 336 607 7500

**NEW YORK**
31 West 52nd Street, 14th Floor, **New York**, NY 10019
**Tel:** 212 775 8700   **Fax:** 212 775 8800

International Offices in London and Stockholm

KILPATRICK
STOCKTON LLP
Attorneys at Law

# KING & SPALDING LLP

## THE FIRM

**Chairman:** Robert D Hays
**Managing Partner, Atlanta:** Mason W Stephenson
**Managing Partner, Houston:** Robert E Meadows
**Managing Partner, London:** John L Keffer
**Managing Partner, New York:** Michael J O'Brien
**Managing Partner, Washington:** J Sedwick Sollers

**Number of partners:** 240
**Number of other lawyers:** 560

**FIRM OVERVIEW:** King & Spalding LLP is an international law firm with more than 800 lawyers in Atlanta, Houston, London, New York, and Washington, DC. The firm represents more than 250 public companies, including over half of the *Fortune* 100.

## MAIN AREAS OF PRACTICE:

**Antitrust:** King & Spalding's antitrust lawyers are trial lawyers who know how to litigate in 'bet the company' situations. The firm has been counsel for clients in numerous antitrust litigation settings, ranging from class actions and multi-district litigation to disputes between particular suppliers and their customers or competitors.

**Financial Transactions:** The practice group provides legal services for domestic and non-US banks and other financial institutions. It handles all aspects of credit-facilities and financial products.

**Construction:** Today, the Construction and Procurement Practice Group represents some of the world's largest organizations involved in global construction projects. King & Spalding was one of the first large, general practice firms in the nation to establish a practice devoted to construction and procurement law.

**Corporate/M&A:** Consistently ranks among the leading M&A practices in the United States in terms of aggregate deal value and total number of transactions handled.

**Corporate Finance:** The firm represents issuers, underwriters, investors, and other corporate finance participants, and provides corporate advice to public and private companies.

**Employment & Labor Law:** The firm defends *Fortune* 500 corporate defendants against complex claims of unlawful employment policies and conduct involving allegations of discrimination under federal and state non-discrimination statutes.

**Energy:** The firm's energy attorneys have been involved in transactions throughout the world related to energy and natural resources. King & Spalding's experience includes developing project structures as well as the drafting and negotiating of project agreements, contracts and documentation. Additionally, King & Spalding lawyers have been active advisors to the Liquefied Natural Gas (LNG) marketplace for the last 30 years. As pioneers on this legal scene, the internationally recognized group of lawyers have been key participants in LNG export, transport, and import projects . Today, King & Spalding's team is sought after by LNG players worldwide owing to depth of experience, knowledge, skill, and determination.

**Environment:** King & Spalding is recognized as one of the leading environmental firms and combines substantive expertise, technical knowledge and litigation experience on numerous environmental issues.

**Insolvency/Corporate Recovery:** The Financial Restructuring Group at King & Spalding provides valuable knowledge and experience in the areas of corporate reorganizations, commercial debt restructuring, workouts, bankruptcy, and insolvency litigation.

**Intellectual Property:** The firm's IP lawyers concentrate on acquiring, creating, licensing, protecting, and litigating intellectual property rights, both domestically and internationally.

## HEAD OFFICE

**GEORGIA**
1180 Peachtree Street, **Atlanta**, GA 30309-3521
**Tel:** 404 572 4600  **Fax:** 404 572 5100
**Email:** kingspalding@kslaw.com
**Website:** www.kslaw.com

## BRANCH OFFICES

**NEW YORK**
1185 Avenue of the Americas, **New York**, NY 10036-4003
**Tel:** 212 556 2100  **Fax:** 212 556 2222
**Email:** kingspalding@kslaw.com

**TEXAS**
1100 Louisiana, Suite 4000, **Houston**, TX 77002-5213
**Tel:** 713 751 3200  **Fax:** 713 751 3290
**Email:** kingspalding@kslaw.com

**DISTRICT OF COLUMBIA**
1700 Pennsylvania Avenue, N.W., **Washington**, DC 200006-4706
**Tel:** 202 737 0500  **Fax:** 202 626 3737
**Email:** kingspalding@kslaw.com

## INTERNATIONAL OFFICES

King & Spalding International LLP, London.

**Litigation & Arbitration:** The firm provides litigation services in the areas of antitrust, appellate, class action, commercial disputes, product liability, shareholder and securities litigation, trade and customs, and toxic tort. The firm also has a substantial international arbitration practice.

**Real Estate:** The firm's real estate practice includes acquisition, development, financing and leasing of commercial real estate primarily for nationally recognized developers, and non-US institutional and private investors.

**Tax:** The firm works with clients on the planning and execution of business transactions of all sizes and types arising in domestic and cross border settings, including acquisitions, disposition, joint ventures, and financing transactions.

**CLIENTS:** 3M, Brown & Williamson Tobacco Corporation, Chevron Corporation, The Coca-Cola Company, Credit Suisse First Boston LLC, The Dow Chemical Company, Ernst & Young LLP, ExxonMobil Corporation, General Electric Company, General Motors Corporation, Georgia-Pacific Corporation, GlaxoSmithKline, Goldman Sachs & Company, The Home Depot, Inc., Honeywell International Inc., KPMG LLP, Lehman Brothers Inc., Lockheed Martin Corporation, Merrill Lynch & Co., Inc., Morgan Stanley Capital Group, Inc., Purdue Pharma L.P., Scientific-Atlanta, Inc., Shell Oil Company, Sprint Nextel Corporation, SunTrust Banks Inc., Turner Broadcasting System, Inc., UCB Inc., UPS.

# KING & SPALDING

# MCKENNA LONG & ALDRIDGE LLP

## THE FIRM

**Chairperson:** Jeffrey K Haidet

**FIRM OVERVIEW:** McKenna Long & Aldridge LLP is an international law firm comprised of approximately 400 lawyers and public policy advisors with offices in Atlanta, Brussels, Denver, Los Angeles, Philadelphia, San Diego, San Francisco and Washington, DC. The firm's range of services fall into three broad categories: transactional, litigation and government/regulatory. Within these categories, the firm has extensive experience in over 90 practice area specializations including services in: corporate, environmental, government contracts, intellectual property, international, litigation, public policy and regulatory affairs, real estate finance and development, and restructuring and bankruptcy.

## MAIN AREAS OF PRACTICE:

**Corporate:** The Corporate Practice predominately handles transactions involving public and private corporate finance, mergers and acquisitions, tax planning and governance. Its lawyers focus on helping clients meet their business objectives, while minimizing legal costs and complications.

**Real Estate Finance & Development:** The Real Estate Finance and Development Practice represents developers, entrepreneurs, institutional lenders and investors.

**Restructuring & Bankruptcy:** The Restructuring and Bankruptcy Practice helps clients structure and consummate workouts of all types, including traditional economic restructurings, collateral recovery/liquidation workouts, and prepackaged bankruptcy plans. The firm's restructuring lawyers have resolved in excess of $10 billion in problem loans.

**Litigation:** The Litigation Practice offers experience, depth and high degrees of specialization. Areas of specialization include: product liability and toxic tort litigation, white collar crime, and complex business litigation. The firm's litigation expertise derives from its strong background in corporate and regulatory law. Its depth of experience means that the firm handles everything from routine commercial disputes in local courts to high profile cases in the highest state and federal appellate courts.

**Toxic Torts & Product Liability:** The Toxic Torts and Product Liability Practice has successfully defended numerous product liability and environmental tort actions such as chlorinated solvents, pesticides, PCBs, mercury and other materials released from or used at facilities, as well as pesticides, pharmaceuticals and consumer products released into the stream of commerce.

**Government Relations:** The government relations lawyers and policy advisors provide extensive legislative and regulatory counsel on behalf of clients who have issues with local, state and federal governments.

**Government Contracts:** The firm's Government Contracts Practice is the first of its kind and continues as the leading practice in this field in the country. Its lawyers focus on clients who provide the government with highly technical, sophisticated and complex products and systems.

**Intellectual Property & Technology:** The intellectual property lawyers have extensive experience in representing domestic and international clients in all aspects of intellectual property protection and licensing both in the US and abroad.

**Environmental Practice:** The Environmental Practice handles all traditional areas of environmental law, structuring its client services in light of a single, guiding principle: environmental solutions must reflect a sound business perspective. With more than 40 lawyers practicing in the environmental field, the firm helps its clients shape the law through litigation, legislative and administrative action.

## US OFFICES

**CALIFORNIA**
444 South Flower Street, 8th Floor, **Los Angeles**, CA 90071
**Tel:** 213 688 1000   **Fax:** 213 243 6330
**Website:** www.mckennalong.com

Suite 3300, Symphony Towers, 750 B Street, **San Diego**, CA 92101
**Tel:** 619 595 5400   **Fax:** 619 595 5450

101 California Street, Floor 41, **San Francisco**, CA 94111
**Tel:** 415 267 4000   **Fax:** 415 267 4198

**COLORADO**
Suite 200, 1875 Lawrence Street, **Denver**, CO 80202
**Tel:** 303 634 4000   **Fax:** 303 634 4400

**DISTRICT OF COLUMBIA**
1900 K Street, NW, **Washington**, DC 20006
**Tel:** 202 496 7500   **Fax:** 202 496 7756

**GEORGIA**
Suite 5300, 303 Peachtree Street, NE, **Atlanta**, GA 30308
**Tel:** 404 527 4000   **Fax:** 404 527 4198

**PHILADELPHIA**
28 South Waterloo Road, Suite 101, **Devon**, PA 19333
**Tel:** 610 687 9750   **Fax:** 610 687 9755

## INTERNATIONAL OFFICES

The firm also has an office in Brussels, Belgium.

**International:** The International Practice assists clients in all aspects of moving goods, services, capital and technology across national boundaries as well as in all aspects of their global enterprises. The firm's clients range from large multinationals to companies that are engaging in international joint ventures, contracts of sale, use of foreign business representatives and other partnering and commercial arrangements.

**Homeland Security:** The Homeland Security Practice is a leading practice of its kind, having helped draft national legislation, regulations and policy impacting product liability, biodefense, and public health with the homeland security field.

**Compliance & Investigations:** The Compliance and Investigations Practice helps companies promote corporate integrity by designing and evaluating compliance programs based on an up-to-date review of both legal requirements and the risks inherent in the company's business. They conduct internal audits and investigations and counsel companies on the best way to respond to government inquiries and the advantages and disadvantages of making a voluntary disclosure.

**Military Bases & Communities:** The Military Bases and Communities Practice provides assistance to communities and their local redevelopment authorities that are facing closure, realignment, or expanding missions. For the private sector, the practice addresses the real estate assets and human capital represented by these bases. In particular, they have pioneered the Transition Benefit Corporation model that may allow civilian jobs to be retained even in a closure situation.

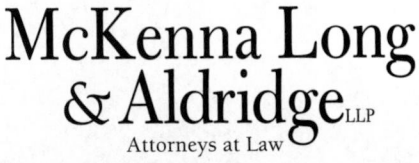

McKenna Long & Aldridge LLP
Attorneys at Law

# OGLETREE, DEAKINS, NASH, SMOAK & STEWART, P.C.

## THE FIRM

**Managing Shareholder:** L Gray Geddie, Jr
**Number of shareholders:** 160
**Number of other lawyers:** 142

**Website:** www.ogletreedeakins.com

**FIRM OVERVIEW:** Ogletree, Deakins, Nash, Smoak & Stewart, P.C. (Ogletree Deakins) is one of the nation's largest labor and employment law firms, representing management in all types of employment-related legal matters. The firm has more than 300 labor and employment lawyers located in 24 offices and has thriving practices focused on business immigration, employee benefits, and workplace safety and health law. The firm represents a diverse range of clients, including more than half of the Fortune 50 corporations in the United States. Ogletree Deakins is proud to have more lawyers who are Fellows in the College of Labor and Employment Lawyers and listed in Best Lawyers in America than any other labor and employment specialty firm in the United States. Ogletree Deakins' primary focus is client service, a message that is emphasized in the firm's tagline: "Employer and Lawyers, Working Together." Lawyers remain on call 24 hours a day, seven days a week to provide prompt and, most importantly, effective legal advice over the phone, through a computer, or in the field. They regularly conduct comprehensive employment audits with their clients to expose problem areas before they become legal nightmares and conduct management training seminars to equip supervisors to handle tough workplace issues. Often, firm attorneys are called upon to prepare and review employment policies and procedures manuals to ensure compliance with federal and state laws. This combination of educating supervisors on employment issues and giving employees notice of company expectations results in very real cost savings, as well as intangible personnel benefits.

## MAIN AREAS OF PRACTICE:

**Labor & Employment:** Ogletree Deakins' dedicated focus on the practice of labor and employment law enables the firm to maintain both 'bench strength' and depth of expertise in all areas of the practice, including counseling, training, preventive and proactive workplace strategies, litigation, and diversity management. Because the firm's lawyers are focused on, and prepared to deliver, this full range of labor and employment representation, Ogletree Deakins provides the 'continuity of care' that ensures knowledgeable and client-centered solutions and consistent attorney–client relationships. Ogletree Deakins has years of experience with and regularly practices before both the federal and state agencies that regulate the workplace. In fact, some of the firm's attorneys have held high level positions within several governmental agencies, providing them with the type of access few firms possess. Ogletree Deakins regularly files amicus curiae briefs with the United States Supreme Court on behalf of the US Chamber of Commerce and other organizations on important labor and employment matters. The firm's attorneys are asked by Congress, as well as by state legislatures, to testify on matters in which Ogletree Deakins concentrates its practice.

## OFFICES

**ALABAMA**
**Birmingham: Tel:** 205 328 1900 **Fax:** 205 328 6000

**ARIZONA**
**Phoenix: Tel:** 602 778 3700 **Fax:** 602 778 3750

**CALIFORNIA**
**Los Angeles: Tel:** 213 239 9800 **Fax:** 213 239 9045

**Torrance: Tel:** 310 217 8191 **Fax:** 310 217 8184

**FLORIDA**
**Miami: Tel:** 305 374 0506 **Fax:** 305 374 0456

**Tampa: Tel:** 813 289 1247 **Fax:** 813 289 6530

**GEORGIA**
**Atlanta: Tel:** 404 881 1300 **Fax:** 404 870 1732

**ILLINOIS**
**Chicago: Tel:** 312 558 1220 **Fax:** 312 807 3619

**MISSOURI**
**Kansas City: Tel:** 816 471 1301 **Fax:** 816 471 1303

**INDIANA**
**Indianapolis: Tel:** 317 916 1300 **Fax:** 317 916 9076

**NEW JERSEY**
**Morristown: Tel:** 973 656 1600 **Fax:** 973 656 1611

**NORTH CAROLINA**
**Charlotte: Tel:** 704 342 2588 **Fax:** 704 342 4379

**Greensboro: Tel:** 336 375 9737 **Fax:** 336 375 4430

**Raleigh: Tel:** 919 787 9700 **Fax:** 919 783 9412

**SOUTH CAROLINA**
**Charleston: Tel:** 843 853 1300 **Fax:** 843 853 9992

**Columbia: Tel:** 803 252 1300 **Fax:** 803 254 6517

**Greenville: Tel:** 864 271 1300 **Fax:** 864 235 8806

**TENNESSEE**
**Nashville: Tel:** 615 254 1900 **Fax:** 615 254 1908

**TEXAS**
**Austin: Tel:** 512 344 4700 **Fax:** 512 344 4701

**Dallas: Tel:** 214 987 3800 **Fax:** 214 987 3927

**Houston: Tel:** 713 655 0855 **Fax:** 713 655 0020

**San Antonio: Tel:** 210 354 1300 **Fax:** 210 277 2702

**DISTRICT OF COLUMBIA**
**Washington: Tel:** 202 887 0855 **Fax:** 202 887 0866

## INTERNATIONAL OFFICES

The firm also has an office in the Virgin Islands.

## ADDITIONAL INFORMATION

For more information on these office locations, visit www.ogletreedeakins.com

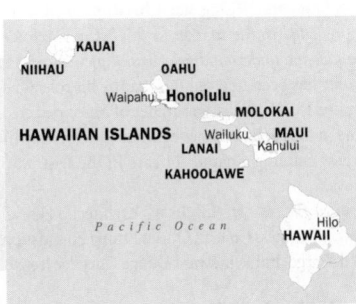

## How lawyers are ranked

Every year we carry out thousands of in-depth interviews with clients and lawyers in order to assess the reputations and expertise of business lawyers across the USA. Chambers rankings and editorial are referred to extensively by General Counsel and other purchasers of legal services who look to our recommendations when choosing their lawyers.

# BANKRUPTCY/RESTRUCTURING

### Bankruptcy/Restructuring
#### Leading Firms

1. **CADES SCHUTTE** *Honolulu*
   **CASE LOMBARDI & PETTIT** *Honolulu*
   **GELBER, GELBER, INGERSOLL** *Honolulu*
   **MOSELEY BIEHL TSUGAWA LAU** *Honolulu*
   **RUSH MOORE LLP** *Honolulu*
   **WAGNER CHOI EVERS** *Honolulu*

#### Leading Individuals

1. **CHOI Chuck** *Wagner Choi Evers*
   **DREHER Nicholas** *Cades Schutte*
   **GELBER Don** *Gelber, Gelber, Ingersoll*
   **GUBEN Jerrold** *Reinwald O'Connor & Playdon*
   **PETTIT Ted** *Case Lombardi & Pettit*
   **TIUS Susan** *Rush Moore LLP*
   **WAGNER James** *Wagner Choi Evers*
2. **DUCA James** *Kessner Duca Umebayashi Bain*
   **KLEVANSKY Simon** *Gelber, Gelber, Ingersoll*
   **MUZZI Christopher** *Moseley Biehl Tsugawa Lau*

#### Up-and-coming individuals
   **PIPER Alika** *Gelber, Gelber, Ingersoll*

## Band 1

### Cades Schutte

**The Firm:** One of the state's oldest and largest firms, Cades Schutte earned enthusiastic praise for its creditors' rights and bankruptcy practice. The Honolulu-based team enjoys a leading position and boasts considerable expertise spanning a variety of sectors, which include real estate and finance. Although the firm earns top marks for its representation of creditors, the group is far from lacking experience of advising major debtors in connection with workouts and restructurings, as well as in Chapter 7 and Chapter 11 bankruptcy matters.

**The Lawyers:** The capacity to *"make a deal, balancing the business and legal issues"* and to *"strike up a good rapport with opposing counsel"* has earned **Nicholas Dreher** a leading position in the market. Described by many as *"one of the best for creditor work"* with *"excellent analytical skills,"* Dreher acted for First Hawaiian Bank, one of the largest creditors in the high-profile Aloha Airlines proceedings. His

debtor work also impressed and includes acting as lead counsel to the debtor in the state's other significant airline bankruptcy, the Hawaiian Airlines case.
**Clients/Work Highlights:** Domestic and international financial institutions, including First Hawaiian Bank, feature in a client list that encompasses debtors and creditors from a range of industries. As Dreher's deal list shows, aviation is one of the foremost among these.

### Case Lombardi & Pettit
See firm details p.755
**The Firm:** *"Whenever there is a decent case, we would naturally go there,"* noted more than one client of this *"resourceful and reputed"* Hawaiian firm. The team's experience of both the debtor and creditor side shone through for clients, who especially appreciated its speedy and prompt handling of matters. Around a third of the 20-attorney firm is dedicated to creditor-debtor relationships. Its broad workload ranges from foreclosure, receivership, collection and enforcement of judgments to reorganizations and liquidation in bankruptcy court. The firm has been particularly active of late in creditor committee work, while its strength on the debtor side is emphasized by its leading role in the Chapter 11 bankruptcy proceedings surrounding Royal Hawaiian Entertainment.
**The Lawyers:** Heading the firm's bankruptcy group is *"one of the leaders in Hawaii,"* **Ted Pettit** (see p.752). He drew enthusiastic praise for his ability to *"look beyond the obvious options,"* and for the *"tremendous experience"* he has gained in high-profile reorganizations. Recent highlights include acting for the unsecured creditors liquidating trust in the H&W Foods/Palama Meat Chapter 11 proceedings. Outside of Hawaii, meanwhile, he has been representing an electrical contractor in the collection of judgment and the prosecution of fraudulent transfer of business assets by a debtor, who had filed a Chapter 11 case in Atlanta, Georgia. April 2005 marked the departure of Christopher Muzzi, who joined other Case Bigelow attorneys to set up Moseley Biehl Tsugawa Lau & Muzzi.
**Clients/Work Highlights:** The firm's extensive clientele includes secured creditors, unsecured creditor committees and landlords. For example, Ted Pettit has been representing Beal Bank of Dallas,

Texas, a secured creditor engaged in multiple commercial foreclosures in Hawaii.

### Gelber, Gelber, Ingersoll & Klevansky, A Law Corporation

**The Firm:** The team of *"bright and thorough attorneys"* at *"this first-rate prime bankruptcy player"* scooped market plaudits for its involvement in many of the state's highest-profile Chapter 11 proceedings and reorganizations. This year, many of these have been in the airline sector, and the 31-year-old firm was involved as lead counsel for Aloha Airlines in its bankruptcy proceedings until May 2005. The seven-lawyer team is able to tap into corporate and tax expertise and has been active in federal and state court litigation.
**The Lawyers:** The *"smart and talented"* **Don Gelber** drew warm praise for his *"excellent intellect, meticulous work"* and *"superb written abilities."* An *"incredibly practical approach"* combined with an *"excellent knowledge of the law"* ensure the entry of newcomer **Simon Klevansky** into the bankruptcy tables. Strong in Chapter 11 matters, he is valued by clients as an attorney who can *"get things done swiftly."* He has been busy of late with the reorganization of a leading wholesale meat-packing business and with work for the major creditors in a hotel bankruptcy case. Significant bankruptcy experience in a junior partner and a strong work ethic drives the up-and-coming **Alika Piper** into the rankings.
**Clients/Work Highlights:** The team has been involved in the H&W Foods and Palama Meat Chapter 11 cases, as well as sizable litigation involving the judicial foreclosure against 240 acres of golf course property. Clients include Casden Properties; MacFarms of Hawaii; National Partnership Investments; Yoshida Kogyo; Kamehameha Schools; Hawaiian Securities & Realty and ResortQuest Hawaii.

### Moseley Biehl Tsugawa Lau & Muzzi

**The Firm:** Created in April 2005 by former Case Bigelow attorneys, this firm has rapidly won a first-class reputation for bankruptcy litigation. The six-lawyer group is notably representing the unsecured creditors in the high-profile Aloha Airlines bankruptcy, the largest pending case in the state. It also boasts experience of assisting secured lenders and advising Chapter 7 trustees on obtaining assets.

**The Lawyers:** Rising star **Christopher Muzzi** is appreciated in the market for his "*strong technical abilities and understanding of bankruptcy issues.*" His profile has been boosted this year by his role as co-counsel for the official committee of unsecured creditors in the Aloha Airlines bankruptcy, currently the largest pending Chapter 11 case in the District of Hawaii.

**Clients/Work Highlights:** Architects Hawaii; Hawaii Business College; Queen Emma Foundation; Wells Fargo and Windward Dodge Chrysler Jeep.

## Rush Moore LLP

**The Firm:** This long-standing firm of around 24 attorneys operates from offices in Honolulu, Maui and on the Big Island, from where it has been involved in most of the state's major Chapter 11 cases. The team is unusual in acting in smaller consumer bankruptcies, which it handles alongside such huge undertakings as the massive reorganization of Hawaiian Airlines. Here it served as local counsel to the unsecured creditors' committee in its first Chapter 11 filing. The team proceeded to act for a Hawaiian bank, a foreign bank and an aircraft lienholder in the second reorganization case of the airline, on which full payment or assumption was made of its clients' claims.

**The Lawyers:** **Susan Tius** offers over 25 years' experience in creditor and debtor bankruptcy litigation, during which time she has developed a "*practical and results-focused approach.*" She regularly represents bankruptcy trustees and creditors in commercial cases.

**Clients/Work Highlights:** The team acts for institutional, real estate and consumer lenders, as well as commercial lessors and other creditor parties. It represented the unsecured creditors' committee in the second reorganization of the shopping center Aloha Tower Marketplace. The firm also served as the Chapter 11 trustee's counsel in the first Chapter 11 case filed by the Marketplace.

## Wagner Choi Evers

**The Firm:** This Honolulu firm enjoys enormous respect for its dedicated practice in bankruptcy, workouts and foreclosures, which it combines with a strong showing in commercial and real estate litigation. Debtor-creditor relations and corporate insolvency work feature prominently in the workload of the four-lawyer team.

**The Lawyers:** The practice's lead pair are seen to focus strongly on debtor representation, though they also win their share of creditor work. Interviewees were full of admiration for "*smart and practical*" **James Wagner**, whose "*excellent courtroom presentation skills*" and "*tremendous common sense and experience*" make him a safe choice for anything tricky

and contentious. As one of the leading figures at the bankruptcy Bar, he was recommended by peers as a "*comfortable and safe referral.*" Also impressing the market is **Chuck Choi**, who enters the tables this year. His client-driven approach is a hit with sources and has helped him to build an extensive practice in workouts and reorganizations.

**Clients/Work Highlights:** The firm acts for a range of debtors and creditors in business reorganizations and bankruptcy proceedings.

## Other Notable Practitioners

"*An excellent intellect*" and "*creative and innovative arguments*" lie behind the success of **Jerrold Guben**, who enters this year's rankings. Interviewees particularly admire the Reinwald O'Connor & Playdon attorney for his representation of debtors. One of the senior members of the bankruptcy Bar, he offers vast experience and can "*recite volume and chapter on any published bankruptcy case.*" Another long-standing member of the bankruptcy Bar is **James Duca** of Kessner Duca Umebayashi Bain & Matsunaga. "*Unafraid of taking on tough cases,*" Duca commands a broad practice, which also spans commercial litigation, banking and real estate.

# CORPORATE/COMMERCIAL

| Corporate/Commercial |
| --- |
| **Leading Firms** |
| [1] CADES SCHUTTE *Honolulu* |
| CARLSMITH BALL LLP *Honolulu* |
| CASE LOMBARDI & PETTIT *Honolulu* |
| GOODSILL ANDERSON QUINN & STIFEL *Honolulu* |
| [2] CHUN, KERR, DODD, BEAMAN & WONG *Honolulu* |
| GELBER, GELBER, INGERSOLL *Honolulu* |
| MCCORRISTON MILLER MUKAI *Honolulu* |

| Leading Individuals |
| --- |
| **Senior Statesmen** |
| CASE Daniel *Case Lombardi & Pettit* |
| CASE James *Carlsmith Ball LLP* |
| [1] KIM Gregory *Vantage Counsel LLC* |
| PRESSMAN Stewart *McCorriston Miller Mukai* |
| REBER David *Goodsill Anderson Quinn & Stifel* |
| SCHULL E Gunner *Cades Schutte* |
| [2] CRIBLEY James *Case Lombardi & Pettit* |
| GELBER Stephen *Gelber, Gelber, Ingersoll* |
| INGERSOLL Richard *Gelber, Gelber, Ingersoll* |
| VAN WINKLE J Thomas *Carlsmith Ball LLP* |

## Band 1

### Cades Schutte

**The Firm:** Corporate, tax and real estate law are the driving forces behind this "*extremely strong*" 70-attorney firm, one of the oldest in the state. Its "*deep and broad expertise*" is split between transactional work and commercial litigation, and the market showered particular praise on the group's skill in healthcare, hospitality and resort work. Interviewees also admired the team of around eight income tax specialists, who are considered by some commentators "*the strongest tax group in the state.*"

**The Lawyers:** For transactional work, the firm's standout corporate name – and, indeed, one of the foremost names on the islands – is the "*honest and trustworthy*" **Gunner Schull**. He has been particularly busy of late negotiating joint venture agreements between parties involved in real property developments. Meanwhile, the "*deal-driven*" **Roger Epstein** earned widespread praise for his successful tax controversy practice. His recent successes include ensuring that the IRS conceded an asserted $85 million claim against a key client, in connection with a complicated corporate liquidation. The team structured and negotiated the client's disposal of a $250 million business. Considered by many to be Epstein's right hand man, **Vito Galati** enters the rankings this year. He was particularly recommended for his knowledge of partnership and real estate tax law, as

well as Hawaii state tax, and also boasts a forte in equipment leasing and low-income housing tax credits.

**Clients/Work Highlights:** Alexander & Baldwin; Aloha Petroleum; First Hawaiian Bank and Outrigger Hotels & Resorts feature in a roster of Fortune 500 clients.

### Carlsmith Ball LLP

**The Firm:** A "*natural depth in the corporate arena*" and a "*long transactional track record*" ensure this high-flying firm a prominent position in our corporate tables. A team of around 50 lawyers operates from five offices across the state, with additional outposts in Guam, Saipan and Los Angeles. It is active in a variety of commercial work for national and international corporate clients, partnerships and joint ventures, including M&A, public offerings and venture capital transactions. Meanwhile, retirement plans and estate planning form part of the expertise of a tax group that is also busy advising on transactional matters. In recent years, healthcare, real estate and tourism have been among the busiest sectors for the firm.

**The Lawyers:** Statesmanlike corporate attorney **James Case** commands market respect for his vast knowledge and experience. He acts as general counsel to many high-profile clients in the tourism, real estate and utilities sectors, recently representing Hamakua Sugar in the formation of a corporation to acquire the assets of an existing company.

**Thomas Van Winkle** also enjoys a broad corporate practice, which includes banking, real estate and antitrust work. Meanwhile, federal income tax and state tax work, tax planning and litigation form the backbone of *"smart tax expert"* **David Wong**'s caseload. His *"determined approach and grasp of the commercial angle"* make him a hit with peers and clients alike. He has been busy negotiating with the Hawai'i Department of Taxation to reduce the proposed general excise tax assessment for work carried out by a multinational engineering firm in a Hawaiian project. Charles Sweet left the firm this year to join McKee Nelson in Washington, DC.

Clients/Work Highlights: Bank of Hawaii; Maui Land & Pineapple; Inter-Island Resorts; Outrigger Hotels & Resorts; American Financial Services of Hawaii and Citizens Utilities.

## Case Lombardi & Pettit

See firm details p.755

**The Firm:** This long-standing, full-service commercial law firm shone through during our research for its friendly atmosphere and *"ability to relate well to Hawaiian clients."* The 22-lawyer outfit includes a broad-based business group, which nicely complements the firm's real estate and commercial litigation teams. The team has counseled clients on M&A, the formation of business entities, UCC-governed transactions, stock transfers and a variety of financings. Interviewees also highlighted a strong ERISA and employee benefits practice as well as a reputation in business licensing.

**The Lawyers:** **Daniel Case** (see p.750), the former president of the Hawaii state Bar, is renowned as the *"dean of business law and estate planning."* His *"hard work"* and *"long track record"* help him *"find convincing answers to complex problems,"* according to clients. Lately he has been increasingly involved in real estate matters, such as representing Grove Farm – which owns approximately 40,000 acres on the island of Kaua'i – in residential, commercial and resort development. **James Cribley** (see p.750) also won widespread respect for his general corporate practice. Lately he has been acting for Ledcor in its acquisition of US Pacific Construction, one of Hawaii's largest construction companies.

Clients/Work Highlights: Ledcor; Kahala Senior Living Community; Chevron USA; Amfac; Bank of Hawaii; Delta Construction; Servco Pacific and Pacific AquaScapes.

## Goodsill Anderson Quinn & Stifel

**The Firm:** A strong reputation in corporate and securities work guarantees this *"highly flexible and collegiate firm"* its place in the foreground of the Hawaiian market. The firm fields more than 70 attorneys, among them an impressive corporate and securities group, which represents domestic and foreign companies in M&A transactions, financing agreements and a range of securities and public offering work. The firm also enjoys a particular niche in the IP area, boasting expertise in negotiating IP licensing agreements and preparing, filing and prosecuting patent and trademark applications.

**The Lawyers:** **David Reber** was highlighted as an *"honest and skilled corporate expert"* whose practice includes M&A transactions, securities law, corporate governance and capital restructurings and reorganizations. He acted for the general partner in reorganizing a series of limited partnerships with real estate holdings in Hawaii and the mainland, resulting in the formation of a holding company. Though a portion of **Miki Okumura**'s time is taken up by her responsibilities as managing partner, she still earns plaudits for her tax practice. She advises clients on a variety of state and local tax matters, including structuring business arrangements and tax controversies. Recent highlights include obtaining a favorable IRS ruling for Family Promise of Hawaii, a new charitable organization providing temporary housing and other assistance to homeless families. The addition of Brad Perkins in May 2005 is expected to enhance the firm's corporate and IP expertise.

Clients/Work Highlights: Bank of Hawaii; Chevron USA; Hawaiian Electric Industries; Hawaiian Electric Company; Hawaii Biotech; Japan Airlines; Hawaii Superferry; New York Life and Wyeth.

## Band 2

## Chun, Kerr, Dodd, Beaman & Wong

**The Firm:** This well-respected, 35-year-old firm participates in substantial corporate and tax work across the islands. More than half of the 12-lawyer outfit operate from the business transactions and organizations group, where they handle a diet of general corporate law and enjoy a particular niche working for Japanese-based clients and nonprofit organizations. The firm has been especially active of late establishing investment entities, LLPs and partnerships, especially in the hi-tech sphere.

**The Lawyers:** The *"knowledgeable and highly skilled"* **Ray Kamikawa** has long been a major force in hi-tech investment work in the state. Here, recent highlights include representing a large mainland fund seeking to invest in Hawaiian technology companies. As a former state tax director, he is one of the best-known and most experienced Hawaiian tax attorneys and is considered especially strong in tax planning. His diverse practice also includes structuring business and real estate transactions and work for nonprofit organizations.

Clients/Work Highlights: The team assisted the buyer, TD Food Group, in its purchase of the Theo Davies Food Service Group. The company bought 85 Pizza Hut and Taco Bell restaurants in Hawaii, Guam and Saipan and two Long John Silver's and A&W All-American Food restaurants on O'ahu. Other clients include Aloha Tower Development; Hawaiian Island Development; Honu Group; Maui Land & Pineapple; Outrigger Enterprises; Outrigger Hotels & Resorts; PacificBasin Communications; Security Alarm Shop; Sanwa Bank and the State of Hawai'i.

## Gelber, Gelber, Ingersoll & Klevansky, A Law Corporation

**The Firm:** The firm is principally renowned for its track record in bankruptcy proceedings; however, its corporate reorganization work underpins a strong and growing general business practice that consumes around half of the group's time. The seven-lawyer team earned plaudits for its expertise in a range of business transactions, and also enjoys a good name for tax controversy work.

**The Lawyers:** **Stephen Gelber** is one of those talented individuals whose reputation is as high in the tax arena as it is for general corporate work. He has been busy of late advising a transportation company and handling the startup and acquisition of a shrimp farming business. Interviewees were also full of admiration for the *"extremely smart"* **Richard Ingersoll**. His corporate workload includes the structuring, buying and selling of businesses in a variety of fields.

Clients/Work Highlights: Casden Properties; MacFarms of Hawaii; National Partnership Investments; Yoshida Kogyo; Kamehameha Schools; Hawaiian Securities & Realty and ResortQuest Hawaii.

## McCorriston Miller Mukai MacKinnon LLP

See firm details p.757

**The Firm:** McCorriston Miller remains one of the outstanding firms in Hawaii for real estate and tourism-driven work. The 16-year-old firm has yet to make quite the same splash in general corporate work; however, a *"young, talented group"* has been rapidly developing a strong reputation in M&A, corporate finance, restructuring and workouts. The group is already considered in some quarters to be *"untouchable"* when it comes to representing Japanese clients in investments into the state. The firm also advises US and foreign companies investing in countries across the Pacific Rim and acts for a number of banks.

**The Lawyers:** Interviewees were full of praise for the *"sharp and excellent"* **Stewart Pressman**. As the firm's standout corporate player, he has earned respect for his handling of corporate agreements and securities issues.

Clients/Work Highlights: A local, national and international clientele includes Cendant; Deloitte & Touche; Fuji Photo Film Hawaii; Philip Morris and Unocal.

## Other Notable Practitioners

**Ron Heller** of Torkildson, Katz, Fonseca, Jaffe, Moore & Hetherington is considered *"an ideal person to bounce ideas off."* His mix of general business knowledge, commercial litigation and tax expertise is considered a great base from which to handle a top-class tax controversy workload. He is active in litigation against the IRS and other state and federal matters. Recent examples include a federal tax case involving the excise tax on sums paid for transportation by air, and one concerning the priority of various liens on real property, including a federal tax lien. **Gregory Kim** is a *"trustworthy, reliable and well-informed"* adviser on corporate, securities, M&A and venture capital work. In October 2004, the former Goodsill Anderson Quinn & Stifel attorney founded Vantage Counsel LLP, a five-attorney firm focused on building emerging companies.

Among his clients are Applied Technology; AssistGuide; Bank of Hawaii; Broadband iTV and Cellular Bioengineering. Another former Goodsill Anderson lawyer, **Jeffrey Piper** of Schlack Ito & Lockwood Piper & Elkind, LLC was described as an *"exemplary"* source for advice on tax and governance issues affecting nonprofits.

# EMPLOYMENT

# MAINLY DEFENDANT

| Employment: Mainly Defendant |
| --- |
| **Leading Firms** |
| [1] MARR HIPP JONES & WANG *Honolulu* |
| TORKILDSON, KATZ, FONSECA, JAFFE *Honolulu* |
| [2] ALSTON HUNT FLOYD & ING *Honolulu* |
| CADES SCHUTTE *Honolulu* |
| GOODSILL ANDERSON QUINN & STIFEL *Honolulu* |
| IMANAKA KUDO & FUJIMOTO *Honolulu* |
| WATANABE ING & KOMEIJI *Honolulu* |

| Leading Individuals |
| --- |
| [1] HIPP Ken *Marr Hipp Jones & Wang* |
| KATZ Robert *Torkildson, Katz, Fonseca* |
| MARR Barry *Marr Hipp Jones & Wang* |
| [2] BANKS David *Cades Schutte* |
| ELENTO-SNEED Anna *Alston Hunt Floyd* |
| KNOREK John *Torkildson, Katz, Fonseca* |
| LEONG Ronald *Watanabe Ing & Komeiji* |
| NAKASHIMA Steve *Marr Hipp Jones & Wang* |
| PETRUS Barbara *Goodsill Anderson Quinn & Stifel* |
| RAND Richard *Torkildson, Katz, Fonseca* |
| WANG Sarah *Marr Hipp Jones & Wang* |
| [3] CONFALONE Perry *Carlsmith Ball LLP* |
| FUJIMOTO Wesley *Imanaka Kudo & Fujimoto* |
| JONES Patrick *Marr Hipp Jones & Wang* |

| Up-and-coming individuals |
| --- |
| GUGELYK Carolyn *Goodsill Anderson Quinn* |
| MUELLER Daniel *Marr Hipp Jones & Wang* |

## Band 1

### Marr Hipp Jones & Wang
See firm details p.756

**The Firm:** This 12-lawyer group remains one of the leaders in the field, and is admired by clients for its *"tremendous experience of the NLRB"* and involvement in the highest-profile employment litigation. *"Aggressive when they need to be"* and *"always results-driven,"* the much-admired boutique also won client plaudits for its comprehensive collective bargaining expertise, especially in the healthcare and transportation industries. Its work for airline clients was boosted by the arrival of former DLA Piper Rudnick lawyer Cynthia Surrisi in June 2004, who brings unique experience of that sector. This doubtlessly assisted the team in its efforts to help United Airlines renegotiate three of its six labor contracts. The group also obtained a federal court injunction to prevent a regional carrier's mechanics from honoring the picket lines of the striking Northwest Airlines mechanics.

**The Lawyers:** Interviewees were unanimous in their praise for the *"immensely professional, smart and top-notch"* **Ken Hipp** (see p.751), who has *"integrity in abundance."* He boasts vast experience of traditional labor law, stemming in part from his time as head of the litigation enforcement division of the NLRB. He has been busy of late representing Northwest's regional partner, Mesaba Aviation, in its dispute with the Aircraft Mechanics Fraternal Association (AMFA), which went on strike in sympathy with the AMFA strike at Northwest. He has also been responding to employment discrimination charges filed with the EEOC against his client, Norwegian Cruise Lines of America. **Barry Marr** (see p.752) has built a *"great reputation"* over more than 25 years in the field. His recent highlights include defending Reliant Pharmaceuticals against a federal court lawsuit brought by a former employee alleging violations of the Pregnancy Discrimination Act, the FMLA and the state's sex discrimination laws. **Steve Nakashima** (see p.752) impressed sources with his *"specialist knowledge and highly approachable demeanor."* He enjoys a strong employment litigation practice, which includes wage and hour disputes and noncompete cases. Lately he has been working on class action FLSA cases, defending the County of Maui and the City and County of Honolulu against claims that they failed to properly pay overtime. The Maui case, which had 125 plaintiffs, settled last year, while the Honolulu case, with more than 2,300 plaintiffs, is in the middle of discovery. Clients applauded the *"active and intelligent"* **Sarah Wang** (see p.753) for her track record in discrimination and sexual harassment cases. A steady stream of cases for national grocery store Safeway has kept her busy recently, and she also devotes a portion of her time to training Hawaii-based employers and supervisors in improved workplace practices. **Patrick Jones** (see p.751) is an *"experienced and diligent"* attorney with a broad labor and employment practice, ranging from union prevention and collective bargaining negotiations to discrimination, OSHA and FMLA issues. Near the forefront of the next generation of attorneys is the energetic and determined **Daniel Mueller** (see p.752). His broad practice spans wrongful discharge, retaliation cases and OSHA matters.

**Clients/Work Highlights:** The team acts for many of Hawaii's most important companies and governmental bodies, including Bank of Hawaii; City and County of Honolulu; County of Maui; State of Hawai`i; Dole Food; General Contractors Association of Hawaii; Hawaii Employers Council; University of Hawai`i and Servco Pacific.

### Torkildson, Katz, Fonseca, Jaffe, Moore & Hetherington Attorneys At Law, A Law Corporation

**The Firm:** With offices on Oahu, Maui and the Big Island, this well-established employment law powerhouse was long considered to be the *"only game in town."* Although the consensus is that it now shares the limelight with Marr Hipp Jones & Wang, the group of around 16 lawyers has lost none of its luster or appeal. The group's expert defense of management in a variety of labor and employment disputes drew widespread praise; clients were impressed with the *"many smart attorneys,"* their *"ability to handle both the small and the complex"* and their *"considerable knowledge of discrimination."*

**The Lawyers:** **Robert Katz** has earned an exalted position as *"the dean of labor and employment law"* in Hawaii over the course of a career spanning almost 40 years. He continues to command a pivotal role, focusing on the big picture surrounding union negotiations, employment discrimination and compliance issues. **John Knorek** is an expert in compliance work with a *"direct, confident and professional"* style. His recent highlights include successfully defending a local hospital on federal court sexual harassment charges. Other clients include condominium associations and nonprofit organizations, while the defense of FMLA and ADA cases also forms a large part of his diverse practice. **Richard Rand** is considered by many to be *"one of Hawaii's recognized wage and hour leaders."* Wage and hour work is certainly a particular forte of his, but he also handles union negotiations and labor arbitrations among other things.

## Band 2

### Alston Hunt Floyd & Ing Attorneys At Law, A Law Corporation
See firm details p.754

**The Firm:** Interviewees praised the five-partner labor and employment team at this full-service firm for its "strategic advice" and "dedicated, team-oriented approach." Working from offices on the Big Island and in Honolulu, the group is active in employment litigation and government contract work: key pillars of its practice and important areas of work in the state. A group of around half a dozen associates assists the partners with a steady stream of litigation, which has recently included an increase in race and national origin cases and a large volume of wrongful termination and sexual harassment disputes.

**The Lawyers:** The team was thought to have benefited greatly from the arrival of the "experienced, competent and hard-working" **Anna Elento-Sneed** (see p.751). "Excellent at technical statutory issues," she has been devoting a portion of her time of late to strategic planning with company management and the design of HR systems. Traditional labor work is handled by Terry Thomason, who previously worked as an adviser for the US army.

**Clients/Work Highlights:** The firm serves the property development, hospitality, insurance and healthcare sectors, among others, in labor and employment issues.

## Cades Schutte

**The Firm:** One of the state's largest and oldest full-service firms, this 70-lawyer outfit is felt to be working hard to raise its profile for labor and employment law. Operating from offices in Kailua-Kona and Honolulu, a team of eight practitioners, including five partners, carries out its share of employment discrimination, harassment, whistle-blower and wrongful termination cases. In line with a market trend, it recently witnessed a considerable rise in the latter type of claim. The team's expertise in OSHA and workers' compensation cases are additional feathers in its cap.

**The Lawyers:** An expert in corporate and securities work, "great lawyer and amiable gentleman" **David Banks** is also the team's leading light in the employment arena. His partial shift into employment work has been well received by the market, and he has been busy assisting employers with workplace train-

ing and devising HR strategies to avoid civil rights complaints and costly litigation. New partner Kristin Shigemura brings unique healthcare employment expertise to the firm's flagship health sector clients.

## Goodsill Anderson Quinn & Stifel

**The Firm:** There was considerable respect for the seven-strong employment team at this much-admired, old-line Hawaii firm. Sources praise the group for producing "top-drawer, high-quality work," and appreciate the "pragmatic and flexible" approach of its lawyers. Typical work ranges from advice on preventative measures and training to representation in wrongful termination, discrimination, sexual harassment and other employment-related civil litigation. Interviewees also commented on the advantage of having a "strong and experienced" commercial litigation team supporting the firm's employment lawyers.

**The Lawyers:** **Barbara Petrus** earns the admiration of the market for her "breadth of experience" and an approach that is "tough but fair and easy to deal with." The pivot of the team, she is particularly appreciated by clients for her "technical excellence, great oral advocacy" and "sound grasp of the avenues employers need to journey down." Her diverse practice leans toward employment litigation and discrimination cases, and she has also been instrumental in building the firm's name for preventative work. Here, she has been acting for the Bank of Hawaii, advising on policies and procedures and training the bank's managers. Junior partner **Carolyn Gugelyk** enters the tables as an up-and-comer. She is considered "well versed in labor and employment law" and was recently involved in a major national origin discrimination case.

## Imanaka Kudo & Fujimoto

**The Firm:** According to market sources, this 18-lawyer Honolulu firm is developing a strong profile on the labor and employment stage. Although it is not among the largest employment groups in the state, it nonetheless offers a broad range of services,

including EEOC compliance on Title VII, ADA and the FMLA. The group also boasts experience of collective bargaining.

**The Lawyers:** **Wes Fujimoto**, the firm's employment group head, has been building a greater market profile of late. This has followed the expansion of his practice from its focus on workers' compensation to include a greater component of general labor and employment work. The former Torkildson Katz attorney won praise for his abilities in litigation defense, counseling and training and, in particular, for his knowledge of compliance issues.

## Watanabe Ing & Komeiji

**The Firm:** Although this "fine and respected" firm has suffered the recent departure of its insurance defense team, this does not seem to have affected the small labor and employment group, which retains the respect of the market. Interviewees highlighted its expertise in counseling clients on a range of workplace issues, including wrongful discharge, harassment and wage and hour disputes.

**The Lawyers:** **Ron Leong** chairs the firm's labor, employment and employee benefits group, and also represents many of its prominent Japanese clients. He is particularly noted for advisory work on employment matters but has also practiced before the NLRB, the National Mediation Board and other state and federal agencies.

**Clients/Work Highlights:** The team acts for a variety of local, national and international clients but was particularly highlighted for its work on behalf of Japanese companies.

## Other Notable Practitioners

The "skilled and experienced" **Perry Confalone** is considered a key force in the rebuilding of Carlsmith Ball LLP's labor and employment practice. Interviewees note that despite changes of key personnel over the years, the firm's commitment to the field has not wavered.

# LAND USE

| Land Use |
| --- |
| Leading Firms |
| 1   BELLES GRAHAM PROUDFOOT AND WILSON *Lihue* |
|     CADES SCHUTTE *Honolulu* |
|     GOODSILL ANDERSON QUINN & STIFEL *Honolulu* |
|     IMANAKA KUDO & FUJIMOTO *Honolulu* |
|     MANCINI WELCH & GEIGER LLP *Kahului* |
|     TSUKAZAKI YEH & MOORE *Honolulu* |
|     WATANABE ING & KOMEIJI *Honolulu* |

## Band 1

### Belles Graham Proudfoot and Wilson

**The Firm:** This respected ten-year-old firm enjoys considerable kudos in the market for its high-class practice. A diverse general workload spans land use,

planning, zoning and subdivisions as well as environmental disputes. Operating from their home on Kaua`i, members of the six-lawyer team boast considerable experience, much of it amassed from lengthy previous stints at a prominent Honolulu practice.

**The Lawyers:** "Honesty, integrity and a high-quality practice" are some of the selling points of this collegiate team. Market sources singled out the "excellent" **Michael Belles** and "highly talented" **Max Graham** for their considerable land use expertise.

**Clients/Work Highlights:** First Hawaiian Bank; Bank of Hawaii; Grove Farm and subsidiaries; Gay & Robinson; Marriott Ownership Resorts; Aetna and General Star.

### Cades Schutte

**The Firm:** With around 60 attorneys and an "excellent market reputation in real estate," this established,

full-service Hawaiian player is unsurprisingly one of the standout firms for land use and environment work. In a state where water is abundant and land is precious, the firm's advice on compliance with hazardous waste, air and water quality laws is regarded as priceless by impressed clients.

**The Lawyers:** **Donna Leong** is said to be "extremely good on Honolulu land use and zoning," particularly in the hospitality area. The "careful and meticulous" real estate and finance partner also enjoys a wider transactional and development-oriented practice. She was recently involved in a complex land use matter, which involved obtaining a special Planned Development-Resort Permit in relation to a 7.7-acre plot in Waikiki. **Patricia McHenry** heads up the firm's environmental work, a role that she combines with commercial litigation and OSHA law.

**Clients/Work Highlights:** Local, national and

## Land Use
### Leading Individuals

[1] **BELLES Michael** *Belles Graham Proudfoot*
**GRAHAM Max** *Belles Graham Proudfoot*
**ING J Douglas** *Watanabe Ing & Komeiji*
**KUDO Benjamin** *Imanaka Kudo & Fujimoto*
**LEONG Donna** *Cades Schutte*
**MANCINI Paul** *Mancini Welch & Geiger LLP*
**MUNGER Lisa Woods** *Goodsill Anderson Quinn*
**TSUKAZAKI Ben** *Tsukazaki Yeh & Moore*

## Land Use: Environment
### Leading Individuals

[1] **MUNGER Lisa Woods** *Goodsill Anderson Quinn & Stifel*
[2] **BAIL Lisa** *Goodsill Anderson Quinn & Stifel*
**HONG Lea Ok Soon** *Alston Hunt Floyd*
**MCHENRY Patricia** *Cades Schutte*
**SANDISON Ian Lorne** *Carlsmith Ball LLP*

international hotels feature prominently in the firm's client roster.

### Goodsill Anderson Quinn & Stifel

**The Firm:** For a number of commentators, Goodsill Anderson is *"the preeminent environment firm in the state."* In addition, the veteran player boasts a *"diverse and broad land use practice"* that can stand alongside the best. As well as handling permits and approvals, rezoning and related litigation, around 12 of the firm's 70-plus lawyers have experience in high-profile land use cases, such as the Waiahole Ditch, Poipu Bay Golf Course, Koa Ridge and Mauna Kea Outrigger telescopes. The team has represented clients in connection with government regulatory disputes, water rights and Native Hawaiian rights cases before administrative agencies, courts and appellate bodies. Environmental impact statements are considered a particular forte of the group.

**The Lawyers:** *"The dean of private practice environmental law,"* **Lisa Munger** is undoubtedly the main attraction here. A *"wonderfully talented, efficient and hard-working"* attorney with a deep background in the field, she and her *"exceedingly smart"* younger colleague, **Lisa Bail**, are considered to have *"written the book on environmental law."* A good team for complex issues, they represent the University of

Hawaii in hazardous waste enforcement matters, and have been busy addressing environmental issues arising from the development of the University's new medical center. They also acted for the Hawaii Superferry in environmental litigation brought by the Sierra Club and others.

**Clients/Work Highlights:** University of Hawai`i, Hawaii Superferry and City and County of Honolulu are among the group's clients.

### Imanaka Kudo & Fujimoto

**The Firm:** Having steadily grown its attorney base, this *"strong and well-connected group"* now numbers around 20 attorneys based in Honolulu. It was specifically praised for its state zoning, land use, planning and infrastructure development finance practice.

**The Lawyers:** Sources admired team head **Benjamin Kudo** for his *"thoroughness and effectiveness"* and his *"expert knowledge"* of land use and local zoning issues. He acts for major resort, commercial, industrial and residential developers throughout Hawaii. As leader of the firm's Pacific-Asia business group, his practice has an international flavor. This was highlighted recently by his involvement in environment work for foreign and US clients in Japan, Scotland and China.

**Clients/Work Highlights:** The group advises a range of local, national and international developers on real estate, land use and environmental issues.

### Mancini Welch & Geiger LLP

**The Firm:** The five-attorney Maui boutique elicited enthusiastic market praise for its *"excellent knowledge of land use in Maui."* The team is busy in a range of commercial and residential developments, and undertakes zoning work for an impressive local clientele.

**The Lawyers:** **Paul Mancini** was recommended to researchers as a skilled attorney who *"knows the ins and outs of the county process"* and is well connected on the island.

**Clients/Work Highlights:** The firm represents a number of local and statewide developers.

### Tsukazaki Yeh & Moore

**The Firm:** This small group is said by market sources to be energetically developing its land use profile. It is typically seen acting for developers before state land and natural resource commissions and other agencies.

**The Lawyers:** The *"talented and experienced"* **Ben**

**Tsukazaki** enjoys a fantastic reputation as one of Honolulu's land use leaders, assisted by good connections at every level. A notable recent case for him was advising the Hawaii Island Economic Development Board (HIEDB) on a plan by the University of Hawai`i to expand an installation of six small telescopes on Mauna Kea.

**Clients/Work Highlights:** HIEDB and Kamehameha Investment are among the group's developer clients.

### Watanabe Ing & Komeiji

**The Firm:** This *"small, flexible and creative"* group of around ten attorneys earned market credit for its strength in a range of areas, including zoning, entitlements, public utilities work and legislative assistance. The departure this year of six attorneys from another part of the firm was not expected to impact on the land use department.

**The Lawyers:** **Douglas Ing** *"seeks to address the hurdles from the outset,"* according to impressed clients. He enjoys a sizable state zoning practice and has been advising a major resort developer on issues related to a number of long-term real estate projects, including a residential development on the island of Kaua`i.

**Clients/Work Highlights:** Local, national and international developers feature in the firm's client list.

### Other Notable Practitioners

**Lea Hong** (see p.751) at Alston Hunt Floyd & Ing Attorneys At Law acts for both plaintiffs and defendants. She earned plaudits for her knowledge of assessment and compliance work. Clients particularly appreciate her understanding of environment impact statements, and she enjoys unique experience of representing Native Hawaiian organizations in environmental compliance matters. **Ian Sandison** is the head of the environment section at Carlsmith Ball LLP. His practice includes civil enforcement actions and obtaining air and waste permits for power plants and metal recycling facilities. For example, he assisted the developer of a medical waste incineration facility with air and solid waste permit negotiations. He is also acting for the owner of a potential Superfund site in cleanup negotiations with the Hawai`i State Department of Health and the EPA.

# LITIGATION

# GENERAL COMMERCIAL

## Band 1

### Goodsill Anderson Quinn & Stifel

**The Firm:** *"Diversity and strength at the partner level"* and *"the ability to handle any big-ticket litigation"* maintain this outstanding firm at the head of the chasing pack. Around half of its 75 attorneys are actively employed in litigation, and it boasts particularly active employment and environmental teams. Sources also highlight the group's expertise in drug and medical devices, product liability, aviation/maritime and IP disputes. In the latter area, the firm handled five copyright infringement matters for long-standing client ASCAP, one of the major music-licensing organizations in the USA.
**The Lawyers:** Corlis Chang's *"highly practical and critical eye"* is employed in products liability, construction and insurance cases, among others. She

has acted as litigation partner for the County of Kaua`i in a wide range of work, defending it and its employees against breach of contract and tort lawsuits, including wrongful termination and defamation cases. Medmarc Insurance Group is another of her key clients. **Jacqueline Earle's** combined healthcare and business litigation expertise has been tested in the course of a very busy year. Clients recommended this *"highly strategic, professional and personable"* attorney for her good connections and *"articulate presentations."* She has been representing drug and medical device manufacturers in product liability and mass tort disputes, as well as defending a major Hawaiian nonprofit health system and several of its subsidiaries in various matters, including a wrongful dismissal suit brought by a former director, a derivative action, a breach of contract lawsuit and an administrative inquiry. Interviewees also admire the *"appropriately aggressive"* **Bruce Lamon**, whose focus of late has been on complex financial disputes and land use litigation. In January 2005, he obtained a Hawaii State Court judgment in favor of his client, the Bank of Hawaii, against plaintiffs who claimed that it had acted in breach of fiduciary duties. **John Lacy** was enthusiastically praised for his *"considerable trial experience."* He has been busy representing The Honolulu Advertiser, the state's largest newspaper, in various commercial disputes involving distribution, publishing and antitrust issues. He also serves as trial counsel for Matson Navigation, Hawaii's largest maritime shipping company, and its subsidiary Matson Terminals. He handles cargo, tariff and contract litigation for them.
**Clients/Work Highlights:** Medmarc Insurance Group; The Honolulu Advertiser; Hawaiian Airlines; American Society of Composers, Authors and Publishers (ASCAP); Matson Navigation; County of Kaua`i; Bank of Hawaii and Historic Hawai`i Foundation.

### McCorriston Miller Mukai MacKinnon LLP
See firm details p.757
**The Firm:** The 20-strong litigation team at this *"top-notch firm"* earned widespread praise from the market for its breadth of experience and trial expertise. Strong in commercial and insurance disputes, the group also boasts considerable skill in products and professional liability, as well as environmental and white-collar litigation. Over the past decade, it has played instrumental roles in many of the key pieces of litigation in the state. For example, it took part in an important antitrust case against major energy companies, and handled the defense of the mayor of the City and County of Honolulu.
**The Lawyers:** Clients were full of praise for the *"excellent and aggressive"* **Bill McCorriston**. A cut above the market, he chairs the firm's litigation group and is highly visible in complex commercial disputes. His broad practice includes insurance cases and government-related litigation. For example, he

continues to defend Jeremy Harris, the former mayor of Honolulu, in a criminal investigation relating to campaign spending. He also represents the owners of Waimea Valley, which is the subject of one of the largest condemnation cases of recent years. Although McCorriston has dominated the team for a long time, other talented litigators have. **Nadine Ando** and **Jon Steiner**, in particular, impressed clients with their *"knowledge of how to take on a fight"* and of *"how to find a solution for their client."* Ando has a mixed business and employment litigation practice, and recently acted for a large local tour bus and travel company in a partnership dispute. This case alleged breach of contract and breach of fiduciary duties among the company's partners in relation to a multi-million-dollar investment venture on Maui. Steiner, meanwhile, has acted for a wholesale food distributor in a case arising from the divestiture of a Hawaii subsidiary, which subsequently filed for bankruptcy protection.
**Clients/Work Highlights:** The firm's local, national and international clients are drawn from a number of industry sectors, such as hotels and leisure, retail, insurance and real estate. It has been acting for a well-known labor leader in federal charges involving tax fraud and money laundering.

## Band 2

### Alston Hunt Floyd & Ing Attorneys At Law, A Law Corporation
See firm details p.754
**The Firm:** This *"solid, flexible and steady"* firm has been busily nurturing a cohort of talented lawyers and rapidly expanding its local clientele. The firm's 40 attorneys practice general litigation in a *"prompt, responsive and innovative way,"* and win particular praise for their work for title insurance companies. Market sources also highlighted multiple lawsuits and class actions as an area of expertise. For example, the team acted in the Vestin Group litigation arising out of the economic collapse of a group of cemeteries and pre-need funeral trusts.
**The Lawyers:** The *"smart and extraordinarily experienced"* **Paul Alston** (see p.750) is considered *"dynamite"* in litigation. Complex commercial disputes, bet-the-company cases and public interest litigation all feature in his practice, and he earned enthusiastic plaudits for professional malpractice and securities fraud. The other half of the *"dynamic duo,"* **Bill Hunt** (see p.751), enjoys a reputation as a *"strong commercial litigator"* and is well respected for medical malpractice and healthcare defense work. He represented Kaiser Foundation Hospital in a federal court medical malpractice action concerning alleged mistakes in the treatment of a premature infant for eye disease, which resulted in total blindness. The *"well-connected"* **Ellen Carson** (see p.750) earned applause for her *"excellent communication skills."* Medical malpractice and employment claims feature prominently in her workload, and she is defending

appeals in two lawsuits filed by a class action of physicians and the state medical society. Another new entrant this year is **David Nakashima** (see p.752), a *"really talented and smart"* generalist who handles commercial and employment disputes, including breach of contract and wrongful termination claims.

Clients/Work Highlights: The team acts for over 5,000 substitute teachers in a class action against the State of Hawai`i claiming unpaid wages totaling more than $25 million. It is also handling the important Hyatt Regency Waikiki Hotel dispute. The group additionally advises Chevron USA; Eaton; Georgia-Pacific; Keene Corporation and Pittsburgh Corning.

## Cades Schutte

The Firm: This full-service firm, the oldest in the state, remains among the leaders in Hawaii for litigation. It employs *"a crop of excellent attorneys,"* according to the market, with good courtroom skills and expertise in a wide range of areas. These include products liability, bankruptcy, real estate disputes, securities litigation and antitrust cases. With considerable bench strength, which includes former federal judges, the group enjoys a breadth of trial and appellate experience that many find hard to match. Interviewees particularly underlined the strength of the midlevel partners, pointing to a promising future for the firm in this area.

The Lawyers: **Jeff Portnoy** chairs the firm's litigation section and is well respected in Hawaii's legal community. *"Bright and extremely smart,"* he boasts over 30 years' experience in the field. Clients are impressed with his *"superb cross-examining skills"* and believe that he wins over judges with his *"sound ethics and credibility."* A talented rainmaker, his diverse practice has recently included media, products liability, employment, securities and insurance coverage disputes. For example, he defended a multi-million-dollar securities brokerage arbitration and obtained a summary judgment in a class action against a local utility, where damages in excess of $17 million were being claimed. **Michael Heihre** is *"superb in the courtroom,"* as well as *"hard-working, tough and great value for money,"* according to clients. Real estate and land use litigation feature prominently in a general commercial caseload. He acted for Yee Hop Realty in proceedings against the City and County of Honolulu over the condemnation of a large industrial area in Honolulu for a rapid transit and bus facility. He is also lead counsel for Pauoa Bay Properties in a case relating to the development of a luxury project on the Kohala Coast of Hawaii. Interviewees recommended **David Schulmeister** as a *"terrific litigator,"* especially for real estate and construction disputes.

Clients/Work Highlights: Norwegian Cruise Lines; SCI Management; Merrill Lynch and Verizon.

## Carlsmith Ball LLP

The Firm: This well-established, old-line Hawaii firm fields a well-respected team of around 25 litigation attorneys. It has an extensive reach, spanning not just the Hawaiian Islands but reaching into Los Angeles, which is an added attraction to clients. During research, the group earned compliments for its track record in a range of litigation, including antitrust, construction and real estate cases, as well as product and professional liability.

The Lawyers: **Gary Grimmer** is a *"capable, efficient and conscientious"* attorney with almost 30 years of experience. Widely considered to be the driving force behind the firm's litigation practice, he is especially active in breach of contract and business torts disputes. Recent highlights include defending a Hawaiian corporation and three majority stockholders in one lawsuit, and in a separate action representing an attorney sued for allegedly breaching his duty to 17 of 176 stockholders.

Clients/Work Highlights: The group acts for local, mainland and international clients. In the current hot real estate market, the team is handling several cases of contract disputes relating to real property deals.

## Kobayashi, Sugita & Goda

The Firm: Although a smaller outfit than some of its rivals, this old-line and *"extremely well-connected"* Honolulu-based firm devotes more than half its resources to commercial litigation. Clients admired not only the strength of the compact group of partners but also the *"strong support from secondary attorneys,"* a combination that together offers clients *"thorough and comprehensive litigation backup."* IP, franchise disputes and white-collar litigation earned specific praise.

The Lawyers: Peers and clients admire *"tenacious battler"* **Bert Kobayashi** for his *"efficiency, work ethic and ability to listen."* Well known at the state Bar, the *"thorough and incisive"* group leader is able to adopt an *"aggressive approach"* when necessary, according to interviewees. His skills have been on show recently in construction litigation on behalf of the City and County of Honolulu and the Board of Water Supply. Interviewees applauded **Lex Smith** for his track record in *"interesting and complex high-end litigation."* A newcomer to the tables, his 20 years of experience hold him in good stead in class actions, antitrust disputes, commercial litigation and IP cases.

Clients/Work Highlights: As well as local corporations, the firm acts for the University of Hawai`i at Manoa; the City and County of Honolulu; the Board of Water Supply and the State of Hawai`i.

## Band 3

## Bays Deaver Lung Rose Baba

The Firm: With real estate such a key driver of growth within the state, this firm's considerable real estate and construction expertise lends it an advantage when developments hit problems. For almost 20 years, the group of around 20 attorneys has been immersed in real estate and construction disputes. It

continues to boast some of the state's top construction litigators and has experience of acting for developers, buyers, sellers, brokers, lenders and other clients in a variety of commercial cases.

The Lawyers: **Crystal Rose** remains the team's outstanding name and was recommended to researchers as an *"awesome problem solver."* Best known as a *"great advocate in real estate disputes,"* she commands a broad practice that also includes construction, trusts litigation and general commercial disputes.

Clients/Work Highlights: The firm acts for a spectrum of clients, such as Amfac Hawaii; Haseko Construction; Lucent Technologies and Xerox.

## Case Lombardi & Pettit

See firm details p.755

The Firm: The seven lawyers in this litigation and alternative dispute resolution group are *"competent, thorough and skilled,"* according to prominent clients. As well as fielding some outstanding partners, the team attracted praise for its *"good associate-level talent."* Real estate and construction litigation are felt to be particular strengths for the group, which also handles a range of general business, commercial and tort disputes.

The Lawyers: Entering the tables this year is the *"responsive, sound and knowledgeable"* **John Zalewski** (see p.753), who is making a good name for himself in the field. He has been busy defending various homeowner, condominium and community associations against claims of wrongful termination, illegal discrimination, and covenant, statute and torts violations.

Clients/Work Highlights: Liberty House; Crazy Shirts; Amfac Hawaii; Bomat; Great Insurance Company and Oahu Construction.

## Paul, Johnson, Park & Niles, Attorneys At Law, A Law Corporation

The Firm: The market respects this *"steady and reliable"* group of around 15 attorneys, many with big-case experience, for their *"good written work and analysis."* From offices in Honolulu and Maui, the group staffs cases leanly and efficiently, picking up compliments along the way for its success in high-end and complex real estate, construction and general commercial disputes. The Maui office was particularly noted for its experience representing the interests of the state's commercial boating community.

The Lawyers: Long-standing experience and an *"efficient, fast and to-the-point style"* are among the reasons **James Paul** is respected by clients, peers and judges alike. The *"good, tough courtroom performer"* handles a variety of cases, and has recently been acting for a law firm in an important legal malpractice case and assisting a large commercial property owner with a piece of complex litigation.

Clients/Work Highlights: The team represents a range of local and national clients in commercial litigation. Recent examples include acting for large resort owners, as well as major Japanese investors, in commercial and real estate litigation in Hawaii.

## Watanabe Ing & Komeiji

**The Firm:** One of the highest-profile events of the year in Hawaii's litigation circles has been the departure of James Kawashima and members of the insurance defense team, who left to establish their own firm late in 2005. Although this undeniably reduces the firm's resources somewhat, its expertise in commercial litigation still elicited the respect of the market.

**The Lawyers:** Among those who remain at the firm is **John Komeiji.** According to clients, he "*comes across as a humble type, but he will then go to court and win*" and, like an excellent poker player, "*he knows when the client needs to fold and when to fight.*" He offers considerable expertise in insurance coverage disputes and enjoys a particular focus on telecommunications law and the defense of commercial and professional malpractice cases.

## Other Notable Practitioners

In the words of one peer, the "*excellent*" **John Nishimoto** at Ayabe, Chong, Nishimoto, Sia & Nakamura is "*arguably the most experienced trial lawyer in the state.*" He boasts a strong track record in litigation, predominantly insurance defense work and medical malpractice, where sources consider him "*absolutely supreme.*" Having left Watanabe Ing & Komeiji this year, **James Kawashima** started nine-attorney Kawashima, Lorusso & Tom. He specializes in insurance defense litigation and also offers expertise in general commercial and construction disputes and professional malpractice cases.

# REAL ESTATE

| Real Estate Leading Firms | |
|---|---|
| 1 | CADES SCHUTTE *Honolulu* |
| | GOODSILL ANDERSON QUINN & STIFEL *Honolulu* |
| | MCCORRISTON MILLER MUKAI *Honolulu* |
| 2 | CARLSMITH BALL LLP *Honolulu* |
| | CASE LOMBARDI & PETTIT *Honolulu* |
| | CHUN RAIR & YOSHIMOTO LLP *Honolulu* |
| | MANCINI WELCH & GEIGER LLP *Kahului* |
| 3 | ASHFORD & WRISTON *Honolulu* |
| | BAYS DEAVER LUNG ROSE BABA *Honolulu* |
| | BROOKS TOM PORTER QUITIQUIT *Honolulu* |
| | CHUN, KERR, DODD, BEAMAN & WONG *Honolulu* |
| | IMANAKA KUDO & FUJIMOTO *Honolulu* |
| | RUSH MOORE LLP *Honolulu* |
| | SCHLACK ITO & LOCKWOOD PIPER *Honolulu* |
| | SCHNEIDER TANAKA RADOVICH ANDREW *Honolulu* |
| | STARN O'TOOLE MARCUS & FISHER *Honolulu* |

## Band 1

## Cades Schutte

**The Firm:** It has been a busy real estate market in Hawaii of late, and this traditional Hawaiian firm has benefited more than most. According to sources, it boasts a bench of "*top-quality, goal-oriented attorneys*" who have amassed a "*wealth of expertise over the decades.*" Clients were also delighted with the depth of support and "*great back-up services*" in ancillary fields. The team enjoyed particularly good feedback for its work in real estate development, finance and leasing, especially in the booming hospitality sector.

**The Lawyers:** Clients showered praise on **Gino Gabrio** for combining "*vast knowledge and top-quality work*" with a "*timely, personable and deal-making approach.*" His practice is split between real estate and banking regulatory matters, and he has served as both lead and local counsel in the acquisition and disposal of hotels, shopping centers and office buildings. The "*articulate, honest and forthright*" **Mark Hazlett** is a name on everyone's lips for his "*excellent knowledge of real estate finance and leasing transactions*" and particularly strong understanding of the condominium market. Completing a trio of top-ranked real estate property experts is the "*first-class*" **Donna Leong.** A wealth of local land use and zoning experience complements a development and leasing workload, making her a top choice. Her "*meticulous and solution-oriented approach*" has benefited clients in many transactions, a major recent example being a massive development project for Outrigger Hotels & Resorts. Outrigger, the largest locally owned company, is in the process of developing an area of approximately 7.7 acres in Waikiki, O`ahu. This will see the creation of a mixed-use entertainment/retail/hotel project, with timeshare and residential components. Interviewees applauded "*extremely smart*" senior attorney **Bernice Littman,** especially for her expertise in financing, development, leasing and the purchase and sale of commercial properties. She has spent a fair amount of time recently on condominium-related work.

**Clients/Work Highlights:** Avalon Development, Outrigger Enterprises and A&B Properties feature in the firm's client roster.

## Goodsill Anderson Quinn & Stifel

**The Firm:** This strongly admired firm instills "*considerable trust*" in its clients through a track record of success in complex real estate transactions. The busy team boasts expertise in all aspects of real property development, financing, leasing and litigation. The team has lost some prominent players in recent years but retains around 18 attorneys.

**The Lawyers:** **Lani Ewart** is said to be a "*bright, practical and pragmatic*" attorney who is "*in tune with the particular needs of banks.*" Clients appreciate her "*succinct writing style*" and knack of "*getting to the heart of issues*" swiftly. She acts for the Bank of Hawaii in connection with the majority of its commercial real estate loans for the acquisition, construction and refinancing of a range of commercial properties. She also acted for Continental Pacific and its affiliates in the acquisition of more than 1,000 acres of land from Campbell Estate in the Kahuku area of O`ahu. Sources also highlighted **Randy Steverson**'s skill in "*identifying critical issues*" for his clients. A "*resourceful*" adviser, his workload leans toward residential and commercial development. He recently completed the restructuring of the ground leases for a regional shopping center, which was connected with its refinancing, and worked on a securitized loan involving five major hotels in three states. The "*top-flight*" **Ray Iwamoto** handles a range of real estate development work. He represented AIG Global Real Estate in the due diligence and negotiations surrounding the acquisition of residential subdivision land in Poipu, Kaua`i, and has also been acting for Moana Pacific condominium development, developer of a large mixed-use condominium project in Honolulu. Interviewees also appreciate the "*easygoing nature*" and experience of **Leighton Yuen,** traits that are said to assist the smooth passage of deals. He represented the owner-developers of the Waikoloa Beach Resort and has been handling all the real estate legal work for several properties within the development. This includes the sale of the leased fee interest in the land under the 1,240-room Hilton Waikoloa Village Hotel and the sale of the 75,000 sq ft resort shopping and dining complex at Waikoloa.

**Clients/Work Highlights:** MacNaughton Group; Waikoloa Beach Resort; AIG Global Real Estate; ConocoPhillips; Bank of Hawaii; Costco Wholesale; Grosvenor Center; Lanai Resorts; Maui Marriott Resort and the Hyatt Regency.

## McCorriston Miller Mukai MacKinnon LLP

See firm details p.757

**The Firm:** Having worked "*all sides of real estate deals,*" this team of around 20 attorneys drew praise for its "*quick responsiveness to clients' demands.*" With a "*number of go-to people,*" this firm is seen to compare favorably with a lot of national mainland outfits. It handles a wide array of real estate finance and development work; however timeshare and condominium deals have featured most prominently of late. Highlights include assisting the owner-developer with the planning, development, finance and construction of the 404 Piikoi Street project, which includes the Nauru Tower condominium project, the 1133 Waimanu Street condominium and the Hawaiki Tower condominium.

**The Lawyers:** Clients appreciate the firm's "*smart and honest*" managing partner **Scott MacKinnon** for his "*extensive experience, easy style and lateral thinking,*" all of which help to make transactions run

## Real Estate

### Leading Individuals

smoothly. Described as *"the voice of reason,"* he offers an *"excellent follow through"* after the deal has been completed. He has spent considerable time of late working in the booming luxury single-family residence and condominium market. **Cliff Miller**, the *"brilliant, knowledgeable and professional"* chair of the firm's business and real estate section, also has a knack for *"getting the parties to agree."* He has been representing the developer of a high-end, single-family residence project in Maui, and also advising a northern California client on the acquisition of 1,600 acres in Mexico. Commentators also think highly of the *"creative"* **Charlie Pear**, who *"speaks fluently the language of timeshare development."* In addition to complex local timeshare work, his expertise has been called on in projects in Las Vegas and New Hampshire. Sources noted the growing reputation of *"sound and bright"* **Randall Sakumoto**, who focuses on real estate and land use matters. He acted recently for Kuilima Resort in connection with a $350 million loan transaction with CSFB. This was to refinance debt and finance a portion of the development and construction costs associated with Kuilima Resort's hotel, the Turtle Bay Resort.

**Clients/Work Highlights:** Starwood Vacation Ownership; Central Pacific Financial; The Mitsubishi Bank; The Long-Term Credit Bank of Japan and Interval International.

## Band 2

### Carlsmith Ball LLP

**The Firm:** This much-admired firm, with offices across the state, fields a team of around 12 real property and land use experts. In addition to work for major landowners, the team enjoys a steady stream of mandates from prominent developers in the high-end resort market across the Islands. For example, it has been providing legal advice on a range of mixed-use residential/hospitality and condominium projects on Kauai and Maui.

**The Lawyers:** **Patricia Devlin** stands out for her *"good sense of how to balance issues"* and her *"impressive guidance to clients."* Her diverse practice spans finance, development and land use matters, and she has assisted major hotel companies with the sale, purchase and operation of their local properties. Commercial leasing forms a large part of the caseload of *"talented and driven"* **Bob Strand**. He focuses on complex real estate transactions, equipment leasing, water law and public utilities issues. In recent months, his talents have been employed in leasing transactions on behalf of Ala Moana Shopping Center. Joining the tables this year is **Eric James**. He offers experience spanning more than 25 years and all phases of the development cycle, and recently acted for Campbell Estate in the development and leasing of the second urban center on O'ahu.

**Clients/Work Highlights:** Ala Moana Shopping Center and Campbell Estate are two of an impressive group of local and national clients.

### Case Lombardi & Pettit

See firm details p.755

**The Firm:** Although smaller than some of its rivals, this well-established firm enjoys a strong profile in the real estate market. Sources say that its success is based on the *"knowledge of the local market"* and *"exceptionally good contacts"* of a team of *"highly responsive and bright attorneys."* The eight-strong group acts for large landowners, home builders and condominium conversion companies in acquisitions, developments and finance transactions in the commercial and residential sectors. However, interviewees did question whether the departures of a number of lawyers, who left to form Schneider Tanaka Radovich Andrew & Tanaka and Moseley Biehl Tsugawa Lau & Muzzi, would impact on the practice.

**The Lawyers:** *"Well-connected"* team leader **Dennis Lombardi** (see p.752) was described as a *"bigger-picture guy"* who *"knows exactly where to hit the diamond."* Particularly strong in entitlement and subdivision work, he continues to advise Schuler Homes, a division of DR Horton and one of the largest home builders in the USA. He is also engaged in acquisitions and sales of resort and commercial properties on O'ahu and other Islands, such as acting in the sale of the Kukui Grove Shopping Center on Kaua'i. **James Cribley** (see p.750) is an *"immensely likeable and capable"* attorney, according to market sources. Perhaps better known as a corporate generalist, he won praise for *"delivering what he promises"* in real estate transactions. Clients also appreciate **Nancy Youngren** (see p.753) for her *"hands-on"* approach and *"sense of timeliness,"* which together help her to lead them *"step by step through transactions."* She worked on the Watermark, a new 212-unit condominium in Waikiki, valued at more than $150 million. Joining them in the tables is the *"bright, prompt and detail-oriented"* **Stacey Foy** (see p.751). She focuses on real estate acquisition, entitlements, development, financing and timeshare registration.

**Clients/Work Highlights:** Bank of Hawaii; Textron Financial; Kahala Senior Living Community; Waipouli Beach Resort and Marriott International.

### Chun Rair & Yoshimoto LLP

**The Firm:** Market sources were full of admiration for this group of five *"service-oriented and deal-making"* lawyers, who spun off into a real estate and finance boutique from Oshima, Chun, Fong & Chung. The recent change to the firm's name took place after its former founder, Alan Oshima, left to take up the role of general counsel at Hawaiian Telecom.

**The Lawyers:** The market was unanimous in praising the *"bright, personable and methodical"* **Deborah Chun** (see p.750), around whom this team revolves. With her financial background, she has a strong grasp of real estate finance issues, including the structuring and drafting of commercial loans, bond issues and financing for complex projects, which she combines with a *"focus on getting the deal done."*

**Clients/Work Highlights:** Local, national and international companies feature strongly in the group's client base. Recent highlights include working on development agreements for a large educational trust.

### Mancini Welch & Geiger LLP

**The Firm:** Commentators highlighted the *"great real estate reputation"* that this smaller, five-lawyer group enjoys on the island of Maui. Here it represents lenders and developers in a variety of transactional, development and land use matters. Especially busy in the second home residential market, the group was deemed to have a wealth of expertise in the municipal permit and zoning process.

**The Lawyers:** Researchers were impressed by the warmth of respect expressed for the seniority and experience of **Paul Mancini** and **Thomas Welch**. Mancini was praised for his *"impressive ability to deal with government bodies and regulations"* as part of a practice that includes land use and condemnation cases. Welch, meanwhile, is considered an *"excellent technical specialist,"* who *"is careful to get a range of matters completed."*

**Clients/Work Highlights:** The team advises a

number of local companies, developers and private individuals, including several movie stars.

## Band 3

### Ashford & Wriston

**The Firm:** Half of this 25-lawyer Honolulu firm is dedicated to real property work, where its transactional expertise wins it considerable compliments. The team's skill has lately been put to good use in the commercial and residential markets, where its broad experience has assisted clients in the development of second cities, resorts, shopping centers, raw land subdivisions and condominiums.

**The Lawyers:** *"One of the best-versed attorneys in ancient Hawaiian real estate law,"* **Bruce Graham**'s *"understanding of all types of title companies"* makes him a *"top guy,"* according to interviewees. He acts for the Kamehameha Schools Bernice Pauahi Bishop Estate on trust law issues, property title and Hawaiian land rights.

**Clients/Work Highlights:** The team advises landowners and developers, including large trusts and corporations. It has advised the Queen Emma Foundation, Hilton Hotels and the Roman Catholic Church in Hawaii on real estate issues.

### Bays Deaver Lung Rose Baba

**The Firm:** Market sources still believe that the firm's forte is on the real estate litigation front. Certainly, many of the firm's 19 lawyers have traditionally acted for developers and investors in land use disputes and statutory and zoning violations. However, the compact team is making efforts to enhance its transactional work and now regularly advises on the negotiation and drafting of agreements to acquire, lease, develop, and finance real estate.

**The Lawyers:** Crystal Rose is at the forefront of the firm's push into the transactional real estate sphere.

### Brooks Tom Porter Quitiquit

**The Firm:** This 24-year-old firm enters the rankings this year following enthusiastic market endorsement of its extensive real estate practice. A group of nine partners and support staff handles a diet of substantial development, land use and zoning work, and counts educational institutions and trusts among its clientele.

**The Lawyers:** Interviewees were full of praise for *"hard-working and bright"* newcomer **Carl Tom**. He mixes real estate work with a general business practice.

### Chun, Kerr, Dodd, Beaman & Wong

**The Firm:** This firm is known for *"punching above its weight"* in the real estate industry. It fields a team of 15 real estate lawyers who handle both quality transactional work and related litigation. In the commercial and residential market, the group undertakes acquisitions, leasing, financing development, sales and title advice. Land use and condominium developments are other areas of strength.

**The Lawyers:** According to sources, **Danton Wong** is the central axis around which this team revolves.

He commands a successful transactional practice and is busy in real estate development work. Recent highlights include acting for HRPT Properties Trust as Hawaii counsel in its $115 million-plus acquisition of 188 acres at Campbell Industrial Park. He also acted in the purchase of warehouse and industrial properties from Damon Estate and the purchase of the Caterpillar heavy equipment division from Theo H Davies.

**Clients/Work Highlights:** The team has acted for a Boston-based REIT, which acquired a real estate portfolio in Hawaii. Further clients include Aloha Tower; Gannett Pacific; Honu Group; Outrigger Hotels & Resorts and Maui Land & Pineapple Company.

### Imanaka Kudo & Fujimoto

**The Firm:** Market commentators identified a small group of *"fine and well-connected practitioners"* at this firm of almost 20 lawyers. Especially noted for its expertise in local land use matters, the team also offers more extensive real estate services, including advice on the acquisition of hotels and resorts, the development of condominiums and vacation ownership programs.

**The Lawyers:** **Mitchell Imanaka** is the *"highly effective"* managing principal here. He joins the tables having been warmly praised for his *"easy to get on with"* style and *"sound niche"* in the timeshare and leisure industries. For more than 24 years he has acted for developers, lenders and other real estate industry players.

**Clients/Work Highlights:** The team represents a number of local and national players in the real estate and development industry.

### Rush Moore LLP

**The Firm:** With offices on Oahu, Maui and the Big Island, this outfit is a growing force in Hawaii's real estate circles. Around half of the firm's 20 attorneys offer expertise in real property matters and related financial advice. The team's practice emphasizes condominium development and sales, as well as leasing and land use and zoning work. It also boasts considerable expertise in the acquisition of hotels and shopping centers.

**The Lawyers:** David Shibata is a contact name in this area and boasts 25 years of experience in real estate transactions.

**Clients/Work Highlights:** Continental Hotels; Marriott International; Halekulani; Bascom Group; Fremont Investment & Loan and Mitsui Fudosan.

### Schlack Ito & Lockwood Piper & Elkind, LLC

**The Firm:** Having spun off from Goodsill Anderson, this *"youthful and experienced"* team of seven respected attorneys is building a strong profile in the market. It boasts considerable experience of acting for developers in a range of acquisitions, sales and joint ventures. Commentators underlined in particular the group's impressive focus on shopping center and office builders and owners, who it regularly serves in commercial leasing transactions.

**The Lawyers:** There was considerable respect for the *"excellent and practical"* **Carl Schlack**, and especially his *"understanding of the bottom line, long experience and deal-closing approach."* In a career spanning 20 years, he has amassed formidable commercial leasing and development expertise, which is offered to the owners and developers of shopping centers, condominiums and offices.

### Schneider Tanaka Radovich Andrew & Tanaka, LLLC

**The Firm:** Interviewees enjoy working with this *"small but high-quality and conscientious"* firm because of its focus on transactional real estate and the *"strong attention to detail"* of its lawyers. Sources also point to a *"good team of associates"* as a key selling point. The group assists a number of investors and landowners in Hawaii with the finance, acquisition and sale of commercial real estate. It has been involved in much of the recent development work on Maui, including the Mauna Lani Resort, and acted on the sale of the Lihue and Kekaha sugar mills.

**The Lawyers:** Sources were full of praise for the *"technical brilliance"* of **Scott Radovich** (see p.753). He commands a broad transactional practice, including condominium and timeshare work. The *"highly competent and pragmatic"* **Bob Schneider** (see p.753) has represented a number of Hawaiian landowners and other investors in acquisition and finance deals, while up-and-comer **David Andrew** (see p.750) joins the tables following praise from well-placed sources for his skill in the condominium field and the state and federal registration of projects.

**Clients/Work Highlights:** The team has been advising on subdivision, entitlement and development matters, including federal and state registration, relating to the Kaanapali Resort. In the office and retail sector, the group has been involved in the acquisition of Waterfront Plaza in Honolulu.

### Starn O'Toole Marcus & Fisher

**The Firm:** This *"increasingly visible"* 11-year-old firm joins the tables on the back of its senior partners' expertise and its particular strength in hotel and tourism work, a field in which it acts for many of the industry's major players. Eight of the firm's 15 attorneys are devoted to real estate transactional work, including development, acquisition and financing. The firm negotiates and drafts ground leases, development leases and leases of retail and office space. It represented the present master developer in its acquisition of the Ko Olina Resort, a 632-acre master-planned resort on the west side of O'ahu.

**The Lawyers:** Having joined the firm in 1999, the *"efficient, smart and hands-on"* **Ken Marcus** is growing in prominence, especially in his hospitality niche. He has been busy representing a merchant bank and hotel developer actively engaged in the development of various hotel projects throughout Mexico. Formerly with Carlsmith Ball, **Peter Starn** boasts *"a top-drawer hotel transactional practice,"* which he has developed over a career spanning 20 years. His workload includes real estate acquisitions and sales, development, financing and restructuring, and he recently advised a consortium of major Japanese lenders on liquidating loans and ownership interests relating to a major hotel.

**Clients/Work Highlights:** Hilton Hotels and subsidiaries; Hilton Waikoloa Village; Ko Olina Development; Princeville Resort and Landmark Hotels.

## Other Notable Practitioners

The "*very impressive*" **John Aube** sits in the banking and real estate group at Watanabe Ing & Komeiji. The former Cades Schutte attorney enters the tables following enthusiastic praise for a practice that is heavy in commercial and construction finance. First Hawaiian Bank and American Savings Bank feature among his clientele, while recent highlights include a $152 million construction loan for the Capitol

Place condominium project and a $135 million loan for the acquisition of the Kahala Mandarin hotel. "*Smart, knowledgeable and technically excellent*" **Wes Chang**, of the eponymous law firm, also enters the tables this year. A talented generalist, the former Carlsmith Ball attorney offers a mixture of traditional real estate projects with expertise in tax and bonds.

# Leaders in Hawaii

### ALSTON, Paul
Alston Hunt Floyd & Ing Attorneys At Law, A Law Corporation, Honolulu
808 524 1888
palston@ahfi.com
*Recommended in Litigation*
**Practice Areas:** State and federal litigation and ADR, emphasizing complex business disputes concerning contracts, securities, real estate, construction defects, insurance coverage, civil rights, professional malpractice, and first amendment rights. Mr Alston represents both plaintiffs and defendants.
**Prof. Memberships:** ABA, Hawaii State Bar Association, American Association of Appellate Attorneys, ABF.
**Career:** Legal Aid Society of Hawaii 1972-77; Private Practice 1977-present. Special Deputy Attorney General for State of Hawaii in selected federal matters.
**Personal:** University So. California JD, 1971; Best Lawyers in America 1995-2005 (Business Litigation, First Amendment Law); Certified Civil Trial Specialist (National Board of Trial Advocacy and Hawaii Supreme Court).

### ANDO, Nadine
McCorriston Miller Mukai MacKinnon LLP, Honolulu 808 529 7300
*Recommended in Litigation*

### ANDREW, David F
Schneider Tanaka Radovich Andrew & Tanaka, LLLC, Honolulu
808 792 4200
dandrew@stratlaw.com
*Recommended in Real Estate*
**Practice Areas:** Real estate acquisitions, development, sales, and regulatory compliance (residential and resort). Extensive experience with State of Hawaii and federal (HUD) land sales registrations. Condominium development and conversions. Master planned community and subcommunity development and associations. General real estate and commercial transactions. Clients include land owners, real estate developers, state regulating authority, community associations.

**Prof. Memberships:** Hawaii State Bar Association.
**Career:** Subdivision Registration Consultant, State of Hawaii Department of Commerce and Consumer Affairs (2001 to present).
**Personal:** Law clerk to Samuel P King, Senior US District Court Judge, 1991-92; JD, University of Hawaii William S Richardson School of Law, 1991; BS, Santa Clara University, 1986.

### AUBE, John
Watanabe Ing & Komeiji, Honolulu
808 544 8300
*Recommended in Real Estate*

### BAIL, Lisa
Goodsill Anderson Quinn & Stifel, Honolulu 808 547 5600
*Recommended in Land Use*

### BANKS, David
Cades Schutte, Honolulu
808 521 9200
*Recommended in Employment*

### BELLES, Michael
Belles Graham Proudfoot and Wilson, Lihue 808 2454705
*Recommended in Land Use*

### CARSON, Ellen Godbey
Alston Hunt Floyd & Ing Attorneys At Law, A Law Corporation, Honolulu
808 524 1800
ecarson@ahfi.com
*Recommended in Litigation*
**Practice Areas:** Healthcare law, alternative dispute resolution, civil rights, constitutional litigation, commercial disputes.
**Prof. Memberships:** ABA, Hawaii State Bar Association, American Health Lawyers.
**Career:** Officer and Director since 1991.
**Personal:** Harvard Law School (1980, JD, cum laude); University of Tennessee (1976, BA, summa cum laude); Best Lawyers in America for Health Law and Alternative Dispute Resolution (2006); President, Hawaii State Bar Association (1996) and recipient of Pro Bono Award for Community Service; President, Hawaii Women Lawyers (1989-90); Presi-

dent, Institute for Human Services (2001-02); YWCA's Outstanding Woman Professional Award (1990); Ronin and counsel for National Council for Japanese American Redress.

### CASE, Daniel H
Case Lombardi & Pettit, Honolulu
808 547 5400
*Recommended in Corporate/Commercial*
**Practice Areas:** Practices in the areas of corporate, business, estate planning and trust law. Senior Director of the firm.
**Prof. Memberships:** Affiliate of the American College of Trust and Estate Counsel. American Bar Association. Hawaii State Bar Association.
**Career:** Bar Admission: Hawaii State, United States District Court for the District of Hawaii. President, Hawaii State Bar Association, 1978.
**Personal:** LLB, University of Denver, 1952. AB, Williams College and University of Denver, 1948.

### CASE, James
Carlsmith Ball LLP, Honolulu
808 523 2500
*Recommended in Corporate/Commercial*

### CHANG, Corlis
Goodsill Anderson Quinn & Stifel, Honolulu 808 547 5600
*Recommended in Litigation*

### CHANG, Wesley
Law Offices of Wesley Y S Chang, Honolulu 808 521 0087
*Recommended in Real Estate*

### CHOI, Chuck
Wagner Choi Evers, Honolulu
808 533 1877
*Recommended in Bankruptcy*

### CHUN, Deborah
Chun Rair & Yoshimoto LLP, Honolulu
(808) 539-0619
dchun@chunrair.com
*Recommended in Real Estate*
**Practice Areas:** Acquisition, development and disposition of real property;

commercial leasing; real estate and asset-based financing.
**Prof. Memberships:** Member and past Chair of the Real Estate and Financial Services Section of the Hawaii State Bar Association; Member and past Treasurer of the Hawaii State Bar Association; ABA.
**Publications:** Editor and contributing author for the 'Hawaii Commercial Real Estate Manual'(1988), the 'Hawaii Real Estate Financing Manual' (1990), and the 'Hawaii Real Estate Law Manual' (1997); contributing author, 'Hawaii's 2000 Report Regarding Lawyers' Opinion Letters in Mortgage Loan Transactions'.
**Personal:** JD, Northwestern University School of Law, 1977; Order of the Coif; BA, Purdue University, magna cum laude, 1974.

### CONFALONE, Perry
Carlsmith Ball LLP, Honolulu
808 523 2500
*Recommended in Employment*

### CRIBLEY, James M
Case Lombardi & Pettit, Honolulu
808 547 5400
jcribley@caselombardi.com
*Recommended in Corporate/Commercial, Real Estate*
**Practice Areas:** Director and Head of the firm's Business Group. He advises clients in the areas of general corporate and business law, corporate finance, business acquisitions and real estate law. His clientele includes domestic as well as foreign owners of businesses and properties.
**Prof. Memberships:** Hawaii State Bar Association.
**Career:** Bar Admission: Hawaii State, United States District Court for the District of Hawaii, United States Court of Appeals, Ninth Circuit.
**Personal:** JD, University of Michigan, 1969. BA, Miami University, 1963.

### DEVLIN, Patricia
Carlsmith Ball LLP, Honolulu
808 523 2500
*Recommended in Real Estate*

**DREHER Nicholas**
Cades Schutte, Honolulu
808 521 9200
*Recommended in Bankruptcy*

**DUCA, James**
Kessner Duca Umebayashi Bain & Matsunaga, Honolulu 808 536 1900
*Recommended in Bankruptcy*

**EARLE, Jacqueline**
Goodsill Anderson Quinn & Stifel, Honolulu 808 547 5600
*Recommended in Litigation*

**ELENTO-SNEED, Anna**
Alston Hunt Floyd & Ing Attorneys At Law, A Law Corporation, Honolulu
808 441 6228
aes@ahfi.com
*Recommended in Employment*
**Practice Areas:** Wrongful termination, employment discrimination, labor unions and collective bargaining, wage and hour law, government contracting, benefits, business transactions, personnel management and training, strategic HR planning, safety and health, proprietary rights, workplace privacy.
**Prof. Memberships:** ABA, Hawaii State Bar Association, Society for Human Resource Management (MAC, Pacific-West Regional Council, Hawaii State Director).
**Career:** Shareholder/Director of the firm. Frequently lectures for universities, business groups, and individual employers.
**Publications:** Written extensively, including articles in The Practical Lawyer, the Hawaii Bar Journal, and The Pacific Employer.
**Personal:** Boalt Hall School of Law, UC Berkeley (JD 1983).

**EPSTEIN, Roger**
Cades Schutte, Honolulu
808 521 9200
*Recommended in Corporate/Commercial*

**EWART, Lani**
Goodsill Anderson Quinn & Stifel, Honolulu 808 547 5600
*Recommended in Real Estate*

**FOY, Stacey W E**
Case Lombardi & Pettit, Honolulu
808 547 5400
sfoy@caselombardi.com
*Recommended in Real Estate*
**Practice Areas:** Real estate acquisition and entitlements; development; financing; time share registration.
**Prof. Memberships:** Hawaii State Bar Association.
**Career:** Bar Admission: Hawaii State, United States District Court for the District of Hawaii.
**Personal:** JD, University of San Francisco, 1989, BA, (Phi Beta Kappa) University of California Davis, 1986.

**FUJIMOTO, Wesley**
Imanaka Kudo & Fujimoto, Honolulu
808 521 9500
*Recommended in Employment*

**GABRIO, Gino**
Cades Schutte, Honolulu
808 521 9200
*Recommended in Real Estate*

**GALATI, Vito**
Cades Schutte, Honolulu
808 521 9200
*Recommended in Corporate/Commercial*

**GELBER, Don**
Gelber, Gelber, Ingersoll & Klevansky, A Law Corporation, Honolulu
808 524 0155
*Recommended in Bankruptcy*

**GELBER, Stephen**
Gelber, Gelber, Ingersoll & Klevansky, A Law Corporation, Honolulu
808 524 0155
*Recommended in Corporate/Commercial*

**GRAHAM, Bruce**
Ashford & Wriston, Honolulu
808 539 0400
*Recommended in Real Estate*

**GRAHAM, Max**
Belles Graham Proudfoot and Wilson, Lihue 808 2454705
*Recommended in Land Use*

**GRIMMER, Gary**
Carlsmith Ball LLP, Honolulu
808 523 2500
*Recommended in Litigation*

**GUBEN, Jerrold**
Reinwald O'Connor & Playdon, Honolulu
808 524 8350
*Recommended in Bankruptcy*

**GUGELYK, Carolyn**
Goodsill Anderson Quinn & Stifel, Honolulu 808 547 5600
*Recommended in Employment*

**HAZLETT, Mark**
Cades Schutte, Honolulu
808 521 9200
*Recommended in Real Estate*

**HEIHRE, Michael**
Cades Schutte, Honolulu
808 521 9200
*Recommended in Litigation*

**HELLER, Ron**
Torkildson, Katz, Fonseca, Jaffe, Moore & Hetherington Attorneys At Law, A Law Corporation, Honolulu
808 523 6000
*Recommended in Corporate/Commercial*

**HIPP, Kenneth B**
Marr Hipp Jones & Wang, Honolulu
808 536 4900
khipp@marrhipp.com
*Recommended in Employment*

**Practice Areas:** Representation of management. Labor law and collective bargaining, arbitration, mediation, administrative agency practice and litigation. Has litigated over 200 cases in the United States Courts of Appeals, as well as numerous cases before airline System Boards of Adjustment and in the Federal District Courts, the Hawaii Circuit Courts and the Hawaii Supreme Court.
**Prof. Memberships:** Hawaii State Bar Association and American Bar Assocation.
**Career:** Partner since 1998. Chairman (1996-97) and Member (1995-98) of the National Mediation Board in Washington DC Former National Labor Relations Board attorney.
**Personal:** University of North Carolina School of Law (JD with high honors).

**HONG, Lea Ok Soon**
Alston Hunt Floyd & Ing Attorneys At Law, A Law Corporation, Honolulu
808 441 6178
lea@ahfi.com
*Recommended in Land Use*
**Practice Areas:** Environmental law (federal and state), water resources, cultural resources (NHPA, burials, access), and land use (zoning, conservation districts, coastlines). Complex commercial litigation.
**Prof. Memberships:** APA; HSBA Natural Resources Section; ABA (Environment, State and Local Government Law, Litigation); Hawaii Women Lawyers; Native Hawaiian Bar Association (Special Member).
**Career:** Partner since 2000; 2005 40-Under-40 Community Leader of the Year; 2004 Outstanding Woman Lawyer; 'One of Hawaii's Best Environmental Lawyers'.
**Publications:** Has lectured and written on environmental and cultural resources law issues. Adjunct faculty, William S Richardson School of Law.
**Personal:** William S Richardson School of Law, JD; Rice University, BA.

**HUNT, William S**
Alston Hunt Floyd & Ing Attorneys At Law, A Law Corporation, Honolulu
808 524 1800
whunt@ahfi.com
*Recommended in Litigation*
**Practice Areas:** Trials in state, federal courts and arbitrations in medical malpractice and personal injury defense, commercial and construction litigation. Clients include ChevronTexaco; Georgia Pacific; Kaiser Permanente; United Technologies.
**Prof. Memberships:** Hawaii State and Federal Courts/9th Cir. 1973; US Supreme Court 1980; ABA Tort and Insurance Section; Hawaii Bar Association; Defense Research Institute.
**Career:** Hart Leavitt Hall & Hunt 1973-80; Paul Johnson Alston & Hunt 1980-91; Alston Hunt Floyd & Ing 1991-present;

Adjunct Professor, Univ. Hawaii Law School 1976-77.
**Publications:** 'Best Lawyers in America' personal injury litigation.
**Personal:** Colgate University, BA 1968; Columbia University School of Law, JD 1972.

**IMANAKA, Mitchell**
Imanaka Kudo & Fujimoto, Honolulu
808 521 9500
*Recommended in Real Estate*

**ING, J Douglas**
Watanabe Ing & Komeiji, Honolulu
808 544 8300
*Recommended in Land Use*

**INGERSOLL, Richard**
Gelber, Gelber, Ingersoll & Klevansky, A Law Corporation, Honolulu
808 524 0155
*Recommended in Corporate/Commercial*

**IWAMOTO, Raymond**
Goodsill Anderson Quinn & Stifel, Honolulu 808 547 5600
*Recommended in Real Estate*

**JAMES, Eric**
Carlsmith Ball LLP, Honolulu
808 523 2500
*Recommended in Real Estate*

**JONES, Patrick H**
Marr Hipp Jones & Wang, Honolulu
808 536 4900
pjones@marrhipp.com
*Recommended in Employment*
**Practice Areas:** Representation of management. Traditional labor and employment, including collection bargaining, arbitration, wrongful termination, discrimination and retaliation claims, FMLA, ADA, WARN and Hawaii Dislocated Workers' laws. Extensive experience in dealing with the EEOC, Hawaii Civil Rights Commission, the Hawaii Department of Labor and Industrial Relations, National Labor Relations Board, and the Office of Federal Contract Compliance Programs.
**Prof. Memberships:** Hawaii State Bar Assocation; American Bar Association; Chamber of Commerce of Hawaii (Public Health Committee).
**Career:** Founding Partner (1995). Private practice since 1986.
**Personal:** Georgetown University Law Center (JD, Cum Laude).

**KAMIKAWA, Ray**
Chun, Kerr, Dodd, Beaman & Wong, Honolulu 808 528 8200
*Recommended in Corporate/Commercial*

**KATZ, Robert**
Torkildson, Katz, Fonseca, Jaffe, Moore & Hetherington Attorneys At Law, A Law Corporation, Honolulu
808 523 6000
*Recommended in Employment*

**KAWASHIMA, James**
Kawashima, Lorusso & Tom, Honolulu
808 275 0300
*Recommended in Litigation*

**KIM, Gregory**
Vantage Counsel LLC, Honolulu
808 780 2495
*Recommended in Corporate/Commercial*

**KLEVANSKY, Simon**
Gelber, Gelber, Ingersoll & Klevansky, A Law Corporation, Honolulu 808 524 0155
*Recommended in Bankruptcy*

**KNOREK, John**
Torkildson, Katz, Fonseca, Jaffe, Moore & Hetherington Attorneys At Law, A Law Corporation, Honolulu 808 523 6000
*Recommended in Employment*

**KOBAYASHI JR, Bert**
Kobayashi, Sugita & Goda, Honolulu
808 539 8700
*Recommended in Litigation*

**KOMEIJI, John**
Watanabe Ing & Komeiji, Honolulu
808 544 8300
*Recommended in Litigation*

**KUDO, Benjamin**
Imanaka Kudo & Fujimoto, Honolulu
808 521 9500
*Recommended in Land Use*

**LACY, John**
Goodsill Anderson Quinn & Stifel, Honolulu 808 547 5600
*Recommended in Litigation*

**LAMON, Bruce**
Goodsill Anderson Quinn & Stifel, Honolulu 808 547 5600
*Recommended in Litigation*

**LEONG, Donna**
Cades Schutte, Honolulu 808 521 9200
*Recommended in Land Use, Real Estate*

**LEONG, Ronald**
Watanabe Ing & Komeiji, Honolulu
808 544 8300
*Recommended in Employment*

**LITTMAN, Bernice**
Cades Schutte, Honolulu
808 521 9200
*Recommended in Real Estate*

**LOMBARDI, Dennis M**
Case Lombardi & Pettit, Honolulu
808 547 5400
dlombardi@caselombardi.com
*Recommended in Real Estate*
**Practice Areas:** Real estate, concentrating in land use and development. Extensive experience in acquisition, permitting, development, financing and sales of master planned residential, resort and commercial communities, centers and projects. He represents not only individuals and firms that are active in the real estate industry but also institutions with real estate business needs such as the purchase or development of headquarters, office building, shopping center, operation site or hotel properties. He is President of the firm and a Member of its Executive Committee.
**Prof. Memberships:** Hawaii State Bar Association, California State Bar Association.
**Career:** Bar Admission: Hawaii State, California State, District of Columbia, United States District Court for the District of Hawaii.
**Personal:** JD (summa cum laude), University of Santa Clara, 1977; BA, University of Hawaii at Manoa, 1974.

**MACKINNON, D Scott**
McCorriston Miller Mukai MacKinnon LLP, Honolulu 808 529 7300
*Recommended in Real Estate*

**MANCINI, Paul**
Mancini Welch & Geiger LLP, Kahului
808 871 8351
*Recommended in Land Use, Real Estate*

**MARCUS, Kenneth**
Starn O'Toole Marcus & Fisher, Honolulu 808 537 6100
*Recommended in Real Estate*

**MARR, Barry W**
Marr Hipp Jones & Wang, Honolulu
808 536 4900
bmarr@marrhipp.com
*Recommended in Employment*
**Practice Areas:** Representation of management in labor and employment disputes. Extensive experience in state and federal litigation and in ADR. Substantial experience in labor relations and collective bargaining.
**Prof. Memberships:** HSBA (Labor and Employment Law); ABA (Litigation, Labor and Employment Law).
**Career:** Counsel to the Chair of the NLRB (1974-76); Private Practice (1976-present); Special Deputy Attorney General for Hawaii in selected employment litigation; Adjunct Professor, University of Hawaii School of Law (1982-86).
**Personal:** LLM, Georgetown University Law Center; JD, Albany Law School of Union University; BA, Hobart College; Hawaii's Best Lawyers (Honolulu Magazine); Best Lawyers in America (1993-present).

**MCCORRISTON, William**
McCorriston Miller Mukai MacKinnon LLP, Honolulu 808 529 7300
*Recommended in Litigation*

**MCHENRY, Patricia**
Cades Schutte, Honolulu
808 521 9200
*Recommended in Land Use*

**MILLER, Clifford**
McCorriston Miller Mukai MacKinnon LLP, Honolulu 808 529 7300
*Recommended in Real Estate*

**MUELLER, Daniel G**
Marr Hipp Jones & Wang, Honolulu
808 536 4900
dmueller@marrhipp.com
*Recommended in Employment*
**Practice Areas:** Representation of management. Labor and employment litigation, including discrimination, harassment, wrongful termination, retaliation, and wage and hour litigation. Counsels employers on employment related issues, including discrimination and harassment prevention and intervention, discipline and discharge, employment agreements, personnel policies and handbooks, FMLA compliance, wage and hour issues, ADA, privacy and internal investigations.
**Prof. Memberships:** Hawaii State Bar Association; American Bar Association.
**Career:** Partner (2005). Private practice since 1996.
**Personal:** William S Richardson School of Law (JD).

**MUNGER, Lisa Woods**
Goodsill Anderson Quinn & Stifel, Honolulu 808 547 5600
*Recommended in Land Use*

**MUZZI, Christopher**
Moseley Biehl Tsugawa Lau & Muzzi, Honolulu 808 531 0490
*Recommended in Bankruptcy*

**NAKASHIMA, David A**
Alston Hunt Floyd & Ing Attorneys At Law, A Law Corporation, Honolulu
808 524 1888
dnakashima@ahfi.com
*Recommended in Litigation*
**Practice Areas:** Business, real estate, ERISA and disability insurance litigation. Mr Nakashima has represented clients in state and federal court, Hawaii and federal appellate courts, as well as in private mediations and arbitrations.
**Prof. Memberships:** Hawaii State Bar Association, ABA and Federal Bar Association.
**Career:** Partner, Alston Hunt Floyd & Ing, 1993-present.
**Publications:** Adjunct Professor, University of Hawaii, William S Richardson School of Law (1997-2001); Adjunct Professor, Kapiolani Community College, Legal Assistant Program (1981-84).
**Personal:** University of Hawaii, William S Richardson School of Law (JD 1977), University of California at Santa Barbara (BA with honors, 1973).

**NAKASHIMA, Steven M**
Marr Hipp Jones & Wang, Honolulu
808 536 4900
snakashima@marrhipp.com
*Recommended in Employment*
**Practice Areas:** Representation of management. Employment discrimination, including race, age, sex, sexual harassment, national origin, arrest and court record, disability, wrongful discharge and non-competition issues. Advises employers on issues such as employment procedures, wage and hour, FLSA, dislocated workers, drug testing, employee handbooks, ADA, and pregnancy.
**Prof. Memberships:** Hawaii State Bar Association; American Bar Association.
**Career:** Partner (1999). State of Hawaii District Court of the First Circuit Judge (1994-99). Lead Civil Judge (1997-99). Law clerk, Ninth Circuit Court of Appeals, the Honorable J Blaine Anderson (1981-99).
**Personal:** Willamette University College of Law (JD); University of Hawaii, BA (Economics).

**NISHIMOTO, John**
Ayabe, Chong, Nishimoto, Sia & Nakamura, Honolulu 808 537 6119
*Recommended in Litigation*

**OKUMURA, Miki**
Goodsill Anderson Quinn & Stifel, Honolulu 808 547 5600
*Recommended in Corporate/Commercial*

**PAUL, James**
Paul, Johnson, Park & Niles, Attorneys At Law, A Law Corporation, Honolulu
808 524 1212
*Recommended in Litigation*

**PEAR, Charles**
McCorriston Miller Mukai MacKinnon LLP, Honolulu 808 529 7300
*Recommended in Real Estate*

**PETRUS, Barbara**
Goodsill Anderson Quinn & Stifel, Honolulu 808 547 5600
*Recommended in Employment*

**PETTIT, Ted N**
Case Lombardi & Pettit, Honolulu
808 547 5400
tpettit@caselombardi.com
*Recommended in Bankruptcy*
**Practice Areas:** Business transactions, business reorganization, creditor workouts, debt restructuring, commercial foreclosure actions, commercial litigation. Extensive experience in large bankruptcy cases.
**Prof. Memberships:** American Bar Association; Hawaii State Bar Association (President, Bankruptcy Law Section, 2001); Federal Bar Association; The Association of Trial Lawyers; American Jurisprudence Society; American Bankruptcy Institute.
**Career:** Bar Admission: Hawaii State, United States District Court for the District of Hawaii, United States Court of Appeals, Ninth Circuit
**Publications:** Hawaii Collection Law Manual, 2002; 'Esquire and Discrimination in the Legal Profession', 2 Haw BJ 22 (1998); frequent lecturer on commercial real estate financing and bankruptcy.
**Personal:** JD, Richardson School of Law, University of Hawaii, 1986 (Executive Editor, Hawaii Law Review); PhD (Med-

ical Physiology), University of Hawaii, 1980; MS (Veterinary Physiology), University of Missouri, 1977.

**PIPER, Alika**
Gelber, Gelber, Ingersoll & Klevansky, A Law Corporation, Honolulu
808 524 0155
*Recommended in Bankruptcy*

**PIPER, Jeffrey**
Schlack Ito & Lockwood Piper & Elkind, LLC, Honolulu 808 523 6040
*Recommended in Corporate/Commercial*

**PORTNOY, Jeffrey**
Cades Schutte, Honolulu
808 521 9200
*Recommended in Litigation*

**PRESSMAN, Stewart**
McCorriston Miller Mukai MacKinnon LLP, Honolulu 808 529 7300
*Recommended in Corporate/Commercial*

**RADOVICH, Scott D**
Schneider Tanaka Radovich Andrew & Tanaka, LLLC, Honolulu
808 792 4200
sradovich@stratlaw.com
*Recommended in Real Estate*
**Practice Areas:** Real estate acquisitions, development and sales, including land use entitlements and regulatory compliance. Extensive experience with bulk land sales and acquisitions; residential, commercial and resort acquisitions, development and sales; retail land sales; condominium development and conversions; master planned community development and associations; time share development and registration; general real estate and commercial transactions. Clients include large land owners, real estate developers, time share operators, community associations.
**Prof. Memberships:** Hawaii State Bar Association.
**Personal:** JD, UCLA, 1984; MBA, University of Colorado, 1981; BS, University of Santa Clara, 1978 (magna cum laude).

**RAND, Richard**
Torkildson, Katz, Fonseca, Jaffe, Moore & Hetherington Attorneys At Law, A Law Corporation, Honolulu
808 523 6000
*Recommended in Employment*

**REBER, David**
Goodsill Anderson Quinn & Stifel, Honolulu 808 547 5600
*Recommended in Corporate/Commercial*

**ROSE, Crystal**
Bays Deaver Lung Rose Baba, Honolulu
808 523 9000
*Recommended in Litigation*

**SAKUMOTO, Randall**
McCorriston Miller Mukai MacKinnon LLP, Honolulu
808 529 7300
*Recommended in Real Estate*

**SANDISON, Ian Lorne**
Carlsmith Ball LLP, Honolulu
808 523 2500
*Recommended in Land Use*

**SCHLACK, Carl**
Schlack Ito & Lockwood Piper & Elkind, LLC, Honolulu 808 523 6040
*Recommended in Real Estate*

**SCHNEIDER, Robert F**
Schneider Tanaka Radovich Andrew & Tanaka, LLLC, Honolulu
808 792 4200
rfs@stratlaw.com
*Recommended in Real Estate*
**Practice Areas:** Real estate development and real estate finance. His practice is transactional, with an emphasis on the acquisition, financing, development and sale of undeveloped lands, residential projects, commercial buildings, shopping centers and resort properties. His work also involves commercial leasing and title analysis. His clients include land owners, developers, investors and lending institutions.
**Prof. Memberships:** Hawaii State Bar Association.
**Publications:** Co-author of the 'Hawaii Real Estate Financing Manual' (1990) and 'Hawaii Real Estate Law Manual' (1997).
**Personal:** JD, McGeorge School of Law, University of the Pacific, 1976. BA, Williams College, with honors, 1973.

**SCHULL, E Gunner**
Cades Schutte, Honolulu
808 521 9200
*Recommended in Corporate/Commercial*

**SCHULMEISTER, David**
Cades Schutte, Honolulu
808 521 9200
*Recommended in Litigation*

**SMITH, Lex**
Kobayashi, Sugita & Goda, Honolulu
808 539 8700
*Recommended in Litigation*

**STARN, Peter**
Starn O'Toole Marcus & Fisher, Honolulu
808 537 6100
*Recommended in Real Estate*

**STEINER, Jonathan**
McCorriston Miller Mukai MacKinnon LLP, Honolulu 808 529 7300
*Recommended in Litigation*

**STEVERSON, Randall**
Goodsill Anderson Quinn & Stifel, Honolulu 808 547 5600
*Recommended in Real Estate*

**STRAND, Robert**
Carlsmith Ball LLP, Honolulu
808 523 2500
*Recommended in Real Estate*

**TIUS, Susan**
Rush Moore LLP, Honolulu
808 521 0400
*Recommended in Bankruptcy*

**TOM, Carl**
Brooks Tom Porter Quitiquit, Honolulu
808 526 3011
*Recommended in Real Estate*

**TSUKAZAKI, Ben**
Tsukazaki Yeh & Moore, Honolulu
808 961 0055
*Recommended in Land Use*

**VAN WINKLE, J Thomas**
Carlsmith Ball LLP, Honolulu
808 523 2500
*Recommended in Corporate/Commercial*

**WAGNER, James**
Wagner Choi Evers, Honolulu
808 533 1877
*Recommended in Bankruptcy*

**WANG, Sarah O**
Marr Hipp Jones & Wang, Honolulu
808 536 4900
swang@marrhipp.com
*Recommended in Employment*
**Practice Areas:** Representation of management. Labor and employment matters, including federal and state court litigation of wrongful termination, harassment, reasonable accommodation, breach of contract, discrimination and harassment cases before administrative agencies, arbitrations and airline System Boards of Adjustment. Training and guidance for employers to assist them in managing personnel issues and in complying with various employment laws. Frequent speaker at labor and employment law seminars.
**Prof. Memberships:** Hawaii State Bar Association; American Bar Association; Hawaii Women Lawyers; Chamber of Commerce of Hawaii (Human Resources Committee).
**Career:** Partner (2001). Private practice since 1995.
**Personal:** University of Virginia School of Law (JD).

**WELCH, Thomas**
Mancini Welch & Geiger LLP, Kahului
808 871 8351
*Recommended in Real Estate*

**WONG, Danton**
Chun, Kerr, Dodd, Beaman & Wong, Honolulu 808 528 8200
*Recommended in Real Estate*

**WONG, David**
Carlsmith Ball LLP, Honolulu
808 523 2500
*Recommended in Corporate/Commercial*

**YOUNGREN, Nancy**
Case Lombardi & Pettit, Honolulu
808 547 5400
nyoungren@caselombardi.com
*Recommended in Real Estate*
**Practice Areas:** Real estate, including acquisitions, condominium development and conversions, leasing, hotel purchases and sales, and general real estate and land development.
**Prof. Memberships:** Hawaii State Bar Association.
**Career:** Bar Admission: Hawaii State, United States District Court for the District of Hawaii.
**Personal:** JD, William S Richardson School of Law, University of Hawaii at Manoa, 1996; MLIS, University of Hawaii at Manoa, 1987; BA, University of Tennessee, 1974.

**YUEN, Leighton**
Goodsill Anderson Quinn & Stifel, Honolulu 808 547 5600
*Recommended in Real Estate*

**ZALEWSKI, John D**
Case Lombardi & Pettit, Honolulu
808 547 5400
jzalewski@caselombardi.com
*Recommended in Litigation*
**Practice Areas:** Civil litigation, commercial litigation, complex litigation.
**Prof. Memberships:** Hawaii State Bar Association, Federal Bar Association, American Bar Association.
**Career:** Bar Admission: Hawaii State, Wisconsin State, United States District Court for the District of Hawaii, United States Courts of Appeals for the Ninth Circuit.
**Personal:** Doctor of Law (JD), University of Wisconsin-Madison, 1986; BS, University of Minnesota, 1980; CPA, Hawaii, 1988; rank in the martial art of Kendo: 5-dan.

# ALSTON HUNT FLOYD & ING

## THE FIRM

**President:** Paul Alston
**Managing Director:** William Hunt

**Number of director-shareholders:** 16

## AREAS OF PRACTICE:

| | |
|---|---|
| Business & Personal Injury Litigation | 35% |
| Real Property & Business Transactions | 15% |
| Healthcare | 15% |
| Labor & Employment | 13% |
| Title & Escrow | 7% |
| Banking & Finance | 7% |
| Environmental & Cultural Resources | 3% |
| Government Affairs & Public Interest | 2% |
| Government Procurement & Grant Compliance | 2% |
| Education | 1% |

**FIRM OVERVIEW:** Alston Hunt Floyd & Ing (AHFI) is a Hawaii-based firm servicing clients throughout the Pacific Region. The firm is known for high quality, fast, creative and cost-effective service. AHFI is very active in community, business and government organizations. These activities give AHFI attorneys a broader perspective on issues, which enables them to better assist clients in achieving their goals.

## MAIN AREAS OF PRACTICE:

**Business & Personal Injury Litigation:** AHFI represents individual and corporate clients in mediation, arbitration, administrative proceedings, litigation and appeals in federal and state courts. The firm has experience in admiralty and maritime law, the Americans with Disabilities Act, antitrust and trade regulation, business torts, communications and media law, construction law, derivative litigation and shareholder disputes, insurance defense and insurance coverage, non-compete and intellectual property disputes, personal injury defense, real property disputes, RICO, and securities litigation.

**Real Property & Business Transactions:** The firm assists individual and corporate clients on acquisition and disposition of real property, real estate financing, real estate development and construction, real estate leasing, landlord-tenant issues, formation of business entities, mergers and acquisitions, and partner disputes. Attorneys also advise on intellectual property, venture capital financing, licensing and strategic ventures, and e-commerce transactions.

**Healthcare:** The firm represents hospitals, health plans, physicians and other health care providers with healthcare litigation, regulatory compliance, and dispute resolution proceedings. Attorneys also advise clients on risk management.

**Labor & Employment:** AHFI provides advice, counseling and litigation representation to employers in matters involving wrongful termination, equal employment opportunity, labor law and collective bargaining, wage and hour law, government contracting compliance, employee benefits, Taft-Hartley trust funds, business transactions, personnel management, safety and health, immigration, proprietary rights, and workplace privacy. The firm also provides management training and strategic planning assistance.

**Title & Escrow:** The firm represents title insurance companies and their insureds in policy coverage issues, quiet title actions, defense of adverse title claims, and defense of bad faith claims. AHFI also assists clients with disputes involving easements, boundaries, access claims, surveyors' errors, forged deeds and mortgages.

**Banking & Finance:** The firm provides advice, counseling and litigation representation in regulatory compliance, lender issues, collections, foreclosures, and bankruptcy to banks, savings and loans, governmental entities, trustees, and judgment creditors.

**Environmental & Cultural Resources:** AHFI provides advice, counseling and litigation representation to public and private sector clients on land use and development, endangered species, environmental impact statements and assess-

## HEAD OFFICE

**HAWAII**
1001 Bishop Street, American Savings Bank Tower, Suite 1800
**Honolulu,** HI 96813
**Tel:** 808 524 1800   **Fax:** 808 524 4591
**Email:** info@ahfi.com
**Website:** www.ahfi.com

## BRANCH OFFICES

**HAWAII**
Palani Court, Suite 104, 74-5620 Palani Road, **Kailua Kona,** HI 96740
**Tel:** 808 326 7979   **Fax:** 808 326 4779
**Kamuela Tel:** 808 885 6762
**Email:** sfloyd@ahfi.com

## CONTACTS

| | |
|---|---|
| **Business & Personal Injury Litigation** | Paul Alston (Honolulu) |
| **Real Property & Business Transactions** | Bruce Noborikawa (Honolulu) |
| **Healthcare** | Ellen Carson (Honolulu) |
| **Labor & Employment** | Anna Elento-Sneed (Honolulu) |
| **Title & Escrow** | Jade Ching (Honolulu) |
| **Banking & Finance** | Louise Ing (Honolulu) |
| **Environmental & Cultural Resources** | Lea Hong (Honolulu) |
| **Government Affairs & Public Interest** | William M Kaneko (Honolulu) |
| **Government Procurement & Grant Compliance** | Terry Thomason (Honolulu) |
| **Education** | Shelby Anne Floyd (Kailua Kona) |

ments, preservation of historic sites, Native Hawaiian cultural issues, air and water pollution, solid and hazardous waste management, water rights, and insurance coverage issues.

**Government Affairs & Public Interest:** The firm provides advice on government and public affairs and represents clients before the state Legislature, county councils and federal, state and local government agencies. This includes bill tracking and monitoring, development of legislative and government relations strategies, drafting of legislation and lobbying.

**Government Procurement & Grant Compliance:** AHFI provides advice, counseling and litigation representation to contracting agencies, contractors and subcontractors involved in federal, state and county government contracts. These services include privatization issues, solicitation analysis and bid preparation, protests against solicitations and awards, contract interpretation and administration, defense of contract terminations, debarment actions, dispute litigation and resolution, and qui tam actions. AHFI also advises clients with federal grants.

**Education:** AHFI provides general business counseling for private schools. The firm also advises on First Amendment, privacy, special education and disability rights with respect to public school systems.

**INTERNATIONAL WORK:** Because of its central location in Hawaii, AHFI represents clients from the US, Europe and Asia who are doing business in the Pacific Region. The firm has language capabilities in English, Japanese, Taiwanese, Spanish and conversational Mandarin.

# CASE LOMBARDI & PETTIT

## THE FIRM

**Executive Committee:** Dennis M Lombardi, Michael R Marsh, Stacey WE Foy
**Managing Director:** Michael R Marsh
**Senior Director:** Daniel H Case

**Number of Directors:** 11
**Number of other lawyers:** 12

**FIRM OVERVIEW:** Case Lombardi & Pettit, A Law Corporation, is a prominent law firm in Hawaii with a diverse civil practice. The firm's attorneys, legal assistants and support staff are committed to client service and quality representation that is efficient and cost-effective. The firm is located in the Pacific Guardian Center in Honolulu on the island of Oahu. Tracing its roots back to 1888, Case Lombardi & Pettit has a history of providing quality legal services throughout Hawaii. To assure the highest quality of service to its clients, the firm's attorneys, legal assistants and support staff are organized into client service groups. The firm presently has three client service groups, which are: business, bankruptcy, estate planning, probate and taxation; litigation and dispute resolution; and real estate.

## MAIN AREAS OF PRACTICE:

**Business, Bankruptcy, Estate Planning, Probate & Taxation:** Business attorneys in this practice group assist clients in the formation and operation of business entities; prepare profit-sharing, pension and other employee benefit plans; assist clients in addressing the opportunities and challenges faced by an ongoing business; and provide advice regarding transactions governed by the Uniform Commercial Code; mergers, acquisitions, dissolutions, asset purchases and financings. In addition to these matters, the firm's corporate attorneys frequently work together with its real estate attorneys with structuring, drafting and closing real estate transactions that are structured as corporate mergers or stock transfers. The firm's Bankruptcy Practice covers all aspects of creditor-debtor relationships ranging from foreclosure, receivership, collection and enforcement of judgments in state and federal court to reorganization and liquidation in bankruptcy court. The firm also represents secured creditors, unsecured creditor committees and landlords in all aspects of bankruptcy proceedings. The firm has a team of creditor counsel experienced in negotiating workouts and restructurings outside of bankruptcy court. The estate planning, probate and taxation attorneys represent a broad spectrum of clients, from small businesses, families and individuals to banks and trust companies. The firm's goal is to design and implement comprehensive business and estate plans and analyze and structure a variety of sophisticated transactions that are designed to fit the client's particular circumstances and concerns. The firm also works to ensure that the business and estate plans it creates are flexible and adaptable to provide for and respond to shifting and unforeseen situations.

**Real Estate:** The firm enjoys a sophisticated and diverse Real Estate Practice. Areas of expertise include the structuring of real estate acquisitions and sales; commercial financing, including complex construction and syndicated loans; loan restructuring; real estate sales and administration; office and retail leasing; condominium and vacation ownership development and licensing; community association formation and administration; residential financing; and land use, zoning and entitlement matters. The firm represents landowners, purchasers, investors and lenders in the acquisition, sale and financing of all types of real estate, including undeveloped land, hotels, shopping centers, office buildings and residential developments. The firm's attorneys in the Real Estate Group take pride in assisting in the consummation of real estate transactions as well as providing creative and cost-effective solutions to the needs of its clients.

**Litigation & Dispute Resolution:** The firm's Litigation and Dispute Resolution Practice Group is led by a team of skillful, experienced and successful litigators and trial lawyers. Attorneys who practice in the litigation and dispute resolution areas are creative and conscientious in their representation of clients in real estate, business, construction, tort, and commercial litigation matters. The attorneys regularly appear in all federal and state courts in Hawaii, both at the trial and appellate levels, and before administrative officers and regulatory agencies. Lawyers in the Litigation and Dispute Resolution Practice Group are committed to efficient dispute resolution through mediation, arbitration, negotiated settlement, and, if necessary, the use of adversary court proceedings.

**CLIENTS:** The firm's clientele is varied. They include large international, national and local corporations and businesses, financial institutions, trusts and non-profit organizations, real estate developers, sole proprietors and individuals.

**INTERNATIONAL WORK:** Case Lombardi & Pettit is counsel to Asian and Pacific Rim based corporations and entities. The firm assists these clients with their transnational real estate sales, acquisitions and development; corporate formations and business transactions. Case Lombardi & Pettit is the exclusive member firm for Hawaii of Lex Mundi, the world's leading association of independent law firms. With more than 15,000 lawyers in 560 offices, Lex Mundi firms are present in more than 160 countries, states and provinces covering virtually every business market worldwide. The firm's membership in Lex Mundi provides it with global reach and access to premiere legal resources that enhance its ability to serve its clients' needs around the world. The firm's attorneys and staff are reflective of Hawaii's ethnic diversity and multi-racial culture and are fluent in Japanese, Chinese, French, and Spanish.

**MEMBER**

LEX MUNDI

**THE WORLD'S LEADING ASSOCIATION OF INDEPENDENT LAW FIRMS**

## HEAD OFFICE

**HAWAII**
Pacific Guardian Center, Mauka Tower, 737 Bishop Street, Suite 2600, **Honolulu,** HI 96813
**Tel:** 808 547 5400  **Fax:** 808 523 1888
**Email:** info@caselombardi.com
**Website:** www.caselombardi.com

## CONTACTS

**Business, Bankruptcy, Estate Planning, Probate & Taxation** ............
................................................................................James M Cribley
**Litigation & Dispute Resolution**...............................Michael R Marsh
**Real Estate** ........................................................Dennis M Lombardi

# MARR HIPP JONES & WANG

## THE FIRM

**Managing Partner:** Barry W Marr

**Number of partners:** 10
**Number of associates:** 4

**FIRM OVERVIEW**: The practice of Marr Hipp Jones & Wang is devoted exclusively to the representation of management in labor and employment law matters. All of the partners and other attorneys in the firm have dedicated their careers to this practice area as they believe their client's interests are best served by attorneys who focus on representing employers. The firm is committed to a diverse workforce, and the diversity of the attorneys reflects that fact. Four of ten partners are women, and five are minorities. All of the partners and other attorneys have either taught at the law school level, written for law review, or served a judicial clerkship.

**Affiliation:** Marr Hipp Jones & Wang is a member of Worklaw Network, a nationwide affiliation of boutique law firms representing employers in labor and employment law and consisting of over 25 law firms with more than 300 attorneys. Network members are linked by both a web-based data bank and daily email forums to ensure efficiency.

## MAIN AREAS OF PRACTICE:

**Labor & Employment:** The firm represents employers in all areas of labor and employment law, including the following:

**Employment Litigation:** The firm's partners have tried multiple cases in federal and state court; have argued numerous cases in the United States Courts of Appeals and before the Hawaii Supreme Court; and have presented or argued cases before the US Supreme Court. The firm has a particularly active federal district court practice defending employers in employment discrimination cases. One partner recently successfully defended an employer in a federal jury trial on ERISA, employment discrimination and whistleblower claims. Another partner is representing two county governments in class action FLSA lawsuits brought by police and firefighters. Two partners recently represented the University of Hawaii in a high-profile matter involving threatened litigation by the University's former president regarding his separation from employment.

**Collective Bargaining & Contract Administration:** The firm's partners have negotiated first-time and successor collective bargaining agreements for hotels, airlines, contractors, and hospitals. They have also served as counsel for multi-employer negotiations in the sugar, pineapple, longshore and construction industries. One partner recently was spokesperson for United Air Lines in its negotiations with its pilots. Another partner was the chief spokesperson in bargaining for a first contract at a Maui Resort. Another partner is the chief spokesperson for a military defense contractor in ongoing negotiations. Three partners are negotiating on behalf of Mesaba Aviation with the four unions representing the company's pilots, flight attendants, mechanics, and dispatchers. In addition, all of the partners have assisted clients with contract administration and have respresented employers in greviance arbitrations.

## HEAD OFFICE

**HAWAII**
1001 Bishop Street, 1550 Pauahi Tower, **Honolulu,** Hawaii 96813
**Tel:** (808) 536 4900   **Fax:** (808) 536 6700
**Email:** bmarr@marrhipp.com
**Website:** www.marrhipp.com

**Employment Counseling & Administrative Practice:** The firm protects the interests of its employer clients through its advice and counseling, training and expertise on alternative dispute resolution. The firm has extensive experience before state and federal administrative agencies that regulate employment.
The firm is often retained to advise companies involved in business transfers regarding the labor and employment aspect of transfers. During the past year, the firm has provided extensive support to Hawaiian Airlines, United Airlines, and Mesaba Aviation in dealing with labor and employment issues during bankruptcy reorganization cases.

**CLIENTS:** The firm's clients include Fortune 500 and local companies in airline, marine and other transportation sectors; finance; banking; military defense contractors; construction; retail; hotels; and healthcare. The firm also represents the State of Hawaii and several of its counties.

MARR HIPP
JONES & WANG
A LIMITED LIABILITY LAW PARTNERSHIP

*Labor and Employment Law*

# MCCORRISTON MILLER MUKAI MACKINNON LLP

## THE FIRM

**Managing Partner:** D Scott MacKinnon

**Number of partners:** 31
**Number of other lawyers:** 9

## HEAD OFFICE

**HAWAII**
Five Waterfront Plaza, 4th Floor, 500 Ala Moana Boulevard
**Honolulu**, HI 96813
**Tel:** 808 529 7300 **Fax:** 808 524 8293
**Website:** www.m4law.com

**FIRM OVERVIEW:** McCorriston Miller Mukai MacKinnon LLP (M4) was formed in 1989 by several experienced lawyers who were partners with established Hawaii law firms but saw a need for a firm which would provide a specialized expertise in real estate and business transactions and expert counsel in a wide range of litigation matters to both domestic and international clients. Through its commitment to excellence, dedication, hard work, and creative and cost efficient legal representation to its many clients, M4 has become one of Hawaii's largest and most respected law firms, with a reputation spreading throughout the Pacific Basin in a very short period of time.

## MAIN AREAS OF PRACTICE:

**Real Estate:** M4 is well recognized for its work involving real estate development and construction of condominiums and resort properties, commercial and construction financing, loan restructurings and workouts, acquisitions and dispositions of real property, commercial leasing, and equity investments. M4 also has extensive experience in timesharing, including work on numerous projects across the US and in other countries. Timeshare expertise extends to property acquisition, product design and structuring, registrations in various jurisdictions, marketing, management, interim financing, and receivables financing.

**Litigation:** M4 has a diverse litigation practice. M4 has handled to a successful conclusion numerous disputes involving complex commercial transactions, technological issues, products liability, environmental matters, corporate disputes, professional liability, defense of persons accused of white collar crime, insurance, and other civil litigation. Many major cases in the State of Hawaii in the past decade have involved members of the firm's Litigation Team, including the Bishop Estate litigation, the state antitrust case against the nation's major energy companies, and defense of the Mayor of the City and County of Honolulu.

**Hospitality:** M4 represents hotel developers and owners, equity investors, ground lessors and lessees, operators, and others involved in the State of Hawaii's principal industry - tourism. Representative transactions include the acquisition, financing and/or development of such well-known hotels as the Kahala Hilton Hotel, Hyatt Regency Hotels - Kaanapali and Waikiki, Ala Moana Hotel, Waikiki Beachcomber, Kona Village Resort, Westin Maui, Kapalua Bay Hotel, Maui Marriott, Kaanapali Embassy Suites Hotel, and Outrigger Prince Kuhio Hotel. M4 also advises clients and has litigated matters concerning hotel management agreements.

**Corporate:** M4 is accomplished in the formation of corporations, limited liability companies, and limited partnerships for its clients. M4 also provides counsel in mergers and acquisitions, corporate finance, financial services, insurance, investment vehicles, and corporate and insurance restructuring and work-outs. Much of this work is in international transactions involving US and foreign companies doing business in Asia and the Pacific Rim.

**Finance:** M4 has extensive experience in handling tax-exempt and taxable bond financing transactions for a wide variety of facilities and projects. The firm's lawyers have served as bond counsel, special counsel to state and local bond issuers, underwriter's counsel, counsel to bond trustees, counsel to non-profit organizations and private developers of bond-financed facilities, and counsel to credit enhancement or liquidity support providers for bond issues.

The firm has recognized expertise in the development of financing plans and structures, compliance with federal and state tax and securities laws, negotiation and preparation of financing and security documents, and preparation of official statements and other bond offering circulars used in the marketing of bond issues.

**Insurance:** M4 represents several major insurers. It has developed a specialty practice in the defense of actions against insurance companies for bad faith and extra-contractual damages. It routinely handles cases involving personal injury, property damage, contracts, products liability, construction issues, employment discrimination, and professional, directors' and fiduciary liability. A considerable part of the practice in this area is devoted to insurance coverage issues, primarily on behalf of insurers. Additionally, M4 has represented the State of Hawaii in the highly specialized field of rehabilitating and/or liquidating insolvent insurance companies.

**Employment:** M4's lawyers have significant experience and expertise in advising employers in connection with employment-related litigation. The firm also regularly provides advice to clients on matters relating to employee handbooks, personnel policies, personnel action and procedures, wage and hour questions, health and safety issues, and a broad range of other subject areas. Such advice is geared toward assisting clients in avoiding litigation where possible.

**Environmental:** M4's lawyers are experts in the handling environmental matters, including preparation of environmental impact statements, permitting, and litigation. M4 represents a diverse mix of clients in environmental matters, including landowners, lessees, financial institutions, construction and design professionals, as well as large and small quantity hazardous waste generators.

**Healthcare:** M4's health care attorneys represent a diverse mix of healthcare clients, including hospitals, healthcare systems, individual doctors, dentists, and other medical practitioners, healthcare payors and insurance companies, pharmaceutical companies, and other participants in the healthcare industry. Each representation is tailored to the client's particular needs and circumstances to ensure that quality service is provided in a timely, responsive, and cost-effective manner.

**CLIENTS:** M4's clients include architects, construction contractors, landowners, developers, banks, major energy companies, property management companies, insurance companies, governmental entities and officials, healthcare organizations, hotel owners and operators, and timeshare operators.

**INTERNATIONAL WORK:** M4 represents many international companies doing business in the United States. The firm is recognized in Hawaii as a leader in representing Japan-based organizations. M4's attorneys are also experienced in doing business in the People's Republic of China and Taiwan. The firm has been involved in a number of joint ventures and other investments in the PRC, including real estate and infrastructure development, telecommunications, and other commercial and industrial projects.

## How lawyers are ranked

Every year we carry out thousands of in-depth interviews with clients and lawyers in order to assess the reputations and expertise of business lawyers across the USA. Chambers rankings and editorial are referred to extensively by General Counsel and other purchasers of legal services who look to our recommendations when choosing their lawyers.

# BANKRUPTCY/RESTRUCTURING

**Bankruptcy/Restructuring**
Leading Firms

1. ELSAESSER JARZABEK ANDERSON *Sandpoint*
   HOLLAND & HART LLP *Boise*
   MOFFATT THOMAS BARRETT ROCK *Boise*

Leading Individuals

1. ELSAESSER Ford *Elsaesser Jarzabek Anderson Marks*
   MEIER Joseph *Cosho Humphrey LLP*
   PETERMAN Randall *Moffatt Thomas Barrett Rock*
   PRINCE Larry *Holland & Hart LLP*
2. CHRISTENSEN Craig *Craig Christensen*
   ROBINSON Brent *Ling, Robinson*
3. GREEN Daniel *Racine Olson Nye Budge*
   KERL Ron *Cooper & Larsen*

## Band 1

### Elsaesser Jarzabek Anderson Marks Elliott & McHugh, Chartered

**The Firm:** Established in 1980, this specialist bankruptcy firm focuses on Chapter 11 proceedings, restructuring and workouts for a range of clients. It is based in Sandpoint and Coeur d'Alene, and comprises six partners.

**The Lawyers:** A former chairman and president of the American Bankruptcy Institute, **Ford Elsaesser** is highly admired not only for his expertise in bankruptcy, but for his understanding of the art of negotiation, and his creative, solutions-focused approach. Sources described him as "*an expert deal-maker*" and endorsed his wide-ranging practice that includes

work for creditors, debtors and trustees.

**Clients/Work Highlights:** Schweitzer Ski Resort/ Pack River Ltd Co; Output, Gulf, Sisco Seeds; AgriBioTech; Myers Financial Group; Bonner Mall Partnership and Summit Securities.

### Holland & Hart LLP

See firm details p.369

**The Firm:** This practice has proved to be a popular choice for clients, in part due to the firm's overall multistate size, and consequently the wealth of resources available. However, clients also benefit from the firm's particular dedication to this area of the law: services include not only bankruptcy and Chapter 11 filings but also restructuring and creditors' rights.

**The Lawyers:** The "*let's work together attitude*" and creative approach of **Larry Prince** (see p.765) has won him a following in the market. He provides "*invaluable information about the bankruptcy world*" and forges an "*exceptional relationship with all parties in court proceedings,*" said clients.

**Clients/Work Highlights:** Prince's team acts for a wide range of clients, mainly creditors, including financial institutions and banks, commercial lenders, landlords, equipment lessors and asset purchasers. Examples include US Bank National Association; Wells Fargo; National Association and Equity; Livestock Corporation and a major insurance company.

### Moffatt Thomas Barrett Rock & Fields

**The Firm:** The creditors' rights and bankruptcy practice at this Idaho firm provides advice on bankruptcy, loan workouts, foreclosures and lender liability.

**The Lawyers: Randall Peterman** dedicates the majority of his time to the restructuring arena, particularly creditor work. Clients praise him for his understanding of their needs, and for doing everything he can to meet them. Peers have also commented on how his understanding of debtors' objectives helps to win cases on behalf of the creditors.

**Clients/Work Highlights:** Clients include creditors and unsecured creditors' committees, especially large banks and financial institutions.

### Other Notable Practitioners

**Joseph Meier** of Cosho Humphrey LLP, represents creditors, debtors and bankruptcy trustees. In addition to advising on federal bankruptcy legislation, he assists clients in loan restructuring and litigation. Also recognized for his work for both creditors and debtors, sole practitioner **Craig Christensen**'s style appeals to clients, as he "*always cuts to the chase.*" A robust courtroom advocate, **Brent Robinson** of Ling, Robinson & Walker has acted in a substantial number of agriculture Chapters 11 and 12 proceedings and business reorganizations. Two of Idaho's leading bankruptcy attorneys are located in Pocatello. At Racine Olson Nye Budge & Bailey, **Daniel Green** specializes in bankruptcy law, creditors' rights and business reorganization, especially for clients involved in farming. Acting for financial institutions and agricultural clients, **Ron Kerl** of Cooper & Larson is an expert in Chapters 11 and 12 bankruptcy reorganizations, and Chapter 7 bankruptcy liquidations.

# CORPORATE/COMMERCIAL

**Corporate/Commercial**
Leading Firms

1. HAWLEY TROXELL ENNIS & HAWLEY LLP *Boise*
   STOEL RIVES LLP *Boise*
2. HOLLAND & HART LLP *Boise*

## Band 1

### Hawley Troxell Ennis & Hawley LLP

**The Firm:** This business and finance department has carved out a strong reputation for corporate and commercial work, including governance and compliance issues that affect clients. The group based in Boise can call upon the support of resources in

Pocatello and in Ketchum.

**The Lawyers: Nicholas Miller** is chair of the business and finance practice group. A "*bright and trusted attorney,*" his expertise lies in corporate and securities issues, particularly bond financings. **Stephen Hardesty** has developed a broad practice that encompasses structured finance and securitizations, M&A and venture capital financings. Interviewees

| Corporate/Commercial | |
|---|---|
| Leading Individuals | |
| [1] BOYD Paul | *Stoel Rives LLP* |
| MILLER Nicholas | *Hawley Troxell Ennis* |
| [2] MACK J Frederick | *Holland & Hart LLP* |
| PRINCE Larry | *Holland & Hart LLP* |
| [3] HARDESTY Stephen | *Hawley Troxell Ennis* |
| JONES Linda | *Holland & Hart LLP* |
| ORMSETH Kris | *Stoel Rives LLP* |
| RILEY Richard | *Hawley Troxell Ennis* |

endorsed him as "*an aggressive lawyer who defends his clients well.*" A skilled technical lawyer and accomplished deal-doer, **Richard Riley** has developed a practice that encompasses loan and credit issues, as well as health care and insurance.

Clients/Work Highlights: The firm acts for public and private companies, particularly those in the banking and accounting industry.

### Stoel Rives LLP

The Firm: This Boise-based team has the distinct advantage of being able to pool support and resources from its offices across the USA. Recent deals include a leveraged buyout of one of the largest medical practices in the state and the acquisition of a major technology license for a new product line.

The team also advises clients on the negotiation of strategic relationships with other financial institutions.

The Lawyers: Many of **Paul Boyd**'s various public and private corporation clients come from the telecom and technology industries. They are attracted by his broad base of business skills, especially in the field of venture capital financing. Boyd's approach is "*friendly and down to earth,*" and clients are impressed by his skills in "*bringing in and coordinating resources from other practices and offices.*" **Kris Ormseth** also specializes in technology-related matters, and clients express great confidence in his "*excellent, thorough and careful*" handling of high-profile matters.

Clients/Work Highlights: Many of the team's public and private corporation clients are within the telecom and technology industries. These include Woodgrain Millwork; American Ecology; Syngenta Seeds; ProClarity; Capital One; GE Capital; Matterhorn Group; Outlook Capital Partners; Futura Corp and Windland.

## Band 2

### Holland & Hart LLP

See firm details p.369

The Firm: One of the largest law firms in the Rocky Mountain West region, this national player fields a Boise team that handles both public and private transactions. Its dedicated and experienced attorneys advise on a range of issues such as M&A corporate governance and compliance.

The Lawyers: Sources described **Frederick Mack** (see p.764) as an "*astute business lawyer who always acts with integrity,*" and highlighted his 28 years of experience in business law as a major drawing card. The "*amiable and well-reputed*" **Larry Prince** (see p.765) mainly focuses on creditors' rights, but also advises on corporate and M&A matters. The "*bright and talented*" **Linda Jones** (see p.764) represents clients in natural resources-related industries such as timber and mining. Her caseload includes environmental compliance work, real estate transactions and financings. While she maintains an enduring reputation for her environmental expertise (particularly in the areas of air, water, contaminated sites and environmental cleanup), of late her practice has had a much broader transactional focus.

Clients/Work Highlights: The team counsels clients in the finance, insurance and retail industries, including WinCo Foods.

# EMPLOYMENT

| Employment: Mainly Defendant | |
|---|---|
| Leading Firms | |
| [1] HALL, FARLEY, OBERRECHT & BLANTON, PA | *Boise* |
| HAWLEY TROXELL ENNIS & HAWLEY LLP | *Boise* |
| MOFFATT THOMAS BARRETT ROCK & FIELDS | *Boise* |
| [2] GIVENS PURSLEY LLP | *Boise* |
| PERKINS COIE LLP | *Boise* |
| STOEL RIVES LLP | *Boise* |

| Leading Individuals | |
|---|---|
| [1] BERENTER Steven | *Hawley Troxell Ennis* |
| DALE James | *Stoel Rives LLP* |
| WAGAHOFF DALE Candy | *Hall, Farley, Oberrecht* |
| [2] LEACHMAN Tamsen | *Hall, Farley, Oberrecht* |
| MUNTHER Merrily | *Penland Munther Goodrum* |
| TOLLEFSON Gregory | *Stoel Rives LLP* |
| WHITE Robert | *Givens Pursley LLP* |

## Band 1

### Hall, Farley, Oberrecht & Blanton, PA

The Firm: This Boise-based team offers a successful and well-respected dispute avoidance and resolution practice, and commentators agree that the attorneys deliver "*hot litigation skills.*" The team also delivers regulatory advice, and policy review and training services. Recent cases have included two summary

judgment dismissals on behalf of Trinity Health and one for US Bancorp in a discrimination claim.

The Lawyers: **Candy Dale** stands out as "*a class act, both expert and experienced.*" She is well versed in business litigation as well as employment law. **Tamsen Leachman** achieves recognition for her energy and commitment to the practice.

Clients/Work Highlights: The Amalgamated Sugar Company; Idaho Power; Blue Cross of Idaho; LandAmerica Financial Group; Sorrento Lactalis and Trinity Health.

### Hawley Troxell Ennis & Hawley LLP

The Firm: The team provides the firm's business clients with employment-related planning and organization advice. It focuses on strategies aimed at preventing disputes, but is "*more than capable of handling litigation*" if it arises. Recent matters have included claims of fraud and wrongful discharge and age, gender and disability discrimination cases.

The Lawyers: **Steven Berenter** is singled out for his litigation expertise and he is perfectly at home before various commissions and both the federal and state court. He also advises his clients on regulatory issues.

Clients/Work Highlights: Washington Group International; J.R. Simplot Company; Alliance Title; Edmark Auto; Primary Health; Alliance Medical Group; Portneuf Medical Center; Bingham Memorial Hospital; Lincare Holdings; St. Luke's Regional Medical Center; Woodgrain Millwork and Futura.

# MAINLY DEFENDANT

### Moffatt Thomas Barrett Rock & Fields

The Firm: This team handles compliance and contentious issues throughout Idaho and also across the country, and offers a well-rounded service in "*just about any issue you can think of.*" The "*smart and confident*" attorneys appear before federal and state courts, and various boards and commissions.

The Lawyers: Employment litigator and preventive counselor Patricia Olsson is a key contact here. Jim Dale has left the firm to join Stoel Rives.

Clients/Work Highlights: Clients include technology, healthcare and retail companies.

## Band 2

### Givens Pursley LLP

The Firm: This relatively small practice provides HR training and compliance advice to help clients avoid litigation. The team is nevertheless experienced in defending clients in disputes before administrative agencies, state and federal courts, using litigation or alternative dispute resolution.

The Lawyers: Expert civil litigator **Robert White** acts in disputes and advises clients on legislation, policy and issues such as risk management.

Clients/Work Highlights: The firm has a healthcare, manufacturing, food production, hi-tech, utilities and construction client base.

### Perkins Coie LLP

**The Firm:** A nationwide network of offices supports the labor and employment practice at this small Boise outfit. The emphasis is very much on keeping clients out of court, and to this end the attorneys focus on policy and training advice.

**The Lawyers:** Shelly Cozakos is the key contact here.

**Clients/Work Highlights:** The Boise office serves private companies and public agencies throughout Idaho, the Intermountain Region and the Pacific Northwest.

### Stoel Rives LLP

**The Firm:** Sources extol this team's expertise in employment law, both in counseling and litigation. It also offers traditional labor services, management training and regulatory advice. It is a significant regional player and draws on support from colleagues in California and Washington as needed.

**The Lawyers:** The arrival of **Jim Dale** from Moffatt Thomas is a coup, agree commentators, and provides a much-needed plug for a gap that had opened in the ranks. He represents clients in the technology, health care and retail industries. **Gregory Tollefson** offers polished litigation and arbitration services, representing employers and management.

**Clients/Work Highlights:** The team acts for clients in various industry sectors including hi-tech, manufacturing, communications, forestry, finance, retail, agriculture and healthcare.

### Other Notable Practitioners

**Merrily Munther** of Penland Munther Goodrum has a diverse business-oriented practice and offers advice in employment and labor law as well as real estate and construction.

# LITIGATION

| | Litigation: General Commercial |
|---|---|
| | **Leading Firms** |
| 1 | HAWLEY TROXELL ENNIS & HAWLEY LLP *Boise* |
| | HOLLAND & HART LLP *Boise* |
| 2 | ELAM & BURKE PA *Boise* |
| | GREENER BANDUCCI SHOEMAKER *Boise* |
| | STOEL RIVES LLP *Boise* |
| 3 | EBERLE, BERLIN, KADING, TURNBOW *Boise* |
| | HALL, FARLEY, OBERRECHT & BLANTON, PA *Boise* |
| | MOFFATT THOMAS BARRETT ROCK *Boise* |
| | PERKINS COIE LLP *Boise* |

| | Leading Individuals |
|---|---|
| | **Senior Statesmen** |
| | BURKE Carl *Greener Banducci Shoemaker* |
| | DINGEL Allyn *Elam & Burke PA* |
| 1 | BITHELL Walter *Holland & Hart LLP* |
| | GREENER Richard *Greener Banducci Shoemaker* |
| | MEADOWS Craig *Hawley Troxell Ennis* |
| | SINCLAIR J Walter *Stoel Rives LLP* |
| 2 | ANDERSEN Steven *Holland & Hart LLP* |
| | BANDUCCI Thomas *Greener Banducci Shoemaker* |
| | CLARK Merlyn *Hawley Troxell Ennis* |
| | SQUYRES Newal *Holland & Hart LLP* |
| 3 | BOARDMAN Richard *Perkins Coie LLP* |
| | DRYDEN William *Elam & Burke PA* |
| | FARLEY Donald *Hall, Farley, Oberrecht* |
| | HALL Richard *Hall, Farley, Oberrecht* |
| | LARUE James *Elam & Burke PA* |

## Band 1

### Hawley Troxell Ennis & Hawley LLP

**The Firm:** This "*mature*" Idaho-centered litigation group also operates an office in Nevada and offers expertise in such areas as construction and medical malpractice. Attorneys work closely with their corporate counterparts to deliver a full commercial service.

**The Lawyers:** Practice chair **Craig Meadows** handles commercial, insurance and bad faith litigation and offers specialty expertise in aviation, products liability, legal malpractice and subrogation cases.

Sources praise his "*good judgment and professionalism.*" **Merlyn Clark** is a distinguished mediator praised for his arbitration and complex civil litigation work.

**Clients/Work Highlights:** Long-standing clients include Idaho Health Facilities Authority; Kerr-McGee; Del Monte Foods; Mayflower Contract Services and some underwriters at Lloyd's. The practice has recently attracted PolyOne; Precision Craft Log & Timber Homes; as well as the following State of Idaho departments: Department of Administration; Division of Purchasing; Risk Management and Health and Welfare.

### Holland & Hart LLP

See firm details p.369

**The Firm:** This firm offers a veritable army of litigators out of 12 offices in six states and is particularly noted for technology and IP expertise. Sources note the team's increasing presence in commercial litigation, and endorse its professional liability and finance capability.

**The Lawyers:** **Walter Bithell**'s (see p.763) litigation workload includes business and commercial matters, personal injury, products and professional liability, insurance and securities. The "*aggressive*" **Steven Andersen** (see p.763) is "*formidable in everything he does.*" He has acted for financial institutions, public bodies, and clients in the automobile, agriculture and construction industries, and interviewees commented on his "*real presence in the courtroom.*" **Newal Squyres** (see p.765) handles judges and juries with aplomb, both at first instance and at appeals.

**Clients/Work Highlights:** Clients are drawn from a range of sectors including construction and design, technology and communications, banking, real estate, energy and healthcare.

## Band 2

### Elam & Burke PA

**The Firm:** This firm has a long and distinguished history and is regarded as one of the more traditional players in this field. The versatile attorneys manage a steady diet of commercial matters including bank-

# GENERAL COMMERCIAL

ruptcies and product liability. In addition to its involvement in litigation the team has recently handled mediation settlements in defective product and breach of contract cases.

**The Lawyers:** **Allyn Dingel** is "*a real character in the community*" and commentators delight in his "*unorthodox but effective and clever*" style. He offers business litigation and insurance defense expertise. **William Dryden** works in environmental and commercial litigation, insurance defense and mediation. The "*well-regarded and experienced*" **James LaRue** acts for insurance companies in defense work and general transactions.

**Clients/Work Highlights:** Farmers; State Farm; DaimlerChrysler; Les Schwab Tire Centers; Bogus Basin Recreational Association; Jerome Urban Renewal Agency; Koch Industries and Lindsay Manufacturing.

### Greener Banducci Shoemaker

**The Firm:** This outfit offers 16 litigators of impeccable pedigree and deep experience harvested from some of Idaho's finest firms. Its bid for marketshare in the state is going well and both plaintiffs and defendants beat a path to the firm's door.

**The Lawyers:** Commentators agree that **Carl Burke** (see p.763) is "*a total legend.*" With half a century's experience under his belt, he is an anchor on numerous committees and advisory boards. He advises on matters including environmental law, business banking and products liability. **Richard Greener** (see p.764) is a staunch litigator praised for his work "*in the trenches,*" particularly for plaintiffs. Having run the litigation department at Stoel Rives for 14 years, the "*exceptionally bright*" **Thomas Banducci** (see p.763) brings "*real wisdom*" to the table.

**Clients/Work Highlights:** The client base consists of corporations, both private and public, based throughout Idaho and the Pacific Northwest.

### Stoel Rives LLP

**The Firm:** Despite losing three litigators to the budding Greener Banducci Shoemaker, commentators argue that the firm is benefiting from the "*fresh approach*" provided by the leadership of Walter

Sinclair. The team deals in complex corporate litigation; recent matters have included defending clients on products liability and breach of duty claims and advising a plaintiff in a case of alleged breach of contract.

**The Lawyers:** **Walter Sinclair** is regarded as the group's "*greatest asset.*" Ambitious and hard-working, he is praised for his "*outstanding organizational and communication skills.*"

**Clients/Work Highlights:** DuPont; Celotex; Albertson's; St. Luke's Medical Center; Cargill; Medtronic; Micron Technology and PacifiCorp.

### Band 3

### Eberle, Berlin, Kading, Turnbow & McIlveen, Chartered

**The Firm:** The heart of this practice is insurance defense work and attorneys are spotted on some of the best cases in the state. The team offers experience in several sectors including aviation, product liability, malpractice and securities.

**The Lawyers:** Warren Jones is experienced in insurance defense litigation.

**Clients/Work Highlights:** Commercial clients include Ada County Highway District; Chase Manhattan; CIT Group; Deloitte & Touche; Prudential Securities; GE; US Steel. Insurance clients include American Manufacturers Mutual Insurance; Chubb Group; Equitable; Farmers; National Indemnity; St. Paul Fire & Marine Insurance and Zurich American Insurance Company.

### Hall, Farley, Oberrecht & Blanton, PA

**The Firm:** Highly respected for its commercial work, this Boise firm offers litigation services across a swathe of business sectors including construction, professional liability, insurance, real estate and health care. It delivers expertise in business, employment and estate planning law, and commentators recommend it for complex litigation and alternative dispute resolution.

**The Lawyers:** **Richard Hall** has particular expertise in defending healthcare clients. The "*talented*" **Donald Farley** specializes in product and auto liability and has a healthy practice in insurance defense work.

**Clients/Work Highlights:** Clients include businesses, professionals, medical insurance companies and healthcare institutions.

### Moffatt Thomas Barrett Rock & Fields

**The Firm:** One of the largest firms in the state, this group offers both breadth and depth out of its four offices across Idaho. Recent highlights have included advising an IT manufacturer on alleged violations of federal and state securities laws and representing a regional bank in a dispute over the purchase of an insurance agency. The team is well versed in IP issues and complex claims of breach of fiduciary duty and fraud.

**The Lawyers:** Stephen Thomas chairs the commercial litigation practice and specializes in products liability, securities and insurance coverage.

**Clients/Work Highlights:** The practice represents a wide range of commercial clients including a major oil company, a medical center, various manufacturers and suppliers and financial institutions.

### Perkins Coie LLP

**The Firm:** The Idaho arm of this regional firm is well supported and resourced by offices in Seattle, Portland, Denver and Anchorage and across the USA. The Boise team is adept in various areas including IP, product liability, insurance and construction.

**The Lawyers:** Managing Partner **Richard Boardman** offers "*a touch of class*" and is "*a pleasure to work with,*" according to sources.

**Clients/Work Highlights:** The practice advises commercial clients from a number of industry sectors.

# NATURAL RESOURCES & ENVIRONMENT

| Natural Resources & Environment Leading Firms | |
| --- | --- |
| 1 GIVENS PURSLEY LLP *Boise* | |
| HOLLAND & HART LLP *Boise* | |
| STOEL RIVES LLP *Boise* | |
| 2 PERKINS COIE LLP *Boise* | |

| Leading Individuals | |
| --- | --- |
| 1 BEATON Kevin *Stoel Rives LLP* | |
| CAMPBELL Scott *Moffatt Thomas Barrett Rock* | |
| FELDMAN Murray *Holland & Hart LLP* | |
| FEREDAY Jeffrey *Givens Pursley LLP* | |
| JONES Linda *Holland & Hart LLP* | |
| MAYNARD Robert *Perkins Coie LLP* | |
| MCINTYRE Krista *Stoel Rives LLP* | |
| MEYER Christopher *Givens Pursley LLP* | |
| MYERS William *Holland & Hart LLP* | |
| 2 BAIRD Joseph *Baird Hanson Williams LLP* | |
| SMITH Bruce *Moore Smith Buxton & Turke* | |

### Band 1

### Givens Pursley LLP

**The Firm:** This proudly homegrown firm is nationally respected for its environmental, water, public lands and natural resources practice; it is particularly commended for its expertise in water law. Working closely with real estate and other colleagues, this team handles a range of complex compliance and liability issues.

**The Lawyers:** Renowned experts in water law, natural resources and public lands, both **Christopher Meyer** and **Jeffrey Fereday** are "*an authoritative combination.*" Meyer has an extensive background in handling water and natural resources cases before the National Wildlife Federation.

**Clients/Work Highlights:** Municipal water suppliers, industrial businesses, irrigators, developers, mining companies and nonprofit organizations comprise the client base.

### Holland & Hart LLP

See firm details p.369

**The Firm:** This long-established natural resources practice handles a wide range of natural resources issues including regulatory work.

**The Lawyers:** **Murray Feldman** (see p.764) is a national authority on endangered species issues and impresses commentators with his "*steady dedication over the years*" to environmental law in general, including public land matters, environmental permitting and environmental insurance. **Linda Jones** (see p.764) has a respected environmental regulatory practice and also offers expertise in real estate, business and financing transactions. **William Myers'** (see p.764) credentials include environmental work for the DOI and high-profile cases before the Supreme Court. He offers specialty federal land advice.

**Clients/Work Highlights:** The original oil, gas and mining clientele has swollen over the years to include clients in the real estate development and ski and recreation sectors.

### Stoel Rives LLP

**The Firm:** This firm offers services across five western states, and the Boise office emphasizes regulatory/compliance issues and any resulting litigation. Areas of focus include air and water quality, waste, wetlands and endangered species protection.

**The Lawyers:** **Krista McIntyre** is an established expert on the CAA. Peers commend her "*rainmaker*" role in developing the practice, while clients extol her "*excellent judgment and creativity in finding solutions.*" The "*pleasant, smart and responsive*" **Kevin Beaton** specializes in the CWA, administrative law and endangered species.

**Clients/Work Highlights:** The team acts for large industrial companies locally, including JR Simplot, Potlatch, Micron and Ash Grove Cement.

### Band 2

### Perkins Coie LLP

**The Firm:** The Boise attorneys are part of a national network that offers transactional advice and counsel on compliance issues, litigation, land use, Native American law and gaming. Natural resources expertise covers the water, minerals and mining, wildlife conservation, marine and energy areas.

**The Lawyers: Robert Maynard** is experienced in environment and energy and natural resources matters including water law and real estate/land use. He acts for high-profile clients such as the USDA Forest Service and is lauded for his *"sensitivity to costs, constraints and business goals."* He recently handled a complex transaction involving the donation of forestland with conservation easement to a

university for research and education purposes.
**Clients/Work Highlights:** Clients include businesses, financial institutions, trade associations, nonprofit organizations, government agencies and individuals. Examples are Ada County Highway District, Coeur D'Alene Mines, Idaho Association of Counties and Calpine.

## Other Notable Practitioners

**Joseph Baird** of Baird Hanson Williams LLP is expert in mining law and acts for base and precious metal production companies, industrial mineral

producers, exploration programs and mineral land management companies. **Scott Campbell** of Moffatt Thomas Barrett Rock & Fields, Chartered practices in environmental, administrative, energy and agriculture law. He is especially rated for his expertise in water law, and his water rights work spans industries including hydroelectric power, agricultural irrigation, commercial mining and fish propagation. **Bruce Smith** of Moore Smith Buxton & Turke is a natural resources specialist who is popular for his water rights work.

# REAL ESTATE

### Real Estate
#### Leading Firms
1. **GIVENS PURSLEY LLP** *Boise*
   **HAWLEY TROXELL ENNIS & HAWLEY LLP** *Boise*
2. **SPINK BUTLER, LLP** *Boise*
   **STOEL RIVES LLP** *Boise*
3. **MEULEMAN MOLLERUP LLP** *Boise*
   **MOFFATT THOMAS BARRETT ROCK & FIELDS** *Boise*

#### Leading Individuals
##### Senior Statesman
**HIGER Dale** *Stoel Rives LLP*
1. **BALLARD Brian** *Hawley Troxell Ennis*
   **BEESON Christopher** *Givens Pursley LLP*
2. **GOWLAND Kimbal** *Meuleman Mollerup LLP*
   **KNIPE Quentin** *Stoel Rives LLP*
   **MOLLERUP Richard** *Meuleman Mollerup LLP*
   **PURSLEY Kenneth** *Givens Pursley LLP*

### Real Estate: Zoning/Land Use
#### Leading Individuals
1. **BUTLER JoAnn** *Spink Butler, LLP*
2. **ALLEN Gary** *Givens Pursley LLP*
   **BRADBURY Steve** *Williams Bradbury*

## Band 1

### Givens Pursley LLP
**The Firm:** This large team offers a full service in this area, and is particularly noted for retail developments. A strong environmental practice complements the real estate offering, and attorneys are well versed in land use issues. The team handles projects including shopping centers, manufacturing plants, offices, residential homes, agricultural properties, nature reserves and leisure resorts. Commentators also flag up a credible finance capability.
**The Lawyers:** Founding partner **Kenneth Pursley** is a veteran of real estate and business law. He represents commercial clients on real estate matters, and has a noted development practice. **Christopher Beeson** acts for shopping centers, offices, hotels and other commercial clients. **Gary Allen** offers impres-

sive environmental credentials and specializes in land use issues concerning industrial, infrastructure and development projects. He recently obtained Planning & Zoning Commission approval on a high-profile condominium project and a $1 billion coal-fired powerplant project.
**Clients/Work Highlights:** The national and regional clientele includes real estate investment companies and developers, title insurance companies, manufacturing firms, financial institutions and venture capital firms. Land use clients include Clark Development/Crescent Rim; the developers of Hidden Springs; Langly Properties; Sempra Generation and Allied Waste Industries.

### Hawley Troxell Ennis & Hawley LLP
**The Firm:** This firm is *"serious about real estate"* and handles a sophisticated workload within Idaho and around the USA. Attorneys offer expertise in many areas including finance, purchase, sale and acquisition, leasing, property management and developments. Sources also indicate a strong land use capability.
**The Lawyers:** The *"experienced and versatile"* **Brian Ballard** is an authority on Section 1031 tax-deferred real estate exchanges and a vigorous lobbyist on public infrastructure financing. The firm's land use and zoning capability owes much to Geoffrey Wardle.
**Clients/Work Highlights:** Real estate developers and corporations comprise the client base.

## Band 2

### Spink Butler, LLP
**The Firm:** Real estate is a large chunk of what this relatively small firm is about. The team offers highly credible services in a range of matters, but is especially distinguished for its land use and development work.
**The Lawyers: JoAnn Butler** is a veritable doyenne in land use and development matters. She also brings expertise in environmental law to the table and advises clients on transactional, business planning and financing arrangements.
**Clients/Work Highlights:** The firm acts for various local government agencies and developers, as well as a range of commercial clients such as realtors, developers, contractors and title companies.

### Stoel Rives LLP
**The Firm:** Attorneys at the Boise office are part of a large regional offering that handles high-profile, complex deals. The team is strong in land use and construction issues, thanks in part to the depth of the firm's environmental practice.
**The Lawyers: Dale Higer** has a broad business practice, of which real estate – including tax issues – is a key part. Clients rate **Quentin Knipe** for his contractual work and expertise in finance and development work; he is adept in the formation of joint ventures.
**Clients/Work Highlights:** Clients include the Simplot Family, FOR 1031 and AEGON USA.

## Band 3

### Meuleman Mollerup LLP
**The Firm:** Attorneys here enjoy a strong reputation in construction law, and practice within a firm that has a long track record as commercial advisers. The team offers transactional and finance advice as well as services in complex litigation and dispute resolution.
**The Lawyers:** The *"thorough and technical"* **Kimbal Gowland** works on leases and sales as part of a thriving general business practice. **Richard Mollerup** is also a respected business attorney. His expertise includes title insurance and escrow matters and judicial and nonjudicial foreclosure of mortgages.
**Clients/Work Highlights:** The client base consists mainly of developers, investors, title insurance companies and commercial clients such as retailers.

### Moffatt Thomas Barrett Rock & Fields
**The Firm:** This Idaho stalwart has a healthy real estate transactions practice and has well-regarded finance expertise. The team offers services in land use and entitlement and dispute resolution.
**The Lawyers:** David Jensen handles real estate finance issues.
**Clients/Work Highlights:** Individual property owners, residential and commercial developers and corporate landowners comprise the client base.

**Other Notable Practitioners**

**Steve Bradbury** at Williams Bradbury, Attorneys at Law, offers real estate, land use and general business expertise. He is a valued land use litigator.

# Leaders in Idaho

**ALLEN, Gary**
Givens Pursley LLP, Boise
208 388 1200
*Recommended in Real Estate*

**ANDERSEN, Steven**
Holland & Hart LLP, Boise
280 342 5000
sandersen@hollandhart.com
*Recommended in Litigation*
**Practice Areas:** Partner practicing in tort and commercial litigation including products liability, professional negligence, and personal injury. Has tried cases involving insurance disputes, partnership dissolution claims by and against banks, patent and intellectual property claims, as well as automobile, medical malpractice and product defects. Has also tried cases involving governmental liability, aviation, agriculture, farming, and construction.
**Prof. Memberships:** American Bar Association (Litigation and Business Sections), Idaho State Bar (Continuing Legal Education Committee, Professional Conduct Board).
**Career:** Admitted to the Idaho Bar (1980), US Court of Appeals, Ninth Circuit (1985). Mr Andersen has been in private practice since 1982 and a Partner with Holland & Hart since 1987. He has lectured statewide on topics of trial preparation and advocacy and has published materials and articles on legal ethics, discovery techniques, and trials.
**Publications:** Author, 'How to Prepare For, Take and Use a Deposition' (James Publishing).
**Personal:** Received a JD (with honors) from Brigham Young University in 1981 and a BA (summa cum laude) from Brigham Young University in 1977.

**BAIRD, Joseph**
Baird Hanson Williams LLP, Boise
208 388 0110
*Recommended in Natural Resources*

**BALLARD, Brian**
Hawley Troxell Ennis & Hawley LLP, Boise
208 344 6000
*Recommended in Real Estate*

**BANDUCCI, Thomas**
Greener Banducci Shoemaker, Boise
208 319 2600
tbanducci@greenerlaw.com
*Recommended in Litigation*
**Practice Areas:** Mr Banducci has considerable expertise in various areas of commercial litigation including complex contractual disputes, unfair business practice claims, products liability and construction litigation. Mr Banducci serves as national litigation counsel for a structural wood products manufacturer. He has had First Chair responsibility for litigation in over 20 states.
**Prof. Memberships:** Idaho State Bar Commissioner, 2004-07; President-elect, Idaho State Bar 2007; Founding Member and Secretary, Federal Bar Association for the District of Idaho; International Association of Defense Counsel (IADC); Faculty IADC Trial Academy, 2005.
**Career:** Tom Banducci founded the Boise office of Stoel Rives, LLP and ran its litigation department for 14 years. He then formed Greener Banducci Shoemaker P.A. in January 2005 and is its current Managing Partner.
**Personal:** University of California, Hastings College of the Law, J, 1979. Editor, Hastings International Law Review; Stanford University, BA with honors, 1976; Executive Committee, Gene Harris Jazz Festival; Board of Directors, Treasure Valley Family YMCA.

**BEATON, Kevin**
Stoel Rives LLP, Boise
208 389 9000
*Recommended in Natural Resources*

**BEESON, Christopher**
Givens Pursley LLP, Boise
208 388 1200
*Recommended in Real Estate*

**BERENTER, Steven**
Hawley Troxell Ennis & Hawley LLP, Boise
208 344 6000
*Recommended in Employment*

**BITHELL, Walter**
Holland & Hart LLP, Boise
208 342 5000
wbithell@hollandhart.com
*Recommended in Litigation*
**Practice Areas:** Partner with practice emphasis on individual and class action tort litigation, including business and commercial, personal injury, products liability, professional liability, commercial, insurance, securities, and general litigation.
**Prof. Memberships:** Fellow of the American College of Trial Lawyers, American Inns of Court No. 130 (Master of the Bench), American Trial Lawyers Association (Board of Governors), Idaho Trial Lawyers Association (past President), Idaho State Bar (past President), University of Idaho Foundation (Board of Directors), The American Society of Writers on Legal Subjects (SCRIBES).
**Career:** Admitted to Idaho Bar (1968), Admitted to Idaho State and Federal District Courts (1968), US Court of Federal Claims (1991), US Court of Appeals, Ninth Circuit (1992), US Supreme Court (1995). Former Idaho Deputy Attorney General, General Counsel for the Idaho State Department of Insurance and General Counsel for the Idaho State Tax Commission.
**Personal:** Received JD from University of Idaho (1968) and a BS from the University of Idaho (1965).

**BOARDMAN, Richard**
Perkins Coie LLP, Boise
208 343 3434
*Recommended in Litigation*

**BOYD, Paul**
Stoel Rives LLP, Boise
208 389 9000
*Recommended in Corporate/Commercial*

**BRADBURY, Steve**
Williams Bradbury, Attorneys at Law, Boise
208 344 6633
*Recommended in Real Estate*

**BURKE, Carl**
Greener Banducci Shoemaker, Boise
208 319 2600
cpburke@greenerlaw.com
*Recommended in Litigation*
**Practice Areas:** Mr Burke has over 50 years of experience practicing law in the federal and state courts, both at the trial and the appellate levels. Mr Burke has spent a considerable amount of time dealing with elected officials in Washington, DC. In Idaho, he has represented clients and client's interests before the legislature, state and US congressional committees, administrative boards, county commissioners, and other state and federal administrators and elected officials. Within the last couple of years he has been involved in trial and appellate work dealing with breach of contracts, real estate and defense of broker/dealers. Mr Burke has also been representing clients in environmental litigation and natural resource damage claims, patent and trademark infringement and constitutional law issues.
**Prof. Memberships:** Founder and first President, Idaho Association of Defense Counsel; Life Fellow of the American Bar Foundation; Boise Bar Association, President 1963-64; Idaho State Bar; American Bar Association; Former state chairman of the Idaho Uniform District Rules Committee; Fellow and three-time Idaho State Chairman of the American College of Trial Lawyers; Idaho Commission on Constitutional Revision, 1965-70.
**Career:** Mr Burke graduated from Stanford in 1950 and then served a clerkship with the United States District Court to the Honorable Chase Clark. He then immediately began his private practice at Elam & Burke. His current law practice, in an of counsel role, consists of advising firm attorneys on a broad variety of trial, mediation and appellate matters, general business law and litigation.
**Personal:** Stanford University, BA, 1947; LLM, 1950; President of the Frank Church Institute; Former Chairman of the US National Parks Advisory Board; chaired all of the senatorial campaigns for Frank Church and his United States presidential campaign in 1976; Idaho State Chairman of the Jack Kennedy and Lyndon Johnson presidential campaigns; served on committees for the reelection of many Idaho state and congressional candidates.

**BUTLER, JoAnn**
Spink Butler, LLP, Boise
208 388 1000
*Recommended in Real Estate*

**CAMPBELL, Scott**
Moffatt Thomas Barrett Rock & Fields, Boise 208 345 2000
*Recommended in Natural Resources*

**CHRISTENSEN, Craig**
Craig Christensen - Attorney at Law, Boise 208 234 9353
*Recommended in Bankruptcy*

**CLARK, Merlyn**
Hawley Troxell Ennis & Hawley LLP, Boise 208 344 6000
*Recommended in Litigation*

**DALE, James**
Stoel Rives LLP, Boise
208 389 9000
*Recommended in Employment*

**DINGEL, Allyn**
Elam & Burke PA, Boise
208 343 5454
*Recommended in Litigation*

**DRYDEN, William**
Elam & Burke PA, Boise
208 343 5454
*Recommended in Litigation*

**ELSAESSER, Ford**
Elsaesser Jarzabek Anderson Marks
Elliott & McHugh, Chartered, Sandpoint
208 263 8517
*Recommended in Bankruptcy*

**FARLEY, Donald**
Hall, Farley, Oberrecht & Blanton, PA,
Boise 208 395 8500
*Recommended in Litigation*

**FELDMAN, Murray**
Holland & Hart LLP, Boise
208 342 5000
mfeldman@hollandhart.com
*Recommended in Natural Resources*
**Practice Areas:** Environmental and
natural resources law, endangered
species, environmental permitting, public
lands, and environmental insurance. Has
represented clients in litigation and
administrative proceedings concerning
endangered species consultation and
habitat protection requirements, National Environmental Policy Act, land use,
contaminated site cleanup, and air and
water quality issues.
**Prof. Memberships:** ABA Section of
Environment, Energy and Resources;
Idaho State Bar, Natural Resources Law
Section Board Member; past President,
University of Idaho College of Natural
Resources Alumni Board of Trustees.
**Career:** Headed firmwide Environmental Practice Group (2001-03); Partner
since 1998.
**Publications:** Frequent speaker and
author on natural resource and environmental topics. Articles published in sever-
al law reviews, Bar publications, and book
chapters.
**Personal:** University of California -
Berkeley (Boalt Hall) School of Law (JD
1988); University of Idaho (MS 1985);
University of California, Berkeley (BS
1982, with high honors).

**FEREDAY, Jeffrey**
Givens Pursley LLP, Boise
208 388 1200
*Recommended in Natural Resources*

**GOWLAND, Kimbal**
Meuleman Mollerup LLP, Boise
208 342 6066
*Recommended in Real Estate*

**GREEN, Daniel**
Racine Olson Nye Budge & Bailey,
Pocatello 208 232 6101
*Recommended in Bankruptcy*

**GREENER, Richard**
Greener Banducci Shoemaker, Boise
208 319 2600
rgreener@greenerlaw.com
*Recommended in Litigation*
**Practice Areas:** Mr Greener's trial experience covers a broad spectrum of substantive law, including securities, construction, environment, employment,
patent infringement, professional legal
and medical malpractice, drug and medical products liability, and general business. During the last ten years, Mr Greener has spent 100% of his time on trial
work. He has litigated in numerous federal district courts, Circuit Courts of
Appeal, and state courts. Approximately
75% of his trials have been tried before
juries.
**Prof. Memberships:** Fellow of American
College of Trial Lawyers; American Board
of Trial Advocates; Boise Bar Association;
Idaho State Bar; Washington State Bar;
American Bar Association; Defense
Research Institute; Idaho Association of
Defense Counsel; Best Lawyers in Ameri-
ca, 1999-Present; Chambers USA Ameri-
can Leading Business Lawyers 2003-04.
**Personal:** University of Idaho, JD, 1968;
University of Washington, BA, 1965.

**HALL, Richard**
Hall, Farley, Oberrecht & Blanton, PA,
Boise 208 395 8500
*Recommended in Litigation*

**HARDESTY, Stephen**
Hawley Troxell Ennis & Hawley LLP,
Boise 208 344 6000
*Recommended in
Corporate/Commercial*

**HIGER, Dale**
Stoel Rives LLP, Boise
208 389 9000
*Recommended in Real Estate*

**JONES, Linda B**
Holland & Hart LLP, Boise
208 342 5000
ljones@hollandhart.com
*Recommended in
Corporate/Commercial, Natural
Resources*
**Practice Areas:** Environmental and
natural resources law; water rights;
secured financing transactions; real estate
transactions, including land use and title
issues; energy and other project development, including permits, environmental
assessments, wetlands, water rights, land
use, financing and other due diligence;
federal and state land matters, including
mineral and geothermal resource leasing;
general business transactions and regulatory matters.
**Prof. Memberships:** Member of the
ABA - Section of Environment, Energy
and Resources and Business Law Section;
Member of the Idaho State Bar - Environment and Natural Resources Section
(past Chair of Governing Council) and

Corporate and Securities Section (Past
Member of Governing Council)
**Career:** Practicing attorney since 1986,
in Idaho since 1989; Partner in Holland &
Hart's Boise, Idaho office
**Publications:** Writes and lectures about
environmental and energy law issues and
about due diligence in real estate and
business transactions.
**Personal:** University of California (MPP
1985); University of California Boalt Hall
School of Law (JD 1985); San Jose State
University (BA 1981, with High Distinc-
tion).

**KERL, Ron**
Cooper & Larsen, Pocatello
208 235 1145
*Recommended in Bankruptcy*

**KNIPE, Quentin**
Stoel Rives LLP, Boise
208 389 9000
*Recommended in Real Estate*

**LARUE, James**
Elam & Burke PA, Boise
208 343 5454
*Recommended in Litigation*

**LEACHMAN, Tamsen**
Hall, Farley, Oberrecht & Blanton, PA,
Boise 208 395 8500
*Recommended in Employment*

**MACK, J Frederick**
Holland & Hart LLP, Boise
208 342 5000
fmack@hollandhart.com
*Recommended in
Corporate/Commercial*
**Practice Areas:** Mr Mack has extensive
experience in all aspects of law relating to
business transactions and regularly consults business clients on such matters. He
represents some of Idaho's largest publicly and privately held companies and
regularly advises clients in contract negotiations and on the formation and development of start-up companies (including
corporations, partnerships, limited partnerships, limited liability partnerships,
and limited liability companies), mergers,
acquisitions, divestitures, share
exchanges, raising capital, and protecting
proprietary interests. Mr Mack also has
25 years of experience in complex wealth
planning. Among other things, he has
prepared both simple and complex wills,
trusts and other wealth planning vehicles.
**Prof. Memberships:** Member of the
American Bar Association; Idaho State
Bar Association, Section on Business and
Corporate Law; and the American Bar
Association, Section of Business Law.
**Career:** Admitted to the Idaho Bar
(1973).
**Personal:** Received a JD (1972) and a BA
(1969) from the University of Idaho.

**MAYNARD, Robert**
Perkins Coie LLP, Boise
208 343 3434
*Recommended in Natural Resources*

**MCINTYRE, Krista**
Stoel Rives LLP, Boise
208 389 9000
*Recommended in Natural Resources*

**MEADOWS, Craig**
Hawley Troxell Ennis & Hawley LLP,
Boise 208 344 6000
*Recommended in Litigation*

**MEIER, Joseph**
Cosho Humphrey LLP, Boise
208 344 7811
*Recommended in Bankruptcy*

**MEYER, Christopher**
Givens Pursley LLP, Boise
208 388 1200
*Recommended in Natural Resources*

**MILLER, Nicholas**
Hawley Troxell Ennis & Hawley LLP,
Boise 208 344 6000
*Recommended in
Corporate/Commercial*

**MOLLERUP, Richard**
Meuleman Mollerup LLP, Boise
208 342 6066
*Recommended in Real Estate*

**MUNTHER, Merrily**
Penland Munther Goodrum, Boise
208 344 4566
*Recommended in Employment*

**MYERS, William**
Holland & Hart LLP, Boise
208 383 3954
wmyers@hollandhart.com
*Recommended in Natural Resources*
**Practice Areas:** Natural resources and
public land law. He advises clients on utilization of federal lands, environmental
compliance, legislative matters, and litigation.
**Prof. Memberships:** Admitted to practice in Idaho, Wyoming, Colorado and
the District of Columbia as well as various federal courts including the United
States Supreme Court; past Vice-Chairman of the American Bar Association
Committee on Public Lands under the
Section of Environment, Energy and
Resources; past Chair of the Federal
Lands Task Force Working Group, chartered by the Idaho State Board of Land
Commissioners to promote improved
management of federal lands in Idaho.
**Career:** Held various federal offices
including Solicitor of the US Department
of the Interior, Deputy General Counsel
for Programs for the US Department of
Energy, Assistant to the US Attorney
General, and Legislative Counsel to US
Senator Alan Simpson (WY).
**Publications:** Extensive writings in areas
of his expertise.
**Personal:** University of Denver College

of Law (JD 1981, Denver Law Journal and Denver Journal of International Law and Policy); College of William and Mary (AB 1977).

## ORMSETH, Kris
Stoel Rives LLP, Boise
208 389 9000
*Recommended in Corporate/Commercial*

## PETERMAN, Randall
Moffatt Thomas Barrett Rock & Fields, Boise 208 345 2000
*Recommended in Bankruptcy*

## PRINCE, Larry E
Holland & Hart LLP, Boise
208 342 5000
lprince@hollandhart.com
*Recommended in Bankruptcy, Corporate/Commercial*

**Practice Areas:** Mr Prince specializes in bankruptcy, commercial litigation, and commercial transactions. He has extensive experience in representing secured creditors and debtors in bankruptcy proceedings and in complex credit transactions. He has represented lenders and borrowers in secured and unsecured credit facilities, ESOP transactions, workout and restructuring of problem loans and leases, multi-bank participations and syndications. His work in real estate law includes real estate acquisition and development and construction and suretyship litigation. His commercial litigation practice includes creditors' rights, contract, construction, Uniform Commercial Code, and real estate litigation.

**Prof. Memberships:** Member of the Idaho State Bar Association, Sections on Commercial Law and Bankruptcy, and Business and Corporate Law; Local Rules Committee, United States Bankruptcy Court for the District of Idaho; American Bankruptcy Institute; and Washington State Bar Association. Appointments: Fellow in the American College of Bankruptcy; Listed in leading American publication.

**Publications:** Mr Prince has published articles and is a lecturer on topics of bankruptcy and commercial law. He also served as a visiting professor at the University of Idaho School of Law.

**Personal:** Received a JD from the University of California, Hastings College of the Law (1975) and a BA (magna cum laude) from Boise State College (1972).

## PURSLEY, Kenneth
Givens Pursley LLP, Boise
208 388 1200
*Recommended in Real Estate*

## RILEY, Richard
Hawley Troxell Ennis & Hawley LLP, Boise 208 344 6000
*Recommended in Corporate/Commercial*

## ROBINSON, Brent
Ling, Robinson & Walker, Rupert
208 436 4717
*Recommended in Bankruptcy*

## SINCLAIR, Walter
Stoel Rives LLP, Boise
208 389 9000
*Recommended in Litigation*

## SMITH, Bruce
Moore Smith Buxton & Turke, Boise
202 331 1807
*Recommended in Natural Resources*

## SQUYRES, Newal
Holland & Hart LLP, Boise
208 342 5000
nsquyres@hollandhart.com
*Recommended in Litigation*

**Practice Areas:** Senior Litigation Partner practicing in a wide variety of complex civil litigation, including False Claims Act, commercial, intellectual property, products liability, construction, insurance coverage and bad faith, employment, aviation, and personal injury. Handled and tried cases before state courts in Idaho and Federal Courts in Idaho, Washington, California, Delaware and Pennsylvania.

**Prof. Memberships:** Member of the American Bar Association (litigation section), and Idaho State Bar (founding member of ADR section).

**Career:** Admitted to the Texas (1972) and Idaho (1974) Bars; the US District Court, District of Idaho (1974); US Court of Appeals, Fifth (1972) and Ninth Circuits (1980); law clerk, US Court of Appeals, 5th Circuit (1972-74); personal staff of US Attorney General Griffin Bell ,in the Office of Legal Counsel (1977-79); Faculty, University of Idaho Law School, Trial Advocacy Clinic. Mr Squyres is a frequent speaker on trial preparation and technique and is the Managing Partner of the Boise office of Holland & Hart LLP.

**Personal:** Received a JD (with honors) in 1972 and a BA in 1968 from Texas Tech University.

## TOLLEFSON, Gregory
Stoel Rives LLP, Boise
208 389 9000
*Recommended in Employment*

## WAGAHOFF DALE, Candy
Hall, Farley, Oberrecht & Blanton, PA, Boise 208 395 8500
*Recommended in Employment*

## WHITE, Robert
Givens Pursley LLP, Boise
208 388 1200
*Recommended in Employment*

## How lawyers are ranked

Every year we carry out thousands of in-depth interviews with clients and lawyers in order to assess the reputations and expertise of business lawyers across the USA. Chambers rankings and editorial are referred to extensively by General Counsel and other purchasers of legal services who look to our recommendations when choosing their lawyers.

# ANTITRUST

### Antitrust
#### Leading Firms

**1** KIRKLAND & ELLIS LLP *Chicago*
MAYER, BROWN, ROWE & MAW LLP *Chicago*
SIDLEY AUSTIN LLP *Chicago*

**2** EIMER STAHL KLEVORN & SOLBERG LLP *Chicago*
FREEMAN, FREEMAN & SALZMAN *Chicago*
MUCH SHELIST FREED DENENBERG *Chicago*
WINSTON & STRAWN LLP *Chicago*

**3** BAKER & MCKENZIE *Chicago*
BELL, BOYD & LLOYD LLC *Chicago*
HOWREY LLP *Chicago*
MCDERMOTT WILL & EMERY *Chicago*
SONNENSCHEIN NATH & ROSENTHAL LLP *Chicago*
SPERLING & SLATER *Chicago*

**4** FREEBORN & PETERS *Chicago*
JENNER & BLOCK LLP *Chicago*
KATTEN MUCHIN ROSENMAN LLP *Chicago*
SCHOPF & WEISS *Chicago*

## Band 1

### Kirkland & Ellis LLP
See firm details p.875

**The Firm:** A "*natural leader*" in the field, this firm generates the type of "*substantive antitrust experience that gets tremendous results for clients.*" The firm's strong suit is litigation, and this group approaches projects with a mentality consistent with its "*top-tier trial expertise.*" Its "*premier litigators*" raise the bar on such cases as cartel competition, monopolization and IP-related issues. The group also takes the lead on criminal defense, handling an abundance of cases with an antitrust element. On the transactional side, the corporate department's glut of private equity and venture capital clients helps produce a substantial amount of M&A-related work, much of it with an international flavor. The group's reach stretches way beyond state borders and forms part of an integrated network that tackles matters nationwide and globally. Clients concur that the firm "*brings to its cases a realistic overview that is both professional and effective.*"

**The Lawyers:** Andrew Langan (see p.840) drew compliments for being a "*fine trial lawyer*" with experience acting on high-stake class actions, multidistrict litigation and products liability cases across the commercial arena. Langan is especially active in antitrust litigation and trade regulation, where his workload includes competition disputes, price-fixing allegations and unfair trading cases. Recently he has acted as lead counsel for GM in five statewide consumer and commercial class actions. Commentators highlighted his "*outstanding level of client responsiveness,*" with one saying: "*He's someone you can rely on to always go the extra mile.*" James Mutchnik (see p.847) springs readily to mind as an "*aggressive, highly ethical*" criminal defense attorney who works on cases with a substantive antitrust element. In addition, he stands out in the commercial field where he enjoys a steady diet of M&A: he represented Bain Capital in securing antitrust clearance of its acquisition of Toys 'R' Us, a deal valued in excess of $8 billion. In a separate matter, Mutchnik led GMT Group in its $350 million sale to First Data Corporation. As well as his "*practically applied, substantive well of knowledge,*" one interviewee appreciated both the way he "*understands what the client needs to solve his problems and his success at interacting with management.*" According to peers, **Robert Robertson** (see p.852) is "*a tough litigator who brings an extra perspective through his strong theoretical bearing.*" His FTC enforcement background, which included a stint as senior litigation counsel for the Bureau of Competition, is highly prized in the industry. Robertson acted as lead trial counsel in the matter of Union Oil Company of California, a standard-setting case based on Unocal's alleged monopolization of the technology market. His civil and criminal range of expertise also covers other unfair competition and merger investigations relating to cruise lines, software, pharmaceuticals and many other industries besides. "*First-rate*" younger partner **Daniel Laytin** (see p.840) impresses on antitrust and competition law while also displaying a comparable expertise in general commercial litigation. High-profile clients acknowledge: "*He's really smart and has a boundless supply of creative, new ideas.*"

**Clients/Work Highlights:** Dow AgroSciences; BP; GM; Illinois Tool Works; Kraft; 3M; Abbott Laboratories and Polaris Industries.

### Mayer, Brown, Rowe & Maw LLP
See firm details p.876

**The Firm:** Mayer Brown's Chicago office remains a firm favorite with clients across the country, not least because of the "*thorough and responsive service afforded by all levels of its antitrust group.*" Its combination of EU and US experience serves to position the firm highly in a competitive market, and its close links with the Washington, DC office contribute to a "*seamless service*" enjoyed by many clients. The group comes up trumps on bet-the-company litigation, including cartel enforcement and government investigations. In terms of its counseling and transactional experience, it is championed for its handling of acquisitions and joint ventures and for its advice on distribution and franchising matters. Drawing upon a robust corporate and M&A practice, the firm generates much work and further benefits from the combined insights of practitioners in related areas such as IP, employment, IT and insurance coverage. Clients relish this "*deep well of antitrust specialists,*" confirming that the lawyers "*really understand all the facets of business inside out.*"

**The Lawyers:** It is clear to clients that **Lee Abrams** (see p.817) is "*a true gentleman of noted brilliance.*" His established antitrust counseling and litigation practice "*has the breadth that others aspire to,*" and he is consistently involved in matters of the highest importance. The undisputed substance of his practice was confirmed by his lead role in the ChoiceParts antitrust litigation, a matter which was ultimately settled in September 2005. Additionally, Abrams defended News Corporation and its subsidiary News America Marketing in a monopolization case. In that instance, he was lead counsel in the trial court and, after four years of litigation, argued the appeal in the Seventh Circuit. Abrams continues to be lead trial counsel for News Corporation in an antitrust case in the District of New Jersey. **Andrew Marovitz** (see p.843), an "*extremely skilful young partner,*" works at the forefront of complex antitrust and commercial litigation. The vigorous enforcement of cartel activity, both private and public, remains a key aspect of his practice. Marovitz represented BASF in the vitamin antitrust litigation, one of the largest price-fixing cases ever filed and an example of the increasingly international and statewide dimensions of his work. He also served as counsel to ANGUS Chemical in its successful defense of Sherman Act litigation, the primary federal antitrust law that was established to put an end to companies conspiring with competitors to fix prices. Clients termed **Mark McLaughlin** (see p.844) a "*dynamic guy with a great courtroom*"

presence." His experience leads him to litigate weighty antitrust cases involving a variety of industries, including monopolization claims, price-fixing and price discrimination matters. He represented Ryerson Tull in defense of a group boycott claim asserted by an aluminum manufacturer. In addition, his general litigation prowess includes securities work for CIBC in connection with its exposure to the collapses of Enron and Global Crossing. Market sources appreciate the pragmatic approach of **Robert Finke** (see p.829), claiming his "*good business sense stands alongside an extensive knowledge of structural antitrust issues.*" He has lately concentrated his efforts in antitrust counseling, with respect to M&A, pricing, distribution and joint ventures, particularly in the steel and marine industries. Finke acted as counsel to Brunswick in its acquisition of several boat companies, including those of Genmar Industries. Clients agree: "*We have a lot of confidence in his opinion.*"
**Clients/Work Highlights:** Angus Chemical; United States Golf Association; Ford; Ryerson Tull and News Corporation.

## Sidley Austin LLP
See firm details p.883
**The Firm:** "*Responsive, skilled and incredibly knowledgeable,*" clients flock to this leading group of antitrust litigators and counselors. As a team, it is looked upon equally favorably for all aspects of antitrust law. Its litigation prowess is well developed in price-fixing, monopolization and price discrimination matters, but the regulatory side is far from neglected with advice being regularly proffered to companies in search of antitrust compliance programs. Clients state the group "*brings a fresh energy to the matter in hand,*" noting that the "*level of communication the lawyers maintain exceeds expectation.*" Among its significant matters, the group represented Citibank in an alleged foreign currency price-fixing case and represented Johnson & Johnson in matters across the USA. It has also advised numerous pharmaceutical companies on pricing, IP and patent-related antitrust work.
**The Lawyers:** The well-respected **Thomas Ryan** (see p.854) won distinction for his antitrust and business counseling and his parallel expertise in litigation. His "*smart and savvy*" manner endears him to clients and peers alike, while the scope of his practice allows him to operate with ease across both geographical borders and diverse subject matters. Clients praised **John Treece** (see p.861) as "*clever and strategic,*" claiming "*he's great with detail and an excellent writer.*" His mastery of monopolization cases has led him to act for such clients as Microsoft, which he represented in a monopolization and patent case brought by an audio-delivery software company. Treece is also currently representing Johnson & Johnson in a series of price-bundling allegations and a separate tying case concerning the vendor practice of requiring customers of one product to buy others. In addition, he has substantial experience in IP litigation and patent antitrust work where he has represented Kimberley-Clark and AT&T. It is recognized that **Jack Bierig** (see p.820) "*inspires confidence with his calm assurance.*" Working in partnership with the client to identify and explain the relevant issues, Bierig concentrates his energy on the representation of trade and professional associations, work which has recently included dealings with realtor associations and the AMA.
**Clients/Work Highlights:** Johnson & Johnson; Microsoft; AT&T; Aon; GlaxoSmithKline and BP.

## Band 2

## Eimer Stahl Klevorn & Solberg LLP
See firm details p.871
**The Firm:** Commentators persistently endorsed the caliber of this firm's antitrust professionals, claiming that "*for a smaller group they are unmatched in the market.*" The boutique practice is "*one of the leaders*" in Chicago, according to clients, a base from where it can mobilize resources to tackle complex cases across the country. Its investment in technology means the firm is well placed to handle multifaceted matters, but commentators note that it still retains the personal touch thanks to the attitude of its "*enthusiastic and helpful*" attorneys. The firm is known for its effective regulatory advice, antitrust litigation and strategic trial strength.
**The Lawyers:** That **Nate Eimer** (see p.828) was a driving force in founding and forging the identity of this firm is "*a testament to his unique skills, abilities and confidence,*" say peers. He continues to be a valuable ingredient in the firm's success, due in part to his "*compelling persona,*" and is agreed to be "*a skilled advocate with pronounced strategic sense.*" An enviable client list includes Union Carbide, for which Eimer has acted as counsel on major multidistrict price-fixing cases. He also recently represented Bank of New York against United Airlines in matters arising from the airline's bankruptcy proceedings. Clients championed **Andrew Klevorn** (see p.839) for his deep litigation experience and his "*calm but compelling demeanor.*" He has recently had a role working with Union Carbide in its claims against shipping companies alleging overcharging. Competitors acknowledge that **David Stahl** (see p.858) can "*really try cases; he is extremely smart and adept in court.*" He enjoys the kudos that 30 years' experience in commercial and antitrust litigation can bring and has worked on a wide variety of matters from price-fixing and securities law violations to class actions and construction disputes.
**Clients/Work Highlights:** Dow Chemical; Corn Products International; Citigroup; Union Carbide; Land O'Lakes and AmerisourceBergen.

## Freeman, Freeman & Salzman
**The Firm:** According to clients, the experienced lawyers of this boutique firm "*have a reputation for producing top-class work.*" A significant string to the firm's bow is provided by its representation of opt-out plaintiffs against manufacturers and producers of, among other things, vitamins, liquid carbon dioxide and sorbates. Significant decisions obtained in such cases have spawned groundbreaking rulings across the country and in foreign jurisdictions. The group also has a successful track record in defending corporations in antitrust cases.
**The Lawyers:** The "*wonderful*" **Lee Freeman** "*has had a great deal of success as a plaintiff's lawyer,*" according to market sources. He remains highly respected in the industry for his antitrust and complex commercial litigation work and is further noted for his appellate advocacy. Attorneys agree that he "*effectively leads the firm*" and many report they would "*happily refer any client to him.*"
**Clients/Work Highlights:** Cargill; Clear Channel; Kraft; Chicago Mercantile Exchange; Boeing; Coca-Cola; Dean Foods and PepsiCo.

## Much Shelist Freed Denenberg Ament & Rubenstein, PC
**The Firm:** According to clients, this is a "*quality firm among the plaintiffs' antitrust Bar.*" Dominance in class action and contingent fee litigation distinguishes a group whose emphasis is on cross-disciplinary work. It has obtained judgments and settlements in fructose litigation, vitamins and brand-name prescription drugs. As a continuation of its specialization, the group has been increasingly involved in the civil side of international cartel cases brought by the federal government. The expansion

of the team and its continually strong national presence augment its success in this field.

**The Lawyers:** Commentators call **Michael Freed** the "*prince of plaintiff antitrust law*," and he is "*highly respected in court for his substance and impressive track record.*" Freed continues to be involved in civil antitrust class actions, having made particular strides in the healthcare industry acting on matters against prescription benefits managers and on a case involving the salary of resident physicians.

**Clients/Work Highlights:** Pharmacy Freedom Fund; Euromarket Designs; Vita Foods; Barry's Drugs and Endler's Pharmacy.

## Winston & Strawn LLP
See firm details p.886

**The Firm:** This "*fine firm*" stands out for its "*commitment to pure antitrust*" and its strong trial abilities. Its modus operandi is litigation, where its reputation is cemented by the presence of Dan Webb, a "*star lawyer*" in the general commercial litigation/white-collar crime section. Antitrust, which falls within the litigation practice group, is one of the firm's most established areas of concentration and competitors are quick to point out that the group is "*more than just one guy.*" Cases are covered on both the criminal and civil side and include monopoly, price-fixing and antitrust claims arising from patent and unfair trade issues.

**The Lawyers:** **Mark McCareins** (see p.844) "*has a fine reputation in big cases due to his excellent advocacy skills.*" Cases of note include his representation of Smurfit-Stone Container, involving price-fixing allegations against it and others in the container industry.

**Clients/Work Highlights:** Marsulex; Smurfit-Stone Container; Abbott Laboratories; Metals Service Center Institute; Wyeth and Chicago Bridge & Iron.

## Band 3

## Baker & McKenzie
See firm details p.866

**The Firm:** According to competitors, the Chicago office of this firm "*now has an antitrust practice to be recognized,*" following the arrival of lawyers from Gardner Carton & Douglas. Overall, its antitrust and competition caseload is substantial and far-reaching with more than 200 lawyers focusing on such matters worldwide. In Chicago itself the team is developing as a cohesive unit, integrating the skills of its incoming attorneys and tackling work across a broad canvas that takes in transactions, anticompetition prevention, strategies for authority investigations and compliance and business policy development. Business disputes are also covered with experts in the litigation department ready to step up to the mark to try cases in a wide variety of industries.

**The Lawyers:** **Roxane Busey** (see p.823) has added a global dimension to her already broad practice with her recent move to Baker & McKenzie. Known and respected as a counselor and strategist, Busey draws

praise for her "*great depth, common sense and judgment,*" all of which are bolstered by her "*outstanding contacts with state antitrust enforcement agencies.*" **Thomas Campbell** is a "*strong litigator with a broad range of skills.*" He concentrates his practice on the trial of antitrust actions and business disputes.

**Clients/Work Highlights:** The firm services clients across the USA and the world, covering all major industries and concerns.

## Bell, Boyd & Lloyd LLC

**The Firm:** This firm offers "*perpetually relevant, wide-ranging antitrust advice*" on both the litigation and counseling fronts. Its group of 22 lawyers scores points for its work on complex class action antitrust lawsuits and other large-scale litigation, including many matters relating to the pharmaceutical industry. Further strength lies in its transactional counseling capability and capacity for handling antitrust cases with an IP flavor. The team has been increasingly focused on work of a substantial cross-border nature, with global distribution issues and international transactions being particularly high on the agenda.

**The Lawyers:** The "*highly respected*" **Michael Sennett** continues to enjoy a "*great career as an antitrust adviser,*" sources ascertain. He counsels on mergers, investigations and acquisitions and is active on a multiplicity of class actions.

**Clients/Work Highlights:** Baxter International; Caremark; Cardinal Health; Fortune Brands; California Dental Association and OfficeMax.

## Howrey LLP

**The Firm:** A "*fine assembly of antitrust lawyers*" sits within this firm's commercial litigation and trial practice. It retains a strong commitment to the upper end of antitrust and business litigation, running an efficient trial shop that tackles a plethora of commercial disputes in federal and state courts. Clients also appreciate the group's ability to advise and counsel on the full gamut of antitrust matters. The team here may be smaller than some but it is part of a wider network of offices. The firm as a whole has an established expertise in Washington, DC and boasts a presence in Europe. It is currently defending a putative nationwide class action alleging antitrust violations in the sale of sulphuric acid. In a separate case, the team is defending the former directors and officers of Divine in regard to fiduciary duty litigation and multiple securities class actions.

**The Lawyers:** "*No question about it,*" sources report, managing partner **Joel Chefitz** is "*smart, knowledgeable and runs things well.*" He splits his time between antitrust and general business litigation. As an illustration of his antitrust commitment, Chefitz acted for State Farm to obtain a defeat of antitrust claims brought by United Airlines and its unsecured creditors' committee in the UAL bankruptcy. His commercial litigation includes acting for Wyeth in defense of a nationwide consumer fraud class action by purchasers of prescription drugs. Chefitz is widely acknowledged by clients to "*take great pains to understand our business and give context to his counseling.*"

**Clients/Work Highlights:** Divine; Wyeth; State Farm; Chicago Board Options Exchange; Koch Industries; marchFIRST and Zebra Technologies.

## McDermott Will & Emery
See firm details p.878

**The Firm:** This group drew commendation for its effective strategy of cross-staffing work via a network of offices across the country. Much of the practice is centered in Washington, DC but a small band of talented lawyers in Chicago drew special mention from commentators. Sources noted that the firm's standout expertise in healthcare informs its antitrust practice; it represents hospitals and integrated healthcare systems, health insurers and physician practice groups among others. The group also deals with a variety of counseling matters, litigation and M&A outside the health arena.

**The Lawyers:** Mostly known to the market as a "*leading healthcare guy,*" **David Marx** (see p.843) takes on substantial antitrust cases in this area, including ongoing matters for West Tennessee Healthcare. However, as head of the Chicago antitrust and competition group, his practice is not limited to healthcare alone. Also active in civil and criminal antitrust litigation and counseling, distribution and trade regulation matters, Marx undertakes matters relating to a variety of industries.

**Clients/Work Highlights:** West Tennessee Healthcare; Stora Enso North America; Mountain View Hospital; Albertsons and Provena Health.

## Sonnenschein Nath & Rosenthal LLP
See firm details p.884

**The Firm:** "*Experts in their field*" who are forthcoming with "*pragmatic advice that is well thought out and perceptive,*" these Chicago antitrust lawyers stand out to their peers. The group has an historic strength in distribution and vertical restraint issues and is a burgeoning presence in mergers and joint ventures. It also garners respect for its development of antitrust compliance programs and advice on federal sentencing guidelines in the light of increased penalties and regulatory scrutiny. Clients admire the lawyers here because they are "*not simply legal theorists but give hands-on directions and input.*" Sources also note the "*great cross-practice communication and support*" that the firm's interlinked offices provide.

**The Lawyers:** Clients praised the wide-ranging experience of **Bob Joseph** (see p.837), a "*skilled antitrust counselor*" whose expertise is also sought in the courtroom. "*He is the best at explaining the vagaries of risk assessment,*" said one client, while others pointed to his professional and practical approach. Joseph takes on distribution and compliance counseling for major clients as part of his generalist antitrust practice and has litigated extensively. **Alan Silberman** (see p.856), the undisputed dean of the firm, is believed by many clients to be "*one of the preeminent antitrust lawyers in the country.*" They say his "*instinctive grasp of the issues enables him to give immediate feedback*" and they appreciate the "*extra layer of credibility he brings to proceedings.*" Though his historic strengths lie in litigation and franchise law, Silberman's practice has evolved to become strongly counsel-based, giving advice and analytical support on potential mergers and the avoidance of antitrust minefields. **Sanford Pastroff** (see p.849) has "*excellent credentials in the industry*" and captures clients' attention with his broad-based litigation and counseling practice. He boasts a range of antitrust expertise from healthcare and insurance to class actions and the structuring of joint ventures.

**Clients/Work Highlights:** Sara Lee; Prudential Real Estate; SE Johnson; McDonald's; Allstate; ChoiceParts and Boeing.

## Sperling & Slater

**The Firm:** This "*small but dedicated*" firm is "*on the way up,*" according to sources. The boutique of around 20 lawyers specializes in litigation and wins distinction in large part due to its "*creative and persistent*" representation of plaintiffs. As well as its antitrust focus the firm also stands out on business litigation, with commentators stating that the lawyers are "*a delight to deal with on either side of the case.*" The team represents retailers, including major grocery store chains, in price-fixing claims against the fees charged by credit card companies. Another notable engagement involves an antitrust and contract dispute on behalf of Bering Truck.

**The Lawyers:** According to sources, **Paul Slater** is a "*lawyers' lawyer and solid as a rock.*" He is equally comfortable working for both plaintiffs and defendants and in all cases "*thinks imaginatively and creatively for his clients.*" In addition to his well-founded practice, Slater has taught antitrust law at Northwestern University School of Law for more than 20 years.

**Clients/Work Highlights:** The firm acts for both plaintiffs and defendants, covering public and private entities and a variety of industry fields.

## Band 4

## Freeborn & Peters

**The Firm:** Described by peers as "*up-and-coming and increasingly involved,*" this strong regional firm scores points across the board in antitrust and trade regulation. The group's scope of practice takes in both litigation and counseling. Clients have been particularly impressed by its "*success in presenting advice that is not simply couched in terms of yes or no; it provides helpful solutions to real life problems.*" Typical matters include distribution and retail strategy, price-fixing, regulatory filings and the implementa-

tion of mergers, strategic alliances and joint ventures. Its lawyers have recently represented Falconbridge, a Canadian mining company, in obtaining US regulatory clearance for its acquisition by Inco, a Canadian minerals company. In the litigation field, the group was defense counsel for companies involved in a class action alleging a price-fixing conspiracy in the sulphuric acid market.

**The Lawyers:** Joining the tables this year, **Jeffery Cross** is described by peers as "*an experienced antitrust lawyer who is first and foremost an effective litigator.*" He represents a variety of corporations throughout the country on antitrust and trade regulation issues. Chair of the group **Eugene Zelek** is rated for his "*collaborative, responsive and energetic communication style.*" Clients add: "*He not only responds to requests for advice immediately, he also provides creative options for addressing the issue at hand.*" His work on mergers and pricing and distribution issues is particularly highlighted.

**Clients/Work Highlights:** Coca-Cola; McKinsey & Company; Holley Performance Products; Nintendo of America and BNSF Railway.

## Jenner & Block LLP

See firm details p.873

**The Firm:** Clients of this full-service national powerhouse are impressed by its litigation prowess and the antitrust expertise that has flowered from it. Its antitrust litigation often involves complex multiparty actions; the group represents US and foreign affiliates of the German Schunk Group in defending class action price-fixing allegations. Compliance counseling also figures for a group whose experience spans industries from healthcare and defense contracting to telecom and manufacturing.

**The Lawyers:** Norman Hirsch is chair of the firm's antitrust and trade regulation practice. He focuses on litigation, both in the field of antitrust and other complex matters, and also counsels businesses on regulatory and compliance requirements.

**Clients/Work Highlights:** Blue Cross and Blue Shield Association; American Maize-Products Company; Mitsubishi Paper Mills; Nippon Denkyoku; Chicago Board of Trade and GE.

## Katten Muchin Rosenman LLP

See firm details p.874

**The Firm:** Although within a firm recognized for its substantial input in the healthcare market, the ten partners here who concentrate on antitrust work drew strong praise from commentators for their work generally. While much of their output has an

undoubted healthcare bias, they have carved a considerable reputation for counseling in various industries and sectors. For example, the team recently represented a French manufacturer of carbon products in a class action alleging price-fixing among various foreign manufacturers. On the compliance front, the firm's expertise involves developing plans for major insurance companies and physician hospitals, as well as representing health systems, technical companies and manufacturing concerns in their regulatory dealings and potential business transactions.

**The Lawyers:** **Laura Keidan Martin** (see p.843), cochair of the group, is "*respected as an antitrust counselor, primarily in the healthcare realm.*" She also takes care of general antitrust transactions, mergers and investigations.

**Clients/Work Highlights:** Among its cadre of clients, healthcare and financial companies dominate.

## Schopf & Weiss

**The Firm:** This "*very successful boutique*" collects praise for its strength in business litigation. The four attorneys specializing in antitrust, part of a wider team of more than 20 general litigators, try cases for both plaintiffs and defendants in federal and state courts in a number of industries. The group earned considerable market respect for its recent $32 million jury verdict and judgment for Goss International against TKS in violations of the Antidumping Act. Its experience includes price-fixing, monopolization cases and breach of contract.

**The Lawyers:** Founding partner **Willam Schopf** (see p.855) is known to clients and peers as a "*consummate trial lawyer; a great strategist and a lawyer capable of making complex matters understandable.*" His experience is not limited to antitrust as he marshals a substantial cadre of general commercial litigation cases.

**Clients/Work Highlights:** Goss International; Crawford Supply; Exide; Air Liquide and Cingular Wireless.

## Other Notable Practitioners

**Randy Hack** of Lord, Bissell & Brook merits a place in the table, according to market sources, for the "*substantial breadth of his practice coupled with an ability to dig into the detail of antitrust matters.*"

# BANKING & FINANCE

| | Banking & Finance<br>Leading Firms |
|---|---|
| 1 | MAYER, BROWN, ROWE & MAW LLP *Chicago*<br>SIDLEY AUSTIN LLP *Chicago* |
| 2 | LATHAM & WATKINS LLP *Chicago*<br>WINSTON & STRAWN LLP *Chicago* |
| 3 | CHAPMAN AND CUTLER LLP *Chicago*<br>GOLDBERG, KOHN, BELL, BLACK *Chicago*<br>KATTEN MUCHIN ROSENMAN LLP *Chicago*<br>KIRKLAND & ELLIS LLP *Chicago*<br>MCDERMOTT WILL & EMERY *Chicago*<br>SKADDEN, ARPS *Chicago*<br>VEDDER, PRICE, KAUFMAN & KAMMHOLZ *Chicago* |
| 4 | BAKER & MCKENZIE *Chicago*<br>DUANE MORRIS LLP *Chicago*<br>NEAL, GERBER & EISENBERG LLP *Chicago*<br>SCHIFF HARDIN LLP *Chicago*<br>SCHWARTZ, COOPER, GREENBERGER *Chicago* |

## Band 1

### Mayer, Brown, Rowe & Maw LLP

See firm details p.876

**The Firm:** This "*remarkable firm*" continues to be a leading light regionally and beyond. Benefiting from an "*enviable global presence,*" in Chicago its "*size and breadth*" allows it to enjoy a diet of "*the largest finance transactions.*" Working "*without pretensions,*" a carefully structured team approach fosters "*a good spirit*" and is one factor in the firm's success. So too is the ability to handle a broad spectrum of work, including secured and unsecured lending, project finance, and international leveraged finance. The group is praised for its flexibility in an evolving Chicago market; it has established itself as "*hands down the best securitization practice,*" with issuances and asset-backed lending making up an increasingly large proportion of the workload. The team's structured finance capacity is "*a cut above,*" according to clients, who particularly value attorneys' expertise on "*the cross-border elements of transactions.*" Work in emerging markets, particularly Latin America, also continues to feature prominently, and the ability to administer cutting-edge regulatory advice was also cited as a major strength.

**The Lawyers:** "*Sharp deal-doer*" **Rob Baptista** (see p.819) brings a "*thoughtful, calm and confident*" manner to bear on a broad spread of general finance transactions that include secured, unsecured and syndicated loans. He is primarily associated with complex multijurisdictional work for lenders, but also has a significant borrower practice and is currently advising a major REIT on its credit facility of over $2 billion, spanning six countries. His ability "*not to over-lawyer, just to get the transaction done,*" delights clients and inspires the respect of contemporaries. The "*weighty*" **Doug Doetsch** (see p.826) is "*simply a great attorney,*" according to sources, who noted his substantial emerging markets expertise.

Focused on restructurings, securitizations and infrastructure financings across Latin America, he followed on from last year's work on the IPO of Mexican homebuilder Homex, the only such company listed on the NYSE, by representing a lender in the financing of the $202 million Corredor Sur toll road project in Panama. Both "*a proactive businessman and an excellent lawyer,*" **Paul Forrester** (see p.830) impresses clients with a range of skills: "*a problem solver;*" "*an effective negotiator;*" "*reality-focused;*" this man "*thinks of everything.*" Dividing his time between CDO and project finance transactions, Forrester has lately been representing a client involved in the proposed $20 billion, 3,000-mile North Slope pipeline in Alaska, and is currently advising Horizon Wind Power on the development and financing of the proposed 400 MW Arrowsmith wind power project at Bloomington, one of the largest such projects in the USA. A composed and thoughtful approach to refinancings and secured and unsecured loan transactions means that the "*wonderful*" **Ami Scott** (see p.855) debuts in the table this year. Peers say: "*She does her job very well,*" and clients "*think the world of her.*"

**Clients/Work Highlights:** Bank of America; JPMorgan Chase; Citigroup; Wachovia; Homex; ABN AMRO; Jefferies; Merrill Lynch; ProLogis; Bank of Montreal; Cohen Bros & Company; Gulf Stream Asset Management and Textron Financial.

### Sidley Austin LLP

See firm details p.883

**The Firm:** Long renowned for its "*top*" finance practice, Sidley once again drew fulsome praise for its "*pervasive*" market reach, true "*breadth of practice*" and "*team-oriented*" feel, leaving "*no question that they belong with the best.*" It is a mark of the esteem in which the team's complement of "*hands-on, together, business lawyers*" are held that a competitor reflected: "*You want the best on the other side and they are the best. If I see I'm against them I know the transaction will go smoothly and cordially.*" Closely associated with the New York and California offices (the latter particularly for hedge fund work), the team excels in representing major banks and lending institutions in highly complex and syndicated financings. JPMorgan Chase, Citibank, Bank of America and ABN AMRO regularly instruct the firm on such matters, which include secured and unsecured loans and other asset-based lending. They are also recognized and respected for possessing "*huge strength*" in securitization matters, and clients told researchers: "*When it comes to multicurrency, multicountry deals, you choose them.*"

**The Lawyers:** Bringing "*thoughtful, responsive and incisive*" qualities to substantial transactions, **James Clark** (see p.824) is praised by clients as "*a world-class lawyer*" and cited by competitors as "*first choice in conflict.*" "*Smart, practical and good with clients,*" assignments of note include a multicurrency letter of credit agreement for Coca-Cola Enterprises, and a credit agreement for a $1.1 billion multicurrency

revolving credit facility for Harley-Davidson Funding. He also continues to advise key client JPMorgan on a range of commercial and financing issues. "*Stellar abilities*" in secured and unsecured syndicated lending, and a fresh approach, define the "*popular*" **Michael Gold** (see p.832), according to a range of sources. He acts for banks and commercial lenders on debt restructurings, acquisition financings and workouts. The "*spectacularly talented*" **James Looman** (see p.841) impresses with his sophisticated work both for banks and corporate borrowers. His practice incorporates equipment leasing transactions. Widely regarded as "*a dean of secured lending,*" senior statesman **Bruce Bernstein** (see p.820) has "*a remarkably active practice*" advising banks and lenders on restructurings, and capital and secured loans. His vast experience allows him to offer impressive risk management and lender liability advice, and peers laud him as "*phenomenal.*"

**Clients/Work Highlights:** The group regularly acts for all the major US banks, including JPMorgan Chase; Bank of America; Citibank and Wachovia; and has a growing range of institutional investor and hedge fund clients. Other clients include GE Capital; Caterpillar; Barclays Bank; Merrill Lynch and Dean Foods.

## Band 2

### Latham & Watkins LLP

**The Firm:** With a finance and bankruptcy team that "*makes a big splash,*" the Chicago office of this international operation is distinguished by its "*broad practice*" and "*involvement in some of the largest transactions.*" It is considered by some to be "*edging toward the top tier,*" and sources were unanimous in the view that the truly distinctive feature of the expanding team is its impressive international capacity. In the past twelve months, lawyers from the state have been involved with matters in the UK, continental Europe, Korea and Australia. Although increasingly occupied by cross-jurisdictional work, at home in the USA the team is "*a major player*" when it comes to lender representation; new instructions from UBS and Goldman Sachs and a resurgence in work for JPMorgan are all recent feathers in the team's cap. The "*very strong*" team of "*characterful*" attorneys is particularly noted for its expertise in advising a variety of lenders on complex loan structurings, and peers were quick to highlight strength in second-lien and mezzanine finance markets. Benefiting from close links with its large New York office, the Chicago group also has an impressive bankruptcy and restructuring practice.

**The Lawyers:** Cochair of the firm's banking practice group and the Chicago finance department, **David Crumbaugh** is hailed as an "*extraordinarily talented finance lawyer.*" Commentators say he is "*focused on being as effective as possible – he clears the obstacles that impede business.*" These characteristics explain a "*loyal client following*" that relies on the "*instant credibility*" he brings to midtier, asset-based lending, commercial finance and insolvency matters. Recently, Crumbaugh advised GE Capital in its $75 million US and European term loans and revolving credit facilities for Lincoln Industrial. Respected as a vastly experienced "*mentor*" figure, senior practitioner **Donald Schwartz** remains active in a wide range of transactions, including structured, lease and project financings. Although he also handles restructuring and insolvency issues, sources reserved especial praise for his work on substantial overseas transactions, including a AUD190 million multi-tranche senior secured credit facility and $35 million senior secured facility from UBS and National Australia Bank. He also recently advised UBS and Goldman Sachs as joint arrangers in a $1.9 billion secured financing to NewPage, relating to the purchase of paper manufacturing facilities and related timberlands. "*First-rate*" **James Doran** is "*good, solid and stands out*" for his skill as an archi-

tect of asset-based lending, structured finance and syndicated loan transactions. Doran has played a crucial role in the consolidation of the firm's relationship with Merrill Lynch. Renowned for his impact in the midmarket, **Philip Perzek** recently advised GE Capital on a $205 million loan and revolving credit facility, as well as Chatham Capital Management II on a $125 million revolving credit facility. He also represents second-tier and mezzanine lenders.

Clients/Work Highlights: Freeport Financial; Goldman Sachs; UBS Investment Bank; Wachovia Capital Finance; Citigroup; RBC Centura; National Australia Bank; Merrill Lynch Capital; GE Capital; ABN AMRO and LaSalle Bank.

## Winston & Strawn LLP

See firm details p.886

**The Firm:** Long recognized for its representation of lenders, the Chicago office of this international firm boasts "*a great team*" with broad experience and an increasing profile among borrowers. A "*robust*" and "*punchy*" group of attorneys impresses clients with its expertise in mid and upper midmarket transactions, particularly when it comes to underwriting, leading and arranging domestic credit facilities or syndicated finance. The team's pragmatic, business-oriented approach allowed it to stand out in the eyes of sources, who commented: "*They recognize that you don't always try to do the perfect deal but you do get results.*" While debt portfolio acquisition and bankruptcies feature large, the team is also developing a burgeoning fund formation practice.

**The Lawyers:** Lauded as "*just the best*," **Greg Murray** (see p.847) handles a variety of commercial finance transactions and complex multicurrency deals for lenders. Peers were swift to praise this "*senior and seasoned*" practitioner, but for clients it is all about Murray's trademark "*creative, bright, thoughtful, practical*" approach; according to them he offers "*the added value of unique ideas and insight.*" Additionally renowned for insurance matters, Murray recently advised long-time clients JPMorgan Chase and JPMorgan Securities as joint lead arrangers on a $2.1 billion letter of credit facility for ING America Insurance Holdings. He also represented JPMorgan Chase on a $1.5 billion acquisition bridge facility and $600 million permanent facility for Wrigley. "*Smart and classy*" **Chuck Boehrer** is admired for his work on syndicated and leveraged loans, particularly those with an international aspect. Representing both borrowers and lenders, in the past year he has advised Deutsche Bank as agent and lead arranger on a $1.3 billion multicurrency, multijurisdictional secured credit facility, and Stryker on its $1 billion revolving and term credit facility. Clients and competitors all agree that **Ron Jacobson** (see p.836) is "*a truly talented guy.*" Predominantly working on midmarket leveraged finance, structured investment and mezzanine financings for agent banks or lenders such as ABN AMRO and LaSalle Bank, he also represents clients in the creation of structured debt vehicles and on debt portfolio acquisitions.

Clients/Work Highlights: Bank of America;

Cinergy; Deutsche Bank; Harley-Davidson; Lear; Stryker; Treehouse Foods; JPMorgan Chase; Freeport Financial; ABN AMRO; LaSalle Bank and Aim Financial Corporation.

## Band 3

### Chapman and Cutler LLP

See firm details p.868

**The Firm:** Carrying a distinguished national reputation for bonds and public finance, lawyers in the Chicago office work closely with their counterparts in San Francisco and Salt Lake City on a whole range of finance-oriented matters, from bonds issuance and sports project financings to securitizations and syndicated loans. Locally, the finance team of roughly 38 "*user-friendly, solutions-oriented*" attorneys takes on securities, bank regulatory compliance and midmarket lender representation (in this instance benefiting from the firm's strong relationships with large insurers). Clients speak highly of the lawyers' close involvement in transactions and "*a mutually rewarding, responsive culture,*" which is characterized by "*technically competent, realistic and real-world business*" advice. Strong relationships with Harris (the primary US subsidiary of Bank of Montreal), ABN AMRO and Fifth Third Bank account for a significant proportion of the team's work, although corporate and sports finance matters also feature regularly.

**The Lawyers:** Sources enthused that "*great business acumen,*" "*outstanding command of legal issues,*" and "*practical creativity*" define **Ronald Rokosz**. He divides his time between work for two key clients. He recently represented Fifth Third Bank on a $350 million multicurrency revolving credit facility for a Cleveland-based US manufacturer. He also has a close relationship with ABN AMRO's national wholesale client services group and takes on highly specialized precious metals-related financings for the bank's New York-based diamond and jewelry group. In the past year, he has advised ABN AMRO on a $50 million secured revolving loan, banker's acceptance and gold consignment. A prominent figure on the Chicago finance scene, **Marc Franson** heads up the consumer banking practice and concentrates on bank M&A and the representation of financial institutions in matters such as consumer credit transactions. A recent highlight has been work on a credit card transaction involving a joint venture between two major banks, which in turn entailed the establishment and chartering of a credit card bank. He also has close relationships with Bank of Montreal and US subsidiary Harris.

Clients/Work Highlights: Other clients include Bank of New York, LaSalle Bank and Allstate Bank.

### Goldberg, Kohn, Bell, Black, Rosenbloom & Moritz, Ltd

**The Firm:** The relatively compact banking and finance team at this established Chicago outfit is widely considered to have "*cornered the market in midrank loan transactions; they're top-flight for*" commercial finance." Attorneys represent predominantly senior lenders on secured, asset and even cash flow-based transactions, drawing praise for their ability to "*work with all types of clients and personalities.*" Satisfied sources particularly valued the team's willingness to "*put all their resources at your disposal.*" The increasing popularity of mezzanine and second lien-financings has seen the team's activities in this area continue to grow, and while senior lending clients such as RBS and Dymas Capital Management have regularly engaged the firm, competitors note a marked increase in instructions from dedicated second-lien and mezzanine lenders.

**The Lawyers:** Principal of the commercial finance group, **David Mason** distinguishes himself as a "*talented, efficient and intelligent*" attorney who completes complex transactions quickly and with a minimum of fuss. Working extensively for key client Merrill Lynch, he has "*great support within the team.*" He also represents a number of midmarket banks and commercial lenders in asset-based and cash flow transactions. Less involved with restructurings and workouts in the past twelve months, Mason has increasingly been active in leveraged recapitalizations and transactions with an international element. **David Dranoff** is trusted by clients "*to get things done,*" and respected by peers for his "*intelligence – he knows his area inside out.*" Able to draw on 20 years of commercial finance experience, his broad practice incorporates cash flow and asset-based transactions for major banks and other financial institutions, as well as mezzanine financings. "*One of the deans of the asset-based finance Bar,*" and the firm's senior principal and chair of its commercial finance group, **Richard Kohn** is widely respected as "*just a terrific, tremendous lawyer.*" A driver behind Goldberg's growing capacity for international transactional work, he has prominence with the Commercial Finance Association, which is the national trade association of commercial finance lenders. He has represented the association in key proceedings before UNCITRAL.

**Clients/Work Highlights:** Madison Capital Funding; Dymas Capital Management; RBS; Antares Capital; Bank of America; Merrill Lynch; LaSalle Bank and GE Capital.

## Katten Muchin Rosenman LLP
See firm details p.874

**The Firm:** This well-regarded firm has seven offices spread across the USA. Its finance group is headquartered in Chicago, where a team of 24 attorneys keep client satisfaction riding high by "*getting deals done and not getting hung up on the details.*" Possessing a distinctively "*accessible culture, style and personality,*" the team primarily represents lenders, with competitors noting that it is highly visible in mid and upper midmarket transactions. One illustrative deal saw attorneys represent Antares Capital as agent and lead arranger on a $35 million revolving loan and $205 million term loan for national outdoor lifestyle products designer and marketer Bushnell Performance Optics. The team has been diversifying its practice over the past year, with a general increase in

mezzanine and second-lien financings prompting a wealth of new instructions from clients such as Caltius Mezzanine, Prism Mezzanine Fund and Midwest Mezzanine Funds. When it comes to such matters, clients reflected that they benefit from the firm's "*keen understanding of our relationship with the borrowers.*"

**The Lawyers:** Despite his being required to devote time to his duties as chair of the commercial finance practice, a wide variety of institutional and entrepreneurial clients "*think highly*" of **Stuart Shulruff** (see p.856) for his no-nonsense, hands-on approach to syndicated loans and mezzanine financings. In 2005, Shulruff led the team's representation of Antares Capital in providing a $13 million revolving loan and $118 million first-lien term loan to Dr. Leonard's Healthcare, and advised long-time client Merrill Lynch on secured revolving credit and term loan facilities for DESA LLC, totalling $210 million. **Michael Jacobson** (see p.836) continues to deserve his up-and-coming ranking, according to clients and competitors; he possesses the valuable "*ability to get parties focused on the point.*" His practice spans a broad range of borrower and senior lender representations, and in the past year he has increasingly taken the lead on mezzanine finance matters.

**Clients/Work Highlights:** Caltius Mezzanine; CapitalSource Finance; Dymas Capital Management; GE Capital; LaSalle Bank; Merrill Lynch Capital; Midwest Mezzanine Funds; Prairie Capital and Prism Mezzanine Fund.

## Kirkland & Ellis LLP
See firm details p.875

**The Firm:** This firm's stellar reputation for corporate and private equity work is widely acknowledged as being at the core of its "*preeminence on the borrower side of bank financing transactions in Chicago.*" Representing LBO and private equity clients, a team of more than 20 attorneys is admired by clients and respected by competitors for its capacity to take a tough stance in negotiations, sometimes bringing a distinctive "*adversarial style to deals.*" Lawyers handle the ongoing financing needs of major clients such as Madison Dearborn Partners, Exide Technologies and Summit Partners, while the presence of the firm's mammoth bankruptcy practice ensures the team is also busy with DIP and exit financing.

**The Lawyers:** **Andrew Kaufman** (see p.838) is head of the firm's financing and secured transactions practice, bringing "*a voice of reason*" as well as "*a knowledge of all the ins, outs and tricks of trade*" to a mix of buyout financing, structured transactions, general corporate and bankruptcy matters. His "*outstanding*" abilities ensure clients "*would use him for every transaction if possible.*" To give some examples of his work, he recently concluded advice to client Exide Technologies on its bankruptcy and continues to assist it in ongoing financing, and he has been representing Joy Global on a major credit facility. Two further Kirkland attorneys join the rankings this year as a result of commendation from competitors who acknowledge that "*they really stand out.*" **Chris**

Butler's (see p.823) practice focuses on secured and unsecured financing transactions, with an emphasis on leveraged financings and acquisitions. He acted for BainCapital in its acquisition of Toys 'R' Us, involving around $3.9 billion of bank financing. Meanwhile, the "*phenomenally talented*" **Maureen Sweeney** (see p.860) was praised for her varied work representing commercial lenders and private equity groups on bankruptcy matters, general corporate work, and secured and unsecured financings.

**Clients/Work Highlights:** Bank One: NRG Energy; Harnischfeger Industries; Greenwich Capital; Madison Dearborn Partners; World Omni Financial and Great Lakes Chemical.

## McDermott Will & Emery
See firm details p.878

**The Firm:** The 11-strong banking and finance team in the Chicago office of this international practice is a "*talented*" group, praised for offering clients "*New York-standard advice without the New York price tag.*" Representing an even spread of borrowers and lenders in midmarket transactions, the team has recently acted for Bank of America in connection with a $350 million syndicated revolving loan facility for Regis Corporation, and a $60 million revolving credit and term loan facility for Scholle and Vacumet. On the borrower side, attorneys represented Actuant on a $500 million credit agreement and The Heico Companies on a $400 million US and Canadian credit agreement, both agented by JPMorgan. In another deal they advised Eby-Brown on a $125 million revolving loan facility provided by LaSalle Bank.

**The Lawyers:** Widely admired as "*a very classy guy,*" **Bob McMenamin** (see p.844) is undoubtedly the engine of the team. After three decades in practice, he is "*experienced, thorough and knowledgeable,*" possessing an ability to be both "*practical and flexible*" that satisfies clients almost as much as his "*creative way of handling problems.*" McMenamin takes on syndicated loans, asset-based financings and leveraged acquisitions for borrowers and lenders. A highlight last year was his representation of air conditioning and bathroom fixtures manufacturer American Standard in connection with a $1 billion syndicated credit agreement.

**Clients/Work Highlights:** First Mercury; Ace Hardware; LaSalle Business Credit; Actuant; Kellwood; The Heico Companies; Northwestern Mutual Life Insurance; Bank of America and American Standard.

## Skadden, Arps, Slate, Meagher & Flom LLP & Affiliates
See firm details p.1557

**The Firm:** Benefiting greatly from the firm's vast securitization capacity in New York, a compact Chicago banking and institutional investor team bears the hallmarks of "*expertise and responsiveness,*" according to sources, who note its involvement in high-profile transactions. Traditionally defined by the "*sophistication and great flair*" it displays in the representation of borrowers on refinancings, restructurings and acquisition financings, the past year has seen the team enjoy an increase in asset-based borrowing work. Even more significantly, it now sees a greater proportion of its instructions come from major lenders such as JPMorgan Chase and Citigroup. The firm's sound reputation for bankruptcy means that workouts feature regularly, while securitization matters also figure in the workload.

**The Lawyers:** **Randall Rademaker** (see p.851) fulfills his role as head of the banking and institutional investing group with aplomb, impressing clients and peers with his detailed, "*almost unparalleled*" knowledge base. Also crucial are the "*strong personal relationships*" he forges with clients. Dealing with borrowers and lenders on a variety of asset-based transactions, secured financings, securitization matters and bankruptcy-related work, he has of late advised Texas Pacific Group on its $4 billion secured financing acquisition of MGM. Rademaker also recently represented ACCO Brands on a $1.2 billion aggregate secured cross-border credit facility and acquisition financing, and JPMorgan Chase on a $400 million securitization of consumer loans and a $2.7 billion securitization of telephone receivables.

**Clients/Work Highlights:** Sara Lee; Solo Cup; Ball Corporation; Koch Industries; JPMorgan Chase; Bank of America; BNP Paribas and Citigroup.

## Vedder, Price, Kaufman & Kammholz
See firm details p.885

**The Firm:** Linked closely to offices in New York and Roseland, New Jersey, this punchy Northeast regional outfit has a team of Chicago finance lawyers who play a key role in maintaining the firm's stellar reputation for niche aircraft, railroad, maritime and equipment financing work. "*Nationally and internationally recognized*" in this capacity, the team is heavily involved in leveraged financings and leasings, and also represents lenders, financial institutions and venture capital funds on midmarket, asset-based lending and other transactions. Researchers also noted that the firm has enjoyed an increase in cash flow-based financings in the past year and possesses a strong bankruptcy practice.

**The Lawyers:** Described as the leading light of Vedder's finance team, **John McEnroe** was praised as a "*wonderful individual*" who brings "*a pleasant, practical demeanor*" to the table and "*doesn't over-lawyer.*" Mainly occupied with asset-based financings, he also takes on secured transactions, LBOs and bankruptcy work, as well as some cash flow financings. He recently represented a major national bank on a $195 million first and second lien financing relating to a multistate bus company. "*The guy for airline finance*" in Chicago, **Dean Gerber** is the foremost figure in a phenomenally strong team that works hand in hand with the New York office. A "*reliable and highly satisfactory*" attorney, he advises lenders on a range of leveraged leasing transactions in the aviation and rail sectors, as well as taking on related tax and regulatory work.

**Clients/Work Highlights:** Export Development Canada; Bank of America; Merrill Lynch Capital; Charter One and GMAC Commercial Finance.

## Band 4

## Baker & McKenzie
See firm details p.866

**The Firm:** In a bid to further enhance its local practice, this global giant continues to beef up the banking and finance team in Chicago. This said, the firm's international links are undoubtedly popular with clients and still a key reason for some to choose the firm over others in Illinois. Over 25 "*professional, knowledgeable and easy to work with*" attorneys represent lenders and borrowers on midmarket finance, restructuring and leasing transactions, such as recent advice to Wells Fargo, as agent, in the $120 million financing of Lerman Enterprises, or the mandate from the lender in a $100 million plus financing for Richardson Electronics. Sources feel "*very positive*" about the team's work, particularly when a transaction involves cross-border elements that bring the firm's international resources into play. The recent advice to Barclays Bank on a $51 million secured term loan facility for a joint venture between English real estate companies and Spanish investment funds perfectly illustrates this point.

**The Lawyers:** The "*terrific*" **Creighton Meland** (see p.845) is at the heart of the firm's finance work in the state. Respected for his "*calming influence,*" "*intense focus*" and "*great deal of integrity,*" his is a general banking and finance practice. Commentators enthused that he "*especially stands out*" when dealing with multicurrency or international credit facilities. Recently arrived from Winston & Strawn, **Bruce Baker** (see p.818) has brought "*fresh thinking*" and "*significant expertise*" to the team and was heavily involved in the $120 million Lerman Enterprises financing for Wells Fargo. Sources anticipate that his presence will help to increase the firm's local visibility.

**Clients/Work Highlights:** BP; Wells Fargo; HSBC Trade Bank; PaR Systems; JPMorgan Chase and Harris Nesbitt.

## Duane Morris LLP
See firm details p.1753

**The Firm:** Small but perfectly formed, the seven-attorney banking and finance team at this reputable Chicago firm features "*strong personalities*" who are "*responsive and get the deal done.*" Primarily representing lenders on refinancings, secured and unsecured loans and acquisitions, the team is also well regarded for its real estate finance capability.

**The Lawyers:** Possessing "*a good bedside manner*" and "*a flair for complex transactions,*" **Brian Kerwin** (see p.838) is a significant factor in the success of the team's carefully targeted midmarket practice. Spending the majority of his time on banking and finance matters (he also mixes in some M&A work), Kerwin represents banks, private equity funds and corporations on a variety of syndicated, mezzanine and acquisition financings. His "*energy and tact*" appeal to a hugely loyal clientele, and in the past twelve months he has represented long-term clients La Salle National Bank – now known as Hometown National Bank – on a complex $225 million refinancing, and Fifth Third Bank on several acquisition financings

totaling $30 million. Characterized by "*good legal knowledge and the ability to translate that into business matters,*" **Kenneth Latimer** (see p.840) is respected among his bank and financial institution clients for being "*a hard-working, nuts-and-bolts lawyer.*" He acts for lenders on asset-based secured loans, unsecured financings and syndicated lending transactions.

**Clients/Work Highlights:** LaSalle Bank; Fifth Third Bank; Northern Trust; AA Capital Partners; Lake Forest Bank & Trust; Wells Fargo Foothill and Alpine Investors.

## Neal, Gerber & Eisenberg LLP
See firm details p.880

**The Firm:** The finance team at this well-established Chicago firm numbers seven attorneys whose solid midmarket practice spans a broad range of finance transactions, from secured and unsecured loans to syndicated financings and workouts. The team has built an impressive reputation for quality among clients and competitors, and represents lenders such as JPMorgan Chase, LaSalle Bank, Wells Fargo and Bank of America in their Chicago operations. Also using the team are notable life insurance and real estate borrowers in syndicated financings, and the firm has additionally been involved in multicurrency, cross-border financings in Japan and Canada of late. An increase in the number of asset-based lending and mezzanine financing instructions received by the firm reflects the successful bedding down of several lateral hires made in 2004 from Jenkens & Gilchrist.

**The Lawyers:** "*Gentlemanly*" attorney **Peter Barrow** (see p.819) displays an "*easygoing style*" and "*thorough knowledge.*" He represents lenders and borrowers across a broad spectrum of midmarket commercial lending and finance matters. As a former assistant general counsel at Bank of America (whom he still advises), clients such as JPMorgan and LaSalle Bank also value his business-oriented perspective. Barrow is heavily involved with the team's cross-border work.

**Clients/Work Highlights:** Other clients include General Growth Properties, National City Bank and First Bank.

## Schiff Hardin LLP
See firm details p.881

**The Firm:** This venerable Chicago firm's finance team "*does a fine job,*" according to sources. Nearly 20 attorneys advise insurance companies, commercial banks and asset-based financiers on midmarket lending transactions. Admired for its strength in real estate and construction financings, the group continues to show improved performance in mezzanine transactions and has good relationships with a number of insurance companies.

**The Lawyers:** Heading up Schiff Hardin's finance group, the "*confident and very capable*" **Scott Pickens** (see p.850) is the main mover in the Chicago team. Admired by peers as "*a methodical business lawyer,*" he is also rated highly by lending clients, who value the "*logical and pragmatic*" approach he brings to all manner of financing transactions and workouts, from mezzanine or aviation finance to asset-based or cash flow loans. Numbering major banks such as LaSalle and Fifth Third among his clientele, he also advises insurance companies and other significant asset-based lenders.

**Clients/Work Highlights:** First Source Financial; RESIDCO; Midwest Mezzanine Funds; One Mezzanine; Prudential Capital Group; Bank of America; Fifth Third Bank and LaSalle Bank.

## Schwartz, Cooper, Greenberger & Krauss, Chartered

**The Firm:** This well-established Chicago firm, widely recognized for its real estate and bankruptcy abilities, fields a team of around 15 banking and finance attorneys. It represents a variety of Midwest regional financial institutions in commercial loan transactions and works on cash flow and asset-based loans, mezzanine financings, and secured and unse-

cured loans. The firm particularly benefits from established relationships with several Chicago banks.

**The Lawyers:** Experienced attorney Martin Salzman is a mainstay of the banking and finance team.

**Clients/Work Highlights:** LaSalle Bank; Oak Brook Bank; Bank One; MB Financial; RBC Builder Finance and Washington Mutual Bank.

# BANKRUPTCY/RESTRUCTURING

## Bankruptcy/Restructuring
### Leading Firms

| | |
|---|---|
| **1** | KIRKLAND & ELLIS LLP *Chicago* |
| | LATHAM & WATKINS LLP *Chicago* |
| | SKADDEN *Chicago* |
| **2** | GOLDBERG, KOHN, BELL, BLACK *Chicago* |
| | SIDLEY AUSTIN LLP *Chicago* |
| **3** | GREENBERG TRAURIG LLP *Chicago* |
| | JENNER & BLOCK LLP *Chicago* |
| | JONES DAY *Chicago* |
| | MAYER, BROWN, ROWE & MAW LLP *Chicago* |
| | SONNENSCHEIN NATH & ROSENTHAL *Chicago* |
| | VEDDER, PRICE, KAUFMAN & KAMMHOLZ *Chicago* |
| **4** | ADELMAN & GETTLEMAN LTD *Chicago* |
| | DLA PIPER RUDNICK GRAY CARY US LLP *Chicago* |
| | FOLEY & LARDNER LLP *Chicago* |
| | KAYE SCHOLER LLP *Chicago* |
| | MCDERMOTT WILL & EMERY *Chicago* |
| | SHAW GUSSIS FISHMAN GLANTZ *Chicago* |
| | WINSTON & STRAWN LLP *Chicago* |

## Band 1

### Kirkland & Ellis LLP
See firm details p.875

**The Firm:** *"Truly a force to be reckoned with,"* this team *"consistently does a phenomenal job"* on the most high-profile restructurings. Considered *"in a league of its own for debtor work,"* its representation of United Airlines continued to draw praise from commentators. At the time of print, the plan of reorganization has just been approved by the bankruptcy court, clearing the debtor to emerge from Chapter 11 protection. As part of the firm's integrated national practice, the Chicago team often works closely with its New York counterparts, most recently to collaborate on the Tower Automotive filing, a matter involving debts of several billion dollars. While most admired for its debtor expertise, the group maintains a healthy creditor practice, continuing to act for the ad hoc committee of lenders in the massive Adelphia Communications bankruptcy. The firm's unparalleled private equity group provides a further stream of work representing hedge funds and other investors in distressed companies.

**The Lawyers:** James Sprayregen (see p.858) is a nationally recognized debtor lawyer who is hailed as *"a trusty guide through the labyrinth of Chapter 11."* Clients applaud his winning interpersonal skills in the boardroom and *"unblinking toughness at the negotiating table."* Peers are equally forthcoming in their praise for this restructuring expert; *"He is brilliantly hardworking and amazingly versatile,"* said one, while another enthused: *"Who else could make conference calls and ski at the same time?"* Marc Kieselstein (see p.838) is a *"smart lawyer who gets great results,"* interviewees say. Counseling several creditor organizations as well as helping other major debtor clients such as TWA and Dade Behring Holdings in their Chapter 11 reorganizations has supplemented his in-depth involvement in the UAL bankruptcy. David Eaton (see p.827) has been singled out for his *"deeply practical and no-nonsense"* style. *"A real class act,"* his restructuring experience includes leading the reorganization of Harnischfeger Industry, a manufacturer worth $2 billion. James Stempel (see p.859) is a *"consistently high performer"* in the bankruptcy arena, while Anup Sathy (see p.854) has a career that many describe as *"locked in an upward trajectory."* A *"fine and thoughtful"* attorney, Sathy's involvement in the Conseco bankruptcy has put him on the map and he manages similar restructurings for numerous other debtors. David Seligman (see p.855) was singled out for his ability to *"coordinate restructurings as if deftly playing with a giant rubix cube."* Clients also appreciate his boundless knowledge, one admiring that *"he can answer any question fired at him off the top of his head."*

**Clients/Work Highlights:** Conseco; UAL; Exide; Trans World Airlines; NRG Energy; Zenith Electronics and The Fleming Companies.

### Latham & Watkins LLP

**The Firm:** Recognized as the leading creditor practice in Chicago, clients select this firm over others for its *"ability to successfully negotiate all parts of the process to make a deal that works."* It acts for an impressive array of financial institutions and asset-management firms as creditors in major filings, as well as in their capacities as lenders to struggling companies. The team represents GECC in three related Chapter 11 proceedings in Atlanta, and has put together DIP loans for both Kaiser Steel and

Owens Corning on behalf of Bank of America. The firm undeniably has growing strength when it comes to representing debtors, and handling the restructuring of AT&T Latin America has given this practice area a boost. Other highlights on the company side include managing the Doctor's Community Hospital recapitalization in a major out-of-court restructuring process. All in all, Latham & Watkins is *"absolutely first choice"* for many impressed clients needing sophisticated bankruptcy expertise.

**The Lawyers:** The team is admired for its impressive collection of lawyers who are *"intelligent, honorable and a pleasure to work with,"* and foremost among these is global cochair David Heller. Clients particularly appreciate his control of antagonistic situations: *"He's always the best negotiator in the room and has no equal when it comes to striking deals."* The constitution of his practice mirrors that of the group's; he leads the representation of many of the firm's major creditor clients, as well as handling the Doctor's Community Hospital case. Josef Athanas is an *"incredibly tenacious advocate"* who conducts business with both intelligence and integrity while Douglas Bacon *"knows where to put your dollars and where not to waste your time."* In addition to managing his caseload of Chapter 11 restructurings for clients such as GECC, he is also currently representing the court-appointed trustee in the forfeiture of Near North Insurance, the largest federal criminal forfeiture in the state. Clients recommended bankruptcy expert Richard Levy because he *"knows the law inside out and can always handle the most complex deals."*

**Clients/Work Highlights:** Black Diamond; GECC; Citicorp; Doctor's Community Hospital; Bank of America and Wachovia Capital Finance.

### Skadden, Arps, Slate, Meagher & Flom LLP & Affiliates
See firm details p.1557

**The Firm:** The group's *"top-drawer bankruptcy practice"* is driven by its exceptional reputation in debtor matters, but commentators insist the group has the depth and diversity that makes it attractive to a large range of clients. Skadden's position as a leading international corporate firm serves as a backdrop to the success of its restructuring department, and it enjoys close ties to the highly respected New York office. The Chicago group lent its considerable weight to the

| Bankruptcy/Restructuring |
|---|
| Leading Individuals |

## Senior Statesman
MUNITZ Gerald *Goldberg, Kohn*

**[1]** BUTLER JR John *Skadden, Arps*
HELLER David *Latham & Watkins LLP*
SPRAYREGEN James *Kirkland & Ellis LLP*

**[2]** BARLIANT Ronald *Goldberg, Kohn*
JACOBSON Fruman *Sonnenschein*
KIESELSTEIN Marc *Kirkland & Ellis LLP*
MILLNER Robert *Sonnenschein*
MISSNER David *DLA Piper Rudnick Gray Cary*
NYHAN Lawrence *Sidley Austin LLP*
POHL Timothy *Skadden, Arps*
SOLOW Michael *Kaye Scholer LLP*
TOWBIN Steven *Shaw Gussis*

**[3]** ADELMAN Howard *Adelman & Gettleman Ltd*
ATHANAS Josef *Latham & Watkins LLP*
BACON J Douglas *Latham & Watkins LLP*
BERKOFF Mark *DLA Piper Rudnick Gray Cary*
BOTICA Matthew *Winston & Strawn LLP*
CONLAN James *Sidley Austin LLP*
EATON David *Kirkland & Ellis LLP*
FISHMAN Robert *Shaw Gussis*
GETTLEMAN Chad *Adelman & Gettleman Ltd*
HARNER Paul *Jones Day*
HEROY David *Bell, Boyd & Lloyd LLC*
IVESTER Eric *Skadden, Arps*
KAPLAN Harold *Gardner Carton & Douglas LLP*
KIRIAKOS Thomas *Mayer, Brown, Rowe & Maw*
KLEIN Randall *Goldberg, Kohn,*
KRAKAUER Bryan *Sidley Austin LLP*
LEVY Richard *Latham & Watkins LLP*
LIPKE Doug *Vedder, Price*
MITCHELL Nancy *Greenberg Traurig LLP*
PANAGAKIS George *Skadden, Arps*
PETERMAN Nancy *Greenberg Traurig LLP*
PETERSON Ronald *Jenner & Block LLP*
ROSENBLOOM Lewis *McDermott Will & Emery*
SHAPIRO Keith *Greenberg Traurig LLP*
SMITH William *McDermott Will & Emery*
SOLOW Alan *Goldberg, Kohn*
SOLOW Sheldon *Kaye Scholer LLP*
STEMPEL James *Kirkland & Ellis LLP*
ZAZOVE Daniel *Perkins Coie LLP*

## Up-and-coming individuals
SATHY Anup *Kirkland & Ellis LLP*
SELIGMAN David *Kirkland & Ellis LLP*

recent Chapter 11 proceedings for Delphi Corporation, and is often enlisted in out-of-court restructurings and debt reorganizations. Experienced creditor lawyers, the group has acted on a number of recent high-profile DIP financings, such as organizing the loan facility for the troubled Solutia on behalf of Citibank. The team also routinely represents large creditor committees.

**The Lawyers:** Hailed by interviewees as a "*phenomenal*" bankruptcy expert who is a "*great intellectual*

lawyer,*" **Jack Butler** (see p.823) cochairs Skadden's global corporate restructuring practice. A man whose courtroom style is thought to be "*not for the faint-hearted,*" he handles numerous Chapter 11 cases on behalf of predominantly large debtor clients. The "*fabulous*" **Timothy Pohl** (see p.850) is recognized for his restructuring expertise and a superior knowledge of the bankruptcy code. He has an impressive pedigree in leading major companies through Chapter 11 reorganizations and out-of-court restructurings, and has particular DIP financing expertise. Market sources recognize that **Eric Ivester** (see p.836) is an "*extremely strong member of the restructuring group.*" He continues to lead the Skadden team involved in the restructuring of Interstate Bakeries Corporation. **George Panagakis** (see p.849) is also acclaimed as a "*quality bankruptcy lawyer,*" his practice having a focus on the retail industry.

**Clients/Work Highlights:** The client roster includes a host of major national and international players, and on the company side includes both Delphi Corporation and Friedmans; CSFB and Verizon Capital are but two examples of major creditor clients.

## Band 2

### Goldberg, Kohn, Bell, Black, Rosenbloom & Moritz, Ltd
**The Firm:** This ten-attorney practice possesses "*immense strength for a smaller player,*" interviewees agree, and it is "*undoubtedly an excellent option for secured creditor work.*" Representing and enforcing creditors' rights is the firm's specialty, the attorneys providing counsel to secured and unsecured creditors, creditors' and equity committees and indenture trustees. The firm has had involvement in major Chapter 11 and restructuring matters, including advice to an equity committee involved in the massive Kmart Corporation case.

**The Lawyers:** The "*venerable*" **Gerald Munitz** is a senior member of the team, known for his tremendous experience in the bankruptcy field. An attorney who "*knows the law inside out,*" he continues to impress clients with his encyclopedic knowledge of his subject: "*You ask him a question, he takes you straight to the page,*" said one interviewee. **Ronald Barliant**'s background on the bench gives him an "*invaluable insight into what judges want.*" With this experience and a burgeoning practice in debtor work, he has "*bolstered the firm's credibility for bankruptcy work.*" "*A class-A guy,*" **Randall Klein** has continued to build his practice apace, winning plaudits for the high quality of his advice and his "*serious and aggressive*" style. He manages a busy practice and acts exclusively for creditors. Chair of the bankruptcy and creditors' rights group **Alan Solow** specializes in representing secured and unsecured creditors. An extremely experienced attorney, he is "*head and shoulders above many of his peers in Chicago.*"

**Clients/Work Highlights:** ABN AMRO; Bank of America; BNP Paribas; Citadel Investment Group;

Congress Financial; Fleet Capital; Foothill Group; GATX Corporation; GE Capital; LaSalle Bank and Merrill Lynch Capital.

### Sidley Austin LLP
See firm details p.883
**The Firm:** According to interviewees, the firm possesses "*specialist lawyers of the highest caliber from top to bottom.*" Clients endorse the attorneys in the corporate reorganization group on the basis that they "*work well together as an effective team*" and are "*cooperative and easy to work with.*" There are 60 bankruptcy lawyers across four offices handling an increasingly balanced workload of creditor and debtor cases. Bankruptcies driven by mass tort litigation are one of the specialties of the practice and lawyers are currently acting for debtors to Owens Corning and Flintcote, both asbestos-related bankruptcy cases.

**The Lawyers:** Group chair **Lawrence Nyhan** (see p.848) possesses "*top-notch knowledge of both legal issues and boardroom business strategies.*" He represents big debtors in the main and chairs the practice group. **James Conlan** (see p.824) provides "*creative counsel combined with great instinct,*" clients applaud. A lawyer with a "*strong courtroom presence,*" he co-manages many of the firm's biggest clients with Nyhan and handles a personal caseload focused on debtor representation. **Bryan Krakauer** (see p.839) is an intellectual attorney with a wide-ranging experience in the bankruptcy and workout field. Hailed by sources as a "*great, great guy,*" he predominantly represents creditor committees and lending institutions.

**Clients/Work Highlights:** On the debtor side the group represents Meridian Automotive, Federal-Mogul and Owens-Corning, and its strong financial grounding means it is a go-to for many major financial institutions.

## Band 3

### Greenberg Traurig LLP
See firm details p.664
**The Firm:** "*A first choice firm for contentious bankruptcy issues,*" expertise in litigation as well as considerable cross-border capacity gives this group an edge over other similarly positioned competitors. The Chicago team forms a considerable part of a nationally operated practice group, and teams networked across offices pool resources and knowledge to work on individual cases. Debtors as well as secured and unsecured creditors, investors and fiduciaries all receive representation from the firm. Lawyers here provide continuing counsel to the trust created under the Chapter 11 reorganization of Conesco Finance, involving creditor claims of more than $6 billion. Other recent projects include advising Mesirow Financial in its acquisition of KPMG's US Corporate Recovery Practice, one of the largest transactions completed by this insolvency client.

**The Lawyers:** The "*terrific*" **Nancy Mitchell** (see p.846) possesses "*excellent business skills in the bankruptcy field,*" according to interviewees. A former investment banker, she has varied experience in corporate finance as well as bankruptcy and restructuring. Entry into the rankings this year for **Nancy Peterman** (see p.850) reflects recognition for her being a *"top talent."* *"There is nobody more dedicated and she is a joy to work with,"* clients say. *"One of the most strategic-thinking lawyers I have come across,"* **Keith Shapiro** (see p.856) is another favorite among clients because he *"stands out for his practicality – he finds the right solution for all parties but he is not afraid to be confrontational when it is needed."* He cochairs the national reorganization, bankruptcy and restructuring practice and devotes a considerable chunk of his time to sitting on a creditor committee for the UAL case.

**Clients/Work Highlights:** A representative sample of recent clients include Crestview Capital Fund, Conesco and Mesirow Financial.

## Jenner & Block LLP
See firm details p.873

**The Firm:** A *"quality firm with plenty of rising talent,"* market sources consider this to be one of the more visible players in the Chicago bankruptcy market. The 22 bankruptcy lawyers here represent a mix of debtor and creditor clients, the latter encompassing creditor committees and secured lenders. There is considerable litigation expertise at the firm, as illustrated by a recent case in which the lawyers secured a permanent injunction in the US Bankruptcy Court against the creditors of British-based client TXU Europe.

**The Lawyers:** Practice cochair **Ronald Peterson** (see p.850) is *"a fiery character in court and at the deal-making table."* Possessing a wealth of experience in bankruptcy and workout matters, he has a growing creditor practice to balance the debtor work on which he traditionally focused. The representation of a secured creditor on a gambling cruise ship bankruptcy is currently occupying much of his time. Jeff Marwil and Mark Thomas recently joined from Katten Muchin Zavis Rosenman and are making their mark in the firm's bankruptcy practice.

**Clients/Work Highlights:** GE Capital; General Dynamics; McDermott International; Tenneco and Pecheny.

## Jones Day
See firm details p.570

**The Firm:** This 12-strong team is *"certainly moving on up"* in the Chicago bankruptcy arena. Meanwhile, the strength of the team is backed up by the firm's reputation as an *"extremely strong national player."* The bankruptcy and restructuring practice is evenly balanced with the lawyers providing counsel to debtors, creditors and parties to distressed transactions on both sides. Both in-court and out-of-court expertise is on offer and current matters in litigation include USG Corp's Chapter 11 cases worth $5 billion. The team is also currently advising Cablevision Systems Corporation as it faces multimillion-dollar claims from an official creditor committee.

**The Lawyers:** **Paul Harner** (see p.834) manages a busy bankruptcy practice and focuses on representing major company debtors.

**Clients/Work Highlights:** Laidlaw; National Century Financial Enterprises; USG Corp and Cablevision Systems.

## Mayer, Brown, Rowe & Maw LLP
See firm details p.876

**The Firm:** This *"very high-quality"* bankruptcy practice is nestled within an international firm that has a major profile for its corporate and commercial work in general. Representing senior lenders is the team's specialty; Canadian Imperial Bank is a valuable client that provides a steady stream of creditor work. The Chicago group of 14 lawyers also handles matters on behalf of debtors including numerous Chapter 11 restructurings.

**The Lawyers:** **Thomas Kiriakos** (see p.838) is considered to be a serious player in the Chicago market. His bankruptcy and restructuring experience is considerable, and both creditor and debtor clients retain him. Bank of America is his flagship client and he has advised this senior lender both in and out of court.

**Clients/Work Highlights:** Bank of America, TransCanada and Bank of Montreal are also clients of the firm.

## Sonnenschein Nath & Rosenthal LLP
See firm details p.884

**The Firm:** The Chicago bankruptcy team has established a strong presence across the Midwest, strengthened by the overlap between the Chicago and New York bankruptcy groups that enables a steady flow of cases and resources to the Illinois practice. Representing the creditor committee in the United Airlines proceedings has undoubtedly raised this firm's profile for bankruptcy, and the lawyers continue to focus on creditor committee work to a large degree. Insurers often seek out the firm for representation and the team is currently acting for the insurer of a Roman Catholic Diocese facing bankruptcy. Clients have faith in the strength and depth of the Sonnenschein's bankruptcy expertise: *"I choose them if I have all my marbles at stake,"* said one.

**The Lawyers:** **Fruman Jacobson** (see p.836) is a *"true scholar and a genuine human being."* Leader of the national bankruptcy practice, he divides his time between Chicago and New York. He has led the firm's involvement in the UAL case and new projects include representing a creditor committee to Wickes Lumber Company in Chicago. Clients applaud **Robert Millner** (see p.846) for being *"highly practical and effective in court."* He is known for his extensive work.

**Clients/Work Highlights:** A cross section of the group's clients include Liberty Mutual, Mesaba Airlines and Wickes Lumber.

## Vedder, Price, Kaufman & Kammholz
See firm details p.885

**The Firm:** The 13-strong practice group focuses squarely on representing secured lenders in troubled workouts and bankruptcy cases. The aircraft industry is where the firm has particularly made a name for itself and representing clients involved in aircraft

and equipment finance bankruptcies and workouts is the most significant aspect of the bankruptcy practice. Lawyers here are currently representing secured creditors facing multibillion-dollar exposures arising from the restructuring of Delta Airlines and Northwest Airlines. The team has also represented creditors in the majority of Chapter 11 cases and restructurings relating to the airline industry in the past 15 years.

**The Lawyers:** The *"wonderful"* **Doug Lipke** is respected for his expertise in the aircraft industry and has numerous workouts and restructurings in this field under his belt. Clients laud his encyclopedic knowledge of the law and the fact that he is *"very results-oriented."*

**Clients/Work Highlights:** ABN AMRO; LaSalle; Merrill Lynch and Bank of Scotland.

## Band 4

### Adelman & Gettleman Ltd
See firm details p.865

**The Firm:** While Adelman & Gettleman may be smaller than some of its direct rivals, this ten-attorney firm more than holds its weight in the Chicago bankruptcy market. The lawyers here exclusively handle bankruptcies and workouts in Delaware and the Midwest, and are respected within the market for their clear focus. The practice is balanced between creditor and debtor clients and recent highlights include representing JPMorgan Chase in a major healthcare case in Chicago. Lawyers are also acting for an affiliate of GM in an out-of-court workout. Bankruptcy-related litigation is also a growing area of expertise at the firm.

**The Lawyers:** **Howard Adelman** (see p.817) is a tremendously experienced bankruptcy specialist who has spent a considerable chunk of the past year serving on the US Advisory Committee to the Supreme Court on the new bankruptcy rules. Fellow partner **Chad Gettleman** (see p.831) formerly practised as a certified public accountant and has won a following for his bankruptcy practice through the provision of high-quality advice.

**Clients/Work Highlights:** Creditors; debtors; insurance companies and boards of directors all receive the benefit of the firm's advice.

### DLA Piper Rudnick Gray Cary US LLP
See firm details p.870

**The Firm:** Clients endorse this bankruptcy practice as an *"excellent and efficient group,"* with the lawyers *"always ready to provide savvy business advice."* The team of ten lawyers at the Chicago office of this international firm takes on all types of bankruptcy-related work and is particularly respected for working with creditor committees and big debtors. The latter is illustrated by the firm's representation of National Steel, which was subsequently sold to US Steel for $1.2 billion. Real estate and insurance are two major areas of practice, and many of the lawyers boast weighty litigation experience in the Bankruptcy Court.

**The Lawyers:** **David Missner** (see p.846) is a

"*bright and effective*" attorney who has lengthy experience in the bankruptcy business. He is known as a debtor specialist and recently guided Help-at-Home through a complex Chapter 11 reorganization. Clients laud **Mark Berkoff**'s (see p.820) "*superb technical knowledge*" of restructuring and bankruptcy issues. He regularly acts as an assignee or trustee and handles an increasing number of 363 Sales and out-of-court workouts. Chairman of the Chicago group, clients consider that he is "*meticulous but has an impressive ability to get things done efficiently.*"

**Clients/Work Highlights:** Air Canada; Business Products Credit Association; High Ridge Partners and National Steel.

## Foley & Lardner LLP
See firm details p.2037

**The Firm:** This respected team handles varied bankruptcy and restructuring matters on behalf of a wide range of clients. Recently, the lawyers acted as official bond committee counsel in the Farmland Industries' Chapter 11 reorganization, the largest-ever cooperative case of its kind. The firm also represented over a dozen airport authorities in the UAL Chapter 11 case and in both US Airways' bankruptcy cases.

**The Lawyers:** Practice leader Michael Small is a key contact for the business reorganizations practice group.

**Clients/Work Highlights:** The firm represents creditor committees; secured and unsecured creditors; bondholders; indenture trustees and numerous debtors.

## Kaye Scholer LLP
See firm details p.1536

**The Firm:** "*Certainly a major player in the Chicago bankruptcy market,*" clients find that this firm "*provides great overall service at competitive rates.*" Not only is the bankruptcy team in Chicago backed up by the firm's tax and litigation experts, it can also draw on the resources and expertise of the firm's New York office. The latter has recently been strengthened by the addition of the majority of Clifford Chance's local restructuring team. The practice focuses squarely on providing counsel to secured creditors, senior lenders and fiduciaries, and current highlights include representing lenders to St Vincent's Catholic Medical Center in New York.

**The Lawyers: Michael Solow** (see p.858) "*integrates business acumen with legal knowledge,*" making him an "*excellent counselor who provides practical, carefully*

*thought-out advice.*" He acts primarily for creditors and his clients include senior lenders in the Aladdin Hotel & Casino reorganization. He divides his time between Chicago and New York and interviewees are of the view that "*he has also successfully penetrated the New York syndicated loans market.*" His brother, **Sheldon Solow** (see p.858), is a "*very robust creditor specialist.*" His clients have included secured lenders, bondholders, fiduciaries and individuals.

**Clients/Work Highlights:** Clients include bank groups, bondholders and senior secured lenders such as Bears Stearns and Morgan Stanley Funds, as well as a growing number of hedge funds and private equity clients.

## McDermott Will & Emery
See firm details p.878

**The Firm:** The bankruptcy and troubled transactions group is part of a national practice, and as such can "*draw effectively on resources from all over the country whenever they are needed.*" A noted area of specialization, the firm represents creditors in the healthcare industry, but the lawyers are also experienced in managing both debtor and creditor cases spanning a range of other fields, including the airline industry.

**The Lawyers:** Corporate restructuring expert **Lewis Rosenbloom** (see p.852) is "*intelligent and easy to work with.*" He has vast experience as debtor counsel, but he increasingly acts for creditors and advises boards of directors of public and private companies. Clients report that **William Smith** (see p.857) is a "*dogged negotiator with a powerful knowledge of the law.*" Possessing a "*unique ability to translate the bankruptcy world to people working in other fields,*" he devotes much of his practice to representing healthcare clients.

**Clients/Work Highlights:** Financial institutions; indenture trustees; institutional investors and debt issuers.

## Shaw Gussis Fishman Glantz Wolfson & Towbin LLC

**The Firm:** "*One of the finest bankruptcy boutiques in town,*" this firm specializes in commercial bankruptcy, restructuring, litigation and real estate. The majority of the firm's 20 lawyers help maintain a very active Chicago-based practice providing counsel to debtors, creditors' committees and unsecured creditors in all aspects of bankruptcy and restructuring, both in and

out of court. What the firm lacks in size, it makes up for in its highly competitive rates and high-quality service: "*They certainly play well with the big boys.*"

**The Lawyers:** An "*excellent negotiator,*" **Steven Towbin** "*consistently provides astute and appropriate advice,*" clients say. His practice has a strong focus on automotive-related cases in Chicago and Detroit. **Robert Fishman** is a "*savvy and capable*" bankruptcy expert who is "*great at getting results.*" Such recommendation gains him a place in the rankings this year.

**Clients/Work Highlights:** Clients range from public companies such as Illinois Toolworks, right down to individual unsecured creditors.

## Winston & Strawn LLP
See firm details p.886

**The Firm:** The bankruptcy team here handles a wide mix of work, mainly on behalf of creditors. Commentators recognize that this firm is "*a huge force in litigation*" and this expertise feeds into the bankruptcy practice, which encompasses in-court work as well as out-of-court matters, Chapter 11 restructurings and workouts. Clients are connected to a wide spectrum of industries ranging from agriculture and construction to manufacturing and telecommunications.

**The Lawyers: Matthew Botica** (see p.821) is an old hand when it comes to bankruptcy and has established "*a truly national practice,*" interviewees claim. He specializes in representing secured creditors, lenders and banks.

**Clients/Work Highlights:** Cisco Systems; CSFB; Deutsche Bank; GE Capital; JPMorgan Chase; LaSalle Bank and Metricom.

## Other Notable Practitioners

Interviewees singled out **David Heroy** of Bell Boyd & Lloyd LCC for his experience in representing equity committees in particular. He chairs the firm's bankruptcy and restructuring group. The "*sharpest mind in the business,*" according to clients, **Harold Kaplan** (see p.837) has an increasingly managerial role at Gardner Carton & Douglas LLP, but maintains a reputable practice focusing on creditors' rights. "*An effective advocate and business man,*" **Daniel Zazove** of Perkins Cole LLP is a vastly experienced bankruptcy practitioner. "*His word is his bond,*" one interviewee remarked.

# CONSTRUCTION

## Band 1

### DLA Piper Rudnick Gray Cary US LLP
See firm details p.870

**The Firm:** Housed in a firm with an internationally renowned real estate practice, it was only ever a matter of time before this 12-lawyer construction team crystalized its reputation as preeminent in the field. Commentators agree that it represents "*a*

*formidable fighting force in a competitive market*" due to the raft of big-name players it fields. One client succinctly summed up the general view by asserting that it is "*a go-to firm for sophisticated construction issues.*"

**The Lawyers: Dan Brennan** (see p.822) is considered "*really excellent, particularly for complex contracts and settlement negotiations.*" Although chiefly a litigator who represents owners in relation

to the termination of contracts, he spends the remainder of his time on transactional work. Recently, Brennan has been engaged on counseling and litigation concerning accessibility for the disabled, but has also found the time to act for the owner of an LNG plant in a claim against an engineer. **Eric Berg** (see p.819) primarily represents owners of all types, whether they be developers, partners in real estate joint ventures or large companies

## Construction

### Leading Firms

1. **DLA PIPER RUDNICK GRAY CARY US LLP** *Chicago*
   **SCHIFF HARDIN LLP** *Chicago*
   **STEIN, RAY & HARRIS LLP** *Chicago*
2. **CONWAY & MROWIEC** *Chicago*
   **LYMAN & NIELSEN** *Oak Brook*
3. **BELL, BOYD & LLOYD LLC** *Chicago*
   **MUCH SHELIST** *Chicago*
   **OGLETREE, DEAKINS** *Chicago*
   **SABO & ZAHN** *Chicago*
   **SACHNOFF & WEAVER LTD** *Chicago*

### Leading Individuals

#### Senior Statesman

**SKLAR** Stanley *Bell, Boyd & Lloyd LLC*

1. **FRIEDLANDER** Mark *Schiff Hardin LLP*
   **LAURIE** Ty *DLA Piper Rudnick Gray Cary US LLP*
   **LURIE** Paul *Schiff Hardin LLP*
   **LYMAN** Bill *Lyman & Nielsen*
   **STEIN** Steven *Stein, Ray & Harris LLP*
2. **ALTMAN** Ross *DLA Piper Rudnick Gray Cary US LLP*
   **BRENNAN** Daniel *DLA Piper Rudnick Gray Cary US LLP*
   **KIKOLER** Stephen *Much Shelist*
   **LEWIS** Charles *Jenkens & Gilchrist*
   **RUFF** Randolph *Ogletree, Deakins*
3. **BERG** Eric *DLA Piper Rudnick Gray Cary US LLP*
   **COLE** Alexandra *Perkins Coie LLP*
   **CONWAY** Timothy *Conway & Mrowiec*
   **DASH** James *Much Shelist*
   **HARRIS** Robert *Stein, Ray & Harris LLP*
   **MROWIEC** John *Conway & Mrowiec*
   **NEWMAN** Margery *Ogletree, Deakins*
   **RAY** Stephen *Stein, Ray & Harris LLP*
   **ROBERTS** Kenneth *Schiff Hardin LLP*
   **SHAPIRO** Clifford *Sachnoff & Weaver Ltd*
   **SINGER** Eric *Wildman Harrold*

#### Up-and-coming individuals

**NIELSEN** Jennifer *Lyman & Nielsen*

---

with significant real estate portfolios. He, too, enjoys a particular niche in federal, state and local disabled accessibility law. **Ross Altman** (see p.817) boasts an international caseload. His work this year has included representing a regional government in China regarding the construction of a large theme park. **Ty Laurie** (see p.840) has a particular expertise in representing owners and developers in large, complex commercial deals. He has advised on sundry developments including stadiums, mixed-use retail projects, high-rise buildings, medical facilities and industrial process plants. Prestigious work this year has included representing the Philadelphia Eagles regarding the construction of Lincoln Financial Field.

**Clients/Work Highlights:** The John Buck Company; Chicago Bears; Equity Office Properties; The Trump Organization; Jones Lang LaSalle; The Related Companies and Sara Lee.

## Schiff Hardin LLP

See firm details p.881

**The Firm:** Chicago's oldest law firm has a construction practice that remains firmly at the head of the market. It is blessed in having attorneys with some of the smartest brains around. As one peer put it: "*It is not only their intellects but their skill sets that impress so much. Every matter I have had with them they have handled with unsurpassed professionalism and exceptional civility.*" The team is considered one of the firm's true gems and has secured a national reputation for itself. A full service is offered, encapsulating every conceivable aspect of construction law, although commentators note that its core strength lies in the energy industry where it could be described as something of a nonpareil.

**The Lawyers:** The "*very widely respected*" **Paul Lurie** (see p.842) has a strong reputation as a mediator and is a member of the CPR Institute for Dispute Resolution, the College of Commercial Arbitrators and the International Academy of Mediators. Cochair of the team **Kenneth Roberts** (see p.851) focuses on providing his clients with procurement and alternative dispute resolution services, and has a particular aptitude for project control. This year, he led a team that assisted Ontario Power Generation on its nuclear refurbishment project. The team provided project oversight and project controls for a unit installation that was hailed as a huge success by Engineering News-Record. Other lead work this year has included representing a nationally renowned real estate developer/REIT as a mediator on a very complex multifamily housing dispute. **Mark Friedlander** (see p.830) is "*well regarded, especially for his representation of architects and engineers.*" His practice is equally divided between litigation and transactional work and he has had involvement in some major construction projects. By way of example, he recently gave advice in relation to the ongoing improvements to the Chicago Bears' Soldier Field Stadium.

**Clients/Work Highlights:** Kiewit; Kansas City Power & Light; Midwest Generation and Nicor.

## Stein, Ray & Harris LLP

**The Firm:** This design and construction industry boutique is "*an excellent firm engaged in sophisticated work.*" As the firm's clients have expanded their businesses out of state, so too have the attorneys at this firm. Much of the practice has a wide geographical reach with many cases having a distinct international flavor; the team has had involvement in matters in Central America, China and Canada, among other regions. At the heart of its success lies its consistency in attracting lawyers of a very fine stamp. On offer are "*accomplished, all-around construction lawyers well able to approach their client's needs holistically.*"

**The Lawyers:** "*Well regarded both regionally and nationally,*" **Steven Stein** has a particularly vibrant litigation and dispute resolution practice. He is especially skilled at the drafting and negotiation of design and construction-related agreements. **Robert Harris** undertakes "*premier work,*" handling significant construction litigation for developers and owners,

general contractors and subcontractors, and design professionals. Also a notable general commercial litigator, he is in a team that includes **Stephen Ray**, the author of a broad-based practice whose "*good wisdom and thoughtful attitude to his work shines through.*" Impressive work this year for the group has included acting in an arbitration involving a power plant in Guatemala; the amounts totalled around $50 million.

**Clients/Work Highlights:** The large international engineering firm, MWH, retained the firm to resolve construction law problems encountered while undertaking work in Guangdong Province, China. Other clients include Fluor; Duke Energy; Taco Bell; Bovis; Graycor and Walsh Construction.

## Band 2

## Conway & Mrowiec

See firm details p.869

**The Firm:** This small but impressive firm is heavily weighted towards construction law. Since splitting from Stein Ray, its attorneys have gone from strength to strength and now constitute a "*hands-on group of very smart, very sharp, very practically minded performers.*" The team offers advice on every shade of construction within the public and private spheres for all types of developments.

**The Lawyers:** **John Mrowiec** (see p.847) focuses on construction and public contracts and undertakes the lion's share of the group's transactional matters while also maintaining a healthy litigation practice. Recently, he orchestrated the successful resolution of a high-value mechanics' lien dispute in favor of an international EPC contractor. **Timothy Conway** (see p.825) has a litigation practice covering complex arbitration, trial and mediation for plaintiffs. His recent work has included prosecuting a priority claim on behalf of an international EPC contractor.

**Clients/Work Highlights:** PCL Constructors; The John Buck Company; American Bridge and Keller Foundations.

## Lyman & Nielsen

**The Firm:** This "*small but extremely sophisticated*" firm of three construction and real estate specialists offers a distinctly personal service. Clients receive advice finely tailored to their needs and enjoy a very close professional relationship with the attorneys on board. As one interviewee stated: "*This team offers a bespoke service and is dedicated to resolving issues in a time and cost-efficient manner.*"

**The Lawyers:** "*Leader at the Bar*" **Bill Lyman** undertakes mechanics' liens and insurance issues in the main. He has been branching out into arbitration lately. The "*very accomplished*" **Jennifer Nielsen** is considered "*energetic, forceful and very practically minded, and an attorney with a superior hold on the law.*"

**Clients/Work Highlights:** A diverse and changing client base including City of Champaign, Thorne Associates and Luhr Bros.

## Band 3

### Bell, Boyd & Lloyd LLC

**The Firm:** Commentators described this firm as having "*a busy construction practice fueled with interesting work.*" The group draws on the firm's expert real estate, corporate finance, securities, loans and bankruptcy departments on an ad hoc basis. This guarantees clients always receive the most appropriately focused service. Particular areas of skill include construction lending, claims prevention and resolution, and mechanics' lien prosecution and defense, to name but a few.

**The Lawyers:** The "*brilliant*" **Stanley Sklar** "*holds a distinguished place in the construction Bar both in Illinois and nationally.*" Although possessing unassailable abilities regarding both the transactional and litigation aspects of construction law, he is increasingly visible as a mediator and arbitrator.

**Clients/Work Highlights:** Real estate developers; owners; lenders; pubic entities; contractors and subcontractors.

### Much Shelist Freed Denenberg Ament & Rubenstein, PC

**The Firm:** This Chicago-based law firm houses a construction litigation group that serves the needs of clients both regionally and nationally. The group has broad capabilities and can take a client from initial contract drafting and negotiating to dispute resolution. The construction litigation practice is intimately connected with the real estate group and, as a result, has a particular reputation for title insurance claims.

**The Lawyers:** **James Dash** cochairs the firm's construction litigation group. He has earned regional renown for his work regarding mechanics' lien claims and title insurance defense work. Dash keeps his litigation skills fresh by representing clients on both sides of the street. As a member of many professional organizations, he serves on the Real Property Law Committee and the Construction and Mechanics' Lien Subcommittee, and is a member of the ABA Forum on the Construction Industry and their Section of Litigation, among others. Where Dash is the litigator, his partner **Stephen Kikoler** focuses

more on transactions. Clients and peers rely on his "*terrific judgment and unparalled strategic awareness.*"

**Clients/Work Highlights:** Notable mechanics' lien work includes representing Continental Community Bank in the successful defense of an appeal against a previously won summary judgment from Tefco.

### Ogletree, Deakins, Nash, Smoak & Stewart, PC

See firm details p.738

**The Firm:** The Chicago office of this titan of the US employment Bar has a particularly notable construction industry practice. The team specializes in representing general contractors and some subcontractors and has been instructed in increasing amounts of litigation this year. At present it represents a small team, but informed sources suggest that may be about to change as the practice looks to expand.

**The Lawyers:** **Randolph Ruff** (see p.853) engenders "*tremendous respect*" for his "*skill and poise.*" He continues to work on a large multiparty case concerning fractured roof trusses in a public school and litigation involving a power generator disaster in Pittsburgh. Ruff has also undertaken a wide range of delay claims this year for a variety of clients from a jail to high-rise condominiums. **Margery Newman** (see p.847) represents everyone in the construction industry from owners and developers to contractors and especially subcontractors. At all stages of proceedings from contract drafting to litigation she "*displays a sure touch.*" This past year has seen Newman undertaking a steady flow of mechanics' lien claims.

**Clients/Work Highlights:** Pepper Construction; McShane Construction; Boller Construction; Weis Builders; Simpson Construction; Bigane Paving Company and WESCO Distribution.

### Sabo & Zahn

**The Firm:** This three-man boutique specializes in owner-architect and designer construction matters. When it comes to designer issues, few teams have more knowledge. Indeed, their expertise in this area is often sought out by other construction attorneys: "*I really appreciated the help and candor they provided – they really deserve the high regard the profession holds them in.*"

**The Lawyers:** Werner Sabo and James K Zahn are both attorney architects, which accounts for the particular focus of their practice. Sabo is the author of the 'Legal Guide to AIA Documents'.

**Clients/Work Highlights:** While it is the first stop for architects, the firm also has owners; contractors; engineers and consultants on its books.

### Sachnoff & Weaver Ltd

**The Firm:** This Chicago firm offers its clients an integrated service, pooling experts from their insurance, real estate, employment, environmental and corporate groups. That said, litigation is the construction group's pièce de résistance, boasting practice areas that include construction defect claims, delay claims and related insurance issues.

**The Lawyers:** **Clifford Shapiro** has a "*distinct expertise in insurance coverage work.*" Pure construction work typically comes out of the Midwest. His more specialized construction insurance practice is conducted nationally.

**Clients/Work Highlights:** Typical clients include owners, developers and contractors.

### Other Notable Practitioners

The "*highly esteemed*" **Alexandra Cole** at Perkins Coie LLP is considered "*a great person to put a deal together owing to the extent of her knowledge, her experience and her affable manner.*" Typically high-profile hotel work this year has included representing DiNapoli Capital Partners regarding its acquisition of Fremont Marriott. Cole was also part of a team instructed by Strategic Hotel Capital to advise it on its secural of the Ritz-Carlton Half Moon Bay in California for $124 million. **Eric Singer** at Wildman Harrold has "*a practical approach to the law underpinned by a firm grip of the substantive issues.*" Construction law and litigation make up a significant part of his broad-based real estate and commercial litigation practice. In particular, his reputation is at its strongest for his work regarding designer liability issues. **Charles Lewis** is head of the construction practice group of Jenkens & Gilchrist's Chicago office. Lewis is a full-service construction lawyer and litigator.

# CORPORATE/M&A & PRIVATE EQUITY

## Band 1

### Kirkland & Ellis LLP

See firm details p.875

**The Firm:** Market sources agree that this firm really "*owns the town*" in the private equity domain. The 500-lawyer Chicago office has captured a national and international profile for fund formations, LBOs and equity investments on behalf of weighty clients the world over. Its work in public M&A should not be overlooked and the smooth handling of the most complex cross-border transactions is assured. As to style, interviewees have highlighted the distinctively

assertive approach taken by the corporate lawyers here, mirroring the hard-hitting reputation of the firm's national litigation practice.

**The Lawyers:** Hailed as a "*real legend in the world of private equity,*" **Jack Levin** (see p.841) is "*a founder of the modern business who has developed many of the legal techniques in the field.*" This senior statesman maintains an active advisory role in the Chicago office and oversees many of the firm's major M&A deals, LBOs and fund formations. In addition to this aspect of his practice, Levin coauthors a leading M&A text and currently advises the President's Advisory Panel on Federal Tax Reform on business and

entity taxation. A current leading light in the private equity world, **Kevin Evanich** (see p.828) manages a practice focused on fund formation and M&A. A forceful man who "*endeavors to pin every point down,*" his major clients include Code, Hennessy & Simmons, Parthenon Capital and Pfingsten Partners. Recent examples of his work include counseling on the acquisition of the world's largest chain of bowling centers as well as structuring captive mezzanine and novel private equity investment funds. **Jeffrey Hammes'** (see p.834) abilities in the private equity arena have also hit the headlines this year. Highlights include acting for BainCapital in the acquisition of

Toys 'R' Us, a deal worth $7.4 billion. Recently admitted to the California Bar, he divides his practice between Illinois and the West Coast, serving a diverse set of domestic and international clients. He is also the relationship partner for some of the firm's marquee clients and, as such, his behind-the-scenes workload is particularly valuable. Kirkland & Ellis has further bolstered its strength in private equity this

year with the addition of **Jon Ballis** (see p.818) from Sidley Austin. "*An all-around great guy,*" he is recognized for the high-quality private equity work that forms the bulk of his practice. He has experience of handling multibillion-dollar strategic mergers in a variety of industries. **Carter Emerson** (see p.828) is a "*skilled, calm and even-handed lawyer*" whose corporate expertise continues to impress. His general corporate practice featured high-level M&A, securities and LBOs. **Sandy Perl** (see p.849) is a "*marvelous man and a trusted adviser for private equity.*" His practice highlights over the past year have included advising GTCR Golder Rauner on the $185 million sale of ATM processor Genpass to a subsidiary of Bankcorp. **Scott Falk** (see p.828) "*shows himself to be a first-class lawyer on every deal,*" agree sources. His depth of experience belies his age, and he is a popular choice among public companies seeking advice on M&A and securities matters. As well as providing counsel to United Airlines on divestitures, the past year has seen Falk closing Adolph Coors's $4 billion merger with brewer Molson Canada. Private equity specialist **Stephen Ritchie** (see p.851) impresses clients with his ability to achieve "*remarkable results on divestitures.*" His busy practice sees him handling a range of LBO, venture capital and M&A transactions. Finally, Kirkland & Ellis is home to one of the most respected fund formation lawyers in the Midwest. **Bruce Ettelson** (see p.828) is considered an authority on private equity and venture capital fund formation, and regularly advises the firm's biggest clients in the structuring and creation of their billion-dollar funds. His considerable expertise also extends to investment management and corporate counseling, making him a valuable draw for private equity clients.

**Clients/Work Highlights:** ABRY Partners; Bain-Capital; Code, Hennessy & Simmons; Golden Gate Capital; Gryphon Investors; GTCR Golder Rauner; Madison Dearborn Partners; Summit Partners; Sun Capital Partners; Swander Pace Capital and Willis Stein & Partners.

## Mayer, Brown, Rowe & Maw LLP
See firm details p.876

**The Firm:** Corporate clients find the "*culture of friendliness*" and an "*absolute lack of arrogance*" here extremely refreshing. Using their tremendous capacity to carry out varied work in large volumes, these talented attorneys handle a broad remit of M&A, securities and private equity deals. Setting it apart from several of its competitors, Mayer Brown is able to offer corporate clients the benefits of a network of offices across the USA and Europe.

**The Lawyers:** Interviewees concur that **Robert Helman** (see p.835) has secured "*an incredible prominence*" in the corporate arena through his almost 40 years of experience. His tremendous capabilities in M&A, securities and other aspects of traditional corporate practice have attracted the market's most sophisticated and demanding clients. **Scott Davis**' (see p.826) "*practical skills and business acumen distinguish him from the pack,*" clients said. A specialist in M&A and related securities matters, his recent major cases include representing Chem-

tura in its $1.8 billion merger with Great Lakes Chemical, a union that forms one of the largest publicly traded chemical companies in the country. A tremendous project manager, he is "*the glue that holds a deal together.*" The "*thorough and highly analytical*" **Richard Shepro** (see p.856) "*can boil problems down to get them solved.*" Shepro's practice focuses on commerce between the USA and France, and involves him working with Mayer Brown's Paris and London offices on large multinational insurance company transactions in particular. He recently handled the LBO of French music company Buffet Crampon on behalf of private equity client Argos Soditic, a case involving a simultaneous buyout of businesses in the UK, USA, Japan and India. Vastly experienced in M&A and general corporate work, **Frederick Thomas** (see p.860) is an "*extremely knowledgeable counsel*" who takes a "*practical and pragmatic approach*" to deals. This year he represented Marconi on US aspects of its £1.2 billion sale of its telecommunications equipment and international services business to Ericsson AB. Capital One also counts among Thomas' clients, and he recently advised the company on two multimillion-dollar acquisitions. Such is the quality of service provided by this corporate expert, one client told researchers: "*He is number two on my speed dial, right after my wife.*" A well-seasoned securities lawyer, **James Junewicz** (see p.837) wins the loyalty of clients through his high standards of service, style and expertise. He is "*excellent at understanding and spotting issues,*" extolled one satisfied customer; "*he covered our back well throughout the deal.*" His practice has a growing focus on securities, high-yield and IPO work, and recent work highlights include representing Wachovia in its high-yield offering for a larger video company. **Edward Schneidman** (see p.855) is "*one of a handful who are at the top of the game,*" clients say. He is a particular force in the field of real estate M&A. A lawyer with a growing following, **Paul Theiss**' (see p.860) corporate and securities practice incorporates IPOs, debt placements, venture capital and M&A for public private companies. He is recognized in particular for his industry expertise in telecom and gaming. An experienced securities attorney, **Edward Best**'s (see p.820) work in this area covers IPO, debt securities, private and Eurobond offerings. He concentrates approximately one third of his time on M&A and also handles a range of general corporate work. Meanwhile, **John Noell**'s (see p.848) caseload has a strong private equity element to it, advising clients on large fund formations, joint ventures and M&A. A recognized leader in the fund formation arena, **Herbert Krueger** (see p.839) is particularly known for his work creating and representing real estate funds and large property investors. "*A great relationship manager and a pleasure to work with,*" his practice also encompasses pension plan investments, executive compensation, ERISA and employee benefit plans. Two newcomers were singled out by impressed clients: **Jennifer Keating** (see p.838) is "*an incredibly dedicated young lawyer who has shown herself more than capable of running the whole show,*"

## Corporate/M&A
### Leading Individuals

### Senior Statesmen

**HELMAN Robert** *Mayer, Brown, Rowe & Maw LLP*
**LEVIN Jack** *Kirkland & Ellis LLP*

[1] **COLE Thomas** *Sidley Austin LLP*
**LOWINGER Frederick** *Sidley Austin LLP*
**MULANEY JR Charles** *Skadden, Arps*
**WALL Robert** *Winston & Strawn LLP*
**WANDER Herbert** *Katten Muchin Rosenman LLP*

[2] **DAVIS Scott** *Mayer, Brown, Rowe & Maw LLP*
**EMERSON Carter** *Kirkland & Ellis LLP*
**EVANICH Kevin** *Kirkland & Ellis LLP*
**GERSTEIN Mark** *Latham & Watkins LLP*
**KUNKEL William** *Skadden, Arps*
**LUBIN Donald** *Sonnenschein Nath & Rosenthal*
**OSBORNE Robert** *Jenner & Block LLP*
**SHEPRO Richard** *Mayer, Brown, Rowe & Maw LLP*
**THOMAS Frederick** *Mayer, Brown, Rowe & Maw LLP*

[3] **CHOI Paul** *Sidley Austin LLP*
**CULLEN Gary** *Skadden, Arps*
**FALK R Scott** *Kirkland & Ellis LLP*
**JUNEWICZ James** *Mayer, Brown, Rowe & Maw  LLP*
**MEADOWS Stanley** *McDermott Will & Emery*
**QASIM Imad** *Sidley Austin LLP*
**SCHREIBER Rodd** *Skadden, Arps*

[4] **AIZENSTEIN Neal** *Sonnenschein Nath & Rosenthal*
**BEST Edward** *Mayer, Brown, Rowe & Maw LLP*
**FRIEDLI Helen** *McDermott Will & Emery*
**FROY Michael** *Sonnenschein Nath & Rosenthal*
**GOODMAN Stuart** *Schiff Hardin LLP*
**GROMACKI Joseph** *Jenner & Block LLP*
**HAHN Arthur** *Katten Muchin Rosenman LLP*
**KITSLAAR Libby** *Jones Day*
**LANDSMAN Stephen** *DLA Piper Rudnick Gray Cary*
**NAPOLITANO Steven** *Winston & Strawn LLP*
**SCHNEIDMAN Edward** *Mayer, Brown, Rowe & Maw LLP*
**THEISS Paul** *Mayer, Brown, Rowe & Maw LLP*
**TOTH Bruce** *Winston & Strawn LLP*

### Up-and-coming individuals

**GUPTA Shilpi** *Skadden, Arps*
**KEATING Jennifer** *Mayer, Brown, Rowe & Maw LLP*
**LIDBURY James** *Mayer, Brown, Rowe & Maw LLP*

---

while **James Lidbury** (see p.841) is recommended as *"an exceptional corporate lawyer – professional, intelligent and friendly."*
**Clients/Work Highlights:** Chemtura; Devon Energy; OshKosh B'Gosh; Swisscom; Argos Soditic; Molex; Baytree National Bank & Trust; Chicago Symphony Orchestra; United Asset Coverage; Mesirow Financial; Everest Reinsurance; Hospira; Whirlpool; Illinois Tool Works; Capital One; Trans-Canada; Ryerson Tull and Home Depot.

### Sidley Austin LLP
See firm details p.883
**The Firm:** This outstanding international firm is placed among *"the best firms for big-ticket clients"* on a national level. The corporate team handles numer-

---

ous multimillion-dollar deals from the Chicago office for both long-standing and one-off clients. The representation of issuers in sales and divestitures forms the backbone of the M&A practice, and the firm is also experiencing a revival of private equity M&A. Recent examples include assisting Exelon in a $22 billion acquisition deal that will create the largest electric utility in the USA. Lawyers here are also employing the firm's extensive resources, including its *"great network of contacts,"* to advise School Specialty's special committee of the board during its $1.5 billion acquisition by BainCapital.
**The Lawyers: Thomas Cole** (see p.824) scores an *"A-plus"* among market sources for his M&A expertise, with clients describing him as a *"superb M&A strategist with an impressive boardroom demeanor,"* skills he regularly puts to use when advising boards and committees on a range of corporate governance matters. Prudential Insurance and Zenith Electronics are among the boards to which Cole has provided counsel. As chair of the firm's executive committee, this *"superb businessman"* has considerable management responsibilities, but is proving highly effective at maintaining the quality and reputation of his own practice. M&A specialist **Frederick Lowinger** (see p.842) is considered an *"excellent team coordinator with great business sense"* by his clients. These clients include brokerage firm Aon, for which he recently handled the sale of its claims processing business to Scandent Group. This year has also seen this talented attorney processing multimillion-dollar M&A matters for West Corporation. **Imad Qasim** (see p.850) is a *"real pleasure to work with"* because of his solutions-oriented approach to deal management. In addition to taking on large public company mergers, he also specializes in securities offerings, both public and private. **Paul Choi** (see p.824) stands out as *"very impressive for someone of his relative youth"* and peers recognize his *"exemplary drafting skills."* His burgeoning M&A and corporate finance practice has recently included advising First Data on its $7 billion acquisition of Concord EFS.
**Clients/Work Highlights:** The group's client base includes an impressive array of companies, as well as utilities, private equity and venture capital funds. A cross-section includes Merrill Lynch; West Corporation; First Data; Aon; Alberto-Culver and Sara Lee.

### Skadden, Arps, Slate, Meagher & Flom LLP & Affiliates
See firm details p.1557
**The Firm:** The *"fabulous"* Chicago office of this international firm is known to *"focus on M&A like nobody's business,"* and interviewees believe it *"definitely deserves distinction"* for its success. This year alone the lawyers here have handled half a dozen multibillion-dollar M&A transactions and the firm can also boast having most private equity investment groups on its books. Corporate clients are highly impressed with the firm's consistency: *"No matter what level of lawyer you talk to, you can rely on always getting top-quality service."*
**The Lawyers: Charles Mulaney** (see p.847) is undoubtedly a *"marquee name"* in the corporate

---

arena. In the past year, he has been a headline name on major M&A deals such as Guidant's acquisition by Johnson & Johnson, a deal worth $21.5 billion. Mulaney has also been involved in representing Scientific-Atlanta in its acquisition by Cisco Systems. **William Kunkel** (see p.839) *"provides reliable guidance through the most complex deals,"* clients say. A *"down-to-earth"* M&A specialist who *"really understands business relationships,"* he recently counseled Wm Wrigley Jr in its $1.5 billion acquisition of several Kraft brands, including Lifesavers and Altoids. He also acted as lead counsel for General Binding in its merger with Acco Brands. Interviewees are convinced that corporate finance and M&A specialist **Gary Cullen** (see p.826) *"always does a fine job for his client."* His recent public M&A accolades include representing National Steel in the $1.05 billion Chapter 11 auction of its assets to United States Steel. Providing strategic corporate governance advice to boards and committees is also a major aspect of Cullen's practice. **Rodd Schreiber** (see p.855) combines practicality, knowledge and a *"smooth and laid back"* style to serve an impressive roster of corporate clients. This M&A specialist's recent highlights include representing real estate investment company LaSalle Partners in its merger with Jones Lang Wooten. His practice generally has a leaning towards the life sciences, healthcare and IT industries. **Shilpi Gupta** (see p.833) has secured a reputation as a hard-working and dedicated corporate practitioner, while the combination of **Peter Krupp** (see p.839) and **Kimberly deBeers** (see p.826) is an impressive draw in the private equity arena. Krupp is admired for his wide-ranging practice and in addition to representing a number of funds, including Brera Capital Partners in recent transactions, he is also working on a major merger in the airline industry. DeBeers has a similarly broad practice, and is experienced in multijurisdictional work having been involved in deals across Europe, Asia and Australia.
**Clients/Work Highlights:** Scientific-Atlanta; Guidant; AMCORE; Anderson-Tully Lumber; FTI Consulting; OAO Severstal; General Binding and Lane Industries.

### Band 2

### Latham & Watkins LLP
**The Firm:** This Chicago corporate team of 35 attorneys displays distinct *"leadership and direction,"* market sources said. Part of a *"great nationwide corporate practice,"* the group takes on a vast swathe of work on behalf of an *"all-star client roster"* of investment banks, public and private companies, private equity sponsors and special committees. With increasingly large deals coming the firm's way, the weight of the M&A practice is growing to match the existing corporate finance expertise. Recent highlights include helping Laidlaw Industries to dispose of its medical response business, a sale worth $820 million. Attorneys also advised Koch Industries on its $1 billion sale of its energy trading business to Merrill

Lynch. These lawyers *"stand behind their advice and actions,"* report clients, and *"inspire confidence with their up-to-date knowledge"* of corporate issues.

**The Lawyers: Mark Gerstein** is considered to be *"at the top of the profession"* in both M&A and private equity work. *"A concise thinker with superior knowledge of this field,"* he cochairs the firm's global M&A practice and spends a large proportion of his time handling private equity transactions for clients such as Glencoe Capital.

**Clients/Work Highlights:** Laidlaw International; ST Engineering; Reliant Pharmaceuticals; CCC Information Services Group; UBS Investment Bank; Accuride Corporation; Merrill Lynch; Nicor and Koch Industries.

## Winston & Strawn LLP
See firm details p.886

**The Firm:** This year has seen expansion of this Chicago-based firm's corporate practice and a major thrust into capital markets, hedge funds, venture capital and other aspects of the financial institutions market. Private equity is the firm's current strongest niche and there is also a trend to representing an increasing proportion of borrowers in large syndicated loan transactions. A sizable team of partners and juniors also maintain the firm's traditional expertise in M&A and securities work. Clients have certainly been impressed, one praising Winston & Strawn lawyers for taking a *"practical and problem-solving approach – they don't just go for glory."*

**The Lawyers: Robert Wall** (see p.862) is a *"leader in corporate securities – he is experienced in the legal issues and their application to business."* He represented AirGate PCS in its merger with Alamosa Holdings, both public traded companies who are affiliates of the Sprint wireless network. IPOs are also one of Wall's specialties and he recently acted for FreightCar America in its IPO and secondary offerings. **Bruce Toth** stands out with his general corporate expertise, and his detailed understanding of M&A and securities law. He led the Winston & Strawn team acting for hedge fund Stark in its formation of Freeport Capital and represented Dean Foods in a spin-out deal worth $800 million. **Stanford Goldblatt** is an experienced practitioner with three decades of *"amazingly good work"* behind him. He focuses his practice on private equity and is well respected within the market for his expertise in acquisitions, divestitures and investments. This year has seen **Steven Napolitano** join the firm from Katten Muchin Zavis Rosenman. Well known for his private equity and M&A expertise, he splits his time between Chicago and New York and represents entities such as Cortec and other leveraged funds. It is not only his legal knowledge that has won him plaudits from clients; he is a *"great business generator,"* said one, *"he is just terrific at getting clients."*

**Clients/Work Highlights:** Motorola; Boeing; Luxottica; Striker Corporation; Nuveen Investments; Morgan Stanley; Reyes Holdings; Citigroup and Deutsche Bank.

## Baker & McKenzie
See firm details p.866

**The Firm:** This firm is a *"juggernaut"* on the international corporate highway and the Chicago office's relatively small but highly respected corporate practice benefits from the firm's global reputation. Once again interviewees recognized Baker & McKenzie's capacity to execute the cross-border and international aspects of corporate transactions, especially relating to private equity, M&A involving LBOs and securities. The team is also focused on representing venture capital funds making investments and venture-backed technology companies focused on their future growth.

**The Lawyers:** Over the past year there have been several changes in the coordinators of the firm's corporate groups. Craig Roeder now chairs the corporate and securities practice in Chicago.

**Clients/Work Highlights:** Abbott Laboratories; CommScope; Gardner Denver; Eaton; Ashland; Sterling Capital Partners; One Equity Partners; EQT and Allianz.

## Jenner & Block LLP
See firm details p.873

**The Firm:** Interviewees singled out this firm for having a corporate practice that is *"on the up."* Following several recent lateral hires, the team has displayed an increased strength in M&A, securities, finance and private equity matters, with General Dynamics and GM counting among the corporate department's flagship clients. Major recent projects include handling an IPO for the Chicago Board of Trade worth $200 million. The firm is also able to capitalize on its well-reputed litigation practice and lawyers here undertake transactional work for many of its high-profile litigation clients such as Sears and Honeywell.

**The Lawyers:** Corporate chair **Robert Osborne** (see p.848) is described as an *"absolutely first-rate"* attorney who is *"capable of building a formidable team."* His practice covers a wide span of transactional matters including a specialist focus on public M&A and securities transactions. **Joseph Gromacki** (see p.833) is cochair of the securities practice and has spent much of the past year on the Chicago Board of Trade case. Together Osborne and Gromacki act as principal outside and securities transaction counsel for GM and this year they have handled a range of matters on the client's behalf.

**Clients/Work Highlights:** High-profile clients include GM, Chicago Board of Trade and General Dynamics.

## Jones Day
See firm details p.570

**The Firm:** Part of a *"great national practice,"* this Chicago corporate team reaps the benefits of being housed within a firm of international reach and reputation. Clients are impressed with the high levels of service; one praised the firm for fielding *"brilliant lawyers who get to the heart of the business issues and come up with business solutions."* Energy and public utility M&A is a particular strength and there is also a drive to build the healthcare expertise within the team. The past year has seen the lawyers here involved in several multimillion-dollar deals, including advising Duchossois Industries in its acquisition of AMX Corporation, a deal worth $288.5 billion.

**The Lawyers:** Client's admire **Libby Kitslaar** (see p.839) for being *"a tough negotiator – she's dynamite."* As head of the Chicago M&A department, she oversees the firm's major deals and is currently acting for The Stanley Works on multiple deals, including a proposed $170 million deal to acquire National Manufacturing. Cross-border work forms around one third of her practice and she is currently assisting a US client with their interests in China.

**Clients/Work Highlights:** Abbott Laboratories; Bridgestone/Firestone; DaimlerChrysler; Duchossois Industries; Entergy; Freescale Semiconductor; JM Smucker; JohnsonDiversey; OGE Energy; Ryder System; Stanley Works and Xcel Energy.

## Katten Muchin Rosenman LLP
See firm details p.874

**The Firm:** *"With great depth on the bench,"* clients value the service provided by this firm's Chicago corporate practice and the depth of talent at all levels. Although there is expertise within the team that spans general corporate, securities and financing matters, several major recent deals speak to the firm's particular strength in private equity investments, M&A and hedge funds. For example, the firm represented Frontenac in its simultaneous acquisitions of Wausau Financial Systems and Kyris Image Software, and lawyers also acted for Prairie Capital in its acquisition of National Industrial Coatings. The firm has also developed a large sport practice with clients including Chicago White Sox, Chicago Bulls and Oakland Athletic baseball team.

**The Lawyers: Herbert Wander** (see p.862) is a *"premier securities lawyer with major standing in the securities regulation world,"* market sources said. A wonderful lawyer with decades of experience behind him, Wander is also an expert in corporate governance and M&A. Recent achievements include being appointed by the SEC to cochair an advisory committee to examine the impact of the Sarbanes-Oxley Act on smaller public companies. Chair of the national financial services practice, **Arthur Hahn** is an expert in corporate finance matters. He has a long pedigree of acting for banks and brokerage firms as well as commodity exchanges and clearing houses such as LIFFE Exchange and LCH Clearnet. On the private equity side, **Craig Bradley** (see p.822) is identified as one of the firm's leading practitioners. He is well known for guiding emerging venture capital companies through their initial financings and subsequent investments, and also offers his clients in-depth knowledge of securities law. *"Reliable and a pleasure to work with,"* **Kenneth Miller** (see p.846) has led many of the firm's recent major private deals in his capacity as cochair of the firm's private equity practice. In addition to acting for Frontenac and Prairie Capital, this year has seen Miller representing portfolio companies such as Ovation Pharmaceutical and he has also financed two portfolio companies for Draupnir Capital. Clients admire **Walter Weinberg** (see p.863) for having "*a great eye for both the detail and the bigger picture.*" Experienced in private equity financing, venture capital and M&A, he is "*a superior adviser who demonstrates real leadership and guidance.*"

Clients/Work Highlights: Caltius Mezzanine; Dolan Media; Draupnir Capital; Frontena; Liberty Group Publishing; Madison Capital Partners; Metropark USA; Midwest Mezzanine; Prairie Capital; Ovation Pharmaceuticals; Pfingsten Partners; Svoboda Collins; WHI Capital Partners and WNC Insurance.

## McDermott Will & Emery
See firm details p.878

The Firm: Clients perceive that this firm "*is small enough to get time with partners and big enough to provide a full sweep of services.*" In addition to handling domestic corporate transactions on behalf of US companies and private equity groups, there is also an increasing cross-border aspect to the Chicago practice. This year McDermott Will represented its key private equity client JW Childs on several major deals including the acquisition of the Sunny Delight and Punica juice brands from Procter & Gamble. Illustrative of the firm's international reach, lawyers advised JH Partners in the lease and acquisition of Frette, an Italian luxury goods firm.

The Lawyers: Clients described **Stanley Meadows** (see p.845) as being a "*business person's lawyer through and through.*" "*Tough and driven,*" he recently represented cross-border private equity group Heico in its acquisition of major Canadian and Chinese assets. Cross-border transactions constitute the bulk of Meadow's practice and he also has a niche specialty in sports finance. **Helen Friedli** (see p.830) is a public and private M&A specialist, who maintains a broad portfolio of corporate and private equity clients. Recent highlights include representing Actuant in its acquisition of Key Components. Private equity and venture capital expert **Timothy Bryant** (see p.822) is revered by clients for being a "*trusted business adviser with a can-do attitude.*" Not only is he "*sensitive to clients' needs,*" he is a "*tough negotiator who copes well with pressure.*" LBO group Dixon Midland and healthcare provider Option Care are two of his clients.

Clients/Work Highlights: Riverlake Partners; Apama; HIG Capital; Dixon Midland; The Edgewater Funds; Paul Royalty Fund; Highland Capital Partners and Signature Capital.

## Schiff Hardin LLP
See firm details p.881

The Firm: Full-service Chicago firm Schiff Hardin adopts a "*solutions-oriented and client-focused*" approach. Clients also recommended the lawyers for their "*very practical approach.*" When it comes to providing M&A, securities and general corporate advice, the firm has attracted a significant number of blue-chip public companies in particular. Newell Rubbermaid is a long-standing client and the past year has seen Schiff Hardin lawyers acquiring Dymo on the

company's behalf, in a deal worth $730 million. As for new clients, the team recently represented Montréal-based Dorel Industries in relation to its acquisition of Pacific Cycle. The firm also holds considerable weight in the private equity sphere, with clients including large institutional investors. Lawyers here are currently managing the major endowment funds of The University of Chicago and Northwestern Hospital.

The Lawyers: **Stuart Goodman** (see p.833) has an exemplary knowledge of securities matters. He has stepped down from his position as head of the corporate group and now focuses on his personal general corporate, M&A and securities practice. Newell Rubbermaid has benefited from Goodman's expertise as principal outside counsel for more than 35 years. **Michael Peck** (see p.849) remains well respected within the market for his corporate practice. Code, Hennessy & Simmons counts among his flagship clients, and he handles M&A and general corporate matters on its behalf.

Clients/Work Highlights: AAR Corp; Intermatic; Anixter; Dorel; Kraft Food Global Industries; Tuthill; Chicago Stock Exchange; Prospect Partners; Wintrust Financial; CIB Marine Bancshares and Trinsic.

## Sonnenschein Nath & Rosenthal LLP
See firm details p.884

The Firm: Interviewees consider this firm to have a "*visibly strengthening global presence,*" particularly in the corporate sphere. One third of the 125 lawyers in the corporate group are based in the Chicago office and clients endorse the quality of the "*effective and detail-oriented*" attorneys they come across. The firm has handled significant public company M&A and financing transactions for clients including Molex and Salton; the recent representation of German company Fresenius in an acquisition worth $4 billion is illustrative of the cross-border expertise on offer. While the firm has a client roster spanning a broad spectrum of industries, lawyers here have niche expertise in healthcare and insurance in particular.

The Lawyers: Corporate veteran **Donald Lubin** (see p.842) handles a range of complex M&A matters and provides business counseling to boards of directors. His deep expertise ensures he takes a 360-degree view of a deal. **Neal Aizenstein** (see p.817), chair of the corporate practice, is a practical, deal-focused attorney. He recently represented Salton in a variety of financings and acquisitions. Interviewees also speak highly of "*smart and savvy*" **Michael Froy** (see p.830), who straddles corporate and private equity work. His recent engagements include acting as lead counsel for Fresenius and handling a variety of matters for Molex. **Michael Rosenthal** (see p.852) excels in private equity and venture capital deals, market sources report, and has taken numerous clients through startups, financing and workout transactions. He also advises on fund formation.

Clients/Work Highlights: Recent headline matters included work for Fresenius, National Bedding/Serta and Molex.

### Band 4

## Bell, Boyd & Lloyd LLC

The Firm: Based in Chicago and Washington, DC, this long-established firm has a respected corporate practice focused on investor and midmarket representation. Its caseload of M&A, private equity investments, corporate governance, fund formation and regulation is complemented by a "*terrific securities practice.*" While this firm may be small compared to many of its rankings rivals, it more than holds its own in the market. Attorneys are able to draw on its strength in practices such as litigation, tax, real estate and bankruptcy to support the corporate expertise on offer.

The Lawyers: Corporate department chair Mark McMillan is a useful contact at the firm.

Clients/Work Highlights: Local, national and multinational businesses seek out this firm for advice, as do private equity and venture funds.

## DLA Piper Rudnick Gray Cary US LLP
See firm details p.870

The Firm: A firm with a global reputation for excellence in corporate and real estate matters, it has made its mark on the Chicago market through the high-quality work of its attorneys. "*At the top of its game nationally,*" according to market sources, the lawyers here possess considerable experience in traditional M&A across a wide industry base, with several deals topping the billion-dollar mark. The team acts for a plethora of public companies and provides M&A, securities, finance and corporate governance expertise. There is also a strong emphasis on developing the private equity element of the practice.

The Lawyers: Clients endorse **Stephen Landsman** (see p.840) for his "*proactive approach*" to deals and client care. Cochair of the M&A practice group, he manages a busy practice with clients including Arthur J Gallagher, Boeing and power utility Avista. Also experienced in business counseling, Landsman has a "*real feel for the details but appreciates that the deal must get done.*"

Clients/Work Highlights: The group has undertaken corporate work for Boeing, Avista and Arthur J Gallagher, and is focusing on an expanding number of private equity clients including Leucadia and One Equity Partners.

## Gardner Carton & Douglas LLP
See firm details p.872

The Firm: Sources recognize that this firm is "*involved in meaningful corporate transactions,*" locally, nationally and on a global scale. The corporate and securities lawyers in Chicago have seen an upswing in M&A transactions over the past year and the firm has acted for local and international clients such as SPX, Sola International and Luminos. Recent highlights include representing German sweet manufacturer Haribo in its acquisition of the Trolli brand from Wrigley. Lawyers here are also acting for the University of Pittsburgh Medical Center in a deal with IBM to update document retention and software equipment.

The Lawyers: David Kay chairs the corporate department. A qualified barrister in England & Wales, his international-oriented practice finds him acting as general counsel to numerous companies and conducting international arbitrations.

Clients/Work Highlights: Perrigo Company; SPX; PBR International; Proudfoot Consulting and CorSolutions Medical.

## Greenberg Traurig LLP
See firm details p.664

The Firm: A relative newcomer on the Chicago corporate scene, this firm has gained a foothold in the Chicago market through the "*consistently high-quality*" work produced by its expanding and "*incredibly professional*" corporate group. A substantial element of the practice involves fund formation and management for private equity, venture capital and hedge fund clients. Lawyers here recently advised on the startup of Internet loan company The Check Giant and negotiated a $50 million receivable loan

from a hedge fund for the company. A further substantial stream of work has come from companies such as Lakeshore Media and 3 Point Media, which the firm helps to purchase, re-engineer and resell radio broadcast stations. These multimillion-dollar deals involve a myriad of elements including negotiating leases, sales, equity placements and senior debt.

The Lawyers: The corporate and securities practice in Chicago is headed by Peter Lieberman, an experienced practitioner in M&A, private equity, startup and venture capital. He is supported by a team of 15 attorneys, a number that is set to grow given the trend of expansion the firm has adopted since the Chicago practice group was established in 1999.

Clients/Work Highlights: Marathon Media; The Check Giant; Mark Goodman & Associates and Devine Racing.

## Sachnoff & Weaver Ltd

The Firm: A Chicago-based firm with a respected corporate practice. Interviewees particularly highlighted the firm's expertise in venture capital and the lawyers here have extensive experience in representing companies and investors in this field. Securities, M&A and corporate governance are also strengths of the firm's business group.

The Lawyers: **Frank Ballantine** can be relied upon to "*get the deal done,*" clients said. A specialist in M&A and corporate finance, he is "*extremely effective at listening and responding to business needs.*" He has considerable experience in representing venture investors and issuers in IPOs. **William Weaver** has a well-respected corporate practice. He has experience in handling complex M&A deals, LBOs and varied clients involved in IPOs. A considerable portion of his practice is devoted to corporate finance matters.

Clients/Work Highlights: The firm represents clients including private equity and venture capital firms; investors; companies and investment banks.

# EMPLOYMENT

### Employment: Mainly Defendant
Leading Firms

1. SEYFARTH SHAW LLP *Chicago*
2. FRANCZEK SULLIVAN *Chicago*
   LANER, MUCHIN *Chicago*
   MECKLER BULGER & TILSON LLP *Chicago*
   MORGAN, LEWIS & BOCKIUS LLP *Chicago*
   VEDDER, PRICE, KAUFMAN & KAMMHOLZ *Chicago*
3. JONES DAY *Chicago*
   LITTLER MENDELSON, PC *Chicago*
   MATKOV SALZMAN MADOFF & GUNN *Chicago*
   SCHIFF HARDIN LLP *Chicago*
   WINSTON & STRAWN LLP *Chicago*
4. BRYAN CAVE LLP *Chicago*
   JENNER & BLOCK LLP *Chicago*
   MAYER, BROWN, ROWE & MAW LLP *Chicago*
   MCDERMOTT WILL & EMERY *Chicago*
   MCGUIREWOODS LLP *Chicago*
   NEAL, GERBER & EISENBERG LLP *Chicago*
   SIDLEY AUSTIN LLP *Chicago*

### Employment: Employee Benefits
Leading Firms

1. MAYER, BROWN, ROWE & MAW LLP *Chicago*
   MCDERMOTT WILL & EMERY *Chicago*
   SONNENSCHEIN NATH & ROSENTHAL *Chicago*
2. GARDNER CARTON & DOUGLAS LLP *Chicago*
   KIRKLAND & ELLIS LLP *Chicago*
   MCGUIREWOODS LLP *Chicago*
   SEYFARTH SHAW LLP *Chicago*
   SIDLEY AUSTIN LLP *Chicago*
   VEDDER, PRICE, KAUFMAN & KAMMHOLZ *Chicago*

## Seyfarth Shaw LLP
See firm details p.882

The Firm: "*The Big Kahuna*" in the Illinois labor and employment market, Seyfarth Shaw has a breadth and depth of talent that ensures clients have access to experts in all areas of employment and employee benefits advice. With close to 300 lawyers in the practice group and about 120 of these in Chicago, the firm has an impressive presence in both the state and across the country. One of the first to develop expertise in this area of law, it continues to attract high-profile clients, many of whom require labor negotiation services and representation in litigation as well as counseling. Indeed, regarding the upsurge in class action cases all over the USA, no other firm is better placed to deal with such challenges. The recent defection of two fine lawyers to rival firms appears to have had only minimal impact and the practice group is still deemed to be "*formidable competition*" by others in the market. Seyfarth lawyers are in evidence at the forefront of new developments in employment law and active in the area of employee benefits and ERISA, moving clients to praise the way they work in unison with them and give "*keen insights that help prioritize the issues ahead.*" Sadly, Michael Warner passed away in late 2005, depriving Illinois of one of its most respected practitioners.

The Lawyers: **Joel Kaplan**, who is "*one of the heavy-weights*" in Illinois, mixes with ease traditional labor work and employment litigation, such as that undertaken on behalf of Merck and Kiewit. One client summarized the feelings of most by saying: "*He has a strong personality and he makes the most of it.*" Accordingly, he is for many their go-to guy. Peers and clients view "*rising star*" **Camille Olson** as a fabulous lawyer. Increasingly, the firm's reputation for class action litigation rests on her work in discrimination, harassment and fraud, as well as the staple of wage

and hour disputes. Olson has developed particular notoriety within the media industry for the restructuring of employment practices and collective bargaining. Clients were particularly impressed with the way she treats them with the utmost respect, taking time to understand their business "*intimately.*" The drive to serve clients well was also one of the traits that drew praise for "*lawyer's lawyer*" **Thomas Piskorski**. Clients pointed to his being a "*consummate professional*" when conducting litigation and negotiations with plaintiffs. Redoubtable traditional labor lawyer **Ken Dolin** works closely with clients such as Pactiv and Pepsi Quaker Oats; he was praised for his prompt and attentive service. Meanwhile, **Gerald Maatman** commands respect from commentators for his work in employment litigation. He has considerable expertise in class actions and EEOC cases. **Ellen McLaughlin** is involved in all manner of litigations and tries many cases. Peers were in no doubt as to her value to the team at this behemoth of a labor and employment firm. The team also depends heavily on the counseling talents of **John Powers**, who has built excellent relations with leading figures in management.

Clients/Work Highlights: Dial; Belo; Motorola; Caterpillar; Pactiv; Abbott Laboratories; Comcast; United Airlines; Merck; City of New York; Federal-Mogal; Lucent Technologies; Beaulieu Group; Costco Wholesale and Kiewit.

## Franczek Sullivan

The Firm: With nearly 50 labor and employment lawyers, boutique firm Franczek Sullivan is amply staffed with talent at all levels. Peers were in no doubt as to its excellence, certain sources remarking on how "*their quality is a cut above the others.*" Of particular note is a strong public sector practice that includes a number of clients such as the fire and police departments of the City of Chicago. Clients were much enamored of the firm, referring to its "*honesty*" and the fact that lawyers here are "*ahead of the pack on problem identification.*"

**The Lawyers:** "*The dean of public bodies,*" **James Franczek** drew praise from clients who appreciated his "*trustworthiness*" and the considered way in which he communicated his advice. The market regards him as "*one of the very best lawyers around*" and "*very smart; simply a very good employment lawyer.*" Franczek has spent much of the past twelve months involved in contract negotiations for the City of Chicago and providing strategic advice to Peoples Energy, the Hotel Employers Labor Relations Association and others. He sets standards that others would be hard pushed to better. Successful trial

lawyer **William Sullivan** commands the respect of fellow attorneys, who hold him "*in the highest regard*" due to his skill in the courtroom, where he continues to represent high-profile clients. One such client labeled him "*the smartest and hardest-working guy I know.*" Clients feel confident when turning to **Anthony Crement**, especially when it concerns litigation, an area in which he has many years of representation to lend weight to his analysis.

**Clients/Work Highlights:** City of Chicago; Chicago Public Schools; McCormick Place; Chicago Park District; Roadway Express; Midwest Generation; Northern Trust; Square D; Dentsply International; Safeway; SBC; Peoples Energy; Oberweis Dairy; Hotel Employers Labor Relations Association and Illinois Hotel and Lodging Association.

## Laner, Muchin, Dombrow, Becker, Levin, Tominberg

**The Firm:** Regarded by clients as being at the top of its game for the defense of employment litigation, this boutique firm can take pride in the level of service provided to clients. Indeed, the response time of lawyers is judged to be "*exceptional*" by some of those who have used the firm. The 42 lawyers here enjoy the respect of the market for their specialist knowledge of labor and employment law, and comparatively low fees enhance their marketability to certain clients. The firm continues to represent large insurers and their clients, with increasing emphasis on arbitrations and some significant work before the NLRB.

**The Lawyers:** Clients admire litigator **Joseph Yastrow** and appreciate his judgment; they feel that they can rely on his good sense of "*when to fight and when to settle.*" Peers admire his attention to detail and the way he never leaves any nasty surprises. A significant amount of his work is litigation conducted on behalf of the insurance industry; however, he is also active in collective bargaining and arbitrations. "*Fabulous litigator*" **Joseph Gagliardo** has a reputation that is envied by many, and his contribution to the Chicago employment legal community is beyond doubt. Clients confirmed he was "*very creative in his approach to the law,*" and that the inclusive nature of his advice and guidance meant that they felt in control at all times. His experience and gravitas benefits several municipal clients.

**Clients/Work Highlights:** Key clients include ATA Airlines; Catholic Charities; Chicago Zoological Society; Chicago Bulls; Chicago White Sox; Harpo Productions; US Cellular; United States Tennis Association; State of Illinois; University of Illinois and YMCA. The firm also advises a variety of leading insurers.

## Meckler Bulger & Tilson LLP

**The Firm:** Despite this being a relatively young practice, the general consensus is that this boutique of 20 lawyers has individuals who are "*among the best in the city.*" Few would dispute the firm's place in the upper echelons of the Chicago labor and employment market and it attracts clients with national and international profiles, from Allstate through to

McDonald's and Starbucks. A number of the partners have strong national practices, and there is a sense that the firm is achieving real success in the areas of class action litigation and collective bargaining.

**The Lawyers:** "*Excellent employment defense lawyer*" **Brian Bulger** "*brings the whole package to the table*" and is well trusted by the market. In addition to his success as a litigator, he focuses on training managers and employees. **Joseph Tilson** impresses peers. Most agree that he is "*a superb lawyer and a very talented guy,*" contributing much to the labor and employment landscape of Chicago. His recent work includes several major class action suits concerning issues such as race discrimination and wage and hour. Additionally, he has led collective bargaining negotiations on behalf of the University of Chicago and Northwestern University.

**Clients/Work Highlights:** Allstate; Archer Daniels Midland; University of Chicago; Cargill; Chicago Board of Trade; International Paper; Loyola University; McDonald's; Northwestern University; Starbucks and Wrigley.

## Morgan, Lewis & Bockius LLP
See firm details p.1758

**The Firm:** The speed with which this national firm is developing a presence in Chicago continues to impress commentators. A strategy of growth through lateral hires has continued with the arrival of Charles Jackson and Philip Miscimarra in the labor and employment group. Clients were keen to speak more generally regarding the "*impressive bench strength*" of a firm that works all over the USA and is deemed excellent in every city in which it operates. It has developed a specialty in EEOC systemic cases for major US clients and continues to be known for class actions and traditional labor work.

**The Lawyers:** "*National star*" **Nina Stillman** (see p.859) is widely recognized for her work on class action litigation, such as that conducted for the Federal Reserve Bank of Chicago, and sexual discrimination defense on behalf of an international client. With a significant portion of her work related to OSHA, she is widely perceived to have "*tremendous expertise in health and safety.*" Clients enjoy the benefit of her "*very broad experience*" and applaud the fact that she will "*get back to you promptly, wherever she is in the world.*" Peers see active member of the ABA **Barry Hartstein** (see p.835) as "*a big guy in the area.*" He heads up the relatively young labor and employment group and, in addition to chairing the Chicago labor practice, is acknowledged as a leading writer. The impressive quality of **Charles Jackson**'s (see p.836) work means he commands much respect among peers. Having moved across from Seyfarth recently, he brings a "*great reputation in class actions, especially the big cases.*" He is also active in the area of employee benefits litigation. "*Most lawyers pale next to* **Philip Miscimarra** (see p.846), according to competitors. Clients admire his "*multilayered abilities and business savvy*" as well as his "*high level of integrity.*" Miscimarra "*provides a national perspective,*" with his recent work largely consisting of labor negotiations for large companies and appearances before the NLRB. He also has "*an extensive network of contacts*" that clients find invaluable. **Grady Murdock** (see p.847) is acknowledged as an accomplished generalist who adds great value to the bench strength of the firm with his skills in "*litigation, counseling and traditional labor.*"

Clients/Work Highlights: RBC Mortgage; Bally Total Fitness; Hooters; McDonald's; sanofi-aventis; Weyerhaeuser; Maytag; Federal Home Loan Mortgage; Dial; University of Chicago; Pepper Construction; Crain Communications; CF Industries; Novartis; Union Pacific and TransCanada Pipelines.

## Vedder, Price, Kaufman & Kammholz
See firm details p.885

The Firm: Traditionally regarded as one of the strongest labor and employment firms in Illinois, this office utilizes its "*strength in depth*" and develops long-term client relationships. Clients spoke of being guaranteed "*practical answers to complex questions*" in a prompt manner, adding they could be certain that their lawyers were fully committed to their business interests. The team offers a broad range of labor and employment services, although particular praise was reserved for its strength in the area of class action litigation. In addition to employment services, a team of executive compensation and benefits lawyers set nationally recognized standards.

The Lawyers: "*Bright, practical and yet still down-to-earth,*" according to his peers, **Edward Jepson** has many of the qualities of the ideal lawyer. The lion's share of his work is class action litigation for large national companies, most recently concerning discrimination issues. "*He can be tough when he needs to be but he doesn't litigate unnecessarily,*" stressed one client. Jepson is also active in labor relations, including collective bargaining. **Richard Schnadig** is a "*big name*" in Illinois employment law. For many years he has enjoyed success litigating complex class action cases, particularly those based on discrimination, and his influence looms large throughout the firm.

His ability to get to the heart of the client's problem engenders much respect among peers. **Robert Stucker** is one of the foremost executive compensation lawyers in the USA. He is perhaps most highly regarded in the market for his work on executive employment agreements, with peers commending his "*original approach*" to problem solving. He works with individual executives, corporate compensation committees and companies in search of new employees. Recognized by commentators as a leading litigator in employee benefits, **Charles Wolf** provides an important service to Vedder's clients. In particular, in a climate of rising costs, he has been redesigning healthcare programs to make them more affordable for companies to operate. "*Unsung hero*" **Tom Hancuch** "*knows ERISA like the back of his hand.*" Clients value his encyclopedic knowledge and he is establishing himself as a vital part of the team. Equally, **Tom Wilde** is carving a good name for himself and is a go-to guy for advice on FLSA.

Clients/Work Highlights: SIRVA; Northern Trust; Novartis; Syngenta; Ciba Specialty Chemicals; Diageo; Rockwell International; RR Donnelley; Sentry Insurance; Burger King; MEBA Benefit Plans and Amsted Industries.

## Jones Day
See firm details p.570

The Firm: With 16 lawyers this is the largest labor and employment office in the Jones Day network. The upswing in class action litigation that is being felt across the USA contributes to the ever-growing reputation of the firm in Chicago. This is particularly the case with regard to the wage and hour actions that make up a large part of the workload. An example of this would be the successful defense of a class action brought against client Scotts this past year. The firm also litigates against former employees of its clients in trade secrets and noncompete cases, and is highly capable in the area of ERISA litigation and executive compensation.

The Lawyers: **Lawrence DiNardo** (see p.826) acts for some of the firm's biggest clients and is held to be "*top-notch*" by commentators. His forte is "*the big, complicated stuff,*" and he is well respected as much for his easy manner as his unquestioned professional prowess. Steven Catlett also works on class action litigation and executive contracts.

Clients/Work Highlights: The firm represents some of the largest companies in the world including Wal-Mart, McDonald's and Scotts.

## Littler Mendelson, PC
See firm details p.333

The Firm: With an office in most cities of note in the USA, this firm offers full national coverage to clients in need of specialist labor and employment advice. Despite only being in Chicago for a short time, the 20-plus lawyers in the city have quickly earned the respect of clients and peers, who noted them for both their litigation work and management training activities. The firm additionally undertakes some employee benefits and executive compensation work, and the firm's broad capabilities have attracted

major clients.

The Lawyers: Much of the growing reputation of the firm in Illinois can be attributed to the excellent stewardship of **David Parsons** (see p.849). Market sources held him in the highest regard, with some suggesting: "*You don't often get the chance to work with someone of David's caliber.*" As "*a very aggressive trial attorney,*" he is as successful in the courtroom as he is effective in arbitration.

Clients/Work Highlights: The firm represents a multitude of Fortune 500 corporations from a number of different industry sectors.

## Matkov Salzman Madoff & Gunn

The Firm: This well-respected boutique firm of 19 attorneys continues to be a beacon of labor and employment law in Chicago, and a number of large corporate and municipal clients are drawn to it. In the context of an economy in which bankruptcies are being filed all over the country, there are few firms better equipped to deal with the associated employment issues than Matkov Salzman, especially if they involve labor negotiations or combating campaigns. The firm has also been doing a lot of work involving the healthcare aspects of employee benefits.

The Lawyers: Commentators were in no doubt that the firms profile rests heavily on the activities of one man – "*terrific lawyer*" **George Matkov**, who is one of the dominant forces in labor and employment law in Illinois. Much of his work consists of traditional labor matters, such as negotiations and arbitrations, although he is also active in employment litigation.

Clients/Work Highlights: The firm represents a great number of corporations from across the length and breadth of the country, as well as major municipal entities in the Northwest.

## Schiff Hardin LLP
See firm details p.881

The Firm: Working as part of a full-service law firm, the group handles the entire spectrum of labor and employment law. A relatively small practice of 16 lawyers advises multinationals and local companies on everything from traditional labor negotiations to employment litigation. Noncompete litigation continues to figure prominently, and in the past year there has been a number of arbitrations.

The Lawyers: **Max Brittain** (see p.822) received a great deal of praise from market sources. "*You think of Schiff and you think of Max,*" said one commentator. The extent of his knowledge of labor and employment law marks him out, and his leadership of the group has been much admired. Recently he has been heavily involved in a multitude of employment cases as well as being active in arbitrations between unions and employers. The reputation of **Patricia Costello Slovak** (see p.825) "*goes beyond the city.*" She is known by peers as an excellent traditional labor lawyer who is "*smart and very dependable.*" She utilizes these characteristics to represent management with efficiency and contributes a tremendous amount to the firm's practice. Known for his sound judgment, **Ralph Morris** (see p.846) is another experienced member of the team. He divides his time between labor negotiations and employment litigation.

**Clients/Work Highlights:** Hamilton Sundstrand; Bank of America; Federal Signal; Delta Air Lines; Dean Foods; NiSource; United Technologies; Owens-Illinois; Circuit City Stores and Fred Meyer.

## Winston & Strawn LLP

See firm details p.886

**The Firm:** *"They're an absolute pleasure to work with,"* was the enthusiastic response of one satisfied client. The firm covers most areas of labor and employment law, including litigation, traditional labor relations and management training. As corporations apply more resources to protecting trade secrets, the team has found itself drafting and litigating over noncompete clauses and deferred compensation matters on a frequent basis. More than 25 labor and employment attorneys are joined by 12 employee benefits and executive compensation lawyers.

**The Lawyers:** **Columbus Gangemi** (see p.831) is a *"strong player"* in the labor relations market and an *"absolute gentleman."* By working with clients such as Caterpillar and American Airlines to help manage their relationships with unions, he establishes himself as one of the most experienced figures in Chicago. During the past year, he represented one of the largest hedge funds in the USA in respect of the protection of trade secrets. Peers were quick to extol the many qualities of **Joseph Torres** (see p.861). Particularly admired for his *"articulacy,"* Torres is making waves in the profession and attracting clients such as Anheuser-Busch. His growing practice includes major class actions and helping to combat the organizing of campaigns. **Michael Melbinger** (see p.845) is heralded by clients as *"one of the leading people in his field,"* and they were especially impressed by the way he handled the complex aspects of their ERISA problems, as well as equity and annual compensation plans. Peers remarked on his *"practicality"* and labeled him *"a top-notch benefits lawyer."* **Mark Weisberg** (see p.863) is also highly regarded by the market for employee benefits and executive compensation advice. His solid work in this area includes updating executive employment agreements and helping companies tackle their fiduciary responsibilities. Much of his recent work pertains to alterations in the rules governing healthcare plans.

**Clients/Work Highlights:** Pfizer; Nuveen Investments; UBS Financial Services; Citadel Investment Group; Cantor Fitzgerald; Boeing; Exelon; Lear; Chicago Mercantile Exchange and Grant Thornton.

## Bryan Cave LLP

**The Firm:** This small team has firmly established itself since its arrival in Chicago a few years ago. It provides advice on the full gamut of labor and employment law, from collective bargaining and arbitration hearings to employment discrimination litigation. Representing some of the largest corporations in the country, the team utilizes many years of combined experience.

**The Lawyers:** **Jules Crystal**'s practice consists of labor relations and employment discrimination matters. He services major clients, helping them with the drafting and review of employment agreements, and representing them in front of the NLRB. Peers regard **Timothy Klenk** with the utmost respect, believing that his considerable experience and ability to attract interesting cases means *"he is still developing after all these years."* Klenk's practice encompasses complex employment and commercial litigation.

**Clients/Work Highlights:** The firm represents a great many multinational and national firms, including several in the Fortune 500.

## Jenner & Block LLP

See firm details p.873

**The Firm:** Although relatively small in Chicago, Jenner & Block undertakes high-quality work for the big, national clients. The 12 lawyers here concentrate their efforts on labor relations and employment litigation. Indeed, recently they were successful in class actions involving retiree healthcare benefits and discrimination issues. The team also advises and litigates on restrictive covenants intended to protect trade secrets, and takes on ERISA matters.

**The Lawyers:** The team is cochaired by David Haase and Carla Rozycki.

**Clients/Work Highlights:** Interpublic Group; Sara Lee Coffee & Tea; University of Illinois; PepsiAmericas and Tenneco.

## Mayer, Brown, Rowe & Maw LLP

See firm details p.876

**The Firm:** The Chicago labor and employment team at this international firm covers the whole spectrum of advice and representation for some of the largest corporations in the USA. As part of a fully integrated national practice, the Illinois group can access vast resources. The employee benefits and executive compensation team is *"top-class,"* according to clients. In particular, lawyers are noted for their efficiency, with one client moved to say *"the speed with which they turn the work around is phenomenal."* Peers are no less convinced of the firm's abilities, commenting that the lawyers can be depended upon to *"exercise sound judgment."* There is a focus on the investment of pension assets and advising boards on executive contracts.

**The Lawyers:** Clients confirmed their satisfaction with the *"fabulous"* **Herbert Krueger** (see p.839), saying that he is *"everything you could want in a lawyer."* They were especially impressed by his ability to condense complex regulatory issues into concise commercial advice. The market admired his *"creativity"* and the good judgment he exercises. His expert opinion on ERISA is much valued. **Wayne Luepker** (see p.842) concentrates his executive compensation practice on advising competition committees, boards and individual executives. Observers noted that he is *"skilled in preventing clients being exposed to nasty surprises"* and knowledgeable on all developments in the law. Recently he has advised boards on how to deal with the new rules

for nonqualified deferred compensation.

**Clients/Work Highlights:** Northern Trust; Ernst & Young; Compensation Committee of the USEC Board of Directors; TIAA-CREF; Kraft; Sears; Hyatt; University of Chicago; City of Chicago; Abbott Laboratories and BNSF Railway.

## McDermott Will & Emery

See firm details p.878

**The Firm:** Clients appreciate the full service on offer at this firm. The fact that *"they anticipate our needs"* encourages clients to trust the labor and employment team implicitly. Lawyers here are especially noted for their work in front of the EEOC, and the employee benefits team commands much respect among peers and clients. Particularly worthy of note is the ERISA litigation expertise for which the firm has a national reputation, and the work on ESOPs that clients felt *"set the firm apart"* from its rivals.

**The Lawyers:** **Jared Kaplan** (see p.837) continues to set the standard regarding ESOPs. Clients are amazed at the level of foresight that he exercises in drafting such plans and found that it becomes clearer over time just *"what a good job he does."* For ERISA litigation, one need look no further than **Bill Boies** (see p.821), who was acknowledged as *"a stellar representative"* by clients. Commentators regarded him as *"top-notch"* on complex and sophisticated cases, including class actions. **Nancy Ross** (see p.853) is very active in benefits litigation and is well known for being determined and *"forceful"* in the courtroom. She also counsels companies on the requirements of ERISA. *"Meticulous lawyer"* **Stephen Erf** (see p.828) is another dominant force. Clients applauded the fact that he worked well with in-house teams and was very flexible in the way that he approached his work. His most recent work has centered on employment litigation.

**Clients/Work Highlights:** Littelfuse; Computer Sciences; Stora Enso; UPM-Kymmene; CHEMCENTRAL; Böwe Bell & Howell; FMC; Condell Health Network; Methodist Medical Centre; Square D; AXA Equitable and BP Amoco.

## McGuireWoods LLP

**The Firm:** This nationwide firm has 25 labor and employment lawyers in Chicago offering a broad range of services, from the employment litigation that accounts for the majority of its workload to helping clients to deal with union-organizing. A 13-strong employee benefits and executive compensation team specializes in healthcare plans and ERISA-based litigation.

**The Lawyers:** **Richard Lieberman** is identified as *"a class act"* by commentators. Recently he has been working on noncompete litigation and high-level executive termination cases, as well as undertaking some labor management matters. He is the vice chair of the firm's labor and employment department and has significant trial experience. Peers admired the level of client care that **Richard Menson** brings to his work on executive compensation and the formulation of retiree healthcare plans. He is highly visible in the market due to his activity in the ABA.

**Clients/Work Highlights:** Manpower; LaSalle National Bank; Siemens; Smurfit-Stone Containers; Trustmark Insurance and Amgen.

## Neal, Gerber & Eisenberg LLP
See firm details p.880

**The Firm:** This team of around 16 lawyers continues to develop its profile. Much of the work is focused on traditional labor issues, including union negotiations and representations in front of the NLRB. However, the firm also prides itself on its employment counseling services, in particular in relation to discrimination in the workplace. Peers were in no doubt as to the quality of this firm's employment and labor work, and the employee benefits and executive compensation team also drew praise from observers for giving "*concise and practical*" advice.

**The Lawyers:** Commentators regarded **Howard Bernstein** (see p.820) as a "*first-rate*" labor lawyer. He counsels companies embroiled in union campaigns and conducts negotiations on their behalf. Recent highlights include successfully representing the Residential Construction Employers Council in their negotiations with a formidable union, and also representing an automotive services company in similar circumstances. **Gerald Golden** (see p.832) is firmly established in Chicago as a generalist who covers many aspects of both labor and employment law. He has years of experience negotiating contracts and representing clients in litigation and in front of the NLRB. The hugely experienced **Harvey Adelstein** (see p.817) engenders a great deal of respect among fellow practitioners. As "*a great traditional labor lawyer,*" and the cochair of the practice group, he is considered a "*go-to guy*" in Illinois.

**Clients/Work Highlights:** The Illinois Association of Healthcare Facilities; Tyson Foods; Automotive Carrier Services and National Gypsum.

## Sidley Austin LLP
See firm details p.883

**The Firm:** The Chicago arm of this international leviathan houses a team that covers the broad spectrum of labor and employment advice as well as employee benefits and executive compensation. Not surprisingly for such a large firm, the clients are among the largest and most profitable companies in the world. Peers respected the "*strength in depth*" of the team.

**The Lawyers:** **Priscilla Ryan** (see p.853) continues to attract market admiration as a "*smart and thoughtful*" employee benefits and executive compensation attorney. Utilizing her background in tax advice, she represents clients in front of various agencies and looks after their interests in respect to ERISA-linked fiduciary duties. She is also active in the ABA. The head of the practice group **Brian Gold** (see p.832) is particularly active in the area of arbitration, although his work also encompasses everything from labor negotiation to employment discrimination litigation. Gold is often to be found assisting on the firm's major corporate transactions.

**Clients/Work Highlights:** The firm represents many of the world's leading companies, as well as midsized, regional entities.

## Sonnenschein Nath & Rosenthal LLP
See firm details p.884

**The Firm:** The labor and employment group at this firm can provide a full range of services to clients, from union-organizing to wage and hour litigation. The "*excellent*" employee benefits and executive compensation group, numbering approximately 18 lawyers, is recognized as fully deserving its national reputation. Clients reported their satisfaction with the lawyers' input on issues such as drafting pension and benefits plans, and counseling boards on compliance with the new deferred compensation rules.

**The Lawyers:** Clients are impressed with the breadth and depth of the practice of **Pamela Baker** (see p.818). She has experience of drafting various plans and utilizes her knowledge of both employee benefits and securities when assisting on transactions conducted by the firm's corporate clients. Such clients report her to be "*creative and proactive,*" and trust that she "*gives everything*" to serving their needs. Peers thought equally highly of her, suggesting that she is "*very smart and has significant experience in sophisticated benefits work.*"

**Clients/Work Highlights:** McDonald's; Prudential; Allstate; Principal Financial Services; EDS; Lincoln Financial Group; Northwestern Memorial Health-Care; WellPoint; University of Chicago Hospitals and Exelon.

## Gardner Carton & Douglas LLP
See firm details p.872

**The Firm:** The employee benefits team at this Illinois-headquartered firm exudes quality. Twenty lawyers are based in the Chicago office, working on retirement plans, nonqualified compensation plans and setting up ESOPs. Clients say the firm is "*proactive*" and in close contact with the IRS in order to keep them informed of new developments. It continues to be the law firm of choice for many in the healthcare sector.

**The Lawyers:** Clients spoke of **Michael Rosenbaum** (see p.852) with a mix of enthusiasm and affection. In particular they stressed how he really understands what it is they want from an adviser. As one adroitly put it: "*He's become a valuable asset because he takes the time to get to know our business and helps us through sticky issues.*" Commentators noted that his advice was every bit as practical as it was technically proficient. He represents healthcare clients, negotiating in IRS audits and working with boards of trustees to comply with fiduciary rules. **David Wolfe** (see p.864) is recognized for his "*broad capabilities*" in benefits work. The strength of his analysis was the subject of considerable admiration and his knowledge of the law in relation to healthcare plans is widely respected. Clients spoke warmly of the closeness with which he worked with them: "*He gets in touch and advises us on how new developments will affect our plans.*" A substantial part of his work concerns nonqualified deferred compensation issues.

**Clients/Work Highlights:** BP; Walgreen; Children's Hospital of Philadelphia; Providence Health System; Banner Health and Decatur Memorial Hospital & Health System.

## Kirkland & Ellis LLP
See firm details p.875

**The Firm:** The employee benefits and executive compensation team at this firm is made up of 13 lawyers, including seven partners. The group handles benefits issues such as 401(k) retirement and deferred compensation plans for clients, and it has a reputation for high-end corporate bankruptcies and acquisitions. The team aggressively pursues the interests of its clients, who in turn appreciate the fact that it keeps costs down. The team is also active in ERISA matters and in the pursuance of retrospective relief.

**The Lawyers:** **Vicki Hood** (see p.835) is highly regarded for her dynamic and aggressive style of representation. Clients are certainly delighted with her efforts regarding their pension plans and found her "*extremely responsive.*" They felt sure she "*knew the law inside out.*" Her recent work has included the reorganization of benefits systems following much-publicized bankruptcies in the airline and automotive industries. She has also worked on a number of acquisitions in the hotel sector and advised private equity firms on how to make newly formed funds compliant with ERISA.

**Clients/Work Highlights:** Aon; Hyatt; Forstmann Little; GM Pension Fund; PwC; Hitachi and National Hockey League Players' Association.

## Other Notable Practitioners

**Ken Lopatka** at Perkins Coie LLP is tremendously well respected in the Illinois labor and employment market, his skills in employment litigation being particularly worthy of note.

# ENERGY & NATURAL RESOURCES

## Energy & Natural Resources
### Leading Firms

**1** FOLEY & LARDNER LLP *Chicago*
JONES DAY *Chicago*
SIDLEY AUSTIN LLP *Chicago*

**2** DLA PIPER RUDNICK GRAY CARY US LLP *Chicago*
LUEDERS, ROBERTSON & KONZEN *Granite City*
MAYER, BROWN, ROWE & MAW LLP *Chicago*
SCHIFF HARDIN LLP *Chicago*
SONNENSCHEIN NATH & ROSENTHAL LLP *Chicago*

## Energy & Natural Resources:
### Regulatory
### Leading Individuals

#### Senior Statesmen
HANZLIK Paul *Foley & Lardner LLP*
READ Sarah *Sidley Austin LLP*
RUXIN Paul *Jones Day*

**1** RIPPIE E Glenn *Foley & Lardner LLP*

**2** FLYNN Christopher *Jones Day*
ROBERTSON Eric *Lueders, Robertson & Konzen*
ROONEY John *Sonnenschein*

**3** GUERRA Michael *Sonnenschein*
MACBRIDE Owen *Schiff Hardin LLP*
ROGERS III John *Foley & Lardner LLP*
STAHL David *Eimer Stahl Klevorn & Solberg*
THOMAS Dale *Sidley Austin LLP*
TOWNSEND Christopher *DLA Piper Rudnick Gray Cary*

## Energy & Natural Resources:
### Transactional
### Leading Individuals

**1** ASTLE Richard *Sidley Austin LLP*
CALLAHAN Timothy *Mayer, Brown, Rowe & Maw*

## Band 1

### Foley & Lardner LLP
See firm details p.2037

**The Firm:** The Chicago team at this national firm is the premier choice for client representation before the Illinois Commerce Commission. Its vast experience of regulatory matters is strengthened and reinforced by a continuing relationship with Commonwealth Edison, the largest utility in the state. Recent work has included representing this client in hearings connected to the changes to power procurement scheduled for 2007. The firm also represents a great many of the local gas and electric utilities in their rate cases, and undertakes a terrific amount of work for clients on the legal aspects of corporate demergers and disposals, such as the recent sale of a stake in a nuclear plant. Competitors were in no doubt that the work of these attorneys is *"exceptional."*

**The Lawyers:** Senior statesman **Paul Hanzlik** (see p.834) continues to shine, applying his years of experience to strategic planning, acquisitions and litiga-

tion for Florida Power & Light and Buckeye Pipe Line among others. As one of the dominant figures in the energy sector, he commands great respect from both peers and clients. Observers commented on **Glenn Rippie**'s (see p.851) extensive knowledge of the Illinois energy industry. A large proportion of his time lately has been occupied by the representation of Commonwealth Edison in front of the Illinois Commerce Commission. The largest and most complicated regulatory issues are invariably passed to him, prompting peers to praise his *"wonderful ability to handle the detail of complex cases."* Clients are no less inclined to heap plaudits upon him, with one suggesting: *"He is bright, extremely knowledgeable on the law, and he works with our interests and needs in mind."* Onlookers acknowledged **John Rogers** (see p.852) as *"a brilliant litigator,"* clients appreciated his efficiency at trial, with one going so far as to say: *"You can't go wrong with John."*

**Clients/Work Highlights:** Airtricity; Corporación EHN; Exelon; Invenergy; Nicor; WPS Resources; Sowood Capital Management and American Transmission.

### Jones Day
See firm details p.570

**The Firm:** The *"terrific"* energy and power lawyers based in the Chicago office of this massive international law firm have attracted the attention of a number of the biggest corporate clients in the USA. The firm can call upon assistance from a network of offices to address a multitude of transactional and regulatory problems. Accordingly, it is well positioned to deal with any possible changes brought about by the repeal of the Public Utility Holding Company Act (PUHCA) and the investment opportunities that this may bring. Recently the team has represented OGE Energy and Enogex in the sale of Enogex Arkansas Pipeline. The regulatory side of the team has continued to develop, thanks to the ever-growing presence of Ameren in the state and the rate work that this entails. Clients were impressed with the punctuality with which the firm turned work around and spoke warmly of its *"dedication to working closely with the client."*

**The Lawyers:** *"Great lawyer"* **Paul Ruxin** (see p.853) clearly has the respect of his peers. He continues to advise electric and gas distribution companies all over the country on matters such as corporate restructuring. In recent times **Chris Flynn**'s (see p.829) workload has been dominated by the all-encompassing needs of Ameren. He has represented the company before state and national regulatory bodies in relation to oncoming power procurement alterations. In his work before the ICC, clients found him *"intelligent, creative and innovative"* and, together with other lawyers, agreed that his sense of humor made him an effective communicator. He is also known as a *"highly credible"* energy M&A attorney.

**Clients/Work Highlights:** AEP; BP; Centerpoint Energy; Dayton Power & Light; Dominion East Ohio; FirstEnergy; SCANA Corporation and Xcel Energy.

### Sidley Austin LLP
See firm details p.883

**The Firm:** This powerhouse of an international firm has once again distinguished itself in the energy sphere due to what observers say is *"an extraordinarily diverse range of clients and work."* To give just one example, the team handles a great deal of regulatory work at the ICC and FERC for Exelon, the giant utility in Illinois. However, it was the transaction practice that drew the most excited responses from commentators, with several pointing to Sidley's undoubted talent for complex projects and transactions. The team works closely with national and state legislatures helping to prepare for the vacuum left by the repeal of PUHCA.

**The Lawyers:** The *"extremely knowledgeable"* **Sarah Read** (see p.851) applies her experience to provide clients with strategic advice encompassing the drafting of legislation, litigation and environmental considerations on renewable energy transactions. Clients said she engaged with their business and provided them with *"creative and workable products."* She divides her time between Illinois and Missouri. Commentators regarded **Richard Astle** (see p.818) as *"a terrific transactional lawyer."* This thorough and meticulous individual also impressed clients with his *"attention to the big picture."* One even remarked: *"He knows our business better than we do!"* Meanwhile, *"sharp and thoughtful"* **Dale Thomas** (see p.860) divides his time between regulatory work and litigation. Clients confirm that he is *"highly capable at juggling complex litigation,"* and identified his skill in preparing witnesses as worthy of particular note. He continues to have a strong presence in the telecom sector.

**Clients/Work Highlights:** The firm attracts work from a multitude of corporations from across the country and continues to act for the major energy players in Illinois.

## Band 2

### DLA Piper Rudnick Gray Cary US LLP
See firm details p.870

**The Firm:** The redoubtable energy team at this global giant represents a number of major energy and utility players in the US market, particularly suppliers. Appearing in front of the ICC and the Illinois General Assembly, it has once more been at the forefront of the constantly changing market within the state. Commentators acknowledged the strong presence of the firm in regulatory proceedings and contract negotiations. The size and scale of the firm's operations mean that the Chicago energy team can draw upon the expertise of lawyers across the international network and across disciplines; accordingly, the team can deal with any manner of energy-related problems, including associated environmental and land use issues.

**The Lawyers:** **Christopher Townsend** (see p.861) is the real force in the team. He leads the representation of energy suppliers in front of the regulatory bodies and heads up many contract negotiations. His work in the area of energy development, his understanding of emerging fuel resources and his *"smart and aggressive"* style keep him at the top of his game.

**Clients/Work Highlights:** The firm represents a number of power suppliers, including Constellation NewEnergy; Direct Energy Marketing; MidAmerican Energy; Peoples Energy Services; US Energy Savings and WPS Energy Services.

### Lueders, Robertson & Konzen

**The Firm:** This quality Granite City firm distinguishes itself from others in the rankings due to its representation of industrial consumers of energy rather than suppliers and generators. It is reasonably certain that if there is a case before the ICC involving industrial consumers then Lueders' lawyers will be involved at some point. The market has warmed to this *"excellent firm,"* with peers respecting the competitive nature of the attorneys.

**The Lawyers:** *"Gentleman and classy trial lawyer"* **Eric Robertson** garnered a tremendous amount of praise from fellow lawyers and other observers. As the chief representative of industrial clients in Illinois, he has built a reputation as a formidable opponent. One particular source referred to him as *"the voice of the large power consumers in Illinois"* and, on account of his extensive legal knowledge and the quality of his preparation, another viewed him as the single most important opponent that energy suppliers might face.

### Mayer, Brown, Rowe & Maw LLP
See firm details p.876

**The Firm:** The huge firm applies its considerable resources to corporate transactions for the energy industry. By concentrating most of their efforts on transaction-led work, the team has developed and refined its reputation for quality in finance and litigation. Accordingly, many clients are drawn to them for use on projects all over the USA including

FirstEnergy, Vestas Americas and Alliant Energy. Much of the group's regulatory work stems from the finance-based elements of these projects. Clients appreciate the *"very high quality work"* and a response time so quick it is *"normally within half an hour."*

**The Lawyers:** Clients commended the commercial skills of **Timothy Callahan** (see p.823) and even more so the fact that he was *"proactive,"* dealing with *"problems before they became problems."* The work that he provided for Vestas Americas is typical in that it involved the drafting of supply and installation agreements in many different jurisdictions. For this and more, commentators were sure that he was among the very best attorneys they had come across thanks to his *"high degree of competency and efficiency."*

**Clients/Work Highlights:** Duke Energy; FirstEnergy; PPL; PSEG Power; Suzlon Energy and ConocoPhillips.

### Schiff Hardin LLP
See firm details p.881

**The Firm:** The firm continues to represent power and energy clients before the ICC and the FERC. It has made some internal reorganizations, including the addition of a number of corporate attorneys to the energy team. This takes the group to around 20 lawyers and hints at a strategy of increased emphasis on the sector. The Chicago lawyers make good use of colleagues in Washington, DC in order to provide an all-inclusive service to national utility and power-producing clients.

**The Lawyers:** Vastly experienced **Owen MacBride** (see p.842) provides electric and gas companies with representation at the ICC on matters that include rate cases and other regulatory functions. He has taken various advisory roles in the past year, including counseling the North American Electric Reliability Organization. Peers considered him to be proficient at designing transaction agreements and in structuring rates *"that satisfy both clients and regulators."*

**Clients/Work Highlights:** Columbia Energy; Consolidated Communications; Dynegy and Dynegy Holdings; McLeodUSA; NiSource; RCN and TDS Metrocom.

### Sonnenschein Nath & Rosenthal LLP
See firm details p.884

**The Firm:** This team specializes in the representation of clients before the ICC and continues to grow in prominence in the market. Largely made up of figures that have at one time or another worked for the commission, the team is well connected and well regarded by the regulatory body. Knowing the ropes so well has attracted the patronage of some of the largest utilities, among them Nicor and ComEd. The former accounts for a considerable proportion of the team's work. Sonnenschein energy lawyers have also represented ReliabilityFirst in its regulatory hearings, and work closely with their corporate colleagues to provide due diligence on energy-related transactions.

**The Lawyers:** At the head of the group is **John Rooney** (see p.852). He commands a great deal of respect among fellow practitioners, who admire *"his pragmatism and his courtroom presence."* One of the leading attorneys appearing before the ICC, he is *"well connected and very knowledgeable."* Some sources suggested there was *"no one better at advising clients in Illinois."* Clients readily acknowledge **Michael Guerra** (see p.833) as an expert in regulatory matters and someone who knows the practice area as well as anybody.

**Clients/Work Highlights:** Clients include a variety of Fortune 500 companies, although much of its work is conducted on behalf of Nicor and ReliabilityFirst.

### Other Notable Practitioners

**David Stahl** (see p.858) of Eimer Stahl Klevorn & Solberg LLP is rated by fellow lawyers as an *"excellent litigator."* He represents significant clients in the energy sector and is widely known for his experience in antitrust issues.

## ENVIRONMENT

### Band 1

### Mayer, Brown, Rowe & Maw LLP
See firm details p.876

**The Firm:** This extensive group is made up of attorneys who practice environmental law exclusively. The group is primarily respected for its great trial experience but also possesses great capability in the transactional and regulatory fields. A formidable foe, it wins the support not just of a host of clients, but of many of its leading rivals. As one peer put it: *"It is an excellent team that I would refer work to without hesitation."*

**The Lawyers:** First among an impressive list of attorneys is the *"undoubtedly first-class"* **Percy Angelo.** He has a high visibility in the market that is matched by colleague **Tim Bishop** (see p.821). Bishop is *"unparalleled in the appellate area of envi-*

*ronmental law"* and, in the words of one commentator, *"is the man to take with you if you're going to the highest court in the land."* The depth of his experience is illustrated by the fact that he has argued the last three CWA cases considered by the Supreme Court and has briefed more than 50 cases there, either as a party or amicus. Recent work has included successfully representing the American Farm Bureau Federation in a challenge to the EPA's new Concentrated Animal Feeding Operation rules in the Second Circuit Court of Appeals. *"One of the best in the state – bright, conscientious and enjoyable to work with,"* **Russell Eggert** (see p.827) has a busy regulatory and litigation advice practice. He leads a team that advises Caterpillar as its primary outside environmental counsel in the USA and sometimes in Europe. Global leader of the firm's environmental

| Environment |
| --- |
| Leading Individuals |

### Senior Statesmen

ANGELO Percy *Mayer, Brown, Rowe & Maw*
KISSEL Richard *Gardner Carton & Douglas*

**[1]** ZABEL Sheldon *Schiff Hardin LLP*

**[2]** BISHOP Timothy *Mayer, Brown, Rowe & Maw*
EGGERT Russell *Mayer, Brown, Rowe & Maw*
FORT Jeffrey *Sonnenschein*
FRANZETTI Susan *Franzetti Law Firm PC*
GRAYSON E Lynn *Jenner & Block LLP*
NIJMAN Jennifer *Winston & Strawn LLP*
OLIAN Robert *Sidley Austin LLP*
WHITE Bruce *Karaganis, White & Magel*

**[3]** BERGHOFF John *Mayer, Brown, Rowe & Maw*
FORCADE Bill *Jenner & Block LLP*
GADE Mary *Sonnenschein*
HARRINGTON James *McGuireWoods LLP*
HODGE Katherine *Hodge Dwyer Zeman*
KARAGANIS Joseph *Karaganis, White & Magel*
OHM Michael *Bell, Boyd & Lloyd LLC*
PERELLIS Andrew *Seyfarth Shaw LLP*
SCHLICKMAN J Andrew *Sidley Austin LLP*
VROMAN James *Jenner & Block LLP*

**[4]** BOYD Eric *Seyfarth Shaw LLP*
CAHAN James *Sidley Austin LLP*
GRAHAM Robert *Jenner & Block LLP*
LYONS Francis *Bell, Boyd & Lloyd LLC*
PRILLAMAN Fred *Mohan, Alewelt*
RUNNING Andrew *Kirkland & Ellis LLP*
RUSSELL James *Winston & Strawn LLP*
SELMAN Russell *Katten Muchin Rosenman LLP*
TER MOLEN Mark *Mayer, Brown, Rowe & Maw*
VIDMAR Jacqueline *Sonnenschein*
WATSON John *Baker & McKenzie*
WEHLAND Chuck *Jones Day*

practice **John Berghoff** (see p.820) has more than 30 years of experience. Working in the industry since its inception, he has the ability to master and litigate large complex cases relating to mining, railroads and insurance. His recent instructions have included the representation of Coeur d'Alene Mines in relation to its contested opening of a gold mine in Alaska. He was commended for his *"utter commitment when serving his clients' interests."* **Mark Ter Molen** (see p.860) has a practice that continues to include more toxic torts and cost recovery work. Particular remediation and restoration matters of note have included the representation of Nicor Gas in class action and federal injunctive litigation regarding injuries and the extent of the cleanup allegedly caused by material left beneath Barrie Park.

**Clients/Work Highlights:** Philips; BNSF Railway; Dow Chemical; Union Carbide; Ryerson Tull and The Alliance of Automobile Manufacturers.

### Sidley Austin LLP

See firm details p.883

**The Firm:** The market continues to be impressed by this *"deep and broad team of key players."* Although arguably best known as environment litigators, clients were eager to point out that the firm's remit is very wide. The sheer number of attorneys on offer here makes Sidley a true one-stop shop with an *"impressive spread of disciplines within the field."*

**The Lawyers:** **Robert Olian** (see p.848) is a *"keen and experienced litigator."* Valued by clients for wielding *"a strong and calming presence in negotiations,"* he has secured a series of prestigious clients such as BP. Peers hold **Andrew Schlickman** (see p.854) in high regard. He has a practice that focuses on environmental enforcement and litigation and is typically engaged in very large and complex cleanup cases, particularly relating to contaminated rivers. In the past year he was involved in a high-profile case in which the interpretation and enforcement of restrictive covenants were at issue. Also present in the team is **James Cahan** (see p.823) who continues to be the proud bearer of a solid reputation for air work and auditing.

**Clients/Work Highlights:** NCR Corporation; Mallinckrodt; BP; Northwestern University; ServiceMaster; Appleton Papers; Sara Lee; Kraft; Exelon and CITGO.

## Band 2

### Jenner & Block LLP

See firm details p.873

**The Firm:** The firm prides itself on having *"a diverse and dynamic environmental practice."* It fields a wide spread of attorneys, some of whom have been in-house government officials, and has an impressive breadth of knowledge. Furthermore, it continues to grow, having increased its size by 20% in recent times through judicious lateral hires. The firm as a whole is admired for its commitment to equality and diversity; it has launched a women's forum dedicated to giving women leadership training and encourages the retention, promotion and advancement of female attorneys.

**The Lawyers:** **Bill Forcade** (see p.829), a presence in environmental compliance work for more than 20 years now, was recommended by one peer as the *"first choice for referral in a conflict."* Enforcement makes up the significant bulk of his practice with the remainder being air and land permitting. **James Vroman** (see p.862) has been conducting more counseling and less litigation of late. Vroman maintains a strong presence in the brownfield arena and has been working with a large Chicago housing association on the conversion of low-income and subsidized housing into mixed-income dwellings. Many of these projects were built on infected soil. The *"very talented"* **Lynn Grayson** (see p.833) has a practice that focuses on CERCLA, Resource Conservation and Recovery Act issues and due diligence work associated with the buying and selling of businesses. Interesting work of late has included involvement on the Omega Superfund site and other such sites in California. The Omega site was ostensibly a soil vapor issue that crossed over into the realms of toxic torts and class actions. **Robert Graham** (see p.833)

heads the environmental group. The scope of his practice is finely balanced, representing big business, major utilities and environmental groups.

**Clients/Work Highlights:** General Dynamics Ordnance and Tactical Systems, NeighborSpace and the Community Economics Development Law Project are clients of the firm.

### Schiff Hardin LLP

See firm details p.881

**The Firm:** Commentators enthused about this team's depth and experience. It is one of the few firms that can claim to have operated an environmental practice since 1969 and has handled issues across many different industries. Taking a hands-on approach to the clients' problems, it has *"attorneys who are not afraid of rolling up their sleeves and getting their hands a little dirty in order to ensure that they fully understand operating practices."* Typical clients are members of the utilities industry who come to this group safe in the knowledge that they will receive first-class counseling and representation for their compliance, permitting, transactional and litigation needs.

**The Lawyers:** The group is headed by star of the Bar **Sheldon Zabel** (see p.864). As one peer said: *"He is tremendous: in my mind he is the best environment lawyer that I know."* Zabel has built his unassailable reputation on a *"thorough nuts-and-bolts understanding of the law that is second to none."* Gifted in all he does, he is particularly expert at CAA cases.

**Clients/Work Highlights:** MidwestGen; Newell Rubbermaid; Chrysler; Ford; HSBC and BP.

### Sonnenschein Nath & Rosenthal LLP

See firm details p.884

**The Firm:** The environmental and energy group at Sonnenschein is set apart from many others in town due to the depth of its contacts with both state and federal administrative agencies. The arrival of Renee Cipriano, the former director of Illinois EPA, seems certain to augment the group's strength in this regard yet further. Rivals praise it as a *"sure-fire winner in a crowded marketplace."*

**The Lawyers:** **Jeff Fort**'s (see p.830) *"keen intellectual capacity"* is readily appreciated by his clients. He has a broad practice base including air credit issues, litigation and internal investigation work. Recent times have also seen Fort engaged in increasing amounts of water quality regulations work. In the past year, he has been engaged in some unique and interesting air credit work such as the negotiation of an amendment to an environmental management system agreement. Fort's client was recognized to have emission reduction credits of 1,000 tonnes of volatile organic compounds, an extraordinary amount by anybody's reckoning. **Mary Gade** (see p.830) is valued by her clients for *"the strength of her advocacy and communication skills, not to mention her creative approach to problem solving and her intimacy with the regulatory agencies."* She focuses on waste and air issues. **Jacqueline Vidmar** (see p.861) concentrates on dealing with the environmental issues that arise out of realty transactions. In particular, she is well known for undertaking air permitting work. Her matters of note have included numerous complex environmental issues relating to the expansion of the Milwaukee Bayshore Mall.

**Clients/Work Highlights:** Sun Chemical; Related Capital; Cargill; McCain Foods; 3M and Wal-Mart.

## Band 3

### Karaganis, White & Magel

**The Firm:** This smaller concern was identified as a *"very good boutique firm that excels in pure environment issues."* Clients of all sizes, both public and private, plaintiff and defendant, seek out this team for their expertise in the full range of environmental issues from Superfund to land use. It also handles some of the more recherché areas such as recycling.

**The Lawyers:** Commentators unanimously agree that **Bruce White** is *"one of the finest environment lawyers in town."* He received particular praise for his *"negotiation skills"* and his *"calming influence in tense situations."* The *"extremely experienced"* **Joseph Karaganis** earns respect for his involvement on the aviation side.

**Clients/Work Highlights:** Typical clients include private landowners, insurance companies, investment funds, real estate developers and state and local governments.

### Seyfarth Shaw LLP

See firm details p.882

**The Firm:** Commentators consider that Seyfarth houses a good all-purpose environment practice with some star performers in its front ranks. The team is made up of 15 lawyers who practice environmental law exclusively and another ten who can be marshaled as backup when needed. The environmental safety and toxic tort group has a dominant OSHA practice.

**The Lawyers:** One peer's *"first choice in a conflict,"* **Andrew Perellis** has a practice that focuses on legacy liabilities, government enforcement and risk allocation. Interesting and challenging work of late has included acting for a large industrial conglomerate in relation to a major diesel spill at an historic railroad. He has also been working on getting a 20-year-old Superfund site removed from the National Priorities List and having the government buy out the liability. An *"exceptionally good lawyer,"* **Eric Boyd** has earned particular market renown for his environmental compliance work, whether in the arena of counseling, enforcement or regulation development. Boyd is both a transactional lawyer and a litigator and has a general toxic practice encompassing air, water and waste issues. Recently, he has been representing a landfill site in a dispute with a now bankrupt company that had been contracted to remove gases from the facility. This was not done and the resultant emissions have caused problems for the client. Boyd is heading up the group's new alternative energy subpractice.

**Clients/Work Highlights:** Typical clients are printers and chemical companies and members of the manufacturing and steel industries. These it represents on various aspects of environmental compliance, especially air emissions and hazardous waste.

### Winston & Strawn LLP

See firm details p.886

**The Firm:** Commentators applauded this group as an *"excellent shop for pure environmental dispute resolution."* The practice is split between 50% litigation, 30% transactional and 20% regulatory work. Both of the team's key players don transactional and litigation hats with equal comfort and form a unit that clients describe as *"totally dependable."* Another busy year has been marked by a resurgence in Superfund litigation.

**The Lawyers:** A *"strong team"* is headed by **James Russell** (see p.853) who has more than 30 years' experience in the field. He works in tandem with **Jennifer Nijman** (see p.848), a *"tremendous talent"* who leads the real estate practice here. She is engaged in the ongoing defense of a toxic tort case; her client, the lessee and operator of an old and now closed landfill site, is facing allegations of property damage and personal injury to do with alleged groundwater contamination. Her team also engages in plaintiff work, most recently handling a contractual dispute over the reneging on an indemnity.

**Clients/Work Highlights:** Amsted Industries; Eaton Corporation; Fortune Brands; Clear Channel Entertainment and Waste Management.

## Band 4

### Baker & McKenzie

See firm details p.866

**The Firm:** Researchers were directed toward **John Watson** by both peers and clients. As one client said: *"When faced with real challenges, Watson has shown himself to be a creative and knowledgeable lawyer who uses his substantial technical knowledge to solve problems. His pleasant demeanor does wonders in overcoming suspicion and hostility from the other side and allowing solutions to be reached that satisfy all parties."* He has recently joined the Chicago office of Baker & McKenzie from Gardner Carton & Douglas and now chairs the firm's North America environmental practice group, which pools this international firm's extensive domestic resources.

### Bell, Boyd & Lloyd LLC

**The Firm:** The environmental team at this firm has benefited from the recent arrival of Francis Lyons, formerly of Gardner Carton & Douglas. Broadly divided between regulatory, transactional and litigation work, this team of nine full-time environment attorneys has displayed a track record in niche specialties such as brownfield sites. Unlike many of the large environmental teams, Bell Boyd has developed a skilled OSHA practice.

**The Lawyers:** Leader of the practice group **Michael Ohm** possesses a broad regulatory advisory practice that features a particular specialty in the CWA. **Francis Lyons** counsels on the full spectrum of environmental issues ranging from regulatory compliance to due diligence to appellate work. Since joining the firm, he has continued to be instructed by both businesses and industry.

**Clients/Work Highlights:** The team impresses many by providing an equality of service to a diverse client base from individuals, municipalities, small companies and big business.

### Gardner Carton & Douglas LLP

See firm details p.872

**The Firm:** This group of environment attorneys is viewed by its clients *"more as business advisers and friends as opposed to legal counsel."* The team holds a strong reputation for being one of the most consistent groups when it comes to the provision of day-to-day environmental counseling, with respect to all state and federal environmental law in the Midwest. The market singled it out, in particular, for conducting environmental audits with aplomb and having strong brownfield expertise.

**The Lawyers:** **Richard Kissel** (see p.839) now holds the position of of counsel in the firm. This allows him to pick and choose which matters he works on, although he is still involved in a sizable amount of litigation.

### Hodge Dwyer Zeman

**The Firm:** Peers judge this to be an *"excellent firm with strong downstate presence."* Situated in Springfield, it enjoys a strong reputation for representing business organizations on the full spread of environmental issues and has particular expertise in the regulatory arena.

**The Lawyers:** **Katherine Hodge** has a reputation for being a strong helmsman. Possessor of a strong administrative practice, she tackles a caseload heavily weighted in favor of regulatory matters.

**Clients/Work Highlights:** Typical clients include industrial entities, agricultural cooperatives, municipalities, individuals and business associations.

### McGuireWoods LLP

**The Firm:** The team is typically engaged by energy and natural resources companies and members of the manufacturing industry. Advisory and litigation work is the team's bread and butter, especially in the fields of regulatory compliance and toxic torts. It operates far beyond state lines and has been engaged in work throughout the USA and overseas.

**The Lawyers:** **James Harrington** is famed for representing significant industry concerns regarding their water and solid and hazardous waste matters. He typically represents members of the steel, oil, chemical, power and manufacturing industries. Some of the year's best work has included acting for Indianapolis Casting in resolving a major air pollution case with the EPA.

**Clients/Work Highlights:** International Truck and Engine; International-Matex Tank Terminals; A Finkle and Sons and Ashland Chemical.

### Other Notable Practitioners

A year after leaving Sonnenschein, the *"fabulous"* **Susan Franzetti** of Franzetti Law Firm PC remains the bearer of an impeccable market reputation, especially for her expertise in water pollution, site remediation, enforcement defense and hazardous waste issues. Clients have shown enormous loyalty to her, one saying that they consider her "*one of the finest environment lawyers in the USA – honest, professional, tactful and a bulldog when the need arises.*" Her representative matters of the past year include her engagement as liaison counsel for Lake Calumet Cluster site PRP group in connection with a demand by EPA for the performance of a remedial investigation/feasibility study at the site. An "*outstanding lawyer with a sterling reputation,*" **Fred Prillaman** heads the environment team at Mohan, Alewelt, Prillaman & Adami. His practice focuses on land pollution and hazardous waste contamination. Prillaman's practice is weighted toward transactional work, although he

is a more than capable litigator when the need arises. One of the year's highlights was the Bi-State Landfill case: a Superfund case involving an old landfill site. Prillaman represented one of the many generators of the waste. **Russell Selman** (see p.855) at Katten Muchin Rosenman LLP specializes in representing public utilities in substantial cost recovery claims, typically where there are just two or three other parties implicated. His significant work has included engagement by KeySpan, one of three companies responsible for one of the world's largest coke plants in Boston. The plant operated from 1890 to 1960 and the cleanup costs are estimated to be in excess of $50 million. Selman represented KeySpan in a federal

court cost recovery action against the two other responsible parties. A fine trial attorney, **Andrew Running** (see p.853) at Kirkland & Ellis LLP has a reputation as a strong commercial litigator with a keen environmental focus. Environmental enforcement, insurance coverage litigation and arbitration take him beyond state lines. **Charles Wehland** (see p.863) at Jones Day is treasured by clients for his "*real feel for the way we work and his ability to put complex legal issues into language that all our staff can understand.*" His practice is dominated by CAA work and cleanup transactional support and litigation.

# HEALTHCARE

## Band 1

### McDermott Will & Emery
See firm details p.878

**The Firm:** "*Constantly in the minds of its competitors,*" according to interviewees, "*no one can touch this team in terms of strength and depth.*" Its decision to interest itself in the healthcare market from its inception decades ago has stood it in good stead. It is now very much at the forefront and continues to gain both more lawyers and greater market share. Its

expertise is wide ranging. While a large percentage of the group's work involves issues relating to the nonprofit sector, it further represents for-profit hospitals and systems. For these it undertakes a healthy diet of joint ventures, corporate restructuring and acquisitions. The firm is further steeped in the regulatory and reimbursement milieu and its litigation prowess is increasingly sought after in a heavily monitored healthcare market. Clients with a long-term involvement in the field "*respect and appreciate its skill,*" noting that it enjoys a "*premier national presence.*" Commentators claim the Chicago group transcends geographic boundaries to benefit from a "*collective richness*" found in the firm's many offices. According to clients, the lawyers are swift to provide "*not just the facts but the full analysis needed to push a matter forward.*"
**The Lawyers:** Clients praised the "*outstandingly knowledgeable*" **Michael Anthony** (see p.818), who remains a significant presence in the firm. "*He's a terrific health lawyer,*" peers reported, singling out his expertise in hospitals and large health systems. General counsel to several major health systems, his transactional work includes the development of managed care programs, acquisitions and joint ventures. **Bernadette Broccolo** (see p.822) is both a "*great strategic partner and a joy to deal with,*" according to clients. She is admired as one of the leading lawyers on the tax regulation of nonprofit healthcare organizations. In addition, she advises on privacy compliance and strategic partnerships in healthcare systems. "*She is diligent, hardworking and one of the first names on anyone's list,*" sources reported. According to clients, **Monte Dube** (see p.827) is an "*absolute gem.*" The head of the health practice is a prominent figure in transactional matters and hospital deals, where his "*brilliant thinking and tactical skill*" are well recognized in the market. He has been especially active in public hospital privatization, the sale of nonprofit hospitals and the facilitation of mergers. Many clients believe **Michael Peregrine** (see p.849) to be one of the leading lawyers in the USA on corporate governance issues in healthcare, in particular the interplay between the various state charitable trust laws and the current best practice in governance that is evolving post-Sarbanes-Oxley. "*He does a tremen-

dous job of maintaining a high profile,*" peers commented, noting his speaking and writing engagements on the issues facing nonprofit entities. "*Excellent strategist*" **Bill Roach** (see p.851) also draws praise for his all-inclusive practice. He acts on the formation of hospital systems, hospital/physician integration arrangements and healthcare M&A. He also advises healthcare providers on the implications of Health Insurance Portability and Accountability Act (HIPAA) compliance matters. "*Terrific*" **Ralph DeJong** (see p.826) merits inclusion for his specialization in executive compensation in tax-exempt agencies, particularly healthcare. He is a member of the health and employee benefits departments and enjoys a considerable crossover practice between these two areas.

**Clients/Work Highlights:** Resurrection Health Care; Provena Health; Tenet Healthcare; The Children's Hospital of Philadelphia; Hillcrest HealthCare System; ProMedica Health System; Omnicare; Northwestern Memorial Hospital; Iowa Health System; Lawrence Hospital Center; Methodist Medical Center of Illinois; PeaceHealth and Consorta.

## Band 2

### Gardner Carton & Douglas LLP
See firm details p.872

**The Firm:** The group's long history in the healthcare arena means "*it understands the business and its morass of regulations exceedingly well.*" Commentators recognize that despite recent changes in personnel the practice "*continues to be solid and impressive*" and has a far-ranging reach of expertise. The group has seen an increase in Medicare fraud and abuse investigations and over-billing issues and continues to play a major role in the many hospital system mergers taking place in the USA. In these and other cross-state deals, the group's national connections come into play and are found by clients to be "*extraordinarily useful.*" Many sources state they have "*absolute faith and confidence in the group's integrity and ability*" and choose them to act on matters ranging from compensation and benefits to corporate compliance and litigation.

The Lawyers: The "*highly regarded and extremely personable*" Ed Bryant (see p.822) is "*undoubtedly one of the deans of healthcare law in the USA*" and a drawing card for the firm. With almost 40 years of experience in the business, he brings a "*unique perspective*" to healthcare law and is seen as a mentor by many younger lawyers. "*He is skilled at counseling at the highest level of an organization but equally at ease communicating with a front line director on the patient care floor,*" said one client. His comprehensive resume covers the whole gamut of healthcare concerns including general counsel work for hospitals and health systems, mergers and consolidations, medical staff issues and fraud and abuse.

Clients/Work Highlights: Northwestern Memorial Hospital; National Center of Healthcare Leadership; Decatur Memorial Hospital; University of Pittsburgh Medical Center; American Health Information Management Association; Healthcare Research & Development Institute and Children's Memorial Medical Center.

## Katten Muchin Rosenman LLP

See firm details p.874

The Firm: Interviewees described this nationally integrated firm as "*a quality practice with many tremendous lawyers.*" The large group is historically provider-based and excels in representing healthcare systems, academic medical centers and large physician groups in the development, delivery and financing of services. The team also brings an expertise in medical products law to the table and has a strong antitrust and reimbursement output. The presence of a regulatory practice dealing with compliance and investigations and a focus on HIPAA matters further contributes to a broad healthcare offering. The group retains its commitment to the Chicago market and clients in the city include most of the major urban and suburban hospitals.

The Lawyers: National chair Steven Olson focuses on M&A transactions and finance in the healthcare arena. Michael Callahan owes much of his success to being "*a terrific counselor, highly respected by his clients.*" He is known as a market leader in medical staffing matters and many interviewees refer to him with respect as "*Mr Community Hospital.*" "*Fabulous young attorney*" Laura Keidan Martin (see p.843) marshals a crossover practice focused on antitrust and healthcare. She spends time on regulatory work, compliance, mergers and joint ventures, and has recently been named president of the Illinois Association of Healthcare Attorneys.

Clients/Work Highlights: Central DuPage Health System; Northwestern Memorial Hospital; Adventist Hinsdale Hospital; Resurrection Health Care and Riverside Health Care.

## Band 3

## Bell, Boyd & Lloyd LLC

The Firm: Peers and clients were full of praise for this "*focused practice,*" which was said to be "*highly successful in the healthcare sphere.*" The scope of its practice is considerable and encompasses the transactional realm of modernization and expansion of hospital premises, M&A and joint ventures alongside litigation and regulatory know-how. Interviewees particularly highlighted the group's established reputation for work in medical staff relations and in new hospital projects. In addition, the firm's expertise in antitrust and litigation is of benefit to the healthcare department with talent shared between these areas when the need arises.

The Lawyers: Jane McCahill is "*an excellent lawyer and well regarded for her physician and hospital-based practice,*" interviewees asserted. She has seen an increased focus on reimbursement work and the Emergency Medical Treatment and Active Labor Act. Clients championed Thomas Shields as "*the cream of the crop*" for healthcare provider issues and medical staffing matters. He has over 20 years' experience in the industry. Corporate lawyer Jeffrey Ladd has a "*significant practice*" in healthcare. He concentrates on the certificate of need area and administration and regulatory planning.

Clients/Work Highlights: The group's clients include hospitals, ambulatory surgical treatment centers, health insurance companies, managed care entities, physicians and nursing homes.

## Hogan Marren Ltd

The Firm: This "*fine boutique*" is prominent in the managed care arena, where it has facilitated a number of HMO strategies, Preferred Provider Organization (PPO) plans and Point of Service options. The lawyers possess the combined experience of many decades and excel at the formation of multihospital systems, the development of relations between physicians and hospitals, regulatory compliance and Medicare representation. Although commentators acknowledge the firm to be relatively small, they readily recognize its "*significant quality*" and depth of input on local and regional projects.

The Lawyers: Clients and peers label John Marren as an "*original thinker*" in the field of managed care. He is the acknowledged leader of the firm's healthcare practice and his experience also includes the representation of hospitals, physicians and HMOs.

Clients/Work Highlights: The team acts for hospitals, physician groups and other nonprofit entities.

## McGuireWoods LLP

The Firm: With a "*successful focus*" and "*good size and capacity,*" this well-known Chicago firm won plaudits for its healthcare output. Its traditional client base is made up of ambulatory surgical centers, ancillary services and dialysis clinics, where its work is nationally recognized. It recently assisted on the sale of a chain of dialysis centers, and is termed "*prominent and visible in joint ventures*" and the drafting of contracts. Alongside this, the group is strong in its ongoing and varied representation of hospitals and systems across the country. Its litigation capability continues to increase, with recent examples of its work including antitrust, fraud and abuse, and pharmaceutical liability and risk management.

The Lawyers: "*Pretty much every ambulatory surgical center in the USA has thought about using*" Scott Becker, sources ascertained. A "*consensus builder*" with a "*strong knowledge base and professional manner,*" he is one of the most widely known healthcare lawyers in the state. His practice is national and includes expertise in joint ventures, securities and regulatory matters. Sources highlighted cochair Jim Riley's national reputation for work with hospitals and health systems and applauded his efforts in the renal dialysis area.

Clients/Work Highlights: The firm's clients include academic medical centers, health insurers, hospices, medical staff, HMOs and multispecialty clinics.

## Ungaretti & Harris

The Firm: This focused boutique is held in high regard by the market for its healthcare expertise. It continues to be prominent in public financing for healthcare entities, where it acts for a range of clients. The firm also stands out for its wide transactional capability, a forte evidenced by its involvement in a series of major hospital sales and mergers. The group continues to assist clients in proceedings before the Illinois Health Facilities Planning Board and in significant transactional and regulatory work. In these matters, its knowledge of state agencies and regulators stands the firm in good stead. The senior-living component of healthcare – increasingly relevant due to population characteristics – rounds out the practice. This is an area the firm has committed itself to through the hire of several new attorneys in the recent past.

The Lawyers: Clients and peers singled out Tom Fahey as the instigator of many positive developments at the firm. "*It's always a good exchange of ideas with him and the transaction is never over the top,*" said one interviewee. Others praised his "*broad base of hospital and public finance knowledge*" and his input on many of the largest transactional deals in Chicago.

Clients/Work Highlights: The group acts as counsel to a variety of clients including hospitals, healthcare associations, clinical laboratories, managed care entities and health insurers.

## Other Notable Practitioners

Louis Glaser (see p.832) has recently moved to Sonnenschein Nath & Rosenthal LLP from Gardner Carton & Douglas where he scooped considerable compliments. He is an "*outstanding lawyer with a truly national practice*" who "*handles complex matters well.*" Jack Rovner (see p.853) of Neal, Gerber & Eisenberg LLP focuses on the payer side of healthcare, representing major health plans and insurers. He is cochair of the newly developing healthcare group, a team that has a strong reputation in HIPAA and health information security. He is described by clients as "*flexible and understanding of the business needs behind transactions.*" He recently developed two unique collaborations among Blue Cross plans to share common needs for legal services. Sources endorsed the "*highly qualified*" Honey Skinner (see p.857) of Sidley Austin LLP for her work in the certificate of need area. Andrew Tecson also stands out as a talented healthcare professional. His practice at Chuhak & Tecson PC includes corporate law as it relates to the healthcare field.

# INSURANCE

## Insurance: Coverage Litigation

### Leading Firms

1. **LORD, BISSELL & BROOK** *Chicago*
2. **JENNER & BLOCK LLP** *Chicago*
   **KIRKLAND & ELLIS LLP** *Chicago*
   **MAYER, BROWN, ROWE & MAW LLP** *Chicago*
3. **BATES & CAREY** *Chicago*
   **MORGAN, LEWIS & BOCKIUS LLP** *Chicago*
   **SCHIFF HARDIN LLP** *Chicago*
   **SIDLEY AUSTIN LLP** *Chicago*
   **SONNENSCHEIN NATH & ROSENTHAL** *Chicago*

### Leading Individuals

1. **FORADAS Michael** *Kirkland & Ellis LLP*
   **GILFORD Steven** *Mayer, Brown, Rowe & Maw*
   **HAARLOW John** *Lord, Bissell & Brook*
   **MATHIAS JR John** *Jenner & Block LLP*
2. **BATES JR Robert** *Bates & Carey*
   **BERKELEY Jill** *Schiff Hardin LLP*
   **HAMM Leisa** *Lord, Bissell & Brook*
   **SHUGRUE John** *Morgan, Lewis*
   **VISHNESKI John** *Mayer, Brown, Rowe & Maw*
3. **BURNS Timothy** *Neal, Gerber & Eisenberg*
   **DICKINSON Christopher** *Jenner & Block LLP*
   **JOHNSON Robert** *Sonnenschein*
   **MARRINSON Thomas** *Morgan, Lewis*
   **MARTIN Alan** *Mayer, Brown, Rowe & Maw*

## Insurance: Transactional & Regulatory

### Leading Firms

1. **LORD, BISSELL & BROOK** *Chicago*
   **SIDLEY AUSTIN LLP** *Chicago*
2. **DLA PIPER RUDNICK GRAY CARY US LLP** *Chicago*
   **FOLEY & LARDNER LLP** *Chicago*
   **MAYER, BROWN, ROWE & MAW LLP** *Chicago*

### Leading Individuals

1. **GOLDMAN Michael** *Sidley Austin LLP*
   **GOODMAN Mark** *Lord, Bissell & Brook*
   **MENDELSOHN David** *DLA Piper Rudnick Gray Cary*
   **SCHWAB Stephen** *DLA Piper Rudnick Gray Cary*
   **WYLIE Kenneth** *Sidley Austin LLP*
2. **SHEPRO Richard** *Mayer, Brown, Rowe & Maw*
   **SPECTOR David** *Schiff Hardin LLP*
   **STINSON James** *Sidley Austin LLP*
   **WATERS Paige** *Sonnenschein*

## Lord, Bissell & Brook

**The Firm:** Sources agreed this national firm "*has been servicing the insurance market excellently for decades – a claim few can make.*" The large group remains an important national player as well as a Chicago standout and its prominence in the London market cannot be ignored. "*It is steeped in history,*" peers maintained, "*with a broad story to tell in terms of its established experience.*" While long-standing, the practice retains its relevance in the most cutting-edge of insurance matters across the transactional, regulatory and litigation spectrum. The group has been working with broker clients on compliance programs and codes of conduct, as well as independent investigations driven by the increased scrutiny of the industry. On the transactional side, the firm has long been a port of call for insurance M&A and corporate insurance issues such as structuring, licensing and formation of insurance companies. Rounding matters off, the firm also has a fine litigation prowess: it is well regarded in both direct coverage and reinsurance disputes and handles a comprehensive range of matters including life and disability claims, property losses, asbestos cases and pharmaceutical issues. "*Their background and knowledge is second to none and they take the inside track to resolve complex issues.*"

**The Lawyers:** On the reinsurance dispute side, **Nick DiGiovanni** is resolutely "*sharp, aggressive and a great advocate for his client.*" He has built up an impressive reputation in the Chicago market, peers say, with his strong client relation skills and experience handling high-profile litigation proving a boon. **Mark Goodman** has seen a surge of activity on the regulatory side and has dealt with the ramifications of many insurance investigations in the Spitzer era. "*He really stands out,*" peers believe. Cochair of the direct insurance practice group, **John Haarlow** is championed for his "*zealous representation of clients' needs*" and for his stature in the London market. He has extensive litigation experience in complex coverage cases, impressing clients due to his "*straightforward, no-nonsense style.*" **Leisa Hamm** is credited with a practice that "*continues to grow stronger and stronger.*" She has handled coverage litigation for insurer clients on an array of issues. These have included health hazard claims such as breast implants, HRT, obesity, silica and tobacco. She also possesses a general advisory and counseling expertise that bolsters her wide-ranging practice.

**Clients/Work Highlights:** Hannover Re; Zurich Re; Amerisure; Genworth Financial; The Hartford; ING America Insurance Holdings; Swiss Re and Union Fidelity Life Insurance.

## Jenner & Block LLP

See firm details p.873

**The Firm:** Competitors are quick to point to the depth of litigation expertise in this "*standout policyholder firm.*" Insurance coverage knowledge is matched by the firm's general commercial litigation success to create a "*top-notch*" service for clients. One enthused: "*They are proactive in anticipation and have a relentless command of the detail of a case.*" The group continues to act for corporate policyholders looking to enforce coverage on numerous issues including asbestos, plastic plumbing, environmental contamination and natural disasters such as Hurricane Katrina. Lawyers from the firm have also worked on matters arising from the events of 9/11. Aside from direct insurance, reinsurance is an increasingly prominent part of the firm's output with arbitration being a fast-growing area. Jenner & Block attorneys are described as "*a creative group of lawyers who bring a lot of experience to the table.*" This accounts for their success in the multifaceted insurance arena.

**The Lawyers:** As a trial lawyer, **John Mathias** (see p.843) is said to possess "*gravitas and presence in the courtroom.*" Although he is described as "*warm, low-key and nonconfrontational,*" clients are confident of his ability to "*pick the right moment to attack the other side.*" Chair of the insurance litigation and counseling practice, he continues to work on behalf of CSX and other household-name clients. **Chris Dickinson** (see p.826) is another "*knowledgeable, effective litigator*" with a focus on complex insurance matters. Clients praised him as "*a highly effective oral advocate and a great counselor.*"

**Clients/Work Highlights:** The group acts for policyholders and includes big-name national companies on its roster.

## Kirkland & Ellis LLP

See firm details p.875

**The Firm:** Interviewees applauded the group's commitment to litigation in the insurance field, an approach they saw as consistent with the powerhouse firm's general trial capabilities. Representing exclusively policyholders, many of whom are drawn from the firm's existing corporate base, the group earned points from clients for its "*tactical and strategic approach*" and its "*intelligent aggressiveness in the face of complex claims.*" An enviable resume includes D&O liability and business interruption work, alongside environmental coverage, toxic torts and products liability litigation. The group represents Union Carbide in connection with asbestos disputes and Republic Engineered Products in business interruption claims.

**The Lawyers:** Clients praised the "*consistent quality*" throughout the group but **Michael Foradas** (see p.829) is singled out as "*a great strategist and always at the top of the list.*" He earns his spurs as a general litigator and tries a broad array of cases, but interviewees markedly appreciated his critical expertise on insurance coverage. "*He takes a lead role on highly significant policyholder matters,*" one noted, "*and he certainly stands out in the field.*"

**Clients/Work Highlights:** Union Carbide; Republic Engineered Products; Bally Total Fitness; Honeywell; Motorola; Alcon; BP; Dow Chemical; Gaylord Container and Raytheon.

## Mayer, Brown, Rowe & Maw LLP

See firm details p.876

**The Firm:** The firm is popular among policyholders looking for top-quality representation in insurance disputes and transactions. It's a "*premier insurance practice,*" clients claimed, with "*more experience than many in Chicago on transactional matters*" and a deep litigation capability. It is perhaps best known for its insurance coverage capability where its team of attorneys is valued for its *"creative yet careful approach."* The group has been increasingly involved in mass tort action. It represented Union Carbide in litigation, arbitrations and mediations concerning $2 billion in insurance coverage. This included a case filed in New York against over 20 insurers for asbestos coverage. The group's transactional output also features in client feedback. Recent projects have included advising CNA Financial on the $700 million sale of its life insurance and annuity business to Swiss Re. Reinsurance is a further specialty: the team handles a number of arbitrations in this area and attends to the needs of captive insurers. In all matters clients *"appreciate the beneficial mutual relationship they have with the firm and look to them for guidance and solid advice."*

**The Lawyers:** While clients praised the team for its *"high degree of talent throughout its ranks,"* **Steven Gilford** (see p.831) shines in his representation of policyholders in reinsurance and coverage disputes. This *"terrific litigator"* has *"the right combination of people-skills and strategy,"* clients reported. He focuses on the representation of Fortune 500 companies and their negotiation, mediation and litigation needs. His recent portfolio includes acting for LaSalle Bank in connection with a claim for fire loss at its Chicago headquarters. He also acted in a case regarding a business interruption and property damage claim involving a chemical reactor. Clients describe **Richard Shepro** (see p.856) as *"thorough, creative and bright."* He specializes in multinational transactions and the structuring of new companies, in particular the formation and combination of insurance and reinsurance entities. He acted for Everest Re

Group in connection with the holding company's migration to Bermuda and subsequent public offerings. A new entrant into *Chambers'* tables, *"high-caliber, efficient young partner"* **Alan Martin** (see p.843) stood out to clients for his *"knowledge of the intricacies of policies and his facilitative style."* One spoke of his *"mastery of issues that could have been lethal if handled differently."* The *"extremely bright"* **John Vishneski** (see p.862) is held to be *"an active and accomplished advocate for policyholders, with a large range of experience."* He has spent a significant amount of time in the mass torts area, predominantly handling pharmaceutical, environmental and asbestos coverage matters.

**Clients/Work Highlights:** Illinois Tool Works; CNA Financial; LaSalle Bank; Union Carbide; Bank of America; BASF; BNSF Railway; Caterpillar; Deutsche Financial Services; Whirlpool and Abbott Laboratories.

## Bates & Carey

**The Firm:** Clients rely on the firm for its technical knowledge and effective representation in a variety of coverage disputes and reinsurance issues. It is *"one of the significant specialist firms in the market and becoming increasingly visible,"* peers added. Its work from a coverage perspective gained positive reviews from interviewees, particularly due to its presence in the area of mass torts and in environmental cases. Reinsurance capabilities also include trying arbitrations and mediating on issues of insolvency, first-party claims and other issues. *"This firm has really developed into something good,"* one client summed up, and its presence is expected to grow.

**The Lawyers:** The *"standout lawyer"* **Robert Bates** steers the course between reinsurance and coverage disputes. He is described as *"determined and hardworking with a great reputation for battling on behalf of his client."*

**Clients/Work Highlights:** American Re; General Re; Swiss Re; Gerling; AIG; XL Capital and Allstate.

## Morgan, Lewis & Bockius LLP
See firm details p.1758

**The Firm:** Clients said this group *"knows all the policies and all the facts, it understands the market and is familiar with the big players."* It has enjoyed a recent spate of successes in environmental, asbestos and D&O cases and also excels in first-party property and business interruption claims. Of particular import is a raft of large-scale loss claims following the high incidence of hurricanes. According to interviewees, the team combines understanding of insurance coverage issues with manpower, diversity of experience and geographical presence. It has a *"great reputation,"* many stated, and is *"extremely knowledgeable in its specialism."*

**The Lawyers:** Clients told us that **John Shugrue** (see p.856) *"brings that intangible extra to his work besides the technical background."* He is variously described as having *"a steady hand on the tiller"* and an *"impressive command of the issues."* He has a significant practice in environmental insurance issues, as well as D&O and first-party claims. *"He is*

*never thrown for a curve, never at a loss,"* one client remarked. Interviewees also recognized **Thomas Marrinson** (see p.843) as a *"first-rate coverage lawyer"* who has significant experience in mass tort claims and bankruptcy-related insurance issues.

**Clients/Work Highlights:** ExxonMobil; Kraft; Sunoco; ConocoPhillips; Nicor Gas and JPMorgan Chase.

## Schiff Hardin LLP
See firm details p.881

**The Firm:** According to clients, the group *"does a fine job in reinsurance"* and it remains a firm favorite for its work in this area. The group has a presence on a large number of disputes and arbitrations in the property/casualty and life and health areas and a concurrent expertise in insurance insolvencies. On the direct insurance side, the bulk of the practice has historically involved coverage litigation with a large portion being directed toward defending insurance companies in class actions. However, the practice has seen an increased leaning toward alternative dispute resolution and other methods of mediation. In all cases the impressive lawyers consult with clients on issues of coverage under all manner of policies. The coverage lawyers also work closely with defense lawyers from other departments to deal with the insurance issues behind large-scale litigation.

**The Lawyers:** To many, the group is of particular note due to the strength of **David Spector** (see p.858) and his focus on reinsurance. Clients reveal the *"top of the shortlist"* lawyer to be *"shrewd, focused and a determined fighter on behalf of his clients."* He also stands out as *"a real expert from a regulatory perspective"* and shines in both this and the area of insurance insolvency. **Jill Berkeley** (see p.820) is celebrated in the market as a *"go-to person in coverage litigation."* Interviewees noted that she *"brings a different perspective to the field"* as a result of her twin experience in insurer and policyholder representation. **Antony Burt** (see p.823) spends a substantial proportion of his time on reinsurance arbitrations. He also has an active presence in court and recently defended the directors and officers of a failed insurance company in breach of fiduciary and disputed reinsurance claims.

**Clients/Work Highlights:** Allstate; Bank of America; Catholic Mutual Group; Gerber Life Insurance; Munich Re; Penn Mutual; Robert Plan; State Farm; Tokio Marine & Nichido Fire Insurance; The Hartford and Farmers.

## Sidley Austin LLP
See firm details p.883

**The Firm:** Many view this firm as *"right at the top and one for others to match in Chicago"* on reinsurance litigation and transactional matters. Its *"large and diversified portfolio of attorneys"* brings a depth and breadth of experience in the courtroom and at arbitration that is hard to beat. Many leading lights in the insurance industry rely on the firm for transactional work where it is deemed *"responsive and knowledgeable about the background to a transaction."* It is active in securitization transactions, alternative risk financing mechanisms and all aspects of work surrounding company formations, demutualizations and reorganizations. The representation of clients in regulatory inquiries represents a further strength with several high-profile attorneys able to advise on SEC investigations and proceedings. For many, however, it's the reinsurance practice that marks the firm out for top-tier status. It's *"clearly strong,"* clients comment, and geared toward litigation and arbitration for companies in domestic and international disputes. While choosing not to focus on direct coverage matters, the group nevertheless offers a service in this area. A particular specialization is the insurance company class action defense group that has defended major claims in federal and state courts. In addition, the insurance practice dovetails with other areas of the firm, such as the environmental sector, to produce a full-coverage service for clients.

**The Lawyers:** Clients are impressed by the *"deep and incisive"* **Michael Goldman** (see p.832). Calling him reassuringly *"bright and client-oriented,"* many interviewees reported he's the *"one real standout for me in transactional matters."* His work, which has been focused on the industry for many years, includes a slew of acquisitions, divestitures and corporate reorganizations. The *"facilitative and personable"* **Jim Stinson** (see p.859) earned universal market respect for his work in insurance and reinsurance insolvency. He represents receivers, reinsurers, ceding insurers and creditors in all manner of disputes, serving by turns as litigator and *"effective"* counselor. **Ken Wylie** (see p.864) delves into the world of the regulator and brings his experience to bear on investigations and transactional inquiries. He also uses his *"sophisticated skills in analysis and argument"* to handle follow-on litigation. He has been occupied particularly with Eliot Spitzer's enquiries into finite reinsurance. **William Sneed** (see p.857) is known for his insight into US ceding companies in litigation and arbitration, especially those in dispute with run-off reinsurers. He is described as *"measured, even-tempered and smart with good judgment"* and has an *"effective way of expressing himself orally."* **Susan Stone**'s (see p.859) experience in the industry is well documented and growing. Clients report: *"When there is a thorny reinsurance problem we will immediately think of her."* She concentrates chiefly on reinsurance disputes but also has a background in insurance insolvency.

**Clients/Work Highlights:** AIG; CNA Insurance Companies; Aon; The Hartford; SCOR Group; Berkshire Hathaway; ACE; Kemper Insurance Companies; JPMorgan Chase; Morgan Stanley; Bear Stearns; Merrill Lynch and Zurich.

## Sonnenschein Nath & Rosenthal LLP
See firm details p.884

**The Firm:** As a new addition to the table, the Chicago group of this strong insurance firm can show capability across the board in dispute resolution, corporate transactions and regulatory matters. *"They stand out as doing a particularly good job for their clients,"* interviewees reported, most notably on litigation. A principal strength in this area lies in class

action defense on behalf of insurance companies such as Allstate whom it represents throughout the country. Further to this, the group of experienced litigators has encountered a broad range of coverage, reinsurance and insolvency issues, and competitors freely concede them to be *"worthy adversaries on the big cases."* The group's regulatory and transactional capabilities are bolstered by the acknowledged strength of the San Francisco and Los Angeles offices. The expertise of such practitioners as Gary Hernandez, former deputy insurance commissioner, brings a luster to its work in insurance company formations, M&A activity and receiverships.

**The Lawyers:** **Paige Waters** (see p.863) excels in regulatory matters and insolvencies. She has been actively involved in insurance company formations and M&A, in particular those involving private equity and hedge funds. Chair of the litigation and business regulation group **Robert Johnson** (see p.837) practices with an emphasis on complex insurance and reinsurance disputes. Much of his practice involves environmental, asbestos, defective construction, class actions and bad faith cases.

**Clients/Work Highlights:** The group represents a range of large and influential insurance and reinsurance clients including ACE; Royal & SunAlliance; Swiss Re; GE Reinsurance; Allstate and St. Paul Travelers.

## Butler Rubin Saltarelli & Boyd

**The Firm:** This compact boutique packs a powerful punch in the reinsurance market, sources agreed. Its focused outlook and attention to detail on the most complex of disputes add up to a *"high-quality service at a good value."* It is first and foremost a firm of trial lawyers with the attorneys having more than 25 years' involvement in litigating and arbitrating reinsurance-related matters. The group has been lead counsel for The Hartford in various contentious matters including London-market litigation concerning the company's casualty program. The attorneys also attract praise for their skill in arbitrations and counseling and their expertise inside the complexities of insolvency issues. Clients were impressed all round with a firm that *"knows the subject inside-out and has technical knowledge second to none."*

**The Lawyers:** More often than not, it's **Jim Rubin** (see p.853) that commentators first mention when speaking about the firm. *"He's just excellent,"* said one. *"He's an extremely accomplished litigator, smart, organized and knowledgeable."* Another stated: *"He's one of the key names in reinsurance."* His strength in arbitrations is illustrated by a number of high-profile roles and he also excels in complex litigation. **Robert Hermes** (see p.835) is deemed *"straightforward and hard-working – just terrific"* by clients. He enjoys a wide practice focused on reinsurance litigation and arbitration.

**Clients/Work Highlights:** CNA Insurance Companies; Fairfax Financial Holdings; Sphere Drake Insurance; TIG Insurance; The Hartford; Liberty Mutual; W. R. Berkley and Zenith Insurance.

## DLA Piper Rudnick Gray Cary US LLP
See firm details p.870

**The Firm:** Clients championed the firm as a *"prime player"* with significant reinsurance, transactional and regulatory capabilities. The group operates under the global umbrella that its merger with the UK's DLA in 2004 provided. It has now sharpened its focus on clients' international needs and continues to grow beyond its US boundaries. For example, the firm is often retained to act for European reinsurance companies in US reinsurance transactions. The *"fine litigators"* possess a *"solid base of experience"* and are *"endlessly accommodating to the client,"* it was reported. Matters of note include advising the reinsurers of 9/11 losses and mediating and arbitrating for international reinsurance intermediaries. Additionally, the team is said to *"do a positive job in regulatory matters"* in the current climate of increased investigation. Attorneys have recently been analyzing finite and structured risk contracts and defending national brokers and leading insurers in state and federal contingent commission investigations and class actions. The group is often engaged on the corporate transactional side of insurance, handling insurance liquidations, demutualizations and restructuring. *"The good thing about them,"* one client reported, is that *"they have a working knowledge of the business from many perspectives – a real advantage."*

**The Lawyers:** **David Mendelsohn** (see p.845) comes to the attention of clients and peers in the realm of advisory and regulatory work where he is recognized as a *"calm, considered man who knows what he's talking about."* His clients number corporations, insurance companies, reinsurers, intermediaries and brokers across the USA, Bermuda and Europe. He has *"a great depth of expertise"* in insurance and reinsurance accountancy-related issues, interviewees noted. The *"smart and approachable"* **Stephen Schwab** (see p.855) *"deserves the particularly good reputation he has"* on both contentious and noncontentious matters, commentators agreed. He is well respected in insurance insolvency, and in addition is seen by many as a *"creative litigator"* who has a handle on some of the most complex disputes in the business.

**Clients/Work Highlights:** The group acts for reinsurers, intermediaries, trade associations and insurers across the USA and internationally.

## Lovells
See firm details p.1543

**The Firm:** This international player is home to a highly regarded insurance department in Chicago whose influence extends beyond state boundaries. The large team is *"genuinely specialized in reinsurance,"* clients enthused, and highly knowledgeable about the issues involved in this heavily regulated area. Work is split equally between life and health and property/casualty work with the group also covering insurance issues that arise from bankruptcies. Illustrative projects include the representation of Aioi Insurance in litigation arising from the collapse of a leading aviation reinsurance pool. The case involved issues of breaches of fiduciary duties, recovery of assets fraudulently converted to third parties, proper accounting for complex financial reinsurance contracts and liability of auditors. The group is currently working on a number of large reinsurance arbitrations in finite reinsurance and financial reinsurance and is also representing clients in asbestos and environmental liability claims. The team in Chicago links with well-established offices in London and New York such that clients report: "*The international aspect is well coordinated and the service is uniformly responsive.*" At the same time, clients placed equal importance on the belief that "*they are as passionate about the issues as we are.*"

**The Lawyers:** The "*eloquent and highly intelligent*" **Gail Goering** (see p.832) is a favorite with clients. She tends to deal with the entire spectrum of reinsurance contracts from property/casualty to life and health. A background in insolvency and a large amount of noncontentious work adds to her broadly scoped practice. The presence of **Eric Haab** (see p.833) "*balances the team to great effect*" with clients seeing him as an "*intelligent, down-to-earth and competent attorney.*" "*Top rainmaker*" **Joe McCullough** (see p.844) heads the firm's US insurance and reinsurance

practice. He has handled litigation and arbitration for high-profile clients across the USA and works closely with the New York team to facilitate the smooth flow of expertise between offices.

**Clients/Work Highlights:** Hannover Re; Equitas; AIG; ACE; SCOR Group; Manulife Financial; London Life Insurance; RGA; Max Re; Tokio Marine & Nichido Fire Insurance and ING.

### Foley & Lardner LLP
See firm details p.2037

**The Firm:** The insurance group of this strong national firm "*continues to augment its solid position in the market,*" according to interviewees. The caliber of its transactional and corporate offering impresses clients and its many years of experience in the industry adds to the group's standing in Chicago. Lawyers have expertise in a range of corporate restructurings, mergers and regulatory compliance as it relates to insurance. In addition, the group's regulatory prowess is well documented and it pays much attention to the relationship between state insurance departments and insurance companies. Its reputation is also linked to the "*quality of its insurance taxa-*

*tion department,*" interviewees agreed. The attorneys in this group regularly counsel in audits and investigations and defend clients in civil and criminal cases.

**The Lawyers:** Richard Bromley cochairs the national insurance industry group and concentrates his practice in the area of insurance taxation. The Chicago team actively works with the Milwaukee office of Foley & Lardner and its cochair Joe Branch.

**Clients/Work Highlights:** Clients include life, health and property/casualty insurance companies, HMOs, captive insurance companies, broker-dealers and mutual funds.

### Other Notable Practitioners

**Tim Burns** (see p.823) of Neal, Gerber & Eisenberg LLP shines brightly in the sensitive and complex area of D&O insurance. "*He is probably the best counselor in the business for the procurement of this insurance,*" interviewees agreed, and is "*a real client magnet in this specialized field.*" He also assists clients in the settlement of securities litigation and in the resolution of disputes with D&O insurers.

# INTELLECTUAL PROPERTY

<table>
<tr><td colspan="2">**Intellectual Property**</td></tr>
<tr><td colspan="2">Leading Firms</td></tr>
<tr><td>[1]</td><td>BRINKS HOFER GILSON & LIONE *Chicago*</td></tr>
<tr><td></td><td>KIRKLAND & ELLIS LLP *Chicago*</td></tr>
<tr><td></td><td>LEYDIG, VOIT & MAYER, LTD *Chicago*</td></tr>
<tr><td></td><td>MCANDREWS, HELD & MALLOY, LTD *Chicago*</td></tr>
<tr><td>[2]</td><td>BANNER & WITCOFF LTD *Chicago*</td></tr>
<tr><td></td><td>JONES DAY *Chicago*</td></tr>
<tr><td></td><td>MARSHALL, GERSTEIN & BORUN *Chicago*</td></tr>
<tr><td></td><td>MAYER, BROWN, ROWE & MAW LLP *Chicago*</td></tr>
<tr><td></td><td>MCDONNELL BOEHNEN HULBERT *Chicago*</td></tr>
<tr><td></td><td>NIRO, SCAVONE, HALLER & NIRO *Chicago*</td></tr>
<tr><td></td><td>SIDLEY AUSTIN LLP *Chicago*</td></tr>
<tr><td>[3]</td><td>HOWREY LLP *Chicago*</td></tr>
<tr><td></td><td>JENNER & BLOCK LLP *Chicago*</td></tr>
<tr><td></td><td>KATTEN MUCHIN ROSENMAN LLP *Chicago*</td></tr>
<tr><td></td><td>MCDERMOTT WILL & EMERY *Chicago*</td></tr>
<tr><td></td><td>PATTISHALL, MCAULIFFE *Chicago*</td></tr>
<tr><td></td><td>WELSH & KATZ LTD *Chicago*</td></tr>
</table>

## Band 1

### Brinks Hofer Gilson & Lione
See firm details p.867

**The Firm:** This "*top-tier, first-class act*" is clearly synonymous with excellence. Clients were quick to comment on the high-caliber service provided, stating: "*The support infrastructure is excellent, the team meticulous and detailed.*" The sheer size of the group – over 150 specialist lawyers – guarantees it promi-

nence in the market. "*Steeped in science and technology,*" the firm takes a full-service approach to the sector and has a particular flair for sophisticated patent matters and high-stakes litigation. The broadest spectrum of IP services is provided, including patent and trademark procurement and litigation, copyright, trade secrets and matters before the ITC. Successes over the past year have included winning 75 out of 76 counts on a patent infringement case involving a German trucking company. The group also obtained a preliminary injunction against a Chinese company seeking to bring in a laser product, and had a major role in the OXO International v Zyliss case, where the federal circuit affirmed the denial of a preliminary injunction regarding brakes for salad spinners.

**The Lawyers:** **Jerome Gilson**'s (see p.832) longevity and experience have earned him the title of "*dean of the trademark Bar,*" and he has crafted the leading treatise on the subject. **Roy Hofer** (see p.835) is similarly distinguished as "*the superb, premier litigator*" and a legend in the field. His "*sound and fair style – litigation minus the personality contest*" has won him a loyal following. Despite his relative youth, **Gary Ropski** (see p.852) has firmly made his mark in the IP market, and is set to take over presidency of the firm this year. Litigation is his forte, especially damage claims, where commentators describe him as "*experienced, articulate and confident.*" Outgoing president **Jerold Jacover** (see p.836) is also a skilled courtroom performer, particularly in patent litigation. He "*develops a great rapport with judges and jury*" and yet has the capacity to "*really dig his heels

in and argue with the best.*" He represented Motorola in a vehicle tracking case. The "*bright, young and energetic*" **Ralph Gabric**'s (see p.830) involvement in the RJ Reynolds case involving over $1 billion in a claim for damages has cast the spotlight on him. **Laura Miller** (see p.846) is noted for her "*mastery of detail*" and "*tremendous amount of intellectual depth*" especially in ITC work and Internet-related issues. She is committed to her clients and places a lot of emphasis on client care. Destined for success is the "*sharply intelligent*" **Meredith Addy** (see p.817). She impresses with her work for Genentech, her experience in appellate matters and her understanding of the federal circuit. Her intellectual strength has instilled such confidence that even her most seasoned rivals stated: "*I'd refer to her before most others.*"

**Clients/Work Highlights:** Motorola; Visteon; United Airlines; Genentech; City of Chicago; Aero Products International; Zyliss; Helman Group and Rival.

### Kirkland & Ellis LLP
See firm details p.875

**The Firm:** For many clients, this "*first-rate litigation powerhouse*" is the one to choose. Rapidly expanding, it has a significant national presence and a growing international reach. Its attorneys are well equipped to handle trademark, copyright, licensing work and trade secrets, but have carved an especially impressive reputation for litigation and patent infringement cases. Its "*excellent in-house litigation training*" has led to the development of a 200-strong

## Intellectual Property
### Leading Individuals

### Senior Statesmen
**GILSON Jerome** Brinks Hofer Gilson & Lione
**HOFER Roy** Brinks Hofer Gilson & Lione
[1] **AMEND James** Kirkland & Ellis LLP
**MALLOY Timothy** McAndrews, Held & Malloy
**MCANDREWS George** McAndrews, Held & Malloy
**NIRO Raymond** Niro, Scavone, Haller & Niro
**ROPSKI Gary** Brinks Hofer Gilson & Lione
**WARNECKE Michael** Mayer, Brown, Rowe & Maw
[2] **BANNER Mark** Banner & Witcoff Ltd
**BOEHNEN Daniel** McDonnell Boehnen
**BORUN Michael** Marshall, Gerstein & Borun
**CEDEROTH Richard** Sidley Austin LLP
**HARTMANN H Michael** Leydig, Voit & Mayer
**HILLIARD David** Pattishall, McAuliffe
**JACOVER Jerold** Brinks Hofer Gilson & Lione
**KOZAK John** Leydig, Voit & Mayer, Ltd
**MANDELL Floyd** Katten Muchin Rosenman LLP
**MCDONNELL John** McDonnell Boehnen
**PRITIKIN David** Sidley Austin LLP
**ROPER Harry** Jenner & Block LLP
**STREFF JR William** Kirkland & Ellis LLP
**WITCOFF David** Jones Day
[3] **BEEN Carol** Sonnenschein
**BROWNE Robert** Neal, Gerber & Eisenberg
**DUNCAN Margaret** McDermott Will & Emery
**FELDMAN Mark** DLA Piper Rudnick Gray Cary
**GABRIC Ralph** Brinks Hofer Gilson & Lione
**KATZ A Sidney** Welsh & Katz Ltd
**MILLER Laura** Brinks Hofer Gilson & Lione
**VEZEAU Timothy** Katten Muchin Rosenman LLP

### Up-and-coming individuals
**ADDY Meredith** Brinks Hofer Gilson & Lione

group of "*creative and gifted*" IP experts, specializing in high-stakes IP litigation. The team achieved a total victory for ConocoPhillips this year in just such a case – a patent infringement bench trial – with an award of $9 million in price erosion and profit damages as well as an immediate injunction in its favor. Similar success was achieved for Amazon.com, obtaining summary judgment in a patent lawsuit, following a compressed 'rocket docket' discovery period, avoiding a $50 million damages pay-out.
**The Lawyers:** Armed with "*strong strategic skills and excellent instincts,*" **James Amend** (see p.817) is quick to grasp facts, which makes him an engaging advocate. His long track record has furnished him with experience in many fields of technology including electronics, computers, chemistry, manufacturing and packaging. Clients highlighted his "*practical perspective*" and creative problem solving among his many attributes. **William Streff** (see p.859) is a client favorite because he is "*personable, sincere and a great listener*" as well as "*committed to building a long-term trustworthy relationship.*" He clearly places clients at the top of the hierarchy, ensuring cases are staffed well and meticulously prepared. In court, however,

the gloves come off to reveal an "*outstanding, dedicated and skilled patent litigator*" committed to the cause.
**Clients/Work Highlights:** Hitachi; Konica Minolta; Amazon.com; Agere Systems; Jays Foods; Oxford Gene Technology; ConocoPhillips and Third Wave Technologies.

### Leydig, Voit & Mayer, Ltd
**The Firm:** This multifaceted group sits at the forefront of Chicago's IP market as "*the quintessential time-honored patent firm.*" It provides advice on trademark, copyright and unfair competition litigation, licensing and franchising, as well as trade secret protection. With two offices in Illinois, and a bank of over 90 IP lawyers, this firm is building on its 100-year foundations to provide a broad and client-focused service. Care is taken to recruit the finest in the field, who can provide not only IP expertise but also experience in supplementary technical fields. As a result, the group is well known for its excellence in niche industries such as biotechnology, pharmaceuticals and software engineering. Clients choose this firm for its "*top-notch and cost-effective service.*"
**The Lawyers: Michael Hartmann** (see p.834) specializes in complex patent litigation, and international technology transfer and patent enforcement. His technical expertise across a range of industries is appreciated, and he recently obtained a reversal for a pharmaceutical company on a decision from the district court regarding a blood pressure product. According to clients, "*he's at ease with technical concepts and exudes a respectful but commanding presence in court.*" **John Kozak** concentrates on IP litigation and counseling, where clients appreciate that his "*vast trial experience and knowledge in the field impart confidence and strength.*" They also highlighted his close control of litigation, happily testifying: "*He spends his client's money carefully, as though he was spending his own.*"

### McAndrews, Held & Malloy, Ltd
See firm details p.877
**The Firm:** With a passion for all things IP, this major firm has grown steadily by hand-picking intelligent and committed attorneys who are experts in science and technology as well as the law. The broad service incorporates patent procurement, counseling, portfolio management and litigation. The group has recently achieved a favorable settlement and dismissal of patent litigation for GE and Home Depot, while ongoing litigations involve lighting apparatus, instant messages and beverage cans. The team advises clients on their business strategies and their efforts to seek early resolution of disputes. However, attorneys here also have a real flair for communicating complex arguments to juries.
**The Lawyers:** Among his many skills, **Tim Malloy**'s (see p.843) courtroom prowess was most highly rated: he displays a "*sharp mind, strong verbal skills and his passion for the case.*" Out of court, clients also endorsed him as "*an intelligent strategist – personable and professional.*" His practice is heavily weighted

toward medical devices, where he obtained for a client one of the highest damages awards ever seen. **George McAndrews** possesses a "*great trial presence that simply cannot be bettered.*" His sharp mind and meticulous preparation are combined with excellent witness-handling skills.
**Clients/Work Highlights:** Laitram; Ford; Goodyear; Cardiac Pacemakers Inc; Kraft; Baxter; Merck and American Chiropractic Association.

### Band 2

### Banner & Witcoff Ltd
**The Firm:** The 80-strong firm has devoted its practice to all things IP, including patent, copyright, trademark, trade secret, and unfair competition matters for a diverse cross-section of industries and clients. What distinguishes this group is its strength in computers and electronics, where it is considered "*one of the best.*" This is evidenced by two recent victories: the first involved a copyright infringement in the resale of freelance authors' articles by periodicals to online databases; the second involved the finding of patent infringement regarding downloading of software from the Internet. This firm is clearly client-focused. It tailors legal strategies to the client's business objectives and provides cost-efficient staffing. Clients appreciated the firm's "*excellent support team*" offering "*courtesy, knowledge and availability.*"
**The Lawyers: Mark Banner** focuses on patent, trademark and copyright litigation, especially in the realm of computer technology. An "*intelligent and energetic*" attorney, he is ideally suited to jury trials, where his versatility and "*detailed, persuasive presentations*" impress. Rivals speak highly of his "*aggressive yet ethical manner*" whereas clients loved his "*honest insights, as well as his firm grasp on the reality of business.*"

### Jones Day
See firm details p.570
**The Firm:** With its 22 offices worldwide, the sheer manpower of this firm makes it an intimidating opponent. It offers the gamut of IP services from complex patent litigation and prosecution to counseling and opinion rendering. This sizable group of IP specialists attracts equally sizable clients of the caliber of Motorola, Micron and IBM, whom it has represented on a number of patent infringement cases relating to monitor graphics, internet credit card purchases and disk drive controllers. Sources rated the team as "*trustworthy and respectable*" and expect great things from this group in the future: "*They're very strong, but not quite stellar... yet.*"
**The Lawyers: David Witcoff**'s (see p.864) many talents as a patent litigator include his "*excellent command of the facts, easy courtroom presence and hard-working go-getter nature.*" He is similarly highly regarded by clients, one of whom described him as someone who "*knows the players and how the game is played. I can rely on him to keep pushing to the goal.*"

## Marshall, Gerstein & Borun

**The Firm:** This boutique firm has nurtured loyal client relationships, which have allowed it to become a serious player on Chicago's IP landscape. In particular, market sources agreed it has established itself as a leader in the field of patent prosecution and biotechnology: it is "*one of the best biotech practices in the entire country.*" The group also advises on licensing, trademarks, trade secrets, copyrights and cyber law services.
**The Lawyers:** **Michael Borun**'s vast experience has earned him "*national and international respect and recognition.*" He focuses on chemical, pharmaceutical and biotechnology IP issues, and is respected as a seasoned litigator.

## Mayer, Brown, Rowe & Maw LLP

See firm details p.876
**The Firm:** This global full-service firm has developed its IP capacity through work on large litigation projects that encompass patents, trademarks and copyright issues as well as providing due diligence and transactional matters. Clients pointed to the group as "*extremely supportive and accessible.*" The team has a particular leaning towards biotechnology, pharmaceuticals and computer technology. Recent successes include the negotiation of a license agreement covering a patent portfolio of over 50 US patents for MetLife.
**The Lawyers:** Clients appreciate that **Michael Warnecke** (see p.862) places their needs first: he is "*a rare find in a lawyer – amiable, smart, outstanding, effective and a pleasure to work with.*" When necessary, he adopts a courtroom style that is "*aggressive and effective without being abrasive,*" and he has the "*ability to make complex issues understandable for a jury.*" In addition, he has specialist expertise in international patents and technology licensing, as evidenced by his work for the Chinese government.
**Clients/Work Highlights:** TriStrata Technology; VLIW Technology LLC; Newell Rubbermaid and Rewards Network.

## McDonnell Boehnen Hulbert & Berghoff LLP

See firm details p.879
**The Firm:** As a relatively young firm in this area, McDonnell has already proved its worth through the successes of its "*outstanding and consistently excellent patent lawyers.*" Its strength and depth is most notable in technology, life sciences, chemistry and pharmaceuticals. Recently, the team worked for Trading Technologies International on a patent that covers a fundamental user interface for trading. It also acted for a biotech company on a lawsuit involving compound screening.
**The Lawyers:** **Daniel Boehnen** (see p.821) impresses with his "*top-flight knowledge, enthusiasm and interest in IP.*" A skilled trial lawyer, his "*strategic mind and articulate, down-to-earth communication skills*" are best utilized in court. One client praised him as an "*excellent mentor who has been instrumental in shaping my company's IP strategy and portfolio*" while others appreciated his "*honesty and integrity.*" Similarly, sources are quick to highlight **John**

McDonnell's (see p.844) outstanding patent practice, and his depth of knowledge in the biotechnology, pharmaceuticals and diagnostics fields.
**Clients/Work Highlights:** Fortune 100 corporations, universities, individuals and startup companies.

## Niro, Scavone, Haller & Niro

**The Firm:** This firm's commitment to plaintiff's contingency patent work has allowed it to forge a formidable reputation in the IP field. It adopts a tough and thorough approach to litigation that has resulted in multimillion-dollar jury verdicts. One such jury trial victory involved willful infringement of a patent for a medical device – a rod for the treatment of shoulder problems. Peers endorsed the group's handling of high-profile cases, while clients spoke of the team's "*comprehensive, efficient and substantive approach to case management.*"
**The Lawyers:** Key to the group's profile is the "*courageous and tenacious*" **Raymond Niro**. Peers warn: "*If you deal with him, get ready for a fight, because few can match him in a courtroom,*" while clients appreciated his persuasive negotiations skills and his clear advice: "*He easily delineates key issues, meets them head on and is even sharper at explaining technicalities to the lay person.*"
**Clients/Work Highlights:** Individuals and smaller companies to Fortune 500 companies including Black & Decker.

## Sidley Austin LLP

See firm details p.883
**The Firm:** The broad trial skills of this nationwide team have resulted in a successful track record of patent litigation. The 25-strong Chicago-based group is split between traditional IP lawyers with technical training and pure litigation attorneys. As such, this firm has nurtured an enviable client base, developed a deep appellate practice, and attracted blue-chip clients. Two recent highlights include representing corporate giant Microsoft, and winning a case for Baxter.
**The Lawyers:** **Richard Cederoth**'s (see p.824) practice focuses on patent litigation concerning the software, computer and semiconductor fields. Not only is he a great advocate with a flair for anything technical, he is also seen as "*a true gentleman*" to work with or against. Clients praised his rational approach, persuasive manner and his "*ability to always keep one eye on the endgame.*" Chair of the firm's national IP practice, **David Pritikin** (see p.850) is an accomplished trial lawyer, equipped to deal with clients from a range of industries including software, semiconductors and chemicals and pharmaceuticals. Market sources spoke of his "*superb intuition and brilliant instincts*" as well as his excellent cross-examination skills, all the while remaining "*approachable and modest.*"

## Band 3

## Howrey LLP

**The Firm:** The Chicago branch is closely integrated into the national and global IP practice that this firm

has developed. The 200-strong group consists of attorneys, patent agents and scientific advisers, and possesses particular strengths in complex multiparty lawsuits as well as all types of IP appeals. While sources were quick to praise the firm as a "*large and distinguished*" IP contender, its work further afield has led to a lower profile in the local market. In the past twelve months, the team has been kept busy on an appeal of a patent infringement suit, worth billions of dollars, regarding a hormone that stimulates the production of red blood cells. In addition, the group achieved a favorable settlement for the patentee of a prostate cancer drug. With its advantage of an enviable client base, clear focus on the sector and national support, rivals see this group as one to watch in Chicago.
**Clients/Work Highlights:** Volvo; Conexant Systems; Dana; Huffy Corporation; Inspire Pharmaceuticals; Monsanto; Protein Design Labs and QUALCOMM.

## Jenner & Block LLP

See firm details p.873
**The Firm:** The firm has successfully integrated a new chair, Harry Roper, whose presence has significantly lifted this national full-service firm's profile in the IP arena. Sources have recognized the wealth of talented younger attorneys housed at the firm, as well as its excellent litigation group. Recent victories include a matter for Johnson & Johnson over an anemia treatment.
**The Lawyers:** Chair of the firm's IP practice, **Harry Roper** (see p.852) specializes in complex patent infringement jury trials on behalf of national and international companies. He has extensive expertise in the areas of biotechnology, medical devices and pharmaceuticals, but is most highly regarded for his successes in oil, gas and chemical work. He brings to the table a combination of "*judgment, analytical thinking and superb intelligence.*" Clients affectionately describe his courtroom performance as "*Columbo-esque in style and effectiveness!*" His recent highlights have included success in the Federal Court of Appeals, which upheld a patent infringement award for over $153 million, for Union Carbide, with a remand for an additional damages award.
**Clients/Work Highlights:** Mitsubishi; SPX; Hitachi; Commonwealth Edison; SkillSoft; Dow Chemical; Johnson & Johnson; ConocoPhillips; Union Carbide; Quebecor World; Ispat Inland and Aladdin Knowledge Systems.

## Katten Muchin Rosenman LLP

See firm details p.874
**The Firm:** This large, full-service national law firm has created a one-stop shop to service its clients' IP needs. The group is most highly regarded for its work in the entertainment industry, where clients range from Universal Studios to music publishers and entertainment channels. In the past year, the team has successfully represented the world's largest battery charger company in a patent infringement dispute, and acted for a major Canadian pharmaceutical company in litigation against generic drug manufacturers.

The Lawyers: National cochair of the firm's IP practice, **Floyd Mandell** is commended for his trademark work. Clients praised his "*accurate assessment of risks, and his common-sense practical approach,*" while peers spoke of his commanding courtroom presence. Recently he achieved a favorable settlement for entertainment giant HBO on the eve of a jury trial. Founding partner of the firm's patent practice, **Timothy Vezeau** has a levelheaded approach or, as one client put it, "*an easygoing style that belies the intensity within.*" He specializes in patent litigation in a diverse range of technical subject matters from particle beam accelerators to human antibody libraries. Clients appreciated his "*wonderful ability to explain highly technical concepts in an understandable way.*"

Clients/Work Highlights: Planet Hollywood; Sears; Bausch & Lomb; Universal Studios; HBO; Chicago White Sox; Chicago Bulls and Sony.

## McDermott Will & Emery
See firm details p.878

The Firm: With a substantial number of IP lawyers spanning the globe, McDermott Will & Emery has the experience to handle IP issues from almost any technical or scientific industry. Its specialist litigation and appellate practice has nurtured a reputation for high-stakes cases. The Chicago office still has room to grow, yet with its proven capabilities in patent, copyright, trademark and prosecution services, and a fully rounded team driving the practice forward, it is clearly one to watch.

The Lawyers: Heading the Chicago IP department, **Margaret Duncan** (see p.827) combines her litigation and prosecution practice with strategic counsel-ing skills. In the patent arena she focuses on life sciences, biotechnology and chemical fields. She successfully defended a patent case for American Express recently, and secured a $2.5 million verdict in a trademark infringement. She is consistently described as "*thoughtful, savvy and persistent.*"

Clients/Work Highlights: Fortune 500 companies, nonprofit trade associations, startups, cooperatives and educational institutes.

## Pattishall, McAuliffe, Newbury, Hilliard & Geraldson LLP

The Firm: This boutique is well respected as one of the most seasoned trademark law specialists in Chicago. The group has attracted a top-flight client base and is one of the market's go-to firms for the range of trademark issues.

The Lawyers: "*Old-school gentleman*" **David Hilliard** is universally admired for his "*polite yet robust advocacy.*" He is a skilled mediator and a deeply experienced trademark lawyer.

Clients/Work Highlights: Clients come from an array of manufacturing industries including automobiles, pharmaceuticals, computer hardware and software, gasoline and oil products. In addition, service industry representations include entertainment, computer networking and publishing companies.

## Welsh & Katz Ltd

The Firm: This firm's experience spans the IP spectrum, and includes patents, trademarks, copyrights and trade secrets. Recently the firm has shifted its emphasis towards pharmaceutical and medical technology while maintaining a strong foothold in electronics and communications systems.

The Lawyers: Veteran **Sidney Katz** was praised as a "*terrific and intelligent strategist.*" His focus remains on copyright laws concerning the protection of computer programs and video games.

Clients/Work Highlights: The firm's distinguished client base includes corporations, universities, and individuals involved in hi-tech fields such as electronics, chemicals, computers and biotechnology as well as those in the entertainment industry.

## Other Notable Practitioners

**Carol Anne Been** (see p.819) of Sonnenschein Nath & Rosenthal LLP impresses with her excellent knowledge of trademark and computer law, as well as her "*efficiency and responsiveness.*" **Robert Browne** (see p.822) of Neal, Gerber & Eisenberg LLP "*possesses good judgment – he can analyze complex issues, set a course of action and carry it through,*" sources agreed. One client pointed to his "*aggressive representation of our business objectives while maintaining a friendly professional demeanor.*" Recent successes include a judgment of noninfringement for Universal Electronics following an eight-day trial, as well as obtaining a favorable settlement for Boeing prior to trial. At DLA Piper Rudnick Gray Cary, **Mark Feldman** (see p.828) is distinguished for his business sense coupled with a "*personable, easygoing*" style. Clients report that he approaches his work with "*alacrity and enthusiasm, is very client-centered, and can be trusted and relied upon for guidance.*" Recently, he successfully represented DHR Cambridge Homes in defeating a motion for preliminary injunction, and ultimately negotiated a favorable resolution after years of dispute.

# LITIGATION

## Litigation: General Commercial
### Leading Firms

| | |
|---|---|
| [1] | **KIRKLAND & ELLIS LLP** *Chicago* |
| | **MAYER, BROWN, ROWE & MAW LLP** *Chicago* |
| [2] | **BARTLIT BECK** *Chicago* |
| | **WINSTON & STRAWN LLP** *Chicago* |
| [3] | **JENNER & BLOCK LLP** *Chicago* |
| | **JONES DAY** *Chicago* |
| | **MCDERMOTT WILL & EMERY** *Chicago* |
| | **SIDLEY AUSTIN LLP** *Chicago* |
| [4] | **BAKER & MCKENZIE** *Chicago* |
| | **KATTEN MUCHIN ROSENMAN LLP** *Chicago* |
| | **SKADDEN, ARPS** *Chicago* |
| [5] | **FREEBORN & PETERS** *Chicago* |
| | **LATHAM & WATKINS LLP** *Chicago* |
| | **SCHIFF HARDIN LLP** *Chicago* |

## Litigation: White-Collar Crime & Government Investigations
### Leading Firms

| | |
|---|---|
| [1] | **COTSIRILOS TIGHE & STREICKER LTD** *Chicago* |
| | **STETLER & DUFFY LTD** *Chicago* |

## Kirkland & Ellis LLP
See firm details p.875

The Firm: This titan of the US legal scene is widely regarded as "*one of the most outstanding litigation groups in the country.*" Strong praise but well deserved, according to clients: "*They have the talent and a long tradition of achieving tremendous results.*" The attorneys win plaudits for their work on product liability, toxic torts, IP, antitrust and other commercial matters and are especially prominent in complex class actions. The firm's bench strength is a compelling point in its favor, with talented associates and young partners augmenting a phalanx of experienced litigators higher up. From its Chicago platform, it reaches out nationally to involve itself in high-stakes representation. This it undertakes on behalf of US and international clients "*assured of a fine service.*"

The Lawyers: **David Bernick** (see p.820) "*clearly has the reputation and the talent*" for big money litigation, clients acknowledged. One noted: "*He has that intelligent aggression that is the trademark of Kirkland & Ellis.*" He wins distinction for his skill in mass tort and products liability trials where he displays a "*remarkable ability to get his arms around the science*" of complex medical and industrial issues. Major matters include the representation of Brown & Williamson Tobacco in the $280 billion RICO action against the tobacco industry. Also notable is his success on behalf of Abbott Laboratories in the Meridia diet drug products liability litigation. In that case and others he exhibited great courtcraft: "*He knows how to handle courtroom dynamics to great effect,*" one interviewee noted. Clients championed **Richard Godfrey** (see p.832) as a "*stellar example of outside counsel.*" He is frequently called upon to take difficult cases to trial all over the country, earning him a reputation as "*the class action specialist in the USA.*" He boasts an undeniably wide-ranging practice that covers matters from discrimination to antitrust, toxic torts to tax, and a thriving appellate section. He represented GM in a multidistrict putative class action filed by Daewoo dealers alleging fraud, tortious interference and violations of various state laws. He also represents Allstate in ERISA litigation and BP in a nationwide class action involving onshore wells. There is a national dimension to **John Hickey**'s (see p.835) work. He is often called upon when a case reaches critical point and is valued for his "*personable approach and great trial presence.*"

Such qualities were evident when he achieved a complete defense verdict for GM in a products liability case challenging the design of the Chevrolet

Suburban roof. Recently he has put more of an emphasis on IP and patent-related cases and has generated a full book of business acting for 3M. "*Tenacious litigator*" **Emily Nicklin** (see p.847) makes an impact in trials across the country. She is a prominent figure in employment litigation and merger-related disputes where she has a significant practice in the representation of directors and consultants. Satisfied clients include accountancy and consulting firms who appreciate her "*outstanding*" service in an increasingly intense regulatory climate. **Stephen Patton** (see p.849) comes across to clients as "*a take-charge type of guy*" who marshals an excellent team around him. His experience as a "*strong litigator with much exposure to complicated and sophisticated matters*" is exemplified by his involvement in tobacco class actions, representing Brown & Williamson Tobacco. He possesses a balanced manner that allows him to be "*impeccably prepared while remaining down to earth.*" "*Impressive*" **Frank Cicero** (see p.824) retains a long-standing reputation at the firm while **Garrett Johnson** (see p.836) earned market respect for his broad-ranging trial practice. "*Johnson is a skilled, on-his-feet lawyer,*" clients asserted. **Steven McCormick** (see p.844) merits inclusion in the table as an "*excellent trial lawyer who is trusted on the most complex of contracts.*" He has over 30 years of experience in state and federal courts along with arbitration panels in the USA, Mexico and Europe.

**Clients/Work Highlights:** Abbott Laboratories; 3M; Allstate; BP; Dow Chemical; GM; Motorola; RJ Reynolds and United Airlines.

## Mayer, Brown, Rowe & Maw LLP
See firm details p.876

**The Firm:** Recognized as a "*wonderfully balanced litigation department that can handle a variety of challenges,*" this outfit boasts a "*hard-working group of lawyers who are problem solvers.*" Its coast-to-coast national scope provides, according to clients, "*a coordinated one-stop shop*" that also covers international ground. It is consequently adept at handling asbestos and tobacco litigation as well as mass torts, securities class actions and antitrust litigation. "*With such a deep bench you always get a high-quality product,*" sources said. The firm's "*tremendous appellate practice*" adds further luster to a team that "*brings together an advocacy package of the highest level to produce an A-plus job.*"

**The Lawyers:** "*If you want fabulous trial expertise, there are few in his league,*" sources said of **Vincent Connelly** (see p.825). According to clients, he has all the expected constituents of a top trial lawyer: "*intelligence, great judgment and strong strategic sense*" as well as a "*uniquely common touch which resonates with a jury.*" With a background in the US Attorney's Office, he also understands the political environment and has the "*ability to boil down complex facts in order to go directly to the critical issues.*" His practice is historically strong in white-collar criminal defense and internal investigations but he further covers general civil matters. "*His mastery of cases and his even temperament make him a formidable opponent,*" said

one client. "*Premier trial lawyer*" **Alan Salpeter** (see p.854) earned considerable market respect, in particular for his significant securities fraud and accounting malpractice work, areas in which clients champion him as a "*master strategist*" both in and out of the courtroom. He was lead trial counsel for CIBC in litigation related to the Enron corporate fraud case recently settled in Houston. He also represents Deloitte & Touche in litigation arising from Italian dairy Parmalat's bankruptcy. Commentators sum up his success by saying: "*He is tenacious, unafraid, creative and, above all, he wins.*" Sources agree that the eminently experienced **Stephen Shapiro** (see p.856), founder of the supreme court and appellate litigation group, possesses a "*sensational appellate practice.*" "*I would consider him at the top of my list for referrals,*" said one source. In a widely followed antitrust case, he represented all the defendants in Empagran v Hoffmann-La Roche in the Supreme Court, obtaining a unanimous victory on appeal. The trial strength of **Thomas Durkin** (see p.827) is well documented, according to peers. He handles state and federal litigation including products liability, securities, patent litigation and malpractice suits. He also includes a significant quantity of criminal defense litigation in his wide-ranging practice. Clients commented on his "*strong practical abilities and easygoing manner.*" The "*incredibly talented*" **Michele Odorizzi** (see p.848) shores up the firm's appellate practice, where her specialty is litigation and brief writing, covering securities and corporate governance, class actions and consumer fraud. Clients were united in their praise of her skills, with one saying: "*She is among the best brief writers I have ever seen, she can cite cases off the top of her head.*" Recent significant work includes acting as appellate counsel on the State Farm v Avery case, in which the Supreme Court recently reversed a $1 billion award against State Farm. She has also recently acted on Philip Morris' appeal against a $10 billion judgment against it in a class action in Illinois. Commentators think highly of **James Ferguson** (see p.829), describing him as a "*sterling lawyer.*" His general commercial practice includes a concentration on patent and IP litigation, especially for pharmaceutical companies. He was lead counsel in the defense of a Fortune 100 company in a patent infringement action that resulted in summary judgment of patent invalidity. **Sheila Finnegan** (see p.829) is "*great on her feet and equally good on paper.*" She has represented companies and individuals in consumer fraud litigation, securities class actions and accounting irregularities. **Jonathan Medow** (see p.845) concentrates his efforts on representing accounting firms, for both plaintiff and defense. Much of his work has resulted from claims of alleged failures in audits made prior to filing for bankruptcy. "*He does a fantastic job – he is capable, smart and works hard,*" say clients. Commentators rate the "*fabulous*" **Stanley Parzen** (see p.849) for his accounts malpractice work and expertise in complex defense litigation. "*He has such a quick mind and he's passionate about his work*" was one commentator's opinion, with another claiming: "*He always finds novel ways to resolve law suits.*" The cochair of international litigation **Herbert Zarov** (see p.864) won backing for his mass torts liability practice. Of late, he has taken a lead role in asbestos and breast implant litigation and has become involved in mass torts relating to benzene exposure.

**Clients/Work Highlights:** BASF; Merrill Lynch; SBC; BellSouth; Qwest; The Kroger Company; GM; Ernst & Young and Deloitte & Touche.

## Bartlit Beck Herman Palenchar & Scott

**The Firm:** This firm is *"first choice for bet-the-company cases"* as commentators believe its relatively modest size has no bearing on its ability to get right to the heart of big-figure litigation. These are *"trial lawyers with the best combination of judgment, presence and skill,"* forming a boutique that is *"the best in the business."* The group has taken a lead role in some of the biggest-profile cases in the country, and has of late acted for pharmaceutical companies in antitrust investigations, chemical companies in toxic torts and accounting firms in commercial fraud. Strength in patent litigation also makes up a large part of the firm's arsenal. Clients say of the firm's success: *"They are trial lawyers in the truest sense of the word."*

**The Lawyers:** Having acted on some of the country's most important cases, **Phil Beck** has a *"record that speaks for itself."* Observers praised his *"immense capability meshed with tactical street smarts."* He scooped plaudits as *"one hell of a cross-examiner, capable of the knockout punch"* in the highest-profile cases. In fact, the only apparent drawback seems to be the difficulty in retaining this incredibly busy attorney. His packed diary includes ongoing responsibility for defending Bayer in the Baycol litigation and representing Merck in the first federal trial over its Vioxx painkiller. The *"sensational and highly experienced"* **Fred Bartlit** *"has an amazing ability to inspire confidence and comfort,"* clients reported. He is a master of big-ticket litigation and recently defeated a damages claim against investment company Forstmann Little. Sources said that *"it's not just a job to him – he truly cares about the case."* **Adam Hoeflich** gained praise for his *"unique collaborative aptitude and ability to coordinate a defense over multiple jurisdictions."* He has a deep practice, acting for pharmaceutical, chemical and other companies and is representing DuPont in class actions across the USA alleging consumer fraud relating to Teflon-coated cookware.

**Clients/Work Highlights:** Bayer; 3M; Merck; DuPont; Reebok; Sears; United Technologies; Hewlett-Packard and Deloitte & Touche.

## Winston & Strawn LLP

See firm details p.886

**The Firm:** Clients agree that this *"terrific group"* remains *"firmly on the shortlist of top trial lawyers in the state."* According to observers, the team excels in white-collar defense and securities litigation and has a presence in major products liability, tobacco and pharmaceutical litigation. Clients championed the raft of *"top talent"* and the firm's *"long tradition of taking on complex cases."* Known largely for superior trial counsel, the firm nevertheless has wide-ranging scope. As an illustration, the Chicago office's book of business includes the corruption trial of the former Governor of Illinois, tobacco litigation, pharmaceutical disputes and corporate compliance matters.

**The Lawyers:** When asked about the reason for much of this firm's success, one source could *"sum it up in two words"* – **Dan Webb**. There are few, if any, rivals to the throne of an attorney known for his tireless trial schedule. He is *"such a superstar,"* peers concurred, *"he can do anything he chooses."* Fêted for his work in white-collar criminal defense, his *"outstanding skills"* are effortlessly transferred to high-stakes commercial litigation. He made his name representing industry giants such as GE and Philip Morris on cases with national significance. At time of press, he is defending former governor George Ryan against federal corruption charges, the first time in more than 30 years that an Illinois governor has been accused of such activities. Commentators agree that *"for a person with such an esteemed reputation Webb is down to earth and humble."* Clients say the *"bright and terrific"* **Brad Lerman** (see p.841) is highly regarded as a *"sensational lawyer with fabulous judgment and great jury persuasion skills."* He represents McDonald's in high-profile obesity and health-related litigation. Peers also noted his expertise in SEC investigations, an arena where he represents big-ticket accounting and financial firms. The *"strong and energetic"* **Bob Sperling** (see p.858) drew generous comments from clients. As well as general commercial matters, his work has a significant bias towards securities litigation. He has recently acted as lead trial counsel for Cisco Systems in a securities fraud class action brought against the company. Veteran trial lawyer **Kimball Anderson** (see p.818) is *"a busy man who is highly regarded."* His diverse workload includes a concentration on patent and trademark infringement, and products and professional liability. Recent highlights include the representation of American Express in a trademark dispute with Blue Cross and Blue Shield Association and involvement in IP disputes for Lear Corporation. **Bruce Braun** joins the rankings on the back of his handling of major cases for clients such as Microsoft and McDonald's. He is described as a *"top-flight trial guy"* with a growing reputation.

**Clients/Work Highlights:** Philip Morris; McDonald's; Abbott Laboratories; Microsoft; Morgan Stanley; Ernst & Young; Grant Thornton and American Express.

## Jenner & Block LLP

See firm details p.873

**The Firm:** This *"terrific litigation firm has always been a powerhouse in Chicago,"* claimed clients and peers alike. With an extensive reach across the USA and a deep pool of attorneys, the group is well positioned to perform on a multitude of cases. The firm has some *"incredible strengths,"* sources remarked, not least in the areas of IP, antitrust, securities and class actions. Clients highlighted the *"consistency of the team"* and peers appreciated that, while the battles were hard-fought, the group remained *"worthy competitors."* In a diverse year, the team has handled an increased amount of IP litigation and a significant number of bankruptcy-related actions while continuing to demonstrate a capacity for white-collar criminal defense work.

**The Lawyers:** *"Standout trial lawyer"* **Jerold Solovy** (see p.858) celebrated his 50th anniversary at Jenner & Block with a major trial win for Coleman against Morgan Stanley. The court entered a $1.58 billion final judgment against Morgan Stanley in a case centered on the investment bank's alleged fraudulent activity in the sale of Coleman to Sunbeam. *"He is as good as it gets on commercial trials,"* sources agreed. **Tony Valukas'** (see p.861) *"genuine and outgoing personality"* helps propel him to the top of many clients' lists. Possessed of *"absolutely top-notch trial skills,"* he can handle cases of any complexity. His diverse workload of late has included the representation of David Radler, one-time lieutenant to newspaper baron Conrad Black, in fraud charges. He also continues to represent committees and auditors and advise boards of directors on investigations and white-collar defense positions. **Barry Sullivan** (see p.859) is credited with being an *"absolutely terrific young lawyer"* who has a practice oriented toward proceedings in the appellate and supreme courts. He represented Air Wisconsin Airlines in issues related to the United Airlines bankruptcy and separately acted on behalf of Commercial Financial Services Inc against Bank of America in insolvency matters. The *"effective and trusted"* **Charles Sklarsky** (see p.857), cochair of the firm's white-collar criminal defense and counseling practice, has seen an increased focus on SEC investigations in the light of Sarbanes-Oxley scrutiny. He earned compliments for his work on such cases ranging from whistle-blower allegations to fraud and bill rigging. In a recent matter, he represented General Dynamics regarding alleged false claims made against their electric boat division. **Thomas Sullivan** (see p.860) garnered respect for his handling of a long-running practice that has been studded with achievements. *"He has a fine reputation,"* one observer noted, *"drawn from his participation in many complex cases."*

**Clients/Work Highlights:** Dell; Dow Chemical; Honeywell; Sara Lee; MCI; PepsiCo; Kellogg; Hitachi and Canada Life.

## Jones Day

See firm details p.570

**The Firm:** This *"fine litigation firm"* continues to impose its presence both in Chicago and on a national basis. Its litigation group owes much of its reputation to practice coordinator and star trial lawyer Dan Reidy. However, sources recognize that one swallow doesn't make a summer and were quick to identify the solid backup he receives from a corps of quality trial lawyers and litigators. This ability to utilize lawyers from disparate specialties has proved a decisive factor in the litigation success of the firm. It has allowed it to become heavily embroiled in white-collar criminal defense, and pharmaceutical and tobacco class actions. It has also forged an "*excellent nationwide reputation in the products liability arena.*"

**The Lawyers:** **Dan Reidy** (see p.851) takes his place in many clients' "*dream team*" of top trial lawyers. His breadth in the white-collar area is well documented and he also scoops praise for his work in patent and pharmaceutical litigation and complex class actions. "*He appreciates the multiple audiences we need to address in court,*" peers said. Many others underlined his "*credibility and technical expertise.*" "*First and foremost an excellent trial lawyer with great judgment,*" he has settled a broad range of cases for TAP Pharmaceutical Products and also handled and won a major patent case for Abbott Laboratories.

**Clients/Work Highlights:** TAP Pharmaceutical Products; Abbott Laboratories; Wyeth; Motorola; Simon Property Group and Duchossois Industries.

## McDermott Will & Emery
See firm details p.878

**The Firm:** This firm is credited with having picked up steam over the years and now represents a "*premier litigation practice*" covering a multitude of commercial disputes. The "*quality of the group's litigators is phenomenal,*" clients stated. Its scope takes in insurance coverage disputes, healthcare, IP and patent work and securities litigation. Clients highlighted the efficient staffing procedures and the "*seamless blending of its talent from across the offices.*" The firm's talent for big-ticket litigation is exemplified by a victory for client Coca-Cola in consumer class action alleging violation of the consumer fraud act. In biotechnology and antitrust matters, the group represents Amgen in seeking to rebut allegations that it is trying to monopolize the market for red blood cell growth factor.

**The Lawyers:** Head of the firm's trial department, **Jeff Stone** (see p.859) has a practice characterized by an equal amount of white-collar defense and civil litigation work. A firm favorite among clients, he is an "*astute, creative thinker,*" a lawyer of "*real depth not bluster*" and a "*great team player who really protects his client's interest.*" **David Rosenbloom** (see p.852) is another "*real talent*" in white-collar and civil litigation matters. A large part of his practice this year has involved class actions against nonprofit hospitals involving allegations made on behalf of uninsured patients. Whistle-blower suits also feature strongly, along with criminal defense, antitrust and healthcare fraud. Products liability and class action champion **Michael Pope** (see p.850) is known to be "*practically oriented with a great business mind.*" He represents State Farm in claims under the Consumer Fraud Act and separately represents Blue Cross and Blue Shield

Association in litigation across the country. "*Bright and quick,*" **Doug Whitney** (see p.863) is a young partner who practices in white-collar criminal defense and complex commercial litigation. Clients appreciate his ability to "*understand the big picture while making sure the small pieces come together.*"

**Clients/Work Highlights:** Allianz; Coca-Cola; DaVita; Nike; RJ Reynolds; State Farm; Trinity Health; ProMedica Health System and Philip Morris.

## Sidley Austin LLP
See firm details p.883

**The Firm:** In the words of clients, this is a "*diverse and talented group that can handle all manner of problems.*" Its expertise ranges from specialized litigation such as products liability, to pharmaceutical, environmental and more general commercial matters. The team has also been acting on significant IP litigation for clients such as Microsoft and has handled antitrust matters for AT&T. It has a further notable presence in complex securities litigation and ERISA-related matters. "*They put together a great strategy,*" sources note, "*and there are any number of fine lawyers there.*"

**The Lawyers:** **William Conlon** (see p.825) collects praise for a diverse practice characterized by a "*high level of experience and practical knowledge.*" Peers stated: "*He comes across as a straightforward, honest man of the people who makes a great impression in the courtroom.*" Recent work has featured an emphasis on ERISA matters and complex civil litigation. **Walter Carlson** (see p.823) is "*absolutely no-nonsense – you can trust anything he says implicitly,*" clients said. Observers have a great deal of respect for the "*smart, creative*" Carlson, particularly in the securities field, where he represents directors and officers, boards and companies in SEC matters and takeover-related litigation. Many point to his "*refined sense of business*" as well as his obvious legal expertise. "*Top-flight and deserving of his reputation,*" **Charles Douglas** (see p.827) stands out to competitors. With a long-standing reputation in antitrust, he has naturally migrated to handle multicase litigation required by clients such as AT&T, Microsoft and Citibank. He recently took a major securities class action to trial for AT&T and has dealt with significant commercial litigation matters for Deloitte & Touche. **Scott Lassar** (see p.840) "*brings great depth to the team – he is a terrific courtroom lawyer,*" peers asserted. His white-collar criminal practice includes internal investigations, securities fraud, pharmaceutical fraud and accounting irregularities. **John Gallo** (see p.831) is a former federal prosecutor and comes to the attention of commentators for his insight and skill in internal investigations and his prosecution of civil fraud cases. **Scott Mendeloff** (see p.845) has handled numerous commercial disputes, although his practice is substantially weighted towards white-collar defense and internal corporate investigations. His time spent as assistant US attorney reinforces his capabilities in these areas. "*Reassuringly well respected,*" **Thomas Ryan** (see p.854) exerts control over a practice with a national scope that is weighted towards complex business litigation and antitrust.

**Constantine Trela** (see p.861) joins the tables on the back of a stellar performance in the Supreme Court and appellate circuit. "*He is a first-class litigator and I frequently recommend him,*" said one commentator. **Linton Childs** (see p.824), though young, "*has the confidence of the client.*" More often than not acting for an accounting firm, underwriter or other defendant in federal securities class actions, "*he has good analytical skills tempered with common sense.*"

**Clients/Work Highlights:** AT&T; Microsoft; Bayer; Citigroup; GE; BP; Aon and Deloitte & Touche.

## Baker & McKenzie
See firm details p.866

**The Firm:** One of the true globally integrated dispute resolution departments in Chicago, this firm's international scope differentiates it from many others in the market. Its access to multiple lawyers in differing locations means that it can mount a coordinated response to matters in multiple jurisdictions. The work it undertakes includes cartel cases, products liability and mass torts defense, and it has further built its white-collar criminal practice under the leadership of Joe Linklater. It is often retained to act for corporations and their officers and directors in international cartel investigations, fraud allegations and other financial and business-related crimes.

**The Lawyers:** **Joe Linklater** (see p.841) "*keeps his eye on the ultimate objective of the client and doesn't get lost.*" Peers note this "*hugely significant*" partner's involvement in counseling and advising as well as trying cases. Much of his time has been spent on major international cartel cases and in federal criminal investigations into financial crime. **Pat Herald** (see p.835) maintains a strong commitment to civil litigation with a practice that encompasses class actions, products liability, internal investigations and IP.

**Clients/Work Highlights:** Crompton; Archer Daniels Midland; Borders Group; Kidde; Mezztech and Turtle Wax.

## Katten Muchin Rosenman LLP
See firm details p.874

**The Firm:** This national firm has a strong portfolio of clients and stands out particularly in the area of securities and financial litigation. It has represented Acceptance Insurance Companies in a securities class action filed by stockholders that was granted summary judgment and upheld in the court of appeal. In a separate case, the team represented individual directors of Boeing in consolidated stockholder derivative actions. Another string to its bow is its involvement in several civil racketeering lawsuits for major insurers including State Farm.

**The Lawyers:** National head of department David Kistenbroker handles complex litigation, while Sheldon Zenner is chair of the white-collar criminal and civil litigation practice. There are around 60 other attorneys practicing in the Chicago office.

**Clients/Work Highlights:** Kmart; State Farm; Accepted Insurance Companies; Boeing and Cerner.

## Skadden, Arps, Slate, Meagher & Flom LLP & Affiliates

See firm details p.1557

**The Firm:** The Chicago office of this international juggernaut is forging a distinct presence in the Midwest. Its visibility is due to expertise in securities litigation, representation before the SEC and other regulatory bodies, products liability and antitrust. Though the team in Chicago is smaller than some, the degree to which the office is integrated within a wider international network pays dividends for its clients. "*They have the confidence of major corporations,*" sources reported. Geographic borders mean little to the group, as evidenced by its work across the country for clients such as GlaxoSmithKline, Aon and McDonald's.

**The Lawyers:** Clients go to **Tina Tchen** (see p.860) for representation on the most complex matters: "*She has the great ability to manage complex, multi-piece puzzles.*" Her practice includes representing boards of directors in stockholder class and derivatives actions. She further handles SEC investigations and the representation of public agencies in state and federal class actions.

**Clients/Work Highlights:** Baxter; Exelon; Intel; General Mills; Wisconsin Energy and American Express.

## Freeborn & Peters

**The Firm:** Litigation remains a key component of this midsize Chicago firm of 120 attorneys. Its prominence lies in securities, complex commercial and antitrust litigation, and the team has also seen a substantial growth in IP-related actions. The team of litigators tries cases across the country, and clients note: "*They bring a common-sense approach to litigation that is straight-shooting and easy to deal with.*" **The Lawyers:** Founding partner Michael Freeborn concentrates on complex commercial and securities litigation. Michael Kelly, the firm's managing partner, is a main contact for the litigation team.

**Clients/Work Highlights:** AEGON USA; BP; Canadian National Railway; Illinois Central Railroad; Citigroup; ExxonMobil; McDonald's; T-Mobile and Boeing.

## Latham & Watkins LLP

**The Firm:** The breadth and depth of this firm's international capabilities put it firmly on the map for litigation. Its Chicago caseload includes antitrust, healthcare,

insurance, IP, energy, utility and business torts. It also undertakes a proportion of work with a criminal defense element. "*Their lawyers are workhorses for big cases and are constantly at trial,*" sources commented. The group recently handled litigation involving design and construction deficiencies associated with a nuclear power plant in the Washington area.

**The Lawyers:** "*Fine, skilled lawyer*" **Bob Tarun** has a widely admired white-collar criminal defense practice. He is known as a tough trial lawyer who "*gets his teeth stuck in*" on complex fraud cases as well as SEC enforcement actions and internal investigations.

**Clients/Work Highlights:** The group acts for major corporations and individuals across the USA.

## Schiff Hardin LLP

See firm details p.881

**The Firm:** Clients notice that this six-office firm has "*developed an outstanding general litigation practice over recent years.*" According to commentators, the Chicago group combines a "*business-minded approach to litigation*" alongside an "*excellent ability to counsel and advise.*" Key areas of expertise relate to IP and technology, securities and commodities, corporate finance and insurance.

**The Lawyers:** While taking on the role of managing partner, **Ronald Safer** (see p.854) remains active in casework with sources singling out his ability to combine both roles. "*He is an outstanding trial lawyer with excellent judgment, one of the best in complex civil and criminal litigation.*"

**Clients/Work Highlights:** Clients across the firm's integrated network of offices include PepsiCo, O-I and Newell Rubbermaid.

## Cotsirilos Tighe & Streicker Ltd

**The Firm:** This six-lawyer litigation boutique retains a strong standing in the market for its expertise in white-collar criminal defense. The "*stellar team*" has experience in both the private and public sectors and in a variety of areas including antitrust, healthcare fraud and abuse, government fraud, securities and internal investigations. "*Whenever they are involved in the case, we know they will do the right thing for their client,*" sources reflected.

**The Lawyers:** **James Streicker** is a "*standout player*" in white-collar criminal defense. His decades of experience lead clients to admire his practice, which is made up of service in federal and state courts in litigation and investigations.

**Clients/Work Highlights:** The firm handles matters for individuals and companies involved in criminal disputes.

## Stetler & Duffy Ltd

**The Firm:** With a reputation for "*formulating effective defense strategies,*" this litigation specialist stands tall on the Chicago legal horizon. Often attracting the highest-profile cases, the group's power lies in its representation of individuals involved in both civil and criminal fraud investigations. Criminal antitrust work has also become a major part of the firm's output. The compact outfit is a popular choice for referrals from larger firms due in part to its "*outstanding trial lawyers and strategic thinkers.*" **The Lawyers:** "*There's nobody better than* **David Stetler**," said one client, referring to his strategic thinking and superior trial skills. "*He can resonate with the jury when he presents the facts – he has the common touch.*"

**Clients/Work Highlights:** The firm acts for company directors and officers and other individuals at public and private companies.

## Other Notable Practitioners

Splitting his time between the business hubs of New York and Chicago, **Steven Molo** (see p.846) of Shearman & Sterling LLP tackles both criminal and civil litigation. Sources call him "*a great commercial litigator – hard-working and always on the go.*" He represents the Dutch accounting partnership KPMG Holding NV in civil securities class action litigation surrounding the overstatement of oil reserves by Royal Dutch Shell. In the white-collar field, he represents the former CFO of Symbol Technologies in a major criminal accounting fraud case. Clients say **Nick Berberian** (see p.819) of Neal, Gerber & Eisenberg LLP is "*detail-oriented, thorough and dogged in getting the best result.*" Deemed "*extremely knowledgeable in the securities area,*" he has represented brokerage firms and their employees before federal and state courts. He represented Lehman Brothers in numerous civil cases, arbitrations and regulatory matters arising out of a fraudulent scheme engaged in by a former broker. **Stephen Novack** of boutique firm Novack & Macey LLP is a popular choice for referrals. He drew praise for his "*impressive, strong-minded stance and fine courtroom skills.*"

# MEDIA & ENTERTAINMENT

# LITIGATION

| Media & Entertainment: Litigation |
| --- |
| Leading Firms |
| **1** JENNER & BLOCK LLP *Chicago* |
| SONNENSCHEIN NATH & ROSENTHAL *Chicago* |
| **2** FOLEY & LARDNER LLP *Chicago* |
| SIDLEY AUSTIN LLP *Chicago* |

## Band 1

### Jenner & Block LLP

See firm details p.873

**The Firm:** This "*accomplished and capable litigation firm*" has a diverse media and entertainment practice covering traditional media matters and First Amend-

ment issues. Expertise in the latter was exhibited when the team represented the video game industry in its concerns relating to the new Safe Games Illinois Act, a law prohibiting the sale or rental of explicit videos to minors. The firm also defends media organizations in libel, defamation and privacy cases and appears in matters relating to the Freedom of Information Act.

The Chicago team draws on expertise from the firm's other regional offices, particularly that in Washington DC, to further its prowess in the field.

**The Lawyers:** *"One of the sharpest lawyers around,"* **David Sanders** (see p.854) is *"an excellent litigator who is extremely attentive to clients,"* according to interviewees. He cochairs the firm's media and First Amendment team and advises a range of media clients on matters such as libel, privacy, news gathering and reporting. He remains popular with clients, who say: *"He is a terrific legal tactician who finds a way to win cases."* New to the tables is **Debbie Berman** (see p.820), an attorney who is building a strong reputation for her First Amendment and defamation work. She acted for Paramount Pictures in a lawsuit brought by an individual who claimed the main character in the film 'Hardball' was based on him. He alleged that the film portrayed him in an unflattering light.

**Clients/Work Highlights:** ABC, Crain Communications and Golfweek Magazine feature on the client list.

## Sonnenschein Nath & Rosenthal LLP
See firm details p.884

**The Firm:** Sources acknowledge this firm to be *"trustworthy, reliable, practical and extremely solid in its advice."* Clients warm to a team that is *"easy to deal with and understands our needs."* One interviewee

outlined the thoughts of many by saying: *"They know how to get the best results at the lowest costs."* The team is one of the most experienced in the field and, accordingly, handles many high-profile cases. For example, it has recently acted for the California Newspapers Partnership and MediaNews Group in a defamation case filed by football star Bo Jackson. The group covers all aspects of broadcast and print media-related work including defamation, advertising and First Amendment issues.

**The Lawyers:** The *"spectacular"* **Sam Fifer** (see p.829) is *"a personable, likable kind of guy."* He handles broadcasting-related matters such as defamation and content liability issues. Lately, he has acted for the Better Government Association in a lawsuit regarding a reporter's privilege to protect the anonymity of sources. **James Klenk** (see p.839) is *"very business minded and always keeps our objectives in mind,"* according to clients. *"A great litigation strategist,"* his skills have recently been utilized in his representation of the Chicago Tribune in a case involving the publication of a photograph featuring a wrongly identified individual.

**Clients/Work Highlights:** Home Shopping Network; NBC; Chicago Tribune; Chicago Magazine and Chicago Cubs.

## Band 2

### Foley & Lardner LLP
See firm details p.2037

**The Firm:** This nationwide firm represents a wide variety of media organizations including print, broadcast and telecom entities. Its team has built a considerable reputation for its specialist First Amendment advice, particularly regarding libel and defamation matters. The group also counsels e-business and multimedia clients on copyright and trademark issues. Recently, the team argued an appellate libel case for broadcaster ABC regarding protection for news content and gathering.

**The Lawyers:** *"Good egg"* **Michael Conway** (see p.825) is praised as *"an excellent lawyer with great judgment."* While he is the chair of the firm's media law group, media work constitutes only one facet of his general commercial litigation practice. According to interviewees: *"He has three key characteristics: honesty, integrity and experience."*

**Clients/Work Highlights:** The Chicago Tribune; ABC; Small Newspaper Group and The Wall Street Journal.

### Sidley Austin LLP
See firm details p.883

**The Firm:** This *"top-quality firm"* is credited by clients for its *"extremely competent lawyers who have a long reputation for achieving great results."* The team covers various aspects of media law including First Amendment, defamation and reporters' privilege issues, as well as the Freedom of Information Act. A highlight for the firm was advising long-standing client the Chicago Tribune on access and reporters' privilege issues in relation to the high-profile criminal case of ex-Illinois governor George Ryan.

**The Lawyers:** **Richard O'Brien** (see p.848) remains the firm's leading light for media and entertainment issues. Clients applaud his *"intelligent and warm manner"* and add: *"He is respectful of our needs."* As well as his vibrant media practice, O'Brien covers invasion of privacy, trademark and trade secrets work. Interviewees further commended him as *"smart but also compassionate."*

**Clients/Work Highlights:** The Chicago Tribune and the Illinois Chamber of Commerce feature on this firm's client list.

# MEDIA & ENTERTAINMENT

# TRANSACTIONAL

## Band 1

### Freeborn & Peters

**The Firm:** This *"efficient"* team of Chicago-based media lawyers is described by observers as both *"capable and knowledgeable."* The group focuses on a broad spectrum of advertising and marketing-related issues including sponsorship, promotions and licensing. This expertise was recently utilized in the team's merchandise licensing work for the new children's electronic learning toy, VSmile, released by VTech Electronics. The team attracts a range of clients across

the country ranging from authors and producers to multimedia companies and motion picture studios.

**The Lawyers:** The *"professional and intelligent"* **Andrew Goldstein** is well regarded for his broad-based IP expertise including his knowledge of entertainment and advertising law. He is recognized as an active member of Lawyers for the Creative Arts, a nonprofit association providing legal advice for artists. **Eugene Zelek** is *"excellent, intelligent and thorough,"* according to clients. Alongside his renowned antitrust practice, he has built a reputation for his marketing, licensing and IP-related work. He is a frequent writer and speaker on such matters.

**Clients/Work Highlights:** Pritzker Military Library; Nintendo; RealNetworks and VTech Electronics North America.

### Holland & Knight LLP
See firm details p.1534

**The Firm:** Clients credit this team as *"an excellent group of people who are conscientious, smart and focused on getting the deals done."* The group is one of the more sizable in Illinois and consequently offers a diverse media practice covering film, music and television. It has become particularly well known for its expertise in independent film production and financing. Major work for the year has included successfully acting for Bunim/Murray Productions when a disgruntled individual, who lived next door to the location for MTV's reality show 'Real World', brought a lawsuit against the company.

**The Lawyers:** In tandem with a strong bankruptcy practice, the *"superlative"* **Robert Labate** (see p.840) has developed a significant reputation for his film and television-related work. As one client confirms, he is a *"low-key and sensible attorney who is one of the best film guys in Chicago."* However, his practice is not limited to film matters as indicated by the fact that he recently defended a modeling agency against sex discrimination charges brought by a former employee. *"Intellectually sharp"* **Peter Strand** (see p.859) is widely praised by interviewees as *"enjoyable* to work with" and an attorney who is "*honest and has a good heart.*" With his previous experience as a recording artist, he is praised by commentators for his expertise in music law.

Clients/Work Highlights: Bunim/Murray Productions; Kartemquin Educational Films; Optomen Productions and New York City Ballet.

## Michael Best & Friedrich LLP
See firm details p.2038

The Firm: This full-service firm enters the tables this year due to the recent addition of entertainment and media authorities Jeffrey Brown and Luke DeMarte. Operating out of the firm's IP department, the team handles a range of concerns including music, film and theater matters. Clients are impressed by the team's expertise, highlighting its "*unique understanding and remarkably extensive knowledge*" as reasons why this is now a go-to firm.

The Lawyers: "*We love him,*" say clients of **Jeffrey Brown**, because "*he cuts through all the thorny talk and legalese to get to the nub of the situation.*" He largely concentrates on music and theater work, although he has recently handled a film concerning a renowned gospel singer. Other highlights include representing EFFEN Vodka in their sponsorship of

events during a recent Rolling Stones tour. The "*top-drawer*" **Luke DeMarte** is "*savvy*" according to clients, while also "*making the legal process affordable and effective.*" A large part of his practice is music oriented involving the representation of recording artists, producers and recording labels. He has handled several large-scale recording agreements for artists signing to major record labels.

Clients/Work Highlights: The firm advises a range of clients including individuals and companies involved in the entertainment industry.

## Winston & Strawn LLP
See firm details p.886

The Firm: The "*great resources*" at this "*bright, energetic and pragmatic*" firm drew consistent praise from interviewees. The firm offers a dedicated media and entertainment team covering everything a company needs to launch its products on to the market. Clients appreciate the "*sound legal advice and business savvy*" the team provides on a range of matters including copyright, trademarks, promotions and advertising. The team also imparts expert sponsorship advice to the likes of car manufacturing giant Honda.

The Lawyers: "*At the top of the game*" is how sources describe **Stephen Durchslag**. He is highly regarded for his specialist advertising, promotions and general entertainment work. **Mary Hutchings Reed** received many compliments for her client-friendly approach. As one interviewee noted: "*She understands our way of doing things.*" She primarily handles marketing and advertising matters. Her expertise in the latter was brought to the fore in her work for Pizza Hut regarding the naming of Pizza Hut Park, a soccer facility in Dallas, Texas. **Brian Heidelberger** (see p.835) "*always pulls through in a crunch with cool, collected strategic counsel*" for clients. He "*operates with the highest integrity and work ethic.*" He has recently assisted the car manufacturer Acura in securing James Spader for a range of endorsements.

Clients/Work Highlights: Pizza Hut; Hoover; Kodak; BBDO; Taco Bell; Wrigley; PepsiCo; Office Depot; DDB Chicago; Carlson Marketing Group and Burrell Communications Group.

## Other Notable Practitioners

Market sources consider **Scott Hodes** of Bryan Cave LLP to be one of the deans of the entertainment Bar in Illinois. Clients say he is "*a joy to work with*" because "*he is a sharp, seasoned attorney who is personally interested and involved in the visual arts.*" Hodes has built a truly nationwide practice dealing with entertainment law as it relates to the visual arts. He represents a range of high-profile clients including artists, dealers and museums. For example, he recently acted for Christo and Jeanne-Claude, handling all the legal issues surrounding their project 'The Gates', located temporarily in New York's Central Park. Sole practitioner **Linda Mensch** is widely admired for her specialist music knowledge. **Peter O'Reilly** of Lea + O'Reilly moves up the tables this year with a great deal of positive feedback from both peers and clients. One interviewee surmised the thoughts of many, noting: "*His advice is always what we need at the right time.*" His practice is focused on sweepstakes and contests. Highlights include helping a telecom company to conduct large-scale promotional activities for the first time. Clients remark: "*He knows the area inside out.*" "*One of the best in town,*" **David Saltiel** of Bell Boyd & Lloyd LLC advises on a range of entertainment topics including film, television and theater. He "*really knows his stuff*" according to commentators. He has been busy recently negotiating agreements for two pilot episodes on network television and an on-air talent agreement for a cable television show. Sole practitioner **Timothy Kelley** focuses on music-related matters. The "*smart as heck*" **Amy Singh** of The Entertainment and Intellectual Property Group enters the tables with recommendations from peers and clients alike. Interviewees praise her "*no-nonsense and business-like*" approach, saying she is "*extremely efficient with tremendous integrity.*" She handles a range of media and entertainment concerns including marketing and advertising. She has recently represented several major motion picture studios regarding talent agreements.

# REAL ESTATE

## Band 1

### DLA Piper Rudnick Gray Cary US LLP
See firm details p.870

The Firm: The Chicago office is the largest of this global firm's and it houses an "*enormously talented*" real estate group, which many consider to be the brightest feather in its cap. Large enough to outgun the majority of its rivals, its standing in the field is beyond doubt. The team's market position is at its strongest for traditional real estate work, although it augments its reputation further with its renowned land use and zoning expertise.

The Lawyers: **Charles Edwards** (see p.827) holds the position of senior counsel and spends a great deal of his time teaching and conducting public engagements on behalf of the firm; he is also the go-to lawyer in the office for all real estate questions. The "*very well-regarded*" **James Beard** (see p.819) is engaged in a lot of joint venture acquisition work, especially for large public real estate investment trusts. This year he has undertaken plenty of financing dispositions and acquisitions in the office sector for Trizec and for Archstone-Smith in the residential sector. **Portia Owen Morrison** (see p.846) has "*high visibility as a developers' lawyer,*" while **David Glickstein** (see

p.832), holder of a truly global practice, is particularly famed for his representation of lenders and borrowers on complex financing transactions and workouts. **Harold Pomerantz**'s (see p.850) large corporate real estate practice sees him representing non-real estate companies for their real estate needs nationally as well as regionally. Companies such as BP regularly turn to him and he has recently acted for the oil giant in selling a refinery and some port facilities. "*An outstanding lawyer and a fine gentleman,*" **David Sickle** (see p.856) has been doing more joint ventures and private equity than development this year. In particular, Sickle is known for representing some of the largest shopping center development clients such as The Mills Corporation. He has further established a niche movie theater practice representing landlords and exhibitors such as Century Theaters. **Mark Yura** (see p.864) has a practice focused on representing and structuring complex acquisition and financing transactions for entrepreneurial companies and fund investors, work he has handled for ECM and Orion Real Estate Company among others. Also present in the group is "*outstanding technician*" **Theodore Novak** (see p.848) who chairs the firm's national land use practice. He dominates the regional market along with Jack Guthman of Shefsky & Froelich and is an all-around real estate lawyer who specializes in entitlements and incentives, land use and development.

Clients/Work Highlights: Boeing; Equity Office Properties/Equity Residential; LaSalle Bank; The Mills Corporation and Transwestern Investment Company.

## Katten Muchin Rosenman LLP

See firm details p.874

The Firm: This "*tremendous group*" provides a wide-ranging set of skills, taking the client from initial fund strategizing right through to the execution of a transaction. Client commentators praised it for its adaptability. As one said: "*The lawyers are tough when they need to be but smart enough to save their bullets for when we really need them; this is a very valuable consideration in many of our transactions and we haven't seen many better at it than Katten.*"

The Lawyers: Head of the group **David Bryant** (see p.822) is the go-to guy for fund structuring. Work this year has included representing the seller of a portfolio of North America properties with a purchase price in excess of $800 million. He also continues to represent sponsors of real estate funds, recently representing one who raised $650 million. "*Bright and thoughtful*" **Kenneth Jacobson** (see p.836) has been involved in

the formation of an investment fund to acquire US timberland and a companion loan facility to assist with the acquisition of the land itself. Jacobson won widespread market support, as did **Daniel Perlman** (see p.849). "*Smart as a whip and fun to work with,*" Perlman has continued to represent LaSalle Investment Management in the formation of an open-ended real estate fund, acquisitions of portfolio assets, joint venture negotiations and financings. "*A great lawyer who undoubtedly deserves his ranking,*" **Mark Simon** (see p.857) typically represents lenders undertaking large loan transactions. His recent sorties have included representing a group of banks financing the development of the shopping mall Pittsburgh Mills, outside of Pittsburgh. Similarly active, **Andrew Small** (see p.857) has been representing The Milestone Group in connection with a joint venture and the acquisition of a multifamily portfolio for a purchase price of over $1 billion. He is joined in the tables by **Marcia Sullivan** (see p.860) whose efforts of late have included representing a lender in making a structured investment in a loan portfolio secured by over 150 golf courses.

Clients/Work Highlights: Jones Lang LaSalle; JPMorgan; Starwood Capital; Blackacre Capital Management and Bank of America.

## Mayer, Brown, Rowe & Maw LLP

See firm details p.876

The Firm: When researchers asked one peer what made the team at Mayer Brown stand out from the pack he replied simply, "*consistency.*" The founding and preeminent office of this global law firm has long been famed for its strength in the finance arena, a factor which explains the real estate group's particular renown within the market when it comes to private equity. One commentator suggested that they were "*probably the best in the state in this field.*"

The Lawyers: "*Top guy*" **John Gearen** (see p.831) has been advising both Deutsche Bank and Oppenheim on the interaction of German and US tax law regarding the acquisition of US assets. He is but one cog in a fine team that includes the "*outstanding*" **Alvin Katz** (see p.838). Katz, who is often handling matters out of state, has been representing a number of private equity providers and has completed between six and seven billion dollars worth of deals in the past year alone. In between this, he has also managed to handle numerous mixed-use developments in New York for CalPERS and acted for The Carlyle Group when it has sought to invest in large condo projects in Florida, Virginia, DC, Arizona, California and Texas. The "*very fine and solid*" **Jeffrey Usow** (see p.861) has been augmenting his career lately with a blossoming private equity practice. Extending his reach well, he is now handling a good degree of cross-border work, especially in Mexico where he has been involved in a $300 million investment fund for Equity International. Primarily recognized as a land use and zoning attorney, **Ivan Kane** (see p.837) enjoys an international practice that goes far beyond these areas. Representing developers, corporations, institutions and individuals in all manner of real estate transactions, his is one of the

busiest practices around. Recent high-profile work has included representing BP with respect to its role as lead investor in and developer of Cantera, a large mixed-use development in Illinois. Kane's involvement has included securing zoning approvals for the overall project and individual end users.

Clients/Work Highlights: The Carlyle Group; Prudential Investment Management; Lehman Brothers and ORIX Real Estate Equities.

## Sonnenschein Nath & Rosenthal LLP

See firm details p.884

The Firm: Research found this team to be comprised of "*terrific real estate lawyers with a broad base of experience operating at a very high level.*" The team has continued to benefit from increased foreign investment and a commensurate need for attorneys who can advise on the interface between different jurisdictions. This is a team with undeniable critical mass and a strength within the junior ranks that promises great things for the future.

The Lawyers: **Patrick Moran** (see p.846) is a "*very fine attorney*" who engenders a lot of respect among clients and peers, especially for his work in the office leasing arena. Lately, Moran has experienced an uptick in engagement on the developers' side of the fence. Representation of The John Buck Company on the disposition of a one million sq ft building is one example of this. His practice is evenly divided between financing outside of Chicago and development work within the city. "*Undoubtedly one of the finest lawyers in the state,*" **Mark Mehlman** (see p.845) focuses his practice on financing, joint ventures, acquisitions and dispositions. This year he has been engaged in plenty of lending for high-end downtown office buildings. Across the country Mehlman has been involved in the acquisition and financing of a number of hotels. In the words of one client, **Eric Schiller** (see p.854) "*has a depth of experience that allows him to move a deal along and advise on important business issues in such a way that improves our business standing.*" Peers agreed that he has a well-deserved name for having an "*appropriately nonconfrontational approach with opposing counsel.*" Commentators deemed the "*business savvy*" **Jana Cohen Blackman** (see p.821) to be "*a real powerhouse who has carved out an enviable niche in tax-advantaged real estate investment deals.*" She has been involved in some cutting-edge inner-city affordable housing projects of late.

Clients/Work Highlights: Metropolitan Life Insurance; Trinity Hotels; PPM America; JPMorgan Chase and Goldman Sachs.

## Band 2

## Barack Ferrazzano Kirschbaum Perlman & Nagelberg

The Firm: This midsized firm is acknowledged by all to be home to some "*exceptional real estate practitioners.*" It boasts a highly specialised 28-lawyer real estate group that typically represents big anchor tenants and REITS. In line with the market as a whole, the real estate team has recently experienced an increase in work from foreign investors, especially from Europe.

**The Lawyers:** The *"enormously talented"* **Dennis Ferrazzano** is renowned throughout the market for his expertise in the areas of commercial and corporate real estate, securities and business planning. **Howard Kirschbaum** focuses his practice on large insurance clients, banks and REITS. Clients value him for acting as both a legal and a business adviser. **Howard Nagelberg** possesses a broad real estate practice that encompasses representation of public real estate companies regarding their acquisition, disposition, joint venture and development needs, both nationally and internationally. His impressive caseload has included leading a team representing First Industrial in a REIT, worth in excess of $1 billion, that covers 227 properties throughout the country. Colleague **Suzanne Bessette-Smith** presides over a broad-based real estate practice with a particular emphasis on publicly traded REITS.

**Clients/Work Highlights:** Ventas; Bank of America; FirstBank; BP Amico; LVMH and Equity Office Properties Trust.

## Sidley Austin LLP
See firm details p.883

**The Firm:** This firm was described by one client as *"the main draw for large, complicated deals with sophisticated elements such as preferred equity and structured mezzanines."* Its 40-strong group engages in a complete spread of real estate work, including buying and selling, development, leasing and zoning. It has considerable synergy with the firm's notable corporate practice and, as such, is considered preeminent for real estate finance.

**The Lawyers:** Peers enthused about firmwide head of real estate **Virginia Aronson** (see p.818). A *"wonderfully gifted lending lawyer and a paragon of first-class client service,"* she works in tandem with **Lee Smolen** (see p.857), head of the Chicago real estate group and a man whose work on structured finance and lending has earned him a national reputation. In the past year, he represented long-standing client Wells Fargo in connection with the financing of an office building portfolio by a large REIT. **Charles Schrank** (see p.855) shares his predilection for finance work, while **Anthony Aiello** (see p.817) has undertaken some interesting work this year, assisting Starwood Hotels & Resorts Worldwide on numerous sales. His other work in the hospitality arena has included advising Deutsche Bank Opportunity Fund on hotel management agreements.

**Clients/Work Highlights:** KKR Financial; Starwood Hotels & Resorts Worldwide; BP; Wells Fargo and Bank One.

## Band 3

## Bell, Boyd & Lloyd LLC

**The Firm:** This firm, with offices in Chicago and Washington, DC, has a full-service team that can provide clients with expertise right across the board. Whether it be acquisitions and sales, zoning, development, design and construction or leasing, this team has something to offer. The thriving condo and mortgage finance markets have proved particularly fertile sources of work in recent times.

**The Lawyers: Thomas Homburger** boasts a practice whose expertise spans all areas of real estate other than zoning and land use. However, it is his aptitude in the areas of financing, development and investment (especially sale/leaseback transactions) that have really earned him the greatest market renown. Such breadth of experience makes Homburger a valuable asset to clients, many of whom seek him out for his business as much as legal advice. Currently chair of the real estate group, **Terrence Budny** has a national practice that encompasses financing, development and investment. Typical clients include buyers, sellers, lenders, borrowers, landlords and tenants. Representative work for both men this year has included a raft of mortgage finance transactions, numerous condominium conversions and the obtaining of a favorable verdict in a major title claim undertaken for a prominent Chicago-based insurance company.

**Clients/Work Highlights:** Pabcor Equities; Oak Brook Bank; Bank Leumi; FirstBank; LaSalle and Lieberman Management Services.

## Jenner & Block LLP
See firm details p.873

**The Firm:** This smaller real estate group provides a broad practice base that takes in mainstream acquisitions, divestitures, financing contracts, development and joint ventures. This team of five partners and six associates works closely with the tax, corporate and environment groups at the firm.

**The Lawyers: Donald Resnick**'s (see p.851) practice has been dominated by selling rather than development. Work regarding the sale of offices continues to come in from long-standing client Jupiter Realty, while Resnick has also acted for Prime Group Realty Trust on the development of a 1.5 million sq ft office block. Before the two companies merged, Resnick represented Sears in its acquisition of 50 sites from Kmart; he continues to represent the Sears holding company.

**Clients/Work Highlights:** Sara Lee; General Dynamics; The John Buck Company and City of Chicago.

## Kirkland & Ellis LLP
See firm details p.875

**The Firm:** Kirkland & Ellis' Chicago office is both the firm's oldest and largest. The team boasts nearly 30 interdisciplinary lawyers who over the past few years have been undertaking increasing amounts of real estate work. With an untarnished reputation in the private equity market, it is the growing interface between private equity and real estate that occupies the thoughts of this real estate department. It will come as no surprise, therefore, that its main areas of expertise include public and private REITs, real estate finance and workouts. The team also boasts a thriving hospitality practice.

**The Lawyers: Stephen Tomlinson** (see p.861) is not a dirt lawyer but focuses on the type of work that straddles the real estate and private equity divide, such as investment fund formation and corporate transactions in the realty industry. Researchers found unanimous support for the assertion that he is *"a very skilled attorney."* He divides his time between seats in the firm's Chicago and New York offices while also having a global practice.

**Clients/Work Highlights:** General Motors Asset Management, LaSalle Investment Management and Starwood Hotels & Resorts Worldwide are among this firm's clients.

## Seyfarth Shaw LLP

See firm details p.882

**The Firm:** This international law firm has ten offices throughout the USA and a European presence, yet it is the Chicago office that wields most muscle. The real estate department here has significant critical mass, being home to more than 30 attorneys, many of whom are also experienced corporate attorneys and add luster to the firm's blossoming investment practice.

**The Lawyers:** Commentators confirm that **Joel Rubin** is very well regarded in the construction Bar. He has a practice that can best be summed up as you name it, he's done it. In particular, he specializes in acquisition and dispositions, nationally and internationally. Clients value his commitment to *"going every step of the way"* with them as they develop their businesses.

**Clients/Work Highlights:** LaSalle Bank; Prudential Real Estate; Merrill Lynch; Home Depot and DB Australia.

## Winston & Strawn LLP

See firm details p.886

**The Firm:** The firm has eight offices across the USA and Europe, with the Chicago office serving as the firm's headquarters and housing more than 350 lawyers. Of these, some 17 band together to form a real estate department whose strength is further augmented by its calling upon the firm's corporate, tax, environmental and litigation groups.

**The Lawyers:** The *"excellent"* **Christopher Murtaugh** (see p.847) is the real estate group's senior figure, boasting 30 years' experience at the real estate Bar. His practice encompasses commercial property investment and disposition, development and lending for a variety of clients. **Mark Henning** (see p.835) is effective at both real estate and financial work and operates a real estate practice that is heavily weighted towards representing investment companies, banks and institutional investors such as US Equities Realty and Bank One. Henning is the head of the real estate side of the firm's leveraged leasing practice and a member of the American College of Real Estate Lawyers.

**Clients/Work Highlights:** Alere Property Group; Ashley Capital; Bayer; CIBC World Markets and GE Asset Management.

## Band 4

## Foley & Lardner LLP

See firm details p.2037

**The Firm:** A presence in many states throughout the country, this firm has signaled the extent of its ambitions by opening offices in cities as far flung as Brussels and Tokyo. Its Chicago office is just one link in the chain but is highly renowned for its *"unstinting*

*efforts in the real estate field."* Particular expertise is boasted in the areas of joint venture partnerships, securitized lending and complex financing.

**The Lawyers:** The team is led by Elizabeth Corey. Her broad-based practice includes the representation of lenders and the developers and managers of shopping centers, hotels and shopping arcades, restaurants, retail businesses, industrial plants, retirement residences, nursing homes and other healthcare facilities.

**Clients/Work Highlights:** Developers; secured lenders; institutional investors and educational institutions all come to this firm for their real estate needs.

## Goldberg, Kohn, Bell, Black, Rosenbloom & Moritz, Ltd

**The Firm:** Although comparatively small, this firm maintains a strong reputation for the quality of its real estate work in general and for its lending expertise in particular. Commentators were quick to praise the team, only sounding one note of caution as to the depth on offer below the two respected senior partners.

**The Lawyers:** **Stephen Bell** chairs the firm's real estate practice and has a workload that focuses on the finance end of the field. **Jim Rosenbloom** boasts extensive experience in the real estate Bar and is renowned for his expertise in the transaction arena. He also has a niche in real estate bankruptcy.

**Clients/Work Highlights:** Chicago Mercantile Exchange; CB Richard Ellis Investors; GE Capital Real Estates and Ventas.

## Greenberg Traurig LLP

See firm details p.664

**The Firm:** This national heavyweight boasts an impressive spread of offices throughout the USA and has a notable European presence by virtue of its strategic alliances with offices in Brussels, London, Rome and Milan. The Chicago real estate practice continues to blossom. The team's size belies its capabilities as its members have expertise in the full spread of real estate work including development, financings, REITs and related environmental matters.

**The Lawyers:** **Michael Fishman** (see p.829) has a market reputation that surpasses the state line and extends into Latin America. His work has included representation of Walton Street Capital and its Mexican partner, Grupo Sadasi, in their acquisition of the Mexican subsidiary of Pulte Homes.

**Clients/Work Highlights:** Archon Group; Kimco Realty; Bally Total Fitness; Saks and Schottenstein Stores.

## Jones Day

See firm details p.570

**The Firm:** The Chicago office of this national heavyweight can call upon 15 talented real estate attorneys. Drawing on the wealth of experience offered by the firm's total of 125 property professionals worldwide, the group further benefits from access to environmental, tax, construction, finance, corporate and dispute resolution experts in other departments. This ensures clients' needs are never left unanswered.

**The Lawyers:** **Robert Lee** (see p.841) presides over a practice focused on the provision of real estate investment representation regionally, nationally and internationally. Typical clients include sponsors and investors in the formation of a panoply of funds. High-profile work this year has included ongoing advisory work for CalEast Industrial Investors in its $3.4 billion acquisition of CenterPoint Properties Trust.

**Clients/Work Highlights:** LaSalle Investment Management; Highcross Group; Orion Capital Management; Great Lakes REIT; CB Richard Ellis Investors; JP Morgan Chase; Washington Mutual and Westbrook Real Estate Funds.

## Neal, Gerber & Eisenberg LLP

See firm details p.880

**The Firm:** One of the smaller real estate groups, the team undertakes the full spread of real estate work from acquisition and financing to development, leasing and disposition. The team engages in a good mix of commercial, industrial and residential projects, yet it is most famous for its work with shopping center REITs.

**The Lawyers:** The Chicago real estate team is chaired by Stephen Berger. Typical work includes the representation of real estate companies and individuals in the acquisition, development and financing of commercial, apartment and hotel and resort properties. Berger has particular expertise in advising owners of hotel, multifamily, shopping center and office properties.

**Clients/Work Highlights:** Local and national corporations; financial institutions; developers and REITs are the group's typical clients.

## Schwartz, Cooper, Greenberger & Krauss, Chartered

**The Firm:** This Chicago firm has a real estate practice that encompasses financing, leasing, development, acquisitions, dispositions, arbitrations and dispute resolution and related litigation.

**The Lawyers:** **Michael Kurtzon** boasts a practice that exceeds state lines and has earned him a national reputation.

**Clients/Work Highlights:** LaSalle Bank National Association; Kaiser Development; Wachovia; The Habitat Company; Equity Residential Properties Trust; Freestone Realty Advisors; ING Realty Partners; Mesirow Stein and Pacific Security Capital.

## Shefsky & Froelich

**The Firm:** As one commentator stated, this team *"has good people and engages in good work."* The group is famed for its land use and zoning work for developers and its representation of private sector interests before government agencies. The team typically acts on residential projects but this year work has also included undertaking the zoning for a development of more than one million sq ft of office space for Hines around the country.

**The Lawyers:** *"Premier practitioner"* **Jack Guthman** has an unassailable reputation for land use and zoning expertise. *"If it's land use and it's in Chicago, Guthman is almost certainly going to be involved."*

**Clients/Work Highlights:** Village of Oak Park; JF

Development; US Equities; LaSalle National Bank and The Rose Group.

## Weinberg Richmond LLP

**The Firm:** The commercial real estate team of this smaller Chicago firm forms the cornerstone of their reputation. It handles a generous spread of real estate work from acquisitions, divestitures, finance, development and construction to leasing and lending.

**The Lawyers:** Mark Richmond is the firm's contact partner. He has a broad-based practice that focuses on development, financing, leasing, construction and other transactional matters. Richmond led a team that closed a $500 million REIT this year.

**Clients/Work Highlights:** CenterPoint Properties Trust; Darwin Realty & Development; The Inland Real Estate Group of Companies; ORIX Real Estate Equities and Residential Homes of America.

## Other Notable Practitioners

**Benjamin Randall** of Randall & Kenig LLP was identified to researchers as "*thoroughly deserving*" of his place in the tables. **Fred Feinstein** (see p.828) at McDermott Will & Emery was found to have a particular reputation for his involvement in development, zoning and environmental matters. **Peter Sarasek** (see p.854) at Quarles & Brady LLP has a practice that focuses on the transactional side of the field, encompassing leasing, acquisition, financing and construction.

# TAX

| | Tax |
|---|---|
| | Leading Firms |
| [1] | **KIRKLAND & ELLIS LLP** *Chicago* |
| | **MAYER, BROWN, ROWE & MAW LLP** *Chicago* |
| [2] | **LATHAM & WATKINS LLP** *Chicago* |
| | **MCDERMOTT WILL & EMERY** *Chicago* |
| | **SIDLEY AUSTIN LLP** *Chicago* |
| | **SKADDEN, ARPS** *Chicago* |
| [3] | **BAKER & MCKENZIE** *Chicago* |
| | **WINSTON & STRAWN LLP** *Chicago* |
| [4] | **JENNER & BLOCK LLP** *Chicago* |
| | **KATTEN MUCHIN ROSENMAN LLP** *Chicago* |
| | **NEAL, GERBER & EISENBERG LLP** *Chicago* |

## Band 1

### Kirkland & Ellis LLP

See firm details p.875

**The Firm:** A team of 20 lawyers ensures the Chicago office contributes significantly to Kirkland & Ellis' worldwide reputation for tax. In particular, the group's work is recognized as preeminent in the private equity and bankruptcy areas. Commentators were in no doubt as to the impressiveness of the "*wonderful*" lawyers here and were envious of the "*strength in depth*" of the all-encompassing tax service on offer to clients. Strong on transactions of many types, the team is perfectly placed to react to the recent increase in LBOs, and it is additionally highly respected in Illinois for its tax controversy practice.

**The Lawyers:** Esteemed adviser **Jack Levin** (see p.841) is widely revered as "*the dean of tax law.*" The influence of this "*fabulous lawyer*" is felt throughout the corporate and transaction-based areas of the firm, and he has many years of experience of complex deals and fund formations. **Jeffrey Sheffield** (see p.856) commands the respect of commentators for his transactional tax advice. A recent highlight was working on the sale of Toys 'R' Us to KKR and others, one of the biggest deals of 2005. Sheffield also represented GM in the sale of one of its interests and has been involved in buyouts around the world. Widely recognized for his expertise in private equity, **Donald Rocap** (see

p.852) is lauded as an excellent corporate lawyer by commentators. People say he is "*very thorough and easy to work with,*" as well as "*flexible*" – often a deciding factor in getting a deal done. "*Smart and thoughtful*" **Todd Maynes** (see p.844) uses his considerable knowledge of tax law to solve bankruptcy and controversy problems for some of the biggest companies in the country. Recent work has included acting as the lead lawyer for United Airlines in its bankruptcy hearings, and successfully representing other airlines in a case that disputed the amount of money that the state authority had taken in fuel tax. Clients referred to **William Welke** (see p.863) as "*an invaluable resource for any team, with an encyclopedic knowledge of the law.*" This "*creative lawyer*" is known for his experience in structuring private equity transactions and represents leading investment funds such as Madison Dearborn Partners.

**Clients/Work Highlights:** Alcoa; American Capital; BainCapital; Conseco Services; GTCR; Goense Bounds & Partners; Northwest Airlines; Parthenon Capital; Sara Lee; ServiceMaster; Summit Partners and Tenet Healthcare.

### Mayer, Brown, Rowe & Maw LLP

See firm details p.876

**The Firm:** At a time when the US government is growing increasingly committed to chasing tax shelters, the controversy group at this global firm has been very busy. The tax controversy and transfer pricing team is separate from the transaction-based practice and is widely recognized as the premier group of its kind in the country. Certainly it is viewed as "*the most consistent in terms of quality.*" Clients appreciated the "*vast resources*" that the team applies to litigation and IRS hearings, and observers noted the tremendous depth of talent available. The transaction team represents large international corporations in cross-border acquisitions and disposals. In the wake of recent accounting scandals and the new standards brought in to counter to them, the group has also seen a rise in work for companies wishing to restructure their accounting procedures.

**The Lawyers:** "*Perhaps the best-known controversy lawyer in the country,*" **Joel Williamson** (see p.863) has been at the forefront of events again over this

past year, representing Tribune in nationally significant litigation. He is much admired in the profession for his ability to identify the issues at hand quickly and incisively. His "*great focus*" and presentation skills are equally acknowledged as instrumental in his success litigating international transfer pricing controversies. "*Super-smart*" tax attorney **Timothy Sherck** (see p.856) is "*very thoughtful and insightful,*" according to his peers. Clients were no less forthcoming with their praise, suggesting that he was "*superb on corporate reorganizations.*" Sherck specializes in separations and acquisitions, and his recent work has included the disposal of a BellSouth subsidiary. International specialist **James Barry** (see p.819) advises mammoth companies on the planning of their worldwide structures. Clients report that he is "*very well versed in this highly technical area*" and are impressed with the way in which he gets to grips with the details of their business and problems. **George Craven** (see p.825) is a fine lawyer who is firmly established at the heart of the corporate tax team. Observers say he is "*at the top of the game*" for insurance and securitized transactions. Peers admired **Bruce Gelman**'s (see p.831) performance despite his relative youth. A "*smart*" lawyer, he is considered especially adept at solving clients' problems, particularly in the structuring of REITs. Capable of achieving "*superb results,*" **William Levy** (see p.841) is one of the state's experts on asset-backed securities. This excellent attorney came highly recommended by clients who applauded him as "*someone you can rely on to get things done.*" Commentators were equally well disposed towards opinion partner **George Luscombe** (see p.842), who was viewed as one of the very best lawyers to turn to for advice on deals involving mineral resources or partnerships. Luscombe is well known for being both "*technically sound and practical,*" and has recently been involved in structuring joint-operation deals for the energy industry.

**Clients/Work Highlights:** Boeing; Developers Diversified Realty; GE Capital; Goodrich; Intel; Lehman Brothers; Mattel; McKesson; Nestlé; Pfizer; Principal America Office Trust; Principal Real Estate Investors; ProLogis; REFCO; Strategic Hotel Capital; Tyco International and UPS.

| Tax |
| --- |
| **Leading Individuals** |
| **Senior Statesman** |
| LEVIN Jack *Kirkland & Ellis LLP* |
| [1] BOWEN Stephen *Latham & Watkins LLP* |
| FREEMAN Louis *Skadden, Arps* |
| SHEFFIELD Jeffrey *Kirkland & Ellis LLP* |
| WILLIAMSON Joel *Mayer, Brown, Rowe & Maw* |
| YODER Lowell *McDermott Will & Emery* |
| [2] BANOFF Sheldon *Katten Muchin Rosenman LLP* |
| LEDUC André *Skadden, Arps* |
| LEMEIN Gregg *Baker & McKenzie* |
| LIPTON Richard *Baker & McKenzie* |
| LYNCH James *Winston & Strawn LLP* |
| ROCAP Donald *Kirkland & Ellis LLP* |
| SHERCK Timothy *Mayer, Brown, Rowe & Maw* |
| ZIMBLER Jay *Sidley Austin LLP* |
| [3] BARRY James *Mayer, Brown, Rowe & Maw* |
| BORDERS Thomas *McDermott Will & Emery* |
| CRAVEN George *Mayer, Brown, Rowe & Maw* |
| GELMAN Bruce *Mayer, Brown, Rowe & Maw* |
| HARRIS Kenneth *Neal, Gerber & Eisenberg* |
| JONES Roger *Latham & Watkins LLP* |
| KIMBALL Christian *Jenner & Block LLP* |
| LEVY William *Mayer, Brown, Rowe & Maw* |
| LUCAS Roger *Winston & Strawn LLP* |
| LUSCOMBE II George *Mayer, Brown, Rowe & Maw* |
| MANDEL Reid *Katten Muchin Rosenman LLP* |
| MAYNES Todd *Kirkland & Ellis LLP* |
| SORENSEN Sharp *Sidley Austin LLP* |
| STEPHENS Thomas *Sonnenschein* |
| WEBER III Louis *Winston & Strawn LLP* |
| WELKE William *Kirkland & Ellis LLP* |

## Band 2

### Latham & Watkins LLP

**The Firm:** Although this firm is strong across the whole of the USA, the Chicago office is deemed to add considerable value to the network. It has long held a good reputation for its corporate transactions practice and the recent boom in restructurings has provided the perfect environment for the Chicago group to shine. The arrival of Roger Jones from Mayer Brown in the past year has allowed the firm to become a major tax controversy player in Illinois within a very short space of time.

**The Lawyers:** *"Top-flight"* **Stephen Bowen** is one of the foremost practitioners in corporate transactional tax law. Variously described as *"wonderful"* and *"superb,"* Bowen concentrates his practice on restructurings. He is also involved in some controversy work in the courts of appeal and is the managing partner of Latham's Chicago office. Having *"intellectual"* **Roger Jones** join the firm has boosted the team and provided it with balance across the practice area. He is hugely experienced in litigation and clients regard him as a *"go-to guy"* for appeals; they like to involve him as early in the process as possible.

**Clients/Work Highlights:** Classic Residence; Comcast; DuPont; Harrah's Entertainment; Hyatt; Koch Industries; Liberty Media; The Pritzker Organization and Sara Lee.

### McDermott Will & Emery

See firm details p.878

**The Firm:** This firm has cultivated a fine reputation for its international work and for its expertise in the complex field of state income tax. Increased M&A activity has boosted the transactional side of the practice and kept attorneys busy. Clients queued up to heap praise on the group, identifying its lawyers' *"great negotiating skills"* and *"extensive knowledge in corporate tax."* They were especially impressed with the extent of their international reach and the efficiency with which the group interacted with affiliated firms and its own overseas offices. Particular note was made of the firm's experience in tax repatriation by way of the homeland dividend relief, which has been a hot topic for multinational companies of late. Observers considered that the firm also has one of the best financial products practices in the country.

**The Lawyers:** Few attorneys can be so well thought of by their clients as **Lowell Yoder** (see p.864). For tax planning he is *"fantastic, on a scale of one to ten he is an 11,"* praised one satisfied customer. This *"smart and creative"* attorney is commended for his ability to grasp the detail of a problem quickly, offer alternative ways of looking at it and, ultimately, solve it. His recent work includes advising Procter & Gamble on the structure of their acquisition of Gillette in a deal worth $50 billion. Peers hold **Thomas Borders** (see p.821) in high regard as a *"thoughtful litigator,"* with one moved to comment: *"You can't go wrong with Borders."*

**Clients/Work Highlights:** Alliant Energy; Baxter; Caterpillar; GATX; Heidrick & Struggles; Mattel; Procter & Gamble and USG.

### Sidley Austin LLP

See firm details p.883

**The Firm:** This firm competes effectively in the international tax market for M&A, commodities pooling and financial products. For one of the smaller teams in the state, this is a considerable achievement and a testament to the *"fine quality"* of the lawyers in the firm's Chicago office. The tax controversy practice is also performing well, focusing as it does on appearances in front of the appeals courts of the IRS. The long-term effects that the retirement of Robert Wootton will have on the firm remain to be seen.

**The Lawyers:** Much of **Jay Zimbler's** (see p.864) recent work has involved the appeals courts of the IRS. His controversy practice continues to add considerable value to the Sidley team, leaning naturally on his extensive experience in complex tax matters. Zimbler specializes in federal income tax and has experience of international transactions. **Sharp Sorenson** (see p.858) heads the tax practice in Illinois and represents many of the firm's key clients in M&A, spin-offs and securitizations. Fellow practitioners found him a pleasure to work with, adding that he *"really knows what he is doing."*

**Clients/Work Highlights:** BNSF Railway; Exelon; First Data; RR Donnelley and Tellabs.

### Skadden, Arps, Slate, Meagher & Flom LLP & Affiliates

See firm details p.1557

**The Firm:** This national law firm has a superb corporate practice, which unsurprisingly has positive knock-on benefits for its tax practitioners. The work of the 20-strong Chicago tax team is bolstered in a large part by the amount of midmarket deals on which its lawyers advise. Clients also identified expertise with regard to REITs and bankruptcies.

**The Lawyers:** Clients singled out **Louis Freeman** (see p.830), whom they regard as *"absolutely brilliant"* and *"a hero"* on acquisitions and disposals. He is acknowledged to be *"unique"* and is apparently noted for his facility for *"memorizing The Wall Street Journal."* **André LeDuc** (see p.840) specializes in bankruptcies and has recently been employed in that capacity by Delphi. Considered by commentators as *"a very brilliant fellow,"* LeDuc is an increasingly essential component of the team.

**Clients/Work Highlights:** Brera Capital Partners; Chicago Mercantile Exchange; Edison Mission Energy; GE Capital; Fortress Investment Group; Insight Venture Partners; Interstate Bakeries and Westfield Holdings.

## Band 3

### Baker & McKenzie

See firm details p.866

**The Firm:** This team of 25 lawyers concentrates its efforts in three main areas of tax: international tax, partnership and real estate, and tax controversy. The firm's extensive international network means it is frequently sought out by multinationals in need of a fully integrated cross-border service. The preeminence of the group in real estate-related matters has seen it take a leading role in the response to recent alterations to the rules regulating tenancy in common transactions. The firm's prominence in transfer pricing was also noted by clients.

**The Lawyers:** *"Knowledgeable and practical"* **Gregg Lemein** (see p.841) is the main man in Chicago for international work. His practice is broad enough to include litigation and controversies as well as the business structuring and transactions. Recent highlights include winning a case on behalf of Jefferson Smurfit in Missouri. Clients appreciate the way in which he engages fully with their problems and provides advice *"consistent with our business needs."* **Richard Lipton** (see p.841) is an expert on partnership and REITs. Clients enthused about his *"comprehensive knowledge"* of those practice specialisms and the speed with which he addressed issues.

**Clients/Work Highlights:** Boehringer Ingelheim; Cisco Systems; Microsoft; Seagate; Square D; Northwestern Mutual; The May Department Stores Company and Pfizer.

## Winston & Strawn LLP

See firm details p.886

**The Firm:** Winston & Strawn continues to have a significant presence in Chicago and the transactions group in particular is benefiting from increased activity in M&A and divestitures. To illustrate, the team recently advised Sara Lee on the spin-off of one of its subsidiaries. The firm is also heavily involved in defending clients from the IRS campaign against tax shelters.

**The Lawyers:** **James Lynch** spends the greater part of his time on litigation in front of the IRS, although he is still an important figure in corporate tax planning. Fellow practitioners admire his *"wealth of experience."* **Roger Lucas** (see p.842) is held to be one of the leaders in Illinois for dealing with private equity clients in need of transactional advice. Meanwhile, clients found **Louis Weber** to be *"terrific"* in his capacity advising on taxable and tax-free M&A. He is also commended for his work on controversies.

**Clients/Work Highlights:** Abbott Laboratories; Allied Waste; Caremark International; Motorola; Sara Lee; SPX and Tribune.

## Band 4

### Jenner & Block LLP

See firm details p.873

**The Firm:** This firm offers a broad range of services to clients, from the structuring of transactions, both international and domestic, to the organization of real estate investments. The separate controversy group came in for especial praise for the quality of its work. Being part of a huge international firm means the team can call upon a vast pool of resources when addressing the needs of its various Fortune 500 and other clients.

**The Lawyers:** Cochair of the tax practice **Christian Kimball** (see p.838) is valued for his responsiveness and the manner in which he explains the law in client-friendly language. He has *"broad expertise,"* although the work he does in IPOs and demutualizations is said to be *"flawless."* Peers consider him a *"thoughtful and bright"* lawyer who has quickly got back into the swing of practicing after time spent in academia.

**Clients/Work Highlights:** General Dynamics; MCI; GMAM and Chicago Board of Trade.

### Katten Muchin Rosenman LLP

See firm details p.874

**The Firm:** Seen to be *"top-notch for M&A,"* the tax team at this full-service law firm has lately been involved in M&A as well as LBOs and joint ventures. The real estate tax practice also came in for strong praise from both peers and clients. In that capacity, the firm advises property companies and investment funds, and is very active in structuring REITs and hedge funds.

**The Lawyers:** Competitors described **Sheldon Banoff** (see p.819) as *"an icon in Chicago"* because of the intellectual weight he lends to the tax arena. This *"outstanding"* attorney is especially knowledgeable on partnerships and federal income taxation, and is *"creative"* in his approach to solving problems. **Reid Mandel** is also tremendously well regarded by his clients. They appreciate his responsiveness and the level of *"technical brilliance"* that he brings to the formulation of their deals and investment funds. His work is primarily focused on REITs and estate planning.

**Clients/Work Highlights:** Atlantic Premium Brands; Denali Capital; Greenfield Partners; iStar Financial; LaSalle Bank; Sterling Capital Partners and Trizec Properties.

### Neal, Gerber & Eisenberg LLP

See firm details p.880

**The Firm:** This fast-growing firm has increased its number of lawyers through lateral hires and is developing a real presence in Illinois tax law. The tax team represents clients in all aspects of taxation, including federal income tax, estate planning and controversies.

**The Lawyers:** **Kenneth Harris** (see p.834) chairs the practice group at the firm and is acknowledged for his capable transactions work.

**Clients/Work Highlights:** The firm's client base boasts several Fortune 500 companies from various industries, including manufacturing, hotels, leisure, securities and commodities.

### Other Notable Practitioners

**Thomas Stephens** (see p.859) of Sonnenschein Nath & Rosenthal LLP has extensive experience advising Fortune 100 companies on transactional tax law and tax planning. He is also highly active in the area of real estate ventures and investment fund formation.

# TECHNOLOGY & IT OUTSOURCING

| Technology & IT Outsourcing |
|---|
| **Leading Firms** |
| 1   **BAKER & MCKENZIE** *Chicago* |
|     **MAYER, BROWN, ROWE & MAW LLP** *Chicago* |
| 2   **KIRKLAND & ELLIS LLP** *Chicago* |
|     **LATHAM & WATKINS LLP** *Chicago* |
|     **SONNENSCHEIN NATH & ROSENTHAL** *Chicago* |
| 3   **DLA PIPER RUDNICK GRAY CARY US LLP** *Chicago* |
|     **GARDNER CARTON & DOUGLAS LLP** *Chicago* |
|     **MCGUIREWOODS LLP** *Chicago* |
|     **NEAL, GERBER & EISENBERG LLP** *Chicago* |

## Band 1

### Baker & McKenzie

See firm details p.866

**The Firm:** It is impossible to consider the strength of the Chicago-based information and technology group in isolation from the firm's immense international and national network. Clients appreciate the *"overall service provided by a great group of attorneys, distinguished by the international reach of the firm."* Much of this growth of late has been driven by the offshore outsourcing market, where the team has represented both purchasers and suppliers in some of the largest outsourcing transactions. For example, it represented Towers Perrin in negotiating a $365 million multijurisdictional IT, network management, software maintenance and help desk outsourcing agreement with EDS. The team is also highly regarded for its work in e-commerce, with clients celebrating its *"absolute command of the data protection area."* Bank of America is another high-profile client and attorneys recently advised it on data protection and privacy issues related to the negotiation of a global BPO agreement.

**The Lawyers:** The *"erudite"* **Michael Mensik** (see p.845) is head of the firm's global IT group and stands out for his leadership abilities. *"He carefully selects and manages his team and projects globally."* His clients include domestic and multinational companies, which he advises on licensing, IT outsourcing and BPO, displaying in all matters an *"unparalleled breadth and depth of knowledge."* **Thomas Smedinghoff**'s (see p.857) broad practice encompasses all aspects of a transaction. An excellent counselor, he employs his *"calm negotiation skills and crystal-clear writing style."* A *"pioneer in the field of electronic commerce law,"* he has served for three years in the Working Group on Electronic Commerce, developing an international convention on electronic contracts, and is a leading authority on electronic and digital signatures. **Ruth Hill Bro** (see p.822) has built up a strong following in the data protection area. Her transactional work has a heavy offshore focus. **Peter George** (see p.831) has a great command of issues arising out of the outsourcing market and his *"diligent and comprehensive drafting"* is a result of his wealth of experience. He recently worked alongside **Sam Kramer** (see p.839) in drafting and negotiating a multivendor strategy for the outsourcing of all of Turtle Wax's manufacturing services for its consumer product lines. Kramer is famed for his personable negotiation style and *"extraordinarily creative approach."* **Jim Stetson**'s reputation as a *"phenomenal drafter"* precedes him. He is active in e-commerce and outsourcing, recent highlights including representing a multinational hardware and services provider in IT outsourcing negotiations.

**Clients/Work Highlights:** Customer Potential Management; ESPN Mobile; G2 SwitchWorks; Hewlett-Packard; Rohm & Haas and Thomson Corporation.

## Mayer, Brown, Rowe & Maw LLP

See firm details p.876

**The Firm:** On a national level and in Chicago, this firm has devoted a great deal of time and resources to the IT outsourcing market, and the results are felt in the high quality and quantity of its workload. The 13-strong group advises on software licensing and e-commerce, and it has an impressive track record in domestic and international outsourcing transactions from both customer and supplier sides. Recent transactional work for key client Procter & Gamble includes a $200 million expansion of an existing outsourcing arrangement, in order to extend coverage to a newly acquired entity. Clients value the commitment and energy of these "*aggressive and passionate*" attorneys: "*They are knowledgeable, constructive and responsive; a pleasure to deal with.*" **The Lawyers:** A name that carries weight far beyond the state lines, **Brad Peterson** (see p.850) is "*accepted in the Chicago legal community as the best of the best.*" In-house counsel spoke of his "*diligent, persistent and persuasive approach in dealing with business teams,*" as well as his capacity to mastermind "*real-world solutions to very complex and difficult issues.*" He recently represented Carlson Companies in a deal with IBM with a contract value in excess of $500 million. Equally popular, **Paul Roy** (see p.853) is an excellent tactician and strategist with "*a unique ability to balance the details and the bigger picture. He is a calming presence at tense points during negotiations.*" His caseload includes a long list of multibillion-dollar outsourcing deals from the customer side, covering sophisticated cross-jurisdictional ITO and BPO arrangements. **Rebecca Eisner** (see p.828) provides expert advice on ITO, BPO, e-commerce and data privacy issues. She is "*a reliable, realistic and invaluable adviser*" with a thoughtful client-focused manner. She has recently been involved in cutting-edge work for Caterpillar in its outbound licensing applications and IT services. **Seth Weinberger**'s (see p.863) "*even-handed, collaborative approach facilitates consensus among differing views*" and ultimately leads to superior supplier/customer relationships. The majority of his time is spent on matters arising out of the airline industry. "*He is a great person with high ethical standards,*" said clients.

**Clients/Work Highlights:** Allegheny Energy Group; Innovene; Marconi Communications; Motorola; Sun Microsystems; Star Alliance; Whirlpool; The Williams Companies; Wolters Kluwer and Yum! Brands.

## Band 2

## Kirkland & Ellis LLP

See firm details p.875

**The Firm:** The firm complements an illustrious history in outsourcing with a workload that includes a wide range of technology-related issues. The impressive resources and reputation of the firm in litigation, private equity and M&A ensures a varied flow of work from high-profile technology companies. A good example of this was the group's recent involvement in the joint venture between AMF and Qubica, which included joining together their multiple hi-tech product lines. For clients: "*It is a top-notch firm with an excellent national reputation in the technology field for strategic alliances and outsourcing.*" **The Lawyers:** Seasoned **Gregg Kirchhoefer** (see p.838) has an extremely broad practice with a strong focus on telecom and technology issues. A "*smart thinker who is always up to speed on changes,*" he is a strong candidate for all manner of technology transactions and advice, as well as outsourcing.

**Clients/Work Highlights:** The firm represents a wide range of clients from many diverse industries, including a number of high-profile national and multinational entities.

## Latham & Watkins LLP

**The Firm:** The firm operates using a truly integrated approach, with attorneys from multiple offices across the USA regularly handling the largest technology and outsourcing transactions. An example of this was its counsel to ORBIMAGE on the IT and IP issues related to its acquisition of Space Imaging. The team was led by Marcelo Halpern and included associates from the firm's New York and DC offices.

**The Lawyers:** Cochair of the firm's global technology transactions group, **Marcelo Halpern** combines knowledge and experience with a "*personable approach to negotiations – he's easy to work with,*" said clients. His broad-ranging practice includes Internet, licensing and outsourcing matters. He also provides general corporate representation to technology companies including M&A and financings. He advised Koch Industries in its acquisition of Georgia-Pacific.

**Clients/Work Highlights:** Bally Total Fitness; Entegra Power Group; Northern Trust; Reliant Pharmaceuticals and Royal Bank of Canada.

## Sonnenschein Nath & Rosenthal LLP

See firm details p.884

**The Firm:** Leading clients such as Accenture and ACS are at the heart of this firm's reputation in the outsourcing market, and the wealth of experience gained has allowed attorneys to expand into customer representation. In addition, the group has carved out a niche representing emerging technology companies: "*it's successfully making a big play in the dotcom arena,*" said sources. The group recently represented the City of Chicago Police Department in negotiating a consulting agreement and license with a large software company for the development of a state-of-the-art law enforcement technology system.

**The Lawyers:** A corporate lawyer with a focus on technology and outsourcing, **Ross Docksey** (see p.826) is regarded by many as "*the most eloquent spokesman for the vendor community.*" Experience with all major clients, including a growing level of customer representation, forms the bedrock of his impressive national reputation. "*Tough but charming, he completely understands transactions and their business implications.*" Clients described **Rosemary Gullikson** (see p.833) as "*an exceptionally well-qualified, imaginative, highly organized lawyer who can coordinate complex technology transactions without ever losing sight of a client's overall goal.*" In addition to many large outsourcing transactions, she recently worked with Publicis in the licensing of Enterprise Resource Planning (ERP) systems in three continents.

**Clients/Work Highlights:** In addition to regular work for outsourcers, the group has also advised various state departments and clients from a range of different industries.

## Band 3

## DLA Piper Rudnick Gray Cary US LLP

See firm details p.870

**The Firm:** Following the merger of late 2004, DLA Piper Rudnick Gray Cary has counterbalanced departures from the team with the increased international force of the integrated practice group. The six-attorney team in Illinois is now part of the firm's wider IT and sourcing group, fielding more than 40 attorneys across the USA. A client list containing a number of Fortune 500 entities is behind a great deal of national technology transactional work and provides a stream of ITO and BPO matters.

**The Lawyers:** Cochair of the technology and sourcing practice, **Vincent Sanchez** (see p.854) is experienced in sophisticated negotiations. "*He is a good judge of character, adept at sizing up opponents.*" Such talents are applied to a variety of technology transactions, including outsourcing, corporate and e-commerce-related issues. The prevailing market view is of an exceptionally talented attorney with knowledge far beyond what could be expected of his years.

**Clients/Work Highlights:** Clients come from within the USA and beyond and include various Fortune 500 entities.

## Gardner Carton & Douglas LLP

See firm details p.872

**The Firm:** "*An excellent resource to any company,*" the nine attorneys comprising the firm's core IT group were praised for their "*sound business and legal skills.*" The team has cornered the market on technology work related to the healthcare industry. A notable representation in this field was its advice to a post-acute care provider in a substantial outsourcing with IBM for clinical information systems. However, the group's remit is wider than this and other highlights include work on a $500 million strategic alliance agreement between a major software vendor and Accenture.

**The Lawyers:** "*Pleasant and personable*" **Cathy Austin** (see p.818) impresses clients with her IT and telecom contracting work, as well as her impeccable understanding of the process of working with the in-house business team. **Pam Walter** (see p.862) has been at the core of the firm's technology group since the very beginning, founding the cyberlaw and IP practice. She represents emerging technology companies, with a particular specialty in cyberlaw and e-business.

**Clients/Work Highlights:** Accenture; Arroweye Solutions; Northern Trust; Rehabilitation Institute of Chicago; Rockford Health Systems and University of Chicago Hospitals.

## McGuireWoods LLP

**The Firm:** Dramatic developments this year have seen the merging of Gordon & Glickson's practice with national giant McGuireWoods. This sees the merging of 25 years' technology-focused experience with depth and breadth of resources of one of the largest firms in the USA. The new technology and business department adopts a multidisciplinary approach and advises on the full range of technology issues, including protection, development and licensing, and financing. Clients spoke of the "*exemplary service*" and overall guidance and support throughout negotiations provided by the lawyers in this group. They were also quick to extol the economic virtues of working with the firm: "*They are very proactive in aligning the right resources to the matter and thus avoiding invoice padding.*"

**The Lawyers:** The "*unshakable*" **Mark Gordon** "*exudes authority,*" said clients. His practice covers reviewing, negotiating and drafting software licenses, M&A and outsourcing issues. He takes on the position of chair of the new department.

**Clients/Work Highlights:** Significant clients of the practice include DiamondCluster; Nextel; United Technologies and the University of Illinois.

## Neal, Gerber & Eisenberg LLP

See firm details p.880

**The Firm:** Since the arrival of Diana McKenzie in May 2004, the firm's IT practice group has grown in prominence and is now widely recognized as a serious contender for the larger transactions, with interviewees predicting further expansion in the future. The team, now comprising seven Chicago-based attorneys, has recently been engaged in a number of ERP deals. The team has also announced its presence in the outsourcing arena on the back of high-value deals such as the closing of a $650 million outsourcing for County of its entire IT and telecom functions.

**The Lawyers:** Practice head **Diana McKenzie** (see p.844) is a "*savvy and aggressive negotiator who brings a multi-industry perspective*" and "*runs a tight deal from RFP to signature.*" Her caseload includes outsourcing and a range of IT transactions, particularly those in the healthcare industry. Credited for putting the firm on the map, she consistently displays a "*superior grasp of technology and current legal standards.*" Alongside her, **Robert Weiss** (see p.863) has built up a practice advising Fortune 500 entities as well as startup companies. A "*shrewd yet fair negotiator pivotal to any team,*" he was praised for his ability to find mutually beneficial solutions.

**Clients/Work Highlights:** Clients are drawn from a wide range of industries from all over the USA, including public sector and Fortune 500 institutions.

# TELECOM, BROADCAST & SATELLITE

# REGULATORY

| Telecom, Broadcast & Satellite: Regulatory Leading Firms |
|---|
| [1] MAYER, BROWN, ROWE & MAW LLP *Chicago* |
| [2] JENNER & BLOCK LLP *Chicago* |
| SIDLEY AUSTIN LLP *Chicago* |
| [3] FOLEY & LARDNER LLP *Chicago* |
| KELLEY DRYE & WARREN *Chicago* |
| MEYER CAPEL, PC *Champaign* |
| SCHIFF HARDIN LLP *Chicago* |

## Band 1

## Mayer, Brown, Rowe & Maw LLP

See firm details p.876

**The Firm:** Clients report that they are "*spoilt for choice with experts of the highest caliber*" in the telecom and broadcast space. Since the group's creation, it has built upon an unrivaled reputation for regulatory matters, both in the Midwest and nationally, and appellate matters. It has been at the forefront of many of the landmark decisions in the area, such as the SBC/AT&T merger in November 2005, where the team acted as lead outside counsel to SBC in gaining approval in its 13 state territories as well as the 14 served by Qwest. The seven-partner team draws strength from its comprehensive coverage of all aspects of telecom transactions and litigation: "*Given

their management of such a large client list and the morass of issues they deal with, I wouldn't be surprised to find out they could dance with an octopus,*" said one impressed client.

**The Lawyers:** "*The guy the clients love,*" **Theodore Livingston** (see p.841) was described by the market as having "*a firmer grasp of telecom issues than just about anyone.*" As head of the group, he has led the team in many of its high-profile representations, such as the SBC/AT&T merger. Also involved in the merger was **Christian Binnig** (see p.820). "*A professional and enthusiastic attorney,*" Binnig acted as national litigation counsel to SBC regarding regulatory issues arising out of its use of public rights of way. **Robert Dow** (see p.827) is "*a terrific lawyer with an equally great acumen for business and people.*" Clients especially endorsed his appellate skills and his rapport with agencies and judges. **Dennis Friedman** (see p.830) has been active in arbitrations arising out of the sector. "*Not only is he a great writer and oral advocate, but he is also good at solving problems where others have failed.*" An excellent draftsman, **Tyson Covey**'s (see p.825) impressive workload includes a number of pricing cases for SBC, which have involved appeals in the federal district court. **Jim Metropoulos** (see p.845), a favorite among clients for appeals proceedings, has the depth of expertise to handle complex matters. He works alongside **John Muench** (see p.847), whose "*incredible constitutional and appellate abili-

ties make him an integral part of the Mayer Brown team.*" Up-and-coming associate **Hans Germann** (see p.831) was the subject of praise for his impressive grasp of the intricacies of the technology market.

**Clients/Work Highlights:** The firm's flagship clients are SBC/AT&T and BellSouth.

## Band 2

## Jenner & Block LLP

See firm details p.873

**The Firm:** This large national firm has developed a substantial telecom practice that handles the whole range of work, including representing telecom companies in general commercial litigation and regulatory matters. It enjoys a particularly strong reputation for asserting IP and privacy rights in the Internet environment, although clients stressed the all-around strength of the team. "*They have enormous capabilities in business strategies, negotiation, patent defenses and any other subject that needs deep and sensitive handling.*" A long relationship with MCI has been maintained since it emerged as a start-up company in the 1970's and through its merger with Verizon in early 2006. The integration of the firmwide practice group, with impressive links on the East Coast through a highly regarded DC team, provides an advantage to clients.

**The Lawyers: John Hamill**'s (see p.834) dedication to his cases is illustrated by his "*willingness to do whatever research is necessary to get the best possible result for the client.*" Complex telecom litigation forms an integral part of his wider litigation practice and he is respected for his courtroom performances across the USA. On behalf on MCI, he has given legal guidance on telecom issues, billing disputes and mediations. Clients, many of whom had sought **John Harrington**'s (see p.834) services for appellate and regulatory litigation, were quick to highlight his "*positive attitude and constructive approach.*" Many see him as offering the complete package, supplementing "*unequaled advocacy*" with great interpersonal skills. "*A powerful, fair and deeply grounded attorney,*" **Chester Kamin** (see p.837) is respected for his wealth of knowledge. According to clients: "*He has an objective understanding of people and the respect he receives from those who are on the other side of the table – including judges – is remarkable.*"

**Clients/Work Highlights:** In addition to MCI, the team's client list includes a range of data center operators and data providers.

## Sidley Austin LLP

See firm details p.883

**The Firm:** This smaller Chicago team forms part of a large national practice that has captured a strong profile across the country. The group has gained prominence through its track record of appearing before the FCC, the US Supreme Court and other regulatory bodies. Its largest client has traditionally been AT&T, who it represented most recently in relation to the merger with SBC.

**The Lawyers:** "*A scholarly, creative appellate lawyer,*" **David Carpenter** (see p.824) is the group's guiding light. Peers spoke of the need to "*keep on your toes when dealing with him, as he can spot the chinks in your armor.*" He has had a long and illustrious career in the industry, including extensive appellate and US Supreme Court advocacy experience.

**Clients/Work Highlights:** The team represents a number of telecom carriers and has also offered advice to government institutions on issues involving regulation, privatization and competition.

## Band 3

### Foley & Lardner LLP

See firm details p.2037

**The Firm:** The great potential of this group was the source of much speculation in the market, with a significant increase in its visibility and expanding practice making it clearly the one to watch. A number of appearances for MCI lie at the heart of these comments and the team has also devoted a lot of time to the area of telecom licensing. Its workload is rooted in representing wireline and wireless telecom carriers in regulatory proceedings, including interconnection agreements.

**The Lawyers:** The "*tenacious*" **Kathy Pasulka-Brown** (see p.849) is an "*intelligent and creative attorney and an excellent communicator,*" said clients. Telecom litigation forms a significant part of her practice, which also includes insurance and energy matters.

**Clients/Work Highlights:** Clients have included MCI, US Cellular and T-Mobile.

### Kelley Drye & Warren

**The Firm:** This compact team represents a range of telecom companies, especially competitive local exchange carriers (CLECs) and new entrants to the market attempting to compete with incumbent companies. The two-attorney group focuses on civil and regulatory litigation at state public service commissions. It works closely with a sizable and highly regarded office in DC, especially on matters at a federal level. Market commentators praised the high standing of the team, which has an influence well beyond what might be expected of its size.

**The Lawyers:** Interviewees praised **Henry Kelly** as "*a worthy and capable adversary who is always keen to resolve issues and listen.*" His experience and wealth of knowledge have attracted many new entrants to the market. He has recently been working on a number of state forums to implement rule changes affecting SBC lease facilities. **Joseph Donovan** was described as "*Henry's lieutenant.*" A significant portion of his time is spent assisting CLEC clients litigate multistate arbitrations.

**Clients/Work Highlights:** Representations have included Kentucky Payphone Association; Level 3 Communications; Talk America and Z-Tel Communications.

### Meyer Capel, PC

**The Firm:** Respected across the state, the three-attorney team at this Champaign-based firm leads the way in the representation of rural local exchange carriers. Its broad client roster also includes independent wireline and wireless carriers and CLECs. The group has built upon expertise in telecom with computer and Internet law work, acting in particular for a number of Internet service providers.

**The Lawyers: Dennis Muncy**'s knowledge of the telecom market and his wealth of experience before the Illinois Commerce Commission stand out. He is a favorite of the incumbents. **Joseph Murphy** brings to the negotiating table a broad skill base and deep experience. He is currently focused on telecom work and IP counseling and litigation.

**Clients/Work Highlights:** The team has acted for Associated Network Partners, Cingular Wireless and SBC Advanced Solutions.

### Schiff Hardin LLP

See firm details p.881

**The Firm:** This firm's impressive reputation in the broader regulated utilities area underpins its strength in telecom matters. Clients routinely seek regulatory and compliance advice from this broad practice. Particularly skilled in the CLEC field, the group is also active in representing incumbent local exchange carriers and interexchange carriers.

**The Lawyers:** "*A great contributor to any negotiations,*" **Owen MacBride** (see p.842) is the backbone of the firm's telecom practice in Chicago. "*A well-respected professional,*" he is known to "*fight hard but fair.*" He has more than 20 years of experience representing telecom carriers before the Illinois Commerce Commission.

**Clients/Work Highlights:** The team has advised a range of carriers concerning interconnection agreement negotiations, rate cases, arbitrations and other dispute resolution proceedings.

## Other Notable Practitioners

**John Rooney** (see p.852) of Sonnenschein Nath & Rosenthal LLP is part of a seven-partner team spanning the firm's Chicago, DC and Kansas offices. In addition to regulatory work and frequent appearances before the Illinois Commerce Commission, he has been involved on the lobbying side through the firm's policy group. Clients described him as "*a great advocate who knows the right line of argument.*" **Warren Lavey** (see p.840) of Skadden, Arps, Slate, Meagher & Flom LLP commands respect within the industry for his "*encyclopedic knowledge*" of regulatory law. "*He is always available to walk his clients through complicated regulatory policies*" and is equally well regarded for his succinct writing skills. He has recently acted for McLeodUSA, Asia Netcom and Alaska Communications Systems.

# Leaders in Illinois

**ABRAMS, Lee N**
Mayer, Brown, Rowe & Maw LLP,
Chicago 312 701 7083
labrams@mayerbrownrowe.com
*Recommended in Antitrust, Sport*
**Practice Areas:** Leading attorney in
antitrust and franchising litigation and
counseling. Has represented numerous
Fortune 500 corporations, including
General Motors, Ford, Eastman Kodak,
Citicorp, Sears, NewsCorp, Capital One,
PitneyBowes, PPG, International Paper,
CompUSA, and the United States Golf
Association. Has frequently litigated
intellectual property and corporate law
cases.
**Prof. Memberships:** American Bar
Association: Chair, Franchising Forum,
1982-85; and Governing Committee
Member, 1978-89; Section of Antitrust
Law: Vice Chair, 1991-92; Financial Offi-
cer and Council Member, 1977-81; Sec-
tion of Business Law: Chair, Antitrust
Committee, 1995-99; Fellow, American
College of Trial Lawyers; Member, CPR
Panel of Distinguished Neutrals; Admit-
ted to practice in Illinois (1957), US
Supreme Court (1961).
**Career:** Joined Mayer, Brown, Rowe &
Maw LLP in 1957; became Partner 1967.
**Publications:** Author of numerous arti-
cles and speeches on antitrust, trade regu-
lation, litigation, and franchising topics.
**Personal:** Born 28 February 1935.
Earned JD with highest distinction from
University of Michigan Law School, 1957;
served on Law Review Board of Editors.
Holds AB from University of Michigan,
1955; elected to Phi Beta Kappa in his
junior year. Winner, Elijah Watt Sells
Award for achieving the highest grade in
the United States on the Uniform CPA
Examination.

**ADDY, Meredith Martin**
Brinks Hofer Gilson & Lione, Chicago
312 321 4280
maddy@usebrinks.com
*Recommended in Intellectual Property*
**Practice Areas:** Appeals before the US
Court of Appeals for the Federal Circuit
and intellectual property litigation in the
biotech, pharmaceutical, chemical, and
electrical arts. Patent prosecution and
portfolio management in the electrical
arts.
**Prof. Memberships:** Advisory Council,
US Court of Appeals for the Federal Cir-
cuit; Editorial Board, AIPLA Quarterly
Journal; Board of Managers, Intellectual
Property Law Association of Chicago;
Member, Federal Circuit Association;
AIPLA, IPO. Barred in Illinois, Georgia,
and DC.
**Career:** Law clerk to the Honorable Paul
R Michel, the now Chief Judge of the US
Court of Appeals for the Federal Circuit

(1997-98). Adjunct Professor, The John
Marshall Law School (2000-present).
**Publications:** Author of articles in
National Law Journal; IP Law Bulletin
Online; Managing IP; IP Strategist; Patent
Strategy & Mgmt; 2003 IP Law Update.
Speaker at Judicial Conference for the US
Court of Appeals for the Federal Circuit,
Advanced Patent Law Institute, Law Sem-
inars International, IPLAC, FCBA, JMLS.
**Personal:** BS, Electrical Engineering, BA,
Art & Art History, Rice University; JD,
cum laude, University of Georgia School
of Law, 1993; LLM, Intellectual Property,
with honors, The John Marshall Law
School, 1997.

**ADELMAN, Howard**
Adelman & Gettleman Ltd, Chicago
312 435 1050
hla@ag-ltd.com
*Recommended in Bankruptcy*
**Practice Areas:** Commercial bankruptcy, reorganization and insolvency matters, and commercial litigation. Has been
involved in major bankruptcy cases since
1977 representing business debtors,
secured creditors, creditors' committees,
sureties and other parties in a variety of
bankruptcy proceedings.
**Prof. Memberships:** Illinois State Bar
Association; Chicago Bar Association –
Bankruptcy and Reorganization Committee; Missouri Bar Association; 7th Circuit Bar Association.
**Career:** Founder, shareholder and member of Adelman & Gettleman, Ltd since
1983. Law clerk to the Honorable Robert
G Dowd, Chief Judge – Missouri Court of
Appeals. Executive Judicial Assistant –
Missouri Court of Appeals. Schwartz,
Cooper, Kolb & Gaynor, 1978-83, Part-
ner, 1982.
**Publications:** 'Mortgage Liens in Bank-
ruptcy' (co-author), Financing Real
Estate Handbook, Illinois Institute of
Continuing Legal Education, 1988; 'Law
of Guaranty' (co-author), 'Secured Trans-
actions Handbook', Illinois Institute of
Continuing Legal Education, 1988;
'Burnside: A Clear and Present Threat to
the Availabilty of Debtor Representation'
(co-author), Bankruptcy Law Advisor,
Norton, 1989.
**Personal:** St Louis University School of
Law (cum laude 1977 JD); Illinois State
University (1974 BS). He has been listed
10 years in Naifeh and Smith's The Best
Lawyers in America, Woodward/White.
He has been chosen as one of the World's
Leading Lawyers by Chambers and Part-
ners 2002-03, and one of America's Lead-
ing Lawyers for Business in 2004 and
2005. He was chosen as one of the top
100 lawyers in 2006 Edition of Illinois
Super Lawyers, and recognized in Illinois
Leading Lawyers Network for Bankrupt-

cy and Workout Lawyers (2004-06); he is
a Fellow of the American College of
Bankruptcy (Twelfth Class). In 1999, Mr
Adelman was appointed by Chief Justice
William Rehnquist to serve as a member
of the Judicial Conference Advisory
Committee on the Federal Rules of Bank-
ruptcy Procedure.

**ADELSTEIN, Harvey M**
Neal, Gerber & Eisenberg LLP, Chicago
312 269 8460
hadelstein@ngelaw.com
*Recommended in Employment*
**Practice Areas:** Labor and employment
law on behalf of management; provides
advice on collective bargaining agreements in both private and public sector,
grievance and arbitration processes,
developing strike contingency plans, representation cases, governmental-agency
proceedings, and decertification process;
has negotiated with many of the major
labor organizations at the local, state and
national level.
**Prof. Memberships:** College of Labor
and Employment Lawyers (Fellow).
**Career:** Senior Counsel; Labor and
Employment Practice Group (Immediate
Past Chair).
**Publications:** Has lectured and written
extensively on labor and employment
matters.
**Personal:** Case Western Reserve University Law School (LLB, 1961); Kenyon
College (AB, 1958).

**AIELLO, Anthony**
Sidley Austin LLP, Chicago
312 853 7128
aaiello@sidley.com
*Recommended in Real Estate*
**Practice Areas:** Partner in the Chicago
office and practices in the Real Estate
Group. His experience includes real estate
acquisition, development and sale
(including office, retail, hotel and industrial properties); office, retail and industrial leasing; real estate loan transactions;
sale/leaseback transactions and lease
financing; and a variety of real estate
transactions for hotel owners and managers as well as heavy industrial and utility companies.
**Personal:** DePaul University College of
Law, JD, 1986, with honors; University of
Notre Dame BBA, 1983. Admission: Illinois, 1986.

**AIZENSTEIN, Neal**
Sonnenschein Nath & Rosenthal LLP,
Chicago 312 876 8938
naizenstein@sonnenschein.com
*Recommended in Corporate/M&A*
**Practice Areas:** Partner with extensive
experience in public and private financings, acquisitions and dispositions,
restructurings, joint ventures and partnerships, securities regulations, venture

capital transactions and general corporate and securities counselling. Has repre-
sented purchasers, sellers and investors in
acquisitions and dispositions; issuers and
underwriters in public and private
financings; borrowers and lenders in
financings such as asset-based loans and
private placements.
**Prof. Memberships:** American Bar
Association, Chicago Bar Association.
**Personal:** Northwestern University
School of Law, JD, cum laude, Dean's List;
University of Illinois, Champaign,
Urbana, BS, Accounting, Member,
Bronze Tablet, CPA, Lowden-Wigmore
Prize recipient.

**ALTMAN, Ross**
DLA Piper Rudnick Gray Cary US LLP,
Chicago 312 368 3442
ross.altman@dlapiper.com
*Recommended in Construction*
**Practice Areas:** Construction; real
estate.
**Prof. Memberships:** Fellow, American
College of Construction Lawyers.
**Career:** Represents clients in drafting
and negotiation of contracts, and in resolution of disputes and claims. Served as
General Counsel for two companies
going through Chapter 11 reorganization, including a global EPC contractor.
Well versed in alternate forms of project
delivery, such as BOT, EPC, CM, D/B and
multiple prime arrangements. Has handled commercial and industrial projects
domestically and overseas. Experienced
in distribution, licensing, warranties, performance guarantees, insurance and
bonds.
**Personal:** JD, George Washington University; BS (Architecture), University of
Michigan. Adjunct Law Professor, University of Miami.

**AMEND, James M**
Kirkland & Ellis LLP, Chicago
312 861 2154
jamend@kirkland.com
*Recommended in Intellectual Property*
**Practice Areas:** Has significant litigation and counseling experience in the following technology-related fields: electronics, computers, automotive, chemistry, manufacturing and packaging. He
has tried many patent infringement cases
to judge and jury and has counseled
clients on patent infringement and validity questions and licensing. He also has
extensive experience in litigating and
counseling in trademark, unfair competition, advertising and copyright fields for
major US and foreign companies.
**Personal:** University of Michigan, BS,
1964; University of Michigan, JD, 1967,
Editor, Law Review, Order of the Coif;
London School of Economics, Fulbright
Scholar, 1967-68. Consulting Professor-

Stanford Law School, 1996-97, Patents and Intellectual Property.

### ANDERSON, Kimball R
Winston & Strawn LLP, Chicago
312 558 5858
kanderson@winston.com
*Recommended in Litigation*
**Practice Areas:** Federal and state court trial practice concentrating in professional liability, product liability, insurance coverage, patent infringement, consumer class actions, and arbitrations.
**Prof. Memberships:** American College of Trial Lawyers; ABA, ISBA, Chicago Bar Association; Federal Circuit Bar Association; Seventh Circuit Bar Assocation,
**Career:** Mr Anderson attended the University of Illinois College of Law (Editor, Law Review; first in class). He presently serves as a member of Winston & Strawn's Executive Committee and as General Counsel of the firm. He has tried numerous cases around the country, including representing large corporations in jury trials lasting many weeks. Mr Anderson also has considerable experience as an appellate advocate, including appearances before the US Supreme Court, Illinois Supreme Court, NJ Supreme Court, NM Supreme Court, Federal Circuit, Seventh Circuit, and Illinois Appellate Court. Mr Anderson is a Laureate of the Illinois Academy of Lawyers and a Distinguished Neutral with the CPR Institute for Dispute Resolution. He was honored in 1996 as the Chicago Magazine Person of the Year. In 2004, Mr Anderson received the ABA's Pro Bono Publico Award. In 2005 and 2006, he was recognized as a Top 100 'Super Lawyer' in Illinois.
**Publications:** See publications at www.winston.com.

### ANGELO, Percy
Mayer, Brown, Rowe & Maw LLP, Chicago 312 782 0600
*Recommended in Environment*

### ANTHONY, Michael F
McDermott Will & Emery, Chicago
312 984 7635
manthony@mwe.com
*Recommended in Healthcare*
**Practice Areas:** Counsel in connection with provider affiliations, integrated delivery system development, formation of HMOs and PPOs, healthcare mergers, acquisitions and affiliations, various joint ventures, joint operating arrangements, reimbursement systems, medical staff matters, Catholic/non-Catholic transactions, medical group representation and other legal and policy issues. Transaction counsel for St David's Health System in combination with local Columbia/HCA facilities in complex and court tested partnership arrangement. Assisted religious congregations in formation of health maintenance organization and preferred provider organization arrange-

ment. Assisted in creating several joint operating entities.
**Personal:** University of Baltimore School of Law (JD); Xavier University (MHA, BS).

### ARONSON, Virginia
Sidley Austin LLP, Chicago
312 853 7741
varonson@sidley.com
*Recommended in Real Estate*
**Practice Areas:** Global Head of the firm's Real Estate Practice and a Member of the firm's Executive and Management Committees. Mrs Aronson has represented lenders, investors and developers in a wide range of commercial real estate transactions including construction and permanent financings, mezzanine financings and sale leasebacks; disposition of portfolios, acquisition and disposition of office buildings and hotels; joint venture formation, REIT formation and financing; and partnership roll-ups, workouts of troubled real estate projects, leasing and vertical subdivisions.
**Prof. Memberships:** Member of the American College of Real Estate Lawyers, the Chicago Mortgage Attorneys Association and The Chicago Network and co-chairs of the Large Law Firm Committee for The Chicago Bar Association. She is on the Board of Directors of the Chicago Central Area Committee and the Leadership Council of the Chicago Public Education Fund.
**Personal:** The University of Chicago Law School, JD, 1975; University of Chicago, MA, 1973; University of Chicago, BA, 1969. Admission: Illinois, 1975.

### ASTLE, Richard W
Sidley Austin LLP, Chicago
312 853 7270
rastle@sidley.com
*Recommended in Energy*
**Practice Areas:** Practice focuses on the analysis and handling of various corporate and securities matters, including disclosure and compliance questions; contract preparation and review; affiliations, joint ventures, acquisitions and dispositions; and financings involving credit facilities and private and public offerings of securities. Mr Astle advises energy companies, including electric and gas utilities and a petroleum refiner/marketer; manufacturers; tax-exempt entities, such as universities and cultural institutions; and a national association. His experience embraces various corporate and financing transactions for public utilities and other businesses, the auction sale of multiple generating plants, and nuclear fuel lease financings; securing tax-exempt status for a national organization formed to aid rural farmers, preparing an agreement for a tax-exempt entity to operate and manage a public zoo, documenting an affiliation/merger of two large tax-exempt healthcare institutions,

and assisting with various tax-exempt financings; and advising the board of directors of a governmental authority on process, compliance, procurement and financing matters.
**Personal:** Georgetown University Law Center, JD, 1980; University of Pennsylvania, MAcc, 1977; University of Pennsylvania, BS 1977. Admission: Illinois, 1980.

### ATHANAS, Josef
Latham & Watkins LLP, Chicago
312 876 7700
*Recommended in Bankruptcy*

### AUSTIN, Cathy Kiselyak
Gardner Carton & Douglas LLP, Chicago
312 569 1455
caustin@gcd.com
*Recommended in Technology*
**Practice Areas:** Ms Austin focuses her practice on business and information technology. She assists established businesses and startup companies to create e-commerce platforms, outsource information services, develop new technology and negotiate agreements for the implementation and operation of computer networks. Ms Austin counsels clients who experience network intrusion, illegal employee downloads and other illegal network activity. She handles a wide range of matters relating to the internet – from online contracting, domain name, privacy and security issues to website service and usage policies and agreements.
**Prof. Memberships:** Executive Club of Chicago, National Association of College and University Attorneys, Software Industry Information Association.
**Career:** Ms Austin was selected by the Leading Lawyers Network as a Leading Lawyer in Computer and Technology Law in 2004 and 2005 and received the 2003 Women in Black award, honoring outstanding women in business technology in Illinois. Ms Austin previously served as General Counsel for an internet catalog company and Assistant General Counsel of Household Finance Corporation.
**Publications:** Frequent author and lecturer on information technology and privacy issues. Previous Co-Editor-in-Chief of CyberStrategies, a quarterly journal published by CCH Incorporated.
**Personal:** Yale University, JD, 1980; Massachusetts Institute of Technology, SB, 1976; Abitur, Heinrich Hertz Gymnasium, 1972.

### BACON, J Douglas
Latham & Watkins LLP, Chicago
312 876 7700
*Recommended in Bankruptcy*

### BAKER, Bruce
Baker & McKenzie, Chicago
312 861 2760
bruce.baker@bakernet.com
*Recommended in Banking & Finance*
**Practice Areas:** He has over 28 years'

experience in a variety of secured and unsecured transactions including acquisitions, divestitures, corporate restructuring, recapitalizations, syndicated and single-bank financing.
**Prof. Memberships:** He is a Member of the American and Chicago bar associations and a Fellow of the American Bar Foundation.
**Personal:** BA in International Relations, Johns Hopkins University, MA from the School of Advanced International Studies, Johns Hopkins University, JD from the University of Chicago Law School. He is a Member of the Board of Managers of the YMCA of Metropolitan Chicago.

### BAKER, Pamela
Sonnenschein Nath & Rosenthal LLP, Chicago 312 876 8989
pbaker@sonnenschein.com
*Recommended in Employment*
**Practice Areas:** Chair and Partner of Employee Benefits and Executive Compensation Group. Focuses on non-qualified deferred compensation, executive equity incentive arrangements for private and public entities, including not-for-profits, and their treatment in corporate transactions. Represents employers and high-level executives in employment agreements, severance arrangements and golden parachute plans; employers in design, implementation and administration of tax-qualified retirement plans; institutional fiduciaries and financial institutions concerning ERISA issues arising in pension fund investing.
**Prof. Memberships:** American Bar Association; American College of Employee Benefits Counsel.
**Personal:** University of Wisconsin Law School, JD, Managing Editor, Wisconsin Law Review; Smith College, AB, with honors.

### BALLANTINE, Frank
Sachnoff & Weaver Ltd, Chicago
312 207 1000
*Recommended in Corporate/M&A: Private Equity*

### BALLIS, Jon A
Kirkland & Ellis LLP, Chicago
312 861 2332
jballis@kirkland.com
*Recommended in Corporate/M&A: Private Equity*
**Practice Areas:** Jon Ballis focuses his practice in the corporate, securities and tax aspects of complex business transactions, including leveraged acquisitions; strategic mergers, acquisitions and joint ventures; and venture capital and PIPE investments. He has structured and closed numerous buyout and private equity related transactions, ranging in size from several million dollars to over $1 billion. Additionally, Mr Ballis has worked on numerous initial and secondary public equity offerings.
**Prof. Memberships:** Leigh University

Political Science Department Visiting Committee; Harvard Law School Society of Illinois.

**Personal:** Harvard Law School (JD, 1994) cum laude; Lehigh University (BA, Soviet Studies, 1991), magna cum laude.

### BANNER, Mark
Banner & Witcoff Ltd, Chicago
312 463 5000
*Recommended in Intellectual Property*

### BANOFF, Sheldon I
Katten Muchin Rosenman LLP, Chicago
312 902 5256
sheldon.banoff@kattenlaw.com
*Recommended in Tax*

**Practice Areas:** Partner, Chicago. Has concentrated in the area of federal income taxation for over 30 years, with particular concentration in investment, real estate, partnership and limited liability company taxation matters. Practice includes the representation of taxable and tax-exempt investors, ventures and professional service firms.

**Prof. Memberships:** A past Chairman of the Chicago Bar Association's Federal Taxation and Large Law Firm Committees. Frequent American Bar Association program speaker on tax planning, partnership, limited liability company, executive compensation, and professional firm matters.

**Career:** Nationally and internationally known author and lecturer. Former Lecturer in Law at the University of Chicago Law School. Co-author of the Journal of Taxation's monthly 'Shop Talk' column since 1985, he has also written over 100 leading articles in the tax area. Has annually been selected by a national poll of lawyers as one of the best lawyers in America and is profiled in several top legal publications, including Chambers Global directory. Elected a Fellow of the American College of Tax Counsel.

**Personal:** Graduated with high honors from the University of Illinois at Chicago (Accounting) and received his Law Degree in 1974 from the University of Chicago Law School, where he was Associate Editor of the Law Review.

### BAPTISTA, Robert C
Mayer, Brown, Rowe & Maw LLP,
Chicago 312 701 7101
rbaptista@mayerbrown.com
*Recommended in Banking & Finance*

**Practice Areas:** Negotiates and documents secured and unsecured lending agreements, debt restructurings, and other financing transactions. Advises in corporate matters such as borrowing transactions, sale agreements, and long-term production and licensing arrangements.

**Career:** Served as judicial clerk to The Honorable R Lanier Anderson III, US Court of Appeals for the Eleventh Circuit, 1982-83. Joined Mayer, Brown, Rowe & Maw LLP in 1983 and became a Partner

in 1989.

**Personal:** JD, summa cum laude, at the University of Illinois in 1982; Editor-in-Chief, Law Review. MA (summa cum laude), Northern Illinois University, 1976. BA, Wheaton College, 1970.

### BARLIANT, Ronald
Goldberg, Kohn, Bell, Black, Rosenbloom & Moritz, Ltd, Chicago
312 201 4000
*Recommended in Bankruptcy*

### BARROW, Peter
Neal, Gerber & Eisenberg LLP, Chicago
312 269 8479
pbarrow@ngelaw.com
*Recommended in Banking & Finance*

**Practice Areas:** Commercial lending and finance transactions, including private banking, middle-market and large corporate financings and debt restructurings, asset-based lending, public finance, secured transactions, syndicated loans, eurodollar, multicurrency and cross-border financings, participations, debt subordinations, aircraft sale, purchase and finance, equipment leasing, transportation-industry lending, regulatory issues, third-party guarantee and support devices, letters of credit and credit training and loan structuring programs; represented vehicle lessors regarding Truth-in-Lending and Regulation Z and M matters.

**Career:** Partner; Finance Practice Group.

**Personal:** Syracuse University (JD, 1976) cum laude, Law Review, Notes and Comments Editor; Washington University (BA, 1972), summa cum laude, Phi Beta Kappa.

### BARRY, James
Mayer, Brown, Rowe & Maw LLP,
Chicago 312 701 7169
jbarry@mayerbrownrowe.com
*Recommended in Tax*

**Practice Areas:** Represent US corporations and individuals in tax planning for foreign operations; foreign corporations and individuals in tax planning for US operations; US and foreign corporations in tax planning for restructuring of existing foreign and US corporate groups, spin-offs, and acquisitions of foreign and domestic corporations, including obtaining private letter rulings from the Internal Revenue Service. Represent offshore insurance companies, investment companies and other foreign entities regarding US taxation of their income and related issues and US investment funds regarding foreign acquisitions.

**Prof. Memberships:** Member University of Chicago Tax Planning Committee.

**Career:** Mayer, Brown, Rowe & Maw LLP, Chicago, 1985 to date. Admitted: Illinois, 1985; US Tax Court, 1986.

**Publications:** 'The Foreign Aspects of Section 382 – Searching for Answers in a Troubled Global Economy', Taxes Magazine (March 2002) and Practicing Law

Institute's 'Tax Strategies Guide'. Presentations: University of Chicago Tax Conference, Tax Executives Institute, OFII, ABA, ATLAS, Strategic Research Institute

**Personal:** DePaul College of Law, JD with honors, 1985. DePaul University, BSc with high honors, 1982.

### BARTLIT JR, Fred
Bartlit Beck Herman Palenchar & Scott,
Denver 303 592 3100
*Recommended in Litigation*

### BATES JR, Robert
Bates & Carey, Chicago
312 762 3100
*Recommended in Insurance*

### BEARD, James
DLA Piper Rudnick Gray Cary US LLP,
Chicago
312 368 2169
james.beard@dlapiper.com
*Recommended in Real Estate*

**Practice Areas:** Real estate; real estate finance; construction; sports facilities development.

**Career:** He concentrates his practice in commercial real estate law and has represented clients in a wide range of commercial real estate transactions, including acquisitions and dispositions, financing, joint venture formation, construction contract negotiation, lease preparation, and government procurement and contracting. He also represents developers and institutional lenders in restructuring and workout of troubled real estate projects.

**Personal:** JD, Chicago-Kent College of Law, Illinois Institute of Technology; BS, University of Illinois at Urbana-Champaign.

### BECK, Philip
Bartlit Beck Herman Palenchar & Scott,
Chicago 312 494 4400
*Recommended in Litigation*

### BECKER, Scott
McGuireWoods LLP, Chicago
312 849 8100
*Recommended in Healthcare*

### BEEN, Carol Anne
Sonnenschein Nath & Rosenthal LLP,
Chicago 312 876 3122
cbeen@sonnenschein.com
*Recommended in Intellectual Property*

**Practice Areas:** Firmwide Practice Chair; focuses on trademark, copyright, advertising, sweepstakes, Internet marketing, software licensing, trade secrets, entertainment, publishing law. Involved in intellectual property counseling, transactions, prosecution, litigation.

**Prof. Memberships:** International Trademark Association committees; Promotion Marketing Association; Board, Lawyers for the Creative Arts; Committee developing trademark jury instructions for the 7th Circuit US Court of Appeals.

**Career:** Joined firm in 1988.

**Publications:** Articles in Intellectual Property Forum (Australia), ABA Forum on Franchising, ABA Intellectual Property Newsletter, IP Litigator.

**Personal:** University of Illinois, JD, magna cum laude; Northwestern University School of Law, visiting student; University of Illinois, BS, Journalism, Bronze Tablet.

### BELL, Stephen
Goldberg, Kohn, Bell, Black, Rosenbloom & Moritz, Ltd, Chicago
312 201 4000
*Recommended in Real Estate*

### BERBERIAN, H Nicholas
Neal, Gerber & Eisenberg LLP, Chicago
312 269 8005
nberberian@ngelaw.com
*Recommended in Litigation*

**Practice Areas:** Class actions, mass actions, lawsuits and arbitrations involving investors and employment practices, CFTC reparations and regulatory matters before the SEC, NYSE, National Association of Securities Dealers, Chicago Board of Options, Chicago Board of Trade, Chicago Mercantile Exchange, Labor Department, and other federal and state agencies.

**Prof. Memberships:** ABA Securities Litigation Committee (Co-Chair, 2003); ABA Subcommittee on Broker-Dealer Litigation (Co-Chair, 1993-2003).

**Career:** Partner; Securities and Commodities Litigation Practice Group Chair; Executive Committee (Member).

**Publications:** Annual Survey of Broker-Dealer Litigation (Co-Editor).

**Personal:** University of Chicago Law School (JD, 1978); University of Chicago (MBA, 1975); Kenyon College (AB, 1974).

### BERG, Eric
DLA Piper Rudnick Gray Cary US LLP,
Chicago 312 368 3448
eric.berg@dlapiper.com
*Recommended in Construction*

**Practice Areas:** Construction; litigation; lodging and timeshare.

**Career:** His practice focuses on construction law in both litigation and transactional work. He has represented owners, contractors, subcontractors, architects, engineers, and lenders. He also has extensive experience in other areas of commercial litigation and alternative dispute resolution. He is well-versed in all facets of the Americans with Disabilities Act and the Fair Housing Act. He has provided counsel on interpretation of and compliance with the ADA, the FHA, and other federal, state and local accessibility statutes.

**Personal:** JD, Northwestern University; BA, Yale University.

## BERGHOFF, John C

Mayer, Brown, Rowe & Maw LLP,
Chicago 312 701 7315
jberghoff@mayerbrownrowe.com
*Recommended in Environment*

**Practice Areas:** Environmental Practice
leader. Litigates in complex environmental trials and appeals before federal and
state courts. Lead lawyer in significant
bench trials and jury cases relating to
class actions, environmental damage and
exposure. Provides counselling and
response to environmental 'crisis' situations.

**Prof. Memberships:** Adjunct Professor,
Northwestern University School of Law,
1996 to date. Lecturer on litigation and
legal ethics.

**Career:** Joined Mayer, Brown, Rowe &
Maw LLP as Partner, 1986.

**Publications:** Articles relating litigation
and environmental law issues.

**Personal:** Earned JD, Northwestern University School of Law; Wigmore Key.
Holds BA, with honors, from Northwestern University. Board of Trustees, Northwestern University, 1988-94. Chairman,
Board of Alumni Regents, Northwestern
University, 1998 to date. Vice Chairman,
Board of Trustees, Ravinia Festival, 1999-
2003.

## BERKELEY, Jill B

Schiff Hardin LLP, Chicago
312 258 5598
jberkeley@schiffhardin.com
*Recommended in Insurance*

**Practice Areas:** Insurance.

**Prof. Memberships:** American Bar
Association – Tort Trial and Insurance
Practice Section, Illinois State Bar Association, Illinois Academy of Laureates,
National Risk Retention Association, Illinois Captive and Alternative Risk Funding Insurance Association, Illinois Association of Defense Trial Counsel, Association of Professional Insurance Women,
Defense Research Institute.

**Career:** Ms Berkeley has extensive experience representating insurers and
insureds in coverage litigation. Has
received several professional awards for
practice excellence.

**Publications:** More than 50 publications
and presentations.

**Personal:** University of Michigan (BA,
magna cum laude, Phi Beta Kappa,
1972), Northwestern University School of
Law (JD, 1975).

## BERKOFF, Mark

DLA Piper Rudnick Gray Cary US LLP,
Chicago 312 368 7090
mark.berkoff@dlapiper.com
*Recommended in Bankruptcy*

**Practice Areas:** Bankruptcy and business reorganization.

**Career:** His practice concentrates on
bankruptcy and creditors' rights. He represents debtors, creditors' committees,
and secured lenders in complex Chapter
11 cases in diverse industries and has
experience in many aspects of this area of
law. He acts as special litigation counsel to
bankruptcy trustees and prosecutes and
defends involuntary petitions in bankruptcy.

**Personal:** JD, University of Chicago; BA,
University of Wisconsin – Madison.

## BERMAN, Debbie

Jenner & Block LLP, Chicago
312 923 2764
dberman@jenner.com
*Recommended in Media &
Entertainment*

**Practice Areas:** Debbie L Berman is a
Partner in Jenner & Block's Chicago
office. She is Co-Chair of the firm's Trade
Secrets and Unfair Competition Practice,
and a Member of the firm's Media and
First Amendment, Litigation and Dispute
Resolution, Government Contracts and
Reinsurance Practices. Ms Berman has
substantial experience representing
clients in trade secrets and unfair competition matters. She litigated the seminal
case involving the inevitable disclosure
doctrine for trade secrets, Pepsico v. Redmond, 54 F3d 1262 (7th Cir 1995), both
on the trial and appellate level. In addition, she has represented other clients in
preliminary injunction and other proceedings concerning the enforcement of
covenants not to compete and related
trade secrets issues, and in Lanham Act
and other unfair competition litigation.
Ms Berman has extensive experience in
the First Amendment and defamation
areas in both state and federal courts. In
particular, Ms Berman has represented
media and non-media clients in more
than 20 separate defamation cases and, in
many of these cases, has successfully
obtained dismissals of these actions. Ms
Berman also represents clients in a variety
of government contracts litigation and
has substantial experience in other areas
of complex civil litigation. She was
recently honored by the JUF/Jewish Federation with its coveted Davis, Gidwitz &
Glasser Award, which recognizes 'young
leaders who represent an ideal of dedication and service to the Jewish community'.

**Personal:** Harvard Law School, JD, 1990,
cum laude.

## BERNICK, David M

Kirkland & Ellis LLP, Chicago
312 861 2248
dbernick@kirkland.com
*Recommended in Litigation, Products
Liability*

**Practice Areas:** National trial Counsel
in mass tort litigation in the areas of
pharmaceutical litigation, asbestos litigation, including the development of a
chapter 11 strategy for companies with
asbestos liabilities, tobacco cost recovery,
holocaust labour, breast implants and
radiation exposure in state and federal
courts. He has also served as trial Counsel
in securities fraud, product liability, leveraged-buyout, trade secret misappropriation, breach of contract, RICO, securities
and monopoly cases. Currently serves on
the Judicial Conference Committee on
the Rules of Practice and Procedure.

**Personal:** University of Chicago, BA,
1974. Yale University, MA, 1975. University of Chicago, JD, 1978.

## BERNSTEIN, H Bruce

Sidley Austin LLP, Chicago
312 853 7635
bbernstein@sidley.com
*Recommended in Banking & Finance*

**Practice Areas:** Member of the firm's
Executive Committee. Concentrates his
practice in secured transactions, commercial finance and restructurings on
behalf of commercial banks and asset-based lenders.

**Prof. Memberships:** Chicago, Illinois
and American Bar Associations. Fellow:
American College of Bankruptcy, American College of Commercial Finance
Lawyers. Member: National Bankruptcy
Conference. 1995 to 2001: General Counsel, Commercial Finance Association.

**Publications:** Frequent lecturer on
secured lending and bankruptcy topics
and has written numerous articles on the
Uniform Commercial Code and Bankruptcy Code.

**Personal:** Cornell University, BA, 1965;
Harvard Law School, JD, 1968. Admission: Illinois, 1968.

## BERNSTEIN, Howard

Neal, Gerber & Eisenberg LLP, Chicago
312 269 8447
hbernstein@ngelaw.com
*Recommended in Employment*

**Practice Areas:** Labor, employment law
and related litigation, with an emphasis
on contract negotiations, arbitrations
and injunction proceedings, NLRB election campaigns, unfair labor practice
cases and employment discrimination
matters; counsels healthcare clients; chief
labor negotiator for multi-employer
nursing home association.

**Prof. Memberships:** ISBA; ABA Labor
Law Section Committee on Development
of the Law Under the NLRA (Chairman);
NLRB (Counsel to the Chairman), 1970-
72.

**Career:** Partner; Labor and Employment
Practice Group (Immediate Past Chair);
Executive Committee (Member).

**Publications:** Author and lecturer on
various labor and employment topics.

**Personal:** University of Texas School of
Law (JD, 1968); University of Texas (BBA,
1965).

## BESSETTE-SMITH, Suzanne

Barack Ferrazzano Kirschbaum Perlman
& Nagelberg, Chicago 312 984 3100
*Recommended in Real Estate*

## BEST, Edward S

Mayer, Brown, Rowe & Maw LLP,
Chicago 312 701 7100
ebest@mayerbrownrowe.com
*Recommended in Corporate/M&A*

**Practice Areas:** Broad securities, M&A
and corporate governance practice with
focus on financial institutions, including
insurance companies, banks and broker-dealers. Also has extensive experience
representing foreign companies, with
focus on financial institutions, in connection with US securities offerings, ongoing
reporting requirements and corporate
governance.

**Career:** Mayer, Brown, Rowe & Maw
LLP, Chicago, 1986 to date; Partner, 1995.

**Personal:** JD (cum laude), Loyola University of Chicago School of Law, 1986;
Research Editor, Law Journal. AB, University of Illinois-Urbana, 1983.

## BIERIG, Jack R

Sidley Austin LLP, Chicago
312 853 7614
jbierig@sidley.com
*Recommended in Antitrust*

**Practice Areas:** Practice focuses on litigation and counseling relating to
antitrust, intellectual property, and regulatory issues for professional associations
in the areas of healthcare and real estate,
healthcare providers, and accreditation
and certification organizations. Mr Bierig
represents clients in government antitrust
and fraud investigations, in private litigation, and in proceedings before agencies
such as the Department of Justice, the
Federal Trade Commission, and the
Department of Health and Human Services. He also counsels clients on a wide
variety of antitrust, association law, and
regulatory issues.

**Prof. Memberships:** Mr Bierig is a lecturer at the University of Chicago School
of Law and the Harris School of Public
Policy. He is a past Chair of the Legal Section Council of the American Society of
Association Executives and past President
of the Illinois Association of Healthcare
Attorneys.

**Publications:** Frequent author and
speaker on antitrust, association, and
healthcare issues.

**Personal:** Harvard Law School, JD, 1972;
Brandeis University, AB, 1968. Admission: Illinois, 1972.

## BINNIG, Christian F

Mayer, Brown, Rowe & Maw LLP,
Chicago 312 701 7079
cbinnig@mayerbrown.com
*Recommended in Telecom, Broadcast
& Satellite*

**Practice Areas:** Litigator specializing in
telecommunications and regulated
industries, particularly gas and electricity.
Experienced in antitrust, mergers and
acquisitions, emergency litigation, appellate work, professional malpractice,
telecommunications and communica-

tions network contract negotiations. **Career:** Joined Mayer, Brown, Rowe & Maw LLP, 1986; became Partner, 1994. Formerly with Troutman, Sanders, Lockerman & Ashmore, Atlanta, 1985-86. **Personal:** University of Michigan Law School, JD, cum laude, 1985. University of Virginia, BA with high distinction, 1982; Phi Beta Kappa.

## BISHOP, Timothy S
Mayer, Brown, Rowe & Maw LLP, Chicago 312 701 7829
tbishop@mayerbrown.com
*Recommended in Environment*
**Practice Areas:** Responsible for arguing four cases and briefing nearly 50 before the US Supreme Court, handling dozens of appeals in federal and state appellate courts, and briefing dispositive dismissal and summary judgment, motions in federal and state trial courts. Experience in Clean Water Act, Endangered Species Act, land use, property rights, and constitutional appeals and litigation, representing property owners, state and local government bodies, and other regulated entities. **Career:** Joined Mayer, Brown, Rowe & Maw LLP, 1991; Partner, 1995. Law clerk to Justice William J Brennan, Jr, US Supreme Court, 1988-89; Judge James L Oakes, US Court of Appeals for the Second Circuit, 1986-87; Staff Counsel and Skadden Fellow, American Civil Liberties Union, Chicago, 1989-91. Adjunct Professor, University of Chicago Law School, 1990-91; Northwestern University School of Law, 1981-83, 1993-96; IIT-Chicago Kent Law School, 1989-91. **Publications:** Recent writings: 'Do Federal Environmental Laws Regulate Commerce?' 17 Natural Resources and Environment 7 (Summer 2002). 'Smart Growth or Dumb Bureaucracy?' 32 Environmental Law Reporter 10822 (July 2002). **Personal:** Northwestern University School of Law, JD magna cum laude, 1985; Articles Editor, Northwestern University Law Review. Oxford University, England, Corpus Christi College, BA in Law, first class honours, 1979; MA, 1983.

## BLACKMAN, Jana Cohen
Sonnenschein Nath & Rosenthal LLP, Chicago 312 876 7967
jblackman@sonnenschein.com
*Recommended in Real Estate*
**Practice Areas:** Real Estate Practice Chair; Tax-Advantaged Investments Practice Chair. Tax-advantaged investments, particularly, low-income housing tax credits, and historic and new market tax credits expert. Transactions include guaranteed investments, fund investments and direct investments in low-income housing tax credit projects; derivative swaps, financial guaranties and surety bonds; low-income housing developments financed in, eg., traditional debt/equity, taxable/tax-exempt bonds

and by US HUD. Collaborates with HUD and Justice Department on affordable or special needs housing issues and federal fair housing claims.
**Prof. Memberships:** Chicago Bar Association, ABA.
**Personal:** University of Chicago Law School, JD; Northwestern University, BA, with honors, Art History.

## BOEHNEN, Daniel A
McDonnell Boehnen Hulbert & Berghoff LLP, Chicago 312 913 2130
boehnen@mbhb.com
*Recommended in Intellectual Property*
**Career:** Daniel A Boehnen is a founder of McDonnell Boehnen Hulbert & Berghoff LLP. His practice focuses primarily on trials, appeals, opposition proceedings, and all forms of disputed patent matters. Clients often seek his counsel on general IP, business, and legal problems because of his keen insight and his ability to create understanding, simplify problems, and innovate solutions. Clients praise Mr Boehnen for crafting aggressive strategies to try cases and settle cases while remaining sensitive to the client's business goals. Mr Boehnen and his team have been praised by clients as the most integrated and efficient attorneys they work with. His litigation experience encompasses a wide range of hi-tech industries in all levels of the federal court system. He has been involved in many notable and precedent-setting cases, such as: (i) landmark biotechnology patent litigation (Amgen v. Chugai Pharmaceuticals and Genetics Institute), (ii) the first decision by any US court that the act of maintaining frozen recombinant host cells comprises an infringing use under 35 U.S.C. §271(a) (Amgen Inc. v. Elanex Pharmaceuticals); and (iii) a decision by the Federal Circuit Court of Appeals establishing that district courts lack the authority to order patentees to file papers on behalf of third parties during Patent Office reexamination proceedings (Emerson Electric v. Davoil). Mr Boehnen was chosen for inclusion in Best Lawyers in America, based upon peer recommendations; the Leading Lawyers Network as a founding member; in Chicago Magazine as one of the top patent trial attorneys in Illinois; in Crain's Chicago Business as one of the top intellectual property lawyers in Illinois; and in the American Bar Association's ABA Foundation Fellow, an honor reserved for the top 1/3 of 1% of all US lawyers. Mr Boehnen is frequently invited as a guest speaker to corporate and professional groups. He is a founder and was an officer of the Association of Patent Law Firms, was a governor for the Federal Circuit Bar Association, and is former Chair of the Cornell Law Alumni Association of Greater Chicago. Mr Boehnen is a contributing author for the ABA Handbook on Patent Litigation Strategies. Mr

Boehnen has a BS in Chemical Engineering from the University of Notre Dame and a JD from Cornell University Law School. He is admitted to practice before the US Supreme Court and many federal courts, and is registered to practice before the US Patent and Trademark Office.

## BOEHRER, Charles B
Winston & Strawn LLP, Chicago 312 558 5989
cboehrer@winston.com
*Recommended in Banking & Finance*
**Practice Areas:** Finance, securities, merger and acquisitions.
**Career:** Mr Boehrer attended the University of Michigan where he served as Editor of the Law Review. He then joined Winston & Strawn as an associate in 1985 and is a Partner in the Corporate Department. Mr Boehrer's extensive experience includes acting as bank counsel for the structuring of senior and senior second lien credit facilities, including leveraged and investment grade transactions, complex international lending transactions, acquisition and going-private transactions, refinancing and repricings, as well as restructuring and workout transactions. He recently represented leading financial institutions and borrowers on over $10 billion of senior debt including his representation of Deutsche Bank on the $2.5 billion credit facility to Huntman International and the $1.3 billion credit facility to Crown Cork and Seal Company; Bank of America on the $600 million credit facility for IDEX Corporation; Lear Corporation in connection with its $2.1 billion senior credit facility; and Nuveen Investments in connection with its $400 million credit facility.

## BOIES, Bill
McDermott Will & Emery, Chicago 312 984 7686
bboies@mwe.com
*Recommended in Employment, ERISA Litigation*
**Practice Areas:** Concentrates on business disputes counseling and business litigation throughout the country, including benefits litigation, securities litigation, financial disputes, class actions, alternative dispute resolution, trials and appeals. Represents benefit plan sponsors and fiduciaries in ERISA class action litigation concerning pension plan administration, fiduciary duty, responsibility for asset losses, and changes in pension and welfare benefits. Defends plan sponsors, company officers and corporate fiduciaries in class actions concerning declining value of employer stock held in 401(k) plans and ESOPs.
**Prof. Memberships:** Chicago Bar Foundation, American Bar Foundation.
**Personal:** Brown University (BA); University of Chicago Law School (JD).

## BORDERS, Thomas
McDermott Will & Emery, Chicago 312 984 7552
tborders@mwe.com
*Recommended in Tax, Tax Litigation*
**Practice Areas:** Areas include federal tax controversies involving audits, administrative appeals and litigation. Also defends companies and individuals in fraud and criminal investigations related to tax and securities matters. Worked on numerous US and international tax cases involving corporate tax matters, valuation, finance and accounting issues.
**Career:** Trial attorney for the Office of Chief Counsel with the Internal Revenue Service for more than eight years. Involved in numerous federal income tax trials and received several Internal Revenue Service awards, which recognized his outstanding trial skills.
**Personal:** St Louis University (BA); Georgetown University Law Centre (JD); Northwestern University (MBA)

## BORUN, Michael
Marshall, Gerstein & Borun, Chicago 312 474 6300
*Recommended in Intellectual Property*

## BOTICA, Matthew J
Winston & Strawn LLP, Chicago 312 558 8095
mbotica@winston.com
*Recommended in Bankruptcy*
**Practice Areas:** Partner, Corporate Department, Chicago office. Practice concentration in insolvency, bankruptcy, and business reorganization. Co-Chair of the Financial Restructuring Group at Winston & Strawn. More than 25 years' experience representing banks, institutional lenders, creditors' committees, trustees, governmental agencies, and other creditors in the bankruptcy, reorganization, and claims trading areas.
**Prof. Memberships:** American College of Bankruptcy.
**Career:** Joined the firm as a Partner in 1999.
**Publications:** Author of a chapter on Chapter 7 business liquidations in the Illinois Institute for Continuing Legal Education (IICLE) 'Bankruptcy Practice Handbook'.
**Personal:** Boston College, 1972, summa cum laude, Phi Beta Kappa. Harvard Law School, 1975.

## BOWEN, Stephen
Latham & Watkins LLP, Chicago 312 876 7700
*Recommended in Tax*

## BOYD, Eric
Seyfarth Shaw LLP, Chicago 312 346 8000
*Recommended in Environment*

## BRADLEY, Craig C

Katten Muchin Rosenman LLP, Chicago
312 902 5353
craig.bradley@kattenlaw.com
*Recommended in Corporate/M&A:
Private Equity*

**Practice Areas:** Partner in the Corporate Department concentrating on the representation of emerging software, life sciences, internet, communications and other technology companies in obtaining angel and venture capital financing and in connection with initial public offerings, compensation arrangements, and mergers and acquisitions. Also represents venture capital firms and private equity funds.
**Prof. Memberships:** Member, Board of Directors, Illinois Information Technology Association; Member, Board of Directors, IBIO; Member, Board of Directors, BioAngels; Adjunct Assistant Professor, Northwestern University Kellogg Graduate School of Business.
**Personal:** JD, cum laude, Indiana University, member, Indiana Law Journal; BS, Finance, summa cum laude, Elmhurst College.

## BRAUN, Bruce

Winston & Strawn LLP, Chicago
312 558 5600
*Recommended in Litigation*

## BRENNAN, Daniel

DLA Piper Rudnick Gray Cary US LLP, Chicago 312 368 4085
daniel.brennan@dlapiper.com
*Recommended in Construction*

**Practice Areas:** Construction; litigation.
**Career:** He concentrates his practice in advising owners, designers, and contractors on risk management in the construction process; prosecuting and defending construction claims including professional negligence, personal injury, and delay claims; drafting construction and design contracts for architects, engineers and owners; and advising clients with respect to design and construction of accessible facilities under Title III of the Americans with Disabilities Act and the Fair Housing Act.
**Personal:** JD, Georgetown University Law Center; BA, University of Notre Dame.

## BRITTAIN, Max

Schiff Hardin LLP, Chicago
312 258 5544
mbrittain@schiffhardin.com
*Recommended in Employment*

**Practice Areas:** Labor and employment.
**Prof. Memberships:** American Bar Association; College of Labor and Employment Lawyers.
**Career:** Mr Brittain leads Schiff Hardin's Labor and Employment Group. He has extensive experience representing management clients in proceedings before the National Labor Relations Board and Equal Employment Opportunity Commission, state and federal courts, and various local, state, and federal agencies.
**Personal:** Bradley University (BS, 1969), Loyola University Chicago School of Law (JD, cum laude, 1976), Managing Editor, Loyola University Chicago Law Review.

## BRO, Ruth Hill

Baker & McKenzie, Chicago
312 861 7985
bro@bakernet.com
*Recommended in Technology*

**Practice Areas:** Privacy, security, e-workplace, e-business. Privacy strategy; global compliance; website, HR, customer, third-party, cross-border, and e-marketing issues; crisis management. Featured speaker: in-house training, conferences. Views noted in WSJ, NY Times, National Law Journal, BNA Privacy and Security Law Report, Bloomberg Radio, CNBC.
**Prof. Memberships:** Secretary, ABA Section of Science and Technology Law. Founder/past-Chair, ABA E-Privacy Law Committee. Editorial boards: Privacy and Data Protection Legal Reporter (Executive Editor), Sci-Tech Lawyer, Internet Law and Strategy.
**Career:** Admitted in Illinois (1994).
**Publications:** Editor, 'The E-Business Legal Arsenal' (ABA, 2004); co-author, 'Online Law' (Addison-Wesley, 1996); numerous privacy/e-business articles.
**Personal:** JD, University of Chicago.

## BROCCOLO, Bernadette

McDermott Will & Emery, Chicago
312 984 6911
bbroccolo@mwe.com
*Recommended in Healthcare*

**Practice Areas:** 26 years of health industry experience. Specialties: federal tax-exemption, not-for-profit corporate governance, privacy, human subject protection and technology contracting. Representative engagements: develop and implement complex relationship formation/realignment (joint ventures, governance restructurings, institutional provider-physician relationships); information technology acquisitions; electronic information networks; comprehensive biomedical research program operations/compliance infrastructure; corporate compliance programs.
**Prof. Memberships:** Leadership positions for American Health Lawyers Association, American Bar Association, Illinois Association of Healthcare Attorneys. Frequent speaker and author.
**Personal:** University of Notre Dame Law School (JD); Boston College (BA).

## BROWN, Jeffrey

Michael Best & Friedrich LLP, Chicago
312 222 0800
*Recommended in Media &
Entertainment*

## BROWNE, Robert E

Neal, Gerber & Eisenberg LLP, Chicago
312 269 5225
rbrowne@ngelaw.com
*Recommended in Intellectual Property*

**Practice Areas:** Represents clients in all aspects of patent, trademark, copyright and unfair competition law and related litigation before the federal district and appellate courts and the ITC; negotiates and drafts patent license, trademark, and merchandise licenses, computer software licenses and development agreements, publishing agreements, technology transfer and development agreements, and video and motion picture distribution agreements.
**Prof. Memberships:** Member, Intellectual Property Law Association of Chicago, International Trademark Association, and American Bar Association.
**Career:** Partner; Intellectual Property Practice Group Co-Chair.
**Publications:** Author and lecturer on intellectual property topics.
**Personal:** University of Wisconsin (JD, 1970); University of Notre Dame (BSCE, 1967).

## BRYANT, David

Katten Muchin Rosenman LLP, Chicago
312 902 5380
david.bryant@kattenlaw.com
*Recommended in Real Estate*

**Practice Areas:** David J Bryant concentrates his efforts in commercial real estate law. He has substantial experience in acquisitions, dispositions and investments in real estate assets, real estate development, real estate finance (including mezzanine financing), joint venture and partnership formation and financing. In addition, Mr Bryant has substantial experience in representing sponsors of real estate funds and in establishing joint ventures and other companies to own, operate, finance and develop real estate.
**Prof. Memberships:** Active Member of the Pension Real Estate Association (PREA) and the Urban Land Institute (ULI).
**Career:** Co-Chair of National Real Estate Practice; Executive Committee; Board of Directors.
**Personal:** Mr Bryant received his Bachelor's Degree from the University of Illinois in 1984 and his JD degree from Northwestern University in 1987.

## BRYANT, L Edward

Gardner Carton & Douglas LLP, Chicago
312 569 1259
ebryant@gcd.com
*Recommended in Healthcare*

**Practice Areas:** Ed Bryant, founder of the firm's Health Law Department in 1979, has participated in more than 230 health industry corporate restructurings, more than 125 hospital mergers/acquisitions, and hundreds of healthcare joint ventures. Ed is a frequent speaker at hospital and health system board retreats on fiduciary duties in light of Sarbanes-Oxley and nonprofit scandals. Other practice areas: integrated delivery systems, hospital closures, managed care arrangements, physician contracts, special risk audits, patient care, medical staff privileges, academic affiliations, corporate governance, federal taxation of exempt organizations, and postmerger reorganizations to implement organizational changes.
**Prof. Memberships:** Public Director, American Board of Medical Specialties; Director, Rehabilitation Institute of Chicago; former Board Chair and Director, Srs of Charity of Leavenworth Health System
**Career:** Faculty member, Kellogg Graduate School of Management of Northwestern University and Loyola University School of Law. Named Illinois Super Lawyer; one of top 100 lawyers in Illinois by SuperLawyers in 2006; one of The Best Lawyers in America for the past 12 years; Best Lawyers in Illinois and Leading Lawyers Network of Illinois. Recipient, James H Douglas, Jr Award for exemplary participation in public and charitable activities.
**Publications:** Speaks/publishes widely within health industry.
**Personal:** Northwestern University, BA, 1963; JD, 1967.

## BRYANT, Timothy

McDermott Will & Emery, Chicago
312 984 2066
tbryant@mwe.com
*Recommended in Corporate/M&A:
Private Equity*

**Practice Areas:** Practice covers the entire spectrum of corporate finance and securities law. Represents public and private companies, as well as the investment banks, private equity funds, and other financial institutions that support them. Represented clients in closing over one hundred transactions, ranging from the venture financing of start-up companies and the representation of executives in their equity and compensation arrangements to the $1.7 billion acquisition of a European engine manufacturer and a $150 million equity investment in a public telecom company.
**Personal:** Northwestern University (BA); Northwestern University School of Law (JD).

## BUDNY, Terrence

Bell, Boyd & Lloyd LLC, Chicago
312 372 1121
*Recommended in Real Estate*

## BULGER, Brian

Meckler Bulger & Tilson LLP, Chicago
312 474 7900
*Recommended in Employment*

## BURNS, Timothy W
Neal, Gerber & Eisenberg LLP, Chicago
312 269 8470
tburns@ngelaw.com
*Recommended in Insurance*
**Practice Areas:** Directors' and Officers' Insurance Practice; counsel clients on purchase and maintenance of D&O insurance, including counseling with respect to the D&O insurance aspects of IPOs, spin-offs, mergers and acquisitions, and bankruptcies; represents clients in their disputes with their insurers.
**Prof. Memberships:** ABA Insurance Coverage Litigation Committee (Co-Chair, 2003-present); ABA Section of Litigation's Task Force on ADR Effectiveness (Member, 2002).
**Career:** Partner; Litigation and Corporate Governance Practice Groups.
**Publications:** Frequent author and lecturer on insurance coverage issues.
**Personal:** University of Missouri-Columbia School of Law (JD, 1991); Weber State University (BA, 1991).

## BURT, Antony
Schiff Hardin LLP, Chicago
312 258 5762
aburt@schiffhardin.com
*Recommended in Insurance*
**Practice Areas:** Litigation, reinsurance.
**Prof. Memberships:** American Bar Association, US Reinsurance and Arbitration Society.
**Career:** Mr Burt focuses on commercial litigation, with a particular concentration in the areas of reinsurance, professional liability, civil fraud investigations, bankruptcy, and antitrust litigation. He has been involved in all aspects of complex civil litigation, including trials, injunctions, appeals, and arbitrations.
**Personal:** Duke University (AB, 1978), Northwestern University School of Law (JD, 1982), Member, Northwestern Law Review.

## BUSEY, Roxane C
Baker & McKenzie, Chicago
312 861 8281
Roxane.C.Busey@bakernet.com
*Recommended in Antitrust*
**Practice Areas:** Partner, Senior Member of Antitrust Practice Group; former Chair of American Bar Association (ABA) Section of Antitrust Law (2001-02); 30 years' experience in antitrust counseling and litigation; Practices before Federal Trade Commission and Department of Justice; substantial experience in antitrust compliance issues and mergers and acquisitions.
**Prof. Memberships:** Currently, Chair, ABA Antitrust Section Task Force on Modernization (2004-present), Co-Chair, Practicing Law Institute Annual Antitrust Institute (Chicago) (2002-present); Previously, ABA Antitrust Section, Chair (2001-02); Officer, Council Member (1992-03); Healthcare Committee

Chair (1989-92); Member, Special Task Force on Competition Policy to Clinton Transition Team (1992), (ex officio) Special Task Force to Bush Transition Team (2000); Chair, Antitrust Committee, Chicago Bar Association (1990); Chair, Illinois State Bar Association Antitrust Council (1984).
**Career:** Joined Baker & McKenzie in 2005 as Partner; previously Partner at Gardner Carton & Douglas (1995-05); Hopkins & Sutter (1975-95).
**Publications:** Frequent author, lecturer on antitrust issues. Recent lecturer at ABA Antitrust Section Masters Program (2004), PLI Annual Antitrust Institute (Chicago) (2005). Testimony before FTC on Healthcare (2003); Intellectual Property (2002); Joint Ventures (1997); Global Competition (1995).
**Personal:** Northwestern University, JD (1975); Miami University (Ohio), BA, cum laude, Phi Beta Kappa (1970).

## BUTLER, Christopher
Kirkland & Ellis LLP, Chicago
312 861 2298
cbutler@kirkland.com
*Recommended in Banking & Finance*
**Practice Areas:** Christopher Butler's practice is concentrated in financing transactions with an emphasis on acquisitions and highly leveraged financings. His financing transaction experience includes representing borrowers and lenders in: structuring secured and unsecured lending transactions; LBO and acquisition financings; restructuring transactions; first and second lien financings; subordinated debt transactions; mezzanine and other private issuances; working capital and letter of credit facilities; DIP financings; 144A debt offerings; and hedging arrangements. His general corporate experience includes: acquisitions; joint ventures and mergers; stock and warrant purchases; business organizations and formations; and general legal counseling.
**Personal:** University of Pennsylvania, BA, 1984; Fordham University, JD, 1988.

## BUTLER JR, John Wm (Jack)
Skadden, Arps, Slate, Meagher & Flom LLP & Affiliates, Chicago 312 407 0730
jbutler@skadden.com
*Recommended in Bankruptcy*
**Practice Areas:** Co-practice Leader, Worldwide Corporate Restructuring Practice. Specializes in troubled company M&A, financing and restructuring situations, including cross-border transactions and advising officers and directors of public companies involved in debt restructuring on matters relating to corporate governance and fiduciary duty. Representative company matters include the restructuring of Delphi Corporation, Friedman's Inc., Kmart Corporation, Rite Aid Corporation, Singer N.V., US Airways Group, Inc. and Xerox Corporation

and special counsel representations of 360/networks, inc., Enron Corporation and The Warnaco Group. in every annual edition of the K&A Restructuring Register, the peer group listing of the top restructuring attorneys and financial advisors in the United States. Eight times named by Turnarounds and Workouts in its annual list of the top dozen restructuring lawyers in America. Named one of the top 25 global restructuring lawyers in the 2005 edition of 'The International Who's Who of Business Lawyers' and listed in the 10th edition (2005) of Global Counsel ('PLC Which Lawyer?'). Named one of the top 10 worldwide restructuring lawyers in 2002 by Global Counsel Magazine. Was named by Euromoney and Legal Media Group as the top restructuring and insolvency expert worldwide after 18 months of research in 2004 and 2005. Recipient of first-ever Chairman's Award from the Turnaround Management Association in 2001 for his contributions to and standing in the corporate renewal industry.
**Prof. Memberships:** Fellow, American College of Bankruptcy and International Insolvency Institute.
**Career:** JD, University of Michigan Law School, 1980; AB, Princeton University, 1977 (magna cum laude).

## CAHAN, James N
Sidley Austin LLP, Chicago
312 853 7750
jcahan@sidley.com
*Recommended in Environment*
**Practice Areas:** Practice focuses in the areas of air pollution, environmental aspects of bankruptcies and transactions, and environmental management. Mr Cahan represents industrial clients in complex air permitting and enforcement matters, including those involving New Source Review and hazardous air pollutants. He also has extensive experience in working with debtors, creditors, banks and other interested parties regarding strategies, negotiations and resolution of a variety of environmental claims and other bankruptcy issues, and also assists corporations with policies and programs for managing their environmental, health and safety problems. He is well versed in the full range of hazardous waste and Superfund issues, asbestos and project management, and the environmental aspects of corporate acquisitions and real estate transactions.
**Personal:** Served in the Office of the General Counsel, Air Division, of the United States Environmental Protection Agency and as an Assistant Attorney General for the State of Illinois in the Environmental Control Division. Washington University School of Law, JD, 1976; Washington University, BA, 1973. Admissions: District of Columbia, 1980 and Illinois, 1976.

## CALLAHAN, Michael
Katten Muchin Rosenman LLP, Chicago
312 902 5200
*Recommended in Healthcare*

## CALLAHAN, Timothy P
Mayer, Brown, Rowe & Maw LLP, Chicago 312 701 7204
tcallahan@mayerbrownrowe.com
*Recommended in Energy*
**Practice Areas:** Project finance/project development/energy: representing owners, developers, lenders, utilities and contractors in all facets of the development, financing, acquisition and disposition of energy and other infrastructure facilities – power plants fired by gas, coal and petroleum coke, electric wind farms, coal gasification plants (including IGCC and SNG projects), hydroelectric, biomass and other renewable facilities, gas and water pipelines, sports stadiums, water and wastewater plants, ethanol plants, oil refineries, and pulp and paper mills. Representation includes the negotiation and preparation of joint venture/development/partnership arrangements, financing documentation, asset and stock sale/purchase agreements, and various project documents. Privatization/public-private partnerships/government negotiation and documentation of complex privatization and public-private partnership arrangements.
**Career:** Mayer, Brown, Rowe & Maw LLP, Chicago, 1994 to date. McHugh Development Co., Vice President/Assistant General Counsel, Chicago, 1992-94. McDermott, Will & Emery, Chicago, 1988-92. Admitted: Illinois, 1988.
**Personal:** University of Michigan Law School, JD, 1988. University of Michigan, BA magna cum laude, 1985.

## CAMPBELL, Thomas
Baker & McKenzie, Chicago
312 861 8800
*Recommended in Antitrust*

## CARLSON, Walter
Sidley Austin LLP, Chicago
312 853 7734
wcarlson@sidley.com
*Recommended in Litigation*
**Practice Areas:** Head of firm's Securities Litigation Practice and has represented numerous clients in a variety of types of specialized and general commercial litigation. Mr Carlson has served as Lead Counsel in numerous federal securities fraud lawsuits. He has handled a large number of cases in state and federal courts involving corporate governance and fiduciary duty issues. He also has frequently represented corporations and individual directors in SEC investigations and in derivative lawsuits and officers' and directors' liability claims. Mr Carlson is a Member of the firm's Executive Committee.
**Personal:** Harvard Law School, JD, 1978; Yale University, BA, 1975. Admissions: US

Supreme Court, 1991; US Court of Appeals, 5th Circuit, 1999; US Court of Appeals, 6th Circuit, 2004; US Court of Appeals, 7th Circuit, 1991; US Court of Appeals, 9th Circuit, 2000; US Court of Appeals, 11th Circuit, 1995; US District Court, ND of Illinois – General, 1980; US District Court, ND of Illinois – Trial Bar, 1991; US District Court, ED of Wisconsin, 1992; Illinois, 1978.

### CARPENTER, David
Sidley Austin LLP, Chicago
312 853 7237
dcarpenter@sidley.com
*Recommended in Telecom, Broadcast & Satellite*
**Practice Areas:** David W Carpenter has extensive experience litigating antitrust and regulatory issues in the telecommunications and energy industries before courts and regulatory commissions, and he specializes in handling appeals of these and other issues. He served as the principal appellate lawyer for AT&T Corp. on antitrust, regulatory, and other issues during the 20 years before it merged with SBC, and he has handled many appeals for other clients. Mr Carpenter has argued five cases in the US Supreme Court and has briefed over 20 additional cases that the Supreme Court decided on the merits. He also has argued over 60 cases in federal courts of appeals and state appellate courts, and briefed numerous other cases on appeal. He has briefed and argued many dispositive motions in federal district courts and state trial courts.
**Personal:** Boston University School of Law, JD, 1975; Yale University, BA, 1972. Served as law clerk to Associate Justice William J Brennan, Jr and to Judge Frank M Coffin of the US Court of Appeals for the First Circuit. Bar Admission: District of Columbia, 1980; Illinois, 1979; Massachusetts, 1975.

### CEDEROTH, Richard A
Sidley Austin LLP, Chicago
312 853 7026
rcederoth@sidley.com
*Recommended in Intellectual Property*
**Practice Areas:** Highly experienced Partner in all aspects of intellectual property, with a focus on litigated patent matters, primarily in the software, computer and semiconductor fields, and related counseling.
**Prof. Memberships:** Mr Cederoth is a Member of the Intellectual Property Section of the American Bar Association and the American Intellectual Property Law Association. He is also a Member of the Bradley University Electrical Engineering Alumni Advisory Board.
**Career:** Adjunct Professor, Patent Law, Northwestern University School of Law.
**Personal:** Mr Cederoth is admitted in several federal courts and registered to practice before the US Patent and Trademark Office and US District Court, ND

of Illinois – General, 1984. He has lectured about patent protection for computer software and intellectual property from the practicing engineer's perspective. University of Illinois College of Law (JD, 1983). Bradley University (BS in Electrical Engineering, 1980). Admission: Illinois, 1983.

### CHEFITZ, Joel
Howrey LLP, Chicago
312 595 1239
*Recommended in Antitrust*

### CHILDS, Linton J
Sidley Austin LLP, Chicago
312 853 2211
lchilds@sidley.com
*Recommended in Litigation*
**Practice Areas:** Partner in the firm's Chicago office. Mr Childs represents accounting firms, underwriters, and other defendants in federal securities class actions and in securities litigation brought by individual shareholders. He has represented accounting firms and other defendants in professional liability and commercial litigation matters, including numerous arbitrations. He has also represented clients in connection with a number of investigations conducted by the SEC's Division of Enforcement. Before joining the firm, he clerked for Judge David A Nelson of the United States Court of Appeals for the Sixth Circuit.
**Prof. Memberships:** Board of Directors of the Chicago Lawyers' Committee for Civil Rights Under Law (Chairman, 2005); American Bar Association; Chicago Bar Association; Chicago Council of Lawyers.
**Personal:** Harvard Law School (JD, 1988, cum laude), Harvard University (AB, 1984, cum laude, Phi Beta Kappa). Admissions: US Supreme Court; US Court of Appeals, 5th Circuit, 6th Circuit, 7th Circuit; US District Court, ND of Illinois – General; US District Court, ND of Illinois – Trial Bar; Illinois, 1988.

### CHOI, Paul
Sidley Austin LLP, Chicago
312 853 2145
pchoi@sidley.com
*Recommended in Corporate/M&A*
**Practice Areas:** Practice focuses on mergers and acquisitions, dispositions, spin-offs and joint ventures, and he counsels clients on takeover defense and proxy contests. He advised First Data Corporation on its $7 billion acquisition of Concord EFS, Inc., advised Barrett Resources in its response to a hostile takeover attempt and in its agreement to merge with The Williams Companies for $2.8 billion, led the representation of KPMG LLP's spin-off of its management and consulting business and represented Conseco, Inc. in its $7.6 billion acquisition of Green Tree Financial Corporation. Mr Choi represents issuers and underwriters on private and public offer-

ings, including IPO's, and subsidiary or 'carve-out' offerings.
**Prof. Memberships:** Board of Directors of the Harvard Club of Chicago, the Chicago Committee of the Chicago Council on Foreign Relations, the American Bar Association, the Illinois Bar Association and the Chicago Bar Association.
**Personal:** Served as a law clerk to the Honorable Laurence H Silberman on the United States Court of Appeals for the DC Circuit from 1989-90. Harvard Law School (JD, 1989). Harvard University (AB, 1986). Admission: Illinois, 1989.

### CICERO JR, Frank
Kirkland & Ellis LLP, Chicago
312 861 2216
fcicero@kirkland.com
*Recommended in Litigation*
**Practice Areas:** Extensive experience in a wide variety of litigation matters. Areas of practice include professional malpractice, admiralty and maritime, antitrust and trade regulation, criminal and civil fraud and securities law, trademark and patent claims, commercial contracts, construction litigation, libel, slander, and First Amendment cases, tax disputes, trade secrets, unfair competition, employment contracts, pollution and toxic substance cases, international arbitrations and litigation, dealer and franchise relationships and terminations, trust, estates and ERISA disputes, divorce and domestic relations law, product liability and warranty claims.
**Personal:** Amherst College, 1953-54. Wheaton College, AB, 1957. Princeton University, MPA, 1962. University of Chicago, JD, 1965.

### CLARK, James
Sidley Austin LLP, Chicago
312 853 7776
jclark@sidley.com
*Recommended in Banking & Finance*
**Practice Areas:** Practice focuses on commercial and banking law and he represents clients in a broad range of financing and lending transactions. He is a Co-Chair of the firm's Professional Responsibility Committee.
**Prof. Memberships:** Mr Clark is a Member of the American, Chicago and Illinois State Bar Associations and a former Chairman of the Acquisition Financing Subcommittee of the Commercial Financial Services Committee of the American Bar Association Business Law Section.
**Publications:** Mr Clark is a Member of the Board of Editors of The Bankruptcy Strategist; co-author of 'Legal Developments in Secured Financing' (1978-94).
**Personal:** University of Chicago (JD, 1976); Brown University (AB, 1970).

### COLE, Alexandra
Perkins Coie LLP, Chicago
312 324 8400
*Recommended in Construction*

### COLE, Thomas A
Sidley Austin LLP, Chicago
312 853 7473
tcole@sidley.com
*Recommended in Corporate/M&A*
**Practice Areas:** Chairman of the firm's Executive Committee and is a Member of its Management Committee. Practices M&A and Corporate Governance transactions. Involved in dozens of public company mergers, including the following, each valued at more than $1 billion: Exelon/PSEG (currently the largest utility merger); Alberto-Culver/Regis (pending); Tellabs/AFC; IMC/Cargill; Williams/Barrett (including the successful defense against Shell); Kimberly-Clark/Scott Paper; Monsanto/DeKalb Genetics; Jefferson Smurfit/Stone Container; Interpublic Group/True North; Wolters Kluwer/CCH; Fred Meyer/QFC; Aon/Alexander & Alexander; IMC Global/Vigoro; Tribune/Renaissance Communications; and LBOs of Northwest Industries and Ohio Mattress. Other significant public company merger transactions include Lyphomed/Fujisawa, Unilever/Helene Curtis, Mercantile/Mark Twain, True North/Bozell (including the successful defense against Publicis), Humana/Emphesys, GE Medical/Marquette and Berisford/Scotsman. Corporate governance assignments have included acting as special counsel to the Boards of Prudential Insurance, Zenith Electronics and other public companies, as well as frequent assignments for audit committees and special transaction, litigation and investigation committees.
**Prof. Memberships:** Member of The American Law Institute; The Economic Club of Chicago; The Commercial Club of Chicago; Board of The University of Chicago; Board of Northwestern Memorial Hospital; the Legal Advisory Committee to the Board of the New York Stock Exchange; Fellow of the American Bar Foundation.
**Personal:** Served on the faculties of the Kellogg Corporate Governance Conference of Northwestern University (NU), the Director's College of The University of Chicago's Graduate School of Business, Tulane Corporate Law Institute, NU's Garrett Securities Law Institute and the Securities Regulation Institute. Mr Cole taught corporate governance at the University of Chicago Law School. University of Chicago Law School (JD, 1975). Johns Hopkins University (AB, 1970). Admission: Illinois, 1975.

### CONLAN, James F
Sidley Austin LLP, Chicago
312 853 6890
jconlan@sidley.com
*Recommended in Bankruptcy*
**Practice Areas:** Partner and Vice - Chairman of the Corporate Reorganization and Bankruptcy Group. Member of the firm's Executive Committee and

Chairman of the Chicago Accounting and Finance Committee. Representative (public) engagements include: Budget Rent A Car Corporation (client, Debtor); Meridian Automotive Systems (client, Debtor); Owens Corning (client, Debtor); Federal-Mogul Corporation, T&N Limited, et al (client, Debtors); Pliant Corporation (client, Debtor); Pegasus Satellite Television (client, Debtor); Dow Corning Corporation (client, Baxter International, Inc., creditor and co-defendant); Florida Coast Paper Company (client, 50% Equity Holder); Pocket Communications, General Wireless, and Nextwave Personal Communications (client, Federal Communications Commission).
**Prof. Memberships:** Director, Heartland Financial USA (Nasdaq: HTLF); Director, Dubuque Bank & Trust Company (Member of Executive Committee and Loan Committee); Director, Citizens Finance; Director, DB&T Insurance.
**Publications:** Lecturer, Legacy Costs: Pension and Healthcare Liabilities', Milken Institute Global Conference 2005; lecturer, 'Cross-Border Insolvency', Insol (Cork, Ireland) 2003; lecturer, 'Bordering on Bankruptcy, Dealing with Troubled Companies in the New Economy', Fall 2001; lecturer, 'What You Need to Know About Internet, eCommerce and Chapter 11, Investment Opportunities In The Distressed Market', Spring 2000.
**Personal:** University of Iowa College of Law (JD, 1988). University of Iowa (BS, 1985). Admission: Illinois, 1988.

## CONLON, William
Sidley Austin LLP, Chicago
312 853 7384
wconlon@sidley.com
*Recommended in Litigation*
**Practice Areas:** Member of the firm's Executive Committee. Has extensive trial experience in commercial, financial, intellectual property, antitrust, and regulatory matters (including SEC and federal criminal). Representative cases have included antitrust, ERISA, securities laws, banking and bank regulatory issues, telecommunications, product liability, insurance and insurance regulatory issues, utilities law, and a variety of complex commercial individual and class action cases. As Assistant United States Attorney in Chicago, prior to joining Sidley, Mr Conlon handled criminal investigations and prosecutions as well as the trial and appeal of a wide variety of civil cases, including class actions. Mr Conlon also served as Chief of the Civil Division of the United States Attorney's Office.
**Prof. Memberships:** Mr Conlon was a Member and Chairman of the Illinois State Board of Ethics from 1982-88, served as Chairman of the Illinois Judicial Inquiry Board 1992-97 and is a Fellow of the American College of Trial Lawyers.
**Publications:** Has served as Adjunct

Professor at Northwestern University Law School since 1991 and has been a co-author of several articles.
**Personal:** University of Illinois College of Law, JD, 1970. Indiana University, AB, 1967. Admissions: Illinois, 1970; Iowa, 1970.

## CONNELLY, Vincent J
Mayer, Brown, Rowe & Maw LLP, Chicago 312 701 7912
vconnelly@mayerbrown.com
*Recommended in Litigation*
**Practice Areas:** Specialises in securities, antitrust, government contract and programme cases, RICO, commercial and financial fraud, and public corruption litigation. Primary trial responsibility in over 70 federal cases, with more than 60 jury trials. Civil litigation representations have included major corporations, corporate directors, and individuals in federal and state court trials, and corporate internal investigations.
**Prof. Memberships:** Member, American College of Trial Lawyers; Blue Ribbon Committee appointed by the Illinois Supreme Court to review the Attorney Registration and Disciplinary Commission. President, Chicago Inn of Court. Lecturer at Chicago Association of Commerce and Industry; Chicago Bar Association; Department of Justice Trial Advocacy Institute; FBI Training Academy; State Bar Antitrust Seminar.
**Career:** Joined Mayer, Brown, Rowe & Maw LLP, Chicago, 1987; became Partner, 1987. Formerly US Attorney's Office, Northern District of Illinois, 1975-87: Chief, Special Prosecutions Division, 1985-87; Chief, Criminal Division, 1983-85.
**Publications:** 'A Dozen Stops on the Grand Jury Road', Litigation. 'Undercover Work at the Exchanges', Chicago Tribune. 'Unconventional Strategies in White-Collar Criminal Investigations', Litigation.
**Personal:** University of Chicago Law School, JD, 1975. University of Notre Dame, BA, summa cum laude, 1972.

## CONWAY, Michael M
Foley & Lardner LLP, Chicago
312 832 4351
mconway@foley.com
*Recommended in Media & Entertainment*
**Career:** Michael M Conway is a Partner at Foley & Lardner LLP. He is the leader of the Chicago office's Litigation Department, former Chair of the firm's Media Law Group and a member of the firm's General Commercial Litigation and Appellate Practices and Entertainment and Media Industry Team. He focuses on media, commercial, corporate and federal tax litigation with a particular emphasis on emergency injunctive cases. Mr Conway is a graduate of Yale Law School (JD, 1973).

## CONWAY, Timothy R
Conway & Mrowiec, Chicago
312 658 1100
trc@cmcontractors.com
*Recommended in Construction*
**Practice Areas:** Construction law.
**Prof. Memberships:** Chicago and American (Member, Fidelity and Surety Law Committee) Bar Associations; Builders Association of Greater Chicago; Fox Valley General Contractors Association; Society of Illinois Construction Lawyers; Leading Lawyers Network.
**Publications:** Author, 'Mechanics Liens and Surety Bonds', Illinois Construction Law, Aspen, 2003. Co-author, 'Requirements for the Original Contractor's Lien on Private Projects', Illinois Institute of Continuing Education, 1994, 2000, 2004 eds.

## COSTELLO SLOVAK, Patricia
Schiff Hardin LLP, Chicago
312 258 5665
pslovak@schiffhardin.com
*Recommended in Employment*
**Practice Areas:** Labor and employment.
**Prof. Memberships:** National Retail Federation, American Bar Association (Chair Elect, Labor and Employment Law Section), Chicago Bar Association, College of Labor and Employment Lawyers, American Bar Foundation.
**Career:** Ms Slovak concentrates in labor and employment law for management. She has extensive experience representing management in all facets of labor and employment relationships. Fellow – College of Labor and Employment Lawyers, Fellow – American Bar Foundation.
**Publications:** Frequent author and lecturer on employment law issues, and has been an Editor of 'The Developing Labor Law'.
**Personal:** St Louis University (BA, 1973), University of Chicago (JD, 1977).

## COVEY, Tyson J
Mayer, Brown, Rowe & Maw LLP, Chicago 312 701 8600
jcovey@mayerbrownrowe.com
*Recommended in Telecom, Broadcast & Satellite*
**Practice Areas:** Specializes in regulated industries litigation and appeals on behalf of telecommunications companies in matters before regulatory agencies and courts. Recent experience includes unbundling disputes, UNE pricing cases, arbitrations, merger approvals, injunction proceedings, and state and federal appeals in several states throughout the country.
**Prof. Memberships:** Admitted in Illinois, 1991; US District Court for the Northern District of Illinois, 1992; US Court of Appeals for the Seventh Circuit, 1992; US Court of Appeals for the Sixth Circuit, 2000.
**Career:** Joined Mayer, Brown, Rowe &

Maw LLP 1996; became Partner 2000. Formerly with Sidley & Austin, Chicago, 1993-96. US Court of Appeals for the Seventh Circuit, Staff Attorney, 1991-93.
**Personal:** Born 1965. University of Illinois College of Law, JD, magna cum laude, 1991; Order of the Coif; Administrative Editor, University of Illinois Law Review. Augustana College, BA, magna cum laude, 1987; Phi Beta Kappa.

## CRAVEN, George W
Mayer, Brown, Rowe & Maw LLP, Chicago 312 701 7231
gcraven@mayerbrown.com
*Recommended in Tax*
**Practice Areas:** Leading authority on tax aspects of financial transactions, cross-border tax arbitrage, offshore insurance arrangements, and deductibility of alternative risk transfer payments, and structuring investments in India. Advises on acquisitions and dispositions of businesses, including structured financings as well as tax aspects of new financial products such as 'Section 483 Notes', and 'Liquid Yield Option Notes'. International tax planning expertise includes Subpart F issues, transactions designed to accelerate or create foreign source income, and redomestication of US insurance companies to foreign jurisdiction.
**Prof. Memberships:** Admitted to practice in Illinois, 1976, and US Tax Court, 1976. Member of the American Bar Association, Section of Taxation; Financial Transactions Committee.
**Career:** Joined Mayer, Brown, Rowe & Maw, LLP Chicago, in 1981 and became a Partner in 1983. Prior to that, had worked for Sidley & Austin, Chicago (1976-80) and Ogden, Robertson & Marshall, Louisville (1980-81).
**Publications:** Lectures widely on tax issues.
**Personal:** Born 11 March 1951. Earned JD, cum laude, from Harvard Law School in 1976 and BA summa cum laude, from the University of Notre Dame in 1973. Also studied at Sophia University, Tokyo (1970-71).

## CREMENT, Anthony
Franczek Sullivan, Chicago
312 986 0300
*Recommended in Employment*

## CROSS, Jeffery
Freeborn & Peters, Chicago
312 360 6000
*Recommended in Antitrust*

## CRUMBAUGH, David
Latham & Watkins LLP, Chicago
312 876 7700
*Recommended in Banking & Finance*

## CRYSTAL, Jules
Bryan Cave LLP, Chicago
312 602 5000
*Recommended in Employment*

**CULLEN, Gary P**
Skadden, Arps, Slate, Meagher & Flom
LLP & Affiliates, Chicago
312 407 0680
gcullen@skadden.com
*Recommended in Corporate/M&A*
**Practice Areas:** Represents Fortune 500,
middle market and emerging companies,
as well as investment banking and other
financial institutions, in a variety of M&A
and corporate finance transactions. Has
worked on behalf of buyers and sellers in
auctions involving public companies,
other stock and asset acquisitions and
dispositions, negotiated and contested
takeovers, proxy contests and joint ventures. Also represents issuers and investment banking institutions in initial and
other public offerings, private placements
of securities, and high-yield debt transactions. Advises on corporate governance
and disclosure issues.
**Career:** JD, Columbia University School
of Law, 1985; BA, University of Illinois,
1982.

**DASH, James**
Much Shelist Freed Denenberg Ament &
Rubenstein, P.C., Chicago
312 521 2000
*Recommended in Construction*

**DAVIS, Scott J**
Mayer, Brown, Rowe & Maw LLP,
Chicago 312 701 7311
sdavis@mayerbrownrowe.com
*Recommended in Corporate/M&A*
**Practice Areas:** Firm Practice Leader of
the Corporate and Securities Group.
Extensive experience in mergers and
acquisitions, corporate governance and
problems arising from real or perceived
conflict of interest between corporate
officers and shareholders. Representative
deals: representation of Chemtura in the
merger in which Great Lakes Chemical
became a subsidiary of Chemtura
(approximate value $1.8 billion as of the
date of announcement), representation
of Devon Energy in the merger in which
Ocean Energy became Devon's subsidiary
(approximate value US$3.1 billion as of
date of announcement), Devon in acquisition of Mitchell Energy and Development (approximate value US$3 billion as
of date of announcement), and Devon in
its acquisition of Anderson Exploration
(approximate value US$3.5 billion). Also
advises in litigation matters involving
derivative, takeover, and securities fraud
litigation.
**Prof. Memberships:** Vice President,
Chicago Police Board.
**Career:** Mayer, Brown, Rowe & Maw
LLP, 1977-present; Partner, 1983.
**Publications:** Author, 'Deal Protection
After Omnicare', 14 International Company and Commercial Law Review 311
(2003).
**Personal:** JD, Harvard University, 1976;
Member of the Board of Editors, Harvard

Law Review. BA, Yale University, 1972.

**DEBEERS, Kimberly A**
Skadden, Arps, Slate, Meagher & Flom
LLP & Affiliates, Chicago 312 407 0982
kdebeers@skadden.com
*Recommended in Corporate/M&A:
Private Equity*
**Practice Areas:** Concentrates practice
in mergers and acquisitions, corporate
and securities law. Regularly represents
private equity funds in aquisitions, dispositions and capital raising as well as companies receiving investments from private
equity funds or other sources. Representations have also included other public
and private acquisitions, debt restructuring and public capital raising representing both issuers and underwriters.
**Career:** JD, DePaul University College of
Law, 1995; BS, University of Illinois, 1990.

**DEJONG, Ralph E**
McDermott Will & Emery, Chicago
312 984 6918
rdejong@mwe.com
*Recommended in Healthcare*
**Practice Areas:** Particular focus on
compensation, executive benefits and
employee benefits of tax-exempt organizations, including designing and preparing deferred and incentive compensation
arrangements, leading governing boards
in independent review and approval of
executive and physician compensation
arrangements, negotiating and preparing
executive and physician employment and
severance agreements, and analyzing the
private inurement and intermediate
sanctions implications of executive and
physician compensation and benefit
arrangements. Practices in full range of
employee benefits issues for various
employers, focusing on analyzing and
minimizing fiduciary liability of employer plan sponsors.
**Personal:** University of Notre Dame Law
School (JD, magna cum laude); Calvin
College (BA).

**DEMARTE, Luke**
Michael Best & Friedrich LLP, Chicago
312 222 0800
*Recommended in Media &
Entertainment*

**DICKINSON, Christopher C**
Jenner & Block LLP, Chicago
312 923 2858
cdickinson@jenner.com
*Recommended in Insurance*
**Practice Areas:** Christopher C Dickinson is a Partner in Jenner & Block's
Chicago office. He is a Member of the
firm's Insurance Litigation and Counseling, and Litigation and Dispute Resolution Practices. Mr Dickinson represents
financial institutions and other corporate
policyholders pursuing insurance recovery for high-stakes claims in such areas as
professional liability, competitive injury,
consumer fraud, directors' and officers'

liability, intellectual property, fidelity and
financial fraud, employment practices
liability, fiduciary liability, catastrophic
bodily injury, product liability and environmental damage. Through litigation,
arbitration or negotiation he has recovered hundreds of millions of dollars for
his clients from virtually all of the major
insurers in the domestic, London and
Bermuda markets. Mr Dickinson also
counsels corporate policyholders on
claims review and management; insurance program design; crafting policy language; and insurer insolvencies. Mr Dickinson serves on the Board of Directors of
the Aids Legal Council of Chicago.
**Personal:** Mr Dickinson graduated with
distinction from the University of Wisconsin – Madison in 1982, and received
his Law Degree cum laude from the University of Wisconsin in 1988. He is admitted to practice in Illinois and Wisconsin,
and in several federal trial and appellate
courts, including the trial bar of the federal district court in Chicago.

**DIGIOVANNI, Nick**
Lord, Bissell & Brook, Chicago
312 443 0700
*Recommended in Insurance*

**DINARDO, Lawrence**
Jones Day, Chicago
312 269 4306
lcdinardo@jonesday.com
*Recommended in Employment*
**Practice Areas:** Particular emphasis on
employment discrimination litigation,
FLSA/wage-hour cases, employee benefits, and executive employment contract
disputes. Extensive experience defending
employers in class actions and individual
cases and representing employers before
the NLRB and labor arbitrations and
negotiations. He has tried more than 35
cases to verdict before juries around the
US and handled an equal number of
cases before federal and state appellate
courts.
**Publications:** Served as a visiting professor of law at Notre Dame Law School and
as a guest lecturer at DePaul University
College of Law. He has published in the
Journal of College and University Law.

**DOCKSEY, Ross**
Sonnenschein Nath & Rosenthal LLP,
Chicago 312 876 8171
jdocksey@sonnenschein.com
*Recommended in Business Process
Outsourcing, Technology*
**Practice Areas:** Partner focusing on
domestic, cross-border and global outsourcing of business functions, including
finance and administration, human
resources, supply chain management,
learning and education, information
technology and services; technology contracting; joint ventures and alliances; and
mergers and acquisitions.
**Prof. Memberships:** Speaks at legal and
outsourcing conferences, including those

by Sourcing Interests Group, Conference
Board, Bureau of National Affairs, Practicing Law Institute, Mealey's Seminars
and Michael Corbett & Associates.
Human Resources Outsourcing Association member. Listed by HRO Today and
FAO Today as a top five US outsourcing
lawyer.
**Personal:** University of Minnesota JD
cum laude. US Military Academy BS.

**DOETSCH, Douglas A**
Mayer, Brown, Rowe & Maw LLP,
Chicago 312 701 7973
ddoetsch@mayerbrownrowe.com
*Recommended in Banking & Finance*
**Practice Areas:** Chicago Office Practice
Leader in Banking and Finance. Partner
in International Corporate and Finance
Practice. Advises on lending for leveraged
buyouts, workouts and project financings, particularly in cross-border transactions. Represents clients in cross-border
securitisation transactions, particularly
future cash flow securitisations, debt
restructuring and debt exchange offers.
Counsels on asset and stock acquisitions
and contract negotiations; joint ventures
emphasising cross-border ventures in
Latin America; Euro-securities offerings,
particularly for emerging market companies, and US equity offerings of foreign
issuers.
**Prof. Memberships:** Director, Chicago
Council on Foreign Relations; Director,
Mid-America Chapter of US-Mexico
Chamber of Commerce.
**Career:** Joined Mayer, Brown, Rowe &
Maw LLP in 1988 and became a Partner
in 1995. Prior to that, worked for Cleary,
Gottlieb, Steen & Hamilton, New York
(1986-88) and, before that, worked as a
Consultant for Data Resources, Inc.
(1979-82).
**Publications:** Frequently writes and
speaks on securitisations by emerging
market issuers, debt restructuring, inter-
national joint ventures, and issuances of
debt securities in the Euro-markets.
**Personal:** JD, Columbia University, 1986;
Editor-in-Chief, Columbia Journal of
Transnational Law. Rotary Graduate Fellow at Universite de Dakar, Dakar, Senegal (1982-83). BA, magna cum laude,
Kalamazoo College (1979); Phi Beta
Kappa. Fluent in French and Spanish.

**DOLIN, Kenneth**
Seyfarth Shaw LLP, Chicago
312 346 8000
*Recommended in Employment*

**DONOVAN, Joseph**
Kelley Drye & Warren, Chicago
312 857 7070
*Recommended in Telecom, Broadcast
& Satellite*

**DORAN, James**
Latham & Watkins LLP, Chicago
312 876 7700
*Recommended in Banking & Finance*

## DOUGLAS, Charles W
Sidley Austin LLP, Chicago
312 853 7706
cdouglas@sidley.com
*Recommended in Litigation*
**Practice Areas:** Partner in the firm's
Chicago office, Member of the firm's
Executive Committee and Member of its
Management Committee. Served as
Chairman of the firm's Management
Committee since 1999. Mr Douglas has
extensive litigation experience in major
antitrust, trade regulation, securities,
product liability and commercial litigation. He recently tried and won a major
securities case for the accounting firm of
Deloitte & Touche, LLP. He also tried a
major securities class action before a jury
in Trenton, New Jersey, in which the
plaintiff sought billions of dollars in
damages but which resulted in a favorable settlement for AT&T Corp. after
three weeks of trial. He lead the successful
defense of G.D. Searle & Co. (now a part
of Pfizer) in an antitrust class action seeking billions of dollars in damages. Following 10 weeks of trial, and before Searle
even had to put on a defense, the Judge
directed a verdict for the defendants. He
also successfully defended AT&T in two
major trials, including one where the
plaintiffs were awarded nothing on their
claims and instead AT&T was awarded
$26 million on its counterclaims against
the plaintiffs. His trial work for AT&T has
spanned two decades, dating back to the
representation of AT&T and the Regional
Bell Operating Companies in various
antitrust actions, including the 1985
damages retrial of MCI's claims in which
MCI received less than one per cent of
the claimed damages. Mr Douglas has
been trial counsel for several of the firm's
clients in a wide range of cases. He successfully tried and won a major case for
IBP, inc. brought by the United States
Department of Agriculture and involving
a novel application of the Packers &
Stockyards Act which would have had
far-reaching consequences for the entire
meat-packing industry.
**Prof. Memberships:** American Bar
Association, Illinois Bar Association,
Chicago Bar Association.
**Personal:** Harvard Law School (JD,
1974); Northwestern University (BA,
1970). Admission: Illinois, 1974.

## DOW, Robert M
Mayer, Brown & Maw LLP,
Chicago 312 701 8441
rdow@mayerbrown.com
*Recommended in Telecom, Broadcast
& Satellite*
**Practice Areas:** General and appellate
litigation, with particular emphasis on
telecommunications, state and federal
constitutional law, jurisdiction, civil procedure, preemption, mass tort and products liability, admissibility of expert testimony and class actions.

**Prof. Memberships:** Admitted: State of
Illinois; United States District Court for
the Northern District of Illinois; United
States Court of Appeals for the Fourth,
Fifth, Sixth, Seventh, Ninth, and Eleventh
Circuits; Supreme Court of the United
States.
**Career:** Mayer, Brown, Rowe & Maw
LLP, Chicago, 1995 to date. Law clerk to
The Honorable Joel M Flaum, US Court
of Appeals for the Seventh Circuit, 1993-
94. Teaching Fellow, Harvard College,
1992.
**Publications:** JE Muench & RM Dow, Jr,
'Invalidation of Ohio Tort Reform Legis-
lation', 2000 International Journal of
Insurance Law 85-88 (January 2000); JC
Schroeder & RM Dow, Jr, 'Arguing for
Changes in the Law', 25(2) Litigation 37-
41, 67-68 (Winter 1999).
**Personal:** University of Oxford, DPhil in
International Relations, 1997. Harvard
Law School, JD cum laude, 1993; Super-
vising Editor, Harvard Journal on Legisla-
tion; Editorial Board, Harvard Human
Rights Journal. University of Oxford,
MPhil in International Relations, 1990;
Rhodes Scholar. Yale College, BA summa
cum laude with distinction, 1987; Phi
Beta Kappa.

## DRANOFF, David
Goldberg, Kohn, Bell, Black, Rosenbloom & Moritz, Ltd, Chicago
312 201 4000
*Recommended in Banking & Finance*

## DUBE, Monte I
McDermott Will & Emery, Chicago
312 984 7549
mdube@mwe.com
*Recommended in Healthcare*
**Practice Areas:** Head of Health Department. Represents hospitals and health
systems nationwide and has served as
counsel in the sale, merger, affiliation and
acquisition of hundreds of hospitals and
academic medical centers, hospital
restructurings, public hospital privatizations, joint ventures, certificate of need
and reimbursement litigation, and hospital and medical staff operational legal
issues of all types. Advises boards on
proper exercise of their fiduciary duties.
**Career:** Regularly lectures and publishes
on hospital-physician relations, hospital
merger and affiliation transactions, fiduciary duties of not-for-profit trustees and
rural healthcare issues.
**Personal:** Benjamin N Cardozo School
of Law (JD); Boston University (AB).

## DUNCAN, Margaret M
McDermott Will & Emery, Chicago
312 984 6476
mduncan@mwe.com
*Recommended in Intellectual Property*
**Practice Areas:** Head of Chicago Intellectual Property Practice. Focuses on IP
litigation, counseling, protection and
transactions. Lead Counsel in federal district courts in patent, trademark, copy-

right, unfair competition, right of publicity, domain name and trade secret cases.
Represents clients in complex technology
areas including chemical formulations,
electronic circuitry, methods for conducting financial transactions and computer programs.
**Career:** Admitted to US District Courts
in Illinois and Wisconsin; US Court of
Appeals, Seventh Circuit; US Court of
Appeals for Federal Circuit and US Patent
and Trademark Office.
**Personal:** Loyola University of Chicago
School of Law (JD); Xavier University
(BS); Indiana University (BS).

## DURCHSLAG, Stephen
Winston & Strawn LLP, Chicago
312 558 5600
*Recommended in Media &
Entertainment*

## DURKIN, Thomas M
Mayer, Brown, Rowe & Maw LLP,
Chicago 312 701 7997
tdurkin@mayerbrownrowe.com
*Recommended in Litigation*
**Practice Areas:** Specializes in complex
civil litigation (including product liability
and patent matters) and criminal
defense. Tried approximately 50 federal
jury trials to verdict.
**Prof. Memberships:** Fellow, American
College of Trial Lawyers. Chicago Board
Options Exchange, Nominating Com-
mittee, 2004-present. DePaul Law School,
Adjunct Professor, Advanced Criminal
Procedure, 1996; 1998. John Marshall
Law School, Adjunct Professor, Trial
Advocacy, 1988-91. Chicago Bar Associa-
tion Judicial Evaluation Committee,
1993-95. Merit Selection Panel for US
Magistrate, Northern District of Illinois,
1994. Assisted Special Counsel Nicholas
Bua, Inslaw Investigation, 1991-92.
**Career:** Joined Mayer, Brown, Rowe &
Maw LLP as Partner, 1993. Assistant US
Attorney, Northern District of Illinois,
1980-93. First Assistant US Attorney,
1990-93. Law clerk to Honorable Stanley
J Roszkowski, Northern District of Illi-
nois, 1979-80.
**Publications:** 'Doing the Right Thing'
(Foreign Corrupt Practices Act), Infra-
structure Finance, September 1996.
Speaker at seminars on Foreign Corrupt
Practices Act. Lecturer, Department of
Justice Trial Advocacy Institute and FBI
Training Academy in Quantico, Virginia.
**Personal:** DePaul University College of
Law, JD with honors, 1978; Illinois Law
Issue Editor, Law Review. University of
Illinois, BS with honors, 1975. Certified
Public Accountant, Illinois, 1975. Excel-
lence in Law Enforcement Award,
Chicagoland Chamber of Commerce,
1993. US Attorney General's John Mar-
shall Award, 1991.

## EATON, David L
Kirkland & Ellis LLP, Chicago
312 861 2066
deaton@kirkland.com
*Recommended in Bankruptcy*
**Practice Areas:** David Eaton concentrates his practice in the representation of
debtors, financial institutions, unsecured
creditors and committees, in domestic
and multinational workout and bankruptcy planning, negotiation and litigation. He also represents purchasers of
financially troubled companies. Mr
Eaton has advised clients including
Collins & Aikman Corp., Harnischfeger
Industries Inc., Federal Communications
Commission, Bank of America, Credit
Suisse First Boston, PPM America, Oaktree Capital, Keystone Consolidated
Industries, Inc., LA Gear, Inc., and Highland Superstores, Inc., among others.
**Personal:** University of Michigan, BA,
1974; University of Illinois College of
Law, JD, 1978.

## EDWARDS, Charles L
DLA Piper Rudnick Gray Cary US LLP,
Chicago 312 368 4010
charles.edwards@dlapiper.com
*Recommended in Real Estate*
**Practice Areas:** Real estate; real estate
finance.
**Prof. Memberships:** Past Chair Chicago
Bar Association Real Property Law Committee and its Real Property Finance Subcommittee, Member of American College
of Real Estate Lawyers and American
College of Mortgage Attorneys.
**Career:** Practice concentrated exclusively
in complex commercial real estate transactions, including purchase and sale;
mortgage financing; leasing; joint ventures and partnerships; condominiums
and cooperatives; general development
and all other aspects of commercial real
estate practice. He is also an adjunct professor and frequently lectures on real
estate finance and leasing subjects.
**Personal:** JD, University of Chicago;
BBA, University of Wisconsin.

## EGGERT, Russell R
Mayer, Brown, Rowe & Maw LLP,
Chicago 312 701 7350
reggert@mayerbrownrowe.com
*Recommended in Environment*
**Practice Areas:** Specializes in trials and
appeals of complex regulatory and environmental tort litigation, and counseling
on environmental compliance. Experienced in responding to environmental
crisis or emergency situations and counseling and strategic management of environmental issues. Tried over 50 environmental cases and argued over 40 appeals
in state and federal courts and administrative agencies.
**Prof. Memberships:** American Bar
Association, Sections on Natural
Resources Law and Litigation.
**Career:** Joined Mayer, Brown, Rowe &

Maw LLP, Chicago, 1987; became Partner 1987. Former Chief (1983-87) and Deputy Chief (1974-79), Environmental Division and Legal Counsel to the Attorney General of Illinois, Chicago. O'Conor, Karaganis & Gail Ltd., Chicago, 1979-83. Graduate Research Associate in Environmental Law, University of Illinois College of Law, 1973-74.
**Personal:** University of Illinois, JD, 1973; University of Illinois, AB, 1970.

## EIMER, Nathan P
Eimer Stahl Klevorn & Solberg LLP, Chicago 312 660 7601
neimer@eimerstahl.com
*Recommended in Antitrust*
**Practice Areas:** Antitrust trial lawyer and counselor. He has handled a large number of grand jury investigations of alleged price fixing, including related criminal proceedings and trial. He has also been involved as trial counsel in numerous civil antitrust cases, particularly class actions related to alleged price fixing. His practice also includes counseling clients regarding the antitrust aspects of mergers and acquisitions, and representation of clients before the Federal Trade Commission, the United States Department of Justice, and in related civil proceedings attempting to enjoin a merger. He has represented a large number of major corporations in antitrust matters, including Union Carbide Corporation, CITGO Petroleum Corporation, Kimberly-Clark Corporation, Borden, Inc., CPC, Inc., International Minerals & Chemicals Corporation, Praxair, Inc., Land O'Lakes Inc., and Corn Products International.
**Prof. Memberships:** Antitrust and Criminal Sections of the American Bar Association.
**Career:** He was one of the founding members of his firm in July 2000. Prior to that he was a member of the Executive Committee, General Counsel, Head of the Commercial and Regulatory Litigation Group, and a Partner of Sidley & Austin. From 1984 until 1990 he was the Head of that firm's New York Litigation Practice.
**Personal:** Born June 26, 1949. Received his JD, cum laude, from Northwestern Universtiy School of Law in 1973, where he was a notes and comments eeditor for the Law Review. Received a BA, magna cum laude, with highest distinction in Economics, from the University of Illinois in 1970.

## EISNER, Rebecca S
Mayer, Brown, Rowe & Maw LLP, Chicago 312 701 8577
reisner@mayerbrownrowe.com
*Recommended in Business Process Outsourcing, Technology*
**Practice Areas:** Specializes in complex global and offshore technology and business process outsourcing transactions, including IT infrastructure, applications

development and maintenance, back office processing, ERP implementations, finance and accounting, payroll processing, call center, HR, technology development, system integration and hosting. Also advises clients in services agreements, strategic alliances, joint ventures, licensing, development and telecommunications agreements, and internet and e-commerce law issues, including data transfer and privacy issues and electronic contracting and signatures.
**Career:** Joined Mayer, Brown, Rowe & Maw LLP, 1989-92; returned, 1996; Partner, 2000. Former Associate Group Counsel and Assistant Vice President, Equifax, Inc., Atlanta, 1993-95. Public Relations and Government Affairs Specialist, The Dow Chemical Company, Midland, Michigan, 1984-86.
**Publications:** Offshore BPO Conference NYC: 'Privacy Issues in BPO'. 'Avoiding Gotchas in Outsourcing', Illinois Institute of Continuing Legal Education, September 2002. 'Making a Good Match: Strategic Alliances In Technology and E-Commerce', i-Street, May 2002. 'Focus on Legal: Smoothing Over the Privacy Potholes in BPO Outsourcing', BPO Outsourcing Journal, March 2002. 'Ignorance Isn't Bliss: What You Need To Know About EU Data Privacy Law', CIO Magazine, February 2002.
**Personal:** University of Michigan Law School, JD cum laude, 1989; Michigan Journal of Law Reform. Ohio State University, BA, cum laude, 1984.

## EMERSON, Carter W
Kirkland & Ellis LLP, Chicago 312 861 2052
cemerson@kirkland.com
*Recommended in Corporate/M&A*
**Practice Areas:** Carter Emerson has extensive experience in counseling public and private corporations on a wide variety of subjects including corporate governance and SEC disclosure matters, securities filings and executive compensation. He also has public offering experience, including 12 initial public offerings (IPOs) for issuers and three for underwriters and many Rule 144A debt offerings. His other principal aspects of practice are corporate transactions such as mergers and acquisitions (including leveraged buyouts), public offerings, debt placements and loans, and venture capital investments.
**Personal:** Miami University (Ohio), BS, 1969. Northwestern University, JD, 1972.

## ERF, Stephen
McDermott Will & Emery, Chicago 312 984 7637
serf@mwe.com
*Recommended in Employment*
**Practice Areas:** Partner in Labor and Employment Group. Concentrates on civil rights and labor/employment counseling and litigation, union organizing,

collective bargaining, arbitration, employment discrimination, wrongful discharge, wage and hour and public accommodations. Has worked with clients in a wide range of industries, including energy, healthcare, education, construction, manufacturing, logistics and distribution, finance, service, food, social service, chemical and transportation.
**Personal:** Loyola University of Chicago School of Law (JD, cum laude); University of Illinois (BA).

## ETTELSON, Bruce
Kirkland & Ellis LLP, Chicago 312 861 2326
bettelson@kirkland.com
*Recommended in Corporate/M&A: Private Fund Formation*
**Practice Areas:** Mr Ettelson's practice focuses on private equity fund formations, private equity and venture capital investments, leveraged buyouts, recapitalisations, mergers and acquisitions and general corporate counseling, with an emphasis on structuring and forming premier private equity funds with commercial and investment banks. He has represented private equity firms in the formation of more than 100 private equity funds.
**Prof. Memberships:** United Jewish Communities Young Leadership Cabinet; Midwest Regional Advisory Board of the University of Pennsylvania; Mount Sinai Medical Institute Council.
**Personal:** University of Chicago (JD, 1989); Wharton School of the University of Pennsylvania (BS, 1986).

## EVANICH, Kevin R
Kirkland & Ellis LLP, Chicago 312 861 2076
kevanich@kirkland.com
*Recommended in Corporate/M&A, Corporate/M&A: Private Equity*
**Practice Areas:** Senior member of Kirkland & Ellis Corporate Group, concentrating in mergers and acquisitions, leveraged buyouts and private equity fund formations. Responsible for structuring, supervising and closing numerous leveraged buyouts and a variety of buyout, venture capital and mezzanine funds. Represents gatekeepers and other major investors in fund investments. Lead Counsel in representation of numerous portfolio companies of private equity funds. Member of firm Management Committee.
**Personal:** University of Wisconsin – Milwaukee, BA, 1976; Northwestern University School of Law, JD, 1980.

## FAHEY, Thomas
Ungaretti & Harris, Chicago 312 977 4400
*Recommended in Healthcare*

## FALK, R Scott
Kirkland & Ellis LLP, Chicago 312 861 2340
sfalk@kirkland.com
*Recommended in Corporate/M&A*
**Practice Areas:** Scott Falk focuses primarily on mergers and acquisitions and securities offerings for public company clients. His broad base of experience includes negotiated mergers, tender and exchange offers, acquisitions and divestitures of subsidiaries and divisions of public companies, private placements and public offerings of securities and securities law counseling. Mr Falk has also structured and negotiated numerous cross-border investments and acquisitions, both inbound and outbound.
**Prof. Memberships:** Member, American Bar Association Section of Business Law.
**Personal:** Harvard University, AB, 1985; Harvard Law School, JD, 1989.

## FEINSTEIN, Fred I
McDermott Will & Emery, Chicago 312 984 7665
ffeinstein@mwe.com
*Recommended in Real Estate*
**Practice Areas:** General transactional and litigation practice with particular emphasis in real estate development, annexation, zoning, environmental and all related facets of acquisition, leasing, financing, bankruptcy and restructuring.
**Prof. Memberships:** Chicago Magazine, Illinois Super Lawyers, Top 10 Regardless of Speciality, 2006. Member American College of Real Estate Lawyers, Illinois State Bar Association, Real Property Section, 1977-83 (Vice Chairman and Chairman, 1980-82) and Legislative Committee, 1984 to present; Lambda Alpha, Beta Gamma Sigma, Beta Alpha Psi, Pi Gamma Mu, Blue Key, Lex Legio, International Association of Attorneys in Corporate Real Estate; Associate Member, American Land Title Association, and Urban Land Institute.

## FELDMAN, Mark I
DLA Piper Rudnick Gray Cary US LLP, Chicago 312 368 7084
mark.feldman@dlapiper.com
*Recommended in Intellectual Property*
**Practice Areas:** Intellectual property; trademark; trademark litigation; domain name; copyrights; M&A.
**Career:** Focusing on trademarks, patents, copyrights, trade secrets, and internet and technology law, he has extensive experience counseling clients on domestic and international intellectual property registration, enforcement, and licensing. He has litigated the protectability of color as a trademark; the enhanced scope of protection for famous trademarks; trademark priority disputes; and protection of the interior design and exterior trade dress of franchised restaurants.
**Personal:** JD, Georgetown University

Law Center; BSIE, University of Illinois at Urbana-Champaign.

## FERGUSON, James R
Mayer, Brown, Rowe & Maw LLP, Chicago 312 701 7282
jferguson@mayerbrownrowe.com
*Recommended in Litigation*

**Practice Areas:** Lead Counsel for major corporations in: all phases of patent, trademark, trade secret and related litigation in the pharmaceutical, medical, diagnostic, healthcare, financial, electronic, textile and food industries; broad range of commercial and white-collar criminal litigation, including healthcare, antitrust, securities, environmental, employment, insurance, tax, civil fraud, RICO, real estate, franchise and breach of contract cases. Tried more than 30 jury trials to verdict; argued more than 35 appeals; conducted numerous corporate internal investigations.
**Career:** Mayer, Brown, Rowe & Maw LLP, Chicago, 2002 to present. Sonnenschein Nath & Rosenthal, 1989-2002. Assistant US Attorney, Northern District of Illinois, 1979-89. Law clerk to The Honorable William J Bauer in the US Court of Appeals, Seventh Circuit, 1977-79.
**Publications:** 'Strengthening Pharmaceutical and Biotechnology Patents', Genetic News (March 1, 2005); 'Clinical Trials As Inside Information', New York Times (Oct 19, 1997). 'Biomedical Research and Insider Trading', New England Journal of Medicine (Aug 28, 1997).
**Personal:** JD, Northwestern University School of Law, 1976; Articles Editor, Law Review. BA, MA, Indiana University, 1972; Director's Award for Superior Performance, Department of Justice; Adjunct Professor, Northwestern Medical School and Law School.

## FERRAZZANO, Dennis
Barack Ferrazzano Kirschbaum Perlman & Nagelberg, Chicago 312 984 3100
*Recommended in Real Estate*

## FIFER, Sam
Sonnenschein Nath & Rosenthal LLP, Chicago 312 876 8000
sfifer@sonnenschein.com
*Recommended in Media & Entertainment*

**Practice Areas:** Intellectual Property and Technology (IP&T), former Group Chair. Experience in obtaining licensing and transferring rights in IP&T, entertainment production and distribution, music, publishing, talent agreements, advertising and promotion law; precedent-setting litigation in defamation, privacy and publicity rights, court access, reporters' rights and subpoena defense. Chair, Firm Ethics Committee.
**Prof. Memberships:** Forum Committee on Communications Law – ABA; INTA; Copyright Society of the United States; Chicago and Illinois Bar Associations;

Media Law Resource Center – Defense Counsel Section; Co-Chair, Pre-Publication Committee; Adjunct Professor, Northwestern University Law School.
**Personal:** DePaul University, JD cum laude; Northwestern University, BS Speech.

## FINKE, Robert F
Mayer, Brown, Rowe & Maw LLP, Chicago 312 701 7110
rfinke@mayerbrownrowe.com
*Recommended in Antitrust*

**Practice Areas:** Specializes in civil, criminal, and antitrust litigation. Represents automotive, chemical, and manufacturing companies in toxic tort, mass disaster, or product liability litigation. Represents financing and financial institutions in general commercial contract and business litigation. Experienced in complex litigation, the proper use of outside counsel and alternative dispute resolution. Counsels on antitrust aspects of acquisitions and mergers, workouts and restructures, distribution, pricing, employee confidentiality, trade secret, and non-competition agreements.
**Prof. Memberships:** American Bar Association, Vice-Chairman, 1976, Council, 1971-75, Section of Legal Education and Admissions to the Bar; Member, Sections of Business, Antitrust, and Litigation; Committee on Corporate Counsel. Economic Club of Chicago. Lawyers Club of Chicago. University Club of Chicago.
**Career:** Joined Mayer, Brown, Rowe & Maw LLP, 1967; became Partner, 1973. Law clerk to The Honorable Richard B Austin, United States District Court for the Northern District of Illinois, 1966-67.
**Publications:** 'Using Expert Testimony in Lender Liability Litigation', The Practical Lawyer, July 1990.
**Personal:** Harvard University, JD, 1966. University of Michigan, AB with distinction and high honors, 1963. Trustee, Rush University Medical Center. President, Lyric Opera Guild Board. Member, Lyric Opera of Chicago Board, ex officio. Director, Chicago Botanic Garden.

## FINNEGAN, Sheila M
Mayer, Brown, Rowe & Maw LLP, Chicago 312 701 8943
sfinnegan@mayerbrown.com
*Recommended in Litigation*

**Practice Areas:** Former federal prosecutor. Extensive trial experience, including over 30 jury trials in federal and state courts. Has conducted numerous corporate internal investigations, and represented corporations and individuals before the SEC, Department of Justice, and State Law Enforcement Agencies in connection with civil and criminal allegations of securities fraud, healthcare fraud, and other wrongdoing. She also has represented major corporations in complex civil litigation, including class actions

alleging product defects, securities fraud, and consumer fraud.
**Career:** Mayer, Brown, Rowe & Maw LLP, Chicago, 2000 to date. Co-Chair of the White-Collar Defense and Corporate Compliance Group. US Attorney's Office for the Northern District of Illinois, 1987-2000: Chief, Criminal Division, 1999-2000; Health Care Fraud Coordinator and Deputy Chief, Special Prosecutions, 1996-99. Law clerk to The Honorable Milton I Shadur, US District Court for the Northern District of Illinois, 1986-87.
**Publications:** 'The First 72 Hours of a Government Investigation: A Guide to Identifying Issues and Avoiding Mistakes' (February 2006, National Legal Center for the Public Interest).
**Personal:** JD, University of Chicago, 1986; Order of the Coif; Member, Law Review. BSFS, Georgetown University, School of Foreign Service, 1982. Adjunct Professor of Trial Advocacy at Northwestern University Law School.

## FISHMAN, Michael T
Greenberg Traurig LLP, Chicago 312 476 5075
fishmanm@gtlaw.com
*Recommended in Real Estate*

**Practice Areas:** Real estate.
**Prof. Memberships:** Member, Urban Land Institute.
**Career:** Listed, Chambers & Partners USA Guide, an annual listing of the leading business lawyers and law firms in the world, 2005-06 edition.
**Publications:** Frequent Lecturer at Urban Land Institute Conferences on Mexican Real Estate.
**Personal:** JD, Cleveland-Marshall College of Law at Cleveland State University, 1995. BA, The Ohio State University, 1991.

## FISHMAN, Robert
Shaw Gussis Fishman Glantz Wolfson & Towbin LLC, Chicago 312 541 0151
*Recommended in Bankruptcy*

## FLYNN, Christopher
Jones Day, Chicago 312 269 4156
cwflynn@jonesday.com
*Recommended in Energy*

**Practice Areas:** Represents electric and gas utilities before federal and state regulatory agencies and courts in commercial transactions and other ventures. Has represented energy companies in mergers, restructurings, transmission unbundling, transmission open access tariff development, wholesale and retail power supply contracts, commercial dispute resolution, and utility rate proceedings. Current practice involves the development of competitive retail markets, including retail access tariffs, stranded cost recovery mechanisms, independent power projects, and wholesale marketing initiatives

and international energy projects. Experienced with energy privatization projects and other commercial projects in Mexico and has spoken before the Spanish National Electricity Commission regarding transmission access issues.

## FORADAS, Michael P
Kirkland & Ellis LLP, Chicago 312 861 2308
mforadas@kirkland.com
*Recommended in Insurance*

**Practice Areas:** Partner in Litigation Group. Extensive experience in commercial, insurance coverage, business torts, mass tort and product liability, trade secret/intellectual property, securities, and antitrust matters. Particular emphasis in representing policy holders in complex insurance coverage litigation, including general and product liability, directors and officers, and business interruption claims. Clients include Dow Chemical, Motorola, ServiceMaster, Brunswick, and other Fortune 500 companies.
**Personal:** AB, College of William & Mary, 1978; (Phi Beta Kappa). JD, Northwestern University School of Law, 1981. (Editor-in-Chief, Northwestern Law Review; Order of Coif; cum laude). Member, Board of Editors, Insurance Coverage Law Bulletin.

## FORCADE, Bill S
Jenner & Block LLP, Chicago 312 923 2964
bforcade@jenner.com
*Recommended in Environment*

**Practice Areas:** Bill S Forcade is a Partner in Jenner & Block's Chicago office. He is a member of Environmental, Energy and Natural Resources Law, Trade Secrets and Unfair Competition, Defense and Aerospace, and Association Practices. Mr Forcade has a wide range of experience in environmental law from the perspective of a scientist, a government regulator, an environmental law judge and as an attorney in private practice. He practices in the area of environmental law, with a focus on air pollution, regulatory and permit compliance, and administrative and judicial enforcement matters. He was appointed by the Governor to serve on Illinois Environmental Regulatory Review Commission (2000-05), which reviewed environmental laws in Illinois and made recommendations to update those laws. He was Chairman of the Groundwater Subcommittee. Mr Forcade has been actively involved in courtroom litigation, client counseling and lobbying. He has represented chemical companies, pulp and paper mills, heavy equipment manufacturers, foundries, smelters, oil and gas production, petroleum refineries, printing and coating companies, natural gas utilities, electric utilities, waste disposal and recycling companies and a variety of industrial manufacturing companies. This representation includes lobbying the legislative and executive branches of state and federal governments, participation in formal and notice and comment rule making at the federal and state level, review of permit applications and negotiations with permitting agencies over the terms and conditions of those permits, client counseling over compliance matters and negotiation and litigation regarding enforcement at the administrative and judicial level.

**Personal:** John Marshall Law School, JD, 1976.

### FORRESTER, J Paul

Mayer, Brown, Rowe & Maw LLP, Chicago 312 701 7366
jforrester@mayerbrownrowe.com
*Recommended in Banking & Finance*

**Practice Areas:** Partner in Corporate Finance Practice. Specialises in structured credit products (including credit derivatives, collateralized debt, fund and swap obligations, and structured investment vehicles) and project financings in oil and gas, energy, transportation, refinery and pipeline industries. Also represents clients in mezzanine financings, high-yield debt financings, structured financings, equity and commodity-linked securities transactions, venture capital investments, interest rate, currency, and commodity swap transactions, restructurings, reorganisations, and workouts.

**Career:** Associate (1980) and Partner (since 1987) with Mayer, Brown, Rowe & Maw LLP, except for one year (1986) as Director of Bildakit Homes Australia. Served variously in Chicago, New York, and London offices. Associate with Allen, Allen & Hemsley, Sydney, 1977-80.

**Publications:** 'Is My SPE a VIE Under FIN46 and, If So, So What?' Journal of Structured and Project Finance, Fall 2003. 'CDOs: Process Not Product', Euromoney's ABS Yearbook 2002. 'Project Finance CDOs: What? Why? Now?', Independent Power Project Finance Yearbook 2001-02. 'Wanted: A New Financing Model (and Acronym?) for Merchant Power Projects', 'Power Economist', February 1997.

**Personal:** JD, Illinois Institute of Technology, Chicago-Kent College of Law, 1985; LLB, University of Sydney, 1976. Admitted in Illinois, 1988; New York, 1984; and New South Wales, Australia, 1978.

### FORT, Jeffrey

Sonnenschein Nath & Rosenthal LLP, Chicago 312 876 8000
jfort@sonnenschein.com
*Recommended in Environment*

**Practice Areas:** Environmental Group Chair. Works with all environmental media, state and federal agencies. Practice includes internal compliance investigations and designing and conducting compliance programs. Experienced in complex air regulatory and permitting

matters and evaluating potential risks associated with chemical exposure in remediation and toxic tort claims. Has successfully litigated before state and federal courts and negotiated with state and federal agencies.

**Prof. Memberships:** Past Chairman Environmental Law Committee – Chicago Bar Association; Past Chairman Lake Michigan States Section – Air and Waste Management Association.

**Personal:** Northwestern University School of Law, JD, cum laude; Monmouth College, BA, Economics.

### FRANCZEK, James

Franczek Sullivan, Chicago
312 986 0300
*Recommended in Employment*

### FRANSON, Marc

Chapman and Cutler LLP, Chicago
312 845 3000
*Recommended in Banking & Finance*

### FRANZETTI, Susan

Franzetti Law Firm PC, Chicago
312 251 5590
*Recommended in Environment*

### FREED, Michael

Much Shelist Freed Denenberg Ament & Rubenstein, P.C., Chicago
312 521 2000
*Recommended in Antitrust*

### FREEMAN, Louis S

Skadden, Arps, Slate, Meagher & Flom LLP & Affiliates, Chicago 312 407 0650
lfreeman@skadden.com
*Recommended in Tax*

**Practice Areas:** Has extensive experience in all aspects of federal tax planning and dispute work, particularly in corporate acquisitions and dispositions, spin-offs, consolidated groups, financings, joint ventures and partnerships, workouts and restructurings, real estate, financial products, and foreign inbound and outbound transactions. Active in the ABA Tax Section, where served as Chair of Committee on Corporate Tax. Is a Fellow in American College of Tax Counsel and a Member of Tax Advisory Group of the ALI Federal Income Tax Project-Subchapter C.

**Career:** LLM (in Taxation), New York University, 1972; JD, Harvard Law School, 1966; BBA, University of Cincinnati, 1963.

### FREEMAN JR, Lee

Freeman, Freeman & Salzman, Chicago
312 222 5100
*Recommended in Antitrust*

### FRIEDLANDER, Mark C

Schiff Hardin LLP, Chicago
312 258 5546
mfriedlander@schiffhardin.com
*Recommended in Construction*

**Practice Areas:** Construction.
**Prof. Memberships:** American Bar Association, Illinois State Bar Associa-

tion, Chicago Bar Association, American Arbitration Association, Design Build Institute of America, American Consulting Engineers Council, National Academy of Science and Engineering, Society of Illinois Construction Attorneys (President), and American College of Construction Lawyers.

**Career:** Co-leads Schiff Hardin's Construction Group. Clients include virtually all construction industry participants. Developed a business structure for design-build projects – the design professional leads the design-build team with a general contractor as subcontractor for construction.

**Publications:** More than 200 publications and speeches.
**Personal:** University of Michigan (BA, 1978), Harvard Law School (JD, 1981).

### FRIEDLI, Helen R

McDermott Will & Emery, Chicago
312 984 7563
hfriedli@mwe.com
*Recommended in Corporate/M&A*

**Practice Areas:** Partner in Corporate and Securities Department and member of the Firm's management and executive committees. Practice focuses on M&A and joint ventures (including public company acquisitions, contested takeovers and proxy contests and cross-border transactions). Recent transactions include a negotiated public tender offer of a Swiss company, the acquisition of Canadian wire and steel products companies and acquisition and financing of businesses engaged in industrial manufacturing. Also focuses on corporate and securities counseling including serving as advisor to boards of directors of public companies.

**Personal:** Indiana University School of Law (JD); Purdue University, (BSIM).

### FRIEDMAN, Dennis G

Mayer, Brown, Rowe & Maw LLP
Chicago 312 701 7319
dfriedman@mayerbrown.com
*Recommended in Telecom, Broadcast & Satellite*

**Practice Areas:** Commercial litigation. Litigator specialising in telecommunications. Experienced in complex litigation and appellate work.

**Prof. Memberships:** Admitted in Illinois, 1982.

**Career:** Joined Mayer, Brown, Rowe & Maw LLP, 1982; became a Partner, 1988. Law clerk to The Honorable Gerald Bard Tjoflat, United States Court of Appeals for the Eleventh Circuit, 1981-82.

**Personal:** Duke University, JD, 1981; graduated first in class. Amherst College, BA, cum laude, 1969.

### FROY, Michael M

Sonnenschein Nath & Rosenthal LLP, Chicago 312 876 8222
mfroy@sonnenschein.com
*Recommended in Corporate/M&A*

**Practice Areas:** Corporate Chair who understands and meets clients' business objectives. Experience includes governance, corporate control/takeover defense, securities regulation and representing purchasers, sellers and investors in M&A transactions valued at $1 million to $1 billion+, involving individuals, public and private companies across a broad array of industries; private companies and institutional and corporate investors in private equity and strategic investments; and issuers and underwriters in public and private financings.

**Prof. Memberships:** Illinois Bar; Chairman, Lex Mundi's Cross-Border Transactions Group; Board Member, Chicago Council on Foreign Relations.

**Personal:** University of Michigan, AB, with honors and high distinction; University of Chicago, JD.

### GABRIC, Ralph J

Brinks Hofer Gilson & Lione, Chicago
312 321 4253
rgabric@usebrinks.com
*Recommended in Intellectual Property*

**Practice Areas:** Patent, trade secrets, copyright, trademark, unfair competition and related antitrust litigation and trials.

**Prof. Memberships:** Illinois Supreme Court; Court of Appeals, Federal Circuit; Federal District Court, Northern District of Illinois; Federal District Court, Western District of Michigan; Registered Attorney before United States Patent and Trademark Office; AIPLA; ABA; FCBA; Chicago Inn of Court; The Lawyers Club of Chicago.

**Publications:** Author, Chapter 2, 'Trade Dress and Product Configuration Law' 'Protecting Trade Dress' (2d ed 1999), published by Aspen Law & Business.

**Personal:** Education: BS, Chemistry, Boston College (1985); JD, DePaul University (1988), Member, DePaul Law Review.

### GADE, Mary A

Sonnenschein Nath & Rosenthal LLP, Chicago 312 876 8934
mgade@sonnenschein.com
*Recommended in Environment*

**Practice Areas:** Has 20-plus years of experience in regulation and enforcement. As Illinois Environmental Protection Agency (EPA) Director, advised governor on state environmental issues. Served as Deputy Assistant Administrator, US EPA, and Office of Solid Waste and Emergency Response and Deputy Director, Waste Management Division, US EPA, Region V.

**Prof. Memberships:** Environmental Council of States; National Academy of Public Administration; Presidential Appointment to Mickey Leland Urban Air Toxics Research Center; Trade and Environment Policy Advisory Committee to US Trade Representative; Environmental Research Institute of the States.

**Personal:** Washington University School of Law JD; University of Wisconsin, BA, Phi Beta Kappa.

### GAGLIARDO, Joseph
Laner, Muchin, Dombrow, Becker, Levin, Tominberg, Chicago
312 467 9800
*Recommended in Employment*

### GALLO, John N
Sidley Austin LLP, Chicago
312 853 7494
jgallo@sidley.com
*Recommended in Litigation*
**Practice Areas:** John Gallo's practice includes conducting internal investigations for institutions, representing criminal defendants and grand-jury targets, and representing parties in complex civil litigation. He has led internal investigations on behalf of institutional clients in the insurance brokerage, airline, university, healthcare, environmental, accounting, regulated-industry, law, and high-technology areas. Mr Gallo has represented a series of clients in grand jury investigations and/or pending criminal matters, and he routinely prosecutes civil cases on behalf of institutional clients seeking redress for having been victimized by fraud. Mr Gallo also has an extensive pro bono practice.
**Personal:** Previously served as Assistant US Attorney in Northern District of Illinois, and as Deputy Chief of the Criminal Division. Currently serves as Adjunct Professor at Notre Dame Law School, and lectures on federal criminal practice. Harvard Law School, JD, 1986; University of Notre Dame, BA, 1983. Admission: Illinois, 1986.

### GANGEMI JR, Columbus R
Winston & Strawn LLP, Chicago
312 558 5811
cgangemi@winston.com
*Recommended in Employment*
**Practice Areas:** Senior Partner, Labor and Employment Practice. Concentrates in all areas of labor and employment relations counseling and litigation, representing clients before federal agencies and courts, US Supreme Court, US Congress.
**Prof. Memberships:** National Labor Relations Board Practice Committee, American Bar Association, 1976-present; Fellow, College of Labor and Employment Lawyers, 1998-present.
**Career:** Joined firm as associate, 1973. Partner, 1979. National Chair, Labor and Employment Group, 1983 to 2005 Member, Executive Committee. Managing Partner, Chicago Office.
**Publications:** 'Labor Disputes Planning Workbook, Labor Policy Association, 1999'; 'The Bargaining Order and Related Remedies Under the NLRA', 'The Labor Law Handbook, IICLE, 1998' (with D Barella); 'The Lockout as an Alternative to Union In-Plant Campaign Tactics', NLRB Watch, LPA, January 1999; 'Retiree

Health Plans: Look Back Before Going Ahead With Changes', Benefits Law Journal,1990/91; 'The Importance of Common Values in Employment Law', Inside the Minds of Leading Labor Lawyers, Aspatore Books, 2002.
**Personal:** Villanova University, AB, 1969; Temple University, Doctoral Fellow-Philosophy, 1970; Villanova University School of Law, JD, 1973, Case and Comments Editor, Villanova Law Review.

### GEAREN, John J
Mayer, Brown, Rowe & Maw LLP, Chicago
312 701 7278
jgearen@mayerbrownrowe.com
*Recommended in Real Estate*
**Practice Areas:** Real estate transactions, representing commercial banks, national insurance companies, and pension funds in negotiating acquisition, construction, and permanent financing for real estate projects and in negotiating workouts. Represents developers of real estate projects in obtaining governmental approvals, financing arrangements, and architectural and construction contracts to develop hotels, offices, residential apartments, and single family residential developments. Represents tenants and landlords in office, commercial, and industrial leases.
**Prof. Memberships:** American College of Real Estate Lawyers. Chicago Bar Association. Chicago Council of Lawyers.
**Career:** Joined Mayer, Brown, Rowe & Maw LLP, 1971; Partner, 1978. Law clerk to The Honorable Spotswood W Robinson, US Court of Appeals, Washington, DC 1970-71.
**Publications:** Frequent speaker and panelist on real estate issues, including panel on lenders' issues at the annual Law Conference of the International Council of Shopping Centers.
**Personal:** Yale University, JD, 1970; Managing Editor, Yale Law Journal. Oxford University, MA, 1967; Rhodes Scholar. Notre Dame, BA, summa cum laude, 1965. Peer selection to several legal publications. Chairman of the Board, Director, Institute for the International Education of Students.

### GELMAN, Bruce L
Mayer, Brown, Rowe & Maw LLP, Chicago 312 701 7288
bgelman@mayerbrownrowe.com
*Recommended in Tax*
**Practice Areas:** Tax Partner with extensive experience advising fund sponsors and investors (taxable and tax-exempt, domestic and non-US) in the organization and structuring of various forms of investment funds and joint ventures, including partnerships, limited liability companies, REITs and insurance company separate accounts. Maintains a broad tax planning practice representing REITs and other investors in real estate. Regularly structures investment vehicles for non-

US investors.
**Prof. Memberships:** Illinois, 1993. US Court of Appeals for the Seventh Circuit, 1993. US Tax Court, 1993.
**Career:** Mayer, Brown, Rowe & Maw LLP, Chicago, 1993 to date; Partner, 2001.
**Publications:** 'The Insurance Company or the Insured: Where Does Defense Counsel's Loyalty Really Lie?' 70 U Det Mercy L Rev 215, 1992. 'Edmonson v. Leesville Concrete Co'. 69 U Det Mercy L Rev 323, 1992.
**Personal:** JD (summa cum laude) University of Detroit School of Law, 1992; Editor, Law Review. BA, Boston College, 1990.

### GEORGE, Peter
Baker & McKenzie, Chicago
312 861 6587
peter.r.george@bakernet.com
*Recommended in Business Process Outsourcing, Technology*
**Practice Areas:** Outsourcing, including business process outsourcing, information technology outsourcing and offshoring; information technology law; complex licensing; intellectual property; and cross-border commercial transactions.
**Prof. Memberships:** Illinois Bar Association. Adjunct Professor, Northwestern University School of Law.
**Career:** Admitted in Illinois 1997.
**Publications:** Changing Landscape: New Legal Issues in Outsourcing; Advisory Board, Northwestern Law School Journal of Technology and Intellectual Property Law.
**Personal:** JD, Northwestern University School of Law.

### GERBER, Dean
Vedder, Price, Kaufman & Kammholz, Chicago 312 609 7500
*Recommended in Banking & Finance, Transportation*

### GERMANN, Hans J
Mayer, Brown, Rowe & Maw LLP, Chicago 312 701 8792
hgermann@mayerbrownrowe.com
*Recommended in Telecom, Broadcast & Satellite*
**Practice Areas:** Litigator specializing in regulated industries, particularly telecommunications. Experienced in administrative proceedings and appellate matters.
**Prof. Memberships:** Illinois, 2001.
**Career:** Mayer, Brown, Rowe & Maw LLP, Chicago, 2001 to date.
**Personal:** JD, Tulane Law School 2001; Order of the Coif; Member, Tulane Law Review. University of Illinois, 1998. Carleton College, 1995.

### GERSTEIN, Mark
Latham & Watkins LLP, Chicago
312 876 7700
*Recommended in Corporate/M&A, Corporate/M&A: Private Equity*

### GETTLEMAN, Chad H
Adelman & Gettleman Ltd, Chicago
312 435 1050
cgettleman@ag-ltd.com
*Recommended in Bankruptcy*
**Practice Areas:** Commercial bankruptcy, reorganization and insolvency matters, and commercial litigation. Has been involved in major bankruptcy cases since 1976 and has confirmed numerous plans of reorganization. Has represented debtors, secured creditors, creditors' committees, sureties and other parties. Recent bankruptcy case involvement includes Armstrong World Industries, Inc., Outboard Marine Corp., Enron Corp., Federal Mogul Corp. Kaiser Aluminum Corp., Kmart Corp., and USG Corp.
**Prof. Memberships:** American Bar Association – Section on Corporation, Banking and Business Law; Illinois State Bar Association; Wisconsin State Bar Association; Chicago Bar Association – Bankruptcy and Reorganization Committee.
**Career:** Founder, shareholder and member of Adelman & Gettleman, Ltd since 1983. Began practicing in 1976 with the United States Securities and Exchange Commission, Branch of Corporate Reorganization.
**Publications:** Co-author, 'Representing the Secured Creditor and Adequate Protection', Business Bankruptcy Practice, 2006 ed, Illinois Institute of Continuing Legal Education.
**Personal:** Marquette University Law School (JD 1976); University of Illinois (BS, Accounting 1973); Certified Public Accountant (State of Illinois 1974). Named Member of Illinois Leading Lawyers Network for Bankruptcy and Workout Lawyers (2004-06); listed in The Best Attorneys Network, and elected as an Illinois Super Lawyer, in the areas of bankruptcy and reoganization (2005).

### GILFORD, Steven R
Mayer, Brown, Rowe & Maw LLP, Chicago 312 701 7909
sgilford@mayerbrownrowe.com
*Recommended in Insurance*
**Practice Areas:** Commercial litigation. International insurance and reinsurance. Coverage disputes. Insurance fraud, regulation and insolvencies. RICO, attorneys' fee and class action litigation. Insurance defense and coordination. Restrictive covenant disputes.
**Career:** Joined Mayer, Brown, Rowe & Maw LLP as Partner, 1987. Formerly with Isham, Lincoln & Beale.
**Publications:** Co-Author: 'After [?] Goes Away', Best's Review (December 2004); Author: 'Insurance Coverage Actions: Who, Where, and When to Sue', The Brief, Fall 1996, Vol. 26, No. 1, ABA Tort & Insurance Practice Section. 'Prior Attention to Arbitration Clauses Help Ensure Fairness', Legal Update, The

Review Worldwide Reinsurance, March 1995. 'Alternatives to Insurance Liquidation: A US Perspective', 7th International Reinsurance Congress, October 1993. 'The Responsibilities and Liabilities of Accountants and Actuaries to Life Insurers and in Life Insurance Insolvencies', ABA National Institute on Life Insurer Insolvency, June 1993.
**Personal:** Duke University, JD, 1978; Order of the Coif; Administrative Law Editor and Member of the Editorial Board, Law Journal. Duke University, MA, 1978. Dartmouth College, AB, summa cum laude, 1974. Member, Board of Education, Evanston Township High School. Director, Metropolitan Family Services.

## GILSON, Jerome
Brinks Hofer Gilson & Lione, Chicago
312 321 4205
jgilson@usebrinks.com
*Recommended in Intellectual Property*
**Practice Areas:** Jerome Gilson is a Senior Partner who has specialized in trademark and unfair competition law for more than 40 years.
**Prof. Memberships:** INTA; ABA; IPLAC. Admitted to practice law in US Supreme Court and eight US Courts of Appeals.
**Publications:** Former author with Anne Gilson LaLonde, 'Trademark Protection and Practice' (standard treatise, supplemented three times annually) and articles in numerous publications. Speaker before ABA, INTA, AIPLA and CBA.
**Personal:** Education: AB, University of Missouri-Columbia (1952); JD, Northwestern University School of Law (1958); Member, Board of Editors, Northwestern Law Review.

## GLASER, D Louis
Sonnenschein Nath & Rosenthal LLP, Chicago 312 876 7525
lglaser@sonnenschein.com
*Recommended in Healthcare*
**Practice Areas:** Healthcare Partner concentrating in health industry joint ventures; M&A; hospital-physician relations; integrated delivery systems; exempt organizations; fraud and abuse and other regulatory compliance; managed care; and other general healthcare corporate issues. He also is a trained healthcare mediator.
**Career:** Named among The Best Lawyers in America, Health (2003-present) in Corporate Counsel; Leading Lawyers Network Health Law (2004-present); Nightingale's Healthcare News – one of the nation's Outstanding Hospital Attorneys (2003), Outstanding Transaction Lawyers (2004).
**Personal:** Loyola University of Chicago, JD, cum laude, 1989, Editor in Chief, Loyola Law Journal; DePauw University, BA, 1984; Ohio State University, MHA (Finance), 1986.

## GLICKSTEIN, David
DLA Piper Rudnick Gray Cary US LLP, Chicago 312 368 7270
david.glickstein@piperrudnick.com
*Recommended in Real Estate*
**Practice Areas:** Real estate; real estate finance.
**Prof. Memberships:** American College of Real Estate Lawyers.
**Career:** He has extensive experience in a broad range of real estate transactions including acquisitions and dispositions, financing, development, joint ventures and leasing. He represents owners and developers on local, national and international projects and has significant experience representing lenders and borrowers on complex financing transactions and workouts. He has been listed for many years in a leading legal publication.
**Personal:** JD, Northwestern University; BBA, University of Wisconsin.

## GODFREY, Richard C
Kirkland & Ellis LLP, Chicago
312 861 2391
rgodfrey@kirkland.com
*Recommended in Litigation*
**Practice Areas:** Senior litigation Partner and member of the firm's Management Committee. He specializes in complex litigation, including jury and bench trials, arbitration, and appellate work in various fields, including class actions, antitrust, environmental contamination claims, franchise and distribution litigation, and business torts and contract disputes.
**Prof. Memberships:** Member, Board of Visitors, Boston University School of Law. Member, Board of Trustees, Augustana College. Member, Lawyers' Committee, National Center for State Courts. Member, American, Illinois, Chicago, Fifth and Seventh Circuit Bar Associations. Member, Board of Governors, The Mid-America Club.
**Personal:** Augustana College, BA, 1976. Boston University School of Law, JD, 1979.

## GOERING, Gail
Lovells, Chicago 312 832 4413
gail.goering@lovells.com
*Recommended in Insurance*
**Practice Areas:** Insurance and reinsurance.
**Prof. Memberships:** American Bar Association; Illinois State Bar Association.
**Career:** Gail's practice is devoted to representing clients in life/health and property/casualty reinsurance disputes in the US and abroad. She regularly assists clients in developing traditional reinsurance products and creating unique risk transfer structures. Gail has particular experience with respect to insurer insolvencies and has been a leading member of Lovells' teams advising on and litigating complex issues in international insurer insolvencies.
**Personal:** The University of Chicago Law School (JD, 1990); Bethel College (BA and BS, 1987).

## GOLD, Brian J
Sidley Austin LLP, Chicago
312 853 2064
bgold@sidley.com
*Recommended in Employment*
**Practice Areas:** Head of the firm's Employment and Labor Group, and counsels and litigates on a wide range of labor and employment matters. On behalf of Fortune 500 employers as well as mid-size manufacturing and service companies, Mr Gold handles industrial labor litigation, arbitrations, unfair labor practice charges, collective bargaining, alternative dispute resolution, and employment discrimination litigation. He advises clients in connection with corporate acquisitions and has successfully litigated union challenges related to such transactions in the courts and before the NLRB and arbitrators. Mr Gold handles labor issues arising from corporate restructurings and business transactions and has successfully represented corporate clients in emergency litigation brought by unions. He represents global companies with operations in the United States and counsels clients in initiating alternative dispute resolution programs in non-union settings.
**Prof. Memberships:** Member of the American Bar Association's Dispute Resolution and the Federal Labor Standards Committees and the ABA's Committee on ADR in Labor and Employment Law, and the Fellows Board of Leadership Greater Chicago.
**Personal:** Georgetown University Law Center, JD, 1982; Miami University – Oxford, AB, 1979. Admission: Illinois, 1982.

## GOLD, Michael
Sidley Austin LLP, Chicago
312 853 7148
mgold@sidley.com
*Recommended in Banking & Finance*
**Practice Areas:** Mr Gold is a Partner in the Chicago office whose area of practice is commercial finance and debt restructurings for banks and commercial finance companies. He focuses on secured and unsecured syndicated financings, workouts and restructurings, and debtor-in-possession financings. Mr Gold also advises investors and companies with respect to acquisition and other financings.
**Prof. Memberships:** Member of American and Illinois Bar Associations.
**Personal:** John Marshall Law School, JD, 1984; University of Illinois, BS, 1981. Admission: Illinois, 1984.

## GOLDBLATT, Stanford
Winston & Strawn LLP, Chicago
312 558 5600
*Recommended in Corporate/M&A: Private Equity*

## GOLDEN, Gerald
Neal, Gerber & Eisenberg LLP, Chicago
312 269 8008
ggolden@ngelaw.com
*Recommended in Employment*
**Practice Areas:** Labor and employment law on behalf of management; collective bargaining, employment discrimination, employment contract disputes, non-competition agreements and other issues that arise between employers, their employees, and union representatives; negotiated labor contracts across the country on behalf of employers in a variety of industries, including manufacturers, service providers, newspapers, hotels, and telecommunications companies.
**Prof. Memberships:** College of Labor and Employment Lawyers (Fellow).
**Career:** Partner; Labor and Employment Practice Group.
**Publications:** Author and lecturer on various labor and employment topics.
**Personal:** DePaul University College of Law (JD, 1972); Northwestern University (MBA, 1968); Washington University in St Louis (AB, 1966).

## GOLDMAN, Michael P
Sidley Austin LLP, Chicago
312 853 4665
mgoldman@sidley.com
*Recommended in Insurance*
**Practice Areas:** Co-Chair of Sidley's Insurance and Financial Services Group. Practice focuses on the corporate representation of insurance companies and other insurance entities, with a focus on acquisitions, divestitures and corporate reorganizations (including demutualization and mutual holding company conversions); the formation, capitalization and corporate financing of insurance companies and related ventures; the regulation of insurance holding company systems; the regulation of insurance company investment practices, including the use of derivative instruments and strategies; the structure and regulation of alternative risk financing mechanisms and complex reinsurance arrangements, including insurance securitization and derivatives, loss portfolio transfers and commutations; the structure of unique marketing and insurance distribution systems; and captive insurance companies, risk retention groups and other alternative market mechanisms. He represents investment and commercial banks, private equity funds, investment advisors and derivatives dealers with respect to insurance company relationships and transactions.
**Prof. Memberships:** Chicago Bar Association's Insurance and Corporate Law Committees and the American Bar Association's (ABA) Tort and Insurance Practice and Business Law Sections.
**Personal:** Loyola University Chicago School of Law JD, 1985; University of Illinois BS, 1982. Certified Public Accoun-

tant (CPA). Admissions: Illinois, 1985; US District Court, ND of Illinois.

## GOLDSTEIN, Andrew
Freeborn & Peters, Chicago
312 360 6000
*Recommended in Media & Entertainment*

## GOODMAN, Mark
Lord, Bissell & Brook, Chicago
312 443 0700
*Recommended in Insurance*

## GOODMAN, Stuart
Schiff Hardin LLP, Chicago
312 258 5711
sgoodman@schiffhardin.com
*Recommended in Corporate/M&A*
**Practice Areas:** Corporate and securities.
**Prof. Memberships:** Chicago Bar Association, American Bar Association, Garrett Corporate and Securities Law Institute.
**Career:** Concentrates in corporate, securities, and mergers and acquisitions, and heads the firm's practice group that includes these areas. Has broad experience in all aspects of representing both privately and publicly owned corporations.
**Personal:** University of Illinois at Urbana-Champaign (BA, with highest honors and with distinction, Phi Beta Kappa, 1960), Harvard Law School (JD, magna cum laude, 1963), Member, Harvard Law Review.

## GORDON, Mark
McGuireWoods LLP, Chicago
312 849 8100
*Recommended in Technology*

## GRAHAM, Robert L
Jenner & Block LLP, Chicago
312 923 2785
rgraham@jenner.co,
*Recommended in Environment*
**Practice Areas:** Robert L Graham is the founder and Chair of Jenner & Block's Environmental, Energy and Natural Resources Law Practice; co-author of the nationally recognized environmental law textbook, 'Environmental Law and Policy: Nature, Law, and Society, Third Edition' (Aspen Publishers, 2004); and member of the firm's Policy Committee. Mr Graham is a nationally recognized authority in environmental, health, safety, natural resources, and energy matters, including disputes involving the National Environmental Policy Act, Superfund, the Resource Conservation and Recovery Act, the Endangered Species Act, the Toxic Substances Control Act, the Clean Air Act, the Clean Water Act, natural resource damages, and toxic torts. Not only did he literally 'write the book' in those areas, but he has also handled numerous cases nationwide involving those types of claims for over 25 years. His environmental and energy law practice has specifically included representation before regulatory agencies, before

courts, and among private parties concerning (i) the location, siting, licensing, permitting, and remediation of plants and facilities; (ii) toxic torts and environmental, health, and safety impacts pertaining to industrial, residential, and commercial developments; (iii) the applicability of federal and state statutes to disputes involving the operation and/or sale of businesses and real estate; and (iv) the handling of chemical spills and industrial accidents. Mr Graham also has broad experience in all types of contractual and business tort disputes, RICO and fraud litigation, securities litigation, and litigation involving the legal protection of computer software, trade secrets, and proprietary rights.
**Personal:** Harvard Law School, JD, 1972.

## GRAYSON, E Lynn
Jenner & Block LLP, Chicago
312 923 2756
lgrayson@jenner.com
*Recommended in Environment*
**Practice Areas:** E Lynn Grayson is a Partner in Jenner & Block's Chicago office. She is a Member of the firm's Environmental, Energy and Natural Resources Law and Defense and Aerospace Practices. Ms Grayson has an extensive environmental law background including both private practice and government service experience. Prior to joining the firm, Ms Grayson was the chief legal counsel for the Illinois Emergency Services and Disaster Agency and the State Emergency Response Commission. She has prosecuted federal and state civil and criminal environmental cases including as an Assistant Attorney General for the State of Illinois. Ms Grayson's national environmental practice and experience includes managing complex CERCLA and RCRA matters, advising clients on critical regulatory concerns, performing environmental due diligence for real estate and corporate transactions, defending against natural resource damage and conducting environmental audits at manufacturing operations. She also has significant experience negotiating agreements to redevelop brownfields sites throughout the United States. Ms Grayson is an authority on federal and state release reporting obligations. Ms Grayson is the past Chairperson for the Environmental, Natural Resources and Energy Law Committee of the American Bar Association, Business Law Section, the Lake Michigan States Section of the Air and Waste Management Association and the Illinois State Bar Association's Environmental Council. She has served as a special liaison from the American Bar Association Standing Committee on Environmental Law to the US Department of Defense addressing regulatory reform.
**Personal:** Indiana University School of Law, JD, 1986, With Distinction.

## GROMACKI, Joseph P
Jenner & Block LLP, Chicago
312 923 2637
jgromacki@jenner.com
*Recommended in Corporate/M&A*
**Practice Areas:** Joseph P Gromacki is a Partner in Jenner & Block's Chicago office. He is a member of the firm's Corporate Practice, Co-Chair of the Securities Practice, and serves on the Management Committee. Mr Gromacki has experience structuring, negotiating and managing public and private mergers, acquisitions, divestitures, public equity offerings and other highly complex corporate finance transactions. He regularly counsels clients regarding corporate governance and disclosure matters and Delaware law issues and other corporation and securities law matters. Mr Gromacki has represented General Motors in the 2003 split-off of Hughes Electronics from GM and the subsequent acquisition by News Corporation of 34% of Hughes for $6.6 billion as part of transactions valued at over $17 billion and GM's 2004 sale of $911 million of News Corporation Preferred ADSs in an underwritten public offering. He also represented GM in several of the world's largest public offerings of equity securities, including the 2000 exchange offer of $9 billion of GM's Class H common stock for $1-2/3 par value common stock. Mr Gromacki has represented the Chicago Board of Trade on a variety of corporate and securities law matters, including its 2005 restructuring and demutualization into a stock, for-profit company as well as its $200 million initial public offering later in 2005. Additionally, he has represented BP in connection with certain significant transactions, including the 2000 and 2001 divestitures of its Alliance refinery and related assets in transactions valued at over $1.2 billion.
**Personal:** University of Virginia School of Law, JD, 1992.

## GUERRA, Michael
Sonnenschein Nath & Rosenthal LLP, Chicago 312 876 8170
mguerra@sonnenschein.com
*Recommended in Energy*
**Practice Areas:** Represents various gas, electric and water utlities and telecommunications carriers with respect to regulatory matters involving both federal and state law. Assists clients with respect to problem solving and strategic planning decisions. Represents these clients before the Illinois Commerce Commission.
**Career:** Joined firm in 2000. Former Administrative Law Judge for the Illinois Commerce Commission, where he presided over numerous contested dockets involving public utilities and telecommunications carriers and conducted evidentiary hearings involving extensive expert testimony and highly technical accounting, economic, engineering and

regulatory policy issues.
**Personal:** John Marshall Law School, Law Review, Moot Court, JD; Loyola University, BBA.

## GULLIKSON, Rosemary L
Sonnenschein Nath & Rosenthal LLP, Chicago 312 876 8963
rgullikson@sonnenschein.com
*Recommended in Business Process Outsourcing, Technology*
**Practice Areas:** A transactional lawyer focusing on strategic alliances, complex technology development and implementation projects, and outsourcing transactions. Negotiates global and cross border services, licensing and technology arrangements, and insurance industry IT and financial/investment industry IT transactions.
**Prof. Memberships:** Director and President, Tim & Tom Gullikson Foundation, a not-for-profit corporation, funding support programs for brain tumor patients and their families.
**Personal:** Northwestern University, JD, cum laude; Northern Illinois University, BS, Nursing, summa cum laude.

## GUPTA, Shilpi
Skadden, Arps, Slate, Meagher & Flom LLP & Affiliates, Chicago 312 407 0738
sgupta@skadden.com
*Recommended in Corporate/M&A*
**Practice Areas:** Advises Fortune 500, middle market and emerging companies and investment banking and other financial institutions in a variety of M&A and corporate finance transactions and other corporate and securities matters. Represents companies acting as acquirors or sellers, as well as investment banking clients, in mergers, stock and asset acquisitions and divestitures, takeovers (negotiated and contested), venture capital transactions, restructurings, joint ventures and other strategic alliances. Also represents issuers and investment banking institutions in initial and other public offerings, private placement of securities and high-yield debt transactions.
**Career:** JD, Georgetown University Law Center, 1994; BS, Columbia University, 1991.

## GUTHMAN, Jack
Shefsky & Froelich, Chicago
312 527 4000
*Recommended in Real Estate*

## HAAB, Eric
Lovells, Chicago
312 832 4403
eric.haab@lovells.com
*Recommended in Insurance*
**Practice Areas:** Insurance and reinsurance.
**Career:** Eric concentrates his practice in the areas of reinsurance, insurance insolvency and financial services litigation. He has represented cedents and reinsurers in the US, Europe and Asia in the litigation

and arbitration of complex reinsurance disputes. Eric has litigated a variety of substantial disputes involving cutting edge reinsurance issues and is experienced in both the property/casualty and life, accident and health reinsurance sectors. In addition, he has authored numerous articles and organized several conferences with regard to reinsurance and insurance insolvency issues.

**Personal:** Harvard Law School (JD, 1989); University of Michigan (AB, 1986).

### HAARLOW, John
Lord, Bissell & Brook, Chicago
312 443 0700
*Recommended in Insurance*

### HACK, Randall
Lord, Bissell & Brook, Chicago
312 443 0700
*Recommended in Antitrust*

### HAHN, Arthur
Katten Muchin Rosenman LLP, Chicago
312 902 5200
*Recommended in Corporate/M&A*

### HALPERN, Marcelo
Latham & Watkins LLP, Chicago
312 876 7700
*Recommended in Technology*

### HAMILL, John J
Jenner & Block LLP, Chicago
312 923 2684
jhamill@jenner.com
*Recommended in Telecom, Broadcast & Satellite*

**Practice Areas:** John J Hamill is a Partner in Jenner & Block's Chicago office. He is a member of the firm's Litigation and Dispute Resolution, Healthcare Law, Appellate and Supreme Court, Telecommunications, and Antitrust and Trade Regulation practices. Mr Hamill practices in a wide range of litigation, focusing particularly on various areas of complex business litigation. Mr Hamill has been extensively involved in complex telecommunications litigation and counseling since his admission to the bar, including appellate, local competition, antitrust, regulatory and class action matters. With colleagues at the firm, he has been at the forefront of representing carriers in local competition litigation since the adoption of the Telecommunications Act of 1996. Representative cases include Mathias v. WorldCom Techs, 121 S Ct 1224 (2001), and Bell Atlantic Tel Cos v. FCC, 206 F 3d 1 (DC Cir 2000), and Illinois Bell Tel Co v. WorldCom Techs, 179 F3d 566 (7th Cir 1999). Mr Hamill also has regularly represented clients in a wide range of antitrust and unfair competition matters, including federal and state court antitrust lawsuits. He routinely counsels clients on complex antitrust issues. He has thought antitrust law at seminars for trade association managers held at DePaul University Law School. Mr Hamill also has repre-

sented clients in a wide range of appellate-style litigation, including telecommunications, trademark, commercial, and criminal litigation.

**Personal:** Harvard Law School, JD, 1993, cum laude.

### HAMM, Leisa
Lord, Bissell & Brook, Chicago
312 443 0700
*Recommended in Insurance*

### HAMMES, Jeffrey C
Kirkland & Ellis LLP, Chicago
312 861 2476
jhammes@kirkland.com
*Recommended in Corporate/M&A: Private Equity*

**Practice Areas:** He has concentrated his practice on structuring and negotiating complex business transactions including domestic and international mergers, acquisitions, leveraged buyouts and recapitalizations, going private transactions, spinoffs, formation of private equity funds, venture capital investments, debt and equity financings and restructurings and workouts and executive compensation, handling transactions which range in size from several million dollars to over $1 billion.

**Personal:** University of Wisconsin, BBA, 1980; Northwestern University School of Law, JD, 1985.

### HANCUCH, Thomas
Vedder, Price, Kaufman & Kammholz, Chicago 312 609 7500
*Recommended in Employment*

### HANZLIK, Paul F
Foley & Lardner LLP, Chicago
312 832 4901
phanzlik@foley.com
*Recommended in Energy*

**Career:** Paul F Hanzlik, a Partner with the Chicago office of Foley & Lardner LLP, is a member of the firm's Management Committee and leads the Energy Regulation Practice. Mr Hanzlik concentrates his practice on energy matters and represents clients before state regulatory agencies and in the courts. His experience includes restructuring electric operations, establishing retail rates for bundled utility services and delivery services, construction of new transmission facilities, evaluation of long-term fuel contracts, generating station operations, litigating construction costs for generating facilities, and demonstrating the reliability of system operations and management prudence before administrative agencies and in the courts.

### HARNER, Paul E
Jones Day, Chicago
312 269 1528
peharner@jonesday.com
*Recommended in Bankruptcy*

**Practice Areas:** Co-chairs Jones Day's firmwide Business Restructuring and Reorganization Practice and also coordi-

nates that practice in the Chicago office. Practice focuses on corporate bankruptcy, restructuring, and other insolvency-related matters. Has been Lead Counsel in several of the nation's largest corporate restructurings. Has extensive experience representing bank groups, institutional investors, secured lenders, and other parties in bankruptcy cases, out-of-court workouts, and related litigation. Substantial experience counseling clients in fraudulent conveyance, illegal dividend, preferential transfer, fiduciary duty, and corporate formalities issues. Regularly speaks on bankruptcy issues.

**Prof. Memberships:** American Bankruptcy Institute; ABA; Illinois State Bar Association; Ohio State Bar Association.

### HARRINGTON, James
McGuireWoods LLP, Chicago
312 849 8100
*Recommended in Environment*

### HARRINGTON, John R
Jenner & Block LLP, Chicago
312 923 2791
jharrington@jenner.com
*Recommended in Telecom, Broadcast & Satellite*

**Practice Areas:** John R Harrington is a Partner in Jenner & Block's Chicago office. He is a member of the Telecommunications, Appellate and Supreme Court, and Litigation and Dispute Resolution Practices. Mr Harrington has represented national and local telecommunications carriers in a wide variety of litigation matters, including matters arising under the Telecommunications Act of 1996. He has represented a client and the client's subsidiaries in the US Supreme Court, in several US Courts of Appeals, and in federal district courts, state appellate courts, and state regulatory commissions around the country. He successfully argued on that client's behalf in the Eighth Circuit in 2004, convincing that court to uphold the ability of state regulatory commissions to enforce reporting requirements on incumbent carriers' federally-tariffed 'special access' services. He also has successfully represented this client and the client's subsidiaries for several years in nationwide litigation concerning 'reciprocal compensation' for the exchange of calls to internet service providers. Mr Harrington also has represented clients in other litigation matters in trial and appellate courts around the country, including class actions, copyright matters and commercial litigation matters.

**Personal:** Indiana University School of Law, JD, 1995, magna cum laude; Order of the Coif. From 1996-97 Mr Harrington served as a law clerk to the Honorable John L Coffey of the United States Court of Appeals for the Seventh Circuit. Prior to that, he served as a law clerk to the Honorable Patrick D Sullivan of the Indiana Court of Appeals.

### HARRIS, Kenneth L
Neal, Gerber & Eisenberg LLP, Chicago
312 269 8410
klharris@ngelaw.com
*Recommended in Tax*

**Practice Areas:** Concentrates on federal income tax aspects of corporate divestitures and acquisitions, partnership transactions and tax planning strategies; advises Fortune 500 companies in structuring tax-free reorganizations, spin-off transactions, partnerships, and LLC joint venture agreements and cross border investments; provides counsel to businesses in all aspects of tax planning.

**Prof. Memberships:** Adjunct Professor of Law, Northwestern University School of Law and IIT/Chicago-Kent College of Law.

**Career:** Partner; Tax Practice Group Chair.

**Publications:** 'Standards of Tax Practice' (co-author, 6th Ed. 2004).

**Personal:** New York University School of Law (LLM, 1987); University of Chicago Law School (JD, 1985); Hamilton College (AB, 1982).

### HARRIS, Robert
Stein, Ray & Harris LLP, Chicago
312 641 3700
*Recommended in Construction*

### HARTMANN, H Michael
Leydig, Voit & Mayer, Ltd, Chicago
312 616 5600
mhartmann@leydig.com
*Recommended in Intellectual Property*

**Practice Areas:** Intellectual property, IP litigation, IP counseling including international.

**Prof. Memberships:** AIPLA, ABA, AIPPI, LES.

**Career:** Mr Hartmann has concentrated his practice in the areas of intellectual property litigation and licensing, including international aspects thereof; and complex patent procurement, including oppositions. He has acted in various technological fields ranging from zeolite catalysis and medical imaging to soft contact lenses and software. He has litigated a number of jury and non-jury patent and trade secret cases in United States district and appellate courts as well as in the International Trade Commission, and has participated in lawsuits, including trials, in Germany, England, and France. He has conducted oppositions before the Japanese and European patent offices.

**Publications:** 'Discovery and Related Motion Practice', 'Winning Strategies in Patent Litigation', Practicing Law Institute, 1995.

**Personal:** Born in Frankfurt, Germany, Mr Hartmann is fluent in the German language. He obtained an engineering degree from the Colorado School of Mines, and a Law Degree, magna cum laude, from the DePaul University College of Law in Chicago. Prior to joining Leydig, Voit & Mayer Ltd, he served on the engineering staff of a major oil company and interned for a European patent firm.

## HARTSTEIN, Barry A
Morgan, Lewis & Bockius LLP, Chicago
312 324 1140
bhartstein@morganlewis.com
*Recommended in Employment*
**Practice Areas:** Mr Hartstein has represented employers around the country in a broad range of employment law matters for nearly 30 years, and handles the defense of both individual and class action claims. He serves as Chicago Practice Leader for the Labor and Employment Law Practice Group (LEPG) and also serves on the LEPG National Leadership Team.
**Prof. Memberships:** For many years, Mr Hartstein has served in a leadership role in the American Bar Association's Section of Labor and Employment Law and recently completely his term as National Co-Chair of the Equal Employment Opportunity Committee. Mr Hartstein also has a leadership role with Cornell University's School of Industrial and Labor Relations and currently serves on the Executive Committee for the School's Alumni Association.

## HEIDELBERGER, Brian L
Winston & Strawn LLP, Chicago
312 558 5897
bheidelberger@winston.com
*Recommended in Media & Entertainment*
**Practice Areas:** Counsels corporations, commerce companies and advertising/promotion agencies on advertising, marketing, and promotional issues, considering copyright, trademark, right of publicity, false advertising, sweepstakes/contest issues, television network guidelines, and the Screen Actors Guild Commercials Contract. Has expertise in talent, music and sponsorship negotiations, and also web development, software licensing, and other related technology agreements.
**Prof. Memberships:** Board of Directors, Kaboom, Inc.
**Publications:** Contributing Author, 'Inside the Minds – Advertising and Promotional Law – Critical Advertising and Promtion Agreements', Aspatore Books (2005).
**Personal:** BS Marketing, Indiana University (1991). JD Chicago Kent College of Law (1994): Law Review, Kent Legal Scholar.

## HELLER, David
Latham & Watkins LLP, Chicago
312 876 7700
*Recommended in Bankruptcy*

## HELMAN, Robert A
Mayer, Brown, Rowe & Maw LLP,
Chicago 312 701 7020
rhelman@mayerbrownrowe.com
*Recommended in Corporate/M&A*
**Practice Areas:** Senior Partner and for-

mer Chairman of Mayer, Brown, Rowe & Maw LLP. Expertise in tender offers, mergers and acquisitions, corporate restructurings, and corporate governance issues. Lecturer, University of Chicago Law School.
**Career:** Joined Mayer, Brown, Rowe & Maw LLP, Chicago, as a Partner in 1967; Chairman, Management Committee, 1984-98. Isham, Lincoln & Beale, Chicago, 1956-66.
**Publications:** Co-author, 'Commentaries on the Illinois Constitution of 1970'; various articles on corporate and public utility matters.
**Personal:** BSL (1954) and LLB (1956), Northwestern University; Order of the Coif; Associate Editor, Northwestern University Law Review. Directorships: Northern Trust Corporation, 1986-present; Dreyer's Grand Ice Cream, Inc., 1998-2003; TC PipeLines GP, Inc., 1999-2004; Chicago Stock Exchange, 1993-2000; Zenith Electronics Corporation, 1995-99; The Horsham Corporation, 1990-96; Alberta Natural Gas Company, 1993-96; Southern Pacific Transportation Co., 1987-88; The Brookings Institution, Emeritus Trustee; Council on Foreign Relations; Museum of Contemporary Art, Trustee, 1996-2003; Aspen Institute, Trustee, 1986-92; Citizens Committee on the Juvenile Court of Cook County, Chairman, 1968-83; The Learned Hand Human Relations Award of the American Jewish Committee, Recipient; 1989; Justice John Paul Stevens Award of the Chicago Bar Association, Recipient, 2001; Legal Assistance Foundation of Chicago, President, 1973-75.

## HENNING, Mark G
Winston & Strawn LLP, Chicago
312 558 5793
mhenning@winston.com
*Recommended in Real Estate*
**Practice Areas:** Head of firm's Chicago-based Real Estate Practice. National practice focused on representing institutional investors, lenders and developers in acquisition, disposition, financing and leasing of commercial real estate and structured financing transactions.
**Prof. Memberships:** Member of the American College of Real Estate Lawyers and the International Council of Shopping Centers.
**Career:** Partner since 1985; associate 1978-85.
**Publications:** 'Lease Financing of Real Estate: Equipment Leasing – Leveraged Leasing' (Practicing Law Institute, 1999).
**Personal:** Loyola University Chicago (JD cum laude, 1978); University of Illinois (BA, magna cum laude with distinction in Economics (Phi Beta Kappa), 1975).

## HERALD, J Patrick
Baker & McKenzie, Chicago
312 861 2830
j.patrick.herald@bakernet.com

*Recommended in Litigation*
**Practice Areas:** Complex commercial litigation trial practice, including but not limited to class actions (consumer, shareholder and derivative claims, environmental, mass tort), internal investigations, unfair competition, SEC and other regulatory agency investigations.
**Prof. Memberships:** The International Academy of Trial Lawyers (Fellow); American College of Trial Lawyers (Fellow); Society of Trial Lawyers; Trial Lawyers Club of Chicago; American Bar Association; Illinois State Bar Association; The Chicago Bar Association; Seventh Circuit Bar Association; International Association of Defense Counsel; and the Defense Research Institute.
**Career:** Illinois (1972), the Federal Trial Bar, Seventh Circuit Court of Appeals and the United States Supreme Court.

## HERMES, Robert N
Butler Rubin Saltarelli & Boyd, Chicago
312 696 4445
rhermes@butlerrubin.com
*Recommended in Insurance*
**Practice Areas:** General commercial and reinsurance litigation and arbitration.
**Career:** Robert Hermes is one of the original lawyers from Winston & Strawn to join Butler Rubin at its inception. He has 25 years of experience as a trial lawyer in all aspects of reinsurance arbitration/litigation and commercial litigation, including jury and bench trials in breach of contract and fraud actions, business torts, trade secret and restrictive covenants, insurance coverage disputes, antitrust and class actions. His appellate experience includes both state and federal courts. Reinsurance experience includes disputes involving the scope and applicability of arbitration clauses, placement disclosures, claim handling, adherence to underwriting guidelines, retrospectively rated business, obligations to follow settlements, allocation of settlements, obligations under surplus share reinsurance contracts, excess of loss contracts, application of ultimate net loss and net retained line clauses, and accounting for premiums and losses. He is also a frequent speaker on reinsurance issues.
**Personal:** JD, DePaul University Law School, 1979, Editor-in-Chief, DePaul University Law Review, 1978-79. BA (Economics), Indiana University, 1976.

## HEROY, David
Bell, Boyd & Lloyd LLC, Chicago
312 372 1121
*Recommended in Bankruptcy*

## HICKEY JR, John T
Kirkland & Ellis LLP, Chicago
312 861 2348
jhickey@kirkland.com
*Recommended in Litigation*
**Practice Areas:** Member of firm's Executive Committee. Lead Trial Counsel in commercial, intellectual property, envi-

ronmental, product liability, consumer fraud, securities, shareholder derivative, antitrust, and contract litigation in state and federal courts, arbitrations and administrative proceedings throughout the US.
**Prof. Memberships:** Fellow, American College of Trial Lawyers; Leading Lawyers Network Advisory Board (top 1% of IL lawyers).
**Personal:** Georgetown University, AB, 1974 magna cum laude, Phi Beta Kappa; University of Chicago, JD, 1977.

## HILLIARD, David
Pattishall, McAuliffe, Newbury, Hilliard & Geraldson LLP, Chicago
312 554 8000
*Recommended in Intellectual Property*

## HODES, Scott
Bryan Cave LLP, Chicago
312 602 5000
*Recommended in Media & Entertainment*

## HODGE, Katherine
Hodge Dwyer Zeman, Springfield
217 523 4900
*Recommended in Environment*

## HOEFLICH, Adam
Bartlit Beck Herman Palenchar & Scott, Chicago 312 494 4400
*Recommended in Litigation*

## HOFER, Roy
Brinks Hofer Gilson & Lione, Chicago
312 321 4204
rhofer@usebrinks.com
*Recommended in Intellectual Property*
**Practice Areas:** Roy Hofer specializes in patent, trademark, trade secret and related contract trials and appeals. He is also a mediator, special master and expert in intellectual property cases.
**Prof. Memberships:** AIPLA; ABA (Litigation, Intellectual Property, Antitrust Sections); FCBA (Board, 1989-95, President, 1993-94); Seventh Circuit Bar Association; IICLE (Board, 1986-88); IPLAC (Board, 1974-76); CBA (President, 1988-89); Law Club of Chicago; Center for Public Resources' Intellectual Property Panel of Distinguished Neutrals; Center for Conflict Resolution (President, 1991-97).
**Personal:** Education: BS, Chemical Engineering, Purdue University (1957); JD, Georgetown University (1961); Member, Board of Editors, Georgetown Law Journal.

## HOMBURGER, Thomas
Bell, Boyd & Lloyd LLC, Chicago
312 372 1121
*Recommended in Real Estate*

## HOOD, Vicki V
Kirkland & Ellis LLP, Chicago
312 861 2092
vhood@kirkland.com
*Recommended in Employment*
**Practice Areas:** Vicki Hood is the Head of Kirkland's Employee Benefits Group.

Her practice focuses on employee/ employee benefits aspects of corporate transactions and restructuring. Vicki also has experience in advising private equity and real estate funds and other clients regarding Department of Labor plan asset rules, prohibited transactions and other fiduciary compliance issues and responsibilities.
**Personal:** Northwestern University, BA, 1974. Northwestern University Kellogg School of Management, MBA, 1977. Northwestern University School of Law, JD, 1977.

### HUTCHINGS REED, Mary
Winston & Strawn LLP, Chicago
312 558 5600
*Recommended in Media & Entertainment*

### IVESTER, Eric
Skadden, Arps, Slate, Meagher & Flom LLP & Affiliates, Chicago
312 407 0920
eivester@skadden.com
*Recommended in Bankruptcy*
**Practice Areas:** Represents clients in business reorganizations, acquisitions and divestitures. Has represented debtors, creditors, investors, sellers, purchasers and other financial advisors in all stages of complex restructuring transactions, from Chapter 11 reorganizations to out-of-court negotiations, workouts and divestitures.
**Career:** JD, University of Oklahoma, 1985 (highest honors; Order of the Coif); BA, University of Oklahoma, 1982.

### JACKSON, Charles C
Morgan, Lewis & Bockius LLP, Chicago
312 324 1156
charles.jackson@morganlewis.com
*Recommended in Employment*
**Practice Areas:** Charles Jackson is a Partner in the Labor and Employment Law Practice Group. Mr Jackson focuses on all facets of employment law and specializes in representing employers in labor, employment and employee benefits litigation, particularly class actions and trials. Mr Jackson has substantial experience with appellate matters, has handled numerous cases before federal and state appellate courts and served as counsel in a number of cases before the US Supreme Court.
**Prof. Memberships:** Admitted to practice in Illinois and numerous federal courts; Member of American Bar Association, Chicago Bar Association, ABA Committee on Labor and Employment Law (Employee Benefits Section), Seventh Circuit Bar Association, College of Labor & Employment Lawyers (Fellow).

### JACOBSON, Fruman
Sonnenschein Nath & Rosenthal LLP, Chicago 312 876 8123
fjacobson@sonnenschein.com
*Recommended in Bankruptcy*

**Practice Areas:** Workout, Reorganisation and Bankruptcy Chair. Represents public/private creditors, debtors, creditors' committees, workout consultants/crisis managers and others with troubled loans/credits. Handles related business issues and litigation in state and federal courts. Represents financial institutions and other lenders; supervises loan/asset reviews; and represents clients in out-of-court workouts or court proceedings. Creditors committees' lead attorney in United Airlines' and Wickes' bankruptcies.
**Prof. Memberships:** Member, ABA's Business Bankruptcy Committee; Faculty, National Institute of Trial Advocacy; Editorial Board, The Bankruptcy Strategist.
**Personal:** BA, University of Illinois, with highest honors; Phi Kappa Phi. James Scholar; Northwestern University School of Law, JD, cum laude.

### JACOBSON, Kenneth M
Katten Muchin Rosenman LLP, Chicago
312 902 5445
Kenneth.Jacobson@kattenlaw.com
*Recommended in Real Estate*
**Practice Areas:** Partner, Chicago. Concentrates on commercial real estate finance and investment in real estate and real estate-related companies (including, multi-family, office, retail, hotel, resort and mixed-use properties) for real estate investment trusts, real estate opportunity funds, commercial banks, insurance companies, finance companies and other lenders and investors, as well as developers and other borrowers. Has been involved in complex financings, including mezzanine financing, multi-asset portfolio financing, permanent and line of credit financing, rated and structured financing and other financing and investment activities in a variety of projects such as shopping centers, hotels, resort facilities, office buildings, build-to-suit distribution facilities and multifamily assets. Represents lenders, loan participants, loan purchasers and sellers, investors and borrowers in unsecured and secured lines of credit, construction and permanent financing, mezzanine financing, portfolio financing, workouts, loan dispositions and acquisitions, distressed property transactions and joint ventures. Regularly represents clients in commercial real estate acquisitions and divestitures.
**Prof. Memberships:** Member of the American College of Real Estate Lawyers, American Bar Foundation and the Chicago Mortgage Attorneys Association. Past President of the Chicago Mortgage Attorneys Association. Chairman of the Legal Opinions in Real Estate Transactions Committee of the Real Property, Probate and Trust Section of the American Bar Association. Past Chair of Investment Entities Committee of American College

of Real Estate Lawyers.
**Career:** Frequent speaker, panelist and author on a variety of topics, including, limited liability companies and partnerships, mortgage finance, attorneys' opinions, portfolio transactions, deeds in lieu of foreclosure and restrictions and easement agreements.
**Publications:** Co-author of 'Illinois Limited Liability Company Forms and Practice Manual'.
**Personal:** Graduated, Phi Beta Kappa, from the University of Illinois in 1976 and received his JD Degree from Stanford Law School in 1979.

### JACOBSON, Michael A
Katten Muchin Rosenman LLP, Chicago
312 902 5443
michael.jacobson@kattenlaw.com
*Recommended in Banking & Finance*
**Practice Areas:** Partner, Chicago. Michael A Jacobson focuses his practice in a wide variety of areas of corporate finance, including both senior and mezzanine financing. His experience includes borrower, senior lender and mezzanine investor representation, cash flow and asset-based transactions, leveraged buyouts and build-ups, restructurings and workouts, addressing and negotiating intercreditor and subordination related issues, equity co-investments and healthcare finance transactions for a wide range of clients in a variety of industries.
**Personal:** Mr Jacobson received his Bachelor of Business Administration Degree in Finance from the University of Iowa and graduated with honors from DePaul University College of Law.

### JACOBSON, Ronald H
Winston & Strawn LLP, Chicago
312 558 5832
rjacobson@winston.com
*Recommended in Banking & Finance*
**Practice Areas:** Partner, Corporate Department, Chicago Office. Practice concentrated in leveraged finance, structured investment, private equity, and debt portfolio purchase matters, including representation of asset managers, banks, financial institutions, funds, institutional investors, and issuers in liquid senior, middle market, hybrid and mezzanine financings, as well as collateralized loan obligations, synthetic transactions, and other structured investment products.
**Prof. Memberships:** Member, American Bar Association Business Law Section, Commercial Finance Association's Education Foundation Founders Leadership Council, Loan Syndications and Trading Association, Inc., Association for Corporate Growth, and Turnaround Management Association.
**Career:** Admitted to Illinois Bar, 1988. Joined Winston & Strawn, 1990; Partner, 1997. Member, Winston & Strawn Income Partner Compensation Committee, Associate Evaluation Committee, and

Billing and Collection Committee.
**Publications:** Co-author of 'The Senior Debt Evolution: A Comparative Analysis of the Cash Flow CLO and the Synthetic Total Return Structure', Journal of Structured Finance, Summer 2005.
**Personal:** Born July 23, 1963. Received BA, 1985, with honors, University of Illinois at Urbana-Champaign. Received JD, 1988, with honors, Loyola University Chicago School of Law; Managing Editor of Loyola Law Journal. Received MBA, 1990, with honors, JL Kellogg Graduate School of Management, Northwestern University, majors in accounting and finance.

### JACOVER, Jerold A
Brinks Hofer Gilson & Lione, Chicago
312 321 4214
jjacover@usebrinks.com
*Recommended in Intellectual Property*
**Practice Areas:** Jerold A Jacover's practice includes much experience in patent, copyright and unfair competition, including litigation and trials. He is the immediate past President of his firm.
**Prof. Memberships:** President: IPLAC (2000-01); IPLAC Educational Foundation (1993-94). Board of Directors: NCI-PLA (2000-01); National Inventors Hall of Fame (2001-02); AIPLA (1994-98). Member: AIPLA; IPLAC; Decalogue Society of Lawyers.
**Publications:** Author, articles in CBA Record, Chicago Lawyer, and AIPLA Bulletin. Speaker, ABA and other bar associations.
**Personal:** Education: BS, Electrical Engineering, University of Wisconsin (1967); JD, Georgetown University (1971); Editor, Georgetown Law Journal.

### JEPSON JR, Edward
Vedder, Price, Kaufman & Kammholz, Chicago 312 609 7500
*Recommended in Employment*

### JOHNSON, Garrett B
Kirkland & Ellis LLP, Chicago
312 861 2268
gjohnson@kirkland.com
*Recommended in Litigation*
**Practice Areas:** His practice focuses on the preparation and trial of cases involving a broad range of business-oriented substantive law issues, including securities and futures (fraud, market manipulation, insider trading), antitrust (monopolization, mergers, price-fixing), environmental tort, products liability, fiduciary responsibilities, breach of contract, defamation and lender liability. He counsels clients on corporate and securities issues such as takeover defense, major corporate transactions, public disclosure obligations, government regulatory matters including futures and securities trading practices, antitrust issues including marketing practices, distribution arrangements, mergers, acquisitions and joint ventures.

**Personal:** Princeton University, AB, 1968; University of Michigan Law School, JD, 1971.

## JOHNSON, Robert C
Sonnenschein Nath & Rosenthal LLP, Chicago 312 876 8155
rjohnson@sonnenschein.com
*Recommended in Insurance*

**Practice Areas:** Practices general litigation with an emphasis in complex insurance and reinsurance litigation, including class actions. Litigates coverage claims, including environmental, asbestos, product liability, construction defect, bad faith and personal injury, including advertising injury.
**Career:** Chair of firm's Litigation Practice. Joined firm in 1973.
**Publications:** 'The Litigator: Advocate and Counselor' (chapter from Inside the Minds: Leading Litigators); 'Making the Jump from Associate to Partner' (The National Law Journal, 2002).
**Personal:** New York University School of Law, JD, Articles Editor-Annual Survey of American Law; Cornell College, BA, magna cum laude, Phi Beta Kappa.

## JONES, Roger
Latham & Watkins LLP, Chicago
312 876 7700
*Recommended in Tax*

## JOSEPH, Robert
Sonnenschein Nath & Rosenthal LLP, Chicago 312 876 8165
rjoseph@sonnenschein.com
*Recommended in Antitrust*

**Practice Areas:** Has 35 years' experience in antitrust and trade regulation litigation and counseling. Handles complex, challenging issues and claims across the antitrust law spectrum (including price-fixing class actions). In connection with distribution matters, counsels and represents franchisors and suppliers in disputes involving claims such as resale price fixing, tying and price discrimination.
**Prof. Memberships:** Served as Chair, ABA Section of Antitrust Law, Chair-Elect, Vice-Chair, Committee Officer, Member, Chair of Franchise and Dealership Committee and Publications Committee.
**Personal:** University of Michigan, JD, cum laude. Member, Michigan Law Review, Alpha Sigma Nu, National Honor Society; Xavier University, AB magna cum laude.

## JUNEWICZ, James J
Mayer, Brown & Maw LLP, Chicago 312 701 7032
jjunewicz@mayebrownrowe.com
*Recommended in Corporate/M&A*

**Practice Areas:** Represents corporations and investment banks in debt and equity financings, including IPOs, high yield securities, US offerings by foreign issuers and private placements. Handles major M&A transactions, corporate restructurings and private equity transactions. Advises boards of directors and executive management teams on the requirements of Delaware law; federal securities laws, particularly regarding the disclosure requirements of the Securities Exchange Act of 1934; corporate governance, including Sarbanes Oxley. Particular industry expertise in telecommunications, consumer products, transportation and natural resources.
**Career:** Joined Mayer, Brown, Rowe & Maw LLP, Chicago, 1984; Partner, 1987. Office of the General Counsel, US Securities and Exchange Commission, Washington, DC, 1979-84; Assistant General Counsel, 1982-84.
**Publications:** 'The SEC's Recent Enforcement Actions Under Regulation FD', Securities & Commodities Regulation, March 2003; 'The SEC Raises the Stakes in Issuer-Analyst Communications', Securities & Commodities Regulation, November 2000.
**Personal:** New York University, LLM, Corporation Law, 1978. Duquesne University, JD, 1976. Georgetown University, BSFS, 1972. Manuel F Cohen Award, given annually to the SEC attorney making an outstanding contribution to the work of the SEC, 1983. Board of Trustees, Chicago Shakespeare Theatre.

## KAMIN, Chester T
Jenner & Block LLP, Chicago
312 923 2795
ckamin@jenner.com
*Recommended in Telecom, Broadcast & Satellite*

**Practice Areas:** Chester T Kamin is a Partner in Jenner & Block's Chicago office. Mr Kamin's trial practice has concentrated on complex cases of strategic significance in diverse subjects. He currently represents long-time client Blue Cross Blue Shield Association in a nationwide RICO physician class action against the Association and most Blue Cross and Blue Shield Plans and also serves as co-liaison defense counsel in the action. In 2005, he represented US Unwired, a former Sprint PCS affiliate, where following a 2 week bench trial of RICO claims against Sprint, Sprint agreed to purchase US Unwired for $1.3 billion. In 2003, he represented long-time client Energy Conversion Devices, Inc. in a lengthy international arbitration hearing against Toyota Corp. and Matsushita Electric Industrial Corp. considering patent infringement claims addressed to nickel metal hydride batteries used in Toyota's hybrid gasoline-electric vehicles. The case was settled before an award. He acted as Lead Counsel to MCI Communications Corp. throughout its lengthy antitrust litigation against AT&T including a 1980 jury trial resulting in a $1.8 billion antitrust judgment for MCI and, on behalf of MCI and industry groups, appeared repeatedly in the related divesti-

ture proceedings. In 1987, he obtained a jury verdict of $105 million on behalf of a Florida real estate developer against a money center bank, the largest lender liability verdict at the time. Mr Kamin also counsels corporate clients on business and legal strategies relating to competitive issues, corporate control and similar controversies.
**Personal:** University of Chicago Law School, JD, 1965.

## KANE, Ivan P
Mayer, Brown, Rowe & Maw LLP, Chicago 312 701 7167
ikane@mayerbrownrowe.com
*Recommended in Real Estate*

**Practice Areas:** Practice concentrates in real estate development and a variety of real estate transactions. Development activity includes representing parties in annexation, zoning and governmental and private agreements related to property development. Development clients include real estate companies and corporate users as well as institutional clients such as universities and hospitals. Experience includes a number of corporate headquarters projects. Transactional work includes both acquisitions and dispositions of a wide variety of property types for both real estate companies and corporate and institutional clients. Financing experience includes representing both lenders and borrowers in a variety of construction, long-term, line of credit, mezzanine and other financing structures, as well as assistance in resolving distressed debt situations.
**Prof. Memberships:** American Bar Association. National Association of Real Estate Investment Trusts. Urban Land Institute.
**Career:** Mayer, Brown, Rowe & Maw LLP, Chicago, 1981 to date; Partner, 1988.
**Personal:** JD, University of Chicago, 1981; Law Week Award, Casper Platt Award, BA, (highest honors) University of Chicago, 1978; Phi Beta Kappa. 2005 BTI Client Service All-Star Team, honoring attorneys identified by their Fortune 1000 clients for outstanding client service.

## KAPLAN, Harold L
Gardner Carton & Douglas LLP, Chicago
312 569 1204
hkaplan@gcd.com
*Recommended in Bankruptcy*

**Practice Areas:** Mr Kaplan has a diverse practice, including regularly representing bondholder and corporate trustee interests, as well as representing or serving on committees, in major national default and bankruptcy cases (including securitization defaults). He is one of the leading lawyers to the corporate trust industry, particularly in the area of default and bankruptcy, as well as being known for healthcare insolvency expertise. His recent cases include, among others, UAL Corp., Northwest Airlines Corp., FLYi,

Inc., Mirant Corp., Loral Orion, USGen New England, ASARCO, Atlas Air, Tower Automotive, WHX Corp., Kaiser Aluminum, HealthSouth, Conseco. He also has extensive experience in regulated industry matters; utility industry matters; securities industry and broker-dealer matters; insurance and bank insolvencies; and healthcare industry matters.
**Prof. Memberships:** Annually chairs two leading industry conferences: the Corporate Reorganizations and Healthcare Transactions conferences both in Chicago; Chair of the Chicago Bar Association Large Law Firm Committee; past Chair of Chicago Bar Association Bankruptcy and Reorganization Committee; Chair of ABA Healthcare-Related and Not-for-Profit Bankruptcy Issues Working Group; Member and former Membership Chair of the American Bar Association Committee on Trust Indentures and Indenture Trustees, as well as serving on several related committees, including the advisory drafting group of the Subcommittee on Revision of the Model Simplified Indenture; Turnaround Management Association's Cornerstone Council.
**Career:** Chair of GCD's Management Committee; Co-Chair of the firm's Corporate Restructuring and Financial Institutions Practice Group; Head of the firm's Corporate Trust and Bondholder Rights Practices; named one of 12 Outstanding Bankruptcy Lawyers in the country for 2003, 2004, and 2005 by Turnarounds & Workouts, and as one of 13 Outstanding Bankruptcy Lawyers in 2001 also by Turnarounds and Workouts.
**Publications:** Mr Kaplan has authored numerous articles and been a presenter at numerous conferences on corporate reorganization, distressed debt, healthcare financing, bond default, and other bankruptcy topics, as well as bondholder/corporate trust topics; Member of Editorial Board of and frequent contributor to the American Bankers Association Trust & Investments magazine; Contributing Editor to the ABI Journal's 'Intensive Care' column; co-author of the 'The Role of the Trustee in Securitization Transactions', Securitization of Financial Assets Treatise.
**Personal:** University of Wisconsin, BA, 1972 and MA, 1975; University of Chicago Law School, JD, 1975.

## KAPLAN, Jared
McDermott Will & Emery, Chicago
312 984 6955
jkaplan@mwe.com
*Recommended in Employment*

**Practice Areas:** Focuses on employee benefits, ERISA, federal tax matters, corporate finance and employee stock ownership plans (ESOPs).
**Career:** Completed a three-year term on Board of Directors of Family Firm Institute, and in 2003 was named its general

counsel. In 2004, elected a Fellow of American College of Employee Benefit Counsel.

**Publications:** Co-author of 'Tax Portfolio on Employee Stock Ownership Plans (ESOPs)', and 'Corporate Portfolio on ESOPs in Corporate Transactions', both published by the Bureau of National Affairs. Editor of The Best of Law, published by the Family Firm Institute.

**Personal:** Harvard Law School (LLB); University of California-Los Angeles (AB).

---

**KAPLAN, Joel**
Seyfarth Shaw LLP, Chicago
312 346 8000
*Recommended in Employment*

---

**KARAGANIS, Joseph**
Karaganis, White & Magel, Chicago
312 836 1177
*Recommended in Environment*

---

**KATZ, A Sidney**
Welsh & Katz Ltd, Chicago
312 655 1500
*Recommended in Intellectual Property*

---

**KATZ, Alvin**
Mayer, Brown, Rowe & Maw LLP,
Chicago 312 701 8285
akatz@mayerbrown.com
*Recommended in Real Estate*

**Practice Areas:** Extensive experience in complex commercial real estate transactions, including partnerships and joint ventures, acquisitions and dispositions, real estate development, finance, management and leasing. He has a widely diversified practice, representing real estate investors and developers in a broad range of transactions across the United States. In recent years his practice has focused on the representation of clients providing equity capital for real estate transactions. Clients include private equity funds, public and private pension funds, investment advisors, developers and real estate investment trusts.

**Prof. Memberships:** American Bar Association. The Economic Club of Chicago. Lambda Alpha International. Pension Real Estate Association. Urban Land Institute. National Association of Real Estate Investment Trusts.

**Career:** Joined Mayer, Brown, Rowe & Maw LLP, Chicago as Partner, 1990. Formerly with Neal Gerber & Eisenberg, Chicago, 1984-90; Levy and Erens, Chicago, 1977-84.

**Publications:** Frequent speaker and panelist at real estate industry and professional conferences, including Information Management Network and Practicing Law Institute programs.

**Personal:** JD, Stanford University Law School, 1977. BA (with high distinction and honors in economics), University of Michigan, 1974.

---

**KAUFMAN, Andrew M**
Kirkland & Ellis LLP, Chicago
312 861 2313
akaufman@kirkland.com
*Recommended in Banking & Finance*

**Practice Areas:** Mr Kaufman's practice focuses principally in the areas of financing and secured transactions, structured and project financings, leasing, workouts and reorganizations, and general corporate practice. He is the senior Partner in the firm's Financing & Secured Transactions Practice. His clients include major private equity firms (as both lenders and borrowers); major national lending institutions; technology, telecom, energy, manufacturing, and financial companies and institutions. He is also an Adjunct Professor of Law at Vanderbilt University Law School, teaching in the areas of finance and commercial transactions.

**Personal:** Yale University, BA, 1971. Vanderbilt University, JD, 1974.

---

**KEATING, Jennifer L**
Mayer, Brown, Rowe & Maw LLP,
Chicago 312 701 8858
jkeating@mayerbrownrowe.com
*Recommended in Corporate/M&A*

**Practice Areas:** Mergers and acquisitions: representation of buyers and sellers in connection with stock and asset acquisitions and divestitures, mergers, tender offers, joint ventures, and similar transactions. Securities: representation of issuers and underwriters in connection with public and private offerings of equity and debt securities. General Corporate: representation of companies in connection with Securities and Exchange Act compliance and reporting and corporate governance.

**Career:** Mayer, Brown, Rowe & Maw LLP, Chicago, 1999 to date. Law clerk to The Honorable James B Loken, United States Court of Appeals for the Eighth Circuit, 1998-99. Admitted: Illinois, 1998; US Court of Appeals for the Eighth Circuit, 1999.

**Personal:** The University of Chicago Law School, JD with honors, 1998; The University of Chicago Law Review. Cornell University, College of Arts and Sciences, BA, 1995.

---

**KELLEY, Timothy**
Timothy S Kelley - Sole Practitioner,
Chicago 312 641 3560
*Recommended in Media & Entertainment*

---

**KELLY, Henry**
Kelley Drye & Warren, Chicago
312 857 7070
*Recommended in Telecom, Broadcast & Satellite*

---

**KERWIN, Brian P**
Duane Morris LLP, Chicago
312 499 6737
bpkerwin@duanemorris.com
*Recommended in Banking & Finance*

**Practice Areas:** Brian Kerwin is a Partner in the Corporate and Finance practice groups and a member of the Management Committee of the Chicago office. Brian has extensive experience representing business entities, lenders, venture capitalists and entrepreneurs in various business and financing transactions, including the buying and selling of companies, acquisition financing arrangements, venture capital transactions, syndicated secured loan transactions, private placements of debt and equity, and intellectual property transfers and licensing arrangements.

**Prof. Memberships:** Chicago Bar Association – Commercial Finance and Transactions Committee and Corporation and Business Law Committee; American Bar Association – Business Law Section.

**Career:** Admitted to practice in the District of Columbia and Illinois.

**Personal:** John Marshall Law School, LLM, Intellectual Property Law, 1996; The National Law Center of The George Washington University, JD, with honors, 1989.

---

**KIESELSTEIN, Marc**
Kirkland & Ellis LLP, Chicago
312 861 3029
mkieselstein@kirkland.com
*Recommended in Bankruptcy*

**Practice Areas:** Mr Kieselstein has extensive experience in complex corporate restructurings, representing debtors and creditors in all aspects of insolvency practice, including Chapter 11 reorganizations, out-of-court workouts, sale of financially distressed companies, distressed debt transactions and Section 363 asset sales and purchases.

**Personal:** University of Chicago Law School, JD, 1988; City University of New York, Queens College, BA, 1985, magna cum laude.

---

**KIKOLER, Stephen**
Much Shelist Freed Denenberg Ament & Rubenstein, P.C., Chicago
312 521 2000
*Recommended in Construction*

---

**KIMBALL, Christian**
Jenner & Block LLP, Chicago
312 923 2662
ckimball@jenner.com
*Recommended in Tax*

**Practice Areas:** All aspects of federal income tax, including business planning, mergers, acquisitions and dispositions, partnerships, financial instruments, executive compensation, and tax controversies.

**Publications:** Co-authored a book on the tax aspects of forming a corporation, and a chapter on entity choice. Has published articles on the tax treatment of convertible debt and the tax treatment of options. Has spoken on numerous subjects related to federal income tax.

**Personal:** Harvard University, BA, 1979, magna cum laude; University of Chicago

Law School, JD, 1983, with honors; Adjunct Professor in the Chicago-Kent College of Law LLM Program (Taxation of Financial Instruments); former Chief Legal Officer and General Counsel for Bcom3 Group and Leo Burnett (1998 to 2002); former Associate Professor at Boston University School of Law (1993-98) (Federal Income Tax; Partnership Tax; International Tax Policy; Taxation of Financial Instruments).

---

**KIRCHHOEFER, Gregg**
Kirkland & Ellis LLP, Chicago
312 861 2177
gkirchhoefer@kirkland.com
*Recommended in Business Process Outsourcing, Technology*

**Practice Areas:** Matters for which Gregg Kirchhoefer has been responsible include: IT outsourcing, business process outsourcing, facilities management, contract and toll manufacturing agreements; sourcing, supply chain management, procurement, and EDI agreements; strategic alliance, joint venture, consortium and teaming agreements; intellectual asset management transactions and counseling; internet/e-commerce agreements and counseling; telecommunications agreements; system development, software licensing, hardware purchase and lease, and other information technology agreements of all types; life sciences, pharmaceutical, medical device and nanotechnology agreements; technology transfer and licensing agreements; university and government research agreements; franchising and distribution arrangements; and mergers, acquisitions, leveraged buyouts and private equity transactions and securities offerings.

**Personal:** Saint Louis University, BSC, 1972; Saint Louis University, cum laude, JD, 1982.

---

**KIRIAKOS, Thomas S**
Mayer, Brown, Rowe & Maw LLP,
Chicago 312 701 7275
tkiriakos@mayerbrownrowe.com
*Recommended in Bankruptcy*

**Practice Areas:** Negotiates and documents loan and corporate restructurings and other workout-related matters, primarily as counsel to senior lenders. Represents acquirors or sellers of assets or businesses of financially distressed companies; corporate banks, commercial banks and other clients in bankruptcy cases, including in appeals of bankruptcy-related lower court decisions and in connection with post-petition financing facilities or securitization transactions; corporations and other business entities in acquiring assets in bankruptcy sales; creditors' committees. Implements public and private disposition of personal and real property collateral, including through sales of financially distressed businesses as going concerns. Represents lenders in litigation matters, including in

connection with UCC issues, possible lender liability claims, or possible borrower fraud; insurance and reinsurance companies in litigation with regulators over insolvency and rehabilitation issues.
**Career:** Joined Mayer, Brown, Rowe & Maw LLP, Chicago, 1982; Partner, 1989. Law clerk to The Honorable William W Thinnes (deceased), US Bankruptcy Judge, Northern District of Iowa, 1981-82.
**Publications:** Co-author: 'Chapter 5: Bankruptcy', of J Kravitt, Securitization of Financial Assets, Aspen Law & Bus. (2d ed.1996). 'Has David Bowie Started a New Era of Celebrity Securitization?', The Financier (December, 1997).
**Personal:** University of Iowa, JD with distinction, 1981. Grinnell College, BA, 1978.

## KIRSCHBAUM, Howard
Barack Ferrazzano Kirschbaum Perlman & Nagelberg, Chicago 312 984 3100
*Recommended in Real Estate*

## KISSEL, Richard J
Gardner Carton & Douglas LLP, Chicago
312 569 1442
rkissel@gcd.com
*Recommended in Environment*
**Practice Areas:** Counsel, Environmental Department, Chairman of department from its inception until 1996; has represented municipal and industrial clients in all aspects of environmental law, including air, water, solid waste, Superfund; extensive litigation and counseling experience in environmental field.
**Prof. Memberships:** Illinois State, Chicago, Lake County Bar Associations; Fellow, International Society of Barristers; Member, Board of Advisors, Northwestern University Law School.
**Career:** Co-drafter of original Illinois Environmental Protection Act, appointed by the late Gov Richard Ogilvie to first Illinois Pollution Control Board (1970); private practice in Environmental Law since 1973; Adjunct Professor at Chicago-Kent College of Law, University of Illinois School of Public Health; recipient, Illinois Award from Illinois Association of Wastewater Agencies.
**Publications:** Frequent writer, lecturer on Environmental Law issues; author, contributor to Illinois Continuing Legal Education series on Environmental Law.
**Personal:** Northwestern University, JD, 1961; Northwestern University, BA, 1958.

## KITSLAAR, Libby
Jones Day, Chicago
312 269 4114
ekitslaar@jonesday.com
*Recommended in Corporate/M&A*
**Practice Areas:** Oversees the Corporate Practice in Jones Day's Chicago office. Her practice is concentrated in M&A, complex financings and restructurings, and securities law. Has been the principal lawyer in a variety of US and international M&A and corporate finance transac-

tions, and serves as outside securities counsel to numerous publicly held companies. In addition, she advises clients on corporate governance matters, including Sarbanes-Oxley, Board of Director, fiduciary duty, takeover preparedness, disclosure policy, and related issues.
**Prof. Memberships:** ABA; Illinois State Bar Association; Chicago Bar Association.
**Publications:** Speaker and author on US securities laws.

## KLEIN, Randall
Goldberg, Kohn, Bell, Black, Rosenbloom & Moritz, Ltd, Chicago
312 201 4000
*Recommended in Bankruptcy*

## KLENK, James
Sonnenschein Nath & Rosenthal LLP, Chicago 312 876 8000
jklenk@sonnenschein.com
*Recommended in Media & Entertainment*
**Practice Areas:** Litigation, Intellectual Property and Technology Partner. Tries in state and federal courts patent, copyright and trademark cases before juries, judges and US Patent and Trademark Office. Litigated novel claims regarding data transmissions over broadcaster television signals; mechanical and electrical patents; companies' damage and valuation claims, tangible and intangible assets; royalties and lost profits for IP intangibles. In antitrust and franchising, has helped companies restructure systems to deliver products/services. Handles libel and privacy matters.
**Prof. Memberships:** Member, Sonnenschein Management Committee.
**Personal:** University of Wisconsin, JD, Order of the Coif, Articles Editor, Wisconsin Law Review; Beloit College, BA, Phi Beta Kappa.

## KLENK, Timothy
Bryan Cave LLP, Chicago
312 602 5000
*Recommended in Employment*

## KLEVORN, Andrew G
Eimer Stahl Klevorn & Solberg LLP, Chicago 312 660 7676
aklevorn@EimerStahl.com
*Recommended in Antitrust*
**Practice Areas:** Commercial litigator with broad trial experience. His practice spans a wide variety of issues, including the defense of class actions, grand jury investigations, construction claims, arbitrations, breach of contract matters, counseling firms with respect to proposed acquisitions, and representation of clients before the Federal Trade Commission and the United States Department of Justice. He has represented a number of leading firms, including, among others, Kimberly-Clark Corporation, Holcim (US), Inc. and CITGO Petroleum Corporation.

**Prof. Memberships:** American Bar Association, Litigation and Antirust Sections; Chicago Bar Association.
**Career:** Admitted to the Illinois Bar, 1987. Member of the trial bar of the United States District Court for the Northern District of Illinois. Partner at Sidley & Austin, 1994-2000.
**Publications:** He has authored a variety of articles in various newspapers and journals, including the Wall Street Journal and the National Law Journal, concerning antitrust and other legal issues.
**Personal:** Born: March 23, 1961. Received his JD, magna cum laude, from the University of Michigan, 1986. Received his AB, with honors, from the University of Chicago, 1983 (economics).

## KOHN, Richard
Goldberg, Kohn, Bell, Black, Rosenbloom & Moritz, Ltd, Chicago
312 201 4000
*Recommended in Banking & Finance*

## KOZAK, John
Leydig, Voit & Mayer, Ltd, Chicago
312 616 5600
*Recommended in Intellectual Property*

## KRAKAUER, Bryan
Sidley Austin LLP, Chicago
312 853 7515
bkrakauer@sidley.com
*Recommended in Bankruptcy*
**Practice Areas:** Partner in the Chicago office. His practice area includes financial restructurings and corporate reorganizations of all types. He has extensive experience in both domestic and international restructurings and proceedings, and in numerous types of regulated and unregulated industries, and has had major representations in some of the largest and most complicated insolvency proceedings filed.
**Prof. Memberships:** American Bar Association Business Bankruptcy Committee.
**Personal:** The University of Chicago Law School, JD, 1981; Duke University, AB, 1978. Admission: Illinois, 1982.

## KRAMER, Samuel
Baker & McKenzie, Chicago
312 861 7960
samuel.g.kramer@bakernet.com
*Recommended in Business Process Outsourcing, Technology*
**Practice Areas:** Partner, Information Technology/Commercial Practice Group. Represents companies on domestic and international technology transactions, including outsourcing, MVNO, complex licensing, and commercial matters.
**Prof. Memberships:** Adjunct faculty member, The John Marshall Law School, Information Technology LLM Program.
**Career:** DeFrees & Fiske 1991-95. Baker & Mckenzie since 1995 (elected Partner 1999). Selected one of '40 Attorneys under 40 in Illinois to Watch' in 2004.

## KRUEGER, Herbert W
Mayer, Brown, Rowe & Maw LLP, Chicago 312 701 7194
hkrueger@mayerbrownrowe.com
*Recommended in Corporate/M&A: Private Fund Formation, Employment*
**Practice Areas:** Advises on the structuring of real estate, private equity and other investment funds, particularly with respect to investments in such funds by ERISA and governmental pension plans and other institutional investors. Advises banks, trust companies, insurance companies, investment managers and plan sponsors with respect to the application of ERISA fiduciary and prohibited transaction rules and the tax treatment of pension plans and other institutional investors. Represents senior executives, compensation committees and corporations with respect to executive compensation, stock incentive programs, employment agreements, change in control matters and severance agreements. Advises on the establishment and operation of pension and 401k plans and other tax-qualified and non-qualified employee benefit arrangements.
**Prof. Memberships:** Pension Real Estate Association Chairman, Governmental Affairs Committee (1995-97). National Advisory Board, NYU Real Estate Institute Pension Fund Investment in Real Estate (1992-95).
**Career:** Mayer, Brown, Rowe & Maw LLP, Chicago, 1975-present; Partner, 1981; management committee, 1989-present.
**Personal:** University of Chicago, JD, 1974; Instructor of Law, University of Miami School of Law, 1974-75.

## KRUPP, Peter C
Skadden, Arps, Slate, Meagher & Flom LLP & Affiliates, Chicago
312 407 0855
pkrupp@skadden.com
*Recommended in Corporate/M&A: Private Equity*
**Practice Areas:** Has an active mergers and acquisitions, private equity and corporate and securities law practice. Regularly represents private equity firms as well as several of the firm's corporate and investment banking clients on a wide variety of acquisition transactions, leveraged buyouts, private equity and venture capital transactions, corporate restructurings and recapitalizations, proxy contests, joint ventures and other financing transactions. Has substantial transactional experience in the healthcare and telecommunications industries.
**Career:** JD, University of Michigan Law School, 1986 (cum laude); BA, Albion College, 1983.

## KUNKEL, William R
Skadden, Arps, Slate, Meagher & Flom LLP & Affiliates, Chicago
312 407 0820
wkunkel@skadden.com

*Recommended in Corporate/M&A*

**Practice Areas:** Advises companies in mergers and acquisitions, corporate finance, and other corporate and securities matters. Represents companies acting as acquirors or sellers, as well as investment and merchant banking clients, in mergers, stock and asset acquisitions and divestitures, takeovers (negotiated and contested), leveraged buyouts, venture capital transactions, restructurings, joint ventures and other strategic alliances. Involved in numerous debt and equity underwritings and private placements, representing companies issuing securities and investment banking firms acting as underwriters or placement agents. **Career:** JD, Harvard Law School, 1981 (cum laude; Editor-in-Chief, Harvard Environmental Law Review); BS, Creighton University, 1978.

## KURTZON, Michael
Schwartz, Cooper, Greenberger & Krauss, Chartered, Chicago
312 346 1300
*Recommended in Real Estate*

## LABATE, Robert J
Holland & Knight LLP, Chicago
312 263 3600
robert.labate@hklaw.com
*Recommended in Media & Entertainment*

**Practice Areas:** Mr Labate concentrates his practice in the areas of corporate restructuring and in developing, financing and distributing feature film and television programming. He teaches a course in Entertainment Law at Marquette University School of Law and annually organizes and teaches film seminars sponsored by Lawyers For the Creative Arts, the Independent Feature Project and Columbia College Film School. Mr Labate's clients include: Bunim Murray Productions (producer of 'Real World'), Yari Film Group, LLC (producer of 'Crash'), Media General, Inc., Steppenwolf Films (a division of Steppenwolf Theatre Company) and Kartemquin Educational Films (producer of 'Hoop Dreams' and 'New Americans').

## LADD, Jeffrey
Bell, Boyd & Lloyd LLC, Chicago
312 372 1121
*Recommended in Healthcare*

## LANDSMAN, Stephen A
DLA Piper Rudnick Gray Cary US LLP, Chicago 312 368 4050
stephen.landsman@dlapiper.com
*Recommended in Corporate/M&A*

**Practice Areas:** Corporate/M&A, private equity, capital markets, healthcare. **Prof. Memberships:** Illinois State Bar Association; Chicago Bar Association **Career:** Co-Chair of the firm's M&A Practice, he engages in a general corporate, business counseling, and tax practice, with special emphasis in mergers and acquisitions. Has extensive experience in numerous industries as Lead Counsel representing both purchasers and sellers in a wide variety of transactions. Clients include LBO and private equity groups, public companies, strategic corporate or institutional entities, investment subsidiaries of public companies, and private investors/owners. **Personal:** JD, University of Michigan Law School; BS, University of Pennsylvania Wharton School of Business.

## LANGAN, J Andrew
Kirkland & Ellis LLP, Chicago
312 861 2064
alangan@kirkland.com
*Recommended in Antitrust*

**Practice Areas:** Experience as litigation and trial counsel in commercial, antitrust, and products liability cases including class actions. He has been principal counsel to major corporate clients in high-stakes class actions alleging violations of the antitrust laws, as well as class actions alleging products liability, mass tort and breach of warranty. Has also been principal counsel in high profile merger investigations and related litigation. He has tried, as lead counsel, seven jury trials, and has been involved in numerous other contested proceedings and appeals. **Personal:** University of Illinois at Urbana-Champaign, AB, 1979; Harvard Law School, JD, 1982.

## LASSAR, Scott R
Sidley Austin LLP, Chicago
312 853 7668
slassar@sidley.com
*Recommended in Litigation*

**Practice Areas:** Scott Lassar's practice includes white-collar criminal defense, representation before the SEC, and class action securities litigation. Mr Lassar has tried over 35 cases in federal court as a prosecutor and in private practice, including trials involving securities and commodity trading, accountant's liability, trade secrets, and federal criminal violations. He often conducts investigations for committees of Boards of Directors. Mr Lassar was the United States Attorney for the Northern District of Illinois in Chicago where he managed a staff of 250 people who handled civil litigation and criminal investigations and prosecutions involving white-collar fraud, public corruption, narcotics trafficking and violent crime. While serving as US Attorney, Mr Lassar personally tried several cases, including the ADM price fixing case, for which he received the Department of Justice's highest award. **Prof. Memberships:** Mr Lassar is a Fellow of the American College of Trial Lawyers. **Personal:** Northwestern University School of Law, JD, 1975; Oberlin College, BA, 1972. Admission: Illinois, 1975.

## LATIMER, Kenneth A
Duane Morris LLP, Chicago
312 499 6730
kalatimer@duanemorris.com
*Recommended in Banking & Finance*

**Practice Areas:** Kenneth A Latimer has represented secured and unsecured lenders in financing transactions including asset based lending, credit enhancements with letters of credit, and real estate and lease financing for more than 30 years. He also has assisted lenders in workout proceedings; represented public and privately held companies in documenting their financial obligations; and has assisted financial institutions in mergers and acquisitions and other regulatory issues. **Prof. Memberships:** American Bar Association – Business Law Section, Banking Law Committee, Commercial Financial Services Committee; Illinois State Bar Association – Committee on Banking (Former Chair); Association of Commercial Finance Attorneys; Commercial Finance Association Education Foundation – Governing Board (Founding Member); American College of Commercial Finance Attorneys; American Bar Foundation – Fellow; Illinois Institute of Continuing Legal Education – author, lecturer (on topics related to secured lending, letter of credit, and the Uniform Commercial Code). **Career:** Admitted to practice in the District of Columbia and Illinois; Duane Morris LLP, Partner, 1999-present; Holleb & Coff, Chicago, Illinois, Partner, 1986-99; Berger, Newark & Fenchel, Chicago, Illinois, Partner, 1975-86. **Personal:** The National Law Center of The George Washington University, JD, 1969.

## LAURIE, Ty D
DLA Piper Rudnick Gray Cary US LLP, Chicago 312 368 2140
ty.laurie@dlapiper.com
*Recommended in Construction*

**Practice Areas:** Construction. **Prof. Memberships:** Fellow of the American College of Construction Lawyers; Incoming Chair of the ABA Forum on Construction Industry (2005-06). **Career:** His representative matters include reconstruction of sports stadiums; capital improvement; replacement of hospitals; construction of high-rises and multiuse complexes. Served as construction counsel for national retailer; chaired zoning appeals board; belonged to governor's commission on Americans with Disabilities Act. Counsels on project delivery methods, negotiates contracts emphasizing dispute avoidance/resolution, ensures ADA compliance, litigates in state and federal courts, and is a certified mediator/arbitrator. **Personal:** JD, University of Michigan Law School; BA, Northwestern University.

## LAVEY, Warren G
Skadden, Arps, Slate, Meagher & Flom LLP & Affiliates, Chicago
312 407 0830
wlavey@skadden.com
*Recommended in Telecom, Broadcast & Satellite*

**Practice Areas:** Advises on regulatory strategies and proceedings before federal, state and municipal regulatory commissions as well as foreign governments; corporate deals involving US and non-US telecommunications ventures and suppliers to telecommunications companies; antitrust issues relating to telecommunications; and technology aspects of Internet, software and computer services transactions. Former special assistant to the chief of the Common Carrier Bureau of the Federal Communications Commission. **Career:** JD, Harvard Law School, 1979 (magna cum laude); Diploma in Economics, Cambridge University, 1976 (first class honors); MS and AB in Applied Mathematics, Harvard University, 1975 (summa cum laude).

## LAYTIN, Daniel E
Kirkland & Ellis LLP, Chicago
312 861 2198
dlaytin@kirkland.com
*Recommended in Antitrust*

**Practice Areas:** Dan Laytin focuses his practice primarily in the areas of commercial, antitrust, and class action litigation in federal and state courts. In the antitrust area, he litigates Sherman Act section conspiracy and conduct cases, as well as state antitrust causes of action, both in commercial cases and consumer class actions. **Prof. Memberships:** 2001-03, Vice Chair of Antitrust Section, Chicago Bar Association; Past Member, Board of Directors of the University of Michigan Alumni Association **Personal:** University of Michigan (AB, 1995) high honors, Phi Beta Kappa; University of Michigan Law School (JD, 1998) magna cum laude, Order of the Coif

## LEDUC, André
Skadden, Arps, Slate, Meagher & Flom LLP & Affiliates, Chicago
312 407 0770
aleduc@skadden.com
*Recommended in Tax*

**Practice Areas:** Has a broad-based federal tax practice. Advises with respect to the federal income taxation of bankruptcy and financial restructurings and tax-advantaged financial products, particularly cross-border transactions. Representative Clients: Comdisco Holding Co., Edison Mission Energy, Friedman's Inc., Interstate Bakeries Corporation, PSEG Resources, Safety-Kleen Corp. **Prof. Memberships:** American Law Institute Federal Income Tax Advisory

Group, 1987-95; Adjunct Professor of Law, University of Miami, 1993-95; Adjunct Professor of Law, Graduate Tax Program, Chicago-Kent College of Law, 1985-90; 1998-present.
**Career:** Counsel, US Senate Committee on Finance, 1981-83. JD, Harvard Law School, 1978 (cum laude); AB, Princeton University, 1975 (summa cum laude).

## LEE, Robert C
Jones Day, Chicago
312 269 4173
rclee@jonesday.com
*Recommended in Real Estate*
**Practice Areas:** Co-Chair of Jones Day's Real Estate Practice. Represents sponsors and investors in the formation of opportunity funds, value-added funds, core funds, and global and geographically focused funds in the US, UK and Europe. Has extensive experience in creating joint ventures, in complex public and private company real estate M&A, in portfolio transactions, and in subscription and property-based financings in the US, Europe, China and Latin America. Selected as an Illinois Super Lawyer and member of the Illinois Leading Lawyers Network in 2005-06. Is a frequent speaker on real estate private equity, cross-border investment, and fund structuring-related topics.

## LEMEIN, Gregg D
Baker & McKenzie, Chicago
312 861 8013
gregg.d.lemein@bakernet.com
*Recommended in Tax, Tax Litigation*
**Practice Areas:** US federal income taxation of corporations, with emphasis on international tax issues. Extensive experience in international tax planning, transfer pricing and tax controversies before the IRS and in court.
**Prof. Memberships:** American Bar Association Tax Section.
**Career:** Joined Baker & McKenzie in 1976 and became a Partner in 1983.
**Publications:** Numerous published articles.
**Personal:** Northwestern University Law School, JD, magna cum laude, Order of the Coif; Kellogg Graduate School of Management, Northwestern University, MM, with distinction; and University of Illinois, BS, with high honors.

## LERMAN, Bradley
Winston & Strawn LLP, Chicago
312 558 7492
blerman@winston.com
*Recommended in Litigation*
**Practice Areas:** Complex commercial litigation, financial and corporate investigations, products liability, white-collar criminal defense.
**Career:** Joined firm as Partner, 1998. Representative clients: Philip Morris, McDonald's, Abbott, Morgan Stanley. Prior experience: Associate Independent Counsel, Madison Guaranty S&L Investi-

gation, Whitewater Investigation, 1994-96; Assistant US Attorney, Northern District of Illinois, 1986-94.
**Personal:** Yale University, BA in Economics, summa cum laude, 1978, Phi Beta Kappa; Harvard Law School, JD, cum laude, 1981.

## LEVIN, Jack S
Kirkland & Ellis LLP, Chicago
312 861 2004
jlevin@kirkland.com
*Recommended in Corporate/M&A, Corporate/M&A: Private Equity, Tax*
**Practice Areas:** Practice concentrates on complex business transactions, including mergers, acquisitions, buyouts, private equity/venture capital investing, private equity fund formations, debt and equity restructurings, and executive compensation, emphasising on tax, corporate, SEC, and structuring aspects, handling transactions ranging in size from several million dollars to over $7 billion.
**Personal:** Northwestern University School of Business, BS, with highest distinction, 1958; Harvard Law School, LLB, 1961 (summa cum laude, ranking 1st in class of 500 and serving as officer of Harvard Law Review). CPA and winner of Illinois gold medal. Teaches at Harvard and University of Chicago Law Schools. Author of five books on M&A and private equity.

## LEVY, Richard
Latham & Watkins LLP, Chicago
312 876 7700
*Recommended in Bankruptcy*

## LEVY, William A
Mayer, Brown, Rowe & Maw LLP, Chicago 312 701 8049
wlevy@mayerbrownrowe.com
*Recommended in Tax*
**Practice Areas:** Specializes in tax-related matters emphasizing structured finance, leveraged leasing, partnership taxation, real estate and real estate investment trusts, and multi-jurisdictional corporate tax planning. Extensive experience in all aspects of mortgage and asset-backed securitization and complex real estate partnerships.
**Career:** Joined Mayer, Brown, Rowe & Maw LLP, Chicago, 1988; Partner, 1997.
**Publications:** Co-author 'The Securitization of Financial Assets', ch. 10 'Tax Issues', Prentice Hall Law & Business, 1994 edition and 'Equipment Leasing-Leveraged Leasing', ch. 30 'Securitization of Equipment and Auto Leases', Practising Law Institute, 2002 edition.
**Personal:** University of Chicago Law School, JD, 1988; Associate Editor, Law Review. University of Pennsylvania, BA magna cum laude, 1984.

## LEWIS, Charles
Jenkens & Gilchrist, Chicago
312 425 3900
*Recommended in Construction*

## LIDBURY, James T
Mayer, Brown, Rowe & Maw LLP, Chicago 312 701 8492
jlidbury@mayerbrown.com
*Recommended in Corporate/M&A*
**Practice Areas:** Mergers, acquisitions and sales of businesses.; leveraged buyouts, recapitalizations; tender and exchange offers.; proxy contests; corporate governance; special board committees; strategic alliances; venture capital investments; private equity investments.
**Career:** Mayer, Brown, Rowe & Maw LLP, Chicago, 1994 to date. US Securities & Ex-change Commission, Washington, DC, Staff Attorney, Division of Corporation Finance, 1992-94. Neal Gerber & Eisenberg, Chicago, 1990-92.
**Publications:** 'How to Buy a US Business; A Guide to Negotiated and Hostile Acquisitions', (London 1999, 2001, 2003); 'Comprehensive Reform of US Takeover Regulations and Regulation of Cross-Border Takeover Bids', (Merrill/Magnus Publishing, November 1999); 'Drafting Acquisition Agreements', PLI Course Handbook, Drafting Corporate Agreements 1998-2000, No. B-1089; 'Acquisition Structuring in the Aftermath of Epstein v. MCA, Inc', Insights, Volume 9, Number 7, July 1995.
**Personal:** Northwestern University School of Law, JD, 1990. Northwestern University, BA, 1987.

## LIEBERMAN, Richard
McGuireWoods LLP, Chicago
312 849 8100
*Recommended in Employment*

## LINKLATER, William J (Joe)
Baker & McKenzie, Chicago
312 861 2794
wjl@bakernet.com
*Recommended in Litigation*
**Practice Areas:** Practice involves criminal and complex civil litigation.
**Prof. Memberships:** American College of Trial Lawyers, Fellow; American Board of Criminal Lawyers, Fellow; American Bar Association, White Collar Crime Committee, Criminal Justice Section; Chicago Bar Association (President 2000-01); Illinois, California, Colorado, Wyoming, Seventh Circuit and Federal Bar Associations; National Association of Criminal Defense Lawyers; The Chicago Inn of Court, Master; The Wong Sun Society of San Francisco, International Proctor; World's Leading White Collar Crime Lawyers (Euromoney).
**Career:** Admitted in Illinois, California, Colorado, Wyoming and various federal District Courts and Court of Appeals.

## LIPKE, Doug
Vedder, Price, Kaufman & Kammholz, Chicago 312 609 7500
*Recommended in Bankruptcy*

## LIPTON, Richard
Baker & McKenzie, Chicago
312 861 7590
richard.m.lipton@bakernet.com
*Recommended in Tax*
**Practice Areas:** Advises on partnerships, LLCs, other pass-through entities, and real estate transactions for multinational corporations and major owners and investors in real estate.
**Prof. Memberships:** Member of Chicago Bar Association (Federal Taxation Committee, Chair, 1991-92) and American Bar Association (section of taxation: Chair, 2001-02); Fellow Regent and Officer, American College of Tax Counsel.
**Career:** Admitted to Illinois Bar and US Tax Court in 1977.
**Publications:** Contributor and Editor to the Journal of Taxation; Journal of Pass-Through Entities; Journal of Real Estate Taxation. Co-author of two treatises. Author of 100+ articles on partnership and real estate taxation.

## LIVINGSTON, Theodore A
Mayer, Brown, Rowe & Maw LLP, Chicago 312 701 7180
tlivingston@mayerbrown.com
*Recommended in Telecom, Broadcast & Satellite*
**Practice Areas:** Specialises in telecommunications and commercial litigation. Lead Counsel for AT&T Inc. (formerly SBC Communications) in regulatory and antitrust litigation under the Telecommunications Act of 1996. Lead Counsel for BellSouth in antitrust litigation under the 1996 Act. Has tried and argued cases in state and federal courts throughout the US.
**Prof. Memberships:** American Bar Association: Administrative Law and Regulatory Practice Section; Antitrust Law Section; Business Law Section; Communications Law Forum; Dispute Resolution Section; Litigation Section; Business Torts Committee of Litigation Section; Public Utilities, Communications and Transportation Law Section (Vice Chairman, Communications Committee); Illinois Supreme Court; US District Court for the Northern District of Illinois, 1973; US Supreme Court; US Court of Appeals for the Seventh Circuit, 1975; Various other US courts of appeals and district courts.
**Career:** Joined Mayer, Brown, Rowe & Maw LLP, 1973; became Partner, 1980.
**Personal:** University of Kansas, JD, 1973; Order of the Coif; Law Review. McPherson College, BA, summa cum laude, 1969.

## LOOMAN, James
Sidley Austin LLP, Chicago
312 853 7133
jlooman@sidley.com
*Recommended in Banking & Finance*
**Practice Areas:** Practice covers a broad variety of corporate and commercial finance transactions, including lending

transactions, securitization, and equipment leasing. Mr Looman represents banks and commercial finance companies in lending transactions, as well as corporate borrowers. His practice ranges from the representation of bank groups and corporate borrowers in large syndicated credit facilities, to the representation of lenders and borrowers in secured credit facilities. In equipment leasing, Mr Looman has represented debt participants, equity sources and lessees in leveraged lease transactions involving railcars, locomotives, aircraft and other equipment. Mr Looman also represents bank-sponsored conduits in the securitization of a variety of financial assets, including auto loans, auto leases, and bank loans.
**Prof. Memberships:** Member of the Bar of Illinois and the American and Chicago Bar Associations and a Fellow of American College of Commercial Finance Lawyers. He is an Associate General Counsel of the Commercial Finance Association. He was Chairman of the Commercial and Financial Transactions Committee of the Chicago Bar Association, 1996-97 and 2002-03.
**Personal:** University of Chicago, JD, 1978; Valparaiso University, BA, 1974. Admission: Illinois, 1978.

### LOPATKA, Kenneth
Perkins Coie LLP, Chicago
312 324 8400
*Recommended in Employment*

### LOWINGER, Frederick C
Sidley Austin LLP, Chicago
312 853 7238
flowinger@sidley.com
*Recommended in Corporate/M&A*
**Practice Areas:** Mr Lowinger is a member of the firm's Executive Committee and the Head of the Chicago office's Corporate Group. He has played a major role in numerous corporate transactions, including: Alberto-Culver Company's spin-off of its beauty supply distribution business and concurrent merger of that business with Regis Corporation (pending); R.R. Donnelley & Sons Company's merger with Moore Wallace Incorporated; First Data Corporation's spin-off of Western Union (pending); First Data's acquisitions of Concord EFS, Inc. and First Financial Management Corporation; Stone Container Corporation's merger-of-equals with Jefferson Smurfit Corporation; Aon Corporation's acquisition of Alexander & Alexander Inc.; and Sara Lee Corporation's sale of its direct selling business. He has represented special committees, including those of Wausau Paper Mills Company, Stauffer Communications and Pittway Corporation. His principal areas of practice are mergers and acquisitions (including contested takeovers), corporate finance and corporate governance.
**Prof. Memberships:** Mr Lowinger is a

Member of the American and Chicago Bar Associations and the Lawyers Club of Chicago.
**Career:** Mr Lowinger served as a law clerk to US Supreme Court Justice William J Brennan, Jr (1981-82) and Judge J Skelly Wright of the US Court of Appeals for the DC Circuit (1980-81).
**Publications:** Mr Lowinger is a Member of the Planning Committee of Northwestern University's Garrett Corporate and Securities Law Institute.
**Personal:** Certified public accountant. University of Chicago (JD 1980). Admission: Illinois, 1982.

### LUBIN, Donald G
Sonnenschein Nath & Rosenthal LLP, Chicago 312 876 8007
dlubin@sonnenschein.com
*Recommended in Corporate/M&A*
**Practice Areas:** Counsels private and public companies' boards and management on restructurings, takeover defense, joint ventures, governance and M&A. Also represents independent directors or committees. Clients include: McDonald's, Molex, Experian.
**Prof. Memberships:** Lawyer's Club, Commercial Club (Executive Committee), Civic Committee (Steering Committee), Fellow-American Bar Foundation. McDonald's: Senior Director, chaired Nominating and Corporate Governance Committee. Molex: Board Member, chaired Audit Committee. Chairman, Chicago Metropolis 2020; Chairman, Renaissance Schools Fund; Trustee, Rush University Medical Center; former Director, Smithsonian Institution, National Museum of American History.
**Personal:** University of Pennsylvania, BS; Harvard Law School, LLB.

### LUCAS, Roger S
Winston & Strawn LLP, Chicago
312 558 5225
rlucas@winston.com
*Recommended in Tax*
**Practice Areas:** Practice concentrated in tax issues related to business planning, mergers and acquisitions, private equity investments, joint ventures, executive compensation, and financings.
**Personal:** BBA, University of Michigan, 1988; JD, University of Michigan Law School, 1992; LLM, New York University School of Law, 1996

### LUEPKER, Wayne R
Mayer, Brown, Rowe & Maw LLP, Chicago 312 701 7197
wluepker@mayerbrownrowe.com
*Recommended in Employment*
**Practice Areas:** Executive compensation and employment: executive employment agreements and separation agreements; retention contracts, including golden handcuffs and stay bonuses; confidentiality and noncompetition agreements and other restrictive covenants; nonqualified deferred compensation

arrangements; executive incentive compensation, including stock-based compensation (stock incentive arrangements, such as stock options and restricted stock), and related insider trading (section 16) issues; executive compensation aspects of corporate transactions; change in control agreements (including rabbi trusts and golden parachute penalty tax matters); $1 million cap on deductible compensation; expatriate and cross-border compensation for executives. Employee benefits: pension plans; profit sharing plans; employee stock ownership plans; welfare benefit plans.
**Career:** Mayer, Brown, Rowe & Maw LLP, Chicago, 1980 to date; Partner, 1986. Peterson, Ross, Schloerb & Seidel, Chicago, 1979-80.
**Publications:** 'Executive Severance Agreements', Executive Compensation (2002). 'Applying the Property-Services Distinction in Corporate Transactions: The New Economy Tests the Limits', 29 Taxes 3 (March 2001). Speaker at seminars for the American Bar Association, Chicago Bar Association, National Association of Stock Plan Professionals, Practicing Law Institute, Profit Sharing Council of America, Southern Employee Benefits Conference, Tax Executive Institute and clients.
**Personal:** University of Chicago, JD, 1979. Grinnell College, BA, 1971.

### LURIE, Paul
Schiff Hardin LLP, Chicago
312 258 5660
plurie@schiffhardin.com
*Recommended in Construction*
**Practice Areas:** Construction.
**Prof. Memberships:** American Arbitration Association, CPR International Institute for Conflict Prevention and Resolution, International Academy of Mediators, College of Commercial Arbitrators, American College of Construction Lawyers.
**Career:** Business/legal Counsel for United States and international development and design firms, advising on project planning, contracting, and dispute avoidance and resolution. His knowledge of design and construction firms has made him a valuable advisor on issues of ownership structure, transition, mergers and acquisitions.
**Publications:** Co-author: 'Ownership Transition Options and Strategies', numerous other publications.
**Personal:** University of Michigan (BA, 1962), University of Michigan Law School (JD, 1965).

### LUSCOMBE II, George A
Mayer, Brown, Rowe & Maw LLP, Chicago 312 701 7099
gluscombe@mayerbrownrowe.com
*Recommended in Tax*
**Practice Areas:** Partner in Corporate Taxation Practice in Chicago. Structures

acquisitions and divestitures, taxable and tax-free, business joint ventures, leveraged buyouts, and leasing transactions; partnership, joint venture, and limited liability company vehicles for real estate, natural resources, and new technologies; investment vehicles and companies in various industries. Represents corporations, partnerships, and limited liability companies in matters related to general corporate, partnership, real estate and natural resources taxation.
**Prof. Memberships:** Admitted to practice in the District of Columbia, 1972, and Illinois, 1969. Adjunct Professor of Taxation, Illinois Institute of Technology/Chicago-Kent College of Law, 1987-93. Member of American Bar Association, Section of Taxation; former Chairman, Committee on Capital Recovery and Leasing; former Editor, 'Tax Notes' column, American Bar Association Journal.
**Career:** Office of Chief Counsel, IRS, Legislation and Regulations Division, Washington, DC, 1969-73. Mayer, Brown, Rowe & Maw LLP, 1973-present; Partner, 1976.
**Publications:** Author of presentations for Illinois Institute for Continuing Legal Education, American Bar Association, University of Chicago Tax Institute, Tulane Tax Institute, and Canadian Petroleum Tax Society and Canadian Property Forum.
**Personal:** LLM, George Washington University, 1972. JD, University of Illinois, 1969; Order of the Coif. BS (honors) University of Illinois, 1966. CPA, Illinois, 1966.

### LYMAN, Bill
Lyman & Nielsen, Oak Brook
630 575 0020
*Recommended in Construction*

### LYNCH, James
Winston & Strawn LLP, Chicago
312 558 5600
*Recommended in Tax*

### LYONS, Francis
Bell, Boyd & Lloyd LLC, Chicago
312 372 1121
*Recommended in Environment*

### MAATMAN JR, Gerald
Seyfarth Shaw LLP, Chicago
312 346 8000
*Recommended in Employment*

### MACBRIDE, Owen
Schiff Hardin LLP, Chicago
312 258 5680
omacbride@schiffhardin.com
*Recommended in Energy, Telecom, Broadcast & Satellite*
**Practice Areas:** Energy, telecommunications, and public utilities.
**Career:** Mr MacBride focuses in regulation, legislation, and transactions affecting suppliers and consumers of electricity, gas, and water. He represents public

utilities and other entities before the Illinois Commerce Commission in various matters including rate and tariff proceedings, certifications, complaint cases and investigations, and rulemakings. He also represents clients in administrative proceedings and litigation involving state and local taxes applicable to utilities and similar businesses, as well as in numerous appeals to the courts from administrative agency decisions.
**Personal:** University of Michigan (BA, Economics, 1971), Yale Law School (JD, 1975).

## MALLOY, Timothy J
McAndrews, Held & Malloy, Ltd, Chicago
312 775 8000
tmalloy@mhmlaw.com
*Recommended in Intellectual Property*

**Practice Areas:** Litigation and trial of high technology matters, including jury and bench cases, arbitrations, and mediations involving patent and other intellectual property law matters throughout the United States.
**Prof. Memberships:** Admitted to practice in Illinois and is a member of the bars of many US district and appellate courts, and the US Supreme Court, and registered to practice before the US Patent and Trademark Office.
**Career:** As a lead trial counsel, Mr Malloy has obtained numerous multi-million dollar verdicts, awards, and settlements for his clients, including $166 million in Advanced Cardiovascular Systems, Inc. v. Medtronic, Inc., Civil Action No. 99-05393. ('Top Ten IP Damage Awards For All Time', Intellectual Property Today, March 2003, p 43). He prepared and argued before the Supreme Court the case of Eli Lilly and Company v. Medtronic, Inc., 496 US 661 (1990) involving patent protection for medical devices. For defendants, he has obtained numerous verdicts and judgments of invalidity and noninfringement.
**Personal:** Mr Malloy holds BSEE and JD degrees from the University of Notre Dame; elected to the National Register of Who's Who, Chamber's USA – America's Leading Lawyers, Strathmore's Who's Who, and Top 100 Illinois Super Lawyers.

## MANDEL, Reid
Katten Muchin Rosenman LLP, Chicago
312 902 5200
*Recommended in Tax*

## MANDELL, Floyd
Katten Muchin Rosenman LLP, Chicago
312 902 5200
*Recommended in Intellectual Property*

## MAROVITZ, Andrew S
Mayer, Brown, Rowe & Maw LLP, Chicago 312 701 7116
amarovitz@mayerbrownrowe.com
*Recommended in Antitrust*

**Practice Areas:** Chicago Litigation Practice Co-Leader. Specializes in

antitrust litigation and high-stakes commercial litigation. Represents national and multinational corporations in monopolization, attempted monopolization, price fixing, market allocation and conspiracy cases. Counsels on general antitrust issues.
**Prof. Memberships:** Admitted: Illinois, 1989. US District Court for the Northern District of Illinois, 1989. US District Court for the Central District of Illinois, 1995. US Court of Appeals for the Fourth Circuit, 1994. US Court of Appeals for the Seventh Circuit, 1990. US Court of Appeals for the Eighth Circuit, 1998. US Court of Appeals for the DC Circuit, 2000. US Supreme Court, 2004.
**Career:** Joined Mayer, Brown, Rowe & Maw LLP, Chicago, 1990; Partner, 1998. Law clerk to The Honorable Richard D Cudahy, US Court of Appeals for the Seventh Circuit, 1989-90.
**Publications:** 'Empagran and the Globalization of the Sherman Act', Business Law Int'l 197 (Sept 2003); 'Snapshots After Kodak', Of Interest (March 1993) (co-authored with Mark McLaughlin); 'Casting a Meaningful Ballot', 98 Yale LJ 1193 (1989).
**Personal:** Yale Law School, JD, 1989; Potter Stewart Prize, Best Team in Moot Court Competition; Notes Editor, The Yale Law Journal. Amherst College, BA with honors, 1986; Phi Beta Kappa; Harry S Truman Scholar.

## MARREN, John
Hogan Marren Ltd, Chicago
312 946 1800
*Recommended in Healthcare*

## MARRINSON, Thomas A
Morgan, Lewis & Bockius LLP, Chicago
312 324 1120
tmarrinson@morganlewis.com
*Recommended in Insurance*

**Practice Areas:** Thomas A Marrinson is a Partner in the Chicago office of Morgan, Lewis & Bockius LLP. His practice focuses on both commercial litigation and insurance coverage counseling and litigation. His insurance experience spans a broad range of matters, including environmental clean-up, asbestos and other mass tort claims, as well as professional liability and first-party property insurance coverage. He frequently counsels Fortune 500 companies on insurance-related matters and has significant experience in bankruptcy-related insurance issues. Mr Marrinson is active in the leadership of the American Bar Association's Section of Litigation and writes and lectures frequently on insurance coverage issues.

## MARTIN, Alan J
Mayer, Brown, Rowe & Maw LLP,
Chicago 312 701 7266
amartin@mayerbrownrowe.com
*Recommended in Insurance*

**Practice Areas:** Representation in: com-

plex insurance coverages; general commercial litigation, including joint venture agreements, bank LOCs, service agreements, breach of warranty and supply agreements; civil RICO and fraud claims; product liability; healthcare; toxic torts. Insurance/Reinsurance including antitrust, asbestos, bodily injury and wrongful death, class actions, construction defects, coverage placement, captive programs, directors and officers, employment practices, entertainment, environmental, errors and omissions (professional services), ERISA and fiduciary duty claims, financial institutions, fraud and RICO claims (including qui tam actions), healthcare (hospital, nursing facility, physician groups, review firms, support services and products); insolvency and regulatory, intellectual property, mass liability, products liability, large-scale property damage and business interruption/extra expense claims and toxic torts.
**Career:** Mayer, Brown, Rowe & Maw LLP, Chicago, 1987 to date. Isham, Lincoln & Beale, Chicago, 1985-87. United States Department of State, Bureau of Intelligence and Research, Office of Politico-Military Analysis, 1981.
**Publications:** Co-author: ABA publication, 'Putting Your Attorney On The Witness Stand And His Advice At Issue: The Perils Of Selective Waiver of Privilege'.
**Personal:** University of Virginia, JD, 1985; Managing and Executive Editor, Journal of Law and Politics. University of Illinois, BA summa cum laude, 1982; Phi Beta Kappa, Bronze Tablet, Merriam Scholar.

## MARTIN, Laura Keidan
Katten Muchin Rosenman LLP, Chicago
312 902 5487
laura.martin@kattenlaw.com
*Recommended in Healthcare, Antitrust*

**Practice Areas:** Specializing in healthcare law and antitrust. Healthcare law practice includes mergers and acquisitions, physician integration strategies, provider joint ventures and regulatory compliance, with particular expertise in stark/fraud and abuse compliance. Clients include hospitals, outpatient facilities, medical supply vendors, therapy management companies, managed care entities and venture capital firms. Antitrust practice includes HSR issues, merger investigations, counseling and compliance plan development for clients in hi-tech, healthcare, financial services and manufacturing industries.
**Prof. Memberships:** President and Board Member of the Illinois Association of Healthcare Attorneys; former Chair (2005), Antitrust Law Committee, Chicago Bar Association; American Bar Association; American Health Lawyers Association.
**Career:** Named one of '40 Under Forty Attorneys to Watch' in 2004 by Law Bul-

letin Publishing.
**Publications:** 'OIG Special Advisory Bulletin Attacks Certain Contractual Joint Ventures', Hospitals & Health Systems (Summer 2003) (co-author); 'Not So Fast, It's Regulated', Business Law Today, (September/October 2000); 'Antitrust Guidelines Impact CPA Firm Alliances', CPA Administrator's and Manager's Report, (September-September 2000) (co-author); 'Antitrust Guidelines for Competitor Collaborations', Outside Counsel, (Summer, 2000) (co-author); past Articles Editor, ABA Antitrust Law Section's Antitrust Health Care Chronicle.
**Personal:** Harvard University (JD cum laude 1989); University of Michigan (BA with high distinction 1986).

## MARX, David
McDermott Will & Emery, Chicago
312 984 7668
dmarx@mwe.com
*Recommended in Antitrust*

**Practice Areas:** Partner in Litigation Department. Concentrates practice in civil and criminal antitrust litigation and counseling, and trade regulation matters. Responsible for Chicago antitrust practice. Serves corporate and healthcare industry clients, and individuals who are the subjects or targets of investigations or enforcement proceedings initiated by federal or state antitrust agencies, and in private civil litigation. Develops, implements and monitors antitrust and trade regulation compliance programs for a variety of corporate clients.
**Personal:** Syracuse University College of Law (JD); Amherst College (BA, cum laude).

## MASON, David
Goldberg, Kohn, Bell, Black, Rosenbloom & Moritz, Ltd, Chicago
312 201 4000
*Recommended in Banking & Finance*

## MATHIAS JR, John H
Jenner & Block LLP, Chicago
312 923 2917
jmathias@jenner.com
*Recommended in Insurance*

**Practice Areas:** John H Mathias, Jr is a Partner in Jenner & Block's Chicago office. He is Chair of the firm's nationally prominent Insurance Litigation and Counseling Practice, and Co-Chair of its Professional Liability Litigation Group. He is also a member of the Class Action Litigation, Arbitration: Domestic and International, Reinsurance and Litigation and Dispute Resolution Practices. Mr Mathias is a veteran trial lawyer concentrating on business litigation with particular emphasis upon insurance coverage litigation, reinsurance arbitration, contract litigation, directors and officers litigation, class actions, professional liability litigation, and intellectual property disputes. He has co-authored over 20 legal publications, including Insurance Coverage Disputes (Law Journal Press 1996) and Directors and Officers Liability: Prevention, Insurance and Indemnification (Law Journal Press, 2000.) Mr Mathias is a frequent lecturer on insurance coverage litigation topics. He has been an active member of the American Bar Association's Section of Litigation, where he has served on the Section's Leadership Council. Mr Mathias also has co-chaired various Section committees, including the Insurance Coverage Litigation Committee and its bipartisan Task Force on Environmental Insurance Coverage.

**Personal:** Mr Mathias is a graduate of Dartmouth College (1969) and Harvard Law School (1972). He is a founder of the Dartmouth Lawyers Association, and currently serves on its Board of Directors.

## MATKOV, George
Matkov Salzman Madoff & Gunn, Chicago 312 332 0777
*Recommended in Employment*

## MAYNES, Todd F
Kirkland & Ellis LLP, Chicago
312 861 2485
tmaynes@kirkland.com
*Recommended in Tax*

**Practice Areas:** Todd Maynes focuses his practice in the areas of tax litigation and the tax aspects of bankruptcy, including the handling of federal and state contested tax matters for corporations and individuals. He has represented clients before the US Supreme Court, the Courts of Appeals, Tax Court, federal district court and various state courts. He is Co-Chairman of the Chicago-Kent Federal Tax Institute and is a Member of the University of Chicago Federal Tax Conference Planning Committee.

**Personal:** Brigham Young University, BA, 1984; Brigham Young University, JD, 1987.

## MCANDREWS, George
McAndrews, Held & Malloy, Ltd, Chicago
312 775 8000
*Recommended in Intellectual Property*

## MCCAHILL, Jane
Bell, Boyd & Lloyd LLC, Chicago
312 372 1121
*Recommended in Healthcare*

## MCCAREINS, R Mark
Winston & Strawn LLP, Chicago
312 558 5902
rmccareins@winston.com
*Recommended in Antitrust*

**Practice Areas:** Antitrust, trade regulation, intellectual property litigation.

**Prof. Memberships:** American, Federal and Seventh Circuit, Chicago, and California Bar Associations; American Inns of Court; American Bar Foundation Fellow.

**Career:** Associate, 1981. Partner, 1988. Litigation Department Advisory Committee.

**Publications:** Senior Editor, 'Antitrust Discovery Handbook', ABA Antitrust

Section, 2003; Vice-Chair, ABA Antitrust Section Civil Practice and Procedure Committee; Adjunct Professor of Antitrust, Northwestern University Kellogg Graduate School of Management; Chairman of Advisory Board, Center for Inter-disciplinary Studies, Washington University School of Law.

**Personal:** Northwestern University, BA, with honors, 1978; Washington University, JD, 1981, Editor in Chief, Washington University Law Quarterly.

## MCCORMICK, Steven D
Kirkland & Ellis LLP, Chicago
312 861 2246
smccormick@kirkland.com
*Recommended in Litigation*

**Practice Areas:** Commercial litigation, international arbitration, civil and criminal antitrust, product liability, mass tort and intellectual property litigation.

**Career:** 35 years of experience in state and federal courts, and domestic and international arbitrations. Cases tried as lead counsel in 20 different federal and state courts in every region of the country, as well as to arbitration panels in the US, Mexico, and Europe.

**Personal:** Head of Kirkland & Ellis in-house trial advocacy program since 1993. Adjunct Professor, Northwestern University School of Law, Integrated Trial Advocacy course, since 1997. Instructor, National Institute for Trial Advocacy, Chicago and Boulder, Colorado, 1989-98.

## MCCULLOUGH, Joe
Lovells, Chicago 312 832 4401
joe.mccullough@lovells.com
*Recommended in Insurance*

**Practice Areas:** Insurance and reinsurance.

**Career:** Joe has devoted his practice to representing insurance and reinsurance companies. He has acted as counsel to insurers and reinsurers in numerous arbitrations and court proceedings across the US, as well as the Carribean and Europe, including some of the highest profile cases in the industry. Joe is a frequent contributor to various insurance industry publications and has organized, chaired and spoken at numerous reinsurance seminars and conferences around the globe.

**Personal:** Northwestern University School of Law (JD, 1985); University of Ghent, Belgium (MA European Law, 1982); Georgetown University (BA, 1979).

## MCDONNELL, John J
McDonnell Boehnen Hulbert & Berghoff LLP, Chicago 312 913 2110
McDonnell@mbhb.com
*Recommended in Intellectual Property*

**Career:** John J McDonnell is a founder of McDonnell Boehnen Hulbert & Berghoff LLP. His patent practice primarily focuses on biotechnology, pharmaceuticals, diag-

nostics, and related healthcare matters, with a particular focus on advising emerging high-technology companies and groups investing in such companies. Noted for his creative strategies and alternative approaches to intellectual property business objectives, he has extensive experience in complex lawsuits involving major biotechnology products. Dr McDonnell has more than 30 years of experience in pharmaceutical and diagnostic patent matters. He was formerly chief patent and trademark counsel at G.D. Searle and Company, where he secured a five-year extension of the Aspartame patent and directed the brand ingredient strategy for NutraSweet. He was also Head of the diagnostic patent operations at Abbott Laboratories for five years. Before entering the practice of law, he was an assistant professor of chemistry at the Illinois Institute of Technology. He is a Member of the American Intellectual Property Law Association and the Association of Corporate Patent Counsels, and he has spoken widely on many aspects of biotechnology related to intellectual property issues in the United States and abroad. Dr McDonnell earned a PhD in Organic Chemistry from Iowa State University and a JD from Chicago-Kent College of Law. He is admitted to practice in Illinois and before the US Patent & Trademark Office.

## MCENROE, John
Vedder, Price, Kaufman & Kammholz, Chicago 312 609 7500
*Recommended in Banking & Finance*

## MCKENZIE, Diana
Neal, Gerber & Eisenberg LLP, Chicago
312 2698093
dmckenzie@ngelaw.com
*Recommended in Technology*

**Practice Areas:** Nationwide practice focused on significant information technology transactions including: outsourcing, business process outsourcing, ASP, ERP, healthcare technology, licensing, distribution, development, consulting and other services, support and maintenance, integration, strategic alliances, privacy, internet and e-commerce, and other information technology related matters.

**Prof. Memberships:** Advisory Board, Computer Law Association (2003-present), President (2002-03), Officer (2000-03), Board of Directors (1997-2003); Senior Member, Healthcare Information & Management Systems Society (2002-present).

**Career:** Partner; Information Technology Practice Group Chair.

**Publications:** Noted author and lecturer (100+ speeches) on information technology and electronic commerce law topics.

**Personal:** Emory University (JD, 1985; MBA, 1985); Kenyon College (BA, 1981).

## MCLAUGHLIN, Ellen
Seyfarth Shaw LLP, Chicago
312 346 8000
*Recommended in Employment*

## MCLAUGHLIN, T Mark
Mayer, Brown, Rowe & Maw LLP, Chicago 312 701 7066
mmclaughlin@mayerbrownrowe.com
*Recommended in Antitrust*

**Practice Areas:** Litigation and counseling on antitrust and other distribution matters. Has litigated substantial antitrust cases involving a variety of industries and issues, including monopolization claims, challenges to acquisitions, and group boycott, exclusive dealing, sham litigation and price discrimination claims, and claims involving practices in foreign commerce.

**Prof. Memberships:** Part-time Faculty, Loyola University of Chicago School of Law (antitrust courses), 1983, 1986, 1988-90. Governing Committee, ABA Forum on Franchising, 1992-95. ABA Section of Antitrust Law, Chair, Membership Committee, 1993-96. American Bar Association, Section of Antitrust Law, Forum on Franchising. Chicago Bar Association. Commercial Arbitration Panel. American Arbitration Association. Illinois, 1978. US District Court for the Northern District of Illinois and Trial Bar, 1978. US Court of Appeals for the Seventh and Eleventh Circuits, 1982; Eighth Circuit, 1998; Tenth Circuit, 2004. US District Court for the Central District of Illinois, 1992. US District Court for the Eastern District of Wisconsin, 1992.

**Career:** Mayer, Brown, Rowe & Maw LLP, 1978-present; Partner, 1985.

**Personal:** University of Notre Dame, JD, magna cum laude, 1978; Law Review. University of Notre Dame, BA, summa cum laude, 1975. Board of Directors, American Diabetes Association, Northern Illinois Affiliate, Inc., 1985-94; Chairman, 1990-92.

## MCMENAMIN, J Robert
McDermott Will & Emery, Chicago
312 984 3618
rmcmenamin@mwe.com
*Recommended in Banking & Finance*

**Practice Areas:** Previously Chair of firm's Finance Group. Currently Senior Counsel in Corporate Department. Experience includes syndicated loans, restructurings, securitisations, project financing, leveraged acquisition financing, capital financing, asset-based lending, subordinated debt and mezzanine financing, ESOP lending, credit enhancement, and workouts, both in private and public markets.

**Prof. Memberships:** American Bar Association; The Lawyers Club of Chicago; and The Economic Club of Chicago. Past President, The Lawyers Club of Chicago. Past Chairman, Advisory Board of Holy Trinity High School. Past Direc-

tor, Saints Scholistica Academy.
**Career:** Clerked in US Court of Appeals, 7th Circuit (1971-72).
**Personal:** University of Notre Dame (JD, BA).

### MEADOWS, Stanley
McDermott Will & Emery, Chicago
312 984 7570
smeadows@mwe.com
*Recommended in Corporate/M&A*
**Practice Areas:** Practices acquisitions and dispositions of businesses, public and private financings and business counseling. Clients include companies whose securities are publicly traded, buyout funds, entrepreneurs and other buyers of financially distressed companies. Matters include acquisitions and financings of businesses engaged in telecommunications, software development, sports and entertainment, restaurant management, pharmaceutical distribution, manufacturing, insurance and real estate activities. Counseled purchasers of professional sports franchises, including financing of purchase and development of new sports venues. Represented clients in establishing manufacturing, technology and trading ventures in Asia and Latin America.
**Personal:** University of Illinois (BS); University of Chicago Law School (JD).

### MEDOW, Jonathan C
Mayer, Brown, Rowe & Maw LLP, Chicago 312 701 7060
jmedow@mayerbrown.com
*Recommended in Litigation*
**Practice Areas:** Extensive experience litigating complex commercial disputes across the country, particularly in the areas of securities regulation, professional malpractice and bankruptcy. Has served as lead trial counsel for several major accounting firms in numerous complex, high-stakes disputes.
**Career:** Mayer, Brown, Rowe & Maw LLP, Chicago, 1983 to date. Law clerk to The Honorable Susan Getzendanner, US District Court for the Northern District of Illinois, 1981-83.
**Personal:** Harvard Law School, JD magna cum laude, 1981; Board of Editors, Law Review. Stanford University, BA with distinction, 1978; Phi Beta Kappa.

### MEHLMAN, Mark
Sonnenschein Nath & Rosenthal LLP, Chicago 312 876 8023
mmehlman@sonnenschein.com
*Recommended in Real Estate*
**Practice Areas:** Experience includes financing (including conduit lending), troubled loan workouts, acquisitions and dispositions, partnerships and joint ventures, and hotel transactions.
**Prof. Memberships:** Secretary, ABA's Executive Committee of the Real Property, Probate and Trust Section; Member and Vice President of the Executive Committee, American College of Real Estate

Lawyers; Member, Anglo-American Real Property Institute; Honorary Life Member, Anti-Defamation League; Vice Chairman, Board of Trustees, Spertus Institute of Jewish Studies; Member, Sonnenschein Policy and Planning Committee.
**Personal:** University of Michigan, LLB; Administrative Editor, University of Michigan Journal of Law Reform; University of Illinois, BA.

### MELAND, Creighton
Baker & McKenzie, Chicago
312 861 2990
creighton.r.meland@bakernet.com
*Recommended in Banking & Finance*
**Practice Areas:** Corporate finance and lending for senior and subordinated debt, including bank debt and private placements; leveraged leasing; acquisition finance; cross-border lending and foreign currency, denominated credits; multibank, agented and syndicated credits and loan participations.
**Prof. Memberships:** Financial Institutions Committee, The Chicago Bar Association (Chairman: 2000-01, Vice Chairman: 1999-2000 and Legislative Liaison: 1998-99).
**Publications:** Has written and presented extensively on a variety of financial topics.
**Personal:** Received his BS Degree (Finance), University of Pennsylvania, cum laude, and is a graduate of University of Michigan Law School, magna cum laude (where he was a Michigan Law Review Articles Editor).

### MELBINGER, Michael S
Winston & Strawn LLP, Chicago
312 558 7588
mmelbinger@winston.com
*Recommended in Employment*
**Practice Areas:** Executive compensation, retirement and welfare benefit plans and related tax, securities and litigation issues.
**Prof. Memberships:** NASPP, NACD, ABA, American College of Employee Benefits Counsel Fellow.
**Career:** Partner and Chair: Executive Compensation and Employee Benefits Department, Winston & Strawn LLP, 1997-present; Adjunct Professor, Northwestern University Law School, 2003-present; Partner, Schiff Hardin; associate/Partner, McDermott Will & Emery.
**Publications:** 'Executive Compensation, CCH; Guide to Employee Benefit Trusts', ABA; more than fifty articles on employee benefits and executive compensation topics. Contributing editor: CompensationStandards.com.
**Personal:** BA University of Notre Dame, 1980; JD University of Illinois College of Law, 1983.

### MENDELOFF, Scott T
Sidley Austin LLP, Chicago
312 853 7362
smendeloff@sidley.com

*Recommended in Litigation*
**Practice Areas:** Scott Mendeloff's work includes civil and criminal trial practice and internal corporate investigations. Mr Mendeloff's civil and criminal practice has ranged from representation of Fortune 100 companies to individuals. He served as primary trial counsel in a numerous commercial disputes focusing upon allegations of healthcare fraud and abuse, accounting fraud, contract interpretation, and civil RICO. He has handled numerous substantial internal corporate investigations for the nation's largest corporations and academic institutions as well as for local charities. Mr Mendeloff served as one of the primary trial lawyers in the government's prosecution of Timothy McVeigh for the Oklahoma City bombing. The United States Justice Department awarded Mr Mendeloff one of its highest honors, the Attorney General's Award.
**Prof. Memberships:** Treasurer of the Federal Bar Association (Chicago); Secretary of the Chicago Crime Commission; and Chairman of a blue ribbon panel selected to examine ethics in Cook County government.
**Career:** As an Assistant US Attorney in Chicago, Mr Mendeloff supervised hundreds of cases in the Criminal and Special Prosecutions Divisions of that office.
**Personal:** Georgetown University Law Center, JD, 1983; Georgetown University, MS, 1986; University of Wisconsin Madison, BA, 1979. Admission: Illinois, 1983.

### MENDELSOHN, David
DLA Piper Rudnick Gray Cary US LLP, Chicago 312 368 7272
david.mendelsohn@dlapiper.com
*Recommended in Insurance*
**Practice Areas:** Insurance and reinsurance.
**Prof. Memberships:** Associate of Fellows and Legal Scholars of the Center for International Legal Studies.
**Career:** Handles insurance and reinsurance, and structured finance and alternative risk, transactions and regulatory matters, as well as mediations and arbitrations. He also conducts internal investigations and compliance reviews, and counsels clients on compliance, E&O risk management, ethics, IT and e-commerce, and information management matters, such as records management and retention, contracts management, money laundering, and data privacy and security.
**Personal:** JD, Chicago-Kent College of Law, Illinois Institute of Technology; Lancaster Gate School of Law; LLB, University College London.

### MENSCH, Linda
Linda S Mensch PC - Sole Practitioner, Chicago 312 922 2910
*Recommended in Media & Entertainment*

### MENSIK, Michael S
Baker & McKenzie, Chicago
312 861 8941
michael.s.mensik@bakernet.com
*Recommended in Business Process Outsourcing, Technology*
**Practice Areas:** Focus: outsourcing; information technology; privacy; e-commerce. Advises companies on doing business in global environment, physically and electronically, particularly intellectual property protection. He counsels multinationals on how to structure their outsourcing arrangements, from ITO to BPO, and creating background to vendor-to-vendor strategic alliances that support such customer offerings.
**Prof. Memberships:** Global Co-Coordinator, Baker & McKenzie IT/Communications Practice; Editor, Global e-Law Alert, and Outsourcing Legalbytes.
**Career:** Admitted in Illinois (1980).
**Publications:** 'Legal Briefs – Top Outsourcing Lawyers Give Advice to Buyers', Outsourcing Essentials (Spring 2005); 'Building Trust', EquaTerra Equips Newsletter, Volume 10 (May 2005); 'Global Data Transfers and the European Directive – A Practical Analysis of the New ICC Contract Clauses', Privacy & Security Law, Vol. 4, No. 6 (February 2005); 'Should Companies Outsource Sarbanes-Oxley Compliance?' Outsourcing Essentials (Winter 2004); 'The Sarbanes-Oxley/Outsourcing Intersection: An Introduction', The Outsourcing Journal (Nov. 2004); 'Outsourcing to India: Key Legal & Tax Considerations for US Financial Institutions', The Outsourcing Journal (August 2004); 'Business Process Outsourcing under Sarbanes-Oxley – Challenges and Complexities', The Outsourcing Journal (April 2004); 'Outsourcing, Offshoring and Employee Privacy Rights', Privacy Litigation Reporter (September 2003).

### MENSON, Richard
McGuireWoods LLP, Chicago
312 849 8100
*Recommended in Employment*

### METROPOULOS, Demetrios G
Mayer, Brown, Rowe & Maw LLP, Chicago 312 701 8479
demetro@mayerbrown.com
*Recommended in Telecom, Broadcast & Satellite*
**Practice Areas:** Jim has devoted the majority of his practice to communications-related litigation for over nine years. He has served both as lead trial counsel (in numerous proceedings before state regulatory commissions) and lead appellate counsel (in state and federal courts). Jim has also represented clients with respect to insurance coverage, products liability, and antitrust.
**Career:** Mayer, Brown, Rowe & Maw LLP, Chicago, 1994 to date; Partner, 2002. Law clerk to The Honorable Joseph T

Sneed, US Court of Appeals for the Ninth Circuit, 1993-94. Coopers & Lybrand, Certified Public Accountants, Detroit, 1985-90.

**Publications:** 'Constitutional Dimensions of the North American Free Trade Agreement', 27 Cornell Int'l LJ 141, 1994. Note, 'Human Rights, Incorporated: The European Community's New Line of Business', 29 Stan J Int'l L 131, 1993. Note, 'Son of COBRA: The Evolution of a Federal Malpractice Law', 45 Stan L Rev 263, 1993. Co-author: 'Putting Attorneys on the Witness Stand and Their Advice at Issue', The Attorney-Client Privilege in Civil Litigation, Vincent S. Walkowiak, ed., American Bar Association, 2004.

**Personal:** JD, Stanford Law School, 1993; Order of the Coif; Senior Editor, Stanford Law Review. BBA, University of Michigan, 1985; Phi Beta Kappa.

## MILLER, Kenneth W
Katten Muchin Rosenman LLP, Chicago
312 902 5261
ken.miller@kattenlaw.com
*Recommended in Corporate/M&A:*
*Private Equity*
**Practice Areas:** Partner, serves as Chairman of national private equity practice. Practice focuses on representing private equity firms and other private investors in equity and debt financings, leveraged buyouts and other acquisitions, dispositions and recapitalizations. Advises portfolio companies of private equity firms in financings, acquisitions, sales and other transactions. Also advises executives in compensation and equity related matters. Has represented private equity funds in numerous investments and acquisitions, including investments in technology, healthcare and services companies; leveraged buyouts of retailers, distributors, manufacturers and service businesses; and the formation, financings, acquisitions and sales of emerging growth companies.

## MILLER, Laura B
Brinks Hofer Gilson & Lione, Chicago
312 321 4715
lmiller@usebrinks.com
*Recommended in Intellectual Property*
**Practice Areas:** Laura Beth Miller has litigation experience involving a variety of internet-related issues, as well as in traditional areas of intellectual property including patent, trademark, unfair competition, trade secret and copyright law.
**Prof. Memberships:** Illinois Supreme Court; United States Supreme Court; Court of Appeals, Federal Circuit and the Seventh Circuit; Federal District Court: Northern District of Illinois, Southern District of Indiana, Western District of Michigan, Eastern District of Wisconsin; Registered Attorney before the United States Patent and Trademark Office.
**Publications:** 'Enforcing and Defending Against Patent Rights Through Litiga-

tion', Intellectual Property Law, ICLE 2005. 'Copyright Law in the Digital Age', Business, Law and the Internet: Essential Guidance For You, Your Clients and Your Firm, ICLE 2002. 'IP: Trademarks/Unfair Trade Practices', Business Law and the Internet: Essential Guidance For You, Your Clients and Your Firm, ICLE 2002.
**Personal:** Education: BA, History, technical background – Chemistry, University of Virginia (1982); JD, College of William and Mary (1985).

## MILLNER, Robert
Sonnenschein Nath & Rosenthal LLP, Chicago 312 876 7994
rmillner@sonnenschein.com
*Recommended in Bankruptcy*
**Practice Areas:** Practices bankruptcy and commercial litigation. Represents financial institutions and insurance companies in bankruptcy litigation and lenders, other creditors and debtors in complex reorganization real estate matters. Has handled significant cross-border matters for both debtors and creditors.
**Prof. Memberships:** Fellow, American College of Bankruptcy; Past Co-Chair, Bankruptcy and Insolvency Committee, Litigation Section of the American Bar Association; Honorary Overseas Member, Commercial Bar Association (London); Past Trustee, Anshe Emet Synagogue; Vice President, American Jewish Congress (Midwest).
**Personal:** University of Chicago, JD, University of Chicago Law Review; Wesleyan University, BA magna cum laude, Phi Beta Kappa.

## MISCIMARRA, Philip A
Morgan, Lewis & Bockius LLP, Chicago
312 324 1165
pmiscimarra@morganlewis.com
*Recommended in Employment*
**Practice Areas:** Mr Miscimarra represents management in all aspects of labor and employment law, including employment litigation, collective bargaining, and traditional labor matters. He also Co-Chairs Morgan Lewis' Workforce Change Practice, which addresses employment, labor, benefits and related issues associated with mergers, acquisitions, workforce reductions and other types of business restructuring. Mr Miscimarra is also a Senior Fellow with the Center for Human Resources at the University of Pennsylvania's Wharton School of Business, and he is Managing Director of the Center's Research Advisory Group ('RAG'), consisting of many of the country's largest manufacturing, service and retail companies.
**Prof. Memberships:** Admitted to practice in Illinois, Wisconsin and Pennsylvania.

## MISSNER, David
DLA Piper Rudnick Gray Cary US LLP, Chicago 312 368 2170
david.missner@dlapiper.com

*Recommended in Bankruptcy*
**Practice Areas:** Bankruptcy reorganization, commercial transactions and banking law.
**Prof. Memberships:** American Bar Association; Illinois State Bar Association; Chicago Bar Association.
**Career:** He is a frequent lecturer on banking and bankruptcy-related topics for the Chicago Bar Association, Illinois Institute for Continuing Legal Education and other professional and trade organizations.
**Publications:** 'Chapter 11', and 'Representing the Debtor and Representing the Creditor with a Secured Claim', both published by Illinois Institute for a Continuing Legal Education.
**Personal:** BA, Miami University, Oxford, Ohio; JD, Northwestern University School of Law.

## MITCHELL, Nancy
Greenberg Traurig LLP, Chicago
312 456 5107
mitchelln@gtlaw.com
*Recommended in Bankruptcy*
**Practice Areas:** Reorganization, bankruptcy and restructuring, public finance, corporate and securities, energy and natural resources.
**Career:** Executive Director, CIBC World Market Corp., 1999-2001; listed, Chambers & Partners USA Guide, an annual listing of the leading business lawyers and law firms in the world, 2005-06 edition; recognized as an Illinois Super Lawyer, 2006.
**Publications:** Co-author, 'Ancillary Proceedings – Should the Tail Wag the Dog?' Canadian-American Symposium on Cross-Border Insolvency Law, Toronto, Ontario, February 11, 2005.
**Personal:** JD, cum laude, University of Michigan Law School, 1987. Contributing Editor, The Michigan Law Review. BA, with honors, English and History, Indiana University Bloomington, 1984.

## MOLO, Steven F
Shearman & Sterling LLP, New York
212 848 4000
*Recommended in Litigation*
**Practice Areas:** Partner in Shearman & Sterling's Litigation Group. Active trial and appellate practice in complex business litigation, regulatory matters and white-collar criminal matters, including corporate internal investigations, throughout the United States and abroad.
**Prof. Memberships:** Member, Illinois Supreme Court Rules Committee; Programs and Membership Chair, Seventh Circuit Bar Association; Fellow, American Academy of Appellate Lawyers.
**Career:** Assistant Attorney General, Chicago (1982-86); associate, Partner, Winston & Strawn (1986-2004).
**Publications:** Co-author of 'Corporate Internal Investigations' (1989, updated semi-annually) and 'Your Witness:

Lessons on Cross-examination from Great Chicago Trial Lawyers' (forthcoming).
**Personal:** BS (1979) and JD (1982), University of Illinois.

## MORAN, Patrick G
Sonnenschein Nath & Rosenthal LLP, Chicago 312 876 8132
pmoran@sonnenschein.com
*Recommended in Real Estate*
**Practice Areas:** Handles various commercial real estate and related financing matters, emphasizing development, leasing and financing. Works with major office landlords and tenants in developing and leasing more than 10 million square feet of office space. Financing practice focuses on multistate secured and unsecured revolving credit loans to REITs and other real estate companies and traditional project loans secured by office buildings, apartment projects, shopping centers, golf courses, hotels and mixed-use projects.
**Prof. Memberships:** American College of Real Estate Lawyers; ABA Committee on Commercial Leasing.
**Personal:** Georgetown University, JD; Harvard College, BA.

## MORRIS, Ralph A
Schiff Hardin LLP, Chicago
312 258 5553
rmorris@schiffhardin.com
*Recommended in Employment*
**Practice Areas:** Labor and employment.
**Prof. Memberships:** American Bar Association, Chicago Bar Association, College of Labor and Employment Lawyers.
**Career:** Mr Morris represents management in both traditional labor matters and employment disputes. He provides presentations on harassment issues and measures employers can take to prevent employment-related litigation, and he has acted as an independent investigator on harassment complaints. He also serves as a mediator on employment issues.
**Personal:** Valparaiso University (BA, 1967), University of Michigan (JD, magna cum laude, Order of the Coif, 1970), Associate Editor, Michigan Law Review.

## MORRISON, Portia Owen
DLA Piper Rudnick Gray Cary US LLP, Chicago 312 368 4013
portia.morrison@dlapiper.com
*Recommended in Real Estate*
**Practice Areas:** Real estate; lodging and timeshare; real estate finance.
**Prof. Memberships:** American College of Real Estate Lawyers.
**Career:** She represents investors, developers, and lenders in multi-family, office, retail, hotel, and industrial development and redevelopment projects; construction of infrastructure and buildings; sales and leasing activities; and construction

and permanent financing. She has an extensive practice in real estate investment and finance, representing lenders, investors, and borrowers in structuring financing through traditional mortgage loans, joint venture formations, structured debt placements, mezzanine loans, and other financing and investment mechanisms.
**Personal:** JD, University of Chicago; MA, University of Wisconsin; BA, Agnes Scott College.

### MROWIEC, John S
Conway & Mrowiec, Chicago
312 658 1100
jsm@cmcontractors.com
*Recommended in Construction*
**Practice Areas:** Construction law.
**Prof. Memberships:** Chicago (Mechanics Lien) and American (Construction Industry Forum, Public Contracts and Litigation Sections) Bar Associations; Builders Association of Greater Chicago; Fox Valley Contractors Association; Associated General Contractors; American Institute of Architects; Society of Illinois Construction Lawyers.
**Publications:** Law Columnist, Midwest Construction News (McGraw-Hill), May, 2000 to present; instructor and author: 'Construction Law & Contracts', Real Estate Center, DePaul University (Mar. 2005, Mar 2004, Mar 2003, Dec. 2002); co-author: 'Requirements for the Original Contractor's Lien on Private Projects', in Illinois Mechanics Liens, IICLE (1994, 2000, 2004 eds.); co-author, 'Changes that Result from Delays and Interferences' in 'Construction Change Order Claims 2d' (Aspen, 2005); author and speaker, 'AIA Documents' (Sept. 2005, Sept. 2004); 'Public Construction Contracting' (Oct 2004, Mar 2002, Aug 2001, Mar 2001); 'Fundamentals of Construction Contracts: Understanding the Issues', (Mar 2006, Mar 2005, Mar 2004, Oct 2002, May 2002, Mar 2002, Feb 2002, Feb 2001, 2000); 'Construction Management & Design-Build: Contracting & Claims Avoidance', (Apr 2005, Nov 2004, Apr 2004, Apr 2003, Apr 2002, Mar 2002, Nov 2001, Nov 2000); 'Construction Delay Claims' (Jan 2006, May 2005, June 2004, Aug. 2002, Sept. 2000).

### MUENCH, John E
Mayer, Brown, Rowe & Maw LLP, Chicago 312 701 7059
jmuench@mayerbrown.com
*Recommended in Telecom, Broadcast & Satellite*
**Practice Areas:** General and appellate litigation specializing in telecommunications, constitutional law, civil procedure, antitrust, and tort law.
**Prof. Memberships:** Admitted in Illinois, 1976. US District Court for the Northern District of Illinois, 1976; US Supreme Court, US Courts of Appeals for the Fourth, Fifth, Sixth, Seventh, Ninth,

Eleventh, and District of Columbia Circuits.
**Career:** Joined Mayer, Brown, Rowe & Maw LLP, 1983; became Partner, 1985. Assistant Professor of Law, University of Illinois College of Law, Champaign, 1978-83. Law clerk to The Honorable John Paul Stevens, Associate Justice, Supreme Court of the United States, Washington, DC, 1977-78. Law clerk to The Honorable Robert A Sprecher, US Court of Appeals for the Seventh Circuit, 1976-77.
**Personal:** Northwestern University School of law, JD, magna cum laude, 1976; Order of the Coif; Editor-in-Chief, Northwestern Law Review. College of the Holy Cross, AB, magna cum laude, 1970.

### MULANEY JR, Charles W
Skadden, Arps, Slate, Meagher & Flom LLP & Affiliates, Chicago
312 407 0500
cmulaney@skadden.com
*Recommended in Corporate/M&A*
**Practice Areas:** Concentrates on mergers and acquisitions (both friendly and hostile), joint ventures, divestitures and spin-offs, corporate financings, restructurings and general corporate governance. Counsels on a range of securities, corporate and business related matters, including disclosure issues, directors' duties and responsibilities, corporate governance and internal investigations.
**Prof. Memberships:** Lecturer, Corporate Counsel Institute sponsored by Northwestern University School of Law. Member, Executive Committee, Ray Garrett, Jr Corporate and Securities Law Institute.
**Career:** JD, Yale Law School, 1974 (Editor, Yale Law Journal); AB, Georgetown University, 1971 (summa cum laude).

### MUNCY, Dennis
Meyer Capel, PC, Champaign
217 352 1800
*Recommended in Telecom, Broadcast & Satellite*

### MUNITZ, Gerald
Goldberg, Kohn, Bell, Black, Rosenbloom & Moritz, Ltd, Chicago
312 201 4000
*Recommended in Bankruptcy*

### MURDOCK JR, Grady B
Morgan, Lewis & Bockius LLP, Chicago
312 324 1105
gmurdock@morganlewis.com
*Recommended in Employment*
**Practice Areas:** Grady B Murdock, Jr is a Partner in the Labor and Employment Law Practice with over 30 years of experience. His practice focuses on management representation in nationwide and other class actions, collective actions, pattern and practice actions and individual actions from various federal and state employment laws. Mr Murdock practices traditional labor law leading numerous labor arbitrations. Mr Murdock formerly

served as Chief Labor Counsel for a large fast food chain.
**Prof. Memberships:** National Bar Association, American Bar Association, National Employment Law Council, EEOC Liaison Committee – Chicago Bar Association, Federal Bar Association, American Employment Law Council.

### MURPHY, Joseph
Meyer Capel, PC, Champaign
217 352 1800
*Recommended in Telecom, Broadcast & Satellite*

### MURRAY, Gregory S
Winston & Strawn LLP, Chicago
312 558 5669
gmurray@winston.com
*Recommended in Banking & Finance*
**Practice Areas:** Partner concentrating in syndicated leveraged finance representing numerous prominent US and foreign lending institutions in a variety of senior and subordinated credit facilities, cross-border facilities and structured finance transactions. Extensive experience in structuring multi-tiered acquisition and tender facilities. In recent years has represented agent bank in US and London-based financings aggregating in excess of US$50 billion. Has particular experience in insurance-related transactions.
**Career:** Joined Winston & Strawn in 1974 after attending the University of Notre Dame and the University of Virginia Law School. Partner since 1980; served as Member of the firm's Compensation Committee and Executive Committee.

### MURTAUGH, Christopher D
Winston & Strawn LLP, Chicago
312 558 5798
cmurtaugh@winston.com
*Recommended in Real Estate*
**Practice Areas:** Partner and former Chairman of the Real Estate Department. More than 30 years' experience focusing on national practice in commercial property acquisition and disposition, real estate development, and lending activities.
**Prof. Memberships:** Member of the American College of Real Estate Lawyers, Order of the Coif, Fellow of the American Bar Foundation, Chicago, Illinois, Florida, and American Bar Associations. Member of the International Council of Shopping Centers.
**Career:** Joined as associate, 1974. Partner, 1979. Member of the Billing and Collections Committee and Insurance Committee.
**Personal:** University of Illinois, 1967. JD, University of Illinois College of Law, 1970.

### MUTCHNIK, James
Kirkland & Ellis LLP, Chicago
312 861 2350

jmutchnik@kirkland.com
*Recommended in Antitrust*
**Practice Areas:** Represents corporate and individual clients in antitrust, white-collar crime, commercial, bankruptcy, and patent litigation in federal and state courts throughout the United States and before a variety of federal and state investigative agencies. In the antitrust area, litigates various matters, from alleged price fixing to price discrimination, and representing clients in dealing with the antitrust aspects of mergers, acquisitions and joint ventures. Counsels a wide range of small and large companies in diverse industries on pricing, marketing, distribution and dealer termination issues.
**Personal:** University of Pennsylvania, BS, May 1986. Northwestern University School of Law, JD, May 1989.

### NAGELBERG, Howard
Barack Ferrazzano Kirschbaum Perlman & Nagelberg, Chicago 312 984 3100
*Recommended in Real Estate*

### NAPOLITANO, Steven
Winston & Strawn LLP, Chicago
312 558 5600
*Recommended in Corporate/M&A, Corporate/M&A: Private Equity*

### NEWMAN, Margery
Ogletree, Deakins, Nash, Smoak & Stewart, PC, Chicago
312 558 1258
margery.newman@ogletreedeakins.com
*Recommended in Construction*
**Practice Areas:** Construction law, business litigation.
**Prof. Memberships:** Chicago Bar Association, Illinois State Bar Association, American Bar Association (Forum on Construction), Women Construction Owners & Executives.
**Career:** Admitted to practice in Illinois, Northern District of Illinois, US Court of Appeals (Seventh Circuit). Served as Corporate Counsel to the Federation of Women Contractors. Chairperson of Chicago Bar Association Subcommittee on Mechanics Liens. Professional Councils (ASA, LCCA, UCA).
**Publications:** Has lectured and written extensively on mechanic's liens and construction disputes.
**Personal:** Brooklyn College (BA, 1969), Roosevelt University (MA, 1973), John Marshall Law School (JD with high distinction, 1983).

### NICKLIN, Emily
Kirkland & Ellis LLP, Chicago
312 861 2387
enicklin@kirkland.com
*Recommended in Litigation*
**Practice Areas:** Has been lead trial counsel in cases (both individual and class action) in a number of areas including: professional liability for accountants and consultants, securities, contract, tort (including product liability and personal

injury), employment discrimination, constitutional law and municipal law. Trials have included both jury and bench trials, as well as arbitrations, in various state and federal venues including Arkansas, California, Delaware, Idaho, Illinois, Iowa, Michigan, Missouri, Nebraska, Nevada, New York, Pennsylvania, Texas, Wisconsin, and Washington, DC.
**Personal:** University of Chicago, BA, 1975 (Junior year, Phi Beta Kappa); University of Chicago, JD, 1977 (Order of the Coif)

### NIELSEN, Jennifer
Lyman & Nielsen, Oak Brook
630 575 0020
*Recommended in Construction*

### NIJMAN, Jennifer T
Winston & Strawn LLP, Chicago
312 558 5771
jnijman@winston.com
*Recommended in Environment*
**Practice Areas:** Enforcement, including toxic tort, private cost recovery, and Superfund; permitting and siting, compliance issues, and transactions.
**Prof. Memberships:** President, Chicago Bar Association (2002-03); American Bar Association; Illinois State Bar Association; Public Interest Law Initiative (Board), Center for Conflict Resolution (Board President).
**Career:** Joined 1994; Practice Group Chair; Diversity Committee Co-Chair; Hiring Committee.
**Publications:** 'Environmental Law', Illinois Institute of Continuing Legal Education, April 2005; 'Coordination of a Large Environmental Permitting Effort', Natural Resources & Environment, Spring 2001 (winner of 2002 Burton Award).
**Personal:** University of Illinois, 1984; University of Chicago Law School, JD, 1987, The Legal Forum.

### NIRO, Raymond
Niro, Scavone, Haller & Niro, Chicago
312 236 0733
*Recommended in Intellectual Property*

### NOELL, John W
Mayer, Brown, Rowe & Maw LLP, Chicago 312 701 7179
jnoell@mayerbrownrowe.com
*Recommended in Corporate/M&A: Private Equity*
**Practice Areas:** Works with issuers sponsoring real estate and investment funds for tax-exempt institutional investors. Active joint venture practice, representing buyers and sellers of professional service companies, investment management firms and other companies. Experienced in initial public offerings and debt and common stock offerings.
**Career:** Mayer, Brown, Rowe & Maw LLP, Chicago, 1985-90; 1997 to date. General Counsel, JMB Institutional Realty Corporation, 1990-94. Heitman Capital Management Corporation, 1994-97.

**Personal:** Loyola University of Chicago, JD, cum laude, 1985; Editor-in-Chief, Law Journal. University of Notre Dame, BBA cum laude, 1978.

### NOVACK, Stephen
Novack & Macey LLP, Chicago
312 419 6900
*Recommended in Litigation*

### NOVAK, Theodore
DLA Piper Rudnick Gray Cary US LLP, Chicago 312 368 4037
theodore.novak@dlapiper.com
*Recommended in Real Estate*
**Practice Areas:** Real estate; governmental affairs, zoning, land use, public incentives and eminent domain.
**Prof. Memberships:** Member, American College of Real Estate Lawyers (ACREL).
**Career:** He has been instrumental in the acquisition, disposition, public financing, condemnation, rezoning, and development of all types of property. He has extensive litigation experience in trial and appellate courts. He is a lecturer at the University of Chicago Law School and is an Adjunct Professor at Northwestern University School of Law, teaching a course on land use, zoning, and condemnation.
**Personal:** JD, Chicago-Kent College of Law, Illinois Institute of Technology; BS, University of Illinois.

### NYHAN, Lawrence
Sidley Austin LLP, Chicago
312 858 7710
lnyhan@sidley.com
*Recommended in Bankruptcy*
**Practice Areas:** Chairman of the firm-wide Corporate Reorganization and Bankruptcy Group and a Member of the firm's Executive Committee. Representative engagements include: Adelphia Communications; AmeriServe Food Distribution, Inc.; Bethlehem Steel Company; Birch Telecommunications; Budget Group, Inc.; Centennial Coal Company; Choice One Communications; Devon Convenience Stores, Inc.; Federal Mogul Corporation; LaClede Steel Company; London Fog Industries, Inc.; Lone Star Steel Company; Malden Mills, Inc.; Meridian Automotive Systems, Inc.; New World Pasta, Inc.; Outboard Marine Corporation; Owens Corning Fiberglass; Murray, Inc.; Pegasus Satellite Television; Recoton Corporation; Pacific Trail, Inc.; Venture Holdings Company, Inc.; and Zenith Industries, Inc.
**Personal:** Loyola University Chicago School of Law (JD, 1980); University of Chicago (BA, 1977). Admission: Illinois, 1980.

### O'BRIEN, Richard
Sidley Austin LLP, Chicago
312 853 7283
robrien@sidley.com
*Recommended in Media & Entertainment*
**Practice Areas:** Richard J O'Brien has a diverse media law and intellectual property practice. Mr O'Brien has handled matters involving defamation, invasion of privacy, reporter's privilege, access and FOIA issues, copyright, trademark, misappropriation of ideas, false advertising, and trade secrets. Mr O'Brien's defense of defamation cases have all virtually resulted in a defense victory, with no payment of any amount to the plaintiffs. Mr O'Brien has been lead trial lawyer for cases in federal and state courts in Chicago and around the country. Many of his cases have involved injunction or other emergency proceedings.
**Personal:** Georgetown University Law Center JD, 1979; St Louis University BA, 1976. Admission: Illinois, 1979. Clerked for United States District Court Judge Abraham L Marovitz 1979-81.

### ODORIZZI, Michele L
Mayer, Brown, Rowe & Maw LLP, Chicago 312 701 7309
modorizzi@mayerbrown.com
*Recommended in Litigation*
**Practice Areas:** Specializes in both appellate litigation and brief-writing at the trial court level. Areas of expertise include class actions, federal securities law and shareholder derivative claims, accountants' liability, consumer fraud, and general commercial litigation.
**Prof. Memberships:** Admitted: Illinois, 1976; US Supreme Court, 1980; US Courts of Appeals for the Second, Third, Fourth, Sixth, Seventh, Eighth, Ninth and Tenth Circuits; Northern District of Illinois.
**Career:** Clerked for Justice John Paul Stevens, 1979-80 and for Judge Philip W Tone, Seventh Circuit Court of Appeals, 1976-77. Joined Mayer, Brown, Rowe & Maw LLP, Chicago, 1977-79, 1980; Partner, 1983.
**Personal:** University of Chicago Law School, JD cum laude, 1976; Order of the Coif; Articles Editor, The University of Chicago Law Review. Northwestern University, BA, 1973; Phi Beta Kappa.

### OHM, Michael
Bell, Boyd & Lloyd LLC, Chicago
312 372 1121
*Recommended in Environment*

### OLIAN, Robert
Sidley Austin LLP, Chicago
312 853 7208
rolian@sidley.com
*Recommended in Environment*
**Practice Areas:** Robert M Olian Co-Heads the firm's national Environmental Practice. Mr Olian works primarily on contested matters involving compliance

and civil or criminal enforcement proceedings. He also manages complex legal projects, including environmental impact statement proceedings and the siting of waste disposal facilities. He has represented: a refinery in federal class action litigation and state court jury trial alleging property value diminution; a waste disposal company in class action jury trial alleging health impacts (including cancer) and property value diminution (settled pre-verdict); an electric utility resisting successor liability for manufactured gas plant remediation (verdict of no liability for our client); a major waste disposal company concerning a criminal investigation of the company's recycled drum transportation procedures (US Attorney's Office declined to seek indictment); and a transportation company in connection with internal investigations of potential criminal conduct.
**Prof. Memberships:** ABA (Litigation Section, Environment, Energy & Resources Section).
**Publications:** Editor, 'Illinois Environmental Law Handbook' (1st ed.).
**Personal:** Harvard Law School, JD, 1977; Harvard University, MPP, 1977; Harvard University, AB, 1973. Admission: Illinois, 1977.

### OLSON, Camille
Seyfarth Shaw LLP, Chicago
312 346 8000
*Recommended in Employment*

### O'REILLY, Peter
Lea + O'Reilly, Chicago
312 755 9127
*Recommended in Media & Entertainment*

### OSBORNE, Robert Stephen
Jenner & Block LLP, Chicago
312 923 2690
rosborne@jenner.com
*Recommended in Corporate/M&A*
**Practice Areas:** Robert S Osborne is a Partner in Jenner & Block's Chicago office and Chair of the firm's Corporate Practice. Mr Osborne has a broad-based practice encompassing most of the department's practice groups, with particular focus on representing public companies in M&A and securities transactions as well as counseling clients on corporate governance and disclosure matters. Mr Osborne has represented General Motors in many strategic transactions, including the disposition of Hughes Electronics (DirecTV) in 2003, previous spin-offs of EDS, Hughes Defense and Delphi Automotive Systems, and the sale of National Car Rental and other operating units. He has also represented General Motors in public offerings of common stock, straight and convertible preferred stock, and straight and convertible debt securities that in each case were among the largest securities transactions of their kind. Mr Osborne has represented an

investment management subsidiary of GM in a variety of private equity transactions involving fund participations and direct investments. Mr Osborne served in an outside capacity as General Counsel of Lands' End from its initial public offering in 1986 until 1995, and continued to serve as Special Counsel to its Board of Directors through the sale of the company to Sears in 2002. He has also represented numerous other public companies in M&A and securities matters, including General Dynamics and the Chicago Board of Trade. Mr Osborne has frequently represented committees of independent directors, including audit, compensation, special investigative, litigation and going private committees.
**Personal:** Harvard Law School, JD, 1979, magna cum laude.

### PANAGAKIS, George N
Skadden, Arps, Slate, Meagher & Flom LLP & Affiliates, Chicago
312 407 0638
gpanagak@skadden.com
*Recommended in Bankruptcy*
**Practice Areas:** Represents clients in complex business reorganizations, debt restructurings and insolvency matters. Advises debtors, creditors, investors, sellers, purchasers and other parties in all stages of restructuring transactions, from Chapter 11 reorganizations to out-of-court negotiations, workouts and divestitures.
**Career:** JD, Northwestern University School of Law, 1990; BA, Northwestern University, 1987.

### PARSONS, David
Littler Mendelson, PC, Chicago
312 372 5520
dparsons@littler.com
*Recommended in Employment*
**Practice Areas:** Focuses on employment discrimination and employment-related litigation. Represents clients in federal and state trial and appellate courts, federal and state administrative agencies, and labor arbitration. Has substantial jury trial experience, and practice emphasizes employment discrimination, wrongful discharge cases, arbitration proceedings, and litigation regarding covenants not to compete. Admitted to practice in Illinois, before United States Supreme Court, and various other district courts.
**Prof. Memberships:** Member, American Bar Association (Trial Practice Committee, Litigation Section and Labor and Employment Law Section), the Defense Research Institute, and the Seventh Circuit Bar Association.
**Personal:** University of Illinois (JD, 1971); Denison University (BA).

### PARZEN, Stanley J
Mayer, Brown, Rowe & Maw LLP, Chicago 312 701 7326
sparzen@mayerbrownrowe.com
*Recommended in Litigation*

**Practice Areas:** Complex litigation in federal and state courts, including appeals. Focus on representing accounting firms in cases relating to failed savings and loan institutions, banks, insurance companies, investor class actions and malpractice claims brought by clients.
**Career:** Mayer, Brown, Rowe & Maw LLP, Chicago, 1977 to date. Law clerk to The Honorable Harrison L Winter, US Court of Appeals for the Fourth Circuit, Maryland, 1976-77.
**Personal:** Harvard University, JD cum laude, 1976; Harvard Law Review. Earlham College, BA, 1973.

### PASTROFF, Sanford
Sonnenschein Nath & Rosenthal LLP, Chicago 312 876 3170
spastroff@sonnenschein.com
*Recommended in Antitrust*
**Practice Areas:** Focuses on antitrust and trade regulation counseling and litigation, including numerous class actions. Significant experience with criminal and civil investigations by federal and state antitrust authorities. Substantial work on mergers, joint ventures and other competitor collaborations. Extensive involvement in healthcare, distribution and intellectual property antitrust matters.
**Prof. Memberships:** Member, ABA Section of Antitrust Law; leadership positions included: Chair, Robinson-Patman Act Committee; Vice-Chair, Insurance Industry and Publications Committees; Member, Public Service Task Force.
**Personal:** Northwestern University School of Law, JD, cum laude, Journal of Criminal Law and Criminology, Moot Court Board; University of Michigan, BBA with High Distinction.

### PASULKA-BROWN, Kathleen
Foley & Lardner LLP, Chicago
312 832 5164
kpasulka-brown@foley.com
*Recommended in Telecom, Broadcast & Satellite*
**Career:** Kathleen Pasulka-Brown, a Partner in the Chicago office of Foley & Lardner LLP, is a member of the firm's Insurance Dispute Resolution, Business Reorganizations, and Energy Regulation Practices, as well as the Energy and Insurance Industry Teams. Ms Pasulka-Brown is regularly involved in both litigation and regulatory proceedings pertaining to insurance coverage, telecommunications, and energy matters. In addition, she is involved in a variety of general commercial litigation matters. Ms Pasulka-Brown is a graduate of Harvard Law School (JD, 1986).

### PATTON, Stephen
Kirkland & Ellis LLP, Chicago
312 861 2406
spatton@kirkland.com
*Recommended in Litigation, Products Liability*
**Practice Areas:** Mr Patton has practiced

with Kirkland & Ellis since 1978 and has been a Partner since 1984. He currently serves as Chairman of Kirkland's firmwide Litigation Management Committee. Mr Patton has extensive trial experience in a wide variety of complex commercial litigation, including contract, antitrust, and product liability cases. In addition to his active trial practice, Mr Patton has served as an advisor to senior management in connection with a number of 'bet the company' exposures.
**Personal:** Indiana University, BA, 1975; Georgetown University Law Center, JD, 1978

### PECK, S Michael
Schiff Hardin LLP, Chicago
312 258 5811
speck@schiffhardin.com
*Recommended in Corporate/M&A: Private Equity*
**Practice Areas:** Private equity and venture capital, corporate and securities.
**Career:** Mr Peck concentrates in leveraged buyouts and other merger and acquisition transactions, as well as general corporate, investment, and financing matters. He principally represents private equity funds in their merger and acquisition activity, as well as the representation of the portfolio companies they acquire with respect to acquisitions, divestitures, public offerings, restructurings, recapitalizations, and general corporate activities. He has handled transactions in a wide variety of industries.
**Personal:** University of Chicago (BA, 1969), University of Michigan Law School (JD, cum laude, 1972).

### PEREGRINE, Michael W
McDermott Will & Emery, Chicago
312 984 6933
mperegrine@mwe.com
*Recommended in Healthcare*
**Practice Areas:** Represents nonprofit healthcare facilities and systems and other charitable organizations, with focus on corporate, fiduciary duty, tax and charitable trust issues facing such organizations. Experience includes representation of nonprofits in connection with the organization and operation of healthcare systems, including related governance issues and parent/subsidiary relationships. Has experience with complex business transactions such as mergers, consolidations and acquisitions and corporate and charitable trust law issues associated therewith.
**Career:** Frequent author and speaker on legal topics affecting tax exempt, nonprofit corporations.
**Personal:** Northwestern University School of Law (JD); Texas Christian University (BA).

### PERELLIS, Andrew
Seyfarth Shaw LLP, Chicago
312 346 8000
*Recommended in Environment*

### PERL, Sanford E
Kirkland & Ellis LLP, Chicago
312 861 2291
sperl@kirkland.com
*Recommended in Corporate/M&A: Private Equity*
**Practice Areas:** Mr Perl concentrates on the corporate, securities and tax aspects of complex business transactions, including leveraged buyouts of public and private companies; mergers and acquisitions; venture capital and minority equity investments; initial public offerings; private equity fund formations; executive compensation; and restructurings and workouts. Mr Perl has led transactions in a wide variety of industries, including healthcare, manufacturing, distribution, insurance, biotechnology and media. Mr Perl represents numerous private equity funds and their portfolio companies.
**Personal:** University of Illinois, BS, Accountancy, high honors; University of Michigan Law School, magna cum laude, JD, Order of the Coif. Certified Public Accountant.

### PERLMAN, Daniel J
Katten Muchin Rosenman LLP, Chicago
312 902 5532
daniel.perlman@kattenlaw.com
*Recommended in Real Estate*
**Practice Areas:** Concentrates his practice in real estate, primarily in the area of fund and venture formation, conventional, securitized and mezzanine financing, commercial development and commercial acquisitions and dispositions. Client types include pension funds and their advisors, foreign institutions, national developers and retailers, public and private real estate investment trusts, investment banks, securitized lenders, insurance companies and national banking associations. Mr Perlman has extensive experience in representing sponsors of real estate investment funds and structuring tax efficient investment vehicles and addressing the sponsor's and investors' ERISA concerns. Mr Perlman has been lead counsel on some of the nation's highest profile retail developments. His extensive development experience includes municipal and state incentive financings, joint venture equity investments and construction financings. Mr Perlman also represents several 'Wall Street' securitized lenders and has an in-depth knowledge of the CMBS industry.
**Prof. Memberships:** Chairman of the American Cancer Society Greater Chicago Downtown Board, Member of the Law Committee of the International Council of Shopping Centers.
**Career:** Member of the firm's Board of Directors.
**Publications:** Frequent lecturer and author of articles on issues ranging from REITs portfolio transactions to joint venture strategies.
**Personal:** Graduated from the University

of Michigan with a Bachelor of Arts Degree in Political Science and earned his Law Degree in 1985 from Northwestern University School of Law.

## PERZEK, Philip
Latham & Watkins LLP, Chicago
312 876 7700
*Recommended in Banking & Finance*

## PETERMAN, Nancy A
Greenberg Traurig LLP, Chicago
312 456 8410
petermann@gtlaw.com
*Recommended in Bankruptcy*
**Practice Areas:** Business reorganization and bankruptcy.
**Prof. Memberships:** American Bankruptcy Institute; Former Chair, Chicago Bar Association's Bankruptcy & Reorganization Committee; former President/former Board Member, Women's Health Executive Network, 2001-02.
**Career:** Board Certified Business Bankruptcy Lawyer, American Board of Certification; listed, Illinois Super Lawyers; Member, Leading Lawyers Network; listed, one of the 'Top Bankruptcy Lawyers', The Deal, 6/04.
**Publications:** Assistant Editor, West's Norton Bankruptcy Law & Practice treatise co-author, 'Section 506: A Five-Year Look Back', Norton's Annual Survey of Bankruptcy Law, 2005 edition.
**Personal:** JD, University of Michigan Law School, 1991; BA, University of Michigan, 1988.

## PETERSON, Brad L
Mayer, Brown, Rowe & Maw LLP, Chicago 312 701 8568
bpeterson@mayerbrownrowe.com
*Recommended in Business Process Outsourcing, Technology*
**Practice Areas:** Information technology and business process outsourcing. Onshore and offshore sourcing transactions. Information technology transactions such as software licensing and development. Supplier relationship management, including restructurings, resourcings and insourcings. Collaborative transactions including joint ventures and strategic alliances. Corporate and commercial transactions.
**Prof. Memberships:** Admitted in Illinois, 1988.
**Career:** Joined Mayer, Brown, Rowe & Maw LLP, 1995; became Partner, 1998. Formerly at Wildman, Harrold, Allen & Dixon, Chicago, 1992-95; Kirkland & Ellis, Chicago, 1988-92. International Business Machines Corporation, Marketing Representative, Chicago, 1982-85.
**Publications:** 'The Smart Way to Buy Information Technology: How to Maximize Value and Avoid Costly Pitfalls' (AMACOM Books, New York, 1998, 250 pages). Author of dozens of articles on outsourcing, alliances, and technology transactions.
**Personal:** Harvard Law School, JD with

honors, 1988; Managing Editor, Harvard Journal of Law and Public Policy. University of Chicago Graduate School of Business, MBA, cum laude, 1982; Beta Gamma Sigma. Northwestern University, Computer Studies, 1977-80; Phi Beta Kappa.

## PETERSON, Ronald R
Jenner & Block LLP, Chicago
312 923 2981
rpeterson@jenner.com
*Recommended in Bankruptcy*
**Practice Areas:** Ronald R Peterson is a Partner in Jenner & Block's Chicago office and a member of the firm's Bankruptcy, Workout and Corporate Reorganization Practice. He is also a member of the Construction Law and Corporate and Commercial Finance practices. Mr Peterson has concentrated his practice in the areas of commercial, insolvency and bankruptcy law, focusing primarily on representing debtors, trustees, creditors' committees, landlords and secured lenders in Chapter 11 cases. Mr Peterson represents the creditors' committees in the bankruptcies of Anicom Inc., Access Air Inc. and Charter Behavioral Health Systems Inc. He was counsel to the creditors' committees in the Chapter 11 cases of Handy Andy Home Centers, a chain of 88 hardware stores, and Payless Cashways Inc., a chain of 100 hardware stores. He was the attorney for the debtor in the bankruptcy cases of Harrah's Jazz Company, The Rath Packing Company and Armstrong's, Inc. Mr Peterson also counsels clients on a variety of transactional issues. He represented the commercial paper holders in an out-of-court restructuring of Mercury Finance, a substandard lender of automobile loans, and was involved in the restructuring of the law firms of Keck, Mahin & Cate and Spicer & Oppenheim. He represented Norand Corporation in a successful workout with a Chicago bank group. Mr Peterson has been a member of the panel of Chapter 7 Trustees for the Northern District of Illinois, Eastern Division, since 1987. He presides over approximately 100 consumer bankruptcy cases per month. Mr Peterson is a Fellow of the American College of Bankruptcy, and a Member of the American Bankruptcy Institute, the Business Bankruptcy Committee of the Business Law Section of the American Bar Association, Commercial Law League of America and the International Association of Restructuring Insolvency and Bankruptcy Professionals.
**Personal:** University of Chicago Law School, JD, 1973.

## PICKENS, Scott E
Schiff Hardin LLP, Chicago
312 258 5515
spickens@schiffhardin.com
*Recommended in Banking & Finance*
**Practice Areas:** Finance, corporate and

securities.
**Career:** Mr Pickens concentrates in the areas of corporate, securities, and commercial law, especially in the representation of creditors in financing transactions. He represents major insurance companies, commercial banks, asset-based lenders, and virtually every other type of participant in the finance markets in a variety of financing transactions and workouts. A past-managing Partner of the firm and a Member of the firm's Executive Committee.
**Personal:** University of Illinois at Urbana-Champaign (BS, 1972), University of Chicago (MBA, 1976), Loyola University Chicago School of Law (JD, cum laude, 1978).

## PISKORSKI, Thomas
Seyfarth Shaw LLP, Chicago
312 346 8000
*Recommended in Employment*

## POHL, Timothy R
Skadden, Arps, Slate, Meagher & Flom LLP & Affiliates, Chicago
312 407 0772
tpohl@skadden.com
*Recommended in Bankruptcy*
**Practice Areas:** Represents a variety of clients in complex business reorganizations, debt restructurings and distressed mergers and acquisitions. Advises companies in both chapter 11 and out-of-court restructurings. Also advises lenders to, creditors and purchasers of or investors in distressed companies.
**Career:** JD, University of Chicago, 1991; BA, Amherst College, 1988 (magna cum laude).

## POMERANTZ, Harold B
DLA Piper Rudnick Gray Cary US LLP, Chicago 312 368 4036
Harold.pomerantz@dlapiper.com
*Recommended in Real Estate*
**Practice Areas:** Real estate.
**Prof. Memberships:** Active Member of the International Council of Shopping Centers.
**Career:** Concentrates his practice in the area of complex commercial real estate transactions, including acquisitions and dispositions of various types of real estate assets; commercial financing; syndications; partnership and joint ventures; development, operations and management; and commercial leasing transactions. He lectures frequently on commercial real estate issues to both bar associations and real estate industry trade groups.
**Personal:** JD, Washington University; MBA, Washington University; BA, Washington University.

## POPE, Michael
McDermott Will & Emery, Chicago
312 984 7780
mpope@mwe.com
*Recommended in Litigation, Products*

Liability
**Practice Areas:** Heads international Product Liability Practice, including complex class action lawsuits. Currently represents nation's largest automobile insurer in two national class actions challenging the company's claims policies and 17 Blue Cross/Blue Shield plans on HMO litigation. Has extensive experience handling reinsurance disputes, in interpretation of excess and umbrella liability insurance policies, and in professional liability and complex business litigation. Active in ADR, both as advocate and arbitrator.
**Prof. Memberships:** Former President: International Association of Defense Counsel, 7th Circuit Bar Association, and Illinois Equal Justice Foundation.
**Personal:** Loyola University of Chicago (BS); Northwestern University School of Law (JD, cum laude).

## POWERS, John
Seyfarth Shaw LLP, Chicago
312 346 8000
*Recommended in Employment*

## PRILLAMAN, Fred
Mohan, Alewelt, Prillaman & Adami, Springfield 217 528 2517
*Recommended in Environment*

## PRITIKIN, David T
Sidley Austin LLP, Chicago
312 853 7359
dpritikin@sidley.com
*Recommended in Intellectual Property*
**Practice Areas:** David Pritikin chairs the firm's national Intellectual Property Practice and has an active trial practice concentrated in that field. Mr Pritikin has represented companies in major patent cases in a range of industries. He has handled cases in the federal district courts and in the International Trade Commission as well as appeals before the Court of Appeals for the Federal Circuit. He has served as lead counsel in a number of high profile cases tried before judges and juries. In 2004, Mr Pritikin was inducted into the American College of Trial Lawyers. He is a member of the firm's Executive Committee.
**Prof. Memberships:** ABA, AIPLA.
**Personal:** Harvard Law School (JD, 1974); Cornell University (AB, 1971).

## QASIM, Imad
Sidley Austin LLP, Chicago
312 853 7094
iqasim@sidley.com
*Recommended in Corporate/M&A*
**Practice Areas:** Focuses on mergers and acquisitions, corporate finance, corporate governance, securities law compliance, public and private securities offerings including high yield, joint ventures and cross-border transactions. He played a major role in a number of public company mergers, including the acquisition of True North Communications by Inter-

public Group, Tellabs' proposed merger with CIENA Corporation, Tellabs' acquisition of Advanced Fibre Communications, Quality Food Centers' acquisition by Fred Meyer, Mark Twain Bancshares' acquisition by Mercantile Bancorporation, Kimberly Clark's acquisition of Tecnol Medical Products, Jacor Communications' acquisition by Clear Channel Communications, Concord EFS's acquisitions of Star Systems and Electronic Payment Services, and the acquisition of The Cherry Corporation by the Cherry family. He represented Concord EFS, Inc. in two public offerings in excess of one billion dollars in proceeds. He represents private equity and strategic investors, advises public companies and their Boards of Directors on corporate governance matters.

**Prof. Memberships:** Member of the securities law section of American Bar Association.

**Personal:** Georgetown University, JD, 1982; Hamilton College, AB, 1979. Admissions: Illinois, 1987; New York, 1983.

## RADEMAKER, Randall J
Skadden, Arps, Slate, Meagher & Flom LLP & Affiliates, Chicago
312 407 0930
rrademak@skadden.com
*Recommended in Banking & Finance*

**Practice Areas:** Concentrates in banking and financing transactions, including asset-backed financings and asset-securitization transactions, acquisition financings, structured products, financial restructurings and debtor-in-possession financings. Active in acquisition financings involving cross-border and multi-currency borrowings. In 2005, represented equity sponsor group in connection with the $4 billion financing for the acquisition of MGM. Led the financial restructuring of many companies on both the lender and the borrower side.

**Career:** JD, University of Chicago, 1982; BA, Knox College, 1979 (summa cum laude).

## RANDALL, Benjamin
Randall & Kenig LLP, Chicago
312 845 2510
*Recommended in Real Estate*

## RAY, Stephen
Stein, Ray & Harris LLP, Chicago
312 641 3700
*Recommended in Construction*

## READ, Sarah
Sidley Austin LLP, Chicago
312 853 2171
sread@Sidley.com
*Recommended in Energy*

**Practice Areas:** Energy, legislation, regulatory, and alternative dispute resolution. Ms Read has advised both utility and nonutility companies on a wide variety of complex regulatory, legislative,

strategic planning and ADR issues. Representations include work as a resolution counsel on complex multi-party commercial and regulatory matters; negotiation counsel on various transactional matters; consulting on regulatory and strategic issues; legislative drafting and lobbying (particularly with regard to industry restructuring legislation); regulatory litigation; and coordination of local counsel on multistate transactional matters. Ms Read has tried cases before the Illinois, Missouri, Nevada and Ohio public utility commissions, argued related appeals, and assisted in the design and implementation of collaborative and other dialogue processes.

**Prof. Memberships:** American Arbitration Association, national panel of neutrals; ABA, Public Utility Section; Chicago Bar Association; Missouri Bar Association; Co-Chair, ADR Committee; Wisconsin Bar Association.

## REIDY, Daniel
Jones Day, Chicago 312 269 4140
dereidy@jonesday.com
*Recommended in Litigation, Products Liability*

**Practice Areas:** Litigation Practice Coordinator in the Chicago office and oversees the firm's Corporate Criminal Investigations Practice. Divides his time evenly between civil and criminal litigation. He has extensive trial and appellate experience as lead counsel in civil and criminal matters in state and federal court. He has handled numerous high profile corruption and complex financial crime cases. He has taught trial practice and has spoken on criminal defense and civil litigation issues at various seminars.

**Prof. Memberships:** Fellow, American College of Trial Lawyers and the International Academy of Trial Lawyers.

## RESNICK, Donald I
Jenner & Block LLP, Chicago
312 923 2656
dresnick@jenner.com
*Recommended in Real Estate*

**Practice Areas:** Donald I Resnick is a Partner in Jenner & Block's Chicago office. He is Chair of the firm's Real Estate Practice, Co-Chair of Real Estate Securities Practice, and member of Management Committee. Mr Resnick focuses his practice in the area of commercial real estate, on both national and local basis, having significant experience in real estate transactions, financing, development and construction and corporate real estate services. His practice also encompasses real estate-related loan and equity restructuring and workouts and the hospitality, gaming and entertainment industry. Mr Resnick represents clients in connection with all types of real estate transactions, including acquisitions and dispositions, leasing, joint ventures and like-kind exchanges involving office

buildings, multi-family apartment projects, retail projects, hotels and industrial facilities. He counsels clients on all facets of real estate transactions, including contract and financing issues, due diligence, lease negotiations, operational and management issues, ownership and equity structures and tax issues. Mr Resnick represents national banks, REITS, pension funds and other institutions in connection with all aspects of real estate financing, including both secured and unsecured credit facilities and construction and permanent financing. He has significant expertise in Tax Increment Financing (TIF) and in advising clients with respect to tax exempt bond financing. He counsels both lenders and borrowers in connection with all aspects and types of real estate and commercial credit facilities. Mr Resnick counsels numerous corporate clients, including Fortune 500 companies, in connection with all of their corporate real estate needs.

**Personal:** Harvard Law School, JD, 1975.

## RILEY JR, James
McGuireWoods LLP, Chicago
312 849 8100
*Recommended in Healthcare*

## RIPPIE, E Glenn
Foley & Lardner LLP, Chicago
312 832 4910
grippie@foley.com
*Recommended in Energy*

**Career:** E Glenn Rippie is a Partner in the Chicago office of Foley & Lardner LLP. He is a member of the Regulatory Department and Energy Regulation Practice Group. He advises clients on gas and electric issues and represents industry clients before regulatory agencies including state public utility commissions and the Federal Energy Regulatory Commission, and state and federal courts. Mr Rippie's practice focuses on complex strategic, restructuring, operations, and rate matters, and includes both counseling and litigation. Mr Rippie received his Law Degree from the Yale Law School.

## RITCHIE, Stephen L
Kirkland & Ellis LLP, Chicago
312 8612210
sritchie@kirkland.com
*Recommended in Corporate/M&A: Private Equity*

**Practice Areas:** Mr Ritchie's practice focuses on complex business transactions, including mergers, acquisitions, buyouts, recapitalizations, divestitures, venture capital and growth equity investing, and executive compensation. He has handled many private equity, LBO, venture capital and merger and acquisition transactions for clients including GTCR Golder Rauner, Code, Hennessy & Simmons, William Blair Capital Partners, Leeds Weld & Co., Evergreen Pacific Partners, Chicago Growth Partners, AEA

Investors, Inc., HIG Capital, Wind Point Partners, Bain Capital, Adams Street Partners and their respective portfolio companies.

**Personal:** University of Virginia, BA, 1985; University of Chicago, JD, 1988.

## ROACH JR, William H
McDermott Will & Emery, Chicago
312 984 6941
wroach@mwe.com
*Recommended in Healthcare*

**Practice Areas:** Experience includes the formation of regional and national hospital systems, mergers, acquisitions, affiliations and dispositions of healthcare facilities and systems, joint sponsorship of faith-based healthcare facilities and systems, corporate reorganizations, hospital/physician integration arrangements, health industry joint ventures, creation and implementation of corporate compliance plans, focused compliance reviews, tax-exempt organizations, health information privacy and regulation, and medical staff organization, credentialing and contracts. Represents institutions of higher education in matters relating to governance, mergers/acquisitions, student records, joint ventures and faculty organization.

**Personal:** Vanderbilt University (JD); University of Pittsburgh (MS); Columbia University (AB).

## ROBERTS, Kenneth M
Schiff Hardin LLP, Chicago
312 258 5704
kroberts@schiffhardin.com
*Recommended in Construction*

**Practice Areas:** Construction.

**Prof. Memberships:** Society of Illinois Construction Attorneys, Society of American Military Engineers, American Bar Association.

**Career:** Co-leads Schiff Hardin's Construction Group. Concentrates in representing owners and architects/engineers in construction law, contracting/procurement, dispute resolution, and insurance issues. National/international practice. Particular focus on project controls counseling. Mr Roberts' expertise in tracking large and complex construction projects progress is confirmed by his selection by owners and governmental agencies as their independent 'eyes and ears' for monitoring budget and schedule of ongoing work.

**Personal:** University of Iowa (BGS, with honors, 1982), University of Iowa (JD, with distinction, 1985).

## ROBERTSON, Eric
Lueders, Robertson & Konzen, Granite City 618 876 8500
*Recommended in Energy*

## ROBERTSON, Robert
Kirkland & Ellis LLP, Chicago
312 861 2225
rrobertson@kirkland.com
*Recommended in Antitrust*

**Practice Areas:** Mr Robertson is a Litigation Partner with over 20 commercial or antitrust trials before federal and state courts, administrative agencies, and arbitration panels. From July 2002 through January 2004, Mr Robertson served as the Senior Litigation Counsel for the Bureau of Competition at the Federal Trade Commission in Washington, DC.
**Personal:** Virginia Military Institute, BA, 1977. University of Chicago Law School, JD, 1990.

## ROCAP, Donald
Kirkland & Ellis LLP, Chicago
312 861 2266
drocap@kirkland.com
*Recommended in Tax*

**Practice Areas:** His practice focuses on the tax aspects of complex business transactions, including mergers, acquisitions, leveraged buyouts, formation of private equity funds, and debt and equity restructurings and workouts. Is a lecturer at the University of Chicago Law School and is a volume co-author of 'Mergers, Acquisitions, and Buyouts', by Martin Ginsburg and Jack Levin, and a Special Editor of 'Structuring Venture Capital, Private Equity, and Entrepreneurial Transactions', by Jack Levin.
**Personal:** Duke University, BA, 1977. University of Virginia School of Law, JD, 1980.

## ROGERS III, John L
Foley & Lardner LLP, Chicago
312 832 4915
jrogers@foley.com
*Recommended in Energy*

**Career:** John L Rogers III is a Partner in the Chicago office of Foley & Lardner LLP. He is a member of the firm's Energy Regulation and Securities Litigation, Enforcement and Regulatory Practice Groups. He is also a member of the Energy Industry Team. Mr Rogers focuses on representation of clients in SEC enforcement proceedings, as well as clients in the fields of energy and financial services. Mr Rogers is a law graduate of Harvard University (JD, magna cum laude, 1973).

## ROKOSZ, Ronald
Chapman and Cutler LLP, Chicago
312 845 3000
*Recommended in Banking & Finance*

## ROONEY, John E
Sonnenschein Nath & Rosenthal LLP, Chicago 312 876 8925
jrooney@sonnenschein.com
*Recommended in Energy, Telecom, Broadcast & Satellite*

**Practice Areas:** A Partner in the Energy and Telecommunications practice. He works on utility regulatory matters and

related legislative issues. He has successfully represented clients before the Illinois Commerce Commission on complex issues, including rate cases, rulemakings, and audits and investigations. He also represents clients involved in competitive marketplace development issues for energy and telecommunications service providers. He has worked on electric regional reliability council oversight matters and transactions involving electric generation and transmission assets.
**Prof. Memberships:** Chicago Bar Association; Past Chairman, Public Utilities Law Committee.
**Personal:** The John Marshall Law School, JD, Law Review; Loyola University, BBA.

## ROPER, Harry J
Jenner & Block LLP, Chicago
312 923 8303
hroper@jenner.com
*Recommended in Intellectual Property*

**Practice Areas:** Harry J Roper is a Partner in Jenner & Block's Chicago office, Chair of the firm's Intellectual Property Practice and Member of the firm's Management Committee. He is nationally recognized as one of the foremost trial and appellate lawyers in the intellectual property field and has extensive trial experience with complex patent litigation cases. Mr Roper has tried numerous patent infringement jury trials on behalf of such companies as The Dow Chemical Company, Johnson & Johnson, Medtronic and Phillips Petroleum Company. He was recently Lead Trial Counsel for Union Carbide Corporation in a patent infringement case in which it obtained a $152 million jury verdict against Shell Oil Company. In a cross-appeal of that case, in 2005, he was successful in extending the reach of patent damages to include foreign activities under 35 USC § 271(f). Also in 2005 he was lead trial counsel in a case where he successfully defended an inventorship claim against a major anti-cancer drug. Mr Roper has represented clients in substantial computer-related litigation such as in the field of word processing software used by Microsoft Word and other leading manufacturers. Mr Roper has written and lectured extensively concerning patent infringement, trade secret and antitrust litigation matters. He is a Member of, among others, the American Intellectual Property Law Association; Intellectual Property Law Association of Chicago; Barristers of the Patent Law, and a Fellow of the American Bar Foundation.
**Personal:** New York University School of Law, LLB, 1966. Rensselaer Polytechnic Institute, EEE, 1962.

## ROPSKI, Gary
Brinks Hofer Gilson & Lione, Chicago
312 321 4216
gropski@usebrinks.com

*Recommended in Intellectual Property*

**Practice Areas:** Gary Ropski's practice includes litigation in patents, trademarks, trade dress, copyright, trade secrets, right of publicity, and related unfair competition and antitrust matters in federal and state courts.
**Prof. Memberships:** AIPLA; International (Chair, Patent Subcommittee 1993-96), American, and Chicago Bar Associations; INTA; IPO; LES; IPLAC (Chair, Antitrust Committee 1995-97). Adjunct Professor, Northwestern University School of Law (1981-97).
**Publications:** Editor, Butterworths' 'Patent Litigation: Enforcing A Global Patent Portfolio'.
**Personal:** Education: BS, Physics, Carnegie-Mellon University (1972); JD (cum laude), Northwestern University School of Law (1976); Executive Editor, Journal of Criminal Law & Criminology (1975-76).

## ROSENBAUM, Michael D
Gardner Carton & Douglas LLP, Chicago
312 569 1308
mrosenbaum@gcd.com
*Recommended in Employment*

**Practice Areas:** Partner, Chairman, HR Law Department; practice includes employee benefit, executive/physician compensation matters; extensive experience: designing, implementing tax-qualified retirement plans; designing, implementing, funding executive compensation plans; addressing health and welfare plan design, compliance, operational issues; advising on workers' classification; advising on employee benefit arrangements for executives, physicians of tax-exempt organizations.
**Career:** Mr Rosenbaum has been with Gardner Carton & Douglas since 1987, is Chairman of the firm's HR Law Department (which includes the Employee Benefit Practice) and is a member of the firm's Operating Committee.
**Publications:** Co-author, Employee Benefit Plan Review Journal's 'Regulatory Update' column; articles published in Journal of Accountancy, Employment Relations Today, Medical Practice Management Journal, CCH Tax Transactions healthcare industry book, Callaghan's legal checklist, Illinois Institute for Continuing Legal Education manual. Frequent speaker on employee benefits, executive/physician compensation issues to national conferences of such organizations as Profit-Sharing Council of America, Enrolled Actuaries, American Institute of Certified Public Accountants, American Bar Association, American Medical Association, Chicago Bar Association, Michigan, Illinois CPA Societies, Strategic Research Institute, Institute for International Research, Employers Summit on Healthcare.
**Personal:** University of Wisconsin, JD, 1987, cum laude; Michigan State University, BA, 1984.

## ROSENBLOOM, David
McDermott Will & Emery, Chicago
312 984 7759
drosenbloom@mwe.com
*Recommended in Litigation*

**Practice Areas:** Head of the firm's White-Collar Criminal Defense Practice. Practices white-collar criminal defense, qui tam litigation, healthcare fraud and abuse compliance, internal investigations, and class actions and other complex commercial litigation. Represented numerous corporations and individuals in connection with civil and criminal allegations of misconduct. Extensive experience in representing healthcare providers and manufacturers. Has represented clients in various industries, including securities, insurance, manufacturing and energy, both in response to specific allegations of misconduct and as part of preventive compliance programs.
**Personal:** Harvard Law School (JD, magna cum laude); Colorado College (BA, magna cum laude)

## ROSENBLOOM, James
Goldberg, Kohn, Bell, Black, Rosenbloom & Moritz, Ltd, Chicago
312 201 4000
*Recommended in Real Estate*

## ROSENBLOOM, Lewis S
McDermott Will & Emery, Chicago
312 984 6943
lrosenbloom@mwe.com
*Recommended in Bankruptcy*

**Practice Areas:** Senior Partner, Corporate Department, leading the corporate finance, M&A, restructuring, governance and corporate advisory practices focused on distressed business and financial marketplace. Recognized among nation's leading corporate restructuring advisors, represented virtually every possible stakeholder or participant in major bankruptcy, corporate restructuring, finance, merger and acquisition, and multi-district class litigation matters during his 29 years of practice. Served as Board Member and general counsel of several public and private companies and has managed purchase, sale and financing of many billions of dollars of distressed company assets and securities.
**Personal:** Lake Forest College (BA); DePaul University (JD, summa cum laude).

## ROSENTHAL, Michael D
Sonnenschein Nath & Rosenthal LLP, Chicago 312 876 3180
mrosenthal@sonnenschein.com
*Recommended in Corporate/M&A: Private Equity*

**Practice Areas:** Corporate and Securities Partner. Represents private equity and venture capital funds, and target companies in investments from seed to late stage and in buyouts, leveraged recapitalizations and workouts; M&A; joint ventures; securities; general corpo-

rate counseling. Represents funds in hedge, venture and private equity fund formation and investment structuring and limited partners in fund investments.
**Prof. Memberships:** Venture Capital and Private Equity Committee, ABA's Business Section; Planning Committee of Illinois Business & Investor Forum.
**Personal:** University of Michigan Law School, JD magna cum laude, Law Review, Order of the Coif; Washington University, AB, magna cum laude, Phi Beta Kappa.

### ROSS, Nancy
McDermott Will & Emery, Chicago
312 984 7743
nross@mwe.com
*Recommended in Employment, ERISA Litigation*
**Practice Areas:** Practices primarily in employee benefits class action litigation and counseling under the Employee Retirement Income Security Act of 1974 (ERISA). Experience in counseling and representing employers, plan fiduciaries and trustees concerning pension and welfare benefit plans. Representation of pension plans, ESOPs, trustees and employers in litigation concerning their administration of plan assets and fiduciary responsibilities, directors and officers named as defendants in ERISA litigation over 401(k), ESOP plans and other employee benefit plans.
**Prof. Memberships:** Co-Chair, Fiduciary Responsibility Committee of the ABA Employee Benefits Committee.
**Personal:** Loyola University of Chicago School of Law (JD); University of Colorado (BA).

### ROVNER, Jack A
Neal, Gerber & Eisenberg LLP, Chicago
312 269 8014
jrovner@ngelaw.com
*Recommended in Healthcare*
**Practice Areas:** Focuses on health law, antitrust, business counseling and transactions, and commercial litigation; experience covers health insurance and healthcare financing, health information technology, hospital systems and alliances, and group purchasing; counsels on anti-fraud and abuse laws, HIPAA privacy, security and transaction standards, and Medicare private health plans.
**Prof. Memberships:** ABA (Sections on Health Law, Antitrust, and Litigation); ISBA; American Health Lawyers Association.
**Career:** Partner; Health Law Practice Group C-Chair.
**Publications:** Author and lecturer on health law topics; Member, Advisory Board, BNA, Inc's Health Law Reporter (2005-present).
**Personal:** Boston University School of Law (JD, 1976); Brandeis University (BA, 1968).

### ROY, Paul J N
Mayer, Brown, Rowe & Maw LLP, Chicago 312 701 7370
proy@mayerbrownrowe.com
*Recommended in Business Process Outsourcing, Technology*
**Practice Areas:** Partner in Corporate, Information Technology, Telecommunications and Outsourcing Practices. Represents corporate clients in a broad range of information technology, telecommunications and outsourcing transactions, including the outsourcing of data and voice networks, data centers, personal computers, help desks, applications development and maintenance, call centers, finance and accounting functions, logistics, human resources and other business process functions. Representative transactions also include software and systems development and implementation, systems integration, strategic alliances and joint ventures. Clients include domestic and international corporations of various sizes, and in a variety of industries, including chemicals, telecommunications, software and computer equipment manufacturing, pharmaceutical, life sciences, banking and finance, securities trading, insurance, professional associations, auditing, consulting, consumer products, and distribution.
**Prof. Memberships:** Admitted to practice in Illinois. Member of the American Bar Association.
**Career:** Joined Mayer, Brown, Rowe Maw LLP, 1985. Formerly with The Associates Commercial Corporation, Chicago, manager, personal computer software development, business systems analyst, 1982-85. Borg Warner Corporation, Automotive Parts Division, warehouse department manager, financial analyst, 1979-82.
**Personal:** Loyola University of Chicago, JD, 1985. Northwestern University, MBA, 1982. Colby College, BA, 1978.

### RUBIN, James
Butler Rubin Saltarelli & Boyd, Chicago
312 696 4443
jrubin@butlerrubin.com
*Recommended in Insurance*
**Practice Areas:** Reinsurance litigation and arbitration.
**Career:** James Rubin is a trial lawyer, founding Partner and Head of Reinsurance Litigation and Arbitration Practice Group. He has represented insurance and reinsurance companies in over 200 complex reinsurance disputes and he counsels insurers and reinsurers regarding transactions, reinsurance wordings, and commutations. His experience includes matters in litigation, arbitration and mediation, involving disparate issues such as the proper allocation of losses, fraud, contract interpretation, finite contract disputes, the authority of agents, the conclusiveness of commutations, and claims by and against companies in receivership

or operating under schemes of arrangement. He is a frequent speaker on reinsurance issues and has spoken at numerous industry programs. He sits on ARIAS ethics and editorial committees. With two other industry representatives, he co-authored ARIAS's Code of Conduct for Arbitrators.
**Personal:** JD, Loyola University Law School, 1971, Member, Loyola University Law Review, 1970-71. AB, University of Illinois, 1967.

### RUBIN, Joel
Seyfarth Shaw LLP, Chicago
312 346 8000
*Recommended in Real Estate*

### RUFF, Randolph E
Ogletree, Deakins, Nash, Smoak & Stewart, PC, Chicago 312 558 1220
randolph.ruff@ogletreedeakins.com
*Recommended in Construction*
**Practice Areas:** Mr Ruff heads the Construction Law and Litigation Practice Group at Ogletree Deakins. He represents national and regional general contractors, subcontractors, specialty contractors and suppliers in all phases of the construction process. Mr Ruff handles all manner of construction claims, disputes, litigations, arbitrations and mediations, including design and construction defect, delay, acceleration, extra work, and mechanics lien matters.
**Prof. Memberships:** Society of Illinois Construction Attorneys, ABA Construction Industry Forum, CBA Construction and Mechanics Lien Committee (past Chairperson).
**Publications:** Has lectured and written extensively on construction processes and disputes.
**Personal:** University of Colorado (BA, 1981), Valparaiso University (JD, 1986).

### RUNNING, Andrew R
Kirkland & Ellis LLP, Chicago
312 861 2412
arunning@kirkland.com
*Recommended in Environment*
**Practice Areas:** Extensive experience in bankruptcy, environmental, insurance, toxic tort and general commercial litigation. He has tried numerous environmental lawsuits involving claims of property damage and alleged regulatory violations, as well as litigation over the allocation of responsibility for the cleanup of hazardous waste sites. He has successfully defended product liability actions involving allegations of hazardous substance contamination. His arbitration experience includes the trial of cases involving commercial breach of contract claims, disputes between international joint venture partners, non-compete clause disputes, biotechnology licensing disputes and reinsurance and insurance fraud claims.
**Personal:** University of Chicago, AB, 1979. Yale University JD, 1982.

### RUSSELL, James H
Winston & Strawn LLP, Chicago
312 558 6084
jrussell@winston.com
*Recommended in Environment*
**Practice Areas:** Environmental law and environmental litigation: administrative, civil, and criminal environmental enforcement litigation and cost recovery litigation before state and federal courts and agencies; rulemakings before state agencies and USEPA; permit appeals, permit negotiations, and regulatory counseling; all environmental aspects of corporate transactions, corporate successor liability and lender liability.
**Prof. Memberships:** Chicago Bar Association; American Bar Association.
**Career:** Joined as Partner, 1986.
**Publications:** 'Avoiding Corporate Successor Environmental Liability', Chemical Waste Litigation Reporter, 1987; 'Basic Principles of Superfund Litigation', Regulatory Toxicology and Pharmacology, 1985; 'A Proposal to Repeal the Illinois Pollution Control Board's Construction Permit Regulations', Chicago Bar Record, 1980; 'Water Pollution', Chapter VI of Handbook on Environmental Law, Illinois Institute for Continuing Legal Education, 1978; 'Aircraft and Airport Noise: Current Legal Remedies and Future Alternatives', Insurance Counsel Journal, 1975; 'Inverse Condemnation of Air Space', Journal of Air Law and Commerce, 1973.
**Personal:** Ohio Wesleyan University, BA, 1965; The Ohio State University Moritz College of Law, JD, 1969.

### RUXIN, Paul
Jones Day, Chicago
312 269 1546
paultruxin@jonesday.com
*Recommended in Energy*
**Practice Areas:** Represents natural gas, pipeline, electric, and telephone public utilities before state and federal regulatory bodies and courts. Regularly involved in the development, acquisition, and sale of energy resources and independent power and energy-related projects, the structure and restructuring of public utility and other energy businesses, the impact of the antitrust laws on regulated utilities, and the general litigation and commercial problems of the energy and public utility industries. For 25 years he served as Chairman of Jones Day's specialized Energy Industry Practice. He is a frequent speaker at utility industry meetings and seminars.

### RYAN, Priscilla E
Sidley Austin LLP, Chicago
312 853 7072
pryan@sidley.com
*Recommended in Employment*
**Practice Areas:** Concentrates her practice in employee benefits matters, including fiduciary issues that arise under

ERISA and executive compensation, and she provides litigation support in ERISA class action lawsuits. She represents clients on a variety of matters before the Treasury Department, the Internal Revenue Service, the Department of Labor and the Pension Benefit Guaranty Corporation. Ms Ryan is Co-Chair of the firm's Insurance Committee, which is responsible for the administration of all the firm's insurance policies (other than malpractice insurance).

**Prof. Memberships:** Member of the Section of Taxation of the American Bar Association and serves as the Chair of its Employee Benefits Committee. She is a Member of the ABA Joint Committee on Employee Benefits, the IRS Great Lakes Area Tax Exempt and Government Entities Council and a Fellow of the American College of Employee Benefits Counsel.

**Career:** Served as an attorney-advisor in the Office of Tax Policy of the US Treasury Department, advising the Assistant Secretary of Tax Policy.

**Publications:** Ms Ryan has lectured and written many articles on tax and employee benefit issues.

**Personal:** Loyola University Chicago School of Law, JD, 1982; Marquette University, AB, 1969. Admission: Illinois, 1982.

### RYAN, Thomas F
Sidley Austin LLP, Chicago
312 853 7497
tryan@sidley.com
*Recommended in Antitrust, Litigation*

**Practice Areas:** Thomas F Ryan serves on the firm's Executive and Finance Committees. He focuses on antitrust and business counseling, arbitration and alternative dispute resolution, and trials before State and Federal Courts. Mr Ryan engages in litigation in several areas including antitrust, class actions, commercial, environmental and securities, and was named to the BTI Consulting All-Star Team for Client Service.

**Prof. Memberships:** Mr Ryan has served as a Member of the Advisory Committee on Circuit Rules for the Seventh Federal Circuit Court of Appeals and as President of the Seventh Circuit Bar Association.

**Personal:** Wayne State University Law School, JD, 1971; Ferris State University, BS, 1965. Admission: Illinois, 1972.

### SAFER, Ronald S
Schiff Hardin LLP, Chicago
312 258 5500
rsafer@schiffhardin.com
*Recommended in Litigation*

**Practice Areas:** Litigation, white-collar defense, corporate compliance

**Prof. Memberships:** Federal Bar Association, Center on Wrongful Convictions, American College of Trial Attorneys (Fellow)

**Career:** Leads Schiff Hardin's White Collar Criminal Defense Group and is very

active in the firm's Tax Litigation and Civil Litigation Practices. Serves as the firm's Managing Partner and Executive Committee Member. Former Assistant US attorney in the Northern District of Illinois, where he was Chief of the Criminal Division.

**Personal:** University of Pennsylvania (BS, Economics, cum laude, 1979), Georgetown University Law Center (JD, magna cum laude, 1983)

### SALPETER, Alan N
Mayer, Brown, Rowe & Maw LLP, Chicago 312 701 7051
asalpeter@mayerbrownrowe.com
*Recommended in Litigation*

**Practice Areas:** Senior litigator with approximately 70 bench and jury trials and 20 appeals. Commercial cases focus on alleged malpractice suits against lawyers, accountants and consultants; alleged securities fraud; multiple kinds of class actions, including shareholder and consumer class actions; disputes over information technology; contested mergers or acquisitions; business torts; and actions involving corporate governance and alleged breach of fiduciary duties.

**Career:** Joined Mayer, Brown, Rowe & Maw LLP, Chicago, 1972; became Partner, 1979. Co-Leader Litigation Department, 1994-2000.

**Publications:** Co-author of a number of articles and chapters in books on a range of litigation issues. Speaker at numerous programs sponsored by Swiss Reinsurance New Markets, Practicing Law Institute, NERA Conference, American Bar Association, The Garrett Institute and Boalt Hall School of Law (University of California at Berkeley).

**Personal:** Villanova University, JD, 1972; Managing Editor, Villanova Law Review. The American University, BS in Political Science with highest honors, 1969.

### SALTIEL, David
Bell, Boyd & Lloyd LLC, Chicago
312 372 1121
*Recommended in Media & Entertainment*

### SANCHEZ, Vincent
DLA Piper Rudnick Gray Cary US LLP, Chicago 312 368 3420
vincent.sanchez@dlapiper.com
*Recommended in Technology*

**Practice Areas:** Technology transactions; outsourcing, electronic commerce and privacy.

**Career:** Co-Chair of the firm's Technology Transactions Practice, where he represents companies in acquisitions, divestitures, joint ventures, strategic alliances, equity investments, and licensing arrangements involving some form of technology or intellectual property. His practice also includes representing companies in the outsourcing of business processes and operations and advising companies with respect to the legal and

regulatory issues and risks regarding the use and security of data and other information as well as transacting business through the internet or in other networked environments.

**Personal:** MBA, Northwestern University; JD, University of Notre Dame.

### SANDERS, David P
Jenner & Block LLP, Chicago
312 923 2963
dsanders@jenner.com
*Recommended in Media & Entertainment*

**Practice Areas:** David P Sanders is a Partner in Jenner & Block's Chicago office. Mr Sanders is Co-Chair of the firm's Media and First Amendment Practice, and a member of the firm's Litigation and Dispute Resolution and Class Action Litigation Practices. Mr Sanders has served as regular outside counsel to several media clients, including a national broadcast network, Crain Communications Inc, Chicago magazine and Golfweek, and has represented numerous other national publishers, broadcasters, and others in the news and entertainment businesses. Mr Sanders provides litigation and counseling services to clients on a wide range of media law and First Amendment issues. He has successfully defended dozens of libel and privacy cases on behalf of media clients. Recently, he successfully handled, on behalf of several major news organizations, the appeal of a high profile libel action brought by an Islamic charity. Other cases have included the successful defense of Forbes in a libel case brought by a prominent business executive; the defense of a television network in a libel and invasion of privacy case challenging a hidden camera investigative news report; and the appeal of the then-largest damage award in the history of American libel law. Mr Sanders regularly handles other types of litigated matters involving First Amendment and press issues for his media clients, and counsels media and non-media clients on a broad range of problems involving defamation, privacy, newsgathering, Freedom of Information Act, copyright, advertising, promotion, insurance and related business/legal issues.

**Personal:** Georgetown University Law Center, JD, 1974.

### SARASEK, Peter A
Quarles & Brady LLP, Chicago
312 715 5035
psarasek@quarles.com
*Recommended in Real Estate*

**Practice Areas:** Real estate, financial institutions.

**Prof. Memberships:** Associations: Chicago Bar, Illinois State Bar (Real Property Section, Federal Taxation Section), Wisconsin Bar, American Bar; Building Owners and Managers (Chicago Chapter); Lender's Counsel Group, American

Land Title; American College of Real Estate Lawyers.

**Career:** Partner since 1980.

**Publications:** Co-authored: 'Cash, Car Keys and Other Collateral', Chicago BOMA Report 1995; 'When Your Building is a Star', Journal of Property Management 1994; 'Who Foots The Bill for Capital Costs?' Commercial Investment Real Estate Journal 1993.

**Personal:** University of Wisconsin (JD, 1974); Catholic University of America (MA, 1968; BA, 1967).

### SATHY, Anup
Kirkland & Ellis LLP, Chicago
312 861 2046
asathy@kirkland.com
*Recommended in Bankruptcy*

**Practice Areas:** Anup Sathy concentrates his practice in matters relating to corporate restructurings, workouts and Chapter 11 reorganizations. He has substantial experience representing companies, buyers and lenders in all aspects of distressed situations.

**Personal:** University of Illinois at Urbana-Champaign, BS, Finance, 1992, highest honors. Northwestern University School of Law, JD, 1995, cum laude.

### SCHILLER, Eric M
Sonnenschein Nath & Rosenthal LLP, Chicago 312 876 8015
eschiller@sonnenschein.com
*Recommended in Real Estate*

**Practice Areas:** Real Estate and Finance Partner with 25+ years representing corporate and institutional clients nationwide in real estate and commercial finance matters. Specializes in financing, joint ventures, commercial leases, real estate acquisition and sales and workouts. Matters include multi-state, multi-asset real estate and commercial transactions involving office buildings, industrial buildings, shopping centers, hotels and apartment complexes. Counsels lenders in syndication groups in loans, as agent and co-lender.

**Prof. Memberships:** Elected to American College of Real Estate Lawyers; Member, Chicago and American Bar associations.

**Personal:** Northwestern University School of Law, JD, Editorial Board, Law Review; Indiana University, BA with honors.

### SCHLICKMAN, J Andrew
Sidley Austin LLP, Chicago
312 853 7404
jaschlickman@sidley.com
*Recommended in Environment*

**Practice Areas:** J Andrew Schlickman's practice involves complex environmental enforcement and litigation matters, with an emphasis on contaminated river and sediment cases, natural resource damages cases, disputes between buyers and sellers of contaminated properties, diminution in property value cases, and defense of governmental enforcement actions. He has tried complex environmental cases, handled appeals of such cases, negotiated a wide variety of consent decrees and settlements, and participated in hearings on the fairness of settlements. Named twice to BTI Consulting's All-Star Team for Client Service.

**Prof. Memberships:** American Bar Association, section of Environment and Natural Resources, and the Chicago Bar Association.

**Career:** Mr Schlickman has practiced in the environmental litigation field for almost 20 years, and before then focused on complex civil litigation. He has been with Sidley Austin LLP his entire career and a Partner of the firm since 1988.

**Personal:** The University of Chicago Law School (JD, 1978); Georgetown University (BA, 1974). Admission: Illinois, 1978.

### SCHNADIG, Richard
Vedder, Price, Kaufman & Kammholz, Chicago 312 609 7500
*Recommended in Employment*

### SCHNEIDMAN, Edward J
Mayer, Brown, Rowe & Maw LLP, Chicago 312 701 7348
eschneidman@mayerbrownrowe.com
*Recommended in Corporate/M&A*

**Practice Areas:** Mergers of publicly and privately held corporations, partnerships, limited liability companies and other entities. Stock and asset acquisitions and divestitures. Corporate and partnership liquidations and reorganizations. General corporate governance and compliance. Public and private offerings. Real estate investment trusts and other public and private real estate-related entities. Limited partnerships, mortgage pools and institutional funds, including group trusts, separate accounts, and tax-exempt title-holding corporations. Federal and state securities law compliance.

**Prof. Memberships:** Illinois, 1980. US District Court for the Northern District of Illinois, 1980.

**Career:** Joined Mayer, Brown, Rowe & Maw LLP, Chicago, 1980; became Partner 1987. Corporate Practice Area Administrator since 1996-2002.

**Publications:** Illinois Continuing Legal Education Seminars, 'Partnership Law and Aspects of Oil and Gas Law'. American Association of Equipment Lessors Lawyer Forum.

**Personal:** Duke University School of Law, JD with honors, 1980. University of Pennsylvania, BSE magna cum laude, 1977.

### SCHOPF, Willam G
Schopf & Weiss, Chicago
312 701 9300
schopf@sw.com
*Recommended in Antitrust*

**Practice Areas:** Over 30 years of successful verdicts and settlements, including Lead Trial Counsel role in numerous jury

trials involving issues such as international trade, civil RICO, legal malpractice, price-fixing, deceptive practices, breach of contract, fraud, product liability, toxic torts and negligence. Recognized in 2004 by the National Law Journal as one of the top 10 'Winning Trial Lawyers' in the United States.

**Prof. Memberships:** American Bar Association; Chicago Bar Association; Union Internationale des Avocats

**Career:** Founded Schopf & Weiss, 1987; Partner: Isham, Lincoln & Beale; Reuben & Proctor 1979-87.

**Publications:** See www.sw.com.

**Personal:** Cornell Law School (JD, 1973); Princeton University (AB, 1970).

### SCHRANK, Charles E
Sidley Austin LLP, Chicago
312 853 4140
cschrank@sidley.com
*Recommended in Real Estate*

**Practice Areas:** Charles E Schrank is a Partner in the Chicago Real Estate Group and primarily represents investment banks and other institutional lenders and investment funds in connection with loan origination for commercial mortgage-backed securitization programs, mezzanine and A/B note financing, preferred equity investments, warehouse repurchase and credit facilities and other debt and debt-like capitalization structures, servicing agreements, fund venture agreements, construction loans, and debt restructurings and workouts. Mr Schrank has also represented operating companies and investors in connection with sales and acquisitions, equity investments, joint ventures, sale-leasebacks, and commercial and industrial leasing and development.

**Personal:** University of Wisconsin Law School, JD, 1986; University of Wisconsin – Madison, BBA, 1983. Admission: Illinois, 1990.

### SCHREIBER, Rodd M
Skadden, Arps, Slate, Meagher & Flom LLP & Affiliates, Chicago 312 407 0531
rschreib@skadden.com
*Recommended in Corporate/M&A*

**Practice Areas:** Concentrating in mergers and acquisitions, corporate financings and other corporate and securities matters. Has represented corporate clients and financial advisors in a wide variety of domestic and international transactions, including public and private acquisitions and divestitures, negotiated and contested takeovers, leveraged buyouts, spin-offs, joint ventures and other strategic alliances and public and private debt and equity financings. Provides continuing counseling to a number of corporate clients regarding general corporate and securities matters, including governance, securities law compliance and disclosure issues.

**Career:** JD, University of Michigan, Ann

Arbor, 1987 (cum laude); BA, University of Michigan, 1984 (with distinction).

### SCHWAB, Stephen W
DLA Piper Rudnick Gray Cary US LLP, Chicago 312 368 2150
stephen.schwab@dlapiper.com
*Recommended in Insurance*

**Practice Areas:** International commerce and litigation; insurance and reinsurance.

**Career:** He is a commercial litigator who concentrates his practice in the areas of insurance and reinsurance, litigation, arbitration and mediation, transactions and regulation. He has published and addressed audiences throughout the world on topics analyzed in an extensive list of book chapters, law review articles, and pieces for trade publications on insurance and reinsurance-related subjects.

**Personal:** JD, The Dickinson School of Law of Pennsylvania State University; BA, Northwestern University.

### SCHWARTZ, Donald
Latham & Watkins LLP, Chicago
312 876 7700
*Recommended in Banking & Finance*

### SCOTT, Ami G
Mayer, Brown, Rowe & Maw LLP, Chicago 312 701 8478
agscott@mayerbrownrowe.com
*Recommended in Banking & Finance*

**Practice Areas:** Represents financial institutions and borrowers in a variety of secured and unsecured lending transactions, including acquisition financings, working capital financings and private lending transactions.

**Prof. Memberships:** National Black MBA Association. Alumni Society Board, Fisher College of Business at The Ohio State University.

**Career:** Mayer, Brown, Rowe & Maw LLP, Chicago, 1999 to date. Dickinson Wright PLLC, 1997-98.

**Personal:** The University of Michigan Law School, JD, 1997. The Ohio State University, MBA, 1994. The Ohio State University, BSBA magna cum laude, 1994.

### SELIGMAN, David R
Kirkland & Ellis LLP, Chicago
312 861 2463
dseligman@kirkland.com
*Recommended in Bankruptcy*

**Practice Areas:** Mr Seligman concentrates his practice in all aspects of corporate restructuring, bankruptcy, and insolvency. He primarily represents reorganizing companies, but has significant experience representing creditors, creditors committees, asset purchasers, and trustees. Mr Seligman has special expertise in labor and pension restructuring, particularly in the airline industry. He also has significant experience in complex cross-border creditors' rights matters.

**Prof. Memberships:** American Bankruptcy Institute; Dartmouth Lawyers Association; Chicago Bench and Bar Liaison Committee, Founding Member; Anti-Defamation League.

**Personal:** London School of Economics, 1991; Hebrew University of Jerusalem, 1992; Dartmouth College, AB, 1993; University of Miami School of Law, JD, 1996.

### SELMAN, Russell
Katten Muchin Rosenman LLP, Chicago
312 902 5390
russell.selman@kattenlaw.com
*Recommended in Environment*

**Practice Areas:** Department Chair. Practices in corporate, real estate, electric and gas utilities environmental compliance and litigation matters. Represents leading parties seeking cost recovery at several sites with remedial costs exceeding $100 million in Illinois, Massachusetts and Minnesota. Defense of a multi-million dollar wetland penalty case in Chicago. Defends toxic tort cases associated with manufactured gas plants and releases of solvents in Chicago. Counsels on matters involving hazardous waste control (Superfund), chemical regulation, worker protection and federal wetlands law. Prepares RCRA compliance plans, Clean Air Act permits, and overall environmental permitting plans for power plant operations. Successful negotiation and litigation with the US Environmental Protection Agency ('EPA') for the cleanup of the largest PCB disposal site in the nation. Clients include KeySpan (New York), Boston Gas, SEMCO, ONEOK, PCB Treatment, Inc. Steering Committee, AIG Environmental, GKN North America and Park District of Oak Park, IL.

**Prof. Memberships:** American Bar Association, American Gas Association, Chicago Bar Association, Midwest Gas Association.

**Career:** Joined Katten in 1993. Served as Special Assistant to the General Counsel (Superfund) and Acting Assistant Enforcement Counsel for the US Environmental Protection Agency, Washington, DC. Developed legal and enforcement policies for EPA environmental programs and worked on the reauthorization of the Superfund statute. Received the EPA's 'Special Achievement' award for litigation. Member of the Bar in Illinois, Missouri and Washington, DC.

**Publications:** Restaurant critique columnist for Chicago Lawyer.

**Personal:** Washington University (JD 1979); Syracuse University, Maxwell School (MPA 1978); New College, Sarasota, Florida (BA 1975).

### SENNETT, Michael
Bell, Boyd & Lloyd LLC, Chicago
312 372 1121
*Recommended in Antitrust*

## SHAPIRO, Clifford
Sachnoff & Weaver Ltd, Chicago
312 207 1000
*Recommended in Construction*

## SHAPIRO, Keith
Greenberg Traurig LLP, Chicago
312 456 8405
shapirok@gtlaw.com
*Recommended in Bankruptcy*
**Practice Areas:** Reorganization, bankruptcy and restructuring.
**Prof. Memberships:** Member, Board of Directors, INSOL International. Member, American Bankruptcy Institute. Fellow, American College of Bankruptcy.
**Career:** Listed, Chambers & Partners 2005-06 listed, Best Lawyers, 2001-present; listed, Who's Who in Business, Crain's Chicago Business, 2005.
**Publications:** Co-Editor-in-Chief, Wiley's annual Bankruptcy Law Update. Contributing author, West's Norton 'Bankruptcy Law and Practice treatise and Wiley's Advanced Chapter 11 Bankruptcy Practice' treatise. Authored two editions of the book 'Guide to Core vs. Noncore Jurisdiction Under the Bankruptcy Code'.
**Personal:** JD, Emory University School of Law, 1983; BS, Finance, University of Illinois at Urbana-Champaign, 1980.

## SHAPIRO, Stephen R
Mayer, Brown, Rowe & Maw LLP, Chicago 312 701 7327
sshapiro@mayerbrown.com
*Recommended in Litigation*
**Practice Areas:** Founder and Senior Member, firm's Supreme Court and Appellate Litigation Practice Group, the largest in the country. Has argued 24 cases in the US Supreme Court and large number of appeals in federal and state courts nationwide. Co-Head of firm's Telecommunications Practice Group. Served on firm's management committee. Clients represented on appeal include General Motors, SBC Corp., BellSouth, BASF Corp., Merrill Lynch, ChevronTexaco, ITT Hartford, and the National Association of Manufacturers.
**Prof. Memberships:** Board of Directors, New York University Law School, Institute of Judicial Administration. Member, American Law Institute, American Academy of Appellate Lawyers. Former trustee of Product Liability Advisory Foundation.
**Career:** Mayer, Brown, Rowe & Maw LLP, Chicago, 1972-78; 1983-date; Partner, 1978. Deputy Solicitor General, US Department of Justice, 1981-83. Assistant to the Solicitor General, DOJ, 1978-80. Law clerk to The Honorable Charles M Merrill, US Court of Appeals, Ninth Circuit, 1971.
**Publications:** Prolific writer. Numerous publications include standard treatise on litigation before US Supreme Court, R Stern, E Gressman, S Shapiro and K

Geller, 'Supreme Court Practice' (2002).
**Personal:** Yale Law School, JD, 1971; Board of Editors, Yale Law Journal. Yale College, BA magna cum laude, 1968; honors with exceptional distinction; Phi Beta Kappa.

## SHEFFIELD, Jeffrey
Kirkland & Ellis LLP, Chicago
312 861 2454
jsheffield@kirkland.com
*Recommended in Tax*
**Practice Areas:** Mr Sheffield concentrates his practice in the areas of business planning; mergers, acquisitions and venture capital investing; tax planning for public and closely-held entities; and executive compensation.
**Publications:** He has authored or co-authored several articles, including 'Monetization Strategies in Corporate Spin-Offs' 81 Taxes 287 (March 2003).
**Personal:** University of Chicago, BA, 1976, Phi Beta Kappa; Harvard Law School, JD, 1979. Editor, Harvard Law Review.

## SHEPRO, Richard Warren
Mayer, Brown, Rowe & Maw LLP, Chicago 312 701 7007
rshepro@mayerbrownrowe.com
*Recommended in Corporate/M&A, Insurance*
**Practice Areas:** Chicago Office Practice Leader for Corporate and Securities Law. Represents and counsels on acquisitions, restructurings, and securities law; negotiation/planning for acquisitions; offshore corporations; international investment; insurance and reinsurance companies; venture capital, private equity fund work; proxy, consent solicitations; public, private offerings; broker-dealer, investment advisor regulation.
**Career:** Served as law clerk to The Honorable Judge James R Browning, Chief Judge, US Court of Appeals for the Ninth Circuit, 1979-81. Joined Mayer, Brown, Rowe & Maw LLP in 1981 and became Partner in 1986. Lecturer, University of Chicago Law School. Former Visiting Professor, Northwestern University School of Law. Lectured at the London Business School, Ecole des Hautes Etudes Commerciales, and at professional associations. Taught at Harvard University.
**Publications:** Co-author, 'Bidders & Targets: Mergers and Acquisitions in the US' (1990). Articles on mergers, corporate law, and securities law for such publications as Financial Times, Harvard Business Review, and Business Lawyer.
**Personal:** JD (cum laude), Harvard University, 1979; Supreme Court Note Editor, Law Review. MSc (1976), The London School of Economics; AB magna cum laude (1975), Harvard University. Special Assistant Attorney General of the State of Illinois, 1981-82. Staff Member, US Senate Judiciary Committee, 1978-79. Speaks French and Russian.

## SHERCK, Timothy C
Mayer, Brown, Rowe & Maw LLP, Chicago 312 701 7148
tsherck@mayerbrownrowe.com
*Recommended in Tax*
**Practice Areas:** Represents and counsels on all tax aspects of acquisitions and dispositions of business, including consolidated return, carryforward, spinoff and asset basis issues; tax-free reorganisations; corporate joint ventures; tax aspects of business financial restructurings, workouts, and bankruptcy, including debt exchanges and modification, cancellation of indebtedness income, loss carryforwards, and related matters such as tax liens and tax-related aspects of bankruptcy law; acquisitions of financially troubled business; and preparation and handling of requests for private letter rulings before the IRS National Office.
**Career:** Served as law clerk to The Honorable Walter R Mansfield, US Court of Appeals for the Second Circuit, New York, 1974-75. Joined Mayer, Brown, Rowe & Maw LLP in 1975 and became Partner in 1981.
**Publications:** Author of 'Treatment of Options in Applying Stock Ownership Tests in the Corporate World', 66 Taxes 935 (1988); 'Restructuring Today's Financially Troubled Corporation', 68 Taxes 881 (1990); 'Applying the Property- Services Distinction in Corporate Transactions: The New Economy Tests the Limits', 68 Taxes 120 (2001) (co-author).
**Personal:** JD, cum laude, from Harvard Law School, 1974; Comment Editor, Law Review. BA, cum laude (1971), Northwestern University.

## SHIELDS, Thomas
Bell, Boyd & Lloyd LLC, Chicago
312 372 1121
*Recommended in Healthcare*

## SHUGRUE, John
Morgan, Lewis & Bockius LLP, Chicago
312 324 2535
jshugrue@morganlewis.com
*Recommended in Insurance*
**Practice Areas:** John Shugrue is a Partner in the Litigation Practice, with a focus on insurance recovery. He is experienced in all aspects of litigation, mediation, and arbitration with Lloyd's of London, London and Bermuda market insurers, and all major domestic insurers. He has substantial experience in handling complex litigation and insurance coverage matters involving Commercial General Liability (CGL), Directors & Officers (D&O), Errors & Omissions (E&O), First Party Property and Fidelity policies. He is co-author of the treatise 'Insurance Coverage Disputes' and is past Co-Chair of the ABA Litigation Section's Insurance Coverage Litigation Committee.
**Prof. Memberships:** American Bar Association.

## SHULRUFF, Stuart P
Katten Muchin Rosenman LLP, Chicago
312 902 5694
stuart.shulruff@kattenlaw.com
*Recommended in Banking & Finance*
**Practice Areas:** Partner, Chicago; Chair of Commercial Finance Practice. Concentrates practice in corporate finance (senior financing, second lien/term B financing, mezzanine financing, equity co-investments) for institutional and entrepreneurial clients including Ableco Finance LLC, Antares Capital Corporation, CapitalSource Finance LLC, Dymas Capital Management Company LLC, General Electric Capital Corporation, LaSalle Bank National Association, Prairie Capital, Madison Capital Funding LLC, Merrill Lynch Capital, Midwest Mezzanine Fund, and Norwest Mezzanine Partners, LP.
**Prof. Memberships:** Illinois Bar Association, Chicago Bar Association.
**Personal:** BS, Accountancy (high honors) from the University of Illinois at Urbana-Champaign, 1981. CPA, 1981. JD (cum laude) from Loyola University School of Law, 1984.

## SICKLE, David B
DLA Piper Rudnick Gray Cary US LLP, Chicago 312 368 4081
david.sickle@dlapiper.com
*Recommended in Real Estate*
**Practice Areas:** Real estate; landlord leasing.
**Career:** His practice concentrates in transactional real estate and finance. He represents a wide variety of REITs, banks, and developer and institutional clients and has particular experience in shopping center finance, acquisition, development, leasing, and dispositions. He has recently written and published on the topic of loan workouts and deeds in lieu of foreclosures.
**Personal:** JD, University of Michigan; BS, University of Pennsylvania.

## SILBERMAN, Alan H
Sonnenschein Nath & Rosenthal LLP, Chicago 312 876 8103
asilberman@sonnenschein.com
*Recommended in Antitrust*
**Practice Areas:** Antitrust, Marketing Practices, Franchising and Distribution Chair with 40 years of experience in antitrust, franchising and general commercial litigation, counseling and related transactions. Represents franchisors in negotiated, litigated and arbitrated disputes with franchisees and third parties and domestic and international activities. Acts for McDonald's and other significant franchisors and manufacturers.
**Prof. Memberships:** Illinois Franchise Advisory Board; Co-Chair, Practising Law Institute's Annual Antitrust Law Institute; Former Chair, ABA's Section of Antitrust Law, ABA House of Delegates member; Illinois, US Supreme Court,

various US Courts of Appeal and district Court bars.

**Personal:** Yale University, LLB; Northwestern University, BA, with Distinction.

### SIMON, Mark C
Katten Muchin Rosenman LLP, Chicago
312 902 5301
Mark.Simon@kattenlaw.com
*Recommended in Real Estate*

**Practice Areas:** Partner, Chicago. Represents banks, pension fund advisors and developers financing, acquiring, leasing and developing real estate. Frequently acts as agent's counsel on large syndicated REIT credit facilities. Substantial experience documenting mezzanine loans and joint ventures. Has handled a considerable number of workouts for both lending institutions and developers, including restructuring the indebtedness of entire real estate companies.

**Prof. Memberships:** Past Chair of the Chicago Bar Association Real Estate Finance Subcommittee. Board Member of the Community Economic Development Law Project. Represents not for profit organizations redeveloping urban sites on a pro bono basis.

**Personal:** Graduated magna cum laude from Carleton College in 1976 and with honors from the University of Michigan Law School in 1979.

### SINGER, Eric
Wildman Harrold, Chicago
312 201 2000
*Recommended in Construction*

### SINGH, Amy
The Entertainment & Intellectual Property Group, Chicago 312 357 1401
*Recommended in Media & Entertainment*

### SKINNER, Honey J
Sidley Austin LLP, Chicago
312 853 7577
mskinner@sidley.com
*Recommended in Healthcare*

**Practice Areas:** Represents healthcare providers before government agencies both in Illinois and Washington, DC. She assists hospitals, health systems and physician practices in gaining government approval for the expansion of their services and in their efforts to achieve equitable Medicaid reimbursement.

**Prof. Memberships:** Ms Skinner is actively involved in numerous civic endeavors, and serves as a Director of the Chicago Area Foundation for Legal Services and a Director of the Northern Funds.

**Personal:** Northwestern University School of Law, JD, 1981; Harvard University, BA, 1978. Admissions: District of Columbia, 1990; Illinois, 1981.

### SKLAR, Stanley
Bell, Boyd & Lloyd LLC, Chicago
312 372 1121
*Recommended in Construction*

### SKLARSKY, Charles B
Jenner & Block LLP, Chicago
312 923 2904
csklarsky@jenner.com
*Recommended in Litigation*

**Practice Areas:** Charles B Sklarsky is a Partner in Jenner & Block's Chicago office. He is Co-Chair of the firm's White-Collar Criminal Defense and Counseling Practice and member of the Conflicts Resolution and the Pro Bono Committees. Mr Sklarsky counsels individuals and companies on a wide range of issues involving litigation or potential litigation, including fraud and abuse, conflicts of interest, public corruption, criminal tax matters, criminal antitrust, theft of trade secrets, securities fraud and regulatory matters. He has substantial experience in representing individuals and entities in grand jury investigations, SEC investigations, criminal trials, SEC enforcement actions, qui tam litigation, complex civil litigation and appearances before regulatory bodies. Mr Sklarsky counsels individuals and companies involved in the gaming industry in Illinois and elsewhere and represents clients before the Illinois Gaming Board. He counsels companies on compliance issues, conducts compliance audits and assists companies in the drafting and implementation of codes of conduct and compliance programs. Mr Sklarsky joined the Firm in 1986 after serving for over eight years as an Assistant US Attorney for the Northern District of Illinois and over four years as an Assistant State's Attorney of Cook County, Illinois. At the US Attorney's Office, he held the positions of Deputy Chief of Criminal Litigation and later Chief of Criminal Receiving and Appeals. He was one of the architects of Operation Greylord, an unprecedented undercover probe of corruption in the Cook County Judiciary.

**Personal:** University of Wisconsin Law School, JD, 1973; American College of Trial Lawyers, Fellow.

### SLATER, Paul
Sperling & Slater, Chicago
312 641 3200
*Recommended in Antitrust*

### SMALL, Andrew
Katten Muchin Rosenman LLP, Chicago
312 902 5489
Andrew.small@kattenlaw.com
*Recommended in Real Estate*

**Practice Areas:** Partner, Chicago. Concentrates on real estate primarily in the areas of commercial development, structured finance, joint ventures and acquisitions and dispositions. Development practice is focused primarily on ground up development, redevelopment, capital raising, venture formation and financing of retail, hotel, golf course and urban mixed use (office, hotel and residential) projects. Lending practice includes conventional, mezzanine and securitized

financing matters, construction loans and preferred equity matters. Has substantial experience representing lenders and borrowers in connection with loan modifications and workouts, public and private developers, public and private REITs, golf course owners and operators, institutional lenders, opportunity funds, insurance companies and securitized lenders. A significant portion of practice relates to the acquisition, disposition, financing and development of golf course projects throughout the country.

**Prof. Memberships:** Member of the International Council of Shopping Centers where he is a frequent lecturer and contributor.

**Career:** Co-Hiring Partner for Katten Muchin Rosenman LLP.

**Personal:** Graduated from the University of Michigan with a Bachelor's Degree in Business Administration and obtained his Law Degree in 1989 from the University of Chicago Law School. Completed the Certified Public Accountant's examination in 1987.

### SMEDINGHOFF, Thomas J
Baker & McKenzie, Chicago
312 861 8670
smedinghoff@bakernet.com
*Recommended in Technology*

**Practice Areas:** Information law; e-business; information security; privacy; digital signatures and PKI; information technology. Acts as e-business counsel for clients worldwide; internationally recognized for leadership in addressing legislative and public policy issues relating to information security and electronic signatures.

**Prof. Memberships:** Member, US Delegation to United Nations Commission on International Trade Law (UNCITRAL); Chair, ABA Section of Science & Technology Law (1999-2000); Chair, ABA E-Commerce Law Division (1995-2003); Chair, Illinois Commission on Electronic Commerce (1996-98).

**Career:** Admitted Illinois (1978).

**Publications:** Editor and primary author, 'Online Law' (Addison-Wesley, 1996); numerous e-transaction, security, and IT articles.

**Personal:** JD University of Michigan (1978).

### SMITH, William P
McDermott Will & Emery, Chicago
312 984 7588
wsmith@mwe.com
*Recommended in Bankruptcy*

**Practice Areas:** Head of the Distressed Transactions and Bankruptcy Practice Group. Practices restructuring troubled financial transactions and defaulted securities, especially tax-exempt bonds. Represents indenture trustees, institutional investors, credit enhancers, commercial banks, and debt issuers (principally healthcare) in resolution of a broad vari-

ety of troubled debt financings in the United States, Canada and Germany. Has extensive experience in bankruptcy-related matters.

**Career:** Is recognized as one of the leading practitioners on tax-exempt and healthcare-related defaults.

**Personal:** University of Cincinnati College of Law (JD); Cornell University (BA).

### SMOLEN, Lee M
Sidley Austin LLP, Chicago
312 853 7823
lsmolen@sidley.com
*Recommended in Real Estate*

**Practice Areas:** Lee M Smolen is Head of Sidley's Chicago Real Estate Group and Co-Chair of the firm's Practice Development Committee. His practice has an emphasis on debt and equity financing and structured finance. Mr Smolen has represented institutional investors, commercial banks, investment banks, insurance companies, pension funds and opportunity funds. He has represented these clients in the full range of loan origination activity, including CMBS, construction, permanent and interim financing arrangements, fee and leasehold financings, sale-leaseback financings, mezzanine financings and structured finance transactions. The loans have involved all asset types. Mr Smolen has also represented lenders in connection with loan workouts and restructurings. He has represented both the master and the special servicer in connection with the administration of securitized loans. Mr Smolen has also represented lenders in connection with the development of their form loan documents and the administration of their loan programs.

**Personal:** The University of Chicago Law School, JD, 1985; University of Illinois, BS, 1982. Mr Smolen is a CPA and received the Elijah Watt Sells Award the year he took the CPA exam (top 100 scores in the nation; 7th highest score in the State of Illinois). Admission: Illinois, 1985.

### SNEED, William M
Sidley Austin LLP, Chicago
312 853 7899
wsneed@sidley.com
*Recommended in Insurance*

**Practice Areas:** William Sneed has extensive experience arbitrating and litigating international and domestic reinsurance disputes on behalf of ceding companies, reinsurers, and receivers. His practice encompasses the property and casualty and life and health areas. He has arbitrated dozens of reinsurance disputes, addressing such issues as allocation of loss payments, aggregation of claims, late notice, ECO/XPL coverage, follow the fortunes, pre-hearing security, cessions of declaratory judgment expenses, and retention warranties. He has tried

jury and non-jury cases in state and federal courts, including civil rights, tort, tax, and commercial disputes.
**Personal:** Northwestern University School of Law, JD, 1987; Northwestern University, MM, 1987; Stanford University, AB, 1983. Admission: Illinois, 1987.

### SOLOVY, Jerold S
Jenner & Block LLP, Chicago
312 923 2671
jsolovy@jenner.com
*Recommended in Litigation*
**Practice Areas:** Jerold S Solovy, the Chairman of Jenner & Block and a member of its Policy Committee, is widely regarded as one of the preeminent appellate and trial lawyers in the country. Since 1991, he has been regularly cited in the National Law Journal as one of the 100 most influential lawyers in America. Mr Solovy has extensive experience in state and federal litigation, both at the trial and appellate levels. He has argued several cases before the United States Supreme Court. Mr Solovy focuses on litigating complex business matters and insurance coverage issues. In addition, he has handled many high profile intellectual property and securities cases. Most recently, Mr Solovy successfully served as Co-Lead Counsel for Coleman (Parent) Holdings (CPH) in its fraud suit against securities firm giant Morgan Stanley. In May of 2005, the Florida jury unanimously awarded $604.33 million in compensatory damages and $850 million in punitive damages to CPH. The Court entered final judgment, including prejudgment interest, in the amount of $1.58 billion against Morgan Stanley for aiding and conspiring with Sunbeam Corp. to defraud CPH into selling CPH's interest in The Coleman Co. Inc. to Sunbeam, a client of Morgan Stanley. In addition, Mr Solovy successfully represented the Illinois Attorney General in reducing the fees paid to law firms that had represented the State in the nationwide tobacco industry litigation from the requested $780 million to a total of $67.5 million.
**Personal:** Harvard Law School, LLB, 1955, cum laude; American College of Trial Lawyers, Fellow.

### SOLOW, Alan
Goldberg, Kohn, Bell, Black, Rosenbloom & Moritz, Ltd, Chicago
312 201 4000
*Recommended in Bankruptcy*

### SOLOW, Michael
Kaye Scholer LLP, Chicago
312 583 2310
msolow@kayescholer.com
*Recommended in Bankruptcy*
**Practice Areas:** Partner, Co-Chair, Business Reorganization and Creditors' Rights Group. Has over 20 years' experience representing creditors, trustees and governmental agencies and other parties in the bankruptcy and insolvency area.

He has counseled and represented clients in a variety of industries, including energy, gaming, finance as well as manufacturing.
**Prof. Memberships:** Member of the Bars of the States of Illinois and New York, Northern District of Illinois (Trial Bar), Southern District of New York, District of Arizona, Northern District of Texas, Western District of Michigan and admitted to practice before the Fourth, Sixth, Seventh and Eighth Circuit Courts of Appeals and the US Supreme Court.
**Career:** JD, Harvard Law School; BA (summa cum laude), University of Illinois, Phi Beta Kappa; Bronze Tablet.
**Publications:** 'Sarbanes-Oxley and the US Bankruptcy Code', INSOL 2005 World Congress (co-author); 'Lease Terminations and Mortgage Foreclosures as Fraudulent Conveyance'; 'Buying Assets in Bankruptcy: A Guide to Purchasers' (co-author); 'Considerations in Dealing with the Federal Savings & Loan Insurance Corporation in Chapter 11' (co-author); 'Lender Liability and Equitable Subordination in the Illinois Institute for Continuing Legal Education's Secured Transactions 2001' (co-author).

### SOLOW, Sheldon L
Kaye Scholer LLP, Chicago
312 583 2320
ssolow@kayescholer.com
*Recommended in Bankruptcy*
**Practice Areas:** Partner, Business Reorganization and Creditors' Rights Group. Represents a wide variety of constituencies in the bankruptcy process, including secured lenders, purchasers of businesses, bondholders, fiduciaries, special litigation committees and debtors, as well as individual clients.
**Prof. Memberships:** Member of the Bars of the State of Illinois and the Northern District of Illinois and admitted to practice before the Seventh and Eighth Circuit Courts of Appeals, Customs Court and the US Supreme Court.
**Career:** JD, Harvard Law School.
**Publications:** 'Bankruptcy Litigation: A Secured Creditor's Perspective', Trial Diplomacy Journal, Summer, 1988, and 'Trustees Avoiding Powers' (co-author) in the 1990 edition of the Illinois Institute for Continuing Legal Education's Bankruptcy Handbook.

### SORENSEN, Sharp
Sidley Austin LLP, Chicago
312 853 7151
ssorensen@sidley.com
*Recommended in Tax*
**Practice Areas:** Sharp Sorensen heads Sidley's Tax Practice in Chicago. He concentrates in federal tax matters, and focuses principally on domestic and foreign transactions, including mergers and acquisitions, spin-offs, securitizations, joint ventures, foreign and domestic securities offerings, and financial prod-

ucts. Mr Sorensen was the lead outside tax advisor to Exelon Corporation in its negotiations to acquire PSEG, to First Data Corporation in its acquisition of Concord EFS, to Wallace Computer Services in its cross-border acquisition by Moore Corporation Limited and in turn to RR Donnelley in its cross-border acquisition of Moore Wallace, and to Tellabs in its acquisition of Advance Fibre Communications. He has represented numerous corporate and non-corporate clients in non-public transactions using a wide range of structures. Mr Sorensen has significant experience in the taxation of investment units, integrated securities, convertible debt and other securities. He has also advised on the structuring of a variety of securitization arrangements.
**Personal:** Northwestern University School of Law (JD, 1985, with honors; Order of the Coif; Managing Editor, Northwestern University Law Review); University of Utah (BS, 1982). Admissions: Illinois, 1992; New York, 1986.

### SPECTOR, David
Schiff Hardin LLP, Chicago
312 258 5552
dspector@schiffhardin.com
*Recommended in Insurance*
**Practice Areas:** Reinsurance and insurance litigation.
**Prof. Memberships:** American Bar Association.
**Career:** Co-leads Schiff Hardin's Insurance Group. For more than 25 years, Mr Spector has ranked among the preeminent American practitioners in the insurance field. His expertise encompasses a variety of complex matters, including reinsurance litigation and arbitration, insurance company insolvencies, business counseling, and coverage litigation. Numerous national and international practice excellence honors.
**Publications:** Numerous articles and speeches.
**Personal:** Northwestern University (BA, 1968), University of Michigan Law School (JD, magna cum laude, Order of the Coif, 1971), Notes Editor, Michigan Law Review.

### SPERLING, Robert Y
Winston & Strawn LLP, Chicago
*Recommended in Litigation*
**Practice Areas:** Complex litigation with an emphasis on securities litigation and commercial litigation, including class actions.
**Prof. Memberships:** American Bar Association, Illinois State Bar Association, Chicago Bar Association.
**Career:** Has extensive experience representing financial services clients in securities actions, including class actions. Has represented the directors of various companies in derivative shareholders actions and ERISA actions that related to securities claims filed against those companies.

Has extensive experience in national class actions that involved alleged violations of various federal consumer protection statutes.
**Personal:** DePaul University School of Law, JD, DePaul Law Review, University of Illinois, AB in History.

### SPRAYREGEN, James HM
Kirkland & Ellis LLP, Chicago
312 861 2481
jsprayregen@kirkland.com
*Recommended in Bankruptcy*
**Practice Areas:** Experience includes the representation of significant companies including United Airlines, Chiquita and TWA, as debtors in bankruptcy proceedings or in non-bankruptcy fora and large creditors in bankruptcy and insolvency proceedings. Mr Sprayregen has handled a wide variety of matters involving such issues as deleveraging, fraudulent conveyances, equitable subordination, substantive consolidation, preferences, and successor liability. In addition, he has extensive experience in representing Boards of Directors in troubled situations, the acquisition of companies and assets of companies out of bankruptcy proceedings or from insolvent debtors.
**Personal:** University of Michigan, BA, 1982; University of Illinois College of Law, JD, 1985.

### STAHL, David M
Eimer Stahl Klevorn & Solberg LLP, Chicago 312 660 7602
dstahl@EimerStahl.com
*Recommended in Antitrust, Energy*
**Practice Areas:** Antitrust, commercial and energy litigation with broad trial experience in state and federal courts and regulatory agencies, and in arbitrations. His practice encompasses Sherman Act (§ 1 and § 2) and Robinson-Patman Act litigation and counseling, acquisitions, securities litigation, breach of contract, products liability and toxic tort, professional malpractice defense, and a wide variety of electric power litigation. He has represented a number of leading firms including, among others, CITGO Petroleum Corporation, Kimberly-Clark Corporation, Praxair, Inc., Abbott Laboratories, Holcim (US) Inc., Midwest Generation EME, LLC, the former Central and South West Corporation (now part of American Electric Power), Exelon Corporation, and Consumers Energy.
**Prof. Memberships:** American Bar Association, Litigation and Antitrust Sections; Chicago Bar Association; Chicago Inn of Court.
**Career:** Admitted to the Illinois Bar, 1972. Member of the trial bar of the United States District Court for the Northern District of Illinois. Partner at Isham, Lincoln & Beale, 1979-88. Partner at Sidley & Austin, 1988-2000. Head of Regulatory/Litigation Group, 1995-2000. Co-founder of his firm, 2000.

**Personal:** Born: September 22, 1946. Received his JD, magna cum laude, from the University of Michigan, 1971. Member, Michigan Law Review, Order of the Coif, 1971. Received his MA (History) from the University of Michigan, 1971. Received his BA from the University of Illinois (Chicago), 1968 (History).

## STEIN, Steven
Stein, Ray & Harris LLP, Chicago
312 641 3700
*Recommended in Construction*

## STEMPEL, James A
Kirkland & Ellis LLP, Chicago
312 861 2440
jstempel@kirkland.com
*Recommended in Bankruptcy*

**Practice Areas:** James Stempel concentrates his practice in counseling debtors in all aspects of Chapter 11 cases, purchasers of distressed companies inside and outside of bankruptcy, investors in distressed debt and claims market, companies and boards of directors in out-of-court workouts and restructurings, secured and unsecured lenders to bankrupt companies. Mr Stempel was named as one of the Outstanding Young Bankruptcy Lawyers of 2002 by Turnarounds & Workouts Magazine.
**Personal:** University of Michigan, BGS, 1985; IIT/Chicago-Kent College of Law, JD, 1989.

## STEPHENS, Thomas M
Sonnenschein Nath & Rosenthal LLP, Chicago 312 876 7485
tstephens@sonnenschein.com
*Recommended in Tax*

**Practice Areas:** Nationally recognized in partnership taxation; Head of Tax in Affordable Housing Investment Practice. Focuses on tax planning and transaction structuring for partnerships, limited liability companies, corporations and individuals. Advises for M&A, spin-offs, other restructurings, joint ventures, alliances, organizational structuring, compensation, real estate ventures, investments and workouts, including low-income housing tax credits, developments, offerings, venture capital investments and issuance and holding of financial instruments.
**Prof. Memberships:** ABA; Advisory Board, Journal of Passthrough Entities.
**Personal:** New York University, LLM in Taxation; Catholic University School of Law, JD, 1982; University of Connecticut, BA.

## STETLER, David
Stetler & Duffy Ltd, Chicago
312 338 0200
*Recommended in Litigation*

## STETSON, Jim
Baker & McKenzie, Chicago
312 861 8800
*Recommended in Technology*

## STILLMAN, Nina G
Morgan, Lewis & Bockius LLP, Chicago
312 324 1150
nstillman@morganlewis.com
*Recommended in Employment*

**Practice Areas:** Ms Stillman focuses on labor and employment, equal employment opportunity, and occupational safety and health law matters. She has successfully represented corporations and institutions in large employment class actions, individual employment, health and safety-related cases. Ms Stillman counsels employers nationwide on cross-border workplace issues and counsels international clients on US employment and workplace safety and health law.

## STINSON, James R
Sidley Austin LLP, Chicago
312 853 7203
jstinson@sidley.com
*Recommended in Insurance*

**Practice Areas:** Co-Chairs the firm's Insurance and Financial Services Group, which includes approximately 60 lawyers in the US and England. Represents ceding insurers and reinsurers in reinsurance disputes and handles all manner of domestic and non-US insurer insolvency matters, representing receivers, reinsurers, ceding insurers and creditors. Has served as an administrative hearing officer, and as an arbitrator, umpire and mediator in reinsurance and insurance arbitrations.
**Prof. Memberships:** ARIAS-US, the American Bar Association, International Association of Insurance Receivers, Insol.
**Career:** Established the firm's Insurance Insolvency, Insurance Regulatory and Reinsurance Dispute practices. Publications: He is a past Director and Vice-President of the International Association of Insurance Receivers (IAIR) and edits the Legal Chapter of the National Association of Insurance Commissioner's (NAIC) 'Receivers' Handbook for Insurance Company Insolvencies'. He also assisted in drafting the Interstate Insurance Receivership Compact and chaired the Compact Commission's Receivership Law Advisory Committee, which drafted the Uniform Receivership Law.
**Personal:** University of Illinois College of Law, JD, 1977; Indiana University, AB, 1973. Admissions: US Court of Appeals, 7th Circuit, 1978; US Court of Appeals, 10th Circuit, 1982; US District Court, ND of Illinois – General, 1977; US District Court, ND of Illinois – Trial Bar; Illinois, 1977.

## STONE, Jeffrey E
McDermott Will & Emery, Chicago
312 984 2064
jstone@mwe.com
*Recommended in Litigation*

**Practice Areas:** Head of firm's Trial Department. Concentrates on white-collar criminal defense, complex commercial litigation, internal investigations and RICO. Represents individuals and corporations in criminal prosecutions and complex commercial litigation.
**Prof. Memberships:** Fellow of American College of Trial Lawyers. Member of American Bar Association, Chicago Council of Lawyers and Board of Directors of Harvard Law Society of Illinois. National Chairman, Stanford Fund. Vice Chair, Stanford's Campaign for Undergraduate Education.
**Career:** Served as law clerk to Chief Judge Robert F Peckham of US District Court, San Francisco.
**Personal:** Stanford University, (BA with honors and distinction); Harvard Law School, (JD, cum laude).

## STONE, Susan
Sidley Austin LLP, Chicago
312 853 2177
sstone@sidley.com
*Recommended in Insurance*

**Practice Areas:** Susan A Stone is a Litigation Partner focusing on commercial and financial litigation matters. She has significant trial experience in both state and federal courts, and practices in the areas of insurance insolvency, reinsurance disputes, environmental coverage litigation, white-collar criminal defense and sensitive investigations. Prior to joining the firm, Ms Stone was an Assistant United States Attorney in Los Angeles. She serves as a Co-Chair of the firm's Practice Development Committee.
**Publications:** Ms Stone was named by the Chicago Lawyer as one of the '40 Attorneys Under 40'.
**Personal:** Harvard Law School, JD, 1987; Yale University, BA, 1983. Served as an Adjunct Professor teaching Trial Practice at DePaul University College of Law. Law clerk for District Court Judge William J Orrick of the Northern District of California. Admissions: Illinois and California.

## STRAND, Peter
Holland & Knight LLP, Chicago
312 263 3600
peter.strand@hklaw.com
*Recommended in Media & Entertainment*

**Practice Areas:** Mr Strand is a Senior Counsel in the firm's Business Section. His practice comprises entertainment and intellectual property law. He represents artists, songwriters, recording artists, musicians, television and film writers, independent record labels, publishing companies, production companies and authors in litigation and transactional matters. He assists clients in protecting and enforcing copyrights and trademarks and licensing or exploiting their creative works. Strand is an Adjunct Professor of law at DePaul University Law School teaching entertainment and music law.

## STREFF JR, William A
Kirkland & Ellis LLP, Chicago
312 861 2126
wstreff@kirkland.com
*Recommended in Intellectual Property*

**Practice Areas:** William A Streff, Jr has been practicing intellectual property law for 32 years, concentrating on intellectual property litigation, including jury trials, and transactions, including international strategic alliances, involving computer hardware, firmware, software and systems; semiconductor processing technology and circuitry, including DRAMs, CCDs and MPUs; optical networks; satellite and cable communications systems; avionics; high definition and satellite television systems; and digitally-controlled fuel systems. He is one of the leaders of the firm's 250-member Intellectual Property Department and is a member of the firm Management Committee.
**Personal:** Northwestern University, BSME, 1971. Northwestern University School of Law, JD, 1974.

## STREICKER, James
Cotsirilos Tighe & Streicker Ltd, Chicago
312 263 0345
*Recommended in Litigation*

## STUCKER, Robert
Vedder, Price, Kaufman & Kammholz, Chicago 312 609 7500
*Recommended in Employment*

## SULLIVAN, Barry
Jenner & Block LLP, Chicago
312 923 2652
bsullivan@jenner.com
*Recommended in Litigation*

**Practice Areas:** Barry Sullivan is a Partner in Jenner & Block's Chicago office. He is Co-Chair of the Firm's Appellate and Supreme Court Practice, and member of Litigation and Dispute Resolution, Labor and Employment, and Bankruptcy, Workout and Corporate Reorganization Practices. Mr Sullivan has litigated cases at all levels of the judicial system since joining the firm in 1975, but he is particularly known for his expertise in appellate litigation. He began his career as a law clerk to Judge John Minor Wisdom of the US Fifth Circuit Court of Appeals and later served as an assistant to the US Solicitor General. Mr Sullivan has briefed and argued cases in the US Supreme Court, and in state and federal courts across the country. His appellate cases have included constitutional and administrative law, commercial law, bankruptcies and business restructurings, corporate and securities law, labor and employment, school and university law, and local government law, among others. He was Dean of Washington and Lee University Law School, 1994-99. He also was a Fulbright professor at Warsaw University and a visiting fellow of London University. Mr Sullivan frequently writes and lectures on a variety of legal topics. He serves on the ABA Standing Committee on Amicus Briefs, the Visiting Committee of the University of Chicago's Graduate School of Public Policy Studies, and the Editorial Board of the Dublin University Law Journal. He was elected to the American Law Institute in 1983.

**Personal:** University of Chicago Law School, JD, 1974; Middlebury College, AB, 1970.

## SULLIVAN, Marcia W
Katten Muchin Rosenman LLP, Chicago
312 902 5535
Marcia.Sullivan@kattenlaw.com
*Recommended in Real Estate*

**Practice Areas:** Partner, Chicago. Concentrates on commercial real estate finance and structured finance for commercial banks, insurance companies, finance companies and other lenders. Has been involved in complex financing for a variety of projects across the nation – shopping centers, hotels, office buildings, build-to-suit, golf courses, apartments and for-sale residential. Has represented lenders and investors in unsecured and secured lines of credit, permanent financing, workouts and foreclosures. Has also represented lenders, investors, servicers, trustees and borrowers in loan securitizations, as well as in portfolio transactions and structured finance. In conjunction with real estate financing, represents lenders in loan participations and co-lender arrangements. Regularly represents developers and investors in real estate acquisitions and divestitures, development and financing.

**Prof. Memberships:** Served as President and Member of Chicago Real Estate Executive Women and Chicago Real Estate Education Initiative, Co-Chaired the 13th National Forum for Women Corporate Counsel.

**Personal:** Graduated, Phi Beta Kappa, from DePaul University in 1972 and received her JD Degree from the Indiana University School of Law, where she was an Associate Editor of the Indiana Law Review.

## SULLIVAN, Thomas
Jenner & Block LLP, Chicago
312 923 2928
tsullivan@jenner.com
*Recommended in Litigation*

**Practice Areas:** Thomas P Sullivan is a Partner in Jenner & Block's Chicago office. With the exception of an almost four year period (July 1977 to April 1981) when he served as the United States Attorney for the Northern District of Illinois, Mr Sullivan has practiced law at Jenner & Block since 1954. At Jenner & Block, Mr Sullivan has established himself as one of the nation's most outstanding civil and criminal trial lawyers. He has been called upon to represent some of the most prominent international corporations, governmental entities and individ-

uals. He has tried scores of major cases, both civil and criminal, and has established himself as a premier counselor to clients from every point on the economic spectrum. As the United States Attorney in Chicago from 1977-81, Mr Sullivan was known for his fairness, his devotion to the pursuit of justice and for his initiation of Operation Greylord, the single most wide-ranging investigation of judicial corruption in the nation's history. Mr Sullivan served as Co-Chair of the then Governor George Ryan's Commission on Capital Punishment. The Commission issued its widely-acclaimed report with 85 significant recommendations for reform of the death penalty process in Illinois. As a result of all of his efforts, he received the prestigious 2003 American Bar Association's John Minor Wisdom Award, and in December 2004 was selected as Chicago Lawyer Magazine's Person of the Year for 2004.

**Personal:** Loyola University Chicago School of Law, LLB, 1952, cum laude, Alpha Sigma Nu, Delta Theta Phi.

## SULLIVAN, William
Franczek Sullivan, Chicago
312 986 0300
*Recommended in Employment*

## SWEENEY, Maureen E
Kirkland & Ellis LLP, Chicago
312 861 2190
msweeney@kirkland.com
*Recommended in Banking & Finance*

**Practice Areas:** Maureen Sweeney focuses her practice on debt financing transactions. She represents private equity groups, commercial lending institutions and other private and public companies in connection with the negotiation, structuring and documentation of secured and unsecured financing transactions for both borrowers and lenders, including senior, mezzanine and subordinated debt transactions; acquisition financings; and loan workouts and restructurings, including debtor-in-possession financings.

**Personal:** University of Michigan (BS, Mathematics, 1993); University of Michigan Law School (JD, 1996), cum laude.

## TARUN, Robert
Latham & Watkins LLP, Chicago
312 876 7700
*Recommended in Litigation*

## TCHEN, Christina M
Skadden, Arps, Slate, Meagher & Flom LLP & Affiliates, Chicago
312 407 0518
ttchen@skadden.com
*Recommended in Litigation*

**Practice Areas:** Has broad litigation experience at all levels of the state and federal courts, and has represented clients in various types of lawsuits and arbitrations, including shareholder, takeover, securities, fraudulent conveyance, intel-

lectual property, constitutional, executive compensation, accounting, insurance, real estate, and breach of contract litigation. Has represented companies, officers and directors in shareholder class and derivative actions, and has handled a wide range of commercial, intellectual property and employment-related litigation. Has also represented public agencies in state and federal class actions.

**Career:** JD, Northwestern University School of Law, 1984; BA, Radcliffe College, Harvard University, 1978.

## TECSON, Andrew
Chuhak & Tecson PC, Chicago
312 444 9300
*Recommended in Healthcare*

## TER MOLEN, Mark R
Mayer, Brown, Rowe & Maw LLP, Chicago 312 701 7307
mtermolen@mayerbrownrowe.com
*Recommended in Environment*

**Practice Areas:** Toxic tort trials and appeals in state and federal courts. National Counsel for corporations facing significant asbestos liabilities. Complex environmental litigation. Environmental regulatory hearings and appeals before state and federal agencies. General corporate counseling on environmental compliance issues and environmental concerns in the context of corporate transactions. Supervising environmental remediations pursuant to various state and/or federal requirements. Condemnation and property valuation actions. Defended and prosecuted trials and appeals in state and federal courts, including Lead Counsel in People v. Jimerson, established innocence of man on death row for 11 years, and Jimerson v. Capelli, et al, resulting in a $36 million settlement from Cook County for malicious prosecution.

**Career:** Mayer, Brown, Rowe & Maw LLP, Chicago, 1988 to date; Partner, 1997. Law clerk to The Honorable Charles Levin, Michigan Supreme Court, Southfield, Michigan, 1987-88.

**Publications:** 'Environmental Law for Transactional Attorneys', Illinois Institute of Continuing Legal Education.

**Personal:** JD, University of Chicago Law School, 1987. AB (magna cum laude), Cornell University, 1984. Illinois State Bar Association John C McAndrews Pro Bono Service Award, 1996. President of the Board, Baker Demonstration School, 2005-present.

## THEISS, Paul W
Mayer, Brown, Rowe & Maw LLP, Chicago 312 701 7359
ptheiss@mayerbrownrowe.com
*Recommended in Corporate/M&A*

**Practice Areas:** Chicago Office Practice Leader for Corporate and Securities Group. Emphasizes mergers and acquisitions, securities offerings, and corporate governance matters. Mergers and acquisitions work has included both public and

private transactions. Represents both issuers and underwriters in public debt and equity offerings and Rule 144A private placements, with recent emphasis on equity and high-yield debt issuances. Other specialties include private equity, outsourcing transactions and domestic and international joint ventures.

**Prof. Memberships:** Admitted in Illinois, 1985.

**Career:** Mayer, Brown, Rowe & Maw LLP, Chicago, 1985 to present.

**Personal:** JD, University of Chicago, 1985. BA, Amherst College, 1982.

## THOMAS, Dale E
Sidley Austin LLP, Chicago
312 853 7787
dthomas@sidley.com
*Recommended in Energy*

**Practice Areas:** Dale E Thomas advises electric utilities, internet/telecommunications providers, and AT&T on a wide variety of matters, and represents them in state and federal administrative and court proceedings and appeals. Mr Thomas has represented a major utility client in a range of matters, including: rate case and prudence proceedings; a $1.2 billion settlement of five interrelated legal actions involving the utility's rates; the decision to retire a nuclear generating plant; and the transfer of cutting-edge technology to an unregulated subsidiary for further development and commercialization. Mr Thomas has represented internet/telecommunications providers on FCC and related matters, including: requirements to obtain broadband spectrum licenses from the FCC; obtaining certification to provide telecommunications services at state and federal levels; and adopting corporate structures to limit potential regulatory and tax burdens. He has extensive experience in telecommunications antitrust litigation and in follow-on litigation concerning the interpretation and application of the AT&T Consent Decree. He has represented AT&T in connection with contract negotiations under, and FCC litigation concerning, the Telecommunications Act of 1996.

**Personal:** Yale Law School, JD, 1974; Yale Divinity School, MDiv, 1973; Princeton University, AB, 1969. Mr Thomas clerked for Judge Robert P Anderson of the US Court of Appeals, Second Circuit.

## THOMAS, Frederick B
Mayer, Brown, Rowe & Maw LLP, Chicago 312 701 7035
fthomas@mayerbrownrowe.com
*Recommended in Corporate/M&A*

**Practice Areas:** Partner in Corporate Practice in Chicago. Advises clients on acquisitions, mergers, joint ventures, strategic alliances, financings, shareholder arrangements, and a variety of other transactions involving US, foreign and multinational corporations and other entities, both public and private. Provides

advice to Boards of Directors, committees of Boards of Directors, and management regarding corporate governance, securities, and other matters. Extensive representation of clients in technology businesses.
**Career:** Served as law clerk to The Honorable John C Godbold, US Court of Appeals for the Fifth Circuit, Montgomery, AL, from 1974-75. Joined Mayer, Brown, Rowe & Maw LLP, Chicago, in 1975. Served in London office from 1978-81; became Partner in 1981. Serves on Management Committee of Mayer, Brown, Rowe & Maw LLP.
**Personal:** JD, University of Chicago, 1974; Joseph Henry Beale Prize; Comment Editor, University of Chicago Law Review. AB, magna cum laude, Dartmouth College, 1971; Phi Beta Kappa. Board of Managers of the YMCA of Metropolitan Chicago; Board of Trustees of LaRabida Children's Hospital; Chair, Planning Committee of 2006 Ray Garrett, Jr, Corporate and Securities Law Institute. Adjunct Professor of Law (teaching Corporations) at the University of Notre Dame, London Law Center, 1980-81.

**TILSON, Joseph**
Meckler Bulger & Tilson LLP, Chicago
312 474 7900
*Recommended in Employment*

**TOMLINSON PC, Stephen G**
Kirkland & Ellis LLP, Chicago
312 861 2386
stomlinson@kirkland.com
*Recommended in Real Estate*
**Practice Areas:** Stephen G Tomlinson, PC, the senior Partner in Kirkland & Ellis' Global Real Estate Practice Group, focuses on complex business transactions in the hospitality and real estate industries for real estate private equity sponsors, institutional investors, real estate investment trusts (REITs) and real estate operating companies engaged in mergers and acquisitions, and dispositions, operating company investments and formations, and multi-investor fund formations and investments. He is resident in the Firm's Chicago and New York offices.
**Personal:** University of Michigan, AB, 1981; University of Michigan, JD, 1984.

**TORRES, Joseph J**
Winston & Strawn LLP, Chicago
312 558 7334
jtorres@winston.com
*Recommended in Employment*
**Practice Areas:** Labor, employment and employee benefits litigation before trial and appellate courts; collective bargaining and labor disputes; labor and employment aspects of corporate mergers, acquisitions and divestitures; trade secrets and non-competition disputes.
**Prof. Memberships:** Member, American Bar Association, Labor and Employment Section; Member, Hispanic National Bar

Association; Chairman, Hispanic Lawyers Scholarship Fund of Illinois.
**Career:** Joined firm in 1990; became Partner, 1998; Co-Chair of firm Diversity Committee; member of Hiring Committee.
**Publications:** Associate Editor, 'The Developing Labor Law' (BNA), contributing Editor, 'Employment Discrimination Law' (BNA).
**Personal:** University of Chicago, 1985; University of Illinois College of Law, 1990.

**TOTH, Bruce**
Winston & Strawn LLP, Chicago
312 558 5600
*Recommended in Corporate/M&A*

**TOWBIN, Steven**
Shaw Gussis Fishman Glantz Wolfson & Towbin LLC, Chicago
312 541 0151
*Recommended in Bankruptcy*

**TOWNSEND, Christopher**
DLA Piper Rudnick Gray Cary US LLP, Chicago 312 368 4039
christopher.townsend@dlapiper.com
*Recommended in Energy*
**Practice Areas:** Energy; environmental.
**Career:** He has experience in all aspects of energy, public utility, communications, and environmental law and regulation and regularly counsels clients, including independent power producers, competitive suppliers, and customers, in strategic analyses and structuring transactions to conform to legal and regulatory requirements. He has been involved in a wide variety of regulatory proceedings and related appeals, emphasizing matters related to restructuring in the electric and natural gas industries. He frequently assists consumers in negotiating natural gas, electric, on-site generation, chilled water supply, and cable and telecommunications contracts.
**Personal:** JD, University of Iowa; BA, Augustana College.

**TREECE, John**
Sidley Austin LLP, Chicago
312 853 2937
jtreece@sidley.com
*Recommended in Antitrust*
**Practice Areas:** Substantial experience in multidistrict class actions alleging horizontal price-fixing as well as monopolization and price discrimination cases. He coordinated the successful defense of G.D. Searle & Co. in In Re Brand Name Prescription Drugs Antitrust Litigation, a class action price-fixing trial in which plaintiffs sought $1.1 billion in damages from Searle. He also represented Kimberly-Clark in In Re Commercial Tissue Paper Antitrust Litigation, a multidistrict price-fixing action settled in 2000, and the only defendant to obtain summary judgment in In Re Cement and Concrete Antitrust Litigation in the early 1980's. He recently represented Microsoft against

charges of monopolization brought by a company that made software for the delivery of audio-video content over the internet. Mr Treece has been closely involved in many state 'indirect purchaser' actions and is experienced with the relevant class certification issues. He is familiar with healthcare antitrust cases, and represented the plaintiff in the first case to consider the antitrust implications of preferred provider organizations. He frequently counsels clients on merger matters and on Robinson-Patman price discrimination issues.
**Prof. Memberships:** American and Chicago Bar Associations.
**Personal:** Columbia University School of Law, JD, 1978; Harvard University, BA, 1975. Admission: Illinois.

**TRELA JR, Constantine L**
Sidley Austin LLP, Chicago
312 853 7293
ctrela@sidley.com
*Recommended in Litigation*
**Practice Areas:** Mr Trela is one of the co-ordinators of the firm's national Appellate Practice Group. His practice covers a broad range of areas, including financial, product liability, insurance, environmental and patent. For example, Mr Trela has persuaded the Seventh Circuit to overturn a $3.4 million jury verdict in a propane gas explosion case and a $2.4 million jury verdict in a dealership termination dispute. He won a unanimous decision from the Illinois Supreme Court on behalf of chemical manufacturers in a case alleging that the plaintiffs suffered from acquired chemical sensitivity. In the patent area, Mr Trela has handled cases involving everything from disposable diapers to semiconductor chips to computer operating systems to plastic moldings. Most recently, Mr Trela convinced the Federal Circuit to vacate one of the largest infringement verdicts in history, a $565 million award against Microsoft based on claims that its Windows®operating system infringed the plaintiffs' patent.
**Career:** Law clerk, Justice John Paul Stevens (1980-81), Judge Robert A Sprecher (1979-80).
**Personal:** Northwestern University, JD, 1979, BA, 1976. Admissions: US Supreme Court; US Court of Appeals, 3rd Circuit, 5th Circuit, 6th Circuit, 7th Circuit Federal Circuit; US District Court, ND of Illinois.

**USOW, Jeffrey A**
Mayer, Brown, Rowe & Maw LLP, Chicago 312 701 8612
jusow@mayerbrownrowe.com
*Recommended in Real Estate*
**Practice Areas:** Represents real estate operating companies, private investment funds and real estate investment trusts in broad range of matters, including purchases and sales, joint ventures, financing,

leasing and other transactions. Also represent non-domestic investors in US real estate and domestic investors in cross border real estate investments.
**Career:** Mayer, Brown, Rowe & Maw LLP, Chicago, 1996 to date. Keck, Mahin & Cate, Chicago, 1990-96. Miller, Shakman, Nathan & Hamilton (formerly Devoe, Shadur & Krupp), Chicago, 1977-90.
**Personal:** Harvard Law School, JD cum laude, 1977. University of Wisconsin, BA, 1974.

**VALUKAS, Anton B**
Jenner & Block LLP, Chicago
312 923 2903
avalukas@jenner.com
*Recommended in Litigation*
**Practice Areas:** Anton R Valukas is Chair of Jenner & Block's White Collar Criminal Defense and Counseling Practice and serves on the Firm's Policy Committee. He is a Fellow of the American College of Trial Lawyers. He is a former US Attorney. Mr Valukas has been Lead Counsel for numerous boards of directors and audit committees in a variety of matters relating to corporate governance and litigation relating to these issues. He has assisted many corporations in developing their corporate compliance policies. He has represented many Fortune 500 companies regarding potential conflicts of interest, ethics violations and internal corporate investigations. And he regularly counsels clients in connection with SEC and grand jury investigations. Mr Valukas's experience as a trial lawyer includes numerous complex civil and criminal cases. Most recently, he won a $76 million arbitration award on behalf of a global company involved in a long-standing dispute over a petrochemical supply agreement by establishing the opposing party's manipulative pricing practices. Other recent notable cases include the defense of a major food manufacturer in the class action and criminal litigation cases stemming from an outbreak of listeria.
**Personal:** Northwestern University School of Law, JD, 1968.

**VEZEAU, Timothy**
Katten Muchin Rosenman LLP, Chicago
312 902 5200
*Recommended in Intellectual Property*

**VIDMAR, Jacqueline M**
Sonnenschein Nath & Rosenthal LLP, Chicago 312 876 7436
jvidmar@sonnenschein.com
*Recommended in Environment*
**Practice Areas:** Environmental Practice Vice-Chair. Provides advice on all aspects of environmental law, including regulatory compliance, internal auditing, investigations, enforcement defense strategies, permitting, remediation and redevelopment of contaminated properties. Appears before state and federal courts and administrative bodies. Transactional

practice includes due diligence for corporate and real estate transactions, and property management compliance assistance for a myriad of issues, including indoor air quality, mold, asbestos and lead-based paint.

**Prof. Memberships:** ABA Section on Natural Resources and Environmental Law; Vice Chairperson, Board Member, Chicago Committee on Minorities in Large Law Firms; Board Member, Asian American Bar Association for Greater Chicago.

## VISHNESKI, John S

Mayer, Brown, Rowe & Maw LLP, Chicago 312 701 7210
jvishneski@mayerbrownrowe.com
*Recommended in Insurance*

**Practice Areas:** Represents policyholders in complex insurance coverage litigation. Special emphasis on environmental and intellectual property insurance coverage disputes, having represented clients before numerous courts in many jurisdictions, including the Supreme Court of Illinois and the Supreme Court of Connecticut. Has represented policyholders in insurance coverage disputes involving diverse types of insurance, including first party property policies, general liability policies, directors and officers liability policies and employment practices liability policies. Practice is nationwide and has also involved Lloyds and the London Market.

**Career:** Mayer, Brown, Rowe & Maw LLP, Chicago, 2001 to date; Partner, 2001. Neal, Gerber & Eisenberg, Chicago.

**Publications:** Representative articles/presentations: 'The Plain Meaning Of Wrongful Entry or Eviction or Other Invasion of the Right of Private Occupancy: Why Standard-Form Personal Injury Insurance Coverage Applies to Pollution Claims', Environmental Claims Journal (Winter 1999). 'Insurance Coverage for Internet Liabilities', A Presentation To Members of the Chicago Bar Association (June 23, 1998). 'The Illinois Estoppel Doctrine: Illinois Courts Make It Costly For Insurers To Breach Their Duty To Defend', Environmental Claims Journal (Autumn 1995).

**Personal:** JD, University of Virginia, 1988. University of Virginia, BA magna cum laude, 1985; Phi Beta Kappa.

## VROMAN, James A

Jenner & Block LLP, Chicago
312 923 2836
jvroman@jenner.com
*Recommended in Environment*

**Practice Areas:** James A Vroman is a Partner in Jenner & Block's Chicago office. He is Co-Chair of the firm's Environmental, Energy and Natural Resources Practice. Mr Vroman has extensive experience in a wide variety of environmental and toxic tort matters. He has represented litigation clients in

CERLA cost-recovery actions, both as plaintiffs and defendants. In these matters he has encountered issues ranging from environmental 'stigma' to technical impracticability to human health and environmental exposure risks. He has defended clients in RCRA, Clean Water Act and TSCA enforcement actions and in Superfund proceedings initiated by the EPA under Sections 106, 107 and 122 of CERCLA. Mr Vroman negotiated on behalf of a major client of the firm a ground breaking CERCLA administrative order on consent which governed the remediation of 38 PCB-contaminated sites located in five EPA regions and nine states. He has also represented and advised a major client as this client remediated a former Manufactured Gas Plant site under the Illinois Site Remediation Program. The remediation of this MGP site has become the largest cleanup project under the voluntary Illinois remediation program. Mr Vroman has represented clients in dispute resolution proceedings involving allocation issues before mediators and arbitrators. He has counseled transactional clients on environmental considerations in corporate and real estate matters and has supervised environmental due diligence efforts for significant acquisitions and divestitures. He has extensive experience in counseling clients remediating or marketing 'brownfield' properties.

**Personal:** University of Illinois College of Law, JD, 1977, magna cum laude.

## WALL, Robert F

Winston & Strawn LLP, Chicago
312 558 5699
rwall@winston.com
*Recommended in Corporate/M&A*

**Practice Areas:** Senior Partner in Corporate Department. Concentration in mergers and acquisitions and corporate finance for public companies. Represented clients in these areas since 1977. Recently, represented Keebler Foods Company in sale to Kellogg Company; represented Airgate PCS, Inc. in connection with merger involving Alamosa Holdings, Inc.; represented special committee of Board of Directors of Orbitz, Inc. in connection with Cendent Corporation's acquisition of Orbitz; and represented Reyes Holdings, Inc. in connection with its acquisition of Reinhart FoodService, Inc.; represented Morgan Stanley in secondary stock offering of CDW Corporation. Frequent speaker at seminars and member of various securities and merger and acquisition organisations.

**Prof. Memberships:** Member, Editorial Board, Mergers and Acquisitions and Corporate Control Law Reporter; Chair, Northwestern University's Ray Garrett Securities Institute.

**Career:** Joined firm as associate, 1977. Partner, 1984.

**Personal:** University of Virginia, 1970;

Northwestern University, BA, with distinction, 1973; Santa Clara University, JD, summa cum laude, 1977, Comments Editor, Santa Clara Law Review.

## WALTER, Priscilla A (Pam)

Gardner Carton & Douglas LLP, Chicago
312 569 1475
pwalter@gcd.com
*Recommended in Technology*

**Practice Areas:** Ms Walter focuses her practice on information technology and e-business, including assisting clients in the development or acquisition of complex information systems and in the protection and distribution of software, databases and multimedia products. Ms Walter also negotiates technology-focused joint venture and strategic partnering relationships and counsels clients on issues such as website development, privacy and security. Her clients include major banks and other financial institutions, governmental entities, equipment manufacturers and early-stage e-commerce ventures.

**Prof. Memberships:** Computer Law Association; American Bar Foundation; Society for Information Management; Information Integrity Coalition; Named to Leading Lawyers and Illinois Super-Lawyers. Community/Civic Organizations: Chairman of Board of Directors, Chicago Shakespeare Theater; Board of Trustees and Executive Committee, Illinois Institute of Technology; Board of Overseers, Chicago-Kent School of Law; Board of Governors and Executive Committee, Metropolitan Planning Council; The Chicago Network.

**Career:** Founded firm's Cyberlaw and Intellectual Property Practice, which is part of Technology Department; served for six years on firm's Management Committee.

**Publications:** Frequent author, lecturer in cyberlaw, technology area.

**Personal:** Northwestern University, JD, 1978, magna cum laude; London School of Economics, MSc, 1967; Wellesley College, BA, 1965. Law clerk to Judge Walter J Cummings, Seventh Circuit Court of Appeals, 1978-79.

## WANDER, Herbert S

Katten Muchin Rosenman LLP, Chicago
312 902 5267
hwander@kattenlaw.com
*Recommended in Corporate/M&A*

**Practice Areas:** Partner, Chicago. Concentrates on all aspects of business law, especially corporate governance, securities law and M&A transactions. Has been the chief legal architect for many major M&A transactions, both negotiated and hostile. The SEC Chairman appointed him to Co-Chair the SEC's Advisory Committee on Smaller Public Companies. The SEC also selected him to be one of two securities lawyers to make a presentation at the SEC's April 2001 Regulation FD Roundtable.

**Prof. Memberships:** Served as Chair of the ABA's 53,000 member Business Law Section. Appointed by the President of the American Bar Association to serve on the Commission on Multidisciplinary Practice and the Task Force on Attorney Client Privilege. Past-President of the Jewish Federation of Metropolitan Chicago and the Jewish United Fund; Trustee and Vice-Chair of the Michael Reese Health Trust; Director of Telephone & Data Systems Inc., a $4 billion market cap telecommunications company. He is serving his second term as a member of the Legal Advisory Committee to the New York Stock Exchange Board of Governors. In 2002, he was nominated by his peers as one of the world's leading practitioners in the field of corporate governance and is listed in The International Who's Who of Corporate Governance Lawyers.

**Publications:** Has authored numerous articles and book reviews in various publications including the Yale Law Journal, the Business Lawyer, the Northwestern University Law Review, and INSIGHTS. He was the first Editor of the Business Law Section's magazine, Business Law Today and was the Editor of Volume 49 (1993-94) of The Business Lawyer. Frequently speaks at institutes and programs of various business and legal organizations.

**Personal:** BA Degree from the University of Michigan and a Law Degree from Yale Law School, where he was on the Board of Editors of the Yale Law Journal.

## WARNECKE, Michael O

Mayer, Brown, Rowe & Maw LLP, Chicago 312 701 8602
mwarnecke@mayerbrownrowe.com
*Recommended in Intellectual Property*

**Practice Areas:** First Chair in numerous major patent litigation cases. Experienced in international patent, technology licensing, and other IP matters. Frequent expert witness, arbitrator, and mediator.

**Prof. Memberships:** Fellow, American College of Trial Lawyers. American Bar Association.

**Career:** Joined Mayer, Brown, Rowe & Maw LLP, Chicago, 1996; became Partner 1996. Formerly with Keck, Mahin & Cate, Chicago, 1991-96; Neuman, Williams, Anderson & Olson, Chicago, 1967-91; US Patent and Trademark Office, US Patent Examiner, Group 350, Washington, DC, 1963-67.

**Publications:** Frequent lecturer. Selected by the People's Republic of China trade delegation to host two-day seminar for American automotive and after-market companies and the Chinese delegation on the legal aspects of doing business in China. Frequent lecturer and speaker, nationally and internationally, on intellectual property law, including Federal Court of Australia, IP Colloquium II, Melbourne, Australia, March 2001; Presenta-

tion to Federal Bench on United States litigation on how to determine issues to litigate and the conducting of Markman hearings on claim construction.
**Personal:** George Washington University, JD, 1967. Purdue University, BS, 1963.

### WATERS, Paige D
Sonnenschein Nath & Rosenthal LLP, Chicago 312 876 2545
pwaters@sonnenschein.com
*Recommended in Insurance*
**Practice Areas:** Insurance Regulatory and Public Law and Policy Partner. Handles transactional, regulatory, litigation and insolvency matters involving national and international insurance, HMO, reinsurance and healthcare clients. Represents private equity and hedge funds in acquisitions of, and investments in, insurers and similarly regulated entities. Assists international and domestic assuming and ceding insurers in mergers and acquisitions, entity formations and reinsurance transactions.
**Prof. Memberships:** Chicago Bar Association; International Association of Insurance Receivers; NCOIL-Industry Education Council; NAIC Insolvency Working Groups.
**Personal:** IIT Chicago-Kent College of Law, JD; Miami University, BA.

### WATSON, John
Baker & McKenzie, Chicago
312 861 8800
*Recommended in Environment*

### WEAVER, William
Sachnoff & Weaver Ltd, Chicago
312 207 1000
*Recommended in Corporate/M&A: Private Equity*

### WEBB, Dan
Winston & Strawn LLP, Chicago
312 558 5600
*Recommended in Litigation, Products Liability*

### WEBER III, Louis
Winston & Strawn LLP, Chicago
312 558 5600
*Recommended in Tax*

### WEHLAND, Chuck
Jones Day, Chicago 312 269 4388
ctwehland@jonesday.com
*Recommended in Environment*
**Practice Areas:** Represents clients nationwide in matters including greenhouse gas emissions from electric power plants, Clean Air Act permits, and responsibility for the cleanup of contaminated drinking water wells and river sediments. His experience with rules for hazardous waste management, air permits, and water permits allows him to prepare creative and competitive management solutions and apply this experience to help obtain complex construction and operating permits for clients. In transactions, he is well versed in negotiating

agreements and directing due diligence.
**Prof. Memberships:** Environmental Law Institute; ABA (Environment, Energy and Resources Section).
**Publications:** Regularly writes and lectures on environmental subjects.

### WEINBERG, Walter S
Katten Muchin Rosenman LLP, Chicago
312 902 5405
walter.weinberg@kattenlaw.com
*Recommended in Corporate/M&A: Private Equity*
**Practice Areas:** Partner and Chair of the Chicago Corporate Practice. Private equity and venture capital (including portfolio equity and mezzanine debt investments and recapitalizations, management representation, portfolio company representation, and fund formation; early stage to leveraged buyouts); mergers and acquisitions; general corporate counseling.
**Prof. Memberships:** American Bar Association; Chicago Bar Association.
**Publications:** Speaker at ABA's Venture Capital and Private Equity Committee meetings and Chicago Bar Association seminars; Guest Lecturer at Northwestern University Kellogg School of Business.
**Personal:** University of Chicago, BA (general honors), Economics (Phi Beta Kappa); Northwestern University, JD, cum laude (Order of the Coif).

### WEINBERGER, Seth J
Mayer, Brown, Rowe & Maw LLP, Chicago 312 701 7257
sweinberger@mayerbrownrowe.com
*Recommended in Technology*
**Practice Areas:** Advises both vendor and customer clients on IT and outsourcing transactions, including application development and maintenance, call center, network, and business process transactions. Represents global IT joint ventures, including in the aviation, chemical and steel industries. Represents venture capital firms and companies seeking private equity or venture capital funding in various industries, including information technology, telecommunications and biotechnology. Also advises on general corporate matters, including mergers and acquisitions.
**Career:** Mayer, Brown, Rowe & Maw LLP, Chicago, 1982 to date; Partner, 1986. Pitney, Hardin, Kipp & Szuch, Morristown, NJ, 1980-82.
**Personal:** University of Michigan Law School, JD cum laude, 1979. University of Michigan, BA with high honors, 1977. Founder of Innovations for Learning, a not-for-profit corporation that develops software for teaching reading in urban centers.

### WEISBERG, Mark S
Winston & Strawn LLP, Chicago
312 558 8070
mweisberg@winston.com
*Recommended in Employment*

**Practice Areas:** Design, establishment and administration of retirement benefit, welfare benefit, and non-qualified deferred compensation and equity compensation plans. Negotiation and drafting of executive employment agreements on behalf of companies and their compensation committees, individual executives and management teams. ERISA litigation.
**Prof. Memberships:** American Bar Association; National Association of Stock Plan Professionals.
**Career:** Previous Partner and Co-Chair of ERISA Group, KMZ Rosenman; to Winston as Partner, 2004.
**Publications:** Co-author of numerous articles in the Benefits Law Journal; frequent speaker on noteworthy topics.
**Personal:** University of Pennsylvania, 1985; University of Pennsylvania Law School, 1988; Trustee, Evanston Police Pension Fund.

### WEISS, Robert M
Neal, Gerber & Eisenberg LLP, Chicago
312 269 8455
rweiss@ngelaw.com
*Recommended in Technology*
**Practice Areas:** Specializes in complex technology transactions; experience includes systems integrations, technology development and licensing projects, ERP implementations, infrastructure and business process outsourcings, and telecommunications procurements; provides counsel to clients on e-commerce, corporate finance and joint venture transactions.
**Prof. Memberships:** Computer Law Association; Chairman, Computer Law Committee; Member, Chicago Council on Foreign Relations.
**Career:** Partner, Information Technology Practice Group; named to '40 Under 40' most accomplished Illinois attorneys, Chicago Daily Law Bulletin (2003).
**Publications:** Author and lecturer on information technology law issues; U.S. Developments Editor, 'Bulletin' (Computer Law Association Journal).
**Personal:** Stanford Law School (JD, 1990); Dartmouth College (AB, 1987).

### WELKE, William R
Kirkland & Ellis LLP, Chicago
312 861 2143
wwelke@kirkland.com
*Recommended in Tax*
**Practice Areas:** Mr Welke focuses his practice on the tax aspects of complex business transactions and entities, including: mergers, acquisitions, and leveraged buyouts; venture capital and other private equity investments; formation of private equity funds; joint ventures and partnerships; debt and equity restructurings; and executive compensation.
**Personal:** Massachusetts Institute of Technology, SB, 1980. University of Michigan Law School, JD, 1983.

### WHITE, Bruce
Karaganis, White & Magel, Chicago
312 836 1177
*Recommended in Environment*

### WHITNEY, Douglas
McDermott Will & Emery, Chicago
312 984 6991
dwhitney@mwe.com
*Recommended in Litigation*
**Practice Areas:** Partner in Trial Department. Practices in the areas of complex commercial litigation and white-collar criminal defense. Represented numerous individuals and professional service firms in litigation and investigations relating to tax shelters, securities fraud, healthcare fraud, defense contracting, and antitrust. Tried numerous cases in state and federal courts, and has argued several cases before US Courts of Appeals. Editorial Board Member of ABA Criminal Justice Section Newsletter.
**Personal:** New York University School of Law (JD, magna cum laude); Yale University, (BA, cum laude); law clerk, Hon Phyllis A Kravitch, US Court of Appeals for the Eleventh Circuit.

### WILDE, Thomas
Vedder, Price, Kaufman & Kammholz, Chicago 312 609 7500
*Recommended in Employment*

### WILLIAMSON, Joel V
Mayer, Brown, Rowe & Maw LLP, Chicago 312 701 7229
jwilliamson@mayerbrownrowe.com
*Recommended in Tax, Tax Litigation*
**Practice Areas:** Firm Practice Leader, Tax Controversy. Tried 50+ tax cases. Represented clients in six major international transfer pricing cases; financial products cases; captive insurance; Subpart F issues; constructive triangular dividends; R&D moratorium; Brazilian foreign tax credits; Iranian losses and foreign tax credits; tax accounting; sale and leaseback transactions; foreign source income on export sales; IRC Section 338 liquidations; trademark valuation; sale of assets for preferred stock, reorganization versus taxable sale treatment; and proper role of IRS trial counsel in audit examination process and summons enforcement; R&D allocation to DISC.
**Career:** Mayer, Brown, Rowe & Maw LLP as Partner, 1986-present. Special Trial Attorney, Chief Counsel's Office, US Department of Treasury, 1972-85.
**Publications:** 'The Corporate Tax Director: Responsibilities in the New Era of Increased Corporate Accountability', Taxes, March 2005. 'Litigating Transfer Pricing Cases' and 'Tax-Advantaged Transactions', co-author, Practicing Law Institute, 2001, 2002; 'Mrs. Gregory's Great-Grandchildren: The Lost Generation', Journal of Taxation of Global Transactions (Summer 2002) (with Thomas C Durham and Stuart E Thiel).
**Personal:** JD, University of Kentucky,

1970; Order of the Coif; Law Review; Moot Court Board; National Moot Court Team. BA (1967), Davidson College. Officer, US Army, Ft. Bragg, NC; Republic of South Vietnam, 1970-72.

**WITCOFF, David L**
Jones Day, Chicago
312 269 4259
dwitcoff@jonesday.com
*Recommended in Intellectual Property*
**Practice Areas:** Specializes in litigating and resolving complex patent and other intellectual property disputes, particularly in high-technology matters. Counsels on all aspects of intellectual property matters across a broad spectrum of technologies, including semiconductor products and processing, internet and world wide web systems and protocols, computer hardware and software, electronic commerce systems, cellular telephones, paging control systems, pharmaceuticals, medical devices, and diagnostic equipment, among others. Admitted to practice before various US District Courts, the US Court of Appeals for the Federal Circuit, and the US Patent and Trademark Office. Recognized in various publications as a leading intellectual property lawyer.

**WOLF, Charles**
Vedder, Price, Kaufman & Kammholz, Chicago 312 609 7500
*Recommended in Employment, ERISA Litigation*

**WOLFE, David L**
Gardner Carton & Douglas LLP, Chicago
312 569 1313
dwolfe@gcd.com
*Recommended in Employment*
**Practice Areas:** Partner, HR Law Department; practice covers tax-qualified plans, health and welfare arrangements, executive compensation; benefits issues in corporate acquisitions and divestitures, benefits issues for tax-exempt clients, US benefits for international clients, ERISA fiduciary issues and litigation, cash balance and other hybrid pension arrangements, legal compliance reviews and non-qualified deferred compensation arrangements.
**Prof. Memberships:** Named to The Best Lawyers in America (1993-2004).
**Career:** Member, firm Management Committee; frequent lecturer, including before ABA, ISBA, CBA, IICLE.
**Publications:** Contributor, DePaul Law Review, Akron Law Review, CCH Financial and Estate Planning Reporter, The Practical Lawyer, Legal Checklists, Chicago Bar Record, IICLE Handbooks (on S Corporations and Employee Benefits Law), IICLE, ISBA and ABA outlines, ISBA Employee Benefits Section Newsletter; Contributor, 'Healthcare Industry', CCH Tax Transactions Library; co-author, 'Compensation in 2003', Employee Benefit Plan Review, January 2003; co-

author, 'Expensing Stock Options: Ten Predictions for 2003 and Beyond', Employee Benefit Plan Review, March 2003; co-author, 'Internal Fiduciaries Gain New Roles Post-Enron', Employee Benefit Plan Review, January 2003; co-author, 'Current Considerations and New Challenges for ERISA 404(c) Compliance', BNA's ERISA Enforcement Strategy & Compliance Guide 2004.
**Personal:** University of Michigan, JD, cum laude, 1976; University of Illinois, BS, 1973; CPA (IL-1993).

**WYLIE, Kenneth R**
Sidley Austin LLP, Chicago
312 853 7157
kwylie@sidley.com
*Recommended in Insurance*
**Practice Areas:** Kenneth R Wylie concentrates his practice in insurance law with emphasis on insurance regulatory matters that affect insurance companies, agents and brokers, and other insurance entities. Mr Wylie has provided legal and counseling services on corporate, commercial and regulatory matters for insurance industry organizations, including the organization and acquisition of insurance companies, the evaluation of captives and alternative risk transfer vehicles, and insurance risk securitizations. He has extensive experience representing insurance guaranty funds, insureds, reinsurers, reinsureds, claimants and other parties involved in insurance company insolvencies. Mr Wylie handles reinsurance arbitrations, including disputes involving reinsurance pools and finite reinsurance.
**Prof. Memberships:** Federation of Regulatory Counsel, AIDA Reinsurance and Insurance Arbitration Society (US), and the Chicago and American Bar Associations, including the respective insurance committees of these two associations.
**Publications:** 'Finite Risk Reinsurance: The Spitzer Fallout', Sidley Reinsurance Law Report (2006); 'Insurance Products as Credit Enhancement Devices', Mealey's Reinsurance Law Reporter (2003); 'Regulatory and Structural Aspects of Insurance Exit Strategies', Sidley Reinsurance Law Report (2001).
**Personal:** The University of Michigan Law School (JD, 1977), Michigan State University (BS in Mechanical Engineering, 1973, high honors). Admissions: US District Court, ND of Illinois, General, 1977; Illinois, 1977.

**YASTROW, Joseph**
Laner, Muchin, Dombrow, Becker, Levin, Tominberg, Chicago 312 467 9800
*Recommended in Employment*

**YODER, Lowell D**
McDermott Will & Emery, Chicago
312 984 7523
lyoder@mwe.com
*Recommended in Tax*
**Practice Areas:** Partner in Tax Depart-

ment; Co-Chair of International Tax Practice. Focuses on international tax planning for multinationals. Advises on cross-border acquisitions, mergers, financings, restructurings and repatriation. Advises on foreign tax credits, expense allocations, sourcing of income, Subpart F and passive foreign investment companies.
**Career:** Frequent speaker for Practising Law Institute, Tax Executives Institute and International Fiscal Association. Adjunct Professor of International Tax Law.
**Publications:** Author of four treatises on Subpart F (rules that apply to foreign operations of US multinationals); author of numerous articles on international tax topics.
**Personal:** University of Illinois College of Law (JD, magna cum laude).

**YURA, Mark**
DLA Piper Rudnick Gray Cary US LLP, Chicago 312 368 4084
mark.yura@dlapiper.com
*Recommended in Real Estate*
**Practice Areas:** Real estate.
**Career:** Concentrates his practice in real estate transaction matters with clients including lenders, investors, and developers. He is a frequent speaker before trade and professional groups on matters of state and federal legislation, multi-family housing financing and commercial real estate lending topics and has taught real estate finance law at the University of Michigan Law School and in the LLM Program in Real Estate Law at The John Marshall Law School.
**Personal:** JD, University of Michigan; BA, University of Michigan.

**ZABEL, Sheldon**
Schiff Hardin LLP, Chicago
312 258 5540
szabel@schiffhardin.com
*Recommended in Environment*
**Practice Areas:** Environmental.
**Prof. Memberships:** American Bar Association.
**Career:** Chairs Schiff Hardin's Environmental Group. Concentrates in environmental, natural resources, and public utility law. Has principal responsibility for environmental matters for major energy company clients. Has principal representation of the Steering Committee at the Rose Chemical Site, Holden, Missouri, one of the largest US PCB CERCLA sites. Has participated in significant natural resource matters, including contract preparation and negotiation and litigation primarily involving fossil fuel contracts and related transportation contracts.
**Personal:** Princeton University (AB, Economics, cum laude, 1963), Northwestern University Law School (JD, cum laude, 1966).

**ZAROV, Herbert L**
Mayer, Brown, Rowe & Maw LLP, Chicago 312 701 7317

hzarov@mayerbrownrowe.com
*Recommended in Litigation, Products Liability*
**Practice Areas:** Senior litigator and co-firm practice leader in litigation. Extensive experience in mass torts, federal securities law class actions, and complex commercial litigation. Served as National Counsel for The Dow Chemical Company in multi-district breast implant litigation and currently ational Co-Counsel for Union Carbide Corporation in asbestos litigation. Also experienced in securities, appellate, and tax litigation.
**Prof. Memberships:** Admitted in Illinois, 1979; US Supreme Court, 1996; US District Court for the Northern District of Illinois, 1979; US Court of Appeals for the Third Circuit, 1992; US Court of Appeals for the Sixth Circuit, 1995; US Court of Appeals for the Seventh Circuit, 1981; US Court of Appeals for the Ninth Circuit, 1991; US Tax Court, 1984; US Court of Claims, 1985.
**Career:** Joined Mayer, Brown, Rowe & Maw LLP, 1986; became Partner in 1987. member of management committee and is Co-Chairman of the Litigation Group. Prior firm: Friedman & Koven, Chicago, 1977-86. Taught English and American Studies at Smith College from 1973-76. Also taught at Washington University of St Louis, University of Missouri, Roosevelt University, Wilson Junior College (now Kennedy-King), pre-1973.
**Personal:** JD, University of Chicago, 1979. MA, University of Chicago, 1968. BA, Columbia University, 1967.

**ZAZOVE, Daniel**
Perkins Coie LLP, Chicago
312 324 8400
*Recommended in Bankruptcy*

**ZELEK, Eugene**
Freeborn & Peters, Chicago
312 360 6000
*Recommended in Antitrust, Media & Entertainment*

**ZIMBLER, Jay**
Sidley Austin LLP, Chicago
312 853 2232
jzimbler@sidley.com
*Recommended in Tax*
**Practice Areas:** Practice focused on Federal Income Taxation. Experienced in the taxation of foreign related transactions, mergers and acquisitions, and contested tax matters. Has handled complex cases with IRS Appeals for a variety of multinational corporations nationwide, as well as litigated cases in the US Tax Court, the US Court of Federal Claims, and the Seventh Circuit Court of Appeals.
**Prof. Memberships:** 1975-96, Hopkins & Sutter; 1996-present, Sidley Austin LLP.
**Personal:** Harvard Law School, JD, 1975; University of Michigan, BA, 1972. Certified Public Accountant. Admission: Illinois, 1975.

# ADELMAN & GETTLEMAN, LTD.

## THE FIRM

**Firm Size:** 8

**Website:** www.adelmangettlemanlaw.com

**FIRM OVERVIEW:** Adelman & Gettleman, Ltd. was founded in March, 1983 by Howard L Adelman and Chad H Gettleman, both of whom have devoted their entire professional career to the areas of bankruptcy, corporate reorganization and insolvency, and commercial litigation. The firm presently has six principals, including: Howard L Adelman, Chad H Gettleman, Henry B Merens, Brad A Berish, Mark A Carter and Adam P Silverman, all of whom have devoted their entire professional careers to the foregoing areas of concentration.

The firm is the only Chicago bankruptcy boutique firm having its lawyers recognized in 'Illinois Super Lawyers 2006', 'Illinois Leading Lawyers Network', 'Best Lawyers in America', Woodward/White, 'World's Leading Lawyers' by Chambers and Partners, Legal Publishers 2002-03, 'America's Leading Lawyers for Business', Chambers & Partners, Legal Publishers 2004 and 'Chambers USA, America's Leading Lawyers for Business', Chambers & Partners, Legal Publishers 2005. Two of the firm's attorneys, Chad H Gettleman and Brad A Berish, are also non-practicing Certified Public Accountants. In October of 1999, Chief Justice William Rehnquist appointed Howard L Adelman to serve as a Member of the Judicial Conference Advisory Committee on the Federal Rules of Bankruptcy Procedure. Mr Adelman is also a Fellow of the American College of Bankruptcy, as part of its Twelfth Class.

## MAIN AREAS OF PRATICE: Insolvency, bankruptcy and reorganization law, commercial and corporate litigation.

**Specialty:** In addition to commercial litigation in the State and Federal Courts, the firm has participated in many major bankruptcy and reorganization cases, representing debtors, trustees, secured creditors and committees. Approximately 75% of the firm's matters consist of litigation in the bankruptcy courts. The firm has an extensive internal continuing legal education program. Members of the firm participate as speakers in seminars and commercial litigation programs, and offer articles on areas of their concentration.

The firm's Bankruptcy and Commercial Litigation Practice is highly regarded and respected in bankruptcy courts throughout Illinois, Indiana, and Wisconsin. The firm seeks innovative approaches and solutions in the workout context, but stands prepared to draw upon its substantial litigation experience in complex bankruptcy litigation when necessary. The firm is experienced in resolving the business and legal problems that arise when commercial transactions, credit agreements, business plans and mortgages fail to proceed as intended. The firm's bankruptcy attorneys routinely handle the following matters for its clients: advising management, boards of directors, and committees of directors of troubled companies before and during Chapter 11 proceedings, including counseling financially distressed companies of viable alternatives to commencing a bankruptcy case; identifying problems and solutions which may arise in bankruptcy cases and structuring the potential resolution of same prior to their emergence; handling cash collateral negotiations and debtor-in-possession financing arrangements; structuring and implementing the purchase and sale of businesses and assets from Chapter 11 debtors; handling complex Chapter 11 plan negotiations and the litigation of contested plan confirmation issues; prosecuting and defending preference litigation and fraudulent conveyance litigation; enforcing the rights of secured creditors; handling single asset real estate partnership cases; providing corporate restructuring advice.

## HEAD OFFICE

**ILLINOIS**
53 West Jackson Blvd., Suite 1050, **Chicago**, IL 60604
**Tel:** 312 435 1050   **Fax:** 312 435 1059
**Website:** www.adelmangettlemanlaw.com

# BAKER & MCKENZIE

## THE FIRM

**Chairman of the Executive Committee:** John J Conroy
**NA Managing Partner:** David P Hackett

**Number of North American partners:** 195
**Number of other lawyers in North America:** 468
**Number of partners worldwide:** 658
**Number of other lawyers worldwide:** 2707

**Email:** info@bakernet.com
**Website:** www.bakernet.com

**FIRM OVERVIEW:** For more than 50 years, Baker & McKenzie has provided sophisticated legal advice and services to many of the world's most dynamic global organizations. Helping clients understand and thrive in diverse legal, political, social and economic systems made Baker & McKenzie one of the world's largest law firms and the first to be truly global. With a network of more than 3,300 locally qualified, internationally experienced lawyers in 38 countries, the firm has the knowledge and resources to deliver the broad scope of quality legal services required to respond effectively to both international and local needs – consistently, confidently and with sensitivity for cultural, social and legal practice differences. The 9,000 professionals of Baker & McKenzie share common values of integrity, personal responsibility and tenacity in an enthusiastic client-service culture. The firm is still guided by the entrepreneurial spirit and demanding standards of its founders, and since its earliest days, it has worked to forge close personal relationships among its professionals in order to foster the responsiveness and accountability clients rightfully expect. The firm has a diverse and welcoming culture with a global mindset. The lawyers and other professionals in its network are citizens of more than 60 countries, are admitted to practice in nearly 250 jurisdictions and have been educated at more than 1,200 institutions, including nearly all of the world's leading law schools. More than 60 languages are spoken, with English being the firm's common language. The firm's teams are supported by advanced technologies and sophisticated global management systems. These include a single, shared global technology platform, including client intake, financial and billing systems, e-mail, intranet and client extranets as well as global practice standards, a quality audit program and a worldwide conflicts policy based on the standards of the American Bar Association.

**MAIN AREAS OF PRACTICE:** Core global areas of practice include antitrust/competition and trade; banking and finance; international commercial; employment; intellectual property; litigation and dispute resolution; M&A, securities and private equity; real estate; and tax. Core global industries include, among others, energy, chemicals, mining and infrastructure; technology, media and telecommunications; and pharmaceuticals and healthcare.

**CLIENTS:** Baker & McKenzie provides exceptional service to domestic and international clients in a wide variety of industries and sectors by forming multi-disciplinary teams that share the clients' interests. The firm's extensive client list includes multinational and domestic entities, a great many of which engage the firm on a multi-jurisdictional basis. Clients include major corporations, financial institutions and other business entities, as well as governments and other organizations. Baker & McKenzie also provides pro bono legal services to clients worldwide and supports the community through leadership activities, public service and charitable giving.

**INTERNATIONAL WORK:** Baker & McKenzie provides legal services to most of the world's largest corporations as well as a broad spectrum of regional and local organizations. The firm is widely recognized as a pre-eminent provider of legal services by leading publications, professional organizations and research institutions. Among its honors: *Corporate Board Member* magazine rates it

## UNITED STATES

### CALIFORNIA
660 Hansen Way, **Palo Alto**, CA 94304
**Tel:** 650 856 2400   **Fax:** 650 856 9299
**Email:** peter.j.engstrom@bakernet.com

101 West Broadway, 12th Floor, **San Diego**, CA 92101
**Tel:** 619 236 1441   **Fax:** 619 236 0429
**Email:** charles.h.dick@bakernet.com

12544 High Bluff Drive, Suite 150, **San Diego**, CA 92130
**Tel:** 858 523 6200   **Fax:** 858 259 8290
**Email:** charles.h.dick@bakernet.com

Two Embarcadero Center, 24th Floor, **San Francisco**, CA 94111
**Tel:** 415 576 3000   **Fax:** 415 576 3099
**Email:** peter.j.engstrom@bakernet.com

### DISTRICT OF COLUMBIA
815 Connecticut Avenue, NW, **Washington**, DC 20006
**Tel:** 202 452 7000   **Fax:** 202 452 7074
**Email:** thomas.j.egan@bakernet.com

### FLORIDA
Mellon Financial Center, 1111 Brickell Avenue, Suite 1700, **Miami**, FL 33131
**Tel:** 305 789 8900   **Fax:** 305 789 8953
**Email:** roy.larson@bakernet.com

### ILLINOIS
One Prudential Plaza, 130 East Randolph Dr, **Chicago**, IL 60601
**Tel:** 312 861 8000   **Fax:** 312 861 2899
**Email:** chicago.information@bakernet.com

### NEW YORK
1114 Avenue of the Americas, **New York**, NY 10036
**Tel:** 212 626 4100   **Fax:** 212 310 1600
**Email:** gerald.j.hayes@bakernet.com

### TEXAS
2300 Trammell Crow Center, 2001 Ross Avenue, **Dallas**, TX 75201
**Tel:** 214 978 3000   **Fax:** 214 978 3099
**Email:** david.parham@bakernet.com

Pennzoil Place, South Tower 711 Louisiana, Ste 3400, **Houston**, TX 77002
**Tel:** 713 427 5000   **Fax:** 713 427 5099
**Email:** n.susan.stone@bakernet.com

## INTERNATIONAL

Baker & McKenzie has over 60 offices in more than 35 countries outside of the United States.

among the 10 most admired corporate law firms in the United States. The firm also ranked #1 for the second year running in the *PLC Which Lawyer?* awards 2004 and consistently ranks highly in PLC's Global 50 rankings. In addition, numerous offices, practices and individuals have been named as leaders in their respective areas by a wide variety of organizations.

**BAKER & McKENZIE**

*Baker & McKenzie LLP is a member firm of Baker & McKenzie International, a Swiss Verein with member law firms around the world. In accordance with the common terminology used in professional service organizations, reference to a "partner" means a person who is a partner, or equivalent, in such a law firm. Similarly, reference to an "office" means an office of any such law firm.*

# BRINKS HOFER GILSON & LIONE

## THE FIRM

**President:** Gary M Ropski

**Number of partners:** 65
**Number of other lawyers:** 82

**FIRM OVERVIEW:** Founded in 1917, Brinks Hofer Gilson & Lione is one of the largest intellectual property law firms in the United States and is at the cutting edge of intellectual property law. With approximately 150 attorneys, supported by a full complement of scientific advisors, patent agents and paralegals, the firm specializes in intellectual property litigation and all aspects of patent, trademark, copyright, trade secret, unfair competition, intellectual asset management, and technology and licensing agreements. Brinks routinely handles assignments in fields as diverse as electrical, chemical, mechanical, biotechnology, pharmaceutical, nanotechnology, internet and computer technology, as well as in trademarks or brand names for a wide variety of products and services. The firm is repeatedly ranked by Chambers & Partners as the number one IP firm in Chicago and the Midwest and is ranked fourth among ALM's law firms representing the IP needs of the most companies in the Fortune 250.

## MAIN AREAS OF PRACTICE:

**Patents:** Brinks patent lawyers have experience prosecuting patents in every major technical field and help clients obtain and license patents, enforce them against infringers, and defend against charges of infringement. Managing Intellectual Property magazine ranked the firm among the top 10 law firms for patent litigation in the United States.
**Trademarks:** The Trademark Group at Brinks performs the full range of trademark-related services in the United States and abroad, including registering, enforcing, opposing, and defending trademark rights. Managing Intellectual Property magazine ranked the firm among the top 20 firms in the US for both contentious and non-contentious trademark work.
**Trade Secrets:** Brinks lawyers regularly advise clients on the application of individual state trade secret laws and represent plaintiffs and defendants in a wide variety of trade secret disputes.
**Copyrights:** Brinks attorneys assist both artists and businesses in the preparation and filing of domestic and foreign applications to register copyrights in many fields, including book, magazine and music publishing; photocopying; sound recordings; the visual arts; television and motion pictures; theater and dance; compilations and databases; computer software; video games; multimedia, virtual reality and the internet; and international treaties.
**Unfair Competition:** Brinks represents victims and alleged infringers in the resolution of unfair competition disputes in multiple areas, including trade-dress infringement, counterfeit products, dilution, unfair trade practices and right of publicity.

**CLIENTS:** Brinks represents a wide range of major US and international corporations, including Deere & Company, The Progressive Corporation, United Air Lines, Inc. and Visteon Corporation, to name a few.

## HEAD OFFICE

### ILLINOIS
NBC Tower, Suite 3600, 455 N. Cityfront Plaza Drive,
**Chicago**, IL 60611-5599
**Tel:** 312 321 4200  **Fax:** 312 321 4299
**Website:** www.usebrinks.com

## BRANCH OFFICES

### INDIANA
One Indiana Square, Suite 1600, **Indianapolis**, IN 46204-2033
**Tel:** 317 636 0886  **Fax:** 317 634 6701

### MICHIGAN
524 S. Main, Suite 200, **Ann Arbor**, MI 48104
**Tel:** 734 302 6000  **Fax:** 734 994 6331

### VIRGINIA
Crystal Plaza One, Suite 208, 2001 Jefferson Davis Highway,
**Arlington**, VA 22202-3603
**Tel:** 703 415 0303  **Fax:** 703 415 0304

**BRINKS
HOFER
GILSON
& LIONE** ®

**Intellectual Property
Law Worldwide**

# CHAPMAN AND CUTLER LLP

## THE FIRM

**Chief Executive Partner:** Richard A Cosgrove
**Chief Operating Partner:** Steven L Clark
**Number of partners:** 117
**Number of other lawyers:** 88

**FIRM OVERVIEW:** Founded in 1913, the firm has focused on finance. The firm is one of the country's preeminent law firms in banking, bankruptcy and financial litigation, corporate finance and securities, public finance and tax. This focus enables the firm to consistently develop innovative and practical legal solutions for complex financial transactions. To complement that focus, the firm maintains a substantial corporate practice representing business entities in administrative and regulatory matters, commercial litigation, divestitures, employee benefits, intellectual property, joint ventures, and mergers and acquisitions. The firm also provides sophisticated trust and estate planning services for high net worth individuals.

## MAIN AREAS OF PRACTICE:

**Asset Securitization:** The firm represents clients in domestic and cross-border asset-backed and mortgage-backed securities, tax-exempt and CDO transactions. Asset classes financed include traditional trade receivables, student loans, tobacco settlements, meal credits, timeshares, leases, and 12b-1 fees.

**Banking, Bank Regulatory & Consumer Financial Services:** The firm has a comprehensive banking practice, with emphasis on syndicated bank credits, asset-based lending transactions, bank mergers and acquisitions, real estate finance, lease finance (including synthetic leases), credit enhancement, swaps and derivatives, consumer financial services, bank regulatory compliance and examination activities, cash management, payment systems and technology and securitization of receivables as well as other traditional commercial bank lending activities.

**Bankruptcy, Workouts & Commercial Litigation:** The firm is nationally recognized as one of the leading creditors' counsel in bankruptcy, restructuring and workouts and has been involved in many of the largest bankruptcies in the United States, including major airline, utilities, retail and manufacturing cases. In addition, the firm maintains a strong commercial, financial and consumer finance litigation and dispute resolution practice.

**Corporate Counseling, Employee Benefits & Intellectual Property:** The firm provides general corporate counseling to a variety of domestic and international corporate clients.

**Corporate Finance & Securities:** The firm represents financial institutions and issuers in connection with public and private offerings of debt and equity securities, including domestic and cross-border private placements and Rule 144A offerings, public offerings, private equity, mezzanine and project finance. The firm also counsels issuers with respect to disclosure requirements, stock exchange rules and compliance with the requirements of the Sarbanes-Oxley Act.

**Investment Companies & Investment Partnerships:** The firm serves as counsel to investment companies, sponsors and advisors to investment companies, and the independent members of investment company boards of directors.

**Lease Finance:** The firm is a market leader in representing a wide range of lessees, lessors, capital providers and underwriters in lease finance transactions with extensive experience with all types of lease finance structures. The firm also represents leasing companies in portfolio management, financing and joint venture transactions.

**Public Finance:** The firm has been one of the country's preeminent law firms in state and municipal finance and has consistently served as bond counsel on more municipal bond issues each year than any other law firm in the country.

**Tax:** The firm is nationally recognized for its advice on tax issues involved in corporate and municipal finance transactions, with particular emphasis on the representation of state and local governments and financial institutions.

## HEAD OFFICE

**ILLINOIS**
111 West Monroe Street, **Chicago**, IL 60603
**Tel:** 312 845 3000   **Fax:** 312 701 2361
**Website:** www.chapman.com

## BRANCH OFFICES

**CALIFORNIA**
595 Market Street, **San Francisco**, CA 94105
**Tel:** 415 541 0500   **Fax:** 415 541 0506

**UTAH**
201 South Main Street, **Salt Lake City**, UT 84111
**Tel:** 801 533 0066   **Fax:** 801 533 9595

## CONTACTS

**Head Office Contacts** .....................Ronald E Rokosz, Marc P Franson

**Trust Counsel & Estate Planning:** The firm represents the corporate and personal trust departments of financial institutions and provides estate and gift planning and probate services.

**CLIENTS:** US commercial banks, many of the world's largest foreign banks, insurance companies, investment banks, corporate and governmental issuers, investors and credit providers including: ABN AMRO, Allstate Bank, American General Finance, Bank of America, Bank of Montreal, Bank of New York, Bank of Tokyo-Mitsubishi, Bayerische Landesbank, Citizens Financial Group, Depfa Bank, Dredsner, BNP Paribas, First Midwest Bank, Fifth Third Bank, GE Capital, H&R Block Mortgage, Harris Bank, HypoVereinsbank, Landesbank Hessen Thuringen, JPMorgan Chase, LaSalle Bank, Mizuho Bank, Moneris Solutions, National Australia Bank, National City Bank, Option One Mortgage, Provident Bank, Rabobank, Royal Bank of Scotland, SunTrust, State Street, Toronto Dominion, Wachovia, Washington Mutual, Westdeutsche Landesbank, US Bancorp and Wells Fargo.

**INTERNATIONAL WORK:** Due to the international operations of many of the firm's clients, the firm has extensive experience in structuring cross-border financial transactions. This experience includes acting as agent bank and lead investor counsel in structuring LIBOR-based and multi-currency financings involving foreign obligors and collateral to structuring Eximbank and other financings backed by other export credit agencies or private insurers, letters of credit or bank guarantees. Further, the firm participates in cross-border institutional private placement transactions involving issuers and guarantors domiciled in numerous foreign jurisdictions, including England, Canada, Australia, New Zealand, Ireland, Finland, Sweden, Bermuda, the Cayman Islands, the Netherlands, Germany, Norway, Finland, Switzerland, Malta and Luxembourg. The firm represented institutional investors in the first Rule 144A styled private placement debt transaction and has acted as designated special investor's counsel in numerous additional Rule 144A and like private placement transactions. The firm acted as special issuer's counsel to the first Irish, German and Finnish corporations to close US private placements, as well as counsel to one of the largest corporations in Norway and many corporations listed on the Financial Times FT-SE 100 Index.

# CONWAY & MROWIEC

## THE FIRM

**Partners:** Timothy R Conway
John S Mrowiec
Edward B Keidan

**Number of other lawyers:** 3

### AREAS OF PRACTICE:
Construction Litigation, Contract
Negotiation & Consultation ............................ 100%

### HEAD OFFICE
**ILLINOIS**
20 South Clark, Suite 750, **Chicago**, IL 60603
**Tel:** 312 658 1100  **Fax:** 312 658 1201
**Website:** www.cmcontractors.com

**FIRM OVERVIEW:** Conway & Mrowiec concentrates its practice in construction and public contracts law and litigation. Conway & Mrowiec has broad experience in achieving successful, cost-effective results for contractors, construction managers, design/builders, trade contractors, architects, engineers, owners and sureties, in litigation, arbitration, contract drafting, bidding, and performance issues through claim prosecution or defense. Conway & Mrowiec's goal is to build longstanding relationships with its clients. In that spirit, Conway & Mrowiec employs its extensive mediation, litigation and arbitration experience to provide its clients with special insight in contract drafting, project administration assistance, and project personnel education, as well as in claims prosecution and resolution.

**MAIN AREAS OF PRACTICE:** Examples of recent issues litigated:
**Delay Claims – Gasoline Refinery:** Successfully defended design-builder of gasoline refinery from multi-million dollar claims of piping subcontractor for alleged delays, reduced labor productivity and changes at jury trial. The dispute involved a fixed price subcontract based on schematic design with detailed change methodology once the design was completed, the effect of numerous signed change orders thereafter and fraudulently overstated lien clam.
**Mechanics Lien Claims – Lien Drafting & Enforcement:** Conway & Mrowiec has drafted hundreds and litigated over 100 mechanics lien claims on public and private projects in Illinois and throughout the United States in the last five years. Among the complex issues addressed include the lienability of various services, multiple contracts, fraudulent overstatement, 'last day of work', the allocation of amounts due and completion dates on complex multi-owner projects such as mixed use condominiums, tower, hotel, retail, office buildings.
**Bidding Disputes:** Obtain favorable judgment after trial on tortious interference and other claims brought by contractor against competing contractor.
**Differing Site Condition – Bridge:** Represented foundation contractor in successful recovery of claims of unpaid lump sum payments and Type II differing site condition and defended against defense and counterclaim of alleged overpayment of unit prices and delay on highway bridge construction project.
**Cost Plus with GMP Contracts – Retail/Hotel Complex:** Litigated and successfully mediated on behalf of owners dispute with contractor under GMP contract and against architect for construction of an upscale retail/hotel complex. Issues involve acceleration, scope of the GMP, owner direct payment to subcontractors and structural design.
**Public Contract Bid Protest – Hospital:** Successfully protested award of contract to apparent low bidder on competitively bid public hospital project.
**Bankruptcies – Construction:** For EPC contractor of power plant, recovered on $16 million dollars plus lien claim after litigating priority over lender and disputes with subcontractors to agreed judgment of foreclosure and allowed secured claim and preparing detailed written bid in bankruptcy court auction sale. For design-builder of telecommunictions facilities, recovered on mechanics liens filed in 11 different states despite bankruptcy of customer.

**Design Errors & Omissions – Hotel:** Mediated, on behalf of architectural and engineering firm, hotel owner's delay and defective design claims.
**Insurance Claims – Crane Collapse:** Represented concrete contractor on tender of defense and indemnity to Owner-Controlled Insurance Program's liability insurer, contractor's comprehensive general liability insurer and property insurer including prosecution of coverage action against property insurer for claims by crane supplier to contractor of destruction and rent, prosecution of contractor's acceleration and payment claim and litigating with OCIP builder's risk carrier regarding delayed and inadequate payment after crane collapse and suspension of work by governing authorities on mixed-use highrises.
**Reported Cases:** Builders Association of Greater Chicago v City of Chicago, 298 F.Supp.2d 725 (N.D. Ill. 2004); Builders Association of Greater Chicago v County of Cook, 256 F.3d 642 (7th Cir. 2001); Mellon Stuart Construction, Inc. v Metropolitan Water Reclamation District, 1995 US Dist. LEXIS 5376 (N.D.Ill. 1995); Builders Association of Greater Chicago v County of Cook, 2000 US Dist. LEXIS 144 (N.D.Ill. 2000); 1998 US Dist. LEXIS 2991 (N.D.Ill. 1998); 1996 US Dist. LEXIS 13142 (N.D.Ill. 1996); Amalgamated Trust & Savings Bank v Silha, 460 N.E.2d 372 (1984); Prisco Serena Sturm Architects, Ltd. v Liberty Mutual Insurance Co., 1995 US Dist. LEXIS 9904 (N.D.Ill. 1995); 1996 US Dist. LEXIS 7278 (N.D.Ill. 1996); US Dist. LEXIS 4350, 3021, 2216 (N.D.Ill. 1996); Downey, Inc. v Bradley Center Corp., 524 N.W.2d 915 (Wis.Ct.App. 1994); Mellon Stuart Construction, Inc. v MWRDGC, 1995 US Dist. LEXIS 3493 (N.D.Ill. 1995); Southwest Financial Bank & Trust Co. v George Hyman Construction Co., 940 F.Supp. 1331 (N.D.Ill. 1996); United States f/u/b DJM Construction, Inc. v Rust Engineering Co., 1996 WL 204318 (N.D.Ill. 1996); Mellon Stuart Construction, Inc. v MWRDGC, 1990 US Dist. LEXIS 7669 (N.D.Ill. 1990); Acme Metals, Inc. v Raytheon Engineers & Constructors, Inc. (In re Acme Metals, Inc.), 257 B.R. 714 (Bankr. Ct. D. Del.2000); Delaney v DeTella, 123 F.Supp.2d 429 (N.D.Ill. 2000); Chase Commercial Corp. v Brandt, 1999 US Dist. LEXIS 16441 (N.D.Ill. 1999).

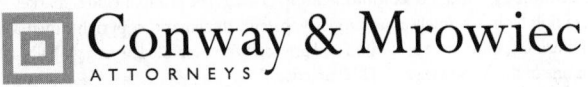

# DLA PIPER RUDNICK GRAY CARY US LLP

## THE FIRM

**Chairman:** Senator George J Mitchell
**Joint Chief Executive Officers:** Francis B Burch Jr, Nigel Knowles
Lee I Miller
**Executive Director:** Stephen R Colgate

**Number of partners worldwide:** 1142
**Number of other lawyers worldwide:** 2044

**FIRM OVERVIEW:** The firm are relationship-driven lawyers who meet the ongoing legal needs of our clients wherever they choose to do business. Operating across the US, Europe and Asia, they offer more than 3,000 lawyers in 58 cities in 22 countries. The firm acts for enterprises across the full spectrum of business, including local, national and multinational companies in a wide range of business sectors. Its clients range from single-owner startups to household name companies known worldwide. The firm commits to being a long-term partner with its clients on a day-to-day basis, year after year, and is there for the important everyday business issues that its clients face, as well as 'bet the company' transactions and lawsuits that might come just once in a business lifetime. As an organization, DLA Piper places the highest value on building close working relationships with its clients. To accomplish that, they offer lawyers who are culturally attuned to the business demands and legal requirements of their countries, who have excellent legal skills, and who are totally committed to its client service ethic. Their clients say that this commitment is what really sets the firm apart.

**MAIN AREAS OF PRACTICE:** The firm's practice is focused on:
**Corporate & Finance:** On the corporate and finance side, the firm operates significant transactional based practices and serves not only some of the world's largest companies but numerous middle and upper-mid market clients. The firm is on the panels of a number of major banks and financial institutions and has a substantial bankruptcy and restructuring practice.
**Litigation:** The group brings together more than 800 top litigators in the US, Europe and Asia and offers lawyers experienced in patent, class action, securities, antitrust, banking and finance, technology, telecommunications and insurance disputes.
**Real Estate:** With 500 lawyers globally, the firm's real estate practice is the largest and one of the most highly ranked in the world, serving the needs of owners, investors, developers, and corporations from straightforward transactions to complicated, multifaceted projects and sophisticated financings.
**Legislative & Regulatory:** At the federal and state level in the US, and in the individual countries of Europe as well as the EU, its people understand the legislative and regulatory process. To the strengths of its team, which includes chairman Senator George J Mitchell, is added the firm's alliance with The Cohen Group, the international business consulting firm.
**Human Resources:** With more than 250 lawyers located in key jurisdictions around the world, its human resources and labor lawyers are equipped to handle both local employment issues and complex cross-border transactions.
**Commercial:** A market leader in Public Private Partnerships and the provision of infrastructure and project finance services to sponsors and funders internationally, the group has lawyers who are particularly experienced in energy, sports, water, defense, health care and transportation, and is also recognized worldwide for its top-ranked franchise and distribution practice.
**Technology, Media & Communication (TMC):** The group includes market-leading teams in intellectual property, patent, trademark, copyright, media, e-business, sport, data protection and privacy. With over 420 lawyers, globally it is one of the world's leading TMC practices.

## HEAD OFFICE

### ILLINOIS
**Chicago** — Tel: 312 368 4000  Fax: 312 236 7516
**Email:** info@dlapiper.com
**Website:** www.dlapiper.com

## BRANCH OFFICES

### CALIFORNIA
| | | |
|---|---|---|
| **Los Angeles** (Century City) | Tel: 310 595 3000 | Fax: 310 595 3300 |
| **Los Angeles** (Downtown) | Tel: 213 330 7700 | Fax: 213 835 6001 |
| **Sacramento** | Tel: 916 930 3200 | Fax: 916 930 3201 |
| **San Diego** (Golden Triangle) | Tel: 858 677 1400 | Fax: 858 677 1401 |
| **San Diego** (Downtown) | Tel: 619 699 2700 | Fax: 619 699 2701 |
| **La Jolla** | Tel: 858 638 6806 | Fax: 858 456 3654 |
| **San Francisco** (Townsend St) | Tel: 415 836 2500 | Fax: 415 836 2501 |
| **San Francisco** (Market St) | Tel: 415 659 7000 | Fax: 415 659 7300 |
| **East Palo Alto** (Silicon Valley) | Tel: 650 833 2000 | Fax: 650 833 2001 |

### DISTRICT OF COLUMBIA
**Washington** — Tel: 202 861 3900  Fax: 202 223 2085

### FLORIDA
**Tampa** — Tel: 813 229 2111  Fax: 813 229 1447

### MARYLAND
| | | |
|---|---|---|
| **Annapolis** | Tel: 443 482 3830 | Fax: 443 482 3848 |
| **Baltimore** (Mt Washington) | Tel: 410 580 3000 | Fax: 410 580 3001 |
| **Baltimore** (Downtown) | Tel: 410 580 3000 | Fax: 410 580 3665 |

### MASSACHUSETTS
**Boston** — Tel: 617 406 6000  Fax: 617 406 6100

### NEVADA
**Las Vegas** — Tel: 702 737 3433  Fax: 702 737 1612

### NEW JERSEY
A New Jersey Limited Liability Partnership
(Robert A Assuncao, Managing Partner)
**Edison** — Tel: 732 590 1850  Fax: 732 590 1860

### NEW YORK
**New York** — Tel: 212 835 6000  Fax: 212 835 6001

### PENNSYSVANIA
**Philadelphia** — Tel: 215 656 3300  Fax: 215 656 3301

### TEXAS
| | | |
|---|---|---|
| **Dallas** | Tel: 214 743 4500 | Fax: 214 743 4545 |
| **Austin** | Tel: 512 457 7000 | Fax: 512 457 7001 |

### VIRGINIA
**Reston** — Tel: 703 773 4000  Fax: 703 773 5000

### WASHINGTON
**Seattle** — Tel: 206 839 4800  Fax: 206 839 4801

# EIMER STAHL KLEVORN & SOLBERG LLP

## THE FIRM

**Managing Partner:** Nathan P Eimer

**Number of partners:** 8
**Number of other attorneys:** 21

**FIRM OVERVIEW:** Eimer Stahl Klevorn & Solberg LLP engages in complex litigation throughout the United States. The firm is dedicated to providing top quality legal services in a cost-effective manner. With a commitment to client service, advanced technology and diversity, the firm partners with clients to obtain creative solutions to complex legal problems. The firm is proud to serve as trial counsel to many leading companies and organizations.

**MAIN AREAS OF PRACTICE:** The firm concentrates on complex litigation across a variety of subject areas, including antitrust, environmental, securities, energy, unfair competition, product liability, toxic torts, construction, and general commercial disputes. The firm has particular expertise relating to the defense of class action lawsuits, particularly in the securities, mass tort, and antitrust fields. Matters on which the firm has recently worked include government investigations and private suits relating to energy prices, defense of several securities class actions and related SEC investigations, defense of mass tort claims alleging injuries arising from the use of fuel additives, multimillion dollar breach of contract claims in the paper and cement industries, and defense of price-fixing claims in the chemical, dairy, pharmaceutical, and paper industries. The firm also engages in antitrust counseling, including obtaining government antitrust clearance of proposed mergers and acquisitions. Members of the firm have provided advice regarding such matters  across a wide variety of industries, including consumer goods, paper, chemicals, commercial printing, cosmetics, telecommunications, crop nutrients and fertilizers, foodstuffs, and automotive parts.

**CLIENTS:** The firm serves clients across a wide array of industries, including CITGO Petroleum, Hollinger, Inc., Abbott Labs, HSBC, Kimberly-Clark, Dow Chemical, Land O' Lakes Dairy, Corn Products International, Praxair, Holcim (US) Inc., Midwest Generation, Smurfit-Stone Container, and McGladrey & Pullen. Superior client service is a hallmark of the firm's operating philosophy and principles.

## HEAD OFFICE

**ILLINOIS**
224 S. Michigan Avenue, Suite 1100, **Chicago**, IL 60604
**Tel:** 312 660 7600   **Fax:** 312 692 1718
**Website:** www.eimerstahl.com

## CONTACTS

**Antitrust/Commercial Litigation** ..Nathan P Eimer, Andrew G Klevorn
**Energy/Commercial Litigation** ....................................David M Stahl

EimerStahl

Eimer Stahl Klevorn & Solberg LLP

# GARDNER CARTON & DOUGLAS LLP

## THE FIRM

**Chairman:** Harold L Kaplan

**Number of partners worldwide:** 130
**Number of other lawyers worldwide:** 95

**FIRM OVERVIEW:** Founded nearly 100 years ago, Gardner Carton & Douglas LLP (GCD) is a leading national law firm with offices in Chicago, Washington DC, New York City, Milwaukee, and Albany. The firm has more than 230 lawyers and advisors practicing in corporate law, corporate restructuring, customs & international trade, government relations, health law, HR law (employee benefits and labor and employment), intellectual property, litigation and dispute resolution, real estate and environmental law, and wealth planning and philanthropy.

## MAIN AREAS OF PRACTICE:

**Corporate Law:** GCD's Corporate Law Department offers legal counsel in financial and investment services; business transactions, including M&A; securities; and tax law, representing clients ranging from multinational corporations, local businesses and money center banks to privately held companies. The group includes one of the country's most active hedge fund practices, which advises commodity pool operators and management companies that act as investment advisors or operate offshore investment funds. The Indian Tribal Governments Practice represents tribes and tribal organizations in every region of the United States.

**Corporate Restructuring:** GCD's Corporate Restructuring Group represents clients in large-scale, complex restructurings; insolvencies; workouts and bankruptcies, including creditors and indenture trustees with more than $10 billion in defaulted corporate debt. The group also represents numerous creditors' committees in bankruptcy proceedings. Clients include a wide range of industries – from claims trading, manufacturing, transportation, securities and financial services, to oil and gas, retail, hospitality, telecommunications, and healthcare.

**Customs & International Trade:** GCD's Customs and International Trade Group provides advice on a wide variety of regulatory, policy and compliance issues to clients participating in the global marketplace, including global trade compliance, supply chain management, import/export compliance, trade remedies and litigation. Clients comprise a wide array of industries including aerospace, automotive, electronics, heavy machinery, chemicals, pharmaceuticals, healthcare, food and agriculture, textiles, consumer products and retail.

**Government Relations:** GCD's Government Relations Group provides advocacy advice and assistance to a wide array of clients, including healthcare providers, corporations, academic institutions, trade associations, nonprofits, telehealth networks, governmental entities and coalitions.

**Health Law:** The Health Law Group represents academic medical centers; faculty practice plans; foundations; hospital and licensed professional associations; hospital systems and integrated health systems; long-term care providers; managed care and disease management organizations; medical schools and university healthcare programs; the pharmaceutical industry; physician practice groups; and public and private hospitals. The firm also represents clients in industries closely tied to the healthcare industry, such as healthcare venture capital funds, financial services companies that lend to healthcare organizations, technology companies, insurance companies, and healthcare REITs, as well as tax-exempt organizations in their compliance with tax laws, fiduciary laws, and other laws relating to their tax-exempt status. Innovative Health Strategies LLC, a wholly owned subsidiary of GCD, advises hospitals, health systems and academic medical centers on matters of procurement and outsourcing strategies.

**HR Law/Wealth Planning & Philanthropy:** GCD's HR Law Practice covers employee benefits, executive compensation, ESOPs and stock-based compensation plans, ERISA counseling and litigation, retirement plans, international benefits, labor and employment counseling, litigation, and wealth and estate planning and philanthropy.

**Intellectual Property:** GCD's IP Practice helps clients identify, protect and exploit their full range of intellectual capital and helps them enhance their competitive position in the marketplace. The group counsels clients regarding patents, brands, information technology, unfair competition, copyrights, trade secrets or other proprietary rights. With experience in a wide range of industries and scientific disciplines, the firm's IP practitioners are litigators, transactional specialists, registered patent attorneys and counselors. GCD's IP litigators have long represented clients in complex intellectual property disputes, winning in court or leveraging viable business resolutions. GCD's transactional attorneys concentrate in complex outsourcing, information technology, research and development, technology transfer and in-bound and outbound licensing arrangements. They also guide clients through the complex world of new media, branding, technology and advertising.

**Litigation & Dispute Resolution:** GCD's Litigation Practice includes complex commercial litigation, antitrust and IP work, class action securities, products liability defense, healthcare litigation, and international and domestic arbitrations. Within this practice, the Financial Markets/Insurance and Reinsurance Litigation Group represents brokers, investment advisors, specialists and broker-dealers in federal and state courts, and industry arbitration forums, including SEC, NASD, CFTC, and other regulatory organizations.

**Real Estate & Environmental:** GCD's real estate and environmental attorneys work with developers, lenders, and investors whose primary business is real estate, in addition to corporate, governmental entities and nonprofits for which real estate is an important asset. The group focuses on development, land use and zoning; real estate investment and finance; leasing and property management; nonprofit institutions; business services; and environmental matters. Its environmental lawyers have counseled corporate, municipal and individual clients through the development and implementation of every major federal and state environmental regulatory initiative for more than 30 years. The scope of its environmental legal services includes all aspects of compliance counseling, transaction counseling and litigation.

# JENNER & BLOCK LLP

## THE FIRM

**Managing Partner:** Gregory S Gallopoulos
**Chairman:** Jerold S Solovy

**Number of partners:** 218
**Number of other lawyers:** 221

**FIRM OVERVIEW:** Jenner & Block LLP is a national full-service law firm with offices in Chicago, Dallas, New York, and Washington, DC. Founded in 1914, the firm has over 400 attorneys offering significant experience in virtually every area of the law. The firm consistently delivers outstanding representation of clients in corporate transactions and secures victories from the trial level through the United States Supreme Court. Jenner & Block's clients range from large international conglomerates to smaller, family-owned businesses, including industrial, commercial, telecommunications, research and development, technology, and utility companies, as well as financial and service enterprises. In the public sector, the firm represents a variety of state and local governmental entities. In January of 2006, Jenner & Block placed among the top five litigation departments in the United States in *The American Lawyer* magazine's biennial 'Litigation Department of the Year' award competition. The firm was lauded for "astonishing" victories, "hard-fought" settlements and courtroom wins for their clients. The magazine also praised the firm's "extraordinary efforts" in providing pro bono services to the needy. Jenner & Block is an Illinois Limited Liability Partnership including professional corporations. For more information, please visit www.jenner.com.

## MAIN AREAS OF PRACTICE:

**Business Transaction:** Jenner & Block has substantial business and financial transactions practices, with experienced groups focusing on corporate and commercial transactions including mergers and acquisitions, corporate governance, securities, corporate finance, tax, government contracts, real estate, environmental, insurance, commercial law, technology and intellectual property, bankruptcy and reorganization, benefits, employment, labor and executive compensation, healthcare and associations. The firm's lawyers have authored books and treatises in many of these areas, most recently on such topics as director and officer liability, securities, environmental law, insurance coverage, intellectual property and the Uniform Commercial Code. Jenner & Block handles transactional work for a wide range of large public corporations as well as privately held businesses, financial institutions, prominent trade associations, nonprofit organizations, new ventures, and individuals. The firm's lawyers represent many international and domestic clients in connection with mergers and acquisitions, joint ventures, strategic alliances and dispositions of businesses. Jenner & Block attorneys regularly advise clients in connection with public and private securities offerings and financings. The BTI Consulting Group, Inc. interviewed 329 corporate counsel at Fortune 1000 companies and large organizations and found that Jenner & Block is a premier 'Bet the Company' firm in the eyes of these world-class clients.

**Litigation:** Jenner & Block has one of the most prominent and successful litigation practices in the country. The firm's more than 250 litigators have won impressive victories in a broad range of complex and challenging civil and criminal cases before federal, state and administrative courts. Jenner & Block regularly represents clients before the United States Supreme Court, in all of the 13 United States Circuit Courts of Appeals, and in federal district courts and state courts nationwide. The quality and competence of the firm's trial lawyers is well known. Among them are two partners who are former United States Attorneys, many former Assistant US Attorneys, a former Chair of the ABA Litigation Section, and numerous leaders of national, state and local bar associations. Currently, 11 partners in the firm are Fellows of the American College of Trial Lawyers, the country's most prestigious trial group. Many of the firm's trial lawyers clerked for judges in the federal and state systems, including 11 who clerked for one or more United States Supreme Court Justices. In addition,

several former partners now serve as federal judges, maintaining a remarkable history of judicial service by members of the firm.

**Public Service:** Public service is part of the fabric of Jenner & Block. Throughout its history, the firm has served as a national leader in pro bono advocacy and continues to run one of the strongest and largest public service programs in the nation. The firm's lawyers contribute tens of thousands of their billable hours annually to pro bono work. In 2004, its attorneys logged more than 55,000 pro bono hours firm-wide. Of the nation's largest law firms, Jenner & Block is continually ranked among the very top in pro bono work by *The American Lawyer* magazine. The firm received *The National Law Journal*'s 2002 Pro Bono Award for its remarkable representation of clients in capital punishment cases. In 2004 Jenner & Block was awarded the Illinois State Bar Association's prestigious John C McAndrews Pro Bono Award for its remarkable record of accomplishments on behalf of those in greatest need of free legal assistance in the district. In addition, the firm's DC office was the recipient of District of Columbia Bar's 2005 Pro Bono Law Firm of the Year Award (large firm category).

## HEAD OFFICE

**ILLINOIS**
One IBM Plaza, **Chicago**, IL 60611
**Tel:** 312 222 9350   **Fax:** 312 527 0484
**Website:** www.jenner.com

## BRANCH OFFICES

**DISTRICT OF COLUMBIA**
601 Thirteenth Street, NW, Suite 1200 South, **Washington**, DC 20005
**Tel:** 202 639 6000   **Fax:** 202 639 6066

**NEW YORK**
919 Third Avenue, 37th Floor, **New York**, NY 10022
**Tel:** 212 891 1600   **Fax:** 212 891 1699

**TEXAS**
1717 Main Street, Suite 3150, **Dallas**, TX 75201
**Tel:** 214 746 5700   **Fax:** 214 746 5757

# JENNER & BLOCK

# KATTEN MUCHIN ROSENMAN LLP

## THE FIRM

**Managing Partner:** Vincent AF Sergi
**Number of partners:** +250
**Number of other lawyers:** +350

**FIRM OVERVIEW:** Katten Muchin Rosenman LLP is a full-service law firm with offices in the nation's largest centers of business, government, finance and technology and an associated entity in London, England. The firm's 600 attorneys in more than 40 practice areas provide timely and cost-effective counsel to clients in numerous industries. They are business advisors and advocates for a wide range of public and private companies – from entrepreneurial, emerging-growth, and middle market firms to global Fortune 100 corporations – as well as government entities and major universities, museums and other charitable and cultural organizations. In addition to the practice areas listed below, the firm maintains many highly focused practices, including: antitrust, customs and international trade, employee benefits and executive compensation, labor and employment, life sciences and public finance.

## MAIN AREAS OF PRACTICE:

**Litigation:** The firm's trial lawyers handle cases ranging from contract disputes and regulatory matters to securities class action lawsuits, antitrust matters and other complex commercial and criminal litigation. The Securities Litigation Practice is nationally recognized for successfully representing corporations and their officers and directors in shareholder class actions, derivative actions, SEC investigations and federal and state criminal investigations. They also represent clients in corporate control disputes and mergers and acquisitions litigation. The White Collar Criminal and Civil Litigation Practice is led by highly respected former federal prosecutors and law enforcement officers with broad investigative, trial and appellate experience. The Environmental Practice handles some of the largest and most complex environmental litigation in the country involving soil contamination and hazardous waste and substances.

**Corporate:** The Corporate Practice provides sophisticated transactional representation and business counseling on a national basis across a broad range of concentrations. The Mergers and Acquisitions Practice is involved in all aspects of public and private mergers, acquisitions and divestitures, representing both targets and bidders in negotiated and hostile takeovers. The nationally recognized Private Equity Practice represents leveraged buyout funds, mezzanine debt funds and venture capital funds in acquisitions, divestitures and financing transactions, as well as general partners and institutional limited partners in all aspects of private equity fund formation. The Securities Practice assist clients with public and private offerings of equity and debt securities, tender offers, proxy contests and going private transactions. They also provide corporate governance counseling to public and private companies, boards of directors and board committees. The Entertainment and Media Practice provide transactional, general corporate, and litigation representation to the entertainment and media industry. The Healthcare Practice represents healthcare systems, hospitals, academic medical centers, physician groups, ancillary care providers, integrated delivery systems, and managed care organizations.

**Real Estate:** The Real Estate Practice, widely recognized as a national leader, has built one of the largest and broadest practices in the country and serves clients in virtually every aspect of real estate law, including acquisitions, dispositions, developments and financings, along with establishment of joint ventures, real estate investment trusts, real estate opportunity funds and other real estate investment vehicles. Property types include office, retail, hotel, multi-family, industrial and mixed-use and resorts.

**Financial Services:** The Financial Services Practice regularly advises a broad range of participants in the financial services arena, including broker-dealers, futures commission merchants, investment advisors, finance companies, investment bankers, futures and securities exchanges, commodity trading advisors, pension funds, banks and insurance companies, as well as investment vehicles such as hedge funds, commodity pools, venture capital funds and private equity funds, securitization vehicles, mutual funds and bank collective investment funds. Attor-

neys apply an interdisciplinary approach in providing comprehensive legal services, including: regulatory and transactional advice, tax and ERISA counsel and domestic and foreign litigation.

**Commercial Finance & Reorganization:** The Commercial Finance Practice represents a broad range of financial institutions in a wide variety of senior secured commercial loan transactions, including lenders, investors and borrowers in conventional asset-based and cash-flow loans. Attorneys regularly represent financial institutions, investors and borrowers in mezzanine investments and Term B Loans and Second Lien Term Loans, including secured and unsecured mezzanine debt investments, direct mezzanine equity investments and warrant purchases and issuances, related equity co-investments and stand-alone equity investments, one-stop senior and mezzanine facilities, and first lien and second lien credit facilities.

**Intellectual Property:** The Intellectual Property Practice secures, protects and enforces patents, trademarks, trade secrets and other intellectual property. It has represented plaintiffs and defendants in some of the most significant intellectual property cases (i.e., patents, trademarks, trade secrets, copyrights and unfair competition) of the last 20 years, for some of the world's most prominent corporations. They also work with its corporate technology lawyers, in exploiting intellectual property rights through licensing, joint venture and technology transfer agreements.

**Tax:** The Tax Practice handles US and international tax planning and advises clients on the tax aspects of mergers and acquisitions, recapitalizations, reorganizations, spin-offs, venture capital and LBO transactions and financings, investment fund formation, securitizations of debt, equipment leasing, real estate transactions, hedge funds, public and private partnerships, limited liability companies, and closely-held and multinational corporations.

**Trusts & Estates:** The Trusts and Estates Practice develops and implements sophisticated estate, tax, business succession and charitable plans on the state, federal and international levels. They handle all aspects of the administration of estates and trusts, as well as probate, accounting, tax and other litigation on behalf of both fiduciaries and beneficiaries of complex estates and trusts.

# Katten Muchin Rosenman LLP

# KIRKLAND & ELLIS LLP

## THE FIRM

**Number of partners:** 505
**Number of other lawyers:** 621

**FIRM OVERVIEW:** For nearly 100 years clients have called upon Kirkland & Ellis to handle complicated litigation, corporate, intellectual property, restructuring, tax, and counseling matters for major national and international clients. Today, Kirkland & Ellis continues to work with a long-standing base of clients engaged in industries as varied as manufacturing, transportation, telecommunications, private equity/venture capital, pharmaceutical, technology, energy, health care, real estate, chemicals, food products, finance, insurance, e-commerce, advertising, sales and marketing, and accounting.

## MAIN AREAS OF PRACTICE:

**Litigation & Arbitration:** Kirkland & Ellis has earned a reputation as trial lawyers, not just 'litigators', by successfully defending companies with business-threatening lawsuits and class actions in such diverse legal areas as securities, defamation, antitrust, mass torts, product liability, insurance coverage, construction, environmental and commercial, handling the trial, appellate and Supreme Court phases. This trial-ready reputation has been the impetus for favorable and prompt results for the firm's clients through settlements, as well as the various Alternative Dispute Resolution (ADR) mechanisms employed whenever practicable and desired by the client. In 2005, Kirkland was named the number one 'go-to' firm for litigation in the Corporate Counsel survey, 'Who Represents America's Biggest Companies?' Additionally, Chambers & Partners named Kirkland the '2004 USA Litigation Law Firm of the Year.'

**Transactional:** Kirkland & Ellis is known for its ability to negotiate and close highly sophisticated transactions, representing venture capital investors and public and private companies in merger and acquisition, securities, spin-off and split-off, private equity, and real estate transactions. The firm has a premier private equity practice, having represented private investment funds, the private equity groups at several major money center banks and other participants in this industry for more than 25 years. For two years in a row, Chambers & Partners chose Kirkland as the Private Equity Law Firm of the Year. The prestige of this award signifies the strength and scope of the firm's Private Equity Practice Group.

**Intellectual Property:** The lawyers of Kirkland & Ellis have been recognized for their experience in litigation, transactional, counseling and administrative matters involving areas of intellectual property. The Intellectual Property Practice Group includes engineers and scientists trained in a variety of technical disciplines. Kirkland's lawyers regularly conduct trials of patent, trademark and copyright infringement, trade secret misappropriation and other intellectual property claims in federal and state courts throughout the United States. On the transactional side, Kirkland lawyers concentrate on domestic and international business transactions that are driven by the acquisition, use or divestiture of rights in technology, trademarks and other intellectual property. In addition, clients receive counseling in all aspects of intellectual property acquisition, transfer, protection and enforcement, both domestic and foreign, including related issues such as US and EC antitrust concerns.

**Restructuring:** Kirkland & Ellis' Restructuring Practice Group provides a broad range of business advisory and crisis management skills with extensive experience in US, UK and international insolvency matters to navigate clients through the turmoil of situations involving financially troubled companies. The group has earned a distinguished national and international reputation for providing outstanding legal advice and judgment to all constituencies in situations where companies face impending insolvency. The firm acts for a varied range of national and international clients: debtors; financial institutions; secured creditors; insurance companies; bondholders; lessors; unsecured creditors; investors; and board/creditor and equity committees in complex corporate restructuring, workout and bankruptcy planning, negotiation and litigation.

## BRANCH OFFICES

**ILLINOIS**
Aon Center, 200 East Randolph Drive, **Chicago**, IL 60601-6636
**Tel:** 312 861 2000   **Fax:** 312 861 2200
**Email:** dbernick@kirkland.com

**CALIFORNIA**
777 S. Figueroa Street, **Los Angeles**, CA 90017-5800
**Tel:** 213 680 8400   **Fax:** 213 680 8500
**Email:** jdavidson@kirkland.com

555 California Street, **San Francisco**, CA 94104
**Tel:** 415 439 1400   **Fax:** 415 439 1500
**Email:** jhammes@kirkland.com

**DISTRICT OF COLUMBIA**
655 Fifteenth Street NW, **Washington**, DC 20005-5793
**Tel:** 202 879 5000   **Fax:** 202 879 5200
**Email:** tyannucci@kirkland.com

**NEW YORK**
Citigroup Center, 153 East 53rd Street, **New York**, NY 10022-4611
**Tel:** 212 446 4800   **Fax:** 212 446 4900
**Email:** kradke@kirkland.com

**Tax:** The firm's Tax Practice Group provides its clients with the most creative tax planning available in a responsive and cost-efficient manner. The practice has developed a strong international reputation for providing sophisticated tax counseling on both US, foreign and state tax issues, and effectively representing its clients in tax disputes worldwide. Kirkland's tax practice can be divided broadly into two areas: (i) tax planning in connection with mergers, acquisitions, buyouts, restructurings, financings, executive compensation plans, and other sophisticated transactions; and (ii) contested tax matters. The firm's goal in both types of matters is the same: to achieve the best possible tax results in the most efficient manner.

**INTERNATIONAL WORK:** The European Practice Group consists of approximately 50 lawyers practicing English, German and international law, with several lawyers experienced in the international application of US law as well. During the last six years, Kirkland's private equity practice has represented over 50 different clients in hundreds of leveraged acquisitions and other types of transactions and has been principal counsel in over US$70 billion in fund formations. In the M&A and securities area, Kirkland has recently represented clients ranging from some of the world's largest corporations to major banks and investment banks in some of the world's largest and most complex M&A transactions and securities offering. Lawyers at Kirkland & Ellis are fluent in English, Chinese, French, German, Greek, Hebrew, Hindi, Italian, Japanese, Korean, Russian and Spanish.

# KIRKLAND & ELLIS LLP

# MAYER, BROWN, ROWE & MAW LLP

## THE FIRM

**Chairman:** Tyrone C Fahner
**Managing Partner:** Debora de Hoyos
**Number of partners in US offices:** 425
**Number of other lawyers in US offices:** 584

**Website:** www.mayerbrownrowe.com
**Email:** info@mayerbrownrowe.com

## AREAS OF PRACTICE:

Litigation & Arbitration . . . . . . . . . . . . . . . . . . . . . . . . . . . . . . . . . 32%
Corporate & Securities . . . . . . . . . . . . . . . . . . . . . . . . . . . . . . . . . 22%
Finance, Banking & Insurance . . . . . . . . . . . . . . . . . . . . . . . . . . . . 22%
Tax. . . . . . . . . . . . . . . . . . . . . . . . . . . . . . . . . . . . . . . . . . . . . . . . 9%
Oil, Gas & Real Estate . . . . . . . . . . . . . . . . . . . . . . . . . . . . . . . . . . 8%
Antitrust . . . . . . . . . . . . . . . . . . . . . . . . . . . . . . . . . . . . . . . . . . . . 7%
Other . . . . . . . . . . . . . . . . . . . . . . . . . . . . . . . . . . . . . . . . . . . . . . 1%

**FIRM OVERVIEW:** Mayer, Brown, Rowe & Maw LLP is the sixth largest law firm in the United States and among the dozen largest law practices in the world. The practice has more than 1,300 lawyers in seven US cities and six European cities. Mayer, Brown, Rowe & Maw is a combination of two limited liability partnerships, each named Mayer, Brown, Rowe & Maw LLP, one established in Illinois, USA, and one incorporated in England. A full-service law firm, Mayer, Brown, Rowe & Maw is renowned in the US for its appellate, corporate, banking and finance, litigation, ERISA, outsourcing, and tax practices.

**MAIN AREAS OF PRACTICE:** The practice handles appellate and litigation, finance, structured bank finance, corporate and M&A, outsourcing, asset securitizations, capital markets and securities, fund management and financial services regulation, commodities and derivatives, international arbitration, global trade.

**CLIENTS:** Mayer, Brown, Rowe & Maw serves 65 of the Fortune 100 companies, one out of every three US banks, and ranks ninth in both the Financial Times Stock Exchange 100 Index principal advisors survey and its most-used law firm survey. Clients include Abbott Laboratories, Banc One, Bank of America, BASF, Bertelsmann, Brunswick Corporation, Deutsche Bank, Dow Chemical, EMI, General Electric, ICI, Morgan Stanley, Nestlé, Pfizer, Starwood Hotels & Resorts, State Farm Insurance Companies, Unilever, and United Air Lines.

## INTERNATIONAL WORK:

**Latin American Telecom:** Advised BellSouth Corp. in an agreement with Telefonica Móviles to sell its interests in its 10 Latin American operations.
**Appellate Strength:** Argued nine cases before the US Supreme Court in two latest terms.
**Privatized US Toll Bridge:** Acted as principal counsel for the City of Chicago on the a $1.83 billion privatization of the Chicago Skyway Toll bridge – the first such deal in the United States.
**Outsourcing:** Advised TXU Corp. in a $3.5 billion outsourcing deal with CapGemini – believed to be largest reported deal in the energy industry.
**International Price-Fixing:** Won 8-0 US Supreme Court decision in F. *Hoffmann-LaRoche Ltd.* v *Empagram, SA*, involving international claims in a multibillion-dollar vitamins case.
**Spin-Off:** Represented Abbott Laboratories in its $2.5 billion spin-off of Global Hospital Products Company.
**Oracle Case:** Won summary judgment in favor of Oracle's chairman and CEO and CFO in a derivative action alleging insider trading.
**Acquisition:** Advised ProLogis in connection with its partnership's $1.6 billion acquisition of Keystone Property Trust.

## OFFICES

### CALIFORNIA

350 South Grand Avenue, 25th Floor, **Los Angeles**, CA 90071-1503
**Tel:** 213 229 9500  **Fax:** 213 625 0248

555 College Avenue, **Palo Alto**, CA 94306-1433
**Tel:** 650 331 2000  **Fax:** 650 331 2060

### DISTRICT OF COLUMBIA

1909 K Street, N.W., **Washington**, DC 20006-1157
**Tel:** 202 263 3000  **Fax:** 202 263 3300

### ILLINOIS

71 South Wacker Drive, **Chicago**, IL 60606-4637
**Tel:** 312 782 0600  **Fax:** 312 701 7711

### NEW YORK

1675 Broadway, **New York**, NY 10019-5820
**Tel:** 212 506 2500  **Fax:** 212 262 1910

### NORTH CAROLINA

214 North Tryon Street, Suite 3800, **Charlotte**, NC 28202-2137
**Tel:** 704 444 3500  **Fax:** 704 377 2033

### TEXAS

700 Louisiana Street, Suite 3600, **Houston**, TX 77002-2730
**Tel:** 713 221 1651  **Fax:** 713 224 6410

## INTERNATIONAL OFFICES

Mayer, Brown, Rowe & Maw LLP has offices in Belgium, France, Germany and the United Kingdom. The firm also has two associated offices in China (MBP Consulting Limited LLC) and an independent correspondent firm, Jáuregui, Navarrete & Nader, in Mexico.

**Pharma Case:** Won summary judgment on behalf of Novartis AG in multi-district products liability litigation concerning products containing phenylpropanolamine.
**Maritime Acquisition:** Advised TAL International Group, Inc., in connection with its $1.2 billion acquisition of Transamerica Maritime Containers from AEGON N.V.
**Ryerson:** Represented Ryerson Tull, Inc. in its purchase of Integris Metals, Inc., a joint venture between Alcoa Inc. and BHP Billiton.
**London Real Estate:** Advised longstanding client, Unilever, on its sale of Unilever House to Sloane Blackfriars Limited – one of the most significant London real estate transactions of 2004.
**Hydroelectric:** Advised TransCanada in connection with its purchase of USGen New Englands hydroelectric assets for $505 million.
**Agribusiness:** Advised Monsanto Company and its subsidiaries on the disposal to RAGT Génétique S.A. of its European wheat and barley seed business.
**Natural Gas:** Advised Devon Energy Corporation in stock-for-stock merger (enterprise value $5.3 billion at signing) with Ocean Energy, Inc., making Devon one of the largest independent oil and natural-gas producers in the United States.
**Food:** Advised Nestlé S.A. in its $2.6 billion acquisition of Chef America.
**Suez:** Advised Suez on the $4.2 billion sale of its US industrial water treatment services subsidiary to a consortium of private equity sponsors – The Blackstone Group, Apollo Management and Goldman Sachs Capital Partners.

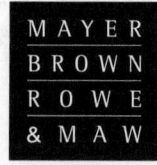

# MCANDREWS, HELD & MALLOY, LTD.

## THE FIRM

**Founding Partners:** George P McAndrews, John J Held, Timothy J Malloy, Lawrence M Jarvis, Gregory J Vogler

**Senior Partner:** George P McAndrews

**Number of lawyers:** 91

**FIRM OVERVIEW:** McAndrews, Held & Malloy is one of the nation's preeminent legal resources for intellectual property and technology matters. The firm's attorneys serve as counsel of choice for companies and institutions ranging from major multinationals and start-ups to world-class colleges and universities. The firm's reputation, founded upon an unparalleled record of litigation successes before juries, as well as in bench trials and ADR proceedings, encompasses a full range of legal services. The firm's attorneys are known for their clear and effective communication skills, expertise and training in engineering and science, their passion for technology law, their command of winning business strategy and their tenaciousness – both inside and outside of the courtroom.

## MAIN AREAS OF PRACTICE:

**Litigation (Patent, Trademark, Copyright, Antitrust, Trade Secret, Unfair Competition & Other Technology):** Includes the firm's primary practice in all areas of intellectual property and complex technology litigation, including jury and bench trials, appeals, practice before the International Trade Commission, as well as ADR proceedings. The firm is strategically located so that its nationwide litigation practice measures up with its coast to coast clientele.

**Patent & Trademark Procurement & Portfolio Management:** Includes the prosecution of patents (ranging from simple mechanical devices to complex electrical systems) and trademarks, obtaining and maintaining intellectual property assets, and management of overall corporate or institutional holdings.

**Patent Interferences:** Includes all aspects of these complex, highly specialized proceedings, including pre-interference investigation and patent prosecution.

**Trademark Oppositions & Cancellations:** Includes all contested administrative proceedings before the Trademark Trial and Appeal Board.

**International Practice:** Includes all aspects of international intellectual property litigation, foreign prosecution, global transactions, licensing, appeals of patents and trademarks in other jurisdictions, and all issues related to foreign patents.

**Intellectual Property/Technology Opinions & Investigations:** Includes highly specialized strategic investigations, counsel and opinion analysis.

**Due Diligence & M&A Support:** Includes merger and acquisition counsel and support involving due diligence processes, investigations regarding asset quality and potential infringements.

**Technology Licensing & Joint Ventures:** Includes counsel regarding a wide variety of revenue-generating opportunities related to intellectual property holdings.

**Technology Transfers & Donations:** Includes the donation of intellectual property assets as charitable gifts.

## HEAD OFFICE

**ILLINOIS**
500 West Madison Street, **Chicago**, IL 60661
**Tel:** 312 775 8000　**Fax:** 312 775 8100
**Website:** www.mhmlaw.com

**CLIENTS:** The firm's clients represent a diverse group of domestic and international clients covering a broad range of technology and proprietary rights. Clients include many leading companies in such diverse industrial and commercial fields as chemical, mechanical, and electrical manufacture, processing and use; such as, cell biology, angioplasty catheters, kidney dialysis equipment, medical imaging, pharmaceuticals, petrochemicals, digital cellular telephony, electronic games, computer memories and other hardware, software, satellite communications, fuel cells, power sources, industrial equipment (from paving equipment through mining equipment through papermaking machinery), printing equipment, sporting goods equipment (such as basketballs, softballs, golf balls and golf clubs), giftware, heating and air-conditioning, measurement instruments, appliances, furniture, aviation, avionics, transportation, confections and foodstuffs, and financial instruments.

# MCDERMOTT WILL & EMERY LLP

## THE FIRM

**Managing Partner:** Harvey W Freishtat
**Number of partners:** 608
**Number of other lawyers:** 418

**FIRM OVERVIEW:** McDermott Will & Emery is an international law firm with more than 1,000 lawyers in five European and nine US offices. The firm represents a wide range of industrial, financial and commercial enterprises, both publicly and privately held.

**INTERNATIONAL EXPERIENCE:** Firm lawyers have been involved in cross-border matters on every continent and in virtually every sector of business. International matters include cross-border mergers and acquisitions; joint ventures; financings; corporate restructuring and reorganizations; the structuring of distributorship, licensing and agency arrangements; the negotiation of commercial contracts; compliance with investment laws; privatization; cross-border tax planning; international litigation and dispute resolution; public law; environmental; real estate; banking; anti-competition; e-business and intellectual property, acquisitions, dispositions and financings. The firm has represented clients from more than 70 countries.

**MAIN AREAS OF PRACTICE:** Agribusiness, alcohol beverages and products, antitrust and competition, biotech and life sciences, bankruptcy, construction, corporate, responsibility, e-business, employee benefits and pensions, energy, environmental, executive compensation, finance and banking, financial products, food and beverage, health, hospitality, insurance, intellectual property, international, labour and employment, government strategies, mergers and acquisitions, OSHA, pharmaceutical, private clients, products liability and regulation, real estate, securities, sports and entertainment, taxation, technology, telecommunications, transportation, trial, utilities, venture capital/private equity, white collar criminal defence.

**Antitrust & Competition:** The practice is comprised of approximately 60 lawyers, many of whom have prior government experience with the European Commission, Federal Trade Commission, the Antitrust Division of the Department of Justice or the office of a State Attorney General.

**Finance & Banking:** The firm has an integrated finance and banking team of more than 70 lawyers, with recognised experience in all areas of US, UK, German, Italian and international corporate finance.

**Bankruptcy:** The firm represents debtors, trustees, and various creditor and equality constituencies on a regular basis, including banks, bondholders, trade creditors, credit corporations and acquirers.

**Employee Benefits & Pensions:** There are approximately 50 lawyers who practice exclusively in employee benefits and compensation, providing counsel in the international planning, implementation and administration of a wide range of compensation and benefit plans and programs. The employee benefits lawyers advise corporations, partnerships and organizations from all business sectors.

**Health:** With an over 50-year history of serving the healthcare industry, the firm has one of the United States' largest and most prestigious health law departments. The health lawyers counsel leading organizations in every major sector of the healthcare industry on regulatory and business transaction issues.

**Labour, Employment & OSHA:** The practice has considerable experience in all employment-related matters, both contentious and non-contentious. Its lawyers advise on wrongful and unfair dismissal, executive severance, confidentiality and restrictive covenants, breaches of fiduciary duty, fraud by employees, sex/race/disability discrimination, early retirement program, development of employee manuals, wage-hour compliance, workers' compensation, substance abuse programs, drug testing, equal pay, Working Time Regulations, union recognition and works councils, industrial disputes, EU employment law, TUPE, employment aspects of acquisitions and OSHA.

**Intellectual Property:** The firm's IP lawyers hold degrees in a wide variety of technical and scientific fields and are uniquely capable of handling intellectual property matters in virtually every technical or scientific discipline. The firm offers comprehensive legal services in every aspect of intellectual property law. Among these services, the firm's IP Practice is renowned for its trial and appellate experience. The IP Practice includes client counseling, procurement, and licensing in the patent, trademark, trade dress, copyright, trade secret, entertainment and computer law areas. The firm's IP lawyers undertake all forms of IP litigation, and have assisted clients with oppositions in the European Patent Office and the Community Trade Mark Office.

**M&A:** The firm's lawyers have extensive experience and advise on the purchase, sale and merger of businesses. The firm handles take-overs, acquisitions and disposals, MBOs and MBIs, LBOs and LBIs, and reorganisations and restructurings.

**Private Client:** The Estate Planning Practice is one of the largest and best-known departments of its kind in the United States. The firm's lawyers represent families and individuals, family offices, closely held businesses, foundations, estates, trusts and special purpose asset transfer and investment management entities providing a spectrum of estate, succession, gift transfer and wealth planning services. Their experience covers all significant facets of wealth planning.

**Tax:** The firm advises clients on all tax-related areas, including corporate, employee benefits, private clients, state and local taxation, and international matters. The core of the tax practice deals with thousands of statutory tax requirements imposed at international, federal, state and local levels. The firm represents more than half of the Fortune 100 companies in tax matters on a regular basis.

**Trial:** The trial lawyers are regularly engaged in all aspects of civil, regulatory and white-collar criminal defence litigation in US and international forums. Experience includes handling emergency situations such as temporary restraining orders and preliminary injunctions, bench and jury trials, arbitrations and alternative dispute resolution, including mediations and summary jury trials.

## HEAD OFFICE

**ILLINOIS**
227 West Monroe Street, **Chicago**, IL 60606-5096, USA
**Tel:** 312 372 2000   **Fax:** 312 984 7700
**Website:** www.mwe.com

## BRANCH OFFICES

**CALIFORNIA**
18191 Von Karman Avenue, Suite 500, **Irvine**, CA 92612-0187
**Tel:** 949 851 0633   **Fax:** 949 851 9348

4370 La Jolla Village Drive, **San Diego**, CA 92122
**Tel:** 858 535 9001   **Fax:** 858 597 1585

2049 Century Park East, 34th Floor, **Los Angeles**, CA 90067-3208
**Tel:** 310 277 4110   **Fax:** 310 277 4730

3150 Porter Drive, **Palo Alto**, CA 94304-1212
**Tel:** 650 813 5000   **Fax:** 650 813 5100

**DISTRICT OF COLUMBIA**
600 13th Street NW, **Washington**, DC 20005-3096
**Tel:** 202 756 8000   **Fax:** 202 756 8087

**FLORIDA**
201 South Biscayne Boulevard, **Miami**, FL 33131-4336
**Tel:** 305 358 3500   **Fax:** 305 347 6500

**MASSACHUSSETTS**
28 State Street, **Boston**, MA 02109-1775
**Tel:** 617 535 4000   **Fax:** 617 535 3800

**NEW YORK**
340 Madison Ave, **New York**, NY 10017
**Tel:** 212 547 5400   **Fax:** 212 547 5444

## INTERNATIONAL OFFICES

The firm also has offices in Düsseldorf, London, Munich, Rome and Brussels.

# MCDONNELL BOEHNEN HULBERT & BERGHOFF LLP

## THE FIRM

**FIRM OVERVIEW:** McDonnell Boehnen Hulbert & Berghoff LLP is a progressive, mid-size intellectual property law firm focusing on the needs of technology-driven companies. MBHB's clients range from *Fortune* 100 companies to entrepreneurial start-ups, in industries such as biotechnology, pharmaceuticals and medical devices, chemical, telecommunications, electrical, computing, and mechanical and materials. MBHB attorneys are experienced in procurement, licensing, enforcement, and defense of patents, trademarks, and copyrights in a number of technological disciplines and product categories. Virtually all of the firm's attorneys are registered to practice before the Patent and Trademark Office, and more than half of their professionals have Masters or PhD degrees. The firm's attorneys have been recognized as leaders in their fields by Leading Lawyers, Best Lawyers in America, Chambers USA, *Chicago* magazine, *Crain's Chicago Business*, and many other publications and groups.

## MAIN AREAS OF PRACTICE:

**Aggressive Litigation:** The firm's attorneys represent clients aggressively, effectively, and efficiently in all types of intellectual property litigation before all forums, including the federal courts, the International Trade Commission, the Patent and Trademark Office, and private mediations. Even in the heat of litigation, the firm keeps its focus on the clients' business goals. MBHB always understands what is truly important to its clients.

**Focused Prosecution:** As with its litigation strategy, MBHB crafts prosecution strategies designed to further the clients' business goals. The firm is highly adept in patent and trademark procurement, including drafting applications and prosecuting them before the United States Patent and Trademark Office and internationally. MBHB is also skilled in other aspects of prosecution, including patent interference, re-examination, reissue, and opposition proceedings, and trademark opposition and cancellation proceedings.

**Insightful Counseling:** Sound, creative advice and the skills to implement it are the most important benefits the firm provides to its clients. MBHB advises clients on the management and development of their intellectual property assets by counseling them on issues of patentability, freedom-to-operate, patent validity, and infringement. The firm's experience in business consulting is yet another valuable resource for its clients as they negotiate licensing transactions.

### INDUSTRY-FOCUSED TECHNOLOGY GROUPS

**Biotechnology:** Spearheaded by attorneys, agents, and law clerks with advanced degrees (including 22 PhD's) in such areas as biochemistry, molecular biology, immunology, and plant sciences, the firm's practice has the combination of technical expertise and legal experience that enables it to represent clients in the most sophisticated arenas. MBHB works extensively in cutting-edge sub-specialties, such as the production and use of RNAi, recombinant genes, proteomics, monoclonal antibodies, gene-gun applications, pharmaceutical products for disease treatment and diagnosis, and apparatuses and techniques for isolating, labeling, and detecting molecules of biological importance. The firm's focus on the burgeoning field of nanotechnology is one of the most comprehensive in the legal profession. MBHB understands the far-reaching implications of nanotechnology and its potential to transform technology as we now know it.

**Pharmaceuticals, Medical Devices & Diagnostics:** Drawing on the firm's strengths in biomedical and chemical matters, MBHB has prosecuted, licensed, and litigated a wide variety of patents in the pharmaceutical and medical devices fields, including such technologies as target discovery, high-throughput screening, combinatorial chemistry, drug-delivery systems, therapeutic small molecules, and drug and antibody assay devices, methods, and reagents.

**Chemical:** The firm has experience prosecuting and litigating cases involving industrial chemicals, consumer-product compositions, processes and methods of manufacture and catalysis, waste management technology, process chemistry, surfactants and detergents, and organic synthesis of both small molecules and polymers.

**Telecommunications:** MBHB also represents a broad range of clients in the rapidly expanding area of telecommunications. The firm has extensive experience handling patent matters in both analog and digital communications, including cellular wireless communications, digital signal processing, modulation and coding techniques, real-time media transmissions, internet communications, wireless intelligent networks, policy-based networking, and satellite communications.

**Computing:** The exponential growth of computing and the internet have made this aspect of intellectual property an active and important field. MBHB's attorneys have litigated and prosecuted cases for clients relating to such matters as computer architecture, computer networking, software, data compression, data mining, cryptography, and programming languages.

**Electrical:** Innovations in the field of electrical devices and systems are closely related to developments in computing and telecommunications. MBHB has applied its expertise in these areas to cases involving signaling formats, semiconductors, power regulation systems, high-definition television, biomedical instrumentation, optics and imaging devices, digital video compression, optical and magnetic storage devices, and circuit board and chip manufacturing.

**Mechanical & Materials**: The strong engineering background of the firm's attorneys has helped MBHB's clients secure and protect their rights concerning such mechanical and manufacturing techniques and products as medical devices, industrial controls, hot-runner and injection molding systems, recycling technology, plastic extrusion techniques, horizontal directional drilling, large scale polymer synthesis, and offset printing. MBHB attorneys also have strong backgrounds in materials sciences, including polymers and alloys.

## HEAD OFFICE

**ILLINOIS**
300 South Wacker Drive, **Chicago**, IL 60606-6709
**Tel:** 312 913 0001   **Fax:** 312 913 0002
**Website:** www.mbhb.com

# NEAL, GERBER & EISENBERG LLP

## THE FIRM

**Managing Partner:** Jerry H Biederman
**Senior Partners:** Marshall E Eisenberg, Phil C Neal

**Number of partners:** 109
**Number of other lawyers:** 67

**HEAD OFFICE**

**ILLINOIS**
Two North LaSalle Street, Suite 2200, **Chicago**, 60602-3801
**Tel:** 312 269 8000  **Fax:** 312 269 1747
**Website:** www.ngelaw.com

**FIRM OVERVIEW:** Neal Gerber Eisenberg LLP is a Chicago-based law firm providing legal services to a diverse group of clients in a wide array of domestic and global business transactions and litigation matters. The firm's clients include privately and publicly held companies, financial institutions, non-profit organizations and high net worth individuals. The firm's client base reflects virtually every business industry, including a number of Fortune 100 companies. Founded in 1986, the firm enjoys a reputation as one of the fastest growing law firms and is recognized throughout the Chicago area and nationally for its expertise in a number of key practice areas. The firm's mission is to deliver superior individualized client service in a thoroughly integrated manner that exceeds expectations.

## MAIN AREAS OF PRACTICE:

**Associations & Not-For-Profit Organizations:** The firm represents international, national, state and local organizations of all sizes including trade associations, professional societies, educational foundations and charities.

**Bankruptcy, Reorganization & Creditors' Rights:** National in scope, the firm's bankruptcy practice encompasses the full range of insolvency matters, from out-of-court restructurings to formal reorganization and liquidation proceedings.

**Commercial Leasing:** The firm handles a broad range of leasing and leasing-related matters in the retail, office and industrial areas with a national client base that includes large publicly traded REITs and private companies.

**Corporate & Securities:** Addressing all areas of business and transactional law, the firm handles complex acquisition and financing transactions and provides general corporate counseling to a diverse client base that includes public and private local, regional, national and international businesses in a wide variety of industries.

**Corporate Governance:** Be it best practices in corporate governance or defense of potential claims, the firm provides counsel to boards of directors, committees (including audit committees), directors, officers and others with oversight responsibilities.

**Employee Benefits & Executive Compensation:** The firm advises a variety of clients on employee pension plans; development and implementation of executive compensation arrangements; negotiation and preparation of executive employment contracts and termination/severance arrangements; design and administration of health, welfare and other fringe benefit plans; and employee benefits aspects of corporate transactions.

**Environmental:** The firm has extensive experience in environmental litigation, government enforcement actions, corporate and real estate transactions, solid and hazardous waste landfill regulation, air quality regulation and general regulatory compliance.

**Finance:** The firm represents borrowers and lenders of secured and unsecured commercial loans providing a full range of financial legal services including the structuring, negotiation and documentation of new and refinanced credit facilities, the workouts of distressed credits, representations in foreclosure and pre-bankruptcy cases and certain banking regulatory matters.

**Health Law:** The firm represents a broad range of healthcare organizations, including Blue Cross and Blue Shield Plans, other health insurance and managed care organizations, hospital systems and academic medical centers, health industry associations, long-term care, hospice and home health providers, health industry suppliers and group purchasing organizations, clinics, group practices and professional practitioners.

**Information Technology:** Regarding technology related contracting needs, the firm has negotiated the full gamut of information technology transactions with nearly every major industry player, including negotiating some of the largest technology deals of their respective types ever concluded in the US and abroad.

**Intellectual Property:** The firm handles a wide variety of strategic intellectual property counseling, litigation and prosecution matters, involving patents, trademarks, service marks, domain names, trade dress, trade secrets, copyrights and advertising claims.

**Labor & Employment:** The firm advises a myriad of clients on how to encourage a union-free workplace, litigate employment-related claims, develop employee-friendly yet effective employment policies, legal risks and liabilities, and negotiating contracts.

**Litigation:** Advocating for individuals and businesses across industries, the firm's litigators bring depth of experience to all forms of alternative dispute resolution, including arbitration, and represent clients before administrative agencies and tribunals. Litigation members are broadly interdisciplinary, working closely with attorneys in all other substantive practice areas.

**Private Wealth Services:** The firm represents high net worth clients and their families in providing the full range of tax, estate planning and corporate issues that have an impact on business value and personal worth, and the development, preservation, maximization and transfer of a client's wealth.

**Real Estate:** The firm's diverse client base includes REITs, local and national corporations, partnerships, entrepreneurs, financial institutions, multi-project builders, management companies, operators, developers and individuals with significant real estate holdings.

**Real Estate Tax:** While the firm's practice is concentrated in Cook County (Chicago) and the surrounding 'collar' counties, their practice is national in scope with over 10,000 tax parcels under management. The firm maintains a significant property tax foreclosure and exemption practice coupled with extensive work in all aspects of state and local property tax, including assessment appeals.

**Securities & Commodities Litigation:** The firm represents many of the major national, regional and local broker-dealers and commodities firms, as well as affiliated individuals. The firm has been successful in advising and defending clients in the full range of customer disputes, employment disputes and regulatory matters. The firm has in-depth knowledge of the financial services industry and regulatory environment coupled with their extensive, national courtroom and arbitration trial experience.

**Tax:** The firm represents clients in a multitude of tax-oriented areas, including domestic and international income tax and business planning, estate, gift and generation-skipping taxation, the tax aspects of executive compensation arrangements, and the successful resolution of federal and state tax controversies.

**CLIENTS:** The firm's client base reflects virtually every business industry, including a number of Fortune 100 companies. Examples: Citigroup Global Markets Inc.; Lehman Brothers Inc.; Boeing Company; Disney Enterprises Inc.; McDonald's Corp.; United Parcel Service of America, Inc.; Waste Management, Inc.; Ford Motor Company; JPMorgan Chase & Co.; and Hyatt International Corp.

NEAL ▪ GERBER ▪ EISENBERG

# SCHIFF HARDIN LLP

## THE FIRM

**Managing Partner:** Ronald S Safer

**Number of partners worldwide:** 186
**Number of other lawyers worldwide:** 164

**FIRM OVERVIEW:** Schiff Hardin LLP, founded in 1864, is a general practice firm with local, regional, national, and international clients.

## MAIN AREAS OF PRACTICE:

**General Litigation:** The firm is especially active in the trial of complex matters before state and federal courts, as well as administrative agencies nationwide and abroad. Schiff Hardin's General Litigation Practice includes commercial disputes, product liability, class actions, securities, construction, labor and employment, antitrust and trade regulation, franchising, environmental and natural resources, bankruptcy and creditors' rights, real estate, energy, sports, government contracts, and white-collar criminal defense.

**Intellectual Property:** Schiff Hardin provides litigation, counseling, and transactional services involving patents, trademarks, trade dress, trade secrets, copyrights, software, computers, internet, electronic commerce, technology transfers, joint ventures, strategic alliances, licensing, technology protection programs, international technology applications, and federal and state regulations.

**Reinsurance/Insurance:** Schiff Hardin attorneys have decades of experience in reinsurance litigation. This includes scores of reinsurance arbitrations and lawsuits involving practically the entire scope of the insurance industry.

**Corporate & Securities:** Schiff Hardin represents a broad range of business organizations and individuals engaged in national, international, regional, and local business. Services involve corporate transactions of every variety, mergers and acquisitions, reorganizations, public and private offerings, private equity and venture capital, corporate governance, government contracts, and international business activities. Schiff Hardin's Corporate Practice also includes securities and futures market regulation, public law and public finance, financial institutions, taxation, employee benefits and executive compensation, telecommunications, energy and utilities, and sports and entertainment.

**Finance:** Schiff Hardin represents lenders, institutional investors, placement agents, borrowers, and lessors/lessees in various commercial and corporate debt financing contexts.

**Estate Planning & Administration:** Schiff Hardin has one of the most prominent Estate Planning and Administration Practices in the US. The firm's practice also includes trust and fiduciary litigation.

**Real Estate:** Schiff Hardin represents clients in the purchase, sale, leaseback, exchange, and leasing of commercial, office, retail, industrial, and residential properties, vacant land, and community investment and development. The firm also assists clients with construction, permanent, asset-based, and other complex types of financing.

**Construction:** Schiff Hardin has particular strengths in construction contracting, litigation, and alternative dispute resolution, including a focus on designer-led/design build construction and major energy project controls counseling.

**INTERNATIONAL WORK:** Schiff Hardin services international clients in all of its practice disciplines. Main international practice areas include general litigation, intellectual property, reinsurance, corporate and securities, mergers and acquisitions, finance, and financial institutions. Schiff Hardin is a member of two referral networks – TerraLex and the US Law Firm Group.

## HEAD OFFICE

**ILLINOIS**
6600 Sears Tower, **Chicago**, IL 60606
**Tel:** 312 258 5600   **Fax:** 312 258 5600
**Website:** www.schiffhardin.com

## BRANCH OFFICES

**GEORGIA**
One Atlantic Center, Suite 2300, 1201 West Peachtree Street
**Atlanta**, GA 30309
**Tel:** 404 437 7000   **Fax:** 404 437 7100

**ILLINOIS**
One Westminster Place, **Lake Forest**, IL 60045
**Tel:** 847 295 9200   **Fax:** 847 295 7810

**NEW YORK**
623 Fifth Avenue, **New York**, NY 10023
**Tel:** 212 753 5000   **Fax:** 212 753 5044

**DISTRICT OF COLUMBIA**
1101 Connecticut Avenue, NW, Suite 600, **Washington**, DC 20036
**Tel:** 202 778 6400   **Fax:** 202 778 6480

## INTERNATIONAL

The firm also has an office in Dublin, Ireland.

## CONTACTS

| | |
|---|---|
| **General Litigation** | Thomas B Quinn (Chicago) |
| **Intellectual Property** | Paula J Morency (Chicago) |
| **Product Liability** | Robert H Riley (Chicago/New York City) |
| **Class Actions** | Marci A Eisenstein (Chicago) |
| **Construction** | Mark C Friedlander (Chicago) |
| | Kenneth M Roberts (Chicago) |
| **Labor & Employment** | Max G Brittain, Jr (Chicago) |
| **Environmental** | Sheldon A Zabel (Chicago) |
| **Insurance/Reinsurance** | David M Spector (Chicago) |
| | Marci A Eisenstein (Chicago) |
| **Antitrust & Trade Regulation** | William M Hannay (Chicago) |
| **Bankruptcy** | J Mark Fisher (Chicago) |
| **White Collar Criminal Defense** | Ronald S Safer (Chicago) |
| **Corporate & Securities** | Stephen J Dragich (Chicago) |
| **Securities & Futures Regulation** | Howard Kramer (Washington ,DC) |
| **Finance** | Scott E Pickens (Chicago) |
| **Public Law & Public Finance** | Bruce P Weisenthal (Chicago) |
| | James M Kane (Chicago) |
| **Financial Institutions** | Christopher J Zinski (Chicago) |
| **Taxation** | Robert R Pluth, Jr (Chicago) |
| **Employee Benefits** | David H Williams (Atlanta) |
| | Edward Spacapan, Jr (Chicago) |
| **Energy/Utilities/Telecommunications** | |
| | Barbara K Heffernan (Washington, DC) |
| | Patricia Dondanville (Chicago) |
| **Government Contracts** | Garry S Grossman (Chicago) |
| **Estate Planning & Administration** | David R Hodgman (Chicago) |
| **Real Estate** | David A Grossberg (Chicago) |
| **International** | Robert S Appel (Chicago) |
| | Hans F Kaeser (New York City) |

# SEYFARTH SHAW LLP

## THE FIRM

**Managing Partner:** J Stephen Poor
**Number of partners:** 318
**Number of other lawyers:** 353

**FIRM OVERVIEW:** For over 60 years, Seyfarth Shaw LLP has represented clients throughout the United States and in every industry of the global economy. As a full service law firm with over 650 attorneys, Seyfarth Shaw's practice offerings, capabilities and geographic locations allow the firm to respond quickly and effectively to the critical legal and business issues clients face each day. Clients include companies in the financial, media, hospitality, insurance, manufacturing, professional services, retail, technology and telecommunications industries. The firm also represents a number of federal, state, and local governmental and educational entities.

## MAIN AREAS OF PRACTICE:

**Corporate & Securities:** Offering focused, sophisticated and efficient attention to client matters, delivered with the resources of a full service national practice, the firm's attorneys effectively blend broad knowledge of corporate law with extensive experience in key subdisciplines. Representing individuals, closely held companies, multinational corporations, investment companies, financial institutions, investment banking firms and others – on both sides of the dealmaking table – they understand the unique legal, regulatory, economic and competitive forces their clients face.

**Employee Benefits:** Through their consultative, business-oriented approach and efficient staffing, they can quickly respond to client needs in all areas of employee benefits and executive compensation law, including retirement plans, welfare benefit plans, retiree medical issues, deferred compensation, incentive arrangements and equity compensation, ESOPs, corporate transactions, restructurings and severance plans, multi-employer plans and employee benefits litigation.

**Labor & Employment:** With one of the largest national labor and employment practices, Seyfarth Shaw is able to offer its clients sophisticated global employment law solutions. Clients regularly seek the firm's counsel on workplace issues ranging from hiring, firing and disciplining employees, application of the ADA and FMLA, corporate reorganization and workforce reductions, traditional labor relations and union issues, business immigration, affirmative action and administrative agency and court litigation. The firm's attorneys have extensive experience defending class and collective action cases in jurisdictions across the country under wage and hour statutes, ERISA and practice suits brought by the EEOC. In addition, Seyfarth Shaw at Work, a subsidiary of the firm, is one of the nation's leading legal compliance and management training companies, providing highly engaging and interactive employment law related training over a variety of platforms.

**Commercial Litigation:** The firm offers a full service commercial and corporate litigation practice, and has particular experience in the following areas: bankruptcy, class action, construction, government contracts, trade secrets and unfair competition, intellectual property, product liability and securities. Many of the group's attorneys are recognized for their subject matter expertise in their respective practice areas, both locally and nationally.

**Real Estate:** Seyfarth Shaw provides comprehensive legal solutions for real estate companies, investors and organizations of all types for which real estate is an important asset in the course of their daily operations. Their clients include institutional lenders, real estate developers, management companies, privately held and public investors, government entities, not-for-profits, and those in the retail and shopping center industry.

**INTERNATIONAL WORK:** In addition to the extensive experience of the firm's attorneys in the international labor, employment and employee benefits practice – based throughout the US and in the firm's office in Brussels, Belgium – they have

## HEAD OFFICE

**ILLINOIS**
55 East Monroe Street
**Chicago**, IL 60603-5803
**Tel:** 312 346 8000   **Fax:** 312 269 8869
**Website:** www.seyfarth.com

**Effective September 1, 2006**
**New Address:**
131 S. Dearborn Street, Suite 2400
**Chicago**, IL 60603-5577

## BRANCH OFFICES

**CALIFORNIA**
One Century Plaza, 2029 Century Park East, Suite 3300
**Los Angeles**, CA 90067-3063
**Tel:** 310 277 7200   **Fax:** 301 201 5219

400 Capitol Mall, Suite 2350
**Sacramento**, CA 95814-4428
**Tel:** 916 448 0159   **Fax:** 916 558 4839

560 Mission Street, Suite 3100
**San Francisco**, CA 94105-2930
**Tel:** 415 397 2823   **Fax:** 415 397 8549

**DISTRICT OF COLUMBIA**
815 Connecticut Avenue, NW Suite 500
**Washington**, DC 20006-4004
**Tel:** 202 463 2400   **Fax:** 202 828 5393

**GEORGIA**
One Peachtree Pointe, 1545 Peachtree Street, NE, Suite 700
**Atlanta**, GA 30309-2401
**Tel:** 404 885 1500   **Fax:** 404 892 7056

**MASSACHUSETTS**
World Trade Center East, Two Seaport Lane, Suite 300
**Boston**, MA 02210-2028
**Tel:** 617 946 4800   **Fax:** 617 946 4801

**NEW YORK**
1270 Avenue of the Americas, Suite 2500
**New York**, NY 10020-1801
**Tel:** 212 218 5500   **Fax:** 212 218 5526

**TEXAS**
700 Louisiana Street, Suite 3700
**Houston**, TX 77002-2797
**Tel:** 713 225 2300   **Fax:** 713 225 2340

## INTERNATIONAL

The firm also has an office in Brussels, Belgium.

developed a seamless network of international contacts and resources. The cornerstone of these relationships is its membership in *ius laboris*, the International Employment Law, Pensions and Employee Benefits Alliance.

# SIDLEY AUSTIN LLP

## THE FIRM

**Chairman of Executive Committee:** Thomas A Cole
**Chairman of the Management Committee:** Charles W Douglas
**Vice-Chairman of Management Committee:** Theodore N Miller

**Number of partners:** 595
**Number of other lawyers:** 1,010

**FIRM OVERVIEW:** With over 1,600 lawyers and 15 offices in North America, Europe and Asia, Sidley Austin LLP is one of the world's largest law firms. Sidley combines experience, in-depth knowledge and quality to provide a broad range of legal services to meet the needs of its clients. Sidley's global network of offices provides integrated multi-jurisdictional and cross-jurisdictional legal services, while respecting local sensibilities. Sidley lawyers are able to work collaboratively to offer outstanding service to the firm's local, regional, national and international clients.

Sidley has a major capital markets practice and a broad transactional practice. Major practice disciplines include corporate and securities, mergers and acquisitions, securitization, intellectual property, funds and other pooled investments, bankruptcy and corporate reorganization, bank and commercial lending, public finance, real estate, project finance, tax and employee benefits, as well as trusts and estates.

Sidley offers clients extensive litigation experience in regulatory, trial and appellate matters spanning virtually every area of substantive law. Main practice areas include general and commercial litigation, regulatory and financial litigation, antitrust, white collar criminal defense, environmental, life sciences, patent and other intellectual property litigation, product liability and mass tort litigation, international commercial arbitration and dispute resolution, and international trade law.

The firm has been recognized by clients and by the media for leadership in its transactional, litigation and international practices. In 2005, the BTI Consulting Group named Sidley to its Client Service Hall of Fame as one of only two law firms to rank in its Client Service Top 10 for five years in a row. For the past four years, Thomson Financial has ranked Sidley in the top two for both issuer's counsel and underwriter's counsel in the US.

Over the past five years, the firm's recruitment and retention efforts have been both innovative and progressive, demonstrating a commitment to increasing the number of diverse lawyers in the firm. In recognition of a firmwide diversity initiative, Sidley received the 2005 Catalyst Award presented by Catalyst, the leading research and advisory organization dedicated to expanding opportunities for women and business.

Sidley has a long tradition of providing pro bono services. The firm's pro bono policy strongly encourages all lawyers to devote time to pro bono legal matters, including legal assistance to the poor and to charitable, community or other organizations that serve the indigent, who would otherwise be unable to afford legal representation. For example, in 2005, Sidley lawyers worked more than 50,000 hours on pro bono matters. In recognition of this work on behalf of homeless individuals and groups working to end homelessness, the firm received the 2004 Pro Bono Counsel Award from the National Law Center on Homelessness & Poverty.

**CLIENTS:** Sidley's strong, diverse client base includes Fortune 100 and 500 companies in a wide range of industries and business sectors, investment banks, commercial banks, public utilities, mutual funds, entrepreneurs and executives, insurance and financial institutions, professional firms, venture capital/private equity firms, partnerships, foundations, non-profit organizations, individuals and government agencies.

## US OFFICES

### CALIFORNIA
555 West Fifth Street, **Los Angeles**, CA 90013
**Tel:** 213 896 6000  **Fax:** 213 896 6600

555 California Street, **San Francisco**, CA 94104-1715
**Tel:** 415 772 1200  **Fax:** 415 772 7400

### DISTRICT OF COLUMBIA
1501 K Street, NW, **Washington**, DC 20005
**Tel:** 202 736 8000  **Fax:** 202 736 8711

### ILLINOIS
One South Dearborn Street, **Chicago**, IL 60603
**Tel:** 312 853 7000  **Fax:** 312 853 7036

### NEW YORK
787 Seventh Avenue, **New York**, NY 10019
**Tel:** 212 839 5300  **Fax:** 212 839 5599

### TEXAS
717 N Harwood, Suite 3400, **Dallas**, TX 75201
**Tel:** 214 981 3300  **Fax:** 214 981 3400

## INTERNATIONAL OFFICES

The firm also has offices in Beijing, Brussels, Frankfurt, Geneva, Hong Kong, London, Shanghai, Singapore and Tokyo.

**INTERNATIONAL WORK:** With one of the world's leading capital and financial market practices, Sidley represents sovereign and corporate securities issuers and borrowers, financial intermediaries, derivative parties, credit-enhancers and fiduciaries in structuring and developing innovative capital and financial products, and executes a broad range of capital and financial transactions involving Asia, America and Europe. Sidley also provides advice on local corporate and securities law and stock exchange listings for financial transactions involving US, English and Hong Kong law. Sidley has extensive experience in a broad range of debt and equity capital markets transactions, including SEC-registered as well as privately-placed offerings. Sidley lawyers have established impressive track records in handling IPOs with international placements, and listings on the New York Stock Exchange, NASDAQ, the Stock Exchange of Hong Kong, the London Stock Exchange, the Luxembourg Stock Exchange and, in conjunction with local advisers, the Jakarta, Korea and Singapore Stock Exchanges. The firm has been international counsel to the PRC Ministry of Finance since the PRC entered the international debt capital markets in 1994. Sidley's International Trade and Dispute Resolution group was recently recognized by *American Lawyer-Focus Europe* magazine. Additionally, its Global Securitization Practice received honors in 2005, on three continents, for its work on behalf of its international clients.

# SONNENSCHEIN NATH & ROSENTHAL LLP

## THE FIRM

**Chairman:** Duane C Quaini
**Number of partners:** 366
**Number of other lawyers:** 361

**FIRM OVERVIEW:** With some 700 attorneys in nine US offices and a global reach, Sonnenschein serves many of the world's largest and best-known businesses, nonprofits and individuals.

## MAIN AREAS OF PRACTICE:

**Antitrust, Marketing Practices & Franchising/Distribution:** Counsels and litigates on antitrust, distribution, licensing, franchise and dealer law, marketing, franchisee relations and supplier arrangements.

**Bankruptcy & Restructuring:** Represents official unsecured creditors, equity committees, Chapter 11 debtors/debtors-in-possession, insurers, indenture trustees, asset acquirers and secured creditors.

**Biotech/Life Sciences:** Counsels in scientific environment; backgrounds: genetics, organic chemistry, biochemistry, molecular and cellular biology.

**Asia Pacific:** Extensive understanding of US and Chinese laws/cultures; well positioned to advise US and European clients on business in China and Chinese enterprises on business in US.

**Communications & Media:** Advises on federal and state regulation, procurement, outsourcing of telecom/IT services; general counsel to public cable and broadcast TV companies; represents media, publishing, entertainment, sports firms and talent in IP litigation, securities, commercial matters, First Amendment cases, labor and employment.

**Corporate & Securities:** Advises on M&A; joint ventures, strategic alliances; technology investment; licensing; outsourcing; securities offerings and compliance; private equity transactions; commercial financing; corporate control, takeover defense; corporate governance.

**Corporate Diversity Counseling:** Assists organizations with demographic shifts in global marketplaces; diversity laws and regulations.

**Employee Benefits & Executive Compensation:** Negotiates executive agreements, change-in-control compensation strategies, equity plans. Counsels in developing, managing tax-qualified retirement plans, deferred compensation, welfare plans, HIPAA; class action defense of ERISA fiduciary, benefit claims.

**Environmental/Energy:** Counsels on avoiding/minimizing liability; litigates government, private-party suits; negotiates alternative agreements; develops plans for managing liability, facilitating new projects, product development, structuring, supporting management programs; develops energy policy and legislation.

**Government Regulation & Enforcement:** Counsels through government contracts process and regulatory bodies, especially in healthcare, before agencies such as the CPSC, FDA and FTC.

**Healthcare:** Extensive experience in healthcare law, including joint ventures, M&A, e-health, managed care transactions, healthcare financing and Medicare/Medicaid reimbursement.

**Information Security & Internet Enforcement:** Advises on safeguarding information, investigates and seeks redress for computer-based misconduct, including IP piracy, unsolicited commercial email, proprietary information theft; provides immediate legal response to unlawful Internet-based conduct.

**Insurance:** Counsels in crisis management, complex commercial litigation; provides legal solutions, including in major class actions, constitutional cases, coverage disputes, employment, regulatory and compliance matters.

**Intellectual Property & Technology:** Counsels, litigates on development, use, protection of IP; electronics, computers, telecommunications, aerospace, mechanical design, engineering arts, chemistry, pharmaceutical science, biotech; patent and trademark rights, applications and protections.

**International & International Trade:** Counsels on laws governing movement of goods, technology across borders. Advises on trade policy, customs regulation, export controls, enforcement, penalties, boycotts, sanctions, embargoes, import relief investigations, including antidumping, countervailing duty scope deter-

## OFFICES

**ILLINOIS**
7800 Sears Tower, 233 South Wacker Drive, **Chicago**, IL 60606-6404
**Tel:** 312 876 8000    **Fax:** 312 876 7934
**Website:** www.sonnenschein.com

**MISSOURI**
4520 Main Street, Suite 1100, **Kansas City**, MO 64111
**Tel:** 816 460 2400    **Fax:** 816 531 7545

One Metropolitan Square, Suite 3000, **St Louis**, MO 63102
**Tel:** 314 241 1800    **Fax:** 314 259 5959

**CALIFORNIA**
601 South Figueroa Street, Suite 1500, **Los Angeles**, CA 90017
**Tel:** 213 623 9300    **Fax:** 213 623 9924

685 Market Street, 6th Floor, **San Francisco**, CA 94105
**Tel:** 415 882 5000    **Fax:** 415 543 5472

**NEW YORK**
1221 Avenue of the Americas, **New York**, NY 10020
**Tel:** 212 768 6700    **Fax:** 212 768 6800

**NEW JERSEY**
101 JFK Parkway, **Short Hills**, NJ 07078
**Tel:** 973 912 7100    **Fax:** 973 912 7199

**DISTRICT OF COLUMBIA**
1301 K Street NW, Suite 600, East Tower, **Washington**, DC 20005
**Tel:** 202 408 6400    **Fax:** 202 408 6399

**FLORIDA**
Phillips Point, West Tower, 777 South Flagler Drive, Suite 1102
**West Palm Beach**, FL 33401
**Tel:** 561 833 2410    **Fax:** 561 833 8387

minations, unfair trade practices; develops export/import management systems and internal controls.

**Labor & Employment:** Counsels on compliance issues, including training, internal investigations; representation in single employee litigation, arbitrations, administrative investigations, class actions, corporate transactions, including M&A and downsizings.

**Litigation & Business Regulation:** Services encompass class action defense, insurance, white collar crime, product liability, IP, technology, real estate, construction, financial transactions, securities, antitrust, franchising, distribution and government contracts.

**Public Law & Policy Strategies:** Focuses on issues, strategies before Congress, Executive Branch, national policymakers, state legislators and regulators; assists in direct advocacy, budget, appropriations, grass-roots communications, marketing, crisis management, coalition and partnership development and international government relations.

**Real Estate:** Advises in complex multi-state purchases, dispositions; constructions; financing; equity investment; commercial, multifamily development; leasing; affordable housing; hotels and hospitality.

**Taxation:** Structures, advises on corporate acquisitions, dispositions involving US and non-US entities, financing techniques, US and non-US planning for USMNCs, partnerships, other joint ventures, real estate, foreign transactions; exempt organizations and tax litigation controversies.

**Training Solutions:** Develops, implements compliance and training programs for *Fortune* 500 companies, government agencies, small businesses, nonprofits.

**Trusts & Estates:** Counsels wealthy individuals on tax, estate planning, related litigation; administers estates, trusts and fiduciary accountings.

**Venture Technology:** Represents emerging growth, *Fortune* 500 clients; counsels management and boards; robust relationships with investment banks and VC firms on the West and East coasts.

# VEDDER, PRICE, KAUFMAN & KAMMHOLZ, P.C.

## THE FIRM

**Chairman:** Robert J Stucker
**President:** Michael A Nemeroff
**Managing Shareholder:** Douglas M Hambleton
**Managing Director:** Bruce E Brown

**Number of Attorneys:** 225

**FIRM OVERVIEW:** Established in 1952, Vedder Price is a general practice law firm best viewed in terms of three core areas of client service: Corporate Services (Jonathan H Bogaard); Labor and Employment Services (Bruce R Alper); and Litigation Services (James S Montana, Jr). Within each of these core service areas are a number of significant boutique practices whose reputations are national and even international in scope. Within the corporate area, for instance, the firm enjoys a world-class reputation in important areas of practice including asset-based finance; banking; executive compensation; investment services (mutual funds); and aircraft and equipment finance.

## MAIN AREAS OF PRACTICE:

**Finance & Transactions:** Michael Nemeroff, President of Vedder Price, chairs the firm's Finance and Transactions Practice, which is comprised of more than 60 attorneys who concentrate in M&A, corporate finance, corporate reorganization, securities and general corporate reorganization. The members of this team counsel and advise the buyers and sellers of businesses, emerging growth and technology companies, financiers and lenders, venture capital and equity funds and investment banks and corporate issuers on a broad range of corporate transactions.

**Equipment & Structured Finance:** Jon Bogaard, Dean Gerber and Ron Scheinberg lead a team of more than 35 structured finance specialists who are consistently ranked among the top aircraft finance and maritime lawyers in the world. This group represents lessees, lessors, financiers, and related parties – both domestic and international – in a broad range of equipment finance transactions, including those involving aircraft, railcars, vessels and marine terminals, computers, industrial equipment, satellites, cars and trucks.

**Investment Services:** Cathy O'Kelly and David Sturms direct 25 attorneys in the firm's Investment Services Practice. This group represents some of the world's largest mutual funds, their managers and boards of directors. The group also represents the leading trade organization for the mutual fund industry, as well as leading investment advisers and broker-dealers.

**Financial Institutions:** The firm and its Financial Institutions Group, headed by Jim Kane, was named as one of the top ten banking firms in the nation by the editors of Bank Director magazine. The group is comprised of more than 20 professionals and represents public and private financial institutions ranging in size from de novo banks to those with more than $500 billion in assets.

**Labor & Employment:** In the area of labor and employment, Vedder Price is recognized as one of the premier law firms in the nation, representing public and private sector management clients in all areas of labor and employment law. The firm's practice is national in scope, combining both counseling and litigation. Integrated with the Labor and Employment Practice is the firm's Employee Benefits Group led by Paul Russell, Chuck Wolf, Tom Desmond and Phil Mowery. Members of this group are responsible for the design, implementation and legal compliance of profit-sharing, pension, welfare and executive compensation programs of all types. In the area of executive compensation, Bob Stucker, Chairman of Vedder Price, heads a 15-person team of lawyers who advise the world's leading companies, compensation committees and executives in analyzing, negotiating and documenting employment and compensation agreements for senior executives.

## OFFICES

The firm has offices in Chicago, New York and New Jersey.

**Website:** www.vedderprice.com

## CONTACTS

| | |
|---|---|
| Bankruptcy & Insolvency | Douglas J Lipke |
| Banking | James M Kane |
| Construction | Karen P Layng |
| Employee Benefits | Philip Mowery |
| Employment & Labor | Bruce Alper |
| Equipment Finance | Dean Gerber |
| | Ron Scheinberg |
| Estate Planning | Igor Potym |
| Executive Compensation | Robert J Stucker |
| Health Law | Richard H Sanders |
| Intellectual Property | Angelo Bufalino |
| International | Gabrielle Buckley |
| Investment Services | David Sturms |
| Litigation | James S Montana |
| M&A & Finance | Michael Nemeroff |
| Real Estate | Pearl Zager |
| Taxation | Daniel Sherlock |
| Trade & Professional Associations | Michael Reed |

**Litigation:** The firm's litigation attorneys are responsible for handling client matters in trial and appellate courts, before administrative agencies, and in arbitration and comparable alternative dispute resolution contexts. Trial attorneys work closely with fellow Vedder Price attorneys in various substantive legal areas. While the general philosophy is toward minimal staffing at levels necessary to achieve effective and efficient results, the Litigation Practice area has the resources to staff the most complex litigation matters and has substantial experience in trying lengthy, multiparty cases involving computerized depositions, massive document management and sophisticated discovery and trial techniques. Within the Litigation Practice, there are a number of industry-specific practice areas for which the firm is well known. These include Accounting Law, chaired by Dan Goldwasser in the firm's New York office and the Construction Law Group, chaired by Karen P Layng in Chicago. The firm's Accounting Law Practice Group represents more than 100 accounting firms in professional liability matters. Members of the firm's Construction Law Group provide a complete range of services to the construction industry including the negotiation of contract documents and the representation of contractors in breach of contract, fraud, errors and omissions, delay damage and mechanics liens claims.

# VEDDER PRICE

# WINSTON & STRAWN LLP

## THE FIRM

**Managing Partner:** James M Neis (until Aug 2006)
Thomas P Fitzgerald (from Aug 2006)
**Senior Partner:** James R Thompson (Chairman)
Paul Hensel (Administrative Partner)

**Number of partners in US:** 362
**Number of other lawyers in US:** 448
**Number of lawyers worldwide:** 861

**FIRM OVERVIEW:** Founded in 1853. One of the oldest and largest US law firms with more than 850 attorneys in Chicago; New York; Washington, DC; Los Angeles; San Francisco; Paris, France; London, England; Geneva, Switzerland; and Moscow, Russia.

## MAIN AREAS OF PRACTICE:

**Litigation:** Winston & Strawn's litigators are consistently entrusted with some of corporate America's highest stakes litigation, and they have tried major jury and bench trials in virtually every significant federal and state venue. They handle appeals and critical motions before the United States Supreme Court, the US Court of Appeals, and numerous state appellate courts. Winston also has an active International Arbitration Practice before the ICC, ICSID, UNCITRAL, AAA, and other arbitral institutions. Substantive areas of litigation work include: antitrust, trade regulation, and unfair competition; construction, technology, and other contractual disputes; class actions; internal investigations and white-collar criminal defense; patent/trademark/copyright infringement; securities; product liability; employment and ERISA; environmental; tax controversy; and professional liability.

**Corporate & Financial:** The Corporate and Financial Practice Group provides a range of transaction-related legal services to enterprises of all types and sizes. Corporate attorneys advise on mergers and acquisitions, securities transactions and regulation, corporate governance, commercial lending, private equity, leasing, asset securitization, project finance, public finance, financial services regulatory, and bankruptcy, workout, and financial restructuring.

**Labor & Employment Relations:** The firm counsels major employers and a variety of closely held business enterprises on labor and employment relations programs and policies, as well as employment, labor, and ERISA litigation in state and federal courts throughout the country. It also represents clients before federal, state, and local administrative agencies, including the EEOC and the NLRB.

**Real Estate:** Real estate attorneys counsel all types of sophisticated real estate market participants in the acquisition, financing, sale, development, and leasing of commercial, industrial, and multifamily properties.

**Intellectual Property:** IP lawyers provide general IP counseling; litigation throughout the United States and before the US Patent and Trademark Office and the Federal Circuit Court of Appeals; management of trademark, patent, and copyright portfolios; and patent, trademark, and copyright prosecution and licensing.

**Tax:** The Tax Practice assists in virtually every area of corporate tax law, from planning through audit as well as appeals and litigation. Its transactional attorneys are known for innovation in domestic and cross-border structured finance transactions, particularly in leasing and asset securitization. Tax controversy attorneys represent clients in judicial and administrative proceedings at both the state and federal levels.

**Governmental Relations & Regulatory Affairs:** Led by former four-term Illinois governor James R Thompson, this group includes attorneys and advisors who have held major positions with national trade associations, congressional committees, and congressional leaders. Work includes legislative and regulatory representation, counseling and bill analysis, congressional lobbying, executive branch advocacy on policy questions, legislative drafting, and preparation and presentation of congressional testimony.

## HEAD OFFICE

**ILLINOIS**
35 West Wacker Drive, **Chicago** IL 60601
**Tel:** 312 558 5600   **Fax:** 312 558 5700
**Email:** info@winston.com
**Website:** www.winston.com

## OTHER OFFICES

**CALIFORNIA**
333 South Grand Avenue, **Los Angeles** CA 90071
**Tel:** 213 615 1700   **Fax:** 213 615 1750

101 California Street, **San Francisco** CA 94111
**Tel:** 415 591 1000   **Fax:** 415 591 1400

**DISTRICT OF COLUMBIA**
1700 K Street, N.W., **Washington**, DC 20006
**Tel:** 202 282 5000   **Fax:** 202 282 5100

**NEW YORK**
200 Park Avenue, **New York** NY 10166
**Tel:** 212 294 6700   **Fax:** 212 294 4700

## CONTACTS

| | |
|---|---|
| **Litigation** | Thomas J Frederick |
| **Corporate & Financial** | Steven J Gavin |
| **Labor & Employment Relations** | Rex L Sessions |
| **Real Estate** | Corey A Tessler |
| **Intellectual Property** | Stephen P Durchslag, Virginia R Richard |
| **Tax** | Robert F Denvir |
| **Governmental Relations & Regulatory Affairs** | James R Thompson |
| **Energy** | James R Curtiss |
| **Environmental** | Jennifer T Nijman, William N Hall |
| **Employee Benefits & Executive Compensation** | Michael S Melbinger |
| **Healthcare/Maritime & Admiralty** | Thomas L Mills |
| **Trusts & Estates** | Christine A Albright |

**Energy:** This practice ranks among the largest in the nation, representing entities engaged in all aspects of the energy industry, including production, transmission, and distribution of electricity and natural gas.

**Environmental:** This practice encompasses all aspects of environmental law, including litigation matters, corporate transactions, and regulatory issues. The Paris practice includes regulatory, transactional, and litigation aspects of environmental law of the European Community.

**Employee Benefits & Executive Compensation:** The firm advises on issues regarding compensation of employees and the planning and administration of employee benefits. It also assists in the design and drafting of all forms of executive compensation plans.

**CLIENTS:** Significant relationships with companies including Abbott Laboratories, American Airlines, AON Corporation, Barr Laboratories, Deutsche Bank AG, Exelon Corporation, J.P. Morgan Chase, Lear Corporation, McDonald's Corporation, Microsoft Corporation, Morgan Stanley, Motorola, Inc., PPG Industries, Philip Morris USA Inc., Salomon Smith Barney, and Smurfit-Stone Container.

**INTERNATIONAL WORK:** Clients include: Albemarle Corporation, Alstom Group, Bavaria International Aircraft Leasing Group, Deutsche Bank AG, FAGE Dairy Industry SA, Fleet Bank, N.A., Foot Locker France, Francaise des Jeux SA, General Electric Capital Corporation, IPOC International Growth Fund Limited, NKAZ, Pentair, Inc., Phillip Morris USA, Rhodia, Soitec SA, Veolia Proprete.

## How lawyers are ranked

Every year we carry out thousands of in-depth interviews with clients and lawyers in order to assess the reputations and expertise of business lawyers across the USA. Chambers rankings and editorial are referred to extensively by General Counsel and other purchasers of legal services who look to our recommendations when choosing their lawyers.

# CORPORATE/M&A

### Corporate/M&A
#### Leading Firms

1. **BAKER & DANIELS** *Indianapolis*
   **BARNES & THORNBURG** *Indianapolis*
   **ICE MILLER LLP** *Indianapolis*
2. **SOMMER BARNARD PC** *Indianapolis*
3. **BOSE MCKINNEY & EVANS LLP** *Indianapolis*
   **KRIEG DEVAULT LLP** *Indianapolis*

#### Leading Individuals

1. **ASCHLEMAN James** *Baker & Daniels*
   **HUMKE Steven** *Ice Miller LLP*
   **STRAIN James** *Sommer Barnard PC*
   **WORRELL David** *Baker & Daniels*
2. **BOEGLIN Daniel** *Baker & Daniels*
   **BRIDGE Catherine** *Barnes & Thornburg*
   **BROWN J Jeffrey** *Baker & Daniels*
   **HACKMAN Stephen** *Ice Miller LLP*
   **HICKS Robert** *Sommer Barnard PC*
   **MILLARD David** *Barnes & Thornburg*
   **SWHIER Claudia** *Barnes & Thornburg*
   **THORNBURGH John** *Ice Miller LLP*
   **THRAPP Richard** *Ice Miller LLP*
3. **BUTCHER David** *Bose McKinney*
   **CROSS Patrick** *Baker & Daniels*
   **DENSBORN Donald** *Sommer Barnard PC*
   **GREISING Robert** *Krieg DeVault*

#### Up-and-coming individuals

**CARUSO II Ralph** *Sommer Barnard PC*
**LONG Christine** *Baker & Daniels*
**MILLIKAN Michael** *Ice Miller LLP*
**SHARROW Regina** *Sommer Barnard PC*

## Band 1

### Baker & Daniels
See firm details p.902

**The Firm:** An increase in the capital available for acquisitions and investments in the Indiana market has caused an upsurge in M&A and financing work for this "*wonderful, diverse law firm.*" Clients agree: "*There is no better operation in Indianapolis*" for M&A when it comes to delivering "*value for money,*" and it enjoys a tremendously loyal following as a result. The firm is the market leader in fund formation and has been putting together a series of hedge funds for Oxford Financial Group, raising approximately $149 million over two years. It was also significantly involved in the merger of Anthem with WellPoint Health Networks, which led to the formation of a health benefits company serving the needs of approximately 28 million medical members nationwide. In both areas of work, clients give this firm an "*A-plus.*" As one interviewee remarked: "*I feel comfortable that we're getting better legal advice than anyone else.*"

**The Lawyers:** "*I would go to him first for anything to do with securities or corporate,*" said one client of the "*tremendous*" **Jim Aschleman** (see p.894), a view that echoes his burgeoning popularity in the marketplace. He goes beyond the call of duty with "*unbelievable, proactive customer care,*" and is credited with a "*practical, common-sense approach.*" He represented Priority Healthcare in Florida in its $1.3 billion sale to Express Scripts. **David Worrell**'s (see p.901) "*outstanding*" abilities win him promotion to the top tier this year. His 25 years of experience and "*exceptional*" quality of service impressed peers and clients alike. Researchers were also told that he had a "*unique ability to make you feel like the only client he's working for.*" He acts for a number of public companies based in Indiana, and represented the Simon Property Group in 144A offerings to the tune of $1 billion in June 2005. The "*cerebral*" **Dan Boeglin** (see p.894) has a well-deserved reputation as "*one of the best corporate lawyers in town.*" One client enthused: "*You can trust him 100% to look after your interests; in fact you can trust him even more than you trust yourself!*" His practice centers on the life sciences industry, particularly the field of proteomics, where he is engaged in collaborative transactions for the commercialization and development of research technologies. He also represents Zimmer, a leading manufacturer of orthopedic products, in an array of strategic partnering transactions. The "*great and creative*" **Jeff Brown** (see p.895) heads the firm's private capital and venture group. Lauded as "*the best lawyer I've ever seen,*" interviewees admire his "*driven, East Coast approach*" and describe how he will "*work through the night*" to close a transaction. He completed the formation of various private investment funds lately, including the $4 million Indiana Seed Fund managed by Indiana's life sciences consortium BioCrossroads. As well as venturing into the life sciences field, **Pat Cross** (see p.895) continues to specialize in healthcare. He assisted Clarian Health Partners in the creation of several hospital joint ventures involving complex corporate, securities and regulatory issues. Clients like his "*client-friendly, well-informed*" approach and "*superb, diplomatic negotiation skills.*" Clients find partner **Christine Long** (see p.897) "*unbelievably knowledgeable*" and "*very accessible.*" She focuses on general corporate and securities law, and assists clients on corporate governance matters, including compliance with the Sarbanes-Oxley Act.

**Clients/Work Highlights:** The Indiana Proteomics Consortium; Indiana Centers for Applied Protein Sciences; Priority Healthcare; Great Lakes Chemical; Steak n Shake; Quality Dining; Patton Fund Management; Triton Pacific Investment Management; American Commercial Lines; WellPoint; ITT Educational Services; Shoe Carnival; Kimball International and Eli Lilly.

### Barnes & Thornburg
See firm details p.903

**The Firm:** This firm has been "*running away from its peers in the market*" and duly joins the top tier. Clients are impressed with the quality of work here and "*would recommend the firm to anyone!*" The past year has seen an increase in its M&A workload, which comprised more than 200 acquisitions for high-profile consumer brands such as BISSELL, Woolite, Ford Motor Credit and Hat World. It has an outstanding securities practice and currently dominates the market for bank mergers. This last point is reflected in the firm's representation of City Holding Company – a $2.2 billion bank holding company based in Charleston, West Virginia – in its $77.4 million acquisition of Classic Bancshares. Members of the firm also advise an increasing number of publicly traded companies on compliance issues stemming from Sarbanes-Oxley legislation. Other innovative matters where the firm was involved include a reverse/forward stock split for Northeast Indiana Bancorp.

**The Lawyers:** **Cathy Bridge** (see p.895) and **Claudia Swhier** (see p.899) form the upper echelon of lawyers at the firm and both generate an "*exquisite*" work product." The "first-rate" Cathy Bridge chairs the business, tax and real estate department and in 2005 acted for engineering group Tomkins in its acquisition of Milcor and LE Technologies. Swhier is perceived as a market-leading securities lawyer who concentrates on M&A transactions involving financial institutions. Clients appreciate her "knowledge and thoroughness" coupled with a "100% business approach." "Client magnet" **David Millard** (see p.898) is promoted in the table and chairs the firm's entrepreneurial services group. He focuses on smaller, emerging growth companies and peers regard him as "having made a valuable contribution to advancing the interests of the business community in this state." He was further described as a wonderful lawyer and "tireless worker" who "lives and breathes" his vocation.

**Clients/Work Highlights:** Indiana Secondary Market for Education Loans; Union Community Bancorp; NorthWest Indiana Bancorp; LSB Financial; Vectren and DowAgro Sciences.

## Ice Miller LLP

See firm details p.904

**The Firm:** Market opinion places the "excellent" Ice Miller firmly in the first tier. It is distinguished by its heavy workload and ability to handle large, complex cases. The outfit commands client loyalty because of its "24/7 response rate" and ability to understand clients' business needs: "The approach was very professional and focused on the issues that were key to getting the deal done," reported one client. During the past year, the firm has closed numerous private equity transactions, representing both investors and the target companies.

**The Lawyers:** Clients see **Steven Humke** (see p.896) as the "go-to guy" for all corporate issues. He is a "successful, efficient negotiator who instinctively takes the best path to closing a transaction." He has won "a boatload of business" for the firm, including representing Baker Hill – one of the largest IT firms in Carmel, Indiana – in its acquisition by California-based information services provider Experian, a subsidiary of GUS. Venture capital expert **John Thornburgh** (see p.899) is a "superlative lawyer," who is constantly in demand. As well as chairing the private equity and venture capital group, he chairs the firm's sports and entertainment law practice. Peers admire his "brilliant" navigation of complex cases. Meanwhile, clients enthuse over the "wonderful" **Richard Thrapp** (see p.900), and as one stated: "I would give him a call anytime – he really is amazing." Peers were impressed above all by his intellect, and he represents midsized public companies on transactions throughout Indiana and the Midwest. He was also lead counsel in the sale of Fastec Industrial – a company engaged in the distribution of products such as fasteners and screws worldwide –

to Wesco. Thrapp cochairs the firm's corporate/M&A group with **Stephen Hackman** (see p.896), a "shining star" of M&A and securities work. Clients describe Hackman as a "business-oriented practitioner whose approach combines just the right quantities of innovation and common sense." One client said: "I've worked with a lot of attorneys and he is one of the best." He has had an active year, which included completing a public offering for the reorganized super alloy manufacturer Haynes International, as well as a number of acquisitions for ADESA, the second largest automobile redistribution company in the USA. **Michael Millikan** (see p.898) enters the tables as a "strong" up-and-comer who provides his clients with "excellent customer service." He was active in the firm's representation of Reynolds in its sale to Layne Christensen, a public Kansas-based company.

**Clients/Work Highlights:** Monument Capital Partners; hhgregg; ADESA; Cook Group; Haynes International; Lumina Foundation for Education; Citizens Gas & Coke Utility; Wal-Mart; Morgan Foods and The Indiana Rail Road Company.

## Band 2

### Sommer Barnard PC

See firm details p.906

**The Firm:** Clients say of this firm: "All of its lawyers are excellent." The legal work they produce is "consistently of a superior quality and timely too." The business law group concentrates on transactions involving midmarket companies and is famed for acting on behalf of an Indiana-based private equity fund. It is involved in a growing number of acquisitions and is increasingly snapping at the heels of the top three firms in the state. Highlights of the year have involved the acquisition of companies throughout the USA for a healthcare management firm and representing the acquirers and developers of a historic hotel and casino project.

**The Lawyers:** **Jim Strain** (see p.899) and **Bob Hicks** (see p.896) "lead the charge" at this firm in terms of corporate/M&A work. Peers admire the "excellent" Jim Strain for his "intellectual strength" and "sophisticated advice." Nationally renowned as an expert in public company and corporate governance work, he worked on the restructuring of commercial vehicle manufacturer Utilimaster. Clients like what "straight-shooting" Bob Hicks has to offer and are impressed by the results he achieves. His "understanding of clients' objectives" earns him praise as a "motivated, aggressive deal-maker" with a "brilliant and creative mind." "One of the leading acquisition lawyers around," **Donald Densborn** (see p.895) is admired by market commentators for his "pragmatic and efficient approach, excellent negotiating skills and

high integrity." He is actively involved in advising start-up companies, including one in the ethanol industry. Advising hi-tech companies on finance matters is another of his fortes. Of the firm's younger lawyers moving up through the ranks, **Ralph Caruso** (see p.895) works side by side with Bob Hicks and won praise from peers for his involvement in high-profile M&A transactions. Peers also respect **Regina Sharrow** (see p.899) for her M&A and securities law practice.

**Clients/Work Highlights:** Utilimaster; Vectren; Hammond Kennedy Whitney; Maxon Corporation; Reinhold Industries; Cook Group and Standard Management.

## Band 3

### Bose McKinney & Evans LLP

**The Firm:** The firm is credited with a heavy transactional diet and several promising young lawyers who may emerge as the "stars" of the future. The business services group has grown, picking up several lawyers following the dissolution of Henderson Daily Withrow & DeVoe.

**The Lawyers:** Chair of both the business services and financial institutions groups, peers recognize **David Butcher** as a "fine banking lawyer," as well as a leader in M&A. He acts for the largest locally controlled bank, First Indiana Bank.

**Clients/Work Highlights:** The firm represents financial institutions and a variety of businesses, including First Indiana Bank and media company Emmis Communications.

### Krieg DeVault LLP

**The Firm:** With "one of the strongest securities teams in town," this firm attracts its fair share of "sophisticated deals" and a broad range of clients to boot. It has represented financial institutions for many years and clients hold its leading lending practice in high regard. Clients are also impressed by the firm's wealth of corporate experience.

**The Lawyers:** Interviewees describe **Bob Greising** as a "terrific lawyer," who is "detail-oriented and great to work with." He represented United Student Aid Funds – a student loan guarantor – in the takeover of a loan association, and acted for Bridgestone/Firestone in its acquisition of Copper Sales.

**Clients/Work Highlights:** First Indiana Bank; Old National Bancorp; First Merchant Bank; Fifth Third Bank; United Student Aid Funds; Bridgestone/Firestone; Sisters of St Francis Health Services; Rolls-Royce and Chromcraft Revington.

# EMPLOYMENT

## MAINLY DEFENDANT

## Band 1

### Baker & Daniels

See firm details p.902

**The Firm:** This large labor and employment practice provides "*excellent advice and great representation*." Billed as a "*well-run and responsive organization*," it inspires loyalty nationwide, as clients feel confident that the firm is on the cutting edge when it comes to the latest developments in the field. The team's recent focus on client development has been rewarded with a growth in work for both existing and new clients. Indeed, the firm acts for entities from states such as Texas, Michigan and Georgia. It has also witnessed a large increase in employment law litigation, while its level of involvement in traditional union work remains constant. Healthcare sector matters further occupy the firm, especially where nursing homes are concerned, and the team represents one of the nation's top five healthcare companies on union avoidance work throughout the USA.

**The Lawyers:** Peers "*think the world*" of **David Miller** (see p.898), who is considered "*a wonderful communicator*" and, according to some, "*far and away the best in the state*." He was heavily involved in strategic planning and union management issues for regional and national clients, including Tenneco Automotive, a \$3.5 billion global manufacturing company based in Lake Forest, Illinois. This has incorporated issues such as collective bargaining and strikes. With 30 years' experience, this year **Greg Utken** (see p.900) is promoted to tier one. Clients

describe him as a "*fantastic individual*" who has "*done a tremendous job*" for them, while peers "*would not hesitate to hire him personally*." The "*absolutely wonderful*" **John Neighbours** (see p.898) is "*a pleasure to work with*" and has a formidable reputation, both in and out of the Hoosier State. He successfully secured multiple labor agreements in the USA on behalf of a Canadian company for which he acted as chief spokesperson in collective bargaining negotiations. Head of the firm's employment litigation group, **Ellen Boshkoff** (see p.894) is renowned nationwide for speaking on employment law issues. Her recent highlights include successfully defending a New York investment banking company against a multimillion-dollar promissory estoppel claim. **Todd Nierman** (see p.898) focuses on obligations faced by employers under the NLRA, the FLSA and equal employment opportunity legislation. He is the coauthor of a specialist employment handbook for Indiana. At time of going to press, Todd announced his intention to join Littler Mendelson in Chicago.

**Clients/Work Highlights:** Children's Courtyard; Knowledge World Learning Centers; Pearson Education; Indiana University; hhgregg; Roll Coater; Cognis; ArvinMeritor; BorgWarner; EaglePicher Automotive; City of Indianapolis; Emmis Communications; Extendicare; Guidant; MasterBrand Cabinets; Ryder Logistics; Superior Essex; Eli Lilly and Zimmer.

### Barnes & Thornburg

See firm details p.903

**The Firm:** Clients describe this "*excellent*" team as "*practical, thorough and very effective*." The group has been asked to assist the US Chamber of Commerce and a consortium of employers with amending ADA guidelines, which necessarily involves a great deal of collaboration with the firm's Washington, DC office. The workload has been punctuated by four favorable decisions from the Seventh Circuit Court of Appeals through the year, including those involving the FMLA and the Worker Adjustment and Retraining Notification Act (WARN). Its continued expansion most recently involved two new lawyers joining the Grand Rapids office in Michigan.

**The Lawyers:** The firm's labor and employment group centers on its chairman **Ken Yerkes** (see p.901), a lawyer of impressive stature, not to mention "*extremely smart, creative and hard-working*." One interviewee said of him: "*He is one of the finest employment lawyers I have ever met*." Yerkes recently completed a series of contract negotiations in several different states, focusing on employee cost-sharing and insurance. **Doug Heckler** (see p.896) rises in the rankings having made a significant impact on the market with his experience in the labor litigation arena. His "*intuitive feel for the subtlest legal nuances*" and "*impressive client list*" means he is held in particularly high regard. Heckler has also negotiated successor contracts throughout the USA.

**Clients/Work Highlights:** Wal-Mart; Georgia-Pacific; Johnson & Johnson; Finish Line; Roche

Diagnostics; WellPoint; Bristol-Myers Squibb; Indianapolis Power & Light and Hillenbrand Industries.

### Ice Miller LLP

See firm details p.904

**The Firm:** Clients appreciate the "*diligence*" shown by this firm in "finding solutions" to any potential labor issues that need remedying. Peers say it is "*probably the best in the state*" for construction sector issues. The firm recently negotiated a labor agreement for the construction of the Indianapolis Colts football stadium in downtown Indianapolis, and it continues to advise the Canadian-based multinational Court Holdings on labor law matters across the USA.

**The Lawyers:** The "*outstanding*" **Samuel Born** (see p.894) is admired by peers for being "*smart and practical*," while his "*thoroughness, attention to detail*" and 35 years of experience inspire client loyalty. He is involved in industrial labor union negotiations and has been busy drawing up large contracts, each involving between 400 and 600 employees. Clients value **Michael Boldt** (see p.894) for his "*creativity in understanding the business side of a collective agreement*." He is described as a "*great business man*," who will "*dot every 'i'*" and is "*exceptionally articulate*." He is renowned for his expertise in the construction industry and the majority of his work involves collective bargaining and arbitration work for manufacturing clients. Peers respect **Martin Klaper** (see p.897) for "*representing some of the best clients in Indiana*," and he is active in advising the State of Indiana on HR matters.

**Clients/Work Highlights:** Court Holdings; Visteon Systems; Eli Lilly; Emmis Communications; Brightpoint; ITT Educational Services; Coachmen Industries; Citizens Gas and Coke Utility; Chemtura; McDonald's; Butler University; Taylor University and Indiana University.

### Ogletree, Deakins, Nash, Smoak & Stewart, PC

See firm details p.738

**The Firm:** This dedicated national labor and employment law firm retains its status as a top-tier player in Indiana. Clients discern an "*outstanding operation that consistently provides quality representation*," and "*wouldn't hesitate to recommend its lawyers*." The firm's network of offices is expanding rapidly throughout the USA, and the Indianapolis office can call on an army of 300 experts for support as required. Over the past year, the number of attorneys in Indiana has more than doubled, a development fueled in part by an increase in class action activity. The group has also won new clients, including a large national retailer with more than 500 outlets.

**The Lawyers:** Managing stockholder **Kim Ebert** (see p.895) is highly respected in his field as a "*top-notch lawyer*." He "*engages with his client as a partner, listens, appreciates business realities and helps the client realize business goals at the same time as providing thorough and reasonable advice*." He has recently led several successful campaigns to prevent union formation for a variety of clients, including for a Japanese company. **Charles Baldwin** (see p.894) is a successful litigator with a substantial client list, and described by clients as "*thorough and professional.*" He handles depositions around the USA, with a recent focus on Ohio, and is experienced in acting against national counsel in employment litigation cases. **Brian McDermott** (see p.897) is one of the firm's younger lawyers, who clients say does a "*quality job.*" He has represented and provided advice to public and private employers on a variety of labor and employment issues.

**Clients/Work Highlights:** Federal Home Loan Bank; Hillenbrand Industries; Clarian Health; Kraft;

Kroger; National Wine & Spirits; BMG Columbia House and BAA Indianapolis.

## Band 2

### Bose McKinney & Evans LLP

**The Firm:** Its small labor and employment group has a reputation for providing clients with an excellent service. The team has been successful in defeating union organization efforts for large businesses and runs in-house workshops for both public and private companies interested in recent legal developments. The group also defends management in employment litigation cases.

**The Lawyers:** Group chair **David Swider** is a "*strong labor lawyer*" with a firm reputation in employment law, including discrimination and affirmative action matters. **Daniel Emerson** is highly respected by peers and renowned for his work with UPS and the Indianapolis Colts. He has extensive experience of trade secret matters and represents employers throughout the USA on labor and employment issues.

**Clients/Work Highlights:** Eli Lilly; WellPoint; Thomson; UPS; Pfizer; Coca-Cola; National City Bank and the Indianapolis Colts.

# LITIGATION

| Litigation: General Commercial |
|---|
| **Leading Firms** |
| [1] **BAKER & DANIELS** *Indianapolis* |
| **BARNES & THORNBURG** *Indianapolis* |
| [2] **BINGHAM MCHALE LLP** *Indianapolis* |
| **ICE MILLER LLP** *Indianapolis* |
| **MCTURNAN & TURNER** *Indianapolis* |
| **SOMMER BARNARD PC** *Indianapolis* |
| [3] **BOSE MCKINNEY & EVANS LLP** *Indianapolis* |
| **LOCKE REYNOLDS LLP** *Indianapolis* |

| Leading Individuals |
|---|
| ★ **FICKLE** Stanley *Barnes & Thornburg* |
| [1] **CAMPBELL** David *Bingham McHale LLP* |
| **ELBERGER** Ronald *Bose McKinney & Evans LLP* |
| **MCTURNAN** Lee *McTurnan & Turner* |
| **SCANLON** Chris *Baker & Daniels* |
| **TITTLE** David *Bingham McHale LLP* |
| **WHISTLER** Philip *Ice Miller LLP* |
| **YEAGER** Jay *Baker & Daniels* |
| [2] **BROWN** Alan *Locke Reynolds LLP* |
| **DEPREZ** Anne *Barnes & Thornburg* |
| **HARRIS** Edward *Sommer Barnard PC* |
| **HERZOG** David *Baker & Daniels* |
| **MACGILL** Robert *Barnes & Thornburg* |
| **MITCHELL** Marvin *Mitchell Hurst Jacobs* |
| **PENCE** Linda *Sommer Barnard PC* |
| **SHOCKLEY** Steven *Sommer Barnard PC* |
| **STANLEY** Robert *Baker & Daniels* |
| **TURNER** Wayne *McTurnan & Turner* |
| [3] **BENNETT** Jackie *Sommer Barnard PC* |
| **DETHERAGE** Andrew *Barnes & Thornburg* |
| **HOKANSON** Jeffrey *Ice Miller LLP* |
| **KASPER** David *Locke Reynolds LLP* |
| **WELCH** Brian *Bingham McHale LLP* |
| **WILKINS** Michael *Ice Miller LLP* |

## Band 1

### Baker & Daniels

See firm details p.902

**The Firm:** With the strength and depth to tackle just about any type of civil litigation, the firm's "*organized and confident*" team has attracted a loyal client following and will do "*everything possible to keep the pressure on*" in the courtroom. Clients describe its litigators as "*wonderfully talented.*" The practice comprises five discrete units, including the "*excellent*" IP litigation group, enabling specialists to respond effectively to clients' needs. The firm has seen a significant increase in bankruptcy litigation and has been involved in some of the state's most high-profile cases, including representing barge operator American Commercial Lines in a US Bankruptcy Court. Overseas highlights include several class action victories in the Indian Supreme Court.

**The Lawyers:** Baker & Daniels is renowned for being home to the best litigators in Indiana. Securities expert **Chris Scanlon** (see p.899) has a "*first-rate*" reputation and is admired for being "*intelligent, aggressive and thoughtful.*" Clients place absolute trust in **Jay Yeager** (see p.901), who has an "*incredible presence in the courtroom and really takes the client's cause to heart.*" He represents businesses and individuals in a wide variety of lawsuits and arbitrations. Head of business litigation **Bob Stanley** (see p.899) is an "*impressive commercial litigator.*" He defended PSI Energy, an electric utility owned by Cinergy, in a case that led to a change in the law relating to premises liability for asbestos exposure. **David Herzog** (see p.896) moves up the table and does a "*marvelous job*" for clients. Peers hold this "*thorough, engaging, aggressive and creative*" lawyer in extremely high regard. After returning from his position as executive vice president and general counsel at Conseco, he has rebuilt an impressive practice and won a sophisticated client base. Clients described head of IP litigation **Nancy Tinsley** (see p.900) as "*a great personality, very intelligent and highly ethical.*" She has been involved in a patent case concerning electronic catalogs in Texas, which featured famous brands

such as AOL, Amazon.com, Sears, Lands' End, Victoria's Secret, eBay and IBM as defendants. **David Irmscher** (see p.897) has devoted much of his time to settling IP cases involving financial transaction software in San Francisco, Los Angeles and Texas.

**Clients/Work Highlights:** Medco Health Solutions; Kerasotes Theatres; Guidance Corporation; ATA Airlines; GM and WellPoint.

### Barnes & Thornburg

See firm details p.903

**The Firm:** "*High-quality*" lawyers and "*competitive and fair*" prices make this firm a favorite among clients. One of the largest firms in Indiana, it provides a full range of litigation services at both trial and appellate levels. It has particularly strong expertise in IP and securities. In 2005, the firm formed a new nonlegal subsidiary, ThemeVision LLC, a trial consulting firm that offers jury research and advocacy analysis services to law firms and litigants throughout the USA.

**The Lawyers:** **Stan Fickle** (see p.896) is hugely in demand as an appellate lawyer of national renown at the pinnacle of his career. This "*terrific*" attorney inspires awe in his peers, who "*can say with confidence he's a wonderful scholar.*" **Anne DePrez** (see p.895) is one "*real smart*" lawyer, and "*among the top*" securities litigators in the state. Acting for broker-dealers and investment managers in connection with customer disputes forms the bulk of her workload. **Rob MacGill**'s (see p.897) practice covers the gamut of commercial litigation. He is famed for being "*extremely aggressive, as well as highly organized and effective,*" and turns over a large volume of work. **Andrew Detherage** (see p.895) has advised numerous clients on insurance coverage issues and enjoys a fine reputation among peers. Billed as a "*clear, critical thinker*" and "*splendid writer,*" **Don Knebel** (see p.897) is considered the state's leading IP litigator. He has represented the likes of Eli Lilly and Dow Agro-Sciences in patent infringement cases, and is supported by a team of junior lawyers who clients appreciate for being able to "*carry out helpful analysis without getting bogged down in unnecessary detail.*"

Clients/Work Highlights: Dow AgroSciences; Beazer Homes; DePuy Orthopaedics; Georgia-Pacific; Dow Chemical; 3M; Whirlpool and Eli Lilly.

## Band 2

### Bingham McHale LLP

The Firm: This "*fantastic, timely and thorough*" business litigation group acts for clients in state and federal courts throughout the USA, and represents businesses and individuals as both defendants and plaintiffs. It is particularly well regarded for its insurance defense practice, which has a track record stretching back over 75 years. With many "*technically excellent, strong performers,*" this operation is perceived as a force to be reckoned with in Indiana.

The Lawyers: **David Campbell** has concentrated on general corporate litigation and professional liability defense of late. Clients say he "*sees the issues and resolves them; he always has the right answer.*" He represented clients in several cases involving trust administration and fiduciary duties. The "*tremendously experienced, thoughtful and thorough*" **David Tittle** joins the ranks of Indiana's top advocates, and is praised as an "*energetic, well-rounded practitioner.*" Chair of business litigation **Brian Welch** sustains a wide-ranging practice and recently advised on matters relating to the export of military technology.

Clients/Work Highlights: Saint-Gobain; Thomson; National City Bank of Indiana; Gatorade Trust; Indiana Horse Racing Commission and Xerox.

### Ice Miller LLP

See firm details p.904

The Firm: A deep bench of "*quality*" lawyers, who are "*willing, able and effective*" when it comes to negotiating, sustains the litigation practice at Ice Miller. A wide range of cases is handled, with an increasing emphasis on IP litigation. The firm prides itself in helping clients to avoid court action and has successfully resolved a raft of arbitration proceedings involving more than 100 claims against Merrill Lynch, of which only 20 ended up in court. The team is also extremely active in representing pharmaceutical and medical device companies on both a national and regional basis.

The Lawyers: "*Outstanding legal strategist*" **Philip Whistler** (see p.900) took a lead role in the series of Merrill Lynch cases, as well as acting for DuPont in

asbestos litigation in Indiana. **Jeffrey Hokanson** (see p.896) focuses on bankruptcy litigation, where he acts for both creditors and debtors, while **Michael Wilkins** (see p.900) is a "*first-rate*" lawyer who peers regard highly for his technical abilities. In addition to settling cases for DIRECTV, he has an enviable appellate practice.

Clients/Work Highlights: Wyeth; Eli Lilly; St Jude Medical; Emerson Electric; Procter & Gamble; Merrill Lynch and Indianapolis Motor Speedway.

### McTurnan & Turner

See firm details p.905

The Firm: This "*excellent boutique*" specializes exclusively in litigation. The lawyers have "*sparkling resumes*" and are involved in complex litigation matters for high-profile clients. Highlights include defending global sonic innovator Onkyo against fraudulent transfer and negligent representation claims in Michigan and Florida courts. The team is also acting as defense counsel for GM in an action over alleged injuries and cleanup costs relating to alleged PCB contamination in soil and groundwater near a plant in Bedford, Indiana.

The Lawyers: **Lee McTurnan** (see p.898) comes highly recommended as a "*wonderful attorney,*" and one who interviewees would expect to make most shortlists drawn up by large companies requiring a litigator in the state. Fellow name partner **Wayne Turner** (see p.900) is praised as a "*talented, thorough lawyer who has a broad range of experience.*" The firm also benefits from having a number of "*energized, assertive and smart*" younger lawyers in its ranks who "*appear to love what they do.*"

Clients/Work Highlights: Indianapolis Life; SBC; PwC; Salomon Smith Barney; CitiFinancial; ProLiance Energy; Wachovia; Earlham College; DIRECTV and McGraw-Hill.

### Sommer Barnard PC

See firm details p.906

The Firm: The firm has an "*excellent reputation*" for litigation and a particularly strong class action practice. The group is also involved in the antitrust, securities, environmental and real estate arenas, where its lawyers appear in actions throughout the USA.

The Lawyers: **Ed Harris** (see p.896) inspires admiration among peers as a "*bright, thorough, engaging and creative practitioner.*" He acts for both plaintiffs and defendants in antitrust cases and has represented several large corporations across a variety of industries in class actions. **Linda Pence** (see p.898) is an acknowledged leader in terms of general commercial litigation and criminal white-collar defense. **Steve Shockley** (see p.899) is both a "*tremendous advocate*" and a "*true lawyer's lawyer,*" who is "*extremely thorough*" in his work. Peers admire him for his impressive skills as a "*thinker and writer.*" **Jackie Bennett**

(see p.894) is building a reputation as "*one of the leading business litigators in town.*" Like Pence, he covers both general commercial litigation and criminal white-collar defense.

Clients/Work Highlights: The team represents publicly traded companies, including those in the healthcare and manufacturing sectors.

## Band 3

### Bose McKinney & Evans LLP

The Firm: Its notable depth of experience in complex litigation matters makes this firm an important player in the market. In addition to four existing offices in the state, it is planning to open a new branch in the Purdue Research Park, West Lafayette, in order to expand its IP services.

The Lawyers: The "*top-notch*" **Ron Elberger** was described as a "*charming and passionate advocate, who wholeheartedly fights for his client's best interests – whatever he's working on becomes the most important thing in the world to him.*" His is an expansive practice but, above all, Elberger stands out as the state's premier lawyer for defending other attorneys in professional malpractice suits.

Clients/Work Highlights: Emmis Communications; Emmis Publishing; Chip Ganassi Racing Teams and SABCO Racing.

### Locke Reynolds LLP

The Firm: This well-established litigation practice has an especially good reputation for products liability and asbestos litigation, as well as insurance defense. Midsized commercial disputes remain the order of the day, with appellate, business and torts groups all continuing to win their fair share of cases.

The Lawyers: Peers admire the all-around strength of the lawyers hired by this firm. Both **Alan Brown** and **David Kasper** are highly respected in the market. Observers reserved special praise for Kasper's "*ability to find practical solutions.*"

Clients/Work Highlights: Citizens Insurance, Phoenix Aviation and Utica National Insurance Group feature on the firm's list of clients.

### Other Notable Practitioners

**Marvin Mitchell** at Mitchell Hurst Jacobs & Dick is "*the kind of person you could turn an important matter over to and be confident that he'd do a super job.*" His practice centers on business and real estate litigation. **Spiro Bereveskos** at Woodard, Emhardt, Naughton, Moriarty, McNett & Henry has a fine reputation for his IP litigation practice and is praised for his "*aggressive and colorful*" approach.

# REAL ESTATE

## Band 1

### Baker & Daniels
See firm details p.902

**The Firm:** This "*excellent practice*" has a number of "*top-quality*" attorneys and is promoted to the top tier, in the context of which some interviewees consider it as being first among equals. The team has been heavily involved in M&A transactions, especially on behalf of Max convenience stores, a client it has represented in acquiring numerous gas stations. On the development side, residential and mixed-use developments have come to the fore, including the conversion of the Athletic Club into condominiums in downtown Indianapolis. The firm is also counsel to Indiana's capital improvement board, and in a separate instance it advised on the construction of a $500 million stadium project for the Indianapolis Colts.

**The Lawyers:** Chairman of the real estate and land use team **Joe Scimia** (see p.899) is famed for his zoning work and is highly respected by peers. "*Phenomenal lawyer*" **Mary Lisher** (see p.897) continues to work on projects for Eli Lilly and Clarion Health Partners, assisting the former with acquisitions and advising both on leasing matters. The team also has several younger lawyers who are beginning to make their mark.

**Clients/Work Highlights:** The Sterling Group; Browning Investments; Hearthview Residential; Equity Investment Group; Zimmer; Paragon Properties; Andy Mohr Automotive; UBS Realty Investors and the City of Indianapolis.

### Barnes & Thornburg
See firm details p.903

**The Firm:** The true forte of this firm's "*high-caliber*" team is real estate finance, according to sources. In this respect, the group has a truly nationwide appeal and services a large base of banking clients. The Indianapolis office has closed loans in 32 different states throughout the past year. Further highlights include extensive involvement in a 1,700-acre mixed-use development in northwest Indianapolis. Clients value highly the team's negotiating skills, the "*clear and reasonable*" advice it provides and its "*accommodating*" approach. The "*cooperative, thorough and responsive*" approach of the team members supporting the firm's lead lawyers received further praise.

**The Lawyers:** One of the younger top-tier practitioners, **David Warshauer** (see p.900) has amassed a great deal of experience relatively early on in his career, and clients are impressed by the "*team spirit*" that he fosters. He acted for Beazer Homes on a variety of developments, litigation and zoning work relating to one of Noblesville's largest real estate projects. The "*well-rounded*" **Richard Johnson** (see p.897) is increasingly involved in out-of-state matters. Highlights include acting for a syndicate of banks in financing a $220 million shopping center in Kansas City. Viewed by peers and clients alike as "*bright and thorough*," **Stephen Lee** (see p.897) provides a level of service that inspires great confidence in his clients. He has been working on the development of condominiums and multifamily residential projects in Indianapolis, Ohio and North Carolina. **Dennis Johnson** (see p.897) boasts a wealth of real estate experience. He represented a national lender on two syndicated loan transactions for regional shopping centers in Indiana and Pennsylvania, and acts for financial clients in Chicago, Cleveland and New England. Newly ranked up-and-comer **John Baxter** (see p.894) has made waves with his real estate lending work. He closed several loans for high-profile projects, including one involving the Conrad Indianapolis hotel. Clients describe him as a "*brilliant supporting attorney*" but are also confident that he can handle transactions single-handedly.

**Clients/Work Highlights:** Hokanson Companies; Flaherty & Collins Properties; KeyBank National Association; Zeta Tau Alpha National; National City

Bank of Indiana; Martin Marietta Materials; Eli Lilly; Georgia-Pacific and Whirlpool.

### Ice Miller LLP
See firm details p.904

**The Firm:** An "*outstanding*" group of lawyers and an extensive client list that includes some of the most active real estate developers in Indiana and across the USA make this firm a definite leader in the field. It is representing the stadium authority in the land acquisition and development of the new Indianapolis Colts stadium – a project worth in excess of $500 million. The team also acted for the Lauth Group in a multimillion-dollar joint venture with the Cook Group concerning the development of the French Lick Springs Resort & Casino.

**The Lawyers:** Market leaders **Phillip Bayt** (see p.894) and **Zeff Weiss** (see p.900) are admired as "*incredibly bright, sophisticated lawyers who understand the real estate business.*" Managing partner Phillip Bayt took a lead role in the development of the luxury Conrad Indianapolis, due for completion in March 2006, and advised on the conversion of two factory buildings into condominium lofts. Meanwhile, Zeff Weiss represents some of the firm's most significant clients on large development projects. He has handed over the chair of the real estate group to Sarah Funke.

**Clients/Work Highlights:** Kite Realty Group; HDG Mansur Capital Group; Pulte Homes; Whiteco Industries; Blue Sky Casino and the City of Indianapolis.

## Band 2

### Bose McKinney & Evans LLP

**The Firm:** Market commentators hold this "*super*" real estate practice in high regard and reserve special praise for its "*fine young lawyers.*" The team can provide clients with full support both locally and nationally, and recently received a boost following the recruitment of lawyers from leading firm Ice Miller.

**The Lawyers:** "*Hugely experienced zoning lawyer*" **Phil Nicely** makes the top tier for the first time, and his "*reputation for getting things done*" together with his "*practical*" approach means he is much in demand. **Jim Carlino** stands out for his extensive experience, which covers secured lending, construction and environmental law. Clients particularly appreciate "*the way he puts things down on paper and makes things easy to understand from a layman's standpoint.*" Peers "*think very highly*" of **Angela Tempel**, formerly of Ice Miller, and describe her as "*hard-working, knowledgeable and easy to work with.*"

**Clients/Work Highlights:** Skinner & Broadbent; New Boston Fund; Maefield Development and BP America.

## Wallack Somers & Haas PC
See firm details p.75284

**The Firm:** This dedicated real estate boutique continues to rival and share clients with some of Indiana's larger firms. The team provides a hands-on service to entrepreneurial clients, including developers and lenders. Clients say they *"wouldn't hesitate to recommend"* this firm and are impressed by its *"immediate responses"* and ability to *"get all the people to the table."*

**The Lawyers:** The firm boasts a triumvirate of top tier practitioners. **Karl Haas** (see p.896) has a superb reputation and a flourishing practice that covers acquisitions as well as development, leasing and financing matters. His colleague **George Somers** (see p.899) has led the charge in a variety of public-private redevelopments. Clients appreciate receiving the *"undivided attention"* of the *"insightful"* **Barry Wallack** (see p.900), who was described as *"a great facilitator and negotiator, with a real knack for direct communication."* Among other projects, Wallack advised on the formation of shopping centers in Indiana and Illinois. Recent recruits of note include Mark Boos from Baker & Daniels and William Carson, who was previously recognized in *Chambers* as a leader in real estate in Memphis, Tennessee.

**Clients/Work Highlights:** Republic Services; City of Carmel, Indiana; Fifth Third Bank; Kite Realty Group Trust and REI Investments.

## Band 3

### Bingham McHale LLP

**The Firm:** The real estate group at Bingham McHale has grown significantly during recent years and has made lateral hires from several Indiana law firms. The team won a number of new clients this year, including Duke Realty. It covers all services relating to real estate law and is particularly well renowned for its construction expertise.

**The Lawyers:** The *"well-connected"* **Mary Solada** anchors the firm's real estate practice and has represented Gershman Brown & Associates in a joint venture with Simon Property Group for the development of a lifestyle center in Noblesville. She also serves as outside general counsel to the Capital Improvement Board of Marion County, the public entity that owns and operates public property. This recently involved advising the board on negotiations

with the State of Indiana and the Indianapolis Colts relating to the development of a new downtown stadium. *"Impressive"* up-and-comer **Steve Hardin** *"has done a good job of carving out a zoning practice"* in Indiana and has impressed clients with his *"excellent negotiating style."* He is active in Hamilton County and represented a number of residential developers, including KB Home and M/I Homes, seeking land use approvals.

**Clients/Work Highlights:** Bremner Healthcare; Davies Homes; First Industrial Realty Trust; Sun Development & Management and Thomson Consumer Electronics.

### Dann Pecar Newman & Kleiman, PC

**The Firm:** Clients admire the *"technically fine lawyers"* who make up this firm's team. The number of practitioners involved now stands at ten, and the firm has sufficient resources to assist substantial developer clients. In this respect, the retail sector has been a focus area for recent work. Acting for banks also accounts for a significant part of the firm's practice, while with regard to out-of-state matters, there has been an emphasis on projects taking place in Texas.

**The Lawyers:** Peers admire **Jeff Abrams** for his strong real estate practice, and while he remains an acknowledged leader in the field, he also devotes portions of his time to corporate and specialized alcohol beverage law issues. Highlights for Abrams include working on leases for a 300,000 sq ft retail center. **Jim Schwarz** is praised for being exceptionally capable and offers a particular depth of experience where retail sector developments are concerned.

**Clients/Work Highlights:** Mann Properties; Simon Property Group; First Indiana Bank; Muncie Housing Authority; Emmis Communications; Sunbeam Development; Equicor Companies; Colliers Turley Martin Tucker and OB Development Services.

### Wooden & McLaughlin LLP
See firm details p.908

**The Firm:** This real estate group moves up the table in recognition of its depth of experience, representation of significant clients, and peers' admiration for its *"knowledgeable and accomplished practitioners."* The team is extremely active on behalf of developers and also represents lenders.

**The Lawyers:** Interviewees agree that **Tom Dinwiddie** (see p.895) has *"been through every kind*

*of deal there is"* and uses his *"creative and practical"* approach to good effect. He frequently applies his impressive negotiating skills to real estate finance and development matters. Peers also enjoy working with **John Hamilton** (see p.896), who advises several institutional investors and private developers.

**Clients/Work Highlights:** Skinner & Broadbent; Indiana University; Indianapolis Neighborhood Housing Partnership and Lauth Property Group.

## Band 4

### Sommer Barnard PC
See firm details p.906

**The Firm:** In September 2005, the firm brought in a small group of lawyers who specialize in putting together conservancy districts, providing the resources to continue serving existing clients while at the same time attracting new ones. The operation has also expanded its zoning and land use practices. The firm continues to represent one of the major retail developers in Indianapolis and is involved in the acquisition and development of regional shopping centers.

**The Lawyers:** **Erick Ponader** (see p.899) assisted CFC, a real estate development and management company, with land and facilities acquisitions for the casino project in French Lick, Indiana. Clients describe his work as *"outstanding"* and are impressed by his skill at working on complex transactions.

**Clients/Work Highlights:** CFC; Skinner & Broadbent; Gateway Shoppes and Cook Group.

### Other Notable Practitioners

**Rory O'Bryan** of Harrison & Moberly LLP moves up to the top tier of real estate lawyers in Indiana. Interviewees describe him as a *"smart, practical, knowledgeable and experienced practitioner,"* with an *"impressive demeanor"* and a reputation as an academic. The Fort Wayne-based **Jack Lawson** of Beckman Lawson, LLP is one of Indiana's leading zoning lawyers. He is renowned for speaking at the Indiana State Bar Association's legal seminars and is hired by clients throughout the state who *"seek out Jack for his expertise."* The *"smart"* **Barbara Wolenty** of Robinson Wolenty & Young, LLP acts for a broad range of clients and is renowned for her no-nonsense approach to work.

# Leaders in Indiana

**ABRAMS, Jeffrey**
Dann Pecar Newman & Kleiman, PC,
Indianapolis 317 632 3232
*Recommended in Real Estate*

**ASCHLEMAN, James A**
Baker & Daniels, Indianapolis
317 569 4883
jim.aschleman@bakerd.com
*Recommended in Corporate/M&A*
**Practice Areas:** Jim Aschleman has represented various issuers (corporations, real estate investment trusts, master limited partnerships, and investment companies) in public offerings of debt and equity securities. He has extensive experience in securities laws aspects of demutualizations of insurance companies, including federal and state securities laws exemptions for the conversion and representation in the initial public offerings and other capital raising transactions. Jim also has extensive experience representing large and small public and private companies in mergers, acquisitions, and stock or asset sales, including 'squeeze out' mergers, tender offers, and leveraged buyouts. In addition to representing special committees of the Board of Directors of public companies in internal investigations and in management leveraged buyouts, Jim also represents public companies in their disclosure and reporting obligations.
**Prof. Memberships:** Indianapolis, Indiana State, and American Bar Associations. Fellow, Indiana Bar Foundation.
**Personal:** Manchester College, BA, summa cum laude, 1966; Harvard University, JD, 1969. Recognized in Chambers USA 2003, 2004, 2005 and 2006 editions, Corporate/M&A; named member of The BTI Client Service All-Star Team for Law Firms, 2005; Voted one of 'Top 50 Indiana SuperLawyers', 2004 and 2005; voted best corporate and best securities lawyer in Indianapolis, 1993.

**BALDWIN, Charles B**
Ogletree, Deakins, Nash, Smoak & Stewart, PC, Indianapolis 317 916 1300
charles.baldwin@ogletreedeakins.com
*Recommended in Employment*
**Practice Areas:** Employment law, labor law, litigation.
**Prof. Memberships:** Board of Directors, Indiana Chamber of Commerce; US Chamber of Commerce Labor Relations Committee.
**Career:** Admitted in Indiana; Ohio; various US District Courts and US Courts of Appeals. Selected as Counsel for Amici Curiae 7th Circuit Court of Appeals concerning case of 1st impression under ADA. Selected as an 'Indiana Super Lawyer' (2004-06).
**Publications:** Contributing author, ABA's 'Model Jury Instructions-Employ-

ment Litigation'; Seventh Circuit editor, ABA's Employment & Labor Relations Litigation Newsletter; co-author, 'Indiana Guide to Preventing Workplace Harassment'.
**Personal:** Valparaiso University (BS, 1980), University of Dayton (JD, 1983).

**BAXTER, John B**
Barnes & Thornburg LLP, Indianapolis
317 231 7533
john.baxter@BTLaw.com
*Recommended in Real Estate*
**Practice Areas:** Commercial real estate; leases and leasing; real estate banking law; represents construction and permanent real estate lenders, commercial real estate developers, developers of multi-family and single-family residential projects, and single-family residential builders.
**Prof. Memberships:** Indianapolis, Indiana, and American Bar Associations.
**Career:** Admitted to practice in the state of Indiana.
**Personal:** Miami University (BA, 1994); Indiana University (JD, cum laude, 1997).

**BAYT, Phillip**
Ice Miller LLP, Indianapolis
317 236 2396
phillip.bayt@icemiller.com
*Recommended in Real Estate*
**Practice Areas:** Mr Bayt is a Managing Partner of Ice Miller with a primary practice concentration in real estate law. He assists clients in finance, development, real estate taxes, workouts and foreclosures, mineral law, construction law, leasing and gaming. Mr Bayt is a Member of the Board of Directors for the Greater Indianapolis Chamber of Commerce, the Indy Partnership and the Greater Indianapolis Progress Committee.
**Prof. Memberships:** Member of the American College of Real Estate Lawyers, the Indianapolis Bar Association, the Indiana State Bar Association, and past Chairman of the board of the Near North Development Corporation.

**BENNETT, Jackie**
Sommer Barnard PC, Indianapolis
317 713 3500
jbennett@sommerbarnard.com
*Recommended in Litigation*
**Practice Areas:** Member of Sommer Barnard's Litigation Department. Represents corporate and individual clients in grand jury and regulatory investigations, criminal trials, internal investigations, and civil litigation in state and federal courts.
**Prof. Memberships:** Indianapolis, Indiana State, American and Seventh Circuit Bar Associations; Indianapolis Law Club.
**Career:** Admitted to Indiana Bar (1983). Served as Assistant US Attorney for the Southern District of Indiana from 1985 to 1988. From 1988 to 1995, was Trial

Attorney and Senior Trial Attorney in the Public Integrity Section of the Justice Department's Criminal Division in Washington, DC. Served from 1995 to 1999 as Associate Counsel and principal Deputy to Independent Counsel Kenneth W Starr in the Whitewater Investigation. Recipient of the Attorney General's John Marshall Award 'For Outstanding Legal Achievement' in 1994.
**Personal:** Received a BA from Hanover College (1980) and JD from Indiana University School of Law (1983). Was Note and Development editor of the Indiana Law Review, 1982-83.

**BEREVESKOS, Spiro**
Woodard, Emhardt, Naughton, Moriarty & McNett, Indianapolis 317 634 3456
*Recommended in Litigation*

**BOEGLIN, Daniel L**
Baker & Daniels, Indianapolis
317 569 4644
dan.boeglin@bakerd.com
*Recommended in Corporate/M&A*
**Practice Areas:** Dan Boeglin assists clients in the life sciences industry with the formation of strategic alliances and joint ventures, including research and development collaborations, licensing transactions, commercialization and distribution arrangements, and similar matters. His experience includes development and commercialization of drugs, tissues, biologics, medical devices, surgical techniques and research tools. He completed the Biotechnology for Business program at Duke University in 2004. He has been lead counsel in the formation of numerous multi-party joint ventures in fields such as proteomics research, health informatics and protein analysis. Having started his career in the firm's Corporate Finance and M&A practices, Dan also brings that background and experience to clients engaged in capital formation and acquisition transactions. He is Chair of the firm's Business Department, which encompasses all of the Business, Finance, Commercial and Transactional Practice Groups and includes approximately half of the firm's professionals.
**Personal:** Indiana University, BS in Accounting, with highest distinction, 1982; University of Virginia, JD, 1985. Recognized in three leading legal publications, including 'America's Leading Business Lawyers' and 'The Best Lawyers in America'.

**BOLDT, Michael**
Ice Miller LLP, Indianapolis
317 236 2327
michael.boldt@icemiller.com
*Recommended in Employment*
**Practice Areas:** Representing employers

regarding employment issues generally, with extensive experience concerning collective bargaining, arbitration, union organizing drives, construction labor law, and equal employment opportunity law.
**Prof. Memberships:** Member: Indianapolis, Indiana and American Bar Associations. Member, Board of Directors: Brooke's Place for Grieving Young People, Inc.; Highland Golf & Country Club. Recognized in 'Who's Who in American Law' and 'The Best Lawyers in America'.
**Publications:** Author of numerous employment related articles/books on collective bargaining and construction labor law. Faculty member for numerous labor-management and collective bargaining seminars for national organizations.
**Personal:** Wayne State University (BA), University of Michigan (JD).

**BORN II, Samuel**
Ice Miller LLP, Indianapolis
317 236 2305
born@icemiller.com
*Recommended in Employment*
**Practice Areas:** Represents management in labor relations including labor litigation, arbitration and negotiations. He advises employers in arbitration proceedings before the NLRB and the EEOC. Recently, he negotiated a collective bargaining agreement in a 600 person bargaining unit. Mr Born is a certified civil mediator.
**Prof. Memberships:** Past President of the Indiana State Bar Association (1997-98) and the Indianapolis Bar Association. Member: the American Bar Association House of Delegates; US Chamber of Commerce employer labor relations and OSHA committees.
**Publications:** Author of Indiana OSHA 'Guidebook For Employers' (5th ed., 2004).

**BOSHKOFF, Ellen**
Baker & Daniels, Indianapolis
317 237 1266
ellen.boshkoff@bakerd.com
*Recommended in Employment*
**Practice Areas:** Ellen Boshkoff leads the firm's Employment Litigation Practice Group which currently consists of 14 members. For well over a decade, she has represented employers exclusively (both public and private) and has defended and tried employment cases in federal and state courts. Her experience includes defending class actions and wage/hour collective actions. Ellen's depth of experience, focus, and tenacity allow her to bring practical strategies and desired results to clients. She has been recognized by businesses and peers as one of the 'go to' lawyers in her field. She also regularly

makes presentation to businesses, organizations and fellow lawyers on employment law issues and litigation.

**Prof. Memberships:** Indianapolis, Indiana State, and American Bar Associations.

**Publications:** Chapter editor, 'Employment Law Handbook: A Business Guide to Indiana and Federal Discrimination Laws', 5th Edition (2005); co-author, 'Survey of Employment Law Developments for Indiana Practitioners, 36 Ind L Rev 1035 (2003); co-author, Survey of Employment Law Developments for Indiana Practitioners', 35 Ind L Rev 1369 (2002).

**Personal:** Swarthmore College, BA, with high honors, 1983; Indiana University School of Law, JD, summa cum laude, 1990. Recognized in Chambers USA 2005 and 2006 editions.

### BRIDGE, Catherine
Barnes & Thornburg LLP, Indianapolis
317 231 7255
catherine.bridge@BTLaw.com
*Recommended in Corporate/M&A*

**Practice Areas:** Mergers, acquisitions and divestitures; securities, initial public offerings; corporate law; corporate finance; insurance regulation; represents clients in insurance regulatory and other matters including incorporation, licensing, changes in control, and redomestications, as well as reinsurance and formation of captive insurance companies.

**Prof. Memberships:** American Bar Association and its Committee on Negotiated Acquisitions and Committee on Federal Regulation of Securities.

**Career:** Admitted to practice in Indiana and the US District Court for the Southern District of Indiana.

**Personal:** Fordham University (AB, 1972); Columbia University (JD, 1975).

### BROWN, Alan
Locke Reynolds LLP, Indianapolis
317 237 3800
*Recommended in Litigation*

### BROWN, J Jeffrey
Baker & Daniels, Indianapolis
317 569 4613
jeff.brown@bakerd.com
*Recommended in Corporate/M&A*

**Practice Areas:** Jeff Brown is a member of the firm's Private Capital Group. He has a diverse practice that is principally devoted to financing and acquisition transactions. He commonly represents corporate issuers in connection with securities offerings, acquisitions and corporate governance matters, and represents both financial investors and management participants in venture capital transactions, leveraged buy-outs, recapitalizations and other complex transactions. He represents a number of investment advisers, broker-dealers and other financial institutions in connection with the structuring and offering of various

investment vehicles, including private investment funds, mutual funds and asset-backed securities. He also represents investment banks generally, both in connection with their own legal needs and as counsel to underwriters in securities offerings and financial advisors in acquisitions of private and publicly held companies. While his practice is largely devoted to financing and acquisition transactions, Jeff also represents a number of private companies on a day to day basis in all aspects of their business law needs.

**Personal:** Indiana University, BA, 1982; Georgetown University, MBA, 1984; University of Virginia, JD, 1987. Recognized in Chambers USA 2005 and 2006 editions.

### BUTCHER, David
Bose McKinney & Evans LLP, Indianapolis 317 684 5000
*Recommended in Corporate/M&A*

### CAMPBELL, David
Bingham McHale LLP, Indianapolis
317 635 8900
*Recommended in Litigation*

### CARLINO, James
Bose McKinney & Evans LLP, Indianapolis 317 684 5000
*Recommended in Real Estate*

### CARUSO II, Ralph A
Sommer Barnard PC, Indianapolis
317 713 3500
rcaruso@sommerbarnard.com
*Recommended in Corporate/M&A*

**Practice Areas:** Member of the Business Practice Group, focusing on mergers and acquisitions, joint ventures, and related financing transactions; significant experience in private equity and gaming transactions.

**Prof. Memberships:** Indianapolis and Indiana State Bar Associations.

**Career:** Admitted to Indiana Bar (1994).

**Personal:** University of Notre Dame, JD, 1994; LeMoyne College, BS, magna cum laude, 1991.

### CROSS, Patrick
Baker & Daniels, Indianapolis
317 569 4844
patrick.cross@bakerd.com
*Recommended in Corporate/M&A*

**Practice Areas:** Pat Cross leads the firm's Life Sciences Practice. He advises life sciences, healthcare and technology clients on mergers, acquisitions, joint ventures, research and development collaborations, technology transfer and licensing issues, and corporate governance, regulatory and compliance matters. He counsels pharmaceutical and medical device companies on structuring strategic alliances and related licensing arrangements. He recently advised Indiana's largest healthcare system on the creation and funding of three physician joint ventures to develop and operate three new acute care hospitals. Pat served as

counsel to a joint venture organized by some of Indiana's leading public and private healthcare institutions to develop and operate a groundbreaking regional health information exchange. Pat also regularly counsels BioCrossroads, a non-profit organization focused on the life sciences economy in Indiana.

**Prof. Memberships:** Indianapolis and Indiana Bar Associations; American Health Lawyers Association.

**Personal:** Indiana University, BA, 1987; Indiana University School of Law, JD, magna cum laude, 1993; Editor-in-Chief, Indiana Law Journal; Indiana Governor's Fellow; 'The Best Lawyers in America', Chambers USA 2005 and 2006 editions, and 'Guide to Leading U.S. Healthcare Lawyers', 2006.

### DENSBORN, Donald
Sommer Barnard PC, Indianapolis
317 844 4744
ddensborn@sommerbarnard.com
*Recommended in Corporate/M&A*

**Practice Areas:** Partner focusing on business law, mergers and acquisitions law.

**Prof. Memberships:** Admitted to Indiana, (1976). Uniform Law Commission (Drafting Committee, Limited Liability Company Act); Indianapolis, Indiana State and American Bar Associations.

**Career:** Listed: 'Best Lawyers in America'; 'Who's Who in Finance' in Indianapolis Business Journal; 'Indiana Super Lawyer' in Indianapolis Monthly Magazine. Named: 'Who's Who in Law' in Indianapolis Business Journal.

**Publications:** Numerous articles on topics including negotiating business acquisitions and negotiating venture capital funding.

**Personal:** JD (magna cum laude), Indiana University (Indianapolis), 1976; BS (magna cum laude), Indiana University, 1973. Beta Gamma Sigma Academic Honorary Fraternity.

### DEPREZ, Anne
Barnes & Thornburg LLP, Indianapolis
317 231 7264
anne.deprez@BTLaw.com
*Recommended in Litigation*

**Practice Areas:** Securities litigation; business litigation; commercial litigation; class action defense; civil RICO; commodities litigation; complex and multi-district litigation; represented clients in arbitrations under the auspices of the New York Stock Exchange, National Association of Securities Dealers, National Futures Association, American Arbitration Association, and Center for Public Resources.

**Prof. Memberships:** American and Indiana Bar Associations.

**Career:** Admitted to practice in Indiana, United States District Courts for the Southern and Northern Districts of Indiana, Western District of Michigan, and

the Seventh and Sixth Circuit Courts of Appeals.

**Personal:** Smith College (BA, 1977); Indiana University (JD, magna cum laude, 1981).

### DETHERAGE, Andrew
Barnes & Thornburg LLP, Indianapolis
317 231 7717
andy.detherage@btlaw.com
*Recommended in Litigation*

**Practice Areas:** Insurance coverage; insurance bad faith; trade secrets; commercial litigation; complex litigation; toxic tort defense.

**Prof. Memberships:** Indianapolis and American Bar Associations.

**Career:** Admitted to practice before the state of Indiana, the US District Court, Northern and Southern Districts of Indiana; and the US Court of Appeals, Seventh Circuit.

**Personal:** Indiana University (BA, with highest distinction, 1987; JD, summa cum laude, 1990).

### DINWIDDIE, Thomas
Wooden & McLaughlin LLP, Indianapolis
317 639 6151
tdinwiddie@woodmclaw.com
*Recommended in Real Estate*

**Practice Areas:** Business-related matters with an emphasis on real estate finance and real estate development, both single-family and multi-family mortgage banking, federal and state mortgage licensing and regulation, tax exempt financing, conduit lending, mortgage backed securities and structured lending with government sponsored entities.

**Prof. Memberships:** Indianapolis and Indiana State Bar Associations. Past Chair of the Indiana State Bar Association Corporation, Banking and Business Law Section and the Real Property Division of the Business Law Section of the Indianapolis Bar Association.

**Personal:** Admitted to Indiana Bar, 1973. Education: DePauw University (AB, 1969) and Indiana University (JD, 1973).

### EBERT, Kim F
Ogletree, Deakins, Nash, Smoak & Stewart, PC, Indianapolis
317 916 1300
kim.ebert@ogletreedeakins.com
*Recommended in Employment*

**Practice Areas:** Represents employers in the full range of labor and employment matters, including litigation, administrative proceedings, collective bargaining, union contract administration, and union avoidance.

**Prof. Memberships:** ABA (past Chair, Employer-Employee Relations Committee, TTIPS), Indiana Chamber of Commerce, Indiana Manufacturers Association.

**Career:** Listed in 'The Best Lawyers in America' since 1995. Fellow in The College of Labor and Employment Lawyers.

**Publications:** Has lectured and written

extensively on labor and employment subjects at local, regional and national programs. Co-author of 'Indiana Employer's Guide to the ADA and FMLA'. **Personal:** Wabash College (BA cum laude, 1972), Indiana University (JD cum laude, 1976).

## ELBERGER, Ronald
Bose McKinney & Evans LLP, Indianapolis 317 684 5000
*Recommended in Litigation*

## EMERSON, Daniel
Bose McKinney & Evans LLP, Indianapolis 317 684 5000
*Recommended in Employment*

## FICKLE, Stanley
Barnes & Thornburg LLP, Indianapolis 317 231 7240
stan.fickle@BTLaw.com
*Recommended in Litigation*
**Practice Areas:** Litigation; appellate practice; civil appeals.
**Prof. Memberships:** Member of American Academy of Appellate Lawyers and the Indiana Supreme Court's Committee on Rules of Practice and Procedures; former member of the Rules Advisory Committee for the United States Court of Appeals for the Seventh Circuit; former Member and Chairman of the Rules Advisory Committee for the United States District Court for the Southern District of Indiana.
**Career:** Admitted to practice in the state of Indiana.
**Personal:** Indiana University (AB, 1966; MBA, 1968; JD, summa cum laude, 1974).

## GREISING, Robert
Krieg DeVault LLP, Indianapolis 317 636 4341
*Recommended in Corporate/M&A*

## HAAS, Karl P
Wallack Somers & Haas PC, Indianapolis 317 231 9000
kph@wshlaw.com
*Recommended in Real Estate*
**Practice Areas:** Partner at Wallack, Somers & Haas, concentrating in a broad range of real estate and redevelopment projects representing developers, lenders, investors and municipalities. These projects include purchasing, financing, developing, leasing, refinancing and selling office, retail, industrial, hotel and residential properties. In addition, he has provided counsel for numerous urban renewal projects, including Conseco Fieldhouse, home of the Indiana Pacers.
**Career:** Indiana State Bar admission 1985; Baker & Daniels (associate 1985; Partner 1992-99).
**Personal:** Indiana University (BS, highest distinction, 1982); Indiana University School of Law, Indianapolis (JD, graduated first in class 1985); Recognized in 'Best Lawyers in America'.

## HACKMAN, Stephen
Ice Miller LLP, Indianapolis 317 236 2289
stephen.hackman@icemiller.com
*Recommended in Corporate/M&A*
**Practice Areas:** Stephen Hackman is Chairman of Ice Miller's Corporate Practice Group. His practice focuses on federal and state securities law, mergers/acquisitions, structured finance, commercial lending and general corporate matters. He regularly provides sound, practical advice to public and large private companies in connection with strategic acquisitions and dispositions, public/private financings, securities law disclosure and compliance issues and corporate governance matters. His clients are involved in a variety of industries, including medical devices, chemical manufacturing, healthcare, finance, contract research and automobile redistribution.
**Prof. Memberships:** Member: Indianapolis, American Bar Associations; Indianapolis Lawyers Club; past Chair, Indianapolis Bar Association's Business Section.

## HAMILTON, John W
Wooden & McLaughlin LLP, Indianapolis 317 639 6151
jhamilton@woodmclaw.com
*Recommended in Real Estate*
**Practice Areas:** Represents institutional investors, commercial banks, finance companies and private developers; lenders and borrowers in commercial lending transactions; and commercial developers in the acquisition, sale and leasing of real estate.
**Prof. Memberships:** Indiana and Indianapolis Bar Associations.
**Publications:** CLE lectures including Financing the Deal, Insurance Issues in Commercial Real Estate Lending, Co-Lending and Participation Arrangements. Co-authored commercial law survey for Indiana from 1998 to 1999 that was published in the Indiana Law Review.
**Personal:** Admitted to Indiana Bar, 1996. Davidson College (BA, 1986); Washington & Lee University (JD, cum laude, 1993). Editor, Washington & Lee Law Review.

## HARDIN, Steven
Bingham McHale LLP, Indianapolis 317 635 8900
*Recommended in Real Estate*

## HARRIS, Edward W
Sommer Barnard PC, Indianapolis 317 713 3500
eharris@sommerbarnard.com
*Recommended in Litigation*
**Practice Areas:** Chair of the firm's Litigation Department and represents clients in a wide range of business disputes, practicing mostly in federal court. He is particularly experienced in antitrust and class action disputes, representing both plaintiffs and defendants in cases in federal trial and appellate courts throughout the United States.
**Prof. Memberships:** Indianapolis, Indiana State, American and Seventh Circuit Bar Associations.
**Career:** Admitted to Indiana Bar (1968).
**Personal:** BA from Amherst College in 1964 and JD from University of Michigan University in 1967. Note, Comment and Recent Developments editor, Michigan Law Review, 1966-67. Teaching Fellow, Stanford Law School, 1967-68.

## HECKLER, Douglas
Barnes & Thornburg LLP, Indianapolis 317 231 7528
doug.heckler@BTLaw.com
*Recommended in Employment*
**Practice Areas:** Collective bargaining; labor arbitration; management labor law; counsels clients concerning personnel practices, wage and hour laws, workplace health and safety matters, and individual employment contracts; provides supervisor training.
**Prof. Memberships:** Advisory board member and instructor for the annual National Labor Relations Board—I.U. School of Law Seminar on Labor-Management Relations.
**Career:** Admitted to practice before the US District Courts for the Northern and Southern Districts of Indiana and the US Court of Appeals for the Sixth and Seventh Circuits.
**Personal:** Valparaiso University (BA, 1979); Indiana University (JD, 1982).

## HERZOG, David K
Baker & Daniels, Indianapolis 317 237 1240
David.Herzog@bakerd.com
*Recommended in Litigation*
**Practice Areas:** David Herzog concentrates his practice in business and commercial litigation in both trial and appellate courts. He has had extensive experience in securities, banking, business-tort, hedge-fund, and shareholder derivative litigation, and has represented defendants in numerous class actions involving claims under the securities laws, the Truth in Lending Act, and various consumer contracts. David has also represented defendants in a number of cases involving mass torts.
**Prof. Memberships:** Indianapolis, Indiana State, Seventh Circuit, and American Bar Associations.
**Career:** Partner since 1987; Indianapolis Managing Partner, 1998-2000; Executive Vice President, General Counsel and Secretary of Conseco, Inc., September 2000-February 2003.
**Personal:** Wabash College, AB, summa cum laude, 1977; Vanderbilt University, JD, 1980. Recognized in Chambers USA 2005 and 2006 editions and in 'Indiana Super Lawyers' 2006 edition.

## HICKS, Robert J
Sommer Barnard PC, Indianapolis 317 713 3500
bhicks@sommerbarnard.com
*Recommended in Corporate/M&A*
**Practice Areas:** Firm Managing Director focusing practice on complex business and commercial transactions, private equity and venture capital transactions, business advisory services, and tax and estate planning matters. Lead Counsel to sellers and buyers in numerous merger and acquisition transactions and in several private equity and joint venture transactions.
**Prof. Memberships:** Indianapolis, Indiana State, and American Bar Associations. Indiana Certified Public Accountant Society.
**Career:** Admitted, Indiana Bar (1987); Certified Public Accountant.
**Personal:** BS, (highest honors) Butler University, 1984; JD, Marshall-Wythe School of Law; College of William & Mary, 1986. Order of the Coif, William & Mary Law Review, 1985-86.

## HOKANSON, Jeffrey
Ice Miller LLP, Indianapolis 317 236 2185
jeff.hokanson@icemiller.com
*Recommended in Litigation*
**Practice Areas:** Jeff is a member of its Bankruptcy and Commercial Law and Private Equity/Venture Services Groups. Jeff, a Partner, concentrates his practice on commercial and debtor/creditor law, bankruptcy and related commercial litigation, and private equity transaction work representing and protecting debtor and creditor-clients in judicial proceedings and out of court workouts. He assists parties with leases, supply agreements, other contracts involved in bankruptcy proceedings, and advises corporate management on the duties and obligations of management of businesses facing threatened or mounting insolvency.
**Prof. Memberships:** Indianapolis and Indiana State Bar Associations; American Bankruptcy Institute, Indiana Association for Corporate Renewal.

## HUMKE, Steven
Ice Miller LLP, Indianapolis 317 236 2394
steven.humke@icemiller.com
*Recommended in Corporate/M&A*
**Practice Areas:** Founding Partner of Ice Miller's Private Equity/Venture Services Group. Concentrates in capital raising strategies, mergers and acquisitions and general corporate matters. During 2005 represented HHGregg and former shareholders in recapitalization transaction financed by Freeman Spogli; served as counsel to Monument Capital Partners in its investments in Separators, Inc. Represented: Baker-Hill Corporation in sale to Experian; Reynolds, Inc. in sale to Layne Christensen; and State of Indiana in 15

year lease of Indiana Toll Road.

**Prof. Memberships:** Director: The Villages; Indiana Humanities Council; TechPoint Foundation. President-elect, Association for Corporate Growth, Alumni of Stanley K Lacy Executive Leadership Series.

### IRMSCHER, David
Baker & Daniels, Fort Wayne
219 424 8000
*Recommended in Litigation*

**Practice Areas:** David Irmscher concentrates his practice in intellectual property litigation, focusing primarily on patent litigation. He has litigated patent matters involving diverse technologies, including orthopedic implants of various types, electric motors, valves, roof vents and case-ready meat packaging. David also has handled an assortment of trade secret, trademark and unfair competition cases. Additionally, he has extensive experience with alternative dispute resolution, including commercial arbitrations. In 2004, David prevailed twice before the US Court of Appeals for the Federal Circuit.
**Prof. Memberships:** Allen County, Indiana State, and American Bar Associations; American Intellectual Property Law Association.
**Personal:** Dartmouth College, AB, cum laude, 1979; University of Michigan Law School, JD, 1982. Recognized in Chambers USA 2005 and 2006 editions, IP Litigation; Recognized in 'Indiana Super Lawyers' 2004, 2005 and 2006.

### JOHNSON, Dennis
Barnes & Thornburg LLP, Indianapolis
317 231 7736
dennis.johnson@btlaw.com
*Recommended in Real Estate*

**Practice Areas:** Real estate; commercial finance law; represents construction and permanent real estate lenders, commercial real estate developers, developers of multi-family and single-family residential projects and single-family residential builders.
**Prof. Memberships:** Former Chair of the Business Section of the Indianapolis Bar Association and a former Member of the Board of Directors of the Community Organization Legal Assistance Project.
**Career:** Admitted to practice in the state of Indiana.
**Personal:** Indiana University (BS, 1982; JD, cum laude, 1985).

### JOHNSON, Richard
Barnes & Thornburg LLP, Indianapolis
317 231 7787
rjohnson@btlaw.com
*Recommended in Real Estate*

**Practice Areas:** Real estate; represented financial institutions in commercial real estate transactions for over 28 years; been involved in many high-profile projects in Indiana, including Hamilton Proper, Circle Centre Mall, Conrad Hotel and French Lick Springs Resort and Casino;

projects in 33 states, including Mall of America, The Legends at Village West Shopping Center in Kansas City, the Houston Orthopaedic Hospital and assisted in the sale of the Indian Wells Country Club and Royal Kenfield Golf Club in Las Vegas.
**Personal:** University of North Dakota (BA, 1965); Whittier College (MEd, 1968); Hastings College of Law, University of California (JD, 1972).

### KASPER, David
Locke Reynolds LLP, Indianapolis
317 237 3800
*Recommended in Litigation*

### KLAPER, Martin
Ice Miller LLP, Indianapolis
317 236 2322
martin.klaper@icemiller.com
*Recommended in Employment*

**Practice Areas:** Martin concentrates on labor contract administration and negotiation; arbitration and NLRB matters; administrative and civil court discrimination matters; OFCCP matters; and union-free maintenance programs. He is a certified mediator.
**Prof. Memberships:** Bar of the Supreme Court of the United States; College of Labor and Employment Lawyers; Labor Relations Committee of the United States of Commerce; National Labor Relations Board and Equal Employment Opportunity Sub-committees of the United States Chamber of Commerce; Indiana and American Bar Associations. Recognized in: '2004 Super Lawyers', 'Who's Who in America', 'Who's Who in American Law' and 'The Best Lawyers in America'.

### KNEBEL, Donald
Barnes & Thornburg LLP, Indianapolis
317 231 7214
donald.knebel@btlaw.com
*Recommended in Litigation*

**Practice Areas:** Intellectual property; intellectual property litigation; patent litigation; federal civil litigation; antitrust and trade regulation; unfair trade.
**Prof. Memberships:** Co-author of the Indiana chapter of State Antitrust Practice and Statutes, published by the American Bar Association; immediate past President of TechLaw Group, an international network of law firms having significant technology practices; on the Executive Committee of TechPoint, a statewide technology advocacy organization in Indiana
**Career:** Admitted to practice in Indiana and before the First, Third, Fourth, Sixth, Seventh and Federal Circuits.
**Personal:** Purdue University (BSEE, with highest distinction, 1968); Harvard University (JD, magna cum laude, 1974).

### LAWSON, Jack
Beckman Lawson, LLP, Fort Wayne
219 422 0800
*Recommended in Real Estate*

### LEE, Stephen W
Barnes & Thornburg LLP, Indianapolis
317 231 7200
stephen.lee@btlaw.com
*Recommended in Real Estate*

**Practice Areas:** Real estate; commercial real estate; construction law; zoning; planning and land use; eminent domain; all aspects of commercial real estate acquisition, development, construction, financing, leasing, disposition and related litigation, including condemnation proceedings.
**Prof. Memberships:** Indianapolis and Indiana State Bar Associations.
**Career:** Admitted to practice before the Supreme Court of Indiana, the US District Court for the Southern District of Indiana, the US Court of Appeals for the Seventh Circuit and the Supreme Court of the United States.
**Personal:** Ball State University (BS, 1971); Indiana University (JD, summa cum laude, 1977).

### LISHER, Mary
Baker & Daniels, Indianapolis
317 237 1081
mary.lisher@bakerd.com
*Recommended in Real Estate*

**Practice Areas:** Mary Lisher has over 20 years of concentrated real estate experience. Areas of expertise include sales and purchases; ground leases; leasing of improved retail, commercial, and industrial properties; preparation of easements and other ancillary development agreements; construction and architects agreements and property management agreements; and construction and permanent financing. She serves as attorney for the AmeriPlex Project, a mixed use advanced technology and commerce park in Indianapolis, and as real estate counsel for Eli Lilly and Company and Clarian Health Partners, Inc. In addition, Mary provides legal services of a general business nature to fraternities and sororities and other tax exempt organizations.
**Prof. Memberships:** American (Real Property, Probate and Trust Law Section) and Indianapolis (Business Law Section) Bar Associations; IndyCREW (Indianapolis Commercial Real Estate Women).
**Personal:** Vanderbilt University, BA, cum laude, 1972; Indiana University, JD, summa cum laude, 1975. Named one of the Influential Women in Indianapolis by Indianapolis Business Journal (1999); Voted Top 50 Indiana Super Lawyer (2004) and Top 25 Female Indiana Super Lawyer (2004, 2005, 2006); Recognized in The Best Lawyers in America, Real Estate (2006); Recognized in Chambers USA, Real Estate practice (2003-06); Member, Board of Directors, Lilly Endowment, Inc.

### LONG, Christine
Baker & Daniels, Indianapolis
317 569 4879
Christine.Long@bakerd.com
*Recommended in Corporate/M&A*

**Practice Areas:** Christine Long concentrates her practice in the fields of general corporate and securities law. She represents companies of all sizes, from sole proprietorships to publicly held companies, in mergers, acquisitions and dispositions. Christine counsels publicly held companies with respect to their on-going disclosure and periodic reporting requirements under securities laws, including preparation of reports and other disclosure documents. She assists clients in corporate governance matters, including compliance with the Sarbanes-Oxley Act and stock exchange requirements. Christine has been involved in all aspects of public offerings, private placements and other securities transactions. She has been involved in the preparation, implementation and administration of executive compensation plans, including stock option plans. Christine provides legal counsel in such corporate areas as new business formation, general business planning and contract assistance.
**Prof. Memberships:** Indianapolis and Indiana State Bar Association.
**Personal:** Washington University, BA, with distinction, 1992; Indiana University School of Law, JD, magna cum laude, 1995. Recognized in Chambers USA 2006 edition.

### MACGILL, Robert
Barnes & Thornburg LLP, Indianapolis
317 231 7223
rmacgill@btlaw.com
*Recommended in Litigation*

**Practice Areas:** Intellectual property litigation; commercial litigation; products liability defense; insurance coverage; provides services to numerous US and foreign-owned companies in matters litigated in trial and appellate courts throughout the United States.
**Prof. Memberships:** Chairman, Litigation Department, Barnes & Thornburg LLP; serves as Chairman of the Board of Indianapolis Tennis Championships, Inc. and Indiana Secondary Market for Education Loans, Inc.
**Career:** Admitted to practice in the Northern and Southern Districts of Indiana and the Seventh and Eighth Circuit Courts of Appeals.
**Personal:** Indiana University (BS, with high distinction, 1978; JD, cum laude, 1981).

### MCDERMOTT, Brian L
Ogletree, Deakins, Nash, Smoak & Stewart, PC, Indianapolis 317 916 2170
brian.mcdermott@ogletreedeakins.com
*Recommended in Employment*

**Practice Areas:** Employment law, employment litigation, management labor law, ERISA litigation.

**Prof. Memberships:** Indiana Bar Association (Member Chair, Labor and Employment Section 2003-04), Indianapolis Bar Association (Member Chair, Labor and Employment Section 2004-05).

**Career:** Admitted in Indiana, Iowa. Named as an Indiana Super Lawyer in 2005, 2006; Best Lawyers 2005, 2006.

**Publications:** Co-author of The Indiana Chamber of Commerce's publications: 'The Indiana Employer's Guide to the ADA and FMLA' and 'The Interviewing Guide: Designed to Assist Indiana Employers with Hiring and Retaining Employees'.

**Personal:** University of Iowa (JD, 1991), with Distinction; Judicial Clerk, US District Judge Donald Porter.

### MCTURNAN, Lee B
McTurnan & Turner, Indianapolis
317 464 8181
lmcturnan@mtlitig.com
*Recommended in Litigation*

**Practice Areas:** Business litigation in state and federal trial and appellate courts. For example, corporate securities and corporate governance disputes and breaches of fiduciary duties by directors, officers or employees; defending class actions involving securities, employment discrimination and various fraud claims; other employment matters; defending accountants, lawyers and securities broker-dealers; utility regulation litigation; restraint of trade and antitrust litigation; a wide variety of contract and business tort disputes; First Amendment media issues.

**Prof. Memberships:** Indianapolis, Chicago (Member, Board of Managers, 1977-78), Indiana State, Illinois State, Seventh Circuit and American Bar Associations; Indianapolis American Inn of Court (Master); Indianapolis Law Club (President, 1988-90); Local Rules Advisory Committee for Southern District of Indiana (1995-2000).

**Career:** Admitted to practice in Illinois in 1965 and Indiana in 1978. Law clerk to Justice Goldberg, US Supreme Court, 1963-64. Practiced business litigation with: Sidley & Austin, Chicago, Illinois, as an associate from 1964-69 and as a Partner from 1970-78; and with Smith Morgan & Ryan (later Hackman McClarnon & McTurnan), Indianapolis, Indiana, as a Partner from 1978-88. Co-Founder of McTurnan & Turner 1989.

**Personal:** Reared in Bloomington, Illinois. Received AB magna cum laude in 1959 from Harvard University; Diploma in Law from Oxford University (Lincoln College) in 1961; JD, cum laude from University of Chicago Law School in 1963. Was Phi Beta Kappa; Editor-in-Chief of the 'University of Chicago Law Review' from 1962-63; Order of the Coif.

### MILLARD, David
Barnes & Thornburg LLP, Indianapolis
317 231 7803
david.millard@btlaw.com
*Recommended in Corporate/M&A*

**Practice Areas:** Business law; contracts; corporate finance; mergers, acquisitions and divestitures; counsels middle-market and high-growth businesses.

**Prof. Memberships:** Served as President of The Venture Club of Indiana and the Entrepreneur's Alliance of Indiana; is chairman of the Indiana Chamber of Commerce Business Council; serves on the Indiana Chamber of Commerce Board and Executive Committee.

**Career:** Admitted to practice in the state of Indiana.

**Personal:** Indiana University School of Business (BS, with highest distinction, 1977); Indiana University School of Law (JD, magna cum laude, 1979).

### MILLER, David W
Baker & Daniels, Indianapolis
317 237 1316
david.miller@bakerd.com
*Recommended in Employment*

**Practice Areas:** David Miller represents management clients in matters of employment law with particular emphasis on union avoidance, handling charges before Federal and State Fair Employment Practice Agencies and the National Labor Relations Board, and defending employers in federal and state court discrimination suits. He also participates in the negotiation and administration of collective bargaining agreements, including arbitration of grievances. A substantial portion of David's time is devoted to day to day counseling of clients on issues involving compliance with federal wage and hour laws, hiring, disciplining, and terminating employees.

**Prof. Memberships:** Admitted: Indiana; US Court of Appeals for the Fourth, Fifth, Sixth, Seventh and Tenth Circuits.

**Publications:** 'It's the Law' Federal employment law training modules (2003), National Child Care Association; Co-author, 'The Indiana Guide to Hiring & Firing' (2001 & 1997), Indiana State Chamber of Commerce.

**Personal:** Indiana University, AB, 1971; JD, summa cum laude, 1976. Listed in Chambers USA 2003, 2004, 2005 and 2006 editions, Employment. Recognized in 'The Best Lawyers in America' for 10 years.

### MILLIKAN, Michael E
Ice Miller LLP, Indianapolis
317 236 5965
michael.millikan@icemiller.com
*Recommended in Corporate/M&A*

**Practice Areas:** Michael is a Partner and founding member of the firm's Private Equity/Venture Services Group. He concentrates in venture capital and private equity financing and mergers and acqui-

sitions. He also focuses on representing high energy entrepreneurial companies in strategic planning, raising money and achieving growth through acquisitions. Michael's experiences include representing private equity clients in numerous equity and mezzanine investments, serving as general counsel to many of his private equity clients' portfolio companies and assisting family-owned businesses in succession planning including sale transactions.

**Prof. Memberships:** Michael is the Board Chairman of the ALS Association of Indiana.

### MITCHELL, Marvin
Mitchell Hurst Jacobs & Dick, Indianapolis 317 633 7680
*Recommended in Litigation*

### NEIGHBOURS, John T
Baker & Daniels, Indianapolis
317 237 1325
john.neighbours@bakerd.com
*Recommended in Employment*

**Practice Areas:** John Neighbours represents employers throughout the country in all aspects of labor and employment law, including collective bargaining and administration of collective bargaining contracts, employment litigation, employment discrimination issues, and day to day administration of employee relations. Additionally, he is nearly continuously involved in advising employers throughout the United States concerning maintaining union free work places, particularly as organized labor looks for new ways to reinvent itself in the 21st century.

**Prof. Memberships:** Member of College of Labor and Employment Law Lawyers; Member, American Bar Association (Council Member, Section on Labor and Employment Law; Chair, Developments Under the National Labor Relations Act Committee, 1997-2000; editor, 4th Edition, 1997-2000, assistant editor, 1990-96, and contributing editor, 1985-89, Developing Labor Law. Fellow, Indiana Bar Foundation.

**Publications:** Editor, 'Indiana Employment Law Letter', M Lee Smith publisher (1992-present).

**Personal:** DePauw University, BA, 1971; Indiana University, JD, 1974. Recognized in: Chambers USA 2003, 2004, 2005 and 2006 editions; 'The Best Lawyers in America' (listed for past 10 years); 'The International Who's Who of Business Lawyers', Labor and Employment; and Euromoney's 'Best Labor and Employment Lawyers in the World'.

### NICELY, Philip
Bose McKinney & Evans LLP, Indianapolis 317 684 5000
*Recommended in Real Estate*

### NIERMAN, Todd
Baker & Daniels, Indianapolis
317 237 1312
todd.nierman@bakerd.com
*Recommended in Employment*

**Practice Areas:** Todd Nierman has a diversified practice representing and counseling employers in labor and employment matters, especially matters regarding obligations under the National Labor Relations Act, the Fair Labor Standards Act, and Equal Employment Opportunity legislation, including the ADA. His counsel is sought concerning union organizing efforts, National Labor Relations Board representation elections and proceedings, collective bargaining negotiations, construction industry labor relations, wage and hour compliance matters (private and public sector), and discrimination charges. He has represented clients before the Indiana Supreme Court, the Indiana Court of Appeals, Indiana trial courts, the Seventh Circuit Court of Appeals, the Sixth Circuit Court of Appeals, Federal District Court in Indiana, Ohio, Illinois and Texas, the National Labor Relations Board, the Equal Employment Opportunity Commission, the United States and Indiana Departments of Labor, and the Indiana Civil Rights Commission.

**Personal:** University of Michigan, BBA, with distinction, 1983; Vanderbilt University, JD, 1986. Certified Public Accountant, Illinois, 1983. Recognized in Chambers USA 2004, 2005 and 2006 editions - Employment.

### O'BRYAN, Rory
Harrison & Moberly LLP, Indianapolis 317 639 4511
*Recommended in Real Estate*

### PENCE, Linda L
Sommer Barnard PC, Indianapolis
317 713 3500
lpence@sommerbarnard.com
*Recommended in Litigation*

**Practice Areas:** Co-Chairs Litigation Department and Head of the White Collar Criminal Practice. Concentrates practice on federal white-collar criminal defense and complex civil litigation, including government procurement contract fraud, tax fraud, violations of securities laws, antitrust violations, and other related matters.

**Prof. Memberships:** National Association of Criminal Defense Lawyers; American and Indiana State Bar Associations.

**Career:** Admitted to Indiana Bar (1974); District of Columbia Bar (1982). Nine years with US Department of Justice as Chief, Special Projects Branch; Deputy Chief, Government Fraud Section, Criminal Division; and Trial Attorney, Civil Division.

**Personal:** BA and JD, Indiana University, 1971 and 1974.

## PONADER, Erick
Sommer Barnard PC, Indianapolis
317 713 3500
eponader@sommerbarnard.com
*Recommended in Real Estate*

**Practice Areas:** Chairman of the firm's Real Estate Group. Represents clients in real estate development, acquisition, sale, leasing and financing. Extensive experience in commercial transactions, including the sale and purchase of businesses, intellectual property licensing, construction law, aviation law, and medical device and pharmaceutical law.
**Prof. Memberships:** Indianapolis (President-Business Law Section), Indiana State and American Bar Associations.
**Career:** Admitted to Indiana Bar, 1989 and Illinois Bar, 1985.
**Personal:** JD, Indiana University (Bloomington), 1985; AB, (Chemistry and Biology), Indiana University, 1982.

## SCANLON, Chris
Baker & Daniels, Indianapolis
317 237 1253
chris.scanlon@bakerd.com
*Recommended in Litigation*

**Practice Areas:** Chris Scanlon concentrates his practice in the area of business and commercial litigation involving a broad range of substantive areas, including contract, insurance, business tort, RICO, trade secret, accountants liability and environmental liability. He has extensive experience in securities litigation under both state and federal securities laws, including securities class actions. Chris also regularly represents business insureds in Indiana and elsewhere in insurance coverage disputes arising from products liability, environmental, and other large loss liabilities.
**Prof. Memberships:** Indianapolis, Indiana State, Seventh Circuit and American Bar Associations. Local Rules Committee, US District Court, Southern District of Indiana.
**Personal:** Indiana University, BS, 1977; Indiana University, JD, cum laude, 1980. Recipient, 1996 Pro Bono Publico Award, and Distinguished Fellow, Indiana Bar Foundation. Recognized in: Chambers USA 2003 through 2006 editions, Litigation; 'The Best Lawyers in America' (since 1987); and 'Indiana Super Lawyers', 2004 through 2006.

## SCHWARZ, James
Dann Pecar Newman & Kleiman, PC, Indianapolis
317 632 3232
*Recommended in Real Estate*

## SCIMIA, Joseph
Baker & Daniels, Indianapolis
317 569 4680
joseph.scimia@bakerd.com
*Recommended in Real Estate*

**Practice Areas:** Joe Scimia is the Chairman of the firm's Real Estate Group and represents developers, contractors,

lenders, landlords, tenants and property owners in a variety of real estate transactions. His areas of expertise include construction and permanent financing of commercial, office, retail, industrial and residential developments; and the acquisition, development, leasing and disposition of office, retail, commercial, industrial and residential properties. His practice also includes securing necessary land use approvals from local units of government for commercial, industrial, residential and mixed use projects.
**Prof. Memberships:** Indiana and Arizona State Bar Associations.
**Personal:** Indiana University, BS, with high distinction, 1982; Indiana University, JD, magna cum laude, 1985. Recognized in 'The Best Lawyers in America' and Chambers USA 2003, 2004, 2005 and 2006 editions.

## SHARROW, Regina
Sommer Barnard PC, Indianapolis
317 713 3500
rsharrow@sommerbarnard.com
*Recommended in Corporate/M&A*

**Practice Areas:** Practices in areas of general corporate law, mergers and acquisitions, securities law and executive compensation, including equity-based plans and packages for executives.
**Prof. Memberships:** Indianapolis, Indiana State (ISBA) and American Bar Associations; Past chair, ISBA Business Section.
**Career:** Admitted to California Bar, 1991, Admitted to Indiana Bar, 1996; Lecturer: Golden Gate University School of Law, San Francisco, Executive Compensation and ERISA Basics Classes; speaker at various seminars on general business agreements and securities matters.
**Personal:** JD, University of California at Berkeley, 1991; BS, University of Michigan, Ann Arbor, 1987.

## SHOCKLEY, Steven C
Sommer Barnard PC, Indianapolis
317 713 3500
sshockley@sommerbarnard.com
*Recommended in Litigation*

**Practice Areas:** Member of the Litigation, Appellate Practice (Chair) and Governmental Affairs Departments. Represented State Bar Association in original actions in Indiana Supreme Court to enjoin unauthorized practice of law. Represented state circuit court judge in original actions in the Indiana Supreme Court seeking jurisdictional writs.
**Prof. Memberships:** Indiana and Indianapolis Bar Associations.
**Career:** Admitted in Indiana (1984) and Florida (1986) (inactive). Associate, Holland & Knight, 1986-88. Law clerk, Indiana Court of Appeals, 1984-1986. Indiana Law Review, 1983-84.
**Personal:** Indiana University (BA, 1978; JD, 1984, magna cum laude).

## SOLADA, Mary
Bingham McHale LLP, Indianapolis
317 635 8900
*Recommended in Real Estate*

## SOMERS, George W
Wallack Somers & Haas PC, Indianapolis
317 231 9000
gws@wshlaw.com
*Recommended in Real Estate*

**Practice Areas:** Partner at Wallack, Somers & Haas, concentrating in all types of real estate development. He has provided counsel to local, regional and national developers regarding the acquisition, construction, leasing, financing and disposition of retail, office and mixed-use developments.
**Career:** Indiana State Bar admission 1979; Baker & Daniels (associate 1979; Partner 1985-99), Wallack Somers & Haas PC (1999-present).
**Personal:** Graduated St Olaf College (BA, 1969, Phi Beta Kappa); Harvard University (MTS, 1971); Duke University (MA, 1974, James B Duke Fellow); University of Chicago (JD, 1979); recognized in 'Best Lawyers in America', 1997-2006.

## STANLEY, Robert K
Baker & Daniels, Indianapolis
317 237 1254
Robert.Stanley@bakerd.com
*Recommended in Litigation*

**Practice Areas:** For more than 20 years, Bob Stanley has concentrated his practice in business and commercial civil litigation at both the trial and appellate levels. Bob's principal focus in recent years has been prosecuting or defending private arbitrations and civil suits in federal and state courts involving antitrust claims; business-related torts, including unfair competition, false advertising and product disparagement claims; probate-related litigation, including will contests, will/trust construction disputes, and breach-of-trust claims; bankruptcy litigation, including adversary proceedings; and contract disputes, including breach of contract claims and contract construction disputes.
**Prof. Memberships:** Admitted to practice in all courts of the State of Indiana, US Supreme Court, and US Courts of Appeals for Sixth, Seventh and Eighth Circuits; Member, American, Indiana State and Indianapolis Bar Associations.
**Personal:** Ball State University, AB, summa cum laude, 1978; Indiana University School of Law (Bloomington), JD, summa cum laude, 1981. Recognized in 'The Best Lawyers in America' (2003-06) and Chambers USA (2004-06).

## STRAIN, James A
Sommer Barnard PC, Indianapolis
317 713 3500
strain@sommerbarnard.com
*Recommended in Corporate/M&A*

**Practice Areas:** Director and Chairman of Business Law Practice Group with

extensive experience in mergers and acquisitions matters.
**Prof. Memberships:** The American Bar Association, Seventh Circuit Bar Association (President, 1995-96 term), Indiana State Bar Association.
**Career:** Admitted to practice in Indiana (1969). Law clerk to Judge John S Hastings, US Court of Appeals for Seventh Circuit, 1970-71 and to then Associate Justice William H Rehnquist, US Supreme Court, October Term 1972. A Partner of Sommer Barnard PC since joining the firm in 1996.
**Personal:** JD (cum laude), Indiana University School of Law, 1969 and AB, Indiana University, 1966.

## SWHIER, Claudia
Barnes & Thornburg LLP, Indianapolis
317 231 7231
CSwhier@BTLaw.com
*Recommended in Corporate/M&A*

**Practice Areas:** Banks and banking; securities; initial public offerings; mergers, acquisitions and divestitures; corporate finance; serves a number of banks, thrifts, and credit unions, many of which are publicly traded; provides the full spectrum of legal services in the bank and securities regulatory compliance area; handles public offerings, mergers and acquisitions, holding company formations, financings and stock conversions of mutual thrifts for client financial institutions.
**Prof. Memberships:** American, Indiana State, and Indianapolis Bar Associations.
**Career:** Admitted to practice in the state of Indiana.
**Personal:** Yale University (BA, 1972); Harvard University (JD, cum laude, 1975).

## SWIDER, David
Bose McKinney & Evans LLP, Indianapolis 317 684 5000
*Recommended in Employment*

## TEMPEL, Angela E
Bose McKinney & Evans LLP, Indianapolis 317 684 5000
*Recommended in Real Estate*

## THORNBURGH, John
Ice Miller LLP, Indianapolis
317 236 2405
john.thornburgh@icemiller.com
*Recommended in Corporate/M&A*

**Practice Areas:** Chairman of Ice Miller's Private Equity/Venture Services and Sports and Entertainment Groups, John focuses on general corporate matters, mergers and acquisitions, private equity fund formation, and venture finance transactions. In 2005, John represented CID Capital, Centerfield Capital and Argo Partners in a number of investment and buy-out transactions. He also represented Heron Capital in fund formation and several clients in private acquisition transactions.

**Prof. Memberships:** Board of Directors, Indianapolis Symphony Orchestra; Chairman of the Board of Directors, IM Sports Services, LLC; Board of Advisors: CID Capital, Inc.; Major Tool and Machine, Inc.; and Western Reserve Partners, LLC.

## THRAPP, Richard
Ice Miller LLP, Indianapolis
317 236 2442
richard.thrapp@icemiller.com
*Recommended in Corporate/M&A*
**Practice Areas:** Co-Chair of Ice Miller's Corporate/M&A Group, his primary practice areas are in general corporate, mergers and acquisitions, business finance, corporate and commercial law, nonprofit organizations, and shareholder rights.
**Prof. Memberships:** Member: Indiana Corporate Law Survey Commission; Indiana State and American Bar Associations; Board of Directors, Indianapolis Bar Foundation. Distinguished Fellow, Indianapolis Bar Foundation; Served on the task force for Limited Liability Companies and on the drafting committee for the Indiana Nonprofit Corporation Act. Member: Board of Governors, Child Advocates, Inc.; Board of Directors, Indianapolis Zoological Society; Board of Directors, Geist Christian Church.

## TINSLEY, Nancy
Baker & Daniels, Indianapolis
317 237 1245
nancy.tinsley@bakerd.com
*Recommended in Litigation*
**Practice Areas:** Nancy Tinsley leads the firm's Intellectual Property Litigation Group and represents clients in intellectual property litigation and counsels clients in intellectual property matters. She has litigated patent cases across the country in a variety of technological areas including medical devices, chemical processing, fluid handling, consumer products, and software. Nancy has extensive experience in alternative dispute resolution and is a registered civil mediator. She is an inventor with three US patents and is registered to practice before the Patent and Trademark Office.
**Prof. Memberships:** Indianapolis (Member, Women in the Law Executive Committee, 1998-99); Indiana State (Member, Women in the Law Committee, 1997-present); Seventh Circuit, Federal Circuit and American Bar Associations. American Intellectual Property Lawyers Association.
**Career:** Prior to becoming an attorney, Nancy worked at a major pharmaceutical company as a research chemist.
**Personal:** Purdue University, BS in Chemistry, 1982; Indiana University School of Law, JD, cum laude, 1990. Recognized in 'The Best Lawyers in America', 2005 and 2006; 'Indiana Super Lawyers', (Law & Politics) 2004 and 2005; and

Chambers USA 2005 and 2006 editions.

## TITTLE, David
Bingham McHale LLP, Indianapolis
317 635 8900
*Recommended in Litigation*

## TURNER, Wayne C
McTurnan & Turner, Indianapolis
317 464 8181
wturner@mtlitig.com
*Recommended in Litigation*
**Practice Areas:** Business litigation in state and federal trial and appellate courts. For example, corporate securities and corporate governance disputes and breaches of fiduciary duties by directors, officers or employees; defending class actions involving securities, employment discrimination and various fraud claims; other employment matters; defending accountants, lawyers and securities broker-dealers; utility regulation litigation; restraint of trade and antitrust litigation; a wide variety of contract and business tort disputes; First Amendment media issues.
**Prof. Memberships:** Indianapolis, Indiana State, Seventh Circuit and American Bar Associations; Indianapolis Law Club; Defense Research Institute; Indianapolis Bar Foundation (Distinguished Fellow).
**Career:** Admitted to practice in Indiana in 1985. Associate at Smith Morgan & Ryan (later Hackman McClarnon & McTurnan), Indianapolis, Indiana, from 1985-88. Co-founder of McTurnan & Turner in 1989.
**Personal:** Reared in Rising Sun, Indiana. Received BS in Economics, with highest distinction, in 1982 from Purdue University (GA Ross Outstanding Graduate); JD, magna cum laude, in 1985 from Indiana University. Was Note and Development editor of the 'Indiana Law Review', 1984-85. Order of Barristers.

## UTKEN, Gregory
Baker & Daniels, Indianapolis
317 237 1327
greg.utken@bakerd.com
*Recommended in Employment*
**Practice Areas:** Greg Utken is Chair of the firm's Advocacy Department which consists of nine practice groups. He represents management only in labor and employment law matters and litigation throughout the United States. Among the areas are: assisting employers in maintaining their non-union status; strategizing on work consolidation/relocation issues, reorganizations and reductions in force; matters before the National Labor Relations Board; negotiation of collective bargaining agreements; labor arbitrations; affirmative action; equal employment law; wrongful discharge; and strategic counseling. With over 30 years of experience, Greg is able to be both practical and creative in developing strategies with clients on managing through the often complex labor and employment

issues they face. He has been recognized as one of the leading management labor and employment lawyers by peers and businesses in multiple publications.
**Prof. Memberships:** Indiana State, Michigan State, and American Bar (Labor and Employment Law Section) Associations; past President, Indiana University School of Law Indianapolis Alumni Association.
**Personal:** Indiana University, AB, 1971; JD, magna cum laude, 1974. Recognized in 'The Best Lawyers in America', Chambers USA 2003, 2004, 2005 and 2006 editions, and 'Indiana Super Lawyers,' 2004 and 2005 (Law & Politics).

## WALLACK, Barry Z
Wallack Somers & Haas PC, Indianapolis 317 231 9000
bzw@wshlaw.com
*Recommended in Real Estate*
**Practice Areas:** Partner at Wallack, Somers & Haas, concentrating in leasing, lending, borrowing, development, and operation. He has represented clients in public debt offerings, sales and purchases of real estate projects, development of apartment projects, leasing of office buildings and shopping centers, and lender representation.
**Career:** Indiana State Bar admission 1965; Baker & Daniels (associate 1965-69); Klineman Rose Wolf & Wallack (Partner 1969-93; Managing Partner 1986-93); Wallack & Wallack (Partner 1994-99).
**Personal:** Graduated University of Wisconsin (BS, 1962; JD, 1965, Order of the Coif). Board Member, St Vincent Hospital Foundation (2000-05): Recognized in 'Best Lawyers in America', 2001-06.

## WARSHAUER, David
Barnes & Thornburg LLP, Indianapolis
317 231 7346
david.warshauer@BTlaw.com
*Recommended in Real Estate*
**Practice Areas:** Real estate; zoning; planning and land use; represents a broad range of clients in connection with financing and secured lending, real estate development, acquisition, and leasing; has worked on real estate issues for some of Indiana's largest industrial development projects, including the Subaru-Isuzu automotive facility in Lafayette, Indiana; the Toyota plant in Princeton, Indiana; and the Steel Dynamics mill in Butler, Indiana.
**Prof. Memberships:** American College of Real Estate Lawyers.
**Personal:** Washington University (BA, 1980); Indiana University (JD, magna cum laude, 1984).

## WEISS, Zeff
Ice Miller LLP, Indianapolis
317 236 2319
zeff.weiss@icemiller.com
*Recommended in Real Estate*
**Practice Areas:** Zeff, a Partner in Ice

Miller's Real Estate Section, concentrates in real estate development, finance and taxation. He is also involved in complex equity and debt structuring, complex tax and workout matters, as well as eminent domain, sports stadiums and private/public partnership matters.
**Prof. Memberships:** Recognized in: 'Best Lawyers in America'; 'International Who's Who of Real Estate Lawyers'; Indianapolis Business Journal's 'Who's Who in Commercial and Residential Real Estate'. Member of: American College of Real Estate Lawyers; Indianapolis and Indiana State Bar Associations. Executive Committee Member, Board of Directors, The Jewish Federation of Greater Indianapolis, Inc.

## WELCH, Brian
Bingham McHale LLP, Indianapolis
317 635 8900
*Recommended in Litigation*

## WHISTLER, Philip
Ice Miller LLP, Indianapolis
317 236 2349
philip.whistler@icemiller.com
*Recommended in Litigation*
**Practice Areas:** Primary practice concentration in civil litigation, including, antitrust, trade regulation, corporate and securities, distribution and franchising, class actions, and intellectual property. Over 25 years of trial experience, numerous jury and non-jury trials in state and federal courts, and arbitrations before NASD and AAA.
**Prof. Memberships:** Listed in 'Best Lawyers in America'. Member of the Indianapolis, Indiana State, and American Bar Associations. Member of the ABA: Forum Committee on Franchising; Antitrust Section; and Litigation Section. Local Rules Advisory Committee for the US District Court, Southern District of Indiana. Board of Directors, Indianapolis Legal Aid Society.

## WILKINS, Michael
Ice Miller LLP, Indianapolis
317 236 2395
mike.wilkins@icemiller.com
*Recommended in Litigation*
**Practice Areas:** Michael has a uniquely diverse practice, with a focus on appellate advocacy, media law, and family law. He spends the majority of his time representing clients in state and federal appellate courts, but his practice covers all aspects of litigation. He represents media clients on a variety of issues, including pre-publication review, access issues, and defense of defamation and other related suits. He also devotes significant time to representing families in the adoption process and in all other aspects of family law.
**Prof. Memberships:** Member, Indianapolis and Indiana State Bar Associations. Advisory Council, St Elizabeth's/Coleman Pregnancy Services.

## WOLENTY, Barbara
Robinson Wolenty & Young, LLP,
Indianapolis 317 587 7820
*Recommended in Real Estate*

## WORRELL, David
Baker & Daniels, Indianapolis
317 237 1110
david.worrell@bakerd.com
*Recommended in Corporate/M&A*
**Practice Areas:** Represents issuers and
underwriters on IPOs, private placements, and hedge fund and other venture
capital transactions. Advises public companies on compliance with Sarbanes-
Oxley Act, corporate governance requirements, reporting obligations, proxy solicitations and tender offer requirements.
Counsels financial institutions (formations, acquisitions, holding companies,
regulatory compliance and securities
offerings) and directors on fiduciary
duties and regulatory responsibilities.
Counsels companies on mergers, acquisitions or sales of assets or securities,
restructurings and defensive measures on
takeover offers.
**Prof. Memberships:** American Bar
Association.
**Personal:** Wabash College, AB, summa
cum laude, 1973; University of Chicago,
JD, 1976. Recognized in 'The Best
Lawyers in America'; Chambers USA
2004 and 2005 editions,
Corporate/M&A; and 'Indiana Super
Lawyers' 2004 and 2005 editions (Law &
Politics).

## YEAGER, Jay
Baker & Daniels, Indianapolis
317 237 1278
jay.yeager@bakerd.com
*Recommended in Litigation*
**Practice Areas:** Jay Yeager has represented businesses and individuals in a
wide variety of lawsuits and arbitrations,
including aviation litigation, business and
securities fraud, class actions, contract
actions, corporate governance disputes,
international litigation and sale of business disputes. He has tried numerous
bench and jury trials in state and federal
courts, including United States Bankruptcy Court, and has prosecuted and
defended appeals at all levels of both systems. He is also an instrument-rated
commercial pilot.
**Prof. Memberships:** Indianapolis (former Litigation Section Chair), Indiana
State and Seventh Circuit Bar Associations; Member, ISBA House of Delegates;
Member, Indiana Continuing Legal Education Commission.
**Personal:** Harvard University, BA, cum
laude, 1979; Indiana University, JD, cum
laude, 1983. Recognized in 'The Best
Lawyers in America'; Chambers USA
2003, 2004, 2005 and 2006 editions, Litigation; and 'Indiana Super Lawyers' 2004
and 2005 editions (Law & Politics).

## YERKES, Kenneth
Barnes & Thornburg LLP, Indianapolis
317 231 7513
ken.yerkes@btlaw.com
*Recommended in Employment*
**Practice Areas:** Employment law;
employment litigation; management
labor law; collective bargaining; union
elections; wrongful termination; experience includes federal and state court litigation involving discrimination and
wrongful discharge claims, representation in alternative dispute resolution proceedings; supervisor training; union
avoidance planning; collective bargaining; contract administration and representation in arbitration proceedings
**Prof. Memberships:** Indiana State and
American Bar Associations.
**Career:** Admitted to practice before the
US Supreme Court; US Courts of
Appeals for the Sixth, Seventh, and
Eighth Circuits and several district
courts.
**Personal:** Earlham College (BA, 1980);
Indiana University School of Law (JD,
1983).

# BAKER & DANIELS LLP

## THE FIRM

**CEO/Chair:** Brian K Burke

**Number of partners:** 148
**Number of other lawyers:** 164

**FIRM OVERVIEW:** Since 1863, Baker & Daniels has served clients across the country and around the world. With 400 professionals in eight offices in Indiana, Washington, DC and China, Baker & Daniels offers integrated business and legal counsel through legal personnel and the firm's affiliated company, B&D Consulting.

## MAIN AREAS OF PRACTICE:

**Business & Finance:** Baker & Daniels represents business enterprises, from start-ups to large multinational companies on issues including business planning; tax planning; raising capital; employee incentives; contract negotiations and dispute resolution; joint ventures; governmental incentives and public/private venture; purchase or sale of business; licensing, franchise, development and distribution agreements; succession planning; buy-sell and service agreements.

**Healthcare/Medical Technology:** The firm represents hospitals, national and multi-state healthcare systems, nursing and retirement homes, community mental health centers, ambulatory surgery centers, HMOs, PPOs, physicians and other health professionals and trade associations. It also represents medical device and drug companies with intellectual property, FDA, reimbursement, compliance/marketing, liability, clinical trials management and other issues.

**Intellectual Property:** With 49 attorneys, including 34 registered patent attorneys, Baker & Daniels represents clients around the world in the creation of commercial property rights, as well as the protection and leverage of rights in the patent, trademark, copyright and trade secret area. Professionals have technical and legal expertise in the applied sciences, including electronic and mechanical technologies, chemistry, and computer science.

**Labor/Employment & Benefits:** Baker & Daniels' Labor, Employment and Employee Benefits Practice is national in scope. Members of these practice groups have represented employers in all 50 states. While the firm provides services in every aspect of labor, employment and benefits law, it is best known for its traditional labor law practice and employment litigation defense.

**Life Sciences:** With experience, expertise, and industry knowledge to advise businesses shaping the future of life sciences, the firm helps new ventures find resources, market leaders stay ahead of the competition, and research universities move new technologies. They help state and local governments create environments that foster targeted growth, and structure and support the complex alliances among industry, academia, government and non-profits that are at the heart of much of the industry's growth. In addition, Baker & Daniels conceived, organized, and structured the Indiana Future Fund, one of the most innovative funding mechanisms in the life sciences industry. This $73 million fund-of-funds resulted from unprecedented collaboration and has invested in regional and national venture capital funds, thereby attracting capital to emerging Indiana life sciences companies.

**Litigation:** More than 60 litigators and paralegals represent clients in state and federal cases in Indiana and throughout the United States, and serve as national counsel to clients in complex multistate litigation. Product liability team members represent international, national and local manufacturers and distributors in a diverse range of industries, including the medical device, automotive and industrial equipment industries.

**Real Estate:** The firm represents a diverse group of clients on all aspects of real estate, zoning and land use law. Real estate members plan and develop strategies, negotiate and structure essential terms of a transaction, draft or review agreements and instruments, develop zoning regulations, and obtain zoning approvals.

**Tax:** Baker & Daniels represents individuals, corporations, partnerships, tax-exempt organizations, financial institutions, trusts/estates, and specialized entities such as real estate investment trusts, with federal, state and local taxation issues.

## HEAD OFFICE

**INDIANA**
300 N Meridian Street, Suite 2700, **Indianapolis**, IN 46204
**Tel:** 317 237 0300   **Fax:** 317 237 1000

**Website:** www.bakerdaniels.com

## BRANCH OFFICES

**INDIANA**
600 E 96th Street, Suite 600, **Indianapolis**, IN 46240
**Tel:** 317 569 9600   **Fax:** 317 569 4800

111 East Wayne Street, Suite 800, **Fort Wayne**, IN 46802
**Tel:** 260 424 8000   **Fax:** 260 460 1700

First Bank Building, 205 West Jefferson Boulevard, Suite 250,
**South Bend**, IN 46601
**Tel:** 574 234 4149   **Fax:** 574 239 1900

317 West Franklin Street, **Elkhart**, IN 46515
**Tel:** 574 296 6000   **Fax:** 574 296 6001

**DISTRICT OF COLUMBIA**
805 15th Street, NW, Suite 700, **Washington**, DC 20005
**Tel:** 202 312 7440   **Fax:** 202 312 7441

## INTERNATIONAL OFFICES

The firm also has law offices in Beijing and Qingdao, PR China.

**CLIENTS:** Representative clients include Eli Lilly and Co; Zimmer, Inc; WellPoint, Inc.; JP Morgan Chase Bank; ArvinMeritor; Mittal Steel USA, Inc.; Tecumseh Products Company; Roche Diagnostics Corporation; Wabash National Corporation; Mac's Convenience Stores; Kimball International; Cinergy Corporation and American Commercial Lines.

**INTERNATIONAL WORK:** The international team represents clients around the world regarding all business and legal issues. The firm provides business and legal counsel regarding joint ventures; wholly foreign owned enterprises; international arbitration/litigation; trade disputes; distribution and licensing agreements; protection of intellectual property rights; identification of business partners; foreign governments; negotiations; immigration and emigration; international trade tax issues; government affairs; and venture capital and IPOs. China practice professionals in Beijing and Qingdao provide American, Chinese and international clients with comprehensive service including the identification of business partners, manufacturing sources, key personnel and plant site locations. Baker & Daniels is one of only 40 US law firms licensed to practice in China. Networks: Exclusive Indiana member of Lex Mundi and participating member of TAGLaw.

## BAKER & DANIELS LLP

A firm understanding of your legal needs

# BARNES & THORNBURG LLP

## THE FIRM

**Managing Partner:** Alan A Levin
**Number of partners:** 191
**Number of other attorneys:** 204

**FIRM OVERVIEW:** With more than 450 attorneys and other legal professionals, Barnes & Thornburg LLP is one of the Midwest's largest firms. The firm provides legal services to a diverse group of clients ranging from entrepreneurial growth companies to Fortune 500 corporations. Firm attorneys represent clients in many industries, including financial services, technology, international business, life sciences, healthcare, government, higher education, manufacturing, and nonprofit organizations and foundations, among others.

## MAIN AREAS OF PRACTICE:

**Business Transactions & Counseling:** Made up of approximately 150 professionals, the firm's Corporate Group has experience in merger, acquisition, joint venture and capital raising transactions of all types, and in working with entrepreneurial companies. Attorneys counsel corporate clients in the areas of governance, shareholder relations, antitrust planning, distribution, tax and securities matters. The firm's transactional attorneys handle a spectrum of financing matters, including, among others, public and private equity and debt placement, conventional and asset-based lending, commercial real estate finance, structured and asset-backed financing and securitization, and leveraged Employee Stock Ownership Plans (ESOPs), as well as industrial revenue bonds.

**Creditors' Rights:** Attorneys handle all aspects of representation of secured and unsecured creditors, borrowers, guarantors, trustees, and creditors' committees, including negotiating and drafting loan agreements, negotiable instruments, and other commercial transactions in both litigation and transactional aspects of the practice. They also represent creditors and obligors nationally in out-of-court workouts and refinancings, as well as in various state and federal courts, including bankruptcy proceedings, repossessions, and foreclosures.

**Energy, Telecommunications, Transportation & Public Utilities:** The firm serves investor-owned, municipal, and other utilities; telecommunications companies; energy providers; and large consumers in a wide array of regulatory, adversarial, and transactional matters. Attorneys seek to find solutions on both state and federal regulatory challenges in areas such as electricity, gas, internet, telecommunications, high-speed rail, water and waste management.

**Environmental:** Attorneys assist clients with a variety of issues, including compliance counseling, obtaining and negotiating permits, business transactions and planning, facility cleanups, and administrative adjudication before federal and state agencies. The department also has a national water practice that assists clients with a broad range of issues that arise for the regulated community, from policies and rulemaking to permitting and enforcement.

**Governmental Services & Finance:** Firm attorneys regularly represent government issuers and underwriters in government bond financings and many other public finance projects in several states. Attorneys also assist a variety of clients at the local, state and national levels through lobbying and public affairs efforts. The firm serves clients on a variety of business, government and trade association issues and in regulatory and administrative matters, including licensing, rate, finance, contracting with the federal government and complaint proceedings before federal regulatory agencies.

**Healthcare:** The firm's healthcare attorneys represent physicians, medical groups, managed care organizations, hospitals, nursing homes, and national healthcare-related associations located around the country. Attorneys deliver guidance on complex healthcare legal issues, including long-term-care facilities, managed care networks, medical staff issues, medicare and medicaid, mergers and acquisitions, physician-hospital contracting, physician practice groups, provider, joint ventures, reimbursement disputes and audits, and tax exemption issues.

**Intellectual Property:** This department ranks among the largest in the nation for full-service law firms and handles important IP matters domestically and abroad. The group has experience in several facets of intellectual property law, from patent and trademark prosecution to franchising, from antitrust and unfair trade practices to technology development and deployment, and from life sciences and biotechnology to "bet the company" patent infringement litigation. The firm's life sciences and biotech practice includes nine lawyers and patent agents who have earned PhDs in areas such as biology, chemistry, microbiology and pharmacology.

**Labor & Employment:** This group is one of the largest in the Midwest and spans the country in geographic reach. It is dedicated solely to proactively representing the interest of employers. Attorneys routinely defend clients against claims of wrongful discharge, harassment, discrimination, workplace defamation, breach of contract, invasion of privacy, ERISA violations, illicit drug testing and other federal and state law claims, and enforce non-competition and non-solicitation agreements. The firm also has an extensive traditional labor practice, which encompasses defending against unfair labor practice charges and union organizing campaigns, negotiating and administrating union contracts, and coaching and training on lawful union-avoidance techniques.

**Litigation:** More than 130 of the firm's attorneys concentrate their practices resolving disputes through negotiation, arbitration or litigation. Barnes & Thornburg's litigators have represented businesses in controversies in all 50 states and before most of the US federal courts, as well as before various international and multi-jurisdictional tribunals.

**Real Estate Services:** The firm's real estate attorneys offer all of the legal services necessary to take a parcel of land from initial purchase through the completion of a real estate project. These services include rezoning and land-use planning; negotiation of financing; project development; organization of owners' associations and development of architectural standards; leasing, sale, or tax-free exchange of the completed project; and any other matters, including litigation, which may be encountered before, during, and after the completion of a project.

## OFFICES

### DISTRICT OF COLUMBIA
750 17th St., NW, Suite 900, **Washington**, DC 20006-4675
**Tel:** 202 289 1313   **Fax:** 202 289 1330
**Website:** www.btlaw.com

### ILLINOIS
One North Wacker Dr., Suite 4400, **Chicago**, IL 60606-2833
**Tel:** 312 357 1313   **Fax:** 312 759 5646

### INDIANA
121 W.Franklin, Suite 200, **Elkhart**, IN 46516
**Tel:** 574 293 0681   **Fax:** 574 296 2535

600 One Summit Square, **Fort Wayne**, IN 46802-3119
**Tel:** 260 423 9440   **Fax:** 260 424 8316

11 S.Meridian St., **Indianapolis**, IN 46204-3535
**Tel:** 317 236 1313   **Fax:** 317 231 7433

100 N.Michigan, 600 1st Source Bank, **South Bend**, IN 46601-1632
**Tel:** 574 233 1171   **Fax:** 574 237 1125

### MICHIGAN
300 Ottawa Ave., NW, Suite 500, **Grand Rapids**, MI 49503
**Tel:** 616 742 3930   **Fax:** 616 742 3999

# BARNES & THORNBURG LLP
**btlaw.com**

# ICE MILLER LLP

## THE FIRM

**Managing Partners:** Phillip Bayt, Byron Myers, Melissa Proffitt Reese

**FIRM OVERVIEW:** Founded in 1910, Ice Miller LLP is one of the largest law firms in Indiana with a national reputation in many of its practice areas. The firm's main office is in Indianapolis, Indiana, and it maintains additional offices in Chicago, Illinois; Naperville, Illinois; and Washington, DC. The firm has over 225 lawyers, 40 paraprofessionals and 250 staff members. Their lawyers and business professionals, through their understanding of businesses, industries and government entities, help simplify the complexities faced by the firm's clients. They are committed to helping clients achieve their legal and business goals.

## MAIN AREAS OF PRACTICE:

**Colleges & Universities:** Public and private colleges and universities can be confronted by unique legal issues. The firm utilizes a multidisciplinary team that understands how an institution's legal and strategic needs can differ from those in the world of business and corporations. To fully understand and address an institution's needs, attorneys serve as directors and trustees of colleges and universities as well as teach as adjunct faculty at area law schools. They also participate in organizations such as the National Association of College and University Attorneys (NACUA) to gain further insight, and are well positioned to react quickly and effectively, offering institutions creative solutions.

**Corporate and Business Transactions:** Ice Miller is one of the most experienced and widely recognized firms in the United States in general corporate matters and in structuring, negotiating and documenting all types of business transactions. They assist growing companies in acquiring businesses or product or service lines of businesses, and help companies streamline their organizations by selling operations or assets they no longer need. The firm's attorneys also have significant experience with joint ventures, licensing and franchise transactions.

**Litigation:** Ice Miller litigators have represented thousands of clients before state and federal courts throughout the nation. Each litigator concentrates in two or three substantive areas of law and, when necessary, consults with other attorneys to capitalize on Ice Miller's broad range of knowledge and diverse experience.

**Private Equity/Venture Services:** Ice Miller is known throughout the United States as a significant player in the private equity fund and venture services arena. For more than 25 years, its attorneys have represented private equity funds and provided fund formation, structuring and investment transaction services to funds that focus on equity and debt investments in private companies, including seed, venture, mezzanine, buy-out, "crossover" investment and broad-based private equity funds. They also provide comprehensive legal services to high growth companies, with a particular emphasis on assisting with venture finance.

**Real Estate:** Ice Miller's real estate attorneys act as "legal architects," putting to use all of the tools in today's regulated business environment to creatively pursue client's goals. They represent developers, landlords, financial institutions, and others who regularly engage in real estate transactions, as well as clients who only occasionally need the firm's services to lease, construct, buy or sell facilities.

**Tax:** Ice Miller's Tax Practice is dedicated to providing clients with timely and efficient solutions that enhance economic return by reducing tax expense. The firm's knowledge of federal, state and local tax issues provides comprehensive coverage for clients, whether they are individual entrepreneurs or domestic and foreign multinational corporations.

## EMPLOYMENT SERVICES

**Benefits:** Current economic pressures and the aging of the work force have made employee benefits a focal point for employers and employees in the public and private sector. Lawyers and consultants in the Ice Miller's Benefits Practice advise businesses, governments, churches, and plan trustees on how to handle retirement plans, health plans, compensation packages, and other fringe benefits.

## HEAD OFFICE

### INDIANA
One American Square, Suite 3100, **Indianapolis**, IN 46282-0200
**Tel:** 317 236 2100   **Fax:** 317 236 2219
**Email:** info@icemiller.com
**Website:** www.icemiller.com

## BRANCH OFFICES

### ILLINOIS
200 West Madison, Suite 3500, **Chicago**, IL 60606-3417
**Tel:** 312 726 1567   **Fax:** 312 726 7102

568 South Washington Street, **Naperville**, IL 60540
**Tel:** 630 527 2315   **Fax:** 630 527 2417

### DISTRICT OF COLUMBIA
1090 Vermont Ave. NW, Ste. 920, **Washington**, DC 20005
**Tel:** 202 824 8600   **Fax:** 202 824 8601

**Labor:** In choosing labor and employment counselors to satisfy business objectives, the client first needs to know what Ice Miller believes in and what they stand for. Whether in a union or non-union environment, the firm's chief goal is to work with clients to create a work force that is world-class in all respects.

## HEALTH SERVICES

**Drug, Device & Chemical Exposure Litigation:** Ice Miller has decades of experience in drug, device and chemical exposure claims and litigation. Their attorneys have served as national, regional, and local counsel in drug, device and chemical exposure litigation where they regularly address scientific, epidemiologic and complex medical issues in multi-jurisdictional litigation. They also conduct audits of pharmaceutical products both before and after product launch, and provide counseling on preventative measures and risk management.

**Healthcare:** Ice Miller has substantial experience in the business and regulatory aspects of healthcare. Their clients can be found in all branches of the healthcare industry, including hospitals, multi-specialty physician clinics, physician groups, individual physicians, health maintenance organizations, retirement centers, medical research organizations, and suppliers of medication and medical equipment. The firm's attorneys provide advice in solving technical as well as practical problems, and, when necessary, thorough representation in litigation, business transactions and municipal finance transactions.

**CLIENTS:** CID Equity Partners, Community Hospitals of Indiana, Inc., Eli Lilly and Company, Haynes International, Inc., Hoffmann-LaRoche Inc., Howard Regional Health System, Indiana Bond Bank, Indiana University, Indianapolis Motor Speedway, Kite Realty, L'Oreal USA, Merrill Lynch, Remy, Inc., and Under Armour, Inc.

**INTERNATIONAL WORK:** The firm's International Practice addresses the business and legal needs of clients around the world including export consultation and licensing, foreign investment in the United States, immigration and international employees, international agreements and antitrust issues, tax and export/import matters. They have personnel fluent in Japanese, Chinese, Spanish, French, Russian, German, Persian and Greek.

# McTURNAN & TURNER

## THE FIRM

**Managing Partners:** Lee B McTurnan, Wayne C Turner

**Number of partners:** 4
**Number of other lawyers:** 9

### AREAS OF PRACTICE:
Business Litigation . . . . . . . . . . . . . . . . . . . . . . . . . . . . . . . . . 100%

**FIRM OVERVIEW:** McTurnan & Turner concentrates in relatively complex business litigation. The firm's goal is to provide the high quality of representation expected from the largest firms with the responsive and efficient services that distinguish the best small firms. The firm has assembled a group of unusually talented lawyers who work closely with the client or corporate counsel to plan and implement strategies throughout pre-trial and trial proceedings.

**MAIN AREAS OF PRACTICE:** The firm's lawyers have litigated issues concerning:

**Corporate Securities/Governance:** Fraud or misstatements in sales of securities or financial statements; shareholder derivative claims; breaches of fiduciary duties of directors, officers and employees and of corporate governance provisions; tender offers/takeover.

**Class Actions:** Representing defendants in alleged class actions related to securities laws, equal employment opportunity laws (race, sex and age), consumer fraud, product liability, and federal and state taxation.

**Employment/Discrimination Matters:** Race, sex and age discrimination; employment contracts; covenants not to compete.

**Professional Responsibility:** Defending professionals such as accountants, lawyers and securities broker-dealers against claims of negligence or misconduct.

**Competition/Regulation:** Restraints of trade, antitrust; regulation of utilities (telephone, electric, natural gas).

**Contracts:** Sales of goods, equipment, or services; insurance; franchises; commissions; guarantees; leases; construction.

**Business Torts:** Product liability; consumer fraud; lender liability; trade secrets; unfair competition; environmental liability; tortious interference.

**First Amendment:** Defamation; protection of free speech and press; third-party discovery from media; newsgatherers' rights and privileges; access to public records and proceedings.

**Reported Cases:** Some reported cases handled by the firm include: Gold Seal Termite And Pest Control Co., et al., on behalf of themselves and others similarly situated, v PrimeTV, LLC and DIRECTV, Inc., Marion Superior Court (defense counsel for DIRECTV in 2005 nationwide class action settlement of multi-billion dollar claims for alleged violation of the Telephone Consumer Protection Act with respect to unsolicited fax advertisements); M-Plan, Inc., et al. v Indiana Comprehensive Health Insurance Association and Sally McCarty, 809 N.E. 2d 834 (Ind.2004) (requiring exhaustion of administrative remedies for claims against Indiana Insurance Commissioner and involuntary association created by statute); Polinsky and Sutker v Violi, 803 N.E. 2d 684 (Ind. Ct. App. 2004) (addressing issue of first impression concerning mandatory arbitration for claims against controlling shareholders in privity with corporation that entered agreement to arbitrate); Indiana Comprehensive Health Insurance Association, et al. v Avemco Insurance Company, et al., 812 N.E. 2d 108 (Ind. Ct. App. 2004) (affirming injunction forcing approximately $8 million in funding for Indiana's high risk health pool, by companies claiming not to meet the statutory criteria for assessment); Midwest Gas Services, Inc., et al. v Indiana Gas Co., Inc. and ProLiance Energy, LLC, 317 F.3d 703 (7th Cir. 2003) (affirming dismissal of multiple Sherman Act claims); United States Gypsum Inc. v Indiana Gas Co., Inc., ProLiance Energy LLC, et al., 735 N.E.2d 790 (Ind. 2000) (opinion affirming ruling by the Indiana Utility Regulatory Commission that client ProLiance Energy LLC, a natural gas marketer, is not a public utility subject to state regulation); Indianapolis Newspapers v Indiana State Lottery Comm'n and James F. Maguire, 739 N.E.2d 144 (Ind.Ct.App. 2000) (reversing trial court's decision that would have eliminated client Indianapolis Newspapers' statutory right to recover attorneys' fees if it substantially prevails on the merits of its claim for public access to Lottery sales records); Adams v Indiana Bell Telephone Co., Inc. and Ameritech Services, Inc., 2 F. Supp. 2d 1077- 1134 (S.D. Ind. 1998) (summary judgment in favor of client Ameritech Services, Inc. against class and individual claims of age and pension discrimination in downsizing; affirmed as to pension claims and reversed as to age claims, 231 F.3d 414 (7th Cir. 2000)); Indiana Wholesale Wine & Liquor Co., Inc. v State of Indiana ex rel. Indiana Alcoholic Beverage Commission, 695 N.E.2d 99-108 (Ind. 1998) (opinion upholding client Indiana Wholesale's liquor distribution permits on statutory ground; Court of Appeals had ruled for Indiana Wholesale on U.S. constitutional Commerce Clause and 21st Amendment bases, 662 N.E.2d 950-970 (Ind.App. 1996)); In re WTHR-TV and McGraw-Hill Broadcasting Company, Inc. d/b/a WRTV-6; State of Indiana v Krista M. Cline, 693 N.E.2d 1-16 (Ind. 1998) (Indiana Supreme Court's opinion of first impression on Indiana third-party discovery and access to television out-takes); IPALCO Enterprises, Inc. v PSI Resources, Inc., 148 F.R.D. 604-608 (S.D. Ind 1993) (discovery/privilege issues in merger/tender-offer dispute).

**CLIENTS:** The firm's corporate clients include AT&T Inc (formerly SBC Communications, Inc.); PricewaterhouseCoopers LLP; Wachovia Corporation; ProLiance Energy LLC; CitiFinancial; General Motors Corporation; Salomon Smith Barney, Inc.; Western Newspaper Publishing Co.; Earlham College; Redcats USA, LP; and McGraw-Hill Broadcasting Co., Inc. (WRTV-6). The firm is regularly employed by corporate counsel or through other law firms to represent corporate or individual clients in substantial, non-recurring litigation matters.

**INTERNATIONAL WORK:** The firm has represented a number of non-US clients in litigation within the United States. These clients include: Onkyo Japan; Shell International BV; Langen Packaging, Inc.; Molins PLC; Autoliv; Euribrid, Inc.; Sleeman Breweries, Inc; and Tagsys Q.

# SOMMER BARNARD PC

## THE FIRM:

**Number of Partners:** 51
**Number of Other Lawyers:** 42

**FIRM OVERVIEW:** Sommer Barnard has been serving the legal needs of business clients for over 35 years. Headquartered in Indianapolis, its primary practice areas include litigation, business law, business workouts, bankruptcy and creditors' rights, environmental law, government services, health and life sciences, intellectual property, labor and employment, real estate, tax and trusts and estates.

## MAIN AREAS OF PRACTICE:

**Business Workouts, Bankruptcy & Creditors' Rights:** The firm has extensive experience representing businesses in Chapter 11 bankruptcy. The firm also has one of the largest practice groups in Indiana dedicated to assisting businesses in their reorganization activities outside Chapter 11. It also represents creditors in the bankruptcy and reorganization process.

**Business Law:** The firm assists clients in the pursuit of business strategies, including their acquisition, disposition, financing and licensing activities. Members of its business group have guided companies through some of the largest public company mergers and initial public offerings within in the state, routinely serve middle market companies, and have assisted in the start-up and growth of numerous emerging companies, including high-tech ventures.

**Environmental Law:** The firm's experience includes all areas of environmental law. The firm represents clients in environmental litigation before state and federal courts and in administrative proceedings throughout the United States.

**Government Services:** The firm's practice involves a wide range of legislative and regulatory activities at the local, state and federal levels, representing business, trade associations and governmental entities.

**Health & Life Sciences:** The firm's practice group includes a diverse legal team representing health industry clients across the state and beyond. The firm advises clients on rapidly changing legal, regulatory and business developments in the health and life sciences field.

**Intellectual Property:** The firm's IP practice group provides full intellectual property services in the traditional areas of patent, trademark, copyright and trade secret law, and counsel for new technology transactions, advertising, privacy and e-commerce.

**Labor & Employment Law:** The firm is well experienced in representing both employers and employees in employment litigation, counseling in traditional labor law areas, and advising employers on various issues concerning their employee benefits.

**Litigation:** The firm represents plaintiffs and defendants in its nationwide commercial and class action litigation practice. The practice encompasses complex cases involving antitrust, securities, environmental, real estate and other commercial issues, as well as white collar criminal litigation.

**Real Estate:** The firm's real estate attorneys have experience in all aspects of complicated real estate transactions, as well as business transactions involving real estate, including representation of developers in the acquisition, zoning, financing and development of real estate in both local and multi-state transactions. The firm's Real Estate Group often acts as special counsel for the purpose of rendering opinions for borrowers and lenders in connection with complex financing transactions.

**Tax:** The firm provides a wide range of tax services for individual clients and businesses and represents taxpayers in administrative and judicial proceedings.

**Trusts & Estates:** The firm counsels individuals and families on estate planning needs, assists fiduciaries in the administration of estates and trusts, counsels on many business succession planning issues, and assists clients in charitable planning.

# SOMMER BARNARD PC

# WALLACK SOMERS & HAAS P.C.

## THE FIRM

**Senior Partners:** Barry Z Wallack
George W Somers
Karl P Haas

**Number of partners:** 6
**Number of other lawyers:** 2

## AREAS OF PRACTICE:

| | |
|---|---|
| Commercial Real Estate Development | 40% |
| Municipal Redevelopment | 25% |
| Commercial Leasing | 15% |
| Commercial Real Estate Lending | 15% |
| Commercial Real Estate Litigation | 5% |

**FIRM OVERVIEW:** Wallack Somers & Haas, P.C. is an Indianapolis, Indiana-based boutique law firm concentrating its practice in all aspects of commercial real estate development, leasing, and financing. Comprised of experienced and innovative attorneys, the firm provides legal advice to local, regional and national clients.

## MAIN AREAS OF PRACTICE:

**Commercial Real Estate Development:** The firm's attorneys have extensive experience in assisting commercial real estate developers in achieving their goals, including the development and redevelopment of shopping malls, retail centers, business campuses, industrial facilities, hotels, sports centers, office buildings and multi-family housing.

**Municipal Redevelopment:** The firm has an established municipal redevelopment practice, focusing on the unique requirements of urban and suburban mixed, public/private redevelopment projects.

**Commercial Leasing:** The firm represents both landlords and tenants in office, retail and industrial leasing.

**Commercial Real Estate Lending:** The firm represents local and national borrowers and lenders for construction and permanent lending, tax credit transactions, mezzanine financing, syndications and securitized lending.

**Commercial Real Estate Litigation:** The firm acts as counsel to clients in a limited array of commercial real estate disputes, including landlord-tenant disputes and mechanic's liens.

**CLIENTS:** The firm's clients include a publicly-traded REIT, commercial banks, insurance and other financial institutions, developers, landlords, tenants, non-profit organizations, municipal entities and individual entrepreneurs and investors.

## HEAD OFFICE

**INDIANA**
One Indiana Square, Suite 1500, **Indianapolis**, IN 46204
**Tel:** 317 231 9000  **Fax:** 317 231 9900
**Website:** www.wshlaw.com

## CONTACTS

| | |
|---|---|
| **Commercial Real Estate Development** | George W Somers |
| **Municipal Redevelopment** | Karl P Haas |
| **Commercial Leasing** | Barry Z Wallack |
| **Commercial Real Estate Lending** | Barry Z Wallack |
| **Commercial Real Estate Litigation** | Michael S Wallack |

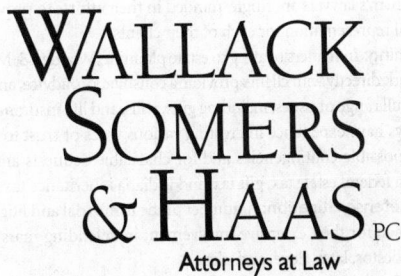

WALLACK
SOMERS
& HAAS PC
Attorneys at Law

# WOODEN & MCLAUGHLIN LLP

## THE FIRM

**Management Committee:** Tom Dinwiddie, Dale Eikenberry, Kent Broach

**Number of partners:** 17
**Number of other attorneys:** 18

**FIRM OVERVIEW:** Founded in Indianapolis in 1970, Wooden & McLaughlin offers its clients a high level of experience, knowledge, and accessibility. It is a law firm that strives to exceed the commonly accepted standards of professionalism and client service. The phrase 'raising the bar' is used to describe this philosophy. The phrase 'raising the bar' embodies the philosophy that guides and motivates the lawyers at Wooden & McLaughlin. It is not about the firm's image, but about its identity. It is not a slogan, but a pledge. Most importantly, it is the clients' assurance that when they call Wooden & McLaughlin, they will receive legal representation that is thoughtful, professional, efficient, and, above all, effective.

## MAIN AREAS OF PRACTICE:

**Commercial Litigation:** The firm's trial and litigation attorneys regularly handle all types of commercial litigation including: antitrust, business torts such as trade secrets, interference with business relations and fraud cases, contract disputes, employment matters, eminent domain, insurance matters, intellectual property, lease and mortgage matters, and professional liabilty.

**Complex Environmental, Product Liability & Tort Litigation:** A significant part of the firm's Litigation Practice includes matters in this area such as: aviation cases, environmental litigation, medical device cases and a wide variety of product liability cases.

**Employment Litigation:** In the area of employment law, large and small companies alike have benefited from Wooden & McLaughlin's thoughtful approach and dedicated counsel. From the administration of union contracts (including negotiation, arbitration, and contract interpretation issues) to the defense of employment discrimination cases (such as race, sex and age discrimination claims), the firm's lawyers are single-minded in their efforts to provide the best possible legal representation for each of their clients.

**Estate Planning:** In matters relating to estate planning, Wooden & McLaughlin's attorneys work directly with clients providing consultation, advice, and assistance regarding a full range of issues, including gifts, wills, and life insurance planning. Our attorneys have experience in creating various types of trust to provide for all types of possible contingencies and for charitable bequests and gifts, and assisting with federal estate tax, gift tax, and Indiana inheritance tax matters.

**Mass Tort Defense Litigation:** A number of the firm's trial and litigation attorneys are known for their extensive involvement in defending mass tort claims including: asbestos, latex glove, and silica.

**Corporate:** Entity selection and formation, along with all possible operational advice needs; mergers and acquisitions; and tax.

**Lender Finance:** Documentation and negotiation of all types of real estate secured financings, including acquisition, construction, land development and permanent mortgage loans; documentation and negotiation of all types of commercial and asset-based financings; advise on current methods and alternatives in real estate financing and assisting in the structuring and documentation of real estate mortgages and other financing transactions.

**Real Estate:** Includes representing clients in development, construction, syndication, taxation, financing, leasing, condemnation, litigation, and zoning. Clients include local and regional retail, residential, commercial, and industrial real estate developers; state, regional and national financial institutions; real estate trade associations; architectural firms; general construction contractors; not-for-profit low income housing lenders; and real estate brokerage firms.

## HEAD OFFICE

**INDIANA**
One Indiana Square, Suite 1800, **Indianapolis**, IN 46204
**Tel**: 317 639 6151  **Fax**: 317 639 6444

**Website:** www.woodmdaw.com

## CONTACTS

| | |
|---|---|
| **Commercial Litigation** | Dale W Eikenberry |
| | John D Nell |
| **Complex Environmental, Product Liability & Tort Litigation** | Daniel D Trachtman |
| | Dale Eikenberry |
| **Mass Tort Defense Litigation** | Douglas B King |
| | Dan Trachtman |
| **Corporate** | Kent M Broach |
| | Ronald G Salatich |
| **Lender Finance** | John W Hamilton |
| | Thomas M Hanahan |
| **Real Estate** | Thomas W Dinwiddie |
| | E Joseph Kremp |

**CLIENTS:** AIG Aviation, Inc., American State Bank, Apartment Association of Indiana, Inc., AT&T, Barrett & Stokely, Inc., Bechtel Corporation, BP Products North America, Inc., CB Richard Ellis, CNA Insurance Companies, Comerica Bank, Cranfill & Company, CVS Pharmacy, Delphi Corporation, Delta Airlines, Inc., FCCI Insurance Group, Fifth Third Bank, Fleet Mortgage Corp., HP Products Corp., Hughes Group Incorporated, Huntington National Bank, Indiana Beer & Wine Distributors, Inc., Indiana Land Title Association, Indiana Mortgage Bankers, Inc., Indiana Soc. of Prof. Land Surveyors, Indiana University, Indianapolis Neighborhood Housing Partnership, Irwin Mortgage Corp., Irwin Union Corporation, J.C. Hart Company, Inc., Lauth Properties, Lucent Technologies, MEDMARC, Inc., Metropolitan Life Insurance Company, National Bank of Indianapolis, National City Trust, NiSource, Northrop Corporation, Olympia Partners Ltd., P/R Mortgage & Investment Corporation, Peabody Coal Co., Shiel Sexton Co., Inc., Terre Haute Regional Hospital, The May Department Stores Company, The Skinner & Broadbent Company, Trustcorp Mortgage Company, U.S. Aviation Insurance Group, U.S. Bank, United States Aviation Underwriters.

**WOODEN & McLAUGHLIN** LLP

Attorneys At Law

RAISING THE BAR SM

**CONTENTS:**

## How lawyers are ranked

Every year we carry out thousands of in-depth interviews with clients and lawyers in order to assess the reputations and expertise of business lawyers across the USA. Chambers rankings and editorial are referred to extensively by General Counsel and other purchasers of legal services who look to our recommendations when choosing their lawyers.

# CORPORATE/M&A

| Corporate/M&A |
| --- |
| Leading Firms |

| 1 | BELIN LAMSON MCCORMICK *Des Moines* |
| --- | --- |
| | DAVIS, BROWN, KOEHN, SHORS *Des Moines* |
| | NYEMASTER, GOODE, WEST *Des Moines* |
| 2 | LANE & WATERMAN LLP *Davenport* |
| | SHUTTLEWORTH & INGERSOLL PLC *Cedar Rapids* |
| 3 | BRADLEY & RILEY, PC *Cedar Rapids* |
| | BRADSHAW, FOWLER, PROCTOR *Des Moines* |
| | BROWN, WINICK, GRAVES *Des Moines* |
| 4 | AHLERS & COONEY PC *Des Moines* |
| | MOYER & BERGMAN, PLC *Cedar Rapids* |

| Leading Individuals |
| --- |

**Senior Statesmen**

| | BROWN Donald *Davis, Brown, Koehn* |
| --- | --- |
| | RILEY Byron *Bradley & Riley, PC* |
| 1 | CARROLL Frank *Davis, Brown, Koehn* |
| | HANSELL Edgar *Nyemaster, Goode, West* |
| | KRAMBECK James *Belin Lamson McCormick* |
| | STREIT Gary *Shuttleworth & Ingersoll* |
| | ZUMBACH Steven *Belin Lamson McCormick* |
| 2 | CORTESIO John *Bradshaw, Fowler* |
| | DICKINSON Mark *Nyemaster, Goode* |
| | NEUMANN Gordon *Nyemaster, Goode* |
| | REASONER Carroll *Shuttleworth & Ingersoll PLC* |
| | SHORS John *Davis, Brown, Koehn* |
| | WATERMAN III Dana *Lane & Waterman LLP* |
| 3 | ADAMS Garth *Belin Lamson McCormick* |
| | BERENSTEIN Marvin *Berenstein, Moore* |
| | BOYKEN Quentin *Belin Lamson McCormick* |
| | BROWN William *Brown, Winick, Graves* |
| | CAMPBELL Bruce *Davis, Brown, Koehn* |
| | LAMSON Jeffrey *Belin Lamson McCormick* |
| 4 | BLASER Michael *Brown, Winick, Graves* |
| | GROSS Doug *Brown, Winick, Graves* |
| | HINTZE John *Ahlers & Cooney PC* |
| | HOCHSTETLER William *Shuttleworth & Ingersoll* |

**Up-and-coming individuals**

| | REAMES Wayne *Belin Lamson McCormick* |
| --- | --- |
| | SACKETT Christopher *Brown, Winick, Graves* |

## Band 1

### Belin Lamson McCormick Zumbach Flynn, PC

**The Firm:** Benefiting from the regional omnipotence of one of the most *"creative and smart"* teams in the state, this firm enjoys a pan-market reputation for depth and quality. A plentiful diet of midsized M&A work has been supplemented over the past year by acting in the $44.9 million sale of Integrated Distribution Solutions, an Omaha-based software business that was acquired by an Israeli company listed on the Israeli stock exchange and NASDAQ. Clients were consistently impressed by the firm's *"unbelievable knowledge and dedication."*

**The Lawyers:** A team of *"stellar individuals"* is headed by rainmaker **Steve Zumbach**, the market's *"clear leader."* Contemporaries say he is *"in a class of his own"* and highlight his particular expertise in estate planning and transactional work. Described as *"bright and articulate,"* **Jim Krambeck** is another of the firm's major assets; he received accolades from sources that deem him *"one of the top corporate lawyers in Iowa and highly respected by everyone."* Clients appreciate that Krambeck *"really knows how to get a deal done."* He has lately closed nearly 20 transactions valued between $5 million and $75 million. **Quent Boyken**'s ranking results from a growing acknowledgment of his *"talent, diligence and brightness."* Clients were impressed by his *"wonderful"* tax and pensions knowledge, in addition to his *"great time management."* Boyken recently represented a company engaged in the distribution of manufacturing equipment in an asset purchase agreement by a Mississippi-based corporation. **Jeff Lamson** is regarded as *"a gentleman and a fine lawyer,"* while *"super, young guy"* **Garth Adams** has a reputation for *"industriousness and intelligence;"* clients view him as *"competent, creative and compatible."* He acts as external counsel to a variety of clients, but has a notable number in the construction industry. Adams recently undertook a private placement for a healthcare company. Newcomer to the tables **Wayne Reames** joins as a reflection of clients' admiration for his *"technical competency and problem-solving approach."*

**Clients/Work Highlights:** Hallett Materials; RSM McGladrey; Integrated Distribution Solutions; Cityview; Central Bancshares; RUAN Transportation Management Systems and Meredith Corporation.

### Davis, Brown, Koehn, Shors & Roberts, PC

**The Firm:** Acknowledged as having a *"long history of fine corporate work,"* Davis Brown possesses *"true expertise"* and earns *"a huge amount of admiration"* from the market. It currently has around 25 attorneys in the group, many of whom have specialist skills in addition to providing general corporate counseling. Said one long-standing client: *"The firm is comprehensive and has very well-trained attorneys. They are reliable and I have a tremendous amount of confidence in them."* The firm worked in conjunction with the Iowa Bankers' Association on a proposal to the federal government for $70 million worth of new market tax credits, and helped a technology company on a common and preferred stock offering. Other work includes a management transition matter that involved the repurchasing of stockholder stock and mobilization of the new management team.

**The Lawyers:** Displaying extensive tax and employee benefits knowledge as well as more general corporate skills, **Frank Carroll** is widely looked upon as *"one of the best tax lawyers in the state."* His peers acknowledge that he is *"solution-oriented"* and *"doesn't get carried away with advocacy."* Meanwhile, *"measured and thoughtful"* **John Shors** ascends the tables this year. In the area of venture capital, he helped to set up the Iowa Fund of Funds, during which he was instrumental in changing state legislation to allow the operation of the fund. Several commentators testify that *"he has considerable experience and is really attuned to clients' needs,"* and clients appreciate that he *"is an expert at finding a middle ground and an amenable solution to difficult problems."* **Bruce Campbell** is a new entrant following positive client endorsement. Rising to the category of Senior Statesman in this year's rankings is *"conscientious, capable and thorough"* **Don Brown**. His practice centers on governance, and he serves as outside counsel to a board of directors of one of the top 50 construction companies in the USA. Although now semi-retired, Brown commands marketwide admiration for his *"outstanding level of expertise."*

Clients/Work Highlights: Mg Biologics; Edge Technologies; Mercy Hospital Medical Center and Iowa Capital Investment Corporation.

## Nyemaster, Goode, West, Hansell, and O'Brien

The Firm: With a *"high-quality"* team of 30, the largest corporate practice in the state retains its top spot in the tables thanks to abundant praise for its *"exceptionally talented attorneys."* It represents a broad cross-section of corporate clients in a swath of diverse M&A work, which this year included assisting a client in acquiring a publicly traded company in Denmark. It was heavily involved in the demutualization of an insurance company, and regularly undertakes private equity raising for businesses, while also advising clients on Sarbanes-Oxley compliance and other regulatory matters. It interfaces between state government and startup businesses in raising venture capital and this year secured a $6 million state grant for a biotech company. Clients view this multidisciplinary outfit as *"a one-stop shop."*

The Lawyers: Known affectionately as *"the market's patriarch,"* **Edgar Hansell** spends a large portion of his time representing health and dental insurance companies. In particular, he has been involved in contracting and physician relationship work on behalf of McFarland Clinic PC. Peers consider him *"a bulldog,"* confirming their universal respect for his *"astuteness and energy."* With his background in the Iowa State Bar Association, his depth of experience is undisputed. **Rick Neumann** and **Mark Dickinson** ascend the rankings this year on the basis of an expanding acknowledgment of their *"gentlemanly demeanor"* and *"capable, competent"* approach. Neumann represents several healthcare entities and commands respect from clients for his *"prompt and conscientious"* attitude, while Dickinson is an insurance and securities expert, admired for his *"fine work."*

Clients/Work Highlights: EMC Insurance Companies; American Republic Insurance; Ames National Corporation; Wellmark; Delta Dental Plans Association; The Lauridsen Group and McFarland Clinic PC.

## Band 2

## Lane & Waterman LLP

The Firm: At over 150 years old, this firm has a sterling reputation for unmatched quality and depth in the Davenport area. Its 25-strong business law team is involved in all manner of corporate work and several members of the team are qualified to undertake work in Illinois as well as Iowa. As the fastest growing part of the firm, the corporate practice represents regional and super-regional banks, such as Wells Fargo, in addition to smaller banks in credit and corporate undertakings. The team has been helping one client establish a joint venture in China and another Indiana-based client expand into Florida and the West Coast. Clients say the firm's name is synonymous with *"a fine tradition"* and

*"substantial, highly regarded"* individuals.

The Lawyers: An ongoing relationship with Lee Enterprises has seen **Dana Waterman** this year act in the $1.45 billion acquisition of Pulitzer newspapers. Alongside Ed Carroll, he handled the related syndicated financing and refinancing of existing debt with a new credit agreement following the acquisition, which has now made Lee Enterprises the fourth largest newspaper company in the USA. Clients pinpoint his *"outstanding expertise and highly professional manner."*

Clients/Work Highlights: The firm acts for major countrywide banks, medium-sized local banks and other firms such as Deere & Company, Ryan Companies US and Genesis Health System.

## Shuttleworth & Ingersoll PLC

The Firm: As *"the leading firm in Cedar Rapids,"* this practice undertakes the full range of corporate work; indeed, clients say it is *"fluent in the A-Z of legal services,"* both transactional and contentious. It recently handled complex estate issues involving multiple assets, charity remainder and tax aspects in the USA and Canada. Also on the books were two complex asset purchases of out-of-state manufacturing concerns for a local client. Peers view Shuttleworth as a *"high-quality and well-respected"* competitor, while its clients are more than satisfied with the *"competent, professional and creative thread that runs through the entire firm."*

The Lawyers: **Gary Streit**'s performance has prompted some very positive comments from peers who say he is *"extremely well respected"* by the local legal and business communities. Client approval underlines his *"good understanding of business needs"* combined with a *"down-to-earth, jargon-free approach."* The first and still the only female president of the Iowa State Bar Association, **Carroll Reasoner**, *"works creatively to find the right solutions."* Contemporaries rate her as *"an excellent, very personable lawyer."* Newcomer to the tables **Bill Hochstetler**'s areas of specialism include estate planning and business planning. He was highly acclaimed by interviewees, who deemed him *"professional and creative in his approach."*

Clients/Work Highlights: The firm works on behalf of many high-profile clients including national banks, food suppliers and insurers.

## Band 3

## Bradley & Riley, PC

The Firm: Despite its comparatively small size, this firm maintains a reputation for *"high-quality and reliable work."* It advises startup businesses on their responsibilities and has expertise in debt and equity work. It has a prominent place in the Cedar Rapids market through its representation of lenders and venture capital firms.

The Lawyers: Seasoned attorney **Buck Riley** commands *"tremendous respect"* from clients and admiring fellow practitioners.

Clients/Work Highlights: Alliant Energy; Mount

Mercy College; Heartland Inn; Merit Construction and MidAmerica Housing Partnership.

## Bradshaw, Fowler, Proctor & Fairgrave, PC

The Firm: A *"detail-oriented and reliable"* practice, this firm's corporate group has considerable experience of the insurance market. Over the past year, it was involved in defending a class action in addition to its regular business law, antitrust and trade regulation undertakings. The team is able to draw upon the expertise of other specialists within the firm and clients are appreciative of this.

The Lawyers: The practice group is led by the *"extremely detail-oriented"* **John Cortesio**, who in many commentators' eyes is *"very bright and has an ethical approach"* and *"a wealth of experience."* Cortesio is supported by other attorneys, including bankruptcy specialist Donald Neiman and Gregory Kenyon, who heads the transaction practice and is a recognized expert in estate planning.

Clients/Work Highlights: The firm advises a variety of corporate and other clients.

## Brown, Winick, Graves, Gross, Baskerville and Schoenebaum PLC

See firm details p.923

The Firm: Regularly *"exceeding expectations,"* this 20-strong corporate practice attracted plenty of favorable comments from competitors and clients. It recently broadened its capabilities to include capital markets and advice to the agriculture industry for the first time. To this end, it worked on over $600 million in equity and debt financing for agricultural processing facilities. Other notable matters include representing a startup wine cooperative, a large-scale biodiesel production facility, and two companies seeking to establish operations in China. It also acts for numerous corporate clients in an advisory capacity, dealing with matters such as Sarbanes-Oxley compliance. Lawyers assisted a nonprofit company when the IRS asserted that excess compensation was paid to a former executive – a case which made the front page of the Wall Street Journal.

The Lawyers: **Bill Brown**'s (see p.920) practice encompasses estate planning and M&A. He was recently involved in the acquisition of group foster care providers in Arizona and Wyoming for an Iowa-based client. **Doug Gross**'s (see p.920) connections with state government *"have earned him great respect in Iowa,"* according to peers. Clients say: *"He works really hard to get a resolution in everybody's interests."* With emphasis on the representation of agribusinesses such as cooperatives, hog processors, poultry farms and egg processors, **Mike Blaser** (see p.919) joins the rankings this year. He was formerly general counsel to Iowa Select Farms and is known as a *"helpful and astute"* attorney. Another newcomer to the tables, **Christopher Sackett** (see p.921) prompted a wave of praise for his *"great energy and buckets of common sense."* He is currently representing a Canadian manufacturing company in a joint venture with a US materials producer. Clients like the fact that *"he makes us feel we're a priority."*

**Clients/Work Highlights:** Harvest Capital Asset Management; Lisle; EZ Way; Hagie Manufacturing; Stellar Industries; United Equipment Accessories; Interpower; Wright Welding Supply; Clarke County Development Corporation; Iowa Wine Cooperative; Southern Iowa BioEnergy and Wells Fargo Home Mortgage.

## Band 4

### Ahlers & Cooney PC

**The Firm:** With its core in transactional work, Ahlers & Cooney also has *"a wonderful reputation"* for its municipal bond work. The firm's finance and business departments work closely together, recently completing the $30 million sale of a meat-packing company, undertaking State Employees Combined Campaign compliance work on behalf of various clients, and working extensively with state and local governments on the negotiation of urban renewal development projects. A significant amount of time

is spent representing lenders, insurance companies and banks in preparing documents for commercial lending transactions.
**The Lawyers:** Head of the practice **John Hintze** is much admired by peers, who say he is *"a fine fellow and a very capable lawyer."*
**Clients/Work Highlights:** The firm represents several banks and publicly traded companies, including the State of Iowa Board of Regents, Iowa Student Loan Liquidity Corporation and Principal Financial Group.

### Moyer & Bergman, PLC

**The Firm:** This eight-strong Cedar Rapids practice focuses on business acquisitions, disposals and reorganizations. While the majority of the work is undertaken locally, it is sometimes hired by large, out-of-state entities for transactions elsewhere. While seven-figure deals are the usual upper echelons of its work, the firm has been known to undertake deals in the eight-figure range. Recently it assisted a group of employees in the successful acquisition of a manu-

facturing business, and was also engaged in a stockholder dispute between related families.
**The Lawyers:** The corporate practice is led by Phil Brooks.
**Clients/Work Highlights:** American Family Insurance; CRST International; Ag Services of America; State Farm; TrueNorth Companies; Westfield Insurance and GreatAmerica Leasing.

### Other Notable Practitioners

*"Bright and capable"* **Marvin Berenstein** of Berenstein, Moore, Berenstein, Heffernan & Moeller is thought of as *"the leading attorney in Sioux City."* In that part of the state, he represents some significant clients and has been involved in major transactions alongside Omaha and Chicago law firms. His area of expertise is principally trusts and estates work as it relates to corporate, and to this end he has acted as the coordinator between client and M&A counsel in helping a client to sell a significant family business. Berenstein is active in the Iowa State Bar Association.

---

# EMPLOYMENT

# MAINLY DEFENDANT

| Employment: Mainly Defendant |
|---|
| **Leading Firms** |
| [1] AHLERS & COONEY PC *Des Moines* |
| DICKINSON, MACKAMAN, TYLER *Des Moines* |
| NYEMASTER, GOODE, WEST *Des Moines* |
| [2] BELIN LAMSON MCCORMICK *Des Moines* |
| DAVIS, BROWN, KOEHN, SHORS *Des Moines* |
| SHUTTLEWORTH & INGERSOLL PLC *Cedar Rapids* |
| [3] BRADLEY & RILEY, PC *Cedar Rapids* |
| BRADSHAW, FOWLER, PROCTOR *Des Moines* |
| SIMMONS PERRINE ALBRIGHT *Cedar Rapids* |
| WHITFIELD & EDDY, PLC *Des Moines* |

## Band 1

### Ahlers & Cooney PC

**The Firm:** A pillar of the employment community in Des Moines, this 11-strong practice *"does a stellar job"* covering the range of employment and labor work in both the public and private sectors. Clients confirm that it *"staffs cases accurately and correctly and never overcharges."* Its public sector practice recently saw it advising schools and school districts on teacher terminations, policy reviews and litigation. In the private sector, it represents many high-profile employers in discrimination cases in the state and federal courts. Lawyers additionally counsel employers on how to prevent litigation, touching on contracts; harassment; severance deals; terminations; drug testing policies and collective bargaining agreements. A notable case from the past year involved the representation of a CEO of a company in a dispute over claims relating to contracts.
**The Lawyers:** A favorite among peers and clients, **Elizabeth Kennedy** has earned a reputation for

providing *"practical and candid"* advice and possessing a *"thoughtful and careful manner."* Clients say she *"can tell you frankly things that you do and don't want to hear,"* and she possesses *"a depth of knowledge that gives her great credibility."* In addition to undertaking more standard labor and employment matters, she is carving out a niche mediation practice. As her right-hand man, *"analytical and intellectual"* **Nathan Overberg** is gaining a following. He provides *"clear advice that's free from lawyer-type confusion."* **James Hanks** enters the tables this year as a consequence of the recognition he gained for his schools defense practice. This past president of the National School Attorneys Association is recognized as a well-established expert.
**Clients/Work Highlights:** Employers in the public and private sectors across the state.

### Dickinson, Mackaman, Tyler & Hagen, PC

**The Firm:** Ten attorneys form the heart of this *"reputable"* employment practice which, according to client consensus, is *"one of the most highly sought-after teams in the Midwest."* It works with employers on all types of issues inside and outside the state, including: OSHA; workers' compensation; consulting; training; litigation and traditional labor matters. The firm has particular expertise in ADA and FMLA cases and is seeing a surge in noncompete and wage and hour litigation. Recent highlights include obtaining summary judgment for Pioneer Hi-Bred International on an age discrimination claim from the Southern District Court of Iowa. It also won summary judgment for Des Moines Water Works in a race and disability discrimination case. Clients note that the team *"really understands our business and can explain the law in clear terms."*

**The Lawyers:** *"The anchor of the practice,"* **Helen Adams** devotes a significant portion of her time to litigation and played key roles in the cases mentioned above. Clients prize highly her *"knowledgeable and approachable"* demeanor, which they say *"makes people feel comfortable."* Invaluable experience is coupled with *"an ability to communicate with people at all levels,"* equipping her with *"simply a great presence."* **Russ Samson's** practice falls into the more traditional domain of labor work, in which he is viewed as *"the guru."* The focus of his work is helping clients to avoid problems with unions, but he also worked extensively on a recent ERISA case that emanated from the $26.8 million demutualization of an insurance company. Clients say he is *"a key person to have in your corner."* Debuting in *Chambers'* tables, the *"just fabulous"* **Bridget Penick** received many recommendations. She specializes in immigration law as it relates to employment and receives work from across the country. Clients are struck by her *"terrifically knowledgeable and thorough approach."*
**Clients/Work Highlights:** Adventureland Park; Cahaba Government Benefit Administrators; Des Moines Water Works; Exceptional Persons Inc.; FCStone; Grinnell Regional Medical Center; MCI; Merit Resources; Pioneer Hi-Bred International; Verizon Wireless and US Cellular.

### Nyemaster, Goode, West, Hansell, and O'Brien

**The Firm:** With a team of ten dedicated lawyers, this celebrated practice handles all types of labor and employment law, undertaking a *"phenomenal"* amount of work and drawing upon an *"impressive breadth"* of skills. It has seen a rise in the number of discrimination cases, coupled with an upturn in the amount of sophisticated and complex class actions undertaken. Significant involvement with IP issues as an offshoot of employment law is similarly a growth area, and the firm has handled a number of noncompete matters. It attracts praise from competitors who admire its *"fine reputation,"* while clients regard it as *"first-class, ethical and exceptional in every way."*

**The Lawyers:** The practice is led by **Frank Harty,** who this year completed his 40th jury trial: a sexual harassment case that was the first one of its kind under the Iowa Civil Rights Act. Fervent admiration from clients assures his continued presence at the top of the *Chambers* tables; they confirm that he is *"sincere, prompt and personable, with a great sense of humor."* **Thomas Foley** focuses mainly on employment discrimination defense work and, thanks to a background in commercial litigation, he is viewed as a key operator in this domain. **Thomas Cunningham'**s regional labor and employment practice has seen him represent a large building products manufacturer in a labor lawsuit across seven Midwest states. He is also regional counsel for a large convenience store chain. Contemporaries regard him as *"tenacious,"* while clients note that he is *"very bright and a great strategist."* **Randall Armentrout** specializes in the defense of wrongful termination, breach of contract, sexual harassment and other discrimination cases. He recently obtained summary judgment in a large breach of contract case while representing a clinic that was sued for fraud by a former employee contract. Clients confirm that his strengths in advocacy can be put down to *"a strong commitment to his clients and to his work."* **Mary**

**Funk** joins the tables this year. She has been working on a significant case for an employer who terminated an employee's contract for sending risqué e-mails; she also obtained summary judgment when a court threw out a claim of wrongful termination of a railroad worker who alleged that federal railroad law had preempted the claim. This was only the second case in the USA to deal with this point of law. According to peers, Funk is *"tremendously bright."*
**Clients/Work Highlights:** The firm acts for a wide range of corporate clients inside and outside the state.

## Band 2

### Belin Lamson McCormick Zumbach Flynn, PC

**The Firm:** This group of *"well-educated professionals"* has consistently impressed its clients with its *"focus on business issues."* It aids clients who find themselves in hostile work environments, both through involvement in employment disputes and trials, and through sharing its expertise in the area of labor relations. Last year it acted for Prairie Meadows Casino in an FMLA claim and for FedEx in a promissory estoppel claim. Both resulted in summary judgment in favor of the firm's client. Lawyers regularly defend harassment and discrimination suits.

**The Lawyers:** **Jim Swanger'**s traditional labor law practice was praised by commentators, who saw him as dextrously combining *"a tenacious courtroom presence"* with *"a calming effect on his clients."* Others pointed out his ability *"to see the silver lining in every cloud."* Clients tell of the *"seasoned and experienced"* air he exudes – one that belies his age – and of the *"terrific advice and great direction"* he gives. Employment litigator **Michael Reck** possesses *"a great intellect and a mind that works faster than anyone else's,"* giving him *"fluency and fluidity on his feet."* Clients admire him for being *"a great tactician."* **Holly Logan** is newly ranked following client validation of her *"detailed, go-getting approach,"* which she manages to blend with a *"calm and collected"* manner.
**Clients/Work Highlights:** The team represents clients from a variety of industries.

### Davis, Brown, Koehn, Shors & Roberts, PC

**The Firm:** An upturn in litigation following an increase in claims under the FLSA has allowed this firm to take key roles in some significant disputes. It is additionally handling two wage and hour cases that relate to the payment of overtime on behalf of Winnebago Industries and West Liberty Foods, and has advised on the acquisition of a tire plant with 730 employees covered by a collective bargaining agreement. Clients proclaim it *"one of the best employment firms in Iowa,"* and say: *"It has the breadth and talent to handle just about anything."*
**The Lawyers:** Rising through the rankings to take up a place in the top tier, **Gene La Suer** has *"a signif-*

*icant presence"* in the employment community, which clients put down to his *"extraordinary intelligence and experience."* Client loyalty is assured by the fact he *"really gets results."* Dividing her time evenly between litigation and employment work, **Deborah Tharnish** was also the subject of significant client praise. Displaying characteristic *"good common sense and competence,"* she has been playing a major role in various complex class actions and cases filed under the FLSA. **Sharon Malheiro'**s recent successes include winning summary judgment on a sexual harassment case, though a large part of her practice is devoted to helping clients with prevention and training policies. Market sources applaud her *"expertise and knowledge."*
**Clients/Work Highlights:** Clients from a variety of industry sectors are represented, including hospitals and other medical facilities; factories and other manufacturers; publishing houses and nonprofit organizations.

### Shuttleworth & Ingersoll PLC

**The Firm:** This is a fairly traditional labor and employment practice which encompasses the usual litigation and arbitrations, plus counseling and preventive advice. In a recent case the firm won summary judgment on behalf of an Egyptian dismissed from his workplace in the wake of 9/11; it also represented an African-American federal probation officer who was passed over for promotion – the resultant ruling deemed that this was race-related. The firm also helps local companies being bought by out-of-state firms on the modifications of their human resources procedures and policies in the event of potential claims by employees, and is seeing an increase in IP work such as trade secrets as it relates to employment.
**The Lawyers:** Widely considered to be *"one of the state's best lawyers,"* **Mark Zaiger** is the key figure here. Cerebral in nature, he impresses many with his *"scholarly approach and deep knowledge of the subject."* His expertise lies in employment law and union negotiations, an area in which he is viewed as *"a problem solver, not a problem creator."*
**Clients/Work Highlights:** The firm represents many small regional companies and better-known names such as Quaker Oats, Swiss Valley Farms and Cargill.

## Band 3

### Bradley & Riley, PC

**The Firm:** Clients from both private and public sectors are represented by this small but renowned firm. It undertakes a variety of work on its clients' behalf, including collective bargaining negotiations, union organizing and election campaigns, strikes and picketing, immigration, unlawful discrimination, unemployment compensation and OSHA complaints.
**The Lawyers:** With the bulk of the practice resting on his shoulders, *"calm and decisive"* **Kelly Baier** is rated as *"the best employment lawyer in Cedar*

Rapids." His strengths lie across the range of employment and labor law, and he inspires admiration for his *"diligence, knowledge and confidence."*

**Clients/Work Highlights:** Woodward Communications; Alliant Energy; Kirkwood Community College and Chubb Group.

## Bradshaw, Fowler, Proctor & Fairgrave, PC

**The Firm:** The ripening employment and labor practice is an adjunct to the sophisticated litigation division of this firm. The team represents both defendants and plaintiffs, and was hired recently to represent the insurer of a landfill site in a lawsuit in which the site's owner was accused of raping a female member of staff. Motion for summary judgment was filed and the case was settled. In another case, it is representing a plaintiff who was fired from an advertising agency when she was several months pregnant. The case will go to trial in 2006.

**The Lawyers:** **Gordon Fischer** is acclaimed as *"smart and savvy"* by observers. He acted in the cases mentioned above.

## Simmons Perrine Albright & Ellwood PLC

**The Firm:** Offices in Iowa City and Cedar Rapids ensure a steady stream of work into the employment practice. It regularly represents clients in claims of unlawful discrimination, unemployment compensation, occupational health and safety, unfair labor practice charges and wrongful discharge claims in both the private and public sectors. On the labor side, work includes collective bargaining agreements and arbitrations.

**The Lawyers:** The *"terrific"* **Iris Muchmore** was described to researchers as *"smart and careful"* with a *"levelheaded and personable"* approach to her work. Market recognition has pushed her into the top tier this year.

## Whitfield & Eddy, PLC

**The Firm:** A *"good all-around"* firm, this compact Des Moines-based unit covers the complete range of employment issues for both plaintiffs and defendants. Its market visibility has been enhanced by the publication of the firm's labor and employment peri-

odical, and the regular appearance of its lawyers on the lecture circuit.

**The Lawyers:** A *"recognizable"* name, **Greg Naylor** is known to *"keep up to date with all the fast-changing moves in employment law."* His colleague **Jaki Samuelson** is a *"sharp and articulate"* attorney who has impressed a number of her peers.

**Clients/Work Highlights:** Clients include Wells Fargo, American Equity Investment Life Insurance and Midwest Heritage Bank.

## Other Notable Practitioners

Heading up a four-strong team at Brown, Winick, Graves, Gross, Baskerville and Schoenebaum PLC, **Jim Gilliam** (see p.920) has an employment and labor practice that is primarily litigation-oriented. The majority of his time over the past year has been spent defending discrimination, wage and hour, and workers' compensation cases. He is recommended by clients for his *"professional and strategic"* approach.

# LITIGATION

## Litigation: General Commercial
### Leading Firms

| 1 | AHLERS & COONEY PC *Des Moines* |
| | BELIN LAMSON MCCORMICK *Des Moines* |
| | LANE & WATERMAN LLP *Davenport* |
| | NYEMASTER, GOODE, WEST *Des Moines* |
| 2 | FINLEY, ALT, SMITH, SCHARNBERG, *Des Moines* |
| | SHUTTLEWORTH & INGERSOLL PLC *Cedar Rapids* |
| | WHITFIELD & EDDY, PLC *Des Moines* |
| 3 | BRADSHAW, FOWLER, PROCTOR *Des Moines* |
| | DAVIS, BROWN, KOEHN, SHORS *Des Moines* |
| | DUTTON, BRAUN, STAACK & HELLMAN *Waterloo* |
| | ELDERKIN & PIRNIE PLC *Cedar Rapids* |
| | SIMMONS PERRINE ALBRIGHT *Cedar Rapids* |
| 4 | BRADLEY & RILEY, PC *Cedar Rapids* |
| | BROWN, WINICK, GRAVES, GROSS *Des Moines* |
| | HANSEN, MCCLINTOCK & RILEY *Des Moines* |

## Band 1

### Ahlers & Cooney PC

**The Firm:** *"An excellent firm with excellent lawyers,"* was the market's view on this midsized practice. Described by clients as *"a wonderful firm"* that is *"always able to help us and very easy to trust,"* Ahlers & Cooney has expiated the departure of Dave Swinton by further strengthening its core specialties. Under the umbrella of business and commercial litigation, it recently took on an array of complex and high-profile cases, including defending a clothing manufacturer in a products liability lawsuit brought by a plaintiff whose 100% cotton garment was set alight by a candle and who alleged that the fact the

garment was not flame-retardant was not made explicit by its manufacturer. The firm works closely with school districts and recently emerged from a successful representation of one school district in trial with a building contractor, in addition to several other pieces of litigation brought by disgruntled ex-employees of schools and colleges. Its skills are being called upon with increasing frequency for IP and antitrust cases. The firm's reputation is enhanced further by strong Bar association connections.

**The Lawyers:** The fulcrum of the practice, **Rick Santi** enjoys *"a tremendous reputation"* throughout the state, especially since his tenure as president of the Iowa Defense Counsel Association. Exalted by his peers as *"an exceptional litigation lawyer,"* he is likewise recognized by clients as *"bright, fair and innovative."* Santi recently acted in a fatality case in which an aircraft crashed, killing its pilot, and the maintenance company responsible for the upkeep of the aircraft was sued by the pilot's estate. A member of the American College of Trial Lawyers, **Ed Remsburg** has a following that declares he is *"one of the state's best trial lawyers."* Recent work includes trade secrets and trademark cases. Although relatively young, **Randall Stefani** has already accumulated a coterie of admirers, who have warmed to his *"honesty and thoroughness."* They say he is *"very easy to work with and always tells you exactly what he's thinking."* Stefani is *"aggressive and smart"* – qualities that cement his reputation as *"an exceptional litigator."* He has become more involved in the firm's education practice of late. **Wade Hauser** earns recognition for his *"sharp and smart"* approach to litigation.

**Clients/Work Highlights:** Corporate entities from a variety of industry sectors and geographical locations make up a loyal client base.

# GENERAL COMMERCIAL

## Belin Lamson McCormick Zumbach Flynn, PC

**The Firm:** Clients do not hesitate to proclaim this firm *"a first-class operation with high-caliber associates,"* and its litigation practice has endeared itself to an ever-growing circle of fellow practitioners. It enjoys something of a celebrity status in the state thanks to the late founding partner David Belin, who was on the Warren Commission. The group has been fortified this year with the addition of Dave Swinton, formerly of Ahlers & Cooney, in a move which will bring another area of expertise to the practice. The firm takes a spot in the top tier of the rankings this year in recognition of these developments. For some this is *"probably the best litigation firm in Des Moines;"* it has a long-standing relationship with Iowa State University and this year was involved in a dispute over whether the university's records are subject to public disclosure. It successfully acted in an IP matter for Midwest Oilseeds, which netted a $43 million judgment in its favor from the Federal Court of Appeals. The firm handles all major commercial litigation for MidAmerican Energy, in addition to servicing several other notable clients. It draws admiring words from market commentators: *"Their clients are impressive and the work they do is complex."*

**The Lawyers:** **Mark McCormick**'s time is increasingly being taken up in engagements as expert witness in legal negligence cases. *"A lawyer's lawyer,"* he is also heavily involved in arbitrations, mediations and appellate cases. McCormick's *"cerebral, bright and ethical"* manner has made such an impact on fellow practitioners and clients that one rated him *"the smartest guy I have ever met."* Despite his authority, clients say he is *"softly spoken yet forceful"* in trial,

| Litigation: General Commercial |
| --- |
| Leading Individuals |

**Senior Statesmen**

ELDERKIN David *Elderkin & Pirnie PLC*
JAMES Dwight *The James Law Firm PC*
MCCLINTOCK John *Hansen, McClintock & Riley*
★ DUTTON David *Dutton, Braun, Staack & Hellman PLC*

[1] FANTER Robert *Whitfield & Eddy, P.L.C*
FIGENSHAW Michael *Bradshaw, Fowler, Proctor*
FINLEY Thomas *Finley, Alt, Smith, Scharnberg, Craig*
MCCORMICK Mark *Belin Lamson McCormick*
PHIPPS David *Whitfield & Eddy, P.L.C*
ROBY Patrick *Elderkin & Pirnie PLC*
SANTI Richard *Ahlers & Cooney PC*
SAPP Richard *Nyemaster, Goode, West*
WATERMAN Thomas *Lane & Waterman LLP*
WATERMAN JR Robert *Lane & Waterman LLP*

[2] BROWN David *Hansen, McClintock & Riley*
COLLINS Kevin *Shuttleworth & Ingersoll PLC*
COOK Guy *Grefe & Sidney, P.L.C.*
CRITELLI JR Nicholas *Law Chambers of*
HAYES James *Hayes Lorenzen*
HILMES Jack *Finley, Alt, Smith*
HOUGHTON Robert *Shuttleworth & Ingersoll*
LEDERER Gregory *Simmons Perrine Albright*
REMSBURG Edward *Ahlers & Cooney*
STEFANI Randall *Ahlers & Cooney*
SWINTON David *Belin Lamson McCormick*
THARNISH Deborah *Davis, Brown, Koehn*
THOMPSON Donald *Bradley & Riley*
TRIPP Mark *Bradshaw, Fowler*

[3] APPEL Brent *Wandro, Baer & Appel*
BICKEL John *Shuttleworth & Ingersoll*
DRAPER Hayward *Nyemaster, Goode, West*
GAFFNEY Todd *Finley, Alt, Smith, Scharnberg*
GUNDERSON Joseph *Gunderson, Sharp & Walke*
HAUSER III Wade *Ahlers & Cooney PC*
MANSFIELD Edward *Belin Lamson McCormick*
TANK David *Davis, Brown, Koehn*
WEINHARDT Mark *Belin Lamson McCormick*

[4] BRALEY Bruce *Dutton, Braun, Staack*
DRISCOLL Kevin *Finley, Alt, Smith, Scharnberg*
REYNOLDS Kevin *Whitfield & Eddy, P.L.C*
SCHARNBERG Steven *Finley, Alt, Smith, Scharnberg*
SMITH Glenn *Finley, Alt, Smith, Scharnberg*
WOODBURN III Chester *Hansen, McClintock & Riley*

and his *"prestigious credentials"* go a long way toward earning him *"enormous respect in the community."* Such comments have allowed him to move up to the top of the table. **Dave Swinton**'s arrival at the firm is widely seen as *"strengthening its litigation impact."* He recently represented a life insurance company in defense of securities and contracts claims. *"Bright and brilliant"* **Ed Mansfield** recently represented Fortune 500 company Kaydon in an indemnification case involving the failure of a hydraulic cylinder. He also represented a subsidiary of Monsanto in a lawsuit brought by former regional managers, and a

printing company in a multimillion-dollar products liability claim. Clients are comfortable in the knowledge that his *"law professor demeanor"* will help him *"deal with difficult situations practically and intellectually."* Another attorney possessing a *"smart legal mind,"* **Mark Weinhardt** consistently impressed clients with his *"professionalism and experience."* As a former DOJ federal prosecutor, he has *"great advocacy skills"* and performs well in sizable and complex cases, *"which he is able to make comprehensible to juries."*

**Clients/Work Highlights:** Midwest Oilseeds; Kaydon; Mediacom Communications; MidAmerican Energy; Unisys and Maytag.

## Lane & Waterman LLP

**The Firm:** Cast as *"a model litigation practice"* in the eyes of many interviewees, this general litigation unit is seen as *"the only one in the east of the state that can handle complex business."* Long established, and living up to its tradition of *"high-quality and high-volume"* work, a recent key success was its achievement of the largest class action settlement recovery in state court history – a $100-200 million settlement payout to 300,000 policyholders of Allied Mutual Insurance. The firm is retained as state counsel for Glaxo-SmithKline and is also involved in parts of the OxyContin litigation, adding to the growing amount of pharmaceutical products liability litigation on its books.

**The Lawyers:** **Tom Waterman** was lead counsel on the Allied Mutual case, and his successes have not gone unnoticed by fellow practitioners. *"He's top-notch and has broad experience,"* they told researchers, while clients reported it was his *"strong relationships with federal court judges"* that set him apart. With a wealth of medical malpractice expertise, *"honorable"* **Bob Waterman** has a marketwide reputation for doing *"a wonderful job."* Commentators say his *"analytical"* approach is one of his best assets.

**Clients/Work Highlights:** The firm represents a cross-section of financial institutions; media companies; railroads; manufacturers; utilities; contractors and retailers.

## Nyemaster, Goode, West, Hansell, and O'Brien

**The Firm:** The state's largest firm boasts a 35-strong litigation team, which this year raised its game through state representation of the manufacturer of the painkiller OxyContin in the trial that made headlines worldwide. In addition to performing well in products liability, healthcare and medical malpractice litigation, it is developing niche expertise in ERISA cases. Clients like the fact that it is able to draw on in-depth expertise when needed: for example, it retains a bank of medical experts to whom it refers in cases such as the OxyContin litigation.

**The Lawyers:** *"Superb"* **Richard Sapp** is lead defense attorney for Purdue Pharma, the manufacturer of OxyContin, and is also the products liability lawyer for Deere & Company, on whose behalf he regularly defends agricultural and recreational equipment claims. His *"absolutely first-class"* stand-

ing in the market is corroborated by clients, who say he not only has *"a sharp understanding of the law and expert handling of very sensitive issues,"* but a *"shrewd judgment and a wealth of experience that enable him to predict in what direction a case is heading."* Other clients appreciate the fact they can call upon him as *"a source of input and comment – he always gives good feedback."* Opinion deems Sapp *"top of the talent pole."* He is backed up by an able team of litigators that includes **Hayward Draper**, described as *"a bright, fine attorney."* Historically, Draper's practice has been based on professional liability defense and commercial fraud, but he has become increasingly involved in contentious matters arising from medical malpractice, ERISA and healthcare work.

**Clients/Work Highlights:** Clients include major national manufacturers such as Deere & Company and Purdue Pharma, in addition to other Fortune 500 companies and local entities.

## Band 2

## Finley, Alt, Smith, Scharnberg, Craig, Hilmes & Gaffney PC

**The Firm:** Acting in the Enron litigation as well as tobacco and asbestos cases typifies the class of work that this capacious boutique takes on. In addition to prowess in regular commercial litigation, it boasts a *"superb"* track record in medical malpractice, the core of which is the defense of hospitals, clinics and medical practitioners across the state. It also undertakes the defense of insurance, construction, railroad and manufacturing companies. Work is not restricted to Iowa, but is in much of the Midwest, and lawyers regularly undertake work in Chicago, Minneapolis and Kansas. The firm is currently representing a railroad company in a case involving a man who lost his leg while coupling defective cars, and recently acted in a successful products liability case involving the manufacturer of a toilet valve that failed, allowing several thousand gallons of water to damage a home.

**The Lawyers:** A unit of ten trial lawyers is headed by **Tom Finley**, who is described as *"the tsar of medical malpractice"* by his peers. His clients credit him with being *"extremely bright, likable and competent,"* and acknowledge his *"superb statewide reputation"* as *"a real specialist."* Making a name for himself in railroad defense, medical malpractice and product liability, **Jack Hilmes** puts clients at ease with his *"even-keel demeanor and great judgment."* Peers with experience of his courtroom presence say he is *"bright and well prepared."* Also undertaking a significant amount of products liability and railroad litigation, **Todd Gaffney** is gaining a following. There are three new additions to *Chambers'* tables this year. **Kevin Driscoll** has been included thanks to growing recognition of his aptitude, and undertakes construction litigation representing insurers, contractors and architects. The *"terrifically bright"* **Steve Scharnberg** concentrates on medical malpractice, a field in which he has *"a very good name"* and *"handles work with great aplomb."* **Glenn Smith**

received praise for the "*sharp, ethical, old-school*" style he brings to his commercial litigation practice.

Clients/Work Highlights: A substantial portion of the firm's clients are in the healthcare sector, but it also works for clients in manufacturing, construction and financial services.

## Shuttleworth & Ingersoll PLC

The Firm: Engaged in more business emanating from the eastern part of the state than any other local firm, the "*top-notch*" litigation practice here offers comprehensive representation in several areas of dispute resolution. Regularly trying cases before federal and state court, court of appeals and US Supreme Court, its name is synonymous with an august reputation and long, illustrious history. Some 14 attorneys comprise the litigation practice, their recent work including the conclusion of a business fraud case that went to the US Supreme Court in which they represented an Israeli client. Another matter was a $40 million trademark and copyright infringement case that was tried in Washington state; a third involved the representation of a group of hospitals in reimbursement claims in federal programs. Its IP, medical device and drug work take it to all parts of the country, and it represents local physicians, lawyers, engineers, architects and hospitals in all types of litigation. Clients place it at the forefront of the local competition: "*It is an excellent law firm and the best known in Cedar Rapids for this kind of work.*"

The Lawyers: Fêted by clients as "*an awesome litigator,*" Kevin Collins can "*impress a jury*" and relate to clients in an "*understanding, energetic*" way. As former president of the Iowa State Bar Association, he is perceived as "*the cornerstone of most complex litigation at the firm.*" Bob Houghton is a "*talented, well-prepared and smart*" attorney whose practice is mainly concentrated in the areas of medical malpractice and medical device litigation, in which he "*does a really nice job.*" Broad litigation experience is what "*seasoned and dedicated*" John Bickel has to offer. He provided litigation support to The Schneider Group following multimillion-dollar losses resulting from a fire, and represented Gazette Communications in general litigation and First Amendment matters.

Clients/Work Highlights: Clients include many local and regional businesses in addition to larger international companies.

## Whitfield & Eddy, PLC

The Firm: Made up of 15 "*fabulous trial lawyers,*" the litigation team here is licensed to practice in 12 different states and represents clients in federal courts, administrative hearings and alternative dispute resolution on a variety of different matters. Work has traditionally sprung from "*big, bad*" products liability cases, and it has also been active outside the USA, wherever its clients have been embroiled in overseas disputes. Recent work has involved the proprietary rights of various product lines, covering issues of patents and copyright on behalf of a design firm that services the petrochemical business. Clients

value the lawyers for their "*broad, dependable*" expertise. The Lawyers: "*A prestigious and impressive problem solver,*" Bob Fanter is admired for his "*masterly*" ability to bring about resolution between seemingly irreconcilable parties. His practice has recently been more concentrated on products liability work. Peer testimonies highlight the "*rock-solid and capable*" nature of David Phipps who has "*a tremendous amount of good courtroom experience.*" Despite his savoir faire, clients attest that his manner is "*never flamboyant or flashy.*" Phipps' work includes a lot of insurance defense and business litigation, domains in which he is considered "*one of the best lawyers in the state.*" Another "*excellent defense attorney,*" Kevin Reynolds was also highlighted to researchers this year. In addition to being very active in the Defense Research Institute, he handles a number of high-profile products liability cases.

Clients/Work Highlights: A diverse range of clients is represented by the firm, including those in the manufacturing, petrochemicals and technology industries.

## Band 3

## Bradshaw, Fowler, Proctor & Fairgrave, PC

The Firm: Primarily known for its medical malpractice work, this "*reliable and straightforward*" firm also conducts products liability and insurance defense. Its diet of medical malpractice trial work has been complemented this year with an employment injury case. Lawyers have earned a high degree of respect from the state's medical community as well as fellow practitioners.

The Lawyers: "*Talented and experienced*" Michael Figenshaw ascends the tables following the praise he received from peers, who reckoned him a "*very reassuring and pragmatic*" presence. Clients feel that they "*get good representation from him,*" and can depend on his "*sound judgment.*" Mark Tripp moves up the rankings following widespread approval of his "*low-key yet effective*" style. Often engaged in products liability defense, he is seen as an "*outstanding trial lawyer blessed with a ton of common sense.*" Clients warm to his "*compelling, bright and innovative*" approach.

## Davis, Brown, Koehn, Shors & Roberts, PC

The Firm: The civil litigation practice here has "*tentacles in a lot of complex work.*" It defends pharmaceuticals giant Wyeth in the ongoing Fen-Phen diet drug litigation, which is expected to reach a conclusion over the next year, and has widened its focus on IP-related trial work with extensive involvement in patent litigation and business trade secret cases. Other litigation includes property tax assessment and insurance defence. Clients are increasingly calling upon the firm to act for them in mediations and arbitrations, and commentators spoke of the "*impressive amount of brainpower*" on offer.

The Lawyers: An "*outstanding and wonderful*" team

includes Deborah Tharnish, whose bifurcated practice encompasses employment law as well as business litigation. Client appraisal deemed her "*a pleasure to work with,*" while peers recognized her as "*procedurally very knowledgeable.*" Impressing clients with his "*confidence and intellect*" is "*young, bright spark*" David Tank. He has showcased on a number of patent disputes lately.

Clients/Work Highlights: Clients include commercial banks; nonprofit organizations; national and international corporations and insurance companies.

## Dutton, Braun, Staack & Hellman PLC

The Firm: "*The premier firm in Waterloo*" has had a busy year, with its team of seven litigation lawyers occupied in a variety of trial matters for prestigious clients. Latterly, it represented the CEO of an agricultural lending institution in connection with violations of federal law, and provided counsel for a prisoner serving a life sentence in a federal habeas corpus matter. Lawyers recently concluded the trial of a bank fraud case involving the transfer of $1 million between a debtor and his wife, and are working on a trade secrets case involving the former president and vice president of a university, due to go to trial in 2006. Even though the firm is characterized by the fact it "*juggles many balls at the same time,*" clients reported that they never felt any less than top priority.

The Lawyers: Senior partner David Dutton is at the apogee of state litigation, according to interviewees. As a "*top-quality, tough-guy*" former prosecutor, he has the armor to "*try a million cases.*" Peers spoke of his "*fabulous, professional and ethical*" approach, something which prompted one client to tell researchers: "*He has restored my faith in lawyers.*" An attorney of statewide renown, Dutton was praised for "*not misleading clients in any way – he tells you the truth straight up,*" and his "*boundless energy*" was felt to be unmatched. Another "*outstanding trial lawyer,*" Bruce Braley joins the tables this year. He is running for Congress this year.

Clients/Work Highlights: GE; PepsiCo; Sears; TEREX; St. Paul Travelers; Kemper Insurance Companies; Upper Iowa University and Principal Financial Group.

## Elderkin & Pirnie PLC

The Firm: At this "*small, excellent*" boutique 15 lawyers take on a variety of work over a range of business sectors.

The Lawyers: David Elderkin's "*legendary and unbeatable*" reputation as one of the state's litigation forefathers is at the heart of this firm's profile. Now into his nineties, he still has gravitas and is remembered by peers as "*a lion in the courtroom.*" Superlatives also abounded for "*bright and aggressive*" Patrick Roby, who is quite simply "*an outstanding lawyer.*" His presence is said to "*elevate the firm,*" and his peers describe him as "*full of dynamite and fun to work with.*" In the courtroom, he "*prevails through his sheer ability to command attention.*"

**Clients/Work Highlights:** Cessna Aircraft, Mercy Medical Center and American Funeral Home are among the firm's clients.

## Simmons Perrine Albright & Ellwood PLC

**The Firm:** Steady growth and solid performance have marked out this broad-based defense firm as a dependable fixture in the eastern Iowa marketplace. Twenty trial lawyers defend clients in many types of litigation, with the commercial practice covering employment, antitrust and contract cases that flow in from across the region. Recent work includes successfully defending BMW in a trial following a motor vehicle crash in which a driver was rendered quadriplegic.

**The Lawyers:** As the current president of the International Association of Defense Counsel, *"tremendously experienced"* **Greg Lederer** is increasingly active on a nationwide stage, while also managing to maintain a presence in the state. He is known for his *"zealous representation of his clients"* and his *"professional and collegial business relationships."* Lederer is supported by partners James Shipman, Stephen Holtman and James Gerk.

**Clients/Work Highlights:** Local, national and multinational companies are represented by the firm.

## Band 4

## Bradley & Riley, PC

**The Firm:** A cadre of eight attorneys makes up the *"excellent"* commercial litigation practice at this Cedar Rapids-based firm. Its undertakings are many, including construction and employment litigation. It does a significant amount of alternative dispute resolution work too, the most recent being arbitrations on behalf of Interstate Power and Light. Don Thompson acted as lead counsel representing the power company and Alliant Energy in the arbitration of several claims arising from the construction of a combined natural gas facility.

**The Lawyers:** **Don Thompson's** alternative dispute resolution work is winning him admirers. In particular, client interviewees praised his *"top-notch"* credentials.

**Clients/Work Highlights:** United Fire & Casualty, Knutson Construction Services and Cole + Russell Architects are among the firm's clients.

## Brown, Winick, Graves, Gross, Baskerville and Schoenebaum PLC

See firm details p.923

**The Firm:** Recent successes for this 15-strong litigation team include an appeal to the Federal Circuit Court regarding a preliminary injunction, obtaining a jury verdict declaring that their client, Pigmentos Vegetales del Centro, did not infringe a patent claiming a composition of the antioxidant lutein. It also won an appeal before the Iowa Court of Appeals on behalf of Nationwide Mutual Insurance against Polk County in a case relating to the allocation of compensation owed to the insurer. An increase in IP litigation has allowed the practice to diversify its offering.

**The Lawyers:** Scott Long, Brian Rickert and Mike Dee form the core of the litigation practice, which also has a strong focus on agricultural work.

## Hansen, McClintock & Riley

**The Firm:** *"Small and powerful,"* this mature boutique practice consists of seven *"high-quality"* attorneys who are active across a variety of disputes, such as professional negligence, products liability, personal injury, workers' compensation, appellate practice, and corporate and real estate litigation. Activity extends to state and federal courts as well as administrative agencies, and certain lawyers have a high profile in the American Bar Association and Iowa State Bar Association.

**The Lawyers:** An attorney with *"a great history,"* **John McClintock** is widely viewed as an *"exceptional and influential"* individual, despite nearing retirement. *"Lawyers' lawyer"* **David Brown's** impressive extracurricular achievements were also the subject of consistent acclaim from peers and client interviewees: *"If there is a lawyer who has given so much of himself to improving the profession at local and national level, it is him."* Brown regularly serves on commissions appointed by the Supreme Court to revise administrative law and rewrite jury instructions, and has also served in political capacities. He undertakes a substantial amount of business and commercial litigation in which he *"gets fantastic results,"* and in the estimation of observers is *"an amazing guy who knows so much."* Partner **Trip Woodburn** makes his debut in the rankings this year in light of the impact he has made on fellow practitioners, who are envious of his ability to *"think on his feet"* and approach cross-examination with *"bullet-like conciseness."*

## Other Notable Practitioners

**Dwight James** of Des Moines-based The James Law Firm PC enjoys pan-market recognition for his *"sheer dedication to his profession."* An influential and ubiquitous figure in the state's litigation community, James is highly respected for his *"genteel and committed"* approach to work, both within his own plaintiffs' PI firm as well as in state matters. *"One hell of a good attorney with great common sense,"* **Guy Cook** of Grefe & Sidney, PLC ascends the tables following client support. This *"tenacious and creative"* trial lawyer, whose civil litigation expertise includes white-collar defense work, is currently president of the Polk County Bar Association. Cook recently defended a company in a wrongful termination case, and regularly defends a large amusement park in claims brought against it. Barrister **Nicholas Critelli** of Law Chambers Nicholas Critelli PC rises through the tables in recognition of his *"trailblazing"* practice. His stint as president of the Iowa State Bar Association recently came to an end, enabling him to focus on more casework. Critelli was instructed to defend a major defamation case, Park v Hill, and also acted in a case in Gibraltar on the subject of attorney fees. Having qualified in England, he is one of very few lawyers in the USA equipped to advise on English law. Commentators place him *"at the cutting edge,"* and clients say he *"is a wonderful trial lawyer."* Personal injury specialist and *"a real gentleman,"* **James Hayes** of Hayes Lorenzen Lawyers PLC represents plaintiffs in PI cases, many of which emanate from medical malpractice. Contemporaries are impressed that he has accomplished what they saw as the rare feat of being *"a highly respected and well-liked plaintiffs' lawyer."* Formerly at Dickinson Mackaman Tyler & Hagen, **Brent Appel** joined plaintiffs' firm Wandro, Baer & Appel, PC in Des Moines. He wins market approval from commentators who affirm, *"he is a talented and bright lawyer."* **Joe Gunderson** of Gunderson, Sharpe & Walke works mainly in plaintiff class actions covering antitrust, oil and gas, wage and hour, insurance and health. Taking his slice of defense work, he defended a bank caught up in Enron-related litigation. Commentators pointed out that he *"is an absolutely meticulous lawyer who can master complex situations easily."*

# REAL ESTATE

## Real Estate
### Leading Firms

**1**   **BELIN LAMSON MCCORMICK** *Des Moines*
    **CONNOLLY, O'MALLEY, LILLIS** *Des Moines*
    **NYEMASTER, GOODE, WEST** *Des Moines*

**2**   **BRADSHAW, FOWLER, PROCTOR** *Des Moines*
    **DAVIS, BROWN, KOEHN, SHORS** *Des Moines*
    **DICKINSON, MACKAMAN, TYLER** *Des Moines*
    **LANE & WATERMAN LLP** *Davenport*

**3**   **BRADLEY & RILEY, PC** *Cedar Rapids*
    **BROWN, WINICK, GRAVES, GROSS** *Des Moines*
    **MEARDON, SUEPPEL & DOWNER** *Iowa City*
    **MOYER & BERGMAN, PLC** *Cedar Rapids*
    **SHUTTLEWORTH & INGERSOLL PLC** *Cedar Rapids*
    **SIMMONS PERRINE ALBRIGHT** *Cedar Rapids*

### Leading Individuals

**1**   **BARTINE William** *Belin Lamson McCormick*
    **COLACINO Antonio** *Nyemaster, Goode, West*
    **DETTMANN David** *Lane & Waterman LLP*
    **ERICKSON David** *Davis, Brown, Koehn*
    **HOLCOMB James** *Bradshaw, Fowler*
    **KUBICEK David** *Simmons Perrine Albright*
    **LILLIS William** *Connolly, O'Malley, Lillis*
    **SHARPE Jeremy** *Belin Lamson McCormick*
    **TYLER Paul** *Dickinson, Mackaman*

**2**   **DOUGLAS Robert** *Davis, Brown, Koehn*
    **LEFF Philip** *Leff, Haupert, Traw*
    **MOORE Dan** *Berenstein, Moore, Berenstein*
    **NELSON Stephen** *Moyer & Bergman*
    **POSE Christopher** *Connolly, O'Malley, Lillis*
    **SULLIVAN Jon** *Dickinson, Mackaman, Tyler*

**3**   **ANDEWEG Robert** *Brown, Winick, Graves*
    **MCMENIMEN Dennis** *Shuttleworth & Ingersoll*
    **MONSON Terry** *Nyemaster, Goode, West*
    **PROWELL William** *Shuttleworth & Ingersoll PLC*
    **SARCONE James** *Belin Lamson McCormick*
    **SEYFER Greg** *Bradley & Riley, PC*
    **WINE James** *Nyemaster, Goode, West*

**4**   **AUSTIN Brad** *Nyemaster, Goode, West*
    **CAMERON Streetar** *Connolly, O'Malley, Lillis*
    **DOWNER Robert** *Meardon, Sueppel & Downer*
    **GREEN Mike** *Brown, Winick, Graves*
    **NEPPL William** *Bradley & Riley, PC*

### Up-and-coming individuals
    **HURLEY Cynthia** *Bradshaw, Fowler, Proctor*

## Band 1

### Belin Lamson McCormick Zumbach Flynn, PC

**The Firm:** Consistently hailed as a superior outfit due to the scale and scope of the work it takes on, this six-strong team covers real estate across the state for developers, lenders, investors and users. It has developed good working relationships with county councils and cities, with whom it deals on zoning issues, approvals for development and measures to prevent or rectify environmental problems. Clients speak extremely positively of these attorneys and are well aware that the firm's name is synonymous with "*great credibility among lawyers and local business-people.*" With an increasing number of clients wishing to take advantage of tax-free exchanges, the firm has acted in several transactions driven by tax concerns. It is involved in a sizable project alongside a Washington, DC-based firm to facilitate syndications of investors wishing to invest in real estate for tax-free exchange completion.

**The Lawyers:** With his signature "*calm demeanor and strong work ethic,*" **Bill Bartine** works for developers on zoning changes and the construction of properties to lease to commercial tenants. Clients are impressed with his dedication and rare ability to "*take a complicated issue and explain it so that everyone understands.*" Someone who is "*great on document review*" is **Jeremy Sharpe**, whose expertise is characterized by his "*detail-oriented intelligence and efficiency.*" Clients are conscious of his "*quick understanding of the issues and the processes we go through.*" As the number of tax-free exchanges rises, Sharpe has found himself acting for an increasing number of investors wishing to take advantage of the current conditions. In addition to his diet of regular real estate work, he is engaged in a large project on behalf of a Washington state-based company that facilitates the syndication of investors looking at real estate for tax-free exchange completion. The "*very effective*" **James Sarcone** has been undertaking a considerable volume of foreclosure work on behalf of major banks and advising various companies on relocation matters.

**Clients/Work Highlights:** Knapp Properties; Mid-America Group; GuideOne Insurance; Iowa Health System; General Growth Properties and Science Center of Iowa.

### Connolly, O'Malley, Lillis, Hansen & Olson LLP

**The Firm:** With a reputation as a traditional and well-connected Des Moines boutique which is "*good to work with,*" this firm has eight real estate attorneys who work with developers and landowners on zoning and land use work. Recently it was successful in its representation of a landowner seeking to obtain a district court ruling allowing it to build a hospice on the eastern side of Des Moines. The firm has real kudos in clients' eyes: "*They're a major presence in this area.*" Rivals note: "*They are well known for working with cities on rezoning and Board of Adjustment matters, and when we have conflict of interest then we would go to them.*"

**The Lawyers:** "*The premier attorney for zoning matters in Des Moines,*" **William Lillis** is well recognized for his deep knowledge of zoning and experience working with local governments and developers. "*He has great credibility and is very effective.*" His protégé **Christopher Pose** is widely regarded as "*a bulldog*" who is well on his way to becoming a zoning expert in his mentor's mold.

Clients say he is "*confident and knowledgeable*" and appreciate that he "*just gets things done.*" Described as "*practical and easy to deal with,*" **Streetar Cameron** focuses on commercial development and working with city councils, a domain in which clients highlight his "*attention to detail*" and his forte for closing difficult transactions.

**Clients/Work Highlights:** The firm represents a selection of government bodies, corporate developers and landowners.

### Nyemaster, Goode, West, Hansell, and O'Brien

**The Firm:** This name is a byword for "*thorough, courteous and conservative excellence.*" This firm straddles Des Moines and Ames and has forged strong links with law firms outside Iowa, enabling it to undertake work across the country. Its repertoire covers estate exchanges, development, condominium conversions, loan financing, tax appeals and foreclosures, and "*the firm is very responsive in terms of its legal expertise and timeliness of its work product.*" Recent matters of note include acting alongside the state university in a $20 million land sale, an ongoing project with Employers Mutual Casualty involving the sale of parking lots, and working on a $75 million multistate financing project for wind farms. Client testimonies confirm that Nyemaster lawyers are "*very professional and knowledgeable,*" as well as being "*easy to get an answer from without a lot of billing hours or legalese.*" Clients also say that "*efficiency and responsiveness*" filter through the team from top to bottom.

**The Lawyers:** For some, "*the most detailed and technical lawyer on the team*" is **Tony Colacino**. He ascends the tables on a wave of enthusiastic feedback from clients who point to his "*trustworthiness and organizational skills.*" With a background in boom-and-bust land work, **Terry Monson**'s practice has recently become more focused on the wind power industry. In addition to leading the wind farm financing mentioned above, Monson recently conducted two highly complex land acquisitions. Clients portray him as "*dedicated and very pleasant to work with,*" with one saying: "*He understands my style of business and knows how to keep me away from the landmines.*" **James Wine** concentrates on financing and represents many of Iowa's life insurance companies and lenders. He recently closed a $127 million apartment financing deal and a $120 million portfolio of office properties across the country. He also secured a $12 million loan for the Iowa Heart Center. Contemporaries highlight Wine's "*deep understanding of the clients' position, the city and the developers that approach it.*" **Brad Austin** represents insurance companies, both in Iowa and internationally, on long-term deals on properties such as shopping centers and industrial warehouses across the country. His work comprises a high number of midvalue transactions, of which he undertakes approximately 200 each year. Clients confirm that he is "*knowledgeable and likeable.*"

**Clients/Work Highlights:** The firm represents public utilities; power producers; insurers; developers; local governments and lenders.

## Band 2

### Bradshaw, Fowler, Proctor & Fairgrave, PC

**The Firm:** One of the dominant firms in the eastern Iowa market, this practice has come to be known as a *"go-to"* firm for complex real estate transactions. It handles major projects for Principal Financial Group on national acquisitions and dispositions of commercial property, and represents some of the country's largest lenders. The team has steadily built a reputation for integrity and a strength that belies the size of the nine-lawyer team.

**The Lawyers:** With 30 years' experience of handling large commercial transactions, **Jim Holcomb** rises to the top of the tables in recognition of his prestigious client base and ability to *"make deals happen."* Strong on detail and technicalities, Holcomb is considered *"affable and courteous"* and *"extremely competent with sophisticated work"* by clients, among whom he inspires *"a high degree of confidence."* **Cynthia Hurley** works closely with Principal Financial Group on estate planning, an area in which she is gaining favorable recognition.

**Clients/Work Highlights:** AmerUS Leasing, Earlham Savings Bank and Wells Fargo are among the clients.

### Davis, Brown, Koehn, Shors & Roberts, PC

**The Firm:** Underpinned by its representation of lending institutions such as Wells Fargo and Citibank, this firm undertakes high-volume commodity work and boasts strong ties with debtors and creditors in foreclosure and title transactions. It acts for BH Management, a large countrywide apartment developer, and recently represented Iowa Lottery Authority on the acquisition of a new building. As a general real estate practice it offers advice to borrowers and lenders at all points on the scale, from an individual wishing to buy a house to corporate entities involved in multi-million-dollar transactions.

**The Lawyers:** **David Erickson**'s ascent through the rankings is a reflection of the respect fellow practitioners have for him. Described consistently as *"having an excellent understanding of real estate law,"* gleaned from many years' experience, Erickson is also admired within the wider legal community for *"putting his professional knowledge to good use"* in the courses and seminars he organizes for Drake University in Des Moines. Clients are impressed by how he *"expertly handles several complex matters simultaneously."* **Bob Douglas** undertakes a substantial number of commercial transactions, and among clients he has earned himself a reputation as a *"thorough and competent"* attorney.

**Clients/Work Highlights:** Iowa Manufactured Housing Association; Wells Fargo Home Mortgage;

Des Moines Area Metropolitan Planning Organization and BH Management.

### Dickinson, Mackaman, Tyler & Hagen, PC

**The Firm:** A distinguished client base is served by an increasingly prolific full-service team of real estate lawyers. The firm advised Life Care Retirement Communities on a project to extend a care facility and build an on-site infirmary, and regularly undertakes significant work for developers and residential subdivisions in Des Moines. It also remains busy with the documentation and foreclosure of secured loans.

**The Lawyers:** *"Class act"* **Paul Tyler** takes a top spot in the rankings due to his long presence *"at the forefront of real estate law in Des Moines."* His work with financial institutions such as Wells Fargo has allowed this *"affable"* figure to carve a niche for himself as *"an excellent and very detailed lawyer."* Foreclosure and bankruptcy specialist **Jon Sullivan** was singled out for his *"scholarly and courteous"* manner. He recently represented the construction lender and letter of credit bank in connection with a $5 million bond project involving the construction of a 60-unit independent living facility. Sullivan also represented a mortgage lender in a state court receivership and foreclosure proceedings. Interviewees commend him for being *"highly capable and competent."*

**Clients/Work Highlights:** Gratias Construction; Merrill Lynch; Life Care Retirement Communities; First American; Hills Bank & Trust; Waukee State Bank and Iowa State Savings Bank.

### Lane & Waterman LLP

**The Firm:** Lane & Waterman is based in Davenport where it has a commanding presence on Iowa's eastern edge. The firm has had an active year, one major matter being the acquisition of Pulitzer newspapers on behalf of client Lee Enterprises, in which the *"high-quality"* real estate practice was called upon to handle the property elements of the purchase. In other transactions, the team represented a local hospital and orthopedic group in the development of an outpatient facility and is working with Fry Development on plans to build a shopping mall.

**The Lawyers:** Heading up the practice is **David Dettmann**, a *"multitalented and bright"* attorney held in high esteem by his peers and clients. *"He does everything and does an excellent job,"* according to commentators. Dettmann is visible on the lecture circuit and has even been instrumental in reviewing and proposing legislation.

**Clients/Work Highlights:** Lee Enterprises; Russell Construction; Quad City Bank & Trust; Deere & Company; Sears Manufacturing; Farm Bureau Mutual Insurance; Verizon Wireless and iWireless.

## Band 3

### Bradley & Riley, PC

**The Firm:** Casting its net over the whole of the eastern Iowa marketplace, this practice offers the

complete range of services, including advising on Section 1031 tax-deferred exchanges, financing and development. It represents several developers involved in residential subdivisions at the top end of the market and has been advising the developer of a somewhat controversial project involving a multi-million-dollar home scheme that has encountered zoning problems. A thriving market for residential and commercial development has led to a consequential rise in the amount of lending work undertaken at the firm.

**The Lawyers:** **Greg Seyfer** combines *"a great personality"* with an *"exact and businesslike"* approach to his work. Clients appreciate his promptness and professionalism, and his standing within the market is underlined by *"the high degree of respect the real estate community and the realtors have for him."* Zoning don **Bill Neppl** is engaged by a client aiming to penetrate the corridor connecting Waterloo, Cedar Rapids and Iowa City with residential and commercial developments. Clients value his input, saying they *"trust his judgment and have confidence he is doing what is in our best interests."*

**Clients/Work Highlights:** Regency Land Company; Cedar Rapids Bank & Trust; Guaranty Bank and Trust; United Fire & Casualty and McLeodUSA.

### Brown, Winick, Graves, Gross, Baskerville and Schoenebaum PLC

See firm details p.923

**The Firm:** Boosted by favorable conditions for investment in real estate, this practice has seen an upturn in complex commercial transactions, including the buying and selling of tax exchanges. It has specialist experience in tax assessment protest cases, in which it has acted in recent sizable disputes concerning the value of warehouses and other industrial properties. *"It does a fine job of getting the work done accurately,"* say clients.

**The Lawyers:** Described by clients as *"a deal-maker, not a deal-breaker,"* **Bob Andeweg**'s (see p.919) *"care and attention to detail"* have endeared him to a growing circle in this arena. Noted for being *"diligent and not overly confrontational,"* his work is also characterized by the *"personal interest he takes in his clients' business."* Seen as *"quite simply the backbone of the practice,"* **Mike Green**'s (see p.920) work with developers is also much admired.

**Clients/Work Highlights:** Hurd Real Estate Services; Ruhl & Ruhl Commercial; Grubb & Ellis Mid-America Pacific; Stateside Capital and Westown Association.

### Meardon, Sueppel & Downer

**The Firm:** *"Leading the way in Iowa City,"* this six-lawyer team is experiencing an explosion in activity thanks to its location, where – bucking the general trend for the Midwest – the economy is growing. Generated increasingly by the nearby University of Iowa, recent work has included funding issues and land acquisitions. The firm is advising a developer on a $150 million proposal to build an indoor rainforest and aquarium complex in a suburb of Iowa City. In addition, it is in the preliminary stages of a 500-acre residential development to the north of the city and a 240-acre residential development in Coralville. The firm has "*always played an important part in the community,*" say clients.

**The Lawyers:** Former president of the Iowa State Bar Association **Bob Downer** has a national reputation as "*a key figure in the market.*" The depth of his knowledge and experience is undisputed, while his broad "*business generalist*" skill set has impressed many. His involvement in sizable and multidimensional projects in this part of the state has cemented his reputation as "*an attorney of high quality and great knowledge.*"

## Moyer & Bergman, PLC

**The Firm:** "*One of the top Cedar Rapids firms,*" Moyer & Bergman's real estate practice is an adjunct to its business and tax department. Though only two lawyers strong, the practice has "*top-notch*" expertise, which it usually applies to the representation of developers, though it also advises lenders. Additionally, a small proportion of its time is devoted to tax-deferred exchanges and zoning work. Transactions of note in the past year have included retail subdivisions and ten condominium projects.

**The Lawyers:** **Stephen Nelson**'s affable manner and considerable experience were brought to researchers' attention; he is considered one of the most "*highly respected and qualified*" attorneys in the area. "*Nelson can handle anything in the real estate arena,*" commented one interviewee. He is supported by real estate and business law attorney Matt Adam.
**Clients/Work Highlights:** Bankers Trust; Fauser Oil; Great America Leasing; Omega Communications and State Farm.

## Shuttleworth & Ingersoll PLC

**The Firm:** Interviewees repeatedly highlighted the unfussy and pragmatic manner in which this firm conducts business. In its representation of lenders on commercial transactions it has caught the attention of peers, who comment that Shuttleworth lawyers "*have a depth of understanding of clients' needs that allows them to be met more efficiently.*" Recently, the firm has been involved in significant due diligence work and was the catalyst behind an office condominium project. The disposition of industrial premises also forms a substantial portion of its workload and a growing area of activity is agriculture-related. Lately the group has acted in several acquisitions of livestock facilities.

**The Lawyers:** **Dennis McMenimen**'s expanding practice is the subject of warm client feedback. Many testified to him being "*extremely thorough and conscientious.*" Others highlighted his "*real gift for language*" and corroborated the view that he is "*diligent and knowledgeable.*" Clients applied many of these same comments to **Bill Prowell**, whose ability to "*understand transactions and accomplish them well*" was also praised.
**Clients/Work Highlights:** The firm represents midsized companies in the $10-100 million range; real estate investors; agricultural organizations and local firms.

## Simmons Perrine Albright & Ellwood PLC

**The Firm:** This Cedar Rapids-based firm has a two-pronged practice that covers both commercial and residential real estate work. It recently represented the developer of a warehouse facility alongside its regular diet of work for local clients involved in buying, selling or leasing property. Lawyers undertake significant foreclosure work and offer litigation services relating to the enforcement of leases, assessment disputes and other related matters.

**The Lawyers:** As chairman of the Title Standards Committee, "*first-rate*" **David Kubicek** is a prominent figure. Clients say he is "*dedicated and proficient*" in his approach, and meticulous in the execution of his work. Kubicek heads up the real estate practice and concentrates on commercial matters, while Nick Abou-Assaly covers the residential side.
**Clients/Work Highlights:** The firm represents mortgage lenders; residential and commercial real estate brokers; landlords and tenants; developers and property managers.

## Other Notable Practitioners

"*Always a pleasure to work with,*" **Philip Leff** of Leff, Haupert, Traw & Willman LLP picked up a number of recommendations on account of his "*even-tempered manner and technical expertise.*" He is well known in the Iowa City marketplace, where he represents the city's Association of Realtors as well as developers of residential and commercial properties. In the past year, he represented the developer of a downtown high-rise condominium. Leff has taught real estate law at the state's law school, a post he will retire from this year, and one peer commented that Leff is "*as close to being universally respected as anyone I know.*" In the western part of the state, **Dan Moore** of Berenstein, Moore, Berenstein, Heffernan & Moeller is "*energetic and committed*" to his real estate practice. This former chair of the real estate section of the Iowa Bar Association received abundant praise for his "*excellent handling of transactions.*" By way of example, Moore engineered a partnership between Sioux City Community School District and Morningside College over the ownership of Roberts Stadium, and is representing a client in the process of purchasing historic landmark site Badgerow Building in order to rehabilitate it.

# Leaders in Iowa

## ADAMS, Garth
Belin Lamson McCormick Zumbach Flynn, PC, Des Moines
515 243 7100
*Recommended in Corporate/M&A*

## ADAMS, Helen
Dickinson, Mackaman, Tyler & Hagen, PC, Des Moines 515 244 2600
*Recommended in Employment*

## ANDEWEG, Robert
Brown, Winick, Graves, Gross, Baskerville and Schoenebaum PLC, Des Moines 515 242 2438
rda@ialawyers.com
*Recommended in Real Estate*
**Practice Areas:** Extensive experience in all aspects of commercial real estate law, including: development and land use; tax assessment protests and eminent domain proceedings; acquisition, sale and financing of commercial real estate; and com-

mercial leasing.
**Prof. Memberships:** Iowa Commercial Real Estate Association (Board Member). Polk County, Iowa State (Member, Real Estate and Title Law Section) and American Bar Associations. Iowa and National CCIM (Certified Commercial Investment Member) Chapters. All coursework completed for CCIM designation.
**Career:** Joined BrownWinick in 1987; became Partner in 1992.
**Publications:** Note, 35 Drake Law Review 365, 1985-86; Case Note, 35 Drake Law Review 433, 1985-86.
**Personal:** Currently Mayor of the City of Urbandale, Iowa. Past member of the Urbandale Planning & Zoning Commission and Urbandale City Council.

## APPEL, Brent
Wandro, Baer & Appel, PC, Des Moines
515 281 1475
*Recommended in Litigation*

## ARMENTROUT, Randall
Nyemaster, Goode, West, Hansell, and O'Brien, Des Moines
515 283 3100
*Recommended in Employment*

## AUSTIN, Brad
Nyemaster, Goode, West, Hansell, and O'Brien, Des Moines
515 283 3100
*Recommended in Real Estate*

## BAIER, Kelly
Bradley & Riley, PC, Cedar Rapids
319 363 0101
*Recommended in Employment*

## BARTINE, William
Belin Lamson McCormick Zumbach Flynn, PC, Des Moines
515 243 7100
*Recommended in Real Estate*

## BERENSTEIN, Marvin
Berenstein, Moore, Berenstein, Heffernan & Moeller, Sioux City
712 252 0020
*Recommended in Corporate/M&A*

## BICKEL, John
Shuttleworth & Ingersoll PLC, Cedar Rapids 319 365 9461
*Recommended in Litigation*

## BLASER, Michael R
Brown, Winick, Graves, Gross, Baskerville and Schoenebaum PLC, West Des Moines
515 242 2480
blaser@ialawyers.com
*Recommended in Corporate/M&A*
**Practice Areas:** Corporate transactions, including entity structuring and private placements, mergers and acquisitions. Workouts of distressed companies. Environmental and administrative agency

representation. Extensive agricultural entity work, including compliance with corporate farming laws in Iowa and other states.

**Prof. Memberships:** ABA, Iowa State Bar Association (Agricultural Law Section - Council Member), Iowa Society of CPAs. Environmental Committee, National Pork Producers Council, Iowa Association of Business and Industry, Agribusiness Association of Iowa, American Agricultural Law Association.

**Career:** Partner since 1988. In-house Counsel to Iowa Select Farms, LLP from 1995-2000.

**Publications:** Has written extensively and lectured on limited liability companies and laws and regulations affecting production agriculture.

**Personal:** University of Iowa School of Law, with distinction (1985); University of Iowa School of Business (BBA, Accounting, 1982); Certified Public Accountant, Iowa (1983).

**BOYKEN, Quentin**
Belin Lamson McCormick Zumbach Flynn, PC, Des Moines
515 243 7100
*Recommended in Corporate/M&A*

**BRALEY, Bruce**
Dutton, Braun, Staack & Hellman PLC, Waterloo 319 234 4471
*Recommended in Litigation*

**BROWN, David**
Hansen, McClintock & Riley, Des Moines
515 244 2141
*Recommended in Litigation*

**BROWN, Donald**
Davis, Brown, Koehn, Shors & Roberts, PC, Des Moines 515 288 2500
*Recommended in Corporate/M&A*

**BROWN, William**
Brown, Winick, Graves, Gross, Baskerville and Schoenebaum PLC, Des Moines 515 242 2412
brown@ialawyers.com
*Recommended in Corporate/M&A*

**Practice Areas:** Vice-Chair of Brown, Winick, Graves, Gross, Baskerville & Schoenebaum, PLC. Focuses on a corporate transactional and business planning practice, concentrating on acquisitions, divestitures, capital formation, financing and tax planning. Also has been active in legislative matters affecting small business and has successfully lobbied for several business and tax initiatives benefiting closely held business.

**Prof. Memberships:** American Bar Association Section on Taxation, S Corporation Committee; Iowa State Bar Association, Tax Section Council.

**Career:** Has been active in a wide variety of civic leadership positions with organizations such as the Iowa Association of Business and Industry, the Iowa Taxpayers Association, the Polk-Des Moines Taxpayers Association and the United

Way of Central Iowa.

**Publications:** 'Evaluating a Subchapter S Conversion', 37 Drake Law Review 395, 1989.

**Personal:** BA with honors in Psychology 1974, University of Iowa; JD with high distinction 1977, University of Iowa.

**CAMERON, Streetar**
Connolly, O'Malley, Lillis, Hansen & Olson LLP, Des Moines
515 234 8157
*Recommended in Real Estate*

**CAMPBELL, Bruce**
Davis, Brown, Koehn, Shors & Roberts, PC, Des Moines 515 288 2500
*Recommended in Corporate/M&A*

**CARROLL, Frank**
Davis, Brown, Koehn, Shors & Roberts, PC, Des Moines 515 288 2500
*Recommended in Corporate/M&A*

**COLACINO, Antonio**
Nyemaster, Goode, West, Hansell, and O'Brien, Des Moines
515 283 3100
*Recommended in Real Estate*

**COLLINS, Kevin**
Shuttleworth & Ingersoll PLC, Cedar Rapids 319 365 9461
*Recommended in Litigation*

**COOK, Guy**
Grefe & Sidney, PLC, Des Moines
515 245 4300
*Recommended in Litigation*

**CORTESIO, John**
Bradshaw, Fowler, Proctor & Fairgrave, PC, Des Moines 515 243 4191
*Recommended in Corporate/M&A*

**CRITELLI JR, Nicholas**
Law Chambers Nicholas Critelli PC, Des Moines 515 243 3122
*Recommended in Litigation*

**CUNNINGHAM, Thomas**
Nyemaster, Goode, West, Hansell, and O'Brien, Des Moines
515 283 3100
*Recommended in Employment*

**DETTMANN, David**
Lane & Waterman LLP, Davenport
563 324 3246
*Recommended in Real Estate*

**DICKINSON, Mark**
Nyemaster, Goode, West, Hansell, and O'Brien, Des Moines
515 283 3100
*Recommended in Corporate/M&A*

**DOUGLAS, Robert**
Davis, Brown, Koehn, Shors & Roberts, PC, Des Moines 515 288 2500
*Recommended in Real Estate*

**DOWNER, Robert**
Meardon, Sueppel & Downer, Iowa City
319 338 9222
*Recommended in Real Estate*

**DRAPER, Hayward**
Nyemaster, Goode, West, Hansell, and O'Brien, Des Moines
515 283 3100
*Recommended in Litigation*

**DRISCOLL, Kevin**
Finley, Alt, Smith, Scharnberg, Craig, Hilmes & Gaffney PC, Des Moines
515 288 0145
*Recommended in Litigation*

**DUTTON, David**
Dutton, Braun, Staack & Hellman PLC, Waterloo 319 234 4471
*Recommended in Litigation*

**ELDERKIN, David**
Elderkin & Pirnie PLC, Cedar Rapids
319 362 2137
*Recommended in Litigation*

**ERICKSON, David**
Davis, Brown, Koehn, Shors & Roberts, PC, Des Moines 515 288 2500
*Recommended in Real Estate*

**FANTER, Robert**
Whitfield & Eddy, PLC, Des Moines
515 288 6041
*Recommended in Litigation*

**FIGENSHAW, Michael**
Bradshaw, Fowler, Proctor & Fairgrave, PC, Des Moines 515 243 4191
*Recommended in Litigation*

**FINLEY, Thomas**
Finley, Alt, Smith, Scharnberg, Craig, Hilmes & Gaffney PC, Des Moines
515 288 0145
*Recommended in Litigation*

**FISCHER, Gordon**
Bradshaw, Fowler, Proctor & Fairgrave, PC, Des Moines 515 243 4191
*Recommended in Employment*

**FOLEY, Thomas**
Nyemaster, Goode, West, Hansell, and O'Brien, Des Moines
515 283 3100
*Recommended in Employment*

**FUNK, Mary**
Nyemaster, Goode, West, Hansell, and O'Brien, Des Moines 515 283 3100
*Recommended in Employment*

**GAFFNEY, Todd**
Finley, Alt, Smith, Scharnberg, Craig, Hilmes & Gaffney PC, Des Moines
515 288 0145
*Recommended in Litigation*

**GILLIAM, James H**
Brown, Winick, Graves, Gross, Baskerville and Schoenebaum PLC, Des Moines 515 242 2446
gilliam@ialawyers.com
*Recommended in Employment*

**Practice Areas:** General practice including but not limited to labor and employment law, civil rights and discrimination and litigation, including advice to private and public sector employers in collective bargaining and employment transactions

of all types.

**Prof. Memberships:** ABA (State Labor Law Developments Subcommittee), SHRM, IPMA-HR.

**Career:** US Army Judge Advocate General's Corps (1980-84); Iowa Public Employment Relations Board, General Counsel (1984-88); BrownWinick (1988-present), Partner since 1991.

**Personal:** University of Iowa (JD, 1980); University of Iowa (BA, 1977).

**GREEN, Mike**
Brown, Winick, Graves, Gross, Baskerville and Schoenebaum PLC, Des Moines 515 242 2431
mgreen@ialawyers.com
*Recommended in Real Estate*

**Practice Areas:** Real estate and corporate transactional.

**Prof. Memberships:** American, Iowa and Polk Couty Iowa Bar Associations and respective sections.

**Career:** Concentrated practice in all aspects of the above areas from 1976 to present. Client real estate transactions exceeded ten million dollars in 2005.

**GROSS, Doug**
Brown, Winick, Graves, Gross, Baskerville and Schoenebaum PLC, Des Moines 515 242 2410
gross@ialawyers.com
*Recommended in Corporate/M&A*

**Prof. Memberships:** United States District Court, Southern District of Iowa; American Bar Association; Iowa State Bar Association; Polk County Bar Association.

**Career:** Member of Brown, Winick, Graves, Gross, Baskerville & Schoenebaum, P.L.C.; Chief of Staff to Governor Terry Branstad; Director of Business and Finance, Iowa State Board of Regents; Administrative Assistant to Governor Robert D Ray; 2002 Republican nominee for Governor of Iowa.

**Personal:** BA, summa cum laude, Iowa Wesleyan College; Lydia C Roberts Fellow, Columbia University School of International Affairs; JD with honors, Drake University.

**GUNDERSON, Joseph**
Gunderson, Sharp & Walke, Des Moines
515 288 0219
*Recommended in Litigation*

**HANKS, James**
Ahlers & Cooney PC, Des Moines
515 243 7611
*Recommended in Employment*

**HANSELL, Edgar**
Nyemaster, Goode, West, Hansell, and O'Brien, Des Moines
515 283 3100
*Recommended in Corporate/M&A*

**HARTY, Frank**
Nyemaster, Goode, West, Hansell, and O'Brien, Des Moines
515 283 3100
*Recommended in Employment*

**HAUSER III, Wade**
Ahlers & Cooney PC, Des Moines
515 243 7611
*Recommended in Litigation*

**HAYES, James**
Hayes Lorenzen Lawyers PLC, Iowa City
319 887 3688
*Recommended in Litigation*

**HILMES, Jack**
Finley, Alt, Smith, Scharnberg, Craig,
Hilmes & Gaffney PC, Des Moines
515 288 0145
*Recommended in Litigation*

**HINTZE, John**
Ahlers & Cooney PC, Des Moines
515 243 7611
*Recommended in Corporate/M&A*

**HOCHSTETLER, William**
Shuttleworth & Ingersoll PLC,
Cedar Rapids 319 365 9461
*Recommended in Corporate/M&A*

**HOLCOMB, James**
Bradshaw, Fowler, Proctor & Fairgrave, PC,
Des Moines 515 243 4191
*Recommended in Real Estate*

**HOUGHTON, Robert**
Shuttleworth & Ingersoll PLC,
Cedar Rapids 319 365 9461
*Recommended in Litigation*

**HURLEY, Cynthia**
Bradshaw, Fowler, Proctor & Fairgrave, PC,
Des Moines 515 243 4191
*Recommended in Real Estate*

**JAMES, Dwight**
The James Law Firm PC, Des Moines
515 246 8484
*Recommended in Litigation*

**KENNEDY, Elizabeth Gregg**
Ahlers & Cooney PC, Des Moines
515 243 7611
*Recommended in Employment*

**KRAMBECK, James**
Belin Lamson McCormick Zumbach
Flynn, PC, Des Moines
515 243 7100
*Recommended in Corporate/M&A*

**KUBICEK, David**
Simmons Perrine Albright & Ellwood PLC,
Cedar Rapids 319 366 7641
*Recommended in Real Estate*

**LA SUER, Gene**
Davis, Brown, Koehn, Shors & Roberts, PC,
Des Moines 515 288 2500
*Recommended in Employment*

**LAMSON, Jeffrey**
Belin Lamson McCormick Zumbach
Flynn, PC, Des Moines  515 243 7100
*Recommended in Corporate/M&A*

**LEDERER, Gregory**
Simmons Perrine Albright & Ellwood
PLC, Cedar Rapids
319 366 7641
*Recommended in Litigation*

**LEFF, Philip**
Leff, Haupert, Traw & Willman LLP,
Iowa City 319 338 7551
*Recommended in Real Estate*

**LILLIS, William**
Connolly, O'Malley, Lillis, Hansen &
Olson LLP, Des Moines
515 234 8157
*Recommended in Real Estate*

**LOGAN, Holly**
Belin Lamson McCormick Zumbach
Flynn, PC, Des Moines
515 243 7100
*Recommended in Employment*

**MALHEIRO, Sharon**
Davis, Brown, Koehn, Shors & Roberts, PC,
Des Moines 515 288 2500
*Recommended in Employment*

**MANSFIELD, Edward**
Belin Lamson McCormick Zumbach
Flynn, PC, Des Moines
515 243 7100
*Recommended in Litigation*

**MCCLINTOCK, John**
Hansen, McClintock & Riley, Des Moines
515 244 2141
*Recommended in Litigation*

**MCCORMICK, Mark**
Belin Lamson McCormick Zumbach
Flynn, PC, Des Moines
515 243 7100
*Recommended in Litigation*

**MCMENIMEN, Dennis**
Shuttleworth & Ingersoll PLC, Cedar
Rapids
319 365 9461
*Recommended in Real Estate*

**MONSON, Terry**
Nyemaster, Goode, West, Hansell, and
O'Brien, Des Moines
515 283 3100
*Recommended in Real Estate*

**MOORE, Dan**
Berenstein, Moore, Berenstein, Heffernan & Moeller, Sioux City
712 252 0020
*Recommended in Real Estate*

**MUCHMORE, Iris**
Simmons Perrine Albright & Ellwood PLC,
Cedar Rapids 319 366 7641
*Recommended in Employment*

**NAYLOR, Greg**
Whitfield & Eddy, P.L.C.,
West Des Moines 515 558 0111
*Recommended in Employment*

**NELSON, Stephen**
Moyer & Bergman, PLC, Cedar Rapids
319 366 7331
*Recommended in Real Estate*

**NEPPL, William**
Bradley & Riley, PC, Cedar Rapids
319 363 0101
*Recommended in Real Estate*

**NEUMANN, Gordon**
Nyemaster, Goode, West, Hansell, and
O'Brien, Des Moines
515 283 3100
*Recommended in Corporate/M&A*

**OVERBERG, Nathan**
Ahlers & Cooney PC, Des Moines
515 243 7611
*Recommended in Employment*

**PENICK, Bridget**
Dickinson, Mackaman, Tyler & Hagen, PC,
Des Moines 515 244 2600
*Recommended in Employment*

**PHIPPS, David**
Whitfield & Eddy, PLC, Des Moines
515 288 6041
*Recommended in Litigation*

**POSE, Christopher**
Connolly, O'Malley, Lillis, Hansen &
Olson LLP, Des Moines
515 234 8157
*Recommended in Real Estate*

**PROWELL, William**
Shuttleworth & Ingersoll PLC,
Cedar Rapids 319 365 9461
*Recommended in Real Estate*

**REAMES, Wayne**
Belin Lamson McCormick Zumbach
Flynn, PC, Des Moines
515 243 7100
*Recommended in Corporate/M&A*

**REASONER, Carroll**
Shuttleworth & Ingersoll PLC,
Cedar Rapids 319 365 9461
*Recommended in Corporate/M&A*

**RECK, Michael**
Belin Lamson McCormick Zumbach
Flynn, PC, Des Moines
515 243 7100
*Recommended in Employment*

**REMSBURG, Edward**
Ahlers & Cooney PC, Des Moines
515 243 7611
*Recommended in Litigation*

**REYNOLDS, Kevin**
Whitfield & Eddy, PLC, Des Moines
515 288 6041
*Recommended in Litigation*

**RILEY, Byron**
Bradley & Riley, PC, Cedar Rapids
319 363 0101
*Recommended in Corporate/M&A*

**ROBY, Patrick**
Elderkin & Pirnie PLC, Cedar Rapids
319 362 2137
*Recommended in Litigation*

**SACKETT, Christopher R**
Brown, Winick, Graves, Gross,
Baskerville and Schoenebaum PLC,
Des Moines 515 242 2470
sackett@ialawyers.com
*Recommended in Corporate/M&A*
**Practice Areas:** Practice focuses pri-
marily on domestic and international

business/transactional, corporate and
securities matters, including: organiza-
tion/formation and management; debt
and equity financing including public
and private securities offerings; mergers
and acquisitions; joint ventures; real
estate; and franchise/dealer/distributor
issues. Primary industries include manufacturing, biofuels, publishing, consumer
lending, agribusiness, grape and wine
industry.
**Prof. Memberships:** ABA (Business Law
Section; Forum on Franchising); ISBA
(Corporate, Trade Regulation and
Antitrust, and Real Estate Sections).
**Career:** Joined BrownWinick in 1994.
Made Partner in 1998. Member of firm's
Management Committee since 2001.
**Personal:** BA, magna cum laude, Central
College; JD, with distinction, University
of Iowa.

**SAMSON, Russell**
Dickinson, Mackaman, Tyler & Hagen, PC,
Des Moines 515 244 2600
*Recommended in Employment*

**SAMUELSON, Jaki**
Whitfield & Eddy, PLC, Des Moines
515 288 6041
*Recommended in Employment*

**SANTI, Richard**
Ahlers & Cooney PC, Des Moines
515 243 7611
*Recommended in Litigation*

**SAPP, Richard**
Nyemaster, Goode, West, Hansell, and
O'Brien, Des Moines 515 283 3100
*Recommended in Litigation*

**SARCONE, James**
Belin Lamson McCormick Zumbach
Flynn, PC, Des Moines
515 243 7100
*Recommended in Real Estate*

**SCHARNBERG, Steven**
Finley, Alt, Smith, Scharnberg, Craig,
Hilmes & Gaffney PC, Des Moines
515 288 0145
*Recommended in Litigation*

**SEYFER, Greg**
Bradley & Riley, PC, Cedar Rapids
319 363 0101
*Recommended in Real Estate*

**SHARPE, Jeremy**
Belin Lamson McCormick Zumbach
Flynn, PC, Des Moines
515 243 7100
*Recommended in Real Estate*

**SHORS, John**
Davis, Brown, Koehn, Shors & Roberts, PC,
Des Moines 515 288 2500
*Recommended in Corporate/M&A*

**SMITH, Glenn**
Finley, Alt, Smith, Scharnberg, Craig,
Hilmes & Gaffney PC, Des Moines
515 288 0145
*Recommended in Litigation*

**STEFANI, Randall**
Ahlers & Cooney PC, Des Moines
515 243 7611
*Recommended in Litigation*

**STREIT, Gary**
Shuttleworth & Ingersoll PLC,
Cedar Rapids 319 365 9461
*Recommended in Corporate/M&A*

**SULLIVAN, Jon**
Dickinson, Mackaman, Tyler & Hagen, PC,
Des Moines 515 244 2600
*Recommended in Real Estate*

**SWANGER, James**
Belin Lamson McCormick Zumbach
Flynn, PC, Des Moines
515 243 7100
*Recommended in Employment*

**SWINTON, David**
Belin Lamson McCormick Zumbach
Flynn, PC, Des Moines
515 243 7100
*Recommended in Litigation*

**TANK, David**
Davis, Brown, Koehn, Shors & Roberts, PC,
Des Moines 515 288 2500
*Recommended in Litigation*

**THARNISH, Deborah**
Davis, Brown, Koehn, Shors & Roberts, PC,
Des Moines 515 288 2500
*Recommended in Employment,
Litigation*

**THOMPSON, Donald**
Bradley & Riley, PC, Cedar Rapids
319 363 0101
*Recommended in Litigation*

**TRIPP, Mark**
Bradshaw, Fowler, Proctor & Fairgrave, PC,
Des Moines 515 243 4191
*Recommended in Litigation*

**TYLER, Paul**
Dickinson, Mackaman, Tyler & Hagen, PC,
Des Moines 515 244 2600
*Recommended in Real Estate*

**WATERMAN, Thomas**
Lane & Waterman LLP, Davenport
563 324 3246
*Recommended in Litigation*

**WATERMAN III, Dana**
Lane & Waterman LLP, Davenport
563 324 3246
*Recommended in Corporate/M&A*

**WATERMAN JR, Robert**
Lane & Waterman LLP, Davenport
563 324 3246
*Recommended in Litigation*

**WEINHARDT, Mark**
Belin Lamson McCormick Zumbach
Flynn, PC, Des Moines
515 243 7100
*Recommended in Litigation*

**WINE, James**
Nyemaster, Goode, West, Hansell, and
O'Brien, Des Moines
515 283 3100
*Recommended in Real Estate*

**WOODBURN III, Chester**
Hansen, McClintock & Riley, Des Moines
515 244 2141
*Recommended in Litigation*

**ZAIGER, Mark**
Shuttleworth & Ingersoll PLC,
Cedar Rapids 319 365 9461
*Recommended in Employment*

**ZUMBACH, Steven**
Belin Lamson McCormick Zumbach
Flynn, PC, Des Moines
515 243 7100
*Recommended in Corporate/M&A*

# BROWN, WINICK, GRAVES, GROSS, BASKERVILLE & SCHOENEBAUM, P.L.C.

## THE FIRM

**Number of partners:** 38
**Number of associates:** 15

**FIRM OVERVIEW:** Founded in 1951 as a tax law firm, the firm's mission is to attract, retain and add value to clients by providing them with effective and innovative legal solutions. The firm offers its clients a comprehensive range of legal services, covering all aspects of business in Iowa, on a state, regional and national basis. The firm prides itself on providing aggressive, effective and innovative legal solutions to its clients. The firm has grown significantly in the last four years, both by the addition of top graduates from area law schools and by the addition of a significant number of lateral attorneys with diverse practices and skills.

## MAIN AREAS OF PRACTICE:

**Agribusiness:** The firm serves trade associations, commodity producers, cooperatives, seed companies, genetics companies, chemical companies and biotech companies. The practice group assists clients navigating diverse federal, state and local issues such as entity organization, financing, securities laws, environmental compliance, corporate farming laws, contracts, mergers, acquisitions, joint ventures and estate and family business succession planning.

**Construction Law:** The firm provides legal advice and representation to all facets of the construction industry. The firm's representation includes bidding; document preparation; contract negotiation, formation, and performance; warranty issues; OSHA compliance; liens; and litigation and dispute resolution. The firm also represents a number of construction-related trade associations.

**Corporate & Securities:** The firm represents buyers, sellers and investors in mergers, acquisitions, business combinations, leveraged buy-outs, ESOPs and recapitalizations. The firm advises clients regarding federal and state securities laws in connection with public offerings and private placements, annual and other periodic reports and proxy statements. The firm also advises borrowers, banks and other financial institutions on all aspects of lending transactions and various regulatory issues. The firm provides advice and consultation on choice of entity, joint venture arrangements and a wide variety of operational and strategic issues.

**Employee Benefits:** The firm assists clients with a wide range of benefit-related matters, including the design, establishment and maintenance of qualified retirement plans, including pension, profit sharing, ESOP and 401(k) plans.

**Employment:** The firm counsels public and private employers on employment issues such as discrimination in employment, termination and layoffs, wage and hour disputes, individual disciplinary problems, drug testing, employment and severance contracts, covenants not to compete and employee handbooks. The firm advises clients on compliance with federal and state workplace laws, including workers compensation, occupational safety and health, wage and hour, and anti-discrimination statutes. The firm defends employers before a variety of local agencies, and federal and state courts, as well as representing employers in alternative dispute resolution proceedings, including mediation and arbitration.

**Environmental:** The firm assists clients in dealing with the wide variety of environmental challenges that face businesses and individuals. The group assists real estate developers attempting to develop former industrial sites and also provides advice to lenders, sellers and purchasers of properties affected by potential environmental concerns. The firm provides counsel to regulated companies facing permit issues and enforcement actions; helps agricultural businesses meet air permitting and water discharge challenges, and also helps ethanol and biodiesel clients meet regulatory compliance requirements.

**Estate Planning/Retirement:** The firm provides sophisticated estate and retirement planning advice, assisting clients with respect to wills; living trusts; life insurance trusts; irrevocable trusts; gifting programs; family limited partnerships; deferred compensation arrangements; gift and estate tax planning for retirement benefits; charitable planning and planning for the transition of a family or closely-held business. Members of the firm are also experienced in the administration of estates, conservatorships, and guardianships, and trust and estate litigation.

**Governmental Relations:** The firm represents business, agricultural and individual interests before the Iowa Legislature, the Governor's Office and numerous state, federal and local agencies and governmental subsidiaries. The firm's lobbying team has considerable prior experience in all three branches of state government, as well as service in county and city government.

**Health Law:** The firm represents healthcare clients, including multi-hospital systems, community hospitals, nursing homes, physicians and physician groups. The group provides representation on a full range of health law issues, such as tax exemption, Certificate of Need, reimbursement, licensure and regulatory matters, fraud & abuse, managed care, mergers and acquisitions and physician relations.

**Intellectual Property/Franchising:** The firm provides a range of intellectual property services and consultation pertaining to traditional copyright, trademark, patent and trade secret law. In addition, this group provides counsel on the developing e-commerce, internet and biotechnology law along with licensing and litigation expertise in these areas. The firm has an extensive franchise practice, representing franchisors and franchisees throughout the United States.

**Litigation:** The firm represents clients in civil and commercial litigation in state and federal courts, appellate advocacy, arbitration/alternative dispute resolution, and administrative agency proceedings. This practice group covers a broad range of substantive areas including business torts, contracts, intellectual property, securities, employment, healthcare, real estate, environmental, agricultural and construction.

**Real Estate:** The firm provides a broad range of services to organizations and individuals who are in the business of purchasing, developing, managing, leasing and selling real estate. Clients retain the firm to guide them through the many title, environmental, land use and zoning issues involved in real estate transactions and to assist them in all legal areas relating to the utilization and management of real property and improvements, including but not limited to, taxation, tenant relations and governmental compliance.

**Renewable Fuels:** The firm is a leading provider of legal services to ethanol and biodiesel manufacturing companies throughout the Midwest. It develops capitalization and operating strategies for development-stage and functioning plants. The firm has assisted dozens of ventures in nine states. It is an active member of the Renewable Fuels Association, and its lawyers are in demand to speak on legal topics of interest to the industry.

**Tax:** The firm provides federal, international, state and local tax consulting and routinely advises clients on tax issues related to business transactions, choice of entity, mergers, acquisitions, sales, and liquidations. The firm provides tax compliance services and represents clients before the IRS, state and local tax authorities, and in all courts. The firm also represents insurance companies in complex tax matters.

## HEAD OFFICE

**IOWA**
666 Grand Avenue, Suite 2000, **Des Moines**, IA 50309
**Tel:** 515 242 2400   **Fax:** 515 283 0231
**Email:** info@ialawyers.com
**Website:** www.ialawyers.com

## BRANCH OFFICES

**IOWA**
616 Franklin Place, **Pella**, IA 50219
**Tel:** 641 628 4513   **Fax:** 641 628 8494

Regency West 5, 4500 Westown Parkway, Suite 277,
**West Des Moines**, IA 50266
**Tel:** 515 242 2400   **Fax:** 515 242 2448

## How lawyers are ranked

Every year we carry out thousands of in-depth interviews with clients and lawyers in order to assess the reputations and expertise of business lawyers across the USA. Chambers rankings and editorial are referred to extensively by General Counsel and other purchasers of legal services who look to our recommendations when choosing their lawyers.

# CORPORATE/M&A

| Corporate/M&A |
| --- |
| **Leading Firms** |

**1** BLACKWELL SANDERS PEPER *Overland Park*
FOULSTON SIEFKIN LLP *Wichita*
STINSON MORRISON HECKER LLP *Overland Park*

**2** LATHROP & GAGE L.C. *Overland Park*
POLSINELLI SHALTON WELTE *Overland Park*
SHUGHART THOMSON & KILROY *Overland Park*

**3** FLEESON, GOOING, COULSON & KITCH *Wichita*
SHOOK, HARDY & BACON LLP *Overland Park*
TRIPLETT, WOOLF & GARRETSON LLC *Wichita*

| **Leading Individuals** |
| --- |

**1** ADAMS Stephen *Blackwell Sanders*
ENGSTROM Eric *Fleeson, Gooing, Coulson & Kitch*
MARVIN Jack *Stinson Morrison Hecker LLP*
SORENSEN Harvey *Foulston Siefkin LLP*
SWAIN Lawrence *Shughart Thomson & Kilroy*

**2** GARRETSON Thomas *Triplett, Woolf & Garretson*
PISHNY Lyle *Lathrop & Gage L.C.*
TRENKLE William *Foulston Siefkin LLP*
TRIPLETT Thomas *Triplett, Woolf & Garretson*
WOOD William *Foulston Siefkin LLP*

## Band 1

### Blackwell Sanders Peper Martin LLP
See firm details p.1212

**The Firm:** Although predominantly visible in the Missouri market, this large firm still remains the first port of call for many Kansas-based peers looking to refer out work when conflicted. Corporate law dominates the firm and is the preserve of a talented group of lawyers who have crafted a particularly strong reputation for representing banks.

**The Lawyers:** **Stephen Adams** (see p.1203) is an *"excellent and experienced lawyer"* who *"enjoys a well-deserved reputation at the corporate Bar."* Clients commend him *"for always having our interests at the top of his list."* Although a brilliant all-around corporate attorney, he is especially prized for his expertise in the fields of healthcare, contracts, compliance, real estate and transactions. Recently, Adams has tackled numerous general corporate acquisitions and joint ventures while also organizing a series of divestitures

for healthcare providers.

**Clients/Work Highlights:** Recent work has included the completion of two IPOs for Tortoise Capital Advisors, worth $400 million and $115 million respectively. For John Q Hammons, the majority shareholder, founder and CEO of John Q Hammons Hotels, the team created and completed a series of tax-advantaged, joint venture structures totaling $1.2 billion. Other clients include American Italian Pasta; MC Real Estate Services; Applebee's International; Saint Luke's Health System and Aquila.

### Foulston Siefkin LLP
See firm details p.935

**The Firm:** *"Experienced, confident and professional,"* Foulston Siefkin wins fierce loyalty from its clients. The reasons for this were summed up by one commentator: *"We feel we are represented by the best in the profession: always knowledgeable, prompt and professional. They also add value by being honest with us about any given situation and lend business advice as well."* The team is proficient in all aspects of corporate law but taxation undoubtedly proves a core strength.

**The Lawyers:** *"Top-flight"* **Harvey Sorensen** (see p.933) is appreciated by clients for *"understanding the dynamics of business as well as he understands business law."* Sorensen represents clients, often with a Kansas connection, all over the USA and has undertaken international work. **William Trenkle** (see p.933) is renowned for being particularly strong in the taxation arena but is strong on corporate matters generally. Focusing largely on the highly regulated healthcare field, he recently advised on the private acquisition of around 25 surgical hospitals across the USA. General counsel **William Wood** (see p.934) has an excellent reputation for representing banks.

**Clients/Work Highlights:** The firm mainly represents midmarket companies such as LodgeWorks and American Restaurant Partners.

### Stinson Morrison Hecker LLP
See firm details p.1220

**The Firm:** A few years on from the merger of Morrison & Hecker and Stinson Mag & Fizzell, the resultant firm continues to arrest the attention of the market. While some question whether the merger has yet bedded down properly, most agree that, as an

entity, the firm has signal strength. Stinson Mag & Fizzell was notoriously robust when it came to corporate law and the new firm has played on this to consolidate its position in the market. With a following wind, many feel the best could be yet to come.

**The Lawyers:** **Jack Marvin** (see p.932) brought a loyal client following with him. Of his many votaries, one stated: *"We have used Marvin for over ten years. He provides valuable legal advice and counsel regarding complex commercial loan transactions, including problem loan resolution and bankruptcy representation. He is an outstanding attorney in his chosen field."* Marvin works predominantly in the field of finance transactions, representing lenders making loans to multifarious commercial entities including real estate development, oil and gas companies and manufacturers. He also does a small amount of mortgage foreclosure litigation.

**Clients/Work Highlights:** Of late, the team has continued to work on multistate hotel financings for a new hotel chain across the USA. These involved several hotel construction and apartment complex construction loans with bond financing features. The team also represented a foreign bank in a multinational aircraft financing involving parties from South Africa, Canada, the USA and Poland. Representative clients include Commerce Bank; Central Bank & Trust; Haldex; Hillcrest Bank; Security Savings Bank and United Missouri Bank.

## Band 2

### Lathrop & Gage L.C.
See firm details p.1214

**The Firm:** Situated in Johnson County, this firm is known throughout Kansas as *"a tough nut to crack on the local scene."* Benefiting from a continuing and rapid expansion of corporate law, it increasingly serves the needs of clients in outlying regions whose needs have surpassed the expertise of the small local firms available to them. As one client said: *"It is the depth of their in-house expertise on myriad aspects of the law that makes them such a valuable resource to us."*

**The Lawyers:** **Lyle Pishny** (see p.932) is appreciated by clients for his *"professional and unflappable demeanor when faced with sensitive or controversial issues and challenging personalities."* Among other

things, Pishny has been representing tax-exempt organizations that need corporate work, in particular advice regarding the application of the Sarbanes-Oxley Act. He is the lead attorney representing Kansas State University Foundation on a $300 million corporate matter regarding governance, contract, human resources and related matters.
**Clients/Work Highlights:** The caseload includes advising on a $12 million loan for a banking client looking to develop a shopping center.

### Polsinelli Shalton Welte Suelthaus PC
See firm details p.1217
**The Firm:** This firm rightly prides itself on being one of the fastest-growing practices in the Midwest. Constantly evolving, it has now set up offices in locations as diverse as Kansas City, Overland Park, Edwardsville, New York and Washington, DC to name but a few. The firm's "*savvy*" corporate group is reputed to serve its clients with vigor, representing them "*zealously and aggressively.*"
**The Lawyers:** Stanley Woodworth's business practice focuses on corporate finance and M&A. In addition to this, he bears a particular reputation among peers for providing a high-class service in the area where corporate and real estate development meet. Woodworth is situated in the firm's Overland Park office and is licensed to practice in both Kansas and Missouri.
**Clients/Work Highlights:** Clients range in size from local entrepreneurial firms to Fortune 50 companies. These are drawn from industries as diverse as construction, retailing and telecom.

### Shughart Thomson & Kilroy PC
See firm details p.1219
**The Firm:** A "*first-rate local firm*" with a formidable Midwest presence, this outfit has offices in Springfield and St Joseph, Missouri, Denver, Colorado and Phoenix, Arizona in addition to those in Kansas City and Overland Park. A full-service business and litigation firm, it is heavily weighted toward its corporate department.

The Lawyers: Bearer of a "*sterling reputation,*" **Lawrence Swain** (see p.933) engages in the full gamut of general corporate transactional work and issues arising out of contracts between companies. Much of his work is centered on IP, computer software and some general copyright and trademark work. It is his knowledge of the crossover between IP and corporate matters that really distinguishes Swain in the marketplace.
**Clients/Work Highlights:** Swain is currently closing a $3.5 billion software deal for a major food distribution company. Other clients include Associated Wholesale Grocers; GEAR for Sports; Crane Plumbing and Applebee's.

## Band 3

### Fleeson, Gooing, Coulson & Kitch, LLC
**The Firm:** This long-standing law firm has an outstanding client list and an irrefutable reputation in the Wichita market for being home to some outstanding litigators. Commentators alluded to the fact that the firm could do with some beefing up in the junior ranks but were quick to point out that, in the upper reaches, it "*has some of the finest attorneys in the state.*"
**The Lawyers:** **Eric Engstrom** is considered by peers to be "*the team's leading light.*" His corporate and transactional practice covers the purchase and sale of corporations in the USA and abroad. His reputation is strongest in the field of bankruptcy where he is engaged by creditors and unsecured creditors' committees.
**Clients/Work Highlights:** American Airlines; Fidelity Bank; INTRUST Bank and Grant Thornton.

### Shook, Hardy & Bacon LLP
See firm details p.1218
**The Firm:** The Kansas branches of this international firm are best known for defending the largest tobacco companies against all manner of litigation.

That said, observers agree that its team offers a very fine corporate service that spans all the major facets of the discipline.
**The Lawyers:** Bob Grossman is currently on the firm's executive committee and specializes in employee benefits and employee stock ownership plans. Alson Martin's main area of expertise is closely held businesses. An expert in this relatively recherché area of corporate law, he has recently represented the seller of a window manufacturer, 98% of which is ESOP-owned. He is further possessed of expertise in each of the tax, corporate and healthcare sectors and was praised by clients for having "*a matchless understanding of our unique demands.*"
**Clients/Work Highlights:** Clients range from large multinational public companies to early-stage private firms. Examples include Kansas City Orthopaedic Institute and Building Material Distributors.

### Triplett, Woolf & Garretson LLC
**The Firm:** Researchers were left in no doubt that this is a "*very fine Wichita firm*" to which peers are more than happy to refer clients. Its corporate team continues to attract a panoply of clients including corporations, partnerships, limited liability companies and proprietorships of differing sizes. With more than 15 partners, the firm provides a complete service to business clients, covering everything from formations and acquisitions to liquidations and beyond.
**The Lawyers:** **Thomas Triplett** represents several large trusts and is considered "*the dean of tax and estate planning lawyers.*" The "*excellent*" **Thomas Garretson** has an especially strong reputation for the quality of his securities and bond finance work.
**Clients/Work Highlights:** Small entrepreneurial firms and large businesses with both a regional and a national presence are equally well catered for here.

# EMPLOYMENT

# MAINLY DEFENDANT

| Employment: Mainly Defendant |
|---|
| Leading Firms |
| [1] FOULSTON SIEFKIN LLP *Wichita* |
| KUTAK ROCK LLP *Wichita* |
| MARTIN, PRINGLE, OLIVER, WALLACE *Wichita* |
| MORRIS, LAING, EVANS, BROCK *Wichita* |
| [2] MARTIN & CHURCHILL CHARTERED *Wichita* |
| STINSON MORRISON HECKER LLP *Wichita* |

## Band 1

### Foulston Siefkin LLP
See firm details p.935
**The Firm:** This "*very well-respected, old Kansas law firm*" provides a complete labor and employment law service to both private and public clients of all sizes. Attorneys defend employers in the full range of employment law actions in front of administrative tribunals and state and federal courts. They are also increasingly engaged in employment discrimination class actions, and provide high levels of advice to employers seeking to institute procedures likely to prevent future litigation against them. On the labor law front, the firm's breadth of experience is such that "*there is no situation a union could present that the team*

*would not be able to handle.*" Its team's standing is well illustrated by its unique association with the Employers Counsel Network (ECN). This is a group of law firms, one from each state, that advises and represents employers in workplace-related issues and disputes.
**The Lawyers:** "*A brilliant man and an excellent attorney,*" Douglas Stanley (see p.933) is widely respected as a traditional labor lawyer. His caseload includes representing employers on every conceivable employment issue that comes before state and federal administrative agencies. In addition, he has conducted a sizable number of labor arbitrations of late and is also highly regarded for his work advising employers in respect to union efforts to organize employees. **Kathleen Babcock** (see p.931) is the star employment lawyer here and has a particular repu-

## Employment: Mainly Defendant
### Leading Individuals

[1] **BABCOCK Kathleen** *Foulston Siefkin LLP*
**MANN Terry** *Martin, Pringle*
**RUPE Alan** *Kutak Rock LLP*
**SCHECK Stephanie** *Stinson Morrison Hecker LLP*
**STANLEY Douglas** *Foulston Siefkin LLP*
**WORTH Diane** *Morris, Laing*
[2] **CHURCHILL Stanley** *Martin & Churchill Chartered*
**OVERMAN Robert** *Morris, Laing*
**PETERSON Ken** *Morris, Laing*
[3] **HILL Donald** *Martin & Churchill Chartered*
**MACKAY Douglas** *Kutak Rock LLP*

tation as an appellate lawyer: "*An excellent courtroom communicator,*" she acts for both private and public entities and recently represented Boeing in class action litigation in Kansas and Oklahoma.
**Clients/Work Highlights:** Boeing; Spirit AeroSystems; AT&T; Via Christi Health System and Coleman.

## Kutak Rock LLP

**The Firm:** This firm enjoys a strong reputation locally, coupled with a notable presence in surrounding states. It has 16 offices covering an impressive spread of the USA but it is the Wichita office that acts as headquarters for a labor and employment group headed by managing partner Alan Rupe. The team's main strength lies with its talented cadre of excellent employment litigators who constitute "*a formidable fighting unit.*"
**The Lawyers:** "*Excellent on his feet and a man who clearly relishes the trial process,*" **Alan Rupe** has a particular reputation for carrying out incisive cross-examinations. He is currently acting for a chain of Kansas nursing homes in defending a string of allegations brought by 16 plaintiffs relating, inter alia, to race and age discrimination. "*Bright, enthusiastic and pleasant to work with,*" **Douglas Mackay** is felt to be a fine foil to Rupe. Mackay offers his clients a particularly valuable service as he is licensed to practice in Kansas, Missouri and Oklahoma. The continuing national trend away from litigation in favor of settlement has affected the balance of Mackay's practice and he has been conducting more counseling recently.
**Clients/Work Highlights:** The group has been engaged in 180 discrimination cases since late 2004.

## Martin, Pringle, Oliver, Wallace & Bauer, L.L.P.

**The Firm:** Operating from offices in Wichita, Overland Park and Kansas City, this firm represents a formidable presence in the region. Its team prides itself on trial avoidance and is always looking for a swift resolution to the client's problems. Cost-effectiveness and efficient staffing are the watchwords, but commentators are in no doubt that, should matters go to trial, this group can put up as stiff a fight as anyone.
**The Lawyers:** Esteemed throughout the state, **Terry Mann** is considered an "*astute and experienced employment lawyer who enjoys immense respect from her clients.*" She also undertakes traditional labor law and much of her recent work has been dealing with manufacturers and subcontractors in the aircraft industry. As the most senior employment attorney in the group, Mann is generally in charge of discrimination cases. Primarily a litigator, Roger McClellan has been doing a little more medical malpractice of late. One peer informed researchers that McClellan was their "*first port of call when conflicted.*"
**Clients/Work Highlights:** Raytheon Aircraft; AIG; Abercrombie RTD; Aladdin Petroleum; Backwoods Equipment and Wichita Iron & Metals.

## Morris, Laing, Evans, Brock & Kennedy, Chartered

**The Firm:** Despite being formed into a relatively small group, the lawyers here have "*excellent credentials*" for providing assistance to small and midsized businesses throughout the Midwest and beyond. The firm has offices in both Wichita and Topeka and delivers a full traditional labor and employment service.
**The Lawyers:** **Diane Worth** undertakes the full range of employment work. One satisfied client told researchers that she is "*very professional, considerate and sensitive to the issues faced by the employer as well as the employee. She is insightful, reads people very well and is very much alive to time issues, meeting deadlines ahead of schedule.*" She recently resolved a sex discrimination retaliatory discharge case for Anthony Hospital. "*Excellent trial lawyer*" **Ken Peterson** has been litigating at both the state and federal level for over 30 years. He is part of a group led by the "*very experienced*" **Robert Overman**, a traditional labor lawyer of some repute. Recently he has represented Iowa Central Community College and has also acted for the Wichita Symphony Orchestra conducting

management negotiations in relation to collective bargaining agreements. On the employment side, Overman's work has included wrongful discharge litigation for Martin K Eby Construction.
**Clients/Work Highlights:** Dillon Companies, Cargill Meat Solutions and Midwest Drywall are among the firm's clients.

## Band 2

## Martin & Churchill Chartered

**The Firm:** Acknowledged by all as very strong in the labor field, this firm has a long history of success. Although observers fear that the recent trend for dealing with labor relations issues in-house may impact upon its business, they were happy to acknowledge it as a major force in the area. Perhaps not as long in numbers as some others, its team makes up for any lack of depth through the sheer quality of the lawyers in its upper echelons.
**The Lawyers:** **Stanley Churchill** and **Donald Hill** are both considered by peers to be "*long-term practitioners with excellent reputations who undoubtedly do a great job.*"
**Clients/Work Highlights:** Bombardier Learjet and Presbyterian Manors of Mid-America feature on the client list.

## Stinson Morrison Hecker LLP

See firm details p.1220

**The Firm:** The firm is well known in the Midwest, having numerous offices in the region, while also extending its tentacles to Phoenix and Washington, DC where it has a couple of sister branches. The Wichita team itself is relatively small but able to draw on expertise across the firm's network of offices to provide a full service. Clients say that there is rarely an employment issue that one or other of its attorneys is incapable of handling.
**The Lawyers:** The "*impressive*" **Stephanie Scheck** (see p.933) has had a successful employment practice for years that continues to grow. Head of the Wichita employment department, her areas of expertise are discrimination, harassment, Title VII, FMLA and FLSA issues. Her nonlitigation work includes advising companies on affirmative action plans. Scheck engages in a little labor law and has two unionized clients.
**Clients/Work Highlights:** Wesley Medical Center is a key client of the firm.

# LITIGATION

## GENERAL COMMERCIAL

### Litigation: General Commercial
#### Leading Firms

1. **FOULSTON SIEFKIN LLP** *Wichita*
   **HITE, FANNING & HONEYMAN LLP** *Wichita*
   **SHOOK, HARDY & BACON LLP** *Overland Park*
   **STINSON MORRISON HECKER LLP** *Overland Park*
2. **LATHROP & GAGE L.C.** *Overland Park*
   **SHUGHART THOMSON & KILROY PC** *Overland Park*
3. **REBEIN BANGERTER PA** *Dodge City*
   **SPENCER FANE BRITT & BROWNE** *Overland Park*
   **WRIGHT, HENSON, SOMERS, CLARK** *Topeka*

#### Leading Individuals

1. **HINDERKS Mark** *Stinson Morrison Hecker LLP*
   **HITE Richard** *Hite, Fanning & Honeyman*
   **REBEIN David** *Rebein Bangerter PA*
   **STOUT Mikel** *Foulston Siefkin LLP*
2. **BADGEROW J Nick** *Spencer Fane Britt & Browne*
   **BATH Thomas** *Bath & Edmonds, P.A*
   **FOCHT Jack** *Foulston Siefkin LLP*
   **FOWLER Jay** *Foulston Siefkin LLP*
   **HATLEY Joseph** *Lathrop & Gage L.C.*
   **HONEYMAN Richard** *Hite, Fanning & Honeyman*
   **MUSIL Greg** *Shughart Thomson & Kilroy*
   **SAMPSON William** *Shook, Hardy & Bacon LLP*
   **WARTA Darrell** *Foulston Siefkin LLP*
   **WRIGHT Thomas** *Wright, Henson*

## Band 1

### Foulston Siefkin LLP
See firm details p.935

**The Firm:** The largest firm in Kansas, Foulston Siefkin has a big presence in the east of the state with offices in Topeka and Overland Park. The group is led from the Wichita branch and constitutes "a band of very well-regarded commercial litigators." Indeed, competitors assured researchers that they "were happy to refer clients in the case of conflict because we know they will be well taken care of."

**The Lawyers:** The group boasts an impressive catalog of lawyers. Competitors enthused about **Mikel Stout** (see p.933), one remarking that they were "proud to be in the same profession as him: he is an excellent trial lawyer with impeccable professional standards." Clients commend him for being "responsive, very intelligent and, most importantly, a very convincing advocate at trial – he has provided excellent legal services to my company for over 25 years and has been a pleasure to work with on many difficult matters." Highlights of the past year have included representing Coleman on a trademark violation case. Stout defended the action with a counterclaim for which the jury gave them judgment – the court then trebled it. "A dean of Kansas trial lawyers," **Jack Focht** (see p.931) is a former president of the Kansas Bar Association. A deft exponent of dispute resolution, he is currently reaping praise for his representation of lawyers in ethics complaints. The relatively junior

**Jay Fowler** (see p.931) is considered "a very fine trial lawyer on a rising path." His practice focuses on contract and breach of fiduciary duty matters, as well as related commercial torts for both plaintiff and defendant businesses. It is clear to all that the "highly respected and quick-witted" **Darrell Warta** (see p.933) has enormous experience and enjoys the trial process. His practice is truly diverse but he enjoys a signal reputation in healthcare, where he can count Via Christi Health System among his clients.

**Clients/Work Highlights:** American General Finance; Catholic Mutual Group; Johnson & Johnson; Boeing; Spirit AeroSystems and Koch Industries.

### Hite, Fanning & Honeyman LLP

**The Firm:** This Wichita litigation boutique consistently commands respect from competitors for being the home of some of the state's best litigators and distinguished mediators and arbitrators. This group of smart civil litigators possesses broad practices with notable specializations in insurance, workers' compensation, oil and gas litigation, and medical malpractice work, to name but a few.

**The Lawyers:** Admiring words abounded for "commercial litigation guru" **Richard Hite**. His position at the top of the Kansas Bar is undoubted: "Outstanding – whenever we have conflicts he is the first guy I think of. He is a smart, determined and tenacious trial lawyer," said one peer. Hite continues to be engaged in major contract disputes, though he is increasingly acting as an agreed mediator. He enjoys considerable public standing and is a chair of the Supreme Court Nominating Committee. "An extremely experienced defense lawyer," **Richard Honeyman** is undertaking more work in the area where commercial litigation and general civil litigation meet. For instance, his past year's work included suing a railroad company after a derailment in which Honeyman's client's property sustained damage worth approximately $3 million. Historically, the firm's reputation was based on the level and quality of insurance carrier work it undertook. This is still partly true of Honeyman who continues to have a number of such clients on his books.

**Clients/Work Highlights:** Vulcan Chemicals; Nowak Construction; Cox Communications and Quick Trip Convenience Stores.

### Shook, Hardy & Bacon LLP
See firm details p.1218

**The Firm:** The Kansas branch of Shook, Hardy & Bacon sits in Kansas City and, as such, their lawyers have as much fame in Missouri as Kansas. The law firm was established in Kansas City at the end of the 19th century and remains one of the state's giants. Expansion over the years now means they have a significant national and international presence with offices in Geneva, Houston, Kansas City, London, Miami, Orange County, Overland Park, San Francisco, Tampa, and Washington, DC. It is in the area of products liability that this law firm really comes into its own.

**The Lawyers:** The "highly respected" **William Sampson** (see p.1210) is considered a keen defense advocate: "He is a great and experienced trial lawyer who commands a lot of respect from opposition counsel." Sampson tries cases at both the state and federal level and, in addition to the standard fare of commercial litigation, has made a name for himself of late in fraud cases. He recently represented the plaintiff Total in a breach of contract action in the federal court in which he defeated the defendant's summary judgment motion. Securities and antitrust litigation are also within his demesne. Sampson draws on his extensive experience by teaching trial practice, litigation strategy and legal writing. He is also former president of the Defense Research Institute.

**Clients/Work Highlights:** The team acts for a host of major businesses and commercial concerns.

### Stinson Morrison Hecker LLP
See firm details p.1220

**The Firm:** The firm continues to sit comfortably in the first tier, bearing a formidable presence throughout the Midwest. The business litigation division is the firm's largest and is its crowning glory. Clients especially value the team's determination to nip things in the bud through wise mediation and arbitration. That said, there is little doubt that the firm houses a group of "sharp and imaginative litigators who do one hell of a job for their clients."

**The Lawyers:** The quality of a firm is only ever as good as the quality of their individuals and you will not find anyone much better than **Mark Hinderks** (see p.932). Peers consider him a "lawyer's lawyer" and regular clients make him a "first choice for litigation in Kansas." Indeed, it was noted by many that Hinderks delivered a level of service that compared favorably to that found at many New York firms. This has not gone unnoticed in the community: Hinderks earned membership of the Association of Trial Lawyers of America last fall. His practice is focused on complex litigation for both businesses and public entities. For example, the past year has seen Sprint Nextel continue to instruct him in the defense of large class actions throughout the country.

**Clients/Work Highlights:** Clients include Sprint Nextel and Garman International. Work is also undertaken for several local government entities, including the Unified Government of Wyandotte and Kansas City.

## Band 2

### Lathrop & Gage L.C.
See firm details p.1214

**The Firm:** The group conducts the full range of commercial litigation with a slight emphasis on real estate-related litigation. The continuing growth of Kansas City's suburbs has brought with it a concomitant rise in commercial transactions and subsequent litigation. This trend is felt to have been of great benefit to a firm always happy to fight for its client. The Lawyers: Research found that the "*outstanding*" **Joseph Hatley** (see p.931) kept his clients very pleased. One enthused: "*He handles our complex deals with capability and precision, cutting through the law to focus on the real issues. He is especially good at reading and understanding people.*"

Clients/Work Highlights: Clients include PMI Mortgage Insurance. The firm represented Bank of America against an allegation of breach of contract in a loan participation agreement. It also successfully defended Developers Diversified Realty against an allegation of breach of covenant.

## Shughart Thomson & Kilroy PC
See firm details p.1219

The Firm: The firm has a significant presence in the Midwest with offices in Kansas, Missouri, Colorado and Arizona. The market considers this group to be wholly deserving of its place in the table. As one peer said: "*When you think about Kansas City litigators, Shughart will always come to mind.*"

The Lawyers: **Greg Musil** (see p.932) is the star name in this group. He is considered a "*great, solid lawyer who is truly excellent on his feet.*" Musil is as famous locally for his active involvement in politics as his skill in the courtroom. In terms of the law, he commands an impressive and diverse practice representing big, national names and smaller, local concerns in both Kansas and Missouri.

Clients/Work Highlights: The firm acted for Learjet in a suit relating to the design and quality of a component they use in their models. Other clients include La Petite Academy and HCA.

## Band 3

### Rebein Bangerter PA
See firm details p.936

The Firm: This Dodge City group has an excellent reputation for being the commercial litigator of the High Plains. It continues to have a very active class action litigation defense practice and is particularly well known for its involvement in cattle industry litigation.

The Lawyers: President-elect of the Kansas Bar Association, **David Rebein** (see p.932) is renowned as "*a very fine and thorough lawyer with a very busy practice all around the state.*" A former partner at Foulston Siefkin, Rebein can handle the full spectrum of general business litigation but has made a particular name for himself representing the Kansas Livestock Association.

Clients/Work Highlights: Excel; National Beef; Cargill and Archer Daniels Midland.

### Spencer Fane Britt & Browne LLP

The Firm: This historic Midwest firm of litigators is primarily famed for its employment work, yet Spencer Fane also has a busy and "*well-respected*" litigation practice with most depth at its Overland Park office. The group has earned a particular reputation for its expertise in construction and real estate litigation, alongside general commercial work. The team's members are litigators in the broadest sense, being keen arbitrators engaged in much dispute arbitration.

The Lawyers: Commentators praised **Nick Badgerow** for his stellar involvement in "*first-rate litigation.*" Although a consummate general commercial litigator, Badgerow specializes in employment and construction litigation, in which he has a near unique insight having worked as a construction worker through college. His practice is conducted largely but not exclusively in the Midwest.

Clients/Work Highlights: Home Depot, Kansas Power & Light and Honeywell are among the team's clients.

### Wright, Henson, Somers, Clark & Bake LLP

The Firm: Relatively small in comparison to some of the other firms listed, Wright, Henson, Somers, Clark & Bake has greatest prominence in Topeka and the west of the state. The group is best known for servicing the banking, business litigation and advisory needs of its extensive bank and insurance client list.

The Lawyers: Fellow of the Association of Trial Lawyers of America, **Thomas Wright** is viewed by the market as the firm's "*big gun.*" When it comes to the field of professional liability, he is considered "*truly first rate.*" Wright is also a renowned mediator.

### Other Notable Practitioners

Unanimous agreement was forthcoming that **Thomas Bath** is "*the premier white-collar criminal defense attorney in the state – the leading guy, for sure.*" A founding partner of the criminal defense specialists Bath & Edmonds PA, he represents individuals and corporations in the full range of white-collar proceedings, from allegations of bank fraud to public corruption. Bath enjoys considerable standing in the community and, in 2004 alone, was both awarded the outstanding service award by the Kansas Bar Association and elected for the second time to the Kansas Supreme Court Nominating Commission.

# LITIGATION

## Litigation: Environmental
### Leading Firms
| 1 | FOULSTON SIEFKIN LLP *Wichita* |
| | LATHROP & GAGE L.C. *Kansas City* |
| | SHOOK, HARDY & BACON LLP *Kansas City* |
| | SPENCER FANE BRITT & BROWNE *Kansas City* |
| | STINSON MORRISON HECKER LLP *Kansas City* |

### Leading Individuals
| 1 | EFFLANDT Charles *Foulston Siefkin LLP* |
| | ERICKSON David *Shook, Hardy & Bacon LLP* |
| | FORD JR William *Lathrop & Gage L.C.* |
| | PRICE James *Spencer Fane Britt & Browne* |
| | TRIPP David *Stinson Morrison Hecker LLP* |

## Band 1

### Foulston Siefkin LLP
See firm details p.935

The Firm: The largest law firm in Kansas has an environmental law group based in its Wichita office. The group concentrates primarily on representing clients in litigation and administrative proceedings. However, it is increasingly expert at designing and implementing appropriate and cost-effective environmental due diligence strategies for business acquisition and merger transactions.

The Lawyers: **Charles Efflandt** (see p.931) is the practice group leader of the firm's environmental and natural resources team. His practice is evenly weighted between litigation, administrative proceedings and the provision of support to some of the firm's other departments. He is acclaimed by clients for providing "*precise and accurate legal advice, enhanced by a thorough understanding of the business culture in which we operate. He represents our interests to others with a courteous manner, having excellent

# ENVIRONMENTAL

working relationships with regulators and administrators. A man of a calm and professional demeanor, he can be tough when necessary.*" In addition to the clients he generates himself, Efflandt provides an invaluable service to many of the firm's real estate clients involved in environmental due diligence. He is also engaged in transactional work carried out in conjunction with the firm's corporate team.

Clients/Work Highlights: Recently, Efflandt has been involved in a multimillion-dollar Superfund case involving complex causation covers. The case is particularly interesting for involving unique issues of modeling and time dating. Other clients include Coleman; McAndrews & Forbes; Boeing and Spirit AeroSystems.

### Lathrop & Gage L.C.
See firm details p.1214

The Firm: A presence in both Kansas and Missouri, this truly broad-based team is subdivided into practice groups covering solid and hazardous waste, insurance coverage, transactional representation, federal and state Superfund matters, toxic torts, air regulation, water regulation and chemical regulation.

**The Lawyers:** Current chair of the environment practice, **William Ford** (see p.1205) has earned the respect of his peers for being "*an outstanding litigator.*" Clients praise him for providing a truly comprehensive service: "*He exhibits a great combination of excellent legal thinking, practical advice and the command of a great legal network, a holy trinity that is very rarely come across.*" The bulk of his practice is made up of solid and hazardous waste, chemical exposure and toxic tort litigation. Ford presides over a growing team that looks set to increase its influence in the coming years. In a busy last year, many of its members have been engaged in environmental insurance recovery work, acting for holders of historic policies.

**Clients/Work Highlights:** Alliant Techsystems; Cargill; GM and AMC Theaters.

### Shook, Hardy & Bacon LLP

See firm details p.1218

**The Firm:** Straddling the divide between Kansas and Missouri, the environmental group of this Kansas City firm is comparatively large, being comprised of approximately 15 lawyers. Such depth allows it to handle very large toxic tort and environmental cases, while also giving it the scope to undertake other areas such as transactional work, regulatory compliance and government investigations.

**The Lawyers:** A "*truly top-flight, principled and effective litigator,*" **David Erickson** (see p.1205) has "*a reputation for getting straight to the facts and not engaging in histrionics.*" "*A great aid to his clients,*" he was further described by peers as "*the type of lawyer*

you really want to work with: bursting with common sense, he aggressively pursues strong points but does not labor after weak ones.*" In the past year, Erickson has undertaken a marked increase in toxic tort and chemical exposure litigation, but he continues to engage in a wide variety of matters, many of them transactional in nature.

**Clients/Work Highlights:** Wal-Mart; DuPont; Lockheed Martin; Morton Salt and North American Salt.

### Spencer Fane Britt & Browne LLP

**The Firm:** The firm has offices in Kansas, Missouri and Nebraska, and represents clients throughout the USA. The environmental practice is run largely from the Kansas City office that is the home of group chair James Price. This is a full-service team able to advise clients on environmental laws, regulations and liabilities. The team is particularly well known for its competent handling of brownfield issues.

**The Lawyers:** An "*excellent attorney,*" **James Price** was described by one peer as "*the very first person I would send a client to in a conflict.*" His practice covers the full gamut of environmental work, with a particular emphasis on regulation and compliance, insurance and business litigation, and business transactions with environmental overtones.

**Clients/Work Highlights:** The group boasts a comprehensive list of public and private clients, ranging from municipal landfills and retail department stores to concerns in many different industries, not least agriculture and mining.

### Stinson Morrison Hecker LLP

See firm details p.1220

**The Firm:** This firm's environment and natural resources division continues to expand its practice areas. In the past year, for example, it has witnessed a marked increase in electric utility work. As is increasingly common with many such practice groups, its expertise is far from confined to the litigation arena. Other work typically involves the drafting and negotiation of environmental provisions in transactional documents, and a good deal of Superfund work. Peers laud it as a group with a healthy future.

**The Lawyers:** **David Tripp** (see p.1210) was described by one peer as "*a top-notch environment lawyer and one of those guys who you can rely on to be honest – when he tells you something, it's the truth!*" Others suggested that he had a "*greater extent of expertise than the other attorneys in the state.*" Apart from experiencing the steady increase in work that many fellow environmental litigators have seen, Tripp has been inundated with matters relating to the replacement of old-style, combined sewer systems for the City of Cincinnati, the Washington, DC metropolitan area and Kentucky. This constitutes big-bill work as the expense and social disruption of replacement is extensive: replacement itself can exceed $1 billion, the work takes years to negotiate and the overall schedule for such a project is 20 years or more.

**Clients/Work Highlights:** The group provides representation for the full range of environmental issues at both a regional and national level. Clients are drawn from the public and private sectors.

# REAL ESTATE

| **Real Estate** |
|---|
| Leading Firms |
| **1** ADAMS & JONES CHARTERED *Wichita* |
| FLEESON, GOOING, COULSON & KITCH *Wichita* |
| FOULSTON SIEFKIN LLP *Wichita* |
| HINKLE ELKOURI LAW FIRM LLC *Wichita* |
| LATHROP & GAGE L.C. *Overland Park* |
| POLSINELLI SHALTON WELTE *Overland Park* |
| STINSON MORRISON HECKER LLP *Wichita* |
| **2** MORRIS, LAING, EVANS, BROCK *Wichita* |
| TRIPLETT, WOOLF & GARRETSON LLC *Wichita* |

## Band 1

### Adams & Jones Chartered

**The Firm:** This Wichita firm has been heavily involved in real estate throughout its history and is "*home to some of the biggest names at the Kansas real estate Bar.*" Its team undertakes the full gamut of work in this sector from across the region. Although home to busy business and estates practices, the name of the game here is real estate.

**The Lawyers:** **Mert Buckley** heads up an eminent collection of attorneys whose "*breadth of knowledge mirrors the breadth of their experience.*" Buckley is admired by peers for his "*technical excellence*" and his "*straightforward and honest approach to negotiation.*" His practice focuses on transactions, development and leasing. A diverse and impressive portfolio has recently included the $14 million redevelopment of an old manufacturing building into a Marriott hotel in downtown Wichita. He has also been involved in the ongoing $20 million development of Wild West World, a western theme park just outside Wichita. **Monte Vines** consistently wins the esteem of his clients, with one commenting: "*Of his many admirable qualities, the things that I, as his client, value most are his measured and comprehensive approach to a case and his ability to steer the ship calmly through the storm.*" An "*honest and committed litigator with a brilliant mind,*" **Philip Bowman** is still considered a "*dean of the Kansas real estate Bar*" and has the finest of reputations in the finance area, representing lenders in the litigation of real estate transactions. **Roger Hughey** is deemed an "*extremely intelligent and methodical negotiator.*" His main areas of focus

are purchase transactions, loan transactions and distressed real estate. For RiverWalk LLC, he worked on a $6.3 million financing to facilitate the purchase of a large apartment complex in Wichita. Hughey has no single type of client and has engaged in work for an office, a retail store, a radio station office and a convenience store this past year alone.

**Clients/Work Highlights:** INTRUST Bank; Regency Bank; First American Title Insurance; Slawson Companies; AG Holdings and Sedgwick County.

### Fleeson, Gooing, Coulson & Kitch, LLC

**The Firm:** This top Wichita firm has been considered a first-class firm for oil and gas litigation for some time. Its ascendancy into the top tier of the rankings is a result of the increasing visibility and industry of its real estate attorneys. These lawyers are part of a team that operates as a subunit of the firm's overall business department and are kept busy by a client base typically made up of Kansas-based entities. Such clients are active both regionally and nationally, and many of them are major commercial developers of shopping centers, offices and the like.

## Real Estate
### Leading Individuals

**Senior Statesman**

BOWMAN Philip *Adams & Jones Chartered*

[1] BUCKLEY Mert *Adams & Jones Chartered*

HARNDEN Ronald *Triplett, Woolf & Garretson*

HEAVEN JR Lewis *Lathrop & Gage L.C.*

PETERSEN John *Polsinelli Shalton Welte Suelthaus*

WOODWORTH Stanley *Polsinelli Shalton Welte Suelthaus*

[2] DOERR Brian *Duggan, Shadwick, Doerr*

GOODELL Gerald *Goodell, Stratton*

HUGHEY Roger *Adams & Jones Chartered*

MARVIN Jack *Stinson Morrison Hecker LLP*

SCHRAG Donald *Morris, Laing*

SHORTLIDGE Neil *Stinson Morrison Hecker LLP*

STALLINGS John *Hinkle Elkouri Law Firm LLC*

STARK Stephen *Fleeson, Gooing, Coulson & Kitch*

VINES Monte *Adams & Jones Chartered*

WINN III Larry *Polsinelli Shalton Welte Suelthaus*

WOOD William *Foulston Siefkin LLP*

**The Lawyers:** *"First-rate"* **Stephen Stark** practices both real estate transactional work and environmental law. A veteran of a long and varied career, his experience ranges from zoning, development and sale to commercial leasing and landlord and tenant disputes. It is, however, in the field of real estate financing that he particularly shines.

**Clients/Work Highlights:** Zilkha Renewable Energy; NMF America; Bank of America; City of Wichita and GMAC.

## Foulston Siefkin LLP
See firm details p.935

**The Firm:** Based in Wichita, with a smaller office in Kansas City, this full-service real estate group is eyed by peers with admiration and envy. The team prides itself on being able to deliver a personal and complete service to fulfill the needs of all real estate clients, whether developer, investor, lender, borrower, seller, purchaser, landlord, tenant, landowner or entrepreneur. Work is undertaken throughout the USA with an emphasis on Kansas and the rest of the Midwest.

**The Lawyers:** The *"eminently capable"* **William Wood** (see p.934) is considered by peers to be as *"bright as can be and set to make advances in his career."* Real estate is not the only string to Wood's bow as he also enjoys thriving practices in the areas of M&A, franchise, banking and financing, securities and general business law.

**Clients/Work Highlights:** Featured on the client list are Total Entertainment Restaurant, Freddy's Frozen Custard & Steakburgers and BeautyFirst.

## Hinkle Elkouri Law Firm LLC

**The Firm:** This *"first-line firm in Wichita"* has a real estate group that is renowned for being particularly strong. The team rightly prides itself on its expertise in the field of large commercial developments such as hotels, shopping centers, offices, warehouses,

apartment complexes and residential and business condominiums. Representative clients include investors, developers, lenders, governmental organizations and individuals.

**The Lawyers:** None in the field doubt **John Stallings'** expertise. Impressed peers informed researchers that he *"has a large stable of real estate developer clients and undertakes a ton of related work for lenders."* This reflects the fact that his practice is not limited to real estate but also includes corporate work.

**Clients/Work Highlights:** Farm Credit Bank of Wichita; Chisholm Trail State Bank; AG Edwards & Sons and Stifel Nicolaus.

## Lathrop & Gage L.C.
See firm details p.1214

**The Firm:** The real estate group here has a strong Kansas City presence and a particular strength on the transactional side. Its members differentiate themselves from the majority of others in the field by taking a multidisciplinary approach – typically, each attorney runs his real estate practice alongside at least one other area of law. This ensures that the 25-strong team can provide a full selection of real estate and related services as part of a practice that extends well beyond state boundaries. At present the team is engaged in a good deal of work in Colorado.

**The Lawyers:** *"Top of the Kansas real estate Bar,"* **Lewis Heaven** (see p.932) was described as a *"fabulous, articulate lawyer with a lot of substance"* whom others really enjoy working with. Residential property forms the key element of Heaven's practice and, in recent times, he has been engaged in an increasing amount of consultation work, advising cities regarding master plan development. He is still a big name in the golf club development arena where he has an in-depth knowledge of the specialist liability issues that arise.

**Clients/Work Highlights:** Rodrock Development; Acuff & Rhodes; Clarkson Construction and Heritage Development.

## Polsinelli Shalton Welte Suelthaus PC
See firm details p.1217

**The Firm:** The firm is hailed as the second fastest-growing firm in the USA and the fastest-growing in the Midwest with multiple offices in Kansas, Missouri, Illinois, New York and Washington, DC. In terms of the real estate market, it is a development-heavy team with a zoning practice that excites all-around admiration.

**The Lawyers:** The *"extremely effective"* **John Petersen** (see p.932) is renowned throughout the community for being a particularly skilled land use attorney. His work of late has included the initial stages of the redevelopment of the Sunflower Army Ammunition Plant, a 9,000-acre site. Once remediated, a third of the land will be transferred to the public benefit transferors and the remaining two-thirds will be used for mixed-use projects including a bioscience research park. It is felt by **Stanley Woodworth's** (see p.934) peers that he has a *"particular aptitude for the technical aspects of real estate law."*

The *"wonderful and well-connected"* **Larry Winn** (see p.933) continues to thrive in this busy market. His practice revolves almost exclusively around land use, zoning, planning and the use of economic development incentives. His recent highlights have included working on a 1,000-ft tall replica of a tornado and the proposed development of a $300 million theme park.

**Clients/Work Highlights:** The team has been involved in the approval of a 1.1 million sq ft regional shopping center for Cormac Development. Other clients include AG Spanos; Home Depot; Sprint and NASCAR.

## Stinson Morrison Hecker LLP
See firm details p.1220

**The Firm:** A *"very good firm with enviable involvement in substantial transactions,"* this outfit has a large real estate practice divided into three subgroups: development, lending and litigation. This approach allows the firm to field attorneys sufficiently specialized to fulfill the exact needs of the client. The operation is large enough, however, to allow individual lawyers to seek advice from colleagues in related departments such as environmental and natural resources, general business and public law. The result is that *"there is really nothing within the field of real estate law that this team cannot do."*

**The Lawyers:** **Jack Marvin** (see p.932) is *"an outstanding real estate lawyer who is truly first-rate."* Marvin's practice encompasses both real estate and banking and he has established an unshakable reputation as a leader in bank financing. **Neil Shortlidge** (see p.933), meanwhile, has a practice dominated by development, redevelopment and the representation of public sector entities. A maven when it comes to land use decisions, Shortlidge continues to be engaged by Verizon Wireless, specifically in relation to the leasing of their cell tower sites. Recently he has also been serving as city attorney for Roland Park, Kansas, regarding a redevelopment project in the downtown area.

**Clients/Work Highlights:** Representative clients include the City of Overland Park, the City of Lansing and the City of St Joseph, Missouri.

### Band 2

## Morris, Laing, Evans, Brock & Kennedy, Chartered

**The Firm:** Despite the presence of two offices in Kansas and one in Topeka, this firm has its roots in Wichita, an area where it continues to have its largest presence. The real estate group, however, operates across all its offices and can cater to virtually every whim of the entrepreneurs, real estate developers and financial institutions that make up its client base. Services it offers range from acquisition and divestiture to land use and zoning, with much in between.

**The Lawyers:** *"A very fine lawyer with an excellent mind,"* **Donald Schrag** has a practice that covers both real estate and banking. He possesses a particular reputation for representing financial institutions engaged in commercial lending.

**Clients/Work Highlights:** Michaelis Real Estate, Homestead Affordable Housing and Anderson Investment are clients of the firm.

### Triplett, Woolf & Garretson LLC

**The Firm:** Described by one peer as "*my first port of call when conflicted,*" the firm's real estate group is well placed to represent its many and varied clients on a full range of matters. Developers in all fields are represented at every stage of the purchase, sale, leasing and development of properties. The team is well known, in particular, for having a thriving real estate financing practice.

**The Lawyers:** Bearer of a "*fine and long history in*

*this market,*" **Ron Harnden** is considered to be one of the finest real estate lawyers in Kansas, "*especially at the entrepreneurial end of the field.*" In addition to his real estate practice, Harnden is a successful corporate and M&A lawyer who has a particular reputation for financing work. His longevity in the market means that he can offer his clients a wealth of advantageous contacts.

**Clients/Work Highlights:** Ritchie Development; Ablah Enterprises; Flint Hills Rural Development; Key Construction; BAT and Central Mechanical Wichita.

### Other Notable Practitioners

**Gerald Goodell** of Goodell, Stratton, Edmonds & Palmer LLP commands the respect of the market through his wealth of experience and his work within the legal community. When sporting his real estate hat, he represents real estate brokers, developers and lenders. He has a particular aptitude for condemnation proceedings having been counsel to the Urban Renewal Agency of the City of Topeka. **Brian Doerr** at the law firm Duggan, Shadwick, Doerr & Kurlbaum, PC is greatly admired for his all-around real estate practice; however, sources particularly endorsed his expertise on zoning issues.

# Leaders in Kansas

### ADAMS, Stephen
Blackwell Sanders Peper Martin LLP, Kansas City 816 983 8000
*Recommended in Corporate/M&A*
*Please see Missouri for profile*

### BABCOCK, Kathleen
Foulston Siefkin LLP, Wichita
316 291 9588
kbabcock@foulston.com
*Recommended in Employment*
**Practice Areas:** Employment and labor, education/public entity, and mediation/dispute resolution. Ms Babcock advises public and private employers on the entire spectrum of employment legal issues. She regularly defends federal discrimination cases and represents public employers in First Amendment, Fourteenth Amendment, and other § 1983 litigation. Ms Babcock also serves as general counsel to school districts and represents both schools and parents in special education litigation. In addition, her services as a mediator frequently are sought by litigants.
**Prof. Memberships:** Kansas Bar Association, Board of Governors, Secretary, Board of Discipline of Attorneys, Chair; Wichita Women Attorneys Association; Kansas School Attorneys Association.

### BADGEROW, Nick
Spencer Fane Britt & Browne LLP, Overland Park 913 345 8100
*Recommended in Litigation*

### BATH, Thomas
Bath & Edmonds, P.A, Overland Park
913 652 9800
*Recommended in Litigation*

### BOWMAN, Philip
Adams & Jones Chartered, Wichita
316 265 8591
*Recommended in Real Estate*

### BUCKLEY, Mert
Adams & Jones Chartered, Wichita
316 265 8591
*Recommended in Real Estate*

### CHURCHILL, Stanley
Martin & Churchill Chartered, Wichita
316 263 3200
*Recommended in Employment*

### DOERR, Brian
Duggan, Shadwick, Doerr & Kurlbaum, P.C., Overland Park 913 498 3536
*Recommended in Real Estate*

### EFFLANDT, Charles
Foulston Siefkin LLP, Wichita
316 291 9551
cefflandt@foulston.com
*Recommended in Litigation*
**Practice Areas:** Environmental law. Mr Efflandt is the Practice Group Leader of the firm's Environmental and Natural Resources Team. His practice encompasses environmental and toxic tort litigation, environmental regulatory enforcement and compliance matters and environmental issues related to business acquisitions, mergers and property transactions. Mr Efflandt represents and advises a wide variety of clients including large corporations, small and medium-sized businesses, lenders and trusts, and individuals.
**Prof. Memberships:** American Bar Association, Member of Section of Environment, Energy and Resources; Kansas Bar Association; Wichita Bar Association, Fee Disputes Committee; Kansas Association of Defense Counsel; Defense Research Institute.

### ENGSTROM, Eric
Fleeson, Gooing, Coulson & Kitch, LLC, Wichita 316 267 7361
*Recommended in Corporate/M&A*

### ERICKSON, David
Shook, Hardy & Bacon LLP, Kansas City
816 474 6550
*Recommended in Litigation*
*Please see Missouri for profile*

### FOCHT, Jack
Foulston Siefkin LLP, Wichita
316 291 9519
jfocht@foulston.com
*Recommended in Litigation*
**Practice Areas:** Commercial and complex litigation, health law, mediation/dispute resolution, white-collar crime/professional responsibility, and employment and labor. Mr Focht has more than 40 years of experience as an attorney, and is a Fellow of the American College of Trial Lawyers. His practice has ranged from high profile criminal cases to complex civil litigation. Mr Focht has directed the defense of numerous individuals and companies targeted for investigation by agencies of the state and federal government.
**Prof. Memberships:** American Bar Foundation, Fellow; Wichita Bar Association, President; Kansas Bar Association, President 1989-90; National Association of Criminal Defense Attorneys.

### FORD JR, William
Lathrop & Gage L.C., Kansas City
816 292 2000
*Recommended in Litigation*
*Please see Missouri for profile*

### FOWLER, Jay
Foulston Siefkin LLP, Wichita
316 291 9541
jfowler@foulston.com
*Recommended in Litigation*
**Practice Areas:** Commercial and complex litigation, professional malpractice, insurance defense, and products liability. Mr Fowler's trial practice emphasizes trial of lawsuits involving commercial relationships, professional malpractice and

tort defense. He frequently handles complex commercial lawsuits, intellectual property and employment disputes. He has tried high-exposure professional negligence cases and has built an extensive and respected civil litigation practice in state and federal court. He has taken in excess of 175 jury cases to verdict.
**Prof. Memberships:** American College of Trial Lawyers, Fellow; Kansas Bar Foundation, Fellow; American, Kansas and Wichita Bar Associations; Defense Research Institute; Kansas Association of Defense Counsel.

### GARRETSON, Thomas
Triplett, Woolf & Garretson LLC, Wichita
316 630 8100
*Recommended in Corporate/M&A*

### GOODELL, Gerald
Goodell, Stratton, Edmonds & Palmer, LLP, Topeka 785 233 0593
*Recommended in Real Estate*

### HARNDEN, Ronald
Triplett, Woolf & Garretson LLC, Wichita
316 630 8100
*Recommended in Real Estate*

### HATLEY, Joseph
Lathrop & Gage L.C., Overland Park
913 451 5134
jhatley@lathropgage.com
*Recommended in Litigation*
**Career:** Hatley's experience spans across a range of legal disciplines. He successfully represented the following clients: a telecommunications firm in a landmark case challenging efforts by a local city to require that firm to obtain a municipal franchise; another telecommunications firm in enforcing covenant not to compete signed by its Chief Technology Officer; an operator of motion picture theatres in a multimillion dollar suit for liquidated damages arising from construction delays; 100 corporate defendants in defeating class certification in a toxic tort

suit arising from an abandoned hazardous waste site. He was selected as a Leading Lawyer by Chambers USA, 2003-06.

## HEAVEN JR, Lewis
Lathrop & Gage L.C., Overland Park
913 451 5119
lheaven@lathropgage.com
*Recommended in Real Estate*
**Practice Areas:** Real estate; land use; construction law.
**Career:** Heaven has represented the most prominent residential and commercial real estate developers in the Midwest for over 25 years. He also serves as counsel to a number of regional contractors, handling contract negotiation, bidding and construction issues. He currently represents the developers of almost ten separate golf course community projects across the country, requiring extensive knowledge of restrictive covenants, homes associations and golf course liability issues. Heaven served as City Attorney of the City of Merriam, Kansas, for 18 years. He is the recipient of numerous honors and awards.

## HILL, Donald
Martin & Churchill Chartered, Wichita
316 263 3200
*Recommended in Employment*

## HINDERKS, Mark
Stinson Morrison Hecker LLP,
Overland Park 913 451 8600
mhinderks@stinsonmoheck.com
*Recommended in Litigation*
**Practice Areas:** Successful prosecution and defense of cases (in court proceedings and arbitrations) involving tens and hundreds of millions of dollars on behalf of business and governmental clients, including contract disputes, telecommunications, construction, intellectual property and license disputes, tort actions, and land claims. Defense of class actions across the United States for major client. Co-General Counsel for the firm. Frequent speaker and author on professional responsibility, trial practice and construction topics.
**Prof. Memberships:** American College of Trial Lawyers, Fellow; Kansas Bar Association.
**Personal:** JD, University of Kansas (1982); BA, University of Kansas (1979).

## HITE, Richard
Hite, Fanning & Honeyman LLP, Wichita
316 265 7741
*Recommended in Litigation*

## HONEYMAN, Richard
Hite, Fanning & Honeyman LLP, Wichita
316 265 7741
*Recommended in Litigation*

## HUGHEY, Roger
Adams & Jones Chartered, Wichita
316 265 8591
*Recommended in Real Estate*

## MACKAY, Douglas
Kutak Rock LLP, Wichita
316 609 7900
*Recommended in Employment*

## MANN, Terry
Martin, Pringle, Oliver, Wallace & Bauer, L.L.P., Wichita
316 265 9311
*Recommended in Employment*

## MARVIN, Jack
Stinson Morrison Hecker LLP, Wichita
316 265 8800
jmarvin@stinsonmoheck.com
*Recommended in Corporate/M&A, Real Estate*
**Practice Areas:** Jack has served as counsel for numerous financial institutions for over 25 years. His experience includes commercial financing transactions, industrial revenue bond workouts, foreclosure/receivership litigation and bankruptcy, including Chapters Seven, 11 and 12. He also has significant experience with real estate transactions.
**Prof. Memberships:** American College of Mortgage Attorneys, Wichita Bankruptcy Council, American Bar Association.
**Career:** Jack is a frequent speaker on commercial finance, workouts and real estate. He is also listed in the current edition of Kansas Super Lawyers (Banking) and Best Lawyers in America (Real Estate).
**Personal:** JD, BS, University of Kansas.

## MUSIL, Greg L
Shughart Thomson & Kilroy PC, Overland Park
913 451 3355
gmusil@stklaw.com
*Recommended in Litigation*
**Practice Areas:** Business litigation, land use, zoning and real estate development; property taxation. Greg L Musil served on US Sen Nancy Kassebaum's staff (R-Kansas) from 1983-87 and on the Overland Park, Kansas City Council from 1993-2001. He is active in government affairs, public service and political activities in the State of Kansas.
**Prof. Memberships:** Admitted 1983, District of Columbia (Inactive); 1987, Kansas; 1989, Missouri. Order of the Coif. Member, Editorial Board, University of Virginia Law Review, 1981-82. Three-year term appointment by the Kansas Supreme Court to the Kansas Continuing Legal Education Commission, responsible for establishing and administering the CLE rules and regulation requirements for members of the Kansas bar (2003-06); appointed by the Kansas Supreme Court to the Client Protection Fund Commission. (Chair, 2001-02); awarded Martindale-Hubbell AV rating; Kansas Bar Association; Missouri Bar Association; Johnson County (Kansas) Bar Association; American Trial Lawyers Association; Member, US District Court

for the District of Kansas Civil Justice Reform Act Advisory Committee (1993-96); Johnson County Bar Association Board of Directors (1994-96).
**Career:** Joined Shughart Thomson & Kilroy PC (1987); shareholder (1992); served as a lead legislative assistant to US Senator Nancy Kassebaum Baker (R-Kansas) 1983-87; appointed by Kansas Supreme Court to the Client Protection Fund Commission (1996-2002; Chair 2001-02) and to the Continuing Legal Education Commission (2003-present); recognized in Best Lawyers in America (2005/06 edition); recognized in Chambers USA Client's Guide to America's Leading Business Lawyers (2003, 2004 and 2005); KC Magazine in 2005 recognized Greg as a Missouri/Kansas Super Lawyer.
**Publications:** Co-author: 'Kansas Property Tax, Surviving Reappraisal and Reassessment', Journal of the Kansas Bar, March, 1988. Author: Kansas Chapter, 'ABA Property Tax Handbook' (1995-present) and the Institute of Property Taxation annual update (1995-2002).
**Personal:** Born Marysville, Kansas, May 23, 1957. University of Virginia, JD (1983). Kansas State University, BS, cum laude (1980).

## OVERMAN, Robert
Morris, Laing, Evans, Brock & Kennedy, Chartered, Wichita
316 262 2671
*Recommended in Employment*

## PETERSEN, John
Polsinelli Shalton Welte Suelthaus PC, Overland Park
913 451 8788
jpetersen@pswslaw.com
*Recommended in Real Estate*
**Practice Areas:** Real estate development, including zoning and land use; financing incentives; state and federal regulatory approvals; economic development initiatives; litigation.
**Career:** Real Estate Development Practice (1989-present). Governmental experience, Chief Counsel to Governor Mike Hayden (1987-89); Deputy Chief Counsel to US Senator Bob Dole (1983-86). Litigation Practice, 1978-83.
**Personal:** JD, Washburn University, cum laude.

## PETERSON, Ken
Morris, Laing, Evans, Brock & Kennedy, Chartered, Wichita
316 262 2671
*Recommended in Employment*

## PISHNY, Lyle D
Lathrop & Gage L.C., Overland Park
913 451 5101
lpishny@lathropgage.com
*Recommended in Corporate/M&A*
**Career:** Pishny has been in practice for over 25 years. He has a Master of Laws in taxation and concentrates his practice on

designing creative solutions to business and personal situations. Pishny has represented clients in structuring their business and real estate sales, acquisitions and leases, and in planning their business organizations and estate affairs. He was the Co-Managing Partner of the Bennett Lytle law firm, which joined Lathrop & Gage in 1998. He was selected in Best Lawyers in America, 2003-06.

## PRICE, James
Spencer Fane Britt & Browne LLP, Kansas City 816 474 8100
*Recommended in Litigation*

## REBEIN, David
Rebein Bangerter PA, Dodge City
316 267 6371
drebein@rebeinbangerter.com
*Recommended in Litigation*
**Practice Areas:** Rebein has extensive legal experience, having represented clients in workers compensation, estate and probate, employment law, discrimination litigation, personal injury, oil and gas litigation, construction law litigation, professional malpractice litigation and class actions. Rebein concentrates his practice in the areas of commercial and complex litigation and personal injury. He regularly defends agricultural entities against negligence and contract claims, has defended oil companies against mismeasurement and underpayment claims, and has developed a strong personal injury practice.
**Prof. Memberships:** President-Elect of the Kansas Bar Association; International Association of Defense Counsel; Defense Research Institute; Kansas Association of Defense Counsel; American Trial Lawyers Association; Kansas Trial Lawyers Association; American Bar Association, Fellow; Kansas Supreme Court Nominating Commission.
**Publications:** 'Achilles' Heel: Employer's Knowledge of Employee's Preexisting Handicaps in Workers Compensation Cases' 57JBAK21 (1988); 'An Overview of the 1993 Amendment to the Kansas Workers Compensation Act' 62JBAK30 (1993); 'Supreme Court Nominating Commission Goes to Work: Are you the next Kansas Supreme Court Justice?' 71JBAK16 (2002).
**Personal:** Rebein received his BA, summa cum laude, from Washburn University in 1977 and his JD from the University Of Kansas School of Law in 1980.

## RUPE, Alan
Kutak Rock LLP, Wichita
316 609 7900
*Recommended in Employment*

## SAMPSON, William
Shook, Hardy & Bacon LLP, Kansas City
816 474 6550
*Recommended in Litigation*
*Please see Missouri for profile*

## SCHECK, Stephanie
Stinson Morrison Hecker LLP, Wichita
316 265 8800
sscheck@stinsonmoheck.com
*Recommended in Employment*
**Practice Areas:** Practice concentrated in the field of employment law litigation and advising. Represents employers on employment law matters in administrative proceedings and in federal and state courts. Provides consulting, training, and audits on a variety of employment law compliance issues, including consultation in the development and implementation of affirmative action plans, personnel policies and procedures.
**Prof. Memberships:** Admitted to practice in Kansas and the Tenth Circuit Court of Appeals.
**Personal:** JD, University of Kansas (1996); BS, Business Administration, Human Resources Management, Kansas State University (1993). Selected to the Wichita Business Journal's 2003 class of '40 Under 40'.

## SCHRAG, Donald
Morris, Laing, Evans, Brock & Kennedy, Chartered, Wichita
316 262 2671
*Recommended in Real Estate*

## SHORTLIDGE, Neil
Stinson Morrison Hecker LLP,
Overland Park 913 451 8600
nshortlidge@stinsonmoheck.com
*Recommended in Real Estate*
**Practice Areas:** Vice-Chair of the firm's Public Law/Finance Division. Serves as special counsel for a number of municipalities on issues relating to land use and development, development/redevelopment incentives, annexation, public infrastructure financing and eminent domain.
**Prof. Memberships:** International Municipal Lawyers Association (Regional Vice President); ABA; Kansas Bar Association; Missouri Bar; Missouri Municipal Attorneys Association, City Attorneys Association of Kansas (President, 2000-01); KCMBA, Local Government Law Committee (Chair 2004); Johnson County Bar Association.
**Publications:** Frequent speaker and author on issues of interest to local governments.
**Personal:** JD, University of Kansas, 1976; BA, University of Kansas, 1973.

## SORENSEN, Harvey
Foulston Siefkin LLP, Wichita
316 291 9774
hsorensen@foulston.com
*Recommended in Corporate/M&A*
**Practice Areas:** Taxation, estate planning, mergers and acquisitions, general business, private equity and venture capital, and family business enterprise. Mr Sorensen's practice focuses on mergers and acquisitions, private equity transactions and venture capital investments,

income tax planning and inter-generational tax planning. His practice includes advising family-owned businesses through the life cycle of the business and the family.
**Prof. Memberships:** American College of Tax Counsel, Fellow; American Bar Association, Member, Tax Section, Agriculture Committee on Business Cooperatives, Chair-Elect; Kansas Bar Association, Member, Tax Section; Wichita Bar Association; Lex Mundi, Inc., State and Local Tax Committee, Chair; World Services Group, Chairman.

## STALLINGS, John
Hinkle Elkouri Law Firm LLC, Wichita
316 267 2000
*Recommended in Real Estate*

## STANLEY, Douglas
Foulston Siefkin LLP, Wichita
316 291 9502
dstanley@foulston.com
*Recommended in Employment*
**Practice Areas:** Employment and labor. Mr Stanley is Team Leader for one of the firm's two employment litigation teams. He has served as chief negotiator of numerous collective bargaining agreements and advised employers in union attempts to organize groups of employees. Mr Stanley also has extensive experience in responding to unfair labor practice charges, wage and hour disputes, and employment discrimination charges before state and federal administrative agencies. Mr Stanley has tried numerous employment arbitrations in both union and non-union settings.
**Prof. Memberships:** American, Kansas and Wichita Bar Associations; Employment Law Section of the Kansas Bar Association, past President.

## STARK, Stephen
Fleeson, Gooing, Coulson & Kitch, LLC,
Wichita 316 267 7361
*Recommended in Real Estate*

## STOUT, Mikel
Foulston Siefkin LLP, Wichita
316 291 9516
mstout@foulston.com
*Recommended in Litigation*
**Practice Areas:** Commercial and complex litigation, environmental law, employment and labor, and mediation/dispute resolution. Mr Stout handles employment and complex commercial cases. He specializes in high-exposure litigation with an emphasis on trial practice. He is one of the most well-known trial lawyers in Kansas and has tried many of the region's high-profile employment, environmental and commercial cases. His practice includes consultation on litigation problem solving and alternative dispute resolution.
**Prof. Memberships:** American College of Trial Lawyers, Fellow and Board of Regents; Kansas Bar Foundation; Ameri-

can, Kansas and Wichita Bar Associations; Kansas Association of Defense Counsel.

## SWAIN, Lawrence
Shughart Thomson & Kilroy PC,
Overland Park 816 395 0677
lswain@stklaw.com
*Recommended in Corporate/M&A*
**Practice Areas:** Corporate law; business contracts; intellectual property; mergers and acquisitions. Lawrence A Swain is Partner in Charge of the Overland Park office, a member of the firm's Board of Directors, Business Department Chair and Co-Chair of the Intellectual Property and Technology Practice Group. Larry's rare combination of business law and intellectual property expertise make him a unique fit for technology companies. His clients include locally based companies with regional or national scope, including Associated Wholesale Grocers, Gear For Sports, MidAmerica Neuroscience, Black & Veatch, Jack Henry Software and Blue Springs Ford. He also represents national entities located outside the Kansas City area, such as Crane Plumbing, The Major League Baseball Players Association, Woodstock Ventures and Community Foundations of America.
**Prof. Memberships:** Admitted to practice in Missouri and US Tax Court (1977); Kansas (1985). Member of The Missouri Bar (Patent, Trademark and Copyright Law Committee); Software Patent Institute's Past President; Licensing Industry Merchandisers' Association, past Vice President.
**Career:** Joined Shughart Thomson & Kilroy PC (1989); shareholder (1996). Executive Committee. Partner in Charge of the Overland Park office. Co-Chair, Intellectual Property and Technology Practice Group. Listed in Chambers USA: America's Leading Lawyers for Business (2005); KC Magazine in 2005 recognized Larry as a Missouri/Kansas Super Lawyer.
**Personal:** Born Brookfield, Missouri, October 7, 1952. University of Kansas, JD (1977). University of Kansas, BS, with distinction (1974). Phi Theta Kappa. Beta Gamma Sigma. Summerfield Scholar.

## TRENKLE, William
Foulston Siefkin LLP, Overland Park
913 498 2100
btrenkle@foulston.com
*Recommended in Corporate/M&A*
**Practice Areas:** Corporate, general business, taxation, banking and financial services, estate planning and probate, and health law. Mr Trenkle practices as a general business lawyer with an emphasis in taxation. Businesses he represents range from large agri-business enterprises to a healthcare facility developer. This representation includes commercial transactions, entity formation, tax planning and estate planning. He is a frequent speaker

on taxation, estate planning and business topics.
**Prof. Memberships:** American Bar Association; Southwest Kansas and Johnson County Bar Associations; Kansas Bar Association, Tax Section - Executive Committee and past President, Corporation and Banking Section - past President.

## TRIPLETT, Thomas
Triplett, Woolf & Garretson LLC, Wichita
316 630 8100
*Recommended in Corporate/M&A*

## TRIPP, David
Stinson Morrison Hecker LLP,
Kansas City 816 842 8600
*Recommended in Litigation*
*Please see Missouri for profile*

## VINES, Monte
Adams & Jones Chartered, Wichita
316 265 8591
*Recommended in Real Estate*

## WARTA, Darrell
Foulston Siefkin LLP, Wichita
316 291 9514
dwarta@foulston.com
*Recommended in Litigation*
**Practice Areas:** Commercial and complex litigation, professional malpractice, products liability, and mediation/dispute resolution. Mr Warta has spent 33 years successfully trying civil lawsuits in Wichita and throughout the state of Kansas. Mr Warta is lead trial counsel specializing in defending high-exposure personal injury, products liability and professional liability cases. He also serves as corporate litigation counsel in business-related trials and arbitration proceedings.
**Prof. Memberships:** American College of Trial Lawyers, Fellow; Federation of Defense and Corporate Counsel; Kansas Association of Defense Counsel; American, Kansas and Wichita Bar Associations.

## WINN III, Larry
Polsinelli Shalton Welte Suelthaus PC,
Overland Park
913 451 8788
lwinn@pswslaw.com
*Recommended in Real Estate*
**Practice Areas:** During his 37 years of practicing law, Winn has shepherded the approval of the original Sprint Campus plan, two regional malls, more than a dozen regional office facilities, and residential subdivsidens, as well as a number of high profile projects in which he was successful in obtaining substantial economic benefits either through local or county governments.
**Prof. Memberships:** Kansas State Bar Association; Johnson County Bar Association; admitted to practice in Kansas (1968).
**Publications:** Frequent presenter and author in seminars and continuing legal

education programs involving land use and public law.
**Personal:** University of Kansas (BS, 1966, JD, 1968).

## WOOD, William
Foulston Siefkin LLP, Wichita
316 291 0772
bwood@foulston.com
*Recommended in Corporate/M&A, Real Estate*

**Practice Areas:** Mergers and acquisitions, securities, real estate, franchise, banking and financial services, private equity and venture capital, and general business. Mr Wood has a comprehensive business practice representing public and private companies in mergers and acquisitions, creation and termination of business entities, business entity ownership issues, securities transactions, real estate transactions, franchising, private equity transactions and venture capital investments, financing, contract negotiations and preparation, and general business matters.
**Prof. Memberships:** American, Kansas and Wichita Bar Associations; President and Member of Executive Committee, Kansas Bar Association Corporate Banking and Business Law Section.

## WOODWORTH, Stanley N
Polsinelli Shalton Welte Suelthaus PC, Overland Park
913 451 8788
swoodworth@pswslaw.com
*Recommended in Real Estate*

**Practice Areas:** Residential real estate development and construction; limited liability companies; joint ventures; franchising; capital formation; partnerships.
**Prof. Memberships:** Kansas Bar Association; The Missouri Bar.
**Career:** Joined Polsinelli as a Shareholder/Director in 1992 after being with another large area firm for 12 years.
**Publications:** Co-author, 'Limited Liability Companies', Kansas Bar Association.
**Personal:** University of Kansas (JD, 1978); Kansas State University (BS, 1975); past President of Kansas City Businessmen's Club.

## WORTH, Diane
Morris, Laing, Evans, Brock & Kennedy, Chartered, Wichita
316 262 2671
*Recommended in Employment*

## WRIGHT, Thomas
Wright, Henson, Somers, Clark & Bake LLP, Topeka 785 232 2200
*Recommended in Litigation*

# FOULSTON SIEFKIN LLP

## THE FIRM

**Managing Partner:** Richard D Ewy
**Number of partners:** 53
**Number of other attorneys:** 26

**FIRM OVERVIEW:** Foulston Siefkin LLP is the largest, and one of the oldest law firms in Kansas, tracing its origins to 1919. Today the firm has over 75 attorneys, with offices in Wichita, the state's largest city, Topeka, the state's capital, and Overland Park, the heart of commerce in the Kansas City area. Foulston Siefkin is the only Kansas member of Lex Mundi, the world's most prestigious international organization of independent law firms.

## MAIN AREAS OF PRACTICE:

**Administrative & Regulatory:** Team members represent telecommunications companies, and gas and electric utilities, with special emphasis on rate cases and other proceedings before the Kansas Corporation Commission.
**Agribusiness:** Foulston Siefkin attorneys have provided counsel to the agricultural industry for more than 75 years, handling the issues that clients face in all sectors of the agribusiness industry. Clients include ranchers, farmers, meat packers, coops, and ag product suppliers and lenders.
**Appellate:** Foulston Siefkin attorneys have an established reputation for incisive legal writing and determined advocacy. The firm's attorneys have been counsel of record in far more reported federal and state cases in Kansas than any other firm. The appellate attorney team is experienced in complex cases and knows how to work with teams of corporate counsel and co-counsel to coordinate strategy, work allocation, and quality control.
**Banking, Financial Services & Bankruptcy:** Foulston Siefkin has extensive experience representing lenders, financial institutions, and other creditors in lending transactions, disputes, securities issues, loan enforcement, creditors' rights litigation, bankruptcy and bankruptcy litigation. Clients range from some of the largest financial institutions and lenders in the state to smaller community banks.
**Commercial & Complex Litigation:** The firm handles every variety of commercial litigation from the simple contract dispute to complex litigation, including class action, qui tam and white collar criminal defense cases. The Litigation Group includes five members of the American College of Trial Lawyers.
**Construction:** Attorneys assist construction industry clients with a wide range of construction projects, from conception through completion and any dispute resolution. One attorney is a graduate architect and brings unique expertise and understanding to the problems facing the construction industry.
**Employment, Labor & Workers Compensation:** Employment and labor law is one of the firm's core practice areas, with 23 attorneys that advise and represent employers in the full range of issues arising from the employer/employee relationship. The team includes a past President of the Kansas Bar Association Employment Law Section and the co-editors of the Kansas Employment Law Letter, the largest circulation employment law newsletter in Kansas.
**Energy:** Throughout its history, Foulston Siefkin has handled the full spectrum of legal matters relating to purchase and sales, exploration, production, marketing, transportation, financing and regulation of energy and natural resources. Clients range from individual land and mineral owners, to independent oil and gas operators, both large and small, to some of the world's largest major integrated oil and gas companies.
**Environmental & Water Rights:** Foulston Siefkin has substantial experience in all areas of environmental law, related toxic tort litigation, regulatory and transactional areas, and water rights issues in Kansas. As important as the scope of its substantive expertise is its attorneys' practical experience and the relationships they have built with regulators, environmental consultants and other counsel on local, state, regional and national levels.
**Franchise:** The firm has represented local, regional and national franchisors, franchisees and franchise associations in the full range of franchise law issues. Clients have included some of the best known names in the franchise business.

## US OFFICES

**KANSAS**
1551 N Waterfront Parkway, Suite 100, **Wichita**, KS 67206
**Tel:** 316 267 6371   **Fax:** 316 267 6345
**Email:** info@foulston.com
**Website:** www.foulston.com

9 Corporate Woods, Suite 450, 9200 Indian Creek Parkway,
**Overland Park**, KS 66210
**Tel:** 913 498 2100   **Fax:** 913 498 2101

555 S Kansas Ave., Suite 101, **Topeka**, KS 66603
**Tel:** 785 233 3600 **Fax:** 785 233 1610

**General Business:** The firm's experience in representing a diverse range of business clients, ranging from industry leading companies, to private equity firms, to sole proprietors, in local, state, regional, national, and international transactions provides a wide-ranging perspective allowing the business attorneys to find creative and resourceful solutions to business issues.
**Health Law:** The firm's Health Law Practice Group guides healthcare providers through the increasingly complex maze of federal and state regulations, and its relationship with the other practice groups, including taxation, general business, employment, and commercial litigation, enhances the team's ability to provide a complete solution to healthcare providers' legal requirements.
**Insurance Defense:** Foulston Siefkin's insurance defense attorneys have decades of experience and one of the most active trial practices in the region, defending medical malpractice actions, product liability and personal injury claims.
**Mergers & Acquisitions:** The firm's depth and experience in the structuring, financing and successful completion of acquisitions, divestitures, joint ventures, and other business transactions rivals that of any law firm in the region.
**Taxation & Employee Benefits:** The team assists individuals and businesses alike by helping to interpret, apply, and utilize the complicated rules of ERISA, the Internal Revenue Code, and applicable state laws. Foulston Siefkin's taxation services include representation before the IRS, Kansas Department of Revenue and other taxing authorities and tax agencies, including all matters of tax litigation. Seven team attorneys hold an LLM in taxation.

**CLIENTS:** The firm represents a broad range of clients, including major financial institutions, corporations, public utilities, insurance companies, healthcare providers, manufacturers, franchisors and franchisees, agricultural and natural resource producers and processors, professional entities, construction companies and contractors, and service providers. Clients include: AmerUs Annuity Group, Bank of America, N.A, The Boeing Company, Bombardier Aerospace Learjet, Capitol Federal Financial, Cargill Meat Solutions Corporation, Cessna Aircraft Company, The Coleman Company, Inc., Cox Communications, Delta Dental Plan of Kansas, Inc., Engenio Information Technologies, Inc., Fox & Hound Restaurant Group, Galichia Medical Group, P.A., Integra Technologies LLC, Invista, Koch Industries, Inc., Neuterra Healthcare, Schaefer Johnson Cox Frey Architecture, Shelter Insurance Companies, Spirit AeroSystems, Inc., Wichita Area Chamber of Commerce, and Via Christi Health System.

FOULSTON SIEFKIN LLP

ATTORNEYS AT LAW

# REBEIN BANGERTER PA

## THE FIRM

**Contact Partner:** David J Rebein

**Number of other attorneys:** 4

**FIRM OVERVIEW:** Rebein Bangerter PA has a long and respected history of providing legal services to Kansans. Located in Dodge City, Kansas, the firm is one of the largest in the western half of the state and is located in the heart of the Kansas agriculture industry.

## MAIN AREAS OF PRACTICE:

**Agribusiness:** Rebein Bangerter attorneys have a long tradition of service to the agriculture industry. In the last year, firm attorneys defended numerous agriculture related matters, including a Food Security Act claim; agister's liens; fence repair disputes; crop damage claim stemming from chemical application; fraud claims relating to the purchase and feeding of cattle; and negligence and contract claims stemming from feed and care provided for dairy cattle. The firm serves farmers, ranchers, meat packers, feed yards and many others in the agriculture industry.

**Commercial & Complex Litigation:** The firm handles commercial litigation at every level. In the last year, firm attorneys defended numerous agriculture related matters. Firm attorneys have also defended a gas mismeasurement class action and a vitamin class action, and a major product liability lawsuit. David J Rebein served as special master in a tobacco class action.

**Workers Compensation:** The firm defends the workers compensation claims against two of the major packers in the area and for numerous other businesses.

**General Business:** The firm assists individuals and local businesses with general business, corporate, and real estate transactions, including entity formations and start-ups, mergers and acquisitions, distributorship arrangements, exchanges, employment agreements, and tax-driven business transactions. In addition, the firm frequently assists small business owners with succession planning and business transition issues.

## HEAD OFFICES

**KANSAS**
810 West Frontview, **Dodge City**, KS 67801
**Tel:** 620 227 8126
**Email:** info@rebeinbangerter.com
**Website:** www.rebeinbangerter.com

## How lawyers are ranked

Every year we carry out thousands of in-depth interviews with clients and lawyers in order to assess the reputations and expertise of business lawyers across the USA. Chambers rankings and editorial are referred to extensively by General Counsel and other purchasers of legal services who look to our recommendations when choosing their lawyers.

# CORPORATE/M&A

### Corporate/M&A
### Leading Firms

1. **FROST BROWN TODD LLC** *Louisville*
   **GREENEBAUM DOLL & MCDONALD PLLC** *Louisville*
   **STITES & HARBISON PLLC** *Louisville*
   **WYATT, TARRANT & COMBS, LLP** *Louisville*
2. **REED WEITKAMP SCHELL & VICE PLLC** *Louisville*
   **STOLL KEENON OGDEN PLLC** *Lexington*

### Leading Individuals

1. **BRADLEY JR Craig** *Stites & Harbison PLLC*
   **CONNER Stewart** *Wyatt, Tarrant & Combs, LLP*
   **GLASSCOCK C Edward** *Frost Brown Todd LLC*
   **HELM III Kennedy** *Stites & Harbison PLLC*
   **STRAUS R James** *Frost Brown Todd LLC*
2. **LESTER David** *Stoll Keenon Ogden PLLC*
   **LYNDRUP Peggy** *Greenebaum Doll & McDonald*
   **MACDONALD Alan** *Frost Brown Todd LLC*
   **MATTINGLY Patrick** *Wyatt, Tarrant & Combs, LLP*
   **NORTHAM Patrick** *Greenebaum Doll & McDonald*
   **STRENCH William** *Frost Brown Todd LLC*
   **WILLIAMS Ernest** *Stoll Keenon Ogden PLLC*
   **YOUNG Cynthia** *Wyatt, Tarrant & Combs, LLP*
3. **BECK JR Robert** *Stites & Harbison PLLC*
   **BECKMAN David** *Frost Brown Todd LLC*
   **CROMER Brian** *Stites & Harbison PLLC*
   **DIAMOND Ivan** *Greenebaum Doll & McDonald*
   **DOLSON Scott** *Frost Brown Todd LLC*
   **GIESEL James** *Frost Brown Todd LLC*
   **HABLE Kevin** *Wyatt, Tarrant & Combs, LLP*
   **HALLOS Jeffrey** *Frost Brown Todd LLC*
   **KEETON Charles** *Frost Brown Todd LLC*
   **KING June** *Greenebaum Doll & McDonald PLLC*
   **RUTLEDGE Thomas** *Stoll Keenon Ogden PLLC*
   **SCHELL Ivan** *Reed Weitkamp Schell & Vice PLLC*
   **SEIFFERT James** *Stites & Harbison PLLC*
   **STEENROD Ralston** *Stites & Harbison PLLC*
   **WEITKAMP Gary** *Reed Weitkamp Schell & Vice PLLC*

### Up-and-coming individuals
**MATTINGLY Bryan** *Frost Brown Todd LLC*

## Band 1

### Frost Brown Todd LLC
See firm details p.954

**The Firm:** This national firm has seven offices located across Ohio, Kentucky, Indiana and Tennessee, and attracts major clients from various industries, including several Fortune 500 companies. While its Lexington office is dedicated to M&A work, the large Louisville team specializes in a broad range of corporate services. In addition to an increase in M&A over the past year, venture capital transactions were a major focus. The healthcare sector is an important area for the firm, where recent highlights include closing a $100 million merger between SHPS and eBenX, and handling the acquisition of Advanced Imaging Concepts.

**The Lawyers:** The highly efficient **Ed Glasscock** (see p.947) frequently represents major financial institutions in M&A transactions, and also represents emerging companies in venture capital transactions. His prominence in the field is believed to stem in large part from "*having his finger on the pulse of what's going on in the city,*" and clients rate Glasscock not only as "*one of the most influential attorneys in Kentucky,*" but as "*a superb business lawyer.*" One enthusiastic client remarked: "*He's like a great athlete with a smile on his face: he isn't satisfied with anything but the best,*" while another emphasized that "*he is one of the hardest-working lawyers around, and extraordinarily energetic.*" Interviewees frequently referred to his "*steel trap memory*" and his charming manner: "*He makes you feel comfortable in his presence and comes across as a true gentleman.*" **James Straus** (see p.952) has won huge respect in the business community for his representation of financial institutions as well as private and public companies. A significant proportion of his clientele hails from the food and restaurant industry, where Straus is renowned for his handling of complex relationships between franchisees and company suppliers. Clients commented that "*he has mastered a vast body of knowledge, and yet remains eminently practical.*" **Alan MacDonald** (see p.949) is best known for assisting public companies with securities transactions and acting for private companies on corporate/M&A matters. Clients greatly value his knowledge of the SEC and his approach: "*He gets the job done without the fanfare.*" In addition to acting for public and private companies, the "*technically accomplished*" **William Strench** (see p.952) represents mutual funds, investment advisory firms and venture capital funds. **David Beckman** (see p.945) is considered to have emerged as an influential M&A lawyer relatively early on in his career, particularly when it comes to representing financial institutions. Though **Scott Dolson** (see p.946) majors as a tax lawyer, he is heavily involved in M&A, and acts for limited liability companies, partnerships and corporations in various industry sectors. **James Giesel** (see p.947) handles securities matters and investment management, and is praised by peers for his way with clients and his ability to manage under pressure. The Lexington-based **Jeffrey Hallos** (see p.948) represents borrowers and lenders in both international and domestic transactions. **Charles Keeton** (see p.949) is identified as being particularly strong in representing financial institutions on commercial transactions, financial restructuring and e-commerce. Another Lexington lawyer, **Bryan Mattingly** (see p.950) was praised for his "*phenomenal case management skills and amenability.*" He advises on M&A, emerging businesses, venture capital and securities transactions and general business law.

**Clients/Work Highlights:** ResCare; LG&E Energy; Steel Technologies; RxCrossroads; Jewish Hospital; Texas Roadhouse and Yum! Brands.

### Greenebaum Doll & McDonald PLLC
See firm details p.955

**The Firm:** The operation comfortably retains its top-tier status. Of the firm's eight offices, four are in Kentucky, in Louisville, Lexington, Covington and Frankfort. Its corporate and commercial department is subdivided into separate practices covering everything from M&A to IP and economic development issues to emerging technologies law. Separate corporate and securities, bankruptcy, tax, and finance and development departments provide supporting firepower as required.

**The Lawyers:** The "*bright and well-respected*" **Peggy Lyndrup** offers corporate services to clients from a wide range of industries. **Patrick Northam** practices in the areas of corporate/M&A and general business law. Clients particularly emphasize his "*extraordinary attention to detail,*" and compliment him on his handling of complex issues, not to mention his *"unrivaled work ethic."* *"Colorful character"* **Ivan Diamond** has over 40 years of experience, and sustains a strong reputation for his work in corporate, securities, bank acquisition and regulatory matters. **June King** covers a range of corporate law matters, including those relating to the healthcare sector, and was cast during research as a valuable member of the team. She often works alongside Diamond and is perceived as a *"a reliable attorney who can be counted on by clients."*

**Clients/Work Highlights:** The team acts for all manner of public and private companies and partnerships.

### Stites & Harbison PLLC

See firm details p.959

**The Firm:** Spread across five eastern states, the firm has Kentucky offices located in Louisville, Lexington and Frankfort. While this firm is particularly known for its litigation capabilities, it deals with all manner of corporate matters, including M&A, trade association law, securities, and corporate governance and disclosure. One long-standing client said of the attorneys there: *"They always do their research thoroughly, instead of simply churning the case out."*

**The Lawyers:** The *"personable and easygoing"* **Kennedy Helm** (see p.948) is not only *"a real spokesman for the firm,"* but highly rated for his strategic planning. His *"great confidence is backed up by a high level of professional knowledge,"* according to sources. At the same time, he is perceived to be *"extremely ethical, and always takes into consideration the practical consequences."* He specializes in business law and banking and finance, and is also well versed in aviation law. The *"meticulous"* **Craig Bradley** (see p.945) was billed as *"probably the most knowledgeable securities lawyer in the state."* He represents public companies, investment banking firms and institutional investors. **Robert Beck** (see p.944) has a strong corporate practice in Lexington. He is well known for representing clients in the equine industry, although he also acts on behalf of a range of different domestic and international clients. **Brian Cromer** (see p.946) practices in a range of corporate disciplines, including M&A, securities, venture capital and real estate. Working closely with Bradley, **James Seiffert** (see p.951) focuses on tax, limited partnerships and M&A. Clients were impressed by his *"concise and immediate responses."* **Ralston Steenrod** (see p.952) is well regarded for advising on securities, M&A and general corporate law issues.

**Clients/Work Highlights:** CompuDyne; Steel Technologies; Onex Partners; University of Louisville Foundation; Louisville Regional Airport Authority; Yum! Brands and Stock Yards Bank.

### Wyatt, Tarrant & Combs, LLP

See firm details p.962

**The Firm:** This firm is distinguished from competitors by its depth of involvement in the local and regional community. In addition to offices in Louisville, Lexington and Bowling Green, it boasts two Tennessee branches and a further office in Indiana. The *"well-rounded"* 34-strong team offers a comprehensive range of expertise covering M&A, securities, corporate finance, venture capital, banking and insurance. It caters for many different kinds of clients, from public companies to closely held businesses.

**The Lawyers:** *"Classic southern gentleman lawyer"* **Stewart Conner** (see p.945) concentrates on banking, securities, M&A and corporate finance. He is chair of the firm's executive committee but sustains an active practice, albeit as a senior adviser providing strategic insight rather than being involved on a day-to-day basis. Sources praise **Patrick Mattingly** (see p.950) for providing an excellent service and generating clients for the firm. Based in Louisville, he concentrates on general business law, venture capital and M&A. **Cynthia Young** is well regarded by peers and clients alike for her banking and M&A work. Her new position as president of the LBA Bar further enhances her credentials. Managing partner **Kevin Hable** proves popular among interviewees, and is referred to as *"an extremely strong corporate lawyer."*

**Clients/Work Highlights:** The team's client base includes various healthcare clients such as Norton Healthcare, a number of coal industry players, and a range of other corporations such as Churchill Downs and Ashland.

## Band 2

### Reed Weitkamp Schell & Vice PLLC

See firm details p.957

**The Firm:** This Kentucky-based firm of 15 attorneys may only have a relatively small corporate practice, but peers identify it as *"fielding first-class lawyers."* Closely held businesses make up an important part of the outfit's client base.

**The Lawyers:** In addition to specializing in employee benefits work, **Ivan Schell** (see p.951)

represents medical professional groups on a variety of corporate matters. A popular choice among peers for referrals, the *"excellent"* **Gary Weitkamp** (see p.952) focuses on business and taxation, both nationally and in other jurisdictions such as Canada and Mexico. In a recent transaction he advised a public body on a $175 million senior credit facility.

**Clients/Work Highlights:** The corporate client base covers a wide range of public and private corporations, partnerships, LLCs, institutions and professional practice groups, including ResCare, Jones Plastic & Engineering and Lantech.

### Stoll Keenon Ogden PLLC

See firm details p.960

**The Firm:** This newly merged firm combines the general business, banking and corporate department from Lexington-based Stoll, Keenon & Park with the business law practice from Louisville-based Ogden Newell & Welch. The new firm boasts a total of almost 140 lawyers. The Ogden Newell side, which accounts for about a third of the overall number of lawyers, was noted as having a particularly strong M&A and securities practice. A recent highlight involved representing Brown-Forman in a €61 million acquisition to gain full control over a liqueur-producing company. The team represented the same client in its acquisition of Finlandia Vodka.

**The Lawyers:** Based in Lexington, **David Lester** (see p.949) specializes in corporate law, secured transactions and healthcare law. Peers enjoy working with him, describing him as a *"canny and real sharp guy,"* and a *"good negotiator who produces quality work: if he tells you that something will get done, it will get done."* Clients complimented *"experienced"* M&A lawyer **Ernest Williams** (see p.952) for *"proving every bit as skilled as some of the top Wall Street lawyers, whether drafting documents or in negotiations."* **Thomas Rutledge** (see p.951) sustains an expansive practice and was identified by clients as *"the leading expert in the state on limited liability law."*

**Clients/Work Highlights:** The client base consists of a wide range of corporate clients, including financial institutions and federal regulatory agencies. Brown-Forman; ISCO Industries; Newcomb Oil; United Medical; Bramco; Publishers Press; Sodrel Truck Lines and Jewish Hospital HealthCare Services all feature in the firm's roster.

# EMPLOYMENT

## MAINLY DEFENDANT

## Band 1

### Frost Brown Todd LLC

See firm details p.954

**The Firm:** This large regional firm is spread across four eastern states, with offices in both Louisville and Lexington. Clients showered its well-connected and resourceful team with praise, and described the overall outfit as *"a great firm to do business with."* The sheer size of its labor and employment law practice reflects the importance the firm attaches to the practice area. It covers the full range of issues, from employment litigation to collective bargaining and class actions to union contract negotiations. Expertise in discrimination, sexual harassment, ADA issues and wrongful discharge is also on offer.

**The Lawyers:** Popular among clients and peers alike, **Patton Pelfrey** (see p.950) was referred to as *"bright, energetic, outspoken, professional and caring about his clients,"* not to mention *"ethical, hard-working and up to speed on the latest legal developments."*

A veteran at the firm, he cochairs the practice and concentrates more on counseling than litigation. **James Cockrum** (see p.945), the *"number two guy behind Pelfrey,"* defends employers in the manufacturing and services sector. He covers both employment-related issues and labor proceedings. **Tony Coleman** is a labor expert with particular depth of knowledge of both the NLRA and the Railway Labor Act. The dedicated and *"well-seasoned"* **John Lovett** (see p.949) is extremely well regarded in the field. One client commented: *"When delivering legal advice, he recognizes the need to develop practical solutions,"* while another commented on his *"subtle, nonaggressive approach to problem solving."* **Laurence Woods** was praised for the *"close and professional relationships he forms with his clients,"* and another client commented how *"it's unusual to do business with someone who is so pleasant, and competent at the same time!"* He was also complimented for drafting *"fair and equitable contracts."*

**Clients/Work Highlights:** UPS; American Synthetic Rubber; WAVE 3 and Kentucky Manufacturing.

### Greenebaum Doll & McDonald PLLC

See firm details p.955

**The Firm:** The firm's sizable labor and employment team represents both regional and national employers across several industry sectors, with an emphasis on automotive manufacturers and aluminum and steel producers. It is known for its *"slightly more aggressive approach,"* though the team endeavors to avoid litigation where possible, and focuses on preventive counseling and training. ERISA, noncompete agreements, employment litigation and labor relations are all core areas for the practice.

**The Lawyers:** Peers enjoy working with the *"conscientious"* **Richard Cleary**, who specializes in both employment and labor law, and chairs the practice group. Clients emphasize how *"he always gets right to the point."* With comments like *"he is outstanding in every respect"* and *"I have never had a complaint about him in over 26 years,"* clients are clearly delighted with the service he provides. Also practicing in both labor and employment spheres is **Thomas Birchfield**, who specializes in mediation. **Jeffrey Savarise** is well regarded by peers, and referred to as an *"extremely skillful lawyer."* He represents Toyota on a regional level. **Wendy Becker** deals with employment issues such as disability, harassment and discrimination, while **Philip Eschels** handles a broad range of labor and employment matters.

**Clients/Work Highlights:** Active clients include Toyota; Texas Roadhouse; American Standard; Aleris; LG&E Energy; DuPont Performance Elastomers and National Tobacco.

## Band 2

### Smith & Smith Attorneys

See firm details p.958

**The Firm:** The 11-strong team at Kentucky's leading employment boutique is credited with *"producing a high-quality work product"* and *"lawyers who are extremely talented at handling traditional labor law."* Providing small and medium-sized employers with litigation avoidance advice is considered the outfit's true forte, though it is more than adequately equipped with litigators to handle contentious cases as the need arises.

**The Lawyers:** Clients described **James Smith** as *"experienced, bright and ethical,"* and remarked that he *"shows great sensitivity toward the issues involved."* **John Sheller** was billed as *"one of the brightest lawyers in this area,"* and both he and James Smith are perceived as heavyweight employment litigators. Meanwhile, **Kevin Smith** is better known for drafting labor and employment documents, and sustains his market profile.

**Clients/Work Highlights:** The majority of the firm's clients are small to midsize companies, though it is also known for acting for the likes of Chubb Group and Churchill Downs.

### Stoll Keenon Ogden PLLC

See firm details p.960

**The Firm:** Following a recent merger, this new firm brings together the former labor and employment group at Ogden Newell & Welch, which operated principally out of Louisville, and the former employment relations department at Stoll, Keenon & Park, which was based in Lexington. One recent highlight involved defending a media company in a case pertaining to wage and hour issues. The team has also counseled defendants in discrimination cases concerning national origin and disability as well as issues arising from breach of contract and the FMLA.

**The Lawyers:** As a result of the merger, the firm boasts an impressive triumvirate of top-tier lawyers. Clients expressed great confidence in both the *"hardworking and bright"* **Richard Griffith** (see p.947) and **Thomas Williams** (see p.952), who clients described as *"professional, attentive and responsive."* Williams came in for further praise as *"an excellent source of information and a lawyer who is aggressive in finding solutions."* He handles employment litigation, in addition to counseling on employment-related issues. **Walter Sales** (see p.951) is an experienced labor and employment practitioner who is held in particularly high regard for his strong knowledge of substantive law.

**Clients/Work Highlights:** LG&E Energy; Water Works Supplies; Doe Anderson; Roll Forming Corporation; Kentucky Housing Corporation; Center for Nonprofit Excellence; Jim Beam Brands; Lexmark International and Parker Hannifin.

## Wyatt, Tarrant & Combs, LLP

See firm details p.962

**The Firm:** The litigation department at Wyatt Tarrant includes a large subgroup of litigators from across the firm's four Kentucky offices who devote a substantial proportion of their time to labor and employment cases. The firm has a particularly impressive track record in discrimination and wage and hour disputes. In addition to seeking advice on contentious matters, a client base of major regional and national clients spanning a range of different industries calls upon the firm for assistance with personnel training, regulatory issues and union prevention programs.

**The Lawyers:** Having practiced labor law for 30 years, **Edwin Hopson** (see p.948) is well known and well respected in this field. The "*extremely bright*" **Debra Dawahare** (see p.946) in Lexington cochairs the firm's labor and employment practice group. Involved both in litigation and counseling, she was praised for her "*excellent performances in front of a jury.*" **Michael Kirk** (see p.949) wins his fair share of market recommendation while **George Miller** (see p.950) makes an entry in the table for the first time in recognition of his involvement in contentious labor and employment matters.

**Clients/Work Highlights:** GE; American Red Cross Blood Services; Appalachian Regional Healthcare; 3M; Papa John's International; Asbury College;

James River Coal; Chubb Group; Knox County Hospital and Argonaut Insurance.

### Band 3

## Dinsmore & Shohl LLP

See firm details p.1645

**The Firm:** This Cincinnati-headquartered firm is best known for acting on behalf of employers in the newspaper, media and communications sectors. Its lawyers offer wide-ranging experience, which covers an array of matters, from religious and disability discrimination cases to wage and hour claims.

**The Lawyers:** **Jon Fleischaker** (see p.947) has a high profile as a First Amendment lawyer, representing various media outlets. For employment issues, clients cite him as "*thorough*" and "*responsive.*" He is particularly strong on dealing with contentious issues.

**Clients/Work Highlights:** Clients include Gannett (The Courier-Journal); Jewish Hospital HealthCare Services; L'Oréal; AstraZeneca and the Presbyterian Church.

## Woodward, Hobson & Fulton LLP

**The Firm:** While this firm is best known in the market for its professional malpractice defense work, its attorneys also handle discrimination claims and

provide human resources departments with day-to-day employment counseling. Regular appearances before the NLRB, in cases relating to unfair labor practice charges and contract negotiations for example, further contribute to the workload.

**The Lawyers:** Managing partner **Donna Perry** sustains her sophisticated dispute resolution practice, which in addition to a heavy general commercial litigation caseload involves a significant labor and employment element. "*Well liked by clients,*" **Raymond Haley** is complimented for his "*strong personal presence*" and his intelligence. **Kathryn Quesenberry** is hailed as an emerging talent and handles employment law issues such as severance packages and sexual harassment. Peers admire her style in the courtroom, especially her handling of witnesses and her use of "*appropriately aggressive cross-examination techniques.*" Sources also comment: "*She is able to get to the bottom of an issue quickly.*"

**Clients/Work Highlights:** Clients include Norton Healthcare, the University of Louisville and Louisville Water.

### Other Notable Practitioners

**Shannon Hamilton** (see p.948) of Stites & Harbison PLLC is renowned for her lead trial counsel experience in employment litigation.

# ENVIRONMENT, NATURAL RESOURCES & REGULATED INDUSTRIES

| Environment, Natural Resources & Regulated Industries |
| :--- |
| **Leading Firms** |
| **1** GREENEBAUM DOLL & MCDONALD *Lexington* |
| STITES & HARBISON PLLC *Lexington* |
| STOLL KEENON OGDEN PLLC *Lexington* |
| WYATT, TARRANT & COMBS, LLP *Lexington* |
| **2** DINSMORE & SHOHL LLP *Lexington* |
| FROST BROWN TODD LLC *Lexington* |

### Band 1

## Greenebaum Doll & McDonald PLLC

See firm details p.955

**The Firm:** This national firm ensures its dominance in Kentucky with "*well-run and capable*" offices in Louisville, Lexington, Covington and Frankfort. It offers a range of services in environmental compliance, covering such matters as air, water, waste and minerals. Its deep natural resources capability includes specialty expertise in limestone and coal. The team handles major transactions across the region, recently acting on the purchase of a large mining complex, four medium-sized coal operations and an oil company. The bill of fare here includes volumes of M&A, development and construction work.

**The Lawyers:** The vastly experienced **Bruce Cryder**'s practice covers mineral and environmental law, and he is "*the guy you want on your side*" in commercial litigation. He is "*probably the best known coal attorney for both litigation and transactions,*" according to sources. The "*practical, helpful and extremely smart*" **Jack Bender** advises utilities on their environmental concerns. Skilled finance and corporate lawyer **Patrick Northam** is a familiar figure on the natural resources scene and is portrayed as the firm's primary utilities lawyer. Commentators commend his negotiation skills, and clients are bowled over by his "*unrivaled work ethic*" and "*superb attention to detail.*"

**Clients/Work Highlights:** The team advises public and private entities in diverse industries. These include Peabody Coal, Consul Energy and LG&E Energy.

## Stites & Harbison PLLC

See firm details p.959

**The Firm:** The energy law team here handles restructuring, development and finance deals for developers, investors and operators of power plants and synthetic fuel production facilities. It is a major player in the utilities sector and offers potent regulatory capability; this was demonstrated recently by the purchase of smelter power rates in the wake of the restructuring of a large electric corporation. The environmental compliance team gets involved in

prestigious transactions such as the recent acquisition of surface rights in southern Appalachia for a timber investment management client. On the CWA side the team advised a thoroughbred racetrack facility operator.

**The Lawyers:** **David Brown** (see p.945) is "*experienced, bright and a hard worker,*" who specializes in utility regulation. **Mark Overstreet** (see p.950) represents utilities such as Kentucky Power in regulatory and litigation matters. **William Gorton**'s (see p.947) work spans natural resources, including land and water, as well as environmental regulation.

**Clients/Work Highlights:** Clients include Alcan Aluminum; Century Aluminum; Kroger; New York Department of Insurance and Magna Entertainment.

## Stoll Keenon Ogden PLLC

See firm details p.960

**The Firm:** Clients welcome the merger of Stoll, Keenon & Park and Ogden Newell & Welch, anticipating a quantum leap in natural resources and utilities services throughout Kentucky, Indiana, Tennessee, Virginia and DC. The Stoll, Keenon & Park contingent's recent successes have included several proceedings before the Kentucky Public Service Commission in matters such as gas and electric rates, gas regulation and merger approvals. The former Ogden Newell & Welch element brings to the table a sterling track record in providing regulatory and corporate services in the energy, natural gas and

---

| Environment, Natural Resources<br>& Regulated Industries: Utilities |
| --- |
| Leading Individuals |

**Senior Statesman**

NEWELL Richard *Stoll Keenon Ogden PLLC*

[1] BROWN David *Stites & Harbison PLLC*

HATFIELD C Kent *Stoll Keenon Ogden PLLC*

INGRAM JR Lindsey *Stoll Keenon Ogden PLLC*

NORTHAM Patrick *Greenebaum Doll & McDonald*

OVERSTREET Mark *Stites & Harbison PLLC*

RIGGS Kendrick *Stoll Keenon Ogden PLLC*

WATT Robert *Stoll Keenon Ogden PLLC*

**Up-and-coming individuals**

BRENT Douglas *Stoll Keenon Ogden PLLC*

CORNETT J Gregory *Stoll Keenon Ogden PLLC*

| Environment, Natural Resources<br>& Regulated Industries: Natural Resources |
| --- |
| Leading Individuals |

[1] CRYDER Bruce *Greenebaum Doll & McDonald*

CURTZ Chauncey *Dinsmore & Shohl LLP*

GORTON William *Stites & Harbison PLLC*

HOFFMANN Warren *Frost Brown Todd LLC*

INGRAM JR Lindsey *Stoll Keenon Ogden*

NORTHAM Patrick *Greenebaum Doll & McDonald*

RHORER John *Dinsmore & Shohl LLP*

WARD Richard *Wyatt, Tarrant & Combs*

[2] DAVIS R Eberley *Stoll Keenon Ogden*

| Environment, Natural Resources<br>& Regulated Industries: Environment |
| --- |
| Leading Individuals |

[1] BENDER Jack *Greenebaum Doll & McDonald*

CRYDER Bruce *Greenebaum Doll & McDonald*

GORTON William *Stites & Harbison PLLC*

[2] CONNIFF Dennis *Frost Brown Todd LLC*

WARD Richard *Wyatt, Tarrant & Combs, LLP*

telecommunications industries. Recent work has included representing Louisville Gas and Electric Company and Kentucky Utilities Company in various matters, including a bid to disengage from a regional transmission organization, applications for environmental compliance approval and concerns related to a proposed increase in gas and electric rates.

**The Lawyers:** Corporate expert **Eberley Davis'** (see p.946) in-house experience at a coal company stands him in good stead in his natural resources and environmental law practice, and sources declare: "*He has integrity and is a great character.*" Regarded as a "*fine litigator and all-around attorney,*" **Kent Hatfield** (see p.948) is a popular choice for referrals on energy and utilities-related work and clients praise his "*excellent judgment.*" **Lindsey Ingram** (see p.948) specializes in litigation and public utility law and represents various gas, water, electric and communications companies before the Public Service Commission. Fans of **Kendrick Riggs** (see p.951) and **Robert Watt** (see p.952) deem them "*the best utilities lawyers in the state,*" and clients declare them "*skilled strategists and technicians – talented, capable and thorough.*" Both excel in transactional work and they also litigate in state and federal courts. Riggs acts for energy and telecommunications companies and is "*formal and sophisticated in approach.*" **Richard Newell** (see p.950) has nearly half a century's experience in regulatory and administrative matters to offer. **Douglas Brent** (see p.945) is a regulatory specialist in the telecommunications sector and has useful in-house experience in the industry. He also has a good line in utilities law. **Gregory Cornett** (see p.946) specializes in litigation and alternative dispute resolution and dedicates a significant portion of his practice to utility and regulatory law.

**Clients/Work Highlights:** Clients include Louisville Gas & Electric; Kentucky Utilities; Delta Natural Gas; Cinergy; Equitable Gas; Equitable Production; Williams Telecommunications and Duke Energy North America.

## Wyatt, Tarrant & Combs, LLP

See firm details p.962

**The Firm:** This is a full-service outfit that offers bespoke multidisciplinary services in environmental, mineral and energy matters. Best known for its litigation and regulatory advice, the well-rounded team also provides transactional counsel. There is also a dedicated mine safety group that is active nationally.

**The Lawyers:** **Richard Ward** is a respected commercial litigator with specialty expertise in minerals, energy and environmental law.

## Band 2

### Dinsmore & Shohl LLP

See firm details p.1645

**The Firm:** This revered Lexington-based team is especially identified with minerals and mining work. The versatile lawyers offer polished skills in many areas, including development, transportation and ownership/leasing of natural resources. Naturally enough, the practice includes a sturdy vein of environmental law and attorneys are familiar with Superfund and toxic tort issues.

**The Lawyers:** Both ranked lawyers enjoy close ties to the coal industry. The "*phenomenal*" **Chauncey Curtz** (see p.946) has a nationwide reputation for transactional and litigation services to coal lessors and operating companies. Clients appreciate his strategic abilities and his awareness of business risks. The "*extremely capable*" **John Rhorer** (see p.951) focuses on transactional work and documentation for lenders and borrowers.

**Clients/Work Highlights:** Clients include Arch Coal; Peabody Energy; Kentucky Berwind Land and Madison Capital Investors.

### Frost Brown Todd LLC

See firm details p.954

**The Firm:** This firm is a serious regional player across the energy, natural resources and environmental board. It draws deep on the capabilities of a large and experienced stable of attorneys and offers powerful commercial litigation services in addition to adroit transactional counsel. Clients particularly note the group's environmental cleanup expertise and heartily endorse the firm's fluid multidisciplinary resources.

**The Lawyers:** "*Excellent strategist*" **Warren Hoffmann** (see p.948) has a thriving general corporate practice with a strong niche acting for clients in the coal and utility industries. Clients rely on **Dennis Conniff** (see p.945) for his "*impressive understanding*" in transactional and contentious environmental matters.

---

# LITIGATION

## Band 1

### Frost Brown Todd LLC

See firm details p.954

**The Firm:** This recognized regional heavyweight has a particularly "*strong and broad-based*" commercial litigation group that is thoroughly "*at home on sizable and complex deals*" in just about any sector. Clients comment that the team has "*just the right*" levels of associates and the right mix of skills," and sources agree that the lawyers "*cover every kind of litigation.*" Recent cases include one that involved pharmaceuticals companies being sued by several states over their pricing, and a high-profile antitrust suit in the stock car racing industry.

**The Lawyers:** "*Constitutional scholar*" **Sheryl Snyder** (see p.951) is "*expert in complex strategy and handling political developments,*" and widely agreed

# GENERAL COMMERCIAL

to be "*the state's premier appellate lawyer.*" His "*consummate oratorical skills*" are in high demand, and he recently defended the Governor of Kentucky in an investigation into political hiring procedures. **Carl Henlein** (see p.948) is "*as good as it gets in mass tort litigation*" and enjoys a reputation that extends well beyond Kentucky. Constantly engaged in impressive matters, "*he always has an interesting story to tell.*" **Winston Miller** (see p.950) handles various

## Litigation: General Commercial

### Leading Firms

**1** FROST BROWN TODD LLC *Louisville*
GREENEBAUM DOLL & MCDONALD PLLC *Louisville*
STITES & HARBISON PLLC *Louisville*
WYATT, TARRANT & COMBS, LLP *Louisville*

**2** MIDDLETON REUTLINGER PSC *Louisville*
REED WEITKAMP SCHELL & VICE PLLC *Louisville*
STOLL KEENON OGDEN PLLC *Lexington*

**3** BOEHL STOPHER & GRAVES, LLP *Louisville*
DINSMORE & SHOHL LLP *Louisville*
WOODWARD, HOBSON & FULTON LLP *Louisville*

### Leading Individuals

#### Senior Statesman

BALLANTINE John *Stoll Keenon Ogden PLLC*

**1** CRONAN IV Charles *Stites & Harbison PLLC*
HAYNES Greg *Wyatt, Tarrant & Combs, LLP*
HINKLE IV Samuel *Stoll Keenon Ogden PLLC*
REED John *Reed Weitkamp Schell*
SNYDER Sheryl *Frost Brown Todd LLC*
STOPHER Edward *Boehl Stopher & Graves, LLP*

**2** COLLIER Philip *Stites & Harbison PLLC*
HENLEIN Carl *Frost Brown Todd LLC*
KING W Gregory *Stoll Keenon Ogden PLLC*
MILLER Winston *Frost Brown Todd LLC*

**3** CASSIS Charles *Frost Brown Todd LLC*
CLAY Richard *Woodward, Hobson & Fulton LLP*
CONNOLLY Robert *Stites & Harbison PLLC*
CORYELL II Cornelius *Wyatt, Tarrant & Combs, LLP*
DOHENY JR Frank *Dinsmore & Shohl LLP*
ELY III Hiram *Greenebaum Doll & McDonald*
HOVIOUS R Gregg *Tachau Maddox Hovious*
ISON Eric *Greenebaum Doll & McDonald*
JAKUBOWICZ Janet *Greenebaum Doll & McDonald*
MONOHAN David *Woodward, Hobson & Fulton*
PITT M Stephen *Wyatt, Tarrant & Combs, LLP*
SHIVEL JR Charles *Stoll Keenon Ogden PLLC*
SNELL Virginia *Wyatt, Tarrant & Combs, LLP*
TACHAU David *Tachau Maddox Hovious*
THOMPSON B Todd *Thompson Miller & Simpson*

**4** BALLANTINE Douglas *Stoll Keenon Ogden PLLC*
BUSH John K *Greenebaum Doll & McDonald*
FENZEL Mark S *Middleton Reutlinger PSC*
GREENWELL Charles *Middleton Reutlinger PSC*
GRIFFITH Robert *Stites & Harbison PLLC*
HALE David *Reed Weitkamp Schell & Vice*
KAPLAN David *Frost Brown Todd LLC*
LEET Byron *Wyatt, Tarrant & Combs*
LINDSAY Colin *Dinsmore & Shohl LLP*
MILLIMAN James *Middleton Reutlinger PSC*
MURPHY Marc *Stites & Harbison PLLC*
ROBINSON III Wm *Greenebaum Doll & McDonald*
ROYSE David *Stoll Keenon Ogden PLLC*

types of litigation including products liability, mass tort, fire and explosion, employment and business. **Charles Cassis** (see p.945) is an *"excellent business generator"* for the firm, and clients commend his

wealth of knowledge and credibility in the courtroom. **David Kaplan** (see p.949) *"clearly stands out"* among his contemporaries for his talent and intelligence as a litigator. Clients declare him *"confident, capable and responsible"* and are especially keen on his *"excellent judgment."*

**Clients/Work Highlights:** Clients include LG&E Energy; Equitable Resources; Churchill Downs; NASCAR; AstraZeneca; Anthem Insurance Companies; UPS; ICI and Yum! Brands.

### Greenebaum Doll & McDonald PLLC

See firm details p.955

**The Firm:** The name of the game here is the provision of a well-rounded and integrated service to business clients, crowned by a litigation capability that packs *"a heck of a punch."* The team is adept in all forms of dispute resolution, whether the courts are involved or not. Commentators identify the practice's sheer depth of specialty expertise (such as environmental and corporate) and the consistently high quality of the litigators as defining characteristics.

**The Lawyers:** **Hiram Ely** is effective keeping clients out of court, but will litigate with focus and verve when necessary. His practice includes alternative forms of dispute resolution and he is a certified mediator and arbitrator. **Eric Ison** is a stalwart of the Kentucky scene and offers niche expertise in products liability, class actions and appeals as well as more general litigation services. Sources extol **Janet Jakubowicz**'s *"intelligence, common sense and credible demeanor."* She acts for financial institutions and clients in the manufacturing, service and retail industries in commercial litigation and arbitration, securities and class action defense. Corporate lawyer **John Bush** focuses on complex issues, often at an appellate level. His range takes in antitrust, securities, finance, IP and products liability. The *"insightful"* **Bill Robinson** is based in the north of the state and is often found on governmental matters and appeals.

### Stites & Harbison PLLC

See firm details p.959

**The Firm:** Lawyers here offer a staunch civil litigation service and notably strong products liability and IP capability. The team defends clients in various industries including aviation, utilities and energy, healthcare, finance and commercial real estate. It was recently involved in construction litigation concerning a water tank project in Massachusetts. Other successes include defending an industrial safety equipment manufacturer against allegations of a breach of a sales contract, and litigating on a complex breach of fiduciary duty claim.

**The Lawyers:** Endorsement for the *"absolutely top-notch"* **Charles Cronan** (see p.946) streams in from all quarters and he *"engenders respect in the judiciary itself."* Described as *"thorough, capable, intelligent and insightful,"* clients emphasized his qualities as *"an extremely wise counselor as well as a fine litigator."* **Philip Collier** (see p.945) is *"extraordinarily thorough and bright"* and reputed to be something of *"a bulldog in terms of preparation."* **Robert Connolly** (see p.946) chairs the group and his commercial liti-

gation workload is studded with products liability and construction cases. **Marc Murphy** (see p.950) deals with both commercial and white-collar criminal litigation. His high-profile crime prosecution is recognized far afield. **Robert Griffith** (see p.947) is *"one heck of a litigator,"* say sources, and handles a large volume of work for the aviation industry.

### Wyatt, Tarrant & Combs, LLP

See firm details p.962

**The Firm:** This firm offers broad and significant litigation capability across the region and particular expertise in banking and finance. It fields a large team out of offices in Kentucky, Indiana and Tennessee, and offers solid ancillary expertise in areas such as employment, construction and healthcare.

**The Lawyers:** *"Clever and fast on his feet,"* **Greg Haynes** (see p.948) enjoys a reputation as *"a brilliant cross-examiner"* and receives plaudits for his effective leadership of the team. **Virginia Snell** (see p.951) is regarded as *"more of a motions lawyer than a trial lawyer"* and makes up a formidable double act with Haynes. She specializes in appellate work and handles securities fraud, class action, business tort and legal malpractice cases. *"Smart guy"* **Corky Coryell** counsels and litigates as part of a practice that covers banking, UCC and consumer protection, products liability and personal injury. **Byron Leet** (see p.949) is *"an accomplished litigator and a seasoned lawyer"* who acts for both public and private clients in tort and insurance cases as well as more general areas. **Stephen Pitt** specializes in complex commercial and toxic tort litigation and his practice extends to environmental and criminal law.

## Band 2

### Middleton Reutlinger PSC

See firm details p.956

**The Firm:** This is a smaller team than the state heavyweights, but it is home to *"seriously fine lawyers."* IP is a particular strength here, including patent and trademark infringement and trade secret litigation. A discrete practice is dedicated to insurance litigation, covering such areas as personal injury, professional negligence, labor and employment and toxic torts.

**The Lawyers:** **James Milliman** (see p.950) adopts an aggressive stance in general commercial and IP litigation on behalf of high-profile clients. **Mark Fenzel** (see p.946) represents insurance companies and self-insured corporations, schools and local businesses in their various requirements. The forceful **Charles Greenwell** (see p.947) handles an impressive banking litigation caseload.

### Reed Weitkamp Schell & Vice PLLC

See firm details p.957

**The Firm:** The quality and profile of the litigation work handled by this small outfit is extremely high and the market endorses it as a *"reliable and sophisticated"* group. A mixed bag of work includes notable IP, antitrust and employment litigation. Recent matters include a federal antitrust case brought by the DOJ against the Commission, and suing a pharmaceutical manufacturer on behalf of the Kentucky attorney general.

**The Lawyers:** The "*poised*" **John Reed** (see p.950) "*doesn't lose his cool when under fire*." He springs immediately to commentators' minds as "*someone you'd go to in difficult, high stakes cases where not only courtroom skills but a great deal of thinking are required*." **David Hale** (see p.947) has a fine reputation in complex high-profile cases. He represents the State Treasurer, for whom he recently litigated on matters concerning a budget stalemate and Kentucky's prepaid college tuition savings plan.

**Clients/Work Highlights:** Clients include Northwestern Mutual; State Treasurer of the Commonwealth of Kentucky; Dees Crafts; Kentucky Real Estate Commission and Jones Day.

### Stoll Keenon Ogden PLLC
See firm details p.960

**The Firm:** The merger of Ogden Newell & Welsh and Stoll, Keenon & Park has created a formidable firm with deep roots in Kentucky's legal marketplace. Its capabilities have been boosted in a number of areas, and nowhere more so than in quality litigation. The former Ogden team recently defended various medical practitioners against allegations of malpractice, and handled a complex action against a stock insurance company in Federal Court regarding the distribution of its stock.

**The Lawyers:** Revered veteran **John Ballantine** (see p.944) now spends most of his time in mediation. **Sam Hinkle** (see p.948) is praised for his calm approach to litigation, and described as "*a warrior, but not warlike*." Focused on medical malpractice defense and products liability, **Greg King** (see p.949) has a firm grasp of complex issues; clients are impressed, saying: "*He is assertive and aggressive, but with an easy, believable manner*." **Charles Shivel** (see p.951) is first and foremost "*an extremely skilled and seasoned commercial litigator*," renowned for his expertise in commercial lending and coal matters. **David Royse**'s (see p.951) "*thorough and effective*" approach is a hit with clients who are drawn to his

great track record in the courtroom. He offers specialty expertise in zoning and planning, eminent domain and media matters. **Douglas Ballantine** (see p.944) is "*well received by the jury*," observe commentators. His specialty areas include IP, professional malpractice, environmental and toxic torts, personal injury and products liability.

**Clients/Work Highlights:** Former Ogden clients include AP Capital Insurance; Preferred Physicians Insurance; Professional Risk Management Service; American Healthcare Indemnity; Chubb Insurance; Norton Hospitals of Louisville; Papa John's International; LG&E Energy; Brown-Foreman and Anthem Health Plans of Kentucky. The former Stoll client base is also impressive and adds a number of Lexington-based businesses to the list.

## Band 3

### Boehl Stopher & Graves, LLP
See firm details p.953

**The Firm:** This civil litigation boutique enjoys strong market recognition and has "*been around forever, doing great stuff*." The team offers advice on cases and transactions across the region and is particularly noted for insurance defense, products liability and personal injury matters.

**The Lawyers:** The "*high-energy*" **Ed Stopher** (see p.952) is regarded as "*the consummate litigator*" and handles sophisticated products liability and medical malpractice issues. Clients cheer him on as "*a gifted orator and a no holds barred litigator*" who "*really goes for the jugular*."

### Dinsmore & Shohl LLP
See firm details p.1645

**The Firm:** This large Ohio-rooted regional player continues its inexorable march into Kentucky's markets. The relatively small litigation group here is centered on offices in Louisville and Lexington and is growing steadily. Sources clearly identify some "*important individual players*" who offer services in an impressive range of areas and up to a high level of complexity.

**The Lawyers:** **Frank Doheny** is "*extremely effective in front of juries*" and acknowledged as "*a premier medical practice litigator*" and products liability expert. **Colin Lindsay** (see p.949) is a respected advocate and particularly well regarded for products liability matters.

### Woodward, Hobson & Fulton LLP

**The Firm:** This group offers commercial litigation services across the firm's sector specialties, which include professional liability, products liability, labor and employment, business organization and estate planning. Lawyers operate out of offices in Louisville and Lexington.

**The Lawyers:** **Dick Clay** is recommended for sensitive matters and acts for institutions jealous of their reputations; by all accounts he does "*a masterful job of shielding clients from the public eye*." He is a capable and experienced trial lawyer with a "*spot-on sense of the big picture*" and a flourishing caseload that includes pharmaceutical and medical device litigation, constitutional issues and defamation. **David Monohan**'s "*effective advocacy*" has stood many a client in good stead. He is "*always well prepared*" and defends a range of clients that includes hospitals, architects, engineers, construction companies and maritime organizations.

### Other Notable Practitioners

Thompson Miller & Simpson PLC's **Todd Thompson** is an experienced trial lawyer with a sterling reputation for medical malpractice and hospital liability work. He also handles general commercial litigation for significant clients such as Ford. **David Tachau** (see p.952) and **Gregg Hovious** (see p.948) of Tachau Maddox Hovious & Dickens PLC are "*formidably aggressive*" litigators and win praise as "*talented and intelligent*" lawyers who "*can handle just about any type of litigation that comes their way*."

# REAL ESTATE

| Real Estate | |
|---|---|
| **Leading Firms** | |
| 1 | **FROST BROWN TODD LLC** *Louisville* |
| | **STITES & HARBISON PLLC** *Louisville* |
| | **WYATT, TARRANT & COMBS, LLP** *Louisville* |
| 2 | **GREENEBAUM DOLL & MCDONALD** *Louisville* |

| Real Estate: Zoning/Land Use | |
|---|---|
| **Leading Firms** | |
| 1 | **GREENEBAUM DOLL & MCDONALD** *Louisville* |

### Frost Brown Todd LLC
See firm details p.954

**The Firm:** This is a large, diverse and versatile practice that offers a full range of real estate services to clients of all stamps. Sources report: "*They have the full suite – you can take anything to them*," and clients value the team's compelling regional standing. The group is particularly well regarded for its representation of local, regional and national developers. Recent projects include the relocation of a heavy lift cargo carrier from Dayton, Ohio, to a new $45 million facility in Louisville and the acquisition and leasing of hospital facilities in nine states for a local healthcare provider.

**The Lawyers:** **Dale Ahearn** (see p.944) has a nice line of work representing clients in the shopping center and retailing industry. He handles leasing and development transactions across the country. Clients extol **Timothy Martin**'s (see p.949) thoroughness and responsiveness, declaring him "*an effective negotiator who doesn't allow himself to get ruffled*." He handles a small volume of lending work but is most closely identified with his work for developers, which includes zoning and land use matters. **Jude Clark** (see p.945) "*understands corporate business needs*" and concentrates on lending work for institutional lenders. He has a useful background in city planning and a sideline in zoning issues. **Marshall Polk**

## Real Estate
### Leading Individuals

**Senior Statesman**

JOSEPH III Alfred *Stites & Harbison PLLC*

**1** AHEARN Dale *Frost Brown Todd LLC*

HADEN JR William *Stites & Harbison PLLC*

HINES Barry *Stites & Harbison PLLC*

MARTIN Timothy *Frost Brown Todd LLC*

VINCENTI Michael *Wyatt, Tarrant & Combs*

**2** CAMP Leo *Wyatt, Tarrant & Combs*

CLARK JR L Jude *Frost Brown Todd LLC*

ELDRED JR Marshall *Frost Brown Todd LLC*

GATHRIGHT JR Joseph *Weber & Rose*

LOBB James *Weber & Rose*

SAFFER David *Stites & Harbison PLLC*

VICE Robert *Reed Weitkamp Schell & Vice*

### Real Estate: Zoning/Land Use
### Leading Individuals

**1** BARDENWERPER William *Bardenwerper, Talbott*

PRICE Glenn *Greenebaum Doll & McDonald*

**Eldred** (see p.946) has *"a gift for identifying the important issues."* He has a long experience of real estate projects and now works on a part-time basis. **Clients/Work Highlights:** Jefferson Development; UPS; Renaissance Development; General Growth Properties and Oakland Hills Development.

### Stites & Harbison PLLC
See firm details p.959
**The Firm:** This group has a thriving practice in redevelopment, conservation easements and community development and revitalization. With a considerable number of major lenders and financial institutions on its client roster, it offers dedicated real estate

finance expertise. Clients emphasize the lawyers' *"fast and detailed work"* and rate their diligence and cost effectiveness as major draws.
**The Lawyers:** With more than 35 years of experience in all areas of real estate transactions, **Alfred Joseph** (see p.949) has cut back much of his practice and focuses on strategic counsel and education programs. **Bill Haden** (see p.947) specializes in credit enhancement and acts mainly for banks and life assurance companies. **Barry Hines** (see p.948) has achieved regional and even national recognition for his conduit loans and real estate finance expertise. Handling finance work for institutional lenders, **David Saffer** (see p.951) is described as *"a hard worker, with a great personality."*
**Clients/Work Highlights:** Regions Bank; Fidelity Bank; Main Street Bank and JPMorgan.

### Wyatt, Tarrant & Combs, LLP
See firm details p.962
**The Firm:** Acting for a range of commercial clients, notable lenders and developers, this team has a solid reputation in the community for the *"strength, size and quality"* of its team. Real estate capability is concentrated in Louisville and Lexington, and the firm offers support services in litigation and finance to boot.
**The Lawyers:** Interviewees recommend **Michael Vincenti**'s (see p.952) expertise in high-rise office leasings and development. Clients appreciate the way he *"offers genuinely different options, with pros and cons clearly identified,"* and his knack for getting *"right to the meat of the problem."* **Leo Camp** focuses on corporate transactions, including real estate finance.
**Clients/Work Highlights:** Examples of the team's varied client base are Main Street Realty; Faulkner Real Estate; Regions Bank; Bank One and Houchens Industries.

### Greenebaum Doll & McDonald PLLC
See firm details p.955
**The Firm:** This regional corporate player's real estate and construction practice is subsumed under the litigation and dispute resolution group. Lawyers handle a healthy diet of general commercial real estate and are credited with a real forte in zoning.
**The Lawyers:** Tandy Patrick chairs the real estate development and construction team and specializes in retail leasings and acquisitions and disposals. **Glenn Price** is the key contact for land use and zoning matters.
**Clients/Work Highlights:** Clients span various industries, including healthcare, education and real estate development.

### Other Notable Practitioners
**Joseph Gathright** of Weber & Rose specializes in commercial real estate, advising banks and other lenders on development and term financing issues. Clients praise **James Lobb**, also at Weber & Rose, for his *"magnificent skill at negotiating loan agreements."* He works on development, lending and condominium law. Reed Weitkamp Shell & Vice PLLC's **Robert Vice** (see p.952) works in the public finance and historic tax credits area. **William Bardenwerper** of Bardenwerper, Talbott & Roberts practices exclusively in the zoning and land use area and is hailed as *"absolutely at the top of his game."*

# Leaders in Kentucky

## AHEARN, Dale
Frost Brown Todd LLC, Louisville
502 568 0275
dahearn@fbtlaw.com
*Recommended in Real Estate*
**Practice Areas:** Lead counsel in development of 100+ regional shopping centers and many major industrial facilities.
**Prof. Memberships:** Kentucky Bar Association, 1978; International Council of Shopping Centers; CoreNet Global.
**Publications:** University of Kentucky, 'Use Restrictions on Real Estate'; Commercial Leasing Law and Strategy, 'Require Sublease that Protects Your Interests' (2001), 'Essential and Advanced Protections for Landlords in Subleases' (2001), 'Dealing with Landlord Default: An Introduction' (1999), 'Lessors Beware: Rejection of Lease By Lessee in Bankruptcy May Not Terminate Sublessee's Interest' (1999), 'Risk Allocation for Haz-

ardous Substances' (1998).
**Personal:** Michigan State University, BA, 1975, University of Michigan, JD, 1977.

## BALLANTINE, Douglas C
Stoll Keenon Ogden PLLC, Louisville
502 560 4247
douglas.ballantine@skofirm.com
*Recommended in Litigation*
**Practice Areas:** Concentration in commercial, intellectual property, and environmental litigation, including superfund and toxic tort matters. Experience with professional negligence litigation, especially defense of medical malpractice cases, and defense of personal injury and products liability actions.
**Prof. Memberships:** American, Kentucky (Chair, Continuing Legal Education Commission; Ethics Committee), and Louisville Bar Associations; Advisory Committee on Local Rules of the United States Court of Appeals for the Sixth Cir-

cuit; Kentucky Supreme Court Civil Rules Committee; Defense Research Institute; Kentucky Defense Counsel, Inc.
**Personal:** Indiana University (Bloomington) (JD, 1988); American University (BA, 1984). Listed in 'Best Lawyers in America', Business Litigation.

## BALLANTINE, John T
Stoll Keenon Ogden PLLC, Louisville
502 560 4213
john.ballantine@skofirm.com
*Recommended in Litigation*
**Practice Areas:** Civil, personal injury, and commercial litigation with concentration on professional liability and medical malpractice defense cases; mediation and arbitration of all types of civil cases and claims.
**Prof. Memberships:** Fellow, American College of Trial Lawyers; Life Member, Judicial Conference of US Court of Appeals, Sixth Circuit; Federation of

Defense and Corporate Counsel; Kentucky Defense Counsel, Inc.
**Personal:** Harvard Law School (LLB, 1957); University of Kentucky (AB, high distinction, 1952). Listed in 'Best Lawyers in America', Personal Injury Litigation; recipient of Kentucky Bar Association Outstanding Lawyer Award (2003) and Louisville Bar Association Judge Shobe Civility and Professionalism Award (2006).

## BARDENWERPER, William
Bardenwerper & Talbott PLLC, Louisville
502 426 6688
*Recommended in Real Estate*

## BECK JR, Robert M
Stites & Harbison PLLC, Lexington
859 226 2336
rbeck@stites.com
*Recommended in Corporate/M&A*
**Practice Areas:** Business Service Group. Member of Management Committee.

Emphasis in equine, general corporate, commercial finance, mergers and acquisitions.
**Prof. Memberships:** Admitted to practice in Kentucky (1975) and United States Supreme Court. Member of American, Kentucky and Fayette County Bar Associations. President, Founder and Director, American College of Equine Attorneys.
**Career:** Member, Stites & Harbison.
**Publications:** Co-author, 'Developments in Equine Breeding Syndications,' University of Kentucky CLE publications, 1999.
**Personal:** JD, Vanderbilt University, 1975; BA, Economics, Vanderbilt University, 1971.

### BECKER, Wendy
Greenebaum Doll & McDonald PLLC, Lexington 859 231 8500
*Recommended in Employment*

### BECKMAN, David
Frost Brown Todd LLC, Louisville
502 568 0374
dbeckman@fbtlaw.com
*Recommended in Corporate/M&A*
**Practice Areas:** Extensive experience in mergers and acquisitions, joint ventures, franchising, financial institutions law, and general commercial and business transactions.
**Prof. Memberships:** Admitted Kentucky Bar 1988. Member of American Bar Association Sections on Business Banking, Tax and Forum on Franchising.
**Career:** Frost Brown Todd LLC; Vice-Chair Corporate/Business Department.
**Personal:** JD (cum laude), Northwestern University, 1988; AB (cum laude), Harvard College, 1985.

### BENDER, Jack
Greenebaum Doll & McDonald PLLC, Lexington 859 231 8500
*Recommended in Environment*

### BIRCHFIELD, Thomas
Greenebaum Doll & McDonald PLLC, Louisville 502 589 4200
*Recommended in Employment*

### BRADLEY JR, Craig C
Stites & Harbison PLLC, Louisville
502 681 0411
cbradley@stites.com
*Recommended in Corporate/M&A*
**Practice Areas:** Business Service Group. Practice emphasis in securities and corporate finance.
**Prof. Memberships:** Admitted to practice in Kentucky (1980). Member of American, Kentucky and Louisville Bar Associations, Kentucky Securities Law Legislative Advisory Committee and Drafting Committee for Kentucky Business Corporation Act.
**Career:** Member of Stites & Harbison. With the firm since 1980.
**Personal:** JD, University of Kentucky, 1980; BA, University of Virginia, 1977.

### BRENT, Douglas F
Stoll Keenon Ogden PLLC, Louisville
502 568 5734
douglas.brent@skofirm.com
*Recommended in Environment*
**Practice Areas:** Concentration in telecommunications, public utility and common carrier regulation and administrative law, with more than 15 years of experience in state and federal telecommunications regulatory matters.
**Prof. Memberships:** Louisville, Kentucky and Federal Communications Bar Associations.
**Personal:** University of Kentucky, Honors Program with Departmental Honors in Business (BBA, 1982); University of Kentucky College of Law (JD, 1986).

### BROWN, David C
Stites & Harbison PLLC, Louisville
502 681 0421
dbrown@stites.com
*Recommended in Environment*
**Practice Areas:** Kentucky Public Service Commission Practice, commercial and business transactions and energy regulatory transactions. Certified Mediator, Private Adjudication Center, Duke University School of Law, 2002.
**Prof. Memberships:** Admitted to practice in Kentucky. Member of American, Kentucky and Louisville Bar Associations.
**Career:** Counsel, Stites & Harbison. Former Managing Partner. With the firm since 1964.
**Personal:** JD, University of Virginia, 1964; BA, Kenyon College, 1961.

### BUSH, John
Greenebaum Doll & McDonald PLLC, Louisville 502 589 4200
*Recommended in Litigation*

### CAMP, Leo
Wyatt, Tarrant & Combs, LLP, Louisville
502 589 5235
*Recommended in Real Estate*

### CASSIS, Charles
Frost Brown Todd LLC, Louisville
502 568 0233
ccassis@fbtlaw.com
*Recommended in Litigation*
**Practice Areas:** Mr Cassis is a member in the Litigation Department. His practice involves general trial litigation and appellate practice.
**Prof. Memberships:** Kentucky Bar Foundation, Founding Member; American Bar Foundation, Fellow; US Law Firm Group, President, 1995; appointed to special commissions by the Governor for changes in Kentucky Legislation; Jefferson County Police Merit Board, Chairman; Federation of Defense and Corporate Counsel.
**Career:** One of the founding Partners of Brown, Todd & Heyburn PLLC, one of the legacy firms to Frost Brown Todd LLC. Instrumental in forming the Litigation Department and served as its Chair-

man for several years.
**Personal:** JD, University of Kentucky, 1963; BS, University of Kentucky, 1960.

### CLARK, Bruce
Stites & Harbison PLLC, Frankfort
502 223 3477
*Recommended in Environment*

### CLARK JR, L Jude
Frost Brown Todd LLC, Louisville
502 568 0260
jclark@fbtlaw.com
*Recommended in Real Estate*
**Practice Areas:** Real estate finance; commercial finance; real estate acquisitions, dispositions, leasing and development; affordable housing tax credit investments; zoning and land use.
**Prof. Memberships:** Fellow, American College of Mortgage Attorneys; American Bar Association, Real Property Probate and Trust Law Section; American Bar Association Forum on Affordable Housing; Kentucky and Indiana State Bar Associations.
**Career:** Member, Frost Brown Todd, LLC, joined 1999. Vice-Chair, Commercial Transactions and Real Estate Department.
**Publications:** 'Between a Rock and a Hard Place: Representing Owners in SNDA Negotiations', ICSC Publications.
**Personal:** Born 8 August 1955; JD University of Louisville, 1981; BS University of Kentucky, 1977.

### CLAY, Richard
Woodward, Hobson & Fulton LLP, Louisville 502 581 8000
*Recommended in Litigation*

### CLEARY, Richard
Greenebaum Doll & McDonald PLLC, Louisville 502 589 4200
*Recommended in Employment*

### COCKRUM, James
Frost Brown Todd LLC, Louisville
502 568 0317
jcockrum@fbtlaw.com
*Recommended in Employment*
**Practice Areas:** Mr Cockrum practices management-side labor and employment law representing employers before federal and state courts and administrative agencies.
**Prof. Memberships:** Kentucky Bar Association; Louisville Bar Association.
**Career:** Mr Cockrum has been a member of Frost Brown Todd LLC since its inception. He joined Brown, Todd & Heyburn in 1987.
**Publications:** Mr Cockrum has authored private seminar publications for seminars sponsored by the Kentucky Chamber of Commerce, the University of Louisville, the University of Kentucky and other organizations.
**Personal:** Born 16 August 1958. JD - Indiana University (Bloomington) 1987. BA - Kentucky Wesleyan College (cum laude) 1980.

### COLEMAN, Tony
Frost Brown Todd LLC, Louisville
502 568 0354
tcoleman@fbtlaw.com
*Recommended in Employment*

### COLLIER, Philip W
Stites & Harbison PLLC, Lexington
502 681 0415
pcollier@stites.com
*Recommended in Litigation*
**Practice Areas:** Business, insurance and class action defense litigation.
**Prof. Memberships:** Admitted to practice in Kentucky and United States Supreme Court. Member of American and Kentucky Bar Associations.
**Career:** Member, Stites & Harbison. Presented oral arguments before United States Supreme Court in Itel Containers International Corp. v Huddleston, 113 S.Ct. 1095 (US 1993). Appellate arguments before Kentucky Court of Appeals, Tennessee Supreme Court and United States Court of Appeals for the 6th Circuit.
**Publications:** Lecturer, Kentucky Bar Association Convention, 'Disputes in Closely Held Businesses', June 2003.
**Personal:** JD, University of Kentucky, 1979; BA, with high distinction, University of Kentucky, 1976.

### CONNER, Stewart
Wyatt, Tarrant & Combs, LLP, Louisville
502 562 7223
sconner@wyattfirm.com
*Recommended in Corporate/M&A*
**Practice Areas:** Managing Partner and Chair of the firm's Executive Committee (1988-2000). He concentrates his practice in the corporate finance, securities, and banking areas and is a frequent lecturer on securities and banking law.
**Prof. Memberships:** He serves on the Board of Directors of the DNP Select Dream Fund, and Lousiville Water Company, Boy Scouts of America. He is a Fellow of the American and Kentucky Bar Foundations.
**Publications:** He has authored numerous articles and handbooks for practitioners.
**Personal:** Mr Conner received his BSC Degree in 1963 and his JD Degree (cum laude) in 1966 from the University of Louisville.

### CONNIFF, Dennis J
Frost Brown Todd LLC, Louisville
502 568 0398
dconniff@fbtlaw.com
*Recommended in Environment*
**Practice Areas:** Reprsentation and counseling of clients with respect to issues concerning permitting and compliance with the state, federal, and local programs regulating air emissions, waste management and water quality.
**Prof. Memberships:** Louisville and Kentucky Bar Associations; admitted to practice in Kentucky, the Federal Courts for the Eastern and Western Districts of Ken-

945

tucky, and the Sixth Circuit Court of Appeals.
**Personal:** Chair, Greater Louisvile Inc., Air Toxics Task Force.

### CONNOLLY, Robert M
Stites & Harbison PLLC, Louisville
502 681 0424
rconnolly@stites.com
*Recommended in Litigation*
**Practice Areas:** Product liability and construction litigation. Over 80 trials and numerous appellate arguments.
**Prof. Memberships:** Admitted to practice in Kentucky, US 6th Circuit. Member of American, Kentucky Bar Associations, Louisville Bar Foundation, Inc., DRI, Kentucky Defense Council.
**Career:** Member, Stites & Harbison. Chair, Litigation Section.
**Publications:** Reported cases: Marley Cooling Tower v Caldwell Energy & Environmental, Inc., 280 F Supp 2d 651 (WD Ky 2003); Southeastern United Medigroup, Inc. v Hughes, et al., Ky, 952 SW2d 195 (1997); and others.
**Personal:** JD, Washington and Lee University, 1980. BA, Dartmouth College, Government (Honors), magna cum laude with high distinction, 1977.

### CORNETT, J Gregory
Stoll Keenon Ogden PLLC, Louisville
502 560 4210
greg.cornett@skofirm.com
*Recommended in Environment*
**Practice Areas:** Concentration in utility and energy regulatory and litigation work, representing clients in matters such as rate proceedings, applications for certificates of convenience and necessity, applications for construction certificates, fuel adjustment proceedings, territorial disputes, consumer complaints, and contract and personal injury disputes. Represents other businesses and professionals in business and professional liability and licensure matters.
**Prof. Memberships:** American, Kentucky and Louisville Bar Associations; Energy Bar Association; Defense Research Institute; Kentucky Defense Counsel, Inc.
**Personal:** University of Kentucky College of Law (JD, 1995); University of Kentucky (BA, 1992).

### CORYELL II, Cornelius
Wyatt, Tarrant & Combs, LLP, Louisville
502 589 5235
*Recommended in Litigation*

### CROMER, Brian A
Stites & Harbison PLLC, Louisville
502 681 0440
bcromer@stites.com
*Recommended in Corporate/M&A*
**Practice Areas:** Business and Finance Service Group. Practice emphasis in business law, international law, secured transactions, commercial law, banking, real estate law, mergers and acquisitions, securities law and general corporate matters.
**Prof. Memberships:** Admitted to practice in Kentucky, 1990. Member of American, Kentucky and Louisville Bar Associations.
**Career:** Member of Stites & Harbison. With the firm since 1993. Served as a commercial banking officer prior to law school.
**Personal:** JD, with high distinction, University of Kentucky, 1990; Editor-in-Chief, Kentucky Law Journal; Order of the Coif. BA, Business Administration, Bellarmine University, 1983.

### CRONAN IV, Charles J
Stites & Harbison PLLC, Louisville
501 681 0430
ccronan@stites.com
*Recommended in Litigation*
**Practice Areas:** Business litigation. General civil, medico-business and products liability litigation.
**Prof. Memberships:** Admitted to practice in Kentucky (1970). Fellow of the American College of Trial Lawyers, Member of Federation of Defense and Corporate Counsel and Defense Research Institute, Member of American, Kentucky and Louisville Bar Associations, and Kentucky Bar Foundation.
**Career:** US Navy Judge Advocate General's Corps, 1970-74. Joined Stites & Harbison in 1974. Managing Partner, 1994-97. Listed in The Best Lawyers in America, 1989-present.
**Personal:** JD, cum laude, University of Louisville, 1970. BA, Government, Wesleyan University, 1967. Married, four grown children.

### CRYDER, Bruce
Greenebaum Doll & McDonald PLLC, Lexington 859 231 8500
*Recommended in Environment*

### CURTZ, Chauncey SR
Dinsmore & Shohl LLP, Lexington
859 425 1035
curtz@dinslaw.com
*Recommended in Environment*
**Practice Areas:** Mineral law; Chairman of Natural Resources Practice Group of Dinsmore & Shohl LLP; arbitration of commercial contracts relating to production and sale of coal.
**Prof. Memberships:** Trustee, Energy and Mineral Law Foundation, Trustee Natural Council of Coal Lessors.
**Career:** Counsel, Dinsmore & Shohl LLP; President, Coal, Energy Investments & Management, LLC; Chairman, United American Resources, LP.
**Publications:** Author: 'Market Price Reopeners in Long Term Coal Supply Contracts' (EMLF Annual Proceedings, 1994); 'The Applicant Violator System Under SMCRA Ownership and Control Regulations' (U.K. Journal of Mineral Law and Policy, 1990); Responsive Pleadings (UK/CLE Practitioners Manual, 1989).

### DAVIS, R Eberley
Stoll Keenon Ogden PLLC, Lexington
859 231 3087
eberley.davis@skofirm.com
*Recommended in Environment*
**Practice Areas:** Concentration in areas of bankruptcy, environmental and natural resources, and general business and corporate law.
**Prof. Memberships:** Fayette County, Kentucky and American Bar Associations.
**Personal:** University of Kentucky (BA, high distinction, 1979; Phi Beta Kappa; MBA, 2000); University of Kentucky College of Law (JD, with distinction, 1982; Order of the Coif, Kentucky Law Journal). Admitted to practice in 1982.

### DAWAHARE, Debra
Wyatt, Tarrant & Combs, LLP, Lexington
859 288 7617
ddawahare@wyattfirm.com
*Recommended in Employment*
**Practice Areas:** Co-Chair of the firm's Labor and Employment Group.
**Career:** She was co-counsel in the landmark case of Rose v Council for Better Education, which declared Kentucky's school finance system unconstitutional. She speaks on employment issues, conducts training seminars, counsels management about employment issues of all kinds, and defends employers in state, federal, and local forums.
**Publications:** She contributed to the Kentucky Chamber of Commerce's 'The Kentucky Employer's Guide to Hiring and Firing' (1999), and has published numerous articles on employment law.
**Personal:** BA, Centre College; MA and JD, University of Kentucky.

### DIAMOND, Ivan
Greenebaum Doll & McDonald PLLC, Louisville 502 589 4200
*Recommended in Corporate/M&A*

### DOHENY JR, Frank
Dinsmore & Shohl LLP, Louisville
502 540 2300
*Recommended in Litigation*

### DOLSON, Scott
Frost Brown Todd LLC, Louisville
502 568 0203
sdolson@fbtlaw.com
*Recommended in Corporate/M&A*
**Practice Areas:** Firm Practice Leader in corporate/M&A and tax. Practice emphasis includes business and tax planning for business start-ups and joint ventures, representing buyers or sellers in negotiated transactions, and representing shareholders and LLC members in freeze-out transactions and owner disputes. Experience handling federal and state civil tax controversies.
**Prof. Memberships:** Admitted to practice in Kentucky (1982). Member of the Kentucky and Louisville Bar Associations.
**Career:** Frost Brown Todd LLC Member.
**Publications:** 'Kentucky Limited Liability

Companies', 'Business Succession Planning' and 'Kentucky Corporations Handbook.'
**Personal:** UVA Law, Harvard College.

### ELDRED JR, Marshall Polk
Frost Brown Todd LLC, Louisville
502 568 0262
meldred@fbtlaw.com
*Recommended in Real Estate*
**Practice Areas:** Member of Commercial Transaction/Real Estate Department. He concentrates in areas of real estate acquisition, zoning, financing, development, construction, lease/sale of the finished project and certain real estate related litigation, such as condemnation, receiverships and leasehold disputes.
**Prof. Memberships:** Louisville, Kentucky and American Bar Associations. past President and current Board Member Legal Aid Society and Isaac W Bernheim Foundation; serves as General Counsel for Home Builders Association of Louisville for the past 23 years.
**Personal:** Vanderbilt University BA, 1960; University of Kentucky JD, 1963 (Order of the Coif, Kentucky Law Journal).

### ELY III, Hiram
Greenebaum Doll & McDonald PLLC, Louisville 502 589 4200
*Recommended in Litigation*

### ESCHELS, Philip
Greenebaum Doll & McDonald PLLC, Louisville 502 589 4200
*Recommended in Employment*

### FENZEL, Mark S
Middleton Reutlinger PSC, Louisville
502 584 1135
mfenzel@middreut.com
*Recommended in Litigation*
**Practice Areas:** Mr Fenzel specializes in insurance defense, professional errors and omissions, school law and commercial litigation. He is Chair of the firm's Insurance Practice.
**Prof. Memberships:** Admitted to practice in United States Supreme Court and Kentucky. Member of National School Board Association, American Bar Association, Torts and Insurance Section; Louisville Bar Foundation; Citizens for Better Judges.
**Career:** Mr Fenzel was involved in a landmark negligence case (Kirschner v Louisville Gas & Electric Company)and McGinnis v Taitano, involving federal procedure and international jurisdictional issues. He also handled cases involving important school law and constitutional issues. (Blau v Fort Thomas Schools, Beckham v Jefferson County Schools and Cornett v Jefferson County Schools). Mr Fenzel was an attorney with the Judge Advocate General's Corps of the US Navy. For two years he was a trial attorney at Subic Bay Naval Base in the Phillipines, handling complex criminal court martials and trying cases on board ships in the Indian Ocean. Mr Fenzel was the first

Special Assistant to consolidate Navy prosecution of federal crimes in San Diego County. Military awards include Navy Achievement Medal, Navy Expeditionary Ribbon and Meritorious Unit Citation. **Personal:** University of Louisville School of Law; University of Kentucky (BS Accounting).

### FLEISCHAKER, Jon
Dinsmore & Shohl LLP, Louisville
502 540 2319
jon.fleischaker@dinslaw.com
*Recommended in Employment*
**Practice Areas:** Practice emphasizes communications law as well as employment law. Has been actively engaged with counseling and defending newspapers, radio stations and television stations. Has extensive employment law practice including litigation in numerous state and federal forums. **Prof. Memberships:** Admitted in Kentucky. Member of American Bar Association, Louisville Bar Association, Kentucky Bar Association, Kentucky Press Association, The Fellows of the American Bar Foundation, The Media Law Resource Center, Life Fellow, Kentucky Bar Association. **Career:** Joined Dinsmore & Shohl as Partner in 1997. **Personal:** JD, University of Pennsylvania Law School, magna cum laude (1970); BA, Swarthmore College (1967).

### GATHRIGHT JR, Joseph
Weber & Rose, Louisville
502.589.2200
*Recommended in Real Estate*

### GIESEL, James A
Frost Brown Todd LLC, Louisville
502 568 0307
jgiesel@fbtlaw.com
*Recommended in Corporate/M&A*
**Practice Areas:** Practicing in the general corporate, transactional and securities law areas, with significant experience involving corporate governance, public offerings, banking and investment management. **Prof. Memberships:** Member of Kentucky and Louisville Bar Associations; Louisville Bar Foundation, Fellow and Board Member. **Personal:** Mr Giesel received his JD degree (cum laude) in 1985 from Harvard Law School and his BA degree (magna cum laude) in 1982 from Yale University.

### GLASSCOCK, C Edward
Frost Brown Todd LLC, Louisville
502 568 0230
eglasscock@fbtlaw.com
*Recommended in Corporate/M&A*
**Practice Areas:** Co-Chairman of Mergers and Acquisitions Section. Has extensive experience in mergers and acquisitions, joint ventures and venture capital

transactions. **Prof. Memberships:** Admitted to practice in Kentucky (1969); Chambers & Partners, Chambers USA, ranked number one Corporate/M&A attorney in Kentucky; selected and listed in Naifeh and Smith, The Best Lawyers in America (1991-2005); Kentucky Bar Association, Past Chairman, Corporations, Banking and Business Law Section; American Bar Association, Member, Mergers and Acquisitions Committee; Louisville Bar Association, past Chairman, Corporations, Banking and Business Law Section. **Career:** Joined Frost Brown Todd (FBT), formerly Brown, Todd & Heyburn,1969; Member, 1974; Managing Partner, Brown, Todd & Heyburn, 1977-2001; Co-Managing Member, FBT (2001-present); Member, Compensation Committee, FBT. **Publications:** Glasscock, Lester, Lyndrup and Tannon, 'Buying and Selling a Business in Kentucky', 1974 & 1975, (1993, University of Kentucky College of Law/Office of Continuing Legal Education); Dolson, Glasscock, et al, 'Buying and Selling a Business in Kentucky', 1972, (2002, University of Kentucky College of Law/Office of Continuing Legal Education, 2d ed); Dolson, Glasscock, et al, 'Kentucky Corporation Law', Chapter 6, (1997, University of Kentucky College of Law/Office of Continuing Legal Education). **Personal:** JD with high distinction, University of Kentucky, 1969; Order of The Coif; Kentucky Law Journal, Member of Staff; Recipient, Outstanding Student Award, University of Kentucky, Phi Delta Phi, Graduate of the Year; BS Civil Engineering, 1966.

### GORTON, William T
Stites & Harbison PLLC, Lexington
859 226 2241
wgorton@stites.com
*Recommended in Environment*
**Practice Areas:** Environmental, natural resources, agriculture, energy and surety law, environmental audits and due diligence related to environmentally sensitive commercial transactions. **Prof. Memberships:** Admitted to practice in Kentucky, Pennsylvania and federal courts. Member of American, Kentucky and Pennsylvania Bar Associations. **Career:** Member, Stites & Harbison. University of Kentucky, assistant professor in Environmental Law, College of Agriculture, Natural Resources Conservation, 1998-present. Associate, Buchanan-Ingersoll, Philadelphia, 1989-93. Manager, Skelly and Loy Engineers - Consultants, 1976-85. **Publications:** 'A Primer for Engineering and Technical Professionals Regarding Reclamation and Environmental Surety Bonds.' **Personal:** JD, with distinction, University of Kentucky, 1988; BS, Pennsylvania State University, 1976.

### GREENWELL, Charles D
Middleton Reutlinger PSC, Louisville
502 584 1135
cgreenwell@middreut.com
*Recommended in Litigation*
**Practice Areas:** Mr Greenwell concentrates in litigation arising from complex disputes involving banking, insurance, medical and railroad industries. **Prof. Memberships:** Admitted to practice in US Supreme Court. Member of Kentucky and Louisville Bar Associations; Kentucky Bar Foundation; American Bar Association, Business Law and Tort Trial and Insurance Sections; National Association of Railroad Trial Counsel, former Executive Board Member; American Trial Lawyers Association; Kentucky Academy of Trial Attorneys. **Career:** Mr Greenwell won multi-million dollar recoveries for wrongful deaths for mothers and babies against three pharmaceutical manufacturers. He represented patients in Sisters of Charity Health Systems, Inc. v Raikes, KY, (Kentucky Supreme Court recognized an exception to statutory peer review privilege). Mr Greenwell was lead counsel in Kentucky's landmark lender liability and punitive damages case, (Hanson v American National Bank & Trust Co.). His experience in insurer insolvencies and liquidations includes organization, representation and successful recovery for a multi-member, multi-state creditors' group of financial institutions from thirteen states. Mr Greenwell represented American International Group in a multi-district liquidation of Delta America Re Insurance Company (Stephens v American Home Assurance Company). And is presently lead counsel for trustees in rehabilitation and class action proceedings concerning a major self insurance group. He successfully defended banks and insurance companies against claims of bad faith (Baldwin v North American Company for Life and Health Insurance).

### GRIFFITH, Richard
Stoll Keenon Ogden PLLC, Lexington
859 231 3036
rick.griffith@skofirm.com
*Recommended in Employment*
**Practice Areas:** Concentration in the area of labor and employment law and is one of the seven persons identified as the leading employment law attorneys in Kentucky in 2005. Regularly counsels employers and litigates all types of employment law disputes. **Prof. Memberships:** Fayette County, Kentucky and American (Member, Labor and Employment Law Section) Bar Associations. **Personal:** University of Kentucky (BA, History with distinction, 1980; Phi Beta Kappa); University of Kentucky College of Law (JD, 1983; staff member, Kentucky Law Journal; Moot Court Board). Listed

in 'Best Lawyers in America', labor and employment.

### GRIFFITH, Robert W
Stites & Harbison PLLC, Louisville
502 681 0422
rwgriffith@stites.com
*Recommended in Litigation*
**Practice Areas:** Business Litigation Service Group. Focus on corporate, commercial and real estate litigation. **Prof. Memberships:** Admitted to practice in Kentucky and New York. Member of American, Kentucky and Louisville Bar Associations. **Career:** Member of Stites & Harbison. With the firm since 1982.

### HABLE, Kevin
Wyatt, Tarrant & Combs, LLP, Louisville
502 589 5235
*Recommended in Corporate/M&A*

### HADEN JR, William H
Stites & Harbison PLLC, Louisville
502 681 0473
bhaden@stites.com
*Recommended in Real Estate*
**Practice Areas:** Real estate lending, commercial leasing, tax exempt financings. **Prof. Memberships:** Admitted to practice in Kentucky. Member of American and Kentucky Bar Associations; National Association of Bond Lawyers; International Council of Shopping Centers. **Career:** Member, Stites & Harbison. Law Clerk, Kentucky Supreme Court, 1972-73. **Publications:** 'Limited Liability Company Annotated Forms Compendium', 1995; ccontributing editor, Kentucky, 'State By State Guide to Commercial Real Estate Leases', Aspen Publishers, 2006; 'Implied Covenants of Continuous Operation in Percentage Leases: Was Charles Dickens Right', Commercial Leasing Law & Strategy, November 1999. **Personal:** JD, University of Kentucky, 1972. BA, History, University of Kentucky, 1969.

### HAGERTY, Timothy
Frost Brown Todd LLC, Louisville
502 589 5400
*Recommended in Environment*

### HALE, David J
Reed Weitkamp Schell & Vice PLLC, Louisville 502 657 1356
dhale@rwsvlaw.com
*Recommended in Litigation*
**Practice Areas:** Litigation Section. Business, insurance and governmental litigation in state and federal trial and appellate courts; administrative law. **Prof. Memberships:** Kentucky, Louisville, American and Federal Bar Associations. **Career:** Admitted to practice in Kentucky, 1992. Member, Reed Weitkamp Schell & Vice PLLC. Assistant US Attorney, US Attorney's Office for the Western District of Kentucky (civil and criminal divisions), 1995-99.

**Publications:** Kentucky Chapter, Business Torts Desk Reference, Aspen 2006
**Personal:** BA, Vanderbilt University, 1989; JD, University of Kentucky (National Moot Court Team), 1992; US Department of Justice Civil Trial School, 1995; Leadership Kentucky, 2002; Member, Executive Committee, Louisville Urban League.

## HALEY III, Raymond
Woodward, Hobson & Fulton LLP, Louisville 502 581 8000
*Recommended in Employment*

## HALLOS, Jeffrey L
Frost Brown Todd LLC, Lexington
859 244 3256
jhallos@fbtlaw.com
*Recommended in Corporate/M&A*
**Practice Areas:** Vice-Chair of the Corporate Department and Co-Chair of the firm's Mergers and Acquisitions and International Practice Groups. Advises clients regarding mergers and acquisitions, corporate finance transactions, domestic and international financing transactions, and private equity investments.
**Prof. Memberships:** Admitted to practice in California (1989) (currently inactive), District of Columbia (1991), Kentucky (1996).
**Career:** Joined Frost Brown Todd LLC, 1996; Member, 1998. Previously practiced in the Los Angeles, Washington DC and Hong Kong offices of Latham & Watkins.
**Personal:** Born 18 July 1963; JD (cum laude) Cornell Law School, 1988; BA Bucknell University (magna cum laude, Phi Beta Kappa), 1985.

## HAMILTON, Shannon Antle
Stites & Harbison PLLC, Louisville
502 681 0469
shamilton@stites.com
*Recommended in Employment*
**Practice Areas:** Labor and Employment Law Service Group (Co-Chair). Emphasis in litigation of complex employment law issues.
**Prof. Memberships:** Admitted to practice in Kentucky. Member of American, Kentucky and Louisville Bar Associations.
**Career:** Member of Stites & Harbison. Co-Chair of the firm's Diversity Committee. Lead trial counsel experience in employment litigation and has tried numerous employment cases to verdict.
**Publications:** 4th Annual Kentucky Human Resources Seminar, Kentucky Chamber of Commerce, Louisville, Ky and Lexington, Ky, June 8-9, 2005 and June 21-22, 2005.
**Personal:** JD, University of Louisville, 1988; BSBA, University of Louisville, 1985.

## HATFIELD, C Kent
Stoll Keenon Ogden PLLC, Louisville
502 568 5745
kent.hatfield@skofirm.com
*Recommended in Environment*

**Practice Areas:** Concentration in antitrust and trade regulation, public utility law, telecommunications regulation and corporate law and litigation. Corporate practice involves financing mergers and acquisitions, restructuring, corporate valuations and shareholder disputes. Corporate secretary to a large manufacturing joint venture and serves as principal outside counsel to a number of corporations.
**Prof. Memberships:** Louisville, Kentucky, American and Energy Bar Associations.
**Personal:** University of Kentucky (BS, 1970); University of Kentucky College of Law (JD, with high distinction, 1973); Trial Attorney, Antitrust Division, US Department of Justice, Washington, DC, 1973-78. Listed in 'Best Lawyers in America', energy law.

## HAYNES, Greg
Wyatt, Tarrant & Combs, LLP, Louisville
502 562 7363
ghaynes@wyattfirm.com
*Recommended in Litigation*
**Practice Areas:** Is a member of the firm's Executive Committee and is Co-Chair of the firm's Litigation Department. He concentrates his practice in the area of commercial litigation.
**Prof. Memberships:** He is a Fellow of the American College of Trial Lawyers and a Master and past President of The Brandeis Inn of Court.
**Career:** Mr Haynes has also served on numerous civic and charitable boards.
**Personal:** He received his BA Degree from Davidson College and his JD Degree from the University of Kentucky.

## HELM III, Kennedy
Stites & Harbison PLLC, Louisville
502 681 0449
khelmiii@stites.com
*Recommended in Corporate/M&A*
**Practice Areas:** Business, airport law, project finance and transportation law. Lead counsel to the $780 million Louisville Airport Improvement Program.
**Prof. Memberships:** Admitted in Kentucky (1968) and United States Supreme Court. Member of American, Kentucky and Louisville Bar Associations. Member of Outstanding Lawyers of America. Listed in Best Lawyers in America.
**Career:** Member of Stites & Harbison. Chairman of Stites & Harbison since 1997. Joined the firm in 1974.
**Publications:** Guest Lecturer, Aviation Law, Embry-Riddle Aeronautical University, 2000-04.
**Personal:** JD, University of Virginia, 1974; Order of the Coif. MA, Indiana University, 1970. BA, cum laude, Yale University, 1968.

## HENLEIN, Carl
Frost Brown Todd LLC, Louisville
502 568 0348
chenlein@fbtlaw.com
*Recommended in Litigation*

## HINES, Barry A
Stites & Harbison PLLC, Louisville
502 681 0525
bhines@stites.com
*Recommended in Real Estate*
**Practice Areas:** Real estate financing.
**Prof. Memberships:** Admitted to practice in Kentucky (1993). Member of American, Kentucky and Louisville Bar Associations; Mortgage Bankers Association of America; American College of Real Estate Lawyers; Commercial Mortgage Securities Association.
**Career:** Member, Stites & Harbison. Farm Credit Administration, Louisville Office, 1987-90, Bank Examiner for the Federal Regulatory Agency of the Farm Credit System.
**Publications:** 'Service Contracts: Protecting Real Estate Lenders', Probate & Property, March/April 1997 (co-author).
**Personal:** JD, cum laude, University of Louisville, 1993. BS, University of Kentucky, 1987.

## HINKLE IV, Samuel D
Stoll Keenon Ogden PLLC, Louisville
502 568 9100
sam.hinkle@skofirm.com
*Recommended in Litigation*
**Practice Areas:** Member of the firm's Litigation and General Business, Banking and Corporate Departments, concentrating in matters involving contracts and commercial matters, securities, bankruptcy issues, environmental law, unfair competition, IP, land use disputes and equine law.
**Prof. Memberships:** Louisville, Kentucky and American Bar Associations, including ABA sections on antitrust law, litigation, health law, natural resources, energy and environmental law.
**Personal:** Washington & Lee University (BA, 1969); Yale Law School (JD, 1972). Listed in 'Best Lawyers in America', Commercial Litigation.

## HOFFMANN, Warren
Frost Brown Todd LLC, Lexington
859 244 3220
whoffmann@fbtlaw.com
*Recommended in Environment*
**Practice Areas:** Corporate and commercial law emphasizing coal and electric utility industry.
**Prof. Memberships:** Admitted to practice, Kentucky, 1984. Energy and Mineral Law Foundation (Trustee); Kentucky Coal Association; Generation and Transmission Lawyers' Association; Western Kentucky Coal Association, Southern Coals, Lexington Coal Exchange.
**Career:** Joined firm in 1984. Expertise regarding acquisitions and dispositions of coal companies; utility generation, transmission and distribution; sales and leases of coal reserves; coal supply agreements and related transportation matters; coal company reorganizations, permitting, financing, and other operational issues.

## HINES, Barry A
**Personal:** Born: Newark, New Jersey, 1957; JD University of Kentucky, 1984; BA University of Kentucky, 1979

## HOPSON, Edwin
Wyatt, Tarrant & Combs, LLP, Louisville
502 562 7360
ehopson@wyattfirm.com
*Recommended in Employment*
**Practice Areas:** Member of the firm's Labor and Employment Practice Group.
**Prof. Memberships:** Mr Hopson is a Fellow of the College of Labor and Employment Lawyers, Inc.
**Career:** He began his career, with the US Department of Labor, and later became a field attorney with the National Labor Relations Board in Baltimore, Maryland. He returned to Louisville in 1974 and became associated with the firm.
**Personal:** He received a BSL Degree, and JD Degree from the University of Louisville School of Law, and an LLM degree (with highest honors), from George Washington University.

## HOVIOUS, R Gregg
Tachau Maddox Hovious & Dickens PLC, Louisville 502 588 2010
ghovious@tmhd.com
*Recommended in Litigation*
**Practice Areas:** General commercial and healthcare litigation.
**Career:** In 2004, a Kentucky municipality engaged him to investigate improprieties by previous counsel, resulting in a substantial settlement. Previously, he successfully represented banks in lender liability actions, contract disputes and corporate takeover litigation; 40 Kentucky hospitals in successful class action against a regional insurer; obtained a $550,000 insurance settlement for destruction of warehoused goods in Vietnam; and obtained over $1 million in a terminated employee's arbitration. He is panel counsel for two national life insurers for ERISA and contract matters.
**Personal:** University of Alabama (BS, 1982); University of Kentucky (JD, 1986).

## INGRAM JR, Lindsey W
Stoll Keenon Ogden PLLC, Lexington
859 231 3033
lindsey.ingram@skofirm.com
*Recommended in Environment*
**Practice Areas:** Member of the firm's Litigation and General Business Departments, concentrating in the areas of litigation, environmental law and public law utility.
**Prof. Memberships:** Fayette County (President, 1978), Kentucky and American Bar Associations; Chairman of the Kentucky Bar Association Attorney Advertising Commission and a Member of the Kentucky Bar Association Task Force on Lawyer Advertising; Deputy Secretary and General Counsel of the Kentucky Natural Resources and Environmental Protection Cabinet.
**Personal:** Duke University (AB, 1961); Duke University College of Law (LLB,

1964). Listed in 'Best Lawyers in America', Energy Law.

### ISON, Eric
Greenebaum Doll & McDonald PLLC, Louisville 502 589 4200
*Recommended in Litigation*

### JAKUBOWICZ, Janet
Greenebaum Doll & McDonald PLLC, Louisville 502 589 4200
*Recommended in Litigation*

### JOSEPH III, Alfred S
Stites & Harbison PLLC, Louisville
502 681 0465
fjoseph@stites.com
*Recommended in Real Estate*
**Practice Areas:** Real estate law.
**Prof. Memberships:** Admitted to practice in Kentucky (1968). Member of American, Kentucky and Louisville Bar Associations and American College of Real Estate Lawyers. Listed in 'The International Who's Who of Business Lawyers'.
**Career:** Counsel, Stites & Harbison. Listed in the 'Real Estate Lawyers' section of The Best Lawyers in America.
**Publications:** Author, Kentucky Chapter, State-By-State Guide to Commercial Real Estate Leases, Mark Senn, editor, 2004; co-author, 'Certificates of Insurance: The Illusion of Protection,' Probate & Property, Jan/Feb 1995.
**Personal:** JD, University of Michigan, 1968. BA, cum laude and Honors, Wesleyan University, 1965.

### KAPLAN, David
Frost Brown Todd LLC, Louisville
502 568 0356
dkaplan@fbtlaw.com
*Recommended in Litigation*
**Practice Areas:** Commercial, regulatory, and administrative agency litigation.
**Prof. Memberships:** Kentucky and Louisville Bar Associations.
**Career:** Member in the Commercial Litigation and Appellate Groups. Specializes in commercial and regulatory matters, representation before state and federal agencies, and advising clients on administrative law and constitutional questions. Former Assistant Attorney General and counsel to the Department of the Treasury. Law clerk to Judge John Heyburn II of the US District Court for the Western District of Kentucky.
**Personal:** MPP, Harvard University, 1997; JD, Harvard Law School, magna cum laude, 1997; BA, University of North Carolina at Chapel Hill, 1993.

### KEETON, Charles R
Frost Brown Todd LLC, Louisville
502 568 0257
ckeeton@fbtlaw.com
*Recommended in Corporate/M&A*
**Practice Areas:** Co-Chair of Commercial Transactions, Financial Restructuring and Information Technology and Internet Commerce Practice Groups.
**Prof. Memberships:** Member American

Bar Association, American Bankruptcy Institute, Kentucky Bar Association (past Chair, Commercial Law Section), and Louisville Bar Association (past Chair, Business Law Section).
**Career:** Joined predecessor of Frost Brown Todd LLC in 1975, became Partner January 1981.
**Publications:** Author, articles in various publications, recently, '10 Ways Revised Article 9 Will Change Your (Lending) Life', July 2000 Kentucky Banker; frequent seminar speaker, including sponsored by Practicing Law Institute, Kentucky Bar Association, University of Kentucky College of Law, and Louisville Bar Association. Adjunct Instructor of Law, Secured Transactions, Brandeis School of Law, University of Louisville, last taught Fall 1999.
**Personal:** Born 8 November 1949. Order of the Coif, 1975; JD (With High Distinction), University of Kentucky, 1975; AB (summa cum laude), Marshall University, 1971.

### KING, June
Greenebaum Doll & McDonald PLLC, Louisville 502 589 4200
*Recommended in Corporate/M&A*

### KING, W Gregory
Stoll Keenon Ogden PLLC, Louisville
502 560 4284
greg.king@skofirm.com
*Recommended in Litigation*
**Practice Areas:** Concentration in defense of medical malpractice, and product liability, as well as will and trust contests, and general civil litigation. Has extensive jury trial experience, including defense of professional negligence, and plaintiff's personal injury and business fraud.
**Prof. Memberships:** American, Kentucky, and Louisville Bar Associations (President, 2000; Distinguished Service Award, 2005); Kentucky Academy of Trial Attorneys; Association of Trial Lawyers of America; Kentucky Defense Counsel, Inc.; Defense Research Institute.
**Personal:** University of Kentucky (JD, 1982); Kentucky Wesleyan College (BA, 1979). 'Best Lawyers in America', Personal Injury Litigation; Board Certified, National Board of Trial Advocates.

### KIRK, Michael K
Wyatt, Tarrant & Combs, LLP, Louisville
502 562 7306
mkirk@wyattfirm.com
*Recommended in Employment*
**Practice Areas:** Labor and employment.
**Prof. Memberships:** Louisville, Kentucky, New York, and American Bar Associations, the bars of the United States District Courts for Eastern and Western Kentucky and the United States Court of Appeals for the Sixth Circuit.
**Career:** Assistant District Attorney for Ulster County, NY (1985-87).
**Personal:** He received his BA Degree in 1980 from Colgate University, his JD Degree in 1983 from the University of Louisville Brandeis School of Law, and

his LLM Degree in 1985 from Georgetown University School of Law.

### LEET, Byron E
Wyatt, Tarrant & Combs, LLP, Louisville
502 562 7354
bleet@wyattfirm.com
*Recommended in Litigation*
**Practice Areas:** Civil trial, litigation and commercial law.
**Prof. Memberships:** Member of the Defense Research Institute, Federalist Society, and the Louisville, Kentucky, and American Bar Associations.
**Personal:** Mr Leet received his BA Degree in 1980 from the University of Louisville, cum laude, and his JD Degree in 1983 from Vanderbilt University, where he was a Member of the National Moot Court Team.

### LESTER, David
Stoll Keenon Ogden PLLC, Lexington
859 231 3082
david.lester@skofirm.com
*Recommended in Corporate/M&A*
**Practice Areas:** Practices in the areas of corporate law, business acquisitions, secured transactions and healthcare law.
**Prof. Memberships:** Fayette County, Kentucky and American Bar Associations.
**Personal:** Western Kentucky University (BS, 1970); University of Kentucky College of Law (JD, with high distinction, 1975). Listed in 'Best Lawyers in America', corporate law.

### LINDSAY, Colin Hugh
Dinsmore & Shohl LLP, Louisville
502 540 2312
colin.lindsay@dinslaw.com
*Recommended in Litigation*
**Practice Areas:** Litigation and trial practice, including commercial, intellectual property, product liability, pharmaceutical and mass tort. Member of Firm's Recruiting & Retention Committee, and Diversity Subcommittee
**Prof. Memberships:** American, Kentucky, New York, and Louisville Bar Associations (Board of Directors, Diversity Committee, and Committee on Judicial Integrity and Independence).
**Career:** Substantial trial experience in state and federal courts. Adjunct Instructor of Advanced Trial Practice at University of Louisville Law School.
**Publications:** 'Human Trafficking, the New Face of Slavery' (author). 'Advanced Trial Advocacy in Kentucky' (contributing author). 'Gaining the Competitive Edge: Litigating to Win Through Advanced Trial Advocacy in Kentucky' (contributing author).

### LOBB, James
Weber & Rose, Louisville
502 589 2200
*Recommended in Real Estate*

### LOVETT, John T
Frost Brown Todd LLC, Louisville
502 568 0263

jlovett@fbtlaw.com
*Recommended in Employment*
**Practice Areas:** Employment litigation, unions, and union avoidance.
**Prof. Memberships:** Charter Member, American Employment Law Council; Chairperson, Labor Lawyers Advisory Committee for the Council on Union-Free Environment (CUE); Kentucky Bar Association; Listed in the Best Lawyers in America; Kentucky Association General Contractors Award for Excellence; US District Court, Southern District of Indiana.
**Career:** Law clerk, US District Court, Western District of Kentucky (1981-82); Partner, Lovett & Lamar (1982-95); Member, Frost, Brown, Todd (1995-present).
**Personal:** JD with Distinction, Order of the Coif, University of Kentucky College of Law (1981); BA, Indiana University (1978); wife, Melissa, four daughters.

### LYNDRUP, Peggy
Greenebaum Doll & McDonald PLLC, Louisville 502 589 4200
*Recommended in Corporate/M&A*

### MACDONALD, Alan
Frost Brown Todd LLC, Louisville
502 568 0277
amacdonald@fbtlaw.com
*Recommended in Corporate/M&A*
**Practice Areas:** Co-Chair, firm's Public Companies and Securities Practice. Advises on securities offerings and compliance, corporate governance, mergers and aquisitions and corporate law.
**Prof. Memberships:** Admitted to the Kentucky Bar (1985). Member, American Bar Association, Section on Corporation, Banking and Business Law; Kentucky Bar Association, Business Law Section (Chair 2000-02); Louisville Bar Association, Business Law Section (Chair 1997).
**Career:** Joined Frost Brown Todd, 1985; became member 1993.
**Publications:** Co-author: 'Kentucky Corporate Law' (1997); 'Limited Liability Companies in Kentucky' (2nd ed. 2000); 'Business Succession Planning' (1998).
**Personal:** Born 8 June 1955. JD, Vanderbilt University, 1985; AB, Dartmouth College, 1977.

### MARTIN, Timothy
Frost Brown Todd LLC, Louisville
502 568 0274
tmartin@fbtlaw.com
*Recommended in Real Estate*
**Practice Areas:** Acquisition, zoning, land use, financing, leasing and development of commercial, retail, residential, industrial and office properties.
**Prof. Memberships:** Admitted to practice in Kentucky (1972). Member, American College of Real Estate Lawyers; International Council of Shopping Centers; American, Kentucky and Louisville Bar Associations.
**Career:** Joined Brown, Todd & Heyburn (now Frost Brown Todd LLC), 1972; became Partner, 1979; Chair of Frost

Brown Todd LLC Compensation Committee.
**Publications:** 'Federal Regulations Affecting Real Estate' published by University of Kentucky ('Kentucky Real Estate Law and Practice Handbook').
**Personal:** Born April 9, 1947. JD, University of Kentucky, 1972; BA, University of Kentucky, 1969.

## MATTINGLY, Bryan K
Frost Brown Todd LLC, Lexington
859 244 3235
bmattingly@fbtlaw.com
*Recommended in Corporate/M&A*
**Practice Areas:** Mergers and acquisitions; business law; corporate law.
**Prof. Memberships:** Admitted to practice law in Kentucky 1994.
**Career:** Mr Mattingly assists foreign and domestic clients in negotiating, structuring, financing and documenting mergers, acquisitions, dispositions and other business transactions. Regularly advises clients in connection with formation, venture capital and securities matters, as well as other general corporate transactions.
**Personal:** Born: Springfield, Kentucky, 1966. JD University of Kentucky, with distinction, 1994; BA Transylvania University, cum laude, 1989

## MATTINGLY, Patrick W
Wyatt, Tarrant & Combs, LLP, Louisville
502 562 7294
pmattingly@wyattfirm.com
*Recommended in Corporate/M&A*
**Practice Areas:** Member of the firm's General Business Practice Group. Concentrating his practice in the areas of start-up and emerging companies, general business, venture capital and private equity financings and mergers and acquisitions.
**Prof. Memberships:** He is a member of the Louisville (Corporate Practice Section) and American (Business, Banking & Corporate Law Section Venture Capital Committee) Bar Associations.
**Career:** He served as Chairman of the Firm's General Business group (1990-96).
**Personal:** He received his (BA, 1974) from Miami (of Ohio) University and his (JD, 1980) from the University of Louisville, (cum laude).

## MILLER, George
Wyatt, Tarrant & Combs, LLP, Lexington
859 288 7640
gmiller@wyattfirm.com
*Recommended in Employment*
**Practice Areas:** Labor and employment.
**Prof. Memberships:** American, Kentucky, and Fayette County Bar Associations.
**Career:** Mr Miller is a past Secretary and President of the Labor and Employment Law Section of the Kentucky Bar Association.
**Publications:** He is a frequent speaker and a published author on topics related to labor and employment law.
**Personal:** Mr Miller received a BA from Bloomsburg University of Pennsylvania

(1975), AM (1978) and PhD(1981) from Brown University, and a JD from the University of Kentucky College of Law (1984).

## MILLER, Winston
Frost Brown Todd LLC, Louisville
502 568 0296
wmiller@fbtlaw.com
*Recommended in Litigation*
**Practice Areas:** Civil litigation including diversified experience in products liability, mass tort, fire and explosion, employment and business litigation.
**Prof. Memberships:** American, Kentucky and Louisville Bar Associations, Defense Research Institute, and CPR.
**Career:** Defending complex multi-party cases arising out of catastrophic losses and serial litigation. Examples (San Juan DuPont Plaza Hotel Fire, The Breast Implant Litigation, The Station Night Club Fire and the West Pharmaceutical Fire, NC). Represents manufacturers of various products, devices, drugs, appliances, and materials. Represents area's largest employer in employment and business litigation.
**Personal:** JD University of Kentucky, 1970.

## MILLIMAN, James E
Middleton Reutlinger PSC, Louisville
502 584 1135
jmilliman@middreut.com
*Recommended in Litigation*
**Practice Areas:** Commercial litigation.
**Prof. Memberships:** Admitted to practice in United States Supreme Court. Member of Louisville Bar Association; Kentucky Bar Association; American Bar Association.
**Career:** James E Milliman engages in a diversified litigation practice with broad experience in commercial and intellectual property litigation. Mr Milliman has argued before the United States Supreme Court. He represented Brown & Williamson Tobacco Company in a highly publicized case, (Brown & Williamson Tobacco Company v Wigand) against a whistle blower in which he upheld the right of the company to protect its confidential information. Recently, Mr Milliman has handled extensive election litigation. He has experience dealing with media in high profile cases, including the Brown & Williamson case and his successful representation of the Governor of Kentucky in an action to disqualify him during the primary as a candidate. Mr Milliman's cases have been featured in 'Time', 'Newsweek', 'Forbes', 'Business Insurance', 'The Wall Street Journal', 'USA TODAY', 'The Sporting News', and 'ESPN's Outside the Lines'. Mr Milliman currently serves as a commentator on a weekly political television program, 'Hot Button' on WAVE 3, the NBC affiliate in Louisville.

## MONOHAN, David
Woodward, Hobson & Fulton LLP,

Louisville 502 581 8000
*Recommended in Litigation*

## MURPHY, Marc S
Stites & Harbison PLLC, Louisville
502 681 0536
mmurphy@stites.com
*Recommended in Litigation*
**Practice Areas:** Jury trial and commercial litigation. Practice emphasis on white collar criminal litigation and complex commercial and class action defense.
**Prof. Memberships:** Admitted to practice in Indiana (1984) and Kentucky (1988). Member of American, Kentucky and Louisville Bar Associations.
**Career:** Member of Stites & Harbison. Former military prosecutor, Judge Advocate General's Corps; former Commonwealth's Attorney. Joined the firm in 1997. Seasoned trial lawyer with over 20 years of courtroom experience, including military, handling challenging, high-profile, and complex commercial and white collar criminal cases.
**Personal:** JD, University of Louisville, 1984. BA, cum laude, University of Notre Dame, 1981.

## NEWELL, Richard F
Stoll Keenon Ogden PLLC, Louisville
502 560 4233
rick.newell@skofirm.com
*Recommended in Environment*
**Practice Areas:** Concentration on utility and energy matters, regulatory and other administrative hearings and practiced before state and federal agencies, and related appellate practice in both Kentucky and federal courts.
**Prof. Memberships:** American, Kentucky and Louisville Bar Associations; Energy Bar Association; American Judicature Society; Association of Life Insurance Counsel of America; Trial Commissioner for Kentucky Attorney Disciplinary Procedures.
**Personal:** Harvard Law School (LLB, 1956); Georgetown College (AB, 1953).

## NORTHAM, Patrick
Greenebaum Doll & McDonald PLLC, Louisville 502 589 4200
*Recommended in Corporate/M&A, Environment*

## OVERSTREET, Mark R
Stites & Harbison PLLC, Frankfort
502 209 1219
moverstreet@stites.com
*Recommended in Environment*
**Practice Areas:** Civil and administrative litigation with emphasis on business litigation, representation of utilities and other businesses before administrative agencies.
**Prof. Memberships:** Admitted to practice in Kentucky. Member of Kentucky Bar Association.
**Career:** Member, Stites & Harbison. Trial practice before state and federal courts in Kentucky. Appellate arguments before

Supreme Court of Kentucky, Court of Appeals of Kentucky and US Court of Appeals for the 6th Circuit.
**Publications:** 'Preclusive Effect of Administrative Agency Determinations in Subsequent Court Proceedings,' Kentucky Bar Association's Bench & Bar, March 2004.
**Personal:** JD, University of Kentucky, 1980; BA, University of Kentucky, 1976.

## PELFREY, D Patton
Frost Brown Todd LLC, Louisville
502 568 0252
ppelfrey@fbtlaw.com
*Recommended in Employment*
**Practice Areas:** Mr Pelfrey is Co-Chair of Frost Brown Todd's Labor and Employment Law Department and specializes in representing management.
**Career:** He has vast experience negotiating collective bargaining agreements, handling union avoidance campaigns and litigating cases involving all types of employee relations issues.
**Publications:** Mr Pelfrey recently authored chapters in 'The Developing Labor Law', (various editions) - considered to be the most authoritative treatise in the field of labor relations.
**Personal:** He earned the distinction of being included in all editions of Naifeh and Smith's 'The Best Lawyers in America' and is a Fellow of the College of Labor and Employment Lawyers.

## PERRY, Donna
Woodward, Hobson & Fulton LLP, Louisville 502 581 8000
*Recommended in Employment*

## PITT, Stephen
Wyatt, Tarrant & Combs, LLP, Louisville
502 589 5235
*Recommended in Litigation*

## PRICE, Glenn
Greenebaum Doll & McDonald PLLC, Louisville 502 589 4200
*Recommended in Real Estate*

## QUESENBERRY, Kathryn
Woodward, Hobson & Fulton LLP, Louisville 502 581 8000
*Recommended in Employment*

## REED, John S
Reed Weitkamp Schell & Vice PLLC, Louisville 502 657 1313
jreed@rwsvlaw.com
*Recommended in Litigation*
**Practice Areas:** Litigation Section. Practice includes business litigation in state and federal courts, antitrust counseling and litigation, and intellectual property litigation.
**Prof. Memberships:** American, Kentucky and Louisville (past President) Bar Associations.
**Career:** Admitted to practice in Kentucky, 1974. Partner in other firms, 1979-96. Founded Reed Weitkamp Schell & Vice PLLC in 1996.

**Publications:** Kentucky Chapter, Business Torts Desk Reference, Aspen 2006.
**Personal:** JD, University of Virginia, 1974. AB, University of Kentucky, with highest distinction, Phi Beta Kappa, 1971. Has served on a number of civic boards and is a founder and Chair of Leadership USA, Inc. Married, two children.

### RHORER, John R
Dinsmore & Shohl LLP, Lexington
859 425 1015
john.rhorer@dinslaw.com
*Recommended in Environment*
**Practice Areas:** Real estate, energy law, corporate.
**Prof. Memberships:** Trustee, Energy and Mineral Law Foundation; Kentucky Bar Association, Fayette County Bar Association; Lexington Coal Exchange.
**Career:** Partner, Dinsmore & Shohl LLP; Partner, Wyatt, Tarrant & Combs (1981-97).
**Personal:** JD with Distinction, Order of the Coif, University of Kentucky College of Law (1981); BA, Government, Centre College of Kentucky (1978).

### RIGGS, Kendrick R
Stoll Keenon Ogden PLLC, Louisville
502 560 4222
kendrick.riggs@skofirm.com
*Recommended in Environment*
**Practice Areas:** Vice-Chair of the firm's Management Committee and member of the Finance Committee. Concentrates on representing energy and telecommunications clients before Kentucky and Virginia regulatory agencies and courts. Extensive administrative trial experience involving all phases of representation, appearing before state and federal courts representing energy and telecommunications clients in commercial and industry disputes.
**Prof. Memberships:** Kentucky and Virginia Bar Associations; Energy Bar Association; Energy and Mineral Law Foundation.
**Personal:** University of Kentucky (JD, 1982); Wittenberg University (BA, cum laude, 1979). 'Best Lawyers in America', Public Utility Law, since 1997-98; Martindale-Hubbell AV Rating since 1996; 2006 Louisville Magazine's 'Top Lawyer'.

### ROBINSON III, Wm
Greenebaum Doll & McDonald PLLC, Covington 859 655 4200
*Recommended in Litigation*

### ROYSE, David T
Stoll Keenon Ogden PLLC, Louisville
859 231 3681
david.royse@skofirm.com
*Recommended in Litigation*
**Practice Areas:** General litigation practice involving broad range of subject matters. Extensive experience in real estate litigation, eminent domain/condemnation, and planning and zoning. Handles significant estate and fiduciary litigation, equine-related litigation, large commercial disputes and administrative/regulato-

ry proceedings.
**Prof. Memberships:** Fayette County, Kentucky (Former Member, Executive Committee, Young Lawyers Section) and American Bar Associations; Association of Trial Lawyers of America.
**Personal:** Birmingham-Southern College (BA, cum laude, 1995); University of Kentucky College of Law (JD, cum laude, 1998).

### RUTLEDGE, Thomas E
Stoll Keenon Ogden PLLC, Louisville
502 560 4258
thomas.rutledge@skofirm.com
*Recommended in Corporate/M&A*
**Practice Areas:** Business and securities law with a focus on the law of business organizations.
**Prof. Memberships:** ABA Committee on Partnerships and Unincorporated Business Organizations and the Ad-Hoc Committee on Entity Rationalization. Section of Business Law Advisor to NCCUSL project to update Uniform Liability Company Act as well as drafting committees for Model Entity Transactions Act and Uniform Statutory Trust Act. Member of American Law Institute.
**Publications:** A national authority on business entity law, he has been published in the Kentucky Law Journal, Business Entities, The Business Lawyer, and Delaware Journal of Corporate Law.

### SAFFER, David
Stites & Harbison PLLC, Louisville
502 681 0547
dsaffer@stites.com
*Recommended in Real Estate*
**Practice Areas:** Concentrates practice in real estate and lending and regularly represents institutional lenders and borrowers in all types of commercial loan transactions including complex conduit-lending transactions.
**Prof. Memberships:** Member of the Louisville, Kentucky, and American Bar Associations. Member of the American College of Mortgage Attorneys.
**Career:** Member, Stites & Harbison. Joined the firm in 2004.
**Publications:** Co-author, 'Mortgages', UK/CLE Kentucky Real Estate and Practice Handbook, 2d Ed, 1996.
**Personal:** JD, cum laude, University of Louisville, 1995; BLS, summa cum laude, University of Evansville, 1992.

### SALES, Walter L
Stoll Keenon Ogden PLLC, Louisville
502 560 4252
walter.sales@skofirm.com
*Recommended in Employment*
**Practice Areas:** Concentration in labor and employment and commercial litigation with regular representation of both employers and employees in cases contesting the enforcement of covenants-not-to-compete, employee breach of fiduciary duty, and employee breach of confidentiality. Has tried several cases

including class action employment discrimination cases against the Equal Employment Opportunity Commission ranging from age discrimination to race, sex, sexual harassment, equal pay act, and ADA cases.
**Prof. Memberships:** American, Kentucky, and Louisville Bar Associations.
**Personal:** University of Kentucky (JD, 1973); Washington & Lee University (BA, 1970). Listed in 'Best Lawyers in America', labor and employment.

### SAVARISE, Jeffrey
Greenebaum Doll & McDonald PLLC, Louisville 502 589 4200
*Recommended in Employment*

### SCHELL, Ivan J
Reed Weitkamp Schell & Vice PLLC, Louisville 502 657 1341
ischell@rwsvlaw.com
*Recommended in Corporate/M&A*
**Practice Areas:** Member of Health Law, Corporate and Estate Planning Sections. His practice includes management and intergenerational transition planning for closely held businesses, medical corporation contract negotiation and government compliance, and wealth transfer planning.
**Prof. Memberships:** Member of American, Kentucky, Illinois and Louisville Bar Associations.
**Career:** Admitted to practice in Illinois, 1974, Kentucky, 1976; founding member Reed Weitkamp Schell & Vice 1996.
**Personal:** JD, University of Michigan, 1974. BS, Butler University 1968. Phi Eta Sigma. Chair, Buckhorn Children's Foundation.

### SEIFFERT, James C
Stites & Harbison PLLC, Louisville
502 681 0519
jseiffert@stites.com
*Recommended in Corporate/M&A*
**Practice Areas:** Mergers and acquisitions, corporate, taxation.
**Prof. Memberships:** Admitted to practice in Kentucky and Iowa. Member of American, Kentucky and Iowa Bar Associations.
**Career:** Member of Stites & Harbison.
**Publications:** 'Physicians Beware! Dealing with Tax-Exempt Healthcare Organizations Can be Hazardous to One's Financial Health', Journal of Kentucky Medical Association, February 1998; 'Man-O-War Restaurants, Inc. v John Martin, Jr, Ky Supreme Court Deals a Severe Blow to Compensatory Restricted Stock Arrangement', Louisville Bar Association Bar Briefs, May 1997.
**Personal:** JD, with high distinction, University of Louisville, 1980. LLM, Taxation, University of Miami, 1981. BA, American History, University of Iowa, 1977.

### SHELLER, John
Smith & Smith Attorneys, Louisville
502 587 0761
*Recommended in Employment*

### SHIVEL JR, Charles
Stoll Keenon Ogden PLLC, Lexington
859 231 3039
charles.shivel@skofirm.com
*Recommended in Litigation*
**Practice Areas:** Member of the firm's Litigation Department, concentrating in the area of business and complex commercial litigation, with a focus on commercial claims, including lender liability claims, fiduciary duties, intentional torts, contract disputes and matters involving all aspects of the coal industry.
**Prof. Memberships:** Fayette County, Kentucky, and American Bar Associations.
**Personal:** Berea College (AB, 1966); University of Kentucky College of Law (JD, with high distinction, 1972). Elected to Order of the Coif and was a member of the Kentucky Law Journal. Listed in 'Best Lawyers in America', Commercial Litigation.

### SMITH, Kevin
Smith & Smith Attorneys, Louisville
502 587 0761
*Recommended in Employment*

### SMITH III, James
Smith & Smith Attorneys, Louisville
502 587 0761
*Recommended in Employment*

### SNELL, Virginia
Wyatt, Tarrant & Combs, LLP, Louisville
502 562 7366
vsnell@wyattfirm.com
*Recommended in Litigation*
**Practice Areas:** Chair of the firm's Appellate Practice Group; member of the firm's Commercial Litigation Group.
**Prof. Memberships:** Formerly, Judicial Clerk, United States Court of Appeals, Fifth Circuit; Currently Member, Kentucky Supreme Court Civil Rights Committee; Currently, Vice President, Board of Trustees, Oldham County Public Library, and Member, State Advisory Council on Libraries.
**Personal:** BA Degree, University of Texas Plan II Honors Program, with highest honors and special honors in History; Member, Phi Beta Kappa; JD Degree, with honors, University of Texas Law School, 1981; Member, Order of the Coif, and articles editor, Texas Law Review.

### SNYDER, Sheryl
Frost Brown Todd LLC, Louisville
502 568 0247
ssnyder@fbtlaw.com
*Recommended in Litigation*
**Practice Areas:** Chair of Appellate Practice Group. Extensive experience in constitutional law, state and federal; antitrust, securities, trademark, copyright and other complex business litigation.
**Prof. Memberships:** Bars of the Supreme Courts of the United States, Kentucky, Tennessee, Texas, and Missouri; United States Courts of Appeals for the Third, Fourth, Sixth, Seventh, Eighth, Tenth and Eleventh Circuits. Past President, Ken-

tucky and Louisville Bar Associations.
**Career:** Joined Frost Brown Todd (then Brown, Todd & Heyburn) 1994. Executive Vice President and General Counsel, ICH Corporation (1990-94). Wyatt Tarrant & Combs (1973-90).
**Personal:** Born 11 October 1946. University of Kentucky, BA 1968, JD 1971.

### STEENROD, Ralston W
Stites & Harbison PLLC, Louisville
502 681 0436
rsteenrod@stites.com
*Recommended in Corporate/M&A*
**Practice Areas:** Practice includes corporate mergers, taxable acquisitions, tax-free reorganizations, contested takeovers and general corporate. Also includes bank holding company formations, rights of dissenting shareholders and securities registration and exemptions.
**Prof. Memberships:** Admitted to practice in Kentucky. Member of the American, Kentucky and Louisville Bar Associations.
**Career:** Member of Stites & Harbison. Joined the firm in 1971.
**Personal:** JD, University of Louisville, 1968; AB, cum laude, English, Princeton University, 1959.

### STOPHER, Edward H
Boehl Stopher & Graves, LLP, Louisville
502 589 5980
estopher@bsg-law.com
*Recommended in Litigation*
**Practice Areas:** Civil litigation and trial practice with emphasis on corporate law, Insurance law, product liability, legal malpractice and negligence matters.
**Prof. Memberships:** Mr Stopher is a Member of the Louisville Bar Association; Kentucky Bar Association; American Bar Association; Fellow, American College of Trial Lawyers; Fellow, International Society of Barristers; Association of Defense Trial Attorneys; Fellow, American Bar Foundation; National Association of Railroad Trial Counsel; Kentucky Defense Counsel; The Law Club; The Lawyers Club. He is listed in 'The Best Lawyers in America' 1989-2005.
**Career:** Mr Stopher was law clerk to Hon James F Gordon, United States Judge Western District of Kentucky, 1968-69. He joined Boehl Stopher & Graves, LLP, in 1969 and became Partner in 1970.
**Personal:** BA with honors, Davidson College, 1965; JD, University of Virginia, 1968.

### STRAUS, R James
Frost Brown Todd LLC, Louisville
502 568 0221
jstraus@fbtlaw.com
*Recommended in Corporate/M&A*
**Practice Areas:** Firm Practice Chair, Financial Institutions and Franchising. Has extensive experience in banking, distribution, purchasing groups and mergers and acquisitions.
**Prof. Memberships:** Admitted to practice in Kentucky (1974). Member of American Bar Association Sections on

Business, Banking and AntiTrust Law, and Forum on Franchising.
**Career:** Joined Frost Brown Todd 1974, became Partner, 1980. Corporate Department Chair.
**Personal:** Born 17 August 1946. JD, University of Chicago, 1974; BA, Yale University (cum laude), 1968; Captain USMC, Vietnam Veteran; Legal Aide Society Board of Directors.

### STRENCH, William
Frost Brown Todd LLC, Louisville
502 568 0207
wstrench@fbtlaw.com
*Recommended in Corporate/M&A*

### TACHAU, David Brandeis
Tachau Maddox Hovious & Dickens PLC, Louisville 502 588 2015
dtachau@tmhd.com
*Recommended in Litigation*
**Practice Areas:** General commercial, insurance, estate and employment litigation.
**Career:** Recent engagements include representation of PricewaterhouseCoopers in state government procurement litigation; dismissal of a RICO and fraud class action, Pratt v Ventas, Inc., 365 F3d 514 (6th Cir. 2004); federal jury trial yielding $28 million judgment, Monumental Life Insurance v Nationwide Retirement Solutions (WDKy 2003); and serving as litigation counsel for corporate fiduciary administering $30 million estate involving spousal renunciation, sale of closely-held business, pursuit of legal malpractice claims, and defense of action to remove executor.
**Personal:** Harvard College (AB, magna cum laude, 1978); University of Michigan (JD, 1982).

### THOMPSON, B Todd
Thompson Miller & Simpson PLC, Louisville 502 585 9900
*Recommended in Litigation*

### VICE, Robert B
Reed Weitkamp Schell & Vice PLLC, Louisville 502 589 1000
rvice@rwsvlaw.com
*Recommended in Real Estate*
**Practice Areas:** Real estate finance, taxation and development; partnership law and taxation.
**Prof. Memberships:** American, Kentucky and Louisville Bar Associations.
**Career:** Reed Weitkamp Schell & Vice and predecessor since 1990; Managing Director of Corporate Finance for an affiliate of PNC Financial Corp; President, Hilliard Lyons Real Estate Finance, real estate investment banking; legal practice in corporate, real estate and securities with Wyatt, Tarrant & Combs.
**Publications:** 'Kentucky Partnership Law', University of Kentucky College of Law, co-author.
**Personal:** JD, 1978, University of Kentucky College of Law, Order of the Coif; BA, 1975, University of Kentucky, with

high distinction, Honors Program.

### VINCENTI, Michael
Wyatt, Tarrant & Combs, LLP, Louisville
502 562 7518
mvincenti@wyattfirm.com
*Recommended in Real Estate*
**Practice Areas:** Co-Chair of the firm's Business Law Deparment and member of the Real Estate and Lending Practice Group.
**Prof. Memberships:** Mr Vincenti is a member of the American College of Real Estate Lawyers, the American College of Mortgage Attorneys, the International Council of Shopping Centers, the American Land Title Association (Lender's Counsel Group), Kentucky and Illinois Bar Associations.
**Publications:** He has written and lectured extensively on commercial leasing, mortgages, e-commerce's impact on real estate, loan documentation, workouts, title insurance, and real estate development matters.
**Personal:** Mr Vincenti received his BA from Johns Hopkins University in 1972 and his JD from New York University in 1975.

### WARD, Richard
Wyatt, Tarrant & Combs, LLP, Lexington
859 233 2012
*Recommended in Environment*

### WATT, Robert M
Stoll Keenon Ogden PLLC, Lexington
859 231 3043
robert.watt@skofirm.com
*Recommended in Environment*
**Practice Areas:** Member of the Litigation, General Business, Banking and Corporate Departments, concentrating on utility regulation and business and complex commercial litigation. Areas of particular substantive focus include utility rate and other regulation, contract disputes, intentional torts, corporate law disputes, securities laws and equine law matters.
**Prof. Memberships:** American, Kentucky and Fayette County Bar Associations.
**Personal:** Duke University (BA, 1969); University of Kentucky College of Law (JD, with distinction, 1973).

### WEITKAMP, Gary R
Reed Weitkamp Schell & Vice PLLC, Louisville 502 657 1312
gweitkamp@RWSVlaw.com
*Recommended in Corporate/M&A*
**Practice Areas:** Representing purchasers and sellers of operating businesses, with extensive experience in the healthcare industry and contracting and mining industries; advising and structuring business and tax aspects of transactions and new ventures; representing parties in aircraft sale transactions. Has represented taxpayers in federal and state tax controversies.
**Prof. Memberships:** ABA; KBA; and LBA (Business and Taxation Sections).
**Career:** Member in current and prede-

cessor firms since 1985.
**Publications:** Has written and lectured regarding business and taxation matters for local, regional and national organizations.
**Personal:** University of Cincinnati (JD 1979 - Order of the Coif); Wittenberg University (BA 1976)

### WILLIAMS, Ernest W
Stoll Keenon Ogden PLLC, Louisville
502 560 4243
ernest.williams@skofirm.com
*Recommended in Corporate/M&A*
**Practice Areas:** Concentration in the area of business acquisitions with regular representation of both buyers and sellers of businesses, including asset acquisitions, stock acquisitions, mergers, supply and distribution agreements, employment agreements, service agreements, and business planning for closely-held businesses. In an international context, has represented local businesses acquiring businesses or establishing joint venture arrangements in foreign countries, as well as representing foreign businesses seeking to acquire or establish local operations.
**Prof. Memberships:** Kentucky and Louisville Bar Associations.
**Personal:** Harvard Law School (JD, 1975); Murray State University (BA, 1975). Listed in 'Best Lawyers in America', Corporate Law.

### WILLIAMS, Thomas M
Stoll Keenon Ogden PLLC, Louisville
502 560 4279
tom.williams@skofirm.com
*Recommended in Employment*
**Practice Areas:** All aspects of employment litigation, counseling, and supervisor training, including class action defense and ERISA litigation.
**Prof. Memberships:** American Bar Association (Employment Rights and Responsibilities Subcommittee since 1999); Louisville Bar Association (President-Elect, Board of Directors, past Chair of Labor & Employment Section); Louisville Society for Human Resources Management (Labor Relations Chair); Society for Human Resources Management (SPHR designation).
**Personal:** University of Cincinnati (JD, 1990); College of William & Mary (BA, 1986). Listed in 'Best Lawyers in America', labor and employment; 2002 Award for Professional Excellence by the Louisville Society for Human Resources Management.

### WOODS III, C Laurence
Frost Brown Todd LLC, Louisville
502 589 5400
*Recommended in Employment*

### YOUNG, Cynthia
Wyatt, Tarrant & Combs, LLP, Louisville
502 589 5235
*Recommended in Corporate/M&A*

# BOEHL STOPHER & GRAVES LLP

## THE FIRM

**Executive Committee:** Edward H Stopher, Richard W Edwards, Jefferson K Streepey, Robert E Stopher, Raymond G Smith, Phillip J Reverman, Jr
**Partners:** 26
**Lawyers:** 50

**FIRM OVERVIEW:** Since 1895, Boehl Stopher & Graves LLP, has represented a wide variety of businesses all across Kentucky in State and Federal Courts. The firm's philosophy is simple: Though the firm is highly effective in the courtroom, it is more concerned with bringing matters to a satisfactory conclusion, whether it be through negotiation, mediation, arbitration, or litigation. From insurance to energy, from workers' compensation to mergers and acquisitions, the diversity of the firm's experience in civil litigation has given it depth and breadth in the areas in which it practices.

## MAIN AREAS OF PRACTICE

**Civil Litigation:** The firm represents clients in civil matters in just about every arena. The majority of its work has focused on product liability, toxic torts, contract disputes, corporate disputes, employment disputes, professional negligence, facility negligence, intellectual property law, and personal injury.
**Workers' Compensation:** The firm represents clients in the defense of workers' compensation claims.
**Corporate:** The firm represents buyers and sellers in various transactions including mergers, buy-outs, and other business combinations.
**Trust & Estates:** The firm represents individuals in the area of trust and estate planning, will preparation, execution and probate.

**CLIENTS:** Boehl Stopher & Graves LLP has successfully defended corporations such as Eli Lilly and Company, CSX Transportation, Bristol-Myers Squibb, Ford, Tricon, and NCAA in high-risk, high-visibility cases. The firm has successfully defended insurance companies such as AIG, Coregis, Old Republic Companies, State Farm, and Ohio Casualty. Boehl Stopher & Graves LLP has also defended individuals and non-profit organizations.

## HEAD OFFICE

**KENTUCKY**
2300 AEGON Center, 400 W. Market Street, **Louisville**, KY 40202
**Tel:** 502 589 5980   **Fax:** 502 561 9400
**Email:** Louisville@bsg-1aw.com
**Website:** www.BSG-Law.com

## BRANCH OFFICES

**INDIANA**
Elsby East - Suite 204, 400 Pearl Street, **New Albany**, IN 47150
**Tel:** 812 948 5053   **Fax:** 812 948 9233
**Email:** Indiana@bsg-in.com

**KENTUCKY**
444 West Second Street, **Lexington**, KY 40507-1009
**Tel:** 859 252 6721   **Fax:** 859 253 1445
**Email:** Lexington@bsglex.com

410 Broadway, **Paducah**, KY 42001
**Tel:** 270 442 4369   **Fax:** 270 442 4689
**Email:** rwalter@bsgpad.com

137 Main Street, Suite 200, PO Box 1139, **Pikeville**, KY 41502
**Tel:** 606 432 9670   **Fax:** 606 432 9680
**Email:** tanderson@bsgeast.com

## CONTACTS

| | |
|---|---|
| Litigation | Edward H Stopher |
| Workers' Compensation | Philip J Reverman, Jr |
| Corporate/Trust & Estates | Jefferson K Streepey |

## US OFFICES

### NEW ALBANY
**Managing Partner:** Jeffrey L Hansford
**Number of Lawyers:** 6
**Office Profile:** The New Albany, Indiana office is an integral part of the Greater Louisville metropolitan area providing defense representation of medical malpractice, products liability, workers' compensation, personal injury, professional liability and other litigation matters.

### LEXINGTON
**Managing Partner:** Ronald L Green
**Number of Lawyers:** 9
**Office Profile:** The Lexington office is strategically located 20 minutes from the state capital, Frankfort, Kentucky, and approximately 75 miles from both Louisville and Cincinnati. The office has provided a broad range of trial and appellate services since 1943.

### PADUCAH
**Managing Partner:** Richard L Walter
**Number of Lawyers:** 6
**Office Profile:** The Paducah office has an active practice in western Kentucky and southern Illinois, including all State and Federal Courts in both jurisdictions. The Paducah office handles a wide variety of litigation, including professional liability, construction, personal injury and maritime matters.

### PIKEVILLE
**Managing Partner:** C Tom Anderson
**Number of Lawyers:** 3
**Office Profile:** The Pikeville office handles a significant amount of workers' compensation defense cases in the heart of eastern Kentucky's coal mining region. This office's practice also includes auto and coal truck defense, school board matters and professional, products and premises liability cases.

# FROST BROWN TODD LLC

## THE FIRM

**Managing Partners:** Richard J Erickson, C Edward Glasscock

**Number of partners:** 190
**Number of lawyers:** 193

**FIRM OVERVIEW:** Located in Ohio, Kentucky, Indiana and Tennessee, Frost Brown Todd is an innovative business partner providing legal solutions that rival major law firms around the United States. The firm has built a solid reputation by helping its clients solve the legal challenges that can affect their long-term success. With over 370 lawyers and nearly a centry of combined experience, the firm is routinely advancing the business interests of clients, from small business startups to corporate mergers to business succession, providing them with unmatched connections, legal skill and business resources.

## MAIN AREAS OF PRACTICE:

**Business & Corporate:** Over 70 attorneys provide a full range of transactional, regulatory and other advisory services to the firm's regional, national and multi-national business clients. The firm handles mergers and acquisitions, public companies and securities, tax, emerging business and venture capital, international, e-Business and technology, employee benefits and executive compensation, health law, financial institutions, investment management, public finance and governmental.

**Commercial Transactions/Real Estate:** The firm offers significant experience in the areas of commercial finance, financial restructuring and real estate, including financial institution regulation, equipment leasing, asset securitization, land use, economic development incentives and shopping centers/retail development.

**Environmental:** With one of the largest and most diverse environmental practices in the region, the firm helps clients navigate through federal, state and local environmental regulations, and assists clients in creating solutions that achieve their business objectives, avoid disputes and minimize transactional costs.

**Intellectual Property:** From litigation to licensing, from prosecution to unfair competition, the firm is ready to serve its clients in developing, obtaining, protecting and enforcing creative assets. After handling intellectual property litigation throughout the US for a variety of Fortune 500 clients, the firm was named one of the top 10 patent litigation firms in the US by Managing Intellectual Property Magazine.

**Labor & Employment:** Over 40 attorneys handle labor and employment issues, such as collective bargaining, employment discrimination, sexual harassment, OSHA inspections, workers' compensation, arbitration, alternative dispute resolution, wage and hour, common law employment claims and immigration.

**Litigation:** The firm counsels and represents a variety of clients, and has extensive experience in complex litigation, multi-party cases and class actions. The firm also has experience in the following areas: antitrust, appellate practice, banking/commercial, catastrophic loss, construction, surety and real estate, drug and medical device, fire and explosion, First Amendment, franchise and distribution, government enforcement and compliance, insurance coverage, fraud and bad faith, personal injury and tort defense, product liability, securities and professional liability, toxic tort/chemical exposure, trucking and commercial transportation and unfair competition.

**Personal Planning & Family Business:** The firm counsels individuals in the areas of wealth preservation and wealth transfer matters involving estate, income tax, retirement, charitable and business succession planning. Closely held businesses are served in all tax matters, ranging from choice of business structure and operational issues to the transfer, sale or liquidation of the business.

**International:** Frost Brown Todd provides a wide range of legal services required by international businesses as they expand into the US and by US businesses as they market and operate abroad. The firm handles various international transactions, including direct investments, mergers and acquisitions, joint ventures, licensing, trade law compliance, as well as international commercial dispute resolution. The group's international practice concentrates on corporate, commer-

cial, tax, intellectual property, labor and immigration law, as well as litigation and arbitration services. The firm recently received an Export Achievement Award from the US Department of Commerce in recognition of its involvement with export focused organizations.

## HEAD OFFICES

**KENTUCKY**
400 West Market Street, 32nd Floor, **Louisville**, KY 40202-3363
**Tel:** 502 589 5400   **Fax:** 502 581 1087
**Email:** info@fbtlaw.com
**Website:** www.frostbrowntodd.com

**OHIO**
2200 PNC Center, 201 East Fifth Street, **Cincinnati**, OH 45202-4182
**Tel:** 513 651 6800   **Fax:** 513 651 6981

## BRANCH OFFICES

**DISTRICT OF COLUMBIA**
923 Fifteenth Street NW, **Washington**, DC 20005
**Tel:** 202 662 9700

**INDIANA**
120 West Spring Street, Suite 400, **New Albany**, IN 47150-3655
**Tel:** 812 948 2800   **Fax:** 812 948 7994

**KENTUCKY**
Lexington Financial Center, Suite 2700, 250 W Main Street,
**Lexington**, KY 40507-1749
**Tel:** 859 231 0000   **Fax:** 859 231 0011

**OHIO**
One Columbus, Suite 2300, 10 West Broad Street,
**Columbus**, OH 43215-3467
**Tel:** 614 464 1211   **Fax:** 614 464 1737

300 North Main Street, Suite 200, **Middletown**, OH 45042-1919
**Tel:** 513 422 2001   **Fax:** 513 422 3010

**TENNESSEE**
424 Church Street, Suite 1600, **Nashville**, TN 37219-2308
**Tel:** 615 251 5550   **Fax:** 615 251 5551

## CONTACTS

| | |
|---|---|
| **Business & Corporate** | R James Straus |
| **Commercial Trans/Real Estate** | P Reid Lemasters |
| **Environmental** | Paul W Casper Jr |
| **Intellectual Property** | Steven J Goldstein |
| **Intellectual Property Litigation** | David E Schmit |
| **International** | Joseph J Dehner, Jeffrey L Hallos |
| **Labor & Employment** | Robert A Dimling, D Patton Pelfrey |
| **Litigation** | Winston E Miller, David C Olson |
| **Personal Planning & Family Business** | F Gerald Greenwell |

Lawyers : Business partners.

# GREENEBAUM DOLL & MCDONALD PLLC

## THE FIRM

**Chairman:** P Richard Anderson, Jr

**Number of lawyers:** 185

**FIRM OVERVIEW:** For more than 50 years, Greenebaum has distinguished itself as a progressive business law firm committed to the practice of breakthrough law. Clients rely on Greenebaum to break through stalemates and find creative solutions to complex legal and business issues. The firm is known for getting the deal done. The firm's attorneys are licensed in more than 25 states and several international jurisdictions, and it also provides unmatched international representation through its unique TerraLex® alliance, an association of independent law firms in 87 countries.

## MAIN AREAS OF PRACTICE:

**Regulatory & Administration:** Energy; environmental and natural resources; governmental affairs; intellectual property; land use.

**Corporate & Commercial:** Antitrust; banking and financial companies; China; economic development and incentives; immigration; international; Japan; mergers and acquisitions; product distribution and franchising; real estate development and construction; securities; telecommunications and technology.

**Estate Planning, Health & Insurance:** Employee benefits; family business; general and captive insurance; health, health insurance and life sciences; privacy; wealth transfer.

**Labor & Employment:** Automotive; collective and class action; covenant not to compete and trade secrets; employment practices liability; labor management relations; workplace safety and health.

**Litigation & Dispute Resolution:** Appellate practice; alternative dispute resolution; beverage alcohol; class action defense; construction litigation law; environmental and toxic tort defense; equine; products liability; white collar crime.

**Tax & Finance:** Bankruptcy; bond; ERISA controversy; federal tax; finance; state and local tax; tax exempt organizations.

## HEAD OFFICE

**KENTUCKY**
3500 National City Tower, 101 South Fifth Street, **Louisville**, KY 40202-3197
**Tel:** 502 589 4200   **Fax:** 502 587 3695
**Website:** www.greenebaum.com

## BRANCH OFFICES

**KENTUCKY**
300 West Vine Street, Suite 1100, **Lexington**, KY 40507-1665
**Tel:** 859 231 8500   **Fax:** 859 255 2742

50 East RiverCenter Blvd, Suite 1800, **Covington**, KY 41011-2673
**Tel:** 859 655 4200   **Fax:** 859 655 4239

229 West Main Street, Suite 101, **Frankfort**, KY 40601-1879
**Tel:** 502 875 0050   **Fax:** 502 875 0850

**OHIO**
2800 Chemed Center, 255 East Fifth Street, **Cincinnati**, OH 45202-4728
**Tel:** 513 455 7600   **Fax:** 513 455 8500

**TENNESSEE**
700 Two American Center, 3102 West End Avenue, **Nashville**, TN 37203-1397
**Tel:** 615 760 7100   **Fax:** 615 760 7300

**DISTRICT OF COLUMBIA**
1146 19th Street, NW, Suite 250, **Washington**, DC 20036-3726
**Tel:** 202 293 7000   **Fax:** 202 293 9700

**GEORGIA**
1175 Peachtree Street, NE, 100 Colony Square, Suite 780, **Atlanta**, GA 30361
**Tel:** 770 933 6270   **Fax:** 770 675 3490

## CONTACTS

**Regulatory & Administration**................................Carolyn M Brown
**Corporate & Commercial**..........................................Peggy B Lyndrup
**Estate Planning, Health & Insurance**...................John R Cummins
**Labor & Employment**.................................................Richard S Cleary
**Litigation & Dispute Resolution**.............................Mark S Riddle
**Tax, Benefits & Finance**...........................................Mark F Sommer

GREENEBAUM®
BREAKTHROUGH LAW

# MIDDLETON REUTLINGER

## THE FIRM

**Managing Partner:** Charles G Middleton III
**Senior Partner:** Kenneth S Handmaker, James E Milliman

**Number of partners:** 26
**Number of other attorneys:** 20

**AREAS OF PRACTICE:**
Litigation . . . . . . . . . . . . . . . . . . . . . . . . . . . . . . . . . . . . . . . . . . . . 40%
Business Transactions . . . . . . . . . . . . . . . . . . . . . . . . . . . . . . . . 30%
Intellectual Property (patents, trademarks, copyrights) . . . . . . . . 30%

**FIRM OVERVIEW:** Middleton Reutlinger attributes its continued success to a steadfast team of attorneys who provide quality service while maintaining personalized contact. The firm's attorneys are as diverse in background as the fields of law in which they practice or the clients they represent. Yet, they share the common goals and unity of purpose which turned individual lawyers into one of Kentucky's oldest law firms. Middleton Reutlinger offers a comprehensive range of services to meet the legal needs of individuals and corporations. The firm's practice groups consistently work together to provide clients quality, full service legal representation at the most efficient cost.

## MAIN AREAS OF PRACTICE:

**Litigation:** Middleton Reutlinger has a broad litigation practice with extensive experience including complex commercial litigation, torts litigation, intellectual property, employment law, tax and class actions, foreclosure, eminent domain, construction law, lender liability, products liability, medical malpractice, and utility regulatory. Middleton Reutlinger counsels clients on litigation issues in Kentucky, across the nation and internationally. The firm's attorneys have represented clients in many cases which have resulted in reported decisions setting legal precedent or a benchmark in the law. In one notable case, Middleton Reutlinger attorneys represented Kentucky tax payers in a class action in which the Kentucky Supreme Court held the Kentucky intangible tax on stocks and deposits (a tax enacted in 1907) discriminatory and unconstitutional. Determined under the Commerce Clause of the United States Constitution, it resulted in refunds to Kentucky taxpayers of more than $180,000,000.
**Intellectual Property:** The firm's Intellectual Property Practice consists of trademark, copyright, patent, trade secrets, and internet issues. Middleton Reutlinger's patent services include evaluation of inventions for patent protection and practice before the US Patent Office, from preparation of applications through post-filing prosecution and amendments, to interferences and appeals (including the Board of Patent Appeals). In one notable case, Middleton Reutlinger secured a $28 million jury verdict, sustained in appeal, in a patent infringement action. The firm's trademark attorneys counsel clients in trademark development, clearance, and registration strategies, including preparation and assessment of trademark searches. Middleton Reutlinger files and prosecutes applications in the US Trademark Offices and in various state trademark offices. One of the firm's most recent well known trademark cases was Moseley v V Secret Catalogue, Inc., 123 S. Ct. 1115 (2003), in which the firm presented a case to the United States Supreme Court on an issue of national importance on federal trademark dilution. The firm prevailed with a 9-0 decision. The firm's copyright attorneys advise clients regarding 'fair use,' 'work made for hire,' and other copyright ownership issues, including cases involving computer software infringement.
**Business Transactions:** Middleton Reutlinger's attorneys have significant experience in business transactional issues including real estate, zoning, construction and land use issues, contracts, succession planning, environmental law and safety management and alcohol/beverage licensing. The firm has assisted clients with various issues at state and federal levels.

## HEAD OFFICE

**KENTUCKY**
2500 Brown & Williamson Tower, **Louisville**, KY 40202
**Tel:** 502 584 1135   **Fax:** 502 561 0442
**Email:** skang@middreut.com
**Website:** www.middreut.com

**CLIENTS:** Middleton Reutlinger's clients include a wide array of commercial entities for which legal services are performed in the United States and abroad. Among them is Genlyte Thomas Group LLC, Papa John's International Inc., Hillerich & Bradsby Co. (Louisville Slugger and Powerbuilt), HCA-The Healthcare Company, The Kroger Co., DESA US, LLC, Rexam Closures, and AAF-McQuay, Inc.

**INTERNATIONAL WORK:** Although Middleton Reutlinger provides various legal services to clients in numerous countries, the firm is most recognized for its international work in the area of intellectual property law. The firm regularly works in obtaining patent protection in such countries as Canada, Australia, the European Patent Office, the Pacific Rim countries (including Japan, Taiwan, China, Indonesia, and Korea), Russia and many others.

MIDDLETON
REUTLINGER

# REED WEITKAMP SCHELL & VICE PLLC

## THE FIRM

**Number of members:** 9
**Number of lawyers:** 16

**FIRM OVERVIEW:** Reed Weitkamp Schell & Vice PLLC offers its business, individual, institutional and public agency clients a broad range of legal services to support, enhance and protect their strategic interests. From its offices in Louisville, Kentucky, the firm represents a diverse client base across Kentucky, the region, and beyond. Many of its lawyers have practiced in large, traditional law firms and bring to the firm a broad range of experience representing clients from family-owned businesses to Fortune 500 companies. The firm is dedicated to providing all of its clients with the highest quality legal service in a timely and efficient manner.

## MAIN AREAS OF PRACTICE:

**Litigation:** The firm's litigation lawyers engage in a wide range of trial, appellate and administrative practice and alternative dispute resolution before federal courts, state courts, administrative tribunals, arbitration panels and mediators throughout Kentucky and across the country. The firm's lawyers practice in the areas of complex commercial litigation and business disputes, trade secret litigation, business torts, intellectual property disputes, civil and criminal antitrust litigation, contract disputes, insurance defense and insurance coverage disputes, healthcare, professional liability defense, federal and state tax litigation, employment matters, regulatory compliance, white-collar crime and government investigations.

**Corporate/M&A/Tax:** Public and privately held corporations, partnerships, limited liability companies, and professional practice groups call on the experience and skill of the firm's lawyers in general corporate law, mergers, acquisitions, divestiture and reorganization, tax-exempt status, joint ventures, venture capital funding, federal and state tax planning, private and government employee benefit plans, securities compliance, antitrust, and trade regulation. The firm also advises individuals in the organization of new businesses.

**Finance/Real Estate:** The firm's Financial Practice encompasses a varied range of services including representation of financial institutions, developers, title companies, businesses, and government agencies in corporate loan transactions, commercial real estate loan and partnership transactions, mortgage warehouse lending and other asset-securitizations, tax-credit transactions, and community-based developments. The firm's Real Estate Practice includes representing developers, holders of coal and other mineral interests, and commercial landlords and tenants.

**Healthcare:** The firm serves as counsel for the leading publicly held company in the field of disabilities, training and youth services. The firm also represents over 120 physician groups and individual physicians throughout the region. In addition to general corporate and transactional work for a leading residential care company, attorneys in the firm's Healthcare Group advise and represent clients in various facets of healthcare law, including the defense of physicians and physician practice groups in a variety of litigation contexts, Medicare/Medicaid reimbursement, physician recruitment, physician noncompetition agreements, practice formation and acquisition, state and federal regulatory compliance, preferred provider agreements, and employment matters.

**Estate Planning, Probate & Estate Administration:** The firm's Estate Planning, Probate and Estate Administration Practice encompasses a wide variety of tax and planning services in estate and closely held business transition planning, as well as estate and trust administration. The firm's lawyers assist clients in the preparation of wills and trusts (including both living and testamentary trusts), powers of attorney, advanced directives (living wills), charitable giving, family partnerships and limited liability entities, grantor retained annuity trusts and charitable remainder trusts.

## HEAD OFFICE

**KENTUCKY**
500 West Jefferson Street, Suite 2400, **Louisville**, KY 40202-2812
**Tel:** 502 589 1000   **Fax:** 502 562 2200
**Website:** www.rwsvlaw.com

## CONTACTS

| | |
|---|---|
| Litigation | John S Reed |
| Corporate/M&A/Tax | Gary R Weitkamp |
| Estate Planning | Ivan J Schell |
| Financial/Real Estate | Robert B Vice |
| | Jeffrey A Hamilton |
| Employment | Michael W Oyler |
| Employee Benefits/ERISA | Alan D Pauw |
| Healthcare | Ivan J Schell |
| | Gary R Weitkamp |
| Antitrust | John S Reed |
| | David J Hale |
| Insurance | Ridley M Sandidge |
| Government | David J Hale |
| | Robert B Vice |
| Bankruptcy/Creditors' Rights | Trevor L Earl |

**CLIENTS:** Abbott Laboratories Inc.; Aspen Healthcare Investors, LLC; ATS Construction; AU Associates, Inc.; Barton Brands, Ltd.; Bizzack I, Inc.; Central Bank; Citizens Union Bank of Shelbyville; Commonwealth of Kentucky; Connected Learning.Network, Inc.; Diageo North America, Inc.; Diesel Injection Service Co., Inc.; Downtown Development Corporation; Fifth Third Bank; First Capital Bank of Kentucky; Giles Industries, Inc.; Hanson Aggregates Midwest, Inc.; Horton Fruit Co., Inc.; The Housing Partnership, Inc.; Humana Inc.; Jones Plastic & Engineering Company, LLC; Kindred Healthcare, Inc.; Lantech.com, LLC; Main Street Realty, Inc.; MainSource Bank; Massie-Clarke Development Company; Measured Progress, Inc.; Mountain-Elkhorn, Inc.; National Biodiesel Board; National City Bank of Kentucky; National City Community Development Corporation; Northwestern Mutual Life Insurance Company; OPM Services, Inc.; Res-Care, Inc.; UST Inc.; ZirMed, Inc.

**INTERNATIONAL WORK:** The firm represents US businesses operating and selling abroad and provides its full range of transactional and litigation services to international businesses with interests in the US.

# REED WEITKAMP
# SCHELL & VICE PLLC

# SMITH & SMITH, ATTORNEYS

## THE FIRM

**Managing Partner:** James U Smith, III

**Number of partners:** 4
**Number of other lawyers:** 6

### AREAS OF PRACTICE:
Employment Litigation . . . . . . . . . . . . . . . . . . . . . . . . . . . . . . . . . . . . 45%
Labor Law . . . . . . . . . . . . . . . . . . . . . . . . . . . . . . . . . . . . . . . . . . . . . 35%
Employment Law/Preventive Counseling . . . . . . . . . . . . . . . . . . . . . 20%

**FIRM OVERVIEW:** Smith & Smith, Attorneys was founded in 1946 and has been at the forefront in the region in counseling public and private sector employers in all facets of labor and employment law. The firm's comprehensive labor and employment law practice includes: union avoidance; employment litigation; traditional labor law; wage and hour; in-house training; employment discrimination; and employment contracts and policies. The firm couples its goal of providing the highest quality representation of its clients with a commitment to responsive and efficient service and attention to client matters that distinguish the best small firms. The firm emphasizes consulting and advising its clients on labor and employment-related matters in an effort to avoid litigation, and on vigorously defending its clients when they are embroiled in controversies or lawsuits. Smith & Smith also is a member of Worklaw Network®, a nationwide network of independent law firms practicing exclusively in the areas of labor and employment law. Worklaw Network has 26 member firms whose approximately 340 attorneys practice in 41 states, the District of Columbia and Canada.

### MAIN AREAS OF PRACTICE:

**Labor Law:** Smith & Smith advises and represents its clients in all phases of labor relations under the NLRA and RLA. The firm's attorneys regularly guide clients through union organizing campaigns and decertification procedures, as well as adversarial proceedings before the National Labor Relations Board. The firm also handles collective bargaining negotiations, contract administration matters and arbitrations, and other issues arising out of application of state and federal labor laws.

**Employment Law/Preventive Counseling:** The firm advises its clients with respect to wage and hour laws, civil rights laws, discrimination issues, wrongful discharge, employment-related torts, and employment and independent contractor agreements. Clients also seek counsel from the firm's attorneys in matters of compliance with the Americans with Disabilities Act, the Occupational Safety and Health Act, the Family and Medical Leave Act, and other federal and state employment statutes and regulations. The firm assists clients in the development and implementation of employment policies and procedures, and conducts preventive training for supervisory personnel in all aspects of the employment relationship.

**Employment Litigation:** Smith & Smith has an extensive Civil Litigation Practice, which encompasses representation of clients in employment law matters in state and federal trial courts, before administrative agencies, appellate advocacy, arbitration and other forms of alternative dispute resolution. A principal focus of Smith & Smith is avoiding protracted litigation and its attorneys are leaders in developing innovative defense strategies to end lawsuits at their early stages, as well as implementing preventive strategies for its clients.

## HEAD OFFICE

**KENTUCKY**
300 South, First Trust Centre, 200 South Fifth Street,
**Louisville**, KY 40202
**Tel:** 502 587 0761   **Fax:** 502 589 5345
**Email:** firm@smithandsmithattorneys.com
**Website:** www.smithandsmithattorneys.com

## CONTACTS

Labor Law . . . . . . . . . . . . . . . . . . . . . . . . . . . . . . . . . . . . . . . . . . . . . . . . . . James U Smith III
**Employment Law/Preventive Counseling** . . . . . . . . . . . . . . . W Kevin Smith
**Employment Litigation** . . . . . . . . . . . . . . . . . . . . . . . . . . . . . . . . . John O Sheller

**CLIENTS:** Smith & Smith represents clients in a broad range of industries, such as utility, construction, manufacturing, retail, healthcare, education, chemical, banking, insurance, and transportation. The firm represents clients of every size, from small, single-site employers to large national companies. Representative clients of Smith & Smith include: Arch Chemicals, Inc.; Associated Builders & Contractors, Inc.; The Chubb Group; Churchill Downs, Inc.; Papa Johns International, Inc.; James N. Gray Company; 84 Lumber Company L.P.; Disabled American Veterans; Lindsey Wilson College; R.C. Bigelow, Inc.; Wehr Constructors, Inc.; Whayne Supply Company; Louisville Water Company; Louisville Gas & Electric Co.; United Methodist Hospital of Kentucky, Inc.; ResCare, Inc.; and T & WA, Inc.

# SMITH & SMITH
ATTORNEYS

# STITES & HARBISON, PLLC

## THE FIRM

**Chairman:** Kennedy Helm, III

**Number of partners:** 115
**Number of associates:** 95
**Number of counsel:** 42

**Email:** general@stites.com
**Website:** www.stites.com

**FIRM OVERVIEW:** Stites & Harbison, PLLC is a preeminent law firm based in strategic Southeastern locations and sought by business and institutional clients nationwide for sophisticated transactions, difficult litigation and complex regulatory matters. Stites & Harbison is a full service firm practicing through departmental groupings with specialty and industry teams whose eight locations function as a single law office.

**MAIN AREAS OF PRACTICE:** Business and finance; business litigation; construction; creditors' rights and bankruptcy; employment; environmental; intellectual property and technology; liability defense; personal services; real estate.

## CLIENTS:

**REPRESENTATIVE CLIENTS:** Aegon USA Investment Management, Inc.; A.H. Belo Corporation; Alcan, Inc.; Alcoa Fujikura Ltd.; Alstom Power; Ambrake Corporation; American Electric Power Service Corporation (Kentucky Power Co.); American General Corporation; American Institute of Steel Construction, Inc.; Anthem Inc.; Bank One, Kentucky, N.A.; Baptist Healthcare System; The Beck Group; BellSouth Telecommunications, Inc.; Beverly Enterprises, Inc.; Brainstorm USA LLC; Bridgestone/Firestone, Inc.; Brown-Forman Corporation; Brown & Williamson Holdings, Inc.; Caldwell Tanks, Inc.; CHA HMO, Inc.; Countryside Commercial Real Estate Finance, Inc.; Dynergy Power Corp.; Electrolux LLC; Fidelity National Bank; Fleet Financial Corp.; Fortune Brands; Frontier Insurance Corporation; GE Capital Corporation; GlaxoSmithKline; The Goodyear Tire & Rubber Company; International Port of Kentucky; James N. Gray Company; Holder Construction Company; ITT Financial; J.P. Morgan Chase Bank, Inc.; Kajima Construction Services, Inc.; Kentucky Economic Development Finance Authority (KEDFA); KFC Corporation; Lexington-Fayette Urban County Airport Board; Life Insurance Company of Georgia; Louisville Regional Airport Authority; Metropolitan Nashville Airport Authority; Microsoft; Modis Professional Services, Inc.; National City Bank of Kentucky; National Health Investors, Inc.; National Renal Alliance, LLC; New Life Corporation of America; New York Department of Insurance; Northern Life Insurance Company; Pfizer, Inc.; Presco Steel, Inc.; Purdue Pharma LP; Regions Bank; Lin R.Rogers Electrical Contractors; Russell Athletic Corporation; Southern Land Company; Steel Technologies, Inc.; Stock Yards Bank & Trust Co.; SunTrust Bank; Synaxis Group, Inc.; ThermoView Industries, Inc.; Tricon Global Restaurants, Inc.; Tyson Foods, Inc.; Union Planters Bank, N.A.; University Medical Center, Inc.; University of Kentucky; University of Louisville; Vanderbilt University; Whayne Supply Company; Yum Brands, Inc.; Zurich American Insurance Companies.

## OFFICES

### KENTUCKY
400 W. Market St, Suite 1800, **Louisville**, KY 40202
**Tel:** 502 587 3400   **Fax:** 502 587 6391

250 W. Main St, Suite 2300, **Lexington**, KY 40507
**Tel:** 859 226 2300   **Fax:** 859 253 9144

421 W. Main St, **Frankfort**, KY 40602
**Tel:** 502 223 3477   **Fax:** 502 223 4124

### DISTRICT OF COLUMBIA
1200 G St, NW, Suite 800, **Washington**, DC 20005
**Tel:** 202 434 8968   **Fax:** 202 737 5822

### GEORGIA
303 Peachtree St, NE, 2800 SunTrust Plaza, **Atlanta**, GA 30308
**Tel:** 404 739 8800   **Fax:** 404 739 8870

### INDIANA
323 E. Court Ave, **Jeffersonville**, IN 47130
**Tel:** 812 282 7566   **Fax:** 812 284 5519

### TENNESSEE
424 Church St, Suite 1800, **Nashville**, TN 37219
**Tel:** 615 244 5200   **Fax:** 615 782 2371

### VIRGINIA
1199 N.Fairfax St, Suite 900, **Alexandria**, VA 22314
**Tel:** 203 739 4900   **Fax:** 203 739 9577

## CONTACTS

| | |
|---|---|
| **Business & Finance** | Robert M Beck, Jr (Lexington) |
| | W Thomas Halbleib, Jr (Louisville) |
| | Brian A Cromer (Louisville) |
| | A Stuart Campbell (Nashville) |
| **Business Litigation** | Phillip W Collier (Louisville) |
| | T Morgan Ward Jr (Louisville) |
| | J Clarke Keller (Lexington) |
| | Dianna B Shew (Nashville) |
| **Construction** | Anne Gorham (Lexington) |
| **Creditors' Rights & Bankruptcy** | W Robinson Beard (Louisville) |
| | Elizaeth Thompson (Lexington) |
| **Employment, Labor & Immigration** | Shannon A Hamilton (Louisville) |
| | Stephen H Price (Nashville) |
| **Environmental** | W Patrick Stallard (Louisville) |
| **Intellectual Property & Technology** | Jack A Wheat (Louisville) |
| **Liability Defense** | John L Tate (Louisville) |
| | John M Famularo (Lexington) |
| **Estate Planning** | J David Porter (Lexington) |
| **Real Estate** | Richard W Stephens (Atlanta) |
| | William H Haden, Jr (Louisville) |
| | Stephen M Ruschell (Lexington) |
| | Julian Bibb (Nashville) |

**STITES & HARBISON** PLLC

ATTORNEYS

# STOLL KEENON OGDEN PLLC

## THE FIRM

**Managing Member:** William M Lear, Jr

**Number of Attorneys:** 140

**FIRM OVERVIEW:** Stoll Keenon Ogden provides the wide ranging resources of a large Midwestern law firm, yet takes pride as the law firm of choice for clients who define the economy and culture of the Kentucky region. With 140 lawyers in four Kentucky cities, SKO built the firm reputation representing all types of businesses in Kentucky, the Midwest and beyond. SKO's work includes representation before all state and federal courts and numerous administrative agencies. In addition to serving as legal counsel for businesses, the firm's lawyers have held leadership positions at every level of state and local government. The firms of Stoll, Keenon & Park and Ogden Newell & Welch merged in January 2006. Beginning in the 1890s, both firms established regional reputations representing Kentucky's signature industries in wine and spirits, the thoroughbred industry, and energy. The firm has maintained its leadership as legal counsel to clients in these industries, and today these clients operate on a global basis. SKO also represents major national and international clients in healthcare, technology, manufacturing, telecommunications, utilities and financial services. SKO is exclusively affiliated with Meritas, the world's largest network of independent law firms.

**MAIN AREAS OF PRACTICE:** Corporate/mergers and acquisitions; business litigation; utility and energy law; corporate finance and lending; labor and employment; employee benefits; professional liability defense; state and federal tax; intellectual property; bankruptcy; real estate finance and development; mineral and environmental law; healthcare law; estate planning and administration; family law; immigration, government relations and equine law.

**CLIENTS:** Representative clients include: Brown-Forman Corporation, E.ON U.S., Lexmark International, Inc., Keeneland Association, Jewish Hospital & St. Mary's Healthcare, Norton Healthcare Inc., St. Joseph HealthCare, Baptist Healthcare System, Central Bank, Fifth Third Bank, Papa John's International, Inc., Genlyte Thomas Group LLC, Caterpillar, Inc., ISCO Industries, Inc., Kentucky American Water Company, and Fireman's Fund Insurance Company.

**INTERNATIONAL WORK:** SKO has represented local businesses that are acquiring businesses outside of the United States or establishing distribution or joint venture arrangements in foreign countries. The firm has also represented foreign businesses seeking to acquire or establish local operations. In the area of immigration, SKO represents companies based outside of the United States in obtaining investor visa status to facilitate direct investment and transfer of personnel to US markets, and also represents companies in international assignments to offices overseas.

## US OFFICES

**KENTUCKY**
300 West Vine Street, Suite 2100, **Lexington**, KY 40507
**Tel:** 859 231 3000   **Fax:** 859 253 1093
**Email:** sko@skofirm.com
**Website:** www.skofirm.com

2000 PNC Plaza, 500 West Jefferson Street, **Louisville**, KY 40202
**Tel:** 502 582 1601   **Fax:** 502 581 9564

307 Washington Street, **Frankfort**, KY 40601
**Tel:** 502 875 6220   **Fax:** 502 875 6235

201C North Main Street, **Henderson**, KY 42420
**Tel:** 270 831 1900   **Fax:** 270 827 4060

## CONTACTS

| | |
|---|---|
| **Corporate/Mergers & Acquisitions** | Ernest W Williams |
| **Business Litigation** | Charles E Shivel Jr |
| **Utility & Energy Law** | C Kent Hatfield |
| **Corporate Finance & Lending** | Scott W Brinkman |
| **Labor & Employment** | Richard G Griffith |
| **Employee Benefits** | Joseph C Beavin |
| **Professional Liability Defense** | W Gregory King |
| **State & Federal Tax** | Timothy J Eifler |
| **Intellectual Property** | P Douglas Barr |
| **Bankruptcy** | Lea Pauley Goff |
| **Real Estate Finance & Development** | Richard A Nunnelley |
| **Mineral & Environmental Law** | David H Thomason |
| **Healthcare Law** | James S Goldberg |
| **Estate Planning & Administration** | James E Hargrove |
| **Family Law** | Anita M Britton |
| **Immigration Law** | Charles R Baesler, Jr |
| **Government Relations** | B Riggs Lewis |
| **Equine Law** | William T Bishop III |

STOLL · KEENON · OGDEN

# TACHAU MADDOX HOVIOUS & DICKENS PLC

## THE FIRM

**Founding Members:** David Tachau, Victor Maddox, R Gregg Hovious
**Managing Member:** Benjamin C Fultz

**Number of members:** 7
**Number of other attorneys:** 11

### AREAS OF PRACTICE:

| | |
|---|---|
| Commercial Litigation | 60% |
| Healthcare Litigation & Advising | 10% |
| Plaintiff's Personal Injury Litigation | 10% |
| Personal Injury Litigation Defense | 10% |
| Corporate & Real Estate Transactions | 10% |

**FIRM OVERVIEW:** Tachau Maddox Hovious & Dickens PLC was opened in 1995 by three litigation partners from a large regional law firm, and has steadily grown by focusing on commercial litigation for businesses and individuals in Kentucky and southern Indiana. The firm also handles constitutional and public interest litigation, as well as employment matters and personal injury litigation for plaintiffs and defendants, and has several substantial healthcare clients for whom it does litigation and business counseling. The firm has enjoyed remarkable success at trials and in appeals; all seven of its partners have tried or arbitrated cases to successful awards in the last three years, and have won state or federal appeals during that period. The firm has also developed a sophisticated Corporate and Real Estate Transactional Practice with the recent addition of experienced attorneys. The firm compensates its attorneys well, and has attracted exceptionally talented lateral associates from a number of large regional and national firms.

## MAIN AREAS OF PRACTICE:

**Corporate/Real Estate Transactions:** Tachau Maddox Hovious & Dickens advises clients and manages commercial transactions including mergers, acquisitions and dispositions, commercial finance and real estate financing. The firm also handles emerging business and venture capital transactions, product distribution and franchising matters.

**Commercial Litigation:** Tachau Maddox Hovious & Dickens handles numerous kinds of business litigation for regional and national clients.

**Financial Institutions:** The firm has recently represented the leading banking firms in the Kentucky market in complex litigation matters, including JPMorgan Chase, National City Bank, PNC Bank, Wachovia Bank, Huntington National Bank, BB&T, Wells Fargo and Stock Yards Bank, in disputes involving consumer regulatory, UCC, lender liability, contract formation/breach, estate and trust/breach of fiduciary duty, letter of credit and guaranty, property rights and claims, fraud, bankruptcy and general banking matters.

**General Commercial Entities:** The firm handles contract performance and breach litigation, bankruptcy, commercial partnership disputes, securities and other fraud litigation, class action claims, procurement litigation, commercial tort, and zoning and property disputes, for publicly-traded companies and other businesses such as Aegon, CTB-McGraw Hill, General Electric, Papa John's Pizza, PricewaterhouseCoopers, ResCare and Ventas.

**Insurance Firms:** The firm has served as primary litigation counsel on various commercial, administrative and employment matters in the past decade for Neace Lukens, the largest insurance agency in the Kentucky/Indiana/Ohio region. The firm has also been engaged in other contract and insurance coverage matters for other clients, including two specialty lines managing general agents who underwrite and administer intellectual property insurance and public employee benefits, and three substantial life and health insurers (Principal Life Insurance Co., Time Insurance Co., and Aegon/Life Investors Insurance Co.). The firm's

agency-related work has included the successful defense of multiple errors and omissions claims, the successful prosecution and defense of multiple noncompetition covenant claims, the successful representation of various contract actions, and the successful representation of administrative matters before the Kentucky Office of Insurance.

**Labor & Employment Clients:** The firm provides counseling and litigation services for employers and employees on matters involving ERISA and benefits, race and gender and disability discrimination, employment contracts, independent contractor issues, restrictive covenants and non-competition agreements, and employment-related torts including defamation, interference with contractual relations and breach of fiduciary duty.

**Constitutional & Public Interest Litigation:** The firm has represented the state House of Representatives Minority Leader in a challenge to the constitutionality of legislative redistricting under the state constitution, successfully opposed a certiorari petition to the United States Supreme Court on behalf of the Kentucky Registry of Election Finance to defend the constitutionality of public financing of gubernatorial elections, and successfully sued the Governor and General Assembly to vindicate equal protection rights of voters to legislative redistricting, among other matters.

**Healthcare Firms:** The firm represents various healthcare entities, including a number on a national basis. The firm's representation includes administrative issues and Certificate of Need proceedings, government investigations and qui tam matters, physician practice issues, commercial litigation and bankruptcy matters. The firm also provides business counseling on restructuring, regulatory (including Stark and Anti-Kickback) analysis, and reimbursement issues. The firm's clients include Kindred Healthcare (NYSE: KND), RehabCare Group (NYSE: RHB) and Jewish Hospital & St Mary's Healthcare.

**Personal Injury Litigation:** The firm represents injured plaintiffs as well as serving as national coordinating counsel for certain General Electric Co. product liability litigation.

### HEAD OFFICE

**KENTUCKY**
2700 National City Tower, **Louisville**, KY 40202-3116
**Tel:** 502 588 2000   **Fax:** 502 588 2020
**Email:** bfultz@tmhd.com
**Website:** www.tmhd.com

# WYATT, TARRANT & COMBS, LLP

## THE FIRM

**Managing Partner:** J Larry Cashen

**FIRM OVERVIEW:** With over 200 attorneys in six offices, Wyatt, Tarrant & Combs, LLP offers a full range of legal services in Kentucky, Indiana and Tennessee. By leveraging the firm's rich heritage and tradition of excellence, the Wyatt firm has been able to continually attract top legal talent and grow its business. Attorneys in the Wyatt firm adhere to their core principles of integrity, zealous representation and absolute loyalty to clients. This discipline, combined with an overriding dedication to client service, an uncompromising commitment to quality legal work and an old fashioned work ethic are the hallmarks of the firm.

## MAIN AREAS OF PRACTICE:

**Business Law:** Wyatt has active practices in the areas of banking, tax, public finance, venture capital, environment, real estate and lending, securities compliance, executive compensation, employee benefit plans and labor law. Wyatt counsels its clients over the entire life of the business – from selecting the form of business entity, to raising capital and financing growth (both public and private offerings), to taxation issues, to acquisition and sale transactions and other exit strategies. The firm represents a wide range of established companies (both public and closely held) and start-ups. It also represents directors, officers, majority/minority owners and entrepreneurs in connection with a wide range of business issues.

**Commercial Litigation:** Wyatt handles all types of business litigation, including class actions, multi-district litigation and other complex litigation as well as more routine matters of business litigation in both jury and non-jury settings. The firm regularly represents the interests of major businesses, individuals, professional firms and governmental entities in all varieties of disputes, including those involving contracts, antitrust, fiduciary duties, toxic torts, tortious interference with contracts, franchises, unfair competition, regulatory law, bankruptcy, and creditors' rights.

**Healthcare:** Wyatt has significant experience in all aspects of the healthcare industry including: (i) regulatory, administrative and accreditation matters such as certificates of need, licensure, HIPAA, Medicare, Medicaid and third-party reimbursement, (ii) planning and implementation regarding corporate structure, joint ventures, sales and acquisitions and tax-exempt status, and (iii) hospital/physician/patient relationships.

**Mineral & Energy:** Wyatt represents owners, producers and distributors of coal, oil and gas, energy facility operators and those who provide financing, technical assistance, equipment and insurance to the mineral and energy industries. The firm handles a broad range of matters such as acquisitions and divestitures, mineral leasing, supply contracts, real and personal property issues, labor and employment, taxes, mining agreements, and disaster response consultation. The firm also frequently handles litigation matters in these areas before state and federal courts and regulatory agencies.

**International Trade:** Wyatt's Immigration Practice is very active, providing assistance with immigration, naturalization and visas. The firm also has experience with international business negotiations, acquisitions, and joint ventures, as well as multi-national sales, distribution and licensing arrangements, protection of intellectual property, and tax issues related to the foregoing.

**Estate Planning:** Wyatt has a large estate planning practice helping clients plan for the disposition of assets during their lifetime and at death. Primary emphasis is placed on preparation of wills, revocable and irrevocable trust agreements, prenuptial agreements and other documents that are necessary for wealth preservation, the orderly transfer of assets and the mitigation of federal and state taxes.

**CLIENTS:** Representative clients include: Churchill Downs Incorporated; E.I. duPont de Nemours; General Electric Company; Heaven Hill Distilleries; Jefferson County Public Schools; JPMorgan Chase Bank, N.A.; LG&E Energy Corp.; Norton Healthcare; Regions Bank; Thornton Oil Corporation; Union Underwear Company; Wal-Mart Stores, Inc.

### OFFICES

**KENTUCKY**
PNC Plaza, 500 West Jefferson Street, Suite 2800,
**Louisville**, KY 40202-2898
**Tel:** 502 589 5235   **Fax:** 502 589 0309

Lexington Financial Center, 250 West Main Street, Suite 1600,
**Lexington**, KY 40507-1746
**Tel:** 859 233 2012   **Fax:** 859 259 0649

918 State Street, **Bowling Green**, KY 42101-1220
**Tel:** 270 842 1050   **Fax:** 270 842 4720

**TENNESSEE**
1715 Aaron Brenner Drive, Suite 800, **Memphis**, TN 38120-4367
**Tel:** 901 537 1000   **Fax:** 901 537 1010

2525 West End Avenue, Suite 1500, **Nashville**, TN 37203-1423
**Tel:** 615 244 0020   **Fax:** 615 256 1726

**INDIANA**
The Community Bank Building, 101 West Spring Street, Suite 500
**New Albany**, IN 47150-3610
**Tel:** 812 845 3561   **Fax:** 812 949 2524

**Website:** www.wyattfirm.com

### CONTACTS

| | |
|---|---|
| Business Law | Robert A Heath (Louisville) |
| Commercial Litigation | Cornelius E Coryell (Louisville) |
| Healthcare | Carole D Christian (Louisville) |
| | Theodore T Myre (Louisville) |
| Mineral & Energy | Joseph J Zaluski (Lexington) |
| International Trade | Jeffrey E Wallace (Louisville) |
| Estate Planning | Bruce K Dudley (Louisville) |

WYATT, TARRANT & COMBS, LLP

## How lawyers are ranked

Every year we carry out thousands of in-depth interviews with clients and lawyers in order to assess the reputations and expertise of business lawyers across the USA. Chambers rankings and editorial are referred to extensively by General Counsel and other purchasers of legal services who look to our recommendations when choosing their lawyers.

# BANKING & FINANCE

**Banking & Finance**
Leading Firms

1. JONES WALKER *New Orleans*
   LISKOW & LEWIS PLC *New Orleans*
   PHELPS DUNBAR LLP *New Orleans*
2. CARVER DARDEN KORETZKY TESSIER *New Orleans*
   CORRERO FISHMAN HAYGOOD *New Orleans*
   MCGLINCHEY STAFFORD *New Orleans*
   PETTIETTE, ARMAND, DUNKELMAN *Shreveport*

Leading Individuals

1. CLAVERIE SR Philip *Phelps Dunbar LLP*
   STUCKEY James *Phelps Dunbar LLP*
2. TESSIER Frank *Carver Darden Koretzky Tessier*
   WILLIS Sterling *Correro Fishman Phelps*
3. CROMWELL David *Pettiette, Armand, Dunkelman*
   PAGE Marshall *Jones Walker*
   ROBERSON JR Thomas *Jones Walker*
   RUBIN Michael *McGlinchey Stafford*
   WILLENZIK David *McGlinchey Stafford*
   WOGAN John *Liskow & Lewis PLC*

Up-and-coming individuals
   LELONG Rivers *Jones Walker*

## Band 1

### Jones Walker Waechter Poitevent Carrère & Denègre, LLP

See firm details p.994
**The Firm:** This large, full-service firm was widely praised for the "*capability, knowledge and integrity*" of its banking attorneys. As one client remarked: "*They are so professional that it is effortless to deal with them.*" The group has many clients from outside Louisiana and works closely with the firm's corporate section, as well as with its offices in other cities. Recent highlights include representing Ventura Foods in the negotiation of a $105 million acquisition facility provided by CoBank.
**The Lawyers:** Marshall Page (see p.984) was recognized for his ability in private credit facility transactions, structured finance and venture capital work. He acted for key client CenturyTel as lead counsel in the refinancing of the company's credit facilities. The

"*extremely astute*" Thomas Roberson (see p.985) won praise for his "*intelligent, creative approach to problems*" and "*straightforward, down-to-earth manner with clients.*" He represents many publicly held clients in syndicated finance work, including Ruth's Chris Steak House, on behalf of which he negotiated a $55 million syndicated working capital facility arranged by Wells Fargo. Up-and-comer Rivers LeLong (see p.983) impressed clients by supplementing legal expertise with knowledge of the wider subject matter, according to the case in hand.
**Clients/Work Highlights:** Freeport-McMoran Copper & Gold; JPMorgan Chase; Stewart Enterprises and Tidewater.

### Liskow & Lewis PLC

**The Firm:** The market resounds with praise for the firm's impressive track record in representing lenders in financing transactions. While New Orleans and Lafayette are the key offices involved, the client roster includes companies hailing from far beyond Louisiana. The group participates in a diverse range of work and was heavily involved in municipal bond financings in the wake of the hurricanes.
**The Lawyers:** Billed as a "*lawyer who is able to provide banks and trust companies with all the services they could possibly require,*" John Wogan comfortably sustains his position in the table. "*He knows exactly what he is talking about and is very versatile, so he always keeps opposing counsel on their toes,*" said one client.
**Clients/Work Highlights:** The team advises regional and national banks, as well as many of the firm's high-profile energy industry clients.

### Phelps Dunbar LLP

See firm details p.997
**The Firm:** It is the "*quality of practitioners*" at this large multiservice firm's highly regarded finance practice that sets it apart, according to sources. Clients were quick to expound the benefits of working with "*likable and trustworthy attorneys who show a high level of commitment and personal interest in the success of your company.*" The team is particularly renowned for the caliber of its work on the lending side and represents a number of large financial institutions.
**The Lawyers:** Peers and clients alike applauded the impressive contributions made by this "*highly

respected team*" to the banking and finance arena. Jim Stuckey (see p.987) combines "*first-rate insight,*" gained through a wealth of experience working on various legislative committees, with an "*impressive intellect.*" Working alongside him in the New Orleans office, Philip Claverie (see p.978) has also been at the forefront of legislative activity in the state. His transactional expertise covers finance and real estate work, and his recent highlights include involvement in the financing of a new coffee silo in Florida and of an alligator farm in Louisiana. "*He is easy to deal with, can be trusted and always does a good job for the client,*" say sources.
**Clients/Work Highlights:** AmSouth Bank; Audubon Capital Fund; Hibernia National Bank; IBERIABANK and Whitney National Bank.

## Band 2

### Carver Darden Koretzky Tessier Finn Blossman & Areaux LLC

**The Firm:** This compact New Orleans-based firm is said to provide an impressive roster of lending institutions with "*truly top-notch counsel.*" Whitney National Bank is a major client, which it recently advised on the financing of many real estate transactions. The firm also plays a prominent role in the oil and gas industries and is renowned for its energy financing work.
**The Lawyers:** The firm's managing partner, Frank Tessier, was highly praised for his work on both real estate and finance fronts. In addition to being retained as regular counsel for Whitney National Bank, Tessier acted as lead bank counsel to Bank Group in the $40 million construction of The Astor Crowne Plaza.
**Clients/Work Highlights:** AmSouth Bank; Hibernia National Bank; LATTER & BLUM; Rathborne Group; Regions Bank and STANDARD Mortgage.

### Correro Fishman Haygood Phelps Walmsley & Casteix LLP

See firm details p.992
**The Firm:** The "*first-rate banking practice*" at this corporate boutique is involved in a variety of work on behalf of both borrowers and lenders. The firm has been particularly active in large energy sector

deals and represented a private company in connection with the development of a $400 million underground natural gas storage facility. A further highlight involved assisting a landowner in the lease of his property for the construction of a $500 million Cheniere LNG terminal.

**The Lawyers:** "*A great teacher who has created rather than hired a superb team,*" **Scott Willis** (see p.988) was commended by clients for the quality of his performances on both sides of lending transactions. He advised Amedisys on a $75 million revolver and term loan facility from Wachovia.

**Clients/Work Highlights:** AmSouth Bank; ASCO plc; First Bank & Trust; JPMorgan Chase; Offshore Logistics; OMNIBANK; Robinson Lumber; Sprint and Whitney National Bank.

## McGlinchey Stafford

See firm details p.996

**The Firm:** Having one of the largest devoted financial services groups in the state has won the firm a national reputation in the field and, as such, clients include Fortune 500 entities of the likes of The Bank of New York and Fannie Mae. Commentators unanimously agreed that regulatory compliance work is the team's true forte, though members of the firm handle a diverse range of cases pertaining to consumer finance and commercial lending.

**The Lawyers:** **David Willenzik** (see p.988) heads up the firm's business law section and is identified as one of the principal drivers behind the firm's national reputation. He focuses on commercial and consumer financing, real estate lending and bank regulatory work. Willenzik has published numerous texts and has been intimately involved in the initiation and drafting of statutory provisions relating to banking and commercial finance in Louisiana. Research indicated **Michael Rubin** (see p.986) as "*the name on everyone's lips,*" and he enters the rankings accordingly. A highly regarded appellate lawyer and commercial litigator, Rubin has enjoyed involvement in some of the frontline finance and secured lending cases of recent times.

**Clients/Work Highlights:** American Express; Bank of America; Citibank; DaimlerChrysler Services; Ford Motor Credit; GM Finance; Merrill Lynch; Wachovia and Wells Fargo.

## Pettiette, Armand, Dunkelman, Woodley, Byrd & Cromwell LLP

**The Firm:** This ten-attorney firm based in Shreveport sets the standard for transactional work in north Louisiana. The team offers "*exceptional service*" to banks on a range of corporate, banking and real estate transactions.

**The Lawyers:** "*Commanding much respect in the banking community,*" **David Cromwell** was the first name to come to mind for many satisfied customers. "*He has the best legal brain for sophisticated projects that I have ever come across,*" said one client. In addition to transactional and litigation work for his many bank clients, Cromwell has recently assisted with financings relating to local motion pictures.

**Clients/Work Highlights:** The firm's client list includes JPMorgan Chase and AmSouth Bank, as well as many regional banks.

# CORPORATE/M&A

| Corporate/M&A Leading Firms | |
|---|---|
| 1 | CORRERO FISHMAN HAYGOOD *New Orleans* |
| | JONES WALKER *New Orleans* |
| 2 | KANTROW SPAHT WEAVER *Baton Rouge* |
| | KEAN, MILLER, HAWTHORNE *Baton Rouge* |
| | PHELPS DUNBAR LLP *New Orleans* |
| | STONE PIGMAN WALTHER WITTMANN *New Orleans* |
| 3 | ADAMS AND REESE LLP *New Orleans* |
| | LISKOW & LEWIS PLC *New Orleans* |
| | MCGLINCHEY STAFFORD *New Orleans* |
| | TAYLOR, PORTER, BROOKS *Baton Rouge* |

## Band 1

### Correro Fishman Haygood Phelps Walmsley & Casteix LLP

See firm details p.992

**The Firm:** This boutique houses "*the most distinguished roster of corporate lawyers in the state,*" and is so well renowned for its "*top-draw work product*" that many satisfied clients believe it "*merits consideration alongside the top New York firms.*" Prioritizing quality over quantity, corporate and securities matters account for the great majority of the workload for the 15-lawyer firm. In the past twelve months, the team represented clients in mezzanine investments, acquisitions and stock offerings, as well as a number of PIPE transactions. Specific highlights include acting as company counsel for US Unwired in its acquisition by Sprint, a deal valued at an excess of $1 billion. One client summed up the operation as follows: "*Its lawyers offer the complete package – impeccable knowledge, outstanding negotiation skills, a proactive*

approach to getting things done and the ability to make every client feel like their number-one priority.*"

**The Lawyers:** Peers have huge respect for senior partners **Anthony Correro** (see p.978), **Louis Fishman** (see p.980) and **Paul Haygood** (see p.981), who continue to be billed as "*Louisiana's three wise men of corporate law.*" As one commentator remarked: "*They kick-started corporate and securities work in New Orleans and anyone worth their salt these days was trained by one of them.*" Correro drew effusive praise on all sides for his "*unparalleled knowledge of securities law,*" not to mention his ability to "*cut right to the chase of any matter.*" Focusing more heavily on M&A work, the "*extremely diplomatic*" Fishman was also a firm favorite among interviewees: "*He has excellent people skills, which he uses to maximize his position in negotiations.*" Commentators described Haygood as "*a man of integrity who knows the ins and outs of Louisiana law.*" Hot on the heels of the firm's foremost practitioners, **Robert Walmsley** impressed the market with his M&A and financing work. A "*personable and consummate professional,*" he represents a diverse range of business clients, which have recently included a number of real estate holding companies and the State of Louisiana. One of the highlights of a busy year for "*client-oriented*" **John Werner** (see p.987) came when he represented Jefferson Capital Partners in connection with two mezzanine investments to fund the acquisitions of a hardware company and a cosmetics manufacturer.

**Clients/Work Highlights:** Amedisys; Chaffe & Associates; The Department of Treasury for the State of Louisiana; Laitram; MidSouth Bank; Offshore Logistics; Pennington Medical Foundation; Petro-Com; Riverlake Properties; Sanderson Farms; SMG; Stewart Enterprises and Times-Picayune Publishing.

### Jones Walker Waechter Poitevent Carrère & Denègre, LLP

See firm details p.994

**The Firm:** For many observers, this is "*the biggest and the best group in the state,*" and it clearly leads the pack in terms of the sheer volume of high-profile corporations among its clientele. Members of the firm focus on the larger transactions, which recently included representing the buyout group composed of employees of Howard Weil and led by its CEO in negotiating the purchase of all of its stock from Citigroup. The group's "*careful negotiators*" are "*individually and collectively known for their experience and integrity.*" Furthermore, they were praised for their commitment and dedication to a transaction: "*Their engagement goes far beyond the expected lawyer-client relationship.*" The firm represents public and private companies as well as directors and investors in all matters relating to federal and state corporate and securities laws.

**The Lawyers:** "*So outstanding that you always want him involved,*" **Rick McMillan** (see p.984) sustains his top-tier status. Interviewees "*think the world of him*" and agree: "*He is a hugely significant figure in the corporate arena.*" His complete mastery of corporate finance and governance, securities law and M&A allows him to "*quote laws off the cuff and then restate them, using accessible language, in terms of practical consequences.*" Commentators note that **Curtis Hearn** (see p.981) has added to his large stable of active M&A clients and is increasingly operating on a national level. One satisfied client noted: "*You could not expect a higher level of professional performance or competency.*" Elsewhere, Hearn was labeled as a "*highly experienced and highly qualified, get-the-job-done type of individual.*" Lead counsel in the Howard

## Corporate/M&A
### Leading Individuals

**1** CORRERO III Anthony *Correro Fishman Haygood Phelps*
   FISHMAN Louis *Correro Fishman Haygood Phelps*
   MCMILLAN II L Richards *Jones Walker*

**2** FULLMER Mark *Phelps Dunbar LLP*
   HAYGOOD Paul *Correro Fishman Haygood Phelps*
   HEARN Curtis *Jones Walker*
   KANTROW Lee *Kantrow Spaht Weaver & Blitzer*
   WOLFE Richard *Jones Walker*

**3** CAVERLY Joseph *Stone Pigman Walther Wittmann LLC*
   MASTERS William *Jones Walker*
   MILLER JR Ben *Kean, Miller, Hawthorne, D'Armond*
   WALMSLEY Robert *Correro Fishman Haygood Phelps*
   WHITTAKER Scott *Stone Pigman Walther Wittmann*

**4** AGUILAR JR Rodolfo *McGlinchey Stafford*
   BOULET Virginia *Adams and Reese LLP*
   BUTLER JR Patrick *Phelps Dunbar LLP*
   CAMPBELL JR John *Taylor, Porter, Brooks*
   CLARK JR Blane *Kean, Miller, Hawthorne, D'Armond*
   DILEO Anthony *Sole Practitioner*
   FANTACI James *McGlinchey Stafford*
   KLEIN Steven *Sher Garner Cahill Richter Klein*
   NORTON William *Baker, Donelson*
   SNYDER Charles *Milling Benson Woodward LLP*
   WERNER John *Correro Fishman Haygood Phelps*
   WOGAN John *Liskow & Lewis PLC*

### Up-and-coming individuals
   CURRAULT II Douglas *Jones Walker*
   ROUSSEAU Dionne *Jones Walker*

## Corporate/M&A: Bankruptcy
### Leading Individuals

**1** DRAPER Douglas *Heller, Draper, Hayden*
   PATRICK III William *Heller, Draper, Hayden*
   VANCE R Patrick *Jones Walker*

**2** BARRIERE Brent *Phelps Dunbar LLP*
   CERONE Rudy *McGlinchey Stafford*
   FORSYTH J David *Sessions, Fishman*
   HAYDEN Jan *Heller, Draper, Hayden*
   JONES JR Philip *Liskow & Lewis PLC*

**3** CHEATHAM Robin *Adams and Reese LLP*
   DUCK John *Adams and Reese LLP*
   GOODMAN Alan *Lemle & Kelleher, LLP*
   HOOTSELL III Sessions *Phelps Dunbar LLP*
   WAGUESPACK David *Lemle & Kelleher, LLP*

Weil transaction, **Dick Wolfe** (see p.988) also represented the majority shareholder of the New Orleans/Oklahoma City Hornets in the buyout of a 35% minority holding. "*He is adept at understanding the complex details of transactions and capable of providing multiple solutions from multiple perspectives,*" say sources. **Bill Masters** (see p.983) is highly regarded for his experience in public and private offerings but has a broad focus that incorporates M&A, corporate finance and energy sector matters. Head of litigation **Patrick Vance** (see p.987) was named "*one of the best bankruptcy litigators around.*"

His enviable caseload includes some of the biggest cases in the state, such as the Hollywood Casino Shreveport bankruptcy and the post-Katrina Entergy filing. With regard to the firm's up-and-coming practitioners, **Douglas Currault** (see p.979) was singled out for his work on behalf of public companies, while **Dionne Rousseau** (see p.985) won the respect of clients for being "*a very skilled lawyer and an adept communicator, both on paper and orally.*"

**Clients/Work Highlights:** CenturyTel; Elliott Associates; Enhanced Capital Partners; Freeport-McMoRan Copper & Gold; Horizon Offshore; Stewart Enterprises; SCP Pool Corporation and Superior Energy Services.

### Band 2

### Kantrow Spaht Weaver & Blitzer

**The Firm:** This modestly sized Baton Rouge boutique is promoted in the rankings on account of its "*stellar client list and dominance of the local market.*" Loyal clients return to the firm time and again for its "*top-quality attorneys and equally high-quality work product.*" The 23-attorney firm is committed to commercial litigation and transactional work with a heavy corporate and securities focus.

**The Lawyers:** "*An outstanding lawyer and gentleman,*" **Lee Kantrow** is highly respected by his peers. Interviewees singled him out for his valuable negotiation skills: "*He only says what needs to be said and engages with an opponent in negotiations without being confrontational.*" Kantrow is active in M&A, securities and general corporate work.

**Clients/Work Highlights:** The firm has a varied client roster of public and private companies, which has included Allied Waste; American Excess Underwriters; CIGNA; Citizens Bank; First American Title Insurance; The Shaw Group and Whitney National Bank.

### Kean, Miller, Hawthorne, D'Armond, McCowan & Jarman, LLP
See firm details p.995

**The Firm:** According to clients, the Capital Region's largest firm is home to "*an extremely competent group of lawyers, who sustain a comprehensive corporate practice.*" The business and corporate practice group is traditionally renowned for the strength of its corporate finance and M&A work in the chemical and refining industries, though recent downturns in these areas have corresponded with increased activity for the team in a variety of other areas. Close links with the real estate group helped its representation of Shell Pipeline in corporate acquisitions linked to pipeline extensions in Louisiana. Another active client is Lamar Advertising, which the team represented in renegotiating a $1.3 billion credit agreement with JPMorgan Chase.

**The Lawyers:** Commentators unanimously agree that **Ben Miller** (see p.984) is the standout corporate attorney at the firm. A founding member and "*one of the leading practitioners in Baton Rouge for many years,*" he supplements his corporate finance and M&A work with expertise in tax and real estate. **Blane Clark** (see p.978) enters the rankings amid endorsement from clients and peers alike. His recent representations have included acting for a local industry support company and its shareholders in the sale of stock to a global service provider.

**Clients/Work Highlights:** Albemarle; Associated Grocers; DSM; SGS Petroleum Services Corporation; Regions Bank; The Shaw Group and The Williams Companies.

### Phelps Dunbar LLP
See firm details p.997

**The Firm:** Clients showered praise upon a team that was dubbed "*absolutely painless to deal with.*" The effort its lawyers invest in educating and informing clients, particularly when it comes to securities, M&A and venture capital financing, was repeatedly identified as the firm's unique selling point. As one commentator remarked, its attorneys "*excel both professionally and personally and go beyond the call of duty to help.*" Strong links with the Houston office mean the firm is able to retain a strong client roster of public and private companies across the Gulf Coast. In the past twelve months the team acted as local counsel to Hibernia Corporation in its multi-billion-dollar acquisition by Capital One.

**The Lawyers:** Securities and M&A expert **Mark Fullmer** (see p.980) enjoys extensive market support for his transactional expertise: "*He is a unique talent with a well-honed business instinct,*" and has acted in various high-profile acquisitions and issuances by national banks and holding companies. **Patrick Butler** (see p.977) has increasingly focused on M&A and general corporate work. Managing an acquisition and divestiture program for a major client has taken up much of his time recently. Litigator **Brent Barriere** (see p.977) was applauded for his "*rare combination of legal knowledge, business savvy and command of the courtroom.*" He is heavily involved in both general commercial and bankruptcy cases, and has a niche practice representing litigation trusts and trustees in cases against officers and directors in Chapter 11 proceedings. Working alongside him, **Ault Hootsell** (see p.982) joins the rankings upon receiving extensive praise from clients and peers: "*He is one of the most practical trial lawyers I have ever worked with – he has a tremendous work ethic.*"

**Clients/Work Highlights:** Audubon Capital Fund; Edison Chouest Offshore; Hibernia National Bank; INNOVUS; Isle of Capri Casinos; L&B Consulting; Waste Management and Whitney National Bank.

### Stone Pigman Walther Wittmann LLC
See firm details p.999

**The Firm:** This "*tremendous law firm*" houses a "*broad practice with expertise across the board.*" The team has built upon a diverse regional client list with a number of national and international clients. Of particular note, it represented a local service company when it was acquired for $600 million. On the purchaser side, the group advised an important client on acquisitions in the USA and Canada.

The Lawyers: Chair of the firm's corporate and securities practice group, **Joseph Caverly** (see p.978) was the subject of effusive market praise. Since joining the firm 20 years ago, he has been at the forefront on many of the group's most significant transactions. Interviewees also celebrated the talents of **Scott Whittaker** (see p.988), chair of the business section of the firm. He predominantly focuses on M&A and "*employs a nice soft style that avoids confrontation in negotiations.*"

Clients/Work Highlights: The firm represents a range of acquiring companies, investment bankers, venture capitalists and institutional private investors, as well as partnerships, limited partnerships and trusts.

## Band 3

### Adams and Reese LLP

See firm details p.989

The Firm: The sizable corporate and securities team at this large multiservice firm has an impressive reach across the southern states, where it benefits from an extensive network of offices. The team advises private and publicly held organizations on securities offerings and M&A transactions, as well as the negotiation of credit facilities and venture capital financing. It is perceived to be expanding apace.

The Lawyers: There is a strong consensus that **Virginia Boulet** (see p.977) is the firm's leading corporate lawyer. An active figure in the local market for many years, she is currently special counsel to the firm. Elsewhere, **Robin Cheatham** (see p.978) and **John Duck** (see p.979) were described as "*big players*" in bankruptcy work. They have both represented a wide range of parties from various industry sectors in assorted bankruptcy proceedings across the southern states and beyond.

Clients/Work Highlights: The firm represents clients from a vast array of industries, ranging from airline and pharmaceutical to catering and broadcasting sectors.

### Liskow & Lewis PLC

The Firm: Primarily known for its strength in real estate and the oil and gas industry, Liskow & Lewis is also highly regarded for the financing and M&A work it undertakes. "*The firm offers attorneys who are easy to work with; it has a strong practice, there's no question,*" said one client, summing up the general view of the market. The practice centers on New Orleans and Lafayette offices, and the group has significant regional reach.

The Lawyers: The "*versatile*" **John Wogan** was described as a "*great all-around business lawyer.*" In addition to a strong reputation for banking and finance work, he is also a player in the M&A market. Commercial litigator **Philip Jones** cements his position in the rankings following his representation of the creditors in a number of high-profile bankruptcy filings. This included a nine-day confirmation hearing following the bankruptcy of a Fortune 500 oil company and an appearance in the Entergy filing.

Clients/Work Highlights: BP America; Chevron; Columbian Chemicals; Harrah's Entertainment; Hibernia National Bank; Hunt Oil; JPMorgan Chase; Shell and Whitney National Bank.

### McGlinchey Stafford

See firm details p.996

The Firm: The sizable corporate group at this large full-service firm provides "*tremendous resources and support staff,*" according to sources. Clients commented favorably on its "*intelligent and streetwise attorneys*" who are "*adept at getting deals done.*" A broad focus incorporates the full spectrum of corporate work, and recent highlights include representing Analytic Stress in the acquisition of a division of The Shaw Group. The team has also assisted a manufacturing company with creating an insurance network.

The Lawyers: "*An incredibly hard worker and quick study,*" **Rudy Aguilar** (see p.976) was described by one interviewee as "*an absolute gem to work with.*" Based in Baton Rouge, he is the first port of call at the firm for many satisfied clients. Leading the charge in New Orleans, **Jim Fantaci** (see p.979) was afforded much praise for his M&A work. His practice also involves business formation, restructuring and general corporate work. Largely focusing on representing creditors, **Rudy Cerone** (see p.978) received much praise for his work in Chapter 11 bankruptcy proceedings. He has a subspecialization in casino bankruptcies and recently represented significant bondholders in the Hollywood Casino Shreveport bankruptcy.

### Taylor, Porter, Brooks & Phillips, LLP

The Firm: A "*well-known and established name*" in Baton Rouge, the firm is home to a "*solid corporate practice.*" However, it does not have formalized departments and as such the ten attorneys devoting a significant proportion of their time to corporate work all bring significant experience from other disciplines to the table. Members of the firm have recently advised on the transfer of responsibility for managing 70,000 acres of wetland and on the transfer of ownership of two motor vehicle distributorships.

The Lawyers: General business and finance practitioner **John Campbell** has a caseload that includes gaming, real estate lending, and public and private finance work. Market commentators agreed: "*He is very personable and represents his clients well.*"

Clients/Work Highlights: Alma Plantation; AEP; Argosy Gaming; Chemical Waste Management; Chevron Products; Dixie Plantation; Dow Chemical; Parish Water and Shell Pipeline.

## Other Notable Practitioners

The "*honest and personable*" **Anthony DiLeo**, formerly of Stone Pigman, established himself as a sole practitioner in October 2005. His focus is on business, corporate and partnerships work, with a heavy emphasis on the healthcare sector. The prevailing view among a large client following is that "*he is a terrific guy doing an outstanding job.*" **Steven Klein**, of Sher Garner Cahill Richter Klein & Hibbert LLC, was praised for the structuring and investment work which flows from his first-rate tax practice. At Baker, Donelson, Bearman, Caldwell & Berkowitz, PC, the "*highly competent*" **William Norton** (see p.984) is perceived as spearheading the national giant's efforts to push into the Louisiana market. Recent highlights for him include involvement in the leveraged lease financing of an offshore drilling platform. "*True professional*" **Charles Snyder** of Milling Benson Woodward LLP has acquired a staunch client following during his lengthy legal career. Meanwhile, **Doug Draper**, **William Patrick** and **Jan Hayden** at "*premier bankruptcy boutique*" Heller, Draper, Hayden, Patrick & Horn, LLC lead the way where Louisiana's bankruptcy work is concerned. The market views the trio as "*the preeminent debtor counsel in Louisiana,*" although their involvement in all the major bankruptcy cases in the state has included significant creditor representation too. Draper and Patrick were also the names most often cited by peers as the first choice of attorneys to refer work to in a conflict. The "*competent and thorough*" **David Forsyth** of Sessions, Fishman & Nathan LLP is said to "*excel in the courtroom.*" He specializes primarily in real estate litigation, with an emphasis on the retail sector. **Alan Goodman** and **David Waguespack** of Lemle & Kelleher, LLP enter the rankings in recognition of their activity in the bankruptcy arena. Goodman was described as "*one of the best attorneys when negotiations become combative,*" while Waguespack was labeled "*a promising up-and-comer.*"

# EMPLOYMENT

## MAINLY DEFENDANT

## Band 1

### Jones Walker Waechter Poitevent Carrère & Denègre, LLP

See firm details p.994

**The Firm:** Observers unanimously agreed that this firm, which enjoys a well-respected national presence, thoroughly deserves its top-tier ranking. It has tremendous strength in depth with which to press the interests of its clients across the region and throughout the USA. Indeed, clients say they "*revel in the attention*" given to their cause by the attorneys at "*this outstanding firm.*" Its membership of the Employers Counsel Network, a national coalition of firms, further enhances the firm's profile. The practice encompasses traditional labor and employment litigation as well as OSHA matters, and the team comprises 18 attorneys, of whom nine are partners. **The Lawyers:** Head of labor and employment, **Mark Adams** (see p.976) has been especially busy

recently, assisting employers and employees in coming to terms with the aftermath of Hurricane Katrina. In this respect he advised clients on coping with reductions in force and relocation programs, as well as amending severance plans so that employees can take advantage of their benefits. Prior to the storms he was involved in defending employment litigation such as noncompetition and EEOC disputes, and counseled Sodexho through a DOL investigation. Traditional labor specialist **Clyde Jacob** (see p.982) is actively involved in union elections as a negotiator and counsels companies on the effects of terminations and reductions in force. Commentators regard him as a "*fine labor lawyer,*" and his recent successes include representing Sanderson Farms in one of the largest union elections of the year. Clients rate **Sidney Lewis** (see p.983) highly for both labor relations and employment litigation. One in particular noted that Lewis is "*good at problem-solving and likes rolling up his sleeves and getting stuck in to the detail.*" He is renowned for his performance in EEOC matters, where he is valued for "*aggressively pursuing*" his client's interests and avoiding damaging litigation. **Cornelius Heusel** (see p.982) is principally a litigator and represents clients in cases involving discrimination of all types, as well as in wage and hour class actions. His recent highlights include getting a wage and hour class action dismissed, defeating offshore-based immigrant workers claiming entitlement to US fair pay laws. **Clients/Work Highlights:** Capital City Press; Flying J; Home Depot; Ruby Tuesday Restaurants; Ruth's Chris Steak House; Morrison Management Services; Turner Industries; Wells Fargo and Freeport McMoRan.

### The Kullman Firm PLC

**The Firm:** This boutique labor and employment firm has been at the forefront of the practice area for 60 years. During this time, it has been instrumental in the development of labor law in Louisiana and built up a client base hailing from across the USA. Members of the firm represent some of the largest regional employers in employment litigation, and observers remark the firm is also a market leader in terms of traditional labor-relations work. As such, it is especially active in the fields of arbitration, campaigns and elections, RICO and collective bargaining. The firm is structured in such a way as to manage day-to-day counseling alongside emergencies as and when they arise. **The Lawyers:** The "*outstanding*" **Ernest Malone** "*excels at everything,*" say sources. Commentators note his clients always feel well attended by him and admire his "*common-sense approach*" to any problem that he faces. Malone's practice centers on counseling employers in strategic planning and employment policy. He also represents employers in collective bargaining and in contract negotiations. "*One of the best labor practitioners in the state,*" was how one market source described **Howard Linzy**. He is

particularly active in negotiations, especially when it comes to union election matters, as well as being closely tied to some major regional employers. **Bob Spencer** is another of the firm's leading labor attorneys. He frequently appears in front of the NLRB on behalf of management in cases relating to union organizing, elections and defending unfair labor practice charges.
**Clients/Work Highlights:** The firm represents clients from many different industry groups including banking and finance, oil and gas, construction, aviation and manufacturing.

## Band 2

### Fisher & Phillips LLP

See firm details p.732

**The Firm:** A devoted labor and employment giant, it is perceived to have benefited hugely from a string of lateral hires over the last few years. With 15 offices nationwide, the firm can compete with the best in the field when it comes to employment discrimination litigation and traditional labor relations. The 18-lawyer team in Louisiana excels in its own right by representing Fortune 500 employers in negotiations and before the NLRB.
**The Lawyers:** Commentators have nothing but respect for the abilities of **Robert McCalla** (see p.983). His practice covers the broad sweep of labor and employment issues and he has many years of experience negotiating collective bargaining agreements as well as handling discrimination class actions. In a recent highlight he managed to have a class action dismissed that could otherwise have potentially involved thousands of plaintiffs. One source summed up McCalla as being "*among the best labor and employment lawyers in the whole country and a perfect gentleman.*" Observers agree that **Keith Pyburn** (see p.985) is a "*key figure*" in the state where labor negotiations are concerned. He recently negotiated new contracts with a number of unions on behalf of a major oil and gas client. **Michael Mitchell** (see p.984) impressed clients as an excellent union negotiator. Special praise was reserved for the effort he goes to in order to minimize the exposure of clients to EEOC claims, which sources said they "*would be lost without.*"
**Clients/Work Highlights:** The firm acts for major companies such as the likes of ConocoPhillips and Pan-American Life.

## Band 3

### Adams and Reese LLP

See firm details p.989

**The Firm:** The sophistication of its employment insurance practice marks this firm out from others in the field. The group also maintains its solid reputation in the Gulf region for discrimination litigation and advising on labor relations. As a large firm it can call upon an impressive depth of resources with which to service clients throughout the USA. Since the storms its lawyers have been active in EEOC and wage and hour litigation cases.

**The Lawyers:** Well regarded by market sources for his skills across the practice area, **Brooke Duncan** (see p.979) recently represented Freeman Decorating in contract negotiations with unions. He has also appeared many times before the NLRB on behalf of management.

**Clients/Work Highlights:** The firm represents clients from a wide variety of industries, including some of the leading companies in the Southeast states.

### Breazeale, Sachse & Wilson, LLP

**The Firm:** Commentators admire this *"fiercely competitive"* outfit for its success in employment discrimination litigation. As a stalwart of Baton Rouge the firm prides itself in either forcing settlement before trial or straining every sinew to achieve the optimum result when the courts cannot be avoided.

**The Lawyers:** Chairman of the firm's labor and employment practice, **Murphy Foster** is widely regarded as a litigator of considerable repute for discrimination cases. Commentators value his *"bullishness"* and his determination to push cases hard.

**Clients/Work Highlights:** Clients come from all manner of industries including banking, construction, manufacturing, transport and retail.

### Frilot, Partridge, Kohnke & Clements LC

**The Firm:** Peers and clients alike were quick to point out that the firm should be recognized due to the strength of its employment litigation practice. The team handles complaints before the EEOC, OFCCP and various other agencies as well as litigation in state and federal courts. Clients praised the firm's *"real go-to lawyers"* for endeavoring to quickly resolve cases wherever possible.

**The Lawyers:** Robert McNeal and Walter Christy are the key contacts here.

**Clients/Work Highlights:** AutoZone; Sears Roebuck; Murphy Oil and Alliance Mortgage Company.

### Kean, Miller, Hawthorne, D'Armond, McCowan & Jarman, LLP

See firm details p.995

**The Firm:** There was strong consensus that this 11-attorney group punches well above its weight and frequently competes with much larger firms for big oil and gas clients. Indeed, the team represents international and national clients in federal and state courts, as well as handling the employment aspects of corporate acquisitions and divestitures. Clients were entirely satisfied with the litigation services provided by the firm and found its lawyers to be *"very diligent"* over billing.

**The Lawyers:** While **William D'Armond** (see p.979) continues to have contact with clients, he has withdrawn significantly from the frontline and acts as of counsel. However, this *"bright and trustworthy guy"* is still a major resource for the firm. Employment litigator **Melanie Hartmann** (see p.981) comes highly commended for her work in the federal courts. Clients remarked: *"Her work is excellent, she is very professional and her opponents respect her."*

**Clients/Work Highlights:** American Gateway Bank; City of Baton Rouge; ExxonMobil; IBM and Vulcan Materials.

### McGlinchey Stafford

See firm details p.996

**The Firm:** With a network of eight offices in five states, this *"superior"* firm is well equipped to cover both employment litigation and traditional labor matters throughout Louisiana and beyond. Particular emphasis is placed on the prevention of litigation and members of the firm channel considerable resources into training management to avoid EEOC claims. In the wake of the storms the firm has been active in addressing the implications of the Warren Act for employers in the New Orleans area. Clients value the level of communication sustained by lawyers here too: *"They keep us aware of what is going on every step of the way."*

**The Lawyers:** Clients agree that given **Fredrick Preis'** (see p.985) ability to interact with opposing parties and his fast response times, litigation is that much easier to avoid. The *"highly credible"* **Mark Mallery** (see p.983) represents employers in complex whistle-blower cases, EEOC class actions and collective actions under the FLSA. He also performs some collective bargaining and represents management in union campaigns.

**Clients/Work Highlights:** ARAMARK; Interstate Warehousing; Louisiana Hotel & Lodging Association; Martin & Bayley; Namasco; Officemax; Target and Winn-Dixie.

### Phelps Dunbar LLP

See firm details p.997

**The Firm:** A seven-office network throughout the Gulf region makes the firm a valuable resource for employers involved in litigation in one or more of the Southern states. The team is experienced in representing clients before the EEOC, NLRB and OFCCP as well as state and federal courts. Providing alternative dispute resolution services is also high on the firm's agenda.

**The Lawyers:** Owing to her *"overwhelming knowledge of the law,"* **Nan Alessandra** (see p.976) is a popular choice among clients, and she spends most of her time counseling employers. Policy advice is considered one of her fortes, and she is perceived as being at the forefront of developments in the handling of cases concerning communicable illnesses. Alessandra also handles a hefty employment discrimination and harassment litigation caseload. Market sources hold **Thomas Kiggans** (see p.982) in high regard for *"always being well prepared"* in contentious contexts. He has increasingly specialized in racial and nationality-based harassment claims of late.

**Clients/Work Highlights:** City of New Orleans; City of Baton Rouge; Dow Chemical; Georgia Gulf; Laitram; Louisiana Lottery; Turner Industries; Vertex Aerospace and Domino's Pizza.

### Taylor, Porter, Brooks & Phillips, LLP

**The Firm:** This ten-lawyer employment, labor and benefits group is best known for its prowess in contentious settings and is well regarded for its track record in overseeing union elections. One of the oldest firms in the state, it has been instrumental in significantly reducing the presence of the unions over the last few decades.

**The Lawyers:** *"Bright and well-prepared"* discrimination litigator **Vicki Crochet** was billed as a *"truly excellent lawyer."* Despite a year disturbed by illness she is now back up to speed again, advising clients in the construction industry among others on how to avoid discrimination violations and claims. Clients repeatedly call upon **Michael Pharis** (see p.984) for assistance during labor negotiations.

**Clients/Work Highlights:** Clients include Blue Cross and Blue Shield of Louisiana, Head and Enquist Equipment and Louisiana State University.

### Other Notable Practitioners

**Thomas McGoey** of Liskow & Lewis PLC enters the table as a leading employment discrimination lawyer. He has successfully litigated cases in trial and appellate courts at both state and federal levels, and is also well regarded for his arbitration practice.

# ENERGY & NATURAL RESOURCES

**Energy & Natural Resources**
Leading Firms

1. GORDON, ARATA, MCCOLLAM *New Orleans*
   JONES WALKER *New Orleans*
   LISKOW & LEWIS PLC *New Orleans*
2. CARVER DARDEN KORETZKY TESSIER *New Orleans*
   KEAN, MILLER, HAWTHORNE *Baton Rouge*
   PHELPS DUNBAR LLP *New Orleans*
   SCHULLY, ROBERTS, SLATTERY *New Orleans*
   STONE PIGMAN WALTHER WITTMANN *New Orleans*

**Leading Individuals**

1. ARNOLD III Edward *Baker, Donelson*
   CARVER Hampton *Carver Darden Koretzky Tessier*
   DUPLANTIS BJ *Gordon, Arata, McCollam*
   FONTHAM Michael *Stone Pigman Walther Wittmann*
   HUNTER Jonathon *Liskow & Lewis PLC*
   KING Katherine *Kean, Miller, Hawthorne*
   MCCOLLAM John *Gordon, Arata, McCollam*
   ROSENBLUM Carl *Jones Walker*
   WOLF Alan *Phelps Dunbar LLP*

**Energy & Natural Resources:**
**Marine Finance**
Leading Individuals

1. BENNETT Blake *Liskow & Lewis PLC*
   BRODERS John *Jones Walker*
   KING Henry *King, LeBlanc & Bland*
   ROUSSEL James *Baker, Donelson*

## Band 1

### Gordon, Arata, McCollam, Duplantis & Eagan LLP

**The Firm:** This firm's impressive domestic reputation centers on its oil and gas work, and its large energy practice houses *"some senior practitioners who are very well respected and among the most knowledgeable in the state."* Matters handled include gas purchase contract disputes, mineral leases, seismic permits, onshore and offshore joint operating agreements and pipeline construction projects. In addition, the group offers expertise in personal injury and property damage claims arising from oil and gas operations and also handles a diverse range of corporate work in the energy sector.

**The Lawyers:** Interviewees singled out the *"extremely talented"* Bob Duplantis in Lafayette for his prowess in litigation. He routinely represents many different clients before the Louisiana Office of Conservation and Office of Mineral Resources. *"An institution in his own right,"* John McCollam in New Orleans was the subject of extensive market praise, in which his *"devastating combination of abilities"* came in for special commendation. Peers branded him *"the dean of the practice area,"* and his broad practice embraces transactional and regulatory energy work, as well as related litigation and arbitration.

**Clients/Work Highlights:** The firm represents an array of oil and gas producers, onshore and offshore operators, pipeline companies, seismic companies and financial institutions.

### Jones Walker Waechter Poitevent Carrère & Denègre, LLP

See firm details p.994

**The Firm:** The market resounded with praise for this large, broad-based firm, which is able to draw upon vast resources in order to compete with the specialist firms in the market. A large team comprises attorneys who are experienced in a range of areas, making for a diverse practice. Its lawyers are said to *"put the client first, roll up their sleeves and get things done."* Recent representations have hinged on class actions and force majeure issues in the wake of the hurricanes.

**The Lawyers:** A well-regarded litigator who covers a variety of areas, Carl Rosenblum (see p.985) heads up the energy litigation practice. Clients described him as a *"go-to guy for big problems,"* because *"he takes a client's case personally and hates to lose."* Admiralty expert John Broders (see p.977) boasts an extensive track record in the field and vast experience of maritime transactions and related mortgage, lien, insurance and property issues.

**Clients/Work Highlights:** American Commercial Barge Line; Global Industries; JM Huber; Massey Energy; McMoRan Oil & Gas; Sundown Energy; TGS-NOPEC Geophysical; Tidewater and Trico Marine Assets.

### Liskow & Lewis PLC

**The Firm:** Its long and successful history as an oil and gas firm is perceived to stand this operation in good stead. Well-regarded teams focusing on transactions on the one hand and litigation on the other mean the firm has *"a lot of lawyers in the trenches."* Its consistent involvement in significant property restoration cases further defines the practice and clients repeatedly remarked upon the advantages of working with a *"service-oriented firm where the lawyers have a superior approach to understanding a business from the client's perspective."* Highlights of the past twelve months include a number of significant national pipeline financings.

**The Lawyers:** Jonathon Hunter is billed as a *"top-tier"* litigator in the energy field. *"An exceptionally talented lawyer, he offers a lot of bang for your buck,"* sources confirm. On the admiralty side, the *"truly outstanding"* Blake Bennett is recommended for his marine finance expertise and regularly handles the finance and maritime components of offshore operations. Bennett also offers niche expertise in riverboat gaming.

**Clients/Work Highlights:** An impressive and extensive client list includes both independent and major oil companies, among which feature BP, Chevron and Shell.

## Band 2

### Carver Darden Koretzky Tessier Finn Blossman & Areaux LLC

**The Firm:** Now over ten years old, this firm has fast gained a reputation among peers for representing energy and exploration clients with considerable aplomb. Its work for oil and gas companies has earned it a place in this year's rankings. Above all, clients singled out the *"considerable experience"* of its lawyers in disputes relating to contracts and to exploration issues, as well as in oil and gas title transactions.

**The Lawyers:** One of the founders of the firm, Hampton Carver impressed fellow practitioners with his *"good instincts and wide-ranging knowledge."* Much of his work relates to the Outer Continental Shelf and related leases, federal regulations, disputes, contract negotiations, oil and gas transportation issues and deepwater operations.

**Clients/Work Highlights:** Bass Enterprises Production; Chevron Pipe Line; Nexen Petroleum Offshore USA and Shell Offshore.

### Kean, Miller, Hawthorne, D'Armond, McCowan & Jarman, LLP

See firm details p.995

**The Firm:** The firm works closely with the Louisiana Department of Natural Resources, the Mineral Board and the Office of Coastal Restoration and Management in representing the interests of the many large oil and gas companies. The energy team at the firm handles a variety of matters including contract negotiation, transactions, oil and gas litigation and regulatory issues that involve the transportation of oil and gas.

**The Lawyers:** Market commentators admire Katherine King (see p.982) for her *"thoroughness and depth of knowledge,"* especially where public utilities are concerned. Her recent highlights include renegotiating a power supply contract, representing clients successfully in rate cases and involvement in alternative-fuel generation projects.

**Clients/Work Highlights:** ExxonMobil; Chevron; ConocoPhillips; Shell; BP and CITGO.

### Phelps Dunbar LLP

See firm details p.997

**The Firm:** This perennial performer offers extensive expertise in public utility law with an overwhelming emphasis on the electricity sector. Although best known as an important player in the shipping sector, the team has also shown itself to be adept in handling gas utility and wider administrative and energy law issues.

**The Lawyers:** Sources waxed lyrical about Alan Wolf (see p.988), who is *"even-handed and professional to a fault,"* according to commentators. The director of the firm's public utilities and electric power practice *"does a great job for his clients"* and is often associated with long-standing client Cleco. According to rivals this *"superior"* attorney is *"a pleasure to work with."*

**Clients/Work Highlights:** Cleco Corporation and Cleco Power can both be counted as clients.

## Schully, Roberts, Slattery, Jaubert & Marino

**The Firm:** Commentators were quick to praise this boutique environmental law firm for its work in the oil and gas sector. Its ten-strong team is praised as "*a great bunch of guys for transactional work.*"

**The Lawyers:** Anthony Marino is a key contact at the firm for oil and gas transactions.

**Clients/Work Highlights:** Amerada Hess; Apex Oil & Gas; Constellation Energy Group; Energy Partners; Energy Resource Technology; ExxonMobil; Fidelity Exploration & Production; Gryphon Exploration and Swift Energy.

## Stone Pigman Walther Wittmann LLC

See firm details p.999

**The Firm:** For nearly 30 years this firm has acted as special counsel to the Louisiana Public Service Commission (LPSC) in major rate cases and litigation involving charges paid for utilities by Louisiana companies. Regulatory compliance is its forte, and the team frequently defends clients from a range of industries against lawsuits brought by the DOJ, the EPA and the Louisiana Department of Environmental Quality.

**The Lawyers:** The "*excellent*" Michael Fontham (see p.980) is said to "*know the regulatory arena better than anyone,*" and clients and peers alike applaud his tremendous reputation in the field of public utility regulation. Fontham chairs the regulatory practice group of the firm and lectures extensively on public utility law.

**Clients/Work Highlights:** LPSC is the firm's major client, though construction, public service and transportation entities also contribute to its workload.

## Other Notable Practitioners

Interviewees singled out **Hank Arnold** (see p.977) as the leading attorney in a promising group at Baker, Donelson, Bearman, Caldwell & Berkowitz, PC. His transactional focus has led to him being heavily involved in new projects, as well as representing a vessel-operating company and a bank in energy-related transactions. A recent highlight was his participation in the $300 million sale of an offshore platform. Arnold has now been joined by **James Roussel** (see p.985), a former Phelps Dunbar lawyer. As a maritime specialist, he covers collisions, class actions and large marine financings, with a recent highlight involving an oil pollution case. **Henry King** is a newcomer to this year's rankings. A partner at King, LeBlanc & Bland, PLLC, he was praised for his high-profile marine finance activity and impressive client base, which includes some large financial institutions.

# ENVIRONMENT

## Environment
### Leading Firms

1. **ADAMS AND REESE LLP** *New Orleans*
   **JONES WALKER** *New Orleans*
   **KEAN, MILLER, HAWTHORNE** *Baton Rouge*
   **LISKOW & LEWIS PLC** *New Orleans*
   **PHELPS DUNBAR LLP** *New Orleans*
   **TAYLOR, PORTER, BROOKS & PHILLIPS** *Baton Rouge*

### Leading Individuals

1. **CHERNEKOFF Michael** *Jones Walker*
   **DICHARRY Paul** *Taylor, Porter, Brooks*
   **HARBOURT Maureen** *Kean, Miller, Hawthorne*
   **HOLDEN Robert** *Liskow & Lewis PLC*
   **KILGORE III Leonard** *Kean, Miller, Hawthorne*
   **LEVINE Steve** *Phelps Dunbar LLP*
   **MCCOWAN Charles** *Kean, Miller, Hawthorne*
   **NOSEWICZ Thomas** *Jones Walker*
   **PILIE Glen** *Adams and Reese LLP*

## Band 1

### Adams and Reese LLP

See firm details p.989

**The Firm:** While Adams and Reese offers a full-service environment practice, it is the team's strength in litigation that steals the limelight for commentators. Hazardous waste cases are a specialty, but these impressive advocates have represented a range of clients in tort and contractual matters. The group also applies its mastery of international, federal and state laws to dealing with regulatory issues. In this respect, a recent highlight was the defense of a major client against a class action involving a substance carried by a pipe owned by the company.

**The Lawyers:** Commentators credited litigator **Glen Pilié** (see p.984) with "*having gotten clients out of a lot of jams.*" A renowned expert in defending major oil companies in class actions and remediation cases, he also offers extensive knowledge of naturally-occurring radioactive material or NORM issues. Pilié is currently defending a class action brought against a major client as a result of Hurricane Katrina, where it is alleged that oil and gas work in the marshes damaged the natural protection offered by the site against the disaster.

**Clients/Work Highlights:** The firm's client roster includes oil and gas companies, financial institutions, chemical companies and manufacturers.

### Jones Walker Waechter Poitevent Carrère & Denègre, LLP

See firm details p.994

**The Firm:** With 15 dedicated environment lawyers across the state, Jones Walker possesses a depth of talent that few other firms in Louisiana can match. Many of its attorneys are former regulators and prosecutors, and several serve as law professors. The diverse backgrounds of its practitioners enable the team to provide a unique insight into complex environmental issues and regulatory disputes. In addition to abundant experience in class actions and enforcement cases, the firm is also talented in the transactional arena. It has been active in the legal issues surrounding the cleanup after Hurricane Katrina.

**The Lawyers:** "*If I were a client with a big case, Mike would be on the list,*" enthused one source commenting on **Michael Chernekoff** (see p.978). Environmental and toxic torts litigation accounts for most of this experienced attorney's time, particularly those cases involving the contamination of property by oil and gas companies. Chernekoff is currently advising several clients in New Orleans on the cleanup and disposal of debris and waste after Hurricane Katrina. Also renowned for his defense of class action lawsuits is **Thomas Nosewicz** (see p.984). His most significant transaction of late is the defeat of a huge class action regarding waste management at a hazardous waste site.

**Clients/Work Highlights:** The firm's clients range in size from Fortune 500 companies to the owners of small businesses.

### Kean, Miller, Hawthorne, D'Armond, McCowan & Jarman, LLP

See firm details p.995

**The Firm:** This relatively young firm is noted for its thriving Baton Rouge presence and coveted relationship with the Louisiana Chemical Association. Superfund cases and remediation strategy in the context of hazardous and non-hazardous waste issues are where these "*focused*" attorneys excel. The team was recently engaged as state and federal environmental counsel for Louisiana in a case relating to an LNG regasification-receiving terminal in Cameron Parish. It has also successfully obtained air and water permits on behalf of a large energy company for a greenfield merchant power plant in Lincoln Parish, in the face of significant opposition in the local community.

**The Lawyers:** The "*fabulous*" **Charles McCowan** (see p.984) is celebrated for his appearances in high-profile cases and his "*wonderful way with juries.*" He represents several companies in the petrochemical industry in toxic tort and commercial class actions involving thousands of class members. McCowan is also noted for his enviable position as counsel to the Louisiana Chemical Association. Equally talented is the "*trustworthy and knowledgeable*" **Leonard Kilgore** (see p.982). Praised for his ability to "comprehend the technical and legal issues involved and understand the ins and outs," Kilgore's true strength lies in Superfund litigation. He has represented clients in relation to state and federal Superfund sites including Shoreline Refinery Site, Dutchtown Site and Line Avenue Creosote Site. Kilgore is also sought out for his expertise in defending class actions. **Maureen Harbourt** (see p.980) lends her "steel-trap mind" to representing industrial and commercial clients in a variety of environmental regulatory issues. She has counseled a national chemical company on environmental issues relating to the multimillion-dollar acquisition of a Lake Charles facility, and has advised several clients in the energy industry.

**Clients/Work Highlights:** The Louisiana Chemical Association is the firm's most prominent client, but it attracts other Louisiana-based businesses and several Fortune 500 companies.

### Liskow & Lewis PLC

**The Firm:** Liskow & Lewis continues to impress market commentators and is nationally recognized for its environmental prowess at state and local levels. Collaboration between the firm's environment lawyers and white-collar criminal attorneys has led to the formation of the environmental criminal defense practice group, which has successfully defended corporate and individual clients in internal and grand jury investigations. It also assists with the drafting of compliance programs. Elsewhere, the firm handles coverage litigation against insurance carriers relating to issues such as pollution and waste disposal. It has undertaken numerous tort cases in Louisiana courts concerning allegations of damage done to land caused by industrial operations.

**The Lawyers: Robert Holden** is "great at advising on sophisticated regulatory issues." Energy and chemical companies frequently retain him as defense counsel in civil and criminal enforcement cases. He handled a nationally prominent controversy involving a major chemical company's attempts to obtain permits for the construction of an integrated polyvinyl chloride manufacturing complex near St James Parish. Holden has also represented energy and sulfur companies in various regulatory matters before the Minerals Management Service and the Interior Board of Land Appeals.

**Clients/Work Highlights:** The firm has garnered a host of national and international clients, but also represents numerous local organizations on a pro bono basis.

### Phelps Dunbar LLP

See firm details p.997

**The Firm:** The firm has been around for over 150 years and is one of the oldest in the state. The technical expertise of its environmental team is supplemented by close collaboration with industry experts specializing in a diverse range of disciplines, including toxicology and hydrology. Clients are counseled on permitting and compliance as well as the drafting of documents and site assessments. On the litigation front, the firm tries cases before judicial and administrative bodies, and recent highlights include successfully representing two waste management companies in an environmental damages and trespass suit arising from alleged oil field waste contamination. Judicial review proceedings further contribute to the firm's workload in the field.

**The Lawyers:** The "steadfast" **Steve Levine** (see p.983) is described as being "assertive without being aggressive." Commentators applauded his "collaborative approach" and "resilience when approaching an issue with a radical solution." Clients say Levine's scientific background is invaluable for analyzing cases and communicating with experts. His practice comprises both contentious and noncontentious regulatory matters, with a bias toward permitting issues. He recently handled a significant trial involving environmental trespass.

**Clients/Work Highlights:** Clients include financial institutions, healthcare systems, insurance companies, educational institutions, partnerships and governmental agencies.

### Taylor, Porter, Brooks & Phillips, LLP

**The Firm:** Commentators praised this firm for its solid regulatory practice and talented team of litigators. Its team is presently acting as counsel to a corporation involved in the remediation process surrounding one of the largest Superfund sites in the country. Other significant matters include obtaining an operating permit for the largest commercial hazardous waste treatment, storage and disposal facility in the state and representing local government bodies in the privatization of municipal landfill sites.

**The Lawyers:** A prominent new recruit for the firm, **Paul Dicharry** is renowned for his robust regulatory practice. He has served as lead counsel in obtaining permits for several industrial facilities and headed litigation teams defending cases involving Superfund and remediation sites.

**Clients/Work Highlights:** Chemical Waste Management; Entergy Corporation; City of Baton Rouge and the State of Louisiana.

# GAMING & LICENSING

| Gaming & Licensing Leading Firms | |
|---|---|
| **1** | JONES WALKER *New Orleans* |
| | MCGLINCHEY STAFFORD *Baton Rouge* |
| **2** | PHELPS DUNBAR LLP *New Orleans* |

| Leading Individuals | |
|---|---|
| **1** | DUNCAN J Kelly *Jones Walker* |
| | WEST Paul *McGlinchey Stafford* |
| **2** | BLACKBURN Frank *Sole Practitioner* |
| | HARKINS Deborah *McGlinchey Stafford* |
| **3** | BENNETT Blake *Liskow & Lewis PLC* |
| | RESTER Daniel *Adams and Reese LLP* |
| | WALLACE Brian *Phelps Dunbar LLP* |

| Up-and-coming individuals | |
|---|---|
| | BARBIN Jeffrey *Phelps Dunbar LLP* |

## Band 1

### Jones Walker Waechter Poitevent Carrère & Denègre, LLP

See firm details p.994

**The Firm:** Clients applaud this team's sophisticated licensing attorneys, who can tap into the firm's substantial resources as necessary, and have become a powerful force in the Southern gaming arena. The group has been at the forefront of the gaming industry since it arrived in Louisiana, representing casino companies and financial institutions in relation to the development, operation and financing of gaming facilities. As such, it played a key role in the recent consolidation of the major casino companies, which included representing Columbia and an affiliate in the acquisitions of the Belle of Orleans and Belle of Baton Rouge riverboat casinos. For many satisfied clients, "what sets the firm apart is the way its lawyers work with you and always apply their knowledge in a proactive manner."

**The Lawyers:** Chair of the firm's gaming practice **Kelly Duncan** (see p.979) is widely respected in the market for his regulatory and transactional know-how. "His lengthy experience of working with all the leading players on both sides of the table means he knows who to go to and how to get things done," say sources. Duncan's constant interfacing with the regulatory agencies was put to good use when he handled the gaming and regulatory matters arising out of the restructuring, bankruptcy and sale of Hollywood Casino Shreveport.

**Clients/Work Highlights:** Columbia Entertainment; GTECH; Konami Gaming and Spielo Manufacturing.

### McGlinchey Stafford

See firm details p.996

**The Firm:** The regulatory strength of this firm's sizable gaming practice is scarcely matched anywhere in the state. A strong focus on the sector over a period of many years has led to the team forming unique relationships with gaming boards and commissions. Its well-regarded practice covers all aspects of gaming work associated with representing casino operators, investors, lenders and suppliers.

The team recently acted as bond counsel on the Hollywood Casino Shreveport transaction.

**The Lawyers:** *"A certain leader in the field,"* **Paul West** (see p.988) represents clients on a range of regulatory, transactional and litigation issues. His position in the rankings reflects the high esteem in which he is held within the industry: as one market observer remarked, *"his word carries a lot of weight with the regulatory bodies."* **Deborah Harkins** (see p.981) was singled out for her excellent work as *"a regular in the trenches."* She focuses mostly on the regulatory and legislative process, and is credited with initiating many instrumental legislative changes in the area.

## Band 2

### Phelps Dunbar LLP
See firm details p.997

**The Firm:** Home to a diverse gaming group, Phelps Dunbar is *"among the few large firms that do full-service gaming work."* Benefiting from offices in Louisiana and Mississippi, the practice has an enviable reach across the Southern states. Its lawyers frequently win lead roles in major transactions and represented Eldorado Casinos in the acquisition of Hollywood Casino Shreveport.

**The Lawyers: Brian Wallace** (see p.987) represents numerous gaming institutions in M&A, financing, licensing and litigation matters. He divides his time between admiralty and gaming, and combined his skills in both areas when acting as national maritime finance counsel for Penn Gaming in its merger with Argosy. Working out of the Baton Rouge office, **Jeffrey Barbin** (see p.977) continues to carve a reputation out for himself for

representing gaming companies in larger transactions.

### Other Notable Practitioners

Monopolizing the video poker scene in the state, sole practitioner **Frank Blackburn** was generously praised by interviewees for his prominence in licensing work. He focuses exclusively on the gaming industry and his client roster includes one of the largest slot machine manufacturers in the world. *"A super nice guy and a very good lawyer,"* **Blake Bennett** of Liskow & Lewis PLC originally entered the gaming arena through ship financing and maintains an emphasis on riverboat gaming. Recent undertakings include acting as an agent for title insurers of a number of riverboat vessels and, elsewhere, gaming work with a Native American bent. **Daniel Rester** (see p.985) enters the rankings this year as the attorney to watch at Adams & Reese LLP. His broad transactional focus encompasses licensing and finance work related to gaming.

# LITIGATION

## Band 1

### Barrasso Usdin Kupperman Freeman & Sarver LLC
See firm details p.990

**The Firm:** The firm's 20 lawyers all specialize in complex commercial litigation, forming a team noted for its combination of youthful vigor and the presence of some of Louisiana's top litigators. Centering on a core group of ex-Stone Pigman attorneys, the firm represents an impressive array of clients in the region and its lawyers are frequently involved in litigation throughout the USA. It is renowned for its bold approach to cases and its willingness to go to trial. In the wake of the recent storms, the firm has spearheaded the defense of several class actions relating to coverage issues for insurers and is involved in counseling clients on many others.

**The Lawyers:** One commentator summed up **Judy Barrasso** (see p.977) as having a *"pleasant, understated demeanor"* underwritten by a *"toughness and a smartness that makes her hard to beat."* She has earned a reputation among competitors as an aggressive and bright practitioner who gives *"tremendous attention to detail"* throughout the litigation process. Barrasso represents insurers in class actions involving credit scoring and preferred provider issues. Clients feel confident in hiring **Richard Sarver** (see p.986) on the basis that he is *"thoughtful, well prepared and loved by juries."* Much of his time is spent representing companies in the throes of products liability litigation, with recent highlights including the successful defense at trial of a case relating to a welding rod, and representing Clear Channel in a major piece of commercial litigation. **Steven Usdin** (see p.987) is a strong trial lawyer who represents insurers in class action litigation and, since the storms, has been heavily involved in coverage cases. Commentators acknowledge the speed with which he picks up a case and admire the way he *"gets into the detail without ever losing sight of the big picture."*

**Clients/Work Highlights:** Chubb Group; Allstate; Liberty Mutual; MetLife; Wachovia and BOC.

### Jones Walker Waechter Poitevent Carrère & Denègre, LLP
See firm details p.994

**The Firm:** As one of the biggest law firms in the Gulf region this practice has particularly impressive firepower with which to protect the interests of clients all over the Southeastern states. Approximately 60 lawyers in Louisiana are involved in commercial litigation on behalf of clients from a broad spectrum of industries, and the firm can handle many different complex litigation cases at once. The firm's market-

leading corporate group provides the litigation department with work from major national and international corporations. Clients appreciate the way members of the firm interact with them in terms of getting to know their business and assisting them in achieving their aims.

**The Lawyers: Pauline Hardin** (see p.980) has honed her great courtroom style over many years, not least during her career as a first assistant US attorney. Market sources commented that she has a reputation for representing big business in white-collar crime matters that is second to none. She also benefits from having excellent working relationships with the DOJ. **Patrick Vance** (see p.987) is widely viewed in the market as a *"force to be reckoned with in the courtroom."* His litigation practice revolves around representing companies in Chapter 11 bankruptcy proceedings, which most recently meant acting for a large local utility company. Elsewhere he made an appearance in complex class action litigation on behalf of Louisiana clients. Peers acknowledge and clients are grateful for the fact that **Harry Hardin** (see p.981) *"doesn't see litigation as the only solution."* At the same time as being one of the state's *"most effective courtroom lawyers,"* his advice on how to avoid litigation where possible is much sought after by clients. He heads up the firm's appellate litigation group and represents many large clients ranging from investment banks to railroad entities.

**Clients/Work Highlights:** Aegon USA; Allied Waste Industries; BellSouth; ExxonMobil; GM; Marriott International; Ralph Brennan Restaurant Group; Universal Studios and Cisco Systems.

## Litigation: General Commercial
### Leading Individuals

★ WITTMANN Phillip *Stone Pigman Walther*

1. BARRASSO Judy *Barrasso Usdin Kupperman Freeman*
   BARRIERE Brent *Phelps Dunbar LLP*
   CHEATWOOD Roy *Baker, Donelson*
   HERMAN Russ *Herman, Herman, Katz*
   MEUNIER Gerald *Gainsburgh, Benjamin, David*
2. ABAUNZA Donald *Liskow & Lewis PLC*
   BROWN James *Liskow & Lewis PLC*
   GARNER James *Sher Garner Cahill Richter*
   LAFITTE Gene *Liskow & Lewis PLC*
   MCCOLLAM John *Gordon, Arata, McCollam*
   SARVER Richard *Barrasso Usdin Kupperman*
   SWANSON James *Correro Fishman Haygood Phelps*
   VANCE R Patrick *Jones Walker*
3. ASHE Barry *Stone Pigman Walther*
   EAGAN Ewell *Gordon, Arata, McCollam*
   FRILOT George *Frilot, Partridge, Kohnke*
   HARDIN III Harry *Jones Walker*
   JARMAN William *Kean, Miller, Hawthorne*
   KERRIGAN JR Robert *Deutsch, Kerrigan*
   KOHNKE IV Edward *Frilot, Partridge, Kohnke*
   LUND Daniel *Montgomery, Barnett, Brown*
   MARTZELL Jack *Martzell & Bickford, APC*
   PHILIPS Harry *Taylor, Porter, Brooks*
   ROSENBERG Harry *Phelps Dunbar LLP*
   USDIN Steven *Barrasso Usdin Kupperman*

## Litigation: White-Collar Crime & Government Investigations
### Leading Individuals

1. BECKER Walter *Chaffe McCall, LLP*
   CLARKE Shaun *Liskow & Lewis PLC*
   HARDIN Pauline *Jones Walker*
   ROSENBERG Harry *Phelps Dunbar LLP*

## Liskow & Lewis PLC

**The Firm:** This operation continues to appear at the forefront of major commercial litigation in Louisiana. It has a group of around 30 lawyers at its disposal, *"every one of which inspires confidence"* according to clients, whether it be commenting on courtroom proceedings or in negotiations. In the aftermath of Hurricane Katrina the firm's caseload has included representing parties to a claim that a barge caused damage to the levees in New Orleans. Before the storm the firm was involved in class action litigation on behalf of many clients retained by the firm due to its close ties to the oil and gas industry.
**The Lawyers:** Many clients consider themselves fortunate to have found **Shaun Clarke** to defend them in white-collar crime cases. He has extensive trial experience and is considered a past master in handling government investigations on behalf of a nationwide clientele. He is described as *"diligent, personable and effective."* The head of the firm's admiralty group, **Donald Abaunza**, has over 30 years of experience in the courtroom and in arbitrations. He enjoys a stellar reputation as a maritime

specialist among fellow practitioners, and clients characterize him as *"very persuasive"* and an *"excellent negotiator."* That Abaunza is a *"homespun, down-to-earth kind of guy"* was also said to count in his favor, making him particularly easy to work with. **James Brown** is regarded as a *"savvy lawyer"* who is both *"dogged and articulate"* in his representation of clients. His practice largely consists of the realization of insurance proceeds and claims but also takes in the full scope of commercial litigation from class actions to white-collar crime and legal malpractice suits. Peers are united in praising **Gene Lafitte** for his *"commanding presence"* in the courtroom. This *"wonderful statesman"* for the Louisiana Bar remains very active and maintains well-developed relations with oil and gas companies, to which he lends all the benefits of his 50-year trial experience.
**Clients/Work Highlights:** Bank One; Chevron; ExxonMobil; Gaylord Chemical; Forest Oil; Nissan North America and Shell.

## Phelps Dunbar LLP
See firm details p.997
**The Firm:** A stalwart of the state's legal scene, its two offices in Louisiana play a vital role in this outfit's extensive network of offices, which covers the whole of the Gulf region. The firm's lawyers regularly appear before federal, state and appellate courts in matters ranging from major bankruptcies and securities litigation to midrange breaches of contract. Observers note that this team of *"superb commercial litigators"* upholds the highest standards of professionalism. Current work includes defending oil companies that are being sued for alleged damage to land to which they once had a proprietary right.
**The Lawyers:** Bankruptcy cases have come to the fore of **Brent Barriere**'s (see p.977) recent caseload in which he has represented the interests of many corporations, including a troubled sports company in Alabama. Peers consider his national reputation for complex commercial litigation to be well deserved and brand him a *"wonderful trial lawyer"* with a *"strong and engaging personality."* **Harry Rosenberg** (see p.985) *"zeros in on the issues and conducts himself with impeccable style in court,"* according to sources. This *"smart and highly capable"* lawyer is greatly admired by peers for his federal court practice and is deemed especially adept in cases involving a civil rights or white-collar crime bent.
**Clients/Work Highlights:** Chubb Group; Dominion Exploration & Production; GATX; International Paper; The Shaw Group and Wells Fargo.

## Stone Pigman Walther Wittmann LLC
See firm details p.999
**The Firm:** The firm maintains its status as one of the dominant forces in the field by continuing to attract some of the most complex high-end cases in the region. Undoubtedly this is in part due to the presence of one of the most capable litigators in the USA, Phillip Wittmann. The team behind him is constantly developing and represents major clients in high-profile matters such as State Farm in complex class action litigation.

**The Lawyers: Phillip Wittmann** (see p.988) stands out as the *"best litigator in the state by a long way."* He benefits from rich and varied experience in a vast array of commercial areas and is generally regarded as the *"dean of the litigation Bar"* in Louisiana. As a *"venerable old warhorse"* in the courtroom, he is believed to be *"fearless."* One observer noted that he *"brings the full weight of his substantial intellectual capabilities to solving complex problems all the while remaining charming and generous and never veering from a preeminently practical approach."* **Barry Ashe** (see p.977) sustains an expansive practice that includes products liability and breach of contract disputes as well as personal injury and negligence claims.
**Clients/Work Highlights:** Chevron Phillips Chemical; Endo Pharmaceuticals; Kaiser Aluminum; Louisiana Public Service Commission; New Orleans Saints and Purdue Pharma.

## Band 2

## Baker, Donelson, Bearman, Caldwell & Berkowitz, PC
See firm details p.1819
**The Firm:** Banking and finance, oil and gas and maritime sector disputes all enter into the practice here, as do contentious environmental matters. Recent work has included representing Union Pacific in a multitude of cases nationwide. Clients adjudge the team to be *"impressive across the board"* and appreciate the firm's regional reach as well as its responsiveness to client needs. Indeed, one commented that, *"in contrast to previous experiences, I never for a moment felt this firm had lost track of the case."*
**The Lawyers: Roy Cheatwood**'s (see p.978) aggressive pursuit of his clients' interests in the courtroom is much admired among competitors: *"Ever thorough and charismatic, he can stand up to anybody."* Clients appreciate his willingness to work closely with them in an effort to keep costs down.
**Clients/Work Highlights:** Entergy; Hibernia National Bank; Texas Gas Transmission and Union Pacific.

## Gainsburgh, Benjamin, David, Meunier & Warshauer
**The Firm:** Plaintiff representation in personal injury claims is considered to be where the firm's strongest suit lies. Indeed, it is renowned throughout the region for offering *"some of the most prominent plaintiff lawyers in the state."* Admiralty and maritime, products liability and class action suits are also covered.
**The Lawyers:** *"Excellent trial lawyer"* **Gerald Meunier** is noted for his brilliant manner before juries when acting for plaintiffs. Special praise was reserved for his *"conversational style"* and peers consider him a *"wonderful professional to have on the other side."*

## Gordon, Arata, McCollam, Duplantis & Eagan LLP

**The Firm:** The group here has considerable experience of representing both plaintiffs and defendants before federal and state courts, administrative bodies and in alternative dispute resolution contexts. In accordance with general market trends, class actions are a growth area in which members of the firm have defended clients in the tobacco, oil and gas, insurance and pharmaceutical industries. Niche areas of expertise include construction litigation.

**The Lawyers:** **John McCollam** has many years of experience representing oil and gas clients in complex litigation relating to matters such as take-or-pay gas purchase and sale contracts, operating agreements and farm-out agreements. He also has impressive credentials when it comes to defending class actions, particularly on behalf of tobacco and oil and gas clients or where pharmaceutical products liability is concerned. **Ewell Eagan** represents energy, construction, securities and banking sector clients in a variety of complex litigation before trial and appellate courts at both state and federal level. Market sources rate him highly for his *"affable and smooth"* courtroom style.

**Clients/Work Highlights:** Biloxi Marsh Land; Burlington Resources Oil; Dominion Exploration & Production; Northrop Grumman; Shaw Environmental; Chevron and Swift Environmental.

## Kean, Miller, Hawthorne, D'Armond, McCowan & Jarman, LLP

See firm details p.995

**The Firm:** Baton Rouge's leading litigation firm offers a team of about 30 lawyers involved in disputes. The department is often fed work via the firm's existing clients, which include an impressive contingent of large oil and gas companies among others. Over the last 20 years or so the firm has cultivated a special focus on Louisiana-based clients and those Fortune 500 companies wishing to expand their operations in the Gulf region.

**The Lawyers:** **William Jarman** (see p.982) is deeply experienced in acting on behalf of energy companies including Shell and Chevron. His recent highlights include representing Shell in acquiring the right of way for a 75-mile pipeline that was delivered on time and under budget. Observers note that he does an *"excellent job for his clients"* and is remarkably *"good on his feet"* in the courtroom.

**Clients/Work Highlights:** BASF; Black & Decker; ConocoPhillips; ExxonMobil; IBM; Microsoft; The Shaw Group and Shell.

## Band 3

## Correro Fishman Haygood Phelps Walmsley & Casteix LLP

See firm details p.992

**The Firm:** This compact five-lawyer team attracts significant cases from some of the state's big-name clients, including key finance sector entities and municipalities. It is currently involved in some of the biggest arbitrations in the region and was recently hired by the State of Louisiana to advise on income tax disputes.

**The Lawyers:** *"Talented, astute and an expert performer before the jury"* was how interviewees summed up **James Swanson** (see p.987). He heads the litigation practice at the firm and has acted for the likes of The Times-Picayune.

**Clients/Work Highlights:** First Bank; JMH Realty; SMG; State of Louisiana; The Times-Picayune; US Unwired and Sabin, Bermant & Gould.

## Frilot, Partridge, Kohnke & Clements LC

**The Firm:** The firm is credited with considerable *"strength in depth"* and its lawyers frequently try significant cases. The team's national work in products liability is complemented by strength in insurance coverage, defense matters, medical malpractice and toxic tort cases.

**The Lawyers:** *"A terrific lawyer,"* **George Frilot** has applied his extensive experience, which stretches back over 45 years, to a case concerning the big oil spill that occurred in the Gulf following the storms. He sustains his position in the table along with **Edward Kohnke**, who won special praise for communicating clearly and effectively in court.

**Clients/Work Highlights:** Chevron; ExxonMobil; GE; Medical Malpractice Insurance; Nintendo; Nokia and Tidewater.

## Herman, Herman, Katz & Cotlar LLP

See firm details p.993

**The Firm:** This firm maintains its reputation as a top-notch plaintiff operation at state and federal level as well as before appellate courts. Its standing in the field stems largely from its huge success in class actions, particularly those launched against the tobacco industry.

**The Lawyers:** **Russ Herman** (see p.981) is without question one of the leading attorneys in the state and enjoys a nationwide reputation as an *"extraordinary trial lawyer."* Commentators were united in acknowledging him as a *"bright and bullish"* courtroom performer, with one going so far as to say that he *"works with juries better than anyone else."*

## Sher Garner Cahill Richter Klein & Hilbert LLC

See firm details p.998

**The Firm:** An ability to utilize the latest technology to the advantage of clients was discerned as distinguishing this firm from competitors. A major full-service player in the Gulf region and beyond, commentators speak of *"never being less than impressed"* with the firm's work product. The full range of commercial litigation, from banking and finance through to personal injury and insurance disputes, is covered.

**The Lawyers:** *"Extremely bright, never caught short and quick on his feet,"* is how onlookers described **James Garner** (see p.980), who has developed a reputation as an aggressive and tenacious trial lawyer. Clients find his communication skills particularly appealing and appreciate the lengths he goes to in order to achieve the best possible result on their behalf. He represented Deutsche Bank in an attempt to enforce a mortgage claim in the Entergy bankruptcy filing.

**Clients/Work Highlights:** AXA Corporate Solutions; First Bank; National Trust New Orleans; International Rivercenter; Murphy Oil USA; Touro Infirmary; Trinity Industries and University of New Orleans Foundation.

## Taylor, Porter, Brooks & Phillips, LLP

**The Firm:** The *"highly competent"* team of litigators continues to shine at this firm, which is one of the longest established outfits in Louisiana, having sustained a practice there for the best part of a century. Close ties with municipalities and state universities as well as corporations such as JPMorgan Chase shape the workload. Insurance and bankruptcy practices that are widely respected throughout the region also help to determine the caseload.

**The Lawyers:** **Harry Philips** handles coverage cases for insurers, corporate work for nonprofit organizations and regularly represents banks and financial institutions. Recent highlights include defending the directors of a healthcare company against professional liability claims in three states.

**Clients/Work Highlights:** Argosy Gaming; Baton Rouge Water Works; Bank One; BP; Entergy; Liberty Mutual; Louisiana State University; Dow Chemical and Yamaha Motor USA.

## Other Notable Practitioners

Before joining the firm of Chaffe McCall, LLP, **Walter Becker** spent many years as a state and federal prosecutor, and clients find his unique experience in this respect a major benefit. **Robert Kerrigan** of Deutsch, Kerrigan & Stiles, LLP is heavily involved in major insurance cases for significant regional clients. Market sources suggest he is a *"smart and savvy"* trial lawyer with a great deal of experience and is aggressive in his defense of clients. **Daniel Lund** of Montgomery, Barnett, Brown, Read, Hammond & Mintz, LLP is particularly well renowned in Louisiana for his involvement in professional malpractice suits, while **Jack Martzell** of Martzell & Bickford, APC has a broad practice covering commercial as well as civil and criminal matters.

# REAL ESTATE

## Band 1

### Liskow & Lewis PLC

**The Firm:** The real estate practice at this large broad-based operation won the firm both promotion in the table and the respect of interviewees for its "*capacity to deal with the most complex deals.*" It came in for further praise for the encyclopedic knowledge of its practitioners. The group benefits from the firm's unrivaled reputation for oil and gas work, and is often involved in related acquisitions and developments. A diverse client list includes The National D-Day Museum, which the team advised on architectural and contractual issues surrounding its $180 million expansion program.

**The Lawyers:** Billed as "*a top attorney leading an excellent team,*" **Leon Reymond** was the subject of widespread acclaim from interviewees: "*He combines a total command of Louisiana law with a great deal of personal integrity.*" Along with the firm, Reymond also enters the top tier of the tables, with interviewees reserving special praise for strength in leasing matters.

**Clients/Work Highlights:** Belle Meade Shopping Center; DR Horton; Harrah's Entertainment; North American Petroleum; Rushton Industries and Tammany Oil & Gas.

### Phelps Dunbar LLP

See firm details p.997

**The Firm:** Its "*commitment to client service*" is considered to have been central to the firm consolidating its top-tier status. Spanning both the New Orleans and Baton Rouge offices, the practice is particularly well regarded on the developer front. A recent highlight in this respect involved overcoming land use planning restrictions in order for the development of the old plantation site at Willow Grove to go ahead. Close links between real estate and banking practices make the firm particularly appealing to lenders partaking in real estate transactions.

**The Lawyers:** "*A high-quality lawyer who has all the right credentials,*" **Philip Claverie** (see p.978) impressed clients with his "*great grasp of Louisiana law and high level of commitment to clients.*" He primarily represents lenders, though his practice also encompasses work on behalf of a range of developers. **Randy Roussel** (see p.986) was the name interviewees singled out in Baton Rouge. Dedicating his practice to commercial real estate, Roussel has recently represented developers of shopping centers, apartment buildings and offices.

**Clients/Work Highlights:** AmSouth Bank; Audubon Capital Fund; JPMorgan Chase; Ghk Developments; Hibernia National Bank and Rubicon.

### Sher Garner Cahill Richter Klein & Hilbert LLC

See firm details p.998

**The Firm:** Commentators largely agree that the real estate practice remains the bedrock of this firm's impressive reputation, though several clients cited the "*diversity of services on offer*" as a winning feature of the overall outfit. Both the quantity and quality of real estate work here attracted praise, and the group competes for work on a national basis. Clients range from international corporations to local purchasers and sellers of property, and the practice covers the full spectrum of real estate transactions from acquisitions to development plans.

**The Lawyers:** "*One of the top real estate lawyers in Louisiana,*" **Lee Sher** (see p.986) enjoys a sterling reputation with clients on all sides. "*A classy and consummate professional,*" he was further praised for maintaining a dialogue with clients throughout negotiations and consistently responding to their needs. Interviewees were quick to give credit to the "*industrious*" **Elwood Cahill**. A "*safe pair of hands*" in any transaction, he is valued for "*his incredible patience, even when dealing with the most difficult people.*" The team's standing is further enhanced by **Neal Kling**, who represents developers, lenders and debtors in developments ranging from hotels to manufacturing facilities and power plants.

**Clients/Work Highlights:** Burger King; Burrus Investment Group; Cracker Barrel Old Country Store; Greystar Development & Construction; The Hertz Investment Group; Marrero Land & Improve-ment Association; MetLife; PMAT Real Estate Investments; Realm Realty & Management; Sizeler Property Investors; Southern Homes and University of New Orleans Foundation.

### Stone Pigman Walther Wittmann LLC

See firm details p.999

**The Firm:** Stone Pigman is home to a "*first-class*" real estate team, renowned by peers for the caliber of its work and the amenity of its practitioners, and by clients for its "*can do*" attitude. It has built a strong reputation for representing both developers and lenders in a wide range of development projects. Of particular note in the past year, members of the firm acted for a fast food franchisee in the restructuring of its affiliated real estate holdings, which included over 200 units in eight states.

**The Lawyers:** An impressive level of client endorsement and a high profile, both in terms of caseload and appearances on legislative committees, means **Susan Talley** (see p.987) cements her position at the top of the rankings. Interviewees generally cast her as "*a fantastic draftsperson and an extremely clear thinker,*" while clients say that "*she is more like a colleague than outside counsel.*" Talley is consistently to be found at the center of the firm's real estate lending activity. Cochair of the real estate practice **Michael Schneider** (see p.986) plays a similar role to Talley on the developer side. The market resounded with praise for his practice, which includes acting for the likes of Pinnacle Entertainment and The Berger Company.

**Clients/Work Highlights:** Criimi Mae; EnCana Gas Storage; National Gypsum and Pyramid Hotel Opportunity Venture.

### The Steeg Law Firm, LLC

**The Firm:** Commentators were quick to pay tribute to the lengthy history behind what some interviewees deem to be "*the premier real estate boutique in Louisiana.*" The firm is renowned for "*keeping all eyes on the clients' goals and closing deals quickly and effort-lessly.*" As one client remarked: "*The best way of finding a route through the most complicated of real estate transactions is to get The Steeg Law Firm involved.*" The group advises on a wide spectrum of real estate transactions, including commercial loans, acquisitions and leases.

**The Lawyers:** **Robert Steeg**, who was applauded by clients for being "*accessible, hard working and a consummate deal-maker,*" spearheads the team. Primarily known for his expertise in representing developers, clients were quick to comment on the pleasure they experience in working with him: "*He is a man of integrity with an unrivaled instinct for real estate.*" **Jon Leyens** enters the rankings on the strength of substantial client endorsement for his work in sophisticated loan transactions and large-scale property acquisitions.

**Clients/Work Highlights:** Chevron USA; Corporate Realty; Entergy; First American Title Insurance;

Hibernia National Bank; Historic Restoration; Lauricella Land; Loeb Partners Realty; Magnolia Marketing Group; Tulane University and Whitney National Bank.

## Band 2

### Jones Walker Waechter Poitevent Carrère & Denègre, LLP

See firm details p.994

**The Firm:** The real estate practice at Louisiana's largest firm centers on the Baton Rouge office. It is a substantial, full-service operation and its attorneys have enjoyed involvement in a series of retail developments lately, having represented the developers of three new retail sites in Baton Rouge. Moreover, it has acted as Louisiana counsel to Wal-Mart for a number of years. For clients, *"the overall knowledge and attention to detail of its practitioners is what sets the group apart."*

**The Lawyers:** Interviewees singled out managing partner **Charles Landry** (see p.983) as a leader in his field. Landry's practice incorporates real estate development and finance, as well as land use and zoning issues, for which he won particularly high praise: *"He is an outstanding negotiator with a great deal of knowledge of local ordinances as they apply to real estate."*

**Clients/Work Highlights:** Columbus Properties; Department of Natural Resources; Department of Wildlife and Fisheries; ExxonMobil Pipeline; Fletcher Bright; Hexion Specialty Chemicals; Hunt Forest Products; International Paper; Piccadilly Cafeterias; State of Louisiana and Tonti Management.

## Band 3

### McGlinchey Stafford

See firm details p.996

**The Firm:** Its strong domestic profile is complemented by close links with real estate attorneys in the firm's offices across the Gulf South region. A diverse clientele includes developers, lenders, landlords and tenants, many of which were quick to expound the benefits of working with this *"ever-accessible and highly knowledgeable"* team. In addition to domestic entities, the firm also acts for multinationals such as Verizon and DaimlerChrysler.

**The Lawyers:** An *"effective and fair deal-maker,"* **Keith Colvin** (see p.978) is held in high esteem by clients and peers alike for his commercial real estate practice. Primarily known for representing developers, he was recently involved in a $90 million project to build a film studio and a $50 million retirement community project.

**Clients/Work Highlights:** Boyd Gaming; Cendant Timeshare Resort Group; Federal National Mortgage Association; Occidental Chemical; PNC Business Credit; Toyota Motor Credit and Whitney National Bank.

## Band 4

### Chaffe McCall, LLP

See firm details p.991

**The Firm:** Satisfied clients laud this firm as *"one of the older and most highly regarded outfits in the state,"* while also noting the strength of its members' polit-ical and legal connections. The lean commercial real estate team is involved in a range of development work but also dovetails nicely with the firm's banking practice. As such, it is renowned for acting as lender's counsel, as in a recent example where attorneys were involved in the construction of a power plant on the Gulf Coast.

**The Lawyers:** **Howell Crosby** (see p.979) is head of the firm's corporate section and has accrued a comprehensive knowledge of commercial transactions over a period of 20 years. He is considered well connected with city and state officials, which clients agree *"enables him to cut through the red tape and get things done."*

**Clients/Work Highlights:** Al Copeland Enterprises; Amsdell; Baker Hughes; Home Depot; Kimpton Hotel & Restaurant Group and Monarch Real Estate Advisors.

## Other Notable Practitioners

**Mack Gregorie** (see p.980) is a newcomer to the rankings upon being heavily endorsed as a leader. He practices in the Baton Rouge office of Kean, Miller, Hawthorne, D'Armond, McCowan & Jarman, LLP where he represents international petrochemical and energy clients, financial institutions, landlords and tenants. Up-and-comer **Justin Schmidt** (see p.986) continues to impress the market following his move to Adams and Reese LLP. Within the context of a broad real estate practice, he has a particular emphasis on land use and zoning matters.

# Leaders in Louisiana

### ABAUNZA, Donald
Liskow & Lewis PLC, New Orleans
504 581 7979
*Recommended in Litigation*

### ADAMS, H Mark
Jones Walker Waechter Poitevent
Carrère & Denègre, LLP, New Orleans
504 582 8258
madams@joneswalker.com
*Recommended in Employment*
**Practice Areas:** Partner and Founder of Jones Walker's Labor Relations and Employment Practice. Counsels employers on development of practical and preventive strategies for reducing risks of workplace claims. For more than 20 years has successfully represented employers in all types of employment and labor relations litigation and dispute resolution. 'A lawyer's area of practice as stated here is one to which (s)he devotes a substantial portion of his/her professional practice and should not be considered a 'specialization' unless certified by the Louisiana Board of Legal Specialization (or similar body in any other state in which such lawyer is licensed to practice)'.

**Prof. Memberships:** American Bar Association, Labor and Litigation Sections; Louisiana and Mississippi State Bars; Also admitted: United States Supreme Court; United States Courts of Appeal, Second, Fifth, Sixth, Eighth, and Eleventh Circuits; all United States District Courts in Louisiana and Mississippi. Louisiana representative to Employers Counsel Network, an association of leading labor and employment law firms in the United States and Canada.
**Career:** Joined Jones Walker, 1981; Partner since 1986; Member of firm's Executive Committee from 2001 to 2006; chaired firm's Labor Relations and Employment Practice for more than 20 years. Recent accomplishments include counseling numerous employers through employment-related disaster recovery issues following Hurricanes Katrina and Rita and successful defense of several multi-plaintiff, class action, and representative employment discrimination lawsuits by individual employees and the EEOC.
**Publications:** Editor, 'Louisiana Employment Law Letter' (the leading Louisiana

authority on developments and emerging trends in labor and employment law), since 1992.

### AGUILAR JR, Rodolfo J
McGlinchey Stafford, Baton Rouge
225 382 3625
rudyaguilar@mcglinchey.com
*Recommended in Corporate/M&A*
**Practice Areas:** Managing Partner of the firm; maintains a Corporate, Business, and Insurance Regulatory Practice; handles corporate transactions, commercial financing transactions, transactions relating to real estate development and general business matters; represents physician groups and organizations in their internal corporate structure, joint ventures and healthcare related matters; represents clients in the acquisition and formation of health, property, casualty and life insurance companies; represents developers and owners in the negotiation, documentation, acquisition, financing and management of various mixed use developments including hotel, retail and condominium developments.
**Prof. Memberships:** Louisiana State Bar

Association, American Bar Association.
**Personal:** Speaks conversational Spanish.

### ALESSANDRA, M Nan
Phelps Dunbar LLP, New Orleans
504 584 9297
alessann@phelps.com
*Recommended in Employment*
**Practice Areas:** Ms Alessandra is a Partner and the practice co-ordinator of the Employment Law Group in the New Orleans office. She practices in the areas of labor and employment, civil rights, constitutional law, consumer credit litigation, and general business litigation. Her employment litigation practice includes representing employers in discrimination claims for age, sex, disability, race, religion, and workplace harassment, and handling EEOC charges and other administrative complaints through the administrative and judicial process. She also advises clients on a variety of human resource issues and assists in developing employee policies and procedures. Ms Alessandra has been awarded the 'AV' rating by the Martindale-Hubbell Law Directory, which is the highest possible

rating for legal ability and ethical standards. She is listed in the 2003-04 and 2005-06 editions of the Best Lawyers in America. Ms Alessandra is also among a select group of employment lawyers listed in a nationwide client survey published in Chambers USA, America's Leading Lawyers for Business for 2003 and 2004. Ms Alessandra writes and speaks often on behalf of management interests on employment-related topics and frequently provides training to clients on corporate compliance issues under a host of federal and state laws, such as workplace harassment and supervisory training. She is also the managing editor of the firm's monthly HR Alert. Recently, she co-authored a law review article entitled 'Drafting Non-Competition Agreements in Louisiana: A Drafter's Dilemma', 49 Loyola Law Review 809 (2003). Prior to joining the firm, Nan was Judicial Clerk to the Honorable AJ McNamara and Judicial Extern to the Honorable Martin LC Feldman, both of the United States District Court for the Eastern District of Louisiana.
**Personal:** Loyola University, JD, cum laude, 1985; Loyola Law Review. Hunter College in New York; University of New Orleans, BA, 1982.

### ARNOLD III, Edward H (Hank)
Baker, Donelson, Bearman, Caldwell & Berkowitz, PC, New Orleans
504 566 5204
harnold@bakerdonelson.com
*Recommended in Energy*
**Practice Areas:** Extensive experience in commercial, marine and energy finance and real property acquisitions and leases. Represents owners, shipyards and lenders regarding construction, financing and operation of documented vessels. Representation of creditors, bankruptcy trustees and official committees before bankruptcy courts in Louisiana, Texas and Mississippi. Assists developers, lenders and licensed vendors regarding finance and regulatory matters in the riverboat gaming, video gaming and casino industries.
**Prof. Memberships:** Board Member and President, Turnaround Management Association Louisiana Chapter. Member, American Bankruptcy Institute. Member, Louisiana Bankers Association. Member, Maritime Law Association. Member, American, Federal and Louisiana Bar Associations.
**Career:** Licensed in Louisiana 1988.

### ASHE, Barry W
Stone Pigman Walther Wittmann LLC, New Orleans 504 593 0843
bashe@stonepigman.com
*Recommended in Litigation*
**Practice Areas:** Commercial litigation; products liability; maritime; appellate practice.
**Prof. Memberships:** Lawyers Advisory

Committee, US Court of Appeals for the Fifth Circuit. Fellow of the Louisiana Bar Foundation, serving on its Education Committee. New Orleans Chapter Board Member of the Federal Bar Association. A Member of the Maritime Law Association of the United States, the Federal Fifth Circuit Court of Appeals Bar, the American Bar, Louisiana State Bar, and the New Orleans Bar Associations.
**Career:** Law clerk to the Honorable Carolyn Dineen King, Judge, US Court of Appeals for the Fifth Circuit, 1984-85. JD (magna cum laude), Tulane School of Law, 1984. Order of the Coif; Senior Managing Editor, Tulane Law Review, 1983-84, and member of the Board of Editors, 1982-83. BA, (summa cum laude), Tulane University, 1978. Phi Beta Kappa.
**Publications:** The Fifth's Circuit's War Against Religion in the Public Square (47 Loyola Law Review 973, 2000); Incidental Demands in Louisiana Civil Pretrial Procedure (American Inns of Court Series, 1998); Disciplining Maritime Pilots: A Review of State and Federal Pilotage Regulation (58 Tulane Law Review 1460, 1984); Admiralty - Determining LHWCA Coverage Seaward of the Water's Edge (57 Tulane Law Review 682, 1983).

### BARBIN, Jeffrey M
Phelps Dunbar LLP, Baton Rouge
225 376 0243
barbinj@phelps.com
*Recommended in Gaming & Licensing*
**Practice Areas:** Mr Barbin is an associate in the business group in the Baton Rouge office. His practice consists primarily of business transactional and regulatory matters with emphasis on commercial real estate and gaming. In particular, Mr Barbin specializes in gaming transactions requiring local gaming regulatory approvals and in commercial lease transactions representing both landlords and tenants in drafting office building leases, shopping center leases and ground leases. His practice also includes representing lenders and borrowers in commercial loan closings, development of Louisiana banking forms, business entity formation, stock sales and entity mergers, Louisiana gaming regulatory matters, and other general business matters. Mr Barbin has been a guest lecturer on leases in an office practice course at LSU Law School.
**Personal:** Louisiana State University, JD, 1998, BS in Finance, 1992.

### BARRASSO, Judy Y
Barrasso Usdin Kupperman Freeman & Sarver LLC, New Orleans 504 589 9700
JBarrasso@barrassousdin.com
*Recommended in Litigation*
**Practice Areas:** Ms Barrasso represents clients in commercial litigation matters, including unfair trade practices, trade secret, professional liability, securities and banking, class actions, insurance coverage and insurance bad faith claims.

**Career:** Ms Barrasso is a founding member of Barrasso Usdin Kupperman Freeman & Sarver, L.L.C.
**Personal:** JD, summa cum laude, Tulane University 1981, Order of the Coif; Articles Editor, Tulane Law Review; 'Best Lawyers in America'; a Fellow of the International Society of Barristers; Tulane University Law School Trial Advocacy Adjunct faculty (1993 - present)

### BARRIERE, Brent B
Phelps Dunbar LLP, New Orleans
504 584 9210 barrierb@phelps.com
*Recommended in Corporate/M&A, Litigation*
**Practice Areas:** Mr Barriere is a Partner and the practice co-ordinator of the Commercial Litigation Group in the New Orleans office. He represents clients in a wide variety of commercial disputes, including bankruptcy and creditors' rights, securities litigation, breach of contract, business valuation disputes, and class actions. Mr Barriere has been named one of Louisiana's top 10 litigators by the National Law Journal, rated as a top litigator by Chambers USA: America's Leading Business Lawyers (2004-2005), and one of the Best Lawyers in America.
**Personal:** Tulane University, JD, magna cum laude, 1981; Order of the Coif; Board of Editors and Articles Editor, Tulane Law Review. Hamilton College, BA, with honors, 1977.

### BECKER, Walter
Chaffe McCall, LLP, New Orleans
504 585 7000
*Recommended in Litigation*

### BENNETT, Blake
Liskow & Lewis PLC, New Orleans
504 581 7979
*Recommended in Energy, Gaming & Licensing*

### BLACKBURN, Frank
Frank D Blackburn - Sole Practitioner, Baton Rouge 225 756 9696
*Recommended in Gaming & Licensing*

### BOULET, Virginia
Adams and Reese LLP, New Orleans
504 585 0331
virginia.boulet@arlaw.com
*Recommended in Corporate/M&A*
**Practice Areas:** Special Counsel: corporate, securities and banking law. Authored numerous Louisiana banking and corporate statutes. Represented numerous banks, securities firms and corporate firms in Louisiana and Mississippi in mergers/acquisitions, corporate restructurings, takeovers and defenses, raising capital and making investments.
**Prof. Memberships:** American and Louisiana Bar Associations; Association of Louisiana Bank Counsel.
**Career:** Admitted to Louisiana bar in 1983. From 1983 to March 2002, served as associate, then Partner of New Orleans based firms. Director of CenturyTel, Inc,

a NYSE corporation headquartered in Monroe, Louisiana.
**Personal:** JD (cum laude), Tulane University Law School, 1983; BA Yale University, 1975.

### BRODERS, John J
Jones Walker Waechter Poitevent Carrère & Denègre, LLP, New Orleans
504 582 8172
jbroders@joneswalker.com
*Recommended in Energy*
**Practice Areas:** Partner concentrating in all aspects of maritime and marine energy related matters with an emphasis on marine transactions, including construction of vessels, charters, services agreements, acquisitions and sales, financing and mortgages, flagging and manning, marine insurance and arbitration and related matters. 'A lawyer's area of practice as stated here is one to which (s)he devotes a substantial portion of his/her professional practice and should not be considered a 'specialization' unless certified by the Louisiana Board of Legal Specialization (or similar body in any other state in which such lawyer is licensed to practice)'.
**Career:** Joined Jones Walker in 1971, Partner in 1976, Senior Partner in 2000.
**Personal:** Tulane University (BA 1971, JD 1971).

### BROWN, James
Liskow & Lewis PLC, New Orleans
504 581 7979
*Recommended in Litigation*

### BUTLER JR, Patrick J
Phelps Dunbar LLP, New Orleans
504 584 9298 butlerr@phelps.com
*Recommended in Corporate/M&A*
**Practice Areas:** Mr Butler is a Partner in the Business Group in the New Orleans office. He practices primarily in the areas of corporate and securities law and mergers and acquisitions. Mr Butler has extensive experience in the purchase and sale of businesses (both asset and stock transactions) for large, publicly-traded corporations and for smaller, privately-held firms. He also handles federal and state securities law matters, including the registration of offerings with the Securities and Exchange Commission and state securities regulators, private placements and other transactions exempt from registration under the securities laws, disclosure requirements for companies registered under the Securities Exchange Act of 1934 and proxy contests. Mr Butler also represents issuing companies and investors in venture capital transactions, assists in the formation of joint ventures and advises clients on general corporate matters.
**Personal:** Duke University, JD, with honors, 1986. University of Notre Dame, BA, cum laude, 1983.

**CAHILL JR, Elwood**
Sher Garner Cahill Richter Klein &
Hilbert LLC, New Orleans
504 299 2100
*Recommended in Real Estate*

**CAMPBELL JR, John**
Taylor, Porter, Brooks & Phillips, LLP,
Baton Rouge 225 387 3221
*Recommended in Corporate/M&A*

**CARVER, Hampton**
Carver Darden Koretzky Tessier Finn
Blossman & Areaux LLC, New Orleans
504 585 3800
*Recommended in Energy*

**CAVERLY, Joseph L**
Stone Pigman Walther Wittmann LLC,
New Orleans 504 593 0845
jcaverly@stonepigman.com
*Recommended in Corporate/M&A*
**Practice Areas:** Corporate; mergers and
acquisitions; securities law. Chair of the
firm's Corporate and Securities Practice
Group.
**Prof. Memberships:** Admitted to prac-
tice in Louisiana, 1985. Member of the
American and Louisiana State Bar Asso-
ciations and the French-American
Chamber of Commerce.
**Career:** Joined Stone Pigman in 1985;
became member in 1991.
**Personal:** JD (magna cum laude), Tulane
University School of Law. Member of
Order of the Coif and Tulane Law Review.
Undergraduate and advanced Degrees,
the University of Notre Dame (with high
honors), 1978; the London School of Eco-
nomics and Political Science, 1980; the
University of Oxford, 1982.

**CERONE, Rudy**
McGlinchey Stafford, New Orleans
504 596 2786
rcerone@mcglinchey.com
*Recommended in Corporate/M&A*
**Practice Areas:** Bankruptcy, litigation,
gaming.
**Prof. Memberships:** American Bank-
ruptcy Institute, American College of
Bankruptcy, Bar Association of the Fifth
Federal Circuit, Federal Bar, International
Association of Gaming Attorneys,
Louisiana Bankers Association, American
Bar Association, California State Bar,
Louisiana State Bar, Louisiana New
Orleans Bar.
**Career:** Bankruptcy and litigation; certi-
fied specialist in business bankruptcy by
American Board of Certification and LA
State Bar Association Board of Legal Spe-
cialization.

**CHEATHAM, Robin B**
Adams and Reese LLP, New Orleans
504 585 0411
robin.cheatham@arlaw.com
*Recommended in Corporate/M&A*
**Practice Areas:** Partner: commercial
restructuring and bankruptcy, energy and
environmental, bankruptcy, oil and gas
contracts, construction law, commercial
litigation.

**Prof. Memberships:** American Bankruptcy Institute, Mid-Continent Law
Association, Commercial Law League of
America.
**Career:** Experienced in commercial litigation, construction law, asset acquisitions, general business counseling and
complex commercial financial transactions as well as various aspects of oil and
gas transactions. He has appeared on
behalf of creditors, committees and
trustees and has also litigated various
construction law issues.
**Personal:** JD Loyola University New
Orleans School of Law, 1979; BS University of New Orleans, 1976.

**CHEATWOOD, Roy C**
Baker, Donelson, Bearman, Caldwell &
Berkowitz, PC, New Orleans
504 566 5266
rcheatwood@bakerdonelson.com
*Recommended in Litigation*
**Practice Areas:** Practice focused in
commercial litigation including corporate and securities, banking and financial
services, oil/gas, energy and minerals,
construction, trade secrets and legal mal-
practice. Representation of local, national
and international concerns before trial
and appellate courts, regulatory bodies
and ADR forums.
**Prof. Memberships:** Member, Louisiana
Board of Legal Specialization; American,
Federal, Louisiana State and New Orleans
Bar Associations. Faculty Member,
National Institute for Trial Advocacy,
Trial and Deposition Programs. Master
Barrister, Tulane Inn of Court. Co-
author, Louisiana Courtroom Evidence.
**Career:** Louisiana license, 1974. Served
US Army (First Lieutenant).
**Personal:** Tulane University, JD, 1974.
University of South Florida, BA, 1968.

**CHERNEKOFF, Michael A**
Jones Walker Waechter Poitevent Carrère & Denègre, LLP, New Orleans
504 582 8264
mchernekoff@joneswalker.com
*Recommended in Environment*
**Practice Areas:** Environmental and
toxic torts, class action defense, and energy. 'A lawyer's area of practice as stated
here is one to which (s)he devotes a substantial portion of his/her professional
practice and should not be considered a
'specialization' unless certified by the
Louisiana Board of Legal Specialization
(or similar body in any other state in
which such lawyer is licensed to practice)'.
**Prof. Memberships:** Louisiana State Bar
Association (Environmental Law Section,
Chairman, 1993-94), American Bar Association (Sections on Environment, Energy and Resources, Vice-Chair, Environmental Enforcement and Crimes Committee, 2005-06; Torts and Insurance
Practice - Toxic Tort and Environment
Law Committee; Litigation - Environmental Litigation Committee); DRI

(Toxic Torts and Environmental Law
Committee); District of Columbia Bar;
New Orleans Bar Association.
**Career:** Mr Chernekoff started his career
at the US Environmental Protection
Agency in Washington, DC as an attorney
advisor in the Office of Air, Mobile
Source Enforcement from 1981 until
joining the firm in May 1982.
**Publications:** Mr Chernekoff has written and presented on a variety of environmental topics including: criminal
enforcement; civil enforcement; compliance auditing; due diligence; Brownfield
reclamation projects; CERCLA, RCRA
and Clean Water Act programs.
**Personal:** Admitted to Bar, 1980, District
of Columbia; 1982, Louisiana.

**CLARK JR, Blane**
Kean Miller Hawthorne D'Armond
McCowan & Jarman, LLP, Baton Rouge
225 382 3414
blane.clark@keanmiller.com
*Recommended in Corporate/M&A*
**Practice Areas:** Business, banking, real
estate.
**Prof. Memberships:** Louisiana Law
Institute; Baton Rouge, Louisiana and
American Bar Associations.
**Career:** Blane Clark has 20 years of experience in corporate law. He works with
clients on commercial lending transactions and has experience in the preparation and review of commercial loan documents for asset-based and real estate
loans, consumer loans, title policies and
closing opinions. He is one of the region's
leading lawyers in the area of mergers and
acquisitions, and corporate finance. He
has experience in merger transactions
and represents acquiring and acquired
parties in the petrochemical, energy,
healthcare and construction industries.

**CLARKE, Shaun**
Liskow & Lewis PLC, New Orleans
504 581 7979
*Recommended in Litigation*

**CLAVERIE SR, Philip deV**
Phelps Dunbar LLP, New Orleans
504 584 9223
claverip@phelps.com
*Recommended in Banking & Finance,
Real Estate*
**Practice Areas:** Mr Claverie is a Partner
in the firm's Business Group in the New
Orleans office. His business practice
includes banking, commercial, real estate
and probate. Mr Claverie represents various financial institutions in dozens of
transactions involving financing of real
estate construction, mergers and acquisitions and working capital. He also represents several real estate developers in connection with various development projects, from major office buildings to
shopping centers. Mr Claverie represents
as general counsel a large petrochemical
manufacturer in connection with all
aspects of business, from contract prepa-

ration and review to financing and real
estate matters, to corporate formation
and restructuring, and also supervised for
the manufacturer other activities, such as
environmental, personal, tax, and
employee benefit matters.
**Personal:** Tulane University, JD, 1966;
Index Editor, Associate Editor, Tulane
Law Review; Order of the Coif; Phi Delta
Phi; Omicron Delta Kappa. Princeton
University, AB, magna cum laude, 1963.

**COLVIN, R Keith**
McGlinchey Stafford, New Orleans
504 596 2730
kcolvin@mcglinchey.com
*Recommended in Real Estate*
**Practice Areas:** Manager of Real Estate
section concentrating in commercial real
estate; represents developers, owners, and
lenders in projects including industrial
plants, shopping centers and malls, apartment complexes, hotels, office buildings,
condominium, townhome and timeshare
developments and golf course and resort
developments. President, MACSTAM Title
Company; licensed title insurance agent.
**Prof. Memberships:** American College
of Real Estate Lawyers, Vice-Chairman,
Title Insurance Committee; American
College of Mortgage Attorneys, Board of
Regents; Urban Land Institute, Louisiana
Council Executive Committee; Coalition
to Restore Coastal Louisiana, Board of
Directors; New Orleans Regional Leader-
ship Institute, Board of Directors.
**Personal:** LSU Law School, JD (1979),
Managing Editor, 'Louisiana Law Review',
Volume 39; LSU, BS (1976)

**CORRERO III, Anthony J**
Correro Fishman Haygood Phelps Walmsley & Casteix LLP, New Orleans
504 586 5253
acorrero@cfhlaw.com
*Recommended in Corporate/M&A*
**Practice Areas:** His primary practice
areas include corporate and securities
law, mergers and acquisitions and banking. In particular, he helps clients with
SEC compliance, public and private securities offerings, the regulation of financial
institutions and the buying and selling of
businesses. He has advised clients in a
variety of transactions, ranging in size
from $3.1 billion to $100,000, including
the $3.1 billion sale of First Commerce
Corporation to Bank One; the $1.3 bil-
lion sale of U.S. Unwired Inc. to Sprint
Corporation; the $500 million purchase
of Zapata Corporation by Tidewater, Inc.;
the $119.4 million acquisitions by
Amedisys, Inc. of the home healthcare
operations of Housecall Medical
Resources, Inc. and SpectraCare Home
Health Services, Inc.; the sale of VitaRx to
McKesson Corporation for $62 million;
the public offerings of oil and gas interests for a single client aggregating $1 bil-
lion; the $75.9 million stock offering by
Amedisys, Inc.; and the private offering of

oil and gas interests for a single client of $100,000; as well as initial public stock offerings for several companies.

**Career:** Andy has served as Chairman of the Corporate Laws Committee of the LSBA Section on Corporate and Business Law since 1998, and is a former Chairman of the Section. He has also been a Member of the Board of Directors of several private and public companies. He is a Member of the American Law Institute and Louisiana Bankers Association. He is an adjunct faculty Member of both the Tulane and LSU Law Schools, where he teaches the courses in Securities Registration and Corporation Finance. He also spent eight years as a Member of the Planning Committee of the Tulane Corporate Law Institute.

**Publications:** He has been the editor of the Louisiana Corporate Newsletter and co-editor of Basic Forms for Louisiana Corporations, has been listed in a leading legal publication in America, in corporate law, since that publication's inception in 1983 and has been ranked by New Orleans Magazine as one of the city's top lawyers in banking, securities and corporate law.

**Personal:** Andy graduated from Northeast Louisiana State College in 1962 and got his LLB degree from LSU in 1965, where he was a Member of the Order of the Coif and Associate Editor of the 'Louisiana Law Review'.

### CROCHET, Vicki
Taylor, Porter, Brooks & Phillips, LLP, Baton Rouge 225 387 3221
*Recommended in Employment*

### CROMWELL, David
Pettiette, Armand, Dunkelman, Woodley, Byrd & Cromwell LLP, Shreveport 318 221 1800
*Recommended in Banking & Finance*

### CROSBY, E Howell
Chaffe McCall, LLP, New Orleans 504 585 7212
crosby@chaffe.com
*Recommended in Real Estate*
**Practice Areas:** Partner in Real Estate Section concentrating in commercial real estate; represents developers, owners, tenants and lenders in projects including office buildings, shopping centers and malls, apartment complexes, hotels, and condominium developments.
**Prof. Memberships:** Past President - American College of Mortgage Attorneys; American College of Real Estate Lawyers; International Association of Attorneys and Executives in Corporate Real Estate; International Council of Shopping Centers; New Orleans Regional Leadership Institute.
**Career:** Joined Chaffe McCall in 1984 and became a Partner in 1988. Was appointed and served as an interim New Orleans City Council Member in 1999-2000.

**Personal:** Tulane Law School, JD 1984; Tulane Freeman School of Business, MBA 1983; Admitted in Louisiana and Mississippi

### CURRAULT II, Douglas N
Jones Walker Waechter Poitevent Carrère & Denègre, LLP, New Orleans 504 582 8412
dcurrault@joneswalker.com
*Recommended in Corporate/M&A*
**Practice Areas:** Mr Currault's practice includes handling corporate and securities law matters for public and private companies. His practice focuses on SEC reporting, corporate finance, mergers and acquisitions, and corporate governance and compliance. 'A lawyer's area of practice as stated here is one to which (s)he devotes a substantial portion of his/her professional practice and should not be considered a 'specialization' unless certified by the Louisiana Board of Legal Specialization (or similar body in any other state in which such lawyer is licensed to practice)'.
**Prof. Memberships:** New Orleans Bar Association, Louisiana State Bar Association, Louisiana State Board of CPAs.
**Career:** Partner of the firm since 1997. Tulane University (JD, cum laude, 1989; Order of the Coif). Loyola University (BS, cum laude, Mathematics 1986).
**Personal:** Mr Currault and his wife, Donna, have been married since 1988 and have two children, Katharine and Nicholas.

### D'ARMOND, William
Kean Miller Hawthorne D'Armond McCowan & Jarman, LLP, Baton Rouge 225 382 3403
bill.d'armond@keanmiller.com
*Recommended in Employment*
**Practice Areas:** Labor and employment, union negotiations.
**Prof. Memberships:** Baton Rouge, Louisiana State and American Bar Associations; State Bar of Texas; Labor and Employment Law Section, American and Louisiana Bar Associations.
**Career:** Bill D'Armond is Of Counsel to Kean Miller. He advises clients on compliance with state and federal labor and employment laws, and actively represents employers in court, administrative and arbitration proceedings. He has experience with the major federal agencies with employment related jurisdiction, including the NLRB, EEOC, OFCCP, and OSHA. He also assists employers in negotiation of collective bargaining agreements and with labor contract interpretation and grievances.

### DICHARRY, Paul
Taylor, Porter, Brooks & Phillips, LLP, Baton Rouge 225 387 3221
*Recommended in Environment*

### DILEO, Anthony
Anthony DiLeo - Sole Practitioner, New Orleans 504 274 0087

*Recommended in Corporate/M&A*

### DRAPER, Douglas
Heller, Draper, Hayden, Patrick & Horn, LLC, New Orleans 504 581 9595
*Recommended in Corporate/M&A*

### DUCK, John M
Adams and Reese LLP, New Orleans 504 585 0226
john.duck@arlaw.com
*Recommended in Corporate/M&A*
**Practice Areas:**
Corporate/securities/mergers and acquisitions, commercial restructuring/bankruptcy, banking/ finance, general business/transactions.
**Prof. Memberships:** American, Louisiana, and Fifth Federal Circuit Bar Associations, Louisiana Bar Foundation, American Bankruptcy Institute, Chairman Urban League of New Orleans Nominating Committee, Executive Committee New Orleans Ballet, Vice-Chair Committee for a SECURE Louisiana, Committee of 100 and Committee for Economic Development for Louisiana.
**Career:** Partner: Complex corporate restructuring matters both bankruptcy and non-bankruptcy contexts. Advises/represents clients in connection with the acquisition/disposition of corporate assets, commercial lending matters, including debtor-in-possession financing transactions.
**Personal:** JD Tulane University Law School, 1980; BS University of Southern Mississippi, 1977.

### DUNCAN, J Kelly
Jones Walker Waechter Poitevent Carrère & Denègre, LLP, New Orleans 504 582 8218
kduncan@joneswalker.com
*Recommended in Gaming & Licensing*
**Practice Areas:** Gaming Law: Serves as Jones Walker's Gaming Practice Chair concentrating in the representation of major casino companies, domestic and international manufacturers and suppliers, and financial institutions in connection with licensing, compliance, statutory and regulatory interpretation, administrative hearings, acquisitions, operations and financings. Admiralty, maritime and international and customs law: 25 years of experience in handling marine regulatory matters, acquisitions, financings, contracts, vessel constructions, lien enforcement and foreclosure, customs rulings, protests, seizures and classification disputes. 'A lawyer's area of practice as stated here is one to which (s)he devotes a substantial portion of his/her professional practice and should not be considered a 'specialization' unless certified by the Louisiana Board of Legal Specialization (or similar body in any other state in which such lawyer is licensed to practice)'.
**Prof. Memberships:** Founding Member and Director of the International Masters of Gaming Law; past Chairman of the

New Orleans Bar Association Maritime and International Law Committee; Member of the following: International Association of Gaming Attorneys; American Bar Association — Sections on Admiralty and Maritime Law and Business Law - Maritime Financing and Gaming Law Committees; Maritime Law Association of the United States - Maritime Financing and Carriage of Goods Committees; New Orleans Maritime Seminar Advisory and Planning Committees; Southeastern Admiralty Law Institute; American Association of Exporters and Importers; and Association of Average Adjusters
**Career:** Georgetown University (AB, cum laude, 1976); Tulane University (JD, 1979).
**Publications:** Member, Editorial Board, Gaming Law Review.
**Personal:** Born, New Orleans, Louisiana, February 22, 1954.

### DUNCAN III, Brooke
Adams and Reese LLP, New Orleans 504 585 0220
brooke.duncan@arlaw.com
*Recommended in Employment*
**Practice Areas:** Partner: special business services, labor and employment, management counseling, labor relations, collective bargaining, employment discrimination - agency practice, OSHA.
**Prof. Memberships:** Louisiana State Bar; Chairman, Louisiana State Police Commission; Louisiana Civil Service League; Each One Save One Board.
**Career:** Proactive consulting with managers about problematic labor and employment issues to achieve positive employee relations. Counsels employers on maintaining union-free status, defending job discrimination claims, wage-hour issues, OSHA, reduction-in-force questions, compliance with workplace regulations and miscellaneous state law issues, for public and private employers. Represents management before National Labor Relations Board, defends union grievances, and negotiates union contracts.
**Personal:** JD, Tulane University Law School, 1986; AB, Vassar College, 1974.

### DUPLANTIS, BJ
Gordon, Arata, McCollam, Duplantis & Eagan LLP, New Orleans 504 582 1111
*Recommended in Energy*

### EAGAN, Ewell
Gordon, Arata, McCollam, Duplantis & Eagan LLP, New Orleans 504 582 1111
*Recommended in Litigation*

### FANTACI, James
McGlinchey Stafford, New Orleans 504 596 2791
jfantaci@mcglinchey.com
*Recommended in Corporate/M&A*
**Practice Areas:** Practice includes negotiation and preparation of asset purchase, stock purchase, and merger agreements for transfers of businesses; confidential private placement memoranda; franchise

agreements and disclosure documents; formation of corporations, limited liability companies and partnerships; and business restructuring. Advises on liquidations, shareholder (buy-sell) agreements, non-competition contracts, and other business oriented documents.
**Prof. Memberships:** American Bar Association, Forum on Franchising; Louisiana and Virginia Bar Associations; Jefferson Chamber of Commerce; Jefferson Parish Economic Development Commission.
**Publications:** Louisiana Limited Liability Company Forms and Practice Manual (1996).
**Personal:** Received JD from University of Virginia (1971) and BA from University of Rochester (1968).

## FISHMAN, Louis Y
Correro Fishman Haygood Phelps Walmsley & Casteix LLP, New Orleans
504 586 5255
lfishman@cfhlaw.com
*Recommended in Corporate/M&A*
**Practice Areas:** Louis Fishman has since 1966 represented a variety of business clients in numerous transactions that have included mergers and acquisitions and public and private offerings of securities. He also counsels clients on business, securities and corporate law matters, including corporate governance.
**Career:** Louis was a founder in 1988 of Tulane's Corporate Law Institute and still serves on its Planning Committee. He has served since 1991 as a member of the Advisory Board of Editors of the 'Tulane Law Review'. He has held several key posts, including Chairman, of the Louisiana State Bar Association's Section on Corporation and Business Law and has served as a Member of that Section's Corporate Laws Committee. Louis has taught 'Corporate Governance Post Enron' at Tulane Law School, and 'Judaism and Christianity' at a Presbyterian church in New Orleans.
**Publications:** Louis has been listed as a top corporate lawyer in a leading legal publication in America, since that publication's first edition in 1983, and has been ranked by 'New Orleans Magazine' as one of the city's top lawyers.
**Personal:** Louis received his Undergraduate Degree in Business Administration from Tulane University in 1963. He received his LLB Degree in 1965 from Tulane Law School, where he was a Member of the Order of the Coif and Editor-in-Chief of the 'Tulane Law Review'. He earned a Master of Laws Degree in 1966 from Yale Law School, where he was a Sterling Fellow.

## FONTHAM, Michael R
Stone Pigman Walther Wittmann LLC, New Orleans 504 593 0810
mfontham@stonepigman.com
*Recommended in Energy*

**Practice Areas:** Public utility regulation and commercial litigation.
**Prof. Memberships:** American Academy of Appellate Lawyers; Delegate, 2005 National Conference on Appellate Justice.
**Career:** Joined Stone Pigman in 1971; became Member in 1975. Teaching: Visiting Professor, University of Virginia Law School 1982-83; Adjunct Professor, Tulane University Law School, 1987-present; Adjunct Professor, Louisiana State University Law School, 1974-present; Faculty Member, Trial Advocacy Institute, University of Virginia, 1983-present. Academic subjects: Evidence, Appellate Advocacy, Problems of Proof, Antitrust, Constitutional Law.
**Publications:** Books: Trial Technique and Evidence 2d ed (Lexis Nexis 2002); Persuasive Written and Oral Advocacy: In Trial and Appellate Courts (Aspen, 2002); and Written and Oral Advocacy (John Wiley and Sons, 1985).
**Personal:** JD, University of Virginia School of Law, 1971. Member of the Order of the Coif and the Virginia Law Review. Undergraduate Degree from Louisiana State University.

## FORSYTH, J David
Sessions, Fishman & Nathan LLP, New Orleans 504 582 1500
*Recommended in Corporate/M&A*

## FOSTER, Murphy
Breazeale, Sachse & Wilson, LLP, Baton Rouge 225 387 4000
*Recommended in Employment*

## FRILOT, George
Frilot, Partridge, Kohnke & Clements LC, New Orleans 504 599 8000
*Recommended in Litigation*

## FULLMER, Mark A
Phelps Dunbar LLP, New Orleans
504 584 9324
fullmerm@phelps.com
*Recommended in Corporate/M&A*
**Practice Areas:** Mr Fullmer is a Partner in the Business Group in the New Orleans office. He represents start-up companies as well as companies in the mature stages of their growth cycle. His practice in the area of corporate and securities includes all aspects of public and private company representation, including public offerings, private placements, and mergers and acquisitions. He has also represented both venture capital funds and investors in private equity transactions. He is recognized as a leading practitioner in New Orleans in the area of corporate and securities law in The Best Lawyers in America and Chambers USA, America's Leading Lawyers for Business.
**Personal:** Louisiana State University, JD, 1976; Order of the Coif; Louisiana Law Review. University of New Orleans, BS in Accounting, 1976.

## GARNER, James
Sher Garner Cahill Richter Klein & Hilbert LLC, New Orleans
504 299 2102
jgarner@shergarner.com
*Recommended in Litigation*
**Practice Areas:** Mr Garner, a Member of the firm, is a trial lawyer specializing in commercial and complex litigation. He has been lead counsel in cases in New Mexico, Kansas, Arizona, Indiana, Arkansas, Mississippi, Louisiana and Texas. He is admitted to practice before the federal courts in Arkansas and Mississippi and all courts in Texas and Louisiana.
**Prof. Memberships:** Professional and civic activities include: American (Member); Louisiana (Member) and Federal (Director, Membership Chair, Member) Bar Associations; Defense Research Institute (Member); Louisiana Association of Business and Industry (Member); Louisiana Bankers Association (Member); Holy Cross High School (Board Member); Our Lady of Holy Cross College (Development Board); Tulane University (Admissions Council and Externship Committee); Tulane Law Review Board of Advisory Editors; St. Catherine of Siena Cub Scout Pack 230 Den Leader.
**Publications:** 'The Public Documents Hearsay Exception for Evaluative Reports: Fact or Fiction?', 63 Tul L Rev 121, 63, 1988 The Louisiana 1988 Products Liability Reform Act: The Changes and Their Effects, 5 Tul Civ L Forum 129, 5, 1990 Federal Bar Association, New Orleans Chapter, Advocate, Volume 12, 2002

## GOODMAN, Alan
Lemle & Kelleher, LLP, New Orleans
504 586 1241
*Recommended in Corporate/M&A*

## GREGORIE JR, Isaac McPherson
Kean Miller Hawthorne D'Armond McCowan & Jarman, LLP, Baton Rouge
225 382 3411
mack.gregorie@keanmiller.com
*Recommended in Real Estate*
**Practice Areas:** Commercial and industrial real estate, business and corporate, finance.
**Prof. Memberships:** Baton Rouge, Louisiana and American Bar Associations. Fellow, American College of Mortgage Attorneys.
**Career:** Mack Gregorie represents clients in business transactions including complex commercial and industrial real estate finance. He represents petrochemical clients, energy producers, banks and financial institutions, buyers and sellers, landlords and tenants, and lenders. A certified public accountant, he lectures frequently on real estate topics such as sales, leases, property law, purchase and sale agreements, and recent developments in real estate law. He is also a title agent for First American Title Insurance Company.

## HARBOURT, Maureen N
Kean Miller Hawthorne D'Armond McCowan & Jarman, LLP, Baton Rouge
225 382 3412
maureen.harbourt@keanmiller.com
*Recommended in Environment*
**Practice Areas:** Environmental regulation.
**Prof. Memberships:** Baton Rouge, Louisiana (Environmental Law Committee) and American (Section on Energy/Environmental Resources) Bar Associations; Air and Waste Management Association.
**Career:** Maureen Harbourt represents industrial and commercial clients in a variety of environmental areas such as Title V and PSD air permitting, RCRA/HSWA hazardous waste and remediation, RECAP, water and wetland issues, stratospheric ozone regulation, underground injection wells, environmental compliance and audits, assistance in mergers, acquisitions and reorganizations, defense of state and federal enforcement actions, criminal enforcement issues, and regulatory/legislative development. A member of the Management Committee, she represents the Louisiana Chemical Association.

## HARDIN, Pauline
Jones Walker Waechter Poitevent Carrère & Denègre, LLP, New Orleans
504 582 8110
phardin@joneswalker.com
*Recommended in Litigation*
**Practice Areas:** Commercial litigation, white-collar crime and corporate compliance, and environmental and toxic torts. 'A lawyer's area of practice as stated here is one to which (s)he devotes a substantial portion of his/her professional practice and should not be considered a 'specialization' unless certified by the Louisiana Board of Legal Specialization (or similar body in any other state in which such lawyer is licensed to practice)'.
**Prof. Memberships:** Louisiana State Association; American Bar Association; American College of Trial Lawyers; Louisiana Association of Criminal Defense Lawyers.
**Career:** Ms Hardin has been a Partner in the firm's Litigation Section since 1990. She has 31 years of experience litigating criminal matters and 19 years of experience litigating business, commercial and labor matters. She served as the former Head of the Litigation Section at Jones Walker for four years. Prior to joining Jones Walker, Ms Hardin was with the United States Attorney's Office for the Eastern District of Louisiana and served as both First Assistant United States Attorney and Chief of the Criminal Division. Prior to that time, she served as an Assistant District Attorney in charge of the Orleans Parish's Fraud and White Collar Crime Unit.
**Personal:** Born in New Orleans,

Louisiana; admitted to Bar, 1974, Louisiana; Loyola University of New Orleans (BA, 1971); Tulane University (JD, 1974).

### HARDIN III, Harry S
Jones Walker Waechter Poitevent Carrère & Denègre, LLP, New Orleans
504 582 8170
hhardin@joneswalker.com
*Recommended in Litigation*

**Practice Areas:** Senior Partner concentrating in commercial business litigation, contract, railroad, antitrust, trademark, copyright, professional responsibility and environmental law. 'A lawyer's area of practice as stated here is one to which (s)he devotes a substantial portion of his/her professional practice and should not be considered a 'specialization' unless certified by the Louisiana Board of Legal Specialization (or similar body in any other state in which such lawyer is licensed to practice).'

**Prof. Memberships:** Fellow, American College of Trial Lawyers; American Judicature Society Board of Directors (2003-06); American Bar Association: Board of Governors (2005-08), Louisiana State Delegate (1994-2003), Fifth Circuit Representative to Standing Committee on Federal Judiciary (1998-2002), Sections of Litigation, Antitrust, Patent Trademark & Copyright, Tort & Insurance Practice; Louisiana State Bar Association, past President; Louisiana Bar Foundation, past President; International Association of Defense Counsel; National Association of Railroad Trial Counsel.

**Career:** 1971 Jones Walker, (1973-77 1st Lt. JAG US Army), Partner, 1976; Chair, Appellate Practice; speaks on ethics, professionalism and malpractice avoidance; Louisiana Supreme Court: Chair, Judicial Campaign Oversight Committee, Advisory Committee for Revision of Code of Judicial Conduct.

**Publications:** Managed Care and Antitrust: The PPO Experience, ABA Press (contributing author); 'Pitfalls for In-House Counsel', The Brief, ABA Press.

**Personal:** New Orleans native; BA Harvard (cum laude); JD Tulane University.

### HARKINS, Deborah
McGlinchey Stafford, New Orleans
504 596 2799
dharkins@mcglinchey.com
*Recommended in Gaming & Licensing*

**Practice Areas:** Environmental, gaming, government relations, healthcare, insurance regulation and compliance.

**Prof. Memberships:** Louisiana healthcare Commission, Louisiana Hospital Association, Louisiana Lobbyist Association, National Health Lawyers Association, New Orleans Film and Video Corporation, Women Health Executive Network, Committee of 21, French Market Corporation Board, Vieux Carre Alliance, Lower Quarter Crime Watch, Louisiana

Bar Association.

**Career:** Registered lobbyist; industries represented include healthcare, insurance, environment, banking, gaming, and pharmaceutical; works with Louisiana Department of Insurance on matters including licensure, insurance regulation and compliance, managed care plans, independent review organizations and third party administrators; represents Louisiana Healthcare Commission for Commissioner of Insurance; appears before Louisiana Gaming Control Board and Louisiana State Racing Commission, Public Service Commission and Louisiana Used Motor Vehicle Commission.

### HARTMANN, Melanie
Kean Miller Hawthorne D'Armond McCowan & Jarman, LLP, Baton Rouge
225 382 3422
melanie.hartmann@keanmiller.com
*Recommended in Employment*

**Practice Areas:** Labor and employment law, litigation.

**Prof. Memberships:** Baton Rouge, Louisiana (Employment Law Section) and American Bar Associations.

**Career:** Melanie Hartmann represents clients in employment litigation. She represents management with regard to compliance with state and federal labor laws. She actively represents employers in court and administrative proceedings and has experience with federal agencies including the EEOC and the Department of Labor. She has more than 16 years of experience in employment law litigation including employment discrimination, EEOC issues, ADA, sexual harassment, and wrongful termination. Melanie has represented clients in bench and jury trials in state and federal court.

### HAYDEN, Jan
Heller, Draper, Hayden, Patrick & Horn, LLC, New Orleans 504 581 9595
*Recommended in Corporate/M&A*

### HAYGOOD, Paul M
Correro Fishman Haygood Phelps Walmsley & Casteix LLP, New Orleans
504 586 5263
phaygood@cfhlaw.com
*Recommended in Corporate/M&A*

**Practice Areas:** Mr Haygood practices in the areas of mergers and acquisitions, corporate law, securities law, probate, estate planning and trust law. He has represented clients in a variety of corporate finance and planning matters, including representing numerous financial institutions in connection with acquisition transactions involving more than $1 billion in assets; acting as lead outside counsel in connection with the corporate and securities aspects of the reorganization of a large publicly-held enterprise in what was the largest financial reorganization up to that time of a Louisiana-based company; acting as lead outside counsel in connection with the financial and cor-

porate restructuring of a Louisiana-based, publicly-traded entity with assets in excess of $500 million; representation of an international oil and gas service company in connection with the acquisition of assets located on three different continents and totaling in excess of $40 million; and structuring estate plans for individuals having an estimated combined net worth in excess of $150 million.

**Career:** Like his partners, Andy Correro, Louis Fishman, and Robert Walmsley, Mr Haygood is a former Chairman of the Corporate and Business Law Section of the Louisiana State Bar Association. He also chaired for many years the Association's Bar Admission Committee that prepares the Louisiana corporation law portion of the Louisiana Bar Examination, as well as chairing for 10 years the Association's Corporate Laws Committee, which monitors the Louisiana Business Corporation Law and makes recommendations to the Louisiana Legislature with respect to changes in the Louisiana Business Corporation Law.

**Publications:** Mr Haygood is listed in a leading legal publication in America as one of the best lawyers in America in the area of corporate law. He has retained that listing since 1983, when that publication was first published.

**Personal:** Mr Haygood graduated from Louisiana State University in 1964 and received his LLB from Harvard Law School in 1967. In addition to the practice of law, Mr Haygood also has played an active role in the civic affairs of New Orleans and Louisiana, having served as President of the Council for a Better Louisiana, as President of the New Orleans Bureau of Governmental Research, and as an active board member of a number of philanthropic organizations. In 1991 he chaired the New Orleans Conference on North American Free Trade. Mr Haygood also is a former member of the Board of Supervisors of Louisiana State University and a former member of the Board of Advisors of the National Trust for Historic Preservation.

### HEARN, Curtis R
Jones Walker Waechter Poitevent Carrère & Denègre, LLP, New Orleans
504 582 8308
chearn@joneswalker.com
*Recommended in Corporate/M&A*

**Practice Areas:** Mergers and acquisitions; corporate and securities; healthcare transactions. 'A lawyer's area of practice as stated here is one to which (s)he devotes a substantial portion of his/her professional practice and should not be considered a 'specialization' unless certified by the Louisiana Board of Legal Specialization (or similar body in any other state in which such lawyer is licensed to practice).'

**Prof. Memberships:** Member, American Bar Association, Negotiated Acquisitions Committee of Business Law Section.

**Personal:** Adjunct Professor, Law, Mergers and Acquisitions, Tulane University Law School.

### HERMAN, Russ M
Herman, Herman, Katz & Cotlar, New Orleans 504 581 4892
rherman@hhkc.com
*Recommended in Litigation*

**Practice Areas:** Business and commercial law; class actions/complex multi-district litigation; construction litigation; explosions and fires; maritime; HMO litigation; medical negligence; motor vehicle litigation; personal injury; pharmaceutical litigation; professional negligence; railroad litigation; tobacco litigation.

**Prof. Memberships:** Admitted Louisiana (1966); American Board of Professional Liability Attorneys (Diplomate), International Academy of Trial Lawyers (Fellow), National College of Advocacy (Diplomate), American Board of Trial Advocates, American Society of Barristers (Fellow), International Society of Barristers (Fellow), Louisiana Trial Lawyers Association (past President); Association of Trial Lawyers of America (past President), Civil Justice Foundation (past President), Roscoe Pound Foundation.

**Career:** Senior Partner in the firm of Herman, Herman, Katz & Cotlar of New Orleans, Louisiana. Awards: LTLA President's Outstanding Louisiana Trial Lawyer Award (1977); ATLA's Lifetime Achievement (1999); ATLA's Leonard M Ring Champion of Justice Award (2001); Best Lawyers In America (20+ Years); Pursuit of Justice Award (2005), American Bar Association Tort Trial & Insurance Practice Section (TIPS); and City Business' Leadership in Law (2005); The Lawdragon 500 Leading Lawyers in America (2005).

**Publications:** 'Courtroom Persuasion, Winning with Art, Drama & Science', Clark-Boardman Thompson and West Group (1997); 'West Group Practice Series: Louisiana Personal Injury, Volumes I & II', West Group (1999); ATLA Press, 1992: 'The Art of Courtroom Persuasion' (Video-Six Volumes); Louisiana Damages, 'For the Plaintiff: Determining and Proving Damages; For the Defense: Limiting Damages', co-author with Melville Z Wolfson, PhD, National Business Institute, Inc. 12/12/85; 'Successful Trial Techniques of Expert Practitioners', 1990 Supplement, 'Opening Statement' 'Personal Injury Review' - 1990, 'Preparing the Difficult Medical Causation Case and the Cross-Examination of Physicians from Medical Texts', p. 781, 1990 Ed.; Contributing Author: 'Best of Trial Products Liability', ATLA Press, 1991; Civil Trial Practice - 2000 and Beyond, Lawyers & Judges Publishing Co., March 2000; Civil Trial Practice - Winning Techniques of Successful Trial Attorneys, The Lawyers & Judges Publishing Company, 2000.

**Personal:** Tulane University, New Orleans, Louisiana, BA Degree, 1963; Tulane University School of Law, New Orleans, Louisiana, LLB Degree (now JD), 1966.

### HEUSEL, Cornelius
Jones Walker Waechter Poitevent Carrère & Denègre, LLP, New Orleans
504 582 8148
nheusel@joneswalker.com
*Recommended in Employment*

**Practice Areas:** Partner in Jones Walker's Labor Relations and Employment and White Collar Crime and Corporate Compliance Practices. 'A lawyer's area of practice as stated here is one to which (s)he devotes a substantial portion of his/her professional practice and should not be considered a 'specialization' unless certified by the Louisiana Board of Legal Specialization (or similar body in any other state in which such lawyer is licensed to practice)'.

**Career:** Mr Heusel served three years as a Special Agent with the Federal Bureau of Investigation before serving as Executive Assistant District Attorney for Orleans Parish in charge of capital cases. In 1972, he joined the US Attorney's Office in New Orleans, serving as Criminal Division Chief and First Assistant US Attorney. In 1976, he received the US Attorney General's Exceptional Service Award. Beginning in 1977, he headed the Department of Justice Organized Crime and Racketeering Strike Force with jurisdiction over Texas, Louisiana, Arkansas, Mississippi, and Alabama. He also served as an Assistant Special Prosecutor appointed by the federal courts to investigate allegations of corruption involving members of the White House staff. Mr Heusel has been a guest lecturer at the US Department of Justice Trial Advocacy Institute on Trial Tactics and a member of the Tulane University School of Law Panel of Instructors on Trial Advocacy. Since 1979, he has primarily represented management in the field of labor relations. Joined Jones Walker in 1999.

**Personal:** Native of New Orleans; Loyola University (BBA, 1967; JD, 1967).

### HOLDEN, Robert
Liskow & Lewis PLC, New Orleans
504 581 7979
*Recommended in Environment*

### HOOTSELL III, Sessions Ault
Phelps Dunbar LLP, New Orleans
504 584 9371
hootsela@phelps.com
*Recommended in Corporate/M&A*

**Practice Areas:** Mr Hootsell is a Partner in the Commercial Litigation Group in the New Orleans office. For more than 18 years, he has counseled corporate and individual clients on a full range of business related disputes, both in litigation and planning. Mr Hootsell's practice includes the handling of complex com-

mercial litigation matters in both federal and state court, including contract and lease disputes, construction disputes, supplier disputes, surety matters, intellectual property disputes, business torts, lender liability, director and officer matters, insurance regulatory matters, franchisor/franchisee disputes, and the protection and enforcement of debtor's and creditors' rights generally in the non-bankruptcy context. Within the past year alone, he has represented clients in matters before courts in California, Indiana, Kansas, Delaware, New Jersey, Texas, Mississippi and Louisiana. With regard to the latter, Mr Hootsell is Board Certified at both the national and state level in the area of business bankruptcy, and is the Chairman of the Bankruptcy Committee of the New Orleans Bar Association.

**Personal:** Louisiana State University, JD, 1986; BS in Finance, 1983

### HUNTER, Jonathon
Liskow & Lewis PLC, New Orleans
504 581 7979
*Recommended in Energy*

### JACOB, Clyde
Jones Walker Waechter Poitevent Carrère & Denègre, LLP, New Orleans
504 582 8230
cjacob@joneswalker.com
*Recommended in Employment*

**Practice Areas:** Clyde Jacob is a Partner in the firm's Labor Relations and Employment Law Practice. He represents employers in the field of labor relations and has assisted employers in responding to union organizing, boycotts, strikes, collective bargaining, National Labor Relations Board representation cases, and corporate campaigns throughout the United States and in Puerto Rico, Norway, and the United Kingdom. He also defends employment claims. He has spoken on a national basis to employers, employer associations, and bar associations including the Inter American Bar Association and the US Chamber of Commerce. He has twice testified as an expert before the US Congress, and has worked with and spoken before the United States Council for International Business. 'A lawyer's area of practice as stated here is one to which (s)he devotes a substantial portion of his/her professional practice and should not be considered a 'specialization' unless certified by the Louisiana Board of Legal Specialization (or similar body in any other state in which such lawyer is licensed to practice)'.

**Prof. Memberships:** American Bar Association, Labor Section; Louisiana Bar Association; Virginia Bar Association; Louisiana Association of Defense Counsel; US Chamber of Commerce, Labor Relations Committee, Washington, DC; admitted to bar, 1975, Virginia; 1976, Louisiana; also admitted: US Supreme Court; Virginia and Louisiana Supreme

Courts; and numerous Federal appellate and district courts.

**Career:** Law clerk, US District Court, Eastern District of Virginia; joined Jones Walker in 1999.

**Personal:** Native of Norfolk, Virginia; resides in New Orleans; University of Virginia (BA, 1971; JD, 1975).

### JARMAN, William
Kean Miller Hawthorne D'Armond McCowan & Jarman, LLP, Baton Rouge
225 382 3405
bill.jarman@keanmiller.com
*Recommended in Litigation*

**Practice Areas:** Litigation, oil and gas, energy law, products liability.

**Prof. Memberships:** Baton Rouge, Louisiana and American Bar Associations; Louisiana Association of Defense Counsel; State Bar of Texas; Louisiana Law Institute; Institute for Energy Law; Fellow, American College of Trial Lawyers; Fellow, International Oil and Gas Foundation; Member, Advisory Board, Center for American and International Law (Institute for Energy Law); Member, MidContinent Oil and Gas Association.

**Career:** Bill Jarman represents Fortune 100 clients in energy litigation, pipeline expropriation, environmental litigation, toxic tort, product liability, NORM, and commercial litigation. He is a widely respected trial strategist and a renowned negotiator.

### JONES JR, Philip
Liskow & Lewis PLC, New Orleans
504 581 7979
*Recommended in Corporate/M&A*

### KANTROW, Lee
Kantrow Spaht Weaver & Blitzer, Baton Rouge 225 383 4703
*Recommended in Corporate/M&A*

### KERRIGAN JR, Robert
Deutsch, Kerrigan & Stiles LLP, New Orleans 504 581 5141
*Recommended in Litigation*

### KIGGANS, Thomas H
Phelps Dunbar LLP, Baton Rouge
225 376 0247
kigganst@phelps.com
*Recommended in Employment*

**Practice Areas:** Mr Kiggans is a Partner and the practice co-ordinator of the Employment Law Group in the Baton Rouge office. He also practices labor and employment law out of the firm's Houston, Texas office. He has practiced labor and employment law almost exclusively since 1984. He represents primarily employers in both litigation and counseling in all areas of labor and employment, including discrimination, ERISA, sexual harassment, employee defamation, and other employment-related tort claims, employment contracts, OSHA, union matters, wage and hour, drug testing, and drafting and implementing employment

policies. Mr Kiggans represents employers in a wide variety of industries, including construction, equipment rental, banks, maritime, petrochemical, oil and gas exploration and production, insurance, gaming, governmental entities, educational institutions and restaurants, and has extensive trial experience in both federal and state courts.

**Personal:** Louisiana State University, JD, 1984; Board of Editors, Louisiana Law Review. Louisiana Tech University, BA, magna cum laude, 1981.

### KILGORE III, Leonard L
Kean Miller Hawthorne D'Armond McCowan & Jarman, LLP, Baton Rouge
225 382 3406
len.kilgore@keanmiller.com
*Recommended in Environment*

**Practice Areas:** Environmental regulation, toxic tort litigation, environmental litigation.

**Prof. Memberships:** Baton Rouge, Louisiana (Environmental Law Section) and American (Land and Natural Resources Section; Vice-Chair, Committee on Environmental and Toxic Torts, 1989-90) Bar Associations; Defense Research Institute; Louisiana Association of Defense Counsel; Fellow, Louisiana Bar Foundation.

**Career:** Len Kilgore has 25 years of experience in environmental regulation and litigation, including class action, multiple joinder, and toxic tort cases. He represents energy, chemical and industrial clients in litigation involving toxic tort claims, property damage claims, Superfund sites, RCRA, environmental remediation, class actions, RECAP, environmental releases and reporting, and permitting.

### KING, Henry
King, LeBlanc & Bland, New Orleans
504 582 3800
*Recommended in Energy*

### KING, Katherine
Kean Miller Hawthorne D'Armond McCowan & Jarman, LLP, Baton Rouge
225 382 3436
katherine.king@keanmiller.com
*Recommended in Energy*

**Practice Areas:** Energy, utilities regulation, cogeneration projects.

**Prof. Memberships:** Baton Rouge, Louisiana and American Bar Associations; Association of Energy Engineers; Co-Chair, Public Utility Section, Louisiana State Bar Association.

**Career:** Katherine King has more than 15 years of experience in the regulation of Louisiana's telecommunications, pipeline, and electric industry. She represents utilities and industry before the Louisiana Public Service Commission and the Federal Energy Regulatory Commission. She serves as lead counsel to the Louisiana Energy Users Group and represents electric generators and project developers in regulatory proceedings before the LPSC and in individual contract negotiations.

### KLEIN, Steven
Sher Garner Cahill Richter Klein & Hilbert LLC, New Orleans
504 299 2100
*Recommended in Corporate/M&A*

### KLING, Neal
Sher Garner Cahill Richter Klein & Hilbert LLC, New Orleans
504 299 2100
*Recommended in Real Estate*

### KOHNKE IV, Edward
Frilot, Partridge, Kohnke & Clements LC, New Orleans 504 599 8000
*Recommended in Litigation*

### LAFITTE, Gene
Liskow & Lewis PLC, New Orleans
504 581 7979
*Recommended in Litigation*

### LANDRY, Charles
Jones Walker Waechter Poitevent Carrère & Denègre, LLP, Baton Rouge
225 248 2020
clandry@joneswalker.com
*Recommended in Real Estate*
**Practice Areas:** Real estate: land use, development and finance; project development and finance. 'A lawyer's area of practice as stated here is one to which he devotes a substantial portion of his professional practice and should not be considered a 'specialization' unless certified by the Louisiana Board of Legal Specialization (or similar body in any other state in which such lawyer is licensed to practice)'.
**Prof. Memberships:** Urban Land Institute; Council for a Better Louisiana; East Baton Rouge Parish Planning Commission Zoning Ordinance Task Force; LSU Foundation; Pennington Biomedical Foundation.
**Career:** Mr Landry has been the Managing Partner of the firm's Baton Rouge office since 1996. He has represented a wide range of real estate transactions, including office buildings, shopping malls and centers, hotels, medical facilities, golf courses and golf course communities, as well as industrial and residential developments. He has also been very involved in advancing the Greater Baton Rouge's high-tech, information and entrepreneurial economic sector. He was instrumental in the formation of the Louisiana Technology Park, and serves as General Counsel to Research Park Corporation. Since 1993, Mr Landry has been listed in The Best Lawyers in America (Woodward/White, Inc.) in real estate law. He was selected as the 2006 Businessperson of the Year by the Baton Rouge Business Report and Junior Achievement, as the first attorney to receive this award.
**Publications:** 'The Foreign Investor's Guide to the Legal Aspects of Doing Business in Louisiana', co-editor.

**Personal:** Louisiana State University Law School (JD, 1977); (BS (Business), 1975).

### LELONG, Rivers
Jones Walker Waechter Poitevent Carrère & Denègre, LLP, New Orleans
504 582 8378
rlelong@joneswalker.com
*Recommended in Banking & Finance*
**Practice Areas:** Mr Lelong's practice involves a variety of commercial transactions involving secured finance, real estate, acquisitions and divestitures of privately held companies and their assets, and the negotiation of sophisticated commercial contracts. 'A lawyer's area of practice as stated here is one to which (s)he devotes a substantial portion of his/her professional practice and should not be considered a 'specialization' unless certified by the Louisiana Board of Legal Specialization (or similar body in any other state in which such lawyer is licensed to practice)'.
**Prof. Memberships:** Louisiana State Bar Association
**Career:** Admitted to Bar, 1990, Louisiana; Partner at Jones Walker since 1998.
**Personal:** Born New Orleans, Louisiana, February 14, 1965; Amherst College (BA, summa cum laude, 1987); Stanford Law School (JD 1990).

### LEVINE, Steve J
Phelps Dunbar LLP, Baton Rouge
225 376 0220
levines@phelps.com
*Recommended in Environment*
**Practice Areas:** Mr Levine is a Partner and the practice co-ordinator of the Litigation Group in the Baton Rouge office. His practice consists of environmental counseling and litigation. He routinely interacts with the Environmental Protection Agency and the state Department of Environmental Quality in matters relating to litigation, permitting, compliance orders, and penalty orders in various areas of Louisiana. Additionally, he counsels lending and real estate institutions on such matters as environmental assessments, contractual arrangements, and wetlands issues. Before entering law school he gained substantive educational and practical experience in the areas of fisheries biology, water resources, conservation, and resource management.
**Personal:** Louisiana State University, JD, 1984; managing editor, Louisiana Coastal Law Journal, Louisiana State University, MS in Fisheries Biology, 1977, University of Maryland, BS in Conservation and Resource Development, 1974.

### LEWIS, Sidney
Jones Walker Waechter Poitevent Carrère & Denègre, LLP, New Orleans
504 582 8352
slewis@joneswalker.com
*Recommended in Employment*
**Practice Areas:** Mr Lewis is a Partner and Chair of the firm's Labor Relations

and Employment Law Practice Group. He is an experienced litigator in federal, state and administrative judicial forums. A large part of his practice is devoted to advising and counseling employers with respect to union organizing drives and in the development, maintenance and administration of personnel policies, procedures and employee relations to minimize exposure to litigation and union organizing. Mr Lewis regularly conducts supervisor and management training programs. He is a frequent speaker for human resource associations, and has authored numerous articles for professional journals and other publications on a wide range of labor and employment law topics. 'A lawyer's area of practice as stated here is one to which (s)he devotes a substantial portion of his/her professional practice and should not be considered a 'specialization' unless certified by the Louisiana Board of Legal Specialization (or similar body in any other state in which such lawyer is licensed to practice)'.
**Prof. Memberships:** American Bar Association Labor and Employment Law Section; Louisiana State Bar Association.
**Career:** Admitted in Louisiana, 1985; Joined Jones Walker as Partner in 1999; Tulane School of Law (JD, 1985); University of Alabama (BA, 1982).
**Publications:** 'Sexual Harassment in Employment Law', BNA Books (contributing author); 'Louisiana Employment Law Letter' (associate editor); 'Jones Walker Labor and Employment Tip Sheet' (electronic newsletter) (co-editor).
**Personal:** Native of New Orleans, Louisiana.

### LEYENS, Jon
The Steeg Law Firm, LLC, New Orleans
504 582 1199
*Recommended in Real Estate*

### LINZY, Howard
The Kullman Firm PLC, New Orleans
504 596 4105
*Recommended in Employment*

### LUND, Daniel
Montgomery, Barnett, Brown, Read, Hammond & Mintz LLP, New Orleans
504 585 3200
*Recommended in Litigation*

### MALLERY, Mark
McGlinchey Stafford, New Orleans
504 596 2736
mmallery@mcglinchey.com
*Recommended in Employment*
**Practice Areas:** Labor and employment.
**Prof. Memberships:** Program Chair, Committee on Employment Rights and Responsibilities, ABA Labor and Employment Section.
**Career:** Defends employers in employment litigation, including acting as lead counsel in class actions, Sarbanes-Oxley whistleblower claims, class based EEOC

claims, pattern and practice cases prosecuted by the US Department of Labor's Civil Rights Center, wage and hour collective actions, hundreds of employment termination lawsuits, and prosecuting injunction proceedings against former executives and salespeople to protect trade secrets and proprietary information.
**Publications:** Editor-in-Chief, Employment Termination Treatise, BNA/ABA, 2003 Supplement.
**Personal:** JD University of Mississippi, 1986. BBA Mississippi State University, 1983.

### MALONE JR, Ernest
The Kullman Firm PLC, New Orleans
504 596 4105
*Recommended in Employment*

### MARTZELL, Jack
Martzell & Bickford, APC, New Orleans
504 581 9065
*Recommended in Litigation*

### MASTERS, William B
Jones Walker Waechter Poitevent Carrère & Denègre, LLP, New Orleans
504 582 8278
bmasters@joneswalker.com
*Recommended in Corporate/M&A*
**Practice Areas:** Mr Masters has a broad business practice in the areas of corporate finance, mergers and acquisitions and energy. His clients include public and privately owned companies engaged in virtually all areas of the energy industry, with an emphasis on service providers, private capital portfolio companies and other businesses in a variety of industries, including banking. Mr Masters has extensive experience in public and private offerings of debt and equity securities and acts as general counsel for several public and private companies. Mr Masters also routinely structures and negotiates acquisitions and financing transactions. 'A lawyer's area of practice as stated here is one to which (s)he devotes a substantial portion of his/her professional practice and should not be considered a 'specialization' unless certified by the Louisiana Board of Legal Specialization (or similar body in any other state in which such lawyer is licensed to practice)'.
**Prof. Memberships:** American Bar Association, Louisiana State Bar Association and Society of Corporate Secretaries.
**Career:** Joined Jones Walker law firm in 1982.
**Personal:** London School of Economics; Tulane University, BA, 1979; George Washington University, JD, 1982.

### MCCALLA, Robert
Fisher & Phillips LLP, New Orleans
504 522 3303
rmccalla@laborlawyers.com
*Recommended in Employment*
**Practice Areas:** Bob McCalla is a Senior Partner in the New Orleans office of the

national law firm of Fisher & Phillips LLP, practicing exclusively in labor and employment law representing management. He has handled numerous complex individual and class action discrimination cases and Fair Labor Standards Act collective action cases and has extensive experience handling both judge trials and jury trials. McCalla has negotiated many labor agreements and is experienced in advising clients in connection with strikes and corporate campaigns. He received a JD from the University of Nebraska College of Law, graduating Cum Laude, Order of the Coif.

### MCCOLLAM, John
Gordon, Arata, McCollam, Duplantis & Eagan LLP, New Orleans 504 582 1111
*Recommended in Energy, Litigation*

### MCCOWAN, Charles
Kean Miller Hawthorne D'Armond McCowan & Jarman, LLP, Baton Rouge
225 382 3404
charles.mccowan@keanmiller.com
*Recommended in Environment*
**Practice Areas:** Environmental litigation.
**Prof. Memberships:** DRI; Louisiana Law Institute; American Board of Trial Advocates; Baton Rouge, Louisiana, and American Bar Associations; Judicial Liaison Committee, Louisiana Bar Foundation; Fellow, International Society of Barristers.
**Career:** Charles McCowan has more than 35 years of experience with petrochemical, energy, industrial clients in a variety of disputes. His experience includes class action, toxic tort, construction, environmental, commercial, and massive tort litigation. He is a respected litigation strategist for Fortune 500 companies with Louisiana operations. He is General Counsel to the Louisiana Chemical Association and a member of the American Board of Trial Advocates.

### MCGOEY II, Thomas
Liskow & Lewis PLC, New Orleans
504 581 7979
*Recommended in Employment*

### MCGUIRE, Robin
Independent or In Limbo, Unionville
*Recommended in Energy*

### MCMILLAN II, L Richards
Jones Walker Waechter Poitevent Carrère & Denègre, LLP, New Orleans
504 582 8188
rmcmillan@joneswalker.com
*Recommended in Corporate/M&A*
**Practice Areas:** Corporate, securities, corporate finance, mergers and acquisitions, corporate governance. 'A lawyer's area of practice as stated here is one to which he devotes a substantial portion of his professional practice and shouldn't be considered a 'specialization' unless certified by the Louisiana Board of Legal Specialization (or similar body in any other state in which such lawyer is licensed to practice)'.

**Prof. Memberships:** Past Chairman, Corporate Law Section, Louisiana State Bar Association; former Member, Committee on Negotiated Acquisitions, American Bar Association.
**Career:** He joined Jones Walker in 1976 after serving three years in the Navy JAG Corps and became a Partner in 1979. He served as Head of the firm's Corporate and Securities Practice (1987 to 2002) and as a member and Chairman of the firm's Executive Committee for most of the period from 1990 through 2002. He has broad industry experience, with significant representations of clients in banking, chemical manufacturing, computer technology, consumer services, defense contracting, manufacturing, mining, ocean shipping, offshore construction, oil and gas exploration and production, oil and gas services, and retailing. He also has business operational experience, having served as Chairman, from 1986 through the current date and as President from 1989 through 1999, of a privately held integrated manufacturing company producing water purification equipment.
**Personal:** Born New Orleans, Louisiana, 1947; Washington and Lee University (BS, 1969); Tulane University School of Law (JD, 1972); Order of the Coif; US Navy Judge Advocate General's Corps (1972-75); New York University School of Law (LLM in Taxation, 1976).

### MEUNIER, Gerald
Gainsburgh, Benjamin, David, Meunier & Warshauer, New Orleans
504 522 2304
*Recommended in Litigation*

### MILLER JR, Ben R
Kean Miller Hawthorne D'Armond McCowan & Jarman, LLP, Baton Rouge
225 382 3401
Ben.Miller@KeanMiller.com
*Recommended in Corporate/M&A*
**Practice Areas:** Business, corporate, banking, real estate, estate planning.
**Prof. Memberships:** Baton Rouge, Louisiana and American Bar Associations. Past Fellow, American College of Trust and Estate Counsel; Member, Louisiana Bar Foundation.
**Career:** Ben Miller has more than 40 years of experience in complex commercial and industrial transactions, tax and corporate law in Louisiana. His experience includes industrial acquisitions, mergers and acquisitions, and real estate. He represents clients in the finance, acquisition, construction, purchase, refinancing, management, leasing and sale of various types of real estate developments, including office buildings, shopping malls, manufacturing parks, retail centers, industrial facilities, and commercial developments.

### MITCHELL, Michael S
Fisher & Phillips LLP, New Orleans

504 529 3830
mmitchell@laborlawyers.com
*Recommended in Employment*
**Practice Areas:** Michael S Mitchell is a Partner in the New Orleans office of the national law firm of Fisher & Phillips LLP, practicing exclusively in labor and employment law representing management. His practice emphasizes traditional labor law matters such as union avoidance, collective bargaining, arbitration, and unfair labor practice proceedings before the NLRB. With more than 30 years of experience, he has successfully argued major cases in the Third, Fourth, Fifth, and Seventh Circuit US Courts of Appeals. Mitchell performs preventive training and has addressed conferences and trade associations across the country on labor and employment topics.

### NORTON, William N
Baker, Donelson, Bearman, Caldwell & Berkowitz, PC, New Orleans
504 566 5297
wnorton@bakerdonelson.com
*Recommended in Corporate/M&A*
**Practice Areas:** Practice concentrated in corporate and business transactions, mergers and acquisitions and finance. He has particular experience in entity formation, capital formation, acquisitions of financial institutions, service companies and energy concerns, defense of unwanted takeovers, business reorganizations and financings.
**Prof. Memberships:** Former Chair, Louisiana Bar Association and New Orleans Bar Association, Corporate and Business Law Sections. Board of Directors, Louisiana Bar Foundation. Member, American Bar Association, Negotiated Acquisitions Committee and Small Business Committee.
**Career:** Licensed in Mississippi since 1972 and in Louisiana since 1977.

### NOSEWICZ, Thomas
Jones Walker Waechter Poitevent Carrère & Denègre, LLP, New Orleans
504 582 8178
tnosewicz@joneswalker.com
*Recommended in Environment*
**Practice Areas:** Mr Nosewicz is a Senior Partner concentrating in environmental, business and product liability litigation. In 1979, he began representing a large asbestos manufacturer and has continued to represent other manufacturers, plant owners and defendants in building/asbestos litigation and varied chemical exposure claims. He has successfully defended several Agent Orange claims arising out of service-related claims from Viet Nam and Korea. He has handled the defense and trial of lengthy environmental and toxic tort claims before juries involving multiple plaintiffs and class actions claiming the full spectrum of tort damages. He has successfully tried cases in Louisiana, Arkansas, Flori-

da, and Virginia. 'A lawyer's area of practice as stated here is one to which (s)he devotes a substantial portion of his/her professional practice and should not be considered a 'specialization' unless certified by the Louisiana Board of Legal Specialization (or similar body in any other state in which such lawyer is licensed to practice)'.
**Prof. Memberships:** New Orleans Association of Defense Counsel, Board of Directors and President; International Association of Defense Counsel, member, Toxic Tort Subcommittee; American Bar Association, Member, Section on Litigation; Torts & Insurance Practice, Toxic Torts & Environmental Law Committee, Vice-Chair, newsletter editor; and Section on Natural Resources, Energy, Environmental Law; and Products Liability
**Career:** Joined firm in 1974, Partner in 1979; former Chair of firm's Casualty Practice Group.
**Personal:** Native of Detroit, Michigan; resides in New Orleans, Louisiana; Tulane University (BA 1968; JD 1973).

### PAGE, Marshall
Jones Walker Waechter Poitevent Carrère & Denègre, LLP, New Orleans
504 582 8248
mpage@joneswalker.com
*Recommended in Banking & Finance*
**Practice Areas:** Corporate finance; international; venture capital. 'A lawyer's area of practice as stated here is one to which (s)he devotes a substantial portion of his/her professional practice and should not be considered a 'specialization' unless certified by the Louisiana Board of Legal Specialization (or similar body in any other state in which such lawyer is licensed to practice)'.
**Prof. Memberships:** Louisiana State Bar Association (Chairman, International Section).
**Career:** Partner since 1996; University of Virginia (JD, 1988; BA, with distinction, 1985), Virginia Law Review; Jefferson Scholar; Echols Scholar; one of 50 fourth year students to live on the Lawn; Omicron Delta Kappa; listed in The Best Lawyers in America (Woodward/White, Inc.) in the area of Financial Institutions Law.

### PATRICK III, William
Heller, Draper, Hayden, Patrick & Horn, LLC, New Orleans 504 581 9595
*Recommended in Corporate/M&A*

### PHARIS, Michael
Taylor, Porter, Brooks & Phillips, LLP, Baton Rouge 225 387 3221
michael.pharis@taylorporter.com
*Recommended in Employment*

### PHILIPS, Harry
Taylor, Porter, Brooks & Phillips, LLP, Baton Rouge 225 387 3221
*Recommended in Litigation*

### PILIE, Glen
Adams and Reese LLP, New Orleans

504 585 0260
glen.pilie@arlaw.com
*Recommended in Environment*
**Practice Areas:** Partner: environmental and toxic tort, energy and environmental, environmental regulatory and litigation.
**Prof. Memberships:** Mid Continent Oil and Gas Association, American Society of Civil Engineers, Louisiana Society of Professional Engineers.
**Career:** Centers around environmental issues, co-chaired industry committee formed under the Mid Continent Oil and Gas Association to review/comment on General Environmental Impact Statement addressing offshore oil and gas operations in coastal waters, varied permitting/compliance issues, EPA remediations, and complex PSD air permitting.
**Personal:** JD Loyola University New Orleans School of Law, 1982; MS University of New Orleans, 1977; BSCE University of Southwestern Louisiana, 1973.

## PREIS JR, E Fredrick
McGlinchey Stafford, New Orleans
504 596 2716
epreis@mcglinchey.com
*Recommended in Employment*
**Practice Areas:** Senior member of national Labor/Employment Practice; as trial lawyer and advisor serves as lead counsel for Fortune 500 companies, trade associations and businesses throughout the United States.
**Prof. Memberships:** Charter member National Academy of Hospitality Industry Attorneys; treasurer of Louisiana Association of Business and Industry and Chairman of New Orleans Chamber of Commerce; board of editors of The Corporate Counselor national newsletter.
**Career:** Co-argued 2002 case before Louisiana Supreme Court urging New Orleans attempt to adopt minimum wage be nullified - court overwhelmingly agreed.
**Personal:** Prior to military service, received degrees from Louisiana State University Business Administration School and Law School.

## PYBURN JR, Keith M
Fisher & Phillips LLP, New Orleans
504 522 3303
kpyburn@laborlawyers.com
*Recommended in Employment*
**Practice Areas:** Keith Pyburn is the Managing Partner in the New Orleans office of the national law firm of Fisher & Phillips LLP, practicing exclusively in labor and employment law representing management. He has represented management in labor relations and employment law since 1975. A former Chairman of the Labor and Employment Section of the Louisiana State Bar Association and a fellow of the College of Labor and Employment Lawyers, he is a contributing editor to Employment Discrimination Law, published by the American Bar Association's Section of Labor and Employment Law. Pyburn received a JD from Louisiana's Tulane Law School.

## RESTER, Daniel K
Adams and Reese LLP, Baton Rouge
225 336 5200
daniel.rester@arlaw.com
*Recommended in Gaming & Licensing*
**Practice Areas:** Partner: gaming, commercial litigation, general corporate, energy and environmental, real estate, forestry law.
**Prof. Memberships:** International Association of Gaming Attorneys, Louisiana Land Title Association, Rotary Club.
**Career:** Practice has been predominately in business, commercial, real estate transactional and construction litigation, including emphasis on gaming and entertainment law and financial transactions. His current representation of clients includes ongoing gaming licensing and financial transactions, commercial lease negotiations, corporate and partnership matters, various commercial loan transactions, construction and commercial litigation, and pipeline right-of-way negotiations and condemnations.
**Personal:** JD Tulane University Law School, 1971; BS Louisiana State University, 1969.

## REYMOND JR, Leon
Liskow & Lewis PLC, New Orleans
504 581 7979
*Recommended in Real Estate*

## ROBERSON, JR, Thomas Y
Jones Walker Waechter Poitevent Carrère & Denègre, LLP, New Orleans
504 582 8382
troberson@joneswalker.com
*Recommended in Banking & Finance*
**Practice Areas:** Mr Roberson's primary focus has been in the areas of commercial and corporate finance. He represents many of the firm's publicly-held clients in connection with structuring, negotiating and documenting syndicated credit facilities, public debt offerings and project financings. Mr Roberson has worked extensively with the treasury group of one of the firm's largest clients in connection with (among other things) a $1 billion secured working capital facility and the financing of various infrastructure projects in support of an Indonesian mining operation. He has also worked on several domestic and cross-border leveraged acquisitions. Mr Roberson also has significant experience with structured financing transactions representing various firm clients in sale/leasebacks, inventory and accounts receivable financings/securitizations and other asset monetizations. He has also worked on, and is familiar with, standard ISDA and IFEMA agreements (and related schedules) for hedging interest rate and foreign exchange risk. 'A lawyer's area of practice as stated here is one to which (s)he devotes a substantial portion of his/her

professional practice and should not be considered a 'specialization' unless certified by the Louisiana Board of Legal Specialization (or similar body in any other state in which such lawyer is licensed to practice)'.
**Prof. Memberships:** Louisiana State Bar Association; American Bar Association.
**Career:** Admitted to bar, 1988, Louisiana; joined Jones Walker in 1988, Partner since 1996.
**Personal:** Born Lexington, Kentucky, January 25, 1958; University of Delaware (BS, 1980); Tulane University (JD, cum laude, 1988).

## ROSENBERG, Harry
Phelps Dunbar LLP, New Orleans
504 584 9219
rosenbeh@phelps.com
*Recommended in Litigation*
**Practice Areas:** Mr Rosenberg is a Partner in the New Orleans Commercial Litigation Practice. He concentrates his practice in the areas of business torts, trial practice, civil rights, and criminal law. Prior to joining Phelps Dunbar in 1974, he served as a judicial clerk to The Honorable Jack M Gordon, Judge, US District Court, Eastern District of Louisiana. Mr Rosenberg also served as the United States Attorney for the Eastern District of Louisiana from 1990 through 1993.
**Personal:** Tulane University, JD, 1972; Board of Editors and editor, Tulane Law Review. Case Western Reserve University, BA, 1969.

## ROSENBLUM, Carl D
Jones Walker Waechter Poitevent Carrère & Denègre, LLP, New Orleans
504 582 8296
crosenblum@joneswalker.com
*Recommended in Energy*
**Practice Areas:** Senior Litigation Partner and Chair of firm's Energy Practice Group. He devotes his time primarily to the representation of entities and individuals involved in significant oil and gas disputes. He represents independent producers, major producers, pipeline companies, oilfield service companies, seismic exploration companies, oil and gas management companies, financial institutions and significant landowners. He has handled numerous disputes concerning the rights and obligations of parties to joint operating agreements, oil and gas leases, royalty matters, exploration agreements, gas purchase contracts, drilling contracts, pipeline right-of-way agreements, farmout agreements, gas balancing agreements, seismic permitting and exploration agreements, and the enforcement of oil and gas liens, as well as the recognition and protection of those rights when an operator files for protection under the US Bankruptcy Code. 'A lawyer's area of practice as stated here is one to which (s)he devotes a substantial portion of his/her professional practice

and should not be considered a 'specialization' unless certified by the Louisiana Board of Legal Specialization (or similar body in any other state in which such lawyer is licensed to practice)'.
**Prof. Memberships:** Admitted to the State Bars of Louisiana and Texas; American Bar Association; Louisiana State Bar Association; Texas State Bar Association; Federal Energy Bar Association.
**Career:** Joined Jones Walker, 1983; Partner since 1990.
**Personal:** Born 1955; married, two teenage daughters; resident of New Orleans since 1983.

## ROUSSEAU, Dionne M
Jones Walker Waechter Poitevent Carrère & Denègre, LLP, New Orleans
504 582 8338
drousseau@joneswalker.com
*Recommended in Corporate/M&A*
**Practice Areas:** Corporate, securities, corporate finance, mergers and acquisitions, venture capital and corporate governance matters for public and private companies. 'A lawyer's area of practice as stated here is one to which (s)he devotes a substantial portion of his/her professional practice and should not be considered a 'specialization' unless certified by the Louisiana Board of Legal Specialization (or similar body in any other state in which such lawyer is licensed to practice)'.
**Career:** She joined Jones Walker in 1990 and became a Partner in 1998; Investment banker with Paine Webber Capital Markets, New York, 1985-87.
**Publications:** 'Overview of Recent SEC and Stock Market Rules', 2004 Burkenroad SEC Conference; 'Corporate Governance Reform', 2003 New Orleans Does Business Right Conference; 'Corporate Goverance in the Headlines', 2003 UNO Energy Accounting and Technology Conference.
**Personal:** University of Chicago (JD 1990, Order of the Coif, Law Review); Georgetown University (BA 1985, magna cum laude, Phi Beta Kappa).

## ROUSSEL, James H
Baker, Donelson, Bearman, Caldwell & Berkowitz, PC, New Orleans
504 566 5278
jroussel@bakerdonelson.com
*Recommended in Energy*
**Practice Areas:** Of Counsel in the New Orleans office. He practices in the areas of marine insurance coverage disputes, cargo damage claims, maritime allisions and collisions, maritime commercial transactions, ship construction, salvage drilling and sales contracts, and charter agreements, and litigating matters arising from these transactions. He represents general liability, marine, and P&I underwriters in regard to coverage issues involving a broad range of marine, energy, general liability, excess and umbrella forms of coverage, including representa-

tion of underwriters interest in litigation arising out of coverage disputes.
**Personal:** Tulane University, JD, 1964; Phi Delta Phi; Dartmouth College, AB in History, 1961.

## ROUSSEL, Randy P
Phelps Dunbar LLP, Baton Rouge
225 376 0234
rousselr@phelps.com
*Recommended in Real Estate*
**Practice Areas:** Mr Roussel is a Partner in the Business Group in the Baton Rouge office. His general business practice is concentrated in the areas of real estate, banking, and commercial transactions. He has represented Wampold Companies, Waffle House, AmSouth Bank, Whitney National Bank, Gross Builders, Inc, and a variety of multifamily and commercial developers.
**Personal:** Louisiana State University, JD, 1984; Louisiana Law Review; Order of Coif; Beta Alpha Psi; Louisiana Bar Association Civil Law Award for the highest grade point average in Louisiana Civil Law courses. Louisiana State University, BS, 1977. Board member for the Louisiana Land Title Association, Baton Rouge Growth Coalition and Adjunct Professor at Louisiana State University Law School and Southern University Law School.

## RUBIN, Michael H
McGlinchey Stafford, Baton Rouge
225 382 3623
mrubin@mcglinchey.com
*Recommended in Banking & Finance*
**Practice Areas:** Banking and finance; appellate law; commercial litigation.
**Prof. Memberships:** American College of Real Estate Attorneys (President-Elect, 2006); past President of: US Fifth Circuit Bar Association, Louisiana State Bar Association, and Southern Conference of Bar Presidents. Member: American Academy of Appellate Lawyers; American Law Institute; Anglo-American Real Property Institute; American College of Commercial Finance Lawyers; and American College of Mortgage Attorneys.
**Publications:** Author, co-author, and contributing writer to 11 books and more than 30 law review articles and periodicals. An award-winning writer, Mr Rubin's publications on finance have been cited as authoritative by state and federal courts. Mr Rubin has presented over 200 papers in the US and Canada on finance, real estate, appellate litigation, and legal ethics. In addition to the full-time practice of law, Mr Rubin continues his more than two decades work as an adjunct professor teaching courses in finance and real estate and in legal ethics at LSU Law School and Tulane Law School.
**Personal:** Amherst College (BA 1972); LSU Law School (JD 1975).

## SARVER, Richard E
Barrasso Usdin Kupperman Freeman & Sarver LLC, New Orleans
504 589 9700
rsarver@barrassousdin.com
*Recommended in Litigation*
**Practice Areas:** Mr Sarver specializes in defending toxic tort, environmental and product liability cases. He has served as lead trial counsel in numerous class actions and mass joinder cases involving products liability and environmental issues. Mr Sarver also teaches trial skills and serves as an adjunct faculty member of Tulane University Law School.
**Career:** Mr Sarver is a founding member of Barrasso Usdin Kupperman Freeman & Sarver, L.L.C. and a former trial attorney for the US Department of Justice. He has served as lead trial counsel in jury trials in eleven different states.
**Personal:** JD magna cum laude, University of Michigan School of Law, 1982, Order of the Coif, Michigan Law Review. LLM, University of Virginia Law School, 1990.

## SCHMIDT, Justin B
Adams and Reese LLP, New Orleans
504 585 0361
justin.schmidt@arlaw.com
*Recommended in Real Estate*
**Practice Areas:** Real estate, acquisition, development /finance, mortgage lending, zoning/permitting, land use matters, estate planning.
**Prof. Memberships:** New Orleans, Louisiana and American Bar Associations; International Council of Shopping Centers; Board of Directors YMCA; Putnam Cultural Endowment Trustee/Officer; Building Committee World Trade Center, NOLA; Trustee, Louis S McGehee School, NOLA.
**Career:** Focuses on real estate, emphasis on land use/zoning matters, representing companies/individuals in commercial transactions, business development and landlord/tenant negotiations and lenders and developers with the acquisition, divestiture, development, leasing and financing of developments.
**Personal:** JD Louisiana State University Paul M Hebert Law Center 1998; BBA University of Mississippi, 1992.

## SCHNEIDER, Michael R
Stone Pigman Walther Wittmann LLC, New Orleans 504 593 0835
mschneider@stonepigman.com
*Recommended in Real Estate*
**Practice Areas:** Real estate law; finance law; environmental law; construction law. Co-chairs the firm's Real Estate Practice Group and has extensive experience in the area of sophisticated commercial real estate transactions with an emphasis on the representation of developers and owners and local counsel for national lenders.
**Prof. Memberships:** Admitted to practice in Louisiana, 1983. Member of the

American, Louisiana, and New Orleans Bar Associations, and the International Council of Shopping Centers.
**Career:** Joined Stone Pigman, 1984; became member, 1990. Law clerk to Honorable Walter Marcus, Louisiana Supreme Court, 1983-84.
**Personal:** JD (magna cum laude), Tulane University, 1983. Member of Order of the Coif and Tulane Law Review. BA, Stanford University, 1980.

## SHER, Leopold
Sher Garner Cahill Richter Klein & Hilbert LLC, New Orleans
504 299 2101
lsher@shergarner.com
*Recommended in Real Estate*
**Practice Areas:** Mr Sher is a business lawyer whose practice is concentrated in commercial real estate and business and finance law. He also practices in the areas of: commercial litigation, creditors' rights, workouts and foreclosures, commercial bankruptcy, arbitration and mediation, secured finance and asset based lending. Along with his practice, Mr Sher is actively involved with many professional and trade organizations, including the American College of Real Estate Lawyers, where he served as Treasurer and a member of the Executive Board; the Anglo American Real Property Institute (an organization limited in its membership to the top 50 real estate practitioners in the United States and the top 50 real estate practitioners in the United Kingdom) where he served as a member of the Governing Board; the Lenders' Counsel Group of the American Land Title Association (ALTA), which is a group limited to 75 lending lawyers who meet in conjunction with the ALTA, which is the title insurance industry trade association; the Real Property Section of the American Bar Association, where Mr Sher has served in many positions, including the Section's governing Counsel; the American College of Commercial Finance Lawyers, which selects its members (Fellows) from those attorneys in the United States who serve the asset based lending industry; the American College of Mortgage Attorneys; the Business Section of the American Bar Association, particularly the Commercial Financial Services Committee of the Section; and the International Council of Shopping Centers, a trade association that represents the interests of those involved in the shopping center industry, including lenders, tenants, owners and developers. Mr Sher is an arbitrator for the American Arbitration Association, with a special designation for arbitrating Commercial Disputes. Mr Sher also serves on the Tulane Law School Dean's Advisory Board, whose purpose is to serve as an advisory and consultative group to the Dean of the Law School, bringing the perspective of alumni and other friends

of the Law School to bear on matters of Law School policy, activities, programs and goals, and acts as an advocate to assist the Dean in advancing the interest of the school. Over the years, Mr Sher has been actively involved in virtually every type of major business, real estate and finance transaction representing various and diverse interests as follows: major lenders, including life insurance companies, banks, finance companies and other asset based lenders, savings and loans and other lenders such as Real Estate Investment Trusts (REITS) and Real Estate Mortgage Investment Conduit (REMICS) [conduit lending], for all categories of loans and lending arrangements including private and public financing (industrial development bond financing, public/private partnerships and urban development action grants); commercial developers, including developers of shopping centers, hotels, office buildings, apartment complexes, free standing retail establishments, industrial properties, condominiums, golf courses, planned unit developments, historic rehabilitations, mixed-use projects, conversions, parking lots and garages, warehouses, and other traditional and nontraditional (facade donations, air rights transactions, etc) real estate projects; businesses, including representation related to the buying and selling of businesses, structuring transactions, joint ventures and other combinations, general business advice and major contracts; landlords and tenants, which representation includes drafting of form leases and negotiation of lease agreements, construction, operation and reciprocal easement (servitude) agreements and other agreements that affect real property; owners and purchasers, which representation includes drafting and negotiation of purchase and sale agreements, construction contracts and development agreements. Mr Sher has also represented major national and international clients in the food service, hospital, title insurance and oil and gas industries. On behalf of clients of the firm, Mr Sher regularly practices before and works closely with political entities and public administrative boards and agencies, at the local, parish (county) and state levels. Mr Sher has spoken extensively, both locally and nationally, on many diverse subjects including environmental law, limited liability companies, workouts, leases, title insurance, lender liability, civil forfeiture, distressed real estate, brokerage agreements, and other areas related to his practice.
**Prof. Memberships:** American College of Real Estate Lawyers, Board of Governors, Treasurer Member; American College of Mortgage Attorneys Member-American Arbitration Association, Panel of Arbitrators Member; Anglo American Real Property Institute, US Group Trea-

surer Lender's Counsel Group of the American Land Title Association (ALTA) Member; American Bar Association, Real Property Section, Governing Counsel Member; American College of Commercial Finance Lawyers MemberAmerican Bar Association, Business Section, Commercial Financial Services Committee Member; International Council of Shopping Centers Member; American Bar Foundation Member; Academy of Hospitality Industry Attorneys Member Association of Commercial Finance Attorneys, Inc. Member; American Bankruptcy Institute Member; Tulane Dean's Advisory Board Member.

### SNYDER, Charles
Milling Benson Woodward LLP, New Orleans 504 569 7000
*Recommended in Corporate/M&A*

### SPENCER, Bob
The Kullman Firm PLC, New Orleans 504 596 4105
*Recommended in Employment*

### STEEG, Robert
The Steeg Law Firm, LLC, New Orleans 504 582 1199
*Recommended in Real Estate*

### STUCKEY, James A
Phelps Dunbar LLP, New Orleans 504 584 9239
stuckeyj@phelps.com
*Recommended in Banking & Finance*
**Practice Areas:** Mr Stuckey is a Partner in the Business Group in the New Orleans Office. He practices in the areas of commercial finance, real estate, banking, and leasing. His lending practice includes representing lenders in oil and gas loans, real estate and construction financings, leveraged leases, and secured working capital loans. He advises clients in negotiations of a wide variety of contracts, including major lease development agreements. Prior to joining Phelps Dunbar in 1984, Mr Stuckey served as a judicial clerk to the Honorable Walter Marcus, Louisiana State Supreme Court Justice.
**Personal:** Tulane University, JD, magna cum laude, 1983; editor, Tulane Law Review; Order of the Coif. Davidson College, AB, magna cum laude, 1980; judicial clerk to the Honorable Walter Marcus, Louisiana State Supreme Court Justice, 1983-84.

### SWANSON, James R
Correro Fishman Haygood Phelps Walmsley & Casteix LLP, New Orleans 504 586 5267
jswanson@cfhlaw.com
*Recommended in Litigation*
**Practice Areas:** Mr Swanson is the Head of the firm's Litigation Section. He represents clients in a broad range of business litigation matters. He regularly represents The Times-Picayune Publishing Corporation, SMG and others. Mr Swanson has recently represented The

Times-Picayune and The Associated Press in access litigation arising out of the trial of former Governor Edwin Edwards; SMG, in an arbitration brought by the New Orleans Saints alleging breaches of the Saint's lease of the Superdome; Manpower, defending hundreds of millions of dollars of claims, including class action claims, arising out of the Kaiser Plant explosion; the State of Louisiana, prosecuting corporate tax claims against Tennessee Gas, Texaco and International Paper and obtaining a $26 million jury verdict against Tennessee Gas; IBM, working with New York counsel to defend it in multidistrict patent litigation; and HPI, in the successful defense of an offshore service company in a lengthy jury trial arising out of an offshore rig explosion which caused over $20 million in property damage.
**Career:** Mr Swanson serves as a Director of the Louisiana Freedom of Information Coalition.
**Personal:** Mr Swanson received his JD, magna cum laude, from Tulane Law School, where he was a Member of the Order of the Coif and an Associate Editor of the 'Tulane Law Review'. Mr Swanson was also winner of the Tulane Moot Court Appellate Competitions in 1986 and 1987.

### TALLEY, Susan G
Stone Pigman Walther Wittmann LLC, New Orleans 504 593 0828
stalley@stonepigman.com
*Recommended in Real Estate*
**Practice Areas:** Real estate; finance; banking.
**Prof. Memberships:** Admitted to practice in Louisiana, 1981. Member of the Board of Governors of the American College of Real Estate Lawyers. Supervisory Council Member of the Real Property, Probate and Trust Law section of the American Bar Association; Vice-Chair of its Publications Committee; and a member of its CLE Committee, Committee on Workouts, Foreclosures and Bankruptcies and Committee on Mortgage Loan Structure and Origination. Member and US Secretary of the Anglo American Real Property Institute. Founding member of New Orleans CREW and a member of its Board of Directors. Co-Chair of the New Orleans Bar Association Real Property Committee. Member of the American College of Mortgage Attorneys, the Council of the Louisiana State Law Institute, the Louisiana Bankers Association Bank Counsel Section and the International Council of Shopping Centers.
**Career:** Joined Stone Pigman, 1981; became member, 1987. Member of the firm's Management Committee.
**Personal:** JD (summa cum laude), Tulane University, 1981. Phi Kappa Phi, Order of the Coif, and Tulane Law Review Board of Editors, 1979-81, and Business Manager, 1980-81. BS (summa cum

laude), Louisiana State University, 1978.

### TESSIER, Frank
Carver Darden Koretzky Tessier Finn Blossman & Areaux LLC, New Orleans 504 585 3800
*Recommended in Banking & Finance*

### USDIN, Steven W
Barrasso Usdin Kupperman Freeman & Sarver LLC, New Orleans 504 589 9721
susdin@barrassousdin.com
*Recommended in Litigation*
**Practice Areas:** Mr Usdin has over 20 years of experience in all types of commercial litigation matters, including intellectual property, unfair trade practices, securities, antitrust, unfair competition, insurance coverage, and oil and gas. He has extensive experience in representing clients in class actions and complex litigation and has been named one of the Best Lawyers in America since 2001.
**Career:** Mr Usdin is a Founding Member of Barrasso Usdin Kupperman Freeman & Sarver, L.L.C.
**Personal:** JD, University of Virginia School of Law, 1980; clerk, Honorable Adrian G Duplantier, United States District Court, Eastern District of Louisiana.

### VANCE, R Patrick
Jones Walker Waechter Poitevent Carrère & Denègre, LLP, New Orleans 504 582 8194
pvance@joneswalker.com
*Recommended in Corporate/M&A, Litigation*
**Practice Areas:** Commercial litigation, bankruptcy, and creditors-debtors rights. As a trial lawyer he has handled over three hundred plus commercial disputes in a wide variety of practice areas: antitrust, RICO, copyright infringement, Lanham Act, securities litigation, defense of class actions, foreclosures, fraud, lender liability, ERISA, dealer-distributor disputes, successions, legal malpractice, expropriation, partnership and utility regulation. He has over 60 reported decisions. He regularly represents debtors, secured and unsecured creditors in all types of business bankruptcy cases involving banks, telecommunications, utilities, maritime, oil and gas, the music industry, casinos and insurance companies. 'A lawyer's area of practice as stated here is one to which (s)he devotes a substantial portion of his/her professional practice and should not be considered a 'specialization' unless certified by the Louisiana Board of Legal Specialization (or similar body in any other state in which such lawyer is licensed to practice)'.
**Prof. Memberships:** National Bankruptcy Conference; Fellow, American Law Institute and American College of Bankruptcy; past Chairman of the following: Louisiana Bankers Association, Bank Counsel Committee; Bankruptcy Litigation Subcommittee, ABA; CLE Planning

Committee, LSBA.
**Career:** Louisiana State University (BA, 1970; JD 1975); Phi Beta Kappa Faculty Group Award; Louisiana Law Review, 1973-75; admitted to Bar, 1975, Louisiana; Section Head, Commercial Litigation (1986-91; 2003-); Chair, Executive Committee (1994-95; 1999-2000; 2004)
**Publications:** Mr Vance has written 50-plus articles or seminar outlines on topics such as commercial litigation, lender liability and bankruptcy.
**Personal:** Born Birmingham, Alabama, 1948.

### WAGUESPACK, David
Lemle & Kelleher, LLP, New Orleans 504 586 1241
*Recommended in Corporate/M&A*

### WALLACE, Brian D
Phelps Dunbar LLP, New Orleans 504 584 9204
wallaceb@phelps.com
*Recommended in Gaming & Licensing*
**Practice Areas:** Mr Wallace is a Partner in the Admiralty Group in the New Orleans office, concentrating on ship financing and admiralty litigation. His practice in the area of ship financing involves commercial transactions and representing vessel owners, lenders, and shipyards in ship construction, ship sales and financing, lien enforcement, and charters. His admiralty litigation practice includes representing vessel owners and underwriters in matters involving personal injury, collision, cargo, commercial disputes, construction, and mortgage foreclosure. Mr Wallace also practices in the area of gaming law, representing casino owners, operators, and lenders in complex financial transactions, licensing, and litigation.
**Personal:** Tulane University, New Orleans, Louisiana, LLM in Admiralty, with distinction, 1985; Dalhousie University, Halifax, Nova Scotia, LLB, 1984; Saint Mary's University, Halifax, Nova Scotia, BS magna cum laude, 1980.

### WALMSLEY, Robert
Correro Fishman Haygood Phelps Walmsley & Casteix LLP, New Orleans 504 586 5252
*Recommended in Corporate/M&A*

### WERNER, John D
Correro Fishman Haygood Phelps Walmsley & Casteix LLP, New Orleans 504 586 5252
jwerner@cfhlaw.com
*Recommended in Corporate/M&A*
**Practice Areas:** Corporate; securities; M&A; commercial transactions.
**Prof. Memberships:** Louisiana and American Bar Associations, Louisiana Bankers Association, Association for Corporate Growth.
**Career:** Partner since 2001.
**Personal:** Born Dallas, TX, November 4, 1965; admitted to Bar - 1994; Education:

Duke University (BA 1988), Tulane University (JD 1994); law clerk to Hon Donald E Walter, US District Court, WD LA.

## WEST, Paul
McGlinchey Stafford, Baton Rouge
225 382 3636
pwest@mcglinchey.com
*Recommended in Gaming & Licensing*
**Practice Areas:** Gaming, business litigation, class action defense, and corporate.
**Prof. Memberships:** American Bar Association, Baton Rouge Bar Association, International Association of Gaming Attorneys, Louisiana Bar Foundation, Louisiana State Bar Association.
**Career:** Experienced commercial litigator and one of the most recognized casino gaming attorneys in the industry; matters include riverboat and land-based casinos; racinos and video poker; represents casino owners, operators and financiers; handles negotiations between suppliers, municipalities and gaming companies; major commercial trials (bench and bar) have involved finance companies, Fortune 500 companies, landowners, developers and growing businesses; AV rated; annually listed in 'Best Lawyers in America' by Woodward White.

## WHITTAKER, Scott T
Stone Pigman Walther Wittmann LLC,
New Orleans 504 593 0836
swhittaker@stonepigman.com
*Recommended in Corporate/M&A*
**Practice Areas:** Corporate; mergers and acquisitions; securities laws; real estate. Chair of the firm's Business Section.
**Prof. Memberships:** Admitted to practice in Louisiana, 1984. Member of the Louisiana State Bar Association, Section on Corporate and Business Law, and served as Chairman of the governing council of the Section in 1991-92. Chairman of the Louisiana Supreme Court Committee on Bar Admissions. From 1991 through 2004, served as Director of Testing and Examiner for the subjects of Business Entities and Negotiable Instruments on the Louisiana Supreme Court Committee on Bar Admissions. An active member of the Negotiated Acquisitions Committee of the American Bar Association. Chairman of the Subcommittee on M&A Jurisprudence, and Member of the Editorial Working Group of the Task Force on the Model Stock Purchase Agreement. Frequent lecturer and author in the area of business mergers and acquisitions.
**Career:** Joined Stone Pigman in 1984; became member in 1990.
**Personal:** JD (magna cum laude), Tulane University. Order of the Coif and Tulane Law Review Board of Editors. BA (cum laude), Tulane University, 1982.

## WILLENZIK, David S
McGlinchey Stafford, New Orleans
504 596 2708
dwillenzik@mcglinchey.com
*Recommended in Banking & Finance*
**Practice Areas:** Heads Business Law Practice and focuses on banking, commercial finance, asset based lending, equipment leasing, consumer finance, and UCC litigation, defense of lender liability, consumer credit and class action claims. Clients include banks, finance companies, mortgage bankers, manufacturers, equipment lessors, insurers, venture capital companies and project finance lenders. Negotiates commercial loans, real estate, aircraft, and vessels, project finance, equipment leases, acquisition financings and letters of credit. Drafter of multistate sales, commercial and consumer finance and equipment lease documents. Initiator and primary drafter of numerous laws that apply to banking, commercial finance and consumer credit transactions. Lead effort to enact UCC Article 9 in Louisiana.
**Prof. Memberships:** ABA Business Law Section, Commercial Financial Services, Consumer Financial Services, Banking Law, and UCC Committees; American College of Commercial Finance Lawyers (co-founder and past President); American College of Consumer Financial Services Attorneys; American College of Mortgage Attorneys; American Law Institute; Consumer Banker's Association Lawyers Committee (past Chair); Association of Commercial Finance Attorneys (past Director); Louisiana State Law Institute UCC Committee; Louisiana Bankers Association Bank Counsel Section (past Chair); International Lawyers Network (Director).
**Publications:** West, 'Louisiana Secured Transactions'.
**Personal:** LSU Law School Board of Trustees.

## WILLIS, Sterling Scott
Correro Fishman Haygood Phelps Walmsley & Casteix LLP, New Orleans
504 586 5264
swillis@cfhlaw.com
*Recommended in Banking & Finance*
**Practice Areas:** Mr Willis heads the Real Estate and Commercial Finance Groups. He practices primarily in the areas of commercial transactions, secured lending, oil and gas and commercial real estate. Mr Willis has counseled business clients in a variety of matters, including a $3 billion bank note securitization; a $150 million secured oil and gas revolving credit facility; numerous helicopter financings; the acquisition, merger and sale of numerous private and public companies; a $400 million high yield bond offering; numerous bank mergers and branch transactions; and the acquisition of the Canal Place mixed-use development in New Orleans.

**Career:** Mr Willis is a Member of the New Orleans, Louisiana State, and American Bar Associations. He is the past Chairman of the ABA Real Property, Probate and Trust Law Section Committee on Legal Opinions. Mr Willis was a Member of the drafting group for the ABA/ACREL Real Estate Opinion Letter Guidelines 38 REAL. PROP. PROB. & TR. J. 241 (2003). Mr Willis is a Member of the Louisiana Bankers Association Bank Counsel Committee and a Member of the Board of Directors of the New Orleans Bureau of Governmental Research.
**Publications:** Mr Willis is the author of 'Article 9 Remedies' in 'West's Louisiana Statutes Annotated Code of Civil Procedure'.
**Personal:** Mr Willis graduated from Louisiana State University in 1980 and received his JD Degree from LSU in 1983, where he was a Member the Order of the Coif, and also served as an associate eeditor of the 'Louisiana Law Review'.

## WITTMANN, Phillip A
Stone Pigman Walther Wittmann LLC,
New Orleans 504 593 0804
pwittmann@stonepigman.com
*Recommended in Litigation*
**Practice Areas:** Commercial litigation; class actions and complex litigation; products liability; antitrust; toxic tort litigation.
**Prof. Memberships:** Admitted to practice in Louisiana, 1961. Served as President of the New Orleans Bar Association in 2004. Served as a Member of the Civil Rules Advisory Committee of the Judicial Conference of the United States and as a Member of the House of Delegates of the American Bar Association. Chaired the Louisiana State Board of Legal Specialization and is a Member of the House of Delegates, the Continuing Legal Education Committee and the Antitrust Section of the Louisiana State Bar Association. Fellow of the American College of Trial Lawyers, the American Academy of Appellate Lawyers and the International Society of Barristers. He is the 2005 recipient of the American Inns of Court Professionalism Award and the 2000 recipient of the G Duffield Smith Outstanding Publication Award from the Defense Research Institute.
**Career:** Joined Stone Pigman, 1961; became member, 1963. Chair of the firm's Management Committee.
**Personal:** LLB, Tulane University School of Law, 1961. Phi Beta Kappa, Order of the Coif, Omicron Delta Kappa and Tulane Law Review Board of Editors. BA, Tulane University, 1956.

## WOGAN, John
Liskow & Lewis PLC, New Orleans
504 581 7979
*Recommended in Banking & Finance, Corporate/M&A*

## WOLF, Alan C
Phelps Dunbar LLP, New Orleans
504 584 9316
wolfa@phelps.com
*Recommended in Energy*
**Practice Areas:** Mr Wolf is a Partner in the Business Group in the New Orleans office. He practices in the areas of administrative law, electric utilities, gas utilities, and energy law, and directs the firm's Energy and Utilities Practice. Prior to joining Phelps Dunbar, Mr Wolf was Senior Trial Attorney at the Office of General Counsel - Electric Rates Section, Federal Energy Regulatory Commission, and Vice President and General Counsel, Mid Louisiana Gas Company, New Orleans, Louisiana. He has over 30 years experience in gas and electric utility matters and is a former chair of the Electric Power Committee of the American Bar Association's Section on Natural Resources, Energy and Environmental Law and a former Chairman of the Natural Gas Rates Committee of the Federal Energy Bar Association. Mr Wolf is also a Member of the Legal Committee of the Edison Electric Institute.
**Personal:** University of Alabama, JD, 1971; National Moot Court Team. Birmingham-Southern College, AB, 1968.

## WOLFE, Richard
Jones Walker Waechter Poitevent Carrère & Denègre, LLP, New Orleans
504 582 8182
rwolfe@joneswalker.com
*Recommended in Corporate/M&A*
**Practice Areas:** Mr Wolfe's concentration is in corporate and securities law, particularly mergers and acquisitions He has over 35 years experience in corporate matters, including representing issuers and underwriters in initial and subsequent public equity offerings and advising public and private companies in matters involving tender offers, proxy contests, venture capital transactions, spin-offs, private offerings of securities, special litigation committees in derivative stockholder suits, foreign joint ventures, and related matters. 'A lawyer's area of practice as stated here is one to which (s)he devotes a substantial portion of his/her professional practice and should not be considered a 'specialization' unless certified by the Louisiana Board of Legal Specialization (or similar body in any other state in which such lawyer is licensed to practice)'.
**Career:** Joined Monroe & Lemann, New Orleans, in 1963, Partner in 1968, headed Corporate Department 1974-96; joined Jones, Walker, Waechter, Poitevent, Carrère & Denegre, LLP as Partner, 1997; Special Counsel as of January 2006.
**Personal:** Princeton University (AB, magna cum laude, 1959); Harvard University (JD 1962); Tulane University (M Civ L 1965); Phi Beta Kappa.

# ADAMS AND REESE LLP

## THE FIRM

**Managing Partner:** Charles P Adams, Jr
**Number of partners in US offices:** 168
**Number of other lawyers in US offices:** 132

**FIRM OVERVIEW:** Adams and Reese is a fast-growing multi-disciplinary firm with over 300 attorneys in nine offices throughout the South Central United States and the District of Columbia. By offering legal services on a regional basis, this AmLaw 200 firm provides its clients with localized control over their legal matters, and access for clients to multiple markets where they have interests. The firm prides itself on its dedication and reputation for providing superior client service. The firm's primary commitment is to provide clients with the highest quality legal service in the most prompt, cost-effective and efficient manner possible. Adams and Reese strives to foster a working environment of inclusion, understanding, respect and opportunity for all. Enriched by a diversity of backgrounds and experiences within the firm, Adams and Reese attorneys and staff are committed to helping improve the communities where they live and work. The firm dedicates time, talent and financial resources to many community outreach projects, as well as to civic and professional organization. In recognition of these efforts, the firm was the first law firm recipient of the Excellence in Corporate Volunteerism Award presented by the Points of Light Foundation and was also honored as Outstanding Corporate Philanthropist by the Greater New Orleans Chapter of the Association of Fundraising Professionals.

## MAIN AREAS OF PRACTICE:

**Litigation:** Both of the firm's founding partners were widely respected litigators involved in some of the most momentous court decisions of their time. As the firm grew, Adams and Reese earned a national reputation for outstanding trial work. Adams and Reese represents its clients before all courts, governmental regulatory bodies, tribunals, as well as alternate dispute resolution, including arbitration and mediation. The firm is experienced in an ever-increasing variety of litigation matters ranging from the simplest forms of court action, to multi-district litigation, complex/class action claims, and mass tort litigation. Adams and Reese litigators represent clients in the following areas: commercial disputes; banking and financial matters; professional liability/D&O; antitrust and unfair competition; products liability; asbestos; pharmaceuticals; insurance; pesticides; energy and environmental; maritime; healthcare; transportation; real estate and construction; technology and telecommunications; state and local taxation; class action; appellate; arbitration and alternate dispute resolution.

**Corporate/Transactions:** Adams and Reese provides advice to privately and publicly held business organizations including corporations, general partnerships, limited partnerships, limited liability companies, limited liability partnerships and proprietorships. The firm counsels clients in all phases of business development and continuation, such as business organization, choice of entity, choice of jurisdiction, organizational documentation, state and federal filings, general securities, and tax issues bearing upon these types of entities. The firm also advises clients on day-to-day operations, from meetings of equity holders and management, to loans and credit facilities, to compensation and benefits. Adams and Reese clients also rely on the firm's advice on issues pertaining to directors' liability, privilege, and consulting agreements, as well as all types of commercial and financial transactions and negotiations, and the drafting and execution of all necessary documentation. The firm's corporate practice areas include: banking and finance; tax; general corporate; securities; mergers and acquisitions; bankruptcy and commercial restructuring; public finance; economic development; forestry; and real estate.

**Special Business Services:** Adams and Reese attorneys partner with their clients to develop and execute creative and insightful strategies which will assist in accomplishing the goals of the organization. The firm's Governmental Relations Team provides detailed representation in the public sector by integrating clients' federal, state and local business goals and participating in the legislative and executive branch processes. The team crafts and implements clear strategies and employs a

## OFFICE

**LOUISIANA**
One Shell Square, 701 Poydras St, Suite 4500, **New Orleans**, LA 70139
**Tel:** 504 581 3234   **Fax:** 504 566 0210
**Website:** www.adamsandreese.com
**Email:** info@arlaw.com

**ALABAMA**
Concord Center 2100 Third Ave North, Suite 1100, **Birmingham**, AL 35203
**Tel:** 205 250 5000   **Fax:** 205 2505034

One St Louis Street, Suite 4500 (36602), PO Box 1348, **Mobile**, AL 36633
**Tel:** 251 433 3234   **Fax:** 251 4387733

**DISTRICT OF COLUMBIA**
Market Square North, 401 9th Street, NW, Suite 610 South,
**Washington**, DC 20004
**Tel:** 202 737 3234   **Fax:** 202 737 0264

**LOUISIANA**
450 Laurel Street, Suite 1900, **Baton Rouge**, LA 70801
**Tel:** 225 336 5200   **Fax:** 225 336 5220

**MISSISSIPPI**
111 East Capitol Street, Suite 350 (39201), PO Box 24297,
**Jackson**, MS 39225
**Tel:** 601 353 3234   **Fax:** 601 355 9708

**TENNESSEE**
Financial Center, 424 Church Street, Suite 2800, **Nashville**, TN 37219
**Tel:** 615 259 1450   **Fax:** 615 259 1470

Music Row, 901 18th Avenue South, **Nashville**, TN 37212
**Tel:** 615 341 0068   **Fax:** 615 341 0596

**TEXAS**
One Houston Center, 1221 McKinney, Suite 4400, **Houston**, TX 77010
**Tel:** 713 652 5151   **Fax:** 713 652 5152

## CONTACTS

**Senior Partner in Charge, New Orleans** .............Mark C Surprenant
**Partner in Charge, New Orleans** .........................Charles A Cerise, Jr
**Partner in Charge, Washington, DC** .........................B Jeffrey Brooks
**Partner in Charge, Houston** .............................................Mark F Elvig
**Partner in Charge, Mobile** .....................................W David Johnson
**Partner in Charge, Birmingham** .................Morris Wade Richardson
**Partner in Charge, Jackson** .......................................A Jerry Sheldon
**Partner in Charge, Baton Rouge** .......................................B Troy Villa
**Partner in Charge, Nashville** .....................Cynthia Mitchell Barnett
**Partner in Charge, Nashville, Music Row** ...........Linda Edell Howard

broad range of public policy tools to achieve its clients objectives. On the labor and employment front, Adams and Reese clients turn to the firm to tailor policies and procedures specific to their organization. The firm represents management in all areas of employment and traditional labor law, including, employee benefits and compensation; litigation; administrative proceedings; contract compliance; and labor/management relations. Adams and Reese attorneys also represent clients in protecting their assets. The firm's Intellectual Property Team is experienced in handling all of the following: copyrights; commercial litigation; contractual negotiation, development and litigation; computer and software protection; software technology; communications law; entertainment; internet and cyberspace issues; patents; international protection; trademarks; and trade secrets.

# BARRASSO USDIN KUPPERMAN FREEMAN & SARVER, L.L.C.

## THE FIRM

**Number of members:** 7
**Number of other lawyers:** 13

**Managing Member:** Steven W Usdin
**Members:** Judy Y Barrasso, Stephen H Kupperman, George C Freeman III, Richard E Sarver, H Minor Pipes, III, Celeste Coco-Ewing.

## AREAS OF PRACTICE:
Litigation ............................................. 100%

**FIRM OVERVIEW:** Founded by experienced litigators departing from an established firm, Barrasso Usdin concentrates on litigating complex civil cases throughout the Gulf South Region. The firm provides the high quality of representation expected from large firms together with responsive and efficient services provided by top tier smaller firms. The firm's lawyers are well equipped to handle complex civil cases because they always have excelled. More than 75 percent served as members of law reviews. More than half clerked for federal judges, both at the appellate and district levels.

## MAIN AREAS OF PRACTICE

**Class Actions/Complex Litigation:** The firm regularly represents clients in a wide variety of class actions and other types of complex litigation, including mass tort cases and multidistrict litigation.
**Commercial Litigation:** Their attorneys have prosecuted and defended every type of commercial dispute.
**Construction Litigation:** Their attorneys represent general contractors, subcontractors, owners and architects in large and small disputes.
**Environmental/Product Liability:** The firm has successfully represented clients in environmental and product liability disputes in a myriad of forums nationwide.
**Insurance Coverage & Bad Faith:** Their attorneys regularly represent numerous insurers in complex declaratory judgment actions, class actions, significant first party coverage disputes and bad faith litigation, including excess judgment cases and institutional bad faith claims.
**Securities Litigation & Enforcement:** Their lawyers are active in every major area of securities litigation and enforcement and represent clients in federal and state courts as well as before regulatory organizations throughout the Gulf South.

**CLIENTS:** The firm's clients include: 3M Company, Allstate Insurance Company, Blanchard & Company, Inc., BP Corporation N.A, Inc., Chubb and Son, Clear Channel Broadcasting, Inc., CNA Insurance, Deutsche Bank Securities, Laitram L.L.C., Liberty Mutual Insurance Corporation, Lincoln Electric Company, Merrill Lynch, Pierce, Fenner & Smith, Inc., Metropolitan Property & Casualty Ins. Co., Morgan Keegan & Company, Inc., Smith Barney, Inc. and UBS Financial Services.

## HEAD OFFICE

**LOUISIANA**
909 Poydras Street, Suite 1800 **New Orleans**, LA 70112
**Tel:** 504 589 9700   **Fax:** 504 589 9701
**Website:** www.barrassousdin.com

## CONTACTS

| | |
|---|---|
| **Class Actions** | Stephen H Kupperman |
| **Commercial Litigation** | Steven W Usdin |
| **Construction** | H Minor Pipes,III |
| **Environmental** | Richard E Sarver |
| **Insurance Coverage & Bad Faith** | Judy Y Barrasso |
| **Product Liability** | Richard E Sarver |
| **Securities Litigation/Enforcement** | George C Freeman, III |

BARRASSO · USDIN · KUPPERMAN
FREEMAN & SARVER, L.L.C.
- COUNSELLORS AT LAW -

# CHAFFE MCCALL L.L.P.

## THE FIRM

**Managing Partner:** Corinne A Morrison
**Number of members:** 28
**Number of other lawyers:** 36

**FIRM OVERVIEW:** More than 64 attorneys strong, Chaffe McCall is a progressive law firm headquartered in New Orleans. Chaffe McCall has always provided high quality representation in an efficient client focused manner. Chaffe McCall's record of success in landmark litigation, as well as its political and civic endeavors, sets it apart as the exceptional New Orleans law firm, a position the firm has continually earned since 1826.

## MAIN AREAS OF PRACTICE

**Real Estate:** Chaffe McCall's Real Estate Section represents clients in a full array of real estate transactions throughout the Gulf South, including acquisitions and sales, construction and permanent financing, joint ventures and leasing transactions, as well as development, construction and real estate management, for clients such as financial institutions, investors, developers and corporations. Chaffe McCall also represents these clients in commercial real estate workouts and the enforcement of rights and remedies in foreclosure, eviction and bankruptcy and other real estate related litigation.

**Business & Taxation:** Chaffe McCall's Business and Taxation Section provides advice and representation in traditional areas including business formation, mergers, dispositions, stock and asset acquisitions, corporate reorganizations, dissolutions, federal and state regulations, bank governance, corporate management, franchising, entertainment law, estate planning and administration, wills, trusts, and all areas of federal, state, and local tax matters and representation in federal, state and local governmental relations, including zoning and expropriation matters and federal, state, and local constitutional and charter issues.

**Labor & Employment:** Chaffe McCall's Labor and Employment Law Section is a recognized leader in the field and represent clients in all aspects of employment relations law. The attorneys appear before not only state and federal courts but also before labor arbitrators and federal boards and agencies.

**Commercial Litigation:** Chaffe McCall's Commercial Litigation Section includes client representation in cases that arise from anti-trust, civil RICO, securities fraud, patent and trademark infringement, intellectual property disputes, unfair trade practices, dealer terminations, lender liability, professional liability, bankruptcy, mergers and acquisitions, minority shareholder rights, lease disputes, secured transactions, real-estate, fidelity and surety bonds, foreclosure and collections, tortious interference, and contract breach.

**Litigation:** Chaffe McCall's Litigation Section represents clients in personal injury and commercial litigation from one-plaintiff casualty cases to mass torts and class actions, representing national retailers, insurers, railroads, petrochemical companies, businesses, and individuals. A significant part of the practice is products liability litigation which includes the defense of products manufacturers.

**International:** Chaffe McCall's practice is international as well as national and has assisted domestic corporations in conducting business transactions abroad, and foreign corporations and law firms with business dealings in the United States.

**HEAD OFFICE**

**LOUISIANA**
2300 Energy Centre, 1100 Poydras Street,
**New Orleans**, LA 70163-2300
**Tel:** 504 585 7000  **Fax:** 504 585 7075
**Website:** www.chaffe.com

**BRANCH OFFICE**

**LOUISIANA**
202 Two United Plaza, 8550 United Plaza Blvd,
**Baton Rouge**, LA 70809
**Tel:** 225 922 4300  **Fax:** 225 922 4304

**Health Law:** Chaffe McCall's Health Law Section has been involved in nearly every aspect of this technical and heavily regulated field of law.

**Admiralty:** Chaffe McCall's Admiralty Section has served the international and domestic shipping communities since the 1820s. Chaffe McCall attorneys represent US clients in other countries, and foreign interests in the US with a staff that is multicultural and multilingual.

**Appellate:** Chaffe McCall's Appellate Section represents clients at all levels of Louisiana and Federal appellate courts, including the United States Supreme Court. The section's attorneys work closely with fellow litigators within the firm, and co-draft appellate briefs and writ applications with other lawyers and firms who have tried cases independently.

**CLIENTS:** Chaffe McCall's representative client list includes major financial institutions, developers, public companies, life insurance companies, tenants, transportation and property management companies, REITS, major pharmaceutical and medical manufacturers and tobacco companies.

C H A F F E M c C A L L
L. L. P.

# CORRERO FISHMAN HAYGOOD PHELPS WALMSLEY & CASTEIX, L.L.P.

## THE FIRM

**Number of partners:** 8
**Number of other lawyers:** 9

**FIRM OVERVIEW:** Correro Fishman Haygood Phelps Walmsley & Casteix, L.L.P., was founded in the mid-1990's by the leading business and litigation lawyers from three of the largest law firms in Louisiana. Its corporate lawyers have been repeatedly recognized in national and regional publications as among the best. It regularly represents public and private companies in a variety of corporate and securities matters. It also has an extensive general business law practice that focuses on real estate, commercial transactions, commercial finance, banking, bank regulation and general contractual matters. The firm has a higher percentage of its New Orleans lawyers listed in a leading American publication of 'best lawyers' than any other firm. Four of the firm's partners are former Chairmen of the Corporate and Business Law Section of the Louisiana State Bar Association. One partner was Chair of the ABA Business Law Section's Committee on Corporate Laws, and another was Chair of the ABA Real Property Section's Committee on Legal Opinions. Two partners have served, and one currently serves, on the Planning Committee of the Tulane Corporate Law Institute. One partner teaches corporate finance at Louisiana State University's Law School and securities registration at Tulane University's Law School and has taught securities regluation at Loyola University Law School. Another partner teaches a corporation and securities law course at Tulane University's Law School. The firm's litigators have handled some of the most challenging and interesting business litigation in their region, including representing SMG, the world's largest facilities manager, in a challenge by the New Orleans Saints of their lease of the Louisiana Superdome; IBM, in multi-district patent litigation; Manpower Inc., in the defense of class action claims arising out of the Kaiser plant explosion; The Times-Picayune and The Associated Press, in numerous First Amendment cases including access issues arising out of the trial of former Louisiana Governor Edwin Edwards; and the State of Louisiana, in actions to collect tens of millions of dollars of disputed taxes.

## MAIN AREAS OF PRACTICE

**Corporate, Securities & Corporate Finance:** The firm regularly represents public and private companies in corporate and securities matters, such as public and private offerings, mergers and acquisitions, proxy contests, periodic reporting, corporate governance and general SEC compliance.

**Banking:** The firm is a leader among law firms representing financial institutions in Louisiana. Three partners have served on the Bank Counsel Committee of the Louisiana Bankers Association. For two years in a row the firm was ranked no. 1 in the Southwest by The Merger Strategy Report and Shushunoff Information Services in the handling of legal work associated with acquisitions of financial institutions. The firm's lawyers have been involved in at least 50 of these transactions, more by far than any other group of lawyers in the state, including the four largest bank mergers in Louisiana. The firm also routinely counsels clients regarding regulatory compliance and reorganisations, and has handled branch purchases and sales, commercial financing transactions, S-corp reorganizations, oil and gas financings, secured transactions and structured financings. Its banking clients include AmSouth Bank, Coastal Commerce Bank, First Bank & Trust, First Community Bank, First Guaranty Bank, Gulf Coast Bank, Liberty Bank, MidSouth Bank, Omni Bank, Parish National Bank, People's Bank of Louisiana, Resource Bank and Whitney National Bank.

**Mergers & Acquisitions:** The firm's corporate lawyers handle mergers and acquisitions of private as well as public companies involving both negotiated and unsolicited acquisitions, going-private transactions and acquisitions of minority interests. Lawyers in the firm have been involved in some of the largest M&A transactions in Louisiana as well as numerous others, both large and small.

## HEAD OFFICE

**LOUISIANA**
201 St. Charles Avenue, 46th Floor, **New Orleans**, LA 70170-4600
**Tel:** 504 586 5252   **Fax:** 504 586 5250
**Website:** www.cfhlaw.com

**Real Estate:** The firm handles all aspects of commercial real estate transactions, including commercial and industrial leasing, acquisitions, financings, condominium conversions, commercial developments, oil and gas tranfers and encumbrances, timber developments and large tract opportunities. It is also experienced in transactions involving historic and low-income housing tax credits and public and private issues of development bonds. Lawyers in the firm routinely advise clients on all aspects of real estate leasing, and often represent landlords and tenants in lease negotiations, including representing the landlord in major league sports leases with the NFL New Orleans Saints and the NBA New Orleans Hornets.

**Litigation:** The firm's litigators regularly represent The Times-Picayune L.L.C. in libel, defamation and invasion of privacy cases and public record and access disputes, as well as The Associated Press and Capital City Press L.L.C. in various access disputes. They also represent defendants in class action litigation, including mass tort and securities litigation; clients in contract disputes of various kinds, including options, purchase agreements and leases; clients in products liability and tort actions in federal and state courts throughout Louisiana and elsewhere relating to the oil industry and the various large industrial facilities located in this region; plaintiffs and defendants in securities litigation and arbitration, including broker-dealer disputes and public company disclosure; clients involved in arbitrated disputes, including proceedings administered by the American Arbitration Association, National Association of Securities Dealers and the New York Stock Exchange; and the State of Louisiana in corporate income and franchise tax matters, including obtaining a $26 million jury verdict awarding taxes, interest and penalties that is believed to be the largest jury award of its kind in Louisiana history.

**Other:** The firm has extensive experience in estate planning and the acquisition, sale and financing of motion picture tax credits. It has recently been active in advising clients, both large and small, on the myriad of issues arising out of the incredible devastation brought by Hurricane Katrina in August 2005.

**CLIENTS:** Some clients that have entrusted legal matters to the firm are: Amedisys, Inc., AmSouth Bank, ASCO plc, The Associated Press, Autodesk, Inc., Biloxi Marsh Lands Corporation, Blue Cross of Louisiana, Capital City Press, L.L.C., Carbo Chlorination Technologies, L.L.C., Chaffe & Associates, Inc., Enterprise Products Operating, L.P., Entergy Corporation, FBT Investments, Inc., First Bank and Trust, First Guaranty Bank, Great Lakes Chemical Corporation, Gulf Coast Bank, Hibernia Southcoast Capital, Inc., High Pressure Integrity, Inc., Hirsch Investment Management, L.L.C., International Business Machines Corporation, Jefferson Capital Management, L.L.C., Kinder Morgan Energy Partners, Ltd., Laitram, L.L.C., Liberty Bank, Louisiana Companies, Mac-Re, LLC, MidSouth Bancorp. Inc., New Orleans Metropolitan Convention and Visitors Bureau, Inc., OCA, Inc., Offshore Logistics, Inc., Pennington Medical Foundation, Petrocom LLC, Resource Bankshares, Inc., Robinson Lumber Company, Inc., Sanderson Farms, Inc., SMG, Stewart Enterprises, Inc., The Times-Picayune L.L.C., T.L. James & Company, Inc., Tulane University, Turbo Squid, Inc., Waters Parkerson & Co., Inc., Whitney National Bank and Wyndham International, Inc.

# HERMAN, HERMAN, KATZ & COTLAR

## THE FIRM

**Managing Partner:** Steven J Lane, Esq
**Partners:** Russ M Herman, Maury A Herman, Morton H Katz, Sidney A Cotlar, Steven J Lane, Leonard A Davis, James C Klick, Stephen J Herman, Brian D Katz

**Number of Attorneys:** 13

**FIRM OVERVIEW:** Since opening its doors in 1942, Herman, Herman, Katz & Cotlar has earned a reputation for promoting the rights of all citizens. The firm has become more diverse and sophisticated with time, and is committed to promoting the good of the public, which has always been the cornerstone of the firm. Herman, Herman, Katz & Cotlar's expertise allows them to skillfully represent each of its clients, whether representing a single injured individual or thousands of plaintiffs in a class action, and the firm believes that each case it litigates has the potential to open the door to a new avenue of justice. In many cases, the firm has been able to create legal precedent that has changed the face of the law. The firm works closely with its clients to provide them with the highest level of satisfaction and legal representation available.

Herman, Herman, Katz & Cotlar is a member of Herman, Mathis, Casey, Kitchens & Gerel, LLP.

**Herman, Mathis, Casey, Kitchens & Gerel, LLP:** Herman, Mathis, Casey, Kitchens & Gerel, LLP is a partnership comprised of five nationally prominent law firms and their members. The firm represents consumers across the nation, drawing on the substantial expertise of its member firms' partners. It specializes in significant national class actions, mass torts and other complex cases consistent with its mission of representing consumers, pursuing the public justice, and protecting the rights of families, children, and the elderly. This approach, unique among plaintiff firms, provides plaintiffs with the same access to national representation that large defense firms have long made available to corporations. **Partner firms:** Herman, Herman, Katz & Cotlar, L.L.P., of New Orleans, Louisiana; The Mathis Law Firm, P.C. of Atlanta, Georgia; Casey, Gerry of San Diego, California; Kitchens & Ellis of Jackson, Mississippi; and Ashcraft & Gerel of Washington DC, Maryland, Virginia and Massachusetts. The central office is located in Atlanta, Georgia.

## MAIN AREAS OF PRACTICE:

**Business & Commercial Law:** Throughout the firm's history, business executives and owners have called upon HHK&C for a variety of business and commercial litigation needs. In this capacity, the firm has litigated several cases of national note.
**Class Actions:** The firm has represented clients in numerous class actions, including the national tobacco litigation, improper hiring and commission practices, mass disaster, various business class action cases, products liability and HMO litigations.
**Complex Multi-District Litigation:** HHK&C and members of the national firm Herman, Mathis, Casey, Kitchens & Gerel serve as co-lead counsel in MDLs involving the drugs Propulsid and Vioxx, litigation involving HMO subscribers and Pharmacy Benefit Managers.
**Construction Litigation:** HHK&C has expertise in contract negotiations, contract disputes and performance, architectural omissions, quality of work issues, construction bonds and zoning. The firm is also one of the few local law firms that handles disputes over workers' compensation insurance premiums.
**Explosions & Fires:** The firm has been heavily involved in a number of diverse cases involving mass explosions and fires throughout the Gulf Coast Region and the South. For years, it has litigated cases involving catastrophes connected with refineries, chemical facilities and industrial plants.
**Family Law:** The firm's attorneys handle complex and significant asset family law cases.

## HEAD OFFICE

**LOUISIANA**
201 St. Charles Ave., Suite 4310, **New Orleans**, LA 70170
**Tel:** 504 581 4892   **Fax:** 504 561 6024
**Website:** www.hhkc.com
**Email:** hhkc@hhkc.com

**Fall 2006 Address:** 820 O'Keefe Ave, **New Orleans**, LA 70113

**HMO Litigation:** HHK&C, through the national firm of Herman, Mathis, Casey, Kitchens & Gerel, LLP, is confronting managed healthcare organizations in the interest of patient rights. The national firm of Herman, Mathis, Casey, Kitchens & Gerel, LLP, has the resources and experience in complex class action litigation to effectively represent a large number of plaintiffs in pursuing their claims against multiple HMOs.
**Insurance Claims:** The firm is actively pursuing thousands of claims for damages related to Hurricanes Katrina and Rita including homeowners, flood and business interruption claims.
**Medical Negligence:** HHK&C has been representing victims of medical negligence for over half a century and handles a full range of claims arising from medical negligence and medical product liability cases. The firm has handled cases in many states, including Louisiana, Alabama, Mississippi and Oklahoma, and have on staff a neurosurgeon/attorney who has been board certified for over 20 years.
**Personal Injury:** HHK&C handles various personal injury cases including catastrophic injury, electrocutions, explosions and fires, highway liability, maritime personal injury, medical negligence, motor vehicle collisions, premises liability, product liability, railroad crossing and derailment, toxic torts and wrongful death cases.
**Pharmaceutical Litigation:** HHKC has earned a nationwide leadership role in the complex litigation involving drug reaction and interactions.
**Professional Negligence:** HHK&C represents clients in cases that encompass a full spectrum of professions, including medical, architectural, legal, accounting and engineering professions. For both individuals and professionals, the firm offers its years of experience working professional negligence cases along with its innovative law practice in an attempt to achieve a favorable outcome.
**Railroad Litigation:** For years, the attorneys at HHK&C have aggressively and tactfully represented clients against railroad companies in pedestrian, derailment and collision cases.
**Tobacco Litigation:** In 1994, HHK&C, along with 60 other law firms, brought tobacco companies to court to recover Medicare costs and other economic damages resulting from tobacco-related deaths and disease. In addition, Russ Herman is lead counsel for the Louisiana trial team that is currently litigating Scott v American Tobacco Co., the only viable class action in the United States concerning individuals affected by tobacco addiction and tobacco-related disease.

**Representative Cases:** HHK&C has obtained numerous significant judgments ranging from $1,000,000 to $25,550,000. Specific information is available on the firm's website.

HERMAN, HERMAN, KATZ & COTLAR
L.L.P.
Attorneys at Law

# JONES WALKER WAECHTER POITEVENT CARRÈRE & DENÈGRE, LLP

## THE FIRM

**Management by Board of Directors**
**Number of partners:** 113
**Number of other lawyers:** 98
**Website:** www.joneswalker.com
**Email:** info@joneswalker.com

**FIRM OVERVIEW:** The firm is one of the most distinguished law firms in the Gulf South with nearly three dozen practice areas. Over 200 attorneys are located in Baton Rouge, Houston, Lafayette, Miami, New Orleans, The Woodlands, and Washington, DC. Businesses routinely call on Jones Walker to handle matters of local, regional, national and international interest. The firm's continued expansion enables it to better serve the needs of clients, while maintaining its mission of rendering the highest standards of legal service. By understanding its clients' business and building strong, personal relationships with them, Jones Walker creates a working partnership that is concentrated on getting the best results in the most efficient manner.

**Client Services:** Corporate America, money center financial institutions, worldwide insurers, and small to mid-size businesses rely on the firm's creative and innovative delivery of legal services and a personalized client service approach. Jones Walker strikes a balance between the traditional one-on-one relationship of attorney and client and the demands of today's increasingly complex legal problems that often require the attention of a team of attorneys.

**The Attorneys:** Jones Walker attorneys are licensed to practice in multiple states, the District of Columbia, the Republic of Colombia, and the United Mexican States. The firm's attorneys are regularly published in legal, commercial, and industry journals. They are featured as speakers for professional, trade and business seminars, as well as instructing law school courses. Jones Walker attorneys are committed to improving their communities by dedicating time, talent and financial resources to many community, civic and professional organizations.

**MAIN AREAS OF PRACTICE:** Admiralty and maritime; antitrust and trade regulation; appellate litigation; aviation; bankruptcy, restructuring and creditors-debtors rights; business and commercial litigation; class action defense; commercial lending and finance; construction; corporate and securities; employee benefits, ERISA and executive compensation; energy; environmental and toxic torts; gaming; government relations; healthcare; insurance, banking and financial services; intellectual property; international; labor relations and employment; mergers and acquisitions; products liability; professional liability; project development and finance; public finance; real estate: land use, development and finance; tax (international, federal, state and local); telecommunications and utilities; trusts, estates and personal planning; venture capital and emerging companies; white collar crime and corporate compliance.

**CLIENTS:** Banking and finance; communications and technology; energy, environmental, and mining; healthcare; maritime; media/advertising; manufacturing/industrial; public sector; sports, entertainment and gaming; real estate; transportation; wholesale/retail/service industries.

**INTERNATIONAL WORK:** The firm's international attorneys have significant experience in foreign investment, corporate, commercial, financial, tax, and administrative laws and regulations relevant to global operations. Jones Walker represents clients in all forms of international transactions, including and in connection with: joint ventures; international capital markets (including issuers and underwriters on debt and equity offerings); project finance (including developers, borrowers, lenders and the World Bank); mergers and acquisitions; real estate; energy; maritime; telecommunications; international tax, tax compliance and planning; intellectual property; healthcare; antitrust and unfair trade practices; export controls; government regulation; environmental; labor and employment; and arbitration and dispute resolution. The firm has handled transactions in some 30 countries in Latin America, Europe, Asia, and Africa.

## OFFICES

**LOUISIANA**
201 St Charles Avenue, **New Orleans**, LA 70170-5100
**Tel:** 504 582 8000    **Fax:** 504 582 8583

8555 United Plaza Boulevard, **Baton Rouge**, LA 70809-7000
**Tel:** 225 248 2000    **Fax:** 225 248 2010

500 Dover Boulevard, Suite 120, **Lafayette**, LA 70503-5269
**Tel:** 337 406 5610    **Fax:** 337 406 5620

**DISTRICT OF COLUMBIA**
499 South Capitol Street SW, Suite 600, **Washington**, DC 20003-4013
**Tel:** 202 203 1000    **Fax:** 202 203 0000

2600 Virginia Avenue, N.W., Suite 1113, **Washington**, DC 20037
**Tel:** 202 944 1100    **Fax:** 202 944 1109

**FLORIDA**
601 Brickell Key Drive, Suite 500, **Miami**, FL 33131
**Tel:** 305 679 5700    **Fax:** 305 679 5710

**TEXAS**
10001 Woodloch Forest Drive, Suite 350, **The Woodlands**, TX 77380
**Tel:** 281 296 4400    **Fax:** 281 296 4404

600 Travis Street, Suite 6601, **Houston**, TX 77002
**Tel:** 713 437 1800    **Fax:** 713 437 1810

# KEAN MILLER HAWTHORNE D'ARMOND MCGOWAN & JARMAN, LLP

## THE FIRM

**Managing Partner:** Gary A Bezet
**Number of partners:** 68

**FIRM OVERVIEW:** With more than 120 lawyers, Kean Miller is the largest law firm in the capital region and one of the largest in Louisiana. The firm maintains two offices in Baton Rouge (Downtown and Bluebonnet Boulevard), as well as offices in New Orleans, Lake Charles and Plaquemine.

The firm serves clients in numerous industries including energy, petrochemical, chemical, information technology, telecommunications, shipping and transportation, drilling and exploration, pipelines, media, advertising, financial services, insurance, gaming, government, education, healthcare, manufacturing, real estate, retail, construction, and leasing.

Kean Miller works with clients in a wide variety of practice areas, including: environmental regulation, permitting, commercial litigation, admiralty and maritime, products liability, business transactions, real estate, intellectual property, chemical exposure litigation, toxic tort defense, oil and gas, healthcare, medical malpractice, bankruptcy and reorganization, utilities regulation, labor and employment, technology, state and local tax, administrative matters, lobbying, estate planning, probate, and insurance coverage litigation.

Whether the firm is helping its clients defend lawsuits, raise capital, comply with regulatory requirements, enter new markets, obtain and defend intellectual property rights, develop and distribute products and services, or acquire or divest businesses, the firm understands that its client's goals are paramount. When clients are faced with disputes, the firm assists them in identifying and pursuing the fastest and most effective solutions.

The firm has a particular dedication to working closely with Louisiana-based businesses and *Fortune* 500 companies with significant operations in the state of Louisiana – ensuring that they have the legal resources they need to grow into leaders in the region. The firm's 23-year history is one of lasting alliances with its clients. Its client partnerships are based on value, service, and Louisiana know-how.

**MAIN AREAS OF PRACTICE:** Admiralty and maritime; banking and finance; bankruptcy and business reorganization; business, corporate and real estate; class action defense; construction; energy law; environmental regulation; environmental litigation; estate planning; expropriation, land use and wetlands; health law; intellectual property, trademarks and copyright; labor and employment; litigation; mass tort defense; medical malpractice; oil and gas; pipelines; products liability; retail and casualty litigation; state and local taxation; toxic tort defense; utilities regulation; white collar criminal defense; and workers compensation.

**Key Industries:** Energy, petrochemical, chemical, pipelines, trucking and transportation, retail, forest products, marine, drilling and exploration, and healthcare.

**CLIENTS:** Kean Miller works with Louisiana-based businesses and *Fortune* 500 companies with significant operations in the Bayou state. The firm provides advice to major energy and petrochemical companies, manufacturers, distributors, transportation companies, construction companies, shipping companies, drilling and exploration contractors, retail and food service companies, and healthcare providers. The firm serves as general counsel to the Louisiana Chemical Association and the Louisiana Municipal Association.

## OFFICES

**LOUISIANA**
22nd Floor, One American Place, PO Box 3513, **Baton Rouge**, LA 70821
**Tel:** 225 387 0999   **Fax:** 225 388 9133
**Email:** client_services@keanmiller.com
**Website:** www.keanmiller.com

## BRANCH OFFICES

**LOUISIANA**
5035 Bluebonnet Blvd, Suite B, **Baton Rouge**, LA 70809
**Tel:** 225 387 0999   **Fax:** 225 388 9133

Suite 1600, One Lakeshore Drive, **Lake Charles**, LA 70629
**Tel:** 337 430 0350   **Fax:** 337 436 5566

LL&E Tower, Suite 1450, 909 Poydras St, **New Orleans**, LA 70112
**Tel:** 504 585 3050   **Fax:** 504 585 3051

Suite 10, 23425 Railroad Avenue, **Plaquemine**, LA 70764
**Tel:** 225 687 9845   **Fax:** 225 382 3445

KEAN MILLER
FROM MAIN STREET TO WALL STREET
KEAN MILLER HAWTHORNE D'ARMOND McCOWAN & JARMAN LLP

# MCGLINCHEY STAFFORD

## THE FIRM

**Managing Partner:** Rodolfo J Aguilar, Jr
**Number of partners:** 96
**Number of other lawyers:** 91

### AREAS OF PRACTICE:

| | |
|---|---|
| Commercial & Business Litigation (Defense) | 22% |
| Financial Services | 15% |
| Products Liability, Pharmaceutical & Medical Devices | 14% |
| Class Action Defense & Consumer Finance Litigation | 11% |
| Employment Law (Defense) | 7% |
| Healthcare | 5% |
| Public Law | 5% |
| Real Estate (Commercial) | 4% |
| Insurance Regulation, Compliance & Defense | 3% |
| Admiralty | 3% |
| Bankruptcy | 3% |
| Environmental Law | 3% |
| Corporate & Business Transactions | 1% |
| Estate/Probate/Trust | 1% |
| Government Contracts/Relations | 1% |
| Taxation | 1% |
| Casino Gaming | 1% |

## MAIN AREAS OF PRACTICE

**Commercial & Business Litigation:** Advises clients in matters involving antitrust and trade regulation laws; pricing and product distribution; dealer terminations; unfair competition; deceptive acts and practices; advertising; patent abuse; franchising; complex multi-district and class action litigation; RICO; DOJ, and FTC investigations.

**Banking & Commercial Finance:** Represents financial institutions in matters involving federal and state banking laws/regulations; asset-based lending; equipment leasing; commercial loan closings; workouts; bankruptcies; loan and deposit account agreements; real estate and personal property security interests; bank holding company formations; M&A; trust powers; investment and securities activities; new product development; bank-sponsored mutual funds; insurance and annuity products.

**Consumer Financial Services:** Counsels the world's leading financial institutions on compliance under federal and state consumer finance laws and regulations. Services include multi-state legal surveys; design of mortgage, automobile and manufactured housing finance credit products and agreements; compliance audits and training; defense of regulatory enforcement actions and consumer credit litigation, including class actions. Affiliate MS&YB serves the residential mortgage lending industry offering outsourcing of mortgage banking functions.

**Class Action Defense & Consumer Finance Litigation:** Defends banks; consumer finance companies; mortgage companies; specialty and non-prime equity lenders; retailers; credit card issuers; credit insurers; property and casualty insurers; life insurers; consumer leasing companies; payday lenders; auto finance companies; insurance premium finance companies; service companies; and other consumer financial services providers in class action and multidistrict litigation involving the entire range of causes of action and emerging legal theories.

**Employment Law:** Representation includes affirmative action; arbitration; collective bargaining; communications and employee motivation; compensation and benefits; compliance audits; discrimination; contracts; immigration compliance; labor disputes including industry-wide, multi-state strike; management training; OSHA; personnel policies and practices; strikes and labor injunctions; unfair labor practice proceedings before the NLRB; union organizing and election proceedings; Wage and Hour investigations, and wrongful discharge.

**Healthcare:** Represents clients in matters involving compliance with federal and state healthcare laws and regulations, including fraud and abuse, Stark and False Claims; hospital operational and medical staff issues; licensing, including Board matters; contract matters; M&A; Medicare and other third party payor reimbursement issues; legislation/regulation; litigation, including professional liabil-

ity; risk management and loss control, and managed care.

**Real Estate:** Represents developers; landlords; tenants; lenders; individual and corporate landowners; financial institutions; insurance and mortgage companies, and institutional investors. Transactions involve historical renovation and low income housing tax credits. Projects include industrial plants; merchant power and cogeneration plants; office buildings; gaming; retail and restaurant chains; wireless network sites; hotels; golf course developments; planned unit, condominium, and timeshare. Owns MACSTAM Title Company LLC, a licensed title insurance agency, and provides title abstract services through its subsidiary, Abstracts by Godail, LLC.

**Products Liability:** Represents foreign and domestic insurers; manufacturers and distributors in defense of manufacturer and design liability cases involving motor vehicles; electrical appliances, and chemical and industrial products. Coordinates products liability litigation for businesses regionally and nationally.

**Pharmaceutical & Medical Devices:** Represents major prescription pharmaceutical manufacturers and distributors in defense of claims involving prescription and over-the-counter drugs; medical and surgical devices, and implantable contraceptives. Defends clients in putative class action suits involving pharmaceutical products and in medical device litigation.

## HEAD OFFICE

**LOUISIANA**
643 Magazine Street, **New Orleans**, LA 70130
**Tel:** 504 586 1200 **Fax:** 504 596 2800
**Email:** info@mcglinchey.com
**Website:** www.mcglinchey.com

## BRANCH OFFICES

**TEXAS**
1001 McKinney, Suite 1500, **Houston**, TX 77002
**Tel:** 713 520 1900 **Fax:** 713 520 1025

2711 N. Haskell Ave, Suite 2700, LB 25, **Dallas**, TX 75204
**Tel:** 214 257 1700 **Fax:** 214 257 1717

**LOUISIANA**
One American Place, 14th Floor, 301 Main Street, **Baton Rouge**, LA 70825
**Tel:** 225 383 9000 **Fax:** 225 343 3076

1811 Tower Drive, Suite A, **Monroe**, LA 71201
**Tel:** 318 651 0807 **Fax:** 318 651 0809

**MISSISSIPPI**
200 South Lamar Street, Suite 1100, City Centre, **Jackson**, MS 39201
**Tel:** 601 960 8400 **Fax:** 601 960 8406

**NEW YORK**
194 Washington Avenue, Suite 600, **Albany**, NY 12210 (Albany Co.)
**Tel:** 518 432 1200 **Fax:** 518 432 8711

**OHIO**
25550 Chagrin Boulevard, Suite 406, **Cleveland**, OH 44122-4640
**Tel:** 216 378 9905 **Fax:** 216 378 9910

## CONTACTS

| | |
|---|---|
| Banking & Commercial Finance | David S Willenzik |
| Commercial & Business Litigation | B Franklin Martin III |
| Consumer Financial Services | Bennet S Koren |
| Class Action & Consumer Finance Litigation | Anthony Rollo |
| Employment Law | E Fredrick Preis, Jr |
| Healthcare | Donna Guinn Klein |
| Real Estate | R Keith Colvin |
| Pharmaceutical & Medical Devices | Henri Wolbrette III |
| Products Liability | Michael M Noonan |

**MCGLINCHEY STAFFORD** PLLC

# PHELPS DUNBAR

## THE FIRM

**Managing Partner:** Richard N Dicharry
**Number of partners:** 104

**FIRM OVERVIEW:** Founded in 1853 in New Orleans, Phelps Dunbar is one of the oldest law firms in continuous practice in the South. The firm is a progressive and diverse partnership, with a practice that is international in scope. Phelps Dunbar has offices in New Orleans and Baton Rouge, Louisiana; Jackson, Tupelo, and Gulfport, Mississippi; Houston, Texas; Tampa, Florida; and London, England. Through the firm's network of regional offices, clients have access to more than 250 attorneys representing an extensive range of talent and experience. No matter how intricate a client's legal needs, the firm's professional depth and experience offer accessible, cost-effective, and reliable service. The firm continually refocuses the major practice areas to serve the changing needs of its client community. Attorneys in all practice areas work together to provide a broad base of legal services to institutions and individuals. Phelps Dunbar handles virtually every type of civil case in federal and state courts across the region. The firm was recognized in 2002 for its efforts in diversity by receiving the Defense Research Institute (DRI) National Diversity Award. The firm was also ranked first in the nation in 2002 and 2004 and among the top three in 2003 and 2005 in percentage of African-American lawyers by the Minority Law Journal.

**CLIENTS:** Clients include public and private companies, financial institutions, insurance companies, healthcare systems, educational institutions, partnerships, estates, governmental agencies and individuals.

## US OFFICE CONTACTS

### NEW ORLEANS

Canal Place, 365 Canal Street, Suite 2000, New Orleans, 70130-6534

**Office Profile:** As the firm's administrative and headquarters office, the New Orleans office is the largest of Phelps' regional legal practices. Over 85 attorneys represent a wide range of practice areas within six key groups: admiralty, business, commercial litigation, employment law, insurance and reinsurance, and tort litigation.

### BATON ROUGE

City Plaza, 445 North Boulevard, Suite 701, Baton Rouge, LA 70802-5707

**Office Profile:** The firm's Baton Rouge office was the first regional office of Phelps Dunbar, opening in 1984. With over 40 attorneys, the Baton Rouge office has become one of the largest law offices in the state capital. The firm's attorneys support clients with a full-service litigation and business practice, as well as counseling on employment, regulatory, environmental and intellectual property matters.

### JACKSON

111 East Capitol Street, Suite 600, Jackson, MS 39201

**Office Profile:** The Jackson office opened in 1986, and now, with more than 50 attorneys, provides full-service litigation and traditional business practice for a diverse clientele. The office also has a labor and employment practice and gaming practice.

### TUPELO

One Mississippi Plaza, 201 S. Spring Street, Seventh Floor, Tupelo, MS 38804

**Office Profile:** Phelps Dunbar is the only law firm with substantial offices in Tupelo, Jackson, and Gulfport, Mississippi. The offices coordinate projects for

## HEAD OFFICE

**LOUISIANA**
Canal Place, 365 Canal Street, Suite 2000, **New Orleans**, LA 70130-6534
**Tel:** 504 566 1311   **Fax:** 504 568 9130
**Email:** info@phelps.com
**Website:** www.phelpsdunbar.com

## BRANCH OFFICES

**LOUISIANA**
City Plaza, 445 North Bvd, Suite 701, **Baton Rouge**, LA 70802-5707
**Tel:** 225 346 0285   **Fax:** 225 381 9197

**MISSISSIPPI**
NorthCourt One, 2304 19th Street, Suite 300, **Gulfport**, MS 39501
**Tel:** 228 679 1130   **Fax:** 228 679 1131

111 East Capitol Street, Suite 600, **Jackson**, MS 39201
**Tel:** 601 352 2300   **Fax:** 601 360 9777

One Mississippi Plaza, 201 S. Spring Street, Seventh Floor,
**Tupelo**, MS 38804
**Tel:** 662 842 7907   **Fax:** 662 842 3873

**TEXAS**
700 Louisiana Street, Suite 2600, **Houston**, TX 77002
**Tel:** 713 626 1386   **Fax:** 713 626 1388

**FLORIDA**
100 South Ashley Drive, Suite 1900, **Tampa**, FL 33602-5311
**Tel:** 813 472 7550   **Fax:** 813 472 7570

many clients with legal business throughout the state. As the center of the firm's thriving healthcare practice, the Tupelo office employs attorneys well-versed in the subtleties of this constantly evolving field of law. The firm's health law attorneys represent hospitals, physicians, managed care organizations and other healthcare providers throughout the Southeast as counsel on corporate, tax and health law matters. In addition, it maintains a business and a litigation practice.

### GULFPORT

NorthCourt One, 2304 1th Street, Suite 300, Gulfport, MS 39501

**Office Profile:** Phelps Dunbar opened its Gulfport office on December 1, 2000. The office handles business litigation, construction, real estate, financing, products liability, insurance, environmental and tort litigation.

### HOUSTON

700 Louisiana Street, Suite 2600, Houston, TX 77002

**Office Profile:** Opened in 1990, the Houston office has attorneys with extensive trial, appellate and business experience supplemented by excellent academic and professional backgrounds.

### TAMPA

100 South Ashley Drive, Suite 1900, Tampa, FL 33602-5311

**Office Profile:** Phelps Dunbar extended its legal services from Texas to Florida by opening its eighth office in Tampa on April 1, 2001. The Tampa office handles admiralty and tort litigation, business, real estate, commercial litigation, construction, insurance and reinsurance, labor and employment and petroleum marketing litigation.

# SHER GARNER CAHILL RICHTER KLEIN & HILBERT, L.L.C.

## THE FIRM

**Co-Managing Partners:** Leopold Z Sher, James M Garner
**Number of partners:** 18
**Number of other lawyers:** 20

**FIRM OVERVIEW:** Sher Garner Cahill Richter Klein & Hilbert, L.L.C. practices a wide variety of business and litigation disciplines and serves a multi-jurisdictional clientele. Its talented team of attorneys provides its clients with sophisticated legal services common to a large firm practice, but with responsiveness, personal attention and sensible staffing of a smaller firm. The firm's lawyers are committed to working with one another, with experienced support staff and clients as a team to deliver legal services of unsurpassed quality, effectiveness and efficiency. All of the firm's attorneys seek continuous professional and personal advancement and adhere to the highest ethical standards. The firm is dedicated to the betterment of its community and is committed to diversity. Everyone within the firm shares a common dedication to these principles. The firm encourages active participation by all of its attorneys in professional activities as well as civic, charitable, political and educational endeavors.

**MAIN AREAS OF PRACTICE:** Administrative law, admiralty and maritime law, advertising and marketing, agency and distributorships, agricultural law, alternative dispute resolution, antitrust and trade regulation, appellate practice, aviation and aerospace, bankruptcy, banks and banking, biotechnology, business law, casinos and gambling, civil practice, civil rights, class actions, collections, commercial law, commercial real estate, communications and media, complex and multi-district litigation, computers and software, constitutional law, construction law, contracts, copyrights, corporate law, education law, election, campaign and political law, eminent domain, employee benefits, energy, entertainment and the arts, environmental law, equipment finance and leasing, fidelity and surety, finance, franchises and franchising, fraud and deceit, general practice, government, government contracts, healthcare, historic preservation, hospital law, insurance, insurance defense, intellectual property, international law, investments, labor and employment, leases and leasing, legal ethics and professional responsibility, libel, slander and defamation, litigation, media law, debtor and creditor, medical malpractice, medicare and medicaid, mergers, acquisitions and divestitures, mortgages, municipal law, natural resources, negligence, nonprofit and charitable organizations, occupational safety and health, partnership law, personal injury, premises liability, products liability, professional liability, property law, public finance, real estate, resorts and leisure, RICO, securities, sports law, taxation, technology and science, torts, toxic torts, trade and professional associations, trade secrets, trademarks, unfair competition, utility law, workers compensation, zoning, planning and land.

Capdevielle Title Corporation, an affiliate of the Sher Garner law firm, provides a full spectrum of commercial title insurance services through all major title insurance companies.

**CLIENTS:** Sher Garner's clients include a wide array of public and private companies, educational institutions, banking and financial institutions, insurance companies, healthcare systems, governmental agencies, real estate groups and individuals.

**HEAD OFFICE**

**LOUISIANA**
909 Poydras Street, 28th Floor, **New Orleans**, LA 70112-1033
**Tel:** 504 299 2100   **Fax:** 504 299 2300
**Email:** matters@shergarner.com
**Website:** www.shergarner.com

Law Offices of
## SHER GARNER CAHILL RICHTER KLEIN & HILBERT, L.L.C.

# STONE PIGMAN WALTHER WITTMANN LLC

## THE FIRM

**Chair of the Management Committee:** Phillip A Wittmann
**Number of members:** 30
**Number of lawyers:** 51

**FIRM OVERVIEW:** The New Orleans law firm of Stone Pigman Walther Wittmann LLC is an important resource for national corporations doing business in the Gulf South. With over 75 years of practicing law, Stone Pigman has the experience on which corporate counsel can rely. The firm possesses a deep reservoir of talent and experience in handling litigation and business matters across a wide range of industries consisting of banking and finance, construction, education, energy and natural resources, healthcare and pharmaceutical, insurance, manufacturing, media and entertainment, real estate, service, tax-exempt organizations, technology, telecommunications, transportation and utilities.

## MAIN AREAS OF PRACTICE

**Commercial Litigation:** The firm represents defendants and plaintiffs in a variety of complex litigation matters in both state and federal courts. Firm lawyers have represented clients in cases involving class actions, multi-district litigation, professional liability, appellate procedures and other complicated cases arising from mass torts, environmental and toxic tort claims, product liability actions, consumer fraud, antitrust claims, securities claims, bankruptcy and creditors' rights, bank regulation, employment claims, healthcare regulation, utility regulation, state and federal taxation, construction, insurance regulation, gaming regulation and intellectual property disputes.

**Corporate & Securities/Mergers & Acquisitions:** Firm lawyers have experience in all types of corporate finance transactions, including mergers and acquisitions, reorganizations, public offerings and private placements of common and preferred stock, subordinated debentures, partnership or LLC interests, and commercial paper, medium term notes and other types of securities. The firm also has extensive experience with non-corporate entities including partnerships, limited partnerships, LLCs, registered limited liability partnerships and trusts.

**Real Estate, Finance & Construction:** As counsel for real estate developers, buyers, sellers, institutional lenders and major tenants, Stone Pigman lawyers have been involved in most of the commercial real estate developments that have occurred in the greater New Orleans metropolitan area over the last several decades, as well as many significant projects throughout the rest of Louisiana, the Gulf South and the United States. For owner clients, the firm offers expertise in zoning and land use, leasing, environmental matters, construction issues, acquisition techniques and cross-easements and restrictive covenants. For borrowers and lenders, Stone Pigman lawyers are proficient in current lending techniques and have an in-depth understanding of the unique issues in Louisiana lending law.

**Intellectual Property & Technology:** Firm lawyers advise clients in a broad range of technology-related legal services, including trademarks, copyrights, patent litigation, trade secrets and other related legal issues including unfair competition, unfair trade practices, non-competition, employee raiding, confidentiality agreements, fiduciary duties and anti-trust matters. The firm represents a diverse group of clients, from local start-ups to established international clients, in various industries.

**Tax:** The firm's tax practice encompasses federal, state and local taxation, and focuses on tax planning and dispute resolution. The federal Tax Practice covers corporate, partnership, limited liability company, nonprofit organization, Employee Retirement Income Security Act and executive compensation matters as well as international taxation. Stone Pigman represents taxpayers in administrative proceedings before the Internal Revenue Service and in litigation before the United States Tax Court and other federal courts. The state and local tax practice covers corporate income and franchise tax, sales and use tax, ad valorem tax and mineral severance tax. Firm lawyers represent taxpayers in administrative proceedings before the Louisiana Department of Revenue, the Louisiana Board of Tax Appeals and the Louisiana Tax Commission, and in litigation before Louisiana state courts.

## HEAD OFFICE

**LOUISIANA**
546 Carondelet Street, **New Orleans**, LA 70130-3588
**Tel:** 504 581 3200   **Fax:** 504 581 3361
**Website:** www.stonepigman.com

## CONTACTS

| | |
|---|---|
| **Commercial Litigation** | James C Gulotta Jr |
| **Corporate & Securities/M&A** | Scott T Whittaker |
| **Real Estate, Finance & Construction** | Susan G Talley |
| **Intellectual Property & Technology** | Stephen G Bullock |
| **Tax** | John W Colbert |
| **Probate, Trusts & Estate Planning** | Hirschel T Abbott |
| **Healthcare** | Michael D Landry |
| **Insurance Coverage & Regulation** | Wayne J Lee |
| **Public Utility Regulation** | Michael R Fontham |

**Probate, Trusts & Estate Planning:** Stone Pigman has an extensive probate, trust and estate practice, which involves a full range of estate planning, representation of trust beneficiaries and fiduciaries, and the establishment, qualification and representation of public and private charitable organizations.

**Healthcare:** Firm lawyers handle a full spectrum of litigation and business matters related to healthcare and the pharmaceutical industry for hospitals and hospital service districts; diagnostic and treatment ancillary facilities; large and small physician groups and sole practitioners; nursing homes and continuing care retirement communities; home health agencies; pharmaceutical companies; academic institutions; healthcare insurers; and medical research organizations.

**Insurance Coverage & Regulation:** Stone Pigman has insurance-related litigation experience with both American and London companies. Firm lawyers also have experience in insurance regulatory matters.

**Public Utility Regulation:** The firm's lawyers have practiced before the Louisiana Public Service Commission, United States Supreme Court, United States district and appellate courts, Federal Energy Regulatory Commission, other state public service commissions, the Securities and Exchange Commission, Federal Communications Commission and Louisiana state courts. The rate cases and other litigation have involved numerous utilities and electric, gas and telecommunications carriers.

### How lawyers are ranked

Every year we carry out thousands of in-depth interviews with clients and lawyers in order to assess the reputations and expertise of business lawyers across the USA. Chambers rankings and editorial are referred to extensively by General Counsel and other purchasers of legal services who look to our recommendations when choosing their lawyers.

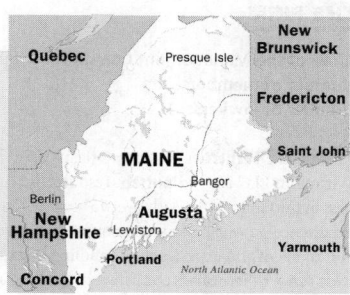

## CORPORATE/M&A

### Corporate/M&A
### Leading Firms

1. **PIERCE ATWOOD LLP** *Portland*
   **VERRILL DANA, LLP** *Portland*
2. **BERNSTEIN SHUR** *Portland*
   **DRUMMOND WOODSUM & MACMAHON** *Portland*
3. **EATON PEABODY** *Bangor*
   **PRETI FLAHERTY BELIVEAU & PACHIOS** *Portland*
   **RUDMAN & WINCHELL LLC** *Bangor*

### Leading Individuals

★ **ZIMPRITCH James** *Pierce Atwood LLP*
1. **FRYER Gregory** *Verrill Dana, LLP*
   **HIGH Michael** *Drummond Woodsum & MacMahon*
   **MCKAY Daniel** *Eaton Peabody*
2. **CHAMPOUX David** *Pierce Atwood LLP*
   **EATON II George** *Rudman & Winchell LLC*
   **SAUNDERS Eric** *Bernstein Shur*
3. **CARPENTER John** *Bernstein Shur*
   **GOOGINS Mark** *Verrill Dana, LLP*
   **LOGIUDICE Susan** *Preti Flaherty*
   **MACEWAN Alan** *Verrill Dana, LLP*
   **TUMLIN Wayne** *Bernstein Shur*

### Corporate/M&A: Bankruptcy
### Leading Individuals

1. **AMORY Daniel** *Drummond Woodsum & MacMahon*
   **CLEMENT JR Roger** *Verrill Dana, LLP*
   **KEACH Robert** *Bernstein Shur*
   **MANHEIMER Jacob** *Pierce Atwood LLP*
   **MARCUS Benjamin** *Drummond Woodsum & MacMahon*
   **MARCUS George** *Marcus, Clegg & Mistretta*
2. **ALLEN Gayle** *Verrill Dana, LLP*
   **BOPP III Fred** *Perkins, Thompson*
   **MCVEIGH John** *Preti Flaherty*
   **MORRELL Stephen** *Eaton Peabody*

### Up-and-coming individuals

**FAGONE Michael** *Bernstein Shur*

## Band 1

### Pierce Atwood LLP

See firm details p.1022

**The Firm:** Sources assert that this team, "*on a person-for-person basis, is easily as good as any in the country.*" It is made up of "*dedicated, high-quality*" corporate attorneys engaged in a striking transaction-focused practice. In a busy year, they have handled several large private transactions. The group serves both regional and national institutional clients. Peers agree that its sheer depth ensures its status as an "*always strong player in the market.*" It has an "*impeccable*" M&A reputation, particularly representing buyers and sellers in the technology, manufacturing and service sectors.

**The Lawyers:** The "*absolutely outstanding*" **Jim Zimpritch** (see p.1017) is hailed as "*the dean of corporate lawyers in Maine.*" Sources portray him as "*a smart and careful draftsperson*" well able to "*gauge a deal and not overplay his hand.*" He has a broad practice advising financial institutions on bank and insurance regulation, acquisitions and permitted activities. He also handles M&A for privately held companies, corporate governance issues and general commercial transactions. Seasoned bankruptcy practitioner **Jack Manheimer** (see p.1014) is "*a gifted advocate in the courtroom.*" He represents debtors, creditors and operating trustees in Chapter 11 reorganizations, debtor-creditor relations and a string of commercial transactions. Displaying "*strong analytical skills,*" he earns praise as a smart and personable attorney who is just the thing for large-scale matters. **David Champoux** (see p.1011) has a knack for "*taking his client's position and riding it hard.*" He has a reputation as a sharp and articulate negotiator who is "*aggressive, but neither obstructionist nor nit-picky.*" His workload consists of corporate, finance and M&A matters, as well as securities law and SEC reporting and compliance issues. He recently represented BlueTarp Financial in a $15 million venture capital financing.

**Clients/Work Highlights:** MEMIC; Dexter Enterprises; FNB Bankshares; Eaton Vance; Maine Mutual Group; First National Bank of Damariscotta; Casella Waste Systems; American Skiing; Fraser Timber; First National Lincoln; UCompareHealthCare and BiODE.

### Verrill Dana, LLP

See firm details p.1024

**The Firm:** This firm offers the largest business and securities law group in the state, earning a reputation as "*the obvious one-stop shop for corporate matters.*" Sources are impressed with the attorneys' "*judgment and collegiality,*" declaring them "*as skilled and as friendly as any in Maine.*" The focus is on general corporate law, tax, and securities involving a substantial amount of spin-off corporate work. Financial institutions drive much of the load. On the bankruptcy side, six lawyers are experienced in all types of business bankruptcy proceedings, typically representing debtors, creditors, landlords and owners of IP in the restructuring of companies in financial distress.

**The Lawyers:** Chairing the bankruptcy and commercial law department, **Roger Clement** (see p.1011) is a "*thoroughly prepared and very constructive problem solver.*" He specializes in troubleshooting distressed companies. An expert in Chapter 11 proceedings, he also has a niche in debtor-side workouts and restructuring. Up-and-comer **Gayle Allen** (see p.1010) is one of the Chapter 7 liquidation trustees nominated by her peers to handle trustee work. Sources confirm her "*strong background and great skills.*" Preeminent securities lawyer **Greg Fryer** (see p.1012) co-heads the securities law practice. He also handles venture capital work and is known for drafting legislation. The "*terrific*" **Mark Googins** (see p.1012) enters *Chambers'* tables this year in recognition of his involvement in commercial finance and corporate transactions for businesses. He serves as general counsel for public and private companies such as Devine Tarbell, and is portrayed as a "*solid, collegial lawyer who is easy to work with and knows how to get a deal done.*" **Alan MacEwan** (see p.1013) is a "*practical deal lawyer*" who specializes in business acquisitions and sales, corporate finance and contract work. Interviewees find him a pleasure to work with, saying: "*He really strives to impress.*"

**Clients/Work Highlights:** Diversified Communications; Agfa-Gevaert; Presidential Financial; Bangor Hydro Electric; Village Ventures; EMSOURCE; Grimmel Industries; ViA Marketing & Design; Devine Tarbell & Associates; HighPoint Capital; Orion Ropeworks/Canada Cordage; Speltz & Weis; IntelliCare; JobsInTheUS.com; Seabrook International; Firstmark Corporation; ImmuCell and Time Wise Management Systems.

## Band 2

### Bernstein Shur
See firm details p.1018

**The Firm:** Though smaller than its competitors, this group of "*bright sparks*" has the capacity to handle sizable projects and prides itself on its "*entrepreneurial style.*" In addition to a preeminent litigation practice, the firm offers an excellent broad-based business service that includes the formation of corporate entities, M&A, joint ventures, equity financing and partnership advice. Work is allocated to deal attorneys spread throughout the firm, and observers admit the group's success at "*choosing the personalities for a case.*" The thriving bankruptcy practice is a power in northern New England, with eight attorneys counseling clients in complex reorganizations and liquidations under Chapter 11 and Chapter 7, large commercial insolvencies, and insolvency-related litigation. Recent highlights include acting as co-counsel for the debtor-in-possession in the largest Chapter 11 reorganization in Maine's history, involving Pegasus Satellite Television and twenty affiliates.
**The Lawyers:** "*Aggressive courtroom advocate*" **Bob Keach** (see p.1013) handles debt work in and out of court, representing upper to midmarket companies in the region; the other facet of his practice centers on distressed M&A, acting buyer-side for national parties looking for targets. **Eric Saunders** (see p.1016) "*covers a lot of ground,*" say sources, with "*a personal touch that is perfect for family-owned businesses.*" He also represents clients in the medical sector. Rising star **John Carpenter** (see p.1011) is "*a kind of junior Eric Saunders,*" according to sources. As well as his excellent bedside manner, he brings impressive drafting skills and judgment to deals that often have an IP twist. **Wayne Tumlin** (see p.1017) is said to be "*the best of the bunch*" on the securities end, impressing sources with his intelligence and technical proficiency. Up-and-coming bankruptcy specialist **Michael Fagone** (see p.1012) is "*good at details,*" say observers, and rapidly making his mark in this field.
**Clients/Work Highlights:** UnumProvident; Principal Financial Services; Waynflete School; Georgia-Pacific; Great Northern Paper; Androscoggin Energy; Irving Tanning; Lincoln Paper and Tissue; Anthem Blue Cross and Blue Shield; RJ Reynolds; Rite Aid; Northwest Airlines; McDonald's; Ford; University of Maine System; State Street Capital Markets; Citizens Financial Group and Citizens Bank New Hampshire.

### Drummond Woodsum & MacMahon
See firm details p.1019

**The Firm:** This firm's strength lies in the great volume of deals its attorneys handle. The lawyers "*excel at everything they put their minds to,*" interviewees report. The "*fascinating practice*" is fed by certain deep specialties, such as a nationally recog-

nized Indian law offering and a strong bankruptcy team. This year the group has seen an increase in the number of gaming transactions and work for privately held businesses. Highlights include representing long-standing client Binax in a $44 million sale to Inverness Medical Innovations.
**The Lawyers: Dan Amory** (see p.1010) is a seasoned member of the bankruptcy Bar and "*an extremely smart man,*" according to peers. His judgment and courtroom skills make him a firm favorite for Chapter 11 proceedings. He is experienced in commercial law and has carried out a substantial amount of gaming work this past year. **Ben Marcus** (see p.1014) has a niche in insolvency law and is described as "*a well-rounded commercial lawyer – incredibly intelligent, articulate and pragmatic.*" His clients include commercial lenders in Maine and beyond, as well as Canadian businesses in the aquaculture industry. **Michael High** (see p.1012) garners praise as "*a real high-end Renaissance lawyer.*" He has a broad and busy practice representing banks doing commercial financings. He demonstrates an effective and pleasant approach to peers and clients alike.
**Clients/Work Highlights:** Portsmouth Paper; Foxwoods Development; Stonewall Kitchen; CEI Ventures; Maine Trailer; Rich Technology International; Stormwater360; local venture capital firms and investors and a number of Latin American aquaculture companies.

## Band 3

### Eaton Peabody
See firm details p.1020

**The Firm:** This "*gang of talented lawyers*" dominates business in Bangor, representing clients ranging from small businesses in Maine to midsized and publicly held companies elsewhere. Given its location in the Northeast's timberland, the group's Canadian-American focus is a unique selling point: it has a niche representing Canadian entities in cross-border transactions involving large tracts of land. Clients also come from the fishing and agriculture industries. Notable projects include representing a large Canadian aquaculture firm in the acquisition of two US aquaculture companies, and the representation of a consortium of 170 Maine communities in a PPP for a regional waste-to-energy facility. On the bankruptcy side, three lawyers represent debtors and creditors, trustees and creditors' committees in a range of insolvency matters. Clients praise the team as "*always willing to give us anything we need, and identify any trends.*"
**The Lawyers:** Managing partner **Dan McKay** (see p.1014) is revered as "*the best in Bangor*" for general corporate work, healthcare and antitrust matters. Sources admire his professional demeanor and local business sense. Epitomizing client comments, one source declared: "*He's probably the most gifted attorney I've ever worked with at finding compromises,*" and "*he early identifies ways to eliminate costs.*" **Steve Morrell** (see p.1015) divides his time between bankruptcy and business disputes and litigation.

**Clients/Work Highlights:** Eastern Maine Healthcare Systems; The Municipal Review Committee; Bangor Savings Bank; Bar Harbor Bankshares; Kmart and Ames Department Stores.

### Preti Flaherty Beliveau & Pachios, LLP
See firm details p.1023

**The Firm:** This firm impresses with "*the maturity and seriousness of a firm several times its size,*" according to clients. Peers add: "*It is a classic personality firm with an extraordinarily successful lobbying practice.*" Traditionally strong in litigation, legislative lobbying and healthcare practices, the team is particularly suited to transactional work with a public-private element. "*The caliber of the staff is second to none – they are certainly at the top of their game,*" clients report. This year the group has seen fewer intricate corporate transactions, more real estate matters and significant volumes of M&A. Recent highlights include representing the owner in the $100 million-plus sale of an 'inside-the-fence' power generating facility. It also handled the corporate restructuring and related refinancing of a 71-unit residential senior housing and assisted living community housing project in Maine.
**The Lawyers:** Bankruptcy litigator **John McVeigh** (see p.1014) is "*very constructive in terms of problem solving,*" say sources. He concentrates on creditors' rights, commercial disputes and bankruptcy matters. **Susan LoGiudice** (see p.1013) is a "*conscientious and technically gifted*" lawyer who specializes in M&A and outside general counsel. She strikes clients as "*extremely capable and willing,*" and "*able to see both the big and the small picture.*"
**Clients/Work Highlights:** Hussey Seating; Kingspan Group; Mid-Maine Communications; SurePoint Reinsurance Advisors; Maine Turnpike Authority; Bath Iron Works; Elmet Technologies; KeyBank National Association; Boothbay Harbor Shipyard; PowerPay; UBS Financial Services and University of Maine System.

### Rudman & Winchell LLC
**The Firm:** This midsized firm is a force in Bangor, sought out by clients who like its "*down-to-earth, not at all stuffy*" style. A "*superstar*" team of seven is involved in transactions of all sizes, from local deals to million-dollar cases for clients in Maine and beyond. Attorneys handle a substantial amount of work for nonprofit organizations. Because of its location, the group has a significant timberland practice and a substantial Canadian client base. It can draw on experience in the energy, hospitality, automobile and yacht-building sectors. Recent highlights include the completion of a $12 million acquisition for Village Car Company. The group also counseled a construction company in the acquisition of a competitor.
**The Lawyers: George Eaton** "*can take a tough deal,*" agree sources. His diverse practice covers M&A, venture capital financings and consulting services for family-owned enterprises, including corporate governance and compliance work. Peers are reassured by his knowledge, admitting: "*He can take complex issues*

*on his shoulders and say you're OK!"*

**Clients/Work Highlights:** Village Car Company; Prentiss & Carlisle; Sargent Corporation; Lafayette Hotels; James W. Sewall; Stillwater Scientific Instruments and Gagne Precast.

## Other Notable Practitioners

*"Phenomenal"* lawyer **George Marcus** of Marcus, Clegg & Mistretta PA has over 30 years of experience in corporate commercial matters. Sources praise him as *"a business-savvy, goal-oriented guy with street-smart skills."* He has seen fewer Chapter 11 proceedings this year, but has instead been busy handling substantial deals, out-of-court workouts and commercial litigation matters. **Fred Bopp** of Perkins, Thompson, Hinckley & Keddy, P.A. is *"developing into a very strong bankruptcy practitioner,"* according to sources, who admire his *"congenial style,"* declaring him *"accommodating and cooperative."*

# EMPLOYMENT

### Employment: Mainly Defendant
**Leading Firms**

| | |
|---|---|
| 1 | MOON, MOSS & SHAPIRO, P.A. *Portland* |
| | PIERCE ATWOOD LLP *Portland* |
| 2 | DRUMMOND WOODSUM & MACMAHON *Portland* |
| | EATON PEABODY *Bangor* |
| | RUDMAN & WINCHELL LLC *Bangor* |
| 3 | BERNSTEIN SHUR *Portland* |
| | PRETI FLAHERTY BELIVEAU & PACHIOS *Portland* |
| | VERRILL DANA, LLP *Portland* |

**Leading Individuals**

| | |
|---|---|
| 1 | MCGILL Linda *Bernstein Shur* |
| | MOON Richard *Moon, Moss & Shapiro* |
| 2 | ERWIN James *Pierce Atwood LLP* |
| | JACOBS Peter *Pierce Atwood LLP* |
| | JOHNSTON Thomas *Eaton Peabody* |
| | LEPAGE Margaret *Pierce Atwood LLP* |
| | MCGUIRE Frank *Rudman & Winchell LLC* |
| | MESSERSCHMIDT Michael *Preti Flaherty* |
| | PAYNE Clare *Eaton Peabody* |
| | PRINGLE Harry *Drummond Woodsum & MacMahon* |
| | SHAPIRO Jonathan *Moon, Moss & Shapiro* |
| 3 | BENNETT Peter *The Bennett Law Firm PA* |
| | CURRIER Douglas *Verrill Dana, LLP* |
| | DEROSBY Anthony *Pierce Atwood LLP* |
| | HEWEY Melissa *Drummond Woodsum & MacMahon* |
| | O'BRIEN Timothy *Verrill Dana, LLP* |
| | OLIVIER Elisabeth *Preti Flaherty* |
| | UHL Eric *Moon, Moss & Shapiro* |

**Up-and-coming individuals**

| | |
|---|---|
| | STOREY Anne-Marie *Rudman & Winchell LLC* |

### Employment: Employee Benefits
**Leading Individuals**

| | |
|---|---|
| 1 | BACHELDER Stephen *Moon, Moss & Shapiro* |
| | EINSIEDLER JR Charles *Pierce Atwood LLP* |
| | GINN Greg *Verrill Dana, LLP* |
| | SHAPIRO Jonathan *Moon, Moss & Shapiro* |
| | SINGER Brent *Rudman & Winchell LLC* |
| | WAKELIN David *Wakelin, Hallock & O'Donovan* |

## Band 1

### Moon, Moss & Shapiro, P.A.

See firm details p.1021

**The Firm:** This five-partner boutique is *"well known as one of the premier employment defense firms in northern New England."* Central to its success is its ability to cover matters comprehensively due to the manifest expertise of all its lawyers. The firm handles the full spectrum of employment matters and is well known for its representation of companies in the hospitality and insurance industries, such as Starwood Hotels and Resorts, for which it has been handling grievance arbitrations. The recent departure of Linda McGill from the team has been viewed as regrettable but unlikely to adversely affect the fortunes of the firm. As one commentator stated: *"You cannot knock the amount of talented individuals they have in all areas – they can more than absorb the blow."* Clients stated that they choose the firm for its *"creativity, high standard of service and cost-effective rates."* Catering to every conceivable facet of the subject, including employee benefits, this is a firm whose *"high level of responsiveness and impressive know-how"* make it catnip to the discerning customer.

**The Lawyers:** Interviewees have high regard for **Richard Moon**'s (see p.1014) *"judgment and legal ability."* He is one of the premier employment lawyers in the state because he is *"tough-minded, creative, always responsive and does a good job"* for his clients. He has been involved in cutting-edge work before the NLRB on the issue of unions enforcing card-signing recognition agreements, and also co-counseled Bowater Paper on its successful defense of a class action healthcare benefits claim. Sources revealed that *"seldom with him do you get the sense that he has not come across an issue before."* He continues to advise on union-related matters for clients such as Blethen Maine Newspapers and Smiths Tubular System, and defends technology clients on immigration matters. *"Detail-oriented"* **Jonathan Shapiro** (see p.1016) oversees litigation matters while also counseling and planning strategies for companies nationwide. Advice on handbooks and policies is his forte, and he has clients ranging from private equity firms and publishing companies to hotels and large financial institutions. Further praised for his work on wage and hour issues, he is a *"careful and analytical attorney who gets things done."* Clients spoke of an attorney with *"good business sense and judgment"* who *"it pays to take seriously."* Employee benefit matters provide an additional aspect to Shapiro's practice, and he regularly handles the litigious elements associated with benefit claims. Trial lawyer **Eric Uhl** (see p.1017) has the *"ability to be imaginative and look for solutions that are not necessarily litigation-focused."* As his profile increases in the industry he is regularly receiving referrals and is *"definitely a name to look out for."* Recently he won a $1.2 million disability religious discrimination jury trial. **Stephen Bachelder** (see p.1010) is one of the key figures on the employee benefits and executive compensation side. *"Combining technical proficiency with a wealth of experience,"* he was lauded for his work negotiating contracts, designing and implementing plans and advising on compliance with tax issues.

### Pierce Atwood LLP

See firm details p.1022

**The Firm:** This *"well-structured"* Portland-based firm has 14 attorneys engaged in the full spectrum of employment services, with specific expertise in benefits, workers compensation, tax and litigation. The group is widely admired for the *"number of leading professionals who can sort out the task at hand,"* all of whom *"work in the interest of its clients."* As one of the largest full-service firms in Maine, it attracts fine clients and has the luxury of being able to call upon specialist practitioners in the areas of corporate, tax and immigration to support its employment department.

**The Lawyers:** Commentators enthusiastically recommended **Margaret Coughlin LePage** for *"litigation work of the highest quality."* *"Fair-minded and with a great demeanor,"* she practices all aspects of employment law including discrimination and harassment, wrongful discharge, drug testing, employee benefits and union management disputes. In recent years she has been focusing on sexual harassment and disability discrimination matters and is now *"assuredly one of the stars of the team."* **Peter Jacobs** (see p.1012) is an excellent lawyer who represents a number of large hospitals and healthcare providers. He handles discrimination complaints, collective bargaining, union negotiations, organizing campaigns and NLRB proceedings. **Anthony Derosby** (see p.1011) has a niche practice in OSHA and immigration law. He represents multinational business organizations that need to move workers from one country to another and is increasingly advising healthcare organizations in the northern Maine borders. **Charles Einsiedler** chairs the firm's employee benefits practice team. Displaying an active practice, he advises employers on a wide range of compliance issues such as COBRA, the Health Insurance Portability and Accountability Act, the Uniformed Services Employment and Reemployment Rights Act and FMLA. He has also led court challenges to statutes and regulations intended to restrict employer flexibility. "*Terrific*" **James Erwin** (see p.1011) is chair of the firm's employment and eemployee benefit group and is a highly regarded trial lawyer. He has extensive experience in litigating before the state and federal courts, at trial, appellate and administrative levels. He is "*talented and always does a great job.*" He also counsels clients on labor issues and conducts investigations into sexual harassment claims for employers. He is described as "*intellectually strong, with a sharp mental ability to match.*"

## Band 2

### Drummond Woodsum & MacMahon
See firm details p.1019

**The Firm:** This firm has ten lawyers specializing in various areas of employment and labor law. The team has a renowned public sector practice and dominates the field of school law, but also has an interesting list of private sector clients, mainly in the technology field. Additionally it represents Native American tribes. This "*wonderfully slick*" group is highly recommended because it is "*approachable, knowledgeable and clients feel they receive added value by virtue of the attention given by the lawyers.*" One such client noted that: "*The team is worth every penny we budget for it.*"

**The Lawyers:** A "*fine consultative lawyer,*" **Harry Pringle** (see p.1015) is a good strategist who, while not being afraid of a fight, regularly settles cases, thus avoiding litigation and public scrutiny for his clients. Many of his cases relate to issues concerning highly paid executives but he is also noted as a leader in school law. "*Inventive,*" he "*looks at the needs of the situation and knows how to apply the law in a savvy way.*" Clients love him because "*he works hard at establishing relationships that are grounded in respect.*" "*Superstar*" **Melissa Hewey** (see p.1012) is noted for her strength in employment litigation where she proves "*capable in the courtroom, able to keep her composure and professional at all times.*" She has been seeing an increase in matters involving school and other public sector employees suing their employers and a rise in retaliation claims. Her recent cases include representing the schools in Coal v SAB no1, a case where a teacher claimed he had suffered professionally following his complaints about the curriculum.

### Eaton Peabody
See firm details p.1020

**The Firm:** Sources consider this Bangor-based firm to be one of the leading players in the northern Maine region. With five offices in the state, it is able to provide both a community-based and statewide legal service. The employment group is made up of some "*very capable lawyers*" who enjoy a good reputation in the field. It works with employers on a broad range of employment issues such as ADA, FMLA, disability, sexual harassment and municipal labor law. It also provides advice to clients with regards to employment handbooks.

**The Lawyers:** **Thomas Johnston** (see p.1013) is an "*excellent negotiator who is able to think outside the box.*" He concentrates on employment relations and employee benefits and represents management in both the private and public sectors. Commentators think well of him because he is "*easy to work with and cuts through everything with the minimum of posturing.*" **Clare Payne** (see p.1015) is "*particularly strong at advising clients.*" She has been handling sexual harassment investigations for some time now but is increasingly focusing on FMLA work. She represents a broad spectrum of clients including public, private and nonprofit employers.

### Rudman & Winchell LLC

**The Firm:** This "*stellar*" Bangor-based firm serves a wide range of clients and is well regarded for its litigation skills. The employment group has three generalists: two senior litigation lawyers principally handling workers' compensation and OSHA issues, and an ERISA expert. Clients trust the firm because it "*has a certain integrity, professionalism and confidentiality that inspires confidence.*" Interviewees also praised its responsiveness and helpfulness, with one stating: "*The lawyers always get back to us immediately and would come to our location at the drop of a hat.*" The team also offers additional services in the form of monthly seminars and annual all-day training sessions.

**The Lawyers:** "*Truly dedicated and conscientious,*" **Frank McGuire** is an employment law generalist with a great wealth of experience. His litigation practice has grown substantially and he has been defending several cases relating to sex discrimination and whistle-blowing. He is a "*very thorough and careful lawyer,*" much patronized by healthcare organizations, public utilities, hospitality firms and commercial enterprises. He also handles administrative complaints for the Maine Human Resources Association. "*Energetic*" **Anne-Marie Storey** practices general employment and labor law. Sources say she is "*conscientious and a person who attends to the utmost detail. She will go through everything to ensure she comes to the right decision for her clients.*" Storey is also a frequent speaker at seminars on employment-related topics. **Brent Singer** is recognized for his strength in the employee benefits and executive compensation field. However, sources pointed to his handling of ERISA and ERISA-related litigation as being his strongest suit.

## Band 3

### Bernstein Shur
See firm details p.1018

**The Firm:** Renowned for its "*tremendous book of corporate clients*" and municipalities work, this well-supported employment practice has been growing steadily since the arrival of Linda McGill from Moon, Moss & Shapiro. The group now has five senior lawyers each focusing on specific areas of employment law. Areas of concern include disability and age discrimination cases and general labor law for schools in Maine. Attorneys also focus on private sector work, advising businesses on IP and noncompete matters, and prove particularly effective at employee benefits and executive compensation work. Also, as litigation becomes more and more expensive and protracted, the team has taken to providing seminars dedicated to dispute prevention for its business clients.

**The Lawyers:** "*Clearly an outstanding name in the field,*" **Linda McGill**'s (see p.1014) practice continues to cover the full range of labor and employment law, representing both private and public sector employers. She is well thought of in the industry for her work for municipalities, towns and counties, an area in which she is widely held to be the best around. Her interests also lie in sexual harassment, whistle-blower retaliation and disability matters, and she has experience in handling litigation before the Maine Human Rights Commission. "*One of the state's finest practitioners,*" she is also tackling an increasing amount of work in the labor management area and has been negotiating a series of collective bargaining agreements with an array of unions.

**Clients/Work Highlights:** Bath Iron Works; Maine Community College System; Community Counseling Center; UNUMProvident; Wright Ryan Construction; Waynflete School and University of Maine Systems Office.

### Preti Flaherty Beliveau & Pachios, LLP
See firm details p.1023

**The Firm:** Eight attorneys provide general counsel on a wide range of employment law issues and advise on day-to-day management and employee relations. The group includes a union expert, an immigration specialist and an employee benefits guru, allowing it to offer a truly diverse service. It also represents employers in unfair labor practice charges and union election proceedings before the NLRB. Clients appreciate the team philosophy on show, asserting that "*when you work with the firm you are not getting one attorney's opinion but the expertise of the whole firm.*" They also welcome the fact that "*the fees are incredibly reasonable and the service is wonderful.*"

**The Lawyers:** Practice chair **Michael Messerschmidt** (see p.1014) is well regarded throughout the state as "*smart, intelligent and dependable.*" Involved in arbitration, litigation and negotiations, he has niche specialties in downsizing issues and internal company investigations where he represents both unionized and nonunionized clients. His votaries appreciate his personal approach: "*He notifies me of* *any new changes in the laws and immediately makes me feel as if I am his only client,"* said one interviewee. Peers are similarly impressed with his work and ethics, with more than one referring to the fact that they would like him on their team. **Elisabeth Oliver** (see p.1015) is a healthcare and employment specialist who regularly advises hospitals and other healthcare providers on a variety of employment-related matters. She is highly rated by peers for having *"firm grounding in the law and a good sense of what employers should and should not do."* Clients are fond of her because she is *"attentive, responsive and gets results."* **Clients/Work Highlights:** The firm has advised an employer operating several private schools on how to avoid unionization by the State Employees' Association of New Hampshire and assisted an industrial employer through a wage and hour audit. In other matters, it has advised manufacturing clients on the downsizing of supervisory ranks, performing risk and demographic analyses of those individuals whose positions were to be eliminated.

## Verrill Dana, LLP

See firm details p.1024

**The Firm:** This well-rounded team has nine lawyers involved in a variety of employment law issues. It has strengths in a series of industries, including the sport, nursing home, construction and hospitality sectors,

and has one of the biggest employee benefits and executive compensation practices in the state. Interviewees have been *"favorably impressed"* with this team of strong lawyers.

**The Lawyers: Douglas Currier** (see p.1011) has been in the employment and immigration fields for a long time, litigating and providing counsel to management. Described as *"really easy to work with,"* one highlight of his work has been winning against a union campaign relating to a healthcare facility in Maine. He is also very active in the area of whistleblower discrimination and is felt to be a *"nice guy who does a fine job."* *"Wonderful lawyer"* **Tim O'Brien** (see p.1015) has 20 years' experience representing management in a wide variety of labor and employment issues. Interviewees found him to be *"a good thinker who cuts through the garbage and focuses on getting results."* A lawyer who *"gets it spot on,"* he also represents the public sector and has acted for York County regarding both general employment and union issues. With a niche practice in sports law, he also handles employment contracts for athletes, coaches and organizations. *"Really smart and clued up"* **Greg Ginn** (see p.1012) generated praise across the board for his *"undeniable presence in the market."* Chair of the firm's employee benefits group, he concentrates his practice on the design, drafting and operation of qualified and nonqualified retirement

plans, ERISA welfare benefit plans and executive compensation agreements.

**Clients/Work Highlights:** Kennebec Savings Bank; Bowdoin College; First Atlantic Healthcare; LL Bean; Timberland; Hannaford Bros; TD Banknorth; IDEXX Laboratories and Wright Express.

## Other Notable Practitioners

Assisting management throughout New England in dealing with union issues, **Peter Bennett** of The Bennett Law Firm PA is *"absolutely masterful."* He has a traditional labor law practice but specializes in collective bargaining and contract administration. He represented Lepage Bakeries and Bellavance Beverage in defeating Teamster Union Local 633's attempt to represent its employees. Commentators say he is a *"a knowledgeable lawyer able to handle sophisticated work."* A number of institutional clients stay loyal to him because he is a *"good and tenacious negotiator who inspires enormous confidence."* **David Wakelin** is managing partner of Wakelin, Hallock & O'Donovan, a three-member firm located in Portland. A *"superb attorney,"* peers were quick to label him as one of the leading employee benefits and ERISA practitioners in the state, averring that his *"knowledge of the intricacies of the area is phenomenal."*

# ENVIRONMENT

| Environment |
| --- |
| Leading Firms |
| [1] PIERCE ATWOOD LLP *Portland* |
| [2] BERNSTEIN SHUR *Portland* |
| EATON PEABODY *Bangor* |
| PRETI FLAHERTY BELIVEAU & PACHIOS *Portland* |
| VERRILL DANA, LLP *Portland* |

| Leading Individuals |
| --- |
| [1] AHRENS Philip *Pierce Atwood LLP* |
| DOYLE Thomas *Pierce Atwood LLP* |
| HAMILTON P Andrew *Eaton Peabody* |
| TAYLOR William *Pierce Atwood LLP* |
| VAN SLYKE David *Preti Flaherty* |
| [2] BROWNE Juliet *Verrill Dana, LLP* |
| KILBRETH James *Verrill Dana, LLP* |
| MAHONEY Sean *Verrill Dana, LLP* |
| THALER Jeffrey *Bernstein Shur* |

## Band 1

### Pierce Atwood LLP

See firm details p.1022

**The Firm:** This firm fields the largest environmental group in the state, offering *"phenomenal resources,"* according to sources. Lawyers represent national and regional corporations in a wide range of environmental, land use, natural resource, energy,

and toxic tort issues. The firm assembles *"cutting-edge"* lawyers on cases and has seen a rise in waste management matters. Highlights include representing US Functional Foods in its efforts to license a 25 to 30-acre greenhouse project powered by an adjacent wood biomass cogeneration facility.

**The Lawyers:** Group head **Chip Ahrens** (see p.1010) earned his spurs as chief of the Natural Resources Division of the Maine attorney general's office. He counsels clients on complex regulatory and enforcement issues, land issues and waste management, winning praise as *"a thoughtful listener and proactive strategist who is strong on his feet."* Meanwhile, **Tom Doyle** (see p.1011) is a *"hands-on and aggressive"* lawyer involved in complex regulatory and corporate matters. Doyle is a heavy hitter who clients find *"excellent at dealing with boards and decision-makers."* A veteran in solid waste, he recently led proceedings to increase the disposal capacity at a state-owned secure solid waste landfill. He is currently defending the license on two appeals in the Maine Superior Court. **Bill Taylor** (see p.1017) is a water guru and handles all aspects of water and wetland regulation. Dubbing him *"the state expert on wetlands permitting,"* sources describe *"a straight shooter with great judgment – he really knows how to work with people."* He regularly represents clients before local, state and federal administrative agencies.

**Clients/Work Highlights:** Rockwell Collins; TRC Companies; SAPPI/SD Warren; OSRAM; Georgia-Pacific; Casella Waste Systems; FMC; New England

Organics; Domtar Industries and Maine Pulp & Paper Association.

## Band 2

### Bernstein Shur

See firm details p.1018

**The Firm:** This *"small but aggressive"* team of five works in tandem with the firm's environmental engineering affiliate Stratex, handling diverse work for developers, energy companies, municipalities, nonprofit organizations and small businesses. In the past busy year, the team has seen an increase in instructions for large projects, particularly in the energy area. The team is prominent in the municipal arena: it has a large and respected municipal law practice possessing *"excellent relations with regulators."* Case highlights include working on Quoddy LNG – an LNG permitting project in Quoddy Bay, and on a boat launch facility for the town of Brunswick.

**The Lawyers: Jeff Thaler** (see p.1017) is a *"skilled and aggressive trial lawyer,"* who shares his time between environmental work and a full-trial practice. He is expert in complex permitting procedures and *"knows exactly what he's doing"* before regulatory boards, according to clients.

**Clients/Work Highlights:** Endless Energy; FPL Energy; Town of Wells, Maine; Topsham Hydro; Irving Tanning and Beazer East.

## Eaton Peabody

See firm details p.1020

**The Firm:** "*Bangor's finest*" fields five lawyers in its environmental and land use group, which focuses on natural resource protection and permitting matters. It also offers expertise in wetlands and water discharge permitting and compliance, oil and hazardous waste management and solid waste. Attorneys represent private and municipal clients in state and municipal land use regulatory matters. The group took on a number of large development projects over the last year, involving permitting and approvals. For example, the team assisted the Maine Department of Inland Fisheries and Wildlife in a heavily contested proceeding before the Maine Board of Environmental Protection.

**The Lawyers:** **Andy Hamilton** (see p.1012) is celebrated as a "*thorough and smart guy who can secure his clients' interests without alienating people.*" His practice includes brownfields redevelopment counseling and he is an acknowledged expert on state and federal hazardous substance proceedings.

**Clients/Work Highlights:** The Richmond Company; Eastern Maine Healthcare Systems; Ocean Properties & Management; Grant Trailer Sales; First Hartford Corporation; City of Brewer and City of Bangor.

## Preti Flaherty Beliveau & Pachios, LLP

See firm details p.1023

**The Firm:** This large and varied practice is well known for lobbying and is a familiar name on the environmental circuit. Nine lawyers counsel Fortune 500 companies, financial institutions and developers on a range of concerns including pollution prevention and community right-to-know issues. Experts are on offer in practically every area from air, water and noise pollution to waste management, chemical regulation and land use controls.

**The Lawyers:** Group chair **David Van Slyke** (see p.1017) put in time at the US EPA, and is praised for his "*great background in government law.*" An experienced compliance lawyer, Slyke directs the firm's work in hazardous waste matters. His practice also takes him into the transactional and litigation arenas, where he handles a range of Superfund matters. "*He brings to his practice a keen understanding of private business concerns,*" note sources.

**Clients/Work Highlights:** Clients are Fortune 500 companies, financial institutions and developers.

## Verrill Dana, LLP

See firm details p.1024

**The Firm:** The team is renowned for its handling of permits for large, complex industrial projects in Maine. It is perceived as "*highly credible with the authorities,*" interest groups and citizens who oppose projects. Six attorneys concentrate mainly on permitting compliance, development and litigation. Together with the corporate group, the team negoti-

ated an agreement, the first of its kind, between one of the nation's largest utilities and its opponents to allow the restructuring of a hydropower development on the Penobscot River.

**The Lawyers:** "*Knowledgeable and capable*" group head **Juliet Browne** (see p.1010) is a "*savvy and strategic analyst and counselor,*" who devotes most of her time to the permitting of linear development projects and compliance matters. She recently obtained permits for an electric transmission line crossing New England to Canada. Former chief deputy attorney general **Jamie Kilbreth**'s (see p.1013) diverse practice covers environmental matters, securities, antitrust and complex commercial and regulatory litigation. Sources extol him as "*a thoughtful adviser and a skilled litigator.*" **Sean Mahoney** (see p.1014) is a "*proactive specialist*" in laws controlling water pollution, hazardous waste and endangered species. He is heavily involved in projects that need water quality certification from the state and also represents clients in environmental litigation.

**Clients/Work Highlights:** Bangor Hydro-Electric Company; Bowdoin College; Duke Energy; Emera; EMSOURCE; Evergreen Power/UPC Wind Management; GAC Chemical; International Paper; Loring Development Authority; Maine Audubon; Maine Community College System; Maine Department of Transportation; Maritimes & Northeast Pipeline; Natural Resources Council of Maine; Noranda; Portland Water District; Prime Tanning; Verizon Wireless; Waste Management and York County.

# LITIGATION

<table>
<tr><td colspan="2">Litigation: General Commercial</td></tr>
<tr><td colspan="2">Leading Firms</td></tr>
<tr><td>1</td><td>PIERCE ATWOOD LLP Portland</td></tr>
<tr><td>2</td><td>BERMAN & SIMMONS Portland</td></tr>
<tr><td></td><td>BERNSTEIN SHUR Portland</td></tr>
<tr><td></td><td>HARVEY & FRANK Portland</td></tr>
<tr><td></td><td>PRETI FLAHERTY BELIVEAU & PACHIOS Portland</td></tr>
<tr><td>3</td><td>EATON PEABODY Bangor</td></tr>
<tr><td></td><td>NORMAN, HANSON & DETROY, LLC Portland</td></tr>
<tr><td></td><td>RUDMAN & WINCHELL LLC Bangor</td></tr>
<tr><td></td><td>VERRILL DANA, LLP Portland</td></tr>
</table>

## Band 1

### Pierce Atwood LLP

See firm details p.1022

**The Firm:** "*If you look across the board for a general service law firm, it's the best in the state,*" agreed sources. Litigation is the largest practice area at the firm and it offers "*substantial depth and sophistication.*" A team of 35 attorneys, several of them deemed "*stellar,*" are skilled in complex commercial litigation, particularly class actions. Other areas of involvement include representing both plaintiffs and defendants in personal injury actions, insurance defense, and environmental, employment and antitrust litigation.

The firm has a blossoming IP group which advises startups and Fortune 500 companies on a full range of legal issues relating to patents, trademarks, copyrights and trade secrets. Attorneys throughout the firm are seeing an increasing volume of work outside Maine. For instance, the litigation group recently represented the State of California in the renegotiation and litigation of power contracts with a total value in excess of $43 billion.

**The Lawyers:** "*Leader of the pack*" **Bill Kayatta** (see p.1013) wins praise for his "*phenomenal*" litigation experience and commercial outlook. Clients say he is "*a strategic expert who has the ability to address simultaneous problems on a number of levels.*" Clients outside the state increasingly seek him out for his complex litigation and class action expertise. Highlights from his caseload include acting as lead counsel for the California energy regulators in a multibillion-dollar action against energy sellers. Kayatta also acts as lead counsel to the defendants in a series of ERISA class actions pending in Tennessee, and as lead defense counsel in several pending Qui Tam and class actions in Massachusetts and New York. Highly respected litigator **Peter Culley** (see p.1011) is "*organized, succinct and well liked by the jury,*" report sources, who add: "*He has a wry sense of humor and doesn't try to be flashy.*" With extensive trial experience in a range of civil and white-collar

matters, Culley typically represents financial institutions. Sources extol his capacity for complex cases: "*He knows how to weave his way through sticky situations.*" **Bob Stier** (see p.1016) enters the tables this year and is widely acknowledged as "*the main guy for patent litigation.*" Interviewees commend his intellect and "*great way with juries,*" and single out his deep specialization in patent and IP litigation. He has an international practice that finds him representing a number of European and Scandinavian clients. Recent triumphs include acting as lead trial counsel for the accused in a chromatography patent infringement action. There is a strong body of opinion that regards "*fierce trial lawyer*" **John Aromando** (see p.1010) as "*possibly the best lawyer there.*" He has a diverse litigation practice that covers the environmental, commercial, construction, insurance and personal injury areas. "*Clever and tough,*" Aromando inspires the deepest respect in peers. The popular, IP heavyweight **Jeff White** (see p.1017) heads up the practice and is also expert in civil and business litigation. Sources pay tribute to his calm approach and excellent judgment.

**Clients/Work Highlights:** Harley-Davidson; GE; Dragon Products; Toys 'R' Us; Central Maine Power; On Target Utility Services; UnumProvident; Olympia Equity Investors; MaineHealth and Hannaford Brothers.

## Band 2

## Berman & Simmons

**The Firm:** This firm has risen to fame as "*the premier personal injury litigation firm in the state,*" according to sources. Despite its compact size, it deploys attorneys who are "*highly skilled*" and "*easily able to bring the necessary resources to bear.*" The group's sole emphasis is civil litigation, which generally encompasses personal injury, medical malpractice, legal accounting and business litigation. A team of 15 attorneys takes on work via a prodigious referral network in the state, and generally on a contingency fee basis; since they habitually win seven-figure medical malpractice cases every year, this suits all concerned. Recent highlights include winning a $635,000 medical malpractice case against a well-known neurosurgeon in Maine.
**The Lawyers:** **Bill Robitzek** is recommended as "*an excellent, tenacious lawyer, who keeps fighting and doesn't give up.*" He devotes his time to personal injury work and medical malpractice, in addition to commercial litigation for individuals or small companies battling larger corporations. Peers describe him as "*a real professional,*" and "*one of the most efficient and direct trial lawyers there is.*" Trial lawyer **Jay Sweet** is "*preeminent*" in the medical malpractice market, and won the largest ever plain-tiff's verdict in a case of medical negligence in Maine. A gifted advocate who presents effectively, Sweet "*can motivate juries and get across a complex case simply,*" observe sources. He only takes on major cases and enjoys a strong reputation among insurance companies. **Steve Silin** is an effective personal injury specialist who also handles products liability, professional negligence and civil rights litigation. He impresses sources with his "*smooth and graceful approach to people: more balletic than pugnacious.*"
**Clients/Work Highlights:** The firm represents numerous local businesses, insurance companies and individuals.

## Bernstein Shur

See firm details p.1018
**The Firm:** Commenting on this "*enviably good commercial firm,*" sources cite depth and entrepreneurial spirit as reasons for its success. The litigation group houses about 30 attorneys who, though they do not all spring immediately to mind as trial attorneys, "*sure know how to write a brief.*" They represent plaintiffs and defendants in a range of commercial disputes, securities and antitrust matters. The team has a long history of success in energy and waste-related litigation, and acts as defense counsel in thousands of personal injury cases for clients across the country. Niche areas of expertise include transportation, criminal and construction litigation. For example, the group recently negotiated with four insurance carriers and obtained coverage in a claim alleging that a client was responsible for the failure of a skylight system at an airport in Virginia.
**The Lawyers:** Commentators tag firm president **Peter Rubin** (see p.1016) as a senior trial lawyer who "*stands head and shoulders above the rest.*" He has a national reputation for complex litigation in products liability, business litigation, personal injury and, especially, medical malpractice. Sources also praise his "*wealth of experience in asbestos litigation.*" The "*smart and responsive*" **Jeff Thaler** (see p.1017) is recommended on the basis of a successful trial practice with an environmental twist. Besides permitting and litigation, Thaler also undertakes commercial litigation, medical and legal negligence, insurance disputes and personal injury. Sources declare that he "*knows exactly what he is doing.*"
**Clients/Work Highlights:** IDEXX Laboratories; Owens-Illinois; Trico Mechanical; Radiology Specialists of Maine and Resort Sports Network.

## Harvey & Frank

**The Firm:** Two lawyers form the core of this esteemed litigation boutique. Commentators distinguish it from garden-variety firms, declaring it "*very witty and excellent for small cases.*" The team handles general commercial and IP litigation, as well as some employment and antitrust regulation issues. Medical malpractice and healthcare litigation is a significant part of the practice, the team's reputation having been boosted since acting for MaineHealth. The "*dynamic duo*" work with three support staff, bringing in outside resources as needed. Recent highlights include representing the plaintiffs in a national class action against a major automobile manufacturer, alleging an unlawful agreement to restrain the importation of Canadian automobile imports into the USA.
**The Lawyers:** **Bob Frank** is "*an incredibly strong analyst who can wrestle his way through very complicated regulatory antitrust issues.*" An expert in antitrust law and trade regulation, he has a reputation for being "*an accomplished persuader.*" **Chuck Harvey** is "*real good at his game,*" according to the market. He specializes in medical malpractice and commercial litigation, and is fast developing a name for himself as a mediator and arbitrator. "*He's a smart, clever, personable guy who uses humor to great effect,*" say sources.
**Clients/Work Highlights:** The State of Maine; Johnson Outdoors; FPL Energy; Iworx; Selfworx; Dead River; Spectrum Medical Group and the Maine Community College System.

## Preti Flaherty Beliveau & Pachios, LLP

See firm details p.1023
**The Firm:** Clients endorse the "*top quality*" litigation offered here, observing: "*They handle our needs with great skill, getting us out of nasty scrapes and keeping us informed and up to date.*" Trial lawyers dominate the substantial group. It has a varied practice with a generous volume of medical malpractice defense work. Lawyers pride themselves on their relationships with healthcare personnel and their familiarity with the latest scientific developments. In addition, the group has considerable expertise in complex business litigation and runs a dynamic First Amendment practice. Construction, securities and products liability litigation are also undertaken by the firm.
**The Lawyers:** Group chair **Jon Piper** (see p.1015) wins praise for his "*impressive business and communication skills,*" and for his "*ability to put himself in his clients' shoes.*" Clients find him "*aggressive, but not overly so – he gets excellent outcomes without damaging relationships.*" Arguably "*the top First Amendment lawyer in Maine,*" Piper has cornered the market in libel and communications litigation, but his principal focus is on business litigation. He achieved a record $40 million for Kingspan Group in claims of common law fraud and securities violations, and successfully defended Forbes magazine in a $10 million libel action. "*Very professional*" **Fred Frawley** (see p.1012) is acknowledged this year as "*one of the highest IP litigators in the state.*" Other areas of practice include complex business litigation, antitrust and trade regulation. Peers noted that he was an experienced speaker on trademark and employment issues and he easily won the confidence of his clients. **Rob Newton** (see p.1015) enjoys a sterling profile as a trial attorney. He concentrates on healthcare and carefully selected plaintiff work in products liability and hospital malpractice. In the past year, Newton acted as chief trial counsel for the defendant in a large, multi-plaintiff toxic tort action. **Chris Nyhan** (see p.1015) is a distinguished trial lawyer who is credited with developing the firm's healthcare group. He assists Maine hospitals and other healthcare providers on

medical staff, credentialing and employment-related issues.

**Clients/Work Highlights:** Peoples Heritage Savings Bank; Bath Iron Works; Compañia Chilena de Fósforos; Coldwell Banker Residential Brokerage; Portland Press Herald/Maine Sunday Telegram and RE/MAX By the Bay.

## Band 3

### Eaton Peabody
See firm details p.1020
**The Firm:** Market sources agree: "*If you want to try a case in Bangor, they're the firm of choice.*" Ten highly skilled attorneys in the litigation/dispute resolution practice group offer a deep pool of experience and expertise. "*They do a sterling job*" acting for both plaintiffs and defendants in antitrust and trade regulation, and contract and commercial disputes. Bankruptcy and real estate matters are key areas, and the team counts a number of insurance companies and self-insured entities as its clients. Consistent with the market trend against trials, the group is developing its alternative dispute resolution practice.
**The Lawyers:** Group chair **Bernie Kubetz** (see p.1013) is "*thorough, very sound in the law and great at evaluating cases,*" according to interviewees. His practice includes commercial disputes, products liability, employment discrimination and personal injury claims.
**Clients/Work Highlights:** Clients consist of individuals, small businesses and large companies from Maine and throughout the USA and Canada.

### Norman, Hanson & DeTroy, LLC
**The Firm:** This group built its reputation on insurance defense and personal injury litigation. It defends claims against healthcare professionals and hospitals such as the Maine Medical Center. Besides this, attorneys represent clients in every kind of civil dispute, from claims relating to business and construction, to employment, bankruptcy securities and domestic relations. The firm is also known for undertaking white-collar criminal work and has strong employment and workers' compensation practices.
**The Lawyers:** The "*entirely fabulous*" **Peter DeTroy** is celebrated for his "*versatility and great instincts.*" Sources describe him as "*a real humanist – he gets to the heart of the matter.*" DeTroy is well versed in all

kinds of civil litigation, criminal defense, professional liability and insurance matters. With a growing focus on alternative dispute resolution, he is fast developing a reputation as "*a superb mediator.*" **Mark Lavoie** is said to do "*a superlative job in complex cases.*" He has a prodigious workload centered on complex civil litigation, with particular emphasis on professional liability and discipline matters. He is equally adept in the healthcare field, with one source suggesting that Lavoie had "*tried more cases in the past year than most have tried in their careers.*" Peers highlighted his "*very keen sense of humor.*"
**Clients/Work Highlights:** Acadia Insurance; AIAC; Bath Iron Works; Boise Cascade and Maine Medical Center.

### Rudman & Winchell LLC
**The Firm:** Sources dub this "*the premier firm north of Portland,*" highlighting the group's strength in the commercial litigation market in Bangor and beyond. A ten-strong team of "*very sound*" attorneys "*do a little of everything,*" claim sources. Personal injury actions for plaintiffs and defendants and insurance defense are strong areas for the group, as are products liability law, business and employment litigation and construction claims. According to market sources, the team is adept in arbitration and mediation.
**The Lawyers:** "*If I had a matter in Bangor, I'd refer it to David King*" is the unequivocal opinion proffered by many sources around the state. He is "*certainly in the top three for insurance defense in that part of the state.*" King mainly advises healthcare providers on insurance defense, personal injury and products liability law. Fellow colleague **John McCarthy** has a broad caseload that includes tort claims, fire losses, employment disputes, products liability and first-party insurance claims.
**Clients/Work Highlights:** Webber Oil; Vermont Mutual; Husson College; Bank of America; LandAmerica and a number of individuals.

### Verrill Dana, LLP
See firm details p.1024
**The Firm:** Best known for its real estate and corporate expertise, this firm fields 25 litigators in matters ranging from bankruptcy and employment to civil rights and criminal litigation. Recent matters include negotiating the dismissal of criminal charges brought against two Rhode Island businessmen allegedly

scheming to gain entry to Martha Stewart's home. Sources acknowledge efforts to increase the depth of the trial experience here. In the past twelve months, the team has seen an increase in personal injury and products liability work. Yet it is in contract disputes, securities and antitrust class actions that the group shines. The firm has a mushrooming IP litigation practice, which has handled a number of high-profile cases this year, including the representation of BioPay in a patent litigation battle over biometric financial transactions.
**The Lawyers:** According to commentators, the heart of the team is **Jamie Kilbreth** (see p.1013), a smart lawyer who "*can handle both witnesses and arguments skillfully.*" He specializes in complex commercial and regulatory litigation, including securities, antitrust and environmental matters. The market appreciates his "*personable and nonconfrontational*" style. Sources singled out **Jim Goggin** (see p.1012) for his intellectual property expertise. A "*great trial lawyer who prepares well and wins,*" he acts as head litigator in the firm for all IP matters, including trademark, broadcast licensing fee agreements, copyright infringements, and patent litigation. He recently represented BioPay, and in a separate matter, got a jury verdict of willful trademark infringement for a local kitchen goods store against Maytag Corporation.
**Clients/Work Highlights:** Jasper Wyman & Son; BioPay; Broan-NuTone; TD Banknorth; Doten's Construction; ASCAP; Attrezzi; Black Diamond Sportswear; Chamilia; Remstar International and Sagoma Plastics.

### Other Notable Practitioners
"*Smart, organized and professional,*" **Gerry Petruccelli** of Petruccelli Martin & Haddow LLP is a popular choice for trial and appellate work. He "*walks and talks like a lawyer,*" say clients, adding that he "*makes the best statements.*" His varied practice covers anything from stockholder disputes and insurance defense work to construction law and products liability. For nearly a decade, Petruccelli has represented a class of 850 adults with mental retardation in order to force the State of Maine into compliance with an existing consent decree.

# REAL ESTATE

## Band 1

### Bernstein Shur

See firm details p.1018

**The Firm:** This well-known group boasts 13 full-time members and further draws on resources from the firm's litigation and taxation departments. Clients remarked that "*the depth demonstrated by the team gives it the capacity to deal with all real estate issues without exception.*" Collecting praise for expertise in the property sales, acquisitions, financings and leasing areas, it is said to possess a commercial development practice that is "*a cut above the rest.*" According to one interviewee, team members "*really make things happen rather than being obstructive,*" and "*always leave favorable impressions.*" The group represents many small and midsize businesses in addition to a number of Maine's largest developers and big businesses. It recently carried out the permitting, acquisition and development of numerous New England site development projects as regional coun-

sel for a significant 'big-box' retailer. Sources also noted the team's strength in the easements area, especially with regards to the forestry industry.

**The Lawyers:** Despite being managing shareholder of the firm, **Charles Miller** (see p.1014) still possesses a vibrant real estate practice according to interviewees. His caseload incorporates all elements of real estate law but he was distinguished as being a specialist in the complex commercial ground leases area, a sector in which he carries out more leasing work than any other practitioner in Maine. He recently carried out the leasing requirements for the first residential facility on the waterfront in Portland. His national reputation precedes him and he often undertakes work outside the state for Maine clients who want to expand their operations. His "*tenacity and diligence*" in practice were noted by one client who commented that he never allows "*anything to fall through the cracks.*" An "*incredibly bright gentleman,*" he is "*without question, the best real estate lawyer I have ever dealt with.*" "*Down-to-earth*" **Jamie Schwartz** (see p.1016) combines the role of chair of the real estate group with a practice spanning areas such as the acquisition, disposition, financing, management and development of real estate. He attributes a particular focus to the representation of landlords and tenants in the sphere of commercial leasing transactions. "*Approaching transactions from all sides,*" commentators felt him to be "*wonderful at understanding the nuances of the agreement even if not apparent at first blush.*" A recent highlight saw him involved in the negotiation and completion of the first phase of development with the City of Bangor in relation to Maine's first casino. **Nathan Smith** (see p.1016) remains a popular choice among sources for his commercial real estate expertise and additional environmental and land conservation skills. Appearing in large hydroelectric, waste, energy and other power projects, he was welcomed by clients for "*really knowing the ins and outs of the area.*" Large-scale transactions involving commercial development projects and multifamily housing also form a portion of his practice and, moreover, he was touted as "*one of the state's title experts.*" He recently represented various conservation organizations in fee acquisitions of more than 35,000 acres in Maine's northern forest.

**Clients/Work Highlights:** Wal-Mart; General Signal; Montreal Maine & Atlantic Railway; Florida Power and Light; The Ram Companies; First American Title Insurance; The Lyme Timber Company; New England Forestry Foundation; Waterview Development; Lincoln Paper and Tissue; University of Maine System and Maine Medical Center.

### Jensen Baird Gardner & Henry

**The Firm:** "*Mature and thoughtful attorneys*" provide counsel and represent clients on a wide variety of projects including shopping centers, malls, office buildings, housing, commercial and industrial buildings and condominiums. Commentators complimented the team on its weighty involvement

in land use and permitting issues relating to real estate transactions, where it often assists clients in proceedings before municipal boards and federal agencies. Speedy response times and lawyer availability were additional characteristics of this practice extolled by clients.

**The Lawyers:** **Kenneth Cole** has a flourishing niche practice representing municipalities in their real estate, land use and title needs. Described by sources as being "*practical, diligent and professional,*" he "*dives through the complexities of matters with ease*" and possesses skills contingent upon his "*abundant experience*" and years of practice in the field. Positive feedback from market sources resulted in **Lee Lowry**'s entrance in this year's table. "*If I had a real estate matter he is the man I would go to,*" stated one peer. He represents clients in all aspects of real estate and land use planning and is a dab hand at securing municipal, state and federal regulatory approvals. A "*no-ego type of guy*" who exhibits a "*calming aura,*" he is most recognized for his work in the commercial field regarding shopping centers. **Walter Webber** continues to gain acclaim for his years of real estate expertise. "*A name to reckon with,*" he now takes on a role as senior counsel within the group.

**Clients/Work Highlights:** The team caters to major real estate developers, lending institutions, commercial landlords and tenants in addition to individual sellers and buyers. Clients include Stewart Title Guaranty; Banknorth; Packard Development and Commonwealth Land Title Insurance.

### Pierce Atwood LLP

See firm details p.1022

**The Firm:** This heavyweight Maine firm has a "*solution-oriented*" real estate team comprising 12 "*technically solid*" attorneys. They smoothly handle the full range of land use, permitting, title, conveyancing, development and transactional matters arising in the field. Commentators cited "*wonderful local and industry knowledge*" as reasons for choosing them in large-scale transactions, particularly acquisitions and developments in the office, retail center and warehouse area. Of late, the team's caseload has included representing landlords and tenants in several large office leases such as the sale/leaseback of office headquarters for a national environmental company in Portland. Strength in the retail sector was another highly praised feature of the practice, with the team continuing to represent a major supermarket with operations spanning Maine, New Hampshire, Massachusetts, New York and Vermont on issues concerning four new sites.

**The Lawyers:** Market commentators identify group chair **Dennis Keeler** (see p.1013) as this team's leading light. Reverently described as "*one of the top in the state,*" he maintains a dynamic practice within commercial real estate, focusing on development, permitting, financing and leasing. His "*pragmatic and thoughtful stance*" in matters makes him a frequent choice as local counsel for large multistate lending transactions. In keeping with the high-profile office acquisition work undertaken by the group, he recently acted for a major office/hotel developer in the permitting, financing, leasing and development of three office buildings. His practice and reputation extend beyond the confines of the state and a portion of his workload is carried out in New Hampshire and New York. A popular attorney among clients, he was said to exhibit "*a certain magic in getting deals done.*" **Judith Woodbury** (see p.1017) counts real property title work, title insurance claims and easements among her expertise. Highly endorsed by sources for her work in complex multi-state projects within Maine and northern New England, she was further commended for the "*technical skills she brings to the table*" in transactions.

**Clients/Work Highlights:** Among recent highlights, the team is lead counsel for the seller of over $100 million of air cargo facilities in seven states. These include ground-leased facilities on major airports and fee-owned air cargo distribution facilities. The real estate team continues to represent a host of significant developers, landowners, tenants and businesses throughout Maine and New England.

### Verrill Dana, LLP
See firm details p.1024

**The Firm:** Venerated as "*one of the leading real estate groups in the state,*" this practice gathered praise for its sophisticated attorneys who "*have experience of every legal issue.*" It counsels and advises individuals, businesses and professional groups on real estate law, land use and zoning, financing, developments and leasing. Members were lauded for being "*great at finding the middle ground*" and "*realizing client objectives.*" Covering a broad scope of industry sectors and drawing on the firm's corporate, securities and banking resources if necessary, this team also provides "*quality advice even in obscure situations.*" Market sources approved of the talented younger attorneys here, feeling sure that they will guarantee strength and dominance for the firm in years to come.

**The Lawyers:** Clients value **Charles Oestreicher** (see p.1015) for his "*gentlemanly manner*" and the "*refined edge*" he brings to matters. Utilizing years of experience in the field, "*he can comfortably deal with any issue*" but, of late, has tended to act in the more high-end residential deals. He also undertakes a sizable amount of work in the easements area both for and against state agencies, especially with regards to negotiating and restricting. "*Valued partner*" **Christopher Coggeshall** (see p.1011) has a "*strong grip on leasing matters,*" say commentators. In the past year, he carried out substantial commercial leasing work throughout the state for client Aniford Brothers, a large national grocery food chain with headquarters in Maine. Clients were as one in commenting on "*the depth of analysis*" he brings to any discussion.

**Clients/Work Highlights:** GMO Renewable Resources; LandVest; Plum Creek Timber; Verizon Wireless; JM Huber; Loring Development Authority of Maine and Great Island Development Group.

### Band 2

### Eaton Peabody
See firm details p.1020

**The Firm:** Renowned for its focus on timberland issues, this well-established real estate team offers a high-quality work product to clients. Considered by some sources to be the "*best in Bangor,*" its six-strong team is known for its "*intelligent and thorough handling of matters*" and "*the wonderful local industry knowledge.*" Sales and acquisitions of numerous timberlands form a large portion of the practice, but development and commercial lending projects also feature prominently. In the past year the team has carried out a wealth of commercial lending and loan workouts.

**The Lawyers:** "*One of the state's finest,*" **Edward Leonard** (see p.1013) was deemed by peers to be a "*source of invaluable advice.*" Specializing in real estate law, he has expertise in commercial lending and loan workouts and represents a number of Maine's chief banks and developers. His work remit also encompasses natural resources law, a skill making him "*a first port of call*" in dealing with the real estate matters relating to the timber, mining, crops and aquaculture arena. Colleague **Karen Huber** (see p.1012) is most recognized for her extensive work in the timberland area where she regularly handles complex transactions. "*Always on top of things,*" market sources commended her for "*impressing when on the other side of the table.*" Banks also feature within her extensive client list.

**Clients/Work Highlights:** International Paper; Wagner Forest Management; Seven Islands Land; Prentiss & Carlisle; Pingree Associates; Bangor Savings Bank; Merrill Bank; Machias Savings Bank and United Kingfield Bank.

### Perkins, Thompson, Hinckley & Keddy, P.A.

**The Firm:** Despite the retirement of lead partner Bruce Leddy last year, this firm holds a practice of a sufficient size to ensure the full scope of issues is handled. Clients rate the team for its "*well-versed and thoroughly prepared*" members. Seeing plenty of activity on the acquisition, selling, developing and leasing front, work within the agricultural and retail spheres was highlighted as a particular strength of this team's practice. Working closely with the firm's land use team, clients further applauded the team's management of projects "*in a timely and economical fashion.*"

**The Lawyers:** The past year has seen **Paul Pietropaoli** expand his more recognizable landlord representation, office, retail and agricultural leasing practice to include tenants with matters concerning retail leasing. Distinguished for his "*technical skills,*" his "*down-to-earth nature*" was classed by clients as one of the reasons to keep going back. He was recently involved in the real estate aspects of the redevelopment of a former industrial plant into a mixed-use office and residential project, and undertook the leasing work for a 3000-acre project in Maine. Advising a host of lenders, borrowers, businesses and municipalities, **Gordon Scannell** was highlighted by interviewees for "*the wonderful thought process he

employs*" in a range of development, land use and commercial lending matters.

**Clients/Work Highlights:** The team advises numerous businesses, developers and municipalities.

### Band 3

### Drummond Woodsum & MacMahon
See firm details p.1019

**The Firm:** Situated within the firm's business service group, this commercial real estate team works closely with its corporate, tax and environmental colleagues to provide "*a flawless service, really focused on clients' needs.*" The bread and butter of the practice includes the sale, acquisition and leasing of commercial, residential and industrial real property. Another distinct niche lies in Native American law with the lawyers having represented various tribes throughout the country in a wealth of tribal housing financings. The firm is now hoping to extend its geographic remit with the opening of a new office in New Hampshire.

**The Lawyers:** "*Worthy of merit,*" **Richard Shinay** (see p.1016) is "*always good to work with.*" Demonstrating wide-ranging expertise, he particularly impresses through his understanding of complex condominium law, an asset that allows him to "*easily identify the pitfalls in any given case.*" An attorney who can "*calmly negotiate out of any problem, no matter how heated it gets,*" he has worked recently on a number of residential subdivision and condominium projects. He is also lauded for his advice to municipalities and school districts and recently acted for Colby College in the leasing of a facility for its students. In other matters he has acted for the Appalachian Mountain Club and Maine Appalachian Trail Land Trust in acquiring easements protecting wild parts of Maine.

**Clients/Work Highlights:** The team has recently acted in the conversion of the Bangor Water Works site to a low-income housing project and was also involved in the Stone Arch Village project.

### Preti Flaherty Beliveau & Pachios, LLP
See firm details p.1023

**The Firm:** Much of this team's time is taken up with sales and acquisitions, but it also regularly assists clients with advice on real estate developments, leasing and financings. "*Firmly in control in all that it does,*" it operates out of offices in Portland and Augusta.

**The Lawyers:** Commentators point to **Michael Sheehan** (see p.1016) as one of the attorneys here "*best equipped to deal with real estate matters.*" He recently acted for Harpers Development, a real estate development company, in all its real estate transactions across the state. The "*incredibly sharp*" **Michael Lane** (see p.1013) debuts in the table this year thanks to glowing feedback he received from the market. "*He always catches something that may have been missed*" say commentators.

**Clients/Work Highlights:** The team recently handled real estate transactions in Maine for Cardente Properties and its affiliates. These included the bulk sale of several blocks of property on the

Portland Peninsula, property acquisitions, large commercial leases and refinancings.

## Rudman & Winchell LLC

**The Firm:** Emitting a *"welcoming atmosphere,"* the less formal nature of this firm was perceived to be an attractive quality by clients quick to appreciate the *"high levels of attention"* they receive. Its six lawyers are located within the Bangor area and *"answer clients' problems with ease and fluidity."* They regularly deal with matters arising in the timberland industry, acting for leading paper and pulp companies, but generally demonstrate a comprehensive coverage of real estate matters. Other clients include developers, landlords and tenants, with banks and lending institutions proving particularly regular visitors to their door.

**The Lawyers: Winfred Stevens** is one of the region's leading players who peers *"have no hesitation in recommending to a client when a conflict arises."* An experienced practitioner possessing over 30 years of experience in the field, he is noted for his *"palpable know-how"* when dealing with real estate transactions, financings and title work. Active in alternative dispute resolution, he has further created a niche for himself by acting as mediator in real estate disputes, an area where his *"excellent judgment"* is particularly valued. The past twelve months have also seen him carry out substantial work for long-standing client Irving Paper. Joining him is **Hans Peterson**, who was exalted as *"one of the state's finest young lawyers."* He carries out substantial work in the commercial bank lending area and is, as one client reported, *"in the midst of a career that is set to soar in years to come."*

**Clients/Work Highlights:** JD Irving; Merrill Bank; Bangor Savings Bank; Chicago Title Insurance; McDonald's; Husson College; Quirk Auto Park and McPherson Timberlands.

## Other Notable Practitioners

**Drew Anderson** from Portland firm Murray, Plumb & Murray joins the rankings this year following widespread praise for his expertise in the area. He is a regular adviser on the purchase and sale of commercial, industrial and multifamily apartment buildings and further represents lenders and borrowers in loan transactions. Recommended by sources for his *"pragmatic approach,"* peers held him out as *"a highly skilled lawyer who is always a pleasure to deal with."*

# Leaders in Maine

### AHRENS, Philip FW
Pierce Atwood LLP, Portland
207 791 1298
pahrens@pierceatwood.com
*Recommended in Environment*
**Practice Areas:** Has concentrated on environmental matters almost exclusively since 1977. Counsels clients on complex permitting and enforcement matters before the Maine Department of Environmental Protection, the Maine Land Use Regulation Commission, and other state and federal environmental agencies. Recent successful client representation includes developers of three natural gas-fired electric generating facilities; a large-scale wind energy project; a significant expansion of a major shipyard; an airport expansion; 20-year expansion of a commercial solid waste disposal facility; and a major bottled water facility. Current client representation includes developers of a new large-scale wind energy project, a new bottled water facility and associated spring water sources, and a LNG facility.
**Prof. Memberships:** ABA, Section of Environment, Energy and Resources, Vice-Chair, State and Regional Environmental Cooperation Committee; Maine Bar Association.
**Career:** Deputy Attorney General and Chief, Natural Resources Section, Maine Attorney General's Office (1977-90).
**Publications:** 'Maine Environmental and Land Use Statutes Deskbook'.
**Personal:** JD, University of Michigan Law School, 1975; BA, Amherst College (cum laude), 1968; US Navy, 1968-72.

### ALLEN, Gayle H
Verrill Dana, LLP, Portland
207 774 4000
gallen@verrilldana.com
*Recommended in Corporate/M&A*
**Practice Areas:** Bankruptcy and commercial law; litigation.

**Prof. Memberships:** Maine, Massachusetts and California State Bar Associations; American Bankruptcy Institute; Turnaround Management Association.
**Career:** Ms Allen's practice focuses on restructuring and bankruptcy, regularly representing debtors, creditors, official committees of unsecured creditors, trustees and secured lenders. She has appeared in proceedings before the District of Massachusetts, the Southern District of New York, the District of Delaware and the District of Maryland. Ms Allen also has significant litigation experience. Ms Allen is a frequent panelist on bankruptcy related topics.
**Personal:** Education: Golden Gate University School of Law (JD, 1991); Simmons College (BA, 1982).

### AMORY, Daniel
Drummond Woodsum & MacMahon, Portland 207 772 1941
damory@dwmlaw.com
*Recommended in Corporate/M&A*
**Practice Areas:** Business disputes, workouts, commercial bankruptcy proceedings and bankruptcy litigation, focusing on business reorganization, lender liability, fraudulent transfer and related issues; also has expertise in Indian law and Indian gaming.
**Prof. Memberships:** Fellow, American College of Bankruptcy and Member, American Bankruptcy Institute; listed in Best Lawyers in America since 1987 in the field of creditors' rights.
**Career:** He joined the firm in 1973; was Chair of the Bankruptcy and Reorganization Section of the Maine Bar Association 1984-85; assisted in the enactment of the Uniform Fraudulent Transfer Act and various UCC articles by the Maine legislature; and has lectured in the field of insolvency law. He served on the Committee on Local Rules, United States Dis-

trict Court for the District of Maine, 1985-93, and the Committee on Local Rules, United States Bankruptcy Court for the District of Maine (1995-2000).
**Personal:** Yale Law School, JD 1973; Harvard College (magna cum laude) 1967; active in civic affairs.

### ANDERSON, Drew
Murray, Plumb & Murray, Portland
207 773 5651
*Recommended in Real Estate*

### AROMANDO, John J
Pierce Atwood LLP, Portland
207 791 1302
jaromando@pierceatwood.com
*Recommended in Litigation*
**Practice Areas:** Litigation: complex commercial, healthcare, suretyship, environmental, and insurance. Experience defending class actions.
**Prof. Memberships:** American Bar Association, Fidelity & Surety Law Committee; Maine State Bar Association; Maine Trial Lawyers Association; Cumberland County Bar Association.
**Career:** Boston College Law School, 1984. Clerk to Honorable Elmer H Violette, Maine Supreme Judicial Court, 1984-85. Associate at Hewes, Beals & Douglas, 1985-86. Pierce Atwood 1987-present, Partner since January 1, 1993.
**Publications:** 'The Surety's Liability for Bad Faith', 47 Me L Rev 389 (1995). Maine Chapter for ABA FSLC Payment Bond Manual 3rd ed. (to be published April 2006).
**Personal:** Born Worcester, MA June 10, 1959. University of Massachusetts, BS Zoology, 1981. Resident of Cumberland, ME, where he serves on the Board of Directors for Maine School Administrative District No 51.

### BACHELDER, Stephen G
Moon, Moss & Shapiro, P.A., Portland
207 775 6001
info@moonmoss.com
*Recommended in Employment*
**Practice Areas:** Of Counsel to Moon, Moss & Shapiro, he practices in the areas of executive compensation, related corporate transactions, and employee benefits.
**Prof. Memberships:** Admitted to practice in District of Columbia (1977); New York (1980); Maine (1987). Member: Maine State, New York State and American Bar Associations.
**Career:** Office of the Solicitor of Labor (DC); Office of Pension & Welfare Benefit Programs, US DOL (DC); Cadwalader, Wickersham & Taft (NY); Moon, Moss & Shapiro (ME); Bachelder & Dowling (ME).
**Personal:** Born Pullman, Washington, 24 August 1949. JD, Washington & Lee University (1976); AB (with honors), Middlebury College (1971).

### BENNETT, Peter
The Bennett Law Firm PA, Portland
207 773 4775
*Recommended in Employment*

### BOPP III, Fred
Perkins, Thompson, Hinckley & Keddy, P.A., Portland 207 774 2635
*Recommended in Corporate/M&A*

### BROWNE, Juliet T
Verrill Dana, LLP, Portland
207 774 4000
jbrowne@verrilldana.com
*Recommended in Environment*
**Practice Areas:** Environmental permitting, compliance and litigation. Chair, Environmental Group. Vice-Chair, Trial Department.
**Prof. Memberships:** Admitted to Bar: 1990, California; 1996, Maine. MSBA Natural Resources and Environmental Law Section.

**Career:** Skadden, Arps, Slate, Meagher & Flom (1990-93); Assistant Attorney General, Republic of Palau (1993-95); Verrill Dana (1996-present).
**Publications:** 'Brownfields: A Comprehensive Guide to Redeveloping Contaminated Property', Maine Chapter, ABA Section of 'Natural Resources, Energy and Environmental Law' (1997).
**Personal:** University of Michigan (BA, 1984); University of California, Boalt Hall School of Law (JD, 1990). Articles Editor, California Law Review, 1989-90. Trustee, Unity College.

### CARPENTER, John L
Bernstein Shur, Portland
207 774 1200
jcarpenter@bernsteinshur.com
*Recommended in Corporate/M&A*
**Practice Areas:** Co-Chair Commercial Department. John concentrates his practice in the areas of corporate law and commercial transactions such as business formations, sales, mergers and acquisitions, and debt and equity financings. He also advises clients in the area of trademark, copyright, and product distribution agreements and licensing.
**Prof. Memberships:** American, Maine State, and Cumberland County Bar Associations.
**Personal:** JD, Washington & Lee University (1984, magna cum laude); AB, Colby College (1980, cum laude).

### CHAMPOUX, David
Pierce Atwood LLP, Portland
207 791 1100
DChampoux@PierceAtwood.com
*Recommended in Corporate/M&A*
**Practice Areas:** Concentrates in corporate, finance, and general transactional representation, including all aspects of corporate, securities, and commercial law, focusing on representing corporations and individuals in a wide variety of transactional settings. Experience includes securities law, special purpose entities such as limited liability companies, M&A, venture capital financing, and SEC reporting and compliance.
**Prof. Memberships:** New York Bar (1985); Maine Bar (1987). Chair, Maine Bar's Business Law Section (2001).
**Career:** Partner, (1993-). Listed in a leading legal publication, 2003-06 editions, for corporate, M&A, and securities.
**Personal:** University of Virginia School of Law, JD 1984; Harvard College, AB (cum laude) 1981.

### CLEMENT JR, Roger A
Verrill Dana, LLP, Portland
207 774 4000
rclement@verrilldana.com
*Recommended in Corporate/M&A*
**Practice Areas:** Chair, Bankruptcy and Commercial Law Department. Extensive experience in representing Chapter 11 debtors-in-possession, trustees, creditors' committees, secured creditors, and land-

lords in local, regional and national Chapter 11 cases. Clients include railroads, healthcare institutions, technology companies, manufacturers, service companies, timber companies, landlords, acquirers of assets, banks, utilities and insurance companies in bankruptcy cases, restructurings and liquidations.
**Prof. Memberships:** Admitted to Bar: 1991, Maine. American Bankruptcy Institute.
**Career:** Partner since 1997.
**Publications:** 'Going For Broke With Intellectual Property', 17 Maine Bar Journal 178 (2002).
**Personal:** Bowdoin College (AB, 1986); University of Maine School of Law (JD, 1991); Notes Editor, Maine Law Review.

### COGGESHALL, Christopher J W
Verrill Dana, LLP, Portland
207 774 4000
ccoggeshall@verrilldana.com
*Recommended in Real Estate*
**Practice Areas:** Focuses on commercial real estate transactions, including negotiating, structuring and documenting commercial, retail and industrial developments, shopping centers, and office and apartment buildings. Has an extensive practice in drafting and negotiating commercial leases, acquisition documents and government-assisted housing projects.
**Prof. Memberships:** Admitted to Bar: 1970, Maine; 1969, New Hampshire.
**Career:** Partner, practicing at Verrill Dana for over 30 years.
**Personal:** Born: Brattleboro, Vermont, April 2, 1940. Education: Harvard Law School (LLB, 1968); Cornell University (BMetE, 1965).

### COLE III, Kenneth
Jensen Baird Gardner & Henry, Portland
207 775 7271
*Recommended in Real Estate*

### CULLEY, Peter
Pierce Atwood LLP, Portland
207 791 1288
pculley@pierceatwood.com
*Recommended in Litigation*
**Practice Areas:** Extensive experience in representing corporate interests in jury trials in all courts. Represents manufacturers, financial institutions, and professional service firms in a broad range of matters, including business litigation, professional liability and product liability actions.
**Prof. Memberships:** International Association of Defense Counsel; American Board of Trial Advocates; Fellow, American College of Trial Lawyers.
**Career:** Jacobson v Raytheon Aircraft Company: judgment for defendant client in air-crash case; Davric v Rancourt, et al: successful defense of client in conspiracy and antitrust case; Guitard v Gorham Savings Bank: judgment for bank on all claims in a class action lawsuit; and Haines, et al v Great Northern Paper

Company: successful defense of one of Maine's largest landowners in breach of contract claim seeking unlimited access to 600,000 acres of Maine forest lands.
**Personal:** Boston University, JD 1968; University of Maine, AB 1965.

### CURRIER, Douglas P
Verrill Dana, LLP, Portland
207 774 4000
dcurrier@verrilldana.com
*Recommended in Employment*
**Practice Areas:** Chair, Labor and Employment Law Department. Immigration.
**Prof. Memberships:** Admitted to Bar: 1985, Maine; US District Court, District of Maine. Maine State Bar Association Labor and Employment Law Section; National Association of College and University Attorneys.
**Career:** Having practiced law at Verrill Dana since 1985, Mr Currier has extensive experience representing employers, unionized and non-unionized, in all aspects of labor and employment law, including litigation and personnel counseling.
**Personal:** Born: Cleveland, Ohio, September 15, 1959. Education: Middlebury College (BA, cum laude, 1982); Ohio State University College of Law (JD, with honors, 1985).

### DEROSBY, Anthony R
Pierce Atwood LLP, Portland
207 791 1343
aderosby@pierceatwood.com
*Recommended in Employment*
**Practice Areas:** Directs firm's Immigration Practice Group. Practice includes all aspects of employment and immigration law. Extensive experience in business and employment immigration as well as DOL, WHA, OSHA, and IRCA compliance, inspections and enforcement.
**Prof. Memberships:** Admitted in Maine (1988) and Massachusetts (1995). Member of American Bar Association, Labor and Employment Law Committee; American Immigration Lawyers Association; American Bar Association, Occupational Safety and Health Law Committee; Massachusetts State Bar Association, Employment Law Section; and Maine State Bar Association, Employment Law Committee.
**Career:** Joined Pierce Atwood, 1988; became Partner, 1995.
**Publications:** Section Editor, 'Wage and Hour Laws: A State-by-State Survey' (ABA/BNA 2004 and 2005-06 Supplements).
**Personal:** JD (cum laude), University of Maine School of Law, 1988; University of North Carolina, Chapel Hill, 1980-81; BA (cum laude), Bates College, 1980.

### DETROY, Peter
Norman, Hanson & DeTroy, LLC,
Portland 207 774 7000
*Recommended in Litigation*

### DOYLE, Thomas R
Pierce Atwood LLP, Portland
207 791 1214
tdoyle@pierceatwood.com
*Recommended in Environment*
**Practice Areas:** Environmental and land use law, including complex adjudicatory proceedings and corporate transactions.
**Prof. Memberships:** Vice-Chair, ABA's Environmental Transactions and Brownfields Committee.
**Career:** Successfully licensed major semiconductor fabrication facility, largest industrial investment in Maine's history; successfully licensed several high profile development projects, including energy, manufacturing, and waste facilities.
**Publications:** 'A Developer's Dream or Nightmare: Maine's Site Location, Storm Water, and Traffic Permitting Laws', MSBA (2004); co-author: 'Listing Distinct Population Segments of Endangered Species: Has it Gone Too Far?', ABA's Natural Resources & Environment (2001).
**Personal:** Yale University, BA 1975; Suffolk University Law School, JD (cum laude) 1982.

### EATON II, George
Rudman & Winchell LLC, Bangor
207 947 4501
*Recommended in Corporate/M&A*

### EINSIEDLER JR, Charles
Pierce Atwood LLP, Portland
207 791 1100
*Recommended in Employment*

### ERWIN, James R
Pierce Atwood LLP, Portland
207 791 1237
jerwin@pierceatwood.com
*Recommended in Employment*
**Practice Areas:** Chair, Employment Group. Represents management in adversary proceedings and preventative services.
**Prof. Memberships:** Employment Law Alliance; ABA (Employment and Labor Relations Committee, Litigation Section); American Judicature Society (Director 2001-04); National Advisory Council 2004-); American Counsel Association (Director 2002-); Alliance for Maine's Future (Director 2005-); Maine State Bar Association
**Career:** Assistant Attorney General, Maine (major prosecutions) (1978-83); Commissioner, Maine Human Rights Commission (1985-87).
**Publications:** 'Model Jury Instructions, Employment Litigation', 2nd ed. (ABA 2005) (Board of Editors); 'Employment Litigation Handbook' (ABA 1998) (chapter author).
**Personal:** Boston University School of Law, JD 1978; Dartmouth College, AB (cum laude, high distinction) 1975.

## FAGONE, Michael A
Bernstein Shur, Portland
207 774 1200
mfagone@bernsteinshur.com
*Recommended in Corporate/M&A*

**Practice Areas:** Mike's practice focuses primarily on the representation of debtors, secured and unsecured creditors, purchasers, and other parties in bankruptcy cases, in other types of insolvency proceedings, and in out-of-court workouts. He also represents businesses and individuals in a wide range of commercial transactions, as well as in business litigation in state and federal courts.
**Prof. Memberships:** Maine State Bar Association; New Hampshire Bar Association; American Bankruptcy Institute; Turnaround Management Association
**Personal:** JD, University of Maine School of Law (1997, summa cum laude); BA, Amherst College, 1993

## FRANK, Robert
Harvey & Frank, Portland
207 775 1300
*Recommended in Litigation*

## FRAWLEY, Alfred
Preti Flaherty Beliveau & Pachios, LLP, Portland 207 791 3000
afrawley@preti.com
*Recommended in Litigation*

**Practice Areas:** Intellectual property litigation and counseling, including advice on trademark and copyright registration, licensing and management of IP assets; complex litigation.
**Prof. Memberships:** INTA, AIPLA, ABA
**Career:** Partner since 1998; Brann & Isaacson, Lewiston, Maine 1982-98; Howry & Simon, Washington, DC 1978-82.
**Publications:** Has lectured and written extensively on IP issues throughout the United States.
**Personal:** Georgetown University School of Law (LLM 1980); University of Maine School of Law (JD 1976); Dartmouth College (AB 1973).

## FRYER, Gregory
Verrill Dana, LLP, Portland
207 774 4000
gfryer@verrilldana.com
*Recommended in Corporate/M&A*

**Practice Areas:** Securities, corporate, venture capital. Has represented bidder or target in every major takeover battle in Maine since 1985.
**Prof. Memberships:** Admitted to Bar: 1981, New York; 1983, Georgia; 1985, Maine. Maine State Bar Association: Chair, Business Law Section, (1991 and 1992); Chair, Securities Law Subcommittee (1993-present); Boston Bar Association (2004-present); Drafting Committee, Maine Business Corporation Act and Maine Uniform Securities Act; Board of Directors, Maine Bar Foundation (2004-present).
**Personal:** Dartmouth College (AB, magna cum laude, 1976); Cornell University (JD, cum laude, 1979); editor, Cornell Law Review.

## GINN, Gregg H
Verrill Dana, LLP, Portland
207 774 4000
gginn@verrilldana.com
*Recommended in Employment*

**Practice Areas:** Employee Benefits and Executive Compensation.
**Prof. Memberships:** Maine State Bar Association.
**Career:** Mr Ginn is a Partner and Chair of the Employee Benefits and Executive Compensation Group and has practiced exclusively in the areas of employee benefits and executive compensation, concentrating on the design, drafting, and operation of qualified and non-qualified retirement plans, ERISA welfare benefit plans, and executive compensation arrangements.
**Personal:** Education: Harvard Law School (JD, 1981); Columbia University (MA, 1976); United States Air Force Academy (BS, 1971).

## GOGGIN, James G
Verrill Dana, LLP, Portland
207 774 4000
jgoggin@verrilldana.com
*Recommended in Litigation*

**Practice Areas:** Intellectual property and technology; litigation.
**Prof. Memberships:** Maine State Bar Association; Maine Trial Lawyers Association; American Intellectual Property Law Association.
**Career:** Over 25 years of experience litigating in the intellectual property area throughout the United States, including trademarks, copyrights, broadcast licensing fee agreements, trade secrets and patents. Admitted to Maine Bar; United States Supreme Court; First, Second, Seventh and Tenth Circuit Courts of Appeal; United States District Courts of Colorado, Delaware, Illinois, Maine, Massachusetts, New Hampshire, New York, Utah and Vermont.
**Personal:** Education: Stanford University (JD, 1979) Phi Beta Kappa; Georgetown University (BA, magna cum laude, 1975).

## GOOGINS, Mark K
Verrill Dana, LLP, Portland
207 774 4000
mgoogins@verrilldana.com
*Recommended in Corporate/M&A*

**Practice Areas:** Represents clients in the sale and acquisition of businesses and of assets, in complex commercial negotiations, and in a wide variety of lending transactions, including equipment leasing, leveraged buyouts and sale-leasebacks.
**Prof. Memberships:** Admitted to Bar: 1984, Maine; 1983, New York; American Bar Association; Maine State Bar Association; New York State Bar Association.
**Career:** Partner in Verrill Dana's Business Law Group; practiced with Milbank, Tweed, Hadley & McCloy in New York before joining Verrill Dana.
**Personal:** New York University School of Law (JD, 1982), Articles Editor, 'Annual Survey of American Law', 1981-82; Tufts University (BA, 1977).

## HAMILTON, P Andrew
Eaton Peabody, Bangor
207 992 4332
ahamilton@eatonpeabody.com
*Recommended in Environment*

**Practice Areas:** Assists clients with state and federal natural resource permitting, siting of major developments under environmental siting laws, and land use permitting under local zoning. Environmental counseling and representation of businesses in proceedings under state and federal hazardous substance and waste laws. Provides representation of developers, municipalities, and utilities before the Maine Department of Environmental Protection, Maine Public Utilities Commission, and Maine Department of Human Services.
**Prof. Memberships:** Maine and American Bar Associations (Natural Resources and Environmental Law Sections), US District Court, and District of Columbia.
**Personal:** University of Maine School of Law, 1984; Wesleyan University, BA, 1981

## HARVEY, Charles
Harvey & Frank, Portland
207 775 1300
*Recommended in Litigation*

## HEWEY, Melissa
Drummond Woodsum & MacMahon, Portland 207 772 1941
mhewey@dwmlaw.com
*Recommended in Employment*

**Practice Areas:** Complex civil litigation including school law and employment matters, defense against discrimination, sexual harassment and civil rights claims. Also has experience in a variety of forms of alternative dispute resolution.
**Prof. Memberships:** She is a Member of the Maine Trial Lawyers Association as well as the Maine State and Cumberland County Bar Associations. She serves on the Local Rules Committee of the United States District Court and is a Member of the Gignoux Inn of Court.
**Career:** Joined Drummond Woodsum and MacMahon in 1987 and is Chair of the Trial Services Group.
**Publications:** Wrote and produced training videos entitled, 'Harassment: It's About More Than Just Sex', 'Effective Staff Evaluations: A Legal Perspective', and 'Student Expulsions: Effective Practice and Procedures'. She is a contributing author to 'Maine School Law, Third Edition.'
**Personal:** University of Maine School Law (magna cum laude) JD 1987; Wesleyan University, BA 1980.

## HIGH, Michael E
Drummond Woodsum & MacMahon, Portland 207 772 1941
mhigh@dwmlaw.com
*Recommended in Corporate/M&A*

**Practice Areas:** Represents business entities, investors, lenders and borrowers in a wide range of corporate and commercial matters, including mergers and acquisitions, corporate finance, shareholder matters, private placements, venture capital financing, loan transactions, technology licensing and transfers, and intellectual property.
**Prof. Memberships:** Massachusetts Bar Association, 1983; Maine Bar Association, 1985; listed in a leading US legal publication; served as Chair of the Business Law Section of the Maine State Bar Association; Co-Chair of a Bar Subcommittee that oversaw the adoption of Revised Article 9 in Maine, and on the Corporate Law Revision Committee of the Business Law Section that revised and recommended the adoption of the Maine Business Corporation Act.
**Career:** Practiced in Boston, MA for several years before joining Drummond Woodsum; Chair of the firm's Business and Commercial Services Group.
**Personal:** Cornell Law School (1983); articles editor of the International Law Journal.

## HUBER, Karen A
Eaton Peabody, Bangor
207 947 0111
khuber@eatonpeabody.com
*Recommended in Real Estate*

**Practice Areas:** Real estate practice includes clients in the title insurance, banking and timberland industries, and individuals. Extensive experience with complex commercial and timberland transactions, including underwriting commercial and timberland titles.
**Prof. Memberships:** Maine State Bar Association (member of Title Standards subcommittee), US District Court.
**Personal:** University of Maine School of Law, 1984; University of Maine, BA, 1981.

## JACOBS, Peter
Pierce Atwood LLP, Portland
207 791 1353
pjacobs@pierceatwood.com
*Recommended in Employment*

**Practice Areas:** Labor and employment.
**Prof. Memberships:** Maine Bar Association.
**Career:** With 30 years experience, Peter represents both unionized and non-unionized employers, including a large number of hospitals and other healthcare providers, representing employers in union organizing campaigns, union contract negotiations, unfair labor practice proceedings, grievance arbitration cases. Peter also practices in the field of discrimination law before the EEOC and state discrimination agencies.

**Publications:** A twice published author, Peter is the Editor of 'Maine Business and Employment Law'.
**Personal:** Peter attended Brown University; London School of Economics; Cambridge University; and Harvard Law School, JD 1974.

### JOHNSTON, Thomas
Eaton Peabody, Bangor
207 947 0111
tjohnston@eatonpeabody.com
*Recommended in Employment*

**Practice Areas:** Chair of Employment Law Group. Represents management in a full range of employment matters, providing practical advice and legal representation regarding employment discrimination; wrongful discharge; compensation, benefits and wage and hour laws; union campaigns; labor contract negotiations and arbitration; and employee safety and health (workers' compensation, OSHA, and drug testing). Provides training to managers and supervisors on sexual harassment, negotiating skills, union organizing, hiring and interviewing, and creativity.
**Prof. Memberships:** American, Maine State and Penobscot Bar Associations, HR Association of Eastern Maine, and Society of HR Management.
**Personal:** Boston College Law School, JD 1973; Middlebury College, AB, 1970.

### KAYATTA JR, William
Pierce Atwood LLP, Portland
207 791 1100
wkayatta@pierceatwood.com
*Recommended in Litigation*

**Practice Areas:** Complex civil litigation; class actions; life and disability.
**Prof. Memberships:** Fellow, American College of Trial Lawyers; Member, American Law Institute; President, Maine Bar Foundation (2004).
**Career:** Successfully defended $846 million asset purchase deal in FPL Energy v CMP; recovered $58 million in actions concerning nuclear plant decommissioning; either lead or liaison defense counsel in 3 pending MDL class proceedings; twice argued to US Supreme Court
**Personal:** Harvard Law School, 1979 (Harv L Rev 1978-79); Amherst College, 1976; clerk, Chief Judge Frank Coffin, US 1st Circuit Court of Appeals (1980).

### KEACH, Robert J
Bernstein Shur, Portland
207 774 1200
rkeach@bssn.com
*Recommended in Corporate/M&A*

**Practice Areas:** Chair of the Business Restructuring and Insolvency Practice Group. His practice focuses on representing parties in workouts and bankruptcy cases, including debtors, creditors, creditors' committees, lessors and third parties acquiring troubled companies and/or their assets.
**Prof. Memberships:** Maine State Bar Association (Committee on Bankruptcy and Reorganization); American Bar Association (Sections on Business, Banking and Corporations, and Real Estate, Probate and Trust Law); American Bankruptcy Institute (Vice President, Education; Certified Specialist, Business Bankruptcy Law, American Bankruptcy Board of Certification).
**Personal:** University of Maine School of Law (JD, cum laude, 1980); Univesity of Vermont (BA, magna cum laude, 1977).

### KEELER, Dennis C
Pierce Atwood LLP, Portland
207 791 1331
dkeeler@pierceatwood.com
*Recommended in Real Estate*

**Practice Areas:** Chair, Real Estate Group. Practices primarily in the real estate development area, with emphasis on representing developers and owners of retail centers, office buildings, commercial projects and large residential/resort developments throughout New England and the East Coast.
**Prof. Memberships:** Colorado Bar (1981); Maine Bar (1984); Secretary and Member, Board of Directors of Maine Real Estate Development Association; Member, International Council of Shopping Centers.
**Career:** Partner (1990-). Practiced in Denver, Colorado. Selected for inclusion in a leading legal publication, 2003-04 and 2004-05 editions, for real estate law.
**Personal:** University of Denver, JD 1981; University of Maryland, BA 1975.

### KILBRETH, James
Verrill Dana, LLP, Portland
207 774 4000
jkilbreth@verrilldana.com
*Recommended in Environment, Litigation*

**Practice Areas:** Chair, Trial Department. Complex commercial litigation, antitrust, securities, and class actions; white-collar crime; environmental.
**Prof. Memberships:** Admitted to Bar: 1976, District of Columbia; 1980, US Supreme Court; 1984, Maine; 1991, US District Court, District of Maine; US Court of Appeals for the DC Circuit, First, Fifth, and Eleventh Circuits. Maine State and American Bar Associations; Maine Trial Lawyers Association; Maine Equal Justice Partners Legal Panel; Gignoux Inn of Court.
**Career:** State of Maine, Chief Deputy Attorney General (1987-90), Deputy Attorney General (Chief, Litigation Division, 1985-86), Assistant Attorney General (Environmental Division, 1983-85); Associate, Wilmer, Cutler & Pickering, 1976-83.
**Publications:** 'Brownfields: A Comprehensive Guide to Redeveloping Contaminated Property', Maine Chapter, ABA Section of 'Natural Resources, Energy and Environmental Law' (1997); 'Minimizing Environmental Liability for Lenders and Corporate Fiduciaries in Maine', NBI (1993).
**Personal:** Education: Harvard College (BA, cum laude, 1970); Northeastern University (MA, 1974); American University School of Law (JD, magna cum laude, 1976). Director and past President, Southern Africa Legal Services and Legal Education Project.

### KING, David
Rudman & Winchell LLC, Bangor
207 947 4501
*Recommended in Litigation*

### KUBETZ, Bernard J
Eaton Peabody, Bangor
207 947 0111
bkubetz@eatonpeabody.com
*Recommended in Litigation*

**Practice Areas:** Practice includes: commercial disputes, product liability, First Amendment, employment discrimination, malpractice and personal injury. Recently chaired the Maine Bar Association's Commission on Alternative Dispute Resolution. Clients include individuals, businesses, insurance companies and self-ensured entities in both the United States and Canada.
**Prof. Memberships:** Maine Bar Association, Massachusetts Bar Association, US Supreme Court, US First Circuit Court of Appeals, Maine Trial Lawyers Association (Member, Board of Governors), Association of Trial Lawyers of America (Member), and Maine Supreme Court appointed Alternative Dispute Resolution Commission (Chair).
**Personal:** University of Syracuse School of Law, 1973; Bowdoin College, BA, 1970.

### LANE, Michael L
Preti Flaherty Beliveau & Pachios, LLP, Portland 207 791 3000
mlane@eatonpeabody.com
*Recommended in Real Estate*

**Practice Areas:** Real estate; land use and zoning; commercial and public financing. Title and conveyancing in complex timberland transactions, including operating agreements, underwriting timberland titles; LURC development, compliance and permitting. Land conservation. Representation for compliance with and applications for Tree Growth and Open Space programs.
**Prof. Memberships:** American, Maine State (Title Standards subcommittee) and Penobscot County Bar Associations.
**Personal:** University of Maine School of Law, cum laude, 2001; University of Maine, BA, summa cum laude, 1996, Phi Beta Kappa.

### LAVOIE, Mark
Norman, Hanson & DeTroy, LLC, Portland 207 774 7000
*Recommended in Litigation*

### LEONARD III, Edward D
Eaton Peabody, Bangor
207 947 0111
tleonard@eatonpeabody.com
*Recommended in Real Estate*

**Practice Areas:** Specializes in real estate law, including complex conveyancing and ownership restructuring, commercial lending, commercial loan workouts and banking law and regulation. Practice encompasses all aspects of Natural Resources Law, including timber, mining, crops and aquaculture, environmental and land-use law, conservation law and timberland law.
**Prof. Memberships:** Maine Bar Association and United States Federal Courts.
**Career:** Real Estate Department Chair; Head of Real Estate; Natural Resources and Timberlands; and Financial Services Practice Groups.
**Publications:** 'The Coast Guard: Always Ready, Sometimes Careful', Maine Law Review, 1969.
**Personal:** University of Maine School of Law, 1969; University of Maine, BA, 1965.

### LEPAGE, Margaret
Pierce Atwood LLP, Portland
207 791 1100
*Recommended in Employment*

### LOGIUDICE, Susan E
Preti Flaherty Beliveau & Pachios, LLP, Portland 207 791 3000
sel@preti.com
*Recommended in Corporate/M&A*

**Practice Areas:** Concentrates practice in business organizations and commercial transactions, including mergers and acquisitions, entity formation and governance, corporate finance, joint ventures, private placements and venture capital financings. She also advises family owned and closely held businesses through the life cycle of the business and on succession planning.
**Prof. Memberships:** Admitted to practice in Maine (1985); Maine State Bar Association, Corporate Law Section; American Bar Association, Business Law Section.
**Career:** Joined Preti Flaherty in 1985. Became Partner, 1992, Member, Preti Flaherty Management Committee.
**Personal:** Born 22 November 1957. Northeastern University JD (1985), State University of New York at Binghamton (1979).

### LOWRY, Leslie
Jensen Baird Gardner & Henry, Portland
207 775 7271
*Recommended in Real Estate*

### MACEWAN, Alan D
Verrill Dana, LLP, Portland
207 774 4000
amacewan@verrilldana.com
*Recommended in Corporate/M&A*

**Practice Areas:** Business acquisitions and sales; contracts; general corporate.

Has represented domestic and foreign companies, public and private, in the acquisition or divestiture of companies and divisions.
**Prof. Memberships:** ABA, MSBA, ABA Negotiated Acquisitions Committee. Currently serves on the Editorial Committee, ABA Model Stock Purchase Agreement Revision Task Force; served on the Committee to Revise Maine's Business Corporation Act. Admitted in New York and Maine.
**Career:** Partner since 1993. Chair, Business Law Department. Former Legal Counsel, Maine Governor John R McKernan, Jr (1988-91).
**Publications:** Has lectured and written on mergers, acquisitions and contracts. Author, Blue Sky Regulation of REG D Offerings, The Review of Securities & Commodities Regulation (1985).
**Personal:** Syracuse University (JD, 1981); editor, Syracuse Law Review; Colby College (BA, 1978).

### MAHONEY, Sean
Verrill Dana, LLP, Portland
207 774 4000
smahoney@verrilldana.com
*Recommended in Environment*
**Practice Areas:** Environmental permitting and litigation. Represents clients before state and federal courts and administrative agencies focusing on solid and hazardous wastes and Clean Water Act permitting and enforcement actions.
**Prof. Memberships:** Admitted to Bar: 1992, California; 1998, Maine; 2005, US Supreme Court; past President, MSBA Natural Resources and Environmental Law Section; Maine Trial Lawyers Association; ABA Environment, Energy, and Natural Resources Law Sections.
**Career:** Clerk, Judge Fred I Parker, US District Court of Vermont (1992-93); Morrison & Foerster, LLP, San Francisco, CA (1993-97); United States Peace Corps, Sri Lanka (1986-89).
**Publications:** 'Superfund Contribution Protection After The Seventh Circuits, Akzo v. Aigner', 9 Toxics Law Reporter 17.
**Personal:** Bowdoin College (AB, magna cum laude, 1986); University of Virginia (JD, 1992).

### MANHEIMER, Jacob A
Pierce Atwood LLP, Portland
207 791 1338
jmanheimer@pierceatwood.com
*Recommended in Corporate/M&A*
**Practice Areas:** Bankruptcy and reorganization; creditors' rights; commercial finance.
**Prof. Memberships:** American Bankruptcy Institute; Maine State Bar Association.
**Career:** Associate, Fried Frank Harris Shriver & Jacobson (1983-86); associate, Pierce Atwood (1986-90); Partner, Pierce Atwood (1991-date).
**Personal:** Fordham University School of Law, JD 1983; Dartmouth College, AB 1978.

### MARCUS, Benjamin E
Drummond Woodsum & MacMahon, Portland 207 772 1941
bmarcus@dwmlaw.com
*Recommended in Corporate/M&A*
**Practice Areas:** Represents lenders, businesses, investors and other stakeholders in connection with troubled business enterprises, including workouts, restructurings and proceedings under Chapter 11 of the US Bankruptcy Code. Serves as general outside counsel to numerous businesses in a variety of industries including oil and gas, aquaculture, light manufacturing, automotive, insurance and hospitality.
**Prof. Memberships:** Maine Bar Association; American Bar Association, International Law Section; Local Rules Committee, United States Bankruptcy Court, District of Maine.
**Career:** Clerk, Honorable Joseph L Tauro, Chief Judge, US District Court, District of Massachusetts; joined Drummond Woodsum & MacMahon in 1997; serves on the firm's Management Committee.
**Personal:** Cornell Law School (magna cum laude) JD 1986; Order of Coif; Editor in Chief of the Cornell Law Review

### MARCUS, George
Marcus, Clegg & Mistretta PA, Portland
207 828 8000
*Recommended in Corporate/M&A*

### MCCARTHY, John
Rudman & Winchell LLC, Bangor
207 947 4501
*Recommended in Litigation*

### MCGILL, Linda D
Bernstein Shur, Portland
207 774 1200
lmcgill@bernsteinshur.com
*Recommended in Employment*
**Practice Areas:** Her practice covers all aspects of public and private sector employment law; labor-management negotiations; union avoidance; discrimination claims defense; counsel on best practices and compliance; non-competition; intellectual property.
**Prof. Memberships:** US Supreme Court, First Circuit; Maine State and American Bar Associations, Labor and Employment and Women's Law Sections; Maine Bar Foundation Fellow; International Senior Lawyers Program.
**Career:** Chief Counsel, Governor's Office of Employee Relations (1979-84); Perkins, Thompson, Hinckley, Keddy (1984-89); Founding Partner, Moon, Moss, McGill (1989); adjunct faculty, University of Maine Law School (1994-present).
**Personal:** JD, Northeastern University, 1978; BS (magna cum laude), Randolph-Macon Woman's College, 1971.

### MCGUIRE, Frank
Rudman & Winchell LLC, Bangor
207 947 4501
*Recommended in Employment*

### MCKAY, Daniel G
Eaton Peabody, Bangor
207 947 0111
dmckay@eatonpeabody.com
*Recommended in Corporate/M&A*
**Practice Areas:** Practice concentrates on representation of small and medium sized entities in a variety of corporate and transactional matters. Broad-based transactional practice with specialized expertise in mergers and acquisitions, securities, antitrust, healthcare and international transactional matters. Clients include a variety of business sectors, including hi-tech manufacturing, software, seafood, forest products, healthcare and banking.
**Prof. Memberships:** American Bar Association (Business Law, Healthcare Law, International Law Sections), Maine State Bar Association (Business Law, Health Law, International Practice Sections), American Health Lawyers Association.
**Personal:** Boston University School of Law, 1977; Princeton University, AB, cum laude, 1974.

### MCVEIGH, John P
Preti Flaherty Beliveau & Pachios, LLP, Portland 207 791 3000
jmcveigh@preti.com
*Recommended in Corporate/M&A*
**Practice Areas:** Bankruptcy, commercial litigation, energy litigation, water rights. Representation of major secured or unsecured creditors in bankruptcy proceedings; litigation of a wide variety of commercial disputes, including all manner of contract, commercial landlord/tenant, internal governance and close corporation, and mechanic's lien issues. Significant litigation experience representing industrial energy consumers and other parties to energy contracts. A substantial element of practice is structuring transactions in advance to avoid litigation and bankruptcy pitfalls. Practice is in all state and federal courts. Admitted to the United States Supreme Court.
**Prof. Memberships:** American Bankruptcy Institute; Maine State Bar (1987), Cumberland County Bar.
**Career:** Member, Preti Flaherty, 1996.
**Personal:** Born 31 July 1947, BA University of Virginia, 1969, English Dept U Va, 1972-83, JD University of Virginia, 1987.

### MESSERSCHMIDT, Michael
Preti Flaherty Beliveau & Pachios, LLP, Portland 207 791 3000
mmesserschmidt@preti.com
*Recommended in Employment*
**Practice Areas:** Chair of firm's Labor and Employment Law Practice Group. Focuses his practice on advising and defending management in employment discrimination, harassment, and civil

rights claims, including federal and state court litigation. Also has extensive experience counseling employers on EEO compliance and risk management issues, and has handled numerous arbitrations under collective bargaining agreements as well as executive compensation agreements.
**Prof. Memberships:** Admitted to practice in Maine (1978); Maine State Bar Association, Labor and Employment Section; American Bar Association, Labor and Employment Law Section.
**Career:** Assistant Attorney General, State of Maine (Criminal Division) (1978-80); Joined Preti Flaherty 1980. Became Member, 1987. Managing Partner 1991-92.
**Personal:** Born 22 June 1953. University of Maine School of Law, JD, 1978; Harvard College, BA (Cum Laude), 1975.

### MILLER, Charles E
Bernstein Shur, Portland
207 774 1200
cmiller@bernsteinshur.com
*Recommended in Real Estate*
**Practice Areas:** Managing shareholder. His practice incorporates all elements of real estate law, including the acquisition, disposition, financing, leasing, management and development of real estate. He also focuses on corporate planning, including asset and stock transactions, investment banker selection, formation of business structures, entity planning and strategy.
**Prof. Memberships:** American Bar (Business and Real Estate Law Section; Subcommittee on Commercial Leases), Maine State Bar (Member, Real Estate Section), and Cumberland County Bar Associations.
**Personal:** University of Maine School of Law (JD, cum laude, 1979); Managing Editor, Maine Law Review (1978-79); University of Maine (MEd, 1973); Colby College (AB, 1969).

### MOON, Richard G
Moon, Moss & Shapiro, P.A., Portland
207 775 6001
rmoon@moonmoss.com
*Recommended in Employment*
**Practice Areas:** Firm practice leader in private sector employment and labor law emphasizing advice on all employment issues and collective bargaining, arbitrations, mergers and acquisitions. Extensive national experience in all employment discrimination litigation and trials, including class action employee benefits and wage and hour matters. National practice in H1-B and related business immigration matters for technology and financial sectors.
**Prof. Memberships:** Admitted to practice in New York (1975); Maine (1978). American Bar Association, Labor and Employment Law Section; Maine State and Cumberland County Bar Associations; Fellow, American College of Labor and Employment Lawyers. Listed in sev-

eral leading US legal publications for labor and employment law and litigation expertise.
**Career:** Joined Carter Ledyard & Milburn (New York 1975); joined Perkins Thompson Hinckley & Keddy (Maine 1978); Founding Partner, Moon Moss (1989).
**Publications:** 'Winning the Battle of the Experts: Strategies for Employers in the Wake of Faragher and Ellerth', Practising Law Institute, 2000; 'Wage and Hour Class Actions: Update & Current Hot Topics', Georgetown University Law Center's 23rd Annual Employment & Litigation Institute, 2005.
**Personal:** Born Detroit, Michigan, 18 January 1947. JD, University of Michigan (1974); AB, Dartmouth College (1969).

### MORRELL, Stephen G
Eaton Peabody, Brunswick
207 729 1144
smorrell@eatonpeabody.com
*Recommended in Corporate/M&A*
**Practice Areas:** Insolvency law specialist, board certified in the field of business bankruptcy by American Board of Certification. Works closely with firm's business planners and trial attorneys. Seasoned courtroom advocate and an experienced business advisor.
**Prof. Memberships:** Maine and American Bar Associations; admitted to bars of US District Court, US Court of Appeals (First Circuit), US Supreme Court; Edward T Gignoux Inns of Court (Senior Attorney), American Bankruptcy Institute; Maine Trial Lawyers Association.
**Career:** Joined Eaton Peabody 1978, elected shareholder 1984, Board of Directors 1992.
**Personal:** University of Maine School of Law, JD, 1978; Bowdoin College, BA, magna cum laude, 1975.

### NEWTON, Robert O
Preti Flaherty Beliveau & Pachios, LLP, Portland 207 791 3000
rnewton@preti.com
*Recommended in Litigation*
**Practice Areas:** Extensive experience before State and Federal Courts and regulatory agencies in discovery and trial of complex cases involving medical, health and environmental issues. Has acted as litigation counsel for manufacturer in extensive FIFRA action by EPA (2003); plaintiff's counsel in wrongful death action by widow of environmental engineer (2003); chief trial counsel in defense of Maine's largest toxic tort case, involving 18 plaintiffs alleging brain cancer and related diseases (2002); trial counsel in defense of product liability action by consumers alleging repetitive stress injury by use of computer and data entry keyboards (1998).
**Prof. Memberships:** Admitted to practice in Colorado (1971), Maine (1996) and New Hampshire (1997). Member,

Maine and New Hampshire Bar Associations, Maine Trial Lawyers Association; admitted to practice before the United States District Courts for Colorado, Maine and New Hampshire, and 10th Circuit Court of Appeals.
**Career:** Partner of Myrick, Newton & Sullivan, Denver, CO (1973-81); professional furniture maker and cabinetmaker, Yarmouth, ME (1981-95); became Of Counsel to Preti Flaherty in 1996, became Member, 1999. Member, Preti Flaherty Recruitment Committee, 2001-present.
**Personal:** Born 3 April 1946. JD, University of Denver College of Law, 1971, BA Duke University, 1968.

### NYHAN, Christopher D
Preti Flaherty Beliveau & Pachios, LLP, Portland 207 791 3000
cnyhan@preti.com
*Recommended in Litigation*
**Practice Areas:** Chair of the firm's Medical Liability Group. Extensive experience in complex medical, antitrust and products liability. Tried over 100 jury trials in state and federal courts. Has argued over 20 cases to Maine Supreme Court.
**Prof. Memberships:** Admitted in ME (1976), District of Columbia (1998) and various federal trial and appellate courts. Maine State Bar Association liaison to Model Professional Liability Demonstration Project of Maine State Legislature.
**Career:** Joined firm in 1976, became Partner in 1980. Member or Chair, Management and Hiring Committees. Frequent lecturer to medical and professional risk associations throughout New England. Listed in The Best Lawyers in America.
**Personal:** Born 4 February 1946; JD, University of San Francisco (1976); MA, University of California, Berkeley (1973); BA, Boston College (1968).

### O'BRIEN, Timothy J
Verrill Dana, LLP, Kennebunk
207 774 4000
tobrien@verrilldana.com
*Recommended in Employment*
**Practice Areas:** Labor and employment law; sports law.
**Prof. Memberships:** Maine State Bar Association; American Bar Association Sections on Labor Law; Litigation; Equal Employment Opportunity Committee.
**Career:** For the past 20 years, Mr O'Brien has represented management on a wide variety of labor and employment issues and defended cases brought on an individual and class action basis.
**Publications:** Contributing author to 'Employment Discrimination Law', Schlei & Grossman, 3rd Edition; co-author of 'Managing Legal Issues in College Athletics', LRP Publications (2004).
**Personal:** Born: June 5, 1958. Education: New England School of Law (JD, 1983); University of Notre Dame (AB, 1980).

### OESTREICHER, Charles R
Verrill Dana, LLP, Portland
207 774 4000
coestreicher@verrilldana.com
*Recommended in Real Estate*
**Practice Areas:** Real estate; real estate brokerage; land use and zoning; conservation easements. Timberland acquisitions and sales.
**Prof. Memberships:** Admitted to Bar: 1968, Maine. Memberships: Maine State Bar Association Real Estate and Title Section; Cumberland County Bar Association (President, 1992); New England Land Title Association; ABA Real Property, Probate & Trust Section; Member, American College of Real Estate Lawyers (ACREL).
**Publications:** Author, 'Maine Supplement to Principles of Real Estate Law', Castle Publishing, 1986, and updates.
**Personal:** Born: Pittsburgh, Pennsylvania, April 8, 1942. Education: Indiana University of Pennsylvania (BS, 1964); Case Western Reserve University (JD, 1968). Phi Alpha Delta.

### OLIVIER, Elisabeth
Preti Flaherty Beliveau & Pachios, LLP, Portland 207 791 3000
eolivier@preti.com
*Recommended in Employment*
**Practice Areas:** Employment and health law, with extensive experience counseling employers on discrimination laws, compliance and risk management, contracting and non-competition. Also represents employers in employment disputes before courts, EEOC and Maine Human Rights Commission.
**Prof. Memberships:** Admitted to practice in Maine in 1987; First Circuit; Maine and American Bar Associations (Labor and Employment and Health Law Sections); American Health Lawyers Association
**Career:** Joined firm in 1987; became Partner in 1995.
**Personal:** Born Leominster, Massachusetts; JD Suffolk University Law School, 1987; BS, University of Maine 1978.

### PAYNE, Clare
Eaton Peabody, Bangor
207 947 0111
cpayne@eatonpeabody.com
*Recommended in Employment*
**Practice Areas:** Represents a broad spectrum of employers, including public, private, and non-profits. Provides representation before arbitrators, NLRB, MLRB, MHRC and Unemployment Commission. Prepares personnel handbooks and policies. Advises on FMLA, return-to-work, discipline, discharge, Wage and Hour, sexual harassment investigations, and other employment matters. Frequent speaker on employment issues.
**Prof. Memberships:** Maine Board of Bar Examiners (1988-2000), ABA, Maine and Penobscot Bar Association.
**Career:** Joined 1979; Shareholder 1986.

**Publications:** 'New USERRA Notice/Poster Requirement', Maine Business & Employment Law (March, 2005).
**Personal:** Villanova University School of Law, 1979; Trinity College (CT), BA, 1973; The Madeira School, 1970.

### PETERSON, Hans
Rudman & Winchell LLC, Bangor
207 947 4501
*Recommended in Real Estate*

### PETRUCCELLI, Gerald
Petruccelli Martin & Haddow LLP, Portland 207 775 0200
*Recommended in Litigation*

### PIETROPAOLI, Paul
Perkins, Thompson, Hinckley & Keddy, P.A., Portland 207 774 2635
*Recommended in Real Estate*

### PIPER, Jonathan S
Preti Flaherty Beliveau & Pachios, LLP, Portland 207 791 3000
jpiper@preti.com
*Recommended in Litigation*
**Practice Areas:** Chair of the firm's Litigation Practice Group. Extensive experience in complex litigation, international and domestic arbitration, commercial litigation, securities litigation, and libel defense work for the media.
**Prof. Memberships:** Admitted to practice in Maine (1976); United States District Court, District of Maine (1976); United States Court of Appeals, First Circuit and Third Circuit. Fellow, Maine Bar Foundation (since 1996); counsel Member of Media Law Resource Center; Maine Civil Rules Advisory Committee (1999-2000).
**Career:** Law clerk, Honorable Edward S Godfrey, Maine Supreme Judicial Court, 1976-77. Joined Preti Flaherty, 1977; became Partner, 1982. Member, Preti Flaherty Management Committee; Managing Partner, 1995-99.
**Publications:** Comment, 'The Repair Rule: Maine Rule of Evidence 407(a) and the Admissibility of Subsequent Remedial Measures in Proving Negligence', 27 Maine Law Review 255 (1975); article, 'Subpoenas on the Press: The Constitutional Privilege Not to Produce', Maine Bar Journal, Vol. 2, No. 2 (1987); contributor: 'Annual 50-State Survey of Libel and Privacy, Media Law Resource Center' (1986-present); 'How to Avoid Covering Your Own Trial', Maine State Bar Association Media/Law Guide (1990).
**Personal:** Born 7 April 1950; JD, University of Maine School of Law (Portland), 1976; BA (magna cum laude), Bowdoin College, 1972.

### PRINGLE, Harry R
Drummond Woodsum & MacMahon, Portland 207 772 1941
hrpringle@dwmlaw.com
*Recommended in Employment*
**Practice Areas:** Has extensive experience in employment litigation, labor

negotiations, National Labor Relations Board and Maine Labor Relations Board proceedings, Title VII litigation, and discrimination cases before the courts, the Equal Employment Opportunity Commission and the Maine Human Rights Commission.

**Prof. Memberships:** Has been a Member of the Board of Directors of the National School Board Association Council of School Board Attorneys. He has been listed in labor and employment law by a leading US legal publication for over 10 years, and is a Fellow of the College of Labor and Employment Lawyers.

**Career:** Past President of the Maine Council of School Board Attorneys. He joined the firm in 1973, is the firm's Managing Director, has served as lead instructor for school law courses at two area universities, and is a frequent lecturer on employment law issues.

**Publications:** Editor of 'Maine School Law, Third Edition' co-author of 'Significant Cases in Maine School Law,' and has authored numerous articles on school and employment law issues.

**Personal:** Harvard Law School (1973 cum laude); Princeton University (1968 magna cum laude, Phi Beta Kappa).

### ROBITZEK, William
Berman & Simmons, Portland
207 774 5277
*Recommended in Litigation*

### RUBIN, Peter J
Bernstein Shur, Portland
207 774 1200
prubin@bernsteinshur.com
*Recommended in Litigation*

**Practice Areas:** Rubin's practice concentrates on complex cases involving product liability, business litigation, malpractice/PI claims, and defense of asbestos claims at the national level.

**Prof. Memberships:** Fellow, American College of Trial Lawyers and American Academy of Appellate Lawyers; Advocate, American Board of Trial Advocates; member of American, Maine State, and Cumberland County Bar Associations.

**Publications:** Harvard Law Review and Maine Law Review.

**Personal:** Harvard Law School (JD, magna cum laude, 1970); Member, Harvard Law Review (1969-70); Duke University (AB, 1967); law clerk to the Honorable Edward T Gignoux, USDC Judge for the District of Maine, September 1970-August 1971.

### SAUNDERS, Eric F
Bernstein Shur, Portland
207 774 1200
esaunders@bernsteinshur.com
*Recommended in Corporate/M&A*

**Practice Areas:** Eric practices business law with an emphasis on shareholder and partnership disputes, housing law with an emphasis on the acquisition and refinancing of federally subsidized housing

projects, and health law with an emphasis on the structuring of multi-party transactions.

**Prof. Memberships:** American, Maine State, and Cumberland County Bar Associations.

**Personal:** Boston University (JD, 1973); Member Boston University Law Review (1972-73); Harvard University (AB, 1969).

### SCANNELL, Gordon
Perkins, Thompson, Hinckley & Keddy, P.A., Portland 207 774 2635
*Recommended in Real Estate*

### SCHWARTZ, Jaimie Paul
Bernstein Shur, Portland
207 774 1200
jschwartz@bernsteinshur.com
*Recommended in Real Estate*

**Practice Areas:** Chair of the Real Estate Practice Group. He practices in several areas of real estate law, including the acquisition, disposition, financing, management and development of real estate, with particular focus on representation of landlords and tenants in commercial leasing transactions.

**Prof. Memberships:** Maine State Bar Association; American Bar Association (Real Property, Probate and Trust Law, Natural Resources, Energy and Environmental Law Sections).

**Personal:** Ohio State University College of Law (JD, with honors, 1991); Member, Order of the Coif; Ohio State University (BA, Journalism, 1984).

### SHAPIRO, Jonathan
Moon, Moss & Shapiro, P.A., Portland
207 775 6001
jshapiro@moonmoss.com
*Recommended in Employment*

**Practice Areas:** Firm Practice Leader in private sector employment law with extensive experience defending management in agency and court litigation and counseling management and high net worth individuals; safeguarding corporate property and information, including intellectual property, and enforcing restrictive covenants; internal investigations; and defending DOL, OFCCP, Immigration and other government agency audits/investigations.

**Prof. Memberships:** Admitted to practice in Massachusetts (1987); District of Columbia (1988); Maine (1992); New York (1997). Member: New York State and American Bar Associations (Labor and Employment Law Section; Equal Employment Opportunity Committee); District of Columbia Bar.

**Career:** Joined Akin Gump Strauss Hauer & Feld (Washington, DC 1987); joined Moon Moss (1992); became Partner (1996) and Managing Partner (1997) Moon, Moss & Shapiro.

**Publications:** Contributing Author, 'Cathcart and Dichter 1992 Employment at Will, State by State Survey', National

Employment Law Institute.

**Personal:** Born Montreal, Canada, 4 October 1962. JD (with honors), Duke University (1987); BA, (with distinction) McGill University (1984).

### SHEEHAN, Michael L
Preti Flaherty Beliveau & Pachios, LLP, Portland 207 791 3000
msheehan@preti.com
*Recommended in Real Estate*

**Practice Areas:** Real estate (including low-income housing tax credits); federal, state and local taxation; corporate/commercial transactions (including business acquisitions and dispositions); estate planning.

**Prof. Memberships:** Maine State Bar; American Bar (taxation; real property, probate and trust, and business law sections).

**Career:** Joined firm in 1986. Law clerk to the Honorable Thomas J Lydon, US Court of Federal Claims, Washington, DC.

**Publications:** Co-author of the Maine chapter of the American Bar Association's 'Sales and Use Tax Desk Book'. Contributing author since 1988.

**Personal:** JD, University of Maine, 1985 (Cum Laude); BSCE, New Jersey Institute of Technology, 1981 (magna cum laude).

### SHINAY, Richard
Drummond Woodsum & MacMahon, Portland 207 772 1941
rshinay@dwmlaw.com
*Recommended in Real Estate*

**Practice Areas:** Represents individuals, businesses, developers, lenders, municipalities and schools in the acquisition, development, financing and sale of real estate. Also represents clients in land conservation efforts. Serves as President of Classic Title Co., a subsidiary of Drummond, Woodsum & MacMahon, overseeing the issuance of title insurance.

**Prof. Memberships:** American Bar Association; Maine State Bar Association; Title Standards Subcommittee, MSBA; Committee on Condominiums, Cooperatives and Associations of Co-Owners, Real Property, Probate and Trust Law Section, ABA; American Land Title Association, New England Land Title Association and the Maine Land Title Association. Legislative Committee, Maine Real Estate & Development Association.

**Career:** Manager/Attorney, Lawyers Title Insurance Corporation, Portland, Maine (1980-85); Drummond Woodsum & MacMahon (1985 -); Former Member, South Portland Planning Board (1989-93; Chair, 1991-93) and Scarborough Planning Board (1995-2003; Chair 2000-03); past Co-Chair, Scarborough Open Space Committee and Scarborough Growth and Services Committee; past Chair, Scarborough Intermediate School Land Search Committee; Co-Chair, Scarborough Comprehensive Plan Revision Committee; Trustee; Scarborough Land

Conservation Trust and Portland Stage Company.

**Personal:** University of Maine School of Law, JD 1980; Boston College, AB 1977.

### SILIN, Steven
Berman & Simmons, Portland
207 774 5277
*Recommended in Litigation*

### SINGER, Brent
Rudman & Winchell LLC, Bangor
207 947 4501
*Recommended in Employment*

### SMITH, Nathan H
Bernstein Shur, Portland
207 774 1200
nsmith@bernsteinshur.com
*Recommended in Real Estate*

**Practice Areas:** Nathan Smith has a broad practice which includes acquisition, development, real estate leasing and financing with particular focus on larger scale transactions, including housing projects, commercial buildings, railroads, waste-to-energy plants, hydro-electric facilities, forest land conservation and estate properties.

**Prof. Memberships:** American, Maine State, and Cumberland County Bar Associations.

**Career:** Former Mayor and City Councilor, Portland, Maine; Commissioner, Maine State Housing Authority; lecturer on real estate law at Maine Law School.

**Personal:** Washington & Lee University (JD, cum laude, 1982); Omicron Delta Kappa; McMaster University (MA, 1975); University of North Carolina (BA, 1971), Phi Beta Kappa.

### STEVENS, Winfred
Rudman & Winchell LLC, Bangor
207 947 4501
*Recommended in Real Estate*

### STIER JR, Robert H
Pierce Atwood LLP, Portland
207 791 1163
rstier@pierceatwood.com
*Recommended in Litigation*

**Practice Areas:** Jury trials of cases involving complex scientific or technical subject matter, particularly patent litigation and products liability defense, but also copyright, trademark, trade secret and other complex commercial litigation.

**Prof. Memberships:** AIPLA; Products Liability Advisory Council (Sustaining Member); State Bar Associations in Maine, Massachusetts and Virginia

**Career:** Piper & Marbury, Baltimore and Washington, DC (1980-87); Bernstein, Shur, Sawyer & Nelson, Portland, ME (1987-98); Pierce Atwood, Portland, ME (since 1998); adjunct faculty, University of Maine School of Law (patent law, since 2000)

**Publications:** 'Revisiting the Missing Witness Inference,' 44 Md L Rev 137 (1985); 'Proving Infringement,' in Grossman and Hoffman, eds., 'Patent Litigation Strategies Handbook' (BNA Books with the American Bar Association Section of Intellectual Property Law, 2nd ed. 2005); 'Economic Damages', in Black and Lee, eds., 'Expert Evidence: A Practitioner's Guide to Law, Science and the FJC Manual' (West Group, 1997); numerous presentations on trial advocacy and intellectual property issues

**Personal:** Harvard College, AB (honors) 1975; University of Gothenburg, Sweden (non-degree) 1977; Harvard Law School, JD (honors), 1980.

### STOREY, Anne-Marie
Rudman & Winchell LLC, Bangor
207 947 4501
*Recommended in Employment*

### SWEET, Julian
Berman & Simmons, Portland
207 774 5277
*Recommended in Litigation*

### TAYLOR, William E
Pierce Atwood LLP, Portland
207 791 1213
wtaylor@pierceatwood.com
*Recommended in Environment*

**Practice Areas:** Partner, Environmental Practice Group. Represents clients before local, state, and federal administrative agencies. Practice has been devoted to matters related to water law, waste discharge, wetland and natural resource licensing, compliance counseling, rulemaking, auditing, and enforcement.

**Prof. Memberships:** Commissioner for State of Maine, New England Interstate Water Pollution Control Commission. Member of the Maine NPDES Advisory Group, the Maine State Wetlands Task Force, and the American and Maine State Bar Associations Natural Resourses Sections.

**Publications:** Authored 'Major Land Use Laws Affecting Industrial, Commercial and Residential Development in Maine', National Business Institute, 1990, and 'Wetland Permitting in Maine', Maine Bar Journal, September 1997. Co-authored 'A Wetlands Primer', Natural Resources & Environment, 1992, and 'The Watershed Protection Approach', Water Resources, Natural Resources & Environment, 1996.

**Personal:** Vermont Law School, JD and Masters in Environmental Law 1983; University of Massachusetts, BA (cum laude), 1980.

### THALER, Jeffrey A
Bernstein Shur, Portland
207 774 1200
jthaler@bernsteinshur.com
*Recommended in Environment, Litigation*

**Practice Areas:** His practice includes environmental permitting and litigation, as well as litigation for commercial and professionsl disputes, insurance coverage, personal injury, and toxic tort problems.

**Prof. Memberships:** American Bar,

Maine State Bar, and Cumberland County Bar Associations; Maine Trial Lawyers Association: Board of Governors; American Trial Lawyers Association; State Land for Maine's Future Board.

**Publications:** He lectures frequently and has written extensively for state and national publications on such topics as toxic torts, environmental permitting, court decisions, and legal ethics.

**Personal:** Yale University Law School (JD, 1977); Williams College (BA, magna cum laude with highest honors, 1974).

### TUMLIN, Wayne E
Bernstein Shur, Portland
207 774 1200
wtumlin@bernsteinshur.com
*Recommended in Corporate/M&A*

**Practice Areas:** Leads the Securities and Private Equity and Mergers and Acquisitions Groups. His practice focuses on negotiated transactions and reorganizations, commercial lending, public and private offerings of securities, and securities and financial institution regulatory compliance.

**Prof. Memberships:** American, Maine State, Cumberland County, District of Columbia, Connecticut, and Maryland Bar Associations.

**Personal:** LLM, Securities Law and Financial Regulation, Georgetown University (1996); JD, New York Law School (1992, cum laude); AB, Economics, University of North Carolina (1981).

### UHL, Eric J
Moon, Moss & Shapiro, P.A., Portland
207 775 6001
euhl@moonmoss.com
*Recommended in Employment*

**Practice Areas:** Concentrates practice in the areas of employment and labor law and business litigation, defending management against wrongful termination, discrimination, compensation, employee benefits and other employment-related claims. Also engages in general commercial litigation, including unfair competition, restrictive covenants and intellectual property.

**Prof. Memberships:** Admitted to practice in California (1987); Maine (1991); Massachusetts (2004). Member: Maine State (currently Co-Chairperson of the MSBA's Labor and Employment Law Section) and American Bar Associations; New England Chapter, Association for Conflict Resolution; Maine Association of Dispute Resolution Professionals.

**Career:** Clerk, Justice Stanley Mosk, California Supreme Court (1987); joined San Francisco City Attorney's Office (1988); joined Lambert, Coffin, Rudman & Hochman (Portland, ME 1991); joined Moon, Moss & Shapiro (1993); became Partner (2000).

**Personal:** Born Monroe, Michigan, 31 January 1960. JD, University of California, Hastings College of Law (1987); BA,

University of Michigan (1983).

### VAN SLYKE, David
Preti Flaherty Beliveau & Pachios, LLP, Portland 207 791 3000
dvanslyke@preti.com
*Recommended in Environment*

**Practice Areas:** Chair of firm's Environmental Law Practice Group. Focuses his practice on due diligence in business and lending transactions, project siting and permitting, environmental risk management and compliance counseling, and defense of governmental enforcement actions and toxic tort suits.

**Prof. Memberships:** Admitted to practice in the District of Columbia (1982), Maine; (1992), US District Court (DC 1982, Maine 1992); US Court of Appeals (First Circuit 1998). Member of Maine State Bar Association (and Natural Resources Section), American Bar Association (and Section on Environment, Energy and Natural Resources). State Law Editor, BNA Environmental Due Diligence Guide.

**Career:** Booz-Allen & Hamilton 1982-83; US EPA: Enforcement Attorney 1983-87, Section Chief 1987-89, Deputy Director, Hazardous Waste Division 1989-90, Director, Superfund Division, 1990-92. Preti Flaherty: Of Counsel 1992-94, Partner since 1994, Environmental Practice Group Chair since 1995.

**Personal:** Born 21 September 1954. JD, Syracuse University Law School 1981; BS, St Lawrence University 1976. EPA awards: Department of Justice Commendation for Outstanding Service (1991); Assistant Administrator's Enforcement Award for Excellence (1990); Special Achievement Silver Medal (1990) and two Bronze Medals (1986 and 1988); six Superior Performance and Outstanding Achievement Awards (1984-89).

### WAKELIN, David
Wakelin, Hallock & O'Donovan LLP, Portland 207 774 3595
*Recommended in Employment*

### WEBBER, Walter
Jensen Baird Gardner & Henry, Portland
207 775 7271
*Recommended in Real Estate*

### WHITE, Jeffrey M
Pierce Atwood LLP, Portland
207 791 1292
jwhite@pierceatwood.com
Recommended in Litigation

**Practice Areas:** Pierce Atwood Litigation Group Leader; complex, commercial, antitrust, trade regulation and intellectual property litigation.

**Prof. Memberships:** Fellow, Maine Bar Foundation; former Chair, Maine Bar Association CLE Committee and Director, NE Bar Association.

**Career:** US v American Skiing Company (merger litigation); FPL Energy v CMP (defense judgment on $846 million asset

purchase contract); Maine v Sears Roebuck & Co. (defense judgment on Unfair Trade Practice claims involving service agreements and sales practices); Net 2 Press v 58 Dix Ave. Corp. (defense judgment on business sale contract and fraud claims); Colt Defense v Bushmaster Firearms (successful trademark litigation defense).

### WOODBURY, Judith Fletcher
Pierce Atwood LLP, Portland
207 791 1386
jwoodbury@pierceatwood.com
*Recommended in Real Estate*

**Practice Areas:** Partner, Real Estate Group; Manager, Bigelow Title Company. Representation for title and conveyancing in complex commercial transactions.

**Prof. Memberships:** Leadership Gift Co-Chair, Campaign for Justice (2005-06); Maine State Bar (Chair, Real Estate (1999-2000); Women's Law and Environmental Law Sections) and Cumberland Bar Associations; Maine Land Conservation Attorney's Network; Maine Society of Land Surveyors.

**Career:** Assistant Attorney General, Maine (1980-83); Lawyers Title Insurance Corporation (1983-84); President, Casco Bay Title Company (1984-86); Atlantic Title Company (1986-91).

**Personal:** Friends of Casco Bay, Board of Directors. University of Maine Law School, JD (1980); University of Maine, BA (highest distinction) (1976).

### ZIMPRITCH, James B
Pierce Atwood LLP, Portland
207 791 1270
jzimpritch@pierceatwood.com
*Recommended in Corporate/M&A*

**Practice Areas:** Broad corporate experience. Active M&A practice. Extensive experience in corporate and securities, banking, insurance, shareholder disputes, director duties, structuring investments and general commercial law. Involved in nearly every takeover fight in Maine in last 20 years. Represents emerging, middle-market, and large publicly held companies.

**Prof. Memberships:** American Law Institute; ABA Corporate Laws Committee; Maine: Chair, Corporate Law Revision Committee (2000-); past Chair, Business Law Section; frequent lecturer.

**Career:** Partner, Pierce Atwood LLP (1978-).

**Publications:** 'Maine Corporation Law & Practice', the definitive treatise.

**Personal:** Duke Law School, JD 1973; Duke Law Journal, 1972-73; Dartmouth College, AB 1970.

# BERNSTEIN SHUR

## THE FIRM

**Managing Shareholder:** Charles E Miller
**Senior Shareholder:** Leonard M Nelson
**President:** Peter J Rubin

**Number of Shareholders:** 58
**Number of Lawyers:** 83

**FIRM OVERVIEW:** Bernstein Shur is one of northern New England's largest full-service law firms, with more than 80 attorneys in Portland and Augusta, Maine and Manchester, New Hampshire. Established in 1915, the firm provides practical legal counsel to a diverse group of public and private clients throughout the region and around the world.

## MAIN AREAS OF PRACTICE

**Business Law:** Attorneys in the firm's Business Law Group have the advanced training and business experience required to effectively address client legal needs pertaining to operational matters, commercial planning, contract negotiations, regulatory compliance, and general company legal compliance. The firm is a leader in structuring ownership perpetuation plans, as well as related contractual arrangements and financing strategies.

**Business Restructuring & Insolvency:** Bernstein Shur has the largest business restructuring and insolvency practice in northern New England. The group's attorneys provide practical counsel to clients in complex reorganizations and liquidations under Chapter 11 and Chapter 7, large commercial insolvencies, and related litigation in state, federal, and bankruptcy courts.

**Construction Law:** The firm's Construction Law Group provides legal services to contractors, subcontractors, suppliers, insurers, bonding companies, and developers of construction projects. The practice covers all aspects of construction law from contract drafting, negotiation, and competitive bidding issues to the development and presentation of claims, mediation, arbitration and litigation, mechanics' liens, and insurance coverage issues.

**Energy:** The Energy Practice Group represents regional and international clients on issues relating to energy generation and distribution. Its clients are independent power producers (IPP's), small power producers, co-generators that produce electricity from renewable resources, and financial institutions . The group also represents contractors and subcontractors that are building IPP facilities, large consumers of electricity such as paper companies, water districts, and manufacturing facilities, and municipalities.

**Environmental & Natural Resources:** The Environmental and Natural Resources Practice Group represents individuals, businesses, and municipalities who are trying to comply with or enforce local, state, or federal environmental and land use laws, as well as acquiring other businesses or large land parcels. The group deals with issues involving land use permitting and development, remediation, conservation easements, wetlands, waste disposal or recycling, toxics, and insurance coverage.

**Healthcare:** The firm's Healthcare Group represents physicians and other healthcare professionals, physical group practices and associations, hospitals, nursing homes, health agencies, pharmacies, and other healthcare providers throughout northern New England.

**Immigration:** Bernstein Shur represents clients from around the world in immigration issues that include business and employment, foreign investor, family, citizenship, asylum, and deportation. The group's members conduct business in a variety of foreign languages.

**Intellectual Property:** Bernstein Shur's Intellectual Property Practice Group consists of corporate, commercial, and trial attorneys experienced in assisting clients with obtaining, managing, licensing, and enforcing intellectual property rights. The group handle matters involving utility and design patents, trademarks and service marks, copyrights, and trade secrets.

**Labor & Employment:** The Labor and Employment Group represents employers of all sizes in northern New England. The group defends employer clients in the state and federal courts, the Maine Human Rights Commission, and all other state and federal agencies that oversee labor and employment laws and regulations.

**Legislative & Regulatory Affairs:** Bernstein Shur understands that changing the law in the legislature and through agency rulemaking is often more cost-effective for clients than litigating current law. Headquartered in the capitol of Augusta, the firm's Legislative and Regulatory Affairs Group represents clients before the Maine Legislature and before various state and federal agencies.

**Litigation:** Bernstein Shur's Litigation Practice is broad-based, with representation for both plaintiffs and defendants. The firm is involved in litigation for domestic and foreign clients, including commercial disputes, securities litigation, antitrust, business torts, energy, products liability, personal injury, real estate transactions, education, intellectual property infringement, criminal cases, constitutional issues, health, insurance, and environmental matters.

**Mergers & Acquisitions:** Bernstein Shur's M&A Group represents bidders, targets, investors making financial acquisitions, founders of companies, financial advisers, and other parties in privately negotiated transfers of securities or assets, leveraged buyouts, public-company combinations, and takeovers.

**Municipal Law:** Bernstein Shur's Municipal Law Group currently serves as general counsel or special counsel to more than 125 Maine municipalities. Group attorneys frequently serve as special counsel to governmental entities including towns, cities, counties, school districts, sanitary and sewer districts, regional planning commissions, regional waste disposal groups, and other quasi-municipal agencies.

**Real Estate:** Bernstein Shur's real estate attorneys have expertise in all aspects of commercial real estate and a record of creating practical solutions to complex transactional issues. The firm has negotiated and closed development and value-added transactions for privately and publicly held businesses, individuals, trusts, and investment partnerships involving both public and private land ownership.

**Tax:** The Tax Group provides clients with clear approaches to the most complicated tax, estate planning, business planning, and succession issues, in addition to controversies with the IRS. Bernstein Shur finds practical solutions to issues involving federal, state, and international taxes, estate planning matters, and probate.

**Technology:** Bernstein Shur's Technology Group focuses its expertise on the evolving legal issues surrounding today's developing business and consumer technologies and the parties that develop and use them. The group represents technology developers, as well as parties using new technologies to improve their business processes.

**INTERNATIONAL WORK:** The professional scope of Bernstein Shur's international practice is as multi-faceted as its geographic scope, with attorneys engaging in dispute resolution, commercial negotiation, and government relations throughout the industrial and developing world.
**Languages:** Spanish, French, German, Italian, Japanese, Chinese, and Russian.

## HEAD OFFICE

**MAINE**
100 Middle Street, PO Box 9729, **Portland**, ME 04104-5029
**Tel:** 207 774 1200   **Fax:** 207 774 1127
**Email:** info@bernsteinshur.com   **Website:** www.bernsteinshur.com

## BRANCH OFFICES

**MAINE**
146 Capitol Street, **Augusta**, ME 04330
**Tel:** 207 623 1596   **Fax:** 207 626 0200

**NEW HAMPSHIRE**
Jefferson Mill Building, 670 North Commercial Street, Suite 108
PO Box 1120, **Manchester**, NH 03104
**Tel:** 603 623 8700   **Fax:** 603 623 7775

# DRUMMOND WOODSUM & MACMAHON

## THE FIRM

**Managing Director:** Harry R Pringle

**Number of shareholders:** 27
**Number of associates and consultants:** 14

**FIRM OVERVIEW:** Founded in 1965, Drummond Woodsum & MacMahon is one of Maine's largest and most well respected law firms. The firm's attorneys have earned a reputation for providing high quality counsel to clients across a wide spectrum of legal practice areas. Drummond Woodsum's philosophy of quality, responsiveness and efficiency in the delivery of legal services to firm clients has led to the development of some of the best lawyers in the United States. The reputation of the firm's attorneys was recently recognized nationally when, in 2001 and 2002, then firm member Robert E Hirshon became the first Maine lawyer in nearly 100 years to serve as President of the American Bar Association.

## MAIN AREAS OF PRACTICE:

**Public Sector Group:** The firm offers expertise in municipal and school law in areas including labor relations, employment matters, special education, finance, construction, employee benefits and litigation, and has litigated numerous precedent-setting cases on behalf of public sector clients. The school practice is widely recognized as pre-eminent in Maine and the school law website is nationally known.

**Employment Services:** The Employment Group consists of attorneys and highly skilled consultants who defend both private and public sector employers' interests. The practice includes substantial litigation in federal and state courts along with an active practice before all relevant federal and state agencies including the National Labor Relations Board, the Equal Employment Opportunity Commission, the Maine Labor Relations Board, the Maine Human Rights Commission, and other administrative bodies.

**Business Services:** The Business Group handles a full range of corporate and securities matters, advising clients on acquisitions and mergers, corporate tax planning and financing, multi-state financings, venture capital and private placements, and international trade. Attorneys in the firm are approved 'Red Book' bond counsel and have extensive experience in public utility law, franchising, executive compensation, foreign investment regulation, bankruptcy and securities matters, and other areas of corporate and business law.

**Trial Services:** The firm is involved in every type of civil litigation in federal and state courts and administrative agencies, including the United States Supreme Court. Recent cases fall into a broad range of areas including business and commercial litigation, employment, securities, intellectual property, antitrust, real estate and land use, construction disputes, product liability, bankruptcy and Native American tribal rights.

**Indian Law:** The Indian Practice provides legal services to Native American tribes, tribal businesses, and select developers and businesses working with tribes in the United States. Legal services include litigation in tribal, federal and state courts, economic development strategies, business transactions by and with tribes or tribal entities, tribal employment law and personnel management, developing tribal laws and governmental processes, Indian housing, federal contracting, and tribal gaming.

**CLIENTS:** Clients include Fortune 500 and private corporations throughout the US and in Canada and Great Britain, US insurance companies, commercial banks and institutions, public utilities, municipalities, private and public schools, and Native American tribes.

## HEAD OFFICE

**MAINE**
245 Commercial Street, PO Box 9781, **Portland**, ME 04104-5081
**Tel:** 207 772 1941
**Email:** info@dwmlaw.com
**Websites:** www.dwmlaw.com; www.SchoolLaw.com

## BRANCH OFFICES

**NEW HAMPSHIRE**
85 Merrimac Street, PO Box 460, **Portsmouth**, NH 03802
**Tel:** 603 433 3317

## CONTACTS

| | |
|---|---|
| **Business Services** | Michael E High |
| **Indian Services Group** | Gregory Sample |
| **Public Sector Group** | Eric R Herlan |
| **Trial Services** | Melissa A Hewey |

**INTERNATIONAL WORK:** The firm is the only Maine firm to be a member of Meritas, a worldwide organization that offers high-quality legal services through an integrated, yet independent, group of full-service law firms which provides clients a local contact for obtaining reliable legal services throughout the country and around the world. Membership in Meritas is by invitation only and requires firms to adhere to rigorous quality standards and a stringent code of ethics.

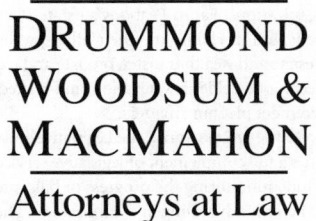

DRUMMOND
WOODSUM &
MACMAHON
Attorneys at Law

# EATON PEABODY

## THE FIRM

**Managing Partner:** Daniel G McKay
**Number of shareholders:** 24
**Number of other lawyers:** 20

**FIRM OVERVIEW:** Founded in 1917, Eaton Peabody is one of Maine's oldest and most widely recognized law firms. The firm strives to provide sophisticated legal services emphasizing constructive and cost effective problem resolution, whether through negotiation, development of creative alternatives or litigation. Service teams assure that all client matters receive thorough consideration by lawyers with specialized knowledge of the matter at hand. Through its subsidiary, Eaton Peabody Consulting Group, Eaton Peabody also offers professional consulting services in such areas as legislative lobbying, political campaign management and economic development.

## MAIN AREAS OF PRACTICE:

**Business Planning:** Eaton Peabody's Business Planning Group serves a diverse, statewide clientele. Their dynamic team helps clients navigate through all phases in the life of a business, including choice of entity, formation, raising capital, mergers and acquisitions, ownership succession, commercial transactions, taxation, government regulation, business disputes, dissolution, liquidation and bankruptcy. The Business Planning Group serves businesses of all sizes, from small start-ups to publicly held companies. It has unique experience in several specialties tied closely to the Maine economy, including aquaculture, and representation of large timberland owners and Canadian companies establishing US operations.

**Employee Relations & Benefits:** Eaton Peabody's Employee Relations and Benefits Group represents employers in response to organization campaigns, strikes and other concerted employee action, in collective bargaining negotiations and in proceedings before state and federal labor tribunals. The group positions its clients to minimize more acute labor issues by developing employment manuals and policies, employment agreements, and training programs on such topics as work-place harassment and employer-employee rights and responsibilities. Attorneys practicing in the areas of taxation and intellectual property join the group to develop employee benefit plans, anticipate and respond to questions concerning the ownership and use of intellectual property, and resolve disputes between employer and former employee.

**Environmental & Land Use:** Eaton Peabody's Environmental and Land Use Group advises private and municipal clients in state, federal and municipal environmental matters. Working regularly with an array of environmental consultants, they can quickly organize a team of professionals to address an environmental issue efficiently and effectively. They also provide legal assistance on state and municipal land use regulatory matters. These services include drafting ordinances, preparing and presenting permit applications, responding to enforcement proceedings, participating in rulemaking, and representing clients in appeals of local and state agency decisions before state and federal court.

**Estate Planning & Probate:** Focusing on individuals, closely held businesses and charitable organizations, Eaton Peabody's Estate Planning and Probate Group works closely with its clients and their other professional advisors to provide advice on estate and wealth transfer, probate and trust administration, charitable giving techniques, elder law, taxation, and related types of sophisticated trust and retirement planning matters.

**Legislative & Government Relations:** The Legislative and Government Relations Group provides a full complement of legislative services tailored for each client. Services include monitoring the progress of bills, preparing legislation and testimony, and actively advocating in the legislature. The group also assists other attorneys handling client matters before various agencies of local and state governments. Services include preparing and presenting applications for permits and licenses, participating in rule-making, responding to agency investigations and enforcement proceedings, and representing clients in appeals of agency decisions before state and federal courts.

**Litigation/Dispute Resolution:** Eaton Peabody's Litigation/Dispute Resolu-

## HEAD OFFICE

**MAINE**
80 Exchange Street, PO Box 1210, **Bangor**, ME 04402-1210
**Tel:** 207 947 0111   **Fax:** 207 942 3040
**Email:** inquiry@eatonpeabody.com
**Website:** www.eatonpeabody.com

## BRANCH OFFICES

**MAINE**
77 Sewall Street, Suite 3000, PO Box 5249, **Augusta**, ME 04330-5249
**Tel:** 207 622 3747   **Fax:** 207 622 9732

167 Park Row, PO Box 9, **Brunswick**, ME 04011
**Tel:** 207 729 1144   **Fax:** 207 729 1140

148 East Main Street, PO Box 460, **Dover-Foxcroft**, ME 04426
**Tel:** 207 564 8378   **Fax:** 207 564 7059

204 Maine Street, PO Box 119, **Ellsworth**, ME 04605
**Tel:** 207 664 2900   **Fax:** 207 667 3550

## CONTACTS

**Corporate Law & Business Planning** .........................Daniel G McKay
**Employee Relations & Benefits** ...........................Thomas C Johnston
**Environmental & Land Use** .................................P Andrew Hamilton
**Estate Planning & Probate** ....................................Calvin E True
**Legislative & Government Relations** .............William V Ferdinand, Jr
**Litigation/Dispute Resolution** .................................Bernard J Kubetz
**Municipal Law & Finance** ....................................P Andrew Hamilton
**Real Estate** ....................................................Edward D Leonard
**Tax** ........................................................Dorrance Sexton, Jr

tion Group provides representation in all the state courts of Maine and at all levels of the federal system from the United States District Courts to the Supreme Court. It is also experienced in various forms of alternative dispute resolution. Its attorneys are equipped by experience to handle virtually every variety of plaintiff and defendant representation. Clients include individuals, small businesses, and large companies.

**Municipal Law & Finance:** Eaton Peabody's Municipal Law and Finance Group provides a full spectrum of legal services to Maine's town and city governments, zoning and planning boards, school administrative districts, water and sewer utility districts, local development corporations, inter-local agencies, and other quasi-municipal entities. The firm also represents non-municipal clients and individuals in their dealings with government agencies at all levels.

**Real Estate:** Eaton Peabody's Real Estate Group provides a full range of legal services including title, lease, sale, acquisition, resolution of real estate disputes, like-kind exchanges, commercial and residential condominiums, planned unit developments, road associations, and advice and documentation regarding natural resource based land ownership issues, including Maine timberland ownership. The firm owns and operates Dirigo Title Company, a respected agent for four major national title insurance companies.

**Tax:** The Tax Group provides experienced advice to business and individual clients in federal, state, and local tax planning, ERISA issues, estate and gift tax planning and nonprofit organization tax issues. The group also provides tax planning for settlements and judgments, employee benefit plans, assistance with federal and state tax audits, like-kind exchanges and crossborder transactions.

**INTERNATIONAL WORK:** Eaton Peabody is proud to be the only Maine firm to be a member of TAGLaw, an international association of top independent law firms. This membership has created working relationships with over 130 firms worldwide providing the firm's clients with access to local contacts throughout the world. The firm has extensive experience with clients residing in Atlantic Canada in the areas of general commercial practice, cross border trade, economic development and timberlands management.

# MOON, MOSS & SHAPIRO, P.A.

## THE FIRM

**Managing Partner:** Jonathan Shapiro
**Senior Partner:** Richard G Moon

**Number of partners:** 5
**Number of other lawyers:** 3
**Number of Of Counsel lawyers:** 5

## HEAD OFFICE

**MAINE**
Ten Free Street, **Portland**, ME 04101
Mailing Address: PO Box 7250, Portland, ME 04112-7250
**Tel:** 207 775 6001  **Fax:** 207 775 6407
**Website:** www.moonmoss.com

**FIRM OVERVIEW:** Since1989, Moon Moss has concentrated its practice in labor and employment law on behalf of management.

**MAIN AREAS OF PRACTICE:** The firm's exclusive goal is to provide the best counseling and representation to its clients to help them achieve all their business goals. To achieve that purpose, the firm's practice is organized as follows: advice concerning labor and employment law matters on behalf of unionized and non-unionized private and public sector employers, including corporate planning in mergers and acquisitions; litigation of all employment and labor related matters on behalf of management; and employee benefits and executive compensation including methods of compensation, health and retirement plan design and compliance.

**Labor Relations:** Moon Moss is committed to the practice of preventive labor relations through issue assessment, compliance analysis, supervisory training, policy development, and positive communications. The preservation of management rights is the firm's goal, whether prior to a union offensive or during a union-organizing campaign. The firm has assisted many employers in winning NLRB elections or in avoiding union elections altogether. Moon Moss attorneys have appeared before the National Labor Relations Board, state labor boards, and state and federal courts and have preserved operational flexibility in contract negotiations, contract administration, and grievance and arbitration proceedings. The firm has also assisted corporations in improving labor and employee relations through the creation of better policies, supervision and communication systems.

**Employment:** The firm's Employment Practice includes training employers and their employees in the proper handling of all employment matters, designing and implementing policies and practices, providing sound, practical advice on day-to-day personnel matters, guiding businesses through governmental audits, inspections and investigations, conducting internal corporate audits and investigations, assisting companies in safeguarding corporate property and information (including enforcing non-competition and non-solicitation agreements against former employees and competitors), as well as counseling employers on immigration matters and the employment aspects of mergers, acquisitions and divestitures.

**Litigation:** The attorneys at Moon Moss have been particularly successful in helping their clients in the litigation process. The firm has broad-ranging civil litigation experience. This includes all employment-related civil litigation, including class actions under state and federal laws. The firm's practice also regularly encompasses claims relating to breaches of employment contracts and restrictive covenants, breaches of an employee's fiduciary duties, Sarbanes-Oxley and other whistleblower claims, and theft and/or misuse of confidential information and trade secrets. A substantial portion of litigated matters involve claims of discrimination arising out of terminations or other adverse personnel decisions as well as wage and hour disputes.

**Employee Benefits & Executive Compensation:** Moon Moss' Employee Benefits Practice offers a full range of legal services to its clients involving plan design and administration of pension, profit sharing, and other retirement and deferred compensation plans for both public and private employers. Moon Moss attorneys assist management in hiring and maintaining the best and the brightest executives and professionals with state-of-the-art compensation packages. The firm also advises employers when severing their relationship with top-level personnel. The firm also drafts and reviews contracts for both corporate (publicly traded and private) and individual clients.

**CLIENTS:** The firm's clients range from sole proprietorships to multi-state publicly traded corporations with over 100,000 employees, and include virtually every sector of the economy, from banks and hospitals to corporations involved in manufacturing, construction, transportation, public utilities, hospitality and retailing, as well as high technology companies, grocery chains, insurance companies and other service industries (including law firms). Because of the firm's reputation, several national corporations use Moon Moss for their legal work throughout New England.

MOONMOSS

*Workplace Guidance
and Solutions*

# PIERCE ATWOOD LLP

## THE FIRM

**Managing Partner:** Bruce A Coggeshall
**Senior Partner:** Ralph I Lancaster, Jr
**Number of partners:** 70
**Number of other lawyers:** 49

**FIRM OVERVIEW:** Pierce Atwood LLP is a leading New England law firm, recognized nationally and internationally for expertise in commercial law. The firm strives to deliver the highest level of service and meet the changing and increasingly complex needs of its clients, who range from entrepreneurs and individuals to members of the Fortune 500 and foreign governments, and span a variety of traditional and emerging business sectors. Clients derive superior value from the firm's location and its high level of sophistication. Pierce Atwood Consulting provides governmental relations, public relations, and economic development.

## MAIN AREAS OF PRACTICE:

**Commercial Finance & Bankruptcy:** Known for sophistication in complex financing transactions, leadership in creative public policy solutions to business and economic problems, and expertise in restructuring financially distressed businesses, the firm has premier practices in commercial lending, public finance and bankruptcy.

**Corporate & Tax:** Leading practice in acquisitions and sales of businesses, venture capital, private equity and other financing transactions, entity formation, federal and state tax, and representation of owners, directors and officers.

**Employment & Employee Benefits:** The group seeks to build expertise in its clients through counseling and training. Representation of management in state and federal trial, appellate, administrative and ADR proceedings; in matters arising under the NLRA and RLA (bargaining, arbitrations, board proceedings, organizing and labor disputes); in specialty areas such as benefits, immigration, FLSA, OSHA, and workers compensation; and in government relations.

**Energy:** The firm has built a national and international reputation serving domestic utilities, deregulated enterprises such as major merchant plants, and foreign emerging economies' need for energy market expertise. Clients are regional, national (utilities, independent project developers, lenders and investors in over 20 states), and international, including foreign governments and international financial institutions.

**Environmental:** The regional leader with national clients in all areas of environmental law and regulation, including land use, wastewater discharge, air emissions, solid waste, hazardous waste, chemical disclosure, wetlands, endangered species, and all other natural resources law.

**Governmental Relations:** In conjunction with Pierce Atwood Consulting, they combine substantive legal expertise, access to governmental leadership and a comprehensive, integrated array of complementary services such as public relations, traditional lobbying, media relations, campaigns, and stakeholder education, designed to further clients' public policy initiatives.

**Intellectual Property:** Intellectual property, technology, e-commerce and internet-related matters for emerging and established companies with national and international business interests. The firm manages national and international patent and trademark portfolios and litigates claims of infringement and misappropriation of all types of intellectual property.

**Litigation:** National and regional practice in business litigation including energy, intellectual property, white collar, products liability, environmental, ERISA, insurance and many other areas. Members include the two most recent Chief Justices of the Maine Supreme Judicial Court, a former Independent Counsel, and a past President and four Fellows of the American College of Trial Lawyers.

**Real Estate:** Sophisticated commercial practice includes development, financing, entity creation, taxation leasing, land use permitting and conveyancing of retail, commercial, industrial, and energy facilities and timberlands.

**Retail Financial Services:** Provides transactional, regulator, compliance, operations, and dispute resolution services to lenders, deposit takers, non-deposit investment providers, and insurance producer. Also serve vendors who support these types of retail financial service companies (e.g., software companies and loan servicers).

## HEAD OFFICE

**MAINE**
One Monument Square, **Portland**, ME 04101
**Tel:** 207 791 1100   **Fax:** 207 791 1350
**Email:** info@pierceatwood.com   **Website:** www.pierceatwood.com

## BRANCH OFFICES

**MAINE**
77 Winthrop Street, **Augusta**, ME 04330
**Tel:** 207 622 6311   **Fax:** 207 623 9367

**MASSACHUSETTS**
225 Franklin Street, Suite 1740, **Boston**, MA 02110
**Tel:** 617 426 1367   **Fax:** 617 426 2321

**NEW HAMPSHIRE**
One New Hampshire Avenue, Suite 350, **Portsmouth**, NH 03801
**Tel:** 603 433 6300   **Fax:** 603 433 6372

114 North Main Street, **Concord**, NH 03301
**Tel:** 603 223 0360   **Fax:** 603 223 0312

## CONTACTS

| | |
|---|---|
| **Commercial Finance & Bankruptcy** | Jacob A Manheimer |
| **Corporate & Tax** | David J Champoux |
| **Employment & Employee Benefits** | James R Erwin, Charles S Einsiedler, Jr |
| **Energy** | John W Gulliver |
| **Environmental** | Dixon P Pike |
| **Governmental Relations** | Christopher E Howard |
| **Intellectual Property** | Gloria A Pinza |
| **Litigation** | Jeffrey M White |
| **Real Estate** | Dennis C Keeler |
| **Retail Financial Services** | Richard P Hackett |
| **State Tax** | James G Good |

**State Tax:** Expertise covers corporate structuring, M&A and other transactions, business planning, succession and estate planning, and IRS controversies, as well as all forms of taxation, including personal and corporate income tax, sales and use tax, property tax, excise tax, multistate taxation and related services such as tax controversies, transactional advice, planning, ruling requests and legislative.

**CLIENTS:** Include Advanced Cell Technologies, Angela Adams Design, Anthem Blue Cross & Blue Shield, TD Banknorth, Brascan, Casella Waste Systems, Calypte Biomedical Corporation, Central Maine Power Corporation, Chittenden Bank, Cianbro Corporation, City of Portland, DaimlerChrysler, Dead River Company, DuPont, Energy Easy, Environmental Power Corporation, FPL Energy, Fairchild Semiconductor, The First Marblehead Corporation, Georgia Pacific Corporation, Hannaford Bros. Inc., IDEXX Laboratories, Immucell Corporation, J.D. Irving, Ltd., Key Bank N.A., Mercy Hospital, Nestle Waters N.A./Poland Spring, Sappi Fine Paper N.A., Sprague Energy Corporation, State of California, Tom's of Maine, University of New England, UNUMProvident, USAID, Verizon, World Bank, Wright Express Corporation.

**INTERNATIONAL WORK:** Encompasses multilateral transactions; cross-border financings; enterprise restructuring; energy and environmental law; EU compliance; regulatory reform and compliance; competition; privatization; litigation; arbitration; cross-border boundary dispute resolution; intellectual property licensing and transfer; defense and litigation. Attorneys have worked in 50 countries.

PIERCE
ATWOOD
LLP
*ATTORNEYS AT LAW*

# PRETI FLAHERTY BELIVEAU PACHIOS & HALEY LLP

## THE FIRM

**Managing Partner:** Harold C Pachios

**Number of partners:** 48
**Number of other lawyers:** 31

**FIRM OVERVIEW:** Preti Flaherty answers the call of a diverse business community with a sophisticated practice, international reach and multi-state experience. One of Northern New England's largest law firms, it is known for high-powered legal talent and exceptional credentials working with state and local governments.

## MAIN AREAS OF PRACTICE:

**Business Law:** Preti Flaherty advises clients in every stage of business development. For businesses that are just beginning, the firm's attorneys have broad ranging experience navigating business formation, securities offerings, technology protection and venture capital financing. The firm can also adroitly counsel clients on the added challenges that come with growth and success such as, technology licensing, executive compensation, debt financing and counseling Boards. Those businesses that find themselves poised to move onto the regional, national or global level also turn to Preti Flaherty for counsel on mergers and acquisitions, franchising, joint ventures and strategic alliances, international transactions, commercial contracts, and tax planning.

**Energy:** Preti Flaherty is a national leader in the rapidly evolving US – Canada energy marketplace. The firm counsels industrial consumers, energy project developers, energy cooperatives and aggregators, energy service companies and state and local governments on the reduction of risk and cost through deregulation. The firm provides counsel on rate reductions, special rate contracts, cost of service, rate structures, customer relations and competitive relationships with, from and among utilities, energy suppliers and customers. Its attorneys also assist in the structuring of entities to finance, build, license and operate renewable and natural gas powerplants and large and small transmission lines. The firm is the national leader in the development of Regional Transmission Organizations and Independent System Operators which are responsive to the needs of customers and consumer groups.

**Environmental:** Preti Flaherty has one of the region's largest and most diverse environmental practices. The firm's environmental litigators, transactional attorneys and regulatory specialists advise clients on legal issues related to all aspects of environmental regulation, compliance and due diligence, including air and water pollution, hazardous waste, chemical regulation and land use controls. The firm offers in-depth experience in all phases of Federal, State and local administrative and civil judicial enforcement proceedings.

**Health Law:** Preti Flaherty counsels hospitals, nursing homes, home health agencies, rehabilitation centers and other healthcare facilities, as well as insurers and individual practitioners. The firm has encompassing experience dealing with emerging healthcare issues and their legal ramifications and works hard to adjust regulations and advance laws and interpretations in support of its clients' interests. Preti Flaherty provides extensive services to institutions facing increasingly complex state regulatory issues. It has represented hospitals at hearings and proceedings before the Department of Human Services and the Federal Provider Reimbursement Review Board.

**Intellectual Property:** The firm works with clients to develop creative and cost-effective strategies for securing, maintaining, exploiting, and enforcing a company's intellectual property assets. Trademarks, copyrights, patents or licensing issues can arise in the United States, worldwide and via the internet. The firm's attorneys register companies' assets, provide regular portfolio reviews and offer experienced insight to help make sensible decisions based on a solid understanding of the business' goals and competitive position.

**Labor & Employment:** Preti Flaherty helps businesses, both in non-union and unionized settings, avoid potentially damaging situations by developing, implementing and communicating sound workplace policies and strategies. In addition to the counseling and risk prevention work the group provides, it also has

## HEAD OFFICE

**MAINE**
One City Center, PO Box 9546, **Portland**, ME 04112-9546
**Tel:** 207 791 3000  **Fax:** 207 791 3111
**Email:** info@preti.com
**Website:** www. preti.com

## BRANCH OFFICES

**MAINE**
45 Memorial Circle, PO Box 1058, **Augusta**, ME 04332-1058
**Tel:** 207 623 5300  **Fax:** 207 623 2914

Thirty Front Street, PO Box 665, **Bath**, ME 04530-0665
**Tel:** 207 443 5576  **Fax:** 207 443 6665

**NEW HAMPSHIRE**
57 North Main Street, PO Box 1318, **Concord**, NH 03302-1318
**Tel:** 603 410 1500  **Fax:** 603 410 1501

**MASSACHUSETTS**
10 High St, **Boston**, MA 02110
**Tel:** 617 226 3800  **Fax:** 617 226 3801

## CONTACTS

| | |
|---|---|
| Business Law | Susan LoGiudice |
| Energy | Anthony Buxton |
| Environmental | David Van Slyke |
| Health Law | John Doyle |
| Intellectual Property | Alfred Frawley |
| Labor & Employment | Michael Messerschmidt |
| Legislative, Regulatory & Governmental Services | Severin Beliveau |
| Litigation | Jonathan Piper |

extensive experience litigating claims in State and Federal courts, representing management in National Labor Relations Board proceedings and arbitrations under collective bargaining agreements, and defending charges of discrimination before the Equal Opportunity Commission and the Maine Human Rights Commission.

**Legislative, Regulatory & Governmental Services:** Preti Flaherty has an extensive legislative/regulatory practice. The firm's inside knowledge of public policy and the legislative process, combined with legal skills both traditional and groundbreaking, combine to create a wide range of approaches to resolving issues and influencing legislation. Many of the firm's attorneys have actively participated in the legislative process at both State and Federal levels.

**Litigation:** Preti Flaherty boasts one of the largest and most respected litigation groups in northern New England. Recognizing that success is often the result of pre-litigation counseling, the Litigation Group is nonetheless equipped to advocate for its clients wherever necessary, including consensual or mandatory mediation, domestic or international arbitration, and trials in State or Federal court. The group's experience is varied and extensive, including noteworthy successes in such matters as toxic tort litigation, securities claims, professional liability litigation, construction claims, lender liability claims, injunction of governmental agencies on constitutional grounds, and libel defense of national publications. Members of the litigation group are licensed in over a dozen states and numerous Federal courts.

**INTERNATIONAL WORK:** Preti Flaherty works with foreign-based companies seeking to do business in the United States whether it is a straightforward joint venture or a more complex acquisition. The firm helps companies navigate the local, state and Federal legal and regulatory landscape.

# VERRILL DANA, LLP

## THE FIRM

**Managing Partner:** David E Warren
**Senior Partner:** Peter B Webster

**Number of partners:** 58
**Number of other lawyers:** 44

**FIRM OVERVIEW:** Verrill Dana, LLP is widely known for delivering high quality legal services in a thoughtful and responsive manner that regularly exceeds our clients' expectations. The only Maine firm with offices in Boston, Hartford and Washington DC, Verrill Dana is a dynamic firm that provides sophisticated legal representation to businesses and individuals in every area of the law. It is the only law firm in Northern New England to be selected for the BTI Consulting Group's '2006 Survey of Client Service Performance for Law Firms.' This singular honor was based on independent client feedback from corporate counsel at large and Fortune 1000 organizations.

## MAIN AREAS OF PRACTICE:

**Litigation:** Verrill Dana's Litigation Group is comprised of experienced and skilled advocates who provide superior legal representation across a broad range of subject areas. What sets the Litigation Group apart is its commitment to client service and its track record of success in matters ranging from the most straightforward to the complex. The Litigation Group knows that disputes are fought and won outside as well as inside the courtroom. The group's trial lawyers understand that disputes do not arise in a vacuum, and develop strategies to solve clients' business and personal objectives as well as their legal needs.

**Business Law:** The Business Law Group is highly respected throughout the region for its specialized knowledge and experience, and for its ability to provide the resources of a large law firm while providing the attentiveness and accessibility of a smaller firm. In addition to advising clients in their role as general counsel, attorneys in the Business Law Group offer expert representation in a wide variety of matters, including mergers and acquisitions; reorganizations; joint ventures; securities offerings; SEC reporting; proxy contests; takeover defenses; and related issues.

**Bankruptcy & Commercial Law:** Verrill Dana's Bankruptcy and Commercial Law Group has extensive experience in all types of business bankruptcy proceedings, representing both debtors and creditors in Chapter 11 business reorganizations, Chapter 7 business liquidations, and Chapter 13 cases that involve business issues. Over the past 20 years, the group's lawyers have represented clients in virtually every significant bankruptcy case in the District of Maine, as well as other significant filings throughout the US.

**Employee Benefits & Executive Compensation:** The Employee Benefits and Executive Compensation Group counsels many of Maine's largest employers, as well as a growing number of employers outside of Maine, regarding all aspects of compliance with ERISA, the Internal Revenue Code and other laws that govern the form and administration of all types of retirement plans, health plans, executive compensation programs and fringe benefit plans. The group also represents employers in audits, investigations and proceedings conducted by various governmental entities.

**Environmental:** Verrill Dana's Environmental Law Group is an experienced team that provides clients with proactive advice to successfully manage the full range of their environmental permitting, compliance, development, and litigation needs. While not the largest, the practice is the most successful in Maine, and the group's lawyers have been involved in virtually every major permitting project or environmental issue in Maine over the last several years. Its breadth of experience uniquely positions the group to work collaboratively with diverse stakeholders and obtain favorable results before local, state and federal regulatory agencies as well as in the courtroom.

**Labor & Employment:** Verrill Dana's labor and employment lawyers practice on a national stage representing businesses in a wide array of industries. In addition to regular appearances in state and federal courts, they often appear before state

## HEAD OFFICE

**MAINE**
One Portland Square, **Portland**, ME 04112
**Tel:** 207 774 4000   **Fax:** 207 774 7499
**Email:** info@verrilldana.com
**Website:** www.verrilldana.com

## BRANCH OFFICES

**CONNECTICUT**
1028 Boulevard #201, **West Hartford**, CT 06119
**Tel:** 860 228 1023   **Fax:** 860 228 2583

**DISTRICT OF COLUMBIA**
400 North Capitol Street NW, Suite 585, **Washington**, DC 20001
**Tel:** 202 624 1466   **Fax:** 202 393 5218

**KANSAS CITY AREA**
1900 W. 47th Place, Suite 130, **Westwood**, KS 66205
**Tel:** 913 722 9555   **Fax:** 913 722 9559

**MAINE**
45 Memorial Circle, **Augusta**, ME 04332
**Tel:** 207 623 3889   **Fax:** 207 622 3117

403 Lafayette Center, **Kennebunk**, ME 04043
**Tel:** 207 985 7193   **Fax:** 207 985 3957

**MASSACHUSETTS**
One Boston Place, Suite 2330, **Boston**, MA 02108
**Tel:** 617 309 2600   **Fax:** 617 309 2601

## CONTACTS

| | |
|---|---|
| Litigation | James T Kilbreth |
| Business Law | Alan D MacEwan |
| Bankruptcy & Commercial Law | Roger A Clement, Jr |
| Employee Benefits | Gregg H Ginn |
| Environmental | Juliet T Browne |
| Labor & Employment | Douglas P Currier |
| Real Estate | James C Palmer |

and federal agencies that regulate the employer/employee relationship. Whether involving preventative counseling or active litigation, areas of expertise include all aspects of personnel law relevant to both private and public sector employers. Affirmative action, employment discrimination, OSHA and wage and hour laws are just a few examples. The group's lawyers are also active in labor management relations, union negotiations, representation elections and arbitrations.

**Real Estate:** Lawyers in Verrill Dana's Real Estate Group are widely regarded as premier practitioners in the state. The Real Estate Practice includes, but is not limited to, counseling and advising individuals, businesses, and professional groups with respect to the ownership, purchase, development and sale of real estate, boundary disputes, easements, real estate trusts and zoning matters. The group's lawyers also represent lenders and developers in negotiating, structuring, and documenting commercial, retail, residential, and industrial transactions and developments including manufacturing facilities, shopping centers, office and apartment buildings, timberlands, telecommunication towers, hotels and business and industrial parks.

## How lawyers are ranked

Every year we carry out thousands of in-depth interviews with clients and lawyers in order to assess the reputations and expertise of business lawyers across the USA. Chambers rankings and editorial are referred to extensively by General Counsel and other purchasers of legal services who look to our recommendations when choosing their lawyers.

# CORPORATE/M&A

| Corporate/M&A |
|---|
| **Leading Firms** |
| 1 · DLA PIPER RUDNICK GRAY CARY *Baltimore* |
|    HOGAN & HARTSON LLP *Baltimore* |
|    VENABLE LLP *Baltimore* |
| 2 · MILES & STOCKBRIDGE PC *Baltimore* |
|    WILMERHALE *Baltimore* |
| 3 · OBER KALER GRIMES & SHRIVER *Baltimore* |
|    WHITEFORD, TAYLOR & PRESTON *Baltimore* |

| Leading Individuals |
|---|
| **Senior Statesman** |
|   LOHR JR Walter *Hogan & Hartson LLP* |
| ★ SMITH JR Robert *DLA Piper* |
| 1 · COOK Bryson *Venable LLP* |
|    HANKS James *Venable LLP* |
|    KAHN Henry *Hogan & Hartson LLP* |
|    SILVER Michael *Hogan & Hartson LLP* |
|    WATKINS John *WilmerHale* |
| 2 · BAADER Michael *Venable LLP* |
|    FRISCH John *Miles & Stockbridge PC* |
|    WASHBURNE Thomas *Venable LLP* |
|    WEBB Thompson *Miles & Stockbridge PC* |
| 3 · ABEL Kenneth *Ober Kaler Grimes* |
|    CURRAN Bob *Whiteford, Taylor* |
|    POLIAKOFF Abba *Gordon, Feinblatt, Rothman* |
| **Up-and-coming individuals** |
|   CHALK David *DLA Piper* |
|   HARMON Jason *DLA Piper* |
|   HILL Eva *Whiteford, Taylor* |
|   MARTIN Thene *Hogan & Hartson LLP* |

## Band 1

### DLA Piper Rudnick Gray Cary US LLP
See firm details p.870

**The Firm:** *"Nothing but great quality work comes out of DLA Piper,"* say clients of this top-flight firm. As well as being an international player, it boasts a stalwart regional corporate and securities practice, with the DC, Baltimore and Northern Virginia offices working closely together for a long-standing group of sophisticated clients. Highlights of the year include a $1 billion joint venture and finance transaction for Marriott International and the $313 million sale of Columbia Bancorp to Fulton Financial.

**The Lawyers:** Clients have *"nothing but superlatives"* for the *"fantastic"* **Jay Smith** (see p.1044), cochair of the firm's national corporate and securities group. Widely considered to be the *"most efficient and well-rounded corporate lawyer"* in the state, Smith is a *"calming influence,"* while his tremendous experience and excellent judgment are evident in his extremely practical advice. Up-and-comer **Jason Harmon** (see p.1040) was also recommended as a *"go-to lawyer"* for public company securities. He provides strategic advice to clients, who describe him as *"incredibly responsive, hard-working, thoughtful, resourceful and able to handle matters normally requiring more experienced lawyers – he's that good."* **David Chalk** (see p.1038) has a reputation for his venture capital and investment banking practice. Clients enthuse that *"he's a terrific lawyer – excellent across the board in his business and legal judgment."*

**Clients/Work Highlights:** Human Genome Sciences; Legg Mason Wood Walker; Marriott International; PHH Corporation; T Rowe Price Group; McCormick; Educate; Laureate Education and Grotech Capital Group.

### Hogan & Hartson LLP
See firm details p.568

**The Firm:** This international firm is at the top of the market in Baltimore, and was described by sources as *"the very best"* in the region for public company representation and securities expertise. The team inspires high confidence in clients, who are delighted with the lawyers' *"excellent, first-rate, professional and responsive"* attitude and their collaborative approach. The firm has a number of star attorneys and a respected cluster of associates supporting the constellation. Its recent highlights include acting for Guilford Pharmaceuticals in its acquisition by MGI Pharma, part of a plan to build a leading biopharmaceutical company focused on oncology and acute care. The group also represented ABS Capital Partners in its $20 million Series A equity investment in WhenU.com, a provider of software-based online advertising.

**The Lawyers:** The *"exceptional"* **Duke Lohr** (see p.1041) has been working on transactions in California and the areas surrounding Baltimore. His work in recent months has been increasingly strategic in nature. The global head of the firm's capital market practice, **Mike Silver** (see p.1044), was highlighted by clients as another exceptional attorney. Peers described him as *"sharp, intense, no-nonsense and of pristine quality."* During 2005 he represented Martek Biosciences in connection with an $86.3 million common stock offering. *"Just an outstanding lawyer,"* **Henry Kahn** (see p.1041) impresses clients with his *"hands-on business and legal advice"* in complex transactions. His recent highlights include advising SevenSpace on its acquisition by Sun Microsystems. **Thene Martin** (see p.1041) was recommended by clients as *"terrific, detail-oriented, extremely practical and a fine negotiator."* She acted for Arcadian Management Services in its sale of $19 million of equity securities to an investor group.

**Clients/Work Highlights:** Avalon Pharmaceuticals; Martek Biosciences; Guilford Pharmaceuticals; Wabash National; Fieldstone Investment; ABS Capital Partners; LabCorp; American Public University System; Colfax; Ciena and Camden Partners.

### Venable LLP

**The Firm:** This firm's corporate group is admired in particular for its excellence in closely held private company work. Clients are impressed with the *"high quality"* of the attorneys' work in restructuring matters, and note that they are *"extremely practical, understand the law completely and are able to work through a complicated problem and come up with solutions."* Among a number of impressive deals from the past year, Venable represented Susquehanna Pfaltzgraff in the sale of the nonmanufacturing assets of its Pfaltzgraff division to Lifetime Brands, a transaction valued at around $34 million.

**The Lawyers:** **Jim Hanks** has done an *"excellent job in making himself a leading expert on corporate law issues,"* and is an excellent choice to advise companies on the nuances of Maryland law. He was also singled out for the representation of REITs. The *"excellent and innovative"* **Bryson Cook** has built up a sizable practice, and clients benefit from the *"creative structures he comes up with."* As a *"sharp tax attorney,"* he is deemed a first port of call for issues combining tax and corporate law. Highlights of his year include the restructuring of governance arrangements for CareFirst and a leveraged recapitalization for consumer products company Vector Products. **Tuck Washburne** is highly respected for his work for public companies. Clients particularly appreciate his *"experience and client focus."* He represented MBNA America Bank in its acquisition of Nexstar Financial, a portfolio company of private equity firm KKR. He also represented Mercantile Bankshares in its acquisition of Community Bank of Northern Virginia. Now the partner in charge of the firm's Baltimore office and chair of its corporate transactions group, **Michael Baader** is a *"great lawyer and a wonderful guy,"* according to peers. He recently represented Ritz-Carlton in negotiating development, financing, managements and joint venture agreements for mixed-use resorts worldwide, each costing $300 million or more.

**Clients/Work Highlights:** The Ritz-Carlton Hotel Company; Marriott International; Rewards Plus of America; EMG and Federalist Group.

## Band 2

### Miles & Stockbridge PC
See firm details p.1050

**The Firm:** This Baltimore-based firm was complimented for *"bending over backward"* to create multi-disciplinary teams of attorneys that are flexible enough to work around clients. Interviewees describe these teams as *"effective in understanding us and working with us on a day-to-day basis,"* and recommend the firm precisely for this responsiveness and focus on clients' needs. The high quality of the associates was another factor highlighted by interviewees.

**The Lawyers:** **John Frisch** (see p.1039) is chairman of the firm and a prominent figure in the local legal market. He focuses on M&A and securities transactions. **Topper Webb** (see p.1045) was recommended to researchers as *"extremely attentive to clients' needs. He works hard to determine how best to serve them."* Clients particularly admire his skill at *"taking legalese down to a simple articulate level."*

**Clients/Work Highlights:** Clients are drawn from a variety of sectors, such as manufacturing, financial

services, real estate and life sciences. Examples include US Foodservice, Norsk Hydro and Black & Decker.

### WilmerHale
See firm details p.580

**The Firm:** Wilmer Cutler's merger with Hale and Dorr has brought greater breadth and resources to the corporate team in Maryland, improving its services to clients. This was brought out strongly in research; as one source noted: *"We are extremely pleased with their accessibility, diligence and critical response time. They work through the night and are methodical and helpful, thinking through all the ramifications."* Another client added: *"These guys are excellent – extremely responsive and competent, and can give advice on a timely basis."* Peers also express a great deal of respect for this relatively small but *"excellent, high-quality"* team. Highlights of the year include M&A buyout work for a private equity fund and SEC filing and tax structuring for a real estate fund.

**The Lawyers:** **Jay Watkins** (see p.1045) was described to researchers as *"an excellent attorney, always approachable and responsive."* He is not only *"technically savvy"* but also offers practical business advice in a constructive way that makes him *"outstanding, impressive and easy to work with."*

**Clients/Work Highlights:** Legg Mason; Danaher; Sinclair Broadcast Group; Camden Partners Holdings and Manugistics.

## Band 3

### Ober Kaler Grimes & Shriver

**The Firm:** The firm's business and tax group focuses on midmarket transactions for entrepreneurial companies, but also regularly assists public company community banks with day-to-day corporate governance. It has concentrated a large amount of time of late on revising corporate charter documents for a mutual fund complex.

**The Lawyers:** **Ken Abel** is the *"standout lawyer"* here for many interviewees because he is *"extremely smart, mature beyond his years, reflective and has great judgment."* Cochair of the firm's business and tax

group, he concentrates on M&A, securities issues and general business advice.

**Clients/Work Highlights:** Clients include institutional and entrepreneurial companies in a variety of industries such as banking, healthcare, financial services, media and entertainment, technology, advertising, wholesale and distribution, and construction.

### Whiteford, Taylor & Preston LLP
See firm details p.1052

**The Firm:** Clients were full of praise for the excellent attorneys at this firm and their *"outstanding effectiveness and astuteness."* Their practical, detail-oriented approach particularly stood out. Peers, meanwhile, acknowledge the firm as a *"formidable competitor."* The firm's three offices work closely together to provide teams tailored to the specific needs of clients. Highlights of the year include an unusual leveraged buyout using an ESOP.

**The Lawyers:** Interviewees described **Bob Curran** (see p.1038) as *"an extremely fine attorney"* who is *"very thorough and practical."* Although the bulk of his practice involves M&A and strategic corporate advice, he also frequently consults on ERISA litigation. **Eva Hill** (see p.1040) impresses sources with her well-honed negotiation skills. She provides a *"terrific viewpoint,"* say clients, which gives them the information they need to make effective decisions. Interviewees also recommended her as *"astute, confident and detail-oriented with a sound understanding of business principles."*

**Clients/Work Highlights:** Clients are mostly private companies in industries such as construction, chemical distribution, engineering and services.

### Other Notable Practitioners

**Abba Poliakoff** of Gordon, Feinblatt, Rothman, Hoffberger & Hollander, LLC is respected for his securities practice. He has handled a number of equity financings for technology and biotech companies as well as representing venture investors making investments in developing companies. Clients find him *"thorough, honest and easy to work with."*

---

# EMPLOYEE BENEFITS & EXECUTIVE COMPENSATION

| Employee Benefits & Executive Compensation Leading Firms | |
|---|---|
| [1] | DLA PIPER RUDNICK GRAY CARY *Baltimore* |
| | VENABLE LLP *Baltimore* |
| [2] | MILES & STOCKBRIDGE PC *Baltimore* |
| [3] | OBER KALER GRIMES & SHRIVER *Baltimore* |
| | WHITEFORD, TAYLOR & PRESTON *Baltimore* |

## Band 1

### DLA Piper Rudnick Gray Cary US LLP
See firm details p.870

**The Firm:** This firm has a terrific broad-based practice doing sophisticated work for national and international clients *"at the cutting edge"* of employee benefits work. The strong team in Baltimore can draw upon the support of offices around the country. Clients are delighted with its *"thorough, responsive, proactive approach to solving problems"* and find the lawyers *"great at not being overly*

legalistic; they break down complex issues into terms HR people understand."* The firm covers just about every legal issue in this specialist area, from regulatory compliance to advice on complex pension fund investments and help in administering nonqualified deferred compensation and stock option plans. For ERISA litigation, clients dub the group *"aggressive, and good at laying it all out clearly,"* with one noting: *"This is exactly what I want."* The firm recently acted as employee benefits counsel to Whirlpool in connection with its $1.7 billion bid to acquire Maytag, addressing issues related to Maytag's underfunded pension liability.

**The Lawyers: Mark Muedeking** (see p.1042) is lauded by clients as a *"terrific litigator with great experience from beyond the law firm world."* Peers, meanwhile, agree *"He is the most innovative lawyer doing cutting-edge stuff."* His experience covers, among other things, all aspects of ERISA and ESOP law. The *"smart and sophisticated"* **John Kratz** (see p.1041) has been working in this area since the enactment of ERISA legislation in 1974. His depth of experience led interviewees to say that he *"understands everything,"* while clients appreciate that he is *"calm, doesn't get rattled easily, and is extremely responsive – I don't think 24 hours go by without him getting back to me."* **Linda Thomas** (see p.1044) deals in the specialized area of nonstatutory stock options and executive compensation, for which she is described as *"extremely knowledgeable on the intricacies of this type of law."* Clients say: *"She's great; she has lots of expertise and people like working with her."*

Clients/Work Highlights: Most of the team's work originates with publicly traded companies, although it also represents small private businesses, tax-exempt entities, trade associations, insurers, government retirement plans, healthcare organizations, and employee benefit and executive compensation consulting firms. Clients include Agilent Technologies; CareFirst BlueCross BlueShield; Leucadia National; Massachusetts Mutual Life Insurance; Maxtor; MCI; Profit-Sharing/401K Council of America and Zurich American Insurance Company.

## Venable LLP

**The Firm:** According to clients this is a first-class employee benefits team. Many claimed that they *"couldn't be more satisfied"* with the lawyers: *"They are extremely thorough, timely and outstandingly available."* The group has been busy this year handling a major workforce reduction program for a leading international financial services company. It has also been reviewing and redrafting welfare benefits contracts for a defense industry contractor, and lobbying for large supermarkets with respect to multiemployer pension liabilities.

**The Lawyers:** Clients find the head of the employee benefits group, **Barbara Schlaff**, to be *"attentive, knowledgeable, easygoing, levelheaded and intelligent; she always has an answer for us."* Peers also described her work as *"terrific,"* admiring her depth of experience and ability to *"boil complex issues down to a simple level."* Her practice includes work on qualified and nonqualified deferred compensation retirement plans, executive compensation and welfare plans. **Ken Hoffman** was also recommended to researchers as *"excellent, technically skilled and extremely thorough."*

Clients/Work Highlights: MBNA; Mercantile Bankshares; Sprint Nextel; General Dynamics and Legg Mason.

## Band 2

### Miles & Stockbridge PC
See firm details p.1050

**The Firm:** Miles & Stockbridge enjoys a strong name for employee benefits and executive compensation work, and covers the full spectrum of services in this practice area. The team has recently been focusing on nonqualified deferred compensation plans because of changes in legislation, and has consequently been heavily involved in compliance activities. Clients find its lawyers *"absolutely excellent and extremely responsive."*

**The Lawyers: Edward Adkins** (see p.1037) was described by a number of interviewees as simply *"the best – a smart guy with an enormous amount of experience."* Clients rely on this *"extremely articulate, tremendously knowledgeable"* attorney to return calls promptly and have the correct answers at his fingertips. He has recently been busy consolidating 411K retirement plans for the US subsidiary of a German company. **Thomas St. Ville**'s practice is focused on employee benefits law and executive compensation under ERISA and the Internal Revenue Code.

Clients/Work Highlights: Black & Decker; US FoodService; MG North America Holdings; Calvert County Maryland and a number of foreign companies with US subsidiaries.

## Band 3

### Ober Kaler Grimes & Shriver

**The Firm:** This regionally focused team boasts a broad practice covering most areas of employee benefits and executive compensation work. It is a popular choice with clients, who admire the *"excellent quality of work"* and *"rely on the team to dot the 'i's and cross the 't's"* in ERISA documents. The group's lawyers are felt to be particularly experienced writing ERISA plans and interpreting regulations.

**The Lawyers: Marika Ostendorf** spends 100% of her time on employee benefits law, and is proclaimed *"ERISA counsel number one"* by satisfied clients. Her *"personable"* manner puts clients at their ease, while her *"technical skill and breadth of knowledge"* – supplemented by an accounting background –

encourage them to rely on her advice. In recent months she has been handling a considerable volume of restructuring and compliance work.

Clients/Work Highlights: Clients include an international food servicing company, a construction company with employees on the East Coast, and a number of healthcare entities.

### Whiteford, Taylor & Preston LLP
See firm details p.1052

**The Firm:** The firm enjoys a *"prestigious presence"* in the local corporate community, with clients praising this two-person team for conducting *"outstanding work in a number of areas."* They were particularly impressed with the *"in-depth knowledge"* and an ethos of *"responsiveness, overlaid with a practical perspective."* The team is held to be particularly experienced in issues surrounding 411K plans, including their establishment and monitoring. It has lately been looking hard at IRS and DOL rules and regulations concerning retirement and health benefits provided by employers.

**The Lawyers:** *"Excellent with the governmental employers,"* **Paul Madden** (see p.1041) is a highly respected expert in the field. **Mary Claire Chesshire** (see p.1038) represents a number of counties in Maryland, regularly advising on retirement benefits. Both are admired by clients for their *"great interpersonal skills and high technical competence."*

Clients/Work Highlights: The firm's client roster includes a large utility with a national presence, governmental organizations including 21 counties in Maryland, engineering firms and hospitals. It has recently been busy with employee benefits work for a large nonprofit community association.

### Other Notable Practitioners

**Barry Berman** at Thomas & Libowitz PA is described by interviewees as an *"extremely knowledgeable attorney who knows how to get to the meat of the question; he reads a statute, understands it and relates it in normal terms, without losing any of the nuances."* He has a strong command of the benefits arena, and is ahead of the game when it comes to pension plans. Clients also consider him a great source of advice on employee benefits law in the context of mergers. **Henry Smith** of boutique law firm Smith & Downey PA is a respected authority on executive compensation. One interviewee described him as *"one of the most intelligent people I know; he really can dissect these issues."* He is particularly appreciated for the combination of an *"extremely effective and detail-oriented"* approach and a *"vivacious, sometimes aggressive"* style. **Katrina Kamantauskas-Holder** of husband and wife team Holder Law Group LLC is *"as smart as can be – she devours the regulations."* Peers recommended her as a good port of call for conflict work.

# EMPLOYMENT

## Band 1

### DLA Piper Rudnick Gray Cary US LLP
See firm details p.870

**The Firm:** Clients find this nine-lawyer labor and employment group to be *"responsive, practical, professional, thorough and knowledgeable."* It consistently delivers *"outstanding successes,"* sources agree, developing a track record of achievement that guarantees its top-tier status. The firm continues to represent management in a variety of labor and employment matters, acting for large corporations on a regional and national basis and, with its increasingly international outlook, it is said to be *"going everywhere and anywhere."* It recently won summary judgment on behalf of Cisco Systems in the US District Court for the Eastern District of Virginia. This case alleged violations of Title VII (sex harassment, sex discrimination and retaliation), assault and battery, tortious interference and civil conspiracy.

**The Lawyers:** *"Premier"* attorney **Rich Hafets** (see p.1040) recently defended a client in a government-initiated class action concerning its hiring practices. He has dealt with a slew of labor disputes nationwide, and handled major collective bargaining negotiations with the Teamsters. **Russ Gardner** (see p.1039) was described by peers as *"always polished and well prepared,"* while the *"terrific"* **Emmett McGee** (see p.1042) is highly recommended for high-stakes lawsuits: *"He's extremely aggressive and thorough in complex litigation; there's no one I'd rather have – he's an outstanding lawyer."* He has a strong regional practice, and has earned enormous loyalty from clients who say he is *"creative, fast and discreet – great at protecting the company and the feelings of the individuals involved."* He has recently prevailed in cases involving sex, race and disability discrimination claims. Up-and-comer **Larry Seegull** (see p.1044) has also been involved in a variety of discrimination cases. He is described by clients as a *"hard-working, thorough and aggressive"* attorney who *"leads cases well, with knowledge and experience beyond his age."*

**Clients/Work Highlights:** Accredited Home Lenders; Aon; Avon; Cisco Systems; Computer Sciences; E*TRADE Financial; GE; McAfee; MCI; MGM Mirage; Nestlé USA; Saks; UPS; US Cellular and Xerox.

### Miles & Stockbridge PC
See firm details p.1050

**The Firm:** This regionally strong firm has an extremely powerful labor group and is seen by market commentators as *"a real player"* in employment litigation. Clients express themselves delighted with the *"outstanding, first-class treatment"* they have received at all levels of the firm, from leading partners to young associates. They also benefit from being able to call upon resources from the firm's other offices. Alongside court and tribunal work in all areas of the employment and labor field, the firm regularly sends out teams to conduct investigations and is often called in to give secondary opinions, for

example reinvestigating cases of alleged sex discrimination.

**The Lawyers:** **Steve Silvestri** is admired for his command of traditional labor law, and is also experienced in handling employment discrimination matters. Clients say that he is *"the real deal: cool under pressure, experienced, savvy, superb."* He has been busy supervising labor work for a Scandinavian multinational across the USA. Practice group leader **Kathy Pontone** (see p.1043) has been handling a number of employment-related torts, such as assault and battery, as well as working on noncompete cases. Much of her time is spent on OSHA work. Clients describe her as *"responsive, articulate and astute."* **Steve Frenkil** (see p.1039) moves up the table this year after clients queued up to praise him as *"a really outstanding lawyer – thorough, methodical, strategic, cost-conscious and good at serving our needs in the most efficient and effective ways."* They were particularly impressed by his *"extraordinary verbal negotiating skills."* He specializes in high-level noncompete cases and represents a number of clients in the education sector.

**Clients/Work Highlights:** The team represents public sector clients, healthcare providers, educational institutions, and companies from the food service distribution, manufacturing and processing industries, among others.

### Shawe Rosenthal LLP
See firm details p.1051

**The Firm:** Sources agree that this is *"head and shoulders the leading labor boutique"* in the city, as well as being renowned nationwide for its *"terrific practice"* in employment law. Clients, in particular, laud it as *well versed in the law, knowledgeable, practical and results-oriented."* Although smaller than many of its rivals, it boasts a nationwide roster of clients who enjoy *"service with a personal touch."* Work is split between employment litigation and traditional labor law, the latter increasing due to the growing unionization of the healthcare industry, and the firm has recently been involved in a number of class actions relating to the FLSA. The group continues to grow and diversify, and it made two recent lateral hires at associate level.

**The Lawyers:** **Mike McGuire** (see p.1042) is an *"excellent, polished and gifted"* attorney, who interviewees say is *"absolutely preeminent at Shawe Rosenthal."* His *"incredible breadth of knowledge"* was particularly singled out for praise. McGuire focuses on traditional labor law, with a third of his practice involving employment discrimination, in which field he is described as a first-class litigator. **Steve Shawe** (see p.1044) also has *"tremendous experience"* of both traditional labor law and employment discrimination matters. He is *"smart, analytical and considerate"* with an impressive demeanor and, according to one satisfied client: *"He's among the best lawyers I've ever worked with – his combination of skill and personality makes him a top negotiator."* He represented May Department Stores when the business was acquired by Federated Department Stores in 2005. **Bruce Harrison** (see p.1040) heads up complex nationwide class actions for GEICO Insurance. Clients describe him as *"top-drawer, extremely knowledgeable on all employment law issues and litigation matters, thorough, aggressive and attentive."* They also appreciate his outstanding accessibility, noting that he *"gives us whatever we need wherever he is."* Traditional labor lawyer **Gary Simpler** (see p.1044) is on the road much of the year, representing clients in various different states. His knowledge of the field is highly respected, and clients appreciate an approach that is *"calm, thoughtful and focused."* Indeed, one client even said: *"I've been in this business 25 years and he's the best I've seen."* Up-and-comer **Elizabeth Torphy-Donzella** (see p.1045) is a new entrant to the tables after her *"hard-hitting and knowledgeable"* advice and excellent service impressed a number of clients.

**Clients/Work Highlights:** Government Employees Insurance; May Department Stores; Legg Mason; McDonald's; Genesis HealthCare; Danaher; Chubb Group and Reliant Energy.

### Venable LLP

**The Firm:** Clients find this labor and employment group to be *"extremely responsive."* With its close relationship between the Towson and Baltimore offices, and additional resources on hand in Rockville and DC, the firm assembles cross-disciplinary teams with ease, offering clients the resources of a large firm with the feel of a boutique. As a full-service firm, many companies will use Venable across a number of different practice areas. However the employment group also boasts a number of standalone clients. It assists management in most aspects of employment law, providing proactive advice to help clients avoid claims, and representing them before a variety of courts and tribunals where necessary.

**The Lawyers:** The *"terrific and top-flight"* **Jeff Ayres** was described by clients as a *"tenacious and skillful"* advocate. His recent successes include obtaining summary judgment on behalf of Marriott International in a discrimination lawsuit. **Ron Taylor**'s niche practice is focused on occupational safety and health work nationwide. He is regarded as one of the *"foremost experts"* on OSHA matters in the state, if not the country, and has taught the subject at Johns Hopkins University. Peers describe him as *"terrific, extremely pragmatic and he doesn't make a mountain out of a molehill,"* while clients find that when they follow his *"excellent judgment"* they end up *"with the best result."* Department chair **Bob Ames** is felt by many to be *"the preeminent labor attorney in Maryland."* He *"achieves business-oriented results"* for clients and is famed for his broad practice and particular focus on the healthcare industry. **George Johnston** is lauded as a *"real scholar and great for esoteric points of law."* Clients particularly appreciate his *"experience, focus and judgment."* This year he has been working on a large class action discrimination claim involving over 100,000 employees. New to the table, **Todd Horn** was described by peers as the *"brightest light"* coming up in the team. Admired as a *"fantastic litigator – one*

of the best in the courtroom, with a tremendous presence,"* his skills have been employed by such sophisticated clients as Marriott International and Sodexho. Clients themselves like the fact that he is a *"straightforward problem solver"* and consider him a *"business partner."* **Pat Clancy** is also said to be top-notch for complex litigation. He specializes in disability-related claims and acts for one of the largest nonprofit medical research organizations in the region.

**Clients/Work Highlights:** Marriott International; Sodexho; Whiting-Turner Contracting; Mercantile Bank & Trust; MBNA; Wal-Mart; Pizzagalli Construction; PEMCO; National Aquarium in Baltimore; WR Grace; Johns Hopkins University; Raytheon; MileOne Automotive and St Mary's Hospital.

## Band 2

### Kollman & Saucier PA

**The Firm:** This boutique firm is said to be increasingly visible in Baltimore's labor and employment circles. According to clients, a group of *"young, hungry, hard-working"* attorneys provides a *"high caliber"* of work. The firm has brought in several new associates this year and its *"first-class lawyers"* are handling matters for larger clients than before. This has made for an active year, with an increasing number of union avoidance situations, a successful trial in the DC Supreme Court, several major noncompete lawsuits and a role in an important racial and sexual harassment case in California.

**The Lawyers:** President of the firm **Darrell VanDeusen** was recommended by interviewees as an *"exceptionally bright, accomplished, extremely efficient and fact-oriented"* adviser. This *"straight shooter"* impresses clients with his high level of *"practical business advice."* He represents management in all areas of labor and employment law, often at the national level. The *"intellectual and creative"* **Eric Paltell** has spent a lot of time this year negotiating collective bargaining agreements, including four new employment contracts for a municipality. He has also been involved in labor negotiations for a client in the public utilities field. On the employment side, he handled a multimillion-dollar sexual harassment case, while ERISA litigation also makes up about 20% of his practice.

**Clients/Work Highlights:** Clients include private and public companies, government entities, education institutions; healthcare companies; financial institutions and public utilities.

## Band 3

### Gordon, Feinblatt, Rothman, Hoffberger & Hollander, LLC

**The Firm:** This small employment and labor team remains busy representing clients in a variety of issues. The team has been successful this year in several collective bargaining negotiations, but the

majority of its time has been spent on employment-related issues, such as defense of discrimination claims and advice on restrictive covenants, restructuring and downsizing.

**The Lawyers:** **Bob Kellner** was described by peers as an *"excellent lawyer: practical, thorough and a cut above the rest."* He *"knows the law and pays close attention to detail."* As well as handling a stream of employment law issues, Kellner also helps clients to modify employee benefits plans.

**Clients/Work Highlights:** Mid-Atlantic Permanente Medical Group; Kennedy Krieger Institute; Henderson-Webb and Merchants Terminal.

### Hogan & Hartson LLP
See firm details p.568

**The Firm:** This large, international firm has a small but *"tremendous"* labor and employment team in Baltimore. It handles a wide variety of employment matters for major clients, and is also seeing an increase in traditional labor work. Hogan & Hartson's international reach was recently demonstrated by a case involving a journalist from the Russian service of Radio Free Europe/Radio Liberty who crossed into Chechnya and interviewed Chechen terrorist Shamil Basayev. The Maryland team liaised with the firm's Moscow office over disciplinary issues when the screening of this interview on ABC's Nightline gave rise to an international incident. This extremely sensitive case involved foreign policy matters and issues under both US and Russian law.

**The Lawyers:** A *"fine gentleman – one of the local deans of the Bar,"* **Gil Abramson** (see p.1037) handles a variety of complex cases for sophisticated clients, including several household-name multinationals. According to clients, he is a *"combination of being highly expert, extremely confident and very thorough."*

**Clients/Work Highlights:** Johns Hopkins University Applied Physics Laboratory; Baltimore Ravens; Guilford Pharmaceuticals; La Petite Academy; Martek Biosciences; Radio Free Asia and Radio Free Europe/Radio Liberty.

### McGuireWoods LLP

**The Firm:** McGuireWoods' sizable labor and employment practice includes a unit in Baltimore that focuses on labor-management relations and employment discrimination issues. The team's recent highlights include representing a major defense contractor and acting both regionally and nationally for a French company.

**The Lawyers:** **Doug Topolski** was described as *"extremely smart, hard working"* and even *"like a whirling dervish!"* Interviewees praised his *"experienced and effective"* style and appreciated his degree of specialization in the field. His real forte is said to be union avoidance and union organization issues, for which he travels all over the USA representing clients. Here, recent successes include concluding a collective bargaining contract in Virginia for a foreign multinational.

**Clients/Work Highlights:** Clients include a variety of national and international companies, including DAP and Nexion Health.

## Ober Kaler Grimes & Shriver

**The Firm:** This firm's labor and employment department has enjoyed a busy year, representing healthcare providers across the USA. It has also been seeing an increase in work defending management against claims under the ADA, which is a growing source of potential disputes between employees and employers.

**The Lawyers:** **Pam White** chairs the firm's labor and employment group and is a designated arbitrator and mediator for the employment and commercial panels of the AAA. She was described as a *"hard-hitting advocate"* for both management and plaintiffs, and interviewees acknowledged that *"she's terrific for an aggressive approach."*

**Clients/Work Highlights:** Clients are drawn from the financial and professional services, and healthcare and construction industries, among others.

## Saul Ewing LLP

See firm details p.1763

**The Firm:** This sizable firm has a team of highly regarded lawyers in its Baltimore office, who are particularly famed for their work in noncompete issues. The group is also well versed in the defense of discrimination claims, such as diversity, sexual harassment and disability cases. On the traditional labor side, it offers experience of negotiating collective bargaining agreements and overseeing the management response to union organization campaigns. The team also has the capacity to deal with issues relating to employee benefits law.

**The Lawyers:** Department chair **Harriet Cooperman** (see p.1038) is a *"tough negotiator and business-getter,"* who wins considerable loyalty with her *"thorough and aggressive"* approach to protecting her clients' interests. During 2005 she was reappointed to the Maryland State Higher Education Labor Relations Board. Well versed in noncompete issues, **Gary Eidelman** (see p.1038) is said by market sources to *"really focus on the issues. He's smart, good to work with and great with clients."*

**Clients/Work Highlights:** Clients range from owner-managed businesses to Fortune 500 companies, and include nonprofit organizations, public entities and federal contractors. Industries represented include manufacturing; wholesale; automobile; technology; financial services; entertainment and retail.

## Serotte, Rockman & Westcott

**The Firm:** This boutique firm focuses on representing midsized local businesses. Interviewees recommended the team for offering clients a value-for-money service with impressive and reliable attorneys. Typical work includes advising clients on labor relations and defending management against claims involving restrictive covenants, wrongful discharge, OSHA and equal opportunities law.

**The Lawyers:** **Neal Serotte** is described by interviewees as *"terrific for traditional labor law,"* because of his *"practical and results-oriented"* approach. **Jeff Rockman** also enjoys a well-deserved reputation in the state and was enthusiastically recommended to researchers.

**Clients/Work Highlights:** Baltimore Aircoil; Baltimore Blast; Baltimore Spice; 1st Mariner Bank; Continental Realty; Fila USA; Griffith Energy Services; Health Facilities Association of Maryland; Leaseway Transportation; Locke Insulators; Merrill Lynch; S3 Technologies and Shopco Management.

## Whiteford, Taylor & Preston LLP

See firm details p.1052

**The Firm:** This well-established firm benefits from fielding a number of experienced, distinguished and high-quality lawyers. Its labor and employment group continues to represent clients in major discrimination defense claims. Meanwhile, in the traditional labor law arena the team has been assisting management in preventing unionization in West Virginia, Baltimore and Columbia, Maryland.

**The Lawyers:** **Jeanne Phelan** (see p.1043) is highly thought of by clients for her *"successful advice and sure handling of sensitive issues."* Interviewees particularly admire her courtroom skills and *"terrific and thorough"* presentation of cases. Experienced management-side labor attorney **Larry Wolf** (see p.1046) is a *"brilliant lawyer who has a scholarly bent that enhances his practice."* He handles some of the most significant appellate-level employment matters in the region. Senior counsel **Joe Pokempner** (see p.1043) is described as *"old school"* in his approach. He has a varied practice spanning all aspects of employment law, and advises premier clients, including one of the municipalities in Maryland. *"Quality attorney"* **Peter Guattery** (see p.1040) acts for a number of EU companies with US operations. Primarily known as a labor lawyer, his practice also encompasses immigration work. New to the firm, the *"quite excellent"* **James Gillece** (see p.1039) brings an impressive client base with him.

**Clients/Work Highlights:** Clients include employers in many industry sectors, including manufacturing, distribution; retail; professional and financial services and healthcare.

# HEALTHCARE

| Healthcare | | |
| --- | --- | --- |
| **Leading Firms** | | |
| [1] | OBER KALER GRIMES & SHRIVER *Baltimore* | |
| | VENABLE LLP *Baltimore* | |
| [2] | GALLAGHER, EVELIUS & JONES, LLP *Baltimore* | |
| | GORDON, FEINBLATT, ROTHMAN *Baltimore* | |
| | HOGAN & HARTSON LLP *Baltimore* | |
| [3] | GOODELL, DEVRIES, LEECH & DANN *Baltimore* | |
| | WHITEFORD, TAYLOR & PRESTON LLP *Baltimore* | |

## Band 1

## Ober Kaler Grimes & Shriver

**The Firm:** With more than 20 attorneys in its Baltimore office, this firm has a large and diverse healthcare practice. The *"excellent and exceptional"* team is focused principally on representing providers, including sole practitioners, nursing homes, clinical laboratories, hospitals and pharmaceutical manufacturers. This is a truly national practice, with clients in every state of the USA, 80% of them based outside Maryland. A third of the caseload involves fraud and abuse allegations, and the team has been involved in some of the largest healthcare fraud settlements of the past five years. For the 30th anniversary of the healthcare practice, the firm is in the process of establishing the Leonard C Homer Ober Kaler Law and Healthcare Fund at the University of Maryland School of Law, to help educate the next generation of healthcare lawyers.

**The Lawyers:** *"Major national player"* and chair of the firm's health law department, **Sanford Teplitzky** brings valuable government experience and an excellent reputation to the healthcare team. He has a national practice centered around fraud and abuse cases, and typically deals with federal rather than state law. **Howard Sollins** was described as an *"extremely knowledgeable"* attorney with a good name for representing clients in the senior living industry. He has obtained a number of certificate of need approvals, including one connected to an expansion at Shady Grove Adventist Hospital. He also represented a client in the acquisition of 18 adult day care centers across four states.

**Clients/Work Highlights:** Clients include ancillary service providers, pharmacy and biotech companies, healthcare management and billing companies and healthcare trade organizations.

## Venable LLP

**The Firm:** This broad practice evolved out of the firm's work for major healthcare providers in the region. It is now one of the most respected in the field, with clients queuing up to praise *"the full gamut of resources"* on offer. The team's work is evenly split between advising community hospitals and large academic health centers, and doing diverse work for hospitals and physicians in joint ventures. The team also represents clients in the pharmaceutical industry, for example advising wholesalers and manufacturers on drugs marketing. Much of the group's

| Healthcare |
| --- |
| Leading Individuals |
| ★ **TEPLITZKY** Sanford *Ober Kaler Grimes* |
| 1 **ADELMAN S Allan** *Adelman, Sheff* |
| **ROSEN Barry** *Gordon, Feinblatt, Rothman* |
| 2 **BAKER Constance** *Venable LLP* |
| **IMMELT Stephen** *Hogan & Hartson LLP* |
| **MERKLE Craig** *Goodell, DeVries, Leech* |
| **PRESTON Susan** *Goodell, DeVries, Leech* |
| **SARBANES John** *Venable LLP* |
| **SOLLINS Howard** *Ober Kaler Grimes* |
| **TRANTER Jack** *Gallagher, Evelius* |
| 3 **MATRICCIANI Rose** *Whiteford, Taylor* |
| **PARVIS Peter** *Venable LLP* |

work is in the regulatory arena, navigating governmental regulations at both state and federal levels. This includes obtaining certificates of need, and advising on fraud, abuse and antireferral prohibitions. The team has also been active in M&A involving healthcare providers.

**The Lawyers: Connie Baker** is sought out by physicians and hospitals for her regulatory experience and skill in credentialing. Her practice is focused on Maryland and surrounding states. **John Sarbanes** is active in the senior living industry, representing assisted living providers, retirement communities, multistate and sole providers. He also handles tax-exempt financing advice for nonprofit hospitals. Clients describe him as *"talented, thoughtful and responsible."* **Peter Parvis** has a diverse practice, but is especially well known for his regulatory expertise and niche in planning law.

**Clients/Work Highlights:** Clients include acute care, chronic and specialty hospitals; hospital networks; physician groups; nursing homes and continuing care retirement communities; a professional liability insurance company; self-insurance trusts; pharmaceutical manufacturers and wholesalers.

## Band 2

### Gallagher, Evelius & Jones, LLP

**The Firm:** This firm enjoys a stalwart reputation for its healthcare practice. Much of its focus is on the regulatory and transactional sides, with the group handling a range of issues from Medicare and Medicaid fraud and abuse law compliance, to mergers and affiliations of healthcare entities. One long-term project has involved assisting in the development of the Weinberg Center for Baltimore's Mercy Medical Center, providing state-of-the-art women's health services.

**The Lawyers: Jack Tranter** is an active player in the healthcare community and is renowned for his certification expertise. He recently helped Washington County Hospital Association to obtain approval from the Maryland Health Care Commission for the relocation of a hospital to a new site, in the face of considerable opposition.

**Clients/Work Highlights:** Clients include hospitals; nursing homes; physicians and professional corporations.

### Gordon, Feinblatt, Rothman, Hoffberger & Hollander, LLC

**The Firm:** This busy group focuses on work in Maryland, typically representing healthcare providers and those in the payment arena. Examples of recent work include M&A in the hospital sector, the development of medical waste facilities and surgical centers, and advice on joint ventures between physicians and hospitals.

**The Lawyers:** The highly respected and experienced **Barry Rosen** heads the firm and its healthcare practice group. He spends much of his time in front of the Maryland Health Care Commission obtaining certificates of need, and the HSCRC (Health Services Cost Review Commission), where he has been successful in increasing hospital rates. He has also been before a variety of licensing regulatory boards for doctors and nurses, and provided advice on joint ventures between hospitals and physicians.

**Clients/Work Highlights:** Clients include physicians; dentists; hospitals; professional associations; nursing homes; continuing care retirement communities; home health agencies; managed care companies; HMOs; insurers; manufacturers of medical equipment and suppliers throughout the mid-Atlantic region.

### Hogan & Hartson LLP

See firm details p.568

**The Firm:** Although Hogan & Hartson doesn't have a distinct healthcare department in Baltimore, a formidable group of leading attorneys from the office's corporate and litigation teams effectively forms an extension of the firm's strong national healthcare practice. Recent highlights include the $200 million sale of biotech company Guilford Pharmaceuticals to MGI PHARMA in a cash and stock deal. The firm is also defending seven hospitals that have been sued by the government under the False Claims Act for allegedly improper billings relating to the use of investigational devices in the treatment of Medicare patients.

**The Lawyers: Steve Immelt** (see p.1040) is a commercial litigator with a diverse practice, who was singled out by commentators as *"excellent and extremely knowledgeable"* when it comes to healthcare work. Particularly respected for his representation of medical device companies, he has been busy of late resolving a False Claims Act matter for Cornell University arising from federally funded research. He is also advising a group of 40 hospitals in a false claims investigation into a medical device, and acts for a large pharmaceutical client in marketing issues. Immelt cochairs the healthcare team with corporate star Mike Silver, while Henry Kahn, Gil Abramson, Mark Gately and Thene Martin are also part of this group.

**Clients/Work Highlights:** Guilford Pharmaceuticals; Martek Biosciences; Avalon Pharmaceuticals; Laboratory of America Holdings and Novartis.

## Band 3

### Goodell, DeVries, Leech & Dann, LLP

See firm details p.1047

**The Firm:** This firm is famed for its strong medical malpractice defense team. Here a recent highlight was obtaining a defense verdict after three days of trial in a malpractice case concerning the postoperative management of a patient following a hysterectomy. It also regularly advises clients on credentialing and medical staff issues.

**The Lawyers:** According to at least one client, **Susan Preston** (see p.1043) is *"one of the smartest lawyers I've come across."* One of the founding partners of the firm, she has a strong reputation in the professional negligence and malpractice arena. **Craig Merkle** (see p.1042) impresses clients with his *"tremendous ability"* and success in winning medical malpractice cases. They particularly appreciate his constructive approach, prompt turnaround times and knack of *"zeroing in on the main issues."*

**Clients/Work Highlights:** The Doctors Company; University of Maryland Medical System; Mercy Medical Center; The Medical Protective Company; Upper Chesapeake Health; Ascension Health; St. Agnes HealthCare; Wyeth; Bayer and Pfizer.

### Whiteford, Taylor & Preston LLP

See firm details p.1052

**The Firm:** This small healthcare group focuses on regulatory matters, including fraud and abuse, HIPAA compliance, practitioner licensing, disciplinary proceedings and Medicare audits. It also handles contract negotiations and the development of healthcare facilities, and advises on mergers and joint ventures. In recent months the group has been increasing its involvement and visibility in the senior living arena. The team is most active in the regional market, venturing further afield when dealing with Medicare and in the continuing care sector.

**The Lawyers: Rose Matricciani** (see p.1042) is particularly active in the fraud and abuse arena. She was recently the senior regulatory counsel for a $185 million retirement community condominium project, and the health regulatory counsel in the bond financing for the renovation of a healthcare system involving two hospitals. Clients describe her as an attorney who is *"always responsive, knowledgeable and experienced,"* and who *"lays out the full spectrum of possibilities, zeroing in on a range of choices."*

**Clients/Work Highlights:** Clients include hospitals, ambulatory care facilities, university healthcare systems and physician groups.

### Other Notable Practitioners

**Allan Adelman** of Adelman, Sheff & Smith LLC is extremely active in the national healthcare arena, and is the current president of the American Health Lawyers Association. He is highly respected for his representation of hospitals, and interviewees described him as an *"excellent, standout attorney."*

# LITIGATION

## Litigation: General Commercial
### Leading Firms

### Leading Individuals

#### Senior Statesmen

#### Up-and-coming individuals

## Band 1

### DLA Piper Rudnick Gray Cary US LLP
See firm details p.870

**The Firm:** This *"excellent international firm"* offers clients the full range of litigation services. These include securities class actions, appellate work, Sarbanes-Oxley-related claims, bankruptcy litigation and professional negligence defense for law firms and other professionals. The group is also increasingly moving into international arbitration. Clients describe it as a *"terrific law firm with terrific lawyers and strength through the ranks,"* and particularly appreciate its provision of *"specialized advice in complex litigation cases."* The fact that it obtains *"great results"* while remaining *"cost-effective"* is also a considerable drawing card. Recent highlights include defending a major bank against a nationwide class action relating to its lending practices, and advising defense contractors on the procurement of materials.

**The Lawyers:** Joint global leader and chair of the firm's US litigation practice, **Bob Mathias** (see p.1042) was described by clients as *"extremely smart, knowledgeable, practical and modest."* This *"outstanding trial lawyer gets results; with a terrific combo of brains and guts he will adapt to any kind of case."* He spends a considerable portion of his time on the West Coast and overseas. Clients also praised **Neil Dilloff** (see p.1038) for his *"cutting-edge"* work and direct approach. Peers, meanwhile, consider him a *"long-time cantankerous battle lawyer; a tenacious bulldog; an extremely aggressive litigation star, who commands instant confidence in front of a jury and has total mastery in the courtroom."* He *"tells you exactly what he thinks with no sugar coating."* **Frank Burch** (see p.1037) is also considered a *"real star."* He has not been taking depositions recently but has instead been focusing on providing strategic advice to clients. They are impressed by his *"results-oriented"* approach and consider him *"terrific – as an adviser and strategist he is the tops; extraordinary, bright and savvy."* As managing partner, meanwhile, he is described as *"a quintessential leader; he has vision, is decisive, charismatic and perfect at running the firm."* Interviewees admire **George Nilson** (see p.1043) as a *"fine litigator with excellent judgment." "Smart, effective and someone who dominates the room,"* he represents CareFirst of Maryland in connection with continuing issues with regulators in Maryland and DC. Clients appreciate his business knowledge and describe him as *"totally timely and aggressive without being overbearing." "One of the smartest guys around,"* **Charles Scheeler** (see p.1044) is a *"truly outstanding"* lawyer who establishes *"excellent"* rapport with the judge and jury and is formidable in cross-examinations. He has had a tremendous year, successfully representing MCI against a nationwide class action in which the plaintiff alleged over-billing.

**Clients/Work Highlights:** MCI; St. Paul Travelers; Computer Sciences; Marriott International; National Aquarium in Baltimore and Amtrak.

# GENERAL COMMERCIAL

### Hogan & Hartson LLP
See firm details p.568

**The Firm:** This international firm has a strong Baltimore-based litigation team made up of *"excellent lawyers."* The group works closely with attorneys from across the network, recently collaborating with lawyers from its New York, Asian and European offices to successfully handle a fiercely contested securities action in the US District Court for the Southern District of New York on behalf of Harmony Gold Mining. The team has also obtained several important victories for a Fortune 500 biotech company in states across the USA.

**The Lawyers:** **George Beall** (see p.1037) is described as *"the distinguished face of the firm."* He has been spending time this year on a matter involving the owner of the Baltimore Ravens professional football club, and has also conducted a number of white-collar criminal investigations. **Mark Gately** (see p.1039) represents a number of sophisticated clients, as part of a practice that is becoming increasingly international in scope. Interviewees described the experienced litigator as a *"great, straightforward, high-integrity attorney"* with *"an engaging personality – he's a crackerjack."* The multitalented **Steve Immelt** (see p.1040) is a litigator with a stellar reputation and diverse practice. He represents a number of clients in the healthcare industry, including hospitals and pharmaceutical companies. The majority of his work is on the East Coast and includes regulatory compliance issues and fraud. A recent example was resolving a matter for Cornell University involving False Claims Act issues arising from federally funded research. Commentators say: *"He is one of the smartest people I've ever met; he has common sense and is effective at solving problems."*

**Clients/Work Highlights:** The Johns Hopkins University; The Johns Hopkins Hospital; Martek Biosciences; Fieldstone Investment; Sizeler Property Investors; Royal Ahold; Deutsche Bank Alex. Brown; T Rowe Price; Medtronic Sofamor Danek and LabCorp.

### Kramon & Graham, PA
See firm details p.1048

**The Firm:** Clients appreciate the *"top-notch service and excellent business sense"* of these Baltimore litigators: *"They really understand our operations and what's important to us."* The firm maintains a strong focus on commercial and white-collar criminal litigation, while at the same time growing its corporate and real estate transactional capabilities. It boasts some of the *"most experienced trial lawyers"* in the state, who are renowned for their *"smart and solution-oriented"* approach and for giving *"sound advice before you get to the courtroom."* Clients also find them to be *"upfront, forthcoming, expedient, articulate and clear on the interpretation of the law."* The firm's work is increasingly reaching beyond Baltimore to the national and international spheres.

**The Lawyers:** *"Lawyers' lawyer"* **Andy Graham** (see p.1040) was described by clients as *"a highly ethical* *person who leaves small talk aside and gets right to the facts.*" In the words of one interviewee: "*He is one of the most professional lawyers I've worked with and one of the most intelligent.*" **Jim Ulwick** (see p.1045) is another "*wonderful*" attorney and "*right up there*" in the top tier. Interviewees praise his "*phenomenal*" criminal defense skills and clients find him "*extremely professional and client-oriented.*" This year he has spent much of his time in commercial litigation involving the horse racing and media industries, though he also handles a fair amount of medical malpractice defenses, as well as IP and products liability cases. New up-and-comer and a principal of the firm, **Geoffrey Genth** (see p.1039) is "*mature, steady, tenacious and practical.*" He has been involved in litigation for Deutsche Bank Securities.

**Clients/Work Highlights:** BAA; Deutsche Bank Securities; Goodyear; Gulf Insurance Group; North American Bus Industries; Pepsi Bottling Group; RadioShack; Siemens Power Ventures and Streuver Bros Eccles & Rouse.

## Venable LLP

**The Firm:** This long-established "*high-quality*" Baltimore firm has enjoyed a busy year with success in a variety of trials. Clients appreciate a "*thorough, professional, client-oriented and technically talented*" team that takes a holistic approach, forming multi-disciplinary groups to solve different types of commercial dispute. For example, a team of trial, bankruptcy and transactional attorneys recently won a significant victory in Enron Corp v JPMorgan Securities, Inc, et al. The firm has also had clusters of cases in the products area in which the Virginia and New York offices have become involved.

**The Lawyers:** Managing partner **Jim Shea** is an "*extraordinarily well-spoken individual,*" say interviewees. An "*extremely smart, straightforward litigator who fights hard but fair,*" he is admired by clients for his "*unwavering, consistently strong advice.*" His main focus of late has been on representing Maryland's largest health insurer, CareFirst Blue Cross Blue Shield, in a multijurisdictional dispute. A portion of his time is also given over to advising global clients on complex and politically sensitive issues. **Jim Archibald** was described as "*organized, methodical and effective.*" The author of a well-known and much-used guide on pleading in Maryland, he is respected by both judges and practitioners, especially in the products liability field. "*Smart, thorough and extremely forceful,*" **Jim Gray** has a practice spanning Maryland, DC and Virginia. Clients find him to be "*experienced, professional and skillful,*" while peers say he "*makes you go through every single step and work for all you've got.*" He recently defended a large financial institution from a wrongful termination suit brought by an executive in the Maryland state court, and was involved in an extensive counterclaim by the institution, settled in Spring 2005. **Michael Schatzow** is renowned for his criminal defense expertise but has also proved himself an effective general commercial litigator, representing Enron in complex cases. Interviewees say: "*He will dive into a case and become a really passionate believer in his client's*

cause.*" **Paul Strain** handles complex matters on a local and national basis, trying cases across the USA. He was recently involved in a major patent case in Chicago. Clients describe him as the classic Venable attorney: "*Prepared and charismatic – he deals with situations with confidence and grace.*"

**Clients/Work Highlights:** Cardinal Health; Ford; Labcorp; Marriott International; MBNA; Navistar; Royal Ahold; SafeNet; US Foodservice; Wachovia; Watts Water Technologies and The Whiting-Turner Contracting Company.

## Band 2

### Goodell, DeVries, Leech & Dann, LLP
See firm details p.1047

**The Firm:** This "*excellent litigation firm*" moves up the rankings table this year following consistent praise for its strong team of "*great trial lawyers.*" The single-site outfit competes with larger, top-tier Baltimore firms in products liability and has a great reputation for insurance defense work. It is also often seen in the medical malpractice field and offers experience in class actions and commercial and business tort litigation. The team represents clients regionally, nationally and internationally.

**The Lawyers:** **Charles Goodell** (see p.1039) is "*superb in the courtroom,*" according to commentators. Clients find him "*tremendous, successful and prompt*" and appreciate his ability to "*zero in on the main issues.*" Well respected for his medical malpractice and products liability work, he served as national coordinating counsel for Vermont Talc, a subsidiary of Pluess-Staufer Industries, in connection with 3,500 suits alleging lung injury from commercial talc. The "*talented and terrific*" **Craig Merkle** (see p.1042) concentrates on professional malpractice defense, pharmaceutical and medical device litigation, hospital litigation and professional disciplinary and licensing actions. In Disney v McClain, et al, he obtained a defense verdict for an obstetrician in a $6 million claim for alleged medical malpractice after cerebral palsy and brain damage followed a preterm delivery. He also has extensive appellate experience and represents individuals, partnerships and corporations in a variety of tort and contract disputes.

**Clients/Work Highlights:** Clients include pharmaceutical and medical-device companies; healthcare providers; academic and community healthcare systems; and companies in the chemical, manufacturing and consumer products industries.

### Miles & Stockbridge PC
See firm details p.1050

**The Firm:** This "*fine firm*" is respected in the market for its high-caliber attorneys. It is renowned especially for insurance defense litigation but has been involved in an increasing breadth of work, particularly class actions concerning consumer banking. The team continues to represent Calvert County, obtaining summary judgment in three lawsuits relating to its right to supply water to its citizens. The firm also handles internal investigations for companies

and public bodies relating to accounting, tax issues, and best practice under Sarbanes-Oxley. Other areas of expertise include real estate litigation, representing developers in land use disputes and trademark, patent and copyright cases.

**The Lawyers:** **Jeff Wright** (see p.1046) heads the firm's commercial and business litigation group, and was described by interviewees as a "*quality trial lawyer.*" He has recently been involved in litigation over ATM bank machines. Alongside financial services, other clients are drawn from the telecom, IT, manufacturing, insurance and real estate sectors.

**Clients/Work Highlights:** Bank of America; Citi-Financial; Black & Decker; Provident Bank of Maryland; Niro; Mercy Medical Centre; M&T Bank; Verizon; US Foodservice; Lowe's; QuadraMed; SunTrust Banks; Stewart Title Guarantee; Gambro Healthcare and MBNA.

### Rosenberg, Martin, Funk, Greenberg, LLP

**The Firm:** This specialist operation is particularly well esteemed for its business and white-collar criminal defense litigation. It has chalked up an impressive list of trial successes which this year include representing the bankruptcy trustee for Inphomation Communications, a Pikesville-based company that owned and operated the Psychic Friends Network. The firm negotiated $4.1 million in a cash and stock settlement with MCI after three years of litigation, for what they claim was an inability to properly bill and collect on calls as promised.

**The Lawyers:** Veteran litigator **Ben Rosenberg** was described by clients as "*excellent – he could not be any better.*" Also highly regarded is **Gerry Martin**, who has a terrific white-collar criminal defense practice, effective litigation skills and excellent judgment. He has handled an internal investigation for a large client involving a large number of interviews and analysis of five years of e-mails and environmental data. In the past year he has also taken two pieces of business litigation to verdict and handled several appeals.

**Clients/Work Highlights:** Clients include financial institutions, commercial and residential real estate developers and large nonprofit organizations. Examples include The Harrison Group, MS Willett and Landex.

### Zuckerman Spaeder LLP

**The Firm:** This excellent litigation firm, with its network of offices from New York to Florida, has a solid and capable team in Baltimore which was described as having "*some really terrific lawyers.*" Its strong suit is in white-collar criminal defense work, for which it enjoys a wonderful reputation and wins a wealth of client referrals.

**The Lawyers:** Former public defender **Greg Bernstein** is "*top-notch and extremely effective*" in the area of white-collar criminal defense. Interviewees also described him as a good choice for general commercial matters. **Martin Himeles** is a "*terrific attorney doing a damn good job*" in the white-collar criminal defense and investigation sector, while **Herb**

**Better** was also highlighted to researchers as a strong all-rounder with good experience in complex civil and criminal litigation.

**Clients/Work Highlights:** Clients included Fortune 500 companies, small and midsized public and privately held businesses, and individuals.

## Band 3

### Brault Graham Scott & Brault LLC

**The Firm:** This Rockville-based litigation firm boasts particular expertise in insurance, concentrating its efforts on medical and professional malpractice defense. According to peers, its 14-strong team does an excellent job in the field, litigating throughout Maryland, DC and Northern Virginia.

**The Lawyers:** **Al Brault** is admired as a *"hard-working, tough breed"* of lawyer. He has a stellar reputation among peers, who say that as a pure trial lawyer he has an *"almost magical courtroom skill."* His high level of preparation and ability to connect with juries are *"what you need in insurance defense."*

**Clients/Work Highlights:** American Express Property and Casualty companies; Coakley & Williams Construction; Sterling Jewelers; GAB; Colonial Penn; Medstar Health; Prudential Financial; Lerner; Washington Hospital Center; Georgetown University Hospital; United Services Automobile Associates; Sentry; North American Risk Services; Natelli Communities; Nations Bank; The Equitable Bank; Sherwood Brands; Pohanka Automotive Group and OMS National Insurance.

### Gordon, Feinblatt, Rothman, Hoffberger & Hollander, LLC

**The Firm:** This *"strong, business-oriented"* firm has a deep litigation bench covering a broad array of issues. These include handling commercial litigation, construction disputes, government contracts, antitrust claims and real estate and environmental law problems. Freedom of Information Act, civil RICO, IP, and criminal and civil tax issues also form part of a challenging workload.

**The Lawyers:** Lawrence Fletcher-Hill, former assistant attorney general and chief of litigation for the State of Maryland, chairs the firm's litigation group.

**Clients/Work Highlights:** Clients include public and private entities, many of them existing corporate clients of the firm. The team represents several healthcare insurance companies including United-Healthcare and CareFirst Blue Cross Blue Shield.

### Murphy & Shaffer

**The Firm:** According to the market, this is a small but *"very fine firm"* with five *"high-quality lawyers."* They focus on a range of business litigation which spans products liability, antitrust, real estate, defamation, consumer protection, employment and white-collar criminal defense. Recent highlights include representing a retailer of alcoholic beverages who is challenging Maryland's pricing regulations in an antitrust case.

**The Lawyers:** The *"hard-working"* **Bill Murphy** was consistently recommended by interviewees. He regularly acts for attorneys in professional malpractice and professional responsibility matters and has been representing witnesses in Enron securities litigation.

**Clients/Work Highlights:** Clients include Fortune 500 companies acting in the region and small and midsized local and regional businesses.

### Saul Ewing LLP

See firm details p.1763

**The Firm:** This sizable firm boasts eight offices spread throughout the mid-Atlantic region, including a prestigious location in Baltimore Inner Harbor's Lockwood Place. The office's *"strong and solid"* litigation team enjoys a particular reputation for representing debtors in large bankruptcy cases.

**The Lawyers:** **Charlie Monk** (see p.1042), managing partner of the firm's Baltimore office, was described by commentators as a *"fine lawyer"* and a *"great human being."* His practice is focused on business disputes, IP, insolvency, antitrust and securities litigation, and he regularly appears for securities and financial services companies.

**Clients/Work Highlights:** The Daily Record; The Frederick News-Post; Avir Corporation and Newsweek magazine.

### Whiteford, Taylor & Preston LLP

See firm details p.1052

**The Firm:** This firm has three offices in Maryland, one in Washington, DC and another in Alexandria, Virginia. The litigation team in Baltimore offers clients extensive trial experience and is extremely active in a range of commercial litigation, with a particular reputation for insurance defense work. Clients expressed their admiration for these *"great general litigators"* and the range of skills available within the department.

**The Lawyers:** **Jim Chason** (see p.1038) has been working on tough professional negligence cases in Baltimore, obtaining two defense verdicts last year for the same physician. The bulk of his time is spent on medical malpractice but he has also been branching out into other forms of professional negligence work. Clients say he *"produces tremendous results, doesn't miss a thing and has a comfortable jury style."* **Bill Ryan** (see p.1043) has been pursuing a multi-million-dollar claim in Alabama following the failure of retailer Just For Feet, representing the trustee appointed as the receiver. He also handles a heavy dose of IP work, often for software companies.

**Clients/Work Highlights:** Rainforest Café (in Houston, Texas – a subsidiary of Landry's Restaurants); City of Baltimore; Just For Feet trustee and MySQL.

### Other Notable Practitioners

Self-proclaimed superhero **Steve Snyder** of Snyder Slutkin & Snyder is a *"terrifyingly effective negotiator"* and *"an extremely talented, formidable adversary."* His practice is centered on medical malpractice and complex business fraud. *"Legend"* **Arnold Weiner** of Weiner & Weltchek is described as *"extremely creative, smart and one of the absolute best plaintiff business litigators."* The Murphy Firm's **Billy Murphy** was recommended as *"a flamboyant, brilliant trial lawyer"* with considerable experience of representing plaintiffs. According to clients, *"he connects with jurors like nobody I've ever seen; he has a sophisticated understanding of the law and is great at gaining the confidence of everyone, from the bottom to the top of the company."* His criminal defense background comes across in court, where he is said to have an *"unconventional"* approach.

# REAL ESTATE

## Real Estate
### Leading Firms

1. **BALLARD SPAHR ANDREWS & INGERSOLL** *Baltimore*
   **DLA PIPER RUDNICK GRAY CARY US LLP** *Baltimore*
   **VENABLE LLP** *Baltimore*
2. **GALLAGHER, EVELIUS & JONES, LLP** *Baltimore*
   **GORDON, FEINBLATT, ROTHMAN** *Baltimore*
   **LINOWES AND BLOCHER LLP** *Bethesda*
   **WILMERHALE** *Baltimore*
3. **LENROW, KOHN & OLIVER** *Baltimore*
   **ROSENBERG, MARTIN, FUNK** *Baltimore*
   **SHULMAN, ROGERS, GANDAL, PORDY** *Rockville*
   **WHITEFORD, TAYLOR & PRESTON LLP** *Baltimore*

### Leading Individuals

1. **FISHER** Morton *Ballard Spahr*
   **FISHMAN** David *Gordon, Feinblatt, Rothman*
   **LEVIN** Edward *DLA Piper*
   **OLIVER** James *Lenrow, Kohn & Oliver*
   **POLLAK** Mark *WilmerHale*
   **SHEPHERD** Kevin *Venable LLP*
   **WINSTON** Roger *Linowes and Blocher LLP*
2. **CHRISS** Timothy *Gordon, Feinblatt, Rothman*
   **FISH** Ronald *Ballard Spahr*
   **MACHEN** John *DLA Piper*
   **RENO** Russell *Venable LLP*
   **SHULMAN** Lawrence *Shulman, Rogers, Gandal*
   **TRUITT** Raymond *Ballard Spahr*
   **WRIGHT** James *Venable LLP*
3. **GREENBERG** Barry *Rosenberg, Martin, Funk*
   **KOCHANSKI** David *Shulman, Rogers, Gandal*
   **LEVINE** Richard *DLA Piper*
   **MILLSPAUGH** Thomas *WilmerHale*
   **SEARS** Barbara *Linowes and Blocher LLP*
4. **BARBUTI** Thomas *Whiteford, Taylor*
   **COHEN** David *Linowes and Blocher LLP*
   **GOLDSTEIN** Andrew *Linowes and Blocher LLP*
   **GUBEN** Jan *Venable LLP*
   **ISAACSON** Andrew *Linowes and Blocher LLP*
   **KEENER** Mark *Gallagher, Evelius*
   **LEWIS** Thomas *Gallagher, Evelius*
   **REED** Matthew *WilmerHale*
   **SHELLEY** Patrick *McGuireWoods LLP*

### Up-and-coming individuals

**LARIA** Jon *Ballard Spahr*
**TOTTEN** Thomas *DLA Piper*
**WILSON** Jane *DLA Piper*

## Band 1

## Ballard Spahr Andrews & Ingersoll LLP

See firm details p.1746

**The Firm:** The talented group of Baltimore real estate lawyers at this multioffice firm is renowned for its delivery of *"quality"* work. *"Creative in complex transactions,"* these attorneys are noted for finding *"uncomplicated ways of solving complicated issues."* Clients are also impressed by their *"conscientious"* approach to acquainting themselves with companies' needs and personalities, which includes both anticipating problems and discovering potential opportunities. The firm has been working of late on the Arundel Preserve development, a mixed-use project with over 1,000 residential units and two million square feet of office space. This is one of the first developments submitted under Anne Arundel County's new mixed-use zoning laws. Successes such as this ensure that the team has been able to expand steadily, with two new partners added this year.

**The Lawyers:** **Morty Fisher** (see p.1038) is a high-flier in Baltimore's real estate market who is admired for his *"total knowledge and ability to do complex deals"* and for being *"pleasant to work with."* **Ray Truitt** (see p.1045), managing partner of the Baltimore office, has extensive experience in real estate. He was described by clients as a *"wonderful"* adviser who is *"always thinking ahead,"* and by peers as *"of the Morty mold: excellent, extremely knowledgeable and a straight shooter."* He represents national lenders, including life insurance companies and pension funds. Much of his time is also spent working on real estate matters for a large Baltimore healthcare company. Senior counsel **Ron Fish** (see p.1038) was described by interviewees as an *"excellent lawyer who never gets rattled."* Clients consider him to be *"as good as it gets – great at handling difficult situations."* He represents a number of local developers and banks, and has been working on the conversion of an old public housing site into a commercial center. Up-and-comer **Jon Laria** (see p.1041) enters the table following praise for his *"thorough knowledge of real estate, tax and business issues."* Clients are impressed with his *"calm presence"* and his problem-solving abilities.

**Clients/Work Highlights:** The team is real estate counsel for Loews Cineplex throughout the USA, and represented an affiliate of the University of Baltimore in the development of a large biotech park.

## DLA Piper Rudnick Gray Cary US LLP

See firm details p.870

**The Firm:** Loyal clients use the Baltimore branch of this rapidly expanding international law firm for all their real estate needs, including advice on financing and tax issues. The 13-strong team is famed for representing national clients in multimillion-dollar transactions across the region. Recent examples include advising Struever Bros Eccles & Rouse on the adaptive reuse and redevelopment of industrial projects in Maryland, Rhode Island and North Carolina. The latter project concerned 628,000 sq ft of the American Tobacco Historic District.

**The Lawyers:** Clients enthuse about the *"extremely smart, hard-working and wonderful"* **Ed Levin** (see p.1041), whose hands-on approach was especially appreciated. As one interviewee noted: *"When you give him a task he doesn't stop until it's finished. He keeps you informed, solves the problem and is always on top of things."* **Jack Machen** (see p.1041) was described by clients as *"easy to work with, experienced, practical and focused,"* while peers call him a *"straight shooter who knows the law inside-out."* He splits his practice evenly between work for institutional lenders and work for local developers, including Struever Bros Eccles & Rouse. **Rich Levine** (see p.1041) has his feet planted in the worlds of both real estate and tax, while *"fantastic"* up-and-comer **Tom Totten** (see p.1045) was also singled out by clients. He represents local developers and has acted for lenders on large transactions involving loan portfolios, as well as handling several multiple site sales for a national hotel chain. **Jane Wilson** (see p.1045) focuses on real estate finance, representing financial institutions. She recently acted for M&T Bank in arranging a $72 million revolving line of credit for the acquisition and development of 1,950 residential building lots.

**Clients/Work Highlights:** The team has represented AEGON USA Realty Advisors in many commercial mortgage loan transactions throughout the Northeast and Midwest. Other clients include Continental Realty, M&T Bank and Ryland.

## Venable LLP

**The Firm:** This excellent, full-service firm is respected for producing *"top-band real estate work."* The team acts for local, regional and national clients in every sort of real estate transaction. Recent highlights include representing the sellers of a large undeveloped tract of land alongside the I-270 corridor in Montgomery County. This was eventually sold for $137 million. The team also acted for the City of Rockville in a multidisciplinary project involving the redevelopment of the town center.

**The Lawyers:** **Kevin Shepherd** co-chairs the firm's real estate group. A *"splendid and diligent"* adviser, he *"does a great job"* for his clients. In May 2005 his talents were employed by Boston Properties in a $237 million disposition in Baltimore. *"Delightful, open and quick-minded,"* **Ronnie Reno** was described by interviewees as *"terrific – one of the deans of real estate law."* According to market sources, he has *"seen virtually everything, is great with the fundamentals"* and masterminds *"creative solutions to difficult problems."* **Jim Wright** is also highly regarded by peers as a *"wonderful attorney – one of the best in Baltimore."* He recently led a team of 20 attorneys representing Marriott International in the acquisition of a $1.5 billion portfolio of hotels throughout the USA and worldwide. New to the table, **Jan Guben** is admired for his *"organizational and drafting abilities, great judgment and common sense."*

**Clients/Work Highlights:** Marriott International; Alexandria Real Estate Equities; City of Rockville; Mercantile Bank & Trust and Boston Properties.

## Band 2

### Gallagher, Evelius & Jones, LLP

**The Firm:** This *"substantial and impressive"* boutique practice boasts 35 lawyers in its transactional group. They focus mainly on development work, but also represent lenders and investors. Said to be a *"locally oriented"* group, the firm has *"shone of late"* with its involvement in a number of exciting projects, including the $130 million Four Seasons Hotel in the mixed-use waterfront development of Harbor East. The firm has also been working on conversions of historic buildings, including the Abell Building and the Congress Hotel. Clients find the team *"extremely responsive."*

**The Lawyers:** **Tom Lewis** is an *"extremely fine lawyer,"* according to market sources. He has been busy representing clients on the development side. New to the table, **Mark Keener** impresses clients with *"expertise and practical knowledge that reflects on the firm as a whole."* He has taken a leading role in a number of major development projects in Baltimore.

**Clients/Work Highlights:** Clients include lenders, real estate developers, equity investors, health systems, colleges and universities.

### Gordon, Feinblatt, Rothman, Hoffberger & Hollander, LLC

**The Firm:** This full-service Baltimore firm has a small but excellent real estate practice with a *"number of strong lawyers."* Interviewees are especially impressed by the *"high caliber"* of the team's work. As well as handling acquisitions, dispositions, leasing and zoning matters, these lawyers are experienced in all aspects of project financing and tax matters relating to real estate.

**The Lawyers:** **David Fishman**'s excellence is widely appreciated and he was described as *"one of the deans of real estate law"* in Maryland. The chair of the firm's real estate group, he is *"extremely knowledgeable about all aspects of whatever project he's involved with,"* as well as being *"an excellent drafter."* His knowledge and experience of complex real estate transactions was highlighted by numerous commentators. **Tim Chriss** inspires confidence in clients, who describe him as *"able to handle any real estate transaction that comes along."* His efficiency is particularly admired by interviewees: *"He knows the law and doesn't waste time."*

**Clients/Work Highlights:** Clients include real estate developers, owners and investors, local and national commercial lenders, and condominium and homeowners' associations.

### Linowes and Blocher LLP

**The Firm:** Clients particularly appreciate this Montgomery County firm for its *"thorough, practical, business-oriented approach,"* and the real estate team's *"extraordinary availability, interest and dedication"* inspire great loyalty. As one client said: *"They take good care of us in complex transactions,"* thus encouraging a feeling of mutual trust. With its deep bench, this firm has the resources to assist clients in all aspects of the field. This has recently included handling the land use and transactional aspects of a number of mixed-use projects. Public-private ventures for suburban regeneration schemes, including the redevelopment of Silver Spring in Maryland, have been another keynote of the year. The firm's reach has spread beyond the local area and it represents some large developers in the Washington, DC region.

**The Lawyers:** **Roger Winston** is an expert in condominium and community association law. According to market commentators, *"he is superb, hard working and also has a terrific national reputation. There is nobody better than him and he's a lot of fun to deal with."* **Andrew Isaacson** handles a wide variety of transactions for clients who describe him as *"aware of our business plan, wise, experienced and practical."* They also appreciate his style of communication; as one remarked: *"In my mind he's the consummate gentleman in personality, demeanor and dedication."* *"The land use lawyer in Montgomery County,"* **Barbara Sears** is recommended by interviewees for her exceptional knowledge and commitment. Practice group chair, **David Cohen**, is a highly respected transactional lawyer with a focus on tax. The highly experienced **Andy Goldstein** also impresses interviewees: *"He just wants to get the deal done, is great at negotiating, and knows what's important and what's not."*

**Clients/Work Highlights:** Percontee; Potomac Investors; Penrose; Federal Realty Investment Trust; Stonebridge Associates; Ross Development & Investment and Oxbridge Development.

### WilmerHale

See firm details p.580

**The Firm:** The 2004 merger of Wilmer Cutler Pickering LLP and Hale and Dorr LLP has continued to create opportunities for this group to impress new clients with its *"diligence and critical response times."* The team is a favorite with clients, who feel that this large national firm delivers a *"responsive personal service."* Its *"methodical approach"* and *"global thought processes"* were also enthusiastically praised. Over the past year, the team has handled a large number of acquisitions and dispositions of properties for national clients, including REITs and investment banks.

**The Lawyers:** **Mark Pollak** (see p.1043) is admired for his *"strength and excellence"* in the field. He recently finalized agreements between the State of Maryland, Baltimore County and a private developer for the creation of a $400 million mixed-use town center project. Clients find **Ted Millspaugh** (see p.1042) *"personable, approachable and responsive."* Highlights of his year include multimillion-dollar sales and acquisitions in many states, including Hawaii, California, Texas, Florida, New York and Maryland. One client described **Matt Reed** (see p.1043) as *"a real bulldog"* in negotiations, and his *"great turnaround time"* also met with widespread approval. His expertise lies in the public financing of real estate projects and PPPs.

**Clients/Work Highlights:** US RE Investing Division; Morgan Stanley; The Shelter Group; Maryland Department of Transportation; Baltimore National Aquarium; LaSalle Investment Management; Alex Brown Realty and Legg Mason.

## Band 3

### Lenrow, Kohn & Oliver
### A Professional Corporation

**The Firm:** This five-strong firm commands respect well beyond its size in Baltimore's real estate circles. Its range of services includes advice on the construction, leasing, acquisition, disposition and development of all types of real estate project. It provides services to a client base that ranges from individuals to major businesses, including, for the sweet-toothed, such household names as Baskin-Robbins and Dunkin' Donuts.

**The Lawyers:** **Jim Oliver** moves up to the top tier this year following a deluge of praise from peers and clients. Interviewees enthuse: *"He is one of the best real estate lawyers I've ever seen; an attorney's attorney, smart, industrious, knowledgeable and detail-oriented."* He also *"understands all the business aspects of any real estate transaction, is extremely practical and accomplishes the goals of his clients."*

**Clients/Work Highlights:** Chelsea Property; Prime Retail; Giant Food; Brookstone; Brick Bodies Health & Fitness; Johns Hopkins University; Boggs & Partners; Maryland Economic Development and Stanley Halle Communities.

### Rosenberg, Martin, Funk, Greenberg, LLP

**The Firm:** This real estate practice enjoys an especially strong reputation for local zoning work, where clients expressed a *"high level of confidence in their user-friendly legal staff."* In the past year the team has been busy representing local and national home-builders in land acquisitions and developments where its skills have been to the fore. A highlight was representing the developer in the leasing and financing of a large mixed-use project in Howard County, Maryland.

**The Lawyers:** **Barry Greenberg** was recommended to researchers as a *"consistently strong"* lawyer, with particular expertise in land use. Clients were full of praise for a *"problem solver who takes a prudent and practical approach to any issue,"* and particularly valued the perspective he brings to transactions and his skill at *"fitting pieces into the puzzle."* As well as land use, he serves as counsel to developers, investors and builders in all aspects of real estate projects.

**Clients/Work Highlights:** Mercantile Bank & Trust; Tousa Homes; Greenebaum & Rose; Time Group; Macks; B&B Realty; Manekin; Obrecht Commercial Real Estate and Preakness Homes.

### Shulman, Rogers, Gandal, Pordy & Ecker, PA

**The Firm:** This Montgomery County firm has a respected real estate department. According to clients, its lawyers possess *"fine judgment and strong negotiation skills,"* along with an ability to bring

parties together on significant issues. The team has been busy this year representing clients in acquisitions, dispositions and a large amount of commercial leasing. The group also has a distinct financing team working with all types of real estate loans for mixed-use, commercial and residential projects.
**The Lawyers:** *"Fine lawyer"* **Larry Shulman** is known as a go-to real estate attorney. His expertise lies in commercial real estate and leasing work, and he is also famed for hosting annual Georgetown seminars. **David Kochanski** is a former chair of the Maryland state Bar Real Estate Property, Planning and Zoning Section. He was singled out by interviewees for his technical expertise.

**Clients/Work Highlights:** Clients include retailers, residential developers and homebuilders, financial institutions, educational institutions, municipalities and nonprofit entities.

## Whiteford, Taylor & Preston LLP
See firm details p.1052
**The Firm:** This locally strong real estate practice has experience of a variety of complex commercial real estate matters. However, it is particularly known for its zoning and land use expertise, an area in which it fields a dedicated group.
**The Lawyers:** Chair of the Maryland state Bar Real Estate Property, Planning and Zoning Section, **Tom**

**Barbuti** (see p.1037) is highly respected for his experience and expertise. Priscilla Carroll has now left the firm for an in-house position at Struever Bros Eccles & Rouse.
**Clients/Work Highlights:** Clients include property developers, educational institutions, retailers, financial institutions and utilities.

## Other Notable Practitioners
**Pat Shelley** of McGuireWoods LLP is rated by clients as *"extremely diligent, a creative problem solver, responsive and professional."* They also admire the way he seamlessly integrates business needs with legal requirements.

# Leaders in Maryland

## ABEL, Kenneth
Ober Kaler Grimes & Shriver, Baltimore
410 685 1120
*Recommended in Corporate/M&A*

## ABRAMSON, Gil
Hogan & Hartson LLP, Baltimore
410 659 2723
gaabramson@hhlaw.com
*Recommended in Employment*
**Practice Areas:** EEO litigation, wrongful discharge, protection of intellectual property, trade secrets, and restrictive covenants, wage and hour, injunctions against strikes and picketing. Counsels on employment practices and policies, workplace training, arbitrations, collective bargaining, union campaigns. International and multijurisdictional employment counseling.
**Prof. Memberships:** ABA; MDBA; FBA (former Chairman, Labor and Employment Law Section).
**Career:** Partner since 1993.
**Publications:** 'Religious Practices in the Workplace' (24 January 2006); 'They're Baaaaak: New Union Organizing Approaches and Employee Responses' (9 April 2005).
**Personal:** Boston University School of Law (JD, 1969); State University of New York, University at Buffalo (BA, 1966).

## ADELMAN, Allan
Adelman, Sheff & Smith LLC, Annapolis
410 224 3000
*Recommended in Healthcare*

## ADKINS, Edward J
Miles & Stockbridge PC, Baltimore
410 385 3500
eadkins@milesstockbridge.com
*Recommended in Employee Benefits*
**Practice Areas:** Head of the Employee Benefits and Executive Compensation Practice Group, specializing in ESOPs; ERISA compliance, fiduciary responsibility and plan asset management; health

and welfare plans/HIPAA; non-qualified deferred compensation, Code Section 409A compliance and executive compensation; tax-deferred plans for governments and non-profit organizations and tax-qualified pension, savings, profit-sharing & 401(k) plans. Represents small and large businesses located in the US and internationally; expertise in benefits matters for US subsidiaries of international companies.
**Prof. Memberships:** American Bar Association, Employee Benefits Committee of the Tax Section; District of Columbia Bar Association; Maryland State Bar Association; Worldwide Employee Benefits Network (WEB); The Group, Inc.; Trained Mediator for Employee Benefits and Executive Compensation; Listed in 2005 in The Best Lawyers in America.
**Career:** Venable, Baetjer & Howard in Baltimore, Maryland (associate 1975-79; Partner, 1980); Yaffe & Offutt, Inc. in Baltimore, Maryland (Senior Benefits Consultant, 1981-82). Miles & Stockbridge P.C. (Partner/Principal, 1982 to Present).
**Personal:** Born: October 18, 1947, Annapolis, Maryland. Juris Doctor Degree, 1972, University of Maryland School of Law (Order of the Coif and with honors); AB Degree, University of North Carolina (Chapel Hill), 1969. Married. Fluent in Spanish.

## AMES, Robert
Venable LLP, Baltimore 410 244 7400
*Recommended in Employment*

## ARCHIBALD, James
Venable LLP, Baltimore 410 244 7400
*Recommended in Litigation*

## AYRES, Jeffrey
Venable LLP, Towson 410 494 6200
*Recommended in Employment*

## BAADER, Michael
Venable LLP, Baltimore 410 244 7400
*Recommended in Corporate/M&A*

## BAKER, Constance
Venable LLP, Baltimore 410 244 7400
*Recommended in Healthcare*

## BARBUTI, Thomas
Whiteford, Taylor & Preston LLP,
Baltimore 410 347 8719
tbarbuti@wtplaw.com
*Recommended in Real Estate*
**Practice Areas:** Sophisticated, transactional commercial real estate, including purchase and sale agreements, leases, subleases, covenants, conditions and restrictions, easements, reciprocal easements, development agreements, construction contracts and financing with a concentration in development, construction and leasing of residential, commercial, retail and mixed-use projects.
**Prof. Memberships:** American College of Real Estate Lawyers; International Council of Shopping Centers; Urban Land Institute; National Association of Industrial and Office Properties; Maryland State Bar Association (Chair, 2005-06, Section of Real Property, Planning and Zoning). Admitted in Maryland and Washington, DC.
**Personal:** JD, Rutgers University, 1974; BA, University of Maryland, 1970.

## BEALL, George
Hogan & Hartson LLP, Baltimore
410 659 2715
gbeall@hhlaw.com
*Recommended in Litigation*
**Practice Areas:** Focuses on civil and criminal litigation in state and federal courts. Involved in every major contested takeover of a Maryland corporation between 1975 and 1990. Handles regulatory, compliance and criminal matters involving 'white-collar' offenses.
**Prof. Memberships:** Fellow, American

College of Trial Lawyers; Chairman, US District Court for Maryland Magistrate Selection Panel; Co-Chairman Maryland Judicial Election Conduct Commission; permanent member of the Judicial Conference for the Fourth US Circuit Court of Appeals and of the American Law Institute.
**Career:** Presidential appointment as US Attorney for the District of Maryland (1970-75).
**Personal:** University of Virginia School of Law (JD).

## BERMAN, Barry
Thomas & Libowitz PA, Baltimore
410 752 2468
*Recommended in Employee Benefits*

## BERNSTEIN, Greg
Zuckerman Spaeder LLP, Baltimore
410 332 0444
*Recommended in Litigation*

## BETTER, Herbert
Zuckerman Spaeder LLP, Baltimore
410 332 0444
*Recommended in Litigation*

## BRAULT, Albert
Brault Graham Scott & Brault LLC,
Rockville 301 424 1060
*Recommended in Litigation*

## BURCH JR, Francis B
DLA Piper Rudnick Gray Cary US LLP,
Baltimore 410 580 4040
frank.burch@dlapiper.com
*Recommended in Litigation*
**Practice Areas:** Litigation; class action; patent litigation; securities litigation.
**Prof. Memberships:** Fellow of the American College of Trial Lawyers; Member of The American Law Institute.
**Career:** He is joint CEO of the firm and has been listed in leading legal publications for over 10 years. He focuses on defense and prosecution of claims under federal securities laws; corporate control-

related litigation; and a broad spectrum of business litigation, including intellectual property matters.

**Personal:** JD, University of Maryland; AB, Georgetown University; serves on the Boards of Johns Hopkins University and Johns Hopkins Medicine and The University of Maryland Baltimore Foundation.

## CHALK, Wm David
DLA Piper Rudnick Gray Cary US LLP, Baltimore 410 580 4120
david.chalk@dlapiper.com
*Recommended in Corporate/M&A*

**Practice Areas:** Corporate/M&A, capital markets.

**Prof. Memberships:** ABA; Maryland State Bar Association.

**Career:** Co-Chair of the Capital Markets Practice, his emphasis is on public and private M&A and public offerings. Advises on disclosure, corporate governance, shareholder relations, compliance with Sarbanes-Oxley Act and rules and regulations of the SEC, National Association of Securities Dealers, and major stock exchanges. Counsel in more than 75 public and private offerings, tender offers, and other transactions involving equity and debt securities and counsel to buyers and sellers in more than 50 M&A transactions.

**Personal:** JD, University of Maryland; BS, University of Baltimore

## CHASON, James R
Whiteford, Taylor & Preston LLP, Towson 410 832 2020
jchason@wtplaw.com
*Recommended in Litigation*

**Practice Areas:** Mr Chason has represented plaintiffs and defendants in complex professional liability cases in healthcare, product design, engineering, accounting and insurance. He has served as national counsel for several products liability cases and has represented one of the country's leading medical institutions. He has handled over 100 jury trials.

**Prof. Memberships:** Fellow, American College of Trial Lawyers; Maryland Defense Council; Board Member, Carson Scholarship Fund. Admitted in Maryland, United States District Court for the District of Maryland, US Court of Appeals for the Fourth Circuit.

**Personal:** JD, with honors, University of Baltimore, 1976; BA, University of Maryland, 1973.

## CHESSHIRE, Mary Claire
Whiteford, Taylor & Preston LLP, Baltimore 410 347 9465
mchesshire@wtplaw.com
*Recommended in Employee Benefits*

**Practice Areas:** Partner in the firm's Employee Benefits Practice Group. Substantial experience advising organizations ranging from small firms to Fortune 500 companies with respect to retirement, welfare and executive compensation plan

design and ERISA and Internal Revenue Code compliance. Experience also includes fiduciary training and counseling and guiding clients through government agency audits and correction programs. Practice extends to advice regarding employee benefit matters in bankruptcy, litigation and corporate transactions.

**Prof. Memberships:** Maryland State Bar Association; National Association of Public Pension Attorneys.

**Personal:** JD (with honors), University of Baltimore School of Law, 1993; BA, The Johns Hopkins University, 1989.

## CHRISS, Timothy
Gordon, Feinblatt, Rothman, Hoffberger & Hollander, LLC, Baltimore
410 576 4000
*Recommended in Real Estate*

## CLANCY, Patrick
Venable LLP, Rockville 301 217 5600
*Recommended in Employment*

## COHEN, David
Linowes and Blocher LLP, Bethesda 301 654 0504
dcohen@linowes-law.com
*Recommended in Real Estate*

**Practice Areas:** Real estate transactions; business transactions.

**Career:** Partner in the firm's Business and Real Estate Transactions Groups and Chairs the Business Practice Group. Practice emphasizes business and tax planning for real estate developers and investors, and entrepreneurs both in and outside of the real estate industry, particularly in the areas of real estate acquisitions/dispositions, structuring equity and debt financing, business entity formation and reorganization, workout and asset protection strategies, business succession, and family trusts and partnerships.

**Personal:** BS, Wharton School, University of Pennsylvania; MS Wharton School, University of Pennsylvania; JD, University of Maryland; Certified Public Accountant.

## COOK, Bryson
Venable LLP, Baltimore 410 244 7400
*Recommended in Corporate/M&A*

## COOPERMAN, Harriet E
Saul Ewing LLP, Baltimore
410 332 8974
hcooperman@saul.com
*Recommended in Employment*

**Practice Areas:** Partner/Co-Chair of Saul Ewing's Labor and Employment Practice. Extensive experience in collective bargaining/NLRA, discrimination, harassment, tort, non-compete, and litigation. Represents private, public and nonprofit employers.

**Prof. Memberships:** Admitted to practice in Maryland, US Supreme Court, Fourth Circuit, US District Courts - Maryland and DC; Former Chair, Labor Section, Maryland Bar, Employer-

Employee Relations Committee, ABA-TIPS.

**Career:** Former Vice Chair, State Higher Education Labor Relations Board; Adjunct Professor, Labor and Employment Discrimination, University of Baltimore Law School.

**Publications:** 'Discovery in Employment Cases', 'Unresolved Arbitration Issues', 'Evidentiary Issues in Sexual Harassment Litigation'.

**Personal:** JD, University of Maryland, BS, Cornell University.

## CURRAN, Bob
Whiteford, Taylor & Preston LLP, Baltimore 410 347 9472
rcurran@wtplaw.com
*Recommended in Corporate/M&A*

**Practice Areas:** Business and corporate law; mergers and acquisitions; leveraged buyouts; formation and structuring of business entities including corporations, partnerships, joint ventures, and limited liability companies; corporate succession planning; ESOP transactions; employee benefits and executive compensation.

**Prof. Memberships:** American Bar Association, Maryland State Bar Association (Chair, Section of Taxation 1987-88). Admitted in Maryland.

**Personal:** JD, with honors (Order of the Coif), University of Maryland School of Law, 1974; BA, University of Delaware, 1971.

## DILLOFF, Neil
DLA Piper Rudnick Gray Cary US LLP, Baltimore 410 580 4138
neil.dilloff@dlapiper.com
*Recommended in Litigation*

**Practice Areas:** Insurance litigation and coverage, litigation, professional liability, construction.

**Career:** Experience includes significant professional malpractice liability litigation, particularly on behalf of lawyers, extensive construction litigation experience, and roles as lead counsel in many large, complex commercial litigation matters. He has tried more than 100 cases in state and federal courts and has won two of the largest plaintiffs' verdicts in Maryland history. He also has achieved over a dozen recoveries in excess of $1 million. He has also successfully defended law firms, insurance companies and other organizations.

**Personal:** JD, Georgetown University; BA, University of North Carolina.

## EIDELMAN, Gary B
Saul Ewing LLP, Baltimore
410 332 8975
geidelman@saul.com
*Recommended in Employment*

**Practice Areas:** Partner in Saul Ewing's Labor and Employment Practice. Represents management in labor and employment law and litigation matters, including employment discrimination, sexual harassment, disability and leave, wrong-

ful discharge, breach of contract, noncompetition agreements, wage and hour, occupational safety and health, affirmative action compliance and audits, and fair housing.

**Prof. Memberships:** Admitted to practice in DC and Maryland; Management Co-Chair, Employment At-Will Subcommittee, American Bar Association, Labor and Employment Law Section, Employment Rights and Responsibilities Committee.

**Career:** Vice Office Managing Partner of Baltimore Office. Lecturer on employment law.

**Personal:** JD, Widener University (magna cum laude), BA, University of Maryland.

## FISH, Ronald
Ballard Spahr Andrews & Ingersoll LLP, Baltimore 410 528 5617
fish@ballardspahr.com
*Recommended in Real Estate*

**Practice Areas:** Focuses on commercial real estate acquisition, development, financing, leasing and restructuring, and represents developers, lenders, investors, landlords, tenants, and users in all areas of the real estate market.

**Prof. Memberships:** Member, American College of Real Estate Lawyers since 1984. Member, American Bar Association and Maryland Bar Association. Lecturer, real estate law for the Maryland Institute for Continuing Professional Education of Lawyers. Adjunct Professor, Allen Berman Real Estate Institute of Johns Hopkins University.

**Career:** Admitted to the Maryland Bar (1964).

**Personal:** LLB, cum laude, University of Maryland (1964); AB, Williams College (1961).

## FISHER, Morton
Ballard Spahr Andrews & Ingersoll LLP, Baltimore 410 528 5615
fisher@ballardspahr.com
*Recommended in Real Estate*

**Practice Areas:** Focuses on real estate transactions, representing developers, lending institutions, department stores, and other big box users and tenants.

**Prof. Memberships:** Former President, American College of Real Estate Lawyers, former Chair, ABA Section of Real Property Probate and Trust Law, Instructor, University of Maryland School of Law. Charter Member, American College of Construction Lawyers, Member, The American Law Institute, The Counselors of Real Estate, and the Anglo-American Real Property Institute. Served on Mayor's Advisory Council for the Downtown, the Baltimore County Economic Development Commission, and the Greater Baltimore Committee Economic Development Committee. Member, Board of the Baltimore Downtown Partnership. Member of the Board of Trustees

of the University of Maryland (Baltimore) Foundation, Chair of the Campus and Community Enterprise Committee. Member, Board of the Johns Hopkins University Real Estate Institute.
**Career:** Admitted to Maryland Bar (1961); District of Columbia Bar (1978).
**Publications:** Author, 'The Journal of the Section of Real Property', 'Probate and Trust Law', 'Probate & Property', 'The Practical Real Estate Lawyer', contributing author to 'A Practical Guide to Commercial Real Estate Transactions' published by ABA Publishing.
**Personal:** LLB, Yale Law School (1961); AB, Dartmouth College (1958).

### FISHMAN, David
Gordon, Feinblatt, Rothman, Hoffberger & Hollander, LLC, Baltimore
410 576 4000
*Recommended in Real Estate*

### FRENKIL, Steven
Miles & Stockbridge PC, Baltimore
410 385 3758
sfrenkil@milesstockbridge.com
*Recommended in Employment*
**Practice Areas:** Advises and defends employers in all aspects of employment law and human resource matters, including discrimination, harassment, wage and hour, non-competition, trade secrets, wrongful discharge, employment agreements, defamation and employment torts, ADA, leave issues, OSHA, and arbitration.
**Prof. Memberships:** American Bar Association (EEO Committee); National Association of College and University Attorneys; Society for Human Resource Management; Maryland State Bar Association, Section of Labor and Employment Law (Member, Section Council); Howard County Human Resources Society (Board of Directors, Legislative Chair).
**Career:** Recognized by Chambers USA as a leading management lawyer in 2004 and 2005. Selected by Who's Who Legal USA 2006 as a leader in management labor and employment law. Principal at Miles & Stockbridge P.C., 1992 to present. Previously Partner and associate, Semmes, Bowen & Semmes, 1977-1992.
**Publications:** Published numerous articles and books. Frequently presents seminars for clients, industry groups and others.
**Personal:** Graduated from George Washington University (BA, 1974 with Distinction; Phi Beta Kappa), and University of Maryland School of Law (JD, 1977 with honors; Law Review). Member of Board of Directors of the Howard County Human Resources Society (SHRM affiliate); Friends School of Baltimore (Development and Finance Committees); Villa Julie College, President's Advisory Committee.

### FRISCH, John B
Miles & Stockbridge PC, Baltimore
410 385 3507
jfrisch@milesstockbridge.com
*Recommended in Corporate/M&A*
**Practice Areas:** In addition to serving as the Chairman and Chief Executive Officer of the firm, he specializes in mergers and acquisitions, securities and other business transactions. He has been responsible for acquisitions and dispositions of businesses by public and private enterprises, including the disposition of substantial international businesses. He provides general business counseling to businesses and their officers and directors, including counseling concerning fiduciary duty, corporate governance and related matters.
**Career:** Principal since 1990.
**Personal:** University of Maryland (JD, 1983); Dickinson College (BA, 1980).

### GARDNER, Russell H
DLA Piper Rudnick Gray Cary US LLP, Baltimore 410 580 4154
russell.gardner@dlapiper.com
*Recommended in Employment*
**Practice Areas:** Labor and employment law; class action litigation.
**Career:** His practice encompasses all areas of management-side labor and employment discrimination. He regularly advises on union-avoidance matters, including representation before the National Labor Relations Board, employment discrimination and OSHA matters, and defense of employment claims, including ERISA claims, in state and federal courts across the nation. He has experience in drafting and enforcing employment agreements and non-competition agreements. He has written and lectured extensively on a variety of employment topics, particularly for the Americans with Disabilities Act.
**Personal:** JD, Syracuse University; BA, Alfred University.

### GATELY, Mark
Hogan & Hartson LLP, Baltimore
410 659 2742
mdgately@hhlaw.com
*Recommended in Litigation*
**Practice Areas:** Focuses on complex commercial and corporate litigation, particularly in the antitrust and securities law area, and products liability. Handles significant post-closing disputes involving claims arising from large corporate transactions and hostile takeover and proxy related litigation. National products liability counsel for a major pharmaceutical company.
**Prof. Memberships:** Fellow, American College of Trial Lawyers; Fellow, International Academy of Trial Lawyers (Maryland State Chair); Member, Product Liability Advisory Counsel; Member, The American Board of Trial Advocates, Listed in Best Lawyers in America.

**Career:** Former Chair of the Litigation Department of a large Baltimore firm. Former law clerk Judge C Stanley Blair, US District Court for the District of Maryland.
**Publications:** 'Direct and Derivative Actions of Maryland Corporation Stockholders', The Maryland Bar Journal (2/18/2004).
**Personal:** University of Maryland School of Law (JD, with honors, Order of the Coif).

### GENTH, Geoffrey H
Kramon & Graham, PA, Baltimore
410 752 6030
ggenth@kg-law.com
*Recommended in Litigation*
**Practice Areas:** Civil Business Litigation. Mr Genth also practices in the areas of insurance coverage, professional liability, securities litigation, general civil litigation, and mediation.
**Prof. Memberships:** Mr Genth is Chairperson of the Maryland Chapter of the Federal Bar Association and a permanent Member of the Fourth Circuit Judicial Conference. He has served on the Section Council of the Alternative Dispute Resolution Section of the Maryland State Bar Association, and on local Bar committees relating to ethical matters. Mr Genth is an active Member of the American Bar Association, the Maryland State Bar Association, and the Baltimore City and Baltimore County Bar Associations.
**Career:** From 1990-92, Mr Genth served as a law clerk to the Honorable Alexander Harvey, II on the United States District Court for the District of Maryland. From 1992 to the present, Mr Genth has practiced with Kramon & Graham, P.A.
**Personal:** Mr Genth was born September 3, 1964. He graduated from Yale University with high honors in 1987, and with honors from the University of Michigan Law School in 1990. Mr Genth is an active member of the boards of various non-profit organizations serving the Baltimore community.

### GILLECE JR, James P
Whiteford, Taylor & Preston LLP, Baltimore 410 347 9470
jgillece@wtplaw.com
*Recommended in Employment*
**Practice Areas:** Mr Gillece is an experienced trial lawyer and has practiced in all areas of labor and employment law, including union avoidance, union representation elections, civil rights litigation, defamation, wrongful discharge, covenants not to compete, wage and hour, and DOL investigations. He is primary labor counsel to numerous businesses, including many in the healthcare industry.
**Prof. Memberships:** American, Maryland, and Baltimore City Bar Associations; Law Advisory Council, University of Notre Dame (1983 to present).

**Personal:** University of Notre Dame (JD, 1969); University of Notre Dame Law Review LaSalle University (AB, 1966).

### GOLDSTEIN, Andrew M
Linowes and Blocher LLP, Bethesda
301 654 0504
agoldstein@linowes-law.com
*Recommended in Real Estate*
**Practice Areas:** Real estate transactions.
**Career:** Serves as the firm's Managing Partner. Concentrates in the areas of real estate acquisitions and sales, commercial leasing and real estate finance. Represents builders, developers, tenants and institutional users of real property with particular expertise in land development matters. Has also represented national and regional retailers in site acquisition and leasing activities in the Washington/Baltimore region.
**Personal:** BA, University of Pennsylvania; JD, Washington College of Law, American University.

### GOODELL JR, Charles P
Goodell, DeVries, Leech & Dann, LLP, Baltimore 410 783 4001
cpg@gdldlaw.com
*Recommended in Litigation*
**Practice Areas:** Mr Goodell has 34 years of experience in litigation and litigation management on a national, regional and local level. He has counseled clients on various aspects of individual and mass litigation. He has served as National Counsel on matters such as pacemaker leads, tainted blood products used by hemophiliacs, statins for treatment of cholesterol, PPA and lung injuries claimed from talc. He has been a member of national trial teams for companies making drugs to treat diabetes, heart valves, COX-2 pain medications and hormone replacement therapy. He has tried complex pharmaceutical and other cases in various jurisdiction in the US, including Florida, Pennsylvania, Missouri, Maryland, Rhode Island and Indiana. He has also served as Regional Counsel in the southeast, the midwest and the mid-Atlantic US for litigation involving contraception, diabetes medication and hormone replacement therapy. His representative clients include Pfizer, Inc., Bayer Corporation and Wyeth.
**Prof. Memberships:** American Bar Association; Advocate, National Board of Trial Advocates; Maryland State Bar Association; Federal Bar Association; Defense Research Institute; National Institute of Trial Advocacy; Federation of Defense and Corporate Counsel; Product Liability Advisory Council (PLAC); International Association of Defense Counsel (IADC).
**Career:** Goodell, DeVries, Leech & Dann, LLP, 1988-present. One of the founding partners of law firm devoted to representation of clients in litigation and litigation management. Semmes, Bowen

& Semmes, 1972-1988, Partner and associate in Litigation Department of large, full-service law firm.

**Publications:** 'Keys to Winning' Network of Trial Law Firms, 2003: 'Preventing Litigation'; Network of Trial Law Firms, 2003: 'Lesson for Mass Tort Litigation'; Judicial Institute of Maryland, 1995: 'Theories of Recovery and Proof of Causation in Cases Involving Exposure to Hazardous Substances'; Defense Research Institute, February 1994: 'Electromagnetic Fields'; Defense Research Institute, May 1993: 'The Concept of Acceptable Risk'; Defense Research Institute, November 1992: Maryland Judicial Institute, 1991: 'Warnings in Product Liability'; Regulatory Affairs Professional Society Annual Meeting, 1989: 'Products Liability'; Defense Research Institute 1988 Product Liability Seminar: 'Recalls in Products Liability'.

**Personal:** Johns Hopkins University (BA, 1969); George Washington University (JD, with honors, 1972).

## GRAHAM, Andrew Jay
Kramon & Graham, PA, Baltimore
410 752 6030
agraham@kg-law.com
*Recommended in Litigation*

**Practice Areas:** Civil Business Litigation. Mr Graham also practices in the areas of professional liability matters, white-collar criminal litigation, trade secrets litigation, antitrust litigation, securities litigation, general civil litigation, and mediation. A lawyer's area of practice as stated here is one to which he devotes a substantial proportion of his professional practice and should not be considered a 'specialization'.

**Prof. Memberships:** Mr Graham is a Fellow of the American College of Trial Lawyers, and was its Maryland State Chairman from 1996-98. He is a Member of the Association of Professional Responsibility Lawyers. He is a Fellow of the American Bar Foundation. Mr Graham is a Member of, and has held various offices and board and committee positions with, the American Bar Association, the Federal Bar Association, and the Maryland and Baltimore City Bar Associations. He is the Chairman of the Maryland Bar, Ethics 2000 Committee. He is a permanent Member of the Fourth Circuit Judicial Conference. He is a founding Member of Maryland ADR Services, Inc., a nonprofit forum for alternative dispute resolution. He is a Member of Bars of Maryland, New York and the District of Columbia.

**Career:** Mr Graham served as a law clerk to the Honorable Alexander Harvey, II on the United States District Court for the District of Maryland. He was an assistant United States attorney for the District of Maryland from 1971 through 1974. Mr Graham is an active member of the Bars of Maryland, New York and the District

of Columbia. He is admitted to practice before the United States Supreme Court, the United States Court of Appeals for the Fourth Circuit, and the United States District Courts for the District of Columbia, the District of Maryland, the Eastern District of New York, and the Southern District of New York.

**Publications:** 'The Significance of Civility', published in The Maryland Bar Journal, Volume XXXVI, Number 5, September/October 2003; 'Changes in Maryland's Rules of Professional Conduct on Horizon', published in the Bar Bulletin, December 15, 2004.

**Personal:** Mr Graham was born February 21, 1943. He graduated from Yale University (BA 1965) and received his Law Degree from the New York University School of Law (JD 1968).

## GRAY, James
Venable LLP, Baltimore 410 244 7400
*Recommended in Litigation*

## GREENBERG, Barry
Rosenberg, Martin, Funk, Greenberg, LLP, Baltimore 410 727 6600
*Recommended in Real Estate*

## GUATTERY, Peter
Whiteford, Taylor & Preston LLP, Baltimore 410 347 9431
pguattery@wtplaw.com
*Recommended in Employment*

**Practice Areas:** Advice and counsel to public and private employers in employment related matters, including defense of discrimination, harassment and other employment claims; employment documentation and drafting of contracts; wage and hour; immigration and nationality law, including employer compliance, DOL investigations, and employment of foreign nationals.

**Prof. Memberships:** Maryland State Bar Association; American Bar Association; American Immigration Lawyers Association. Admitted in Maryland.

**Personal:** JD, University of Pennsylvania, 1987; BA, Johns Hopkins University, 1984.

## GUBEN, Jan
Venable LLP, Baltimore 410 244 7400
*Recommended in Real Estate*

## HAFETS, Richard J
DLA Piper Rudnick Gray Cary US LLP, Baltimore 410 580 4168
richard.hafets@dlapiper.com
*Recommended in Employment*

**Practice Areas:** Labor and employment law; class action litigation.

**Career:** He practices in all areas of labor and employment law, including union avoidance, traditional labor-management relations, employment litigation, EEO and affirmative action, OSHA, and general personnel. He is primary labor counsel to many Fortune 500 companies, healthcare institutions, charities, and civic orga-

nizations, and represents many of the firm's significant clients. Prior to joining DLA Piper, he worked with the National Labor Relations Board.

**Personal:** JD, American University; BS, American University.

## HANKS, James
Venable LLP, Baltimore 410 244 7400
*Recommended in Corporate/M&A*

## HARMON, Jason C
DLA Piper Rudnick Gray Cary US LLP, Baltimore 410 580 4170
jason.harmon@dlapiper.com
*Recommended in Corporate/M&A*

**Practice Areas:** Corporate/M&A; private equity; capital markets; life sciences

**Career:** His practice includes public and private equity and debt offerings, mergers and acquisitions, and other corporate matters, emphasizing high technology and emerging growth companies, including Internet, communications, and biotech companies. His M&A experience includes both serving as buyer's counsel and seller's counsel. In his equity offering and debt offering experience, he has been both Company Counsel and Banker's Counsel.

**Personal:** JD, Washington and Lee University; BA, University of Pittsburgh

## HARRISON, Bruce S
Shawe Rosenthal LLP, Baltimore
410 752 1040
harrison@shawe.com
*Recommended in Employment*

**Practice Areas:** Employment discrimination litigation; employment tort and contract litigation; wage and hour laws; class action litigation; family and medical leave act (FMLA); employment agreements, policies, and procedures.

**Prof. Memberships:** Bar Admissions: Maryland; District of Columbia; Pennsylvania; US Courts of Appeals for the 1st, 2nd, 3rd, 4th, 5th, 9th, 11th, and DC Circuits. Professional Associations: Fellow, College of Labor and Employment Lawyers, 1999-present; American Bar Association; Maryland State Bar Association.

**Career:** Before joining the Firm in 1971, Bruce served as a senior attorney at the Equal Employment Opportunity Commission's headquarter offices.

**Publications:** Bruce is editor of the 'Employment Law Deskbook' (Lexis/Matthew Bender) and has also co-authored three monographs published by Matthew Bender: 'Avoiding Employment Discrimination Charges', 'Employer Discipline and Discharge', and 'Responding to Employment Discrimination Charges'. Other publications include: 'Sexual Harassment and Related Torts: The Employer's Perspective', American Bar Association. Contributing author: 'Age Discrimination: A Legal and Practical Guide for Employers', BNA Special Report. Contributor: 'Workplace Privacy',

Thompson Publishing Group. Case note editor and Contributing Author: 'Sexual Harassment & Discrimination Reporter', James Publishing, Inc. Board of Editors: 'Model Jury Instructions: Employment Litigation', Section of Litigation, American Bar Association. Contributor: 'Employment Litigation Handbook', Section of Litigation, American Bar Association. Member of Editorial Board and Contributor: Bender's Labor & Employment Bulletin, Matthew Bender, Publishers; contributing editor: Maryland and Federal Employment Law Manual, American Chamber of Commerce Publishers. Contributor: 'Workplace Privacy', Thompson Publishing.

**Personal:** George Washington University School of Law, JD, cum laude, 1971; LLM Labor Law, 1975; Case Western Reserve University, BA, 1967.

## HILL, Eva H
Whiteford, Taylor & Preston LLP, Baltimore 410 347 8798
ehill@wtplaw.com
*Recommended in Corporate/M&A*

**Practice Areas:** Eva Hill's practice encompasses mergers and acquisitions; business and corporate law; corporate governance; business and succession planning; executive compensation; structuring of business entities including corporations, partnerships, limited liability companies, and joint ventures; equipment leasing; and commercial contracting.

**Prof. Memberships:** American, Maryland and Baltimore City Bar Associations.

**Career:** Ms Hill is the Head of the Corporate and Securities Department.

**Publications:** Co-author: 'Recent Trends in Psychiatric Liability', Volume 3, Review of Clinical Psychiatry and the Law.

**Personal:** University of Maryland School of Law (JD, Order of the Coif, 1990); Loyola University of New Orleans (BA, magna cum laude, 1987).

## HIMELES, Martin
Zuckerman Spaeder LLP, Baltimore
410 332 0444
*Recommended in Litigation*

## HOFFMAN, Kenneth
Venable LLP, Baltimore
410 244 7400
*Recommended in Employee Benefits*

## HORN, Todd
Venable LLP, Baltimore
410 244 7400
*Recommended in Employment*

## IMMELT, Stephen
Hogan & Hartson LLP, Baltimore
410 659 2757
sjimmelt@hhlaw.com
*Recommended in Healthcare, Litigation*

**Practice Areas:** White-collar criminal litigation; complex litigation in the health and general commercial fields; internal

and congressional investigations, grand jury practice, defense of qui tam cases, and development of compliance plans.
**Prof. Memberships:** Member, Fourth Circuit Judicial Conference; Association memberships include: ABA Health Law Section and the National Association of College and University Attorneys.
**Career:** Partner, Hogan & Hartson since 1989; private practice from 1983; Assistant US Attorney for the District of Maryland 1979-83.
**Personal:** University of Maryland (JD, cum laude); Yale University (BA, cum laude, 1974).

## ISAACSON, Andrew
Linowes and Blocher LLP, Bethesda
301 654 0504
aisaacson@linowes-law.com
*Recommended in Real Estate*
**Practice Areas:** Real estate transactions.
**Career:** Concentrates in the area of real estate transactions. Represents clients in a wide range of real estate matters, including real estate finance for lenders and borrowers; residential, shopping center, and mixed-use developments; condominium projects; title matters; construction and architect's agreements; workouts; and real estate litigation. Has served as special counsel to a variety of entities, including public redevelopment agencies; local and national residential and commercial builders and developers; local and national real estate lenders and equity investors; and major retailers.
**Personal:** BA, Georgetown University; JD American University, Washington College of Law.

## JOHNSTON, George
Venable LLP, Baltimore
410 244 7400
*Recommended in Employment*

## KAHN, Henry
Hogan & Hartson LLP, Baltimore
410 659 2780
hdkahn@hhlaw.com
*Recommended in Corporate/M&A*
**Practice Areas:** Henry Kahn practices in the areas of merger and acquisition law, securities law and regulation, investment management law, and Maryland corporate law.
**Career:** Henry advises clients on mergers and acquisitions, proxy contests and other matters affecting corporate control, securities offerings, securities regulation matters, and corporate governance matters. He regularly advises corporate boards and special committees. Henry also represents investment management organizations and diversified financial services organizations in structuring investment products and on issues affecting their strategic development.
**Personal:** The George Washington University Law School (JD, 1980); Yale University (BA, 1977).

## KAMANTAUSKAS-HOLDER, Katrina
Holder Law Group LLC, Towson
410 296 9550
*Recommended in Employee Benefits*

## KEENER, Mark
Gallagher, Evelius & Jones, LLP, Baltimore 410 727 7702
*Recommended in Real Estate*

## KELLNER, Robert
Gordon, Feinblatt, Rothman, Hoffberger & Hollander, LLC, Baltimore
410 576 4000
*Recommended in Employment*

## KOCHANSKI, David
Shulman, Rogers, Gandal, Pordy & Ecker, PA, Rockville 301 230 5200
*Recommended in Real Estate*

## KRATZ JR, John E
DLA Piper Rudnick Gray Cary US LLP, Baltimore 410 580 4190
john.kratz@dlapiper.com
*Recommended in Employee Benefits*
**Practice Areas:** Employee benefits.
**Career:** He concentrates in the planning of employee benefits and executive compensation, including all aspects of the Employee Retirement Income Security Act of 1974 (ERISA), and has more than 25 years experience in this area. His employee benefit experience includes designing and drafting all types of employee benefit programs, advising financial institution plan sponsors and other benefit plan fiduciaries on ERISA questions, and dealing with benefit issues in mergers and acquisitions. He is also experienced in designing deferred compensation and other benefit programs for tax-exempt employers.
**Personal:** JD, University of Pennsylvania; BA, Johns Hopkins University

## LARIA, Jon M
Ballard Spahr Andrews & Ingersoll LLP, Baltimore 410 528 5506
laria@ballardspahr.com
*Recommended in Real Estate*
**Practice Areas:** Represents owners, developers, and lenders in all types of commercial real estate transactions, including finance, acquisition, development, leasing, and land use.
**Prof. Memberships:** Faculty, Johns Hopkins University Master's in Real Estate program. Chair, Public Policy Advisory Board of the University of Maryland, Baltimore County and Regional Investment Committee of the Associated: Jewish Community Federation of Baltimore. President, Live Baltimore. Vice President, Baltimore Jewish Council. Board, Healthy Neighborhoods, Inc.
**Career:** Member, American Bar Association. Admitted: Maryland Bar Association (1992), District of Columbia Bar Association (1995), Bar Association of Baltimore City. Served as law clerk to the

Honorable Howard S Chasanow on Maryland's highest court, the Maryland Court of Appeals
**Personal:** JD, with honors, University of Maryland School of Law (1992); BA, Johns Hopkins University (1985).

## LEVIN, Edward J
DLA Piper Rudnick Gray Cary US LLP, Baltimore 410 580 4700
edward.levin@dlapiper.com
*Recommended in Real Estate*
**Practice Areas:** Real estate; real estate finance.
**Prof. Memberships:** Member, American College of Real Estate Lawyers (ACREL).
**Career:** Chair, Section of Real Property, Probate and Zoning, Maryland State Bar Association (MSBA); Chair, ACREL Attorneys' Opinions Committee; Chair, Co-Chair and Steering Committee Member, projects on attorneys' opinions of MSBA, ACREL and American Bar Association (ABA); Chair and lecturer at seminars of ACREL, ABA and MSBA.
**Publications:** Co-author, 'Maryland Real Estate Leasing Forms - Practice'; author of articles on attorneys' opinions and other real property-related matters.
**Personal:** JD, University of Virginia; BA, Johns Hopkins University, with honors.

## LEVINE, Richard E
DLA Piper Rudnick Gray Cary US LLP, Baltimore 410 580 4400
rich.levine@dlapiper.com
*Recommended in Real Estate*
**Practice Areas:** Business tax; real estate; corporate and securities.
**Prof. Memberships:** Fellow of American College of Tax Counsel.
**Career:** He is nationally recognized in the area of partnership and real estate taxation and represents many of the leading real estate entrepreneurs in the Maryland area. He focuses his practice on sophisticated real estate transactions which frequently involve complex tax issues. He is also listed in alternative legal publications.
**Personal:** JD, University of Maryland; LLM, Georgetown University Law Center; BS, Mechanical Engineering, Bucknell University.

## LEWIS, Thomas
Gallagher, Evelius & Jones, LLP, Baltimore 410 727 7702
*Recommended in Real Estate*

## LOHR JR, Walter
Hogan & Hartson LLP, Baltimore
410 659 2764
wglohr@hhlaw.com
*Recommended in Corporate/M&A*
**Practice Areas:** Represents clients in a broad range of transactions, including public and private offerings, mergers and acquisitions, and organization of partnerships and joint ventures. Also provides ongoing representation to corporations, other business enterprises, business own-

ers and executives.
**Career:** Director of a Fortune 500 corporation, where he chaired the Audit Committee and currently chairs the Nominating and Governance Committee. Director of several privately-held corporations and has been a Member of the advisory board of a venture capital firm sponsored by a major US life insurance company.
**Personal:** Princeton University (AB, 1966); Yale University (LLB, 1969).

## MACHEN, John
DLA Piper Rudnick Gray Cary US LLP, Baltimore 410 580 4444
jack.machen@dlapiper.com
*Recommended in Real Estate*
**Practice Areas:** Real estate.
**Career:** He practices in the areas of commercial real estate financing and real estate development, including property acquisition, disposition, and leasing. He has represented lenders and developers in a variety of commercial enterprises, including shopping centers, office buildings, condominiums, townhouses, and apartments, with respect to acquisition, construction and permanent financing, syndication, leasing, sale, foreclosures, and negotiated workouts.
**Personal:** JD, University of Maryland; BA, Princeton University.

## MADDEN, Paul W
Whiteford, Taylor & Preston LLP, Baltimore 410 347 8742
pmadden@wtplaw.com
*Recommended in Employee Benefits*
**Practice Areas:** Partner and Head of the firm's Employee Benefits Practice Group. Regularly advises employers with respect to retirement, welfare and executive compensation plan design and ERISA and Internal Revenue Code compliance. Experience includes fiduciary training and counseling and guiding clients through government agency audits and correction programs. Provides advice regarding employee benefit matters in bankruptcy, litigation and corporate transactions.
**Prof. Memberships:** Maryland State Bar Association, Employee Benefits Subcommittee (Chairman 1995-1996); Co-Chairman: IRS Employee Benefits Conference (1994-2002) National Association of Public Pension Attorneys.
**Personal:** University of Pennsylvania (JD 1975). Catholic University of America (AB, magna cum laude 1969; MA 1970).

## MARTIN, Gerard
Rosenberg, Martin, Funk, Greenberg, LLP, Baltimore 410 727 6600
*Recommended in Litigation*

## MARTIN, Thene M
Hogan & Hartson LLP, Baltimore
410 659 2755
tmmartin@hhlaw.com
*Recommended in Corporate/M&A*
**Practice Areas:** Thene Martin practices

in the areas of corporate, mergers and acquisitions, private equity and venture capital, and securities law. She represents issuers, underwriters and placement agents in public equity offerings, debt offerings, private placements and exchange offers. She also counsels clients on structural, organizational, governance matters, and compliance with federal securities laws.
**Career:** Thene has experience advising clients in a wide variety of industries, including healthcare, education, energy, communications, technology, insurance, manufacturing, marketing, and hospitality.
**Personal:** University of Minnesota (BA, 1986); University of Minnesota Law School (JD, cum laude,1989)

## MATHIAS, Robert
DLA Piper Rudnick Gray Cary US LLP, Baltimore 410 580 4209
robert.mathias@dlapiper.com
*Recommended in Litigation*
**Practice Areas:** Litigation; class action litigation; patent litigation; securities litigation; international arbitration; white-collar.
**Prof. Memberships:** American College of Trial Lawyers, Fellow, Complex Litigation Committee.
**Career:** Co-Chair of the Global Litigation Group, Chair of the US Litigation Group. His primary areas of practice are business litigation, intellectual property litigation and white-collar criminal advice to corporate clients. He has tried cases and argued appeals in the federal and state courts in a number of jurisdictions and has extensive experience with many types of alternative dispute resolution. He is listed in several leading legal publications.
**Personal:** JD, Harvard Law School; BA, Yale University.

## MATRICCIANI, Rose M
Whiteford, Taylor & Preston LLP, Baltimore 410 347 9476
rmatricciani@wtplaw.com
*Recommended in Healthcare*
**Practice Areas:** Health law and corporate.
**Prof. Memberships:** American Health Lawyers Association; American, Maryland, Baltimore City and Baltimore County Bar Associations; Chesapeake Nurse Attorneys.
**Publications:** MedChi's Response to the Challenge of Helping Victims, Maryland Medicine, Summer 2005. Contributing editor, Domestic Violence; Child Maltreatment; Elder/Vulnerable Adult Abuse and Neglect, MedChi, 1994-97. Contributing editor, Guide for Nurses Responding to Domestic Violence, MedChi, July 1995. Contributing editor, Domestic Violence Resource Directory, Baltimore City and Baltimore County Bar Associations.

**Personal:** University of Maryland (JD, 1989); Loyola College (BA, 1983); Essex Community College (AA Nursing, 1973).

## MCGEE JR, Emmett F
DLA Piper Rudnick Gray Cary US LLP, Baltimore 410 580 4211
emmett.mcgee@dlapiper.com
*Recommended in Employment*
**Practice Areas:** Labor and employment law.
**Career:** He represents employers in all aspects of employment law and human resource management, including employment discrimination, wage and hour issues and affirmative action planning. His practice includes litigation in state and federal courts throughout the US, as well as before administrative agencies and arbitration panels. He also has extensive experience in areas of employment contracts, trade secrets and restrictive covenants, and related litigation, as well as the litigation of ERISA claims and stock option claims.
**Personal:** JD, University of Virginia; BA, Johns Hopkins University.

## MCGUIRE, J Michael
Shawe Rosenthal LLP, Baltimore 410 752 1040
mcguire@shawe.com
*Recommended in Employment*
**Practice Areas:** Labor-management relations; practice before the National Labor Relations Board; collective bargaining and labor arbitration representing management; employment discrimination litigation; human resources advice and counsel; employment agreements; employment tort and contract litigation; employment handbooks, policies, and procedures; wage and hour laws; occupational safety and health acts.
**Prof. Memberships:** Bar Admissions: Maryland (State and Federal); US Court of Appeals for the 4th, 9th and 11th Circuits. Professional Associations: American Bar Association; Maryland State Bar Association; Chair, Labor & Employment Law Section of Maryland State Bar Association (2004-06 Term); Maryland Association of Defense Trial Counsel; American Bar Association (EEO & NLRB Practice and Procedure Committees).
**Publications:** Michael has co-authored two books, 'Employee Discipline and Discharge', and 'An Employer's Guide to the Occupational Safety and Health Act', both published by Lexis/Matthew Bender, and numerous articles for the Maryland Bar Journal including 'Jury Trial Waivers' (Vol. 38, 4); 'Acquiring a Unionized Facility' (Vol. 33, 3), and 'Sex Harassment Investigations' (Vol. 35, 1).
**Personal:** University of Maryland School of Law, JD, cum laude, 1978 Recipient, Joseph Bernstein Prize; University of Maryland, BA 1975.

## MERKLE, Craig
Goodell, DeVries, Leech & Dann, LLP, Baltimore 410 783 4007
cbm@gdldlaw.com
*Recommended in Healthcare, Litigation*
**Practice Areas:** Pharmaceutical and medical device litigation – Mr Merkle is actively involved in the firm's Medical Drug and Device Practice. He has been lead trial counsel for multiparty trial groups in the diet drug litigation in the Court of Common Pleas in Philadelphia, Pennsylvania. He has also been involved in the defense of lawsuits arising from prosthetic knee implants and the investigational study of diabetes drugs. Professional Liability Claims – Mr Merkle has represented physicians and healthcare providers in virtually every medical specialty, community hospitals and academic medical centers. He has tried to verdict numerous medical malpractice cases throughout the State of Maryland. Professional Disciplinary, Privileging and Hospital Litigation – Mr Merkle has represented academic and community healthcare systems in matters involving privileging and employment disputes, impaired physicians, boundary violations, and breach of professional and fiduciary obligations.
**Prof. Memberships:** International Association of Defense Trial Counsel; Fourth Circuit Judicial Conference; Maryland Association of Defense Trial Counsel.
**Career:** Goodell, DeVries, Leech & Dann, LLP, 1988-present. Founding Partner. Semmes, Bowen & Semmes, 1982-88. Associate and senior associate. Judicial law clerk, 1981-82, The Honorable Norman P Ramsey, United States District Court for the District of Maryland.
**Publications:** Mr Merkle is the Chair of the Norman P Ramsey Lecture Series, which is held in conjunction with the University of Maryland School of Law. Mr Merkle has frequently been an invited speaker on a broad range of topics in trial practice, risk management, and the application of legal and ethical principles to scientific and medical advances. He has lectured to lawyers and judges on genetics, the human genome project, cloning, and stem cell research. He has also lectured on medical documentation, federal statutory requirements on patient dumping, and numerous topics and trends in medical malpractice.
**Personal:** Western Maryland College (BA, summa cum laude, 1978); Duke University School of Law (JD, with distinction, 1981); Order of the Coif; Duke Law Journal 1979-81.

## MILLSPAUGH, Thomas E D
WilmerHale, Baltimore 410 986 2870
thomas.millspaugh@wilmerhale.com
*Recommended in Real Estate*
**Practice Areas:** Partner, Real Estate

Department. Experience in investment, acquisition, development, leasing, financing, sale transactions for corporations, pension funds, retail organizations, developers and other investors and operators. Negotiates numerous contracts, leases, loan documents; structures joint ventures and other investment partnerships; counsels many non-real estate businesses in connection with real estate matters, both nationally and internationally.
**Prof. Memberships:** Maryland State Bar Committee on Opinions in Commercial Transactions; Urban Land Institute; Pension Real Estate Association; Real Property Section, Maryland State Bar Association; Advisory Board, Chicago Title Insurance Company.
**Personal:** JD, University of Virginia School of Law; BA, University of North Carolina at Chapel Hill.

## MONK II, Charles O
Saul Ewing LLP, Baltimore 410 332 8668
cmonk@saul.com
*Recommended in Litigation*
**Practice Areas:** Managing Partner of Saul Ewing's Baltimore office. Focuses on antitrust, business disputes, insolvency litigation, class actions, and regulatory.
**Prof. Memberships:** Admitted to practice in Maryland and before US Supreme Court; US Courts of Appeals for the Second, Third, Fourth, Fifth, Ninth, and Eleventh Circuits; US Court of Appeals for the District of Columbia; US District Courts for Districts of Columbia and Maryland. Member, American and Maryland State Bar Associations.
**Career:** Served as Assistant Attorney General of Maryland; Chief of the Antitrust Division, Attorney General's Office; Deputy Attorney General of Maryland.
**Personal:** JD, University of Maryland, AB, Brown University.

## MUEDEKING, Mark
DLA Piper Rudnick Gray Cary US LLP, Baltimore 202 861 6258
mark.muedeking@dlapiper.com
*Recommended in Employee Benefits*
**Practice Areas:** Employee benefits and ERISA; tax; sports facilities
**Career:** His practice includes employee benefits and executive compensation; business and tax; and sports law. His employee benefits and executive compensation practice covers all aspects of plan design, operation, assets, audits, and litigation. His business and tax practice includes representation of public and private companies in acquisitions and divestitures. His sports law practice focuses on trademark licensing and enforcement, sponsorship contracts, athlete eligibility, insurance coverage, franchise acquisition, and enforcement of anti-doping regulations.
**Personal:** JD, University of Notre Dame;

LLM, Georgetown University; BA, St John's University

### MURPHY, William
Murphy & Shaffer, Baltimore
410 783 7000
*Recommended in Litigation*

### MURPHY JR, William
The Murphy Firm, Baltimore
410 539 6500
*Recommended in Litigation*

### NILSON, George
DLA Piper Rudnick Gray Cary US LLP, Baltimore 410 580 4227
george.nilson@dlapiper.com
*Recommended in Litigation*
**Practice Areas:** Environmental; litigation; class action litigation; state legislation and public policy; white-collar.
**Career:** He has had significant involvement in environmental controversies (hazardous waste, toxic torts, gasoline contamination, landfill litigation, removal of asbestos products from buildings), public and administrative law, election law controversies, tobacco litigation, cable television controversies, consumer controversies (range of regulatory and litigation issues presented by automobile dealers, condominium developers/sellers, time-share ventures and commercial lenders), zoning and litigation relating to real estate development, and complex civil litigation generally.
**Personal:** LLB, Yale University; BA, Master of Urban Studies, Yale School of Art and Architecture; BA, Yale College.

### OLIVER, James
Lenrow, Kohn & Oliver A Professional Corporation, Baltimore 410 962 0550
*Recommended in Real Estate*

### OSTENDORF, Marika
Ober Kaler Grimes & Shriver, Baltimore
410 685 1120
*Recommended in Employee Benefits*

### PALTELL, Eric
Kollman & Saucier PA, Baltimore
410 727 4300
*Recommended in Employment*

### PARVIS, Peter
Venable LLP, Baltimore
410 244 7400
*Recommended in Healthcare*

### PHELAN, Jeanne
Whiteford, Taylor & Preston LLP, Baltimore 410 347 8738
jphelan@wtplaw.com
*Recommended in Employment*
**Practice Areas:** Management-side advice and counsel and litigation in employment-related areas, including defense of discrimination, harassment and tort claims before courts and administrative agencies; defense of class action employment and pay-related actions, preparation and litigation of employment contracts, non-competition agree-ments, employment documents, and affirmative action plans; federal, state and local statutory compliance and litigation, advice regarding difficult employees.
**Prof. Memberships:** Maryland State Bar Association Section of Labor and Employment Law (Chair 1992-94). American Bar Association Labor and Employment Law Section. Admitted in Maryland.
**Personal:** JD, with honors, University of Maryland School of Law, 1980; BS, University of Maryland, 1977.

### POKEMPNER, Joseph
Whiteford, Taylor & Preston LLP, Baltimore 410 347 8739
jpokempner@wtplaw.com
*Recommended in Employment*
**Practice Areas:** Representation of employers in union-organizing campaigns and collective bargaining. representation of employers in cases before the NLRB, EEOC and other related administrative agencies.
**Prof. Memberships:** Maryland State Bar Association, Section of Labor & Employment (Chair 1982-84), Bar Association of Baltimore City (President 1984-85), Federal Bar Association (MD Chapter President 1979-80).
**Personal:** LLB, University of Maryland School of Law, 1962; BA, Johns Hopkins University, 1957.

### POLIAKOFF, Abba
Gordon, Feinblatt, Rothman, Hoffberger & Hollander, LLC, Baltimore
410 576 4000
*Recommended in Corporate/M&A*

### POLLAK, Mark
WilmerHale, Baltimore
410 986 2860
Mark.Pollak@wilmerhale.com
*Recommended in Real Estate*
**Practice Areas:** Partner in the firm's Real Estate Department, with more than 30 years of experience in real estate development and finance and municipal finance matters. Involved in the public financing of complex real estate projects, major sports stadiums, and the creation of public-private partnerships for development of central business districts.
**Prof. Memberships:** American College of Real Estate Lawyers; National Association of Bond Lawyers; American Planning Association; Board of Directors and Executive Committee for the Baltimore Children's Museum Downtown Partnership of Baltimore, Inc.
**Personal:** Brooklyn College (BA, cum laude, 1968); University of Pennsylvania (JD 1972; Masters in City Planning 1972).

### PONTONE, Kathleen
Miles & Stockbridge PC, Baltimore
410 385 3757
kpontone@milesstockbridge.com
*Recommended in Employment*

**Practice Areas:** Labor and employment law, occupational safety and health, whistleblower, harassment defense and prevention; competition and compensation litigation, ADA and discrimination in housing, lending and public accommodation.
**Prof. Memberships:** American Bar Association; Women's Bar Association; California Bar Association - Labor & Employment Section; US Chamber of Commerce - Labor Relations Committee and its OSHA and Wage & Hour Subcommittees; Securities Industries Association.
**Career:** Labor Counsel for Kaiser Aluminum & Chemical Corporation; Partner at Semmes, Bowen & Semmes (Baltimore, MD); 1992 to present, Principal at Miles & Stockbridge P.C. (Baltimore, MD). In 2004, received Maryland Leadership in Law Award; recognized by Chambers USA as a leading management-side employment lawyer in 2003; Baltimore Business Journal Who's Who in Law, 2003; 2005 Best Lawyers.
**Personal:** Vassar College AB 1972, Duke University School of Law JD 1977; Board of Directors for the Reginald F Lewis Museum of Maryland African American History & Culture; Vice President, The Valleys Planning Council, Inc.; Board of Directors, Ronald McDonald Charities of Maryland, Inc.; Board Miles & Stockbridge, Practice Group Leader - Labor and Employment.

### PRESTON, Susan T
Goodell, DeVries, Leech & Dann, LLP, Baltimore 410 783 4025
stp@gdldlaw.com
*Recommended in Healthcare*
**Practice Areas:** Civil litigation, representing a wide array of medical and nursing specialties, and academic and community hospitals in professional malpractice claims before the Health Claims Arbitration Office of Maryland, The Circuit Courts of Maryland, Superior Court of Washington, DC, and in the United States District Courts for the Districts of Columbia and Maryland.
**Prof. Memberships:** Fellow, American College of Trial Lawyers; associate, American Board of Trial Advocates. Maryland Defense Trial Counsel (President, 1993-94; Executive Committee, 1993-98); Maryland Society for Health Care Risk Management (President, 2000-01; President-Elect 1999-2000; Chairman, Legislative Committee, 1996-99, Member at Large, 1997-99); Maryland State Association; Defense Research Institute; Bar Association of Baltimore City.
**Career:** Partner at Goodell, DeVries, Leech & Dann, LLP, since 1987.
**Publications:** Medical Malpractice: Law Theory and Practice for Attorneys, Physicians, and Risk Managers, Evaluation of a Claim, Settlement and Settlement Negotiations and Structured Settlements,

American Bar Association National Institute on Medical Malpractice, Tort & Insurance Section (1987). Ms Preston has also widely lectured on subjects of professional liability.
**Personal:** American University, BA cum laude 1973; The University of Baltimore, JD, magna cum laude, 1979; law clerk to the Honorable Lawrence F Rodowsky, Court of Appeals of Maryland, 1980-81.

### REED, Matthew
WilmerHale, Baltimore
410 986 2864
Matthew.Reed@wilmerhale.com
*Recommended in Real Estate*
**Practice Areas:** Represents developers, lenders, major corporations, pension funds and other institutional investors, together with their consultants and advisors, in all areas of commercial real estate. Transactional experience is national in scope and includes acquisition, disposition, financing, development, operation, management, work-out and leasing transactions involving office, industrial, mall, hotel, mixed-use, town center, transit-oriented, public-private, military redevelopment, correctional facility, golf course community, multifamily residential and diverse retail projects.
**Personal:** George Washington University Law School (JD 1996); Princeton University (AB 1992).

### RENO, Russell
Venable LLP, Baltimore
410 244 7400
*Recommended in Real Estate*

### ROCKMAN, Jeffrey
Serotte, Rockman & Westcott, Baltimore
410 825 7900
*Recommended in Employment*

### ROSEN, Barry
Gordon, Feinblatt, Rothman, Hoffberger & Hollander, LLC, Baltimore
410 576 4000
*Recommended in Healthcare*

### ROSENBERG, Benjamin
Rosenberg, Martin, Funk, Greenberg, LLP, Baltimore 410 727 6600
*Recommended in Litigation*

### RYAN JR, William F
Whiteford, Taylor & Preston LLP, Baltimore 410 347 8741
wryan@wtplaw.com
*Recommended in Litigation*
**Practice Areas:** Having represented domestic and international clients in federal and many state courts, Mr Ryan concentrates on complex commercial issues including corporate, contract, securities and intellectual property disputes. He recently won a nationally-watched landmark class action housing discrimination case for the City of Baltimore following a month-long trial.
**Prof. Memberships:** Fellow, American College of Trial Lawyers. Admitted in

Maryland, Eastern District of Michigan, US Supreme Court and Circuit Courts of Appeals (2nd and 4th), as well as many state courts pro hac vice.
**Personal:** JD, University of Baltimore, 1979; Editor-In-Chief, Law Review; AB, with honors, Princeton University, 1976.

### SARBANES, John
Venable LLP, Baltimore 410 244 7400
*Recommended in Healthcare*

### SCHATZOW, Michael
Venable LLP, Baltimore 410 244 7400
*Recommended in Litigation*

### SCHEELER, Charles P
DLA Piper Rudnick Gray Cary US LLP, Baltimore 410 580 4250
charles.scheeler@dlapiper.com
*Recommended in Litigation*
**Practice Areas:** Litigation; class action; securities litigation; white-collar.
**Career:** He principally engages in a commercial litigation and white collar criminal defense practice. He has successfully litigated numerous sophisticated commercial and criminal disputes in federal and state courts, as well as in arbitration and mediation. He has represented companies and individuals in white collar criminal investigations and prosecutions and has provided advice on a variety of substantial corporate transactions. His trial experience includes over 25 jury trials and dozens of bench trials and arbitrations.
**Personal:** JD, Harvard Law School; BS, University of North Carolina at Chapel Hill.

### SCHLAFF, Barbara
Venable LLP, Baltimore 410 244 7400
*Recommended in Employee Benefits*

### SEARS, Barbara
Linowes and Blocher LLP, Bethesda 301 654 0504
bsears@linowes-law.com
*Recommended in Real Estate*
**Practice Areas:** Land use.
**Career:** Partner in charge of Land Use Practice Group. Represents land owners, developers and builders in land use, real estate, administrative and municipal law matters before administrative boards and agencies, legislative bodies and state and federal courts. Assists clients in complex matters involving zoning, subdivision, special exceptions, variances, building and other construction permits and approvals, and related facets of the development process. Handles litigation arising from these areas, including administrative appeals and condemnation. Former Associate General Counsel of the Maryland-National Capital Park and Planning Commission.
**Personal:** MA, Catholic University; JD, Catholic University.

### SEEGULL, Larry
DLA Piper Rudnick Gray Cary US LLP, Baltimore 410 480 4253
larry.seegull@dlapiper.com
*Recommended in Employment*
**Practice Areas:** Labor and employment.
**Career:** He represents employers in all areas of labor and employment law. He advises clients on compliance, litigation avoidance, and limiting liability with respect to the full complement of employment decisions, ranging from hiring, leave issues, discipline and termination. He also defends clients in all types of employment-related litigation, arbitration and agency investigations, including claims of discrimination, violations of the ADA/FMLA, claims for wages, claims for breach of contract and employment-related torts.
**Personal:** JD, University of Michigan; BA, Michigan State University.

### SEROTTE, Neal
Serotte, Rockman & Westcott, Baltimore 410 825 7900
*Recommended in Employment*

### SHAWE, Stephen D
Shawe Rosenthal LLP, Baltimore 410 752 1040
sshawe@shawe.com
*Recommended in Employment*
**Practice Areas:** Labor-management relations and NLRB proceedings; collective bargaining; employment discrimination; human resources advice and counsel; employment tort and contract litigation; employment handbooks, policies, and procedures; wage and hour laws; affirmative action programs; Family and Medical Leave Act; Worker Adjustment and Retraining Notification Act; appellate litigation; class actions; alternative dispute resolution.
**Prof. Memberships:** Bar Admissions: Maryland; US Court of Appeals for the 4th Circuit; Supreme Court of the United States. Professional Associations: American Bar Association; Maryland State Bar Association; Fellow, College of Labor and Employment Lawyers.
**Career:** Before joining the Firm in 1966, Stephen served as law clerk to Chief Judge Simon Sobeloff of the United States Court of Appeals for the Fourth Circuit. In 1967, he briefly left the firm when he was appointed an Assistant United States Attorney for the District of Maryland. He held that position until 1970 when he was selected to be the first General Counsel of the Maryland Commission on Human Relations.
**Publications:** Stephen has authored numerous articles on labor and employment matters, including 'An Employer's Duty to Bargain Over a Decision to Subcontract' for the Harvard Legal Commentary. He was co-author of 'Avoiding Employment Discrimination Charges'

for Matthew Bender & Co., Inc., and he has also written articles for the University of Baltimore Law Review on subjects ranging from concession bargaining to employment discrimination.
**Personal:** Education: Harvard Law School, LLB, 1965; Williams College, BA, cum laude, 1962.

### SHEA, James
Venable LLP, Baltimore 410 244 7400
*Recommended in Litigation*

### SHELLEY, Patrick
McGuireWoods LLP, Baltimore 410 659 4000
*Recommended in Real Estate*

### SHEPHERD, Kevin
Venable LLP, Baltimore 410 244 7400
*Recommended in Real Estate*

### SHULMAN, Lawrence
Shulman, Rogers, Gandal, Pordy & Ecker, PA, Rockville 301 230 5200
*Recommended in Real Estate*

### SILVER, Michael J
Hogan & Hartson LLP, Baltimore 410 659 2741
mjsilver@hhlaw.com
*Recommended in Corporate/M&A*
**Practice Areas:** Michael Silver practices in the areas of corporate, securities, mergers and acquisitions, private equity and general business law. He has acted as outside counsel in a wide variety of transactions and in providing ongoing general advice to clients including CIENA Corporation, Laboratory Corporation of America Holdings, Wabash National Corporation, Avalon Pharmaceuticals Inc., ABS Capital Partners and Martek Biosciences Corporation.
**Personal:** Harvard University (AB, magna cum laude, 1977); University of Chicago Law School (JD, 1980).

### SILVESTRI, Stephen
Miles & Stockbridge PC, Baltimore 410 727 6464
*Recommended in Employment*

### SIMPLER, Gary
Shawe Rosenthal LLP, Baltimore 410 752 1040
simpler@shawe.com
*Recommended in Employment*
**Practice Areas:** Labor-management relations; union avoidance; collective bargaining; employment discrimination; human resources advice and counsel; employment tort and contract litigation; covenants not-to-compete litigation; intellectual property and trade secret litigation; wage and hour laws; Family and Medical Leave Act (FMLA); Worker Adjustment and Retraining Notification act (WARN); employment agreements, employment handbooks, policies, and procedures; appellate litigation.
**Prof. Memberships:** Bar Admissions: Maryland; US Courts of Appeals for the

3rd and 4th Circuits. Professional Associations: American Bar Association; Maryland State Bar Association, Member, Labor Law Section.
**Publications:** Gary is a contributing author to the 'Employment Law Deskbook' and 'NLRA Law & Practice', both published by Lexis/Matthew Bender.
**Personal:** University of Maryland School of Law, JD, cum laude, 1985; University of Maryland, BA, cum laude, 1979, Omicron Delta Epsilon, Phi Kappa Phi.

### SMITH JR, Robert (Jay) W
DLA Piper Rudnick Gray Cary US LLP, Baltimore 410 580 4266
jay.smith@dlapiper.com
*Recommended in Corporate/M&A*
**Practice Areas:** Corporate and securities; mergers and acquisitions; life sciences; corporate governance; venture capital and emerging companies.
**Career:** His practice focuses on public and private offerings of debt and equity securities, mergers and acquisitions, and general representation of public and private companies. A significant portion of his practice involves representation of issuers and underwriters in connection with the sale of securities by existing public companies, as well as the initial public offering of securities by emerging companies in the technology, biotechnology and real estate industries.
**Personal:** JD, University of Maryland; BS, The Wharton School of Finance, University of Pennsylvania.

### SMITH III, Henry
Smith & Downey PA, Baltimore 410 321 9000
*Recommended in Employee Benefits*

### SNYDER, Stephen
Snyder Slutkin & Snyder, Baltimore 410 653 3700
*Recommended in Litigation*

### SOLLINS, Howard
Ober Kaler Grimes & Shriver, Baltimore 410 685 1120
*Recommended in Healthcare*

### ST. VILLE, Thomas
Miles & Stockbridge PC, Baltimore 410 727 6464
*Recommended in Employee Benefits*

### STRAIN, Paul
Venable LLP, Baltimore 410 244 7400
*Recommended in Litigation*

### TAYLOR, Ronald
Venable LLP, Baltimore 410 244 7400
*Recommended in Employment*

### TEPLITZKY, Sanford
Ober Kaler Grimes & Shriver, Baltimore 410 685 1120
*Recommended in Healthcare*

### THOMAS, Linda Marotta
DLA Piper Rudnick Gray Cary US LLP, Baltimore 410 580 4271

linda.thomas@dlapiper.com
*Recommended in Employee Benefits*
**Practice Areas:** Employee benefits;
mergers and acquisitions.
**Career:** She counsels companies and
individuals in all aspects of equity-based
and incentive compensation arrangements and has extensive experience
advising clients regarding stock-based
and cash compensation programs. She
focuses on compensation strategies that
position companies in recruiting, retaining and rewarding executive officers and
personnel. She is well experienced in
M&A relative to employee benefits, stock
options, and other compensation
arrangements. She also has a broad range
of experience counseling plan sponsors
and fiduciaries in designing and operating tax-qualified retirement plans.
**Personal:** JD, University of Baltimore;
LLM, University of Baltimore, BS, University of Dayton

### TOPOLSKI, Douglas
McGuireWoods LLP, Baltimore
410 659 4000
*Recommended in Employment*

### TORPHY-DONZELLA, Elizabeth
Shawe Rosenthal LLP, Baltimore
410 752 1040
etd@shawe.com
*Recommended in Employment*
**Practice Areas:** Employment discrimination litigation; employment tort and
contract litigation (including covenants
not to compete); Family and Medical
Leave Act; human resources advice and
counsel; employment law training;
employment agreements; employment
handbooks, policies and procedures;
appellate litigation; alternative dispute
resolution.
**Prof. Memberships:** Bar Admissions:
Maryland; District of Columbia; US
Courts of Appeals for the 3rd, 4th and
DC Circuits. Professional Associations:
American Bar Association; Maryland
State Bar Association; District of Colum-
bia Bar.
**Publications:** Editor of the General
Employment Law Volume of the
Matthew Bender Treatise, Employment
and Labor Law, and contributing eevidi-
tor to the Employment Law Deskbook,
also published by Matthew Bender.
**Personal:** Georgetown University Law
Center, JD, cum laude, 1992; associate
editor, Georgetown Journal of Legal
Ethics; University of North Carolina, BA,
cum laude, 1985.

### TOTTEN, Thomas L
DLA Piper Rudnick Gray Cary US LLP,
Baltimore 410 580 4276
thomas.totten@dlapiper.com
*Recommended in Real Estate*
**Practice Areas:** Real estate; real estate
finance.
**Career:** He practices in the area of real
estate development and finance repre-

senting individuals and private entities,
for-profit real estate developers, nonprofit organizations, distributors and manufacturers, and healthcare institutions in
real property acquisition, disposition,
development, leasing, financing, zoning,
construction, and land use matters. He
also represents commercial banks and
institutional lenders in modifying and
restructuring loans secured by real property and other assets and in portfolio land
sales and underwriters and issuers in tax-
exempt financings.
**Personal:** JD, University of Baltimore;
MA, University of Maryland; BA, Johns
Hopkins University

### TRANTER, Jack
Gallagher, Evelius & Jones, LLP,
Baltimore 410 727 7702
*Recommended in Healthcare*

### TRUITT, Raymond
Ballard Spahr Andrews & Ingersoll LLP,
Baltimore 410 528 5629
truitt@ballardspahr.com
*Recommended in Real Estate*
**Practice Areas:** Managing Partner of
the Baltimore office. Focuses on com-
mercial real estate including
acquisition/disposition, development,
structuring ownership vehicles, financ-
ing, leasing, and restructuring.
**Prof. Memberships:** Member, American
College of Real Estate Lawyers (ACREL),
American Bar Association (ABA), Mary-
land State Bar Association (MSBA), and
International Council of Shopping Cen-
ters. Former Chair, Section Council of the
Section of Real Property, Planning, and
Zoning of the MSBA, and former Chair,
Code Revision Committee of the Section.
**Career:** Admitted to Maryland Bar
(1982); Frequent speaker for ICSC,
MSBA and other professional organiza-
tions; former adjunct faculty member,
University of Baltimore School of Law
and The Allen Berman Institute of Johns
Hopkins University; faculty member and
advisory board member, Georgetown
University Law School's Advanced Com-
mercial Leasing Institute.
**Publications:** Author and contributing
author to various ABA, MSBA, and ICSC
periodicals.
**Personal:** JD, University of Virginia
School of Law (1982); BA, magna cum
laude, Loyola College (1979).

### ULWICK, James P
Kramon & Graham, PA, Baltimore
410 752 6030
julwick@kg-law.com
*Recommended in Litigation*
**Practice Areas:** Litigation. Mr Ulwick's
litigation practice is wide-ranging,
including criminal and civil litigation of
all kinds. Mr Ulwick has tried many cases
in state and federal courts, including:
banking, criminal defense, class actions,
contracts, personal injury, legal and medical malpractice, RICO, construction,

equal employment, real estate, securities,
toxic tort, and other cases. He has extensive experience in complex cases, and he
frequently appears in multidistrict litigations. In addition to trial work, he frequently briefs and argues appeals in both
federal and state courts of appeals. He is
listed in more than 625 published cases. A
lawyer's area of practice as stated here is
one to which he devotes a substantial
proportion of his professional practice
and should not be considered a 'specialization'.
**Prof. Memberships:** Mr Ulwick is a fellow in the American College of Trial
Lawyers and a permanent member of the
Judicial Conference for the United States
Court of Appeals for the Fourth Circuit.
He is a member of the Bars of Maryland,
New Jersey and the District of Columbia,
and is admitted in numerous federal
courts.
**Career:** Upon graduation from law
school, Mr Ulwick served as a judicial
clerk for The Honorable Edward S
Northrop, Chief Judge, United States Dis-
trict Court for the District of Maryland.
Mr Ulwick then spent six years as a feder-
al prosecutor; three years as an Assistant
United States Attorney for the District of
New Jersey (1978-81) and three years as
an Assistant United States Attorney for
the District of Maryland (1981-84). He
joined Kramon & Graham in 1984, and
became a member of the firm in 1986.
**Publications:** 'Producing by Mistake',
Vol. 18, No. 3, Litigation, Spring 1992;
'Bank Fraud, Chapter 88, Criminal
Defense Techniques', Vol. IV, Matthew
Bender & Co., New York, 1991; 'The Bail
Reform Act of 1984: Fundamental
Changes in the Conditions and Availabil-
ity of Release', 3 Barrister 16, 1985.
**Personal:** Mr Ulwick was born July 20,
1952. He is a 1974 graduate of the Uni-
versity of Massachusetts, and a 1977
graduate of the Columbus School of Law,
Catholic University of America.

### VANDEUSEN, Darrell
Kollman & Saucier PA, Baltimore
410 727 4300
*Recommended in Employment*

### WASHBURNE, Thomas
Venable LLP, Baltimore 410 244 7400
*Recommended in Corporate/M&A*

### WATKINS, John
WilmerHale, Baltimore 410 986 2820
John.Watkins@wilmerhale.com
*Recommended in Corporate/M&A*
**Practice Areas:** Practice focus: securities offerings transactions, equity and
debt investments, mergers and acquisitions, real estate investment trusts
(REITs). Advises wide range of clients on
complex corporate and securities matters, and handles acquisitions, securities
offerings transactions for public and private companies. Represents numerous

investment banking firms, merchant
banking, private equity, venture capital
funds in connection with securities offer-
ing matters, acquisitions of controlling
interests, debt and equity investments.
**Prof. Memberships:** ABA Business Law
Section (Venture Capital and Private
Equity, Federal Regulation of Securities
and Partnerships and Unincorporated
Business Organizations Committees).
**Personal:** Johns Hopkins University, BA;
University of Michigan Law School, JD.

### WEBB, Thompson
Miles & Stockbridge PC, Baltimore
410 385 3501
twebb@milesstockbridge.com
*Recommended in Corporate/M&A*
**Practice Areas:** Topper Webb represents
publicy and privately held entities in a
general business and transactional practice, including mergers and acquisitions,
joint ventures, a variety of financial transactions and private equity. He frequently
counsels boards of directors of REITs and
other publicly held companies organized
under Maryland law, as well as special
committees of boards, regarding corporate governance issues, antitakover
defenses and Maryland corporate laws
generally. Mr Webb heads the firm's Corporate and Securities Practice Group.
**Personal:** Williams College (AB, 1977);
University of Virginia (JD, 1980).

### WEINER, Arnold
Weiner & Weltchek, Lutherville
410 769 8080
*Recommended in Litigation*

### WHITE, Pamela
Ober Kaler Grimes & Shriver, Baltimore
410 685 1120
*Recommended in Employment*

### WILSON, Jane A
DLA Piper Rudnick Gray Cary US LLP,
Baltimore 410 580 4285
jane.wilson@dlapiper.com
*Recommended in Real Estate*
**Practice Areas:** Real estate; real estate
finance.
**Career:** Ms Wilson practices primarily in
real property law, including real estate
financing, leasing, and land acquisition
and disposition. Her clients include commercial banks and other lending institutions in acquisiton, construction, or permanent real estate financings, and she
also has extensive experience in representing private lenders in multi-layered
affordable housing finance.
**Personal:** JD, University of Maryland;
MA, University of Pittsburgh; BA, Elmira
College

### WINSTON, Roger
Linowes and Blocher LLP, Bethesda
301 654 0504
rwinston@linowes-law.com
*Recommended in Real Estate*
**Practice Areas:** Condominium and
common interest development.

**Career:** Concentrates practice on the representation of developers, builders, and lenders in connection with the development of common interest projects. Member, American College of Real Estate Lawyers. Officer within the Real Property, Probate and Trust Law Section of the American Bar Association and the Washington District Council of the Urban Land Institute. Listed in Best Lawyers in America, The International Who's Who in Real Estate Law and the Guide to the World's Leading Real Estate Lawyers.

**Personal:** BA, University of Maryland; LLM, Georgetown University School of Law; JD, University of Maryland Law School.

## WOLF, Larry

Whiteford, Taylor & Preston LLP, Baltimore 410 347 8747
lwolf@wtplaw.com
*Recommended in Employment*

**Practice Areas:** Labor-management relations; NLRB ULP defense; collective bargaining negotiations and arbitration; local government labor relations; EEO/Discrimination claim representation; union avoidance strategies; employment claim prevention strategies.

**Prof. Memberships:** Maryland State Bar Association, American Bar Association; Bar Association of Baltimore City. Admitted in Maryland, US Circuit Court of Appeals (DC, 3rd and 4th) and US Supreme Court.

**Career:** Private practice representing management since 1961. Adjunct lecturer in labor law and collective bargaining, 1965-70, 1972-80.

**Personal:** LLB, Yale University, 1961; AB, Johns Hopkins University, 1958.

## WRIGHT, James

Venable LLP, Baltimore 410 244 7400
*Recommended in Real Estate*

## WRIGHT, Jefferson V

Miles & Stockbridge PC, Baltimore
410 385 3600
jwright@milesstockbridge.com
*Recommended in Litigation*

**Practice Areas:** Commercial and business litigation, involving the litigation and arbitration of disputes concerning business contracts and torts, class actions, securities, RICO and other fraud claims, intra-corporate and partnership disputes, internal corporate investigations, claims against or among financial institutions (lender liability, enforcement actions, inter-creditor disputes, and claims under FCRA, FDCPA, ECOA, HOEPA, TILA, UDAP and other consumer protection statutes), privacy claims, constitutional challenges, IP disputes and claims seeking injunctions or other emergency relief. He also furnishes advice to lawyers both inside and outside of his firm on matters relating to professional ethics, professional liability and corporate responsibility and liability, and occasionally serves as an expert on matters relating to business litigation and professional ethics or responsibility.

**Prof. Memberships:** Admitted to practice in the state and federal courts of Maryland (1981), the United States Court of Appeals for the 4th Circuit (1981) and the US Supreme Court (1995). Mr Wright is a Member of the American Bar Association, Maryland State Bar Association (Chair, Committee on Ethics, 1985), Bar Associations of Baltimore City and Baltimore County. Member, Judicial Nominating Commission of Maryland, as well as various professional organizations and societies.

**Career:** Law clerk to J Dudley Digges of the Court of Appeals of Maryland (1979-81).

**Personal:** Georgetown University Law Center (JD, 1980, with honors); Tufts University (BA, 1977, with honors). Mr Wright has served as a Member of his firm's Board of Directors, and as General Counsel and as Chair of his firm's Ethics Committee for many years.

# GOODELL, DEVRIES, LEECH & DANN LLP

## THE FIRM

**Managing Partner:** Linda S Woolf
**Senior Partner:** Charles P Goodell Jr
**Number of partners:** 21
**Number of other lawyers:** 31

### AREAS OF PRACTICE:

| | |
|---|---|
| Pharmaceutical & Medical Device Litigation | 35% |
| Medical Institutions | 25% |
| Corporate/Commercial/Insurance | 20% |

**FIRM OVERVIEW:** Goodell, DeVries, Leech & Dann, LLP ('GDLD') was founded in 1988 by 16 lawyers who left one of Baltimore's largest firms to practice in an environment that fostered the highest quality legal representation, client service, collegiality and professionalism. The firm has expanded to over 50 lawyers without sacrificing these values. GDLD has a depth of real experience in the trial and management of complex litigation that is found in few other firms. Since the firm's inception, its attorneys have been involved in the defense and trial of pharmaceutical and medical device, healthcare, and commercial actions (including class actions and mass tort litigation) on behalf of national, regional and local clients. The firm's 'litigation-only' practice allows it to avoid many of the conflicts of interest that arise in firms with extensive corporate and transactional practices. GDLD has trial lawyers admitted to practice in Maryland, Virginia, the District of Columbia, New York, Pennsylvania and Tennessee.

The firm's lawyers appear in court in numerous jurisdictions, from the northeast to the mid-west and throughout the south. Corporate clients frequently request that the firm staff trial teams in complex national litigation. GDLD counsels clients when sensitive business issues intersect with the company's interest in defending itself in court. The firm has been instrumental in helping its clients protect and achieve their business objectives in the course of litigation related to the acquisition or divestiture of businesses, disputes involving directors and officers, shareholders, contracts, insurance and similar matters. From its earliest days, GDLD invested significant resources and technology in order to streamline the practice of law and enhance the communications between client and counsel. GDLD's Information Service Department supports the firm's attorneys with advances in technology that extend the 'office' to wherever its lawyers need to manage large volumes of information and documents. In sum, GDLD's wealth of trial experience, central East Coast location and utilization of technology enable it to field a team of lawyers uniquely suited to achieving excellent results for its corporate clients in a cost-effective manner.

## MAIN AREAS OF PRACTICE:

**Pharmaceutical & Medical Device Litigation:** The firm's lawyers have represented major pharmaceutical and medical device companies in product liability, class action and mass tort litigation since the 1970s. The firm has been responsible for developing successful defense strategies and nationally recognized experts in the fields of drug safety, biostatistics, health economics, epidemiology, engineering and metallurgy, protein biochemistry, hematology, toxicology, regulatory affairs and labelling. Members of the firm have served as national counsel in litigation involving pacemakers, pacemaker leads, defibrillators, HIV tainted blood products, Hepatitis C, Cipro/Avelox and other mass tort claims. They have served as regional counsel in litigation involving the Dalkon Shield, Rezulin, hormone replacement therapy medications, artificial knees, hips, and spinal devices and HIV tainted blood products. The firm's lawyers have served on national trial teams in litigation involving breast implants, the Dalkon Shield, heart valves, Rezulin, hormone replacement therapy, PPA, Baycol and diet drugs.
**Medical Institutions:** GDLD represents health systems, medical institutions and individual hospitals on a regional and local basis. Its work for these institutions includes defending claims of professional negligence, credentialing disputes and commercial matters.

## HEAD OFFICE

**MARYLAND**
One South Street 20th Floor, **Baltimore**, MD 21202
**Tel:** 410 783 4000   **Fax:** 410 783 4040
**Email:** info@gdldlaw.com.com
**Website:** www.gdldlaw.com

## CONTACTS

| | |
|---|---|
| Pharmaceutical & Medical Device Litigation | Charles P Goodell Jr |
| Medical Institutions | Donald L DeVries Jr |
| Corporate/Commercial/ Insurance | Linda S Woolf |

**Corporate/Commercial/Insurance:** The firm's attorneys have represented local, national and international clients in litigation arising from the sale of subsidiaries and business units, antitrust, non-competition agreements, theft of technology, shareholder derivative suits, claims against corporate directors and officers, trustees, securities brokers, and fiduciaries, ERISA class actions, defamation, tortious interference with contract and other business torts. It regularly represents national and international insurers in complex insurance coverage disputes involving directors and officers, errors and omissions, excess and surplus lines, and other insurance products. The firm also represents securities brokers/dealers and registered representatives in NASD proceedings and SEC audits.

**CLIENTS:** The firm represents the largest pharmaceutical companies in the United States on a national and regional basis. It also represents medical systems and individual medical institutions in a variety of litigation contexts. The firm represents international, national and local corporations in commercial litigation and international and national insurance companies in coverage litigation. Finally, it represents numerous national and local companies in toxic tort litigation.

**INTERNATIONAL WORK:** The firm serves as international counsel for a medical device manufacturer, Accufix Research Institute, Inc. ('ARI'). The international defense of ARI by the firm has included a class action and other isolated cases pending in Canada (working with Fraser Milner Casgrain LLP), a defibrillator case in the United Kingdom (working with Taylor Wessing) and many product liability matters in France (working with Bouckaert Ormen Passemard Sportes and Proskauer Rose LLP). The firm has also assisted ARI in matters pending in Hong Kong, Israel, Japan and Australia (working with Phillips Fox and Freehills). Finally, the firm advised the officers of ARI in connection with negotiations involving agreements entered into by ARI with related corporations. The firm has represented Pacific Dunlop Limited (n/k/a Ansell Limited), an Australian corporation, in litigation arising from the sale of certain worldwide subsidiaries, including litigation in Illinois state court, federal court and bankruptcy court. The firm represents both an international mining company and one of the world's largest producers of cement and ready mix products in connection with asbestos liabilities throughout the United States. The firm represented Fireman's Fund Insurance Company in a multi-million dollar fidelity bond claim brought in Greece by a Greek subsidiary of Marriott Corporation.

# KRAMON & GRAHAM P.A.

## THE FIRM

**Managing Principal:** Philip M Andrews

**Number of Members:** 14
**Number of other lawyers:** 13

**FIRM OVERVIEW:** Kramon & Graham, P.A., was founded in 1975 by two former Assistant United States Attorneys to handle complex commercial litigation and significant white collar criminal matters. The firm, which has enjoyed continual growth and success since then, currently has 27 lawyers. As the firm has grown, its practice areas have expanded as well, and now include commercial real estate, corporate, insurance coverage, executive employment, and administrative law matters. In addition to their professional commitments, Kramon & Graham lawyers are actively involved in state and local civic, cultural, charitable, and political activities, and serve in leadership roles on a wide range of outside boards and committees.

## MAIN AREAS OF PRACTICE:

**Civil Litigation:** A major portion of Kramon & Graham's practice is concentrated in business litigation, a field in which the firm is preeminent. The firm's lawyers have extensive trial and appellate experience at all levels of the federal and state court systems, as well as before administrative agencies. They have tried innumerable significant matters, involving virtually every kind of business and commercial issue. Three of the firm's members are Fellows in the American College of Trial Lawyers; four are former Assistant United States Attorneys; and three other members are former Assistant Attorneys General for the State of Maryland. Among the myriad business cases handled by Kramon & Graham lawyers are commercial disputes concerning contract, securities, fiduciary duty, unfair competition, commercial construction and residential development, trademark and copyright, trade secret, professional malpractice, technology, and attendant matters. In addition, the firm is retained to represent many lawyers and law firms on a regular basis.

**Real Estate:** The firm represents developers and entrepreneurs in connection with complex real estate transactions, large scale development projects, zoning and land use issues, financings, environmental issues, lending matters, and litigation involving real estate, zoning, land use, condemnation and construction matters.

**Insurance Coverage & Advice:** The firm maintains a sophisticated insurance practice that includes insurance coverage disputes and advice concerning general liability, excess, and umbrella policies. Kramon & Graham represents insurers in matters arising out of construction, environmental, products liability, professional liability, and other commercial disputes. The firm's practice in this area is national. It has acted as insurance liaison counsel in coverage disputes involving more than $100,000,000.00. The firm also represents insurance carriers, agents and brokers in regulatory matters before state insurance departments.

**Administrative Law:** Among the firm's long-standing clients are entities that do business with state and local governments. Several of the firm's principals are former Assistant Attorneys General with extensive knowledge of, and familiarity with, state agencies that award contracts for privatized services, construction work, and the supply of goods and materials. The firm routinely represents clients before various state agencies in licensing and regulation matters, as well as before the Maryland State Board of Contract Appeals, which has exclusive jurisdiction of procurement disputes and state contract claims.

## HEAD OFFICE

**MARYLAND**
One South Street, Suite 2600, **Baltimore**, MD 21202-3201
**Tel:** 410 752 6030  **Fax:** 410 539 1269
**Website:** www.kramonandgraham.com

## CONTACTS

**Administrative Law** ................................................Philip M Andrews
**Civil Litigation** .............................Andrew Jay Graham, James P Ulwick
**Criminal Litigation** .......................Andrew Jay Graham, James P Ulwick
**Insurance Coverage & Advice** ......................................Lee H Ogburn
**Real Estate & Corporate** ...........................................Jeffrey H Scherr

**Corporate/Commercial:** The firm represents many national and international entities, as well as regional and local businesses and entrepreneurs, in all matters relating to every kind of corporate law and business transaction. The firm's clients include professional practices such as architectural firms, law firms, medical practices, real estate services, internet services firms, wholesale distributors, manufacturers, and retail companies. The firm handles transactions that concern equity investments in businesses and real estate ventures. Kramon & Graham lawyers also do a significant amount of corporate legal planning, particularly with respect to family and closely-held businesses.

**Criminal Litigation:** The firm frequently represents companies, or their officers and directors, involved in federal and state criminal investigations in Maryland and other jurisdictions. Since the firm's founding, Kramon & Graham lawyers have served as lead defense counsel in many of the largest white collar criminal investigations and trials conducted in federal and Maryland courts.

# LINOWES AND BLOCHER LLP

## THE FIRM

**Managing Partner:** Andrew M Goldstein
**Number of partners:** 36
**Number of other lawyers:** 27

**FIRM OVERVIEW:** Linowes and Blocher LLP is one of the leading local law firms in the Washington DC region. Since its founding in 1956, the firm has focused its primary attention on real estate law and exists today as a full-service real estate firm, capable of providing the complete spectrum of services to clients acquiring, developing, financing, leasing, or disposing of real estate. For the past five decades, its attorneys have played a key role in many of the major real estate projects that have been undertaken in the Washington DC metropolitan area. The firm's clients include developers, investors, lenders, and institutional users of real property. In recent years, the firm's practice areas have significantly broadened and the firm now offers services in the areas of commercial litigation, bankruptcy, business planning, taxation, and corporate transactions that are characterized by the same sophistication that mark its traditional real estate services. Linowes and Blocher LLP is known for its comprehensive, team-oriented approach to the legal matters it handles – an approach that consistently produces successful results for its clients.

## MAIN AREAS OF PRACTICE:

**Land Use:** The firm's lawyers are experienced in the entire range of private and public sector land use issues. Beginning with planning and zoning and extending through the processes of subdivision, site planning and permitting, the firm guides development projects through the full range of requisite land use approvals. It also works on matters such as: transferable development rights; affordable housing regulations; municipal growth regulations; adequate public facilities ordinances and exactions; impact fees and linkage fees; code enforcement; special districting; and myriad zoning devices, including floating, overlay, use-it-or-lose-it, planned and mixed-use development, central business district and performance zones.

**REAL ESTATE TRANSACTIONS:** The firm's lawyers have extensive experience in negotiating and documenting every phase of commercial real estate transactions, including the financing, acquisition, disposition, construction, leasing and management of office, retail, industrial, residential, and mixed use projects.

**Development & Financing:** The firm prepares and negotiates purchase and sales contracts, ground leases, joint venture agreements, and multi-party development and easement agreements; review survey, title and environmental matters; and assist borrowers and lenders in negotiating and closing acquisition, construction and permanent loans. Its lawyers have particular experience in the negotiation and structuring of agreements with local governmental authorities relating to public/private development ventures and to alternative financing techniques, such as tax increment financing and tax development districts.

**Real Estate Closings:** The firm's settlement attorneys assist in closing large-scale commercial and residential transactions in the Greater Washington region. The firm is an authorized agent for several nationally known title insurance carriers and maintains close working relationships with the professional staffs of these companies.

**Leasing:** The firm assists clients in leasing matters for office buildings, shopping centers, and industrial properties, including providing advice as to problems arising in the landlord-tenant relationship. Its lawyers have worked extensively in large-scale governmental leasing transactions at the federal, state and local levels.

**Common Interest Development:** The scope of the firm's representation includes the preparation and registration of public offering statements for condominiums, the compilation of disclosure statements for residential community associations, and the preparation of documentation necessary to establish

## HEAD OFFICE

**MARYLAND**
7200 Wisconsin Avenue, Suite 800, **Bethesda**, MD 20814
**Tel:** 301 654 0504   **Fax:** 301 654 2801
**Email:** agoldstein@linowes-law.com
**Website:** www.linowes-law.com

## BRANCH OFFICES

**MARYLAND**
145 Main Street, **Annapolis**, MD 21401
**Tel:** 301 261 1668   **Fax:** 301 261 2603
**Email:** dplott@linowes-law.com

## CONTACTS

| | |
|---|---|
| Business Transactions | David M Cohen |
| Common Interest Development | Roger D Winston |
| Environmental | James B Witkin |
| Land Use | Barbara A Sears |
| Business Controversies | Bradford F Englander |
| Real Estate Transactions | Richard M Zeidman |

and operate residential, commercial and mixed-use condominiums, community associations, business parks and merchant associations. The firm has particular experience in dealing with master-planned communities, neo-traditional communities and golf course communities in addition to land condominiums, marina condominiums, two-tiered condominium regimes, and private associations for environmental and conservation purposes. A separate division of the group focuses exclusively on the representation of condominium and home-owner associations.

**Environmental:** The firm's environmental attorneys assist clients in performing environmental due diligence and assessing the environmental risks involved in transactions. It represents buyers and sellers and borrowers and lenders in negotiating transactional documents dealing with environmental matters. Where contaminated properties are involved, the firm's lawyers negotiate remediation agreements that allow the parties to allocate liability and permit transactions to close. The firm counsels clients on a range of environmental compliance issues affecting property owners and managers, including regulations dealing with underground storage tanks, asbestos, PCBs, radon, lead-based paint and indoor air quality.

**Business Controversies:** The group handles complex commercial and business litigation in state and federal trial and appellate courts in Maryland, the District of Columbia and Virginia. In addition to real estate-related litigation, the firm also represents clients in all aspects of business and commercial litigation. The firm represents both debtors and creditors and are engaged in resolving transactions in the region. Additionally, it represents banks and other creditors with diverse loan portfolios as well as a wide range of borrowers in both non-bankruptcy workouts and bankruptcy cases. The firm's bankruptcy lawyers provide advice to clients with respect to collections and related litigation; reorganization and liquidation; loan modification and restructuring; construction litigation and insolvency; acquisition of troubled assets; enforcement of guarantees; landlord and tenant bankruptcies; foreclosures and receiverships; lender liability; tax considerations in workouts; and environmental issues in workouts.

**Business Transactions:** The firm's lawyers assist in a variety of commercial transactions, including business formations, mergers, acquisitions, financings and reorganizations. Lawyers in the group are well versed and highly experienced in corporate, securities, tax and commercial finance law. Using the full breadth of business experience within the firm, the group structures transactions that fulfill business goals, comply with local, state and federal regulations, and take full advantage of tax laws.

# MILES & STOCKBRIDGE

## THE FIRM

**Chairman:** John B Frisch

**Number of partners:** 104
**Number of other lawyers firm wide:** 97

**FIRM OVERVIEW:** For more than 70 years Miles & Stockbridge has brought a deep personal commitment to serving business, corporate, non-profit and individual clients. Today the firm's 200 lawyers are both generalists – with the capacity to meet nearly every legal need – and specialists who understand the technical aspects of demanding and complex practice areas. Its eight Mid-Atlantic offices have comprehensive capabilities to deliver quality work and quality service, yet are part of a humanly scaled, accessible organization with many long-term client relationships that illustrate a rare ability to walk in the clients' shoes.

**MAIN AREAS OF PRACTICE:** The firm's comprehensive business and commercial practice encompasses 15 practice groups that among them have well over 120 practice subspecialties. The broadest description of its legal services emphasize these wide-ranging areas of focus:

**Finance:** From general corporate and securities counsel to in-depth services for banks and financial institutions, the firm handles a full spectrum of transactional and capital markets needs for their clients. Its experience includes assistance with tax and creditors' rights concerns, and advice to individuals and family-owned businesses on wealth and estate management.

**Human Resources:** The firm assists employers of all sizes and in all industries with the legal dimensions of human resources management in the areas of employment and labor, employee benefits and executive compensation. Although emphasizing proactive problem avoidance, they vigorously defend clients in court and before regulatory agencies.

**Litigation:** Comprehensive services offered by nearly 100 litigators throughout all firm offices address general business torts and trade regulation disputes, as well as areas of emphasis like products liability, mass torts and insurance recovery. The firm's lawyers also are skilled at domestic and international alternative dispute resolution.

**Real Estate:** Miles & Stockbridge assists developers, lenders, lessors, contractors and other real estate clients throughout the greater Baltimore/Washington region, from Northern Virginia to Pennsylvania. The firm gets deals done using unsurpassed market knowledge and close working relationships with governmental entities and commercial finance institutions.

**Technology:** From locations in the heart of dynamic centers of biotechnology and telecommunications activity, the firm offers intellectual property, business law and dispute resolution counsel to emerging companies and established multinational giants alike.

**Government Contracts:** The firm puts broadly based experience to work for clients that do business with government agencies and organizations at all levels. They help businesses of every size with contract dispute resolution (including an impressive record of bid protest success), and provide effective guidance on RPPs and procurement law compliance.

**Biotechnology:** The firm gives life sciences, biotech and pharmaceutical clients the financial market access, management skill and operational guidance they need for commercial success. Its multi-disciplinary business and technical counsel and strategically placed office sites – including UMB BioPark, Maryland's newest life sciences complex – help emerging and mature companies take products from the laboratory to final production.

## HEAD OFFICE

**MARYLAND**
10 Light Street, **Baltimore**, MD 21202-1487
**Tel:** 410 727 6464   **Fax:** 410 385 3700
**Website:** www.milesstockbridge.com

## BRANCH OFFICES

**MARYLAND**
300 Academy Street, **Cambridge**, MD 21613-1865
**Tel:** 410 228 4545   **Fax:** 410 228 5652

10490 Little Patuxent Parkway, **Columbia**, MD 21044
**Tel:** 410 381 6000   **Fax:** 410 381 6430

101 Bay Street, **Easton**, MD 21601
**Tel:** 410 822 5280   **Fax:** 410 822 5450

30 West Patrick Street, **Frederick**, MD 21701
**Tel:** 301 662 5155   **Fax:** 301 662 3647

11 North Washington Street, **Rockville**, MD 20850
**Tel:** 301 762 1600   **Fax:** 301 762 0363

One West Pennsylvania Ave, **Towson**, MD 21204
**Tel:** 410 821 6565   **Fax:** 410 823 8123

UMB BioPark, 800 West Baltimore Street, **Baltimore,** MD 21201
**Tel:** 410 500 5000   **Fax:** 410 385 3700

**VIRGINIA**
1751 Pinnacle Drive, **McLean**, VA 22102
**Tel:** 703 903 9000   **Fax:** 703 610 8686

**CLIENTS:** Miles & Stockbridge is widely regarded a leading law firm in the mid-Atlantic region that encompasses Maryland, Northern Virginia and Washington, DC. They are the choice of Fortune 500 industrial giants, major financial institutions, privately owned businesses as well as national and local not-for-profit organizations, and the firm's services in key litigation and transactional areas extend well beyond its immediate geographic base. Clients encompass 14 different industry groups, including the services sector (construction, consulting, distribution, hospitality), finance and investment, manufacturing (from consumer and industrial goods to biotechnology) and nonprofit providers of health, charitable and governmental services. Among these clients are such household names as: The Black & Decker Corporation, a global consumer products manufacturer; major financial firms like Bank of America and SunTrust Bank; retailing giant Lowe's Companies, Inc.; and such high-profile technology leaders as Verizon Communications and Hitachi, Ltd.

**INTERNATIONAL WORK:** Miles & Stockbridge advises US and multinational corporations on their transactional, investment and trade concerns worldwide, and has longstanding relationships representing non-US companies in direct investment and general business activities within the United States and North America. As a member of TerraLex®, a worldwide network of independent law firms comprising 10,000 lawyers in nearly 100 countries, there are few global jurisdictions where the firm cannot provide the assistance that its clients need.

M I L E S & S T O C K B R I D G E P.C.

# SHAWE ROSENTHAL, LLP

## THE FIRM

**Managing Partners:** Stephen D Shawe/Bruce S Harrison
**Partner:** J Michael McGuire

**Number of partners:** 11
**Number of other lawyers:** 5

**HEAD OFFICE**

**MARYLAND**
20 S. Charles Street, 11th Floor, **Baltimore**, MD 21201
**Tel:** 410 752 1040  **Fax:** 410 752 8861
**Website:** www.shawe.com

**FIRM OVERVIEW:** One of the first law firms in the country devoted exclusively to the representation of management in labor and employment matters, Shawe Rosenthal LLP was founded in 1947 by Earle K Shawe. Shawe Rosenthal's practice involves both traditional labor and employment law matters, including claims brought under the Civil Rights Act, Age Discrimination in Employment Act, and the Americans with Disabilities Act. The firm defends claims involving employment discrimination, wrongful termination, defamation, ERISA, wage and hour, and occupational safety and health matters before state and federal agencies and in the courts. It represents management in NLRB hearings, representation campaigns and collective bargaining negotiations. The firm provides advice and assistance in the formulation of covenants not to compete and trade secret protection commitments, and is active in litigation associated with disputes over restrictive covenants and trade secrets. The firm also provides advice and counsel in the creation of affirmation action plans and compliance with OFCCP regulations. From its inception in 1947, Shawe Rosenthal decided to remain a boutique practice (16 labor and employment attorneys), select and centralized rather than expand into regional offices. This philosophy has contributed to a professional excellence that has attracted clients from across the nation. The firm has for decades represented many Fortune 500 companies, including some of the country's largest manufacturing, public utility, retail, healthcare and insurance concerns. Over the past four years the firm has handled two labor cases in the United States Supreme Court (Allentown Mack v NLRB, 118 S.Ct. 818 (1998) and Kolstad v American Dental Association, 527 U.S. 526 (1999)). Shawe Rosenthal is an efficient well managed organization, and is therefore able to provide clients with uniform and consistent advice, greater efficiencies in rendering services, and greater capabilities in providing short and long-term strategic planning. All of the firm's clients are represented in their general business affairs by other law firms, indeed some of the largest law firms in the country. Many of these other law firms now have their own labor law sections. The firm's clients have, nonetheless, continued to turn to Shawe Rosenthal for advice and counsel in the labor and employment field because of the firm's specialized knowledge and experience, and capability to provide advice quickly and efficiently. Members of the firm have written many publications in the employment field, including the 'Employment Law Deskbook' (1989) and two chapters in 'NLRA Law & Practice' (1991), both published by Mathew Bender. The firm also wrote the 'Maryland and Federal Employment Law Manual' (2001), published by the American Chamber of Commerce Publishers.

**MAIN AREAS OF PRACTICE:** Employment law including defense of statutory and common law employment discrimination claims; labor management relations including collective bargaining, and proceedings before the NLRB; human resources advice and counsel; employment tort and contract litigation; covenants not-to-compete litigation; intellectual property and trade secret litigation; wage and hour laws (FLSA, Portal to Portal Act); Occupational Safety and Health Acts (OSHA); Affirmative Action Programs (AAPs); Family and Medical Leave Act (FMLA); Workers' Adjustment and Retraining Act (WARN); Employee Benefits/ERISA; emploment policy and document review and drafting, including employment agreements, employment handbooks, policies and procedures; appellate litigation; class actions defense.

**CLIENTS:** The firm represents clients in all sectors of the economy including major manufacturing concerns such as Black & Decker, Danaher Corporation and Pepsi Bottling, Inc.; hospitals and other healthcare providers including MedStar Health and Genesis HealthCare Corporation; service industry corporations including McDonald's Corporation and Sylvan Learning Center.; business and financial services such as GEICO, Legg Mason and the Federal Reserve Bank of Richmond; and retailers including May Department Stores, Inc. and Rite Aid Corporation. Shawe Rosenthal also represents numerous mid-size and smaller employerss in each of these sectors.

**International Clients:** Bermuda Hotel Association. For more than 20 years, Stephen Shawe served as chief spokesman for the Association in its collective bargaining negotiations with the union representing the Island's 3000 hotel employees. When Bermuda passed legislation requiring interest arbitration to resolve unresolved collective bargaining negotiations, Stephen presented the hotel employers' position at interest arbitration hearings in Hamilton, Bermuda.

# WHITEFORD, TAYLOR & PRESTON, L.L.P.

## THE FIRM

**Managing Partner:** Albert Mezzanotte, Jr
**Number of partners:** 94
**Number of other lawyers:** 62

**FIRM OVERVIEW:** Closing a transaction, resolving a dispute, litigating or settling a claim, planning a company's future – since 1933, clients have come to Whiteford, Taylor & Preston for representation and guidance on a wide range of issues critical to achieving their business goals.

WTP is one of Maryland's largest law firms. With three offices in Maryland, as well as Washington, DC, and northern Virginia, the firm serves clients throughout the mid-Atlantic region, as well as national companies and law firms needing representation in Maryland, DC or Virginia.

Community oriented and culturally diverse, the firm's attorneys practice in every area of the law that is important to its clients. In business matters ranging from acquisitions to real estate, and litigation ranging from antitrust to bankruptcy to zoning, Whiteford, Taylor & Preston assert their clients' rights and advance their interests through vigorous and creative legal action.

## MAIN AREAS OF PRACTICE:

**Business & Corporate:** The firm's services range from starting a business – such as choosing and forming the appropriate form of entity – to those needed at the end of its life, such as succession planning, sale of business, or liquidation. The firm also handles everything in between, including financing, securities offerings, stockholder and employment agreements, stock incentive programs and tax planning.

**Bankruptcy & Creditors' Rights:** The Bankruptcy Group is among the largest and most accomplished in the region, with many cases that are national in stature. The firm represents debtors and debtors in possession, creditors and creditors' committees, lenders and trustees in all types of debt restructuring and bankruptcy reorganization proceedings, including out-of-court workouts. The firm has worked in industries as diverse as real estate development, retail and wholesale, transportation, healthcare, manufacturing, telecommunications, agribusiness and a host of other industries. The members of the group include a former Justice Department litigator, Chapter 7 and 11 trustees, career Chapter 11 specialists and a former in-house counsel of a financial institution.

**Healthcare:** The Healthcare Group provides counsel on all aspects of health law ranging from fraud and abuse and corporate practice of medicine to government regulation and privacy. The group counsels clients on HIPAA compliance as well as federal and state laws regulating managed care, Medicare and Medicaid. The group also counsels clients on matters related to compliance with anti-kickback statutes, self-referral legislation (the 'Stark Law') and defending against False Claims Act actions.

**Litigation:** The firm's Litigation Department practices before a wide range of tribunals, including all state and federal trial and appellate courts in the region as well as a wide variety of administrative agencies, and alternative dispute resolution forums. One of the strengths of the firm is the substantial 'in-court' trial experience of its attorneys. The firm's extensive trial experience greatly enhances its ability to evaluate a case, develop it in a manner that will appeal to a judge and/or jury, and, if appropriate, ultimately go to trial with the confidence and skill that only comes with actual trial experience.

**Labor & Employment:** The firm helps its clients create a practical platform on which to base labor and employee relations decisions. The team includes attorneys formerly with the Department of Labor and the National Labor Relations Board, along with those whose careers have been devoted to representing and counseling management in labor relations issues. Clients represent virtually every area of business and industry, and range in size from Fortune 500 companies with thousands of employees in various locations to small, closely held businesses.

**Real Estate & Land Use:** The firm's lawyers have extensive experience in virtually all types and variations of complex commercial real estate matters, including commercial and residential development, commercial leasing, complex easement

agreements, sales agreements, condominium development, construction contracts, environmental, real estate finance, and zoning and land use.

**Technology & Intellectual Property:** The firm's Technology and Intellectual Property Group handles a full range of technology and intellectual property matters for its clients, including domestic and foreign patents, trademark and copyright applications and related opinion matters, domestic and international technology and content licenses, research and development agreements, technology transfer agreements, strategic alliances, joint ventures and other innovative 'partnering' agreements; and a wide range of software, computer and internet law matters, including web site audits, e-commerce issues, domain names, database protection matters, ASPs, open source and other innovative distribution models.

**CLIENTS:** Clients range from *Fortune* 500 companies to small businesses and start-up enterprises. They are engaged in technology and e-commerce, banking, finance, healthcare, insurance, transportation, communications, real estate, securities and manufacturing.

**INTERNATIONAL WORK:** The firm's Technology and Intellectual Property Group is experienced in international transactions, both in-bound and out-bound. It protects the intellectual property rights of US companies abroad and represents foreign companies expanding into the US market.

## HEAD OFFICE

### MARYLAND
7 St. Paul Street, **Baltimore**, MD 21202-1626
**Tel:** 410 347 8700   **Fax:** 410 752 7092
**Website:** www.wtplaw.com

## BRANCH OFFICES

### DISTRICT OF COLUMBIA
1025 Connecticut Avenue, NW **Washington**, DC 20036-5405
**Tel:** 202 659 6800   **Fax:** 202 331 0573

### MARYLAND
210 West Pennsylania Avenue, **Towson**, MD 21204-4515
**Tel:** 410 832 2000   **Fax:** 410 832 2015

10420 Little Patuxent Parkway, **Columbia**, MD 21044-3528
**Tel:** 410 381 6000   **Fax:** 410 381 6430

### VIRGINIA
115 Oronoco Street, **Alexandria**, VA 22313-1685
**Tel:** 703 836 5742   **Fax:** 703 836 3558

## CONTACTS

| | |
|---|---|
| **Business & Corporate** | Eva H Hill (Baltimore) |
| | William M Davidow, Jr (Baltimore) |
| **Bankruptcy & Creditors' Rights** | Paul M Nussbaum (Baltimore) |
| **Healthcare** | Rose M Matricciani (Baltimore) |
| **Litigation** | Ward B Coe III (Baltimore) |
| **Labor & Employment** | Kevin C McCormick (Baltimore) |
| **Real Estate** | Joseph N Schaller (Baltimore) |
| **Land Use** | G Scott Barhight (Towson) |
| **Technology & Intellectual Property** | Frank S Jones, Jr (Baltimore) |

## How lawyers are ranked

Every year we carry out thousands of in-depth interviews with clients and lawyers in order to assess the reputations and expertise of business lawyers across the USA. Chambers rankings and editorial are referred to extensively by General Counsel and other purchasers of legal services who look to our recommendations when choosing their lawyers.

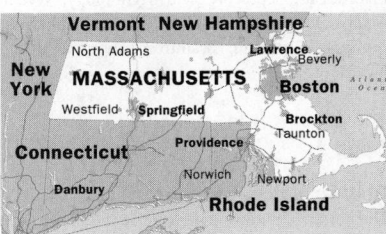

# ANTITRUST

### Antitrust
### Leading Firms

1. **BINGHAM MCCUTCHEN LLP** *Boston*
   **NUTTER, MCCLENNEN & FISH, LLP** *Boston*
   **WILMERHALE** *Boston*
2. **CHOATE HALL & STEWART** *Boston*
   **EDWARDS ANGELL PALMER & DODGE** *Boston*
   **FOLEY HOAG LLP** *Boston*
   **ROPES & GRAY LLP** *Boston*

### Leading Individuals

#### Senior Statesman
**CURTIN JR** John *Bingham McCutchen LLP*

1. **BURLING** James *WilmerHale*
   **GOLDBERG** Daniel *Bingham McCutchen LLP*
   **MILLER** Michelle *WilmerHale*
   **MOTENKO** Neil *Nutter, McClennen & Fish*
   **SCOTT** Thane *Edwards Angell Palmer*
2. **ARMISTEAD** Cary *Ropes & Gray LLP*
   **BUCHANAN JR** Robert *Choate Hall & Stewart*
   **PATTON** William *Ropes & Gray LLP*
   **SAVRIN** Daniel *Bingham McCutchen LLP*
   **WOOD** Lisa *Foley Hoag LLP*
3. **CONDE** Kathryn *Nutter, McClennen & Fish*
   **MARTLAND** David *Nixon Peabody LLP*

#### Up-and-coming individuals
**DOWNEY** Alicia *Bingham McCutchen LLP*
**WILLIS** Jane *Ropes & Gray LLP*

## Band 1

### Bingham McCutchen LLP
See firm details p.1110

**The Firm:** This "*hugely efficient*" firm maintains its reputation as "*a genuine national player*" in the US antitrust league. Attorneys of "*an extremely high quality*" are popular with clients because "*they gets the results we want,*" claimed enthusiastic sources. Though primarily renowned for its expertise in antitrust litigation, the group offers a range of services including advice on complex M&A transactions. The firm is also well regarded for its expertise on matters relating to criminal investigations including bid rigging and international cartel activity.

**The Lawyers:** Senior statesman **John Curtin** (see p.1091) continues to be well respected by peers and clients alike. His contribution to the Boston antitrust market is widely acknowledged across the region. The "*sharp and extremely knowledgeable*" **Daniel Goldberg** (see p.1093) is a long-term member of the Boston Bar and is hailed as "*a superb lawyer*" by clients. He is recommended for his litigation prowess and is a well-known personality in the sports sector. Interviewees rate **Daniel Savrin** (see p.1105) for his experience in handling class action work. Sources praise him for his ability to "*focus on the target in order to develop effective strategies.*" Rising star **Alicia Downey** (see p.1091) demonstrates "*real potential*" as an antitrust specialist. Her ability to handle franchising matters impresses commentators.

**Clients/Work Highlights:** The team continues to act for BMW North America in a state-level multi-district class action relating to the alleged inhibition of exports from Canada to the USA. It is currently representing Marsh in the defense of matters arising in relation to contingent commission payments and alleged bid rigging in the brokerage of insurance. Additional clients include GM; eBay; Stop & Shop; Toyota; Mitsui; Nissan North America; Freightliner; FLEXcon; Toyo Tanso and Detroit Diesel.

### Nutter, McClennen & Fish, LLP

**The Firm:** This firm enjoys a long history of antitrust prowess in the region and has successfully maintained its reputation as the state's go-to firm for healthcare-related matters. Sources recommend a "*compact but significant*" team that boasts well-respected attorneys and high-quality work. Lawyers are experienced in counseling hi-tech and emerging companies and have recently undertaken a significant amount of joint venture work. In 2005 the team also applied its governmental experience when undertaking work for a trade association, which involved approaching an antitrust enforcement agency.

**The Lawyers:** According to market observers, the 2004 departure of Lisa Wood has not disadvantaged the team, which continues to house significant bench strength. The "*exceptionally bright*" **Neil Motenko** is the team's "*key individual*" with a "*great courtroom presence for oral argument,*" according to interviewees. A popular referral among peers, sources enthuse: "*He is a very fine lawyer whose ability and reputation have made the firm what it is today.*" Onlookers assert that **Kathryn Conde** has benefited from Motenko's mentoring over the years and is now "*developing extremely well in her own right.*" A "*bright and diligent lawyer,*" she is valued for her background in economics, which enables her to "*speak the same language*" as her clients.

**Clients/Work Highlights:** Clients include ambulance companies, physicians, various healthcare organizations, hospitals, Fortune 500 companies, and a range of manufacturers, retailers and distributors.

### WilmerHale
See firm details p.1119

**The Firm:** This well-established firm offers clients a range of high-quality legal services and is renowned for its focus on life sciences and IT. The Boston antitrust practice is divided primarily between litigation, merger clearance and additional government-initiated matters. The "*extremely talented*" team contains highly knowledgeable lawyers with a "*great sense of judgment,*" say commentators. Sources told researchers of "*softly spoken*" litigation specialists who are "*well prepared and respectful to judges,*" but who have "*backbones of steel*" Several US offices, in addition to overseas resources in London, Brussels, Berlin and Beijing, support the Massachusetts practice.

**The Lawyers:** Interviewees admire capable and thorough **James Burling** (see p.1089) for his strategic ability and "*sheer experience*" in the antitrust field. He wins plaudits for his "*command of the courtroom*" and for his "*wise use of resources – he will really listen to the client in order to deal with issues effectively,*" says one onlooker. "*Smart, responsive and likable,*" **Michelle Miller** (see p.1100) is "*extremely capable at a variety of work,*" according to sources. She has a strong talent for co-coordinating large groups in class action disputes and also wins praise for her client counseling skills.

**Clients/Work Highlights:** Highlights in 2005 included defending Ocean Spray Cranberries in three related monopolization cases, including a California class action. The team represented Akamai Technologies in connection with the acquisition of its competitor, Speedera. It also acted for Lionbridge Technologies in obtaining clearance from the FTC for its $180 million acquisition of Bowne Global Solutions. Additional clients include Penwest Pharmaceuticals; Sepracor; Avid Technology; Wyeth; Analog Devices; Biogen Idec; CollaGenex Pharmaceuticals; Cephalon; Braintree Laboratories and EMC.

## Band 2

### Choate Hall & Stewart

**The Firm:** The business group at this impressive outfit expanded with the arrival of lawyers from imploded firm Testa Hurwitz & Thibeault in 2005. Notwithstanding the bolstering of the antitrust team, clients continue to highlight "*driving force*" Robert Buchanan as the group's key player. Particularly adept at handling antitrust litigation, the team's courtroom experience and general counseling ability are highlighted by sources. The group regularly offers clients mergers and transactional advice and continues to enjoy success in healthcare-related matters.

**The Lawyers:** The "*smart and capable*" **Robert Buchanan** continues to shine as a leading light of the firm's antitrust practice. Interviewees also note his experience in commercial litigation, where class action disputes are among his specialty areas.

**Clients/Work Highlights:** The team successfully defended Hewlett-Packard in a suit brought by Boston Scientific for attempted monopolization and breach of contract. Lawyers also acted for Cape Cod Healthcare against allegations by EasCare that the health service provider conspired with one ambulance company to exclude another. Additional clients include Agfa-Gevaert; PwC; Blue Cross Blue Shield of Massachusetts; Boston Ventures; Cambridge Health Alliance; Dana-Farber Cancer Institute; Massachusetts Medical Society and UCB Chemicals.

### Edwards Angell Palmer & Dodge LLP
See firm details p.1112

**The Firm:** According to onlookers, this firm is "*well regarded for its academic ability*" and maintains a fine reputation for its work in the antitrust field. The Palmer & Dodge arm enjoys a fine reputation for its tradition of work in multiparty private litigation and government enforcement work. Its recent merger with Edwards & Angell has increased both the size of its antitrust team and the breadth of its business-counseling scope. Previously noted for its advisory work with higher education institutions, the firm's evolving client base now includes those in the media and telecom sectors.

**The Lawyers:** Commentators laud **Thane Scott** (see p.1105) as an "*intelligent and humorous*" character who is capable of demonstrating "*profound judgment and intelligence*" as a lawyer. "*He has the rare ability to successfully capture a situation in a succinct sentence,*" explains one source.

**Clients/Work Highlights:** Fidelity; Genzyme; Risk Management Foundation; Parametric Technology and the Consortium on Financing Higher Education are among the firm's antitrust client base.

### Foley Hoag LLP

**The Firm:** The arrival of Lisa Wood from Nutter McClennen & Fish has placed this well-established outfit firmly on the Massachusetts antitrust radar. In addition to litigation and merger expertise, the team is capable of advising clients on a broad range of antitrust matters, as well as trade and consumer protection issues. The group also has the capability to conduct internal investigations when illegal activity is suspected in the defense, mutual fund and healthcare sectors. Clients are based in a broad swathe of sectors, including the manufacturing, chemical and hi-tech industries, as well as insurance and financial services.

**The Lawyers:** Interviewees recommend **Lisa Wood** for her knowledgeable work in the antitrust field. She also boasts experience in securities, accounting and malpractice defense work.

**Clients/Work Highlights:** The team represented a mutual fund trader in a putative class action claiming antitrust and commodities fraud violations in 2005. It also defended a national specialty retailer in enforcement action initiated by the Massachusetts Attorney General regarding the retailer's discounting claims and compliance with consumer protection laws. Additional clients include trade associations, telecom companies and physician groups.

### Ropes & Gray LLP
See firm details p.1117

**The Firm:** According to sources, "*by history and reputation, this firm is great,*" and the Boston antitrust team is no exception. The group works closely with its Washington, DC office to provide an interdisciplinary approach to client needs. The antitrust team interacts with the firm's highly regarded corporate, litigation and IP teams to provide advice on a broad spectrum of matters, including global merger reviews and competition counseling. In addition to public and private antitrust litigation, the team is also renowned for its government enforcement and trade association work.

**The Lawyers:** **Cary Armistead** (see p.1086) is co-head of the international practice group and vice chairman of the corporate department. Sources rate him for his "*valuable industry experience*" and "*vast strength*" when dealing with merger-related matters. **William Patton** (see p.1102) is particularly experienced in patent infringement matters and associated antitrust counterclaims. Commentators identify him as an "*outstanding litigator.*" **Jane Willis** (see p.1109) continues to attract attention for her developing antitrust litigation practice and effective client-counseling skills.

**Clients/Work Highlights:** The firm acts for a diverse range of clients, including those in the pharmaceutical, healthcare, private equity and sports industries.

## Other Notable Practitioners

Praised for his "*low-key manner and sense of humor,*" **David Martland** (see p.1099) of Nixon Peabody LLP is favored by clients and peers alike. His "*flexible and collaborative*" approach enables him to "*get to the point quickly*" and "*truly understand the bigger antitrust picture,*" market sources told researchers.

# BANKING & FINANCE

## Band 1

### Bingham McCutchen LLP
See firm details p.1110

**The Firm:** Revered as "*one of the traditional US banking powerhouses,*" this tremendous firm enjoys an outstanding national reputation in the finance arena. Its "*absolutely first-rate*" domestic and international debt financing practice "*clearly has the resources*" to handle sizable deals and complex syndicated loans, according to sources. Clients attribute its success to a team of "*high-quality, creative thinkers*" with an "*incredible depth of knowledge.*" The group wins plaudits for its ability to handle sophisticated financing and traditional lending transactions in equal measure. It also continues to be noted for its expertise in corporate and regulatory work, where it has displayed "*a long history of M&A know-how.*" The team offers expertise in acquisition and recapitalization financings, asset-based lending and secured mezzanine loans, alongside securitizations and other structured finance products. The firm's lawyers have also contributed to the national development of finance and secured transactions law, including the UCC.

**The Lawyers:** Peers describe **Neal Curtin** (see p.1091) as "*top of the list for referrals*" and "*a true mentor*" in the field. Clients value his rounded approach to corporate and regulatory work, particularly noting his experience in bank litigation. The "*practical and intellectual*" **Edwin Smith** (see p.1106) is "*one of the world's premier experts*" on the UCC, according to sources. His "*rare*" all-around lending capability and expertise in the field of bankruptcy litigation combines to make him "*great on both the front and back of a transaction.*" Commentators recommend the excellent finance lawyer **Amy Kyle** (see p.1097) for her deal experience and "*sheer breadth of knowledge.*" Alongside her ability to lead transactions successfully, she is also commended for generating "*genuine client loyalty.*"

**Clients/Work Highlights:** The firm's clients include banks, credit providers, investment banks, financial institutions and investment companies within a range of industry sectors. Its portfolio includes Bank of America; GE Capital; FleetBoston Financial; Deutsche Bank; UBS Financial and Wells Fargo. Retail financing work in 2005 included acting for lead arrangers Banc of America Securities on a $750 million deal for Staples. It represented Bank of America NA as administrative agent on a $225 million loan for Moran Transportation Company.

The team also advised JPMorgan Chase on a syndicated warehouse loan to a real estate investment trust.

## Edwards Angell Palmer & Dodge LLP
See firm details p.1112

**The Firm:** The market observes the recent merger between these established regional players with interest. Prior to the alliance, both firms were well regarded for their private equity capabilities and for advising clients across the state on a range of finance-related matters. Edwards & Angell had traditionally been recognized for its long history within corporate and regulatory banking, boasting established relationships with regulatory agencies in the region and expertise in handling transactions within the Massachusetts healthcare industry. By contrast, Palmer & Dodge had been noted for its lending expertise, particularly in specialized technology areas such as media and communications sector financings. Commentators herald the newly branded firm's debt finance capabilities spread across multiple US offices, offering interdisciplinary teams that can advise clients on banking matters of a multijurisdictional nature. Clients praise a solid bench of responsive attorneys for producing "*high-quality, tailored*" finance work across New England. Additional areas of combined finance expertise include bond work and securitizations.

**The Lawyers:** "*Extraordinary lending lawyer*" **George Ticknor** (see p.1107) has developed "*an excellent practice*" and wins plaudits for his "*keen business sense and judgment.*" Interviewees say "*he knows how to get a transaction done,*" while also commending his drafting ability. Previously with Palmer & Dodge, Ticknor cochairs the firm's newly formed debt finance and capital markets group with **Susan Siebert** (see p.1106) from Edwards & Angell. Siebert owes her reputation as a wonderful corporate banking lawyer to her ability to "*solve problems effectively,*" say sources. She also garners praise for "*fiercely protecting*" clients' interests by articulating their positions assertively without "*dominating negotiations by virtue of being a bully!*" **Bruce Raphael** (see p.1103) continues to win market approval for his regulatory expertise. He is also recommended for M&A-related banking matters. An expert in bond financing, **Jonathan Harris** (see p.1094) is identified by sources as "*the person that we turn to in the event of a big healthcare deal.*" Clients praise him for his "*focus on closing a deal*" and for "*understanding all of the business intricacies that matter to us as clients.*"

**Clients/Work Highlights:** Major clients include Bank of America; HSBC; John Hancock Life Insurance; JPMorgan Partners; Wells Fargo; Bear Stearns; UBS Financial Services; Brown Brothers Harriman; NewStar Financial; Sankaty Advisors and Massachusetts Financial Services. Lawyers closed a $400 million syndicated financing for JPMorgan and acted for Bank of America in its recent acquisition of an insurance broker in 2005. The team also represented an agent bank in arranging a $300 million multicurrency cross-border syndicated financing to a public company.

## Goodwin Procter LLP
See firm details p.1114

**The Firm:** According to onlookers, this is an excellent firm with "*real strength and depth*" in the corporate banking sphere. An increasingly national player, the Boston, New York and Washington, DC offices work closely together on complex regulatory, product and deal matters across the USA. Despite having "*taken its show on the road around the country,*" the firm continues to offer advice to a loyal client base in Massachusetts. Clients value the banking team's ability to find "*creative solutions*" to acquisition finance and securitization matters and speak of "*quality legal work allied with great business judgment.*" Lawyers' advisory work in relation to domestic bank and thrift deals is also particularly admired. The financial services group consists of distinguished specialists who are "*true leaders in their fields*" and who "*complement one another effectively.*" Clients told researchers: "*The team-spirited working environment singles this firm out.*" In addition to its banking expertise, onlookers also highlight the seamless integration between the firm's investment management, consumer finance, and compliance management divisions.

**The Lawyers:** The "*strong, experienced*" **Lynne Barr** (see p.1086) is recommended for her solid background in all areas of consumer banking. She "*knows her lending relations stuff extremely well,*" clients enthuse. Lauded for his "*enormous breadth of knowledge and experience*" of US banking regulations, **Gregory Lyons** (see p.1098) enjoys a reputation as "*one of the country's preeminent lawyers*" in the field and is admired for his contribution to raising the firm's national profile. Financial institutions continue to recommend **William Mayer** (see p.1099) for his familiarity with all aspects of M&A transactions. A noted figure in the corporate sphere, he is perceived as one of the state's acquisition finance experts. Notwithstanding her position as managing partner of the firm, "*strategic thinker*" **Regina Pisa** (see p.1102) continues to impress clients with her hands-on involvement in corporate and regulatory banking work. "*A great person to have at the negotiation table,*" she is said to be "*extremely smart,*" with "*practical judgment*" and "*astounding knowledge*" of the financial services industry. The market continues to endorse the work of the "*highly professional*" **William Stern** (see p.1107), who is valued for "*his ability to internalize the facts surrounding a transaction.*"

**Clients/Work Highlights:** The firm's financial services portfolio includes banks, thrifts, funds, investors and financial holding companies. Key clients include State Street Bank & Trust; Citizens Financial Group; Bank of America; Boston Private Financial Holdings; Massachusetts Bankers Association and American Express. The team advised Boston Private Financial Holdings in the $246 million acquisition of Gibraltar Financial in 2005. Lawyers also acted for Chart Bank regarding its $46.5 million acquisition by Benjamin Franklin Bancorp, and for Washington Trust Bancorp in its $20 million acquisition of Weston Financial Group.

## Band 2

### Foley Hoag LLP

**The Firm:** This impressive outfit continues to win market approval within Massachusetts for its regulatory banking expertise. In a climate where its competitors are increasingly looking outside of the region to develop a national footprint, commentators praise the firm for its focus on New England clients. In particular, the banking and finance team maintains a niche in community bank representation. It advised Eastern Bank on its merger with Plymouth Savings Bank in 2005.

**The Lawyers:** Sources continue to recognize the "*exceptionally bright*" **Peter Coogan** as the banking and finance team's highest-profile individual. The "*great deal-manager*" **Carol Hempfling Pratt** strikes "*a nice balance between her knowledge of securities law and bank regulations,*" say commentators. She was primary securities counsel on Benjamin Franklin Bancorp's mutual-to-stock conversion and simultaneous acquisition of Chart Bank.

**Clients/Work Highlights:** The firm acts for a range of community banks, as well as thrift and holding companies. It is currently handling regulatory aspects of the mutual holding company reorganization of Salem Five Cents Savings Bank and the simultaneous merger of Salem Five with Heritage Co-operative Bank.

### Goulston & Storrs

**The Firm:** Regional middle-market clients continue to recognize this "*consistently strong*" player for its work on asset-based lending and acquisition finance deals. The firm belies its relatively compact size by providing a streamlined, "*nimble*" service, according to sources. The "*smart, resourceful*" banking team is particularly renowned for its transactional know-how, but maintains the breadth and ability necessary to meet wide-ranging client needs. Indeed, the "*level of attention and engagement of partners differentiates this firm from its competitors,*" clients tell researchers. Notable experience in the private equity arena enables lawyers to handle multilayered debt and equity financings. The group works closely with its real estate counterpart, allowing interdisciplinary teams to offer seamless advice to clients in the retail and hospitality sectors.

**The Lawyers:** The "*smart and resourceful*" **Philip Herman** garners respect for his experience in debt finance. "*Easygoing but by no means a pushover,*" clients appreciate the sense of humor he brings to his work.

**Clients/Work Highlights:** Clients include commercial banks, thrifts, credit unions, investment funds and trust companies, as well as officers and directors. Examples include Citizens; Bank of America; GMAC and KeyBank.

### Nutter, McClennen & Fish, LLP

**The Firm:** This "*ultra-responsive*" team continues to gain recognition for the "*strength in depth*" of its well-regarded finance division. In addition to regular lending work, the firm excels at corporate and regulatory banking advice. Sources especially recommend lawyers for their experience of working with community and mutual banks. Clients from such institutions comment on the team's "*genuine understanding of the business problems we face.*" Significant securities law expertise within the team has also enabled the firm to develop an impressive portfolio of publicly held banking clients.

**The Lawyers:** "*Rainmaker*" **Kenneth Ehrlich** is said to be "*driving the growth*" of the firm's finance department and is a popular referral amongst peers. Lauded as "*bright, thorough and client-driven,*" he is "*extremely strong on the regulatory side,*" sources enthuse. Clients recommend **Michael Krebs** for being "*a calming influence*" in negotiations. He is respected for his regulatory work, along with his notable securities and transactional expertise. As part of a team, Krebs and Ehrlich's "*differing areas of expertise serve to complement one another very well,*" according to sources.

**Clients/Work Highlights:** Notable clients include Massachusetts Bankers Association; TD Banknorth; Bank of New York; Mellon Financial; Service Bancorp; Commerce Bank & Trust; Westborough Bank and Fall River Five Cents Savings Bank.

### Ropes & Gray LLP

See firm details p.1117

**The Firm:** This high-quality, full-service firm wins plaudits for its finance capabilities, garnering praise for both its bank lending and broad transactional experience. The group represents lender, borrower and fund clients on a range of matters from large capitalizations to middle-market debt. It offers expertise on structured and asset-based loans, as well as securitization-related matters. The group works closely with the firm's outstanding private equity team and also benefits from its well-respected investment management capabilities. Lawyers are highly visible in national leveraged acquisition financings and accordingly represented CIT Group as lead senior lender in a financing enabling a financial sponsor to acquire clothing retailer Loehmann's.

**The Lawyers:** Head of the debt finance practice, **Thomas Draper** (see p.1092) is "*a supremely capable transactional attorney,*" particularly on behalf of private equity firms, according to interviewees. Senior lawyer **Philip Smith** (see p.1107) is also recommended for his experience in the acquisition finance field.

**Clients/Work Highlights:** The firm's clients include commercial banks, specialized finance institutions and borrowers. It also advises financial sponsors and represented private equity fund Monitor Clipper Partners regarding the Medical Services Company acquisition financing in 2005. Additional clients include Berkshire Partners; Boston Ventures; BainCapital; Nortek; Loews; Riddell Bell and Fenway Partners; Santaky Funds and Windjammer Capital and Brown Brothers Harriman & Co.

## Band 3

### Choate Hall & Stewart

**The Firm:** According to sources, this "*fabulous*" firm boasts top-level personnel and a well-established client base. Appreciated for being "*a nice bunch of people to work with,*" the specialty finance group also wins plaudits for its technical ability. The group offers expertise in securitization lending, communications financing, sports and retail lending to a variety of banks, funds and institutional investors. In 2005 it represented a syndicate of banks including Fleet National Bank, Sumitomo Mitsui Banking and Israel Discount Bank of New York in connection with a $100 million credit facility established for Phillies Ballpark. It also assisted Wells Fargo Retail Finance in the $76 million financing of a national furniture retailer.

**The Lawyers:** **James McDaniel** is terribly well regarded within the state for his regulatory finance and securities-related experience, sources report. He is renowned for his work with banks and bank holding companies.

**Clients/Work Highlights:** Key clients include Citizens Bank; Wells Fargo; MassMutual; State Street Bank & Trust; Foothill Capital; Bank of America; John Hancock Life Insurance and Massachusetts Mutual Life Insurance.

### Gallagher, Callahan and Gartrell, PC

**The Firm:** This "*helpful and responsive*" firm is still establishing itself in Massachusetts, but already offers a regional alternative to many of the state's more nationally driven players. A "*first-rate*" office in New Hampshire and additional resources in Maine support the growing prowess of the firm's banking group. While traditionally very strong in the community banking market, the group is also recommended for its experience in working with New England's financial institutions in connection with energy, affordable housing and new markets tax credit investments. Clients also praise lawyers for their advisory work, particularly in the field of regulatory compliance and enforcement.

**The Lawyers:** The "*pragmatic*" **Kevin Handly** (see p.1094) has "*an excellent appreciation of banking law,*" clients state. His "*knowledgeable and skilled*" approach is backed-up with strong relationships with government and regulatory officials. "*Laid-back and affable, but extremely efficient,*" **Stephen Coukos** (see p.1090) wins plaudits for his ability to focus on a deal. Sources commend him for "*cutting to the chase without dumbing things down*" when explaining matters in the boardroom. The two men bring considerable strength from their experience at other firms in the region, according to interviewees.

**Clients/Work Highlights:** The firm's Boston office represents a wide range of both publicly traded and privately held New England-based community banks. These include mutual holding companies such as Enterprise Bancorp; LSB Corporation; BankNewport; MountainOne Financial Partners and the Rockland Trust Company. It also advises larger national and international financial institutions, such as State Street Bank & Trust and Anglo Irish Bank. In 2005 work highlights included advising Community Bank on its acquisition of a Massachusetts insurance agency and completing the mutual holding company reorganization of BankNewport.

## Riemer & Braunstein LLP

**The Firm:** This respected outfit houses a well-established banking and finance team, which enjoys a solid reputation across the region and beyond. Lacking the market profile of larger firms in Massachusetts, it is said to be *"somewhat underrated"* compared to some of its regional counterparts.

While the firm's reach extends across several industry sectors, sources put it forward as a leader in the field of retail finance. Noted for its asset-based work, the group is especially strong in Boston's middle-market, where it is a popular choice as lender counsel. An office in New York enables the firm to handle debt transactions of a more complex nature. Additional areas of expertise include real estate lending and workouts.

**The Lawyers:** Alongside continued respect for his middle-market loan abilities, **David Berman** also wins client endorsement for his asset-based financial expertise. He acted as lead counsel for the bank behind the financing of the Boston Red Sox.

## Other Notable Practitioners

Sources continue to commend Kirkpatrick & Lockhart Nicholson Graham LLP's **Stanley Ragalevsky** for his work with community banks in the region. Interviewees praise his practice for its *"sheer number of quality clients."* **Chris McCarty** (see p.1099) at Holland & Knight LLP's Boston office, having been in Providence, has recently become a partner at the firm. He represents regional and national lenders in banking transactions, as well as secured creditors in receiverships and bankruptcies, and was said to *"grasp the problems very quickly."*

# BANKRUPTCY/RESTRUCTURING

## Bankruptcy/Restructuring
### Leading Firms

**1** GOODWIN PROCTER LLP *Boston*
   HANIFY & KING *Boston*
   MINTZ LEVIN *Boston*
   WILMERHALE *Boston*

**2** CHOATE HALL & STEWART *Boston*
   COHN WHITESELL & GOLDBERG LLP *Boston*
   GOULSTON & STORRS *Boston*
   ROPES & GRAY LLP *Boston*

**3** BROWN RUDNICK BERLACK ISRAELS *Boston*
   DUANE MORRIS LLP *Boston*
   FOLEY HOAG LLP *Boston*
   GADSBY HANNAH LLP *Boston*
   NIXON PEABODY LLP *Boston*

## Band 1

### Goodwin Procter LLP

See firm details p.1114

**The Firm:** This *"top-quality"* firm has a *"professional, responsive"* house style and an excellent insolvency and business reorganization team, according to its clients. Fielding a group of *"smart but human"* individuals with strong business acumen, the group provides strategic advice that is *"truly rendered in the context of what clients do, not just in the jurisdiction of law."* The firm regularly handles complex matters for high-profile clients, including Fortune 100 businesses and top-tier banks, across the region and beyond. Its expertise ranges from workouts of specific debt default to general reorganizations and liquidations of substantial businesses. It was particularly recommended for handling debtor work, defending bankruptcy avoidance actions and managing international insolvency cases. It also advises on distressed company lending, investment and acquisitions. *"Incredibly high standards"* of recruitment are felt to have achieved an ideal mixture of *"sophisticated"* partners and promising talent at junior level.

**The Lawyers:** **Daniel Glosband** (see p.1093) is noted for the national scope of his work. He handles a wide variety of bankruptcy matters and currently sits *"at the top of his game,"* say commentators. *"Thoughtful and analytical"* in his approach, he is an *"acute technician"* who fosters an *"academic sense of law that translates well to daily practice."* He is especially valued for his ability to *"navigate the uninitiated through bankruptcy proceedings in complex situations."* **Michael Pappone** (see p.1101) is a *"provider of excellent service and strategy"* who is well known for his work with creditor groups. A *"masterful negotiator,"* he wins plaudits for his ability to *"quickly grasp all kinds of issues – neither size nor complexity of instrument confounds him."* *"Smart, practical and efficient"* **Jon Schneider** (see p.1105) was praised for his *"careful listening and skillful analysis."* A *"brilliant presence in any meeting,"* he is also a *"tough advocate"* on behalf of secured creditors.

**Clients/Work Highlights:** The group acts for a diverse client base, including debtors, secured and unsecured creditors, lenders, private equity and other investors, the buyers of troubled businesses and assets, real estate owners and operators, and officers and directors. It recently represented Landmark Growth Capital Partners, which negotiated and financed the purchase of a call center through a Section 363 sale, as part of Abacus Communications' Chapter 11 proceedings in the Eastern District of Virginia.

### Hanify & King

See firm details p.1115

**The Firm:** Hanify & King is a *"different breed"* to its top-tier competitors, say interviewees. This *"premier"* boutique is renowned as *"one of the best bankruptcy outfits in Boston,"* and is highly visible despite – or perhaps because of – its *"relatively small size and narrow focus"* when compared to many of the general service firms. The focused firm handles a range of insolvency matters, enjoying especially great success in landing the debtor work for which it is renowned. Indeed, it is felt to have been *"on a roll"* in

the past year, and was singled out as one of the *"busiest and most esteemed"* practices in the state during 2005. Admired for its work on high-profile cases across the region, the group is characterized by its *"practical approach to getting things done."* Clients especially value the lawyers for their skill in remaining *"several moves ahead of the opposition,"* and for *"knowing the drill and getting to heart of the issues."*

**The Lawyers:** **Harold Murphy** (see p.1100) is heralded as *"a master – one of the best and busiest bankruptcy lawyers in the city."* He commands a huge level of respect for his track record of successes, which are attributed to his *"huge intellect and creative style."* A *"tenacious negotiator,"* he has the ability to *"push through all the posturing"* and is *"highly effective in the courtroom."* **Charles Bennett** (see p.1087) is *"about as tough as they come,"* according to commentators. An esteemed bankruptcy litigation specialist, he is said to be *"very smart with a good use of imagination"* and a high level of technical accuracy. Clients also value his *"marvelous ability to motivate the other side – he is never blinded by the chase but always understands the goal."* **Ethan Jeffery** (see p.1095) is *"showing himself to be capable and well versed in a wide range of bankruptcy-related matters."* He is tipped as the firm's rising star, and was recommended for his *"good all-around skill set"* and effective client handling. *"Smart and industrious"* **Andrew Lizotte** (see p.1098) is also popular among clients, who recognize him as an up-and-coming individual in the bankruptcy field.

**Clients/Work Highlights:** The team acted for debtors owning two of Boston's main office towers, One and Two International Place, in their Chapter 11 reorganizations in the US Bankruptcy Court for the District of Massachusetts. It represented the creditors' committee as special counsel in the Chapter 11 of Plassein International and six of its eight subsidiaries, and also advised the creditors' committee in the shut-down and subsequent liquidation of Boston Regional Medical Center. The group is also advising law firm Testa Hurwitz & Thibeault following its dissolution in 2005. Having successfully

## Bankruptcy/Restructuring
### Leading Individuals

### Senior Statesman

MCCARTHY William *Ropes & Gray LLP*

[1] COHN Daniel *Cohn Whitesell & Goldberg*
GLERUM Charles *Choate Hall & Stewart*
GLOSBAND Daniel *Goodwin Procter LLP*
MIKELS Richard *Mintz Levin*
MURPHY Harold *Hanify & King*
PAPPONE Michael *Goodwin Procter LLP*
SCHWARTZ Andrew *Foley Hoag LLP*

[2] BENNETT JR Charles *Hanify & King*
BERMAN Mark *Nixon Peabody LLP*
BLECK Daniel *Mintz Levin*
DALE III Charles *Gadsby Hannah LLP*
DALEY Paul *WilmerHale*
GOODING Douglas *Choate Hall & Stewart*
MONAGHAN John *Holland & Knight LLP*
MOORE Paul *Duane Morris LLP*
ROSNER Douglas *Goulston & Storrs*
SCHNEIDER Jon *Goodwin Procter LLP*
WALLACK James *Goulston & Storrs*

[3] APPELBAUM Mitchel *WilmerHale*
BALDIGA William *Brown Rudnick*
DOUGHERTY Charles *Foley & Lardner LLP*
GOLDBERG Michael *Cohn Whitesell & Goldberg*
HOORT Steven *Ropes & Gray LLP*
JEFFERY D Ethan *Hanify & King*
KANNEL William *Mintz Levin*
LEONETTI Kenneth *Foley Hoag LLP*
LEVINE Richard *The Law Office of Richard Levine*
LIZOTTE Andrew *Hanify & King*
SIGEL John *WilmerHale*
SWAIM Hall *WilmerHale*
VENTOLA John *Choate Hall & Stewart*
WALSH Kevin *Mintz Levin*

### Up-and-coming individuals

LYNCH Christine *Goulston & Storrs*
MORRIER John *Mintz Levin*

---

gained an order from the Bankruptcy Court dismissing the Chapter 11 case, it is now assisting in the liquidation of its assets and the distribution of the proceeds to its creditors and other parties.

## Mintz Levin Cohn Ferris Glovsky and Popeo PC

**The Firm:** This *"incredibly strong and complex"* firm remains an active player in Massachusetts' bankruptcy market. Following a very active year, its enormous department has continued to grow while maintaining *"true breadth and depth throughout the ranks,"* according to clients. Peers, meanwhile, commend a team structure that places *"premier"* senior lawyer Richard Mikels at the forefront of the practice while surrounding him with *"talented and dependable lieutenants"* who can manage caseloads efficiently. The group is well known for its Chapter 11 work and was particularly recommended for representing debtors and bondholders. It enjoys a

strong national profile, and clients were impressed by the *"importability"* of the Massachusetts-based bankruptcy lawyers on matters occurring outside of the state.

**The Lawyers:** A popular choice for debtor work, **Richard Mikels** (see p.1099) *"always gets things done and has met with a lot of success"* in 2005. An *"incredibly impressive individual,"* he *"carries a real presence in the courtroom,"* where he is *"pleasant, but tough when he needs to be."* Clients also appreciate his *"practical, savvy and diplomatic"* approach and his ability to *"come up with unique solutions that no one else has tapped into."* **Daniel Bleck** (see p.1087) is a *"sharp lawyer and a great negotiator"* who *"can handle virtually any matter in bankruptcy."* He and Mikels *"make a great team,"* clients enthuse. **William Kannel** (see p.1096) continues to be endorsed for his work on a national scale. He is especially admired for his litigation work, in which arena he is considered *"one of the best in the business."* **Kevin Walsh** (see p.1108) employs a *"pleasant demeanor,"* but clients note that *"he can be tough when he needs to be."* *"Rising star"* **John Morrier** (see p.1100) wins plaudits as *"an incredible work force"* with *"all the core qualities."* His tireless enthusiasm is matched by an application of *"practical business sense, effective courtroom skills and drafting skill."*

**Clients/Work Highlights:** The team recently represented Liberty Mutual in asbestos and other mass tort-related Chapter 11 proceedings. It advised an affiliate of Tishman Speyer Properties as secured creditor in the International Place Chapter 11 proceedings, and also acted for the bondholders in the Delta Air Lines Chapter 11 proceeding.

## WilmerHale

See firm details p.1119

**The Firm:** This blue-chip firm enjoys a reputation as *"one of the preeminent bankruptcy outfits in town."* The office attracted praise from regional and national clients for the can-do approach of its lawyers and the high quality of their technical expertise. Clients also value the expertise available across the network of offices, and particularly the *"great stable of resources"* in New York. Enthusiastically recommended for its representation of bondholders and debtors, the group's client base includes a number of mutual funds and hedge funds. It is a natural choice for *"complicated, brainteaser"* matters, owing to the intellectual capabilities of its *"extremely smart, well-educated"* lawyers. Clients were also keen to highlight the group's *"communicative, human"* style.

**The Lawyers:** *"A pearl's pearl,"* **Paul Daley** (see p.1091) is a major force in the bankruptcy field, according to sources. His success has been premised on a mixture of a *"congenial and businesslike"* manner with *"old-school common sense and courtesy,"* and excellent negotiating skills. Although he is perceived to be less active than some of his competitors, clients continue to instruct him on important matters. **Hall Swaim** (see p.1107) is known in the market as a *"technically skilled"* lawyer and *"tough negotiator."* He is particularly admired for his expe-

rience of reorganizations and workouts. *"Quick thinker"* **Mitchel Appelbaum** (see p.1086) is *"definitely on the rise,"* say market observers. *"Capable, hard-working and increasingly knowledgeable,"* he was tipped by sources as *"the Mark Polebaum of the future!"* *"Smart"* **John Sigel** (see p.1106) is co-vice chair of the bankruptcy and commercial department. Recommended for his work on Chapter 11 cases, his experience at handling general finance matters is also valued by clients. Mark Polebaum, a leading light at the firm for a number of years, has recently gone in-house.

**Clients/Work Highlights:** The team recently completed the successful Chapter 11 reorganization of KB Toys, representing the mall-based retailer in the sale of its Internet business and the closure of approximately 600 stores. In the restructuring of McLeodUSA, the group acted for funds managed by its largest creditor, Fidelity Investments. It is also assisting the former directors of Polaroid, following its Chapter 11 filing in Delaware. Other clients include Arch Wireless; PSINet; Bradford & Bigelow; GEM Gravure; Muro Pharmaceutical; Slattery Brothers; Genaissance Pharmaceuticals and Verizon.

## Band 2

## Choate Hall & Stewart

**The Firm:** This firm boasts a great bankruptcy practice and its lawyers won plaudits for achieving *"spectacular"* results this year. The group was singled out for work on complex fiduciary matters and large mass tort bankruptcy cases. In particular, it received considerable acclaim for its work as counsel for the Chapter 11 trustee of High Voltage Engineering Corporation and its various debtor affiliates. It has also represented insurers in mass tort-related bankruptcy litigation throughout the country, including cases in Delaware, Louisiana, Ohio, Illinois and California. Clients are impressed by the *"smart, practical, down-to-earth"* approach of the team and the *"depth, breadth and delivery of its service."* They also praised the group for working effectively with other departments: *"We can rely on the firm's business segments pulling together when we need them to,"* noted one source.

**The Lawyers:** **Charles Glerum** is a *"great diplomat"* who has *"seen and done it all"* in the bankruptcy arena. Much admired for his deal-making ability, he is a skilled negotiator who was recommended for producing excellent work with creditors' committees. *"Tough but reasonable"* **Douglas Gooding** is respected for his experience in debtor work and insurance matters. Commentators particularly value the *"imagination and innovation"* he brings to cases. Junior partner **John Ventola** is *"progressing nicely,"* say sources. He *"is not afraid to tackle issues independently,"* clients enthuse, and is respected for his *"smart and thorough"* approach.

**Clients/Work Highlights:** The group was appointed as examiner in the Chapter 11 case of Gitto/Global, in order to consider allegations of fraud. It has continued to advise ACT Manufacturing and its affiliates on its wind-up. Additional clients include Bank of America Business Capital; Citizens Bank; Computer Associates International; Harvard Pilgrim Healthcare; Hewlett-Packard; Liberty Mutual; St. Paul Travelers; State Street Global Markets and Wausau Insurance Companies.

## Cohn Whitesell & Goldberg LLP

See firm details p.1111

**The Firm:** This *"small but unique"* firm specializes in bankruptcy and restructuring work. It houses a group of *"excellent and dedicated"* attorneys, which has recently been bolstered by the addition of seasoned practitioner Michael Goldberg. Though this boutique is smaller than many of its competitors, its quality was emphasized by sources, who stressed its experience of working in a range of industries. Chapter 11 reorganizations form a keynote of its practice, especially on the debtor side; however the team is also skilled in acting for investors, lenders, suppliers, creditors' committees and trustees.

**The Lawyers: Daniel Cohn** (see p.1090) is widely recognized as the central force behind the firm's bankruptcy strength. Valued for his experience in *"high-class cases,"* he is a popular point of referral for debtor work. The addition of **Michael Goldberg** (see p.1093) *"will make a positive difference to the practice,"* onlookers predict. Previous work for heavyweight Massachusetts firms has earned him a great reputation among peers. He is admired for his diverse experience in the field, and his impressive performances in the courtroom.

**Clients/Work Highlights:** The team is advising DB Companies on its Chapter 11 plan and distributions to creditors. Acting for BioTransplant in Chapter 11 proceedings, it succeeded in paying the creditors in full during 2005. The firm was also appointed as an arbitrator to resolve issues among partners arising from the dissolution of Testa Hurwitz & Thibeault.

## Goulston & Storrs

**The Firm:** This well-respected firm boasts a skilled bankruptcy team, which was roundly praised for its constructive teamwork. According to sources, the lawyers here are *"highly skilled practitioners each and every one."* Recommended for representing corporate debtors and creditor committees, the group is visible both in and outside of the state, across New England and beyond. Given the firm's real estate prowess, it is unsurprising to see it working for developers and companies acquiring assets out of bankruptcy. It also represents landlords, secured and unsecured lenders, institutional and private investors and court-appointed trustees.

**The Lawyers:** An *"increasingly regular player in the most significant bankruptcy cases,"* **Douglas Rosner** is *"becoming a force in his own right."* Applauded for his work with creditors, he is said to be *"intellectually smart, innovative and determined."* Senior lawyer **James Wallack** is *"a great strategist"* who is valued for his experience in handling a range of bankruptcy cases. *"Practical, thorough and tenacious,"* his *"confident but laid-back"* manner is popular with sources.

Up-and-comer **Christine Lynch** is also establishing a name for herself in this field.

**Clients/Work Highlights:** The team is acting as counsel to debtors in the Omni Facility Services Chapter 11 reorganization pending in the Southern District of New York. It counseled the secured lender in the Chapter 11s of Merrimac Paper and Holyoke Card, and assisted the reorganized companies upon exit from bankruptcy. Additional clients include High Voltage Engineering Corporation, Gordon Brothers Group and DJM Asset Management.

## Ropes & Gray LLP

See firm details p.1117

**The Firm:** Ropes & Gray is *"one of the oldest, largest and most prestigious firms in the city,"* and remains well respected for its bankruptcy expertise. Viewed as *"a strong player on the national level,"* the excellent group boasts a broad range of bankruptcy capabilities offered by *"great, highly qualified attorneys"* who know their way around both transactional matters and litigation. The team was recommended to researchers for its expertise in handling Chapter 11 reorganizations, restructurings, liquidations and workouts. Other specialties include insolvency litigation, troubled loan syndications and bond defaults.

**The Lawyers:** Although **William McCarthy** (see p.1099) officially stepped down as head of the bankruptcy and business restructuring department in 2004, he remains *"the most recognized name in the group."* In his capacity as senior counsel to the firm, he advises both debtors and creditors on a national scale. *"Tremendous advocate"* **Steven Hoort** (see p.1095) is co-head of the bankruptcy team. *"Cerebral and efficient,"* he is rated highly as a *"strategic thinker"* with a good, detailed knowledge of the bankruptcy code. He was also recommended by market sources as a *"tough and articulate"* negotiator who *"doesn't waste any time."*

**Clients/Work Highlights:** The team represented the first and second lien holders in the Chapter 11 of High Voltage Engineering Corporation, providing DIP financing as a bridge to a successful sale by the trustee. It advised the independent directors before and during the Chapter 11 of Trump Hotel & Casino Resorts, and advised on the Baupost Group's acquisition of General Roofing Company and its affiliates in the Chapter 11 of CEI Roofing. The team assists a number of other private equity and hedge funds, distressed companies, investors, major retailers, claims purchasers, bondholders, banks and financial institutions.

## Band 3

### Brown Rudnick Berlack Israels LLP

**The Firm:** This firm is *"well respected in town,"* say sources, with a strong market profile across New England for bankruptcy work. While New York remains the firm's focus, supporting offices in Massachusetts and New Hampshire are also developing a national reputation for their restructuring experience. The group enjoys a particularly strong name for

representing creditors (especially banks) and bondholders, and it is said to have *"capped some significant work"* in the past year. Commentators also report an *"articulate and combative"* negotiation style.

**The Lawyers: William Baldiga** was recommended by clients as *"a skilled bankruptcy attorney"* with a *"forthright"* manner. He offers considerable experience of handling Chapter 11 cases.

**Clients/Work Highlights:** The group recently acted for the unsecured creditors in the high-profile reorganization of International Place. Areas of industry expertise include aviation, retail and gaming.

## Duane Morris LLP

See firm details p.1753

**The Firm:** Duane Morris commands a *"substantial bankruptcy practice"* across the region, combining strength in Boston with a sizable presence in other areas of the country. Sources particularly recommended the group for its expertise in business reorganization and financial restructuring matters. It is justly renowned for its representation of debtors; however the team also acts for a range of other clients, including secured lenders, creditors' committees and trustees.

**The Lawyers:** The *"extremely smart"* **Paul Moore** (see p.1100) is widely acknowledged as the force behind this firm's success in the bankruptcy arena. Admired for his skill in acting for debtors, his *"take no prisoners"* style is a hit with clients, especially since it is combined with a deep vein of pragmatism.

**Clients/Work Highlights:** The team is currently acting for United Shoe Machinery in its Chapter 11 proceedings. It recently represented Canusa Corporation of Baltimore in the Chapter 11 of Bay State Paper Company. Other clients include MacLean's Seafood, Foss Manufacturing and Greenleaf IV Inc.

## Foley Hoag LLP

**The Firm:** This well-regarded firm has earned itself a reputation for being *"tenacious and dedicated"* in the bankruptcy field. Sources highlight the strength of the practice, which is predominantly litigation-driven but maintains recognized expertise in transactional matters. The group was especially recommended for its work on behalf of creditors' committees, but has recently expanded to include a variety of work for international clients with interests in the USA. It also represents debtors, equity holders, the purchasers of assets, and defendants in avoidance actions.

**The Lawyers: Andrew Schwartz** is a talented attorney who has enjoyed *"a meteoric rise in the last five years,"* according to market sources. An impressive advocate, he is widely admired for his expertise in bankruptcy litigation. Clients value his *"tremendous efficiency"* and *"upfront"* style of communication. **Kenneth Leonetti** is an *"established and knowledgeable"* member of the state's bankruptcy community. His ability to achieve excellent results in negotiations *"seemingly effortlessly"* has won him the respect of clients.

**Clients/Work Highlights:** The team acted for real estate developer Don Chiofaro in the Chapter 11 reorganization of International Place. It represented the creditors' committee, and later the liquidating supervisor and creditor trust, in the bankruptcy of Engage Inc. Other representative clients include the creditors' committee for Richard-James Inc; the claims committee for Malden Mills Industries; Media/Communications Partners and representative bodies of various developing nations.

## Gadsby Hannah LLP

**The Firm:** This *"up-and-coming"* firm was tipped by some sources to be *"one of the region's major bankruptcy outfits in five to ten years."* Clients value the *"solid support"* on restructuring matters of a team that *"effortlessly pulls successful business thinking, negotiation and strategy together."* Having cut its teeth on smaller cases in the state, the group is now increasingly recommended for sophisticated matters. It was singled out to researchers for its work with distressed companies in the technology and life sciences sectors, alongside those in retail and energy. It also advises creditors' committees, debtors, trustees and investors.

**The Lawyers: Charles Dale** is *"intelligent, direct and practical:"* he *"cuts right to the heart of the issue,"* clients claim. Dale is widely felt to be the driving force behind the firm's bankruptcy and restructuring practice. He is admired for having *"a broader range of experience"* than many competitors, as well as excellent communication skills: *"He knows when*

*to use pleasant cajoling and when confident aggression works best!"*

**Clients/Work Highlights:** During 2005 the group represented The Art Store throughout its Chapter 11 proceedings. It acted for two New York-based retail clothing chains, selling the more distressed chain and recapitalizing the other. It is also advising California-based chain Prints Plus on Chapter 11 proceedings pending in Boston, and represents the official committees of unsecured creditors for United States Mineral Products (USM) and Harvard Clinical Technology.

## Nixon Peabody LLP

See firm details p.1546

**The Firm:** The Boston office of this terrific firm continues to win market endorsement as *"a major bankruptcy law outfit"* within the state. The firm's lawyers were praised for being *"responsive and consistent,"* and producing high-quality work. They handle a wide range of restructuring-related matters on all sides of proceedings; however they were particularly singled out this year for handling a high volume of creditor work.

**The Lawyers: Mark Berman** (see p.1087) is the firm's leading light in Boston, and was widely admired as *"a tremendous resource for clients."* According to interviewees, he is *"a plain-speaking guy who really knows his stuff"* when it comes to the bankruptcy code. A *"tough negotiator and a zealous*

*advocate,"* he is also admired for his professionalism: *"He never hits below the belt but always gets his points across."*

**Clients/Work Highlights:** The group continues to represent PUMA North America in a variety of bankruptcy-related matters. During United Airlines' recent Chapter 11 proceedings, the group acted for a provider of services to United Airlines. Through its association with the Gerson Lehrman Group's Law Council, the team has also advised a variety of companies on potential Chapter 11 cases, including Kmart, Friedman's Jewelers and Interstate Bakeries.

## Other Notable Practitioners

*"Hands-on"* **Richard Levine**, at the eponymous law office, specializes in complex workout and Chapter 11 cases. He is especially recommended for his experience of acting for lenders. **John Monaghan** (see p.1100) also maintains an excellent reputation in the Massachusetts bankruptcy courts. An *"enormously capable wordsmith,"* the Holland & Knight LLP attorney also possesses *"an elegant style in the courtroom"* and is praised for building *"an easy rapport with laypeople."* **Charles Dougherty** (see p.1091) stands out at Foley & Lardner LLP for his skill in this practice area. He is highly rated for representing the creditors and equity holders of troubled companies.

# CORPORATE/M&A

| Corporate/M&A |
| Leading Firms |

| 1 | GOODWIN PROCTER LLP *Boston* |
| | ROPES & GRAY LLP *Boston* |
| | WILMERHALE *Boston* |
| 2 | BINGHAM MCCUTCHEN LLP *Boston* |
| | MCDERMOTT WILL & EMERY *Boston* |
| | SKADDEN, ARPS *Boston* |
| | WEIL, GOTSHAL & MANGES LLP *Boston* |
| 3 | CHOATE HALL & STEWART *Boston* |
| | EDWARDS ANGELL PALMER & DODGE *Boston* |
| | FOLEY HOAG LLP *Boston* |
| | GOULSTON & STORRS *Boston* |
| | MINTZ LEVIN *Boston* |

## Band 1

## Goodwin Procter LLP

See firm details p.1114

**The Firm:** This *"outstanding"* firm continues to garner praise for its corporate expertise and enjoys an increasingly national profile in the M&A sphere. Clients agree that the firm does an *"unbelievable job"* on complex transactions, while maintaining an *"entrepreneurial"* edge, particularly through its work with spin-off companies. Sources rate the team's

*"experienced individuals, quick turnaround and leveled advice."* Benefiting from the arrival of some *"strong players"* from dissolved firm Testa Hurwitz & Thibeault, the team's *"deep bench"* of lawyers covers a broad spectrum of skills. Areas of expertise include securities and corporate governance. The team is also noted for its REIT knowledge and is well positioned to assist the state's thriving life sciences industry.

**The Lawyers:** *"Upfront and genuine,"* **Stuart Cable** (see p.1089) wins plaudits for his professional integrity and straight-talking approach; *"he doesn't beat around the bush!"* claimed one source. He remains a key figure for major M&A transactions on behalf of an enviable client list. The *"clever"* **Gilbert Menna** (see p.1099) continues to win acclaim for his nationally renowned REIT expertise. Clients express confidence in his abilities and particularly value the speed of his responsiveness. **Ettore Santucci** (see p.1105) is a *"smart and experienced"* corporate specialist noted for making *"sound business decisions."* His *"careful, detail-oriented"* style wins favor among clients who appreciate his drafting and negotiating ability. *"A superstar in the making,"* **Mark Bettencourt** (see p.1087) is *"incredibly bright but practical at the same time"* and his work is informed by *"excellent legal judgment."*

**Clients/Work Highlights:** The team acted for Gables Residential Trust in its $2.8 billion acquisition by ING Groep and for Ionics in its $1.3 billion

merger with GE Infrastructure. Lawyers advised Boston Private Financial Holdings regarding its $246 million acquisition of Gibraltar Financial. The firm also acted for the company and founders in the $250 million buyout of Webloyalty.com. Additional clients include Fidelity Investments; AEW Partners; DDJ Capital Management; Highfields Capital Management; K Capital Partners; Stride Rite; Citrix Systems and Agfa-Gevaert.

## Ropes & Gray LLP

See firm details p.1117

**The Firm:** This *"large, powerful"* firm continues to enjoy a stellar reputation in the M&A market for its *"intelligent, creative and responsive"* style. With a long history in Massachusetts, it is noted for its long-standing relationships with many of the state's institutional clients. Alongside its M&A profile, the group is also respected for its securities-related and corporate governance advice to prominent public and private clients. Sources praise the *"smart, capable"* team for its excellent breadth of knowledge, experience and business sense. Individual lawyers *"understand the problem from our perspective, not just from a strictly legal angle,"* clients say.

**The Lawyers:** Sources commend **Keith Higgins** (see p.1095) for being *"one of Boston's top securities lawyers"* and value his *"straightforward and constructive"* ability to lead transactions. He is lauded as a

## Corporate/M&A
### Leading Individuals

### Senior Statesman
| | |
|---|---|
| | KELLER Stanley *Edwards Angell Palmer* |

**[1]**
| | |
|---|---|
| | BORDEN Mark *WilmerHale* |
| | CABLE Stuart *Goodwin Procter LLP* |
| | GOODMAN Louis *Skadden, Arps* |
| | HIGGINS Keith *Ropes & Gray LLP* |
| | REDLICK David *WilmerHale* |
| | SINGER Steven *WilmerHale* |
| | WIESEN Jeffrey *Mintz Levin* |

**[2]**
| | |
|---|---|
| | ASHER JR William *Choate Hall & Stewart* |
| | BROWNE Steven *Bingham McCutchen LLP* |
| | CHAPIN David *Ropes & Gray LLP* |
| | MALT R Bradford *Ropes & Gray LLP* |
| | MENNA Gilbert *Goodwin Procter LLP* |
| | NUTT Robert *Ropes & Gray LLP* |
| | RONDEAU Patrick *WilmerHale* |
| | ROSENBLUM Peter *Foley Hoag LLP* |
| | WESTRA James *Weil, Gotshal & Manges LLP* |

**[3]**
| | |
|---|---|
| | BOTHWICK Jay *WilmerHale* |
| | BRIGHAM Johan *Bingham McCutchen LLP* |
| | BROWN Margaret *Skadden, Arps* |
| | FELDMAN Roger *Fish & Richardson P.C.* |
| | KOLB William *Foley Hoag LLP* |
| | LEIBOWITZ Hal *WilmerHale* |
| | SANTUCCI Ettore *Goodwin Procter LLP* |
| | UTZSCHNEIDER John *Bingham McCutchen LLP* |
| | WHITE Dennis *McDermott Will & Emery* |
| | WILLIAMS Samuel *Brown Rudnick* |

### Up-and-coming individuals
| | |
|---|---|
| | BETTENCOURT Mark *Goodwin Procter LLP* |

"*calm, knowledgeable and clear-headed*" individual to work with. **David Chapin** (see p.1089) continues to be well regarded for his M&A expertise. He boasts experience as lead adviser to some of the state's key corporate clients, including Reebok and Gillette. Sources value his terrific business judgment, negotiation skills and client orientation. Predominantly renowned in the private equity field, **Bradford Malt** (see p.1098) also enjoys an "*extremely strong reputation*" in the corporate arena. He is widely perceived to "*hold the key*" to the firm's prolific relationship with BainCapital. Interviewees recommend **Robert Nutt** (see p.1101) for his advisory experience, particularly in the field of corporate governance. He also heads up the firm's representation of the Merrill Lynch Diversified Private Equity Program as a fund of funds and direct private equity investor.

**Clients/Work Highlights:** The group led a team of R&G public company and insolvency lawyers in guiding the independent directors on the board of Trump International through the restructuring and recapitalization of its casino enterprise in 2005. Other key clients include BainCapital; Berkshire Partners; EMC; Putnam Investments; Mizuho Corporate Bank and Fenway Partners.

## WilmerHale
See firm details p.1119

**The Firm:** This firm retains both regional clients and national respect for its "*customer service orientation*" and "*broad-based knowledge*" in the corporate sphere. According to onlookers, the firm's 2005 merger has bedded in well and, while the firm's client base has broadened as a result, the team remains "*Boston's primary technology specialist.*" "*High-quality*" attorneys win plaudits for being "*smart, skilled and pleasant*" practitioners with "*key industry experience,*" particularly in the life sciences market. Accordingly, the team acted for Alnylam Pharmaceuticals on its $700 million collaboration with Novartis in the field of RNAi therapeutics.

**The Lawyers:** The "*extraordinarily talented*" and **Mark Borden** (see p.1088) is seen as "*one as the deans*" of the Massachusetts corporate community. He also maintains a top-drawer securities practice. According to one observer: "*He is a real pro who has been everywhere and seen everything in this field.*" Clients regard him as "*a first-class adviser,*" while peers welcome his "*collaborative and focused*" approach to negotiations. **David Redlick** (see p.1103) applies a "*pragmatic and solution-focused*" approach to his nationally regarded work in the life sciences field. Sources value his ability to handle IPO, M&A and licensing deals in equal measure. He "*never loses his cool*" and is able to "*break down complicated issues into simple ideas,*" commentators state. With "*many years of credibility and effectiveness*" in the biotech field, **Steven Singer** (see p.1106) is well regarded for his work with corporate clients in the region. He combines "*exceptional knowledge*" of the life sciences industry with broad transactional and licensing experience and a "*pragmatic, low-key*" style. **Patrick Rondeau** (see p.1104) is praised by sources for being "*intellectual and responsive*" in his work. He wins plaudits for his "*practical, clear and concise*" handling of IPOs and is also rated for his ability in private equity matters. Clients especially value his ability to "*articulate complex issues succinctly.*" **Jay Bothwick** (see p.1088) continues to win client endorsement in both the M&A and private equity markets. He is recommended for his work with venture-backed companies. Interviewees hail **Hal Leibowitz** (see p.1097) for his "*wealth of corporate experience.*" Sources enthuse: "*He is incredibly committed to his work and extraordinarily dedicated to client needs, he is just available all of the time!*"

**Clients/Work Highlights:** Lawyers advised Icagen on its IPO and assisted American Superconductor regarding its $48.3 million follow-on public offering in 2005. In the M&A field, key transactions included the representation of DoubleClick in its $1.1 billion acquisition by Hellman & Friedman. Other notable clients include Adams Harkness & Hill; America's Growth Capital; Legacy Partners; Needham; Bio-Sphere Medical; Transkaryotic Therapies; Millennium Pharmaceuticals; Sepracor and SkillSoft.

## Band 2

## Bingham McCutchen LLP
See firm details p.1110

**The Firm:** This ever-expanding firm's "*national depth*" has enabled the Boston office to establish a solid reputation within the region. The financial powerhouse is recommended for its seasoned transactional expertise, particularly in the M&A field. Its "*stellar*" corporate team garners praise for producing work of an "*extremely high quality.*" The group acts for NASDAQ and NYSE-listed clients, and is particularly renowned for its work with entrepreneurial hi-tech and biotech clients. Interviewees commend the team for its ability to provide tailored business advice on corporate governance and strategic matters: "*It is as if we have our own in-house counsel.*" Clients also highlight lawyers' "*broad and accessible skill sets,*" stressing the team's effective interfacing with other departments.

**The Lawyers:** The "*technically sound and creative*" **Steven Browne** (see p.1088) "*understands what really matters in a deal,*" according to sources. His negotiation skills and "*business-oriented approach*" are valued by clients, who report that he is "*assertive in a noncombative way*" with a refreshing ability to "*lighten the atmosphere when it gets a little tense.*" "*Deal-doer*" **Johan Brigham** (see p.1088) is well regarded for his focus on "*getting the transaction done.*" Sources also identify experienced corporate figure **John Utzschneider** (see p.1108) as "*a highly intellectual but practical lawyer.*"

**Clients/Work Highlights:** The team represented Concord Communications on its $337 million acquisition by Computer Associates. It also assisted Tempur-Pedic International in connection with a secondary public offering of approximately $235 million of common stock. Additional clients include Boston Scientific; Cytyc; Citrix Systems; Oracle; Cognos and Raytheon.

## McDermott Will & Emery
See firm details p.878

**The Firm:** This firm is internationally regarded for the breadth of its legal advice and the quality of its attorneys. Commentators commend its Boston arm for the ability to source "*highly integrated*" teams to meet client needs on cross-border deals, especially involving Europe. Sources value the "*collaborative*" nature of the corporate group's interaction with other departments within the firm. Notwithstanding several departures from the private equity group in 2005, clients continue to rate the firm's transactional ability in the healthcare industry. For example, the team recently represented Clinical Data on its pending acquisitions of Icoria and Genaissance Pharmaceuticals.

**The Lawyers:** **Dennis White** (see p.1109) has "*a high degree of integrity and genuine concern for the well-being of the client,*" sources said. With "*his ego firmly locked in a drawer,*" he is "*a pleasure to deal with*" and works hard to ensure that negotiations run as smoothly as possible.

**Clients/Work Highlights:** In collaboration with

the London office, lawyers represented Apama in its merger with Progress Software, a Massachusetts-based software company. It coordinated with its Chicago, London, Munich and Silicon Valley counterparts to advise American Healthways on the establishment of a structure for its international operations. The Boston team also assisted Gorton's in the acquisition of King & Prince Seafood and represented Novamerican Steel in connection with a secondary public offering of its shares. Additional clients include Castile Ventures; Fidelity Capital Investors; Gemini Investors; Highland Capital Partners; i-Hatch Ventures; Oxford Bioscience Partners; SV Life Sciences; Tuckerman Capital; Coley Pharmaceutical and Velocity Equity Partners.

## Skadden, Arps, Slate, Meagher & Flom LLP & Affiliates
See firm details p.1557

**The Firm:** While the Boston office undoubtedly benefits from the firm's prowess in New York and an enviable global network, sources specifically commend the ability of the *"extremely capable"* Massachusetts-based group. With *"an impressive depth of knowledge,"* the *"small but well-formed"* team is *"easy to work with,"* owing to its *"flexible and accommodating"* approach to client needs. *"Thorough and skillful experts"* with decades of experience are visibly *"operating at a high transactional level"* while serving as *"sound strategic counselors"* to existing clients, according to commentators. Observers particularly value the firm's success at combining *"expert technical knowledge with practical business sense."*

**The Lawyers:** *"Proactive, savvy and experienced,"* **Louis Goodman** (see p.1093) is a *"'get it done' kind of guy"* who is solution-focused in his work: *"He covers the necessary theoretical issues but always pushes for completion,"* claimed one source. Goodman draws on his *"huge knowledge base and pure intelligence"* to provide advice that is *"framed in a business-oriented way."* He also wins plaudits for maintaining a *"high level of integrity"* and *"an incredible balance of expertise and wisdom."* **Margaret Brown** (see p.1088) is praised for being *"an incredible technical drafter"* whose analytical ability serves her well in M&A and securities transactions. Clients value her *"creative solutions"* and overall coordination skills.

**Clients/Work Highlights:** The Boston team represented Ascential Software in its $1.1 billion acquisition by IBM. It is also advising Esselte Group Holdings in the pending sale of its DYMO unit to Newell Rubbermaid for $730 million. Lawyers acted for Boise Cascade in the $3.7 billion sale of its paper and forest products businesses to an investor group led by Madison Dearborn Partners, and assisted EMC in its acquisition of Rainfinity. Additional clients include Biogen Idec; Citigroup; Fidelity Investments; JW Childs; OfficeMax; Peter Kiewit Sons'; Putnam Investments; Regeneron Pharmaceuticals; Spectrum Brands; Sycamore Networks and Textron.

## Weil, Gotshal & Manges LLP
See firm details p.1565

**The Firm:** This strong outfit is primarily renowned for its prowess in the private equity field and enjoys an international reputation for its acquisition finance expertise. Consequently, sources also note the Boston office for its M&A capabilities, particularly in the technology and telecom sectors. The expanding corporate team is developing a reputation across the region, aided by the firm's recently opened office in Providence.

**The Lawyers:** The *"fabulous lawyer"* **James Westra** (see p.1109) continues to shine as the firm's leading light in Boston's private equity market. He is also lauded for his *"star quality"* in the M&A field.

**Clients/Work Highlights:** Thomas H Lee Partners; Vivendi Universal; Koch Industries; Pfizer; Highland Capital Partners; MCI; Millennium Chemicals; Estée Lauder; Global Crossing and Reuters.

## Band 3

### Choate Hall & Stewart

**The Firm:** Following the 2005 dissolution of Testa Hurwitz & Thibeault, this *"utterly capable"* firm has been bolstered by the arrival of a significant number of its attorneys. The list of new arrivals includes some that are well known to the Boston M&A market and, according to sources, a *"more active corporate practice"* has ensued. Noted for its advice to privately held clients in the midmarket, the group is especially recommended for its advice to startup businesses in the region. It also garners praise for its *"broad corporate capability"* and can *"handle public company transactions of a significant size."* The team benefits from the firm's recognized private equity and specialty finance capabilities.

**The Lawyers:** Renowned for his position as managing partner at Testa Hurwitz & Thibeault, *"smart"* senior lawyer **William Asher** is a respected player in the corporate field.

**Clients/Work Highlights:** Major clients include Blue Dolphin Group; Conjoin; E5 Systems; Hammerhead Networks; Linden Technologies; Pegasystems; Platypus Technology; VenturCom and VistaCare.

### Edwards Angell Palmer & Dodge LLP
See firm details p.1112

**The Firm:** The 2005 merger with Edwards & Angell has bolstered Palmer & Dodge's already impressive reputation in the region. Observers comment on an overall broadening of skills within the team, citing the firm's combined ability to offer acclaimed corporate and private equity advice. The synergy of Palmer & Dodge's experience in the life sciences industry with Edwards & Angell's profile in media and telecoms is also expected to fortify the team's reputation among regional clients. The firm is most visible in the midmarket, where sources rate its *"responsive and knowledgeable"* corporate team and recommend lawyers for their work on behalf of emerging companies.

**The Lawyers:** Senior statesman and securities expert **Stanley Keller** (see p.1096) garners praise for accumulating four decades of practical experience and *"inspired"* academic credentials. His declining profile in deals is offset by his reputation as *"the professor who has all the answers."* A regular commentator in the press, he *"really knows the law in a way that makes a difference"* and is consulted as *"a community adviser,"* claim corporate peers.

**Clients/Work Highlights:** The team acted in the $255 million acquisition of Idenix by Novartis. It also advised Upstate on its $205 million sale to Serologicals. Additional clients include Axcelis Technologies; Radianse; Target Partners; Dyax; TriPath Imaging; Cerimon Pharmaceuticals; Genzyme and Magellan Biosciences.

### Foley Hoag LLP

**The Firm:** This firm continues to be recognized primarily across the state for its work within the technology sector. Maintaining a loyal client base of public and private businesses in the midmarket, the corporate team offers a range of services in the M&A field in addition to IPO and MBO advice. Sources rate the *"dedicated"* client orientation and counseling expertise of a team of *"profoundly capable"* lawyers.

**The Lawyers:** **Peter Rosenblum** continues to shine as the firm's leading corporate light. Peers recognize his work as lead counsel in the firm's major deals of 2005 and clients rate his expertise at handling M&A transactions. **William Kolb** is coordinator of the firm's business department and chair of the firm's M&A practice group. His work with emerging companies is noted by onlookers.

**Clients/Work Highlights:** The team has recently assisted management in the MBO of Boston Trust and Investment Management Company from Citizens Financial Group. Additional clients include CRA International; Crossbeam Systems; the Special Committee of the Board of Directors of Concerto Software; Inverness Medical Innovations; Numeric Investors and YDI Wireless.

### Goulston & Storrs

**The Firm:** While this *"well-run, friendly"* firm is primarily renowned for its real estate expertise, it also offers *"uniquely efficient and cost-effective"* corporate advice. Its developing client base is noted by sources who also highlight the firm's capability in the private equity field. A variety of businesses in the region's midmarket rate the corporate team's ability to provide *"an extremely helpful combination of legal skills and business judgment."* In particular, its *"technical experts"* are reputed for being *"thorough and detailed"* in their work. Noted for cross-border experience, the Boston team benefits from the firm's additional offices in London, New York and Washington, DC. It recently acted for Massachusetts-based rapid prototyping technology company Zcorp on its acquisition by Danish firm Contex Scanning Technology. It has also represented venture-backed telecommunications software firm eDial in its $27 million acquisition by Alcatel.

The Lawyers: Kitt Sawitsky and Lester Fagen are among the corporate group's driving forces.

Clients/Work Highlights: The team has represented Boston-based Jasmine Company in its acquisition by New York & Company. It also advised venture capital firm Greylock in its initial investment in China in FibreXon. Additional clients include Old Mutual (US) Holdings; Oxfam America; Tweeter Home Entertainment; Not Your Average Joe's; Victory Supermarkets; LeMaitre Vascular and Partners HealthCare Systems.

## Mintz Levin Cohn Ferris Glovsky and Popeo PC

The Firm: The Boston office of this *"accessible"* firm maintains its national reputation in the biotech and healthcare industries. It continues to offer consistent service to clients, although sources suggested that the corporate team's *"middle ranks could do with beefing up."* The team boasts some excellent life sciences attorneys who offer a *"smart, experienced and practical"* approach to transactions. For example, the team acted for TransForm Pharmaceuticals in its acquisition by Johnson & Johnson. It also advised MPM Capital, Burrill and SV Life Sciences in the formation and funding of Alinea Pharmaceuticals.

The Lawyers: The *"phenomenal"* **Jeffrey Wiesen** (see p.1109) brings *"a win-win philosophy"* and a *"hands-on"* approach to his work, according to interviewees. A *"wise but tough negotiator"* and a *"top-notch"* adviser, he is lauded as *"an all-around expert"* in the life sciences field. Corporate clients attribute his ability to *"represent clients so efficiently"* to his *"genuinely understanding our position from a business angle."*

Clients/Work Highlights: Notable clients include Biogen Idec; CuraGen; Archemix; Dynogen Pharmaceuticals; Hypnion; ARIAD Pharmaceuticals; Paratek Pharmaceuticals; Targacept Pharmaceuticals and OXiGENE.

## Other Notable Practitioners

Despite the distinctly IP focus of Fish & Richardson P.C., **Roger Feldman** (see p.1092) enjoys a reputation as *"a highly capable corporate lawyer."* He acted for National Instruments in the acquisition of Measurement Computing. Clients continue to endorse the work of **Sam Williams** at Brown Rudnick Berlack Israels LLP, whose national practice covers the gamut of corporate and M&A matters.

# EMPLOYEE BENEFITS & EXECUTIVE COMPENSATION

Employee Benefits
& Executive Compensation
Leading Firms

| | |
|---|---|
| 1 | **GOODWIN PROCTER LLP** *Boston* |
| | **ROPES & GRAY LLP** *Boston* |
| 2 | **WILMERHALE** *Boston* |
| 3 | **MCDERMOTT WILL & EMERY** *Boston* |
| | **MINTZ LEVIN** *Boston* |
| | **PARKER & BROWN** *Boston* |

Leading Individuals

| | |
|---|---|
| 1 | **CLEARY John** *Goodwin Procter LLP* |
| | **ISAIA Russell** *Bingham McCutchen LLP* |
| | **SCHMIDT William** *WilmerHale* |
| | **TSE Marian** *Goodwin Procter LLP* |
| | **ZORN Jonathan** *Ropes & Gray LLP* |
| 2 | **BIANCHI Alden** *Mintz Levin* |
| | **CAPORIZZO A William** *WilmerHale* |
| | **GAUDREAU JR Russell** *Ropes & Gray LLP* |
| | **HUGG Joseph** *DLA Piper* |
| | **LIAZOS Andrew** *McDermott Will & Emery* |
| | **NULL Amy** *WilmerHale* |
| | **RAISH David** *Ropes & Gray LLP* |

## Band 1

## Goodwin Procter LLP

See firm details p.1114

The Firm: This firm's important ERISA and employee benefits group was highlighted by market sources for the *"sophisticated practice and depth of expertise"* it offers. Experienced in all aspects of ERISA and the International Code, its attorneys are said to be *"providers of practical and informed advice"* to clients from an array of industries. The full range of benefit plans are handled, including tax, acquisitions and sureties law issues, and the group also offers advice on areas such as retirement and welfare plans. Associated dispute resolution expertise is also available. The firm's substantial corporate base regularly involves the team in M&A transactions, and clients perceived the *"whole-scale group"* to be *"one of the finest in the state."*

The Lawyers: This team houses two of the leading players in the state. **John Cleary** (see p.1090) is *"a real people person,"* say sources, *"who is always ready to help clients understand the nuances of the legal arguments he employs."* He has particular experience in dealing with the DOL in respect of ERISA matters, and frequently advises fiduciaries and trustees on their responsibilities. A recent highlight saw him advise The Charles Stark Draper Laboratory on a defined benefit plan, several retirement plans and welfare plan administration. **Marian Tse** (see p.1108) chairs the group and focuses primarily on executive compensation. Commentators described her as a *"smart and tenacious lady,"* who can provide *"quick, concise answers."* She also advises clients on employee benefit matters, including qualified retirement plans and ESOPs.

Clients/Work Highlights: The team advises Blue Cross Blue Shield of Massachusetts and the Rogers Corporation on design and compliance for qualified plans and deferred compensation plans. A highlight was handling a host of employee benefit issues, such as qualified and nonqualified retirement plans, split dollar life insurance arrangements and Voluntary Employee Beneficiary Association (VEBA), for Partners HealthCare System.

## Ropes & Gray LLP

See firm details p.1117

The Firm: This tax and benefits group houses *"some of the top practitioners in the state,"* according to the market. Clients were quick to praise the team, with more than one source reporting: *"We get finely tuned advice, tailored to each of our interests, which at the end of the day really makes us feel special."* The group offers expertise in the more traditional aspects of the area, such as qualified plans, health and welfare benefits and the implications of M&A, as well as representing tax-exempt organizations in their unique compensation and benefit matters. Investment management and private equity clients also employ the team's knowledge and skill in the ERISA area, where attorneys regularly assist employers in benefit claims and appeals under retirement and welfare plans, up to litigation if necessary.

The Lawyers: **Jonathan Zorn** (see p.1109) practices *"at the highest stratum,"* say market sources. He has years of experience dealing with executive compensation arrangements, and regularly advises financial services clients on stock options and restrictive stock. **Russell Gaudreau** (see p.1093) spearheads the group, enjoying a national reputation for his work. Primarily focused on the benefits aspects of the practice, he was admired for *"always immersing himself in the details of the matter."* **David Raish** (see p.1103) debuts in the rankings following enthusiastic market feedback. He is busy on the employee benefits side, where he boasts particular expertise in dealing with tax-exempt employers, such as hospitals and universities. His intelligence and *"personable nature"* make him a popular choice with peers and clients.

Clients/Work Highlights: BainCapital; Millipore; Genzyme; Gillette; Timberland; Silver Lake Partners; State Street Bank & Trust and Harvard Management.

## Band 2

## WilmerHale

See firm details p.1119

The Firm: A four-strong employee benefits team operates from this growing international firm. With *"a thriving practice going from strength to strength"* under the leadership of Bill Caporizzo, the group was praised by clients for its responsiveness, availability and attention to their needs. As one said, the lawyers *"always produce great results, and more importantly do so on a timely basis."* It handles the gamut of employee benefit and executive compensation matters; however, with the firm's strong corporate client base, it displays particular strength in managing transactional work, especially in the hi-tech and biotech areas.

**The Lawyers:** **William Schmidt** (see p.1105) has a corporate law practice with a focus on employee benefit plans and executive compensation matters. *"An excellent negotiator,"* he was praised by sources for his willingness to accommodate other perspectives without compromising his clients' interests. Of late, he has been more involved in the transactional side of the practice, but he continues to advise a number of technology companies on their benefit plans. **Amy Null** (see p.1101) possesses broad experience of advising financial institutions, benefit plan service providers and employers on ERISA, federal income tax and other rules and regulations. With *"a good head on her shoulders,"* she was touted by sources as a future star. She recently advised several mutual fund complexes on the ERISA implications of their in-house retirement plans. Heading the team, **Bill Caporizzo** (see p.1089) is *"always ready to fight the client's corner without hesitation,"* agree sources.

**Clients/Work Highlights:** Among its clientele, the team acts for a host of technology and life science entities on a national and global scale.

## Band 3

### McDermott Will & Emery

See firm details p.878

**The Firm:** This employee benefits and executive compensation group works with the firm's corporate and tax departments to provide *"a seamless service"* that even the most demanding client *"would find difficult to fault."* Clients also appreciate the group's cutting-edge knowledge; in the words of one: *"They are continuously picking up new trends and identifying ways to cope with new hurdles."* Benefit compli-

ance, employee claims and litigation, ESOPs and welfare benefit plans fall within the team's remit; this breadth, and its ability to handle international work, are singled out as important attractions by clients.

**The Lawyers:** Heading both the Boston employee benefits practice and the firm's national executive compensation group is the *"excellent and conscientious"* **Andrew Liazos** (see p.1098). In recent months he has acted for a number of boards of directors in compliance reviews and IRS scrutiny procedures related to compensation plans. Other typical work includes designing long-term incentives, equity compensation, nonqualified deferred compensation and golden parachutes.

**Clients/Work Highlights:** The team represents financial institutions, public companies including many from the Fortune 500, cooperatives, nonprofit organizations, closely held businesses and executives.

### Mintz Levin Cohn Ferris Glovsky and Popeo PC

**The Firm:** According to market sources, this firm is *"certainly raising its game"* in the employee benefits arena. Commentators laid the credit for its success at the feet of a *"capable team who can handle incredibly thorny issues."* It is experienced in the design, development and implementation of employee benefits and executive compensation programs, dealing frequently with compliance and operational issues arising under ERISA and the Internal Revenue Code. Particular note was made of the transactional side of the practice, where sources were impressed by the focus on addressing benefit issues in planned corporate acquisitions.

**The Lawyers:** Sources point to **Alden Bianchi** as this team's standout name. A *"careful practitioner,"* he heads the group and was highlighted for being *"well versed in the complexities of the area."*

**Clients/Work Highlights:** The team acts for healthcare providers, hospitals, educational institutions, banks, insurance companies and mutual fund groups.

### Parker & Brown

**The Firm:** This Boston-based boutique debuts in the rankings after receiving enthusiastic praise from market sources. It concentrates exclusively on employee benefits law and ERISA, which gives it an enviable focus and understanding of the area's highly technical regulations. This proved popular with clients, who appreciate its skill in *"helping to guide us through the field."* Typical work includes the design and implementation of plans, IRS audits, hiring and terminating contracts, claims and litigation under benefit plans, and the obtaining of IRS approvals or amendments.

**The Lawyers:** Name partners Carol Brown and Stephen Parker are the firm's leading practitioners in this field.

**Clients/Work Highlights:** The team represents a range of clients, from family-owned businesses to large multinationals, located throughout the state. These are drawn from a variety of industries, such as medicine, aerospace, media, Internet services, banking, manufacturing and chemicals. A number of nonprofit organizations also figure in its client roster.

### Other Notable Practitioners

**Russell Isaia** (see p.1095) from Bingham McCutchen LLP clearly enjoys a leading position in the Massachusetts market. His *"tremendous judgment"* is placed at the disposal of a variety of clients, who value his advice on the securities, ERISA and tax implications of the design, implementation, documentation and termination of all forms for benefit program. The *"incredibly bright"* **Joseph Hugg** (see p.1095) operates out of DLA Piper Rudnick Gray Cary US LLP's Boston tax group. He concentrates on executive compensation issues, and offers experience in tax-qualified and nonqualified compensation agreements and ERISA compliance, among other things. According to clients, his popularity stems from the fact that *"he omits all the legal jargon that most lawyers love to play on, and tells us the facts straight."*

# EMPLOYMENT

## Band 1

### Foley Hoag LLP

**The Firm:** Sources were quick to credit this team for its *"across-the-board excellence in labor and employment matters."* Positioned firmly as clear leader in the field, the 25-strong team undertakes a broad spectrum of matters with *"the requisite aptitude and expertise to get the job done to the highest standards."* Although traditional labor law remains the focus of the group's activities, with much of the work consisting of general counseling and union negotiations, clients appreciate the added dimension of its employment litigation service. Noncompete and trade secret litigation were other key features of the team's workload in 2005.

**The Lawyers:** The *"ferociously smart, ethical and aggressive"* **Arthur Telegen** chairs the firm's employment group. A veteran in the field, he wields tremendous clout and *"brings a remarkable degree of business acumen to the table,"* say interviewees. Labor issues form the lion's share of his practice. **William Koffel** is an *"intellectually outstanding"* practitioner who is dedicated to his clients and who *"displays an unmatched level of finesse."* This former trial attorney for the DOL represents clients before state and federal agencies and is renowned for always being on the cutting edge of developments within the law. **James Bucking** practice is heavily focused on traditional labor law and he is famed for his knack for handling litigious matters. His clients singled him out for his *"extensive knowledge of labor relations"* and

# MAINLY DEFENDANT

his ability to come up with *"pragmatic solutions to problems."* **Michelle Whitham** combines her role as managing partner of the Boston office with a practice that is heavily focused on employment litigation. She drew positive feedback from peers and clients, who believe *"you can really rely on her,"* particularly in complex wage and hour class action litigation and matters involving the theft of electronic information.

**Clients/Work Highlights:** Clients within the industrial, medical, retail, technological, financial, academic and governmental communities are all beneficiaries of this group's work. Major clients of the group include Verizon; General Dynamics; Anheuser-Busch; Polaroid; Genzyme; Intel and Bath Iron Works.

## Ropes & Gray LLP

See firm details p.1117

**The Firm:** This team remains a principal player within the Massachusetts market, with commentators highlighting the team's "*undeniable presence*" in all aspects of the practice area. There is an even split in the group's workload between conventional labor relations work and a spectrum of employment-related litigation. However, clients were quick to point out that "*emerging concerns facing employers are also a part of the group's comprehensive service.*" The past year has seen this "*finely tuned*" group of 20 lawyers carry out substantial work in noncompete litigation and class actions regarding wage and hour claims, where one client remarked: "*They really know the ins and outs of the law.*" Work within the hospital and medical sector is a particular forte of this group's repertoire.

**The Lawyers:** **Robert Gordon** (see p.1094) position as "*premier lawyer*" within this team was consistently echoed by impressed sources, who enthused over his "*intense, intellectual and driven nature.*" The bread and butter of his practice involves counseling and litigation where his consideration of "*all angles in the case – and then some*" continues to earn him respect as one of the leading players in the field. As one client put it, what distinguishes Gordon from the rest is "*his wonderful relationships with his clients and his knack of staying one step ahead of the game.*" He recently acted for a large financial institution in a trial involving a complex sex discrimination charge. **Richard Ward** (see p.1108) is highly regarded for his prestigious practice and undertakes work predominantly in the employment litigation and labor arbitration arenas. Peers held him out to be "*the guy we all want to be,*" while clients were particularly appreciative of the "*tremendous judgment he exhibits each and every time.*" Despite his relative youth, **Anthony Rizzotti** (see p.1103) is an accomplished individual who commentators characterize as a real force to be reckoned with. "*Bright and upbeat,*" he has been busy advising on the labor and employment issues relating to the mergers and acquisitions of corporate entities, and in one instance, the impact of a merger between two unions. Clients praised his creativeness in problem solving, stating: "*You can really see the wheels turning as he processes the matter.*"

**Clients/Work Highlights:** Caritas Christi healthcare, Reebok and Partners HealthCare feature in a diverse client list that includes Fortune 500 companies from a range of industries. The group also acts for educational and nonprofit entities.

## Seyfarth Shaw LLP

See firm details p.882

**The Firm:** Clients are drawn to this group on account of its "*dedicated and intelligent collection of lawyers.*" It covers the gamut of labor and employment matters and can draw on the resources of nine offices nationwide. It has secured a loyal following of clients who are confident that "*the team can handle any problem we bring to the table.*" A large percentage of the group's caseload consists of employment litigation where it acts for employers against an individual or multiclass action. Highlights from the past year include a raft of class action trials challenging the distribution of tips and service charges in the hospitality industry and an increasingly prevalent number of wage and hour disputes. Interviewees also recommended its strong labor law practice, with clients praising the "*consistent and invaluable advice*" members give. Respected throughout the state, the team acts as outside counsel to the University of Massachusetts and has represented it in arbitrations, negotiations and unfair labor practice proceedings.

**The Lawyers:** "*Always first choice in a line-up,*" state-renowned **Richard Alfred** is prized for his premier labor and employment work. His sophisticated practice involves acting for employers in a range of disputes, and he has recently represented clients before state and federal courts in complex, multi-plaintiff wage and hour disputes. He has also handled several complex whistle-blowing cases under Sarbanes-Oxley legislation and is renowned for his "*up for a challenge*" attitude and his "*unreserved commitment to his clients' cause.*" **Lisa Damon** attracted praise from peers and clients alike for her "*fantastic judgment.*" She combines her role as managing partner with a vigorous labor and employment practice. Sources highlighted her particular emphasis on discrimination litigation, where she is widely regarded as "*one of the best in the field.*" Her recent highlights include acting in the age and sex discrimination case of Sullivan v Liberty Mutual, which established a new standard for discrimination in the context of a reduction of force. **Joseph Ambash** is an authority in the area of traditional labor law and was warmly recommended by clients as "*a source of originality in negotiations.*" He has an impressive stable of clients and continues to act as outside labor law counsel to both the City of Boston and Boston Red Sox. **Ariel Cudkowicz** debuts in the rankings this year following staunch support for his employment litigation practice. He has been busy representing clients from the hospitality industry in collective actions, challenging the distribution of tips and service charges under Massachusetts law.

**Clients/Work Highlights:** The team's high-profile cases include acting in the Motorola v Casa Systems, in which an injunction was secured to protect the firm's client from alleged theft of trade secrets and violation of the former employees' noncompete agreement. Other work includes acting for a host of large national companies and institutions, including Yale University in its labor relation matters.

**Band 2**

## Goodwin Procter LLP

See firm details p.1114

**The Firm:** *Chambers*' interviewees enthusiastically reported that "*the lawyers pay you so much attention you feel as if you are their only client!*" The group is home to "*a collaborative team of top lawyers,*" who advise the firm's larger corporate clients on their labor and employment issues. The team also has a standalone component to its practice, counseling local, regional and national companies from a spectrum of industries. Its strengths include whistle-blower litigation, affirmative action and OSHA issues in addition to matters involving the FMLA and FLSA. The team's other recent matters include challenging discrimination, wage and hour and harassment suits where clients found the "*levels of support they offer as a team are great.*"

**The Lawyers:** Interviewees believe **James Nagle** (see p.1101) "*plays the law like a chess match and is always three moves ahead.*" He leads the group and combines work in the traditional labor arena with a high-profile employment litigation practice. Although he has been involved in a number of important whistle-blower cases, sources assert that it is in union negotiations that he really shines. Here he is well respected for "*always conjuring creative answers and ensuring the main issues are broached.*" According to the market, **Wilfred Benoit** (see p.1087) is a "*real straight shooter*" who maintains an "*aura of thoughtfulness*" and is committed to the careful preparation of his cases. His recent workload has included several cases under Sarbanes-Oxley legislation, employment discrimination matters for a high-profile financial service firm and work within the noncompete arena. He has also represented a number of clients in the technology sector, who found "*his up-to-date knowledge of the law*" a real asset. **Bradford Smith** (see p.1106) is a "*rising star among the troops*" who impressed clients with his work in the employment discrimination, collective bargaining and arbitration fields.

Clients/Work Highlights: Boston Scientific; Beacon Capital Partners; Hewlett-Packard; Fidelity Investments and Invensys.

## Littler Mendelson, PC

See firm details p.333

**The Firm:** This labor and employment boutique continues to consolidate its position within the Massachusetts market and fields a team of 12 specialized individuals who are "*each fully committed to the cause.*" The Boston office acts for clients from the healthcare, financial services and technology sectors. They rely on the team for its "*first-class*" employment litigation practice, which is complemented by expertise in traditional labor law. The team can call on additional resources from the firm's nationwide network, comprising over 400 lawyers, which in interviewees' minds ensures it "*strength and depth in all quarters.*" Clients were particularly impressed by the team's "*efficient delivery of a work product that one can't fault.*"

**The Lawyers:** **David Casey** (see p.1089) is held in high esteem by the market, particularly for his skills as a trial lawyer, and was described by several clients as "*our first port of call.*" Chambers' researchers heard that he exhibits a "*killer combo of intellect and facts*" and that he is "*one of the best at getting what the client wants.*" **Adam Forman** (see p.1092) wins respect for his flexible and creative thinking, while his colleague **Christopher Perry** (see p.1102) picked up praise for the breadth of his employment litigation expertise. His recent caseload has included several trade secret

and noncompete disputes. **Greg Keating** (see p.1096) is a new entrant to the tables and has recently successfully acted for WellCare in a noncompete case in the Supreme Court of New York. Clients agree that he "*is making a real name for himself*" and rated him as a "*savvy individual.*"

Clients/Work Highlights: Aspen Technology; Hewlett-Packard; Lowe's; State Street; Taco Bell; Viacom; Zurich North America; Abbott Laboratories; Allmerica Financial; Bose; Buckingham Browne & Nichols; Cisco Systems; Compass Group; El Paso; EMC; Emerson Hospital; General Mills; Infinity Pharmaceuticals and US Airways.

## Morgan, Brown and Joy LLP

See firm details p.1116

**The Firm:** This high-quality boutique gained plaudits from the market for successfully building up a group that has "*experts throughout its hierarchy who provide an all-encompassing service.*" The team of 32 lawyers is popular among clients for its "*more personal service*" than some of its larger competitors, and has built up a nationwide profile. This is evidenced by the fact that the team handled employment litigation for Home Depot in six New England states. Labor law issues remain the heart of this team's practice and it recently advised on the police union negotiations for the City of Boston.

**The Lawyers:** **Robert Joy** boasts a name and reputation that "*pulls clients in.*" Interviewees heaped praise on his litigation skills, describing him as "*masterful in court*" and an expert in the construction of detailed and complex arguments. **William Joy** has "*really honed his skills*" and was lauded by sources for his work within the labor relations arena. Recently he successfully concluded a number of high-profile union contracts for clients within the retail industry in New York and Massachusetts. Clients appreciated his responsiveness, and claim: "*He is always available in our hour of need.*" **Laurence Donoghue** debuts in the rankings this year, having received recommendations from sources for "*always seeing the big picture.*"

Clients/Work Highlights: The team has been busy representing Federated Department Stores in employment litigation and labor relation issues. Other notable clients of the firm include GE; Harvard University; Amica Mutual Insurance; Bloomingdale's; Boston Scientific; Oracle; Lucent Technologies; Macy's and South Shore Hospital.

## WilmerHale

See firm details p.1119

**The Firm:** Clients believe "*the seamless provision of services nationally and internationally*" sets this group apart from some of its competitors. The ten-member team in Boston acts closely with the firm's nationwide offices to advise on a catalog of employment and labor matters. "*We can always rely on their terrific judgment calls and wisdom gained from their cumulative experience,*" clients stressed. The group boasts an impressive record of victories before state and federal agencies and courts, particularly in the discrimination area where it has successfully

defended clients in numerous cases before the EEOC. Although success at trial is a notable feature of this group's repertoire, clients also appreciate the lawyers' "*detailed analysis of ways to avoid litigation if possible.*" Clients also stay loyal to the group because "*they always accommodate us, no matter how big or small the problem.*"

**The Lawyers:** **Joan Lukey** (see p.1098) is a "*supreme litigator*" who also devotes some of her time to general commercial litigation. Although in previous years she has concentrated on plaintiff work, she has shifted her focus towards defendant representation in the last year. Headline cases include defending the City of Cambridge in a five-week race discrimination suit and continuing to represent the Massachusetts Bay Transportation Authority in its federal case in Boston. The "*brilliant*" **Neil Jacobs** (see p.1095) has enjoyed a fruitful year having successfully represented toy manufacturer Hasbro in a major discrimination dispute. Much of his time is also devoted to acting for clients in major wage and hour class actions throughout the state and beyond. **Jonathan Rosenfeld** (see p.1104) chairs the group and counsels clients on the full range of issues. They warmly reported that "*he really makes an effort to understand the history and culture of our company – so much so, we consider him part of our organization.*"

Clients/Work Highlights: The team successfully argued on behalf of Pioneer Group for the dismissal of a former employee's claim of race discrimination from the Federal District Court of Massachusetts. In another highlight, lawyers represented Bull HN Information Systems in a federal age discrimination suit. Clients also pointed to the group's flourishing immigration practice.

## Band 3

## Bello, Black & Welsh LLP

**The Firm:** This labor and employment boutique was singled out for its "*cost-effectiveness and high levels of partner-client interaction.*" A collection of practitioners, formerly from some of the state's largest full-service firms, makes up this team, which was praised for the depth of its experience and expertise. Recent work has included averting a major strike by a large company's employees. Its other niche strengths include defending labor cases before the NLRB and dealing with complex Sarbanes-Oxley matters.

**The Lawyers:** **John Welsh** is an experienced and "*intellectually strong*" litigator who "*really sees the big picture and always opts for the most practical solutions to the problems.*" His colleague **Kenneth Bello** is adept at dealing with the complexities arising from traditional labor law issues. He impressed clients with his knack of "*sensing out our opposition and adopting the best approach*" and also earned plaudits for his "*tough and unfaltering negotiation skills.*"

Clients/Work Highlights: American Personnel; Malden Mills; Keane; ARIAD; Agfa-Gevaert; Biogen Idec and Pegasystems.

## Jackson Lewis

**The Firm:** The Boston office of this nationwide labor and employment boutique secured plaudits for the quality of its work. Sources recommended the team for its *"great service and incredible value for money"* and for the range of issues that it is able to cover. The group has carried out substantial work for insurance companies and was lauded for its *"invaluable work on behalf of management."* Clients are also impressed by the team's ability to draw on the national resources of the firm.

**The Lawyers:** The go-to name within the group is Boston managing partner **Andrew Pickett** (see p.1102), who handles employment litigation matters, noncompete agreements and arbitrations. Market sources described him as a *"polished performer with the raw talent to match."* He recently acted for a client in a major dispute involving severance pay issues and matters relating to reductions in force. Interviewees tipped **Tom Royall Smith** (see p.1104) as *"the driving force behind the team"* and characterized him as an astute rainmaker. They recognized him for his *"brilliance"* in major labor cases and referred to his *"terrific book of clients."* **Joan Ackerstein** (see p.1085) has an active litigation caseload and is another of the group's *"sharp tools within the box."*

## Mintz Levin Cohn Ferris Glovsky and Popeo PC

**The Firm:** This Boston team *"displays real energy and enthusiasm when it comes to labor and employment issues,"* commentators report. Its lawyers scored highly for their commitment to client service and for *"never trying to sugar-coat the situation – they always give us a balanced and pragmatic view."* The team regularly advises clients on wrongful termination suits, discrimination claims and wage and hour disputes. It also has an active employment counseling service and advises clients on their employment policies and contracts.

**The Lawyers:** **Robert Gault**'s (see p.1093) clients report that *"he is adroit at making judgment calls and always ensures that we understand the complex matters under consideration."* He advises the firm's corporate clients on the employment issues associated with M&A deals but also handles a busy caseload of discrimination claims. Litigation is at the heart of **Bret Cohen**'s (see p.1090) practice although peers also rated the caliber of his advice in the coun-

seling arena. He is widely tipped as *"a real rising star with a terrific manner"* who has won the adoration of his clients through his string of excellent results in court.

**Clients/Work Highlights:** The team continues to cater to the needs of the firm's corporate client base in all aspects of their M&A activities. A variety of industry and sector clients are represented including hi-tech and biotech, financial and professional services, hospitality, manufacturing and education.

## Robinson & Cole LLP

**The Firm:** The group debuts in the rankings this year following the impressive weight of feedback it received from the market. Much of its work is undertaken on behalf of healthcare sector clients including community healthcare centers and nursing homes. They are attracted to the team because its lawyers are *"always willing to help and will not rest until they are sure you understand what matters,"* say sources. The practice covers employment litigation, labor relations, immigration and employee benefits.

**The Lawyers:** A *"terrific lawyer and gentleman,"* **Jeffrey Hirsch**'s forthrightness and *"ability to get to the heart of the matter"* make him indispensable to clients. He is well known for his careful consideration of the dynamics of issues rather than just the legal angles and is *"a walking textbook for labor relations."* He recently acted for a large hospital in Connecticut as chief negotiator in union negotiations and bargaining agreements. According to one client, **Cathy Reuben** is *"straightforward to talk to and it's easy to formulate a strong working relationship with her."* She provides counseling, training and litigation defense for a host of employers and recently represented a healthcare-related company in a federal whistle-blower claim brought by a former employee.

## Other Notable Practitioners

**Judith Malone** (see p.1098) is a partner and member of Edwards Angell Palmer & Dodge LLP's litigation group. Clients praised her for *"her agreeable nature"* which they believe allows her to resolve issues with *"less hostility and better results."* She achieves statewide recognition for her work within the school and colleges field and represents clients such as Boston College, Northeastern University and Williams College. **Ilene Robinson Sunshine** of Sulli-

van & Worcester LLP is *"sharp as a knife"* and was highlighted by sources for her resourceful and pragmatic advice. As one interviewee commented: *"She looks for different avenues that will really help the client with their case."* Although she handles a varied caseload, discrimination work, particularly within the disabilities area, is the hallmark of her work. **Sharon Burger** from Nutter, McClennen & Fish, LLP received warm praise for her litigation-oriented practice. *"A sensible and knowledgeable practitioner who knows how to put the client at ease,"* she has undertaken a number of high-level noncompete litigation cases. She also continues to act for clients in other equal employment disputes involving claims of disability, age and race discrimination. **Lou Rodriques** (see p.1104) of Bingham McCutchen LLP is a name that sits comfortably with other leading players in the field, say sources. He frequently counsels clients on human resource matters, including the drafting and enforcement of noncompetition and confidentiality agreements and employment contracts. He is also involved in labor and employment mediation and arbitration. **Jay Shepherd** (see p.1106) at the Shepherd Law Group, P.C. is a *"strong lawyer who is really making his way up in this world."* He continues to impress sources for his expertise in the noncompete arena where he always *"cuts to the chase."* At Sullivan Weinstein & McQuay, **Jerome Weinstein** stood out as a *"thoughtful, earnest and mature"* labor and employment attorney. Particularly noted for his expertise in the healthcare sector, many sources dubbed him as their first port of call for dealing with the complex issues involving healthcare unions. Peers were quick to endorse the *"wisdom and terrific judgment he displays and his immense experience in the field."* **Ellen Kearns** (see p.1096) is of counsel at Foley & Lardner LLP and represents management in the full range of traditional labor and employment issues. These include NLRB proceedings, employment discrimination cases, wrongful discharge and wage and hour matters. Interviewees admire her as *"an experienced and thoroughly able practitioner."* **Sara Goldsmith Schwartz** (see p.1105) is managing partner of the employment law boutique Schwartz Hannum PC in Andover. She generated impressive feedback from sources, who cast her as a *"smart and tenacious lawyer. She has the drive and determination to succeed."*

# ENVIRONMENT

## Band 1

### Foley Hoag LLP

**The Firm:** "*Probably the premier environmental firm in the city,*" say market sources, agreeing that this group is a "*dominant force*" in the region. Maintaining its pole position, the team is admired for its "*strength, depth and sophistication,*" and the broad environmental expertise of its "*terrific lawyers.*" Clients profit from the group's flair in litigation, clean water and air, Superfund and brownfield redevelopment. This was evident throughout 2005, as the team handled some of the most important cases in the state. In this it works closely with the firm's real estate department, bringing an integrated approach to client needs. The group's considerable experience of advising on work in the energy sector is another drawing card for clients.

**The Lawyers:** **Laurie Burt** is one of the "*first generation of environmental lawyers in Boston,*" and remains a dean of the field. Her broad experience in federal and state hazardous waste, Superfund and redevelopment work makes her a "*first-class, worthy adviser*" in the eyes of peers. "*Top-notch*" **Seth Jaffe** is recommended as a "*talented litigator who is not afraid to take risks.*" Market sources point to his flair in hazardous waste and state regulatory matters, and clients particularly value his "*dynamic and creative*" style. **Adam Kahn** wins plaudits for his work on Superfund, permitting and energy matters: "*He really does his homework!*" say sources. **Martin Pentz** joins the team from Nutter, McClennen & Fish, bringing with him niche expertise in dovetailing insurance coverage litigation with environmental work. **Robert Sanoff** is a "*good strategist and negotiator*" who is recommended for litigious matters, particularly in Superfund work.

**Clients/Work Highlights:** Verizon; National Energy & Gas Transmission; The Newark Group; Allied Waste; American Ref-Fuel; Cornell Dubilier Electronics; NiSource and the Institute of Contemporary Art.

## Band 2

### Goodwin Procter LLP

See firm details p.1114

**The Firm:** This "*strong, capable*" group has risen to prominence on the strength of its skill in environmental litigation and a much-praised national reach. The workload straddles contaminated urban industrial sites, permitting, brownfield projects and environmental insurance work. The team was also noted for its expertise in the energy arena, and has proved to be particularly adept in nuclear power issues. It demonstrated its expertise recently acting for Cabot on the hazardous waste Ashtabula River and Fields Brook sites, the former a nationally important contaminated sediment site. It has also been involved in strategic development for negotiations with the state and federal trustees on natural resource damages. Other major highlights from 2005 include successfully negotiating groundwater contamination claims between two abutting landowners.

**The Lawyers:** The market consensus is that the "*outstanding*" **Christopher Davis** (see p.1091) thoroughly deserves his top spot in the table. Peers enjoy working with this "*smart and articulate*" individual who "*is constructive and excels in seizing the issues quickly.*" He has carved a particular reputation in federal and state Superfund and site remediation matters, and boasts experience in issues involving Chapter 21E, Massachusetts Contingency Plan and greenhouse gas initiatives. **Elise Zoli** (see p.1109) was recommended in this area for her work as an energy specialist, especially in connection with the nuclear power industry.

**Clients/Work Highlights:** The team has recently advised on a $900 million offshore LNG terminal project. Lawyers also represented a major private equity firm in its sale of a national laboratory company. Clients include Cabot; GE; Hewlett-Packard; Honeywell; Kraft; Newmont Mining; Prudential Financial; UniFirst; Unisys; Watts Water Technologies; Partners HealthCare System; SUEZ LNG; Entergy and Public Service of New Hampshire.

### McDermott Will & Emery

See firm details p.878

**The Firm:** McDermott Will & Emery is renowned for its work, not just across the country, but on an international plane. This "*top-shelf*" team navigates clients around an obstacle course of issues, including toxic tort and Superfund matters. The group was particularly recommended for its work in regulatory compliance, and this mixes well with a national OSHA practice. A "*firm and persuasive*" stance reinforces client confidence and helps this practice to stand out as "*impressive all the way around.*"

**The Lawyers:** "*One of the brightest around,*" **Jeffrey Bates** (see p.1086) enjoys an international standing in the environmental field. He is especially recognized for his work on insurance matters and valued for his "*practical, smart judgment.*" "*Low-key, patient, and precise*" **Susan Cooke** (see p.1090) commands the respect of contemporaries as "*one of the last generalists in environment.*" She continues to impress market sources with her skill in handling regulatory and environmental due diligence work.

**Clients/Work Highlights:** The team represents a diverse set of clients, from individuals and small businesses, to US and foreign multinationals, governments and NGOs. It is currently acting for Banca Arner in litigation against Argentina connected with that country's $150 billion sovereign debt default.

### Mintz Levin Cohn Ferris Glovsky and Popeo PC

**The Firm:** In the environmental sphere this superb firm is "*uniformly good in all aspects,*" say interviewees. Its growing practice is admired for doggedly and intelligently "*furthering the ultimate goal – rather than being caught up in the natural inertia, they bring a strategic view to problems.*" The group of "*detail-oriented*" lawyers handles a range of environmental work. It focuses on regulatory issues, federal and state permitting, and insurance matters, including issues related to brownfield sites and pipeline projects. It has been handling environmental matters in Massachusetts and Rhode Island for Cargill that are connected with the former operations of petroleum storage facilities. Another highlight was acting as primary environmental counsel to the drug store chain CVS in its national expansion plan, and the team also advises Mirant on complex permitting renewals relating to cooling water discharges from its Massachusetts power plants.

**The Lawyers:** Ralph Child (see p.1089) is regarded as an "*eminent lawyer*" whose forte lies in environmental regulatory work. Acclaimed for permitting, compliance and regulatory advice, his prominence is founded upon the combination of an "*extremely methodical and detail-oriented*" approach with "*great connections to the regulators*" from his previous position at the Massachusetts Department of Environmental Protection. He has counseled Duke Energy on interstate natural gas pipelines in Massachusetts, including complex federal and state permitting issues related to the offshore HubLine and Northeast Gateway lateral projects. According to peers **Jeffrey Porter** (see p.1102) is "*assertive on behalf of his clients.*" Clients themselves applaud a "*thoughtful and sharp*" stance that, coupled with an "*ability to grasp complex issues and distill them down,*" makes him "*excellent at moving deals forward.*" He is recommended for his regulatory expertise, particularly in relation to brownfield, Superfund, cleanup and redevelopment matters.

**Clients/Work Highlights:** GE; CVS; Mirant; Cargill; Duke Energy; Allied Domecq; Colony Realty Partners; Dunkin' Brands; Jefferson Properties (JPI) and Rohm and Haas.

## WilmerHale

See firm details p.1119

**The Firm:** This environmental practice provides clients with a national platform, and is especially admired for its expertise in a fusion of government enforcement and regulatory matters, alongside facilities development and permitting. Superfund and hazardous waste cases feature regularly in the workload, and environmental litigation also remains a forte. Of late, the team has been busy in investigation and remediation issues for National Grid, connected with former manufactured gas plant facilities and fly ash landfills. It advised Cape Wind Associates on environmental regulatory issues surrounding the development of the nation's first offshore wind energy generation facility. Other work includes acting for Nyacol Nano Technologies in the EPA's claim for past and future response costs at the Nyanza Superfund site in Ashland.

**The Lawyers:** Chairing the environmental group is the "*wonderful*" **Robert Kirsch** (see p.1096). The engine room of the practice, he is popular with peers, who value his "*reliable and forthright*" style and hail him as a "*fabulous litigator.*" Here, his skill is said to lie in "*bringing an effective voice of reason to potentially difficult conflicts.*" Kirsch's focus is on enforcement and related strategy work, and he commands particular respect for his mastery of Superfund and hazardous waste matters.

**Clients/Work Highlights:** The group acted for Massachusetts Technology Collaborative on the structuring and implementation of its Community Wind Collaborative, and continues to represent MSM Industries in cleanup issues. Other clients include Lowe's; Weaver's Cove Energy; Cabot; Casella Waste Systems; SUEZ Energy Generation and Trigen Energy.

## Band 3

## Anderson & Kreiger LLP

**The Firm:** Experience and commitment to environmental, land use and municipal law push this "*high-quality, respectable environment boutique*" up the tables this year. Best known for its work on the plaintiff side, the group attracts praise from the market as "*the go-to firm for any citizen's group for environmental concerns.*" Superfund, Chapter 21E, hazardous waste and oil contamination, insurance and wetlands matters are bread-and-butter work for these "*skilled litigators.*"

**The Lawyers:** "*If there's one lawyer in a boutique firm that I'd go to first, it's*" **Arthur Kreiger**, one source told researchers. A "*smart, sharp litigator,*" he is a fixture in the market, particularly when it comes to representing municipalities. Contemporaries were full of praise for his "*low-key, collegial and dogged*" approach to a variety of environmental matters, from Superfund to Chapter 21E work, and he duly rises in this year's rankings.

**Clients/Work Highlights:** The City of Cambridge and the towns of Acton, Wrentham, Norfolk, Belmont and Wakefield feature on the client list. The firm also acts for a number of oil companies.

## Goulston & Storrs

**The Firm:** Dovetailing nicely with the firm's top-class real estate practice, this Boston group was recommended for its excellence in brownfield redevelopment and environmental insurance work. Its focus remains heavily on the transactional side, including sales and purchases of contaminated property for large developers and institutions. Other typical work spans risk management of hazardous waste site cleanups, property damage and toxic tort claims. The team continues to provide environmental counsel to the Boston Redevelopment Authority with respect to the Boston Convention & Exhibition Center project, and represents National Development Associates in relation to the acquisition of significant portions of the Industri-Plex Superfund site.

**The Lawyers:** This team's driving force is the "*savvy*" **Ned Abelson**, who earns widespread recognition for his prowess in the cleanup of brownfield sites – for many he is "*the first name that comes to mind*" in this area. A "*diplomatic and polished*" demeanor and an informed business approach ensure him continuing top position. He is also recommended for his work in the insurance sector. **William Seuch** was lauded as "*second to none in asserting new issues to do with large projects.*" He wins applause for his transactional and redevelopment expertise.

**Clients/Work Highlights:** AvalonBay Communities; Beacon Capital Strategic Partners; Citizens Bank; Joan Fabrics Corporation; Lincoln Property; Nordblom Company and SR Weiner & Associates.

## Moehrke, Mackie & Shea, P.C.

**The Firm:** This "*small but highly regarded boutique*" effectively handles a wide range of environmental

issues. In particular, market sources identified the group as a dominant player in the field of solid and hazardous waste. Here, the Massachusetts-based firm recently won damages in the region of $3.2 million for KR Rezendes, for the unlawful prevention of a structural fill land-filling project. The firm has also been active in site hearings related to a construction and demolition debris recycling and processing facility, and has negotiated settlements for the remediation of a solid waste disposal site, to allow its redevelopment into residential condominiums.

**The Lawyers:** "*Practical and savvy*" **Thomas Mackie**'s standing in the sector depends largely on his skill in the landfill permitting and solid waste domains, where he is deemed an "*energetic litigator.*" His expertise was effectively utilized recently in the acquisition of buildings for Boston's largest recycling facility. He also negotiated Host Community Agreements for solid waste landfill expansion. **John Shea** is highly visible in land use matters, which encompass developing, permitting and wetlands work. He is admired by clients for his "*good counseling skills before local boards.*" This year he acted for the town of Cohasset and the Sandy Beach Association in settling a Department of Environmental Protection administrative enforcement action, which had threatened residential use of the beach. He has also advised on the environmental aspects of affordable housing projects for Beacon Residential Properties.

**Clients/Work Highlights:** Casella Waste Systems; Gypsum Recycling International; Allied Waste; Toll Brothers and Prolerized New England.

## Nutter, McClennen & Fish, LLP

**The Firm:** This solid, broad-based team handles a variety of environmental work, offering particular depth in litigation, enforcement, regulatory permitting and compliance matters. The firm's specialty in land use involves its environmental lawyers in close cooperation with the real estate team. Other typical work includes Superfund cases, brownfield redevelopment, and the restructuring of power plant facilities.

**The Lawyers:** Litigation specialist **Mary Ryan** is widely acknowledged as "*one of the most experienced environmental practitioners in the state.*" She is respected for her expertise at handling Superfund cases, as well as hazardous waste issues, enforcement actions, insurance coverage cases and land use matters. Sources consider her a "*sharp and dedicated*" attorney and "*a zealous advocate*" in the courtroom. Also highlighted during research was the "*careful and detail-oriented*" **Michael Leon**. He is recognized for his work on environmental regulatory, Superfund, and land use development issues, which is combined with strength in permitting.

**Clients/Work Highlights:** The team represents a mixture of public and private clients, predominantly based in the New England region. They range from municipalities and nonprofit institutions to manufacturers and national and international conglomerates. Its work with petroleum companies was particularly noted.

## Band 4

### Bernstein, Cushner & Kimmell PC

**The Firm:** Best known for its work for public interest groups, the firm's strength resides in a mixture of environmental, land use law and litigation expertise. This spans regulatory, permitting, risk counseling, brownfield development and municipalities issues. Recent highlights have included successfully representing a hazardous waste recycling company in an administrative lawsuit challenging its right to expand its operations.

**The Lawyers:** Dubbed *"very smart and very quick,"* **Kenneth Kimmell** is well recognized for his work on behalf of citizens' groups. Sources also appreciate him as a *"skilled advocate"* in land use matters.

**Clients/Work Highlights:** The firm acts for businesses, landowners/developers, towns and cities, state governments, environmental groups and other nonprofit organizations.

### Bowditch & Dewey LLP

**The Firm:** This team of *"impressive, capable attorneys"* continues to offer strength in environmental compliance work, government enforcement issues, litigation, and permitting associated with acquisitions. Noted for its strong relationship with regulators, the group regularly employs its expertise, which includes brownfield and remediation work, on behalf of both the nonprofit organizations of colleges and universities, and large corporate clients.

**The Lawyers: Robert Cox** is an *"astute"* attorney, adept at handling litigation and administrative appeals. He was especially recommended for his skill in Chapter 21E cleanup and brownfield matters. *"Deeply knowledgeable"* **Lauren Stiller Rikleen** is gaining profile for her compliance and enforcement expertise. *"One of the familiar faces"* in this market, she is well known in government circles.

**Clients/Work Highlights:** Harvard University; Boston College; Boston University; Children's Hospital Boston and Wyman-Gordon are among the group's representative clients.

### Brown Rudnick Berlack Israels LLP

**The Firm:** This group boasts expertise in a range of matters, with a focus on environmental development, due diligence, cleanup and remediation. It cooperates closely with the firm's energy practice, winning mandates to represent energy companies in facility expansions and other work. Regulatory enforcement also forms a portion of the workload, especially land use matters on wetlands. During the past year, highlights have included successfully representing the Massachusetts Bay Transportation Authority in front of the District Court in relation to decisions to construct sidewalk facilities for the disabled, and resolving environmental enforcement cases related to commuter railroad construction, for Jay Cashman and Balfour Beatty.

**The Lawyers: Stephen Leonard** is the bedrock of the firm's environmental practice. He brings with him a talent for complex government regulatory matters, and draws acclaim as *"an excellent litigator and compliance lawyer."* He recently acted for Alliance of Automobile Manufacturers in challenging the Commonwealth of Massachusetts' attempt at adopting carbon dioxide vehicle emission standards.

**Clients/Work Highlights:** The firm represents a mixture of clients, including developers, state agencies, manufacturers, municipalities and individuals.

### Other Notable Practitioners

DLA Piper's loss is Sugarman, Rogers, Barshak & Cohen, PC's gain in the form of **Lisa Goodheart**, who has established a name as a *"terrific litigator."* Admired for her persistent and aggressive style, *"she is the quintessential advocate for your position,"* clients enthuse. She has cultivated a particular niche in cost recovery actions, enforcement matters, permit appeals, and insurance coverage disputes. **Donald Anglehart** of Gadsby Hannah LLP is also recognized for his skill in litigation and extensive experience in enforcement actions, permitting and remediation of contaminated property. This includes acting for the US EPA, Massachusetts Department of Environmental Protection, and Massachusetts Office of the Attorney General in the defense of enforcement cases. Previously the leading light of Choate Hall & Stewart's environment team, **Hamilton Hackney** (see p.1094) has recently joined the Boston office of Greenberg Traurig LLP. He is known in the market as a *"solid, knowledgeable"* attorney, who *"asks great questions and focuses on the right things."*

# HEALTHCARE

## Band 1

### McDermott Will & Emery

See firm details p.878

**The Firm:** The firm is credited with housing *"one of the nation's finest healthcare practices,"* a reputation which is upheld by this *"redoubtable"* ten-member team operating out of the Boston office. Each attorney has a *"different and unique practice,"* which ensures that the group can provide services across the gamut of industry issues. Clients point to the team's *"local industry familiarity"* as well as its ability to draw on nationwide resources, stating: *"It has successfully formulated a winning combination."* Regulatory and transactional work for a sophisticated clientele of leading healthcare providers forms the bedrock of the practice. The team also advises on cutting-edge issues such as concierge medicine, e-health technology and financings, and is seen acting for academic medical and research centers. Clients are united in praising the team's *"extremely responsive and accessible"* members, asserting that the proactive group *"always ensures we are kept ahead of the curve."*

**The Lawyers:** Although he is capable of *"wearing many hats,"* **Michael Blau**'s (see p.1087) signature area is currently concierge medicine. He represents for-profit and nonprofit healthcare organizations, bringing a *"creative approach"* to the table. A *"first-class lawyer who always fights a good fight,"* he is also experienced in organizing and financing health-related companies. He recently acted for a major national health insurer in rewriting its entire insurance policy to be implemented in 50 states. **Chris Jedrey** (see p.1095) is billed as *"one of the most pragmatic and well-rounded healthcare attorneys in the city – if not nationally."* A lawyer who *"knows how to close a deal without floundering,"* he advises clients on a range of regulatory matters, with a focus on federal, state and local tax exemption requirements, charitable trust matters and corporation law. He also represents a variety of academic medical centers. Market observers emphasize *"his charming character, veracity and high standard of ethics."* **Stephen Bernstein** (see p.1087) shines as an *"extraordinarily responsive"* lawyer who can guide clients through the minefield of health law issues. He specializes in e-health, where his *"resourceful mind"* is best put to the test. For example, he acted for Massachusetts eHealth Collaborative and carried out work for Harvard University. He also advises academic medical centers, hospitals and multispecialty physician practice groups (including tax-exempt organizations) on transactional and other matters. An adviser who *"always keeps his eye on the client's goals and the best way to achieve them,"* **Peter Braun** (see p.1088) is *"down-to-earth, pragmatic and reasonable."* Recent matters include corporate restructurings, joint ventures and tax-exempt bond financings. New entrant to the tables **Charles Buck** (see p.1088) is identified as a promising talent with an ability that belies his age. In a unique venture, he assisted Quality Health Solutions in designing and developing a central command center staffed by physicians to remotely monitor intensive care unit patients through real-time video connections.

**Clients/Work Highlights:** Genentech; IMS Health; Harvard University; Pediatric Physicians' Organization at Children's; Massachusetts Eye and Ear Infirmary; Caritas Medical Group; Dana-Farber/Partners CancerCare; HealthOne Care System; Saint Peter's University Hospital and ChartOne.

## Ropes & Gray LLP

See firm details p.1117

**The Firm:** *"One of the state's finest"* is the market summary of this nationally renowned healthcare practice. The firm's regional strength is enhanced by its national capabilities and it enjoys well-established relationships with prestigious clients such as Children's Hospital Boston and NYU Medical Center. It has built up a formidable reputation for advising on managed care plans and provider networks, alongside expertise in bond financing, disaffiliations and joint ventures. In addition to counseling hospitals and physician practices on corporate and regulatory affairs, the team also advises a range of nonprofit entities. Its workload in this field amounts to one of the largest tax-exempt organization practices in the USA, where clients include academic medical centers and troubled institutions. The firm also offers a well-regarded HIPAA compliance service. Clients praise the *"exceptionally well-seasoned"* team, citing the diversity of its expertise and its experience representing institutions on a national scale as *"huge advantages."*

**The Lawyers:** Chair of the healthcare group **Michele Garvin** (see p.1093) *"practices at the highest echelons of the field,"* according to sources. Clients say her reputation as a leader derives from *"knowledge acquired from years of experience, the highest standards of professionalism and ethics and a real sense of social consciousness."* She is noted for the *"intelligent approach"* she brings to problems, and she advises numerous children's hospitals in the state. **Jeffrey Heidt** (see p.1094) possesses *"a boundless level of knowledge and expertise,"* which he put into play advising on the Tufts healthcare and transitional plan. Community hospitals and for-profit hospital chains are also the beneficiaries of his *"creative mode of thinking."* **William Knowlton** (see p.1097) is described as *"extremely smart and capable"* by clients, who also say: *"He really understands the social implications of the work he carries out."* He brings his corporate background and his nonprofit tax law expertise to bear on regulatory and other healthcare matters, working with state medical centers and physician groups. **Anne Ogilby** (see p.1101) is *"incredibly sharp when it comes to the law, as well as being pleasant to deal with,"* say clients. Well connected in charitable circles, she carried out tax-exempt financings for numerous organizations last year. Her long history of carrying out hospital work is admired by market sources, who also highlight her advocacy skills. **Eve Brunts** (see p.1088) specializes in reimbursement and compliance matters for the pharmaceutical industry. She debuts in the rankings this year as a *"cordial, technically proficient and professional adviser."* **Dan Roble** (see p.1103) enjoys a preeminent reputation in the field and is labeled by clients and peers alike as *"a force to be reckoned with."* He focuses on the nonprofit sector and the past twelve months have seen him undertake numerous Medicare appeals.

**Clients/Work Highlights:** The team recently acted in a breakthrough Medicare reimbursement matter, enabling Caritas St. Elizabeth's Medical Center and Milton Hospital to qualify for exemption as new skilled nursing facilities. Other clients include academic medical centers, managed care organizations, physician practice groups, healthcare technology, biomedical companies and community hospitals.

## Band 2

## Brown Rudnick Berlack Israels LLP

**The Firm:** This healthcare team *"never gives you reason to look elsewhere,"* according to clients. A *"well-rounded"* practice is complemented by an eight-member team, highly endorsed by clients, who were quick to point to the clearly visible *"breadth and depth in the team's members."* Strong work within the regulatory arena was an aspect of the practice highlighted by sources, while specialties that gained further acclaim were M&A, affiliations and joint ventures for private medical institutions, public entities and tax-exempt. With the group's ability to call on resources in Boston, Providence and Hartford, clients were particularly impressed with its *"responsiveness and ability to solve all problems."*

**The Lawyers:** *"One of the best and brightest,"* **Lawrence Litwak** has *"the sort of personality that is really skewed toward the interests of the clients."* He has been busy acting for major client Boston Medical Center, handling an assortment of issues, including physician contracts and relationships, affiliation agreements with other hospitals and complex physician conduct issues. Other matters include determining federal and state funding of intergovernmental structures. He was distinguished for his experience in the field, with peers stating: *"He is definitely one of the lawyers of the old school."* He has also been involved in negotiating the sale of two nursing homes to a nonprofit company. **Paul Shaw** enters the rankings this year due to his work in the regulatory litigation side of the practice. He represents healthcare clients involved in criminal, civil and administrative fraud and abuse investigations and was praised by clients for the *"careful consideration he puts into our issues."*

**Clients/Work Highlights:** Community and academic hospitals; clinics and community health centers; home health providers; physician group practices; long-term care and assisted living facilities; medical billing companies; ambulance companies and integrated healthcare networks and systems.

## Mintz Levin Cohn Ferris Glovsky and Popeo PC

**The Firm:** *"A true forerunner in the area,"* this healthcare group was received in high esteem by the market for its work in the sector. Both for-profit and nonprofit companies providing healthcare services are devoted to this group, on both a local and a national level. Clients were quick to point out the *"creative and strategic mindset"* that the lawyers exhibit and the *"deep relationships they have constructed,"* particularly in the hospital systems, managed care organizations and long-term care provider professions. Of further appeal were the team's expertise and relationships with state and federal agencies that regulate the industry, making them *"always in the loop with the latest developments."*

**The Lawyers:** **Stephen Weiner** is an *"exceedingly smart and savvy lawyer."* Extolled for the diversity of clients he represents, he was moreover recommended as an *"incredibly effectual"* attorney, particularly in the representation of large healthcare organizations. He frequently advises on hospital structuring and restructuring work.

**Clients/Work Highlights:** Brigham and Women's/Faulkner Hospitals; Massachusetts General Hospital; North Shore Medical Center; Newton-Wellesley Hospital; McLean Hospital; Spaulding Rehabilitation Hospital Network; Dana-Farber/Partners CancerCare and Partners Community Healthcare.

## Other Notable Practitioners

**Christine Solt** was regarded as the *"anchor of the healthcare practice"* at Choate Hall & Stewart. She predominantly services the needs of the firm's large corporate and litigation clients, who regarded her *"sharp intellect and broad-ranging knowledge"* of healthcare matters as appealing. Noted for her ability with mental health privacy information, she focuses upon government enforcement matters and has recently advised on human research issues, including clinical trials. **David Spackman** (see p.1107) exhibits *"fantastic collegial skills"* according to commentators. Housed in Greenberg Traurig LLP's Boston office he possesses extensive regional and national experience representing healthcare clients involved in organization changes and joint ventures statewide. Sources articulated his expertise includes dealing with hospital system mergers, sales, acquisitions and reorganizations.

# INTELLECTUAL PROPERTY

## Band 1

### Fish & Richardson P.C.
See firm details p.1113

**The Firm:** This specialist IP outfit is holding its own as one of the most successful boutiques remaining in the region. In *"a market that lacks an abundance of highly trained IP lawyers,"* its outstanding experts *"fill a niche"* in Massachusetts, onlookers remarked. With a *"well-earned reputation for technical skill,"* the IP team contains lawyers of *"an extremely high caliber"* who *"can handle a deep bench of cases."* A network of offices across the USA supports these *"established and experienced"* Boston players. The group was especially commended for its excellent work on patent applications and prosecutions, and in patent infringement litigation. It offers an impressive range of experience in the life sciences, electronics and biotechnology sectors.

**The Lawyers:** **Robert Hillman** (see p.1095) is a *"very methodical, highly intelligent engineer."* Lauded for his *"intellectual and strategic"* approach, he is admired for his scientific knowledge and *"remains the dean of the pure patent litigators in Boston."* *"One of the best IP attorneys in the USA,"* **Frank Porcelli** (see p.1102) is *"an absolute class act,"* sources enthuse. *"Very, very smart,"* he enjoys an excellent reputation for his knowledge of a range of IP matters. **Frank Scherkenbach** (see p.1105) is a *"terrific"* lawyer who is *"making his mark"* in the field of patent infringement litigation. He was especially recommended for his experience of representing clients in the medical devices industry. **Gilbert Hennessey** (see p.1094) is also well known and well reputed in the market.

**Clients/Work Highlights:** Mayo Foundation for Medical Education and Research; Intel; SeaChange International; Rollerblade and Massachusetts General Hospital.

### WilmerHale
See firm details p.1119

**The Firm:** This excellent firm enjoys *"great brand recognition"* among clients in the life sciences and technology arenas; its *"stellar"* IP group is no exception. The team is primarily recommended for its work in patent litigation, with clients praising the courtroom skills of attorneys who are *"litigators first and technical experts second."* Its patent lawyers were particularly valued for their ability to *"explain complicated issues very simply;"* one source even claimed that they could *"take off the judge's head, pour in the technical knowledge and screw it back on!"* With its high number of technically trained IP experts in-house, the department also picked up plaudits for its *"strong level of patent expertise and knowledge."* In 2005 the group was lead litigation counsel in patent trials in federal courts in Delaware, California, Massachusetts, Texas, Nevada and New York, and in the ITC in Washington, DC. It has also coordinated patent litigation in the UK, Japan and Germany.

**The Lawyers:** *"True star player"* **William Lee** (see p.1097) continues to enjoy overwhelming market approval for his skill in patent infringement litigation. An *"outstanding and exceptionally smart"* practitioner, he enjoys *"a high level of success"* on a global scale. This is attributed to his knack of *"relating to judges and juries"* with his *"incredible ability to take complex situations and distill them into simple explanations."* Clients also dubbed him a *"great strategist"* with an *"easygoing and accessible approach."* *"Skilled and talented"* **David Bassett** (see p.1086) is admired for his experience in pharmaceutical biotech cases and ANDA patent litigation. Interviewees commended his courtroom skills and the *"quality of his briefs."* **Peter Dichiara** (see p.1091) is chair of the firm's Nanotechnology Practice Group and offers specialized expertise in the electronics, communications, storage and computer industries. He wins plaudits for his ability to litigate patents and trade secrets. **Wayne Stoner** (see p.1107) co-heads the IP litigation group. A *"straight shooter who speaks in simple terms,"* he is *"smart and experienced"* with good judgment and a *"client-focused but laid-back"* style. **Mark Selwyn** (see p.1106) also won praise for his client communication skills: *"He pulls everything together in ways that we can understand."* **Donald Steinberg** (see p.1107), meanwhile, is known for his work with patents, and is especially well regarded in the fields of computing and electrical engineering.

**Clients/Work Highlights:** The team recently won a summary judgment for GlaxoSmithKline in the US District Court for the District of New Jersey, in a Hatch-Waxman Act case. It also won an appeal before the Federal Court of Appeals for Gen-Probe, which invalidated a patent issued to Enzo for DNA probe testing. Other clients include Wyeth; Intel; Procter & Gamble; GM; EMC; Boston Scientific; GE; Disney; Biogen; Nantero; Broadcom; STMicroelectronics and Analog Devices.

## Band 2

### Foley Hoag LLP

**The Firm:** This established firm is renowned for its *"deep technical expertise"* in the life sciences sector. Its strong IP team specializes in the biotech field, where it advises important clients in the region and beyond. The group also offers advice to clients in the hi-tech, telecom and retail industries. Sources rated the firm especially highly for its patent prosecution application and opinion expertise, and it also undertakes some patent infringement litigation work.

**The Lawyers:** Having started as a general commercial litigator 20 years ago, **Donald Ware** now knows so much about biotechnology that *"people assume he has a PhD."* Commended as *"a pleasure to deal with,"* he was described to researchers as *"a great all-around lawyer"* who is *"smart, creative and persistent."* **Beth Arnold** is a *"top-notch"* patent prosecutor who is admired for her *"wonderful biotech expertise."* Her strong leadership skills and efficient approach were also highlighted, and she is a popular point of referral among peers. **Claire Laporte** was visible in the medical devices and technology arena during 2005. She is credited with building up that practice and achieving good results in recent biotech cases.

**Clients/Work Highlights:** Becton, Dickinson and Company; Genzyme; Pfizer; CR Bard; Harvard University; Biogen Idec; QLT Inc and MIT.

### Goodwin Procter LLP
See firm details p.1114

**The Firm:** Goodwin Procter *"fields an excellent team"* in the IP arena, according to interviewees. The *"responsive"* group is especially recommended for its patent litigation practice, while clients spoke highly of lawyers who are *"exceptional in the courtroom"* and skilled at *"simplifying complex terms."* In 2005 the department was boosted by the arrival of patent prosecution specialists from Testa Hurwitz & Thibeault, alongside lateral hires from other firms across the region. The group advises on electrical, computer science, software, chemistry and biology-related matters, among others, and it was particularly recommended for its work with generic companies in the pharmaceutical industry. For example, the team recently demonstrated noninfringement of Teva's generic fosinopril after a bench trial. The case bears upon a market worth $500 million. Owing to the firm's strong finance prowess, the IP group also regularly provides advice to players in the financial services sector.

**The Lawyers:** *"A good writer who is excellent in the courtroom,"* **Douglas Kline** (see p.1096) *"converses equally well with the board of directors and the jury."* Valued by clients for his background in mechanical engineering, he is *"quick to grasp key concepts"* and wins praise for his strategic approach. **Paul Ware** (see p.1108) is recommended for his industry experience and strong presence in the courtroom. Sources value his *"tough"* response to opposing counsel and his *"concise delivery of arguments."* **Stephen Charkoudian** (see p.1089) is *"extremely good"* at a range of technology matters. He acts for a range of pharmaceutical companies and is also noted for handling IP aspects of the firm's corporate transactions. *"Hands-on litigator"* **John Englander** (see p.1102) also attracted praise for his technical engineering knowledge, while his *"intellectual capacity and presentation skills are top-notch,"* say interviewees. In particular, sources highlight his ability to *"fathom out key arguments and deliver them cohesively to management teams."* **Steven Frank** (see p.1092) continues to be endorsed by the market for his *"great business sense."* He is especially recommended for his work in IP licensing matters.

**Clients/Work Highlights:** The group successfully represented Inverness Medical Innovations in a series of injunctive actions against Pfizer for, among other things, infringement of patents related to pregnancy test strips. In a recent jury trial, it successfully defended Applied Materials against allegations that its new ion implantation machine infringed Axcelis' patent. It also obtained summary judgment for Chase Manhattan in a case involving its use of the mark Chase Freedom. Other clients include GE; Teva Pharmaceuticals; Boston Scientific; VICOR; Hewlett-Packard; PepsiCo; Cartier; Montblanc; Colgate-Palmolive; ViaCell; Patlex; Henkel and Roll Systems.

## Band 3

### Choate Hall & Stewart

**The Firm:** This firm is said to be *"making strides"* across the region in a number of areas, due in part to its absorption of lawyers from the now defunct Testa Hurwitz & Thibeault. The IP group continues to win plaudits for its *"high technical ability"* and for *"effectively utilizing its scientifically trained lawyers"* to the clients' advantage. The team's diet includes biotechnology, chemistry, engineering and materials science cases, and it also works closely alongside the firm's corporate and litigation experts. It was primarily recommended for its patent prosecution work, although market sources encounter the group *"more and more"* in patent litigation matters, and it also offers trademark expertise.

**The Lawyers:** *"Esteemed litigator"* **Robert Frank** is a *"smart and thorough"* attorney who is especially admired for his excellent judgment and attention to detail. *"Outstanding"* in the courtroom, his patent infringement expertise and experience of cases in the life sciences and pharmaceutical sectors were particularly highlighted. **Sam Pasternack**, the department founder, is commended for his patent prosecution work and noted for his strength in materials science cases. He *"understands the technology,"* say sources, and has enormous experience in writing patent applications and dealing with the patent office. A *"great scientist with a nice practice,"* **Brenda Jarrell** is *"smart and well regarded in the chemistry field."* Her patent prosecution counseling skills impressed interviewees. **John Lanza** brings a good reputation with him from his time at Testa Hurwitz & Thibeault. An active patent prosecutor, he is lauded by clients for his *"technology know-how"* and personable approach.

**Clients/Work Highlights:** MIT; Microsoft; Hewlett-Packard; EMC; Harvard University and Massachusetts General Hospital.

### Proskauer Rose LLP

See firm details p.1551

**The Firm:** Following the 2004 arrival of Steven Bauer, this focused IP team continues to expand, along with the firm's Massachusetts presence. The team in Boston is noted for its emphasis on patent and trademark protection and litigation in the technology sector. Its portfolio includes work for companies in the electronics, semiconductor, medical device, biotechnology, alternative energy, software, financial services, and textile industries. The depart-

ment is also noted for its ability to handle technology collaboration and dispute resolution matters. Clients value the support of a national network of offices offering an extensive range of IP-related expertise.

**The Lawyers:** **Steven Bauer** (see p.1086) remains the *"number-one choice"* of a number of companies in the region. *"Results-oriented, pragmatic and flexible,"* he was recommended by clients for being *"in tune with our needs,"* while peers admire a combative courtroom style that, many believe, makes him *"the litigator that clients really want."* *"User-friendly and responsive,"* **Joseph Capraro** (see p.1089) is said to be a technically strong and *"client-oriented"* attorney, who is also *"a great advocate."*

**Clients/Work Highlights:** RSA Security; Descartes Systems Group; Bessemer Venture Partners; Helicos Biosciences; MKS Instruments; Hypertherm and Candela.

### Wolf, Greenfield & Sacks PC

**The Firm:** This traditional IP boutique boasts well-respected practitioners and *"a good spectrum of clients"* at the midmarket level. The group covers a wide range of sectors, offering advice on matters related to biotechnology, electrical and mechanical engineering, chemical technologies, computer science and medicine. Interviewees were impressed with the *"high technical quality"* on offer, and the seamless way the group combines engineers, scientists and lawyers on IP transactions, patent prosecutions and litigation. It is also rated for its expertise in trademarks, copyright and licensing strategy.

**The Lawyers:** Jason Honeyman is the firm's managing partner. He also chairs its mechanical practice group and is a member of the IP transactions, litigation and trademark and copyright groups.

**Clients/Work Highlights:** The firm acts for a range of clients including those providing athletic equipment; bioinformatics; clinical diagnostics; computer software; electromechanical devices; medical devices; nanotechnology pharmaceuticals and immunology.

### Other Notable Practitioners

**Thomas Turano** continues to enjoy a good profile in the region. His firm, Kirkpatrick & Lockhart Nicholson Graham LLP, increased its IP workload during 2005; however, market sources consider him to be far and away its *"standout individual"* in the field, and *"in a league of his own there."*

# LITIGATION

# GENERAL COMMERCIAL

| Litigation: General Commercial |
| --- |
| **Leading Firms** |

**1** GOODWIN PROCTER LLP *Boston*

   ROPES & GRAY LLP *Boston*

   WILMERHALE *Boston*

**2** BINGHAM MCCUTCHEN LLP *Boston*

   FOLEY HOAG LLP *Boston*

   GOULSTON & STORRS *Boston*

   MCDERMOTT WILL & EMERY *Boston*

   TODD & WELD LLP *Boston*

**3** CHOATE HALL & STEWART *Boston*

   FOLEY & LARDNER LLP *Boston*

   HOLLAND & KNIGHT LLP *Boston*

   MINTZ LEVIN *Boston*

   NUTTER, MCCLENNEN & FISH, LLP *Boston*

   SHERIN AND LODGEN LLP *Boston*

| Leading Individuals |
| --- |

**Senior Statesmen**

  GALVANI Paul *Ropes & Gray LLP*

  MAHONY Gael *Holland & Knight LLP*

  POPEO R Robert *Mintz Levin*

  RENEHAN Richard *Goulston & Storrs*

**1** DONOVAN John *Ropes & Gray LLP*

  KEATING Michael *Foley Hoag LLP*

  LUKEY Joan *WilmerHale*

  TODD Owen *Todd & Weld LLP*

  WARE JR Paul *Goodwin Procter LLP*

**2** FELTER John *Goodwin Procter LLP*

  KOCIUBES Joseph *Bingham McCutchen LLP*

  LEIBENSPERGER Edward *McDermott Will & Emery*

  MONTGOMERY John *Ropes & Gray LLP*

  PEARLSTEIN Mark *McDermott Will & Emery*

  PIERCE Rudolph *Goulston & Storrs*

**3** ARROWOOD Lisa *Todd & Weld LLP*

  BARSHAK Edward *Sugarman, Rogers*

  CARROLL James *Skadden, Arps*

  DOWNS J Anthony *Goodwin Procter LLP*

  FABIANO John *WilmerHale*

  GLEASON Daniel *Nutter, McClennen & Fish*

  HALSTON Daniel *WilmerHale*

  LANE Roger *Greenberg Traurig LLP*

  MULDOON JR Robert *Sherin and Lodgen LLP*

  PARSIGIAN Kenneth *Goodwin Procter LLP*

  POSS Stephen *Goodwin Procter LLP*

  TUTEUR Michael *Foley & Lardner LLP*

## Band 1

### Goodwin Procter LLP

See firm details p.1114

**The Firm:** This top-notch player boasts a strong litigation presence across the region and beyond. Clients rate the team for its *"adept handling of complex matters,"* including sophisticated securities, white-collar crime and products liability cases. *"Skilled and seasoned"* partners employ a *"well-prepared, methodical"* approach, and sources also reserved much praise for the large team of efficient and motivated junior lawyers supporting them behind the scenes. Together these *"talented"* attorneys know *"what we need and get to the heart of the issue,"* enthuse clients, with one even claiming that they are *"beyond crossing."* While a proportion of its caseload spins off from Goodwin Procter's excellent transactional practice, the team attracts a great deal of work on the merit of its courtroom skills and *"creative"* approach to contentious matters. Typical work includes conducting trials, hearings and arbitrations; it also defends clients in enforcement matters and investigations, and provides counsel on alternative dispute resolution, litigation avoidance and risk management.

**The Lawyers:** *"Extremely bright and capable,"* **Paul Ware** (see p.1108) remains this team's *"banner trial man."* He has built an impressive track record of success in nationally important cases, and is valued by clients for his previous experience in the US Attorney's office. **Kenneth Felter** (see p.1092) has a *"low-key, careful"* style, and an *"extraordinarily thorough and methodical"* approach. Sources highlighted his skill in *"addressing litigation needs with the greatest insight,"* and providing support in a professional and efficient manner. He recently acted for the Boston Professional Hockey Association in a case concerning the authority of Massachusetts to tax the Boston Bruins' revenues from gate receipts, broadcast rights and logos and trademark licenses. **Anthony Downs'** (see p.1091) ability to *"out-maneuver the other side"* was brought to the attention of researchers. A lawyer who *"easily absorbs the details of a case,"* his speed in *"understanding the really complicated financial aspects"* of disputes is particularly valued by clients. Recent work has included successfully representing an affiliate of Wheelabrator Technologies in a complex contract suit against the Connecticut Resources Recovery Authority. **Kenneth Parsigian** (see p.1101) wins plaudits for his skill in handling mass tort actions, which often take him outside of the state. Particularly noted for his work in complex class actions involving unions and groups of hospitals, he has been representing approximately 300,000 individuals in Massachusetts who purchased Marlboro Lights cigarettes during the 1990's. **Stephen Poss** (see p.1103) is admired for his work in complex commercial contract disputes and practice breaches, including the theft of trade secrets. He also wins praise for his work on securities litigation and corporate governance matters, particularly those relating to Sarbanes-Oxley. In the field of white-collar crime litigation, **David Apfel** (see p.1085) is a *"hard-working and detail-oriented"* attorney who provides a *"good mix of the intellectual and the practical."* He acted for Harvard University in a major civil FCA case, which began in 1999 and resulted, in 2005, in the government's decision not to bring criminal charges against the original targets. **Joseph Savage's** (see p.1105) *"wonderfully seasoned judgment"* is a major drawing card for clients.

Another white-collar crime expert, equally adept at the defense and prosecution sides, Savage is admired for his *"wealth of experience"* and *"ability to put clients at ease."* **Brian Pastuszenski** (see p.1102) is recognized for his work on securities class action and stockholder litigation defense. He has been busy of late representing numerous publicly traded companies that were sued, along with roughly 300 other issuers, in the IPO Allocation Class Action Litigation, currently pending in New York City's federal court. **James Dittmar** (see p.1091) is the third of a trio of highly regarded securities litigators at the firm. He is experienced at handling fraud class action work, and represents a slew of financial services firms, including a number of prominent players in the mutual funds industry. A recent highlight was defending Gables Residential Trust and its Board of Trustees in securities class action litigation brought in Maryland State Court, challenging the $2.8 billion acquisition of Gables by ING Clarion Partners.

**Clients/Work Highlights:** The litigation group represents leading companies in the financial services, life sciences, technology, software, manufacturing, mining, defense, consumer products, communications and real estate sectors. It has also acted for prominent REITs and mutual fund groups during 2005.

### Ropes & Gray LLP

See firm details p.1117

**The Firm:** This firm is one of the top three in Boston that rise *"head and shoulders above the rest"* in litigation. The team at Ropes & Gray is well regarded for its *"great depth of experience"* in a range of matters, provided by a deep bench of excellent trial lawyers. Clients appreciate these partners for their *"integrity and professionalism."* As one source put it, they are *"both sensitive and wise,"* with a *"great way of communicating to clients."* In addition to handling general commercial disputes, the department offers expertise in government enforcement, securities and insurance litigation. It is commended for its ability to collaborate effectively with the firm's other departments and its wider network of offices. These include bases in Washington, DC and New York, which help to ensure that clients are well served in matters requiring attention outside of the state.

**The Lawyers:** **John Donovan** (see p.1091) is lauded for his general commercial litigation expertise, and is also known as a specialist in securities-related matters. Recommended for his knack of *"genuinely understanding the problem from the client's perspective,"* his *"calm, professional"* manner is matched by *"excellent business sense."* He is particularly rated for his advisory work with boards of directors, and sources note that *"his persuasive skills on paper are just terrific."* **John Montgomery** (see p.1100) brings *"a calm, smooth"* demeanor and *"great judgment"* to the table – *"he maintains his perspective at all times,"* say interviewees. His easygoing style translates well to the courtroom where he has achieved some phenomenal results, peers admit, owing in part to his *"exceptionally thorough preparation."* Veteran litigator **Paul Galvani** (see p.1093) is widely acknowledged as *"one of the deans of the Boston commercial litigation Bar."* Admired for his outstanding trial experience, he is dubbed *"the real deal"* in the courtroom, particularly for environmental matters such as contaminated brown water and cleanup cases. He is also noted for his arbitration work. **Michael Fee** (see p.1092) maintains a great reputation in the field of white-collar crime and government investigations. A *"highly effective lawyer,"* he regularly defends both individuals and institutions, including manufacturers, hospitals and pharmaceutical companies. *"Topnotch"* **Joan McPhee** (see p.1099) is also highly regarded for her government enforcement and white-collar crime practice. She acts for a broad range of institutional clients, including those in the healthcare and financial services sectors. **Brien O'Connor** (see p.1101) garners praise for his *"creative and tenacious"* approach to securities litigation. Particularly recommended for his experience with clients in the pharmaceutical sector, his experience of working for the US Attorney's office was also highlighted to researchers. Sources also rate his *"easy manner"* and *"excellent client relation skills."* Up-and-coming individual **Joshua Levy** (see p.1098) is an *"able young trial lawyer"* whose *"dogged tenacity"* and *"creative approach"* are winning him fans in the white-collar crime sphere.

**Clients/Work Highlights:** The team regularly acts for clients in the healthcare and life sciences sectors, including academic medical centers. It also has a strong base in the financial services industry, where it is increasingly visible, acting for funds and other heavyweight names, including Allianz, Putnam, Scudder, Pimco, MFS and American Express. In 2005, the team successfully assisted Lloyd's against

the owner of the World Trade Center in a New York jury trial. As was widely reported, this saved Lloyd's the sum of $3.5 billion. It also represented Blue Cross & Blue Shield of Rhode Island in high-profile state and federal investigations into relationships between corporate organizations and Rhode Island lawmakers.

## WilmerHale
See firm details p.1119

**The Firm:** This firm is *"on top of its game,"* sources enthuse, with some even considering it the *"center of gravity"* for litigation in the Boston market. Onlookers are impressed by the group's *"strong bench of trial lawyers"* and the depth of knowledge possessed by its senior partners. In the words of one, the litigation team comprises *"extremely bright, strategic and practical"* lawyers who can be relied upon to *"put up a good fight"* in the courtroom. They also win plaudits for being *"skilled writers."* As one client noted, *"their first drafts are equivalent to the final versions produced by some other firms!"* The firm is especially well known for work in the life sciences, pharmaceuticals and technology sectors. Renowned for its prowess in the IP field, it has a *"strong trial presence"* in a range of litigation matters, including white-collar crime, government enforcement and securities matters.

**The Lawyers:** **Joan Lukey** (see p.1098) is an enormous force in the courtroom, according to interviewees, and was highly recommended for her corporate governance advisory work. An *"articulate and persuasive"* advocate, she is much admired in the fields of general commercial litigation and employment law. **John Fabiano** (see p.1092) is *"flash on his feet"* but keeps his *"eye on the ball,"* claim market sources. He was recommended as a *"solid and trustworthy"* choice for a range of commercial disputes. **Daniel Halston** (see p.1094) is admired as a great communicator who *"takes the time to explain things concisely."* His *"logical"* approach to securities fraud, class actions and fiduciary claims is popular with clients. **Karen Green** (see p.1094) combines a *"brilliant and focused"* approach to federal crime investigations with a *"matter-of-fact"* style. She is particularly renowned for her work on alleged healthcare frauds. **Robert Keefe** (see p.1096) is *"an incredibly dedicated"* white-collar crime specialist whose *"easygoing and friendly"* manner is much appreciated by sources. He promotes a *"calm, practical"* approach, which *"takes the emotion out"* of stressful matters. His impressive track record of success in cases against the government was noted by interviewees. *"Effective litigator"* **John Batter** (see p.1086) was highlighted for his skill at handling disputes related to complex securitizations. Clients value his ability to *"distill a lot of information into the points he wants the judges to focus on."* He is also rated for being *"tough when he needs to be and measured when appropriate."* *"Fabulous advocate"* **Jeffrey Rudman** (see p.1104) is *"a great strategist"* who also enjoys a *"tremendous reputation"* for his experience in the securities field. *"Bright, entertaining and confident,"* his *"flamboyant"* style in the courtroom is matched by *"an impressive understanding of the judiciary"* and an appreciation of the perspective from

the boardroom.

**Clients/Work Highlights:** The team recently defended a $2.1 million libel case against The Boston Globe and one of its reporters. It continues to defend Commonwealth Automobile Reinsurers in various cases relating to the provision of automobile insurance in Massachusetts, and is also representing Network Engines in a securities fraud class action. Other representative clients include John Hancock; Sonus Networks; Red Hat and Fidelity Investments.

## Band 2

## Bingham McCutchen LLP
See firm details p.1110

**The Firm:** This *"top firm"* boasts *"extremely high-quality"* attorneys within its Boston litigation department, who achieve *"great results"* for their clients. Seasoned trial lawyers handle a variety of litigation, often on a national scale. The team has a particularly strong name for banking and finance-related work, and is well regarded for its handling of contentious securities, broker-dealer and mutual fund matters. The firm's antitrust litigation expertise is a major drawing card for clients and the team wins plaudits for interfacing effectively with its other departments and the multistate network of offices.

**The Lawyers:** **Joseph Kociubes** (see p.1097) manages to be both *"pragmatic and aggressive,"* a rare combination that is a hit with clients. Peers also admit they would *"turn to him in a minute"* for referrals, due to his broad expertise and experience in the courtroom. His skill in cross-examinations was particularly noted, and he also wins plaudits for his arbitration work.

**Clients/Work Highlights:** Recent work includes an arbitration for GE Credit Corporation related to a power plant in Mississippi. Other clients include Bain & Company and Boston Scientific, along with a raft of other businesses, nonprofits and government entities.

## Foley Hoag LLP

**The Firm:** This firm enjoys a long history in the state and boasts a wide range of litigation expertise. Although the department's bench strength is perhaps less deep than the market leaders', this doesn't seem to be holding it back, as onlookers highlighted the *"exceptional"* ability of its key individuals and the *"amazing"* service on offer to clients. In addition to its prowess in the IP arena, the group has developed considerable expertise in environmental and white-collar crime disputes. It was particularly admired for its experience at handling class action litigation and for advising accountancy firms on contentious securities-related matters.

**The Lawyers:** *"Hard-working and capable,"* **Michael Keating** is lauded as the firm's *"shining star"* in a range of litigation matters. A powerful force in the courtroom, he is *"a pleasure to try cases against,"* say peers, and stands out as one of the state's *"outstanding players"* in the field.

**Clients/Work Highlights:** Representative clients

include Baxter; Varian Semiconductor; Boston Communications Group and Electro Scientific Industries.

## Goulston & Storrs

**The Firm:** This well-regarded firm has a sizable litigation group catering for clients across the state and beyond. Sources believe that it has benefited greatly from the 2003 lateral hire of a much-admired litigation team from the now defunct Hill & Barlow. Having previously been regarded as a real estate outfit, this move catapulted it strongly into the litigation firmament. While the firm is still perhaps better known for its transactional work, the litigation department is increasingly coming to the fore, and boasts a number of trial lawyers with enviable experience. Its close cooperation with the real estate team has enabled the group to attain a particularly strong name for real estate litigation.

**The Lawyers:** Senior statesman **Richard Renehan** is lauded as *"a first-rate trial lawyer – juries are putty in his hands."* With his decades of experience behind him, he is renowned as one of the state's finest litigators and maintains some visibility in the courtroom. **Rudolph Pierce** is another *"highly rated trial lawyer,"* particularly recommended for his skill in real estate litigation. A former justice of the Massachusetts Superior Court, he now divides his time between the Massachusetts and DC offices.

**Clients/Work Highlights:** Clients include US and foreign individuals, corporations and business entities of all sizes. Manufacturers, Internet companies and software developers are represented by the team, in addition to institutional lenders and investors, governmental agencies, nonprofit organizations and educational institutions. In addition, the firm's specialty in real estate ensures a high proportion of property-related clients.

## McDermott Will & Emery

See firm details p.878

**The Firm:** Clients were full of enthusiasm for the *"high level of expertise"* that this team offers in areas like financial litigation and white-collar crime. The group's trial experience was highlighted by sources, who recommend it for complex litigation, especially in the field of professional malpractice defense. Also recommended for its experience in matters relating to the healthcare and life sciences sectors, the firm's growing network of international offices was another attraction for clients.

**The Lawyers:** **Edward Leibensperger** (see p.1097) is said to be an *"astute"* lawyer who approaches his work from a practical perspective. Although a master of the fine points, he also *"has the ability to see the big picture and not to get caught up in the detail,"* sources explained. He was particularly recommended for his niche expertise in handling malpractice issues in the accountancy arena. With his skill, intelligence and *"great judgment,"* **Mark Pearlstein** (see p.1102) is reputedly *"as smart as they come."* He has experience of working in government, and is particularly skilled in financial crime and tax-related matters. His white-collar expertise dovetails with a general commercial

litigation practice, where he handles a varied workload, spanning products liability and general business disputes.

**Clients/Work Highlights:** The team successfully acted for the Massachusetts Port Authority (Massport) against the town of Hull in litigation over allegations that Massport defrauded environmental regulators in an effort to avoid noise mitigation for the town and was operating at Logan Airport as a public nuisance. It has also recently acted for Deloitte & Touche; Arthur Andersen; Concentra; GE and Dynamics Research.

## Todd & Weld LLP

**The Firm:** This fine litigation boutique offers clients a high level of trial advocacy expertise in an extensive range of areas. Founded in 1992 by attorneys from Hale and Dorr, the team remains relatively compact, but this clearly isn't holding it back, as sources acknowledge it *"tries an awful lot of cases"* in the region, achieving *"excellent"* results. Sources praised the group's breadth and depth, noting the *"bunch of talented young lawyers"* who are expected to propel the firm forward in the future. The firm acts for both defendants and plaintiffs, with specialist expertise in white-collar crime, IP, products liability, construction and real estate disputes. It also has a well-respected appellate practice and is visible in arbitration and mediation.

**The Lawyers:** *"Phenomenal trial lawyer"* **Owen Todd** remains an active player and popular referral choice. One of the state's *"big names,"* he has been a senior partner at Hale and Dorr, and assistant justice in the Massachusetts Superior Court. **Lisa Arrowood** was recommended as *"a dynamic courtroom attorney,"* with one source even describing her as *"a force of nature."* She is particularly admired for her ability to *"promote a case to a jury"* and her *"tremendous talent"* in cross-examination, especially in medical malpractice cases.

**Clients/Work Highlights:** The litigation team represents individuals, partnerships, limited liability entities, publicly held corporations, close corporations, trusts and joint ventures.

## Band 3

## Choate Hall & Stewart

**The Firm:** According to market sources, this well-established team enjoys a *"well-earned reputation for its intellectual approach"* to complex legal matters. Another drawing card for clients is the *"great depth of resources"* on offer here, which makes this a good choice for a range of large and sophisticated commercial disputes. The firm offers specialist advice on financial litigation, government defense work and products liability matters, among other things.

**The Lawyers:** Mark Cahill is the chair of the office's litigation department.

**Clients/Work Highlights:** The team acts for a range of business entities within the state and beyond. Institutional lenders and investors also

feature in its client list, in addition to government agencies.

## Foley & Lardner LLP

See firm details p.2037

**The Firm:** Foley & Lardner is rapidly establishing a base in Boston, following the Milwaukee firm's decision to expand beyond Wisconsin. Although its litigation bench in Massachusetts is not yet as deep as some of its competitors, the merger with Epstein Becker & Green has already given it a sound foothold in the region. According to market sources, the team houses some *"exceptional"* attorneys, who offer expertise in securities, white-collar crime and government enforcement work, as well as IP litigation. Its particular experience in the life sciences, technology and environmental sectors was also highlighted to researchers.

**The Lawyers:** The *"tremendously smart"* **Michael Tuteur** (see p.1108) was recommended to researchers for his *"experience and judgment."* Clients appreciate both his general commercial know-how and practical approach – in the words of one source, he *"understands the results that businesses want."* White-collar crime is an area of particular expertise.

**Clients/Work Highlights:** Harvard University; Blue Cross Blue Shield of Massachusetts; CareGroup; McKinsey & Co; MassHousing Finance Agency; The Boston Consulting Group; Mutual of America Life Insurance; CIGNA; Stewart Title Insurance Company and Kirwan Surgical Products.

## Holland & Knight LLP

See firm details p.1534

**The Firm:** The Boston office of this expanding global firm handles a broad mixture of local and national work in the litigation field. Typical examples include advising clients on class actions, securities disputes and insurance litigation. The well-connected team also offers strength in white-collar crime and government investigations. Clients wax lyrical about the firm's *"refreshing culture,"* praising its capable attorneys for being on top of all the issues, while not being *"as pretentious as some of their competitors."*

**The Lawyers:** *"Superb trial lawyer"* **Gael Mahony** (see p.1098) is universally respected as *"a titan of the Bar."* Unquestionably one of Boston's leading litigators, he is among the field's charmed circle of senior statesmen, and is greatly valued by clients for his expert strategic advice and perceptive judgment.

**Clients/Work Highlights:** Fortune 500 companies, government bodies and nonprofit organizations feature on this group's client list.

## Mintz Levin Cohn Ferris Glovsky and Popeo PC

**The Firm:** This excellent firm maintains a strong foothold in the Massachusetts litigation market. Although some sources questioned the depth of the team behind leading light Bob Popeo, all acknowledge that he has built a *"fabulous"* practice, which continues to boast good lawyers and a good name. The team advises clients on a range of litigation matters, including class action disputes in various sectors, environmental cases and white-collar crime defense.

**The Lawyers:** President and chairman of the firm, **Bob Popeo** (see p.1102) enjoys *"name recognition across America"* for his *"terrific trial experience."* Many years of experience give the veteran litigator a knowledge of the law and courts that is hard to equal.

**Clients/Work Highlights:** The firm is renowned for its work with biotech, healthcare, pharmaceutical and life sciences businesses. It also assists clients in the construction, IT, retail and manufacturing sectors, as well as insurance and financial services companies.

### Nutter, McClennen & Fish, LLP

**The Firm:** This well-regarded department is rated for its *"effective, tenacious and creative"* approach to litigation. The group enjoys a national profile, and clients particularly rate the advice of its *"excellent"* white-collar crime group. Other typical work includes general business disputes, securities litigation, environmental claims, insurance coverage, IP and products liability litigation.

**The Lawyers:** **Daniel Gleason** combines *"a fine intellect"* with *"the ability to see a case as a whole."* An active trial lawyer with a track record of success in jury trials, he is also well-regarded for his experience at handling business disputes outside the courtroom in his work as an arbitrator.

**Clients/Work Highlights:** The group acts for a range of clients, including public and private companies; law and accountancy firms; universities and hospitals; investment advisers and governmental entities, such as the Commonwealth of Massachusetts.

### Sherin and Lodgen LLP

**The Firm:** This focused firm continues to win market endorsement for its litigation expertise. The team has a marked interdisciplinary approach, working closely with other departments in the firm to advise on professional liability, environmental and real estate litigation, among other things. Complex business litigation is clearly a strong suit, and here it has recently represented hi-tech companies in stockholder disputes. Commentators also detect a growing profile in the IP field.

**The Lawyers:** **Robert Muldoon** is said to be an *"outstanding"* choice for civil litigation and intercorporate disputes.

**Clients/Work Highlights:** Representative clients include Teva Pharmaceuticals; Haemonetics; The Beal Companies; Stop & Shop; Volvo North America; Royal Ahold and Wachovia.

### Other Notable Practitioners

Sugarman, Rogers, Barshak & Cohen, PC's *"accomplished"* **Edward Barshak** continues to win plaudits for his trial experience in the commercial arena. Also admired for his commercial litigation skills is **James Carroll** (see p.1089) of Skadden, Arps, Slate, Meagher & Flom LLP & Affiliates. Clients appreciate the *"sound, practical"* advice he offers in relation to consumer products and insurance litigation. Also at Skadden, **Thomas Dougherty** (see p.1091) enters the rankings in recognition of his experience in securities litigation. *"One of the big names in this field,"* he focuses on defending companies, their officers, directors, underwriters and auditors. **Roger Lane** (see p.1097) at Greenberg Traurig LLP is *"extraordinarily patient and thorough,"* with a good record of *"getting clients out of sticky situations."* He advises executives and stockholders on a range of commercial litigation matters.

---

# PRIVATE EQUITY

# BUYOUTS & VENTURE CAPITAL INVESTMENT

| Private Equity: Buyouts & Venture Capital Investment Leading Firms |
| --- |
| **1** GOODWIN PROCTER LLP *Boston* |
| ROPES & GRAY LLP *Boston* |
| WEIL, GOTSHAL & MANGES LLP *Boston* |
| WILMERHALE *Boston* |
| **2** CHOATE HALL & STEWART *Boston* |
| EDWARDS ANGELL PALMER & DODGE *Boston* |
| MCDERMOTT WILL & EMERY *Boston* |
| **3** BINGHAM MCCUTCHEN LLP *Boston* |
| FOLEY HOAG LLP *Boston* |
| MORSE, BARNES-BROWN & PENDLETON *Waltham* |

## Band 1

### Goodwin Procter LLP

See firm details p.1114

**The Firm:** As lateral hires from McDermott Will & Emery and Testa Hurwitz & Thibeault bed into this already impressive private equity outfit, sources anticipate that the firm will further strengthen its hold on the market. The *"diligent"* private equity team is admired for its *"extremely flexible"* approach and *"swift response rate."* Clients continue to value the combination of *"terribly smart and creative"* partners and a developing midlevel tier of associates. Particularly favored by startup, venture-backed companies, public companies, buyout firms, later-stage investors and funds also benefit from the lawyers' *"impeccable*

*service standards."* The team maintains an active profile in a range of market sectors including computer technology, life sciences, media and telecom.

**The Lawyers:** *"Fantastically successful"* and *"great fun to work with,"* **John LeClaire** (see p.1097) is *"first pick"* for later-stage buyout and investment clients in the state. He is valued for his *"outstanding"* knowledge and appreciation of the intricacies of private equity matters. Interviewees also revere him for *"steering clients from a business-oriented viewpoint"* and *"processing information quickly, without unnecessary fuss."* The *"deal-savvy"* **John Egan** (see p.1092) garners praise for his *"profound experience"* and *"high-level strategizing."* Clients value his *"cool, calm and collected"* approach and ability to think on his feet – *"He comes up with great ideas on the fly!"* **Laura Hodges Taylor** (see p.1095) is commended for her problem-solving skills and the cordial relations that she maintains with opposing counsel: *"She doesn't browbeat the other side or waste time trying to prove how smart she is,"* according to commentators. New arrival from Testa Hurwitz & Thibeault **William Schnoor** (see p.1105) is a seasoned and respected figure in early-stage and venture capital work. The *"flexible"* **Anthony Medaglia** (see p.1099) is rated for his ability to *"take total control of a situation"* while remaining cool-headed. His hands-on approach to client care inspires sources to report: *"He rolls his sleeves up and does the work himself."* **Michael Kendall** (see p.1096) continues to develop a profile in this market for being *"exceptionally quick on his feet."* His *"articulate and likable"* style ensures that he

is *"exceptionally good at client interaction."* **James Curley** (see p.1090) is another *"first-rate lawyer in the making,"* according to onlookers, who regard him as *"great backup"* for John LeClaire.

**Clients/Work Highlights:** The team acted for New Radio Group and its partners in a $100 million merger with Waitt Media and advised Florida Career College on its $53 million recapitalization. Lawyers also represented Art.com and its investors in the merger with AllPosters, which created the largest online art and poster company in the world. Additional clients include TA Associates; AIG; Alta Communications; Matrix Partners; Charlesbank Capital Partners; Behrman Capital; Polaris Venture Partners; Prism Venture Partners and Fidelity Investments.

### Ropes & Gray LLP

See firm details p.1117

**The Firm:** This heavyweight corporate player is *"always first on everyone's list of the region's top firms – they are so well known that the business comes to them,"* market sources enthuse. Notwithstanding the close relationships it enjoys with key blue-chip clients at the higher end of the market, the firm is also recommended for its work with early-stage hi-tech companies. The *"top-notch"* private equity team maintains a *"professional, can-do"* approach to representation of debt and equity financers and managements in private equity transactions. Within minority investments, the group acts for minor and majority investors, as well as for issuers.

| Private Equity: |
|---|
| **Buyouts & Venture Capital Investment** |
| Leading Individuals |

**1** BORDEN Mark *WilmerHale*
  CHAPIN David *Ropes & Gray LLP*
  LECLAIRE John *Goodwin Procter LLP*
  WESTRA James *Weil, Gotshal & Manges*

**2** EGAN III John *Goodwin Procter LLP*
  HESSION John *McDermott Will & Emery*
  HODGES TAYLOR Laura *Goodwin Procter LLP*
  MALT R Bradford *Ropes & Gray LLP*
  MEREDITH Stephen *Edwards Angell Palmer*
  RONDEAU Patrick *WilmerHale*
  ROSENBLUM Peter *Foley Hoag LLP*
  SCHNOOR William *Goodwin Procter LLP*
  WOLF Robert *Bingham McCutchen LLP*

**3** CHORY John *WilmerHale*
  COHEN Stephen *Choate Hall & Stewart*
  LENIHAN Brian *Choate Hall & Stewart*
  MEDAGLIA Anthony *Goodwin Procter LLP*
  MOORE Gregory *Ropes & Gray LLP*
  MORREALE Justin *Bingham McCutchen LLP*
  PENDLETON Lea *Morse, Barnes-Brown & Pendleton*
  ROSE Alfred *Ropes & Gray LLP*
  SMALL Richard *Edwards Angell Palmer*
  STILLWELL R Newcomb *Ropes & Gray LLP*

| Up-and-coming individuals |
|---|
| CURLEY James *Goodwin Procter LLP* |
| FRENCH Marilyn *Weil, Gotshal & Manges* |
| KENDALL Michael *Goodwin Procter LLP* |

**The Lawyers:** The "*smart, experienced and pragmatic*" **David Chapin** (see p.1089) "*focuses on the greater view, rather than trying to win every point in an argument,*" say sources. He displays particularly "*rock-solid judgment*" on behalf of public companies. Though more active in private equity fund formation during 2005, **Brad Malt** (see p.1098) remains visible in the transactional market while also playing a management role at the firm. He is considered "*the point man*" for the team's "*pivotal*" relationship with BainCapital. Market observers recommend **Gregory Moore** (see p.1100) for his work with venture capital investors. He is well regarded for his familiarity with clients in the computer and technology industry. The "*experienced and pragmatic*" **Alfred Rose** (see p.1104) wins plaudits for his "*collaborative, cooperative attitude.*" In 2005 he acted in the consortium acquisition of SunGard Data Systems. "*He certainly is a problem solver*" and "*doesn't waste time on posturing,*" interviewees enthuse. Sources continue to endorse co-head of the private equity transaction group **Newcomb Stillwell** (see p.1107).

**Clients/Work Highlights:** The group recently represented the Silver Lake Partners, BainCapital, The Blackstone Group, Goldman Sachs Capital Partners, Providence Equity Partners, KKR, and TPG consortium in their $11 billion acquisition of SunGard Data Systems. Another of the firm's key clients is Fenway Partners.

## Weil, Gotshal & Manges LLP
See firm details p.1565

**The Firm:** Notwithstanding the undeniable support of the firm's nexus in New York, the "*robustly strong*" private equity group in Boston "*runs a great operation independently,*" claim market sources. Lawyers regularly act for blue-chip clients on complex, "*big-ticket*" deals, prompting interviewees to recognize that it "*undoubtedly has more of a Wall Street practice than any of the other firms in town.*" Sources unanimously agree that James Westra's "*outstanding*" leadership, combined with the breadth and depth of a sprawling international network, is crucial to the firm's continued success. The firm is recommended for its later-stage representation of major funds, especially on acquisitions.

**The Lawyers:** The "*wonderful*" **James Westra** (see p.1109) "*tops the charts on so many levels*" and remains "*one of the best later-stage buyout lawyers in the country,*" according to sources. "*Excellent judgment and unflappable composure*" allied with "*incredible preparation*" make him a "*formidable opponent*" in the eyes of peers. The up-and-coming **Marilyn French** (see p.1093) continues to win market endorsement for her developing expertise in this market. She is predominantly known for her involvement in a range of private equity deals but also assists clients with fund formation and M&A work on a regular basis.

**Clients/Work Highlights:** Major clients include Summit Partners; Highland Capital Partners; Thomas H Lee Partners; Providence Equity Partners and Berkshire Partners.

## WilmerHale
See firm details p.1119

**The Firm:** A "*phenomenal*" hi-tech practice that was established in the 1970's has enabled the firm to do "*a great job of cultivating key relationships*" in the private equity and venture capital space. The private equity team represents a "*well-respected brand name*" for clients and is perceived as "*the gold standard*" among peers. Sources especially recommend the group for its expertise on the company side, while also noting the "*sheer quality*" of its transactional work.

**The Lawyers:** **Mark Borden** (see p.1088) continues to enjoy a "*terrific*" reputation for his great client base and significant level of experience in the private equity arena. A popular referral among peers, he is recommended for his early-stage expertise. The "*smart*" **Patrick Rondeau** (see p.1104) is a "*pragmatic*" individual with a "*tremendous*" ability to distinguish between important and trivial issues, state sources. A valued opponent across the negotiation table, Rondeau is "*capable of being aggressive*" on behalf of his clients while also understanding "*exactly when to back off.*" Commentators praise **John Chory** (see p.1089) for his "*practical and businesslike*" handling of early-stage financings. He is particularly valued for maintaining a "*focus on the bigger picture*" throughout transactional proceedings.

**Clients/Work Highlights:** The firm continues to represent many venture-backed companies and venture capital firms in the software, semiconductors and electronics, telecom and networking, life sciences and medical devices industries.

## Band 2

## Choate Hall & Stewart

**The Firm:** This well-established state player has "*always provided work of the highest quality*" and "*successfully moved with the times,*" interviewees report. According to onlookers, the business division has significantly developed its private equity capabilities to become "*up there with the very best in Boston.*" In 2005, the firm was bolstered by the arrival of attorneys, and associated clients, from Testa Hurwitz & Thibeault and is "*clearly a better firm as a result.*" Sources especially recommend lawyers for their early-stage and acquisition work.

**The Lawyers:** **Stephen Cohen** spearheads the private equity team. He is "*fantastic to work with*" and possesses key leadership skills, making him a popular referral among peers. The "*extremely responsive*" **Brian Lenihan** is valued for "*coping with anything that you hurl at him.*" Because he "*understands how deals really work,*" Lenihan "*never gives legal advice in a vacuum, instead it is always practical,*" clients enthuse.

**Clients/Work Highlights:** The team represented Heritage Partners in the $640 million sale of Skilled Healthcare Group, Inc. to Onex Partners in 2005. It also acted for Boston Ventures in its recapitalization of Harron Communications, and similarly for Summit Partners in its recapitalization of Tivoli Audio. Additional clients include Riverside Partners, Spectrum Equity Investors and Celtic House Venture Partners.

## Edwards Angell Palmer & Dodge LLP
See firm details p.1112

**The Firm:** This already prolific player in the private equity arena bolstered its ranks by merging with Palmer & Dodge in 2005. Its "*fantastic*" private equity team is well regarded for its ability to "*deal effectively with the most complicated issues*" and later-stage work. Sources wax lyrical about the team's representation of both lenders and sponsors in acquisitions. The team is also admired for "*staffing its transactions very effectively*" and remains a key outfit for media work. Recent highlights in this area include representing M/C Venture Partners, Bank of America Capital and Columbia Capital in a $125 million equity investment in joint venture with Warner Bros. to produce and own Hollywood films. Following its recent merger, the firm has also been acting for clients in the life sciences and telecom industries.

**The Lawyers:** The "*astute*" **Steve Meredith** (see p.1099) is valued for his problem-solving skills and tendency to "*cut to the chase.*" His "*easygoing personality*" and "*dry, witty*" style are popular among clients. **Richard Small** (see p.1106) is the relationship manager responsible for some of the firm's key clients and he "*absolutely knows his business,*" according to sources. Clients respect his "*steady hand, calm *persona and great practicality."*

**Clients/Work Highlights:** The group advised Great Hill Partners in both the formation and $225 million sale to The Blackstone Group of Global Towers in 2004/5. It also represented Columbia Capital in the $60 million startup investment in SiTV, a Latino-themed cable television channel. Additional clients include Bank of America Capital; Brynwood Partners; JPMorgan Partners; Alta Communications; Spectrum Equity Investors and M/C Venture Partners.

### McDermott Will & Emery
See firm details p.878

**The Firm:** Benefiting from an international network of offices, the firm continues to be well regarded in the state and beyond for its work with clients in the healthcare and technology sectors. Clients praise the level of *"partner attention,"* while also noting that a clutch of talented associates should further strengthen the team in the future. The group is recommended for its early-stage work with venture-backed companies.

**The Lawyers:** The combination of **John Hession's** (see p.1094) *"no-nonsense"* approach and *"great business sense"* finds favor with sources. Entrepreneurs and investors alike value his ability to *"cut to the chase"* in negotiations connected to a range of private equity matters. He also boasts experience advising emerging companies in the state.

**Clients/Work Highlights:** Key venture fund clients include Velocity Equity Partners; Highland Capital Partners; Castile Ventures; Polaris Ventures and Brook Venture Fund. Private companies featuring in the firm's roster include Ion Signature Technology;

WhyData; Nomir Medical Technologies; Longwatch; Feanix; InBoxer; Nexaweb Technologies; Powerspan; ToolsGroup and TCI Technologies Consulting International.

## Band 3

### Bingham McCutchen LLP
See firm details p.1110

**The Firm:** This *"strong"* firm continues to be well regarded in the state for its transactional experience. An international network of offices ensures a broad geographical client reach encompassing leading private equity firms, investment banks and institutional investors. Private equity specialists work closely with the firm's corporate lawyers to deal with the gamut of M&A and private equity matters.

**The Lawyers:** Commentators identify **Bob Wolf** (see p.1109) as the firm's key player in private equity matters. His practice encompasses leveraged acquisitions, recapitalizations, mezzanine financings and equity investments. The *"trusted adviser"* **Justin Morreale** (see p.1100) is credited with building the firm's hi-tech practice.

**Clients/Work Highlights:** Clients include Banc-Boston Capital, Bunker Hill Capital and Weston Presidio.

### Foley Hoag LLP

**The Firm:** The private equity team here is admired for its *"thorough and academic"* approach to transactions, in which lawyers *"think through all the issues and put them into a broader context."* The group is popular among venture capital firms and is recom-

mended for its early-stage experience with companies in the technology arena. Sources also note the firm for its PIPE expertise and work with hedge funds. Lawyers recently undertook a $70 million PIPE for Inverness Medical Innovations. Clients express satisfaction with the balanced mix of experienced partners and able associates on transactions.

**The Lawyers:** **Peter Rosenblum** boasts a *"tremendous breadth"* of experience in the private equity industry. He combines great business sense with a *"calm and commanding"* negotiation style, report clients.

**Clients/Work Highlights:** Notable clients include Polaris Ventures; Global Forest Partners; Common-Angels; Still River Fund; Ascent Venture Partners; Atlas Venture; BioVentures; Charles River Ventures; Galen Partners; Golub Capital; IDG Ventures; Masthead Venture Partners; Prism Venture Partners and Skyline Ventures.

### Morse, Barnes-Brown & Pendleton PC

**The Firm:** This private equity team is *"big on personalized service,"* in spite of its impressive size, say commentators. Predominantly recognized for its venture capital work, 2005 also saw the firm involved in work on funds and later-stage transactions, including LBOs and MBOs.

**The Lawyers:** The *"enthusiastic and dedicated"* **Lea Pendleton** is *"totally comfortable with assisting entrepreneurs and startups,"* according to sources.

**Clients/Work Highlights:** Major clients include TechTarget; Egan-Managed Capital; Dragonvest Partners; Genzyme; OATSystems; Axia Partners; Windspeed and Julius Koch USA.

# PRIVATE FUND FORMATION

## Band 1

### Proskauer Rose LLP
See firm details p.1551

**The Firm:** Following the 2005 dissolution of Testa, Hurwitz & Thibeault, the firm's former private equity team has developed a successful practice here. Maintaining its position at the forefront of the Massachusetts fund formation market, the experienced group of practitioners successfully held on to its loyal client base and expanded its reach. The growing team's representation of private equity funds has benefited from its new firm's deeper geographical and regulatory footprint and an international plat-

form. Previously noted for its focus on venture capital funds, the group increased its representation of buyout and mezzanine funds in 2005. The breadth and scope of the fund formation department has also been improved by an extension of the firm's hedge fund capability. Well-regarded ERISA, tax and securities lawyers at the firm support the group.

**The Lawyers:** The *"extremely competent"* **Robin Painter** (see p.1101) is a well-known figure on the venture capital scene and wins praise for her global knowledge of the fund formation industry. Commentators report that **Daniel Finkelman** (see p.1092) *"has always been a great lawyer"* for significant fund formation matters. He combines experience in venture capital and buyout funds to act for clients in the USA and Israel. *"As effective as ever,"* **David Tegeler** (see p.1107) continues to win warm endorsement from peers and clients alike. Sources value his experience of classic private equity fund formation, alongside secondary fund and investment activity work. **Malcolm Nicholls** (see p.1101) belies his years by impressing onlookers: *"For his age, he has done extremely well for himself,"* said one market source.

**Clients/Work Highlights:** The team represents a range of international general and limited partners, as well as institutional investors. The team assisted Ares Capital Management in its $1 billion buyout fund. It also acted for Abbott Capital Management on its $750 million fund of funds and Columbia Capital Equity Partners IV on its $500 million venture capital fund in 2005.

### Ropes & Gray LLP
See firm details p.1117

**The Firm:** Sources laud this well-established firm as one of Massachusetts' leading players for its *"absolutely top-notch"* private equity expertise. In particular, the Boston fund formation team is recommended for its significant experience in handling private investment funds, including venture capital, CDO and buyout funds. The team is also noted for its experience in offshore funds and in advising clients on structuring the internal management of sponsors. The firm remains familiar with the life sciences industry, and a raft of the state's largest investors, including Harvard University and Bain-Capital, contribute to the firm's enviable client base.

| Private Fund Formation |
| --- |
| **Leading Individuals** |

| | |
| --- | --- |
| [1] | **MALT R Bradford** *Ropes & Gray LLP* |
| | **PAINTER Robin** *Proskauer Rose LLP* |
| | **ROWE Larry** *Ropes & Gray LLP* |
| [2] | **BEAUDOIN Thomas** *WilmerHale* |
| | **FINKELMAN Daniel** *Proskauer Rose LLP* |
| | **ROTHERMEL Sarah** *WilmerHale* |
| | **TEGELER David** *Proskauer Rose LLP* |
| | **WATSON David** *Goodwin Procter LLP* |
| [3] | **KREISLER David** *Weil, Gotshal & Manges* |
| | **MILNER Ann** *Ropes & Gray LLP* |
| | **NICHOLLS III Malcolm** *Proskauer Rose LLP* |

Its fund formation and investment group works closely with a well-regarded transactions team. While *"it goes without saying that the Boston private equity attorneys are of an exceptionally high quality,"* sources view the firm's New York office as an effective counterpart to the Massachusetts group.

**The Lawyers:** One of the market's most visible experts, **Larry Jordan Rowe** (see p.1104) continues to impress onlookers with his *"smart"* approach and *"practical"* style. He is recommended for his ability to represent investors. **Bradford Malt** (see p.1098) continues to enjoy *"a great reputation"* across the region in all facets of the private equity sphere. His new role as chairman of the firm has shifted his focus to predominantly acting for funds, although he remains an impressive transactional lawyer. The *"exceptionally bright"* **Ann Milner** (see p.1100) enters the *Chambers* table in 2005 on the basis of her investment knowledge and experience in raising funds for significant clients in the state.

**Clients/Work Highlights:** BainCapital; Fenway Partners; Thomas H Lee Partners; Welsh, Carson, Anderson & Stowe; Saunders Karp & Megrue; Goldman Sachs and Merrill Lynch.

## Band 2

## Goodwin Procter LLP
See firm details p.1114

**The Firm:** Known across the region for its business acumen and finance skill, *"this is clearly a firm that is doing things right,"* market sources told researchers. The firm's private fund formation team is no exception and is recommended for its work at general partnership level. It is particularly well established in real estate funds, although it also offers expertise in private equity, venture capital and hedge funds. Lawyers represented Advent International in the formation of a $3.3 billion global private equity fund that raised capital in the USA and throughout Europe. The team also acted for BayNorth Capital Partners in the formation of a $430 million real estate opportunity fund for investments in North America. The group is supported by the firm's respected investment management practice.

**The Lawyers:** **David Watson** (see p.1108) shines as the firm's leading light in the fund formation market. He is admired for his skill at handling both private equity and real estate funds.

**Clients/Work Highlights:** Representative real estate fund clients include AEW Capital Management; Beacon Capital Partners; Fidelity Real Estate Group; Lend Lease; Prudential Real Estate Investors; RREEF and TA Associates Realty. The team has undertaken international fund work for a range of clients including ABN AMRO; Allied Irish Banks; Crédit Agricole Indosuez; Fidelity; Putnam Investments; Scudder and State Street.

## Weil, Gotshal & Manges LLP
See firm details p.1565

**The Firm:** This *"well-rounded"* firm is recognized on a global scale for its private equity transactional expertise. Sources also note lawyers' handling of key Massachusetts fund formation work. The Boston team works closely with the New York and Dallas offices, pooling significant resources in order to create a national footprint. Respected for its capacity to deal with complex buyout funds, the firm was involved in megafunds in 2005, while maintaining regular client relationships at state level. The fund formation team regularly interfaces with the firm's esteemed tax lawyers.

**The Lawyers:** Handling some of the state's notable private equity fund formation work, the *"understated"* **David Kreisler** (see p.1097) is the standout individual at this firm. He *"clearly knows what he is doing and commands respect for his expertise, rather than his back-slapping ability,"* say interviewees. Sources also note him for his buyout transactional experience.

**Clients/Work Highlights:** Berkshire Partners, TH Lee Putnam Ventures and Thomas H Lee Partners are key clients of this firm.

## WilmerHale
See firm details p.1119

**The Firm:** This impressive outfit is a key player in the state's corporate finance scene, and is primarily recommended for its venture capital and investment work. With a developing reputation in fund formation, the growing team has made a name for itself across the state and beyond. Its diverse international reach saw the firm advising clients on Vietnamese, Italian and English venture capital funds in 2005. Commentators recommended the team for its work on behalf of general partners in the middle-market, especially in connection with the technology sector. Lawyers advised Silicon Valley-based Canaan Partners on raising their Fund VII. The team also acted for Israeli firm Carmel Ventures in raising Carmel Ventures II.

**The Lawyers:** The *"resoundingly solid"* **Thomas Beaudoin** (see p.1087) heads the firm's private equity practice and has established a *"great name"* for himself in the venture capital funds market, according to sources. Popular among clients, he is recommended for his *"strategically aggressive"* style: *"He has a take-no-prisoners approach!"* claimed one source. The *"level-headed"* **Sarah Rothermel** (see p.1104) successfully combines *"common sense, business knowledge and hard work,"* clients told researchers. She is also *"tied into the Boston venture capital community, which is a plus,"* peers said.

**Clients/Work Highlights:** Alongside a range of international projects, Massachusetts-based work included representing North Bridge Venture Partners in raising North Bridge Venture Partners VI and acting for WestView Capital Partners (a Boston-area firm) in raising WestView Capital Partners I.

# REAL ESTATE

### Real Estate
#### Leading Firms

1. **DLA PIPER RUDNICK GRAY CARY** *Boston*
   **GOODWIN PROCTER LLP** *Boston*
   **GOULSTON & STORRS** *Boston*
2. **WILMERHALE** *Boston*
3. **NUTTER, MCCLENNEN & FISH, LLP** *Boston*
4. **BINGHAM MCCUTCHEN LLP** *Boston*
   **BROWN RUDNICK BERLACK ISRAELS** *Boston*
   **EDWARDS ANGELL PALMER & DODGE** *Boston*

#### Leading Individuals

1. **FISHMAN Robert** *Nutter, McClennen & Fish*
   **GLAZER Michael** *Goodwin Procter LLP*
   **KRASNOW Jordan** *Goulston & Storrs*
   **ROTTENBERG Alan** *Goulston & Storrs*
   **SIRKIN Joel** *WilmerHale*
   **SURKIN Elliot** *DLA Piper*
2. **BACHMAN Katharine** *WilmerHale*
   **BARKER Christopher** *Goodwin Procter LLP*
   **HAROZ Michael** *Goulston & Storrs*
   **KAY Minta** *Goodwin Procter LLP*
   **KWASNICK Raymond** *Goulston & Storrs*
   **O'REILLY JR William** *WilmerHale*
   **RATTIGAN John** *DLA Piper*
   **RUDMAN Richard** *DLA Piper*
   **SCHWARTZ Paul** *Goodwin Procter LLP*
   **SULLIVAN John** *DLA Piper*
3. **CHRISTIAN Joseph** *WilmerHale*
   **GREEN Barry** *Goulston & Storrs*
   **JAKUBOWSKI Paul** *WilmerHale*
   **MITCHELL Beth** *Nutter, McClennen & Fish*
   **MOFFATT Maura** *Goodwin Procter LLP*
   **RECK Joel** *Brown Rudnick*
   **ROBINSON Marcia** *Bingham McCutchen LLP*
   **TOELKE Richard** *Bingham McCutchen LLP*

#### Up-and-coming individuals
**TRIBUSH Bruce** *Goodwin Procter LLP*

### Real Estate: Zoning/Land Use
#### Leading Individuals

1. **BIALECKI Gregory** *DLA Piper*
   **FISHMAN Robert** *Nutter, McClennen & Fish*
   **HALEY Joseph** *Goodwin Procter LLP*
   **HEALY Martin** *Goodwin Procter LLP*
   **HUSID Douglas** *Goulston & Storrs*
   **KIEFER Matthew** *Goulston & Storrs*
   **LYMAN R Jeffrey** *Goodwin Procter LLP*
   **NYLEN JR Richard** *Lynch DeSimone & Nylen*
   **PUTZIGER Myrna** *Rubin and Rudman LLP*
   **TWOHIG John** *Goulston & Storrs*

## Band 1

### DLA Piper Rudnick Gray Cary US LLP
See firm details p.870

**The Firm:** Commentators agree that this "*sterling group*" continues to power forward in the market. A "*top-flight*" 24-attorney team balances "*business judgment and sensitivity with strong technical skills*" according to clients. It is frequently seen on major projects for its developer client base, and is also prominent in the representation of institutional investors, including pension funds. Real estate is an essential component of the firm's growth plan and consequently its Boston hub is a "*nationally formidable*" player at the center of a substantial network of linked groups. The recent series of mergers have added to its international reach and strengthened the firm's platform in Europe and Asia. This is a drawing card for clients, many of whom enjoy the benefits of retaining not just a regional standout but also a "*major player in the real estate world.*"

**The Lawyers:** Leading commercial development lawyer **Elliot Surkin** (see p.1107) possesses an "*uncanny ability to defuse the most difficult of situations,*" according to clients. Having acted on many of the largest developments in Boston and the surrounding area, he is acknowledged to have "*great experience to draw on that gives him perspective and vision.*" Recent highlights include acting for an affiliate of Hyatt Development in connection with the $115 million sale of the Fan Pier project. **John Rattigan** (see p.1103) arrives at the firm from Palmer & Dodge, bringing "*significant real estate force*" to the team, particularly in urban development. He has a focus on projects with a public sector component, often representing public authorities, lenders and developers in major schemes. The development and financing of airports is a particular niche, and he has recently been assisting Millennium Partners with the sale of a high-rise office building in Boston for just under $500 million. According to clients, **Richard Rudman** (see p.1104) uses his "*tremendous intellect*" to "*cut right to the heart of issues.*" Along with his "*tough and articulate negotiation skills,*" this stands him in good stead in the field of real estate development and financing. He concentrates on sophisticated development projects and acquisitions, large leasing work and joint venture investments, recently completing a 320,000 sq ft lease to a major Boston law firm. "*Skilled negotiator*" **John Sullivan** (see p.1107) concentrates on representing funds, advisers and other investors in real estate transactions. His clients tend to have nationwide interests, such as AEW Capital Management and its pension fund clients, who he recently advised on the acquisition of more than $500 million of office, industrial and residential properties throughout the USA. **Gregory Bialecki** (see p.1087) was recommended for his skill in the land use arena. An "*excellent resource for his clients,*" his work encompasses the permitting, construction and development of large-scale projects.

**Clients/Work Highlights:** The Congress Group; The Davis Companies; Tishman Speyer Properties; Lyme Properties; AEW Capital Management; Fidelity Investments and Charlesbank Capital Partners.

### Goodwin Procter LLP
See firm details p.1114

**The Firm:** According to interviewees, this is first and foremost a "*great firm for real estate capital markets,*" although the group also scored points for its more traditional real estate offering. The team is widely acknowledged as top for tax, securities and corporate advice to REITs and for its capital raising activity in the real estate arena. Interdisciplinary teams of "*strong and capable*" lawyers focus on issues relating to investment management, funds, leasing, joint ventures, and sales and acquisitions, while the firm's depth in tax, ERISA and bankruptcy makes it a first choice for a variety of cross-disciplinary matters. Of particular note is the group's long-standing experience in the hospitality industry, where it has served as general counsel to Wyndham International in its domestic and foreign hotel mergers and acquisitions.

**The Lawyers:** **Michael Glazer** (see p.1093) chairs the firm's real estate investment management practice, and enjoys a "*first-rate reputation*" among clients and peers. He is particularly admired for his advice on investment opportunities for investor, pension fund and real estate adviser clients. He has handled over 40 major transactions for BlackRock's investment funds, totaling over $1 billion, and represented Citigroup Property Investors in two major joint venture developments on the West Coast and in Washington, DC. Clients describe **Christopher Barker** (see p.1086) as a "*terrific lawyer – confident, smart and able to run major transactions,*" while peers rate him as "*thoughtful, creative and great to work with.*" He takes the lead in representing tax-exempt entities in a variety of real estate investments. Further specialized in the hospitality field, he has recently acted for HEI Hospitality in a number of large hotel acquisitions and financings in Florida, California and Maryland. **Minta Kay** (see p.1096) has built a reputation for "*incredibly sharp and tenacious*" work in real estate securities and capital markets. She represented Prudential Real Estate Investors in negotiations surrounding a $17 million mezzanine loan to affiliates of Trammell Crow Residential, which was used to finance a portion of the development costs of the Harborview Point condominiums. Clients say she "*gains respect by creating an atmosphere of consolidation not contention.*" The "*enormously bright*" **Paul Schwartz** (see p.1105) delivers on private market finance projects associated with the real estate industry, including joint ventures, fund formations, mezzanine debt and REIT investments. Clients appreciate his "*thoughtful*" approach and "*ability to structure complex transactions.*" "*Rising star*" **Maura Griffith Moffatt** (see p.1100) has a wide-ranging practice emphasizing real estate investment management and finance. Her client list includes pension fund advisers, banks, insurance companies and real estate investors. **Bruce Tribush** (see p.1108) maintains his position as an up-and-comer in this market. He is recognized for building up broad transactional experience and has recently worked with construction and development clients. **Joseph Haley** (see p.1094) was recommended to researchers as a "*highly respected practitioner*" with a long career in development and permitting. His experience spans retail, industrial, residential and mixed-use real estate development, planning and financing. **Martin Healy** (see p.1094) chairs the firm's real estate development and permitting practice group. He is highly regarded in all matters relating to zoning, subdivision and land use. **Jeffrey Lyman** (see p.1098) is another beacon for clients looking for advice on development and permitting matters. His clients include public and private development firms, investors and institutional owners across the region.

**Clients/Work Highlights:** AEW Capital Management; Fidelity Investments; The Wilder Companies; Four Seasons; Prudential Real Estate Investors; La Quinta Corporation; Beacon Capital Partners; Equity Office Properties; HEI Hospitality; Leggat McCall Properties; BlackRock Realty Investors and Cabot Properties.

## Goulston & Storrs

**The Firm:** Interviewees were unequivocal about this firm's market-leading position, believing it to be "*well known for its core real estate commitment and clearly at the highest level in the market.*" The large group of "*pragmatic, responsive and creative*" real estate attorneys wins particular praise for its handling of development issues, an area in which clients describe its expertise as "*second to none.*" It is, however, a broad practice that is also involved in sophisticated construction, acquisition and leasing matters across the state and beyond. Another area of niche strength for the group is its "*tremendous retail practice,*" acting for shopping center owners, lenders and investors. The team has recently been active in the sale and acquisition of several portfolios of office buildings and development properties across Massachusetts and the USA, on behalf of a number of high-profile clients. It also boasts a substantial financing side to its business, along with a strong REIT practice and skill in joint ventures and tax planning.

**The Lawyers:** According to admiring sources, **Jordan Krasnow** is "*rightfully at the top of the list*" in real estate. His enthusiastic client following appreciates his "*outstanding*" input on many of the most complex transactions in the region and beyond. His core expertise lies in acquisitions, disposals and development work, plus real estate finance. Krasnow continues to represent Beacon Capital Partners on transactions across the country, including the purchase of a portfolio of office buildings valued at $950 million in Arlington and Fairfax County, Virginia. Other highlights include acting in the sale of 47 properties in New England for CrossHarbor Capital Partners. "*Strong senior attorney*" **Alan Rottenberg** handles a broad mix of real estate

matters, such as national real estate development, acquisitions, leasing and financing transactions. Clients particularly appreciate his willingness to "*take time to personalize the relationship.*" As a "*phenomenal listener,*" he is also said to get swiftly to the heart of issues. **Michael Haroz** "*couldn't be better*" for commercial real estate finance and development. He maintains a split lender/developer practice, with clients on both sides admitting their "*respect for his intelligence and integrity.*" He was recently involved in a $125 million fund financing for a major healthcare facility in the Boston area. **Raymond Kwasnick** impresses by being "*energetic in his representation of clients' interests,*" and by "*focusing on everyone's needs so that he ultimately gets to a place everyone is comfortable with.*" "*One of the top leasing lawyers in the city,*" he acts on many of the largest transactions in this field, a recent example being the 311,000 sq ft research and laboratory facility for Beth Israel Deaconess Medical Center. His practice also includes acquisitions, dispositions and construction. Clients described **Barry Green** as "*knowledgeable and quick.*" His broad-ranging practice is focused on complex transactions, including work for international clients investing in the USA. He represented Boston Properties in negotiating $130 million of construction and permanent financing for office building in Washington, DC, and also advised IBUS Company on a joint venture for the development of townhouses in Atlanta. **Douglas Husid** stands out as a "*detail-oriented guy who focuses on the nitty-gritty.*" His background in government gives him extra insight into the complexities of land use and permitting, and his portfolio includes acting on many large-scale projects. Sources also championed **Matthew Kiefer** as a "*deep thinker*" focused on complex urban projects, such as affordable housing, commercial and mixed-use developments, and educational, cultural and nonprofit ventures. **John Twohig**, meanwhile, "*does a great job*" of zoning and permitting matters, according to sources. He is often retained by real estate developers in connection with land acquisitions, title issues and financing.

**Clients/Work Highlights:** The firm has recently brought its expertise to bear on a complex laboratory relocation deal for Schlumberger Technology. Other clients include Boston Properties; S.R. Weiner & Associates; The Green Company; Beacon Capital Partners; AvalonBay Communities; CrossHarbor Capital Partners; Tishman Speyer; Samuels & Associates; Boston Redevelopment Authority; Winn Development Company and Northland Investment Corporation.

## Band 2

## WilmerHale

See firm details p.1119

**The Firm:** This recently merged powerhouse fields a substantial real estate offering from its Boston office. Although this is not seen as the firm's primary focus, the group nevertheless gets involved in "*many sophisticated matters*" and has a lineup of "*great*

names.*" Its institutional debt and equity practice is especially well respected, as is the development and capital management arm. Retail development, especially work in New England for major store clients, remains strong and the group represents Wal-Mart in multiple land assemblies and ground leases. The firm's full-service capability remains a drawing card for clients who appreciate the added input they can receive from the tax, litigation, environment and other practice groups. In addition its national reach and growing international presence are well documented. Clients are also impressed by the group's ability to "*understand the intricacies of real estate negotiation,*" which one summed up by saying "*we view them less as a law firm and more as an extension of our own department.*"

**The Lawyers:** **Joel Sirkin** (see p.1106), the chair of the firm's real estate practice, is one of Boston's leading real estate lights. A combination of "*efficiency and tenacity,*" and a "*great personality*" get the deal done quickly and effectively. As commentators note, "*he is not willing to waste clients' time.*" He recently represented the US subsidiary of a UK biotech startup in lease negotiations for the creation of a research and pharmaceutical manufacturing facility in the Boston area. Sirkin has also acted for Fidelity Management Trust Company pension funds in a number of joint venture investments and mezzanine financings of apartments and condominiums. Sources describe **Katharine Bachman** (see p.1086) as a "*proficient and experienced real estate lawyer*" who handles a range of development and finance transactions. She acted for Equity Office Properties Trust in the redevelopment of Russia Wharf, Boston, into a mixed-use complex and has also assisted Trinity Financial with major housing projects in Boston, New Haven and Newport. **William O'Reilly** (see p.1101) is deemed "*smart and pleasant to deal with – he doesn't make an issue out of every little thing.*" His expertise and "*wonderful judgment*" are deployed on development projects and financing arrangements in Boston and the surrounding region. Typical work includes retail sales and acquisitions, condominium developments, and residential and office developments. Clients and peers describe **Joseph Christian** (see p.1089) as a "*solid attorney with good judgment and experience.*" He has acquired a reputation for the management of real estate assets across the country and overseas, representing real estate advisers, operating companies, financial institutions and REITs. As evidence of his international links, he recently assisted in establishing an international school in the master-planned development in Incheon, South Korea. **Paul Jakubowski** (see p.1095) is known to be "*fully up to speed*" on a range of real estate deals. Interviewees praised his approach to sales and acquisitions, and his sure touch on finance, development and leasing transactions. Recent highlights include the acquisition, joint venture, financing and partial lease of a life sciences campus in Lexington.

**Clients/Work Highlights:** New institutional clients include LaSalle Investment Management. Members of the firm have now represented LaSalle and its pension fund clients in billions of dollars' worth of property transactions across the USA. Recent development highlights include acting for Equity Office Properties Trust in the redevelopment of Russia Wharf, a mixed-use waterfront complex in Boston. Campanelli Companies and Trinity Financial also feature in the team's client roster.

## Band 3

### Nutter, McClennen & Fish, LLP

**The Firm:** According to interviewees, the attorneys at this respected firm are "*highly regarded and intelligent*." The 25-plus real estate team is actively involved in a variety of issues for a client roster that is evenly divided between developers and institutional lenders. On the finance side, the group acts for life insurance companies, pension funds, banks and investment trusts. A recent example was representing Connecticut General Life Insurance and Wachovia in the $69 million construction and permanent financing of the ArborPoint at Seven Springs apartment project in Burlington. Real estate expertise is coupled with excellent land use and permitting capabilities, alongside a solid environmental department. Recently the "*strong group*" has been growing in profile, "*bringing on clients and attracting new ones,*" sources say.

**The Lawyers:** Chair of the land use practice group, **Robert Fishman** receives high marks for his across-the-board real estate practice. "*He is a master of the details,*" sources stated, as well as a "*smart, experienced client manager.*" He has represented developers, lenders and corporate, municipal and nonprofit clients in the development and financing of office, industrial, retail and residential buildings. He is equally renowned for being "*right up there for land use matters*" and boasts a busy permitting and contractual practice. **Beth Mitchell** is also considered "*strong and capable.*" She has been especially busy of late representing South Shore Tri-Town Development in the redevelopment of the former South Weymouth Naval Air Station. This involves considerable zoning and mixed-use development work. Her practice also increasingly includes a substantial component of real estate finance-related work.

**Clients/Work Highlights:** Connecticut General Life Insurance; Wachovia Bank and New York State Teachers' Retirement System.

## Band 4

### Bingham McCutchen LLP
See firm details p.1110

**The Firm:** This multioffice firm has leveraged well off the strength of its corporate department to develop what interviewees describe as an "*extremely well-regarded*" real estate practice. The group offers a broad spectrum of expertise, including acquisitions and disposals, development, leasing and joint ventures, mainly on the owner-developer side. Areas of particular focus include project development, construction and land use law. Among a number of recent highlights, the group acted on the master development and sale of a mixed-use waterfront project.

**The Lawyers:** **Marcia Robinson** (see p.1103) wins praise from the market for her work in the field of commercial real estate and finance. Her remit is wide and she offers considerable experience in acquisitions, lending and leasing matters. **Richard Toelke** (see p.1108) is recognized for his relationship with key clients in Massachusetts including The Berkshire Group and Berkeley Investments. His experience is also recognized outside of the region.

**Clients/Work Highlights:** The firm advises lenders, developers, pension fund advisers, REITs, banks and corporations on a range of transactions and property types. Recent examples include representing Advanced Bionics in its acquisition of 63 acres in California for development into a life sciences manufacturing, warehouse and office facility.

### Brown Rudnick Berlack Israels LLP

**The Firm:** This excellent and cohesive team is skilled in a broad array of development, real estate finance, housing and retail matters. The group represents clients from a variety of sectors, including the energy, telecommunications, healthcare, finance and real estate development industries. Recent highlights include advising Antares Real Estate Partners on the acquisition of a development site in Connecticut involving substantial environmental cleanup issues. The group also acted for a retail development fund in the acquisition and sale of shopping centers across the country for more than $150 million. Ongoing work includes representing the developer of a 1,400-acre military base in the cleanup, transfer and redevelopment of the site. Traditionally strong in the region, the real estate group enjoys a burgeoning national presence and an increasingly sophisticated mix of development activity, tax-structured finance, and securitizations.

**The Lawyers:** Generalist **Joel Reck** stands out as a "*smart, practical and highly personable lawyer*" with a substantial amount of experience. He deploys his skills in a range of work, such as representing Target Corporation throughout New England in a variety of development transactions, dispositions and acquisitions, and acting for Teradyne in real estate dispositions across the country.

**Clients/Work Highlights:** Spaulding & Slye Colliers; KBS Realty Advisors; Teradyne; Brooks Automation; Kendall Companies; Tyco; Sun Microsystems; Boston, Cambridge and Somerville housing authorities; East Boston Community Development Corporation and Rogerson Communities.

### Edwards Angell Palmer & Dodge LLP
See firm details p.1112

**The Firm:** The merger of general practice firms Edwards & Angell and Palmer & Dodge in November united two strong regional players. The merged firm may be best known for its strength in IP and finance but its real estate capability is also expected to grow, particularly in the public-private enterprise sphere, which was an established strong point of Palmer & Dodge's Boston office. The group represents developers in major projects, ranging from waterfront developments to residential condominiums, biotechnology facilities and rental housing. Attorneys also regularly act for national and regional lenders and borrowers in real estate finance transactions.

**The Lawyers:** The loss of John Rattigan to DLA Piper Rudnick Gray Cary may prove a blow to the newly integrated team. However, clients see other members of the team coming through, and appreciate the group's "*business-oriented, creative and responsive*" ethic and its skill in generating consensus in deals.

**Clients/Work Highlights:** The firm advises public authorities, businesses, institutional landowners and private developers. Examples include Port Authority of Oakland; Millennium Partners-Boston; Hines; Massachusetts Port Authority; Edens & Avant and Massachusetts Convention Center Authority.

### Other Notable Practitioners

Sources explained **Richard Nylen** of Lynch DeSimone & Nylen LLP's appeal: "*He is great on the complex, esoteric permitting issues that arise in suburban and urban projects.*" He also stands out for his work on the environmental side of land use and real estate, gaining particular plaudits for his wetlands and rare species knowledge. "*Focused*" zoning lawyer **Myrna Putziger**, of Rubin and Rudman LLP, won considerable praise for her development and finance practice. She enjoys a particularly strong profile in large Boston-based projects.

# TAX

## Band 1

### Goodwin Procter LLP

See firm details p.1114

**The Firm:** Venerated as "*one of the best tax groups in the state*," this team wins praise for a transaction-oriented practice which is the "*envy of many.*" The group caters to the gamut of tax-related matters but is particularly noted for its provision of services to the firm's corporate and real estate client base on a state, federal and international level. Sources praise the team's private equity work and REITs expertise for being "*easily some of the state's finest.*" Commentators attribute the team's "*culture of looking out for the interests of the client*" to its "*knowing the law like the back of its hand.*" Lawyers additionally boast niche expertise in controversy work, where the team was busy representing the IRS in 2005.

**The Lawyers:** Chair of the tax practice **Howard Cubell** (see p.1090) "*thinks outside the box,*" say commentators. While noted for being aggressive in his approach, "*he walks right up to the line but never crosses it.*" Cubell focuses his practice on developing innovative tax strategies for various domestic and international business transactions and acts for a number of high-profile private equity sponsors. In 2005, he carried out a significant volume of work for TA Associates in structuring its investment ventures. Clients admire **William Whitledge** (see p.1109) for being a "*real problem solver*" who is "*completely dedicated to our cause.*" His "*innovative judgment and widespread experience*" are particularly applied to structuring domestic and international transactions. He represented Charlesbank Capital Partners in the LBO of Walco Holdings in 2005. New entrant to the tables **Neal Sandford** (see p.1104) garnered praise for his work representing clients in the private equity and real estate fund formation arenas, including a particular focus on REITs.

**Clients/Work Highlights:** Lawyers acted for The Prudential Insurance Company of America regarding its $705 million recapitalization of International Place in downtown Boston. Other notable clients include Beacon Capital Partners: Morgan Stanley; Citizens Financial Group; Kimco Realty and Boston Properties.

### Ropes & Gray LLP

See firm details p.1117

**The Firm:** The team's "*clear and consistent demonstration of excellence*" in the tax field was continually highlighted by sources who agree that "*Ropes & Gray deserve the highest accolades.*" This national heavyweight houses a "*raft of excellent individuals,*" with a 50-member tax and benefits group in Boston catering to the full range of tax matters. A sophisticated transaction-related practice predominantly provides tax planning advice and representation to domestic and international investors and business entities. Commentators recommend this team for having "*lawyers of the highest caliber, all of whom are profound industry experts*" in their ability to work in tandem with the firm's nationally reputed private equity practice.

**The Lawyers:** "*International tax law veteran*" **Stephen Shay** (see p.1106) "*has a way of elucidating complex matters into their most uncomplicated forms,*" say impressed sources. Noted for his superior handling of work in the international tax sphere, he earned plaudits for his "*formidable ability to stay on the cutting edge of the law.*" The past year has seen him act in a number of transfer pricing and foreign tax credit matters. The combination of "*outstanding analytical skills, creativity and practical business judgment*" stands **Eric Elfman** (see p.1092) out from the crowd. Particular praise was reserved for his work representing and advising corporate clients on tax issues related to M&A, restructurings and financings. Sources describe **Susan Johnston** (see p.1095) as "*one of, if not the, leading authority in the country for fund formation work.*" Clients were impressed with her recognition and assessment of the risks posed in complicated transactions and her ability to "*bring matters alive and into the real world.*" Her knowledge of "*every case and every ruling*" makes her "*someone you constantly want to go back to,*" according to interviewees. **Rom Watson**'s (see p.1108) international tax law practice is highlighted for being "*a barrel of originality.*" In 2005 he represented a multitude of clients in the tax issues concerning securities lending and financial products. Clients prize him for his ability to "*make matters simple.*" **Christopher Leich** (see p.1097) has an "*excellent understanding of tax rules and how to relate them to the business objectives of the client in transactions,*" according to sources.

**Clients/Work Highlights:** Key clients include BainCapital; Millipore; Genzyme; Gillette; Timberland; Silver Lake Partners; Fenway Partners; SOFTBANK Capital Partners; Brooks Automation; EMC; Barclays Global Investors; Columbia Management Group; State Street Bank & Trust and Harvard Management Solutions.

## Band 2

### Bingham McCutchen LLP

See firm details p.1110

**The Firm:** Commentators lavish praise on this impressive outfit for its tax controversy work on behalf of clients in court and administrative proceedings. As well as being respected leaders in federal and state litigation work, the team also boasts a smaller transactional practice supporting a highly regarded corporate department. A "*hard-working and intelligent*" team "*resolves to handle matters with minimum fuss,*" according to clients.

**The Lawyers:** **John Brown**'s (see p.1088) sheer experience in the field is allied with "*a tremendous business brain,*" say sources. His reputation as "*the best in the country for controversy work*" is buttressed by a succession of unbroken wins, both on a federal and state level. Brown is a key provider of tax planning advice connected with structuring organizations and transactions. The "*incredibly smart*" **Donald-Bruce Abrams** (see p.1085) "*really digs into all aspects of the case rather than taking the straight legal route,*" clients report. In 2005 he was kept busy with intricate project financings and energy-related transactions. Sources identify the "*diligent and responsive*" **Matthew Schnall** (see p.1105) as "*an expert at looking for the corporate angles of tax transactions.*" He recently acted for an international medical products client in a mixed domestic and cross-border tax transaction. **George Mair**'s (see p.1098) debut in the tables is based on his widely admired work in estate planning matters.

**Clients/Work Highlights:** New client GE Capital joins an impressive roster of clients including Boston Scientific; PerkinElmer; Harvard University; Raytheon; National Grid; Bank of America and Invensys.

### WilmerHale

See firm details p.1119

**The Firm:** The firm continues to make waves in the area thanks to "*a selection of impressive names on its bench.*" Clients praise the transaction-focused team for "*really looking at us as business partners as opposed to just giving us the legal language.*" The group primarily concentrates on supporting the firm's corporate and real estate departments, including a heavy volume of fund formation and partnership tax work, although lawyers offer clients significant knowledge and expertise in the international arena. Junior members of the team were singled out for being able to "*communicate even the most complex of matters.*"

**The Lawyers: William Benjamin** (see p.1087) has "*the business insight and the knowledge of US tax codes to give you all the strategic guidance you need,*" report sources. He provided advice in relation to the US tax treatment of international shipping operations for a large international company in 2005. Other facets to his practice include advising both domestic and overseas clients on the legal and tax aspects of international transactions. Renowned for his impressive international practice, **Roger Ritt** (see p.1103) focuses predominantly on the tax elements of corporate M&A transactions, including taxable and tax-free M&A and federal and state controversies, although he is also active in bankruptcies and workouts. Sources testified to him being "*without a doubt, a name that conjures up respect.*" The "*creative and resourceful*" **Robert Burke** (see p.1088) is "*among the best in the land for partnership work,*" according to sources. His practice includes representations of limited liability partnerships regarding tax matters related to venture capital and hedge fund activities. **Richard Giuliani** (see p.1093) "*takes an innovative and meticulously detailed stance*" on corporate, partnership and individual state and federal matters. He is involved in tax aspects of transactions, controversies and mutual fund matters.

## Band 3

### Foley Hoag LLP

**The Firm:** This compact, transaction-oriented group is capable of offering an innovative approach to tax questions, claim interviewees. Key areas of expertise include international tax planning and advice to hedge and other investment funds, as well as to high net worth individuals. The team also boasts a distinctive niche in representing US entities investing in forestry plantations and other natural resources in the southern hemisphere.

**The Lawyers:** In international tax planning, **Leonard Schneidman** is "*a true expert in the field, with the capacity to deal with any matter that falls his way,*" according to commentators. He is often found assisting US clients doing business abroad, particularly in Europe, as well as counseling in-bound foreign clients.

**Clients/Work Highlights:** Notable clients include Millicom International Cellular and Global Forest Partners LP.

### Sullivan & Worcester LLP

**The Firm:** This East Coast firm "*really understands the client's aims,*" say sources. The 30-strong team "*has a firm grip on tax work*" concerning Fortune 500 corporations, closely held businesses and individuals. With offices in Boston, New York and Washington, DC, the resourceful and multitalented group handles a host of matters ranging from corporate taxation and cross-border planning to federal and state controversy work, as well as planning for charitable trusts. The firm also boasts a separate trusts and estates practice that is "*hard to fault,*" say clients.

**The Lawyers: Michael Davis** is a "*truly exceptional lawyer,*" say sources, who praise the group head for his wealth of experience, particularly in the income tax and estate planning sector. His clients tend to be owners of closely held businesses, as well as those

with large holdings of real estate and S corporation stock. "*A rising star among the ranks,*" co-director of the group **Ameek Ponda** debuts in the tables on the basis of his "*well thought-out*" handling of the tax elements of M&A and REIT transactions.

**Clients/Work Highlights:** Fortune 500 companies; entrepreneurs; financial institutions; closely held businesses; hedge funds; LBO and venture capital funds, and REITs all feature in a solid portfolio of clients.

## Other Notable Practitioners

Sources recommend **Louis Marett** of Choate Hall & Stewart for his work in the transactional arena. Clients like the fact that he "*won't enter into a transaction without considering all the aspects first.*" He acts primarily for technology companies and associated investors, providing domestic and cross-border transactional support. He also advises on executive compensation issues. Marett acted for Sand Video during its acquisition by Broadcom and advised Bessemer Venture Partners on the formation of Bessemer Venture Partners VI in 2005. Market feedback confirmed the "*quick and creative*" **Arnold May** (see p.1099) of Proskauer Rose LLP as "*a force to be reckoned with*" in the fund formation market and the private equity field. "*You trust him because he knows what he is talking about,*" reported one client. May handled tax aspects of the formation of the Latin Power Fund and assisted long-standing client The Wellcome Trust in the past year. Private equity expert **Joe Newberg** (see p.1101) of the Boston office of Weil, Gotshal & Manges LLP is able to "*juggle a number of competing interests and find a common ground.*" Of late, his practice has included acting for a number of foreign investors with their investments in limited liability companies. He is appreciated by clients for his "*accessibility and a nonadversarial approach that always looks after the best interests of the client.*"

# Leaders in Massachusetts

### ABELSON, Ned
Goulston & Storrs, Boston
617 482 1776
*Recommended in Environment*

### ABRAMS, Donald-Bruce
Bingham McCutchen LLP, Boston
617 951 8584
don.abrams@bingham.com
*Recommended in Tax*

**Practice Areas:** Primarily devoted to advising corporations, partnerships and individuals on federal, state and international tax controversy and transactional tax planning matters. Transactional practice includes providing advice on structuring and negotiation of mergers and acquisitions, equity and debt financing transactions, real estate and project finance transactions, bankruptcy and restructuring transactions, leveraged leas-

es and structured finance transactions. Controversy practice includes extensive representation of clients in administrative and federal and Massachusetts court proceedings. Represents clients in obtaining administrative rulings from both the Internal Revenue Service and Massachusetts Department of Revenue.

**Personal:** Harvard Law School, JD, 1987; MIT, MBA,1984; MIT, BS, 1982.

### ACKERSTEIN, Joan
Jackson Lewis, Boston
617 367 0025
ackerstj@jacksonlewis.com
*Recommended in Employment*

**Practice Areas:** Employment litigation and counseling on behalf of management, including discrimination, contract and tort claims, reductions in force, ADA and FMLA leaves, non-competition agreements and ERISA litigation. Chair

of Employment Litigation Practice.

**Career:** Associate, Goodwin, Procter & Hoar, Boston (1977-83); Assistant US Attorney, Office of the United States Attorney, Boston (1983-86); Partner, Jackson Lewis, Boston (1987 to present).

**Publications:** 'The Americans With Disabilities Act – What Supervisors Need to Know', Business Skills Express Series, 1994.

**Personal:** Georgetown University Law Center, JD, 1977; editor, Georgetown Law Journal; 2004-05 Massachusetts Super Lawyer; Recommended Attorney in 'PLC Which Lawyer? Yearbook 2006.'

### ALFRED, Richard
Seyfarth Shaw LLP, Boston
617 946 4800
*Recommended in Employment*

### AMBASH, Joseph
Seyfarth Shaw LLP, Boston
617 946 4800
*Recommended in Employment*

### ANGLEHART, Donald
Gadsby Hannah LLP, Boston
617 345 7000
*Recommended in Environment*

### APFEL, David J
Goodwin Procter LLP, Boston
617 570 1000
dapfel@goodwinprocter.com
*Recommended in Litigation*

**Practice Areas:** Mr Apfel is an experienced trial lawyer who defends individuals and entities in criminal and complex civil litigation. His areas of expertise are white-collar crime, including insider trading and money laundering; government investigations, especially Department of Justice, US Attorneys Offices, SEC and NASD investigations; the federal False Claims Act; the federal Racketeer Influenced and Corrupt Organizations Act (RICO); and multi-dimensional business litigation. He also specializes in land use litigation.

**Prof. Memberships:** Massachusetts State 'Murder List': Member Attorney; US District Court's 'CJA Panel': Member Attorney.

**Personal:** JD, Northeastern University School of Law, 1987; BA, Swarthmore College, 1974.

## APPELBAUM, Mitchel
WilmerHale, Boston
617 526 6713
mitchel.appelbaum@wilmerhale.com
*Recommended in Bankruptcy*

**Practice Areas:** Practice focuses on matters involving the financial restructuring of corporate clients, including the use of Chapter 11, secured lending, lease arrangements and other commercial transactions for clients. Advises variety of clients on acquisition of troubled companies through section 363 sales, and has counseled various secured and unsecured creditors with respect to bankruptcy, workout and restructuring matters.

**Prof. Memberships:** Turnaround Management Association; American, Massachusetts and Boston Bar Associations; Board of Directors, The Lawyers Clearinghouse for Homelessness and Affordable Housing, Inc.

**Career:** Admitted to Massachusetts Bar. Joined firm in 1991.

**Personal:** Boston University School of Law (JD); Brandeis University (BA).

## ARMISTEAD, Cary
Ropes & Gray LLP, Boston
671 951 7832
cary.armistead@ropesgray.com
*Recommended in Antitrust*

**Practice Areas:** Counsels domestic and multinational corporations regarding corporate legal matters, the antitrust laws of the US, and the competition laws of European Union and other nations in: joint ventures, mergers, acquisitions, and divestitures; acquisition and licensing of intellectual property rights; distribution of products and services. Assists high technology and other clients with domestic and international commercial matters including technology transfers, distribution and licensing agreements, and other complex business arrangements.

**Career:** District of Columbia Bar (1970); Massachusetts Bar (1979); Partner, Ropes & Gray (1996).

**Personal:** JD, cum laude, Columbia Law School (1970); BA, Economics, Michigan State University (1967).

## ARNOLD, Beth E
Foley Hoag LLP, Boston
617 832 1000
*Recommended in Intellectual Property*

## ARROWOOD, Lisa
Todd & Weld LLP, Boston
617 720 2626
*Recommended in Litigation*

## ASHER JR, William
Choate Hall & Stewart, Boston
617 248 5000
*Recommended in Corporate/M&A*

## BACHMAN, Katharine E
WilmerHale, Boston
617 526 6216
katharine.bachman@wilmerhale.com
*Recommended in Real Estate*

**Practice Areas:** Vice-Chair of Wilmer-Hale's Real Estate Department. Practice covers broad spectrum of real estate development and financial transactions, including representation of investors and developers in office, industrial, R&D facilities and residential developments. Represents institutional lenders in loan collection matters and landlords and tenants in commercial leasing matters (including high technology and biotechnology facilities). Special interest in projects involving public/private partnerships and affordable housing.

**Prof. Memberships:** New England Regional Advisory Committee of The Trust for Public Land; Trustee, Dickinson College.

**Career:** Admitted to Massachusetts Bar.

**Personal:** New York University School of Law (JD); Dickinson College (BA, summa cum laude).

## BALDIGA, William
Brown Rudnick Berlack Israels LLP, Boston 617 856 8200
*Recommended in Bankruptcy*

## BARKER, Christopher B
Goodwin Procter LLP, Boston
617 570 1000
cbarker@goodwinprocter.com
*Recommended in Real Estate*

**Practice Areas:** Mr Barker has particular expertise in representing tax-exempt entities in structuring and implementing debt and equity investments in real estate and in real estate operating companies. His practice, national in scope, involves representing institutional investors, public and private real estate operating companies and lenders in a wide range of real estate activities. Clients include: Charlesbank Capital Partners, AEW Capital Management, Westcor Partners, Beacon Capital Partners, AMB Properties, La Quinta Hotels, Wyndham Hotels, Leggat McCall Properties and Liberty Properties.

**Personal:** JD, Harvard Law School, 1985; BA, Brown University, 1982 (magna cum laude).

## BARR, Lynne B
Goodwin Procter LLP, Boston
617 570 1000
lbarr@goodwinprocter.com
*Recommended in Banking & Finance*

**Practice Areas:** Ms Barr advises banks,

bank holding companies, brokerage concerns, mortgage companies, trade associations and other entities on general corporate matters, including the operation and offering of their products and services, particularly in the context of federal and state regulation of financial institutions and their activities. She has extensive experience in credit and mortgage lending matters, fair lending and equal credit opportunity issues, credit and deposit services, electronic banking and Internet services, and insurance products.

**Personal:** JD, George Washington University, 1975 (with honors); BA, George Washington University, 1972.

## BARSHAK, Edward
Sugarman, Rogers, Barshak & Cohen, PC, Boston 617 227 3030
*Recommended in Litigation*

## BASSETT, David
WilmerHale, Boston 617 526 6259
david.bassett@wilmerhale.com
*Recommended in Intellectual Property*

**Practice Areas:** Practice concentrates on intellectual property litigation, particularly biotechnology and pharmaceutical patent disputes. Represents clients in variety of other business disputes, including breach of contract, Lanham Act and Internet-related claims. Covers all facets of litigation, including discovery, settlement, alternative dispute resolution, trials and appeals.

**Prof. Memberships:** American and Massachusetts Bar Associations; Co-Chair, Intellectual Property Litigation Committee of the Boston Bar Association.

**Career:** Admitted to Massachusetts Bar and Indiana Bar. Joined firm in 1989.

**Personal:** Harvard Law School (JD, cum laude); Editor, 'Harvard Law Review'; Finalist, Ames Moot Court Competition; Indiana University (BA, with Honors and Distinction National Merit Scholarship).

## BATES, Jeffrey
McDermott Will & Emery, Boston
617 535 4068
jbates@mwe.com
*Recommended in Environment*

**Practice Areas:** Practices international and environmental law. Provides counsel to corporations, environmental organizations and governments in connection with international law, environmental litigation, due diligence, product roll-outs, compliance, cleanups, brownfields development, insurance coverage and products, corporate and governmental policy, and legislation and rulemaking worldwide. Has considerable experience with high profile, complex litigation and controversies.

**Prof. Memberships:** Admitted to US Supreme Court, US District Court for the District of Massachusetts, US Court of Appeals for the First Circuit, US Court of Appeals for the District of Columbia,

Supreme Judicial Court of Massachusetts.

**Personal:** Colgate University (BA); University of Virginia Law School (JD).

## BATTER III, John F
WilmerHale, Boston
617 526 6754
john.batter@wilmerhale.com
*Recommended in Litigation*

**Practice Areas:** Partner in Wilmer-Hale's Securities Department and Litigation Department. Mr Batter's practice focuses on the defense of public and private companies and their directors and management against breach of fiduciary duty claims and securities fraud allegations, including those arising out of IPOs and in SEC investigations.

**Prof. Memberships:** Mr Batter has served as a panelist for Massachusetts Continuing Legal Education programs and is a visiting teacher at MIT's Sloan School of Management, co-teaching since 1984 'The Manager's Legal Function'.

**Career:** Joined the firm in 1982. Admitted to Massachusetts Bar.

**Personal:** Harvard Law School (JD); Massachusetts Institute of Technology (SB).

## BAUER, Steven M
Proskauer Rose LLP, Boston
617 526 9700
sbauer@proskauer.com
*Recommended in Intellectual Property*

**Practice Areas:** Mr Bauer is a Partner in Proskauer Rose's Patent Litigation and Dispute Resolution Group, Head of the firm's Boston office, and on the firm's Policy Committee. He has practiced over 20 years exclusively in complex patent and other intellectual property enforcement, litigation and dispute resolution, and has substantial trial and appellate experience. He has been lead counsel in matters ranging from siRNA, genetic testing and medical devices; software, encryption and business method processes; high-energy plasma systems and high-temperature superconductors; telecommunications, digital compression and cable industry technology; and nanotechnology and polymer chemistry.

**Prof. Memberships:** Roster of Neutrals, American Arbitration Association; Vice-Chair, Litigation Committee of the Intellectual Property Owners' Association; Past Editor, AIPLA Quarterly Journal.

**Publications:** He speaks regularly to leading patent law and industry groups (eg, The Sedona Conference, MIT Sloan School, National Bureau of Economic Research), and has been quoted often in the national press on intellectual property issues (eg, The Economist, Associated Press, InfoWorld, Boston Business Journal).

**Personal:** Boston University School of Law, JD cum laude, 1983. Massachusetts Institute of Technology, MS (Electrical

Engineering), 1980. Massachusetts Institute of Technology, BS (Electrical Engineering & Computer Science), 1979.

### BEAUDOIN, Thomas A
WilmerHale, Boston
617 526 6661
thomas.beaudoin@wilmerhale.com
*Recommended in Private Fund Formation*
**Practice Areas:** Firm's Fund Formation Group Chair. Advises US and non-US fund managers, institutional investors and investment advisors on broad range of issues, including capital formations, secondary transactions, portfolio investments, internal governance and administration, and divestments and distributions.
**Prof. Memberships:** American Bar Association; Massachusetts Bar Association; Boston Bar Association.
**Career:** Admitted to Massachusetts Bar. Partner at Testa, Hurwitz & Thibeault, LLP before joining firm in 2004.
**Publications:** Frequent lecturer and panelist at private equity industry-sponsored events (US and abroad); writes for several prominent private equity publications.
**Personal:** George Washington University Law School (JD, with Honors); Boston University (BA, cum laude).

### BELLO, Kenneth
Bello, Black & Welsh LLP, Boston
617 247 4100
*Recommended in Employment*

### BENJAMIN, William
WilmerHale, Boston
617 526 6318
william.benjamin@wilmerhale.com
*Recommended in Tax*
**Practice Areas:** Advises on legal and tax aspects of international business transactions. Represents US companies in connection with their activities outside the US, and foreign businesses and individuals with respect to their activities in the US.
**Prof. Memberships:** New England Regional Council of the International Fiscal Association; Editorial Advisory Board of Practical US/International Tax Strategies; and the International, American, Massachusetts and Boston Bar Associations.
**Career:** Admitted to Massachusetts Bar, New York Bar, United States Tax Court. Joined firm in 1982.
**Personal:** Harvard Law School (JD, cum laude); Graduate Institute of International Studies, Fulbright Scholar; Princeton University (BA, summa cum laude).

### BENNETT JR, Charles R
Hanify & King, Boston 617 423 0400
crb@hanify.com
*Recommended in Bankruptcy*
**Practice Areas:** Complex commercial litigation involving financial institutions

and corporations, including directors' and officers' claims and insolvency. The current focus of his practice is on rights and remedies for debtors and creditors in corporate Chapter 11 cases. Mr Bennett has substantial experience in banking and lending litigation representing both borrowers and banking institutions in commercial disputes. He has tried numerous jury and jury-waived cases concerning business torts, unfair trade practices, and insolvency issues.
**Prof. Memberships:** American Bankruptcy Institute, Massachusetts and Boston Bar Associations.
**Career:** Massachusetts Bar, New Hampshire Bar, Rhode Island Bar.
**Personal:** JD, Boston College Law School (1974); BA, cum laude, Boston College (1970).

### BENOIT, Wilfred J
Goodwin Procter LLP, Boston
617 570 1000
wbenoit@goodwinprocter.com
*Recommended in Employment*
**Practice Areas:** Mr Benoit has represented management in all types of labor and employee relations disputes since 1975. He also has extensive employment litigation and alternative dispute resolution experience. He has successfully defended companies across a broad spectrum of industries in suits involving a wide variety of wrongful discharge and employment discrimination issues, including disparate treatment, sexual and racial harassment, equal pay, reasonable accommodation of disabilities and age discrimination claims arising out of reductions in force.
**Personal:** JD, University of Michigan Law School, 1973 (cum laude); BA, University of Notre Dame, 1970 (cum laude).

### BERMAN, David
Riemer & Braunstein LLP, Boston
617 523 9000
*Recommended in Banking & Finance*

### BERMAN, Mark N
Nixon Peabody LLP, Boston
617 345 6037
mberman@nixonpeabody.com
*Recommended in Bankruptcy*
**Practice Areas:** Chapter 11 reorganizations, Chapter 7 liquidations, out-of-court workouts, securitizations, intercreditor issues in the structuring and documentation of financing transactions.
**Prof. Memberships:** Admitted to practice in MA, US District Court (MA), US Court of Appeals (First Circuit), US Supreme Court. Fellow, American College of Bankruptcy; Boston Bar Association (former Chair Business Law Section and Bankruptcy Committee); American Bar Association; American Bankruptcy Institute (Ed. ABI World; Co-Chair Northeast Bankruptcy Conference); Loan Syndications and Trading Association; Client Security Board (former Vice

Chairman, Secretary, and Treasurer); Instructor in Business and Credit Law for National Association of Credit Management.
**Career:** Partner, Nixon Peabody LLP; Hutchins & Wheeler; Widett, Slater & Goldman, P.C. Legal Assistant, Office of the District Attorney for Suffolk County.
**Publications:** 'Buying and Selling a Distressed Business' a chapter in a book entitled 'Buying and Selling a Privately Owned Business', published by Massachusetts Continuing Legal Education (MCLE), November, 2005; 'Not So Fast! Delaware Court Reigns in Creditor Suits Against Ds & Os' published in the American Bankruptcy Institute Journal, May, 2005; 'Plain Meaning and the Assumption (OR NOT) of a License of Copyrighted Software' published on ABI World, May, 2004.
**Personal:** Boston College, JD; Northwestern University, BA.

### BERNSTEIN, Stephen W
McDermott Will & Emery, Boston
617 535 4062
sbernstein@mwe.com
*Recommended in Healthcare*
**Practice Areas:** Co-Chair: Health Transactions Practice, and HIPAA Practice. Specializes in health information, e-health, privacy/security/HIPAA, electronic health records, clinical trials and patient registries as well as healthcare merger/acquisitions, affiliations and joint ventures. Works with pharmaceutical/biotech companies, healthcare providers, universities and insurers concerning uses of health information and tissue samples for clinical and database research, patient registries and marketing matters. Representative clients include: Harvard University, Massachusetts eHealth Collaborative, Cardinal Health.
**Personal:** Boston College Law School (JD, cum laude), Duke University (AB, magna cum laude).

### BETTENCOURT, Mark T
Goodwin Procter LLP, Boston
617 570 1000
mbettencourt@goodwinprocter.com
*Recommended in Corporate/M&A*
**Practice Areas:** Mr Bettencourt concentrates his practice on general corporate and securities law and has extensive experience in mergers and acquisitions, public offerings, private placements of debt and equity securities, securities law compliance, and technology transfer and licensing. He represents start-up, private and public companies in a wide range of industries, including software, hardware, networking equipment, information services and healthcare. He has worked with numerous companies from their initial financing through successful initial public offerings or acquisitions.
**Personal:** JD, New York University

School of Law, 1994 (cum laude); BA, University of Notre Dame, 1991 (with high honors).

### BIALECKI, Gregory P
DLA Piper Rudnick Gray Cary US LLP, Boston 617 406 6019
gregory.bialecki@dlapiper.com
*Recommended in Real Estate*
**Practice Areas:** Real estate; state legislation and public policy.
**Career:** His practice is focused on permitting, construction, and development of large mixed-use urban redevelopment projects. His work frequently involves technical and strategic advice on sophisticated land use and environmental regulation matters. His clients include nonprofit organizations and governmental agencies engaged in land conservation and open space protection.
**Personal:** JD, Harvard Law School; BA, Harvard University.

### BIANCHI, Alden
Mintz Levin Cohn Ferris Glovsky and Popeo PC, Boston 617 542 6000
*Recommended in Employee Benefits*

### BLAU, Michael L
McDermott Will & Emery, Boston
617 535 4010
mblau@mwe.com
*Recommended in Healthcare*
**Practice Areas:** Chairs Health Department's planning committee. Represents for-profit and non-profit healthcare organizations. Advises corporate and regulatory matters, including mergers, acquisitions and affiliations, managed care contracting, and forming provider groups, networks, alliances, health plans and joint ventures.
**Prof. Memberships:** Co-Chairs Boston Bar Association's Child Mental Health Task Force. Chairman, Project HEALTH, a national charity that operates volunteer programs in conjunction with academic institutions improving the health status of impoverished children with chronic medical conditions.
**Career:** Recognized among the top 10 health attorneys by Nightingale's Healthcare News.
**Personal:** Georgetown University Law Center (JD, cum laude); Harvard College (AB, magna cum laude).

### BLECK, Daniel
Mintz Levin Cohn Ferris Glovsky and Popeo PC, Boston 617 348 4498
dsbleck@mintz.com
*Recommended in Bankruptcy*
**Practice Areas:** Bankruptcy, restructuring and commercial law.
**Prof. Memberships:** Daniel is a member of various associations including the Turnaround Management Association and the American Bankruptcy Institute.
**Career:** Daniel is a member in the Boston office of Mintz Levin, practicing in the Bankruptcy, Restructuring and

Commercial Law Section. He specializes in insolvency, workouts, bankruptcy and creditors' rights. Daniel represents debtors, secured and unsecured creditors, and trustees in all aspects of Chapter 7 and 11 proceedings, as well as advising clients in out-of-court debt restructurings. He also represents bondholders and indenture trustees in various workouts as well as bankruptcy proceedings. In addition to advising clients in troubled debt transactions, Daniel also represents institutional leaders in various financing matters and represents insurers in mass tort bankruptcies as well as clients in bankruptcy acquisitions.

**Publications:** Daniel has published various articles associated with insolvency matters and has also been featured as a lecturer in various forums.

**Personal:** He received his BA, cum laude, from Boston College (1986), and his JD, cum laude, from Boston University Law School (1989).

### BORDEN, Mark
WilmerHale, Boston
617 526 6675
mark.borden@wilmerhale.com
*Recommended in Corporate/M&A, Private Equity*

**Practice Areas:** Member of the firm's Management Committee and Co-Chair of the Corporate Department. Practice concentrates primarily in the areas of securities law, corporate finance and acquisitions; has over 25 years' experience in representing public companies; represented companies and underwriters in over 100 public offerings; has extensive experience both in structuring acquisitions and in designing defenses against unsolicited takeovers.

**Career:** Admitted to Massachusetts Bar. Joined firm in 1976.

**Publications:** Co-author of 'Start-up Companies – Planning, Financing and Operating the Successful Business', published by Law Journal Seminars Press.

**Personal:** Harvard Law School (JD); Yale University (BA, summa cum laude).

### BOTHWICK, Jay
WilmerHale, Boston
617 526 6526
jay.bothwick@wilmerhale.com
*Recommended in Corporate/M&A*

**Practice Areas:** Member of the firm's Executive Committee and Chair of the firm's Mergers and Acquisitions Group. Practice focuses on mergers and acquisitions and has significant experience in venture capital and corporate finance transactions. Advises public and private companies, both domestically and overseas, in mergers and acquisitions, tender and exchange offers, proxy contests and public and private offerings.

**Prof. Memberships:** American, Massachusetts and Boston Bar Associations; Negotiated Acquisitions Committee of

the Business Law Section of the American Bar Association.

**Career:** Admitted to Massachusetts Bar. Joined firm in 1981.

**Personal:** Columbia Law School (JD); Bowdoin College (AB).

### BRAUN, Peter
McDermott Will & Emery, Boston
617 535 4032
pbraun@mwe.com
*Recommended in Healthcare*

**Practice Areas:** Has significant experience in general counsel, corporate and regulatory matters affecting hospitals and other aspects of the healthcare industry. Has assisted in a substantial number of corporate restructurings, joint ventures and tax-exempt bond financings involving healthcare industry clients.

**Personal:** Franklin Pierce Law Center (JD), Oberlin College (BA).

### BRIGHAM, Johan V
Bingham McCutchen LLP, Boston
617 951 8351
johan.brigham@bingham.com
*Recommended in Corporate/M&A*

**Practice Areas:** Maintains general corporate and securities practice, with concentrations in the representation of technology companies, particularly in the medical device and biotechnology areas, and in mergers and acquisitions, including representation of both financial and strategic acquirors. Has represented numerous public and private companies and debt and equity financing sources, including investment banks, private equity firms and venture capital firms in mergers and acquisitions, leveraged buyouts, joint ventures and other corporate partnering transactions, as well as private and public offerings of debt and equity and restructurings.

**Personal:** University of Michigan Law School, JD, 1991; Yale University, BA, 1988.

### BROWN, John S
Bingham McCutchen LLP, Boston
617 951 8252
john.brown@bingham.com
*Recommended in Tax*

**Practice Areas:** Maintains practice devoted primarily to federal and state tax matters. Provides tax-planning advice in connection with structuring organizations and transactions. Handles federal and state tax controversies, involving both administrative proceedings and litigation.

**Career:** Served as special assistant to the assistant attorney general in the Tax Division of the US Department of Justice. Also spent four years as an assistant and then associate professor of law at Cornell University Law School.

**Personal:** Cornell Law School, LLB, with distinction, 1965; Villanova University, BA, 1957.

### BROWN, Margaret A
Skadden, Arps, Slate, Meagher & Flom LLP & Affiliates, Boston
617 573 4815
mabrown@skadden.com
*Recommended in Corporate/M&A*

**Practice Areas:** Counsels on a wide variety of corporate matters, concentrating on merger and acquisition transactions, corporate financings and corporate governance matters. Represents various venture capital investors and start-up companies and has been underwriter's and issuer's counsel in a number of public offerings of debt and equity securities. Has also worked on a number of proxy contests and consent solicitations, as well as restructurings of publicly held debt securities.

**Career:** JD, Boston College Law School, 1979 (cum laude; Articles Editor, Boston College Law Review); BA, Holy Cross College, 1976.

### BROWNE, Steven C
Bingham McCutchen LLP, Boston
617 951 8124
steven.browne@bingham.com
*Recommended in Corporate/M&A*

**Practice Areas:** Serves as Co-Chair of Corporate Mergers & Acquisitions and Securities Group. Has extensive experience in mergers and acquisitions, leveraged buyouts, corporate finance, private equity financing transactions, public offerings, SEC compliance, and technology transfer and licensing. Serves as general counsel to public and privately held companies in a variety of industries. Also represents private equity firms in complex structured finance transactions as well as early and later-stage financings. Serves as counsel to boards of directors on corporate governance matters.

**Personal:** Cornell Law School, JD, cum laude, 1988; University of Rhode Island, BA, cum laude, 1985.

### BRUNTS, Eve M
Ropes & Gray LLP, Boston
617 951 7911
eve.brunts@ropesgray.com
*Recommended in Healthcare*

**Practice Areas:** Advises on Medicare and Medicaid coverage, claims and payment requirements for various services; reimbursement for healthcare services in clinical trials; Medicaid drug rebate program and other drug pricing programs; regulation and contracting for Medicare, Medicaid and commercial managed care; federal and state fraud and abuse laws; healthcare regulatory compliance policies. Assists in corporate transactions and government investigations involving healthcare manufacturers, providers or insurers by providing regulatory and reimbursement advice.

**Career:** Massachusetts Bar (1995); Partner, Ropes & Gray (2004).

**Personal:** JD, Yale Law School (1995);

BA, magna cum laude, Yale University (1992); LLM, Cambridge University (1997).

### BUCHANAN JR, Robert
Choate Hall & Stewart, Boston
617 248 5000
*Recommended in Antitrust*

### BUCK, Charles
McDermott Will & Emery, Boston
617 535 4151
cbuck@mwe.com
*Recommended in Healthcare*

**Practice Areas:** Specializes in healthcare transactions, affiliations, and joint ventures; federal and state regulatory matters, including anti-kickback and Stark law; health privacy and HIPAA; federal tax-exemption; and state insurance law. Representative clients include: Dana-Farber Cancer Institute, Blue Cross and Blue Shield of Massachusetts, and the Massachusetts e-Health Collaborative.

**Career:** Professional Staff of the United States Senate Finance Committee, with responsibility for Medicare Part A (1994-96); law clerk to the Honorable Charles R Breyer, Northern District of California (2001-02).

**Personal:** Stanford Law School (JD, Order of the Coif); Middlebury College (BA, magna cum laude).

### BUCKING, James
Foley Hoag LLP, Boston
617 832 1000
*Recommended in Employment*

### BURGER, Sharon
Nutter, McClennen & Fish, LLP, Boston
617 439 2000
*Recommended in Employment*

### BURKE, Robert
WilmerHale, Boston
617 526 6470
robert.burke@wilmerhale.com
*Recommended in Tax*

**Practice Areas:** Practice concentrates on the taxation of partnerships and limited liability companies engaged in investment activities (including real estate, venture capital and 'hedge fund' activities) and business operations as well as on corporate restructurings, acquisitions, and dispositions and the taxation of financial instruments.

**Prof. Memberships:** Member of the American Bar Association's Section on Taxation; serves on its Committee on Partnerships and Subcommittee on Partnership Allocations.

**Career:** Admitted to Massachusetts Bar.

**Personal:** Williams College (BA, magna cum laude, Phi Beta Kappa); Cornell University Law School (JD, magna cum laude); Boston University School of Law (LLM in taxation).

## BURLING, James
WilmerHale, Boston
617 526 6416
james.burling@wilmerhale.com
*Recommended in Antitrust*
**Practice Areas:** Co-Chair of firm's Antitrust and Competition Department. Concentrates in antitrust litigation and merger clearance for high technology clients, particularly in computer, Internet, biotech and pharmaceutical industries. Represents clients in private litigation, in responding to government antitrust investigations, and before the Department of Justice and Federal Trade Commission in Hart-Scott-Rodino review of mergers and acquisitions.
**Prof. Memberships:** American Bar Association Antitrust Section; Boston Bar Association Antitrust Committee; Massachusetts Bar Association.
**Career:** Admitted to Massachusetts Bar, United States Supreme Court. Joined firm in 1978 after two years with the Federal Trade Commission.
**Personal:** Harvard Law School (JD); Grinnell College (AB).

## BURT, Laurie
Foley Hoag LLP, Boston
617 832 1000
*Recommended in Environment*

## CABLE, Stuart M
Goodwin Procter LLP, Boston
617 570 1000
scable@goodwinprocter.com
*Recommended in Corporate/M&A*
**Practice Areas:** Mr Cable represents as outside general counsel a wide array of public and private companies involved in diverse businesses, including those involving life sciences, optical components, semiconductors, professional services, alternative energy and software. His transactional practice is focused on public offering transactions, negotiating, structuring and implementing strategic acquisitions and private placements of equity and debt.
**Prof. Memberships:** The Buckingham, Browne and Nichols School: Chairman of the Board of Trustees; Beth Israel Hospital: Trustee.
**Personal:** JD, Columbia Law School, 1979; MBA, Amos Tuck School of Business Administration at Dartmouth College, 1976; AB, Dartmouth College, 1975 (magna cum laude).

## CAPORIZZO, A William
WilmerHale, Boston
617 526 6411
william.caporizzo@wilmerhale.com
*Recommended in Employee Benefits*
**Practice Areas:** Bill Caporizzo is Co-Chair of the Tax Department of Wilmer-Hale and a certified public accountant. He focuses his practice on the taxation of domestic and cross-border corporate mergers, acquisitions and dispositions, as well as international restructurings. His practice also includes the taxation of partnerships and limited liability companies engaged in investment activities and real estate activities. Mr Caporizzo is a member of the firm's Joint Venture and Fund Formation Group.
**Prof. Memberships:** Member of the Tax Sections of the American, Massachusetts, and Boston Bar Associations.
**Personal:** Boston University School of Law (JD); University of Pennsylvania (BS).

## CAPRARO JR, Joseph A
Proskauer Rose LLP, Boston
617 526 9800
jcapraro@proskauer.com
*Recommended in Intellectual Property*
**Practice Areas:** Partner in the Patent Law and Intellectual Property Practice Groups at Proskauer Rose. Provides clients with practical legal advice across the spectrum of intellectual property areas. Represents technology start-ups and private and public emerging technology companies. Works closely with clients in developing national and international patent and trademark portfolios. Experience in the area of patent prosecution includes strategic portfolio prosecution development, patent reissue and re-examination proceedings in the US, and patent opposition proceedings throughout the world. Has extensive experience in technology and intellectual property licensing, and has also participated in numerous intellectual property litigations and in alternative dispute resolution of intellectual property matters.
**Personal:** Suffolk University Law School, JD, cum laude, 1993. Tufts University, BS, magna cum laude, 1985.

## CARROLL, James R
Skadden, Arps, Slate, Meagher & Flom LLP & Affiliates, Boston
617 573 4801
jcarroll@skadden.com
*Recommended in Litigation*
**Practice Areas:** Has experience in mutual fund, insurance and securities class action defense as well as a broad array of complex civil litigations. He is currently national coordinating counsel for a major New York-based life insurer and is defending a variety of purported class and individual actions in the life, disability and casualty insurance contexts. He regularly represents individuals and corporations in SEC enforcement matters. Has tried cases to verdict in the areas of alleged securities fraud, theft of trade secrets and covenant-not-to-compete disputes.
**Career:** JD, Harvard University, 1989; BA, Niagara University, 1985 (summa cum laude; Presidential Scholar).

## CASEY, David
Littler Mendelson, PC, Boston
617 378 6000
dccasey@littler.com
*Recommended in Employment*
**Practice Areas:** Focused on defending management in employment law including individual and class-wide claims involving discrimination and harassment, wage and hour, ERISA, wrongful termination, fiduciary duty, unfair competition and disclosure of proprietary information. Counsels employers on a daily basis in many aspects of the employment relationship including litigation avoidance, terminations, diversity and safeguarding proprietary information. Admitted to practice in all the federal and state courts of Massachusetts.
**Prof. Memberships:** Has co-chaired the Boston Bar's Labor and Employment Section; served as adjunct member, Northeastern Law School's Faculty, and on its Dean's Committee.
**Personal:** Northeastern University (JD, 1979); Brown University (BA, 1976).

## CHAPIN, David C
Ropes & Gray LLP, Boston
617 951 7371
david.chapin@ropesgray.com
*Recommended in Corporate/M&A, Private Equity*
**Practice Areas:** Member of the firm's Policy Committee and the Strategic Development Partner at Ropes & Gray. Specializes in private equity transactions, securities law and mergers and acquisitions involving public companies. Practice includes representing private equity sponsors, issuers of high-yield debt, underwriters of debt and equity securities, and purchasers of high-yield '144A' debt offerings. Broad experience representing clients in financial and strategic transactions.
**Career:** Massachusetts Bar (1980); Partner, Ropes & Gray (1989).
**Personal:** JD, cum laude, Harvard Law School (1980); BA, summa cum laude, Lafayette College (1976).

## CHARKOUDIAN, Stephen G
Goodwin Procter LLP, Boston
617 570 1000
scharkoudian@goodwinprocter.com
*Recommended in Intellectual Property*
**Practice Areas:** Mr Charkoudian's practice encompasses a broad range of intellectual property and technology matters, including advising clients on intellectual property protection, technology licensing and transfers, product development and distribution, mergers and acquisitions of technology companies, technology joint ventures, and venture capital transactions. He has represented hi-tech, life sciences, private equity and venture capital firms, emerging growth companies and other clients in intellectual property matters, including issues relating to patents, trademarks, copyrights and trade secrets.
**Personal:** JD, American University, Washington College of Law, 1992 (cum laude); BA, Boston College, 1987 (cum laude).

## CHILD, Ralph
Mintz Levin Cohn Ferris Glovsky and Popeo PC, Boston 617 542 6000
rchild@mintz.com
*Recommended in Environment*
**Practice Areas:** Environmental law.
**Career:** Mr Child is the senior member of Mintz Levin's Environmental Section. Major clients include energy project developers, manufacturers, and real estate developers. Ralph previously served as General Counsel to the Massachusetts Department of Environmental Protection, the principal environmental regulatory agency in Massachusetts with over 50 regulatory programs. Ralph graduated from Dartmouth College, held a fellowship at the Massachusetts legislature, and graduated from Harvard Law School, where he was an editor of the Harvard Law Review. He also was a Luce Scholar, providing counsel on legal reform efforts in Indonesia.

## CHORY, John
WilmerHale, Waltham
718 966 2001
john.chory@wilmerhale.com
*Recommended in Private Equity*
**Practice Areas:** Partner in charge of the firm's Waltham office. Member of the Corporate Department and Chair of WilmerHale Venture Group. Advises both private and public companies in the areas of initial- through late-stage venture capital financings, public offerings of securities, mergers and acquisitions, technology licensing and securities law. Also advises entrepreneurs in early-stage company formation and strategy.
**Publications:** Lectures frequently and has had several articles published on legal issues facing emerging companies.
**Personal:** Harvard Law School (JD 1988); Golden Gate University (MBA 1984); US Military Academy, West Point (BS 1980).

## CHRISTIAN, Joseph J
WilmerHale, Boston
617 526 6947
joseph.christian@wilmerhale.com
*Recommended in Real Estate*
**Practice Areas:** Chair of firm's Real Estate Capital Management Group. Has handled acquisition, management and disposition of real estate assets in all major US markets, representing investment advisory firms, operating companies, pension and profit-sharing plans, financial institutions and real estate investment trusts. Has also represented a US real estate operating company in the acquisition and development of a 1,500-acre parcel in Incheon, South Korea.

Areas of legal expertise include joint ventures, debt financings, real estate and land use law, environmental law, insurance company separate accounts, taxation of tax-exempt entities, and rules governing real estate investment trusts.

### CLEARY, John J
Goodwin Procter LLP, Boston
617 570 1000
jcleary@goodwinprocter.com
*Recommended in Employee Benefits*
**Practice Areas:** Mr Cleary specializes in all aspects of ERISA and employee benefits. He represents numerous employers in connection with their employee benefit requirements, including qualified and nonqualified retirement plans, welfare plans and executive compensation. Mr Cleary has particular experience with respect to issues arising in connection with corporate and real estate transactions and under Title I of ERISA, including fiduciary, investment and prohibited transaction matters.
**Prof. Memberships:** Government Affairs Committee of the Pension Real Estate Association: Member.
**Personal:** JD, Harvard Law School, 1974 (magna cum laude); MA, Yale University, 1970; BS, Massachusetts Institute of Technology, 1968.

### COHEN, Bret A
Mintz Levin Cohn Ferris Glovsky and Popeo PC, Boston 617 348 3089
bcohen@mintz.com
*Recommended in Employment*
**Practice Areas:** Bret is a member of the firm and practices in the Employment, Labor and Benefits Section. His practice includes representing employers in labor and employment litigation, including claims arising under FLSA, Title VII, ADA, ADEA, Mass. Gen. Laws ch. 151B, Massachusetts Wage Act, as well as state common law, breach of contract, wrongful termination and defamation claims. Bret has extensive experience litigating non-competition and non-solicitation agreements and executive compensation agreements. He frequently lectures on practice before the Massachusetts Commission Against Discrimination and on practice before the state and federal courts. He is a Fellow of the Massachusetts Bar Foundation. In August 2000, he was selected by the Massachusetts Lawyers Weekly as one of the top five up-and-coming lawyers in the state. More recently, Bret was ranked as one of Massachusetts' top employment defense attorneys by Chambers USA.
**Prof. Memberships:** The labor and employment law sections of the American Bar Association, the Bar Associations of Massachusetts, Illinois, Missouri, New Hampshire, Virginia, and Washington, DC. Bret is also admitted to practice before the US District Court for the District of Massachusetts, and the First Cir-

cuit Court of Appeals.
**Career:** Admitted to the state and federal Bars in Illinois (1993), Missouri (1994), Massachusetts (1997), New Hampshire (2004), Virginia (2006) and the District of Columbia (2006). A Partner at Mintz Levin since joining the firm in 2004. Frequently lectures on practice before the Massachusetts Commission Against Discrimination and Massachusetts civil practice. Past Chair of the New Lawyers Section of the Massachusetts Bar Association (1998-2000), MBA's Labor and Employment Law Section Council (2001-present) and a Fellow of the Massachusetts Bar Foundation. In August 2000, the Massachusetts Lawyers Weekly selected him as one of the top five up-and-coming lawyers in Massachusetts. Member of the Joint Bar Committee (2002-03); Chair of the Joint Bar Committee (2003-present), which reviews judicial nominations. Chair of American Bar Association's Business Law Section's subcommittee on employment litigation.
**Publications:** Bret has written and lectured extensively on employment law issues. He is a contributory author to the American Bar Association's Annual Review of Developments in Business and Corporate Litigation (2004 and 2005 editions). His speaking engagements include presentations at the SES Seminar (on Harassment and Discrimination, as well as Management Leave and Substance Abuse), 2004 Annual Meeting of the American Bar Association, MCAD Trial Training Seminar, and CEM Seminar (on 'Anatomy of a Discrimination Lawsuit from Both Sides'). Bret is the former Chair of the Joint Bar Committee for Judicial Appointments, and currently Chairs the American Bar Association's Subcommittee on Employment Litigation. Bret is the President of the Board of Directors of the Natick Montessori School. He has also published 'Ten Commandments to Practicing Before the Attorney Assisted Unit of the Massachusetts Commission Against Discrimination', MBA's Section Review (Feb 2003); '2004 Review of in Business and Corporate Litigation – Employment Law', American Bar Association (Jan 2004).
**Personal:** BA from the University of Illinois (1989). JD from St Louis University (1993) where he was awarded a Certificate in Labor and Employment Law and received the American Jurisprudence Award and the Everett E Hullverson Award.

### COHEN, Stephen
Choate Hall & Stewart, Boston
617 248 5000
*Recommended in Private Equity*

### COHN, Daniel
Cohn Whitesell & Goldberg LLP, Boston
617 951 2505
cohn@cwg11.com

*Recommended in Bankruptcy*
**Practice Areas:** Focuses on financially distressed companies. Clients include debtors in out-of-court restructurings and Chapter 11 reorganizations, acquirers of distressed businesses and assets, other parties with a stake in the troubled company, and defendants in bankruptcy-related litigation. Industry experience includes manufacturing, retail, healthcare, environmental, technology, plastics, automotive components, broadcasting, advertising and real estate. Also serves as mediator/arbitrator.
**Prof. Memberships:** Fellow of the American College of Bankruptcy; Member: American Bankruptcy Institute; American Bar Association.
**Career:** Admitted 1978. Practiced at Hale and Dorr. Founded CWG in 1990.
**Personal:** JD (cum laude) Cornell Law School 1978. BA Yale University 1975. Married with four children.

### CONDE, Kathryn
Nutter, McClennen & Fish, LLP, Boston
617 439 2000
*Recommended in Antitrust*

### COOGAN, Peter
Foley Hoag LLP, Boston
617 832 1000
*Recommended in Banking & Finance*

### COOKE, Susan
McDermott Will & Emery, Boston
617 535 4012
scooke@mwe.com
*Recommended in Environment*
**Practice Areas:** Heads Environmental Practice Group and Boston Office. Practice covers regulatory analysis and counseling in US and EU jurisdictions, enforcement actions, permitting activities, brownfields redevelopment, EHS due diligence and audits, and legislative and regulatory proposals, including cleanup and liability negotiations at major contaminated sites, development of environmental opinion format for transactions, interpretation of complex regulatory requirements for chemicals use and waste management, emission trading, and procurement of first waivers under federal and state chemical regulation laws.
**Publications:** Editor-in-Chief and principal author of leading treatise, 'The Law of Hazardous Waste'.
**Personal:** Emmanuel College (MA); Boston University (JD).

### COUKOS, Stephen J
Gallagher, Callahan and Gartrell, PC, Boston 617 426 5347
coukos@gcglaw.com
*Recommended in Banking & Finance*
**Practice Areas:** Advises public and private companies on strategic transactions, corporate and regulatory matters, securities law compliance and corporate governance issues.

**Prof. Memberships:** American and Boston Bar Associations; Co-Chair of Banking and Financial Services Committee of Business Law Section of Boston Bar Association.
**Publications:** Frequent author and speaker on corporate and banking topics; recent articles and presentations have addressed mergers and acquisitions, strategic thinking for mutual institutions, recent developments in banking regulation, credit union conversions and compliance obligations of Board of Directors and senior management.
**Personal:** Stanford Law School, JD, 1986; Trinity College (CT), BA, 1981 (Phi Beta Kappa).

### COX JR, Robert
Bowditch & Dewey LLP, Worcester
508 791 3511
*Recommended in Environment*

### CUBELL, Howard A
Goodwin Procter LLP, Boston
617 570 1000
hcubell@goodwinprocter.com
*Recommended in Tax*
**Practice Areas:** Mr Cubell's practice focuses on the development of innovative tax strategies for various domestic and international business transactions and collective investment vehicles. He has been at the forefront in developing creative structures for private equity funds to use in doing leveraged buyouts overseas and for making investments in domestic pass-through entities such as Subchapter S corporations, partnerships and LLCs.
**Personal:** JD, Boston University School of Law, 1973; BA, University of Michigan, 1970; New York University Graduate Tax Program.

### CUDKOWICZ, Ariel
Seyfarth Shaw LLP, Boston
617 946 4800
*Recommended in Employment*

### CURLEY, James M
Goodwin Procter LLP, Boston
617 570 1000
jcurley@goodwinprocter.com
*Recommended in Private Equity*
**Practice Areas:** Mr Curley's practice focuses primarily on corporate finance, mergers and acquisitions and the general representation of private equity firms, venture capital firms and early- and later-stage growth companies. He has represented a number of leading private equity and venture capital firms. Mr Curley has represented a variety of early- and later- stage growth companies in various industries, including financial services, healthcare, manufacturing, retail and technology.
**Personal:** JD, Boston University School of Law (magna cum laude; Distinguished Scholar); BA, Brandeis University (magna cum laude; Phi Beta Kappa).

### CURTIN, Neal J
Bingham McCutchen LLP, Boston
617 951 8437
neal.curtin@bingham.com
*Recommended in Banking & Finance*
**Practice Areas:** Involved in bank and
bank holding company mergers, acquisitions, conversions and restructurings.
Has been involved in international transactions in sub-Saharan Africa, South
America and the Caribbean and has represented banks and other international
companies establishing operations or
making acquisitions in the US. Regulatory experience involves practice before the
Federal Reserve System, Federal Deposit
Insurance Corporation, Comptroller of
the Currency and the Securities and
Exchange Commission as well as the
Office of the Commissioner of Banks of
the Commonwealth of Massachusetts
and the bank regulators of other states.
**Personal:** Fordham University School of
Law, JD, 1968; Harvard College, BA, 1965.

### CURTIN JR, John J
Bingham McCutchen LLP, Boston
617 951 8325
john.curtin@bingham.com
*Recommended in Antitrust*
**Practice Areas:** Former Chairman of
the firm's Litigation Department. Has
served as trial counsel in many complex
commercial and criminal jury and non-
jury trials, and appeals in state and federal
courts.
**Career:** Received Lifetime Achievement
Award from The American Lawyer.
Served as President of the American Bar
Association and President of the Boston
Bar Association. Inducted as a fellow of
the American College of Trial Lawyers.
**Personal:** Georgetown University Law
Center, LLM, 1959; Boston College Law
School, JD, 1957; Boston College, BA,
magna cum laude, 1954.

### DALE III, Charles
Gadsby Hannah LLP, Boston
617 345 7000
*Recommended in Bankruptcy*

### DALEY, Paul
WilmerHale, Boston
617 526 6720
paul.daley@wilmerhale.com
*Recommended in Bankruptcy*
**Practice Areas:** Concentrates practice
in bankruptcy and commercial law,
including the representation of boards of
directors, debtors, creditors' committees,
trustees and secured and unsecured creditors in Chapter 11 reorganizations, Chapter 7 liquidations, and parties to § 363
sales.
**Prof. Memberships:** Fellow, American
College of Bankruptcy; International,
American, Massachusetts and Boston Bar
Associations; American Bankruptcy
Institute; Commercial Law League; Legal
Fee Arbitration Board (MBA); Associate
Editor, Massachusetts Law Review.

**Career:** Admitted to Massachusetts and
New York Bar; First, Second and Fifth
CCA; and United States Supreme Court.
**Personal:** Harvard Law School (JD);
Harvard Business School (MBA); Boston
College (AB); Captain, USNR (Ret.).

### DAMON, Lisa
Seyfarth Shaw LLP, Boston
617 946 4800
*Recommended in Employment*

### DAVIS, Christopher P
Goodwin Procter LLP, Boston
617 570 1000
cdavis@goodwinprocter.com
*Recommended in Environment*
**Practice Areas:** Mr Davis is a nationally
recognized Superfund practitioner and
environmental litigator, who has represented potentially responsible parties at
more than 50 federal and state Superfund
sites throughout the northeastern United
States. He served as trial counsel in the
first governmental and private Superfund
trials and has litigated a number of
prominent CERCLA cases and had mediated complex, multiparty environmental
disputes.
**Prof. Memberships:** Keystone Conference on Environmental Law: Chair;
Massachusetts Waste Cleanup Advisory
Committee: Member; Toxics Law
Reporter: Advisory Board Member.
**Personal:** JD, Harvard Law School, 1980;
AB, Dartmouth College, 1976.

### DAVIS, Michael
Sullivan & Worcester LLP, Boston
617 338 2800
*Recommended in Tax*

### DICHIARA, Peter M
WilmerHale, Boston
617 526 6466
peter.dichiara@wilmerhale.com
*Recommended in Intellectual Property*
**Practice Areas:** Chair of WilmerHale's
Nanotechnology Practice Group. Practice
focuses on obtaining and enforcing intellectual property rights, with an emphasis
on the electronics, communications and
computer industries. Has litigated patents
and trade secrets relating to communication systems, computer software, storage
systems, electronic circuits and semiconductor manufacturing equipment. Has
prepared infringement and validity opinions and has advised clients on portfolio
strategy, risk assessment and design-
around strategies.
**Prof. Memberships:** Mass Nanotech
Exchange, Board Member.
**Career:** Admitted to Massachusetts Bar,
United States Patent and Trademark
Office. Joined firm in 1997.
**Personal:** Boston University School of
Law (JD); Boston University (BS, Computer Engineering).

### DITTMAR, James S
Goodwin Procter LLP, Boston
617 570 1000
jdittmar@goodwinprocter.com
*Recommended in Litigation*
**Practice Areas:** Mr Dittmar focuses his
practice on complex business litigation
with particular emphasis on securities litigation; civil litigation and regulatory
investigations and enforcement proceedings involving asset management and
other capital markets financial services;
civil litigation and regulatory investigations and enforcement proceedings
under ERISA; and corporate transaction,
control and governance disputes. His
practice concentrates on class actions,
derivative actions, and multi-proceeding
litigations including federal multi-district
litigation and simultaneous federal and
state court actions.
**Personal:** JD, Harvard Law School, 1972
(cum laude); MSc, London School of
Economics, 1967; BA, Amherst College,
1966 (magna cum laude).

### DONOGHUE, Laurence
Morgan, Brown and Joy LLP, Boston
617 523 6666
*Recommended in Employment*

### DONOVAN, John D
Ropes & Gray LLP, Boston
617 951 7566
john.donovan@ropesgray.com
*Recommended in Litigation*
**Practice Areas:** Business litigation,
including corporate and securities matters, class actions, disputes in connection
with mergers and acquisitions, and other
complex business transactions. Expertise
in corporate and securities litigation as a
result of successfully defending hi-tech
corporations, 'old economy' issuers,
underwriters and financial services companies in litigation. Appeared and argued
such cases in dozens of state and federal
jurisdictions, producing successful results
at both trial and appellate court levels.
**Career:** Massachusetts Bar (1981); New
York Bar (2003); Partner, Ropes & Gray
(1990).
**Personal:** JD, summa cum laude, Boston
College Law School (1981); Undergraduate Degree, cum laude, Harvard College
(1975).

### DOUGHERTY, Charles R
Foley & Lardner LLP, Boston
617 342 4053
cdougherty@foley.com
*Recommended in Bankruptcy*
**Career:** Charles R Dougherty, a Partner
with the Boston office of Foley & Lardner
LLP, is a member of the firm's Business
Reorganizations and Private Equity &
Venture Capital Practice Groups, and the
Emerging Technologies Industry Team.
Mr Dougherty is a business lawyer whose
practice focuses on working with troubled companies. In addition to assisting
companies facing serious financial and

structural challenges, he advises creditors
and equity holders of troubled companies. Mr Dougherty received his JD from
Boston University School of Law in 1980,
magna cum laude.

### DOUGHERTY, Thomas J
Skadden, Arps, Slate, Meagher & Flom
LLP & Affiliates, Boston
617 573 4820
dougherty@skadden.com
*Recommended in Litigation*
**Practice Areas:** Heads the Litigation
Department in the firm's Boston office.
Has been active in many major control
contests and other court and SEC challenges to company disclosures and officer/director conduct. Has been heavily
involved in litigating key cases that have
fashioned the standards by which subsequent cases have been governed, including cases involving The Boston Company,
Computervision, Continental Cablevision, EMC, Erco, General Electric,
Guardian, Hycor, Instron, Interco, Lotus,
MacMillan, Polaroid, Prospect Street,
Stratus and Unitrode.
**Career:** JD, Harvard University, 1976
(cum laude); BPhil in Economics, Oxford
University, 1973 (Marshall Scholar); BA,
Holy Cross College, 1970 (magna cum
laude).

### DOWNEY, Alicia L
Bingham McCutchen LLP, Boston
617 951 8187
alicia.downey@bingham.com
*Recommended in Antitrust*
**Practice Areas:** Has extensive litigation
and counseling experience in competition, franchise, fiduciary and business law
matters as well as government investigations, mergers and joint ventures. Has litigated complex contract, business tort,
antitrust and unfair competition cases in
federal and state courts and in various
arbitration settings, including the International Chamber of Commerce, American Arbitration Association, National
Association of Securities Dealers and the
NYSE. Practice includes defense of firms
in private customer arbitrations and regulatory investigations of sales practices.
**Personal:** Boston College Law School,
JD, magna cum laude, 1993; Harvard
University, MA, 1984; Harvard College,
BA, magna cum laude, 1984.

### DOWNS, J Anthony
Goodwin Procter LLP, Boston
617 570 1000
jdowns@goodwinprocter.com
*Recommended in Litigation*
**Practice Areas:** Mr Downs practices
general civil litigation, with specialization
in patent, copyright, antitrust/competition law, securities and other complex
commercial litigation. He has represented
individuals and entities in a wide variety
of commercial disputes and business litigation. He also has extensive experience
in arbitration and other alternative dis-

pute resolution procedures. Clients include General Electric, Applied Materials, Inverness Medical Innovations and Boston Scientific.

**Personal:** JD, University of Chicago Law School, 1986 (cum laude); AB, Princeton University, 1982 (magna cum laude).

## DRAPER, Thomas B
Ropes & Gray LLP, Boston
617 951 7430
thomas.draper@ropesgray.com
*Recommended in Banking & Finance*

**Practice Areas:** Broad range of experience in financing transactions. Coordinator for firm Debt Financing Practice Group. Represents lenders and borrowers in many large financings, with emphasis on leveraged acquisitions and financial sponsor transactions. Also represents collateralized loan obligation funds and venture capitalists in investments in start-up and middle-market companies. Has taught commercial lending at Boston University School of Law and has chaired panels for numerous continuing legal education programs about financing transactions.

**Career:** Texas Bar (1979); Massachusetts Bar (1980); Partner, Ropes & Gray (1989).

**Personal:** JD, University of Texas School of Law (1979); Undergraduate Degree, cum laude, Yale University (1975).

## EGAN III, John J
Goodwin Procter LLP, Boston
617 570 1000
jegan@goodwinprocter.com
*Recommended in Private Equity*

**Practice Areas:** Mr Egan's practice involves early- and late-stage venture financings, leveraged recapitalizations and buyouts, IPOs, mergers and acquisitions, joint ventures, strategic licensing and the general representation of public and private emerging growth companies in industries ranging from enterprise software, networking, security and business services to communications, media and life sciences. He also represents numerous venture capitalists, private equity investors and investment banks and has extensive experience in intellectual property and licensing issues.

**Personal:** JD, Boston University School of Law, 1984; AB, Brown University, 1981.

## EHRLICH, Kenneth
Nutter, McClennen & Fish, LLP, Boston
617 439 2000
*Recommended in Banking & Finance*

## ELFMAN, Eric M
Ropes & Gray LLP, Boston
617 951 7298
eric.elfman@ropesgray.com
*Recommended in Tax*

**Practice Areas:** Federal and Corporate Tax Practice focusing on transactions, planning, tax audit and controversy matters; extensive experience in structuring

acquisitions, mergers, leveraged buyouts, recapitalizations, preferred stock financings and spin-off transactions, venture capital and private equity deals, technology licensing transactions for biotechnology and life science companies.

**Career:** Certified Public Accountant (Pennsylvania, 1977); California Bar (1980); Massachusetts Bar (1986); Partner, Ropes & Gray (1989); Previously Attorney-Advisor in the US Treasury's Office of Tax Policy.

**Personal:** JD, George Washington University Law School (1980); MS, Accounting, University of Pennsylvania Wharton Graduate School (1976); BS, Economics, University of Pennsylvania Wharton Graduate School (1975).

## ENGLANDER, John C
Goodwin Procter LLP, Boston
617 570 1000
jenglander@goodwinprocter.com
*Recommended in Intellectual Property*

**Practice Areas:** Mr Englander's practice focuses on complex commercial litigation, with an emphasis on patent litigation. He also has extensive experience in banking and financial services litigation, including in particular class action defense. He has litigated cases involving all manner of commercial disputes, business torts, and unfair trade practices claims. In addition, Mr Englander has been counsel in patent infringement cases involving clients including Applied Materials, Inc., Brooktrout Technology, Inc. and GE-Interlogix and has represented various medical/pharmaceutical companies including ViaCell and TEVA Pharmaceuticals, USA Inc.

**Personal:** JD, Boston University Law School, 1983; BS, Cornell University, 1980.

## FABIANO, John G
WilmerHale, Boston
617 526 6612
jack.fabiano@wilmerhale.com
*Recommended in Litigation*

**Practice Areas:** Has tried more than 100 jury and non-jury cases before state and federal courts, and administrative hearings and arbitrations in both the US and the UK. Specializes in complex commercial litigation and has trial experience in a variety of areas including wrongful death and personal injury, medical malpractice, legal malpractice, insurance, strategic consulting, securities, fraudulent conveyance, ERISA, oil and gas, partnership disputes, employment disputes, banking, real estate, insurance, professional baseball, professional hockey and academic tenure.

**Prof. Memberships:** Fellow of the American College of Trial Lawyers.

**Career:** Admitted to Massachusetts Bar.

**Personal:** Harvard Law School (JD); Harvard College (AB).

## FEE, Michael K
Ropes & Gray LLP, Boston
617 951 7607
michael.fee@ropesgray.com
*Recommended in Litigation*

**Practice Areas:** Represents clients in criminal litigation and counsels clients in federal and state investigations. Handles civil litigation matters, many of which are related to government enforcement. Defended numerous clients in matters involving healthcare, securities, investment advisor regulation, export law, public corruption and campaign finance law.

**Career:** Massachusetts Bar (1985); Prosecutor, Public Integrity Section, Criminal Division, US Department of Justice (1985-89); Partner, Ropes & Gray (1993).

**Personal:** JD, magna cum laude, Boston College Law School (1984); AB, magna cum laude, Boston College (1981).

## FELDMAN, Roger D
Fish & Richardson P.C., Boston
617 542 5070
feldman@fr.com
*Recommended in Corporate/M&A*

**Practice Areas:** Principal of Fish & Richardson P.C. Member of the Corporate and Securities Group with practice emphasizing mergers and acquisitions, public and private securities offerings, and general corporate transactions. He has served as corporate counselor and advisor to a broad range of clients from entrepreneurs to maturing companies to major corporations.

**Prof. Memberships:** American Bar Association; Massachusetts Bar Association; Boston Bar Association.

**Personal:** Harvard College BA 1967; Boston University School of Law JD 1970.

## FELTER, John Kenneth
Goodwin Procter LLP, Boston
617 570 1000
kahuna@goodwinprocter.com
*Recommended in Litigation*

**Practice Areas:** Mr Felter is an experienced trial attorney who has tried numerous cases in federal and state trial courts. He has also frequently presented oral arguments before federal and state appellate courts. Mr Felter's practice is concentrated in the areas of complex commercial, land use, products liability, sports and entertainment, and college and university law litigation.

**Prof. Memberships:** American College of Trial Lawyers: Fellow; National Association of College and University Attorneys: Member; Massachusetts Bar Foundation: Fellow; Greater Boston Legal Services: Board of Directors.

**Personal:** JD, Harvard Law School, 1975 (cum laude); MA in Economics, Boston College, 1972; BA, Boston College, 1972 (magna cum laude).

## FINKELMAN, Daniel P
Proskauer Rose LLP, Boston
617 526 9755
dfinkelman@proskauer.com
*Recommended in Private Fund Formation*

**Practice Areas:** Partner at Proskauer Rose. Member of the Firm's Corporate Department and the Private Equity Group. Over 25 years of experience in the private equity field. He concentrates on representation of private equity funds, including venture capital, buyout, corporate-sponsored, offshore and multinational funds, and fund-of-funds. He also represents institutional investors. His principal activities include fund formations, portfolio investments, sales and distributions, internal governance, secondary transactions, and administration.

**Personal:** Columbia University School of Law, 1972; Harlan Fiske Stone Scholar. Columbia University, MBA, 1972. Clark University, AB, cum laude, 1968; Phi Beta Kappa.

## FISHMAN, Robert
Nutter, McClennen & Fish, LLP, Boston
617 439 2000
*Recommended in Real Estate*

## FORMAN, Adam
Littler Mendelson, PC, Boston
617 378 6000
aforman@littler.com
*Recommended in Employment*

**Practice Areas:** Advises and represents employers in a broad range of employment law matters, including discrimination, harassment and wrongful discharge litigation; non-competition and trade secret litigation; the drafting of employment related documents such as employment agreements and personnel policies; and litigation avoidance training. His practice also focuses on employment related transactions and injunction proceedings. Mr Forman is admitted to practice in Massachusetts and in Pennsylvania.

**Prof. Memberships:** Mr Forman is an active Member of the American Bar Association; Massachusetts Bar Association; and the Boston Bar Association.

**Personal:** Georgetown University Law Center (JD, cum laude, 1987); Pennsylvania State University (Bachelor's, 1984).

## FRANK, Robert
Choate Hall & Stewart, Boston
617 248 5000
*Recommended in Intellectual Property*

## FRANK, Steven J
Goodwin Procter LLP, Boston
617 570 1000
sfrank@goodwinprocter.com
*Recommended in Intellectual Property*

**Practice Areas:** Mr Frank focuses on advising clients in all areas of intellectual property law, with emphasis on patent prosecution, analysis of infringement and related issues, copyright questions, and

the drafting and negotiation of agreements relating to the transfer or license of intellectual property. He has significant experience with general IP diligence, both in investment and M&A contexts. Mr Frank has negotiated multimillion-dollar domestic and cross-border licenses, as well as technology-transfer agreements involving leading universities and research institutions.
**Personal:** JD, Harvard Law School (cum laude), 1986; ScB in Chemistry, Brown University (magna cum laude), 1983.

### FRENCH, Marilyn
Weil, Gotshal & Manges LLP, Boston
617 772 8319
marilyn.french@weil.com
*Recommended in Private Equity*
**Practice Areas:** Marilyn French's practice focuses on private equity, fund formation, mergers and acquisitions. She represents several of the country's leading private equity firms, including Thomas H. Lee Partners, Texas Pacific Group, Providence Equity Partners, Berkshire Partners and Summit Partners. Recent transactions include acquisitions of or investments involving Sungard, Citizens of Humanity, Waterworks, Certegy, Sedgwick Holdings, Michael Foods and Simmons. She also represents portfolio companies in connection with corporate counseling, acquisitions and liquidity events.
**Personal:** Hofstra University, BA, 1987; Boston College Law School, JD, 1990.

### GALVANI, Paul B
Ropes & Gray LLP, Boston
617 951 7543
paul.galvani@ropesgray.com
*Recommended in Litigation*
**Practice Areas:** Extensive practice in environmental law, commercial litigation, and intellectual property matters. Experienced trial lawyer who has served as defense counsel in complex commercial and white-collar litigation, including in securities, patent, and natural resource damage cases. Represented potentially responsible parties in numerous CERCLA matters. Written and lectured extensively on litigation.
**Career:** Former law clerk and assistant United States Attorney in the Southern District of New York. Massachusetts Bar (1964); New York Bar (1965); Partner, Ropes & Gray (1975).
**Personal:** JD, cum laude, Harvard Law School (1964); Undergraduate Degree, magna cum laude, Phi Beta Kappa, Williams College (1960).

### GARVIN, Michele M
Ropes & Gray LLP, Boston
617 951 7495
michele.garvin@ropesgray.com
*Recommended in Healthcare*
**Practice Areas:** Focused on general federal and state regulatory compliance and transactional matters including clinical joint ventures, governance, physician integration and managed care issues. Practiced in the health law field since 1987 and has represented a wide range of healthcare industry representatives including health plans, academic medical centers, community hospitals, physician group practices, faculty practice plans, and pharmaceutical manufacturers.
**Career:** Massachusetts Bar (1988); Partner, Ropes & Gray (1996).
**Personal:** JD, Suffolk University Law School (1987); PhD, Boston College (1981); BA, College of William and Mary (1974).

### GAUDREAU JR, Russell A
Ropes & Gray LLP, Boston
617 951 7261
russell.gaudreau@ropesgray.com
*Recommended in Employee Benefits*
**Practice Areas:** Concentrates on retirement plan and executive benefit matters in Boston and Washington, DC. Maintains close contacts with Internal Revenue Service (IRS) and Department of Labor (DOL) representatives. Frequently obtains private letter rulings, closing agreements, and advisory opinions for clients from the IRS and DOL. Has concentrated in employee benefits law for 35 years and teaches retirement plan law at Georgetown Law Center and Boston University Law School.
**Career:** Massachusetts Bar (1968); District of Columbia Bar (1991).
**Personal:** LLM (Tax Law), New York University School of Law (1969); JD, Suffolk University Law School (1968); BA, University of Massachusetts (1965).

### GAULT, Robert M
Mintz Levin Cohn Ferris Glovsky and Popeo PC, Boston
617 348 1643
rgault@mintz.com
*Recommended in Employment*
**Practice Areas:** Employment: counseling and litigation for employers and senior executives, including employment agreements; M&A transactions; noncompetes; trade secrets; discrimination; discipline, separations, investigations, codes of conduct, and WARN. Labor: represents management in organizing drives, arbitrations and litigation.
**Prof. Memberships:** Boston Bar Association; Massachusetts Bar Association; ABA.
**Career:** Law clerk, USDC (WD Wa) 1971-73; Mintz Levin 1973, Member of the Firm 1978; Chair/Manager of 37 member Employment, Labor & Benefits Section; counsel in numerous published decisions.
**Publications:** Has published numerous articles; frequently lectures; interviewed on employment topics.
**Personal:** Williams College, BA 1968; U. of Michigan Law School, JD with honors 1971; former Member of the Board,

Greater Boston Legal Services and Law Firm Resources Project; current Member of the Board, Greater Boston Food Bank.

### GIULIANI, Richard
WilmerHale, Boston
617 526 6435
richard.giuliani@wilmerhale.com
*Recommended in Tax*
**Practice Areas:** WilmerHale's State and Local Tax Group Chair. Experienced in all areas of tax law including federal and state income taxation and state sales and use taxes. Handles corporate, partnership and individual federal and state tax matters; tax dispute advocacy in administrative and judicial forums; tax planning. Represented clients before the Internal Revenue Service Appeals Office; US Tax Court; Massachusetts Appellate Tax Board; Massachusetts courts.
**Prof. Memberships:** Extensive work with Boston Bar Association, Massachusetts Taxpayers Foundation, Massachusetts Department of Revenue.
**Career:** Admitted to Massachusetts Bar. Joined firm in 1970.
**Personal:** Harvard Law School (JD); Harvard College (BA, cum laude).

### GLAZER, Michael H
Goodwin Procter LLP, Boston
617 570 1000
mglazer@goodwinprocter.com
*Recommended in Real Estate*
**Practice Areas:** Mr Glazer specializes in real estate, commercial finance, joint ventures and leasing. He has developed special expertise in the areas of joint ventures, creative debt structuring and investments by tax-exempt investors, such as pension funds and endowments. In addition, he helps clients structure complex debt and equity transactions specifically targeted to the needs of these institutional investors and has extensive leasing experience representing both landlords and tenants of office, flex, industrial and retail space.
**Personal:** JD, Boston University Law School, 1973; BS, in Economics, Wharton School, University of Pennsylvania, 1970.

### GLEASON, Daniel
Nutter, McClennen & Fish, LLP, Boston
617 439 2000
*Recommended in Litigation*

### GLERUM, Charles
Choate Hall & Stewart, Boston
617 248 5000
*Recommended in Bankruptcy*

### GLOSBAND, Daniel M
Goodwin Procter LLP, Boston
617 570 1930
dglosband@goodwinprocter.com
*Recommended in Bankruptcy*
**Practice Areas:** Mr Glosband's primary areas of practice are insolvency and reorganization. He represents secured and unsecured creditors, committees and debtors in workouts and proceedings under the Bankruptcy Code. Mr Glosband also acts as an advisor to the US State Department and the American Law Institute on international insolvency projects. He has worked with lenders and debtors in major real estate, retail and technology-oriented reorganizations; parties to significant contracts with debtors in reorganization; and defendants in complex bankruptcy court litigation.
**Personal:** JD, Cornell University, 1969; BA, University of Massachusetts, 1966.

### GOLDBERG, Daniel L
Bingham McCutchen LLP, Boston
617 951 8327
daniel.goldberg@bingham.com
*Recommended in Antitrust, Sport*
**Practice Areas:** Focuses on antitrust, IP and franchise cases. Has served as national and regional counsel in complex franchise matters and is lead litigation counsel for several Boston-area sports teams. Has tried cases in state and federal courts and before arbitration panels and administrative agencies. Counsels clients on antitrust and trade regulation matters. Was the primary draftsman of the Massachusetts Antitrust Act.
**Personal:** Harvard Law School, JD, cum laude, 1971; Trinity College, BA, cum laude, 1968.

### GOLDBERG, Michael
Cohn Whitesell & Goldberg LLP, Boston
617 951 2505
goldberg@cwg11.com
*Recommended in Bankruptcy*

### GOODHEART, Lisa
Sugarman, Rogers, Barshak & Cohen, PC, Boston 617 227 3030
*Recommended in Environment*

### GOODING, Douglas
Choate Hall & Stewart, Boston
617 248 5000
*Recommended in Bankruptcy*

### GOODMAN, Louis A
Skadden, Arps, Slate, Meagher & Flom LLP & Affiliates, Boston
617 573 4830
lgoodman@skadden.com
*Recommended in Corporate/M&A*
**Practice Areas:** Head of Skadden's Boston office. Advises on a wide range of corporate matters, from financings, acquisitions and restructurings to white-collar criminal defense. For many years, has represented clients in some of their most significant transactions – many that have industry-wide and sometimes worldwide significance.
**Career:** JD, Harvard Law School, 1969; MA, Harvard University, 1966; AB, Columbia College, 1965.
**Publications:** Author, 'Takeover Strategies & Responses: The Battle for Corporate Control'.

## GORDON, Robert B
Ropes & Gray LLP, Boston
617 951 7442
robert.gordon@ropesgray.com
*Recommended in Employment*
**Practice Areas:** Advising, defending management in employment discrimination, wrongful discharge, employee privacy, defamation, employee benefits, wage and hour, non-competition, trade secret litigation. Counsels on employee discipline and discharge, reductions in force, executive employment/separation agreements, sexual harassment and other internal investigations, compliance issues under Americans with Disabilities Act, Family and Medical Leave Act, Worker Adjustment Retraining and Notification Act, Fair Labor Standards Act.
**Career:** Massachusetts Bar (1986); Rhode Island Bar (1991); Connecticut Bar (1995); Partner, Ropes & Gray (1995); New Hampshire Bar (2005).
**Personal:** JD, cum laude, University of Michigan Law School (1986); BA, Phi Beta Kappa, Wesleyan University (1983).

## GREEN, Barry
Goulston & Storrs, Boston
617 482 1776
*Recommended in Real Estate*

## GREEN, Karen F
WilmerHale, Boston
617 526 6207
karen.green@wilmerhale.com
*Recommended in Litigation*
**Practice Areas:** Co-Chair of firm's Litigation Department; member of firm's Executive Committee. Practice concentrates on complex business litigation, including the defense of white-collar criminal investigations and litigation. Extensive experience representing companies and corporate officers and directors in parallel civil and criminal proceedings alleging healthcare fraud, securities fraud, government contracting fraud, consumer fraud and mail and wire fraud. Has conducted corporate internal investigations, and provided advice on establishment of corporate compliance programs.
**Prof. Memberships:** Fiduciary Trust Company, Director.
**Career:** Admitted to Massachusetts Bar. Joined firm in 1982.
**Personal:** Harvard Law School (JD, cum laude); Radcliffe College (AB, magna cum laude).

## HACKNEY, Hamilton
Greenberg Traurig LLP, Boston
617 310 6090
hackneyha@gtlaw.com
*Recommended in Environment*
**Practice Areas:** Real estate, environmental.
**Prof. Memberships:** Founding Member and Secretary, National Brownfield Association, Massachusetts/Rhode Island Chapter Member, ABA, Energy, Environ-

ment and Resources Section Member, NAIOP Member, Boston Bar Association.
**Career:** Awarded 2004 Public Affairs Award from the Massachusetts Chapter, National Association of Industrial and Office Properties; listed, 2005 Chambers USA; listed, Super Lawyers of Massachusetts 2004.
**Publications:** 'Liability, Natural Disasters Bring Mold Back to the Fore', Boston Business Journal, 2006; 'Judges Rule Against Local Boards in Permitting Disputes', Boston Business Journal, 2004.
**Personal:** JD, University of Utah College of Law; Order of the Coif; BA, cum laude, Middlebury College.

## HALEY, Joseph W
Goodwin Procter LLP, Boston
617 570 1000
jhaley@goodwinprocter.com
*Recommended in Real Estate*
**Practice Areas:** Mr Haley's practice focuses on real estate development, as well as on acquisitions, dispositions, equity and mortgage financing, master planning, permitting, environmental law and leasing. He has extensive experience in urban and suburban office, retail, industrial, residential, mixed-use and specialty real estate product types. He represents many of the large development firms (both private and public), lenders and institutional owners in Boston, New England and the US.
**Prof. Memberships:** American College of Real Estate Lawyers: Member; Abstract Club of Boston: Member.
**Personal:** JD, Cornell Law School, 1963; BA, University of Maine, 1960.

## HALSTON, Daniel W
WilmerHale, Boston
617 526 6654
daniel.halston@wilmerhale.com
*Recommended in Litigation*
**Practice Areas:** Focuses practice on securities litigation, general commercial litigation and administrative law disputes. Handles wide range of complex litigation matters, including securities fraud class actions, derivative litigation, M&A disputes, investment advisor claims, closely held corporation disputes, proxy contests, non-competition claims, trade secret claims, and wide variety of public law matters. Represents clients in internal investigations and before the SEC, NASD and state regulatory agencies.
**Prof. Memberships:** Director, Massachusetts Appleseed Center for Law and Justice; Supreme Judicial Court Historical Society.
**Career:** Massachusetts Assistant Attorney General, 1991-94.
**Personal:** Boston University School of Law (JD, cum laude); Vassar College (AB, general honors).

## HANDLY, Kevin
Gallagher, Callahan and Gartrell, PC, Boston 617 426 5349
handly@gcglaw.com
*Recommended in Banking & Finance*
**Career:** Assistant District Attorney, Brooklyn, New York, 1979-82; Senior Attorney, Federal Reserve Board, Washington, DC, 1982-87; Partner, Goodwin Procter & Hoar, Boston, MA, 1987-95; Partner, Peabody & Brown, Boston, MA, 1995-2000; Director, Goulston & Storrs, P.C., Boston, MA, 2001-04; Shareholder-Director, Gallagher Callahan & Gartrell, P.C., 2005-present; lecturer on Financial Institutions Mergers & Acquisitions Law, Morin School of Banking and Financial Law, Boston University, 2002-present.
**Publications:** 'Expanding Small-Bank M&A Opportunities', American Banker, Oct. 21, 2005; 'Non-Stock Mutual Holding Companies – Winning Acceptance the Old Fashioned Way', Banker & Tradesman, August 2005; 'Tax-Advantaged Investments for Financial Institutions', Banker & Tradesman, April 2005.

## HAROZ, Michael
Goulston & Storrs, Boston
617 482 1776
*Recommended in Real Estate*

## HARRIS, Jonathan R
Edwards Angell Palmer & Dodge LLP, Boston 617 951 2215
jharris@eapdlaw.com
*Recommended in Banking & Finance*
**Practice Areas:** Jon's practice includes representation of banks, insurance companies and other commercial lenders in a variety of financing transactions which run the gamut from a parking garage to a state-of-the-art laboratory for a biotech company. Other recent transactions include unsecured lending, receivables financings, equipment financings and real estate loans. Jon is skilled in both conventional and tax-exempt financing for senior living facilities, long-term care facilities, educational institutions, non-profit cultural institutions and social service agencies.
**Prof. Memberships:** Boston Bar Association; National Association of Bond Lawyers.
**Personal:** Northeastern University School of Law, JD 1975; Harvard College, AB 1972, magna cum laude.

## HEALY, Martin R
Goodwin Procter LLP, Boston
617 570 1000
mhealy@goodwinprocter.com
*Recommended in Real Estate*
**Practice Areas:** Mr Healy's practice concentrates on providing acquisition, due diligence and permitting advice for complex development projects. His current/past projects include the Boston Logan Airport modernization which has been challenged continuously throughout its lifetime, the permitting of the

Central Artery/Tunnel Project, the renovation of Millennium Place, including the overhaul of the Boston Ritz Carlton and involvement with commercial property projects in and around the Boston area. He is the editor of and a contributing author for the Massachusetts Zoning Manual.
**Personal:** JD, Boston College Law School, 1975 (cum laude); BA, Boston College, 1972 (summa cum laude).

## HEIDT, Jeffrey L
Ropes & Gray LLP, Boston
617 951 7390
jeffrey.heidt@ropesgray.com
*Recommended in Healthcare*
**Practice Areas:** For more than 30 years he has represented hospitals, health systems, academic medical centers and health insurers on complex financial, regulatory and strategic issues including Medicare and Medicaid payment appeals, state and federal fraud and abuse investigations, physician disciplinary matters, mergers and acquisitions and related governance matters.
**Career:** Massachusetts Bar (1970); Partner, Ropes & Gray (2005).
**Personal:** JD, Harvard Law School (1970); AB, high honors in Philosophy, Brown University (1967).

## HENNESSEY, Gilbert
Fish & Richardson P.C., Boston
617 521 7838
hennessey@fr.com
*Recommended in Intellectual Property*
**Practice Areas:** Principal of Fish & Richardson's Boston office. Experience in IP litigation and general IP management involving opinions, patent litigation, ADR and agreements, and IP due diligence, as well as prosecution, with special emphasis on infringement analysis and strategy relating to computer technology and biomedical devices.
**Publications:** Co-author, Patent Practice (ed Kayton), Patent Resources Institute, 1976-95 (7 Vols). Co-author, Compendium of Packaged Software Licensing Provisions (2d ed), American Intellectual Property Law Association, 1988.
**Personal:** Beloit College BA Physics and Mathematics 1966; University of Illinois Law School and George Washington University JD 1969.

## HERMAN, Philip
Goulston & Storrs, Boston
617 482 1776
*Recommended in Banking & Finance*

## HESSION, John
McDermott Will & Emery, Boston
617 535 4460
jhession@mwe.com
*Recommended in Private Equity*
**Practice Areas:** Represents emerging-growth companies, principally in software, medical devices, life sciences, telecommunications and electronic com-

merce fields, as well as venture capital funds in investment process in these sectors. Practice includes start-up and public company work; equity-based compensation strategies; mergers and acquisitions, representing buyers or sellers; public offerings, representing underwriters or companies; corporate partnering, joint ventures and other strategic alliances involving technology transfers; technology license and distribution arrangements, including software, medical devices and biotechnology; and venture capital financings of technology companies.
**Personal:** Boston College Law School (JD, cum laude); University of Notre Dame (BA, summa cum laude, Phi Beta Kappa).

### HIGGINS, Keith F
Ropes & Gray LLP, Boston
617 951 7386
keith.higgins@ropesgray.com
*Recommended in Corporate/M&A*
**Practice Areas:** Over 20 years' experience counseling public companies in securities offerings, mergers and acquisitions and corporate governance. Represents underwriters in public and private securities offerings. Recognized as a top IPO lawyer in the country.
**Career:** Massachusetts Bar (1982); Partner, Ropes & Gray (1991).
**Personal:** JD, summa cum laude, Boston University School of Law (1982); MA, University of Virginia (1975); BA, Phi Beta Kappa, Florida State University (1973).

### HILLMAN, Robert
Fish & Richardson P.C., Boston
617 521 7816
hillman@fr.com
*Recommended in Intellectual Property*
**Practice Areas:** Principal of Fish & Richardson in the firm's Boston office. He is also the firm's Chairman. His practice emphasizes patent litigation in a wide variety of technologies including complex electronics and biotechnology.
**Career:** Joined the firm in 1962.
**Personal:** Earned his Undergraduate Degree in Physics and Economics from the Massachusetts Institute of Technology and his Law Degree from Harvard Law School.

### HIRSCH, Jeffrey
Robinson & Cole LLP, Boston
617 557 5900
*Recommended in Employment*

### HODGES TAYLOR, Laura C
Goodwin Procter LLP, Boston
617 570 1000
lht@goodwinprocter.com
*Recommended in Private Equity*
**Practice Areas:** Ms Hodges Taylor focuses on corporate finance and securities law, as well as on limited partnerships, REITs and business trusts in a variety of industries. She has extensive expe-

rience in representing institutional investors in structuring and effecting investments. She also represented issuers, financial advisors and investors in restructurings such as exchange offers, tender and self-tender offers, going private transactions, rights offerings and leveraged buyouts.
**Personal:** JD, Harvard Law School, 1982; BA, Wellesley College, 1977.

### HOORT, Steven T
Ropes & Gray LLP, Boston
617 951 7470
steven.hoort@ropesgray.com
*Recommended in Bankruptcy*
**Practice Areas:** Representation of institutional creditors, financiers and committees in both the taxable and tax-exempt context, nationwide practice of acquiring businesses, leases and assets out of bankruptcy proceedings, and representation of major parties in contentious insolvency litigation, all in major restructurings or bankruptcy cases. Co-Head of the Bankruptcy and Business Restructuring Department.
**Career:** Michigan Bar (1977); Massachusetts Bar (1978); Partner, Ropes & Gray (1984).
**Personal:** JD, magna cum laude, University of Michigan Law School, Order of the Coif (1975); BA (philosophy), high honors, Grand Valley State College (1972).

### HUGG, Joseph A
DLA Piper Rudnick Gray Cary US LLP, Boston 617 406 6052
joseph.hugg@dlapiper.com
*Recommended in Employee Benefits*
**Practice Areas:** Tax, employee benefits and ERISA.
**Prof. Memberships:** American Bar Association (Tax Section); Massachusetts and Boston Bar Associations.
**Career:** He assists US and international clients in structuring venture capital and other private equity funds to comply with tax and pension regulations, including ERISA. He also advises fund clients on the tax and ERISA aspects of portfolio investments. In addition, he provides advice on executive compensation and employee benefits.
**Personal:** LLM, New York University School of Law; JD, Harvard Law School; BA, Georgetown University.

### HUSID, Douglas
Goulston & Storrs, Boston
617 482 1776
*Recommended in Real Estate*

### ISAIA, Russell E
Bingham McCutchen LLP, Boston
617 951 8427
russell.isaia@bingham.com
*Recommended in Employee Benefits*
**Practice Areas:** Has more than 20 years of experience practicing in the area of executive compensation and employee benefits. Represents a variety of clients on

employee benefits matters and has substantial experience advising on the securities, ERISA and tax implications of the design, implementation, administration and termination of all forms of benefit programs.
**Personal:** Harvard Law School, JD, 1980; University of Illinois, BA, magna cum laude, 1977.

### JACOBS, Neil
WilmerHale, Boston
617 526 6970
neil.jacobs@wilmerhale.com
*Recommended in Employment*
**Practice Areas:** Extensive experience in negotiation and administration of collective bargaining agreements; employment and labor law litigation in state and federal courts; and administrative proceedings before state and federal fair employment agencies. Lead trial or appellate counsel in major employment litigation involving ERISA litigation; unfair labor practice proceedings before the National Labor Relations Board and in US Courts of Appeals; predatory hiring cases; employee theft of trade secrets; wrongful discharge litigation; and discrimination litigation.
**Prof. Memberships:** American Bar Association's Developing Labor Law Committee.
**Career:** Admitted to Massachusetts Bar. Joined firm in 1977.
**Personal:** Harvard Law School (JD); Harvard College (AB).

### JAFFE, Seth
Foley Hoag LLP, Boston
617 832 1000
*Recommended in Environment*

### JAKUBOWSKI, Paul
WilmerHale, Boston
617 526 6948
paul.jakubowski@wilmerhale.com
*Recommended in Real Estate*
**Practice Areas:** Practice focuses on all aspects of real estate law, including sales and acquisitions, joint ventures, financing, development and leasing. Has numerous real estate groups as clients, including national retailers, pension fund advisors, an industrial real estate investment trust (REIT), foreign investors in US real estate, and value-added funds. Counsels many of firm's corporate clients on real estate and leasing matters, including credit tenant leases.
**Prof. Memberships:** Boston, Massachusetts and American Bar Associations; Real Estate Finance Association; National Association of Industrial and Office Properties.
**Career:** Admitted to Massachusetts Bar.
**Personal:** Harvard Law School (JD); University of Pennsylvania (BA).

### JARRELL, Brenda
Choate Hall & Stewart, Boston
617 248 5000
*Recommended in Intellectual Property*

### JEDREY, Christopher M
McDermott Will & Emery, Boston
617 535 4405
cjedrey@mwe.com
*Recommended in Healthcare*
**Practice Areas:** Federal and state healthcare regulatory, corporate and tax matters, including: anti-kickback and Stark law requirements; federal, state and local tax exemption requirements; and charitable trust and corporation law. Notable projects include organizing: HealthOne Care System (non-profit group practices with more than 600,000 patients); Brigham and Women's Physicians Organization (800-physician faculty practice); HMO Blue (non-profit HMO subsidiary); Dana-Farber/Partners Cancer Care (adult medical oncology collaboration); Florida Proton Therapy Institute; and Lasell Village (1st in the nation residential educational community for the elderly).
**Personal:** Boston College Law School (JD); Harvard University (PhD, MA); University of Massachusetts (BA).

### JEFFERY, D Ethan
Hanify & King, Boston
617 226 3410
dej@hanify.com
*Recommended in Bankruptcy*
**Practice Areas:** Practice focuses on representing debtors, creditors' committees, creditors and trustees in complex bankruptcies, non-bankruptcy workouts and other related insolvency proceedings. Mr Jeffery also represents parties in commercial litigation matters relating to the debtor-creditor relationship.
**Prof. Memberships:** American Bankruptcy Institute, Turnaround Management Association; Boston Bar Association.
**Personal:** JD Villanova Law School (1991); BS University of New Hampshire (1987).

### JOHNSTON, Susan A
Ropes & Gray LLP, Boston
617 951 7301
susan.johnston@ropesgray.com
*Recommended in Tax*
**Practice Areas:** Taxation of regulated investment companies, including mutual funds, other pooled investment vehicles, and financial products. Co-author, with James R Brown, Jr, of Taxation of Regulated Investment Companies and Their Shareholders, (Warren, Gorham & Lamont of RIA, 1999); updated with supplements twice annually.
**Career:** Massachusetts Bar (1978); Partner, Ropes & Gray (1987); Member, Investment Company Institute Tax Advisory Board (1988-present); Member, American Bar Association Section of Tax-

ation, Committee on Regulated Investment Companies (Chair, 1987-89); State Tax Committee (1987-89); Head of Ropes & Gray Tax Department (1999-2005).

**Personal:** JD, Harvard Law School (1978); BA, Wellesley College (1975).

## JOY, Robert
Morgan, Brown and Joy LLP, Boston
617 523 6666
*Recommended in Employment*

## JOY, William
Morgan, Brown and Joy LLP, Boston
617 523 6666
*Recommended in Employment*

## KAHN, Adam
Foley Hoag LLP, Boston
617 832 1000
*Recommended in Environment*

## KANNEL, William
Mintz Levin Cohn Ferris Glovsky and Popeo PC, Boston
617 348 1665
Bkannel@mintz.com
*Recommended in Bankruptcy*

**Practice Areas:** Bill Kannel is a member of Mintz Levin's Boston office and practices in the Bankruptcy, Restructuring and Commercial Law Section. He practices primarily in the area of commercial law, workouts and corporate reorganization and has represented various institutional lenders, indenture trustees, bondholders, other creditors, debtors, and trustees in all manner of insolvency proceedings in courts throughout the United States. He has substantial experience in all phases of bankruptcy litigation, practice and case management from both the debtor and creditor's perspective including relief from stay, adequate protection, valuation, preference, fraudulent transfer, subordination and competing plan litigation. He has a specialty in negotiating sales of troubled companies and assets, both in and out of bankruptcy. His practice also includes addressing bankruptcy and documentation issues in securitizations, receivable sales, bond transactions and structured financings generally. Bill is fellow of the American College of Bankruptcy, the Massachusetts Bar Association and is a Member and former Chair of the Bankruptcy Law Section of the Boston Bar Association. He is also active in the American Bankruptcy Institute and the Turnaround Management Association and frequently lectures and writes on insolvency issues in front of these groups and numerous other Bar, trade and industry groups including the National Federation of Municipal Analysts and the Association of Insolvency Accountants. He served as an Editor-in-Chief of the American Bankruptcy Institute Healthcare Insolvency Manual, Second Edition and currently serves as Co-Chair of the American Bankruptcy Institute's health-care insolvency section.

## KAY, Minta E
Goodwin Procter LLP, Boston
617 570 1000
mkay@goodwinprocter.com
*Recommended in Real Estate*

**Practice Areas:** Ms Kay's practice focuses on a variety of commercial real estate transactions, concentrating on real estate securities and capital markets, real estate finance and investment, property acquisitions, leasing and sales, and debt and equity restructuring. She has extensive experience in representing investors in complex joint venture and limited partnership transactions to acquire or develop properties as well as with commercial real estate loan and equity investment restructuring.

**Personal:** JD, Columbia University School of Law, 1986; BA, Barnard College, 1983 (magna cum laude).

## KEARNS, Ellen
Foley & Lardner LLP, Boston
617 342 4023
ekearns@foley.com
*Recommended in Employment*

**Career:** Ellen Kearns is Of Counsel in the Boston office of Foley & Lardner LLP. Ms Kearns is a member of the Labor & Employment Practice Group. She represents management in a full range of traditional labor and employment issues, including NLRB proceedings, negotiations, and arbitration. She has appeared before federal and state courts and administrative agencies with respect to employment discrimination, sexual harassment, wrongful discharge cases, wage and hour matters, and other employment-related litigation. She received her JD from Boston College Law School in 1976.

## KEATING, Gregory C
Littler Mendelson, PC, Boston
617 378 6000
gkeating@littler.com
*Recommended in Employment*

**Practice Areas:** Litigation in federal and state courts. Representation of management in labor issues, during unfair labor practice proceedings before NLRB, obtaining injunctions during employment and labor disputes, negotiating collective bargaining agreements and advising clients during union elections. Representation emphasized in healthcare, education and manufacturing.

**Prof. Memberships:** American Bar Association; Steering Committee of the Boston Bar Association (Labor and Employment Section); Editorial Advisory Board for numerous periodicals.

**Publications:** National treatise entitled 'Retaliation and Whistleblowing: A Guide for Human Resources Professionals and Counsel' (LEXIS, 1st Edition 2005).

**Personal:** Boston College School of Law (JD, 1993); Trinity College (BA, 1987).

## KEATING, Michael
Foley Hoag LLP, Boston
617 832 1000
*Recommended in Litigation*

## KEEFE, Robert D
WilmerHale, Boston
617 526 6334
robert.keefe@wilmerhale.com
*Recommended in Litigation*

**Practice Areas:** Co-Chairman of WilmerHale's Government Investigations and Litigation Group, with a complex general litigation practice that includes internal corporate investigations, extensive white-collar criminal defense work and general commercial litigation.

**Prof. Memberships:** Admitted to practice before the Supreme Judicial Court of Massachusetts; the US Court of Appeals for the First, Second, Fifth, Sixth, Seventh and Ninth Circuits; the US District Court of the District of Massachusetts; and all state courts in Massachusetts.

**Career:** Attorney in the Criminal Division of the Department of Justice before joining the firm in 1974.

**Personal:** Boston College Law School (JD); Harvard College (BA).

## KELLER, Stanley
Edwards Angell Palmer & Dodge LLP, Boston 617 239 0217
stanley.keller@eapdlaw.com
*Recommended in Corporate/M&A*

**Practice Areas:** Stan has extensive, high-level experience in business and securities law matters involving emerging and public companies; financial transactional work involving public and private entities, including representing issuers, underwriters, financial institutions and investors; and mergers and acquisition transactions. He advises companies, boards, board committees and special committees on corporate governance issues, transactional matters and special investigations.

**Prof. Memberships:** American Bar Association; Boston Bar Association.

**Publications:** Stan has written and edited many articles and treatises on corporate and securities law matters. Most recently, he has written a number of articles and chaired several programs on the impact of the Sarbanes-Oxley Act and related SEC and stock exchange initiatives and how they have dramatically changed the landscape for corporate governance and disclosure requirements. He is co-editor of 'The Practitioner's Guide to the Sarbanes-Oxley Act', published by ABA-CLE.

**Personal:** Columbia University, AB, 1959; Harvard Law School, LLB, magna cum laude, 1962.

## KENDALL, Michael J
Goodwin Procter LLP, Boston
617 570 1000
mkendall@goodwinprocter.com
*Recommended in Private Equity*

**Practice Areas:** Mr Kendall focuses his Corporate Finance and Securities Practice on representing private equity and venture capital firms in connection with early- and later-stage investments, leveraged recapitalizations and buyouts, as well as counseling a variety of emerging companies. He has substantial experience representing issuers and underwriters in initial and follow-on public offerings, public and private mergers and acquisitions, and advising public companies on SEC reporting and other general corporate matters.

**Personal:** JD, Boston University School of Law, 1993 (magna cum laude); MBA, Boston University Graduate School of Management, 1994; BA, Tufts University, 1990.

## KIEFER, Matthew
Goulston & Storrs, Boston
617 482 1776
*Recommended in Real Estate*

## KIMMELL, Kenneth
Bernstein, Cushner & Kimmell PC, Boston 617 236 4090
*Recommended in Environment*

## KIRSCH, Robert
WilmerHale, Boston
617 526 6779
rob.kirsch@wilmerhale.com
*Recommended in Environment*

**Practice Areas:** Mr Kirsch is Chair of WilmerHale's Environmental Department and member of its Litigation Department. He represents clients in environmental defense, counseling and permitting contexts, and pursues and defends cost recovery, including defense contractor claims. Mr Kirsch has defended clients in criminal, civil and administrative investigations and enforcement proceedings, and counsels clients in emerging area of nanotechnology and in transactions.

**Prof. Memberships:** Member of the American, Boston and New Hampshire Bar Associations.

**Career:** Admitted to Massachusetts and New Hampshire Bars. Joined firm in 1983.

**Personal:** Cornell Law School (JD, cum laude); Middlebury College (BS, cum laude, Phi Beta Kappa).

## KLINE, Douglas J
Goodwin Procter LLP, Boston
617 570 1000
dkline@goodwinprocter.com
*Recommended in Intellectual Property*

**Practice Areas:** Mr Kline concentrates his practice on all aspects of intellectual property litigation, particularly patent infringement matters and other disputes related to the enforcement of intellectual property rights. He advises inventors, companies, investors and underwriters concerning patent enforcement and infringement risks. He also advises clients regarding technology transfer, including the negotiation and drafting of all forms of related agreements such as patent licenses and technology development and license agreements. Mr Kline also works with clients to develop patent portfolio development strategies, and oversees the preparation and prosecution of patent applications.

**Personal:** JD, Suffolk University Law School, 1990 (magna cum laude); BS, Tufts University, 1984.

### KNOWLTON, William A
Ropes & Gray LLP, Boston
617 951 7496
william.knowlton@ropesgray.com
*Recommended in Healthcare*

**Practice Areas:** Counsels academic medical centers, community hospitals, faculty practice plans, physician groups, managed care organizations, healthcare investment firms, pharmaceutical companies, biotechnology companies, and healthcare information technology companies on business and regulatory matters, helping them find practical solutions to difficult issues in a complex healthcare industry environment.

**Career:** Massachusetts Bar (1982); District of Columbia Bar (1998); Partner, Ropes & Gray (1991).

**Personal:** JD, University of Virginia School of Law (1982); BA, Yale University (1977).

### KOCIUBES, Joseph L
Bingham McCutchen LLP, Boston
617 951 8337
joe.kociubes@bingham.com
*Recommended in Litigation*

**Practice Areas:** Focuses on civil litigation, including commercial, financial services, real estate, securities, insurance, constitutional and products liability litigation, as well as domestic and international arbitrations. Has tried cases in state and federal courts nationally and has appeared before administrative and regulatory agencies, including the Securities and Exchange Commission, Massachusetts Securities Division, Massachusetts Division of Insurance and the Massachusetts Department of Public Health. Inducted as a Fellow of the American College of Trial Lawyers and of the International Academy of Trial Lawyers.

**Personal:** Harvard Law School, JD, cum laude, 1974; University of Pittsburgh, BA, cum laude, 1969.

### KOFFEL, William
Foley Hoag LLP, Boston
617 832 1000
*Recommended in Employment*

### KOLB, William
Foley Hoag LLP, Boston
617 832 1000
*Recommended in Corporate/M&A*

### KRASNOW, Jordan
Goulston & Storrs, Boston
617 482 1776
*Recommended in Real Estate*

### KREBS, Michael
Nutter, McClennen & Fish, LLP, Boston
617 439 2000
*Recommended in Banking & Finance*

### KREIGER, Arthur
Anderson & Kreiger LLP, Cambridge
617 252 6575
*Recommended in Environment*

### KREISLER, David
Weil, Gotshal & Manges LLP, Boston
617 772 8340
david.kreisler@weil.com
*Recommended in Private Fund Formation*

**Practice Areas:** David Kreisler regularly represents a number of private equity sponsors and their investment funds in connection with their organization and administration as well as the acquisition, disposition and financings of their investments. Mr Kreisler represents institutional investors and has been involved in the acquisition of private equity firms and money managers. Mr Kreisler also has a wide ranging corporate and securities law practice, and regularly advises clients on the formation of limited and general partnerships and limited liability companies.

**Personal:** Princeton University, AB, 1988; Syracuse University College of Law, JD magna cum laude, 1991, Order of the Coif.

### KWASNICK, Raymond
Goulston & Storrs, Boston
617 482 1776
*Recommended in Real Estate*

### KYLE, Amy L
Bingham McCutchen LLP, Boston
617 951 8288
amy.kyle@bingham.com
*Recommended in Banking & Finance*

**Practice Areas:** Serves as Deputy Chair of the Finance Area and as a Member of the firm's Management Committee. Represents leading financial institutions in connection with a broad range of finance-related matters, with a particular focus on the transportation industry. Has been actively involved in leveraged finance transactions since the mid-1980s. Experience includes senior and mezzanine financing of private acquisitions and leveraged recapitalizations, including platform companies and roll ups, as well as public mergers and tender offer transactions. Experience also includes loan workouts and debt restructurings.

**Personal:** Columbia University School of Law, JD, 1983; Princeton University, BA, 1980.

### LANE, Roger
Greenberg Traurig LLP, Boston
617 310 6006
laner@gtlaw.com
*Recommended in Litigation*

**Practice Areas:** Litigation; corporate litigation and counseling; shareholder litigation.

**Career:** Listed, Chambers & Partners USA Guide, an annual listing of the leading business lawyers and law firms in the world, 2005-06 edition.

**Publications:** Author, 'Managing Risks in Distressed Companies – Director Duties to Shareholders, Creditors and Employees', The Venture Capital Review, Fall 2001.

**Personal:** JD, cum laude, Harvard University Law School. BA, with high honors, with highest distinction, University of Michigan. Phi Beta Kappa.

### LANZA, John
Choate Hall & Stewart, Boston
617 248 5000
*Recommended in Intellectual Property*

### LAPORTE, Claire
Foley Hoag LLP, Boston
617 832 1000
*Recommended in Intellectual Property*

### LECLAIRE, John R
Goodwin Procter LLP, Boston
617 570 1000
jleclaire@goodwinprocter.com
*Recommended in Private Equity*

**Practice Areas:** Mr LeClaire's private equity work includes leveraged recapitalizations, buyouts and minority investments, both in later stage situations and earlier stage ventures, for leading private equity firms throughout the country. He also specializes in the representation of emerging growth companies in sectors such as technology and information services, healthcare, financial services and consumer products. Involvement with above-mentioned clients focuses on strategic counsel, mergers and acquisitions, equity and executive compensation programs, and going-private transactions.

**Personal:** JD, Boston University School of Law, 1982 (magna cum laude); AB, Brown University, 1979 (magna cum laude).

### LEE, William F
WilmerHale, Boston
617 526 6556
william.lee@wilmerhale.com
*Recommended in Intellectual Property*

**Practice Areas:** Co-Managing Partner; concentrates practice on intellectual property and commercial litigation with extensive trial experience.

**Career:** Served as associate counsel to Independent Counsel Lawrence E Walsh in Iran-Contra investigation; Visiting Professor at Harvard Law School, where he taught intellectual property litigation;

named by chief judge for Court of Appeals for the Federal Circuit to the court's Advisory Committee; elected to the Board of Overseers of Harvard University; member of Visiting Committee at Cornell Law School.

**Personal:** JD, magna cum laude, Cornell Law School, Order of the Coif; MBA, with Distinction, Cornell Business School; AB, magna cum laude, Harvard College.

### LEIBENSPERGER, Edward P
McDermott Will & Emery, Boston
617 535 4046
eleibensperger@mwe.com
*Recommended in Litigation*

**Practice Areas:** Litigation of general business, securities, merger/acquisition and professional liability cases. Experience includes numerous jury cases in both state and federal courts as well as appeals in federal circuit courts and Massachusetts Supreme Judicial Court. Has represented Big Four accounting firms, corporations and individual defendants in private securities litigation and before Securities and Exchange Commission. Has represented plaintiffs in business cases, obtaining settlements and verdicts in multi-million dollar range.

**Prof. Memberships:** President, Boston Bar Association 2005-06; Fellow, American College of Trial Lawyers.

**Personal:** Ohio State University College of Law (JD, summa cum laude); Muskingum College (BA, magna cum laude).

### LEIBOWITZ, Hal J
WilmerHale, Boston
617 526 6461
hal.leibowitz@wilmerhale.com
*Recommended in Corporate/M&A*

**Practice Areas:** Partner in WilmerHale's Corporate Department, Co-Chair of firm's Software and Telecom Corporate Group, and a member of the Mergers and Acquisitions Group. Mr Leibowitz's practice focuses on corporate and securities law matters for technology companies in the software and telecom, services and life sciences industries, with an emphasis on mergers and acquisitions and public offerings.

**Prof. Memberships:** Member of the Board of Directors of the Massachusetts Telecommunications Council, and of the American, Massachusetts and Boston Bar Associations.

**Career:** Joined firm in 1985. Admitted to the Massachusetts Bar.

**Personal:** Suffolk University Law School (JD); Brandeis University (BA).

### LEICH, Christopher M
Ropes & Gray LLP, Boston
617 951 7279
christopher.leich@ropesgray.com
*Recommended in Tax*

**Practice Areas:** Corporate and partnership federal income taxation. Substantial portion of practice devoted to private

equity sponsors and investors including Bain Capital, Silver Lake Partners, Thomas H Lee Partners, Berkshire Partners, Weston Presidio Capital. Regularly advises on domestic and cross-border M&A transactions, joint ventures and spin-offs, and debt and equity offerings. Extensive experience structuring private equity funds, hedge funds, CBO funds, and funds of funds.
**Career:** Massachusetts Bar (1987); District of Columbia Bar (1987); Partner, Ropes & Gray (1996).
**Personal:** JD, cum laude, Harvard Law School (1987); BPhil, with distinction, Oxford University (1977); BA, with high honors, Swarthmore College (1975).

### LENIHAN, Brian
Choate Hall & Stewart, Boston
617 248 5000
*Recommended in Private Equity*

### LEON, Michael
Nutter, McClennen & Fish, LLP, Boston
617 439 2000
*Recommended in Environment*

### LEONARD, Stephen
Brown Rudnick Berlack Israels LLP, Boston 617 856 8200
*Recommended in Environment*

### LEONETTI, Kenneth
Foley Hoag LLP, Boston
617 832 1000
*Recommended in Bankruptcy*

### LEVINE, Richard
The Law Office of Richard Levine, Boston 617 338 8093
*Recommended in Bankruptcy*

### LEVY, Joshua S
Ropes & Gray LLP, Boston
617 951 7281
joshua.levy@ropesgray.com
*Recommended in Litigation*
**Practice Areas:** Defending corporations and individuals in a wide range of civil and criminal matters, including healthcare fraud, tax investigations, Foreign Corrupt Practices Act, securities fraud, environmental crimes and general business crimes. He also conducts internal investigations for numerous organizations.
**Career:** Massachusetts Bar (1993); law clerk, Hon Harold Greene (1992-93); Assistant United States Attorney, District of Massachusetts (1997-2004); Attorney General's Award for Exceptional Service (2000); Partner, Ropes & Gray (2004).
**Personal:** JD, magna cum laude, Georgetown University Law Center, Order of the Coif, Associate Editor, Georgetown Law Journal (1992); BA, Brown University (1987).

### LIAZOS, Andrew C
McDermott Will & Emery, Boston
617 535 4038
aliazos@mwe.com
*Recommended in Employee Benefits*

**Practice Areas:** Chair of Boston Employee Benefits practice and firm's Executive Compensation Group. Focuses on nonqualified deferred compensation, equity incentives, employment agreements, golden parachutes, compensation committees, IRS audits, multinational benefits, employee benefits in bankruptcy, retirement plans and ERISA fiduciary matters. Representative clients include Liberty Mutual, Ocean Spray and Tootsie Roll.
**Prof. Memberships:** Chaired Boston Bar Association's Employee Benefits Committee and ABA Joint Task Force on Split Dollar Life Insurance. John Nolan Tax Fellow of ABA's Tax Section and faculty member of ALI-ABA.
**Personal:** Admitted to Massachusetts (1990), US Tax Court (1991) and Maine (1993). Clerked at IRS National Office (1989).

### LITWAK, Lawrence
Brown Rudnick Berlack Israels LLP, Boston 617 856 8200
*Recommended in Healthcare*

### LIZOTTE, Andrew G
Hanify & King, Boston
617 226 3415
agl@hanify.com
*Recommended in Bankruptcy*
**Practice Areas:** Shareholder in Hanify & King's Bankruptcy and Financial Restructuring Group. Specializes in bankruptcy and commercial law including representation of debtors, creditors committees, and trustees.
**Prof. Memberships:** American Bankruptcy Institute; Boston Bar Association.
**Career:** Shareholder in Hanify & King's Bankruptcy and Financial Restructuring Group. Law clerk to Hon James F Queenan, US Bankruptcy Court, Certified Public Accountant.
**Personal:** JD, Suffolk University Law School (1991); BSBA, Bryant University (1986).

### LUKEY, Joan
WilmerHale, Boston
617 526 6798
joan.lukey@wilmerhale.com
*Recommended in Employment, Litigation*
**Practice Areas:** Concentrates practice in commercial and employment litigation. Highly regarded trial attorney; tried more than 50 federal and state cases, predominantly to juries. Experienced appellate advocate; argued approximately 15 cases before US Court of Appeals for the First Circuit, and approximately 35 cases before state appellate courts in Massachusetts and New Hampshire.
**Prof. Memberships:** Boston Bar Association (President, 2000-01); American College of Trial Lawyers (elected, 1991); International Academy of Trial Lawyers (elected to Fellowship).
**Career:** Admitted to Massachusetts Bar,

New Hampshire Bar and US Supreme Court. Joined firm in 1974.
**Personal:** Boston College Law School (JD); Smith College (BA).

### LYMAN, R Jeffrey
Goodwin Procter LLP, Boston
617 570 1000
rlyman@goodwinprocter.com
*Recommended in Real Estate*
**Practice Areas:** Mr Lyman represents clients in all aspects of commercial real estate development and permitting. His practice often involves cutting-edge permitting and environmental issues and he is widely sought after on complex matters relating to environmental impact assessment, wetlands and waterways work, brownfield redevelopment, regulatory takings litigation, and master plan implementation. He has successfully permitted projects under innovative zoning regulations. Mr Lyman has worked with clients building office, multi-family residential, industrial and recreational facilities in urban, suburban and rural locations.
**Personal:** JD, Vermont Law School, 1993 (magna cum laude); BA, Harvard College, 1986 (cum laude).

### LYNCH, Christine
Goulston & Storrs, Boston
617 482 1776
*Recommended in Bankruptcy*

### LYONS, Gregory J
Goodwin Procter LLP, Boston
617 570 1000
glyons@goodwinprocter.com
*Recommended in Banking & Finance*
**Practice Areas:** Mr Lyons' practice concentrates principally in the banking area, engaging in US and foreign bank regulatory, formation, merger, conversion, structuring and securities work, risk capital and trust matters, as well as general corporate and securities law matters. He has represented financial institutions before the Federal Deposit Insurance Corporation, the Federal Reserve Board, the Office of Comptroller of the Currency, the Office of Thrift Supervision, the Securities and Exchange Commission, and state banking and securities regulatory agencies.
**Personal:** JD, Boston University School of Law, 1990 (magna cum laude); BA, Wesleyan University, 1987.

### MACKIE, Thomas
Moehrke, Mackie & Shea, P.C., Boston
617 266 5700
*Recommended in Environment*

### MAHONY, Gael
Holland & Knight LLP, Boston
617 523 2700
gael.mahony@hklaw.com
*Recommended in Litigation*
**Practice Areas:** Partner in the Litigation Section, specializing in complex business and appellate cases. His high profile clients include such companies as Volvo

and the Hyatt Hotel chain. In a Boston Magazine survey of Boston lawyers he was named the lawyer of choice for 'betting the company' cases. He is Chairman of the ABA Law Library of Congress Advisory Commission, past Chairman of the First Circuit Advisory Committee and a member and former president of the American College of Trial Lawyers, an invitation-only organization of top litigators across the country. He is a graduate of Yale University and Harvard Law School.

### MAIR, George P
Bingham McCutchen LLP, Boston
617 951 8423
george.mair@bingham.com
*Recommended in Tax*
**Practice Areas:** Concentrates on international tax, financial instruments, estate planning and other tax-related matters, including controversy work for both individuals and corporations. Has taught at Harvard Law School and has spoken at the Federal Tax Institute of New England and at various programs sponsored by the Boston Bar Association, Massachusetts Continuing Legal Education and other organizations. Has authored numerous publications on tax-related matters.
**Personal:** Harvard Law School, JD, 1978; Harvard College, BA, 1975.

### MALONE, Judith
Edwards Angell Palmer & Dodge LLP, Boston 617 239 0321
jmalone@eapdlaw.com
*Recommended in Employment*
**Practice Areas:** Judy counsels employers on issues ranging from organizational restructuring to individual termination cases, and on policies and practices dealing with current employment issues. She litigates employment-related claims in both state and federal court, and has represented clients in a variety of discrimination actions, including claims involving race, sex, national origin, disability, sexual harassment, and age discrimination. She represents employers before administrative agencies and conducts employment-law seminars for employers.
**Prof. Memberships:** American Bar Association, Massachusetts Bar Association.
**Personal:** University of Massachusetts, BA, magna cum laude, 1973; Boston College Law School, JD, magna cum laude, 1978.

### MALT, R Bradford
Ropes & Gray LLP, Boston
617 951 7318
bradford.malt@ropesgray.com
*Recommended in Corporate/M&A, Private Fund Formation*
**Practice Areas:** Concentrates in corporate finance and mergers and acquisitions. Represents a variety of private and public equity clients in fundraising and

investment activities. Clients include leveraged buyout funds, hedge funds, CBO funds, fund-of-funds, mezzanine funds, pension funds, alternative investment funds and investors. Expertise advising fund sponsors in connection with fundraising, strategic initiatives, relationships among partners, organizational structure, effective policies and procedures, and operational matters. A founder of the Private Equity Practice at Ropes & Gray.

**Career:** Massachusetts Bar (1979); Partner, Ropes & Gray (1987).

**Personal:** JD, cum laude, Harvard Law School (1979); AB, magna cum laude, Harvard College (1976).

### MARETT, Louis J
Choate Hall & Stewart, Boston
617 248 5000
*Recommended in Tax*

### MARTLAND, David A
Nixon Peabody LLP, Boston
617 345 6145
dmartland@nixonpeabody.com
*Recommended in Antitrust*

**Practice Areas:** Mr Martland has extensive experience advising substantial corporate and healthcare clients on antitrust matters, litigating significant antitrust cases and representing clients in FTC, DOJ and state attorneys general merger and non-merger related investigations. Mr Martland's practice encompasses all aspects of antitrust jurisprudence. He represented Reebok and the Rockport Company in connection with the FTC and NAAG investigations leading to State of New York et al v Reebok International Ltd., et al, 96 F3d 44 (2nd Cir. 1996) and has represented numerous healthcare organizations in merger and other antitrust investigations.

**Prof. Memberships:** Member of the Massachusetts and American Bar Associations.

**Publications:** Writes and lectures extensively on antitrust issues.

**Personal:** Yale Law School, JD, 1985, Senior Editor, Yale Law Journal; Princeton University, BA, cum laude, 1982; clerked for Walter R Mansfield (US Second Circuit Court of Appeals).

### MAY, Arnold P
Proskauer Rose LLP, Boston
617 526 9757
amay@proskauer.com
*Recommended in Tax*

**Practice Areas:** Partner at Proskauer Rose. Member of the Tax Department and Private Equity Group. Concentrates on tax planning for private equity fund managers in connection with fundraising and investments. He advises on international tax issues for investments in the US by non-US investors; investments outside of the US by US persons; structuring tax-free and taxable mergers and acquisitions; equity compensation arrange-

ments; and innovative financing techniques for investments in tax transparent entities.

**Personal:** University of Florida College of Law, LLM, 1994. University of San Diego School of Law, JD, 1993. Rutgers College, BA, 1990.

### MAYER, William P
Goodwin Procter LLP, Boston
617 570 1000
wmayer@goodwinprocter.com
*Recommended in Banking & Finance*

**Practice Areas:** Mr Mayer has handled a wide variety of transactions including mergers, acquisitions, public and private offerings of debt and equity securities, stock conversions, bank and holding company formations and reorganizations of financial institutions and holding companies. He regularly advises clients on bank regulatory matters involving state and federal law.

**Prof. Memberships:** Center for Banking & Financial Law Studies (Boston University): Board of Advisors.

**Personal:** JD, Virginia Law School, 1977; MS, University of Dar es Salaam, Tanzania, 1974; AB, Dartmouth College, 1973 (summa cum laude).

### MCCARTHY, William F
Ropes & Gray LLP, Boston
617 951 7466
william.mccarthy@ropesgray.com
*Recommended in Bankruptcy*

**Practice Areas:** Represents debtors and creditors in reorganization cases throughout the United States and has lectured extensively on debtor/creditor relationships to business and professional groups. Represented debtors in cases in Massachusetts, Delaware and New York; boards of directors; major creditors in Chapter 11 cases; and bidders for assets of Chapter 11 debtors.

**Career:** Massachusetts Bar (1970); Partner, Ropes & Gray (1979).

**Personal:** JD, cum laude, Harvard Law School (1970); BA, College of the Holy Cross (1967).

### MCCARTY, Christopher J
Holland & Knight LLP, Boston
401 824 5137
chris.mccarty@hklaw.com
*Recommended in Banking & Finance*

**Practice Areas:** Partner in the Real Estate Section, practices in the areas of banking, finance, real estate and insolvency law. Mr McCarty has extensive experience representing major US banks and other financial institutions in asset-based and real estate financing transactions, including acquisition, construction and permanent financing of office, retail, hotel and multi-family projects throughout the United States. This experience includes Fannie Mae and Freddie Mac multi-family loan programs, participation and syndicated loan transactions, and work-out and foreclosures. Mr

McCarty also has experience representing the interests of secured creditors and commercial landlords in bankruptcy proceedings and state court receiverships.

### MCDANIEL, James
Choate Hall & Stewart, Boston
617 248 5000
*Recommended in Banking & Finance*

### MCPHEE, Joan
Ropes & Gray LLP, Boston
617 951 7535
joan.mcphee@ropesgray.com
*Recommended in Litigation*

**Practice Areas:** Specializes in white-collar criminal matters and complex civil litigation. Represents clients in criminal litigation, enforcement actions, and federal and state grand jury investigations involving healthcare fraud, securities fraud, bank fraud, contract fraud, RICO violations, mail and wire fraud, and export control violations.

**Career:** Massachusetts Bar (1986); New York Bar (1986); Rhode Island Bar (1991); Partner, Ropes & Gray (1993).

**Personal:** JD, magna cum laude, Harvard Law School (1984); BA, Phi Beta Kappa, Princeton University (1980).

### MEDAGLIA, Anthony J
Goodwin Procter LLP, Boston
617 570 1000
amedaglia@goodwinprocter.com
*Recommended in Private Equity*

**Practice Areas:** Mr Medaglia focuses his practice on the representation of technology companies – both public and private; private equity; mergers and acquisitions; public and private sales of securities; corporate buyouts and reorganizations; and transactions involving intellectual property. He has extensive experience representing hedge funds, investment advisors and venture capitalists. He has structured, negotiated and closed numerous strategic transactions for a diverse group of clients.

**Personal:** LLB, Harvard Law School, 1965; AB, Harvard College, 1959.

### MENNA, Gilbert G
Goodwin Procter LLP, Boston
617 570 1000
gmenna@goodwinprocter.com
*Recommended in Corporate/M&A*

**Practice Areas:** Mr Menna has extensive experience representing public and private issuers (ranging from emerging to NYSE-listed public companies), investors (private and institutional), underwriters and placement agents in all types of equity and debt securities, including sophisticated convertible and exchangeable securities with a broad range of economic, substantive and tax-sensitive terms. He is nationally recognized for his representation of publicly traded real estate operating companies.

**Prof. Memberships:** NYU Real Estate Institute REITs Center: Board of Direc-

tors; NAREIT: Board Member; ULI: Member.

**Personal:** JD, Georgetown University Law Center, 1982; MLT, Georgetown University Law Center, 1983; BA, Syracuse University, 1978 (magna cum laude).

### MEREDITH, Stephen
Edwards Angell Palmer & Dodge LLP, Boston 617 951 2233
smeredith@eapdlaw.com
*Recommended in Private Equity*

**Practice Areas:** Steve has led teams of lawyers in virtually every kind of corporate transaction, both within the US and abroad. His experience includes private equity and venture capital financings, M&A, start-ups, joint ventures, fund formations, buyouts, securities offerings, debt facilities, restructurings and litigation oversight.

**Prof. Memberships:** European Venture Capital Association, Federal Communications Bar Association, American Bar Association, Massachusetts Bar Association, Rhode Island Bar Association.

**Publications:** Steve is the author of a number of articles on private equity and corporate finance and has been quoted in various business publications, including the Wall Street Journal, Venture Capital Journal, The Boston Globe, Private Equity Analyst, and Bloomberg News.

**Personal:** University of Iowa, JD, 1978; Brown University, AB, 1974.

### MIKELS, Richard
Mintz Levin Cohn Ferris Glovsky and Popeo PC, Boston
617 348 1691
RMikels@mintz.com
*Recommended in Bankruptcy*

**Practice Areas:** Bankruptcy, restructuring and commercial law.

**Prof. Memberships:** Rick is a fellow of the American College of Bankruptcy and serves as First Circuit Regent. He is a member of the National Board of Directors of the American Bankruptcy Institute. Rick serves as a director of the New England Chapter of the Turnaround Management Association. He serves on the BU Law School Board of Visitors.

**Career:** Rick is a shareholder of Mintz Levin and serves as Chairman of the Bankruptcy Department. He has practiced in the area of bankruptcy law for over 30 years. He has represented companies both in bankruptcy and in out-of-court restructurings. Additionally, he often represents other constituencies, including secured creditors and acquirers of businesses. Representative Debtor Chapter 11 cases include Malden Mills, ACT Manufacturing, Inc., Filenes Basement, Inc., divine, Inc. and Great Northern Paper, Inc.

**Publications:** Rick is the author of a chapter in Bankruptcy Business Acquisitions and he is a contributing editor to the American Bankrutpcy Institute Journal. He has authored articles regarding the impact of Till, conflicts between bankruptcy law and state law and the proper balance of creditor and equity interests in Chapter 11.

**Personal:** BS in Business Administration, Boston University 1969; JD, cum laude, Boston University 1972.

## MILLER, Michelle
WilmerHale, Boston
617 526 6116
michelle.miller@wilmerhale.com
*Recommended in Antitrust*

**Practice Areas:** Vice-Chair of firm's Litigation Department and Antitrust and Competition Department; member of firm's Executive Committee. Concentrates practice on complex commercial litigation and on providing advice to clients on antitrust compliance issues and strategies for avoiding litigation. Litigates in federal and state courts. Represents clients before the Federal Trade Commission and the Antitrust Division of the Department of Justice in connection with mergers and other government investigations.

**Prof. Memberships:** American Bar Association; former Co-Chair of Boston Bar Association's Antitrust Committee.

**Career:** Admitted to Massachusetts Bar. Joined firm in 1980.

**Personal:** Boston College Law School (JD); Boston University (BA).

## MILNER, Ann L
Ropes & Gray LLP, Boston
617 951 7314
ann.milner@ropesgray.com
*Recommended in Private Fund Formation*

**Practice Areas:** Represents private investment funds, including leveraged buyout, venture, hedge and special focus funds, in their fundraising and ongoing activities. Additionally represents institutional and other investors in alternative investments. Representative clients include Absolute Return Capital, Bain Capital, Brookside Capital, Cayuga Ventures, Parthenon Capital and Verizon Investment Management Corporation.

**Career:** Massachusetts Bar (1986); Partner, Ropes & Gray (1995).

**Personal:** JD, magna cum laude, Boston College Law School, Order of the Coif; Boston College Law Review (1986); BA, highest honors, University of Rhode Island, Phi Beta Kappa/Phi Kappa Phi (1983).

## MITCHELL, Beth
Nutter, McClennen & Fish, LLP, Boston
617 439 2000
*Recommended in Real Estate*

## MOFFATT, Maura Griffith
Goodwin Procter LLP, Boston
617 570 1000
mmoffatt@goodwinprocter.com
*Recommended in Real Estate*

**Practice Areas:** Ms Moffat focuses on a wide variety of commercial real estate transactions, with a particular emphasis on real estate investment management and finance, capital markets and real estate securities. Her national real estate practice includes property acquisitions, leasing and sales, and debt and equity investments of all types, as well as restructurings. Ms Moffatt represents a wide variety of investors, including pension fund advisors and their institutional investors, banking institutions, insurance companies, public and private operating companies and private real estate investors and real estate investment fund sponsors.

**Prof. Memberships:** Urban Land Institute: Member; National Association of Office and Industrial Properties: Member.

**Personal:** JD, Georgetown University Law Center, 1991 (cum laude); BS, Georgetown University's College of Arts and Sciences, 1988.

## MONAGHAN, John J
Holland & Knight LLP, Boston
617 523 2700
john.monaghan@hklaw.com
*Recommended in Bankruptcy*

**Practice Areas:** Practice Group Leader of the firm's National Corporate Restructuring, Bankruptcy and Creditors' Rights Group. His extensive bankruptcy practice has involved representation of a wide range of clients, including Chapter 11 debtors, creditors' committees, equity committees, lenders, landlords, licensors, trustees, parties to prepetition contracts and leases, defendants in adversary proceedings and unsecured creditors. He is particularly focused on representing major case participants in complex commercial Chapter 11 cases. He advises clients on the business aspects of bankruptcy and workouts, and represents clients in matters in the Bankruptcy Court as well as in other state and federal courts.

## MONTGOMERY, John T
Ropes & Gray LLP, Boston
617 951 7565
john.montgomery@ropesgray.com
*Recommended in Litigation*

**Practice Areas:** Complex civil litigation with emphasis on trials and appeals in high profile cases involving novel or publicly sensitive issues. Practice includes a variety of complex matters involving securities, pharmaceutical pricing, intellectual property, insurance coverage, commercial tort, product liability, ERISA, and regulatory matters. Tried cases and argued appeals in state and federal courts in Maine, Massachusetts, Illinois, New York, New Jersey, and Washington, DC. Argued two successful appeals in the United States Supreme Court.

## MORREALE, Justin P
Bingham McCutchen LLP, Boston
617 951 8245
justin.morreale@bingham.com
*Recommended in Private Equity*

**Career:** Massachusetts Bar (1975); Partner, Ropes & Gray (1985); Managing Partner (2004).

**Personal:** JD, Boston College Law School (1975); BA, University of Michigan (1969).

## MOORE, Gregory E
Ropes & Gray LLP, Boston
617 951 7370
gregory.moore@ropesgray.com
*Recommended in Private Equity*

**Practice Areas:** Focuses on representing venture capital investors and advising high technology companies on a broad range of issues including domestic and international distribution, joint ventures, public and private financing, and the protection and licensing of technology. He also advises clients in a variety of industries on intellectual property matters.

**Career:** Massachusetts Bar (1977); Partner, Ropes & Gray (1985); Member, MIT Corporation; Co-Chair of the Venture Capital and Start Up Company Practice Group.

**Personal:** JD, Harvard Law School (1976); SB (Astrophysics), Massachusetts Institute of Technology (1973).

## MOORE, Paul D
Duane Morris LLP, Boston
617 289 9230
pdmoore@duanemorris.com
*Recommended in Bankruptcy*

**Practice Areas:** Paul D Moore focuses his practice on business reorganization, bankruptcy law and litigation and loan workouts. He represents debtors in possession and Chapter 11 trustees in a wide range of reorganization cases under Chapter 11 of the Bankruptcy Code pending in various jurisdictions, including Delaware, as well as Massachusetts. He also represents creditors in bankruptcy and loan workout matters.

**Prof. Memberships:** American Bar Association; Massachusetts Bar Association; Boston Bar Association; American Bankruptcy Institute.

**Career:** Admitted to practice in the Commonwealth of Massachusetts; the Supreme Court of the United States; the United States Court of Appeals for the First Circuit; and the United States District Court for the District of Massachusetts. Duane Morris LLP, Partner, 1999-present; Choate, Hall & Stewart, Boston, Massachusetts, Partner, 1990-99; Foley, Hoag & Eliot, Boston, Massachusetts, Partner, 1982-90, Associate, 1979-82; Testa, Hurwitz & Thibeault, Boston, Massachusetts, Associate, 1976-79.

**Personal:** Boston College Law School, JD, 1976; Boston College, BS, 1973.

## MORREALE, Justin P
Bingham McCutchen LLP, Boston
617 951 8245
justin.morreale@bingham.com
*Recommended in Private Equity*

**Practice Areas:** Focuses on general corporate matters as well as mergers and acquisitions. Serves as corporate counsel to emerging growth and established companies, both public and private, in a variety of fields, including life sciences, software and telecommunications. Formerly served as Chair of the firm's Corporate Area.

**Personal:** Harvard Law School, JD, cum laude, 1968; Syracuse University, BA, magna cum laude, 1964.

## MORRIER, John
Mintz Levin Cohn Ferris Glovsky and Popeo PC, Boston
617 348 3051
JMorrier@mintz.com
*Recommended in Bankruptcy*

**Practice Areas:** John Morrier practices in Mintz Levin's Bankruptcy, Restructuring and Commercial Law section, representing individuals, businesses and pro bono clients in state and federal courts in bankruptcy, business reorganization and business litigation matters including debtors' and creditors' rights, lending and security, workouts and restructurings, as well as representing lenders and borrowers in secured and syndicated financings.

**Prof. Memberships:** Massachusetts and Boston Bar Associations; American Bankruptcy Institute; Turnaround Management Association.

**Publications:** John is a frequent speaker on insolvency and restructuring topics, including recent presentations to the Association of Commercial Finance Attorneys, American Bankruptcy Institute and Boston Bar Association.

**Personal:** Admitted in the state and federal courts of Massachusetts and Maine, John earned his bachelor's (1988), Master of Business Administration (1994) and JD (1994) Degrees from Boston College.

## MOTENKO, Neil
Nutter, McClennen & Fish, LLP, Boston
617 439 2000
*Recommended in Antitrust*

## MULDOON JR, Robert
Sherin and Lodgen LLP, Boston
617 646 2225
*Recommended in Litigation*

## MURPHY, Harold B
Hanify & King, Boston
617 423 0400
hbm@hanify.com
*Recommended in Bankruptcy*

**Practice Areas:** Leads Hanify & King's Bankruptcy and Financial Restructuring Group. Specializes in bankruptcy and commercial law including the representation of debtors, creditors' committees, trustees and creditors in Chapter 11 reorganizations and Chapter 7 liquidations. Mr Murphy has been appointed as trustee, examiner and receiver in various bankruptcy and non-bankruptcy corporate restructurings and liquidations. He

has had considerable experience in the areas of commercial finance and litigation as well as matters involving secured lending, mergers and acquisitions, and the Uniform Commercial Code.
**Prof. Memberships:** American, Boston and Massachusetts Bar Associations; Turnaround Management Association; American Bankruptcy Institute.
**Career:** Founder and Director of Hanify & King's Bankruptcy and Financial Restructuring Group.
**Personal:** JD, Suffolk University Law School (1981); AB, cum laude, Harvard College (1977).

## NAGLE, James W
Goodwin Procter LLP, Boston
617 570 1000
jnagle@goodwinprocter.com
*Recommended in Employment*
**Practice Areas:** Mr Nagle focuses on defending corporations against claims made by employees. He practices in state and federal courts, as well as before a variety of administrative agencies. He is experienced in litigating complex age, sex, race and disability discrimination claims, as well as in defending wrongful discharge, civil rights, employee privacy and drug-testing cases. He also has experience negotiating and litigating issues related to the termination of highly compensated executives.
**Personal:** JD, Georgetown University Law Center, 1980 (magna cum laude); MPA, American University, 1976; BA, Georgetown University, 1974 (magna cum laude).

## NEWBERG, Joseph H
Weil, Gotshal & Manges LLP, Boston
617 772 8350
joseph.newberg@weil.com
*Recommended in Tax*
**Practice Areas:** Joseph Newberg focuses his practice on the sophisticated problems of private equity funds and fund managers, and has particular experience with the international aspects of private equity transactions. He has advised on the formation of private equity funds with over $20 billion of capital commitments, and regularly advises these funds on administrative issues and investment transactions. Mr Newberg's experience includes joint ventures between private equity sponsors and institutions.
**Personal:** University of Michigan, BA, 1969, with High Distinction; Harvard Law School, JD, 1972, magna cum laude.

## NICHOLLS III, Malcolm B
Proskauer Rose LLP, Boston
617 526 9787
mnicholls@proskauer.com
*Recommended in Private Fund Formation*
**Practice Areas:** Partner at Proskauer Rose. Member of the firm's Corporate Department and Private Equity Group. His experience includes representation of

private equity fund managers and investors in both US and non-US fund formation projects, portfolio company investments, and management and governance issues.
**Prof. Memberships:** A Member of the American Bar Association and Boston Bar Association; admitted to the New York Bar in 1995, the US District Court, Southern District of New York, in 1995 and the Massachusetts Bar in 1996.
**Personal:** Boston University School of Law, JD, 1994; University of New Hampshire, BA, magna cum laude, 1991.

## NULL, Amy A
WilmerHale, Boston
617 526 6541
amy.null@wilmerhale.com
*Recommended in Employee Benefits*
**Practice Areas:** Ms Null is a Partner in WilmerHale's Tax Department. She has broad experience advising financial institutions, benefit plan service providers and employers on ERISA, federal income tax law and other rules and regulations applicable to employee benefit plans.
**Prof. Memberships:** Chair of the American Bar Association Tax Section's Subcommittee on Government Plans and past Chair of the Boston Bar Association's ERISA Committee.
**Career:** Prior to joining the firm in 2001, Ms Null was an attorney advisor for the US Department of the Treasury, Office of Tax Policy.
**Personal:** Harvard Law School (JD, cum laude); Haverford College (BA).

## NUTT, Robert L
Ropes & Gray LLP, Boston
617 951 7384
robert.nutt@ropesgray.com
*Recommended in Corporate/M&A*
**Practice Areas:** Transactions lawyer, marshalling the corporate securities and tax law resources of Ropes & Gray in complex capital markets transactions. Represents primarily investment advisors, investment banking firms and private equity clients. Represents committees of public bondholders in large-case debt restructurings and directors of publicly traded companies. Specialist in corporate, commercial, and insolvency law.
**Career:** Massachusetts Bar (1971); New York Bar (1971); Partner, Ropes & Gray (1979).
**Personal:** JD, cum laude, University of Pennsylvania Law School (1970); BA, summa cum laude, Grove City College (1967).

## NYLEN JR, Richard
Lynch DeSimone & Nylen LLP, Boston
617 348 4500
*Recommended in Real Estate*

## O'CONNOR, Brien T
Ropes & Gray LLP, Boston
617 951 7385
brien.o'connor@ropesgray.com

*Recommended in Litigation*
**Practice Areas:** Concentrates on defending against criminal actions against businesses; defending FCA whistle-blower actions and SEC and other civil government actions; defending complex private actions, many of which are related to government enforcement; and conducting internal investigations. Defended well-known clients in healthcare, securities, and other leading economic sectors.
**Career:** Massachusetts Bar (1985); Assistant US Attorney, Boston USAO (1989-99); Chief, Public Corruption and Special Prosecutions, Boston USAO (1996-99); Recipient, John Marshall Award (1997, DOJ's highest recognition for trial work); Partner, Ropes & Gray (1999).
**Personal:** JD, cum laude, University of Pennsylvania Law School (1985); BA, magna cum laude, Yale University (1981).

## OGILBY, Anne Phillips
Ropes & Gray LLP, Boston
617 951 7472
anne.ogilby@ropesgray.com
*Recommended in Healthcare*
**Practice Areas:** Principally responsible for capital financings undertaken on behalf of healthcare and higher education clients, including over 100 tax-exempt and taxable borrowings and associated derivatives transactions. Routinely serves as underwriter's counsel and counsel to financially distressed non-profit corporations. Broadly involved in corporate transactions, including acquisitions and divestitures of healthcare and other non-profit corporations and the development and unwind of multi-provider delivery systems. General corporate counseling for non-profit corporations, including endowment issues.
**Career:** Massachusetts Bar (1985); New York Bar (2004); Partner, Ropes & Gray (1993).
**Personal:** JD, University of Virginia School of Law (1984); BA, Harvard College (1980).

## O'REILLY JR, William R
WilmerHale, Boston
617 526 6210
william.o'reilly@wilmerhale.com
*Recommended in Real Estate*
**Practice Areas:** Vice-Chair of the firm's Real Estate Department. Practice focuses on all aspects of real estate law, including permitting, development, construction, financing, purchase and sales and leasing. Has served as counsel for a broad range of clients, including numerous office, R&D and multi-family developers, retailers, corporations and non-profit institutions for over 25 years.
**Prof. Memberships:** Tufts University (Trustee); The American College of Real Estate Lawyers (Member).
**Career:** Admitted to Massachusetts Bar. Joined the firm in 1980.

**Personal:** Georgetown University Law Center (JD, magna cum laude); Tufts University (BA, summa cum laude with Special Honors).

## PAINTER, Robin A
Proskauer Rose LLP, Boston
617 526 9790
rpainter@proskauer.com
*Recommended in Private Fund Formation*
**Practice Areas:** Partner and Co-Chair of the Private Equity Group at Proskauer Rose. Over 20 years of experience in the private equity field. Concentrates on representation of private equity fund managers in fund formations and management and governance issues, and of institutional investors in their private equity investments.
**Career:** Frequently speaks nationally and internationally on private equity-related issues and is also a frequent contributor to private equity industry publications.
**Personal:** Received her BA, cum laude, from Northwestern University and her JD, cum laude, from Boston College School of Law.

## PAPPONE, Michael J
Goodwin Procter LLP, Boston
617 570 1000
mpappone@goodwinprocter.com
*Recommended in Bankruptcy*
**Practice Areas:** Mr Pappone concentrates in commercial insolvency and reorganization law. His practice spans the spectrum of representing principal parties in large corporate reorganizations to out-of-court workouts for smaller entrepreneurial companies, including representation of equipment lessors, landlords, asset acquirers, creditors' committees or committee members, court-appointed trustees and entities involved in leveraged buyouts. Also advises clients on commercial and insolvency issues arising in corporate restructurings, financings and securitization transactions.
**Prof. Memberships:** American College of Commercial Finance Lawyers: Member; American Bar Foundation: Fellow; American College of Bankruptcy: Fellow.
**Personal:** JD, Harvard Law School, 1973; AB, University of California, Berkeley, 1970.

## PARSIGIAN, Kenneth J
Goodwin Procter LLP, Boston
617 570 1000
kparsigian@goodwinprocter.com
*Recommended in Litigation*
**Practice Areas:** Mr Parsigian represents clients in both civil and criminal matters, with a primary focus on complex products liability, mass tort and RICO litigation. He also advises clients on product warnings and compliance with laws and regulations concerning product safety, import-export procedures and anti-money laundering programs. He has served as Lead Counsel for Philip Morris

USA, and National Coordinating Counsel for the tobacco industry in more than 60 suits across the country involving claims for more than $100 billion in damages.

**Personal:** JD, Boston University School of Law, 1987 (magna cum laude); BA, University of Michigan, 1983.

### PASTERNACK, Sam
Choate Hall & Stewart, Boston
617 248 5000
*Recommended in Intellectual Property*

### PASTUSZENSKI, Brian E
Goodwin Procter LLP, Boston
617 570 1000
bpastuszenski@goodwinprocter.com
*Recommended in Litigation*

**Practice Areas:** Mr Pastuszenski has achieved national prominence in the defense of securities class action and shareholder litigation matters and proceedings brought by the SEC and other regulatory organizations, and the related insurance and indemnification issues that such matters involve. His practice is concentrated in the areas of securities class action and shareholder litigation defense, defense of SEC proceedings, internal corporate investigations, corporate governance and compliance matters, merger and acquisition-related litigation, and other high-stakes business litigation.

**Personal:** JD, Cornell Law School, 1981 (magna cum laude, Order of the Coif); BA, Dartmouth College, 1978 (summa cum laude).

### PATTON, William L
Ropes & Gray LLP, Boston
617 951 7572
william.patton@ropesgray.com
*Recommended in Antitrust*

**Practice Areas:** Extensive experience in general litigation matters, including antitrust and intellectual property litigation. Advises and represents clients in a wide range of antitrust matters including private disputes and Department of Justice, FTC, and state law enforcement investigations. Significant trial and appellate experience before the Supreme Judicial Court, the Federal Courts of Appeals, and the United States Supreme Court.

**Career:** Maine Bar (1969); Massachusetts Bar (1970); Assistant to the Solicitor General of the United States (1973-75); Partner, Ropes & Gray (1977).

**Personal:** JD, Duke University School of Law (1968); BA, Yale University (1965).

### PEARLSTEIN, Mark W
McDermott Will & Emery, Boston
617 535 4425
mpearlstein@mwe.com
*Recommended in Litigation*

**Practice Areas:** Concentrates practice on white-collar criminal defense, the defense of actions brought by the SEC, complex commercial litigation, arbitration and internal investigations. Experi-

ence in corporate criminal investigations. Served as Acting US Attorney responsible for negotiating what was then the largest resolution of a healthcare fraud case.

**Career:** Litigated a range of civil and criminal matters and tried a number of complex white-collar crime cases. Received the Attorney General's Award for Exceptional Service, the highest award presented by the Department of Justice.

**Personal:** University of Michigan (AB, Phi Beta Kappa); Harvard Law School (JD, cum laude).

### PENDLETON, Lea
Morse, Barnes-Brown & Pendleton PC, Waltham 781 622 5930
*Recommended in Private Equity*

### PENTZ, Martin
Foley Hoag LLP, Boston
617 832 1000
*Recommended in Environment*

### PERRY, Christopher
Littler Mendelson, PC, Boston
617 378 6000
cperry@littler.com
*Recommended in Employment*

**Practice Areas:** Represents employers in employment law matters including discrimination, wrongful termination, wage and hour law, contractual issues and sexual harassment and in matters arising from collective bargaining relationships, and union organizing. Litigates cases involving claims of wrongful termination, employee benefits, restrictive covenants, discrimination and breach of contract.

**Prof. Memberships:** Member, Employee Benefits Committee of the ABA's Labor and Employment Section; the Labor and Employment Section of the Boston Bar Association; Member of the Board of Directors of the Robert F Kennedy Children's Action Corps., Inc.

**Personal:** Harvard Law School (JD, 1983); Amherst College, (BA, magna cum laude, 1979).

### PICKETT, Andrew
Jackson Lewis, Boston
617 367 0025
PickettA@jacksonlewis.com
*Recommended in Employment*

**Practice Areas:** Managing Partner, Boston office. Employment litigation and counseling on behalf of management, including discrimination claims, reductions in force, ADA and FMLA leaves, ADR, non-competition agreements and ERISA litigation.

**Prof. Memberships:** Boston, Massachusetts, Vermont and American Bar Associations. Co-Chair, Labor and Employment Law Section, Boston Bar Association, 2000-02.

**Career:** Law clerk, Hon Albert W Coffrin, Chief Judge, USDC VT 1986-87; Ropes & Gray, Boston, MA, 1987-96; Special Assistant District Attorney, Cam-

bridge, MA, 1990-91.

**Personal:** Cornell Law School, JD, cum laude, 1986; Princeton University, AB, magna cum laude, 1983.

### PIERCE, Rudolph
Goulston & Storrs, Boston
617 482 1776
*Recommended in Litigation*

### PISA, Regina M
Goodwin Procter LLP, Boston
617 570 1000
rpisa@goodwinprocter.com
*Recommended in Banking & Finance*

**Practice Areas:** Ms Pisa serves as Chairman and Managing Partner of Goodwin Procter LLP. Her practice focuses on the financial services area, representing banks and investment companies. She has recently concentrated on mergers and acquisitions of banks and financial institutions. She also represents banks and financial institutions on a wide variety of other matters, including corporate and board governance issues, capital raising, and general corporate and securities law issues.

**Prof. Memberships:** Boys and Girls Club of America: Board of Trustees; Easter Seals Society of Massachusetts: Board of Directors and Chair; Simmons College: Board of Trustees.

**Personal:** JD, Georgetown University Law Center; BA, MA, Oxford University, St Hilda's College; AB, Harvard University.

### PONDA, Ameek
Sullivan & Worcester LLP, Boston
617 338 2800
*Recommended in Tax*

### POPEO, R Robert
Mintz Levin Cohn Ferris Glovsky and Popeo PC, Boston
617 348 1716
rropeo@mintz.com
*Recommended in Litigation*

**Career:** Bob is Chairman of Mintz Levin and practices in the Litigation Section which he previously chaired. Bob's distinguished legal career in the public and private sector spans three decades. He has always placed a premium on not only representing his clients to the best of his considerable abilities, but also devoting his singular energy to civic causes. After his early days as a law clerk to a federal judge, he became a Special Assistant Attorney General and was appointed as a United States Commissioner (later known as United States Magistrate Judge). Bob was also an instructor at Boston University School of Law, and a guest lecturer at various law schools. Later he assumed the role as Chairman of Mintz Levin and now has a reputation as one of the region's premier trial attorneys. He represents major corporations and their CEOs and well known political and media figures throughout the country. He has been recognized by the

National Law Journal as one of the country's top 100 lawyers for nine consecutive years, has been featured in the American Lawyer as one of the country's 'heavy hitters'. Bob was Chairman of the task force of the Boston Bar Association that worked with leaders of the Bar, justices of the various courts and the business community to formulate a plan to reform the Massachusetts court system, a plan that was enacted into law. He was a Vice President of the Association and served on the Bar Council. Bob's stature in the field of legal services rests in no small part on the diligent preparation and ingenious strategy for which he is renowned, and on his sound business advice. He lectures widely in the law and continues his studies to remain abreast of the latest legal developments, while finding time for the civic service he pursues so ardently. Bob is admitted to practice in Massachusetts and the District of Columbia and is a member of the American, Massachusetts, District of Columbia, and Boston Bar Associations, as well as the Practising Law Institute. He is also a Fellow of the American College of Trial Lawyers. He received his AB from Northeastern University, and his JD from Boston College Law School.

### PORCELLI, Frank P
Fish & Richardson P.C., Boston
617 521 7808
porcelli@fr.com
*Recommended in Intellectual Property*

**Practice Areas:** Principal of Fish & Richardson in the firm's Boston and Delaware offices. His practice emphasizes patent and trade secret litigation and appellate work.

**Career:** He joined the firm in 1971.

**Publications:** Author of numerous articles on patent damages and other patent litigation and patent law topics, and co-author, with fellow principal John Dragseth, of 'Patents – A Historical Perspective', a casebook on patent law (in progress).

**Personal:** Boston College AB English Literature 1968; Harvard Law School JD 1971; Northeastern University, MS, 1981 Chemistry.

### PORTER, Jeffrey R
Mintz Levin Cohn Ferris Glovsky and Popeo PC, Boston 617 348 1711
jporter@mintz.com
*Recommended in Environment*

**Practice Areas:** Environmental law.

**Career:** Mr Porter leads Mintz Levin's Environmental Law Section from the firm's Boston office. His extensive litigation and transactional experience provides him with unique insight, enabling him to deliver integrated legal, technical and risk management solutions to environmental legal challenges. Mr Porter's clients include Cargill Incorporated, the General Electric Company and Colony Realty Partners, LLC. Mr Porter has been recognized as one of the leading environmental lawyers in the United States by Chambers USA – America's Leading Lawyers for Business, The Best Lawyers in America, Who's Who in American Law and the Guide to the World's Leading Environmental Lawyers. He has also been identified as a Massachusetts Super Lawyer since the inaugural publication of that list. He serves on the Massachusetts Department of Environmental Protection's Waste Site Clean Up Advisory Committee as the representative of Associated Industries of Massachusetts. Mr Porter is also the Vice-Chairman of the Board of Trustees of The Nature Conservancy's Massachusetts Chapter and the Chairperson of the Chapter's Government Relations Committee. He is also the Treasurer and a member of the Board of Directors of the Boston Harbor Island Alliance. Mr Porter is a member of the American, Massachusetts, and Boston Bar Associations. He received his BA, cum laude, from Bates College (1985) and his JD from Cornell University (1988). He is a member of Phi Beta Kappa.

## POSS, Stephen D
Goodwin Procter LLP, Boston
617 570 1000
sposs@goodwinprocter.com
*Recommended in Litigation*
**Practice Areas:** Mr Poss has a national business litigation and counseling practice, particularly in the areas of securities class action defense, SEC disclosure and corporate governance issues, complex business litigation, mergers and acquisitions, contests for corporate control and intellectual property disputes. He represents venture capital and private equity firms in connection with deal protection, IPO issues, shareholder disputes and transactional litigation and also handles complex business litigation and arbitrations.
**Prof. Memberships:** The SEC Institute: National Advisory Board Member.
**Personal:** JD, University of Chicago Law School, 1981; BA, Amherst College, 1978 (magna cum laude).

## PRATT, Carol
Foley Hoag LLP, Boston
617 832 1000
*Recommended in Banking & Finance*

## PUTZIGER, Myrna
Rubin and Rudman LLP, Boston
617 330 7000
*Recommended in Real Estate*

## RAGALEVSKY, Stanley
Kirkpatrick & Lockhart Nicholson Graham LLP, Boston 617 261 3100
*Recommended in Banking & Finance*

## RAISH, David L
Ropes & Gray LLP, Boston
617 951 7253
david.raish@ropesgray.com

*Recommended in Employee Benefits*
**Practice Areas:** For over 25 years has concentrated in retirement plans, deferred compensation, and other employee benefit matters. Represents a broad range of clients with a primary focus on tax-exempt employers, including universities and healthcare organizations.
**Career:** Massachusetts Bar (1975); District of Columbia Bar (1981); Partner, Ropes & Gray (1982); Department Head, Employee Benefits (1990-2001). Books authored: Compensation and Benefits for Key Employees of Tax-Exempt Organizations (Little, Brown & Co.); Tax Management Portfolios on 125 and 401(k) Plans (Tax Management, Inc.).
**Personal:** JD, Harvard Law School, Editor, Harvard Law Review (1973); BA, Yale University (1969).

## RAPHAEL, Bruce W
Edwards Angell Palmer & Dodge LLP, Boston 617 951 2281
braphael@eapdlaw.com
*Recommended in Banking & Finance*
**Practice Areas:** Bruce's practice focuses on mergers and acquisitions and the regulation of financial services firms. His experience includes representing a variety of financial organizations, including bank and financial holding companies, federally and state chartered banks, Edge and Agreement corporations, commercial and consumer finance companies, insurers and producers and companies engaged in e-commerce.
**Prof. Memberships:** American Bankers Insurance Association; Boston Bar Association.
**Publications:** Bruce is the author of a number of articles on a number of business issues including Gramm-Leach-Bliley and Sarbanes-Oxley.
**Personal:** Boston University, LLM, Banking Law, 1996; Boston College, JD, 1989; Colby College, BA,1986.

## RATTIGAN, John
DLA Piper Rudnick Gray Cary US LLP, Boston 617 406 6057
john.rattigan@dlapiper.com
*Recommended in Real Estate*
**Practice Areas:** Real estate; real estate finance; landlord leasing; land use and development.
**Prof. Memberships:** Boston Bar Association; Massachusetts Bar Association.
**Career:** Over 20 years of experience representing property owners in acquisition, financing, and development of major real estate projects. Counsel to national and regional lenders in construction, permanent, and revolving credit loans ranging from $4 million-$300 million and in loan workouts and enforcement of remedies. Represents landowners in development parcel sales, institutions in land acquisition and construction, and public authorities in development of their prop-

erties.
**Personal:** JD, University of Virginia School of Law; AB, Merrimack College.

## RECK, Joel
Brown Rudnick Berlack Israels LLP, Boston 617 856 8200
*Recommended in Real Estate*

## REDLICK, David
WilmerHale, Boston
617 526 6434
david.redlick@wilmerhale.com
*Recommended in Corporate/M&A*
**Practice Areas:** Co-Chair of Wilmer-Hale's Life Sciences Group. Practice focuses on corporate and securities law, with an emphasis on public offerings, corporate collaborations, mergers and acquisitions, and venture capital transactions.
**Prof. Memberships:** Board of Associates, Whitehead Institute for Biomedical Research (affiliated with MIT); Executive Committee of the Board of Directors, Greater Boston Chamber of Commerce; guest lecturer, Kellogg School of Management at Northwestern University, Harvard Law School, and Sloan School of Management at MIT.
**Career:** Admitted to Massachusetts Bar. Joined the firm in 1975.
**Personal:** Harvard Law School (JD, cum laude); University of Wisconsin (BA, Class Valedictorian, Phi Beta Kappa).

## RENEHAN, Richard
Goulston & Storrs, Boston
617 482 1776
*Recommended in Litigation*

## REUBEN, Catherine
Robinson & Cole LLP, Boston
617 557 5900
*Recommended in Employment*

## RIKLEEN, Lauren Stiller
Bowditch & Dewey LLP, Framingham
508 879 5700
*Recommended in Environment*

## RITT, Roger M
WilmerHale, Boston
617 526 6475
roger.ritt@wilmerhale.com
*Recommended in Tax*
**Practice Areas:** Practice focuses on taxable and tax-free mergers and acquisitions, spin-offs, compensation planning, federal and state tax controversies, and bankruptcies and workouts. Successfully represented many of firm's clients at US Tax Court, IRS appeals, Supreme Judicial Court of Massachusetts, Massachusetts Appellate Tax Board and Massachusetts Department of Revenue.
**Prof. Memberships:** American Bar Association's Section on Taxation (Chairman, Committee on Corporate Tax's Carryovers Subcommittee); Executive Committee of the Federal Tax Institute of New England; The Foundation for Tax Education (Co-Founder, Treasurer).

**Career:** Admitted to Massachusetts Bar.
**Personal:** Boston University School of Law (JD, LLM); University of Pennsylvania (BA, with Honors).

## RIZZOTTI, Anthony D
Ropes & Gray LLP, Boston
617 951 7954
anthony.rizzotti@ropesgray.com
*Recommended in Employment*
**Practice Areas:** Maintains broad Labor and Employment Practice including government and administrative litigation (class actions, discrimination, non-compete, trade secret and Sarbanes-Oxley), labor arbitration, and collective bargaining. Conducts internal investigations on issues such as sexual harassment and misappropriation of confidential information. Provides day-to-day advice on a broad range of labor and employment issues, trains clients on issues such as sexual harassment prevention, and assists clients in drafting agreements, handbooks, plans and policies.
**Career:** Massachusetts Bar (1992); New York Bar (2002); Rhode Island Bar (2004); Partner, Ropes & Gray (2003).
**Personal:** JD, cum laude, Boston College Law School (1992); Undergraduate, Boston College (1989).

## ROBINSON, Marcia C
Bingham McCutchen LLP, Boston
617 951 8535
marcia.robinson@bingham.com
*Recommended in Real Estate*
**Practice Areas:** Concentrates practice in commercial real estate law and finance. Handles all aspects of commercial real estate, including acquisitions, dispositions, development, zoning, land use planning and leasing. Has considerable experience in real estate financing, including construction lending, time-share inventory and receivables financing, multi-state portfolio loans, loan restructurings and foreclosures.
**Career:** Served as a law clerk to the justices of the Superior Court of the Commonwealth of Massachusetts.
**Personal:** Suffolk University Law School, JD, cum laude, 1980; Colgate University, BA, cum laude, 1975.

## ROBLE, Daniel T
Ropes & Gray LLP, Boston
617 951 7476
daniel.roble@ropesgray.com
*Recommended in Healthcare*
**Practice Areas:** Specializes in all areas of healthcare law and has represented the full spectrum of providers and payors. Redefining relationships between academic medical centers and their faculty practice plans, creating innovative relationships based on quality initiatives among hospitals, physician groups and managed care organizations, assisting hospitals with governance reconfiguration following Sarbanes-Oxley, dealing with healthcare organizations' fiscal dis-

tress, creating alternative funding sources for lines of businesses of healthcare organizations, and creating joint ventures among a variety of healthcare organizations.
**Career:** Massachusetts Bar (1975); Partner, Ropes & Gray (1984).
**Personal:** JD, University of Virginia School of Law (1975).

## RODRIQUES, Louis A
Bingham McCutchen LLP, Boston
617 951 8340
louis.rodriques@bingham.com
*Recommended in Employment*
**Practice Areas:** Practice involves all aspects of labor and employment law. Counsels on human resource matters, the development and administration of personnel and human resource policies and employee benefit plans, and compliance with statutory and regulatory requirements. Also counsels on drafting and enforcing non-competition and confidentiality agreements, employment contracts and executive compensation plans. Develops litigation-avoidance strategies and advises on government audits, labor-management relations, mediation and arbitration.
**Personal:** Yale Law School, JD, 1978; Yale University, BA, 1975.

## RONDEAU, Patrick J
WilmerHale, Boston
617 526 6670
patrick.rondeau@wilmerhale.com
*Recommended in Corporate/M&A, Private Equity*
**Practice Areas:** Vice-Chair of firm's Corporate Department; Co-Chair, Venture Capital Group. Practice focuses on venture capital and start-up company work, public offerings, mergers and acquisitions, and general corporate and securities work. Advises significant number of venture-backed companies and represents variety of venture capitalists in their investments in portfolio companies. Public offering experience includes variety of types of public offerings, and representation of both issuers and underwriters.
**Prof. Memberships:** National Venture Capital Association task force on Model Financing Documents.
**Career:** Admitted to Massachusetts Bar. Joined firm in 1984 and Partner since 1992.
**Personal:** Harvard Law School (JD); Williams College (BA).

## ROSE, Alfred O
Ropes & Gray LLP, Boston
617 951 7372
alfred.rose@ropesgray.com
*Recommended in Private Equity*
**Practice Areas:** Specializes in leveraged buyouts, mergers and acquisitions and structured financial products. Represented a consortium of seven private equity firms in 2005 (Silver Lake Partners, Bain

Capital, Blackstone, Goldman Sachs Capital Partners, Providence Equity Partners, KKR, and TPG) in their $11 billion acquisition of SunGard Data Systems, at the time the largest buyout since 1989. A featured 'Dealmaker of the Year' by The American Lawyer in 2005.
**Career:** Massachusetts Bar (1984); Partner, Ropes & Gray (1991).
**Personal:** JD, Yale Law School (1982); BA, summa cum laude, Dartmouth College, Phi Beta Kappa (1979).

## ROSENBLUM, Peter
Foley Hoag LLP, Boston
617 832 1000
*Recommended in Corporate/M&A, Private Equity*

## ROSENFELD, Jonathan
WilmerHale, Boston
617 526 6941
jonathan.rosenfeld@wilmerhale.com
*Recommended in Employment*
**Practice Areas:** As Chair of Wilmer-Hale's Labor and Employment Department, Mr Rosenfeld has extensive experience in the practice of labor and employment law. Representing various employers, he has litigated cases of discrimination, wrongful discharge, employee benefit claims under ERISA and other matters in state and federal courts.
**Prof. Memberships:** Mr Rosenfeld is admitted to practice in Massachusetts, Connecticut and California, and before the federal courts of Massachusetts, Connecticut and the Northern District of California and the US Courts of Appeals for the First and Ninth Circuits.
**Personal:** Boston University School of Law (JD); Brandeis University (AB).

## ROSNER, Douglas
Goulston & Storrs, Boston
617 482 1776
*Recommended in Bankruptcy*

## ROTHERMEL, Sarah
WilmerHale, Boston
617 526 6512
sarah.rothermel@wilmerhale.com
*Recommended in Private Fund Formation*
**Practice Areas:** Vice-Chair of Wilmer-Hale's Fund Formation Group; member of the Venture Capital Financing Group. Represents principally private investment entities, including venture capital funds. Also represents LLCs, partnerships, joint ventures and closely held non-corporate businesses engaged in all types of business activities. Advises clients on all aspects of organization, management, operation and regulatory compliance.
**Prof. Memberships:** American Bar Association; Massachusetts Bar Association; Boston Bar Association; Private Equity CFO Organization (Advisory Board Member).
**Career:** Admitted to Massachusetts Bar. Joined the firm in 1981.

**Personal:** Boston University School of Law (JD, magna cum laude); Wellesley College (BA).

## ROTTENBERG, Alan
Goulston & Storrs, Boston
617 482 1776
*Recommended in Real Estate*

## ROWE, Larry Jordan
Ropes & Gray LLP, Boston
617 951 7407
larry.rowe@ropesgray.com
*Recommended in Private Fund Formation*
**Practice Areas:** Specializes in structuring and analyzing private debt and equity investments, investment fund formation and investments, leveraged buyouts, venture capital investments, and international transactions. Extensive experience in organizing funds of funds. Clients include some of the largest endowment funds in the country, funds of funds, investment funds and other institutional investors and advisors.
**Career:** Massachusetts Bar (1985); Partner, Ropes & Gray (1993).
**Personal:** JD, Harvard Law School (1984); MPP, Harvard University (1984); Undergraduate Degree, summa cum laude, Phi Beta Kappa, Dartmouth College (1980).

## ROYALL SMITH, Thomas
Jackson Lewis, Boston
617 367 0025
SmithT@jacksonlewis.com
*Recommended in Employment*
**Practice Areas:** Labor law: NLRB elections and proceedings; contract negotiations; grievance arbitrations and litigation. Employment law: wage-hour; whistleblowing; discrimination; employment tax counseling; workplace torts; OSHA; trials in state and federal courts.
**Prof. Memberships:** Boston Bar Association; Massachusetts Bar Association; American Bar Association, Subcommittee on Practice and Procedure Before the NLRB.
**Career:** Jackson Lewis (1986-present). Managing Partner of Boston office (1986-2004), Siegel, O'Connor and Kainen (1974-86). Admitted in Massachusetts and Connecticut.
**Publications:** Has written extensively on employment and labor law topics.
**Personal:** Lafayette College (AB 1967); Boston University School of Law (JD 1970); Johns Hopkins University (MLA 1975); Captain, US Army JAGC (1971-74).

## RUDMAN, Jeffrey
WilmerHale, Boston
212 295 6307
jeffrey.rudman@wilmerhale.com
*Recommended in Litigation*
**Practice Areas:** Partner in Litigation Department; Co-Chair of the Securities Department. A nationally recognized

authority on defending shareholder class and derivative actions and the related tasks of defending SEC investigations and pursuing directors' and officers' insurance coverage.
**Prof. Memberships:** Trustee of Boston Public Library and Boston Museum Project; served on charitable boards, including the Board of Directors of the Association of American Rhodes Scholars; Boston Public Library Foundation; Buckingham, Browne & Nichols School; and WGBH Advisory Board.
**Career:** Admitted to Massachusetts Bar. Joined firm in 1975.
**Personal:** Harvard Law School (JD); Oxford University (BA, Rhodes Scholar); Columbia College (AB).

## RUDMAN, Richard
DLA Piper Rudnick Gray Cary US LLP, Boston 617 406 6027
richard.rudman@dlapiper.com
*Recommended in Real Estate*
**Practice Areas:** Real estate.
**Prof. Memberships:** American College of Real Estate Lawyers.
**Career:** Focuses his practice on real estate development and finance, property acquisition, leasing, land use and environmental regulation, joint venture arrangements, and construction and design agreements. He has represented the developers of several downtown office towers, and has extensive experience in build to suit developments, hotels, and multi-family apartment projects, including projects with complicated phasing arrangements, environmentally contaminated sites and public/private development agreements. He is listed in a leading American legal directory.
**Personal:** JD, Harvard University; BA, Yale College.

## RYAN, Mary
Nutter, McClennen & Fish, LLP, Boston
617 439 2000
*Recommended in Environment*

## SANDFORD, H Neal
Goodwin Procter LLP, Boston
617 570 1000
nsandford@goodwinprocter.com
*Recommended in Tax*
**Practice Areas:** Mr Sandford specializes in structuring tax-sensitive commercial transactions. His practice includes the organization and operation of REITs, investment funds and other collective investment arrangements; corporate mergers and acquisitions; asset acquisitions and dispositions; the organization and operation of partnerships and joint ventures; transactions involving S corporations; investments by tax-exempt and foreign investors; corporate and partnership restructurings; real estate transactions; equity-based compensation arrangements; international tax issues; and workouts.
**Personal:** JD, University of Virginia Law

School; BA, Yale University (magna cum laude).

## SANOFF, Robert
Foley Hoag LLP, Boston
617 832 1000
*Recommended in Environment*

## SANTUCCI, Ettore A
Goodwin Procter LLP, Boston
617 570 1000
esantucci@goodwinprocter.com
*Recommended in Corporate/M&A*
**Practice Areas:** Mr Santucci's practice focuses on public and private securities offerings, mergers and acquisitions, corporate governance, securities law compliance and cross-border transactions. His specific experience includes representing public and private issuers, underwriters, financial advisors and institutional investors in offerings of a broad range of debt and equity securities, including investment grade and high-yield bonds, and sophisticated convertible and exchangeable securities with a wide spectrum of economic, structural and tax-sensitive features.
**Personal:** JD, Boston University Law School (summa cum laude); JD, Faculty of Jurisprudence of the University of Bologna, Italy (summa cum laude); BA, Manhattanville College.

## SAVAGE, Joseph F
Goodwin Procter LLP, Boston
617 570 1000
jsavage@goodwinprocter.com
*Recommended in Litigation*
**Practice Areas:** Mr Savage concentrates his practice on complex civil litigation, white-collar criminal defense and governmental investigations. His practice involves representing individuals and companies in a variety of fraud, tax, public corruption, healthcare, securities, environmental and other investigations by federal, state and local law enforcement and government regulators. He has handled sophisticated trade secret, Lanham Act, RICO, consumer fraud and other civil litigation, including multi-district class action litigation and has experience in litigating complex white-collar criminal matters.
**Personal:** JD, University of Virginia School of Law, 1981 (Order of the Coif); BA, Harvard College, 1978 (magna cum laude).

## SAVRIN, Daniel S
Bingham McCutchen LLP, Boston
617 951 8674
daniel.savrin@bingham.com
*Recommended in Antitrust*
**Practice Areas:** Represents clients in a wide range of antitrust, white-collar criminal and complex commercial litigation matters. Has litigated matters in federal and state courts throughout the US and in various arbitration venues and has provided counsel with respect to pro-

ceedings outside the US. Antitrust and trade regulation practice includes the representation of individuals and corporations in criminal antitrust matters; civil enforcement matters; individual and class action civil litigation; merger-related proceedings and litigation; and counseling on trade regulation, distribution, and merger and acquisition issues.
**Personal:** University of Virginia School of Law, JD, 1989; Union College, BA, 1984.

## SCHERKENBACH, Frank E
Fish & Richardson P.C., Boston
617 521 7883
scherkenbach@fr.com
*Recommended in Intellectual Property*
**Practice Areas:** Principal in Fish & Richardson's Boston office. Specializes in complex high technology litigation, with particular expertise in computer software, telecommunications, and semiconductors. He has successfully handled cases in state and federal courts and before the US International Trade Commission in Washington, DC, including trials and appeals to the Federal Circuit.
**Prof. Memberships:** Active in Bar organizations including the Federal Circuit Bar Association, the American Bar Association, and the American Intellectual Property Law Association.
**Personal:** Stanford University BS Mechanical Engineering and AB Classics 1986 with distinction; Harvard Law School JD 1989.

## SCHMIDT, William
WilmerHale, Boston
617 526 6946
william.schmidt@wilmerhale.com
*Recommended in Employee Benefits*
**Practice Areas:** Compensation law, including employee benefits plans and executive compensation. Has assisted pension plan providers in structuring investment vehicles and represented many such providers in connection with pension plan investments. Represents clients in financings in which a pension plan provider is party. Expert in matters of professional corporations, personal domestic tax planning and estate planning. Has represented many clients in establishment of employee stock ownership plans (ESOPs).
**Prof. Memberships:** American, Massachusetts, and Boston Bar Associations.
**Career:** Admitted to Massachusetts Bar; United States Tax Court. Joined firm in 1976.
**Personal:** Georgetown University Law Center (JD); University of Chicago (MS); Yale University (BS).

## SCHNALL, Matthew D
Bingham McCutchen LLP, Boston
617 951 8419
m.schnall@bingham.com
*Recommended in Tax*
**Practice Areas:** Handles a diverse range

of business-related tax matters, including tax controversies, transactional planning and advice in areas such as tax-exempt bond financing and the taxation of regulated investment companies. Has experience with a wide variety of issues in the corporate, partnership and international tax areas. State and local tax experience includes constitutional challenges as well as general representation in the areas of personal and corporate income taxes, franchise taxes, sales and use taxes, and property taxes.
**Personal:** Harvard Law School, JD, cum laude, 1993; Harvard College, BA, magna cum laude, 1990.

## SCHNEIDER, Jon D
Goodwin Procter LLP, Boston
617 570 1000
jschneider@goodwinprocter.com
*Recommended in Bankruptcy*
**Practice Areas:** Mr Schneider's practice focuses on creditors' rights, secured transactions, acquisitions and insolvency matters, including representation of lenders in loan transactions, workouts and bankruptcy; bondholders in restructurings; businesses in connection with financial restructurings and acquisitions; investors in connection with buyouts and turn-arounds; and unsecured creditors in connection with bankruptcy proceedings. His practice also involves leveraged buyouts and financially troubled situations.
**Prof. Memberships:** American College of Bankruptcy: Fellow; Massachusetts Certified Development Corporation: Director; American Bankruptcy Institute: Member.
**Personal:** JD, Boston College, 1968; BS, Boston College, 1965.

## SCHNEIDMAN, Leonard
Foley Hoag LLP, Boston
617 832 1000
*Recommended in Tax*

## SCHNOOR, William J
Goodwin Procter LLP, Boston
617 570 1000
wschnoor@goodwinprocter.com
*Recommended in Private Equity*
**Practice Areas:** Mr Schnoor concentrates his practice in the areas of business and securities law, private equity and acquisitions. He has 21 years of experience in representing start-up, private and public companies in a wide range of industries. He has worked with numerous companies from their initial financing through successful initial public offerings or acquisitions. His practice also includes: assisting with cross-border financings and acquisitions; representing investment banks in connection with underwritten offerings and their activities as financial advisors to companies engaged in mergers and acquisitions; and representing numerous private equity clients in connection with their own

fund-raising and organizational issues.
**Personal:** JD, Yale University, 1983; BA, Yale College, 1980 (summa cum laude).

## SCHWARTZ, Andrew
Foley Hoag LLP, Boston
617 832 1000
*Recommended in Bankruptcy*

## SCHWARTZ, Paul D
Goodwin Procter LLP, Boston
617 570 1000
pschwartz@goodwinprocter.com
*Recommended in Real Estate*
**Practice Areas:** Mr Schwartz concentrates on private market finance with emphasis on the real estate industry, including collective investment vehicles for institutional investors, joint ventures, participating and mezzanine debt, and REIT investments. He is familiar with integrating the UBTI, REIT and other tax, ERISA, Investment Company Act, and other securities law aspects of investments by ERISA plans and registered investment companies.
**Prof. Memberships:** Pension Real Estate Association: Voting Member; MIT Center for Real Estate: Voting Member; Real Estate Finance Association: Member.
**Personal:** JD, Harvard Law School, 1978 (magna cum laude); Masters in Architecture, MIT, 1976; BA, Connecticut College, 1973 (magna cum laude).

## SCHWARTZ, Sara
Schwartz Hannum PC, Andover
978 623 0900
schwartz@shpclaw.com
*Recommended in Employment*
**Practice Areas:** Employer representation with respect to labor and employment issues, particularly employment discrimination litigation, traditional labor law issues and non-compete litigation. Expertise in representing multi-state clients with respect to state-specific labor and employment issues.
**Prof. Memberships:** American Bar Association; Boston Bar Association, American Employment Law Council; Massachusetts Bar Association.
**Career:** Firm Founder (1995), President, Co-Managing Partner. Began career with Ropes & Gray in Boston.
**Publications:** Frequent speaker at seminars for attorneys and human resources professionals. Voted Massachusetts Super Lawyer in both 2004 and 2005.
**Personal:** Cum laude graduate of both Yale College and Harvard Law School.

## SCOTT, Thane D
Edwards Angell Palmer & Dodge LLP, Boston 617 239 0154
tscott@eapdlaw.com
*Recommended in Antitrust*
**Practice Areas:** Thane has counseled industry leaders and litigated prominent cases that define modern antitrust law. He has served as lead or liaison counsel in numerous multi-district, complex, or

class action cases, and has represented clients during the course of government investigations. He frequently litigates complex cases among business rivals and defends class actions involving antitrust and business tort claims.

**Prof. Memberships:** American Bar Association, Boston Bar Association, Massachusetts Bar Association.

**Personal:** State University of New York at Albany, BA, cum laude, 1974; Boston College Law School, JD, cum laude, 1980; law clerk to Chief Justice, Massachusetts Supreme Judicial Court.

## SELWYN, Mark D
WilmerHale, Boston
617 526 6923
mark.selwyn@wilmerhale.com
*Recommended in Intellectual Property*

**Practice Areas:** Has represented wide range of commercial interests, concentrating in patent litigation, government investigations, securities and consumer class actions. Also represented clients before the SEC, NASD and state regulatory agencies.

**Career:** Admitted to Massachusetts Bar and New York Bar. Served as a law clerk to Hon Naomi Reice Buchwald on the US District Court for the Southern District of New York prior to joining the firm in 1994.

**Publications:** 'Higher Education Under Fire: The New Target of Antitrust' 26 Colum J L & Soc Probs 117 (1992).

**Personal:** Columbia Law School (JD); Harvard College (AB, magna cum laude).

## SEUCH, William
Goulston & Storrs, Boston
617 482 1776
*Recommended in Environment*

## SHAW, Paul
Brown Rudnick Berlack Israels LLP, Boston 617 856 8200
*Recommended in Healthcare*

## SHAY, Stephen E
Ropes & Gray LLP, Boston
617 951 7302
stephen.shay@ropesgray.com
*Recommended in Tax*

**Practice Areas:** Extensive international tax experience advising clients including large and medium-sized multinational companies, financial institutions, and global investors on issues such as foreign tax credits, deferral of US taxation, foreign currency gains and losses, withholding taxes and financial product issues. Regularly advises clients on transfer pricing issues. Has successfully resolved numerous transfer pricing controversies with the IRS. Advises high net worth clients on cross-border income tax planning.

**Career:** New York Bar (1977); Massachusetts Bar (1991); International Tax Counsel, US Department of the Treasury; Partner, Ropes & Gray (1987).

**Personal:** JD, Columbia Law School (1976); MBA, Columbia Business School (1976).

## SHEA, John
Moehrke, Mackie & Shea, P.C., Boston
617 266 5700
*Recommended in Environment*

## SHEPHERD, Jay
Shepherd Law Group, P.C., Boston
617 439 4200
jay@shepherdlawgroup.com
*Recommended in Employment*

**Practice Areas:** Helps employers succeed by managing their most important assets: their employees. Specializes in strategic employment law and noncompete litigation. Advocates for employers before state and federal courts and administrative agencies.

**Prof. Memberships:** Massachusetts (Chair, Employment Law Practice Group, 2003-04) and Boston (Member, Labor & Employment Law Steering Committee, 2003-05) Bar Associations; ABA.

**Career:** Principal since 1998. Bar admissions: Massachusetts (1994), US District Court (Mass. 1995), First Circuit Court of Appeals (1996), US Supreme Court (2000). Named one of five 'Up and Coming Lawyers' by Massachusetts Lawyers Weekly (2004) and a 'Rising Star' by Law & Politics Magazine (2005).

**Personal:** Boston College Law School (JD, cum laude, 1994); Johns Hopkins University (BA, 1988). Married, two daughters.

## SIEBERT, Susan E
Edwards Angell Palmer & Dodge LLP, Boston 617 951 2220
ssiebert@eapdlaw.com
*Recommended in Banking & Finance*

**Practice Areas:** Susan is a Co-Chair of the Edwards Angell Palmer & Dodge Debt Finance and Capital Markets Group. She represents financial institutions, finance companies, public and private investment funds and insurance companies in syndicated senior, mezzanine, second lien and subordinated debt financings, private equity financings, mergers and acquisitions and debt restructurings. She has represented senior lenders in numerous cross-border, multicurrency financings.

**Prof. Memberships:** Association of Commercial Finance Attorneys, Turnaround Management Association.

**Personal:** Emory University, School of Law, JD, 1978; Wheaton College, BA, high honors, 1975.

## SIGEL, John
WilmerHale, Boston
617 526 6728
john.sigel@wilmerhale.com
*Recommended in Bankruptcy*

**Practice Areas:** Vice-Chair of Wilmer-Hale's Bankruptcy and Commercial Department. Commercial law focus, advising clients on secured and unsecured lending and debt issuance, Chapter 11 reorganizations and Uniform Commercial Code. Expert in matters relating to debt financings of public and private companies and acquisitions and sales of distressed companies. Represented many clients in negotiating credit facilities with institutional lenders, including private placement of debt securities; advised corporate clients in connection with public offering of debt securities.

**Prof. Memberships:** Massachusetts and Boston Bar Associations; American College of Bankruptcy.

**Career:** Admitted to Massachusetts Bar.

**Personal:** Cornell Law School (JD); Middlebury College (BA).

## SINGER, Steven
WilmerHale, Boston
617 526 6410
steven.singer@wilmerhale.com
*Recommended in Corporate/M&A*

**Practice Areas:** Vice-Chair of the firm's Corporate Department; Co-Chair of the firm's Life Sciences Group. Has served as counsel for public and private companies in the life sciences sector, including biotechnology, medical device and pharmaceutical companies. Practice focuses on joint ventures and strategic alliances, corporate and securities laws, public offerings and venture capital transactions.

**Prof. Memberships:** American Bar Association; Massachusetts Biotechnology Council; Biotechnology Industry Organization; Board of Overseers of Beth Israel Deaconess Medical Center.

**Career:** Admitted to Massachusetts Bar. Joined the firm in 1979.

**Personal:** Harvard Law School (JD, magna cum laude); Tufts University (BA, summa cum laude).

## SIRKIN, Joel
WilmerHale, Boston
617 526 6279
joel.sirkin@wilmerhale.com
*Recommended in Real Estate*

**Practice Areas:** Chair of firm's Real Estate Department. Has represented clients in acquisition, development, and financing of apartment projects, hotels, office buildings, assisted living and shopping centers in over 25 states. Major projects include: acquisition, repositioning, and sale of portfolio of 14 Boston office properties for overseas investor group; development of 1 million square feet international research headquarter for multinational drug company and structuring of tax-deferred TIC multi-state office acquisitions. Has been involved in development of Boston office towers and several major suburban office parks.

**Career:** Admitted to Massachusetts Bar.

**Personal:** Harvard Law School (JD); Johns Hopkins University (BA).

## SMALL, Richard G
Edwards Angell Palmer & Dodge LLP, Providence 401 274 9200
*Recommended in Private Equity*

**Practice Areas:** For an extended period of time, Richard has principally focused on handling sophisticated transaction work while serving as counsel to a number of private equity firms, companies backed by private equity firms and management teams backed by private equity firms. Richard also serves as Co-Chair of the firm's Private Equity & Venture Capital Practice Group.

**Prof. Memberships:** Rhode Island and Massachusetts Bar Associations, American Bar Association, Association for Corporate Growth.

**Personal:** Boston University, School of Law, LLM, 1976; Case Western Reserve, School of Law, JD, 1979; Williams College, BA, 1973.

## SMITH, Bradford J
Goodwin Procter LLP, Boston
617 570 1000
bsmith@goodwinprocter.com
*Recommended in Employment*

**Practice Areas:** Mr Smith primarily represents management and institutional clients. His practice includes employment discrimination proceedings before state and federal courts and agencies, wrongful discharge litigation, proceedings before the National Labor Relations Board, labor arbitrations and actions arising under the Occupational Safety and Health Act. He counsels clients on employment-related issues such as employee discipline and termination, development of affirmative action programs and personnel policies, compliance with wage-hour regulations, development and enforcement of employee noncompetition and confidentiality agreements, and compliance with miscellaneous state and federal employment laws and regulations.

**Personal:** JD, Boston University (cum laude); BA, University of Pennsylvania.

## SMITH, Edwin E
Bingham McCutchen LLP, Boston
617 951 8615
edwin.smith@bingham.com
*Recommended in Banking & Finance*

**Practice Areas:** Serves as Co-Chair of the firm's Finance Area. Concentrates on general corporate and commercial law, debt financings, structured financings, workouts, bankruptcies and international transactions. Has actively participated in the drafting of a number of the recent revisions to Uniform Commercial Code. Formerly based in London, where he concentrated in international financing and commercial transactions.

**Career:** Inducted as a fellow of the American College of Bankruptcy.

**Personal:** Harvard Law School, JD, 1974; Yale University, BA, 1968.

**SMITH, Philip J**
Ropes & Gray LLP, Boston
617 951 7744
philip.smith@ropesgray.com
*Recommended in Banking & Finance*
**Practice Areas:** Leveraged buyout and private equity transactions including debt and equity components of these matters. Extensive experience in structuring syndicated bank credits, mezzanine capital transactions, and high-yield debt plus experience with acquisitions and public and private preferred stock financings. Experience in acquisitions and financings on national and international levels in manufacturing, distribution, leasing, motion picture and entertainment industries. Has developed educational seminars and lectured extensively on financing and leveraged buyout transactions.
**Personal:** JD, Order of the Coif, University of Virginia School of Law (1966); Undergraduate Degree, cum laude, Williams College (1963).

**SOLT, Christine**
Choate Hall & Stewart, Boston
617 248 5000
*Recommended in Healthcare*

**SPACKMAN, David G**
Greenberg Traurig LLP, Boston
617 310 6000
spackmand@gtlaw.com
*Recommended in Healthcare*
**Practice Areas:** Health business.
**Prof. Memberships:** Chairman, Boston Bar Association, Health Care Section, 1986-88; Member, American Health Lawyers Association; Member, Massachusetts Hazardous Waste Facility Site Safety Council, 1980-84; Member, Board of Directors, Notre Dame Long Term Care Center, 1996-98; Community Member, Institutional Review Board for Protection of Human Subjects, Education Development Center, 1998-present.
**Career:** Listed, Best Lawyers in America, 2003, 2004, 2005 and 2006 editions.
**Personal:** JD, Suffolk University Law School, 1976; BA, Biology and Education, Beloit College, 1970.

**STEINBERG, Donald R**
WilmerHale, Boston
617 526 6453
donald.steinberg@wilmerhale.com
*Recommended in Intellectual Property*
**Practice Areas:** Chair of WilmerHale's Intellectual Property Department. Practice focuses on advising clients on intellectual property matters, obtaining patent and trademark protection, and intellectual property litigation. Has extensive experience before the Trademark Trial and Appeal Board, including successful trials of opposition and cancellation proceedings involving medical devices and games.
**Prof. Memberships:** Intellectual Property Owners Association's Trademark Law Committee; New England School of Law

(adjunct faculty member).
**Career:** Admitted to Massachusetts Bar and United States Patent and Trademark Office. Joined the firm in 1994.
**Personal:** Harvard Law School (JD, cum laude); Princeton University (BSE, magna cum laude, Phi Beta Kappa).

**STERN, William E**
Goodwin Procter LLP, Boston
617 570 1000
wstern@goodwinprocter.com
*Recommended in Banking & Finance*
**Practice Areas:** Mr Stern works on transactional and regulatory matters with particular emphasis on transactions involving the creation of new bank charters and charter conversions and assisting clients in choosing and structuring the most appropriate bank charter for their business needs. He advises clients on bank regulatory matters relating to domestic and foreign investments and activities, including merchant banking and other types of passive investments, personal and real property leasing, lending, captive reinsurance, trust department and other asset management operations.
**Personal:** JD, George Washington University, 1996 (with high honors); BA, Hamilton College, 1993 (summa cum laude).

**STILLWELL, R Newcomb**
Ropes & Gray LLP, Boston
617 951 7316
newcomb.stillwell@ropesgray.com
*Recommended in Private Equity*
**Practice Areas:** Co-Head of Ropes & Gray's Private Equity Transaction Group. Deep experience in mergers and acquisitions and related financings including cross-border transactions (Canada, Mexico, Europe, Australia). Serves on the Board of Directors and is the Vice-Chairman of the Volunteers of America of Massachusetts, Incorporated.
**Career:** Massachusetts Bar (1984); Partner, Ropes & Gray (1993).
**Personal:** JD, cum laude, Harvard Law School (1984); AB, magna cum laude, Princeton University (1979).

**STONER, Wayne L**
WilmerHale, Boston
617 526 6863
wayne.stoner@wilmerhale.com
*Recommended in Intellectual Property*
**Practice Areas:** Partner in the firm's Litigation Department and Co-Chair of the firm's Intellectual Property Litigation Group. Practice focuses on patent litigation and strategy. Has represented a broad range of clients, including in jury and bench trials and appeals, in diverse technologies such as lasers, medical devices, semiconductor processing, integrated circuits and telecommunications. Practices in courts nationwide and before the US International Trade Commission.
**Prof. Memberships:** Faculty, Harvard

Law School Trial Advocacy Program.
**Career:** Admitted to Massachusetts Bar. Joined the firm in 1986.
**Personal:** University of Pennsylvania Law School (JD); University of Denver (BA, Phi Beta Kappa).

**SULLIVAN, John L**
DLA Piper Rudnick Gray Cary US LLP, Boston
617 406 6029
john.sullivan@dlapiper.com
*Recommended in Real Estate*
**Practice Areas:** Real estate.
**Career:** Broad-ranging practice that encompasses all aspects of commercial real estate, with a particular emphasis on representing public and private pension plans, opportunity funds, investment advisors, and other sophisticated investors in debt, equity, hybrid, and joint venture transactions throughout North America.
**Personal:** JD, Cornell University; BA, College of the Holy Cross.

**SUNSHINE, Ilene Robinson**
Sullivan & Worcester LLP, Boston
617 338 2800
*Recommended in Employment*

**SURKIN, Elliot**
DLA Piper Rudnick Gray Cary US LLP, Boston 617 406 6030
elliot.surkin@dlapiper.com
*Recommended in Real Estate*
**Practice Areas:** Real estate.
**Prof. Memberships:** American College of Real Estate Lawyers; American Law Institute.
**Career:** Real estate development, finance, and taxation. General counsel to many of Boston's significant office, mixed-use, and retail projects. He has taught full-semester courses in real estate development and finance at Harvard Law School and MIT's Center for Real Estate throughout his career.
**Publications:** 'When Joint Venturers Can't Agree: The Buy-Sell Revisited', and 'How Do I Get Out of Here? A Discussion of Exit Strategies in Closely-Held Real Estate LLCs'.
**Personal:** LLB, Harvard Law School; AB, Princeton University.

**SWAIM, Hall**
WilmerHale, Boston
617 526 6716
hall.swaim@wilmerhale.com
*Recommended in Bankruptcy*
**Practice Areas:** Partner in Wilmer-Hale's Bankruptcy and Commercial Department. Practice focuses on commercial law, with an emphasis on Chapter 11 reorganizations, out-of-court restructurings, loan documentation, workouts and contract negotiations, with emphasis on technology-based companies and technology transfer.
**Prof. Memberships:** American, Massachusetts and Boston Bar Associations;

Commercial Law League; American Bankruptcy Institute; New England Chapter of Turnaround Management Association (Board Member, former President).
**Career:** Admitted to Massachusetts, Colorado, New York and Texas Bars; United States Supreme Court; United States Patent and Trademark Office. Joined firm in 1971.
**Personal:** New York University School of Law (JD); Colorado School of Mines (Geophysical Engineer).

**TEGELER, David W**
Proskauer Rose LLP, Boston
617 526 9795
dtegeler@proskauer.com
*Recommended in Private Fund Formation*
**Practice Areas:** Partner and Co-Chair of the Private Equity Group at Proskauer Rose. Concentrates on representation of private equity fund managers in fund formations and regulatory and governance issues, and of institutional investors and investment advisors in their private equity investments.
**Publications:** Frequently speaks nationally and internationally on private equity related issues and is also a frequent contributor to private equity industry publications.
**Personal:** Received his BA from Middlebury College and his JD from Vanderbilt University School of Law.

**TELEGEN, Arthur**
Foley Hoag LLP, Boston
617 832 1000
*Recommended in Employment*

**TICKNOR, George**
Edwards Angell Palmer & Dodge LLP, Boston 617 239 0357
gticknor@eapdlaw.com
*Recommended in Banking & Finance*
**Practice Areas:** George serves as Co-Chair of the firm's Debt Finance Department. He represents banks, finance companies, public and private investment funds, and other financial institutions in financings with emphasis on syndicated acquisition financing. George also represents private equity, sponsor and other investor groups making investments and acquisitions. His experience also encompasses public debt issues and restructurings, securitization, second lien, and mezzanine financings.
**Prof. Memberships:** American Bar Association; Boston Bar Association.
**Personal:** Harvard University, BA, magna cum laude, 1977; University of Virginia School of Law, JD, 1983.

**TODD, Owen**
Todd & Weld LLP, Boston
617 720 2626
*Recommended in Litigation*

## TOELKE, Richard A
Bingham McCutchen LLP, Boston
615 951 8830
richard.toelke@bingham.com
*Recommended in Real Estate*

**Practice Areas:** Represents developers, institutional property owners, pension fund advisors, REITs and lenders in all aspects of transactional real estate practice. Has worked on a wide variety of transactions both regionally and nationally, including acquisitions and dispositions of office, industrial, R&D and multi-family properties; leasing transactions; financing arrangements; and development projects.
**Personal:** Villanova University School of Law, JD, 1989; Boston College, BA, 1986.

## TRIBUSH, Bruce I
Goodwin Procter LLP, Boston
617 570 1000
btribush@goodwinprocter.com
*Recommended in Real Estate*

**Practice Areas:** Mr Tribush represents commercial lenders and borrowers in secured and unsecured credit facilities, construction loans, permanent loans, bridge loans, mezzanine debt transactions, loan participations and loan restructurings; owners and developers in the acquisition, financing and development of real estate; owners, developers, lenders, design professionals and construction professionals in design and construction matters; landlords and tenants in commercial leasing transactions; and institutional and private investors in debt and equity real estate investments.
**Personal:** JD, Fordham University, 1990; BS, Cornell University, 1987.

## TSE, Marian A
Goodwin Procter LLP, Boston
617 570 1000
mtse@goodwinprocter.com
*Recommended in Employee Benefits*

**Practice Areas:** Ms Tse's practice focuses primarily on executive compensation matters. She also advises clients on employee benefits matters, including qualified retirement plans, ESOPs, ERISA fiduciary and prohibited transaction issues, the benefit aspects of mergers and acquisitions, and health and welfare plans.
**Prof. Memberships:** New England Employee Benefits Council: Member; Employee Benefits Committee of the Tax Section of the American Bar Association: Member; Asian American Lawyers Association of Massachusetts: Member; Greater Boston Legal Services: Board of Directors.
**Personal:** JD, Columbia Law School; BA, Vassar College (cum laude).

## TURANO, Thomas
Kirkpatrick & Lockhart Nicholson Graham LLP, Boston 617 261 3100
*Recommended in Intellectual Property*

## TUTEUR, Michael
Foley & Lardner LLP, Boston
617 342 4016
mtuteur@foley.com
*Recommended in Litigation*

**Career:** Michael Tuteur is a Partner with Foley & Lardner LLP and Co-Chair of the Boston office Litigation Department. He is a member of the General Commercial Litigation and White-Collar Defense & Corporate Compliance Practice Groups. Mr Tuteur's practice concentrates on complex commercial litigation, internal investigations and white-collar criminal defense. Mr Tuteur also represents organizations and corporate officers and directors in connection with criminal and civil investigations involving alleged healthcare fraud, securities fraud, mutual fund regulatory violations and banking infractions. Mr Tuteur's JD was conferred magna cum laude from Harvard Law School (1984).

## TWOHIG, John
Goulston & Storrs, Boston
617 482 1776
*Recommended in Real Estate*

## UTZSCHNEIDER, John R
Bingham McCutchen LLP, Boston
617 951 8852
john.utzschneider@bingham.com
*Recommended in Corporate/M&A*

**Practice Areas:** Focuses primarily on mergers and acquisitions and corporate finance. Serves as Deputy Co-Chair of the firm's Corporate Area and as Co-Chair of the firm's Corporate, M&A and Securities Practice Group and the Energy Industry Group. Represents private and public companies, equity and debt financing sources, and underwriters in mergers and acquisitions, leveraged buyouts, joint ventures, private and public offerings, and restructurings.
**Personal:** New York University School of Law, JD, 1986; Dartmouth College, BA, 1982.

## VENTOLA, John
Choate Hall & Stewart, Boston
617 248 5000
*Recommended in Bankruptcy*

## WALLACK, James
Goulston & Storrs, Boston
617 482 1776
*Recommended in Bankruptcy*

## WALSH, Kevin J
Mintz Levin Cohn Ferris Glovsky and Popeo PC, Boston 617 348 1622
KWalsh@mintz.com
*Recommended in Bankruptcy*

**Practice Areas:** Bankruptcy, restructuring and commercial law.
**Career:** Kevin Walsh is a member of Mintz Levin's Boston office, practicing in the Bankruptcy, Restructuring and Commercial Law Section. His practice focuses on all aspects of bankruptcy and commercial law, workouts, restructurings and commercial lending transactions, including negotiating and documenting commercial loans and credits. Kevin represents corporate debtors, secured and unsecured lenders, trustees, bondholders, committees, lessors and lessees and other entities in out-of-court restructuring and bankruptcy proceedings. He has significant experience in distressed acquisitions and divestitures, complex commercial transactions and business litigation.
**Publications:** Kevin has written articles and lectured in a variety of legal and business forums, including Massachusetts Continuing Legal Education, on various topics related to bankruptcies, restructurings and commercial lending, including bankruptcy sales (both buyer and seller perspectives), recharacterization of equity and equitable subordination, negotiating credit agreements and enforcing guaranties.
**Personal:** BA in economics, Trinity College 1988; JD, magna cum laude, New York Law School 1993.

## WARD, Richard P
Ropes & Gray LLP, Boston
617 951 7444
richard.ward@ropesgray.com
*Recommended in Employment*

**Practice Areas:** Provides counsel on employment issues and litigates employment disputes at the trial and appellate level. Specializes in employment litigation, including the trial of discrimination, civil rights, contract and public employment cases, and labor arbitrations. Member of the Labor and Employment Law Section and the Equal Employment Opportunity Committee of the American Bar Association. Elected as a Fellow in the prestigious College of Labor and Employment Lawyers. Writes and lectures on emerging employment law issues.
**Career:** Massachusetts Bar (1967); Partner, Ropes & Gray (1977).
**Personal:** LLB, cum laude, Harvard Law School (1967); AB, magna cum laude, Boston College (1964).

## WARE, Donald
Foley Hoag LLP, Boston
617 832 1000
*Recommended in Intellectual Property*

## WARE JR, Paul F
Goodwin Procter LLP, Boston
617 570 1000
pware@goodwinprocter.com
*Recommended in Intellectual Property, Litigation*

**Practice Areas:** Mr Ware is an experienced trial lawyer, having tried numerous civil and criminal cases to conclusion throughout the country. His principal practice is intellectual property, including patent and other complex technology-related litigation. Mr Ware served as lead trial counsel for the prosecution of the CIA chief of European Operations in the Iran Contra Affair and as Special Counsel to the Massachusetts Commission on Judicial Conduct.
**Prof. Memberships:** American College of Trial Lawyers: Fellow; Supreme Judicial Court Historical Society: Board of Overseers; Social Law Library: Trustee.
**Personal:** LLB, University of Pennsylvania, 1969; AB, University of Notre Dame, 1966.

## WATSON, David W
Goodwin Procter LLP, Boston
617 570 1000
dwatson@goodwinprocter.com
*Recommended in Private Fund Formation*

**Practice Areas:** Mr Watson's practice focuses on public and private securities offerings, private fund formation, partnership law, public and private mergers and acquisitions, securities law compliance for public companies and general corporate matters. His experience in the fund formation area includes establishing private funds through US and international securities offerings, organizing fund manager and sponsor entities, advising fund managers and sponsors in establishing compensation structures and internal operating policies, representing funds and investors and restructuring the terms of existing investment funds.
**Personal:** JD, Harvard Law School, 1988 (cum laude); BA, University of Maine, 1985 (salutatorian).

## WATSON, Rom P
Ropes & Gray LLP, Boston
617 951 7672
rom.watson@ropesgray.com
*Recommended in Tax*

**Practice Areas:** Extensive experience in the international tax area, advising clients including large and medium-sized multinational companies, global investors, and financial institutions. Specializes in the areas of cross-border financial products, transfer pricing, and multinational transactions. Practiced in the Office of Tax Policy at the US Department of the Treasury (1988-91), and was appointed Associate International Tax Counsel.
**Career:** Massachusetts Bar (1985); Partner, Ropes & Gray (1993).
**Personal:** JD, cum laude, Boalt Hall School of Law, University of California at Berkeley (1983); AB, Phi Beta Kappa, Stanford University (1979).

## WEINER, Stephen
Mintz Levin Cohn Ferris Glovsky and Popeo PC, Boston 617 542 6000
*Recommended in Healthcare*

## WEINSTEIN, Jerome
Sullivan Weinstein & McQuay, Boston
617 348 4300
*Recommended in Employment*

## WELSH, John
Bello, Black & Welsh LLP, Boston
617 247 4100
*Recommended in Employment*

## WESTRA, James
Weil, Gotshal & Manges LLP, Boston
617 772 8377
james.westra@weil.com
*Recommended in Corporate/M&A, Private Equity*
**Practice Areas:** Mr Westra's diverse Corporate Practice includes private equity, mergers and acquisitions, financings, general corporate and corporate governance matters. He regularly represents leading private equity and venture firms in acquiring and investing in public and private companies in the US and Europe. He also represents numerous public companies on general corporate matters, financings and merger and acquisition transactions. Mr Westra regularly serves as counsel to boards of directors and board committees with respect to corporate governance matters.
**Personal:** Harvard University, AB, 1973; Boston University School of Law, JD, 1977.

## WHITE, Dennis J
McDermott Will & Emery, Boston
617 535 4011
dwhite@mwe.com
*Recommended in Corporate/M&A*
**Practice Areas:** Partner-in-charge of the Boston Corporate Department. Over 20 years experience counseling companies on mergers and acquisitions, private placements, public offerings of debt and equity, going private transactions and corporate governance matters. Represents emerging and mature companies across a broad range of industries, and private equity investors in the United States and internationally. Regularly counsels companies on cross-border transactions.
**Prof. Memberships:** Global Board of Directors of the Association for Corporate Growth. Negotiated Acquisitions Committee of the Business Law Section of the American Bar Association.
**Personal:** Harvard Law School (JD, cum laude); Holy Cross College (BA, summa cum laude).

## WHITHAM, Michelle
Foley Hoag LLP, Boston
617 832 1000
*Recommended in Employment*

## WHITLEDGE, William H
Goodwin Procter LLP, Boston
617 570 1000
wwhitledge@goodwinprocter.com
*Recommended in Tax*
**Practice Areas:** Mr Whitledge specializes in corporate, partnership, foreign and general business taxation. He spends a substantial amount of time structuring international and domestic business transactions, including mergers, acquisitions, financings, dispositions, reorganizations and other business restructurings, and venture capital investments. He also has extensive experience in structuring collective investment vehicles with tax-exempt, foreign and domestic investors, including RICs, REITs and pension investments from an unrelated business taxable income perspective.
**Personal:** LLM, New York University, 1985; JD, Columbia University, 1980; BA, Michigan State University, 1976.

## WIESEN, Jeffrey M
Mintz Levin Cohn Ferris Glovsky and Popeo PC, Boston
617 348 1759
jwiesen@mintz.com
*Recommended in Corporate/M&A*
**Practice Areas:** Corporate representation of biotechnology and life science companies. Chairman of Biotechnology Practice Group.
**Prof. Memberships:** Jeff serves as General Counsel to the Massachusetts Biotechnology Counsel, and is on the Advisory Board of the Whitehead Institute, the Advisory Council of the MIT-Harvard Health Sciences and Technology Program, and the Board of Directors of the Biomedical Science Careers Program.
**Career:** Jeff is Chair of the firm's Biotechnology Practice, and has been an active participant and much sought-after counsel in the biotechnology industry since its inception. He was involved in the formation of some of the earliest companies and the structuring and negotiation of some of the industry's earliest strategic alliances, venture financings and public offerings. He has led Mintz Levin's Biotechnology Practice to become one of the largest and best known in the country. His clients range from newly-formed start-up ventures to substantial public companies and he assists them with a range of transactions, both domestic and international, including private and public finance, mergers and acquisitions, strategic alliances, joint ventures, technology transfer and cross-transfer agreements, as well as general legal advice. He has successfully structured, coordinated and negotiated technology-based transactions with numerous world-wide pharmaceutical and chemical companies. Jeff is admitted to practice in Massachusetts and the District of Columbia. He is a member of the American, Massachusetts and Boston Bar Associations, as well as the Licensing Executives Society. Jeff received his BS from the Massachusetts Institute of Technology and his LLB from Yale Law School.

## WILLIAMS, Samuel
Brown Rudnick Berlack Israels LLP, Boston 617 856 8200
*Recommended in Corporate/M&A*

## WILLIS, Jane E
Ropes & Gray LLP, Boston
617 951 7603
jane.willis@ropesgray.com
*Recommended in Antitrust*
**Practice Areas:** Focuses on business and commercial litigation. Experienced in antitrust law, securities law, and merger and acquisition-related disputes. Handles active litigation matters and regularly provides advice and counseling regarding fiduciary duty issues and competition law matters. Clients include publicly-traded corporations, privately-held businesses, mutual funds, real estate investment trusts, and private equity funds involved in the consumer products, sports, and financial services industries.
**Career:** Massachusetts Bar (1994); New York Bar (2004); Partner, Ropes & Gray (2003).
**Personal:** JD, magna cum laude, Harvard Law School (1994); Undergraduate Degree, Phi Beta Kappa, Harvard University (1991).

## WOLF, Robert M
Bingham McCutchen LLP, Boston
617 951 8467
robert.wolf@bingham.com
*Recommended in Private Equity*
**Practice Areas:** Serves as Chair of the firm's Corporate Area. Focuses almost exclusively on leveraged acquisitions, recapitalizations, equity investments and mezzanine financings for a variety of private equity firms and financial institutions. Has more than 20 years of experience representing financial sponsors and financial institutions in buyout transactions and related financings.
**Personal:** Boston College Law School, JD, magna cum laude, 1981; Brandeis University, BA, magna cum laude, 1976.

## WOOD, Lisa
Foley Hoag LLP, Boston
617 832 1000
*Recommended in Antitrust*

## ZOLI, Elise N
Goodwin Procter LLP, Boston
617 570 1000
ezoli@goodwinprocter.com
*Recommended in Environment*
**Practice Areas:** Ms Zoli specializes in the areas of energy, environmental and development law. She has extensive experience in the transfer, permitting and development of energy projects, particularly electric-generating and natural-gas-pipeline facilities. Examples of her energy work include strategic development and acquisition advice, compliance counseling and litigation services on behalf of nuclear-powered, fossil-fuel and wind-turbine electric-generating stations and strategic counseling for a leading 'Green tag' provider. She has done work on the assessment and permitting of redevelopment projects involving complex sites, including former nuclear assets.
**Personal:** JD, University of Pennsylvania Law School, 1990; BA, Duke University, 1987 (magna cum laude).

## ZORN, Jonathan M
Ropes & Gray LLP, Boston
617 951 7299
jonathan.zorn@ropesgray.com
*Recommended in Employee Benefits*
**Practice Areas:** Specializes in tax and benefits in the investment management industry. Teaches in the Boston University Graduate Tax Program on employee benefits. Has participated as a speaker in continuing legal education programs for the Boston Bar Association and the Federal Tax Institute of New England, among others.
**Career:** Massachusetts Bar (1982); Partner, Ropes & Gray (1991).
**Personal:** JD, Yale Law School (1982); BA, Indiana University (1972).

# BINGHAM MCCUTCHEN LLP

## THE FIRM

**Chairman:** Jay S Zimmerman
**Vice Chairman:** Donn P Pickett

**Number of partners:** 328
**Number of other lawyers:** 517

## AREAS OF PRACTICE:

Corporate . . . . . . . . . . . . . . . . . . . . . . . . . . . . . . . . . . . . . . . . . .24%
Finance . . . . . . . . . . . . . . . . . . . . . . . . . . . . . . . . . . . . . . . . . . .28%
Litigation . . . . . . . . . . . . . . . . . . . . . . . . . . . . . . . . . . . . . . . . .48%

**FIRM OVERVIEW:** Bingham McCutchen LLP is an international law firm with 850 attorneys in 11 offices. The firm focuses on serving clients in high-stakes litigation, complex financial regulatory and transactional support, and a wide variety of sophisticated corporate and technology matters. Collaboration, focused diversification and growth by merger and acquisition are the corner-stones of Bingham McCutchen's success, resulting in a decade of dramatic growth. Since 1995, Bingham McCutchen has more than quadrupled in size, growing to more than 850 lawyers today. Poised to conduct legal business world-wide, the firm has positioned itself in leading financial centers throughout the world, such as New York, London and Tokyo, while developing a significant and robust East Coast-West Coast presence in the United States.

**CLIENTS:** Adaptec, Inc.; Agrium, Inc.; AIG Highstar, L.P.; Allegheny Technologies Incorporated; Alliance Capital Management Corporation; Alliant Capital, Ltd.; Automatic Data Processing, Inc.; Bank of America; Bechtel Corporation; BMW of North America; BNP Paribas; Cisco Systems, Inc.; Citigroup; Command Audio Corporation; Deloitte & Touche USA; Deutsche Bank AG; eBay; Ernst & Young, LLP; Exxon Mobil Corporation; Fidelity Brokerage Service LLC; First Data Corporation; General Electric Commercial Finance; Globe Newspaper Co.; Goldman Sachs International; Harvard University; Heritage Partners; Heritage Property Investment Trust, Inc.; Hewlett-Packard Company; Humboldt Creamery Association; Hyundai Motor Company; ICU Medical, Inc.; John Hancock Life Insurance Company; JPMorgan Chase; Legg Mason; Lehman Brothers; Louisiana-Pacific Corporation; Los Angeles Department of Sanitation; Lowry Trusts, Denver and Waste Management; Madison Marquette Development Co.; Marsh & McLennan Companies, Inc.; MatlinPatterson Global Advisors; McKesson Corporation; Merrill Lynch, Pierce, et al; Metropolitan Life Insurance Company; Mitsui & Co. (USA), Inc.; Mizuho International plc; Morgan Stanley; National Football League; Nationwide Insurance Companies; Oracle Corporation; Overseas Private Investment Corporation; Parmalat Bondholders; Platinum Equity, LLC; Prudential Financial; Putnam Investments; Raytheon Company; Reliant Resources, Inc.; Roche Molecular Systems; SCS Energy LLC; Shapell Industries of No. California; Sierra National Insurance Holdings, Inc.; Stanford University; State Street Bank; Teachers Insurance and Annuity Association; Tempur World, Inc.; The JBG Companies.

**INTERNATIONAL WORK:** Long recognized for its leading financial restructuring practice, Bingham McCutchen, through its Hartford, New York, London and Tokyo offices, handles some of the world's most high-profile international restructurings and insolvencies. The firm continues to play a key role on the international insolvency front by, among other things, representing the largest group of Parmalat creditors, an assignment that received International Financing Review's 2005 Global Restructuring Deal Award and European Restructuring Deal Award. The firm's growing London office also includes finance, corporate and litigation capabilities as well as a new financial regulatory practice that provides both UK and US-based clients with advice on all aspects of the UK financial services regulatory framework. The Tokyo office has worked on major mergers and acquisitions, litigation, corporate and regulatory matters. Playing a significant role in Japanese insolvency and corporate restructuring matters, Bingham lawyers have advised on strategic and policy issues for Japanese govern-mental agencies. Japanese clients include major financial institutions, corporations and many ministries of the Japanese government. The firm's Securities Regulation Team also provides assistance with FSA regulatory matters in Japan. Attorneys in Bingham's US and Tokyo offices advise and represent major US and European companies in Japan and Asia, as well as nearly 500 Japanese-affiliated companies, including more than 35 of the Fortune Global 500 corporations.

## HEAD OFFICE

### MASSACHUSETTS
150 Federal Street, **Boston**, MA 02110-1726
**Tel:** 617 951 8000   **Fax:** 617 951 8736
**Email:** info@bingham.com
**Website:** www.bingham.com

## BRANCH OFFICES

### CALIFORNIA
600 Anton Boulevard, 18th Floor, **Costa Mesa**, CA 92626
**Tel:** 714 830 0600   **Fax:** 714 830 0700

1900 University Avenue, **East Palo Alto**, CA 94303
**Tel:** 650 849 4400   **Fax:** 650 849 4800

355 South Grand Avenue, **Los Angeles**, CA 900071-3106
**Tel:** 213 680 6400   **Fax:** 213 680 6499

Three Embarcadero Center, **San Francisco**, CA 94111
**Tel:** 415 393 2000   **Fax:** 415 393 2286

1333 North California Blvd., Suite 210, **Walnut Creek**, CA 94596
**Tel:** 925 937 8000   **Fax:** 925 975 5390

### CONNECTICUT
One State Street, **Hartford**, CT 06103-3178
**Tel:** 860 240 2700   **Fax:** 860 240 2800

### DISTRICT OF COLUMBIA
1120 20th Street, N.W., Suite 800, **Washington**, DC 20036
**Tel:** 202 778 6150   **Fax:** 202 778 6155

### NEW YORK
399 Park Avenue, **New York**, NY 10022-4689
**Tel:** 212 705 7000   **Fax:** 212 752 5378

## INTERNATIONAL OFFICES

### LONDON
41 Lothbury, London, **England** EC2R 7HF
**Tel:** 011 44 207 661 530   **Fax:** 011 44 207 661 5400

### TOKYO
Fukoku Seimei Building, 15th Floor, 2-2, Uchisaiwaicho 2-chome Chiyoda-ku, **Japan** 100-0011
**Tel:** 81 3 5521 6870   **Fax:** 81 3 5521 6877

## CONTACTS

Corporate . . . . . . . . . . . . . . . . . . . . . . . . . . . . . . . . . . . . . . . . . . . . . . . . . . . . . Robert M Wolf
Finance . . . . . . . . . . . . . . . . . . . . . . . . . . . . . . . . . . . . . . . . . . . . . . . . . . . . . Edwin E Smith
Litigation . . . . . . . . . . . . . . . . . . . . . . . . . . . . . . . . . . . . . . . . . . . Christopher B Hockett

**BINGHAM McCUTCHEN**

# COHN WHITESELL & GOLDBERG LLP

## THE FIRM

**Chairman:** Daniel C Cohn
**Number of Attorneys:** 6

**FIRM OVERVIEW:** Cohn Whitesell & Goldberg LLP is Boston's leading boutique law firm addressing the problems of distressed companies. Formed in 1990, the firm's practice extends throughout the northeastern United States and includes out-of-court debt restructuring, Chapter 11 reorganizations, acquisition of distressed businesses, all aspects of bankruptcy law and related litigation. The firm also serves as mediator or arbitrator for purposes of alternative dispute resolution.

**MAIN AREAS OF PRACTICE:** Work includes representing debtors, acquirers, creditors' committees, landlords, suppliers, directors, officers and trustees in out-of-court restructurings, Chapter 11 reorganizations and other debtor-creditor proceedings including related litigation.

**Debtors:** Cohn Whitesell & Goldberg LLP represents public and private companies in financial distress, primarily in the middle market (sales of $25 to $500 million). The firm's Debtor Practice includes out-of-court debt restructurings, Chapter 11 reorganizations in courts throughout the eastern United States, and receiverships in federal and state courts. Generally the firm works in association with non-bankruptcy counsel – often the troubled company's long-time corporate counsel – so that the company can combine CWG's unique capabilities, experience and judgment in debt restructuring with the expertise of skilled lawyers in other fields.

**Acquirers/Equity Sponsors:** The firm represents strategic and financial acquirers of troubled companies and assets in balancing the unique opportunities and risks that result from financial distress. The firm also represents equity sponsors with troubled portfolio companies, whether the objective is to reacquire the business or manage risk.

**Committees, Landlords, Suppliers:** Cohn Whitesell & Goldberg LLP represents creditors' committees, landlords, suppliers and others with a stake in distressed businesses. This practice area includes defense of litigation alleging preferential and fraudulent transfers, breaches of fiduciary duties and other insolvency-related matters.

**CLIENTS:** The firm's experience includes manufacturing, retail, healthcare, environmental, technology, plastics, automotive components, broadcasting, advertising and real estate. Sample engagements include:

**Waste Systems International, Inc. et al:** A solid waste disposal company with liabilities of $150 million. CWG represented the company in its successful Chapter 11 reorganization, in which the equity sponsor retained ownership in exchange for an additional investment.

**Wash Depot Holdings, Inc:** A nationwide operator of car washes, quick lube centers, gas stations and convenience stores with liabilities of $130 million. The firm represented the company in its successful Chapter 11 reorganization, in which one of the lenders acquired the equity of the restructured enterprise.

**Diam International, Inc:** A designer and manufacturer of retail product displays with sales of $250 million. CWG represented the company in an out-of-court restructuring whereby almost half of its revolving credit facility of $100 million was forgiven, and the common stock remained in the hands of the equity sponsor.

**Wolverine, Proctor & Schwartz, Inc:** A manufacturer of industrial ovens with sales in excess of $50 million. CWG represented the stockholder in an out-of-court debt restructuring whereby its secured credit facility was discharged in exchange for payment of half of the outstanding amount.

**DB Companies, Inc:** A chain of 150 convenience stores and gas stations in the northeast, with revenues of $175 million. The firm represented the company in selling its retail locations through Chapter 11.

**Plassein International Corp:** A manufacturer of plastic packaging in the United States and Canada with sales of $150 million. CWG represented the company in selling its business, on a going-concern basis, under Chapter 11.

**Acushnet Rubber Co., Inc:** A manufacturer of automotive components with sales of $35 million. The firm represented the company in its successful out-of-court restructuring of its bank loans.

**New Hampshire Electric Cooperative, Inc:** An electric utility with approximately 60,000 customers and 270 million in debt. CWG represented the utility in obtaining confirmation of a Chapter 11 plan that restructured debt resulting from investment in a nuclear power plant while maintaining the utility as an independent company.

**Insurance Holdings of America:** An insurance marketing and technology company with liabilities of $30 million. The firm served as creditors' trustee under an out-of-court wind-down arrangement approved by creditors as a quicker and less expensive alternative to bankruptcy.

**Newcare Health Corporation, et al:** Owners and operators of health-care facilities with revenues of $60 million. In the company's Chapter 11 cases, CWG represented a secured lender which, through a related party, purchased substantially all of the debtors' assets in a bankruptcy sale outside of a plan.

**NordicTrack, Inc:** A manufacturer of exercise equipment with peak sales of $480 million. CWG represented the company in its successful liquidation under Chapter 11.

**Massachusetts Recycling Associates Limited Partnership:** A pulp mill with debts of $180 million. CWG represented the partnership in successfully confirming its Chapter 11 plan.

**P.J. Keating Company:** A producer of asphalt, crushed stone and related materials. In the company's Chapter 11 case, CWG represented an international construction conglomerate in defeating a plan proposed by the company's management and acquiring the company through a competing plan.

**Haskon Corporation:** A manufacturer of components for the aviation industry that was liquidated under the Bankruptcy Code. The firm served as court-approved mediator, successfully resolving disputes between the bankruptcy trustee and the principal secured creditor.

**Standard Box Co., Inc:** A manufacturer of folding paper boxes. The firm represented the Chapter 11 creditors' committee in obtaining confirmation of a liquidating plan providing for full payment to creditors.

**Cape Cod Broadcasting, L.P., et al:** Operator of radio stations in Massachusetts and Florida. CWG represented the state court receiver who sold these stations as going concerns, maximizing the secured creditors' recovery and providing full payment to trade creditors.

**Westra Plastics, Inc:** A specialty plastics manufacturer based in upstate New York. The firm represented the federal court receiver who sold the company as a going concern, maximizing the secured creditors' recovery and providing full payment to trade creditors.

**HEAD OFFICE**

**MASSACHUSETTS**
101 Arch Street, **Boston**, MA 02110
**Tel:** 617 951 2505   **Fax:** 617 951 0679
**Email:** cohn@cwg11.com
**Website:** www.cwg11.com

# EDWARDS ANGELL PALMER & DODGE

## THE FIRM

**Managing Partners:** Charles E Dewitt, Terrence M Finn

**Number of partners:** 232
**Number of other lawyers:** 281

**FIRM OVERVIEW:** Edwards Angell Palmer & Dodge LLP offers a full array of legal services to clients worldwide. Whether the legal issue involves high stakes litigation, complex securities, bankruptcy, intellectual property, real estate development, public finance, estate planning and fiduciary services, tax, or other legal services, the firm's extensive business knowledge of these industry segments makes them value-added members of the client's team. The firm has earned its reputation as a distinguished community leader. The firm's attorneys serve as directors and advisors to numerous community organizations and have been awarded for their pro bono services. The firm has also produced several public and private leaders including US Senators, and Federal and State Judges.

The combination of Edwards & Angell LLP and Palmer & Dodge LLP in the Fall of 2005 blended the distinguished reputations of two century-old leading full-service law firms creating the firm of Edwards Angell Palmer & Dodge LLP. For more information, please visit www.eadplaw.com.

## MAIN AREAS OF PRACTICE:

**Bankruptcy & Creditors Rights:** An interdisciplinary team that assists many of the premier financial institutions, institutional investors, debt investors, finance companies, insurers and sureties to enforce creditors' rights and to achieve strategic goals in the context of commercial litigation, loan workout, debt restructurings and bankruptcy.

**Corporate:** Made up of attorneys who practice in the areas of antitrust, employee benefits and executive compensation, environmental, investment management, licensing, collaborations, joint ventures andstrategic alliances, mergers and acquisitions, private equity, public offerings and public company counseling, start-up companies and venture capital, the hallmark of the firm's Corporate Practice is the shared commitment of both attorneys and clients to find the best possible legal solution to any challenge confronting business today.

**Debt Finance & Capital Markets:** The firm is a national leader in debt finance and capital markets, a practice that has been one of the firm's major strengths for over 100 years. The practice has grown with the world's financial markets to comprise all aspects of banking and finance.

**Insurance & Reinsurance:** One of the leading insurance practices in the country, this department consists of over 50 attorneys who provide a full range of legal services to the global insurance and reinsurance industry. Attorneys enjoy national and international reputations, and have been specifically recognized in Euromoney's 'Guide to the World's Leading Insurance Lawyers', 'The International Who's Who of Insurance and Reinsurance Lawyers', and Chambers USA 'America's Leading Lawyers for Business'.

**Intellectual Property:** This department has extensive experience over many years in establishing, managing, asserting and defending against intellectual property rights. The firm's IP lawyers have handled essentially all business aspects of patents, trademarks, copyrights, trade secrets and related antitrust issues, for the past 35-plus years. The firm has more than 50 intellectual property patent attorneys and agents, of whom 16 have doctorate degrees and an additional 12 have masters degrees in areas of science and engineering.

**International:** The firm represents US clients in their activities in Europe, the Americas, the Middle East, Asia, Australia, and Africa, as well as clients from dozens of countries with respect to activities in nearly all the US states. The firm has an interdisciplinary group of internationally-experienced attorneys, spread throughout its offices. Clients in cross-border matters include public and private companies and entities of all sizes in virtually every type of transaction.

**Litigation:** With more than 150 lawyers handling complex civil and criminal litigation, corporate investigations and regulatory matters, the firm's litigation attorneys represent a wide variety of clients from individuals to closely-held companies to giants in industry, finance, insurance and government entities. Attorneys are admitted to practice in many jurisdictions, regularly litigate cases throughout the country, and have a proven record of success as trial and appellate lawyers.

**Private Client:** An aggregation of people with the skills, talents and experience to provide advice and representation to individuals and families in the world of tax, law and finance. Lawyers, paralegals, tax accountants, investment advisors, trust administrators, and secretaries share the overriding common mission of providing the finest personal service to clients.

**Public Finance:** The firm has a nationally recognized public finance practice serving as bond counsel to governmental entities issuing tax-exempt debt, as well as underwriters' counsel, disclosure counsel and special tax counsel for public debt issues. The firm has the largest bond counsel practice of any New England law firm and is continually ranked among the top 20 bond counsel firms nationally. Each year the firm is involved with hundreds of separate issues of tax-exempt bonds and notes totaling billions of dollars.

**Real Estate:** This department provides comprehensive legal services to developers, lenders, public authorities, businesses, universities and other institutional landowners in connection with the acquisition, sale, development, financing, and operation of real estate projects. Their development, transportation, leasing, and financing practices takes them regularly throughout the United States.

## OFFICES

**CONNECTICUT**
90 State House Square, **Hartford**, CT 06103
**Tel:** 860 525 5065   **Fax:** 860 527 4198

Three Stamford Plaza, 301 Tresser Blvd, **Stamford**, CT 06901
**Tel:** 203 975 7505   **Fax:** 203 975 7180

**DELAWARE**
919 North Market Street, **Wilmington**, DE 19801
**Tel:** 302 777 7770   **Fax:** 302 777 7263

**FLORIDA**
350 East Las Olas Blvd, **Ft Lauderdale**, FL 33301
**Tel:** 954 727 2600   **Fax:** 954 727 2601

One North Clematis Street, Suite 400, **West Palm Beach,** FL 33401
**Tel:** 561 833 7700   **Fax:** 561 655 8719

**MASSACHUSETTS**
111 Huntington Avenue, **Boston**, MA 02199
**Tel:** 617 239 0100   **Fax:** 617 227 4420

101 Federal Street, **Boston**, MA 02110
**Tel:** 617 439 4444   **Fax:** 617 439 4170

**NEW JERSEY**
51 John F Kennedy Parkway, **Short Hills,** NJ 07078
**Tel:** 973 376 7700   **Fax:** 973 376 3380

**NEW YORK**
750 Lexington Avenue, **New York**, NY 10022
**Tel:** 212 308 4411   **Fax:** 212 308 4844

**RHODE ISLAND**
2800 Financial Plaza, **Providence,** RI 02903
**Tel:** 401 274 9200   **Fax:** 401 276 6611

*The firm also has a representative office in London.*

EDWARDS
ANGELL
PALMER &
DODGE LLP

# FISH & RICHARDSON P.C.

## THE FIRM

**Managing Partner:** Peter Devlin
**Chairman:** Robert Hillman

**Number of Principals:** 142
**Total number of lawyers:** 361

**FIRM OVERVIEW:** Fish & Richardson P.C. is a national law firm with over 350 lawyers in ten offices. The firm is one of the largest firms practicing intellectual property, litigation, and corporate law and the only firm with a truly national intellectual property practice. Founded in 1878, the firm represented Thomas Edison, Alexander Graham Bell, and the Wright Brothers. For over 125 years the firm has served great innovators, helping to protect countless ideas, nurture discoveries, and bring new concepts to market. The firm prosecuted and litigated many of the fundamental patents of an industrialized America, serving corporations creating the cutting-edge technologies of the day: the telephone, the air-brake, the steam turbine, the automobile, and the radio. Frederick Fish, the firm's founder, was for many years the acknowledged leader of the patent bar of the entire country at a time when patents were more important than they had ever been. Today, the firm continues to represent great innovators working in cutting-edge technologies. Fish & Richardson files over 4200 patent applications and almost 500 trademark registrations each year. The firm also handles more patent litigation than any other law firm and is the top firm for handling patent cases in the International Trade Commission.

In a survey published in July 2005, *IP Law & Business*, which publishes an annual list of the most active patent litigation firms, found that Fish & Richardson handles more patent litigation than any other firm. Fish & Richardson has ranked number one on the survey for four out of the five years since *IP Law & Business* began publishing its survey of top patent litigation firms. *IP Law & Business* has also named Fish & Richardson the top firm in the country for patent litigation at the International Trade Commission (ITC). In a survey published in September 2005, *IP Law & Business* found that Fish & Richardson handles more ITC patent litigation than any other firm.

## MAIN AREAS OF PRACTICE:
Patents, trademarks, copyrights, trade secrets, intellectual property litigation, corporate and securities, regulatory, ITC proceedings, media and entertainment, labor and employment, general business and commercial litigation, and white-collar criminal defense.

## CLIENTS:
Allergan, Inc.; America Online, Inc.; Bose Corporation; Boston Scientific Corporation; Cargill, Inc.; Dresser, Inc.; Intel Corporation; LeCroy Corporation; Micron Technology; Microsoft Corporation; Power Integrations, Inc.; Princo Corporation; Siemens; OSRAM Opto Semiconductors.

## OFFICES

### CALIFORNIA
500 Arguello Street, Suite 500, **Redwood City**, CA 94063
**Tel:** 650 839 5070   **Fax:** 650 839 5071

12390 El Camino Real, **San Diego**, CA 92130
**Tel:** 858 678 5070   **Fax:** 858 678 5099

### DELAWARE
919 N Market Street, Suite 1100, PO Box 1114,
**Wilmington**, DE 19899-1114
**Tel:** 302 652 5070   **Fax:** 302 652 0607

### DISTRICT OF COLUMBIA
1425 K Street, NW, 11th Floor, **Washington**, DC 20005-3500
**Tel:** 202 783 5070   **Fax:** 202 783 2331

### GEORGIA
1230 Peachtree St NE, 19th Floor, **Atlanta**, GA 30309
**Tel:** 404 892 5005   **Fax:** 404 892 5002

### MASSACHUSETTS
225 Franklin Street, **Boston**, MA 02210
**Tel:** 617 542 5070   **Fax:** 617 542 8906
**Email:** info@fr.com
**Website:** www.fr.com

### MINNESOTA
3300 Dain Rauscher Plaza, 60 South Sixth St, **Minneapolis**, MN 55402
**Tel:** 612 335 5070   **Fax:** 612 288 9696

### NEW YORK
Citigroup Center, 153 East 53rd Street, 52nd Floor,
**New York**, NY 10022-4611
**Tel:** 212 765 5070   **Fax:** 212 258 2291

### TEXAS
One Congress Plaza, 111 Congress Avenue, Suite 810, **Austin**, TX 78701
**Tel:** 512 472 5070   **Fax:** 512 320 8935

1717 Main Street, Suite 5000, **Dallas**, TX 75201
**Tel:** 214 747 5070   **Fax:** 214 747 2091

## CONTACTS

| | |
|---|---|
| **Patent** | Richard Anderson |
| **Trademark & Copyright** | Timothy French |
| **Litigation** | David Barkan |
| **Corporate & Securities** | Eddie Wang Rodriguez |
| **International Regulatory Group** | Terry Mahn |
| **National Marketing Executive** | Kelly Largey |

FISH & RICHARDSON P.C.

# GOODWIN PROCTER LLP

## THE FIRM

**Chairman & Managing Partner:** Regina M Pisa
**Partners nationwide:** 220
**Total attorneys:** 650

**FIRM OVERVIEW:** Goodwin Procter LLP is one of the nation's leading law firms, with 650 attorneys and offices in Boston, New York and Washington, DC. The firm combines in-depth legal knowledge with practical business experience to deliver innovative solutions to complex legal problems. It provides corporate, litigation and real estate services to clients ranging from emerging companies to Fortune 500 multinationals, with a focus on matters involving private equity, technology companies, REITs and real estate capital markets, financial services, intellectual property and products liability. Goodwin Procter understands that people are its most important asset. Consequently, the firm devotes considerable resources to recruiting, training and retaining its lawyers and staff. The firm hires talented, motivated people committed to a culture based on teamwork. It believes that every attorney and staff member deserves a supportive, meritocratic environment in which people of all backgrounds are given the opportunity to excel and thrive. The firm is one of only a handful of comparably sized law firms in the United States to have a woman acting as chairman and managing partner. The firm believes strongly in its obligations as a corporate citizen and is dedicated to community service. Through its longstanding and extensive pro bono program, Goodwin Procter encourages its legal staff to assist those unable to afford legal representation.

**MAIN AREAS OF PRACTICE:** Goodwin Procter's client work includes corporate, litigation, real estate, financial services, intellectual property, products liability, energy, private equity, technology companies, REITs and real estate capital markets, tax, ERISA and employee benefits, labor and employment, environmental and estate planning.

**Business Law:** Goodwin Procter's business law attorneys specialize in transactional work. The firm is respected for its ability to structure, negotiate and close deals that balance its clients' immediate objectives with long-term strategic advantage. Primary areas of industry focus are financial services, technology, life sciences, media and communications, energy, manufacturing, consumer products and real estate. Services range from counseling, financing, fund formation and insolvency work to structuring complex mergers and acquisitions, joint ventures, and private equity deals and capital markets transactions.

**Litigation:** The litigation matters the firm handles are factually and legally complex. The firm's 275 litigators are engaged in high stakes cases across the country, conducting trials, arbitrations, mediations and negotiations, and counseling on litigation avoidance and risk management. These matters primarily involve consumer financial services, intellectual property, multi-district mass tort products liability, white collar defense, securities litigation, commercial litigation and antitrust. Clients include companies in the software, technology, manufacturing, mining, defense, consumer products, life sciences, communications, real estate, healthcare and financial services industries.

**CLIENTS:** Goodwin Procter represents a diverse client base, with clients ranging from entrepreneurial emerging companies to established multinationals. The firm's clients present complex issues and expect cost-effective results to be delivered under tight deadlines. Client service begins with knowing the clients, knowing their business and knowing their competitors. With this information, the firm's attorneys are able to leverage their specialized skills and expertise to deliver responsive, knowledgeable and practical legal advice. The firm maximizes its practice efficiency by focusing on effective use of technology and knowledge management.

## HEAD OFFICE

**MASSACHUSETTS**
Exchange Place, **Boston**, MA 02109
**Tel:** 617 570 1000   **Fax:** 617 523 1231
**Email:** rpisa@goodwinprocter.com
**Website:** www.goodwinprocter.com

## BRANCH OFFICES

**DISTRICT OF COLUMBIA**
901 New York Avenue, NW **Washington**, DC 20001
**Tel:** 202 346 4000   **Fax:** 202 346 4444
**Email:** jaldock@goodwinprocter.com

**NEW YORK**
599 Lexington Avenue, **New York**, NY 10022
**Tel:** 212 813 8800   **Fax:** 212 355 3333
**Email:** asolecki@goodwinprocter.com

## CONTACTS

Boston ....................................................................Regina M Pisa
New York ................................................................Albert J Solecki
Washington, DC ....................................................John D Aldock

GOODWIN

PROCTER

# HANIFY & KING

## THE FIRM

**Managing Partner:** James Coyne King
**Executive Director:** Robert J Perry

**Number of partners:** 12
**Number of lawyers:** 32

**FIRM OVERVIEW:** Since 1980 Hanify & King has met the legal needs of individuals, small businesses and large corporations by delivering on-target solutions in a focused and cost-effective manner. Hanify & King attorneys represent clients in areas ranging from commercial litigation and bankruptcy and financial restructuring to business formation and labor and employment. Clients include private and public corporations, investment partnerships, government agencies, Fortune 500 companies, individuals and non-profit organizations. Hanify & King's sensible approach to legal guidance is embodied in its 12 partners and 20 associates and reflected in its ongoing investment in the most current technology available to the legal profession. This commitment to technology allows Hanify & King attorneys to build evidentiary databases and offer interactive documents that allow for immediate access to critical case information, thereby truncating the time between the onset of a client's problem and its resolution. Exceptional legal talent and catered client service have earned Hanify & King a reputation as a top-notch mid-sized firm.

## MAIN AREAS OF PRACTICE

**Litigation:** Litigation is Hanify and King's largest practice area, and its attorneys appear before state and federal courts and administrative agencies with an 'at trial' success rate of 85 percent or higher. Several cases tried by Hanify and King attorneys have set legal precedents in areas such as intellectual property, business fraud, bankruptcy, leveraged buyouts, professional malpractice and employment. The firm's litigation attorneys, led by co-founder John D Hanify, work with clients outside the courtroom as well, guiding them through critical cost/benefit decisions. The wide-ranging civil litigation practice group offers expertise in the following areas: financial representations, warranty and fraud claims, business divorce and intra-entity disputes, real estate development, ownership and construction disputes, labor and employment, intellectual property claims, insolvency, public and administrative law and fiduciary duty and professional liability claims.

**Bankruptcy & Financial Restructuring:** The Bankruptcy and Financial Restructuring Group represents debtors, creditors and creditors' committees, estate fiduciaries, investors in formal insolvency proceedings and out-of-court workouts throughout the United States. Led by Harold B Murphy, recognized in two leading legal publications including Chambers USA, America's Leading Business Lawyers, Hanify & King bankruptcy lawyers have been nationally recognized for delivering superior results in a timely and cost-effective manner and include former law clerks to bankruptcy judges and attorneys with the Office of the United States Trustee. Hanify and King's Bankruptcy practice is regularly called upon to serve as estate representatives and counsel in Chapter 7 and 11 cases. The group has represented clients in all types of businesses including real estate, hospitality, healthcare, technology, telecommunications, manufacturing, and retail.

**Corporate:** The Corporate Practice at Hanify and King represents clients in mergers and acquisitions and in the purchase and sale of business assets. Hanify and King's corporate attorneys provide counsel to owners and investors in the sale, acquisition, development, zoning, and leasing of commercial real estate. James Coyne King and Robert E Richards, Jr head this practice area and have compiled a team of professionals who are able to negotiate complex transaction documents and navigate due diligence reviews, debt and equity structures, licensing or transfer of intellectual property, business organization and commercial loans. The group also counsels both public and private sector employers to ensure that the myriad legal requirements concerning personnel practices do not distract them from achieving their business objectives.

## HEAD OFFICE

**MASSACHUSETTS**
One Beacon Street, 21st Floor, **Boston**, MA 02108-3107
**Tel:** 617 423 0400   **Fax:** 617 423 0498

**Website:** www.hanify.com

## CONTACTS

| | |
|---|---|
| Litigation | John D Hanify |
| **Bankruptcy & Financial Restructuring** | Harold B Murphy |
| **Corporate** | James Coyne King |
| | Robert E Richards Jr |
| **Alternative Dispute Resolution** | David Lee Evans |

**Alternative Dispute Resolution:** Hanify and King's Alternative Dispute Resolution Practice stems from the firm's expertise inside the courtroom. Hanify and King's attorneys are experienced trial attorneys, however, they understand that not all cases need to be settled in court. The firm encourages clients involved in cases with potential or actual litigation to explore the benefits of alternative dispute resolution. The Alternative Dispute Resolution Group, headed by David Lee Evans, has settled countless business disputes through mediation, arbitration or other informal dispute resolution proceedings, bringing conflicts to a quick and less expensive resolution. Attorneys at Hanify and King have served in approximately 100 cases for the American Arbitration Association's Commercial and Large, Complex Case Panels. The firm also co-founded the Technology Company Mediation Program for the Massachusetts Software and Internet Council. Hanify and King's Alternative Dispute Resolution Group has successfully handled the legal needs of deadlocked corporations, professional malpractice and intellectual property claims and complex business disputes.

# MORGAN, BROWN & JOY, LLP

## THE FIRM

**Managing Partner:** Robert P Joy

**Number of partners:** 16
**Number of other lawyers:** 15

**FIRM OVERVIEW:** Founded in 1923, Morgan, Brown & Joy is New England's oldest and largest management-side employment law firm. The firm's continued success can be credited to its ability to respond rapidly to changes in the law and the workplace. Morgan, Brown & Joy credits its distinguished history and longevity to the value and return on investment that it provides employers. The firm represents clients before courts at all levels, including the United States Supreme Court as well as state and federal agencies. Clients range from Fortune 100 corporations to small businesses and across all sectors of the economy including retailing, technology, biotechnology, healthcare, colleges and universities, utilities, insurance, banking, government and manufacturing. Morgan, Brown & Joy's focus is on anticipating and finding solutions to the ever-expanding range of employment-related legal issues in order to avoid the time and cost of litigation. When litigation becomes necessary, the firm aggressively defends its clients and has a proven record of litigation success.

## MAIN AREAS OF PRACTICE:

**Labor & Employment:** Morgan, Brown & Joy's services include advice on all aspects of workplace discrimination, harassment or retaliation issues; collective bargaining and labor-management relations; reductions in force and terminations; FLSA; NLRA; FMLA; ERISA; OFCCP; worker's compensation; business tort and contract litigation including trade secrets, non-competition agreements and individual employment contracts.

**Employment Counsel & Legal Advice:** Morgan, Brown & Joy focuses on anticipating and finding solutions to the ever-expanding range of employment-related legal issues in an effort to avoid the time and cost of litigation. Its services include: advice on all aspects of workplace discrimination, harassment or retaliation issues; comprehensive counsel on labor-management relationships; advice on reductions in force, terminations and handling employee complaints; expertise on changes in business operations and labor contracts due to mergers and acquisition; counsel on FMLA, wage and hour issues, workers' compensation claims and ERISA, and the ever-increasing list of employment-related laws; guidance on the complex set of laws and regulations governing employee illness, injury, disability and medical leaves; business tort and contract litigation including trade secrets, non-competition agreements and individual employment contracts.

**Litigation:** Morgan, Brown & Joy attorneys are not only expert advisors in employment law, but also experienced litigators. When the same team of attorneys handles the case from inception to the courtroom, they bring complete knowledge of the case along with skills in negotiation, mediation and alternative dispute resolution that can help minimize the most abrasive and expensive litigation. When litigation becomes necessary, the firm aggressively defends its clients in all of the employment areas about which they provide advice and counsel.

**Prevention & Training:** Morgan, Brown & Joy emphasizes the importance of seeking legal advice at the earliest possible time. Because the prevention of claims is preferable to the defense of claims, they offer the following services: its audit and training team reviews clients' policies and practices and provides training to the workforce on how to avoid litigation or other adverse legal consequences; human resource support includes employee handbooks and counsel on a range of personnel policies.

## HEAD OFFICE

**MASSACHUSETTS**
200 State Street, **Boston**, MA 02109-2605
**Tel:** 617 523 6666   **Fax:** 617 367 3125

**Website:** www.morganbrown.com

## CONTACTS

**Head Office** ........................................................Robert P Joy

**Labor Law:** Resolution of labor disputes is its primary objective, and they support employers with counsel and litigation related to: unfair labor practice charges; negotiations of collective bargaining agreements; grievance and arbitration; National Labor Relations Act (NLRA) and state labor law matters, including union organizing issues and union avoidance strategy.

**Employment Law Leadership:** Morgan, Brown & Joy holds the distinction of having two partners who have served as Chairman of the Labor and Employment Law Section of the American Bar Association. Its attorneys are active in the American Bar Association and the Massachusetts Bar Association, as well as national organizations in specific industries such as the National Association of College and University Attorneys and the National Retail Federation. Its attorneys frequently serve as faculty members of educational programs sponsored by these and other organizations. Morgan, Brown & Joy attorneys are members of multiple state bars including California, Connecticut, Georgia, Massachusetts, New Hampshire, New York, Ohio, Pennsylvania, Rhode Island and Vermont.

**CLIENTS:** Representative clients include Federated Department Stores, Inc., Home Depot U.S.A., Inc., General Electric Company, Albertson's, Inc., Harvard University, NSTAR Electric and Gas Corp., EMC Corporation, CVS Corporation, EDS, Boston Scientific Corporation, Serono, Inc, Oracle Corporation, Daimler Chrysler Corporation, Entergy Nuclear Operations, Inc., Kraft, Inc., KeyCorp, Federal Express Corporation, Massport, MBTA, John Hancock Financial Services Inc., WHDH-TV, RadioShack Corporation, Fairmont Hotels, City of Boston, University of Vermont, University of New Hampshire, Shaw's Supermarkets, Inc., among others.

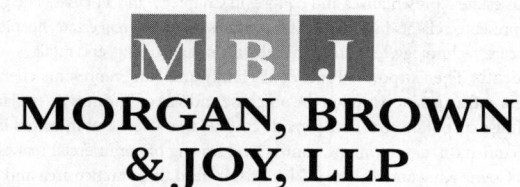

**MORGAN, BROWN & JOY, LLP**

# ROPES & GRAY LLP

## THE FIRM

**Chairman:** R Bradford Malt
**Managing Partner:** John T Montgomery

**Email:** contactus@ropesgray.com
**Website:** www.ropesgray.com

**FIRM OVERVIEW:** Ropes & Gray LLP provides comprehensive legal services to businesses and individuals around the world. Clients benefit from legal expertise enhanced by a culture of collegiality and uncompromising standards of integrity, service, and responsiveness. Clients also appreciate Ropes & Gray's commitment to diversity, which is reflected in consistently high rankings in surveys of workplace diversity.

## MAIN AREAS OF PRACTICE:

**Corporate:** For more than 140 years, the firm has provided effective corporate counsel to its clients, including a number of companies that have been with the firm since the adoption of the Federal Securities Act of 1933. The Corporate Practice, Ropes & Gray's largest practice area, includes debt financing, government relations and regulatory, mergers & acquisition, public finance, real estate, retail and consumer brands, securities and public companies, sports law, technology and venture capital.

**Financial Services & Private Equity:** Ropes & Gray represents leading firms in financial services industries, including investment companies, investment advisers, hedge fund sponsors, depository institutions, insurance companies, private equity and venture capital firms. The firm's Investment Management Practice is among the largest and most diversified of any US law firm, earning top rankings from *The American Lawyer* for more than ten years. The Private Equity Practice consistently ranks #1 nationally for negotiating the most PE or VC funds by *Private Equity Analyst*. The firm serves as transaction counsel to over 50 PE sponsors across all sectors of the marketplace, including many of the most successful and longstanding firms in the industry.

**Government Enforcement:** By quietly defusing potentially ruinous investigations, Ropes & Gray has established one of the leading enforcement defense practices in the country. The practice draws on a deep pool of former prosecutors and other government officials to guide clients through all phases of government investigations.

**Healthcare:** The highly regarded Healthcare Group has provided strategic counsel to industry leaders since the 1970s. Approximately 50 lawyers represent academic medical centers, multiprovider networks, community hospitals, physician organizations, managed care organizations, government agencies and a variety of specialty providers. The group assists with business transactions such as mergers, acquisitions and disaffiliations, and it has deep experience in state and federal regulatory and compliance matters.

**Intellectual Property:** The Fish & Neave IP Group of Ropes & Gray, with more than 200 lawyers, nearly 50 patent agents and technical advisors and more than 30 paralegals, is prepared for any IP challenge, anywhere in the world. The team maximizes IP assets of clients through litigation, rights protection, licensing and transactions. A proven winner in "bet the company" lawsuits, the team has won the largest IP award in history. Attorneys are adept at navigating the legal systems of Europe and Asia, working with multinational clients and their representatives to enhance and protect their patents and other IP rights around the world.

**Life Sciences:** The Life Sciences Practice includes lawyers with diverse expertise, including experience in corporate, intellectual property, healthcare, regulatory, litigation and tax matters. Many of the firm's lawyers and technical specialists hold MDs, PhDs and other advanced degrees in medicine, life sciences and engineering. This unique mix of knowledge and insight allows the firm to understand and anticipate the issues facing clients and craft effective solutions to their most difficult challenges.

**Litigation:** The Litigation Group, which represents clients across the world and in all industry sectors, practices in the following areas: antitrust, bankruptcy, commercial and business, environmental, government contracts, healthcare, insurance, intellectual property and technology litigation, labor and employment, and securities litigation. For example, Ropes & Gray recently successfully represented London and Bermuda insurers in the trial of the World Trade Center coverage action arising out of the events of September 11th.

**Private Client Group:** The Private Client Group is one of the largest practices of its kind in the US. The practice is focused primarily on three areas: estate and gift planning, estate settlement, and trust services, including investment management of trust assets. The group's lawyers are supported by more than 40 professionals, including trust administrators, tax preparers, probate accountants, financial planners, philanthropic advisors, and trusts and estates paralegals.

**Tax & Benefits:** Ropes & Gray's Tax Group has decades of experience guiding clients through complex domestic and international tax matters. The firm regularly represents tax clients in tax controversy matters before the US Congress, Treasury Department, and the National Office of the Internal Revenue Service. The Benefits Group has offered combined legal and benefits consulting under a single umbrella for more than 20 years.

**INTERNATIONAL WORK:** Ropes & Gray represents clients across many industries in cross-border transactions, including mergers and acquisitions, commercial activities, joint ventures, and strategic alliances, as well as in the distribution and licensing of their products. The firm's work is particularly concentrated in Europe, Latin America, Canada, East Asia and Japan. The Fish & Neave IP Group of Ropes & Gray is a worldwide leader in transnational intellectual property matters.

**Languages:** Arabic, Armenian, Bengali, Cantonese, Chinese, Esperanto, French, German, Gujurati, Hebrew, Italian, Japanese, Korean, Mandarin Chinese, Polish, Portuguese, Romanian, Russian, Spanish, Swahili, Tagalog, Telugu, Taiwanese, Urdu.

# SCHWARTZ HANNUM PC

## THE FIRM

**Co-Managing Partners:** Sara Goldsmith Schwartz
William E Hannum III
**Number of partners:** 4
**Number of other lawyers:** 4

**OFFICE CONTACTS**

**MASSACHUSETTS**
11 Chestnut Street, **Andover**, MA 01810
**Tel:** 978 623 0900  **Fax:** 978 623 0908
**Email:** schwartz@shpclaw.com
**Website:** www.shpclaw.com

**FIRM OVERVIEW:** Schwartz Hannum PC is a labor and employment firm that represents businesses and non-profit organizations in a wide variety of industries. Located outside of Boston, the firm represents clients of all sizes throughout New England and nationally, including some of the largest and most sophisticated employers in the United States. The firm is committed to achieving each client's goals as effectively and efficiently as possible. Providing high quality legal representation with excellent client service at cost effective rates have been the firm's priorities since it was founded. Attorneys in the firm are members of the bars of numerous states, including: the District of Columbia, Massachusetts, New Hampshire, New York, Ohio and Texas, and the United States District Court for the Districts of Colorado, Connecticut, Massachusetts and New Hampshire, the Southern and Eastern Districts of New York, the Northern and Eastern Districts of Texas, the Eastern District of Wisconsin, the United States Courts of Appeals for the First, Ninth and Tenth Circuits, and the United States Supreme Court. Schwartz Hannum PC is a woman-owned business. Sara Goldsmith Schwartz founded the firm in 1995 and is its President and Co-Managing Partner.

## MAIN AREAS OF PRACTICE:

**Employment Litigation:** The firm provides employers with a full range of representation in employment litigation before state and federal courts, government agencies and arbitration panels, involving claims of discrimination and retaliation, other statutory claims (e.g., under the Fair Labor Standards Act, Family and Medical Leave Act, Occupational Safety and Health Act, Older Workers Benefit Protection Act, the Sarbanes-Oxley Act and the Worker Adjustment and Retraining Notification Act), as well as state law claims for breach of contract, tort claims of all varieties, breach of non-competition and non-solicitation covenants and misappropriation of trade secrets.

**Labor Relations:** The firm represents unionized and non-unionized employers in a broad range of labor relations matters, including representation campaigns and elections, collective bargaining, arbitrations, strikes, decertifications and unfair labor practice charges. The firm's attorneys have handled labor relations matters for employers in numerous industries, including airlines, construction, distribution, education, health care, manufacturing, retail, social services and trucking, and have negotiated industry-wide, company-wide and site-specific collective bargaining agreements.

**Counseling:** The firm provides counseling with respect to innumerable labor and employment law issues, including hiring, discipline and termination decisions, workplace investigations, reductions in force, plant closings, separation agreements, employment applications and employment and independent contractor agreements.

**Compliance:** The firm conducts a full range of proactive and preventative human resources audits of policies and procedures to evaluate compliance with all applicable state and federal labor and employment laws. The firm counsels employers regarding classification as government contractors, and/or subcontractors, and assists employers in complying with any government contractor obligations, including drafting, implementing and updating affirmative action plans. The firm drafts and reviews employee handbooks, managers' guides, human resources manuals, employment policies, employment applications and other employment-related forms for small businesses and multi-state employers. The firm regularly provides training for managers and employees on topics such as: interviewing and hiring, diversity and sensitivity in the workplace, discipline and discharge, the Family and Medical Leave Act, preventing sexual and other harassment in the workplace, preventing discrimination in the workplace, I-9 Form maintenance, union avoidance and personnel records maintenance.

**Mediation & Arbitration:** The firm represents employers in binding and voluntary alternative dispute resolution efforts such as mediation and arbitration, both with respect to employment and labor disputes.

**Government Audits & Investigations:** The firm represents employers in a broad range of government audits and investigations arising in the arena of labor and employment law, including, for example, audits conducted by the United States Department of Labor, including the Department of Labor's Wage and Hour Division and the Office of Federal Contract Compliance Programs ('OFCCP'), the Massachusetts Attorney General's Office and comparable agencies in other states, the United States Equal Employment Opportunity Commission ('EEOC') and numerous state fair employment practices agencies, and the United States Occupational Safety & Health Administration ('OSHA'). The firm also represents employers with respect to unemployment compensation appeals and investigations of public accommodation issues before state and federal discrimination agencies and state architectural access boards.

**Immigration Law:** The firm assists employers with preparing and processing applications for permanent residence, as well as all types of temporary visa applications including, but not limited to, H-1B, H-2B, L-1 and TN. The firm also counsels employers regarding I-9 procedures and audits by the Department of Labor and USCIS, and handles the special concerns of foreign nationals in planning and executing reductions in force.

**CLIENTS:** Schwartz Hannum PC represents businesses and non-profit organizations in numerous industries, including banking, biotechnology, broadcasting, chemical, construction, data-storage, e-commerce, education, executive search, financial services, hardware design and development, healthcare, hospitality, insurance, lodging, manufacturing, museums, retail, semi-conductors, software design, staffing, technology and telecommunications. The firm's clients include: AMR Research, Inc., Analysis Group, Inc., BladeLogic, Inc., The Children's Museum of Boston, Cognex Corporation, Copyright Clearance Center, Inc., Deploy Solutions, Inc., Fallon Clinic, Inc., Fallon Community Health Plan, Gulf Oil, IBM, InteQ Corporation, Lanier Worldwide, Inc., Lexington Toyota, Inc., Montserrat College of Art, Nantucket Cottage Hospital, OCI Chemical Corporation, Sappi Fine Paper North America, Starwood Hotels and Resorts Worldwide, Inc., SunGard Data Systems Inc., TD Banknorth, N.A., Tenet Healthcare Corporation, The TJX Companies, Inc., Tower Records, WSI Corporation, Welch & Forbes LLC and Wheelabrator Technologies, Inc.

# SCHWARTZ HANNUM PC
LABOR AND EMPLOYMENT LAWYERS REPRESENTING MANAGEMENT

# WILMER CUTLER PICKERING HALE AND DORR LLP

## THE FIRM

**Co-Managing Partners:** William F Lee, William J Perlstein
**Email:** law@wilmerhale.com
**Website:** www.wilmerhale.com

**FIRM OVERVIEW:** WilmerHale offers unparalleled legal representation across a comprehensive range of practice areas that are critical to the success of its clients. The firm has over a thousand lawyers operating in five countries and practices at the very top of the legal profession. With a practice unsurpassed in depth and scope, it has the ability to anticipate obstacles, seize opportunities and get the case resolved or the deal done – and the experience and know-how to prevent it from being undone. WilmerHale was formed in May 2004 through the merger of two of the nation's leading law firms, Hale and Dorr LLP and Wilmer Cutler Pickering LLP. The formation of the new firm fused two storied pro bono and public service traditions. This commitment continues to be an integral part of the cultural fabric of the firm.

## MAIN AREAS OF PRACTICE:

**Antitrust & Competition:** With more than 50 years' experience and over 75 competition lawyers in the US and Europe, the firm has secured antitrust clearance for hundreds of complex mergers and joint ventures, helped clients avoid fines and prison terms in many cartel investigations, and won numerous victories for clients in private and government litigation.

**Aviation:** Regarded as one of the world's premier commercial aviation practices, the firm advises airlines, airports, associations and governments on aviation-specific legal and policy issues, from certification to licensing to enforcement.

**Bankruptcy & Commercial:** Named by *Business Week* as one of the 'top bankruptcy shops' in the United States, the firm has broad experience representing debtors, creditors and creditors' committees in bankruptcy, insolvency and debt restructuring matters, and in related litigation and commercial transactions.

**Communications & E-commerce:** WilmerHale has played a major role in shaping the rules governing the wireline and wireless telecommunications, e-commerce and mass media industries. When important issues and transactions arise, companies turn to them for the highest quality representation and effective problem solving.

**Corporate:** The firm is widely recognized for its preeminence in the representation of technology and life sciences companies in the US and Europe. Its corporate lawyers are renowned for their work in initial public offerings, venture capital and private equity, mergers and acquisitions, strategic alliances, corporate governance matters and the representation of start-up companies.

**Defense, National Security & Government Contracts:** With extensive experience serving in senior national security posts in the US government, the firm's lawyers provide regulatory, legislative, transactional and enforcement advice to clients supplying products and services to military, governmental and commercial customers worldwide.

**Environmental:** Clients rely on the firm to address complex environmental liabilities, permit key operations and understand evolving environmental laws.

**FDA:** The firm's FDA Practice includes considerable experience before the FDA and other administrative agencies, Congress and the federal courts.

**Financial Institutions:** Over the past 30 years, the firm has built a practice of extensive breadth and depth in regulatory, transactional and litigation matters for banks and other financial institutions.

**Intellectual Property:** The Intellectual Property Practice serves as a one-stop solution for clients' IP prosecution, litigation and licensing needs in the US and Europe. *The American Lawyer* recently recognized WilmerHale as having one of the top IP litigation departments in the US.

**International Trade, Investment & Market Access:** Recognized as one of the world's leading trade law firms, WilmerHale represents clients from the US, EU, China, Canada, and more than 30 other countries before administrative, judicial and legislative bodies across the globe, as well as in proceedings under the WTO, NAFTA and the World Customs Organization.

**Labor & Employment:** With capabilities including comprehensive labor and employment law counseling, employment litigation and custom-designed training programs, the firm offers clients in the US and Europe practical solutions for effectively dealing with employment issues and achieving their business objectives.

**Litigation & Arbitration:** The firm's preeminent Litigation Practice is widely recognized for its excellence in civil and criminal trial and appellate litigation, as well as in intellectual property and securities litigation. In addition, it has one of the world's leading international arbitration practices. Many of its litigators formerly held senior government positions and have particular expertise in litigation strategies designed to advance clients' objectives in regulatory and political arenas.

**Private Client:** Attorneys in the Private Client Group advise clients on gift, estate and income taxation, sophisticated gifting and diversification strategies, private philanthropy, trusts and fiduciary investments, and the administration of estates.

**Public Policy & Strategy:** This practice consolidates the extensive work that the firm's lawyers do across the public policy landscape, from providing broad-gauged advice to companies or industries on how to manage public policy risk, to crafting legislative or regulatory solutions to problems, to strategic support for proposed business transactions or initiatives, to crisis management, the response to congressional investigations and advice on multi-state challenges and opportunities.

**Real Estate:** The firm has extensive expertise in real estate capital management, institutional and pension fund equity and debt investment, development and permitting, leasing and foreign investment.

**Securities:** The firm's lawyers have successfully resolved some of the most significant and complex securities investigations and litigation over the last two decades and have established the firm as a leading defender of companies charged with violations of the securities laws and market misconduct.

**Tax:** The firm's top-ranked Tax Practice includes lawyers recognized by 'Who's Who Legal' as among 'the world's leading tax practitioners.' It handles all aspects of domestic and international tax advice for public and private companies, non-profit organizations and individuals.

## OFFICES

**CALIFORNIA**
1117 California Ave., **Palo Alto**, CA 94304
**Tel:** 650 858 6000  **Fax:** 650 858 6100

**DISTRICT OF COLUMBIA**
1875 Pennsylvania Avenue,NW, **Washington**, DC 20006
**Tel:** 202 663 6000  **Fax:** 202 663 6363

**MARYLAND**
100 Light Street, **Baltimore**, MD 21202
**Tel:** 410 986 2800  **Fax:** 410 986 2828

**MASSACHUSETTS**
60 State Street, **Boston**, MA 02109
**Tel:** 617 526 6000  **Fax:** 617 526 5000

WilmerHale Venture Group, Bay Colony Corporate Center,
1100 Winter Street, **Waltham**, MA 02451
**Tel:** 781 966 2000  **Fax:** 781 966 2100

**NEW YORK**
399 Park Avenue, **New York**, NY 10022
**Tel:** 212 230 8800  **Fax:** 212 230 8888

**NORTHERN VIRGINIA**
1600 Tysons Boulevard, Suite 1000, **McLean**, VA 22102
**Tel:** 703 251 9700  **Fax:** 703 251 9797

## INTERNATIONAL OFFICES

The firm has offices in Beijing, Berlin, Brussels, London, Munich and Oxford.

## How lawyers are ranked

Every year we carry out thousands of in-depth interviews with clients and lawyers in order to assess the reputations and expertise of business lawyers across the USA. Chambers rankings and editorial are referred to extensively by General Counsel and other purchasers of legal services who look to our recommendations when choosing their lawyers.

# BANKING & FINANCE

### Banking & Finance
#### Leading Firms

1. **BODMAN LLP** *Detroit*
   **DICKINSON WRIGHT PLLC** *Detroit*
   **MILLER, CANFIELD, PADDOCK AND STONE** *Detroit*
2. **VARNUM, RIDDERING, SCHMIDT** *Grand Rapids*
   **WARNER NORCROSS & JUDD LLP** *Grand Rapids*

#### Leading Individuals

1. **DIEHL JR Robert** *Bodman LLP*
   **SHIELD JR William** *Dickinson Wright PLLC*
   **SHULMAN Larry** *Bodman LLP*
2. **BREAY James** *Warner Norcross & Judd LLP*
   **GREEN Jonathan** *Miller, Canfield, Paddock*
   **HICKEY Kathleen** *Bodman LLP*
   **JOHNSON Donald** *Varnum, Riddering, Schmidt*
   **KOCHANEK Joseph** *Bodman LLP*
   **MCLEOD David** *Miller, Canfield, Paddock*
   **RIBACK Ronald** *Miller, Canfield, Paddock*
   **ROACH Steven** *Miller, Canfield, Paddock*
   **SHEVNOCK Colleen** *Dickinson Wright PLLC*
   **ZABRISKIE Wendy** *Bodman LLP*

#### Up-and-coming individuals
**HERMANN Kristin** *Miller, Canfield, Paddock*

## Band 1

### Bodman LLP
See firm details p.1141

**The Firm:** With over 50 lawyers in the department, this firm is renowned for the strength of its banking practice. The team is well known for its loan origination work on behalf of both borrowers and lenders, and has developed a thriving real estate finance practice. The firm is home to a top-level creditors' rights group that specializes in restructurings and workouts. Its team also includes a number of regulatory specialists who undertake work on behalf of several state banks. The group is popular among clients who spoke warmly of the lawyers' *"unparalleled depth, scope and talent."*

**The Lawyers:** Interviewees crowned **Robert Diehl** (see p.1134) *"the best insolvency lawyer in Detroit."* Peers even acknowledge that *"he's as smart as they come – the definitive go-to guy that everyone looks to for complicated workouts."* He leads the firm's bankruptcy group and has been busy advising lenders on their loans to troubled auto suppliers. He also represented Comerica in relation to a workout filing for Uni Boring, a major supplier to the auto industry. Commercial lenders regard **Larry Shulman** (see p.1139) as *"our secret weapon"* and praised him for his *"truly outstanding"* work. He is the managing partner of the firm and is regarded by many as *"the finest loan origination lawyer in Michigan."* One client even stated: *"He is better than any New York or Chicago lawyer I've worked with."* **Joseph Kochanek** (see p.1136) also *"outstrips any of the big city attorneys"* and is frequently called on for his prowess in big-ticket transactions. He specializes in large multibank syndicated credit facilities and is admired by peers and clients alike for his work on behalf of clients such as Comerica. **Wendy Zabriskie** (see p.1140) cochairs the banking group and specializes in commercial lending, including real estate loans. Her recent highlights include advising on a $90 million syndicated loan for the development of a 'lifestyle' retail center in southeast Michigan. **Kathleen O'Callaghan Hickey** (see p.1135) also cochairs the group and is a loan origination and secured lending specialist who has a strong following among national and international banking clients.

**Clients/Work Highlights:** The group frequently handles loan origination work for Comerica and represents other major banks such as LaSalle and KeyBank, together with a host of smaller financial institutions. Lawyers are also active for automotive suppliers such as Lear and Freudenberg-NOK, and a number of high net worth individuals.

### Dickinson Wright PLLC
See firm details p.1145

**The Firm:** Researchers heard that this is *"one of the premier banking firms in Michigan."* It offers lenders the full range of banking expertise including syndicated lending, securitizations and capital market transactions. The firm also lays claim to one of the largest bankruptcy, debt restructuring and insolvency groups in the state. This group has been especially active recently as a result of the depressed automotive industry. Other areas of expertise include banking regulatory work, asset-based loans and cross-border financings.

**The Lawyers:** **William Shield** (see p.1139) is a firm favorite among lenders: *"He always gives us fast, efficient and value-added service, which is why he is our preferred counsel every time."* He often acts as lead counsel to financial institutions in international syndicated lending and financing transactions involving multiple borrowers and currencies across Europe, Asia and Australasia. **Colleen Shevnock** (see p.1139) is *"an exceptional lawyer,"* who is well known for her work on behalf of banks and institutional lenders. They recommended her because *"it's as if she's part of the bank herself – she really protects our interests."* She also acts for national and international borrowers.

**Clients/Work Highlights:** Lawyers advise major international and national banks on a range of complex and high-value banking deals. Leading clients include JPMorgan Chase; Citibank; LaSalle Bank; National City Bank; Fifth Third Bank and Citizens Bank.

### Miller, Canfield, Paddock and Stone, P.L.C.
See firm details p.1148

**The Firm:** A banking heavyweight in Michigan, the firm closed over $15 billion worth of financing transactions in 2005. The group has a broad geographical reach with offices throughout the state as well as in New York, Florida, Canada and Poland and has advised on a series of transactions in numerous other countries. The team is divided into several subgroups specializing in niche financing areas and includes a number of lawyers who offer expertise in tax-exempt financings.

**The Lawyers:** **David McLeod** (see p.1137) is a lending specialist who has particular expertise in casino-related deals. His workload has a strong international flavor and in one of his recent highlights he advised on a $20 million unsecured ten-year term loan to a private Turkish bank. One of his other key deals involved negotiating a $50 million syndicated line of credit and term loan to a leading waste hauling services provider in New York and New Jersey. **Ronald Riback** (see p.1139) is a seasoned practitioner who boasts over 30 years of transactional experience. He has handled a number of transactions in the health sector including the financing of a facility housing the elderly. **Jonathan Green** (see p.1134) leads the bankruptcy team and advises lenders and financial institutions on secured lending transactions and restructurings. He also acts for high-profile clients such as Ford and garnered support from interviewees as a "*truly talented lawyer and an amazing source of information.*" **Steven Roach** (see p.1139) is "*invaluable in putting together a transaction.*" He concentrates on creditors' rights issues, including offshore assets and troubled loans throughout North America, Mexico and Brazil. He also has a following among diverse entities such as pharmaceutical companies, construction contractors, Internet service providers and automotive electronic assemblers. **Kristin Hermann** (see p.1135) advises financial institutions on lending transactions and "*is at the top of the game for her age and level.*"

**Clients/Work Highlights:** Lawyers advised on the bond financing of the new $168 million state-of-the-art Cardiovascular Center at the University of Michigan Hospital. The team acted for Comerica on the restructuring of an $18.5 million troubled loan to an international company. The group also represents National City Bank; LaSalle Bank; Wells Fargo Bank; Fifth Third Bank; JPMorgan Chase and Ford Motor Credit Company.

## Band 2

### Varnum, Riddering, Schmidt & Howlett LLP
See firm details p.1149

**The Firm:** Interviewees endorsed this group as one of Michigan's key finance firms and praised it for its "*highly specialized core of banking experts.*" The team assists on the formation of bank holding companies and offers clients advice on a spectrum of associated bank regulatory matters. It also has a strong track record in securities law and is popular among lenders and borrowers for its expertise in real estate lending deals. Other areas of expertise include advising financial institutions on issues such as executive compensation, employee relations and banking litigation.

**The Lawyers:** **Donald Johnson** (see p.1135) is the chair of the practice and advises on a host of bank regulatory matters. He has broad experience advising on the formation of banks and bank holding companies. He also has a strong corporate element to his practice and frequently advises banking clients on M&A.

**Clients/Work Highlights:** The group represents many of the state's prominent banks and financial institutions, and is especially prominent in the west of the state.

### Warner Norcross & Judd LLP
**The Firm:** This is one of the largest firms in west Michigan and has developed a sterling reputation in the banking and finance arena. It is steadily expanding its team and has recently hired several lawyers previously based in Chicago. Clients call on the team for its wide-ranging experience that includes advising on banking M&A and litigation, leveraged leasing, commercial lending and regulatory issues.

**The Lawyers:** **James Breay** is best known for his knowledge of banking regulatory matters, and is often called upon to advise on the drafting of new legislation. His recent work has also included preparing amici curiae briefs in cases that are significant to the banking industry and advising on several banking take-private transactions.

**Clients/Work Highlights:** The group has a unique role as general counsel to the Michigan Bankers Association, which it is advising in relation to amendments to the Michigan Banking Code. The firm also regularly acts for a number of prominent banks and other financial institutions.

# CORPORATE/M&A

| Corporate/M&A | |
|---|---|
| **Leading Firms** | |
| 1 | HONIGMAN MILLER SCHWARTZ AND COHN *Detroit* |
| 2 | BODMAN LLP *Ann Arbor* |
| | BUTZEL LONG *Detroit* |
| | DICKINSON WRIGHT PLLC *Detroit* |
| | DYKEMA GOSSETT PLLC *Detroit* |
| | MILLER, CANFIELD, PADDOCK AND STONE *Detroit* |
| 3 | CLARK HILL PLC *Detroit* |
| | MILLER JOHNSON *Grand Rapids* |
| | VARNUM, RIDDERING, SCHMIDT *Grand Rapids* |
| | WARNER NORCROSS & JUDD LLP *Grand Rapids* |
| 4 | BARNES & THORNBURG LLP *Grand Rapids* |
| | FOLEY & LARDNER LLP *Detroit* |
| | JAFFE, RAITT, HEUER & WEISS, PC *Detroit* |

## Band 1

### Honigman Miller Schwartz and Cohn LLP
See firm details p.1146

**The Firm:** This firm stands out for the caliber of its corporate and real estate departments, which form the backbone of its operations. It has offices in Detroit, Lansing and Oakland County but has been busy expanding its practice outside of Michigan by representing national and international clients in high-level and sophisticated deals nationwide. This year has seen an upsurge in private equity transactions, with its lawyers also increasingly called upon to advise on the acquisitions of troubled businesses. Clients praise the team for its ability to "*offer a cost-effective service on a par with the nation's top law firms.*"

**The Lawyers:** **Cyril Moscow** (see p.1137) remains "*a key leader*" and dean of the state corporate Bar. His practice involves advising on major transactions, expert witness work and assisting on the drafting of Michigan general corporate statutes. **David Foltyn's** (see p.1134) national transactional practice includes M&A deals, divestitures, securities offerings and restructurings. He represents a diverse collection of clients including major public companies from the Fortune 500, Michigan-based entities and a number of investment funds. Interviewees recommended him as "*an invaluable business adviser and one of the state's greatest authorities on public companies.*" **Donald Kunz** (see p.1136) heads the corporate department and represents both publicly traded and privately held companies. He was hailed as "*a leading expert in corporate governance,*" and was praised for working "*creatively to get the deal done.*" **Alan Schwartz** (see p.1139) is the firm's managing partner and won praise from sources as "*a tremendous adviser and counselor.*" He specializes in private equity work for a stable of long-term clients but also handles public M&A deals and securities offerings.

**Clients/Work Highlights:** Lawyers advised on the $475 million refinancing of a Detroit-based casino and were involved in the $400 million acquisition of a National Basketball Association franchise. Other highlights include assisting on a $2 billion financing package for a publicly held company. The group also acted as underwriting counsel on the groundbreaking $1.4 billion pension fund securities offering for the City of Detroit. The firm also represents a number of investment funds and local family businesses. Other clients include Pulte Homes, BorgWarner and Ramco-Gershenson Properties.

## Band 2

### Bodman LLP
See firm details p.1141

**The Firm:** This firm has enjoyed a successful year and has maintained a diverse practice representing a wide array of clients. The team has been extensively involved in out-of-state and cross-border activities, and has acted for major European and Indian manufacturers. Its lawyers offer a full range of services including advice on corporate startups, M&A deals and divestitures, venture capital transactions and lending and financing matters.

**The Lawyers:** **Timothy Damschroder** (see p.1133) focuses on corporate finance and M&A deals but also devotes much of his time to venture capital work. Interviewees say he has "*fantastic written and negotiating skills,*" and offers "*superior advice on debt and equity financing agreements.*" **Laurence Deitch** (see p.1134) is "*a creative problem solver and a wonderful negotiator and deal-maker.*" He has a broad, international practice and often acts for

overseas companies on their acquisition of troubled Michigan-based manufacturers. His work also includes advising on recapitalizations and real estate leasing and financing deals. Clients call on him because *"he is an influential person with the political contacts and strength to get things done."* **Terrence Larkin** (see p.1137) heads the corporate group and handles a diverse workload on behalf of large international automotive industry suppliers and other companies involved in beer distribution and city cleaning services. Interviewees praised him as *"a solid practitioner with good instincts. He always maintains an even keel and positive outlook and never misses a trick."* **Thomas Lewand** (see p.1137) specializes in brokering complex deals that unite the public and private sector and is an *"expert in bringing the two together to make a transaction work."* He is a *"magnificent deal-maker"* who has advised on the development of the new Detroit Lions football stadium. He also acted for a client on the $80 million restructuring of the Detroit-Windsor tunnel.
**Clients/Work Highlights:** The firm continues to act for long-term clients Ford and Comerica. Its other key clients include Freudenberg-NOK; Pulte Homes; Lear; Suave Enterprises and a number of wealthy local families.

## Butzel Long
See firm details p.1143
**The Firm:** This is one of the largest groups in the state and recently celebrated its 150th anniversary. The firm has established a strong network of Michigan-based offices and also boasts a presence in Washington, DC and Florida. Its international credentials have also been boosted through the opening of a China office. Traditionally renowned for its strong representation of midmarket companies, the team now handles an increasing percentage of international work. Clients call on the team for assistance on M&A transactions, restructurings and securities offerings.
**The Lawyers:** **Justin Klimko**'s (see p.1136) areas of expertise include M&A transactions, securities deals and corporate governance issues. In one of his headline deals he is advising on the US portion of an international transaction worth $110 million. Peers commended his *"mild-mannered, scholarly approach,"* and regard him as *"a fountain of information."*
**Clients/Work Highlights:** The team typically advises Michigan-based companies on the formation of joint ventures, acquisitions and changes to their corporate structure.

## Dickinson Wright PLLC
See firm details p.1145
**The Firm:** Dickinson Wright is one of Michigan's largest and most prominent firms and offers a full corporate service to many of the state's leading businesses. It has developed wide-ranging sector-specific expertise and is especially well known for its representation of automotive suppliers. Clients frequently choose the firm for assistance on interstate corporate transactions but also rate its lawyers for advice on regulatory compliance, internal audits and shareholder agreements.
**The Lawyers:** **Richard Bolton** (see p.1132) enjoys a strong reputation for his corporate work and acted for a group of stockholders in the divestiture of a $100 million automotive business. He also has a string of big-ticket private equity deals to his name, including several acquisitions and a 'going private' transaction. **Mark High** (see p.1135) is the man to call for cross-border issues. He acts for a number of Canadian, South American and European names in the automotive industry.
**Clients/Work Highlights:** The team represents financial institutions such as JPMorgan Chase and prominent names from the automotive industry including Chrysler and Ford. It also acts for local Michigan-based entrepreneurs and companies.

## Dykema Gossett PLLC
**The Firm:** Although this firm has an established network of offices throughout Michigan, its sphere of influence extends beyond the state's borders thanks to its additional offices in Los Angeles, Washington, DC and Chicago. It is popular with Fortune 500 companies because of its *"high-level of service that you might expect from the largest national firms."* Interviewees highlighted the group's skill in lobbying and public policy, together with its expertise in casino acquisitions as particular areas of strength.
**The Lawyers:** Professor **Lloyd Semple** remains affiliated with the firm, and continues to act on a consultation basis. **Michael Bernard**'s expertise covers asset and stock purchases, corporate securities and large-scale M&A deals. He also serves as attorney for the Detroit Chamber of Commerce. **Aleksandra Miziolek** attracted praise for her performance in M&A deals and knowledge of securities law. She acted as lead counsel in the restructuring of Visteon, which allowed Ford the opportunity to buy back 23 Visteon facilities, and continues to act for Macquarie Bank on various acquisitions. **Paul Rentenbach** represents private equity funds and investment managers and also handles a large number of public M&A deals. One of his most significant recent transactions includes advising a company from India on the acquisition of assets in the USA.
**Clients/Work Highlights:** The firm represents major names in the automotive industry, including Ford and GM. Other clients include the Detroit-Windsor Tunnel, Detroit Medical Center and Parking Company of America.

## Miller, Canfield, Paddock and Stone, P.L.C.
See firm details p.1148
**The Firm:** This is one of Michigan's largest firms and also benefits from additional offices in New York, Washington, DC, Florida, Canada and three locations in Poland. The group is frequently seen acting for both buyers and sellers in complex corporate transactions. Its team of talented lawyers also advises on stock issuances and sales, recapitalizations, joint ventures and private equity investments.
**The Lawyers:** **David Joswick** (see p.1136) is an *"extraordinarily talented lawyer,"* famed for his handling of complex corporate matters. He advised on a recapitalization plan for North Country Financial. **David Parsigian** (see p.1138) is active in the technology arena and recently advised on the $25 million sale of a company that develops technology to treat vascular and coronary artery disease. He was also lead attorney in the sale of a manufacturer of ultra high-speed photoreceivers and instrumentation for the telecom and data communication markets.
**Clients/Work Highlights:** Lawyers advised Arvin-Meritor on the sale of its heavy-duty, offroad brake business, worth $39 million. Other clients include Ford, Numatics and Kongsberg Automotive.

## Band 3

## Clark Hill PLC
See firm details p.1144
**The Firm:** This is a purely Michigan-based firm with a corporate department numbering around 35 attorneys. The team handles sophisticated transactions predominantly in the metropolitan Detroit area, such as acquisitions, divestitures and state planning.

It is a growing practice group, which has developed its expertise and now "*offers a service that rivals any in the state.*" It also wins recommendations for the support provided by additional practice groups such as the IP and bankruptcy departments.

**The Lawyers: Daniel Minkus** has a diverse practice that covers corporate and real estate law. Clients praised his "*magnificent business acumen, which allows him to look at matters from both a legal and a business perspective.*" He has recently handled two multijurisdictional, hi-tech transactions, each worth in excess of $100 million, relating to the US operations of a major European company.

**Clients/Work Highlights:** The firm represents a number of insurance companies such as MetLife, Lincoln Insurance and Massachusetts Mutual Life. Other clients include developers such as Centex Homes and a number of national and international automotive industry suppliers.

## Miller Johnson

**The Firm:** This west Michigan firm fields a team of around 90 lawyers and has offices in both Grand Rapids and Kalamazoo. The team acts for a diverse client base comprising local, family-owned businesses and nationwide, publicly traded companies. Clients recommended it as "*a highly entrepreneurial business group*" that is ably supported by "*a formidable real estate practice and some of the finest litigators in the state.*"

**The Lawyers: Jeffrey Ammon** is "*a true gentleman*" who benefits from "*a fine network of contacts, which helps him facilitate a deal.*" He has been especially busy advising on a series of tax-exempt transactions and has also been selected as managing member of the firm from the start of 2006.

**Clients/Work Highlights:** The group advises a number of affluent western Michigan families, emerging growth businesses and major companies, such as Kellogg.

## Varnum, Riddering, Schmidt & Howlett LLP

See firm details p.1149

**The Firm:** Predominantly based in western Michigan, this firm has recently opened a new office in Novi, just outside metropolitan Detroit, with the intention of further expanding its operations on a statewide level. The team's principal strengths are in corporate law, litigation and labor and employment, with its core clients drawn from the manufacturing sector. It is increasingly being retained by other large, nationwide companies thanks to "*its excellent structure and quality of work.*"

**The Lawyers: Donald Johnson** (see p.1135) is "*one of Michigan's finest,*" and specializes in financial matters, including banking regulatory and structural questions. His work includes advising on the formation of banks and bank holding companies, as well as representing financial institutions in M&A deals. Clients rely on **Carl Oosterhouse** (see p.1138) for his skill in M&A transactions, equity offerings and tax-exempt financings. They described him as "*a wonderful person to work with.*"

**Clients/Work Highlights:** The firm acts for major Michigan-based businesses and prominent names such as Chrysler and Kellogg.

## Warner Norcross & Judd LLP

**The Firm:** This firm is headquartered in Grand Rapids but it is currently growing its practice in the metropolitan Detroit area. The team is keen to develop its international capabilities and has a partner with significant experience working in China who has been charged with building up this side of the practice. Lawyers here are well versed in transactional matters such as M&A deals and financings but are also on hand to advise clients on disclosure and corporate governance issues and executive compensation.

**The Lawyers: Hugh Makens** is the dean of the securities Bar and was warmly endorsed by interviewees as "*a wonderful practitioner.*" With over 35 years of experience in the market, he advises broker-dealers and investors on various regulatory proceedings and compliance matters. **Charles McCallum** heads up the firm's international business practice and advises on acquisitions, disposals and joint ventures. He also represents the US interests of foreign firms, particularly European automotive manufacturers.

**Clients/Work Highlights:** The firm's largest clients are publicly traded entities in the footwear and financial industries. It also acts for companies such as Wolverine World Wide and Muskegon Surgical Associates.

## Band 4

## Barnes & Thornburg LLP

See firm details p.903

**The Firm:** This is one of the Midwest's largest law firms, with offices in Michigan, Indiana, Illinois and Washington, DC. The office in Grand Rapids has marked strengths in corporate law and litigation, but also offers clients a comprehensive legal service that covers labor and employment, IP, tax, banking and real estate law. This office has been the subject of expansion in recent years and is expected to grow further in 2006.

**The Lawyers: Tracy Larsen** (see p.1137) is the managing partner of the Grand Rapids office and specializes in corporate and securities law. Both publicly traded and privately held companies rely on him for advice on M&A, joint ventures, corporate governance and securities matters. He is well regarded by peers who praised him for "*his hard-working and entrepreneurial attitude.*"

**Clients/Work Highlights:** The group's lawyers advise many large foreign corporations on their acquisition strategies throughout the USA, and act for entities based in Canada, Germany, France and the UK. The team also acts for emerging growth and midmarket companies.

## Foley & Lardner LLP

See firm details p.2007

**The Firm:** This large national firm has an extensive network of offices throughout the USA and has a strong international component, thanks in part to offices in Brussels and Tokyo. The size of the team enables it to handle both national and international matters of significant import, and allows lawyers to "*bring great resources to bear when it counts.*" The Detroit office has become "*a growing force*" since its inception in 2000, and now numbers over 40 lawyers.

**The Lawyers: Patrick Daugherty** (see p.1133) is "*a highly knowledgeable securities lawyer with a great entrepreneurial spirit.*" His big-ticket deals include advising on the Euro Currency Trust IPO, which involved $2 billion of SEC-registered shares.

**Clients/Work Highlights:** The team acts for major names in the automotive industry as well as financial service firms, health care entities, transportation groups and other general manufacturers.

## Jaffe, Raitt, Heuer & Weiss, PC

**The Firm:** This firm is well known for its strengths in representing midmarket companies, both within Michigan and on a national and international level. Its team has expertise in an array of corporate and transactional matters including joint ventures, corporate governance and contract law. Its clients also benefit from support provided by lawyers from the antitrust, employment and IP groups.

**The Lawyers: Ira Jaffe** is "*a superlative lawyer who is wonderfully effective for clients.*" He has particular expertise working with closely held businesses, where he was applauded for having "*spectacular business acumen, and a real ability to see the bigger picture.*"

**Clients/Work Highlights:** The firm represents a wide range of clients from individuals to multimillion-dollar enterprises. Its clients are drawn from an array of fields, and include automotive companies and financial institutions.

# EMPLOYEE BENEFITS & EXECUTIVE COMPENSATION

## Employee Benefits & Executive Compensation
### Leading Firms

**1** HONIGMAN MILLER SCHWARTZ AND COHN *Detroit*
MILLER, CANFIELD, PADDOCK AND STONE *Detroit*
STEVENSON KEPPELMAN ASSOCIATES *Ann Arbor*

**2** DYKEMA GOSSETT PLLC *Detroit*
GAMBLE, ROSENBERGER & JOSWICK *Bloomfield Hills*
WARNER NORCROSS & JUDD LLP *Grand Rapids*

### Leading Individuals

**1** BRUSTAD Orin *Miller, Canfield, Paddock*
KEPPELMAN Nancy *Stevenson Keppelman*
SIEBERT Sherill *Honigman*
STEVENSON Robert *Stevenson Keppelman*

**2** HUNTER Margaret *Dykema Gossett PLLC*
JOSWICK Theresa *Gamble, Rosenberger*
LARSON Mary Jo *Honigman*
MCKENDRY JR John *Warner Norcross*
THOMPSON Deborah *Miller, Canfield, Paddock*

## Band 1

### Honigman Miller Schwartz and Cohn LLP
See firm details p.1146

**The Firm:** Within the dedicated employee benefits group, six full-time attorneys advise on a range of issues including retirement plans, welfare matters such as health, life and disability insurance, and executive compensation. The team assists midsized to large employers on the design of programs and advises on legal compliance, tax benefits and healthcare provisions. It is also heavily involved in transactional matters and counsels on the employee benefits implications of corporate sales, acquisitions and purchases. Clients were impressed by the group's "*prompt answers and quick response times, which really help facilitate business.*"

**The Lawyers: Sherill Siebert** (see p.1139) advises on all aspects of employee benefits plans and programs including their creation, termination and operation. She also advises clients that sponsor employee benefit plans, and acts for entities that provide services to the plans such as pension, profit-sharing, medical, life and disability arrangements. Peers hold her in high esteem as "*an experienced attorney who is renowned for her fantastic knowledge and ability.*" **Mary Jo Larson** (see p.1137) leads the department and has over 20 years' experience in the field. She is popular among employers who rely on her for advice on the documentation, operation and compliance of their benefit plans.

**Clients/Work Highlights:** The group represents numerous private and public entities, including automotive manufacturers, educational institutions and healthcare companies, such as DaimlerChrysler; HealthPlus of Michigan; Delta Dental Plan of Michigan and Detroit Diesel.

### Miller, Canfield, Paddock and Stone, P.L.C.
See firm details p.1148

**The Firm:** This vibrant group of five lawyers advises on all types of employee benefits work including pension and profit-sharing plans, governmental retirement and deferred compensation plans and employment contracts. Clients also call on the team for advice on all aspects of their welfare plans including healthcare benefits, disability income and childcare reimbursement. The team is particularly adept at assisting employers on the design, establishment and ongoing management of new plans and provides analysis on the impact of new legislation on existing employee benefits programs. Additionally, lawyers also advise on the employee benefits aspects of M&A deals, securities registrations and labor law issues.

**The Lawyers: Orin Brustad** (see p.1133) acts for a mixed roster of public and private sector clients who rate him for his in-depth knowledge of pensions and other benefit plans, and executive compensation. His highlights include acting as an expert witness for the City of Detroit in arbitration concerning pensions schemes. He is also active on a cross-border basis and has advised on pension matters in relation to international corporate transactions. **Deborah Thompson** (see p.1140) is an employee benefits lawyer who is best known for her niche expertise in tax-related matters. She has been especially busy of late advising the firm's clients on changes introduced by Congress and the IRS.

**Clients/Work Highlights:** Lawyers have advised seven state universities on means of controlling the costs of pensions and benefits for their retired employees. The team also advised the Finance Ministry of the Kingdom of Thailand on proposed changes to the country's public and private pension and social security systems. Other clients include Champion Enterprises; Domino's Pizza; Tecumseh Products; Michigan State University; La-Z-Boy; the City of Detroit and Comerica.

### Stevenson Keppelman Associates

**The Firm:** Interviewees report that this boutique firm has "*an outstanding reputation*" for its employee benefits work. Its attorneys have long-standing experience in the field and offer expertise in areas such as retirement plans, ERISA litigation, executive compensation and the employee benefits ramifications of M&A, bankruptcies and workouts. Clients were impressed with "*the streamlined cost-effective service and rapid response*" they received.

**The Lawyers: Nancy Keppelman** specializes in pension and profit-sharing plans, tax planning, employee benefits and ERISA matters. She is a fellow in the American College of Employee Benefits Counsel and is a past member of the Tax Council of the Michigan State Bar. Commentators enthusiastically endorsed her as "*simply one of the state's leading names on pensions and employee benefit matters.*" **Robert Stevenson** advises on a full range of

employee benefits matters, with clients and peers declaring him "*a fantastic adviser.*" His expertise covers employee benefits, pension plans, federal estate and gift taxation, corporate law and tax planning.

**Clients/Work Highlights:** The team's work has included obtaining pension funding waivers, configuring complex executive compensation arrangements and ensuring clients' retirement and welfare benefit plans remain compliant with all applicable laws. Clients include Ford; ThyssenKrupp USA; Henry Ford Health System; Health Alliance Plan; Blue Cross and Blue Shield Association of Michigan; Detroit Medical Center; Sault Ste. Marie Tribe of Chippewa Indians and Comerica.

## Band 2

### Dykema Gossett PLLC

**The Firm:** This team of seven attorneys handles all manner of employee benefits matters including pension, profit-sharing, severance and medical plans. The team also advises on a spectrum of welfare initiatives such as disability benefits, insured and uninsured medical benefit programs, life insurance and death benefit programs. The group's expertise also extends into the areas of executive and stock compensation issues and incentive plans.

**The Lawyers: Margaret Hunter** leads the employee benefits practice group, and was recommended to researchers as "*a state-renowned expert in the field.*" She advises on the design, implementation and administration of pension plans, welfare plans and executive compensation arrangements. Her workload also includes advising on employee benefits issues in the context of M&A.

**Clients/Work Highlights:** The team acts for major public, nonprofit and governmental employers, as well as some of Michigan's most significant private companies, which are drawn from a wide range of industries.

### Gamble, Rosenberger & Joswick LLP

**The Firm:** This specialist tax and employee benefits boutique has steadily grown since its inception in the mid-nineties and now numbers six attorneys. Its lawyers assist on the design and implementation of retirement and welfare benefit plans, as well as executive compensation arrangements. Interviewees also pointed to the group's skill in counseling on the tax and benefits aspects of corporate transactions and its advice on fiduciary matters.

**The Lawyers: Theresa Joswick** has over 28 years of experience in the areas of ERISA, employee benefits and executive compensation. She has recently helped a number of nonprofit agencies to disaffiliate from their multiemployer plans and advised them on the establishment of their own programs, thus giving them control of their costs, assets and investments.

**Clients/Work Highlights:** The team represents clients of all sizes, including automotive companies and suppliers, banks, insurance companies and nonprofit companies such as hospitals and local governments.

### Warner Norcross & Judd LLP

**The Firm:** This west Michigan firm won recommendations for the breadth of its practice. The group's remit stretches from the design and preparation of retirement plans to corporate and individual income tax planning. Its lawyers also represent clients in administrative proceedings and litigation before the IRS, the DOL and various state and federal courts.

**The Lawyers:** From among a team of around nine lawyers, the chair of the group, **John McKendry**, stood out for his "*exceptional knowledge of retirement pension plans.*" He is also a popular figure among trade and professional associations who call on him for assistance on an array of employee benefits issues.

**Clients/Work Highlights:** The team acts for a wide variety of clients from the public and private sectors and has a following among companies from the footwear and financial industries. Key clients include Wolverine World Wide and Muskegon Surgical Associates.

# EMPLOYMENT

# MAINLY DEFENDANT

## Employment: Mainly Defendant
### Leading Firms

| | |
|---|---|
| 1 | **KIENBAUM OPPERWALL HARDY** *Birmingham* |
| | **MILLER, CANFIELD, PADDOCK AND STONE** *Detroit* |
| 2 | **BRADY HATHAWAY BRADY & BRETZ** *Detroit* |
| | **BUTZEL LONG** *Detroit* |
| | **DICKINSON WRIGHT PLLC** *Detroit* |
| | **DYKEMA GOSSETT PLLC** *Detroit* |
| | **MILLER JOHNSON** *Grand Rapids* |
| | **VARNUM, RIDDERING, SCHMIDT** *Grand Rapids* |
| | **VERCRUYSSE MURRAY & CALZONE** *Bingham Farms* |
| 3 | **CLARK HILL PLC** *Detroit* |
| | **HONIGMAN MILLER SCHWARTZ AND COHN** *Detroit* |
| | **WARNER NORCROSS & JUDD LLP** *Grand Rapids* |

### Leading Individuals

| | |
|---|---|
| ★ | **KIENBAUM** Thomas *Kienbaum Opperwall Hardy* |
| 1 | **BRETZ** Daniel *Brady Hathaway Brady* |
| | **GIVENS** Leonard *Miller, Canfield, Paddock* |
| | **RITOK** Joseph *Dykema Gossett PLLC* |
| | **VERCRUYSSE** Robert *Vercruysse Murray* |
| 2 | **BARNES** Thomas *Varnum, Riddering, Schmidt* |
| | **CALZONE** David *Vercruysse Murray* |
| | **DICKSON** Andrea *Butzel Long* |
| | **HANCOCK JR** John *Butzel Long* |
| | **HARDY** Elizabeth *Kienbaum Opperwall Hardy* |
| | **HOWLETT** Timothy *Dickinson Wright PLLC* |
| | **MARCH** Jon *Miller Johnson* |
| | **MURPHY** Lawrence *Varnum, Riddering, Schmidt* |
| | **MURRAY** Gregory *Vercruysse Murray* |
| | **NORRIS** Megan *Miller, Canfield, Paddock* |
| | **OPPERWALL** Theodore *Kienbaum Opperwall Hardy* |
| | **SARGENT** William *Honigman* |
| | **SERYAK** Richard *Miller, Canfield, Paddock* |
| 3 | **BATTEN** Fred *Clark Hill PLC* |
| | **DONATI** Donna *Miller, Canfield, Paddock* |
| | **HATHAWAY** Thomas *Brady Hathaway Brady* |
| | **KHOREY** David *Varnum, Riddering, Schmidt* |
| | **NIEHOFF** Leonard *Butzel Long* |
| | **WATSON** Jerome *Miller, Canfield, Paddock* |

### Up-and-coming individuals

| | |
|---|---|
| | **THELEN** James *Miller, Canfield, Paddock* |

## Band 1

### Kienbaum Opperwall Hardy & Pelton P.L.C.
See firm details p.1147

**The Firm:** "*One of the best boutiques around,*" this prominent team wins applause for the caliber of its lawyers, who are "*all specialists in their own right.*" It is well known for its strengths in general employment law but is also in high demand for its traditional labor law expertise. The group has been busy acting for clients in a series of sexual harassment and race discrimination cases but also counsels on personnel policies and employment contracts. Clients admire the group's ability "*to muster its resources quickly, and to compete successfully with the larger firms, without any of the inherent complications.*"

**The Lawyers:** The team now numbers around 18 lawyers and includes several individuals who have previously served in-house at large corporations. **Thomas Kienbaum** (see p.1136) was unanimously recommended as one of the state's most accomplished trial lawyers and was the "*obvious top choice*" among peers. He is widely regarded as the dean of the employment Bar, and is frequently engaged in high-profile cases. Researchers heard that he is "*a brilliant strategist who can unravel the most difficult problems — even those that are seemingly irresolvable.*" **Elizabeth Hardy** (see p.1135) has handled several sexual harassment cases before the Michigan Supreme Court in recent times. She also acts as outside labor law counsel to Honigman Miller and devotes part of her time to the niche area of election law, where she has acted for a mayoral candidate. She has earned a reputation in the market as someone who "*is not afraid to take on the difficult cases and who consistently represents top clients.*" **Theodore Opperwall** (see p.1138) "*walks on water*" for his clients. He is a labor law specialist who is a former member of the NLRB. His caseload includes appellant work, labor law arbitrations and collective bargaining. He has an international slant to his practice and has acted for a number of Canadian automotive companies. Clients enjoy working with him because "*he can simplify an issue and present it in a compelling and forceful way.*"

**Clients/Work Highlights:** One of the firm's largest clients is Ford, which lawyers have represented in a series of race-related cases. It also acts for Eaton Corporation; Comcast; Avis; Budget Rent a Car; Alamo; Detroit Edison and Ilitch Holdings.

### Miller, Canfield, Paddock and Stone, P.L.C.
See firm details p.1148

**The Firm:** This is one of the largest labor and employment groups in Michigan with around 30 lawyers, giving the team "*the depth of talent to handle matters at any level.*" It is widely regarded as a leading authority in the labor and employment arena and is the designated Michigan firm in the Employment Law Alliance, an international network of leading labor and employment attorneys. The group's workload includes defending clients against various discrimination and harassment suits before state and federal courts and the EEOC. It has a strong labor law component that encompasses strikes, union elections and reductions in force. Lawyers are also actively involved in academic publishing and are frequent speakers on changes in employment law.

**The Lawyers:** **Leonard Givens** (see p.1134) is co-head of the practice, and a leading figure in traditional labor relations. Some of his time is also devoted to employment litigation and interviewees warmly described him as someone with "*a wonderful breadth of experience, who really understands the bigger picture.*" **Megan Norris** (see p.1138) is the other co-leader of the group and is "*one of the best litigators out there,*" according to sources, who believe her "*common sense and practical approach to employment law issues give her the edge.*" Although she represents employers in a range of cases, she is best known for her expertise in disabilities work. **Richard Seryak** (see p.1139) is a traditional labor relations expert who advises on contracts negotiation, union and collective bargaining and arbitration. His client base has a strong public sector component to it and he is frequently involved in Detroit public school matters and university cases. Commentators tipped him as "*one of the most studious and respectable litigators. He takes a cautious approach and is always most concerned about protecting his client.*" **Donna Donati** (see p.1134) is a tenacious employment litigator who handles discrimination and harassment files for both private and public clients, including schools and universities. Peers remarked "*If you have a very tough case in court, you want her; she can stand up to anybody.*" Interviewees heaped praise on **Jerome Watson** (see p.1140) for his "*amazing skills in front of the judge.*" His practice includes representing employers in wrongful discharge, defamation and discrimination cases. In a recent high-profile matter, he acted for Detroit Edison in a single-plaintiff action, alleging race, age and sex discrimination and harassment. He also acted for a major airline in a national origin discrimination case, brought by an employee claiming to be the victim of wrongful treatment after 9/11. **James Thelen** (see p.1140) is "*a rising star*," and head of the firm's Lansing office. He acts for clients in employment litigation but also counsels them on disciplinary matters, terminations, traditional labor work, collective bargaining and writing employment handbooks.

**Clients/Work Highlights:** Lawyers successfully acted for a large western Michigan employer in two major labor arbitrations in which the unions challenged various outsourcings and privatizations. The team also successfully represented a national retailer against an organizing petition by the Teamsters. Other matters include defending the Lansing School District in a lawsuit that challenges the constitutionality of a special education funding provision of Michigan's schools-of-choice law.

## Band 2

### Brady Hathaway Brady & Bretz

See firm details p.1142

**The Firm:** This specialist boutique firm is home to nine seasoned attorneys who advise on a spectrum of labor and employment matters. The team focuses primarily on employer representation and advises clients on union-organizing campaigns, collective bargaining agreements and employment contracts. On the employment law side, lawyers defend clients against claims of discrimination and harassment, and advise on trade secret, noncompete and wage and hour matters. Competitors view this as a team of "*very fine people who I'd be happy referring clients to in a conflict situation.*"

**The Lawyers:** **Daniel Bretz** (see p.1132) has a mixed labor and employment practice and was recommended to researchers as "*a leading light among litigators.*" His recent highlights include several significant victories over unions against claims of wrongful discharge and breach of contract. **Thomas Hathaway** (see p.1135) "*is a powerful rainmaker for the firm*" who has handled a number of whistle-blower and age discrimination cases. He is currently acting in a high-stakes labor matter for the County of Wayne in which up to $6 million is at stake.

**Clients/Work Highlights:** Lawyers advised Tiffany on an age discrimination case brought by its former director of sales, and represented an individual sued by their employer in relation to a noncompete agreement. The team also advised on the reorganization of a hospital and the related layoffs.

### Butzel Long

See firm details p.1143

**The Firm:** With around 50 attorneys, this is one of the largest labor and employment departments in Michigan. Researchers heard that the firm has always enjoyed a strong reputation for work in this area and

has a knack of attracting big-ticket cases. It focuses heavily on the automotive area, with around half its workload being for clients within this industry. Labor law specialists advise on collective bargaining, union election campaigns and strikes. Interviewees also recommended the team for the quality of its employment law advice and rated it as a leading destination for guidance on immigration law.

**The Lawyers:** **Andrea Roumell Dickson** (see p.1134) is cochair of the labor and employment department and has been particularly busy of late acting for clients in a growing number of reverse discrimination lawsuits. She is "*politically well connected*" and won special recognition for her counseling skills and practical approach to litigation. **John Hancock**'s (see p.1134) clients call on him for both his traditional labor law expertise and his success in employment litigation. He is a "*top-class*" practitioner who has been involved in a number of cases concerning plant closures and is handling ongoing litigation for some of the firm's most long-standing clients. **Leonard Niehoff** (see p.1138) is "*a smooth litigator*" who combines employment work with a specialization in First Amendment work for a large Detroit newspaper. He has acted for the University of Michigan in a class action affirmative action case, which challenged the university's admissions process.

**Clients/Work Highlights:** The firm advises a large number of businesses in such areas as the automotive industry, the hospitality trade, and preeminent state educational institutions. Clients include MGM Grand; the University of Michigan; Michigan Technological University and Marriott Hotels.

### Dickinson Wright PLLC

See firm details p.1145

**The Firm:** Interviewees recommended this group as a full-service labor and employment practice. It has a team of around 30 lawyers who have developed specializations in employment litigation and counseling, union-related work and arbitrations. It has been especially busy acting for employers in union drives and assisting several major automotive suppliers in the negotiation of collective bargaining agreements. The team's other areas of expertise include employee benefits and immigration law.

**The Lawyers:** **Timothy Howlett** (see p.1135) is the chair of the group, and an employment litigator with over 30 years of experience. His practice reflects the current distressed local economy, this year involving much counseling of clients on reductions, and the possible consequences thereof. In litigation matters, his biggest proceeding was a Sarbanes-Oxley whistle-blower case with claims in both state and federal courts. Other cases have included numerous discrimination claims, on the basis of gender, age and race. He was applauded by clients for being "*solid, thoughtful, cerebral and bright; always ahead of trends in the field.*"

**Clients/Work Highlights:** The firm's clients have included some of the most significant names in a number of industries, such as Kmart; Borders Group; Carhartt; Magna International and the University of Michigan.

### Dykema Gossett PLLC

**The Firm:** This group has a strong employment law profile in Michigan but can also call on additional resources from its offices in Chicago and Los Angeles. It represents a broad cross section of private and public sector clients across the Midwest and offers comprehensive employment law advice including litigation support and preventive counseling. Its experts also specialize in traditional labor law, civil rights work and employee benefits.

**The Lawyers:** Interviewees identified **Joseph Ritok** as the leading light of this team of 30 lawyers. He advises clients throughout the USA on traditional labor work and devotes approximately half his time to litigation, although he is also well regarded for his mediation skills. He is popular with clients because "*he walks into negotiations and always ends up getting more than we'd even hoped for.*"

**Clients/Work Highlights:** Eastern Michigan University; UPS; Rite Aid; LaSalle Bank; Citigroup; Marshall Field's; Parking Company of America; Valero; Bank One and Ann Arbor Public Schools.

### Miller Johnson

**The Firm:** A broad range of clients from the private and public sectors flock to the firm for its advice on traditional union-related labor work and for its employment litigation and counseling service. The group's niche areas of strength include defense of wrongful discharge claims and allegations of harassment. Its expertise in other matters such as employment contracts, wage and hour questions and employee benefit disputes led commentators to declare it "*one of the most preeminent teams in the west of the state.*"

**The Lawyers:** **Jon March**'s litigation caseload includes general commercial, construction and employment disputes. He is also a respected mediator who has handled wrongful discharge cases and employment law disputes alleging age, race, gender and national origin discrimination.

**Clients/Work Highlights:** The team serves private and public sector employers, including several from Fortune 500 companies. It acts for automotive parts manufacturers, school districts, universities and municipalities.

### Varnum, Riddering, Schmidt & Howlett LLP

See firm details p.1149

**The Firm:** Principally located in the west of the state, the group has recently opened an office in Novi, just outside metropolitan Detroit, giving it greater access to the east of the state. This office is staffed primarily by labor lawyers and has boosted its profile among large industrial players based there. Indeed, the team is increasingly being retained by larger, more nationally-based companies because of its "*excellent structure and the superior quality of its lawyers.*"

**The Lawyers:** Researchers heard that **Thomas Barnes** (see p.1132) is a leading traditional labor law expert and "*definitely the guy you'd call for help on a complex problem.*" He advises on union-organizing campaigns, particularly those involving the police and fire services, and frequently acts for employers in arbitration cases. **Lawrence Murphy** (see p.1137) is a respected employment law specialist who has handled cases in states stretching from New York to Nebraska. His clients include several Fortune 500 companies that increasingly call on him for his skill in mediations. **David Khorey** (see p.1136) is the chair of the labor group and has devoted much of his time lately to advising on the labor law implications of public sector privatizations. Observers described him as a "*thoughtful and profound lawyer who is a good advocate for his clients.*"

**Clients/Work Highlights:** The team successfully defended DaimlerChrysler against a sexual harassment case and acted for another major client in a series of actions brought in response to the closure of a large manufacturing plant and the transfer of production to China.

### Vercruysse Murray & Calzone, PC

See firm details p.1150

**The Firm:** Since its inception ten years ago, this boutique labor and employment firm has established itself as a key player in the market. The group now numbers about 17 attorneys and has expanded its practice to include immigration law as well as commercial and business-related litigation. Its lawyers attracted praise for their depth of talent and skills in a range of labor and employment law issues and have earned themselves a strong local and national reputation.

**The Lawyers:** **Robert Vercruysse** (see p.1140) combines an active employment discrimination defense practice with expertise in negotiating collective bargaining agreements and other labor law-related matters. This tough attorney is a firm favorite with clients who confided: "*He's someone I trust and who provides us with really good service and advice.*" His colleague, **David Calzone** (see p.1133), was also a popular choice among interviewees. He advises on the full range of employment law but is best known as a leading authority on the FMLA. According to satisfied clients, **Gregory Murray** (see p.1138) is "*unfailingly polite and considerate and is all you could*

*want in a litigator.*" Clients also choose him for his excellent negotiating skills and his ability to help resolve issues before they reach court.

**Clients/Work Highlights:** Lawyers act for prominent companies both in Michigan and nationwide, including DaimlerChrysler; Comerica; Philip Morris; Home Depot and Henry Ford Health System.

### Band 3

### Clark Hill PLC

See firm details p.1144

**The Firm:** The labor and employment group consists of 20 attorneys who represent private, public and nonprofit employers in a variety of union and employment law matters. Its recent workload has been heavy with a spate of discrimination cases, wrongful discharges, wage and hour questions and ERISA claims. The team has the resources to represent employers in multiplaintiff and class actions in federal and state courts.

**The Lawyers:** With over 30 years' experience in the area, **Fred Batten** specializes in representing Fortune 500 companies and other corporate clients in all manner of union negotiations, arbitrations and litigation. Clients have called on him to advise on reductions in force, plant closings and relocations, outsourcing and reallocating health care costs.

**Clients/Work Highlights:** The firm is general counsel to two Michigan employer associations and advises a wide range of businesses, including those from the automotive, chemical, steel, financial, construction and health care industries. Other clients include manufacturers, distributors and retailers, units of government and nonprofit organizations.

### Honigman Miller Schwartz and Cohn LLP

See firm details p.1146

**The Firm:** This is a rapidly expanding department, which now numbers 18 lawyers. The group represents employers from both the public and private sectors and offers expertise in traditional labor-related matters, including proceedings before the NLRB. The team also has a successful track record in a range of employment discrimination cases and also assists clients on litigation avoidance. Work here includes advising on personnel policies, compliance, employment contracts and employee benefits programs.

**The Lawyers:** **William Sargent** (see p.1139) is the department head and has developed a wide-ranging labor and employment practice that includes trade secret matters, discrimination cases, wrongful discharge and collective bargaining agreements. Much of his time is devoted to complex out-of-state work including multiplaintiff cases. Clients warmly described him as "*a great sounding-board, thanks to his wonderful combination of business and legal judgment.*"

**Clients/Work Highlights:** The team advises companies from the financial services, automotive industry, construction and broadcasting sectors. Clients include Fox Broadcasting; Capital Cities/ABC; Viacom International; Quicken Loans; Pulte Homes and Delta Dental Plan of Michigan.

### Warner Norcross & Judd LLP

**The Firm:** This team has gained a strong reputation in western Michigan, where it represents a wide range of local and statewide businesses. Union-related matters account for much of the group's time, with clients calling on the team for advice on organizational questions, collective bargaining negotiations and labor law litigation and arbitration. Employment law is another strong facet of the practice. The recent caseload has included a variety of discrimination suits and wrongful discharge claims. Lawyers also advise clients on OSHA compliance.

# LITIGATION

### Band 1

### Butzel Long

See firm details p.1143

**The Firm:** One of Michigan's heavyweight litigation practices, this firm has expanded its operations beyond the state borders and has domestic offices in Florida and Washington, DC and international operations in China, Canada and Mexico. This has allowed it to penetrate different markets and to profit from the resulting inbound work from foreign companies. Interviewees continue to rate it as a broad and robust practice that acts for clients in a spectrum of litigation and alternative dispute resolution proceedings. In recent times, employment and

IP litigation have featured highly on the caseload.

**The Lawyers:** **Philip Kessler** (see p.1136) is a senior litigator with an active commercial practice that includes a broad array of cases before the supreme and federal courts. His workload includes many IP and patent infringement claims, particularly in relation to the pharmaceutical industry. He has also been involved in stockholder litigation in relation to a squeeze-out and acted for a client in a case concerning claims of improper interpretation of a pension plan. **Richard Rassel** (see p.1138) is chairman of the firm and has a long history as a commercial litigator. He focuses on media law, including libel actions, and has represented a number of prominent media clients. **Edward Kronk** (see p.1136) "*is a smart, ethi-*

*cal and fiercely competitive lawyer*" whose commercial litigation practice centers on products liability defense. Recent work includes tort cases and trade secrets matters as well as a number of arbitration and mediation matters. Peers applauded him for his "*fine blend of intelligence, practical skills and creativity.*" **David DuMouchel** (see p.1134) "*will fight hard but within the rules.*" He is best known for his white-collar work and concentrates on high-profile criminal defense. Clients esteem him as "*a well-connected and preeminent figure in the field.*"

**Clients/Work Highlights:** Lawyers have handled a number of cases for Johnson Controls in the Supreme Court and federal court including a case against a supplier and another against Lear in

Chicago. Other clients include the University of Michigan and the Michigan Press Association.

## Dickinson Wright PLLC

See firm details p.1145

**The Firm:** This is one of Michigan's leading full-service law firms, with offices throughout the state, as well as in Washington, DC. The group comes highly recommended for its prowess in litigation and all forms of alternative dispute resolution and is regarded as *"a standout firm at the forefront of the market."* Its substantial team handles a varied caseload and has niche expertise in areas such as business

and criminal investigations, labor and employment litigation and products liability.

**The Lawyers: Lawrence Campbell** (see p.1133) is *"a go-to trial lawyer"* whose recent work has included a large case concerning the disputed purchase of a business and several major contract cases for SBC. He has been involved in a number of complex commercial arbitrations in Detroit but is best known as a *"highly visible and aggressive litigator, who tries and wins many cases."* **John Scott** (see p.1139) specializes in products liability defense, personal injury and commercial tort cases. He is particularly well known for his work on behalf of the automotive industry and is one of the senior names in the litigation Bar, warmly recommended to researchers as *"a wonderful teacher and lecturer."* Interviewees said that **Edward Pappas** (see p.1138) *"has a great courtroom presence – he's effective with judges and is a calming influence."* His expertise centers on trade secret and noncompete cases, real estate disputes and business torts.

**Clients/Work Highlights:** The team acted in conjunction with a large Chicago-based firm in a software contract case for IDX, which involved a six-week trial. Other clients include JPMorgan Chase; SBC; Chrysler; Ford; Lear; Magna and Northwest Airlines.

## Honigman Miller Schwartz and Cohn LLP

See firm details p.1146

**The Firm:** This is one of the largest litigation departments in Michigan, comprising over 50 lawyers who act for clients in all areas of commercial litigation. It is renowned for its performances in the most significant and complex of cases and is especially adept in representing troubled companies. Well known throughout the USA, clients believe that *"the skill, knowledge and ability of these attorneys make Honigman the natural choice for companies looking for litigation support in Michigan."*

**The Lawyers: Joseph Aviv** (see p.1132) is a towering figure in the field of corporate litigation, where he focuses on stockholder disputes, often of closely held corporations, and issues regarding alleged fraudulent practices. **Norman Ankers** (see p.1132) is chair of the litigation department and specializes in class actions, IP litigation, including trademark and copyright disputes, and securities cases. He recently defended a large pharmaceutical company against a punitive class action relating to one of its products. **Raymond Henney** (see p.1135) is a securities litigation and class action expert who represents many of Detroit's large brokerage houses. His recent cases include a stockholder dispute and ongoing litigation between two Fortune 100 companies. **Richard Zuckerman** (see p.1140) was roundly recommended as *"a top name in white-collar crime litigation."* He is a former prosecutor with the DOJ who now defends individuals and large companies in investigations before bodies such as the SEC.

**Clients/Work Highlights:** Lawyers have secured favorable results for Taubman in two class actions and represented homeowners in arbitration relating

to houses built by a major Detroit developer. Other clients include Philip Morris, Hewlett-Packard, and other major companies throughout the USA.

## Miller, Canfield, Paddock and Stone, P.L.C.

See firm details p.1148

**The Firm:** With around 100 lawyers in the commercial litigation department, this group commands respect from the market. The team *"has the depth and talent to handle any dispute on any level,"* and has expertise in areas such as tort defense, tax litigation and trade secret and noncompete matters. In recent times the group has witnessed an increase in international cases, with attorneys representing a growing number of Canadian clients and acting in cases with filings in multiple jurisdictions. The firm has responded to the recent spate of government investigations through the establishment of its corporate discovery management team, which assists clients with all their discovery needs.

**The Lawyers:** One peer conceded: *"If I were being sued, I'd use* **Carl von Ende** (see p.1140)." He has a wide-ranging portfolio of cases to his name including banking, securities, construction, IP and real estate disputes. One satisfied client described him as *"the consummate trial lawyer. He's first class in everything he does."* **Clarence Pozza** (see p.1138) is *"a preeminent trial lawyer and the leading player in securities litigation in Michigan."* He also focuses on broker-dealer work and products liability cases, where he has acted for Chrysler in a number of cases concerning its Jeeps. **Gregory Curtner** (see p.1133) *"is a major national figure in sports and entertainment cases,"* and is well known for his long-standing representation of the National Collegiate Athletic Association. His work has taken him all over the country and has included cases such as a 47-day trial concerning the safety of aluminum baseball bats and a case in Philadelphia over alleged abuse in summer sports camps. **Thomas Cranmer** (see p.1133) is a highly respected white-collar criminal defense lawyer who represents companies and individuals who are subject to SEC scrutiny, criminal prosecutions and ongoing investigations. He also handles some commercial litigation cases and has recently been elected president of the State Bar of Michigan.

**Clients/Work Highlights:** Lawyers acted for Henry Ford Health System in Detroit in a number of disputes arising out of the acquisition of new businesses. Other clients include Merrill Lynch, as well as several colleges and sports associations.

## Band 2

## Barris, Sott, Denn & Driker, PLLC

**The Firm:** This smaller, closely knit firm has a heavy emphasis on business litigation. The team takes on a spectrum of cases, including products liability defense, real estate, construction and antitrust disputes. The group has an active alternative dispute resolution practice and is home to a number of well-respected arbitration and mediation experts. It also has a flourishing appellate practice and is renowned for the caliber of its trial attorneys.

**The Lawyers: Eugene Driker** "*is the premier business guy in Michigan.*" Interviewees repeatedly referred to him as the dean of the litigation Bar and pointed to his involvement in some of the largest and most significant cases, including securities and antitrust disputes. He has also been called upon to advise on professional liability cases and partnership dissolution matters on behalf of other lawyers and law firms. Clients and peers alike praised his "*wonderful presence,*" and said: "*He walks into the courtroom and judges immediately sit up and take notice.*" **Sharon Woods** chairs the firm's management committee and litigation department. Her clients call on her for her expertise in complex litigation, including IP, employment, securities cases and professional malpractice defense.

**Clients/Work Highlights:** Lawyers act for large automotive manufacturers such as Ford and GM. Other key clients include Michigan Consolidated Gas Company, the State of Michigan and the City of Detroit.

## Bodman LLP

See firm details p.1141

**The Firm:** This is a diverse litigation group comprising around 40 attorneys. The team has built up a loyal and diverse client base that includes automotive manufacturers, insurance companies and sports associations. The firm is particularly renowned for its banking practice and its representation of financial institutions, and this is reflected in the high volume of banking litigation matters that it handles. Work here includes bankruptcy litigation and lender liability suits. Lawyers also have a strong track record in other areas such as healthcare, construction and professional liability litigation.

**Clients/Work Highlights:** Lawyers represented the Detroit Lions in a major arbitration over delays in the construction of their new 65,000-seat stadium, which resulted in a $9 million award for the client. The team, led by Thomas Tallerico, also represented Comerica in a significant international case against a failed Brazilian bank, involving claims of fraud, breach of contract and fiduciary duty. Other cases have included defense of lender liability claims, and work on behalf of advertising and entertainment companies, such as Viacom.

## Dykema Gossett PLLC

**The Firm:** With over 160 lawyers in the litigation group based throughout the firm's offices in the Midwest, this full-service firm has the resources to act in big-ticket cases on a national level. The general litigation practice is divided into subgroups, covering all areas of dispute resolution, and includes a trial lawyer team. Its flourishing arbitration group reflects the growing trend of resolving matters without recourse to a full jury trial.

**The Lawyers: Dennis Haffey** is the firmwide head of litigation, whose caseload covers disputes concerning stockholder rights and failed corporate transactions as well as some arbitration work. Peers

admire him for being "*good on his feet, tastefully aggressive, and adept in presenting a case.*" He has recently been busy defending clients against a number of nationwide products liability claims. **James Feeney** is hired nationwide for "*the toughest of cases,*" and is particularly in demand for his defense of automotive companies in liability suits and class actions. Observers remarked: "*His well-earned reputation as a dedicated trial lawyer has really put him on the map.*"

**Clients/Work Highlights:** The team successfully resolved litigation that had run for several years concerning the purchase of Tampa Bay Lightning. Its other major clients include Ford, GM and Daimler-Chrysler.

## Band 3

## Kerr Russell & Weber

**The Firm:** Although this group is smaller than some of its competitors, it nonetheless continues to handle significant cases on a statewide basis. Its diverse caseload includes personal injury, professional defense and products liability disputes before both federal and state courts. Lawyers here are respected for their trial expertise, but are also accomplished in arbitration and mediation proceedings.

**The Lawyers: William Sankbeil** "*is a terrific lawyer with an excellent courtroom presence.*" He cochairs the firm's litigation practice group and won special recognition for his antitrust expertise and sophisticated work at the federal level. Clients also recommended him for his skill in securities, IP and stockholder disputes.

**Clients/Work Highlights:** The team acts for a wide range of clients including private and publicly held companies, trade and professional organizations, stockholder groups and corporate boards and executives.

## Miller Johnson

**The Firm:** This is a western Michigan firm of around 90 lawyers, many of whom practice in the litigation department. The team is home to "*an admirable number of talented negotiators,*" which affords it "*a wonderful ability to solve disputes without needing to always resort to courtroom proceedings.*" Its varied portfolio of cases includes acting for clients in real estate disputes, IP, construction and antitrust disputes.

**The Lawyers:** Interviewees consistently recommended **Jon Muth** as "*one of the best arbitrators in the state.*" He is a former president of the state Bar who is famed for his mediation skills and his success in complex cases. Researchers also heard that he is "*an excellent litigator*" with the scope to handle a spectrum of cases.

**Clients/Work Highlights:** The team represents a large number of major national and international corporations, local and regional businesses, high net worth individuals and local entrepreneurs.

## Varnum, Riddering, Schmidt & Howlett LLP

See firm details p.1149

**The Firm:** This firm's litigation group comprises over 30 lawyers who are engaged in an array of local and national litigation. The group's work centers on commercial disputes, including securities, antitrust, real estate and products liability litigation. The team also works in conjunction with lawyers from other departments within the firm and has secured a string of victories for clients embroiled in trademark, copyright and patent suits, personal injury cases and labor and employment matters.

**The Lawyers: Richard Kay** (see p.1136) is "*a worthy adversary, who always puts up an excellent fight.*" He is one of the senior partners in the trial practice group and has a particularly impressive track record in products liability matters, construction disputes and employment litigation.

**Clients/Work Highlights:** The group acts for a number of national companies, such as Kellogg and Chrysler, and also counts several financial, healthcare and Michigan-based educational institutions amongst its clients.

## Warner Norcross & Judd LLP

**The Firm:** With offices in Detroit and Grand Rapids, this firm's litigation practice is adept at a spectrum of commercial disputes. The team numbers around 48 litigators, accounting for nearly one-third of the entire firm. Its lawyers have been especially busy of late representing several automotive parts suppliers in price disputes over steel and other commodities. The group represents clients in state and federal courts and also has experience in white-collar crime cases, in addition to environmental and employment disputes.

**The Lawyers: Douglas Dozeman** focuses on IP disputes including patent infringement cases and trademark and copyright litigation. He handled a high-profile patent litigation case for a vision technology manufacturer and acted in a trade secret theft case for the Blue Care Network of Michigan.

**Clients/Work Highlights:** The litigation group has attracted a varied roster of clients including national corporations, Michigan-based entities and smaller partnerships.

## Young & Susser PC Attorneys and Counselors

**The Firm:** This specialist litigation boutique was founded in 1991 and has since established itself as a dynamic outfit, capable of advising on a range of cases. It has offices in Southfield, Michigan and New York City and attracts an ever-expanding client base of both local and national clients. It fields lean and aggressive teams of lawyers who handle high-profile commercial cases, including antitrust, trade secrets and automotive industry disputes.

**The Lawyers: Rodger Young** has experience in large and complex commercial disputes, both within Michigan and beyond. Commentators were impressed by his "*solid track record*" and "*flamboyant, aggressive style.*"

**Clients/Work Highlights:** The team represents a number of automotive suppliers, as well as real estate brokers, manufacturers and accounting institutions. Other clients include Philip Morris; Siemens; AstraZeneca and Pullman Industries.

## Other Notable Practitioners

Market commentators agree that **John Trentacosta** (see p.1140) of Foley & Lardner LLP "*is a phenomenal litigator.*" He is cochair of the firm's automotive industry team and focuses on resolving disputes within this area, particularly those between suppliers

and manufacturers. Clients appreciate his "*savvy advice and careful navigation through complex disputes,*" and praised him for his deep auto industry knowledge, "*which is a rare commodity when packaged with such litigation skills.*"

# REAL ESTATE

| Real Estate |
|---|
| **Leading Firms** |
| **1** HONIGMAN MILLER SCHWARTZ AND COHN *Detroit* |
| MILLER, CANFIELD, PADDOCK AND STONE *Detroit* |
| **2** DAWDA, MANN, MULCAHY *Bloomfield Hills* |
| DICKINSON WRIGHT PLLC *Detroit* |
| DYKEMA GOSSETT PLLC *Detroit* |
| **3** BARRIS, SOTT, DENN & DRIKER, PLLC *Detroit* |
| BUTZEL LONG *Detroit* |
| CLARK HILL PLC *Detroit* |
| JAFFE, RAITT, HEUER & WEISS, PC *Detroit* |
| KERR RUSSELL & WEBER *Detroit* |
| MADDIN, HAUSER, WARTELL, ROTH *Southfield* |

| Leading Individuals |
|---|
| **1** BROMBERG Stephen *Butzel Long* |
| DAWDA Edward *Dawda, Mann, Mulcahy* |
| DUNN William *Clark Hill PLC* |
| MCLAUGHLIN Lawrence *Honigman* |
| **2** BARRIS William *Barris, Sott, Denn & Driker, PLLC* |
| BURSTEIN Richard *Honigman* |
| CANDLER James *Dickinson Wright PLLC* |
| DAWSON Stephen *Dickinson Wright PLLC* |
| HODESS Ronald *Miller, Canfield, Paddock* |
| MADDIN Michael *Maddin, Hauser, Wartell* |
| SALESIN Lowell *Maddin, Hauser, Wartell* |
| SIMPSON James *Miller, Canfield, Paddock* |
| ZUSSMAN Richard *Jaffe, Raitt, Heuer* |
| **3** ADAMS James *Dykema Gossett PLLC* |
| KOLTUN Timothy *Clark Hill PLC* |
| LEWIS Denise *Honigman* |
| MULCAHY Michael *Dawda, Mann, Mulcahy* |
| NIX II Robert *Kerr Russell & Weber* |
| PIGGOTT Cameron *Dykema Gossett PLLC* |
| WINOKUR Laurence *Dickinson Wright PLLC* |

| Up-and-coming individuals |
|---|
| LENNON J Patrick *Miller, Canfield, Paddock* |
| ZELENOCK Katheryne *Miller, Canfield, Paddock* |

## Band 1

### Honigman Miller Schwartz and Cohn LLP

See firm details p.1146

**The Firm:** This is one of the premier real estate firms in the Midwest and enjoys an excellent reputation for its handling of the largest and most complex trans-

actions. The group covers all aspects of real estate, including financings, related environmental matters and tax aspects, and acts for an impressive stable of clients comprising major corporations and developers. The team continues to expand in the wake of the arrival of lawyers from Miro Weiner & Kramer late in 2004 and has attracted a number of new clients to its doors. Lawyers are increasingly active on a national basis and have undertaken projects for mall developers in a number of states.

**The Lawyers: Lawrence McLaughlin** (see p.1137) chairs the real estate group and specializes in complex retail and urban development transactions. This year he has handled two major regional shopping center disposals and advised on the acquisition of a 28-shopping center portfolio, worth in excess of $100 million. Other projects include working on the Detroit Riverfront Conservancy, which is an $80 million project to redevelop a three-mile section of the Detroit River. **Richard Burstein** (see p.1133) is renowned for his transactional prowess and handles major development projects countrywide. He has also been busy representing a number of the firm's largest clients in complex financings of office buildings and retail centers. He is a popular figure who has "*a magical combination of great lawyer skills and an excellent business mind.*" **Denise Lewis** (see p.1137) has national and international components to her practice. She acts for a Canadian company that has real estate interests across the USA, and has recently advised a Detroit-based developer on the divestiture of one of its manufacturing facilities in Africa. Her Michigan-based work includes urban reinvestment and redevelopment, such as the conversion of office buildings into residential condominium units.

**Clients/Work Highlights:** Lawyers assisted on the development and construction of a new $350 million headquarters building for Compuware and advised on the renovation of GM's world headquarters building. The group's workload also included advising on the development of the $600 million rail and truck tunnel under the Detroit River. Other major clients for the firm include Ramco-Gershenson Properties Trust and Taubman Centers.

### Miller, Canfield, Paddock and Stone, P.L.C.

See firm details p.1148

**The Firm:** This team was praised for its success in representing larger financial institutions. It has the skill and infrastructure to handle the most complex transactions and is particularly strong in municipal

deals involving local and state government entities and private developers. Clients believe other key strengths of the team include its ability to bring in-depth tax expertise and strong litigation support to bear when needed. According to sources, this "*really affords the client all the benefits of a top-level law firm.*" Clients also appreciate the firm's innovative use of technology, which allows "*super-fast turnaround*" and rate its lawyers as "*some of the hardest working lawyers in Michigan.*"

**The Lawyers:** This is one of the largest real estate groups in Michigan and has offices in nine locations throughout the state. **Ronald Hodess** (see p.1135) leads the group and often advises on complicated multistate, multimillion-dollar development and construction projects where clients appreciate his "*excellent attention to detail.*" Recent examples include advising on the construction of a $55 million state-of-the-art manufacturing facility in Arkansas and on the $140 million refinancing of the Comerica Park baseball stadium. **James Simpson** (see p.1139) and **Katheryne Zelenock** (see p.1140) jointly lead the firm's capital markets lending group and continue to act for an impressive stable of national lending clients. **Pat Lennon** (see p.1137) spearheads the firm's practice group in Florida and undertakes all aspects of commercial real estate work including sales and acquisitions, financings and zoning and leasing matters. He has been involved in several restructurings and acts as general counsel to several associations of realtors.

**Clients/Work Highlights:** The group acts as primary outside counsel on real estate and construction matters for Siemens, on a national basis. It assisted a developer client on the conversion of more than 2,500 manufactured housing units and advised on a land development project for one of the largest undeveloped tracts of land in southwest Florida. Other clients include the University of Michigan; Ford; Wells Fargo; the Greater Kalamazoo Association of REALTORS and Rite Aid.

## Band 2

### Dawda, Mann, Mulcahy & Sadler PLC

**The Firm:** This smaller niche boutique firm devotes around half of its resources to real estate law, with 17 full-time lawyers concentrating on all aspects of commercial real estate work. Commentators noted that "*the team is able to attract larger clients than its size might otherwise dictate,*" thanks to the "*superior*" *reputation and top-rate service provided for a good fee.*" It also derives strength from the support provided by other members of the firm who advise on tax, corporate, employment and environment matters.

**The Lawyers: Edward Dawda** advises on both real estate and corporate law and represents both private and public companies mainly based in the Midwest. His clients include Wal-Mart, which he represents in all its regional real estate work, including leasing, and retail and commercial developments. Interviewees recommended him as "*an incredibly hard worker, with a consistently strong output.*" **Michael Mulcahy** has a similar practice representing developers and buyers in their real estate acquisitions and advises on the development of retail outlets, office buildings and multiuse projects. He is a popular figure among peers who tipped him as "*a sharp lawyer, who is a delight to deal with.*"

**Clients/Work Highlights:** The team represents several large automotive dealers on a spectrum of real estate issues and handles leasing matters for the major tenants of large retail centers, such as Home Depot and Wal-Mart.

## Dickinson Wright PLLC
See firm details p.1145
**The Firm:** This is a key player in Michigan's real estate market, and has built up a strong group of practitioners who represent corporate lenders, developers and real estate trusts in a range of matters. This includes real estate development and financings, disposals, acquisitions and leasing matters. Interviewees remarked on the great depth and broad skill set among its lawyers – for example, the team is home to several specialized land use litigators, one of whom is currently engaged in a case in the US Supreme Court.

**The Lawyers:** Much of **James Candler**'s (see p.1133) recent time has been spent advising key client MGM Mirage. He assisted the client by successfully arguing against the prevention of the development of casinos in Detroit. He is now coordinating several financings for MGM where he acts as Michigan counsel in the $750 million development of a new casino, which is one of the largest-ever single casino constructions in Detroit. He is a prominent figure in the market whom peers recommended as "*a great technician and one of the big names in the real estate world.*" **Stephen Dawson** (see p.1134) is "*a consummate professional,*" whose work includes advising DaimlerChrysler on its real estate loans and representing local developers and landlords on the creation and negotiation of new leases and sales. He has also acted for a number of Japanese clients on their automotive-related activities. **Laurence Winokur** (see p.1140) "*is one of the best guys around and just gets the job done.*" He is especially active in the retail property arena and advises on leases, financings, refinancings and new projects. He represents the owners and operators of apartment rental housing and regularly acts for a local client buying property in California, Nevada and Hawaii.

**Clients/Work Highlights:** Lawyers represented

Aisin Holdings of America in connection with an 870-acre test-track research facility, which involved issues such as zoning classification, acquisition of property and tax exemptions. The team also advises lenders such as JPMorgan Chase and Pacific Life on their Michigan-based activities, and acts for other large commercial clients, such as Kmart.

## Dykema Gossett PLLC
**The Firm:** This real estate department of around 35 lawyers is based predominantly in the metropolitan Detroit area, and has an evenly balanced practice, representing both lenders and developers. The firm's primary strengths lie in the fields of litigation and corporate law, but it is well regarded among its competitors for the strength of its real estate department. Lawyers tend to concentrate much of their work within Michigan and represent clients from a range of sectors on matters including zoning, land use, planning, tax exemptions and financings.

**The Lawyers: James Adams** leads the real estate department, and acts primarily as developer's counsel in a wide range of transactional construction work. His workload includes representing a major pharmaceutical company on a range of complex matters including the redevelopment of property for new use. He also acts for a nonprofit senior housing development company, and represents a local municipality in large, complex urban development projects. Clients call on **Cameron Piggott** for his "*levelheaded and practical approach*" to public-private projects, including developer and municipality partnerships involved in the buying, selling and leasing of real estate developments. Recent examples include a high visibility $60 million public-private project to develop a parking level to support the downtown area of Detroit.

**Clients/Work Highlights:** Lawyers advised on a $240 million bond issue for Ann Arbor Public Schools. Other clients include Pfizer, Turner Construction Company and Omega Healthcare Investors.

## Band 3

### Barris, Sott, Denn & Driker, PLLC
**The Firm:** This is a medium-sized firm with "*a great real estate pedigree.*" The department covers all areas and commentators note that it is "*regularly engaged on the most complex of matters, which belies its size.*" Clients rely on the team for assistance in development, financing, taxation and real estate litigation matters. The team can also call on support from other departments within the firm including the litigation, business counseling and tax groups.

**The Lawyers: William Barris** is "*a real gentleman,*" with over 35 years of experience in the field. He represents construction lenders and developers, and he has been involved in some of Michigan's largest projects, including retail and shopping centers, office buildings, industrial facilities and hotel projects. Clients were impressed by his "*extensive knowledge and ability to get the deal done.*"

**Clients/Work Highlights:** Lawyers represent two of the big three automobile manufacturers, as well as large gas and electric utilities companies, financial and banking institutions, real estate developers and manufacturers. In the public sector, the team represents governmental entities and agencies, including the State of Michigan and University of Michigan.

## Butzel Long
See firm details p.1143
**The Firm:** This is one of Michigan's most established firms, dating from 1854, and currently numbering over 200 lawyers, who are based in offices statewide. The 20-strong real estate department handles everything from condominium work to environmental and tax matters. The group has been involved in some of Michigan's key projects, representing a range of clients including general contractors, developers and lenders.

**The Lawyers: Stephen Bromberg** (see p.1133) is a high-visibility lawyer renowned for his good judgment. He is popular among constructors and investors, and has recently completed the refinancing of a major hotel, which prompted observers to comment that "*in the current economy, this was a significant achievement and testament to his prowess.*" He is currently in the midst of arranging the structured financing for the largest public housing project in Detroit, and continues to act as general counsel for the Detroit Symphony Orchestra.

**Clients/Work Highlights:** Lawyers represent borrowers, lenders, purchasers and sellers in all aspects of Michigan-based real estate transactions.

## Clark Hill PLC
See firm details p.1144
**The Firm:** This general commercial firm boasts a strong real estate practice, with around 13 attorneys, nestling among the prominent corporate and litigation departments. The group's expertise covers all aspects of real estate law, including leasing, lending, purchasing, acquisitions and development, as well as niche expertise in the construction of low-income housing.

**The Lawyers:** Interviewees attribute much of the group's success to the impressive **William Dunn**. A fellow and past president of the American College of Real Estate Lawyers, he is renowned for his work on ethics committees and has an "*analytical, profound approach to real estate issues.*" **Timothy Koltun** is a real estate transactional attorney who represents clients on land sales and purchases, retail and residential developments and industrial facilities. He advises one of the nation's largest home builders on all aspects of its business and represents it at public hearings and before regulatory bodies.

**Clients/Work Highlights:** The team represented MetLife and MassMutual, who were co-lenders in a $92 million refinancing deal. Lawyers act for a number of other large life insurance companies, such as Northwestern Mutual, as well as constructors and developers, including one of the firm's principal clients, Centex Homes. Other clients include prominent local nonprofit institutions, including a number of Michigan school districts.

### Jaffe, Raitt, Heuer & Weiss, PC

**The Firm:** This group has a broad real estate repertoire and has established a loyal following amongst clients. They use the team for a wide range of matters, including construction, land use and leasing. Lawyers also have expertise in the financing of statewide projects including office and manufacturing facilities, residential developments and retail outlets. The group centers its activity primarily in Michigan, but has been involved in matters throughout the USA.

**The Lawyers:** **Richard Zussman** represents midmarket companies in the acquisition, development, leasing, financing and disposition of numerous real property facilities. His recent work has included advising a client on the purchase of a hospital, and acting for local business entities on M&A.

**Clients/Work Highlights:** The team advises many different middle and large developers such as Sun Communities; Schostak Brothers & Company; Ram Real Estate; Cummings & Associates and Sillman Enterprises.

### Kerr Russell & Weber

**The Firm:** This is a small but successful Michigan law firm that is renowned for its representation of private developers and its skill in business and commercial property work. The team is well respected for the quality of its practitioners, which gives it "*a depth that more than outdoes its size.*" It also offers a broad sphere of expertise, including shopping center development and leasing, construction claims and environmental regulation.

**The Lawyers:** Interviewees widely cited **Robert Nix** as the cornerstone of this group and recommended him for his "*capable manner and tenacious approach.*" His work takes him mostly outside of the metropolitan Detroit area, and includes the leasing and commercial financing of light industrial research and development facilities, as well as shopping centers and office buildings. In 2005 he advised on a $30 million business project in Ann Arbor, and a $20 million development deal for DaimlerChrysler.

**Clients/Work Highlights:** The group is representing Toyota on a large construction project outside Detroit and has advised Volkswagen on its general real estate matters. Other clients include the City of Troy, Somerset Mall and various local councils.

### Maddin, Hauser, Wartell, Roth & Heller PC

**The Firm:** This boutique firm of about 50 lawyers has a sterling reputation for real estate work. The department continues to expand and has gained four new lawyers this year. Based just outside Detroit, the outfit is seen as unique thanks to its "*ability to handle sophisticated work on a par with the larger firms, despite its size.*"

**The Lawyers:** **Michael Maddin** is one of the key figures at the firm, with over 35 years of experience. He principally represents developers in all manner of real estate transactions and has also been involved in estate planning and probate law. Commentators were keen to praise his "*strong client representation and wonderful negotiation skills.*" **Lowell Salesin** is "*a rising star,*" who acts for developers and lenders in the financing, purchase and sale of shopping centers, apartment buildings and manufactured home communities. He has "*an extensive network of contacts within the business community*" and has been busy advising hotel-buyers on a series of hospitality industry transactions in Florida.

**Clients/Work Highlights:** The team advises a number of financial institutions and development companies, such as Grand/Sakwa Properties, RHP Properties and Fifth Third Bank.

# Leaders in Michigan

**ADAMS, James**
Dykema Gossett PLLC, Detroit
313 568 6800
*Recommended in Real Estate*

**AMMON, Jeffrey**
Miller Johnson, Grand Rapids
616 831 1700
*Recommended in Corporate/M&A*

**ANKERS, Norman C**
Honigman Miller Schwartz and Cohn LLP,
Detroit 313 465 7306
NAnkers@honigman.com
*Recommended in Litigation*

**Practice Areas:** Complex commercial litigation, including business torts, securities law, shareholder and partnership litigation and condemnation. National practice in state and federal appellate courts.
**Prof. Memberships:** State Bar of Michigan; Oakland County Bar Association Professionalism Committee; Court Appointed Facilitator for the Oakland County Circuit Court.
**Career:** BA, University of Michigan, 1976; JD, Harvard University Law School; Chairman of Honigman's Litigation Department.
**Publications:** Various, including articles covering Michigan Court Rules Annotated-Evidence multi-volume treatise for West Publishing Company; Civil Procedure sections for the Wayne Law and Detroit College of Law Reviews; and Oppression of Minority Shareholders for the Michigan Bar Journal.

**AVIV, Joseph**
Honigman Miller Schwartz and Cohn LLP,
Bloomfield Hills 248 566 8404
JAviv@honigman.com
*Recommended in Litigation*

**Practice Areas:** Complex corporate, securities, and class action litigation; constitutional law; and non-routine matrimonial and divorce matters involving the valuation of family businesses.
**Prof. Memberships:** State Bar of Michigan; Federal Bar Association; Oakland County Bar Association; American Bar Association; Fellow, American Academy of Matrimonial Lawyers.
**Career:** BA, cum laude, Brandeis University, 1971; JD, cum laude, Boston University School of Law, 1975; shareholder and Head of Litigation, Miro Weiner & Kramer, P.C., 1981-2004; Assistant District Attorney, New York State, 1975-79.
**Publications:** Frequent articles published and lectures at seminars on family law and corporate subjects.

**BARNES, Thomas J**
Varnum, Riddering, Schmidt & Howlett LLP,
Grand Rapids 616 336 6621
tjbarnes@varnumlaw.com
*Recommended in Employment*

**Practice Areas:** Mr Barnes has represented management as an advocate and counselor on a broad range of labor and employoment matters, including union organizing campaigns, labor negotiations, arbitrations, and in matters before the National Labor Relations Board. He

also serves as an arbitrator for employment disputes in reviewing matters from a neutral's perspective. He is listed in 'The Best Lawyers in America'.
**Prof. Memberships:** Member, American Bar Association, NLRB Practice and Procedure Committee; State Bar of Michigan, Labor Relations Law Section; Fellow, The College of Labor and Employment Lawyers and Arbitration Panel Member, Michigan Employment Relations Commission.

**BARRIS, William**
Barris, Sott, Denn & Driker, PLLC, Detroit
313 965 9725
*Recommended in Real Estate*

**BATTEN, Fred**
Clark Hill PLC, Detroit 313 965 8300
*Recommended in Employment*

**BERNARD, Michael**
Dykema Gossett PLLC, Detroit
313 568 6800
*Recommended in Corporate/M&A*

**BOLTON, Richard M**
Dickinson Wright PLLC, Detroit
313 223 3648
rbolton@dickinson-wright.com
*Recommended in Corporate/M&A*

**Practice Areas:** Director: Corporate, M&A, Securities, Private Capital, Corporate Governance, Real Estate, Estate Planning Group. Counsel to private capital funds in numerous venture capital, LBO, recapitalization, and mezzanine finance

transactions. Counsel on numerous public and private corporate finance transactions in numerous industries, including IPOs and secondary offerings, mergers and acquisitions, recapitalizations, tender offers, and going private transactions. Counsel to issuers in 144A private placements of debt followed by registered exchange offers.
**Personal:** Northwestern University School of Law (JD, 1977); Michigan State University, (BA with highest honors, 1974).

**BREAY, James**
Warner Norcross & Judd LLP,
Grand Rapids 616 752 2000
*Recommended in Banking & Finance*

**BRETZ, Daniel**
Brady Hathaway Brady & Bretz, Detroit
313 965 3700
dbretz@bradyhathaway.com
*Recommended in Employment*

**Practice Areas:** Employment law consultation and litigation for management, including discrimination, harassment, retaliation, whistleblower, breach of contract and trade secret claims. Labor law consultation and litigation, including NLRB investigations and trials, union election campaigns, collective bargaining negotiations, grievance arbitrations and contract administration. Extensive defamation and First Amendment trial and appellate experience.
**Prof. Memberships:** ABA (Member EEO

SubCommittee, 1990-present); State Bar of Michigan (Member Labor and Employment Law Section Committee, 2001-present; Officer and Treasurer, 2005-06); American Employment Lawyers Council (Member 1997-present).

**Career:** Founding Partner Brady Hathaway Brady and Bretz, P.C. (1989). Listed in 'Best Lawyers in America' (since 1998) and 'Who's Who Legal: Management Labour and Employment'. 'AV' rated by Martindale-Hubble. Named Barrister of the Year (1987) by the Detroit Metropolitan Bar Association.

**Publications:** Has published various papers and lectured extensively for the ABA, State Bar of Michigan and Michigan ICLE groups. Author: 'FMLA Litigation; Employment Law in Michigan, An Employer's Guide' (ICLE 2nd ed).

**Personal:** University of Michigan, AB; Wayne State University Law School, JD.

## BROMBERG, Stephen A
Butzel Long, Bloomfield Hills
248 258 1616
bromberg@butzel.com
*Recommended in Real Estate*

**Practice Areas:** Represents borrowers and institutional lenders, purchasers and sellers, non-profit entities and contractors and owners in all types of office, commercial, shopping center, apartment and subdivision matters, and major construction and zoning matters and workouts, reorganizations and foreclosures.

**Prof. Memberships:** Past President, American College of Mortgage Attorneys (ACMA). Member: American Judicature Society, American College of Real Estate Lawyers. Past Chair, Real Property Law Section of the State Bar of Michigan.

**Career:** Senior Attorney, Past Director and past President, Butzel Long.

**Personal:** University of Michigan, 1952, with distinction (Phi Beta Kappa). The University of Michigan Law School (JD, 1954).

## BRUSTAD, Orin D
Miller, Canfield, Paddock and Stone, P.L.C., Detroit 313 496 7605
brustad@millercanfield.com
*Recommended in Employee Benefits*

**Practice Areas:** Federal tax and employee benefits; pension and other benefit plans and executive compensation, representing public and private sector clients in connection with qualified retirement plans, retirement incentives, fiduciary liability, non-qualified deferred compensation arrangements for executives, plans involving transfer of employer stock to employees, governmental retirement and deferred compensation plans, employment contracts, cafeteria plans, and various self-insured and insured welfare plans.

**Prof. Memberships:** American Bar Association; State Bar of Michigan; Fellow, American College of Employee Benefits.

**Career:** Joined firm 1968; Principal 1975.
**Personal:** JD, Harvard Law School, 1968; MA, Yale University, 1964; BA, Yale University, 1963.

## BURSTEIN, Richard
Honigman Miller Schwartz and Cohn LLP, Bloomfield Hills 248 566 8430
RBurstein@honigman.com
*Recommended in Real Estate*

**Practice Areas:** Represents and counsels national and regional commercial real estate developers in transactions, investments and development of office complexes, industrial parks, urban redevelopment projects, regional and community shopping centers, and multi family developments. Represents several real estate investment trusts both as primary trust counsel and as local and real estate counsel.

**Prof. Memberships:** State Bar of Michigan; International Council of Shopping Centers (ICSC), Detroit Bar Association, American College of Real Estate Lawyers.

**Career:** BA, University of Michigan, 1966; JD, Wayne State University Law School, 1969.

**Publications:** Frequent lecturer at the ICSC Law Conferences and contributor to real estate publications.

## CALZONE, David B
Vercruysse Murray & Calzone, PC, Bingham Farms 248 540 7030
dcalzone@vmclaw.com
*Recommended in Employment*

**Practice Areas:** Employment discrimination, labor litigation, labor arbitration, appellate litigation, class action litigation. Expertise in ADA and FMLA.

**Prof. Memberships:** Secretary: Labor and Employment Law Section of the State Bar of Michigan. Member: American Bar Association, Federal Bar Association, American Employment Law Council. Fellow: College of Labor and Employment Lawyers and the Michigan State Bar Foundation.

**Career:** Co-founder, shareholder, secretary, Vercruysse Murray & Calzone.

**Publications:** Co-editor and co-author, 'Employment Litigation in Michigan', 2nd ed (ICLE 2004).

**Personal:** University of Michigan Law School (JD, Order of the Coif, 1981); University of Michigan (AB, Phi Beta Kappa, 1978).

## CAMPBELL, Lawrence
Dickinson Wright PLLC, Detroit
313 223 3703
lcampbell@dickinson-wright.com
*Recommended in Litigation*

**Practice Areas:** Experienced in litigation, including accountant malpractice, legal malpractice, contract disputes, employment (including class actions), labor relations and counseling. Extensive experience in handling business and commercial litigation matters, with particular emphasis on securities fraud

defense, as well as accountant malpractice and contract disputes. Broad experience in acquisitions, mergers, and dissolutions of corporations, as well as labor contract negotiations.

**Prof. Memberships:** Member, American College of Trial Lawyers (1992); Panel Member, Large, Complex Case Program, American Arbitration Association; Panel Member, American Arbitration Association's Panel of Employment Arbitrators.

**Personal:** University of Detroit Law School (JD, 1969); Michigan State University (BA, 1962).

## CANDLER, James
Dickinson Wright PLLC, Detroit
313 223 3513
jcandler@dickinson-wright.com
*Recommended in Real Estate*

**Practice Areas:** Real estate experience including development of MGM Grand Detroit Casino, acquisition and sale/leaseback financing, purchase, financing and leasing transactions, lease negotiations, planned unit developments, and co-operative organizations.

**Prof. Memberships:** American College of Real Estate Lawyers; American Land Title Association Real Estate Counsel Group; International Association of Attorneys and Executives in Corporate Real Estate; State Bar of Michigan; Real Property Law Section Council.

**Publications:** 'Condominiums, Planned Communities and Urban Development', Lorman Education Services, 2005; 'Casino Financing', American Land Title Association, 2000.

**Personal:** University of Michigan (JD, 1970); Princeton University (AB, 1965).

## CRANMER, Thomas W
Miller, Canfield, Paddock and Stone, P.L.C., Detroit 313 248 3381
cranmer@millercanfield.com
*Recommended in Litigation*

**Practice Areas:** Representing individual and corporate clients in white-collar criminal defense, corporate compliance, and complex commercial civil litigation, including income tax evasion, fraud, Food and Drug investigations, criminal OSHA, MIOSHA and state/federal environmental matters, criminal antitrust investigations, Customs violations, securities violations, public corruption, police corruption and misconduct, RICO violations, and false claims.

**Prof. Memberships:** Fellow, American College of Trial Lawyers; Fellow, International Academy of Trial Lawyers; Fellow, International Society of Barristers; State Bar of Michigan President, 2005-06; Criminal Defense Attorneys of Michigan.

**Career:** Joined firm as Principal 2005.
**Personal:** JD, Ohio Northern University, 1975; BA, University of Michigan, 1972.

## CURTNER, Gregory L
Miller, Canfield, Paddock and Stone, P.L.C., New York 212 704 4400

*Recommended in Litigation, Sport*
**Practice Areas:** Commercial litigation involving antitrust, class actions, securities, media, and defamation, frequently serving as lead counsel in nationwide antitrust disputes and class actions and appearing pro hac vice in numerous state and federal courts. Former chairman of the Antitrust Section of the State Bar of Michigan, he was a primary drafter of the Michigan Antitrust Reform Act.

**Prof. Memberships:** American Bar Association, State Bar of Michigan, State Bar of New York, Federal Bar Association.

**Career:** Principal, 1977, Managing Partner, 1989-90; Resident Director, New York office, 1996-present.

**Personal:** JD, University of Michigan Law School, 1970; BBA, University of Michigan, 1967.

## DAMSCHRODER, Timothy R
Bodman LLP, Ann Arbor
734 930 0230
tdamschroder@bodmanllp.com
*Recommended in Corporate/M&A*

**Practice Areas:** Practice concentrated in business, securities, corporate finance and tax, which includes advising clients regarding angel and venture capital based financing (representing funds and issuers), business transactions (domestic and international), business formation, corporate governance, and mergers, acquisitions and joint ventures. Specializes in dealing with hi-tech companies from start-up, to venture capital financing, to eventual sale or IPO.

**Prof. Memberships:** State Bar of Michigan (past Chair, Business Law Section); American Bar Association.

**Personal:** JD, University of Detroit Law School; AB, University of Michigan.

## DAUGHERTY, Patrick D
Foley & Lardner LLP, Detroit
313 234 7103
pdaugherty@foley.com
*Recommended in Corporate/M&A*

**Career:** Patrick D Daugherty, a member of the Transactional and Securities Practice Group and Automotive Industry Team, is a Partner in the Detroit office of Foley & Lardner LLP. Mr Daugherty directs multi-office, multi-disciplinary teams of lawyers in the planning and execution of public and private offerings of equity, debt and hybrid securities, structured financings, tender offers, exchange offers, restructurings, recapitalizations, mergers, acquisitions, divestitures, management buyouts, 'going private' transactions and corporate governance assignments. Mr Daugherty received his Law Degree, cum laude, from Cornell University.

## DAWDA, Edward
Dawda, Mann, Mulcahy & Sadler PLC, Bloomfield Hills 248 642 3700
*Recommended in Real Estate*

## DAWSON, Stephen E
Dickinson Wright PLLC, Bloomfield Hills
248 433 7214
sdawson@dickinson-wright.com
*Recommended in Real Estate*

**Practice Areas:** Experienced in real estate development, real estate finance, commercial mortgage lending, and leasing, representing corporations and municipalities. Counsel to DaimlerChrysler Services North America LLC with regard to national real estate activities. Represent various developers in acquisition, development, and leasing of projects. **Prof. Memberships:** Member, American College of Real Estate Lawyers; Member, American Bar Association, Section of Real Estate, Probate and Trust Law; Fellow, Michigan State Bar Foundation; Member, Land Title Standards Committee, State Bar of Michigan. **Personal:** University of Michigan (JD cum laude, 1972); University of Michigan (MA, 1969); Michigan State University (BA magna cum laude, 1968).

## DEITCH, Laurence B
Bodman LLP, Detroit 313 392 1055
ldeitch@bodmanllp.com
*Recommended in Corporate/M&A*

**Practice Areas:** Practice concentrated in corporate law, real estate law and government relations. Substantial experience in corporate governance, mergers and acquisitions (including numerous cross-border transactions), structuring joint ventures, and all legal issues related to real estate development, leasing and finance. Authored the ballot proposal, later enacted into law, which authorized casino gaming in the City of Detroit. **Prof. Memberships:** State Bar of Michigan. **Personal:** JD and BA, University of Michigan. Member, University of Michigan Board of Regents. Director, Detroit Symphony Orchestra. Director, Friends of Modern Art, Detroit Institute of Arts. Member, National Advisory Board, University of Michigan Museum of Art.

## DICKSON, Andrea Roumell
Butzel Long, Detroit 313 983 7440
dickson@butzel.com
*Recommended in Employment*

**Practice Areas:** Employment litigation private and public sector. Emphasis on employment discrimination litigation, related administrative agency procedings, wrongful discharge and whistleblower cases. Preventative counseling and training. **Prof. Memberships:** Member, State Bar of Michigan Judicial Qualifications Committee, past Chair, State Bar of Michigan Labor and Employment Law Council. **Career:** Shareholder, Co-Chair, Labor and Employment Department, Butzel Long. **Publications:** Institute of Continuing Legal Education, Chapter author; 'Employment Law in Michigan: An

Employer's Guide'. **Personal:** Smith College (BA, 1978). Wayne State University Law School (JD, 1981). Judicial clerk to Honorable Robert B Burns of the Michigan Court of Appeals.

## DIEHL JR, Robert J
Bodman LLP, Detroit 313 393 7597
rdiehl@bodmanllp.com
*Recommended in Banking & Finance*

**Practice Areas:** Specializes in complex commercial transactions with a focus on banking, debtor-creditor rights and bankruptcy. Represents lenders in out-of-court workouts and in bankruptcy proceedings involving all types of businesses and collateral, especially automotive, real estate and construction businesses. Documents complex, high risk financial transactions, highly leveraged financings and asset-based loans. Counsels lenders on loan structure and lender liability issues. Defends lenders on lender liability claims. **Prof. Memberships:** State Bar of Michigan; Detroit Metropolitan Bar Association; American Bar Association; Turn-around Management Association. **Personal:** JD, magna cum laude and AB, with high honors and high distinction, University of Michigan.

## DONATI, Donna J
Miller, Canfield, Paddock and Stone, P.L.C., Detroit 313 496 7688
donati@millercanfield.com
*Recommended in Employment*

**Practice Areas:** Trial lawyer representing private and public sector employers in cases alleging all types of discrimination, sex and racial harassment, and wrongful discharge cases in state and federal courts. Experience representing newspapers, radio stations, and magazines in defamation and invasion of privacy lawsuits, and prepublication counseling to avoid litigation. **Prof. Memberships:** American Bar Association, State Bar of Michigan, Federal Bar Association, Association of Trial Lawyers of America, Michigan Trial Lawyers' Association, Michigan Defense Trial Counsel. **Career:** Joined firm 1977; Principal, 1984. **Personal:** JD, University of Michigan Law School, 1977; BA, Wayne State University, 1974.

## DOZEMAN, Douglas
Warner Norcross & Judd LLP, Grand Rapids 616 752 2000
*Recommended in Litigation*

## DRIKER, Eugene
Barris, Sott, Denn & Driker, PLLC, Detroit
313 965 9725
*Recommended in Litigation*

## DuMOUCHEL, David F
Butzel Long, Detroit
313 225 7004
dumouchd@butzel.com

*Recommended in Litigation*

**Practice Areas:** Criminal defense, professional licensure, criminal healthcare matters, internal corporate investigations and compliance. Federal Bar Association Leonard Gilman Award, outstanding criminal law practitioner, Eastern District of Michigan (1986). **Prof. Memberships:** Member: Rules Advisory Committee, US District Court, Eastern District of Michigan; US District Court Committee, Magistrate Program Evaluation; American Law Institute Advisory Committee, Restatement of the Law Governing Lawyers; American College of Trial Lawyers; State Bar of Michigan Criminal Code Revision Committee, US Courts Committee, Grievance Committee; National Association of Criminal Defense Lawyers, Director (1981). Chair: Federal Bar Association Crime Defense Committee; Michigan Attorney Grievance Commission, 1978-85. Master of Bench Emeritus, American Inn of Court Ch. XI. Fellow, American Bar Foundation, Michigan State Bar Foundation. **Career:** Shareholder, Butzel Long. Chair, corporate compliance and criminal defense. **Publications:** 'Grand Jury Practice', Federal Bar Association, 1986-present; 'Grand Jury Practice', US District Court, New Lawyer Seminar, 1986-present. 'Internal Investigations and Corporate Compliance', Mi Assn of CPAs, 2005; speaker, ABA Health Care Law Institute, 2005; speaker, ABA White Collar Crime Practice Institute, 2006. **Personal:** University of Detroit (MA, 1972). Wayne State University Law School (JD, cum laude, 1975).

## DUNN, William
Clark Hill PLC, Detroit 313 965 8300
*Recommended in Real Estate*

## FEENEY, James
Dykema Gossett PLLC, Bloomfield Hills
248 203 0700
*Recommended in Litigation*

## FOLTYN, David
Honigman Miller Schwartz and Cohn LLP, Detroit 313 465 7380
DFoltyn@honigman.com
*Recommended in Corporate/M&A*

**Practice Areas:** Corporate mergers, acquisitions, and divestitures; financial transactions; public offerings and private placements of securities and debt; day to day securities and corporate; business succession and divorces; and corporate governance matters for publicly- and privately-held business clients, boards of directors, and financial services firms. **Prof. Memberships:** State Bar of Michigan, Business Law Section, Immediate Past Chair; Ray Garett Institute, Northwestern University Law School, Planning Committee. **Career:** BBA, with high distinction, Uni-

versity of Michigan, 1977; JD, magna cum laude (Order of the Coif), University of Michigan Law School, 1980. Member, Honigman Board of Directors, Compensation Committee, and Strategic Planning Committee Co-Chair.

## GIVENS, Leonard D
Miller, Canfield, Paddock and Stone, P.L.C., Detroit 313 496 7505
givens@millercanfield.com
*Recommended in Employment*

**Practice Areas:** Labor, employment, and school law, including unfair labor practices, jurisdictional disputes, CBAs, mediation, arbitrations, FLSA, OSHA, wrongful discharge, IEP hearings, teacher tenure, FOIA, and student rights to privacy. Also counsels organizations on minority business issues. **Prof. Memberships:** American Bar Association, State Bar of Michigan, National Bar Association, American and National Labor and Employment Council. Fellow, College of Labor and Employment Lawyers and Michigan State Bar Foundation. **Career:** Joined firm 1971; Principal, 1978; Labor and Employment Group Leader 1982-92, and Co-eader 1995-present; Chief Executive Officer, 1991-94. **Personal:** JD, Howard University School of Law, 1971; BS, Mansfield College, 1965.

## GREEN, Jonathan S
Miller, Canfield, Paddock and Stone, P.L.C., Detroit 313 496 7997
greenj@millercanfield.com
*Recommended in Banking & Finance*

**Practice Areas:** Bankruptcy and debtor-creditor law, representing secured and unsecured creditors, creditors' committees, trustees, debtors, and other interested parties in their debtor-creditor relationships with others. **Prof. Memberships:** American Bar Association, State Bar of Michigan, and Detroit Metropolitan Bar Association. **Career:** Principal since 1992; Leader of Bankruptcy and Workout Practice Group. **Personal:** JD, Cornell University School of Law, 1981; BA University of Michigan, 1977.

## HAFFEY, Dennis
Dykema Gossett PLLC, Detroit
313 568 6800
*Recommended in Litigation*

## HANCOCK JR, John P
Butzel Long, Detroit 313 225 7021
hancock@butzel.com
*Recommended in Employment*

**Practice Areas:** Employment litigation, OSHA litigation, arbitrations, collective bargaining negotiations and counseling for various industries, public schools, municipalities and public utilities. Trials and hearings before the NLRB, multiple state agencies. **Prof. Memberships:** Past Chair, State

Bar of Michigan Labor and Employment Section. Member, American Bar Association, Detroit Bar Association, and Michigan Council of School Attorneys. Fellow, College of Labor and Employment Attorneys. Board Member, National Safety Council of Southeastern Michigan. Best Lawyers of America, and International Who's Who of Business Lawyers.
**Career:** Shareholder, Butzel Long.
**Publications:** Articles/presentations on numerous workplace issues.
**Personal:** University of Notre Dame (BA, 1970). Duke University Law School (JD, 1973).

### HARDY, Elizabeth P
Kienbaum Opperwall Hardy & Pelton P.L.C., Birmingham 248 645 0000
ehardy@kohp.com
*Recommended in Employment*
**Practice Areas:** Employment litigation, preventative counseling and appellate work.
**Prof. Memberships:** Fellow, College of Labor and Employment Lawyers (2005); Member, Model Civil Jury Instruction Committee (Michigan Supreme Court appointee) (2005-); Fellow, Michigan State Bar Foundation (2002); Co-Chair, Judicial Qualifications Committee, State Bar of Michigan (1998-2004).
**Career:** George Washington University (BA, with high honors, 1978); Wayne State University (JD, 1984); Editor-in-Chief, Wayne Law Review (1983-84); 'Best Lawyers in America' (2005); named Lawyer of the Year, Michigan Lawyers Weekly, 2004; named 'One of Detroit's Most Influential Women', Crain's Detroit Business, 1997. Member, 1991-present, Chair, 1995-97, Wayne State University Board of Governors; Chair, 1996-97, Presidential Search Committee, Wayne State University; Member, 2001-03, State Board of Canvassers; Member, 1996-98, Detroit Medical Center Board of Trustees; Member, 1998-2001, Karmanos Cancer Institute Board of Trustees and Executive Committee. Partner, Dickinson Wright Moon Van Dusen & Freeman, 1990-97; Founding Partner, Kienbaum Opperwall Hardy & Pelton, PLC, 1997-present.
**Publications:** Numerous papers and lectures presented on behalf of the National Employment Law Institute and the Michigan State Bar Labor and Employment Law Section.
**Personal:** Born in Traverse City, Michigan; married to Thomas G Kienbaum.

### HATHAWAY, Thomas M J
Brady Hathaway Brady & Bretz, Detroit 313 965 3700
thathawa@bradyhathaway.com
*Recommended in Employment*
**Practice Areas:** National employment law practice, including all discrimination, trade secret, non-compete, breach of contract, whistleblower and civil rights litigation in both federal and state courts,

including the US Supreme court and related administrative agencies. Preventive personnel counseling and training for management. Public and private sector labor law. Facilitator/arbitrator.
**Prof. Memberships:** Charter member, the American Employment Lawyers Council (1993-present); past President, Detroit Metropolitan Bar Association; Past Program Chair EEO Subcommittee, American Bar, Member, Employment Law Section; Chair, State Bar of Michigan Character and Fitness Committee, Wayne District, Member, State Bar of Michigan (Labor and Emplyment Law and Alternate Dispute Sections); Fellow, Michigan State Bar Foundation.
**Career:** Founding Partner and President, Brady Hathaway Brady & Bretz, P.C. (1989); 'AV' rated, Martindale-Hubbell; 'Who's Who Of Legal USA'; speaker, employment law, litigation and ethical issues before the American Bar Association, the Michigan State Bar, the Detroit Bar, ICLE, Council on Education in Management, the MPELRA, the Edison Institute; AB, College of the Holy Cross; JD Vanderbilt Law School.
**Publications:** Contributor, 'Employment Discrimination Law', Schlei and Grossman, second edition 1983 and the third edition, 1997. Authored articles and outlines examining various discrimination claims including age, harrassment and religion, layoffs, damages and breach of contract claims.

### HENNEY, Raymond W
Honigman Miller Schwartz and Cohn LLP, Detroit 313 465 7410
RHenney@honigman.com
*Recommended in Litigation*
**Practice Areas:** Securities litigation cases, including representation of major corporations in class-action shareholder suits, individuals and entities before the Securities and Exchange Commission, and brokerage firms in customer disputes and before regulatory organizations.
**Prof. Memberships:** American Arbitration Association; National Association of Securities Dealers, Inc.; American Bar Association, Securities Arbitration Subcommittee; Securities Industry Association; Oakland County Circuit Court Committee; Oakland County Chapter of American Inn of Courts.
**Career:** BA, with honors (Phi Kappa Phi), Michigan State University, 1980; JD, magna cum laude, Wayne State University Law School, 1983. Ropes & Gray, Boston, 1985-89.
**Publications:** Frequent lecturer at securities seminars.

### HERMANN, Kristin A
Miller, Canfield, Paddock and Stone, P.L.C., Detroit 313 496 8457
hermann@millercanfield.com
*Recommended in Banking & Finance*
**Practice Areas:** Represents institutional

lenders in connection with commercial loan transactions, including real estate, construction and equipment financing, in Michigan and throughout the United States. She is also experienced in various aspects of commercial real estate law including acquisitions, sales, condominium development and commercial leasing.
**Prof. Memberships:** American Bar Association, State Bar of Michigan, State Bar of Texas, Women Lawyers' Association of Michigan.
**Career:** Joined firm 1996; Principal 2005.
**Personal:** JD, University of Michigan Law School, 1996; BA, University of Michigan, 1993.

### HICKEY, Kathleen O'Callaghan
Bodman LLP, Detroit 313 393 7506
khickey@bodmanllp.com
*Recommended in Banking & Finance*
**Practice Areas:** Represents lenders in loan originations. Practice encompasses secured transactions, loan workouts, and counseling on lender liability and loan structure issues. Particular expertise in middle market lending, asset-based loans, private lending, letters of credit, real estate financing, multi-rate, multi-currency loans and facilities and agented and syndicated loan facilities.
**Prof. Memberships:** State Bar of Michigan; American Bar Association; Detroit Metropolitan Bar Association.
**Personal:** JD, cum laude, University of Detroit; BA, Michigan State University. Member, Detroit Community Council, Sister to Sister: Everyone Has a Heart Foundation, Inc.

### HIGH, Mark R
Dickinson Wright PLLC, Detroit 313 223 3650
mhigh@dickinsonwright.com
*Recommended in Corporate/M&A*
**Practice Areas:** Counsel to buyers and sellers in mergers or acquisitions in the manufacturing, retail, food service, real estate, automotive, defense, and natural resource industries. General counsel to small and medium-sized closely-held corporations. Establishing minority business entities. Counsel to domestic offices of foreign businesses in automotive and other industries.
**Prof. Memberships:** Chairman, Business Law Section, State Bar of Michigan.
**Publications:** 'Disney Directors Survive Attack on Magic Kingdom', Business Law Today, ABA, Jan/Feb 2006; 'Looking Under the Rocks: Due Diligence After Sarbanes-Oxley', Business Law Today, ABA, Sept/Oct 2005.
**Personal:** Duke University (JD, 1979); The College of Wooster (BA with honors, 1976).

### HODESS, Ronald E
Miller, Canfield, Paddock and Stone, P.L.C., Troy 248 267 3236
hodess@millercanfield.com
*Recommended in Real Estate*
**Practice Areas:** Commercial real estate,

acquisitions and dispositions, real estate finance, leasing, workouts and foreclosures, title issues, zoning and land use, and all aspects of commercial development. Procurement, negotiation, and consulting for state and local economic development incentives and tax abatements relating to real and personal property. Construction law, construction risk management, construction contracts, architect agreements, construction claims and liens, bonding, surety law, insurance issues and bidding issues.
**Prof. Memberships:** American Bar Association; State Bar of Michigan.
**Career:** Principal, 1996; Leader, Real Estate and Construction Industry groups.
**Personal:** JD, Georgetown University Law School, 1985; BBA, University of Michigan, 1982.

### HOWLETT, Timothy
Dickinson Wright PLLC, Detroit
313 223 3662
thowlett@dickinsonwright.com
*Recommended in Employment*
**Practice Areas:** Director: Labor and Employment, Employee Benefits, Immigration Group. Employment litigation defending wrongful termination, race discrimination, disability discrimination, sex discrimination, and religious discrimination claims.
**Prof. Memberships:** Member, American Employment Law Council, American Bar Association), EEOC Mediation Program Advisory Board, CPR Institute for Dispute Resolution.
**Publications:** Chapter Author: 'Discrimination Claims', Employment Litigation in Michigan, Second Edition (ICLE); 'Garg: Abolishment of the Continuing Violations Doctrine Under Michigan Law', Labor and Employment Lawnotes; 'The Constructive Discharge Doctrine in Michigan: A Need for Clarification', Michigan Bar Journal.
**Personal:** University of Michigan (JD cum laude, 1973); Kalamazoo College (BA, 1970).

### HUNTER, Margaret
Dykema Gossett PLLC, Detroit
313 568 6800
*Recommended in Employee Benefits*

### JAFFE, Ira
Jaffe, Raitt, Heuer & Weiss, PC, Detroit
313 961 8380
*Recommended in Corporate/M&A*

### JOHNSON, Donald
Varnum, Riddering, Schmidt & Howlett LLP, Grand Rapids 616 336 6828
dljohnson@varnumlaw.com
*Recommended in Banking & Finance, Corporate/M&A*
**Practice Areas:** Mr Johnson specializes in a wide variety of bank regulatory and structural matters. He has assisted in the formation of many new banks and bank holding companies throughout the state

of Michigan. He has also represented banking institutions in numerous mergers and acquisitions, including a merger valued over one billion dollars. He is listed in 'The Best Lawyers in America'.
**Prof. Memberships:** American Bar Association; State Bar of Michigan; Michigan Bankers Association; Michigan Association of Community Bankers.
**Career:** Partner, past Chair of Management Committee; past Chair of Corporate Practice Group.

### JOSWICK, David D
Miller, Canfield, Paddock and Stone, P.L.C., Troy 248 267 3252
joswick@millercanfield.com
*Recommended in Corporate/M&A*
**Practice Areas:** Corporate law, including selection of appropriate entity formation, financing, capitalization and allocation of control, relations among shareholders, investors and members, and mergers and acquisitions. Also has extensive experience in securities law and corporate governance.
**Prof. Memberships:** American Bar Association, State Bar of Michigan.
**Career:** Joined firm, 1969; Principal, 1975; Leader, Business and Finance Group, 1997-99. Currently, Adjunct Professor, Wayne State University Law School, and previously, law instructor at the University of Michigan Law School.
**Personal:** JD, magna cum laude, Wayne State University, 1969; BBA, University of Michigan School of Business Administration, 1966.

### JOSWICK, Theresa
Gamble, Rosenberger & Joswick LLP, Bloomfield Hills 248 540 7035
*Recommended in Employee Benefits*

### KAY, Richard A
Varnum, Riddering, Schmidt & Howlett LLP, Grand Rapids 616 336 6730
rakay@varnumlaw.com
*Recommended in Litigation*
**Practice Areas:** Mr Kay has concentrates on commercial/business disputes, construction litigation, employment matters, and product liability. A graduate engineer and registered patent attorney, Mr Kay is qualified in intellectual property litigation. He is listed in 'The Best Lawyers in America'.
**Prof. Memberships:** Fellow, former State Committee Chairman, American College of Trial Lawyers; Member, American Board of Trial Advocates Master of the Bench, American Inns of Court; past President, Federal Bar Association, Western District Michigan; past Chairman, Faculty, Hillman Trial Skills Workshops sponsored by United States District Court, Western District Michigan and Federal Bar Association; Fellow, Michigan State Bar Foundation; Delegate.

### KEPPELMAN, Nancy
Stevenson Keppelman Associates,

Ann Arbor 734 747 7050
*Recommended in Employee Benefits*

### KESSLER, Philip J
Butzel Long, Detroit 313 225 7018
kessler@butzel.com
*Recommended in Litigation*
**Practice Areas:** Prosecution and defense on behalf of individuals, partnerships, private and public corporations. Antitrust litigation, audit malpractice, bankruptcy litigation, contract litigation, corporate control contests, distributorship litigation, false advertising claims, healthcare and pharmaceutical counseling and litigation; intellectual property litigation (including copyright, trademark, trade secrets and unfair competition and patent infringement claims), intra-corporate and partnership disputes, merger and acquisition related litigation, probate and trust litigation and securities fraud claims.
**Prof. Memberships:** Life Member, United States Court of Appeals, Sixth Circuit Judicial Conference. Fellow and Regent, American College of Trial Lawyers. Fellow, International Society of Barristers. Fellow, American Bar Foundation. Fellow, Michigan State Bar Foundation. Member and Chair, Local Rules Advisory Committee, United States District Court for the Eastern District of Michigan.
**Career:** Chairman, Butzel Long.
**Personal:** The University of Michigan (1969, AB, with distinction). School of Law of the University of California at Berkeley (1972).

### KHOREY, David E
Varnum, Riddering, Schmidt & Howlett LLP, Grand Rapids 616 336 6618
dekhorey@varnumlaw.com
*Recommended in Employment*
**Practice Areas:** Mr Khorey's 'client-centered' practice involves a variety of labor and employment issues. He provides practical and confidential advice and consulting on a number of sensitive and complex labor and employment matters including union organizing efforts, negotiations, NLRB proceedings, arbitration, discharge and reduction in force planning, discrimination, employment litigation, union avoidance programs, retiree benefit litigation and preventive employment policies. His representative clients include diverse industries (such as automotive, printing, transportation and hospitals) nationwide. He is listed in 'The Best Lawyers in America'.
**Prof. Memberships:** Member: American Bar Association; State Bar of Michigan; West Michigan Chapter Industrial Relations Research Association.

### KIENBAUM, Thomas G
Kienbaum Opperwall Hardy & Pelton P.L.C., Birmingham 248 645 0000
tkienbaum@kohp.com
*Recommended in Employment*
**Practice Areas:** Employment litigation

with emphasis on complex or class actions; traditional labor relations.
**Prof. Memberships:** State Bars of Michigan and Illinois; Fellow, American and State Bar of Michigan Foundations; College of Labor and Employment Lawyers; Advisory Board, National Employment Law Institute; former President of the State Bar of Michigan.
**Career:** A veteran litigator with over 37 years' experience, Mr Kienbaum has extensive trial experience in Michigan and beyond having practiced before the US Supreme Court, federal trial and appellate courts, and various state courts. He also represents clients before federal and state administrative agencies, as well as in traditional labor relations matters. Mr Kienbaum has been named by 'Best Lawyers in America' for Labor and Employment Law for the past 20 years. BA, University of Michigan, 1965; JD, magna cum laude (Order of the Coif) Wayne State University, 1968; associate, Partner and Chair of Employment Practices Group, Dickinson Wright Moon Van Dusen & Freeman, 1968-97; Founding Partner, Kienbaum Opperwall Hardy & Pelton, PLC, 1997-present.
**Publications:** Various, including papers presented on behalf of the National Employment Law Institute and the Institute of Continuing Legal Education.
**Personal:** Born in Berlin, Germany, 1942; married to Elizabeth Hardy.

### KLIMKO, Justin
Butzel Long, Detroit 313 225 7037
klimkojg@butzel.com
*Recommended in Corporate/M&A*
**Practice Areas:** Securities regulation, corporate financing, mergers and acquisitions and general corporate matters. Biotechnology and life sciences companies. Securities regulation matters for publicly and privately held companies. Planning, negotiating and implementing merger and acquisition transactions. Advising and representing special committees of boards of directors.
**Prof. Memberships:** Past Chair, State Bar of Michigan Business Law Section. Co-Chair, Business Law Section, Corporate Laws Committee. Past Chair, Business Law Section, Ad Hoc Committee on Legal Opinions in Business Transactions. Member, American Bar Association, Legal Opinions Committee, Negotiated Acquisitions Committee, and Federal Regulation of Securities Committee.
**Career:** Shareholder, Butzel Long.
**Publications:** Frequent lectures and articles. Served as general editor of Michigan Business Forms and a contributing author on Michigan contract law.
**Personal:** Ohio University (BA, summa cum laude, 1977). Duke University (JD, with distinction, 1980). Adjunct Professor, University of Detroit Mercy Law School (1990-94).

### KOCHANEK, Joseph J
Bodman LLP, Detroit 313 393 7505
jkochanek@bodmanllp.com
*Recommended in Banking & Finance*
**Practice Areas:** Represents agent, banker and other lenders in secured and unsecured loan originations, including multi-currency loan facilities, syndicated credit arrangements and loans secured by stock and other assets located outside the US, principally in Europe, Mexico, South America and the Pacific Rim. Substantial experience in commercial mortgage financings and other real estate transactions and in representing foundations and community development corporations, public/private partnerships and urban revitalization projects.
**Prof. Memberships:** State Bar of Michigan; American Bar Association; Detroit Metropolitan Bar Association.
**Personal:** JD, magna cum laude and BA, with high distinction, University of Michigan.

### KOLTUN, Timothy
Clark Hill PLC, Detroit 313 965 8300
*Recommended in Real Estate*

### KRONK, Edward M
Butzel Long, Detroit 313 225 7017
kronk@butzel.com
*Recommended in Litigation*
**Practice Areas:** Product liability defense litigation, commercial litigation and automotive regulatory counseling and litigation.
**Prof. Memberships:** State Bar of Michigan; teaching with the Michigan Institute for Continuing Legal Education; faculty of the National Institute of Trial Advocacy; member and past President of the Eastern District of Michigan chapter of the Federal Bar Association; Member and past President of the Michigan Defense Trial Counsel; fellow of the American College of Trial Lawyers; and listed in Best Lawyers in America.
**Career:** Shareholder, Butzel Long.
**Personal:** University of Michigan (JD, 1971); College of the Holy Cross (AB, 1968).

### KUNZ, Donald
Honigman Miller Schwartz and Cohn LLP, Detroit 313 465 7454
DKunz@honigman.com
*Recommended in Corporate/M&A*
**Practice Areas:** Advises corporate clients on business issues, including transactional, financial, operational, and planning matters. Particular experience in the representation of publicly traded corporations, in securities law, venture capital, intellectual property, and in corporate finance matters.
**Prof. Memberships:** State Bar of Michigan, Business Law Section.
**Career:** BSE, summa cum laude (Tau Beta Pi, Alpha Pi Mu), University of Michigan, 1978; JD, magna cum laude, Harvard University Law School, 1981.

Chairman of Honigman's Corporate Department.

**Publications:** Various, including lectures on representing the venture capitalist, corporate stock buy-back programs and associated issues, buying and selling a business, and WKSI offerings.

### LARKIN, Terrence B
Bodman LLP, Troy 248 743 6078
tlarkin@bodmanllp.com
*Recommended in Corporate/M&A*

**Practice Areas:** Corporate law with a focus on mergers and acquisitions. Broad experience representing public and private companies in complex acquisitions, divestitures and joint ventures, including structuring deals, conducting due diligence, preparing definitive documentation, negotiating debt and equity financing, and ensuring regulatory compliance. Expertise includes the organization, financing and general representation of corporations, partnerships and limited liability companies and their shareholders, partners, directors and officers.

**Personal:** JD, cum laude, Wayne State University Law School; BA, with high honors, Michigan State University. Board Member, Detroit Regional Chamber. Advisory Board Member, Detroit Regional Economic Partnership. General Counsel, Better Business Bureau, Detroit/Eastern Michigan.

### LARSEN, Tracy T
Barnes & Thornburg LLP, Grand Rapids
317 742 3931
tracy.larsen@btlaw.com
*Recommended in Corporate/M&A*

**Practice Areas:** Corporate and securities law; mergers and acquisitions; has acted as lead counsel in merger, acquisition and corporate finance transactions worth billions of dollars; significant cross-border experience; has represented many large foreign corporations in their US acquisition strategies, and advises US corporations on cross-border transactions.

**Prof. Memberships:** State Bar of Michigan (Chairman Emeritus, Business Law Section).

**Career:** Admitted to practice in the state of Michigan.

**Personal:** Hope College (BA, summa cum laude, Economics, 1981); Indiana University School of Law (JD, magna cum laude, 1984).

### LARSON, Mary Jo
Honigman Miller Schwartz and Cohn LLP, Detroit 313 465 7458
MLarson@honigman.com
*Recommended in Employee Benefits*

**Practice Areas:** Employee benefits, including ERISA and tax implications of retirement and welfare plans, and executive compensation. Advises plan sponsors and fiduciaries responsible for administering plans or investing plan assets.

**Prof. Memberships:** State Bar of Michigan, Taxation Section - Employee Bene-

fits Committee, former Chair; Michigan Employee Benefits Conference, present Board Member and former Chair and President; American Bar Association, Taxation Section; American College of Employee Benefits Counsel, Fellow.

**Career:** BA, high distinction, University of Michigan, 1979; JD, cum laude, University of Michigan Law School, 1982. Partner and Chair of Honigman's Employee Benefits Department. Frequent speaker and writer on employee benefits.

### LENNON, J Patrick
Miller, Canfield, Paddock and Stone, P.L.C., Kalamazoo 269 383 5870
lennon@millercanfield.com
*Recommended in Real Estate*

**Practice Areas:** Commercial real estate law with extensive experience in transactions, development, construction, land use law, and brokerage. Representing clients in Michigan and Florida in the acquisition, disposition and leasing of virtually all types of real estate including undeveloped land, shopping centers, regional shopping malls, apartment buildings, office buildings and industrial.

**Prof. Memberships:** Michigan, Florida, and Kalamazoo County Bar Associations; International Council of Shopping Center Developers.

**Career:** Principal, 2005; previously: Vice President and Associate General Counsel, WCI Communities, Inc.; and Senior Counsel at Ocwen Federal Bank FSB.

**Personal:** JD, Indiana University School of Law-Bloomington, 1993; BA, Michigan State University, 1990.

### LEWAND, F Thomas
Bodman LLP, Detroit 313 393 7573
tlewand@bodmanllp.com
*Recommended in Corporate/M&A*

**Practice Areas:** Represents corporations and municipalities in complex transactions. Has negotiated numerous public-private partnerships, including a $400 million Detroit stadium complex, $300 million NASCAR track in Kansas and $50 million municipal-assisted Detroit Medical Center restructuring. As Special Master to US District Judge John Feikens on operation of the Detroit Water and Sewer System, has negotiated numerous agreements in the system's seven-county service region.

**Personal:** JD, magna cum laude, Wayne State University. BA, University of Detroit. Chair, Board of Trustees, University of Detroit Mercy. Commissioner, Michigan Civil Service Commission. Director, Wayne County EDC. Treasurer, Governor's Residence Foundation. Chair, Mackinac Island Board of Public Works.

### LEWIS, Denise
Honigman Miller Schwartz and Cohn LLP, Detroit 313 465 7464
DLewis@honigman.com
*Recommended in Real Estate*

**Practice Areas:** Acquisition and sale of

real estate; development agreements; construction; infrastructure development; leasing; environmental assessment; zoning matters; and property management. Assists national and regional developers in securing state and local incentives, including Empowerment Zones, Renaissance Zones, and historic designations; tax abatement and publicly-assisted financing involving tax increment financing and industrial revenue bonds.

**Prof. Memberships:** American College of Real Estate Lawyers; State Bar of Michigan, Real Property Law Section, Governing Council; International Council of Shopping Centers.

**Career:** BA, Columbia University, 1966; MA, Wayne State University, 1969; JD, University of Michigan Law School, 1983. University of Manchester, Ford Foundation Fellowship.

### MADDIN, Michael
Maddin, Hauser, Wartell, Roth & Heller PC, Southfield 248 354 4030
*Recommended in Real Estate*

### MAKENS, Hugh
Warner Norcross & Judd LLP, Grand Rapids 616 752 2000
*Recommended in Corporate/M&A*

### MARCH, Jon
Miller Johnson, Grand Rapids
616 831 1700
*Recommended in Employment*

### MCCALLUM, Charles
Warner Norcross & Judd LLP, Grand Rapids 616 752 2000
*Recommended in Corporate/M&A*

### MCKENDRY, John
Warner Norcross & Judd LLP, Muskegon 231 727 2600
*Recommended in Employee Benefits*

### MCLAUGHLIN, Lawrence
Honigman Miller Schwartz and Cohn LLP, Detroit 313 465 7474
LMclaughlin@honigman.com
*Recommended in Real Estate*

**Practice Areas:** Represents developers of commercial, industrial and residential real estate. Extensive experience in acquisitions, land use, entitlements, development incentives, partnerships and joint ventures, financing, construction, leasing, sales, workouts and restructuring. Special expertise in retail development and complex transactions.

**Prof. Memberships:** American College of Real Estate Lawyers, Program Committee; International Council of Shopping Centers, Program Committee; State Bar of Michigan, Section of Real Property Law, Council Member and former Chairman; Best Lawyers in America since 1991.

**Career:** BSME, General Motors Institute, 1974; JD, magna cum laude, Wayne State University Law School, 1977. Chairman of Honigman's Real Estate Department.

### MCLEOD, David K
Miller, Canfield, Paddock and Stone, P.L.C., Detroit 313 496 7564
mcleod@millercanfield.com
*Recommended in Banking & Finance*

**Practice Areas:** Practice includes all types of commercial transactions, including real estate transactions, banking, and finance.

**Prof. Memberships:** State Bar of Michigan Corporate and Real Estate Sections.

**Career:** Principal, 1997-present; Of Counsel, 1994-96; former Leader, Financial Institutions and Transactions Group.

**Personal:** JD, cum laude, University of Michigan Law School, 1985; BA, magna cum laude, Michigan State University, 1982.

### MINKUS, Daniel
Clark Hill PLC, Birmingham
248 642 9692
*Recommended in Corporate/M&A*

### MIZIOLEK, Aleksandra
Dykema Gossett PLLC, Detroit
313 568 6800
*Recommended in Corporate/M&A*

### MOSCOW, Cyril
Honigman Miller Schwartz and Cohn LLP, Detroit 313 465 7486
CMoscow@honigman.com
*Recommended in Corporate/M&A*

**Practice Areas:** Corporate matters and securities transactions.

**Prof. Memberships:** State Bar of Michigan, Business Law Section and Chairman since 1984 of the Subcommittee on Business Corporation Act Revision; American Bar Association, Business Law Section, Corporate Law Committee.

**Career:** BA, Wayne State University, 1954; JD, University of Michigan (Order of the Coif), 1957.

**Publications:** Various, including 'Michigan Corporation Law and Practice', 'Michigan Securities Regulation', and other articles on corporate and securities law. Adjunct lecturer at the University of Michigan Law School since 1973 as well as a frequent lecturer on securities regulation, business combinations, corporate governance and business planning.

### MULCAHY, Michael
Dawda, Mann, Mulcahy & Sadler PLC, Bloomfield Hills 248 642 3700
*Recommended in Real Estate*

### MURPHY, Lawrence
Varnum, Riddering, Schmidt & Howlett LLP, Grand Rapids 269 553 3511
ljmurphy@varnumlaw.com
*Recommended in Employment*

**Practice Areas:** Mr Murphy represents management clients in labor and employment law, with emphasis on defending management in employment litigation matters. He has extensive experience in employment discrimination; wage and hour; occupational safety and health; sexual harassment; wrongful termination; executive employment contracts; personnel policies and manuals; discipline issues; corporate downsizing; trade secret anti-piracy and non-compete agreements; drug and alcohol testing; and traditional labor law and union avoidance. He is listed in 'The Best Lawyers in America'.

**Prof. Memberships:** Mr Murphy is a member of the Michigan, Indiana, Illinois and Wisconsin Bar Associations and numerous federal district courts throughout the Country.

## MURRAY, Gregory V
Vercruysse Murray & Calzone, PC, Bingham Farms 248 540 7024
gmurray@vmclaw.com
*Recommended in Employment*

**Practice Areas:** Wrongful discharge, employment litigation, civil rights and discrimination litigation.

**Prof. Memberships:** Member: State Bar of Michigan Labor and Employment Law Section and Alternative Dispute Resolution Section, American Bar Association Litigation Section, Federal Bar Association, American Employment Law Council and Oakland County Bar Association. Fellow: College of Labor and Employment Lawyers. Life Fellow: Michigan State Bar Foundation and Oakland County Bar Foundation.

**Career:** Co-Founder, shareholder, Vice President and Treasurer, Vercruysse Murray & Calzone.

**Publications:** Co-author, 'Employment Litigation in Michigan', 2nd ed (ICLE 2004).

**Personal:** Detroit College of Law (JD, cum laude, 1978); University of Michigan (BA, 1971).

## MUTH, Jon
Miller Johnson, Grand Rapids
616 831 1700
*Recommended in Litigation*

## NIEHOFF, Leonard M
Butzel Long, Detroit 734 213 3625
niehoff@butzel.com
*Recommended in Employment*

**Practice Areas:** Litigation, involving media law, higher education law, civil rights, constitutional law, First Amendment business and employment issues.

**Prof. Memberships:** Member of the First Amendment and Media Litigation Section of the American Bar Association and National Association of College and Unviersity Attorneys. Board Member, CS Mott Children's Hospital, the Michigan Theater Foundation and the University Musical Society.

**Career:** Shareholder, Butzel Long.

**Personal:** University of Michigan (JD 1984); University of Michigan (BA 1981).

## NIX II, Robert
Kerr Russell & Weber, Detroit
313 961 0200
*Recommended in Real Estate*

## NORRIS, Megan P
Miller, Canfield, Paddock and Stone, P.L.C., Detroit 313 496 7594
norris@millercanfield.com
*Recommended in Employment*

**Practice Areas:** All aspects of employment and labor, concentrating in the areas of Americans with Disabilities Act, defamation, and employment litigation, including wrongful discharge, sexual harassment, discrimination, and workers' compensation.

**Prof. Memberships:** American Bar Association, State Bar of Michigan, Detroit Metropolitan Bar Association (past President), City of Detroit Board of Police Commissioners (past Chair), Detroit Barristers' Association (past President), Institute of Continuing Legal Education Labor Advisory Board.

**Career:** Joined firm 1986; Principal, 1995; Co-Leader, Labor and Employment Group, 2003-present.

**Personal:** JD, University of Michigan Law School, 1986; BA, Wesleyan University, 1983.

## OOSTERHOUSE, Carl
Varnum, Riddering, Schmidt & Howlett LLP, Grand Rapids 616 336 6818
coosterhouse@varnumlaw.com
*Recommended in Corporate/M&A*

**Practice Areas:** Mr Oosterhouse's corporate and business practice includes mergers and acquisitions, business planning and tax, financing private placement, equity offerings, tax-exempt financing and transportation. He is listed in 'The Best Lawyers in America'.

**Prof. Memberships:** Member, Tax Law and Business Law Sections of the American Bar Association; Real Estate, Business and Tax Sections of the State Bar of Michigan; the Grand Rapids Bar Association and the National Association of Bond Lawyers.

## OPPERWALL, Theodore
Kienbaum Opperwall Hardy & Pelton P.L.C., Birmingham 248 645 0000
topperwall@kohp.com
*Recommended in Employment*

**Practice Areas:** Labor and employment; employee benefits law; appellate practice.

**Prof. Memberships:** American Bar Association (Member, Labor and Employment Law Section: Committee on the Development of the Law under the National Labor Relations Act; Committee on Practice and Procedure under the National Labor Relations Act; Committee on Alternative Dispute Resolution in Labor and Employment Law; Committee on Antitrust, RICO and Labor Law); State Bar of Michigan (Member: Labor and Employment Law Section Council, 1991-95); National and local NLRB Practice and Procedure Committees.

**Career:** With over 30 years' experience in the field, Mr Opperwall specializes in representing management in all facets of traditional labor law, including union organizing, collective bargaining and contract administration, and proceedings before the National Labor Relations Board. A former examiner for the NLRB, Mr Opperwall has a keen understanding of unfair labor practice and union election issues. Listed in 'Best Lawyers in America' and a Fellow of the College of Labor and Employment Lawyers, Mr Opperwall also has extensive experience in wrongful discharge, civil rights, and employee benefits litigation. He is an experienced appellate advocate, admitted to practice before the US Supreme Court and the US Courts of Appeals for the Sixth Circuit and the District of Columbia Circuit. Founding Partner, Kienbaum Opperwall Hardy & Pelton, PLC, 1997-present.

**Publications:** Author of 'Employment Law in Michigan: An Employer's Guide', and 'Buying and Selling a Business in Michigan', published by the Institute of Continuing Legal Education.

**Personal:** Born in Grand Rapids, Michigan, 1951.

## PAPPAS, Edward H
Dickinson Wright PLLC, Detroit
248 433 7228
epappas@dickinsonwright.com
*Recommended in Litigation*

**Practice Areas:** Director: Commercial and Business, Securities Litigation, Alternative Dispute Resolution Group. Business tort litigation, including tortious interference, covenants not to compete, misappropriation of trade secrets, unfair competition, trademark, fraud, business defamation, breach of fiduciary duty, and civil conspiracy claims. Securities fraud, product liability and real estate litigation.

**Prof. Memberships:** Commissioner, Board of Commissioners, State Bar of Michigan; mediator and facilitator, Oakland County Circuit Court; Chairperson, Michigan Attorney Discipline Board Hearing Panel.

**Publications:** 'Michigan Business Torts' (ICLE), co-author, first edition, 2001; second edition, 2003.

**Personal:** University of Michigan Law School (JD cum laude, 1973); University of Michigan (BBA, 1969).

## PARSIGIAN, David N
Miller, Canfield, Paddock and Stone, P.L.C., Ann Arbor 734 668 7117
parsigian@millercanfield.com
*Recommended in Corporate/M&A*

**Practice Areas:** Finance, corporate, and securities law. Emphasis on representing emerging technology companies from inception through acquisition or initial public offering, extensive work in venture capital finance, private placements, joint ventures, technology licensing, strategic alliances, and mergers and acquisitions; representation of hi-technology companies in information technology, e-business, biotechnology and life sciences, advanced manufacturing; and representing institutional venture firm and individual investors in hi-technology investment activities.

**Prof. Memberships:** American Bar Association, State Bar of Michigan, Michigan Economic Development Corporation.

**Career:** Joined firm 1985; Principal 1993.

**Personal:** JD, University of Texas Law School, 1985; BS, Mechanical Engineering, University of Michigan, 1980.

## PIGGOTT, Cameron
Dykema Gossett PLLC, Bloomfield Hills
248 203 0700
*Recommended in Real Estate*

## POZZA JR, Clarence L
Miller, Canfield, Paddock and Stone, P.L.C., Detroit 313 496 7556
pozza@millercanfield.com
*Recommended in Litigation*

**Practice Areas:** Litigation and dispute resolution. Emphasis on commercial, corporate, securities and insurance litigation, regulatory representations, alternative dispute resolution, and preventative and compliance counseling. Experience includes complex trial and appellate work in federal and state courts.

**Prof. Memberships:** American Bar Association, State Bar of Michigan, Federal Bar Association, Detroit Metropolitan Bar Association, National Association of Securities Dealers, American Arbitration Association, Midwest Securities Institute, and ICLE faculty member.

**Career:** Joined firm 1974; Principal, 1981; Litigation Group Leader, 2000-present; Managing Director, 1992-2000.

**Personal:** JD, cum laude, University of Michigan Law School, 1974; BS, University of Michigan, 1971.

## RASSEL, Richard E
Butzel Long, Detroit 313 225 7014
rassel@butzel.com
*Recommended in Litigation*

**Practice Areas:** Business litigation, concentration in media law, libel and slander law, and complex business disputes. Certified Judge Advocate for the US Navy Judge Advocate School.

**Prof. Memberships:** Chair, Multi-Disciplinary Practice Committee, State Bar of Michigan. Past Chair, Media and Law Committee, State Bar of Michigan. Vice-Chair, Media and Law Committee, ABA; Chair, Tort Reform Committee, Media Law Resource Center; Chair, Administrative Committee of Lex Mundi. Fellow, American College of Trial Lawyers.

**Career:** Chairman and CEO, Butzel Long.

**Publications:** Numerous professional publications and presentations.

**Personal:** University of Notre Dame (BA, 1964). University of Michigan Law School (JD, 1966).

## RENTENBACH, Paul
Dykema Gossett PLLC, Detroit
313 568 6800
*Recommended in Corporate/M&A*

## RIBACK, Ronald H
Miller, Canfield, Paddock and Stone, P.L.C.,
Troy 248 267 3233
riback@millercanfield.com
*Recommended in Banking & Finance*
**Practice Areas:** Corporate and securities practice focusing on banking, mergers and acquisitions, commercial and real estate lending transactions, general corporate/business services.
**Prof. Memberships:** American Bar Association, Business Law Section; State Bar of Michigan, Corporate and Banking and Real Estate Sections.
**Career:** Principal, 1990-present.
**Personal:** JD, De Paul University College of Law, 1971; BA, University of Michigan, 1968.

## RITOK, Joseph
Dykema Gossett PLLC, Detroit
313 568 6800
*Recommended in Employment*

## ROACH, Steven A
Miller, Canfield, Paddock and Stone, P.L.C.,
Detroit 313 496 7933
roach@millercanfield.com
*Recommended in Banking & Finance*
**Practice Areas:** Commercial litigation with particular emphasis on creditors' rights, including equipment leases, real estate leases, notes, guaranties, mortgages, UCC Articles 2, 2A and 9, and pre-judgment and post-judgment remedies. Other areas of commercial litigation include property disputes, commercial product liability, shareholder disputes, professional negligence defense, including legal malpractice, accounting malpractice, fiduciary negligence, bankruptcy trustee negligence, and business torts.
**Prof. Memberships:** American Bar Association, State Bar of Michigan, Detroit Metropolitan Bar Association.
**Career:** Joined firm 1986; Principal, 1994; Leader, Financial Institutions and Transactions Group.
**Personal:** JD, University of Michigan Law School, 1986; AB, University of Michigan, 1983.

## SALESIN, Lowell
Maddin, Hauser, Wartell, Roth & Heller PC,
Southfield 248 354 4030
*Recommended in Real Estate*

## SANKBEIL, William
Kerr Russell & Weber, Detroit
313 961 0200
*Recommended in Litigation*

## SARGENT, William D
Honigman Miller Schwartz and Cohn LLP,
Detroit 313 465 7538
WSargent@honigman.com
*Recommended in Employment*
**Practice Areas:** Labor and employment

including labor relations, civil rights, wrongful discharge, and other employment/labor law matters. Single plaintiff litigation to class action and mass plaintiff cases. Assists employers with legal compliance issues related to collective bargaining agreements.
**Prof. Memberships:** State Bar of Michigan; Detroit Metropolitan Bar Association; American Bar Association.
**Career:** BS, summa cum laude (with high honors), Western Michigan University, 1980; JD, magna cum laude (with high honors and Order of the Coif) Wayne State University Law School, 1985; Chairman of Honigman's Labor and Employment Department.
**Publications:** Various, including articles on labor law and related employment issues.

## SCHWARTZ, Alan
Honigman Miller Schwartz and Cohn LLP,
Detroit 313 465 7000
AZSchwartz@honigman.com
*Recommended in Corporate/M&A*
**Practice Areas:** Business and family planning; acquisitions and sales of businesses; and general corporate representation.
**Prof. Memberships:** State Bar of Michigan; Detroit Metropolitan Bar Association; American Bar Association; Board of Directors, Detroit Regional Chamber of Commerce; Vice-Chair, Karmanos Cancer Institute; Board of Governors, Jewish Federation of Metropolitan Detroit.
**Career:** BA, with high distinction and high honors in History (Phi Beta Kappa), University of Michigan, 1965; JD, cum laude, Harvard University Law School, 1968; Chief Executive Officer and Chairman of the Board of Honigman.

## SCOTT, John ES
Dickinson Wright PLLC, Detroit
313 223 3622
jscott@dickinson-wright.com
*Recommended in Litigation*
**Practice Areas:** High stakes litigation, including involvement in or trial of cases involving automotive technologies, such as restraints, fuel tank design and placement issues, roll over and roof crush issues, glass selection and design, seat backs, steering wheel design issues, transmission design issues, metallurgical issues, tire and wheel selection, and design and manufacturing issues.
**Prof. Memberships:** Fellow, American College of Trial Lawyers, International Society of Barristers, and International Academy of Trial Lawyers; Life Member, Sixth Circuit Judicial Conference.
**Personal:** Wayne State University Law School (JD, 1961); Albion College (BA, 1958).

## SEMPLE, Lloyd
Dykema Gossett PLLC, Detroit
313 568 6800
*Recommended in Corporate/M&A*

## SERYAK, Richard J
Miller, Canfield, Paddock and Stone, P.L.C.,
Detroit 313 496 7501
seryak@millercanfield.com
*Recommended in Employment*
**Practice Areas:** Labor and employment practice covers wrongful discharge and employment discrimination civil litigation, NLRB, MERC, EEOC, and Michigan Department of Civil Rights proceedings. Served as lead counsel in numerous reported labor and employment decisions. He also is a member of the firm's Automotive Group.
**Prof. Memberships:** Michigan, Ohio, and Federal Bar Associations; Fellow, College of Labor and Employment Lawyers; Michigan Public Employer Labor Relations Association (MPELRA); former Co-Chair of the Labor and Employment Section of the Federal Bar Association (Detroit Chapter).
**Career:** Joined firm 1978; Principal, 1985.
**Personal:** JD, George Washington University, 1975; BA, University of Notre Dame, 1972.

## SHEVNOCK, Colleen M
Dickinson Wright PLLC, Detroit
734 623 1665
cshevnock@dickinsonwright.com
*Recommended in Banking & Finance*
**Practice Areas:** Extensive experience as counsel to banks and other institutional lenders in commercial lending matters. Negotiation and documentation of wide-range of loan transactions ranging from smaller uncommitted working capital facilities to counsel as agent in connection with large syndicated credit facilities. Experience with foreign currency facilities, acquisition facilities, working capital financing and letters of credit. Secured lending experience in all types of real and personal property. Counsel to various corporations and other entities, as borrowers, in connection with various financing transactions.
**Personal:** Wayne State University (JD cum laude, Order of the Coif, 1989); Michigan State University (BA, 1986).

## SHIELD JR, William P
Dickinson Wright PLLC, Detroit
313 223 3602
wshield@dickinsonwright.com
*Recommended in Banking & Finance*
**Practice Areas:** Counsel in numerous multibank, syndicated credit facilities and cross-border financings. Counsel to senior lenders, subordinated lenders and borrowers in public and private subordinated debt financings. Experience in asset based and other secured lending, including general asset based lending and oil and gas, aircraft and other specialized collateral transactions. Counsel in commercial lending transactions, including restructurings and other refinancings, secured and unsecured credits, acquisi-

tion and spin-off financings, international multiple borrower financings, general working capital facilities, start-up and joint venture financings and construction lending
**Personal:** University of Michigan (JD 1984); University of Michigan (BSEE magna cum laude, 1981).

## SHULMAN, Larry R
Bodman LLP, Detroit 313 393 7503
lshulman@bodmanllp.com
*Recommended in Banking & Finance*
**Practice Areas:** Represents lenders in loan originations and loan workouts and counsels lenders on lender liability issues. Commercial lending experience encompasses leveraged buyout and leveraged recapitalization loans, asset-based loans, letter of credit and bankers acceptance facilities and multi-rate, multi-currency loan facilities. Extensive experience representing lenders providing credit enhancements for commercial paper back-up facilities and municipal bonds.
**Prof. Memberships:** State Bar of Michigan; Detroit Metropolitan Bar Association.
**Personal:** JD, cum laude and BA, University of Michigan. Board of Directors, Downtown Detroit, Inc. Board of Directors, New Detroit. Board of Directors, Forgotten Harvest. Board of Trustees, JARC.

## SIEBERT, Sherill
Honigman Miller Schwartz and Cohn LLP,
Detroit 313 465 7556
SSiebert@honigman.com
*Recommended in Employee Benefits*
**Practice Areas:** Employee benefits, including tax and ERISA compliance and planning issues which arise in connection with all types of employee benefit plans and programs. Advises both sponsors or employee benefit plans and entities providing services to employee benefit arrangements.
**Prof. Memberships:** State Bar of Michigan, former Chair, Taxation Section; ABA, Taxation Section, Committee on Employee Benefits; Michigan Employee Benefits Conference; IRS Great Lakes Area TE/GE Council, Chair; American College of Employee Benefits Counsel, Charter Fellow.
**Career:** BA, UCLA, 1974; JD, cum laude, Wayne State University Law School, 1977. Frequent speaker on various employee benefits topics.

## SIMPSON, James A
Miller, Canfield, Paddock and Stone, P.L.C.,
Troy 248 267 3323
simpson@millercanfield.com
*Recommended in Real Estate*
**Practice Areas:** Experienced in all lending products and real estate. Designed loan processes and documentation for national lending programs; closing or supervising counsel on 1,500+ securitized commercial mortgage loans in all 50 states. Real estate portfolio experience over $4 billion, representing owners,

developers, contractors, syndicators, landlords and tenants.

**Prof. Memberships:** American Bar Association; State Bar of Michigan; Mortgage Bankers' Association of America; Commercial Mortgage Securities Association. **Career:** Joined firm 2003, Principal, 2006, Co-Leader, Capital Markets Lending Group; Previously, Co-Founder, Director, and CSO e-Cognita Technologies, Inc.; Senior Partner Simpson Zelenock. **Personal:** JD, Wayne State University, 1968; BA, Michigan State University, 1965.

## STEVENSON, Robert
Stevenson Keppelman Associates, Ann Arbor 734 747 7050
*Recommended in Employee Benefits*

## THELEN, James B
Miller, Canfield, Paddock and Stone, P.L.C., Lansing 517 483 4901
thelen@millercanfield.com
*Recommended in Employment*
**Practice Areas:** All areas of labor and employment, concentrating in employment discrimination, labor arbitration, state and federal unfair labor practices, and union activities. **Prof. Memberships:** American Bar Association, State Bar of Michigan, Ingham County Bar Association, Human Resource Management Association of Mid-Michigan. Director of Communications, 2005-present. **Career:** Joined firm 1995, Principal, 2005; previously at Western Michigan University as Assistant Vice President for Legislative Affairs and Assistant General Counsel, 1997-99. **Personal:** JD, cum laude, Tulane University Law School, 1995; BA, magna cum laude, Western Michigan University, 1992.

## THOMPSON, Deborah W
Miller, Canfield, Paddock and Stone, P.L.C., Detroit 313 496 7971
thompson@millercanfield.com
*Recommended in Employee Benefits*
**Practice Areas:** Tax-qualified retirement plans, welfare plans, cafeteria plans, nonqualified deferred compensation plans and stock option plans. Particular areas of concentration include defined benefit plans, 401(k) plans, cafeteria plans, healthcare plans (including COBRA continuation coverage) and employee benefit issues in mergers and acquisitions. **Prof. Memberships:** American Bar Association; State Bar of Michigan; Detroit Metropolitan Bar Association; Fellow, American College of Employee Benefits Counsel; Women Lawyers Association of Michigan. **Career:** Joined firm 1989; Principal, 1993; Recruitment Chair, 1995-present. **Personal:** JD, cum laude, Wayne State University Law School, 1978; BA, Michigan State University, 1964.

## TRENTACOSTA, John R
Foley & Lardner LLP, Detroit
313 234 7124
jtrentacosta@foley.com
*Recommended in Litigation*
**Career:** John R Trentacosta is a Partner in the Detroit office Foley & Lardner LLP and leader of the Automotive Industry Team. He is a member of the Distribution and Franchise and Commercial Transactions and Business Counseling Practices, as well as the International Team. Mr Trentacosta has over 20 years of commercial, contract and computer litigation experience and is actively involved in drafting contracts commonly used in the automotive industry. He is also extensively involved in litigating disputes involving automotive concerns. Mr Trentacosta is a 1980 graduate of Georgetown University Law Center.

## VERCRUYSSE, Robert
Vercruysse Murray & Calzone, PC, Bingham Farms 248 540 7011
rvercruysse@vmclaw.com
*Recommended in Employment*
**Practice Areas:** Labor and employment law, ERISA, arbitration, commercial litigation. **Prof. Memberships:** Past Chair: Labor and Employment Law Section, State Bar of Michigan. Member: American Bar Association, American Employment Law Council, Board of the Federal Bar Association. Life Member: Sixth Judicial Conference for the US Court of Appeals. Fellow: College of Labor and Employment Lawyers. Trustee: Historical Society of the US District Court for the Eastern District of Michigan. **Career:** Co-Founder, President, Vercruysse Murray & Calzone. Law clerk to the Honorable Clifford O'Sullivan, US Court of Appeals, Sixth Circuit (1968-69). **Personal:** University of Michigan Law School, Michigan State University.

## VON ENDE, Carl H
Miller, Canfield, Paddock and Stone, P.L.C., Detroit 313 496 7618
vonende@millercanfield.com
*Recommended in Litigation*
**Practice Areas:** Litigation and dispute resolution, with an emphasis on trials and appeals relating to intellectual property, corporate control, securities, banking, taxation, and constitutional litigation. **Prof. Memberships:** State Bar of Michigan; Detroit Metropolitan Bar Association (President 1987-88); American College of Trial Lawyers (Fellow 1994-present, State Chair 1998-99); Faculty Member, Mandatory Continuing Legal Education Program, Michigan Supreme Court; Group Leader, University of Michigan Advocacy Institute; and Instructor, American Arbitration Association. **Career:** Joined firm 1968; Principal, 1975; Litigation Practice Group Leader, 1990-99.

**Personal:** JD, University of Michigan Law School, 1968; AB, University of Michigan, 1964.

## WATSON, Jerome R
Miller, Canfield, Paddock and Stone, P.L.C., Detroit 313 496 7552
watson@millercanfield.com
*Recommended in Employment*
**Practice Areas:** Labor law and litigation, primarily defending employers in discrimination, harassment, breach of contract, wrongful discharge, and retaliation cases. Also experienced in FOIA, OMA, workplace violence, and defending constitutional challenges and employment class actions. **Prof. Memberships:** American Bar Association, State Bar of Michigan, Federal Bar Association, Wolverine Bar Association, National Bar Association. Served as spokesman for Michigan Region of the American Bar Association's Minority Partners in Majority Firms Program. **Career:** Joined firm 1976; Principal, 1983; Managing Director, 2000-present. **Personal:** JD, University of Michigan Law School, 1976; BA, University of Michigan, 1972. Prior experience includes social worker, assessor, and columnist.

## WINOKUR, Laurence
Dickinson Wright PLLC, Detroit
248 433 7263
lwinokur@dickinsonwright.com
*Recommended in Real Estate*
**Practice Areas:** Extensive experience in real estate development, real estate finance and mortgage lending, and leasing. Represent various developers in acquisition, development, and leasing of projects. **Prof. Memberships:** Member, American Bar Association; Member, State Bar of Michigan Real Property Section and Business Law Section. **Personal:** University of Michigan Law School (JD); University of Michigan (BA).

## WOODS, Sharon
Barris, Sott, Denn & Driker, PLLC, Detroit 313 965 9725
*Recommended in Litigation*

## YOUNG, Rodger
Young & Susser PC Attorneys and Counselors, Southfield
248 353 8620
*Recommended in Litigation*

## ZABRISKIE, Wendy L
Bodman LLP, Troy 248 743 6046
wzabriskie@bodmanllp.com
*Recommended in Banking & Finance*
**Practice Areas:** Represents financial institutions in the structuring, negotiation and documentation of real estate and commercial loans, including construction loans, end mortgage loans, working capital arrangements, acquisition and mezzanine facilities, leveraged buyout financings, and agented and syndicated transac-

tions. Represents real estate developers and investors in commercial, industrial and residential acquisitions, sales, developments and financings.
**Prof. Memberships:** State Bar of Michigan; American Bar Association.
**Personal:** JD, magna cum laude, Wayne State University. BA, Michigan State University. Member, City of Birmingham Brownfield Redevelopment Authority. Former Vice Chair, City of Royal Oak Zoning Board of Appeals.

## ZELENOCK, Katheryne L
Miller, Canfield, Paddock and Stone, P.L.C., Troy 248 267 3323
zelenock@millercanfield.com
*Recommended in Real Estate*
**Practice Areas:** Real estate and commercial finance. Representing national and regional lenders, mortgage bankers and loan servicers, emphasis on capital markets, conduit, and bank financing. Litigation counsel to businesses, principally related to real estate and corporate finance matters. **Prof. Memberships:** American Bar Association, State Bar of Michigan, Mortgage Bankers' Association of America, Commercial Mortgage Securities Association, Mortgage Industry Standards Maintenance Organization, Commercial Real Estate Women of Detroit. **Career:** Joined firm 2003, Principal 2006; Co-Leader, Capital Markets Lending Group; previously Co-Founder and President, 1998-2003 e-Cognita Technologies, Inc. **Personal:** JD, University of Notre Dame Law School, 1991; BA, University of Michigan, 1987.

## ZUCKERMAN, Richard
Honigman Miller Schwartz and Cohn LLP, Detroit 313 465 7618
REZ@honigman.com
*Recommended in Litigation*
**Practice Areas:** Federal and state white-collar criminal defense; civil and criminal antitrust and tax litigation; securities fraud defense; and environmental crimes defense. Supervised several Sarbanes-Oxley internal investigations as counsel to the board of directors or audit committee of publicly traded corporations. **Prof. Memberships:** State Bar of Michigan, Judicial Qualifications Committee; State Bar of California; State Bar of Nevada; Federal Bar Association, Committee on Criminal Law; American Bar Association; Michigan Attorney Grievance Committee. **Career:** BA, University of Michigan, 1967; JD, cum laude, Southwestern University School of Law, 1974. US Department of Justice, Organized Crime and Racketeering Section, 1974-77.

## ZUSSMAN, Richard
Jaffe, Raitt, Heuer & Weiss, PC, Detroit 313 961 8380
*Recommended in Real Estate*

# BODMAN LLP

## THE FIRM

**Chairman, Executive Committee:** Larry R Shulman

**Number of partners:** 82
**Number of other lawyers:** 47

**FIRM OVERVIEW:** Bodman LLP offers a broad range of business law services from five Michigan offices located in Detroit, Troy, Ann Arbor, Cheboygan and Lansing. Founded in 1927 by two former Ford Motor Company lawyers, Bodman is one of Michigan's largest law firms. The firm is known for superior service that has led to many significant client relationships that have lasted for decades. For example, Bodman has represented the interests of members of the Ford family continuously since 1927. The firm's relationship with Comerica Incorporated dates to 1933, when it helped establish Comerica's predecessor. Bodman is counsel or special counsel to more than 80 other financial institutions in Michigan and across the nation, including LaSalle Bank Midwest N.A., an affiliate of ABN AMRO. Bodman attorneys also have extensive experience in commercial litigation, alternative dispute resolution, corporate and securities law, probate and estate planning, real estate, debtor-creditor rights and bankruptcy, labor and employment law, tax, intellectual property, environmental issues, municipal finance, and construction law.

**MAIN AREAS OF PRACTICE:** The firm's primary areas of practice are: banking; litigation and alternative dispute resolution; individual clients; business/corporate; real property; debtor-creditor rights and bankruptcy; labor and employment; tax; intellectual property; environmental; construction; municipal law and finance.

**CLIENTS:** Bodman has a diverse client base that includes individuals and businesses in a variety of industries, with emphasis on financial services, automotive, real estate, nonprofit and charitable institutions, high tech, general manufacturing, and other sectors. Representative clients include: Archdiocese of Detroit; Blue Circle America, Inc.; Blue Cross and Blue Shield of Michigan; Booth Newspapers, Inc.; Charles Stewart Mott Foundation; Cheboygan Memorial Hospital; City of Ann Arbor; City of Grosse Pointe Park; Comcast Cablevision; Comerica Bank; CSX Transportation, Inc.; The Detroit Lions, Inc.; Federal National Mortgage Association (Fannie Mae); Financial Institutions Compliance Cooperative; Flagstar Bank F.S.B.; Ford Estates; The Huntington National Bank; LaSalle Bank Midwest N.A.; Lear Corp.; KeyBank National Association; Michigan Insurance Commissioner; Monroe Bank & Trust; Outdoor Advertising Association of Michigan and member companies; PanEnergy Corp.; PricewaterhouseCoopers LLP; Primerica Financial Services; Pulte Homes of Michigan; Saga Communications, Inc.; St. John Health System; Sun America Insurance Company; University of Detroit-Mercy; Wayne County; Jervis B. Webb Company.

**INTERNATIONAL WORK:** Bodman represents many international clients with business interests in Michigan and elsewhere within the United States. Representative international clients include: Bharat Forge Limited; DaimlerChrysler; Freudenberg-NOK General Partnership; Gamebore Cartridge Co., Limited; LaFarge North America, Inc.; St. Marys Cement Corporation, a division of Votorantim; Techform Products Limited; Wahler Metalurgica Ltda.

## HEAD OFFICE

**MICHIGAN**
6th Floor at Ford Field, 1901 St. Antoine Street
**Detroit**, Michigan 48226 USA
**Tel:** 313 259 7777   **Fax:** 313 393 7579
**Email:** info@bodmanllp.com
**Website:** www.bodmanllp.com

## BRANCH OFFICES

Suite 500, 201 West Big Beaver Rd.
**Troy**, Michigan 48084
**Tel:** 248 743 6000   **Fax:** 248 743 6002

Suite 400, 401 East Liberty
**Ann Arbor**, Michigan 48104
**Tel:** 734 761 3780   **Fax:** 734 930 2494

229 Court Street, P.O. Box 405
**Cheboygan**, Michigan 49721
**Tel:** 231 627 8000   **Fax:** 231 627 2802

Suite 2, 721 North Capitol
**Lansing**, Michigan 48906
**Tel:** 517 485 1299   **Fax:** 517 485 1298

## CONTACTS

| | |
|---|---|
| **Banking** | Larry R Shulman |
| | Joseph J Kochanek |
| | Kathleen O'C Hickey |
| | Wendy L Zabriskie |
| **Business/Corporate/M&A** | Terrence B Larkin |
| | F Thomas Lewand |
| | David C Stone |
| | Timothy R Damschroder |
| **Construction** | Harvey W Berman |
| **Debtor-Creditor Rights & Bankruptcy** | Robert J Diehl, Jr |
| **Environmental** | Fredrick J Dindoffer |
| **Individual Clients/Trusts & Estates** | David P Larsen |
| **Intellectual Property** | Susan M Kornfield |
| **Labor & Employment** | John C Cashen |
| **Litigation & ADR** | Thomas J Tallerico |
| | Joseph J Shannon |
| **Municipal Law & Finance** | Jerold Lax |
| **Real Property** | David W Hipp |
| **Tax** | Christopher J Dine |

# bodman

## ATTORNEYS & COUNSELORS

# BRADY HATHAWAY BRADY & BRETZ, P.C.

## THE FIRM

**Founding Partners:** John F Brady, Thomas M J Hathaway, Thomas P Brady, Daniel J Bretz

**FIRM OVERVIEW:** Founded in 1989, Brady Hathaway Brady & Bretz, P.C. ('Brady Hathaway') specializes in counseling and representing management in all aspects of labor and employment law. Brady Hathaway has proven expertise in the areas of employment counseling and litigation, traditional labor law, general litigation and appellate law. The firm has a national reputation as 'The Employer's Lawyer.' In terms of size, the firm is comparable to a labor and employment department found in large 'general practice' law firms. Yet, unlike many big firms, all of the attorneys at Brady Hathaway are specialized litigators with 'first chair' experience in some of the region's most complex and high profile cases. Collectively, the members of Brady Hathaway possess over 140 years of concentrated experience. Clients of all sizes appreciate the value of responsive professionals who have a proven track record in handling their particular employment matter. The firm is committed to premier investigation, reporting and handling of sensitive legal matters. Its goal is a cost-effective deployment of veteran legal talent specializing in a complex and fluid area of the law.

## MAIN AREAS OF PRACTICE:

**Employment Law Experience:** In the area of civil rights and employment litigation, the attorneys at Brady Hathaway have successfully defended lawsuits alleging discrimination, harassment, breach of express or implied contract, public policy discharge, whistleblower, retaliation, defamation, interference with contract, misrepresentation, fraud, and invasion of privacy. Brady Hathaway has represented employers faced with single-plaintiff suits as well as complex multi-plaintiff and class action proceedings. Brady Hathaway has strong credentials at all levels of federal and state trial and appellate courts. The firm has also appeared in other forums such as the EEOC, the Michigan Department of Civil Rights, and various other states' civil rights agencies. The firm counsels clients on a daily basis and has conducted independent investigations in sex harassment and other workplace harassment matters. While the firm's practice is centered in Michigan, it has represented clients nationwide and has rendered employment advice based on the law of other states including Alabama, Arizona, California, Colorado, Florida, Georgia, Illinois, Indiana, Iowa, Kansas, Massachusetts, Minnesota, Missouri, New York, North Carolina, Ohio, Pennsylvania, Texas and Utah. Brady Hathaway develops, drafts, and reviews employment manuals and policies regarding all facets of employment law, including harassment, equal employment opportunity, at-will employment, employee evaluations, fringe benefits, drug testing, sick leave, rules of conduct, attendance control, and the Family and Medical Leave Act. The firm has also worked with management to develop and defend high-level employment contracts, such as stock option agreements, change of control contracts, and covenants regarding confidentiality, trade secrets and competition.

**Labor Law Experience:** Brady Hathaway possesses some of the leading traditional labor lawyers in the region. The firm has extensive trial and investigatory experience before the National Labor Relations Board (NLRB) and the Michigan Employment Relations Commission (MERC). The firm has handled numerous union organizing campaigns, and provided key supervisor training, development of policies, and advice on sound, practical employment relations. Brady Hathaway represents numerous private and public employers in collective bargaining negotiations. In the role of chief negotiator, the firm has negotiated labor contracts that meet the client's economic and efficiency objectives while maintaining labor peace. The firm's attorneys have also handled a broad range of traditional labor matters for governmental and nonprofit entities, including interest-based bargaining, 'Act 312 arbitrations,' mediation-based bargaining, and fact-finding proceedings. The firm also advises clients on the administration of collective bargaining agreements and the drafting of contract language to avoid unnecessary grievances. The firm has tried hundreds of contract interpretation and discipline arbitrations.

**General Legal Experience:** Brady Hathaway is 'AV' rated (the highest rating available) in the Martindale-Hubbell Law Firm Directory. Five of the six shareholders are 'AV' rated, as are two of the firm's associates. Martindale-Hubbell is the facilitator of a peer review process that rates lawyers in two categories – legal ability and general ethical standards. In a recent edition of The Best Lawyers of America, 14 attorneys were listed as 'the best' management and labor employment lawyers in the Metropolitan Detroit area. Two of those 14 are members of Brady Hathaway.

**CLIENTS:** Brady Hathaway has represented a broad range of clients from small local firms to large national and international businesses. The firm has been selected as panel counsel by several insurance firms to defend profit and nonprofit entities under employment practices liability insurance policies. The firm is frequently selected by other attorneys and judges to represent and counsel their law firms and legal entities in labor and employment matters, representing more than 30 law firms. Brady Hathaway has a particular expertise in representing healthcare providers, including acute care hospitals and long term care facilities.

## HEAD OFFICE

**MICHIGAN**
535 Griswold Street, 1330 Buhl Building, **Detroit**, MI 48226
**Tel:** 313 965 3700   **Fax:** 313 965 2830
**Email:** brady@bradyhathaway.com
**Website:** www.bradyhathaway.com

# BUTZEL LONG

## THE FIRM

**Chairman:** Philip J Kessler
**Managing Director of Global Client Relations:** Richard E Rassel
**Chief Marketing Officer:** Joseph J Melnick

**Number of partners:** 119
**Number of other lawyers:** 96

## AREAS OF PRACTICE:
Litigation . . . . . . . . . . . . . . . . . . . . . . . . . . . . . . . . . . . . . . . . . . . . . . . 35%
Corporate/Tax/Real Estate/Wealth Planning . . . . . . . . . . . . . . . . 35%
Labor/Employment/Benefits/Immigration . . . . . . . . . . . . . . . . . . 30%

**FIRM OVERVIEW:** Butzel Long is a leading law firm with offices throughout Michigan, and in strategic locations in Washington DC, Florida and China. The firm's practice ranges from clients on the cutting edge of technology and innovation to traditional industrial and manufacturing giants. The firm strives to be on the cutting edge of significant trends and developments in the business world including advanced technology and manufacturing, e-commerce, internet law, and global operations and transactions. They also have special expertise with global automotive matters, global trade and international business issues. The firm's approach is to provide a personalized attorney-client relationship based on a recognition of, and responsiveness to, each client's unique concerns and requirements. They seek a clear understanding of the business needs of each client through industry-focused research, knowledge management and partnering relationships. Since its founding in 1854, the firm has maintained a commitment to the delivery of consistent excellence in work product and services.

## MAIN AREAS OF PRACTICE:

**Litigation:** Litigation is one of the firm's core practice strengths. Several areas of speciality litigation work provide representation throughout the United States. The firm continues its tradition of landmark, precedent setting matters in litigation. The practice consists of skilled attorneys who by expertise and experience specialize in finding solutions for disputes arising out of business transactions and operations. The range of business matters includes complex business disputes, IP litigation, product liability, class action, corporate compliance and white-collar crime, antitrust and constitutional law.

**Corporate/Tax/Real Estate/Wealth Planning:** The firm has a reputation as leader on all types of transaction and compliance issues. Representative clients include Fortune 500 companies; non-US global concerns; private companies; technology and service companies; business start-ups. The firm maintains a depth of experience in all areas of corporate advice and counsel.

**Labor/Employment/Benefits/Immigration:** The firm is the established leader in all areas of workforce issues. Clients from around the globe are advised on all aspects of employment concerns. Former partner is Chair of the US National Labor Relations Board. The firm maintains the largest immigration and employment benefits practice in Michigan. Employee benefits partner is often asked to testify before the US Congress by business groups.

## HEAD OFFICE

**MICHIGAN**
150 West Jefferson, Suite 100, **Detroit**, MI 48226
**Tel:** 313 225 7000  **Fax:** 313 225 7080
**E-mail:** info@butzel.com
**Website:** www.butzel.com

## BRANCH OFFICES

**DISTRICT OF COLUMBIA**
1747 Pennsylvania Avenue NW, Suite 300, **Washington**, DC 20006
**Tel:** 202 454 2888  **Fax:** 202 454 2805

**FLORIDA**
1200 North Federal Highway, Suite 420, **Boca Raton**, FL 33432
**Tel:** 561 368 2151  **Fax:** 561 368 4668

**MICHIGAN**
350 S. Main Street, Suite 300, **Ann Arbor**, MI 48104
**Tel:** 734 995 3110  **Fax:** 734 995 1777

100 Bloomfield Hills Parkway, Suite 200, **Bloomfield Hills**, MI 48304
**Tel:** 248 258 1616  **Fax:** 248 258 1439

25 West 8th Street, Suite 200, **Holland**, MI 49423
**Tel:** 616 396 8860  **Fax:** 616 396 1771

110 West Michigan Avenue, Suite 1100, **Lansing**, MI 48933
**Tel:** 517 372 6622  **Fax:** 517 372 6672

## INTERNATIONAL OFFICES

The firm also has alliance offices in Beijing and Shanghai.

**INTERNATIONAL WORK:** The firm has broad experience in all matters of international issues. A cross-disciplinary Global Trade and Transactions Group represents client interests throughout the world. The firm has developed a thriving Global Automotive Practice. The firm's lawyers serve as key advisors to automotive companies from Canada, the UK, France, Germany, other European suppliers, Japan, Korea and China. There is a special focus on developing economies of China and Mexico. Recently formed China Alliance provides on-the-ground capabilities in Shanghai and Beijing. Managing Director of the China Alliance is former senior trade official for the White House.

# BUTZEL LONG
ATTORNEYS AND COUNSELORS

# CLARK HILL PLC

## THE FIRM

**Chief Executive Officer:** John J Hern, Jr

**Number of attorneys:** 147
**Number of partners:** 95
**Number of associates:** 50
**Of counsel:** 2

**FIRM OVERVIEW:** Clark Hill PLC combines pre-eminent legal talent with the latest technology to create the efficiency and flexibility today's clients expect. Clark Hill is a diverse group that shares a tradition of integrity, experience, and hard work in the service of its clients and the community. The practice is based on teamwork, with mutual support among lawyers of different specialties and experience levels enabling the firm to meet client needs with the highest proficiency. The firm's clients include publicly held companies, as well as small entrepreneurial startups, sole proprietorships, and individuals. Representative clients include manufacturers, software and internet providers, financial institutions, distributors and retailers, freight associations, hospitals, units of government and non-profit organizations. Clark Hill is utilizing state-of-the-art technology applications, including direct connectivity to client computer networks, advanced systems for document compilation and retrieval, and electronic database research. With more than 135 lawyers, Clark Hill offers clients a complete range of legal services. The firm's diverse practice encompasses all areas of the law, including litigation (business, construction, intellectual property, toxic tort, and product liability), administrative, environmental, energy, business (corporate and partnership, mergers and acquisitions, antitrust, banking, bankruptcy, real estate, and tax-exempt organizations), employment, benefits, immigration, trusts and estates, tax, school and municipal, and family law. The firm combines breadth of experience with depth of specialization to deal with the extraordinary issues and opportunities confronting clients today. Clark Hill PLC faces the challenges of the new millennium with renewed vigor, greater efficiencies, and greater resources, all for the benefit of its clients. The firm remains committed to providing cost-effective legal services that combine the tradition of quality and personal service with the latest innovations in the practice of law.

## MAIN AREAS OF PRACTICE:

**Labor & Employment Law:** Clark Hill labor and employment attorneys offer a full range of employment law services, representing management interests with attorneys specializing in labor relations and its related specialities. The firm represents private, public, and not-for-profit employers of any size. The firm's attorneys specialize in every aspect of the employer-employee relationship: union and non-union employer representation, regulatory matters, and litigation. Employee benefits and immigration law are an integrated component of the firm's full service practice. Three of the practice group members are named in the Best Lawyers in America publication, and another member is the past president of the State Bar of Michigan and currently the president of the National Bar Association. The firm is also general counsel to two Michigan employer associations.

**Bankruptcy & Corporate Restructuring:** The firm specializes in bankruptcy, business reorganization, and insolvency-related matters. The firm regularly represents parties in bankruptcy and other judicial proceedings as well as in out-of-court workouts across the country. Clark Hill PLC represents debtors, unsecured creditors' committees, lenders and other secured parties, bondholders, vendors and trade creditors, asset purchasers, insurance carriers, landlords, equipment lessors, and liquidating agents. The industries in which Clark Hill attorneys have provided representation cover the spectrum of business enterprises, including the automotive, manufacturing, retail, telecommunications, aviation, and real estate industries.

**Business Law:** The firm's business law attorneys are experienced in handling the wide diversity of transactions which come from its location in the nation's tenth most populous metropolitan area and in a state whose economy exceeds

### HEAD OFFICE

**MICHIGAN**
500 Woodward Avenue, Suite 3500, **Detroit**, MI 48226-3435
**Tel:** 313 965 8300   **Fax:** 313 965 8252
**Website:** www.clarkhill.com

### BRANCH OFFICES

**MICHIGAN**
255 S Old Woodward, Third Floor, **Birmingham**, MI 48009
**Tel:** 248 642 9692   **Fax:** 248 642 2174

212 East Grand River Avenue, **Lansing**, MI 48906
**Tel:** 517 318 3100   **Fax:** 517 318 3099

200 Ottawa NW, **Grand Rapids**, MI 49503
**Tel:** 616 233 4822   **Fax:** 616 233 4823

### CONTACTS

| | |
|---|---|
| Business Law | Daniel H Minkus |
| Labor & Employment Law | Fred W Batten |
| Real Estate Law | William B Dunn |
| Real Estate Transactional Matters | Timothy M Koltun |

the gross national product of many nations. The firm deals equally well with its clients' day-to-day affairs and with the extraordinary opportunities and challenges that confront business people. The diversity of transactions reflects the broad pattern of business activity prevalent in Michigan and the Midwest, which brings the firm's clients into contact with the premier law firms in the world in the areas of manufacturing, intellectual property, healthcare, technology transfer, financial institutions, energy, insurance, securities, communications, computer software, pharmaceuticals, corporate finance and mergers and acquisitions.

**Real Estate Law:** Clark Hill's Real Estate Practice is centered in a core group of attorneys who have well developed and recognized skills in representing developers, investors, lenders, public entities, owners and tenants in a broad spectrum of transactions, ranging from the fundamental to the sophisticated in nature. This practice is driven by the firm's dedication to achieve client goals in a practical and solution-directed manner. The Real Estate Group often assists other aspects of the firm's practice in related areas such as finance, litigation, energy and telecommunications; and is the coordinator of the firm's work in such areas as construction and design contracting; eminent domain and valuation matters, including property tax management; environmental; and public support of industrial and commercial development.

**Trial, Litigation & Alternative Dispute Resolution:** Clark Hill litigation attorneys represent a diverse client base, comprised mainly of corporations, directors, officers, shareholders, partnerships, managing partners, limited partners, and limited liability entities. The firm also handle arbitrations, facilitations and mediations. For over 110 years, the firm has provided high quality legal services, and helped solve business problems by effective, economic case management, aggressive advocacy and sensible, timely resolutions. The firm is dedicated to excellent client service and maintain state of the art computerized litigation support systems to enhance efficiency. Throughout all stages of litigation the firm communicates with and informs its clients of case developments to help achieve business driven solutions.

# DICKINSON WRIGHT PLLC

## THE FIRM

**Chairman:** Dennis W Archer
**Chief Executive Officer:** James A Samborn

**Equity members:** 89
**Income members:** 49
**Other attorneys:** 72

**FIRM OVERVIEW:** Dickinson Wright PLLC, founded in 1878, has approximately 210 attorneys and is a full-service law firm with more than 40 practice areas. It provides corporate, commercial litigation, real estate, intellectual property, and employment services, among others, to clients ranging from the Fortune 5 to mid-sized and start ups. The firm is one of the largest operating in Michigan and offers legal assistance locally, regionally, nationally and internationally. Dickinson Wright's attorneys are regularly listed in compendiums of leading firms and belong to many top American Colleges. The firm is a leader in diversity and has been nationally recognized for its commitments in this area.

## MAIN AREAS OF PRACTICE:

**Banking & Financial Services:** The firm provides representation and complete transaction planning advice to both lenders and borrowers in virtually all types of transactions. The firm also offers sophisticated services in commercial bankruptcy, including workouts, insolvency litigation, and refinancing.
**Commercial & Business Litigation:** The firm regularly represents clients in all aspects of litigation, including defense in commercial disputes, class actions and other types of complex litigation, including mass tort and multidistrict litigation.
**Corporate:** The firm offers clients attorneys who are seasoned, talented and exceptionally well versed in all areas related to corporate transactions. Its lawyers handle, on a regular basis, complex issues including mergers and acquisitions, private equity transactions, financings, debt restructurings, joint ventures, securities offerings, and other commercial transactions. The firm also handles SOX-related compliance, corporate governance, SEC and regulatory compliance, and all types of entity formation and contractual arrangements.
**Labor & Employment:** The firm's capabilities extend to areas including employment counseling, immigration, employee benefits and executive compensation, complex employment and employee benefits litigation, wage and hour counseling, non-competition agreements and related obligations, labor management relations and disputes, and ESOP's.
**Real Estate:** The firm represents a clients in a full array of real estate transactions, including acquisitions and sales, joint ventures, permanent financing, construction, development, leasing transactions and real estate management for clients ranging from financial institutions and developers to schools and corporations.
**Additional practice specialties:** Alternative dispute resolution; antitrust and trade regulation; appellate litigation; bankruptcy; biotechnology; business criminal defense/investigations; business technology; construction; corporate finance; corporate governance; employee benefits; energy and public utilities; environmental; estate planning and trusts; family and matrimonial; gaming, immigration; insurance; intellectual property; international; labor and employment relations; medical malpractice defense; mergers and acquisitions; minority business enterprises; municipal law and finance; private capital; product liability litigation; railroads and transportation; regulatory and administrative law; risk management; schools and educational institutions; securities; taxation; telecommunications.

**CLIENTS:** Dickinson Wright maintains in-depth relationships with its extensive client base and handles a wide array of matters. Representative clients include JPMorgan Chase, NA, Ford Motor Company, Blue Cross Blue Shield of Michigan, MGM Grand, AT&T, State of Michigan, DuPont, DaimlerChrysler, Royal Bank of Scotland, Goodyear Tire and Rubber Co., W.Y. Campbell & Co., Dura Automotive Systems, Goldman, Sachs & Co., and Microsoft.

## HEAD OFFICE

**MICHIGAN**
500 Woodward Avenue, Suite 4000, **Detroit**, MI 48226
**Tel:** 313 223 3500    **Fax:** 313 223 3598
**Website:** www.dickinsonwright.com

## BRANCH OFFICES

**MICHIGAN**
301 E. Liberty Street, Suite 500, **Ann Arbor**, MI 48104-2266
**Tel:** 734 623 7075    **Fax:** 734 623 1625

38525 Woodward Avenue, Suite 2000, **Bloomfield Hills**, MI 48304-2970
**Tel:** 248 433 7200    **Fax:** 248 433 7274

200 Ottawa Avenue, NW, Suite 900, **Grand Rapids**, MI 49503-2427
**Tel:** 616 458 1300    **Fax:** 616 458 6753

215 S Washington Square, Suite 200, **Lansing**, MI 48933-1816
**Tel:** 517 371 1730    **Fax:** 517 487 4700

**DISTRICT OF COLUMBIA**
1901 L Street, NW Suite 800, **Washington**, DC 20036 3506
**Tel:** 202 457 0160    **Fax:** 202 659 1559

## CONTACTS

| | |
|---|---|
| **Intellectual Property, Business Technology, Telecommunications, Energy** | Brian R Balow |
| **Corporate, M&A, Securities, Corporate Governance, Private Capital, Real Estate, Estate Planning, Minority Business Enterprises** | Richard M Bolton |
| **Labor & Employment, Employee Benefits, Immigration, Education, Family & Matrimonial** | Timothy H Howlett |
| **Appellate, Products Liability, Class Action, Insurance, Gaming, Environmental, Transportation, Business Criminal Defense** | Kathleen A Lang |
| **Banking, Bankruptcy, Municipal, Taxation** | John K Lawrence |
| **Commercial & Businesss Litigation, Securities Litigation, Construction, Alternative Dispute Resolution, Antitrust** | Edward H Pappas |

**INTERNATIONAL WORK:** Dickinson Wright attorneys regularly handle cross-border transactions and represent a number of international clients, both domestically and abroad. The firm's work on international and foreign projects encompasses corporate and securities transactions, finance matters, antitrust issues, intellectual property, litigation and arbitration, and the design of foreign legal infrastructure. The firm has established an International Task Force which is dedicated to proactively identifying issues which may affect their international clients and finding effective and creative ways to address these issues in advance. The firm has been previously recognized by international publications as a top firm in the United States for corporate transactions and intellectual property-related concerns. Representative clients include Royal Bank of Scotland, Freudenberg-NOK, JPMorgan Europe, USUI International Corporation, Petronas, Sumitomo Wiring Systems, Tachi-S Engineering, Hella North America, Faurecia, and Rofin-Sinar Technologies, Inc.

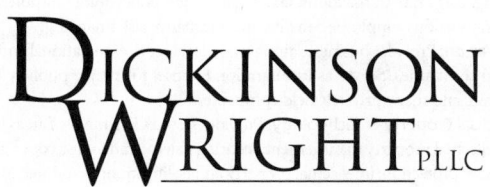

# HONIGMAN MILLER SCHWARTZ AND COHN LLP

## THE FIRM

**Managing Partner:** Alan S Schwartz

**Number of Partners:** 147
**Number of Associates:** 60
**Of Counsel:** 13

### HEAD OFFICE

2290 First National Building, 660 Woodward Avenue, **Detroit**, MI 48226
**Tel**: 313 465 7000 **Fax**: 313 465 8000
**Website:** www.honigman.com

**FIRM OVERVIEW**: Honigman Miller Schwartz and Cohn LLP is a leading business law firm with offices located in Detroit, Lansing and Oakland County, Michigan. For over 50 years, Honigman has been committed to serving its clients with outstanding legal experience and client service. With a total staff of nearly 600 – including 220 attorneys – the firm serves approximately 15,000 clients around the world.

## MAIN AREAS OF PRACTICE:

**Antitrust & Trade Regulation:** A national practice, litigating major cases and representing companies before the federal antitrust agencies. Successfully defended mergers and many class actions, and has been at the leading edge of a number of important legal developments.

**Bankruptcy, Reorganization & Commercial:** Represents secured and unsecured creditors from a variety of industries. It also represents investors both in acquiring financially troubled companies and purchasing assets from bankrupt entities through bankruptcy sales or novel plans of reorganization.

**Corporate & Securities:** Represents clients including entrepreneurs and start up companies, small-cap companies, regional companies, large family-owned companies and multinational publicly traded corporations. Areas of experience include: M&A, capital raising, corporate governance, business planning, SEC reporting and compliance, and business immigration.

**Employee Benefits:** Provides clients with assistance in all areas of the design, establishment, funding, administration and termination of executive compensation, retirement and welfare benefit programs. Represents clients before the IRS, Department of Labor, Pension Benefit Guaranty Corporation, state agencies, and state and federal courts in benefit-related litigation.

**Environmental:** Advises clients in air, land and water quality permit and compliance matters, environmental investigation, and remediation obligations before state and federal environmental agencies. Assist clients in resolving environmental issues raised with the selection and siting of industrial, commercial, and residential projects; and environmental issues related to the purchase and sale of real estate and business assets, including economic incentives to persons who develop or redevelop brownfields in the state.

**Gaming & Hospitality:** Assists gaming and hospitality clients in the gaming and liquor business, from real estate acquisition and zoning work to regulatory compliance with all local, state and federal laws. Represents Native American tribes, licensed casinos and casino related suppliers and employees, and hotels, bars and restaurants buying, selling or transferring liquor licenses.

**Healthcare:** Assists clients in corporate structuring, acquisitions and affiliations, provider integration, tax audits, Medicare and Medicaid payments, managed care contracting, compliance initiatives, disclosures and investigations, including matters of corporate responsibility and ethics, creation and expansion of healthcare systems, mergers and acquisitions, HIPAA compliance and contracting standards, alternative delivery systems, joint ventures, and labor and employee benefits.

**Insurance:** Counsels in a wide range of areas relating to the insurance industry. Represents a wide variety of regulated and captive insurance companies in matters involving: corporate transactions, tax, litigation and policyholder disputes, regulatory transactions, employee benefits, and alternative risk financing.

**Immigration:** Provides business immigration legal services to national and international companies. Serves as immigration counsel for major publicly traded companies and many privately held companies.

**Intellectual Property & Technology:** Provides services in a range of areas including: intellectual property management; securing patent, trademark, copyright and trade secret protection; intellectual property audits; litigation; e-commerce; licensing, distribution and technology transfer and clearance opinions.

**Investment Incentives & Tax Savings:** Assists clients in maximizing their access to, and benefit from, various government-sponsored programs intended to induce businesses to locate or expand in particular geographic areas. The group draws upon the experience of the Corporate, Environmental, Real Estate, Real Estate Tax Appeals, and Tax Departments to cover the full range of local, state and federal programs.

**Labor & Employment:** Defends employers against claims of harassment and discrimination (age, sex, race, national origin, religion and disability), retaliation, wrongful discharge, and employment claims arising under a variety of state and federal laws including FMLA, FLSA, and the WARN Act. Represents clients in non-compete and trade secret litigation; providing policies and procedures, training, employee compensation and severance counseling. Represents clients with unionized work forces, including negotiating collective bargaining agreements, arbitrations, union avoidance counseling, and practices before the NLRB.

**Litigation:** Handles every type of commercial litigation, including defense of nationwide class actions and shareholder lawsuits, breach of contact claims, secured transaction litigation, property disputes and intellectual property claims as well as white-collar criminal defense. Whether the matter is in state or federal court, an arbitration proceeding or an administrative hearing, the department has a demonstrated track record of achieving excellent results through creative resolutions and skilful trial work.

**Real Estate:** Offers an extended range of legal services in every facet of the real estate industry locally and nationally, including acquisitions, development and management, financing, ownership and tax structuring, public/private partnerships, leasing, construction planning, land use, and regulatory and zoning.

**Regulatory:** Handles matters before state administrative agencies and state and federal courts. These include cases before the Michigan Public Service Commission initiated to address energy issues of importance to the State. Represents clients in telecommunications matters; defending complaints filed with regulatory agencies; obtaining licenses or certificates; energy contract negotiations; cable TV rate regulation and drafting legislation.

**Property Tax Appeals:** Offers taxpayers who own, manage or lease commercial, industrial, or personal property, a complimentary review of each assessment and a recommendation about whether an appeal is justified. Have successfully reduced property taxes for clients by hundreds of millions of dollars. The firm has successfully represented taxpayers throughout the country.

**Tax:** Provides services that include the structuring of transactions and business entities, from both a US domestic and international perspective. Experience includes all the areas of mergers and acquisitions, international tax matters; Subchapter S corporations, consolidated income tax returns; real estate transactions, mortgage-backed bonds, REMICs, tax-exempt financing, real estate investment trusts (REITs) and syndications.

**Trust & Estate Planning:** Provides clients with assistance in estate planning, administration of estates and trusts, charitable and business succession planning, and matters related to nonprofit organizations, such as private foundations and support organizations. The firm typically works with Michigan residents having taxable estates of at least $2,000,000 and with the owners of closely-held businesses.

# HONIGMAN

# KIENBAUM OPPERWALL HARDY & PELTON, P.L.C.

## THE FIRM

**Managing Partner:** Thomas G Kienbaum
**Administrative Partner:** Eric J Pelton

**Number of partners:** 4
**Number of other lawyers:** 15

**FIRM OVERVIEW:** Working in partnership with its clients, Kienbaum Opperwall Hardy & Pelton specializes in guiding employers through the challenges of the contemporary workplace. From wrongful discharge claims to traditional union-management matters to preventive advice, the firm's attorneys are all skilled in representing management's interests and perspectives. The firm draws on its attorneys' individual talents, diversity, and wide-ranging experiences in the employment and labor field to deliver large-firm effectiveness at small-firm cost. In addition to competitive hourly rates, the firm derives other efficiencies – which are passed on to their clients – from their specialized boutique practice.

The firm was formed in May 1997 by Thomas G Kienbaum, Theodore R. Opperwall, Elizabeth Hardy, and Eric J Pelton. All were previously partners at a major Detroit law firm, where Mr Kienbaum headed the labor and employment law department. The firm is based in downtown Birmingham, Michigan, and also has an office in downtown Detroit, Michigan.

For several years, Kienbaum Opperwall Hardy & Pelton has been designated in Chambers USA's Client Guide to America's Leading Business Lawyers as one of the top employment and labor law firms in Michigan. Among the firm's members are some of the region's most recognized and successful employment and labor attorneys. A number of their lawyers have been selected by their peers to be listed among the 'Best Lawyers in America' and have been inducted as Fellows of the College of Labor and Employment Lawyers. The firm's lawyers are frequent lecturers for the prestigious National Employment Law Institute and other business education programs.

Their practice spans all aspects of employment and labor law. The firm provides proactive services – counseling employers on avoiding wrongful discharge claims, employment discrimination suits, and all of the potential employee claims that can arise under a myriad of federal and state statutes. Through their in-house seminars and workshops, the firm educates management so that sensitive situations can be prevented or properly handled. The firm conducts on-site investigations of troublesome workplace problems and advises employers on how to deal successfully with the results. But when it becomes necessary, their litigators provide a vigorous defense, based on years of experience before federal and state courts and administrative tribunals. A sizable segment of their practice consists of complex multi-state litigation including class actions. They represent many clients on a regional or national basis. They also have a substantial appellate practice and have been instrumental in establishing legal principles of major significance to employers in Michigan and elsewhere.

The firm's distinctive boutique practice style and philosophy offer their clients a highly focused, proactive, strategic, and resource-conscious approach to avoiding if possible, confronting when necessary, and efficiently resolving the many complex workplace issues facing American employers today. All of the firm's members have devoted their careers to this specialized field, and do not have to 'reinvent the wheel' with each new representation.

**MAIN AREAS OF PRACTICE:** Kienbaum Opperwall Hardy & Pelton provides employment and labor law services in the following areas:

**Preventive Counseling:** Personnel policies and handbooks; workforce reductions; sexual harassment; employee discipline and terminations; workplace investigations; affirmative action; supervisory training; employment contracts; covenants not to compete; arbitration procedures; wage and hour compliance; disability and family leave issues; drug and alcohol issues.

**Employment Litigation:** Wrongful discharge and discrimination suits; defamation and other workplace torts; injunction suits; administrative claims; appeals; alternative dispute resolution.

**Traditional Labor Relations:** Union organizing; collective bargaining; contract administration and arbitration; NLRB matters; specialized labor injunctions; interest arbitrations.

**REPRESENTATIVE CLIENTS:** Amazon.com; Auto Club of Michigan; Avis Rent A Car; Behr America; Blue Cross Blue Shield of Michigan; College for Creative Studies; Comcast Cable Communications, Inc.; Crain Communications, Inc.; DaimlerChrysler Corporation; DaimlerChrysler Services; DaVita Total Renal Care, Inc.; Deloitte & Touche; Detroit Diesel Corporation; DTE Energy; Eaton Corporation; El Paso-Tennessee Pipeline Company; Federal-Mogul Corporation; Ford Motor Company; ING USA Annuity and Life Insurance Company; Pepsi Bottling Group, Inc.; Radio Shack; Sodexho USA; Starwood Hotels and Resorts Worldwide; YUM Brands, Inc.

KIENBAUM OPPERWALL HARDY & PELTON, P.L.C.
ATTORNEYS AND COUNSELORS

# MILLER, CANFIELD, PADDOCK AND STONE, P.L.C.

## THE FIRM

**Chief Executive Officer:** Thomas W Linn
**Deputy CEO:** Beverly Hall Burns
**Attorneys:** 350
**Legal assistants:** 50+
**Support staff:** 300+

**FIRM OVERVIEW:** Founded in 1852, Miller, Canfield, Paddock and Stone, P.L.C., is one of the largest and longest established law firms in Michigan. With offices throughout Michigan, and in New York City, Pensacola, Florida, Windsor, Ontario, Canada, and in Gdynia, Warsaw and Wroclaw, Poland, Miller Canfield provides a broad range of integrated services to meet the needs of clients. Working together with the US offices, the offices in Poland expand the firm's reach to clients throughout Eastern Europe, and the Windsor, Ontario office broadens the firm's ability to offer clients seamless cross-border representation to organizations interested in doing business in North America. Miller Canfield's leadership position is an advantage it shares with each of its clients. Currently, Miller Canfield represents seven of the top 10 Fortune 500 companies and over 20% of the overall list. For nearly 75 years, the firm has served as Martindale-Hubbell's reviser law firm for the state of Michigan's law section. Several of the firm's attorneys belong to prestigious American Colleges, including the College of Labor and Employment Lawyers, and the American Colleges of Bond Counsel, Employee Benefits, Tax Counsel, Trial Lawyers, and Trust and Estate Counsel.

**MAIN AREAS OF PRACTICE:** The practice groups of the firm are: bankruptcy; corporate and securities; environmental and regulatory; federal tax and employee benefits; financial institutions/transactions; healthcare; intellectual property and information technology; international business; labor and employment; litigation, including dispute resolution, product litigation and torts, product safety, and state and local tax; personal services; public law; and real estate. Other specialty areas include antitrust and trade regulation; assisted living facilities; automotive; aviation and transportation; Canadian law; capital markets lending; construction; corporate discovery management; criminal defense; export control; franchise and distribution; governmental entities; high-technology ventures; housing; immigration; insurance; international trade and customs and tax and transfer pricing; minority business; nonprofit and charitable organizations; professional firms; schools; and telecommunications. For contact information, visit www.millercanfield.com.

**CLIENTS:** The firm represents clients diverse in size and character. Attorneys represent individuals in their personal and business concerns, trusts and estates, publicly traded and multinational companies, and many start-up, small- and medium-sized businesses. Clients also include public bodies such as the state of Michigan and many of its agencies, authorities and universities, cities, counties, townships, school and community college districts, and special authorities throughout the state. The firm represents many nonprofit, tax-exempt institutions, such as hospitals, charitable corporations and professional associations.

**INTERNATIONAL WORK:** The firm has dedicated an entire practice group, the International Business Group, to provide legal services to US and foreign multinational companies, banks, and other clients whose business affairs are tied to the increasingly interdependent world economy. The firm handles work in Amharic, Arabic, Danish, Dutch, French, German, Greek, Hebrew, Hindi, Italian, Japanese, Korean, Macedonian, Malaysian, Mandarin, Norwegian, Polish, Portuguese, Punjabi, Russian, Spanish, Swedish, Ukrainian and Yiddish.

## HEAD OFFICE

**MICHIGAN**
150 W. Jefferson, Suite 2500, **Detroit,** MI 48226
**Tel:** 313 963 6420
**Email:** linn@millercanfield.com
**Website:** www.millercanfield.com

## OTHER US OFFICES

**MICHIGAN**
101 North Main Street, 7th Floor, **Ann Arbor,** MI 48104
**Tel:** 734 663 2445

99 Monroe Avenue, NW, Suite 1200, **Grand Rapids,** MI 49503
**Tel:** 616 454 8656

444 West Michigan Avenue, **Kalamazoo,** MI 49007
**Tel:** 269 381 7030

One Michigan Avenue, Suite 900, **Lansing,** MI 48933
**Tel:** 517 487 2070

4800 Fashion Square Blvd, Suite 120, **Saginaw**, MI 48604
**Tel:** 989 791 4646

840 West Long Lake Road, Suite 200, **Troy,** MI 48098
**Tel:** 248 879 2000

**FLORIDA**
25 West Cedar Street, Suite 500, **Pensacola,** FL 32501
**Tel:** 850 469 1088

**NEW YORK**
1450 Broadway, 41st Floor, **New York,** NY 10018
**Tel:** 212 704 4400

## INTERNATIONAL OFFICES

The firm also has offices in Windsor, Ontario, Canada and in Gdynia, Warsaw, and Wroclaw, Poland.

## CONTACTS

| | |
|---|---|
| Detroit | Thomas Parachini |
| Ann Arbor | Joseph Fazio |
| Grand Rapids | Michael Campbell |
| Kalamazoo | John Campbell |
| Lansing | Michael Atkins |
| Saginaw | James Foresman |
| Troy | Kenneth Konop |
| Pensacola | Jerry Rupley |
| New York | Gregory Curtner |

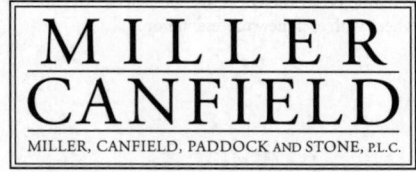

# VARNUM, RIDDERING, SCHMIDT & HOWLETT LLP

## THE FIRM

**Executive Partner:** William J Lawrence III

**Number of partners:** 92
**Number of other lawyers:** 60

**FIRM OVERVIEW:** Founded in 1888, Varnum is a leading Michigan law firm, known for innovation and superior results in the delivery of legal services. With over 150 lawyers practicing in six offices, Varnum is firmly established as one of the region's premier law firms. Varnum's team approach to client service provides an outstanding model for maintaining the close personal relationship that traditionally exists between lawyer and client while ensuring that clients also have available to them the full resources of the firm. Varnum attorneys have distinguished themselves as leaders of state and civic agencies including state employment relations, public service and natural resource commissions. Varnum attorneys are also represented in the American Colleges of Trial Lawyers, Mortgage Attorneys, Real Estate Lawyers, Labor & Employment Lawyers, Trust and Estate Counsel, and Law Practice Management. 33 Varnum attorneys are listed in The Best Lawyers in America® 2006 (Copyright 2005 by Woodward/White, Inc., of Aiken, S.C.), a national peer-review survey.

**MAIN AREAS OF PRACTICE:** A full service provider of legal counsel, Varnum has developed a strong core of experience in many areas.
**Corporate:** A trusted corporate advisor to many of the region's top companies, Varnum has represented local, national and global clients in numerous transactions with values of $100 million or more. The firm advises on mergers and acquisitions, anti-trust and trade regulations, banking and bankruptcy services, bond counsel, securities, corporate governance, intellectual property issues, and more.
**Labor & Employment Relations:** Regarded as a heavyweight in Michigan's competitive labor field, Varnum's Labor and Employment Group is one of the most richly talented and experienced in the state. More than 30 highly-skilled attorneys provide counseling and representation in traditional labor work, employee benefits, employment litigation defense, workplace safety and health, immigration and worker's compensation issues. Varnum has the distinction of having the most listed labor and employment attorneys in Michigan in The Best Lawyers in America ® 2006.
**Environmental Law:** With one of the largest environmental law practices in the Great Lakes Region, Varnum's Environmental Law Group advises clients in matters including air quality issues; land use permitting, due diligence and real estate development; regulatory compliance; waste management; water law; and environmental litigation and administrative enforcement.
**Litigation:** Proficient in a variety of litigation matters, Varnum's trial group has nearly 50 attorneys practicing in more than a dozen focus areas, from business torts and commercial litigation to receivership, securities and RICO matters. Varnum's litigation clients include public and private corporations, municipalities, general and limited partnerships, sole proprietorships and non-profits.
**Trusts & Estates:** Varnum's highly-regarded estate planning team includes attorneys, tax consulting and compliance specialists, and trust administrators.

In addition, the firm has developed practices in response to specific client needs, such as cable and telecommunications law; energy; oil and gas; construction; healthcare; and e-commerce law.

**CLIENTS:** The firm represents a diverse range of clients including manufacturers, banking and financial institutions, municipalities, healthcare providers, colleges and universities, school districts, developers, retailers, utilities, trade associations, and professional groups. Clients include DaimlerChrysler; Kellogg Company; Herman Miller, Inc.; Tower Automotive; and Independent Bank.

## HEAD OFFICE

**MICHIGAN**
333 Bridge Street, NW, **Grand Rapids,** MI 49504
**Tel:** 616 336 6000  **Fax:** 616 336 7000
**Email:** generalinfo@varnumlaw.com
**Website:** www.varnumlaw.com

## BRANCH OFFICES

**MICHIGAN**
1600 S Beacon Blvd, Suite 240, **Grand Haven,** MI 49417
**Tel:** 616 846 7100  **Fax:** 616 846 7101

251 N Rose St, 4th Floor, **Kalamazoo,** MI 49007-3823
**Tel:** 269 382 2300  **Fax:** 269 382 2382

The Victor Center, Suite 810, 201 North Washington Square, **Lansing,** MI 48933
**Tel:** 517 482 6237  **Fax:** 517 482 6937

39500 High Pointe Boulevard, Suite 150, **Novi,** MI 48375
**Tel:** 248 567 7400  **Fax:** 248 567 7440

**WISCONSIN**
PO Box 16549, 3533 North 27th St, Room 663, **Milwaukee,** WI 53216-0549
**Tel:** 414 447 4586  **Fax:** 414 447 4943

## CONTACTS

| | |
|---|---|
| Corporate | Carl Oosterhouse |
| Estate Planning | Tom Kyros |
| Labor | Dave Khorey |
| Trial | Steve Afendoulis |
| Regulatory | Bruce Goodman |

**INTERNATIONAL WORK:** Varnum attorneys have facilitated business all over the world. Recent international legal services include: establishment of maquiladora subsidiaries and relationships in Mexico; acquisition of technology companies in the People's Republic of China; creation of joint ventures throughout Europe, Asia and South America; establishment of subsidiaries or branch offices in Europe, Asia and South America; negotiation and drafting of commercial contracts in such countries as Russia, Spain, the Czech Republic, Brazil, the Union of the Comoros, India, Taiwan, Korea, the People's Republic of China, Germany, Canada and the UK; securing visas and work permits to place key personnel in the US, Canada, Mexico, Brazil, China, Germany, the UK, Spain, Japan, Malaysia and Korea.

# VERCRUYSSE MURRAY & CALZONE, P.C.

## THE FIRM

**Managing Directors:**    Robert M Vercruysse, Chairman
Gregory V Murray, Vice President & Treasurer
David B Calzone, Secretary

**Number of Shareholders:** 12

**FIRM OVERVIEW:** Founded in 1996, the firm quickly established itself both locally and nationally as one of the country's pre-eminent management labor, employment and ERISA litigation law practices. In addition, its commercial litigation and immigration practices allow the firm to assist clients, both large and small, with a wide array of employment, business and personnel legal issues. The firm's national reputation has grown along with its size. Four attorneys – Robert Vercruysse, Gregory Murray, David Calzone, and Virginia Metz (retired) – have been selected by their peers from across the United States as members of the American Bar Association's College of Labor and Employment Lawyers. The same four attorneys are also members of the American Employment Law Council. Four attorneys are listed in various editions of The Best Lawyers in America, and five are Fellows of the Michigan State Bar Foundation. Two have served as Chair of the Labor and Employment Section of the State Bar of Michigan, and David Calzone has served for several years as a member of the Section's governing council and as its current Secretary. The firm's attorneys have a number of publications to their credit, including the monthly Michigan Employment Law Letter, several articles in legal periodicals, and chapter contributions and/or book editing responsibility for the following books: Employment Litigation in Michigan (ICLE 1999), Employment Litigation in Michigan, 2d Ed. (ICLE 2004), Employment Discrimination Law 3d Ed.(BNA 2002), Age Discrimination in Employment Law (BNA 1999), Michigan Wrongful Discharge and Employment Discrimination Law, 2d Ed. (ICLE 1994) and Employment Law in Michigan: An Employer's Guide, 2d Ed. (ICLE 2005). The firm also takes its expertise into the classroom. Several attorneys have taught classes at The University of Michigan Law School, Wayne State Law School and the University of Detroit – Mercy Law School. The firm's attorneys are also frequently featured speakers at American Bar Association, American Employment Law Conference, state and local bar association and Institute for Continuing Legal Education programs and institutes.

## MAIN AREAS OF PRACTICE:

**Labor & Employment Law -Litigation:** The firm has extensive experience representing employers in state and federal courts in age, race, sex, sexual harassment, national origin, religious, and disability/handicap discrimination litigation, non-compete and trade secrets litigation as well as in affirmative action and discrimination matters before administrative agencies such as the Equal Employment Opportunity Commission, the Michigan Department of Civil Rights and the Office of Federal Contract Compliance Programs. The firm also represents employers before state and federal Departments of Labor, and the Department of State; has successfully defended both private and public employers in class action and complex litigation brought in both federal and state court; and is heavily involved in the defense of wrongful discharge cases, including contract and commission claims, implied employment contract claims, slander and libel claims, negligence and negligent retention claims, and whistleblower claims. Trial experience in both judge and jury trials is extensive.

**Labor & Employment Law-Traditional Labor:** In the traditional labor practice, the firm has considerable experience in negotiating collective bargaining agreements on behalf of employers and multi-employer associations in both the public and private sectors. In addition, the firm has defended employers before the National Labor Relations Board throughout the United States and the Michigan Employment Relations Commission in both representation and unfair labor practice proceedings, represented employers in wage and hour, OSHA and MIOSHA matters before both the United States and Michigan Departments of Labor, has represented employers in arbitration matters throughout the United States and has considerable expertise in the use of alternative dispute resolution procedures.

### HEAD OFFICE

**MICHIGAN**
31780 Telegraph Road, Suite 200, **Bingham Farms**, MI 48025-3469
Metropolitan Detroit Area
**Tel:** 248 540 8019   **Fax:** 248 540 8059
**Website:** www.vmclaw.com

### CONTACTS

**Traditional Labor** ....................................................Robert Vercruysse
**Employment Litigation** ...........................................Gregory Murray
**ERISA Litigation** ...........................Robert Vercruysse, William Altman
**Employment Counseling** ......................................David Calzone
**Immigration** ........................................................Dorothy Basmaji

**Labor & Employment Law - Training & Advice:** Vercruysse Murray & Calzone's attorneys have significant experience in counseling employers in a wide variety of human relations and personnel matters such as the Family Medical Leave Act, with the intent of avoiding litigation or unionization. The firm assists employers in the development of personnel policies and procedures, affirmative action plans, disciplinary policies, employee handbooks, drug and alcohol testing programs, and labor and employment issues in sales, mergers and acquisitions.

**ERISA Law & Litigation:** The firm's ERISA law and litigation practitioners have extensive experience providing all facets of ERISA litigation services, from pre-litigation counseling to partnering with in-house ERISA lawyers before and during ERISA litigation, and from serving as mentors or consultants in ERISA litigation to leading the defense of ERISA litigation matters, successfully defending individual and class actions involving challenges to plan design, administration and interpretation, allegations of breach of fiduciary duty, claims of wrongful benefit denial and interference with the attainment of ERISA-governed benefits, challenges to reductions in welfare benefits by current and former participants or retirees, and challenges seeking across-the-board benefit recalculation.

**Immigration:** Vercruysse Murray & Calzone's Immigration Law practice is devoted to I-9 and immigration matters, with an emphasis on business immigration. The firm provides guidance to US and non-US employers who seek to employ foreign nationals in the United States, as well as facilitating the employment of US workers abroad. The firm counsels management on strategic immigration issues related to establishing new US enterprises and provides on-site employer training to human resource personnel and industry groups on issues such as temporary work classifications, student employment, national interest waivers, 'special handling' for university professors, extraordinary ability and outstanding researcher petitions, permanent residence procedures, use of contract employees, I-9 compliance, NAFTA, and IRCA discrimination matters.

**Additionally:** Although best known in the practice areas described above, the firm has also distinguished itself in the following areas: class action, complex and general litigation; executive compensation agreements; securities arbitration; constitutional law; commercial litigation; unfair competition litigation; and trade secret and tortious interference litigation.

**CLIENTS:** Representative clients include: American Axle & Manufacturing, American Red Cross, Campbell Ewald Advertising, Central Michigan University, DaimlerChrysler AG, Detroit Diesel Corporation, Detroit Newspapers, The Detroit News, Detroit Free Press, Faurecia Automotive, Gannett Co., Inc., GlobalHue, Guardian Industries, H&R Block Financial Advisors, Inc., Home Depot U.S.A., Inc., Inergy Automotive Systems (USA), LLC., Mueller Brass, Northwest Airlines Inc., Oakwood Healthcare, Inc., Penske Corporation, Republic Bank, Siemens, SPX Corporation, Sprint Corporation, Starwood Hotels, TRW Automotive, Unique Fabricating, United Auto Group, Walbridge Aldinger Company, Wayne State University and Yazaki North America, Inc.

**VERCRUYSSE MURRAY & CALZONE, P.C.**

## How lawyers are ranked

Every year we carry out thousands of in-depth interviews with clients and lawyers in order to assess the reputations and expertise of business lawyers across the USA. Chambers rankings and editorial are referred to extensively by General Counsel and other purchasers of legal services who look to our recommendations when choosing their lawyers.

# CORPORATE/M&A

| Corporate/M&A Leading Firms |
| --- |
| 1   DORSEY & WHITNEY LLP *Minneapolis* |
|     FAEGRE & BENSON LLP *Minneapolis* |
| 2   FREDRIKSON & BYRON PA *Minneapolis* |
|     KAPLAN, STRANGIS & KAPLAN *Minneapolis* |
| 3   BRIGGS AND MORGAN, PA *Minneapolis* |
|     GRAY, PLANT, MOOTY, MOOTY *Minneapolis* |
|     LEONARD, STREET AND DEINARD *Minneapolis* |
|     LINDQUIST & VENNUM PLLP *Minneapolis* |
|     OPPENHEIMER WOLFF & DONNELLY *Minneapolis* |
| 4   HENSON & EFRON *Minneapolis* |
|     LOMMEN, NELSON, COLE & STAGEBERG *Minneapolis* |

## Band 1

### Dorsey & Whitney LLP
See firm details p.1169

**The Firm:** Increased interest by public companies in the M&A market has meant a busy year for this *"blue-ribbon"* team of around 50 attorneys. It handles advisory work for everyone from NYSE-listed companies to emerging businesses and has brought its expertise to bear on numerous public deals. For example, the team represented SUPERVALU in a $230 million cash-for-stock tender offer for Total Logistics. The firm has proven its ability to compete at national and international level, with 19 offices across the USA, Canada, Asia and Europe. Clients and peers noted the *"depth and breadth"* of the team, taking the time to praise a wide range of associates and partners. Clients value the firm's *"creative"* approach and called it *"every bit as capable as a New York firm."*

**The Lawyers:** *"Analytical skills and drafting ability"* are just two of **Robert Rosenbaum**'s (see p.1166) attributes. Whether carrying out M&A work, advising on corporate governance or acting as external counsel for large public companies, he *"makes sure the critical issues are analyzed."* His client base encompasses everything from technology startups to food service corporations such as Hormel Foods, for whom he closed five transactions totaling more than $350 million in the past year. He also advised Deluxe Corp on a $700 million acquisition of New England

Business Service. **Ken Cutler** (see p.1162) cochairs the firm's emerging companies practice. Cutler works on a national basis, combining venture capital and private equity work with M&A. He recently assisted on the $190 million sale of Arbortext, a Michigan-based publisher, to the Boston software company PTC, closing the deal in just 20 days. His reputation is particularly strong among Minnesota's medical device manufacturers, recently guiding Pulmonetic Systems through its $98 million sale to Viasys. Cutler is particularly admired for his *"phenomenal"* responsiveness, with clients noting that *"he responds to calls within half an hour from anywhere in the country."* It is said that *"straight-shooter"* **Bill Payne** (see p.1165) is a man who *"gets results."* Chair of the M&A practice, he has an *"upfront and direct"* style.

**Clients/Work Highlights:** Trans-Lux; The Mosaic Company; UnitedHealth Group; ADC Telecommunications; Hormel Foods; SUPERVALU and Endocardial Solutions.

### Faegre & Benson LLP
See firm details p.1170

**The Firm:** One of Minnesota's goliaths, this firm boasts a 60-strong corporate team that is highly regarded by clients. *"I know they're going to cover my butt,"* said one; *"It'll be done, and it'll be done right."* With six offices, including three outside the USA, Faegre's client base ranges from Minneapolis startups to multinational financial institutions. It has been representing Crocs Footwear in its IPO, and assisted American Express and US Bancorp in spinning off Ameriprise and Piper Jaffray. Faegre's team is seen as offering *"the best of both worlds: New York quality with a Midwestern culture."* In addition to the depth of experience within the team, clients praised the quality of Faegre's customer service, in particular its willingness to take the time to learn about their business and make unprompted suggestions. *"Technically exceptional and very practical,"* the team was also seen as down to earth and approachable by clients, who noted: *"They don't need to show how smart they are – this leads to efficient and effective negotiations and results."*

**The Lawyers:** *"The dean of securities,"* **Phil Garon**'s (see p.1163) 30 years at the firm have also made him the go-to guy for large, complex M&A work. He

recently conducted a complex $1 billion merger between hi-tech storage manufacturers Entegris and Mykrolis, which included a reincorporation in Delaware. Peers recognized Garon as *"a cut above the rest,"* while clients lauded his ability to *"look at a situation through the eyes of the business"* and to instantly explain complicated developments in accessible language. One client, commenting on his accessibility, declared him *"available 24/7,"* adding: *"I don't know when he sleeps!"* *"Tenacious and creative"* **William Busch** (see p.1162) boasts more than 20 years as a partner in the team. Though his broad practice encompasses everything from M&A to private equity, it has a strong industry focus on the media and professional sport sectors that has seen him representing Minnesota's basketball, hockey and football teams. Recently appointed as the head of the M&A practice, *"problem solver"* **Bruce Engler** (see p.1163) continues to be highly active on private equity transactions for the likes of Norwest Equity Partners and Goldner Hawn. In one recent deal, he represented Pella on the sale of its popular storm doors business to Larson. He is *"excellent, thorough and technical,"* according to clients who note that *"he understands the picture from the business standpoint."* **Andrew Humphrey** (see p.1164) heads the firm's emerging companies practice, offering *"formal legal advice and off-the-record insight,"* particularly in the technology, software and medical device sectors. Typically he steers startups from initial bank and venture capital financings and recapitalizations right through to M&A and public offerings, and clients say: *"He feels more like part of the team than someone from outside."* He is known for his practical approach and is *"focused on navigating problems, not throwing up obstacles."* Gearworks, Optical Solutions and Impres Medical are just a few of Humphrey's local clients; he also serves as corporate counsel for established corporations such as General Mill. Despite devoting much of his time to a new role as head of the corporate group, **Kris Sharpe** (see p.1166) continues to work as disclosure counsel for several large public companies, including Target and Guidant. Clients applauded Sharpe's *"precision"* and *"practical approach,"* explaining: *"He's the detail person; he knows the ins and outs but also has the business orientation."* Meanwhile, *"plugged-in"* **Mike Stanchfield** (see p.1167) rises up the table after

| Corporate/M&A |
| --- |
| **Leading Individuals** |
| **Senior Statesman** |
| EFRON Stanley *Henson & Efron* |
| KAPLAN Samuel *Kaplan, Strangis & Kaplan* |
| LIBBEY Keith *Fredrikson & Byron PA* |
| [1] GARON Philip *Faegre & Benson LLP* |
| ROSENBAUM Robert *Dorsey & Whitney LLP* |
| SCALLEN Timothy *Oppenheimer Wolff* |
| STRANGIS Ralph *Kaplan, Strangis* |
| [2] BUSCH William *Faegre & Benson LLP* |
| CUTLER Kenneth *Dorsey & Whitney LLP* |
| ENGLER Bruce *Faegre & Benson LLP* |
| HUMPHREY Andrew *Faegre & Benson LLP* |
| MACHMEIER Bruce *Oppenheimer Wolff* |
| PAYNE William *Dorsey & Whitney LLP* |
| SHARPE W Smith *Faegre & Benson LLP* |
| SHERMAN Morris *Leonard, Street and Deinard* |
| [3] BROWER John *Gray, Plant, Mooty* |
| COSTLEY Kevin *Lindquist & Vennum* |
| GARTON Thomas *Fredrikson & Byron PA* |
| GORDON Avron *Briggs and Morgan* |
| KAUFMAN D William *Oppenheimer Wolff* |
| KENNEDY Steven *Faegre & Benson LLP* |
| LETSCHER Tom *Oppenheimer Wolff* |
| MOORSE Charles *Lindquist & Vennum PLLP* |
| STAGEBERG Roger *Lommen, Nelson, Cole* |
| STANCHFIELD Mike *Faegre & Benson LLP* |
| **Up-and-coming individuals** |
| SEIDEL Amy *Faegre & Benson LLP* |

*"taking a leading role"* in the M&A team of late. Along with **Steven Kennedy** (see p.1164), head of the firm's public companies practice, Stanchfield represented Minneapolis-based retail software firm RETEK during an international bidding war and its eventual purchase by Oracle for $670 million. In addition, he worked on major M&A transactions for Guidant, Graco and others. Clients expressed admiration for his *"tremendous intellect"* and *"unparalleled knowledge."* Kennedy's 15 years of experience at Faegre is supplemented by executive experience, giving him a commercial mind and approach that is greatly valued by clients. *"You don't just get chapter and verse,"* said one: *"He'll lay out the risks and suggest a course."* His customer service is equally important to them: *"He conducts himself like an in-house lawyer"* and *"works the way I want to be worked with."* Though still an associate, **Amy Seidel** (see p.1166) shows an expertise *"unbelievable for someone her age."* A *"rising star"* in securities work, she represents emerging companies in private and public financing, as well as underwriters in offerings. An expert on SEC reporting requirements, Seidel leads the firm's work on Sarbanes-Oxley compliance and corporate governance, and clients note that she is *"on top of the flood of new requirements."*
**Clients/Work Highlights:** Ameriprise; Bemis; Goldner Hawn Johnson and Morrison; Hutchison Technology; Land O'Lakes; Pella; Piper Jaffray; St. Paul; Target; Tennant and Wells Fargo.

## Band 2

### Fredrikson & Byron PA

**The Firm:** An improved market has allowed this team to expand to more than 50 attorneys providing M&A and securities representation plus corporate governance advice to a range of Midwestern companies. Although the *"talented"* team boasts a *"very strong"* emerging companies practice, its client roster extends to large public companies with international activities. Medical devices manufacturers are central to the firm's client roster, notably Medtronic that recently instructed the firm on several acquisitions and a $1 billion debt offering. The software and retail sectors are also key to the practice. Participation in significant deals has earned Fredrikson a place in the rankings that is close behind the largest firms in the market.
**The Lawyers:** *"Senior figure"* **Keith Libbey** is *"very well regarded in the medical technology sector,"* and leads the firm's work with Medtronic, as well as handling major financial clients such as Ameriprise. *"Excellent and hard-working"* **Thomas Garton** ably employs his tax background to help companies structure M&A deals. As such, he is involved with the firm's major clients and is held in high regard by peers as *"a potential successor"* to Libbey.
**Clients/Work Highlights:** Mayo Foundation; CABG Medical; Cherry Tree Investments; Brightstone and August Technologies.

### Kaplan, Strangis & Kaplan

**The Firm:** Despite fielding a small team of just 14 attorneys, this boutique has acquired *"a stellar reputation"* through involvement in *"large and interesting transactions."* It tackles M&A and securities work for some of Minnesota's largest public and privately held companies, including Allianz Life and UnitedHealth Group.
**The Lawyers:** *"Thoughtful"* founding partner **Samuel Kaplan** combines more than 25 years in practice at the firm with experience both as a corporate board member and as a company owner. Similarly, he is recognized for his extensive community involvement and political interests and his *"outstanding"* track record on M&A and securities law. **Ralph Strangis** is *"as good a corporate lawyer as you're going to find,"* researchers were told. Like Kaplan, he has served as a board member for several local public companies, including TCF Financial, and also as outside general counsel for United Airlines. Peers speak highly of him, some considering him *"the number-one guy for corporate law in Minnesota."*
**Clients/Work Highlights:** Castle Creek Capital; Davisco Foods International; Goldner Hawn Johnson & Morrison; Hajoca; Lupient Automotive Group; Minnesota Twins; Minnesota Wine & Spirits Wholesalers; Polaris Industries; The Good Sam Club and UnitedHealth Group.

## Band 3

### Briggs and Morgan, Professional Association

**The Firm:** Although the team at this midmarket, full-service outfit cannot quite match the giants for sheer manpower, its 35 attorneys have earned a reputation in key areas that belies the firm's size. Considered a go-to player nationally for public finance, it recently acted as bond counsel on offerings worth more than $1 billion. It also provides transactional and general corporate counseling, as well as M&A advice. Clients of all sizes and from most industries turn to the firm, with the changing needs of clients met from startup to IPO and beyond. A national and international profile has enabled Briggs and Morgan to achieve its status of sole Minnesota member of the Lex Mundi international network of law firms.
**The Lawyers:** **Av Gordon**'s 40 years in practice have left him *"very knowledgeable about all aspects of corporate law."* He specializes in representing emerging companies in private and public financings, encompassing securities and venture capital. On securities matters, issuers are particularly drawn from the medical device, transport and food service sectors; however, he also represents underwriters.
**Clients/Work Highlights:** Technology and medical device companies join traditional manufacturers, transportation and food service providers on the team's client roster.

### Gray, Plant, Mooty, Mooty & Bennett, PA

**The Firm:** Incorporating *"the strongest franchise law team in the Midwest,"* the business practice of this 140-year-old firm serves a range of national and international clients, including names as well known as Dairy Queen. The firm has 30 attorneys in this area and fields dedicated M&A and securities teams. Gray, Plant lawyers are admired for their *"business-focused"* and *"responsive"* approach to counseling clients: the team provides *"good advice as well as documentation."*
**The Lawyers:** *"Tenacity and attention to detail"* are seen as **John Brower**'s main strengths, with clients noting that he will *"go the extra mile to get the best deal."* He focuses on long-term relationships with both privately and publicly held clients. Having represented Minnesota-based medical device firm Chronimed since its IPO, he recently guided it through a merger with MIM Corporation to create BioScrip, a new firm with annual revenues of $1 billion. He has represented Carlson Companies, owner of Radisson hotels, through acquisitions and investments for some eight years, and it is said that this long-term approach enables Brower to *"walk in the shoes of his clients,"* who see him as *"the outside backbone"* of their legal departments.
**Clients/Work Highlights:** National retailers and manufacturers such as Ziegler and HNI join smaller regional names on the firm's client roster.

## Leonard, Street and Deinard Professional Association

**The Firm:** In business for over 75 years, this "*true full-service firm*" combines a client base of midmarket and family-owned Minnesota businesses with some national clients, particularly public utilities. Dubbed "*the quiet firm*" for its low-profile approach, Leonard Street was nevertheless lauded for the "*outstanding*" quality of its attorneys. The firm has more than doubled in size in 12 years, and peers were quick to note that "*the quality of its service, not its marketing, has fueled the expansion.*"

**The Lawyers:** "*High-profile*" both in the profession and in the community, **Moe Sherman** this year cemented his reputation with major transactions on the national stage. He represented hi-tech storage company Computer Network Technologies in its $400 million merger with McDATA, including negotiating antitrust issues, and is assisting in the financing of the mammoth Big Stone II coal-fired power station in South Dakota. Like the firm itself, Sherman is praised for his "*low-key, but effective*" approach.

**Clients/Work Highlights:** Allianz Life; Buffets; LodgeNet Entertainment; Marvin Windows and Doors; Michael Foods and McDATA.

## Lindquist & Vennum PLLP

See firm details p.1171

**The Firm:** This midmarket firm has around 100 business lawyers. Life sciences and financial institutions are two sectors in which the firm has a particular interest and its work ranges from private equity to M&A, with a specialty in advising young and entrepreneurial companies. Having counseled Definity Health since its startup phase, the firm recently represented the St Louis Park company in its $300 million acquisition by UnitedHealth Group. Complex M&A transactions are also on the agenda, notably the sale of Transneuronix to Medtronic, the $260 million price of which excludes additional payments attached to significant revenue targets.

**The Lawyers:** **Charles Moorse**'s (see p.1165) broad practice focuses on counseling midmarket public and private companies on everything from M&A to corporate governance. With a "*positive, can-do attitude,*" he recently shepherded Sportsman's Warehouse to its 40th store opening, having represented it since it opened its first store eight years ago. **Kevin Costley** (see p.1162) brings a "*comprehensive understanding*" of the banking sector to his role as head of the firm's financial institutions practice. He works for

local community banks as well as major national institutions. "*An excellent strategist,*" Costley recently represented Marshall Bank in its complex $150 million acquisition of South Dakota's BankFIRST, which included the immediate sale of BankFIRST's $400 million credit card portfolio to a consortium including Merrill Lynch and CompuCredit. He is particularly rated for his regulatory knowledge and his "*good relationships*" with regulatory bodies.

**Clients/Work Highlights:** Young medical device and hi-tech firms, such as CNS and Rimage, feature large in the firm's client base along with venture capital groups such as Churchill and Bayview.

## Oppenheimer Wolff & Donnelly LLP

**The Firm:** After expanding into national and international markets in the area of technology, this 115-year-old firm is now "*back to its roots,*" slimming to a "*core group*" of around 40 attorneys, but "*fighting above its weight.*" Representing a range of clients from startups to Fortune 100 companies, with a renewed focus on its core client base of financial services, manufacturing, and transportation companies, the team remains "*a cut above.*"

**The Lawyers:** **Timothy Scallen** combines his role as chair of the firm's M&A team with a busy securities workload for large public companies such as Ceridian and Ecolab. "*Bright, flexible and imaginative,*" he is praised for a practical and business-minded approach that sees him "*working toward a mutual solution, while promoting his client's interest.*" The "*senior and talented*" **Bruce Machmeier** represents a variety of interests from young companies entering their first share issue to large public companies engaged in significant M&A activity. Considered "*outstanding*" and "*a delight to deal with,*" he has a specialty in private equity work, particularly with medical device and hi-tech companies. **William Kaufman**'s venture capital practice sees him representing both issuers and underwriters. In addition, he has a notable M&A practice. Observers note his pragmatic approach, saying: "*He knows when and when not to dig his heels in.*" "*Talented*" **Tom Letscher** is admired by peers and clients for his bank of knowledge and his "*business-focused*" approach. Although his emerging companies practice lacks the widespread recognition of those at larger firms, peers are quick to observe that this is more to do with Letscher's "*quieter style,*" than the caliber of his work.

**Clients/Work Highlights:** Accenture; ADC Telecommunications; Ceridian; GE Transportation;

Select Comfort; Syngenta International; The Toro Company; UnitedHealth Group and United Airlines.

## Band 4

## Henson & Efron

**The Firm:** This boutique of 32 attorneys – of whom around half are involved in M&A – serves a broad range of midmarket manufacturers, distributors and service providers, in addition to a handful of Fortune 500 companies. The team is currently representing Pentair on an ongoing roll-up of water treatment and disposal firms, with acquisitions totaling more than $3 billion. Its largest clients benefit from its membership of the Legal Netlink Alliance, an international network of affiliated midsized law firms.

**The Lawyers:** **Stanley Efron** is "*the key to the firm's success.*" Although he is increasingly engaged in supplying legal and business counsel to boards and CEOs across Minnesota, he maintains an interest in representing smaller clients in M&A.

**Clients/Work Highlights:** Amjet Aircraft; Minnesota Freezer Warehouse; FORCE America; Medcare Products and Pentair.

## Lommen, Nelson, Cole & Stageberg, P.A.

**The Firm:** This small team of eight attorneys has had a busy year with an array of smaller clients, including a roll-up of funeral homes producing more than 30 acquisitions in two years. Its membership of the International Lawyers Network exposes it to international deals that would otherwise be highly unusual for a firm of its size. For example, in the past year it represented a London-based software company in an international acquisition worth $5 million. The firm is known to excel at the taxation elements of transactions, which is reflective of the support provided by an active and separate team of tax attorneys.

**The Lawyers:** "*Experienced*" **Roger Stageberg** specializes in work for smaller companies and startups. "*Quick and responsive,*" he is applauded by clients for his ability to explain documents in clear language.

**Clients/Work Highlights:** The firm works for startups and privately held midmarket companies, particularly in the software and medical device fields, alongside a handful of international corporations.

# EMPLOYMENT

# MAINLY DEFENDANT

## Band 1

### Dorsey & Whitney LLP

See firm details p.1169

**The Firm:** This Midwestern giant's labor and employment law team "*has very few equals*" in Minnesota, or even nationwide. The team provides counseling, litigation and traditional labor advice for an array of clients ranging from local health care entities to multinational retailers. The team's litigators are "*great in court*," particularly in employee-related noncompete litigation, which has been a busy area of late. The firm secures considerable praise for its service standards from clients who deem it "*very responsive.*"

**The Lawyers:** **Robert Hobbins** (see p.1164) divides his time between employment and labor litigation and arbitration. In the past year, he successfully repelled an attempted class action against Mayo Clinic that challenged its wage and hour policies and sought to represent all salaried employees. He also secured a complete win for Lund Food Holdings in arbitration with United Food and Commercial Workers in a wage and conditions dispute. Hobbins additionally has a significant counseling practice. "*The most well-prepared attorney*" some clients had ever encountered, he was also admired for his "*excellent judgment*" and "*sheer common sense.*" **Robert Reinhart** (see p.1166) represents management in employment litigation and arbitration, and in risk management counseling. He continues to represent Wal-Mart in an array of overtime disputes, from exemption cases to unclaimed hours. Clients spoke of his "*strategic and penetrating*" analysis, and were equally generous about his trial skills calling him "*one of the best public speakers*" they had seen. Although assertive, he is "*not a scorch and burn litigator*," and this approach gives him "*great standing in court.*" Reinhart also impresses with his client service, "*lean staffing and efficient use of time.*" And in perhaps the ultimate accolade, clients noted that his work "*led to better results and lower costs than expected.*" **Doug Christensen** (see p.1162) handles both labor and employment law. Clients remarked on his "*exceptional intelligence*" and "*total command of his area of law*," while also finding him "*approachable and accessible*" and noting: "*He doesn't let ego get in the way.*" **Melissa Raphan** (see p.1166) "*brings a lot of common sense*" to her litigation practice. Her "*quick and to-the-point*" style benefits employers who seek her advice on performance management and termination issues. Fellow litigator **Roy Ginsburg** (see p.1163) specializes in discrimination and harassment and also handles employee-related competition issues, such as trade secrets cases. He is defending Cisco Systems in the appeal of a $450 million lawsuit raised by Storage Technology over the hiring of its employees by a Cisco company. **Steve Gottschalk** (see p.1163) chairs the firm's employee benefits group and represents employers in formulating compensation, welfare and retirement plans. He was recommended to researchers for his work counseling and educating clients on recent amendments to the Inland Revenue Code related to deferred compensation. **Holly Eng** (see p.1163) continues to impress observers with her work on single-plaintiff discrimination actions in both administrative and judicial settings. She has recently been working with other members of the firm on defending a Minneapolis-based Fortune 500 company in an age discrimination class action, potentially affecting thousands of employees.

**Clients/Work Highlights:** Hormel Foods; Xcel Energy; Mayo Clinic; Life Time Fitness; Cisco Systems and HealthPartners.

## Band 2

### Briggs and Morgan, Professional Association

**The Firm:** This midsized, full-service firm divides around 20 "*committed and experienced*" attorneys between its labor law, employment counseling and employment litigation teams. It can also call on a small employee benefits team. Discrimination, ERISA and FLSA claims fuel the litigation practice, along with noncompete agreements and related actions. Counseling covers issues ranging from affirmative action to immigration, as well as training on the basics of employment law for supervisors and managers. The firm's attorneys were seen as "*bright and responsive*" and "*easy for clients to relate to.*"

**The Lawyers:** **Scott Davies** offers "*the whole package – expert knowledge with superb trial skills.*" Although his background is in general litigation, he now focuses on discrimination, wrongful termination and ERISA, as well as some labor matters. Peers note that he "*really knows his stuff.*" Chair of the employment law section, **Ann Huntrods** divides her time between litigation, counseling and training. She "*fills the room,*" whether representing employers in discrimination or harassment litigation, or before government agencies such as the EEOC. "*Client-oriented*" and "*enormously professional,*" she is favored by clients for her "*practical advice*" and constructive approach to litigation: "*She doesn't rely on threats.*" Fellow partner, "*talented and personable*" **Gregory Stenmoe** focuses on discipline, discharge and sexual harassment, with noncompete matters also key to the litigation element of his workload. Expert counselor **Karin Wille** has a niche in advice to higher education institutions. She draws on an in-house background, advising employers on all aspects of employment law from leave to discharge, and with reference to ADA and other relevant legislation. Peers admired her "*great understanding and good judgment,*" particularly with regard to disability discrimination.

**Clients/Work Highlights:** Among the clients are Carlson Companies, Ceridian, AT&T and PepsiCo, plus a variety of state and national businesses as well as health care and educational institutions.

### Faegre & Benson LLP

See firm details p.1170

**The Firm:** Faegre remains "*first-rate for client service and effectiveness,*" and boasts a client base replete with several Fortune 500 companies. The team has a strong labor law practice, and is also active in areas such as discrimination litigation, including some large class actions for national clients. "*Exceptional*" attorneys benefit from Faegre's cross-disciplinary approach, working closely with dedicated employee benefits and immigration teams.

**The Lawyers:** Peers hail **Reid Carron** (see p.1162) as "*the top labor lawyer in Minnesota.*" "*Well-respected in the community,*" his "*exceptional*" practice takes in collective bargaining and union organizing plus

issues arising from M&A and shutdowns. **Mary Stumo's** (see p.1167) litigation practice encompasses all aspects of employment law, with a particular focus on discrimination. Her clients include McDonald's and Wells Fargo. "*Astute and discreet*," she was recommended by peers for her focus on settlement and alternative dispute resolution. "*Straightforward, practical and careful*" **Kathy Noecker** (see p.1165) heads the firm's labor and employment group. She counsels a variety of state and regional enterprises, ranging from schools to Fortune 500 companies and the Minnesota Star Tribune. Her "*great understanding of local issues*" is augmented by her careful approach: "*She makes sure every 'i' is dotted and every 't' is crossed*." This "*prompt and responsive*" lawyer "*never says what you can't do*," and is adept at "*explaining the salient issues to naive legal minds*."
Clients/Work Highlights: Wells Fargo; UPS; Guidant; Minnesota Star Tribune; Target; Hutchinson Technology and McDonald's.

### Felhaber, Larson, Fenlon & Vogt, PC
The Firm: Labor and employment law have been specialties of this firm since it was founded in St. Paul in 1928. It was selected by peers as the best firm operating in the budget area of the market, and is said to provide a variety of simple solutions to the needs of smaller businesses, including a recently introduced one-step compliance audit. Although "*well versed in labor law*," the firm's 25 attorneys also provide counseling on employment matters such as wage and hour and ADA. A particular niche is healthcare, where the team works alongside a health law group with which it shares some members.
The Lawyers: "*Senior and savvy*" labor lawyer **James Dawson** targets health care providers. "*Tough and aggressive*," but always showing "*good judgment*," he also serves as chairman of the firm's board. **Paul Zech** boasts a "*pan-industrial*" practice focused on employment litigation. "*Diligent, productive and high-energy*," he is particularly applauded for his harassment work. Like Dawson, **Jan Halverson** specializes in working for healthcare organizations, providing them with both counseling and representation in labor and employment disputes from collective bargaining to litigation. Sources said of this "*eloquent*" attorney: "*He just deals with what needs to be dealt with*." An expert on FMLA and FLSA matters, **Penny Phillips** is considered "*well organized, thoughtful and highly networked*."
Clients/Work Highlights: The team's broad client base includes Minnesota and Midwestern manufacturers and retailers, as well as healthcare and public sector organizations.

## Band 3

### Fredrikson & Byron PA
The Firm: This team of nine attorneys focuses on employment counseling and litigation, and additionally offers a small but vibrant labor practice. The firm acts as outside counsel for Minnesota clients and as local counsel for larger national clients.
The Lawyers: A former head of the group, **Richard Ross** has extensive experience representing employers in litigation, in union negotiations and before the NLRB. His clients include healthcare institutions as well as manufacturers and retailers. Peers consider him "*top-notch*" for litigation, with a particular knack for securing summary judgments.
Clients/Work Highlights: The firm's broad client base includes many healthcare, financial and educational institutions, as well as manufacturers and retailers.

### Gray, Plant, Mooty, Mooty & Bennett, PA
The Firm: Celebrating its 140th year in business, this is Minnesota's only member of the Employment Law Alliance, a worldwide knowledge-sharing network of employment lawyers. The firm's team of 13 employment attorneys represents both plaintiffs and defendants in employment litigation, as well as counseling a wide range of local manufacturers and technology firms. One high-profile client is Dairy Queen, whose relationship with the firm goes back many years. Clients praise the team for providing "*the full circle*" of service, responding promptly to instructions and "*tactfully and clearly letting us know when we're wrong*."
The Lawyers: **Judith Langevin** is said to be "*one of the wisest people*" around. A former chair of the group, she specializes in discrimination, harassment and wrongful termination. "*Deeply client-focused*," she is capable of "*making sure her work is reflective of our style*," said clients; while in trial her "*objective and compassionate approach*" stands her in good stead. Always "*well prepared*," she "*has the respect of judges*."
Clients/Work Highlights: Ellerbe Becket, Polyphase Electric and Dairy Queen are just three of the larger companies represented by the firm.

### Leonard, Street and Deinard Professional Association
The Firm: This midmarket, full-service Minneapolis firm boasts 19 "*well-intentioned and thorough*" attorneys working on employment and labor law. It has dedicated labor relations and immigration teams, and its client base includes regional and national publicly traded companies in a wide range of industries. Recent changes to overtime regulations continue to be a driver of business, requiring extensive audits of clients' policies.
The Lawyers: **Robert Zeglovitch**, a former chair of the employment practice, specializes in complex employment litigation, taking in discrimination, sexual harassment and wage and hour issues.
Clients/Work Highlights: Land O'Lakes; Canadian Pacific Railway; Honeywell; General Mills; Lexis-Nexis; Taylor; Pentair; Cargill and Allianz Life.

### Other Notable Practitioners
"*Smart and aggressive*," **Barbara D'Aquila** of Flynn, Gaskins & Bennett LLP "*does a great job for her clients*." This "*exceptional strategist*" recently represented clients in two discrimination appeals in the Minnesota Supreme Court. She is admired by peers as "*phenomenal in both preparation and follow through*." Although he is now president of Littler Mendelson PC, the USA's biggest labor and employment law boutique, "*extrovert*" **Marko Mrkonich** (see p.1165) still devotes most of his time to the Minneapolis office. Combining litigation and advisory work with a busy schedule of education and training, he recently won two major discrimination cases in the Eighth Circuit Court of Appeals and in state court in Baltimore. "*Gentleman*" **Joseph Roby** practices at the small Duluth firm of Johnson, Killen & Seiler. Dividing his time between employment litigation and labor law, Roby is an "*effective advocate*" for northern Minnesota companies. **Doug Seaton** heads up the boutique Seaton Beck & Peters PA in suburban Minneapolis. He concentrates on labor relations and is "*well known to the NLRB regionally*." Seaton's practice also incorporates discrimination and harassment investigations. He is seen as a "*good strategic thinker*" who "*can communicate complicated material in a way that's easily understood*." **John Thompson** chairs labor and employment law group at the midsized, full-service Minneapolis firm Rider Bennett LLP. His broad practice encompasses counseling and litigation, and he is deemed "*scholarly and analytical*" yet "*bright and energetic*." Thompson is particularly knowledgeable about workplace violence.

# LITIGATION

## Band 1

### Dorsey & Whitney LLP
See firm details p.1169

**The Firm:** This Minneapolis giant's team of 85 *"bright, articulate"* attorneys *"could take on any case in the country,"* researchers were told. Indeed, with 13 regional offices from San Francisco to Washington, DC, the team's work is national in scope. By way of example, the group recently won almost $1 million for Cargill in a patent jury trial in the Southern Florida District Court. Notable regional clients include Northwest Airlines, which the team successfully defended from privacy and competition claims in federal, district and appellate courts recently. The team's appeal is the depth of its resources and the *"length and strength of its bench,"* however, its attentiveness to clients is also admired. Despite the quality on offer, the team has the flexibility to match its service to a client's resources as well as their needs: *"they can read me,"* said one, *"and they know if I'm anxious about cost."*

**The Lawyers:** Revered by peers and clients as *"the smartest lawyer in town,"* **Roger Magnuson** (see p.1165) *"doesn't miss a point."* His work has included everything from helping the Minnesota Twins obtain permission for a new stadium to defending the directors of a major international bank. He also continues to represent partners in the Mall of America in the follow-up and appellate litigation subsequent to a major victory for the client last year. Observers stress his *"unparalleled"* courtroom skill: *"Judges have a lot of respect for him,"* while juries *"respond to his old-time preacher style."* The *"standout"* attorney **Thomas Tinkham** (see p.1167), who is chair of the commercial litigation practice, has had a busy year. His practice sees him representing some of the Midwest's largest Fortune 500 companies in complex insurance and employment-related litigation. He is currently pursuing a major tax claim for Mayo Clinic, following his successful $50 million claim last year. Clients praised his *"proactive and thematic"* approach and admired *"his ability to quickly grasp issues."* Tinkham is currently collaborating with **Craig Diviney** (see p.1163) on a contract dispute in federal court for SUPERVALU. Diviney, who comes highly recommended for his *"unimpeachable integrity,"* divides his time between complex commercial and IP litigation for large regional public companies such as Land O'Lakes and Fair Isaac. Peers consider him *"a worthy adversary,"* while clients praise his ability to *"anticipate issues and come up with solutions."* His customer service is particularly admired: *"I feel like I'm his only client,"* said one. Formerly ranked Paul Klaas now devotes much of his time to managing the firm's London office. **Marianne Short**'s (see p.1166) 30 years of trial experience includes time as an appellate judge, a background that enables her to offer clients *"excellent advice."* Though her practice encompasses general, IP and appellate work, it is healthcare litigation for which she is best known. She recently defended Medica HealthPlans and its Board in litigation involving governance issues.

**Clients/Work Highlights:** Northwest Airlines; Land O'Lakes; Mayo Clinic; SUPERVALU; 3M; UnitedHealth Group and US Bank.

### Faegre & Benson LLP
See firm details p.1170

**The Firm:** *"If this team were to split into ten firms,"* said one rival lawyer, *"seven or eight of those firms would be in the top tier of your table."* Clients also praised the *"consistent quality"* of the large team of over 50 litigators. Products liability litigation is a particular strength of the practice, which also encompasses securities, antitrust and a growing franchise litigation practice. The firm's *"top-flight"* IP team was additionally singled out for praise by clients. The team was described as *"very attentive to the needs of in-house lawyers;"* it creates *"a real partnership"* with clients and offers *"exceptional value for money."*

**The Lawyers:** **Jerry Snider**'s (see p.1167) practice focuses on complex litigation in areas ranging from antitrust to malpractice. He is widely praised for his *"plainspoken, down-to-earth"* courtroom manner, which gives him *"instant credibility"* with juries. It is said that *"the justice of his cause comes naturally out of the way he speaks."* Another *"big player,"* **Jim Volling** (see p.1167) takes on antitrust, securities and stockholder litigation, in addition to extensive work in white-collar criminal defense. Seen as a *"good strategist"* by peers, he is representing the trustees of a large Minnesota securities clearing firm in a high-profile lawsuit arising out of an alleged stock fraud. With a practice that encompasses commercial, IP and environmental litigation, **Brian O'Neill** (see p.1165) *"cuts a broad swath."* Though best known for representing plaintiffs in the mammoth litigation arising from the Exxon Valdez oil spill, he commonly represents defendants before regulatory authorities. Observers admire his *"creativity"* and note how *"he comes at things from a new direction."* Though his caseload is broad, **Edward Wahl** (see p.1167) is noted for his representation of financial institutions, including Prudential and US Bank Trust. Seen by peers as *"first-rate"* for insurance-related matters, Wahl has also shown his *"special abilities"* on IP cases. **Charles Webber** (see p.1167) is also noted by clients for his creative approach; he has the ability to *"jump in and negotiate the matters that need instant attention."* He recently represented a large Midwestern chemical company in a consumer fraud class action involving several hundred plaintiffs. **Wendy Wildung** (see p.1168) is *"one of the go-to people in the Midwest"* for defending class actions. *"Whip smart"* and *"a quick learner,"* she recently successfully repelled securities claims in both state and federal courts for the directors of notable Minnesota retailers Rural Cellular and Gander Mountain. Wildung is praised for her performance on her feet, whether before a courtroom or a board of directors. *"Laid*

| Litigation: IP | |
|---|---|
| **Leading Individuals** | |
| [1] ALLGEYER David | *Lindquist & Vennum PLLP* |
| CARLSON Alan | *Carlson, Caspers, Vandenburgh* |
| CIRESI Michael | *Robins, Kaplan, Miller & Ciresi LLP* |
| DIVINEY Craig | *Dorsey & Whitney LLP* |
| GROSS David | *Faegre & Benson LLP* |
| HEIN Laura | *Gray, Plant, Mooty* |
| LIEBMAN Kenneth | *Faegre & Benson LLP* |
| MCDONALD Daniel | *Merchant & Gould PC* |
| ROBINER Susan | *Leonard, Street* |
| SCHUTZ Ronald | *Robins, Kaplan, Miller & Ciresi* |
| SINGER Jonathan | *Fish & Richardson P.C.* |
| **Up-and-coming individuals** | |
| KAHNKE Randall | *Faegre & Benson LLP* |

| Litigation: Appellate | |
|---|---|
| **Leading Individuals** | |
| [1] HERR David | *Maslon Edelman Borman* |

back" but nevertheless "*poised and articulate*" in court, and "*well respected by the local judiciary*," she can also "*explain complex securities litigation in a way executives can understand.*" Chair of the firm's IP practice group, **Ken Liebman** (see p.1164) concentrates on life sciences and IT clients, including the University of Minnesota and Guidant whom he is currently representing in patent litigation. **David Gross** (see p.1163) combines academic and practical experience to tackle "*more than averagely complicated cases.*" He boasts 3M as a major client, this year successfully arguing that a competitor's new line of paint spray guns copied 3M's design and securing an injunction against their release. Clients were full of praise for Gross' "*strategic and creative*" approach, noting that "*he's preparing for trial from day one.*" Another standout lawyer is "*young, aggressive and ambitious*" **Randall Kahnke** (see p.1164), whose client base is focused on local medical and IT companies. His ability to "*make things happen*" was illustrated when he defeated a $25 million claim against a leading local software company.

Clients/Work Highlights: IBM; US Bank; Wells Fargo; Koch Industries; Cargill; DuPont; University of Minnesota; Hutchinson Technology; Fair Isaac; Capital One.

### Robins, Kaplan, Miller & Ciresi LLP
See firm details p.1172

The Firm: With support from offices across the country, more than 100 attorneys in Minneapolis work on commercial litigation for clients ranging from Estée Lauder to the Government of India. Although the firm has developed a particular reputation for IP, it has a broad practice that includes bankruptcy, antitrust and products liability. The team is best known for plaintiff work, peers noting how its litigators "*like to be on the attack.*" Clients praised the team's "*terrific trial lawyers,*" who not only stand up well in court but "*also write well.*" Customer service is as much a strength as the quality

of representation. "*Unusually responsive for a litigation firm,*" it "*doesn't overstaff matters*" and permits "*no wild goose chases.*"

The Lawyers: The "*formidable*" **Michael Ciresi** (see p.1162) has a national reputation as "*the paragon of trial lawyers.*" He is established in both general and IP litigation and his client list includes giants such as Pitney Bowes and Estée Lauder. He successfully defended TriStrata in a $26 million patent dispute against cosmetics goliath Mary Kay in federal court in Delaware. In court, Ciresi exhibits "*a toughness and charm that plays well with juries;*" he can "*quickly capitalize on the other side's mistakes.*" Despite his top-flight reputation, clients note that he "*works hard*" and "*doesn't just glide in at the last minute.*" **Martin Lueck** (see p.1165) is also "*a very gifted trial lawyer.*" He combines a strong reputation for IP with substantial experience of antitrust and other commercial litigation. His clients include such giants as Unocal, and he recently prevailed in a major patent dispute between GE and GM. He is praised for his work both before and in trial, clients regarding him "*a skilled cross-examiner.*" Like Ciresi, Lueck "*thinks on his feet*" and, with perhaps a hint of envy, peers remarked that "*juries like him.*" "*Hard-charging*" **Ron Schutz** (see p.1166) chairs the firm's IP practice. He drew the attention of peers with his victories for St. Clair IP Consultants in wide-ranging patent litigation against several major electronics multinationals.

Clients/Work Highlights: The University of California, GE and Pitney Bowes are just some of the household names represented by the firm.

### Band 2

### Anthony Ostlund & Baer

The Firm: Focusing directly on business litigation, for its size this 20-attorney boutique has an impressive reputation. Peers noted the "*top-to-bottom quality*" of the team, which "*does a hell of a job with difficult cases.*" Clients applaud the team's "*passionate*" approach, pointing to low staff turnover which allows long-term relationships to develop.

The Lawyers: "*Appropriately aggressive*" founding partner **Joe Anthony** "*can lead any case.*" He recently successfully represented a former employee of First Albany Corporation in a dispute over compensation and wrongful termination, obtaining nearly $1 million in arbitration, and saw the ruling affirmed in the Eighth Circuit Court of Appeals. Clients lauded Anthony for his "*commanding presence and vigor*" in the courtroom, and for being "*proactive and available*" out of it. Although he normally focuses on stockholder disputes, **Randy Gullickson** grabbed the headlines recently by successfully representing a coalition of tobacco companies opposing a proposed health fee on cigarettes levied by the Minnesota legislature. The 75c-per-pack fee would have amounted to $400 million over the next two years. "*Talented*" **Richard Ostlund** focuses primarily on stockholder and employment litigation, and recently secured $9 million in compensation for a former employee of a

Minnesota motor manufacturer. Praised by peers for his "*attentive, responsive*" style, **Nathan Brenna** is developing a fine reputation for a practice that ranges from securities to fraud.

Clients/Work Highlights: Miller Meester Advertising; Major League Baseball; Piper Jaffrey and Ameriprize.

### Briggs and Morgan, Professional Association

The Firm: The business litigation group at this midsized Minneapolis firm comprises over 60 attorneys and, with a client base that includes several Fortune 500 companies, it rivals the offerings of larger firms. Clients attribute this success to the team's "*outstanding*" attorneys, who "*take great pains to understand each client's business.*" The team's expertise ranges from fraud to products liability cases; however, the team's lawyers are "*flexible enough to approach new areas of law.*" Overall, clients felt the team's performance "*more than vindicates our decision to look beyond the large city firms.*"

The Lawyers: When it comes to antitrust and franchise litigation, **Jeffrey Keyes** is "*the big-picture guy.*" He has vast academic and professional knowledge of these fields, as well as substantial litigation experience. As one source said of his trial skills: "*He has the gray matter, and he can express it.*"

Clients/Work Highlights: The client base stretches from local startups and closely held businesses to national public companies in the manufacturing, medical, technological and financial fields.

### Greene Espel PLLP

The Firm: This "*outstanding*" boutique of 20 lawyers "*does a remarkable job*" on litigation ranging from antitrust to IP matters. The team advises investors, startups, and midsized retailers and financial institutions. It has also served as local trial counsel for Fortune 500 companies. Always "*on top of the facts,*" its lawyers have a particular niche in corporate misconduct, with white-collar crime defense a related specialty.

The Lawyers: "*Straight shooter*" **Andrew Luger** is "*the top choice for white-collar crime,*" however, he also has an active practice in complex business litigation, including securities and IP. Peers cite his New York background as the source of his "*intensity*" of approach, something that allows him to "*get to the bottom of things*" and endears him to juries.

Clients/Work Highlights: Baxter; Cargill; Ceridian; Medtronic; Qwest; Target and US Bank.

### Maslon Edelman Borman & Brand, LLP

The Firm: This team of 43 litigators excels at construction, insurance and products liability cases for a client base of midsized and Fortune 1000 companies. Manufacturers, especially in the pharmaceutical and medical industries, are at the core of the client list, the most significant of these being Medtronic. Peers also note minority stockholder cases as a particular strength of the team. Attorneys are said to "*hone in quickly on the issues,*" with one client describing them as "*the best at cross-examina-*

tion I have seen."

**The Lawyers:** Within **Bill Pentelovitch**'s broad practice, emphasis is placed on trade secrets and competition litigation for life sciences firms. He recently defended Medtronic, successfully repelling a $20 million patent claim, and secured a $3.5 million jury verdict for former Tour de France winner Greg LeMond in breach of contract litigation with PTI Holdings of New York, who had dropped LeMond's name from its merchandise. For clients, Pentelovitch is *"a terrific strategist"* who *"sees the big picture;"* they were also quick to praise his skills in arbitration, saying he is *"incredible on his feet"* and someone who can *"aim and fire at the same time."* A commercial litigation generalist, **Richard Wilson** is noted by observers for his combination of *"excellent preparation and trial skills."* *"Analytical"* and able to *"quickly home in on the issues,"* Wilson can *"present complicated legal arguments simply."* Despite a *"respectful and self-deprecating"* courtroom style, he is *"one of the best at cross-examination"* clients had seen. **David Herr**, who heads the firm's appellate practice, is renowned as *"one of the top appellate lawyers in the Eighth Circuit."* He recently repeated his successful defense of claims against a number of local tobacco companies in federal appeal court. *"Cerebral"* and yet *"a good draftsperson,"* Herr was also noted for his aptitude at working with trial teams from other firms.

**Clients/Work Highlights:** 3M, Medtronic and King Technology are just some of the midsized and major technology, manufacturing and financial companies served by the firm.

## Band 3

### Bassford Remele, A Professional Association

**The Firm:** This boutique of 34 attorneys specializes in insurance, trust and estate litigation. Although Lou Remele is the team's undoubted star, clients note a team-based approach and multidisciplinary support network within the firm. They told researchers: *"We've never had a better relationship with outside counsel."*

**The Lawyers:** Commentators queued up to shower praise on **Lou Remele** (see p.1166), *"one of the best litigators in America."* *"Articulate, incisive and a quick study,"* he is *"phenomenal"* in court. Although increasingly active in mediation and alternative dispute resolution, Remele has an active practice representing trustees, stockholders, insurers and commercial directors and executives. As well as raving about his legal skills, peers considered him *"one of the friendliest people on earth."*

**Clients/Work Highlights:** Metropolitan Council; St. Jude Medical; Wyeth; Chubb Group; Toro and New Access Communications.

### Fredrikson & Byron PA

**The Firm:** Some 65 *"tenacious and zealous"* litigators are gradually expanding their reputation and client base at this midmarket Minnesota firm, which also has offices in Mexico and the UK. Tax law has long been a key area, and tax disputes now fuel the litigation practice. Another area of growth is IP, with six attorneys at the firm specializing in this field. Clients praised the group for its *"unbelievable ability to make complex problems easy to understand."*

**The Lawyers:** Chair of the practice *"likable"* **Tom Fraser** works on everything from stockholder disputes to antitrust. In the past year he has tried trade secrets and breach of contract cases in both state and federal court in Minnesota. *"Smart, resourceful and tough"* as a trial lawyer, Fraser is also increasingly active as a mediator.

**Clients/Work Highlights:** The firm represents regional and national, publicly and privately held manufacturers, banks, financial institutions and utilities.

### Gray, Plant, Mooty, Mooty & Bennett, PA

**The Firm:** More than 40 *"highly strategic"* attorneys are valued for their *"amazing litigation perspective."* The franchising and products liability practices are particularly strong, with the team recently obtaining a crucial summary judgment in favor of a chemical tank manufacturer in litigation arising from a train crash involving one of its tanks. It also represented Xiotech in its high-profile trade secrets dispute with Compellent. A pragmatic and business-focused approach ensures that the lawyers are able to *"see the entire game, not just the current play."* Clients confirmed the team is *"more concerned with getting the right result than generating more fees."*

**The Lawyers:** Labeled *"the intellectual's litigator"* for his mastery of difficult cases, **James Simonson** maintains a successful practice handling complex litigation for both local and national companies. He successfully repelled minority stockholder litigation aimed at preventing the merger of local life sciences manufacturer Chronimed with MIM Corporation, and continues to represent GM as local counsel in a major nationwide class action potentially involving 80 million vehicles. Clients called him both attentive and frank, noting how he *"really listens to what you want"* but *"doesn't just tell you what you want to hear."* Simonson was also rated for his court performance, with clients saying. *"He delivers opinions straight and with confidence."* **Laura Hein**'s IP practice focuses on copyright and trademark cases. A highlight this year was Taylor Corporation v Four Seasons Greetings, in which she successfully demonstrated copyright infringement in the design of Christmas cards. Clients admire her drafting and advocacy skills. *"Talented"* and *"pleasantly aggressive"* in the courtroom and *"adept at writing in non legal language,"* Hein is said to prepare *"the best briefs."* Commenting on her personality, one client called her *"one of my favorite lawyers in the world to work with,"* and others concurred.

**Clients/Work Highlights:** Taylor Corporation; GM; BioScrip; Bridgestone/Firestone; Carlson; Cargill and Tastefully Simple.

### Kelly & Berens PA

**The Firm:** A dozen attorneys strong, this boutique focuses on litigation, and in particular, commercial and securities cases. Although its attorneys have garnered a reputation as *"bulldogs"* in court, alternative dispute resolution is also central to the practice. The team's small size means it *"appreciates every client relationship,"* and enables it to offer *"great service at a reasonable cost."*

**The Lawyers:** As the firm's managing partner and leading light, **Tim Kelly** is simply *"the guy for litigation defense."* *"A great communicator"* in both trial and arbitration, he is also noted for his strategy. Peers remarked on how *"he sees angles no one else does."*

**Clients/Work Highlights:** TCF Financial, Regis, Allianz Life, Guidant and Ceridian are some of the major companies who turn to the firm.

### Leonard, Street and Deinard Professional Association

**The Firm:** With over 20 of its 90 litigators focused on commercial litigation, this *"brilliant"* firm has carved out a strong niche between the Goliaths and the boutiques and represents some of the Midwest's largest corporates, including Honeywell and Allianz Life. It is currently representing Aspen Healthcare in high-profile trade secrets litigation with Guidant. The team emphasizes customer service, leading clients to report: *"We feel like we're its only client."*

**The Lawyers:** **Lawrence Field**'s *"tenacity and creativity"* have been demonstrated by his continuing representation of Simon Property Group in appeals and follow-up cases to the major Mall of America litigation. Field has made some progress in undoing a previously disastrous ruling for his client. He also represents other major companies, including Texas Instruments and Allianz Life, in securities litigation. Clients like his *"detail-oriented"* style, saying: *"He achieves things others would think too difficult."* **Todd Noteboom** this year repeated his successful defense of State Farm in high-profile class action at the appellate level. *"Great on his feet,"* he *"does his homework"* and, as a result, *"he knows the lay of the land before he enters court."* Despite a background in employment law, **Susan Robiner** now chairs the firm's IP practice and, with widespread experience in state and federal appellate courts, she is noted by peers as *"every bit the equal"* of better-known IP litigators.

**Clients/Work Highlights:** Simon Property Group; State Farm; Soo Line Railroad and Texas Instruments.

### Lindquist & Vennum PLLP

See firm details p.1171

**The Firm:** With around 60 litigators, this midmarket firm *"can field a substantial army of good lawyers for complex cases."* Certainly, peers acknowledge that it does *"litigation of major importance."* Although its practice covers all types of commercial disputes, the team is carving out niches in securities and antitrust disputes as well as insurance, where it focuses on representing policyholders and can call on the expertise of a separate insurance law practice. The team serves a wide range of Minnesota-based companies in a wide range of industries, in addition to some national clients.

**The Lawyers:** Litigator **David Allgeyer** (see p.1162) *"gets results."* Active in IP and general commercial litigation, he is particularly active in plaintiff-side work. A *"compelling courtroom presence,"* he is also *"fiercely practical"* and *"good at working out settlements."* This emphasis on resolutions has seen him selected as an arbitrator in disputes across the country. *"Courteous and professional,"* Allgeyer is rated by clients for his customer service as well as his expertise. Active in arbitration, mediation and litigation, *"terrific"* **Terrence Fleming** (see p.1163) is *"a different kind of lawyer."* His specialties are securities and stockholder disputes, and peers say they would *"refer any minority stockholder case to him."* Fleming represents clients before regulatory bodies, and during the past year represented a major broker dealer in arbitration before the National Association of Securities Dealers worth $500 million. **Richard Ihrig** (see p.1164) specializes in all kinds of complex commercial litigation, but he is most recognized for his antitrust work. He recently represented the passengers of Northwest Airlines in a class action challenge to its merger with Republic Airlines. Clients hailed his *"experience and judgment"* and the fact that *"he knows his way around litigation."* They appreciated his sense of when settling or alternative dispute resolution are appropriate, noting that *"he knows what litigation can and can't achieve."*

**Clients/Work Highlights:** General Mills, Walgreen's and Target are among the national retailers, manufacturers and financial institutions that make up the firm's client base.

## Band 4

### Fruth, Jamison & Elsass

**The Firm:** This five-attorney boutique is rated for commercial and securities litigation. Primarily serving Minnesota-based entrepreneurs, stockholders and broker dealers, the team is also often hired as local counsel for national companies, and is currently representing DC-based investment bank Ferris, Baker Watts in high-profile litigation resulting from the collapse of a Minnesota securities broker.

**The Lawyers:** Clients consider **Terence Fruth** *"one of the best lawyers in the Twin Cities."* With a practice that ranges from stockholder disputes to zoning appeals, he is praised for his *"extensive knowledge of the local judiciary."* Making his debut in the table is *"brilliant thinker"* **Tom Jamison**, who brings experience as a former broker to his growing securities practice. He secured a substantial result for dissenting stockholders of eMachines in the Delaware Court of Chancery and at appeal in the Delaware Supreme Court. Jamison is lauded for his *"comprehensiveness and creativity,"* with clients noting that *"he doesn't miss issues."*

**Clients/Work Highlights:** The firm acts for regional manufacturers, retailers and financial institutions.

### Winthrop & Weinstine, A Professional Association

See firm details p.1173

**The Firm:** This growing team recently took on another floor in its downtown Minneapolis building, marking its expansion to over 40 *"superb"* litigators. The firm has developed a niche in stockholder, antitrust and products liability cases and serves major regional clients. In the past year it won over

$100 million for Marvin Windows and Doors in the Eighth Circuit Court of Appeals, the culmination of a long-running products liability dispute with PPG.

**The Lawyers:** **Robert Weinstine** (see p.1167), whose broad practice includes substantial trial activity, was highly praised by clients for his commitment to understanding the details of cases. *"He knows the case better than I do,"* said one, *"and I've been on it five years!"* This ability to understand cases is only rivaled by his capacity to argue them, with clients claiming him *"someone you can be proud of in a court or arbitration setting."*

**Clients/Work Highlights:** Bremer Bank, Marvin Windows and Doors and Wells Fargo are some of the firm's major clients.

## Other Notable Practitioners

**Alan Carlson** is the leading light at 14-attorney Minneapolis IP boutique Carlson, Caspers, Vandenburgh & Lindquist. An *"excellent strategist,"* Carlson tries patent, trade secrets and copyright cases. He dazzled observers with *"a sixth sense of what's needed in the courtroom."* **Daniel McDonald** leads the national IP specialist Merchant & Gould PC's main Minneapolis office. Representing national public companies, including 3M and ADC, in complex patent, trademark, copyright and trade secrets cases, observers called him *"a formidable and respected competitor."* **John Singer** (see p.1167) of national IP specialist Fish & Richardsons Minneapolis office focuses on medical and pharmaceutical patent litigation for regional clients such as Mayo Clinic. He is currently representing MIT and Repligen in a patent infringement case in federal court in Massachusetts. *"Incredibly skilled and knowledgeable,"* clients admiringly observed that Singer can *"walk into court with few notes and pull cases out of nowhere."*

# REAL ESTATE

<table>
<tr><td colspan="2">Real Estate</td></tr>
<tr><td colspan="2">Leading Firms</td></tr>
<tr><td>1</td><td>DORSEY & WHITNEY LLP Minneapolis</td></tr>
<tr><td></td><td>FAEGRE & BENSON LLP Minneapolis</td></tr>
<tr><td></td><td>FREDRIKSON & BYRON PA Minneapolis</td></tr>
<tr><td></td><td>LEONARD, STREET AND DEINARD PA Minneapolis</td></tr>
<tr><td>2</td><td>BRIGGS AND MORGAN, PA Minneapolis</td></tr>
<tr><td></td><td>GRAY, PLANT, MOOTY, MOOTY Minneapolis</td></tr>
<tr><td></td><td>OPPENHEIMER WOLFF & DONNELLY Minneapolis</td></tr>
<tr><td>3</td><td>FELHABER, LARSON, FENLON & VOGT Minneapolis</td></tr>
<tr><td></td><td>LINDQUIST & VENNUM PLLP Minneapolis</td></tr>
<tr><td>4</td><td>FABYANSKE, WESTRA & HART PA Minneapolis</td></tr>
<tr><td></td><td>RAVICH MEYER KIRKMAN MCGRATH Minneapolis</td></tr>
</table>

## Band 1

### Dorsey & Whitney LLP

See firm details p.1169

**The Firm:** Despite some recent departures, this team of 11 attorneys still boasts an *"enviable client list"* that includes local municipal authorities, regional and national developers and financial institutions. Although the team is active in development and other transactional work, financing and land use are particular strengths. It represented McGough Development in gaining approval for Bloomington Central Station, a $700 million high-density, transit-oriented housing development incorporating 1,200 housing units and two million square feet of office space. The deal included negotiating public financing.

**The Lawyers:** Chair of the real estate group **Mark Hamel** (see p.1164) is *"the real deal."* His *"attention to detail"* and *"great technical skill"* stand him in good stead in a practice that focuses on commercial

real estate, including office, hotel and healthcare buildings. **Jay Cook** (see p.1162) brings a *"steady hand"* to his practice counseling developers, financers and buyers in complex transactions. *"Unfazed by difficult projects,"* his expertise extends to office, mixed-use, retail, industrial and resort property. Observers noted that he can *"bring together opposing views and come out with a great deal."* Chair of the firm's urban renewal practice, **Jay Lindgren** (see p.1165) represents both developers and municipal authorities in land use, zoning, public finance and public-private partnerships. Clients admire his writing and negotiating skills, and note that his own experience as former CEO of the Metropolitan Council gives him *"a knowledge others can't match."*

**Clients/Work Highlights:** The firm provides representation to national developers, financial institutions and state municipal authorities, as well as users and owners of real estate from all areas of industry.

## Real Estate
### Leading Individuals

#### Senior Statesman
**ODLAUG Bruce** *Lindquist & Vennum PLLP*

[1] **COOK Jay** *Dorsey & Whitney LLP*
**EIDE David** *Felhaber, Larson, Fenlon & Vogt, PC*
**FERRELL Charles** *Faegre & Benson LLP*
**HAMEL Mark** *Dorsey & Whitney LLP*
**KELLEY David** *Leonard, Street*
**KONECK John** *Fredrikson & Byron PA*
**WHEATON John** *Faegre & Benson LLP*

[2] **CHRISTY Angela** *Faegre & Benson LLP*
**HAYNOR Charles** *Briggs and Morgan*
**KEPPLE Lloyd** *Oppenheimer Wolff*
**MASSOPUST Richard** *Oppenheimer Wolff*
**MAYERLE Thomas** *Faegre & Benson LLP*
**NORWICH Donald** *Oppenheimer Wolff*
**THIEL John** *Gray, Plant*
**WESTRA Mark** *Fabyanske, Westra*

[3] **FINLEY Joseph** *Leonard, Street and Deinard*
**KIRKMAN David** *Ravich Meyer Kirkman McGrath*
**PARSONS Chuck** *Moss & Barnett*
**RAVICH Paul** *Ravich Meyer Kirkman*

## Real Estate: Zoning/Land Use
### Leading Individuals

[1] **HERMAN John** *Faegre & Benson LLP*
**LINDGREN Jay** *Dorsey & Whitney LLP*
**MALKERSON Bruce** *Malkerson, Gilliland, Martin*
**ROM Rebecca** *Faegre & Benson LLP*
**SELLERGREN David** *Fredrikson & Byron PA*

## Faegre & Benson LLP
See firm details p.1170

**The Firm:** As you would expect from a firm with offices as far afield as London and Shanghai, Faegre's real estate practice is "*preeminent in the market well outside Minnesota.*" Its 25 "*extraordinary*" attorneys have been involved in major commercial property sales and acquisitions across the country, and act as national counsel for several large Midwestern insurance companies. The firm's leasing practice represents both landlords and tenants of major commercial centers across the Midwest, and its development practice is active in the highly competitive Chicago market. Clients rated attorneys highly for their "*tenacious*" approach.

**The Lawyers:** "*You frequently hear about other lawyers from clients,*" one peer remarked, "*they'll say, 'He's a great lawyer, but no* **Charlie Ferrell** (see p.1163)'.*" A member of the real estate team for nearly 30 years, Ferrell represents developers in all aspects of a variety of residential and commercial projects, in Minnesota and nationwide. Clients queue around the block to commend his customer service: "*Smart, personable and easy to approach,*" he "*really values the idea of a client relationship.*" Clients turn to **John Wheaton** (see p.1167) "*to get deals done.*" His broad practice encompasses development and finance for projects ranging from entertainment and hotel

complexes to suburban office buildings. Wheaton has lately represented a national retailer acting as primary tenant in the building and redevelopment of malls across the country. His "*sophisticated understanding of the law*" makes him "*invaluable on tough deals,*" and he is frequently brought in at a late stage to close transactions. **Angela Christy** (see p.1162) is "*a national leader*" in her specialized field of affordable housing, which ranges from mixed-income condominiums to projects for chronic alcoholics. She works with government agencies, investors and developers to structure transactions to ensure they are compatible with the mixed funding typical of such projects. Christy has earned the "*great respect*" of her peers for her "*outstanding*" achievements. A former group chair and according to some "*the smartest guy on the team,*" **Tom Mayerle** (see p.1165) "*doesn't miss a thing.*" His practice encompasses leasing and other transactional work on commercial property, with past clients including Piper Jaffray and Arthur Andersen. A key ongoing client is Target, whom he represents on new store and office developments across Minnesota and elsewhere. Faegre's key land use and permitting lawyers, **Rebecca Rom** (see p.1166) and **John Herman** (see p.1164), have had a busy year, spurred on by continuing residential and mixed-use developments in greenfield and former industrial land in suburban Minneapolis. Herman recently secured approval for a controversial mid-rise housing development which will be built on greenfield land in the uptown Lakes area. He is also working on the conversion of abandoned railroad land in Minneapolis as mixed-use office, housing and hotel development. "*Phenomenal*" Rom works "*hand in hand with civil engineers*" to ensure approvals for clients, including Target. "*Technically oriented,*" clients "*never feel anything will get past her.*"
**Clients/Work Highlights:** Cargill; 3M; Target; General Mills and Brookfield Development are just some of the national developers and users of real estate represented by the firm.

## Fredrikson & Byron PA

**The Firm:** In a thriving market, this team has now grown to 18 "*smart and capable*" lawyers. Active in financing, development and land use, the group represents major Minnesota companies in their activities across the USA, including Duke Real Estate, which holds over four million square feet in the Twin Cities. Peers note that the team "*is good at getting deals done,*" and this reputation attracts national players such as The Mills Corporation, which the team represented in its $300 million acquisition of the Southdale Center.
**The Lawyers:** Proficient at both litigation and development, **John Koneck** is noted for his "*tough, hard-nosed and practical*" approach. He brings his "*intellect and energy*" to the representation of major local and national players, including Polaroid. Bankruptcy and workouts are a specialty, and he represents both borrowers and lenders in litigation, often in tandem with his own firm's attorneys or with interfirm teams. **David Sellergren's** land use practice benefits from his environmental law expertise.

His talents proved invaluable on the River's Edge development, a 600-acre housing project on the banks of the Mississippi in southern St. Paul. Sellergren is also skilled at obtaining approvals for suburban subdivisions; his noted "*low-key approach*" sees him "*working with planning commissions, not fighting them.*"
**Clients/Work Highlights:** Liberty Property Trust; The Mills Corporation; DR Horton; Buffalo Wild Wings Bar & Grill and Duke Real Estate.

## Leonard, Street and Deinard Professional Association

**The Firm:** Real estate is becoming a priority for this firm. It now boasts over 35 attorneys who represent commercial and residential developers, with niches in brownfield developments and affordable housing. The team also acts as local counsel for large national REITs on properties across the Midwest, and assists the St. Paul Port Authority on real estate strategy. Another side of the practice is real estate litigation, typically the defense of title insurers and mortgage originators. Clients expressed admiration for the team's "*timely*" service: "*If something needs to be done on a date, it's done,*" and the resulting product is "*always top-notch.*" They also noted the team can be "*very creative on challenging projects.*"
**The Lawyers:** **David Kelley's** practice focuses on lending. This "*practical and personable*" attorney "*helps deals reach conclusions*" for a range of banks and insurance companies from across the Midwest and nationwide, notably Wisconsin's Marshall & Ilsley. "*Careful and non confrontational,*" Kelley "*gets the best result for all parties.*" **Joseph Finley's** reputation as "*a great all-rounder*" is borne out by his recent activity. He advises local corporations, including Target, on zoning and land use issues, and is representing the owners of the Midway Shopping Center in producing a redevelopment plan which relocates a storage facility for over 200 municipal buses. Finley is also active in litigation, leading the defense of a major title insurer against allegations of inconsistency in mortgage charging. Clients praise him for his ability to provide "*plain English*" agreements with a "*fast turnaround.*" He is also admired for his "*highly personalized*" service and ability to explain complex legal and business issues to clients, who consider him "*one of the best, if not the best.*" They wait nervously to see if his new status as managing partner of the firm will limit his ability to practice as much.
**Clients/Work Highlights:** Marshall & Ilsley; St. Paul Port Authority; Canadian Pacific Railway; DR Horton and Quadion.

## Band 2

## Briggs and Morgan, Professional Association

**The Firm:** This midmarket full-service firm boasts a "*substantial*" team of over 20 real estate attorneys, which is noted by peers for a nationwide presence in transactions and financing that belies the firm's size. In addition, the team is active in development and land use. Calling on the support of a ten-person public finance unit, the team's *"excellent"* attorneys specialize in representing both government bodies and developers in setting up publicly supported projects to utilize previously unproductive property. Another busy area is IRC 1031 transactions.

**The Lawyers: Chuck Haynor** represents insurance companies and financial institutions. Real estate finance occupies most of his time, and his practice includes both the structuring of complex loans and the workout and foreclosure of bad debts. *"Bright and responsive,"* Haynor also spends a portion of his time representing local and national developers on acquisitions.

**Clients/Work Highlights:** City governments are a key client for the team, in addition to state and national developers, financial institutions and insurance companies.

## Gray, Plant, Mooty, Mooty & Bennett, PA

**The Firm:** This team of 20 lawyers represents both governmental and corporate clients on all manner of things from finance to land use. It is currently representing the Bloomington Port Authority on the Bloomington Central Station redevelopment project. The firm has a strong environmental practice, representing Real Estate Recycling on the acquisition and redevelopment of contaminated land for companies including Caribou Coffee and Wickes Furniture. Its transactional practice is also strong: lawyers represented Allegheny Energy on the sale of two power stations in deals measured in the hundreds of millions of dollars.

**The Lawyers:** *"Thorough"* **John Thiel**'s practice sees him representing developers, lenders and government agencies on financing, transactions and tax matters. He is acting for the City of Minneapolis on a variety of zoning and land use issues for Midtown Exchange, a mixed-use redevelopment of former warehouse land covering three blocks in Midtown, and he negotiated a tax settlement on behalf of the owners of a regional mall in a first-tier suburb of the Twin Cities. Thiel has carved out a niche in 1031 tax-deferred exchanges, recently representing the sellers of a 130,000 sq ft mall and the buyers of a former library in the Twin Cities in such deals. Clients commend him for giving *"top-notch service with the personal touch."*

**Clients/Work Highlights:** The OPUS Group; Investors Real Estate Trust; Real Estate Recycling; Teachers Insurance and Annuity Association of America; Allegheny Energy; Dairy Queen; Equity Bank; Wells Fargo and Bremer Bank.

## Oppenheimer Wolff & Donnelly LLP

**The Firm:** This Minneapolis firm has undergone some well-publicized challenges in the last few years but real estate has been *"its anchor in difficult times."* Focused on finance, the team has *"the best lending practice in the Twin Cities,"* according to some. Drawing on the strength of its integrated commercial finance and bankruptcy team, these *"great lawyers"* represent national and regional insurance companies

and banks in the working out and foreclosure of distressed properties.

**The Lawyers:** As well as chairing the firm's real estate group, **Lloyd Kepple** has an extensive practice that encompasses equity, acquisition and mortgage lending. *"Personable, responsive and professional,"* he represents major investors in loans and joint ventures, with his knowledge of tax issues identified by peers as a particular skill. However, Kepple also represents Fortune 500 companies and government agencies in development and financing, and peers see him as *"a good all-rounder."* **Richard Massoupust** is *"the classic lender's lawyer."* He has a particular niche working with government and other agencies to set up large-scale conduit financing. *"Thoughtful and client-focused,"* Massopust is admired by peers for his *"substantial expertise"* and envied for his *"great client base."* *"Scrapper"* **Donald Norwich** specializes in syndicated loans for large commercial and industrial projects. His has a national practice, encompassing everything from hotel and resort activity in California to residential construction financing in Florida. Peers note that he *"can get complex deals done expeditiously."*

**Clients/Work Highlights:** Accenture, ADC and United Airlines are among the major public companies that use the team.

## Band 3

### Felhaber, Larson, Fenlon & Vogt, PC

**The Firm:** Around 15 attorneys make up the real estate team at this midmarket general firm. Focused on residential projects, a *"wonderful"* team provides transactional and development support and also boasts a strong lending practice.

**The Lawyers:** Despite his reputation as *"the leading expert on condominiums,"* **David Eide**'s work actually covers other forms of common interest community (CIC), including cooperatives. He is currently working on projects covering six downtown blocks in Minneapolis and two in St. Paul, providing over 1,000 housing units and over 100,000 sq ft of retail space. *"Locally and nationally known for his expertise,"* Eide has written much of the legislation on CICs for the state. He's praised by peers not only for his expertise but his *"prompt turnaround"* on agreements.

**Clients/Work Highlights:** Builders Association of the Twin Cities; Derrick Construction; Opus Northwest; Pratt Homes and Shamrock Development.

### Lindquist & Vennum PLLP

See firm details p.1171

**The Firm:** This team's gradual expansion in recent years sees it now sporting 14 attorneys. Representing users, developers and investors, the firm focuses its attention on commercial and industrial property in the Twin Cities. The team's expertise equips it to structure finance, negotiate acquisitions and leasings, and restructure or workout loans. This core skill set is complemented by construction, land use and environmental expertise.

**The Lawyers: Bruce Odlaug** (see p.1165) remains the practice's leading light. Lauded by peers as *"a great counselor,"* he represents both financial institutions and major regional developers such as United Properties.

**Clients/Work Highlights:** The firm is instructed by midsized Midwestern investors, developers, managers and users.

## Band 4

### Fabyanske, Westra & Hart PA

**The Firm:** Real estate is a key specialty of this boutique, with an 11-attorney real estate practice supplemented by a construction team. *"Strong in the finance area,"* the team works in conjunction with the firm's bankruptcy practice to represent landlords in distressed credit situations. Also active in development, transactions, lending and leasing, the firm has had a hand in commercial, office and residential developments across Minnesota and further afield.

**The Lawyers:** *"Old warhorse"* **Mark Westra** concentrates on financing. *"A great negotiator,"* he is called upon by national lenders and developers to arrange construction loans for commercial, office, residential and industrial projects. He also specializes in representing lenders and borrowers in restructuring and working out bad loans. With over 30 years of local experience, Westra *"knows all the secrets."*

**Clients/Work Highlights:** Cargill; Integroup Realty Trust; Apex Asset Management; Tanurb Developments; Eagle Ridge Partners and Trammell Crow.

### Ravich Meyer Kirkman McGrath & Nauman, PA

**The Firm:** A commercial and real estate boutique like Fabyanske, this firm has developed a strong reputation despite boasting only seven attorneys. Its practice focuses on representing developers of commercial property. The team also draws upon the expertise of the firm's bankruptcy lawyers to represent lenders and borrowers in foreclosures. Peers note that deal structuring is a particular strength: *"They're known for getting deals done."*

**The Lawyers: Paul Ravich** is *"an outstanding lawyer"* and a senior partner at the firm. He focuses on the representation of small to midsized businesses. His capacity as *"the consummate deal-maker"* stands him in good stead when assisting distressed real estate users and working out outstanding loans. Emerging from the shadow cast by his more senior colleague, **Dave Kirkman** was highly recommended by his peers. He is skilled in matters ranging from affordable housing to industrial acquisitions, and he has a particular aptitude for working with municipal authorities on supported financing and land use issues.

**Clients/Work Highlights:** Small and midsized local businesses, financial institutions and lenders make up the firm's clientele.

## Other Notable Practitioners

**Chuck Parsons**, of the midmarket, full-service firm Moss & Barnett is recommended by peers as *"a skilled adviser."* *"Savvy and sage,"* he *"does a great job of representing clients"* ranging from owners and tenants to lending institutions. He is also admired for his work as *"the guardian of the real estate laws"* in the Minnesota legislature. **Bruce Malkerson** of Malkerson, Gilliland, Martin was recommended for his representation of the owners of condemned property. Although he can at times be *"outspoken and combative,"* he has won *"great respect for his skills"* from his peers.

# Leaders in Minnesota

**ALLGEYER, David**
Lindquist & Vennum PLLP, Minneapolis
612 371 3216
dallgeyer@lindquist.com
*Recommended in Litigation*
**Practice Areas:** David practices in the areas of intellectual property litigation, arbitration and commercial litigation. He has successfully litigated cases in the state and federal courts involving patents, trademarks, trade secrets, business torts, contractual obligations, and the Uniform Commercial Code relating to medical devices, software, products and manufacturing equipment in high tech and industrial applications. David helps clients identify and deal with licensing and other intellectual property law matters, contractual issues and business disputes. He is on the American Arbitration Association's commercial roster.
**Personal:** University of Minnesota Law School (JD, magna cum laude, 1980). University of Minnesota (BA, 1975).

**ANTHONY, Joseph**
Anthony Ostlund & Baer, Minneapolis
612 349 6969
*Recommended in Litigation*

**BRENNA, Nathan**
Anthony Ostlund & Baer, Minneapolis
612 349 6969
*Recommended in Litigation*

**BROWER, John**
Gray, Plant, Mooty, Mooty & Bennett, PA, Minneapolis 612 632 3000
*Recommended in Corporate/M&A*

**BUSCH, William**
Faegre & Benson LLP, Minneapolis
612 766 8809
WBusch@faegre.com
*Recommended in Corporate/M&A*
**Practice Areas:** Advertising; corporate and business enterprises; corporate finance and securities; executive compensation; joint ventures; leveraged acquisitions; M&A; private debt and equity financings; stockholder agreements; media and professional sports.
**Prof. Memberships:** American Society of Corporate Secretaries.
**Career:** Current member of firm's Management Committee; acquisition of Minnesota Timberwolves professional basketball franchise from the National Basketball Association; sale of Forward Com-

munications Corporation (including six television stations, eight radio stations and a newspaper) to Wesray Communications, Inc.
**Personal:** BA, University of St Thomas; JD, University of Minnesota, magna cum laude; MBA, University of Minnesota.

**CARLSON, Alan**
Carlson, Caspers, Vandenburgh & Lindquist, Minneapolis
612 436 9600
*Recommended in Litigation*

**CARRON, Reid**
Faegre & Benson LLP, Minneapolis
612 766 7428
RCarron@faegre.com
*Recommended in Employment*
**Practice Areas:** Collective bargaining; opposing union organizing campaigns; unfair labor practice charges; decertification elections; strike planning and operations; labor issues associated with M&A; arbitrations; employment agreements.
**Prof. Memberships:** American Bar Association; Minnesota State Bar Association.
**Career:** Former Head of the Faegre & Benson Labor and Employment Law Group, which offers among the largest teams of full-time labor and employment lawyers and litigators in the Midwest and Rocky Mountain regions.
**Publications:** 'The Employer's Duty to Supply Financial Information to the Union', The Labor Lawyer.
**Personal:** BA, Southeast Missouri State University, magna cum laude; JD, University of Missouri-Columbia, cum laude.

**CHRISTENSEN, Douglas R**
Dorsey & Whitney LLP, Minneapolis
612 340 8875
christensen.doug@dorsey.com
*Recommended in Employment*
**Practice Areas:** All areas of labor and employment law for management, including advice, counseling, training, union organizing attempts, collective bargaining, arbitration, representation before administrative agencies, and litigation.
**Career:** Partner in Dorsey's Labor and Employment Law practice group since 1996, Associate 1988-95.
**Personal:** Duke University School of Law, JD, 1988, Articles Editor 1987-88, Staff Editor 1986-87, Law and Contem-

porary Problems. University of Notre Dame, BA, English Literature, 1984.

**CHRISTY, Angela**
Faegre & Benson LLP, Minneapolis
612 766 6833
AChristy@faegre.com
*Recommended in Real Estate*
**Practice Areas:** Affordable housing; low-income housing tax credit; Indian/tribal law.
**Prof. Memberships:** ABA Forum on Affordable Housing and Community Development Law (Past Chair); Minnesota Certified Real Property Specialist.
**Career:** Angela's practice focuses on affordable housing, particularly tax credit transactions. She has represented non-profit and for-profit developers, investors and governmental entities in more than 150 tax credit transactions throughout the United States. She also has represented numerous contractors and developers regarding construction documents for housing, office buildings and other developments.
**Personal:** BA, North Dakota State University; JD, University of Minnesota, cum laude.

**CIRESI, Michael V**
Robins, Kaplan, Miller & Ciresi LLP, Minneapolis 612 349 8500
mvciresi@rkmc.com
*Recommended in Litigation*
**Practice Areas:** Product liability, intellectual property, and complex commercial litigation.
**Prof. Memberships:** ATLA, MTLA, ABA, IBA, MSBA, Inner Circle of Advocates, International Academy of Trial Lawyers, American Board of Trial Advocates, and the American College of Trial Lawyers.
**Career:** Chairman of the Board since 1995. Partner since 1978.
**Personal:** Honorary Degree of Doctor of Laws, Southwestern University School of Law; University of Minnesota Law School, JD; University of St. Thomas, BA.

**COOK, Jay**
Dorsey & Whitney LLP, Minneapolis
612 340 2922
cook.jay@dorsey.com
*Recommended in Real Estate*
**Practice Areas:** Acquisition, development, construction, financing, sale, leasing and/or securitizing of commercial

real estate, including office, mixed-use, shopping center, and other retail and industrial properties. Financing experience includes multi-state transactions and loan workouts and foreclosures. Townhouse and condominium development, much of it connected with resort development.
**Prof. Memberships:** Member, Minnesota State Bar Association and Hennepin County Bar Association. Member, Mortgage Association of Minnesota. Member, National Association of Industrial and Office Parks. Member, Lambda Alpha International. Fellow, American College of Mortgage Attorneys.
**Personal:** Indiana University School of Law, Bloomington, JD, 1973, magna cum laude. Northwestern University, BS, Journalism, 1970.

**COSTLEY, Kevin**
Lindquist & Vennum PLLP, Minneapolis
612 371 3547
kcostley@lindquist.com
*Recommended in Corporate/M&A*
**Practice Areas:** Kevin specializes in representing financial institutions in mergers and acquisitions, capital financing plans, and business expansion strategies. Most of his clients are independent community banks located in the Upper Midwest.
**Personal:** University of Minnesota School of Law (JD, 1975; Editor, Minnesota Law Review; Order of the Coif). University of California at Los Angeles (BA, summa cum laude, 1971). Before joining Lindquist & Vennum, he clerked for Justice Harry MacLaughlin of the Minnesota Supreme Court.

**CUTLER, Kenneth**
Dorsey & Whitney LLP, Minneapolis
612 340 2740
cutler.ken@dorsey.com
*Recommended in Corporate/M&A*
**Practice Areas:** Emerging growth companies, venture capital financing and corporate finance. Represents private and public companies on general corporate matters, financing transactions, mergers and acquisitions and SEC-registered public offerings.
**Personal:** University of Texas School of Law, JD, 1973, with honors, Order of the Coif. University of Chicago, BA, General Studies, 1970. University of Chicago Graduate School of Business, MBA, 1970.

**D'AQUILA, Barbara**
Flynn, Gaskins & Bennett, Minneapolis
612 333 9500
*Recommended in Employment*

**DAVIES, Scott**
Briggs and Morgan, Professional Association, Minneapolis 612 977 8400
*Recommended in Employment*

**DAWSON, James**
Felhaber, Larson, Fenlon & Vogt, PC,
Minneapolis 612 339 6321
*Recommended in Employment*

**DIVINEY, Craig**
Dorsey & Whitney LLP, Minneapolis
612 340 2993
diviney.craig@dorsey.com
*Recommended in Litigation*
**Practice Areas:** Complex business and
intellectual property litigation, as well as
the development of strategies for the
exploitation and enforcement of clients'
intellectual property. He has tried and
won cases involving a wide variety of
industries and technologies, including life
sciences and medical devices.
**Personal:** University of Iowa College of
Law, JD, 1979, with high distinction.
Augustana College, BA, 1975, cum laude.

**EFRON, Stanley**
Henson & Efron, Minneapolis
612 339 2500
*Recommended in Corporate/M&A*

**EIDE, David**
Felhaber, Larson, Fenlon & Vogt, PC,
Minneapolis 612 339 6321
*Recommended in Real Estate*

**ENG, Holly**
Dorsey & Whitney LLP, Minneapolis
612 343 2164
eng.holly@dorsey.com
*Recommended in Employment*
**Practice Areas:** Labor and employment
law. Litigation, labor arbitrations, and
administrative proceedings. Investigates
or manages investigations of harassment
and other employment-related complaints, and drafts employment agreements and policies.
**Prof. Memberships:** Guardian ad Litem,
Minnesota Guardian ad Litem Program.
Instructor, University of St. Thomas
Graduate School of Business (Center for
Non-Profit Management), 1999-2001.
**Career:** Joined Dorsey in 1993 and
became a Partner in 2001.
**Personal:** Georgetown University Law
Center, JD, 1993. St. Cloud State University, BA degrees in English and Economics,
1989.

**ENGLER, Bruce**
Faegre & Benson LLP, Minneapolis
612 766 8811
BEngler@faegre.com
*Recommended in Corporate/M&A*
**Practice Areas:** Corporate counseling,
finance, securities, debt/equity financing,
institutional private placement financing,

securities issuance, leveraged acquisitions, M&A, public and private securities
offerings.
**Career:** Bruce focuses on M&A, public
and private securities offerings, institutional private placement financing, and
general corporate counseling. Bruce has
represented buyers, sellers and institutional investors in various public and private transactions. He's had primary/significant responsibility for more than 45
acquisition transactions with an aggregate transaction value exceeding 3.5 billion dollars.
**Publications:** 'M&A Auctions: Are You
Ready to Sell Your Company on eBay?'.
**Personal:** BA, Creighton University,
summa cum laude; JD, University of
Michigan, magna cum laude.

**FERRELL, Charles**
Faegre & Benson LLP, Minneapolis
612 766 7531
CFerrell@fagre.com
*Recommended in Real Estate*
**Practice Areas:** Commercial real estate;
sports law; real estate development; debt
and equity financing.
**Prof. Memberships:** American College
of Real Estate Lawyers; Building Owners
and Managers Association.
**Career:** Has represented: US Bank (Minneapolis); Norwest Center (Minneapolis); University of Arizona Science and
Technology Park (Tucson); Niketown
(Seattle); Rich Stadium (Buffalo); Target
Center (Minneapolis); Major Workout
(California, Texas and Pennsylvania). Pro
bono areas include environmental law
and lease representation for civic groups.
**Publications:** 'Form of Commercial
Lease', Minnesota Continuing Legal Education.
**Personal:** BS, Cornell University, with
distinction; JD, University of Michigan,
Law Review, magna cum laude, Order of
the Coif.

**FIELD, Lawrence**
Leonard, Street and Deinard
Professional Association, Minneapolis
612 335 1500
*Recommended in Litigation*

**FINLEY, Joseph**
Leonard, Street and Deinard,
Professional Association, Mankato
507 345 1179
*Recommended in Real Estate*

**FLEMING, Terrence**
Lindquist & Vennum PLLP, Minneapolis
612 371 3248
tfleming@lindquist.com
*Recommended in Litigation*
**Practice Areas:** Terry represents parties
in cases involving commercial fraud
including stockholder derivative and
stockholder class actions, merger and
acquisition litigation, regulatory proceedings, investor-broker and law firm disputes, and minority stockholder disputes.

He also works as an arbitrator, mediator
and expert witness in these areas. He represents parties in regulatory proceedings
involving insider trading, securities fraud,
accounting issues, and investor complaints before the SEC, NYSE, NASD and
state regulatory entities. Terry has represented parties in more than 100 completed jury and court trials, arbitrations,
mediations and regulatory proceedings.
**Personal:** Harvard Law School (JD,
1981). College of St. Thomas (BA, 1978).

**FRASER, Thomas**
Fredrikson & Byron PA, Minneapolis
612 492 7000
*Recommended in Litigation*

**FRUTH, Terence**
Fruth, Jamison & Elsass, Minneapolis
612 344 9700
*Recommended in Litigation*

**GARON, Philip S**
Faegre & Benson LLP, Minneapolis
612 766 8101
PGaron@faegre.com
*Recommended in Corporate/M&A*
**Practice Areas:** Corporate finance and
securities; corporate governance; hostile
takeover defense; M&A.
**Prof. Memberships:** Minnesota State
Bar Association, Business Law Section –
Former Chair.
**Career:** Phil is a Partner in Corporate
Group and is former Chair of the firm's
Management Committee. He focuses
upon corporate matters, public and private mergers and acquisitions, private
financings and hostile takeover defense.
**Publications:** 'Minnesota Corporation
Law and Practice', West Publishing Company.
**Personal:** BA, University of Minnesota,
Phi Beta Kappa, summa cum laude; JD,
University of Minnesota, Law Review
(Associate Editor), Order of the Coif,
summa cum laude.

**GARTON, Thomas**
Fredrikson & Byron PA, Minneapolis
612 492 7000
*Recommended in Corporate/M&A*

**GINSBURG, Roy**
Dorsey & Whitney LLP, Minneapolis
612 340 8761
ginsburg.roy@dorsey.com
*Recommended in Employment*
**Practice Areas:** Employment litigation,
including age, race, sex, and disability discrimination, sexual harassment, and
common law employment claims.
Defends individual, multi-party and
class-wide claims; non-competition
claims, including breach of past employment restrictive covenants, break of fiduciary duty claims; raiding and trade secret
claims. Insurance litigation and general
commercial litigation.
**Prof. Memberships:** Member, American
Bar Association, Litigation Section and
Labor and Employment Law Section.

Member, Minnesota Bar Association and
Hennepin County Bar Association, Litigation Section and Labor and Employment Law Section.
**Personal:** University of Virginia School
of Law, JD, 1980. Carleton College, BA,
1975.

**GORDON, Avron**
Briggs and Morgan, Professional Association, Minneapolis 612 977 8400
*Recommended in Corporate/M&A*

**GOTTSCHALK, Steve**
Dorsey & Whitney LLP, Minneapolis
612 340 2941
gottschalk.steve@dorsey.com
*Recommended in Employment*
**Practice Areas:** Design, formation, IRS
qualification and termination of employee retirement and welfare plans and executive compensation plans. VEBAs,
employee benefits for tax-exempt organizations, leveraged Employee Stock Ownership Plans (ESOPs), employee benefit
problem solving in corporate mergers
and acquisitions.
**Prof. Memberships:** Member, Minnesota State and Hennepin County Bar Associations. Member, Midwest Pension Conference. Employee Plan Member, Central
Mountain Area TE/GE Council. President's Advisory Council, Valparaiso University, 1982-present.
**Personal:** Valparaiso University School
of Law, JD, 1972, with senior honors. Valparaiso University, BS Mathematics,
1969.

**GROSS, David**
Faegre & Benson LLP, Minneapolis
612 766 7804
dgross@faegre.com
*Recommended in Litigation*
**Practice Areas:** Intellectual property litigation, civil trial practice.
**Career:** David was Lead Trial Counsel
for Wyeth in the billion-dollar trade
secret case, Wyeth v Natural Biologics,
Inc. Court granted a permanent injunction prohibiting the defendant from
developing a generic version of Wyeth's
product Premarin. As a result, David was
named one of 15 'Attorneys of the Year'
by Minnesota Lawyer, and the case was
profiled in a page one story in the
National Law Journal.
**Publications:** 'The Power Trial Method'.
**Personal:** BA, University of Minnesota,
Phi Beta Kappa, summa cum laude; JD,
Harvard University, magna cum laude.

**GULLICKSON, Randy**
Anthony Ostlund & Baer, Minneapolis
612 349 6969
*Recommended in Litigation*

**HALVERSON, Jan**
Felhaber, Larson, Fenlon & Vogt, PC,
Minneapolis 612 339 6321
*Recommended in Employment*

**HAMEL, Mark**
Dorsey & Whitney LLP, Minneapolis
612 340 8716
hamel.mark@dorsey.com
*Recommended in Real Estate*
**Practice Areas:** Practices in all aspects
of real property law, focusing on transactions involving the acquisition, development, construction, financing, sale, leasing and/or securitizing of commercial
real estate, including office, mixed-use,
retail, hotel, industrial, healthcare, assisted living and multi-family (including
common interest communities).
**Prof. Memberships:** MNSBA; HCBA;
American College of Real Estate Lawyers;
Executive Committee, Board of Directors
of the Minneapolis Downtown Council.
**Publications:** Contributor: 'Commercial
Landlord/Tenant Law', Minnesota CLE
(2004); author: 'Developing Old McDonald's Farm – 23 Pitfalls to Remember',
Minnesota CLE (2003).
**Personal:** Harvard Law School (JD,
1978); Carroll College (BA, Political Science, 1975).

**HAYNOR, Charles**
Briggs and Morgan, Professional Association, Minneapolis 612 977 8400
*Recommended in Real Estate*

**HEIN, Laura**
Gray, Plant, Mooty, Mooty & Bennett, PA,
Minneapolis 612 632 3000
*Recommended in Litigation*

**HERMAN, John**
Faegre & Benson LLP, Minneapolis
612 766 8908
jherman@faegre.com
*Recommended in Real Estate*
**Practice Areas:** Real estate, development and finance, government relations,
environmental law, land use/zoning/
environmental review, government
regulation of business and commerce.
**Career:** He focuses on real estate development and finance, legislative and government relations and environmental/
land use law. He's been a central figure in
Minnesota real estate development and
environmental policy for more than 25
years. Represents developers of numerous
large commercial projects including
retail, restaurant, entertainment and
office including Block E, City Center,
General Mills Headquarters, Walker Art
Center Complex, Graco Corporate Headquarters, Stinson Technology Corridor,
and Riverplace.
**Personal:** BA, Yale University, cum laude;
JD, Harvard University.

**HERR, David**
Maslon Edelman Borman & Brand, LLP,
Minneapolis 612 672 8200
*Recommended in Litigation*

**HOBBINS, Robert**
Dorsey & Whitney LLP, Minneapolis
612 340 2919
hobbins.robert@dorsey.com
*Recommended in Employment*
**Practice Areas:** Practices in all areas of
labor and employment law for management including labor arbitration,
employment discrimination, union organizing attempts, proceedings before the
National Labor Relations Board, wage
and hour, affirmative action, OFCCP and
common-law employment claims.
**Prof. Memberships:** ABA (Labor and
Employment Law Section, EEO Committee); Minnesota State Bar Association
(Labor and Employment Law Section).
**Personal:** New York University School of
Law (JD, 1973); Creighton University
(BA History, 1970).

**HUMPHREY, Andrew**
Faegre & Benson LLP, Minneapolis
612 766 8816
AHumphrey@faegre.com
*Recommended in Corporate/M&A*
**Career:** Frequently advises public and
private companies in their organization
and corporate governance, ongoing business review and documentation, contractual negotiations, obligations of directors
and officers, relations with stockholders,
capitalization and securities issuances.
Lead Counsel in multiple venture capital
transactions. Member, Management
Committee.
**Publications:** 'Strategies' business column, The Business Journal; Contributing
Editor, Encyclopedia of Venture Capital;
'When the Going Gets Tough', Trends;
'Venture Finance in the 'New' New Economy', Minnesota Technology; 'Antitrust
Jurisdiction and Remedies in an Electric
Utility Price Squeeze', University of
Chicago Law Review.
**Personal:** BA, Amherst College, cum
laude; JD, University of Chicago, Law
Review (Comment Editor).

**HUNTRODS, Ann**
Briggs and Morgan, Professional Association, St Paul 651 808 6600
*Recommended in Employment*

**IHRIG, Richard**
Lindquist & Vennum PLLP, Minneapolis
612 371 3257
rihrig@lindquist.com
*Recommended in Litigation*
**Practice Areas:** Richard resolves commercial disputes, particularly large scale
class actions and multi-party disputes
presenting difficult jurisdiction, liability,
and damage issues. He has particular
expertise in the electric utility, consumer
finance, airline and healthcare industries,
as well as extensive experience in antitrust
matters. Richard is a qualified neutral and
can mediate or arbitrate commercial disputes.
**Personal:** University of Minnesota Law
School (JD, magna cum laude, 1973).

Gustavus Adolphus College (BA, cum
laude, 1970)

**JAMISON, Tom**
Fruth, Jamison & Elsass, Minneapolis
612 344 9700
*Recommended in Litigation*

**KAHNKE, Randall**
Faegre & Benson LLP, Minneapolis
612 766 7658
RKahnke@faegre.com
*Recommended in Litigation*
**Practice Areas:** Complex business and
intellectual property litigation
**Prof. Memberships:** Past President and
Member of the Board of Directors of the
Federal Bar Association, Minnesota
Chapter.
**Career:** Randy focuses his practice on
complex commercial litigation and intellectual property litigation. Randy has
extensive consulting, pretrial, and trial
experience with complex commercial
and intellectual property disputes. Randy
has been the lead attorney at numerous
trials and arbitrations, and is a frequent
lecturer on issues related to complex
business disputes and intellectual property litigation.
**Personal:** BA, University of St. Thomas,
summa cum laude; JD, University of
Minnesota, cum laude, Law Review.

**KAPLAN, Samuel**
Kaplan, Strangis & Kaplan, Minneapolis
612 375 1138
*Recommended in Corporate/M&A*

**KAUFMAN, D William**
Oppenheimer Wolff & Donnelly LLP,
Minneapolis 612 607 7000
*Recommended in Corporate/M&A*

**KELLEY, David**
Leonard, Street and Deinard Professional Association, Minneapolis
612 335 1500
*Recommended in Real Estate*

**KELLY, Timothy**
Kelly & Berens PA, Minneapolis
612 349 6171
*Recommended in Litigation*

**KENNEDY, Steven**
Faegre & Benson LLP, Minneapolis
612 766 8577
skennedy@faegre.com
*Recommended in Corporate/M&A*
**Practice Areas:** Corporate governance
and securities regulation, mergers and
acquisitions, initial public offerings, venture capital financing.
**Career:** Steven represents such publicly
held companies as Archer-Daniels-Midland Company, Fair Isaac Corporation,
Piper Jaffray Companies and Hawkins
Inc. in all areas of corporate governance
and securities law compliance. He also
represents a number of larger private
companies, including United Subcontractors, Inc. and Excel Bank. Steven's
practice also includes merger and acquisi-

tion transactions, representing buyers
and sellers in public and private transactions. He is the Head of the firm's Public
Companies Practice.
**Personal:** BA, St. John's University, cum
laude; JD, University of Virginia

**KEPPLE, Lloyd**
Oppenheimer Wolff & Donnelly LLP,
Minneapolis 612 607 7000
*Recommended in Real Estate*

**KEYES, Jeffrey**
Briggs and Morgan, Professional Association, Minneapolis 612 977 8400
*Recommended in Litigation*

**KIRKMAN, David**
Ravich Meyer Kirkman McGrath & Nauman, PA, Minneapolis 612 332 8511
*Recommended in Real Estate*

**KONECK, John**
Fredrikson & Byron PA, Minneapolis
612 492 7000
*Recommended in Real Estate*

**LANGEVIN, Judith**
Gray, Plant, Mooty, Mooty & Bennett, PA,
Minneapolis
612 632 3000
*Recommended in Employment*

**LETSCHER, Tom**
Oppenheimer Wolff & Donnelly LLP,
Minneapolis 612 607 7000
*Recommended in Corporate/M&A*

**LIBBEY, Keith**
Fredrikson & Byron PA, Minneapolis
612 492 7000
*Recommended in Corporate/M&A*

**LIEBMAN, Kenneth A**
Faegre & Benson LLP, Minneapolis
612 766 8800
KLiebman@faegre.com
*Recommended in Litigation*
**Practice Areas:** Intellectual property;
patent litigation; trade secret litigation;
copyright litigation; trademark litigation;
medical technology; information technology.
**Career:** Chair of the firm's Intellectual
Property Group. His focus is on the representation of companies in the medical
technology and information technology
fields. Was Lead Counsel for the University of Minnesota in its patent licensing litigation against Glaxo Wellcome over the
AIDS drug ZiagenTM. Case settled with
the defendant recognizing the validity of
the University's patents and agreeing to
pay royalties estimated to total $300 million.
**Personal:** BA, Columbia University, Phi
Beta Kappa, summa cum laude; JD, Yale
University.

**LINDGREN, Jay**
Dorsey & Whitney LLP, Minneapolis
612 492 6875
lindgren.jay@dorsey.com
*Recommended in Real Estate*
**Practice Areas:** Partner practicing in
areas of Land Use and Development,
Municipal Law and Public Finance. Represents developers and municipal governments seeking to solve complex land use,
development, and redevelopment issues.
**Prof. Memberships:** MNSBA; HCBA;
NDSBA; National Association of Bond
Lawyers.
**Career:** Former Chief Executive of the
Metropolitan Council, the regional
agency in charge of community develop-
ment, land use planning, transit, open
space and wastewater treatment for the
seven-county Twin Cities, Minnesota
metropolitan area. Former North Dakota
State Representative and Senator.
**Personal:** University of North Dakota
School of Law (JD, 1994); Concordia
College (BA 1984).

**LUECK, Martin**
Robins, Kaplan, Miller & Ciresi LLP,
Minneapolis 612 349 8500
mrlueck@rkmc.com
*Recommended in Litigation*
**Practice Areas:** Trial lawyer experienced
in civil trials and appeals, arbitration and
administrative hearings in commercial
litigation, patent, antitrust, and competi-
tion law.
**Prof. Memberships:** AIPLA, MIPLA,
ABA (Member of the Training the Trial
Lawyer Task Force), IBA, HCBA, Federal
Circuit Bar Association.
**Career:** Chair of the Business Trial and
Litigation Group. Executive Board since
1996. Partner since 1991.
**Personal:** William Mitchell College of
Law, JD, cum laude; Winona State Uni-
versity, BS.

**LUGER, Andrew**
Greene Espel PLLP, Minneapolis
612 373 0830
*Recommended in Litigation*

**MACHMEIER, Bruce**
Oppenheimer Wolff & Donnelly LLP,
Minneapolis 612 607 7000
*Recommended in Corporate/M&A*

**MAGNUSON, Roger**
Dorsey & Whitney LLP, Minneapolis
612 340 2738
magnuson.roger@dorsey.com
*Recommended in Litigation*
**Practice Areas:** Represents clients
throughout the United States and abroad
in high profile litigation spanning a wide
variety of substantive areas, including
class actions, regulatory/white-collar
crime, antitrust, securities/stockholder
cases, and First Amendment litigation,
among others.
**Publications:** Miscellaneous articles in
law reviews and professional journals.

**Personal:** Harvard Law School (JD,
1971); Stanford University (BA).

**MALKERSON, Bruce**
Malkerson, Gilliland, Martin, Minneapolis
612 344 1111
*Recommended in Real Estate*

**MASSOPUST, Richard**
Oppenheimer Wolff & Donnelly LLP,
Minneapolis 612 607 7000
*Recommended in Real Estate*

**MAYERLE, Thomas M**
Faegre & Benson LLP, Minneapolis
612 766 7228
TMayerle@faegre.com
*Recommended in Real Estate*
**Practice Areas:** General commercial
real estate and corporate real estate.
**Career:** Tom is the former head of Faegre's Real Estate Group. He has developed
expertise across the broad spectrum of
commercial real estate, with particular
emphasis on the development, purchase,
sale, leasing and financing of office building and shopping center projects. Tom is
a member of the American College of
Real Estate Lawyers and has been included since 1983 in the listing of Minnesota
real estate lawyers in 'The Best Lawyers in
America.'
**Personal:** AB, Dartmouth College; JD,
University of Minnesota, Law Review,
magna cum laude, Order of the Coif.

**MCDONALD, Daniel**
Merchant & Gould PC, Minneapolis
612 332 5300
*Recommended in Litigation*

**MOORSE, Charles**
Lindquist & Vennum PLLP, Minneapolis
612 371 5771
cmoorse@lindquist.com
*Recommended in Corporate/M&A*
**Practice Areas:** Chuck advises public
and private companies across various
industry groups on matters including
mergers and acquisitions, venture financing, public offerings, corporate governance and securities regulation. On the
M&A side, Chuck represents both buyers
and sellers of privately and publicly held
companies across a range of industry
groups, including high technology, manufacturing, retailing, financial services,
medical devices, OTC products, consulting and contract services. In his general
corporate practice, Chuck serves as outside General Counsel to mid-cap publicly
and privately held companies.
**Personal:** William Mitchell College of
Law (JD, magna cum laude, 1986). Saint
John's University (BS, cum laude, 1981).

**MRKONICH, Marko**
Littler Mendelson, PC, Minneapolis
612 630 1000
mmrkonich@littler.com
*Recommended in Employment*
**Practice Areas:** Member of Class Action
Avoidance and Defense and Traditional

Labor Law Practice Groups. Focuses on
discrimination and other employment
litigation, client counseling, and traditional labor law issues. Represents clients
in federal and state trial and appellate
courts, federal and state administrative
agencies, and labor arbitration. Experienced in mediation and forms of alternative dispute resolution. Counsels clients
on personnel management.
**Prof. Memberships:** Hennepin County
Bar, Minnesota State Bar, Wisconsin State
Bar, and American Bar Associations (Litigation and Labor and Employment Law
Sections); Minnesota Management
Attorneys Association.
**Personal:** Harvard University (JD, with
honors, 1980); Harvard College (AB, with
honors, 1977).

**NOECKER, Kathlyn E**
Faegre & Benson LLP, Minneapolis
612 766 8604
KNoecker@faegre.com
*Recommended in Employment*
**Practice Areas:** International and
domestic labor and employment law and
executive compensation.
**Prof. Memberships:** Kathy leads Faegre's
Labor and Employment Group and practices in Executive Compensation and
Emerging Business Groups. Kathy works
extensively with employers of all sizes to
advise them regarding complex workplace laws. A significant portion of
Kathy's practice involves the negotiation
and preparation of employment, compensation and separation arrangements
for executives. She also counsels clients
on employee discipline and discharge
decisions, personnel policies, disability
accommodation, sexual harassment
investigations, reductions-in-force, and
on employment issues arising out of corporate transactions.
**Personal:** BA, College of St. Catherine;
JD, Georgetown University.

**NORWICH, Donald**
Oppenheimer Wolff & Donnelly LLP,
Minneapolis 612 607 7000
*Recommended in Real Estate*

**NOTEBOOM, Todd**
Leonard, Street and Deinard Professional Association, Minneapolis
612 335 1500
*Recommended in Litigation*

**ODLAUG, Bruce**
Lindquist & Vennum PLLP, Minneapolis
612 371 5792
bodlaug@lindquist.com
*Recommended in Real Estate*
**Practice Areas:** Bruce's practice involves
all aspects of commercial real estate, representing both financial lending institutions and developers. He has counseled
property owners regarding zoning and
land use matters, as well as landlord and
tenant representation, eminent domain
proceedings and real estate tax appeals.

He is a certified real estate specialist.
**Prof. Memberships:** Hennepin County
Bar Association. Minnesota State Bar
Association. American Bar Association.
**Personal:** University of Minnesota Law
School (LLB, 1965). University of Notre
Dame (BBA, 1962).

**O'NEILL, Brian B**
Faegre & Benson LLP, Minneapolis
612 766 8318
boneill@faegre.com
*Recommended in Litigation*
**Practice Areas:** Trial practice and
appellate practice.
**Prof. Memberships:** American College
of Trial Lawyers (State Chair). Board of
Visitors, University of Michigan Law
School, 1994-present. Board of Directors,
Defenders of Wildlife, 1984-present.
**Career:** Significant trials and appeals
include: Peterson v BASF; Pioneer Hi-
Bred International Inc. v Monsanto
Company; Lujan v Defenders of Wildlife,
504 US 555 (1992) (application of
Endangered Species Act to US projects
overseas; standing).
**Personal:** BS, United States Military
Academy, served to Captain, US Army;
JD, University of Michigan, Law Review,
magna cum laude, Order of the Coif.

**OSTLUND, Richard**
Anthony Ostlund & Baer, Minneapolis
612 349 6969
*Recommended in Litigation*

**PARSONS, Chuck**
Moss & Barnett, A Professional Associa-
tion, Minneapolis 612 347 0300
*Recommended in Real Estate*

**PAYNE, William**
Dorsey & Whitney LLP, Minneapolis
612 340 2722
payne.bill@dorsey.com
*Recommended in Corporate/M&A*
**Practice Areas:** Represents buyers and
sellers in the purchase and sale of busi-
nesses.
**Prof. Memberships:** ABA (Editorial
Committee, Task Force Member and
Contributor (2000-05), 'The M&A
Process').
**Publications:** 'Representations, Reliance
and Remedies: The Legacy of Hendricks
v. Callahan', Bench & Bar (September
2005); 'Mergers & Acquisitions – Merrill
Lynch & Co. v Allegheny Energy Inc.:
Lessons for Buyers and Sellers in the Sale
of a Business Unit', Corporate Counsel
Weekly (August 17, 2005).
**Personal:** University of Oklahoma
School of Law (JD, 1968); University of
Oklahoma (BS, 1965)

**PENTELOVITCH, William**
Maslon Edelman Borman & Brand, LLP,
Minneapolis 612 672 8200
*Recommended in Litigation*

**PHILLIPS, Penny**
Felhaber, Larson, Fenlon & Vogt, PC,
Minneapolis 612 339 6321
*Recommended in Employment*

**RAPHAN, Melissa**
Dorsey & Whitney LLP, Minneapolis
612 492 7907
raphan.melissa@dorsey.com
*Recommended in Employment*
**Practice Areas:** Represents employers
in employment litigation matters including class actions, multi-plaintiff actions
and single plaintiff cases nationwide and
in administrative settings including state
and federal agencies. Counsels employers
on issues including, but not limited to,
performance management selection and
termination. Designs and delivers training on every aspect of the employment
relationship.
**Prof. Memberships:** ABA, MSBA,
HCBA (Litigation and Labor and
Employment Section); MNSBA; Minnesota Women Lawyers.
**Personal:** Boston College Law School
(JD, 1987); Duke University (BA, 1982).

**RAVICH, Paul**
Ravich Meyer Kirkman McGrath & Nauman, PA, Minneapolis
612 332 8511
*Recommended in Real Estate*

**REINHART, Robert**
Dorsey & Whitney LLP, Minneapolis
612 340 7835
reinhart.robert@dorsey.com
*Recommended in Employment*
**Practice Areas:** Employment issues as
management advocate, including defense
of class and collective actions, employment policy development, discipline and
discharge advice, equal pay and other
compensation analyses, resolution of
class investigations and DOL, EEOC and
state agency compliance audits.
**Prof. Memberships:** Founder and General Counsel, Minnesota Employment
Law Council; Co-Founder and Co-Chair,
Upper Midwest Employment Law Institute, 1984-present.
**Career:** Past Chair, Labor and Employment Group, Oppenheimer Wolff &
Donnelly.
**Personal:** University of Michigan Law
School (JD, 1971); Northwestern University (BA, 1968).

**REMELE JR, Lewis A**
Bassford Remele, A Professional Association, Minneapolis 612 333 3000
lewr@bassford.com
*Recommended in Litigation*
**Practice Areas:** Civil trial practice
involving commercial litigation including
contract disputes, securities, fiduciary
and stockholder disputes, class actions,
trust and estates litigation, professional
liability, employment, personal injury
and insurance coverage. Clients include
Minnesota Lawyers Mutual Insurance

Company; Illinois Tool Corporation;
Medica Health Plan; URS; American
National Can; Con Agra; Metropolitan
Council; St. Paul Travelers Companies;
and Advance PCS. Appointed Special
Master, United States District Court, Dis-
trict of Minnesota, for In Re Baycol Liti-
gation. Appointed Special Master, Hen-
nepin County District Court, for In Re
Soo Line Derailment Litigation.
**Prof. Memberships:** Minnesota State
Bar Association (past President); Fellow
of the American College of Trial Lawyers,
American Board of Trial Advocates and
American Bar Foundation; Hennepin
County Bar Association (past President).
**Career:** Admitted to Minnesota state and
federal courts, Eighth Circuit Court of
Appeals and United States Supreme
Court. Stockholder with BASSFORD
REMELE since 1989; chief executive offi-
cer, 2001-04. Listed in leading American
publications. Best lawyer in Minnesota by
'Minnesota Law and Politics', 2001-05.
**Personal:** JD, Creighton University (cum
laude); BA, Harvard University (magna
cum laude).

**ROBINER, Susan**
Leonard, Street and Deinard Professional Association, Minneapolis
612 335 1500
*Recommended in Litigation*

**ROBY, Joseph**
Johnson Killen & Seiler, Duluth
218 722 6331
*Recommended in Employment*

**ROM, Rebecca L**
Faegre & Benson LLP, Minneapolis
612 766 7231
rrom@faegre.com
*Recommended in Real Estate*
**Practice Areas:** Becky has practiced
with the real estate, environmental,
administrative law and litigation groups
at Faegre & Benson's Minneapolis office
since 1979. Her practice is focused primarily on commercial real estate.
**Prof. Memberships:** Alaska Coalition of
Minnesota, Founder and Chair 1995-pre-
sent. The Wilderness Society, member,
Governing Council 1996-present, Chair
2002-present.
**Career:** In 1999, Becky was named by
Citybusiness as one of the 25 Most Influential Women in Business in the Twin
Cities. She also received the John C Benson Pro Bono Award.
**Personal:** BA, Mount Holyoke College;
JD, William Mitchell College of Law, cum
laude.

**ROSENBAUM, Robert**
Dorsey & Whitney LLP, Minneapolis
612 340 5681
rosenbaum.robert@dorsey.com
*Recommended in Corporate/M&A*
**Practice Areas:** Practices in the area of
mergers and acquisitions involving publicly and privately held corporations;

advises clients with respect to corporate
governance matters and public reporting
requirements; and is experienced in SEC-
registered public offerings and private
placement transactions.
**Prof. Memberships:** ABA (Business Law
Section); CASBA; MNSBA (Ch. 302A
Sub-Committee of Business Law Section).
**Career:** Formerly Co-Chair of firm-wide
Corporate Group (2002-05), and member of the firm's Management Committee.
**Personal:** Harvard Law School (JD,
1981); Princeton University (AB, Economics, 1978).

**ROSS, Richard**
Fredrikson & Byron PA, Minneapolis
612 492 7000
*Recommended in Employment*

**SCALLEN, Timothy**
Oppenheimer Wolff & Donnelly LLP,
Minneapolis 612 607 7000
*Recommended in Corporate/M&A*

**SCHUTZ, Ronald J**
Robins, Kaplan, Miller & Ciresi LLP, Minneapolis 612 349 8500
rjschutz@rkmc.com
*Recommended in Litigation*
**Practice Areas:** Trial lawyer with experience in complex litigation of patents,
trademarks, copyrights, trade secrets and
unfair competition.
**Prof. Memberships:** University of Minnesota Law Alumni Association, Gover-
nor's Commission on Judicial Selection,
Center of the American Experiment
(Director).
**Career:** Chairs the firm's Intellectual
Property Litigation Department and is a
member of the firm's Executive Board.
Partner since 1989.
**Publications:** Has written and lectured
extensively on intellectual property and
various complex litigation issues for
attorneys, businesses and trade associa-
tions.
**Personal:** University of Minnesota Law
School, JD, with honors, member of Law
Review; Marquette University, magna
cum laude, Mechanical Engineering.

**SEATON, Doug**
Seaton, Beck, Peters, Bowen & Feuss,
Minneapolis 952 896 1700
*Recommended in Employment*

**SEIDEL, Amy**
Faegre & Benson LLP, Minneapolis
612 766 7769
ASeidel@faegre.com
*Recommended in Corporate/M&A*
**Practice Areas:** Securities regulation,
corporate counseling, executive compensation, corporate finance and securities,
mergers and acquisitions.
**Career:** Amy has represented public and
private companies in connection with
securities offerings of both equity and
debt. In public offerings, Amy has repre-

sented both issuers and underwriters.
These offerings have involved compliance
with federal and state securities laws. A
significant portion of Amy's practice
involves advising public companies on
SEC reporting requirements, stock
exchange listing standards, executive
compensation issues, disclosure issues
and general corporate governance matters.
**Personal:** BA, Gustavus Adolphus College, Dean's List, magna cum laude, Phi
Beta Kappa; JD, University of Minnesota.

**SELLERGREN, David**
Fredrikson & Byron PA, Minneapolis
612 492 7000
*Recommended in Real Estate*

**SHARPE, W Smith "Kris"**
Faegre & Benson LLP, Minneapolis
612 766 6828
KSharpe@faegre.com
*Recommended in Corporate/M&A*
**Practice Areas:** Corporate finance and
securities; mergers and acquisitions; private debt and equity financings; venture
capital financing; entrepreneurial and
emerging companies.
**Career:** Kris represents a number of
companies in their development stage
prior to going public. Representation of
such companies involves their formation,
private placement financings, creation of
employee benefit plans, coordination of
other legal service specialties (eg, intellectual property), and general corporate
counseling, including attendance at
board meetings.
**Personal:** BA, Columbia University, Phi
Beta Kappa, summa cum laude; JD, Yale
University.

**SHERMAN, Morris**
Leonard, Street and Deinard Professional Association, Minneapolis
612 335 1500
*Recommended in Corporate/M&A*

**SHORT, Marianne D**
Dorsey & Whitney LLP, Minneapolis
612 340 2833
short.marianne@dorsey.com
*Recommended in Litigation*
**Practice Areas:** Trial and appellate
counsel for a number of major companies
in their most important litigation, includ-
ing antitrust, securities, healthcare, prod-
ucts liability, and class action lawsuits.
**Prof. Memberships:** ABA; MNSBA;
HCBA; American Academy of Appellate
Lawyers; Minnesota Women Lawyers;
National Association of Women Judges.
**Career:** Judge, Minnesota State Court of
Appeals, 1988-2000.
**Personal:** Boston College Law School
(JD, 1976); Newton College of the Sacred
Heart (BA, 1973).

**SIMONSON, James**
Gray, Plant, Mooty, Mooty & Bennett, PA,
Minneapolis 612 632 3000
*Recommended in Litigation*

## SINGER, Jonathan E
Fish & Richardson P.C., Minneapolis
612 337 2534
singer@fr.com
*Recommended in Litigation*
**Practice Areas:** Principal in Fish & Richardson's Twin Cities office. Practice emphasizes all aspects of intellectual property litigation, including patent, trademark, trade secret and trade dress litigation, with an emphasis on the litigation of chemical, pharmaceutical, and biotechnology inventions. Has substantial trial experience, both jury and bench, and has handled numerous Markman hearings in courts across the country.
**Prof. Memberships:** Course faculty Member, 'Biotechnology: Patent Prosecution, Licensing, Litigation, and Hatch-Waxman', Patent Resources Group, Inc.
**Personal:** Dartmouth College AB Chemistry 1986; University of Chicago Law School JD 1992.

## SNIDER, Jerry W
Faegre & Benson LLP, Minneapolis
612 766 7816
jsnider@faegre.com
*Recommended in Litigation*
**Practice Areas:** Antitrust and trade regulation. Civil, commercial and complex employment, Indian/tribal law and intellectual property. Trial and appeals of complex civil cases.
**Career:** Member of firm's Management Committee. Representative clients include Abbott Laboratories, Inc., American Express Financial Corporation, Archer Daniels Midland ('ADM'), Battenfeld of America, Inc., International Business Machines Corp. ('IBM'), Old Republic Title Insurance Company, Parke, Davis & Co., The Pillsbury Company, Target Corporation.
**Personal:** BS, Wake Forest University; JD, University of Houston, Law Review (Articles Editor).

## STAGEBERG, Roger
Lommen, Nelson, Cole & Stageberg, P.A., Minneapolis 612 339 8131
*Recommended in Corporate/M&A*

## STANCHFIELD, Mike
Faegre & Benson LLP, Minneapolis
612 766 7764
MStanchfield@faegre.com
*Recommended in Corporate/M&A*
**Practice Areas:** Corporate, mergers and acquisitions.
**Career:** Mike is a Partner in Faegre's Corporate Group. His practice is focused on the areas of mergers and acquisitions, corporate governance, takeover preparedness, public securities offerings, private financings, and general corporate counseling. Mike has handled major M&A transactions in recent years for companies like Marshall Fields, St. Paul Companies, Guidant, Archer-Daniels-Midland, Graco, ReliaStar, Lutheran Brotherhood, and many others.

**Publications:** 'Voting Lock-Ups and Sales of Partially Owned Subsidiaries: Can Stockholders Love a Deal Too Early and Too Much?' – Winner, 2003 Burton Award for Legal Writing.
**Personal:** BA, University of Minnesota; JD, Harvard University.

## STENMOE, Gregory
Briggs and Morgan, Professional Association, Minneapolis 612 977 8400
*Recommended in Employment*

## STRANGIS, Ralph
Kaplan, Strangis & Kaplan, Minneapolis
612 375 1138
*Recommended in Corporate/M&A*

## STUMO, Mary
Faegre & Benson LLP, Minneapolis
612 766 8115
mstumo@faegre.com
*Recommended in Employment*
**Practice Areas:** Employment and employment litigation.
**Prof. Memberships:** Minnesota Women Lawyers.
**Career:** Mary's practice focuses on employment-related litigation including claims related to all types of discrimination (sexual harassment, age, race, sex and disability), breach of contract, defamation, whistleblowing, and non-compete agreements, up to and including multiple jury trials. Member of firm's Management Committee.
**Publications:** Chapter 21, Using Psychiatric and Psychology Experts at Trial: 'Defense Perspective, Litigating the Sexual Harassment Case' (ABA Book) (1999); 'Forum: Sexual Harassment News for Employers', CityBusiness (1998).
**Personal:** BS, University of Wisconsin, with honors; JD, University of Minnesota, cum laude.

## THIEL, John
Gray, Plant, Mooty, Mooty & Bennett, PA, Minneapolis 612 632 3000
*Recommended in Real Estate*

## THOMPSON, John
Rider, Bennett, Egan & Arundel, LLP, Minneapolis 612 340 7951
*Recommended in Employment*

## TINKHAM, Thomas
Dorsey & Whitney LLP, Minneapolis
612 340 2829
tinkham.tom@dorsey.com
*Recommended in Litigation*
**Practice Areas:** Partner and Chair of the firm's Commercial Litigation Practice Group.
**Prof. Memberships:** MNSBA (past President); HCBA (past President); Volunteer Lawyers Network (past Chair and on Board for 30 years).
**Personal:** Harvard Law School (JD, 1969); University of Wisconsin (BS, 1966).

## VOLLING, James
Faegre & Benson LLP, Minneapolis
612 766 7758
JVolling@faegre.com
*Recommended in Litigation*
**Career:** Jim is the Head of the firm's Business Litigation Group. For more than two decades, he has represented clients in a wide variety of complex commercial disputes valued up to several hundred million dollars. Jim has appeared in state and federal trial courts in every region of the country and has argued appeals in several federal and state appellate courts. His broad-based experience includes extensive work in antitrust, securities and stockholder litigation, consumer class actions, False Claims Act, RICO, lender liability, breach of contract, breach of warranty, and lender liability.
**Personal:** AB, Harvard University; JD, The George Washington University.

## WAHL, Edward T
Faegre & Benson LLP, Minneapolis
612 766 8720
EWahl@faegre.com
*Recommended in Litigation*
**Practice Areas:** Business litigation, commercial litigation.
**Career:** Ned's practice focuses primarily on complex business litigation, often involving financial institutions. Ned has represented indenture trustees, insurance companies and liquidating estates in cases around the country involving breach of fiduciary duty, director and officer claims and fraudulent transfer claims. Ned has extensive experience defending consumer fraud claims and has handled many class actions, including a major defense of a life insurance sales practice class action.
**Personal:** BA, Northwestern University, with honors; MA, University of Virginia; JD, University of Chicago.

## WEBBER, Charles F
Faegre & Benson LLP, Minneapolis
612 766 8719
Cwebber@faegre.com
*Recommended in Litigation*
**Practice Areas:** Bankruptcy litigation; foreclosures and workouts; and receiverships.
**Career:** Chuck Webber is a commercial litigator. He has litigated in a wide variety of commercial contexts, especially the areas of financial services, consumer protection laws, and commercial contracts. Chuck recently successful defended one of the nation's largest refining companies in a whistleblower trial that was named one of the top defense verdicts of the year by The National Law Journal.
**Personal:** BA, University of Minnesota, Phi Beta Kappa, summa cum laude; JD, University of Chicago, Law Review (Associate Managing Editor), Order of the Coif, with honors.

## WEINSTINE, Robert
Winthrop & Weinstine, A Professional Association, Minneapolis
612 604 6613
rweinstine@winthrop.com
*Recommended in Litigation*
**Practice Areas:** Antitrust and trade regulation, litigation business and commercial litigation, securities and directors and officers liability litigation, products liability litigation.
**Prof. Memberships:** American Bar Association, Federal Bar Association, Minnesota State Bar Association, Hennepin County Bar Association, Ramsey County Bar Association, State Bar of Wisconsin, The Minneapolis Club, Board of Directors of The Fund for the Legal Aid Society.
**Career:** Robert R Weinstine, nationally known trial attorney and firm founder, represents clients in commercial litigation, antitrust, securities fraud, products liability and stockholder disputes. Mr Weinstine graduated from the University of Minnesota, Phi Beta Kappa, and the University of Minnesota Law School with honors, including Order of the Coif. Mr Weinstine has been named a 'Super-Lawyer' since its inception and is consistently recognized by The Best Lawyers of America, Minnesota Business Guidebook for Law and Leading Attorneys and Chambers USA, to name a few. Mr Weinstine serves on the Board of Directors of The Fund for the Legal Aid Society.

## WESTRA, Mark
Fabyanske, Westra & Hart PA, Minneapolis 612 359 7600
*Recommended in Real Estate*

## WHEATON, John
Faegre & Benson LLP, Minneapolis
612 766 7761
JWheaton@faegre.com
*Recommended in Real Estate*
**Practice Areas:** Banking; real estate litigation; construction law.
**Prof. Memberships:** Admitted to Practice in Minnesota.
**Career:** Represented a national bank in the sale of its downtown headquarters building in the midst of pending condemnation proceedings. Placement of development and construction loans, and the later closing of securitized, permanent financing, for Dain Bosworth Plaza, a vertical retail and high-rise office project in Minneapolis.
**Publications:** Speeches on various topics at Advanced Legal Education Seminars and Bar Association Groups.
**Personal:** BA, Northwestern University, with honors; JD, University of Minnesota, magna cum laude.

**WILDUNG, Wendy J**
Faegre & Benson LLP, Minneapolis
612 766 7759
WWildung@faegre.com
*Recommended in Litigation*
**Practice Areas:** Business torts; litigation; securities law.
**Prof. Memberships:** American Bar Association; Federal Bar Association; Hennepin County Bar Association; Minnesota State Bar Association; Securities Industry Association Division of Legal and Compliance.
**Career:** Defending securities broker-dealers and financial advisors against claims brought by customers involving purchases and sales of stocks, bonds, mutual funds, option contracts, and commodities futures contracts. Defending corporations against stockholder suits arising out of leveraged buy-outs and going-private transactions. Defending publicly-held corporations, and their officers and directors, in hostile takeover litigation.
**Personal:** BA, University of Minnesota, magna cum laude, Phi Beta Kappa, JD, Harvard University.

**WILLE, Karin**
Briggs and Morgan, Professional Association, Minneapolis 612 977 8400
*Recommended in Employment*

**WILSON, Richard**
Maslon Edelman Borman & Brand, LLP, Minneapolis 612 672 8200
*Recommended in Litigation*

**ZECH, Paul**
Felhaber, Larson, Fenlon & Vogt, PC, Minneapolis 612 339 6321
*Recommended in Employment*

**ZEGLOVITCH, Robert**
Leonard, Street and Deinard Professional Association, Minneapolis
612 335 1500
*Recommended in Employment*

# DORSEY & WHITNEY LLP

## THE FIRM

**Managing Partner:** Peter S Hendrixson

**Number of US partners:** 261
**Number of other US lawyers:** 316

**FIRM OVERVIEW**: Successful companies and organizations around the world collaborate with Dorsey on legal issues that impact success. Dorsey supports a wide range of clients, from life sciences and health to technology and energy; from financial services and investment banking to nonprofits and government; and from manufacturing and agribusiness to media and entertainment.

## MAIN AREAS OF PRACTICE:

**Corporate:** A leader in M&A counsel, Dorsey ranks among the top law firms for completed deals, according to Thomson Financial Securities Data. Dorsey has also ranked among the top 15 firms for initial public offerings (according to IPO Week in Review) and private investment in public equity transactions (according to PrivateRaise L.L.C.). Dorsey clients include: US Bancorp, 3M, UnitedHealth Group, Hormel, Cargill, Buy.com, SUPERVALU, Heartland Payment Systems, Buffalo Wild Wings, Right Now Technologies and Acorn Cardiovascular. Dorsey also provides services in corporate governance, compliance and securities law, Sarbanes-Oxley, SEC regulations and more.

**Commercial Litigation:** Dorsey represents large corporations, medical institutions, small businesses, government entities, exempt organizations, and individuals in all types of dispute resolution. Dorsey lawyers have significant experience in litigation, arbitration, mediation and negotiation concerning financial institutions, commercial, construction/real estate, employment, environmental, ERISA, franchise, fraud, health law, intellectual property, international disputes, products liability, securities, tax, and white collar crime. Recent successes include one of the largest jury awards in Maryland history; a victory in a dispute over management of a nationally known retail/entertainment complex; and the dismissal, for a computer equipment manufacturer, of a competitor's $450 million suit alleging employee raiding.

**Intellectual Property:** With attorneys skilled in technical fields, many holding PhD degrees, the Dorsey Patent group helps companies protect and leverage value-adding intellectual property. Similarly, companies in a wide range of industries rely on the Dorsey Trademark, Copyright and Brand Management group to select, protect and enforce trademarks, copyrights and domain names. Both groups work with companies to build and protect strategic intellectual property portfolios, and defend them against competitors – in the courtroom, if necessary. Dorsey litigators represent clients before judges, juries and regulatory bodies in patent infringement, trade secrets, trademark infringement and dilution, unfair competition, trade dress protection, and copyright infringement cases.

**Labor & Employment Law:** More than 50 attorneys throughout the US offer in-house counsel and HR professionals employment law training, alternative dispute resolution, labor-management relations advice and litigation, administrative audit and crisis management counseling, immigration law counsel and more. The Dorsey team also provides advice on executive and employee compensation law, employee benefits, ERISA compliance, and taxation laws. In 2005, Dorsey litigators won victories on summary judgment motions, securing complete dismissal of clients' cases in 29 employment-related lawsuits.

**INTERNATIONAL WORK:** In more than 60 countries, clients rely on Dorsey for cross-border transactions, corporate advice, complex litigation, corporate finance, mergers and acquisitions, joint ventures, intellectual property, immigration, tax litigation and arbitration, export controls, customs, licensing agreements and international treaties. In London, Dorsey attorneys have deep experience in UK and European law. In Shanghai and Hong Kong, Dorsey native Asian attorneys and American lawyers have extensive region experience. In Canada, Dorsey is the only full-service US firm with two offices (Toronto and Vancouver).

## HEAD OFFICE

50 South Sixth Street, Suite 1500, **Minneapolis**, MN 55402-1498
Tel: 612 340 2600   **Fax:** 612 340 2868
**Website:** www.dorsey.com

## BRANCH OFFICES

### ALASKA
1031 West Fourth Avenue, Suite 600, **Anchorage**, Alaska 99501-5907
**Tel:** 907 276 4557   **Fax:** 907 276 4152

### CALIFORNIA
1717 Embarcadero Road, **Palo Alto**, CA 94303
**Tel:** 650 857 1717   **Fax:** 650 857 1288

555 California Street, Suite 1000, **San Francisco**, CA 94104-1513
**Tel:** 415 781 1989   **Fax:** 415 398 3249

38 Technology Drive, **Irvine**, CA 92618-5310
**Tel:** 949 932 3600   **Fax:** 949 932 3601

### COLORADO
Republic Plaza Bldng, Ste 4700, 370 17th Street, **Denver,** CO 80202-5647
**Tel:** 303 629 3400   **Fax:** 303 629 3450

### IOWA
801 Grand, Suite 3900, **Des Moines**, Iowa 50309-2790
**Tel:** 515 283 1000   **Fax:** 515 283 1060

### NORTH DAKOTA
Dakota Center, 51 Broadway, Suite 402, **Fargo**, ND 58102-1344
**Tel:** 701 235 6000   **Fax:** 701 235 9969

### MONTANA
507 Davidson Building, 8 Third Street North, **Great Falls**, MT 59401-3126
**Tel:** 406 727 3632   **Fax:** 406 727 3638

Millennium Building, 125 Bank St, Suite 600, **Missoula**, MT 59802-4407
**Tel:** 406 721 6025   **Fax:** 406 543 0863

### NEW YORK
250 Park Avenue, **New York,** NY 10177-1500
**Tel:** 212 415 9200   **Fax:** 212 953 7201

### UTAH
170 South Main Street, Suite 900, **Salt Lake City**, Utah 84101-1655
**Tel:** 801 933 7360   **Fax:** 801 933 7373

### WASHINGTON
US Bank Centre, 1420 Fifth Ave, Ste 3400, **Seattle**, WA 98101-4010
**Tel:** 206 903 8800   **Fax:** 206 903 8820

### WASHINGTON, D.C.
1001 Pennsylvania Ave, NW Ste 400, **South Washington,** DC 20004-2533
**Tel:** 202 442 3000   **Fax:** 202 442 3199

## CONTACTS

**Corporate Finance** ......................................Ellen Bancroft
**Corporate Governance & Compliance** ............. Kimberly Anderson
**Mergers & Acquisitions** ..........................................William B Payne
**Litigation** ............................................... Paul Klaas, Roger Magnuson
**Patent** ............................................................................. Lee Osman
**Trademark, Copyright & Brand Management** Elizabeth C Buckingham
**Labor & Employment** ......................................... Robert R Reinhart
**Benefits & Compensation** ..................................... Leslie J Anderson
**Environmental, Natural Resources & Energy** ...... B Andrew Brown

1169

# FAEGRE & BENSON LLP

## THE FIRM

**Managing Partners:** Thomas G Morgan (Chair), John D Shively, Jerry W Snider, Jack M Fribley, Mary E Stumo, William R Busch, Michael S McCarthy, Winthrop A Rockwell, Andrew G Humphrey

**Number of partners in the US:** 250

**Number of other lawyers in US Offices:** 191

**FIRM OVERVIEW:** The firm offers clients more than 475 lawyers in a full range of practice groups, with experience handling legal matters throughout the United States, as well as Europe and Asia. The firm is one of the 100 largest law firms in the world. Independent surveys, from 2003-2005 of corporate counsel in Fortune 1000 companies throughout the US, ranked Faegre & Benson among the top 30 law firms in the country for client service. Faegre & Benson is also a member of two consortiums that provide access to a national and worldwide network of experienced commercial lawyers, the United States Law Firm Group and the World Law Group. Faegre & Benson received several prestigious honors in 2005. The firm scored 100% on the HRC (Human Rights Campaign) Corporate Equality Index. The firm was also ranked in the 'Top 25 Law Firms for Women' list, as reported in Diversity & the Bar.

## MAIN AREAS OF PRACTICE:

**Corporate:** Offering one of the most sophisticated corporate legal teams in the nation, Faegre & Benson regularly handles complex finance, M&A, and securities transactions for leading regional, national, and international companies. Highlights for the firm during 2004-05 include completing more than 120 M&A deals totaling over $33 billion, including high-profile deals for Retek and Entegris, in transactions totaling more than $1.7 billion. The Retek transaction involved a well-publicized bidding war between Oracle and SAP. Other significant M&A transactions included work for Norwest Equity Partners, Goldner, Hawn, Johnson & Morrison Inc., Gambro Healthcare, Optical Solutions, Graco Inc., Fair Isaac Corporation, Digi International, U.S. Bank, Bemis, and Pella Corporation. During 2005, the firm represented issuers and underwriters in over $22 billion in public offerings for clients such as Wells Fargo, Piper Jaffray, Ameriprise, J.P. Morgan, Merrill Lynch, Time Warner Telecom, Crocs and Frontier Airlines, and ADM. The firm offers among the largest and most experienced corporate finance teams in both the Minnesota and Colorado regions and highly regarded corporate experience in London, Frankfurt, Shanghai, and Des Moines.

**Intellectual Property:** Faegre & Benson offers one of the largest teams of intellectual property lawyers in the central US, with experience handling complex litigation and transactions for clients ranging from multinational corporations to high-technology entrepreneurs. The IP Team includes 70 lawyers in the US, Europe, and Asia, including 20 registered patent attorneys. Many of the firm's lawyers offer educational and professional experience unique to the intellectual property needs of specific industries, including backgrounds in chemical and electrical engineering, biotechnology, microbiology, physics, and computer science. The firm's size and depth give it a level of IP expertise that is comparable to leading 'boutique' IP firms, while offering clients the resources of one of the most respected corporate and litigation firms in the US.

**Litigation:** Faegre & Benson offers a large litigation team, with experience litigating at every level of the state and federal court systems, including the US Supreme Court. The firm regularly litigates in product liability, intellectual property, toxic torts, securities, employment law, class actions, multi-district litigation, insurance, antitrust, bankruptcy, franchise and dealer disputes, construction, contract and other commercial litigation. The firm's lawyers have litigated matters in nearly every US state, plus the UK, Europe and Asia. Its team includes highly experienced trial lawyers; litigation managers; lawyers with special expertise with expert witnesses and Daubert challenges; lawyers with extensive experience handling mediations and arbitrations; as well as one of the nation's most advanced in-house technology departments for managing litigation. The firm represented the trustee for the liquidating estate of MJK Clearing, Inc. in four years of investigation and litigation against Deutsche Bank which resulted in a

## HEAD OFFICE

**MINNESOTA**
2200 Wells Fargo Center, 90 South Seventh Street, **Minneapolis,** MN 55402
**Tel:** 612 766 7000 **Fax:** 612 766 1600
**Website:** www.faegre.com

## BRANCH OFFICES

**COLORADO**
1900 Fifteenth Street, **Boulder**, CO 80302
**Tel:** 303 447 7700 **Fax:** 303 447 7800

3200 Wells Fargo Center, 1700 Lincoln Street, **Denver**, CO 80203
**Tel:** 303 607 3500 **Fax:** 303 607 3600

**IOWA**
Suite 3100, 801 Grand Avenue, **Des Moines**, IA 50309
**Tel:** 515 248 9000 **Fax:** 515 248 9010

## INTERNATIONAL OFFICES

The firm also has offices in London, Frankfurt and Shanghai.

## CONTACTS

| | |
|---|---|
| **Finance & Restructuring** | Michael R Stewart |
| **Construction Law** | William R Joyce |
| **Corporate** | W Smith 'Kris' Sharpe |
| **Employee Benefits** | Richard A Nelson |
| **Healthcare/Nonprofit Organizations** | Jay D Christiansen |
| **Intellectual Property** | Kenneth A Liebman |
| **Labor & Employment Law** | Kathlyn E Noecker |
| **Litigation** | James A O'Neal |
| **Real Estate** | Scott A Anderegg |
| **Tax** | Walter A Pickhardt |
| **Trusts & Estates** | David J Shannon |

settlement in 2005 pursuant to which Deutsche Bank paid $147.5 million in cash to the estate of MJK Clearing and caused the withdrawal of an additional $120 million of claims against the estate, for a total settlement value of approximately $270 million.

**CLIENTS:** Faegre & Benson has been a leader in developing the concept of law firm partnering. The firm has for several years been one of a small number of firms selected by DuPont to serve as a preferred legal provider in its innovative 'DuPont Legal Model'. The firm has developed similar relationships on a national and multi-state basis with companies such as Guidant (primary outside counsel), General Mills (preferred provider), Target (primary outside counsel), Ameriprise (preferred litigation and M&A provider), UPS (principal outside counsel for many practice areas in a multi-state region) and Cargill, as one of two national preferred legal providers.

**INTERNATIONAL WORK:** Faegre & Benson offers sophisticated legal counsel for companies doing business around the world and has handled legal matters in more than 60 countries through its offices in the US, London, Frankfurt, and Shanghai. The firm's clients range in size from large, multinational corporations to small and mid-sized companies establishing or expanding their operations overseas. The firm has built close working relationships with local counsel in countries around the world. Faegre & Benson's network of global law firms includes members of the World Law Group (of which Faegre is a member), as well as dozens of lawyers and law firms on every continent with whom the firm has worked directly on international matters.

# LINDQUIST & VENNUM PLLP

## THE FIRM

**Managing Partner:** Daryle L Uphoff
**Number of partners in US office:** 134
**Number of other attorneys in US office:** 55

**FIRM OVERVIEW:** Lindquist & Vennum is a business-oriented, general practice law firm with nearly 200 attorneys in Minnesota and Colorado. The firm is known for its extensive corporate finance, banking and complex commercial litigation practices as well as its agribusiness and life sciences industry-focused groups. Of note are its practices in white collar and regulatory defense, securities litigation and bankruptcy.

## MAIN AREAS OF PRACTICE:

**Corporate & Business:** The firm's corporate business attorneys serve as outside counsel to over 30 public companies in the middle market. In the past 12 months, the group has been involved in a number of IPOs representing both issuers and underwriters. The firm has been very active with its private equity clients and has completed a number of significant M&A transactions.

**Agribusiness & Energy:** Lindquist & Vennum has a national practice representing the interests of agribusinesses and energy producers. Lindquist & Vennum assists traditional agribusiness clients and has helped shape the 'value-added' movement in agriculture, created by agricultural producers seeking new markets for their commodities through ownership of processing and distribution facilities.

**Life Sciences:** The firm's Life Sciences Group provides experienced legal services to clients in the healthcare, pharmaceutical, biotech and device industries. Clients range in size from start-up ventures to mature, publicly traded companies. They work with clients in the areas of private capital, venture finance and public offerings, distribution and licensing, intellectual property protection, non-competition, confidentiality and employment matters, health plans and benefits, regulatory matters and litigation.

**Financial Institutions:** National in scope and serving clients representative of the largest and smallest members of the industry, the firm's Financial Institutions Practice Group has remained on the forefront of issues affecting commercial banks and savings associations in a time of change and challenge. In the last five years, the firm has represented more institutions in mergers and acquisitions than any other law firm in its Federal Reserve District and is among the leading national firms in this practice.

**Commercial Litigation:** The firm's Commercial Litigation Group has extensive experience in the litigation, resolution and prevention of business-related disputes. The firm is particularly well-known for its work in antitrust, insurance coverage, securities fraud and stockholder disputes.

**Securities Litigation:** Lindquist & Vennum represents brokerage firms, brokers and customers in a wide variety of investment and securities-related issues. In addition to arbitration and litigation matters, they counsel clients in regulatory compliance and represent clients in administrative and regulatory matters, including investigations conducted by governmental and self-regulatory organizations.

**Bankruptcy:** The firm is recognized as having one of the premier bankruptcy practices in the Upper Midwest and the Rocky Mountain regions. The group has a wide range of experience including the landmark Marathon Oil and Kaiser Steel/Kaiser Coal cases.

**White Collar & Regulatory Defense:** The White Collar and Regulatory Defense Practice Group is a nationally recognized team of experienced trial lawyers who represent both corporations and individuals involved with increasingly complex criminal, regulatory and civil fraud investigations and lawsuits. Its attorneys include a number of formal federal prosecutors.

**Real Estate:** The firm represents owners, managers, investors and developers of commercial, industrial and mixed-use properties. Projects range from raw land to shopping centers to downtown office complexes. Its practice includes extensive experience in real estate transfers, leasing, financing, land development, construction and environmental compliance.

## HEAD OFFICE

**MINNESOTA**
4200 IDS Center, 80 South Eighth Street, **Minneapolis,** MN 55402
**Tel:** 612 371 3211   **Fax:** 612 371 3207
**Website:** www.lindquist.com

## BRANCH OFFICES

**COLORADO**
600 17th Street, Suite 1800 South, **Denver,** CO 80202
**Tel:** 303 573 5900   **Fax:** 303 573 1956

## CONTACTS

| | |
|---|---|
| Agribusiness & Energy | Mark Hanson |
| Antitrust | James McCarthy |
| Bankruptcy | James Lodoen |
| Commercial Litigation | Wallace Hilke |
| Corporate & Business | Richard Primuth |
| Emerging Companies | Frank Bennett |
| Employee Benefits | Robert Hartman |
| Financial Institutions | Kevin Costley |
| Insurance Coverage | James Reuter |
| Intellectual Property | Bruce Little |
| Labor & Employment | Nancy Vollertsen |
| Life Sciences | Barbara Lano Rummel |
| Litigation | David Allgeyer |
| Mergers & Acquisitions | Richard McNeil |
| Real Estate | Michael Margulies |
| Securities Litigation | William Stute |
| Trusts & Estates | Mavis Van Sambeek |
| White Collar & Regulatory Defense | William Michael |

**Labor & Employment:** The firm provides a wide range of services to businesses concerning employment issues. For several years, the firm's attorneys have collaborated with the state of Minnesota to create the publication, 'An Employer's Guide to Employment Law Issues in Minnesota.' This is one of the premier employment law resources used by Minnesota businesses and state agencies.

**Intellectual Property:** The firm's intellectual property attorneys counsel clients to protect, develop and exploit their intellectual property assets to the fullest. Its practice areas include a full range of protection of rights in copyrights, trademarks, trade names, domain names, advertising compliance, trade secret protection and patent, trademark, copyright, trade secret and related litigation.

**INTERNATIONAL WORK:** Lindquist & Vennum regularly assists clients in the expansion of their international activities. These efforts include: strategic alliances, including joint ventures for product development and distribution; foreign distributors; foreign manufacturing operations; OEM manufacturing; private label manufacturing; raw materials supply; dispute resolution and acquisition of foreign companies and product lines. The firm's reach is extended globally through their membership in TAGLaw. Founded in 1998, TAGLaw is a worldwide network of 125 prominent, high-quality law firms. Lindquist & Vennum has been a member since TAGLaw's initial year.

LINDQUIST&VENNUM PLLP

# ROBINS, KAPLAN, MILLER & CIRESI L.L.P.

## THE FIRM

**Chairman:** Michael V Ciresi
**Managing Partner:** Steven A Schumeister
**Number of partners:** 114
**Number of other lawyers:** 151

**FIRM OVERVIEW:** Founded in 1938, Robins, Kaplan, Miller & Ciresi L.L.P. represents large corporations, insurance companies, other businesses and individuals as both plaintiffs and defendants. The firm is frequently engaged in high stakes, complex litigation. Each matter is approached with the efficiency, focus, and discipline attained through a business which historically has a significant portion of its revenue based on alternative fee arrangements. The firm's Business Practice Group provides a full range of legal services to businesses across the country, serving a broad spectrum of clients from Fortune 500 companies and industry consolidators to emerging companies and individual entrepreneurs.

## MAIN AREAS OF PRACTICE:

**Antitrust & Trade Regulation:** Represents clients in private antitrust litigation, government investigations, mergers, acquisitions and joint ventures, antitrust and intellectual property law, and in antitrust counseling. Cases have included the *Blue Cross Blue Shield of Massachusetts, Blue Cross Blue Shield of Minnesota, Federated Mutual Insurance Company, and Health Care Service Corporation v Mylan Laboratories, Inc.* and Vitamins Antitrust Litigation.

**Business Trial & Litigation:** Represents clients on a national basis in complex business cases. Matters include antitrust and trade regulation, bankruptcy and insolvency, class actions, corporate criminal and regulatory defense, financial litigation, health care litigation, and special business situations, many of which are detailed separately. Cases have included the defense of several large insurers in class actions brought in more than fifteen states that generally allege violations of state antitrust statutes and other state statutes, represented first air carrier to file bankruptcy post 9/11, resulting in sale of airline and its reemergence as a Minneapolis-based, lower-cost carrier and *United States of America ex rel. Brown, et al v AdvancePCS, Inc.*

**Corporate Finance & Securities:** Handles sophisticated finance and securities transactions for private and public companies. Matters have included the completion of Golf Galaxy's initial public offering, Best Buy Co., Inc.'s sale of convertible debentures having $402,400,000 initial aggregate principal amount at maturity, and Crescendo Ventures led a group of institutions in a $9.35 million investment in a Minneapolis software company.

**Financial Litigation:** Represents entities in financial services litigation matters in federal and state courts, and in industry arbitrations not only as defendants, but also as plaintiffs. Represent institutional investors, mutual funds, insurance companies, public pension plans, and hedge funds. Cases have included High-Yield Bond Litigation and In re Workers Compensation Refund Litigation.

**Insurance:** Handles property coverage disputes, subrogation recovery claims, liability policy suits and commercial attacks on a corporate practice. Cases have included Olympic Pipeline subrogation, World Trade Center Towers, *North Dakota State University v Hartford Steam Boiler Inspection & Ins. Co.*, and Super-Valu E-Coli contamination.

**Intellectual Property Litigation:** In 2003, 'The American Lawyer' and 'IP Law & Business' gave the firm the 'IP Litigation Department of the Year' award. Cases have included *Eolas Technologies, Inc. and The Regents of the University of California v Microsoft Corporation, Pitney Bowes Inc. v Hewlett-Packard Co., Intergraph v Dell Inc., Gateway Inc., and Hewlett-Packard Co., St. Clair Intellectual Property Consultants, Inc. v Canon, Inc. et al., TriStrata Technology, Inc. v Mary Kay Inc., Honeywell v Minolta,* and *Unocal Corp. v ARCO, Chevron, Exxon, Mobil, Shell and Texaco.*

**Mass Tort:** Represents consumers injured by defective drugs and medical devices and persons injured or killed by catastrophes, such as the Senator Wellstone airplane crash, and by unfair business practices like fraudulent drug pricing and deceptive marketing and promotion. Have represented clients against

## HEAD OFFICE

**MINNESOTA**
2800 LaSalle Plaza, 800 LaSalle Avenue, **Minneapolis**, MN 55402
**Tel:** 612 349 8500 **Fax:** 612 339 4181
**Website:** www.rkmc.com

## BRANCH OFFICES

**GEORGIA**
2600 One Atlanta Plaza, 950 East Paces Ferry Rd, NE **Atlanta**, GA 30326
**Tel:** 404 760 4300 **Fax:** 404 233 1267

**BOSTON**
800 Boylston, 25th Floor, **Boston**, MA 02199
**Tel:** 617 267 2300 **Fax:** 617 267 8288

**CALIFORNIA**
2049 Century Park East, Suite 3700, **Los Angeles**, CA 90067
**Tel:** 310 552 1030 **Fax:** 310 229 5800

**FLORIDA**
711 Fifth Avenue South, Suite 201, **Naples**, FL 34102
**Tel:** 239 430 7070 **Fax:** 239 213 1970

**DISTRICT OF COLUMBIA**
1801 K Street N.W., Suite 1200, **Washington**, DC 20006
**Tel:** 202 775 0725 **Fax:** 202 223 8604

## CONTACTS

| | |
|---|---|
| Business | Eric O Madson |
| Business Trial & Litigation | Martin R Lueck |
| Insurance Litigation | William H Stanhope |
| IP/General | Ronald J Schutz |
| Individual & Mass Tort | Tara D Sutton |

St. Jude Medical, Inc. in cases that involved the recalled St. Jude 'Silzone' heart valves. Have also represented clients with failed Sulzer hip implants, and are currently representing individuals harmed by the defective drug Vioxx.

## INTERNATIONAL WORK:

**International Arbitration:** Have litigated matters before the International Court of Arbitration of the ICC. Cases have included the representation of a venture-capital fund in an international arbitration in London and Canada commenced by Saudi Arabian investors, representation of a global ice-cream manufacturer and distributor in an international arbitration applying Venezuela law, and representation of international businesses and insurers regarding a subrogation claim in an international arbitration under ICC Rules in Geneva.

**International Litigation:** Extensive experience in international litigation in general. Cases have included the representation of the Government of India in the Bhopal gas leak disaster, representation of US farmers in litigation before the U.S. International Trade Commission, and representation of several domestic and foreign insurance companies in litigation involving a catastrophic explosion.

**Construction Arbitration/Litigation:** Represented numerous international contractors and owners in international arbitrations, including the representation of a large, international architectural firm in "Sick Building Syndrome" case involving DuPage County Government Center in Illinois.

ROBINS, KAPLAN, MILLER & CIRESI LLP

# WINTHROP & WEINSTINE, P.A.

## THE FIRM

**President:** Scott J Dongoske
**Number of stockholders:** 48
**Number of associates:** 35
**Total number of attorneys:** 83

**FIRM OVERVIEW:** Winthrop & Weinstine, P.A., is a successful and growing law firm focused on building strong client relationships. The firm is practical in its approach, responsive to clients and highly competitive by nature. Attorneys rely on innovation rather than outmoded tradition – creativity rather than standard formulas. The firm enjoys steady growth by meeting the diverse needs of clients ranging from individuals and emerging-growth businesses to Fortune 500 companies throughout the Midwest and nationally.

**MAIN AREAS OF PRACTICE:** Winthrop & Weinstine offers a full range of practice areas for each client's legal needs. The firm provides high-quality tailored legal representation that goes beyond an excellent understanding of the law. In-depth experience, cost-effective service, and passionate attention to the details help Winthrop & Weinstine attorneys and staff meet the particular needs of each and every one of its clients.

**Business & Commercial Litigation:** Winthrop & Weinstine's talented trial lawyers tackle complex litigation representing clients from Fortune 100 organizations to closely held businesses and partnerships. With extensive experience in products liability, stockholder disputes, employment law, construction litigation, insurance, securities, fraud, intellectual property, antitrust and unfair business practices, and white color crime, a trusted team directs the best course of action. The firm's litigators appear in state and federal courts at all levels.

**Corporate:** Winthrop & Weinstine provides legal and business counseling services to all sizes and varieties of businesses, representing entrepreneurs and established companies, both privately held and publicly traded. The firm's attorneys are highly experienced in general corporate matters and business transactions, including finance, securities, mergers and acquisitions.

**Banking & Finance:** Throughout the Midwest and nationally, Winthrop & Weinstine represents bank holding companies, national banking associations, state banking institutions, trust companies, mortgage lenders, insurance companies, asset-based lenders and federal savings banks. Whether it is state and federal bank regulatory issues, lending transactions, corporate restructures, bankruptcy and credit transactions issues, mergers and acquisitions, capital raising and expansion activities, Winthrop & Weinstine attorneys keep clients coming back for unparalleled service and advice.

**Intellectual Property & Brand Management:** Winthrop & Weinstine holds a dominant position in the intellectual property field. The Chair of Winthrop & Weinstine's Intellectual Property Group has been a Planner of the Annual Midwest IP Institute since its inception in 2002, and has served as an editor of 'The IP Book' since the 1st Annual Edition in 2003. Attorneys in the firm's IP Group consistently author more chapters in 'The IP Book' than almost any other firm. Winthrop & Weinstine's Trademark and Brand Management Department enjoys a truly prominent reputation of national scope, having special expertise in litigating and resolving registration disputes before the Trademark Trial and Appeal Board, located in Washington, DC, and it remains undefeated in litigating ICANN Domain Name Disputes. Winthrop & Weinstine's Intellectual Property Group is passionate and proactive about protecting its clients' most important assets, whether they be patents, trademarks, copyrights, brands, advertising, rights of publicity, or trade secrets.

**Legislative & Regulatory:** Winthrop & Weinstine has one of the largest and best known practices of this nature in the state. The firm's experienced, senior professionals have built key relationships over 25 years of successfully securing legislative and regulatory outcomes for local, state and national clients. The firm represents clients before the Minnesota Public Utilities Commission, Department of Commerce, Department of Transportation, Department of Revenue, Environmental Quality Board, and the Pollution Control Agency. At the federal level,

## HEAD OFFICE

**MINNESOTA**
225 South Sixth Street, Suite 3500, **Minneapolis**, MN 55402
**Tel:** 612 604 6400 **Fax:** 612 604 6800
**Email:** sdongoske@winthrop.com
**Website:** www.winthrop.com

## CONTACTS

| | |
|---|---|
| Banking & Finance | Edward J Drenttel |
| Business & Commercial Litigation | Brooks F Poley |
| Corporate Law | Mark T Johnson |
| Corporate Finance & Securities | Philip P Colton |
| Emerging Companies | Michele D Vaillancourt |
| Employment Law | Laura A Pfeiffer |
| | Mark A Pihart |
| Estate Planning & Business Succession Planning | Ryan K Crayne |
| Intellectual Property & Brand Management | Stephen R Baird |
| Legislative & Regulatory Law | John A Knapp |
| Mergers & Acquisitions | Scott J Dongoske |
| Real Estate Law | Norman L Jones III |
| Tax Law | Paul W Markwardt |

the firm represents clients before the Environmental Protection Agency, Federal Energy Regulatory Commission and Federal Communications Commission.

**Real Estate & Tax:** The firm represents local and national clients in all aspects of real estate development, investment and operations. The firm provides outstanding service in all matters pertaining to real estate transactions, including land development, common interest communities, affordable housing, land use/eminent domain, financing (both construction and permanent), tax credit syndication, commercial leasing, golf courses, hotels, real estate investment funds, 1031 exchanges, joint ventures, tax-exempt organizations and more. Clients are large and small, and include for-profit and nonprofit developers, investors, lenders, housing authorities, cities and builders.

**CLIENTS:** Aero Systems Engineering; Alliant Techsystems Inc.; Asset Marketing Services; Artspace Projects; Border Foods; Bremer Financial Corporation; Bridgecreek Development; Challenge Printing; COKeM; D'Amico Catering; DECO Inc.; Digital Angel Corporation; Dominium; Dougherty & Co.; Ecolab; Entolo, Inc.; F&A Dairy; Federal Cartridge; First Federal Bancorporation; GMAC Commercial Mortgage; Jazz Pharmaceuticals; LaSalle Bank; M&I Bank; Manitoba Hydro; Marvin Windows; MathStar, Inc.; Medtronic, Inc.; Merrill Lynch; Miller Johnson Steichen Kinnard, Inc.; Navarre Corporation; Orphan Medical; Piper Jaffray & Co.; Prairie Island Indian Community; Pro Staff; Qwest; Robinson Outdoors; Rottlund Homes; Saab Aircraft; Stonebridge Development; Synovis Surgical Innovations; The Cornerstone Group; The Ryland Group; United Properties; US Bank; The Valspar Corporation; Vital Images; Walser; Wal-Mart; Weis Builders; Wells Fargo Bank; Welsh Companies; Winthrop Resources.

**WINTHROP WEINSTINE**

ATTORNEYS AND COUNSELORS AT LAW

A firm difference.®

## How lawyers are ranked

Every year we carry out thousands of in-depth interviews with clients and lawyers in order to assess the reputations and expertise of business lawyers across the USA. Chambers rankings and editorial are referred to extensively by General Counsel and other purchasers of legal services who look to our recommendations when choosing their lawyers.

# CORPORATE/COMMERCIAL

## Corporate/Commercial
### Leading Firms

1. **BRUNINI, GRANTHAM, GROWER & HEWES** *Jackson*
   **BUTLER, SNOW** *Jackson*
   **PHELPS DUNBAR LLP** *Jackson*
2. **BAKER, DONELSON** *Jackson*
   **MCGLINCHEY STAFFORD, PLLC** *Jackson*
   **WATKINS & EAGER PLLC** *Jackson*
   **WATKINS LUDLAM WINTER & STENNIS** *Jackson*
   **WISE CARTER CHILD & CARAWAY** *Jackson*

### Leading Individuals

1. **CANNADA Barry** *Butler, Snow*
   **CHATHAM Henry** *Wise Carter Child*
   **DRINKWATER Robert** *Brunini, Grantham*
   **HISE Daniel** *Butler, Snow*
2. **BUSH F** *Phelps Dunbar LLP*
   **FAIR George** *Watkins & Eager PLLC*
   **GRISHMAN David** *Watkins Ludlam Winter*
   **HAFTER Jerome** *Phelps Dunbar LLP*
   **HODGE E Clifton** *Phelps Dunbar LLP*
   **LAZARUS Robert** *Watkins Ludlam Winter*
   **PAINTER William** *Baker, Donelson*
   **WEEMS Walter** *Brunini, Grantham*
3. **CLARK Donald** *Butler, Snow*
   **JACOBS Gina** *Watkins Ludlam Winter*
   **MARTIN David** *Watkins Ludlam Winter*
   **MENDENHALL William** *McGlinchey Stafford*
   **TAYLOR Zachary** *Watkins Ludlam Winter*
   **WILSON Stephen** *Phelps Dunbar LLP*

## Corporate/Commercial: Gaming & Licensing
### Leading Individuals

1. **ANDRESS Scott** *Balch & Bingham*
   **HISE Daniel** *Butler, Snow*
   **MCDANIEL Dan** *Phelps Dunbar LLP*
   **SHEPHERD Thomas** *Watkins Ludlam Winter*

## Band 1

### Brunini, Grantham, Grower & Hewes, PLLC

See firm details p.1188

**The Firm:** Brunini Grantham handles *"everything from a 'mom and pop' case to serving as local counsel for Fortune 500 companies,"* commentators note. Clients appreciate the firm for its *"broad experience over a huge number of industries,"* and are unanimous in giving it *"a straight A across the board."* The firm operates statewide, regionally and internationally, serving as outside corporate counsel for banks, retailers and hospitals in a variety of corporate and M&A transactions and advisory work.

**The Lawyers:** *"A-plus attorney"* **Bob Drinkwater's** (see p.1183) recent work includes acting as counsel to the lenders, borrowers, credit facility providers and trustees in financings totaling more than $900 million. He has closed over 100 real estate deals and a variety of M&A transactions. Clients claim that he will not only *"defend you till the cows come home"* but that he knows *"how to make things happen for the benefit of all sides; when to push and when to pull."* **Walter Weems** (see p.1187) is known for his expertise in M&A, which he undertakes for clients from a wide variety of industries from banking to broadcasting. He was described to researchers as *"incredibly bright and professional"* and is especially noted for his efforts in fostering good relations between government and business.

**Clients/Work Highlights:** Notable recent work includes negotiating a $15 million construction loan for a large public utility, and providing corporate counsel to real estate developers in the Metro area. Representative clients include AT&T; BanCorp South; Hancock Bank; Motorola; Peco Foods; Trustmark National Bank and Tyson Foods.

### Butler, Snow, O'Mara, Stevens & Cannada, PLLC

See firm details p.1189

**The Firm:** This regional powerhouse is particularly renowned as Mississippi's premier public finance firm. According to clients, it possesses *"the resources to cover all the different issues,"* including *"quality lawyers who always deliver, even on weekends, day and night."* Benefiting from a notable upsurge in investment activity this year, the team has undertaken a large number of refinancing cases along the Gulf Coast in the wake of Hurricane Katrina. Since then it has also been prominent in advising on disaster relief state legislation, and is serving pro bono as general counsel for the Commission on Recovery.

**The Lawyers:** **Barry Cannada's** (see p.1183) previous roles as an investment banker and accountant combine to give his legal practice *"variety and depth of experience."* Clients feel that he *"knows what it's like to be on the inside as well as the outside of a deal,"* and appreciate his *"integrity and creativity"* and *"thoughtful but aggressive"* approach to transactions. He has overseen an upturn in sales of private-equity funds recently, and continues to command a busy finance practice. **Dan Hise** (see p.1184) is closely involved in both gaming law and corporate transactions. Clients report that they *"always start with him"* when considering purchase agreements, while peers value his *"profound reliability and integrity."* On the gaming side, he represents key client Harrah's Entertainment, while elsewhere he has worked on both private equity transactions and PIPEs, particularly in the petroleum industry. **Don Clark** (see p.1183) recently served as bond counsel for the State of Mississippi in a sophisticated futures case. He has also been instrumental in helping gaming companies access incentives, and was closely involved in drafting post-Katrina state legislation. According to clients, he *"engenders great confidence"* thanks to his knack of *"identifying alternative solutions."* Value acquisition cases form a substantial portion of **Stephen Rosenblatt's** (see p.1186) creditor-oriented practice. Clients are hugely impressed with his work; one reported that he is *"quick to learn a lender's hot buttons!"* Also praised for *"knowing the local environment like the back of his hand,"* he is said to be skilled at *"escaping the bureaucratic web to cut to the chase."*

**Clients/Work Highlights:** The firm has been closely involved in helping the State of Mississippi to utilize the federal tax code to secure funding for community reconstruction. It has also handed a steady stream of commercial lending work, typically in the region of $5 million to $50 million. Representative clients include First Commercial Bank; Harrah's Entertainment; Horne CPA Group and U-Save Auto Rental of America.

## Phelps Dunbar LLP

See firm details p.997

**The Firm:** With over 50 attorneys based in offices across Mississippi, Phelps Dunbar continues to maintain a strong presence both statewide and regionally. Clients value the corporate team for offering "*expertise in virtually every field of law you could need*" and appreciate the depth of resources available: in the words of one it has the capacity to bring "*plenty of horses*" to any deal. Its growing profile across the USA was also obvious, as interviewees nationwide attested to the lawyers' "*exemplary work in translating technical knowledge of the law into practical applications.*" The Jackson office provides a full-service business offering, including top-class support in areas like tax and commercial litigation for companies ranging from regional banks to national retailers.

**The Lawyers:** Former law professor and "*masterful lawyer*" **Clifton Hodge** (see p.1184) offers clients an unusual "*breadth of experience.*" Peers acknowledge that, "*not many of us have his versatility,*" while clients declare that he and his team "*never cease to amaze.*" Although a good portion of his time is devoted to business litigation and arbitration, he was also noted for his "*high level of expertise in corporate securities law.*" **James O'Mara**'s (see p.1185) practice is focused on reorganizations and he regularly represents stockholder groups and creditors. In the past year he has devoted the majority of his time to "*the most complex bankruptcy case ever filed in Mississippi,*" in which he was the debtor's primary counsel. Clients appreciate his "*strong work ethic*" and his "*responsiveness and ability to establish a spirit of getting things done.*" **Jerry Hafter** (see p.1184) handles an impressive range of work, acting as general counsel to Delta & Pine Land and recently serving in an interlocutory capacity at the state Supreme Court in connection with a major merger litigation case. The aftermath of Hurricane Katrina has generated a number of interesting mandates such as the relocation of an art auction house from New Orleans to Jackson. Sources describe him as "*well rounded, well regarded and extremely bright.*" **Mike Bush** (see p.1182) is managing partner of the Tupelo office. While his practice centers on healthcare financing and banking work, he also acts as counsel to a number of manufacturing companies. A "*first-rate corporate lawyer*" and a "*real hard negotiator,*" his approach was described as "*extremely detail-oriented.*" **Dan McDaniel** (see p.1185) currently holds the presidency of the International Association of Gaming Attorneys. New work following Hurricane Katrina has included site assessments for new developments and helping clients to navigate the new regulatory process. He

was singled out for his sophisticated understanding of the "*interplay between state rules and local developments.*" Practice coordinator **Stephen Wilson**'s (see p.1187) work consists largely of corporate deals, including a substantial number of joint venture and credit facility cases. Recognized as a "*deal lawyer,*" his handling of M&A tax issues has impressed peers and he was praised for his "*technical expertise and strong judgment in negotiations.*"

**Clients/Work Highlights:** The team has recently overseen the sale of an interest in a manufacturing company, two important bank mergers, and several bank and bond financings in the healthcare sector. It also represented Wal-Mart and regional firm Park Development in connection with state and local tax matters. Other clients include BancorpSouth; Bank of Yazoo; BorgWarner; Callaway Partners; Mississippi Chemical; Neill Farm; Southern Farm Bureau Insurance Companies and West Implement.

## Band 2

## Baker, Donelson, Bearman, Caldwell & Berkowitz, PC

See firm details p.1819

**The Firm:** This full-service regional firm boasts a network that stretches across the Southeast as well as a Washington, DC branch and a representative office in Beijing, China. The Jackson outpost is particularly known to clients and lawyers for its expertise in the healthcare and tax fields, alongside its work on acquisitions and private equity investments. Clients highlight the coherence of the team and the strength of the individual lawyers, citing their "*creativity*" and ability to "*consistently come up with an idea for a solution.*"

**The Lawyers:** **William Painter** (see p.1186) is especially well known for his "*tax-oriented expertise,*" which he employs on behalf of a diverse range of clients from wireless companies to health care providers. Indeed, he is considered an "*absolutely first-rate person in health care,*" particularly when it comes to complex restructurings. "*Aggressive*" in approach with "*lots of expertise on the bigger transactions,*" he ultimately "*knows how to get to the bottom line.*" Clients also drew attention to the strong group of tax-qualified attorneys he has around him, which was praised for its cohesiveness and collective talent.

**Clients/Work Highlights:** Notable recent work includes a sizable purchase for a restaurant chain totaling nearly $100 million. Clients include TLC Vision (USA); McAlister's; Highland Medical Arts and a number of high net worth individuals.

## McGlinchey Stafford, PLLC

See firm details p.996

**The Firm:** This Jackson-based business law group is compact and versatile, with clients appreciating its "*expertise in a wide variety of different fields.*" The team has recently handled a number of sizable transactions including the liquidation of a series of companies. It has advised on lending work for both national and regional banks and automotive compa-

nies, and assists in bond issuances. Corporate real estate work also forms a substantial part of the team's practice.

**The Lawyers:** Peers recommend "*dedicated technician*" **William Mendenhall** (see p.1185) for his "*fine understanding of corporate and LLC law.*" His caseload includes advice on acquisitions and disposals, and insurance regulatory issues. He also assisted the Secretary of State with the navigation of state statutes during an investigation. Clients appreciate his courteousness and responsiveness and are impressed that they can "*explain an issue in two sentences and he drafts the situation immediately.*"

**Clients/Work Highlights:** The team recently advised on lease negotiations and on a client's charitable corporation status. It studied stockholder stock option plans for the board of directors of a large local firm. Clients include Gulf Group; Nissan Motor Acceptance; PolyVulc USA; RPM Pizza; Verizon Wireless and Waggoner Engineering.

## Watkins & Eager PLLC

See firm details p.1191

**The Firm:** Watkins & Eager's acknowledged strong suit is its litigation practice. However it can also lay claim to an active and impressive general business group, which has expanded substantially in recent years. The 15-member team includes qualified tax attorneys and covers a wide range of areas, including financing and real estate transactions. Clients were full of praise for the department's "*superior quality work*" and highlight the "*incredibly practical*" approach taken by its attorneys.

**The Lawyers:** **George Fair** devotes time to a broad range of practice areas combining commercial litigation with M&A, banking law and work with public utilities. He was singled out to researchers as a "*knowledgeable transactional attorney with the highest ethics,*" who is "*highly valued for his level head and good judgment.*"

**Clients/Work Highlights:** Blossman Gas; Knobias Holdings; La-Z-Boy; Pruet Companies and Willmut Gas.

## Watkins Ludlam Winter & Stennis, P.A

**The Firm:** Clients rely on this firm's business solutions practice group "*for any kind of legal advice.*" They claim to be "*satisfied from A to Z*" with the quality of the expertise on offer, and choose the team because it "*really turns work around quickly.*" Especially recognized for its skill in finance transactions, the group's particular forte is public finance, and it undertakes numerous municipal and local redevelopment cases. The firm's gaming practice is felt to be another of its outstanding strengths. An impressive client base includes multinationals of the quality of Nissan.

**The Lawyers:** Franchise work makes up about half of **David Grishman**'s practice. He recently negotiated four franchises for new enterprises in the food, vision and advertising sectors. Clients praise his "*foresight and vision,*" as well as his "*vast knowledge and skill*" in the area, along with his expertise in tax and corporate law. **David Martin** combines strength in insurance regulatory law with a successful corporate and finance practice. A *"bright and aggressive"* lawyer, he is coordinating the defense of a national insurer in the wake of Hurricane Katrina, and represented a client in connection with student loan-related securitized financings worth $250 million. **Zachary Taylor** is in particular demand for his tax expertise. Known for tackling *"challenging and interesting deals,"* his work includes project financings, loan acquisitions and advice on subsidies and tax credits. Securitizing student loans also forms a large part of his practice. Clients go to *"thorough and honest"* **Gina Jacobs** for assistance with M&A and corporate transactions in a variety of sectors. For one client she has been handling syndications worth up to half a billion dollars, and she also undertakes finance work for the Eastern Band of Cherokee Indians of North Carolina. *"Aggressive"* in her approach, she will *"fight for us on every point,"* report clients. The *"well-connected"* **Robert Lazarus** is admired by clients for his *"technical expertise"* in financial transactions. His recent highlights include negotiating an inducement package on behalf of an economic development district and coordinating the state's security position. Corporate work for hospitals and financings for nonprofit companies also feature in his workload, and he managed the financing for national retail chain Belk for the renovation of its state distribution network. Sources describe gaming attorney **Thomas Shepherd** as a *"master of the law, always up to speed on the rules and regulations."* His

recent deals include work on a $290 million notes offering for Majestic Star Casino and a $1.6 billion credit facility for Ameristar Casinos. This *"bright, honest and responsive"* lawyer is also currently representing the purchaser of a gaming property.
**Clients/Work Highlights:** The team advised on a $50 million financing for a large warehousing operation and a major international equity transaction for SeverCorr. On the public finance side, it recently represented a city in the acquisition of a water and sewerage system. Other clients include Caesar's Entertainment; Commercial Developers; Harreld Chevrolet; L & A Contracting; Melvin Entertainment; Mississippi Life & Health Insurance Guaranty Association; Perrett Enterprises; Pinnacle Entertainment and Utility Management.

## Wise Carter Child & Caraway, Professional Association

**The Firm:** Wise Carter's corporate practice covers a variety of commercial transactions and corporate litigation, including M&A and a slew of finance matters. Its stable of clients takes in large national corporations at one end, and small local companies at the other, all of whom praised the skill and dedication of the firm's attorneys.
**The Lawyers:** *"Conscientious, impressive, honorable:"* these adjectives testify to the high esteem in which the market holds **Henry Chatham**. An *"extremely knowledgeable"* adviser, he is a force in corporate law, commercial transactions and business planning.

**Clients/Work Highlights:** The team's client roster includes American Airlines, Sanderson Farms and Twentieth Century Fox.

## Other Notable Practitioners

*"Responsive and professional"* **Scott Andress** (see p.1182) of Balch & Bingham has seen a great deal of interesting work in recent years, including close involvement in House Bill 45 which enabled the 800 ft limit for inland construction. He has also guided the Emerald Star and Silver Slipper casinos through the site approval processes. One source declared to researchers that *"I trust his judgment and analysis of statutes implicitly,"* while another noted that he *"has the confidence of the regulators."* Byrd & Wiser's **Bob Byrd** *"is good to have either on your side or against you"* according to peers, who also praised his *"broad experience in representing the facets of a case."* Alongside a diet of Chapter 11 debtor cases and Chapter 7 panel trust work, he was involved in one of the largest real estate transactions in Mississippi history. Clients report that he is *"always willing to go the extra step."* **Craig Geno** of Harris & Geno PLLC is respected for his hard work and large caseload. He was described to researchers as *"a knowledgeable and experienced bankruptcy practitioner"* who *"knows the judges well and commands their respect."* Geno specializes in Chapter 11 debtor work and this year served as Mississippi counsel for the official committee of unsecured creditors in the largest bankruptcy case in state history.

# EMPLOYMENT

# MAINLY DEFENDANT

| Employment: Mainly Defendant |
| --- |
| **Leading Firms** |
| [1] **PHELPS DUNBAR LLP** *Jackson* |
| [2] **BALCH & BINGHAM** *Jackson* |
| **THE KULLMAN FIRM** *Jackson* |
| **WATKINS & EAGER PLLC** *Jackson* |
| [3] **BUTLER, SNOW** *Jackson* |
| **LEWIS FISHER HENDERSON** *Jackson* |
| **WATKINS LUDLAM WINTER & STENNIS** *Jackson* |
| **WISE CARTER CHILD & CARAWAY** *Jackson* |

## Band 1

### Phelps Dunbar LLP
See firm details p.997
**The Firm:** The state's leading labor and employment team fields an *"impressive line-up"* of 13 lawyers. This sizable group was enthusiastically praised for its *"superb client service,"* and its attorneys were said to *"know how to engage and persuade judges"* and to *"win hands down on cost-benefit analysis."* The team handles a wide variety of work, including EEOC charges, OSHA cases and labor arbitrations, for a client roster that ranges from Fortune 500 companies to local schools. The healthcare, oil, automobile,

manufacturing and chemical industries are especially strong sectors for the firm.
**The Lawyers:** One national client dubbed **Tommy Siler** (see p.1186) the *"best serving lawyer out of the states"* in which it operates. Peers admire his *"common-sense approach to cases"* and *"strong service orientation,"* and interviewees also highlighted his familiarity with the judges and a *"wider-context view of life, which helps him see the clients' perspective"* as major drawing cards. He recently defended Ashley Furniture in the US Supreme Court on a race discrimination charge, and is also representing a large multinational in a race discrimination and unequal pay case brought by 25 plaintiffs. **Gary Friedman** (see p.1184) has a strong niche in representing municipalities, which peers admit *"cannot be matched."* A *"first-class lawyer,"* his *"meticulous presentation of cases and excellent intellect"* are a hit with clients. He is particularly noted for his civil rights work, defending such bodies as the Mississippi Municipal Workers' Compensation Group and the Mississippi Drug Testing Consortium. His private-sector work, meanwhile, includes ERISA cases. **Joseph Adams** (see p.1182) was singled out for his broad range of knowledge, which includes wage and hour collective litigation and race discrimination cases. An *"outstanding attorney with a direct and*

*open"* approach and fearsome skill in the courtroom, his recent highlights include successfully resolving a serious OSHA case brought against Rapid Drilling.
**Clients/Work Highlights:** The team represented True Temper Sports in a nine-plaintiff race discrimination charge, and handled a due process and breach of contract claim against George County Hospital. Other clients include Atmos Energy; BellSouth Telecommunications; Delphi Automotive Systems; Georgia-Pacific; Pruet Oil and numerous municipal government entities.

## Band 2

### Balch & Bingham
See firm details p.161
**The Firm:** This *"seasoned"* firm has this year witnessed an upsurge in proactive consultation in areas such as workforce reduction and product line elimination. Commentators praise the *"exceptionally fine"* labor and employment team, highlighting its breadth and versatility. The traditional labor side has been busy of late, with the group advising on union-organizing campaigns, collective bargaining and labor litigation. Attorneys also regularly appear before the NLRB, OSHA and OFCCP, as well as

various courts, for a client roster including, inter alia, a national hi-tech business, an oil company and a rubber manufacturer.

**The Lawyers:** **Armin Moeller** (see p.1185) is highly regarded for his *"extensive knowledge across the spectrum of labor and employment law."* A *"methodical and scholarly"* style doesn't prevent him from being an *"excellent public speaker."* His recent caseload includes a charge under the FMLA, for which petition for a writ of certiorari has been submitted to the US Supreme Court. He also handled work relating to a pension plan, and managed a collective bargaining agreement. The *"punctual and responsive"* **Pepper Crutcher** (see p.1183) has overseen a large upturn in the firm's FLSA collective action work, as well as tackling wrongful discharge cases, EEOC claims and grievance arbitrations. He is currently taking a dismissal case, worth a quarter of a million dollars, to the state Supreme Court. Clients praised him for doing *"a masterful job"* and always *"striving to give the best advice he can."*

**Clients/Work Highlights:** The firm is currently counseling executives of a technology firm in California on an upcoming buyout and noncompetition agreements. Clients include Delta Air Lines; Eaton Corporation; GlobalSantaFe; Mississippi Power; PCE Constructors; The Clorox Company and Transocean.

## The Kullman Firm A Professional Law Corporation

**The Firm:** This *"pretty much exceptional"* labor and employment boutique is one of the oldest in the country. Highly regarded within the state, not least for its track record of important US Supreme Court work, its lawyers are valued by clients as business partners as much as legal advisers. The group provides advice on a wide variety of labor and employment matters from arbitration to EEOC, OSHA and wage and hour claims, frequently assisting employers with civil rights and safety matters.

**The Lawyers:** *"Dean of the Bar"* **Taylor Smith** is incredibly well respected throughout the state and beyond. He has argued several cases in front of the US Supreme Court and is appreciated by clients for his excellent political sense: he *"knows his way around the legal town."* Major recent matters include a complex labor arbitration case, and he regularly applies his talents to work in numerous sectors from

banking to media and manufacturing.

**Clients/Work Highlights:** As examples of the extensive labor work undertaken by the firm, Taylor Smith has handled union campaigns, contract negotiations and contract and labor agreement arbitrations for AmeriCold Logistics. Other clients include Babcock & Wilcox; Burrows Paper; Grenada Lake Medical Center; Heatcraft and Sanderson Plumbing Products.

## Watkins & Eager PLLC

See firm details p.1191

**The Firm:** The oldest firm in Jackson boasts an impressive and flexible labor and employment group. Its caseload covers a substantial amount of employment discrimination work as well as instructions before the NLRB and an increasing volume of wage and hour litigation. Its client roster runs from a funeral home to two worldwide distribution companies, with sources at both ends of the scale happy to recommend the team for its *"vast experience and willingness to help."*

**The Lawyers:** **Kenneth Milam** commands enormous respect for his *"expert knowledge"* in a number of areas. Clients appreciate him for *"telling you what you need to hear, not what you want to hear,"* while peers declare that he has *"antennae the rest of us don't have."* His alternative dispute resolution practice has almost doubled in size this year, and he is also enjoying an increase in pure labor law work, including union-organizing campaigns. He also spends about a quarter of his time advising on employment contracts and termination compensation. Recent highlights include handling a dispute in Africa for a worldwide construction contractor.

**Clients/Work Highlights:** In one year the firm handled seven EEOC complaints for one business in areas ranging from age to race discrimination. Elsewhere it won an important case in front of the state Supreme Court regarding the employment-at-will doctrine. Clients include Alderwoods; Grenada Stamping and Assembly; La-Z-Boy; Baptist Health Systems; Savings Oil and U-Haul International.

## Band 3

## Butler, Snow, O'Mara, Stevens & Cannada, PLLC

See firm details p.1189

**The Firm:** Clients across the USA described this firm as a *"one-stop shop with expertise in a variety of different disciplines,"* and welcomed the high level of service provided at *"extremely competitive rates."* Its labor and employment practice has been strengthened in recent years by the expansion of its office in Memphis, Tennessee, which caters for north Mississippi. Labor negotiations and advice are a particular feature, and here its success is said to be founded on *"technically superior"* preparatory work.

**The Lawyers:** **Jeffrey Walker** (see p.1186) wins respect for his skill in traditional labor law issues. Clients report that he *"stays focused on the big picture while remaining in control of complex detail"* and

provides *"excellent counsel."* His large portfolio of recent successes includes winning a jury verdict for a regional medical center in a federal disability discrimination case and negotiating an agreement for five years of labor peace on behalf of a local steel industry client. He also advised a casino on non-union status.

**Clients/Work Highlights:** The team defeated an organizing effort for an aerospace industry client. It also obtained a jury verdict on claims for breach of a manager's duty of loyalty, intentional interference with business relationships, and violations of the Uniform Trade Secrets Act, against a former employee and his new employer. Clients include All American Moving & Storage; Alliant Techsystems; Baxter Healthcare; Ergon; MMC Materials; Peavey Electronics; Sara Lee; Tenet Healthcare and The Kroger Company.

## Lewis Fisher Henderson Claxton & Mulroy LLP

**The Firm:** This five-strong labor and employment team *"covers the waterfront"* in terms of services provided. Indeed, it has been so busy of late that it recently brought several new associates on board in response to a growing workload, including in its specialty insurance defence niche. The firm is popular with clients for being *"punctual and highly responsive,"* and for its professed focus on keeping businesses from falling into legal problems, rather than extracting them from lawsuits.

**The Lawyers:** Clients give *"tireless worker"* **Bert Ehrhardt** *"five stars."* They particularly value his hands-on approach to training employees and his *"conscientious efforts at letting you understand the rationale behind his advice."* Among other recent highlights, he has handled an EEOC case for Trustmark.

**Clients/Work Highlights:** The firm appeared for P&S Delivery before the NLRB in a case concerning a contested ballot. It also successfully defended an alleged defamation charge emerging from a wrongful termination claim against the Jubilee Casino. Other clients include Ameristar Casinos; Horne LLP; Migerobe and U-Save Auto-Rental of America.

## Watkins Ludlam Winter & Stennis, P.A

**The Firm:** Clients choose this firm because of its high profile and good service standards, and its lawyers were praised for combining *"first-class advice"* with a sense of the *"overall broad picture."* The team handles traditional labor law, employment litigation, OSHA and ERISA matters, and has particular strength in affirmative action plans. Sources note that, in instances where Hurricane Katrina slowed down casework, especially for Louisiana-based companies, the work was promptly recovered and successfully completed.

**The Lawyers:** Satisfied clients agree that **Peyton Irby** possesses the knack of communicating, in clear and understandable language, the complexities of employment issues facing businesses. This he combines with strength in litigation and the range of labor law to supply *"not one-shot advice, but advice broad enough that you have options, and the information to make the right decision."* Recent work has included three union contract matters along with a host of affirmative action plans and FLSA cases.

**Clients/Work Highlights:** The team has been busy managing employment plans with companies affected by Hurricane Katrina. It has also seen a considerable number of deprocess claims for public entities in recent months. Clients are drawn from the gaming, manufacturing, shipping and finance sectors, among others, and include Boyd Gaming; Brown Bottling Group; City of Olive Branch; Coastal Cargo; Mutual Credit Union and Nissan North America.

## Wise Carter Child & Caraway,

### Professional Association

**The Firm:** The firm fields distinct employment, benefits and workers' compensation teams to supply a strong service spanning labor and employment. It is best known, however, for employment law, where it assists with a steady stream of mediation, litigation and counseling work. Commentators consider Wise Carter a *"well-led practice with just as much talent as any East Coast firm,"* and it remains popular among clients for both its *"cost-effectiveness and strong judgment."*

**The Lawyers:** The *"exceptionally bright"* **Barbara Wallace** counts discrimination law among her strengths. She undertakes a considerable amount of hospital-related work, currently handling a race discrimination charge brought by 89 plaintiffs. Clients value her because she *"removes the burden yet keeps you fully informed,"* while competitors agree that she *"has all the credentials"* and can *"move things forward and take the case on its own terms."* Her handling of cases where employees represent themselves was especially noted.

**Clients/Work Highlights:** The firm is currently handling an important ADA case. It regularly appears in race, age and sex discrimination cases, while recent labor work involved negotiating contracts with a union. Clients include Chubb Group; Entergy Operations; KLLM Transport Services; Neshoba County General Hospital; Pine Belt Mental Healthcare Resources; Mississippi Children's Home Society; Pioneer Aerospace and Sanderson Farms.

# LITIGATION

| Litigation: General Commercial |
| --- |
| Leading Firms |
| [1] PHELPS DUNBAR LLP *Jackson* |
| WATKINS & EAGER PLLC *Jackson* |
| [2] BAKER, DONELSON *Jackson* |
| BRADLEY ARANT ROSE & WHITE LLP *Jackson* |
| BRUNINI, GRANTHAM, GROWER & HEWES *Jackson* |
| BUTLER, SNOW *Jackson* |
| [3] FORMAN PERRY WATKINS KRUTZ *Jackson* |
| MITCHELL, MCNUTT & SAMS PA *Tupelo* |
| [4] LATHAM & BURWELL PLLC *Ridgeland* |
| WATKINS LUDLAM WINTER & STENNIS *Jackson* |
| WISE CARTER CHILD & CARAWAY *Jackson* |

## Band 1

### Phelps Dunbar LLP

See firm details p.997

**The Firm:** This Jackson-based litigation group is often the *"first choice"* to handle complicated matters, say market commentators. The 30-strong team commands a diverse practice covering everything from disputes over commercial contracts to product liability and environmental litigation. The firm also fields a superb team of appellate lawyers which is considered by many to be the *"best in Mississippi."* It has recently been handling an important appeal on behalf of Delta and Pine Land. The group also continues to feature in mass tort actions, which, in recent months, has meant a lot of insurance claims arising from Hurricane Katrina.

**The Lawyers:** **Reuben Anderson** (see p.1182) is a popular lawyer with a superb reputation in the industry. *"A prince of a guy,"* he was a former Supreme Court Justice in Mississippi and so is *"in tune with the political nuances of a particular situation and well liked by the judiciary."* His skill as a writer and thinker, and his ability to see the big picture, attracted praise from interviewees, and he is also

known as an excellent mediator. **Fred Banks** (see p.1182) *"has an excellent understanding of the law and can succinctly put cases into writing."* As a former presiding justice of the Mississippi Supreme Court he has *"clout, experience and strong abilities as a trial lawyer."* He regularly advises other lawyers on appeal cases and has been involved of late in a variety of financial disputes. Also renowned for his financial litigation practice is **Ross Bass** (see p.1182), the firm's managing partner. He has been representing Wachovia this year in a case concerning improvement loans and the indictment of mortgage brokers, and defended a local law firm in a malicious prosecution case. Here he obtained summary judgment in the first instance and is handling the appeal. He was described to researchers as a *"smart, diligent and prepared"* attorney who *"thinks well on his feet and is good in the rough and tumble."* **Clifton Hodge** (see p.1184) is *"charming and personable,"* say sources. His general business disputes and transactional practice includes a slice of fraud, securities and commercial contract litigation. As a former lecturer he *"knows how businesses work and presents complicated financial matters effectively."* He has been busy recently with a complex arbitration. **Luther Munford** (see p.1185) handles appeals and specializes in First Amendment cases. He authored *"the appellate law bible,"* and is admired as *"an excellent legal analyst, persuasive and terrific at putting arguments on paper."* In addition to his news media work he has been handling a medical case in which the attorney general is suing Immunex for allegedly overcharging on Medicaid. In another important case, he convinced the court that damages resulting from a shooting of some colleagues by one employee should be resolved through the workers' compensation system rather than by jury trials. **Michael Wallace** (see p.1187) is another of the leading appellate specialists and is good at writing briefs and presenting oral arguments. Sources consider him an *"excellent strategist with an encyclopedic memory"* who *"can cut to the heart of a matter when everyone else is beat-*

*ing about the bush."* In recent work for Chevron he persuaded the Supreme Court that oilfield pollution cases should be taken before the Oil and Gas Board rather than a civil court.

**Clients/Work Highlights:** BancorpSouth; Wachovia; Chevron; Allstate; North Mississippi Medical Center; Delta and Pine Land; BellSouth; Wells Fargo; St. Paul Travelers and Interstate Fibernet.

### Watkins & Eager PLLC

See firm details p.1191

**The Firm:** Watkins & Eager was singled out by commentators for its wealth of *"bright senior lawyers with deep litigation experience."* In the words of one source, its great selling point is a *"highly competent workforce that is able to cover a wide number of areas simultaneously with an efficient service."* The firm frequently deals with financial institutions, as well as representing energy companies, builders and developers. Pharmaceutical work is another area of expertise, while the products liability group is particularly known for handling automotive, mass tort and medical devices cases.

**The Lawyers:** *"Excellent overall lawyer"* **John Corlew** is active in a broad range of areas. This, combined with his excellent people skills and an *"ability to reach consensus among big egos,"* means that he is considered one of the best jury litigators in the state. Interviewees also drew attention to his *"strong intellect and ability to unravel complicated issues"* as the icing on the cake. **Michael Ulmer** focuses on welding and tobacco cases, and recently led in a welding fume case in Cleveland and a chemical burns case in Alabama. He is admired for his *"great integrity"* and *"tenacity when it comes to defeating the other side's claims."* Commentators also appreciate his ability to take a case from trial to appeal and his knowledge of the various courts and judges throughout the state. *"Rainmaker"* **William Goodman** is renowned as one of the *"preeminent lawyers in Mississippi."* Active in the state for over 50

## Litigation: General Commercial
### Leading Individuals

★ **DRINKWATER Wayne** *Bradley Arant Rose*
   **PERRY Alan** *Forman Perry Watkins Krutz*

[1] **CORLEW John** *Watkins & Eager PLLC*
   **SHAPLEY Christopher** *Brunini, Grantham, Grower*
   **ULMER Michael** *Watkins & Eager PLLC*

[2] **ANDERSON Reuben** *Phelps Dunbar LLP*
   **BASS Ross** *Phelps Dunbar LLP*
   **CAMPBELL Roy** *Bradley Arant Rose*
   **DOVE Luke** *Dove and Chill*
   **FORD Barry** *Baker, Donelson*
   **GALLOWAY Robert** *Butler, Snow*
   **GIBBS Robert** *Brunini, Grantham*
   **GOODMAN William** *Watkins & Eager PLLC*
   **HENEGAN John** *Butler, Snow*
   **HODGE E Clifton** *Phelps Dunbar LLP*
   **JONES Christy** *Butler, Snow*
   **JONES Walker** *Baker, Donelson*
   **KAUFMAN David** *Brunini, Grantham, Grower*
   **KRUTZ Fred** *Forman Perry Watkins Krutz*
   **SAMS L** *Mitchell, McNutt & Sams PA*
   **STEPHENSON III Paul** *Watkins & Eager PLLC*
   **THOMAS Stephen** *Bradley Arant Rose*
   **WALLACE Michael** *Phelps Dunbar LLP*
   **WELCH W Scott** *Baker, Donelson*

[3] **AYERS David** *Watkins & Eager PLLC*
   **EVANS George** *Wise Carter Child & Caraway*
   **GRAHAM D Collier** *Wise Carter Child & Caraway*
   **LATHAM William** *Latham & Burwell PLLC*
   **REED William** *Baker, Donelson, Bearman*

## Litigation: Appellate
### Leading Individuals

[1] **DRINKWATER Wayne** *Bradley Arant Rose*
   **MUNFORD Luther** *Phelps Dunbar LLP*
   **WALLACE Michael** *Phelps Dunbar LLP*

[2] **BANKS Fred** *Phelps Dunbar LLP*
   **HENEGAN John** *Butler, Snow*
   **PERRY Alan** *Forman Perry Watkins Krutz*

## Litigation: Construction
### Leading Individuals

[1] **MOCKBEE David** *Mockbee Hall & Drake*
[2] **PURDY William** *Purdy & Germany PLLC*

years, he was pronounced "*as good as they come*." Goodman advises on business, commercial and banking litigation and is well known in the appellate world. Managing partner **Paul Stephenson** has been spending the bulk of his time litigating insurance fraud cases. He also represents financial institutions charged with negligently laundering insurance money that was fraudulently obtained, assists accounting and legal professionals, and defends class actions on behalf of consumer finance companies. Interviewees describe him as a "*smart attorney who works hard and has good practical sense.*" "*Bright and thorough*" **David Ayers** specializes in products liabil-

ity, mass tort and personal injury claims. He has an impressive roster of international blue chip companies, such as Toyota, and comes highly recommended. In the words of one client he "*will be the best prepared lawyer in the courtroom; he knows the product and his expert witnesses have impeccable credentials.*" He has been winning verdicts on cases concerning faulty brakes, and has a niche in dealing with premises liability.

**Clients/Work Highlights:** The firm has a large market share of the automotive industry in the state, representing Toyota; Nissan; Honda; GM; Ford; Volkswagen and BMW. It also has a niche pharmaceutical practice that has been working with Pfizer.

## Band 2

### Baker, Donelson, Bearman, Caldwell & Berkowitz, PC
See firm details p.1819

**The Firm:** This regional powerhouse has offices throughout the Southeast, including a 35-strong litigation group in Jackson. The primary areas covered by its lawyers include general commercial litigation, products liability, pharmaceutical and medical device cases, and labor, insurance and antitrust disputes. The firm also enjoys nationwide recognition for its healthcare practice and has been defending a number of pharmaceutical companies on cases relating to Medicaid reimbursement. Following Hurricane Katrina, this year has been notable for the volume of insurance liability cases the team has handled. Clients were enthusiastic about the depth of resources on offer here and the group's ability "*to get the job done.*"

**The Lawyers:** **Barry Ford** (see p.1184) leads the group's products liability practice and wows clients with his "*outstanding strength as a trial lawyer.*" He has been defending automotive companies in cases relating to seat belt and glass products, winning several settlements, and also represented 3M in products liability cases brought against the company, proving that the plaintiffs made fraudulent claims and the doctors inaccurate diagnoses. **Walker Jones** (see p.1185) "*loves being in the courtroom,*" say commentators. He has a good understanding of the Mississippi court system and an "*excellent record of success*" based on his skill in "*breaking down cases and communicating to a jury.*" An experienced trial lawyer, he is often involved in high-stakes litigation, primarily in liability and insurance defense. Here he has been working with Lloyd's on environmental liability claims in New York, while other clients include sanofi-aventis, Ford and Philip Morris. "*Smart and responsive*" **William Reed** (see p.1186) is well connected in the legal community. His recent highlights include settling 15 products liability cases for Ford involving SUVs and Ford Explorers. He has also been lead counsel in tobacco litigation, winning a favorable verdict for his clients. **Scott Welch** (see p.1187) recently joined the group from Butler, Snow, O'Mara, Stevens & Cannada, PLLC. A "*thoroughly likable attorney*" with "*the ability to perform at the top*

*level,*" he has been handling commercial litigation for a publishing house and sporting entity in New York against a plaintiff in Mississippi. Other highlights include defending several insurers against a suit bought by the attorney general, who is attempting to rewrite contract flood exclusion clauses in the wake of Hurricane Katrina.

**Clients/Work Highlights:** This year the firm has been handling mass tort work for 3M, which ended in a settlement. Other clients include Ford; Philip Morris; Cendant; sanofi-aventis; Lloyd's; Monsanto and Bristol-Myers Squibb.

### Bradley Arant Rose & White LLP
See firm details p.162

**The Firm:** The firm's 16-lawyer Jackson team is focused heavily on litigation. It may not be the largest in the market but it "*has excellent lawyers*" and enjoys the support of an impressive regional network, with all that this means for resources. Clients were highly impressed by the "*efficient service*" provided. The group's key practice is centered around products liability, contract disputes and negligence claims, with an emphasis on representing financial institutions and large corporate companies. For example, it has been representing GE and Equitable Life recently in various sales assurance practice claims.

**The Lawyers:** "*Brilliant consultant and appellate lawyer*" **Wayne Drinkwater** (see p.1183) is "*hands-down the best trial lawyer in Mississippi,*" according to a number of sources. Not only highly intelligent, he can also take a difficult problem and put it in understandable language. As one interviewee went on to say, he is "*unflappable, eloquent and puts arguments succinctly and persuasively in court.*" This and his many other skills combine to make him "*corporate America's choice.*" Recent successes include getting two $25 million claims dismissed by the Supreme Court and winning favorable rulings in the silica cases in Texas. **Roy Campbell** (see p.1183) is "*conscientious and good at what he does,*" say peers. His highlight of the year was successfully defending Boeing against a class action by plaintiffs alleging exposure to beryllium, a substance used in rocket engines. He also acted for an insurance provider in a class action relating to cancer payments, and was involved in a statewide antitrust suit. "*Talented*" **Stephen Thomas** (see p.1186) is an effective tort lawyer renowned for representing large commercial clients, such as ConAgra Foods, in mass tort cases. In the last year he obtained the dismissal, on behalf of his client, of an environmental pollution claim and acted as lead counsel for Delta and Pine Land in a dispute concerning genetically altered cottonseed.

**Clients/Work Highlights:** The firm has been representing 3M in silica claims and acting for Caterpillar, which is being sued in a welding fumes case. It also works with Georgia-Pacific, RJ Reynolds and BTN.

## Brunini, Grantham, Grower & Hewes, PLLC

See firm details p.1188

**The Firm:** This well-established Mississippi firm continues to be best known for its work defending pharmaceutical companies. Here it boasts a long track record of success; as one impressed source noted, the group *"single-handedly accomplished a virtual shut-down of the OxyContin litigation in the state."* However, there's more to Brunini Grantham than pharmaceutical cases, and clients value its *"excellent attorneys and good, efficient service"* in a wide range of matters. For example, it is defending Koppers and Kerr-McGee in thousands of personal injury and property damage environmental claims in the state and federal courts.

**The Lawyers:** *"Captain of the ship"* **Christopher Shapley** (see p.1186) is renowned as one of the finest litigators in Mississippi because of his *"impeccable judgment and instinct."* He also enjoys *"great jury appeal"* and *"immense credibility with the courts and with his adversaries."* He has been defending Coldwell Banker in dozens of cases in the Mississippi state and federal courts, alleging consumer fraud. Other recent highlights include defending GlaxoSmithKline in personal injury and death claims involving the antidepressant Paxil, as well as playing a central role in the OxyContin cases. Commentators trust **Robert Gibbs** (see p.1184) to *"do an excellent job every time."* A former circuit judge, he *"knows what other judges are thinking"* and is widely respected for the way he *"controls the courtroom."* He has spent a lot of time this year defending consumer fraud cases for a legal services company. **David Kaufman** (see p.1185) has been defending welding rod cases. A *"smart, talented and hard-working"* lawyer who *"knows his way around the courtroom,"* his profile is said to be on the rise.

**Clients/Work Highlights:** Koppers; Kerr-McGee; Trustmark National Bank; Cendant and Caldwell Banker.

## Butler, Snow, O'Mara, Stevens & Cannada, PLLC

See firm details p.1189

**The Firm:** *"Well known for being successful,"* this *"good, solid firm"* operates nationally and is often involved in international cases. It was one of the first firms in Mississippi to establish a products liability practice and this has remained its foremost strength. Its lawyers have been working on several silica and asbestos claims this year and increasingly litigate chemical exposure cases. However, with around 80 litigators, the firm has the resources to offer a diverse range of expertise in areas such as healthcare, labor and general commercial litigation.

**The Lawyers:** *"Low-key"* but effective litigator **Robert Galloway** (see p.1184) is *"smart and deserves his recognition,"* say interviewees. He is *"intellectually honest, researches the issues excellently and briefs well."* Galloway spends around half his time trying products liability cases and the rest litigating general commercial matters. He has been busy this year defending a class action connected with insurance

liability issues, and obtained a summary judgment for State Farm in three companion suits bought by two companies. **John Henegan** (see p.1184) *"is a superb lawyer with a strong intellect and the ability to think through problems."* The lead First Amendment lawyer at the firm, he also litigates antitrust class actions and is a *"terrific appellate attorney – meticulous and with a brilliant legal mind."* Highlights include settling a number of defamation and telecom cases, as well as appellate work involving tortious interference and breach of trust. He was involved in a case for 3M that resulted in the reversal of a $22.5 million judgment. **Christy Jones** (see p.1185) chairs the litigation department and handles drugs and pharmaceutical cases as well as medical devices litigation. She was described to researchers as *"one of the most sought-after pharmaceutical litigators in the USA,"* and one source went on to call her a *"star when it comes to drugs litigation."* Supporting this assessment is her role on the national trial team that won the Vioxx case, and she is also on the national team for the Fen-Phen litigation. During the past year she has also acted as counsel for Johnson & Johnson and Wyeth.

**Clients/Work Highlights:** The firm's diverse client roster includes companies from the banking, financial, telecommunications, healthcare, pharmaceuticals and automotive industries. These include State Farm; SunStates Management; Pinnacle Entertainment; BellSouth; Cingular Wireless; 3M; Merck; Johnson & Johnson; AmSouth Bank; Trustmark National Bank; Baxter; FMC and Edwards Lifesciences.

## Band 3

## Forman Perry Watkins Krutz & Tardy LLP

See firm details p.1190

**The Firm:** For many interviewees this is, first and foremost, *"a good asbestos firm."* Building on this reputation, and following the prevailing trends in the market, it has been successfully moving into silica litigation in recent months. For example, the team handled the Corpus Christi silicosis cases, uncovering mass fraud and changing the way litigation is practiced in mass tort claims. It is also involved in major corporate litigation and has been handling a trade secrets case which was spun off from a mass tort case.

**The Lawyers:** *"Analytical"* **Alan Perry** (see p.1186), with his *"encyclopedic mind,"* has the *"ability to organize and catalog volumes of information."* A strong commercial litigator who also knows his way around the appellate courts, there is *"no action that is too complex for him – he's a good strategist and handles each case superbly."* Indeed, one source went on to describe him as a *"genius when leading cases: if you're looking for brainpower, he's your man."* **Fred Krutz** (see p.1185) is an *"experienced and highly capable"* trial lawyer whose reputation has been on the up since he helped to expose mass fraud in the multidistrict silica cases filed in Corpus Christi, Texas. His

work in this area has led to a marked shift in mass tort litigation in favor of many corporate defendants, and provided the impetus for legislative change to reduce inaccurate diagnoses. Clients praised him as an *"intelligent and personable"* lawyer who *"knows his stuff"* in the courtroom.

**Clients/Work Highlights:** The firm deals primarily with the defense of mass tort and multiple plaintiff claims. It has worked with many impressive clients, including Liberty Mutual; BancorpSouth; Owens-Illinois; BP; Ingersoll Rand; Triumph and The Community Bank.

## Mitchell, McNutt & Sams PA

**The Firm:** This well-known Tupelo firm maintains offices throughout Mississippi. It is a name that repeatedly came to the minds of interviewees for its commercial litigation practice. This encompasses a range of general business disputes, professional liability cases and toxic tort as well as railroad litigation defense and pharmaceutical litigation.

**The Lawyers:** **Sandy Sams** is *"one of the most respected lawyers in the state,"* according to commentators. The *"rock-solid"* Tupelo-based lawyer is often on competitors' referral lists for cases outside Jackson because he is *"extremely hard-working, well prepared, articulate and immediately perceives what the matters are."* He focuses on complex commercial litigation, products liability, construction and professional liability cases.

**Clients/Work Highlights:** BDO Siedman; Harrah's Entertainment; Franklin Corporation; M&F Bank; FL Crane & Sons and North Mississippi Medical Center.

## Band 4

## Latham & Burwell PLLC

**The Firm:** This Ridgeland-based firm is renowned for its bankruptcy practice and remains a force in bankruptcy litigation. It also offers clients considerable expertise in general business litigation including appellate work. Due to its small size the firm is considered a good choice for midsized clients who appreciate a responsive and personalized service.

**The Lawyers:** **William Latham** has an accounting background and has been in private practice for over 30 years. He increasingly serves as a mediator, in which field he enjoys an excellent reputation because of his consensual approach and great understanding of the risks and business imperatives.

**Clients/Work Highlights:** Mississippi Valley Title Insurance; Scott Regional Hospital; State Bank and Trust; LeTourneau; Realty & Mortgage Group; M-I LLC and Lancer Claims Services.

## Watkins Ludlam Winter & Stennis, P.A

**The Firm:** The firm's litigation practice covers, inter alia, premises liability cases, complex commercial litigation, and labor and employment disputes. It has enjoyed a year of considerable success, winning a summary judgment, later upheld on appeal, in a

$90 million rental suit for a casino. Media cases are a niche specialty of the team, and here it recently prevailed in a libel case. The group also represented American Furniture in a business noncompete case, successfully obtaining a preliminary injunction. Other highlights include winning a flood damage insurance case for Wachovia and representing a variety of cough medicine manufacturers in mass tort actions.

**The Lawyers:** Neville Boschert chairs the litigation group here.

**Clients/Work Highlights:** Autoliv; Cooper Tire & Rubber; Empire Fire & Marine Insurance; The Gray Insurance Company; Jackson-Hinds Library System; JC Penney Company; Mack Trucks; MIC Property and Casualty Insurance; Motors Insurance Company; Nissan North America; Royal & SunAlliance; State Bank & Trust Company; Volvo Trucks North America and Washington Mutual Bank.

## Wise Carter Child & Caraway, Professional Association

**The Firm:** This old-line firm has 30 lawyers involved in a wide variety of commercial litigation. It is particularly well known for representing the health care and railroad industries. It also draws its clients from the telecommunications and construction industries and provides alternative dispute resolution services.

**The Lawyers:** **George Evans** is the firm's go-to medical malpractice defense lawyer. As one commentator said: *"For pharmaceutical and drugs cases, he would be first on my list."* According to sources, his *"honesty and tremendous knowledge"* make him a hit with lawyers and judges. **Collier Graham** has been defending a healthcare company in a fraud lawsuit bought by the Federal Government and a whistle-blower, successfully reducing the exposure of his client. He also defended Benjamin Moore, a paint manufacturer, against allegations of injury from lead paint. He was repeatedly recommended because he is *"good at understanding the judges and juries in the Mississippi court system."*

**Clients/Work Highlights:** The firm has worked with clients from the healthcare, insurance, transportation and utilities industries, among others. Examples include sanofi-aventis; Consumer

National Bank; Sprint Communication Systems; Premier Medical Group of Mississippi; Johnson & Johnson and Trustmark National Bank.

## Other Notable Practitioners

**Luke Dove** of Dove and Chill is *"bright and well regarded by the Bar."* He practices commercial litigation, specializing in white-collar crime. Recent highlights include defending a client in a complex tax dispute and playing important roles in a number of high-profile whistle-blower cases. *"Most people would race to hire"* **David Mockbee** of Mockbee Hall & Drake. He specializes in construction and government contracts law and *"knows the industry inside out."* Sources also appreciate the way he *"pays attention to details, which is important in meticulous cases like those in construction."* He is representing Steel Service in a lawsuit over the Cincinnati Reds Ballpark. Mockbee also represents Aceros Prefabricados and acts as defense counsel for a number of engineers and architects, including Johnson Bailey Henderson McNeel. *"Smart and confident"* **William Purdy** of Purdy & Germany *"knows how to win cases."* He also specializes in construction litigation where he primarily represents general contractors.

# REAL ESTATE

| Real Estate |
| --- |
| **Leading Firms** |
| 1 BUTLER, SNOW *Jackson* |
| WATKINS LUDLAM WINTER & STENNIS *Jackson* |
| 2 BRUNINI, GRANTHAM, GROWER & HEWES *Jackson* |
| WATKINS & EAGER PLLC *Jackson* |

| **Leading Individuals** |
| --- |
| 1 CANNADA Don *Butler, Snow* |
| 2 CLEMENT W Rodney *Brunini, Grantham, Grower* |
| DAVIS Mark *Watkins Ludlam Winter & Stennis, P.A* |
| GUNN Paul *Watkins & Eager PLLC* |
| SMITH III William *Watkins & Eager PLLC* |
| TOHILL Jim *Watkins Ludlam Winter & Stennis, P.A* |

## Band 1

### Butler, Snow, O'Mara, Stevens & Cannada, PLLC
See firm details p.1189

**The Firm:** Observers note this firm's strength in handling large sales, purchases, financing and leasing transactions for a range of commercial developers. Its lawyers were praised as *"real deal-makers"* who apply their knowledge of the sector to deliver results for their clients. Clients also note with approval that the firm has the *"back-up to handle what needs to be done."* This includes not just a 12-attorney outfit in Jackson, but a network of offices across the Southeastern USA. Benefiting from Mississippi's active

property market, the team has witnessed steady growth in casino, retail, residential and office developments. Over the last twelve months it has worked with Wal-Mart on a site redevelopment project and is presently advising a utility company looking to build a sanitation and water network in the north of the state.

**The Lawyers:** Valued by clients for *"always responding to our needs in the manner we would expect and want,"* **Don Cannada** (see p.1183) has built a reputation as one of the most experienced real estate lawyers in the state. According to interviewees he is also a *"talented professional"* with a *"wonderful wit and sense of humor."* Cannada recently clinched a $30 million financing deal for Reunion Realty and regularly handles real estate sales and acquisitions for Magazine Street Interests on behalf of drugstore chain Walgreens.

**Clients/Work Highlights:** Wal-Mart; Magazine Street Interests; Luckney; Reunion Realty and Hederman Realty.

### Watkins Ludlam Winter & Stennis, P.A
**The Firm:** This well-organized outfit was recommended for its work with commercial developers across the state. A *"number-one"* firm, it impressed interviewees with the *"important connections and relationships"* it has built up in Mississippi and beyond. The team offers legal representation in both project management and financing work to a range of clients from the public sector to private lenders and borrowers. It takes on cases throughout the

Southeast and has recently been assisting in the development of two large retail sites.

**The Lawyers:** **Mark Davis** was described to researchers as one of the state's *"go-to"* lawyers with strong connections to many of the important actors in the real estate arena. His reputation rests on an approach that *"avoids making too much of a scene"* while attracting clients with solid expertise that saves them from having to *"reinvent the wheel"* with each new transaction. In recent months this expertise has been employed by Ridgeway Lane in the redevelopment of a large tract of land in the state. Sources recommended **Jim Tohill** as an attorney who knows real estate law *"inside out"* and is *"great at dealing with and drafting documents."* His long experience in the industry and regular involvement in some of the state's largest real estate transactions have honed his skill in *"coming up with solutions."*

**Clients/Work Highlights:** State Street Group; Mattiace Properties; Homewood Company; Baptist Health Systems; Reunion Realty; Magazine Street Interests; Pearl River Valley Water Supply District and Underwood Commercial Real Estate.

## Band 2

### Brunini, Grantham, Grower & Hewes, PLLC
See firm details p.1188

**The Firm:** Recommended for handling work swiftly *"without lawyering a deal to death,"* this Jackson-headquartered firm has been doing a lot of work for developers in the office, retail and commercial sectors. The well-qualified, ten-attorney team wins clients through its skill in dealing with a wide range of legal matters including leasing, financing, sales and purchases and managing real estate development projects. It continues to represent some of Mississippi's largest companies from a number of high-profile industries, consistently demonstrating success in dealing with major real estate matters. Brunini also boasts a dedicated zoning and land use regulation practice.

**The Lawyers: Rodney Clement** (see p.1183) is valued by clients for being *"excellent at putting our needs into legal terms and meeting our objectives."* A *"knowledgeable and well-connected"* attorney, with an *"intense and highly detailed"* approach, he is said to be particularly strong at reviewing and drafting documents and assisting in securing project financing. He recently handled the acquisition of a delicatessen chain for a private equity firm, and advised on a finance transaction for a major steel plant on behalf of the State of Mississippi.

**Clients/Work Highlights:** Hillwood Development; Cellular South; Mattiace Properties; St Dominic Health Services; Tyson Foods; Trustmark National Bank and Ingalls Shipbuilding.

## Watkins & Eager PLLC
See firm details p.1191

**The Firm:** This nine-strong practice has gone from strength to strength in recent years. Clients praised the team for its ability to *"apply the law to get the job done,"* and it enjoys a growing reputation for its experience in handling matters within both the mainstream and specialist real estate markets. This includes representing lenders, buyers and investors in urban, retail and office developments, multifamily residential projects, complex commercial proposals and traditional neighbourhood developments. The group has built strong relationships with commercial developers across the state, recently advising on the status of land contracts and projects damaged or postponed in the wake of Hurricane Katrina. It has also acted as counsel for developers of the town of Lost Rabbit as well as those working on a number of rural land projects.

**The Lawyers:** Valued for being *"easy to work with,"* **Paul Gunn** also possesses *"excellent negotiating skills."* A *"highly numerate"* attorney, his in-depth understanding of housing tax credits ensures him a steady stream of mandates from the developers of multifamily-apartment projects. He also regularly assists companies involved in retail, office and condominium developments, as well as those dealing in timber and recreational land. According to sources, **William Smith** communicates well and has a *"likable personality"* while still being the *"most objective-driven lawyer in the state."* One client even likened him to a *"Jedi Master"* for his speed, knowledge and skill in negotiations. His grasp of real estate law extends to such things as securitized financing and complex zoning issues, and he recently acted as counsel to the developers of two major mall projects.

**Clients/Work Highlights:** The Park Companies; Ridgway Lane; BankPlus; One Capital Advisors; SouthTrust Bank; Fleet Morris Petroleum; Cress Realty Group and Neopolis Development.

# Leaders in Mississippi

### ADAMS, Joseph Lee
Phelps Dunbar LLP, Jackson
601 360 9708
adamsjo@phelps.com
*Recommended in Employment*
**Practice Areas:** Mr Adams is a Partner in the Labor and Employment Group in the Jackson office. He has extensive experience in litigating wage and hour collective actions. He practices in the areas of civil rights and Title VII, as well as the Age Discrimination in Employment Act and the Americans with Disabilities Act.
**Personal:** University of Mississippi, JD, cum laude, 1997; associate editor, Mississippi Law Journal. Mississippi State University, BBA, magna cum laude, 1994.

### ANDERSON, Reuben V
Phelps Dunbar LLP, Jackson
601 360 9339
andersor@phelps.com
*Recommended in Litigation*
**Practice Areas:** Mr Anderson, the first African-American Supreme Court Justice in Mississippi, is a Partner in the General Litigation Group in the Jackson office. He practices in the areas of commercial litigation, regulatory and governmental matters and gaming. In addition to his work at the firm, Mr Anderson has cultivated a professional resume spanning three decades of legal service. Key positions have included: Jamie L Whitten Chair of Law and Government at the University of Mississippi, Fall of 1995; Mississippi Supreme Court Justice, 1985-90.

**Personal:** University of Mississippi, JD, 1967. Tougaloo College, BA, 1964.

### ANDRESS, Scott
Balch & Bingham, Jackson
601 965 8160
sandress@balch.com
*Recommended in Corporate/Commercial*
**Practice Areas:** Gaming; litigation.
**Prof. Memberships:** American Bar Association; Mississippi Bar Association; Hinds County Bar Association; International Association of Gaming Attorneys.
**Career:** Scott Andress' practice focuses primarily on gaming law, corporate law, commercial transactions, commercial litigation, intellectual property and environmental law. Mr Andress began his career as a management information consultant in New Orleans, Louisiana, and Washington, DC. Along with the handling of general corporate, transactional, environmental, intellectual property and commercial litigation matters, Mr Andress' practice includes the regular representation of privately owned and publicly traded casino operators, gaming equipment manufacturers and distributors, and landowners in the following areas: gaming compliance, gaming permitting and approvals, gaming litigation.
**Personal:** Born: April 21, 1964; education: Tulane University (JD, cum laude, 1992); Louisiana State University (BS, 1986).

### AYERS, David
Watkins & Eager PLLC, Jackson
601 948 6470
*Recommended in Litigation*

### BANKS JR, Fred L
Phelps Dunbar LLP, Jackson
601 360 9356
banksf@phelps.com
*Recommended in Litigation*
**Practice Areas:** Mr Banks is a Partner in the General Litigation Group in the Jackson office. He is a former Presiding Justice of the Mississippi Supreme Court and retired from that position in October 2001. He was appointed to the Mississippi Supreme Court in 1991 and served on that court for 11 years. He served as a Circuit Judge in Hinds and Yazoo counties for six years before that. From 1976 until 1985, Mr Banks served in the Mississippi House of Representatives where he served as Chair of the Ethics Committee, a Judiciary Committee and the Legislative Black Caucus. Mr Banks also served as a Member of the Mississippi Board of Bar Admissions from 1978-80, and as a member of a number of advisory commissions at the state and federal level. He practices in the areas of commercial litigation, alternative dispute resolution, legislative and governmental relations and appellate law.
**Personal:** Howard University, JD, cum laude, 1968; Civil Rights and Book Reviews editor, Howard Law Journal; Howard University, BA in Administration (Accounting), 1965.

### BASS JR, Ross F
Phelps Dunbar LLP, Jackson
601 360 9332
bassr@phelps.com
*Recommended in Litigation*
**Practice Areas:** Mr Bass is the Managing Partner of the firm's Jackson office and the regional practice co-ordinator for the firm's Commercial Litigation Practice. He practices in the area of complex commercial and product liability litigation. Mr Bass has substantial experience in the representation of financial institutions and the litigation and settlement of class actions, mass tort and other complex matters. He was admitted in Mississippi and Georgia in 1973 and to the US Supreme Court in 1977.
**Personal:** University of Mississippi, JD, with honors, 1973; Editor-in-Chief, Mississippi Law Journal. Vanderbilt University; Belhaven College, BA, 1970.

### BUSH III, F M
Phelps Dunbar LLP, Tupelo
662 690 8136
bushm@phelps.com
*Recommended in Corporate/Commercial*
**Practice Areas:** Mr Bush is the Managing Partner in the Tupelo office. He concentrates in the areas of corporate and business law. He has provided corporate and business representation for many corporations, concentrating primarily in the industries of manufacturing, healthcare, and banking. Mr Bush has served as outside counsel to the largest hospital sys-

tem in Mississippi for over 20 years. In addition, he provides ongoing corporate counsel to approximately 20 business corporations in Mississippi and is local counsel to several large out-of-state public companies. He has represented out-of-state companies in locating or expanding facilities in Mississippi, particularly with a view toward maximizing tax and other incentives offered by the State of Mississippi. Mr Bush has also worked in the area of municipal finance, having served as underwriters' counsel, bond counsel, and trustees' counsel. He has represented both buyers and sellers in a variety of acquisition transactions involving public and private companies in taxable and tax-free transactions.

**Personal:** Harvard University, LLM, 1972; University of Mississippi, JD, 1969; Editor-in-Chief, Mississippi Law Journal. Brown University, BA, 1967.

### BYRD, Robert
Byrd & Wiser, Biloxi 228 432 8123
*Recommended in*
*Corporate/Commercial*

### CAMPBELL, Roy
Bradley Arant Rose & White LLP, Jackson 601 592 9934
rcampbell@bradleyarant.com
*Recommended in Litigation*
**Practice Areas:** Partner in general civil litigation, with emphasis in personal injury and commercial litigation.
**Prof. Memberships:** Admitted, Mississippi (1975) and Tennessee (1999). Fellow, American College of Trial Lawyers. Member, American Board of Trial Advocates, International Association of Defense Counsel, Defense Research Institute, Mississippi Defense Lawyers Association, Board of Governors of Fifth Circuit Bar Association, Mississippi and American Bar Associations.
**Career:** Joined Bradley Arant, 2003. Member, Litigation Practice Group.
**Personal:** Born July 3, 1950. University of Mississippi, JD, 1975; Vice-Chairman, Moot Court Board; Davidson College, BA, 1972.

### CANNADA, Barry
Butler, Snow, O'Mara, Stevens & Cannada, PLLC, Jackson 601 985 4535
barry.cannada@butlersnow.com
*Recommended in*
*Corporate/Commercial*
**Practice Areas:** Business planning, business structure and capitalization and mergers and acquisitions.
**Prof. Memberships:** The Mississippi Bar, National Lawyers Association, American Bar Association.
**Career:** He has extensive experience in various transactional advisory services and has represented numerous businesses in connection with mergers, acquisitions, capital formation, public and private offerings and general transactional advice; listed in 'The Best Lawyers in

America'; former consultant to national investment banking firm; President and general counsel of local, privately-held holding company.
**Personal:** The University of Mississippi, JD, cum laude, 1980 (Farley Award recipient for highest scholastic average in graduating class); BBA, magna cum laude, 1977.

### CANNADA, Don
Butler, Snow, O'Mara, Stevens & Cannada, PLLC, Jackson 601 985 4510
don.cannada@butlersnow.com
*Recommended in Real Estate*
**Practice Areas:** Real estate transactions and financing, commercial law and lending, mergers and acquisitions.
**Prof. Memberships:** The Mississippi Bar; Business Law, Real Property and Probate and Trust Sections of American Bar Association; officer of Tri-County Real Estate Association; International Council of Shopping Centers; American Land Title Association.
**Career:** Chair of Business Department; American College of Real Estate Lawyers; served as Chairman of the Mississippi College School of Law Annual Real Estate Seminar; listed in 'The Best Lawyers in America' and 'Who's Who Legal: USA Real Estate'.
**Personal:** Vanderbilt University, JD, 1978; The University of Mississippi, BBA, 1975.

### CHATHAM, Henry
Wise Carter Child & Caraway, Professional Association, Jackson 601 968 5500
*Recommended in*
*Corporate/Commercial*

### CLARK, Donald
Butler, Snow, O'Mara, Stevens & Cannada, PLLC, Jackson 601 985 4586
don.clark@butlersnow.com
*Recommended in*
*Corporate/Commercial*
**Practice Areas:** Municipal bonds, governmental affairs.
**Prof. Memberships:** Hinds County Bar Association, The Mississippi Bar, Mississippi Association of County Board Attorneys, American Bar Association, National Association of Bond Lawyers.
**Career:** Chairman of Butler Snow; former special assistant attorney general for Mississippi; served on Finance Committee of Governor's Commission on Recovery, Rebuilding and Renewal (following Hurricane Katrina, 2005); serves as bond counsel, underwriters' counsel and trustees' counsel to state and local government entities.
**Personal:** The University of Mississippi, JD, 1973; the University of Southern Mississippi, BS, 1971.

### CLEMENT JR, W Rodney
Brunini, Grantham, Grower & Hewes, PLLC, Jackson 601 960 6850
rclement@brunini.com
*Recommended in Real Estate*
**Practice Areas:** Real estate, land use, secured financing.
**Prof. Memberships:** American College of Real Estate Lawyers (Vice-Chair, Leasing Committee), American College of Mortgage Attorneys (Board of Regents), Joint Editorial Board for Uniform Real Property Acts, Best Lawyers in America (Real Estate).
**Career:** Admitted to The Mississippi Bar in 1983. Brunini, Grantham, Grower & Hewes, PLLC, 1983-present. President of Real Property Section of The Mississippi Bar, 2002-03.
**Publications:** Revised Article 9 and Real Property, 36 Real Property, Probate and Trust Journal 513 (Fall 2001)(co-author); Enforcing Security Interests in Personal Property in Mississippi, 67 Mississippi Law Journal 43 (Fall 1997).
**Personal:** BA, Millsaps College,1980; JD,Washington & Lee University, 1983.

### CORLEW, John
Watkins & Eager PLLC, Jackson 601 948 6470
*Recommended in Litigation*

### CRUTCHER JR, Pepper
Balch & Bingham, Jackson 601 965-8158
pcrutcher@balch.com
*Recommended in Employment*
**Practice Areas:** Labor and employment; litigation; antitrust; intellectual property.
**Prof. Memberships:** Mississippi Bar; Louisiana Bar Association; Federalist Society of Mississippi; Federalist Society for Law and Public Policy Studies; Fifth Circuit Bar Association.
**Career:** R Pepper Crutcher Jr for more than 20 years, has advised and represented employers in defense of their lawful discretion to hire, direct, and discharge their employees. This practice has involved him in continuing litigation in state and federal courts, predominantly in Mississippi and Louisiana, and administrative litigation and investigations conducted by the National Labor Relations Board. Pepper's regular practice includes the drafting and enforcement of confidential non-union employment dispute arbitration agreements, traditional arbitration of union contract grievances, and negotiation of traditional labor agreements. He also frequently presents continuing education programs for clients and industry groups and has testified before subcommittees of the Mississippi Legislature on related topics.
**Personal:** Born: October 12, 1957; education: University of Virginia (JD, 1982); University of Mississippi (BA, magna cum laude, 1979).

### DAVIS, Mark
Watkins Ludlam Winter & Stennis, P.A, Jackson 601 949 4900
*Recommended in Real Estate*

### DOVE, Luke
Dove and Chill, Jackson
601 352 0999
*Recommended in Litigation*

### DRINKWATER, Robert
Brunini, Grantham, Grower & Hewes, PLLC, Jackson
601 960 6852
bdrinkwa@brunini.com
*Recommended in*
*Corporate/Commercial*
**Practice Areas:** Corporations, mergers and acquisitions, securities, real estate, business entities, banking, finance and commercial transactions.
**Career:** Mr Drinkwater has specialized in commercial law since beginning practice in 1977. In recent years his practice has focused on banking, finance and commercial real estate.

### DRINKWATER, Wayne
Bradley Arant Rose & White LLP, Jackson 601 592 9911
wdrinkwater@bradleyarant.com
*Recommended in Litigation*
**Practice Areas:** Senior Partner, general civil litigation. Extensive experience in commercial litigation and appellate practice.
**Prof. Memberships:** Admitted, Mississippi (1974). Member, American College of Trial Lawyers; American Academy of Appellate Lawyers; American Board of Trial Advocates; American Law Institute.
**Career:** Joined Bradley Arant, 2001; Member, Executive Committee and Litigation Practice Group. Former law clerk to Chief Justice Warren E Burger, United States Supreme Court; and Chief Judge William C Keady, United States District Court for Northern District of Mississippi.
**Personal:** Born 20 February 1949. JD (summa cum laude), University of Mississippi, 1974, BA (summa cum laude), University of Mississippi, 1971.

### EHRHARDT, Herbert
Lewis Fisher Henderson Claxton & Mulroy LLP, Jackson 601 360 8444
*Recommended in Employment*

### EVANS, George
Wise Carter Child & Caraway, Professional Association, Jackson 601 968 5500
*Recommended in Litigation*

### FAIR, George
Watkins & Eager PLLC, Jackson 601 948 6470
*Recommended in*
*Corporate/Commercial*

**FORD, Barry W**
Baker, Donelson, Bearman, Caldwell &
Berkowitz, PC, Jackson
601 351 8925
bford@bakerdonelson.com
*Recommended in Litigation*
**Practice Areas:** Practice concentrated in
general civil litigation and white-collar
defense. Prior to joining Baker Donelson,
Judge Ford served three terms as Circuit
Court Judge for the First Circuit Court
District, the largest Circuit Court District
in Mississippi. During this time he served
for approximately five years as the Circuit
Judges' representative on the Board of
Governors, the governing body of all
state, county and youth court judges in
Mississippi.
**Prof. Memberships:** Member, Mississippi Bar Association, Magnolia Bar Association and Hinds County Bar Association.
**Career:** Licensed in Mississippi since
1979.

**FRIEDMAN, Gary E**
Phelps Dunbar LLP, Jackson
601 360 9355
friedmag@phelps.com
*Recommended in Employment*
**Practice Areas:** Mr Friedman is a Partner and practice co-ordinator of the
Labor and Employment Group in the
Jackson office. He is general counsel to
the Mississippi Municipal Liability Plan,
the Mississippi Municipal Workers' Compensation Group, and the Mississippi
Drug Testing Consortium. He has assisted public and private employers throughout the state in matters involving labor
and employment problems.
**Personal:** University of Mississippi, JD,
with distinction, 1982; articles editor,
Mississippi Law Journal; Phi Delta Phi.
Georgia Institute of Technology, BS in
Industrial Engineering, 1971.

**GALLOWAY, Robert**
Butler, Snow, O'Mara, Stevens & Cannada,
PLLC, Gulfport 228 575 3019
bob.galloway@butlersnow.com
*Recommended in Litigation*
**Practice Areas:** Product liability, commercial litigation, maritime litigation, professional liability defense, healthcare law.
**Prof. Memberships:** Harrison County
Bar Association, The Mississippi Bar,
Mississippi Defense Lawyers Association,
American Bar Association, Defense
Research Institute, Maritime Law Association of the United States, International
Association of Defense Counsel.
**Career:** Fellow of American College of
Trial Lawyers, past Chairperson of State
Committee, Fellow and past President of
The Mississippi Bar Foundation, Member of American Board of Trial Advocates
and past President of Mississippi Chapter, frequent law school lecturer, listed in
'The Best Lawyers in America'.
**Personal:** The University of Mississippi,
JD, 1967; BA, 1964.

**GENO, Craig**
Harris & Geno PLLC, Jackson
601 948 0048
*Recommended in
Corporate/Commercial*

**GIBBS, Robert**
Brunini, Grantham, Grower & Hewes,
PLLC, Jackson 601 960 6861
rgibbs@brunini.com
*Recommended in Litigation*
**Practice Areas:** Personal injury, mass
torts and professional product liability;
commercial litigation; environmental litigation; alternative dispute resolution
(ADR); white-collar criminal defense.
**Prof. Memberships:** Mississippi Bar;
Magnolia Bar Association; Hinds County
Bar Association; American Bar Association; National Bar Association; Bar Association of the Fifth Circuit, Governor
(President 2000-02); Charles Clark Chapter of the American Inns of Court (President 2000-02); Mississippi Bar Foundation, Fellow, (President 2004-05); Fellow
of the Mississippi Young Lawyers, President; American Bar Foundation, Fellow;
American College of Trial Lawyers, Fellow; ABA Site Accreditation Team Member; Mississippi Supreme Court appointee
to the Task Force on Gender Fairness;
Mississippi Supreme Court appointee to
the Commission of Bar Admission
Review; Mississippi Supreme Court Complaint Tribunal (1996-2004); Commissioner Mississippi Bar (2001-04).
**Career:** Robert has worked as staff attorney for Southeast Mississippi Legal Services, Assistant District Attorney for the
Eleventh Circuit District, and Deputy
Attorney General for the State of Mississippi. In 1991, Robert became Hinds
County Circuit Court Judge, a position
he held until 1998. In 1998 he joined the
Brunini firm, practicing areas including
alternative dispute resolution, criminal
litigation, mass tort litigation, product
liability and white-collar criminal
defense.
**Publications:** On Faculty Excellence in
Judicial Education, 1996, National Council of Juvenile and Family Court Judges,
Reno Nevada.
**Personal:** Tougaloo College (BS, cum
laude, 1975; University of Mississippi (JD,
1979); National Judicial College, Reno,
Nevada (Graduate 1991, 1993).

**GOODMAN, William**
Watkins & Eager PLLC, Jackson
601 948 6470
*Recommended in Litigation*

**GRAHAM, Collier**
Wise Carter Child & Caraway, Professional Association, Jackson
601 968 5500
*Recommended in Litigation*

**GRISHMAN, David**
Watkins Ludlam Winter & Stennis, P.A,
Jackson 601 949 4900
*Recommended in
Corporate/Commercial*

**GUNN, Paul**
Watkins & Eager PLLC, Jackson
601 948 6470
*Recommended in Real Estate*

**HAFTER, Jerome C**
Phelps Dunbar LLP, Jackson
601 360 9347
hafterj@phelps.com
*Recommended in
Corporate/Commercial*
**Practice Areas:** Mr Hafter is a Partner
in the Business Group in the Jackson
office. He practices in the areas of business and corporate law, agricultural law,
biotechnology, acquisition transactions,
bankruptcy, taxation, casinos and gaming
law, intellectual property licensing, commercial litigation and employment advice
and litigation. Mr Hafter served as a law
clerk to the Honorable Charles Clark,
United States Court of Appeals, Fifth Circuit in 1972-73. He is admitted to practice in Mississippi.
**Personal:** Yale University, JD, 1972; associate editor, Yale Law Journal. Oxford
University, MA, 1974, BA, first class honours, 1969. Rice University, BA, summa
cum laude, 1967. Chair, Mississippi
Board of Bar Admissions (1979-2002)
and National Conference of Bar Examiners (1998-99).

**HENEGAN, John**
Butler, Snow, O'Mara, Stevens & Cannada,
PLLC, Jackson 601 985 4530
john.henegan@butlersnow.com
*Recommended in Litigation*
**Practice Areas:** Antitrust and trade regulation, media defamation and privacy
defense, patent and intellectual property,
telecommunications, constitutional law,
complex commercial litigation.
**Prof. Memberships:** Antitrust, Litigation and Patent and Copyright Sections,
Communications Law Forum, American
Bar Association; Mississippi Bar Association; Federal Bar Association; Defense
Counsel Section, Media Law Resource
Center of New York.
**Career:** Commercial Litigation Practice
Group leader; President, Hinds County
Bar Association; executive assistant/chief
of staff, to former Mississippi Governor
William Winter; co-author of several law
review publications; listed 'The Best
Lawyers in America', 'Who's Who in
American Law'.
**Personal:** University of Mississippi, JD,
with honors, 1976; BA, 1972.

**HISE, Daniel G**
Butler, Snow, O'Mara, Stevens & Cannada,
PLLC, Jackson 601 985 4509
dan.hise@butlersnow.com
*Recommended in*

*Corporate/Commercial*
**Practice Areas:** Securities, gaming, corporate transactions.
**Prof. Memberships:** Business Law and
Gaming Law Sections of The Mississippi
Bar, Business Law section of American
Bar Association, International Association of Gaming Attorneys.
**Career:** Listed in 'The Best Lawyers in
America', founding Member and past
Chairman of Secretary of State's Business
Law Advisory Group, Mississippi liaison
to the ABA State Regulations of Securities
Committee, represents the two largest
casino operating companies, Mississippi
College School of Law's Outstanding
Alumnus of 1999.
**Personal:** Mississippi College, JD, 1985;
Tulane University, PhD, 1973; the University of California, Berkeley, BA, 1965.

**HODGE JR, E Clifton**
Phelps Dunbar LLP, Jackson
601 360 9331
hodgec@phelps.com
*Recommended in
Corporate/Commercial, Litigation*
**Practice Areas:** Mr Hodge is a Partner
in the General Litigation Group in the
Jackson office. He practices in the areas of
commercial litigation and business transactions. His litigation practice involves
many types of business disputes and corporate and securities matters, including
securities fraud, financial institution
issues, director and officer liability, and
breach of contracts. He frequently advises
corporate boards of directors concerning
duties and responsibilities of board
members, corporate procedure, and
board decisions concerning pending or
threatened litigation. He has provided
representation for and against securities
broker/dealers in arbitration proceedings
before panels designated by the National
Association of Securities Dealers and also
practices in the area of business and
finance, with an emphasis on mergers
and acquisitions.
**Personal:** Harvard University, LLM
(concentration on corporate law), 1970.
University of Mississippi, JD, 1967; assistant editor, Mississippi Law Journal. University of Mississippi, BBA in Accounting, 1964.

**IRBY, Peyton**
Watkins Ludlam Winter & Stennis, P.A,
Jackson 601 949 4900
*Recommended in Employment*

**JACOBS, Gina**
Watkins Ludlam Winter & Stennis, P.A,
Jackson 601 949 4900
*Recommended in
Corporate/Commercial*

## JONES, Christy

Butler, Snow, O'Mara, Stevens & Cannada, PLLC, Jackson 601 985 4523
christy.jones@butlersnow.com
*Recommended in Litigation, Products Liability*

**Practice Areas:** Drug and medical device litigation, product liability, professional liability, toxic and mass tort.

**Prof. Memberships:** Fellow, American College of Trial Lawyers; American Board of Trial Advocates; International Association of Defense Counsel; Defense Counsel Trial Academy; Trial Attorneys of America; American Bar Association; Mississippi Bar; Mississippi Defense Lawyers Association.

**Career:** Chair of Litigation Department; Fellow, American Bar Association Foundation; listed in 'The Best Lawyers in America,' 'Who's Who Among International Product Liability Lawyers'; former Chair of Drug and Device Committee of the Defense Research Institute; frequent CLE presenter.

**Personal:** University of Arkansas, JD, with high honors, 1977; BA, 1974.

## JONES, Walker

Baker, Donelson, Bearman, Caldwell & Berkowitz, PC, Jackson
601 351 2413
wjones@bakerdonelson.com
*Recommended in Litigation*

**Practice Areas:** Co-Chair of Baker Donelson's Product Liability/Tort Group. Practice concentrated in insurance, commercial and product liability litigation. Extensive experience handling mass tort defense, construction law and chemical/toxic tort litigation.

**Prof. Memberships:** American, Mississippi, Texas and Tennessee Bar Associations (Member, sections on litigation, public contract law, tort and insurance practice). Member, Trial Attorneys of America, The American Board of Trial Advocates and President 2005-06 of its Mississippi Chapter, International Association of Defense Counsel and Maritime Law Association of the United States.

**Career:** Licensed in Mississippi since 1973, Texas since 1996 and Tennessee since 1997.

## KAUFMAN, David

Brunini, Grantham, Grower & Hewes, PLLC, Jackson 601 960 6873
dkaufman@brunini.com
*Recommended in Litigation*

**Practice Areas:** General civil litigation, including complex business and mass tort cases, antitrust, toxic exposure, business torts, product liability, and premises liability.

**Prof. Memberships:** American College of Trial Lawyers; American Board of Trial Advocates; International Association of Defense Counsel; Hinds County Bar Association (secretary).

**Career:** He has been practicing litigation

exclusively since joining the Brunini firm in 1978.

**Publications:** He has spoken at a number of trial practice and toxic exposure seminars and has been an invited lecturer at a number of trial practice classes at area law schools.

**Personal:** University of Mississippi (BBA, 1975); University of Mississippi (JD, 1978).

## KRUTZ, Fred

Forman Perry Watkins Krutz & Tardy LLP, Jackson 601 960 8600
fred@fpwk.com
*Recommended in Litigation*

**Practice Areas:** Mr Krutz has many years of experience in defending thousands of mass tort and multiple plaintiff cases in state and federal courts, including asbestos, silica, noise-induced hearing loss, personal injuries from alleged pollution of air and surface waters, and consumer finance cases; He also has extensive experience in defending multi-defendant litigation (MDL) cases, including asbestos, silica, and pedicle screw cases.

**Prof. Memberships:** Served on the Mississippi Law Journal, Editorial Board; The Mississippi Bar.

**Career:** Founding Partner of Forman Perry Watkins Krutz & Tardy, LLP, 1986; Butler, Snow, O'Mara, Stevens & Cannada – associate (1978-82), Partner (1982-86).

**Publications:** Silicosis: Explaining the Inconsistency Between Declining Public Health Statistics and the Epidemic in Litigation, Chest 128, Suppl. 4:2145, 2005; MEALEY'S LITIGATION REPORT: Silica, Commentary - In The Wake Of Silica MDL 1553, Vol. 4, No. 5 (January 2006); Federal Jurisdiction - Civil Rights Jurisdiction Under 28 USC §1349(3) Not Available When Equitable Monetary Relief, Sought Under 42 USC §1983, Would Stem Directly From Municipal Funds, Miss L J, Vol. 47 (1976).

**Personal:** Graduated from University of Mississippi Law School, December 1977 with highest honors; admitted to the Bar in 1978; Received the Phi Delta Phi Award for the outstanding law school graduate in 1977; he was Chairman of the Defendants' Steering Committee in the Silica MDL 1553 in Corpus Christi, TX, which litigation ended with an historic order and opinion by Judge Janis Jack as reported in numerous media, including the New York Times, Fortune Magazine, and The Wall Street Journal.

## LATHAM, William Larry

Latham & Burwell PLLC, Ridgeland
601 981 4470
*Recommended in Litigation*

## LAZARUS, Robert

Watkins Ludlam Winter & Stennis, P.A, Jackson 601 949 4900
*Recommended in Corporate/Commercial*

## MARTIN, David

Watkins Ludlam Winter & Stennis, P.A, Jackson 601 949 4900
*Recommended in Corporate/Commercial*

## MCDANIEL JR, Dan M

Phelps Dunbar LLP, Jackson
601 360 9367
mcdaniel@phelps.com
*Recommended in Corporate/Commercial*

**Practice Areas:** Mr McDaniel manages the firm's Gaming Practice in Mississippi, Louisiana, Texas and Florida. He is a Partner in the firm's Jackson office. Currently President for the International Association of Gaming Attorneys, he represents both domestic and international clients (including casinos, manufacturers, distributors, lessors, shareholders, officers, directors, key employees and other persons) before gaming authorities with regard to licensing, registration, findings of suitability, transfers of ownership, work permits, patron disputes, investigations, disciplinary proceedings and other regulatory matters. He has also represented clients in several other states regarding proposed gaming legislation and has testified as an expert witness before numerous legislative committees.

**Personal:** University of Mississippi, JD, 1973. University of Southern Mississippi, BS, 1971.

## MENDENHALL, William

McGlinchey Stafford, PLLC, Jackson
601 960 8400
bmendenhall@mcglinchey.com
*Recommended in Corporate/Commercial*

**Practice Areas:** Partner in the Business Section concentrating in corporate practice, business transactions, commercial real estate and insurance regulatory matters.

**Prof. Memberships:** The American Bar Association, the Hinds County Bar Association, and the Mississippi Bar.

**Career:** Admitted to the Mississippi Bar in 1984. Former Chariman of Mississippi Law Institute. In 1993, appointed by Secretary of State Dick Molpus to the Secretary of State's Business Law Advisory Group and currently serves as Chairman of Corporate Laws Subcommittee.

**Personal:** Received a JD (cum laude) in 1984, and a BBA (magna cum laude) in 1980 from the University of Mississippi. Named in leading US legal publication.

## MILAM, Kenneth

Watkins & Eager PLLC, Jackson
601 948 6470
*Recommended in Employment*

## MOCKBEE, David

Mockbee Hall & Drake, Jackson
601 353 0035
*Recommended in Litigation*

## MOELLER JR, Armin J

Balch & Bingham, Jackson
601 965 8156
amoeller@balch.com
*Recommended in Employment*

**Practice Areas:** Labor and employment; healthcare; litigation; technology.

**Prof. Memberships:** Mississippi Defense Lawyers Association; Mississippi Bar; American Bar Association Developing Labor Law Committee; College of Labor and Employment Law.

**Career:** Armin J Moeller, Jr's practice concentrates on labor relations and the defense of adverse employment decisions; litigation; drafting and negotiating contracts, including information technology project agreements; and litigation cliams against information technology companies. Mr Moeller represents employers in maintaining non-union status; collective bargaining negotiations and arbitration; race, sex, religion, age, disability, sexual/workplace harassment discrimination and retaliation claims; handling EEOC, NLRB, OSHA and other administrative claims through judicial process; drafting employment, severance, noncompetition and confidentiality contracts; and affirmative action and OFCCP compliance. Mr Moeller has been listed in 'The Best Lawyers' in America since 1989.

**Personal:** Born: June 18, 1947; education: Louisiana State University (JD, Phi Alpha Delta, 1972); Tulane University (BA, 1989).

## MUNFORD, Luther T

Phelps Dunbar LLP, Jackson
601 360 9364
munfordl@phelps.com
*Recommended in Litigation*

**Practice Areas:** Mr Munford works in the General Litigation Practice Group in the Jackson office. He handles appeals and represents news media clients. He clerked for Judge Paul H Roney, US Court of Appeals, Fifth Circuit, from 1976-78; and to Justice Harry A Blackmun, US Supreme Court, from 1978-79. Prior to joining Phelps Dunbar, he was a Partner at another Jackson law firm and taught constitutional law and other subjects full time for three years at Mississippi College School of Law. He still teaches an Appellate Practice and Procedure course as an Adjunct Professor at Mississippi College School of Law.

**Personal:** University of Virginia, JD, 1976; Oxford University, BA, 1973; Princeton University, AB, 1971.

## O'MARA, James W

Phelps Dunbar LLP, Jackson
601 360 9720
omaraj@phelps.com
*Recommended in Corporate/Commercial*

**Practice Areas:** Mr O'Mara is a Senior Partner in the Business Group in the

Jackson office. He practices in the areas of bankruptcy and creditors' rights, loan workouts, secured lending, commercial litigation and business transactions.
**Personal:** University of Mississippi, JD, with distinction, 1967; Editor-in-Chief, Mississippi Law Journal; Phi Delta Phi; Phi Kappa Phi; Omicron Delta Kappa. University of Mississippi, BA, 1962.

### PAINTER, William S

Baker, Donelson, Bearman, Caldwell & Berkowitz, PC, Jackson
601 351 2425
wpainter@bakerdonelson.com
*Recommended in Corporate/Commercial*

**Practice Areas:** Practice concentrated in corporate transactions, tax and healthcare restructuring. Extensive experience in employee benefits and deferred compensation; federal, state and local taxation; securities and trusts and estates.
**Prof. Memberships:** Fellow, American College of Trust and Estate Counsel. Fellow, American College of Tax Counsel. Former Chair, Mississippi Secretary of State's Task Force on Business Law Reform. Former Chair, Mississippi Secretary of State's Business Law Advisory Group. Member, American, Mississippi and Hinds County Bar Associations.
**Career:** Licensed in Mississippi since 1974 and US Tax Court since 1975.

### PERRY, Alan W

Forman Perry Watkins Krutz & Tardy LLP, Jackson 601 960 8600
aperry@fpwk.com
*Recommended in Litigation*

**Practice Areas:** Mr Perry is involved in a wide variety of complex commercial and corporate litigation, including disputes related to environmental matters, trade secrets, antitrust, banking, public utilities, professional liability of accountants and lawyers, and the obligations of corporate directors and officers. He frequently advises corporate boards of directors on corporate governance matters and potential litigation.
**Prof. Memberships:** Member, Lawyers Advisory Committee, United States Court of Appeals, Fifth Circuit; Former member, Standing Committee of Rules and Procedure of the Judicial Conference of the United States.
**Career:** Clerked for Judge Charles Clark, United States Court of Appeals, Fifth Circuit (1972-73); Butler, Snow, O'Mara, Stevens & Cannada - associate/Partner (1973-86); Founding Partner of Forman Perry Watkins Krutz & Tardy, 1986.
**Publications:** 'Partnerships and Tax Shelters: The Crane Rule Goes Public', 27 'Tax Law Review' 525 (1972); 'The Model Business Corporation Act: Does the Mississippi Version Lime the Bushes?', 46 Miss L J 371 (1975) (with E Clifton Hodge).
**Personal:** Awarded JD, magna cum

laude, Harvard Law School, 1972, receiving the Fay Diploma as first in class. Served as editor and senior editor, Harvard Law Review. Awarded BBA (Accountancy), summa cum laude, University of Mississippi, 1969. Awarded Silver Medal for second highest grade in the United States on CPA Examination. Director of BancorpSouth, Inc.; Trustee of The Robert M Hearin Foundation and The Robert M Hearin Support Foundation.

### PURDY, William R

Purdy & Germany PLLC, Jackson
601 969 4140
*Recommended in Litigation*

### REED, William N (Bill)

Baker, Donelson, Bearman, Caldwell & Berkowitz, PC, Jackson 601 351 2410
wreed@bakerdonelson.com
*Recommended in Litigation*

**Practice Areas:** Practice concentrated in products liability, toxic tort, insurance and franchise litigation. Mr Reed has tried commercial and tort cases in federal and state courts in 10 states and has handled appeals in Mississippi and four federal circuits.
**Prof. Memberships:** Fellow, Mississippi Bar Foundation. Member, Defense Research Institute, Mississippi Defense Lawyers Association, Bar Association of the Fifth Federal Circuit and International Association of Defense Counsel. Board of Directors, Mississippi World Trade Center.
**Career:** Licensed in Mississippi since 1977.

### ROSENBLATT, Stephen W

Butler, Snow, O'Mara, Stevens & Cannada, PLLC, Jackson 601 985 4504
steve.rosenblatt@butlersnow.com
*Recommended in Corporate/Commercial*

**Practice Areas:** Bankruptcy; creditors' rights; commercial litigation; loan workouts and restructuring; commercial transactions; corporate law; alternative dispute resolution.
**Prof. Memberships:** The Mississippi Bar; American Bar Association; American Bankruptcy Institute; Association of Insolvency & Restructuring Advisors; Turnaround Management Association.
**Career:** Chairman, Butler Snow (1998-2005); 'The Best Lawyers in America' 10+ years; 'Who's Who Legal USA: Insolvency & Restructuring 2006'; lecturer and panelist, various CLE programs; Founding Member and past President, Mississippi Bankruptcy Conference; Fellow, The Mississippi Bar Foundation; former President, Mississippi Young Lawyers Association and Jackson Young Lawyers Association.
**Personal:** University of Mississippi, JD, with honors, 1975; Vanderbilt University, BA, 1970.

### SAMS, L F

Mitchell, McNutt & Sams PA, Tupelo
662 842 3871
*Recommended in Litigation*

### SHAPLEY, Christopher

Brunini, Grantham, Grower & Hewes, PLLC, Jackson 601 960 6875
cshapley@brunini.com
*Recommended in Litigation*

**Practice Areas:** General civil litigation, including environmental, pharmaceutical, business, healthcare, mass torts and personal injury.
**Prof. Memberships:** American College of Trial Lawyers (1995); American Board of Trial Advocates (2000); International Association of Defense Counsel (2001).
**Career:** He has been practicing litigation exclusively since joining the Brunini firm in 1976.
**Publications:** 'ABA Antitrust Law Sections, State Antitrust Practice and Statutes (1990)', Chapter 26 - Mississippi, p 26-1.
**Personal:** Mississippi State University (BS cum laude 1973); University of Mississippi (JD 1976).

### SHEPHERD, Thomas

Watkins Ludlam Winter & Stennis, P.A, Jackson 601 949 4900
*Recommended in Corporate/Commercial*

### SILER JR, W Thomas

Phelps Dunbar LLP, Jackson
601 360 9357
silert@phelps.com
*Recommended in Employment*

**Practice Areas:** Mr Siler is a Partner and the regional practice co-ordinator of the firm's Labor and Employment Group. Since 1983, his practice has been concentrated in the representation of management in labor and employment law matters, and in the defense of civil rights issues. Among other matters, Mr Siler has represented employers in Title VII, ADEA, ADA, FLSA, FMLA, OSHA, ERISA, as well as matters involving the NLRA and LMRA. He also has handled a variety of issues arising under the United States Constitution. During almost 20 years of practice he has litigated numerous jury trials in the Federal Court system and arbitrated many disputes regarding the interpretation of collective bargaining agreements.
**Personal:** University of Mississippi, JD, with distinction, 1983; assistant editor, Mississippi Law Journal; Millsaps College, BBA, 1979; past President of the Mississippi Defense Lawyer's Association and Vice-Chairman of the IADC's Employment Law Committee.

### SMITH, Taylor

The Kullman Firm A Professional Law Corporation, Columbus 662 244 8824
*Recommended in Employment*

### SMITH, William

Watkins & Eager PLLC, Jackson
601 948 6470
*Recommended in Real Estate*

### STEPHENSON, Paul

Watkins & Eager PLLC, Jackson
601 948 6470
*Recommended in Litigation*

### TAYLOR, Zachary

Watkins Ludlam Winter & Stennis, P.A, Jackson 601 949 4900
*Recommended in Corporate/Commercial*

### THOMAS, Stephen

Bradley Arant Rose & White LLP, Jackson 601 592 9912
sthomas@bradleyarant.com
*Recommended in Litigation*

**Practice Areas:** Complex civil litigation. Extensive experience in agricultural litigation, intellectual property, toxic tort, environmental and products liability litigation and white-collar crime.
**Prof. Memberships:** Admitted, Mississippi (1973). Fellow, American College of Trial Lawyers. American Board of Trial Advocates (Advocate). International Association of Defense Counsel. Defense Research Institute. Mississippi and American Bar Association.
**Career:** Joined Bradley Arant, 2001. Member, Litigation Practice Group.
**Personal:** Born December 17, 1948. JD, University of Mississippi, 1973. BA, University of Mississippi, 1970.

### TOHILL, Jim

Watkins Ludlam Winter & Stennis, P.A, Jackson 601 949 4900
*Recommended in Real Estate*

### ULMER, Michael

Watkins & Eager PLLC, Jackson
601 948 6470
*Recommended in Litigation*

### WALKER, Jeffrey A

Butler, Snow, O'Mara, Stevens & Cannada, PLLC, Jackson 601 985 4558
jeff.walker@butlersnow.com
*Recommended in Employment*

**Practice Areas:** Collective bargaining, labor arbitration, union organizing campaigns, unfair labor practice charges, preventive labor relations, fair employment practices litigation, wage and hour, non-competition, trade secret litigation.
**Prof. Memberships:** Labor and Employment Law Section of The Mississippi Bar, Mississippi Defense Lawyers Association, Labor and Employment and Litigation sections of American Bar Association, Defense Research Institute.
**Career:** Listed in 'The Best Lawyers in America', Fellow of College of Labor and Employment Lawyers, frequent speaker at labor and employment seminars, presentations at Mississippi Manufacturers Association and Mississippi Bankers Association seminars.

**Personal:** The University of Mississippi, JD, 1978; University of Wisconsin-Madison, BS, 1975.

## WALLACE, Barbara
Wise Carter Child & Caraway, Professional Association, Jackson
601 968 5500
*Recommended in Employment*

## WALLACE, Michael B
Phelps Dunbar LLP, Jackson
601 352 2300
wallacem@phelps.com
*Recommended in Litigation*
**Practice Areas:** Mr Wallace is a Partner in the General Litigation Group in the Jackson office. He was admitted to the Mississippi Bar in 1976. In 1999, he served as Special Impeachment Counsel to Senate Majority Leader Lott for the impeachment trial of President Clinton. His practice is concentrated in commercial litigation at the trial and appellate levels. He also has wide experience in litigating constitutional claims and election disputes. Prior to joining Phelps Dunbar, Mr Wallace served as a law clerk to Justice Harry G Walker, Supreme Court of Mississippi, from 1976-77, and to Associate Justice William H Rehnquist, Supreme Court of the United States, from 1977-78. From 1980-83 he served as counsel to Trent Lott, who was then Republican Whip of the United States House of Representatives. He is general counsel of the Mississippi Republican Party.
**Personal:** University of Virginia, JD, 1976; Law Review; Order of the Coif. Harvard University, BA in Government, cum laude, 1973.

## WEEMS, Walter S
Brunini, Grantham, Grower & Hewes, PLLC, Jackson 601 960 6863
wweems@brunini.com
*Recommended in Corporate/Commercial*
**Practice Areas:** Corporate; mergers and acquisitions; real estate.
**Prof. Memberships:** American Bar Association; Mississippi Bar.
**Career:** With Brunini Grantham Grower & Hewes from 1978-present.
**Personal:** JD from Vanderbilt Law School 1977 (first honors; Order of Coif). BA from Vanderbilt University 1974 (magna cum laude; Phi Beta Kappa).

## WELCH, W Scott
Baker, Donelson, Bearman, Caldwell & Berkowitz, PC, Jackson 601 351 2440
swelch@bakerdonelson.com
*Recommended in Litigation*
**Practice Areas:** Commercial transportation, insurance coverage, environmental, commercial and product liability litigation.
**Prof. Memberships:** Fellow - American College of Trial Lawyers, The Mississippi Bar, American Board of Trial Advocates, American Bar Association, International Association of Defense Counsel, Trucking Industry Defense Association, Trial Attorneys of America, Bar of United States Supreme Court.
**Career:** Past President of American Board of Trial Advocates and The Mississippi Bar, State Delegate - ABA House of Delegates, listed in 'The Best Lawyers in America,' (10 years), 40+ years' trial and appellate experience.
**Personal:** The University of Mississippi, LLB; The University of the South, BA, cum laude.

## WILSON, Stephen M
Phelps Dunbar LLP, Jackson
601 360 9701
wilsons@phelps.com
*Recommended in Corporate/Commercial*
**Practice Areas:** Mr Wilson is a Partner and the practice co-ordinator of the Business Group in the Jackson office. His practice consists largely of corporate transactional work, business and tax planning, and lending transactions. He represents buyers and sellers in asset purchase, stock purchase, and merger transactions; corporations with ongoing contractual, tax, and business planning needs; and financial institutions in corporate and regulatory matters, and commercial lending transactions. Mr Wilson also serves as bond counsel, trustee counsel, issuer's counsel, and company counsel on a number of bond issues, both taxable and nontaxable, including state economic development incentive financing and planning issues.
**Personal:** New York University, LLM in Taxation, 1992; University of Mississippi, JD, 1991; Northeast Louisiana University, BBA in Marketing, 1982.

# BRUNINI, GRANTHAM, GROWER & HEWES, PLLC

## THE FIRM

**Managing Partner:** Walter S Weems
**Number of partners:** 42
**Number of other lawyers:** 27

**FIRM OVERVIEW:** A singular focus on Mississippi makes the Brunini firm unique among many of the law firms with offices in Mississippi and its capital city, Jackson. The firm was founded in the 1880s, and it has long been recognized as being at the top of the legal profession in Mississippi. In addition to being a well established firm, the Brunini firm is also dynamic, having made significant strides towards achieving the diversity necessary to reflect Mississippi's populace. The firm's clientele includes numerous Fortune 500 companies, as well as many of Mississippi's largest employers, its largest bank and its largest health insurer. The Brunini firm knows and understands Mississippi's legal and business environment.

## MAIN AREAS OF PRACTICE:

**General & Commercial Litigation:** Chambers USA recognizes Brunini trial lawyers Chris Shapley, Robert Gibbs and David Kaufman as three of the best litigators in Mississippi. Brunini's trial lawyers handle a wide range of matters, including litigation involving complex commercial transactions, mass torts, environmental issues, pharmaceutical products, consumer fraud, construction disputes, employment discrimination, products liability, medical malpractice, nursing homes, breach of contract, antitrust, securities fraud, business torts, taxation, and white collar crime. The firm's trial lawyers have extensive experience in state and federal trial and appellate courts in Mississippi and have served as lead counsel in some of Mississippi's largest and most complex litigation.

**Environmental Law & Litigation:** The firm's Environmental Practice Group is acknowledged as a statewide leader. One of the firm's attorneys currently serves as chair of the environmental section of the Mississippi Bar. The firm's attorneys have extensive experience in both environmental litigation and regulatory proceedings and have defended numerous enforcement actions instituted by the United States Department of Justice, Region IV of the Environmental Protection Agency, and the Bureau of Pollution Control. The firm has also obtained numerous environmental permits for its clients in proceedings before the Mississippi Environmental Quality Permit Board. The firm also has extensive experience in defending multi-plaintiff and class action lawsuits alleging harm from releases of hazardous substances, hazardous waste, and petroleum products.

**Healthcare Law & Litigation:** The firm has a comprehensive healthcare practice, representing hospitals, physician groups, nursing homes, and other healthcare providers. The firm has broad experience in administrative proceedings and litigation concerning Certificates of Need, Medicaid fraud, nursing home care, fraud and abuse-Stark II, private inurement, and other legal issues facing the healthcare industry.

**Business & Commercial:** Chambers USA recognizes Robert Drinkwater, Walter Weems and Rodney Clement as leading Mississippi business lawyers. Other Brunini business lawyers are recognized among their peers as leaders in their respective areas of business expertise. The firm's expertise includes general corporate law, mergers and acquisitions, public and industrial development financing and tax incentives, securities regulation, banking, real estate transactions, insurance regulation, syndication, estate planning, and corporate and personal taxation.

**Public Industrial Development & Tax Incentives:** The firm's representation in tax-exempt financing has included bonds issued by the State of Mississippi and various instrumentalities of the State, municipalities, counties, junior and senior colleges, and public school districts. In addition, the firm has extensive experience in state and local industrial and economic development financing with state and federal tax incentives.

## HEAD OFFICE

**MISSISSIPPI**
248 East Capitol Street, **Jackson**, MS 39201
**Tel:** 601 948 3101   **Fax:** 601 960 6902
**Website:** www.brunini.com

## CONTACTS

| | |
|---|---|
| **General & Commercial Litigation** | Chris Shapley, Robert Gibbs |
| | David Kaufman |
| **Business & Commercial** | Robert Drinkwater, Walter Weems |
| | Rodney Clement, Leigh Allen |
| **Taxation** | Louis Fuller, Jody Varner |
| **Labor & Employment** | Anne Sanders, Stephen Carmody |
| **Construction** | Ron Yarbrough, Samuel Kelly |
| **Public Industrial Development & Tax Incentives** | Wilson Montjoy |
| | Louis Fuller |
| **Environmental Law & Litigation** | John Milner, Trudy Fisher |
| | Chris Shapley, David Kaufman |
| **Healthcare Law & Litigation** | Edmund L Brunini, Jr, Chris Shapley, |
| | John E Wade, Kathryn R Gilchrist |
| **Public Utilities & Telecommunications** | Wilson Montjoy, |
| | James L Halford, Charles L McBride, Jr |

**Public Utilities & Telecommunications:** The firm serves as corporate counsel to the largest privately held wireless carrier in the United States. Its practices extensively before the Mississippi Public Service Commission, representing a number of intrastate pipeline companies and telecommunications, gas, water and sewer companies. The firm has served as counsel in administrative proceedings and litigation regarding rates and service and application for certificates of public convenience and necessity for the construction of electric generation facilities, natural gas transmission and distribution facilities, underground natural gas storage facilities and telecommunications facilities.

**Labor & Employment:** The firm's labor and employment attorneys represent employers' interests both in litigation and in a broad array of state and federal administrative settings. In addition, the firm's employment attorneys advise and assist employers with a variety of other employment issues.

**Construction Law & Litigation:** The firm's construction attorneys have a vast range of experience representing owners, contractors, subcontractors, and sureties in the construction industry. Specifically, the firm's experience includes drafting and negotiating contract agreements, preparing and presenting construction claims, bid protests, business consultation, project workouts and mediation, arbitration or litigation of claims and disputes which arise in the course of construction projects.

**CLIENTS:** Trustmark National Bank; Northrup Grumman (Ingalls Shipbuilding); Blue Cross Blue Shield of Mississippi; Kerr-McGee Corporation; Purdue Pharma, L.P.; Cendant Corporation; Cellular South, Inc.; St. Dominic Health Services, Inc.; CenterPoint Energy; Choctaw Maid Farms, Inc.; Textron; Beverly Enterprises; Duke Energy; and El Paso Energy.

# BUTLER, SNOW, O'MARA, STEVENS & CANADA PLLC

## THE FIRM

**Firm Chair:** Donald Clark, Jr

**Number of partners:** 76
**Number of other lawyers:** 75

**FIRM OVERVIEW:** For 50 years, Butler Snow has been a leading presence in the field of law. With offices in Jackson, Mississippi, on the Gulf Coast of Mississippi, and in Memphis, Tennessee, Butler Snow provides legal services to many of the nation's leading businesses, as well as to individuals. Butler Snow represents a variety of clients across a multitude of industry sectors in both the litigation and business practice areas.

## MAIN AREAS OF PRACTICE:

**Appellate & Written Advocacy:** Since the firm's inception, Butler Snow has enjoyed an extensive federal and state appellate practice, often involving cases raising novel or complex legal issues, in all fields of law.

**Commercial Litigation:** Butler Snow's Commercial Litigation Group is led by some of the firm's most experienced trial lawyers. Although the firm's size and formidable litigation resources attract a significant number of representations in large commercial disputes involving complex issues such as antitrust, basic contract and business dissolution matters continue to be a significant part of the commercial litigation practice.

**Health Litigation:** Butler Snow's Health Litigation Group regularly represents pharmaceutical and medical device manufacturers and professionals, providers and businesses in the healthcare field on a national, regional and statewide basis, including physicians and medical practices, hospitals and hospital systems and companies providing products and services. In addition to product liability and medical negligence, this group is involved with government compliance, regulatory and industry counseling and defense.

**Product Liability:** Butler Snow has a long history of representing both manufacturers and sellers in product liability litigation in the state and federal courts of the United States and abroad. Butler Snow attorneys have experience that permits them to work equally well with the design engineers and the operators in the field. From dioxin to PCBs, HCL, agricultural chemicals and other substances, Butler Snow has successfully defended toxic exposure cases across the United States. The firm has tried many cases to verdict, and trials range from one plaintiff to several thousands.

**General Tort, Insurance & Transportation Litigation:** Butler Snow's General Litigation Group represents a wide variety of clients in litigated matters in both state and federal court, including personal injury, insurance coverage/bad faith, trucking and motor home matters.

**Government Compliance & White Collar Crime:** A former US attorney leads Butler Snow's criminal and government compliance team that works regularly with other groups to provide counseling and defense to corporate clients and individuals.

**Business Services:** The firm's business attorneys are regularly engaged in offering counsel regarding the formation and operation of and transactions involving corporations and other business entities. Clients include entities of widely varying sizes and sophistication.

**Financial Services:** Butler Snow's Banking and Financial Services Group serves a large and growing number of financial services providers throughout Mississippi and the nation. Butler Snow attorneys have wide-ranging experience as in-house bank lawyers and with the Comptroller of the Currency. They serve as counsel to the Mississippi Regulatory Compliance Group and the Mid-South Regulatory Compliance Group (coalitions of some 40 banks and 34 banks, respectively).

**Government & Administrative:** Butler Snow has extensive experience in representing governmental entities and officials in a variety of matters at the local, state and federal levels of government. Further, the firm regularly assists private clients in solving problems through the regulatory process and legislative process.

## HEAD OFFICE

**MISSISSIPPI**
AmSouth Plaza, 17th Floor, 210 East Capitol Street,
PO Box 22567, **Jackson**, MS 39225
**Tel:** 601 948 5711   **Fax:** 601 985 4500
**Email:** info@butlersnow.com
**Website:** www.butlersnow.com

The firm's lawyers are able to provide effective representation to both public and private clients in government related matters due to their actual experience in government service and their representation of governmental entities and officials.

**Health & Technology:** Butler Snow's Health Group regularly represents a wide variety of professionals, providers and businesses in the healthcare field on a national, regional and statewide basis. As relates to the firm's Technology Practice, Butler Snow's attorneys are experienced in computer software and technology licensing, electronic commerce, multimedia issues and technology transfer issues.

**Labor & Employment:** Butler Snow represents private and public sector employers in every aspect of the employment relationship. The firm represents clients in employment-related matters throughout the United States and adheres to a philosophy that preventive advice and action are the most efficient means for resolving and preventing workplace disputes.

**Public Finance:** Butler Snow enjoys a comprehensive and diverse public finance practice ranging from all forms of state and municipal bonds and obligations to the full complement of techniques available to finance healthcare, industrial/economic development, exempt facilities, utilities and housing.

**Real Estate:** Butler Snow has maintained a substantial and diverse real estate practice since the inception of the firm. The firm provides a full range of services to clients, from the initial purchase of real property to the development, financing and leasing stages and through the sale or syndication of such real property.

**Trust & Estate:** Butler Snow advises fiduciaries involved in the administration of estates and trusts. Two of the firm's attorneys in this practice area have been honored by induction into the prestigious American College of Trust and Estate Counsel.

**CLIENTS:** Butler Snow represents a wide range of clients which includes pharmaceutical companies, healthcare providers, insurance companies, government and government-related entities, transportation and financial services organizations.

**INTERNATIONAL WORK:** Butler Snow attorneys have represented clients in trade matters before the US International Trade Commission, the US Department of Commerce and have been involved in disputes in the World Trade Organization. The firm's network of foreign associates enables them to coordinate their clients' legal and regulatory needs. Butler Snow also serves as national counsel for some clients whose businesses are conducted internationally and has represented clients in various parts of the world.

**BUTLER, SNOW,
O'MARA, STEVENS
& CANNADA, PLLC**

ATTORNEYS AT LAW

# FORMAN PERRY WATKINS KRUTZ & TARDY LLP

## THE FIRM

**Firm Management:** Executive Committee: Richard L Forman, Walter G Watkins Jr, Fred Krutz, Steven M Hendrix
**Number of partners:** 29
**Number of other lawyers:** 90

**FIRM OVERVIEW:** Forman Perry Watkins Krutz & Tardy LLP is a general civil practice firm with a strong emphasis in tort, environmental and commercial litigation. Founded in Jackson, Mississippi in 1986, Forman Perry has grown to more than 100 lawyers in four cities. Forman Perry litigates throughout the United States for both local and national clients, handling virtually every type of litigation from simple negligence claims to complex commercial litigation and mass tort claims involving thousands of plaintiffs. Lawyers within the firm also provide a wide spectrum of legal services in a number of other areas, including corporate law, commercial lending, bankruptcy, securities, commercial real estate, public utilities, antitrust and administrative law. Forman Perry utilizes the latest technology to handle all aspects of litigation, from discovery through trial, and maintains an extensive medical library and expert deposition depository. The firm has a strong belief in obtaining the best possible results for its clients at the lowest possible cost, and all management decisions are made with that goal in mind.

## MAIN AREAS OF PRACTICE:

### LITIGATION

**Class Actions:** Forman Perry's attorneys have extensive experience in class action litigation, litigating the issues of class certification, class and merits discovery, and negotiating and obtaining approval for class settlements. Forman Perry's attorneys also have extensive experience in appellate practice involving all aspects of class action litigation.

**Commercial Disputes:** Attorneys in the firm are experienced in handling a full range of complex commercial disputes, and understand and appreciate the factually complex business, financing and operational issues which are at the core of most commercial disputes. Forman Perry has extensive experience representing individuals, partnerships, and publicly-traded and privately-held corporations, and represents clients involved in: lending and public finance, transportation, telecommunications, real estate, public utilities, securities, technology, manufacturing and distribution, and others. Forman Perry regularly represents clients in state and federal courts and before administrative agencies in matters involving lender liability claims, contract disputes, shareholder disputes, securities fraud, trade regulation, antitrust claims, debtor-creditor disputes, and others.

**Drugs & Medical Devices:** Attorneys in the firm have been involved in all aspects of drug and medical device litigation, defending a broad array of pharmaceutical claims, and acting as national coordinating counsel in medical device litigation.

**Environmental & Toxic Torts:** Forman Perry is actively involved in defending numerous environmental and toxic torts including asbestos, silica, welding rod, lead paint, mold, PVC, PCB and wood preservation. Forman Perry's presence in asbestos litigation on the local and national fronts is unparalleled. The firm represents over 180 asbestos clients in Mississippi and is handling more than 250,000 individual claims nationwide, representing clients in 23 states, with particular emphasis in Texas and Louisiana. Forman Perry lawyers serve as national counsel and national trial counsel to a number of asbestos defendants. Forman Perry is also extensively involved in silica litigation nationally, representing numerous defendants and acting as national counsel for several silica defendants. Forman Perry's successes in silica litigation have been documented in many publications, including Wall Street Journal, New York Times, Fortune Magazine and National Law Journal. Forman Perry's litigation experience also includes defense of claims of alleged environmental contamination from industrial and oilfield operations involving various chemicals, including PCBs, BTEX/TPH, heavy metals, saltwater and naturally-occurring radiation materials (NORM). Forman Perry also represents clients in litigation arising out of exposure to wood preservative chemicals (creosote, pentachlorophenol and copper chromated arsenate (CCA), dioxins and polycyclic aromatic hydrocarbons (PAHs).

## HEAD OFFICE

**MISSISSIPPI**
City Centre, 200 South Lamar Street, Suite 100, **Jackson**, MS 39201
**Tel:** 601 960 8600   **Fax:** 601 960 8613
**Website:** www.fpwkt.com
**Mailing Address:** PO Box 22608 Jackson, MS 39225-2608

## BRANCH OFFICES

**LOUISIANA**
1515 Poydras Street, Suite 1300, **New Orleans**, LA 70112
**Tel:** 504 799 4383   **Fax:** 504 799 4384

**TEXAS**
Bryan Tower, Suite 1300, 2001 Bryan Street, **Dallas**, TX 75201
**Tel:** 214 905 2924   **Fax:** 214 905 3976

1717 St. James Place, Suite 600, **Houston**, TX 77056
**Tel:** 713 402 1717   **Fax:** 713 621 6746.

## CONTACTS

| | |
|---|---|
| Mass Tort Litigation | |
| | Richard L Forman, Walter G Watkins, Jr, Fred Krutz |
| Commercial Litigation | Alan W Perry |
| General Litigation | Fred Krutz |
| Toxic Tort & Environmental Litigation | |
| | Thomas W Tardy, III, Walter G, Watkins, Jr, Fred Krutz |
| Business & Corporate Practice | Steven M Hendrix |

**Insurance:** Forman Perry represents insurance companies in many different facets, including third-party and first-party claims, coverage-related issues, claims involving commercial general liability (CGL), property, casual, automobile, environmental and fleet insurance.

**Products Liability:** From the firm's inception, Forman Perry has enjoyed a close working relationship with manufacturers and insurers in defending products liability cases, successfully defending a full spectrum of products liability cases.

**Professional Negligence:** The firm handles professional negligence claims including claims alleging accounting, legal and medical malpractice. The firm's litigation attorneys who handle accounting negligence claims are certified public accountants who have practiced in major public accounting firms.

## BUSINESS & CORPORATE PRACTICE

**General:** Forman Perry's Business and Corporate Practice includes representation of both privately-held and publicly-traded corporations in a wide variety of industries. The firm regularly provides counsel to banks and financial institutions, institutions of higher learning, REITs, manufacturers and distributors, private foundations, public utilities, telecommunications companies and other businesses, working closely with clients to understand and analyze the legal and business issues behind a deal to provide clients with creative, cost-effective strategies and solutions for complex transactions.

**Lending:** The firm regularly represents community, state and national banking institutions in connection with commercial lending activities, including large multi-state financings. Forman Perry also represents insurance companies and other national financing institutions as both lead and local counsel with respect to loans in Mississippi.

**Real Estate:** Forman Perry's Commercial Real Estate Practice is national in scope, the firm regularly represents NYSE-listed REITs and other companies in connection with acquisitions, development, dispositions and financings. Forman Perry attorneys also have extensive leasing expertise representing publicly-traded companies on a national basis.

**Transactions/Securities:** Forman Perry has substantial experience representing buyers and sellers in major transactions ranging from asset and stock transactions to mergers, acquisitions and corporate reorganizations, including experience in both registered and exempt offerings.

# WATKINS & EAGER PLLC

## THE FIRM

**Managing Member:** Paul H Stephenson III
**Senior Member:** William F Goodman Jr

**Number of members:** 46
**Number of other lawyers:** 32

## OFFICE

**MISSISSIPPI**
The Emporium Building, Suite 300, 400 East Capitol Street,
**Jackson**, MS 39205
**Tel:** 601 948 6470   **Fax:** 601 354 3623
**Website:** www.watkinseager.com

**FIRM OVERVIEW:** Watkins & Eager PLLC is a full service, diversified law firm. The firm began in 1895 when William Hamilton Watkins became the twentieth lawyer at the Jackson Bar. The influential career of Will Watkins spanned 64 years during which he argued over 20 cases before the Supreme Court of the United States. Pat H Eager Jr joined Will Watkins in 1916 and practiced with the firm until his death in 1970. Pat Eager was recognized as a premier trial lawyer who served as president of the International Association of Defense Counsel (1943-44) and who was Mississippi's initial invitee into the American College of Trial Lawyers. For several decades the image of the firm was heavily influenced by two of Will Watkins' children. Elizabeth Watkins Hulen, an outstanding appellate advocate, was the first woman in Mississippi history to argue before the Supreme Court of the United States. Thomas H Watkins earned a national reputation in the representation of corporate and governmental clients. Will Watkins' grandson, William F Goodman Jr, is the firm's senior member and is one of only a few Mississippi lawyers who is a member of both the American College of Trial Lawyers and the American Academy of Appellate Lawyers. Charles Clark, another active member, is the retired Chief Judge of the United States Court of Appeals for the Fifth Circuit and is also a member of both the American College of Trial Lawyers and the American Academy of Appellate Lawyers. Four other members are also Fellows in the American College of Trial Lawyers. Others are fellows of the American College of Trust and Estate Counsel and American College of Employment Lawyers. Many others have contributed and continue to contribute to the growth and progress of the firm that now enjoys an extensive corporate and business practice in addition to its broad trial and appellate practice.

## MAIN AREAS OF PRACTICE:

**Commercial & Business Litigation:** The firm's involvement in the rapidly expanding areas of contract and business litigation and arbitration addresses a large variety of commercial controversies and business tort disputes as well as litigation involving issues of antitrust, lender liability, consumer fraud, and securities. Several members of the firm have served as arbitrators and mediators of various business disputes.

**Tort/Mass Tort Litigaton:** Firm lawyers defend tort claims of all types. A substantial part of the firm's tort practice is the defense of product liability actions, representing a number of manufacturers of aircraft, automotive products, chemicals, farm implements, firearms, heavy equipment, tires, tools, medical devices, and pharmaceuticals throughout the state and beyond its borders. The firm's lawyers have also assumed key defense roles on a local, regional and national basis, in mass tort litigation of matters such as pharmaceutical products, breast implants, dioxin, asbestos, and welding. The defense of professional malpractice claims against doctors, dentists, lawyers, architects, engineers and accountants is another significant segment of the firm's tort practice.

**Banking & Consumer Finance:** The firm has represented various financial institutions both in and out of state, maintaining a regular clientele of the state's leading financial institutions. The firm's banking work includes litigation, transactional advice and counsel, opinions and drafting bank forms and loan workouts.

**Corporate:** The firm's Corporate Practice covers a wide range of areas including mergers and acquisitions, commercial finance, the formation of and counsel to business entities, and the drafting of commercial contracts.

**Tax:** The firm has five lawyers who are experienced tax attorneys. Two lawyers are also CPAs. In addition to providing tax counsel and advice to businesses and individuals, firm members have also represented clients in tax disputes before the IRS, the State Tax Commission and local public bodies.

**Wills, Trusts & Estates:** Estate planning, wills, trusts and probate are an integral part of the firm's practice.

**Public Utility Law:** The firm has historically represented utilities before the Public Service Commission, which regulates public utilities in Mississippi.

**Construction Law:** The firm has represented owners, architects and engineers, contractors and sureties in construction disputes and projects and their business activities.

**Bankruptcy:** The firm has represented various lenders and other creditors in workouts and in bankruptcy proceedings.

**Labor & Employment:** The firm possesses considerable experience in representation of management in various employer related transactions and disputes, including, day to day employment issues, litigation, collective bargaining and proceedings before the federal and state regulatory bodies.

**Environmental:** The firm's environmental practice includes representation of clients in litigation in both federal and state courts, as well as before the MS Department of Environmental Quality, the EPA and other administrative agencies. Representation includes the defense of toxic claims, environmental permitting and compliance matters, and negotiating and drafting of environmental related contract provisions.

**Real Estate:** The firm has a broad real estate practice. In January 2004, the members of Taylor, Covington & Smith, P.A., a firm known for its real estate practice, joined the firm and added extensive expertise in real estate matters. The real estate practice now includes representation of local residential and commercial developers, and involves new urbanism, multifamily and commercial developments in Mississippi and neighboring states. The firm also serves as local counsel for numerous out of state lending institutions.

**Insurance:** The firm has considerable experience in insurance matters. Firm members possess experience in handling claims involving fire, property, casualty, workers' compensation, fidelity and surety, officers and directors, errors and omissions, as well as life, health and accident matters/insurance.

**Government:** The firm has traditionally represented a number of governmental bodies on various matters, including annexation, public finance and housing.

**CLIENTS:** Watkins & Eager's client base includes major manufacturers, employers, contractors, real estate developers, public utilities, oil and gas producers and refiners, banks and financial institutions, timber companies, pharmaceutical companies, insurers and government entities on the federal, state, county and municipal levels.

*Free background information is available upon request from M Binford Williams, Jr. at the above address.*

## How lawyers are ranked

Every year we carry out thousands of in-depth interviews with clients and lawyers in order to assess the reputations and expertise of business lawyers across the USA. Chambers rankings and editorial are referred to extensively by General Counsel and other purchasers of legal services who look to our recommendations when choosing their lawyers.

# CORPORATE/M&A

### Corporate/M&A
### Leading Firms

**1** BLACKWELL SANDERS PEPER *Kansas City*
BRYAN CAVE LLP *St Louis*
SONNENSCHEIN NATH & ROSENTHAL *Kansas City*
STINSON MORRISON HECKER LLP *Kansas City*
THOMPSON COBURN LLP *St Louis*

**2** ARMSTRONG TEASDALE LLP *St Louis*
LATHROP & GAGE L.C. *Kansas City*

**3** HUSCH & EPPENBERGER, LLC *Kansas City*
POLSINELLI SHALTON WELTE *Kansas City*
SHOOK, HARDY & BACON LLP *Kansas City*
SHUGHART THOMSON & KILROY *Kansas City*
SPENCER FANE BRITT & BROWNE *Kansas City*

## Band 1

### Blackwell Sanders Peper Martin LLP

See firm details p.1212

**The Firm:** Known for its strength in corporate/M&A, this regional giant represents sophisticated clients across the USA, working on a coordinated basis across its six offices. In a combined effort, the Kansas City and Springfield teams concluded a successful multimillion-dollar joint venture and a going-private tender offer for John Q Hammons Hotels. The team has seen continued growth in the mutual fund and fund management area, primarily in the energy sector, and represented Tortoise Energy in several financings in 2005. Clients find the firm *"thorough, terrific – one of the top Midwestern corporate securities transactional firms"* and appreciate its *"value-for-money"* service.

**The Lawyers:** Jim Ash (see p.1203) is admired for his technical abilities and lauded by interviewees for being *"extremely knowledgeable, experienced, diligent and as good as it gets,"* particularly in relation to securities work. He represented TCG International in the sale of its Canadian glass operations to Belron Canada. *"Top-tier"* attorney **Gary Gilson** (see p.1206) centers his practice on M&A, public securities and private equity formation. He works across the USA representing investment banks, private equity firms and a number of manufacturers, including working on acquisitions for elevator companies.

**Stephen Adams'** (see p.1203) practice is focused on representing clients in the healthcare industry, both in terms of corporate/M&A work and real estate, while **Steven Carman** (see p.1204) has a strong practice in public company securities and drives the firm's mutual fund work. Interviewees see him as a *"rising star."* **Jason Reschly** (see p.1209) is famed for his expertise in tax law and is also active in strategic corporate planning. He has a national practice in representing cooperatives. Senior statesman **Ralph Wrobley** (see p.1211) has a strong practice in strategic advice for both midmarket and large publicly traded companies. He is highly respected in the field for his experience and expertise.

**Clients/Work Highlights:** Applebee's International; American Italian Pasta; Tortoise Energy; MC Real Estate Services; St. Luke's Health System; Aquila; Ash Grove Cement; Associated Wholesale Grocers; Energy West; Huntco Steel; Kansas City Royals; Lady Baltimore Foods; Stifel Nicolaus; Edward Jones and Kansas Farm Bureau.

### Bryan Cave LLP

**The Firm:** This heavyweight Missouri firm continues to dominate the legal marketplace in St. Louis, regularly representing companies involved in the largest M&A transactions. Clients remain loyal to an experienced team that provides *"high-quality service."* They appreciate the team's ability to be *"continually on top of what you are doing and their understanding that we're trying to make a deal, not a kill."* In addition to the star partners, this department also fields a number of younger attorneys, who are described by clients as *"bright, experienced, extremely dedicated and hard-working."* The firm has had a busy year in M&A transactions, representing GameStop in a $1.3 billion acquisition. Other deals include advising Monsanto on its $1.5 billion acquisition of fruit and vegetable seed company Seminis; and Brown Shoe in its $205 million acquisition of Bennett Footwear.

**The Lawyers:** *"Dean of corporate practice"* **Thomas Van Dyke** is described by clients as a lawyer who *"never loses his cool – he remains objective and principled."* His forte lies in both public company securities and M&A transactions, and he has been representing investment company C3 Capital Partners. Chairman of the firm **Don Lents** concentrates

his practice on corporate governance, providing advice on issues such as fiduciary duties. **James Nouss** is described by clients as *"bright, complete in his work and an excellent business attorney."* He practices a combination of corporate finance and securities – working on behalf of underwriters and issuers – and M&A. He also does a significant amount of venture capital work. Highlights include his involvement in the acquisition of Legg Mason's capital markets arm by Stifel Financial. 2005 was a particularly active year in terms of M&A for **Bill Seabaugh**. Among numerous sizable transactions, he advised footwear wholesaler Brown Shoe in its $205 million acquisition of Boston-based Bennett Footwear and also represented Emerson Electric in three multimillion-dollar acquisitions. **Fred Bartelsmeyer** had an impressive year, working with a team of nearly 50 lawyers and professionals, advising long-time client Sigma-Aldrich in its $378 million acquisition of JRH Biosciences, a deal involving multiple jurisdictions.

**Clients/Work Highlights:** Emerson Electric; Ralcorp Holdings; NS Group; Monsanto; Sigma-Aldrich; Stereotaxis; AG Edwards & Sons; Oakwood Medical Investors; Lockton Companies; GameStop; H&R Block and C3 Capital Partners.

### Sonnenschein Nath & Rosenthal LLP

See firm details p.884

**The Firm:** This Chicago-based firm has a large corporate and securities presence in Kansas City and St. Louis, advising a national client base on complex M&A deals. Clients are *"extremely happy"* with this team of *"great, professional transactional lawyers."* The team has expanded its Kansas City office with several lateral hires. Recently the team advised clients on numerous acquisitions, financings and international transactions, including representing Kansas City Southern in the purchase of the principal Mexican railroad, a deal in excess of $1 billion. The team also worked on a number of both common and secure stock offerings for the same railway company.

**The Lawyers:** **Bob Fisher** (see p.1205) moves into the top tier with a fantastic reputation among peers as a quality lawyer with years of experience in M&A. In the past year he was involved in more than 30 deals for midmarket clients, including sales, purchases and related financings. Clients find managing partner **James Heeter** (see p.1206) *"thorough and conscien-*

## Corporate/M&A

### Leading Individuals

#### Senior Statesmen

**NIXON** Richard *Stinson Morrison Hecker*
**WROBLEY** Ralph *Blackwell Sanders*

[1] **ASH** James *Blackwell Sanders*
**FISHER** Robert *Sonnenschein*
**GILSON** Gary *Blackwell Sanders*
**GRANDA** John *Stinson Morrison*
**MEDVED** Joseph *Lathrop & Gage*
**VAN DYKE** Thomas *Bryan Cave LLP*

[2] **ADAMS** Stephen *Blackwell Sanders*
**EVANS** Craig *Shook, Hardy & Bacon*
**HEETER** James *Sonnenschein*
**HUNTER** Robert *Stinson Morrison Hecker*
**JONES** Steve *Armstrong Teasdale*
**LAUSE** Michael *Thompson Coburn*
**LENTS** Donald *Bryan Cave LLP*
**LITZ** Thomas *Thompson Coburn LLP*
**MARVIN** John *Sonnenschein*
**MONROE C** Robert *Stinson Morrison Hecker*
**NOUSS** James *Bryan Cave LLP*
**O'CONNELL** Mary Anne *Husch & Eppenberger*
**SEABAUGH** William *Bryan Cave LLP*

[3] **BARTELSMEYER** Fred *Bryan Cave LLP*
**CARMAN** Steven *Blackwell Sanders*
**FITZGERALD JR** Robert *Shughart Thomson*
**FRETWELL** Norman *Spencer Fane Britt*
**FRIZELL** Edward *Polsinelli Shalton Welte*
**KEIM** Robert *Kutak Rock LLP*
**LAROSE** Robert *Thompson Coburn LLP*
**MINOGUE** Thomas *Thompson Coburn LLP*
**POLSINELLI** James *Polsinelli Shalton*
**RESCHLY** Jason *Blackwell Sanders*
**STAHL** Thomas *Lathrop & Gage L.C.*
**WERTS** Dale *Lathrop & Gage L.C.*

### Up-and-coming individuals

**SWEENEY** Kevin *Sonnenschein*

---

tious." He has, among other transactions, been working on an acquisition and a disposition worth approximately $200 million for a client in Kansas City. **John Marvin** (see p.1208) is seen by interviewees as a *"strong, experienced leader"* in both securities and M&A. Clients find him *"terrific – a man of great character and a top securities lawyer."* He has worked on complex transactions for both Kansas City Southern and DST Systems, as well as representing clients in New York and Chicago on Sarbanes-Oxley matters. The firm hired the *"strong, bright and hardworking"* **Kevin Sweeney** (see p.1210) from Shook, Hardy & Bacon. He is known for his national practice and experience in M&A . He was involved in the representation of Kansas City Southern in a $1 billion joint venture with the Norfolk Southern Railway.

**Clients/Work Highlights:** H&R Block; Monsanto; American Safety Razor; Waddell & Reed; Pliant; DST Systems; Westar Energy; Boulder Capital and Jordan Industries.

## Stinson Morrison Hecker LLP

See firm details p.1220

**The Firm:** This *"terrific"* law firm has a strong hold on the Kansas City corporate market and a statewide presence with more than 30 attorneys focusing on M&A. Clients are impressed with these *"technically skilled"* attorneys who handle the full range of corporate services, from M&A and securities to venture and private equity capital. The team served as Kansas counsel in the complex $36 billion Sprint-Nextel merger, creating a new wireless phone powerhouse in the USA. The team also acted for LabOne in the $934 million sale of the company to Quest Diagnostics.

**The Lawyers:** *"Top lawyer"* **John Granda** (see p.1206) leads on a significant number of the firm's complex M&A and securities transactions. **Rob Hunter** (see p.1207) splits his practice between venture capital and M&A work. He represented INVISTA in its spin-off of IP assets and acquisition of Series A Preferred Stock, a matter involving cross-license issues. **Bob Monroe** (see p.1208) is a *"leader on banking"* and focuses his practice both on M&A and regulatory matters for financial services clients. Senior statesman **Richard Nixon** (see p.1209) is described by interviewees as *"extremely knowledgeable."* He worked on a number of acquisitions for propane distributor Inergy and was also involved in representing Quest Resource in its $126 million acquisition of oil and gas companies.

**Clients/Work Highlights:** AMCON Distributing; Cerner; Duckwall-ALCO Stores; Euronet Worldwide; Exchange National Bancshares; Gold Banc; Great Plains Energy; Interstate Bakeries; Kinder Morgan Energy Partners; LabOne; Layne Christensen; Leggett & Platt; The Monarch Cement Company; Pioneer Financial; Quest Resource; Seaboard; Sprint and UMB Financial.

## Thompson Coburn LLP

See firm details p.1221

**The Firm:** Clients are happy with this *"value-added"* firm and appreciate *"the way they build a team in a non hierarchical manner and the way the relationship person is the person who does the work,"* adding: *"At this firm, institutional knowledge translates to better value."* The team provides a full range of corporate legal services, including complex private equity work, securities and M&A, as well as advising clients on their acquisition of foreign companies. The team has grown, solidifying its presence in St. Louis with the addition of two lateral hires and two new graduates to the corporate and securities practice. Clients describe these new additions as *"excellent, highly responsive, attentive, knowledgeable and they have the ability to provide great legal advice complemented by general business judgment."* The firm has been representing Engineered Support Systems in its $1.9 billion acquisition by defense contractor DRS Technologies.

**The Lawyers:** Administrative head of the corporate department, **Michael Lause** (see p.1207) is highly respected in the marketplace. This leader in municipal finance has been working on a $300 million bond issue for the University of Missouri, as well as a $200 million bond issue for the Missouri Higher Education Loan Authority. Corporate and securities department cochair **Tom Litz** (see p.1208) is praised by clients for his *"compatible approach and ability to work seamlessly with others, bringing them in where necessary."* He *"makes complex things simple and mixes business sense with legal."* Acting on a range of corporate and securities matters, he focuses particularly on representing public sector companies in private equity and venture capital. Chairman of the firm **Tom Minogue** (see p.1208) handles the firm's relationships with both Enterprise Rent-A-Car and bottling company Barry-Wehmiller. Clients find him *"thoughtful;"* he *"takes a business approach, is not overly enamored with wordsmithing, gets the deal done and helps us assess the risks and stay focused."* Department cochair **Bob LaRose** (see p.1207) is lauded by clients for his *"strong client-orientation, business sense and practicality – he doesn't get bogged down in legal minutiae."* His practice focuses on M&A transactions and he represents large publicly traded clients, including RehabCare in St. Louis.

**Clients/Work Highlights:** AG Edwards & Sons; BUNZL USA; Charter Communications; Stifel Nicolaus; Pepsi Bottling Group; Missouri State Employees' Retirement System; US Bank; Enterprise Rent-A-Car; Maritz; Bethesda Health Group; Insituform Technologies; President Casinos; United Van Lines; Federal Signal; Huttig Building Supply and Bunge North America.

## Band 2

## Armstrong Teasdale LLP

**The Firm:** A *"strong"* presence in St. Louis, this firm represents midmarket companies in M&A transactions. The M&A group of nine attorneys draws on the firm's expertise in other areas, including the securities and government and compliance groups, in order to provide clients with the full set of skills needed for complex transactions. Highlights of 2005 include representing a public company in the acquisition of multiple geotextiles converting and distribution businesses.

**The Lawyers:** **Steve Jones** has garnered an enormous amount of respect from peers. He is a member of the firm's business services department and concentrates his practice on M&A and real estate.

**Clients/Work Highlights:** Clients include businesses in industries such as broadcasting, financial services, information technology, retailing, manufacturing, distribution, utilities, wireless communications, chemicals and real estate.

## Lathrop & Gage L.C.

See firm details p.1214

**The Firm:** With four offices in Missouri, this firm has a significant regional presence and also represents companies internationally. Interviewees praise the Kansas City corporate department's *"sharp, professional"* attorneys, who advise clients in both M&A and securities transactions. Highlights include representing an insurance company in the recapture of $9 million of policies that had been co-insured to a reinsurer. The team also acted for a utilities company in its $3 million sale of assets.

**The Lawyers:** **Joseph Medved**'s (see p.1208) practice leans toward representing the larger clients in complex transactions, ranging from the $200 million to the billion-dollar range. Recently he has been doing a lot of work for GE Insurance, GEAR For Sports and a waste haulage company. Chair of the corporate department, **Dale Werts** (see p.1211) represents both public and private clients in a wide variety of industries for their finance, operational and transactional needs. Adding to the team, **Thomas Stahl** (see p.1210) joined the firm in September 2005 from Armstrong Teasdale. He focuses his practice on representing small and large businesses in corporate governance, regulatory issues and M&A. Clients appreciate his integrity, pragmatism and business sense.

**Clients/Work Highlights:** AMC Entertainment; AT&T; Bank of America; Butler Manufacturing; MGP Ingredients; Sprint Nextel; Time Warner Cable; Zimmer; CST Industries; GE Insurance Solutions; Waddell & Reed; Shinn Fu; GEAR For Sports and Whitman's Candies.

## Band 3

### Husch & Eppenberger, LLC

**The Firm:** Market commentators agree that this is a fine regional firm, with a strong corporate presence in St. Louis and Kansas City. With attorneys in eight cities across the Midwest and mid south, the group has a pool of more than 50 corporate lawyers from which to draw expertise.

**The Lawyers:** Member of the corporate and securities team, **Mary Anne O'Connell** is lauded by interviewees for her experience and technical skills, acting out of both the Kansas City and St. Louis offices. She represents businesses and equity funds in corporate transactions and securities, including public offerings, private placements and other capital structurings.

**Clients/Work Highlights:** Clients include closely held businesses, entrepreneurs, private clients, mature midmarket companies and national and multinational companies.

### Polsinelli Shalton Welte Suelthaus

See firm details p.1217

**The Firm:** This impressive Kansas City-based corporate practice is known for its representation of midmarket companies, including healthcare and non profit clients. The *"efficient and effective"* team is also known for its strong leaning toward real estate. The team has a group of over 20 lawyers who spend more than half of their time on midmarket M&A transactions, representing regional clients both regionally and nationally. The firm represented a special committee of the board of directors that approved the AMC going-private transaction. The team also acted for an insurance company in a restructure transaction in excess of $500 million.

**The Lawyers:** Rainmakers **Trip Frizell** (see p.1206) and **Jim Polsinelli** (see p.1209) *"take good care of their clients."* Frizell has been working on around a dozen acquisitions in the past year for a privately held engineering company and also leads on acquisitions for several privately held companies in Kansas City. Polsinelli concentrates his practice in the area of corporate law, with an emphasis on M&A and business succession planning. Clients find him *"thoughtful and well prepared."*

**Clients/Work Highlights:** Stowers Institute for Medical Research; Lockton Companies; Sprint Nextel; KeyBank; Bayer HealthCare; University of Kansas Hospital Authority; TranSystems and LCC International.

### Shook, Hardy & Bacon LLP

See firm details p.1218

**The Firm:** The Kansas City branch of this international firm, renowned for its top-flight litigation group, also has a 13-strong corporate team. Highlights of the year include representing Cerner in its $100 million acquisition of the medical division of VitalWorks. The team also acted for Premium Standard Farms in an IPO of common stock.

**The Lawyers:** Chair of the firm's corporate finance and banking group, **Craig Evans** (see p.1205) glides up the ranks, described by interviewees as a *"wonderful corporate lawyer."* He leads on complex M&A and securities transactions for sophisticated clients.

**Clients/Work Highlights:** Bank of America; Barkley Evergreen & Partners; BAT; Business Men's Assurance Company of America and Deutsche Financial Services.

### Shughart Thomson & Kilroy PC

See firm details p.1219

**The Firm:** This is a strong litigation firm with a significant corporate practice. The team concentrates its work on securities law matters, including initial and secondary public offerings of corporate common stock, debt securities, REIT interests and cattle program interests. The group has been involved in a number of M&A transactions for clients in a wide variety of industries.

**The Lawyers:** **Robert Fitzgerald** (see p.1205) is known for his great real estate work and is the *"go-to"* lawyer at the firm for corporate work. He represents clients in business transactions ranging from corporate acquisitions to regulatory enforcement.

**Clients/Work Highlights:** Carondelet Health; Chicago Title Insurance; Commerce Bank; Dickinson Financial; DST Realty; Kansas City Southern; Stormont-Vail HealthCare; Mission Bank; United Missouri Bank and Walton Construction.

### Spencer Fane Britt & Browne LLP

**The Firm:** This regional firm has a sizable business transactions group in Missouri, with 18 attorneys in Kansas City and ten in St. Louis. The team represents a range of clients, from entrepreneurial businesses to large public companies from many different industries. The firm also advises local and national trade associations and other non profit organizations.

**The Lawyers:** Leader of the financial services group, **Norm Fretwell** represents financial institutions alongside other corporate and business entities. He is admired for his expertise on the banking side and is described by interviewees as *"an extremely bright, honorable guy whose word is his bond – he doesn't play games."*

**Clients/Work Highlights:** Allied Waste Industries; American Century Investments; Birch Telecom; Commerce Bank; Gannett Satellite Information Network; Kansas City Power & Light and Procter & Gamble.

### Other Notable Practitioners

**Robert Keim** of Kutak Rock LLP has been structuring a number of significant joint ventures and continues to be the outside general counsel for several corporations.

# EMPLOYMENT

## MAINLY DEFENDANT

## Band 1

### Blackwell Sanders Peper Martin LLP

See firm details p.1212

**The Firm:** With recognized expertise in both labor law and employment litigation across both the Kansas City and St. Louis offices, this firm is a leader in Missouri. The team has handled several FLSA class actions. These have typically involved large numbers of employees claiming millions of dollars in overtime. These cases have been on a national basis, stretching to California and Washington, DC.

**The Lawyers:** The *"excellent"* **John Phillips** (see p.1209) has negotiated several significant labor agreements in Milwaukee, Kansas City, New Jersey and Wisconsin. He has regularly acted as an arbitrator and mediator in the past year, resolving multimillion-dollar cases in the healthcare, manufacturing, engineering, publishing and leisure industries.

Managing partner of the firm's St. Louis office, **Robert Tomaso** (see p.1210) is respected as a *"great"* traditional labor lawyer. He also has extensive experience in employment law, especially in obtaining summary judgment in discrimination defense cases.

**Clients/Work Highlights:** American Water Company; Applebee's International; Argosy Gaming; CCP Industries; Casey's General Stores; Chubb Group; Commerce Bank; Forest Pharmaceuticals; Hallmark Cards; Harcros Chemicals; Heartland Automotive; Jacobs Engineering; The Kansas City Star; Maytag; Smurfit-Stone Container; St. Luke's Health System; Waddell & Reed Financial and Walgreen.

### Bryan Cave LLP

**The Firm:** This firm has a *"great"* and sizable labor and employment group. A *"dominant player"* it has a host of experienced attorneys, providing a full service to clients. With a decline in unionization, the team has been doing more employment litigation than traditional labor law. However, it also spends a fair amount of time on union avoidance, injunction proceedings, advising clients on contract negotiations and defending or filing lawsuits under Section 301 of the Labor Relations Act. In employment litigation, the team has a steady track record in obtaining summary judgments for clients nationwide. It represents employers in a variety of industries, including manufacturing, retail, university education, entertainment and broadcasting.

**The Lawyers:** Interviewees harbor great respect for the *"superb"* **Dennis Donnelly**. He was involved in a case for Union Pacific. He is praised as *"a fine man, totally professional, extremely bright and knowledgeable."* The *"standout"* attorney **Jerry Hunter** is described by market commentators as *"a great guy to work with, tough and down to earth."* His practice is split evenly between labor law and employment litigation and he handles discrimination cases in both Missouri and Arkansas federal courts. Interviewees say that his government experience adds to his business acumen. Up-and-comer **Danny O'Keefe** is described by interviewees as a *"wonderful trial lawyer, a real star."* He focuses on employment discrimination litigation and was involved in several class actions.

**Clients/Work Highlights:** ABB; Waste Management; State Farm; Wells Fargo Home Mortgage and Lyondell-CITGO Refining.

## Band 2

### Lathrop & Gage L.C.

See firm details p.1214

**The Firm:** This Kansas City-based firm has five offices across the State of Missouri and counts a large number of household names among its clients. The labor and employment team consists of 36 attorneys spread across the state, the Kansas City office providing the most strength and depth. In John Snyder v

Yellow Freight, the team successfully defended a transportation services provider against claims of age discrimination and retaliation in federal court. The team also defeated class certification in a suit against one of the world's largest fast-food restaurant chains, in which plaintiffs claimed violation of the FLSA.

**The Lawyers:** **Jack Rowe** (see p.1209) is highly respected as a leader in both labor and employment law. He acts for management in equal employment opportunity, personnel relations and traditional labor matters, including federal, state and local agency investigations and hearings, court actions and day-to-day advice. **Rosalee McNamara** (see p.1208) is well regarded in the field of employment law. She represents clients in matters throughout the USA, successfully defending a number of employment discrimination claims and acting in trials in federal and state courts.

**Clients/Work Highlights:** Allied Waste Industries; AMC Entertainment; Burger King; Butler Manufacturing; Cargill; Colgate-Palmolive; Faultless Linen; GM; Hallmark Cards; Harley-Davidson; Hilton Hotels and McDonald's.

### Shook, Hardy & Bacon LLP

See firm details p.1218

**The Firm:** Interviewees admire the *"great set of both young and senior partners"* in the firm's labor and employment group. A firm with offices from coast to coast and overseas, the group represents corporate employers, including a number of Fortune 500 companies, throughout the USA.

**The Lawyers:** The *"excellent"* **Bill Martucci**'s (see p.1208) experience, judgment and ability to handle the most complex and sophisticated matters are renowned throughout the market; he is *"clearly the top"* in Missouri employment law. He represents management in national employment litigation and policy matters.

**Clients/Work Highlights:** Verizon, Honeywell and Centerpulse feature on the client list.

### Spencer Fane Britt & Browne LLP

**The Firm:** A large team with plenty of expertise in the labor and employment arena, this *"great"* Midwestern firm moves up the rankings table. The team represents both regional and national clients, including some of the Midwest's largest utilities and healthcare providers and several of the nation's largest retailers, trucking companies and construction firms.

**The Lawyers:** Leading labor lawyer **David Wing** is described by interviewees as *"smart, professional and extremely engaging."* A *"standout"* for clients, **Denise Drake** heads up the team. She enters the table with a reputation for *"excellence"* and experience in the courtroom. Clients appreciate the fact that *"she knows all the judges and relevant people in this area."*

**Clients/Work Highlights:** Clients include those in the trucking; airline; construction; retail; distribution; manufacturing; healthcare; utility; food processing and service industries; as well as state and local governments, municipal corporations, school districts and state agencies.

## Stinson Morrison Hecker LLP

See firm details p.1220

**The Firm:** This 37-strong outfit, divided into employment litigation and labor law teams, also has a significant employee benefits team. The firm has had an ongoing relationship with Chubb Group and represented more than 50 insurers in employment litigation, ranging from charges of discrimination to civil action for violations of Title VII, ADA, FMLA and state torts. In Rogers v US Bank, the team had a summary judgment affirmed in the Eighth Circuit Court of Appeals in a disparate treatment case.

**The Lawyers:** Chair of employment litigation and top attorney, **Paul Donnelly** (see p.1204) is the key relationship partner for Chubb Group and Deluxe. He defended the latter against race discrimination claims concerning pay, promotion and training. Clients enjoyed his *"calm, practical problem-solving approach"* to complex cases.

**Clients/Work Highlights:** American Academy of Family Physicians; American Airlines; Bunge North America; Cerner; City of Overland Park; DeBruce Grain; Deluxe; Hallmark Cards; Kansas City Royals; MCI and Papa John's.

## Thompson Coburn LLP

See firm details p.1221

**The Firm:** This 27-strong labor and employment group concentrates its practice not only on union avoidance and employment litigation, but also has a strong focus on employee benefits. Clients appreciate the team's *"responsive, creative and meticulous style – cutting through and boiling down issues,"* especially on ERISA matters. The team has also seen an increase in the amount of litigation relating to immigration issues. Work on issues relating to the rail industry has picked up with new client Kansas City Southern, which rides the rails from Missouri to Mexico.

**The Lawyers:** **Clifford Godiner** (see p.1206) spends a significant amount of his time representing two giant railroad companies in traditional labor matters, while the rest of his practice centers on employment discrimination defense. Clients say he is a *"pleasure to work with – extremely bright and hard-working."* Highlights include obtaining summary judgment for a client, based on the plaintiff's failure to disclose that she had filed for bankruptcy. The *"fine lawyer"* **Richard Jaudes** (see p.1207) is respected by interviewees for being extremely knowledgeable and having *"great management skills."* With a national practice, he spends the majority of his time outside the state. Among other highlights of 2005, he worked on the labor issues relating to Bunzl's acquisition of US Foodservice's New York-based SOFCO division.

**Clients/Work Highlights:** ACF Industries; Baldor Electric; Bunzl Distribution; Chubb Group; Energizer Holdings; Insituform Technologies; Johnson & Johnson; Kansas City Southern; Saint Louis

Symphony Orchestra; Stifel Nicolaus; Union Pacific and US Bank.

## Band 3

## Armstrong Teasdale LLP

**The Firm:** This firm's employment and labor team has a strong presence in St. Louis with 14 dedicated attorneys. Four of the team left at the start of 2005 to join Ogletree Deakins' new Kansas City office. However, the employment group retained its longstanding clients, has made one lateral hire from Lathrop & Gage and is making full use of its litigation team to support its workload. The team has an active noncompete practice.

**The Lawyers:** Chair of the labor and employment group, peers cite **John Vering** as a *"leading employment lawyer."* The majority of his practice involves defending employers in noncompete discrimination matters. One highlight involved obtaining summary judgment in a same-sex harassment case, which was approaching Supreme Court level. He also spends time as a mediator and arbitrator.

**Clients/Work Highlights:** Columbia Public Schools; IBM; UPS; Lear Corporation; North Kansas City Hospital; Cintas and Kforce.

## Constangy, Brooks & Smith, LLC

**The Firm:** This national labor and employment boutique *"really knows its stuff"* in Missouri. Clients describe the Kansas City team as *"great."* The team has seen a number of victories, representing clients in the traditional labor arena. The team has a significant presence in the healthcare market, representing a number of acute care centers and successfully handling a union NLRB deauthorization election for one healthcare client. The team also handled complex labor negotiations in California for construction and entertainment industry clients involving geographic jurisdictional issues.

**The Lawyers:** The *"top-flight"* traditional labor lawyer **Robert Janowitz** is described by clients as *"extremely knowledgeable and personable."* His practice spans the USA and he handled NLRB charges for management in Ohio, Indiana, New York and California.

**Clients/Work Highlights:** HCA; Farmland Foods; LaserCycle; Woodbridge Corp-Kc Foam; Fairmont Hotels & Resorts; The Raphael Hotel; Toyo Tires; Tanner Health System; Russell-Stanley; Federal Home Loan Bank of Topeka; Innovia Films; Motion Control Engineering; Imperial Electric and Communication Service for the Deaf.

## Fisher & Phillips LLP

See firm details p.732

**The Firm:** Fisher & Phillips' expansion into Kansas City with the merger of Bioff Finucane Coffey Holland & Day in March 2005 brought a national labor and employment law firm into the state. Representing employers throughout the USA, this boutique has a lot to offer clients. The team practices a mix of traditional labor law and employment law,

particularly litigation. Highlights of the year include the successful handling of several collective and class actions. A respected team including several dynamic lawyers, the Kansas City office is one to watch.

**The Lawyers:** The *"excellent"* **Brian Finucane** (see p.1205) is described by interviewees as a top of the line employment lawyer with a strong work ethic. Managing partner of the Kansas City office, he handles a variety of traditional labor law matters and employment discrimination cases.

**Clients/Work Highlights:** DST Systems; Kansas City Power & Light; Interstate Bakeries; American Ingredients; Sutherland Lumber; Farmers; Prudential Financial of America; Deffenbaugh Industries; GE; Neighbors Construction; Aramark; Tamko Asphalt Products and Deutsche Bank.

## Greensfelder, Hemker & Gale, P.C.

**The Firm:** A full-service firm based in St. Louis, this outfit is renowned for labor relations work and its representation of healthcare clients. These *"extremely knowledgeable labor and employment lawyers"* represent management in all aspects of the employer-employee relationship.

**The Lawyers:** Chair of the labor and employment group and described by interviewees as a *"top guy,"* **Dennis Collins** has a great reputation for union relations work. He also defends clients throughout the USA against employment discrimination claims. *"As bright as they come,"* **Mary Beth Ortbals** represents employers in matters before federal and state courts, the NLRB, the EEOC, and the DOL. She also advises clients on human resources issues and helps in the development of employment policies.

**Clients/Work Highlights:** Clients are drawn from a variety of industries including healthcare; grocery; manufacturing; technology; education and nonprofit organizations.

## McMahon Berger Hanna Linihan Cody & McCarthy, A Professional Corporation

See firm details p.1216

**The Firm:** For almost half a century this 24-strong St. Louis firm has been dedicated to labor and employment law. The team has a reputation for being *"great and aggressive"* in both traditional labor law and employment litigation. The firm has handled several discrimination charges and obtained two summary judgments in cases brought by the EEOC, where attorneys' fees were also awarded.

**The Lawyers:** **Thomas McCarthy**'s practice is mainly focused on litigation before federal and state courts and the NLRB. He is described by interviewees as a *"leading labor lawyer,"* and frequently conducts seminars on labor and employment law for employer organizations.

**Clients/Work Highlights:** Sigma Chemicals; Cox Communications; Enterprise Leasing; Bodine Aluminum; Brinker International; Cooper Industries; Dana; EDS and Emerson Electric.

### Other Notable Practitioners

**David Yates** (see p.1211) at Polsinelli Shalton Welte Suelthaus PC in St. Louis enters the table this year with 35 years of experience representing management in all aspects of labor and employment matters. Interviewees describe him as an *"excellent lawyer and litigator."* **Jack Yates** of Husch & Eppenberger LLC is highly respected for his experience and employment law practice.

# LITIGATION

| Litigation: General Commercial |
| --- |
| Leading Firms |
| [1] ARMSTRONG TEASDALE LLP *St Louis* |
|     BERKOWITZ OLIVER WILLIAMS SHAW *Kansas City* |
|     BRYAN CAVE LLP *St Louis* |
|     ROUSE HENDRICKS GERMAN MAY PC *Kansas City* |
|     SHOOK, HARDY & BACON LLP *Kansas City* |
|     SHUGHART THOMSON & KILROY PC *Kansas City* |
|     THOMPSON COBURN LLP *St Louis* |
| [2] BLACKWELL SANDERS PEPER MARTIN *Kansas City* |
|     HUSCH & EPPENBERGER, LLC *St Louis* |
|     KOHN, SHANDS, ELBERT, GIANOULAKIS *St Louis* |
|     LATHROP & GAGE L.C. *Kansas City* |
|     STINSON MORRISON HECKER LLP *Kansas City* |
| [3] DEACY & DEACY LLP *Kansas City* |
|     LEWIS, RICE & FINGERSH LC *St Louis* |
|     POLSINELLI SHALTON WELTE *Kansas City* |
|     SONNENSCHEIN NATH & ROSENTHAL *Kansas City* |
|     SPENCER FANE BRITT & BROWNE *Kansas City* |
|     WYRSCH HOBBS & MIRAKIAN *Kansas City* |

## Band 1

### Armstrong Teasdale LLP

**The Firm:** A regional leader, this firm boasts three Missouri offices and is praised for its strong litigation group. This is evidenced by a team of more than 75 litigators, with at least 30 practicing general commercial litigation and seven Fellows of the American College of Trial Lawyers. Clients appreciate the *"outstanding"* work delivered by a team of *"intelligent, diligent and creative"* problem solvers. The team's *"attention to detail and willingness to roll up their sleeves"* was also noted by clients. Recently the team has obtained a number of summary judgments in both Missouri and Illinois, as well as several appellate court successes. With the hire of top white-collar crime expert Jeffrey Demerath from Greensfelder, Hemker & Gale in May 2005, and the addition of a former US attorney for the Eastern District of Missouri, the firm anticipates further growth in this particular practice area.

**The Lawyers:** Cochair of the litigation department, **James Virtel** is cited as a *"wonderful and excellent lawyer"* by market commentators. Clients find him *"frank, astute, responsive"* and attuned to their own objectives. He *"lulls the opposition into a false sense of security."* The team has gained the skills of the *"extraordinary"* **Jeffrey Demerath**, who concentrates his practice on criminal defense and compliance. He is described by interviewees as *"extremely experienced, cooperative, has great judgment"* and delivers these attributes with a calm demeanor.

**Clients/Work Highlights:** Clients include those from the banking and finance; IT; healthcare; manufacturing and transportation sectors.

### Berkowitz Oliver Williams Shaw & Eisenbrandt LLP

**The Firm:** A 30-strong litigation boutique, this firm represents clients on both sides of the state line, in both state and federal courts. Clients include some of the largest household names in the retail and automotive industries. The team worked on a number of large class action defense cases, and was successful in obtaining summary judgment for a client in an antitrust case involving the manufacture of limousines. Clients put the firm *"right up there at the top of the list"* for its *"strong work ethic, commitment and client orientation."*

**The Lawyers:** The *"splendid"* **David Oliver** spends much of his time on class action defense work and recently went to Taiwan in order to gather evidence to use in a trial involving the use of aftermarket parts manufactured there. He has also mediated a case between a Taiwanese company and a Kentucky-based chainsaw manufacturer. *"Terrific"* senior statesman **Barney Berkowitz** is an extremely experienced litigator who is moving into the mediation arena, recently arbitrating and mediating securities and construction disputes both in Kansas City and New Mexico. He also represents architects and building owners in construction litigation. *"Probably the best white-collar criminal defense lawyer in Kansas City,"* **Jim Eisenbrandt** is described as *"one of the deans of the Bar"* who has refined the way white-collar criminal defense law is practiced. His trial work is concentrated in federal courts, representing companies and individuals who are under investigation for issues such as antitrust, tax, healthcare and general business fraud. New up-and-comer for white-collar crime, **Jeffrey Morris** has come into his own of late, and is described by interviewees as *"first class"* in the courtroom and *"exceptionally well prepared."* He was involved in a federal court case representing the president of a Kansas-based energy company.

**Clients/Work Highlights:** Ford; BMW North America; Morgan Stanley; KPMG; Prudential Securities; Kawasaki Motors Manufacturing USA; UBS Financial Services and H&R Block.

### Bryan Cave LLP

**The Firm:** Both the large St. Louis office and the sizable Kansas City office of this international heavyweight are described as *"excellent"* by market commentators. The biggest law firm headquartered in Missouri, clients say this is a *"go-to"* firm for large class action defense cases. The team undertook a products liability class action in the field of aviation, reducing by $100 million the amount of damages claimed by the plaintiffs against the aircraft manufacturer. The team also took on a class action lawsuit concerning H&R Block's refund anticipation loan program, alleging violation of West Virginia consumer protection statutes and various common law causes of action.

**The Lawyers:** *"Top lawyer"* **Dan Ball** is group leader of the products liability client service group and specializes in class and derivative actions. Managing partner of the Kansas City office and co-leader of the commercial litigation group, **Irvin Belzer** impresses clients and peers alike. **Craig O'Dear** tries cases nationwide and is involved in cases for H&R Block and Teledyne. *"One of the leading appellate lawyers in the county,"* **Thomas Walsh** represented comic book artist Todd McFarlane in appealing a $15 million damage award made to former professional hockey player Tony Twist, who contended that McFarlane's depiction of a villain named Tony Twist in a comic book misappropriated the plaintiff's right of publicity and damaged his future earning capacity. **Laurence Frazen** is renowned for his expertise in the area of bankruptcy and represents one of the world's preeminent financial services companies. **Edward Dowd** has a reputation for *"excellence"* in the white-collar criminal defense field and is prominent in the area of healthcare defense.

**Clients/Work Highlights:** Sprint; Bank of New York; Boeing; DaimlerChrysler; Ford; Bank of America; Monsanto; Wells Fargo; Commerce Bank; Lucent Technologies; Pulitzer Publishing; Merck; Teledyne; Barnes & Noble; HCA and GMAC.

### Rouse Hendricks German May PC

**The Firm:** A *"small but great"* boutique, this firm is highly favored by interviewees and lauded as *"terrific."* Clients use the team for a variety of multi-state litigations and find them *"extremely helpful, intelligent and creative."* Highlights include obtaining a $452 million jury verdict for Kansas City Power & Light in products liability claims arising out of a power plant explosion. The team also represented Lyondell in antitrust class actions brought by purchasers of polyurethane chemical products.

**The Lawyers:** Interviewees describe **Charles German** in superlatives: he is *"top-flight, excellent, top of the line, a leading light of the firm"* and *"first class"* in white-collar crime *"He is terrific and he makes the firm terrific."* Peers turn to him for advice on sophisticated federal criminal and civil litigation matters. He represented clients in several antitrust class actions in Kansas City.

**Clients/Work Highlights:** American Century;

## Litigation: General Commercial
### Leading Individuals

**Senior Statesman**

BERKOWITZ Lawrence *Berkowitz Oliver Williams Shaw*

★ WARD R Lawrence *Shughart Thomson & Kilroy PC*

[1] BROWN Spencer *Deacy & Deacy LLP*

EVERSON David *Stinson Morrison Hecker LLP*

GERMAN Charles *Rouse Hendricks German May PC*

GRIFFIN James *Blackwell Sanders Peper Martin LLP*

SAMPSON William *Shook, Hardy & Bacon LLP*

[2] ADAMS Robert *Shook, Hardy & Bacon LLP*

BALL Dan *Bryan Cave LLP*

BELZER Irvin *Bryan Cave LLP*

DALGLEISH Douglas *Lathrop & Gage L.C.*

DEAN Cathy *Polsinelli Shalton Welte*

GIANOULAKIS John *Kohn, Shands, Elbert*

KOHN Alan *Kohn, Shands, Elbert*

O'DEAR Craig *Bryan Cave LLP*

OLIVER David *Berkowitz Oliver Williams Shaw*

PRICE James *Spencer Fane Britt*

SHORT Barry *Lewis, Rice & Fingersh LC*

TRIPP David *Stinson Morrison Hecker LLP*

VIRTEL James *Armstrong Teasdale LLP*

VOIGTS Gene *Shook, Hardy & Bacon LLP*

WALSH Thomas *Bryan Cave LLP*

WOLF Jerome *Sonnenschein*

[3] BASH Roy *Shughart Thomson*

BECK William *Lathrop & Gage L.C.*

CARNEY Thomas *Husch & Eppenberger, LLC*

FRAZEN Laurence *Bryan Cave LLP*

KAPLAN Harvey *Shook, Hardy & Bacon LLP*

KOKORUDA Thomas *Shughart Thomson*

MASSEY Raymond *Thompson Coburn LLP*

NEWBOLD J William *Thompson Coburn LLP*

REBEIN Joseph *Shook, Hardy & Bacon LLP*

WELSH W Russell *Polsinelli Shalton Welte*

## Litigation: White-Collar Crime & Government Investigations
### Leading Individuals

[1] AISENBREY John *Stinson Morrison Hecker LLP*

ANKNEY Gordon *Thompson Coburn LLP*

BRADSHAW II Jean Paul *Lathrop & Gage L.C.*

DEMERATH Jeffrey *Armstrong Teasdale LLP*

DOWD JR Edward *Bryan Cave LLP*

EISENBRANDT James *Berkowitz Oliver Williams Shaw*

GERMAN Charles *Rouse Hendricks German May PC*

HOBBS James *Wyrsch Hobbs & Mirakian PC*

SHORT Barry *Lewis, Rice & Fingersh LC*

WYRSCH James *Wyrsch Hobbs & Mirakian PC*

[2] HILL Stephen *Blackwell Sanders Peper Martin LLP*

### Up-and-coming individuals

MORRIS Jeffrey *Berkowitz Oliver Williams Shaw*

Commerce Bank; Deloitte & Touche; Great Plains Energy; Hutchens Industries; Lyondell; Southwestern Bell Yellow Pages; Sprint; Stowers Institute; US Central; US Salt and Westar Energy.

## Shook, Hardy & Bacon LLP
See firm details p.1218

**The Firm:** This *"truly wonderful"* litigation team belongs to a *"powerhouse"* of a firm that clients believe *"sends a signal to the other side that we're a force to be reckoned with."* Praised by clients for its *"superb thoroughness, professionalism and responsiveness,"* this team thinks ahead and follows through for clients. The firm handles clients' litigation matters on a nationwide basis, including work on products liability cases for Tyco, consolidating the company's work throughout the USA out of the Kansas City office. The team is also renowned for its strong suit in tobacco and products litigation. As one client summed up, this firm offers a rare combination of *"litigation talent, savvy, ethics, cogent advice, prompt service and reasonable Midwest billings."*

**The Lawyers:** **Bill Sampson** (see p.1210) is lauded by market commentators for his no-nonsense approach. Clients said he displayed absolute *"complex mastery of the facts, which he was prepared to discuss at any time."* He represented a chemical company in Alabama against the French corporation Total and its US subsidiary, successfully obtaining summary judgment in a breach of contract action and defeating the defendant's motion for summary judgment on a fraud claim. **Rob Adams** (see p.1203) is renowned for his expertise in products liability defense and recently defended Ford in trials in New Jersey and Missouri. Interviewees say he is *"energetic, smart and one of the most experienced people in the community who actually tries cases."* **Gene Voigts** (see p.1210) is the firm's vice chairman and general counsel and a member of the firm's executive committee. **Harvey Kaplan** (see p.1207) chairs the firm's pharmaceutical and medical device litigation division and has tried cases in a variety of jurisdictions. **Joe Rebein** (see p.1209) chairs the firm's general litigation division and serves as lead trial counsel in complex matters, including antitrust and securities class actions. He represented a pharmaceutical company in the resolution of a multidistrict patent-related litigation in federal court in New Jersey. Clients say he provides them with *"consistently outstanding results."*

**Clients/Work Highlights:** Eli Lilly; DuPont; Sanofi-Synthelabo; sanofi-aventis; Miller Brewing; Capitol One; Lowe's Companies; Toshiba International; Jarden Corporation; BAT; Pfizer and Pharmacia.

## Shughart Thomson & Kilroy PC
See firm details p.1219

**The Firm:** This large and *"quality"* firm has a *"strong"* litigation team of *"lawyers' lawyers."* The business litigation department covers a wide range of matters, including financial, antitrust, breach of contract, securities, director liability and class action litigation. Highlights include representing Viacom Outdoor in a two-week jury trial in federal court in the defense of a breach of contract. The team also represented Sprint Nextel, winning an evidentiary class certification hearing in Dallas, Texas and also obtaining a reversal on appeal of a class certification in Louisiana in Chiarella v Sprint.

**The Lawyers:** A true *"star"* and *"dean of the Bar,"* **Larry Ward** (see p.1210) is admired for his strong presence in the courtroom, where he is described by interviewees as *"superb and extraordinary."* Chair of the firm's construction group, **Roy Bash** (see p.1203) is lauded as *"the best construction litigator in the city – as smart as can be."* Executive vice president of the firm, **Thomas Kokoruda** (see p.1207) chairs the litigation department and the healthcare litigation group. His practice is focused on hospital liability, physician malpractice and medical staff privilege litigation, and interviewees describe him as a *"great"* lawyer.

**Clients/Work Highlights:** HCA; H&R Block; Black & Veatch; BlueCross and BlueShield of Kansas City; JE Dunn Construction; Kansas City Power & Light and Burns McDonnell.

## Thompson Coburn LLP
See firm details p.1221

**The Firm:** This *"excellent"* St. Louis-based firm has one of the largest litigation teams in the region with close to 200 lawyers. The department is divided into 13 practice areas and a strong focus is placed on business litigation, IP, complex torts, products liability and railroad and admiralty issues. In 2005, the firm successfully represented American Commercial Barge Line in suing an insurance company in Jefferson, Indiana. The team also handled the litigation issues involved in the sale of client Astaris, a major US producer of specialty phosphates, to Israel Chemicals, a multinational fertilizer and specialty chemicals company.

**The Lawyers:** **Ray Massey** (see p.1208) is valued by clients as a *"wise"* lawyer who *"only acts if it will advance the case."* Among other highlights he represents Insituform in litigation matters regionally, locally and nationally. Senior counsel **Bill Newbold** (see p.1209) was successful as lead counsel in a nine-month trial involving tobacco companies. **Gordon Ankney** (see p.1203) is cited by interviewees as *"first rate"* for white-collar crime and government investigations and is highly respected for his experience and sound judgment. He was involved in several federal criminal cases, defending clients in government investigations and also assisting the government in several cases. Clients find him *"focused, detailed and helpful."*

**Clients/Work Highlights:** American Commercial Barge Line; Lorillard Tobacco; Cargill; Union Pacific; Charter Communications; DaimlerChrysler; SBC Communications; Bunzl USA; Insituform and Federal Signal.

## Band 2

## Blackwell Sanders Peper Martin LLP
See firm details p.1212

**The Firm:** With some 70 litigators in Kansas and 40 in St. Louis, this firm has a deep litigation presence in Missouri. The Kansas City office deals primarily with commercial litigation, the majority of which involves class action defense and also several plaintiff cases. Clients appreciate *"expert"* advice from this team. A highlight of the year was obtaining a summary judgment for client Aquila in a class action lawsuit alleging securities violations. Another jewel of the year was representing a coalition of insurance receivers across several states, recovering in excess of $9 million from Martin Frankel in the form of currency and diamonds.

**The Lawyers:** *"Top of the line trial lawyer"* **James Griffin** (see p.1206) recently obtained a defense verdict for a feed manufacturer in a jury trial. He worked on a number of class action defense cases, including high-profile lawsuits against charitable hospitals. Former US attorney for the Western District of Missouri, **Steve Hill** (see p.1206) is described by interviewees as *"an outstanding younger trial lawyer."* His practice involves defending criminal and regulatory actions, counseling businesses on internal investigations and the development of proactive compliance.

**Clients/Work Highlights:** AG Edwards & Sons; Stifel Nicolaus; The Kansas City Star and Saint Luke's-Shawnee Mission Health System.

### Husch & Eppenberger, LLC

**The Firm:** This firm has a *"strong"* outfit of litigators in St. Louis made up of *"fine"* attorneys. With four offices spread throughout the state and more than 150 litigators, the business litigation team has a deep pool of resources to draw on. The department represents clients in both state and federal courts in a full range of cases. Market commentators particularly noted the firm's skill at insurance defense litigation.

**The Lawyers:** *"Wonderful litigator"* **Thomas Carney** chairs the firm's general business litigation group and concentrates his practice on products liability, toxic torts and environmental litigation.

**Clients/Work Highlights:** Monsanto, Olin Corporation and various local and national financial and healthcare institutions are clients of the group.

### Kohn, Shands, Elbert, Gianoulakis & Giljum,LLP

**The Firm:** *"Kohn Shands is a different animal – it is small but wonderful."* This 15-strong St. Louis firm continues to be busy, getting great results for sophisticated clients. The team represents a number of local school districts. A highlight of the year was obtaining summary judgment in a case for a school district client in a multimillion-dollar litigation, the plaintiff being a teachers' union. Interviewees describe the lawyers as *"excellent and of high quality."*

**The Lawyers:** With a stellar reputation as a *"wonderful trial lawyer"* for business litigation, **John Gianoulakis** also represents public school districts, both as a counselor on a wide variety of issues from employee and student problems, and in the courtroom. **Alan Kohn** is described as an *"excellent trial lawyer with many skills and common sense."* A highlight of his year was a case involving the transportation of students, where the school district is suing the State of Missouri. He has also emerged victorious from arguing a case in the Eighth Circuit Court of Appeals involving a complex business transaction.

**Clients/Work Highlights:** Clients include a number of Fortune 500 companies, St. Louis businesses, school district clients and individuals.

### Lathrop & Gage L.C.

See firm details p.1214

**The Firm:** With 180 litigators and five offices in Missouri, this firm offers a large pool of expertise. Clients appreciate an *"economical operation"* coupled with *"high-quality"* work. The team has gone to great lengths to take advantage of this, coordinating its Missouri offices with those in Kansas, Colorado and New York. The firm has made a substantial investment in IP and obtained significant patent case wins in cases concerning medical devices. The team is also renowned for its successes in environmental litigation. The team defended insurers and represented businesses on a number of commercial claims resulting from a Mississippi river flood more than ten years ago. In another flood-related case, a Kansas district court jury found client BNSF Railway not liable for $15 million worth of damages to Everseal when a 1998 Kansas City flood trapped one of its trains in the Turkey Creek area.

**The Lawyers:** **Douglas Dalgleish** (see p.1204) is described by interviewees as *"extremely smart and results-oriented."* He was involved in a complex contract dispute arbitration involving intermodal transportation for client BNSF Railway. He was also involved in a maritime case and has two international clients. *"Fine lawyer"* and environment litigator **William Beck** (see p.1203) continues to successfully defend clients in Superfund matters, closing landfill sites throughout the USA. He also undertakes insurance and toxic tort cases. A *"sharp, knowledgeable lawyer who gets great results for his clients,"* **Jean Paul Bradshaw** (see p.1203) successfully concluded the defense of one of the largest privately held US companies in an environmental criminal investigation in St. Louis in a pollution claim. His workload also includes defending clients in the healthcare industry against claims of fraud.

**Clients/Work Highlights:** Allied Waste Industries; American Multi-Cinema; Ash Grove Cement; Deere & Company; Extended Stay America; Fortis Benefits Insurance; Payless ShoeSource; Marillac Centre; O'Reilly Automotive; State of Kansas; Shinn Fu; Parmelee Industries and GM.

### Stinson Morrison Hecker LLP

See firm details p.1220

**The Firm:** This quality firm has a number of strong litigators in its *"superb"* Kansas City office, with *"not just one star, but a host of smart and accomplished trial lawyers."* The team was highly successful in IP and antitrust cases, and obtained summary judgment for Aventis Pharmaceuticals in a multidistrict case involving a challenge to the settlement of patent litigation. The firm is also representing the same client in Alameda County, California, in a multiparty case alleging an antitrust conspiracy involving the pricing of pharmaceuticals. Great results for reasonable costs impressed clients.

**The Lawyers:** Excellent litigator **David Everson**

(see p.1205) is renowned for his prowess in antitrust cases, continuing to win judgments in his clients' favor. Clients find his *"storytelling"* approach a pleasure to work with. **David Tripp** (see p.1210) is a leader in environmental law, dealing with cases on clean air, water and toxic substances. He represented a coalition of electric utilities and has begun representing a Fortune 100 company in a toxic tort defense case. Interviewees *"think the world"* of the *"outstanding trial lawyer"* **John Aisenbrey** (see p.1203), who is described as *"smart, aggressive and tough competition."* In addition to his white-collar crime and government investigations practice, he also takes on business litigation, recently leading on a multimillion-dollar dispute between reinsurance companies.

**Clients/Work Highlights:** GE Insurance Solutions; Hallmark Cards; Sprint Nextel; Aventis Pharmaceuticals; S&M NuTec and Big Dog Motorcycles.

## Band 3

### Deacy & Deacy LLP

**The Firm:** This Kansas City litigation boutique is home to a number of respected trial lawyers. The nine-strong team offers clients its expertise in a variety of matters, including antitrust, banking and railroad law. It is particularly renowned for its skills in insurance defense work.

**The Lawyers:** *"Awesome"* attorney **Spencer Brown** is famed for his *"outstanding"* abilities in the courtroom. Business torts, securities and asbestos litigation cases are among his repertoire.

**Clients/Work Highlights:** BellSouth; BNSF Railway; Cessna; Continental Western Insurance; Hyatt; Illinois Central Railroad; CIGNA; Lexington Insurance; Missouri Insurance Guaranty Association; Pitney Bowes and Southwestern Bell.

### Lewis, Rice & Fingersh LC

See firm details p.1215

**The Firm:** Market commentators praise this *"wonderful"* team of litigators, with 60 dedicated attorneys and six offices throughout the state. The team represents clients in a wide variety of commercial disputes, including claims brought under general contract law, business tort law, insurance policies, the Uniform Commercial Code, federal and state securities laws, lender liability, and class action representations.

**The Lawyers:** The *"superb"* lawyer **Barry Short** is particularly admired for *"not being afraid to try a case."* He is lauded for both his general commercial litigation skills and his expertise in white-collar crime. His practice also involves antitrust and environmental, chemical and toxic tort litigation.

**Clients/Work Highlights:** Bank of America; DaimlerChrysler; Doe Run; St. Louis Post-Dispatch; The Stanley Works; RightCHOICE Managed Care; Pioneer Hi-Bred International; True Fitness Technology and Owens Corning.

## Polsinelli Shalton Welte Suelthaus

See firm details p.1217

**The Firm:** This Midwestern firm has three offices in the state and a large litigation team experienced in arbitration, mediation, trial and appellate work. The group represents clients in a full range of litigation services, from breaches of contract to complex antitrust and RICO actions. Highlights of the year include class actions relating to pharmaceutical products and products liability cases in the automotive industry.

**The Lawyers:** Chair of the litigation department **Cathy Dean** (see p.1204) is known for her work on trials relating to the pharmaceutical sector. She is well versed in products liability, antitrust and taxation disputes. Chairman and CEO of the firm **Russell Welsh** (see p.1211) is admired for his integrity and charisma in the courtroom. His practice includes products liability, business torts and bankruptcy litigation.

**Clients/Work Highlights:** Bayer; Bristol-Myers Squibb; Honeywell; University of Kansas Hospital Authority and the Stowers Institute for Medical Research.

## Sonnenschein Nath & Rosenthal LLP

See firm details p.884

**The Firm:** A Chicago-based outfit, with offices in San Francisco, Los Angeles, New York, Washington, DC and St. Louis, this firm has a significant presence in Kansas City and has hired more than ten lawyers over the past year. The firm has a multioffice coordination work ethic and the litigation department is divided into seven specific subgroups. The firm

settled a case for Lafarge North America, the world's largest supplier of construction materials, to the tune of more than $300 million. The firm also represented two minority shareholders, negotiating a favorable buyout from a company in financial trouble.

**The Lawyers:** Head of the Kansas City litigation group, **Jerome Wolf** (see p.1211) is a highly respected trial lawyer with a full litigation docket. His practice covers environmental, antitrust, IP, construction litigation and alternative dispute resolution issues.

**Clients/Work Highlights:** CNA Insurance Companies; Sun Microsystems; Lafarge North America; Wolfe Automotive; Mediacom Communications and Duke Energy.

## Spencer Fane Britt & Browne LLP

**The Firm:** Market commentators praise this regional firm for its *"fine negotiators and litigators."* The litigation and dispute resolution group is described as *"intellectually strong and having great client advocates."* The group endorses mediation and arbitration as a means of resolving disputes and also puts together focus teams to serve clients' needs.

**The Lawyers:** Chair of the environmental law group, **Jim Price** stands out for his *"excellence"* in environmental litigation. His practice concentrates on environmental regulation and compliance, environmental litigation, insurance coverage litigation and business transactions involving environmental issues.

**Clients/Work Highlights:** Attorneys act for clients in the telecom, environmental, media and manufacturing sectors.

## Wyrsch Hobbs & Mirakian PC

**The Firm:** This boutique litigation firm is highly respected by other litigation teams, who turn to them for their expertise in white-collar crime: this *"excellent"* outfit is *"probably the best for criminal litigation."* The firm does a significant amount of healthcare defense litigation and a highlight of the year was the conclusion of the representation of Dan Anderson, former CEO of Baptist Medical Center, a hospital in Kansas City. The team is also recognized for its defense of attorneys involved in disciplinary and criminal proceedings.

**The Lawyers:** Premier attorney **James Hobbs** deals mainly in criminal defense litigation and earns the respect of both judges and prosecutors with his *"gentle-mannered, understated, well-prepared"* approach in court, obtaining excellent results for clients. He was involved in a fraud case in New York and Kansas City based on a claim that consumers were being tricked into buying highly priced pornography on the Internet. Excellent lawyer and *"dean of the Bar"* **James Wyrsch** (see p.1211) splits his practice between civil and criminal litigation. He is praised for his involvement in *"tremendous cases"* and his role in changing the way white-collar criminal law is practiced. He shined for clients with his elephantine memory.

**Clients/Work Highlights:** Clients include a variety of individuals and business organizations, including those in the moving and storage, healthcare and petroleum industries.

# REAL ESTATE

## Real Estate
### Leading Firms

| | |
|---|---|
| [1] | BLACKWELL SANDERS PEPER MARTIN *St Louis* |
| | BRYAN CAVE LLP *St Louis* |
| | LEWIS, RICE & FINGERSH, L.C. *Kansas City* |
| | STINSON MORRISON HECKER LLP *Kansas City* |
| [2] | LATHROP & GAGE L.C. *Kansas City* |
| | POLSINELLI SHALTON WELTE *Kansas City* |
| | WHITE GOSS BOWERS MARCH *Kansas City* |
| [3] | ARMSTRONG TEASDALE LLP *St Louis* |
| | GREENSFELDER, HEMKER & GALE *St Louis* |
| | HUSCH & EPPENBERGER, LLC *St Louis* |
| | KING HERSHEY, PC *Kansas City* |
| | SHUGHART THOMSON & KILROY PC *Kansas City* |
| | THOMPSON COBURN LLP *St Louis* |

## Band 1

### Blackwell Sanders Peper Martin LLP

See firm details p.1212

**The Firm:** With 16 attorneys in the St. Louis office,

14 in Kansas City and three in Springfield, the firm's real estate team spans Missouri. Interviewees are impressed with the *"high standard of real estate expertise"* at this *"outstanding household name."* The Kansas City team has an excellent reputation for zoning and land use work, while in St. Louis the diverse team represents lenders across the USA, in addition to undertaking leasing work and representing the firm's corporate clients in acquisitions and dispositions. Highlights include Project Renov8, an $80 million renovation and expansion plan to enhance the downtown presence of the Federal Reserve Bank of St. Louis. The team also represented Axa Equitable Life Insurance in a $40 million financing for the Grand Traverse Resort in Michigan, a 660-acre development including a high-rise hotel, convention center, condominiums, a health club and three golf courses. The borrower was the Grand Traverse Band of Ottawa and Chippewa Indians, recognized by the federal government as a Native Sovereign Nation.

**The Lawyers:** *"Fine attorney"* and chairman of the firm's real estate department, **John McNearney** (see p.1208) continues to focus his practice on real estate

finance and acts for some of the largest investment banks in the USA, doing loan workout transactions for many projects, including high-rise condominiums, retail centers and a Californian winery. **Kathleen Mueller** (see p.1209) has concentrated a substantial amount of her practice on handling the needs of the firm's corporate clients both locally and nationally, helping them to lease office, warehouse and laboratory space. She has also helped manufacturing facilities obtain zoning permits. **Lon Brincks** (see p.1204) is described by market commentators as a *"leading real estate attorney."* He is renowned for his leasehold work and has also closed numerous lender financings. **David Fenley** (see p.1205) is described by interviewees as *"one of those leading the development folks in Kansas City"* and a *"smart"* zoning and land use attorney.

**Clients/Work Highlights:** Aquila; AXA; AG Edwards & Sons; Federal Reserve Bank of St. Louis; H&R Block; Highwoods Properties; JC Nichols; Jacobs Engineering; Keystone Bank; National City Bank and Tyco International.

## Real Estate
### Leading Individuals

1. **CARR William** *Lewis, Rice & Fingersh, L.C.*
   **DIGIOVANNI Peter** *Lewis, Rice & Fingersh, L.C.*
   **FRANTZE David** *Stinson Morrison Hecker LLP*
   **KING Richard** *King Hershey, PC*
   **MILLER Charles** *Lewis, Rice & Fingersh, L.C.*

2. **BRINCKS Lon** *Blackwell Sanders*
   **DAGENAIS Don** *Lathrop & Gage L.C.*
   **FITZGERALD JR Robert** *Shughart Thomson & Kilroy*
   **HAINES Lisa** *Polsinelli Shalton Welte*
   **MCNEARNEY John** *Blackwell Sanders*
   **MUELLER Kathleen** *Blackwell Sanders*
   **MURRAY George** *Bryan Cave LLP*
   **SHALTON Lonnie** *Polsinelli Shalton Welte*
   **SPARKS Stephen** *Bryan Cave LLP*

3. **FLANIGAN Daniel** *Polsinelli Shalton Welte*
   **HAUBER Catherine** *Stinson Morrison Hecker LLP*
   **SHTEAMER Michael** *Shughart Thomson & Kilroy*
   **TRYNIECKI Timothy** *Armstrong Teasdale LLP*

### Up-and-coming individuals

**LASALA Todd** *Stinson Morrison Hecker LLP*

## Real Estate: Zoning/Land Use
### Leading Individuals

1. **FENLEY David** *Blackwell Sanders*
   **KING Richard** *King Hershey, PC*
   **WHITE Michael** *White Goss Bowers*

2. **BOWERS James** *White Goss Bowers*
   **MARCH Aaron** *White Goss Bowers*
   **NESTER Daniel** *Bryan Cave LLP*
   **RIFFEL Jerome** *Lathrop & Gage L.C.*

### Up-and-coming individuals

**JENSEN Patricia** *White Goss Bowers*

## Bryan Cave LLP

**The Firm:** This international firm has a strong real estate presence in Missouri and is admired for its *"excellent lawyer base, great clients, wonderful work and a can-do attitude."* Much of the work they do is local, but this team has the benefit of drawing on the firm's pool of expertise from Los Angeles to New York. The team is representing the City of Kansas in its downtown revitalization, including a new multi-purpose arena, an entertainment district and a new world headquarters for H&R Block. In St. Louis, the team handled the $50 million financing of the acquisition and renovation of five apartment complexes in the city for Delphi Affordable Housing Group.

**The Lawyers:** **George Murray** has a national and regional practice encompassing the full breadth of real estate work including finance, leasing, acquisition and construction. His knowledge and broad range of experience are highly respected by market commentators. Kansas City-based **Steve Sparks** is involved in the downtown redevelopment and is recommended for zoning and land use work. Zoning and land use attorney **Dan Nester** represented City Beverages on the $19 million acquisition and construction of an Anheuser-Busch beer distribution

and warehouse facility on the outskirts of Seattle.

**Clients/Work Highlights:** Aimco; Sara Lee; Emerson Electric; Merrill Lynch; Lucent Technologies; Watson Pharmaceuticals; Rave Motion Picture Theaters; Sunrise Assisted Living; West Pointe Bank; Forever Enterprises and Monsanto.

## Lewis, Rice & Fingersh, L.C.
See firm details p.1215

**The Firm:** This regional firm boasts six offices spread throughout Missouri and is involved in real estate projects throughout the state. The *"strong"* real estate department has added several lawyers at associate level to its 28-strong team. Viewed by market commentators as *"a real player,"* the team has worked on large regional mixed-use projects. One highlight includes representing Copaken in the $400 million development of Lenexa City Center, which aims to provide a unified focal point for an expanding suburb outside Kansas City. The team also represented clients in residential condominium projects and handled the leasing of movie theaters nationwide.

**The Lawyers:** **Bill Carr** (see p.1204) has been working on an innovative way of financing charter schools. He also represented the Landmark Theatre Corporation in its expansion across Los Angeles, Denver, Baltimore and Indianapolis. Clients found him *"forthright, honest and reliable."* Head of real estate in Kansas City, **Charles Miller** (see p.1208) has *"a quiet way of getting things accomplished – the work gets done with Charlie."* Interviewees find him *"first rate."* Clients say of **Peter DiGiovanni** (see p.1204): *"Few have his expertise and knowledge in the shopping center industry – he is first class."* In 2005, he concluded the sale of three regional malls to a REIT in a $500 million transaction.

**Clients/Work Highlights:** American Multi-Cinema; Sprint Spectrum; Mills Corporation; Westfield Corporation; Helzberg's Diamond Shops; Sprint; Landmark Theatre Corporation; Copaken, White & Blitt; Dreiseszun and Morgan; VeriSign; AMLI Residential Properties and Pulte Homes.

## Stinson Morrison Hecker LLP
See firm details p.1220

**The Firm:** This *"great"* real estate practice has a large and diverse group comprising 31 lawyers. It was a busy year for the team, involving work on $1 billion worth of projects in downtown Kansas City. This included representing The Cordish Company in its Kansas City Live downtown retail entertainment district in the South Loop area of the city. The team has also acted for the Unified Government of Wyandotte County/Kansas City, Kansas in all phases of legal work for the $250 million International Speedway Corporation 75,000-seat NASCAR auto racetrack. They forge close relationships with clients, who find them *"extremely thorough, high quality and devoted to representing our interests."*

**The Lawyers:** Chair of the real estate division, **Dave Frantze** (see p.1206) is lauded by interviewees as *"an incredible lawyer – open-minded, sharp, great at finding creative solutions, interested in keeping deals alive*

*and a pleasure to work with."* He handles economic development incentives as well as being a transactional lawyer. The experienced **Kate Hauber** (see p.1206) offers clients a full range of real estate services, including conservation easements and environmental liability issues. Interviewees admire her as a *"responsive and accomplished real estate lawyer."* New up-and-comer **Todd LaSala** (see p.1207) is described by interviewees as *"extremely bright and hard-working."* He is lauded by clients as *"dedicated, timely and a great presence."* He concentrates his practice on representing commercial real estate owners, brokers and developers. He played a key role in the development of Village West, the 400-acre retail and entertainment district next to the Kansas Speedway.

**Clients/Work Highlights:** Anschutz Entertainment Group; Briarcliff Development; DST Realty; PETsMART; DeBruce Grain; Federal Reserve Bank of Kansas City; The Cordish Company; Entertainment Properties Trust; Kansas City Art Institute; Clay Blair Services; Home Decorators Collection; Swope Community Builders; Union Hill and Union Station.

## Band 2

## Lathrop & Gage L.C.
See firm details p.1214

**The Firm:** This 25-strong regional outfit is active in Kansas City's downtown development. The firm represented the Kansas and Missouri Union Station Bistate Commission to fund $118 million of a $256 million project to renovate Kansas City's historic Union Station and create a world-class science museum. The team also represented a large developer in a complex project involving water rights and treatment issues in Taney County, Missouri. The firm also has a significant zoning and land use presence in Springfield, where the team of four real estate lawyers were active in a high-end PPP financing. The merger of Lathrop & Gage with insurance law firm Craft Fridkin & Rhyne in 2004 has brought the group several sophisticated clients with a high level of interest in government regulations. Clients found the firm populated with *"excellent legal advisors with a strong commitment to customer service,"* and one client commented: *"They are respected and know the right people; we wouldn't have made it without them."*

**The Lawyers:** *"Principled and efficient,"* **Don Dagenais** (see p.1204) continues to represent developers and acts for lenders in loans for conversions of buildings into condominiums. Zoning and land use attorney **Jerry Riffel** (see p.1209) has worked on two $300 million mixed-use projects for Pinnacle Entertainment in downtown St. Louis and in the suburb of Lemay, involving retail outlets, a hotel and casino. He provides *"invaluable advice"* to clients and brings a *"broad base of legal knowledge and political insight"* to the table.

**Clients/Work Highlights:** AMC Entertainment; Zimmer Development; Hilton Hotels; Children's Mercy Hospitals & Clinics; Kansas City Area Transportation Authority; Bank of America; DST Realty;

Hallmark Cards; Lafarge; T-Mobile; Russell Stovers Candies and Union Hill.

## Polsinelli Shalton Welte Suelthaus

See firm details p.1217

**The Firm:** *"A great school of lawyers,"* this outfit provides clients with expert representation in real estate financing. Highlights include handling the issuance of a cutting-edge substantive consolidation opinion for PNC. The firm also boasts a growing defeasance practice and a successful transactional practice, representing the New York-based Extell Development nationwide. In the largest residential land sale in US history, the team acted for Extell in the $1.8 billion purchase of a 77-acre group of properties along the Hudson River waterfront, bought from Donald Trump and a Chinese investment consortium. Clients' verdict was *"responsive, affordable and thorough."*

**The Lawyers:** **Lonnie Shalton** (see p.1210) is lauded as *"one of the premier transactional lawyers in the nation when it come to buying, selling and financing."* Interviewees admire his *"pragmatism."* Chair of the firm's real estate and financial services department, **Daniel Flanigan** (see p.1205) is described by interviewees as *"extremely bright"* when it comes to representing national lenders in financing activities and acts for big-name clients. **Lisa Haines** (see p.1206) is praised for her skills in loan work. In addition to the Extell transaction, highlights include a $500 million water park and retail river walk facility in Kansas City, Kansas.

**Clients/Work Highlights:** KeyBank; Wells Fargo; Extell Development; Developers Diversified Realty; Bridger Commercial Funding; Credit Suisse Group and AG Spanos.

## White Goss Bowers March Schulte & Weisenfels, A Professional Corporation

**The Firm:** This boutique law firm in Kansas City is praised by interviewees as *"top of the class"* on land use, zoning and economic development incentives. Clients appreciate its *"creative, aggressive"* approach: *"The team know how to get results and the attorneys are top notch."* The firm also has four partners in the area of general real estate.

**The Lawyers:** Government incentives specialist **Michael White** is *"a cut above, with a combination of skills and knowledge."* Praised by clients as *"excellent and scholarly,"* he is *"the original real estate development lawyer in the region."* **James Bowers** focuses on zoning matters throughout Missouri and also handles public financing. *"Deal-maker and effective negotiator"* **Aaron March** is known for charming those in the public sector. In 2005, he concentrated on sizable economic development projects in the metropolitan area and in Springfield, Missouri, representing the City of Springfield in the financing of a mixed-use, lifestyle retail center with loft and residential use. **Patricia Jensen** concentrates her practice on zoning and was involved in condominium conversions throughout Kansas City. Her

*"technical knowledge and diligence"* are appreciated by interviewees.

**Clients/Work Highlights:** Knight Ridder; Home Depot; Wal-Mart and Jackson County Sports Complex Authority.

## Band 3

### Armstrong Teasdale LLP

**The Firm:** This real estate group boasts more than 30 attorneys across its three Missouri offices, with the mainstay of the practice in St. Louis. Continuing the firm's cross-departmental culture, the real estate transactional team worked with the firm's incentives practice group on the development of a shopping center. The team continues to work on the development of the Cardinals' new downtown stadium and also represented BJC HealthCare in the development of new facilities.

**The Lawyers:** Transactional attorney **Tim Tryniecki** *"does a fine job"* for clients and is admired for being *"practical and knowledgeable."* He is leader of the firm's real estate group and is a member of both the ACREL and the International Council of Shopping Centers.

**Clients/Work Highlights:** Mills Properties; BJC HealthCare; Ameren; Centocor; Pfizer and Harman Kardon.

### Greensfelder, Hemker & Gale, P.C.

**The Firm:** This firm's real estate team is divided between Illinois and Missouri, with eight attorneys in the St. Louis office. The firm has a strong reputation for its skills in construction law and has a team of 13 lawyers dedicated to this practice.

**The Lawyers:** Thomas Story heads the real estate team and represents clients in a full range of services, from parcel assemblage, construction and financing to leasing and sale. He has particular expertise in real estate tax planning and creative financing.

**Clients/Work Highlights:** Clients include developers; investors; landlords; property managers; local and national retailers; for profit and nonprofit property owners, tenants, lenders and borrowers.

### Husch & Eppenberger, LLC

**The Firm:** This land use development and financing group is recognized by interviewees as *"experienced, practical and not trying to showboat or grandstand."* The firm has also made an impact both in Missouri and nationally with its *"premier"* construction group. Clients find the construction team *"bright, diligent, responsive and really on top of all the modern issues."* The firm is also lauded for being *"great value for money."*

**The Lawyers:** Chair of the land use development and financing group, St. Louis-based Gary Feder concentrates his practice on real estate law, including acquisition, zoning and condemnation issues. He also practices school law, corporate law and related litigation. Susan Linden McGreevy chairs the construction team. Her practice involves advising construction companies and she is also a member of

the firm's business transactions group in Kansas City.
**Clients/Work Highlights:** Clients include construction companies; national, regional and local enterprises and developers; landlords; tenants; community banks; regional banks; money center institutions; asset-based lenders and life insurance companies.

### King Hershey, PC

See firm details p.1213

**The Firm:** This Kansas City firm has a niche practice, specializing in structuring public-private financing for development. Interviewees admire this team of *"accomplished attorneys."* The firm represented clients in a number of mixed-use assignments. Highlights of the year include putting together a $300 million financing project for Bass Pro sporting goods shops in the city of Independence, Missouri. The team also worked on the conversion of office buildings for residential use and the financing of a hospital.

**The Lawyers:** Chairman and CEO of the firm, **Richard King** (see p.1207) is famed for his work in the suburb of Independence and recognized as *"top notch for zoning."* He is described by interviewees as *"extremely bright"* and peers find him to be a *"challenging opponent."*

**Clients/Work Highlights:** City of Boonville; City of Fulton; Clay County, Missouri; Economic Development Corporation of Kansas City; Land Clearance for Redevelopment Authority of Kansas City, Missouri; Quality Hill Redevelopment; Hospital Corporation of America; Ameristar Casinos and Security Bank of Kansas City.

### Shughart Thomson & Kilroy PC

See firm details p.1219

**The Firm:** This real estate team has a significant presence in Kansas City, with a 13-strong outfit, and two attorneys based in St. Joseph, Missouri. The group works closely with the firm's sizable construction department to provide clients with representation in all phases of real property acquisition, entitlement, construction, operation, sale and financing. Development projects taken on by the team include retail, industrial, multifamily, hospitality, medical, entertainment and recreational facilities.

**The Lawyers:** Business, tax and real estate lawyer **Robert Fitzgerald** (see p.1205) is praised by interviewees as a *"fine attorney."* He has more than 30 years' experience in representing clients in Kansas City. **Michael Shteamer** (see p.1210) has a diverse practice including banking, healthcare, corporate and business law alongside his real estate expertise.

**Clients/Work Highlights:** Capital Electric; DST Realty; Landmark Mortgage; Sutherland Lumber and Sunway Hotel Group.

### Thompson Coburn LLP

See firm details p.1221

**The Firm:** This increasingly busy real estate team hired two new law graduates in the fall of 2005, bringing the department in St. Louis to more than 20 attorneys. The firm represents a number of St.

Louis-based clients in both local and regional projects. Highlights of the year include a $200 million undertaking converting more than 15,000 apartments into condominiums in the Central West End in St. Louis. Clients found the team's work to be timely and of high quality.

**The Lawyers:** Daniel Engle and Paul Macon chair the real estate group. Engle represents commercial property owners, developers and borrowers in complex transactions. Macon complements his real estate expertise with work in the banking and finance and construction arenas.

**Clients/Work Highlights:** Barry-Wehmiller; Commercial Development; Mills Properties; US Bank; Hardee's; Savvis Communications and Clayco Construction.

# Leaders in Missouri

## ADAMS, Robert
Shook, Hardy & Bacon LLP, Kansas City
816 474 6550
rtadams@shb.com
*Recommended in Litigation*
**Practice Areas:** Practices in products liability litigation, intellectual property litigation, insurance coverage litigation, and tort litigation. Has tried more than 30 jury trials in several different states, primarily in the areas of automobile litigation, patent litigation and insurance coverage litigation. Has made numerous appellate arguments in appellate courts throughout the country.
**Prof. Memberships:** Admitted to practice in Missouri and before the US Court of Appeals for the Fourth and Eighth Circuits. Member of Federation of Defense and Corporate Counsel and Board Member of Missouri Organization of Defense Lawyers.
**Career:** Joined Shook, Hardy & Bacon, 1987; became Partner, 1994. Chair, Shook, Hardy & Bacon Tort Section. Member, Shook, Hardy & Bacon Executive Committee.
**Publications:** 'Juror Non-Disclosure', MODL Journal (April 2000); 'Practical Aspects of the Revisions to the Federal Rules of Civil Procedure', Journal of the Missouri Bar (1994).
**Personal:** JD, University of Missouri-Columbia Law School, 1987; BA, University of Kansas, 1984.

## ADAMS, Stephen
Blackwell Sanders Peper Martin LLP, Kansas City 816 983 8173
sadams@blackwellsanders.com
*Recommended in Corporate/M&A*
**Practice Areas:** Commercial transactions; healthcare; mergers and acquisitions; real estate.
**Prof. Memberships:** Admitted to practice in Kansas (1970) and Missouri (1971). Member, American Bar Association; American Health Lawyers Association; Greater Kansas City Society of Health Care Attorneys; Johnson County Bar Association; Kansas Bar Association; Kansas Hospital Attorneys Association; Lawyers Association of Kansas City; the Missouri Bar; and Missouri Society of Hospital Attorneys.
**Career:** Joined firm, 1970; named Partner, 1976.
**Personal:** JD, University of Kansas Law

School, 1970; Order of Coif, Member, 'Kansas Law Review', 1968-70; BS, University of Kansas, 1967.

## AISENBREY, John C
Stinson Morrison Hecker LLP, Kansas City 816 842 8600
jaisenbrey@stinsonmoheck.com
*Recommended in Litigation*
**Practice Areas:** Focuses on commercial litigation and white-collar crime. Provides representation in complex commercial, civil RICO and fraud matters, federal criminal investigations and prosecutions, and internal investigations. Also defends manufacturers in product liability actions.
**Prof. Memberships:** Admitted in Missouri and Kansas; IADC, National Association of Criminal Defense Lawyers, American Bar Association.
**Career:** Former assistant United States attorney, District of Columbia. Was law clerk to Judge Roger Robb, US Court of Appeals for DC Circuit. Former Adjunct Law Professor at University of Missouri-Kansas City School of Law.
**Personal:** JD, Georgetown University, 1977; AB, Cornell University, 1969.

## ANKNEY, Gordon L
Thompson Coburn LLP, St Louis
314 552 6003
gankney@thompsoncoburn.com
*Recommended in Litigation*
**Practice Areas:** Co-Chairman of firm's White Collar Practice. Has extensive experience as a trial lawyer in white-collar criminal cases, as well as civil commercial litigation.
**Career:** Spent 12 years as special prosecutor in St. Louis, Missouri. In private practice, he has tried cases to juries involving allegations of fraud, securities violations, false test reports, nuisance, anti-trust, government false claims, taxation, negligence, bid-rigging and whistleblower claims. His trials have taken place in federal and state courts, including: Missouri, Illinois, Kansas, Alabama and Maryland. Has made extensive use of computers in trials, especially in US v Thermal Science, Inc., USDC Maryland.

## ASH, James
Blackwell Sanders Peper Martin LLP, Kansas City 816 983 8137
jash@blackwellsanders.com
*Recommended in Corporate/M&A*

**Practice Areas:** Mergers and acquisitions; securities.
**Prof. Memberships:** Admitted to practice in Missouri (1981). Listed: 'Best Lawyers in America'.
**Career:** Joined firm as Partner, 1993. Chair, Blackwell Sanders Peper Martin Corporate Department, 2000-present.
**Personal:** JD, University of California at Los Angeles, 1981; Member, Order of the Coif and Law Review; editor, University of California at Los Angeles 'Alaska Law Review'; BA, University of California at Los Angeles (with honors), 1978.

## BALL, Dan
Bryan Cave LLP, St Louis
314 259 2000
*Recommended in Litigation*

## BARTELSMEYER, Fred
Bryan Cave LLP, St Louis
314 259 2000
*Recommended in Corporate/M&A*

## BASH, Roy
Shughart Thomson & Kilroy PC, Kansas City 816 395 0633
rbash@stklaw.com
*Recommended in Litigation*
**Practice Areas:** Litigation; construction law; professional liability. Roy Bash Chairs the firm's Construction Practice Group. He represents numerous constituents in the industry with an emphasis on those entities with general construction, CM, EPC and design-build responsibilities. He has also represented many architectural/engineering firms with design liability issues. He also serves as an arbitrator and mediator in construction disputes.
**Prof. Memberships:** American Arbitration Association. Has served as arbitrator or mediator on a number of occasions, including arbitration of a commercial dispute regarding an international licensing agreement for computer software. American Bar Association Forum on the Construction Industry. The Missouri Bar.
**Career:** Joined Shughart Thomson & Kilroy in 1990 as Shareholder/Director. Chair, Construction Practice Group. Member, Executive Committee. 1974 court admissions in Iowa and Missouri. Missouri & Kansas Super Lawyers and KC Magazine in 2005 recognized Roy as a Top 50 Super Lawyer. Listed in 'Chambers USA: America's Leading Lawyers for

Business' (2005).
**Personal:** Born in Oklahoma City, Oklahoma. University of Iowa, BBA with High Distinction, 1971. University of Iowa, JD 1974. Phi Delta Phi, President, 1973-74.

## BECK, William G
Lathrop & Gage L.C., Kansas City
816 460 5811
bbeck@lathropgage.com
*Recommended in Litigation*
**Practice Areas:** Environmental, insurance and other complex litigation.
**Career:** Beck devotes his practice to resolving complex environmental liabilities and insurance claims. His environmental experience includes matters relating to the generation, transportation, treatment, storage, disposal, cleanup and taxation of hazardous and solid waste, including acquisition, permitting, operational, corrective action, closure, financial assurance and post-closure issues for both sanitary landfills and hazardous waste facilities. He successfully represents policyholders seeking to enforce coverage for environmental damages and defends toxic tort lawsuits claiming personal injury, death and property damage due to chemical exposure. He has experience in insurance archeology, claims resolution and coverage litigation.

## BELZER, Irvin
Bryan Cave LLP, Kansas City
816 374 3200
*Recommended in Litigation*

## BERKOWITZ, Lawrence
Berkowitz Oliver Williams Shaw & Eisenbrandt LLP, Kansas City
816 561 7007
*Recommended in Litigation*

## BOWERS, James
White Goss Bowers March Schulte & Weisenfels, A Professional Corporation, Kansas City 816 753 9200
*Recommended in Real Estate*

## BRADSHAW II, Jean Paul
Lathrop & Gage L.C., Kansas City
816 460 5507
jpbradshaw@lathropgage.com
*Recommended in Litigation*
**Career:** Bradshaw's practice includes white-collar criminal defense, healthcare fraud and abuse, internal corporate investigations, the establishment of corporate preventative law programs that comply

with federal requirements and complex commercial litigation. His experience includes: United States Attorney, Western District of Missouri, 1989-93; formed first healthcare fraud task force in Missouri in 1992; Chairman-Elect and Member, United States Attorney General's Advisory Committee - Subcommittees on Sentencing Guidelines, Office Management and Budget, 1991-93; Member, Economic Crimes Council, US Department of Justice, 1989-93; and Member, Governor's Commission on Crime, 1989-93. He was selected as 'Leading Lawyer' by Chambers USA, 2005-06.

### BRINCKS, Lon
Blackwell Sanders Peper Martin LLP, Kansas City 816 983 8184
lbrincks@blackwellsanders.com
*Recommended in Real Estate*
**Practice Areas:** Real estate; commercial transactions.
**Prof. Memberships:** Admitted to practice in Missouri (1989) and Arizona (1987). Member, American Bar Association, Real Property Section; Chair, Kansas City Bar Association, Real Estate Law Committee.
**Career:** Joined firm as Partner, 2002.
**Personal:** JD, University of Iowa, Order of Coif, 1986; Associate Editor, 'Iowa Law Review'; BA, University of Iowa, honors program, 1983

### BROWN, Spencer
Deacy & Deacy LLP, Kansas City
816 421 4000
*Recommended in Litigation*

### CARMAN, Steven F
Blackwell Sanders Peper Martin LLP, Kansas City 816 983 8153
scarman@blackwellsanders.com
*Recommended in Corporate/M&A*
**Practice Areas:** M&A, securities, general corporate.
**Prof. Memberships:** The Missouri Bar.
**Career:** Joined firm as Partner, 1995. In recent years, Mr Carman has been asked by clients to devote increasing amounts of his time to issues impacting registered investment companies (including business development companies), unregistered investment funds and investment advisors.
**Personal:** JD, University of Pennsylvania, 1985; MBA, Wharton School of Business at the University of Pennsylvania, 1985; BA, Hamilton College, 1981.

### CARNEY, Thomas
Husch & Eppenberger, LLC, St Louis
314 421 4800
*Recommended in Litigation*

### CARR, William E
Lewis, Rice & Fingersh, L.C., Kansas City
816 472 2503
wecarr@lrf-kc.com
*Recommended in Real Estate*
**Practice Areas:** Recognized as a leader in the practice of commercial real estate,

including finance, development, acquisitions and sales, joint ventures and leasing; worked on projects throughout the United States and in Europe and Asia.
**Prof. Memberships:** Admitted to practice in Missouri and Kansas (1971). Member, Kansas and Missouri Bar Associations; Member, Kansas City Metropolitan Bar Association (past Chairman, Real Estate Section and Managing Partners Section); Member, American College of Real Estate Lawyers (past Chairman, Leasing Committee; Board of Governors 2006-09); Member of Advisory Board, Georgetown University Law School Advanced Commercial Leasing Institute.
**Career:** Joined Brown, Koralchik & Fingersh, predecessor to Lewis, Rice & Fingersh in 1973; former Chairman, Real Estate Department 1983-96; Managing Member of Kansas City office, 1997 to present.
**Publications:** Co-author, 'The International Practice of Real Estate,' Probate & Property, September/October 1996, The Magazine of Real Property, Probate and Trust Law Section of the American Bar Association (recipient of the 1996 Excellence in Writing Award). Author, 'Negotiation of Commercial Leases', the Commercial Property Lease, 1993 American Bar Association Section of Real Property, Probate and Trust Law. Author, 'Boxed In: The Rise of the Box Store and the Downfall of the Traditional Shopping Center Lease', American College of Real Estate Lawyers, Spring 2001, Williamsburg, VA, published as part of the ACREL Papers by ALI-ABA.
**Personal:** Born July 20, 1946, JD, University of Chicago Law School, 1971; AB, University of California at Berkeley, 1968.

### COLLINS, Dennis
Greensfelder, Hemker & Gale, P.C., St Louis 314 241 9090
*Recommended in Employment*

### DAGENAIS, Don F
Lathrop & Gage L.C., Kansas City
816 460 5715
ddagenais@lathropgage.com
*Recommended in Real Estate*
**Practice Areas:** Real estate and financial institutions.
**Career:** Dagenais handles real estate and other asset-based lending work for banks, savings and loan associations, savings banks and other commercial lenders. The types of projects involved in this work include apartment complexes, shopping centers, office buildings, warehouse/industrial projects, retail stores and nursing homes. He also practices construction law, zoning, foreclosures and loan workouts, ADA requirements pertaining to commercial space, and other related issues. He was selected as 'Best of the Bar', Kansas City Business Journal, 2003-05; a 'Leading Lawyer' by Chambers USA, 2003-06; and for Missouri/Kansas Super

Lawyers, 2005.

### DALGLEISH, Douglas
Lathrop & Gage L.C., Kansas City
816 460 5708
ddalgleish@lathropgage.com
*Recommended in Litigation*
**Practice Areas:** Tort litigation, business litigation, personal injury/products liability.
**Career:** Dalgleish has tried numerous jury cases, and argued appellate cases in the US Court of Appeals for the Eighth and Seventh Circuits, the Court of Appeals for the Eastern and Western Districts of Missouri, the Third Circuit of Louisiana and the Missouri Supreme Court. Dalgleish is an experienced trial attorney and a member of the American Board of Trial Advocates. He was named 'Best Lawyers in America', 2005-06; 'Best of the Bar' by the Kansas City Business Journal, 2004-05; and was a 'Top Lawyer Under 40' by Missouri Lawyers Weekly.

### DEAN, Cathy J
Polsinelli Shalton Welte Suelthaus PC, Kansas City 816 360 4317
cdean@pswslaw.com
*Recommended in Litigation*
**Practice Areas:** Trial practice; commercial litigation; class actions; antitrust. Tries cases in various state and federal courts. Defends trial results in state and federal courts of appeal. Represents individuals, publicly traded companies, closely held companies and not for profit entities in various types of disputes, including claims of antitrust, breach of contract, breach of fiduciary duty, negligence, fraud and product liability.
**Prof. Memberships:** The United States Supreme Court; The Missouri Bar; Missouri Bar Board of Governors; Trustee of The Missouri Bar Foundation; Association for Women Lawyers of Greater Kansas City (president 1987); American Bar Association; Kansas City Metropolitan Bar Association (executive committee).
**Career:** Law clerk to the Honorable D Brook Bartlett, United States District Court, Western District of Missouri (1982-84). Joined Polsinelli firm (1985); shareholder (1989); previously Chair of Commercial Litigation, currently Chairperson of Litigation Department.
**Personal:** University of Missouri (BA 1970, JD 1982). Holds Missouri lifetime teaching certificate.

### DEMERATH, Jeffrey
Armstrong Teasdale LLP, St Louis
314 621 5070
*Recommended in Litigation*

### DIGIOVANNI, Peter
Lewis, Rice & Fingersh, L.C., Kansas City
816 472 2504
pmdigiovanni@lrf-kc.com
*Recommended in Real Estate*
**Practice Areas:** Development, acquisi-

tion and disposition of commercial real estate, including regional malls, office buildings and mixed use projects. Has extensive experience in negotiation of regional mall department store REA's and substantial retail and office leases.
**Prof. Memberships:** Admitted to practice in Missouri (1977) and Kansas (1983). Member of the American College of Real Estate Lawyers; Member, Missouri Bar Association, Kansas Bar Association, Kansas City Metropolitan Bar Association (former Chair of the Real Estate Section).
**Career:** Joined Brown, Koralchik and Fingersh (predecessor to Lewis, Rice & Fingersh) in 1976, became Partner in 1980; Adjunct Professor of Law (real estate development and finance), University of Kansas School of Law, 1985-87 and 2000-02.
**Publications:** 'Alternate Methods of Financing the Sale and Purchase of Single Family Residences: Representing the Buyer and the Seller', Journal of the Kansas Bar Association, Fall, 1981.
**Personal:** Born June 5, 1948; JD University of Kansas School of Law (Order of the Coif and Law Review) 1976; BA University of Kansas 1971.

### DONNELLY, Dennis
Bryan Cave LLP, St Louis
314 259 2000
*Recommended in Employment*

### DONNELLY, Paul
Stinson Morrison Hecker LLP, Kansas City 816 842 8600
pdonnelly@stinsonmoheck.com
*Recommended in Employment*
**Practice Areas:** Donnelly serves as lead counsel in both jury and bench trials in federal and state courts throughout the multi-state region, representing employers in federal discrimination class actions and individual and multi-plaintiff actions. He regularly counsels employers and senior management with respect to executive compensation issues as well as basic employment law issues. He also represents a prominent agricultural, non-profit organization. Donnelly is Chair of the firm's Employment Litigation Division.
**Prof. Memberships:** American Employment Law Council; Federal Practice Committee, Western District of Missouri; The Missouri Bar.
**Personal:** JD, St Louis University (1973); BA, St Louis University (1970).

### DOWD, Edward
Bryan Cave LLP, St Louis
314 259 2000
*Recommended in Litigation*

### DRAKE, Denise
Spencer Fane Britt & Browne LLP, Kansas City 816 474 8100
*Recommended in Employment*

## EISENBRANDT, James

Berkowitz Oliver Williams Shaw & Eisenbrandt LLP, Kansas City 816 561 7007
*Recommended in Litigation*

## ERICKSON, David

Shook, Hardy & Bacon LLP, Kansas City
816 474 6550
*Recommended in Litigation*
**Practice Areas:**Has devoted most of the past 15 years to environmental litigation, toxic tort litigation, environmental regulatory issues, and environmental transactional issues. Has filed and defended CERCLA allocation actions involving the government and private parties. Has first-chaired trials in state and federal courts.
**Prof. Memberships:**Admitted to practice in Missouri, Kansas and Wisconsin and before the US District Court for the Western District of Missouri, the District of Kansas and the Eastern District of Wisconsin, and the US Court of Appeals for the Eighth and Tenth Circuits. Member of American Bar Association's Section of Litigation, Section of Tort and Insurance Practice, and Section of Environment, Energy and Resources and Defense Research Institute.
**Career:**Joined Shook, Hardy & Bacon, 2000 (as partner). Chair, Shook, Hardy & Bacon Environmental Section.
**Publications:**Missouri Environmental Law, Toxic Substances Chapter 13, 2002 Supplement; (August 2002)
**Personal:**JD, with distinction, University of Iowa College of Law, 1981; BA, with high honors, University of Texas at Arlington, 1978.

## EVANS, Craig

Shook, Hardy & Bacon LLP, Kansas City
816 474 6550
cevans@shb.com
*Recommended in Corporate/M&A*
**Practice Areas:** Practice focuses on mergers and acquisitions involving public and private companies, public and exempt offerings of securities, securities law compliance, technology driven joint ventures, and strategic alliances and corporate governance matters, including takeover defense planning and implementation for public companies.
**Prof. Memberships:** Admitted to practice in Missouri and Texas.
**Career:** Joined Shook, Hardy & Bacon, 2002 (as Partner). Chair, Corporate Finance and Banking Practice Group.
**Publications:** Co-author, Developing a Flexible and Reliable Crisis Management Plan, 'The Metropolitan Corporate Counsel' (October and November 2004). What You Need to Know About the Sarbanes-Oxley Act, 'The Metropolitan Corporate Counsel' (October 2002). The Uniform Commercial Code - Article 8 - Investment Securities, 'West Missouri Practice Transaction Guide' (2001).
**Personal:** JD, University of Kansas

School of Law, 1985; BA, William Jewell College, 1982.

## EVERSON, David

Stinson Morrison Hecker LLP,
Kansas City 816 842 8600
deverson@stinsonmoheck.com
*Recommended in Litigation*
**Practice Areas:** Everson handles a wide range of civil and criminal business litigation, including antitrust and intellectual property and has successfully tried civil and criminal cases in state and federal courts. He has lectured and appeared on panels across the country, having made presentations at the ABA Antitrust Meeting, the New England Conference on Antitrust and the Southeastern Criminal Defense Seminar.
**Prof. Memberships:** President, Midwestern Forensic Society; University of Michigan Board of Visitors.
**Personal:** JD, University of Michigan (1971); AB, University of Missouri (1966).

## FENLEY, David A

Blackwell Sanders Peper Martin LLP,
Kansas City 816 983 8134
dfenley@blackwellsanders.com
*Recommended in Real Estate*
**Practice Areas:** Real estate.
**Prof. Memberships:** Admitted to practice in Missouri (1979), US District Court, District of Western Missouri (1979), and US Tax Court (1980). Member, American Bar Association, Sections on Real Property, Probate & Trust Law, and Taxation; American College of Real Estate Lawyers; Kansas City Metropolitan Bar Association; Lawyers Association of Kansas City; and the Missouri Bar.
**Career:** Joined firm, 1980; named Partner, 1985; named firm Chairman, 2000.
**Personal:** JD (with honors), Washburn University, 1979, assistant notes editor, 'Washburn Law Journal'; BBA (cum laude), Washburn University, 1976; Certified Public Accountant (Missouri), 1980.

## FINUCANE, Brian J

Fisher & Phillips LLP, Kansas City
816 842 8770
bfinucane@laborlawyers.com
*Recommended in Employment*
**Practice Areas:** Brian Finucane is Managing Partner of the Kansas City Regional Office of Fisher & Phillips LLP, a national law firm practicing exclusively in labor and employment law representing management. He represents employers before state and federal courts and administrative agencies, including the Equal Employment Opportunity Commission, Department of Labor, and National Labor Relations Board. He served as Chairperson of the Missouri Bar Labor Law Committee, Member of the Heartland Labor and Employment Law Institute, and contributing editor to The Developing Labor Law. Finucane received BS and JD Degrees from the University of

Missouri-Columbia (Order of the Coif).

## FISHER, Robert

Sonnenschein Nath & Rosenthal LLP,
Kansas City 816 460 2400
gfisher@sonnenschein.com
*Recommended in Corporate/M&A*
**Practice Areas:** Specializes in corporate and transactional matters, principally M&A. Represents financial and strategic buyers and sellers (including private equity firms) of businesses and product lines, mostly in the private, middle market. Assists in industry roll-up efforts and ownership transitions of family businesses. Represents public companies in reorganizations or domestic or foreign expansion by acquisition and strategic dispositions. Has counseled on M&A transactions in South America, Europe and Asia.
**Prof. Memberships:** ABA; Kansas City Metropolitan Bar Association; Missouri Bar Association; Director, Jordan Industries Inc.
**Personal:** Georgetown University Law School, LLM, Taxation and JD; University of Notre Dame, BA.

## FITZGERALD JR, Robert E

Shughart Thomson & Kilroy PC,
Kansas City 816 374 0534
rfitzgerald@stklaw.com
*Recommended in Corporate/M&A,
Real Estate*
**Practice Areas:** Business law; taxation; real estate; corporate transactions. Has practiced law in Kansas City, Missouri, for more than 31 years. Represents clients in business transactions ranging from corporate acquisitions to regulatory enforcement. Handles major business acquisitions and sales with such divergent projects as real estate general partnerships, dealership purchases and sales, construction business sales, statutory reorganizations of Missouri political subdivisions and real estate venture formations.
**Prof. Memberships:** The Missouri Bar (President's Award for 'Outstanding Contributions' to the Bar [1998]; Vice-Chair, Corporation Committee.) American Bar Association. Kansas City Metropolitan Bar Association. Arbitrator for the American Arbitration Association and the National Association of Securities Dealers. 'Chambers USA 2003-2004 America's Leading Business Lawyers'. Has served extensively on securities and corporate committees with the Missouri Secretary of State's office, especially during the tenure of James Kilpatrick and Roy Blunt.
**Career:** Joined Shughart Thomson & Kilroy PC as a shareholder in 1995. Member of the firm's finance committee. Listed in Chambers USA 2003-04; 2004-05: 'America's Leading Business Lawyers'.
**Publications:** 'Taxes in Your Practice' column, Journal of Missouri Bar, 1982-98.

**Personal:** Born Chicago, Illinois, February 22, 1949. St Louis University, JD (1974). St Benedict's College, AB summa cum laude (1971). Judicial clerkship: Honorable George G Gunn, Jr, Missouri Court of Appeals, St Louis (1972-73).

## FLANIGAN, Daniel J

Polsinelli Shalton Welte Suelthaus PC,
Kansas City 816 753 1000
dflanigan@pswslaw.com
*Recommended in Real Estate*
**Practice Areas:** Chair of the firm's Financial Services and Real Estate Departments. Advisor to lenders for 25-plus years regarding all aspects of debt financing – from secured lending to securitization, from loan origination to loan enforcement and bankruptcy. In recent years he has been intensely involved in the commercial mortgage backed securities industry where he has assisted in the formation and development of two national conduit lenders and supervises a group of lawyers that have documented and closed more than 1200 commercial mortgage loans, $8.5 billion in principal amount, in 48 states and DC. His group also represents loan sellers and servicers in securitizations and related matters including loan sale warranty breach litigation, prepayment premium litigation and all aspects of loan administration and enforcement. He founded and developed the firm's Financial Services Department of 50-plus lawyers dedicated solely to debt financing transactions, comprising corporate banking and regulatory, loan documentation, workouts, loan enforcement litigation, and bankruptcy within the same practice group. He has represented lenders in bankruptcy courts throughout the United States in both large-case and single asset (especially real estate) cases.
**Prof. Memberships:** Missouri and New York Bar Associations; American Bar Association; Commercial Mortgage Securities Association; American Bankruptcy Institute; Turnaround Management Association.
**Personal:** JD, University of Houston; PhD, Rice University; BS, University of Kansas.

## FORD JR, William F

Lathrop & Gage L.C., Kansas City
816 292 2000
*Recommended in Litigation*
**Career** Ford serves as Chair of the firm's Environmental Practice. He has a wide range of litigation experience in environmental, products liability and general business litigation. In the environmental area, Ford successfully represented several national clients as both plaintiffs and defendants in environmental cost recovery litigation. Ford also represented numerous corporations as PRPs in various NPL and other hazardous waste sites in litigation, negotiations, allocations,

PRP searches and remediation coordination. In business litigation areas, Ford successfully represented a major defense contractor in several multi-million dollar claims related to closure of a 9,000 acre Army Ammunition Plant.

### FRANTZE, David
Stinson Morrison Hecker LLP,
Kansas City 816 842 8600
dfrantze@stinsonmoheck.com
*Recommended in Real Estate*

**Practice Areas:** Chairs the Real Estate Practice Division. Represents developers, property owners, tenants, municipalities and non-profits in land use and development, leasing, and real estate lending matters. Expertise in using development incentives such as tax increment financing and tax abatement. Counsels developers and municipalities in forming public/private partnerships.
**Prof. Memberships:** ABA, Real Property Section, Probate and Trust Law; American College of Real Estate Lawyers; The Missouri Bar, Property Law Committee.
**Personal:** JD, University of Missouri – Kansas City, with distinction, 1981; BA, Avila University, magna cum laude, 1976. Adjunct Professor at UMKC School of Law, taught Real Estate Finance and Development Law.

### FRAZEN, Laurence
Bryan Cave LLP, Kansas City
816 374 3200
*Recommended in Litigation*

### FRETWELL, Norman
Spencer Fane Britt & Browne LLP,
Kansas City 816 474 8100
*Recommended in Corporate/M&A*

### FRIZELL, Edward E "Trip"
Polsinelli Shalton Welte Suelthaus PC,
Kansas City 816 753 1000
tfrizell@pswslaw.com
*Recommended in Corporate/M&A*

**Practice Areas:** Corporate/M&A; general business; franchising.
**Prof. Memberships:** The Missouri Bar; Kansas City Metropolitan Bar Association.
**Career:** Joined Morris Larson May 1980; Partner May 1985; Joined Polsinelli as Of Counsel in 1986; Partner 1988; Chair of General Corporate Practice Group.
**Personal:** University of Kansas (JD, 1980, MBA, 1980, BS in Business Administration, 1976).

### GERMAN, Charles
Rouse Hendricks German May PC,
Kansas City 816 471 7700
*Recommended in Litigation*

### GIANOULAKIS, John
Kohn, Shands, Elbert, Gianoulakis & Giljum, LLP, St Louis 314 241 3963
*Recommended in Litigation*

### GILSON, Gary
Blackwell Sanders Peper Martin LLP,
Kansas City 816 983 8141
ggilson@blackwellsanders.com
*Recommended in Corporate/M&A*

**Practice Areas:** Mergers and acquisitions; securities; corporate governance; real estate investment trusts.
**Prof. Memberships:** Admitted to practice in Missouri (1981), Kansas, (1985), Nebraska (1995). Member, American Bar Association - Section of Business Law - Committee on Negotiated Acquisitions; Kansas Bar Association; Missouri Bar; Association for Corporate Growth; National Association of Small Business Investment Companies.
**Career:** Joined firm as Partner, 1993; Founding/Managing Partner, Blackwell Sanders Omaha, Nebraska office, 1995-97.
**Publications:** Author, Chapter 5, General Corporate Actions and Operations, 'Missouri Bar Association Business Organizations Deskbook' (1998).
**Personal:** JD, University of Nebraska at Lincoln, 1981; BS, University of Nebraska at Lincoln, 1978.

### GODINER, Clifford A
Thompson Coburn LLP, St Louis
314 552 6433
cgodiner@thompsoncoburn.com
*Recommended in Employment*

**Practice Areas:** Represents employers in all facets of labor and employment law, including employment discrimination, wrongful discharge, and non-compete litigation. He has handled and tried cases in federal and state courts. Experience in union-managment relations, especially under the Railway Labor Act.
**Prof. Memberships:** Admitted in Missouri. Member of Bar of Seventh, Eighth, Tenth, and DC Circuit Courts of Appeals.
**Career:** Joined Thompson Coburn LLP in 1997 (as a Partner). Adjunct Professor at Saint Louis University School of Law, Center for Employment Law since 1992.
**Personal:** JD, magna cum laude, University of Michigan Law School (1986); BA, Wesleyan University (1983).

### GRANDA, John A
Stinson Morrison Hecker LLP,
Kansas City 816 842 8600
jgranda@stinsonmoheck.com
*Recommended in Corporate/M&A*

**Practice Areas:** Chairman of Corporate Finance Division and Co-Chairman of Corporate Accountability Division. Serves as outside general counsel to a wide range of publicly- and privately-held businesses, including many of Kansas City's largest companies. Extensive experience in large and complex transactions (with size of deals in excess of $5 billion), including public and private offerings of debt and equity securities, mergers, acquisitions, tender offers, proxy contests, takeover defense, spin-offs, recapitalizations, going private, venture capital, joint ventures, strategic alliances, SEC reporting, compliance programs and corporate governance.
**Prof. Memberships:** American Bar Association, The Missouri Bar, Kansas City Metropolitan Bar Association, American Society of Corporate Secretaries, Associate for Corporate Growth, and International Trade Club.
**Career:** Former Counsel to SEC Commissioner and Special Counsel in SEC's Division of Corporation Finance over a five-year period.
**Publications:** Contributing author, 'Missouri Methods of Practice: Transaction Guide'. Numerous papers for programs on securities, mergers and acquisitions and governance sponsored by: Practicing Law Institute; Iowa, Kansas and Missouri Bar Associations; KPMG Audit Committee Roundtable; and several law schools, including Universities of Iowa, Kansas and Missouri.
**Personal:** LLM, Taxation, Georgetown University (1979); JD, University of Iowa, with distinction (1975); Master's (1972) and Bachelor's (1971) in Business Administration, University of Iowa.

### GRIFFIN, James
Blackwell Sanders Peper Martin LLP,
Kansas City 816 983 8199
jgriffin@blackwellsanders.com
*Recommended in Litigation*

**Practice Areas:** Business and commercial litigation; products liability.
**Prof. Memberships:** Admitted to practice in Kansas (1985) and Missouri (1983). Fellow, American College of Trial Lawyers. Member, Defense Research Institute and Kansas Bar Association.
**Career:** Joined firm, 1983; named Partner, 1990; Chair, Litigation Department, 2003.
**Publications:** Author, 'An Analysis of the Admissibility of Expert Opinion Testimony in Kansas State Courts After Kuhn v Sandoz Pharmaceuticals', Journal of the Kansas Bar Association (February 2002); and 'Class Action Trials Commonly Deprive Defendants of Due Process', Washington Legal Foundation (November 2001).
**Personal:** JD, University of Virginia, 1983; BS (cum laude), Kansas State University, 1980.

### HAINES, Lisa
Polsinelli Shalton Welte Suelthaus PC,
Kansas City 816 360 4273
lhaines@pswslaw.com
*Recommended in Real Estate*

**Practice Areas:** General real estate; economic development incentives; public/private partnerships; commerical development; commercial finance.
**Prof. Memberships:** American Bar Association; The Missouri Bar; Kansas City Metropolitan Bar Association; Past Chairman of the Real Property Committee of the KCMBA; Seminar Speaker for ABA, MoBar and KCMBA Seminars.
**Career:** Chairman of the Polsinelli Real Estate Transactions Department. Haines provides a full range of real estate services with an emphasis in commercial development and financing, including mixed-use residential and commercial development projects, complex property assemblages utilizing economic incentive tools for financing, and extensive financing experience from the perspective of both borrowers and lenders.

### HAUBER, Catherine
Stinson Morrison Hecker LLP,
Kansas City 816 691 3207
khauber@stinsonmoheck.com
*Recommended in Real Estate*

**Practice Areas:** Focuses on sales and acquisitions of real estate, secured lender transactions, local counsel opinions and representation, construction, leasing, shopping center financing, reciprocal easement and operating agreements, conservation easements and issues of environmental liability relating to real estate transactions.
**Prof. Memberships:** Missouri and Kansas Bars, Kansas City Metropolitan Bar Association, American Bar Association, American College of Real Estate Lawyers, Association for Women Lawyers of Greater Kansas City, Kansas City CREW.
**Career:** Frequent speaker on various real estate subjects.
**Personal:** JD, University of Kansas, 1983, Order of the Coif; BA, with distinction, University of Kansas, 1976; BS, University of Kansas, 1978.

### HEETER, James
Sonnenschein Nath & Rosenthal LLP,
Kansas City 816 460 2452
jheeter@sonnenschein.com
*Recommended in Corporate/M&A*

**Practice Areas:** 30 years of corporate and healthcare experience. Experience in M&A, debt financings, leveraged buyouts, and start-ups. Works with senior executives, directors, and shareholders as general counsel to diverse businesses, including large privately-held and public companies. Substantial experience with corporate governance and Sarbanes-Oxley compliance and as independent audit committee counsel.
**Prof. Memberships:** Member, ABA, Missouri Bar, and Kansas City Metropolitan Bar Association.
**Personal:** Harvard Law School, JD, cum laude. University of Missouri-Columbia, AB with honors.

### HILL, Stephen L
Blackwell Sanders Peper Martin LLP,
Kansas City 816 983 8162
shill@blackwellsanders.com
*Recommended in Litigation*

**Practice Areas:** Business and commercial litigation; government compliance;

investigations and litigation; healthcare; intellectual property litigation; intellectual property; transportation; white-collar crime; internal investigations.

**Prof. Memberships:** Admitted to practice in Missouri (1987).

**Career:** Joined firm as Partner, 2001. United States Attorney for Western District of Missouri 1993-2001.

**Personal:** JD, University of Missouri at Columbia, 1986; BS Political Science, Missouri State University, 1981; London University, London, England.

### HOBBS, James
Wyrsch Hobbs & Mirakian PC, Kansas City 816 221 0080
*Recommended in Litigation*

### HUNTER, Jerry
Bryan Cave LLP, St Louis
314 259 2000
*Recommended in Employment*

### HUNTER, Robert
Stinson Morrison Hecker LLP, Kansas City 816 842 8600
rhunter@stinsonmoheck.com
*Recommended in Corporate/M&A*

**Practice Areas:** Chairman of the firm's General Business Division. Serves as outside general counsel for several Kansas City-based companies, providing assistance on real estate transactions, commercial leasing, commercial finance, acquisitions and sales, and general corporate matters. Regularly represents entrepreneurs and venture capital investors in structuring venture capital investments. Also represents telecommunications clients in the acquisition and leasing of their communications facilities.

**Prof. Memberships:** ABA, Corporate Law Committee; Kansas Bar Association, Corporate Law Committee; Missouri Bar.

**Career:** Centurions Leadership Training Program (2000); Up and Comers Award (1999).

**Personal:** JD, Kansas University, 1989; BS, Kansas University, 1986.

### JANOWITZ, Robert
Constangy, Brooks & Smith, LLC, Kansas City 816 472 6400
*Recommended in Employment*

### JAUDES, Richard E
Thompson Coburn LLP, St Louis
314 552 6431
rjaudes@thompsoncoburn.com
*Recommended in Employment*

**Practice Areas:** Chairman of firm's Labor and Employment Group. Practice focuses on employment litigation and traditional labor relations. National experience in federal employment litigation, negotiating collective bargaining agreements and union avoidance.

**Prof. Memberships:** Admitted to practice in Missouri.

**Career:** Joined and formed Labor and Employment Department at Peper, Martin, Jensen, Maichel and Hetlage. Joined

Thompson Coburn LLP in 1997 as Partner.

**Personal:** JD (with honors) Saint Louis University Law School, 1968; BS (with honors) Saint Louis University, 1965.

### JENSEN, Patricia
White Goss Bowers March Schulte & Weisenfels, A Professional Corporation, Kansas City 816 753 9200
*Recommended in Real Estate*

### JONES, Steve
Armstrong Teasdale LLP, St Louis
314 621 5070
*Recommended in Corporate/M&A*

### KAPLAN, Harvey
Shook, Hardy & Bacon LLP, Kansas City 816 474 6550
hkaplan@shb.com
*Recommended in Litigation, Products Liability*

**Practice Areas:** Has tried many high profile pharmaceutical cases, and is well-known for defending pharmaceutical and medical device companies in national products liability litigations.

**Prof. Memberships:** Admitted to practice before the US Supreme Court; the US Court of Appeals for the Fifth, Sixth, Eighth, Ninth, and Tenth Circuits; the US Tax Court; the Missouri Supreme Court; and the federal courts of Missouri, Kansas, Arizona, and Nebraska. Fellow of International Academy of Trial Lawyers (board member), International Society of Barristers and American Bar Foundation. Member of International Association of Defense Counsel (IADC).

**Career:** Joined Shook, Hardy & Bacon, 1970; became Partner, 1974. Chair, Shook, Hardy & Bacon Pharmaceutical and Medical Device Litigation Division.

**Publications:** Country Q&A United States, PLC Cross-border Life Sciences Handbook 2005/06; Avoiding/Minimising the Risk of Punitive Damages, Global Legal Group: The International Comparative Legal Guide to: Product Liability 2005, 3rd ed; USA, Chapter 41 in Global Legal Group: The International Comparative Legal Guide to: Product Liability 2005, 3rd ed; Drug Advertising and the Learned Intermediary Doctrine, Global Legal Group: The International Comparative Legal Guide to: Pharmaceutical Advertising 2005, 2nd ed.

**Personal:** JD, University of Missouri-Columbia School of Law, 1968; BS, (Pharm.) University of Michigan, 1965.

### KEIM, Robert
Kutak Rock LLP, Kansas City
816 960 0090
*Recommended in Corporate/M&A*

### KING, Richard A
King Hershey, PC, Kansas City
816 842 3636
rking@kinghershey.com
*Recommended in Real Estate*

**Practice Areas:** Real estate develop-

ment, public/private finance.

**Prof. Memberships:** American Bar Association, National Association of Bond Lawyers, International Association of Gaming Attorneys, Missouri Bar Association, Kansas City Bar Association, Eastern Jackson County Bar Association.

**Career:** Chairman and CEO, King Hershey, Kansas City, Missouri, 1988-date; Partner, Smith Gill Fisher and Butts, Kansas City, Missouri 1985-87; Director of Revenue, State of Missouri 1982-85; Executive Assistant to the Governor of Missouri 1981-82; Partner, Cochran, Kramer, Kapke, Willerth and King, Independence, Missouri, 1979-80; Partner, Constance Slayton Stewart & King, Independence, Missouri 1973-79.

**Personal:** Mayor, Independence, Missouri, 1974-78; President, Missouri Economic Development Financing Association, 1999-2001.

### KOHN, Alan
Kohn, Shands, Elbert, Gianoulakis & Giljum, LLP, St Louis 314 241 3963
*Recommended in Litigation*

### KOKORUDA, Thomas G
Shughart Thomson & Kilroy PC, Kansas City 816 374 0513
tkokoruda@stklaw.com
*Recommended in Litigation*

**Practice Areas:** Healthcare; hospital law; litigation. Focuses his trial practice primarily on commercial healthcare litigation, physician malpractice and medical staff privilege litigation.

**Prof. Memberships:** Admitted to Missouri Bar (1972). Member Kansas City Metropolitan Bar Association (Executive Committee, 1986-94; President, 1993); National Health Lawyer Association; Missouri Society of Hospital Attorneys; American College of Legal Medicine. Fellow, American College of Trial Lawyers. Phi Delta Phi. Member, Board of Governors, University of Kansas School of Law (1991-93); Missouri Supreme Court Civil Jury Study Committee (2000-01). Circuit Court Advisory Committee (past Chair); Hospital-Medico-Legal Committee (past Chair).

**Career:** Joined Shughart Thomson & Kilroy, 1972; shareholder, 1976. Executive Committee (Executive Vice President). Chair, Litigation Department and Healthcare Litigation Group; Vice-Chair, Hospital Law Group. Listed in healthcare section of leading legal publication; KC Magazine in 2005 recognized Tom as one of the Top 10 Super Lawyers in Missouri/Kansas; Best Lawyers In America: Health Care Law and Personal Injury Litigation; KC Business Journal Best of the Bar (highest vote getter Health Care Law); Listed in 'Chambers USA: America's Leading Business Lawyers' as leading individual trial lawyer in Health Care litigation.

**Publications:** Author: 'Pleadings' in Mis-

souri Trial Practice Essays, 57 UMKC Law Review 736, Summer, 1989.

**Personal:** Born Kansas City, Kansas, January 14, 1947. University of Kansas, JD (1972). University of Kansas, BS (1968).

### LAROSE, Robert M
Thompson Coburn LLP, St Louis
314 552 6068
rlarose@thompsoncoburn.com
*Recommended in Corporate/M&A*

**Practice Areas:** Co-Chairman, Corporate and Securities Group; Vice-Chairman, Corporate Department. Over 25 years' experience in M&A, securities disclosure and compliance issues, capital raising and contractual matters for public clients. Experienced in corporate governance counselling and compliance.

**Prof. Memberships:** Admitted to practice in Missouri and Minnesota.

**Career:** Joined Thompson Coburn LLP in 1983 after three years in St. Paul, MN firm.

**Personal:** JD (cum laude), Northwestern University School of Law (1980); BA (with honors), The Johns Hopkins University (1977).

### LASALA, Todd A
Stinson Morrison Hecker LLP, Kansas City 816 842-8600
tlasala@stinsonmoheck.com
*Recommended in Real Estate*

**Practice Areas:** Counsel to private developers and municipalities in using public incentives to stimulate real estate development and redevelopment. Representation of commercial real estate owners, brokers, and lenders. Expertise in commercial leasing matters, conveyance, and loan issues and drafting and negotiating transactional real estate documents.

**Prof. Memberships:** ABA, Real Property Section, Missouri and Kansas Bars, Kansas City Metropolitan Bar Association, International Council of Shopping Centers.

**Career:** Lead counsel in the development of Village West, a major retail and entertainment district spanning 400 acres in Kansas City, Kansas.

**Personal:** JD, University of Kansas, 1996; BS, Regis University, cum laude, 1993.

### LAUSE, Michael F
Thompson Coburn LLP, St Louis
314 552 6069
mlause@thompsoncoburn.com
*Recommended in Corporate/M&A*

**Practice Areas:** Chairman of firm's Corporate Department. Legal practice is focused in areas of finance and corporate law. He has special concentrations in areas of public finance and in the representation of governmental and non-profit entities and of financial institutions interacting with such entities.

**Career:** Thompson Coburn LLP (1973-present). He serves as outside general counsel to various entities.

**LENTS, Donald**
Bryan Cave LLP, St Louis
314 259 2000
*Recommended in Corporate/M&A*

**LITZ, Thomas A**
Thompson Coburn LLP, St Louis
314 552 6072
tlitz@thompsoncoburn.com
*Recommended in Corporate/M&A*
**Practice Areas:** Co-Chairman of firm's
Corporate and Securities Group; member of firm's Management and Executive
Committees. Concentrates practice in
corporate and securities law, and mergers
and acquisitions. Over 20 years of experience representing issuers and underwriters in public and private offerings of
securities, and public and privately held
companies in mergers, acquisitions and
securities law compliance. Experience
representing private equity funds in syndication and portfolio investments and
dispositions.
**Prof. Memberships:** Admitted to practice in Missouri and Illinois.
**Career:** Thompson Coburn LLP (1982-
present).
**Personal:** JD, cum laude, Georgetown
University Law Center (1982); BSBA
Finance, magna cum laude, Georgetown
Univeristy (1979).

**MARCH, Aaron**
White Goss Bowers March Schulte &
Weisenfels, A Professional Corporation,
Kansas City 816 753 9200
*Recommended in Real Estate*

**MARTUCCI, William**
Shook, Hardy & Bacon LLP, Kansas City
816 474 6550
wmartucci@shb.com
*Recommended in Employment*
**Practice Areas:** Practice focuses on
complex class action litigation, employment discrimination, wage and hour litigation, ERISA litigation, and covenants
not to compete. Has successfully defended various employment lawsuits and
written and lectured extensively on
employment law issues throughout the
country. Practices exclusively on behalf of
management in connection with national
employment litigation and policy matters.
**Prof. Memberships:** Member of Eighth
Circuit Model Federal Civil Jury Instructions Subcommittee and National
Human Resources Policy Board of Commerce Clearing House (CCH). Listed in
'The Best Lawyers in America.'
**Career:** Joined Shook, Hardy & Bacon,
2000 (as Partner). Practice leader, Shook,
Hardy & Bacon National Employment
Litigation and Policy Group.
**Personal:** Executive Education, Harvard
Business School, 1997; LLM, Georgetown
University Law Center, 1981; JD, with
honors, Leflar Law Center, University of
Arkansas, 1977; AB, magna cum laude,
Rutgers College, 1974.

**MARVIN, John**
Sonnenschein Nath & Rosenthal LLP,
Kansas City 816 460 2513
jmarvin@sonnenschein.com
*Recommended in Corporate/M&A*
**Practice Areas:** Has 40+ years of experience, primarily in securities and general
corporate law, encompassing IPOs, aftermarket trading and control compliance,
proxy solicitation, takeover defense and
corporate transactions. Counsels public
company boards and management governance.
**Prof. Memberships:** Law Professor at
two law schools; State Board of Law
Examiners; Director, Chamber of Commerce of Greater Kansas City; Member,
several bar associations.
**Personal:** University of Missouri at
Kansas City, BBA, JD, with distinction,
Omicron Delta Kappa, Law Review Editor, National Moot Court Team; New
York University, LLM, honors.

**MASSEY, Raymond L**
Thompson Coburn LLP, St Louis
314 552 6075
rmassey@thompsoncoburn.com
*Recommended in Litigation*
**Practice Areas:** Chairman of firm's Litigation Department and Admiralty
Group. Concentrates on litigation affecting business, including heavy industry
and manufacturing. Much of his litigation involves vessels, marine contracts,
serious personal injuries, complex tort
and environmental issues. Taken significant jury and non-jury trials to verdict in
state and federal courts and is often
selected by the assured as counsel where a
loss is subject to insurance in complex litigation matters.
**Prof. Memberships:** Admitted to practice in Missouri, Illinois and Texas. Proctor Member and past Director of Maritime Law Association of the United
States. Frequent speaker at industry and
business seminars.

**MCCARTHY, Thomas**
McMahon Berger Hanna Linihan Cody &
McCarthy, A Professional Corporation,
St Louis 314 567 7350
*Recommended in Employment*

**MCNAMARA, Rosalee M**
Lathrop & Gage L.C., Kansas City
816 460 5604
rmcnamara@lathropgage.com
*Recommended in Employment*
**Practice Areas:** Employment litigation,
labor law, general employment counseling.
**Career:** McNamara represents clients in
employment matters throughout the US.
She has defended complaints of alleged
employment discrimination and has
handled court and jury trials in federal
and state court. Her litigation and counseling experience includes sexual harassment, ADA, race, age, sex, national origin,
religious discrimination, FMLA, wage

and hour laws, hiring and reference procedures, employee discipline/termination, and employee drug/alcohol testing
policies and procedures. She was selected
as 'Leading Lawyer' by Chambers USA,
2004-06; selected for Missouri/Kansas
Super Lawyers, 2005; and has received
Martindale Hubbell's highest rating, the
'AV Rating'.

**MCNEARNEY, John**
Blackwell Sanders Peper Martin LLP,
St Louis 314 345 6415
jmcnearney@blackwellsanders.com
*Recommended in Real Estate*
**Practice Areas:** Real estate; creditors'
rights; financial institutions.
**Prof. Memberships:** Admitted to practice, Illinois (1984), Missouri (1983).
ABA; Bar Association of Metropolitan St.
Louis; Illinois Bar Association; Missouri
Bar. Board of Directors, Life Skills Foundation; Forest Hills CC. Listed, 'Best
Lawyers in America', 2005-06.
**Career:** Named Partner, 1993; Chair,
Real Estate Department.
**Publications:** Author, 'Did Your Construction Leader Ask for That?', ABA
Property Journal, 2004. 'Anatomy of a
Mortgage: A Primer on Real Estate
Finance', ABA (2000); Real Estate Financing, Chapter 9, 'Missouri Real Estate
Practice', Fourth Edition (2000).
**Personal:** JD, Northwestern University,
1983; BA, University of Virginia, 1979.

**MEDVED, Joseph W**
Lathrop & Gage L.C., Kansas City
816 460 5824
jmedved@lathropgage.com
*Recommended in Corporate/M&A*
**Career:** Medved represents clients in
transactions in mergers/acquisitions and
corporate finance, including asset purchases/sales, stock purchases/sales, mergers, joint ventures, tender offers, bank
financings, public/private stock offerings,
and public/private debt offerings. His
transactions range from the $200 million
range to the billion dollar range. He is
engaged in a broad corporate and business practice, representing public and
private companies. Medved is a member
of the firm's Executive Committee and
Chairman of the Greater Kansas City
Foreign Trade Zone. He was selected for
Missouri/Kansas Super Lawyers, 2005
and as a Leading Lawyer by Chambers
USA, 2003-06.

**MILLER, Charles F**
Lewis, Rice & Fingersh, L.C., Kansas City
816 472 2512
cfmiller@lrf-kc.com
*Recommended in Real Estate*
**Practice Areas:** Real estate law, including acquisition, sales, financing, leasing,
construction, development, redevelopment, incentives, zoning, other governmental approvals and joint ventures.
**Prof. Memberships:** American College
of Real Estate Lawyers; Missouri Eco-

nomic Development Finance Association; NAIOP Association of Commercial
Real Estate, local Board of Directors; Missouri Bar Association, Property Law
Committee; Kansas City Metropolitan
Bar Association, Real Estate Law Committee (past Chairman); Board of Editors
(past), Shopping Center Legal Update;
International Council of Shopping Centers; Greater Kansas City Chamber of
Commerce, Kansas City, Missouri Committee; Downtown Council of Kansas
City (Executive Committee Member)
and other civic and professional organizations.
**Career:** Joined Brown, Koralchik & Fingersh 1979 (predecessor to Lewis, Rice &
Fingersh, L.C.); Chairman of Real Estate
Department; Member of Executive Committee; past Adjunct Professor of law,
UMKC Law School; regular speaker at
legal and real estate industry events and
seminars, including Are Easements Easy,
and Case Study of Missouri and Kansas
Development Incentives.
**Publications:** Include Missouri Provides
Condemnation Powers and Real Estate
Tax Abatement for Developers, 'Shopping
Center Legal Update', Summer, 1986, and
'Landlord's Duty to Relet When a Tenant
Abandons Leased Property', 43 Missouri
Law Review 359, among others.
**Personal:** JD University of Missouri Law
School, 1979, Law Review Board of Editors; AB Political Science, University of
Missouri, 1976 (summa cum laude), Phi
Beta Kappa.

**MINOGUE, Thomas J**
Thompson Coburn LLP, St Louis
314 552 6080
tminogue@thompsoncoburn.com
*Recommended in Corporate/M&A*
**Practice Areas:** Chairman of Thompson Coburn LLP. Legal practice principally concentrated in the areas of corporate
law and finance. Over 25 years of experience in mergers and acquisitions, leveraged buyouts, joint ventures, shareholder
relations and redemptions, commercial
finance (representing borrowers and
lenders), private placements, secured and
unsecured lending and lease financing.
Successfully concluded multiple transactions involving dollar amounts in excess
of $1 billion.
**Prof. Memberships:** Admitted to practice in Missouri and Illinois.
**Career:** Thompson Coburn LLP (1979-
present); Acting General Counsel, Mercantile Bancorporation (1990).
**Personal:** JD, cum laude, Harvard Law
School (1979); BA Economics, summa
cum laude, UM-St. Louis (1976).

**MONROE, C Robert**
Stinson Morrison Hecker LLP,
Kansas City 816 842 8600
bmonroe@stinsonmoheck.com
*Recommended in Corporate/M&A*
**Practice Areas:** Chairman of the firm's

Financial Services Division. Counsel to over 100 financial institutions and financial holding companies. Has significant experience in company mergers, bank and bank holding company formations, branch acquisitions, converting to S-Corporations, regulatory orders and bank examination issues.
**Prof. Memberships:** ABA, Banking Law Committee; Admitted in Missouri and Kansas; Missouri Bankers Association, Kansas Bankers Association, Illinois Bankers Association, and New York Bankers Association.
**Career:** Listed in 'Best Lawyers in America.'
**Publications:** Frequent lecturer and author on banking issues.
**Personal:** JD, St Louis University School of Law, cum laude, 1975; BA, Westminster College, 1968.

### MORRIS, Jeffrey
Berkowitz Oliver Williams Shaw & Eisenbrandt LLP, Kansas City 816 561 7007
*Recommended in Litigation*

### MUELLER, Kathleen T
Blackwell Sanders Peper Martin LLP, St Louis 314 345 6491
kmueller@blackwellsanders.com
*Recommended in Real Estate*
**Practice Areas:** Real estate, finance and lending, closely held businesses.
**Prof. Memberships:** American Bar Association, Bar Association of Metropolitan St. Louis, International Association of Attorneys and Executives in Corporate Real Estate (AECRE), The Missouri Bar, St. Louis Leadership Program.
**Career:** Joined firm as associate, 1980; named Partner, 1987.
**Personal:** JD, Washington University 1980, Order of the Coif. Washington University Law Quarterly; BA, Maryville University, summa cum laude, 1976.

### MURRAY, George
Bryan Cave LLP, St Louis
314 259 2000
*Recommended in Real Estate*

### NESTER, Daniel
Bryan Cave LLP, St Louis
314 259 2000
*Recommended in Real Estate*

### NEWBOLD, J William
Thompson Coburn LLP, St Louis
314 552 6088
wnewbold@thompsoncoburn.com
*Recommended in Litigation*
**Practice Areas:** For over 38 years, he has tried complex cases for major companies before state and federal courts. He is one of the lead trial counsel in United States of America v Philip Morris USA Inc., f/k/a Philip Morris Inc., et al., which awaits a decision after a nine-month trial.
**Prof. Memberships:** Admitted to practice in Missouri, Illinois and various federal and appellate courts. Member, American College of Trial Lawyers and Inter-

national Society of Barristers and listed in 'The Best Lawyers in America' (2005-06).
**Career:** Thompson Coburn LLP (1979-present).
**Personal:** JD, University of Missouri-Columbia School of Law, 1967.

### NIXON, Richard
Stinson Morrison Hecker LLP,
Kansas City 816 842 8600
dnixon@stinsonmoheck.com
*Recommended in Corporate/M&A*
**Practice Areas:** Serves clients in general business matters, including organizational and financing matters, day to day operational/legal issues, acquisitions and selling the business. Represents private and publicly held companies in acquisitions, dispositions, debt and equity financing, and joint ventures. Has worked extensively with not-for-profit and co-operative organizations.
**Prof. Memberships:** ABA, Business Law Committee; Missouri Bar, Business Law Committee.
**Career:** Has served as general counsel to several of the firm's mid-sized clients. Listed in 'Best Lawyers in America' since 1987; held several leadership roles with the firm.
**Personal:** JD, University of Missouri, 1969; MA, Florida State University, 1966; AB, William Jewell College, 1964.

### NOUSS, James
Bryan Cave LLP, St Louis 314 259 2000
*Recommended in Corporate/M&A*

### O'CONNELL, Mary Anne
Husch & Eppenberger, LLC, Kansas City
816 421 4800
*Recommended in Corporate/M&A*

### O'DEAR, Craig
Bryan Cave LLP, Kansas City
816 374 3200
*Recommended in Litigation*

### O'KEEFE, Daniel
Bryan Cave LLP, St Louis
314 259 2000
*Recommended in Employment*

### OLIVER, David
Berkowitz Oliver Williams Shaw & Eisenbrandt LLP, Kansas City 816 561 7007
*Recommended in Litigation*

### ORTBALS, Mary Beth
Greensfelder, Hemker & Gale, P.C.,
St Louis 314 241 9090
*Recommended in Employment*

### PHILLIPS, John R
Blackwell Sanders Peper Martin LLP,
Kansas City 816 983 8119
jphillips@blackwellsanders.com
*Recommended in Employment*
**Practice Areas:** Labor and employment; alternative dispute resolution.
**Prof. Memberships:** Admitted to practice, Missouri (1971); US Supreme Court (1976). Fellow, American College of Trial Lawyers. Fellow, International Academy

of Mediators. Member, ABA; Kansas City Metropolitan Bar Association; Lawyers Association; Missouri Bar.
**Career:** Joined firm, 1971; named Partner, 1976.
**Publications:** Co author/director, Mediation Madness (ABA Video 2004); author, 'Mediation from the Perspective of Defense Counsel', Journal, Kansas Trial Lawyers Association (2003); 'Mediation, One Step in Adversarial Litigation', Journal of Dispute Resolution (2002).
**Personal:** JD (cum laude), University of Missouri at Columbia, 1971; BS (cum laude), University of Missouri at Columbia, 1968.

### POLSINELLI, James A
Polsinelli Shalton Welte Suelthaus PC,
Kansas City 816 753 1000
jpolsinelli@pswslaw.com
*Recommended in Corporate/M&A*
**Practice Areas:** Corporate/M&A; business succession planning. Often acts in the role of corporate general counsel by assisting clients with a variety of tax, shareholder, and ongoing day to day corporate matters.
**Prof. Memberships:** American Bar Association; The Missouri Bar; Kansas City Metropolitan Bar Association; Admitted to practice in Missouri, US District Court, Western District of Missouri, and US Tax Court.
**Career:** Founding member of Polsinelli Shalton Welte Suelthaus. Past Chairman of Business Law Department. Outstanding Career Achievement Award Recipient from University of Missouri Kansas City. Listed in 'Best Lawyers in America' (2000-present).

### PRICE, James
Spencer Fane Britt & Browne LLP,
Kansas City 816 474 8100
*Recommended in Litigation*

### REBEIN, Joseph
Shook, Hardy & Bacon LLP, Kansas City
816 474 6550
jrebein@shb.com
*Recommended in Litigation*
**Practice Areas:** Specializes in complex litigation. Lead trial counsel in complex cases, including antitrust and securities class actions. Has tried federal and state trials, NASD arbitrations, general civil arbitrations, administrative proceedings before state and federal regulatory bodies, and CFTC enforcement actions.
**Prof. Memberships:** Admitted to practice in Missouri and before US Court of Appeals for the Sixth, Seventh, Eighth, and Tenth Circuits and the US District Court for the Western District of Missouri, District of Kansas, Eastern District of Michigan, Eastern and Western Districts of Wisconsin, Southern and Northern Districts of Mississippi, Northern District of Illinois, and District of Connecticut. Member of Defense Research Institute and American Bar Association's

Antitrust and Securities Litigation Sections.
**Career:** Joined Shook, Hardy & Bacon, 1985; became Partner, 1992. Chairman, Shook, Hardy & Bacon General Litigation Division. Firm's member of CPR Institute for Dispute Resolution.
**Publications:** Author, 'Winning Legal Strategies for Alternative Dispute Resolution', 'ADR Best Practices for Arbitration, Mediation and Contract Resolution' (2005); co-author, 'Derail the Runaway Jury by Promoting Jury Service within Corporate America: Employers Should Support Jury Service - Here Is How', The Metropolitan Corporate Counsel (2003).
**Personal:** JD, University of Kansas School of Law, 1985; BS, University of Kansas, 1982.

### RESCHLY, Jason
Blackwell Sanders Peper Martin LLP,
Kansas City 816 983 8170
jreschly@blackwellsanders.com
*Recommended in Corporate/M&A*
**Practice Areas:** Taxation; agribusiness; energy and public utility.
**Prof. Memberships:** Admitted to practice in Missouri (1981). Member of American Bar Association and the Missouri Bar.
**Career:** Joined firm as Partner, 2002. Certified Public Accountant (Missouri).
**Personal:** JD (cum laude), University of Missouri at Columbia, 1981, Order of the Coif; BS (magna cum laude), University of Colorado, 1977.

### RIFFEL, Jerome
Lathrop & Gage L.C., Kansas City
816 460 5712
jriffel@lathropgage.com
*Recommended in Real Estate*
**Career:** Riffel is one of the most experienced real estate attorneys in the region. He serves on organizations such as the Executive Committee of the Downtown Council and is former City Councilman for Kansas City, Mo. Riffel handles Tax Increment Financing Development, urban redevelopment, land clearance, condemnation, special business districts, economic development incentives, and all aspects of land use planning and development. He was honored as Best of the Bar, Kansas City Business Journal, 2003-04; Leading Lawyer by Chambers USA 2004-06; has a Martindale Hubbell AV Rating; and was selected for Missouri/Kansas Super Lawyers 2005.

### ROWE, Jack D
Lathrop & Gage L.C., Kansas City
816 460 5607
jrowe@lathropgage.com
*Recommended in Employment*
**Career:** Rowe represents management and the business sector in equal employment opportunity, personnel relations and traditional labor matters, including federal, state and local agency investigations and hearings, court actions and day

to day counseling. His practice involves consultation concerning and litigation defense of complex employment, personnel and labor relations issues, including union elections, negotiations and arbitrations, reductions in force, discipline and discharge, pay practices, affirmative action, ERISA, OSHA, government complaints, compliance reviews. Honors include Leading Lawyer by Chambers USA, 2003-06; Best Lawyers in America, 2003-06; Missouri/Kansas Super Lawyers, 2005; Best of the Bar, Kansas City Business Journal, 2003-04.

### SAMPSON, William
Shook, Hardy & Bacon LLP, Kansas City
816 559 2482
wsampson@shb.com
*Recommended in Litigation*
**Practice Areas:** Complex litigation, antitrust and business torts. Has tried more than 80 jury cases in federal, state and military courts and tribunals and has been active nationally and internationally in the defense of civil litigation. Listed in 'The Best Lawyers in America'.
**Prof. Memberships:** Admitted to practice in Kansas and Missouri and before the US Court of Appeals for the Eighth and Tenth Circuits and the US District Court for the District of Kansas and the Western District of Missouri. Member of Association of Defense Trial Attorneys and Fellow of American Bar Foundation. Appointments: President, Defense Research Institute, 2003-04.
**Career:** Joined Shook, Hardy & Bacon, 1987; became Partner, 1989. Has an extensive teaching background.
**Publications:** Principal author, 'Kansas Trial Handbook' (1997); Excellence at DRI, 'For The Defense' (November 2003); Shively's Got a Brand New Firm, 'For The Defense' (March 2003).
**Personal:** JD, University of Kansas School of Law, 1971; BA (with honors in History), University of Kansas, 1968.

### SEABAUGH, William
Bryan Cave LLP, St Louis
314 259 2000
*Recommended in Corporate/M&A*

### SHALTON, Lonnie J
Polsinelli Shalton Welte Suelthaus PC, Kansas City 816 753 1000
lshalton@pswslaw.com
*Recommended in Real Estate*
**Practice Areas:** Member and former Chairman of the Real Estate Department with concentration in the representation of national real estate developers.
**Career:** Projects include the Intercontinental Hotel and condo tower on Boston Harbor, bankruptcy purchase and ultimate sale of the Enron Tower in Houston, condo towers in Miami, a major office building in Chicago and several projects in New York City: conversion of the Stanhope Hotel to a co-operative, Ariel condo towers at 99th and Broadway, a $1.76 bil-

lion apartment/land purchase on the Hudson River and the W Hotel and 60-story Orion luxury condo tower in the Times Square area.

### SHORT, Barry
Lewis, Rice & Fingersh LC, St Louis
314 444 7600
*Recommended in Litigation*

### SHTEAMER, Michael B
Shughart Thomson & Kilroy PC, Kansas City 816 374 0586
mshteamer@stklaw.com
*Recommended in Real Estate*
**Practice Areas:** Real estate; banking; corporate law; business law. Michael B Shteamer represents developers and lenders in negotiating and preparing documents for commercial real estate loans, workouts, foreclosures, contracts, leases and analyzing and resolving environmental problems relating to real estate. Mike also represents large and small corporate clients. His corporate practice encompasses all facets of corporate organization, including shareholder, stock and employment agreements for general and professional corporations.
**Prof. Memberships:** The Missouri Bar; Kansas City Metropolitan Bar Association.
**Career:** Joined Shughart Thomson & Kilroy PC as a shareholder in 1995. Listed in 'Chambers USA: America's Leading Lawyers for Business' (2005).
**Personal:** Born Kansas City, Missouri July 7, 1951. Tulane University, JD, 1973; BA, 1976.

### SPARKS, Stephen
Bryan Cave LLP, Kansas City
816 374 3200
*Recommended in Real Estate*

### STAHL, Thomas H
Lathrop & Gage L.C., Kansas City
816 460 5821
tstahl@lathropgage.com
*Recommended in Corporate/M&A*
**Career:** Stahl concentrates his practice in corporate and business services, which includes business formation, business planning, mergers and acquisitions, board of directors, employment and shareholders issues. He has provided counsel to large and small business entities in a multitude of areas including general corporate governance, corporate planning and organization, international, banking, healthcare, professional corporations, federal and state regulations and business litigation. Stahl served as assistant US attorney general, Western District of Missouri from 1971-73; and served as assistant Missouri attorney general from 1970-71. He was selected as America's Leading Business Lawyers, 2003-06 and for Missouri/Kansas Super Lawyers, 2005.

### SWEENEY, Kevin R
Sonnenschein Nath & Rosenthal LLP, Kansas City 816 460 2456
krsweeney@sonnenschein.com
*Recommended in Corporate/M&A*
**Practice Areas:** Has over 20 years' experience leading merger and acquisition transactions, public and private securities offerings, joint ventures and strategic alliances, venture capital investments and other finance transactions. His practice focus includes bio-tech, hi-tech, emerging growth companies and corporate governance, as well as amateur sports organizations.
**Prof. Memberships:** Adjunct Professor of Law at the University of Missouri, Columbia.
**Personal:** University of Missouri, Columbia, School of Law, with Honors. University of Notre Dame, BBA, cum laude, Management Concentration.

### TOMASO, Robert
Blackwell Sanders Peper Martin LLP, St Louis 314 345 6433
rtomaso@blackwellsanders.com
*Recommended in Employment*
**Practice Areas:** Labor and employment; ERISA Litigation.
**Prof. Memberships:** Admitted to practice in Missouri (1989); the District Courts for the Eastern and Western Districts of Missouri as well as the Central and Southern Districts of Illinois; 7th and 8th Circuit Courts of Appeal and the US Supreme Court. Member of American Bar Association and Bar Association of Metropolitan St Louis.
**Career:** Named as Partner, 1997; Member, Advisory Board Committee, 2000-03; Managing Partner of St Louis office, 2003-present.
**Personal:** JD, University of Virginia, 1989; BA (summa cum laude), Washington & Lee University, 1985.

### TRIPP, David
Stinson Morrison Hecker LLP, Kansas City 816 842 8600
dtripp@stinsonmoheck.com
*Recommended in Litigation*
**Practice Areas:** Tripp is Chair of the firm's Environmental Division and has assisted clients in environmental matters including Superfund liability issues and enforcement and permit actions involving air pollution, water pollution, toxic substances, and chemical regulation under federal, state and local laws. His experience and knowledge have been applied to issues in both administrative and judicial tribunals. Prior to joining the firm, Dave was Regional Counsel, US EPA, Region VII, where he worked for 16 years in the Enforcement Division and Office of Regional Counsel.
**Personal:** LLM, University of Missouri-Kansas City (1974); JD and BA, Washburn University, (1971)(1968).

### TRYNIECKI, Timothy
Armstrong Teasdale LLP, St Louis
314 621 5070
*Recommended in Real Estate*

### VAN DYKE, Thomas
Bryan Cave LLP, Kansas City
816 374 3200
*Recommended in Corporate/M&A*

### VERING III, John
Armstrong Teasdale LLP, Kansas City
816 221 3420
*Recommended in Employment*

### VIRTEL, James
Armstrong Teasdale LLP, St Louis
314 621 5070
*Recommended in Litigation*

### VOIGTS, Gene
Shook, Hardy & Bacon LLP, Kansas City
816 474 6550
gvoigts@shb.com
*Recommended in Litigation*
**Practice Areas:** Products liability litigation and business litigation. Has appeared in various civil (products liability, professional liability and commercial litigation) and criminal cases in state and federal courts. Has also argued cases at all levels of the state and federal appellate systems, including the US Supreme Court.
**Prof. Memberships:** Admitted to practice in Missouri and before the US Court of Appeals for the Fifth and Eighth Circuits and the US Supreme Court. Member of American Bar Association, The Missouri Bar, Kansas City Metropolitan Bar Association, The Lawyers Association of Kansas City and Missouri Organization of Defense Lawyers. Appointment: Member, Advisory Group appointed by the US District Court for the Western District of Missouri under the Civil Justice Reform Act of 1990.
**Career:** Joined Shook, Hardy & Bacon, 1973; became Partner, 1975. Firm's Vice Chairman and General Counsel and member of Executive Committee.
**Personal:** LLB, University of Missouri-Kansas City School of Law, 1964; BA, William Jewell College, 1961.

### WALSH, Thomas
Bryan Cave LLP, St Louis
314 259 2000
*Recommended in Litigation*

### WARD, R Lawrence
Shughart Thomson & Kilroy PC, Kansas City 816 374 0571
lward@stklaw.com
*Recommended in Litigation*
**Practice Areas:** Civil trials. R Lawrence Ward is Chairman of the firm and the Business Litigation Group. Larry has spent over 40 years trying cases and arguing appeals in both State and Federal Courts around the country. Substantive areas of trial and appellate experience include antitrust, business tort and commercial claims, fraud, securities, franchise

litigation, fiduciary duty claims, lender liability, shareholder derivative cases, class actions, professional negligence, intellectual property, environmental law, employment law, product liability and personal injury. Client representation includes accounting and law firms, the trucking industry, cable television, the banking industry, national computer companies, pharmaceutical drug manufacturers, utilities and various other manufacturers.

**Prof. Memberships:** Admitted to Missouri Bar (1961); US Supreme Court. The Daily Record inaugural 2004 Top Ten Kansas City Legal Leaders award; University of Missouri at Kansas City, Practitioner of the Year Law Alumni (1996), Law Foundation President (1984-86); Kansas City Metropolitan Bar Association, President (1983); American Bar Association, Fellow, Co-Chairman, Mid-Year Meeting - Kansas City, Missouri (1994), Missouri State Delegate to House of Delegates (1992-98); The Missouri Bar, Board of Governors (1973-77); Judicial Commission for the Sixteenth Judicial Circuit of Missouri in Jackson County, Missouri (1979-85); Appellate Judicial Commission for the State of Missouri (1992-97); Kansas City Metropolitan Bar, Chairman, Foundation Committee for development of the 'Courtroom of the Future' in conjunction with the Sixteenth Judicial Circuit, (1996-97); Herbert Hartley Award, American Judicial Society (2001); selected by the National Law Journal as one of the top 10 trial lawyers in America (1994); listed for many years in the Best Lawyers in America: Business Litigation, Personal Injury Litigation, and Antitrust Law; listed in 'Chambers USA: America's Leading Business Lawyers' as leading individual trial lawyer in general commercial litigation; Lon O Hocker Memorial Trial Lawyer Award, awarded by The Missouri Bar Foundation; The Purcell Professionalism Award, awarded by The Missouri Bar Foundation (1997); KC Magazine in 2005 recognized Larry as one of the Top 10 Super Lawyers in Missouri/Kansas.

**Career:** Joined Shughart Thomson & Kilroy PC (1961); shareholder (1963). Executive Committee (firm Chairman); Chair Business Litigation Group.

**Personal:** Born Kansas City, Kansas, May 19, 1936. University of Missouri at Kansas City, JD (1961). University of Missouri at Kansas City, BBA (1959).

## WELSH, W Russell
Polsinelli Shalton Welte Suelthaus PC, Kansas City 816 753 1000
wrwelsh@pswslaw.com
*Recommended in Litigation*

**Practice Areas:** Business litigation; products liability litigation. Chairman and CEO of firm 1998 to present. Represents corporations and not for profits in commercial, intellectual property and shareholder disputes. Represents manufacturers in catastrophic product liability litigation. Tried cases throughout the United States.

**Prof. Memberships:** American Board of Trial Advocates, Chair, Products Liability Committee TIPS Section; American Bar Association (1993-94); Kansas City Metropolitan Bar Association Board of Directors (2002-present).

**Career:** US Department of Justice, trial attorney (1977-81); Shareholder, Litigation Chairman, firm Chair, Polsinelli Shalton Welte Suelthaus PC (1986-present).

**Personal:** Georgetown University (JD, 1974); University of Kansas (BA, 1971).

## WERTS, Dale A
Lathrop & Gage L.C., Kansas City
816 460 5828
dwerts@lathropgage.com
*Recommended in Corporate/M&A*

**Practice Areas:** Corporate and general business.

**Career:** Werts specializes in corporate and general business, corporate finance, mergers and acquisitions and corporate governance. He represents public and private clients in connection with finance, operational and transactional needs. Werts represents buyers and sellers in connection with their purchases and sales of stock and assets in regulated and unregulated businesses. He handles financing transactions for lenders, investors, borrowers, targets. His corporate finance expertise includes advising clients concerning venture capital/angel investments, PIPEs, private placements of debt and equity, bank financings and asset based lending. He was selected as 'Leading Lawyer' by Chambers USA, 2005-06.

## WHITE, Michael
White Goss Bowers March Schulte & Weisenfels, A Professional Corporation, Kansas City 816 753 9200
*Recommended in Real Estate*

## WING, David
Spencer Fane Britt & Browne LLP, Kansas City 816 474 8100
*Recommended in Employment*

## WOLF, Jerome
Sonnenschein Nath & Rosenthal LLP, Kansas City 816 460 2420
jwolf@sonnenschein.com
*Recommended in Litigation*

**Practice Areas:** Firm Marketing Committee Chair, firm Centennial Committee Chair and Kansas City Litigation Group Head. Concentrates in civil and commercial litigation. Experience in environmental, antitrust, intellectual property, franchise litigation, construction litigation and alternative dispute resolution. Founding Managing Partner of Kansas City office, past Member of firm's Management Committee.

**Prof. Memberships:** Past President, Kansas City Bar Association; Founding President, Kansas City Bar Foundation; Member, Center for Public Resources National Commission to Study Arbitration; Chairman, Civil Justice Reform Act of 1990 Advisory Group, US District Court, Western District of Missouri, Dean of Trial Bar Award, Legal Leader of the Year Award.

## WROBLEY, Ralph
Blackwell Sanders Peper Martin LLP, Kansas City 816 983 8111
rwrobley@blackwellsanders.com
*Recommended in Corporate/M&A*

**Practice Areas:** Commercial transactions; privately held businesses; international; mergers and acquisitions.

**Prof. Memberships:** Admitted to practice in Missouri (1962). Vice-President, Council on Education. Chair, Mid-America Coalition on Healthcare; Citizens Association of Kansas City; and Public Housing Authority of Kansas City. Trustee and Chair, Clearinghouse of Mid-Continent Foundations. Vice-Chair, Center for Business Innovation. Legal Committee Member, National Automated Clearinghouse. Member, Civic Council of Kansas City.

**Career:** Joined firm as Partner, 1992; Member, Blackwell Sanders Peper Martin Executive Committee, 1992-2000; Chair, Blackwell Sanders Peper Martin Corporate Department, 1992-2000.

**Personal:** JD, University of Chicago, 1962; BA, Yale University, 1957.

## WYRSCH, James R
Wyrsch Hobbs & Mirakian PC, Kansas City 816 221 0080
jimwyrsch@whmlaw.net
*Recommended in Litigation*

**Practice Areas:** White-collar criminal defense; complex litigation.

**Prof. Memberships:** Admitted to practice in Missouri, 1966, and numerous federal courts; member, MO Supreme Court Procedures Committee, and Subcommittee to Draft Model Criminal Instructions for 8th Circuit Federal District Courts; Advocate, American Board of Trial Advocates; Fellow, American College of Trial Lawyers; Life Fellow, American Bar Foundation; senior counsel, College of Master Advocates and Barristers; Adjunct Professor, University of Missouri-Kansas City Law School.

**Career:** President, Wyrsch Hobbs & Mirakian, P.C. (and predecessors), 1970 to present.

**Publications:** Co-author, 'Missouri Criminal Trial Practice', 1994, and numerous articles in professional journals.

**Personal:** Born 23 February 1942; BA, Notre Dame University, 1963; JD, Georgetown University, 1966; LLM in Trial Practice, University of Missouri-Kansas City, 1972.

## YATES, David F
Polsinelli Shalton Welte Suelthaus PC, St Louis 314 889 8000
dyates@pswslaw.com
*Recommended in Employment*

**Practice Areas:** Employment; Labor; ERISA, representing management; Alternative Dispute Resolution.

**Prof. Memberships:** Missouri and Illinois; US Supreme Court; Third, Seventh, and Eighth Circuits; Federalist Society; Missouri Bar Association; Illinois State Bar Association.

**Career:** NLRB 1969-70; current firm 1976-90 and 2003-present; Thompson Coburn 1990-2003; 'Best Lawyers' for over 10 years; Mediator USA&M-Midwest.

**Personal:** University of Missouri (JD, 1969); Ohio Wesleyan University (BA, 1966).

## YATES, Jack
Husch & Eppenberger, LLC, Kansas City 816 421 4800
*Recommended in Employment*

# BLACKWELL SANDERS PEPER MARTIN LLP

## THE FIRM

**Chairman:** David A Fenley

**Number of partners:** 155
**Number of other lawyers:** 147

**FIRM OVERVIEW:** With 302 attorneys and over 40 practice concentrations, the firm is one of the leading commercial law firms in the central Midwest and is recognized for its transactional and litigation practices. Corporate Board Member magazine has consistently ranked Blackwell Sanders as one of the 'Best Corporate Law Firms in America'.

**MAIN AREAS OF PRACTICE:** Mergers and acquisitions, corporate finance, business and commercial litigation, labor and employment, intellectual property and intellectual property infringement litigation, real estate, international and governmental affairs.

**Corporate:** Corporate attorneys represent globally known companies, including New York Stock Exchange and NASDAQ listed companies. Because of the diversity of clients and the complexity of their transactions, the firm has nurtured unique legal experiences and earned a national reputation in securities, mergers and acquisitions, and secured and unsecured financing transactions. The sophistication of the firm's transactional work has enabled it to gain distinction in industries such as energy and public utility, agribusiness, healthcare, specialty retailing, manufacturing, financial institutions, telecommunications, franchising and distribution, and transportation.

**Litigation:** The firm's litigation attorneys have attained hard-earned reputations for winning crucial, complex business verdicts. Litigators focus on complex areas of the law, including antitrust, bankruptcy, class actions, corporate governance, securities, intellectual property and white collar crime. Experiences in industry sectors such as energy and public utility, agribusiness, healthcare, construction, transportation, securities and insurance enable the firm's trial attorneys to quickly assess regulatory and operating litigation exposure.

**Labor & Employment:** The firm's Labor and Employment Department is anchored by experienced attorneys. They have guided leading employers, including Fortune 500 companies, both regionally and nationally, in labor and employment matters. Labor and employment representations include traditional labor involving labor negotiations, defense of NLRB allegations, strikes and strike preparation, arbitrations and union prevention, as well as defense of employment discrimination litigation, Wage and Hour audits, OSHA/MSHA safety and OFCCP Affirmative Action program audits.

**Real Estate:** The firm's Real Estate Practice is one of the most diverse in the Midwest. Attorneys represent regional and national clients active in real estate investment, development, financing and leasing. Real estate services range from traditional purchases and sales, leases and financings to complex national mortgage loan and mortgage securitization programs. Real estate attorneys have structured and negotiated developments in the urban core districts of Kansas City, Omaha and St. Louis and secured crucial economic development incentives that serve as the cornerstone for competitive project development.

**CLIENTS:** The firm represents Fortune 500, multi-national and some of the largest privately held companies in the United States. Many of these clients are global leaders in their industries, including agribusiness, energy, finance, manufacturing, specialty retailing, consulting, design and engineering, and real estate lending.

**INTERNATIONAL WORK:** The firm's international practice involves representing United States-based clients with the conduct of their businesses in other countries, including: acquisitions and joint ventures; establishing US subsidiaries in foreign countries; establishing overseas dealerships; and arbitrating international disputes under all major dispute systems (including the rules of the International Chamber of Commerce).

## HEAD OFFICE

**MISSOURI**
4801 Main Street, Suite 1000, **Kansas City**, MO 64112
**Tel:** 816 983 8000   **Fax:** 816 983 8080
**Email:** info@blackwellsanders.com
**Website:** www.blackwellsanders.com

## BRANCH OFFICES

**DISTRICT OF COLUMBIA**
750 17th Street, NW, Suite 1000 **Washington**, DC 20006
**Tel:** 202 378 2300   **Fax:** 202 378 2319

**MISSOURI**
720 Olive Street, Suite 2400, **St Louis**, MO 63101
**Tel:** 314 345 6000   **Fax:** 314 345 6060

901 St. Louis Street, Suite 1900, **Springfield**, MO 65806
**Tel:** 417 268 4000   **Fax:** 417 268 4040

**NEBRASKA**
1620 Dodge Street, Suite 2100, **Omaha**, NE 68102
**Tel:** 402 964 5000   **Fax:** 402 964 5050

## INTERNATIONAL OFFICES

The firm also has an office in London.

## CONTACTS

| | |
|---|---|
| **Corporate Finance & M&A** | Jim Ash |
| | Tom Prince (St Louis) |
| **Litigation** | Doug Schmidt |
| | Jeff Kalinowski (St Louis) |
| **Intellectual Property** | Sam Digirolamo (St Louis) |
| | Michael Kahn (St Louis) |
| **Energy** | William Demarest (DC) |
| **Real Estate** | Dave Fenley |
| | John McNearney (St Louis) |
| **Labor & Employment** | Paul Pautler |
| | John Phillips |
| | Terry Potter (St Louis) |
| **Governmental Affairs** | Steve Kupka (DC) |
| **International** | John Mandelbaum (London) |

BLACKWELL SANDERS PEPER MARTIN
LLP

# KING HERSHEY, PC

## THE FIRM

**Chairman & CEO:** Richard A King

**Number of partners:** 9
**Number of other lawyers:** 10

**FIRM OVERVIEW:** Founded in 1988, King Hershey has developed a reputation as a law firm that finds innovative solutions to complex legal issues facing their clients. Local governments, developers, financial institutions and other businesses bring real estate development, public/private finance, litigation and business challenges to King Hershey. The firm has a diverse practice emphasizing real estate development, public finance and general commercial real estate law.

## MAIN AREAS OF PRACTICE:

**Economic Development Practice:** The firm's Development Practice emphasizes public finance and real estate development. The firm has extensive experience in municipal law, including tax increment financing (TIF) and other forms of municipal finance. King Hershey is known for its ability to assist in the structuring of complex public/private financing partnerships for development projects. The firm has been responsible for several major legislative initiatives in Missouri during the past decade, including an extensive amendment of the Missouri Transportation Development District Act, enactment of the Community Improvement District Act, drafting the Missouri Downtown Economic Stimulus Act and modification of the Missouri Tax Increment Financing Act. These tools are key to the firm's ability to craft innovative public/private financing partnerships for development projects. King Hershey has a unique 'vertical integration' of its practice, allowing the same attorneys to handle planning, structuring and financing complex public/private financed transactions. While most law firms have different attorneys handle zoning and plan approvals, tax increment financing or other public assistance tools and the issuance of municipal bonds related to a project, attorneys in King Hershey's Development Practice handles all aspects of these complex matters, creating efficiency and saving duplication of effort.

**Commercial Real Estate:** The firm maintains one of the Midwest region's most active commercial real estate practices, providing representation in all aspects of real estate law to developers, lenders, landlords, builders, title insurance companies and municipalities. King Hershey is recognized for its expertise in innovative real estate financing techniques and has been instrumental in some of the region's most notable development projects, including Quality Hill, the Jazz District, Park Central Plaza and Ameristar Casino in Kansas City; the Chapel Ridge Business Park in Lee's Summit, Missouri; and Bolger Square, the Independence Regional Medical Center and Hartman Heritage Park in Independence, Missouri. The firm is general counsel to the Land Clearance for Redevelopment Authority of Kansas City and the Kansas City Port Authority, for which it performs urban redevelopment and municipal finance services. King Hershey also represents a number of real estate lending institutions. The firm is experienced in the representation of public agencies and developers in regard to tax increment financing, transportation development districts, neighborhood improvement districts, community improvement districts, Missouri '353' urban redevelopment projects and taxable bonds to fund development. King Hershey also represents owners and managers of real property, including multi-family complexes, golf courses and historic structures.

**Bond Practice:** King Hershey has an active Bond Practice, providing representation in all aspects of municipal bond transactions and other public/private financing transactions. The firm has served as underwriter's counsel and bond counsel on municipal bond offerings as well as acting as issuer's counsel to both public and not-for-profit agencies. King Hershey is listed as nationally recognized bond counsel in the Bond Buyer's Municipal Market Place, commonly known as the 'Red Book.'

### HEAD OFFICE

**MISSOURI**
2345 Grand Boulevard, Suite 2100, **Kansas City**, MO 64108
**Tel:** 816 842 3636   **Fax:** 816 842 2414
**Website:** www.kinghershey.com

**Litigation:** King Hershey provides complete civil federal and state court litigation services in Kansas and Missouri including mediation and appellate practice. The firm provides litigation expertise and representation in administrative hearings in a variety of areas including: banking, bankruptcy, business, commercial, construction law, real estate and taxation.

**Alternative Dispute Resolution:** The firm provides services for any type of alternative dispute resolution and acts as a neutral, including areas of mediation and arbitration.

**CLIENTS:** King Hershey represents a wide variety of both public and private clients including Block & Company, Inc.; City of Boonville, Missouri; City of Fulton, Missouri; City of Hollister, Missouri; City of Neosho, Missouri; Clay County, Missouri; Dial Realty, Inc.; Economic Development Corporation of Kansas City, Missouri; HCA, Inc.; the Jazz District Redevelopment Corporation; McCormack Baron Salazar; Nextel Communications; the Port Authority of Kansas City, Missouri; and Wolfe Automotive Group.

# King Hershey

## ATTORNEYS AT LAW

# LATHROP & GAGE L.C.

## THE FIRM

**Managing Partner:** Thomas S Stewart
**Number of partners worldwide:** 153
**Number of other lawyers worldwide:** 127

**FIRM OVERVIEW:** Lathrop & Gage L.C. offers the depth and strength of a large national firm with the hands-on service, management style and aggressive client service of a smaller regional firm. The firm's attorneys practice in ten offices from Denver to New York, allowing it to respond to all of its clients' legal needs locally, regionally, nationally and internationally. Lathrop & Gage grew in number of attorneys by approximately 20% over the past year alone and jumped to #152 in the *National Law Journal's* list of the top 250 firms in the country. More than half of the firm's attorneys have received *Martindale Hubbell's* highest rating, dozens are listed in *Chambers USA*, *Best Lawyers in America* and are inducted into the prestigious American colleges of their practice areas. Lathrop & Gage consistently ranks as one of the best litigation, intellectual property and corporate firms in the Midwest. Founded in 1873, Lathrop & Gage is considered the oldest firm west of the Mississippi River and still represents its first client, now known as BNSF Railway Company.

## MAIN AREAS OF PRACTICE:

**Litigation:** Lathrop & Gage is one of the largest and most experienced business litigation practices in the region and is the single largest department in the firm. Attorneys represent clients' interests nationally and regionally in all disciplines, including: class action defense, multiparty litigation, intellectual property disputes, trade secret and covenant not to compete enforcement and defense, ERISA and insurance matters, media, accounting professional liability, construction, architects and engineers professional liability, securities, loan enforcement, contract and real estate litigation. The department features many recent successes noted on its litigation website, www.beentherewonthat.com. Of note: Payless ShoeSource in a proxy fight against a group of dissident shareholders; nationwide construction litigation for the leading film exhibition company in the US.; nationwide counsel for class action and commercial matters for a leading automotive manufacturer; national defense of a top ten public accounting firm; national representation of the largest privately held insurance brokerage in the US.

**Intellectual Property:** Lathrop & Gage has one of the largest IP practices in the Midwest with 40 attorneys devoted to this practice who are backed by a general litigation practice with over 180 attorneys. Attorneys practice in every area of IP including litigation, patent, trademark, copyright, trade secret, and licensing law and have helped to shape IP law through their involvement in landmark trademark and false advertising cases involving Thermos®, Monopoly, Eveready Battery and Weight Watchers®. The firm has represented many well-known clients with complex IP issues including Payless ShoeSource, Dear Abby, AMC Entertainment Inc. and Yahoo! Inc. This past year attorneys in this department obtained a multi-million dollar jury verdict for their client by successfully defending its patent for a new and useful de-icing and anti-icing formula.

**Corporate:** During the past year, the firm was involved in transactions with an aggregate value of more than $5 billion dollars. *Corporate Board Member* magazine recently featured Lathrop & Gage among the top corporate practices in the country. The firm represents many of the largest companies headquartered in the region and serves as regional counsel to *Fortune* 500 companies. One of the firm's corporate attorneys in St. Louis was the National Counsel for the Bush-Cheney 2004 re-election campaign. He advised the campaign on national litigation and election law strategies as well as recruited and oversaw local counsel.

**Environmental:** The firm has collected more than $100 million for clients from insurance carriers for historic contamination over the past few years. Additionally, the firm has successfully defended clients in more than 100 Superfund matters, closing landfill sites in 20 states. The firm boasts one of the nation's strongest environmental law practices, providing counsel to businesses on federal and state environmental laws and regulations.

**Labor & Employment:** Lathrop & Gage counsels and represents *Fortune* 500 employers across the country in complex matters. The department obtained several summary judgment and trial successes, including a jury verdict for the employer in a case claiming pregnancy discrimination. Attorneys also defeated class certification in a suit against one of the world's largest fast-food restaurant chains, in which plaintiffs claimed violation of the Fair Labor Standards Act (action pending in federal court).

**Real Estate:** The firm's real estate attorneys have been instrumental in developing and financing numerous local and national commercial projects, including large-scale entertainment complexes, shopping centers, hotels and major business parks. Recently the firm negotiated a process through which the GSA and the IRS were able to achieve congressional authorization and approval for a long-term lease for the IRS Service Center, allowing the Postal Service to find better use for an older facility and the IRS to open a new service center. Additionally, the firm represented the Kansas and Missouri Union Station Bistate Commission to fund $118 million of a $256 million project to renovate Kansas City's historic Union Station and create a world-class science museum. The intermodal portion of the project was funded significantly by federal DOT grants totaling $29 million, together with an additional $10 million from four other federal agencies. The firm participated in all aspects of the project.

## HEAD OFFICE

### MISSOURI
2345 Grand Boulevard, Kansas City, MO 64108

## OTHER OFFICES

### COLORADO
4845 Pearl East Circle, **Boulder**, CO 80301

Republic Plaza, 370 17th Street, **Denver**, CO 80202

### DISTRICT OF COLUMBIA
1300 Eye Street, NW, **Washington, DC** 20005

### KANSAS
10851 Mastin Boulevard, **Overland Park**, KS 66210

### MISSOURI
3610 Buttonwood Drive, **Columbia**, MO 65201 *(by appointment only)*

314 East High Street, **Jefferson City**, MO 65101

1845 South National, **Springfield**, MO 65808

10 South Broadway, **St Louis**, MO 63102

### NEW YORK
230 Park Avenue, **New York**, NY 10169

## AFFILIATE OFFICE

### DISTRICT OF COLUMBIA
Lathrop & Gage DC, PLLC 1300 Eye Street, NW, **Washington, DC** 20005

HROI LLC, Human Resources Return on Investment 2345 Grand Boulevard, **Kansas City**, MO 64108

## FIRM CONTACTS

**Thomas S Stewart**
**Tel:** 800 476 4224  **Website:** www.lathropgage.com

# LEWIS, RICE & FINGERSH, LC

## THE FIRM

**Managing Partner, St Louis:** John K Pruellage
**Managing Partner, Kansas City:** William E Carr

**FIRM OVERVIEW:** The law firm of Lewis, Rice & Fingersh, LC traces its history to the founding of Lewis & Rice in St Louis during 1909 and of Brown, Koralchik & Fingersh in Kansas City during 1948. In August 1989, the two firms merged to form the present organization, having offices in Creve Coeur, Jefferson City, Kansas City, St Louis and Washington, Missouri; Overland Park, Kansas and Belleville, Illinois. With more than 170 lawyers practicing in all of the major legal specialty areas, Lewis, Rice & Fingersh is not only a leading regional firm but has a broad base of national clients as well, who draw upon its talents in such diverse areas as admiralty, antitrust, corporate, heathcare, intellectual property, labor and employment, litigation, estate planning, tax and real estate.

## MAIN AREAS OF PRACTICE:

**Corporate/Business, Tax & Estate Planning:** The firm's Corporate Practice encompasses many disciplines, including banking, securities, corporate finance, mergers and acquisitions, healthcare, bankruptcy, closely-held businesses, employee benefits and e-commerce. The firm serves the diverse needs of public and private businesses of all sizes and in all industries. The attorneys in the firm's Tax Department handle a variety of federal, state and local matters involving tax planning and tax disputes. The firm's estate planning attorneys advise clients regarding individual tax and estate planning, prenuptial agreements, charitable giving and intrafamily wealth transfers.

**Litigation & Labor:** The firm's Litigation Department represents clients in all types of commercial disputes, including claims brought under general contract law, business tort law, insurance policies, the Uniform Commercial Code, federal and state securities laws, lender liability and class action representations. The department has extensive experience in complex litigation, which often requires in-depth review and analysis of thousands of documents, and in alternative dispute resolution techniques. The Labor and Employment Group represents management in employment-related litigation in federal and state courts in actions involving Title VII, the ADA, the ADEA, ERISA, the FMLA, the PDA, state anti-discrimination statutes, and various state law theories, such as wrongful discharge claims and non-competition disputes.

**Real Estate:** The firm's Real Estate Practice includes representation of lenders, developers, institutional investors, contractors, architects, investment advisors, mortgage bankers, brokers and tenants. The department has extensive experience in financing, development, acquisition, joint ventures, taxation, leasing, environmental law, zoning, and work-outs, involving complex, large-scale transactions of all kinds and in nearly every state, as well as several foreign countries. A significant number of attorneys within the department have been recognized by inclusion in, for example, the American College of Real Estate Lawyers, and several leading legal publications, as well as being called upon to teach their specialty at area law schools.

## MAIN OFFICES

**MISSOURI**
500 N Broadway, Suite 2000, **St Louis**, MO 63102
**Tel:** 314 444 7600 **Fax:** 314 241 6056
**Website:** www.lrf.com

1010 Walnut, Suite 500, **Kansas City**, MO 64106
**Tel:** 816 421 2500 **Fax:** 816 472 2500
**Email:** firm@lrf-kc.com

## OTHER OFFICES

**ILLINOIS**
325 S. High Street, **Belleville**, IL 62220
**Tel:** 618 234 8636

**KANSAS**
7015 College Boulevard, Suite 135, **Overland Park**, KS 66211
**Tel:** 913 381 8898

**MISSOURI**
555 N New Ballas Road, Suite 260, **Creve Coeur**, MO 63141
**Tel:** 314 569 2262

221 E Capitol Avenue, **Jefferson City**, MO 65101
**Tel:** 573 893 7724

1200 Jefferson; PO Box 1040, **Washington**, MO 63090
**Tel:** 636 239 7747

10034 N. Ambassador Drive, **Kansas City**, MO 64153
**Tel:** 816 891 9390

## CONTACTS

**Chairman Business, Tax & Estate Planning** .Stanley C Johnston, Kansas City **Chairman Corporate Department** ....Joseph H Weyhrich, St Louis
**Chairman Estate Planning Department** ..Michael D Mulligan, St Louis
**Chairman Litigation & Labor Department** ..Andrew Rothschild, St Louis
**Chairman Litigation Department** ....Robert W Tormohlen, Kansas City
**Chairman Real Estate Department** ..........Charles F Miller, Kansas City
**Chairman Tax Department**...............................William J Falk, St Louis

# MCMAHON, BERGER, HANNA, LINIHAN, CODY & MCCARTHY

## THE FIRM

**Managing Partner:** Thomas O McCarthy

**Number of partners:** 12
**Number of other lawyers:** 12

**FIRM OVERVIEW:** Established in 1955, McMahon, Berger, Hanna, Linihan, Cody & McCarthy is a nationally recognized labor and employment law firm whose practice is devoted to representing management in labor and employment law matters throughout the United States. The firm's philosophy is one of commitment to the highest standards of integrity, quality and service with the achievement of practical, business-oriented results in a cost efficient manner. The firm provides comprehensive labor and employment advice and services to both public and private employers in virtually all areas, including employment litigation, traditional labor matters, employee benefits and health and safety matters.

## MAIN AREAS OF PRACTICE:

**Employment:** McMahon Berger advises clients in establishing policies and procedures to ensure compliance with various federal, state and local non-discrimination laws, as well as assisting them in formulating strategies to maintain a productive workplace environment and minimize the risk of employment litigation. The firm's attorneys regularly teach labor and employment law courses and chair and speak at seminars and workshops on labor, employment and employee benefits topics. McMahon Berger regularly represents clients before federal administrative agencies including EEOC, OFCCP, OSHA and Department of Labor, as well as state and local agencies dealing with the same type issues.

**Traditional Labor:** In court, in negotiations, in arbitration and before government agencies such as the NLRB and NMB, McMahon Berger advises and represents clients in all phases of traditional labor law. Collectively the firm's partners have many years of experience handling and solving the most difficult labor problems faced by employers under the NLRA and RLA. The firm also provides advice on a wide variety of business related labor issues including mergers and acquisitions, relocation and closures.

**Litigation:** McMahon Berger represents clients before state and federal trail and appellate courts throughout the nation, up to and including the United States Supreme Court. The firm's seasoned litigators routinely try to verdict all types of employment cases, including discrimination, harassment, retaliation, wrongful discharge, breach of contract, breach of non-complete agreements, and employee benefit claims. McMahon Berger also has extensive experience representing and defending clients in class actions involving claims of employment discrimination as well as breach of the FLSA, WARN and ERISA.

**Employee Benefits:** McMahon Berger's employee benefits attorneys advise clients on design and implementation of employee benefit plans and compliance with IRS, DOL and PBGC requirements.

**CLIENTS:** Ameren UE; Bodine Aluminum, Inc. (A Subsidiary of Toyota Motor Corporate Services of North America, Inc.) Brinker International; Crane Co.; Emerson Electric Co.; Enterprise Rent-A-Car; Harbour Group Companies; Integram St. Louis Seating, a division of Intier Automotive; Kellwood Co.; Tyco Heathcare/Mallinckrodt, Inc.; Prairie Farms Dairy, Inc.; Ralston Purina; Silgan Plastics Corporation; Sigma-Aldrich Corp; Smurfit Stone Container Corp.; Visant Corporation.

## HEAD OFFICE

**MISSOURI**
2730 North Ballas Road, **St. Louis**, MO 63131
**Tel:** 314 567 7350   **Fax:** 314 567 5968
**Website:** www.mcmahonberger.com

## BRANCH OFFICES

**ILLINOIS**
400 North Bluff Road, **Collinsville**, IL 62234
**Tel:** 618 345 5822   **Fax:** 618 345 6483

# POLSINELLI SHALTON WELTE SUELTHAUS PC

## THE FIRM

**Managing Partner:** W Russell Welsh

**Number of partners:** 108
**Number of other lawyers:** 140

**FIRM OVERVIEW:** With 248 attorneys, Polsinelli Shalton Welte Suelthaus, is a Midwest-based law firm with a national reach that concentrates on business law. In the past two years the firm has grown 60% to meet the needs of its clients. In 2004, the firm was ranked by National Law Journal as the second-fastest growing firm in the US, and in 2005 was ranked 177 in that publication's survey of the nation's largest firms. The firm is a recognized leader in the areas of business law, financial services, real estate and public law, and litigation, providing legal services on a national scale for Fortune 50 companies, investment banks and financial institutions, and on a Midwest regional basis to entrepreneurs, large nonprofit organizations and healthcare organizations. The firm was founded in 1972 in the historic Country Club District of Kansas City and has since grown to nine offices located in Kansas City, St. Louis, Chicago, New York, Washington, DC, Topeka, Kansas, and Edwardsville, Illinois. 70 of the firm's lawyers, who work in the firm's 27 practice groups, have received Martindale-Hubbell's highest rating.

## MAIN AREAS OF PRACTICE:

**Business Law:** The Business Law Department, the firm's largest department, handles a broad spectrum of corporate matters, including mergers and acquisitions, corporate governance, shareholder disputes, tax disputes, intellectual property, tender offers, public offerings and private placements, corporate restructurings, and related succession estate planning and employee benefit programs. The firm's attorneys work extensively with local, state and federal governments and regulatory agencies. The department's clients range in size from national corporations to locally owned entrepreneurial firms and represent a wide variety of industries, including transportation, biotechnology, manufacturing, financial services, healthcare providers, professional service organizations and insurance. Clients include the Stowers Institute for Medical Research, Sprint Nextel, University of Kansas Hospital Authority, TransSystems and Bayer Animal Healthcare.

**Financial Services:** Financial Services, the firm's fastest growing department, now has over 50 lawyers, handling all aspects of debt financing – from secured lending to securitization, from loan origination to loan enforcement – providing a complete 'one-stop shop' for lenders. Clients include several of the major national commercial real estate lenders and servicers, including KeyBank, Midland Loan Services, Barclays, Wells Fargo, Nomura, PNC and Bridger Commercial Funding. The firm's lawyers have documented and closed more than 1,200 commercial real estate loans, $8.5 billion in principal amount, in 48 states and the District of Columbia. The department also has extensive experience in asset based and other commercial lending and securitizations and other capital markets transactions. Its Loan Enforcement and Bankruptcy Group represents lenders and other stakeholders in enforcement, receivership, and bankruptcy proceedings throughout the United States.

**Litigation:** The Litigation Department attorneys represent clients in a variety of industries, including insurance, construction, telecommunications, automotive, pharmaceutical, medical device, public utility, finance, transportation and manufacturing, and across legal areas such as commercial and business, construction, employment, labor and ERISA, intellectual property, toxic and mass tort, products liability and pro bono. Regardless of the nature of a dispute, the depth of experience of the firm's Litigation Department provides its clients with effective representation in attempting to achieve a favorable resolution. Clients include Bayer Animal Healthcare, Bristol-Meyers Squibb, Honeywell, Nissan Motor Company, LTD, University of Kansas Hospital Authority, Easton Technical Products and Aventis.

**Real Estate Development & Transactions:** The firm's Real Estate and Public Law Department is well known as a full-service real estate transaction and zoning and land use firm with extensive specialty practice areas in economic development incentives (including tax increment financing, STAR Bonds, transportation development districts, etc), commercial development, public/private partnerships, like kind exchanges, construction and design, tax credits and commercial lending. The firm represents clients involved in some of the largest projects in the region, including development of a major motor sports facility and adjacent 400-acre retail and destination entertainment complex; zoning, bond and transactional work for the $2 billion Sprint World Headquarters campus. The Transactional Practice includes representation of a New York-based national real estate developer. Their work includes major mixed-use condominium projects in New York, Boston and Miami, a 1.5 million square foot office building in Chicago and a Times Square hotel development.

## HEAD OFFICE

**MISSOURI**
700 West 47th Street, Suite 1000, **Kansas City**, MO 64112
**Tel:** 816 753 1000  **Fax:** 816 753 1536
**Email:** info@pswslaw.com  **Website:** www.pswslaw.com

## BRANCH OFFICES

**ILLINOIS**
180 N. Stetson Avenue, Suite 4525 **Chicago**, IL 60601
**Tel:** 312 819 1900  **Fax:** 312 819 1910

101 W. Vandalia, Suite 225, **Edwardsville**, IL 62025
**Tel:** 618 655 9500  **Fax:** 618 655 9640

**KANSAS**
6201 College Boulevard, Suite 500, **Overland Park**, KS 66211
**Tel:** 913 451 8788  **Fax:** 913 451 6205

555 Kansas Avenue, Suite 301, **Topeka**, KS 66603
**Tel:** 785 233 1446  **Fax:** 785 233 1939

**MISSOURI**
100 S. Fourth Street, Suite 1100, **St. Louis**, MO 63102
**Tel:** 314 889 8000  **Fax:** 314 231 1776

7733 Forsyth Boulevard, Suite 1200, **St. Louis**, MO 63105
**Tel:** 314 889 8000  **Fax:** 314 727 7166

**NEW YORK**
292 Madison Avenue, 17th Floor, **New York**, NY 10017
**Tel:** 212 684 0199  **Fax:** 212 684 0197

**WASHINGTON, DC**
555 12th Street N.W., Suite 710, **Washington**, D.C. 20004
**Tel:** 202 783 3300  **Fax:** 202 783 3535

## CONTACTS

| | |
|---|---|
| Chairman | W Russell Welsh |
| Chair Business | Frank J Ross |
| Chair Litigation | Cathy J Dean |
| Chair Financial Services & Real Estate | Daniel J Flanigan |
| Real Estate Development | John D Petersen |
| Real Estate Transactions | Lisa M Haines |

Polsinelli | Shalton
Welte | Suelthaus PC

LAW IN A NEW LIGHT®

# SHOOK, HARDY & BACON LLP

## THE FIRM

**Chairman:** John F Murphy

**Number of partners & counsel:** 258
**Number of attorneys:** 482

**FIRM OVERVIEW:** Shook Hardy & Bacon (SHB) is widely recognized as a premier litigation firm in the US and abroad. For more than a century, the firm has defended clients in some of the most substantial national and international products liability and mass tort litigations. The firm's attorneys have unparalleled experience in organizing defense strategies, developing defense themes and trying high-profile cases. In 2005, Shook was selected as the 'Global Products Liability Firm of the Year' by *Who's Who Legal*.

## MAIN AREAS OF PRACTICE:

**Products Liablity:** Shook is widely renowned as a 'go-to' firm for products liability litigation. The firm has played a lead role in the largest and most substantial international and national products liability and mass tort litigations, and is proud that it has successfully defended some of the world's largest companies in bet-the-company litigation for more than 40 years. Its clients include the tobacco, pharmaceutical, medical device, automotive, chemical and food industries.

**Antitrust:** SHB antitrust attorneys have represented clients in both civil and criminal litigation and investigations. They have defended numerous civil price-fixing actions, including complex, multidistrict class actions. They have also defended numerous antitrust actions by private plaintiffs challenging mergers, acquisitions and joint ventures in district courts nationwide and before the Federal Trade Commission's administrative law judges.

**Commercial Litigation:** The firm has become many businesses' first choice in handling high-stakes matters regionally and nationally including: antitrust/RICO, banking/financial, bankruptcy/reorganization, class action/complex litigation, contract disputes, design/construction, ERISA litigation, general litigation, insurance coverage, securities/corporate disputes, and uniform commercial code.

**Corporate Finance & Banking:** Attorneys in the firm's Corporate Finance and Banking Practice concentrate on mergers and acquisitions, joint ventures, strategic alliances, securities matters, private equity and financing transactions, commercial finance and banking and the general representation of publicly held and private entities.

**Employment:** The firm represents management's interests in employment disputes and policy matters. Attorneys in this practice represent corporate employers in all types of employment matters including age, sex and race discrimination claims; class action litigation; workplace harassment claims; retaliation and whistle-blower litigation; noncompetition, confidentiality, trade secrets and breach of contract claims; wage and hour claims; ERISA litigation; disability, family and medical leave claims; and other discrimination and wrongful discharge claims.

**Environmental/Toxic Tort:** The firm's Environmental and Toxic Tort Practice offers cutting-edge trial and compliance experience under all federal environmental and safety statutes. SHB's lawyers also have experience in state litigation and compliance matters in more than 30 states.

**Intellectual Property:** Attorneys in this group are proven litigators who regularly handle patent, trademark, copyright and trade secret cases. They are also experienced in the procurement of patent, trademark and copyright protection.

**Public Policy:** The firm's Public Policy Group was formed to help clients respond to the demands of a new and dynamic litigation environment. By combining public policy work with an enormous capacity to defend liability cases nationwide, the firm is able to offer clients a comprehensive set of strategies and tools to navigate the legal landscape.

## HEAD OFFICE

**MISSOURI**
2555 Grand Boulevard, **Kansas City**, MO 64108-2613
**Tel:** 816 474 6550   **Fax:** 816 421 5547
**Website:** www.shb.com

## BRANCH OFFICES

**CALIFORNIA**
Jamboree Center, 5 Park Plaza, Suite 1600, **Irvine**, CA 92614-2546
**Tel:** 949 475 1500   **Fax:** 949 475 0016

333 Bush Street, Suite 600, **San Francisco**, CA 94104-2828
**Tel:** 415 544 1900   **Fax:** 415 391 0281

**DISTRICT OF COLUMBIA**
Hamilton Square, 600 14th Street, NW, Suite 800,
**Washington, DC** 20005-2004
**Tel:** 202 783 8400 **Fax:** 202 783 4211

**FLORIDA**
Miami Center, Suite 2400, 201 South Biscayne Boulevard,
**Miami**, FL 33131-4332
**Tel:** 305 358 5171   **Fax:** 305 358 7470

100 North Tampa Street, Suite 2900, **Tampa**, FL 33602-5810
**Tel:** 813 202 7100   **Fax:** 813 221 8837

**KANSAS**
84 Corporate Woods, 10801 Mastin, Suite 1000,
**Overland Park**, KS 66210-1697
**Tel:** 913 451 6060   **Fax:** 913 451 8879

**TEXAS**
JP Morgan/Chase Tower, 600 Travis Street, Suite 1600,
**Houston**, TX 77002-2911
**Tel:** 713 227 8008   **Fax:** 713 227 9508

## INTERNATIONAL OFFICES

The firm also has offices in Switzerland and the United Kingdom.

**Tort:** The firm's tort attorneys pride themselves on their ability to litigate virtually any matter in any venue. SHB's experience in tort matters encompasses all aspects of litigation in federal and state courts across the country. The firm's collective wealth of experience allows them to successfully transfer litigation tactics and skills across all areas.

# SHUGHART THOMSON & KILROY, P.C.

## THE FIRM

**Chairman:** R Lawrence Ward
**Managing Partner:** John M Kilroy, Jr
**Denver Managing Partner:** G Stephen Long
**Overland Park Managing Partner:** Lawrence A Swain
**Phoenix/Tucson Managing Partner:** Brian M Goodwin
**Springfield Managing Partner:** Thomas J O'Neal
**St. Joseph Managing Partner:** R Dan Boulware

**Shareholders:** 92
**Of Counsel:** 25
**Associates:** 50

**FIRM OVERVIEW:** Shughart Thomson & Kilroy is a full service law firm with 167 attorneys in six offices in the US. Attorneys and staff members from multiple offices work together to serve a broad range of corporate, institutional and individual clients across the US and throughout the world. The firm's affiliation with Mackrell International, a worldwide association of independent law firms, enhances its global reach.

## MAIN AREAS OF PRACTICE:

**Commercial Litigation:** Shughart Thomson & Kilroy is one of the region's best known trial law firms and includes five members of the American College of Trial Lawyers. More than a fourth of the firm's attorneys are involved in business litigation in federal and state courts. The firm is known for its outstanding trial results in all types of commercial disputes, including contract cases, fraud and business torts, and represent plaintiffs and defendants. The firm also has strong appellate and alternative dispute resolution practices.

**Healthcare Business & Litigation:** The firm's trial attorneys include members of the American College of Legal Medicine and healthcare professionals who entered the practice of law after they had established medical careers. The firm's services include: direct representation of healthcare institutions, healthcare labor law and healthcare antitrust. The firm has over 65 years experience developing healthcare organizations and addressing the business challenges in the highly regulated healthcare industry.

**Construction & Real Estate:** The firm's construction attorneys represent several of the top contractors, architects and engineers in the US. The group handles construction business matters as well as multimillion-dollar lawsuits, appeals and arbitration, in state and federal courts, and before government administrative appeals boards. The firm's real estate attorneys serve major developers and lenders nationwide in all phases of real property acquisition, entitlement, construction, operation and sale, and all the interrelated financing that occurs in these transactions.

**General Business:** The firm is highly regarded in general business law, and assists clients with forming business enterprises, employee benefits planning, labor law, commodities and securities, government lobbying, tax, real estate, franchising, insurance, estate and succession planning, public finance and municipal bonds, bankruptcy and reorganization, and mergers & acquisitions.

**Labor & Employment:** Shughart Thomson & Kilroy represents management in all employment issues including union elections, collective bargaining and arbitration, equal employment opportunity litigation, affirmative action, wage and hour, occupational safety and health (OSHA), drug testing, employment contracts and non-compete agreements. The firm advises clients on claim prevention and are experienced employment trial lawyers.

**Tort:** The firm has acted as national counsel for clients involved in environmental litigation, drug litigation and toxic tort defense. It has vast experience in the defense of a wide range of products, from automobiles to aviation and industrial machinery, to biotechnical materials. The firm handles claims involving negligence, products liability, intentional torts and punitive damages exposure.

## HEAD OFFICE

**MISSOURI**
Twelve Wyandotte Plaza, 120 West 12th Street, **Kansas City**, MO 64105
**Tel:** 816 421 3355   **Fax:** 816 374 0509
**Email:** solutions@stklaw.com   **Website:** www.stklaw.com

## BRANCH OFFICES

**ARIZONA**
3636 North Central Avenue, Suite 1200, **Phoenix**, AZ 85012
**Tel:** 602 650 2000   **Fax:** 602 264 7033

**COLORADO**
1050 Seventeenth Street, Suite 2300, **Denver**, CO 80265
**Tel:** 303 572 9300   **Fax:** 303 572 7883

**KANSAS**
9225 Indian Creek Parkway, Suite 1100, **Overland Park**, KS 66210
**Tel:** 913 451 3355   **Fax:** 913 451 3361

**MISSOURI**
901 St. Louis Avenue, Suite 1200, **Springfield**, MO 65806
**Tel:** 417 869 3353   **Fax:** 417 869 9943

3101 Frederick Avenue, **St Joseph**, MO 64506
**Tel:** 816 502 3438   **Fax:** 816 279 3977

## CONTACTS

| | |
|---|---|
| **Commercial Litigation** | R Lawrence Ward |
| **Construction** | Roy Bash |
| **General Business** | Jacob W Bayer, Jr |
| **Healthcare Business** | Randal L Schultz |
| **Healthcare Litigation** | Thomas G Kokoruda |
| **Intellectual Property** | Lawrence A Swain |
| **Intellectual Property Litigation** | Russell S Jones, Jr |
| **Labor & Employment Law** | W Terrence Kilroy |
| **Real Estate** | Daniel T Murphy |
| **Tort** | Robert A Henderson |

**CLIENTS:** Alstom Power, Inc; Associated Wholesale Grocers, Inc; Black & Veatch; Blue Cross and Blue Shield of KC; Burns & McDonnell Engineering Co.; Capital Electric, Inc.; Commerce Bank; Community Health Group (formerly Health Midwest); Crane Plumbing; Dickinson Financial Corporation; DST Realty, Inc.; Heartland Regional Medical Center; HCA, Inc.; H&R Block; J.E. Dunn Construction; Jack Henry & Associates, Inc.; Kansas City Power & Light; Kansas City Public Library; Kansas City Southern Railway; Major League Baseball Players Association; New Directions Behavioral Health, L.L.C.; New Prime, Inc.; Northwest Missouri State University; Olathe Medical Center; Sprint Corp.; St. Joseph Health Center; Stormont Vail Regional Healthcare; Texas Industries, Inc.; United Missouri Bank; U.S. Bank; Swift Transportation; Horizon Organic Holding Corporation.

# STINSON MORRISON HECKER LLP

## THE FIRM

**Managing Partner:** Mark S Foster

**Total number of US partners:** 203
**Number of other lawyers in US offices:** 123

**FIRM OVERVIEW:** Stinson Morrison Hecker is a full-service law firm that represents clients in a variety of corporate, tax, real estate and litigation matters. With more than 325 attorneys in eight offices and five states, the firm can address virtually every legal challenge and opportunity businesses may face. The firm represents local, national and international companies including *Fortune* 500 corporations, municipalities, not-for-profits, small businesses and individuals. The firm's attorneys are recognized leaders in their fields. The firm is ranked among the *National Law Journal*'s Top 250 Law Firms and the *American Lawyer*'s Top 200.

## MAIN AREAS OF PRACTICE:

**Litigation:** With more than 175 skilled litigators, the firm has experience in all aspects of litigation including antitrust, bankruptcy, construction, corporate governance, employment, environmental, federal energy regulatory compliance, patent and trademark litigation, product liability and securities, as well as white collar criminal defense in state and federal courts throughout the nation. Significant litigation includes the representation of General Electric Insurance Solutions (fka ERC) in a reinsurance dispute against Clarendon involving more than $150 million; representation of sanofi-aventis in multidistrict litigation involving a challenge to the settlement of patent litigation in which summary judgment was awarded; and the representation of Sprint Nextel (fka the Sprint Corporation) in a large number of class actions which deal with allegations that they made misleading and deceptive statements regarding limitations on the coverage, capacity and geographic scope of their wireless network. Significant clients include Hallmark Cards, Inc., Sprint Nextel Corporation, Cerner Corporation, Aventis Pharmaceuticals Inc., S&M NuTec and Big Dog Motorcycles.

**Corporate/M&A:** The firm has one of the largest corporate practices in the Midwest. The scope includes financing and securities law compliance, M&A, asset securitizations and structured finance, corporate governance, venture and private equity capital and general corporate matters. They represent several publicly-held companies that run the gamut in size and industry as well as broker/dealer, investment companies, investment advisors, merchant bankers, venture capital and private equity funds, and other participants in the capital markets. Significant accomplishments include serving as corporate counsel for Sprint Corporation in a $36 billion Nextel Communications, Inc. merger and representing H&R Block, Inc. in a $1 billion shelf registration statement and a $400 million public debt offering. Over the last few years, the firm has also assisted Inergy, L.P. in over 50 acquisitions totaling over $1.3 billion. Representative clients include Cerner Corporation, Euronet Worldwide, Inc., Leggett & Platt, Incorporated and LabOne, Inc.

**Banking:** The firm helps all types of financial companies to ensure compliance with federal and state regulations and to achieve their business objectives. This help includes, without limitation, commercial lending matters such as loan syndications and Article 9 of the UCC, M&A transactions, reverse stock splits, bank and holding company formations, succession planning, S-Corp conversions, regulatory issues involving the issuance of trust preferred securities, broker/dealer and insurance networking arrangements, assistance in the negotiation of bank regulatory orders, officer and director training, dealing with corporate governance issues involving financial companies (public and non-public), and federal and state regulatory compliance. The firm's banking division was recognized by *American Banker* as a top legal advisor in M&A for 2004. Significant work includes the formation of a $13.5 million De Novo State Bank in Missouri. Representative clients include US Bank, Bank of America, UMB, Valley View Bancshares and Blue Valley Bank.

**Real Estate:** The Real Estate Practice, which includes more than 25 attorneys, was recently recognized by *Midwest Real Estate News* as one of the 'Best of the Best' transactional real estate firms in the Midwest. The firm focuses on real estate development,

including the use of economic development incentives, acquisitions and sales, mortgage lending, conduit lending and securitization, historic preservation, tax credits, public/private partnerships, leasing (retail/commercial), gaming and liquor licensing issues, real estate litigation and condemnation. Significant work for 2005 includes the representation of the Unified Government of Wyandotte County/Kansas City, Kansas in all phases of legal work for a $400 million water park and a 400-acre retail and entertainment district near the Kansas Speedway (NASCAR), and the development of the Sprint Center (a 19,000 seat state of the art arena) and the Power & Light District (a seven block mixed-use development), both in downtown Kansas City, Missouri. Representative clients include Anschutz Entertainment Group, Inc., Entertainment Properties Trust, The Cordish Company, Midland Loan Services and PetsMart.

**CLIENTS:** Cerner Corporation, Cessna Aircraft Company, H&R Block, Inc., Inergy L.P., Sprint Nextel Corporation.

## HEAD OFFICE

**MISSOURI**
1201 Walnut, Suite 2900, **Kansas City**, MO 64106
**Tel:** 816 842 8600   **Fax:** 816 691 3495
**Email:** info@stinsonmoheck.com

## BRANCH OFFICES

**ARIZONA**
1850 North Central Avenue, Suite 2100, **Phoenix**, AZ 85004
**Tel:** 602 279 1600   **Fax:** 602 240 6925

**KANSAS**
12 Corporate Woods, 10975 Benson, Suite 550, **Overland Park**, KS 66210
**Tel:** 913 451 8600   **Fax:** 913 451 6352

150 North Main, Suite 600, **Wichita**, KS 67202
**Tel:** 316 265 8800   **Fax:** 316 265 1349

**MISSOURI**
230 West McCarty Street, **Jefferson City**, MO 65101
**Tel:** 573 636 6263   **Fax:** 573 636 6231

100 South 4th Street, Suite 700, **St Louis**, MO 63102
**Tel:** 314 259 4500   **Fax:** 314 259 4599

**NEBRASKA**
1299 Farnam Sreet, Suite 1501, **Omaha**, NE 68102
**Tel:** 402 342 1700   **Fax:** 402 930 1701

**DISTRICT OF COLUMBIA**
1150 18th Street, NW, Suite 800, **Washington**, DC 20036
**Tel:** 202 785 9100   **Fax:** 202 785 9163

## CONTACTS

| | |
|---|---|
| Business Litigation | Bruce E Baty |
| Corporate Finance | John A Granda |
| Bankruptcy & Creditors' Rights | Mark Shaiken |
| Employment, Labor & Benefits | Richard L Connors |
| Energy & Telecommunications | Kelly A Daly |
| Environment & Natural Resources | David R Tripp |
| Financial Services | C Robert Monroe |
| General Business | Robert C Hunter |
| IP&T | Penny R Slicer |
| Products Liability | Mark A Kinzie |
| Public Law & Finance | Stephen P Chinn |
| Real Estate | David W Frantze |
| Tax, Trusts & Estates | Paul E McLaughlin |

# THOMPSON COBURN LLP

## THE FIRM

**Chairman:** Thomas J Minogue

**Number of partners:** 175
**Number of other attorneys:** 121

**FIRM OVERVIEW:** Thompson Coburn LLP is a full-service law firm that was established in 1996 with the merger of two of St. Louis' most respected law firms –Thompson & Mitchell and Coburn & Croft. According to the *St. Louis Business Journal*, Thompson Coburn is the largest law firm in the St. Louis metropolitan area. The firm is regularly ranked among top law firms nationwide in the application of client-focused technology and is constantly pursuing initiatives designed to enhance its client service capabilities.

**MAIN AREAS OF PRACTICE:** Through its St. Louis headquarters, Thompson Coburn provides services across a full range of legal specialties and industry sectors, including:
**Corporate & Securities:** For businesses of all sizes, from large publicly owned corporations listed on the New York Stock Exchange to mid- and small-cap companies, the firm provides creative solutions in areas of corporate and securities counseling, public and private offerings of debt and equity securities, and mergers and acquisitions.
**Financial Services:** The firm serves a full spectrum of financial institutions, including commercial banks, investment banks, governmental financial institutions, venture capitalists, pension funds, investment advisors and fund managers. Services cover a complete range of transactional, regulatory and advisory legal matters.
**Healthcare:** The firm provides a full range of legal services to meet the needs of healthcare industry clients, including ambulatory surgery centers, durable medical equipment suppliers, health insurers, hospitals and their medical staffs, managed care organizations, nursing homes, professional associations, staffing agencies and third-party administrators.
**Intellectual Property:** With one of the region's largest IP practices, the firm serves clients in the areas of patent, trademark, copyright, trade secret protection, Internet, electronic commerce, software licensing and false advertising.
**Labor & Employment:** Thompson Coburn has a team of more than 20 attorneys who practice labor and employment law exclusively. This group handles traditional contract negotiations and union organizing matters, as well as provides advice and counsel on issues such as terminations and lay-offs, and protection of intellectual property rights through post-employment restrictions.
**Litigation:** With approximately 150 attorneys and 50 legal assistants, Thompson Coburn's litigation practice has the experience and resources to handle a broad range of business, product and mass litigation matters. The firm's litigation team includes trial lawyers who are skilled in the intricacies of class actions and complex litigation of all types. In the past six years, Thompson Coburn has represented more than 125 Fortune 500 companies and served as national and regional counsel to a wide range of clients in the manufacturing, service and technology sectors. The firm has defended clients in cases involving complex product liability claims, consumer class actions in notoriously difficult jurisdictions, federal prosecution of business owners and cutting-edge environmental issues. In addition to working closely with engineering, technical, medical and other professional experts, the firm's staff includes a physician, registered nurses and a number of PhDs in various disciplines. Thompson Coburn supports its attorneys with a wide range of high-tech resources, including easily searchable electronic discovery tools, advanced document management systems and secure extranets to facilitate client communication.
**Real Estate:** The firm has a strong regional and national real estate practice. Since 2000, the firm has handled transactions for commercial, industrial and multi-family properties in 47 states valued at more than $1 billion.
**Other Practice Areas:** Admiralty; bankruptcy; corporate compliance; construction; employee benefits; environmental; government contracts; private client services; product liability; public finance/law; railroad; tax; tobacco and toxic tort.

## HEAD OFFICE

**MISSOURI**
One US Bank Plaza, **St. Louis**, MO 63101-1611
**Tel:** 314 552 6000  **Fax:** 314 552 7000
**Website:** www.thompsoncoburn.com

## BRANCH OFFICES

**DISTRICT OF COLUMBIA**
1909 K Street, NW, Suite 600, **Washington**, DC  20006-1167
**Tel:** 202 585 6900  **Fax:** 202 585 6969

**ILLINOIS**
525 West Main Street, **Belleville**, IL 62220-1547
**Tel:** 618 277 4700  **Fax:** 618 236 3434

## CONTACTS

| | |
|---|---|
| St. Louis – Corporate | Michael F Lause |
| St. Louis – Litigation | Raymond L Massey |
| Washington, DC | Warren L Dean, Jr |
| Southern Illinois | Thomas W Alvey, Jr |

**Washington, DC Office:** With a strong focus on transportation, the firm's Washington, DC office serves clients throughout the country on matters that involve direct dealings with Federal agencies and the US Congress. Areas of special concentration in the transportation field include marine, aviation, surface, public transit and infrastructure. The firm's Washington, DC office also includes attorneys with experience in litigation, government contracts, international commerce, and postal and utilities regulations.
**Southern Illinois Office:** With only a small fraction of the nation's population, this portion of the country attracts more class actions each year than many of the nation's most populous communities. Attorneys in the firm's Illinois office have experience handling a wide range of class action matters, including product liability, FELA, labor and retaliatory discharge, Railway Labor Act, and matters for insurance companies and financial institutions.

**CLIENTS:** The firm serves a broad spectrum of regional and national clients, including A.G. Edwards & Sons, Inc., Bunzl USA, Inc., Celanese Corporation, Charter Communications, Inc., DaimlerChrysler Corp., Enterprise Rent-A-Car Co., Exxon Mobil Corp., Federal Signal Corp., Kawasaki Motors Corp., KV Pharmaceutical Co., Lorillard Tobacco Co., Maritz Inc., Peabody Holding Co. Inc., SBC Communications, Inc., Scottrade, Stifel Nicolaus & Company, Union Pacific Railroad Co., UniGroup, Inc., University of Missouri, US Bank, N.A., Washington University in St. Louis and Wells Fargo.

**INTERNATIONAL WORK:** Increasingly, Thompson Coburn handles matters for US-based clients that are international in scope. In addition, it is the only firm in the Midwest which is a member of Globalaw Limited, an international network of attorneys and law firms. Through Globalaw, the firm can connect clients with more than 2,600 attorneys in 75 jurisdictions around the world.

THOMPSON COBURN LLP

## How lawyers are ranked

Every year we carry out thousands of in-depth interviews with clients and lawyers in order to assess the reputations and expertise of business lawyers across the USA. Chambers rankings and editorial are referred to extensively by General Counsel and other purchasers of legal services who look to our recommendations when choosing their lawyers.

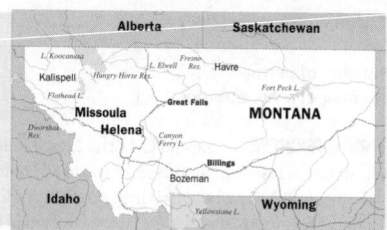

# CORPORATE/M&A

### Corporate/M&A
### Leading Firms

1. CROWLEY, HAUGHEY, HANSON, TOOLE *Billings*
   GARLINGTON, LOHN & ROBINSON, PLLP *Missoula*
2. BOONE, KARLBERG PC *Missoula*
   DORSEY & WHITNEY LLP *Great Falls*
3. CHRISTIAN, SAMSON, JONES *Missoula*
   HOLLAND & HART LLP *Billings*

### Leading Individuals

1. BOONE Thomas *Boone, Karlberg PC*
   CHISHOLM David *Christian, Samson, Jones*
   ELLINGSON Mae *Dorsey & Whitney LLP*
   LAMDIN III William *Crowley, Haughey, Hanson*
   MANNING John *Dorsey & Whitney LLP*
2. CHUMRAU Gary *Garlington, Lohn & Robinson*
   HINGLE Charles *Holland & Hart LLP*
   PETERSEN Larry *Holland & Hart LLP*

## Band 1

### Crowley, Haughey, Hanson, Toole & Dietrich, PLLP

See firm details p.1234

**The Firm:** As Montana's largest law firm, this outfit is a "*one-stop shop*" for clients throughout the northern Rocky Mountain region. The firm has continued to grow over the past year and covers a wide variety of corporate and commercial matters, including M&A, multistate loan transactions and all manner of tax and estate planning issues. The team acts for numerous corporate clients, including many of the state's financial institutions, where interviewees praised the quality of its work product and the professionalism and expeditiousness of its lawyers. Ranchers, farmers and local businesses also feature in the client list and proved to be equally satisfied with the firm's services: "*Even though we are comparatively small fish to them, we never get that feeling – they are always extremely prompt and attentive.*"
**The Lawyers:** Clients describe **Bill Lamdin** as a knowledgeable business lawyer with a lot of common sense: "*He gets the job done without over-lawyering and is tenacious and firm in his convictions without being aggressive or overbearing.*" He repre-

sents financial institutions in a wide range of transactional, regulatory and operational matters. Lamdin is also involved in litigation, real estate and creditors' rights issues as they arise. He recently completed a large financial transaction with a Native American tribe, involving the refinancing of existing obligations totaling $10 million. He further acted on the $20 million financing of a large recreational property in northwestern Montana.
**Clients/Work Highlights:** Blue Cross and Blue Shield of Montana; First Interstate Bank; Rocky Mountain Bank; Stockman Bank; Bank of Baker and Yellowstone Bank.

### Garlington, Lohn & Robinson, PLLP

**The Firm:** This established Missoula-based outfit was described as a "*strong firm*" and is "*highly regarded*" by competitors. It has become the second largest firm in the region and focuses first and foremost on servicing local clientele. The team represents many of the leading businesses in western Montana as well as national corporations and insurance companies.
**The Lawyers:** General commercial lawyer **Gary Chumrau** is experienced in banking and secured transactions as well as real estate law, but he now concentrates principally on hospital and healthcare law. As such, he can count numerous medical care providers as clients.
**Clients/Work Highlights:** Milwaukee Railroad; Mountain Water Company; The Sterling Group and Yellowstone Mountain Club.

## Band 2

### Boone, Karlberg PC

**The Firm:** The firm's commercial practice covers the whole gamut of general commercial matters, from business organization and acquisitions to bankruptcy. Recent focus areas include advising several small businesses on their options with regard to corporate structures and on becoming LLCs. The firm offers related advice on employment matters to both businesses and individuals, and specialist expertise in federal, state and local tax issues is also on offer. The team represents many local and western Montana banks, businesses and individuals.

**The Lawyers:** "*Experienced and smart*" **Tom Boone** is the firm's president. He is involved in business organization and planning, banking, tax and general commercial transactions; however, interviewees reserved special praise for his estate planning expertise. Boone generally sets up 20 to 30 businesses a year and has assisted various corporations in addressing some of their internal problems. Clients trust him implicitly, with one stating: "*He just instills great trust in the client by telling it the way it is.*"
**Clients/Work Highlights:** BJ's Metalworks; First Bank of Lincoln; First Interstate Bank and First Security Bank.

### Dorsey & Whitney LLP

See firm details p.1169

**The Firm:** This national firm's Montana practice focuses largely on corporate, litigation and public finance matters. Indeed, the team is perceived to have cornered the market in Montana where bond transactions are concerned. The firm has two Montana offices, one in Great Falls and another in Missoula, where attorneys can call upon the vast resources of Dorsey & Whitney's domestic and international network of offices as required. It can therefore bring a range of sophisticated expertise to the table, covering areas such as antitrust and IP. Above all, clients valued the outfit's capacity to "*offer the full range of benefits of a large firm and yet remain cost-effective.*"
**The Lawyers:** The "*experienced and hard-working*" **John Manning** (see p.1232) is partner-in-charge of the firm's Montana operation. He is well known for providing emerging companies with securities advice but also represents public companies and investors. Acting for financial institutions on lending and loan workout matters accounts for another portion of his workload. His recent highlights include representing Sammons Trucking of Missoula in its sale to Market Industries and assisting Right-Now Technologies with its acquisition of Convergent Voice. Manning's ability to "*counsel clients on the commercial impact, the real risks and benefits of any course of action,*" also counts in his favor according to sources. **Mae Ellingson** (see p.1231) focuses on tax-exempt finance and bond work. Peers identified her as "*the best bond attorney in the state,*" and she acts for the State of Montana and its various agencies as well as local government.

**Clients/Work Highlights:** Clients include DA Davidson & Co, RightNow Technologies and United Financial Corporation.

## Band 3

### Christian, Samson, Jones & Chisholm, PLLC

**The Firm:** This Missoula-based practice may be younger and smaller than some of its competitors, but its team of *"smart and forceful attorneys"* commands much respect in the market. The firm offers general business and commercial services and is particularly strong in the banking and bankruptcy fields.

**The Lawyers:** **David Chisholm** is *"a technically adept lawyer with a pragmatic streak – a combination that gets deals done."* Acting on behalf of financial

institutions takes up much of his time – he has an enviable track record in banking sector M&A – along with general commercial law and real estate issues. **Clients/Work Highlights:** American Bank Montana; First Interstate Bank; Rocky Mountain Bancorporation; Rocky Mountain Bank and Stockman Bank.

### Holland & Hart LLP

See firm details p.369

**The Firm:** Energy sector matters are perceived as being this national firm's true forte, in which it acts for individuals and companies of all sizes throughout the USA and abroad. The firm boasts the largest operation in the Rocky Mountain region with offices in six mountain states, as well as one in Washington, DC. As such, the team of four in Billings can rely on backup from the firm's out-of-state resources as necessary. Clients particularly value the firm's broad

reach, and the way it channels its abundant resources into providing a cost-effective service.

**The Lawyers:** *"A terrific lawyer and gentleman,"* **Charles Hingle** (see p.1231) focuses on advising businesses in Billings on bankruptcy and creditors' rights. He also offers expertise in banking, real estate and commercial litigation. Interviewees praised his *"meticulous treatment of technical issues and excellent draftsmanship."* Meanwhile, **Larry Petersen** (see p.1232) was described as *"the best corporate lawyer in the state when it comes to smaller M&A deals."* He covers corporate commercial issues surrounding LLCs and advises on natural resource matters. Typical work for Petersen has included advising on a substantial loan facility for a wind energy project and representing the seller in the disposal of a business in the state.

**Clients/Work Highlights:** Clients include Ballard Petroleum, Double D Energy and Wesco Resources.

# EMPLOYMENT

## MAINLY DEFENDANT

| Employment: Mainly Defendant |
| --- |
| **Leading Firms** |
| 1 GARLINGTON, LOHN & ROBINSON, PLLP *Missoula* |
| 2 CROWLEY, HAUGHEY, HANSON, TOOLE *Billings* |
| HOLLAND & HART LLP *Billings* |
| HUGHES, KELLNER, SULLIVAN & ALKE *Helena* |
| 3 BROWN LAW FIRM PC *Billings* |
| DORSEY & WHITNEY LLP *Great Falls* |
| GOUGH, SHANAHAN, JOHNSON *Helena* |
| UGRIN, ALEXANDER, ZADICK & HIGGINS *Great Falls* |
| WORDEN THANE PC *Missoula* |

| Leading Individuals |
| --- |
| **Senior Statesman** |
| THANE Jeremy *Worden Thane PC* |
| 1 BENDER Jeanne *Holland & Hart LLP* |
| FETSCHER Candace *Garlington, Lohn & Robinson* |
| LEHMAN Steven *Crowley, Haughey, Hanson* |
| SULLIVAN John *Hughes, Kellner, Sullivan* |
| 2 HATTERSLEY III Thomas *Gough, Shanahan, Johnson* |
| HERINGER Michael *Brown Law Firm PC* |
| LENNON Maureen *Garlington, Lohn & Robinson* |
| ZADICK Gary *Ugrin, Alexander, Zadick & Higgins* |
| 3 CHRISTENSEN Amy *Hughes, Kellner, Sullivan* |
| FRANCE Lucy *Garlington, Lohn & Robinson* |
| ROBINSON Donald *Poore, Roth & Robinson* |
| **Up-and-coming individuals** |
| WALTER Teri *Gough, Shanahan, Johnson* |

## Band 1

### Garlington, Lohn & Robinson, PLLP

**The Firm:** This leading Missoula firm offers the gamut of employment law services. The nine-attorney team benefits from a trio of standout individuals and counsels employers on various

day-to-day issues in addition to representing them in litigation as it arises. It also offers specialist expertise in workers' compensation and ERISA litigation.

**The Lawyers:** Interviewees describe **Candace Fetscher** as *"one of the best and most experienced employment lawyers in the state."* Her practice encompasses employment law as well as an increasing amount of healthcare and medical malpractice defense law. **Maureen Lennon** is a leading litigator who mainly focuses on employment disputes but also covers personal injury and insurance defense cases. Discrimination matters form a recurring theme for Lennon, who commentators credited with possessing *"a real grasp of the law and the issues."* A younger lawyer who peers *"expect great things of in the future"* is **Lucy France**. She covers both contentious and noncontentious employment matters.

**Clients/Work Highlights:** Beach Transportation; Clark Fork Valley Hospital; Community Medical Center Foundation; Marcus Daly Memorial Hospital; Southgate Mall; Tamarack Management and Yellowstone Club.

## Band 2

### Crowley, Haughey, Hanson, Toole & Dietrich, PLLP

See firm details p.1234

**The Firm:** This full-service regional outfit services clients throughout the northern Rocky Mountain region from offices in Montana and North Dakota. Two partners in the firm's Billings office devote their time exclusively to employment work, primarily acting on the side of the employers. The team offers litigation as well as counseling services and often defends discrimination and wrongful discharge claims.

**The Lawyers:** **Steven Lehman** is active on both employment and labor fronts. He counsels clients on various issues, including union organizing campaigns. Lehman has also defended the likes of Home Depot and Target in contentious settings, and is one of the few lawyers in the state experienced in making appearances before the NLRB. Interviewees describe him as *"a knowledgeable, experienced lawyer with good common sense."*

**Clients/Work Highlights:** MDU Resources Group; Home Depot; First Interstate Bank and Target.

### Holland & Hart LLP

See firm details p.369

**The Firm:** Clients value the service offered by this six-attorney team in Billings and note the advantages of it being able to call upon a rich vein of experience running throughout the national firm's office network. In keeping with the general trend of resolving disputes through mediation, the firm places an emphasis on alternative dispute resolution but covers all aspects of employment and labor law, including where administrative proceedings and trials are involved.

**The Lawyers:** **Jeanne Bender** (see p.1231) was praised for *"making herself available to her clients regardless of the time of day and always providing bulletproof advice."* She is involved in both litigation and counseling as well as training, whether in relation to sexual harassment or other matters of policy. Bender further advises on numerous wage, hour and regulatory matters and has assisted with many disability discrimination and wrongful discharge cases over the past year. She recently obtained a summary judgment in a wage case for a large retail company and represented a transportation company in labor arbitration.

**Clients/Work Highlights:** 3 Rivers Communications; Ballard Petroleum; Security Armored Express; Stillwater Mining; Stockman Bank and Wesco Resources.

## Hughes, Kellner, Sullivan & Alke

**The Firm:** The employment team here devotes a majority of its resources to counseling employers but also litigates claims as necessary. The group acts for many local employers, from small businesses to larger companies in Helena and the surrounding area. Members of the firm are active on the alternative dispute resolution front, both with regard to mediation and arbitration, and labor union work for smaller companies is also covered. Clients particularly value the team's efficiency and responsiveness.

**The Lawyers:** One client remarked that he would give **John Sullivan** "*11 out of ten*" for the level of service he provides, a comment that echoed the effusive praise he garnered from all sides. Sullivan's practice comprises employment as well as professional defense work, and he is involved in counseling, litigation and alternative dispute resolution. He is said to be "*extremely knowledgeable*" and much sought after for the "*depth and diversity of his experience.*" **Amy Christensen**'s practice is equally split between litigation and counseling. Discrimination cases have come to the fore of late and she successfully represented an employee in a matter before the Commission on Political Practices involving allegations of unethical conduct by two leading state employees. Christensen also advised on a case before the Montana Supreme Court involving constitutional issues, which concerned a professor allegedly removed from his department chair as a result of a political speech he gave. She is popular among clients and is described as "*thorough and easy to work with.*"

**Clients/Work Highlights:** Anderson-ZurMuehlen & Co; Carroll College; Mergenthaler Transfer & Storage; Montana Education Association-Montana Federation of Teachers; Montana School Services Foundation; Montana State University; Morrison-Maierle; Shodair Children's Hospital and State of Montana – Risk Management and Tort Defense Division.

## Band 3

### Brown Law Firm PC

**The Firm:** This Montana law firm is well established as one of the state's perennial performers and services clients throughout Montana and the region. Its specialist labor and employment expertise is complemented by niche workers' compensation law know-how.

**The Lawyers:** **Michael Heringer** won praise for being "*an experienced and successful litigator and a very down-to-earth guy: he is a no-nonsense attorney who is practical, straightforward and can get to the root*

of a matter.*" His practice focuses on civil litigation involving employment and workers' compensation issues as well as those pertaining to personal injury and products liability.

**Clients/Work Highlights:** Employee Benefit Management Services; Holland Chemical International; Koch Industries; Montana Silversmiths and United Industries.

### Dorsey & Whitney LLP

See firm details p.1169

**The Firm:** The labor and employment group at this national firm drafts and reviews employment policies and also offers advice on labor law issues, including the interpretation of collective bargaining agreements. In addition, the team can draw on specialist expertise in areas such as employee benefits.

**The Lawyers:** Keith Strong, who is considered one of Montana's leading litigators, has taken over responsibility for the firm's employment work since the departure of John Kutzman. Strong is based in Great Falls but handles matters relating to the whole state.

**Clients/Work Highlights:** The team acts for individuals and local and national businesses in the region.

### Gough, Shanahan, Johnson & Waterman

See firm details p.1235

**The Firm:** Its origins in the natural resources arena go a long way in determining the current clientele of this traditional Montana practice. Its employment group acts on behalf of a variety of clients from mining, timber, oil, gas and utilities industries to hi-tech and public sector employers. With regard to contentious matters, the team primarily litigates wrongful discharge and discrimination cases, but also acts on a variety of other matters concerning wage and hour and safety issues.

**The Lawyers:** The "*faultlessly businesslike*" **Tom Hattersley** sustains a practice that encompasses labor and employment law as well as general litigation. He would be just as likely to handle a workplace tort as a case relating to products liability and insurance coverage. His employment practice spans all aspects of employment law, including wrongful discharge and discrimination claims, wage and hour law and safety compliance. Hattersley recently tried a sex and maternity discrimination case for a communications company and is in the process of taking several wrongful discharge and disability discrimination claims to trial. Often working closely with him is **Teri Walter**, who received numerous

recommendations as an up-and-comer and enters the table accordingly.

**Clients/Work Highlights:** The firm acts for a diverse clientele from a broad range of industry sectors.

### Ugrin, Alexander, Zadick & Higgins, PC

**The Firm:** This emerging Great Falls outfit has developed a wide-ranging general litigation practice. The nine-attorney team acts on a wide range of litigation including employment matters such as wrongful discharge and discrimination cases.

**The Lawyers:** **Gary Zadick** is admired as "*a practical attorney who has a lot of trial experience.*" He acts in cases relating to insurance coverage and personal injury as well as employment law. He is also a well-reputed mediator. Roger Witt is an alternative contact at the firm for employment matters.

**Clients/Work Highlights:** Albertson's; BMC West Poulsens; Herberger's and Smith's Food & Drug Stores.

### Worden Thane PC

**The Firm:** The labor and employment law group at this Missoula-based firm represents both employers and individuals. The caseload features contentious and noncontentious matters relating to wrongful discharge and discrimination as well as labor relations. Members of the firm are regularly involved in negotiations on behalf of management.

**The Lawyers:** **Jeremy Thane** was billed as "*a labor relations guru,*" and he is best known for negotiating collective bargaining agreements on behalf of management. He has appeared before the regional office of the NLRB in Seattle, where he recently represented a cartage company in a dispute between two unions resulting from a takeover attempt and related allegations of unfair labor practice. Further highlights for Thane include obtaining a substantial credit on future insurance premiums as compensation for payments overcharged on insurance plans.

**Clients/Work Highlights:** Bob Ward & Sons; Employers Association of Western Montana; Glendive Medical Center; Missoula Cartage Company and St Patrick Hospital and Health Sciences Center.

### Other Notable Practitioners

Best known as a top-tier litigator with "*a formidable presence in the courtroom,*" **Donald Robinson** of Poore, Roth & Robinson, PC enters the table in recognition of his long-standing presence in the employment field. He is also much in demand where labor relation matters, and union work in particular, are concerned.

# LITIGATION

# GENERAL COMMERCIAL

## Christensen, Moore, Cockrell, Cummings & Axelberg PC

**The Firm:** Above all, this six-attorney firm is said to profit from "*great leadership and an ability to follow through.*" It covers the full spectrum of civil litigation, with an emphasis on complex cases and a recent focus on the defense of class actions. As such, the team currently defends the State of Montana with respect to over 800 asbestos claims arising out of the former mining operations of WR Grace & Company in Libby.

**The Lawyers:** Described both as "*a very impressive individual*" and "*one of the best litigators in the state,*" **Dana Christensen** was showered with praise. He specializes in defending physicians in medical malpractice cases but also handles the defense of class actions and other complex litigation. Interviewees repeatedly highlighted his exceptional courtroom skills, with one stating: "*He has terrific jury appeal and a manner that inspires confidence.*" Christensen is moreover "*exceptionally hard-working, meticulously well prepared, and able to discern and to focus on what is important.*" The "*quietly determined and successful*" **Mikel Moore** covers an array of litigation relating to ski area liability, insurance defense, employment and ERISA disputes. Meanwhile, **Tracy Axelberg** is heavily involved in professional negligence, toxic tort, construction and insurance coverage cases. Mediation is also central to Axelberg's practice and he was described as "*a wonderful mediator with a personality perfectly suited to the role.*"

**Clients/Work Highlights:** AIG; Allstate; CNA Insurance Companies; Ophthalmic Mutual Insurance; Physicians Insurance; State Farm; St. Paul Travelers; The Doctors Company; Unum Life Insurance Company and USAA.

## Garlington, Lohn & Robinson, PLLP

**The Firm:** The first-rate litigators here won considerable praise and are perceived to "*excel when handling complex business litigation.*" About 22 attorneys are more or less intensively involved in disputes, including general litigation, medical malpractice, insurance defense and employment cases. The firm also boasts specialist expertise in areas such as environment and ERISA.

**The Lawyers:** **William Jones** is "*as good as it gets in a courtroom,*" according to sources, and one interviewee stated: "*I don't know anyone who has successfully tried more cases.*" A highly experienced litigator, Jones concentrates mainly on products liability, negligence and insurance bad faith cases. "*The Eminence grise of Montana defense lawyers,*" **Gary Graham** is venerated as "*a straight shooter who combines outstanding ability with scholarship and brings a compelling sense of maturity and perspective to commercial litigation.*" Legal malpractice matters have recently come to the fore in his practice, but Graham acts for a range of clients, from the State of Montana and the state university to pharmaceutical company Amgen. Clients appreciate his easygoing nature and the fact that he "*does not get involved in needless battles.*" **Robert Sheridan** is an experienced attorney "*whose priority is always to get the case resolved.*" He is engaged in a variety of civil litigation relating to railroads, products and other liability, and workers' compensation claims. Mediation accounts for an increasing proportion of Sheridan's time, and interviewees described him as a "*tremendous mediator who is always able to focus on the important issues.*" Managing partner **Lawrence Daly** covers medical malpractice defense, products liability, construction and commercial litigation. He often represents hospitals and medical professionals. Daly is "*a sharp, practical attorney*" who is valued by clients for resolving cases quickly and effectively. **Bradley Luck** is "*a very tenacious, smart and personable guy who gets good results and is good with juries.*" His lengthy experience of defending workers' compensation claims is complemented by a successful track record of defending personal injury and unfair claims practice actions. **Terry MacDonald** received his fair share of commendation for his broad litigation practice, which covers business, toxic tort and personal injury claims.

**Clients/Work Highlights:** Many local businesses as well as national corporations feature in the firm's clientele. Medical and general liability insurers can also be counted as clients.

## Boone, Karlberg PC

**The Firm:** This Missoula-based firm's litigation practice covers most areas of business litigation. About half the firm's attorneys are either entirely or principally devoted to defense litigation, with a particular emphasis on disputes concerning railroads and toxic torts. Clients deem the "*detail-oriented and hard-working*" team to sit comfortably among the upper echelons of Montana's litigation practices.

**The Lawyers:** In accordance with the firm's overall focus in the disputes arena, **Randy Cox** focuses on railroad and toxic tort claims but also covers other complex commercial litigation cases as they arise. Representing the plaintiffs, a fiber optics company, in a multimillion-dollar negligence and breach of contract claim was one recent highlight for Cox, in which he was granted a summary judgment. Among peers he is known to be "*fearless and always willing to take on challenging cases,*" while his thoroughness and excellent communication skills greatly impressed clients. The "*accomplished and highly respected*" **Robert Sullivan** acts on behalf of businesses and individuals in a variety of civil litigation as well as keeping a hand in advising on transactional matters, including those in the banking sector. Products liability cases featured heavily in his workload over the past year. Up-and-coming litigator **Matt Hayhurst** enters the tables this year. He has concentrated on products liability, personal injury and railroad claims of late. This "*hard-working and forceful attorney just doesn't miss anything,*" say clients.

**Clients/Work Highlights:** The client base is statewide, regional and national in scope and includes BNSF Railway; Caterpillar; Farmers Alliance Insurance; First Interstate Bank; Montana Rail Link; Quality Construction; State of Montana and Sterling Savings Bank.

## Crowley, Haughey, Hanson, Toole & Dietrich, PLLP

See firm details p.1234

**The Firm:** As the largest law firm in Montana, this outfit has the bench strength to support a richly varied litigation practice, encompassing almost every kind of litigation and a good number of large and complex cases. Insurance and institution-based litigation is considered one of its key strengths, alongside natural resource sector disputes. Members of the firm recently defended a client in litigation where it was alleged that the houses in Colstrip are splitting in half as a result of water leaking from an artificial cooler lake at a power plant. A dispute concerning an oil pipeline running through North Dakota, Montana and Wyoming further contributed to the workload. Clients particularly value the attorneys' "*depth of understanding and ability to grasp the issues quickly and get it right the first time.*"

**The Lawyers:** Interviewees described **Joe Maynard** as "*Crowley's number one trial lawyer,*" not to mention "*a knowledgeable, rational and trustworthy team player.*" Personal injury is an area in which he holds a particularly strong suit, especially where there is an estate litigation dimension involved. Workers' compensation is another area where he came in for praise from clients and peers alike. Maynard was recently involved in litigation of national significance, that of defending FedEx against the State of Montana. He also acted in reopened litigation concerning the demise of the Montana Power Company, a former Fortune 500 company, and the multimillion-dollar bonuses given to its executives. Peers expect great things of young lawyer **Ian McIntosh**. His practice is largely defense-oriented and focuses mainly on products liability and personal injury matters. However, McIntosh has recently acted for the plaintiff in a number of commercial cases. His recent highlights include obtaining a favorable defense ruling from the Montana Supreme Court in a malicious prosecution case. **Neil Westesen** sustains a practice that centers on construction and Indian law litigation. He often represents professionals such as architects and engineers and recently defended an engineering firm in a suit filed by over 30 homeowners. Westesen also settled a tax dispute between the Fort Peck Indian tribe and the BNSF Railway. Clients value his knowledge of construction law, his manner with clients and the fact that he "*thinks outside the box.*"

**Clients/Work Highlights:** The firm acts for many oil companies and other businesses in Montana, including AIG; Boyne USA Resorts; Chubb Group; Farmers; First Interstate Bank; PPL; Stockman Bank and Zurich.

## Dorsey & Whitney LLP

See firm details p.1169

**The Firm:** This national firm boasts an expansive litigation practice that covers general commercial, securities, insurance, products liability, banking, natural resources and environmental disputes. Its lawyers are also much sought after for their experience of criminal white-collar defense work. While research suggests that the firm's presence in Montana has shrunk, attorneys in Great Falls and Missoula can still rely on nationwide resources for backup and the operation maintains its enviable position in the table.

**The Lawyers:** **Keith Strong** (see p.1232) is said to "*combine brilliant trial skills with the analytical ability required for understanding transactions.*" He is a versatile lawyer who has an eclectic practice that emphasizes complex commercial, natural resources, malpractice, financial institution and white-collar crime litigation. A further subspecialty of his is judicial and lawyer ethics, an area in which he is probably the preeminent lawyer in Montana. "*He is pretty soft-spoken and understated but he wins cases because he knows everything and has a great way of presenting very complicated matters in simple terms,*" remarked one source.

**Clients/Work Highlights:** The firm has a diverse client base and acts for individuals as well as regional and national businesses.

## Brown Law Firm PC

**The Firm:** Deep roots in Billings cultivated over the best part of a century are thought to be what hold this stalwart of Montana's legal scene in good stead. It services clients throughout the state and the surrounding region, covering general civil litigation, insurance coverage, medical malpractice, professional negligence and products liability disputes.

**The Lawyers:** "*Seasoned trial lawyer*" **Guy Rogers** enters the tables this year. According to clients, "*he is very levelheaded and practical and gets excellent results.*" His practice encompasses a variety of general civil litigation, with personal injury defense and insurance coverage cases featuring with particular frequency.

**Clients/Work Highlights:** The firm has a diverse client base that includes a number of insurance companies.

## Browning, Kaleczyc, Berry & Hoven PC

See firm details p.1233

**The Firm:** Clients portray attorneys here as "*diligent, thorough and well attuned to the local business environment in Montana.*" The members of its commercial litigation group are experienced in complex commercial, environmental and general civil litigation. Over the past few years, the firm has raised its game most significantly in the area of business litigation, in terms of both the number and profile of cases where it is engaged. Indeed, litigation now accounts for half of the firm's corporate practice.

**The Lawyers:** Observers note that **Stanley Kaleczyc**, who chairs the firm's commercial group, is involved in almost every large case in Montana. He

came in for praise for his "*great analytical mind,*" and for being "*exceedingly smart and very versatile.*" Insurance and securities disputes supplement his heavy business litigation caseload. Kaleczyc recently represented the Northwestern Corporation in a series of interrelated cases where up to $3.6 billion was at stake. He is also defending Piper Jaffray against allegations of irregularities on the part of a broker, and was hired by Chevron for the purposes of an appeal against a $40 million adverse jury verdict. This "*absolute client magnet*" impresses clients with his "*effectiveness, pragmatism and ability to express himself in a clear and concise way.*"

**Clients/Work Highlights:** Anheuser-Busch; Bearing Point; BNSF Railway; Chevron; Havre Pipeline Company; Montana Hospital Association; Montana Municipal Insurance Authority; Northwestern Corporation; Piper Jaffray and Union Pacific.

## Gough, Shanahan, Johnson & Waterman

See firm details p.1235

**The Firm:** This traditional Helena-based leader has a broad general practice with an emphasis on natural resources. Most of the firm's attorneys are involved in litigation in one way or another, with key strengths lying in the environmental, business, employment and construction arenas.

**The Lawyers:** **Ronald Waterman** was summed up during research as "*a bright, thoughtful and analytical practitioner whose strength lies in his ability to deal with complex litigation.*" A proportion of employment matters round out his business litigation practice.

**Clients/Work Highlights:** The firm represents a wide variety of clients ranging from individuals to corporations.

## Poore, Roth & Robinson, P.C.

**The Firm:** Litigation has long been the core practice area for this small firm. Contract, construction, products liability and other commercial disputes all feature in the workload. The team also undertakes a substantial amount of employment and healthcare law cases and defends healthcare providers in medical liability cases.

**The Lawyers:** **Donald Robinson** is admired for having "*always been on the frontline of plaintiff and defense work in Montana*" and is described as a "*gentleman with the determination of a bulldog.*" He is currently involved in a matter before the Montana Supreme Court that may determine whether a provision in the Montana constitution concerning the right to a clean environment is self-executing. Over the past year, Robinson also represented plaintiffs in a securities case against a broker and defended several employment cases. Interviewees branded **Thomas Welsch** a "*really great lawyer.*" He focuses on personal injury and commercial litigation, and successfully defended a landowner in a jury trial pertaining to a prescriptive easement. Further highlights for Welsch include a successful appearance in a sex discrimination claim before the Montana Human Rights Commission. He also handles insurance disputes and medical malpractice cases.

Clients/Work Highlights: Allstate; Continental Western Insurance; Discover Bank; Montana Municipal Insurance Authority and The Doctors Company.

## Ugrin, Alexander, Zadick & Higgins, PC

The Firm: This ten-attorney firm in Great Falls has "excellent lawyers" and offers expertise in general commercial litigation, medical malpractice and other professional liability defense, as well as disputes over insurance coverage and insurance bad faith. Products liability, personal injury, employment and healthcare litigation round out the caseload.

The Lawyers: "Skilled appellate lawyer and superb mediator" Neil Ugrin focuses on negligence, medical malpractice and personal injury law. "He is respected by the defense and plaintiff Bar alike and has a good sense of cases because of his immense experience," say sources.

Clients/Work Highlights: Brunswick; Chrysler; City of Great Falls and Mountainview Medical Center.

## Holland & Hart LLP

See firm details p.369

The Firm: With over 100 litigators throughout the Rocky Mountain region, this firm has successfully made litigation a core practice area. The Billings office specializes in general commercial, bankruptcy, environmental and natural resources litigation. Another feature of the firm's operation is its separate alternative dispute resolution practice.

The Lawyers: Charles Hingle is involved first and foremost in bankruptcy but also has extensive experience of commercial litigation.

Clients/Work Highlights: The team represents a wide variety of clients from individuals to companies, and from emerging businesses to large public corporations.

## Hughes, Kellner, Sullivan & Alke

The Firm: This eight-attorney general litigation practice is based in Helena. The team sustains a healthy caseload centering on business, personal injury, insurance defense, public utility and employment litigation.

The Lawyers: The "well-respected" Stuart Kellner now specializes exclusively in mediation.

Clients/Work Highlights: Chubb Group; Dick Anderson Construction; Montana Children's Home and Hospital; Montana Department of Commerce and Qwest.

## Edwards Frickle Anner-Hughes & Cook

The Firm: This "tremendous" Billings-based practice is heavily involved in general plaintiff work, especially with regard to environmental matters. The five-attorney team handles a large variety of litigation matters including toxic torts, products liability, professional negligence and insurance bad faith. It is, therefore, often up against major insurance and other national corporations, against which the firm is renowned for having significant success.

The Lawyers: Clifford Edwards is "probably one of the best trial attorneys in the state," and peers respect him as a formidable opponent: "He fights like a bulldog for his clients." His wide-ranging plaintiff litigation practice includes matters such as large-scale pollution cleanups, insurance bad faith, personal injury, wrongful death, products liability and railroad accident and injury claims. The "capable" Roberta Anner-Hughes sustains her market profile.

Clients/Work Highlights: The firm specializes in representing plaintiffs against corporate defendants.

## Goetz, Gallik & Baldwin, PC

The Firm: This "tremendous plaintiff firm" offers a small team that is said to benefit from strong leadership backed up by an "equally bright team." Its varied practice includes business, construction, real estate, professional malpractice and other civil and criminal litigation.

The Lawyers: Observers identify James Goetz as "the best appellate lawyer in the state." He is an "all-around superb trial lawyer" whose eclectic practice involves him acting for both plaintiff and defense. In addition to commercial, environmental and plaintiff personal injury disputes, he also handles constitutional and criminal litigation. "His scholarly approach, brilliant mind and eloquence" combine to make Goetz a top-class practitioner.

Clients/Work Highlights: Blue Cross and Blue Shield of Montana; Confederated Salish and Kootenai Tribes; Edwards Jet Center and Flathead Reservation.

## Hoyt & Blewett

The Firm: This five-attorney Great Falls plaintiff firm specializes in personal injury cases, particularly those involving railroads and railroad companies. However, the group also takes on various other engagements including insurance coverage, products liability and professional malpractice disputes, in which it represents clients throughout Montana and the Northwest.

The Lawyers: Billed as a "wonderful lawyer who is very competitive by nature," Alexander Blewett is

deemed "a formidable opponent who works cases up beautifully." He combines acuity with good judgment and is "both aggressive and effective in equal measure." In addition to railroad law, Blewett covers personal injury, products liability, medical malpractice, environmental and toxic tort disputes.

Clients/Work Highlights: The team assists a wide variety of plaintiffs in cases against companies as well as other individuals.

## Lewis & Slovak PC

The Firm: Market observers agree that this four-attorney plaintiff firm "does a tremendous amount of work and does it well." The workload has been punctuated by recent successes in environmental litigation, and the firm also offers expertise in insurance, general commercial and railroad litigation. Peers admit to its lawyers being "tough fighters, and once up against them, you can expect to be in for a long haul."

The Lawyers: Tom Lewis is perceived to have done much to shape the firm's practice and enjoys a reputation as "an extremely bright, well-seasoned and hard-working lawyer who has a strong loyalty to his clients." Over the past year, Lewis was primarily involved in the appeals of Sunburst School District No. 2 v Texaco, a $40 million groundwater contamination case. Elsewhere, he appeared in Jeremy Parsons v City of Great Falls, an unreported personal injury case concerning a catastrophic head injury. Peers consider him "a worthy opponent and formidable as hell," with one defense attorney stating: "Of all the plaintiff lawyers in the state, he is the one I fear the most."

Clients/Work Highlights: The team acts for a variety of clients but always on the plaintiff side.

## Other Notable Practitioners

Ward Taleff of Alexander, Baucus, Taleff & Paul PC in Great Falls is a highly respected litigator who tries many cases and acts on behalf of both plaintiffs and defendants. Barry O'Connell of Moore, O'Connell & Refling PC won praise for his "pragmatic and efficient approach." The defense of Section 1983 claims constitutes a major part of his practice, but he also handles other cases on the defense side as well as a limited amount of plaintiff work. Clients value Robert Pfennigs of Jardine, Stephenson, Blewett and Weaver, PC for his "calm nature, thoroughness and ability to guide them." His practice focuses on personal injury, medical malpractice and insurance defense as well as employment and real estate litigation. His recent highlights include successfully defending a district court judgment in the Montana Supreme Court.

# NATURAL RESOURCES & ENVIRONMENT

## Band 1

### Browning, Kaleczyc, Berry & Hoven PC

See firm details p.1233

**The Firm:** One client summed up this operation as consisting of *"top-level professionals who adhere to the highest standards of legal and personal ethics, and provide a sterling service founded on solid teamwork."* The five core members of the environmental and natural resource groups cover environmental law issues such as air quality and Superfund sites, and can call upon the support of the firm's litigators as required. The firm is also actively involved in litigation concerning the interpretation of the clean environment provision in the Montana constitution, the outcome of which is expected to have far-reaching consequences. An active lobbying practice further contributes to the firm's profile.

**The Lawyers:** **Leo Berry** is *"politically very well connected, client-oriented and savvy."* He focuses on administrative law and Superfund cleanups. As such he has represented businesses faced with cleaning up sites such as the Silver Bow Creek/Butte Area Superfund site, the Livingston Superfund site and the Kalispell Pole & Timber site. His active lobbying practice won Berry further praise from clients and peers alike. Commentators describe him as *"a forward-thinking strategist who has the ability to predict the outcome of situations with incredible accuracy."* **Steven Wade** *"is extremely capable, thoroughly professional and well versed in the law and politics of Montana."* He has a broad-based practice and acts on all matters environmental, from air and water qual-

ity issues to Superfund cases. He recently settled a dispute on behalf of Rocky Mountain Power, which involved objections raised by the state and an environmental group relating to a coal-powered electrical unit. He also assisted Bull Mountain Energy with procuring an air quality permit for a coal-fired power plant in Montana. Interviewees say of Wade: *"He always delivers no matter how busy he is and makes you feel as if you are the only client he has."*
**Clients/Work Highlights:** Anheuser-Busch; BNSF Railway; Bull Mountain Energy; Centennial Energy; Columbia Falls Aluminum; ConocoPhillips; Great Northern Power Development; Havre Pipeline; International Paper; Logo Signs of America; North-Western Corporation; Pacific Steel & Recycling; SAFECO and Union Pacific.

### Christensen, Moore, Cockrell, Cummings & Axelberg PC

**The Firm:** This Kalispell-based, five-partner firm concentrates on natural resources and environmental as well as general commercial and real estate law. Litigation is considered its foremost strength, though members of the firm are also active on the regulatory front. Clients hail from throughout Montana and the Rocky Mountain region.

**The Lawyers:** **Dale Cockrell**'s wide-ranging practice encompasses environmental and natural resource matters as well as toxic torts and insurance defense law. A *"forceful litigator,"* he defended the State of Montana in approximately 800 asbestos claims that arose out of the mining operations of WR Grace & Co in Libby. Interviewees commented: *"He is one of the hardest-working lawyers I have ever known and excellent at representing his clients."*
**Clients/Work Highlights:** The firm acts for a wide variety of clients including Homestake Mining and Noranda Minerals.

### Crowley, Haughey, Hanson, Toole & Dietrich, PLLP

See firm details p.1234
**The Firm:** The firm handles all aspects of natural resources, from transactional to contentious matters. An upturn in Montana's natural resources sector during the past year has meant continued growth for the team. Its attorneys deal with examination of title issues and natural resource deposits on Indian and federal land. They provide a comprehensive service to oil, gas and mining clients, with a particular emphasis on exploration, development, acquisitions and divestitures. Clients commend the team on its promptness and efficiency: *"Working with Crowley Haughey is quite different to working with a large New York firm in that it cuts out all the superfluous things and gets right to the heart of a matter."*
**The Lawyers:** **Steven Ruffatto** specializes in real estate law with an emphasis on oil, gas and mining sectors. There is often an environmental bent to his caseload and he recently advised on the development of the Bakken oil play. Further examples of typical work for Ruffatto include representing a mining

company in western Montana in transactional matters. He is *"practical, efficient and always ascertains what the client wants to achieve,"* commented one client. **John Lee** is *"technically outstanding,"* particularly where oil and gas matters are concerned. An active regulatory practice sees him represent clients before conservation boards and other regulatory agencies. Title examinations of federal and Indian lands further contribute to his workload. He was recently involved in the development of the Bakken Formation in North Dakota. Clients appreciate that he *"pays attention, listens and makes what we need to happen actually happen."*
**Clients/Work Highlights:** CONSOL Energy; Falconbridge; Headington Oil; Nexen and Lyco Energy.

### Doney, Crowley, Bloomquist, Payne & Uda, P.C.

**The Firm:** Niche water law expertise helps to define the natural resources and environmental practice here. The team is also involved in energy, real estate and litigation matters, while government relations and administrative law support is available as required. The firm is based in Helena but has an additional branch in Dillon to serve the southern part of the state.

**The Lawyers:** Interviewees rate **Frank Crowley** as *"an excellent lawyer."* He gained extensive experience in environmental law as chief legal counsel for the Montana Department of Health and Environmental Sciences. He now concentrates on environmental as well as real estate matters, whether noncontentious or contentious. Administrative and legislative issues also enter into his practice.
**Clients/Work Highlights:** Clients range from ranchers to governmental agencies and from statewide business associations to international corporations.

### Garlington, Lohn & Robinson, PLLP

**The Firm:** Its steadfast presence in Montana and correspondingly solid client base, which includes large national corporations and insurance companies, keep the firm's three-attorney environmental group extremely busy. It is particularly well regarded for its expertise in water rights and regulated utilities.
**The Lawyers:** Interviewees describe **Stephen Brown** as a *"bright, knowledgeable guy and a quality individual."* His practice centers on environmental and natural resources as well as land use law. He is highly regarded by peers, particularly for his niche expertise in water. He acts for industrial corporations as well as state and local government.
**Clients/Work Highlights:** Avista; Bitterroot Resort; Louisiana-Pacific; Mountain Water; Roseburg Forest Products; Spanish Peaks Resort; the State of Montana; The Sterling Group and the Yellowstone Mountain Club.

## Gough, Shanahan, Johnson & Waterman

See firm details p.1235

**The Firm:** The practice area is perceived as this local firm's strong suit and it is renowned for housing "*some outstanding lawyers*" who are "*well connected in Montana and familiar with the state's courts.*" The seven-attorney natural resource team primarily acts for industry clients as well as electricity producers, and covers regulatory, transactional and contentious fronts. Support in areas such as employment is also on hand as necessary. A government relations group offers advice on political and public relations aspects of developments.

**The Lawyers: Alan Joscelyn** has principally made his name in the mining sector, and he offers great depth of experience in mine permitting and closures. Assisting mining companies with domestic and international operations and associated areas such as property rights and water quality issues accounts for the majority of his practice. He has provided ongoing advice on long-running litigation brought by Seven-Up Pete, a mining venture, against the State of Montana, which relates to a dispute over a large gold deposit. Clients value greatly "*his well-researched and thoughtful work and the diversity of his expertise.*" Federal environmental law specialist **Jon Metropoulos** received his fair share of praise, particularly for his work in the coal sector. He has carried out extensive analysis relating to the proposed development of coal bed methane in eastern Montana. Extensive work on Indian water rights has further contributed to his workload. He is also a member of the firm's government relations group.

**Clients/Work Highlights:** The firm acts for the likes of Fidelity Exploration & Production and MDU Resources Group.

## Holland & Hart LLP

See firm details p.369

**The Firm:** A team of five in Billings assists energy companies with various issues including environmental, energy and contract matters. The team can rely on the backup of the firm's litigators in Billings as well as over 70 natural resource and environment attorneys in its other Rocky Mountain offices. The firm's clients are based throughout the Rocky Mountain states, and they value the outfit for "*being able to pool experience and resources from various offices according to the case in hand.*"

**The Lawyers: Don Quander** (see p.1232) concentrates on utility regulatory matters, and especially air quality permitting for power plants. He also works on power generation projects for various clients, including the finance aspects, and is just as well equipped to handle a coal-based project as a wind farm development. Legislative and lobbying activities further contribute to his practice, as a result of which he is "*on top of all the regulations and the politics associated with the field.*" Interviewees described him as "*a very intelligent, forthcoming person who communicates well and treats every party with due respect.*" **Stephen Foster** (see p.1231) is a deeply experienced environmental and commercial litigator who covers toxic torts, products liability and legal malpractice defense cases. Superfund, natural resource damages and cost recovery cases are central to his practice. He was the lead defense counsel in two major federal court cases involving the largest Superfund sites in the USA. Interviewees portray him as "*bright, hard-working, articulate and unfailingly polite,*" and credit him with "*a very good analytical mind.*"

**Clients/Work Highlights:** The firm acts for many of the top-tier regional and national natural resource companies in Montana, including largest oil producer Encore Acquisition, the four large refineries, the largest wood company, the two largest cement refineries and the largest hi-tech manufacturer in the state.

### Other Notable Practitioners

**John Walker Ross** is of counsel at Brown Law Firm PC. He often acts in arbitrations and mediations and is "*very enjoyable to work with.*" His practice encompasses natural resources and environment as well as employment law. Observers count **John Alke** of Hughes, Kellner, Sullivan & Alke as "*one of the state's leading utilities and energy lawyers.*" He has specialized administrative law expertise and is experienced in representing clients involved in litigation. Clients rate him as "*just a superb regulatory lawyer because he understands the energy business and Public Services Commission and can therefore achieve excellent results.*"

# REAL ESTATE

| Real Estate | |
|---|---|
| **Leading Firms** | |
| 1 | BOONE, KARLBERG PC *Missoula* |
| | CROWLEY, HAUGHEY, HANSON, TOOLE *Billings* |
| | GARLINGTON, LOHN & ROBINSON *Missoula* |
| 2 | CHRISTENSEN, MOORE, COCKRELL *Kalispell* |
| | MOULTON, BELLINGHAM, LONGO *Billings* |
| 3 | HEARD & HOWARD *Columbus* |
| | MOORE, O'CONNELL & REFLING PC *Bozeman* |
| | SULLIVAN, TABARACCI AND RHOADES *Missoula* |
| | WORDEN THANE PC *Missoula* |

| Leading Individuals | |
|---|---|
| 1 | CUMMINGS Stephen *Christensen, Moore, Cockrell* |
| | DOCKERY Michael *Crowley, Haughey, Hanson* |
| | KNIGHT Robert *Robert M Knight* |
| | WAGNER William *Garlington, Lohn & Robinson* |
| 2 | BOONE Thomas *Boone, Karlberg PC* |
| | HEARD Richard *Heard & Howard* |
| | JONES John *Moulton, Bellingham, Longo* |
| | KARELL Allan *Crowley, Haughey, Hanson* |
| | MCELYEA Russell *Moore, O'Connell* |
| | STENSLAND Dean *Boone, Karlberg PC* |
| | SULLIVAN Zane *Sullivan, Tabaracci and Rhoades* |

## Band 1

### Boone, Karlberg PC

**The Firm:** This firm sustains its position at the forefront of the real estate and construction markets in Montana. Ranch and residential real estate transactions contribute significantly to the workload of its five-attorney team, which also represents banks in commercial and private lending.

**The Lawyers:** As a result of the current strength in the real estate market, the "*smart and straightforward*" **Tom Boone** has concentrated more and more on real estate transactions, which included significant ranch sales over the past year. Clients value **Dean Stensland** as a "*thorough, smart and approachable practitioner with a lot of common sense and experience.*" His practice encompasses real estate matters as well as construction law and business acquisitions. Stensland recently represented the owners of a 10,000-acre ranch in litigation to obtain a historic easement in order to regain access to their ranch. A further highlight for him was acting for banks that had to take over a development from bankrupt contractors in order to recover their loans.

**Clients/Work Highlights:** Farmers Alliance Insurance; First Interstate Bank; Montana Municipal Insurance Authority; Montana Rail Link and Sterling Savings Bank.

### Crowley, Haughey, Hanson, Toole & Dietrich, PLLP

See firm details p.1234

**The Firm:** Clients value this firm as "*a one-stop shop with departments to cover everything we may need,*" and praise its "*accommodating and expeditious lawyers.*" It boasts a broad depth of experience in all types of real estate matters and can deal with larger, more complex transactions on a regular basis. The team is involved in everything from leasing office buildings to selling agricultural and commercial property. Advising out-of-state clients on buying farms in Montana is considered one of the firm's distinctive strengths.

**The Lawyers: Michael Dockery** was described as "*just a real book of knowledge, he gets to the point quickly and is able to formulate legal documents without unnecessary fanfare.*" His practice spans the gamut of real estate work and includes commercial leasing transactions, the sale and purchase of commercial property, zoning and planning issues, and land use matters. Title insurance work is another of Dockery's specialties, where he has represented several underwriters in related claims. He recently assisted First Interstate Bank with a $10.2 million revenue bond transaction, and represented the banks in a $3.5 million purchase of revenue bonds from a senior housing assistance living project. **Allan Karell**'s practice is largely lending-based and he often appears as local counsel in multistate lending transactions. Representing MetLife in agricultural real estate lending work and advising other clients on significant ranch acquisitions and sales have defined his recent workload. Karell is held in high regard among clients, one of whom gushed: "*He has never done anything that wasn't perfect!*"

Clients/Work Highlights: Big Sky EDA; Chicago Title Insurance; Fidelity National Title Insurance; First American; First Interstate Bank; MetLife and Streeter Brothers Mortgage.

## Garlington, Lohn & Robinson, PLLP

The Firm: This Missoula firm of "*strong lawyers*" has secured a significant presence in the region. It often acts for local businesses but also services major national corporations in purchases, sales and development, land use and zoning issues. The firm's environmental and tax lawyers can be relied upon for support as necessary.

The Lawyers: The "*tremendously talented and knowledgeable*" **William Wagner** retains his position as one of the state's top real estate lawyers with regard to both transactional and contentious matters. Disputes have increasingly become the focus of his practice and Wagner is said to have "*an excellent approach to mediations and other forms of dispute resolution.*"

Clients/Work Highlights: Alternative Service Concepts; Canyon Resources; Maloney Properties and Mountain Water Company.

## Band 2

### Christensen, Moore, Cockrell, Cummings & Axelberg PC

The Firm: Clients throughout Montana and the Rocky Mountain region regularly call upon this Kalispell-based firm for assistance with real estate issues. The six-attorney team provides a range of legal services that cover corporate commercial and litigation matters as well as real estate. Its niche environmental and natural resources expertise often dovetails nicely with its real estate work.

The Lawyers: **Stephen Cummings** enjoys an "*outstanding reputation*" and maintains a diverse practice. Besides advising clients on all manner of real estate law issues, he is experienced in general corporate commercial matters as well as estate planning and probate.

Clients/Work Highlights: AIG; ITT Hartford; The Doctors Company and USAA Insurance.

## Moulton, Bellingham, Longo & Mather, PC

The Firm: This traditional Montana law firm services clients throughout Montana and northern Wyoming, ranging from entrepreneurs to large corporations. The real estate team acts on both small and large-scale transactions relating to condominiums and subdivisions and has tax law experts on hand to advise as required, whether on local, state or federal tax issues.

The Lawyers: Interviewees described **John Jones** as "*a pragmatic lawyer with whom it is easy to put deals together.*" Real estate features heavily in his broad practice, which also covers estate planning and healthcare law as well as business sales and acquisitions. He also offers specialized tax advice.

Clients/Work Highlights: St. Vincent Healthcare, Video Library and West Park Hospital.

## Band 3

### Heard & Howard

The Firm: Real estate is a key practice area for this small Columbus-based practice and its team acts on a variety of transactions and litigation. The firm sustains its position in the table.

The Lawyers: According to commentators **Richard Heard** "*is a wise practitioner with a lot of experience in real estate matters.*" His practice is mainly focused on the transactional side of real estate, with a particular emphasis on the agricultural sector.

Clients/Work Highlights: The firm acts for a variety of clients from Montana and beyond.

### Moore, O'Connell & Refling PC

The Firm: This seven-attorney firm in Bozeman is known for its involvement in real estate development, particularly where large ranches and ski resorts are concerned. Supporting expertise in finance, environment and litigation enables the group to offer clients a comprehensive service.

The Lawyers: Interviewees admire **Russell McElyea** for his "*depth of experience and knowledge.*" His practice is correspondingly broad. Expertise relating to areas such as land use and real estate finance is complemented by his specialized knowledge of conservation easements.

Clients/Work Highlights: The firm can count the likes of Moonlight Basin Ranch and Scottsdale Insurance as clients.

## Sullivan, Tabaracci and Rhoades PC

The Firm: The "*highly competitive*" real estate team here acts on residential as well as commercial transactions and represents clients in negotiations, purchase and sales, leases and easements. Litigation and banking and finance issues are also covered, as are professional liability matters relating to the real estate sector.

The Lawyers: **Zane Sullivan** is a senior member of the firm and an acknowledged leader in the field. He covers the waterfront with regard to real estate and often represents realtors' associations.

Clients/Work Highlights: B&G Log Homes; Charter Construction; Circle H Ranch; Missoula County Association of Realtors; Sage Development and Wesmont Builders-Developers.

## Worden Thane PC

The Firm: A three-pronged approach to real estate means clients can rely on the firm for backup in related tax and contentious issues as well as straight real estate matters. The real estate practice covers residential, commercial and agricultural property transactions and has attracted a varied clientele, including individuals, public and private institutions, insurance companies, hospitals and financial institutions. The firm is a member of Meritas, a worldwide network of independent law firms, and therefore has access to contacts and resources in every US state and many foreign countries.

The Lawyers: Peter Dayton largely concentrates on real estate, while Martin King handles real estate litigation.

Clients/Work Highlights: First American; First National Bank of Montana; Missoula County Public Schools and WGM Group.

## Other Notable Practitioners

Peers acknowledge that sole practitioner **Robert Knight** is a lawyer whose "*depth of experience and knowledge are pretty hard to match in Montana.*" He focuses on large ranch, recreational and commercial property transactions. Last year, Knight represented the buyer in a significant transaction involving the acquisition by stock sale of an industry complex owned by Advanced Silicone Materials.

# Leaders in Montana

**ALKE, John**
Hughes, Kellner, Sullivan & Alke, Helena
406 442 3690
*Recommended in Natural Resources*

**ANNER-HUGHES, Roberta**
Edwards Frickle Anner-Hughes & Cook,
Billings 406 256 8155
*Recommended in Litigation*

**AXELBERG, Tracy**
Christensen, Moore, Cockrell, Cummings
& Axelberg PC, Kalispell 406 751 6000
*Recommended in Litigation*

**BENDER, Jeanne Matthews**
Holland & Hart LLP, Billings
406 252 2166
jbender@hollandhart.com
*Recommended in Employment*
**Practice Areas:** Partner practicing in
commercial and natural resources litigation, and employment counseling and litigation. Has represented commercial and
non-profit entities in a variety of claims
including breach of contract, wrongful
discharge, discrimination, wage and hour
claims and labor issues. Regularly makes
presentations on sexual harassment,
wrongful discharge, discrimination, fair
labor standards and related topics.
**Prof. Memberships:** Member of the
American Bar Association Foundation;
Montana Bar Association; American Bar
Association; ABA Sections on Litigation
and Labor and Employment Law and
Torts and Insurance Law; and the Montana Defense Trial Lawyers Association.
Appointments: past President, Montana
Association of Female Executives.
**Career:** Admitted to the Montana (1985)
and Colorado (1988) Bars, the United
States District Court and the Ninth Cir-
cuit Court of Appeals.
**Publications:** Editor, Montana Employ-
ment Law Letter, published monthly by
M Lee Smith Publishers and Printers
(Nashville). 50-State Survey: Employment Libel and Privacy Law, Montana
chapter, Libel Defense Resource Center,
2004. Included in leading American publication's list of top employment lawyers,
2006.
**Personal:** Received a JD (1985) and a BA
(1965) from the University of Montana.

**BERRY, Leo**
Browning, Kaleczyc, Berry & Hoven PC,
Helena 406 443 6820
*Recommended in Natural Resources*

**BLEWETT, Alexander**
Hoyt & Blewett, Great Falls
406 761 1960
*Recommended in Litigation*

**BOONE, Thomas**
Boone, Karlberg PC, Missoula
406 543 6646
*Recommended in Corporate/M&A,
Real Estate*

**BROWN, Stephen Ross**
Garlington, Lohn & Robinson, PLLP,
Missoula 406 523 2500
*Recommended in Natural Resources*

**CHISHOLM, David**
Christian, Samson, Jones & Chisholm, PLLC,
Missoula 406 721 7772
*Recommended in Corporate/M&A*

**CHRISTENSEN, Amy**
Hughes, Kellner, Sullivan & Alke, Helena
406 442 3690
*Recommended in Employment*

**CHRISTENSEN, Dana**
Christensen, Moore, Cockrell, Cummings
& Axelberg PC, Kalispell
406 751 6000
*Recommended in Litigation*

**CHUMRAU, Gary**
Garlington, Lohn & Robinson, PLLP,
Missoula 406 523 2500
*Recommended in Corporate/M&A*

**COCKRELL, Dale**
Christensen, Moore, Cockrell, Cummings
& Axelberg PC, Kalispell 406 751 6000
*Recommended in Natural Resources*

**COX, Randy**
Boone, Karlberg PC, Missoula
406 543 6646
*Recommended in Litigation*

**CROWLEY, Frank**
Doney, Crowley, Bloomquist, Payne &
Uda, P.C., Helena 406 443 2211
*Recommended in Natural Resources*

**CUMMINGS, Stephen**
Christensen, Moore, Cockrell, Cummings & Axelberg PC, Kalispell
406 751 6000
*Recommended in Real Estate*

**DALY, Lawrence**
Garlington, Lohn & Robinson, PLLP,
Missoula 406 523 2500
*Recommended in Litigation*

**DOCKERY, Michael**
Crowley, Haughey, Hanson, Toole & Dietrich,
PLLP, Billings 406 252 3441
*Recommended in Real Estate*

**EDWARDS, A Clifford**
Edwards Frickle Anner-Hughes & Cook,
Billings 406 256 8155
*Recommended in Litigation*

**ELLINGSON, Mae Nan**
Dorsey & Whitney LLP, Missoula
406 329 5565
ellingson.mae.nan@dorsey.com
*Recommended in Corporate/M&A*

**Practice Areas:** Practices in the area of
tax-exempt finance, acts as bond counsel
to the state, its various agencies and
instrumentalities, local governments and
other political subdivisions, acts as
underwriter's counsel on transactions
and frequently drafts legislation relating
to government finance and other matters
pertaining to state and local government.
**Prof. Memberships:** National Association of Bond Lawyers.
**Personal:** University of Montana School
of Law (JD, 1972); University of Montana
(BA, 1972).

**FETSCHER, Candace**
Garlington, Lohn & Robinson, PLLP,
Missoula 406 523 2500
*Recommended in Employment*

**FOSTER, Stephen H**
Holland & Hart LLP, Billings
406 252 2166
sfoster@hollandhart.com
*Recommended in Natural Resources*
**Practice Areas:** Mr Foster has experience
in environmental and commercial litigation in state and federal courts (jury and
non-jury), and has contested matters
before administrative agencies. His current
practice is heavily focused on CERCLA
natural resource damage and cost-recovery cases. His recent practice has also
included toxic tort, products liability, and
legal malpractice defense. He was lead
defense counsel in US v ARCO and State
of Montana v ARCO, two major federal
court cases involving the largest superfund
sites in the United States.
**Prof. Memberships:** Member of the
American Bar Association, Sections on
Litigation and Natural Resources; State
Bar of Montana; Yellowstone County Bar
Association; American College of Trial
Lawyers; Montana Supreme Court Commission on Rules of Evidence; and the
American Board of Trial Advocates.
**Career:** Prior to joining Holland & Hart,
Mr Foster served as senior counsel for
Atlantic Richfield Company, and as a law
clerk to the Honorable James R Brown-
ing, US Court of Appeals for the Ninth
Circuit.
**Personal:** Received a JD with honors
from the University of Montana (1963),
and a BS from Montana State University
(1960).

**FRANCE, Lucy**
Garlington, Lohn & Robinson, PLLP,
Missoula 406 523 2500
*Recommended in Employment*

**GOETZ, James**
Goetz, Gallik & Baldwin, PC, Bozeman
406 587 0618
*Recommended in Litigation*

**GRAHAM, Gary**
Garlington, Lohn & Robinson, PLLP,
Missoula 406 523 2500
*Recommended in Litigation*

**HATTERSLEY III, Thomas**
Gough, Shanahan, Johnson & Waterman,
Helena 406 442 8560
*Recommended in Employment*

**HAYHURST, Matthew**
Boone, Karlberg PC, Missoula
406 543 6646
*Recommended in Litigation*

**HEARD, Richard**
Heard & Howard, Columbus
406 322 4429
*Recommended in Real Estate*

**HERINGER, Michael**
Brown Law Firm PC, Billings
406 248 2611
*Recommended in Employment*

**HINGLE, Charles**
Holland & Hart LLP, Billings
406 252 2166
chingle@hollandhart.com
*Recommended in Corporate/M&A*
**Practice Areas:** A Partner whose practice focuses on business bankruptcy and
creditors' rights, but with extensive experience in banking and real estate transactions and commercial litigation. He has
been certified as a business bankruptcy
specialist by the American Board of Certification since 1993.
**Prof. Memberships:** Member of the
Louisiana State Bar Association; Montana
State Bar Association; Wyoming State Bar
Association; American Bankruptcy Institute; and the Roster of Neutrals, American Arbitration Association.
**Career:** Admitted to the Louisiana
(1976), Montana (1980), and Wyoming
(1996) State Bars.
**Personal:** Received a JD from Louisiana
State University (1976) and a BA from
Tulane University (1972).

**JONES, John**
Moulton, Bellingham, Longo & Mather,
PC, Billings 406 248 7731
*Recommended in Real Estate*

**JONES, William Evan**
Garlington, Lohn & Robinson, PLLP,
Missoula 406 523 2500
*Recommended in Litigation*

**JOSCELYN, Alan**
Gough, Shanahan, Johnson &
Waterman, Helena 406 442 8560
*Recommended in Natural Resources*

**KALECZYC, Stanley**
Browning, Kaleczyc, Berry & Hoven PC,
Helena 406 443 6820
*Recommended in Litigation*

**KARELL, Allan**
Crowley, Haughey, Hanson, Toole & Dietrich,
PLLP, Billings 406 252 3441
*Recommended in Real Estate*

**KELLNER, Stuart**
Hughes, Kellner, Sullivan & Alke, Helena
406 442 3690
*Recommended in Litigation*

**KNIGHT, Robert**
Robert M. Knight, Missoula
406 721 5440
*Recommended in Real Estate*

**LAMDIN, William**
Crowley, Haughey, Hanson, Toole & Dietrich,
PLLP, Billings 406 252 3441
*Recommended in Corporate/M&A*

**LEE, John**
Crowley, Haughey, Hanson, Toole & Dietrich,
PLLP, Billings 406 252 3441
*Recommended in Natural Resources*

**LEHMAN, Steven**
Crowley, Haughey, Hanson, Toole & Dietrich,
PLLP, Billings 406 252 3441
*Recommended in Employment*

**LENNON, Maureen**
Garlington, Lohn & Robinson, PLLP,
Missoula 406 523 2500
*Recommended in Employment*

**LEWIS, Tom**
Lewis & Slovak PC, Great Falls
406 761 5595
*Recommended in Litigation*

**LUCK, Bradley**
Garlington, Lohn & Robinson, PLLP,
Missoula 406 523 2500
*Recommended in Litigation*

**MACDONALD, Terry**
Garlington, Lohn & Robinson, PLLP,
Missoula 406 523 2500
*Recommended in Litigation*

**MANNING, John**
Dorsey & Whitney LLP, Great Falls
406 727 3632
manning.jack@dorsey.com
*Recommended in Corporate/M&A*
**Practice Areas:** Corporate and securities transactional matters, including venture capital financing, private and public
securities offerings, mergers and acquisitions, SEC regulatory matters and general
corporate advice. Advises financial institutions on lending and loan workout
matters and has experience in public
finance, project finance, cooperative law,
limited partnership and limited liability
company financings, and Indian law.
**Personal:** Stanford Law School, JD, 1975,
note editor, Stanford Law Review, 1973-
75. Dartmouth College, AB, 1972, cum
laude.

**MAYNARD, Joe**
Crowley, Haughey, Hanson, Toole & Dietrich,
PLLP, Billings 406 252 3441
*Recommended in Litigation*

**MCELYEA, Russell**
Moore, O'Connell & Refling PC, Bozeman
406 587 5511
*Recommended in Real Estate*

**MCINTOSH, Ian**
Crowley, Haughey, Hanson, Toole & Dietrich,
PLLP, Bozeman 406 556 1430
*Recommended in Litigation*

**METROPOULOS, Jon**
Gough, Shanahan, Johnson & Waterman,
Helena 406 442 8560
*Recommended in Natural Resources*

**MOORE, Mikel**
Christensen, Moore, Cockrell, Cummings
& Axelberg PC, Kalispell 406 751 6000
*Recommended in Litigation*

**O'CONNELL, Barry**
Moore, O'Connell & Refling PC, Bozeman
406 587 5511
*Recommended in Litigation*

**PETERSEN, Larry**
Holland & Hart LLP, Billings
406 252 2166
lpetersen@hollandhart.com
*Recommended in Corporate/M&A*
**Practice Areas:** Mr Petersen's practice
focuses on tax, estate planning, real estate,
natural resources, mergers and acquisitions. He has extensive experience with
probates; formation of LLC's, partnerships and corporations; coal leasing,
acquisitions, and entity formations; purchase and sale of oil and gas and entity
formation; and healthcare.
**Prof. Memberships:** American Bar
Association, Montana Bar Association,
Yellowstone County Bar Association,
ACTEC.
**Career:** Admitted to Montana Bar
(1967).
**Personal:** Received a JD from University
of Montana (1967), a BS in Economics
from the Wharton School at the University of Pennsylvania (1964), and an LLM
from New York University (Taxation,
1970).

**PFENNIGS, Robert**
Jardine, Stephenson, Blewett and
Weaver, P.C., Great Falls 406 727 5000
*Recommended in Litigation*

**QUANDER, Don**
Holland & Hart LLP, Billings
406 252 2166
DQuander@hollandhart.com
*Recommended in Natural Resources*
**Practice Areas:** Partner addressing full
range of regulatory issues pertaining to
electric power, natural gas and alternative
energy sources, including transmission,
wholesale and retail power contracting,
and construction of generation, production and transmission facilities. Experience in utility proceedings, and in environmental permitting and compliance
for power projects, mining, wood projects, refining and other industrial facilities. Has been instrumental in the draft-

ing of facility siting and environmental
laws in several western states.
**Prof. Memberships:** Member of the
American Bar Association; Montana Bar
Association; Colorado Bar Association;
Montana, Colorado and ABA sections on
Administrative Law and on Natural
Resources, Energy and Environmental
Law; State Industrial Utility Group
Lawyers; Director of the Western Envi-
ronmental Trade Association; Director of
Energy Share Montana.
**Career:** Admitted to the Colorado
(1978) and Montana (1985) Bar Associa-
tions.
**Personal:** Recieved a JD (1978) from
Harvard and the University of Chicago
Law Schools and a BA (1974) from the
University of Chicago.

**ROBINSON, Donald**
Poore, Roth & Robinson, P.C., Butte
406 497 1200
*Recommended in Employment,
Litigation*

**ROGERS, Guy**
Brown Law Firm PC, Billings
406 248 2611
*Recommended in Litigation*

**ROSS, John Walker**
Brown Law Firm PC, Billings
406 248 2611
*Recommended in Natural Resources*

**RUFFATTO, Steven**
Crowley, Haughey, Hanson, Toole &
Dietrich, PLLP, Billings 406 252 3441
*Recommended in Natural Resources*

**SHERIDAN, Robert**
Garlington, Lohn & Robinson, PLLP,
Missoula 406 523 2500
*Recommended in Litigation*

**STENSLAND, Dean**
Boone, Karlberg PC, Missoula
406 543 6646
*Recommended in Real Estate*

**STRONG, Keith**
Dorsey & Whitney LLP, Great Falls
406 771 6806
strong.keith@dorsey.com
*Recommended in Litigation*
**Practice Areas:** Trial and appeal of
commercial, natural resources, malprac-
tice and white-collar criminal matters.
**Prof. Memberships:** American Board of
Trial Advocates (Montana President
2003). National Board of Trial Advocacy
Specialist Certification. Lawyer Member,
United States Judicial Conference for the
Ninth Circuit (2001-present). American,
Montana and Cascade County Bar Asso-
ciations.
**Personal:** University of Montana School
of Law, JD, 1974, high honors. University
of Montana, 1971.

**SULLIVAN, John**
Hughes, Kellner, Sullivan & Alke, Helena
406 442 3690
*Recommended in Employment*

**SULLIVAN, Robert**
Boone, Karlberg PC, Missoula
406 543 6646
*Recommended in Litigation*

**SULLIVAN, Zane**
Sullivan, Tabaracci and Rhoades PC,
Missoula 406 721 9700
*Recommended in Real Estate*

**TALEFF, Ward**
Alexander, Baucus, Taleff & Paul PC,
Great Falls 406 761 4800
*Recommended in Litigation*

**THANE, Jeremy**
Worden Thane PC, Missoula
406 721 3400
*Recommended in Employment*

**UGRIN, Neil**
Ugrin, Alexander, Zadick & Higgins, PC,
Great Falls 406 771 0007
*Recommended in Litigation*

**WADE, Steven**
Browning, Kaleczyc, Berry & Hoven PC,
Helena 406 443 6820
*Recommended in Natural Resources*

**WAGNER, William**
Garlington, Lohn & Robinson, PLLP,
Missoula 406 523 2500
*Recommended in Real Estate*

**WALTER, Teri**
Gough, Shanahan, Johnson & Waterman,
Helena 406 442 8560
*Recommended in Employment*

**WATERMAN, Ronald**
Gough, Shanahan, Johnson & Waterman,
Helena 406 442 8560
*Recommended in Litigation*

**WELSCH, Thomas**
Poore, Roth & Robinson, P.C., Butte
406 497 1200
*Recommended in Litigation*

**WESTESEN, Neil**
Crowley, Haughey, Hanson, Toole & Dietrich,
PLLP, Bozeman 406 556 1430
*Recommended in Litigation*

**ZADICK, Gary**
Ugrin, Alexander, Zadick & Higgins, PC,
Great Falls 406 771 0007
*Recommended in Employment*

# BROWNING, KALECZYC, BERRY AND HOVEN P.C.

## THE FIRM

**Number of partners:** 13
**Number of other lawyers:** 12

**FIRM OVERVIEW:** Browning, Kaleczyc, Berry and Hoven, P.C. (BKBH) is a full-service, twenty-five attorney law firm. With offices in Helena and Missoula, Montana, BKBH provides legal services to businesses and trade associations doing business in Montana. Legislative and public affairs services are also a significant part of the firm's practice – both in Helena and Washington, DC. BKBH works with its clients to create billing arrangements that provide good value both to them and to the firm.

**MAIN AREAS OF PRACTICE:** Commercial law, employment defense, environment and natural resources, government affairs, healthcare, insurance defense, litigation, real estate and taxation.
**Commercial Law:** BKBH offers a complete range of business and commercial services to its clients. The firm is experienced in dealing with the legal problems and opportunities facing organizations of all sizes. BKBH represents small, local businesses and Fortune 500 companies and helps them deal with all types of business transactions.
**Employment Defense:** The defense of Montana employers and their insurers constitutes a significant portion of BKBH's practice. For more than twenty years, the firm has successfully represented employers, insurers, self-insured entities and workers' compensation insurers. BKBH has successfully defended unlawful discrimination, wrongful discharge, claims for unemployment benefits, wage and hour claims, workers' compensation and occupational disease claims.
**Environment and Natural Resources:** BKBH is experienced in assisting clients with complex regulatory issues, including business and real estate transactions complicated by environmental compliance or contamination problems. The firm has successfully guided clients through permitting and compliance projects of all types. With its extensive natural resource and property capabilities, BKBH can provide experienced counsel for all environmental and natural resource matters affecting past, present, and future Montana property owners.
**Government Affairs:** In addition to traditional lobbying activities in Helena and Washington, DC, the firm provides clients with services in a broad array of public affairs projects. BKBH has organized professional campaigns, including policy development, media relations, grassroots communications, and direct advocacy. BKBH also works closely with Montana's powerful Congressional delegation, a service non-Montana firms cannot provide.
**Healthcare:** BKBH attorneys routinely provide a range of services to scores of healthcare providers in Montana. These providers require a variety of services ranging from relatively routine legal questions to complicated legal tasks that address increasingly complex state and federal laws. Compliance with existing state and federal laws is essential to the successful operation of healthcare facilities. BKBH works closely with its healthcare clients to comply with applicable laws.
**Insurance Defense:** Over the past twenty years, BKBH has represented more than one hundred insurance companies, including self-insurers, on issues ranging from coverage determinations to bad faith claims. The firm's representation involves all forums, including state and federal court, administrative proceedings, and claims before the Insurance Commissioner. The firm also provides advice on all insurance related issues directly to its insurance clients and full litigation support.
**Litigation:** BKBH has a substantial litigation department. The firm works in a cooperative, trust relationship with its clients to ensure mutual participation in the strategic defense of each case. BKBH's litigation section has demonstrated a capacity to handle complex lawsuits with multiple parties and tens of thousands of documents. The firm utilizes computerized legal research so that its motions and briefs include the latest in legal developments. BKBH works in cooperation with its clients to determine the appropriateness of alternative dispute resolution mechanisms, including arbitration, mediation and settlement negotiation.

## HEAD OFFICE

**MONTANA**
139 North Last Chance Gulch, PO Box 1697, **Helena**, MT 59624
**Tel:** 406 443 6820  **Fax:** 406 443 6883

## BRANCH OFFICES

**MONTANA**
269 West Front Street, PO Box 8234, **Missoula**, MT 59807
**Tel:** 406 728 1694  **Fax:** 406 728 5475

## CONTACTS

| | |
|---|---|
| Commercial Law | Stan Kaleczyc |
| Employment Law | Oliver Goe |
| Environment & Natural Resources | Leo Berry |
| Government Affairs | Steve Wade |
| Healthcare | Mark Taylor |
| Insurance Defense | Leo Ward |
| Litigation | Dan Hoven |
| Real Estate | Mark Etchart |
| Taxation | Brand Boyar |

**Real Estate:** For more than twenty years, BKBH attorneys have routinely dealt with many of the federal and state laws governing public lands. The firm's public land attorneys are among Montana's most qualified practitioners in this complex area of the law. BKBH also represents Montana's largest private landowner, the railroads and other investor-owned utilities on real estate matters.
**Taxation:** Almost every business transaction is impacted by federal, state, or local taxes. BKBH attorneys knowledgeable in tax matters advise the firm's clients on the tax consequences of proposed transactions and suggest arrangements that will mitigate their impact. The firm's attorneys also have experience representing corporate and other business clients before the Montana Department of Revenue, the Internal Revenue Service, and federal and state tax courts.

**CLIENTS:** Anheuser-Busch Cos. (St. Louis, MO); BNSF Railway Company (Fort Worth, TX); NorthWestern Corporation (Sioux Falls, SD); Union Pacific Railroad (Omaha, NE); Montana Hospital Assn. (Helena, MT); Logo Signs of America (Waite Park, MN); Burlington Resources Oil and Gas Company (Houston, TX); Trinity Industries (Dallas, TX); Pacific Steel and Recycling (Great Falls, MT); Rhodia, Inc. (Princeton, NJ); Corixa (Seattle, WA); BearingPoint, Inc. (Sacramento, CA); Asarco LLC (Tucson, AZ); International Paper (Nashville, TN); Koch Industries, Inc. (Wichita, KS); Huttig Building Products (Stamford, CT); Havre Pipeline Company LLC (Oklahoma City, OK); Devon Energy Corporation (Oklahoma City, OK); Conoco Phillips (Denver, CO); Montana Municipal Insurance Auth; Utah Medical Insurance Association (Salt Lake City, UT); Montana Schools Group Insurance Auth; The Doctors Co. (Napa, CA); Montana Hospital Association Workers' Compensation Trust; Yellowstone Insurance Exchange (Post Falls, ID); Montana State Compensation Mutual Insurance Fund; Travelers Group (Hartford, CT); SISR Services; CNA Surety (Chicago, IL); New West Health Plan (Helena, MT); Penn-America Inc. Co. (Hatsboro, PA); Gallagher Bassett Services (Orlando, FL); General Star Insurance (Chicago, IL); SAFECO Corporation (Chicago, IL).

# CROWLEY HAUGHEY HANSON TOOLE & DIETRICH PLLP

## THE FIRM

**Managing Partner:** Michael S Dockery

**Number of partners:** 49
**Number of other attorneys:** 35

**FIRM OVERVIEW:** Crowley, Haughey, Hanson, Toole & Dietrich P.L.L.P. enjoys a rich history tracing back to 1895, and is the largest law firm in Montana with over 80 attorneys. The firm has offices in Billings, Bozeman, Helena, Kalispell, and Missoula, Montana and Williston, North Dakota. The firm is the reviser for Martindale-Hubbell. The firm provides a full range of legal services and represents an impressive and wide range of clients, including national and international corporations. The firm has a commitment to provide the highest quality legal services and has built upon a strong tradition of legal expertise and high ethical standards.

## MAIN AREAS OF PRACTICE:

**Corporate/Banking & Finance:** The firm handles antitrust, bond offerings, public finance, public utilities, banking, business organizations, corporate, securities, financing transactions, intellectual property, employee benefits, mergers and acquisitions, nonprofit corporations, creditors' rights, real estate, agricultural, regulatory, and immigration.

**Intellectual Property:** The IP Practice Group advises clients on a wide range of matters including patents, copyrights, trademarks, trade secrets, unfair competition, license agreements, nondisclosure agreements, and franchise concerns.

**Labor & Employment Practice:** The firm represents management in all areas of employment law especially employee relations, wrongful discharge and discrimination claims.

**Litigation:** The firm covers all aspects of litigation through its six offices. The Litigation Practice Group handles a wide variety of matters for commercial clients including administrative law, arbitration, condemnation, intellectual property, mediation, insurance defense, personal injury, malpractice, products liability, worker's compensation, commercial litigation, construction law, employment, foreclosures and bankruptcy.

**Natural Resources:** The firm's Natural Resources Practice Group is one of the largest in Montana, specializing in coal, conservation commission hearings, public land issues, regulatory matters, title examinations, utilities, oil and gas, mining, water, energy transmission, environmental compliance and permitting and Indian law.

**Real Estate:** The firm focuses mainly on commercial and agricultural transactions including subdivision, development, finance and bankruptcy proceedings, commonly representing creditors.

**Tax & Estate Planning:** The firm has extensive experience in advising commercial and individual clients in complex probate and estate planning matters.

**CLIENTS:** AIG Life Insurance Co.; Allstate Insurance Co.; The Bank of Baker; Big Sky Economic Development Authority; Billings Clinic; Blue Cross and Blue Shield of Montana; Chicago Title Insurance Co.; Chubb Group of Insurance Cos.; City of Billings; CNA Insurance; Conoco Inc.; Consol Energy; Crawford & Co.; CTA; Decker Coal Co.; The Doctor's Co.; Enerplus; Essex Insurance Company; Farm Credit Bank; Farmers Alliance Mutual Insurance Company; Farmers Insurance Group; Fidelity National Title Insurance Co.; Fireman's Fund Insurance Co.; First American Title Insurance Co.; First Interstate Bank; GAB Robins North America, Inc.; General Motors Acceptance Corp.; Great American Insurance Co.; Hartford Insurance Group; Headington Oil; Holly Sugar Co.; The Home Insurance Cos.; Kemper Insurance Co.; Kennecott Corporation; Liberty Mutual Insurance Co.; Life Investors Insurance Co. of America; MDU Resources Group, Inc.; Inc.; Metropolitan Life Insurance Co.; Millers First Insurance Cos.; Montana State Compensation Insurance Fund; Mutual Life Insurance Co. N.Y.; Natural Gas Processing Company; New York Life Insurance Co.;

## HEAD OFFICE

**MONTANA**
500 Transwestern Plaza II, 490 North 31st Street
**Billings**, MT 59101-1288
**Tel:** 406 252 3441   **Fax:** 406 256 0277
**Email:** crowley@crowleylaw.com
**Website:** www.crowleylaw.com

## BRANCH OFFICES

**MONTANA**
45 Discovery Drive, Suite 200, **Bozeman**, MT 59718-6957
**Tel:** 406 556 1430   **Fax:** 406 556 1433

100 North Park Avenue, Suite 300, **Helena**, MT 59601-6287
**Tel:** 406 449 4165   **Fax:** 406 449 5149

431 First Avenue West, **Kalispell**, MT 59901-4835
**Tel:** 406-752 6644   **Fax:** 406 752 5108

305 South 4th East, Suite 100, **Missoula**, MT 59801-2701
**Tel:** 406 523 3600   **Fax:** 406 523 3636

**NORTH DAKOTA**
111 East Broadway, **Williston**, ND 58802-1206
**Tel:** 701 572 2200   **Fax:** 701 572 7072

## CONTACTS

| Practice | Contact |
| --- | --- |
| Corporate/Banking Finance | William D Lamdin |
| Intellectual Property | Robert C Griffin |
| Labor & Employment | Steven J Lehman |
| Litigation | Joe C Maynard, Jr |
| Natural Resources | John R Lee |
| Real Estate | Michael S Dockery |
| Tax & Estate Planning | Ashley Burleson |

Newton Mining Co.; Nexen Oil & Gas USA; Noranda Minerals Corp.; Northwest Farm Credit Services, ACA; Old Republic Insurance Co.; Peabody Coal Co.; Penn-America Insurance Co.; Petroleum Casualty Co.; PPL Montana, LLC; Prudential Insurance Co.; R.J. Reynolds Tobacco Co., Inc.; Sinclair Oil Corp.; St. Paul Insurance Cos.; Stockman Bank; Streeter Brothers Mortgage Corp.; The Travelers; Turner Enterprises, Inc.; UMC Petroleum Corp.; Wausau Insurance Co.; Zurich American Insurance Group; Yellowstone Banks.

# GOUGH, SHANAHAN, JOHNSON & WATERMAN

## THE FIRM

**Managing Partner:** Jock O Anderson

**Number of partners:** 13
**Number of other lawyers:** 9

**FIRM OVERVIEW:** Established in 1879, Gough, Shanahan, Johnson and Waterman is the oldest and one of the leading law firms in Montana. In addition to the general practice of law, the firm's practice emphasizes natural resources and environmental law, insurance defense and insurance coverage law, commercial litigation, employment counseling and litigation, administrative law, banking law and regulation, government, estate and property law, energy, transportation, product liability and construction litigation. The firm has well established speciality practices in employment, mining, water quality, tribal law, water rights, endangered species, public school districts, patents, state and local taxation. Headquartered in Montana's capital city with a satellite office in Billings, the firm is expert in the workings of the state and federal government at all levels. GSJW is the Montana member firm of the State Capital Law Firm Group.

## MAIN AREAS OF PRACTICE:

**Commercial Litigation:** The firm's Litigation Practice covers state and federal courts including appellate advocacy, especially before the Supreme Court of Montana. The ability to provide effective representation at all phases of litigation assures the client's rights are fully protected, before during and following a trial. The firm also works using mediation and other forms of alternative dispute resolution to resolve matters expeditiously for clients.

**Employment:** The firm represents employers of all sizes, including regular representation of large employers headquartered outside of Montana. With offices in Helena and Billings, the firm's statewide employment practice serves the needs of a diversified clientele including technology, services, telecommunications, manufacturers, mining, energy and oil and gas, as well as agricultural, timber and construction industries.

**Environmental:** The firm's environmental law expertise is applied on behalf of its clients on a daily basis across the spectrum of legal matters, including transactions, regulatory and permitting issues and litigation. The firm has in-depth expertise in surface and ground water quality matters, including the federal Clean Water Act and the Montana Water Quality Acts, and deals regularly with solid hazardous waste issues, facility siting laws, pesticide regulation and environmental regulation specific to areas such as forest products, coalbed natural gas, mining, manufacturing and real estate transactions.

**Government Relations/Regulatory:** The firm has extensive experience in natural resources, public utility regulation, taxation and legislative representation and places an emphasis on cost-effective problem-solving. As a longstanding and respected member of the Montana community, the firm is particularly well-suited to represent diverse corporate clients before Montana local or state government.

**Natural Resources:** The firm's practice encompasses all areas of natural resources law, with an emphasis on mining, coalbed natural gas, water law, water quality and NEPA issues. The firm represents local, national and international clients on air, surface and ground water (both quality and quantity), and waste issues arising from development, operation and reclamation of natural resource projects. The firm represents clients in all local, state and federal contexts, including regulatory agencies, contested case hearings, district and appellate courts, including the Montana Supreme Court, the US Supreme Court, the Ninth Circuit Court of Appeals and the Federal Circuit Court of Appeals. The firm's natural resource team takes a comprehensive approach to addressing its clients' legal, political and public relations needs.

## HEAD OFFICE

**MONTANA**
33 South Last Chance Gulch, PO Box 1715, **Helena**, MT 59624
**Tel:** 406 442 8560   **Fax:** 406 442 8783
**Website:** www.gsjw.com

## BRANCH OFFICES

**MONTANA**
2722 3rd Avenue N., Suite 400, **Billings**, MT 59101
**Tel:** 406 248 3214   **Fax:** 406 245 0627

## CONTACTS

| | |
|---|---|
| Commercial Law | Ronald F Waterman |
| Employment | Thomas E Hattersley, III |
| Environmental | Alan L Joscelyn |
| Government Relations/Regulatory | Jon Metropoulos |
| Insurance Defense | Thomas E Hattersley, III |
| Natural Resources | Jon Metropoulos |
| Real Estate/Banking/Finance | Jock O Anderson |

**Real Estate/Banking/Finance:** The firm's commercial lawyers regularly assist in-state and out-of-state clients in real estate purchases and development and with lending transactions. The firm's banking and lending practice assists both state and federally regulated financial institutions with all aspects of lending transactions, loan workouts, collection and foreclosure litigation, and creditor bankruptcy matters. The firm also assists new and existing financial institutions with regulatory issues including new charters, compliance and acquisitions and mergers in Montana.

## How lawyers are ranked

Every year we carry out thousands of in-depth interviews with clients and lawyers in order to assess the reputations and expertise of business lawyers across the USA. Chambers rankings and editorial are referred to extensively by General Counsel and other purchasers of legal services who look to our recommendations when choosing their lawyers.

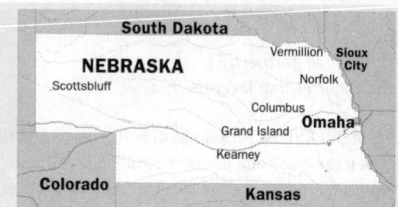

# CORPORATE/M&A

### Corporate/M&A
#### Leading Firms

**1** BAIRD HOLM *Omaha*
   BLACKWELL SANDERS PEPER MARTIN *Omaha*
   MCGRATH NORTH MULLIN & KRATZ PC *Omaha*
**2** ABRAHAMS KASLOW & CASSMAN LLP *Omaha*
   CLINE, WILLIAMS, WRIGHT *Lincoln*
   FRASER STRYKER LAW FIRM *Omaha*
   KOLEY JESSEN P.C. *Omaha*
   KUTAK ROCK LLP *Omaha*
**3** ERICKSON & SEDERSTROM, PC *Omaha*
   WOODS & AITKEN LLP *Lincoln*

#### Leading Individuals

**1** DIXON Joyce *Blackwell Sanders*
   HEFFLINGER David *McGrath North Mullin & Kratz*
   KASLOW Howard *Abrahams Kaslow & Cassman*
   ZEILINGER John *Baird Holm LLP*
**2** BURT Donald *Cline, Williams, Wright*
   FREEMAN Robert *Fraser Stryker Law Firm*
   GEHRING Stephen *Cline, Williams, Wright*
   HANDLOS Bryan *Kutak Rock LLP*
   JESSEN Paul *Koley Jessen P.C.*
   RICHARDSON Todd *Blackwell Sanders*
   TURNER Steven *Baird Holm*
**3** BASS Jo *Kutak Rock LLP*
   GOTSDINER Gary *McGill, Gotsdiner, Workman*
   HERDZINA John *Abrahams Kaslow & Cassman*
   PARSONAGE Ronald *Abrahams Kaslow & Cassman*
   SEDERSTROM Charles *Erickson & Sederstrom, PC*

### Band 1

#### Baird Holm LLP

**The Firm:** This highly respected firm has a long record of excellence in Nebraska, particularly for business advice and transactional support. Interviewees reported that there were "*no weak links,*" while one admitted: "*I know that any lawyer I deal with there is going to be competent, well trained and experienced in the transaction.*" The corporate and M&A group comprises 30 lawyers who serve a diverse client base that includes buyers, sellers, large corporations and small family businesses. Banking and

finance is also traditionally strong, with lawyers excelling in loan issues, foreclosures and banking regulatory issues. Securities law is another area of expertise, and according to clients the firm is "*head and shoulders above the rest for communications.*"
**The Lawyers:** "*Terrific*" attorney **John Zeilinger** is "*a real gentleman to work with.*" Recognized in Nebraska and beyond for financial institutions work, M&A and securities law, clients found him insightful and responsive, asserting that "*he does a great job and isn't contentious.*" **Steve Turner** heads up the firm's finance practice and is deemed "*very influential in the state.*" He handles mainly commercial and agricultural financings and is well versed in bankruptcy workouts and other insolvency matters. He is active in the area of uniform laws and interviewees singled him out as a popular speaker.
**Clients/Work Highlights:** Rabobank; Great Western Bancorporation; River Valley Bancorp; Pinnacle Bancorporation; Bozeman Bancorp and Spectrum Financial Services.

#### Blackwell Sanders Peper Martin LLP
See firm details p.1212
**The Firm:** The geographical reach of this Midwestern giant is one of its distinguishing features. Headquartered in Kansas City, the firm additionally has offices in Omaha, St Louis, Washington, DC and London, England. Clients agreed: "*We use them for everything because they're so diverse – there's no need to go anywhere else.*" In the area of financing, the team represents lenders, institutional clients and, on occasion, borrowers. Asset securitization forms an important part of the practice, while cross-border transactions are carried out between the USA and UK. The firm boasts a venture capital private equity group that works with established and emerging companies. Clients praised a team of "*time-sensitive*" attorneys who are skilled at "*always presenting all the options available.*" Recent highlights include working on a de novo charter for a new bank in Nebraska.
**The Lawyers:** Multitalented attorney **Joyce Dixon** (see p.1244) attracted praise for being "*a very creative problem solver*" who is "*real smooth at dealing with tough situations and difficult people.*" A specialist in financial institutions, regulatory work and compliance matters, clients admired her for "*taking the time on her own nickel to ensure every detail is followed up.*"

**Todd Richardson** (see p.1244) is an excellent younger lawyer who is "*soon to be at the top,*" according to sources. He represents buyers and sellers in M&A and various other types of commercial transaction. Peers pointed to his expertise in general business planning and company formations.
**Clients/Work Highlights:** Diversified Financial Services; InfiBank; World's Foremost Bank; H&R Block; First National Bank of Omaha; Gordmans; West Corporation; Commercial Federal Bank; Empire Fire & Marine Insurance and Government Properties Trust.

#### McGrath North Mullin & Kratz PC
**The Firm:** The second largest firm in Nebraska garnered praise for having "*probably the most M&A experience out of everyone in the state.*" This is in large part due to its long service as general counsel for ConAgra, a company that has acquired 250 businesses since its creation. The group boasts a strong collection of transactional lawyers who are all "*hardworking, aggressive and detail-oriented.*" Peers emphasized the long hours that attorneys would work to get the job done. In addition to its "*superb*" corporate practice, the firm is recommended for its tax work.
**The Lawyers:** "*Outstanding*" lawyer and president of the firm **Dave Hefflinger** has 30 years' experience in business and tax planning. According to sources, he is "*comfortable at handling substantial deals and putting things together,*" including the structure and operation of public and private companies. His practice includes securities as well as corporate and tax advice.
**Clients/Work Highlights:** Valmont Industries; Physicians Mutual Insurance; Creighton University; Omaha Airport Authority; Omaha Chamber of Commerce; First National Bank of Omaha; Peter Kiewit Sons'; Farm Credit Services; Nebraska Medical Center; American Family Insurance; Associated Aviation Underwriters; Blue Cross Blue Shield of Nebraska and GEICO.

## Band 2

### Abrahams Kaslow & Cassman LLP

**The Firm:** This midsized firm excels in commercial business matters and benefits from being "*more tied-in locally than the bigger firms.*" It has a broad, general corporate practice that encompasses employment law, real estate, and IP. Eight "*extremely able*" lawyers handle corporate and securities work, representing privately owned businesses engaged in M&A, company formation and organizational matters.

**The Lawyers:** Peers honored "*shining star*" and "*truly outstanding lawyer*" **Howard Kaslow** as "*one of the great legal minds in the community.*" One interviewee suggested that he would make a fine mentor for many of the younger lawyers in Omaha. Kaslow's practice focuses on corporate and business law, plus estate planning. **John Herdzina** garnered praise for being "*committed and conscientious*" and "*a real gentleman.*" He advises clients, including international companies, in complex business, real estate and energy transactions. Partner **Ron Parsonage** is recognized this year for his corporate work and estate planning; in each area he brings over 30 years of experience to the table and is described as "*a very smooth negotiator.*" Parsonage represents many clients in the farming sector.

**Clients/Work Highlights:** SITEL; First National Bank of Omaha; Tenaska; American National Bank; CSG Systems International and National Equity.

### Cline, Williams, Wright, Johnson & Oldfather LLP

**The Firm:** Peers described this regional law firm as "*the best in Lincoln.*" Though originating in Lincoln, the firm has other offices in Aurora, Scottsbluff and Omaha, where the team is said to be "*right on target.*" Between Lincoln and Omaha, seven attorneys handle a wide variety of corporate and M&A work, including sales and acquisitions of small to midsized businesses. Sources commended the firm's banking practice, noting its "*effective*" style. Highlights from the past twelve months include involvement in the sophisticated $98 million sale of publicly held client Isco, which was acquired by Teledyne Technologies.

**The Lawyers:** **Donald Burt** is "*clearly the top-level lawyer over there,*" reported interviewees. He was highly recommended as someone for corporate, M&A and mutual fund work, with peers endorsing his drafting skills and describing him as "*a cerebral yet comprehensible guy.*" **Stephen Gehring** continues to have an excellent reputation throughout the state, chiefly for his securities work. Clients highlighted his integrity and responsiveness.

**Clients/Work Highlights:** WesterN SizzliN; Ballantyne of Omaha; GM; Cargill and Wells Fargo Bank Nebraska.

### Fraser Stryker Law Firm

See firm details p.1245

**The Firm:** This Omaha firm enjoys an excellent reputation for litigation and has a flourishing business and corporate practice. While not organized along strict departmental lines, the 45-strong operation fields leanly staffed strategic teams on every major matter. "*Truly talented*" attorneys bring diverse expertise to the business arena, where corporate formation, tax law, M&A and divestitures feature with regularity. The firm continues to serve as general counsel for Metropolitan Entertainment & Convention Authority (MECA), the nonprofit agency that manages Qwest Center, Omaha's $280 million convention arena complex.

**The Lawyers:** Partner **Bob Freeman** is "*a very thoughtful, bright and skilled negotiator*" who acts as general counsel for major clients such as the Qwest Center. He is recommended for his strategic planning and contract work.

**Clients/Work Highlights:** Some of the firm's key clients include Omaha Children's Hospital, Oakview Communications and Level 3 Communications.

### Koley Jessen P.C.

**The Firm:** This "*aggressive, visionary*" firm continues to prosper with the arrival of five graduates from Creighton University School of Law in May 2005. Sources agreed that while the group is still young, it is growing in public exposure. "*They are the new kids on the block but they have a good energy and a promising future.*" More than 20 attorneys practice in the business, securities and tax area, advising clients on a range of transactional, regulatory and compliance matters. A smaller group is focused on M&A. Peers endorsed the excellent leadership and training provided to the group.

**The Lawyers:** Managing partner **Paul Jessen** is "*one of the top business lawyers in town.*" He is adept in handling all types of transactional work, as well as estate and business succession planning for closely held businesses. Commentators praised his technical skills and business judgment, observing that "*he focuses on what's important and doesn't get tangled up in humdrum detail.*"

**Clients/Work Highlights:** CitiCapital; First Nebraska Trust; Five Points Bank; Carlson Systems; Security National Bank of Omaha and World Investments.

### Kutak Rock LLP

**The Firm:** The Omaha office of this national heavyweight is the largest firm in Nebraska, boasting 40 lawyers in its corporate department. While sources admitted that the group had "*grown in strength over the years,*" it remained "*a different beast in Omaha*" due to the national and international nature of its practice. Within the corporate department are four work groups specializing in real estate, corporate finance, financial services and health care. Clients valued the "*solid, reliable, consistent work*" carried out

by attorneys, noting in particular their expertise in securitization and compliance work.

**The Lawyers:** Highly regarded lawyer **Bryan Handlos** attracts a loyal client following with his low-key approach to transactions. A specialist in financial institutions and regulatory matters, he is said to be "*the sort of legal counselor you want to have because you can always call on him to handle matters skillfully in a timely way.*" Heading up one of the work groups, **Jo Bass** is "*precise, very thorough and gracious.*" She has a niche in representing public and private companies in asset-backed securitizations, asset acquisitions and dispositions.

**Clients/Work Highlights:** The firm works for many banks and bank service providers, including First National Bank of Omaha and First Data.

## Band 3

### Erickson & Sederstrom, PC

**The Firm:** This firm has an established corporate and business-planning practice and can call upon attorneys in Lincoln and Omaha for a full range of services, including business formation, real estate and franchising. Attorneys are known to be very active in the healthcare sector.

**The Lawyers:** **Charles Sederstrom** remains the most recognized lawyer in the group. A "*good strategic thinker,*" he is celebrated for his corporate and banking expertise, as well as his knowledge of healthcare organizations.

**Clients/Work Highlights:** These comprise healthcare conglomerates, regional manufacturers, retailers and other companies.

### Woods & Aitken LLP

**The Firm:** This "*excellent, full-service*" Lincoln firm was boosted by the opening of an Omaha office in 2004. Nine "*very capable*" lawyers advise a range of banks and financial institutions in various commercial transactions, including secured lending, asset-based and real estate lending, project and acquisition financing, and letters of credit.

**The Lawyers:** Lee Merritt heads up the team. His practice concentrates on business planning, tax and transactional matters.

**Clients/Work Highlights:** HyGain Electronics; Sanitary and Improvement District No. 7; Gateway Realty; J&E Cattle; Rose Equipment; Wanek Furniture and Appliances; ALLTEL and Citizens Communications.

### Other Notable Practitioners

**Gary Gotsdiner** of Omaha firm McGill, Gotsdiner, Workman & Lepp PC LLO is "*very strong on the corporate side. He does a lot, works hard and is very knowledgeable,*" said peers. "*I'd refer work to him, without a doubt,*" one leading commentator confirmed.

# EMPLOYMENT

# MAINLY DEFENDANT

| Employment: Mainly Defendant |
| --- |
| **Leading Firms** |
| 1   **BAIRD HOLM LLP** *Omaha* |
|    **FRASER STRYKER LAW FIRM** *Omaha* |
|    **MCGRATH NORTH MULLIN & KRATZ PC** *Omaha* |
| 2   **BERENS & TATE PC** *Omaha* |
|    **HARDING SHULTZ & DOWNS** *Lincoln* |

| Leading Individuals |
| --- |
| 1   **HEDICAN Chris** *Baird Holm LLP* |
|    **MILLER Roger** *McGrath North Mullin & Kratz PC* |
|    **ROSSITER Robert** *Fraser Stryker Law Firm* |
|    **ROZMARIN George** *Fraser Stryker Law Firm* |
| 2   **BARRETT Patrick** *McGrath North Mullin & Kratz PC* |
|    **BOGUE Stevenson** *McGrath North Mullin & Kratz PC* |
|    **LOUDON Timothy** *Berens & Tate PC* |
|    **STEVENSON Randy** *Baird Holm LLP* |
| 3   **FAHLESON Mark** *Rembolt Ludtke LLP* |
|    **HARDING William** *Harding Shultz & Downs* |
|    **MOORE Scott** *Baird Holm* |
|    **PIGSLEY Jerry** *Harding Shultz & Downs* |
|    **SCHORR Mark** *Erickson & Sederstrom PC* |
|    **SHULTZ Jack** *Harding Shultz & Downs* |

## Band 1

### Baird Holm LLP

**The Firm:** This long-established firm has "*the best employment law group in the state,*" according to clients from both the private and public sectors. A large, "*upfront*" team of 13 has had tremendous success of late in ERISA subrogation and reimbursement cases, including persuading the Nebraska Court of Appeals to uphold a noncompete agreement. Clients praised the firm's responsiveness and cooperative strength, saying: "*We can talk to them about things because they're very open to discussion.*" Several clients drew attention to the firm's employment conferences.

**The Lawyers:** Chief litigator **Chris Hedican** is "*a bright shining star*" who "*sure knows how to present a case.*" A skilled manager and communicator, Hedican is "*levelheaded, professional and always up-to-date.*" **Randy Stevenson** devotes himself to employment counseling, compliance, and OSHA defense. "*There's no one better than Randy for labor relations,*" observed clients. They valued his sound business judgment and resolve, and liked the way "*he will take positions on issues.*" Like Stevenson, **Scott Moore** focuses on everyday employment advice. Clients were impressed with his creativity, one remarking: "*He's one of the most innovative thinkers I've come across.*"

**Clients/Work Highlights:** Modern Equipment; Millard Refrigerated Services; Gordmans; Centris Federal Credit Union; C&A Industries; Vatterott College; Woodmen of the World; Agrium and Wal-Mart.

### Fraser Stryker Law Firm

See firm details p.1245

**The Firm:** The labor and employment section of this firm maintains a relatively low profile, yet those who have encountered it are in no doubt of its excellence. The group's reputation rests largely on the quality of its two leading partners – "*they're definitely top tier.*" They head up a team of six attorneys who are "*highly knowledgeable and full of integrity.*" While litigation is the team's strongest suit, a substantial portion of its work is preventative or labor-related. Attorneys represent a wide range of employers, including large corporations and small, family-owned businesses. The firm is also accomplished in employee benefits, ERISA and executive compensation matters.

**The Lawyers:** Sources heaped praise on **Bob Rossiter** for being "*just a terrific lawyer and fabulous guy.*" Clients found him to have a deep knowledge – "*he knows the law and is a great resource to us*" – and drew attention to his workers' compensation and risk management expertise. Highly respected attorney and "*even-tempered gentleman*" **George Rozmarin** handles traditional labor work, including labor negotiations, elections and arbitrations. While he no longer takes on trials, he brings an impressive breadth of knowledge and skills to his role as adviser. Clients valued his ability to make complex issues easy to understand, calling him "*a delight to work with.*"

**Clients/Work Highlights:** Key clients include Omaha Public Power District, First National Bank of Omaha and Becton Dickinson.

### McGrath North Mullin & Kratz PC

**The Firm:** This is a firm that "*goes the distance,*" clients raved, remarking on how the attorneys were all "*very hard working and willing to put in the hours.*" A team of eight covers the full gamut of labor and employment issues, from preventative trial and appellate work in discrimination cases, to labor relations. Attorneys are well versed in business immigration law, wage and hour disputes, OSHA and supervisory training. While the firm's primary client is ConAgra, it is also known for its plaintiffs work.

**The Lawyers:** Acclaimed lawyer **Roger Miller** is best known for his ConAgra work. "*One of the deans*" of labor law, he "*really knows the ropes,*" proclaimed peers. His practice also includes employment discrimination litigation as well as client training and advice. Experienced attorney **Pat Barrett** is "*a great all-rounder*" who is "*ethical, tenacious and always well prepared,*" according to sources. He concentrates on employment discrimination trial work and has a strong day-to-day advisory practice. Peers confirmed that they would not hesitate to refer work to him. **Steve Bogue** is a "*practical, knowledgeable*" labor attorney with a diverse background that includes time at the NLRB. "*He brings a comprehensive and balanced approach to his work,*" according to clients. They also endorsed his easy manner and his "*judicial temperament*" that ensures he is "*very good at establishing interpersonal relationships.*"

**Clients/Work Highlights:** Sencore; Physicians

Mutual Insurance; Valmont Industries; First Data and Nebraska Medical Center.

## Band 2

### Berens & Tate PC

**The Firm:** This boutique law firm prides itself on being the largest exclusive labor and employment firm in the area. Thirteen "*prompt and pragmatic*" attorneys cover all aspects of employment law, including discrimination, drug testing, policy development, OSHA and safety issues. Traditional labor relations remain the group's best-known area of expertise, featuring both litigation and alternative dispute resolution work. Several commentators remarked on what they saw as a relatively high turnover among associates; however, the firm scored a coup with the hire of distinguished attorney Sam Jensen as counsel. Clients placed the firm "*on the cutting edge, ahead of the curve for new laws and employee news,*" and confirmed that it represented great value for money. They also hoped that it would broaden its range of services even further by entering into the employee benefits area.

**The Lawyers:** **Tim Loudon** is "*a fine lawyer who really knows his stuff.*" His portfolio includes employment discrimination, labor relations and arbitrations, in addition to wage and hour disputes. A distinguished public speaker and article writer, he was lauded by clients for his personal, attentive style: "*He doesn't just tell you what he knows, he goes very slowly and listens carefully.*" One added: "*Tim isn't afraid to tell you when you've screwed up.*"

**Clients/Work Highlights:** SITEL; American National Bank; Nucor Steel; Chubb Group; St. Paul Travelers; Evangelical Lutheran Good Samaritan Society; Leggett & Platt and Atlas Cold Storage.

### Harding Shultz & Downs

**The Firm:** Viewed as "*the leading firm in Lincoln for employment law,*" Harding Shultz has maintained its profile in the employment sector thanks to a handful of specialist lawyers. Three members of the "*professional and courteous*" six-strong team concentrate exclusively on labor and employment, while the other three have an employment law and schools focus.

**The Lawyers:** "*Seasoned attorney*" **Bill Harding** handles a variety of labor and employment issues with a spotlight on public sector work. "*He's done a lot for cities,*" reported peers. Harding has vast experience in traditional labor relations and "*tries to be innovative where he can.*" **Jerry Pigsley** was described as "*a first-class lawyer who does a great job.*" He is renowned for his proficiency in employment discrimination litigation. **Jack Shultz** won plaudits from clients for being "*incredibly ethical, easy to communicate with and fun to argue with.*" As well as labor and employment law, his practice covers transportation and telecommunications.

**Clients/Work Highlights:** AmeriPride; Wells Fargo; Telex and EF Johnson.

### Other Notable Practitioners

Up-and-comer **Mark Fahleson** of Rembolt Ludtke LLP was hotly tipped as "one to watch" by sources this year. Several agreed that "he'll soon be the top employment lawyer in the state." Based in Lincoln, Fahleson enjoys an excellent reputation as an employment litigator and public speaker. **Mark Schorr** is the standout labor and employment lawyer at Erickson & Sederstrom, PC in Lincoln. His practice has an emphasis on employment litigation and discrimination. Peers said they would not hesitate to refer work to him.

# LITIGATION

---

### Litigation: General Commercial

#### Leading Firms

1. **BAIRD HOLM LLP** Omaha
   **CLINE, WILLIAMS, WRIGHT** Lincoln
   **FRASER STRYKER LAW FIRM** Omaha
   **MCGRATH NORTH MULLIN & KRATZ PC** Omaha
2. **LAMSON, DUGAN & MURRAY, LLP** Omaha
3. **BLACKWELL SANDERS PEPER MARTIN** Omaha
   **CASSEM TIERNEY ADAMS GOTCH** Omaha
   **ERICKSON & SEDERSTROM, PC** Omaha
4. **KUTAK ROCK LLP** Omaha

#### Leading Individuals

##### Senior Statesman

**PETERSON Alan** Cline, Williams, Wright

1. **BAUSCH James** Cline, Williams, Wright
   **CULHANE Thomas** Erickson & Sederstrom, PC
   **DITTRICK William** Baird Holm LLP
   **MEUSEY Joseph** Fraser Stryker Law Firm
2. **BLECHA Kirk** Baird Holm LLP
   **BROWNRIGG John** Erickson & Sederstrom, PC
   **DAHLK Thomas** Blackwell Sanders
   **DOMINA David** Domina Law plc LLO
   **FITZGERALD James** McGrath North Mullin & Kratz
   **KAUFFMAN Fred** Cline, Williams, Wright
   **KNOWLES Leo** McGrath North Mullin & Kratz
   **MARK Wayne** Fraser Stryker Law Firm
3. **COLLERAN Kevin** Cline, Williams, Wright
   **HARGENS William** McGrath North Mullin & Kratz
   **LAUGHLIN Gerald** Baird Holm LLP
   **MCLEAY Bartholomew** Kutak Rock LLP
   **O'HARE Terrence** McGrath North Mullin & Kratz
   **SLOVEK Robert** Kutak Rock LLP
   **STROTMAN Andrew** Cline, Williams, Wright
   **WARIN Edward** McGrath North Mullin & Kratz

---

## Band 1

### Baird Holm LLP

**The Firm:** This large, distinguished law firm continues to be a leader in its field; "it really knows what makes businesses tick" and "can find creative solutions to difficult problems." The firm has a wide-ranging litigation practice that focuses on complex commercial litigation and intellectual property. Fourteen "ethical and experienced" lawyers serve a broad client base, taking on large-scale and often long-running cases. They continue to represent Omaha Public Schools in a major school finance case that was filed in 2003 against the state. Other highlights from the past twelve months include the successful resolution through settlement of a major copyright case involving the piracy of an artwork manufactured in China.

**The Lawyers:** Trusted litigator and criminal lawyer **Bill Dittrick** is "a steady performer with a cool head." Peers found him to be honest, thoroughly prepared and "not at all obstreperous." He has lately picked up a good reputation for mediation. His colleague **Kirk Blecha** has a similar practice, handling general commercial litigation with a leaning towards employment cases. Sources admired his personable, down-to-earth style, describing him as "a straight-shooting man of integrity who brings a great personality to the job." "Excellent trial lawyer" **Tom Johnson** has a commercial litigation practice with an emphasis on medical and insurance issues. Bright and diligent, he "always does a great job." Meanwhile, multitalented litigator **Jill Ackerman** has a fine reputation in intellectual property matters, especially in the noncompete covenant area. Proving her flexibility, she has been devoting much of her time to the Omaha Public Schools case. **Gerald Laughlin** is a seasoned attorney with over 40 years of trial experience. "Dogged and very competent," he is said to be particularly effective at the pretrial stage. Up-and-comer **Steve Davidson** has a growing reputation in the field of insurance defense. Sources called him "a persistent collector of facts, who can marshal the evidence and apply it to the law." He is currently handling more than a dozen significant environmental cases.

**Clients/Work Highlights:** Lexington Public Schools; Oriental Trading; Transaction Systems Architects and Iowa West Foundation.

### Cline, Williams, Wright, Johnson & Oldfather LLP

**The Firm:** Sources were full of praise for this, the oldest firm in Nebraska, asserting its "great integrity" and first-rate reputation. It fields 20 "bright and practical" litigators across its two offices in Lincoln and Omaha, and has a particularly strong trial practice with "just fabulous senior lawyers" who are experienced in a range of matters from complex commercial disputes to securities, environmental law and insurance defense. Clients remarked: "They counsel us to see the big picture and help take the emotion out of litigation."

**The Lawyers:** **Alan Peterson** is widely respected as "an effective adversary and outstanding oral advocate." He has gained statewide recognition for his involvement in social issues, handling First Amendment and death penalty cases. Now of counsel, he is "still vigor-ous, extremely quick and thorough" and "known to make fabulous arguments." **Jim Bausch** is a "fair-minded, but well-focused and tough adversary" who opponents consider "a handful when on the other side because of his abilities." Bausch takes on all kinds of business litigation, and sources said: "He can take any lawsuit from A to Z." Similarly, **Fred Kauffman** is "a terrific trial lawyer who can handle any type of litigation." Accordingly, peers put him at the top of their list for referrals. While known as a veteran in medical malpractice defense, he is also renowned for his work for Viacom. "Bright and quick" **Kevin Colleran** enters the tables this year after impressing commentators with his knack for "getting to the heart of the matter." Clients reported that he does an exceptional job, always managing to stay on top even of difficult situations. "Knowledgeable" attorney **Andrew Strotman** is another new entry. He is recognized for complex litigation and white-collar crime, and "does a very good job of counseling the client."

**Clients/Work Highlights:** Viacom; GWR Wealth Management; Securities America and The R.H. Johnson Company.

### Fraser Stryker Law Firm

See firm details p.1245

**The Firm:** This large group of 24 litigators continues to shine. "An excellent insurance defense trial firm," it benefits from relationships with "tremendous clients." For example, it has acted as counsel for the State of Nebraska, successfully removing two of the three main claims against the state involving an outbreak of hepatitis C in Fremont. Attorneys are gifted at handling complex commercial and employment litigation, and do not shy away from trying cases. Notably, the team represented a bank in a case that involved an alleged violation of an employee's First Amendment rights. The case was tried three times: the first trial verdict awarded $1.5 million to the employee, the second was in favor of the bank, and in the third trial the bank also prevailed.

**The Lawyers:** Peers were unanimous in their assessment of **Joe Meusey** as "one of the best and most respected trial lawyers in the state." Described as "top dog" for professional negligence, he has a general practice and often represents closely held businesses and parties involved in class actions. **Wayne Mark** is "a formidable advocate who won't give anything away." He has a broad range of experience in commercial litigation and a niche in construction contracts, but is shifting his focus toward mediation. Peers found him to be ethical and straightforward, calling him "a real honorable guy." **Joe Jones** is a "diligent" trial lawyer who is recognized this year for his involvement in class action defense. Sources remarked: "*He takes care of business and gets things done.*" They also singled out "*aggressive*" up-and-comer **Mike Coyle** for his insurance defense practice. "*You see him in more and more important cases,*" researchers were told. He has additionally had involvement as a plaintiff lawyer in some important personal injury cases, and acts as lead counsel for the State of Nebraska in the hepatitis C litigation. His colleague **Mark Laughlin** is also developing a reputation for insurance defense work. Peers recommended that he be ranked, describing him as "*an intelligent strategist.*"

**Clients/Work Highlights:** The State of Nebraska; Minnesota Lawyers Mutual; Omaha Public Power District; Level 3 Communications; State Farm and Children's Hospital of Omaha.

## McGrath North Mullin & Kratz PC

**The Firm:** This "*hard-working, honest, ethical firm*" has a deep and wide-ranging trial practice that encompasses everything from environmental law to labor and employment law. Commercial disputes, M&A, products liability and insurance defense also feature in the group's caseload. The team of around 40 litigators is "*not afraid of giving you an opinion*" and "*sharper with the pencil than others.*" Clients endorsed the group for being thoroughly prepared and having excellent presentation skills, while peers noted that lawyers were happy to travel and try cases in other cities.

**The Lawyers:** "*Charming and diligent*" attorney **Jim Fitzgerald** is "*the go-to guy for ConAgra,*" according to sources. He has a broad practice that covers complex lawsuits and business disputes. He is currently handling a number of cases involving toxic torts in various parts of the country. Clients reported: "*If he says something you can count on it.*" Highly respected trial lawyer **Leo Knowles** "*has a great record*" in all types of business litigation and products liability, particularly in the area of food safety. "*Passionate but very fair to work with,*" **John**

**Passarelli** heads the firm's intellectual property practice, acting as lead counsel for Rolex and Ford. He has a varied caseload with a heavy focus on trademark litigation and transactional work. He garnered strong praise from his clients, who declared: "*He's got an extremely capable legal mind*" and "*I'd trust my life with him – I wouldn't hesitate to trade my right arm for him!*" **Bill Hargens** has a growing reputation as a talented trial lawyer. He is observed to be "*very meticulous in preparing his cases, and does a nice job in trial.*" According to competitors, **Terrence O'Hare** "*handles tough cases, and handles them well.*" He brings over 30 years of experience to his areas of specialization – class actions, insurance litigation and matters related to the aviation sector. Also rated is former US Attorney for Nebraska **Edward Warin**, who entered private practice some 25 years ago. Since then he has developed "*a great reputation as a trial lawyer*" and specializes in both litigation and government regulatory advice. Peers deemed him "*particularly effective on white-collar crime,*" although this is just one element of his broad caseload.

**Clients/Work Highlights:** ConAgra; American Automobile Association; First National Bank of Omaha; Farm Credits Services of America; Valmont Industries; Physicians Mutual; Omaha Airport Authority and First Data.

## Band 2

### Lamson, Dugan & Murray, LLP

**The Firm:** Sources celebrated this firm for the number and caliber of its trial lawyers, particularly among the younger ranks. A 20-strong team of "*outstanding*" litigators handles a range of work, including commercial and environmental cases and a notable volume of railroad litigation. Insurance defense is the group's crowning glory, and it is expert in medical malpractice matters, encompassing state and federal court trial litigation and appeals, administrative proceedings and arbitrations. Recent highlights include defending the City of Omaha in an annexation case that attracted widespread publicity throughout the state.

**The Lawyers:** "*One of the premier litigators in the state,*" **Bill Lamson** has done much to shape the reputation of the firm. This "*workaholic*" is "*about as good as it gets*" for medical malpractice and commercial disputes. Sources praised him for his courtesy and excellent judgment, calling him "*a fabulous trial lawyer and old warhorse who is still at the top of his game.*" A former managing partner of the firm, "*intelligent and hard-working*" **William Johnson** handles commercial litigation, products liability and professional negligence. "*He's good at analyzing cases and writes good briefs,*" researchers were told.

**Clients/Work Highlights:** As well as the City of Omaha and Union Pacific, the firm represents various medical malpractice insurance companies.

## Band 3

### Blackwell Sanders Peper Martin LLP
See firm details p.1212

**The Firm:** This multifaceted firm fields 120 skilled litigators nationwide, with 15 of them working in Omaha. In a broad practice, there is an emphasis on complex business litigation, securities and regulatory work. Although sources agreed that the Omaha group does not have a long track record in the state, they noted that lawyers were "*professional in their approach*" and "*good at laying out the pros and cons for businesses.*" Clients were impressed with the team's aggressive courtroom style and volunteered this piece of advice on selecting an attorney: "*If you're going to go to war, make sure yours is better than theirs.*" Recent highlights include obtaining a temporary restraining order barring the Missouri Securities Division's suspension of Waddell & Reed's state broker-dealer registration for 14 days, which allowed the company to resume full broker-dealer activities in Missouri.

**The Lawyers:** "*Experienced and smart*" litigator **Tom Dahlk** (see p.1243) specializes in securities cases and divides his time between Omaha and Missouri. Forthright and frank about his recommendations, "*he doesn't pull any punches.*" After seeing him in action, clients branded him an excellent trial attorney and "*quite often a bulldog.*"

**Clients/Work Highlights:** Ag Processing; Gordmans; QA3 Financial; The Gallup Organization; Mutual of Omaha Insurance Company; Waddell & Reed; Ameritrade and Roberts Dairy.

### Cassem Tierney Adams Gotch & Douglas

**The Firm:** This old-line litigation boutique has a niche in insurance defense work. Founded in 1956 as a spin-off from the Nebraska firm Kennedy Holland, the group boasts "*tremendously experienced*" trial attorneys. All 19 of the firm's lawyers work on litigation in some shape or form, either in support or out in the field. Areas of special interest are professional negligence, personal injury and drug and medical device cases; however, all kinds of business and commercial litigation are covered, with products liability and airplane litigation featuring in the group's caseload.

**The Lawyers:** **Mike Kinney** is a "*really knowledgeable*" insurance attorney who has across-the-board expertise in medical malpractice matters. He recently brought to a close a prolonged liver transplant lawsuit in which the Supreme Court affirmed the verdict for the defense given by the jury at trial. "*Outstanding*" **Charlie Gotch** is highly recommended by peers, with one describing him as "*the essence of a trial lawyer – I don't know anyone who tries harder and is more thorough than him.*" He has represented significant pharmaceutical clients on drug liability cases. Like his colleagues, **Jack Douglas** is a courtroom veteran. "*Well prepared*" and highly skilled, he has experience in a wide range of matters.

**Clients/Work Highlights:** COPIC Insurance; Zurich; St. Paul Travelers; Wyeth; CNA Insurance

Companies; Hertz Claim Management and Lindsay Manufacturing.

## Erickson & Sederstrom, PC

**The Firm:** Commercial litigation and insurance defense are the litigation staples of this *"professional"* firm. On the commercial side, 15 practiced attorneys handle a mixture of contract litigation, securities and construction law. From an insurance defense standpoint, personal injury, products liability and workers' compensation all feature.

**The Lawyers:** Leading lawyer **Tom Culhane** is revered for being *"about as buttoned-down, bright and attentive as they come."* He dazzled peers, who judged his professionalism and calm demeanor perfect for insurance litigation. *"He has that great combination of being a very smart person who's impossible not to like,"* they said. *"He makes you feel like he's dealt with you fairly and never gives an inch."* Top-class mediator **John Brownrigg** has *"the best reputation in town"* for complex mediation. Direct and *"full of zip,"* he is known for giving his clients strong opinions on both sides. Sources noted that he was focusing more and more on mediation.

**Clients/Work Highlights:** West Corporation; Berkshire Hathaway Homestate Companies; Columbia Insurance Group; Prairie Construction; Lueder Construction and Upland Construction.

## Band 4

## Kutak Rock LLP

**The Firm:** This firm has a growing litigation practice in Omaha, although it is more commonly viewed in its national context by other lawyers. A team of *"real smart"* attorneys specializes in complex civil litigation, representing corporate and individual clients in courts, arbitrations and mediations throughout the country.

**The Lawyers:** **Bart McLeay** was marked out for being a trial lawyer who *"does a nice job."* Technically proficient, bright and smooth, *"he can definitely work up a big case."* His colleague **Bob Slovek**, who is well respected in the community, has a wide-ranging practice handling commercial litigation and products liability. Peers noted his *"aggressive quality."*

**Clients/Work Highlights:** An excellent client roster

includes Wal-Mart and First National Bank of Omaha.

## Other Notable Practitioners

*"Talented and "intelligent"* **David Domina** of Domina Law plc LLO has an infamous trial practice. Trying cases all over the country, he specializes in high-profile complex litigation that is uncommonly difficult or costly, or that needs to be rescued midstream. *"He'll tackle virtually any case and is prepared to take it as far as he has to,"* researchers learned. One peer reported: *"When you've got him on the other side you know you're in for the long haul as he leaves no stone unturned."* Clearly a pretty unique character, Domina provoked a variety of responses from sources, although mostly they admired his *"classic courtroom skills."* **Dennis Thomte** of Thomte, Mazour & Niebergall, L.L.C. is a well-respected patent litigation lawyer who has earned himself the name *"Mr. Patent"* among his peers. One of a small group in Nebraska, he is very experienced and *"definitely the go-to patent lawyer in town."*

# REAL ESTATE

| Real Estate Leading Firms | |
|---|---|
| 1 | BAIRD HOLM LLP *Omaha* |
| | FULLENKAMP, DOYLE & JOBEUN *Omaha* |
| | PANSING HOGAN ERNST & BACHMAN *Omaha* |
| 2 | BLACKWELL SANDERS PEPER MARTIN *Omaha* |
| | FRASER STRYKER LAW FIRM *Omaha* |
| | KUTAK ROCK LLP *Omaha* |
| 3 | CROKER, HUCK, KASHER, DEWITT *Omaha* |
| | MCGRATH NORTH MULLIN & KRATZ *Omaha* |

## Band 1

## Baird Holm LLP

**The Firm:** *"They don't just pay lip service, they deliver the goods"* was the general view of this firm's real estate practice. A multidisciplinary team of nine lawyers handles a mixture of transactional work, litigation and environmental issues. Sophisticated transactional work constitutes the bulk of the practice, with leasing and mortgage lending being carried out on a national scale. *"Creative"* attorneys incorporate land use, planning and development, and some construction work into their caseloads, drawing from a substantial client base of financial institutions and owners of real estate. *"No 'ifs' or 'buts', they are all excellent lawyers,"* affirmed peers.

**The Lawyers:** *"Effective negotiator"* **Scott Dye** has real breadth of experience; his expertise extends to land use, planning and development, leasing and construction, purchases and sales. Peers reported: *"He's an outstanding academic lawyer who's able to reach practical results,"* conceding that he was patient, approachable, and up-to-date on current trends.

Dye's caseload currently features mixed-use developments and a number of deals for an Omaha client that is leasing office space nationwide. **Larry Kritenbrink** is *"a first-rate person and lawyer."* He too has a national practice which tends to focus on agricultural financing, mortgages and commercial lending. A substantial portion of his work is for the providers of construction loans which are then converted into permanent, long-term loans.

**Clients/Work Highlights:** Rabobank; Omaha Public Schools; Nebraska Methodist Health System; Great Western Bank; Connectivity and MSI Systems Integrators.

## Fullenkamp, Doyle & Jobeun

**The Firm:** This boutique firm is *"still the strongest for bread-and-butter real estate,"* according to sources. Five attorneys specialize in development and regulatory work, incorporating zoning and subdivision matters. The group benefits from a good relationship with the City of Omaha's planning board, enabling it to keep abreast of the current trend toward commercial development, particularly in the downtown area. *"They're at the top for development,"* agreed sources, who prized the team's technical skills.

**The Lawyers:** Highly acclaimed lawyer **John Fullenkamp** is *"the best land use attorney in the city without a doubt – he understands the dynamics as well as anyone."* Honest and experienced, he *"knows the ropes"* and *"gets his projects approved expeditiously."* Up-and-coming lawyer **Larry Jobeun** wins plaudits for having *"really matured over the years."* A talented transactional lawyer in Fullenkamp's mold, sources agreed: *"He'll take that practice and be very successful with it."*

**Clients/Work Highlights:** Hearthstone Homes; Celebrity Homes; KVI and Boyer Young.

## Pansing Hogan Ernst & Bachman LLP

**The Firm:** Commentators praised the *"great depth"* of this firm's real estate practice and acknowledged its sizable share of the local development market. Clients are typically involved in the development of shopping centers, office buildings, residential subdivisions and apartment complexes. The firm also works on sales, purchases, leases and loans. *"They do a great job for their clients,"* reported peers of the 15 *"very capable, straightforward"* attorneys.

**The Lawyers:** **John Bachman** is a *"no-nonsense, get-the-deal-done guy,"* whom peers found easy to work with, as well as being *"conscientious"* and attentive to detail. He has recently been involved in a complex transaction in Texas. **Dennis Hogan** is recognized as *"one of the top names for zoning and land use."* He has a long track record in development and commands the respect of the market. Up-and-comer **Jim Buser** is commended both for his transactional work and for his bank-lending practice. He is said to be an excellent technician who is *"certainly learning the trade well."*

**Clients/Work Highlights:** Lanoha Development; Horgan Development; Lerner; Rogers Development; BHI Development; NP Dodge and CBS Home Real Estate.

## Band 2

## Blackwell Sanders Peper Martin LLP

See firm details p.1212

**The Firm:** Headquartered in Kansas City, this full-service firm has *"a nice presence in Omaha,"* and is *"certainly developing its client base,"* observed interviewees. It has a diverse real estate practice, with six attorneys in Omaha counseling regional and national clients on a range of matters, from purchases and sales to development projects and leasing. The team also represents banks, insurance companies and mortgage lenders on traditional lending, complex mortgage loans and mortgage securitizations. Recent highlights include representing Gallup in the acquisition and development of the new $45 million Gallup University in Omaha.

**The Lawyers:** *"Deal person"* **John Katelman** (see p.1243) *"really understands the dynamics of real estate,"* admired sources. He devotes most of his time to purchase, sale and leasing transactions and has niche expertise in redevelopment projects involving agreements with the City of Omaha. For example, he was key in helping Gallup in its negotiations with the city for the land acquisition, development and financing of its university campus. Peers admired his easygoing, *"low-key, but extremely capable"* personality.

**Clients/Work Highlights:** Mutual of Omaha Insurance; Centris Federal Credit Union; Wells Fargo; First National Bank of Omaha; First Data Resources; Grubb & Ellis/Pacific Realty; No Frills Supermarkets; North Central Group and Pacific Life Insurance.

## Fraser Stryker Law Firm
See firm details p.1245

**The Firm:** Considered one of the top law firms in Omaha, Fraser Stryker is well known for its work in transactional real estate. Four *"high-quality"* attorneys are involved in buying, selling, leasing, financing, and recently some notable development work. With regard to larger, higher profile deals, sources noted it was *"picking up a lot of experience of late."* Highlights include representing the Omaha Performing Arts Society in a $90 million project that opened in October 2005, and involvement in a downtown row house development worth $30 million.

**The Lawyers:** **Bob Rieke** earned accolades for *"working hard to be a deal-maker not a deal-breaker."* An excellent technician and *"a real pusher,"* his strengths lie in the transactional area. Peers praised his ability to connect easily with people.

**Clients/Work Highlights:** Broadmoor Development; Bluestone Development; Noddle; Magnum Resources and Durham Resources.

## Kutak Rock LLP

**The Firm:** Twenty-five *"strong individuals"* practice in the Omaha office of this broad-based national firm. It has a reputation for carrying out complex financial transactions; indeed, these are integral to its real estate practice. Finance aside, local development work is increasingly coming to the fore, with the group taking an active involvement in downtown Omaha redevelopment. Recent national credits for the team include assisting Wal-Mart in its acquisition and development of nearly 50 properties in seven states.

**The Lawyers:** *"Bright guy"* **Mike Curry** enjoys an excellent reputation as the senior lead lawyer in the team. Commentators view him as experienced and knowledgeable.

**Clients/Work Highlights:** Clients include prominent developers, retailers, investment funds and financial institutions, among others.

## Band 3

### Croker, Huck, Kasher, DeWitt, Anderson & Gonderinger, P.C.

**The Firm:** This compact firm is acknowledged for its municipal law, zoning and local development expertise. A team of six is skilled in carrying out transactional work for a range of clients, including mortgage lenders, title companies, builders, real estate brokers and private individuals.

**The Lawyers:** Experienced land use lawyer **Bob Huck** was named by sources as *"the one to go to for large-scale projects."* Well-connected locally, he has gained exposure for carrying out zoning and subdivision work. **Rick Anderson** has a broad practice which includes dealing with a number of Sanitary and Improvement Districts (SIDs), unique to Nebraska. He won praise for being *"diligent and aggressive, but not in an unfriendly way; he pursues his clients' interests without being offensive."*

**Clients/Work Highlights:** Bancroft Property & Casualty; Marathon Realty; Noddle; NP Dodge and Wells Fargo.

### McGrath North Mullin & Kratz PC

**The Firm:** This firm is *"a leading contender for complex real estate transactions,"* according to sources. Seven *"able"* attorneys counsel in various aspects of commercial real estate, including the acquisition and disposition of properties, leasing, title and drafting issues. Development and zoning work constitute a smaller part of the practice. The team's reputation is such that it serves a national client base and is involved in a number of multistate transactions.

**The Lawyers:** *"Practical and visionary"* real estate lawyer **Lee Hamann** won the backing of the market for his ability to negotiate, value, and document complex transactions. *"Bright and softly spoken,"* he impressed peers with his common-sense approach and attention to detail.

**Clients/Work Highlights:** ConAgra; PJ Morgan Real Estate; McCarthy and Valmont Industries.

### Other Notable Practitioners

**Jerry Slusky** brings his skills from Gross & Welch, PC to Slusky Law, LLC, which opened in Omaha in January 2005. Chairman and founder of the firm, he is an expert in land development, zoning, and municipal law. *"Well-connected locally"* and *"not afraid to represent his client, even when he doesn't stand to benefit,"* Slusky impressed sources with his confidence and the commitment to every project he got involved in. He is currently representing the Nebraska Association of Commercial Property Owners on a pending Stormwater Bill.

# Leaders in Nebraska

**ACKERMAN, Jill** Baird, Holm, McEachen, Pedersen, Hamann & Strasheim LLP, Omaha
402 344 0500
*Recommended in Litigation*

**ANDERSON, Richard**
Croker, Huck, Kasher, DeWitt, Anderson & Gonderinger, P.C., Omaha
402 391 6777
*Recommended in Real Estate*

**BACHMAN, John**
Pansing Hogan Ernst & Bachman LLP, Omaha 402 397 5500
*Recommended in Real Estate*

**BARRETT, Patrick**
McGrath North Mullin & Kratz PC, Omaha 402 341 3070
*Recommended in Employment*

**BASS, Jo**
Kutak Rock LLP, Omaha
402 346 6000
*Recommended in Corporate/M&A*

**BAUSCH, James**
Cline, Williams, Wright, Johnson & Oldfather LLP, Omaha 402 397 1700
*Recommended in Litigation*

**BLECHA, Kirk**
Baird, Holm, McEachen, Pedersen, Hamann & Strasheim LLP, Omaha
402 344 0500
*Recommended in Litigation*

**BOGUE, Stevenson**
McGrath North Mullin & Kratz PC, Omaha 402 341 3070
*Recommended in Employment*

**BROWNRIGG, John**
Erickson & Sederstrom, PC, Omaha
402 397 2200
*Recommended in Litigation*

**BURT, Donald**
Cline, Williams, Wright, Johnson & Oldfather LLP, Lincoln 402 474 6900
*Recommended in Corporate/M&A*

**BUSER, James**
Pansing Hogan Ernst & Bachman LLP, Omaha 402 397 5500
*Recommended in Real Estate*

**COLLERAN, Kevin**
Cline, Williams, Wright, Johnson & Oldfather LLP, Omaha 402 397 1700
*Recommended in Litigation*

**COYLE, Michael**
Fraser Stryker Law Firm, Omaha
402 341 6000
*Recommended in Litigation*

**CULHANE, Thomas**
Erickson & Sederstrom, PC, Omaha
402 397 2200
*Recommended in Litigation*

**CURRY, Michael**
Kutak Rock LLP, Omaha 402 346 6000
*Recommended in Real Estate*

**DAHLK, Thomas**
Blackwell Sanders Peper Martin LLP, Omaha
402 964 5031
tdahlk@blackwellsanders.com
*Recommended in Litigation*
**Practice Areas:** Business and commercial litigation; securities industry regulation and litigation.
**Prof. Memberships:** Admitted to practice, Nebraska Supreme Court (1977); US Supreme Court (1992). Member, American Bar Association, Section on Litigation; Nebraska Association of Trial Attorneys; Omaha Bar Association. Fellow, Nebraska State Bar Foundation, 1999.
**Career:** Joined firm as Partner, 1998; Member, Advisory Board, 2000-03; Office Managing Partner, Omaha, 2003-present.
**Publications:** Author, 'Class Actions - The Nebraska Procedure', 'Nebraska Law Review' (1982); and 'Real Estate Partnerships and the Securities Laws: A Primer', 'Creighton Law Review' (1979).
**Personal:** JD (magna cum laude), Creighton University, 1977; BA (with distinction), University of Wisconsin, 1974.

**DAVIDSON, Steven**
Baird, Holm, McEachen, Pedersen, Hamann & Strasheim LLP, Omaha
402 344 0500
*Recommended in Litigation*

**DITTRICK, William**
Baird, Holm, McEachen, Pedersen, Hamann & Strasheim LLP, Omaha
402 344 0500
*Recommended in Litigation*

**DIXON, Joyce A**
Blackwell Sanders Peper Martin LLP, Omaha
402 964 5020
jdixon@blackwellsanders.com
*Recommended in Corporate/M&A*
**Practice Areas:** Finance and lending; mergers and acquisitions; real estate.
**Prof. Memberships:** Admitted to practice in Nebraska (1975), US District Court of Appeals, Eighth Circuit; and US District Court, District of Nebraska. Member, American Bar Association, Nebraska State Bar Association, Committees on Budget and Inquiry for Second Judicial District; and Omaha Bar Association.
**Career:** Joined firm as Partner, 2000; Member, Advisory Board Committee, 2003-present.
**Personal:** JD (summa cum laude), Creighton University, 1975; Editor-in-Chief, 'Creighton Law Review;' BA (with high honors), University of Illinois.

**DOMINA, David**
Domina Law plc LLO, Omaha
402 493 4100
*Recommended in Litigation*

**DOUGLAS, John**
Cassem Tierney Adams Gotch & Douglas, Omaha 402 390 0300
*Recommended in Litigation*

**DYE, Scott**
Baird, Holm, McEachen, Pedersen, Hamann & Strasheim LLP, Omaha
402 344 0500
*Recommended in Real Estate*

**FAHLESON, Mark**
Rembolt Ludtke LLP, Lincoln
402 475 5100
*Recommended in Employment*

**FITZGERALD, James**
McGrath North Mullin & Kratz PC, Omaha 402 341 3070
*Recommended in Litigation*

**FREEMAN, Robert**
Fraser Stryker Law Firm, Omaha
402 341 6000
*Recommended in Corporate/M&A*

**FULLENKAMP, John**
Fullenkamp, Doyle & Jobeun, Omaha
402 334 0700
*Recommended in Real Estate*

**GEHRING, Stephen**
Cline, Williams, Wright, Johnson & Oldfather LLP, Omaha 402 397 1700
*Recommended in Corporate/M&A*

**GOTCH, Charles**
Cassem Tierney Adams Gotch & Douglas, Omaha 402 390 0300
*Recommended in Litigation*

**GOTSDINER, Gary**
McGill, Gotsdiner, Workman & Lepp PC LLO, Omaha 402 492 9200
*Recommended in Corporate/M&A*

**HAMANN, Lee**
McGrath North Mullin & Kratz PC, Omaha 402 341 3070
*Recommended in Real Estate*

**HANDLOS, Bryan**
Kutak Rock LLP, Omaha
402 346 6000
*Recommended in Corporate/M&A*

**HARDING, William**
Harding Shultz & Downs, Lincoln
402 434 3000
*Recommended in Employment*

**HARGENS, William**
McGrath North Mullin & Kratz PC, Omaha 402 341 3070
*Recommended in Litigation*

**HEDICAN, Chris**
Baird, Holm, McEachen, Pedersen, Hamann & Strasheim LLP, Omaha
402 344 0500
*Recommended in Employment*

**HEFFLINGER, David**
McGrath North Mullin & Kratz PC, Omaha 402 341 3070
*Recommended in Corporate/M&A*

**HERDZINA, John**
Abrahams Kaslow & Cassman LLP, Omaha 402 392 1250
*Recommended in Corporate/M&A*

**HOGAN III, Dennis**
Pansing Hogan Ernst & Bachman LLP, Omaha 402 397 5500
*Recommended in Real Estate*

**HUCK, Robert**
Croker, Huck, Kasher, DeWitt, Anderson & Gonderinger, P.C., Omaha
402 391 6777
*Recommended in Real Estate*

**JESSEN, Paul**
Koley Jessen P.C., Omaha
402 390 9500
*Recommended in Corporate/M&A*

**JOBEUN, Larry**
Fullenkamp, Doyle & Jobeun, Omaha
402 334 0700
*Recommended in Real Estate*

**JOHNSON, Thomas**
Baird, Holm, McEachen, Pedersen, Hamann & Strasheim LLP, Omaha
402 344 0500
*Recommended in Litigation*

**JOHNSON, William**
Lamson, Dugan & Murray, LLP, Omaha
402 397 7300
*Recommended in Litigation*

**JONES, Joseph**
Fraser Stryker Law Firm, Omaha
402 341 6000
*Recommended in Litigation*

**KASLOW, Howard**
Abrahams Kaslow & Cassman LLP, Omaha 402 392 1250
*Recommended in Corporate/M&A*

**KATELMAN, John**
Blackwell Sanders Peper Martin LLP, Omaha 402 964 5010
jkatelman@blackwellsanders.com
*Recommended in Real Estate*
**Practice Areas:** Real estate; commercial transactions; financial institutions; mergers and acquisitions.
**Prof. Memberships:** Admitted to practice in Nebraska (1973) and US District Court, District of Nebraska (1973). Member, American Bar Association, Sections on Real Property and Probate and Trust Law; Nebraska State Bar Association; and Omaha Bar Association.

**Career:** Joined firm as Partner, 1996.
**Personal:** JD, Creighton University, 1972; BS, University of Nebraska, 1970.

### KAUFFMAN, Fred
Cline, Williams, Wright, Johnson & Oldfather LLP, Omaha 402 397 1700
*Recommended in Litigation*

### KINNEY, Michael
Cassem Tierney Adams Gotch & Douglas, Omaha 402 390 0300
*Recommended in Litigation*

### KNOWLES, Leo
McGrath North Mullin & Kratz PC, Omaha 402 341 3070
*Recommended in Litigation*

### KRITENBRINK, Lawrence
Baird, Holm, McEachen, Pedersen, Hamann & Strasheim LLP, Omaha 402 344 0500
*Recommended in Real Estate*

### LAMSON, William
Lamson, Dugan & Murray, LLP, Omaha 402 397 7300
*Recommended in Litigation*

### LAUGHLIN, Gerald
Baird, Holm, McEachen, Pedersen, Hamann & Strasheim LLP, Omaha 402 344 0500
*Recommended in Litigation*

### LAUGHLIN, Mark
Fraser Stryker Law Firm, Omaha 402 341 6000
*Recommended in Litigation*

### LOUDON, Timothy
Berens & Tate PC, Omaha 402 391 1991
*Recommended in Employment*

### MARK, Wayne
Fraser Stryker Law Firm, Omaha 402 341 6000
*Recommended in Litigation*

### MCLEAY, Bartholomew
Kutak Rock LLP, Omaha 402 346 6000
*Recommended in Litigation*

### MEUSEY, Joseph
Fraser Stryker Law Firm, Omaha 402 341 6000
*Recommended in Litigation*

### MILLER, Roger
McGrath North Mullin & Kratz PC, Omaha 402 341 3070
*Recommended in Employment*

### MOORE, Scott
Baird, Holm, McEachen, Pedersen, Hamann & Strasheim LLP, Omaha 402 344 0500
*Recommended in Employment*

### O'HARE, Terrence
McGrath North Mullin & Kratz PC, Omaha 402 341 3070
*Recommended in Litigation*

### PARSONAGE, Ronald
Abrahams Kaslow & Cassman LLP, Omaha 402 392 1250
*Recommended in Corporate/M&A*

### PASSARELLI, John
McGrath North Mullin & Kratz PC, Omaha 402 341 3070
*Recommended in Litigation*

### PETERSON, Alan
Cline, Williams, Wright, Johnson & Oldfather LLP, Lincoln 402 474 6900
*Recommended in Litigation*

### PIGSLEY, Jerry
Harding Shultz & Downs, Lincoln 402 434 3000
*Recommended in Employment*

### RICHARDSON, Todd
Blackwell Sanders Peper Martin LLP, Omaha 402 964 5032
trichardson@blackwellsanders.com
*Recommended in Corporate/M&A*
**Practice Areas:** Commercial transactions; closely held businesses; mergers and acquisitions; securities; venture capital/private equity financing and funds.
**Prof. Memberships:** Admitted to practice in Nebraska (1991). Board of Directors, Invest Nebraska and Midlands Venture Forum, and Member of Omaha Chamber of Commerce Target Advisory Group on Entrepreneurship.
**Career:** Joined firm as Partner, 1998.
**Personal:** JD (with highest distinction), University of Nebraska at Omaha, 1991; Editor-in-Chief, 'Nebraska Law Review'; BS and BA (magna cum laude), University of Nebraska at Omaha, 1988.

### RIEKE, Robert
Fraser Stryker Law Firm, Omaha 402 341 6000
*Recommended in Real Estate*

### ROSSITER, Robert
Fraser Stryker Law Firm, Omaha 402 341 6000
*Recommended in Employment*

### ROZMARIN, George
Fraser Stryker Law Firm, Omaha 402 341 6000
*Recommended in Employment*

### SCHORR, Mark
Erickson & Sederstrom PC, Lincoln 402 476 1000
*Recommended in Employment*

### SEDERSTROM, Charles
Erickson & Sederstrom, PC, Omaha 402 397 2200
*Recommended in Corporate/M&A*

### SHULTZ, Jack
Harding Shultz & Downs, Lincoln 402 434 3000
*Recommended in Employment*

### SLOVEK, Robert
Kutak Rock LLP, Omaha 402 346 6000
*Recommended in Litigation*

### SLUSKY, Jerry
Slusky Law LLC, Omaha 402 991 5777
*Recommended in Real Estate*

### STEVENSON, Randy
Baird, Holm, McEachen, Pedersen, Hamann & Strasheim LLP, Omaha 402 344 0500
*Recommended in Employment*

### STROTMAN, Andrew
Cline, Williams, Wright, Johnson & Oldfather LLP, Lincoln 402 474 6900
*Recommended in Litigation*

### THOMTE, Dennis
Thomte, Mazour & Niebergall, L.L.C., Omaha 402 392 2280
*Recommended in Litigation*

### TURNER, Steven
Baird, Holm, McEachen, Pedersen, Hamann & Strasheim LLP, Omaha 402 344 0500
*Recommended in Corporate/M&A*

### WARIN, Edward
McGrath North Mullin & Kratz PC, Omaha 402 341 3070
*Recommended in Litigation*

### ZEILINGER, John
Baird, Holm, McEachen, Pedersen, Hamann & Strasheim LLP, Omaha 402 344 0500
*Recommended in Corporate/M&A*

# FRASER STRYKER

## THE FIRM

**Number of partners:** 28
**Number of other lawyers:** 18

**FIRM OVERVIEW:** Founded in 1898, Fraser Stryker has grown from a small group of dedicated lawyers representing the businesses that fueled Omaha's growth to a nationally-recognized law firm representing local and multinational corporations in all major litigation and commercial practice areas. Whether paving the way for cutting-edge telecommunications networks, defending class actions throughout the country, or working locally to bring a world-class arena and convention center to Omaha, Fraser Stryker is known for its experience, breadth, and vision, and for helping clients build and protect their business interests and assets.

## MAIN AREAS OF PRACTICE:

**Business & Corporate:** The firm's business attorneys are recognized throughout the region for expert advice in all facets of corporate transactions and entity formation, structure, and operation. The firm assists its clients in locating and negotiating venture capital for new businesses. Fraser Stryker has strong expertise in corporate tax law, mergers and acquisitions, and divestitures.

**Litigation:** Litigation has been a cornerstone of Fraser Stryker's practice. The firm handles class action and other complex litigation throughout the country. The firm's success has led to several of its attorneys being selected for the American College of Trial Lawyers and the International Society of Barristers.

**Real Estate:** Fraser Stryker's real estate attorneys represent a broad range of clients in the purchase, sale, and financing of real estate. The firm has been involved in the development of major projects, including corporate business parks, and the Qwest Center Omaha Arena and Convention Center.

**Telecommunications & Technology:** The firm serves as counsel to major domestic and international communications companies, and has assisted its clients in the negotiation of right-of-way, franchise, construction, services, interconnection, and other legal arrangements. The firm also represents established and start-up information technology businesses in capitalization, product development, and sales and licensing. The firm's goal is to help their clients protect and profit from their intellectual property.

**Labor & Employment:** Fraser Stryker is a recognized leader in the area of labor and employment law, representing management. The firm's attorneys handle complex employment litigation in state and federal courts throughout the region and represent clients before the National Labor Relations Board, Equal Employment Opportunity Commission, and Office of Federal Contract Compliance Programs, among others. The firm's preventative counseling includes personnel audits, supervisory training, and employee handbook development.

**Energy & Environmental Law:** Fraser Stryker has represented Nebraska's largest electric utility for more than 60 years. The firm has expertise in the development of nuclear and fossil-fueled generating units, and also has handled complex rate actions for electric and natural gas utilities. The firm's Environmental Practice spans the entire spectrum of federal and state regulation, and includes the acquisition and development of brownfield properties.

**Healthcare:** The firm represents primary care facilities and provides counsel to physicians and other healthcare professionals. The firm regularly represents healthcare clients with respect to federal and state regulatory matters.

## HEAD OFFICE

**NEBRASKA**
500 Energy Plaza, 409 South 17th Street, **Omaha**, NE 68102
**Tel:** 402 341 6000   **Fax:** 402 341 8290
**Website:** www.fraserstryker.com

## CONTACTS

**Business & Corporate** ...............................................Robert L Freeman
**Litigation** .................................................................Joseph E Jones
**Real Estate** ..............................................................Robert W Rieke
**Telecommunications & Technology** ....................Patrick J Duffy
**Labor & Employment** ..............................................Robert F Rossiter
**Energy & Environmental** .....................................Stephen M Bruckner
**Healthcare** ...............................................................James L Quinlan

**CLIENTS:** Fraser Stryker represents domestic and international companies in a wide array of matters, including mergers, acquisitions and divestitures, telecommunications, real estate development, energy, and information technology. The firm's litigation clients include local and national companies involved as plaintiffs and defendants in complex commercial, class action, and personal injury litigation.

**INTERNATIONAL WORK:** Fraser Stryker represents international telecommunications companies and assists other clients as they pursue international trade and investments. The firm advises clients on a wide range of issues that arise in the context of global business.

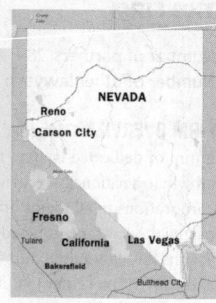

## How lawyers are ranked

Every year we carry out thousands of in-depth interviews with clients and lawyers in order to assess the reputations and expertise of business lawyers across the USA. Chambers rankings and editorial are referred to extensively by General Counsel and other purchasers of legal services who look to our recommendations when choosing their lawyers.

# CORPORATE/COMMERCIAL

### Corporate/Commercial
**Leading Firms**

1. **LIONEL SAWYER & COLLINS** *Las Vegas*
   **SCHRECK BRIGNONE** *Las Vegas*
2. **HALE LANE PEEK DENNISON AND HOWARD** *Reno*
   **JONES VARGAS** *Las Vegas*
   **KUMMER KAEMPFER BONNER** *Las Vegas*
   **WOODBURN AND WEDGE** *Reno*

### Leading Individuals

1. **BONNER Michael** *Kummer Kaempfer Bonner*
   **FOWLER John** *Woodburn and Wedge*
   **SCHULHOFER Ellen** *Schreck Brignone*
   **ZUCKER Jeffrey** *Lionel Sawyer & Collins*
2. **GARCIA David** *Hale Lane Peek Dennison*
   **GOLDSTEIN Mark** *Lionel Sawyer & Collins*
   **JONES Leslie** *Schreck Brignone*
   **WOLOSON Kenneth** *Haney, Woloson & Mullins*
3. **BARNARD Gregg** *Woodburn and Wedge*
   **DOLAN Colleen** *Lionel Sawyer & Collins*
   **DRURY Mary** *Marquis & Aurbach*
   **ETEM Craig** *Lionel Sawyer & Collins*
   **KIM Robert** *Kummer Kaempfer Bonner*
   **KLEGERMAN Neal** *Kummer Kaempfer*
   **NEWMAN James** *Hale Lane Peek Dennison*
   **VERMEYS Sonia** *Schreck Brignone*

### Up-and-coming individuals
**BATTCHER Frederick** *Hale Lane Peek Dennison*

## Band 1

### Lionel Sawyer & Collins

**The Firm:** As part of the largest firm in Nevada, this 19-strong business law group handles a wide variety of corporate finance transactions on behalf of many of the state's largest banks, hotels and casinos. Clients praise the team's ability to "*cater for all our needs*" and to "*bring the full weight of their resources to bear when it counts.*" The firm was particularly active in the luxury condominium market in 2005, acting for major clients in the development and financing of multimillion-dollar tower projects.

**The Lawyers:** Sources recognize **Jeffrey Zucker** as a leader in the corporate and real estate fields. He leads the firm's business law department and chairs the Nevada State Bar Section of Business Law. Interviewees distinguished him as "*one of the top lawyers in Nevada,*" singling out his "*results-oriented approach.*" His work includes representing the developers of the Cosmopolitan Hotel, handling the financing for luxury condominium projects and acting for out-of-state companies purchasing land in Las Vegas. **Mark Goldstein**'s corporate/commercial and real estate transactional practice acts for banks and other lenders in acquisitions and financings for condominium projects. Clients commend him for being "*a bright, super hard-working lawyer who really cares.*" Reno-based **Colleen Dolan** handles corporate matters, including securitizations, real estate acquisitions and residential development work. 2005 saw her involved in a series of casino acquisitions, a transaction on behalf of a local chain of retail outlets, and a number of loans on behalf of both lenders and borrowers. Clients and peers alike rate her "*the best lending counsel in northern Nevada*" for her "*outstanding knowledge of Nevada state law.*" **Craig Etem**'s primary expertise lies in corporate law and the handling of real estate loans and financings for regional banks and developers. He also acts as local counsel to a large number of national firms, particularly in New York, and has served as corporate counsel on a variety of stock offerings. In the past twelve months, Etem has been involved in a plethora of financings and international restructurings. Clients call him "*responsive, accurate and a pleasure to work with,*" while peers describe him as "*a corporate guru*" and "*one of Nevada's finest negotiators.*"

**Clients/Work Highlights:** Lawyers assisted with the sale of Golden Nugget casino and acted for the bank in Donald Trump's Nevada real estate acquisitions. The team also worked on IPOs for Las Vegas Sands and The Venetian. Other clients include Wynn Resorts; Somerset Development; Nevada State Bank; First Republic Bank; Morrison Homes; Cosmopolitan Hotel and Aztar Gaming.

### Schreck Brignone

**The Firm:** This well-established, full-service firm boasts expertise in M&A, project and asset finance. The practice has a particular forte in advising investors on equity public offerings and real estate finance deals in the gaming and hotel sectors. For example, lawyers acted for Wynn Resorts and Harrah's Entertainment in their acquisitions of Las Vegas real estate, and assisted national and international investors with financing and development work in the state.

**The Lawyers:** Interviewees recommend the "*phenomenal*" **Ellen Schulhofer** for her work on corporate and structured finance transactions. She fronts the firm's corporate/commercial group and covers corporate M&A and structured finance. 2005 saw her represent Wynn Resorts in the financing of a Macao-based project involving a number of Nevada properties. She also acted in the Mandalay Resort Group/MGM Mirage and Caesars Entertainment/Harrah's Entertainment mergers. **Leslie Terry Jones** is thought of as a mentor by a number of Nevada attorneys, on the basis of his long-standing experience in M&A and real estate work. He represented Harrah's Entertainment in connection with the purchase of the Horseshoe Hotel and the World Series of Poker, and regularly acts for national construction companies acquiring property in Las Vegas for the development of hotels, condominiums and timeshares. Clients value his "*high ethical standards and fantastic knowledge – he is one of the most down-to-earth practitioners in Nevada.*" **Sonia Church Vermeys**' diverse experience covers M&A, real estate, gaming and liquor licensing, construction and employment. She advised The New Frontier on the development of the Trump International Hotel & Tower. Interviewees commend her for her "*fast turnaround time, great connections and precise, straightforward manner.*"

**Clients/Work Highlights:** The team acted for Harrah's in its acquisition of the Bourbon Street Hotel and Casino, and handled Planet Hollywood's acquisition of the Aladdin Hotel & Casino. In 2005, lawyers also represented Wynn Resorts; Haggar; Station Casinos; Pinnacle Entertainment; Ruffin Gaming and Williams Development.

## Band 2

### Hale Lane Peek Dennison and Howard

**The Firm:** This impressive outfit has grown from its real estate origins to become a full-service, statewide firm with offices in Las Vegas, Reno and Carson City. Its expertise encompasses M&A, securities and tax work. Lawyers are particularly adept at undertaking instructions from developers and publicly traded companies on buyouts and stock purchases.

**The Lawyers:** **David Garcia** is a corporate transaction-focused attorney whose caseload includes M&A, securities law compliance and venture capital financings. Formerly based in Silicon Valley, he has notable experience in structuring technology-related M&A transactions. **James Newman** covers all areas of corporate and real estate work. Commentators commend his *"conscientious and responsive attitude"* when advising technology and manufacturing companies on compliance matters, healthcare law, tax, and licensing and distribution arrangements. The up-and-coming **Frederick Battcher** is known for his M&A and securities work. He regularly advises clients on private equity transactions and venture capital financings, and continues to receive related referrals from Chicago and New York-based firms.

**Clients/Work Highlights:** Key clients include Alere Medical; Haws Corporation; Avalar Network and Nevada Ventures.

### Jones Vargas

**The Firm:** This firm is renowned regionally for the depth of its bench and its capacity to handle all types of local and national financings. Key areas of expertise include M&A, litigation, government relations and gaming. Sources highlight the team for its experience in handling complex finance transactions, multistate litigation and bankruptcy. The first nationally recognized bond counsel firm in Nevada, it continues to advise several local bond issuers and underwriters.

**The Lawyers:** Craig Norville and Jodi Goodheart both command respect from peers: the former for his transactional, securities and corporate finance work, and the latter for her corporate, business and real estate capabilities.

**Clients/Work Highlights:** Notable clients include Harrah's; Business Bank of Nevada; Station Casinos; JPMorgan Securities and Lockheed Martin.

### Kummer Kaempfer Bonner Renshaw & Ferrario

See firm details p.1262

**The Firm:** As one of a small number of Nevada firms specializing in corporate securities and bond counsel work, the firm enjoys national recognition from clients. Notwithstanding such niche expertise, the team is a potent force in M&A, real estate, land use, and gaming and regulatory work. Clients are drawn to the team for its *"prestigious standing and experienced, top-class partners."*

**The Lawyers:** Sources *"think the world of"* **Michael Bonner** (see p.1257), praising his *"great technical abilities and integrity beyond reproach."* His work encompasses business acquisitions, securities, bond financing, private finance and a steady flow of gaming and regulatory work. Interviewees call him *"a rare combination – someone who understands both the intricacies of gaming and the underlying corporate security aspects of a transaction."* The *"young but already sensational"* **Robert Kim** (see p.1259) is the chairman of the Business Law Section Executive Committee of the State Bar of Nevada. A purely corporate lawyer and excellent technician with *"a calm manner and hard-working approach,"* Kim is acknowledged by clients and peers alike as *"a super-star of the future."* **Neal Klegerman** (see p.1259) is a securities lawyer who specializes in corporate transactions and federal securities law. The majority of his time is spent dealing with firms outside of Nevada. He was involved in two sizable stock issuances in 2005, each worth about $200 million.

**Clients/Work Highlights:** Lawyers were involved in a fully registered offering for Diversified Realty worth $190 million, a $200 million sale on behalf of Silver Practice Advisors and a public bond offering for Hooters Las Vegas. Other key clients include Atlantis Casino Resort; Monarch Casino & Resort; Rio All-Suite Hotel & Casino and Gaming Partners International.

### Woodburn and Wedge

**The Firm:** This long-established outfit counsels large corporate clients on business organization, M&A, and real estate and land use law. The firm is

particularly active in representing mining and utility companies, and houses dedicated water rights and environment lawyers. Other key areas of expertise include probate and tax, employment and bankruptcy law.

**The Lawyers:** **John Fowler** *"is among the finest corporate lawyers in Nevada,"* according to interviewees. He boasts US and Canadian law expertise in real estate and corporate financings, as well as niche corporate governance experience, and primarily acts for subsidiaries of major corporations based outside of Nevada. Interviewees acknowledge him to be *"top-notch – he always remains current and abreast of the latest developments."* **Gregg Barnard**'s practice encompasses M&A, long-term financings, corporate restructurings and asset-backed financings. He has also been involved with IPOs and credit card receivables transactions. An impressive roster of clients includes several nationwide commercial lenders and oil and gas corporations, a number of California-based companies and utility entities such as Sierra Pacific Resources.

**Clients/Work Highlights:** Lawyers acted for NYSE-listed Centex, subsidiaries of AGL Resources and the Regional Transportation Commission of Washoe County in 2005. Other major clients include Belco Oil & Gas; Wal-Mart; Shell; Nevada Power and Nevada Bell.

### Other Notable Practitioners

**Kenneth Woloson** of Haney, Woloson & Mullins specializes in business law, acquisitions, corporate formations and reorganizations, and real estate transactions. He also represents a number of casino hotels handling large gaming deals and remains active in construction work, estate planning, and stock and asset purchase transactions. **Mary Drury** of Marquis & Aurbach handles a mixture of corporate, real estate finance, banking and contract law. Peers describe her as *"a smart lady who ranks among Nevada's finest."*

# EMPLOYMENT

## Band 1

### Kamer Zucker & Abbott

**The Firm:** This dedicated employment and labor law firm counsels employers on a wide range of issues, including litigation and alternative dispute resolution. Lawyers cover compliance with federal employment and civil rights statutes, collective bargaining, union avoidance and prevention and remedy of harassment. Commentators affirm: *"The team has always been regarded as one of the state's mainstays – it is simply at the forefront of employment issues."*

**The Lawyers:** **Gregory Kamer** is renowned for his strength in traditional labor matters, representing hotels and casinos, financial institutions, construction companies, and healthcare facilities. As well as litigation, his practice also involves arbitration and mediation in front of bodies including the NLRB and the state's Employee-Management Relations Board. Interviewees praise his *"tenacity, commitment, outstanding knowledge and brilliant mind."* **Carol Zucker** an accomplished employment litigator, who is also heavily involved in advising clients on claim prevention as an alternative to litigation. Peers comment: *"She is obsessive in her attention to detail and has a real passion for the work."* **Scott Abbott** is

| Employment: Mainly Defendant |
| --- |
| **Leading Individuals** |
| **Senior Statesman** |
| EFROYMSON Kevin *Sole Practitioner* |
| [1] COLE Howard *Lionel Sawyer & Collins* |
| KAMER Gregory *Kamer Zucker & Abbott* |
| MOSS Gary *DLA Piper Rudnick Gray Cary* |
| ZUCKER Carol *Kamer Zucker & Abbott* |
| [2] HICKS Patrick *Littler Mendelson, PC* |
| RICCIARDI Mark *Fisher & Phillips LLP* |
| YOUCHAH Elayna *Schreck Brignone* |
| [3] ABBOTT Scott *Kamer Zucker & Abbott* |
| KISHNER Joanna *DLA Piper Rudnick Gray Cary* |
| KOTCHKA Malani *Smith & Kotchka Ltd* |
| MORGAN Ann *Jones Vargas* |
| PAUSTIAN Kathleen *Parsons Behle* |
| SMITH Gregory *Smith & Kotchka Ltd* |
| **Up-and-coming individuals** |
| DORNAK David *Lewis and Roca* |
| KELLER Edwin *Kamer Zucker & Abbott* |

| Employment: ERISA |
| --- |
| **Leading Individuals** |
| [1] BRIGNONE Andrew *Schreck Brignone* |

known for his labor and employment defense work. He handles all aspects of employment law and impresses with his *"thorough, practical knowledge and personable, thoughtful approach."* Up-and-comer **Edwin Keller** *"keeps his head even in the bloodiest of battles,"* according to commentators. His practice covers arbitration, union organizing, labor relations and discrimination claims. Peers admire his *"first-class strategy and communication skills."*

**Clients/Work Highlights:** Lawyers advise most major Nevada hotels and casinos, including the Golden Nugget, Wynn Resorts and MGM Mirage, on all aspects of employment law. Other key clients include BankWest of Nevada, Wells Fargo and Nevada Power.

## Band 2

### DLA Piper Rudnick Gray Cary US LLP
See firm details p.870

**The Firm:** This global giant's Las Vegas office has a strong emphasis on labor, employment and bankruptcy matters. Lawyers act for the majority of the state's major hotels and casinos, and represent key players in the gaming and entertainment industries.

**The Lawyers:** **Gary Moss** (see p.1260) acts for southern California-based clients as well as an array of Nevada-based entities. His expertise includes union labor law, employment laws, state laws, wage and hour matters, and contract and employee benefit negotiations. A key figure for disputes, he regularly appears before the NLRB. He represents a host of major hotels and casinos and also acts for a number of nongaming clients, who describe him as *"the*

*consummate professional; one of the best traditional labor attorneys in town."* **Joanna Kishner** (see p.1259) represents real estate companies, gaming manufacturers and airlines regarding discrimination, wrongful terminations, covenants not to compete and avoidance of class action. She has also appeared in arbitrations and mediations and advised on preventive measures to avoid litigation. Peers comment: *"She commands the respect of the judges, and has a great rapport with them,"* while clients stress that *"she molds herself to what we need, getting tough when she needs to be, and conciliatory otherwise."*

**Clients/Work Highlights:** The team counts major hotels and casinos, including MGM Grand, Stratosphere Las Vegas, Sahara and Station Casinos, among its clientele. Musicians Institute, TEKsystems and United Rentals also feature in an impressive roster of clients.

### Lionel Sawyer & Collins

**The Firm:** This busy outfit acts as labor and employment counsel in a raft of significant matters. The firm has a solid reputation for working on both traditional and more contemporary issues. On the traditional side, lawyers represent clients bargaining with unions, and assist them with all manner of labor grievances, compliance matters and collective bargaining agreement training. Nontraditional work includes all types of discrimination and antiharassment cases, investigations, pre-court administration and lawsuit representation.

**The Lawyers:** **Howard Cole** is *"a gifted speaker and a fierce advocate"* and works exclusively on the management side, representing corporate entities and doing a large share of pro bono work. He handles management election campaigns and dealings with labor unions, lawsuits with the NLRB, terminations, union scares and employment contracts. Clients refer to him as *"an exemplary lawyer with a flamboyant style,"* and applaud his *"sympathetic appreciation of emotional issues."*

**Clients/Work Highlights:** The team represented MGM Mirage in its dispute with the Culinary Workers Union. Lawyers also successfully resolved a sexual harassment case against a golf entity to the amount of $45,000, a significant knockdown from the $1 million demanded by the claimant. Other clients include KLASTV; AT&T; Nathan Adelson Hospice and Konami Gaming.

### Schreck Brignone

**The Firm:** The team counsels major organizations and individuals on all state and federal employment laws. Lawyers undertake negotiations, litigation, mediation and arbitration in state and federal courts, as well as acting for clients in front of the EEOC, the Nevada Equal Rights Commission, the NLRB and the DOL.

**The Lawyers:** Sources continue to regard **Andrew Brignone** as *"the guy to go to in ERISA matters,"* thanks to his *"astute understanding and application of the law."* His practice involves counseling employers on contributions to retirement savings funds, as well as more general employment issues, including

the drafting of Nevada legislation. **Elayna Youchah** works on the management side, covering issues including wrongful terminations, breach of contract, emotional distress, sexual harassment, slander and defamation. She also advises on union-related labor arbitrations and assists in the writing and reviewing of contracts, policies and employee handbooks. Commentators remark: *"She has come a long way in the last five years, making significant advances in litigation and arbitration."* Clients value her *"excellent work product and wonderful understanding of a client's needs."*

**Clients/Work Highlights:** MGM Mirage; Luxor; Excalibur; EG&G; JT3; Home Depot and Pulte Homes.

## Band 3

### Fisher & Phillips LLP
See firm details p.732

**The Firm:** This national firm's labor and employment law focus flavors its Las Vegas office, where the team counsels employers in litigation prevention and defense, as well as pension and benefits, wage and hour disputes and disability law. Lawyers are also involved in the drafting and reviewing of employment contracts, policies and procedures.

**The Lawyers:** **Mark Ricciardi** (see p.1260) is *"an icon in traditional labor law, a great speaker and a fine litigator,"* according to sources. The founding partner of the firm's Las Vegas office, he is credited with bringing outside attention to the Nevada employment market through his strategically integrated national practice. His *"magnificent communication skills and thoroughly pleasant manner"* are often found useful when he's representing gaming companies.

**Clients/Work Highlights:** The firm represents national hotel chains; communications companies; hospitals and healthcare entities, and gaming companies and manufacturers.

### Littler Mendelson, PC
See firm details p.333

**The Firm:** The 18-strong Nevada-based team of this nationally recognized labor and employment law firm has a reputation for its vigorous and aggressive representation of management in complex and high-profile labor and employment matters. Key areas of expertise include litigation, class action avoidance and defense, employee benefits, unfair competition and workers' compensation.

**The Lawyers:** Sources give **Patrick Hicks** (see p.1258) much of the credit for making the firm one of the state's leading outfits for employment law. His work with large national firms has brought growth to the Las Vegas market and his *"affable, cooperative, practical and organized"* approach makes him a favorite with clients.

**Clients/Work Highlights:** The team represents a great number of national entities, including hotel chains, financial institutions and power and construction companies.

## Smith & Kotchka Ltd

**The Firm:** This boutique houses a husband and wife team specializing in management defense. The firm covers employee benefits, wrongful termination, industrial insurance compensation and labor-management relations. Notwithstanding the recent ascendancy of large national firms in the state, the firm maintains a loyal and impressive client base.

**The Lawyers:** **Gregory Smith** practices traditional labor law, with a focus on employment at will, collective bargaining and employment discrimination. **Malani Kotchka** specializes in labor management, employment discrimination, sexual harassment, industrial insurance and collective bargaining. Both enjoy a strong reputation among peers and clients alike.

**Clients/Work Highlights:** The firm handles matters for major names in the gaming, utilities and construction industries, including Boyd Gaming; Las Vegas Valley Water District; City of North Las Vegas and Meadow Valley Contractors.

## Other Notable Practitioners

Sole practitioner **Kevin Efroymson** is widely regarded as *"the dean of Nevada labor law,"* and *"a traditional law guru."* He continues to command respect for his wonderful work representing Las Vegas hotels and casinos. Reno-based **Ann Morgan** of Jones Vargas handles employment law issues, including contracts, human resources matters, violence in the workplace and wage and hour disputes. She represents a large number of local businessmen, as well as Reno-Tahoe International Airport, where she acts as general counsel on employment; Wells Fargo, for whom she does trust work; and Morgan Stanley, for whom she handles general employment matters. **Kathleen Paustian** (see p.1260) of Parsons Behle & Latimer PC is *"a great speaker"* and *"an organized and thoughtful practitioner,"* according to sources. She is active in the defense of employers against claims including discrimination, wrongful termination and emotional distress. Her practice also encompasses training and counseling on matters of preventive work and lawsuit avoidance. The *"absolutely invaluable"* **David Dornak** is *"a star of the future,"* whose move to Lewis and Roca this year has helped to establish him as a force in his own right for employment law. His dedicated labor and employment practice covers preventive work, including injunctions against unions and clients for the prevention of illegal strikes, as well as litigation, arbitrations, contracts and agreements. Clients commend him for being *"always diligent and well up on both state and federal regulatory matters."*

# ENVIRONMENT

## Environment
### Leading Firms

1. **LIONEL SAWYER & COLLINS** *Reno*
   **PARSONS BEHLE & LATIMER PC** *Reno*
   **WOODBURN AND WEDGE** *Reno*
2. **ALLISON, MACKENZIE, RUSSELL** *Carson City*
   **MCDONALD CARANO WILSON** *Reno*
   **SANTORO, DRIGGS, WALCH, KEARNEY** *Las Vegas*

### Leading Individuals

1. **DE LIPKAU Ross** *Parsons Behle & Latimer PC*
   **DEPAOLI Gordon** *Woodburn and Wedge*
2. **BOWMAN Linda** *Law Office of Linda A Bowman*
   **BULLEN Linda** *Lionel Sawyer & Collins*
   **HARRISON Sylvia** *McDonald Carano Wilson LLP*
   **HILL Earl** *Parsons Behle & Latimer PC*
   **PETERSON Karen** *Allison, MacKenzie*
   **WALCH Greg** *Santoro, Driggs, Walch*

## Band 1

## Lionel Sawyer & Collins

**The Firm:** This premier outfit covers a wide range of environmental law matters, including air quality, permitting facilities, hazard and solid waste work, and underground and river pollution. The firm also handles land management, land use and issues concerning the extension of mining, as well as representing clients in all types of environment-related litigation. Lawyers additionally handle transactional work, involving the purchase and sale of land where there are particular environmental concerns or resources.

**The Lawyers:** Formerly of the EPA, **Linda Bullen** brings profound experience in hazardous waste and water and air pollution-related work to the practice. She boasts particular expertise representing clients in environmental litigation in both federal and state courts, where clients value her *"proactive approach; she always remains one step ahead."*

**Clients/Work Highlights:** The firm represents various public authorities and utility companies, including Sinclair Oil, Cendant and Western Exploration Inc.

## Parsons Behle & Latimer PC

See firm details p.1956

**The Firm:** This natural resources group, previously Marshall Hill Cassas & is active in matters concerning environmental and water rights, as well as in mining and public land issues. It works closely with the firm's public utilities practice to cover gas, water, and electricity and cooperative questions, acting as environmental counsel and advising clients on litigation. The team has helped to shape the state's environmental laws through its political and legislative work and a raft of publications on mining and public land law.

**The Lawyers:** **Ross de Lipkau** (see p.1257) is *"one of the top authorities in water rights across the state,"* according to sources. He focuses on environmental permission and litigation, and benefits from the *"strong technical background and historical experience"* he gained from his mechanical and hydraulic engineering background. He is a member of numerous environmental bodies and *"attracts the highest respect from the entire environmental sphere."* **Earl Hill** (see p.1258) specializes in public lands, mining, water law and environmental issues, as well as the niche area of aviation law. His practice includes litigation and advisory work, particularly in mineral mining, where he is seen as *"an undisputed expert and a leading authority."* For the past 20 years he has acted as the Nevada Mining Association's delegate to the board of trustees of the Rocky Mountain Mineral Law Foundation.

**Clients/Work Highlights:** The client roster includes Muddy Valley Irrigation, the City of Las Vegas and Las Vegas Valley Water District.

## Woodburn and Wedge

**The Firm:** The oldest firm in the state advises some of Nevada's largest water users on issues including water supply, irrigation, water settlements and agreements, as well as the implementation of federal acts. Lawyers also boast expertise in land use, geothermal and mining law, where the team supports some of the country's largest mining companies in permission, compliance, hard rock mineral transactions, mineral leases, and exploitation and development agreements. Additionally, the team acts in mediations, hearings and disputes in state and federal courts as well as with the Bureau of Land Management.

**The Lawyers:** **Gordon DePaoli** is *"the best, most knowledgeable and most respected attorney on water law in the state of Nevada,"* interviewees report. He represents clients in complex multijurisdictional arbitration and litigation before legislative committees, as well as in state and federal courts. In 2005, DePaoli was involved in the ongoing mediation of a dispute between the US government and an Indian tribe over 80,000 acres of irrigated Nevada land.

**Clients/Work Highlights:** Lawyers acted on behalf of Truckee Meadows Water Authority in a water settlement agreement involving the states of Nevada and California. Other key clients include Sierra Pacific; Walker River Irrigation District; the City of Reno; Washoe County; Glamis Gold; Placer Dome and AMAX Gold.

## Band 2

### Allison, MacKenzie, Russell, Pavlakis, Wright & Fagan, Ltd

**The Firm:** This Carson City-based group provides wide-ranging expertise in areas including compliance, permitting, regulatory and land use in connection with environmental law and natural resources. Commentators particularly recommend the team for its notable water rights capabilities, where it handles administrative work and represents private customers and municipalities in hearings before the State Engineer. In addition, lawyers act in state and federal trials, as well as administrative hearings, throughout the state. The group was also involved in drafting state regulations governing public utilities and geothermal exploration in 2005.

**The Lawyers:** **Karen Peterson** is an expert in water rights and public utility issues. She acts for private clients as well as water and sewage utilities in hearings, and handles the due diligence and administrative process in front of the Public Utilities Commission.

**Clients/Work Highlights:** The team handles water rights development, and specifically the further economic development of the Lincoln County Water District. Other major clients include Pahrump Utility; Vidler Water; Nevada Land & Resource; Washoe County Utility Operation & Maintenance Division; William Ryan Homes; Calpine Energy Services; Geo-Energy Partners and Northern Nevada Industrial Gas Users.

### McDonald Carano Wilson LLP

**The Firm:** The firm's environmental and natural resources department offers expertise in water, mining and energy law, as well as in all environmental aspects of commercial transactions and air permission. With offices in Reno and Las Vegas, the team represents clients across the state in environmental torts, litigation and appeals to the Interior Board of Land Appeals. Lawyers were also involved in advice on public land law, CERCLA and RCRA enforcement actions, and NEPA and FLPMA (Federal Land Policy and Management Act) compliance in 2005.

**The Lawyers:** Benefiting from a background in geology, environmental and natural resources, **Sylvia Harrison** handles environmental permission, water, mining and public land law, and environmental aspects of complex commercial transactions and bankruptcies. She is also experienced in the prosecution and defense of environmental tort claims.

**Clients/Work Highlights:** The firm's client roster includes Time Oil, State Industries and CH2M HILL.

### Santoro, Driggs, Walch, Kearney, Johnson & Thompson

**The Firm:** This team has built up experience in a broad spectrum of environmental law, including mining, chemical manufacturing, power generation, waste disposal, real estate development, municipal and permission matters. It assists clients in compliance issues, prosecutions and litigation before local governments, southern Nevada authorities and the State Engineer. A particular focus on water law involves the group in the purchase and sale of Nevada groundwater rights, the delivery of fresh or reclaimed water and water supply issues. The firm also advises industrial and municipal clients on all environmental aspects of large transactions.

**The Lawyers:** **Greg Walch** draws from his experience as an agricultural engineer to advise a variety of power, chemical manufacturing and municipal clients. His workload includes environmental, water, land use, mining, eminent domain and administrative law. Peers remark on *"his unique level of expertise; he is the only person of this stature in Las Vegas."*

**Clients/Work Highlights:** The firm acts for a variety of clients, such as agriculture and mining businesses; property developers; waste disposal companies and regulated private water suppliers. Notable clients include America Pacific, Sands Gravel and the Nevada Department of Transportation.

### Other Notable Practitioners

Reno-based sole practitioner **Linda Bowman** earns praise for her work in water issues and environmental cleanup operations. She advises clients on a wide range of environmental law questions including water, mining, hard minerals, natural resources, underground storage tanks, real property, probate administration and Superfunds. She is a member of the Nevada Division of Environmental Protection.

# GAMING & LICENSING

| Gaming & Licensing Leading Firms | |
| --- | --- |
| [1] | LIONEL SAWYER & COLLINS *Las Vegas* |
| | SCHRECK BRIGNONE *Las Vegas* |
| [2] | CURRAN & PARRY *Las Vegas* |
| | GORDON & SILVER LTD *Las Vegas* |
| | JONES VARGAS *Las Vegas* |
| | LEWIS AND ROCA *Las Vegas* |
| | MCDONALD CARANO WILSON LLP *Las Vegas* |

## Band 1

### Lionel Sawyer & Collins

**The Firm:** This extensive gaming and regulatory team houses lawyers representing all the major gaming entities on every level. The 15-strong department commands the respect of those involved in the industry in Nevada, with clients appreciating *"the bottomless depth of talent available,"* and the fact that *"there is not a bad lawyer among them."* The firm takes the lead in the innovation and development of gaming practices, having been heavily involved in the legalization of mobile handheld gaming devices in 2005.

**The Lawyers:** **Bob Faiss** is *"the dean of gaming and the number-one gaming authority in the entire world,"* commentators claim. His practice represents clients in all aspects of gaming, including federal authorities and casino operators. Interviewees unanimously praise him for being *"a legend, a mentor and a diplomat, who is universally well regarded by all regulators and legislators."* 2005 saw Faiss act as lead attorney for Aruze, a Japanese game manufacturer that has become an equal stockholder in the new Wynn resort, making it the largest non-US investor in gaming. Sources report that **Greg Giordano** is *"spectacular and phenomenal – the go-to guy in Nevada."* His specialty is corporate securities, being that he is *"the most knowledgeable expert in that niche area."* Giordano is also involved in substantial volumes of licensing, investment, and regulatory and compliance work with publicly traded companies, and he profits from an extensive network of contacts within the Gaming Control Board and the Gaming Commission. He succeeded in obtaining the appropriate Nevada gaming licenses for Cantor Fitzgerald and Robert Earl, and handled the refinancing for the Lady Luck casino in 2005. Licensing specialist **Paul Larsen** is known as a problem solver for local regulatory bodies and negotiates all the unusual aspects of licensing questions, such as outside restaurants, rooftop bars and privileged licensing for adult nightclubs. Larsen also covers zoning and land use issues, representing clients in public hearings and appearing before the planning commission. Clients appreciate his *"personable, outgoing approach"* and his ability to *"really tap into all the right contacts."* Vice chair of the team **Dan Reaser** *"strikes a solid balance of aggression and dedication, and has a very good legal posture in disputes,"* state interviewees. As well as gaming matters, his Reno-based practice also covers public utilities and related issues, and he is often to be found representing power producers and water companies. Interviewees stress that *"his reputation is such that his integrity is never questioned by any judges or regulators."* The *"knowledgeable and talented"* **Ellen Whittemore** worked on the MGM Mirage/Mandalay Resort Group merger and acted as primary author in a number of Nevada Gaming Commission regulations.

**Clients/Work Highlights:** Lawyers were instrumental in some of the state's most important matters, including handling financings, acquiring license approvals and acting as lead gaming attorneys in the landmark merger of MGM Mirage and the Mandalay Resort Group in 2005. They also assisted in gaining approvals for Las Vegas Sands to go public and managed financings for Aztar Corporation, IGT and ShuffleMaster. Other key clients include The Venetian and Starward Hotels and Resorts.

## Schreck Brignone

**The Firm:** Between them, Schreck Brignone and Lionel Sawyer handle between 80-90% of the state's gaming work. The majority of the state's major gaming parties and publicly traded companies feature in the firm's impressive portfolio of clients and go to the team for assistance on a wide range of matters, including the most complex gaming and licensing questions. The firm has represented key client Wynn Resorts in all manner of cases for 27 years.

**The Lawyers:** **Frank Schreck** enjoys world renown as *"a powerhouse in the political and business spectrum."* His wide network of relationships and influence means that *"he can always get his call answered, whoever he calls."* His key role in licensing questions has seen him acting for key names in the gaming industry and *"licensing more people than anyone on earth,"* according to sources. Schreck is also particularly active in opening up new capital for the gaming industry, which has allowed firms to acquire properties around Las Vegas, including the purchases of the Las Vegas Hilton and a 50% share in Aladdin Hotel & Casino. **David Arrajj** handles corporate matters relating to publicly traded companies, where he demonstrates *"the flexibility to deal with the many different approaches that are needed,"* say commentators. His varied experience includes serving as a regulator in New Jersey and acting as in-house counsel for Hilton Gaming and Park Place and Caesars Entertainment. He is credited with possessing an *"unprecedented understanding of the Gaming Control Act and the licensing and approval processes,"* as well as *"the highest standards of client care."* **Sonia Church Vermeys** prepares the gaming, liquor and other business applications for clients, and assists them through the various regulatory processes involved in the acquisition and establishment of both restricted and non-restricted gaming venues. Her workload includes licensing for Wynn Resorts and the Bourbon Street Hotel & Casino. Clients are impressed with her *"understanding of the law and of how to get applications processed quickly and efficiently."*
**Clients/Work Highlights:** The team acted in a great number of major purchasing and licensing deals in 2005, including Landry's Restaurants' acqui-

sition of the Golden Nugget. Lawyers also represented Mandalay Resort Group in its acquisition by MGM Mirage. Other major clients include Harrah's Entertainment; Sahara Hotel & Casino; Horseshoe Gaming; Park Place Entertainment and Pinnacle Entertainment.

## Band 2

## Curran & Parry

See firm details p.1261
**The Firm:** The team here focuses on two broad areas: contentious and noncontentious corporate law, and administrative law. Corporate work includes significant real estate activity, while administrative work spans issues related to land use, gaming and lobbying. The firm provides construction and development expertise in parallel with gaming and licensing knowledge, advising a wide range of development companies involved in hotel and casino-related projects.
**The Lawyers:** **Bill Curran**'s main strengths are land use, zoning and gaming. His practice includes appearing before county commissions, regulatory authorities and compliance committees, as well as arranging gaming licenses and handling planning approvals, which he has done on behalf of the City of Las Vegas. Curran is the longest serving member and former chair of the Nevada Gaming Commission, and enjoys a strong reputation among his peers: *"He is a class act, a real gent with a lot of credibility."*
**Clients/Work Highlights:** The firm's biggest client is Nevada Power, for which it acts on land use matters. Lawyers also handle a great deal of work for construction giant Sletten Companies, and assist the JW Marriott Hotels & Resorts in licensing proceedings. Other clients include Wynn Resorts; Golden Nugget; The Henry Brent Company; Pinnacle Entertainment; Goldman Sachs and American Golf.

## Gordon & Silver Ltd

**The Firm:** The team represents a range of well-established clients in the gaming industry, based both within Nevada and nationally. The firm adopts an innovative approach to its practice, tackling work for Internet gaming and gaming technologies companies, as well as handling the more traditional needs of the industry, such as liquor licensing, planning and zoning, and contractor issues.
**The Lawyers:** **Jeffrey Silver** boasts 25 years of experience representing major clients such as the Hard Rock Hotel & Casino. In 2005, he obtained zoning and land use approvals for a major mall developer, presented gaming license applications for several resort properties, won approval for new casino game concepts and arranged the individual licensing for key gaming executives.
**Clients/Work Highlights:** Notable clients include The Riviera Hotel and Casino; American Wagering; Gaming Laboratories International (GLI); Tuscany Suites & Casino; Roberts Television and Turnberry Place condominiums.

## Jones Vargas

**The Firm:** This prestigious outfit represents major clients in a range of gaming and regulatory matters, including land use, zoning, licensing and public utilities. The team has experience acting in front of the State Gaming Control Board and the Nevada Gaming Commission among others, as well as appearing in a lobbying capacity when campaigning both for and against proposed legislation on behalf of its clients.
**The Lawyers:** **Michael Alonso** *"has made a great name for himself"* through his work as head of the firm's gaming department, according to sources. His practice covers gaming and regulatory work, lobbying on legislation and local government development work. Alonso is currently acting on behalf of Station Casinos in obtaining approval for a resort hotel in Reno. Clients praise him for his *"acumen, astute political prowess and meticulous attention to detail."*
**Clients/Work Highlights:** Lawyers assisted with Harrah's Entertainment's purchase of Horseshoe Gaming. Other major clients include Silver Club Hotel Casino; Templeton Gaming Corporation; Mandalay Resort Group and Boardwalk Hotel & Casino.

## Lewis and Roca

**The Firm:** Four offices across the Southwest advise clients on issues including interactive and mobile gaming, interstate horse racing and poker. Clients include a wide range of parties with interests in the gaming industry, such as Indian gaming groups, gaming manufacturers and suppliers, investors and casino operators.
**The Lawyers:** Formerly of Lionel Sawyer, **Anthony Cabot** is well known for his niche expertise in the developing area of Internet gaming, where sources acknowledge him as *"the premier world authority in this specialty of the future."* He is also involved in licensing and regulatory work in land-based gaming areas such as sweepstakes, skill games and contests. Clients value him for possessing *"that rare combination of sharp legal skills: current regulatory knowledge and practical business intuition; he is someone who provides clarity where there are areas of gray."*
**Clients/Work Highlights:** Lawyers obtained approvals for Hooters Gaming, assisted in bringing the manufacturer FortuNet public and represented a number of major Internet poker sites on US matters. The team also represented a Nevada association conducting interstate para-mutual account wagering (allowing race bets to be taken across state lines). Other key clients include Playboy Enterprises; US Off-Track; Gaming VC Holdings; SCA Promotions and CryptoLogic.

## McDonald Carano Wilson LLP

**The Firm:** The firm serves corporate clients involved in all aspects of the gaming industry, including gaming manufacturers and Native American gaming operations. With offices based in Reno and Las Vegas, the firm is acknowledged as *"the market leader in northern Nevada."* Lawyers assist with casino acquisitions, hotel developments, regulatory compliance and appearances before various boards and commissions.

**The Lawyers: Bud Hicks** is *"an experienced gaming expert with a solid following,"* say interviewees. A former general counsel of the Gaming Commission, sources regard him as *"one of the longtime deans, and* *the best in the Reno area."* Hicks has represented major names in the gaming world, including operators, manufacturers and suppliers. His practice has also acted as Nevada counsel for a number of investment banks on major transactions and financings involving the gaming industry.

**Clients/Work Highlights:** Lawyers assisted in Harrah's Entertainment's purchase of Horseshoe Gaming. Additional clients include Eldorado Hotel & Casino and the Fort Mojave Indian Tribe.

# LITIGATION

## Litigation: General Commercial
### Leading Firms

| | |
|---|---|
| **1** | **CAMPBELL & WILLIAMS** *Las Vegas* |
| | **HARRISON, KEMP & JONES, LLP** *Las Vegas* |
| | **LIONEL SAWYER & COLLINS** *Las Vegas* |
| | **SCHRECK BRIGNONE** *Las Vegas* |
| **2** | **HALE LANE PEEK DENNISON AND HOWARD** *Reno* |
| | **JONES VARGAS** *Las Vegas* |
| | **KUMMER KAEMPFER BONNER** *Las Vegas* |
| | **MORRIS PICKERING & SANNER** *Las Vegas* |
| **3** | **JOLLEY, URGA, WIRTH** *Las Vegas* |
| | **LAXALT & NOMURA** *Reno* |
| | **LEWIS AND ROCA** *Las Vegas* |
| | **MCDONALD CARANO WILSON LLP** *Reno* |
| | **ROBISON, BELAUSTEGUI, SHARP & LOW** *Reno* |
| | **SANTORO, DRIGGS, WALCH, KEARNEY** *Las Vegas* |

### Leading Individuals

| | |
|---|---|
| **1** | **CAMPBELL Donald** *Campbell & Williams* |
| | **JONES J Randall** *Harrison, Kemp & Jones* |
| | **KENNEDY Dennis** *Lionel Sawyer & Collins* |
| **2** | **FERENBACH Cam** *Lionel Sawyer & Collins* |
| | **HEINZ Von** *Lewis and Roca* |
| | **HEJMANOWSKI Paul** *Lionel Sawyer & Collins* |
| | **JOLLEY R Gardner** *Jolley, Urga, Wirth* |
| | **KUMMER Thomas** *Kummer Kaempfer Bonner* |
| | **LAXALT Bruce** *Laxalt & Nomura* |
| | **MORRIS Steve** *Morris Pickering & Sanner* |
| | **PEEK J Stephen** *Hale Lane Peek Dennison* |
| | **PISANELLI James** *Schreck Brignone* |
| | **SANTORO Nicholas** *Santoro, Driggs, Walch* |
| | **WILLIAMS J Colby** *Campbell & Williams* |
| **3** | **BICE Todd** *Schreck Brignone* |
| | **FERRARIO Mark** *Kummer Kaempfer Bonner* |
| | **GORDON Andrew** *McDonald Carano Wilson LLP* |
| | **LENHARD Kirk** *Jones Vargas* |
| | **ROBISON Kent** *Robison, Belaustegui, Sharp* |
| | **URGA William** *Jolley, Urga, Wirth* |

## Band 1

### Campbell & Williams

**The Firm:** This three-lawyer firm operates at the pinnacle of the Nevada litigation market, specializing in white-collar crime, PI, products liability and commercial litigation. An enviable client base includes major commercial investors and developers, resort hotels and publishing houses.

**The Lawyers:** The former federal prosecutor and *"immensely skilled witness-examiner"* **Donald Campbell** is *"head of the class, and the go-to guy on serious disputes,"* according to sources. He specializes in catastrophic PI, commercial litigation and white-collar criminal defense. Interviewees comment on his *"great criminal experience, extraordinary tenacity and aggressive defense of his clients."* **Colby Williams** is *"a deep thinker and an outstanding writer, capable of delivering a great final work product,"* say commentators. His commercial litigation, PI, First Amendment and appellate expertise prompts sources to predict: *"He will be one of the top guys in time."*

**Clients/Work Highlights:** The Trump Organization; Las Vegas Review Journal; The Wall Street Journal and Coast Resorts.

### Harrison, Kemp & Jones, LLP

**The Firm:** This full-service firm combines litigation expertise with administrative law prowess related to public utilities, licensing and zoning. The litigation practice covers commercial disputes, products liability, insurance defense and PI litigation, and contributes to the firm's strong reputation for construction law. Lawyers are also frequently involved in arbitration and mediation, and both contentious and noncontentious real estate matters.

**The Lawyers: Randall Jones** typically represents plaintiffs in class actions, torts, development cases, PI claims, and real estate and insurance law. He is described as a *"courteous but formidable opponent, who fights hard but always within the lines."* Interviewees also commend him for his *"great courtroom demeanor; he is very good on his feet and very effective before the bench and the jury."* **Kirk Harrison** brings *"a wealth of invaluable trial experience"* to all matters pertaining to the construction industry, especially litigation in cases involving large commercial developments such as The Venetian. He boasts profound experience representing trade and general contractors and is active in mediations and arbitrations. He represented the City of Las Vegas and Mandalay Resort Group in 2005.

**Clients/Work Highlights:** City of Las Vegas; Las Vegas Hilton; Ovation Development; Park Place Entertainment and Pacific Properties and Development.

### Lionel Sawyer & Collins

**The Firm:** Nevada's largest firm boasts an active civil litigation department capable of handling all types of disputes, including employment and labor questions, gaming and regulatory matters, and liability and insurance issues. The team is also adept in alternative dispute resolution, representing clients in arbitrations and mediations. Sources state that the firm is *"nationally renowned for its class action defense abilities,"* pointing to involvement in cases on behalf of gaming manufacturers and major names in the medical industry in 2005. Lawyers were also engaged in a large number of real estate disputes on behalf of property developers, lenders and home builders in the past twelve months.

**The Lawyers:** The chair of the state Bar ethics committee, **Dennis Kennedy**, *"brings focus, dignity and energy"* to his practice, sources report. He specializes in complex litigation and defense of class actions, as well as possessing *"a wonderful knowledge"* of products liability matters. 2005 saw him successfully defend a major hotel chain against gaming manufacturers, and act as lead counsel for GlaxoSmithKline in a national class action against HCA related to uninsured use of the healthcare service provider's hospitals. **Cam Ferenbach**'s business litigation practice covers employment, torts related to business disputes, real estate contracts and collection work. He is also highly regarded for being *"one of the state's top alternative dispute resolution experts."* He worked on disputes over condominium projects, construction contracts and lender liability, and also regularly undertook state Bar and pro bono work in 2005. Market observers describe him as *"a real straight shooter who always gives as good as he gets."* Managing partner **Paul Hejmanowski** is *"a top-class litigator who is particularly adept at delicately positioning a case in order to find a mutually acceptable resolution,"* say commentators. He appears in commercial litigation and contract disputes, often on behalf of codefendants, and recently acted for Don King Productions in a dispute over boxer management. **John Naylor** represents owners and developers of hotels, casinos, and large apartment and condominium projects in disputes with contractors. His work covers litigation, project disputes, dismissal of claims and construction contract administration. He has acted for the Aladdin Resort, Marriott and Las Vegas Sands in cases against contractors, as well as for Pacific Properties and Development in litigation against subcontractors. Interviewees rate his *"calculating, strategic way of getting a positive end result in as short a time as possible."* **Todd Touton**'s expertise centers on real estate project-related commercial construction litigation, but also encompasses arbitrations, partner disputes, bankruptcy and

| Litigation: Construction | |
|---|---|
| Leading Individuals | |
| [1] | HARRISON Kirk *Harrison, Kemp & Jones* |
| | MEAD Leon *Mead Pezzillo LLP* |
| | NAYLOR John *Lionel Sawyer & Collins* |
| | SPANGLER Georlen *Kolesar & Leatham* |
| [2] | HANEY Dennis *Haney, Woloson & Mullins* |
| | PEEL Richard *Peel Brimley LLP* |
| | TOUTON Todd *Lionel Sawyer & Collins* |

general corporate disputes. Although primarily known for owner representation, he also acts for developers and subcontractors. 2005 saw him handle construction issues for the Aladdin Resort and act for Ovation Development and Bright Homes in Reno in the development of residential complexes.

**Clients/Work Highlights:** Lawyers here acted in a stockholders squeeze-out case on behalf of a large hotel group. This was the first case to be tried under recent amendments to Nevada statutes. Other clients include Burke, Blue, Hutchison & Walters; Countrywide Financial; Christian, Smith & Jewell; Fisher & Phillips; Drury Inns; Aztar; The Venetian and Paradise Homes.

### Schreck Brignone

**The Firm:** Lawyers here *"will always try to find a cost-effective solution rather than fight to the bitter end for the sake of billing hours,"* according to interviewees. The firm houses some of the most promising litigators in the state, who are renowned for their *"energy, practicality, determination and tenacity."* Contentious expertise in complex litigation and class actions involves the firm in real estate, commercial, gaming, tort, construction, and labor and employment law disputes. Accordingly, lawyers represented many large local and national businesses, including major hotels and casinos, real estate developers and construction companies in 2005.

**The Lawyers:** James Pisanelli is *"a levelheaded hard worker and a great emerging talent,"* interviewees assert. As a commercial litigator, he handles a wide variety of disputes within real estate, healthcare and construction transactional law, where he represents owners on agreement matters. He successfully represented a major New York real estate developer in a federal court case over a commercial lease, and acted in a bad faith claim for a gaming client in 2005. Sources draw attention to *"his great examining skills and talent for getting things accomplished."* *"You look to* **Todd Bice** *when you really need to get something done,"* say peers. As well as regular corporate and commercial litigation, his caseload also includes some civil rights defense work and contested land use disputes. He recently defended MGM Mirage and Mandalay Resort Group in stockholder litigation, and acted for The Venetian in construction disputes.

**Clients/Work Highlights:** Lawyers played a crucial role in litigation connected to the Harrah's Entertainment/Caesars Entertainment merger and also regularly make trial appearances on behalf of the

City of Las Vegas. Other clients include Wynn Resorts; MGM Mirage; Station Casinos; Mandalay Resort Group; Titanium Metals; Lockheed Martin and EG&G Technical Services.

## Band 2

### Hale Lane Peek Dennison and Howard

**The Firm:** Hale Lane operates a full-service commercial litigation practice, representing major local and national businesses including hotels and casinos, developers, contractors and manufacturers. Lawyers with a reputation for *"determined and aggressive representation of their client,"* and the *"tenacity necessary to fight a matter to the end"* offer expertise in all areas of litigation, arbitration and mediation.

**The Lawyers:** Stephen Peek is *"a fierce, fearless litigator,"* say interviewees. His experience covers corporate and commercial litigation before state and federal courts, where he *"is not afraid to get involved in the grittiest of battles."*

**Clients/Work Highlights:** The firm represents major hotels and casinos such as The Venetian and the Golden Nugget, as well as government entities and utility companies, including Southern Nevada Water Authority.

### Jones Vargas

**The Firm:** The firm acts for clients in a broad spectrum of disputes, including traditional Nevada issues related to real estate, construction and gaming, as well as more general matters such as healthcare and bankruptcy. The firm's corporate client base includes businesses of all sizes, from small local enterprises to large national corporations.

**The Lawyers:** Kirk Lenhard *"will always give you a good fight in the courtroom,"* peers report. He is also a capable mediator and arbitrator, and frequently acts for large corporations, major casino resorts and financial institutions. His clients include Bank of America, for which he has served as counsel for more than 20 years, and the McCarran Airport in Las Vegas. He is described as *"easygoing and a solid man of integrity whose word you can rely on."*

**Clients/Work Highlights:** Harrah's Entertainment; Station Casinos; JPMorgan Securities and Business Bank of Nevada.

### Kummer Kaempfer Bonner Renshaw & Ferrario

See firm details p.1262

**The Firm:** The firm focuses on corporate and commercial disputes, where it provides litigation and alternative dispute resolution experience in construction, real estate, employment and labor law, and gaming and regulatory matters. Lawyers also boast niche expertise in airline litigation, as well as contentious issues surrounding zoning and land use.

**The Lawyers:** Head of the litigation team **Thomas Kummer** (see p.1259) specializes in corporate and commercial law, professional malpractice and avia-

tion litigation. Clients praise his *"wonderful way of managing relationships with clients' opposing counsel."* *"Fearless litigator"* **Mark Ferrario** (see p.1258) represents major names in the gaming and construction industries in civil, commercial and corporate litigation. His *"aggressive yet measured approach"* makes him a favorite with many clients.

**Clients/Work Highlights:** Lawyers represented Southern Nevada Home Builders Association in a number of Nevada Legislature sessions and acted for major insurance companies in disaster litigation in 2005. Other key clients include ITT Corporation; Vidler Water Company; Sierra Health Services and Las Vegas Monorail.

### Morris Pickering & Sanner

**The Firm:** This commercial litigation boutique specializes in antitrust, insurance coverage disputes, securities fraud and employment and labor law. The firm handles matters of stature and importance that belie its size, including acting for hotel chains, pharmaceutical companies and utility entities in significant regional disputes.

**The Lawyers:** The *"outstandingly diligent"* **Steve Morris** enjoys a high standing among his peers. His expertise includes complex commercial and tort litigation, products liability and construction disputes. He acts for hospitals, automobile manufacturers, medical device manufacturers, and insurers.

**Clients/Work Highlights:** Lawyers completed a high-profile case on behalf of a Las Vegas hotel against Rod Stewart, concerning the nonpayment of an advance following the singer's failure to perform at a scheduled concert. Other clients include Las Vegas Convention and Visitors Authority; The Mirage; Sierra Pacific Power Company and Southwest Gas.

## Band 3

### Jolley, Urga, Wirth & Woodbury

**The Firm:** This full-service firm devotes major resources to litigation, notwithstanding its gaming and licensing, probate, estate planning, bankruptcy, construction and banking and finance capabilities. Experienced litigators handle all manner of civil disputes, particularly related to trusts and estates.

**The Lawyers:** *"A real gentleman whose word you can really trust,"* **Gardner Jolley** *"is one of the best in town"* for probate, banking, real estate and litigation work, according to sources. He is especially well known for his trusts and estate capabilities, and also counts banks and large financial entities among his key clients. *"Honest straight shooter"* **William Urga** covers corporate litigation, real estate and administrative law, as well as sophisticated corporate transactions. He *"possesses a great insight into the gaming industry,"* having previously served as a gaming commissioner on the Nevada Gaming Commission for six years.

## Laxalt & Nomura

**The Firm:** This 18-lawyer firm, with offices in Reno and Las Vegas, is known for its representation of national businesses, large insurance companies, manufacturers and banks. Lawyers *"aggressively and effectively defend clients"* in commercial litigation, products liability, construction and employment law, say commentators.

**The Lawyers:** **Bruce Laxalt**'s civil litigation practice covers business litigation, civil rights, tort and legal malpractice defense. He is described as *"a conscientious lawyer with a lot of integrity – an absolute pleasure to work with."*

**Clients/Work Highlights:** Allianz Life Insurance Company of North America; Royal & SunAlliance; Atlantis Hotel and Casino; Hilton Hotels; Mitsubishi Motors North America; Sands Hotel & Casino; Sierra Energy and Wells Fargo.

## Lewis and Roca

**The Firm:** With a presence across the southwest, this impressive outfit is able to bring its full weight to bear on a range of litigation matters. Since the opening of its Las Vegas office, the firm has developed the capacity to handle diverse matters on behalf of a large number of blue-chip defendants, including hotels, casino resorts and large financial services corporations.

**The Lawyers:** **Von Heinz** is active in tort exposure, products liability defense, business malpractice, wrongful death and PI defense disputes. He also acts as local Nevada counsel for a number of large national and international corporations. 2005 saw him appear in defense of a bankruptcy trustees suit, a long-term disability case and litigation related to a large casino corporation's acquisition of a rival. Clients praise him for *"his gracious nature,"* while noting that *"he can be tough and aggressive when the situation demands it."*

**Clients/Work Highlights:** The team has undertaken commercial litigation for JPMorgan Chase; Prudential; MCI; CIGNA and Etna Insurance. Lawyers have also represented Lloyd's underwriters in cases involving Nevada entities.

## McDonald Carano Wilson LLP

**The Firm:** The litigation team here handles both the prosecution and defense of real estate, construction, bankruptcy, insurance, employment and environment-related disputes. Lawyers are also renowned for their skills in alternative dispute resolution and act regularly as arbitrators and mediators in various cases. The firm's client base includes a number of large, multinational corporations, as well as many local businesses and enterprises.

**The Lawyers:** A commercial, construction and employment arbitrator for the AAA, **Andrew Gordon** is known for the breadth of his commercial dispute resolution experience which also covers litigation and mediation. Clients instruct Gordon on the basis of his *"faultless integrity and honesty."*

**Clients/Work Highlights:** Lawyers acted for a number of real estate developers such as Bayer Properties and Centex, as well as significant names in the hotel and casino arena, including Horseshoe Gaming and Eldorado Hotel & Casino, in 2005. Other clients include Associated General Contractors of America, St James Village and First Security Bank.

## Robison, Belaustegui, Sharp & Low

**The Firm:** This Reno-based firm specializes in commercial and civil litigation. Lawyers act for the defense and prosecution in corporate law, real estate transactions, construction, products liability and bankruptcy-related disputes. A varied client base features contractors, developers, investors and financial institutions.

**The Lawyers:** **Kent Robison** is *"a first-rate civil litigator, and an outstanding plaintiff lawyer,"* say sources. His expertise covers contentious aspects of business torts, construction, and commercial and PI law. He is hailed as *"one of the best trial lawyers in Nevada; he is especially good with juries."*

**Clients/Work Highlights:** Specialty Financial; First National Bank of Nevada; Nevada State Bank; Wells Fargo and Alliance Insurance Company.

## Santoro, Driggs, Walch, Kearney, Johnson & Thompson

**The Firm:** Commentators enthuse that *"the firm has a great depth of talent available, no matter how large or small a case."* The team's expertise covers all areas of commercial law, particularly contract and real estate disputes.

**The Lawyers:** *"Litigators don't come much better than"* **Nicholas Santoro**, according to interviewees. His dispute capabilities extend to real estate, contract, business tort, unfair competition and legal malprac-tice defense. In 2005, he acted in a major breach of loan agreement case, which entailed the resolution of a contract dispute over the financing fee of a failed loan transaction. He also appeared in a dispute over the development of a substantial joint venture housing project in Las Vegas. Clients are *"totally satisfied with his representation and trial performance."*

**Clients/Work Highlights:** Gem Homes; Rhodes Design; Howard Hughes Corporation; Pinnacle Entertainment; State of Nevada; American West Homes; Centex and the City of Las Vegas.

## Other Notable Practitioners

**Leon Mead** of Mead Pezzillo LLP covers the whole range of matters that arise in construction projects, including contracts, claims, employment and schedule issues, arbitration and construction licensing. He also counsels clients on insurance liability issues, assists in the collection of payables, and provides interpretations of contracts and new legislation. Acting primarily for contractors and subcontractors, he has represented a number of major developers in Las Vegas, including contract consultation for Caesar's Palace, and handling claims on behalf of subcontractors against Bellagio and Wynn Resorts. Clients value his *"integrity beyond reproach and skill in putting things down in layman's terms."* The *"fair-minded and astute"* **Georlen Spangler** of Kolesar & Leatham Chtd acts for numerous subcontractors in disputes with major hotel-casinos and construction lenders. She also has extensive contract experience, having negotiated in a wide variety of nonstandard construction matters. A member of the AAA for commercial and construction matters, she has arbitrated in a range of cases. **Dennis Haney** of Haney, Woloson & Mullins is *"a superb construction attorney, one of the better litigators and arbitrators out there,"* say sources. He has more than 30 years of experience representing contractors and subcontractors in construction litigation and also acts in contentious aspects of real estate, estate planning and business and corporate law. **Richard Peel** heads specialized construction law outfit Peel Brimley LLP. He possesses more than 20 years of experience acting for public and private clients and subcontractors in connection with construction litigation, arbitration, mediation, licensing and regulatory matters and contracts.

# REAL ESTATE

## Real Estate
### Leading Firms

**1** GOOLD PATTERSON ALES & DAY *Las Vegas*
   JONES VARGAS *Las Vegas*
   LIONEL SAWYER & COLLINS *Las Vegas*
   SCHRECK BRIGNONE *Las Vegas*

**2** HALE LANE PEEK DENNISON AND HOWARD *Reno*
   KUMMER KAEMPFER BONNER *Las Vegas*
   MCDONALD CARANO WILSON LLP *Reno*
   SNELL & WILMER LLP *Las Vegas*

**3** ALLISON, MACKENZIE, RUSSELL *Carson City*
   DEANER, DEANER, SCANN, MALAN *Las Vegas*
   RICE SILBEY REUTHER & SULLIVAN LLP *Las Vegas*
   SANTORO, DRIGGS, WALCH, KEARNEY *Las Vegas*

### Leading Individuals

**Senior Statesman**
   DEANER Charles *Deaner, Deaner, Scann*

**1** BUCKLEY Michael *Jones Vargas*
   GOOLD Barry *Goold Patterson Ales & Day*
   JONES Leslie *Schreck Brignone*
   ZUCKER Jeffrey *Lionel Sawyer & Collins*

**2** CURTIS Patricia *Snell & Wilmer LLP*
   DENNISON Karen *Hale Lane Peek Dennison*
   FRANKOVICH John *McDonald Carano Wilson LLP*
   MACE James *Snell & Wilmer LLP*
   NOVACEK Stephen *Hale Lane Peek Dennison*
   SHARP F DeArmond *Robison, Belaustegui*

**3** BERGIN Leo *McDonald Carano Wilson*
   BUTT Layne *Bailey Merrill*
   DAVIS JR William *Jones Vargas*
   DRIGGS J Douglas *Santoro, Driggs, Walch*
   DUHON Gary *Lionel Sawyer & Collins*
   GOLDSTEIN Mark *Lionel Sawyer & Collins*
   PATTERSON Jeffrey *Goold Patterson Ales & Day*
   RICE Stephen *Rice Silbey Reuther*
   YOKEN Stephen *Snell & Wilmer LLP*

## Real Estate: Zoning/Land Use
### Leading Individuals

**1** FIORENTINO Mark *Kummer Kaempfer Bonner*
   KAEMPFER Christopher *Kummer Kaempfer Bonner*

## Band 1

### Goold Patterson Ales & Day

**The Firm:** This ten-strong boutique focuses exclusively on real estate law. The firm is renowned for the drafting of contracts, easements and covenants, conditions and restrictions documents (CC&Rs). Accordingly, lawyers are frequently involved in the establishment of residential communities, where they act on behalf of homeowner associations and home builders. The team also represents both developers and prospective tenants in the negotiation of leases and construction related to shopping centers. Other key areas of expertise include landlord/tenant and bankruptcy matters.

**The Lawyers:** **Barry Goold** (see p.1258) is *"supremely accomplished in all aspects of the real estate market,"* according to sources. He handles the most complex of issues, including the purchase and sale of real property and real property-secured loans. In this way, Goold routinely represents sellers, buyers, lenders and borrowers. He also boasts niche expertise in negotiating and drafting contracts with architects and contractors. Director of the firm **Jeffrey Patterson** (see p.1260) covers all major areas of real estate law. His practice is distinguished by a well-established bankruptcy element, which sees him represent landlords and secured creditors.

**Clients/Work Highlights:** The firm acts for a raft of local home builders and developers in the negotiation of land acquisitions and subcontractor work.

### Jones Vargas

**The Firm:** Lawyers here are frequently found acting on the most complex cases, including real property, M&A, land use and zoning matters. The firm also boasts profound experience in some of the state's largest, multifaceted financings. Clients include major construction companies, commercial developers and home builders, as well as investment banks and commercial lenders.

**The Lawyers:** **Michael Buckley** *"continues to operate as one of southern Nevada's finest real estate lawyers,"* say corporate clients. Peers recommend him for his high-profile work in planning and zoning. He also has extensive experience representing resort hotel casinos and banks in the purchase and sale of land and commercial developments. He is commended for his *"thoughtful, thorough approach and impeccable judgment."* **William Davis** is an *"innovative and creative talent"* who is capable of *"superior vision and understanding"* in real estate matters, interviewees claim. His practice centers on representing developers, lenders and borrowers in all aspects of complex commercial real estate transactions.

**Clients/Work Highlights:** The firm acts for major real estate companies such as Somerset Development, Gypsum Construction and Reynolds Construction, as well as a number of lenders and investment companies.

### Lionel Sawyer & Collins

**The Firm:** Many commentators regard this outfit as *"the only firm to go to"* for complex financings related to hotel towers and casino resorts in Las Vegas and Reno. Offering a level of service and depth of resources that are *"unparalleled in most other firms,"* the team is also particularly involved in the luxury condominium market, which continues to be a major source of work for the Las Vegas legal community.

**The Lawyers:** **Jeffrey Zucker** is *"a long-standing patriarch and quite simply one of the best real estate lawyers in the USA,"* sources report. As chair of the business law department, he is equally renowned for both real estate and corporate matters. 2005 saw him handle a number of large real estate transactions, including the financing of multimillion-dollar condominium tower projects, which currently make up a substantial part of his practice. Clients rate his *"unbelievable level of service,"* with one claiming: *"He has even been to the office for me at 11pm in the past!"* **Gary Duhon** specializes in real estate sales and acquisitions, leasing, land use, water law and lending, and in the past twelve months he has been heavily involved in residential projects. Clients comment that *"there is no better development lawyer in Reno; we go to him for the hardest, most complicated and stressful transactions."* **Mark Goldstein**'s land business-related practice involves representing lenders in land acquisitions and condominium financing projects, as well as handling real estate sales and performing local counsel and opinion work. He was involved in local security arrangements for a Wynn Resorts project in Macao in 2005, where his advice on the particular aspects of the Nevada legal system was deemed *"invaluable."*

**Clients/Work Highlights:** Lawyers represented the developers of the Cosmopolitan Hotel and handled financings for a number of development companies. The firm also acted for the bank in Donald Trump's Nevada land acquisitions. Other key clients include Pacific Properties and Development; Somerset Development; Barker Coleman Communities; Paradise Homes and Pioneer Companies.

### Schreck Brignone

**The Firm:** This well-established outfit has been instrumental in some of the state's most prominent real estate transactions in recent years. The firm is particularly adept at acting on behalf of the gaming industry, including clients such as Wynn Resorts and Harrah's Entertainment. The team also has experience representing local and national construction and development companies, and assisting in statewide land and property acquisitions.

**The Lawyers:** **Leslie Terry Jones** enjoys the universal respect of peers for his decades of experience in the Nevada property market. In 2005, he acted in the acquisition of land and financing for a large number of high-rise condominium projects and timeshare developments, as well as in significant casino and hotel purchases. Sources tell of *"the highest ethical standards"* of *"the best title and mortgage lawyer in the state."*

**Clients/Work Highlights:** The firm represented Harrah's Entertainment in the purchase of Binion's Horseshoe Hotel & Casino and the World Series of Poker, and also featured in the acquisition of the Bourbon Street Hotel & Casino. Other major clients include Ruffin Gaming; Pinnacle Entertainment; Station Casinos; Hard Rock Hotel & Casino; Wynn Resorts; Sierra Health Services; KB Home and Expedia.

## Band 2

### Hale Lane Peek Dennison and Howard

**The Firm:** This firm continues to stay close to its real estate and property law roots. Lawyers represent a wide range of developers, purchasers, lenders and borrowers in all aspects of real estate transactions, including commercial and residential developments and timeshare properties. The firm also offers more niche expertise in zoning, entitlements and water rights.

**The Lawyers:** Chairperson of the firm's real property and finance practice group **Karen Dennison** has more than 30 years of experience in real property sales and acquisitions, development, leasing and financings. She customarily represents real estate developers, lenders, sellers and purchasers, with a heavy emphasis on transactional work and legislation. Peers highlight her *"top-quality documentation"* and *"magnificent"* work on timeshare projects. **Stephen Novacek** is *"a terrific all-rounder"* who *"regularly handles the most complex cases,"* according to commentators. He enjoys a fine reputation as a lender's lawyer and is recognized among peers for high-level transactional work. His expertise covers real estate financing, real property, and asset secured and unsecured loans.

**Clients/Work Highlights:** Lawyers served as local Nevada counsel in nationwide loan and acquisition transactions for major lending and borrowing institutions in 2005. Other clients include retail and timeshare developers, banks and financial institutions.

### Kummer Kaempfer Bonner Renshaw & Ferrario

See firm details p.1262

**The Firm:** The firm remains the state's leading authority on land use and zoning issues, and accordingly represents clients before the appropriate councils, boards and commissions. Licensing matters, including business, gaming, liquor and privileged licenses, form another key element of the team's representation of a range of commercial and industrial clients.

**The Lawyers:** **Mark Fiorentino** (see p.1258) is one of the state's foremost land use attorneys and a leading light in all zoning and licensing matters. His expertise also covers taxation, construction defects, water rights and administrative law. In addition, he also has extensive experience in drafting ordinances, regulations and legislation. Fiorentino heads the firm's legislative lobbying team, which involves biennial appearances at the Nevada Legislature in Carson City. Founder of the firm's land use and governmental relations department, **Christopher Kaempfer** (see p.1259) remains *"absolutely the attorney to go to"* for his 25 years of experience working on land use questions and influencing land use law today.

**Clients/Work Highlights:** Notable clients include Republic Services; Vidler Water; Sierra Health Services; Focus Property Group; Las Vegas Monorail and DP Partners.

### McDonald Carano Wilson McCune Bergin Frankovich & Hicks LLP

**The Firm:** This 45-lawyer team remains a major force in the Reno market, while also enjoying a recent upsurge in its southern Nevada workload. The firm offers expertise in land use law, entitlement work and zoning, as well as more traditional real estate questions such as real property purchases and sales, financing transactions, and commercial and residential developments.

**The Lawyers:** **John Frankovich** is *"as good as there is in Reno,"* sources state. He is involved in all aspects of real estate, including project approvals, acquisition entitlements, drafting documentation, land use and zoning work. He also cooperates with municipal and government entities, utilizing a *"superb network of contacts and great relations with all the city officials."* Fellow Reno-based partner **Leo Bergin** is involved in the majority of major northern Nevada land deals. His practice involves the representation of agricultural entities such as farming and ranching operations, in particular with respect to the selling of land for conversion to real estate. Bergin is hailed by peers as *"a deal-maker of the highest level."*

**Clients/Work Highlights:** Lawyers have been instrumental in the development of a new shopping center under construction in Reno on behalf of Bayer Properties, and represent Centex on two projects involving over 1,000 houses. Other clients include The Associated General Contractors of America, St James's Village and First Security Bank.

### Snell & Wilmer LLP

See firm details p.200

**The Firm:** The team here benefits from a network of six offices across the west, housing more than 400 attorneys. Lawyers in Las Vegas are known for their handling of complex transactions *"on a scale that few are able to match."* The firm is currently reaping the benefits of the high-rise boom in Las Vegas by playing a key role in mixed-use condominium projects, residential condominiums and casino hotels.

**The Lawyers:** **Patricia Curtis** (see p.1257) handles complex real estate development and finance matters, as well as some corporate acquisition work. 2005 saw her involved in registration and retail office lease work on mixed-use real estate projects such as the Curve, a 47.5-acre residential development of condominium towers, and Streamline Tower. Curtis also featured in a $37 million office condominium acquisition project for Bedford Property Investors. Her practice also covers some finance and charity work. **James Mace** (see p.1259) inspires great client loyalty, with one client commenting: *"We came with him when he moved and would follow him wherever he goes."* His expertise is rooted in complex commercial real estate developments, where he represents major developers in condominium, timeshare and project finance deals. Mace is also very active in the hospitality industry, representing many of Las Vegas' larger hotels. Clients laud him as *"an accommodating and practical problem solver."* An expert in real estate finance, **Stephen Yoken** (see p.1260) handles all types of loans and rights issues. He also boasts expertise in real estate purchasing, sales and leasing, and benefits from his experience at Bank of America by exhibiting great talent in transactional law and lending matters.

**Clients/Work Highlights:** Lawyers acted for Nevada Real Estate council regarding the capture of a $95 million development loan from Deutsche Bank for Town Square, a multiuse regional retail center and luxury hotel joint venture with Turnberry Associates and CENTRA Properties. The team assisted the Falcon Group with the development of the Pinnacle, and acted in the city's redevelopment efforts of Evolution Towers. The firm also obtained an $18 million credit facility for the charity Children's Choice. Other key clients include Lehman Brothers; Bank of America; JPMorgan; MGM; Turnberry Associates and Trump.

## Band 3

### Allison, MacKenzie, Russell, Pavlakis, Wright & Fagan, Ltd

**The Firm:** This Carson City-based outfit features an active real estate team that handles *"matters of significance that belie the firm's size,"* according to sources. The firm represents both state and corporate clients, including major developers, gaming establishments, public utilities and regulatory agencies. Lawyers also feature strongly on lobbying questions, where they are often responsible for the drafting of legislation concerning interval resort projects.

**The Lawyers:** James Cavilia heads the real estate practice here.

**Clients/Work Highlights:** The team handled a number of major development projects in north Nevada, including an interval resort project in Lake Tahoe. Major clients include David Walley's Resort; Quintus Resorts; Resorts West; Vidler Water; Washoe County Utility Division and Carriage House Timeshare Association.

### Deaner, Deaner, Scann, Malan & Larsen

**The Firm:** This six-lawyer firm concentrates on business law, real estate, bankruptcy and commercial litigation. The firm serves local and national clients, which include municipalities, public companies, Nevada businesses and local entrepreneurs.

**The Lawyers:** The firm's founder and senior partner, **Charles Deaner**, is widely regarded as the *"dean of the southern Nevada real estate Bar."* He applies more than 50 years of experience to real property, probate and transactional law and commands great respect among peers, who cite him as *"one of the pioneers of the Nevada legal system."*

**Clients/Work Highlights:** The firm's clients include the City of North Las Vegas; Clark County Credit Union; Land Title of Nevada; Las Vegas Shopping Centers and Nevada Federal Credit Union.

### Rice Silbey Reuther & Sullivan LLP

**The Firm:** This eight-strong boutique devotes its energies to complex real estate transactions. The firm belies its relative youth by enjoying a *"formidable reputation,"* largely thanks to the *"wealth of experience shared between the four founding partners."* The team handles all manner of complex transactions, such as financings, leasing, joint ventures and planned developments on behalf of major Las Vegas real estate developers and businesses.

**The Lawyers:** **Stephen Rice** specializes in real estate acquisitions and dispositions, financings and venture formation. He has a reputation for handling major transactions in a *"confident and technically astute way."* Rice also serves as general counsel to Basic Management, one of Las Vegas' largest landowners.

**Clients/Work Highlights:** The firm acts for a large number of home building and development companies, such as Kimball Hill Homes; Frey Development; Nevada West Development and Avante Homes. Other clients include Dragon Ridge Golf Club, Fortune International and CENTRA Properties.

## Santoro, Driggs, Walch, Kearney, Johnson & Thompson

**The Firm:** Six attorneys cover real property acquisition, land use and environmental and water law. The team also handles real estate financing, planned communities and the booming market in condominium projects. Interviewees comment that *"the team's overall excellence ensures that we can rely on it for all sorts of deals."*

**The Lawyers:** **Douglas Driggs** is credited with maintaining *"a great roster of clients"* and *"an impressive array of contacts"* among Nevada's political and business leaders. Notwithstanding his corporate securities and M&A background, Driggs now focuses on real estate matters. He represents a number of national lenders and local home building and construction companies, and has been instrumental in a number of significant residential, retail and office developments.

**Clients/Work Highlights:** Notable clients include Pinnacle Entertainment; Rhodes Homes; the State of Nevada; American West Homes; Centex and the City of Las Vegas.

### Other Notable Practitioners

The Reno-based **DeArmond Sharp** of Robison, Belaustegui, Sharp & Low handles real estate-related transactional work, including limited liability, loans and syndication. His practice is linked with a major home builder, for which he manages equity, investment and short-term lending. **Layne Butt** of Las Vegas boutique Bailey Merrill is adept at real estate, financial and commercial transactions. He spent a significant period of time at Lionel Sawyer & Collins and carries his big-firm experience and reputation with him.

# Leaders in Nevada

**ABBOTT, Scott**
Kamer Zucker & Abbott, Las Vegas
702 259 8640
*Recommended in Employment*

**ALONSO, Michael**
Jones Vargas, Reno 775 786 5000
*Recommended in Gaming & Licensing*

**ARRAJJ, David**
Schreck Brignone, Las Vegas
702 382 2101
*Recommended in Gaming & Licensing*

**BARNARD, Gregg**
Woodburn and Wedge, Reno
775 688 3000
*Recommended in Corporate/Commercial*

**BATTCHER, Frederick**
Hale Lane Peek Dennison and Howard, Reno 775 327 3000
*Recommended in Corporate/Commercial*

**BERGIN, Leo**
McDonald Carano Wilson McCune Bergin Frankovich & Hicks LLP, Reno
775 788 2000
*Recommended in Real Estate*

**BICE, Todd**
Schreck Brignone, Las Vegas
702 382 2101
*Recommended in Litigation*

**BONNER, Michael**
Kummer Kaempfer Bonner Renshaw & Ferrario, Las Vegas 702 792 7000
mbonner@kkbrf.com
*Recommended in Corporate/Commercial*

**Practice Areas:** Managing Partner. Practice concentration in business transactions, securities and gaming law. Has

acted as counsel on IPOs, follow on offerings, private placements, M&A and restructuring transactions. Has counseled publicly held companies on federal securities law disclosure and corporate governance matters, acquirors and acquirees in M&A, roll-ups and other acquisition-related transactions. Has represented hotel/casino resort operators, including ITT Corporation, Atlantis Casino Resort (Reno), Rio Suite Hotel Casino, Casablanca Resorts, Aladdin Hotel & Casino, as well as manufacturers, suppliers, lenders and officers and directors in transactional and licensing approvals before the Nevada gaming regulatory agencies.
**Prof. Memberships:** Former Chairman, Corporations Sub-Committee, Business Law Committee, State Bar of Nevada; former Vice-Chairman, Southern Nevada Disciplinary Board, State Bar of Nevada; Executive Committee, Nevada Development Authority; Member, International Association of Gaming Attorneys and Young President's Organization.
**Career:** Admitted to Nevada Bar (1981). Founding stockholder of Kummer Kaempfer Bonner Renshaw & Ferrario (1994) and stockholder of predecessor firm.
**Personal:** Las Vegas native; JD, University of California, Los Angeles (1981); BS (high distinction), University of Nevada, Las Vegas (1978).

**BOWMAN, Linda**
Law Office of Linda A Bowman Ltd, Reno
775 335 1700
*Recommended in Environment*

**BRIGNONE, Andrew**
Schreck Brignone, Las Vegas
702 382 2101

*Recommended in Employment*

**BUCKLEY, Michael**
Jones Vargas, Las Vegas
702 734 2220
*Recommended in Real Estate*

**BULLEN, Linda**
Lionel Sawyer & Collins, Las Vegas
702 383 8888
*Recommended in Environment*

**BUTT, Layne**
Bailey Merrill, Las Vegas
702 562 8820
*Recommended in Real Estate*

**CABOT, Anthony**
Lewis and Roca, Las Vegas
702 949 8200
*Recommended in Gaming & Licensing*

**CAMPBELL, Donald**
Campbell & Williams, Las Vegas
702 382 5222
*Recommended in Litigation*

**COLE, Howard**
Lionel Sawyer & Collins, Las Vegas
702 383 8888
*Recommended in Employment*

**CURRAN, William**
Curran & Parry, Las Vegas
702 471 7000
*Recommended in Gaming & Licensing*

**CURTIS, Patricia**
Snell & Wilmer LLP, Las Vegas
702 784 5226
pcurtis@swlaw.com
*Recommended in Real Estate*
**Practice Areas:** Practice concentrated in real estate financing and development. Represents developers of commercial, residential, condominium, hotel-condominium and mixed-use projects and assisted

living communities, as well as a variety of local, regional and national lenders and borrowers in financing transactions.
**Prof. Memberships:** State Bar of Nevada; Clark County Bar Association; American Bar Association (Business Law and Real Estate Sections); Urban Land Institute, Las Vegas Chapter; National Association of Industrial and Office Parks, Las Vegas Chapter; Commercial Real Estate Women of Southern Nevada.
**Personal:** Member of Executive Board, Communities in Schools of Southern Nevada.

**DAVIS JR, William**
Jones Vargas, Reno 775 786 5000
*Recommended in Real Estate*

**DE LIPKAU, Ross E**
Parsons Behle & Latimer PC, Reno
775 323 1601
Rdelipkau@parsonsbehle.com
*Recommended in Environment*
**Practice Areas:** Water law, including governmental permitting and licensing of water projects, due diligence analysis of water rights. Administrative hearings before Nevada State Engineer and judicial matters in state and federal courts.
**Prof. Memberships:** Trustee, Rocky Mountain Mineral Law Foundation. Member, Nevada State Bar.
**Career:** Shareholder, Parsons Behle & Latimer. Before joining the firm, was member of Nevada firm Marshall Hill Cassas & de Lipkau. Served as Deputy Attorney General to Nevada State Engineer. Recognized in Best Lawyers of America, Natural Resources.
**Personal:** BS, Mechanical Engineering, United States Merchant Marine Academy, Kings Point, New York. JD, McGeorge School of Law.

## DEANER, Charles
Deaner, Deaner, Scann, Malan &
Larsen, Las Vegas 702 382 6911
*Recommended in Real Estate*

## DENNISON, Karen
Hale Lane Peek Dennison and Howard,
Reno 775 327 3000
*Recommended in Real Estate*

## DEPAOLI, Gordon
Woodburn and Wedge, Reno
775 688 3000
*Recommended in Environment*

## DOLAN, Colleen
Lionel Sawyer & Collins, Reno
775 788 8666
*Recommended in
Corporate/Commercial*

## DORNAK, David
Lewis and Roca, Las Vegas
702 949 8200
*Recommended in Employment*

## DRIGGS, J Douglas
Santoro, Driggs, Walch, Kearney, Johnson & Thompson, Las Vegas
702 791 0308
*Recommended in Real Estate*

## DRURY, Mary
Marquis & Aurbach, Las Vegas
702 382 0711
*Recommended in
Corporate/Commercial*

## DUHON, Gary
Lionel Sawyer & Collins, Reno
775 788 8666
*Recommended in Real Estate*

## EFROYMSON, Kevin
Kevin C Efroymson, Las Vegas
*Recommended in Employment*

## ETEM, Craig
Lionel Sawyer & Collins, Reno
775 788 8666
*Recommended in
Corporate/Commercial*

## FAISS, Robert
Lionel Sawyer & Collins, Las Vegas
702 383 8888
*Recommended in Gaming & Licensing*

## FERENBACH, Cam
Lionel Sawyer & Collins, Las Vegas
702 383 8888
*Recommended in Litigation*

## FERRARIO, Mark E
Kummer Kaempfer Bonner Renshaw &
Ferrario, Las Vegas 702 792 7000
mferrario@kkbrf.com
*Recommended in Litigation*
**Practice Areas:** Partner and Chair of
Litigation Department. Practice focuses
on general business and commercial litigation with emphasis on business-related
disputes, counsels clients on matters
related to civil litigation involving corporate, real estate, business dissolution,
gaming, entertainment, securities, unfair

competition and intellectual property
issues. Was part of the lead trial team in
the $90 million lawsuit that resulted from
the PEPCON chemical plant explosion in
Henderson, NV (1988); has represented a
major subcontractor in the MGM Grand
and Hilton Hotel fire cases (1980s); Lonnie 'Ted' Binion with Nevada gaming regulators; the Southern Nevada Home
Builders Association during several sessions of the Nevada Legislature.
**Career:** Admitted to Nevada Bar (1983).
University of California, Los Angeles, JD
(1981); University of Nevada, Las Vegas,
BS (1978). Member of both the Nevada
and California Bar and practices in both
jurisdictions.

## FIORENTINO, Mark H
Kummer Kaempfer Bonner Renshaw &
Ferrario, Las Vegas 702 792 7000
mfiorentino@kkbrf.com
*Recommended in Real Estate*
**Practice Areas:** Partner/Head of Land
Use and Government Affairs Practice.
Practices extensively before the Nevada
State Legislature and local government
authorities on land use, zoning, licensing
and general business matters. Substantial
experience with zoning matters, state and
local gaming license and tax matters. Drafts
ordinances, legislation, and regulations on
a variety of zoning, gaming and general
business issues. Represents Focus Property
Group, Howard Hughes Corporation,
Boyd Gaming Corporation, The Related
Companies, Republic Services, Sierra
Health Services, Chelsea Property Group,
Pulte Homes, Astoria Homes, and Lamar
Advertising. Registered lobbyist with the
Nevada State Legislature, Clark County
and Cities of Las Vegas and Henderson.
**Prof. Memberships:** Member, American
Bar Association, Clark County Bar Asso-
ciation, International Association of
Gaming Attorneys. Served as Circuit
Governor, Law Student Division, Ameri-
can Bar Association, Former Member,
Clark County Comprehensive Planning
Steering Committee. Served on Clark
County Committee rewriting the Coun-
ty's Zoning Code and City of Las Vegas
Master Plan Committee.
**Career:** Admitted to Nevada Bar (1992);
Partner, Kummer Kaempfer Bonner Ren-
shaw & Ferrario (1999); former associate,
Lionel, Sawyer & Collins (1992-95).
**Publications:** Member, Drake University
Law Review. Published article on federal
preemption of tobacco litigation. Con-
tributing author to International Casino
Law (1993) and Nevada Gaming Law
(1995).
**Personal:** JS-Drake University (1992);
BS-Arizona State University (1986).

## FOWLER, John
Woodburn and Wedge, Reno
775 688 3000
*Recommended in
Corporate/Commercial*

## FRANKOVICH, John
McDonald Carano Wilson McCune
Bergin Frankovich & Hicks LLP, Reno
775 788 2000
*Recommended in Real Estate*

## GARCIA, David
Hale Lane Peek Dennison and Howard,
Reno 775 327 3000
*Recommended in
Corporate/Commercial*

## GIORDANO, Gregory
Lionel Sawyer & Collins, Las Vegas
702 383 8888
*Recommended in Gaming & Licensing*

## GOLDSTEIN, Mark
Lionel Sawyer & Collins, Las Vegas
702 383 8888
*Recommended in
Corporate/Commercial, Real Estate*

## GOOLD, Barry
Goold Patterson Ales & Day, Las Vegas
702 436 2600
bgoold@gooldpatterson.com
*Recommended in Real Estate*
**Practice Areas:** Barry Goold's practice
is focused on commercial real estate. He
handles a variety of transactions, including purchases and sales of unimproved
real property, shopping centers, apartment complexes and hotels. He also handles landlord/tenant disputes, negotiation
of leases (especially Big Box leases), and
preparation of commercial covenants,
conditions and restrictions. He represents
owners of master-planned communities
and developers of all kinds. (For example,
the firm represents more than a dozen
homebuilders). Mr Goold has an extensive practice representing lenders and
commercial borrowers in loans secured
by real property. Mr Goold also has a
considerable practice in construction law,
negotiating agreements with architects
and contractors for his developer clients.
**Prof. Memberships:** American Bar
Association, State Bar of Nevada, Clark
County Bar Association, State Bar of California (inactive).
**Career:** Barry Goold is the Senior Partner and President of Goold Patterson
Ales & Day, which he co-founded with
Jeffrey D Patterson in 1988. He has practiced in Las Vegas, Nevada for over 25
years. Mr Goold has been named in every
consecutive edition of a leading US legal
publication. He has given many seminars,
and serves as an expert witness in complex real estate litigation.
**Personal:** Barry Goold received his
Undergraduate Degree (with distinction)
from UC Berkeley in 1974 (Phi Beta
Kappa), and his JD Degree from UC
Berkeley (Boalt Hall) in 1977. While
attending Boalt Hall, he clerked for
Melvin Belli, and also clerked for con-
sumer-law specialist Robert A Goldstein.
He is admitted to practice in California
(1977) and Nevada (1978). From Febru-

ary 1978 through July 1982, he was an
associate commercial attorney with
Lionel Sawyer & Collins. He broadened
his commercial practice as a Director in
the firm of Smith, Goold & Kotchka prior
to founding Goold Patterson Ales & Day.

## GORDON, Andrew
McDonald Carano Wilson McCune
Bergin Frankovich & Hicks LLP,
Las Vegas 702 873 4100
*Recommended in Litigation*

## HANEY, Dennis
Haney, Woloson & Mullins, Las Vegas
702 474 7557
*Recommended in Litigation*

## HARRISON, Kirk
Harrison, Kemp & Jones, LLP, Las Vegas
702 385 6000
*Recommended in Litigation*

## HARRISON, Sylvia
McDonald Carano Wilson McCune
Bergin Frankovich & Hicks LLP, Reno
775 788 2000
*Recommended in Environment*

## HEINZ, Von
Lewis and Roca, Las Vegas
702 949 8200
*Recommended in Litigation*

## HEJMANOWSKI, Paul
Lionel Sawyer & Collins, Las Vegas
702 383 8888
*Recommended in Litigation*

## HICKS, Alvin
McDonald Carano Wilson McCune
Bergin Frankovich & Hicks LLP, Reno
775 788 2000
*Recommended in Gaming & Licensing*

## HICKS, Patrick H
Littler Mendelson, PC, Las Vegas
702 862 8800
phicks@littler.com
*Recommended in Employment*
**Practice Areas:** Regularly appears
before all state and federal courts in California and Nevada. He represents
employers before EEOC, the Nevada
Equal Rights Commission and the California Department of Fair Employment
and Housing. Represents employers in
wrongful termination, employment discrimination litigation and trial work;
grievance arbitrations; Title VII proceedings; counsels employers on ADA, FMLA,
employee terminations, workplace violence, and pre-employment screening.
**Prof. Memberships:** Nevada State Bar,
the American Bar Association, the Clark
County Bar Association and the Washoe
County Bar Association.
**Personal:** University of California, Hastings College of the Law (JD, 1987); University of California, Davis (BA, 1984)

## HILL, Earl M
Parsons Behle & Latimer PC, Reno
775 323 1601
EHill@parsonsbehle.com

*Recommended in Environment*

**Practice Areas:** Natural resources, mining law and public lands.

**Prof. Memberships:** Member, State Bar of Nevada. Served as Member of Board of Trustees of Rocky Mountain Mineral Law Foundation for more than 20 years.

**Career:** Of Counsel, Parsons Behle & Latimer. Before joining the firm, was member of Nevada firm Marshall Hill Cassas & de Lipkau and Colorado firm Sherman & Howard. Listed in Best Lawyers in America for Natural Resources every year since beginning of directory. Law clerk to Supreme Court of Nevada in 1962.

**Personal:** BA, University of Washington, 1960. JD, University of Washington School of Law, 1962.

**JOLLEY, R Gardner**
Jolley, Urga, Wirth & Woodbury,
Las Vegas 702 699 7500
*Recommended in Litigation*

**JONES, J Randall**
Harrison, Kemp & Jones, LLP, Las Vegas
702 385 6000
*Recommended in Litigation*

**JONES, Leslie Terry**
Schreck Brignone, Las Vegas
702 382 2101
*Recommended in*
*Corporate/Commercial, Real Estate*

**KAEMPFER, Christopher**
Kummer Kaempfer Bonner Renshaw &
Ferrario, Las Vegas 702 792 7000
ckaempfer@kkbrf.com
*Recommended in Real Estate*

**Practice Areas:** Senior Partner/Founder of the Land Use and Governmental Relations Department. Nearly 25 years representing development clients in Nevada. Personally argued precedent setting land use cases in both state and federal court. Registered lobbyist with the City of Las Vegas and Clark County, Nevada. Representative clients include Wal-Mart, Home Depot, Marnell Corrao, Pulte Homes, Las Vegas 51s Baseball Club, Olympia Group, CamCo, Inc. (SuperPawn) and Atlantic Richfield. Since 1977, represented numerous general contractors and subcontractors in Nevada, including Marnell Corrao (and its predecessor, Corrao Construction Company). As Legal Counsel for Marnell Corrao, negotiated construction contracts totaling nearly $2 billion.

**Prof. Memberships:** Member, American Bar, Clark County Bar, Nevada and California State Bar Associations; admitted to practice in United States District Courts for State of Nevada.

**Career:** Admitted to Nevada Bar (1976); California Bar (1975); Clerked in United States District Court for the Honorable Judge Roger D Foley (1975-76); District Counsel for the State of Nevada for the United States Small Business Administration (1976-77); founding Partner, Kum-

mer Kaempfer Bonner & Renshaw (1993); former Partner, predecessor firm Vargas & Bartlett (1982-93).

**Personal:** JD, University of the Pacific, McGeorge School of Law (1975); BA, University of Nevada, Las Vegas (1971).

**KAMER, Gregory**
Kamer Zucker & Abbott, Las Vegas
702 259 8640
*Recommended in Employment*

**KELLER, Edwin**
Kamer Zucker & Abbott, Las Vegas
702 259 8640
*Recommended in Employment*

**KENNEDY, Dennis**
Lionel Sawyer & Collins, Las Vegas
702 383 8888
*Recommended in Litigation*

**KIM, Robert C**
Kummer Kaempfer Bonner Renshaw &
Ferrario, Las Vegas 702 792 7000
rkim@kkbrf.com
*Recommended in*
*Corporate/Commercial*

**Practice Areas:** Partner. Practice includes general corporate, transactional, securities and gaming law, with focus on corporate governance, entity formation, public company compliance, private placements and contracts. Prior transactions include: VendingData Corporation (2003, $27.5 million equity offering); USA Capital First Trust Deed Fund, LLC (2002, $120 million equity offering); eRoomSystem Technologies, Inc. (2000, IPO); Carefree Holdings Limited Partnership (1999 $60 million roll-up transaction); Rio Hotel & Casino, Inc. (1998, $1 billion acquisition by Harrah's Entertainment, Inc.); and ITT Corporation (1997, takeover defense).

**Prof. Memberships:** Member, State Bar of Nevada, State Bar of California and American Bar Association; Chairman, Executive Committee, Business Law Section, State Bar of Nevada (committee responsible for proposing and preparing amendments to Nevada's business entity statutes). President and Co-Founder, Asian Bar Association of Las Vegas.

**Career:** Admitted to Nevada Bar (1996) and California Bar (1998).

**Publications:** Authored articles for Nevada Business Journal and American Bankruptcy Institute Journal. Speaker at seminars on business entity selection, limited liability companies and venture capital.

**Personal:** JD and MBA, University of Southern California (1996); BA, Government, Cornell University (1992). Born in New York, New York.

**KISHNER, Joanna S**
DLA Piper Rudnick Gray Cary US LLP,
Las Vegas 702 737 3433
joanna.kishner@dlapiper.com
*Recommended in Employment*

**Practice Areas:** Labor and employment law.

**Career:** She counsels clients on cases involving employment discrimination under federal laws as well as state laws in Nevada and California. Also handles cases involving unfair labor practice charges, union organization campaigns, and related administrative proceedings involving the NLRB; advises clients in issues including wrongful termination, wage and hour, personnel policies, privacy, and other state law claims; has litigated and advised clients in common law and statutory claims and in privacy, covenant not to compete, and international employment issues.

**Personal:** JD, University of California School of Law at Los Angeles; BA, Claremont McKenna College.

**KLEGERMAN, Neal**
Kummer Kaempfer Bonner Renshaw &
Ferrario, Las Vegas 702 792 7000
nklegerman@kkbrf.com
*Recommended in*
*Corporate/Commercial*

**Practice Areas:** Of Counsel. 24 years experience in representing companies in a broad range of corporate and securities law matters including counseling, compliance, and transactions (financing and M&A).

**Career:** Admitted to Nevada Bar (1999), New York Bar (1988) and Illinois Bar (1979). 21 years with the law firm of Baker & McKenzie in its Chicago office. During periods of partnership with Baker & McKenzie, was Co-Chair of the Securities Law Subgroup of the national Corporate and Securities Practice and co-coordinator of the Chicago office's Corporate and Securities Practice. Practice included representation of domestic and foreign companies ranging from development stage to Fortune 500 on a variety of corporate and securities matters, including equity and M&A transactions, counseling, compliance, SEC investigations and board of directors matters. Named to list of Illinois Leading Attorneys while with Baker & McKenzie.

**Personal:** Grinnell College, Grinnell, Iowa with honors in Economics and as Phi Beta Kappa in 1979; JD from Columbia University, New York, New York in 1979 and was a Harlan Fiske Stone Scholar in each of 1977, 1978, and 1979.

**KOTCHKA, Malani**
Smith & Kotchka Ltd, Las Vegas
702 382 1707
*Recommended in Employment*

**KUMMER, Thomas F**
Kummer Kaempfer Bonner Renshaw &
Ferrario, Las Vegas 702 792 7000
tkummer@kkbrf.com
*Recommended in Litigation*

**Practice Areas:** Senior Litigation Partner. Practice concentration encompasses business/commercial, professional malpractice, solid waste/resource recovery, aviation and construction litigation. Has

represented ITT Corporation (1997 hostile takeover), Exxon Mobil, Republic Services, Aerospatiale, US Aviation Underwriters, General Growth Properties, Inamed Corporation and Las Vegas Metropolitan Police Department. Has appeared in US and Nevada District Court, the 9th Circuit Court of Appeals, and the Nevada Supreme Court.

**Prof. Memberships:** State Bar of Nevada; American Bar, Clark County Bar and American Trial Lawyers Associations; Defense Research Institute; served for eight years on the Ethics and Professional Responsibility Committee of the State Bar of Nevada, three years as Committee Chair; appointed by the Nevada Supreme Court to act as a Supreme Court Settlement Conference Judge.

**Career:** St Louis University, BSC (1965) and JD (1968). Admitted to Missouri Bar (1968-inactive) and Nevada Bar (1971). Founding Partner, Kummer Kaempfer Bonner & Renshaw (1994); former Partner, predecessor firm (1982-94, Vargas & Bartlett).

**Personal:** Active Member of Las Vegas community, participates in various community and church organizations. Currently serves as Board Member and Legal Counsel to HELP of Southern Nevada.

**LARSEN, Paul**
Lionel Sawyer & Collins, Las Vegas
702 383 8888
*Recommended in Gaming & Licensing*

**LAXALT, Bruce**
Laxalt & Nomura, Reno
775 322 1170
*Recommended in Litigation*

**LENHARD, Kirk**
Jones Vargas, Las Vegas
702 734 2220
*Recommended in Litigation*

**MACE, Jim**
Snell & Wilmer LLP, Las Vegas
702 784 5227
jmace@swlaw.com
*Recommended in Real Estate*

**Practice Areas:** Practice concentrated in complex real estate development, including mixed-use, high-rise condominium and condominium hotel projects.

**Prof. Memberships:** American Bar Association (Business Law Section, Real Property Section, and Probate and Trust Section); New York Bar Association; Florida Bar Association; Nevada Bar Association; Clark County Bar Association.

**Personal:** Director, Nevada Cancer Institute.

**MEAD, Leon**
Mead Pezzillo LLP, Las Vegas
702 233 4225
*Recommended in Litigation*

**MORGAN, Ann**
Jones Vargas, Reno 775 786 5000
*Recommended in Employment*

**MORRIS, Steve**
Morris Pickering & Sanner, Las Vegas
702 474 9400
*Recommended in Litigation*

**MOSS, Gary**
DLA Piper Rudnick Gray Cary US LLP,
Las Vegas 702 737 3433
gary.moss@dlapiper.com
*Recommended in Employment*
**Practice Areas:** Labor and employment.
**Career:** His labor and employment law practice includes federal and state court employment discrimination and wrongful discharge litigation, collective bargaining negotiations, arbitrations, union organizing campaigns, cases before federal and state administrative agencies, wage and hour matters, and labor and employment law issues relating to sales, mergers, acquisitions, shutdown and bankruptcies. He has extensive experience in advising clients regarding strikes and other forms of labor disputes, union organizing attempts, corporate campaigns, and arbitration of disputes arising under collective bargaining agreements.
**Personal:** JD, University of Iowa; BA, University of Illinois.

**NAYLOR, John**
Lionel Sawyer & Collins, Las Vegas
702 383 8888
*Recommended in Litigation*

**NEWMAN, James**
Hale Lane Peek Dennison and Howard,
Reno 775 327 3000
*Recommended in Corporate/Commercial*

**NOVACEK, Stephen**
Hale Lane Peek Dennison and Howard,
Reno 775 327 3000
*Recommended in Real Estate*

**PATTERSON, Jeffrey**
Goold Patterson Ales & Day, Las Vegas
702 436 2600
jpatterson@gooldpatterson.com
*Recommended in Real Estate*
**Practice Areas:** Jeffrey Patterson has practiced in Las Vegas, Nevada for over 23 years, focusing primarily on commercial real estate. He handles a variety of transactions, including the purchase, sale and financing of unimproved real property, shopping centers, apartment complexes and hotels. He also handles lease negotiations and drafting, and landlord and tenant disputes. Mr Patterson also devotes a portion of his practice to representing landlords and lenders in bankruptcy proceedings.
**Prof. Memberships:** American Bar Association, State Bar of Nevada, Clark County Bar Association.
**Career:** Jeffrey Patterson co-founded Goold Patterson Ales & Day with Barry Goold in 1988. Mr Patterson has spoken at a number of seminars on commercial leasing and evictions. Recently, Mr Patter-

son handled two separate hotel transactions.
**Personal:** Jeffrey Patterson received his Undergraduate Degree (with honors) from the University of Michigan in 1978, and his JD from the University of San Diego School of Law in 1981. He was admitted to practice in the State of Nevada in 1981. From September 1981 to December 1982, he was a Nevada Deputy Attorney General. Mr Patterson was the senior commercial associate at Smith Goold & Kotchka from 1983 to 1988, prior to founding Goold Patterson Ales & Day.

**PAUSTIAN, Kathleen M**
Parsons Behle & Latimer PC, Las Vegas
702 384 3877
KPaustian@parsonsbehle.com
*Recommended in Employment*
**Practice Areas:** Employment law, defending management in harassment, discrimination, wrongful termination, wage and hour cases; commercial litigation.
**Prof. Memberships:** Member: American Bar Association; Southern Nevada Association of Women Attorneys; Nevada State Bar; Florida State Bar. North Las Vegas Chamber of Commerce: Board of Directors and co-founder of The Women's Forum.
**Career:** Shareholder, Parsons Behle & Latimer. Lawyer representative, Ninth Circuit Judicial Conference, District of Nevada. Vice-Chair, Nevada Standing Committee on Judicial Ethics and Election Practices. Nevada Supreme Court Settlement Judge. Frequent speaker/trainer on human resource management topics.
**Personal:** JD, University of Florida, 1987. BA, University of South Dakota, 1971.

**PEEK, Stephen**
Hale Lane Peek Dennison and Howard,
Las Vegas 702 222 2500
*Recommended in Litigation*

**PEEL, Richard**
Peel Brimley LLP, Henderson
702 990 7272
*Recommended in Litigation*

**PETERSON, Karen**
Allison, MacKenzie, Russell, Pavlakis,
Wright & Fagan, Ltd, Carson City
775 687 0202
*Recommended in Environment*

**PISANELLI, James**
Schreck Brignone, Las Vegas
702 382 2101
*Recommended in Litigation*

**REASER, Dan**
Lionel Sawyer & Collins, Reno
775 788 8666
*Recommended in Gaming & Licensing*

**RICCIARDI, Mark**
Fisher & Phillips LLP, Las Vegas
702 252 3131
mricciardi@laborlawyers.com

*Recommended in Employment*
**Practice Areas:** Mark Ricciardi is a Partner in the Las Vegas office of the national law firm of Fisher & Phillips LLP, practicing exclusively in labor and employment law representing management. He represents hotels, casinos and other businesses in labor and employment matters and is one of the leading authorities in Nevada on wage-hour law. Ricciardi has successfully tried jury and bench trials in wrongful termination, retaliation, sexual harassment, discrimination, and wage-hour claims. He argued Costa v. Desert Palace, Inc. before the United States Supreme Court and has litigated unfair labor practice charges and union election objections before the NLRB.

**RICE, Stephen**
Rice Silbey Reuther & Sullivan LLP, Las
Vegas 702 732 9099
*Recommended in Real Estate*

**ROBISON, Kent**
Robison, Belaustegui, Sharp & Low,
Reno 775 329 3151
*Recommended in Litigation*

**SANTORO, Nicholas**
Santoro, Driggs, Walch, Kearney, Johnson & Thompson, Las Vegas
702 791 0308
*Recommended in Litigation*

**SCHRECK, Frank**
Schreck Brignone, Las Vegas
702 382 2101
*Recommended in Gaming & Licensing*

**SCHULHOFER, Ellen**
Schreck Brignone, Las Vegas
702 382 2101
*Recommended in Corporate/Commercial*

**SHARP, F DeArmond**
Robison, Belaustegui, Sharp & Low,
Reno 775 329 3151
*Recommended in Real Estate*

**SILVER, Jeffrey**
Gordon & Silver Ltd, Las Vegas
702 796 5555
*Recommended in Gaming & Licensing*

**SMITH, Gregory**
Smith & Kotchka Ltd, Las Vegas
702 382 1707
*Recommended in Employment*

**SPANGLER, Georlen**
Kolesar & Leatham Chtd, Las Vegas
702 362 7800
*Recommended in Litigation*

**TOUTON, Todd**
Lionel Sawyer & Collins, Las Vegas
702 383 8888
*Recommended in Litigation*

**URGA, William**
Jolley, Urga, Wirth & Woodbury, Las
Vegas 702 699 7500
*Recommended in Litigation*

**VERMEYS, Sonia Church**
Schreck Brignone, Las Vegas
702 382 2101
*Recommended in Corporate/
Commercial, Gaming & Licensing*

**WALCH, Greg**
Santoro, Driggs, Walch, Kearney, Johnson & Thompson, Las Vegas
702 791 0308
*Recommended in Environment*

**WHITTEMORE, Ellen**
Lionel Sawyer & Collins, Las Vegas
702 383 8888
*Recommended in Gaming & Licensing*

**WILLIAMS, J Colby**
Campbell & Williams, Las Vegas
702 382 5222
*Recommended in Litigation*

**WOLOSON, Kenneth**
Haney, Woloson & Mullins, Las Vegas
702 474 7557
*Recommended in
Corporate/Commercial*

**YOKEN, Stephen**
Snell & Wilmer LLP, Las Vegas
702 784 5235
syoken@swlaw.com
*Recommended in Real Estate*
**Practice Areas:** Practice concentrated in real estate, including purchases, sales, leasing and development issues; real estate finance, including construction loans, acquisition and development loans, permanent loans, problem loan restructuring, creditors rights issues and foreclosures; affordable housing and redevelopment projects; and other business and contract law matters.
**Prof. Memberships:** State Bar of Nevada; State Bar of California; American Bar Association; Clark County Bar Association.
**Career:** Partner, Snell & Wilmer L.L.P. since 2004. Senior Counsel, Bank of America, 1984-93.
**Personal:** Yale Law School (JD 1979); Harvard University (AB 1975).

**YOUCHAH, Elayna**
Schreck Brignone, Las Vegas
702 382 2101
*Recommended in Employment*

**ZUCKER, Carol**
Kamer Zucker & Abbott, Las Vegas
702 259 8640
*Recommended in Employment*

**ZUCKER, Jeffrey**
Lionel Sawyer & Collins, Las Vegas
702 383 8888
*Recommended in
Corporate/Commercial, Real Estate*

# CURRAN & PARRY

## THE FIRM

**Managing Partners:** William P Curran
                              Stanley W Parry

**Number of partners:** 4
**Number of other lawyers:** 2

**HEAD OFFICE**

**NEVADA**
Bank of America Plaza, 300 South 4th St, Suite 1201, **Las Vegas**, NV 89101
**Tel:** 702 471 7000   **Fax:** 702 471 7070
**Website:** www.curranparry.com
**Email:** curranparry@curranparry.com

**FIRM OVERVIEW:** The attorneys at Curran & Parry collectively boast decades of professional expertise in both the legal and the political environments of the State of Nevada. They are solution-oriented and driven to serve the needs of the client. The firm's culture is its unwavering commitment to the highest standards of service, integrity and professionalism, which is reflected in both its carefully selected staff, as well as in its reputable clientele. Bill Curran's ten years as County Counsel to the Clark County Commission and his subsequent ten-year service after gubernatorial appointment to the Nevada Gaming Commission, including eight years as Chairman, have provided him with invaluable insight into government processes in Nevada. His reputation for ingenuity, integrity and diligence, along with his extensive network of key contacts, enables him to provide uniquely effective representation on matters involving state and local government affairs. His past service as President of the State Bar of Nevada, and current membership on the boards of directors of several corporate and non-profit organizations, reflect his active involvement in the Las Vegas community. He has been selected for inclusion in the publication The Best Lawyers in America. Stan Parry's reputation as a trial attorney in the District Attorney's office, followed by his tenure on the US Department of Justice Organized Crime Strike Force, have earned him countless honors as an aggressive, ethical and successful litigator. Having served as legal counsel to the Clark County Planning Commission for many years, his expertise in real estate matters, eminent domain and construction issues is widely recognized. Susan L Johnson brings years of public sector and private company expertise to the firm. After serving as legal counsel to the Clark County Commission and the Las Vegas Valley Water District, she was appointed Supervising Chief Deputy Attorney General for the State of Nevada. As Assistant General Counsel of Harrah's, General Counsel of Rio Suites Hotels and Casinos, Corporate Counsel of Caesars Entertainment, and part-time professor of Hospitality Law at the University of Nevada Las Vegas, her knowledge of corporate, gaming, transactional and employment issues makes her an invaluable member of the Curran & Parry team. Joshua H Reisman is an active litigator. He has been with Curran & Parry for seven years, having previously been employed as a litigator at a prestigious New York City law firm. After law school he was a law clerk to a federal district court and, subsequently, to the Sixth Circuit Court of Appeals. A native Las Vegan, he has deep roots in the Southern Nevada community. With other firm attorneys having served in a wide variety of community activities, this wealth of government, corporate, political and litigation experience, coupled with a Martindale Hubble A-V rating, assures clients unparalleled legal advocacy enhanced by the personal attention unique to this boutique law firm.

## MAIN AREAS OF PRACTICE:

**Business:** Curran & Parry represents clients on a wide variety of operational and strategic business issues, including the structuring and formation of business entities, land use entitlements, commercial transactions and contracts, real estate transactions, commercial leases, regulatory requirements, and contractual employment matters such as executive employment and severance agreements. Due to the firm's extensive number of clients with gaming and/or liquor licenses, it provides expert operational advice for the complicated regulatory requirements of liquor and gaming related businesses.

**Litigation:** The firm's litigation practice is comprised of predominantly business litigation in state, federal and appellate courts. Litigation areas include real estate litigation, administrative and regulatory matters, business entity member disputes, shareholder derivative lawsuits, business contracts and torts, eminent domain, complex personal injury matters, construction litigation, and title insurance defense.

**Gaming:** The State of Nevada and each local government in Nevada have adopted complex regulatory schemes and procedures for obtaining gaming licenses and for regulatory compliance. Curran & Parry specializes in assisting its clients in navigating this multi-jurisdictional regulatory process, both pre-licensing and post-licensing. Bill Curran has been recognized as one of Nevada's foremost gaming attorneys. In an industry where the value of experience and knowledge of institutional history is critical, his background as Chairman of the Nevada Gaming Commission and as private counsel to gaming licensees makes him one of the most sought after representatives for applicants to the gaming industry. He serves as a member of several casinos' regulatory compliance committees and is frequently called upon to consult with Wall Street investment firms as an expert in gaming matters, and as a consultant for emerging gaming jurisdictions. Susan Johnson's in-house experience with two of the world's largest publicly-traded gaming companies provides a depth of understanding of the issues facing regulated businesses, bringing a unique and invaluable perspective to clients.

**Land Use/Zoning:** With thousands of people moving into Southern Nevada monthly for residential and new commercial opportunities, local municipalities struggle to address growth issues. Curran & Parry is recognized as one of the few local firms specializing in land use matters and represents numerous land owners, investors and developers. The firm's breadth of experience on the "inside" makes it a prudent choice for clients seeking to obtain approvals for land development and related entitlements.

**Administrative & Government Relations:** A significant number of Curran & Parry's clients have matters requiring favorable City Council, County Commission, or State agency action. In addition to privileged licenses such as liquor and gaming, the firm represents corporations and individuals in matters relating to public policy advocacy and legislative relations. Working with other professionals such as corporate counsel, CPA's, architects, engineers, public relations firms and the media is routine.

**Construction & Development:** The firm's clients include real estate developers, general contractors and sub-contractors for whom it provides a wide array of legal advice and services, including zoning applications, contract drafting and review, insurance review and advice, public works bid disputes, construction defect representation, litigation, and alternative dispute resolution. Stan Parry's representation of the local power company on numerous eminent domain cases further strengthens the firm's knowledge and understanding of the issues facing developers in this fast-growing community.

**CLIENTS:** CH2M Hill, Henry Brent Company/Lady Luck Hotel and Casino, Hotspur/JW Marriott Hotel, Interstate Brands Corporation, International Game Technology (IGT), Golden Palm Hotel & Casino, Las Vegas Helicopters, Lawyers Title Company, Meadow Gold Dairy, Nevada Power Company, Sletten Construction Company, Southern California Edison.

# KUMMER KAEMPFER BONNER RENSHAW & FERRARIO

## THE FIRM

**Managing Partner:** Michael J Bonner

**Number of Partners:** 18
**Number of other lawyers:** 27

## AREAS OF PRACTICE:

Corporate/Real Estate/Transactional/SEC & Gaming . . . . . . . . . . 36%
Commercial/Complex Litigation . . . . . . . . . . . . . . . . . . . . . . . . 42%
Governmental Affairs/Zoning/Land Use/Licensing . . . . . . . . . . . 22%

**FIRM OVERVIEW:** Kummer Kaempfer Bonner Renshaw & Ferrario (Kummer Kaempfer) is one of Nevada's largest law firms and a prominent force in the fastest growing state in the US, with offices in Las Vegas as well as Reno/Carson City. The firm's lawyers have had the honor and privilege to counsel many corporations, successful business owners, corporate executives and high-net worth individuals for their legal needs in Nevada. Founded in 1994, the firm's attorneys include a former United States Congressman, a Nevada State Senator, a former Deputy Secretary of State, and one of the state's top litigators who prevailed in one of the largest tort cases ever filed in the United States. Firm attorneys are active members of committees of the State Bar of Nevada, participate in the drafting of new business legislation, and are sought after as lecturers on local, regional and national legal topics. The firm believes that the basic elements of its success – a focus on the client instead of the lawyer and a commitment to results – are values that businesses identify with and share. The firm serves a diverse group of local, regional, national and international clients, including publicly- and privately-held business organizations, institutions, private individuals and non-profit organizations. The industries that the firm serves, among others, include real estate, development, hospitality, gaming, manufacturing, service, high technology and energy.

## MAIN AREAS OF PRACTICE:

**Corporate/Real Estate/Transactional/Securities & Gaming:** Kummer Kaempfer's attorneys are recognized to be among the best corporate and transactional lawyers in Nevada and have participated in a broad range of business transactions including complex merger and acquisition matters. The firm has the premier Nevada-based practice in federal and state securities law representation, having handled initial public offerings, private and public debt and equity securities offerings, development stage and venture capital financings and comprehensive corporate and business entity counseling and representation for issuers, underwriters, investors and lenders. Kummer Kaempfer has represented owners, developers, tenants and financiers in a multitude of real estate transactional and financing matters with significant experience in drafting and negotiating agreements for a variety of clients, projects and industries. Kummer Kaempfer represents clients in all aspects of Nevada's gaming regulatory matters including licensing and disciplinary proceedings.

**Commercial/Complex Litigation:** Kummer Kaempfer's trial and appellate attorneys have reputations for litigation excellence. Litigation areas include business disputes, professional responsibility litigation (including attorney and accountant liability), alternative dispute resolution, employment litigation, administrative and regulatory matters, construction litigation, general insurance litigation (including coverage issues), securities litigation, real estate litigation, receiverships and aviation litigation.

**Governmental Relations, Land Use, Zoning & Licensing, & Public Utilities:** Kummer Kaempfer is the leading Nevada firm representing developers and other businesses before governmental bodies on licensing, planning, zoning and building matters. The firm's Legislative Affairs Team provides select clients with legislative representation before the Nevada State Legislature. The firm also has affiliate relationships in Washington, DC for federal legislative and administrative representation. Kummer Kaempfer's Public Utility Practice includes representation of

## HEAD OFFICE

**NEVADA**
3800 Howard Hughes Parkway, Seventh Floor, Las Vegas, NV 89109-0907
**Tel:** 702 792 7000    **Fax:** 702 796 7181
**Email:** info@kkbrf.com
**Website:** www.kkbrf.com

## BRANCH OFFICES

**NEVADA**
5585 Kietzke Lane, **Reno**, NV 89511-2089
**Tel:** 775 852 3900    **Fax:** 775 852 3982

3425 Cliff Shadows Parkway, Suite 150, **Las Vegas** NV 89129
**Tel:** 702 693 4260    **Fax:** 702 939 8457

clients before the Public Utilities Commission of Nevada on matters that address the purchase, sale and distribution of gas, water and electricity, including all forms of renewable energy such as solar, wind, geothermal and biomass. The firm represents land developers, private individuals and large users and purchasers of water and electricity throughout the state. In addition, the firm represents clients before the State Water Engineer on matters that are exclusively related to the procurement of water.

**Meritas:** Kummer Kaempfer is the Las Vegas, Nevada member firm of Meritas, an international affiliation of business law firms. Meritas is a worldwide alliance consisting of nearly 5,000 lawyers in 200 business law firms located in 50+ countries around the world, each working together to provide clients the best of both worlds: a local legal partner with deep international resources. The alliance has a 12-year record of successful cooperation, offering clients the ability to access high quality legal service worldwide supported by a common technology platform. Membership is by invitation only and firms are subject to a rigorous selection and ongoing monitoring process.

**CLIENTS:** Clients include Archon Corporation; Astoria Homes; Boyd Gaming Corporation; Casablanca Resorts; Chelsea Property Group; Cole Industries; Exxon-Mobil Corporation; Focus Property Group; Gaming Partners International Corp.; General Growth Properties, Inc.; Herbst Gaming, Inc; Kinder Morgan Energy Partners, LP; Lamar Advertising; LS Power Development, LLC; Marnell Corrao Associates, Inc; Marshall Management Company; Molasky Companies; Monarch Casino & Resort, Inc.; Nevada Contractors Insurance Co.; Nevada Development Authority; Newmont Mining Corp.; Pulte Homes; Reading International, Inc.; The Related Companies, L.P.; Republic Services of Southern Nevada; Olympia Land Corporation (Southern Highlands); US Aviation Underwriters; and Zurich-American Insurance Co.

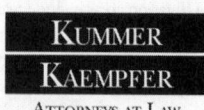

KUMMER KAEMPFER BONNER
RENSHAW & FERRARIO

**CONTENTS:** Corporate/Commercial p.1263; Employment p.1265; Litigation p.1267; Real Estate p.1269; Individuals' Profiles p.1271; Firm' Profiles p.1275.

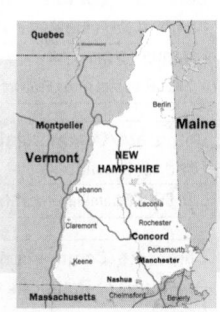

## How lawyers are ranked

Every year we carry out thousands of in-depth interviews with clients and lawyers in order to assess the reputations and expertise of business lawyers across the USA. Chambers rankings and editorial are referred to extensively by General Counsel and other purchasers of legal services who look to our recommendations when choosing their lawyers.

# CORPORATE/COMMERCIAL

### Corporate/Commercial
#### Leading Firms

1. **COOK, LITTLE, ROSENBLATT** *Manchester*
   **MCLANE, GRAF, RAULERSON** *Manchester*
   **SHEEHAN PHINNEY BASS + GREEN PA** *Manchester*
2. **DEVINE MILLIMET & BRANCH PA** *Manchester*
   **NIXON PEABODY LLP** *Manchester*
3. **HINCKLEY, ALLEN & SNYDER LLP** *Concord*
   **ORR & RENO PA** *Concord*

#### Leading Individuals

1. **REISCHE Alan** *Sheehan Phinney Bass + Green*
   **SAMUELS Richard** *McLane, Graf, Raulerson*
2. **BURKE Steven** *McLane, Graf, Raulerson*
   **CASTALDO Neil** *Hinckley, Allen & Snyder LLP*
   **COHEN Steven** *Devine Millimet & Branch PA*
   **COOK James** *Cook, Little, Rosenblatt*
   **HOOD James** *Nixon Peabody LLP*
   **LITTLE Curtis** *Cook, Little, Rosenblatt*
   **MANSON Thomas** *Cook, Little, Rosenblatt*
3. **BURGER Peter** *Orr & Reno PA*
   **DI CROCE Camille** *Devine Millimet & Branch PA*
   **DROOFF Michael** *Sheehan Phinney Bass*
   **ELLISON Scott** *Devine Millimet & Branch PA*
   **MCCUE Mark** *Hinckley, Allen & Snyder LLP*
   **SKLAR Daniel** *Nixon Peabody LLP*
   **TAUB Philip** *Nixon Peabody LLP*

#### Up-and-coming individuals
**NORRIS Daniel** *McLane, Graf, Raulerson*

#### Associates to watch
**BENSON Matthew** *Cook, Little, Rosenblatt*

## Band 1

### Cook, Little, Rosenblatt & Manson PLLC
See firm details p.1275

**The Firm:** Thanks to its "*knowledgeable and capable people,*" larger state and regional firms recognize this corporate boutique as a worthy competitor in the market. While it has particular expertise in representing emerging companies, clients value the team's "*high level of experience in all types of transactions.*" Sources were particularly impressed by its "*incredi-*

ble expertise in the hi-tech sector.*" The firm often acts for entrepreneurial family-owned businesses that are attracted by the firm's practical approach and business insights and connections. Another wing of the practice is high-end corporate lending work, where the firm acts for many of the major banks in the state.

**The Lawyers:** With a diverse practice and an "*eminently good sense of proportion,*" **Curtis Little** (see p.1272) has predominantly been involved in financial transactions and some M&A activity. Clients value his understanding of not only the commercial issues important to them, but also the "*nuances and subtleties required to get a deal done.*" **James Cook** (see p.1271), described as a "*true luminary*" by peers, is recognized as one of the leaders in the state in the technology area. He recently advised on the financing of a hi-tech venture. He is respected for not "*hyping issues and being good at balancing what's practical with what's legally correct.*" "*Quiet star*" **Tom Manson** (see p.1272) represents a number of leading financial institutions in syndicated loan transactions and serves as general counsel to many family-owned businesses. Clients value his "*keen business mind*" and the way he strikes a delicate balance between protecting his clients' interests and "*working well with the other side to achieve a reasonable compromise.*" Clients describe the up-and-coming **Matt Benson** (see p.1271) as a "*joy to work with.*" Peers recognize his prowess and predict his star will continue to rise. His practice comprises work with startup companies in the new technology areas, licensing and IP work.

**Clients/Work Highlights:** Bank of America; Citizens Bank; TD Banknorth; Chittenden Bank; Sovereign Bank; Eastern Propane; Providus Software Solutions; Pragmatech Software; Geophysical Survey Systems; Powerspan and Peterboro Basket.

### McLane, Graf, Raulerson & Middleton Professional Association
See firm details p.1276

**The Firm:** This well-established and respected firm serves a wide variety of clients from a broad range of industry sectors. It has particular strength in the traditional New Hampshire-based industries such as manufacturing, technology, utilities and telecom. Its clients range from small, closely held companies to

large corporations. As one of New Hampshire's largest law firms it offers an entire array of corporate services, including business contracts and formations, M&A, corporate governance and finance. The firm profits from a deep bench of leading experts across the corporate practice and offers particular expertise in securities. The firm's tax and estate planning practice provides added value to clients who report they appreciate the responsiveness and the depth of knowledge of attorneys across the firm.

**The Lawyers:** Heading the corporate department is **Richard Samuels** (see p.1273), whose practice focuses on securities – for both smaller public and nonpublic companies – and on advising utilities on regulatory matters. Peers find him "*extraordinarily disciplined and very detail-oriented, which is why he doesn't make mistakes.*" He represented the Environmental Resource Return Corp in its sale to a regional waste disposal and processing firm, and continues to act for his long-standing client BayCorp Holdings. Clients value his no-nonsense approach and that he "*knows where to draw the line between specific law and business and commercial realities.*" **Steven Burke** (see p.1271) chairs the firm's tax group and divides his practice between tax-related matters and general transactional corporate work, with a specialization in ESOPs. He recently worked on various large ESOP transactions, one involving multiple parties. He also represented one of the largest regional real estate brokerage companies in a joint venture with a Fortune 500 company. As a CPA, Burke "*can see behind the numbers*" and impresses clients with his very deep knowledge: "*He doesn't have to get back to you to look things up.*" Up-and-comer **Dan Norris'** (see p.1273) practice concentrates largely on business combination transactions, corporate restructuring and finance. He recently advised on the sale of a medical products company to a publicly traded medical products industry leader for in excess of $24 million. He also represented a public company borrower in several private loan transactions in excess of $10 million. He is valued for being "*able to address business and legal issues at the same time.*" Regarded as "*one of the top people in the state for estate planning,*" **Bill Zorn** (see p.1274) enters the tax tables. His practice focuses on sophisticated estate planning for executives and business owners, federal and state tax planning and structuring for corporations. "*He is very experienced and confident and grasps the important issues quickly.*"

**Clients/Work Highlights:** BayCorp Holdings; KeyBank; International Paper; Hitchiner Manufacturing; Hanover Water Works; Manchester Water Works; KeySpan Energy Delivery New England; Constellation Energy Group; Algonquin Power Income Fund; Concord Steam; Verizon and Pennichuck Corporation.

## Sheehan Phinney Bass + Green PA
See firm details p.1277

**The Firm:** This full-service regional outfit has an active securities practice and an expertise in privately negotiated, small to mezzanine transactions. Sources report the team benefits from strong leadership and can draw on the support of specialists from other disciplines such as taxation, accountancy and IP. The firm serves a wide variety of clients ranging from small startups to public companies.

**The Lawyers:** Heading the corporate department, **Alan Reische**'s practice is focused on transactional matters including accession and internal planning, equity diversion planning and ESOPs. He recently represented two top-level human capital firms in several acquisitions across the USA and assisted them with their private financing needs. Sources describe him as the "*dean of New Hampshire corporate law*" and credit him with having the "*premier corporate practice in the state.*" Clients value his listening skills intelligence, reporting he "*understands our needs and doesn't just give a legal answer but a practical one.*" "*Bright and reliable*" **Michael Drooff** divides his time between small to mezzanine M&A, private company finance, and venture capital and angel investment work. Last year he represented Choicelinx in their

merger with one of the leaders of the health insurance area. Clients welcome that he is "*extremely responsive*" and "*gives advice straight up.*" "*Very talented tax attorney*" **Peter Beach** enters the tables this year. His practice covers a wide array of tax matters. **Bruce Harwood**, who practices in the bankruptcy and insolvency field, joins him. He has the ability to act as both creditors' and debtors' counsel and is an effective negotiator and litigator. Interviewees commented on his pragmatic approach and that he "*looks for solutions that are efficient for businesses.*"

**Clients/Work Highlights:** The firm acts for a wide selection of clients, from small, private to large, public companies from various industry sectors including manufacturing, IT, temporary staffing, healthcare and insurance.

## Band 2

## Devine Millimet & Branch PA
**The Firm:** With four offices throughout New Hampshire and Massachusetts, this professional and capable full-service firm is well placed to serve clients throughout northern New England. The firm's transactional practice offers general corporate representation including the negotiation of business contracts, organizing startups and the buying and selling of businesses. In addition, the firm has specific strength in state and federal tax planning and finance matters, and is one of only a few firms in New Hampshire that is a recognized bond counsel.

**The Lawyers:** "*Tenacious*" **Steven Cohen** heads the business and tax planning group and focuses his practice on the acquisition and disposition of businesses, business and estate planning, and general corporate representation. As a CPA, he has a good tax background and "*understands financial info and how to structure transactions.*" Recent highlights include advising on the sale of a New Hampshire hi-tech company for $25 million and an outbound call center for $30 million. He is valued for "*seeing all sides of a problem*" and "*understanding how to get a deal done.*" **Scott Ellison** divides his time equally between M&A and general corporate work. He recently advised the acquirers on the financing of their acquisition of the Environmental Resource Return Corp. He also advised on the acquisition of a car dealership franchise and regional car rental business. Peers describe him as a good problem solver and clients value that he is "*always extremely prompt in his response and creative in his solutions.*" Recommended for tax, **Jon Sparkman**'s practice is concentrated on advising small and midsized businesses on tax and general corporate issues. "*Top-notch*" **Camille Di Croce** is a finance attorney and specializes in commercial lending, advising mostly lenders. She is advising on a multimillion-dollar bond financing to a nonprofit corporation. She also recently acted as bank counsel in connection with a multimillion-dollar real estate acquisition. Clients appreciate her problem-solving skills and report she "*is very good at highlighting the issues that are impor-*

*tant to us.*"

**Clients/Work Highlights:** The firm advises a variety of clients including Insight Technology; Rockingham Ventures; Robbins Auto Parts; CB Sullivan; US Trust and Bank of America.

## Nixon Peabody LLP
See firm details p.1546

**The Firm:** Described by clients "*as nothing short of terrific,*" this firm is the only national outfit with a presence in New Hampshire. As such, it has the unique advantage of being able to offer clients a representation in most US jurisdictions. The firm has a wide-ranging corporate practice and is particularly strong on corporate governance issues. With more than 600 attorneys nationwide, the firm has "*great depth of experience and the ability to source experience around the country.*"

**The Lawyers:** **James Hood** (see p.1272) has a generalist corporate practice that comprises corporate governance, M&A and finance work. He has been working on the sale, purchase and development of commercial real estate and recently advised on the purchase and sale of a number of radio stations. He is "*very detail-oriented*" and clients report that he is "*extremely personable and professional at the same time.*" **Daniel Sklar**'s (see p.1273) practice is spread across lending and reorganization in addition to M&A and general corporate work. He acts as debtors' counsel in the $200 million Amherst Technologies bankruptcy, and represented a major aircraft lessor in the Northwest Airlines bankruptcy. Regarded as the preeminent bankruptcy lawyer in the state, he is "*top-notch technically and as a deal-maker.*" Clients applaud his "*ability to explain matters very clearly, almost like a professor.*" **Philip Taub**'s (see p.1274) practice is focused on transactional work such as M&A, leveraged buyouts, startups and venture capital financing. He recently advised the management of Au Bon Pain in a leveraged buyout. Clients value his big-picture thinking and that "*the can coordinate complex deals.*" One client remarked: "*the single thing that stands out most about him is his fantastic level of service to his clients.*"

**Clients/Work Highlights:** The firm represents many of the public and private companies in the state, including Dover Electronics; Brookstone; The Eliot Hospital; North American Industries; Spencer Press of Maine; Orion Seafood International; Excalibur Shelving Systems; Intactis Software; Relyco Sales; Amusement Media; E&R Cleaners and Filterfresh Coffee Service. The firm also acts for a number of the state's large financial institutions such as Eaton Vance, Bank of America and Citizens Bank.

## Band 3

## Hinckley, Allen & Snyder LLP
**The Firm:** This full-service regional firm offers the complete array of corporate services, advising on M&A, finance, restructuring and contractual matters. Moreover, the firm has a widely acknowledged specialty in healthcare law. It acts mostly for

midmarket clients across all industry sectors. The small New Hampshire office draws on the support of the larger Boston and Providence offices for additional specialist capability.

**The Lawyers:** **Neil Castaldo**'s practice encompasses general corporate law such as M&A finance, and legal and business strategy. It further includes a subspecialty in healthcare law. He recently acted for the Frisbie Memorial Hospital in an interest rate swap arrangement. He also represented the New Hampshire Higher Education Loan Corporation in its $150 million financing to fund student loan operations. Clients are full of praise, with one gushing: "*Not only is he one of the best lawyers in the country, he is also genuine, caring and devoted to his clients.*" A new addition to this firm is **Mark McCue**. His practice focus includes M&A, finance, corporate governance, healthcare and business contracts. He often acts for nonprofit entities. Clients commend his "*very pragmatic attitude toward getting solutions to contentious issues,*" which makes him very effective in contract negotiations.

**Clients/Work Highlights:** Dartmouth-Hitchcock Medical Center; Bank of America; Hasbro; Citizens Bank; New Hampshire Higher Education Loan Corporation; CVS; Modern Continental Construction; Textron and Eagle Publications.

### Orr & Reno PA

**The Firm:** This firm's corporate practice comprises eight attorneys and is developing strength representing small, closely held companies. Its diverse list of clients encompasses various industry sectors and includes educational, religious and nonprofit organizations. The firm has particular expertise representing foreign entities.

**The Lawyers:** **Peter Burger**'s practice is concentrated in transactional work with a strong focus in the hospitality area. He recently acted for the stockholders of a firearms company in the disposition of their $40 million interest. He also led on the acquisition and financing of a $20 million redevelopment. Clients appreciate his international expertise – he is fluent in German and acts for various German, Swiss and Austrian businesses – and report that he "*works diligently on the details*" and gets the deal done.

**Clients/Work Highlights:** Lindt & Sprüngli; Audley Construction; Steenbeck & Sons; Ocean National Bank and the Linchris Hotel Corporation.

### Other Notable Practitioners

**Thomas Rath**, founder of firm Rath, Young & Pignatelli PC, is consistently described as a leading government lawyer in the state and the go-to person for government relations work. His practice is at the intersection of law and public policy and he assists clients in all aspects of their relationships with the government. Another strength of the firm is in the area of tax. **William Ardinger** is the head of the firm's tax group and is a very capable tax attorney. At Cleveland, Waters & Bass PA **David Law** is recommended for his tax practice. It encompasses ERISA matters, employee benefits, tax planning and tax-exempt organizations work. He is praised for his exemplary client skills and analytical ability.

# EMPLOYMENT

# MAINLY DEFENDANT

| Employment: Mainly Defendant |
| --- |
| **Leading Firms** |
| 1. **DEVINE MILLIMET & BRANCH PA** *Manchester* |
| **GALLAGHER, CALLAHAN** *Concord* |
| 2. **FLYGARE SCHWARZ & CLOSSON PLLC** *Exeter* |
| **MCLANE, GRAF, RAULERSON** *Manchester* |
| **SHEEHAN PHINNEY BASS + GREEN PA** *Manchester* |
| 3. **ORR & RENO PA** *Concord* |
| **SULLOWAY & HOLLIS PLLC** *Concord* |

| Leading Individuals |
| --- |
| 1. **BROTH Mark** *Devine Millimet & Branch PA* |
| **FLYGARE Thomas** *Flygare Schwarz & Closson PLLC* |
| **FORD Debra** *Devine Millimet & Branch PA* |
| **JOHNSTONE Andrea** *Gallagher, Callahan and Gartrell* |
| 2. **JOHNSON Linda** *McLane, Graf, Raulerson* |
| **KAPLAN Edward** *Sulloway & Hollis PLLC* |
| **MOECKEL Jennifer** *Devine Millimet & Branch PA* |
| **REIDY James** *Sheehan Phinney Bass + Green PA* |
| 3. **BLACKMER Jill** *Orr & Reno PA* |
| **CHATFIELD Andrea** *McLane, Graf, Raulerson* |
| **CLOSSON Tom** *Flygare Schwarz & Closson PLLC* |
| **RICE Emily** *Orr & Reno PA* |
| **Associates to watch** |
| **SHILLING Cameron** *McLane, Graf, Raulerson* |

## Band 1

### Devine Millimet & Branch PA

**The Firm:** This firm has a particularly strong reputation in the employment and labor law field. Its labor, employment and employee benefits practice covers the entire spectrum of employment-related issues and has a particular emphasis on labor law. Interviewees highlight the depth of talent across the team as a key strength: "*They have good leadership and the ability to follow through with a strong bench of associates.*" The firm offers contentious and non-contentious expertise including counseling and training. The past year has seen the team involved in a number of discrimination matters. The team's client base covers a wide spectrum of companies in a variety of industries, from startup businesses to Fortune 500 companies.

**The Lawyers:** **Mark Broth**'s practice encompasses the entire array of labor and employment issues, with a significant focus on traditional labor and union relations work. Among his clients are many public sector employers and municipalities. He recently assisted a municipality in terminating its existing retirement plans and rolling the work force into a state-sponsored employment plan. He also acted for a construction contractor in a contentious retirement plan matter. He "*maintains his calm under fire*" and is a "*good leader in emotional situations.*" Moreover, interviewees consistently highlighted his wealth of knowledge and experience. **Debra Ford** is a seasoned litigator and recently defended a whistleblower case in the federal court. She is also recognized for her counseling ability, particularly on sex discrimination issues. Interviewees stressed that while a "*forceful advocate,*" she remains "*reasonable and practical.*" "*Meticulous and conscientious,*" **Jennifer Moeckel**'s practice concentrates primarily on employer counseling and representing clients before administrative agencies. She acts exclusively for employers, and advises clients from a variety of sectors including manufacturing, automotive, healthcare and education. She "*radiates competence*" and is valued by clients for giving good guidance:

"*She keeps me alert on what's happening and I always feel like she truly cares about us.*"

**Clients/Work Highlights:** Clients range from municipalities to entrepreneurial startup businesses to large Fortune 500 companies from the automotive, biotech, construction, education, energy, healthcare and manufacturing sectors.

### Gallagher, Callahan and Gartrell, PC

**The Firm:** This firm's labor and employment practices continue to expand, offering clients counseling and litigation know-how. The team of seven offers specialist advice on benefits, HR consulting and risk management. The employment team works closely with the tax group to provide comprehensive advice on employee benefits and ERISA matters.

**The Lawyers:** **Andrea Johnstone** (see p.1272) is a standout as a great employment and labor law generalist. Hers is a hybrid practice grounded in both counseling and litigation. Recently her workload has been dominated by a steady flow of employment litigation, primarily in the fields of discrimination and sexual harassment. "*Her client responsiveness is unparalleled, she is intuitive and has a soft way about her that is very effective in getting clients to do what is needed.*" Clients appreciate her practical advice: "*She has a thorough understanding of the workplace and knows how the law translates.*"

**Clients/Work Highlights:** The firm represents a wide variety of clients from an array of industry sectors ranging from large banks to smaller companies, including educational and healthcare institutions, public sector employers and municipalities.

## Band 2

### Flygare Schwarz & Closson PLLC

**The Firm:** The only employment boutique in the tables, this three-partner outfit is focused on employment issues including discrimination claims, wrongful discharge, breach of contract actions, whistle-blower protection and wage claims. It also offers a broad range of labor relations services. Its deep knowledge of labor law in the education sector is a key draw for clients.

**The Lawyers:** *"Knowledgeable and experienced"* **Thomas Flygare** is known for his tremendous strength in labor law, particularly in relation to municipalities. A *"gentleman and very articulate,"* according to peers, he concentrates his practice on labor negotiations and union-related matters. **Tom Closson**'s practice is focused on litigation. Although he usually acts on the employer side, he recently represented a plaintiff in a large discrimination case. He has also recently represented a number of municipalities in arbitration matters. Interviewees report that he has a *"strong sense of realism and understands how juries identify with claimants."*

**Clients/Work Highlights:** The firm often represents public sector employers such as municipalities and educational institutions as well as nonprofit organizations.

### McLane, Graf, Raulerson & Middleton Professional Association

See firm details p.1276

**The Firm:** This premier New Hampshire firm's employment and labor law group offers clients both risk management counseling and litigation expertise, with the added value of benefits and immigration specialists. The firm has extensive experience advising schools and churches, and the employment group is also well versed in serving such clients.

**The Lawyers:** The hugely knowledgeable **Linda Johnson** (see p.1272) is the head of the labor and employment group. She has a diverse practice, counseling clients on risk management issues, and litigating when things get more complicated. She chairs the specialized education law group and has developed a stellar reputation among private school clients. She recently assisted the Diocese of Manchester in its development of training programs for schools and churches. Peers recognize her as a very effective advocate who injects a practical perspective into her legal advice. Clients appreciate that she *"always responds right away"* and *"can be as tough as they get, but is also passionate and a good listener."* A new addition to the tables, **Andrea Chatfield** (see p.1271) heads the

counseling and risk management side of the firm's employment practice and advises clients on workplace policies. Clients praise her responsiveness and report: *"She is very good at focusing on the real implications of the decisions employers make."* Also entering the tables is the chair of the employment litigation group, **Cameron Shilling** (see p.1273). He is recommended for his expertise in trade secrets and noncompetition agreement litigation, and recently obtained an injunction against a former employee of the state's largest architectural and engineering firm, preventing the misappropriation of software. Clients report he *"is always prepared and on top of the material."*

**Clients/Work Highlights:** The group's clients are drawn from medical and dental practices, private schools, manufacturers and hi-tech firms. They include Bauer Nike Hockey; Citronics; Hitchiner Manufacturing; Klüber Lubrication North America; Pennichuck; Polyonics; Poultry Products Northeast; Rock of Ages and St. Paul's School.

### Sheehan Phinney Bass + Green PA

See firm details p.1277

**The Firm:** This seven-attorney group focuses on counseling, training and prevention, in addition to offering litigation services where necessary. Its dedication to advising public sector and private clients on the prevention of claims has led it to create an online resource for employer clients.

**The Lawyers:** *"Energetic"* **James Reidy**'s practice concentrates on counseling, training and risk management work and includes some representation in administrative hearings. *"He constantly puts himself out there for his clients,"* report sources, and is respected for his technical proficiency and his ability to relate easily to clients.

**Clients/Work Highlights:** Avis; Biosan Laboratories; Bottomline Technologies; Colby-Sawyer College; Easter Seals New Hampshire; Elliot Hospital; Felton Brush; Macmillan Construction; Town of Milford; New London Hospital; New Hampshire Retirement System; Nobis Engineering; PC Connections; Rockingham County; Southern New Hampshire University; Stonyfield Farm and Wal-Mart.

## Band 3

### Orr & Reno PA

**The Firm:** This competent and service-oriented, five-lawyer team deals with all employment-related matters including discrimination and harassment claims, wage and hour matters, employment

contracts and workforce reductions. It offers counseling and training as well as dispute expertise. This lean firm offers a surprisingly wide range of services, complementing its employment practice with occupational health and immigration advice as well as a dedicated alternative dispute resolution practice.

**The Lawyers:** **Jill Blackmer**'s practice concentrates on counseling and representing clients before administrative agencies. Her clients are drawn from a wide range of industry sectors and include nonprofit organizations. Interviewees were impressed by her *"no-nonsense and workmanlike approach to the law."* Clients particularly value that she understands their culture and *"can do the work within a corporate value system."* Experienced litigator **Emily Rice** has an eclectic practice that encompasses employment disputes in addition to general commercial litigation and medical malpractice defense. She also brings significant experience as an employment mediator to the table. Her colleague **Martha Van Oot** has mediated a number of complex cases for the state and federal courts, the Human Rights Commission and private parties.

**Clients/Work Highlights:** Blockbuster; Chittenden Corporation; Clear Channel; Laidlaw Transit Services; Lindt & Sprüngli; National Grange Mutual Insurance; Ocean National Bank; Precitech; Rite Aid and Shaw's Supermarkets.

### Sulloway & Hollis PLLC

**The Firm:** The firm offers a wide range of services including developing risk management strategies, implementing retirement plans and employee benefit programs, as well as litigating on a broad range of matters. The employment team undertakes a great deal of contract bargaining and arbitration work for its clients and has developed a particular niche representing municipalities. It often acts for healthcare industry clients as well as school districts. Sources report the firm's *"advice, counsel and knowledge has always been top notch."*

**The Lawyers:** **Edward Kaplan**'s practice has two main areas of focus: he assists companies, municipalities and school districts in contract bargaining negotiations, and also defends employers against various allegations of employment law breaches. He recently defended a hospital in connection with the discharge of a number of physicians.

**Clients/Work Highlights:** The firm often acts for companies, healthcare institutions and hospitals, municipalities and school districts. Further clients include Atlantic Risk Management; Dartmouth-Hitchcock Medical Center; Exeter & Hampton Electric and the Fall Mountain Regional School District.

# LITIGATION

## Band 1

### McLane, Graf, Raulerson & Middleton Professional Association
See firm details p.1276

**The Firm:** This capable and "*very attentive*" outfit gears its litigation services toward business clients. The generalist practice is recognized for its particular strength in environmental, IP, employment, utility and insurance coverage. The team profits from a deep bench of talent from partner through to associate and clients praise its "*hands-on*" attitude. The litigation team is currently representing Bauer Nike Hockey in litigation related to the termination of employment of one of its former CEOs, and is advising on several cases concerning the availability of insurance cover for hazardous waste.

**The Lawyers:** **Bruce Felmly** (see p.1271) makes for a "*formidable opponent*" and is recognized as one of the best trial lawyers in the state. Environmental actions account for a substantial portion of his practice and he continues to act for EnergyNorth in relation to insurance and environmental claims. His litigation abilities allow him to successfully turn his hand to any matter, and he has recently represented Bayer in relation to a products liability claim. Clients report: "*He dedicates himself entirely to a case.*" **Jack Middleton** (see p.1273) is a senior member of the litigation team. He is increasingly focused on alternative dispute resolution and mediation work, but continues to advise long-standing clients such as Verizon, which he is currently representing in a tax abatement matter. His thoroughness, caution and detailed knowledge continues to attract clients, including one who gushed: "*He is legendary, delightful, gracious and brilliant – you couldn't do any better than Jack.*" **Wilbur Glahn** (see p.1272) is "*incredibly thorough and frighteningly clever,*" say clients. While his practice is focused on corporate governance matters, he recently represented a manufacturer of rebuilt automobile parts in a breach of contract matter worth in excess of $3 million. Interviewees describe him as "*conscientious, experienced, friendly and hard-working.*" "*Bright and competent*" **David Wolowitz** (see p.1274) has a diverse practice that includes general commercial as well as employment-related litigation, and is also advising on the Bauer Nike Hockey matter. Clients praise his presentation skills and appreciate that he is "*always prepared and immediately available when needed.*" Mental health care organizations and private schools feature heavily in his client list. **Thomas Donovan**'s (see p.1271) main area of focus is IP law; however he also undertakes general business contract and utility litigation, and continues to advise Pennichuck Water Works in eminent domain proceedings. Clients rate his "*stellar communication skills, personable nature and intricate understanding of the law.*"

**Clients/Work Highlights:** Abbott Laboratories; BAE Systems; Bayer; Chicago Title; Dartmouth College; Irving Oil; KeyBank National Association; KeySpan Energy Delivery and Verizon.

### Orr & Reno PA
**The Firm:** This 15-strong team is primarily defense-oriented and has significant capability in medical malpractice defense and employment litigation. However, market sources report the group more than holds its own across the spectrum of general commercial litigation, with success in land use, IP, personal injury and media law under its belt. The firm's alternative dispute resolution practice also continues to attract attention in the market.

**The Lawyers:** Deeply experienced **Ronald Snow** is the senior litigator at this firm and is "*top of the heap*" according to peers. His practice encompasses general commercial litigation work, with a specialty in aviation and medical malpractice defense. Defending a large class action for an automobile manufacturer has occupied him for most of the year. Clients report he is "*extraordinarily able in the courtroom.*" The "*tenacious*" **Martha Van Oot** has a broad commercial litigation practice and has a particular flair for employment and professional liability defense. She recently represented the State of New Hampshire in a chemical contamination case. First-rate trial attorney **Emily Rice** has an eclectic practice that spans general commercial, employment and professional malpractice defense. Among her instructions recently is a medical malpractice trial. Peers consider **William Chapman** to be preeminent in the field of defamation, and he supplements this practice with medical malpractice defense work. He "*has a magnificent presence in front of a jury.*"

**Clients/Work Highlights:** The Associated Press; Atlantic Trust; Chittenden Bank; Concord Monitor; Dartmouth-Hitchcock Medical Center; Liberty Mutual; Oracle; Pax World Balanced Fund; Presstek; Raytheon Aircraft; Sears; Subaru of New England; University System of New Hampshire and WMUR.

## Band 2

### Devine Millimet & Branch PA
**The Firm:** The firm offers a very broad range of litigation services and has notable strengths in the insurance defense field, which it supplements with a burgeoning commercial and corporate disputes practice. Clients, drawn from local and national businesses, educational and charitable institutions, instruct the team as defense and plaintiff attorneys.

**The Lawyers:** "*Bright and experienced*" **George Moore** divides his time between the Manchester and Andover offices. With broad experience, his focus tends to be on corporate and securities-related litigation, and he has established himself as a superior class action attorney. An "*absolute bulldog in the courtroom,*" he is currently representing Morgan Stanley in a securities fraud matter. Up-and-comer **Alexander Walker**'s practice encompasses general commercial, banking, IP and real estate litigation. With a niche specialty in equine law, he represents many of the leading thoroughbred horse owners in North America.

**Clients/Work Highlights:** The firm acts for a variety of clients including individuals and charitable organizations as well as large corporations.

### Nixon Peabody LLP
See firm details p.1546

**The Firm:** The team of 11 litigators draws on the support offered by this respected national firm, which enjoys a fine reputation for its antitrust, products liability and arbitration work. Focused predominantly on securities and high-end commercial contract litigation, the New Hampshire team also offers two IP specialists.

**The Lawyers: Kevin Fitzgerald** (see p.1272) is the head of the regional office and *"combines big city technical ability with small town responsiveness and client service."* His practice is concentrated in business technology and securities litigation, and he was recently lead counsel for the court-appointed receiver in a matter involving the SEC. **David Vicinanzo**'s (see p.1274) practice stretches across business litigation and government investigations, in addition to white-collar criminal defense. Clients credit his previous experience as a federal prosecutor as contributing to his *"great skill, integrity and very good judgment."*

**Clients/Work Highlights:** Annalee Dolls; Bausch & Lomb; Booth Creek Ski Holdings; Brand Partners; Catholic Diocese of Manchester; Coca-Cola; Corning; E&C Restaurant Management; JetBlue Airways; John Hancock; KeyBank; Kodak; Nordica; Putnam Investments; Riverstone Resources; SIGARMS; Sovereign Bank; St Mary's Bank; Starwood Hotels and the SEC.

## Sheehan Phinney Bass + Green PA

See firm details p.1277

**The Firm:** The litigation practice here is geared toward supporting the firm's core commercial focus, offering litigation expertise in all aspects of its clients' business. Recently the team has flexed its dispute muscle in tax, antitrust, IP, construction, consumer protection and professional malpractice matters.

**The Lawyers:** *"Understated but effective,"* **Michael Harvell** is a *"precise tactician."* With broad business litigation experience, he has earned a reputation as a go-to attorney for small, closely held companies. **James Higgins** is an experienced and effective trial lawyer who is valued by his business clients for being *"bright and efficient, and tough when needed."*

**Clients/Work Highlights:** The firm serves corporate as well as individual clients from a variety of industry sectors including construction, healthcare, insurance, energy, manufacturing, hospitality, technology and transportation.

## Band 3

## Cook, Little, Rosenblatt & Manson PLLC

See firm details p.1275

**The Firm:** This two-attorney team handles business litigation for predominantly entrepreneurial and technology-based companies. The team covers general contract, corporate and partnership, intellectual property and disputes relating to trade secrets and noncompete covenants.

**The Lawyers:** The firm's primary litigator is the very knowledgeable **Arnold Rosenblatt** (see p.1273). Clients report he has an *"exceptional presence in the courtroom"* and *"understands corporate and shareholder disputes better than any other trial lawyer in the state."* His practice is focused on business litigation and he recently obtained a preliminary injunction to stop the use of misappropriated trade secrets.

**Clients/Work Highlights:** Clients range from startups to established businesses and include many technology-based companies.

## D'Amante Couser Steiner Pellerin, P.A.

**The Firm:** Clients reserve high praise for this streamlined team, reporting: *"They are approachable, welcoming and good at putting people at ease."* For both plaintiffs and defense, the team enjoys a solid reputation for its commercial and civil disputes capability.

**The Lawyers:** The *"very logical and supremely intelligent"* **Richard Couser** is the firm's most senior litigator and has a reputation for having the aggression of a pitbull. Apparently, *"once he gets his teeth into your ankle he doesn't let go."* He acts on a variety of matters including eminent domain, environmental and real estate tax matters. According to clients he is always meticulously prepared and *"not only does he give good legal advice but he is also very steady and gracious in the way he handles highly charged situations."*

**Clients/Work Highlights:** BJ's Wholesale Club; Brooks Pharmacy; Burger King; Chicago Title; Concord Hospital; Laconia Savings Bank; Lowes; Pizza Hut; Rite Aid; Shaw's Supermarkets; Target and Toys 'R' Us.

## Gallagher, Callahan and Gartrell, PC

**The Firm:** This full-service litigation practice impresses with its handling of disputes related to commercial contracts, consumer protection, stockholder rights, real estate, environmental, insurance coverage and professional malpractice. It is particularly expert in representing legal and medical professionals before investigative boards in misconduct matters.

**The Lawyers:** The *"capable and quick-witted"* **Michael Callahan** primarily focuses on commercial contract, construction and employment disputes, in addition to a healthy share of white-collar criminal defense work. He often lends his mediation and arbitration skills to private commercial and personal injury disputes. A new addition to the tables is

**David Garfunkel.** His practice encompasses general commercial and employment litigation as well as white-collar criminal defense. He is *"very strategic, a gentleman and technically very good."*

**Clients/Work Highlights:** Bank of New Hampshire; Banknorth Group; BJ's Wholesale Club; Citizens Bank New Hampshire; Concord Monitor; Dartmouth College; Eastern Propane; Elliot Hospital; Fidelity Investments; Frisbie Memorial Hospital; GM; Global Wire Group; Granite State Electric; Lakes Region General Hospital; Merrimack Valley School District; New London Hospital; Northern Utilities; Subaru of America and Wausau Paper Mills.

## Hinckley, Allen & Snyder LLP

**The Firm:** This regional firm's litigation team handles the whole range of civil litigation. From employment to construction, the general commercial expertise is complemented by a significant white-collar defense capability. With offices in New Hampshire, Massachusetts and Rhode Island, the firm can effortlessly serve clients throughout New England.

**The Lawyers: Michael Connolly**'s practice covers general commercial litigation, but he also enjoys a great reputation for government-related work, including white-collar crime. He has a strong advisory practice, assisting clients in the implementation of compliance programs and conducting internal investigations. Clients appreciate his no-nonsense approach: *"His advice isn't sugar coated or politicized and you always know where you stand."* Entering the tables this year is the *"skillful and diligent"* **Christopher Carter**, who is recommended for both his white-collar criminal defense work and commercial litigation ability.

**Clients/Work Highlights:** American Home Industries; Black & Decker; Procter & Gamble; Cookson America; Cytec Industries; ExxonMobil; GAF; GE; JT Baker; Viacom; WR Grace and Wyeth.

## Nelson Kinder Mosseau & Saturley PC

**The Firm:** This boutique lends its dispute resolution skills to an impressive spread of industries, including construction, healthcare and environmental. From its Boston and Manchester offices, the firm has set its stall out to the energy and education sectors, offering these clients not just litigation capability, but the full range of legal services.

**The Lawyers:** *"Tough and smart"* **Peter Mosseau** heads the firm's medical malpractice group and is *"one of the hardest-working and most experienced trial lawyers in the state."* His practice is rounded out by products liability and white-collar defense work.

**Clients/Work Highlights:** The firm represents a variety of national and regional clients.

## Sulloway & Hollis PLLC

**The Firm:** The litigation group here offers the full spectrum of commercial disputes work, in addition to a significant medical malpractice defense practice. Commercially, the group's expertise is utilized most often on general business, employment, real estate, environmental and insurance matters. On the medical front, not only does the team represent healthcare providers at court and regulatory agencies, it also designs risk management and quality assurance strategies for hospitals and physician groups.

**The Lawyers:** As head of the medical malpractice group, **Michael Lehman** is experienced in defending virtually every type of medical malpractice claim. Obstetric injuries and stroke-related problems have dominated his caseload of late. Clients appreciate his collaborative nature and that he is a "*straight shooter.*"

**Clients/Work Highlights:** AIG; Atlantic Risk Management; Amica Mutual Insurance; CNA Insurance; Chicago Title; Citizens Bank New Hampshire; Concord School District; Dartmouth-Hitchcock Medical Center; Keane; Liberty Mutual; Medical Malpractice Joint Underwriting Association; Medical Mutual of Maine; Merrill Lynch; New Hampshire Medical Society; Public Service Company of New Hampshire; Southern New Hampshire Medical Center; Southworth-Milton and Swenson Granite.

### Upton and Hatfield LLP

**The Firm:** Consumer protection and insurance matters are this firm's calling card, in addition to general commercial and liability disputes. As well as representing clients at trial, the team has attracted attention for its dedication to providing alternative dispute resolution services.

**The Lawyers:** "*Very experienced and universally well-regarded,*" **Russell Hilliard** stands out not only for his medical malpractice defense work, but for his all around expertise. "*He has unimpeachable ethics, excellent judgment and is tough, but in a gentlemanly way.*"

**Clients/Work Highlights:** The firm represents a mix of business and individual clients across the state.

### Wadleigh, Starr & Peters PLLC

**The Firm:** The "*responsive*" litigation team is experienced in defending products liability, real estate, land use and construction matters. Professional negligence, particularly medical malpractice, features strongly in the team's workload, which is highlighted by the significant number of hospitals, lawyers, architects and accountants on its client list.

**The Lawyers:** The terrifically experienced **James Wheat** represents both plaintiffs and defendants on a range of general commercial litigation matters, in addition to offering alternative dispute resolution services. **John Friberg** is a "*good people person and an excellent negotiator.*" Defending institutional clients exclusively, his practice encompasses medical malpractice, products liability and environmental matters. Clients point to his attentiveness and responsiveness, and report that "*he is a problem solver. He is quick to sympathize and very honest and candid in his assessments.*"

**Clients/Work Highlights:** Clients include financial and educational institutions, healthcare providers, insurance companies, manufacturers, developers, retailers and local government bodies.

### Wiggin & Nourie

**The Firm:** This generalist team covers the waterfront with business and commercial litigation matters, insurance, and plaintiff personal injury work on its books. Family and domestic relations work rounds out the practice.

**The Lawyers:** **Wright Danenbarger** is the name here, working on commercial and personal injury matters. He recently obtained a $2.8 million medical malpractice verdict for a plaintiff and has a "*very analytical mind that sees through complex business issues.*" Clients described him as an excellent trial attorney: "*He is prompt, attentive, thoroughly prepared and a good strategist.*"

**Clients/Work Highlights:** The firm acts for individuals, businesses, financial institutions, nonprofit organizations and governmental agencies including Allstate; Associated Grocers of New England; Concord Group; Conproco; Crotched Mountain Foundation; Eckman Construction; FleetBoston Financial; Merchants Bank; New Hampshire Automobile Dealers Association; Progressive; Sprague Energy; State Farm and Vermont Mutual.

### Other Notable Practitioners

Also recommended for medical malpractice defense is founding partner **Michael Pignatelli** of Rath, Young & Pignatelli PC. The "*exceptionally bright*" **Andru Volinsky** (see p.1274) of Bernstein Shur practices across general commercial, employment law and civil fraud litigation. He is a "*creative litigator*" and clients remark he has a "*good presence in front of a judge.*"

# REAL ESTATE

## Band 1

### McLane, Graf, Raulerson & Middleton Professional Association

See firm details p.1276

**The Firm:** This commercial lending and real estate team has a broad practice that covers commercial development and land use issues, financing and leasing. Clients are drawn to the considerable resources the firm has on offer, and the team profits from its close relationship with the environmental, tax and bankruptcy practices.

**The Lawyers:** **Peter Rotch** (see p.1273) concentrates his practice in real estate transactions and developments and is currently advising on the sale and tax implications of a commercial property to Wal-Mart. He is always accessible to clients, who remark: "*He can see the forest for the trees and make transactions happen.*"

**Clients/Work Highlights:** BayCorp Holdings; Chicago Title; Community Bank & Trust; Citizens Bank; City of Portsmouth; GE Capital Asset Funding; GE Capital Small Business Finance; Heidelberg Web Systems; Hyundai; Manchester Water Works; Microsoft; Monadnock Paper Mills; Nashua Motor Express; Pfeiffer Vacuum Technology; Sheraton Hotel-Portsmouth; Summit Packaging Systems and Synagro Technologies.

### Sheehan Phinney Bass + Green PA

See firm details p.1277

**The Firm:** A major player in the New Hampshire market, the real estate and commercial lending team here advises on title issues, development, sale and purchase, finance and leasing matters. The three-partner group is bolstered by the considerable resources of the firm's environmental, litigation, zoning and land use capability, and is able to offer clients the added value of an in-house title agent.

**The Lawyers:** The very capable **Susan Manchester** chairs the group and handles a wide range of commercial real estate and lending work as well as land use matters. Her bedside manner is a key draw to clients, who report: "*She can cover all the bases and be confident without over-lawyering.*"

**Clients/Work Highlights:** Commercial lenders, construction companies and nonprofit organizations number among the team's clients, who include ABN AMRO; Bio Energy; Citizens Bank; City of Keene; Families in Transition; The Kane Company; Manchester Neighborhood Housing Services; Maritimes & Northeast Pipeline; Ocean National; Macmillan Construction; Rymes Propane & Oils; Summit Packaging Systems; The Nature Conservancy; The Trust for Public Land and Tyco International.

## Band 2

### D'Amante Couser Steiner Pellerin, P.A.

**The Firm:** This four-attorney real estate team has established itself as "*a force to be reckoned with*" in the market. The lean team punches well above its weight, regularly advising on multimillion-dollar deals. Offering clients a soup-to-nuts service, the team is able to advise clients on finding a property and conducting due diligence through to closing the deal and subsequent sale or leasing.

**The Lawyers:** Ably performing across the full spectrum of real estate-related issues, **Raymond D'Amante** drew particular praise for his regulatory work. Clients report that his affable manner reduces the stress involved in complex deals. Advising developers, owners, contractors, lenders, engineers and architects, he recently advised on a $15 million extension to a local hospital.

**Clients/Work Highlights:** Capital Region Health Care; Grappone Companies; Lowe's Home Improvement Centers and BJ's Wholesale Club.

### Devine Millimet & Branch PA

**The Firm:** This respected firm offers clients of all descriptions assistance in the purchase, sale, leasing and development of land in addition to regulatory, tax abatement and eminent domain advice. Drawing on the finance, environmental, litigation and tax capability of the other respective groups in the firm, the team offers clients a complete service. "*They have a team to take a whole transaction through.*"

**The Lawyers:** Finance attorney Camille Di Croce commands praise for her lending work. Robert Lavoie, of the firm's Andover office, chairs the real estate group.

**Clients/Work Highlights:** Developers, investors, owners, business tenants, lenders and financial institutions such as Bank of America, Citizens Bank and TD Banknorth are among the firm's clients.

### Gallagher, Callahan and Gartrell, PC

**The Firm:** Serving clients from a range of industries, including manufacturing and utilities, the team counsels on development, title insurance and tax abatement issues. With expertise in regulatory, zoning and environmental work, the team leverages the know-how of the firm's municipal law, environment and dedicated condominium practices to offer clients a truly complete service.

**The Lawyers:** **Donald Gartrell**'s practice is concentrated in municipal law and has recently advised on zoning and planning litigation. He lends his "*exceptional technical skills*" to developers and municipalities.

**Clients/Work Highlights:** The firm acts for various clients including BAE Systems; Bank of New Hampshire; Citizens Bank; Concord Monitor; Dartmouth College; Demoulas Super Markets; Granite State Concrete; Manchester Sand & Gravel; Nike; Pike Industries; PNGTS; Providian National Bank; Southern New Hampshire Bank and Trust and Thermal Technology.

### Sulloway & Hollis PLLC

**The Firm:** Commercial development and land use issues dominate this three-partner team's workload, which includes a healthy slice of lending and commercial title work. This group "*always meets deadlines and turns around its service quickly when required*," and serves clients from a diverse range of industries including nuclear power plants, shopping centers, ski resorts and industrial developers.

**The Lawyers:** **Peter Imse**'s practice is centered on development projects and land use matters such as zoning and planning law. "*He thinks outside the box*" and is recommended by clients for his pleasant nature, his thoroughness and efficiency: "*He researches everything and is excellent at looking at the total picture and pulling together all the details.*"

**Clients/Work Highlights:** Androscoggin Valley Regional Refuse Disposal District; Chicago Title; City of Concord; Granite State Management & Resources; John Hancock; Kearsarge/Lake Sunapee Community Center; Konover Development and Northern Equities.

### Upton and Hatfield LLP

**The Firm:** This firm enjoys an excellent reputation for land use and zoning work. This expertise is complemented by its sale, leasing, development and finance capability.

**The Lawyers:** **Robert Upton** attracts market praise for his expertise in municipal statutes, tax and utility matters. In the past year his schedule was dominated by tax abatement work for a number of municipalities and advising the City of Nashua in its effort to acquire by eminent domain the assets of Pennichuck Water Works. **James Raymond**'s practice has a more traditional real estate focus and he advises banks, buyers and sellers on various transactions.

**Clients/Work Highlights:** Clients are drawn from borrowers, lenders, contractors, developers, tenants and landlords, and include many municipalities such as the City of Nashua, the City of Londonderry and the Town of Newington.

### Wadleigh, Starr & Peters PLLC

**The Firm:** Advising clients – both financial institutions and individuals – on the acquisition and financing of major developments is the focus of this firm's real estate offering. Nominated as "*the go-to firm for private commercial work*," the team also advises on zoning, planning and title issues.

**The Lawyers:** "*Great negotiator*" **William Tucker** is rated for his private client and commercial work. He recently advised on a major retail project involving more than two million square feet of space. Clients appreciate his practical approach: "*He gets the job done regardless of how complicated it is and can make both sides agree to get it done directly.*"

**Clients/Work Highlights:** The firm acts for individuals and corporations as well as institutional and private lenders. Further clients include Atlantic Bank & Trust; AutoZone; Bank of New Hampshire; CVS; KeyBank National Association; Packard Development and Pilot Construction.

## Band 3

### Davis & Boghigian, PC

**The Firm:** This real estate boutique concentrates its practice on commercial lending work as well as purchase and sale transactions. The two-attorney team represents small corporations, banks and commercial as well as private lenders.

**The Lawyers:** Hugely experienced, **Jefferson Davis** is "*well grounded and makes transactions happen.*" Clients especially value his expertise in construction loans and his understanding of condominium developments.

**Clients/Work Highlights:** Centrix Bank & Trust; Community Bank & Trust; The First National Bank of Ipswich; Fleet Bank; Lawyers Title Insurance; Southern New Hampshire Bank and Trust; Sovereign Bank and TD Banknorth.

### Donahue, Tucker & Ciandella

**The Firm:** Recognized for its municipal expertise, this firm advises on development, sale and purchase, financing, land use and environmental matters. It acts for both lenders and borrowers on commercial and residential transactions.

**The Lawyers:** Quality operator **Denise Poulos**' practice encompasses development and title issues, particularly for condominiums and timeshare projects. She is additionally rated for her ability to represent both lenders and borrowers in complex financial transactions.

**Clients/Work Highlights:** The firm acts for lenders, borrowers and corporations as well as for individuals and municipalities.

### Winer & Bennett LLP

**The Firm:** This small Nashua-based firm handles an array of real estate-related matters. It conducts the purchase, sale, development and financing of commercial and residential real estate and offers advice on condominium, zoning and planning law.

**The Lawyers:** **Bradford Westgate** "*is always willing to go that extra step.*" Developer clients come to him for top-quality zoning and land use advice.

**Clients/Work Highlights:** The firm advises a mix of local, national and multinational clients.

# Leaders in New Hampshire

**ARDINGER, William**
Rath, Young and Pignatelli PC, Concord
603 226 2600
*Recommended in*
*Corporate/Commercial*

**BEACH, Peter**
Sheehan Phinney Bass + Green PA,
Manchester 603 668 0300
*Recommended in*
*Corporate/Commercial*

**BENSON, Matthew H**
Cook, Little, Rosenblatt & Manson PLLC,
Manchester 603 621 7115
m.benson@clrm.com
*Recommended in*
*Corporate/Commercial*
**Practice Areas:** Represents start-up
companies, privately held companies,
healthcare professionals, and other businesses on a wide variety of corporate legal
issues including entity formation, angel,
venture capital and other debt and equity
financings, securities issues, executive and
employee compensation, contract issues,
equity ownership matters, technology
licensing arrangements, and mergers and
acquisitions.
**Prof. Memberships:** Manchester Bar
Association, New Hampshire and American Bar Associations, Software Association
of NH, NH High Technology Council.
**Career:** Admitted in New Hampshire
(1996).
**Personal:** Brandeis University, BA
magna cum laude 1992; Boston College
Law School, JD 1996; Boston College
Graduate Carroll School of Management,
MBA 1996.

**BLACKMER, Jill**
Orr & Reno PA, Concord 603 224 2381
*Recommended in Employment*

**BROTH, Mark**
Devine Millimet & Branch PA,
North Hampton 603 964 4990
*Recommended in Employment*

**BURGER, Peter**
Orr & Reno PA, Concord 603 224 2381
*Recommended in*
*Corporate/Commercial*

**BURKE, Steven M**
McLane, Graf, Raulerson & Middleton
Professional Association, Manchester
603 628 1454
steve.burke@mclane.com
*Recommended in*
*Corporate/Commercial*
**Practice Areas:** Concentrates on M&As
and business ventures, including tax
implications of transactions, ESOPs, pension plans, ERISA, executive compensation and corporate governance arrangements. Advises on tax and estate planning
for business owners, IRS and state tax
matters. Steve is a CPA.

**Prof. Memberships:** New Hampshire
and Massachusetts Bars, New Hampshire
Society of CPAs, AICPA, American Col-
lege of Tax Counsel.
**Career:** Shareholder, Director, Tax
Department Chair; past President and
Board of Directors, NHSCPA; past Presi-
dent, Tax Section NH Bar; past President
and Treasurer, NH Employee Benefits
Council; Adjunct Professor, Franklin
Pierce Law School. Listed in a leading US
legal publication.
**Personal:** BA, Bates College, 1981; MBA,
University of Lowell, 1984; JD, Franklin
Pierce Law School, 1987; LLM in Taxa-
tion, Boston University School of Law,
1990.

**CALLAHAN, Michael**
Gallagher, Callahan and Gartrell, PC,
Concord 800 528 1181
*Recommended in Litigation*

**CARTER, Christopher**
Hinckley, Allen & Snyder LLP, Concord
603 225 4334
*Recommended in Litigation*

**CASTALDO, Neil**
Hinckley, Allen & Snyder LLP, Concord
603 225 4334
*Recommended in*
*Corporate/Commercial*

**CHAPMAN, William**
Orr & Reno PA, Concord 603 224 2381
*Recommended in Litigation*

**CHATFIELD, Andrea G**
McLane, Graf, Raulerson & Middleton
Professional Association, Manchester
603 628 1341
andrea.chatfield@mclane.com
*Recommended in Employment*
**Practice Areas:** Co-Chair, Employment
Practice – Risk Management. Concentrates on corporate risk management and
employment defense. Formulates
employment policies and handbooks,
advises on discipline, termination, discrimination claims, wage and hour compliance, and other personnel matters.
Conducts harassment and workplace
training and workplace investigations.
Represents employers before administrative agencies.
**Prof. Memberships:** Member, National
Society for Human Resource Management
and local Manchester chapter; National
Human Resource Association; Employment Law Sections of New Hampshire
and American Bar Associations.
**Career:** Of Counsel. Partner at another
large local law firm.
**Personal:** JD, Syracuse University, 1988.

**CLOSSON, Tom**
Flygare Schwarz & Closson PLLC, Exeter
603 778 7300
*Recommended in Employment*

**COHEN, Steven**
Devine Millimet & Branch PA,
Manchester 603 669 1000
*Recommended in*
*Corporate/Commercial*

**CONNOLLY, Michael**
Hinckley, Allen & Snyder LLP, Concord
603 225 4334
*Recommended in Litigation*

**COOK, James G**
Cook, Little, Rosenblatt & Manson PLLC,
Manchester 603 621 7103
j.cook@clrm.com
*Recommended in*
*Corporate/Commercial*
**Practice Areas:** Concentrates on entrepreneurial and technology-based companies throughout their life cycle, including
choice of business form and organization, buy-sell and other ownership agreements, debt and equity financings, joint
ventures and strategic alliances, stock
option and other incentive plans, sales
and distribution agreements, licensing
agreements, mergers and acquisitions,
executive employment agreements, and
other commercial arrangements.
**Prof. Memberships:** New Hampshire,
Manchester and American Bar Associations, NH High Tech Council, NH Charitable Foundation, Leadership New
Hampshire, Computer Law Association.
**Career:** Admitted in New Hampshire
(1978).
**Personal:** University of Iowa, BA, 1973;
University of Michigan, JD, 1978.

**COUSER, Richard**
D'Amante Couser Steiner Pellerin, P.A.,
Concord 603 224 6777
*Recommended in Litigation*

**D'AMANTE, Raymond**
D'Amante Couser Steiner Pellerin, P.A.,
Concord 603 224 6777
*Recommended in Real Estate*

**DANENBARGER, Wright**
Wiggin & Nourie, Manchester
603 669 2211
*Recommended in Litigation*

**DAVIS, Jefferson**
Davis & Boghigian, PC, Nashua
603 595 0210
*Recommended in Real Estate*

**DI CROCE, Camille**
Devine Millimet & Branch PA,
North Hampton 603 964 4990
*Recommended in*
*Corporate/Commercial*

**DONOVAN, Thomas J**
McLane, Graf, Raulerson & Middleton
Professional Association, Manchester
603 628 1337
tom.donovan@mclane.com
*Recommended in Litigation*

**Practice Areas:** Handles intellectual
property litigation and complex commercial disputes, with a focus on patent,
trademark and trade secret litigation
involving computer software and related
businesses. Recent matters have involved
Microsoft, Sandia Laboratories and
Micromuse.
**Prof. Memberships:** Admitted to practice before New Hampshire state and federal courts, as well as federal courts in
Massachusetts, Indiana and Colorado, as
well as the First and Federal Circuits. Former Chair of New Hampshire Bar Association Business Litigation Section. Commercial arbitrator, American Arbitration
Association.
**Career:** Shareholder and Director since
1985; immediate past Chair of Management Committee.
**Publications:** 'Cybersmears and Cyber-
Attacks: Protecting Your Company', Association of Corporate Counsel (2003).
**Personal:** Harvard College, BA magna
cum laude 1975; University of Pennsylvania Law School, JD 1978.

**DROOFF, Michael**
Sheehan Phinney Bass + Green PA,
Manchester 603 668 0300
*Recommended in*
*Corporate/Commercial*

**ELLISON, Scott**
Devine Millimet & Branch PA, North
Hampton 603 964 4990
*Recommended in*
*Corporate/Commercial*

**FELMLY, Bruce W**
McLane, Graf, Raulerson & Middleton
Professional Association, Manchester
603 628 1448
bruce.felmly@mclane.com
*Recommended in Litigation*
**Practice Areas:** Co-Chair, McLane's Litigation Department. Concentrates in
complex commercial defense and plain-
tiff trial practice, including products lia-
bility, environmental, insurance recovery,
employment, and contract claims. Recent
representation of clients has included
Microsoft Corporation, Abbott Labs,
Hyundai Motor Company, Bayer Corporation, Carpet One, Dartmouth College,
Irving Oil Corporation, and KeySpan.
**Prof. Memberships:** Fellow of the
American College of Trial Lawyers (former State Chairman), American and New
Hampshire Trial Lawyer's Associations,
American Law Institute, and a Fellow of
the American and New Hampshire Bar
Foundations.
**Career:** Shareholder and Director since
1979. President of the New Hampshire
Bar Association (1995-96). In 2002, he
received the New Hampshire Bar Associa-
tion's Distinctive Service to the Legal
Profession Award. Listed in a leading US

legal publication. Appointed by the New Hampshire Supreme Court to chair its long-range planning committee for the New Hampshire justice system.
**Personal:** JD, Cornell Law School, 1972.

### FITZGERALD, Kevin M
Nixon Peabody LLP, Manchester
603 628 4016
kfitzgerald@nixonpeabody.com
*Recommended in Litigation*
**Practice Areas:** Litigation Practice Leader; Office Managing Partner; executive committee. Complex and commercial litigation including: M&A, securities, corporate fiduciary duty, D&O liability, insurance, ERISA, employment involving executives. Healthcare: managed care contracting, QA, credentialing. Lead counsel to federal court appointed receiver in $32 million investment fraud recovery action. Secured defendants' verdict in defense of multi-million dollar breach of fiduciary duty claims by minority shareholders against directors and majority shareholders.
**Prof. Memberships:** Admitted in NH, US District Courts for the Districts of NH and Northern NY, First Circuit Court of Appeals, US Supreme Court.
**Personal:** Suffolk University, JD; University of New Hampshire, BA.

### FLYGARE, Thomas
Flygare Schwarz & Closson PLLC, Exeter
603 778 7300
*Recommended in Employment*

### FORD, Debra
Devine Millimet & Branch PA,
Manchester 603 669 1000
*Recommended in Employment*

### FRIBERG SR, John
Wadleigh, Starr & Peters PLLC,
Manchester 603 669 4140
*Recommended in Litigation*

### GARFUNKEL, David
Gallagher, Callahan and Gartrell, PC,
Concord 800 528 1181
*Recommended in Litigation*

### GARTRELL, Donald E
Gallagher, Callahan and Gartrell, PC,
Concord 603 228 1181
gartrell@gcglaw.com
*Recommended in Real Estate*
**Practice Areas:** Counsel to buyers, sellers, developers, investors and lenders in all aspects of real estate ownership and development, including municipal, State and federal regulation, property taxation and business organizations.
**Prof. Memberships:** American, New Hampshire (former Chair, Real Property Probate and Trust Law Section; former Member, Board of Governors) and Merrimack County Bar Associations; Fellow, NH Bar Foundation.
**Publications:** Frequent author and speaker on real estate development, municipal zoning and land use regula-

tion, property taxation and earth excavation.
**Personal:** Vanderbilt University School of Law, LLB, 1965; Ohio Wesleyan University, BA, 1962.

### GLAHN III, Wilbur A
McLane, Graf, Raulerson & Middleton Professional Association, Manchester
603 628 1469
bill.glahn@mclane.com
*Recommended in Litigation*
**Practice Areas:** Business and commercial litigation, including contract disputes, state and local tax matters, securities litigation, issues of corporate governance and control, breaches of fiduciary duty and dissenters' rights litigation. Litigation of state and federal constitutional issues.
**Prof. Memberships:** New Hampshire and American Bar Associations, New Hampshire Trial Lawyers Association.
**Career:** Admitted to practice in the state and federal courts in New Hampshire (1976) and Massachusetts (1972); First Circuit Court of Appeals (1976); US Supreme Court (1978). Former Assistant Attorney General and Head of the Civil Division of the Office of the Attorney General (New Hampshire).
**Personal:** Trinity College, BA with honors 1969 (Phi Beta Kappa); University of Chicago Law School, JD 1972. Recognized in 'Best Lawyers In America'.

### HARVELL, Michael
Sheehan Phinney Bass + Green PA,
Manchester 603 668 0300
*Recommended in Litigation*

### HARWOOD, Bruce
Sheehan Phinney Bass + Green PA,
Manchester 603 668 0300
*Recommended in Corporate/Commercial*

### HIGGINS, James
Sheehan Phinney Bass + Green PA,
Manchester 603 668 0300
*Recommended in Litigation*

### HILLIARD, Russell
Upton and Hatfield LLP, Concord
603 224 7791
*Recommended in Litigation*

### HOOD, James
Nixon Peabody LLP, Manchester
603 628 4051
jchood@nixonpeabody.com
*Recommended in Corporate/Commercial*
**Practice Areas:** Corporate governance, restructuring, acquisitions, mergers, debt/equity financing, shareholder disputes, joint venture/LLC formation and distribution arrangements (domestically, internationally), strategic partnerships. Mortgage and lease-backed securitizations. Water, gas utilities in rate matters; bank holding company regulatory issues.
**Prof. Memberships:** Admitted to prac-

tice in NH, US District Court for the District of NH, First Circuit Court of Appeals. Chairman, New Hampshire International Trade Advisory Committee to the Governor and DRED. Member: Board of Directors of New Hampshire Businesses for Social Responsibility and Manchester Economic Development Corporation.
**Personal:** Georgetown University Law Center, JD; University of New Hampshire, BA, magna cum laude.

### IMSE, Peter
Sulloway & Hollis PLLC, Concord
603 224 2341
*Recommended in Real Estate*

### JOHNSON, Linda S
McLane, Graf, Raulerson & Middleton Professional Association, Manchester
603 628 1267
linda.johnson@mclane.com
*Recommended in Employment*
**Practice Areas:** Chair, Employment Practice. Concentrates on corporate risk management and employment defense. Formulates employment policies and handbooks, advises on discipline, termination, discrimination claims, wage and hour compliance, and other personnel matters. Conducts harassment and workplace training. Defends companies in state and federal courts and before administrative agencies.
**Prof. Memberships:** Past President, Manchester Area Human Resources Association; member, National Society for Human Resource Management; Employment Law Sections of New Hampshire and American Bar; Human Resource Committee, NH Business and Industry Association.
**Career:** Recipient of the 2002 Marilla Ricker Award (NH Women's Bar); 2002 New Hampshire Civil Liberties Union Award; 2006 Outstanding Women in Business; and 2006 Hollman Equality Award. Listed in 'Best Lawyers in America'.
**Personal:** JD, Boston University, 1984.

### JOHNSTONE, Andrea
Gallagher, Callahan and Gartrell, PC,
Concord 603 228 1181
johnstone@gcglaw.com
*Recommended in Employment*
**Practice Areas:** Chair of the firm's Labor and Employment Law and Litigation Departments. Advises management in the development and administration of personnel policies and strategies for handling workplace issues. Represents management in all aspects of labor and employment law, including employment agreements, state and federal employment law compliance, union organizing campaigns, labor negotiations and arbitration and employment litigation.
**Career:** Judicial law clerk, NH Superior Court 1989-90; joined firm of Gallagher, Callahan & Gartrell in 1990; Partner since 1994.

**Publications:** Author of numerous articles on human resource and employment law topics. Co-author of 'Labor and Employment in New Hampshire' (Lexis 2004).
**Personal:** JD, Hofstra University School of Law (1989); BA, Wheaton College (1985). Listed in 'Best Lawyers in America'.

### KAPLAN, Edward
Sulloway & Hollis PLLC, Concord
603 224 2341
*Recommended in Employment*

### LAW, David
Cleveland, Waters and Bass, P.A.,
Concord 603 224 7761
*Recommended in Corporate/Commercial*

### LEHMAN, Michael
Sulloway & Hollis PLLC, Concord
603 224 2341
*Recommended in Litigation*

### LITTLE, Curtis
Cook, Little, Rosenblatt & Manson PLLC,
Manchester 603 621 7104
c.little@clrm.com
*Recommended in Corporate/Commercial*
**Practice Areas:** Represents a broad range of businesses within and outside of New Hampshire, including many of the large financial institutions in New England, with respect to major financings, securities matters, real estate purchases and leases, and forming new companies.
**Prof. Memberships:** New Hampshire and American Bar Association.
**Career:** Began practice at Nixon, Hargrave in Rochester, New York in 1969; served as corporate counsel to Lake Placid Winter Olympics Committee; admitted in New Hampshire (1982).
**Personal:** Dartmouth College, AB magna cum laude 1964 (Phi Beta Kappa); Yale University, LLB 1967.

### MANCHESTER, Susan
Sheehan Phinney Bass + Green PA,
Manchester 603 668 0300
*Recommended in Real Estate*

### MANSON, Thomas P
Cook, Little, Rosenblatt & Manson PLLC,
Manchester 603 621 7105
t.manson@clrm.com
*Recommended in Corporate/Commercial*
**Practice Areas:** Represents a variety of commercial clients and family-owned businesses in entity selection and formation, securities, financing, contract review, technology distribution and licensing and merger, reorganization, and acquisition transactions and has significant experience in assisting financial institutions in commercial lending transactions.
**Prof. Memberships:** New Hampshire Bar Association, New Hampshire High Tech Council, Family Firm Institute.

**Career:** Admitted to practice in New Hampshire (1984).
**Personal:** University of Redlands, BA 1981; Boston University, JD 1984 (Tauro and Liacos Scholar).

## MCCUE, Mark
Hinckley, Allen & Snyder LLP, Concord
603 225 4334
*Recommended in*
*Corporate/Commercial*

## MIDDLETON, Jack B
McLane, Graf, Raulerson & Middleton Professional Association, Manchester
603 628 1446
jack.middleton@mclane.com
*Recommended in Litigation*
**Practice Areas:** Concentrates on arbitration and mediation, utilizing 49 years' trial experience as a trial lawyer and 24 years as a New Hampshire District Court Judge. Jack has a strong trial practice in commercial litigation.
**Prof. Memberships:** Former Secretary, Member, Board of Governors, American Bar Association (ABA); Member, ABA House of Delegates; Fellow, American College of Trial Lawyers; former President, New Hampshire and New England Bar Associations, the National Conference of Bar Foundations and National Conference of Bar Presidents; former Chairman, New Hampshire Bar Foundation.
**Career:** Shareholder and Director (1962). New Hampshire District Court Judge (1964-87). New Hampshire Business Leader of the Year, 2002. Named New Hampshire's Lawyers' Lawyer. Listed in leading US legal publication.
**Personal:** JD, Boston University, 1956.

## MOECKEL, Jennifer Shea
Devine Millimet & Branch PA, North Hampton 603 964 4990
*Recommended in Employment*

## MOORE, George
Devine Millimet & Branch PA, Manchester 603 669 1000
*Recommended in Litigation*

## MOSSEAU, Peter
Nelson Kinder Mosseau & Saturley PC, Manchester 603 647 1800
*Recommended in Litigation*

## NORRIS, Daniel J
McLane, Graf, Raulerson & Middleton Professional Association, Manchester
603 628 1408
daniel.norris@mclane.com
*Recommended in*
*Corporate/Commercial*
**Practice Areas:** Director in the Corporate Department concentrating in merger and acquisition transactions, corporate finance, securities law, and general corporate matters. Advises businesses in negotiating and drafting commercial agreements and in commercial lending and real estate transactions. Recently assisted

client in the alternative energy industry with a $88 million master supply agreement and with the sale of a major regional healthcare business to the leading national provider of home healthcare products.
**Prof. Memberships:** NH and American Bar Association, Business Law Section.
**Career:** Law clerk, New Hampshire Superior Court; Intern, Civil Bureau of the New Hampshire Attorney General's Office. Admitted in NH and MA.
**Personal:** BA, Purdue University, 1992 (with Distinction) Phi Beta Kappa; JD, Northeastern University School of Law, 1995.

## PIGNATELLI, Michael
Rath, Young and Pignatelli PC, Concord
603 226 2600
*Recommended in Litigation*

## POULOS, Denise
Donahue, Tucker & Ciandella, Exeter
603 778 0686
*Recommended in Real Estate*

## RATH, Thomas
Rath, Young and Pignatelli PC, Concord
603 226 2600
*Recommended in*
*Corporate/Commercial*

## RAYMOND, James
Upton and Hatfield LLP, Concord
603 224 7791
*Recommended in Real Estate*

## REIDY, James
Sheehan Phinney Bass + Green PA, Manchester 603 668 0300
*Recommended in Employment*

## REISCHE, Alan
Sheehan Phinney Bass + Green PA, Manchester 603 668 0300
*Recommended in*
*Corporate/Commercial*

## RICE, Emily
Orr & Reno PA, Concord
603 224 2381
*Recommended in Employment,*
*Litigation*

## ROSENBLATT, Arnold
Cook, Little, Rosenblatt & Manson PLLC, Manchester 603 621 7102
a.rosenblatt@clrm.com
*Recommended in Litigation*
**Practice Areas:** Business litigation in state and federal courts and arbitration proceedings including cases in patents, trademarks, trade secrets and other forms of intellectual property, shareholder and partner disputes, non-competition agreements, employment matters, contract actions, lender liability and professional malpractice.
**Prof. Memberships:** American and New Hampshire Bar Associations (Business Litigation Section Chair, 1995-96, 1998-99 and member of Continuing Legal Education Committee and Professional-

ism Committee); American Arbitration Association Panel for Commercial Arbitrators.
**Career:** Admitted in New Hampshire (1987), Massachusetts (1998), New York (1982) and Vermont (2004).
**Personal:** Swarthmore College (BA, with distinction, 1975); Columbia University, JD, 1981 (Harlan Fiske Stone Scholar).

## ROTCH, Peter B
McLane, Graf, Raulerson & Middleton Professional Association, Manchester
603 628 1305
peter.rotch@mclane.com
*Recommended in Real Estate*
**Practice Areas:** Chair of McLane's Real Estate Department. His practice is focused on commercial property development and financing. He works with investors and corporate clients who wish to develop and finance real estate. He is an agent for all of the major title insurance companies. Recent projects include obtaining property and easements for a major gas powered electric generating facility.
**Prof. Memberships:** Fellow of the American College of Real Estate Lawyers, New Hampshire and American Bar Associations.
**Career:** Admitted in New Hampshire, 1966; shareholder and Partner, 1974. Listed in Woodward's 'Best Lawyers In America'.
**Personal:** Dartmouth College (1963-AB), University of Chicago Law School (1966-JD).

## SAMUELS, Richard A
McLane, Graf, Raulerson & Middleton Professional Association, Manchester
603 628 1470
richard.samuels@mclane.com
*Recommended in*
*Corporate/Commercial*
**Practice Areas:** Concentrates practice in corporate and commercial transactions, securities law, banking, and utilities regulatory matters. Advises on merger and acquisition transactions and securities matters, including public and private offerings of securities, entity formation, governance, and commercial matters. An author of New Hampshire's Business Corporation Act and Limited Liability Company Act.
**Prof. Memberships:** Board of Directors and Chair of the Fiscal Policy Committee of the Business and Industry Association of New Hampshire. New Hampshire liaison to the American Bar Associations Business Law Section's Committee on State Regulation of Securities.
**Personal:** BA, Union College, 1974; MA, Duke University, 1976; JD, Cornell University, 1980. Listed in Woodward's 'Best Lawyers in America'.

## SHILLING, Cameron G
McLane, Graf, Raulerson & Middleton Professional Association, Manchester
603 628 1351
cameron.shilling@mclane.com
*Recommended in Employment*
**Practice Areas:** Chair of Employment Litigation. Litigation and counseling on trade secrets, non-compete agreements, unfair competition, electronic data management and discovery, discrimination and harassment, and commercial/ employment contracts.
**Prof. Memberships:** Clerk of Employment Law Section of NH Bar; Chair of ABA Sub-Committee on Trade Secrets and Non-Competition Litigation; Executive Board of Daniel Webster Inn of Court; Admitted in NH and MA.
**Publications:** 'Inevitable Disclosure Doctrine – A Necessary and Precise Tool for Trade Secret Law', ABA 'Best Of' Periodicals (2005); 'The Cutting Edge of Trade Secrets – How Far Should the Law Go to Prevent Misappropriation By Memory and Inevitable Disclosure?', Corporate Counsel Magazine (2003).
**Personal:** Cornell Law School, JD 1995.

## SKLAR, Daniel W
Nixon Peabody LLP, Manchester
603 628 4008
dsklar@nixonpeabody.com
*Recommended in*
*Corporate/Commercial*
**Practice Areas:** Lending transactions, loan workouts/liquidations, bankruptcy reorganizations, lender liability. More than 25 years' experience in corporate law, commercial transactions. Represented debtors, trustees, secured creditors, committees, stockholders, lessors, senior executives in large Chapter 11 cases, several international insolvencies.
**Prof. Memberships:** Admitted to practice before NH state courts, District Court of NH, First and Eleventh Circuit Courts of Appeals, US Supreme Court. Certification, business bankruptcy law, American Bankruptcy Certification Board. American Bankruptcy Institute. NH and American Bar Associations. Fellow, American College of Bankruptcy.
**Career:** Adjunct Professor, Franklin Pierce Law Center.
**Publications:** Co-author, 'What is the Appropriate Statute of Limitations Under Section 723(a) of the Code?' Commercial Law Journal, Volume 104, Fall 1999. Co-author, 'Rewriting Tax History Under the Code'. American Bankruptcy Institute Journal (August 1999). Co-author, 'A Primer for Using the Bankruptcy Code in Analyzing Whether a Payment Constitutes a Preference in the Context of an Insurance Rehabilitation/Liquidation Case'. Mealey's Litigation Report, Insurance Solvency (July 21, 1999). Co-author, 'Single Asset Real Estate – Who Qualified?' 15 American Bankruptcy Institute Journal (April 1996).

**Personal:** Boston University, LLM; Boston College, JD cum laude; University of Pennsylvania, BA.

### SNOW, Ronald
Orr & Reno PA, Concord 603 224 2381
*Recommended in Litigation*

### SPARKMAN, Jon
Devine Millimet & Branch PA, North Hampton 603 964 4990
*Recommended in Corporate/Commercial*

### TAUB, Philip B
Nixon Peabody LLP, Manchester
603 628 4038
ptaub@nixonpeabody.com
*Recommended in Corporate/Commercial*
**Practice Areas:** Partner and Deputy Practice Group Leader of the firm's Business Group. Mr Taub focuses his practice primarily in the area of corporate transactional work, including mergers, acquisitions, leveraged buyouts, start-ups, shareholder disputes and venture capital financing. He has extensive experience in commercial financing having served as counsel to a number of lending institutions.
**Prof. Memberships:** Admitted to practice in New Hampshire, Massachusetts, and the District of Columbia and before the US District Court for the District of New Hampshire. Member of the American, New Hampshire and Manchester Bar Associations.
**Personal:** George Washington University, JD; Boston University, BS.

### TUCKER, William
Wadleigh, Starr & Peters PLLC, Manchester 603 669 4140
*Recommended in Real Estate*

### UPTON II, Robert
Upton and Hatfield LLP, Concord
603 224 7791
*Recommended in Real Estate*

### VAN OOT, Martha
Orr & Reno PA, Concord 603 224 2381
*Recommended in Litigation*

### VICINANZO, David
Nixon Peabody LLP, Boston
617 345 1000
*Recommended in Litigation*
**Practice Areas:** Practices primarily in the area of government investigations and the representation of organizations and individuals in complex civil and criminal matters.
**Prof. Memberships:** Admitted to practice in New York and New Hampshire; the United States Courts of Appeals (First, Second, and District of Columbia circuits); numerous federal district courts.
**Career:** He served as a federal prosecutor in Washington, DC, and New England for 13 years; was as an advisor to the US attorney general, and a chief prosecutor in the campaign finance investigation of the 1996 presidential election.
**Personal:** Fordham University, JD; Harvard University, BA, with honors.

### VOLINSKY, Andru H
Bernstein Shur, Manchester
603 623 8700
avolinsky@bernsteinshur.com
*Recommended in Litigation*
**Practice Areas:** Managing Attorney of Manchester, NH office. His practice focuses on employment law, commercial litigation, and issues of white-collar crime. Mr Volinsky is also lead counsel for the school districts in New Hampshire's landmark school funding cases.

**Prof. Memberships:** New Hampshire Bar Association; New Hampshire Association of Criminal Defense Lawyers; American Association of Criminal Defense Lawyers; Claremont Coalition; New Hampshire Citizens Voice Project; New Hampshire Civil Liberties Union.
**Personal:** JD, George Washington University National Law Center (1980); Certificate in Conflicts Resolution Studied, University of Pittsburgh (1976); BA, Psychology, University of Miami (1976, magna cum laude).

### WALKER JR, Alexander
Devine Millimet & Branch PA, Manchester 603 669 1000
*Recommended in Litigation*

### WESTGATE, Bradford
Winer & Bennett LLP, Nashua
603 882 5157
*Recommended in Real Estate*

### WHEAT, James
Wadleigh, Starr & Peters PLLC, Manchester 603 669 4140
*Recommended in Litigation*

### WOLOWITZ, David
McLane, Graf, Raulerson & Middleton Professional Association, Portsmouth
603 436 2818
david.wolowitz@mclane.com
*Recommended in Litigation*
**Practice Areas:** Concentrates in risk management and litigation on behalf of corporations relating to all aspects of employment law, with a particular focus on mental health issues and difficult employees in the workplace. Recent representation of clients includes BAE Systems, Inc.; Nike, Inc.; Universal Instruments Corp.; as well as healthcare and educational organizations, including St. Paul's School.

**Prof. Memberships:** Admitted to practice before the state and federal courts in New Hampshire and Massachusetts. Member of the New Hampshire, Massachusetts, and American Bar Associations.
**Career:** Shareholder and Director since 1991; guest faculty Harvard Law School, Trial Advocacy Workshop (1984-present). Listed in a leading US legal publication.
**Personal:** 1968, AB, Washington University; 1971, MA, Harvard University; 1975, JD, University of Michigan.

### ZORN, William V A
McLane, Graf, Raulerson & Middleton Professional Association, Manchester
603 628 1340
bill.zorn@mclane.com
*Recommended in Corporate/Commercial*
**Practice Areas:** Mergers and acquisitions involving sophisticated and complex tax issues, allocations and filings. Federal and state tax planning and structuring for corporations, limited liability companies, and partnerships; frequently structures business succession plans for their owners. Advises professional service organizations on the unique aspects created in these mergers and consolidations. Specific transactional experience within the manufacturing industry.
**Prof. Memberships:** NH Bar Association (former Tax Section Chair, Corporate Section Member); MA Bar Association (Member); ABA (Member, Tax Section).
**Personal:** AB, Dartmouth College, 1975; JD, Boston University, 1978; LLM, Taxation, Boston University, 1983. McLane Partner since 1986. Recognized in 'The Best Lawyers in America' in Tax and Employee Benefits Law. Admitted in NH, MA and the US Tax Court.

# COOK, LITTLE, ROSENBLATT & MANSON PLLC

## THE FIRM

**Founding Partners:** James G Cook, Curtis W Little Jr, Arnold Rosenblatt, Thomas P Manson

**Number of partners:** 5
**Number of other lawyers:** 3
**Total number of lawyers:** 8

## AREAS OF PRACTICE:

| | |
|---|---|
| Corporate & Finance | 50% |
| Business Litigation | 35% |
| Real Estate | 10% |
| Employment | 5% |

**FIRM OVERVIEW:** Cook, Little, Rosenblatt & Manson offers commercial law services in the corporate, business litigation and employment areas. The firm has significant expertise in representing entrepreneurial and technology-based companies both within and outside New Hampshire, ranging from start-ups to long established enterprises. The firm has extensive experience in representing businesses in a broad range of commercial matters and transactions, including advising clients in the organization, capitalization and growth of their enterprises. The firm also represents businesses in a broad range of commercial litigation.

## MAIN AREAS OF PRACTICE:

**Corporate:** Cook, Little, Rosenblatt & Manson provides general corporate legal services to a variety of businesses, including entrepreneurial, technology-based companies and family-owned companies. The firm's corporate practice includes advising clients with regard to business formation (including choice of entity), organizational and operational structure (including family participation), protecting trade secrets and other intellectual property, acquiring and licensing of computer software and other technology, distribution arrangements, acquisition and sale of businesses, structuring and establishing joint ventures and other strategic relationships, debt and equity financings (including venture capital), securities matters (including private placements, stock option plans and other incentive and deferred compensation arrangements), agreements between a company's owners (including buy-sell and other arrangements), and purchase, sale and leasing of real estate.

**Business Litigation:** Cook, Little, Rosenblatt & Manson's attorneys have significant experience representing both plaintiffs and defendants in state and federal court as well as in commercial arbitrations. The firm's litigation practice includes representing clients in corporate and partnership disputes, patent, trademark and other intellectual property infringement lawsuits, trade secret misappropriation claims, securities law claims, software and other technology disputes, contract issues, non-compete and other employment issues, as well as other business disputes.

**Banking and Finance:** The firm frequently represents both lenders and borrowers in complex financings, including syndicated loan transactions.

**Employment:** The firm's employment practice includes advising on hiring and termination procedures, drafting employment agreements (including non-disclosure agreements and non-compete agreements), preparing personnel manuals and policies (including harassment policies), handling wrongful termination claims, advising and litigating discrimination claims (including age, gender, race and disability), and counseling on compliance with federal and state laws and regulations.

**CLIENTS:** The firm's clients include high technology clients as well as other entrepreneurial companies from early start up to well established companies. The firm also represents many large financial institutions.

## HEAD OFFICE

**NEW HAMPSHIRE**
650 Elm Street, **Manchester**, NH 03101
**Tel:** 603 621 7100　**Fax:** 603 621 7111
**Website:** www.clrm.com

## CONTACTS

| | |
|---|---|
| Corporate | James Cook |
| Business Litigation | Arnold Rosenblatt |
| Real Estate | Curtis W Little, Jr |
| Securities & Finance | Curtis W Little, Jr |
| Family Enterprises | Thomas P Manson |

# MCLANE GRAF RAULERSON & MIDDLETON, PA

## THE FIRM

**Managing Partner:** Steven V Camerino
**Senior Partner:** Jack B Middleton
**Number of partners:** 35
**Number of other lawyers:** 40

**FIRM OVERVIEW:** 75 lawyers and more than 25 legal assistants advise a wide range of domestic and international corporate clients with their legal needs in the greater New England area. The firm is based in New Hampshire, with locations near the Massachusetts and Maine borders, and is the state's largest full service law firm. The firm counts amongst its lawyers Fellows of the American Colleges of Trial Lawyers, Real Estate Lawyers, Tax Counsel, and Trust & Estates Counsel. The 2006 edition of The Best Lawyers in America recognizes 27 of the firm's lawyers. Firm members have drafted legislation, including the Business Corporation and Limited Liability Company Acts of New Hampshire, and are the authors of the State of New Hampshire's Environmental Law Handbook. McLane's lawyers are licensed in all of the New England states, including Connecticut, as well as in New York, Pennsylvania, Washington, DC, Georgia, Arizona, Missouri, and Nebraska. The firm's lawyers actively participate in service to the public and to the profession. Current members of the firm have served as Attorney General in New Hampshire, as Presidents of the New Hampshire and New England Bar Associations and as Secretary of the American Bar Association. The McLane Law Firm is a member of TerraLex, the premier international and interstate association of independent law firms.

## MAIN AREAS OF PRACTICE:

**Corporate:** The firm's Corporate Department advises clients on merger and acquisition transactions and securities matters, including public and private offerings of equity securities, as well as entity formation, governance, commercial matters and all aspects of corporate finance. The department has industry focus areas in the energy, manufacturing, technology and financial services industries. Recent transaction includes the representation of a publicly traded energy company in connection with the sale of their interests in the Seabrook Nuclear Power Plant, representing 17% of an $800 million transaction.

**Environmental:** The Environmental Practice covers administrative law and litigation under all the major federal environmental laws and their State program analogues. The firm's lawyers have extensive experience in Superfund and State hazardous waste cases, Clean Air Act, Clean Water Act, wetlands, TSCA, EPCRA, NEPA, energy facility siting, and natural resource law, in both permitting and enforcement cases. The firm has handled cases throughout New England, New York, Georgia, South Carolina, and California.

**Commercial Litigation:** The firm's Litigation Department possesses trial experience covering a wide range of cases including: computer software antitrust litigation; disputes over development of software for international businesses; reinsurance contract disputes over asbestos claims; patent infringement litigation; environmental insurance coverage disputes; securities arbitration and litigation; product liability; trademark opposition proceedings; and trade secret and non-competition agreement litigation. A recent case example includes representation of EnergyNorth (ENGI) in EnergyNorth Natural Gas, Inc. v Lloyd's, Underwriters at London in the USDC for the District of New Hampshire, concerning insurance coverage for environmental liabilities at a former manufactured gas plant. EnergyNorth successfully demonstrated that the damage was the result of unintentional leaks and spills that continued for an extended period of time.

**Utility Law:** The firm represent gas, telephone, and water utilities; competitive energy suppliers; small power producers and other wholesale electric generators; wireless communications companies; utility holding companies; municipalitites and industrial and commercial customers of electric utilities. Recent work includes extensive work on restructuring of the electric and gas industries, electric and water municipalization litigation, gas, electric and water rate proceedings and numerous financings.

**Employment:** Representation includes defending and prosecuting claims, workplace audits, managerial and workforce training programs, development of personnel policies and practices, and consultation and advice on the day to day challenges employers face, including internal employee complaints, responding to government investigations, or resolving disability, compensation, benefits, misconduct and termination issues.

**Real Estate:** The firm's Real Estate Practice advises clients on general commercial and construction financing, land use matters, leasing, and other aspects of real estate and business ownership. The firm recently obtained on behalf of a client all permits for an electric generating station producing competitive-cost power. Representation included the acquisition of all real estate, easements for the transmission lines and all environmental and regulatory work for the new 16-mile, interstate gas transmission pipeline.

**Tax:** The firm's Tax Department, the largest in the state of New Hampshire, represents individuals and businesses, buyers and sellers, in a variety of tax-related transactions, planning and issues. McLane's tax lawyers represent clients in every phase of contact with the IRS and state revenue agencies, including audit, collection, appeals, abatement requests and dispute resolution. When necessary, litigation lawyers experienced in tax matters assist in tax matters that require litigation.

**Intellectual Property:** The firm's IP lawyers represent clients on a wide range of US and international intellectual property matters and transactions. In litigated matters, it has helped large software companies, such as Microsoft Corporation, protect their copyright ownership in software against piracy and counterfeiting. The IP Group handles all aspects of IP protection, including patent, trademark, copyright, trade secret, licensing and e-commerce law.

**CLIENTS:** Abbott Laboratories; Algonquin Power Fund; BAUER Nike Hockey U.S.A., Inc.; BayCorp Holdings; El Paso Energy; Hitchiner Manufacturing Co., Inc.; Hyundai Motor Company; Irving Oil, Microsoft Corporation; Synagro Technologies, Inc; and Verizon Communications.

## HEAD OFFICE

**NEW HAMPSHIRE**
City Hall Plaza, 900 Elm Street, **Manchester**, NH 03101
**Tel:** 603 625 6464   **Fax:** 603 625 5650
**Email:** law@mclane.com   **Website:** www.mclane.com

## BRANCH OFFICES

**NEW HAMPSHIRE**
Bicentennial Square, 15 North Main Street, **Concord**, NH 03301
**Tel:** 603 226 0400   **Fax:** 603 230 4448

100 Market Street, Suite 301, **Portsmouth**, NH 03801
**Tel:** 603 436 2818   **Fax:** 603 436 5672

## CONTACTS

| | |
|---|---|
| **Corporate** | Thomas W Hildreth |
| **Environmental** | Gregory H Smith |
| **Commercial Litigation** | Bruce W Felmly |
| **Utility Law** | Steven V Camerino |
| **Employment** | Linda S Johnson |
| **Tax** | Steven M Burke |
| **Real Estate** | Peter B Rotch |
| **Intellectual Property** | Mark A Wright |

McLane, Graf, Raulerson & Middleton
Professional Association

# SHEEHAN PHINNEY BASS + GREEN

## THE FIRM

**Managing Partner:** Joseph A DiBrigida
**Number of partners:** 37
**Number of associates:** 10
**Number of counsel:** 10

## AREAS OF PRACTICE:

Corporate & Finance. . . . . . . . . . . . . . . . . . . . . . . . . . . . . . . . . . . . . . . . . 41%
Litigation. . . . . . . . . . . . . . . . . . . . . . . . . . . . . . . . . . . . . . . . . . . . . . . . . . 36%
Real Estate/Environmental . . . . . . . . . . . . . . . . . . . . . . . . . . . . . . . . . 8%
Labor & ERISA. . . . . . . . . . . . . . . . . . . . . . . . . . . . . . . . . . . . . . . . . . . . . 9%
Trusts & Estates. . . . . . . . . . . . . . . . . . . . . . . . . . . . . . . . . . . . . . . . . . . 6%

**FIRM OVERVIEW:** Sheehan Phinney Bass + Green has been serving clients throughout New England for more than 50 years. While the firm's core clients remain businesses, institutions and municipalities based in New England, the firm also regularly represents the interests of national and international concerns throughout the region and the United States. Sheehan Phinney is known for professional excellence, practical counsel, and commitment to both its clients and the communities it serves. To enhance the services provided to its clients, the firm has expanded beyond its offices in Manchester and Concord by opening an office in the heart of Boston's financial district, and establishing a presence in New Hampshire's technology-rich Upper Valley. The firm's geographic expansion springs from the regional growth and diversity of its clients and their needs, including access to major capital and international markets. These service-oriented developments complement the firm's expansion of its government relations and tax advisory services through its affiliates, the Sheehan Phinney Capitol Group and the Sheehan Phinney Tax Group. The firm is the exclusive member firm for New Hampshire of Lex Mundi, the world's leading association of independent law firms.

## MAIN AREAS OF PRACTICE:

**Corporate:** The firm has particular expertise in mergers and acquisitions, corporate finance, healthcare, real estate, and labor law as well as corporate governance. Areas of practice also include tax matters, public and private securities, bankruptcy and insolvency, business formation, education, the environment and energy, governmental affairs, intellectual property and technology, import/export control and trust and estate planning.

**Litigation:** The firm's Business Litigation Practice is one of the most well respected in Northern New England. Its personal injury litigation practice includes representation of both plaintiffs and defendants. The firm has recently litigated to a successful conclusion or settlement cases involving employment discrimination, securities, class action involving state taxes, contractual disputes, non-competition, stockholder and partnership disputes, and tax matters.

**Banking & Finance:** In addition to its frequent representation of borrowers and lenders in numerous transactions, the firm has served as counsel in more than a billion dollars of tax-exempt financings in New Hampshire and Massachusetts over the past 18 months. The firm's clients in public finance transactions include New Hampshire's largest issuer of tax-exempt bonds, as well as borrowers, underwriters and corporate trustees.

**Labor:** Increasing governmental regulation of the workplace and ever-expanding rights of employees have made 'proactive prevention' the soundest method for avoiding significant liability in employment law. Legal services offered in this area include: developing effective anti-discrimination policies, proper employee screening and verifying procedures, wage and salary administration strategies (FLSA), executive employment agreements, employee handbooks and policies, noncompetition and nondisclosure covenants, employment applications and performance evaluation policies, severance agreements, early retirement programs, reduction in force procedures, substance abuse policies, workplace privacy policies, workplace violence prevention or response plans, leave of absence programs (including FMLA, maternity, military and jury duty), and personnel file record-keeping procedures.

## HEAD OFFICE

**NEW HAMPSHIRE**
1000 Elm Street, **Manchester**, NH 03101
**Tel:** 603 668 0300   **Fax:** 603 627 8121
**Website:** www.sheehan.com

## BRANCH OFFICES

**MASSACHUSETTS**
One Boston Place, **Boston**, MA 02108
**Tel:** 617 897 5600   **Fax:** 617 439 9363

**NEW HAMPSHIRE**
Two Eagle Square, **Concord**, NH 03301
**Tel:** 603 223 2020   **Fax:** 603 224 8899

46 Centerra Parkway, **Lebanon**, NH 03766
**Tel:** 603 627 8140   **Fax:** 603 641 8750

## CONTACTS

| | |
|---|---|
| **Corporate Finance** | Michael J Drooff |
| **Corporate** | Alan L Reische |
| **Healthcare** | Matthew J Lapointe |
| **Labor** | James P Reidy |
| **Litigation** | Peter S Cowan |
| **Real Estate** | Susan A Manchester |
| **Banking** | Kenneth A Viscarello |

**Real Estate:** The firm works with clients in all areas of commercial real estate financing and construction matters, advising and representing developers, lenders and users of commercial properties: office buildings, shopping centers, condominiums, affordable housing projects, corporate headquarters and airports. Representation includes negotiation of purchase, construction and financing documentation (including IRC Section 42 financing), appearance before land use boards and registration of condominiums with State Department of Justice (Consumer Protection Division). Agent for major title insurance companies.

**CLIENTS:** The firm's clients represent a diverse range of industries including: healthcare, education, manufacturing, insurance, import/export, technology, communications, banking and finance, not-for-profit, pension and mutual funds, government relations, religious institutions, commercial lenders and public finance.

ATTORNEYS AT LAW

## How lawyers are ranked

Every year we carry out thousands of in-depth interviews with clients and lawyers in order to assess the reputations and expertise of business lawyers across the USA. Chambers rankings and editorial are referred to extensively by General Counsel and other purchasers of legal services who look to our recommendations when choosing their lawyers.

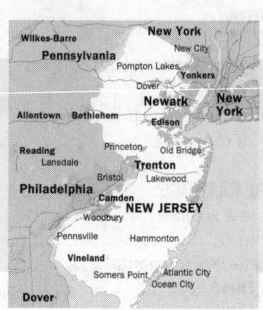

# CORPORATE/M&A

## Corporate/M&A

### Leading Firms

1. **LOWENSTEIN SANDLER PC** *Roseland*
2. **DRINKER BIDDLE & REATH LLP** *Florham Park*
   **MCCARTER & ENGLISH, LLP** *Newark*
   **MORGAN, LEWIS & BOCKIUS LLP** *Princeton*
   **PITNEY HARDIN LLP** *Morristown*
   **SILLS CUMMIS EPSTEIN & GROSS PC** *Newark*
3. **GIORDANO HALLERAN & CIESLA PC** *Middletown*
   **GREENBAUM, ROWE, SMITH & DAVIS** *Woodbridge*
   **NORRIS, MCLAUGHLIN & MARCUS** *Bridgewater*
   **ORLOFF, LOWENBACH, STIFELMAN** *Roseland*
   **RIKER DANZIG SCHERER HYLAND** *Morristown*
   **SONNENSCHEIN NATH & ROSENTHAL** *Short Hills*
   **WILENTZ GOLDMAN & SPITZER, P.A.** *Woodbridge*

### Leading Individuals

1. **AIELLO John** *Giordano Halleran & Ciesla*
   **BOYAJIAN Victor** *Sonnenschein Nath & Rosenthal*
   **EHRENBERG Peter** *Lowenstein Sandler PC*
   **SORIN David** *Morgan, Lewis & Bockius LLP*
2. **COHEN Steven** *Morgan, Lewis & Bockius LLP*
   **DAVIS Alan** *Greenbaum, Rowe, Smith*
   **FELTON W Raymond** *Greenbaum, Rowe, Smith*
   **JANIS Ronald** *Pitney Hardin LLP*
   **KORNSTEIN Alan** *Orloff, Lowenbach, Stifelman*
   **MINION Robert** *Lowenstein Sandler PC*
   **THOMPSON Kenneth** *McCarter & English, LLP*
   **WOVSANIKER Alan** *Lowenstein Sandler PC*
   **ZIMMERMAN Edward** *Lowenstein Sandler PC*
3. **BRODERICK David** *McCarter & English, LLP*
   **CASEY Warren** *Pitney Hardin LLP*
   **GROSS Steven** *Sills Cummis Epstein & Gross PC*
   **HUTCHEON Peter** *Norris, McLaughlin & Marcus*
   **KNEE Stephen** *Greenbaum, Rowe, Smith*
   **LAVEY Stewart** *Drinker Biddle & Reath LLP*
   **STAMELMAN Andrew** *Riker Danzig Scherer Hyland*
   **STODDARD III John** *Drinker Biddle & Reath LLP*
   **SUNBERG Randall** *Morgan, Lewis & Bockius LLP*
   **THEK Raymond** *Lowenstein Sandler PC*

### Up-and-coming individuals

**PERGOLA Anthony** *Lowenstein Sandler PC*

## Band 1

### Lowenstein Sandler PC

See firm details p.1313

**The Firm:** In the corporate arena this firm maintains its primacy; it is "*clearly number one*," most sources acknowledged. One of the largest firms in the state with one of the largest corporate departments, Lowenstein commands respect in all areas of corporate law, from early-stage venture capital to the continued representation of Fortune 500 companies on securities, a field in which it competes with New York firms. Research shows the reputation of the group is based on a strong broad bench, rounded service and good client care: "*It has probably the best client service in the state – the lawyers value their clients.*" Lawyers impress with their "*competent, fast and efficient*" approach, and clients believe them to be "*cost-effective.*"

**The Lawyers: Peter Ehrenberg** (see p.1298) is renowned as "*a star lawyer in the top league.*" The linchpin of the corporate group, his productivity is the object of universal admiration: "*He works a phenomenal amount of time yet is still very accessible,*" say clients. Ehrenberg has played a central role in several of the firm's highlight transactions, including Center Bancorp's merger with Red Oak Bank. The "*outstanding*" **Robert Minion** (see p.1303) leads the firm's national work in investment management and hedge funds and has built up a strong following with clients. "*His approach is personal and he will be the one to watch our backs,*" say clients. **Alan Wovsaniker** (see p.1307) is a general corporate attorney whose market experience and good judgment please clients. "*He's willing to give us a short answer when we need a short answer, and he always has our best interests at heart.*" His clients include public and private companies in the healthcare, transportation and hi-tech sectors, as well as investment banks. An acknowledged star in the venture capital community, "*tireless*" **Edward Zimmerman** (see p.1308) has a towering reputation in New Jersey for technology-driven deals. Clients remark: "*We go beyond the typical lawyer and client relationship; we feel he is part of our team.*" In 2005 Zimmerman acted for Datran Media on the raising of $60 million worth of venture capital, the consolidation of several affiliated entities, and their conversion from LLC to corporation.

**Anthony Pergola** (see p.1304) is also heavily involved in the firm's technology and related venture capital work. His growing reputation extends to securities regulation advice for public companies. **Ray Thek** (see p.1307) is highly regarded for his strong industry focus on biotech matters; he is in his element on startups and has a solid profile in university technology transfers. Thek is characterized as "*a sharp and creative lawyer who solves problems and gets results.*"

**Clients/Work Highlights:** In the venture capital and early-stage arena, the group has undertaken significant work. It represented an investor group led by Aperture Venture Partners on a $30 million financing in the life sciences sector. Clients include both significant private and publicly held companies. In the M&A sector, the firm advised Center Bancorp on its $26 million agreement to acquire Red Oak Bank. Other clients include Lucent Technologies; Cerberus Capital Management; CD&L; Rocker Partners; Inter-Atlantic Group and LibertyHealth.

## Band 2

### Drinker Biddle & Reath LLP

**The Firm:** This Pennsylvania-headquartered firm continues to make inroads into the New Jersey market through its offices in Princeton and Florham Park, the latter garnering particular praise for building on the good name of predecessor firm Shanley & Fisher. The corporate and securities group is "*near the top in terms of depth,*" indeed peers say it is "*a much deeper than average group.*" Recent work has encompassed M&A for publicly held clients and several auction sales by the shareholders of privately held companies.

**The Lawyers:** Renowned lawyer **Stewart Lavey** concentrates on regional M&A, where his experience and transaction skills are highly prized. Peers agree that he is "*a well-rounded corporate lawyer who really knows how to get a deal done.*" **John Stoddard** chairs the firm's venture capital and emerging growth group. He combines more than 20 years of corporate and finance experience with a mix of hi-tech and life sciences work. Stoddard's clients come from industries as diverse as publishing and insurance.

**Clients/Work Highlights:** The team acted for The BISYS Group on the agreement to sell BISYS Information Services to Open Solutions for $470 million. It also assisted The BISYS Group on the purchase of assets from RK Consulting. Among the firm's other New Jersey clients is a NASDAQ-listed financial services company.

## McCarter & English, LLP

**The Firm:** A major presence throughout the northeast, this firm provides an excellent, full corporate service and has a very good reputation acting for public companies. Peers say the "*good breadth and depth of talent*" makes this firm a solid choice in the region. The team is able to provide a multioffice service on major M&A, acting for clients in the technology, pharmaceuticals, manufacturing and insurance industries among others. Strong tax support bolsters the transactional side of the practice, as well as making the firm a sound choice for controversies.

**The Lawyers: Ken Thompson** chairs the corporate team and is the cornerstone of the firm's reputation in this area. "*He is distinguished as a good negotiator who can prioritize well,*" say peers. An M&A expert, Thompson continues to teach at Seton Hall University School of Law as an adjunct professor. "*A seasoned lawyer with a good reputation,*" **David Broderick** co-heads the firm's small business and investment company practice. Sources say he has built a strong base in the venture capital M&A field.

**Clients/Work Highlights:** The team's corporate successes have included acting for RoseArt Industries on its sale to Montreal-based Mega Bloks. This cross-border transaction was reported to be worth in excess of $300 million.

## Morgan, Lewis & Bockius LLP

See firm details p.1758

**The Firm:** The New Jersey contingent of this international firm combines a leading name with a clear market focus, making it tough competition for the other leaders. Clients say the firm is "*without question one of the best,*" acknowledging a surge of activity in the emerging growth market sector and the firm's roster of top lawyers who continue to make their mark in this area. The Princeton office brings together a team of 20 corporate lawyers who are particularly active in the venture capital and private equity financing fields. The office's work on technology and life sciences transactions is considered to be its core strength, although the firm's broad embrace of general corporate work and its international credentials also come in for praise.

**The Lawyers:** "*Big venture capital rainmaker*" **David Sorin** (see p.1306) is one of the firm's most valuable assets. Peers admire his solid reputation in the emerging growth and hi-tech fields. **Steven Cohen** (see p.1297) is another stalwart in the emerging growth area, working with public and private companies. His mature and effective style pleases clients: "*He brought a balanced approach to our needs and he is highly recommended.*" Cohen is particularly active in the life sciences arena and has spoken at major seminars. "*Top-quality technician*" **Randall**

Sunberg (see p.1307) cochairs the firm's life science group, having cemented his reputation in this area over the past decade. His client base consists of large pharmaceutical and biotech companies.

**Clients/Work Highlights:** The team acted for Lighthammer Software Development on its sale to SAP America. It also assisted NexMed on a strategic alliance with Schering and Novartis. Other clients include Aramsco; Barrier Therapeutics; Transwave; Eureka Broadband and TrustWave.

## Pitney Hardin LLP

See firm details p.1316

**The Firm:** This firm has a reputation in New Jersey for creating fine lawyers, and consequently, it comes as no surprise that clients applaud its "*superb quality and service.*" The group's main work is general corporate and securities transactions for public companies, although it continues to impress in the banking sector, with a prestigious list of clients and several notable bank mergers to its name. Abilities in the employment and employee benefits fields complement its full corporate service.

**The Lawyers:** "*An excellent lawyer,*" **Ronald Janis** (see p.1301) is the firm's star for bank M&A work. He combines a knowledge of regulatory issues relating to banks with a deal-focused approach. Chair of the corporate practice group **Warren Casey** (see p.1296) has an impressive practice serving as outside general corporate and securities counsel to a broad range of New Jersey companies. Peers concur that he is "*a smart man with a great client rapport,*" while clients find him "*an excellent, proactive adviser who will explain what you need rather than try to market his response.*"

**Clients/Work Highlights:** The firm acted for Valley National Bank on the $148 million acquisition of the entire stock of NorCrown Bank, a transaction involving complex indemnity and regulatory issues. Other clients include Advantage Bank; Linens 'n Things; Dendrite International; Footstar; Hudson United Bancorp; Agfa-Gevaert and Talbots.

## Sills Cummis Epstein & Gross PC

See firm details p.1319

**The Firm:** This New Jersey outfit has a solid local client base, although its roster also includes Fortune 500 companies throughout the USA. In addition to M&A work, the interdisciplinary group of 40 lawyers is increasingly active on SEC regulatory matters and corporate governance, where the firm positions itself as an attractive alternative to New York players. Moreover, a reputation in the life sciences and healthcare sectors helps the group maintain a steady stream of transactional work, and broad expertise in IP adds further to the team's abilities. Clients say the firm becomes "*a second pair of hands*" and supports them well during complex transactions.

**The Lawyers: Steven Gross** (see p.1299) chairs the corporate department and is the firm's managing partner. Peers and clients agree that he is "*a top name in the community and an extremely well-respected lawyer who has known the market for a long time.*"

**Clients/Work Highlights:** The team's clients

include a major real estate company; a company in the regenerative medicine field; a multinational pharmaceutical company and several healthcare organizations.

## Giordano Halleran & Ciesla PC

**The Firm:** Giordano is headquartered in Middletown with a second office in Trenton, and is best appreciated for its work on behalf of a core New Jersey client base. Drawing positive feedback for its "*outstanding client service,*" this outfit reaps the rewards of a long-term focus on client relationships. Clients enthuse about the approach of the lawyers: "*They are responsive and smart and more like business people than lawyers.*" From venture capital financings to corporate governance advice, the firm has consolidated its reputation in the middle market and has begun to focus on larger transactions, including several cross-border deals of late.

**The Lawyers:** The good standing of veteran lawyer **John Aiello** is one of the firm's chief assets. Peers recognize him as "*a terrific, quality lawyer who is held in the highest esteem.*" In his 30 years at the firm, Aiello has built a loyal following among clients, who agree that he is "*client-focused and always working toward our best interests.*"

**Clients/Work Highlights:** The firm advised a New Jersey company on the sale of its IT consulting division to the subsidiary of a Japanese company. In another matter, it represented a New Jersey manufacturing company on the sale of equity interests to a Hong Kong corporation. The firm also represented a privately held pharmaceutical company in a dual-tranche venture capital financing.

## Greenbaum, Rowe, Smith & Davis LLP

See firm details p.1311

**The Firm:** Having developed a robust practice in New Jersey, this firm acts for a mixture of clients including Fortune 500 companies and private companies at all stages of maturity. The Roseland and Woodbridge offices are one-stop shops for clients, with real estate and litigation specialists complementing the corporate team. Clients praise the firm for its "*responsive, client-oriented*" approach and confirm that the lawyers are thoroughly reliable: "*If you need them, they will be there.*" A diverse client base spans industries including retail, hi-tech and automobiles, and the firm's proven track record in real estate also attracts related corporate work.

**The Lawyers:** The "*extremely hard-working and knowledgeable*" **Alan Davis** (see p.1297) chairs the corporate department. One of the most highly respected figures in the market, Davis has tremendous experience and excellent connections. **Raymond Felton** (see p.1298) is the chair of the technology group and works for a client base of private and public companies. His practice includes private equity and securities matters and his "*good temperament*" impresses peers, who say: "*With him, the deal will be done.*" **Stephen Knee**'s (see p.1301) practice includes international M&A. Clients say that this experienced lawyer "*gets to the root of the transaction and gets it done quicker than many others*," all the while remaining "*a gentleman and a pleasure to work with.*"

**Clients/Work Highlights:** The team recently represented a medical group in a corporate reorganization and worked on partner buyouts in the healthcare sector. A major Dunkin' Donuts franchisee uses the firm for acquisitions, and the group represented Roma Food Enterprises in its sale to VISTAR Corporation. Other clients include Russell-Stanley; Pharmagistics; A.P. Deauville; Tropical Cheese Industries and United Energy.

### Norris, McLaughlin & Marcus, PA, A Professional Corporation

**The Firm:** In business for more than 50 years, this firm attracts respect for the advice and support it gives to its diverse client base. Most visible for general corporate support and midmarket M&A transactions, the group services companies of all types, from early-stage entities to multinationals. The lawyers keep the firm's profile high by participating in Bar association activity and various community events, and the group remains a respected choice.

**The Lawyers:** **Peter Hutcheon** is the fulcrum of the corporate team. Commentators say his "*tremendous intellectual capacity*" is an important asset for the firm.

### Orloff, Lowenbach, Stifelman & Siegel

**The Firm:** This smaller New Jersey player ensures the market has an excellent range of options when choosing a law firm for corporate advice. Founded in 1975, it still adopts a very personalized approach, acting for clients ranging from individual entrepreneurs through to substantial public companies. The firm's reputation for continuity of client relationships remains undented and it is especially noted for the ancillary support it provides on tax and related questions.

**The Lawyers:** Tax expert **Alan Kornstein** is judged to be a "*magnificent*" lawyer. The chair of the New Jersey State Bar Association's Section of Taxation, he combines tax structuring advice with extensive M&A

work. Peers rate his "*ability to speak and be understood – he understands the tax well but can relay anything to the layman.*"

### Riker Danzig Scherer Hyland & Perretti LLP

See firm details p.1318

**The Firm:** A full-service outfit with a proven record, this firm complements its reputation in dispute resolution with an impressive palette of corporate experience. From M&A and private equity transactions to tax and finance, the team has caught the eye of market commentators, who say the lawyers "*do a great job and really cannot be faulted.*" The team's work transcends the core corporate areas to include support on sector-specific work, for example in transportation, retail and food production. In addition, the firm has acted on several cross-border M&A transactions and joint ventures involving Canadian, Indian and Japanese entities.

**The Lawyers:** **Andrew Stamelman** (see p.1306) is head of the tax and corporate practice groups and is an established midmarket corporate counsel. Many of his clients are private and family-owned businesses seeking comprehensive business advice, and to them he is a trusted figure. He is "*very pleasant to deal with, yet speaks with great authority and gets his point across in negotiations,*" report clients.

**Clients/Work Highlights:** The team represented Vitaquest on the sale of a majority stake to private equity fund MidOcean Partners. This was reported as one of the largest transactions of the year to feature a New Jersey firm as lead counsel. Another client is AEON, which the firm assisted on a proposed merger with a global retail business to business network. Other clients include Gerber Products Company; Carbone Lorraine North America; The Meow Mix Company; Wakefern Food; Ahold; Zenith Optimedia Group; Hikma Pharmaceuticals and Primary Energy Ventures.

### Sonnenschein Nath & Rosenthal LLP

See firm details p.884

**The Firm:** Sonnenschein's Short Hills office is reaping the rewards of the booming practice of Victor Boyajian. He has given this national firm a clear New Jersey focus, while taking his own reputation onto the national stage. The team makes its mark with venture capital and emerging growth hi-tech companies, and within this arena it is able to draw on its national resources to impress the fertile New Jersey market. Peers agree this is "*a top firm for emerging growth work,*" and clients praise the team's excellent "*knowledge of critical early-stage venture capital issues.*"

**The Lawyers:** **Victor Boyajian** (see p.1296) chairs the venture capital and emerging growth practice, combining his New Jersey practice with a significant West Coast workload. He is a seasoned player with an impressive list of emerging growth and Fortune 500 clients. An "*excellent communicator,*" Boyajian impresses clients with his focus and depth. Researchers were told: "*He is very attuned to the early-stage venture community and the particular needs of all parts of this ecosystem.*"

**Clients/Work Highlights:** The firm represented Fresenius Medical Care, a medical device company, in its $3.5 billion acquisition of Renal Care Group. Other clients include Management Dynamics; Bell Labs and Identrus.

### Wilentz Goldman & Spitzer, P.A.

**The Firm:** With a heritage stretching back to 1919, this firm combines deep roots in the state with a good up-to-date commercial reputation. From its two New Jersey offices, and with the support of further offices in New York and Philadelphia, it can bring together a team of 50 business lawyers to take on corporate work from M&A to tax and financing. Market sources agree this outfit is "*well respected and reliable.*" The group's work has included syndicated financings across the USA, acting for various lenders.

**The Lawyers:** **Michael Schaff** chairs both the corporate and healthcare teams. Banking and financial services partner **Stuart Hoberman** has become president of the New Jersey State Bar Association.

## EMPLOYEE BENEFITS & EXECUTIVE COMPENSATION

### Band 1

### McCarter & English, LLP

**The Firm:** This firm's top-of-table position is made possible by the existence of an experienced standalone employee benefits and executive compensation group. The view from clients is that this "*high-quality firm provides absolutely excellent service.*" The Newark office is the hub of the practice, although its work spans a number of states and industry sectors, with significant clients including defense contractors, chemicals manufacturers and food processing companies. With organizations

facing ever more complex corporate governance responsibilities, another string to this firm's bow is its reputation for cutting-edge fiduciary duties advice relating to ERISA plans.

**The Lawyers:** **Mark Daniele** is the practice group leader for tax and employee benefits. Peers speak of his "*excellent depth:*" from the design and implementation of plans to regulatory and fiduciary questions, he is a top choice for clients. Said one: "*Mark is knowledgeable on all aspects, keeps abreast of developments and is extremely responsive.*" Admired for his "*fine tax expertise,*" **John Brescher** also focuses on employee benefits and ERISA advice. He has long-

standing relationships with a number of mid-cap companies.

### Pitney Hardin LLP

See firm details p.1316

**The Firm:** Serving the market for over 100 years, Pitney Hardin further proves its full-service credentials with its mature employee benefits and executive compensation team. The eight-lawyer group provides key support to the labor and employment team, and has gained a distinguished reputation of its own. Clients report that "*the lawyers make this firm; they are able to drop everything and take care of*

## Employee Benefits & Executive Compensation

### Leading Firms

1 MCCARTER & ENGLISH, LLP *Newark*
  PITNEY HARDIN LLP *Morristown*
2 LOWENSTEIN SANDLER PC *Roseland*
3 WITMAN, STADTMAUER & MICHAELS *Florham Park*
  WOLFF & SAMSON *West Orange*

### Leading Individuals

1 DANIELE Mark *McCarter & English, LLP*
  GRAW Andrew *Lowenstein Sandler PC*
  LAWLER Kathy *Pitney Hardin LLP*
2 BRESCHER John *McCarter & English, LLP*
  DOYLE David *Pitney Hardin LLP*

*your issues."* Most agree that *"sophistication and size"* are the group's core assets, and that it is flexible enough to provide support to collective bargaining procedures as well as M&A transactions. These lawyers have assisted on several of the firm's highlight corporate transactions and additionally have a good reputation on the issue of executive terminations after acquisitions.

**The Lawyers:** **Kathy Lawler** (see p.1302) is the key figure in the team. She has undertaken significant work on qualified pension plans, as well as ERISA fiduciary issues. Competitors conclude that this highly regarded lawyer is undoubtedly *"one of the best in New Jersey."* Clients find her *"a tremendously helpful resource,"* labeling her as *"one of the top in the country for analytical ability and judgment, while also remaining practical and businesslike."* **David Doyle** (see p.1298) works for a broad client base, from pharmaceuticals to retail companies. He is recognized for his *"highly skilled executive compensation"* focus.

**Clients/Work Highlights:** The team assisted on the sale of Hudson United Bank to TD Banknorth, negotiating both benefits and executive compensation issues. Leading clients include Agfa-Gevaert; Cytec Industries; Lucent Technologies; The New York Times; Valley National Bank; Alpharma; Longwood Industries and Wyeth.

## Band 2

### Lowenstein Sandler PC

See firm details p.1313

**The Firm:** This firm devotes significant resources to providing comprehensive structuring and transactional advice. A team of six lawyers is focused on advising employers, shareholders and fiduciaries, on ESOP transactions and aspects of M&A that are affected by employee benefits. The group is also prominent in benefits disputes, with ERISA litigation and representation before the IRS adding to its comprehensive workload. Worthy of note here is the sterling reputation of the firm's general litigation team in fiduciary matters: it serves to make the specialist employee benefits team all the more attractive. Market sources report that the lawyers are *"working extremely hard"* at building the group's reputation, and an impressive roster of public and private company clients is testament to this.

**The Lawyers:** **Andrew Graw** (see p.1299) heads the group and has 20 years of experience in this field. Clients refer to his *"excellent knowledge of this area, and this includes staying on top of and notifying us of recent developments."* He is also praised for his ability to translate his considerable expertise into *"practical and easy-to-implement advice."*

**Clients/Work Highlights:** The team handled all ESOP aspects in the sale of Geologic Services to another environmental consulting firm, Kleinfelder. Other clients include Phillips-Van Heusen; Vornado

Realty Trust; Apple Bank for Savings; Church & Dwight and Telcordia Technologies.

## Band 3

### Witman, Stadtmauer & Michaels PA

**The Firm:** Tax, pensions and employee benefits lie at the heart of this firm's work. From its Florham Park office it serves a midmarket client base throughout New Jersey and the New York metropolitan area. The team counsels clients on ERISA pension, 401(k) and supplemental executive retirement plans, and provides a comprehensive planning service, short only of administration. Peers see the firm as *"very active in the whole of this practice area."*

**The Lawyers:** Leonard Witman is the leading name at the firm and an adjunct professor at Seton Hall University School of Law. He has prior experience at the IRS in the Employee Plans and Exempt Organizations Division.

### Wolff & Samson, A Professional Corporation

**The Firm:** This West Orange firm has a foothold in the Pennsylvania and New York markets, and it is able to deploy its team to take on pension, profit-sharing, ESOP and 401(k) plan development, implementation and operation. *"Very, very strong"* lawyers attract attention from market commentators and are additionally known to be active on disputes and compliance issues.

**The Lawyers:** Stephen Ferszt is a former chair of the Employee Benefits Committee at the New Jersey State Bar Association. He is a key contact at the firm for ERISA and employee benefits work, as well as tax and trusts matters.

# EMPLOYMENT

# MAINLY DEFENDANT

## Band 1

### McElroy, Deutsch, Mulvaney & Carpenter, LLP

See firm details p.1315

**The Firm:** This firm's rapid ascent has continued to impress the market. The product of a merger in 2004, it combines the core labor and employment assets of the former Carpenter, Bennett & Morrissey firm with the litigation expertise of McElroy, Deutsch & Mulvaney. A group of 45 lawyers provides extensive employment counseling and *"tremendous"* litigation support. Peers concur that this *"terrific group"* is staffed by top lawyers who are *"real competitors and recommended rivals."* A solid traditional labor practice, including appeals of NLRB decisions, adds further strength.

**The Lawyers:** **Frank Dee** continues to be *"one of the best employment litigators in the state."* A *"terrific trial lawyer,"* he is active in discrimination and whistle-

blower cases, as well as OSHA matters. Dee is a former trial attorney for the NLRB, and commentators agree he is *"still marvelous"* on labor counseling. **John Peirano** also combines strong employment litigation and traditional labor practices. Clients agreed he is *"an outstanding trial lawyer"* and his *"extremely attentive client service"* also came in for praise. **Patrick Brady** won commendation this year for his *"smart, hard-working approach and excellent judgment."* Home Depot is a major client of his.

**Clients/Work Highlights:** The firm acted for a Fortune 100 corporation in the defense of nationwide discrimination allegations. It also defended three pharmaceutical companies and a financial organization in whistle-blower actions. In an appellate case the firm was successful in reversing a $2 million verdict against Verizon. Other clients include Johnson & Johnson; Schering-Plough; Telcordia Technologies; Rutgers and Merck.

### Ogletree, Deakins, Nash, Smoak & Stewart, PC

See firm details p.738

**The Firm:** Part of one of America's largest employment firms, the Morristown office houses a group of *"very smart lawyers"* whom peers count as some of the finest in the state. The office's reputation reflects its lineage: it was once the Stanton, Hughes, Diana, Mariani & Margello firm which had a market-leading profile in New Jersey. Now the 15-lawyer team supplements its local talent with resources from across the country; its core client base remains solidly New Jersey, New York and Pennsylvania-rooted. Recent highlight cases have touched on workplace harassment and discrimination, as well as ERISA and employee benefits. Peers agree that this *"excellent firm"* is a top choice in the state, while clients report favorably on attorneys who *"are knowledgeable, responsive and fabulously talented."*

## Employment: Mainly Defendant

### Leading Firms

**1** MCELROY, DEUTSCH, MULVANEY *Newark*
OGLETREE, DEAKINS *Morristown*

**2** BALLARD SPAHR *Voorhees*
GROTTA, GLASSMAN & HOFFMAN *Roseland*
LUM, DANZIS, DRASCO & POSITAN, LLC *Roseland*
PITNEY HARDIN LLP *Morristown*
PROSKAUER ROSE LLP *Newark*

**3** CARMAGNOLA & RITARDI LLC *Morristown*
FISHER & PHILLIPS LLP *Somerset*
GENOVA, BURNS & VERNOIA *Livingston*
JACKSON LEWIS *Morristown*
KIRKPATRICK & LOCKHART *Newark*
LOWENSTEIN SANDLER PC *Roseland*
MCCARTER & ENGLISH, LLP *Newark*
MORGAN, LEWIS & BOCKIUS LLP *Princeton*
RIKER DANZIG SCHERER HYLAND *Morristown*
SILLS CUMMIS EPSTEIN & GROSS PC *Newark*

### Leading Individuals

**1** ALITO Rosemary *Kirkpatrick & Lockhart*
CARMAGNOLA Domenick *Carmagnola & Ritardi LLC*
DEE Francis *McElroy, Deutsch, Mulvaney*
GENOVA Angelo *Genova, Burns & Vernoia*
JACOB Cynthia *Fisher & Phillips LLP*
POSITAN Wayne *Lum, Danzis, Drasco & Positan*
STANTON Patrick *Ogletree, Deakins*
SUFLAS Steven *Ballard Spahr*

**2** FUREY Michael *Riker Danzig Scherer Hyland*
GARLAND David *Sills Cummis Epstein & Gross PC*
KEYSER Denise *Ballard Spahr*
MARIANI Richard *Ogletree, Deakins*
PARLIMAN Gregory *Pitney Hardin LLP*
PEIRANO John *McElroy, Deutsch, Mulvaney*
RIDLEY John *Drinker Biddle & Reath LLP*

**3** BRADY Patrick *McElroy, Deutsch, Mulvaney*
CERASIA Edward *Proskauer Rose LLP*
GOLDSTEIN Marvin *Proskauer Rose LLP*
LESNEWICH Alan *Fisher & Phillips LLP*
OHNEGIAN Scott *Riker Danzig Scherer Hyland*
ROSENBLATT Richard *Morgan, Lewis & Bockius LLP*
SANDAK Lawrence *Proskauer Rose LLP*
SNEIRSON Marilyn *Kirkpatrick & Lockhart*

### Up-and-coming individuals

WEST Richard *Lum, Danzis, Drasco & Positan*

**The Lawyers:** The "*charismatic*" **Patrick Stanton** (see p.1306) is the managing shareholder of the Morristown office. His great reputation stems from a background which includes time spent as director of labor relations at WR Grace. He is also the immediate past chair of the labor and employment law section of the New Jersey State Bar Association. Peers his "*terrific, strong personality,*" and agree he is "*considered a mentor in New Jersey.*" **Richard Mariani** (see p.1302) is heavily involved in employment litigation, a field in which clients judge him to have "*real presence and top-notch capability.*" His recent work

includes major discrimination cases and federal appellate litigation.

**Clients/Work Highlights:** The team recently obtained summary judgment on behalf of a law firm in a long-running malpractice case concerning a missed filing deadline and ERISA withdrawal liability. It also achieved a successful outcome in a collective bargaining arbitration concerning a multinational chemicals manufacturer. Another highlight was defending an allegation of reverse race discrimination concerning claims by white police officers. The firm was successful in obtaining summary judgment in this case. Clients include ABB; BAE Systems; Automatic Data Processing; KPMG; GE; Hachette Filipacchi Media U.S.; CBS; Hertz; Honeywell and Hewlett-Packard.

## Band 2

### Ballard Spahr Andrews & Ingersoll LLP

See firm details p.1746

**The Firm:** This heavyweight regional firm is prominent in southern New Jersey. The Voorhees office has a close synergy with the firm's Philadelphia headquarters, and both offices share significant work. The 12-lawyer New Jersey team is active in litigation and counseling for clients in the chemicals industry, as well as the telecommunications, hospitality and gaming sectors. Peers agree "*the Ballard people have great practices,*" and the office's profile is bolstered by the firm's national reputation. Recent highlights have included whistle-blower and race and sex discrimination cases, as well as OSHA compliance and NLRB representation.

**The Lawyers:** Steven Suflas (see p.1306) is a cornerstone for the firm's employment litigation and labor work. Peers rate this "*heavy-duty litigator*" as "*a high-end lawyer; one of the top names.*" Suflas represented a national corporation in a jury trial, and has also appeared before the NLRB in an unfair labor practice dispute. **Denise Keyser** (see p.1301) is the other half of this firm's "*strong one-two punch.*" Her practice encompasses counseling and litigation, OSHA issues, traditional labor and ERISA litigation. She has lately played a major role in collective bargaining on behalf of DuPont.

**Clients/Work Highlights:** The group acted for a major energy company on an ERISA case, and for another key client in unfair labor practice proceedings before the NLRB. The team's impressive client list includes Sears; Exelon; DuPont; Comcast; Sands Casino Hotel and Penn National Gaming.

### Grotta, Glassman & Hoffman

**The Firm:** "*A standout firm for traditional labor,*" this boutique has offices in California, New York and New Jersey, and is exclusively focused on employment, labor and personnel issues. Clients agreed that labor matters are this firm's strongest suit, saying: "*The team is extremely knowledgeable and has a breadth and depth of understanding of labor in the private and public sectors.*" Nonetheless, "*excellent*" employment litigation abilities and ongoing coun-

seling work on discrimination, harassment and OSHA also help explain the firm's success.

**The Lawyers:** The managing principal of the firm is Theodore Eisenberg, who is active nationally on labor and state and federal compliance issues.

**Clients/Work Highlights:** The group has instituted alternative dispute resolution procedures for many companies. Firmwide, it counts among its clients Princeton University; Morgans Hotel Group; Automated Data Processing; Hackensack University Medical Center and Jersey City Medical Center.

### Lum, Danzis, Drasco & Positan, LLC

See firm details p.1314

**The Firm:** This well-known firm has an excellent pedigree in the state, and has weathered recent changes to remain one of the most highly respected employers' firms. Key figure Domenick Carmagnola left the firm to set up his own boutique, yet competitors assert that "*Lum Danzis still has a terrific practice.*" Clients praise the team for its "*excellent and full service across the board,*" with lawyers "*available and ready to help at any time.*" With notable successes at both trial and appellate levels, as well as a healthy reputation for traditional labor matters, this firm continues to attract good clients and work.

**The Lawyers:** "*Definitely on the first team,*" **Wayne Positan** (see p.1304) is the group's principal name. As well as litigating over discrimination and harassment, his workload includes significant wage and hour disputes and labor negotiations. Peers admire his "*unhesitant and confident*" nature; clients find him easy to work with. "*He is down-to-earth and listens to the whole problem before giving advice,*" they told researchers. **Richard West** (see p.1307) is gaining a reputation as a "*terrific young lawyer*" with a very active employment litigation practice.

**Clients/Work Highlights:** The team successfully represented government entities in two appeals: one a whistle-blower matter concerning a Passaic County employee, the other a federal appeal concerning discrimination and the New Jersey Department of Corrections. Clients include the University of Medicine and Dentistry of New Jersey, Pepsi Bottling Group and Marotta Controls.

### Pitney Hardin LLP

See firm details p.1316

**The Firm:** Headquartered in Florham Park, and with further offices in New York and Brussels, this firm is one of the most active locally for employment litigation. The 11-partner, 15-associate team's major draw is its ability to act on large, multiplaintiff employment cases. Clients declare the firm to be "*professional, reliable, cost-effective and user-friendly.*" Peers say it "*continues to be highly regarded and attractive for high-profile clients.*" A recent highlight for the team was its involvement in a significant class action brought by contract workers seeking equal employee benefits.

**The Lawyers:** **Gregory Parliman** (see p.1303) is a highly experienced litigator who is active on discrimination, harassment and whistle-blower cases. He is *"one of the firm's strongest assets,"* according to clients, and peers concur that he is *"a fine lawyer who does an excellent job."* Other strings to his bow include labor issues concerning illegal picketing and strike violence.

**Clients/Work Highlights:** The team assisted a foreign-owned chemicals company to mediate a favorable settlement in a case of alleged national-origin discrimination. The firm's top clients include AT&T; BASF; BOC; Dassault Falcon Jet; Computer Sciences Corporation; CIT Group; Pfizer and Sony.

## Proskauer Rose LLP
See firm details p.1551

**The Firm:** This outfit combines a sound New Jersey profile with excellent national backup. Primarily recognized for its employment litigation capabilities, the 39-lawyer office is also active in employment counseling and labor advice. Offering what was described by clients as *"first-rate work,"* an *"outstanding and exceptional team"* acts for many of the leading financial institutions in the country, with wage and hour cases playing a particularly significant role. While peers agree that the firm *"clearly has a major New Jersey presence,"* the synergy with the New York office is another attraction to clients. Peers also concede that *"the lawyers have the relationships to keep their clients happy."*

**The Lawyers:** Head of the firm's Newark office, **Marvin Goldstein** (see p.1299) is fêted as an expert on labor relations as well as employment litigation. He has over 35 years of experience, leading competitors to agree that he is *"the right guy for complicated work; he is extremely capable."* **Lawrence Sandak** (see p.1306) earns approval for his *"extremely pragmatic approach and good courtroom manner."* He has 25 years of experience with New York firms, and his trial history attracts acclaim. Known to be *"a real problem solver,"* his client base includes several major financial institutions. **Edward Cerasia** (see p.1296) is recommended by clients for his *"practical and 100%-on-point"* employment and labor advice. He has come of age as a broad-based employers' attorney, and is also an expert on employee benefits litigation.

**Clients/Work Highlights:** Amerada Hess; Bed Bath & Beyond; Bristol-Myers Squibb; NBC Universal; UBS Financial Services; Prudential Financial; Bear Sterns; Citigroup; Pathmark and Polo Ralph Lauren.

## Band 3

## Carmagnola & Ritardi LLC

**The Firm:** This new entrant to the market results from Domenick Carmagnola's move from Lum, Danzis, Drasco & Positan to set up his own firm. It has been in existence only since September 2005, so while it may be somewhat premature to comment on the long-term impact on the market, the venture has attracted plenty of attention. It has opened for business with just two lawyers, but their experience is immense. Peers state that they are *"sure the firm will flourish;"* indeed it has already attracted a good

base of clients, including insurance and healthcare companies and public sector entities.

**The Lawyers:** **Domenick Carmagnola** continues to be praised as one of the foremost labor and employment attorneys in the state. Peers find him a *"dynamite lawyer,"* who has *"the smarts, the civility and the work."* He is respected for his *"ethical"* approach, and his New Jersey focus promotes loyalty in clients.

## Fisher & Phillips LLP
See firm details p.732

**The Firm:** The boutique firm of Collier, Jacob & Mills recently became part of Fisher & Phillips, a Georgia-based specialist firm which has undergone significant expansion. The Somerset office retains some key players at partner level, and there are *"solid associates on the team."* The combination of respected local specialists and the newly acquired backup available in other offices keeps this firm in competition with the market leaders in the state.

**The Lawyers:** **Cynthia Jacob** (see p.1301) has ample expertise stretching back to her days in the New Jersey Office of the Public Defender. A past president of the New Jersey State Bar Association, she commands the utmost respect from peers, who say: *"She handles matters efficiently and effectively."* **Alan Lesnewich** (see p.1302) is a partner with broad litigation experience. Since focusing latterly on employment litigation, his profile as *"an effective trial lawyer"* has remained buoyant.

## Genova, Burns & Vernoia

**The Firm:** This firm has built a solid name for its employment and labor work, which interfaces with the firm's niche expertise in political and election law. Public sector activity is the backbone of its reputation, but the 20-lawyer team also has a growing interest in the private sector. With its work in the labor field being of particular note, the team has played a vital role on behalf of management in private and public sector labor negotiations. Market feedback suggests *"the firm is having a good year."*

**The Lawyers:** **Angelo Genova** is a central figure who stands out for his labor experience, public sector profile and political savvy. A prominent name in election law, and New Jersey politics, peers brand him a *"terrific"* attorney who provides *"excellent counsel."*

## Jackson Lewis

**The Firm:** One of the national leaders for management-side labor and employment representation, Jackson Lewis has worked hard on developing its New Jersey profile and it is gaining visibility. The 28-lawyer Morristown office is active predominantly on litigation but also on labor relations and general counseling. The office has acted for healthcare and hi-tech companies, chemicals manufacturers and financial organizations among others, many of which are referred from the firm's extensive network of offices. Clients like the team's straightforward effectiveness (*"they can answer all the questions"*), and it has also succeeded in attracting the admiration of

peers. Said one: *"From the dealings I've had, I've found them very impressive."*

**The Lawyers:** Richard Schey is the managing partner of the office and an expert on traditional labor matters. He has coauthored a publication on wage and hour issues at the request of the New Jersey State Chamber of Commerce.

## Kirkpatrick & Lockhart Nicholson Graham LLP

**The Firm:** The Kirkpatrick team makeup includes some leading personalities and reflects the firm's commitment to growth in this field; sources agree that *"the team has made a splash."* As well as building on the arrival of employment specialist Rosemary Alito from McCarter & English over a year ago, the firm's merger with established midsized London firm Nicholson Graham & Jones has helped strengthen its international reputation.

**The Lawyers:** **Rosemary Alito** (see p.1296) is a knowledgeable attorney who is praised for her great experience of employment litigation and counseling. Peers call her *"a top defense lawyer in New Jersey,"* adding that *"she wrote the book in this field."* She combines a top-flight trial reputation with a highly respected counseling practice. **Marilyn Sneirson** takes responsibility for many of the firm's clients and is active on employment matters in New York as well as New Jersey. In addition to her employment litigation and counseling, she has contributed to many articles on issues of developing importance, such as blogging and 'love contracts'.

**Clients/Work Highlights:** BMW; Goodyear; E.T. Browne Drug Company and DHL Global Mail.

## Lowenstein Sandler PC
See firm details p.1313

**The Firm:** A corporate law powerhouse, this firm's aim to provide a full-service to its excellent client base is demonstrated by its continuous employment and labor work. The team works across departments, and so it can draw upon very experienced litigators, alternative dispute resolution specialists, employee benefits experts and lawyers from other practice areas to service clients. The strength of the firm's name, its sterling litigators and its ability to provide a one-stop shop service are major attractions. The breadth of the practice goes well beyond litigation to encompass affirmative action plans, disaster planning and OSHA.

**The Lawyers:** The employment group eschews superstars in favor of a team-centric approach. Martha Lester is a member of the corporate group and chairs the employment group.

## McCarter & English, LLP

**The Firm:** This leading regional firm retains an ability in employment litigation. The firm's widespread presence throughout the Northeast gives it access to a deep bench of specialists. Clients confide that *"the group has turned out to be excellent for employment litigation."*

**The Lawyers:** The lawyers are drawn from a number of disciplines, with the firm's excellent litigators carrying a large share of the team's reputation. Partner Adam Saravay is mentioned for his general and employment-related litigation practice.

## Morgan, Lewis & Bockius LLP

See firm details p.1758

**The Firm:** This leading international firm has an impressive practice group that is receiving national recognition. In the Princeton office, the 11-lawyer group makes its mark with a strong litigation focus. This is complemented by impressive appearances before the EEOC and the NLRB. The team is also much admired for its employment counseling.

**The Lawyers:** Based in Princeton, although he also has an office in Philadelphia, *"lawyer's lawyer"* **Richard Rosenblatt** (see p.1305) is *"smart and practical."* He combines employment litigation with experience in labor arbitration, his recent work including defending a call center operator in a series of wage and hour disputes, and defending a women's apparel chain against a nationwide FLSA class action.

## Riker Danzig Scherer Hyland & Perretti LLP

See firm details p.1318

**The Firm:** A well-regarded outfit for litigation, this firm handles a steady flow of employment cases. Impressive clients display intense loyalty to this firm, retaining it not only for litigation but also counseling and workplace investigations. The team was recently involved in a discrimination case for one of

its main clients, and whistle-blower actions relating to Sarbanes-Oxley have also featured prominently. The team recently acted for a major pharmaceutical company in connection with post-employment noncompete issues, by way of assistance to a new employer negotiating a settlement with the former employer.

**The Lawyers:** Leading litigator **Michael Furey** (see p.1298) handles many employment cases. Peers say that this *"top trial lawyer"* is *"smart, good on his feet and good before a jury."* Recent victories have included helping a major national retailer defeat the certification of a class of plaintiff in an overtime case. **Scott Ohnegian** (see p.1303) is rising in prominence at Riker. Dividing his time between litigation and counseling, commentators believe that before long *"he is sure to be Riker's big star."*

**Clients/Work Highlights:** IBM; CIGNA; Amicus Therapeutics; AM Best; Dow Jones; Sun Chemical and Carrier Clinic.

## Sills Cummis Epstein & Gross PC

See firm details p.1319

**The Firm:** The 24-lawyer interdisciplinary group at this firm represents a broad cross-section of New Jersey clients, in industries as diverse as gaming and hospitality, financial services and electronics. The group has fostered an excellent reputation for defending discrimination and hostile work environment claims. It has also arbitrated on issues relating to whistle-blower and CEPA (Conscientious

Employee Protection Act) matters, and represented clients on issues concerning benefits plans. Clients expressed their satisfaction readily. Said one: *"I have been very pleased with the team's service, knowledge and approach – they avoid unnecessary litigation."*

**The Lawyers:** **David Garland** (see p.1298) cochairs the employment and labor group, and is a central figure for litigation. Clients like his *"very personable approach"* and say his style is *"not overly excitable, but very persuasive."* He is particularly busy defending wrongful dismissal actions where a whistle-blower retaliation claim is present.

**Clients/Work Highlights:** The team represented the Atlantic City Hilton in a case decided by the New Jersey Supreme Court, successfully arguing that the company's leave policy was not discriminatory to pregnant employees.

## Other Notable Practitioners

A labor and employment specialist with 25 years of experience, **John Ridley** of Drinker Biddle & Reath LLP cochairs the labor and employment group. He has a string of successes in discrimination cases, including class actions. Clients agree that *"the tricky matters go to this outstanding litigator."* A prolific writer too, his *"highly respected opinions"* have attracted the admiration of many.

# ENVIRONMENT

| Environment | |
|---|---|
| **Leading Firms** | |
| **1** | KIRKPATRICK & LOCKHART *Newark* |
| | LOWENSTEIN SANDLER PC *Roseland* |
| | RIKER DANZIG SCHERER HYLAND *Morristown* |
| **2** | BALLARD SPAHR *Voorhees* |
| | DRINKER BIDDLE & REATH LLP *Princeton* |
| | FARER FERSKO *Westfield* |
| | GIBBONS, DEL DEO, DOLAN, GRIFFINGER *Newark* |
| | GIORDANO HALLERAN & CIESLA PC *Middletown* |
| | GREENBAUM, ROWE, SMITH & DAVIS *Woodbridge* |
| | MCCARTER & ENGLISH, LLP *Newark* |
| | PITNEY HARDIN LLP *Morristown* |
| | PORZIO, BROMBERG & NEWMAN, P.C. *Morristown* |

## Band 1

## Kirkpatrick & Lockhart Nicholson Graham LLP

**The Firm:** Building on the firm's tremendous reputation for Superfund work, this group is currently one of the leaders for contentious environmental law, particularly in relation to hazardous waste sites. It is well positioned to thrive in all areas of New Jersey's aggressive environmental law market, and the lawyers here additionally have experience

throughout the USA. Tracking major developments in the law, the group has been at the forefront of cases concerning natural resources damage and the restoration of urban rivers in and beyond New Jersey. Clients share the opinion that *"this is a very, very good firm,"* and the *"depth and breadth of the environmental law bench"* is beyond question.

**The Lawyers:** **William Hyatt** is undoubtedly one of the greatest assets of the group. As one of the pioneering lawyers in Superfund, he has the respect of the market. Peers acclaim this *"truly fine lawyer"* as *"a real gentleman and a pleasure to work with"* and clients agree that: *"He clearly excels and is first on the list."* **Brian Montag** specializes in environmental litigation, although he also devotes a notable portion of his time to transactional and regulatory advice. Clients praise his *"great credibility and exemplary people skills."* Peers say: *"He is a state leader for environmental justice issues"* and *"a true professional, with a bright future."*

**Clients/Work Highlights:** The group is assisting over companies participating in the Lower Passaic River Cooperating Parties Group. This body is engaged with state and federal agencies in a study of the Lower Passaic River to assess natural resource damages. This pilot study may have important ramifications beyond New Jersey.

## Lowenstein Sandler PC

See firm details p.1313

**The Firm:** A state leader in more than one field, this firm has never neglected the goodwill created by its environmental team. Competitors reveal their admiration for Lowenstein's *"outstanding people"* and agree that the firm has been *"a powerhouse over many years."* Indeed, the leading personalities here are justly viewed as belonging to the vanguard of environmental law. The team's capability stretches beyond litigation to cover extensive counseling and the publication of articles. Furthermore, the firm's corporate preeminence provides it with a platform from which to exercise its environmental transactional strength. Overall, this well-rounded group prompts clients to conclude: *"They have a lot of talented people and can take on almost any type of case, no matter how complex."*

**The Lawyers:** Managing director **Michael Rodburg** (see p.1305) has played a crucial role in the development of environmental law over the last 25 years. This *"brilliant lawyer"* has expanded his litigation portfolio to include expertise in issues analogous to environmental law. He is currently working on a case concerning the alleged causal link between an alcohol-related road accident and the serving of alcoholic beverages. His reputation among clients is as *"a practical and sensible problem solver."* **Michael Dore** (see p.1297) is an experienced practitioner who combines "*a creative and superb courtroom practice*" with impressive academic abilities. His proficiency in toxic torts is reflected in his authorship of three books in this field, and he is also an Adjunct Professor of Environmental Law at Rutgers Law School. Clients agree that he is "*one of the most effective lawyers in New Jersey, and a nationally recognized expert.*" **Richard Ricci** (see p.1305) chairs the environmental department and attracts plaudits for his focused litigation practice. Peers commend this "*outstanding and highly rated litigator.*" His clients have included Exxon Corporation and Rutgers University and his reputation with trade bodies is strong.

**Clients/Work Highlights:** The firm's environmental practice fits well with its mass tort work and related insurance litigation, as well as its real estate practice. The team acted for a retail mall development group on a permitting appeal concerning a high-profile central New Jersey development. Clients include BOC; Georgia-Pacific; Purdue Pharma; Crane Co and Able Energy.

## Riker Danzig Scherer Hyland & Perretti LLP
See firm details p.1318

**The Firm:** Combining a top litigation practice with an experienced specialist environmental group, this firm has struck on a winning formula. It offers a comprehensive litigation service, covering air emissions and Coastal Area Facility Review Act (CAFRA) cases, as well as Superfund and hazardous waste sites. A broad approach makes the firm a first port of call for many matters, and clients confirm the group's "*exceptionally good bench strength never disappoints.*"

Beyond litigation, the team also provides regulatory advice and support on corporate transactions.

**The Lawyers:** **Dennis Krumholz** (see p.1301) is the "*straight shooter*" who over the last 25 years has been instrumental in building the group. Peers and clients say he is an "*excellent*" attorney who is "*always professional and has terrific business and legal judgment.*" **Marilynn Greenberg** (see p.1299) has continued her good work on brownfield redevelopment and mold problems. Although an active litigator, she is well known for her complex regulatory and transactional advice. **Samuel Moulthrop** (see p.1303) was formerly at the EPA and the New Jersey Department of Environmental Protection (NJDEP). Clients enthused about the "*excellent representation*" they receive from this "*top environmental and criminal litigator.*" Another "*impressive*" figure, **Jeffrey Wagenbach** (see p.1307) is particularly active on litigation related to Industrial Site Recovery Act (ISRA) issues. He is also an authority on historic buildings and wetlands.

**Clients/Work Highlights:** The team is working on the appeal of an NJDEP decision concerning CAFRA permitting. A transactional highlight was Vitaquest's sale of a majority stake to MidOcean Partners. Among the firm's clients are JPMorgan Chase; Bristol-Myers Squibb; Lucent Technologies; FirstEnergy; Newport Associates Development Company; Wyeth; Bank of America and Siemens.

## Band 2

### Ballard Spahr Andrews & Ingersoll LLP
See firm details p.1746

**The Firm:** Benefiting from a close synergy with its Philadelphia headquarters, the Voorhees office takes on a broad spread of work in and around the New Jersey-Pennsylvania area. Including specialists experienced in the public sector, the six-lawyer team displays confidence and awareness of all the important issues. Peers are effusive in their praise for the team's "*remarkable success rate*" on wetlands and other matters: "*In southern New Jersey, especially for wetlands, it is a leader,*" they say. The work of the team overlaps with that of land use lawyers at the firm, yet another plus point for a team that is as respected for development work as it is for dispute work.

**The Lawyers:** **Richard Hluchan** (see p.1300) combines land use with environmental work. Former chief counsel to the New Jersey Pinelands Commission, he is an influential figure in the region and has a reputation as one of the foremost environmental experts in New Jersey. He is known for his proficiency in resolving the most complex issues. Commentators also noted the achievements of Glenn Harris, a litigator experienced in Superfund cost recovery and natural resources damages cases.

**Clients/Work Highlights:** The team has worked on large mixed-use (commercial and residential) developments where environmental permitting is an issue. In relation to several hotel and residential projects, the firm's interaction with the Pinelands Commission, and its general wetlands and endangered species expertise, has been of vital importance.

The team has also recently assisted an oil refinery in challenging a municipal ordinance.

## Drinker Biddle & Reath LLP

**The Firm:** From its Princeton and Florham Park offices, this firm has a good grip on the New Jersey market and a 150-year pedigree. Working in conjunction with its Pennsylvania headquarters, the lawyers in the group can provide expertise across all environmental areas. The firm's preeminence in litigation gives it a distinct advantage, and peers agree that the environmental group performs superbly in the realm of hazardous sites from Superfund cost recovery to New Jersey-specific ISRA know-how. Having invested in specialist library resources and databases, the firm's dedication to this area is clear.

**The Lawyers:** Based in Princeton, **William Warren** chairs the firm's New Jersey practice group. This "*veteran*" of Superfund enters the tables on the basis of solid peer recommendations: "*He is an excellent trial lawyer and very efficient,*" researchers were told.

## Farer Fersko

**The Firm:** A boutique focusing on environmental law, land use and specialist litigation, Farer Fersko has earned its stripes. To use the words of a competitor: "*This is the only boutique I would mention – the lawyers are terrific people.*" Its activities center on site remediation and development matters; in particular, ISRA expertise gives this outfit local advantage. Clients regard the firm as "*the premier environmental boutique,*" and the lawyers certainly inspire trust – "*I sleep very well at night knowing our environment ship is kept in good order,*" reported one.

**The Lawyers:** **David Farer** heads the Environmental Department, and is an expert on site remediation. Peers respect his expertise in ISRA, where he is "*considered the state expert*" for his authoritative writings on the subject. His reputation among clients is also enviable, with his "*sharp legal mind*" being the object of praise. While he is less visible in litigation, his tremendous business acumen and academic aptitude continue to draw commendations.

**Clients/Work Highlights:** The team assisted K. Hovnanian on a number of brownfield redevelopments and helped Pulte Homes on a major project to redevelop former landfills in the New Jersey Meadowlands. Other clients include Mack-Cali Realty, Tyco International and L'Oréal.

## Gibbons, Del Deo, Dolan, Griffinger & Vecchione
See firm details p.1310

**The Firm:** Now into its 80th year and with an excellent name in New Jersey, Pennsylvania and New York, this firm continues to grow in stature. The environmental law team makes its mark in litigation with recent cases covering site remediation and cleanup costs, mass torts, and industrywide challenges to NJDEP actions and policies. Beyond contentious matters, the firm provides a comprehensive internal audits service, as well as transactional and facility dismantling advice. Clients commend lawyers for being "*practical, knowledgeable and effective.*"

**The Lawyers: Edward McTiernan** is described by peers as *"the standout person at the firm."* He combines an ISRA counseling practice with a flourishing litigation caseload. Clients concur that *"he is a good thinker and strategist"* and value his *"great nuts-and-bolts environmental knowledge."*

**Clients/Work Highlights:** Unilever turned to the firm on an arbitration concerning the conveyance of contaminated property and the apportionment of liability. Also, the group assisted the New Jersey State Chamber of Commerce in a challenge to NJDEP regulations on groundwater remediation standards. This matter is to be heard by the New Jersey Supreme Court. Other major clients using the firm are Avon Products; Bayer CropScience; sanofi-aventis; Sherwin-Williams; Tiffany & Co; Tyco International; Honeywell; Muralo Paints and Vulcan Construction Materials.

## Giordano Halleran & Ciesla PC

**The Firm:** The six-lawyer team is a major player in issues where environmental matters cross over with real estate and land use law. Relationships with various trade associations remain strong and help define the practice: the team provides wide-ranging regulatory and litigation support to several New Jersey entities. Ronald Heksch, of counsel, joins the firm's litigation department after 30 years working in the public sector. Coming from the New Jersey Department of Law and Public Safety, he adds to the firm's environmental litigation capability and has plenty of enforcement experience.

**The Lawyers: Michael Gross** leads the practice group and offers long experience in this field. Peers label this former deputy attorney general *"an environmental guru"* and *"the best in wetlands."* His knowledge covers areas as diverse as site remediation, CAFRA, stormwater management and air pollution.

**Clients/Work Highlights:** Clients include New Jersey Builders Association; Wesley Lake Associates; Paramount Properties; K. Hovnanian and the New Jersey Shore Builders Association.

## Greenbaum, Rowe, Smith & Davis LLP

See firm details p.1311

**The Firm:** The firm's flagship real estate practice is complemented by a two-partner environmental law team and there is also synergy with the firm's land use team. Together they provide comprehensive transactional support, while also covering areas such as ISRA compliance. Despite suffering a setback when Lloyd Tubman left the firm, Greenbaum has maintained a steady course, keeping its great reputation in property redevelopment and cleanup litigation intact.

**The Lawyers:** Marc Policastro is a land use and environmental specialist.

## McCarter & English, LLP

**The Firm:** This leading regional firm draws upon its network of offices throughout the Northeast to provide a full environmental service. Competitors agree, *"it is doing a good job for its clients."* Most of the group is spread between the Newark and Hartford offices, where it is active in assisting on corporate transactions, giving regulatory advice, and advising on site remediation issues. It continues to play a central role in cases concerning natural resources damages, a field which is growing in importance.

**The Lawyers:** Lanny Kurzweil leads the team in New Jersey. Servicing a client roster of petrochemical and manufacturing companies, he is an active trial attorney as well as an academic.

## Pitney Hardin LLP

See firm details p.1316

**The Firm:** The seven-lawyer team covers a lot of ground to give the practice group its full-service reputation. Well known for CAA and CWA issues, as well as wetlands, brownfields redevelopment and complex CERCLA (Superfund) work, the market views this outfit as a source of great lawyers. The firm has an illustrious history in this area, and the current group combines the best of the established leaders with a steady team at junior level. Highlights have included assisting eight companies to negotiate with the EPA in connection with a Superfund site, and obtaining favorable settlements from the insurers of potentially responsible parties.

**The Lawyers:** *"Smart and hard-working"* Gail Allyn (see p.1296) is commended for her experienced and succinct counsel on subjects as diverse as Superfund, wetlands and the CAA.

**Clients/Work Highlights:** The group assisted a client undergoing an environmental investigation after it had closed a former manufacturing facility and then converted the site for redevelopment and sale. AT&T; Givaudan; International Paper; Coca-Cola; Getty Petroleum Marketing; Schering-Plough and Rexam are among the well-known companies that use the firm.

## Porzio, Bromberg & Newman, P.C.

See firm details p.1317

**The Firm:** A firm with a good following in the chemicals, manufacturing and real estate development industries, this outfit is very capable in many aspects of environmental law. In contentious matters the team covers toxic torts and insurance-driven litigation among other things. Meanwhile, the group dispenses solid advice on redevelopment and regulatory compliance, including occupational safety and health. Clients say they *"would not hesitate to recommend this firm, given its expertise and high-quality service."* Peers, meanwhile, reflect that the firm has created some of the market's finest lawyers.

**The Lawyers: Lisa Bromberg** (see p.1296) is the key player in the group. Other lawyers know her as *"a very, very effective attorney who is courteous and professional at hearings."* Likewise, clients are quick to extol her virtues: *"Lisa is terrific – she's very good on client service."* As well as litigation, her practice includes ISRA compliance and redevelopment advice.

**Clients/Work Highlights:** Clients include Enthone-OMI; Hempel Coatings; Tevco and TriMas Corporation.

## Other Notable Practitioners

**Edward Hogan** of Norris, McLaughlin & Marcus, PA is an *"eminently fair and worthy adversary"* who is an expert on ISRA and brownfields law. He combines prolific writing with his work for a string of manufacturer and industrial landlord clients. **Lloyd Tubman** (see p.1307) attracted attention by moving from Greenbaum, Rowe to Archer & Greiner, A Professional Corporation. While preeminent in wetlands work, she has a broad practice covering all manner of environmental and land use issues. **Peter Herzberg**, now at Wolf, Block, Schorr and Solis-Cohen LLP, was responsible for many of his previous firm Pitney Hardin's Superfund successes. Peers praise this *"very bright and able"* lawyer as one of the original pioneers in New Jersey environmental law. Doing *"excellent work on cutting-edge issues,"* **Steve Picco** (see p.1304) of Reed Smith LLP is a former assistant commissioner at the NJDEP with plenty of experience in energy-related work. He has also been legal adviser to the New Jersey Chemistry Council. **Dennis Toft** of Wolff & Samson enters the tables following strong peer feedback for his hazardous waste and brownfields work: *"He is a very good, careful practitioner,"* sources said. *"Hard-working"* **John McGahren** of Latham & Watkins LLP is a rising star with *"important clients."* He has prior experience as an engineer and spent four years with the EPA.

# HEALTHCARE

## Band 1

### Giordano Halleran & Ciesla PC

**The Firm:** Serving the New Jersey market offices in Middletown and Trenton, this firm has a distinguished reputation for the full service it provides to healthcare clients. The group has grown from strength to strength since its inception 20 years ago, and its reputation is based on combining "*the best of the old guard*" with knowledge of all relevant new legal and market developments. The firm's clients include medical and psychiatric hospitals, ambulance companies and nursing homes, and advice typically extends beyond regulatory opinions to include tax, employment and contractual issues. Clients expressed confidence in the lawyers' capabilities: "*They know healthcare, and all the state and federal regulations, and they are extremely responsive.*"
**The Lawyers:** One definite attraction is the profile of title partner **Frank Ciesla**. He chairs the healthcare group and has developed an expertise in all aspects of its work, including complex business, tax and antitrust advice. His expertise in federal procurement regulations is bolstered by a good knowledge of military contracts. This "*very competent healthcare regulatory and litigation lawyer*" appears to have real influence in the state.
**Clients/Work Highlights:** The group advises around a dozen hospitals and many other healthcare providers. Clients include Saint Barnabas healthcare System; South Jersey Healthcare; Kessler Memorial Hospital; Solaris Health System and Valley Health System.

### Kalison, McBride, Jackson & Murphy PA

**The Firm:** Specializing in healthcare for the last 20 years, this 15-lawyer outfit provides an excellent range of services, from nonprofit organization tax advice and hospital M&A to fraud and malpractice litigation. Based in Warren, and supported by an office in Hauppauge, New York, the firm acts not only for hospitals but also trade associations, insurance carriers and physician practices. The group's niche status and reputation reflects the fact that it takes a lead on many issues, such as patient rights, reimbursement and medical staff relations. The wealth of dedicated and knowledgeable lawyers on offer here convinced peers to "*put the firm on the shortlist.*"
**The Lawyers:** **Andrew McBride** is the cornerstone of the group and peers agree that he "*deserves first mention.*" McBride combines practical corporate experience with a full dispute resolution caseload. Originally trained as a hospital administrator, he has a sure grasp of all the important issues.
**Clients/Work Highlights:** Atlantic Health System; Hackensack University Medical Center; University of Medicine and Dentistry of New Jersey; Valley Emergency Room Associates; Cathedral Healthcare System; Catholic Community Services; Kimball Medical Center.

### Sills Cummis Epstein & Gross PC
See firm details p.1319
**The Firm:** The 25-lawyer, interdisciplinary group is able to turn its hand to all issues in healthcare. The firm's transactional reputation is well established, in part because the healthcare team has a string of successful reorganizations and joint ventures to its name. In the nontransactional area, it has a fertile practice in regulatory litigation, operational issues and employment disputes. Clients say this firm provides "*good bang for your buck*" and praise the "*tremendous*" team for its efficient, no-nonsense approach.
**The Lawyers:** **Gary Herschman** (see p.1300) is the "*very tenacious*" lawyer who is credited with developing the group's profile. Renowned for his transactional experience, clients are fond of his "*thorough and meticulous*" style which he combines with deep regulatory knowledge. Reassured by his effectiveness, clients also say of Herschman: "*Few can protect you in contract better than he.*"

**Clients/Work Highlights:** A broad client base includes ambulatory surgery centers, nursing homes and physician groups as well as hospitals. Several leading New Jersey hospitals and at least one of the leading New York hospitals are on the client roster.

## Band 2

### Gibbons, Del Deo, Dolan, Griffinger & Vecchione
See firm details p.1310
**The Firm:** This large and established firm has a deep background in this area of law and serves a client base of healthcare and life sciences companies. Its strong litigation capability makes it attractive for fraud and abuse cases, and expertise in FDA compliance also proves a draw to its roster of pharmaceutical clients.
**The Lawyers:** The team can draw upon assistance from experts in a wide range of disciplines. For example, Bruce Levy is a defense expert who acts on criminal, civil and administrative cases arising from healthcare and pharmaceutical compliance issues.
**Clients/Work Highlights:** Clients include major pharmaceutical companies, healthcare providers and related entities, such as University Physician Associates of New Jersey.

### McCarter & English, LLP
**The Firm:** One of the largest in the state, this firm has a regional healthcare practice conducted by an interdisciplinary group. It has a good reputation for counseling and administrative law as well as litigation. A group of "*superb attorneys*" are supported by an accomplished corporate department and noted litigators who have had their share of success acting for pharmaceutical companies.
**The Lawyers:** George Kendall and Richard Webb each have deep roots in the New Jersey healthcare sector. They are both partners in the firm's Newark office.

### Other Notable Practitioners
**Morris Bienenfeld** of Wolff & Samson in West Orange is a transactional lawyer who applies his corporate and securities expertise to transactions in the healthcare sector. He impresses peers with his "*brilliant mind and very sharp*" approach to his work.

# INTELLECTUAL PROPERTY

## Band 1

### Lerner David Littenberg Krumholz & Mentlik, LLP
See firm details p.1312

**The Firm:** Judged by peers as *"the leading IP boutique,"* this firm serves a diverse, industry-spanning client base. In both the transactional and contentious areas, it is a dominant force. Over 50 lawyers are drawn from a variety of technical and legal backgrounds, and clients hold them in high esteem and say that *"what makes them outstanding are excellent legal skills in combination with sharp business sense."* This firm is distinguished by its bench strength and its ability to cover the most complex IP questions; for some it is the *"superb hi-tech experience"* of the team that is the real draw.

**The Lawyers:** Joseph Littenberg (see p.1302) has over three decades of experience across the IP spectrum. Respected in particular for patent litigation, clients say *"his accomplishments are well known and he is very influential."* Littenberg also works on major IP portfolio transactions. **William Mentlik** (see p.1303) is also an expert on complex patent litigation, playing a central role in a number of groundbreaking cases. A former patent examiner in the PTO, this *"fine lawyer and very good communicator"* continues to impress at both trial and appellate levels. **Bruce Sales** (see p.1306) is a respected generalist, equally adept in transactions and litigation. His

recent work has included advising on international trademark standards and the effect of the Madrid Protocol.

**Clients/Work Highlights:** Recently, the firm assisted Rutgers in an appeal over whether certain aspects of its patent policy were subject to mandatory negotiation. Also, the team acted for Stryker Trauma in a claim of patent infringement of a medical device – the firm succeeded in defeating a motion for a summary judgment of invalidity. Other clients include IVAX and Hi-Tech Pharmacal Co.

## Band 2

### Lowenstein Sandler PC
See firm details p.1313

**The Firm:** IP assets are a significant element to many of Lowenstein's corporate deals, so it is unsurprising that the firm has increasing involvement in IP work. The high-profile recruitment of technology law expert Mark Kesslen from an in-house role at JPMorgan Chase is one of the most recent developments, and it marks a growth in the firm's transactional focus. Complementing the corporate practice, the IP team provides top-level IP due diligence while still retaining an excellent litigation function. Peers enthuse about the *"top, full-service IP capabilities"* on offer, and the development of both the disputes and transactional sides should prove exciting.

**The Lawyers:** Litigator **David Harris** (see p.1300) regularly handles IP matters. Tried and tested for trademark litigation, he is a seasoned figure who can marshal and lead a team on any type of IP case. A new arrival, *"star player"* **Mark Kesslen** (see p.1301) bolsters this firm's already impressive IP group. At JPMorgan Chase he led a team of 30 lawyers and clients say he has *"the ability to take a big-picture view without leaving out the necessary details."*

### McCarter & English, LLP

**The Firm:** This established northeast player combines its IP lawyers with IT specialists to produce an *"excellent"* and *"highly qualified"* team, especially for hi-tech issues. High-caliber litigation is counterbalanced by pioneering transactional work, such as helping a publicly held company negotiate a secure electronic banking relationship. However, it is not just clients in the hi-tech sector that engage these attorneys: the group is witnessing a boom in work

relating to the arts, with household name clients joining the client roster.

**The Lawyers:** Partner **William Heller** is described by peers as *"smart and pragmatic, and able to reach a sensible resolution."* A litigator with an excellent profile in hi-tech work, he has also secured notable victories elsewhere, one example being for a leading china manufacturer.

**Clients/Work Highlights:** The team represented the late Richard Pryor in relation to the comedian's copyright and trademark infringement claims. It also defended a flash memory device manufacturer against claims of false advertising.

### Sills Cummis Epstein & Gross PC
See firm details p.1319

**The Firm:** This firm provides a comprehensive contentious and transactional IP service. An excellent reputation for technology-related matters is augmented by broad coverage of trademarks issues in several industry sectors. *"The word proactive is top of my mind when I think of Sills Cummis,"* said one client; others valued the group's *"excellent strategic positioning"* in litigation and commercial transactions.

**The Lawyers:** **Marc Friedman** (see p.1296), who has been selected as a specialist IP arbitrator by the American Arbitration Association, is the leading light of the group. Over 30 years he has built up an excellent reputation, particularly on computer issues. Clients appreciate his *"phenomenally good track record."* At the time of going to press, Friedman announced his relocation to the New York office of the firm.

**Clients/Work Highlights:** Alongside patent litigation in the technology and medical devices sectors, the firm has involvement in trademark proceedings across all industries, from cosmetics to real estate. Among its recent highlights was the delivery of publicity rights advice to a former baseball star.

### Other Notable Practitioners

**Robert Schoenberg** (see p.1306) of Riker Danzig Scherer Hyland & Perretti LLP is a *"very smart"* transactional and disputes lawyer who impresses others with his *"excellent analytical skills."* His work includes patent cases for technology and medical device clients, and he has also been assisting the estate of musician Benny Goodman.

# LITIGATION

## Litigation: General Commercial
### Leading Firms

1. **DRINKER BIDDLE & REATH LLP** *Florham Park*
   **GIBBONS, DEL DEO, DOLAN, GRIFFINGER** *Newark*
   **LOWENSTEIN SANDLER PC** *Roseland*
   **MCCARTER & ENGLISH, LLP** *Newark*
   **RIKER DANZIG SCHERER HYLAND** *Morristown*

2. **LATHAM & WATKINS LLP** *Newark*
   **PITNEY HARDIN LLP** *Morristown*
   **SILLS CUMMIS EPSTEIN & GROSS PC** *Newark*

3. **COLE, SCHOTZ, MEISEL, FORMAN** *Hackensack*
   **DUANE MORRIS LLP** *Newark*
   **GREENBAUM, ROWE, SMITH & DAVIS** *Woodbridge*
   **MCELROY, DEUTSCH, MULVANEY** *Morristown*

### Leading Individuals

#### Senior Statesman
**GIBBONS** John *Gibbons, Del Deo, Dolan*

1. **BERRY** Andrew *McCarter & English, LLP*
   **CAMPION** Thomas *Drinker Biddle & Reath LLP*
   **GRIFFINGER** Michael *Gibbons, Del Deo, Dolan*
   **HARRIS** David *Lowenstein Sandler PC*
   **ORLOFF** Laurence *Orloff, Lowenbach, Stifelman*
   **ROLNICK** Lawrence *Lowenstein Sandler PC*
   **ROWE** Paul *Greenbaum, Rowe, Smith*

2. **CLARK** Glenn *Riker Danzig Scherer Hyland*
   **KRAUS** Alan *Latham & Watkins LLP*
   **LILOIA** Gerald *Riker Danzig Scherer Hyland*
   **REILLY** Gregory *Lowenstein Sandler PC*

3. **BUCKLEY** Joseph *Sills Cummis*
   **DEUTSCH** Edward *McElroy, Deutsch, Mulvaney*
   **DRASCO** Dennis *Lum, Danzis, Drasco*
   **EAKELEY** Douglas *Lowenstein Sandler PC*
   **GOLDSTEIN** Arthur *Wolff & Samson*
   **GOLDSTEIN** Bruce *Saiber Schlesinger Satz*
   **GREENBAUM** Jeffrey *Sills Cummis*
   **HAWORTH** Gregory *Duane Morris LLP*
   **LAFIURA** Dennis *Pitney Hardin LLP*
   **LASALA** Joseph *McElroy, Deutsch, Mulvaney*
   **MARCHETTA** Anthony *Pitney Hardin LLP*
   **RIDLEY** John *Drinker Biddle & Reath LLP*
   **ROTHSCHILD** Gita *McCarter & English, LLP*
   **VAN DEVENTER** Kenneth *Riker Danzig Scherer Hyland*

## Litigation: Insurance
### Leading Individuals

1. **ALTIERI** James *Drinker Biddle & Reath LLP*
   **BERRY** Andrew *McCarter & English, LLP*
   **CHESLER** Robert *Lowenstein Sandler PC*
   **KELLY** Shawn *Riker Danzig Scherer Hyland*
   **KIEL** Donald *Kirkpatrick & Lockhart*

## Drinker Biddle & Reath LLP

**The Firm:** Acclaimed as a "*big New Jersey player*" by peers, this first-class team has an excellent market profile and it is active across the board. A winner in all types of civil litigation, the firm has made an impact in products liability, with many pharmaceutical companies taking advantage of the team's full-service offering. From securities and antitrust to insurance litigation, the mark of quality is evident. In all matters, backup from the firm's Philadelphia headquarters provides added depth and strength in numbers when necessary. Overall, the team is highly respected, with the "*to-the-point and incisive*" lawyers securing the unquestioned respect of the market.

**The Lawyers:** Tremendous trial attorney **Thomas Campion** has been an asset to the firm since his arrival in 1962. Peers enthuse about his abilities, calling him "*one of the finest trial lawyers in the state*" because of his long experience and "*smart and focused*" approach. **John Ridley** is an employment litigation specialist who has also caught the attention of peers for his prowess in general disputes, and **James Altieri** is the key figure for insurance company work. An "*extremely knowledgeable, first-class individual*," he has a no-nonsense approach. Meanwhile, **Susan Sharko** is singled out for her products liability work. Clients say the cochair of the practice group is "*visible and well respected across the USA.*" In particular she has a stellar reputation in the pharmaceuticals industry.

**Clients/Work Highlights:** The firm's leading clients include several major pharmaceutical companies.

## Gibbons, Del Deo, Dolan, Griffinger & Vecchione

See firm details p.1310

**The Firm:** This firm is a leader for both criminal and civil disputes. From the 60-lawyer group's superstars down to the most junior names, the "*strong bench of lawyers*" attracts attention. Success in bankruptcy-related asbestos litigation and important mass tort cases have helped the group become known as a go-to team for challenging cases. Intellectual property and general business disputes have also allowed lawyers to show flair and know-how, and clients commend the "*sharp and responsive*" practitioners for their "*New York caliber*" work. The overall impression is one of "*sophistication and effort.*"

**The Lawyers:** There is little doubt about the profile of **John Gibbons**, a senior attorney who has become something of a legend in the state, though he is now seen more as a significant rainmaker. His "*wonderful pro bono work*" was also noted. **Michael Griffinger** is "*one of the deans of the litigation Bar.*" He is renowned for his expertise on issues as diverse as antitrust, securities and bankruptcy; market sources commended his "*incisive and bright*" approach and "*excellent way with people.*" The "*scrupulously honest and fair*" **Lawrence Lustberg** is the firm's prime white-collar criminal lawyer, as well as being a skilled civil litigator. Peers extol the virtues of this "*stand-out*" litigator whose practice has grown increasingly international in scope.

**Clients/Work Highlights:** Clients include Deloitte & Touche and sanofi-aventis, as well as several other pharmaceutical companies plus manufacturers, technology companies and financial institutions.

## Lowenstein Sandler PC

See firm details p.1313

**The Firm:** This firm lives up to its reputation as a full-service market leader. A number of specialists in IP, antitrust, criminal, toxic torts and securities litigation have given the group a reputation for "*sophistication rivaling a New York firm.*" In all areas it has emerged as a significant player, and it has a growing national profile in several fields, for example securities litigation. Clients are impressed by the team's authoritative and confident approach: "*The lawyers gave first-class legal advice and were ethical and disciplined,*" confirmed one client. Meanwhile, the firm's white-collar crime capability – resulting from important lateral hires just over a year ago – puts the group at the head of the pack in that area of practice.

**The Lawyers:** **David Harris** (see p.1300) chairs the litigation department and is, according to clients, an "*outstanding trial lawyer.*" The IP litigator and employment specialist is also said to be "*a lawyer's lawyer*" because of his highly developed strategic and tactical thinking. **Lawrence Rolnick** (see p.1305) has risen to prominence for his securities law expertise. From market-leading plaintiff work to wide-ranging defense assignments, his track record gets him noticed. He is currently active in claims relating to allegations of fraud at Lernout & Hauspie. **Gregory Reilly** (see p.1305) is a broad-based attorney, active on employment, construction and fiduciary duty cases. Peers confirm he is "*a worthy and professional adversary,*" while clients praise his "*excellent judgment.*" Reilly acts for a number of educational institutions, including Rutgers. **Douglas Eakeley** (see p.1298) is a recommended trial and appellate lawyer with a strong profile in complex commercial litigation, including products liability class actions and civil RICO fraud cases. Clients speak of his "*calm demeanor, superior intellect and respect with the judiciary,*" confirming that "*if you walk to court with him it provides you with credibility.*" The "*brilliant*" **Robert Chesler** (see p.1297) is a "*focused and smart*" insurance attorney, who is a dominant force on the policyholder side. Of the white-collar crime lawyers at the firm, **Michael Himmel** (see p.1300) has the highest profile. Since he made the move from Greenbaum, Rowe, Smith & Davis, clients have come to recognize the "*vital*" importance of his presence in the Lowenstein team. Another former Greenbaum lawyer is **Robert Kipnees** (see p.1301), who is a criminal specialist with Department of Justice experience. Finally, **Christopher Porrino** (see p.1304) is a rising star for complex commercial and criminal cases; sources say his future is sure to be bright.

**Clients/Work Highlights:** The team has continued to act for W.R. Huff Asset Management in federal

| Litigation: Products Liability |
| --- |
| **Leading Firms** |
| 1   **DECHERT LLP** *Lawrenceville* |
|     **DRINKER BIDDLE & REATH LLP** *Florham Park* |
|     **MCCARTER & ENGLISH, LLP** *Newark* |
| 2   **LATHAM & WATKINS LLP** *Newark* |
|     **LOWENSTEIN SANDLER PC** *Roseland* |
|     **PORZIO, BROMBERG & NEWMAN, P.C.** *Morristown* |

| Leading Individuals |
| --- |
| 1   **BERRY Andrew** *McCarter & English, LLP* |
|     **SULLIVAN Diane** *Dechert LLP* |
| 2   **EAKELEY Douglas** *Lowenstein Sandler PC* |
|     **PATTERSON Anne** *Riker Danzig Scherer Hyland* |
|     **ROSE Beth** *Sills Cummis* |
|     **ROTHSCHILD Gita** *McCarter & English* |
|     **SHARKO Susan** *Drinker Biddle & Reath LLP* |
|     **TYRRELL James** *Latham & Watkins LLP* |

securities litigation, and a team of lawyers represented Prudential Financial against allegations of anticompetitive behavior. The group also acts for De Beers in an antitrust action. Other clients include Anchor Glass Container, Princeton University and Schering-Plough.

## McCarter & English, LLP

**The Firm:** This firm has kept pace with all the major products liability developments of recent times, and it is considered a leader in this area. Peers describe the group's *"fantastic reputation with pharmaceutical companies,"* confirming that *"it is outstanding on products liability."* Its excellent reputation extends beyond commercial litigation generally, with antitrust, IP and financial litigation core areas of work. Indeed, the leading names display great flexibility, and are a credit to the firm's full-service philosophy. Closely related to the group's products liability and pharmaceuticals work, insurance litigation and acting for policyholders is another forte.

**The Lawyers:** *"Standout"* litigator **Andrew Berry** has distinguished himself with *"top-notch"* insurance, products liability and general commercial litigation. His reputation is cemented by interesting work in international arbitrations and appellate litigation. **Gita Rothschild** is a complex litigation specialist who is highly reputed for her products liability work in the pharmaceuticals industry. Her peers agree that *"she is very smart and a good advocate for her client."*

**Clients/Work Highlights:** The group has been successful in several cases for Novartis, and lawyers helped GE litigate insurance coverage issues relating to toxic torts and environmental liabilities. Pfizer, meanwhile, used the team to defend mass tort cases concerning hormone replacement therapy. Other clients in the pharmaceuticals industry include Wyeth and AstraZeneca.

## Riker Danzig Scherer Hyland & Perretti LLP

See firm details p.1318

**The Firm:** This outfit devotes approximately 50% of its resources to tackling disputes for clients in and beyond New Jersey. The firm has had notable success in all types of commercial cases, from land use disputes and major commercial mortgage foreclosures to partnership and IP cases. Peers reflect that the team is *"a strong litigation outfit, best known for complex cases;"* clients, too, voice their praise for this *"significant, well-connected firm"* which, as an alternative to New York firms, represents *"great value."* It is a major name for insurer representation, with specialists in reinsurance and insurance arbitrations leading the way.

**The Lawyers:** **Glenn Clark** (see p.1297) is the firm's managing partner and one of its leading litigators. Clients point to *"good attention to detail and a creative approach"* as the secrets of his success. Clark has litigated estates and trusts, trade secrets and construction cases. Fellow partner **Gerald Liloia** (see p.1302) has an excellent name as *"an effective attorney"* with *"a tough reputation."* His case history includes the representation of leading banks, including Wachovia and Fleet Bank, and he is much sought after for corporate governance and IP diputes. **Kenneth Van Deventer** (see p.1307) is the linchpin of the complex litigation handled here, particularly cases concerning the financial services sector. Clients praise his ability to stand firm against tough opponents: *"He beats the other side punch for punch, and in our experience his performance has been exemplary."* A *"strong, significant and impressive"* attorney, **Shawn Kelly** (see p.1301) heads the insurance group, taking on coverage disputes and reinsurance cases. His clients include CIGNA, Chubb Group and Gerling Insurance Group. **Anne Patterson** (see p.1304) continues to mark herself out as a leader in products liability. Peers hail her as *"very capable, solid and dependable,"* and she is most active in pharmaceuticals and consumer fraud class actions. Best known for his environmental work, **Samuel Moulthrop** (see p.1303) has also built up a superior profile for white-collar criminal defense. A former federal prosecutor with the EPA, this *"very thorough and knowledgeable"* attorney has caught the attention of the marketplace.

**Clients/Work Highlights:** The firm secured a victory for Harleysville Insurance at the New Jersey Supreme Court and represented AT&T in administrative proceedings before the New Jersey Board of Public Utilities over a merger dispute. Other clients include Bank of America; Lucent Technologies; American Centennial Insurance and Principal Mutual Insurance Company.

## Latham & Watkins LLP

**The Firm:** The Newark office of this leading international firm has captured an impressive share of the market and made inroads into several important areas of work. The group's headline-stealing toxic torts practice is flanked by major commercial cases and class actions. Of particular note, the firm's Agent

Orange litigation for Monsanto has demonstrated the reach and influence of the lawyers, and the group is also involved in several other mass tort cases. An excellent choice for large-scale commercial cases, the office has *"very bright"* attorneys who peers judge will be busy for some time to come. Popular opinion says the New Jersey group is *"here to stay"* as a result of its capacity to combine excellent national and local work.

**The Lawyers:** **Alan Kraus** is renowned for his extensive trial expertise. *"No doubt about it, he is an excellent litigator,"* say competitors. His toxic tort cases have been balanced out by financial disputes and fraud cases. The *"very creative"* **James Tyrrell** is also well versed in toxic torts as well as general commercial cases; in particular his caseload of disaster-related litigation is on the rise. Tyrell has a rich background in major products liability cases, including PCB chemicals and silicone breast implant litigation, and he was chief trial counsel to Monsanto on Agent Orange litigation. Clients conclude that *"he does an extraordinary job."*

**Clients/Work Highlights:** The group achieved a victory for Esso in Puerto Rico on environmental quality concerns. In Monmouth County the team acted for Central Garden & Pet Company in a successful, five-month jury trial. Lawyers have also acted as long-term outside counsel to nonprofit charitable organization, City of Hope, helping it on litigation and organizational issues. Among the firm's other clients are the Township of Montgomery, WR Grace and Monsanto.

## Pitney Hardin LLP

See firm details p.1316

**The Firm:** A stalwart of the New Jersey courtrooms, Pitney Hardin has developed an excellent market presence. The firm has some 70 lawyers active in litigation matters, reflecting the breadth of the work undertaken. The group is active on franchise litigation, white-collar crime and general commercial cases, including mass torts. Appellate appearances round off this firm's full service. Peers acknowledge the group as *"really strong and solid"* for general litigation in New Jersey, and clients rave about the *"high level of expertise and consistent quality"* on offer to them.

**The Lawyers:** **Dennis LaFiura** (see p.1302) is the head of the practice; he has an established profile for automobile industry franchise litigation, as well as real estate and hotel disputes. Clients applaud his *"wonderful way of dealing with adversaries."* **Anthony Marchetta** (see p.1302) possesses a fine reputation for conducting civil jury trials and is active in areas as diverse as IP, bankruptcy, environment, insurance and professional liability. Peers commend his *"smooth"* style, and clients rate his *"exceptional abilities in litigation and management."* **Dennis Kearney** (see p.1301) flies the flag in criminal defense work and has no shortage of cases, in areas including land use, religious institutions and healthcare. Clients are particularly enamored with his *"extremely tenacious and well-prepared"* courtroom performances. Kearney helped Wachovia vindicate itself in a civil RICO fraud case which it had inherited.

**Clients/Work Highlights:** The team acted in a mass tort case concerning the Long Branch Manufactured Gas Plant in New Jersey. This matter involved up to 300 plaintiffs who were claiming personal injury and property damage. Lawyers were active, too, on a complex paternity case concerning the effect of the statute of limitations. The group also acted for International Flavors & Fragrances, defending it against claims of product contamination. Other clients include Coca-Cola; BOC Group; Interpublic Group; Merck; Hunter Douglas and Alpharma.

### Sills Cummis Epstein & Gross PC
See firm details p.1319

**The Firm:** A team of 60 lawyers is equally adept in a contract dispute or in a major financial services case. One highlight is a long-running pharmaceutical products liability case on which the firm displays its reach by acting as national counsel. "*The firm does good work, and I would recommend them,*" said one satisfied client.

**The Lawyers:** "*High-quality commercial litigator*" **Joseph Buckley** (see p.1296) has more than 25 years of trial experience. He leads the firm's banking litigation practice and continues to make a very favorable impression on clients, who say, "*on experience and knowledge alone, he is well worth recommending.*" **Jeffrey Greenbaum** (see p.1299) is the chair of the class action group. He devotes the majority of his time to the defense of class actions of all types, but is particularly well regarded in financial services matters. **Beth Rose** (see p.1305) is acclaimed by sources as a "*tenacious*" products liability lawyer who is "*very attentive to client needs, while knowing exactly what needs to be done.*" Her forte is acting for phar-

maceutical and medical device companies, and she is national counsel to a company involved in phenylpropanolamine (PPA) litigation. Former assistant US Attorney **Lawrence Horn** (see p.1300) is an expert on internal investigations and white-collar crime. Especially excellent for criminal tax matters, sources admire his personable style, saying: "*A nicer guy you wouldn't expect to meet.*"

**Clients/Work Highlights:** Highlights include acting for a bank on a jury trial concerning lender liability. Clients include power companies and pharmaceuticals manufacturers.

### Cole, Schotz, Meisel, Forman & Leonard PA

**The Firm:** From its Hackensack and New York offices, the 35-lawyer team handles an excellent range of disputes, from federal and state litigation to arbitrations and private tribunals. The team has had several notable successes acting for plaintiffs in brokerage and executive compensation cases. Other lucrative areas are partnership and contract disputes. Peers note the caliber of the leading individuals and the firm is viewed as a favorite of the middle market.

**The Lawyers:** Michael Meisel is the department chair and an experienced trial attorney. Steven Klein is a skilled chancery litigator.

**Clients/Work Highlights:** The team dealt with a dispute over commercial brokerage commissions, reaching a successful conclusion for the plaintiffs. The group was also victorious in a significant employment case, with the team representing 22 executives who claimed bonus entitlements.

### Duane Morris LLP
See firm details p.1753

**The Firm:** The Newark office of this national firm is making steady progress in New Jersey. It is very popular with lenders and insurers, and it has taken on prominent cases in class action defense and fraud. Clients are often national in their scope, and several overseas entities are also using the firm. Market feedback supports the group's rising profile, with its core assets being the "*extremely intelligent*" lawyers and the firm's comprehensive geographic footprint.

**The Lawyers:** The "*professional and timely*" **Gregory Haworth** (see p.1300) is respected for banking and insurance cases, including class actions. Clients say he is "*excellent with adversaries – polite, calm and persuasive instead of obnoxious.*"

**Clients/Work Highlights:** The team represented Wachovia on a class action concerning consumer loans. It also helped Taiwan Semiconductor Manufacturing Company settle a dispute over IP licensing. Other clients include Travelers Insurance, Valley National Bank and CitiCapital.

### Greenbaum, Rowe, Smith & Davis LLP
See firm details p.1311

**The Firm:** From the pretrial stage through to appeals, this firm is well staffed and capable of handling any type of dispute. Over 50 of the firm's New Jersey lawyers are litigators, and the "*extremely capable*" group is maintaining a solid market profile.

It is distinguished by the variety of cases it handles, being frequently involved in leading estates matters as well as corporate control battles. Highlights have included stockholder disputes, construction litigation, a patent franchise challenge and a matrimonial dispute. The group is also effective in alternative dispute resolution.

**The Lawyers:** "*Tough and tenacious*" **Paul Rowe** (see p.1306) has a towering reputation for litigation. Peers showed clear enthusiasm for this seasoned trial specialist, calling him "*a super lawyer*" and "*a Renaissance man who can do anything.*" While he is most readily identified for his groundbreaking matrimonial cases, he is also a leader for estates showdowns, bankruptcy litigation, construction cases, antitrust and partnership disputes.

### McElroy, Deutsch, Mulvaney & Carpenter, LLP
See firm details p.1315

**The Firm:** This firm has deep roots in New Jersey and the growing respect of the market. Its reputation has been boosted by office mergers in the last few years – it now has three New Jersey locations in addition to its New York and Denver offices. The group is particularly active on franchise litigation, employment disputes, insurance cases, toxic torts and partnership disputes. Peers confirm of this "*up-and-comer*" that its excellent litigation capabilities are on the rise.

**The Lawyers:** **Edward Deutsch** is the managing partner. "*His litigation skills are excellent and the firm is growing – it's worth watching both,*" researchers learned. Deutsch is experienced in construction, insurance and legal malpractice litigation, but also nurtures a general corporate and real estate practice. **Joseph LaSala** is another "*leading light.*" He has played a key role in several toxic tort cases over the years, and is also a specialist for cases relating to fiduciary duties. Peers rate him as "*a marvelous adversary and a pleasure to deal with.*"

### Dechert LLP
See firm details p.1752

**The Firm:** Indubitably one of the leaders for products liability, Dechert has rightly earned a great name for itself in the pharmaceuticals area. In 2005, the group's reputation skyrocketed when its work for Merck in Vioxx litigation hit the headlines. The team's endeavors have been crucial in stemming a potential flow of litigation, and the consensus is that this "*powerhouse*" firm has now proven beyond question its mastery of pharmaceutical products liability. The office frequently works in conjunction with the Philadelphia headquarters, sharing resources, and for lawyers in each of these locations, 2005 has been a sensational year.

**The Lawyers:** The courtroom performance of "*star lawyer*" **Diane Sullivan** (see p.1307) has put her at the front of a line of top litigators. With her Vioxx trial victory, she has "*risen to the top*" and is now a national leader.

**Clients/Work Highlights:** As well as very favorable verdicts on jury trials for Merck in the Vioxx litigation, the team achieved success for Wyeth in a fen-phen suit. These widely reported cases ensure the group's primacy.

## Porzio, Bromberg & Newman, P.C.
See firm details p.1317

**The Firm:** With 25 years of experience, this group impresses with its environmental and mass tort exposure cases. The 21-lawyer team is also well regarded for its work on pharmaceuticals and medical devices. The group is able to turn its hand to an array of other product areas, for example taking on cases concerning elevators, asbestos and various industrial products.

**The Lawyers:** Lauren Handler and Anita Hotchkiss are the leading names for pharmaceuticals, medical devices and medical malpractice litigation at the firm. **Clients/Work Highlights:** The group represents several pharmaceutical companies in litigation over a polio vaccine, where plaintiffs alleged that the vaccine contained a harmful virus. The firm also helped Wyeth on suits over a diet drug and hormone replacement therapy. Other clients include Ingersoll Rand; Westlake; ITT Industries; Pfizer and Schindler Elevator.

## Walder, Hayden & Brogan P.A.

**The Firm:** This full-service firm is best known for the impressive quality of its principals. The team includes seasoned veterans with public prosecutor experience, and the level of expertise and wisdom on offer marks it out as a state leader. Peers respect the team for the variety and complexity of the cases it takes on, applauding it for its expertise in investigations as well as criminal fraud and corruption issues. Sources also note the firm's successes in attracting high-profile celebrities in need of general criminal defense.

**The Lawyers:** **Joe Hayden** is *"one of the premier white-collar crime litigators,"* and he has the utmost

respect of peers. *"A dean of the defense Bar,"* with a pioneering reputation, his background stretches back to 1970 and his tenure as a Deputy Attorney General. **Justin Walder** is also praised as *"a terrific attorney."* This *"well-prepared and diligent"* lawyer was a former Assistant Essex County Prosecutor.

## Krovatin & Associates LLC

**The Firm:** A relatively young player in the New Jersey market, this firm has made a deep impact since its formation in 1999. It tackles complex civil and criminal cases, with fraud, RICO, civil rights and environmental law ensuring the group covers a broad cross section of work. The firm was retained to defend the CEO of an investment bank in a civil case, a matter which settled on the first day of jury selection. It also represented a real estate developer in a federal criminal trial.

**The Lawyers:** *"Brilliant guy"* **Gerald Krovatin** has a polished, professional edge. Peers say *"Gerry could walk into any Fortune 100 boardroom and fit in — you can't go wrong with him."* The feedback for his courtroom style is equally enthusiastic: *"He is just very smart and very effective with juries."*

## Michael Critchley & Associates

**The Firm:** This West Orange firm concentrates on state and federal criminal cases. Competitors readily concede that *"it has been, is, and probably will continue to be, one of the top choices for white-collar crime."* The firm, which was founded in 1974, complements its criminal workload with complex civil disputes, including products liability. The eponymous principal remains the firm's greatest asset, and his excellent trial skills continue to win the support and respect of both clients and other lawyers.

**The Lawyers:** In court, the *"familiar, simple and direct style"* of **Michael Critchley** leads him to be

known as *"one of the finest pure trial lawyers in the state."* Critchley is especially recommended for major tax, political corruption and fraud cases.

## Other Notable Practitioners

**Laurence Orloff** of Orloff, Lowenbach, Stifelman & Siegel is *"a quality lawyer and a first-class guy."* This senior figure is a very strong chancery litigator. **Dennis Drasco** (see p.1298) of Lum, Danzis, Drasco & Positan, LLC attracts attention for his civil trial experience. Involvement in Bar Association matters and *"a superb courtroom presence"* keep his profile high, and he is also commended for his *"excellent written work."* **Bruce Goldstein** of Saiber Schlesinger Satz & Goldstein, LLC maintains a steady profile. As well as commercial litigation, he is active in white-collar crime, employment and antitrust matters. **Arthur Goldstein** of Wolff & Samson, A Professional Corporation, is gaining a reputation as *"a practical, creative and worthy adversary."* Peers admire his tenacity, and his achievements have included acting as special counsel to Somerset County. For his insurance work on the policyholder side, **Don Kiel** of Kirkpatrick & Lockhart Nicholson Graham LLP earned glowing accolades. *"He is the substantive expert and not just a manager,"* say clients. Kiel is also experienced in environmental law, gun liability, employment and e-commerce. **Kevin Marino** of Marino & Associates PC has built his name on high-level criminal defense and complex civil litigation. *"One of the good guys, and a smart lawyer,"* Marino is widely viewed as a leader among the next generation of white-collar criminal specialists.

# REAL ESTATE

## Real Estate
### Leading Firms

1. GREENBAUM, ROWE, SMITH & DAVIS *Woodbridge*
   SILLS CUMMIS EPSTEIN & GROSS PC *Newark*
2. COLE, SCHOTZ, MEISEL, FORMAN *Hackensack*
   DRINKER BIDDLE & REATH LLP *Florham Park*
   MCCARTER & ENGLISH LLP *Cherry Hill*
   PITNEY HARDIN LLP *Morristown*
   RIKER DANZIG SCHERER HYLAND *Morristown*
   WILENTZ GOLDMAN & SPITZER, P.A. *Woodbridge*
3. FARER FERSKO *Westfield*
   GIBBONS, DEL DEO, DOLAN, GRIFFINGER *Newark*
   GIORDANO HALLERAN & CIESLA PC *Middletown*
   HILL WALLACK *Princeton*
   KELLEY DRYE & WARREN *Florham Park*
   LOWENSTEIN SANDLER PC *Roseland*

### Leading Individuals

1. DOLLINGER Martin *Greenbaum, Rowe, Smith*
   HULL JR Gerald *Drinker Biddle & Reath LLP*
   NEWMAN Jeffrey *Sills Cummis*
2. DOWD Martin *McCarter & English, LLP*
   MORRISON Victoria *Riker Danzig Scherer Hyland*
   RABINOWITZ David *Sutherland Asbill*
   RADZELY Edward *Giordano Halleran & Ciesla*
   SCHACHTER Robert *Greenbaum, Rowe, Smith*
   ZANGARI Ted *Sills Cummis*
3. ABRAMSON Richard *Cole, Schotz, Meisel, Forman*
   BLACK Margaret *Sills Cummis*
   DENITZIO JR Thomas *Greenbaum, Rowe, Smith*
   DIVITA Robert *Sills Cummis*
   GORDON David *Wilentz Goldman & Spitzer*
   KAHN Richard *Winne Banta Hetherington Basralian*
   LI Christine *Greenbaum, Rowe, Smith*
   RACIOPPI JR Nicholas *Riker Danzig Scherer Hyland*
   REILLY Lawrence *Pitney Hardin LLP*
   ROTHPLETZ JR Michael *Drinker Biddle & Reath LLP*
   TOLCHINSKY Harold *Cole, Schotz, Meisel, Forman*

## Real Estate: Zoning/Land Use
### Leading Individuals

1. FERSKO Jack *Farer Fersko*
   GEIGER Glenn *Pitney Hardin LLP*
   PANTEL Glenn *Drinker Biddle & Reath LLP*
2. BARCAN Stephen *Wilentz Goldman & Spitzer*
   BERKLEY Peter *Riker Danzig Scherer Hyland*
   CARROLL Tom *Hill Wallack*
   EISDORFER Stephen *Hill Wallack*
   GIUNCO JR John *Giordano Halleran & Ciesla*
   GOLDSMITH Robert *Greenbaum, Rowe, Smith*
   GONCHAR Meryl *Greenbaum, Rowe, Smith*
   HALL Thomas *Sills Cummis*
   HLUCHAN Richard *Ballard Spahr*
   MEISER Kenneth *Hill Wallack*
   MOORE Kevin *Sills Cummis*
   POLICASTRO Marc *Greenbaum, Rowe, Smith*
   WAEGER Ann *Farer Fersko*

## Band 1

### Greenbaum, Rowe, Smith & Davis LLP
See firm details p.1311

**The Firm:** Further consolidating its top-tier position, this "*premier*" group continues to dominate all the important areas of real estate work. The consensus is that "*Greenbaum is ranked highly, and deservedly so.*" It draws admiration for its prolific office acquisitions, sales and leases, and focuses considerable resources on condominium and redevelopment projects. Clients assert that the "*very responsive, very client-oriented*" lawyers are at the core of this firm's success. With over 15 partners covering the real estate and land use practices, the group is witnessing a growing role in all areas, including major corporate transactions too.

**The Lawyers:** One of the star attractions within the group is **Martin Dollinger** (see p.1297), who has an "*excellent*" transactional practice and real influence in the market. "*Extremely competent*" **Robert Schachter** (see p.1306) chairs the real estate department, and his leasing expertise is the subject of much acclaim. He handles sales and leases throughout New Jersey and his "*practical and no-nonsense way of doing things*" pleases clients enormously. **Robert Goldsmith** (see p.1299) is described as "*a superb redevelopment lawyer;*" he is driving a team of eight lawyers in this area, and has been counsel to the Morristown Parking Authority since 1983. **Meryl Gonchar** (see p.1299) leads the land use group. Her experience has grown vastly since taking over the group more than a year ago, and peers acknowledge her "*very strong*" capability. **Marc Policastro** (see p.1304) covers land use and environmental law. He has achieved early recognition and several sources reported that "*you hear good things about him – he has become established as a land use expert.*" Doing an "*excellent job for his clients*" is **Thomas Denitzio** (see p.1297), a transactional lawyer who also works on disputes concerning mortgages, condemnation and tax. Commentators say he "*handles himself well in all aspects.*" **Christine Li** (see p.1302) enters the tables on the basis of her condominium expertise; her practice is said to be "*flourishing.*"

**Clients/Work Highlights:** The group represented Mack-Cali Realty in the acquisition of a four-building complex in Freehold, New Jersey, for more than $32 million, and on the $329 million acquisition of a limited liability corporation, where the sole asset was a 1.24 million sq ft office building. Apollo Realty used the team to analyze 645 Toys 'R' Us leases as part of its bid to acquire the company for more than $3 billion. A highlight sale was that of 945 Route 10, which was a fully tenanted building sold for $48 million.

### Sills Cummis Epstein & Gross PC
See firm details p.1319

**The Firm:** Already a leader for significant retail and office leasing transactions, this 36-lawyer group is extending its reach in all areas of real estate. Its push into financing work has been rewarded with significant, complex transactions, and in land use and redevelopment it is also a confident player. Clients provide glowing praise for the team's "*superb expertise,*" placing it as a leader for its "*mass, depth and development.*" Peers accept that "*Sills enjoy a sterling reputation for retail real estate,*" and in land use they say, "*the firm definitely has the capacity and is truly excellent.*" The firm's work is frequently national in scale, especially in the flagship leasing practice, where it represents major landlords and corporate tenants. A recent development has been retail guru David Rabinowitz's move to Sutherland, Asbill & Brennan LLP in New York.

**The Lawyers:** "Industry-leading leasing lawyer" **Jeffrey Newman** (see p.1303) is the head of the group and a principal rainmaker. As clients assert: "*You just can't go wrong with him.*" Meanwhile other lawyers agree that "*he knows the ins and outs of the market.*" **Thomas Hall**'s (see p.1299) New Jersey land use practice is booming and he is widely admired for his academic wisdom as well as an impressive roster of developer clients. **Kevin Moore**'s (see p.1303) land use practice is also thriving. Clients credit him with having done "*a good job*" in securing vital entitlements, and from Princeton and Newark his practice is rapidly growing to cover the state. From office, industrial and retail transactions to redevelopment, **Ted Zangari** (see p.1308) makes his mark as an "*extremely polished*" attorney with an "*excellent understanding of political sensitivities.*" His reputation extends beyond the state line. **Margaret Black** (see p.1296) attracts great feedback for her transaction acumen: "*I have a very high regard for her intellect,*" said one key source. **Robert DiVita** (see p.1297), meanwhile, is praised for his "*responsive and meticulous*" approach. A former associate real estate counsel at Toys 'R' Us, he is "*a tough advocate for his client and never misses a thing.*"

**Clients/Work Highlights:** The team acted for a leading financial institution on a portfolio of North American properties. It has also been active on key redevelopment schemes in New Jersey, including resort and academic projects. Among the firm's other clients are a major REIT and a national retailer.

## Band 2

### Cole, Schotz, Meisel, Forman & Leonard PA

**The Firm:** Of this Hackensack firm's 57 lawyers, 28 play a significant role in real estate work. A strong generalist outfit on the transactional side, the group is viewed as a dynamic player on retail transactions and leases. Peers respect the size and expertise of the team, with one commentator remarking: "*I would feel most comfortable referring work to them.*" Rounded off by a broad offering in development, finance and tax, this firm can rightfully claim to be "*a big player*" throughout New Jersey.

**The Lawyers: Richard Abramson** is a renowned commercial leasing lawyer. He has been a partner at the firm for almost 20 years and is also a qualified accountant. His astute business sense attracted many compliments. **Harold Tolchinsky** is acclaimed for his proficiency in all retail matters. A member of the International Council of Shopping Centers, his awareness of the issues and capacity for details has made a good impression on the market.

**Clients/Work Highlights:** The group has represented Vornado Realty Trust in acquisitions and sales of shopping complexes in and beyond New Jersey. It has also assisted Office Depot in its purchase of the Kids 'R' Us portfolio of 124 properties from Toys 'R' Us. Other clients include The Home Depot and Bed, Bath & Beyond.

## Drinker Biddle & Reath LLP

**The Firm:** The real estate practice in the Florham Park office is augmented by an office in Princeton and excellent backup from the firm's headquarters in Philadelphia. The team has attracted a superb client base, including prominent real estate developers and landlords, and unsurprisingly displays good capability in all areas, including land use. Peers are full of admiration for the "*strong, fine real estate department,*" and clients agree the lawyers are "*excellent – very responsive and very efficient.*" The firm has had a busy year on leasing and sales, and its prestige in and beyond the state continues to grow.

**The Lawyers: Gerald Hull**'s long experience puts him in the top bracket, say clients. A co-head of the group, he has an air of authority which clients find reassuring. Researchers were told: "*He is respected by the other side; when they deal with him they know they are dealing with a significant force.*" **Glenn Pantel** is an expert on land use and the effect on commercial transactions of regulatory issues, such as the Industrial Site Recovery Act (ISRA) and wetlands law. Competitors spoke approvingly of his skills: "*I'm impressed by him; he is diligent and understands the process, which makes the project easier,*" said one. "*Respected, credible and convincing,*" **Michael Rothpletz** has played a central role in many of the leasing and financing transactions undertaken by the firm.

**Clients/Work Highlights:** The group represented The Gale Company in the lease of a 700,000 sq ft office complex to sanofi-aventis, to be used by sanofi-aventis as its North American corporate headquarters. Matrix Realty, Trammell Crow Company and CFSB are among the firm's other clients.

## McCarter & English LLP

**The Firm:** This full-service outfit has an excellent roster of business clients to whom a 20-strong team, backed up by colleagues in other Northeast regional offices, offers a broad spread of real estate advice. The lead attorneys have a solid leasing profile, which extends beyond the usual office space to cover a diversity of property classes. The firm's superb reputation for business law ensures that all aspects, from taxation and finance to valuation and condemnation, can be dealt with proficiently. Clients agree that

the team's forte is in handling complex and demanding issues: "*Yes, we used them on a very difficult matter, and they were very good,*" one of them confirmed.

**The Lawyers:** A "*true gentleman,*" **Martin Dowd** earns the respect of the market with his effective yet personable negotiation style. This "*patient and even-tempered*" attorney is more than capable of being assertive for his client, researchers were told. Lois Van Deusen has settled into her role managing the firm, but is still a key contact for some real estate issues.

**Clients/Work Highlights:** The group continues to represent the New York Football Giants on leasing issues relating to a stadium development. Other clients include Prudential, SJP Properties and Phelps Dodge.

## Pitney Hardin LLP

See firm details p.1316

**The Firm:** A dynamic player in New Jersey real estate, this firm represents a good cross section of the state's developers and owners. The 16-lawyer team is well supported by specialists in tax and environmental law who help broaden the firm's appeal. Sources say the team is "*well positioned to capitalize on its long market history and good all-around reputation.*" In the past year lawyers have continued with their involvement in several New Jersey development projects, a skilled land use team also making a valuable contribution.

**The Lawyers: Glenn Geiger**'s (see p.1299) profile goes from strength to strength. Hailed as "*one of the premier land use attorneys in New Jersey,*" he has taken on the chairmanship of the New Jersey State Bar Association's Land Use Law Section. His experience and authoritative manner leave others with "*no hesitancy in recommending him.*" **Lawrence Reilly** (see p.1305) is a prime choice for transactions. This "*very able all-around lawyer*" applies his broad skill set to major leases and other real estate deals.

**Clients/Work Highlights:** The team has continued to assist St Mary's Abbey in connection with a retirement community application in Morris Township. For ExxonMobil the group has been working on the development of a 500-acre research facility. In addition, the team assists Canfield Building Associates in connection with a 700-unit townhouse development. Other clients include: The Gale Company; JPMorgan Investment Management; K. Hovnanian; Citibank; AT&T; Park Avenue Realty Holding and Perimeter Properties.

## Riker Danzig Scherer Hyland & Perretti LLP

See firm details p.1318

**The Firm:** Riker fields a relatively small team of seven partners and ten associates, yet has earned a "*powerhouse*" reputation in the state. On the transactional side, a full caseload of acquisitions, sales, leases and financings is complemented by the activities of a full bench of litigators and capable land use specialists. The firm frequently works on industrial and retail leases in excess of 100,000 sq ft, and it is also working on a major redevelopment project

involving 4 million sq ft of retail and office space. Market sources confirm that the "*the Riker name is treated with respect,*" and is sure to grow in prominence with an increasingly national workload and a lengthening list of international clients.

**The Lawyers: Peter Berkley** (see p.1296), of counsel, is respected for his seniority and recommended for his market knowledge. A veteran in all areas of real estate, his zoning and planning advice is especially admired. **Victoria Morrison** (see p.1303) cochairs the real estate group, has an active transactional practice and is known too for her mortgage work. Peers view her as "*a tough negotiator.*" **Nicholas Racioppi** (see p.1304) covers both transactional real estate and land use. His commercial and industrial property practice inspires positive client endorsements: "*He reaches out and goes above and beyond.*"

**Clients/Work Highlights:** Lucent Technologies; Millennium Towers; The Gale Company; Bed, Bath & Beyond; The Rockefeller Group; The Schultz Organization; Vornado Realty Trust; Ginsburg Development Companies; JPMorgan Chase; Principal Life Insurance; Chicago Title Insurance Company; Independence Bank; Atlantic Mutual Insurance Company; Fleet Bank and Wachovia.

## Wilentz Goldman & Spitzer, P.A.

**The Firm:** Boosted by growth and receiving renewed market attention, this group is attracting work in all areas. The arrival of David Gordon from Reed Smith has provided it with a transactional linchpin, and peers agree the department is now "*strong in general.*" The firm's broad leasing practice – acting for both landlords and tenants – sits side by side with a healthy development and condominiums practice. Clients are drawn from all parts of the real estate world and the firm's work covers the state. Of vital importance is the group's land use capability; it is well versed in everything from riparian permits to land use litigation, at the municipal, county and state levels.

**The Lawyers: Stephen Barcan** is an excellent land use and environmental lawyer. Peers rate him as "*a very thoughtful lawyer who does a good quality job.*" The arrival of **David Gordon** has made an impact on the transactional side. His ability to "*go beyond the theory*" wins him much support.

**Clients/Work Highlights:** The firm represents the Middlesex County Utilities Authority in permitting and land use issues. It has also represented religious institutions, banks, petroleum companies, developers and a newspaper publisher.

## Band 3

## Farer Fersko

**The Firm:** A leader in all matters related to New Jersey environment and land use, this boutique acts for an excellent range of developers, home builders and institutional investors. The team is fully capable on all transactional issues, but it is best recognized for its comprehensive land use work. Expertise in brownfields redevelopment is a key draw for clients, and here the group's synergy with colleagues in the environmental team is of real benefit. This is widely seen as an "*excellent*" group of advisers with the ability to understand all the issues, especially those specific to New Jersey.

**The Lawyers: Jack Fersko** is "*the one to go to*" for any land use question. Highly experienced in redevelopment and most other types of transactions, Fersko is also a leading figure in continuing legal education. **Ann Waeger** is a partner with a rising profile in brownfields redevelopment and the effect of environmental insurance. Her market standing is demonstrated by her appointment to the board of directors of the New Jersey Lawyer magazine.

**Clients/Work Highlights:** Clients include K. Hovnanian; Mack-Cali Realty; Matrix Development Group; Federal Business Centers and Avi Don Management.

## Gibbons, Del Deo, Dolan, Griffinger & Vecchione
See firm details p.1310

**The Firm:** A major player with offices beyond the state in New York and Philadelphia, this firm is building up considerable goodwill in the areas of real estate and land use. The team has assisted its diverse clientele on a series of major developments, with retail and industrial projects proving particularly fertile territory. As evidence of its interest in this work, it recently launched a Web site dedicated to providing advice on redevelopment. Meanwhile, land use and title disputes have allowed the firm to capitalize on its renowned litigation abilities. "*Well respected*" by clients, the team's name is growing for both transactions and disputes.

**The Lawyers:** An adept real estate and finance lawyer, Russell Bershad chairs the real property and environmental group.

**Clients/Work Highlights:** Hilton Hotels; Claremont Construction Group; Home Depot; Honeywell; McDonald's; Mack-Cali Realty; New Jersey Schools Construction Corporation; Staples; Tiffany & Co; Windsor Realty Fund and ITT Industries.

## Giordano Halleran & Ciesla PC
**The Firm:** In this Middletown and Trenton firm of more than 50 attorneys, almost half are significantly involved in real estate, covering not only commercial buildings, but also major historical and residential properties. In addition to leasings, sales and acquisitions, dedicated finance lawyers add another string to the firm's bow. Redevelopment and land use lawyers work hand in glove on a variety of large

projects, particularly in residential property, and the team's work on contested applications is also worthy of note.

**The Lawyers: John Giunco** "*has established himself as a strong figure in land use*" and leads the land use team at Giordano. He has driven many of the firm's top redevelopment deals and is also active with the Institute of Continuing Legal Education and Monmouth University Real Estate Institute. "*Pragmatic*" **Edward Radzely** is "*a pleasure to deal with,*" say peers. He has been assisting several retail and commercial tenants, and has also worked on the sale of a historic building in New York. Clients voiced their approval, saying: "*Edward has done an excellent job in getting deals done on our terms.*"

**Clients/Work Highlights:** The firm is working on a redevelopment project which will involve over 800 residential units as well as water and sewage components, and is acting for a client on a site redevelopment to accommodate 150 luxury, age-restricted housing units. For Sandy Hook Partners the group continued advising on a lease of National Park land at Fort Hancock. Clients include Centex Homes; Orion Enterprises; Paramount Homes and Home Depot.

## Hill Wallack
**The Firm:** This well-regarded firm suffered a considerable loss with the death of one of its founders, the "*land use dean,*" Henry Hill. However, peers confirm that "*the group is still as strong,*" and that the firm has no shortage of talented lawyers. Of particular note, the land use practitioners have an excellent reputation, not least on residential developments and affordable housing projects. The team's involvement in land use litigation has left an extremely positive impression on the market.

**The Lawyers: Tom Carroll's** profile remains high after his recent tenure as chair of the Land Use Law Section of the New Jersey State Bar Association. Peers are especially impressed by his litigation skills. "*Very bright and insightful*" **Stephen Eisdorfer** also attracts attention. Viewed as "*a genius*" by some, his track record on civil rights and affordable housing is impressive. Another "*very capable*" litigator, **Kenneth Meiser** is acclaimed for all aspects of land use litigation.

## Kelley Drye & Warren
**The Firm:** The Parsippany office has continued to develop its experience in the New Jersey real estate market. As part of a well-established national firm, the team of 20 lawyers can call upon excellent backup, particularly from the highly respected New

York office. The group is most prominent in real estate finance and litigation.

**The Lawyers:** Joseph Boyle is the managing partner of the Parsippany office, and a general litigator. Paul Keenan is a real estate finance and capital markets partner who works in both New York and New Jersey.

**Clients/Work Highlights:** Major clients include Bear Stearns, JPMorgan Chase and GMAC.

## Lowenstein Sandler PC
See firm details p.1313

**The Firm:** A leader in corporate matters, this firm also services the real estate needs of its excellent client base. Lawyers counsel Fortune 100 companies on a range of issues, ample transactional ability being backed up by experience in finance, construction and development. Lowenstein has "*a strong stable*" of real estate practitioners, and input from a market-leading environmental team is also invaluable.

**The Lawyers:** Gary Wingens cochairs the department; he is experienced in matters concerning real estate finance.

**Clients/Work Highlights:** A diverse clientele includes Fortune 100 companies and leading educational institutions.

## Other Notable Practitioners
**David Rabinowitz** (see p.1302) of Sutherland, Asbill & Brennan LLP commands immense respect for his nationwide retail and condominiums work. This "*talented, hard-working and thorough*" attorney recently moved from Sills Cummis Epstein & Gross where, clients assert, "*he orchestrated his team like a maestro.*" Although he is now in New York, he retains his superb New Jersey client base. **Richard Hluchan** (see p.1300) of Ballard Spahr Andrews & Ingersoll is a "*terrific*" lawyer with an excellent environmental and land use background. Some 25 years of experience and a high profile gained through Bar Association involvement is matched by superb courtroom skills. The consensus is that Hluchan is "*a very strong adversarial lawyer with great court wins.*" His specialist knowledge on particular regional concerns, such as coastal development, wins him many fans. **Richard Kahn** of Winne Banta Hetherington Basralian & Kahn, PC attracts a good deal of respect for his focused, transactional practice. He is particularly prominent in the office, industrial and retail leasing sectors, and clients attest to his sophisticated style, identifying him as "*an excellent negotiator.*"

# Leaders in New Jersey

**ABRAMSON, Richard**
Cole, Schotz, Meisel, Forman & Leonard
PA, Hackensack 201 489 3000
*Recommended in Real Estate*

**AIELLO, John**
Giordano Halleran & Ciesla PC,
Middletown 732 714 3900
*Recommended in Corporate/M&A*

**ALITO, Rosemary**
Kirkpatrick & Lockhart Nicholson
Graham LLP, Newark 973 848-4022
ralito@klng.com
*Recommended in Employment*
**Practice Areas:** US federal and state
employment law matters, including
advice and litigation in federal and state
courts and administrative agencies. Discrimination, harassment, whistleblowing,
wage and hour and ERISA litigation. Trials and appeals in matters ranging from
single plaintiff cases to class actions and
EEOC pattern and practice cases.
**Prof. Memberships:** Association of the
Federal Bar of the State of New Jersey
(past President); American College of
Employment Lawyers (Fellow); American Bar Foundation (Fellow); International Society of Barristers (Fellow).
**Publications:** Has lectured and written
extensively on employment law issues,
including a treatise, New Jersey Employment Law. Chairman, Editorial Board,
New Jersey Law Journal.
**Personal:** Smith College (BA 1974); Rut-
gers University School of Law Newark
(JD 1978); Law Review.

**ALLYN, Gail H**
Pitney Hardin LLP, Morristown
973 966 8048
gallyn@pitneyhardin.com
*Recommended in Environment*
**Practice Areas:** Environmental matters
including natural resource damages, con-
taminated site remediation, hazardous
waste litigation, and environmental com-
pliance counseling.
**Prof. Memberships:** ABA Natural
Resources, Energy, and Environmental
Law Section; New Jersey State Bar Associ-
ation, Past Chair Litigation Committee.
**Career:** Partner since 1987.
**Publications:** Numerous articles including most recently, 'Third Circuit Affirms
Comprehensive Cleanup Injunction,'
Metropolitan Corporate Counsel, April
2005.
**Personal:** University of Pennsylvania, JD,
1979; Brown University, BA, 1973.

**ALTIERI, James**
Drinker Biddle & Reath LLP,
Florham Park 973 360 1100
*Recommended in Litigation*

**BARCAN, Stephen**
Wilentz Goldman & Spitzer, P.A.,
Woodbridge 732 636 8000
*Recommended in Real Estate*

**BERKLEY, Peter L**
Riker Danzig Scherer Hyland & Perretti
LLP, Morristown 973 451 8403
pberkley@riker.com
*Recommended in Real Estate*
**Practice Areas:** Of Counsel to Real
Estate Practice Group. Specializes in con-
veyancing, leasing, financing, and zoning
and planning matters. Performs work for
major national corporations, local busi-
nesses, real estate developers and lenders.
Featured four times in The Best Lawyers
in America (Woodward/White, Inc.).
**Prof. Memberships:** Member of Ameri-
can College of Real Estate Lawyers; Real
Property Section of the New Jersey State
Bar Association; Real Property, Probate
and Trust Law Section of the American
Bar Association; Past President of the
Harvard Law School Association of New
Jersey.
**Career:** Managing Partner from 1984
through 1995.
**Personal:** Harvard University, JD;
Williams College, BA.

**BERRY, Andrew**
McCarter & English, LLP, Newark
973 622 4444
*Recommended in Litigation*

**BIENENFELD, Morris**
Wolff & Samson, A Professional Corporation,
West Orange 973 325 1500
*Recommended in Healthcare*

**BLACK, Margaret F**
Sills Cummis Epstein & Gross PC,
Newark 973 643 5715
mblack@sillscummis.com
*Recommended in Real Estate*
**Practice Areas:** Margaret F Black is a
Member of the firm's Real Estate Practice
Group. Her Real Estate Practice covers
the gamut of commercial transactions,
from acquisitions, sales and non-taxable
exchanges to leasings and financings.
Those transactions, which often involve
properties nationwide, relate primarily to
shopping centers, office and industrial
buildings and other types of commercial
properties. Ms Black's work includes a
sub-specialty in New Jersey's ISRA statute
and Spill Act and in other environmental
laws that affect real estate transactions.

**BOYAJIAN, Victor**
Sonnenschein Nath & Rosenthal LLP,
Short Hills  vboyajian
973 912 7171
*Recommended in Corporate/M&A*
**Practice Areas:** National Chair, Venture
Capital/Emerging Growth Company
Group. Represents emerging growth and

Fortune 500 companies in broad venture
capital, securities, strategic transactions.
Counsels senior executives of venture-
backed and publicly-traded emerging
growth companies and venture firm
principals. Advises on business strategy,
finance, M&A, executive compensation,
board governance, IP, litigation strategy.
**Prof. Memberships:** Churchill Club, Palo
Alto; NVCA; Executive Council of New
York; Governor's Council of Economic
Advisors; Board Member, New Jersey
Technology Council; NYSBA; ABA;
NJSBA; Board of Governors, University of
Pennsylvania Law Alumni Society.
**Personal:** University of Pennsylvania
School of Law, JD; University of
Rochester, BA, magna cum laude.

**BRADY, Patrick**
McElroy, Deutsch, Mulvaney & Carpenter,
LLP, Newark 973 622 7711
*Recommended in Employment*

**BRESCHER, John**
McCarter & English, LLP, Newark
973 622 4444
*Recommended in Employee Benefits*

**BRODERICK, David**
McCarter & English, LLP, Newark
973 622 4444
*Recommended in Corporate/M&A*

**BROMBERG, Lisa**
Porzio, Bromberg & Newman, P.C., Morristown
973 538 4006
lmbromberg@pbnlaw.com
*Recommended in Environment*
**Practice Areas:** Ms Bromberg specializes in property and Brownfields development and redevelopment, environmental compliance, permitting, property
transfer contracting and litigation, OSHA
issues, auditing and the public relations
aspects of environmental law.
**Prof. Memberships:** NJ State Bar Association (Board of Directors, Past Section
Chair, Environmental Law Section); NY
State Bar Association (Board of Directors, Environmental Law Section);
National Brownfield Association; NJ
Society of Women Environmental Professionals.
**Publications:** Ms Bromberg lectures and
writes extensively on a variety of environmental law issues, including: co-author,
'Surviving Environmental Justice Attacks',
NJ Law Journal; co-author, 'State of the
State Address Sets Environmental Agen-
da', NJ Law Journal.

**BUCKLEY, Joseph L**
Sills Cummis Epstein & Gross PC,
Newark 973 643 5394
jbuckley@sillscummis.com
*Recommended in Litigation*
**Practice Areas:** Joseph L Buckley, Co-

Chair of the firm's Litigation Practice
Group, has over 27 years of trial experience in a wide variety of complex cases in
federal and state courts in New Jersey and
New York. He is considered one of the
leading business litigators in New Jersey.
His practice centers on the representation
of banks and other financial institutions
in large-stakes litigation.

**CAMPION, Thomas**
Drinker Biddle & Reath LLP,
Florham Park 973 360 1100
*Recommended in Litigation*

**CARMAGNOLA, Domenick**
Carmagnola & Ritardi LLC, Morristown
973 267 4445
*Recommended in Employment*

**CARROLL, Tom**
Hill Wallack, Princeton 609 924 0808
*Recommended in Real Estate*

**CASEY, ESQ, Warren J**
Pitney Hardin LLP, Morristown
973 966 8025
wcasey@pitneyhardin.com
*Recommended in Corporate/M&A*
**Practice Areas:** Serves as outside general corporate and securities counsel to
companies in various industries including retail, manufacturing, technology,
and computer services.
**Career:** Partner since 1982; Chair of the
Corporate Group.
**Publications:** Numerous articles including most recently, 'Insider Trading: Food
for Thought,' New Jersey Law Journal -
August 1, 2005.
**Personal:** Notre Dame Law School, JD,
cum laude, 1975, Editor, Law Review;
University of Notre Dame, BA, magna
cum laude, 1972. Finished the 2004 'Ironman Wisconsin' triathlon (2.4 mile swim,
112 mile bike, 26.2 mile run).

**CERASIA, Edward**
Proskauer Rose LLP, Newark
973 274 3224
ecerasia@proskauer.com
*Recommended in Employment*
**Practice Areas:** A Partner in Proskauer's
Labor and Employment Law Depart-
ment, Ed has significant experience handling class/collective actions and complex
employment, wage and hour, and
employee benefits law matters in federal
and state courts for clients in the financial
services, transportation, media, pharmaceutical, telecommunications, and retail
industries. He has a proven record of success handling jury and bench trials. In the
past four years alone, he successfully tried
four cases to verdict. He also counsels
clients on how to avoid litigation.
**Publications:** He has been a contributing author on amicus briefs that
Proskauer submitted to the US Supreme

Court in Burlington Northern & Santa Fe Railway Co. v White, No. 015-259 (2006), and Pennsylvania State Police v Suders, 124 S. Ct. 2342 (2004), and to the NJ Supreme Court in Gerety v Atlantic City Hilton Casino Resort (2005). Editorial Board, ERISA Law Reporter.
**Personal:** University of Bridgeport School of Law, valedictorian and summa cum laude (JD 1991); editor, Law Review. Syracuse University (BS 1987).

## CHESLER, Robert D
Lowenstein Sandler PC, Roseland
973 597 2328
rchesler@lowenstein.com
*Recommended in Litigation*
**Practice Areas:** Robert D Chesler is Chair of the Insurance Law Practice Group. He sues insurance companies and also advises companies with respect to their insurance programs. He represents policyholders in a broad variety of coverage claims against their insurers, including asbestos, silica, D&O, environmental, business interruption and property matters. He has brought coverage complaints in over 20 different states, and currently has matters pending in New Jersey, New York, California, Texas and Indiana.
**Prof. Memberships:** Professor, State University of New York at Purchase (1978-79); Legal Methods Instructor, Harvard University (1981). American Bar Association: Environmental Insurance Subcommittee, Litigation Section, Torts Section, and Insurance Practice Section. New Jersey State Bar Association: Co-Chair, Environmental Insurance, and Committee of the Environmental Section. Essex County Bar Association: Former Co-Chair, Insurance Committee.
**Career:** New York Bar (1983); New Jersey Bar (1984).
**Publications:** Co-author of 'Patterns of Judicial Interpretation of Insurance Coverage for Hazardous Waste Site Liability', which has been cited by six state supreme courts; 'How Not to Be Jilted by Your Insurer', NJBiz; 'As Silica Litigation Moves Forward, Will Defendants Have Insurance Coverage?', National Underwriter Property & Casualty; 'A Risky Business', Corporate Counsel; 'The Absolute Pollution Exclusion at 20 - Continuing Uncertainty', Environmental Claims Journal; 'Managing Your Insurance Broker: Promises & Potential Liability', Commerce Magazine; 'D&O Insurance: Now You See It, Now You Don't', The Metropolitan Corporate Counsel; 'Rolling the Dice: How Many Occurrences Have Occurred?', Environmental Claims Journal; 'Having The Right Insurance', The ICFAI Journal of Insurance Law.
**Personal:** Harvard University School of Law (JD, 1982, cum laude), Princeton University (PhD, 1979), Princeton University (MA, 1976), Rutgers, The State University of New Jersey (BA, 1973, summa cum laude, Phi Beta Kappa).

## CIESLA, Frank
Giordano Halleran & Ciesla PC, Middletown 732 714 3900
*Recommended in Healthcare*

## CLARK, Glenn A
Riker Danzig Scherer Hyland & Perretti LLP, Morristown 973 451 8400
gclark@riker.com
*Recommended in Litigation*
**Practice Areas:** Managing Partner and Member of Executive Committee. Senior litigator, practicing in employment, healthcare, commercial, construction matters, intellectual property and insurance coverage disputes. Extensive experience in arbitration, administrative hearings, jury and non-jury trials and appeals to the US Supreme Court and New Jersey Supreme Court. Has numerous reported decisions in state and federal courts. Successfully argued in the New Jersey Courts to adopt the 'inevitability doctrine' governing disclosure and use of trade secrets.
**Personal:** University of Notre Dame, JD, magna cum laude, executive editor, Notre Dame Law Review, MBA, highest honors; Seton Hall University, BA, summa cum laude.

## COHEN, Steven
Morgan, Lewis & Bockius LLP, Princeton
606 919 6604
scohen@morganlewis.com
*Recommended in Corporate/M&A*
**Practice Areas:** Mr Cohen is a Partner in the Business and Finance Practice. Mr Cohen's practice focuses on advising mid-Atlantic emerging growth companies and the financial institutions that invest in them. He represents companies and investors in venture capital and private equity financings, represents issuers in IPOs and secondary public offerings, and parties to acquisition, divestiture, merger, joint venture and strategic partnership transactions. Mr Cohen has significant experience assisting biotechnology, information technology and other companies in planning for and implementing growth strategies.
**Prof. Memberships:** New Jersey Technology Council (Board of Directors); New Jersey Entrepreneurs Network; and Co-Chair of BioLife Tech Venture Fair.

## CRITCHLEY, Michael
Michael Critchley & Associates, West Orange 973 731 9831
*Recommended in Litigation*

## DANIELE, Mark
McCarter & English, LLP, Newark
973 622 4444
*Recommended in Employee Benefits*

## DAVIS, Alan E
Greenbaum, Rowe, Smith & Davis LLP, Woodbridge 732 549 5600
adavis@greenbaumlaw.com
*Recommended in Corporate/M&A*
**Practice Areas:** Chair, Corporate Department. Represents both publicly

and closely held business enterprises in areas including manufacturing, retailing, distribution and service. Advises clients in financing, supplier relations, customers and non-union staff, securities, business planning, and the purchase and sale of businesses and related business assets. Experience handling franchise, distribution and trade regulation matters, and problems associated with the dissolution of business entities.
**Prof. Memberships:** Chair, Board of Trustees, Monmouth Medical Center; member, Board of Trustees, Monmouth Medical Center Foundation; Member, Board of Trustees, Monmouth University; member, Board of Trustees, Saint Barnabas Corporation.
**Personal:** Columbia Law School (1965), Rutgers College (1962).

## DEE, Francis
McElroy, Deutsch, Mulvaney & Carpenter, LLP, Newark 973 622 7711
*Recommended in Employment*

## DENITZIO JR, Thomas J
Greenbaum, Rowe, Smith & Davis LLP, Woodbridge 732 549 5600
tdenitzio@greenbaumlaw.com
*Recommended in Real Estate*
**Practice Areas:** Partner of the firm. Sale, acquisition, leasing and mortgage financing of commercial and industrial real estate; and real estate-related litigation, such as real estate tax appeals, mortgage foreclosures and workouts, tax sale certificate foreclosures, quiet title actions and condemnation valuation hearings.
**Prof. Memberships:** Member of the American, New Jersey and Middlesex County Bar Associations. Member, Mortgage Bankers Association of New Jersey.
**Personal:** Cornell Law School (1975), Lafayette College (1972).

## DEUTSCH, Edward
McElroy, Deutsch, Mulvaney & Carpenter, LLP, Newark 973 622 7711
*Recommended in Litigation*

## DIVITA, Robert R
Sills Cummis Epstein & Gross PC, Newark 973 643 5782
rdivita@sillscummis.com
*Recommended in Real Estate*
**Practice Areas:** Robert R DiVita is a member of the firm and focuses his practice on commercial real estate transactions, including acquisition, disposition, development, leasing and financing, with a particular specialization in commercial condominiums. Mr DiVita is a frequent moderator and speaker at real estate industry sponsored conferences and at continuing legal education seminars. Prior to joining the firm, he was Associate Real Estate Counsel at Toys "R" Us, Inc. He was admitted to the New Jersey Bar in 1987 and the New York Bar in 1981.

## DOLLINGER, Martin E
Greenbaum, Rowe, Smith & Davis LLP, Woodbridge 732 549 5600
mdollinger@greenbaumlaw.com
*Recommended in Real Estate*
**Practice Areas:** Complex transactional real estate with an emphasis on office, industrial and retail leasing, and corporate matters throughout the United States.
**Prof. Memberships:** Member, American College of Real Estate Lawyers and the American Bar Association and its section on Real Property, Probate and Trust Law. Serves on the Board of Governors of the Ramapo College Foundation.
**Publications:** Author, 'New Jersey Real Estate Leasing Forms: Practice' (Michie 1991, Lexis Law Publishing).
**Personal:** Cornell University (1963), Cornell University Law School (1966), Master of Laws, Georgetown University (1970).

## DORE, Michael
Lowenstein Sandler PC, Roseland
973 597 2344
mdore@lowenstein.com
*Recommended in Environment*
**Practice Areas:** Has more than 25 years of experience representing corporate clients in complex toxic tort and environmental litigation, and counseling. In addition, his experience in handling industrial accidents, fires, explosions and other critical incidents has given him a special understanding of dealing with catastrophe response and crisis management situations. Mr Dore is former counsel for BOC Group, Inc., a Fortune 500 company, where he was responsible for its environmental affairs.
**Prof. Memberships:** Rutgers University Law School, Adjunct Professor of Environmental Law, (1984 - present); Association of Defense Trial Attorneys; Defense Research Institute, Founding Chairman - Environmental Law Committee; International Association of Defense Counsel.
**Career:** Pennsylvania Bar (1975); New York Bar (1976); New Jersey Bar (1980).
**Publications:** 'Law of Toxic Torts: Litigation, Defense, Insurance', four volume treatise published by the West Group; 'Consolidating the Crowd of Cases', New Jersey Law Journal; 'Reforming Mass Tort Coordination Procedures', New Jersey Law Journal; 'Reforming the New Jersey Supreme Court's Procedures for Consolidating Mass Tort Litigation: A Proposal for Disclosing the Rules of the Game', Rutgers Law Review; 'Dealing with Business Emergencies: A Crisis Management Guidebook', Lowenstein Sandler Crisis Management Practice ebook; 'Conducting Internal Corporate Investigations', New Jersey Law Journal; 'Protecting Individual Corporate Executives From Liability - Ten Cardinal Rules For Risk Managers', NJRIMSNews; 'Dealing With Public Relations Concerns in Products Liabil-

ity and Toxic Tort Litigation,' New Jersey Lawyer the Magazine.
**Personal:** Rutgers University School of Law (JD, 1975, editor, Rutgers Law Review, National Moot Court Team); Amherst College (BA, 1972, cum laude).

### DOWD, Martin
McCarter & English, LLP, Newark
973 622 4444
*Recommended in Real Estate*

### DOYLE, David P
Pitney Hardin LLP, Morristown
973 966 8136
ddoyle@pitneyhardin.com
*Recommended in Employee Benefits*
**Practice Areas:** Counsels clients with respect to all aspects of employee benefits, ERISA, and executive compensation matters.
**Prof. Memberships:** ABA Employee Benefits Committee, Tax Section; New Jersey State Bar Association, past Chairperson, Employee Benefits Committee, Tax Section.
**Career:** Partner since 1995.
**Publications:** Numerous articles including most recently, 'EEOC Retiree Medical Exemption Invalidated,' Metropolitan Corporate Counsel, July 2005.
**Personal:** New York University School of Law, LLM, Taxation, 1990; Rutgers University School of Law - Newark, JD, 1985; Emory University, BA, 1982.

### DRASCO , Dennis J
Lum, Danzis, Drasco & Positan, LLC, Roseland 973 228 6770
ddrasco@lumlaw.com
*Recommended in Litigation*
**Practice Areas:** Over 30 years experience in State and Federal litigation in New Jersey and New York. Business litigation, condemnation, construction disputes, appellate practice, arbitration and mediation, NJ court-approved mediator.
**Prof. Memberships:** Admitted to practice in New Jersey and New York; Federal Courts in New Jersey, Southern and Eastern Districts of New York; Second and Third Circuit and US Supreme Court. US Tax Court; ABA House of Delegates (2003-present); Chair ABA Section of Litigation (2004-05); Vice President, Association of the Federal Bar of New Jersey; Fellow, American Bar Foundation; Civil Trial Attorney Achievement Award; Essex County Bar Association (2000); listed in Best Lawyers In America, Superlawyers of New Jersey and Who's Who in American Law.
**Career:** Lum, Danzis, Drasco & Positan, LLC and its predecessors since 1973; Partner/Member since 1980; Chair, Litigation Practice Group.
**Publications:** 'How To Get From The War Room To The Court Room: The Basics For Civil Trial Arguments', 15 New Jersey Lawyer 32 (1993) 'Construction Contracts: Arbitration as a Means of Dispute Resolution in New Jersey', New Jer-

sey Lawyer, February 2003, No. 219.
**Personal:** BA Political Science, Fordham College, 1970; JD Rutgers School of Law, Newark, NJ 1973;

### EAKELEY, Douglas S
Lowenstein Sandler PC, Roseland
973 597 2348
deakeley@lowenstein.com
*Recommended in Litigation*
**Practice Areas:** Mr Eakeley has extensive trial and appellate experience in complex commercial litigation, including securities fraud, antitrust, consumer fraud, class actions, and derivatives. A former Rhodes Scholar and graduate of Yale Law School, he served as First Assistant Attorney General of the State of New Jersey. In 1993 he was appointed by President Clinton to the Board of Directors of the Legal Services Corporation, which he chaired until April 2003. In 1997, he received the John Minor Wisdom Public Service and Professionalism Award from the American Bar Association Section of Litigation.
**Prof. Memberships:** American Bar Foundation, Fellow; Practising Law Institute, Trustee; New Jersey Institute for Social Justice, Trustee; Legal Services Corporation, Chairman (1993-2003); Legal Services of New Jersey, Trustee, Chairman (1982-90), Member (2003-present); New Jersey Law Journal, Editorial Board, Chair (1986-90), Member (1992-96); Association of the Federal Bar of the State of New Jersey, Vice President (1983-90); American Bar Association, Antitrust and Litigation Sections; New Jersey State Bar Association; NJN Public Television and Radio Foundation, Vice-Chair.
**Career:** New York Bar (1973); New Jersey Bar (1979); Admitted to practice before US Supreme Court, US Courts of Appeals for the Second and Third Circuits, US District Courts for New Jersey, Southern and Eastern Districts of New York.
**Publications:** 'The Successful Practitioner of Antitrust Law', in Aspatore Books, The Art & Science of Antitrust Law; 'Defense of Consumer Fraud Class Actions', New Jersey Institute for Continuing Legal Education; 'Defense of Private Treble-Damage Actions', in Hills, ed., Antitrust Adviser; 'Recent Developments in Franchise Litigation', New Jersey Institute for Continuing Legal Education; 'Role of the Legal Services Corporation in Preserving Our National Commitment to Equal Access to Justice', Annual Survey of American Law, New York University School of Law; 'Common Ground', syndicated biweekly column in newspapers published by The Recorder Publishing Company.
**Personal:** Yale Law School (JD, 1972); Oxford University (BA and MA, 1970, in Jurisprudence); Yale University (BA, 1968, summa cum laude, with highest honors in Economics, Rhodes Scholar, Phi Beta Kappa).

### EHRENBERG, Peter H
Lowenstein Sandler PC, Roseland
973 597 2350
pehrenberg@lowenstein.com
*Recommended in Corporate/M&A*
**Practice Areas:** Chair of the Corporate Department and Corporate Finance Practice Group, has extensive experience in securities, mergers and acquisitions, and business law. He represents issuers and investment firms in the private and public offering of debt and equity securities, and participates in complex merger and acquisition transactions, recapitalizations, employee benefit matters, secured and unsecured borrowings and securities offerings. He counsels public companies regarding compliance and public reporting responsibilities, including duties under the Sarbanes-Oxley Act and other corporate governance reforms.
**Prof. Memberships:** New Jersey State Bar Association (Director, Corporate and Business Law Section; past Chair, Securities Law Committee); American Bar Association.
**Career:** 'All-Star Lawyer Deal Makers' by NJBIZ; New Jersey Bar and Federal Courts (1973).
**Publications:** 'Corporate Governance ebook', provides advice regarding Sarbanes-Oxley regulations; 'What to Tell the SEC: The Intricate World of Schedule 13E-3', The M&A Journal; 'SOX and Related Reforms: Where Are We?', The Metropolitan Corporate Counsel; 'LLCs as the New Corporate Order', New Jersey Lawyer; 'Corporate Governance Self-Audits: Policing Yourself Before You Get Policed', Metropolitan Corporate Counsel; 'Structuring the Transaction When the Tax Advisors Leave the Room', New Jersey Lawyer; 'Why Private Companies Should Not Ignore the Sarbanes-Oxley Act', Wall Street Lawyer; 'The Unintended Victim: Ramifications of the Sarbanes-Oxley Act for Private Companies', Metropolitan Corporate Counsel.
**Personal:** Yale Law School (JD, 1973, editor, Yale Law Journal); Trinity College (BA, 1969, Phi Beta Kappa).

### EISDORFER, Stephen
Hill Wallack, Princeton 609 924 0808
*Recommended in Real Estate*

### FARER, David
Farer Fersko, Westfield 908 789 8550
*Recommended in Environment*

### FELTON, W Raymond
Greenbaum, Rowe, Smith & Davis LLP, Woodbridge 732 476 2670
rfelton@greenbaumlaw.com
*Recommended in Corporate/M&A*
**Practice Areas:** Chair, Technology Practice Group. Transactional practice includes mergers and acquisitions, institutional debt and equity financing, private and public offerings, joint ventures and corporate reorganizations. Counsel-

ing includes securities law compliance, business planning and corporate governance.
**Prof. Memberships:** Member, NJ State Bar Association and American Bar Association. Member, Board of Directors, Business Law Section of the NJ State Bar Association, Chair from 2002-04.
**Publications:** Author, 'Organization and Sale of Small Businesses' and numerous articles.
**Personal:** Rutgers Law School, Newark (1981), Research Editor, Rutgers Law Review; Rutgers College, (1978).

### FERSKO, Jack
Farer Fersko, Westfield
908 789 8550
*Recommended in Real Estate*

### FRIEDMAN, Marc
Sills Cummis Epstein & Gross PC, New York 212 643 7000
*Recommended in Intellectual Property*
**Practice Areas:** Marc S Friedman, Chair of the firm's Intellectual Property Practice Group, is resident in the firm's New York office. He has more than 30 years of experience, focusing on complex intellectual property and business matters, and intellectual property and technology litigation, including electronic commerce, patent, copyright, trademark and trade secret matters. He helped pioneer information technology law more than 25 years ago when he won a landmark case of Chatlos Systems v NCR Corporation, one of the most important developments in the history of information technology law.

### FUREY, Michael K
Riker Danzig Scherer Hyland & Perretti LLP, Morristown 973 451 8433
mfurey@riker.com
*Recommended in Employment*
**Practice Areas:** Chair of Labor and Employment Group. Experience in employment and commercial litigation in federal, state courts and before various agencies. Extensive trial experience and certified as a Civil Trial Attorney. Substantial experience arguing before New Jersey Supreme Court and US Third Circuit Court of Appeals.
**Prof. Memberships:** Chairman of the Board of Trustees of the New Jersey Ballet; Trustee of Legal Services of New Jersey and of the Supreme Court Committee on Disciplinary Oversight; Delegate to ABA House; Fellow of ABA Foundation; Member of Litigation Section of ABA.
**Personal:** University of Pennsylvania, JD; Dartmouth College, BA.

### GARLAND, David W
Sills Cummis Epstein & Gross PC, Newark 973 643 6390
dgarland@sillscummis.com
*Recommended in Employment*
**Practice Areas:** David W Garland is Co-Chair of the firm's Employment and

Labor Practice Group. He devotes his practice to defending corporate clients and public entities in employment discrimination, wrongful discharge and other employment-related litigation, including cases involving allegations of sexual harassment, age, disability, gender, pregnancy, race, retaliation, and other discrimination, alleged violations of family leave, whistle blower, equal pay, wage and hour, and other statutes, and contract, public policy and tort claims. He also handles benefits litigation under ERISA, claims based on collective bargaining agreements and NLRA litigation. He has defended lawsuits in courts throughout the United States.

**GEIGER, Glenn C**
Pitney Hardin LLP, Morristown
973 966 8149
ggeiger@pitneyhardin.com
*Recommended in Real Estate*
**Practice Areas:** Land use and transactional real estate matters, with a focus on real estate development matters, including applications for land use and environmental permits and approvals, acquisitions, sales, financing, and leasing.
**Prof. Memberships:** New Jersey State Bar Association, Chairperson, Land Use Law Section; District of Columbia Bar Association; New Jersey Community Builders Association; National Association of Industrial and Office Properties.
**Career:** Partner since 1985.
**Personal:** Seton Hall University Law School, JD, 1976; Georgetown University, BS, 1973.

**GENOVA, Angelo**
Genova, Burns & Vernoia, Livingston
973 533 0777
*Recommended in Employment*

**GIBBONS, John**
Gibbons, Del Deo, Dolan, Griffinger & Vecchione, Newark
973 596 4500
*Recommended in Litigation*

**GIUNCO, John**
Giordano Halleran & Ciesla PC, Middletown 732 714 3900
*Recommended in Real Estate*

**GOLDSMITH, Robert S**
Greenbaum, Rowe, Smith & Davis LLP, Woodbridge 732 549 5600
rgoldsmith@greenbaumlaw.com
*Recommended in Real Estate*
**Practice Areas:** Chair, Redevelopment Practice Group. Concentrates practice in redevelopment and downtown revitalization. Has counseled and consulted with both developers and municipalities for numerous redevelopment projects throughout the state and over 30 Special Improvement Districts.
**Prof. Memberships:** Past President, Downtown New Jersey. Serves on NJ Committee of Regional Plan Association. Member, Main Street NJ Board of Advisors.

**Career:** Clerk, Hon Milton B Conford, Appellate Division and Supreme Court (1977-78). Developed and currently teaches course in redevelopment law at Rutgers Law School, Newark.
**Personal:** Rutgers Law School, Newark (1977), New York University, BA, with honors (1973).

**GOLDSTEIN, Arthur**
Wolff & Samson, A Professional Corporation, West Orange 973 325 1500
*Recommended in Litigation*

**GOLDSTEIN, Bruce**
Saiber Schlesinger Satz & Goldstein, LLC, Newark 973 622 3333
*Recommended in Litigation*

**GOLDSTEIN, Marvin M**
Proskauer Rose LLP, Newark
973 274 3210
mmgoldstein@proskauer.com
*Recommended in Employment*
**Practice Areas:** A Partner in the Labor and Employment Law Department and Head of the firm's Newark office, he has a nationwide practice where he represents employers in all aspects of labor and employee relations in both state and federal courts. He also represents employers in labor arbitration and before administrative boards such as the NLRB and various civil rights agencies. In addition, he represents employers in the securities industry where he regularly arbitrates employment matters before the NASD and the New York Stock Exchange.
**Career:** He has been recognized as one of the 'Best Lawyers in America' for the past 25 years and was ranked among the top five percent of the lawyers in the state of New Jersey by New Jersey Monthly magazine.
**Publications:** An active speaker and writer on labor and employment law issues, he is also co-editor of West Publishing's New Jersey Practice treatise entitled Employment Law, which was published in 1998 and is updated annually.
**Personal:** Boston University School of Law, JD, 1969. Cornell University, BA, 1966.

**GONCHAR, Meryl A G**
Greenbaum, Rowe, Smith & Davis LLP, Woodbridge 732 549 5600
mgonchar@greenbaumlaw.com
*Recommended in Real Estate*
**Practice Areas:** Chair, Land Use Practice Group. Land use, zoning and land use litigation. Represention of developer clients for residential, commercial and industrial projects before planning and zoning boards. Represents clients in land use, condemnation and related litigation before the Superior Court of New Jersey.
**Prof. Memberships:** Past Chair, Board of Directors-Land Use Law Section and member, Legislative Committee, NJ State Bar Association. Member, American Bar Association, Middlesex County Bar Asso-

ciation. Member/Past President, Industrial/Commercial Real Estate Women-NJ.
**Publications:** Co-author, 'Zoning and Land Use Litigation', Chapter 12, New Jersey Land Use and Environmental Law, 1993.
**Personal:** Rutgers School of Law, Newark (1981).

**GORDON, David**
Wilentz Goldman & Spitzer, P.A., Woodbridge 732 636 8000
*Recommended in Real Estate*

**GRAW, Andrew E**
Lowenstein Sandler PC, Roseland
973 597 2588
agraw@lowenstein.com
*Recommended in Employee Benefits*
**Practice Areas:** Andrew E Graw heads the firm's Employee Benefits and Executive Compensation Practice Group. Mr Graw has more than 20 years of experience in executive compensation, employee benefits and employment and labor law. Mr Graw was recognized as a 2005 New Jersey Super Lawyer in the Employee Benefits/ERISA section of the publication.
**Prof. Memberships:** Member, the ESOP Association; New York State Bar Association; Member the National Association of Stock Plan Professionals
**Career:** New York Bar (1984); New Jersey Bar (1999).
**Publications:** 'New Jersey Domestic Partnership Act: Impact On Employer-Sponsored Health Plans', The Metropolitan Corporate Counsel; contributing editor and author, 'A Practical Guide to New Jersey Employment Law: The Employer's Resource'; 'Employee and Benefit Considerations in The Merger and Acquisition Context', New Jersey Law Journal; 'Equity Compensation: Cash-Poor Employers Have Options', The National Law Journal;
**Personal:** Pace University (JD, 1983); State University of New York at Oneonta (BS, 1980).

**GREENBAUM, Jeffrey J**
Sills Cummis Epstein & Gross PC, Newark 973 643 5430
jgreenbaum@sillscummis.com
*Recommended in Litigation*
**Practice Areas:** Jeffrey J Greenbaum, Chair of the firm's Class Action Practice Group, is an active litigator and trial attorney in the Federal and State courts with a specialty in complex business litigation and in defending class action litigation. He has handled cases of national prominence and chaired the ABA Section of Litigation Class Actions and Derivative Suits Committee. He has handled numerous matters involving securities and consumer fraud, class actions and derivative suits, professional liability, antitrust, banking, chancery practice, contracts, real estate, trade secrets and unfair competition.

**GREENBERG, Marilynn R**
Riker Danzig Scherer Hyland & Perretti LLP, Morristown 973 451 8437
mgreenberg@riker.com
*Recommended in Environment*
**Practice Areas:** Partner in Environmental Group. Extensive experience in environmental law, including litigation, transactional matters, permitting, solid waste, indoor air quality (asbestos and mold), defense of enforcement actions, and USEPA Superfund matters. Counsels clients regarding regulatory compliance with state and federal environmental statutes and regulations, with emphasis on site remediation and brownfields redevelopment.
**Prof. Memberships:** Member of New Jersey State Chamber of Commerce's Environmental Committee; Chairs the Township of Livingston's Environmental Commission.
**Career:** Appointed to former Governor James McGreevey's transition team on the environment.
**Personal:** Rutgers University School of Law-Newark, JD, with high honors; University of Wisconsin, BA.

**GRIFFINGER, Michael**
Gibbons, Del Deo, Dolan, Griffinger & Vecchione, Newark 973 596 4500
*Recommended in Litigation*

**GROSS, Michael**
Giordano Halleran & Ciesla PC, Middletown 732 714 3900
*Recommended in Environment*

**GROSS, Steven E**
Sills Cummis Epstein & Gross PC, Newark 973 643 5080
sgross@sillscummis.com
*Recommended in Corporate/M&A*
**Practice Areas:** Steven E Gross is the Co-Chair and Managing Partner of the firm and chairs the Corporate, Banking and Securities Practice Group. His Corporate and Securities Practice is international in scope with client representation and transactional matters conducted across the United States. His Banking Practice involves the representation of institutional creditors in lending transactions, workouts and creditors' rights matters. Mr Gross counsels companies and senior executives in M&A transactions and securities offerings involving multi-million dollar transactions. In addition, Mr Gross advises boards of directors and senior executives on current issues such as fiduciary duties, corporate compliance and Sarbanes-Oxley compliance.

**HALL, Thomas Jay**
Sills Cummis Epstein & Gross PC, Newark 973 643 5738
thall@sillscummis.com
*Recommended in Real Estate*
**Practice Areas:** Thomas Jay Hall is a member of the firm's Real Estate Practice Group and Chair of its Zoning and Land

Use Section. He counsels clients on a variety of land use and environmental issues, including representing them before planning boards and boards of adjustment seeking approval of planned unit developments, subdivisions, site plans and variances; and for permit applications before the Department of Environmental Protection. He has appeared in administrative, trial and appellate courts.

## HARRIS, David L
Lowenstein Sandler PC, Roseland
973 597 2378
dharris@lowenstein.com
*Recommended in Intellectual Property, Litigation*

**Practice Areas:** Chair of the firm's 110-lawyer Litigation Department. He has over 25 years of trial and appellate experience in several jurisdictions, emphasizing intellectual property, trade secrets, antitrust, and other business litigation, insurance coverage for catastrophic events, complex criminal defense, and civil rights cases.

**Prof. Memberships:** American Civil Liberties Union; President 1995-99, Trial Lawyers of New Jersey; Editorial Board 1990-94, New Jersey Law Journal; Commissioner, New Jersey Commission on Racism and Racial and Religious Violence; Rutgers University Law School Alumni Association; President 1989-90, American Bar Association, Intellectual Property Committee, Chair, Subcommittee Trade Secret Damages and Other Remedies; New Jersey State Bar Association; Garden State Bar Association; National Bar Association; President's Advisory Council, Essex County Bar Association; President 1998-2001, Volunteer Lawyers For Justice.

**Career:** Business Litigation; 'Top Ten Litigators in New Jersey', The National Law Journal; NJ Supreme Court (1979), US District Court, District of New Jersey (1979), Pennsylvania Supreme Court (1979), US Court of Appeals, Third Circuit (1982), US District Court, Eastern District of NY (1987), US Court of Appeals, Fourth Circuit (1987), US Court of Appeals, Sixth Circuit (1993), US District Court, Southern District of NY (2001). Rutgers University School of Law, Adjunct Professor - Antitrust 1995-99.

**Publications:** 'Preparing Experts with Kumho in Mind', The Practical Litigator; 'The Absolute Pollution Exclusion: Subterfuge, Confusion and Fair Resolution', ABA Monograph; 'Meet Legal Needs of the Poor Through Organization, Not Mandatory Pro Bono', New Jersey Law Journal; 'Protecting Trade Secrets: Steps to Take When Information is Firmly Lodged in Employees' Heads', NJ Lawyer.

**Personal:** Rutgers University School of Law, (JD, 1979); Pennsylvania State University, (MEd, 1972), (BA, 1970).

## HAWORTH, Gregory R
Duane Morris LLP, Newark
973 424 2014
grhaworth@duanemorris.com
*Recommended in Litigation*

**Practice Areas:** Gregory R Haworth focuses his practice on commercial and business litigation, bankruptcy and banking litigation, commercial real estate disputes, fidelity and surety claims and shareholder and class action disputes.

**Prof. Memberships:** New Jersey State Bar Association - Bankruptcy Law Section, Banking Law Section; Federal Bar Association.

**Career:** Admitted to practice in New Jersey and the United States Court of Appeals for the Third Circuit.

**Publications:** Co-author, 'Collecting Judgments in New Jersey', published by the National Business Institute, 1998; 'Shunning the Errors of the 1980s in Today's Resurging Market', New Jersey Law Journal, March 1995; 'Recent Decisions Favor Lenders Over Borrowers', New Jersey Law Journal, February 1995.

**Personal:** Rutgers School of Law - Newark, JD, 1982; Franklin College, BA, 1977.

## HAYDEN, Joseph
Walder, Hayden & Brogan P.A., Roseland
973 992 5300
*Recommended in Litigation*

## HELLER, William
McCarter & English, LLP, Newark
973 622 4444
*Recommended in Intellectual Property*

## HERSCHMAN, Gary W
Sills Cummis Epstein & Gross PC, Newark 973 643 5783
gherschman@sillscummis.com
*Recommended in Healthcare*

**Practice Areas:** Gary W Herschman is Chair of the firm's Health and Hospital Law Practice Group. His Healthcare Practice experience includes the representation of a diverse group of healthcare providers, including hospitals, ambulatory surgery centers, long-term care facilities, physician groups and various other healthcare facilities and businesses. He represents these clients in connection with a variety of joint ventures, mergers and acquisitions, and contractual arrangements. He also advises on regulatory compliance (federal and state), corporate compliance, HIPAA, government investigations, and civil and administrative healthcare litigation.

## HERZBERG ESQ, Peter
Wolf, Block, Schorr and Solis-Cohen LLP, Roseland 973 228 5700
*Recommended in Environment*

## HIMMEL, Michael B
Lowenstein Sandler PC, Roseland
973 597 6172
mhimmel@lowenstein.com
*Recommended in Litigation*

**Practice Areas:** Chair of the firm's White-Collar Criminal Defense Practice Group. He has developed a national practice in white-collar criminal defense including areas such as tax fraud, securities fraud, political corruption, antitrust, bank fraud, and environmental matters. His clients have included private and public corporations, officers and directors of private and public corporations, professionals and state and federal officials. He also assists corporate clients with internal investigations. A former Assistant US Attorney for the District of New Jersey, Mr Himmel is well known for his work in complex business litigation. He currently represents the State of New Jersey in the prosecution of two multi-billion dollar class action securities fraud cases.

**Prof. Memberships:** American Bar Association, Fellow; New Jersey State Bar Association; New York State Bar Association; Association of the Federal Bar of the State of New Jersey, President 1998-2000; Federal Bar Council; National Association of Criminal Defense Lawyers; New Jersey Association of Criminal Defense Lawyers.

**Career:** New York Bar (1975); US District Court, Southern and Eastern Districts of New York (1975); US Court of Appeals, Second Circuit (1975); US Supreme Court (1980); New Jersey Bar (1981); US District Court, District of New Jersey (1981); US Court of Appeals, Third Circuit (1983); US Court of Appeals, Fifth Circuit (2005).

**Publications:** 'What Lawyers Need to Know About Accepting Cash from Clients', New Jersey Law Journal; 'When an Employee Invokes the Fifth Amendment, the Corporate Employer May Suffer the Consequences', The Metropolitan Corporate Counsel; 'Did You Say Pre-Subpoena Obstruction of Justice?', The Metropolitan Corporate Counsel; 'Victims May "Collude" To Contest Dumping', The National Law Journal; 'The Defense of Criminal Antitrust Prosecutions: Sometimes Half The Battle is Knowing Where To Fight', The Metropolitan Corporate Counsel; 'When the White Collar Criminal Investigation Hits, No Longer Business as Usual', The Metropolitan Corporate Counsel; 'The Parallel Proceedings Pickle: Making the Best of Concurrent Civil and Criminal Federal Cases', Complex Crimes Journal ABA, Section of Litigation; 'Grand Jury Practice', The New Jersey Lawyer.

**Personal:** St Louis University (JD, 1974, Member, St Louis University Law Review); Boston University; New York University (BS, 1971).

## HLUCHAN, Richard M
Ballard Spahr Andrews & Ingersoll LLP, Voorhees 856 761 3420
hluchan@ballardspahr.com
*Recommended in Environment, Real Estate*

**Practice Areas:** Focuses on environmental and land use law, including zoning and regulatory matters. Counsels on hazardous waste clean-ups, wetlands, and land development permits. Assists in land use matters, including CAFRA permitting, waterfront development, riparian matters, rezonings, variances, subdivisions, and site plans. Represents clients in regulatory takings litigation (inverse condemnation).

**Prof. Memberships:** Appointed to Supreme Court of New Jersey's Committee on Environmental Litigation; member, Supreme Court's Committee on Character. Member, New Jersey State Bar Association, Director, Land Use Section, former Chair, 2001-02, former Director, Environmental Section. Leadership New Jersey Fellow in 1994. Member since 2002, American College of Real Estate Lawyers. Master, Delaware Valley Environmental American Inn of Court. Speaks and serves as a panelist at seminars and conferences sponsored by NJ ICLE, the New Jersey Builders Association. Member, Editorial Board of the New Jersey Law Journal.

**Career:** Admitted to California Bar (1975); New Jersey Bar (1975). Law clerk to the Honorable John F Gerry, United States District Court, Camden, NJ. Deputy Attorney General, served as Assistant Chief of the Attorney General's Environmental Section and Chief Counsel to the Pinelands Commission.

**Personal:** JD, magna cum laude, Santa Clara University School of Law (1974); BSFS, Georgetown University (1971).

## HOGAN, Edward
Norris, McLaughlin & Marcus, PA, A Professional Corporation, Bridgewater
908 722 0700
*Recommended in Environment*

## HORN, Lawrence S
Sills Cummis Epstein & Gross PC, Newark 973 643 5484
lhorn@sillscummis.com
*Recommended in Litigation*

**Practice Areas:** Lawrence S Horn is Co-Chair of the firm's Business Crimes and Corporate Internal Investigations Practice Group. His practice consists of defending companies and individuals who are the targets of federal white-collar criminal investigations with a special emphasis on criminal tax cases. Mr Horn is a certified criminal trial attorney and is a frequent lecturer at national seminars and institutes concerning tax fraud and white collar crime defense issues. He was an Assistant United States Attorney for the District of New Jersey from 1971-78 where he specialized in tax fraud prosecutions.

## HULL, Gerald
Drinker Biddle & Reath LLP,
Florham Park 973 360 1100
*Recommended in Real Estate*

## HUTCHEON, Peter
Norris, McLaughlin & Marcus, PA, A Professional Corporation, Bridgewater
908 722 0700
*Recommended in Corporate/M&A*

## HYATT, William
Kirkpatrick & Lockhart Nicholson
Graham LLP, Newark 973 848 4000
*Recommended in Environment*

## JACOB, Cynthia M
Fisher & Phillips LLP, Somerset
732 560 7100
cjacob@laborlawyers.com
*Recommended in Employment*
**Practice Areas:** Cynthia M Jacob is a
Partner in the New Jersey office of the
national law firm of Fisher & Phillips
LLP, practicing exclusively in labor and
employment law representing management. Jacob has extensive trial experience, in both bench and jury trials. She
concentrates on litigating employment-
related cases, including wrongful termination, race, sex and age discrimination,
and other civil rights litigation. A past
President of the New Jersey State Bar
Association (only the second elected
woman officer in the Association's 100-
year history), Jacob received a JD from
Yale Law School.

## JANIS, Ronald H
Pitney Hardin LLP, Morristown
212 297 5813
rjanis@pitneyhardin.com
*Recommended in Corporate/M&A*
**Practice Areas:** Corporate practice with
emphasis on M&A, representing targets,
acquirers and investment banks; advising
banks, broker-dealers, and other financial
institutions with respect to regulatory
issues; and counseling companies with
respect to corporate governance matters.
**Prof. Memberships:** ABA; Association
of the Bar of the City of New York; Financial Services Roundtable; Institute for
International Bankers; Securities Industry Association, Compliance and Legal
Division.
**Career:** Partner since 1994. Managing
Partner of the New York office.
**Publications:** Numerous articles in
American Banker, Bank Director, and
other publications.
**Personal:** New York University School of
Law, JD, 1975; Harvard College, BA, 1970.

## KAHN, Richard
Winne Banta Hetherington Basralian &
Kahn, P.C., Hackensack
201 487 3800
*Recommended in Real Estate*

## KEARNEY, ESQ, Dennis T
Pitney Hardin LLP, Morristown
973 966 8039
dkearney@pitneyhardin.com
*Recommended in Litigation*
**Practice Areas:** Represents corporations, non-profits, and financial institutions in all facets of complex civil and
criminal litigation. Conducted numerous
federal and state jury and non-jury trials
in such areas as RICO, trademark
infringement, bank fraud, and civil rights
violations.
**Prof. Memberships:** ABA; New Jersey
State Bar Association; New Jersey
Supreme Court District X Ethics Committee (Committee Investigator, 1990-94;
Hearing Panel Chairman, 1991-94),
American Health Lawyers Association;
ICLE Panelist healthcare Fraud.
**Career:** Partner since 1988.
**Personal:** University of Notre Dame, JD,
1980; University of Notre Dame, BA,
1976.

## KELLY, Shawn L
Riker Danzig Scherer Hyland & Perretti LLP,
Morristown 973 451 8555
skelly@riker.com
*Recommended in Litigation*
**Practice Areas:** Head of Insurance
Department. Practices commercial litigation and arbitration focusing on reinsurance, insurance and insurance insolvency
matters including complex insurance
coverage disputes, environmental claims
and reinsurance arbitration. Counsels
many major American insurance companies and heads a growing practice in England with several British insurance companies. Substantial record of success
before federal appeals courts.
**Prof. Memberships:** Member of the
Federation of Defense & Corporate
Counsel and Section of Tort and Insurance Practice of the American Bar Association.
**Personal:** Georgetown University Law
Center, JD; Duke University, AB, magna
cum laude.

## KESSLEN, Mark
Lowenstein Sandler PC, Roseland
973 597 2330
mkesslen@lowenstein.com
*Recommended in Intellectual Property*
**Practice Areas:** Mark P Kesslen, Chair
of the Intellectual Property Section of the
firm's Tech Group, provides strategic
guidance to technology-based businesses
in patent strategy (licensing, litigation,
and prosecution), outsourcing and
alliances. Prior to joining Lowenstein
Sandler, Mr Kesslen ran JPMorgan-
Chase's Technology, Sourcing and Intellectual Property Practice Group for the
Legal Department world-wide.
**Career:** New York Bar (1990); US Patent
and Trademark Office (1990).
**Publications:** 'RIM eyeing court show-
down', The Toronto Star; 'BlackBerry

Nation; Patent conflict may trigger
demise of wireless communication link',
The Star Ledger; 'BlackBerry Maker Is
Emboldened By Patent Office', The Wall
Street Journal; 'Blowing Your IP Rights
When Shopping For Venture Funding',
New Jersey TechNews; 'Know your (intellectual property) rights'; The value of a
transaction often resides in the intangible
assets', The Daily Deal.
**Personal:** Case Western Reserve School
of Law (JD, 1989); Tufts University (BS,
Electrical Engineering, 1986).

## KEYSER, Denise M
Ballard Spahr Andrews & Ingersoll LLP,
Voorhees 856 761 3442
keyserd@ballardspahr.com
*Recommended in Employment*
**Practice Areas:** Focuses on representation of management in all phases of labor
and employment matters, including collective bargaining, arbitrations, OSHA,
ERISA, wage and hour, employment-at-
will, wrongful discharge, discrimination,
management training, and affirmative
action.
**Prof. Memberships:** Member, Executive
Committee and co-ordinator on the Disability Discrimination Subcommittee for
the Labor and Employment Law Section of
the New Jersey State Bar Association. Former Co-Chair, Section's Disability Discrimination Committee; former Chair of
the Alternate Dispute Resolution Committee. Member, New Jersey State Bar Association and American Bar Association.
**Career:** Admitted to New Jersey Bar
(1983); Pennsylvania Bar (1983); joined
as Partner (2002).
**Publications:** Contributing author,
ICLE/New Jersey State Bar Association
compendium of New Jersey employment
law, entitled New Jersey Workplace Law.
**Personal:** JD, University of Pennsylvania
Law School, (1983); BA, with high honors, State University of New York at Stony
Brook (1980).

## KIEL, Donald
Kirkpatrick & Lockhart Nicholson
Graham LLP, Newark 973 848 4000
*Recommended in Litigation*

## KIPNEES, Robert J
Lowenstein Sandler PC, Roseland
973 597 6220
rkipnees@lowenstein.com
*Recommended in Litigation*
**Practice Areas:** Concentrates his practice in complex white-collar criminal
cases, including securities fraud, tax
fraud, antitrust and environmental
crimes and political corruption cases. He
brings to bear in defending firm clients
many years of experience, including significant trial experience in both prosecution and defense work. Mr Kipnees also
handles complex civil securities fraud
cases, criminal and civil RICO cases, class
actions and complex civil fraud and
antitrust cases.

**Prof. Memberships:** American Bar
Association, sections of Litigation and
Criminal Justice; Association of the Bar
of the State of New York; New York State
Bar Association; New Jersey State Bar
Association; National Association of
Criminal Defense Lawyers.
**Career:** New Jersey Bar (1981); New York
Bar (1981); US District Court, District of
New Jersey (1981); US District Court,
Eastern and Southern Districts of New
York (1981); US Court of Appeals, Third
Circuit (1985); US Supreme Court
(1992); US District Court, Eastern District of Wisconsin (1995); US Tax Court
(2000).
**Publications:** 'Criminal Trial Preparation', New Jersey Institute of Continuing
Legal Education.
**Personal:** Harvard Law School (JD,
1980, cum laude); Cornell University
College of Arts and Sciences (BA, 1977,
cum laude, with distinction).

## KNEE, Stephen H
Greenbaum, Rowe, Smith & Davis LLP,
Roseland 973 535 1600
sknee@greenbaumlaw.com
*Recommended in Corporate/M&A*
**Practice Areas:** Mergers and acquisitions; corporate law and business counseling; financial services; professional liability counseling and litigation; securities
regulation and litigation; e-commerce
and internet law.
**Prof. Memberships:** Director, Corporate
and Business Law Section, Member,
Banking Law Section and the Bankruptcy
Law Section, NJ State Bar Association.
Member, Section of Business Law, American Bar Association, Committee on
Negotiated Acquisitions; Co-Chair, ABA
Task Force on Acquisitions of Public
Companies. Member, American College
of Investment Counsel; Essex County Bar
Association; founding Member, the Inn
of Transactional Counsel.
**Personal:** New York University School of
Law (1965), Duke University (1962).

## KORNSTEIN, Alan
Orloff, Lowenbach, Stifelman & Siegel,
Roseland 973 622 6200
*Recommended in Corporate/M&A*

## KRAUS, Alan
Latham & Watkins LLP, Newark
973 639 1234
*Recommended in Litigation*

## KROVATIN, Gerald
Krovatin & Associates LLC, Newark
973 424 9777
*Recommended in Litigation*

## KRUMHOLZ, Dennis J
Riker Danzig Scherer Hyland & Perretti
LLP, Morristown 973 451 8454
dkrumholz@riker.com
*Recommended in Environment*
**Practice Areas:** Chair of Environmental
Group. Extensive experience in cost
recovery litigation, brownfields, ISRA

compliance, and consultant malpractice.
**Prof. Memberships:** Held offices in the Environmental Law Section of New Jersey State Bar Association, including Chair of the Section; Past Chair of INFORM, environmental research group; Founding Master of the Stewart G Pollock Environmental American Inn of Court; Founding Chair of Essex County Bar Association's Environmental Law Committee.
**Career:** Served as Deputy Attorney General for the State of New Jersey; Featured in the 1996-2006 editions of The Best Lawyers in America (Woodward/White, Inc.).
**Personal:** Boston College, JD; Oberlin College, BA.

### LAFIURA, ESQ, Dennis R
Pitney Hardin LLP, Morristown
973 966 8068
dlafiura@pitneyhardin.com
*Recommended in Litigation*
**Practice Areas:** Practice focuses on litigation in the following areas: franchising (with particular emphasis on matters involving motor vehicles, hotels, real estate brokerages, and consumer products); officer and director liability; securities; professional liability; consumer; and general equity matters.
**Prof. Memberships:** ABA, Forum on Franchising; New Jersey State Bar Association, Securities Litigation and Franchise Law Committees; Morris County Bar Association; Federal Bar Association; International Franchise Association.
**Career:** Partner since 1985. Managing Partner of firm 2002 - present.
**Personal:** Boston College Law School, JD, 1977; Member and Articles Editor, Boston College Law Review, 1975-77; Duke University, BA, magna cum laude, 1974.

### LASALA, Joseph
McElroy, Deutsch, Mulvaney & Carpenter, LLP, Morristown 973 993 8100
*Recommended in Litigation*

### LAVEY, Stewart
Drinker Biddle & Reath LLP, Florham Park 973 360 1100
*Recommended in Corporate/M&A*

### LAWLER, Kathy A
Pitney Hardin LLP, Morristown
973 966 8172
klawler@pitneyhardin.com
*Recommended in Employee Benefits*
**Practice Areas:** Practice focuses on the design and implementation of pension plans, as well as ERISA. Counsels and advises clients on issues in connection with coordination of benefits under Medicare, COBRA, and NJ Law and on the impact of mergers and acquisitions on employee benefit plans and transition issues.
**Prof. Memberships:** ABA, Employee Benefits Committee, Tax Section; New Jersey State Bar Association, Employee

Benefits Committee, Tax Section; Worldwide Employee Benefits Network, NJ Chapter.
**Career:** Partner since 1991.
**Personal:** New York University, LLM, 1987; The American University, Washington College of Law, JD, 1983; Kent State University, BA, cum laude, 1979.

### LESNEWICH, Alan G
Fisher & Phillips LLP, Somerset
732 560 7100
alesnewich@laborlawyers.com
*Recommended in Employment*
**Practice Areas:** Alan Lesnewich is a Partner in the New Jersey office of the national law firm of Fisher & Phillips LLP, practicing exclusively in labor and employment law representing management. After a varied business career which included law enforcement, he received a JD from Seton Hall University Law School. Following a clerkship with the New Jersey Supreme Court, Lesnewich has represented employers in arbitrations, state and federal court litigation, and before state and federal agencies. His cases have included single plaintiffs through class actions involving allegations of race, sex, age and handicap discrimination, wrongful discharge, and employee benefit disputes.

### LI, Christine F
Greenbaum, Rowe, Smith & Davis LLP, Woodbridge 732 549 5600
cli@greenbaumlaw.com
*Recommended in Real Estate*
**Practice Areas:** Partner, Real Estate Department, specializing in condominiums, planned real estate development, and community association law.
**Prof. Memberships:** Elected to American College of Real Estate Lawyers. Board of Consultors, NJ State Bar Association's Real Property, Probate and Trust Law Section. Listed in National Asian Pacific American Bar Association's Directory of Asian Pacific American Partners and Senior Attorneys in Major US Law Firms.
**Publications:** Co-author, 'New Jersey Condominium and Community Association Law'. Author, 'Real Estate Closing Procedures'. Contributing author, Common Interest Ownership Chapter in 'Commercial Real Estate Transactions in New Jersey'.
**Personal:** University of Pennsylvania Law School (1980), Rutgers College (1977).

### LILOIA, Gerald A
Riker Danzig Scherer Hyland & Perretti LLP, Morristown 973 451 8500
gliloia@riker.com
*Recommended in Litigation*
**Practice Areas:** Head of Litigation Group and Chair of Executive Committee. Focuses on a variety of commercial litigation matters, representing banks and other financial institutions. Has served as lead counsel in many major banking,

insurance, reinsurance, consumer and securities class action and professional liability suits and arbitrations. Represented major New Jersey and money center banks in connection with some of their largest real estate and commercial loan workouts and restructurings. Represented US and international banks in renegotiating and restructuring sovereign and private sector debt in Mexico, Central America and other international venues.
**Personal:** Rutgers University, LLB; Seton Hall University, BA.

### LITTENBERG, Joseph
Lerner David Littenberg Krumholz & Mentlik, LLP, Westfield
908 518 6303
jlittenberg@ldlkm.com
*Recommended in Intellectual Property*
**Practice Areas:** Practice focuses on how to enable clients to best understand and employ patent assets as a source of revenue and support their business. He advises clients on early resolution of patent disputes enabling parties to continue to compete effectively in the marketplace. Throughout Mr Littenberg's career he has advised clients in the areas of complex patent litigation, patent prosecution, licensing and all related aspects on intellectual property law. He has been recognized as one of the top intellectual property law practitioners in the 'Best Lawyers in America' since its inception and has been listed as one of New Jersey's Super Lawyers. He has conducted hearings with patent examiners in substantially all of the major countries, and has assisted a Barrister in a British trial.
**Prof. Memberships:** United States Patent and Trademark Office, Member of the Bars of New York and New Jersey, New Jersey Intellectual Property Law Association, International Association for the Protection of Industrial Property, Licensing Executives' Society, Essex County Bar Association, American Intellectual Property Association.
**Career:** Founding Partner of Lerner David Littenberg Krumholz & Mentlik, LLP.
**Personal:** Seton Hall University (JD, 1964), Rutgers University (BS, Industrial Engineering, 1960).

### LUSTBERG, Lawrence
Gibbons, Del Deo, Dolan, Griffinger & Vecchione, Newark 973 596 4500
*Recommended in Litigation*

### MARCHETTA, Anthony J
Pitney Hardin LLP, Morristown
973 966 8032
amarchetta@pitneyhardin.com
*Recommended in Litigation*
**Practice Areas:** Certified Civil Trial Attorney of the State of New Jersey. Trial and appellate practice encompasses patent and trademark jury trials, complex commercial litigation, products liability, mass torts, and other.

**Prof. Memberships:** US Supreme Court; US Court of Appeals, Second and Third Circuit; US Claims Court; US Tax Court; US District Court for the District of New Jersey; US District Court for the Northern, Southern, and Eastern Districts of New York; Supreme Court of New Jersey; ABA; New Jersey State Bar Association; New York Intellectual Property Law Association.
**Career:** Partner since 1993; member, firm Executive Committee; Partner In-Charge of Marketing; previously, Partner with Hannoch Weisman 1979-93.
**Publications:** Most recent of numerous articles appears in March 20, 2006 Complex Litigation Supplement of the New Jersey Law Journal on the New Jersey Supreme Court's landmark decision in Ayers v Township of Jackson.
**Personal:** Rutgers College, BA, cum laude, 1970; American University, Washington College of Law, JD, 1973.

### MARIANI, Richard C
Ogletree, Deakins, Nash, Smoak & Stewart, PC, Morristown 973 656 1600
richard.mariani@ogletreedeakins.com
*Recommended in Employment*
**Practice Areas:** Extensive experience representing management in all types of employment cases before state and federal trial and appellate courts and administrative agencies, conducting internal corporate investigations and developing/presenting employment training programs.
**Prof. Memberships:** American Bar Association (Equal Employment Opportunity Committee), New Jersey State Bar Association (Labor and Employment Law Section, Trial Practices Subcommittee) and the American Employment Law Council. Fellow of The College of Labor and Employment Lawyers.
**Publications:** Has lectured extensively and has authored numerous articles on employment-related issues.
**Personal:** Boston College (AB, 1968), Villanova University School of Law (JD, 1973). Listed in The Best Lawyers in America.

### MARINO, Kevin
Marino & Associates PC, Newark
973 824 9300
*Recommended in Litigation*

### MCBRIDE, Andrew
Kalison, McBride, Jackson & Murphy PA, Warren 908 647 4600
*Recommended in Healthcare*

### MCGAHREN, John
Latham & Watkins LLP, Newark
973 639 1234
*Recommended in Environment*

### MCTIERNAN, Edward
Gibbons, Del Deo, Dolan, Griffinger & Vecchione, Newark 973 596 4500
*Recommended in Environment*

## MEISER, Kenneth
Hill Wallack, Princeton
609 924 0808
*Recommended in Real Estate*

## MENTLIK, William
Lerner David Littenberg Krumholz &
Mentlik, LLP, Westfield
908 518 6305
wmentlik@ldlkm.com
*Recommended in Intellectual Property*
**Practice Areas:** Practice primarily
focuses on complex patent litigation in
virtually all fields of technology. A major
focus of Mr Mentlik's career has been
appellate practice, in which he has argued
or briefed more than 25 appeals in
numerous US courts, most notably the
US Court of Appeals for the Federal Circuit. Mr Mentlik successfully argued an
appeal on behalf of laser pioneer Gordon
Gould which cleared the way for the
issuance and vindication of four broad
patents arising out of a 1959 patent application, certain of which dominated significant areas of basic laser technology
into the 21st century. He has been recognized as one of the top intellectual property law practitioners in 'Best Lawyers in
America' since its inception and has been
listed as one of New Jersey's Super
Lawyers. He has lso been recognized in
Euromoney magazine's 'Guide to the
World's Leading Patent Law Experts'.
**Prof. Memberships:** United States Patent
and Trademark Office, Member of the
Bars of New York and New Jersey, New
Jersey Intellectual Property Law Associa-
tion, John J Gibbons American Inn of
Court (Master, Intellectual Property Law).
**Career:** Mr Mentlik was a Patent Exam-
iner in the United States Patent and
Trademark Office from 1969-73, and he
also served as a trial attorney with the
United States Department of Justice,
Antitrust Division, Patent Section, from
1973-75. He is a name Partner of Lerner
David Littenberg Krumholz & Mentlik,
LLP and currently serves as the firm's
Managing Partner.
**Personal:** George Washington University
National Law Center (JD, with honors,
1973; Order of the Coif). University of
Pennsylvania (BS, Chemical Engineering,
1969).

## MINION, Robert G
Lowenstein Sandler PC, Roseland
973 597 2424
rminion@lowenstein.com
*Recommended in Corporate/M&A*
**Practice Areas:** Co-Chair of Lowenstein Sandler's Investment Management
Group. He has 20 years of experience in
all aspects of corporate and business law,
with an emphasis in securities law, investment partnerships, mergers and acquisitions and related corporate transactions.
He represents clients throughout the
United States and internationally in a
wide variety of investment, investment

fund, capital formation and corporate
finance transactions (including fund formations, mergers and acquisitions, venture capital, and public and private securities offerings).
**Prof. Memberships:** Mr Minion has
served as an Adjunct Professor at Rutgers
University School of Law, teaching Securities Law and Regulation. He has also
served as the Chairperson of the Corporate Law Committee of the Essex County
Bar Association. He chaired the National
Business Institute Seminar on Negotiating and Drafting Acquisition Agreements, co-chaired The New Jersey Institute for Continuing Legal Education Sale
of Businesses Program, and the Summit
Series on Unlocking Shareholder Value.
He chairs the Annual Lowenstein Sandler
Investment Management Forum and is a
frequent speaker at investment industry
programs, including the 2005 New York
Annual Hedge Fund Regulation and
Compliance Forum, the Bank of America
Fund Manager Conference and the
Emerald Asset Management Investor
Conference. Mr Minion also serves on
the Legal Committee of The Wall Street
Hedge Fund Forum and many other pro-
fessional associations.
**Career:** New Jersey and Federal Bar
(1986); New York Bar (1987).
**Publications:** Mr Minion is a noted
author and lecturer in corporate law,
securities transactions and investment
management. Many of his transactions
have been published in, and/or he has
been quoted in or provided commentary
for, among others, The Wall Street Journal, The Deal, The Deal.com, The PIPEs
Report, The American Lawyer, the New
Jersey Law Journal, and the New Jersey
Lawyer. He is the editor of the Lowenstein
Sandler Investment Management Alert, a
quarterly newsletter of legal issues for the
investment management community.
**Personal:** Stanford University (JD,
1986); Cornell University (AB, 1983, with
distinction in all subjects).

## MONTAG, Brian
Kirkpatrick & Lockhart Nicholson
Graham LLP, Newark 973 848 4000
*Recommended in Environment*

## MOORE, Kevin J
Sills Cummis Epstein & Gross PC,
Newark 973 643 5251
kmoore@sillscummis.com
*Recommended in Real Estate*
**Practice Areas:** Kevin J Moore is a
member of the firm's Real Estate Practice
Group and its Zoning and Land Use Section. He counsels clients on a variety of
redevelopment, land use and environmental issues, including representing
them before planning boards, boards of
adjustment and governing bodies seeking
approval of major mixed use, commercial
and planned unit developments, as well
as subdivisions, site plans and variances;

and for applications for permits before
various state agencies. Mr Moore also
represents golf course developers
throughout the nation in preparing and
revising golf club membership plans and
governing documents.

## MORRISON, Victoria A
Riker Danzig Scherer Hyland & Perretti
LLP, Morristown 973 451 8470
vmorrison@riker.com
*Recommended in Real Estate*
**Practice Areas:** Partner in Real Estate
and Financial Institutions Groups. Commercial real estate experience in acquisition, development, leasing and sale of
commercial, retail, and industrial properties. Represents national and regional
landlords and tenants in leasing transactions. Represents buyers and sellers in
complex commercial transactions,
including sale-leasebacks and build-to-
suits. Represents lenders in real estate
financings. Extensive experience in real
estate partnerships and joint ventures,
federal tax aspects of commercial real
estate transactions and workouts and
foreclosures including bankruptcy.
**Prof. Memberships:** Member of International Council of Shopping Centers;
National Association of Industrial and
Office Parks.
**Personal:** Case Western Reserve University, JD; BA.

## MOULTHROP, Samuel P
Riker Danzig Scherer Hyland & Perretti
LLP, Morristown 973 451 8471
smoulthrop@riker.com
*Recommended in Environment,
Litigation*
**Practice Areas:** Partner in Environ-
mental Group. Focuses on environmental
litigation, permitting, transactional, and
regulatory/compliance, as well as white
collar criminal defense and corporate
investigations.
**Career:** Served in US Attorney's Office
for District of New Jersey as Assistant US
Attorney, Chief of Criminal Division,
Chief of the Appeals Division, Deputy
Chief of Fraud and Public Protection
Division and Chief of Environmental
Section; served as Acting Branch Chief
and as Enforcement Attorney with US
Environmental Protection Agency; Fea-
tured in the 1996-2006 editions of The
Best Lawyers in America
(Woodward/White, Inc.).
**Personal:** Boston University School of
Law, JD; Eckerd College, BA, with honors.

## NEWMAN, Jeffrey H
Sills Cummis Epstein & Gross PC,
Newark 973 643 5788
jnewman@sillscummis.com
*Recommended in Real Estate*
**Practice Areas:** Jeffrey H Newman is a
senior member of the firm, member of
the Management Committee and Chair
of the Real Estate Practice Group. He has
been practicing in the area of real estate

for over 25 years and has focused on the
shopping center industry with emphasis
on the representation of retail tenants
and shopping center developers. He has
developed a national reputation and represents institutional clients on a nationwide basis. This reputation has been
developed through his representation of
numerous retailers, developers, landlords
and lenders, as well as the result of
numerous speaking engagements
throughout the country.

## OHNEGIAN, Scott A
Riker Danzig Scherer Hyland & Perretti
LLP, Morristown 973 451 8551
sohnegian@riker.com
*Recommended in Employment*
**Practice Areas:** Partner in Labor and
Employment Group. Represents clients
in hearings, arbitrations and trials before
federal and state courts, the American
Arbitration Association, and federal and
state agencies in employment-related and
commercial litigation matters. Counsels
clients on a variety of labor and employment issues.
**Career:** Served as a law clerk to Hon
John C Lifland, US District Judge, District of New Jersey; Published employment law articles in state and national
publications as well as given seminars on
various employment law issues.
**Personal:** Rutgers University School of
Law, JD; Amherst College, BA.

## ORLOFF, Laurence
Orloff, Lowenbach, Stifelman & Siegel,
Roseland 973 622 6200
*Recommended in Litigation*

## PANTEL, Glenn
Drinker Biddle & Reath LLP,
Florham Park 973 360 1100
*Recommended in Real Estate*

## PARLIMAN, Gregory C
Pitney Hardin LLP, Morristown
973 966 8015
gparliman@pitneyhardin.com
*Recommended in Employment*
**Practice Areas:** Litigation in defense of
employers in individual plaintiff and class
suits alleging discrimination, whistle-
blower, wrongful discharge, and ERISA
claims. Employer counseling and management training on employee discharge,
discipline, workplace harassment, and
accommodation issues.
**Prof. Memberships:** ABA; New Jersey
State Bar Association; College of Labor
and Employment Lawyers; Association of
the Federal Bar of the State of New Jersey
(Trustee).
**Career:** Partner since 1980. Member,
firm Executive Committee.
**Publications:** 'Gender-Neutral Medical
Leave: In Gender-Specific Situations,'
New Jersey Lawyer, November 2005.
**Personal:** Georgetown University Law
Center, JD, 1973; Rutgers University, BA,
summa cum laude, 1969, Phi Beta Kappa.

## PATTERSON, Anne M
Riker Danzig Scherer Hyland & Perretti LLP, Morristown 973 451 8482
apatterson@riker.com
*Recommended in Litigation*

**Practice Areas:** Partner in Litigation Group. Experience in product liability, including pharmaceutical, tobacco and chemical litigation, and commercial litigation.

**Prof. Memberships:** Member of New Jersey Supreme Court Committee on Character; Chair of Product Liability and Toxic Tort Section of the New Jersey State Bar Association; Trustee of the Association of the Federal Bar of the State of New Jersey; Trustee of Trial Attorneys of New Jersey and Chair of its Education Committee.

**Career:** Served as Special Assistant to the Attorney General and Deputy Attorney General of New Jersey.

**Personal:** Cornell Law School, JD; Dartmouth College, AB, Phi Beta Kappa.

## PEIRANO, John
McElroy, Deutsch, Mulvaney & Carpenter, LLP, Morristown 973 993 8100
*Recommended in Employment*

## PERGOLA, Anthony O
Lowenstein Sandler PC, Roseland
973 597 2444
apergola@lowenstein.com
*Recommended in Corporate/M&A*

**Practice Areas:** Anthony O Pergola is Vice-Chair of Lowenstein Sandler's Tech Group. Mr Pergola's clients create, finance and bring to market new technologies in the communications, software, electronics, financial services and life sciences industries, among others. Mr Pergola is a founding Board Member and currently Co-Chair of AngelVine (www.angelvinevc.com), formerly the Jersey Angel Network, a network of angel investors and more than 20 venture funds dedicated to assisting early-stage ventures in the Mid-Atlantic region.

**Prof. Memberships:** Founder and Co-Chair of the Saint Peter's College Executives and Entrepreneurs Network; Board Member, Rutgers Venture Advisory Council (RVAC); Founding Board Member, AngelVine; NJTC (New Jersey Technology Council), Advisory Board, IT Track; Committee on Internet and Computer Law, New Jersey State Bar Association; Metropolitan Corporate Counsel Law Firm Advisory Committee

**Career:** 'Forty Under 40', NJBIZ, 2005; New Jersey Bar (1995); US District Court, District of New Jersey (1995).

**Publications:** 'Angel Financing: What Entrepreneurs Need to Know', NJBiz; 'Five Ways to Ruin your "B Round" while doing your "A Round"', New Jersey TechNews; 'Bridge Financing Can Be a Salvation or an Albatross', The National Law Journal; 'Raising Capital For the Emerging Private Company: an Introduction to the Inherent Legal Risks and Opportunities of the Capital Raising Process', The healthcare e-Commerce Revolution: Legal, Financial & Regulatory Strategies; When 'Exit' is Not Spelled 'IPO': Protecting Financial and Strategic Investors When A Privately-Held Portfolio Company Is Acquired, Advanced Forum on Business, Selling & Financing Internet Companies, Maximizing Profits in a Volatile Market Place, American Conference Institute; 'Corporate Governance Still Front And Center - And Corporate Counsel's Role Is Critical', The Metropolitan Corporate Counsel; 'Why Private Companies Should Not Ignore the Sarbanes-Oxley Act', Wall Street Lawyer; 'New Jersey Takes Leadership Position in Stem Cell Research and Commercialization', New Jersey TechNews.

**Personal:** Harvard Law School (JD, 1995, cum laude); Saint Peter's College (BA, 1992, summa cum laude).

## PICCO, Steven J
Reed Smith LLP, Princeton
609 514 5970
spicco@reedsmith.com
*Recommended in Environment*

**Practice Areas:** More than 25 years of experience as a regulator and practitioner in administrative environmental and energy law, and land use.

**Prof. Memberships:** Vice-Chair, New Jersey Water Supply Authority; member, New Jersey Economic Development Authority.

**Career:** Assistant Commissioner in both the New Jersey Department of Environmental Protection and the New Jersey Department of Energy. Responsibilities included drafting and enforcing regulations, and co-ordinating lobbying activities in the New Jersey Legislature.

**Personal:** Seton Hall University (JD, 1975); Rider University (BS, 1970); listed in numerous 'Who's Who' and 'Best Lawyers' publications for work in environmental law.

## POLICASTRO, Marc D
Greenbaum, Rowe, Smith & Davis LLP, Woodbridge 732 549 5600
mpolicastro@greenbaumlaw.com
*Recommended in Real Estate*

**Practice Areas:** Partner of the firm. Concentrates his practice in complex environmental, real estate and business transactions, environmental regulatory and redevelopment/zoning matters. Represents developers, lenders, businesses and borrowers in myriad land use contexts, including commercial and residential development.

**Prof. Memberships:** Member, Land Use and Environmental Law Sections, NJ State Bar Association. Member, NJ Builders Association, Mortgage Bankers Association.

**Career:** Selected by the New Jersey Law Journal for inclusion in its top '40 Under 40' list, citing top 40 attorneys under the age of 40.

**Personal:** Seton Hall University School of Law (1990), University of Richmond (1987).

## PORRINO, Christopher
Lowenstein Sandler PC, Roseland
973 597 6314
cporrino@lowenstein.com
*Recommended in Litigation*

**Practice Areas:** Christopher S Porrino is a member of the firm's Litigation Department and White Collar Criminal Defense Practice Group. He concentrates his practice in complex commercial litigation and white collar criminal defense.

**Prof. Memberships:** Supreme Court of the State of New Jersey [Committee on Model Civil Jury Charges (2004-06 term)]; Member of Association of the Federal Bar, State of New Jersey; Member of American Bar Association; Member, Board of Trustees of Summit Speech School.

**Career:** New Jersey Bar: New York Bar; US District Court, District of New Jersey; US District Court, Southern District of New York; United States Court of Appeals for the Third Circuit.

**Publications:** 'Lessons From the Anderson Debacle', The Middlesex Advocate; 'Employer Suffers When Worker Invokes Fifth', New Jersey Lawyer; 'When an Employee Invokes the Fifth Amendment, the Corporate Employer May Suffer the Consequences', The Metropolitan Corporate Counsel; 'Victims May 'Collude' To Contest Dumping', The National Law Journal; 'The Parallel Proceedings Pickle: Making the Best of Concurrent Civil and Criminal Financial Cases', White Collar Crime 1995 at c-12, American Bar Association Section of Criminal Justice.

**Personal:** Seton Hall University School of Law (JD, 1992, with honors); Lehigh University (BA, 1989, high honors).

## POSITAN, Wayne J
Lum, Danzis, Drasco & Positan, LLC, Roseland 973 228 6730
wpositan@lumlaw.com
*Recommended in Employment*

**Practice Areas:** 30 years experience in state/federal litigation of labor and employment matters representing management and defendants; non-compete matters; appellate practice, traditional labor practice; NRLB, collective bargaining; HR counseling; ADR and mediation; NJ Court approved mediator.

**Prof. Memberships:** Admitted: NJ; NY; DNJ; SDNY; EDNY; Third Circuit; US Supreme Court. Member, ABA Board of Governors (2006-09); ABA House of Delegates; President, New Jersey State Bar Association (2006-07); Chair, ABA Commission on MJP (2000-02); ABA Section of Litigation: Council (1997-2000) and Director of Divisions (2001-02); Council, ABA Center for Professional Responsibility (2000-02); Chair, NJSBA Labor and Employment Section (1995-97); DRI. Fellow: College of Labor and Employment Lawyers (1996); ABF; Professional Lawyer of the Year Award (2002), New Jersey Commission on Professionalism; Professional Achievement Award (2001), Essex County Bar Association; 'Top Lawyers' and 'Top 100 NJ Superlawyers', New Jersey Monthly Magazine.

**Career:** Lum, Danzis, Drasco & Positan, LLC since 1974

**Publications:** Editor-in-Chief, 'New Jersey Labor and Employment Law' (NJI-CLE); Board of Editors, 'Jury Instructions in Employment Litigation' (ABA); co-author, 'Employment Torts' in 'Business Torts Litigation' (ABA); co-author, 'Special Evidentiary Concerns' in 'Employment Litigation Desk Reference' (ABA).

**Personal:** BA, Government, magna cum laude, Boston University 1970; JD, NYU 1974.

## RABINOWITZ, David
Sutherland Asbill & Brennan LLP, New York 212 389 5000
*Recommended in Real Estate*

**Practice Areas:** Co-Chair of the firm's Retail Practice Group. Extensive experience in diverse aspects of commercial real estate, including leasing, acquisitions, sales and financing. Focuses on real and office transactions involving nationally located properties, condominion developments and environmental laws that affect real estate transactions. Represented 'big box' users in connection with development of their retail facilities throughout the country, including property acquisitions (including assemblages) for free standing facilities, acquiring and leasing pads within a shopping center, and leasing in-line buildings within a shopping center.

**Prof. Memberships:** Member, American College of Real Estate Lawyers; Member, International Council of Shopping Centers; Member, Section on Real Property, Probate and Trust Law of the American Bar Assoiation.

**Publications:** 'Mall Redevelopment, Phasing and Expansion', International Council of Shopping Centers US Law Conference, October 2005; 'New Bankruptcy Law Benefits Shopping Center Owners', Shopping Center Management Insider, July 2005.

**Personal:** JD, American University, Washington College of Law, 1983; Law Review, associate editor; BA, with distinction, Rutgers University, 1979; Phi Beta Kappa; Henry Rutgers Scholar.

## RACIOPPI JR, Nicholas
Riker Danzig Scherer Hyland & Perretti LLP, Morristown 973 451 8492
nracioppi@riker.com
*Recommended in Real Estate*

**Practice Areas:** Partner in Real Estate and Financial Institutions Practice

Groups. Considerable commercial real estate experience, particularly in the acquisition, development, zoning and planning, leasing and sale of commercial and industrial properties. Represents lenders in real estate financings and has extensive experience in complex real estate workouts and foreclosures. Experience in the formation and structuring of real estate partnerships and joint ventures.
**Prof. Memberships:** Member of New Jersey State and American Bar Associations; Member of National Association of Industrial and Office Parks.
**Personal:** New York University, JD; Rutgers University, BA, with high honors, Phi Beta Kappa.

## RADZELY, Edward
Giordano Halleran & Ciesla PC,
Middletown 732 714 3900
*Recommended in Real Estate*

## REILLY, Gregory B
Lowenstein Sandler PC, Roseland
973 597 2460
greilly@lowenstein.com
*Recommended in Litigation*
**Practice Areas:** Has 30 years of first chair litigation experience representing United States and foreign companies as well as public and private universities. Practice concentrates in federal and state court injunctions and damage actions in such areas as business torts, contract actions, corporate governance, constitutional law, securities, and employment law. He has represented clients at bench trials, jury trials, arbitrations, mediations, administrative proceedings and appeals. He has advised public and private corporations and universities concerning compliance with state and federal legislation and regulations.
**Prof. Memberships:** National Association of College and University Attorneys; American, New Jersey State and Essex County Bar Associations.
**Career:** New Jersey and Federal courts (1973), the US Court of Appeals, Third Circuit and US Tax Court (1975).
**Publications:** 'Managing the Workforce: Private Employees' Right to Organize and the New Jersey Anti-Injunction Act', A Practical Guide to New Jersey Employment Law: The Employer's Resource.
**Personal:** Rutgers University School of Law (JD, 1973); Princeton University (BA, 1967).

## REILLY, Lawrence F
Pitney Hardin LLP, Morristown
973 966 8090
lreilly@pitneyhardin.com
*Recommended in Real Estate*
**Practice Areas:** Transactional real estate matters nationwide. Focus on real estate development, and transactional matters including acquisitions, sales, financing, and leasing. Frequently serves as local counsel to national lenders or borrowers

in multi-state financing transactions. Consultant to firm's Litigation Group in matters including workouts, lease and joint venture disputes, and tax appeals.
**Prof. Memberships:** American Bar Association; New Jersey State Bar Association; Morris County Bar Association; Mortgage Bankers Association of New Jersey.
**Career:** Partner since 1971.
**Personal:** Fordham University School of Law, LLB, 1964; Fordham University, AB, 1961.

## RICCI, Richard F
Lowenstein Sandler PC, Roseland
973 597 2462
rricci@lowenstein.com
*Recommended in Environment*
**Practice Areas:** Richard F Ricci is Chair of the firm's Environmental Department. He has extensive experience in complex negotiations and litigation of environmental and construction issues. Mr Ricci works on a broad range of matters, including, Superfund and toxic tort litigation, injunctive and penalty proceedings, construction, environmental and commercial litigation. He served on an audit team appointed by Governor McGreevey to investigate the State's $500 million auto emissions testing contract as part of McGreevey's pledge to root out waste and mismanagement in state government.
**Prof. Memberships:** New Jersey State Bar Association; American Bar Association.
**Career:** Rhode Island Bar (1982); New Jersey Bar (1984).
**Publications:** 'New Jersey Takes the Lead On Chemical Plant Security', New Jersey Law Journal; 'Interpreting Recent NRD and Brownfield Amendments', Commerce Magazine; 'Cooper Industries Inc. v. Aviall Services Inc.: Whither (Or Is It Wither) Superfund?', The Metropolitan Corporate Counsel; 'Ramifications of Recent NRD and Brownfield Amendments', New Jersey Law Journal; 'The Challenges for Industry in Environmental Law', Inside the Minds: The Art and Science of Environmental Law.
**Personal:** University of Notre Dame (JD, 1982, magna cum laude, associate editor, University of Notre Dame Law Review); Duquesne University (BA, 1979, cum laude).

## RIDLEY, John
Drinker Biddle & Reath LLP,
Florham Park 973 360 1100
*Recommended in Employment,
Litigation*

## RODBURG, Michael L
Lowenstein Sandler PC, Roseland
973 597 2466
mrodburg@lowenstein.com
*Recommended in Environment*
**Practice Areas:** Michael L Rodburg is the firm's Managing Director. He has

more than 30 years experience in complex litigation and has practiced exclusively in environmental law for more than 25 years. Mr Rodburg represents business and industry in connection with significant business transactions, civil litigation and administrative agency proceedings arising out of a wide variety of environmental problems. He concentrates in hazardous waste and substances litigation, mass tort defense, and acquisition counseling.
**Prof. Memberships:** Chemical Waste Litigation Reporter, Editorial Board; The Environmental Claims Journal, Editorial Advisory Board; Environmental Insurance Litigation Institute, Board of Advisors; Hazardous Wastes and Toxic Torts: Law & Strategy, Contributing Editor; New Jersey State Bar Association, First Chair, Environmental Law Section (1984-1985); American Bar Association, Section of Environment, Energy, and Resources; National Conference for Community and Justice, New Jersey Region, Vice-Chairman.
**Career:** New Jersey Bar (1971).
**Publications:** 'New Mexico v. General Electric: A Cautionary Tale', New Jersey Law Journal; 'Groundwater Damages In New Jersey', Superfund and Natural Resource Damages Litigation Committee Newsletter; 'Top Ten Reasons Why New Jersey Businesses Should Be Concerned About Natural Resource Damages', The Metropolitan Corporate Counsel; 'Traps Set for the Unwary - California Supreme Court Invalidates Policy Rights in Corporate Restructuring', Environmental Compliance & Litigation Strategy; 'New Jersey Environmental Law Handbook', (6th Edition), Government Institutes; 'The Large Company with a Small Law Department', co-authored chapter in Successful Partnering Between Inside and Outside Counsel.
**Personal:** Harvard University (JD, 1971, magna cum laude, editor, Harvard Law Review); Massachusetts Institute of Technology (BS, 1968).

## ROLNICK, Lawrence M
Lowenstein Sandler PC, Roseland
973 597 2468
lrolnick@lowenstein.com
*Recommended in Litigation*
**Practice Areas:** Chair of the Securities Litigation Practice. Has extensive experience in complex commercial litigation, with emphasis in securities and class action litigation. Has represented public companies in class action litigation, institutional investors in securities litigation and directors and officers in defense of alleged breach of fiduciary duty claims. Successfully argued before the New Jersey Supreme Court on questions of first impression on securities law issues and defended clients in actions brought by the SEC, NASD and NYSE. Currently representing the Kirch Group in its suit

against Deutsche Bank and Liberty Media.
**Prof. Memberships:** NJ State Bar Association's Securities Litigation and Regulatory Enforcement Committee (Co-founder and Chair); New Jersey and American Bar associations; Trustee of the Federal Bar Association, District of NJ.
**Career:** New York Bar (1985); US District Court, Southern, Eastern and Western Districts of NY (1991); NJ Bar and US District Court, District of NJ (1992); US Court of Appeals, First and Second Circuit (1999); US Court of Appeals, Third Circuit (2000); US Court of Appeals, Fifth Circuit (2001).
**Publications:** 'Complex Litigation: Defending Consumer Fraud Class Actions,' New Jersey Law Journal; 'The Impact of the Kaufman v. i-Stat Corp. Decision', Corporate Officers & Directors Liability.
**Personal:** Rutgers University School of Law (JD, 1984, cum laude) and Officer, Rutgers Law Review; Rutgers University (BA, 1981, with high honors) and Henry Rutgers Scholar.

## ROSE, Beth S
Sills Cummis Epstein & Gross PC,
Newark 973 643 5877
brose@sillscummis.com
*Recommended in Litigation*
**Practice Areas:** Beth S Rose is Co-Chair of the firm's Litigation and Product Liability Practice Groups. She has become a nationally known attorney for her defense of medical device and pharmaceutical companies in mass tort litigation, frequently serving as national counsel. She is the lawyer to whom General Counsel turn when they need an aggressive but practical approach to 'bet the company' product liability matters. She has handled matters involving medical devices, consumer products, pharmaceuticals, foods, chemicals and industrial machines.

## ROSENBLATT, Richard G
Morgan, Lewis & Bockius LLP, Princeton
609 919 6609
rrosenblatt@morganlewis.com
*Recommended in Employment*
**Practice Areas:** Richard G Rosenblatt is a Partner in the Labor and Employment Law Practice. His practice focuses on the representation of employers in a variety of labor and employment-related matters in state and federal courts locally and across the country. In addition to discrimination, non-competition, trade secret, labor-management relations, and other more routine matters arising out of the workplace, his practice is heavily focused on complex wage and hour and employee benefits litigation.
**Prof. Memberships:** Member, American Bar Association, Labor and Employment Section; Executive Committee, New Jersey Bar Association, Labor and Employment Section, former Co-Chair Ethics

and Professionalism and Civil and Personal Rights Committees; Executive Director-South for the Sidney Reitman American Inn of Court.

### ROTHPLETZ, Michael
Drinker Biddle & Reath LLP, Florham Park 973 360 1100
*Recommended in Real Estate*

### ROTHSCHILD, Gita
McCarter & English, LLP, Newark 973 622 4444
*Recommended in Litigation*

### ROWE, Paul A
Greenbaum, Rowe, Smith & Davis LLP, Woodbridge 732 549 5600
prowe@greenbaumlaw.com
*Recommended in Litigation*
**Practice Areas:** Managing Partner; Chair, Litigation Department specializing in complex business and related litigations including construction, partnership and corporate disputes, antitrust, stock fraud and all forms of chancery litigation.
**Prof. Memberships:** Past President, Essex County Bar Association. Fellow-American College of Trial Lawyers, International Academy of Trial Lawyers, American Bar Foundation.
**Career:** 1993 recipient Trial Bar Award, Trial Attorneys of NJ. Admitted New York (1961), New Jersey (1962). Best Lawyers in America – Bet-the-Company Litigation, Business Litigation, Family Law.
**Publications:** Author, 'New Jersey Business Litigation'. Co-author, 'Guidebook to Chancery Practice in New Jersey.'
**Personal:** Columbia Law School (1961), Tufts College (1958).

### SALES, Bruce
Lerner David Littenberg Krumholz & Mentlik, LLP, Westfield 908 518 6311
bsales@ldlkm.com
*Recommended in Intellectual Property*
**Practice Areas:** Practice extends to all areas of intellectual property law with a particular emphasis on patent litigation, trademarks, copyrights, licensing, and intellectual property asset management. He represents a highly diverse client base ranging from sole proprietorships to major corporations throughout the world. His practice also includes worldwide strategic planning for intellectual property assets.
**Prof. Memberships:** United States Patent and Trademark Office, Member of the Bars of New Jersey, California, District of Columbia, American Bar Association, New Jersey Intellectual Property Law Association, Association Internationale pour la Protection de la Propriété Intellectuelle
**Career:** Mr Sales is Partner at Lerner David Littenberg Krumholz & Mentlik, LLP and currently serves on the firm Marketing Committee.
**Personal:** Hofstra University Law School (JD, 1983; Member, National Moot Court

Team) Rutgers University (BS, Biochemistry, with honors, 1977) (MS, Microbiology, 1980).

### SANDAK, Lawrence R
Proskauer Rose LLP, Newark
973 274 3256
lsandak@proskauer.com
*Recommended in Employment*
**Practice Areas:** Has more than 20 years of employment law experience. As a trial lawyer and civil litigator, defends employers accused of discrimination, retaliation, sexual harassment, breach of contract, and wage and hour violations before courts and government agencies. Extensive experience with class and collective actions. Also has substantial experience in arbitrating, mediating and negotiating the settlement of employment disputes. Advises clients on all aspects of the employer-employee relationship, including the creation of sensible personnel and benefit policies and the preparation of employment contracts, policy manuals and employee handbooks. Is frequently called upon to conduct or supervise internal investigations of alleged employee misconduct, including sexual harassment, and to recommend appropriate responses. Has guided clients through significant reductions-in-force and business closures. Extensive experience with financial services, media, banking, insurance and law firm clients.
**Publications:** Frequent commentator for CBS, Court TV, CNN and CNBC. Active speaker and writer on employment and human resources issues.
**Personal:** Brooklyn College of the City University of New York (1975) and Brooklyn Law School (1978). Editor, Brooklyn Law Review.

### SCHACHTER, Robert C
Greenbaum, Rowe, Smith & Davis LLP, Woodbridge 732 549 5600
rschachter@greenbaumlaw.com
*Recommended in Real Estate*
**Practice Areas:** Chair, Real Estate Department. Real estate law specializing in commercial leasing, commercial mortgage financing, real estate brokerage, acquisitions, land use planning and zoning.
**Prof. Memberships:** Elected to American College of Real Estate Lawyers. Listed in International Who's Who of Real Estate Lawyers. Member, Real Property, Probate and Trust Section, NJ Bar Association. Past Vice-Chair, Literature and Publications Committee, Real Property Division of the American Bar Association.
**Publications:** Co-author, 'New Jersey Real Estate Forms: Practice' (Michie 1992, Lexis Law Publishing), Leasing Chapter in Commercial Real Estate Transactions in New Jersey.
**Personal:** Rutgers Law School, Newark (1972), Rutgers College (1967).

### SCHOENBERG, Robert J
Riker Danzig Scherer Hyland & Perretti LLP, Morristown 973 451 8511
rschoenberg@riker.com
*Recommended in Intellectual Property*
**Practice Areas:** Partner in Trademark, Copyright and Computer Law Group. Represents numerous companies in copyright and trademark infringement matters, including a leading software company, a major pharmaceutical company and a company which produces sporting goods and exercise equipment. Represents clients in the entertainment industry. Expertise in computer industry matters and assists clients with protecting contract and property rights arising from the development, licensing, and distribution of computer hardware and software.
**Prof. Memberships:** Member of the Litigation Section and Patent, Trademark and Copyright Law Section of the American Bar Association.
**Personal:** Cornell University, JD, cum laude; Polytechnic University, BS.

### SHARKO, Susan
Drinker Biddle & Reath LLP, Florham Park 973 360 1100
*Recommended in Litigation*

### SNEIRSON, Marilyn
Kirkpatrick & Lockhart Nicholson Graham LLP, Newark 973 848 4000
*Recommended in Employment*

### SORIN, David
Morgan, Lewis & Bockius LLP, Princeton 609 919 6602
dsorin@morganlewis.com
*Recommended in Corporate/M&A*
**Practice Areas:** Mr Sorin is a Partner in the Business and Finance Practice. His practice focuses primarily on corporate transactions, securities law, mergers and acquisitions, and technology. His clients include leading software, information technology, e-commerce, communications and life sciences companies.
**Prof. Memberships:** Director, Co-Founder, Vice-Chair, New Jersey Technology Council.

### STAMELMAN, Andrew J
Riker Danzig Scherer Hyland & Perretti LLP, Morristown 973 451 8515
astamelman@riker.com
*Recommended in Corporate/M&A*
**Practice Areas:** Head of Tax and Corporate Practice Groups. Serves as general counsel for many middle market companies on issues such as tax strategies, mergers and acquisitions, structuring of joint ventures, partnerships and limited liability companies, and developing executive compensation plans. Represents corporations, partnerships and other entities in many corporate transactions including mergers, acquisitions and divestitures. Assists family-owned businesses in succession planning or orchestrating exit strategies, and plan implementation.

**Prof. Memberships:** Member of the New Jersey Bar Association's taxation and corporate law sections.
**Personal:** New York University, LLM, Taxation; Cornell University, JD; University of Virginia, BA, with honors.

### STANTON, Patrick M
Ogletree, Deakins, Nash, Smoak & Stewart, PC, Morristown 973 656 1600
patrick.stanton@ogletreedeakins.com
*Recommended in Employment*
**Practice Areas:** Labor and employment.
**Prof. Memberships:** New Jersey State Bar Association (Immediate Past Chair, Labor and Employment Law Section); NLRB Region 22 Practice and Procedure Committee; Sidney Reitman Employment Law American Inn of Court (Chair, Organizing Committee; President, 1997-2001); Fellow, College of Labor and Employment Lawyers.
**Career:** Admitted: New Jersey, New York, Ohio (inactive), US Supreme Court, US District Courts (DNJ; SDNY; EDNY; SDOH), US Court of Appeals (Third Circuit, and DC Circuit).
**Personal:** St Joseph's (Pa) University (BS, 1969), University of Virginia School of Law (JD, 1972), Fairleigh Dickinson University (Executive MBA Program, 1984).

### STODDARD, John
Drinker Biddle & Reath LLP, Princeton 609 716 6500
*Recommended in Corporate/M&A*

### SUFLAS, Steven W
Ballard Spahr Andrews & Ingersoll LLP, Voorhees 856 761 3466
suflas@ballardspahr.com
*Recommended in Employment*
**Practice Areas:** Focuses on representation of management in all phases of labor and employment matters, including collective bargaining and traditional labor law issues, employment litigation, appearances before administrative agencies, ERISA, and wage and hour law.
**Prof. Memberships:** Past Chair, Labor and Employment Law Section of the New Jersey State Bar Association (1999-2001). Fellow of The College of Labor and Employment Lawyers (1996).
**Career:** Admitted to New Jersey Bar (1976); Pennsylvania Bar (1978); joined as Partner (2002).
**Publications:** Paralegals Are Eligible for Overtime Pay, 'New Jersey Law Journal', Vol. CLXXIX-No. 11, March 14, 2005; Scorecard Redux: Plaintiffs are Still Winners in Employment Cases, 'New Jersey Law Journal', Vol. CLXXIX-No. 7, Index 579 (February 7, 2005); Editor: 'New Jersey Workplace Law', published by The New Jersey Institute for Continuing Education and The NJSBA Labor and Employment Law Section; The New Jersey Labor Letter, Editorial Review Board (1999-2001); Basic Principles for Awarding Attorney's Fees in Discrimination

Cases, 'New Jersey Labor and Employment Law Quarterly', Vol. 26, No. 1 (2002).

**Personal:** JD, with honors, University of North Carolina School of Law (1976); BA, Davidson College (1973).

### SULLIVAN, Diane P
Dechert LLP, Princeton
609 620 3232
diane.sullivan@dechert.com
*Recommended in Litigation, Products Liability*

**Practice Areas:** Ms Sullivan, a Partner in the Mass Torts and Product Liability Group, defends pharmaceutical, medical device, and chemical companies. She has served as one of a group of select national trial counsel in several mass tort litigations, as national and regional counsel for clients in various actions, as court-designated defense liaison counsel, and as a member of national defense steering committees in mass tort litigation.

**Prof. Memberships:** Member, New Jersey Bar and several federal courts; Member, Defense Research Institute and International Association of Defense Counsel.

**Personal:** Fairfield University, BA, 1984; University of Pennsylvania Law School, JD, 1987.

### SUNBERG, Randall B
Morgan, Lewis & Bockius LLP, Princeton
609 919 6606
rsunberg@morganlewis.com
*Recommended in Corporate/M&A*

**Practice Areas:** Randall B Sunberg is a Partner in the Business Transactions Practice and Co-Chair of the firm's Life Sciences Transactions Practice. He has represented pharmaceutical and biotech companies in several of the largest life sciences industry transactions ever completed. Mr Sunberg's clients range from early-stage biotechnology start-ups to global pharmaceutical companies, and medical device and other technology companies. He advises clients on negotiation and structuring of acquisitions, divestitures, joint ventures, corporate partnering, licensing and other complex collaborations, and the equity investments and other securities matters that often accompany such transactions.

**Prof. Memberships:** Member, American Bar Association, Business Law Section.

### THEK, Raymond P
Lowenstein Sandler PC, Roseland
973 597 2574
rthek@lowenstein.com
*Recommended in Corporate/M&A*

**Practice Areas:** Raymond P Thek advises tech and life sciences companies in all aspects of corporate finance, including financing, acquisitions, divestitures and strategic alliances. He has extensive experience in mergers and acquisitions and private equity financings including venture capital investment, tech transfer and strategic partnering. Mr Thek is a mem-

ber of the firm's Corporate Department and the Tech Group.

**Prof. Memberships:** Executive Committee Member of AngelVine - www.angelvinevc.com; Counsel and Director of New Jersey Biotechnology and Life Sciences Coalition; Advisory Board Member of Commercialization Center for Innovative Technologies; Counsel and Member of New Jersey Business Incubation Network; Exclusive On Site 'SPAN' Provider of NJIT-Enterprise Development Center; Guest Lecturer - vSeries MBA program at Lehigh University; High-Tech Program Facilitator of Entrepreneurship Training Institute.

**Career:** New York Bar (1987); New Jersey Bar (2001).

**Publications:** 'NO PAIN - NO GAIN: Five Arguments Not to Have With Your Mezzanine & Late Round VC', LifeSciTech; 'Lowenstein Sandler: Heads Into New Frontier, Picks Up the Stem Cell Gauntlet', New Jersey Business; 'New Jersey Takes Leadership Position in Stem Cell Research and Commercialization', New Jersey TechNews; 'Life on the Creative Edge', Research New Jersey.

**Personal:** Yale Law School (JD, 1986, Director, Yale Law and Technology Association and the Yale Federalist Society); Boston University (BA, 1983, magna cum laude).

### THOMPSON, Kenneth
McCarter & English, LLP, Newark
973 622 4444
*Recommended in Corporate/M&A*

### TOFT, Dennis
Wolff & Samson, A Professional Corporation, West Orange 973 325 1500
*Recommended in Environment*

### TOLCHINSKY, Harold
Cole, Schotz, Meisel, Forman & Leonard PA, Hackensack 201 489 3000
*Recommended in Real Estate*

### TUBMAN, Lloyd H
Archer & Greiner, A Professional Corporation, Flemington
908 788 4311
ltubman@archerlaw.com
*Recommended in Environment*

**Practice Areas:** Ms Lloyd H Tubman is a Partner in Archer & Greiner's Real Estate Department and its Land Use, Environmental Permitting and Compliance Group. She concentrates her practice in zoning approvals and in federal and state environmental compliance, with broad development planning and regulatory enforcement, as well as particular wetlands, water quality, flood hazard area and utility experience.

**Prof. Memberships:** Member, Board of Directors, Land Use Law Section of the NJ Bar Association; Member, New Jersey Tidelands Resource Council.

**Career:** Ms. Tubman was a negotiator and author of the New Jersey Freshwater

Wetlands Protection Act. She is counsel to the New Jersey Chapter of NAIOP, the National Association of Industrial and Office Properties, and has received special recognition awards from NAIOP and the New Jersey Chapter of the National Conference of Christians and Jews for service to the development community.

**Personal:** University of Minnesota Law School (cum laude,1982), University of Minnesota (summa cum laude and Phi Beta Kappa,1979).

### TYRRELL, James
Latham & Watkins LLP, Newark
973 639 1234
*Recommended in Litigation*

### VAN DEVENTER, Kenneth M
Riker Danzig Scherer Hyland & Perretti LLP, Morristown 973 451 8523
kvandeventer@riker.com
*Recommended in Litigation*

**Practice Areas:** Partner in Litigation Group. Represents businesses in complex commercial litigations, arbitrations and appeals. Substantial experience before Federal Courts for District of New Jersey, Southern District of New York, Western District of Virginia, Central District of California, Third Circuit Court of Appeals and US Supreme Court. Appeared before Law and Chancery Divisions of New Jersey Superior Court, New Jersey Appellate Divisions and State Supreme Court. Managed class action litigation for defense and plaintiffs and handled temporary restraining orders and preliminary injunction applications in federal and state courts.

**Personal:** Seton Hall University, JD, Law Review; University of Notre Dame, BA.

### WAEGER, Ann
Farer Fersko, Westfield
908 789 8550
*Recommended in Real Estate*

### WAGENBACH, Jeffrey B
Riker Danzig Scherer Hyland & Perretti LLP, Morristown 973 451 8524
jwagenbach@riker.com
*Recommended in Environment*

**Practice Areas:** Partner in Environmental Group. Extensive experience in regulatory and compliance matters, litigation and transactional matters, and ECRA/ISRA compliance issues.

**Prof. Memberships:** Member of the New Jersey State Bar Association (Environmental Law Section) and the American Bar Association (Natural Resources Section).

**Career:** Frequent speaker and author on environmental topics, including underground storage tanks, water and wetlands compliance and permitting, site remediation procedures and requirements, and ISRA; Named one of The Best Lawyers in America for New Jersey environmental law (Woodward/White, 2003-06 editions).

**Personal:** Syracuse University, College of Law, JD; Dartmouth College, BA, with honors.

### WALDER, Justin
Walder, Hayden & Brogan P.A., Roseland
973 992 5300
*Recommended in Litigation*

### WARREN, William
Drinker Biddle & Reath LLP, Princeton
609 716 6500
*Recommended in Environment*

### WEST, Richard A
Lum, Danzis, Drasco & Positan, LLC, Roseland 973 228 6787
rwest@lumlaw.com
*Recommended in Employment*

**Practice Areas:** Extensive experience in litigated matters, counseling and policy development relating to: federal and state anti-discrimination statutes; whistleblower claims; hostile work environment claims; disability and family/medical leave issues; wage and hour statutes; noncompetition covenants and trade secrets; contractual negotiations and disputes; corporate investigations and training; employee handbooks; and privacy issues.

**Prof. Memberships:** Adjunct Professor, Rutgers School of Law-Newark (2006); New Jersey Law Journal's 'Top 40 Under 40' New Jersey attorneys (2004); Barrister, Sidney Reitman Employment Law American Inn of Court (2002-present); Executive Committee, NJ State Bar Association, Labor and Employment Secton (2005-present); Order of the Coif (1993).

**Career:** Lum, Danzis, Drasco & Positan, LLC, since 1995 (Member since 2001); law clerk, Hon Freda L Wolfson, US District Court for the District of New Jersey, 1994-95.

**Publications:** Managing Editor, 'New Jersey Labor and Employment Law' (NJICLE 2005 Supp.); author, 'No Plaintiff Left Behind: Liability for Workplace Discrimination and Retaliation in New Jersey,' 28 Seton Hall Legislative Journal 127 (2003); author, 'We The People: Limitations on Congressional Term Limits are Unconstitutional Content-Determinative Regulations,' 46 Rutgers Law Review 1787 (1994); contributor, 'Model Jury Instructions: Employment Litigation' (ABA Supp 2005).

**Personal:** JD, with honors, Rutgers School of Law-Newark, 1993.

### WOVSANIKER, Alan
Lowenstein Sandler PC, Roseland
973 597 2564
awovsaniker@lowenstein.com
*Recommended in Corporate/M&A*

**Practice Areas:** Co-Chair of the Closely Held Business Practice, has 25 years of experience in mergers and acquisitions, business planning, securities regulation and corporate finance. He counsels clients on the funding and structuring of business organizations, and the structuring of employment relationships and equity-based compensation plans. In addition, Mr Wovsaniker represents issuers and underwriters in public securities offerings, venture capital and other private securities offerings and periodic reporting requirements.

**Prof. Memberships:** District V-C Ethics Committee, Supreme Court (1994-98) and Chair (1997-98); Trustee of the Essex County Bar Association (1996-99); Chair of the Essex County Bar District V-C Ethics Committee, Supreme Court (1994-98) and Chair (1997-98); Trustee of the Essex County Bar Association's Corporate Law Committee (1999-2002) and Chair of the Essex County Bar Association's Banking Law Committee (1994-97); New Jersey State and American Bar associations; former Adjunct Faculty of Rutgers University Law School and Seton Hall University of Law.

**Career:** New Jersey Bar (1977).

**Publications:** 'Corporate Governance e-book,' provides Sarbanes-Oxley regulations including corporate governance proposals and compliance recommendations; 'SOX and Related Reforms: Where Are We?', Metropolitan Corporate Counsel; 'A New Year's Resolution for Corporate Governance Reform,' Metropolitan Corporate Counsel; 'Ten Ways to Succeed and Prosper When Selling Your Business', Commerce Magazine; 'Equity Compensation: Cash-Poor Employers Have Options', The National Law Journal.

**Personal:** Harvard University (JD, 1977, magna cum laude); Brown University (AB, 1974, magna cum laude, Phi Beta Kappa).

## ZANGARI, Ted
Sills Cummis Epstein & Gross PC,
Newark 973 643 5781
tzangari@sillscummis.com
*Recommended in Real Estate*

**Practice Areas:** Ted Zangari, a member of the firm, concentrates his practice on the development and leasing of commercial real estate throughout the United States. He has extensive experience representing office, shopping center, warehouse and industrial landlords and tenants in transactions ranging from global headquarters, department stores, theatres and container terminals to satellite office locations, mall stores, downtown redevelopment projects, telecomm hotels and storage facilities. His client roster includes many of the country's well-known developers and retailers. He is active in New Jersey policy-making and recently co-chaired the Governor's Business Employment Incentives Study Commission.

## ZIMMERMAN, Edward M
Lowenstein Sandler PC, Roseland
973 597 2568
ezimmerman@lowenstein.com
*Recommended in Corporate/M&A*

**Practice Areas:** Chairs Lowenstein Sandler's Tech Group and has extensive experience representing venture funds and tech-based businesses in their most critical business transactions (venture capital/private equity financings, M&A, securities offerings, going private transactions, strategic alliances, management buyouts, shareholder disputes). He also represents research institutions in tech transfer/spin-offs. Representative clients include: JPMorganChase, Sandoz, Larsen & Toubro, Rutgers University, Princeton University, Stevens Institute of Technology, Datran Media, Edison Venture Fund, Updata Capital, Millennium 3 Capital, Inter-Atlantic Fund, NJTC Venture Fund, RK Ventures, Aperture Venture Partners, AppIntelligence (sold to ISO), Archive Systems, Hotspot FX, dynamicsoft (sold to Cisco Systems), Lamina Ceramics, Hydroglobe (sold to Graver Technology, a Marmon Group company), and many high-net worth individual angel investors.

**Prof. Memberships:** Founder and Co-Chair, Jersey Angel Network; Adjunct Professor of Venture Capital, Rutgers Law School; Member, NVCA Working Group on Model Legal Documents for Venture Capital; Board Member (and Chair, Government Affairs Committee), New Jersey Technology Council; Member, Rutgers University Equity Portfolio Committee; Founder and Chair, Hoop-A-Paluza, Inc.; Founder and Co-Chair, Rutgers Venture Advisory Council; Advisory Board Member (past Board Member), Bill T. Jones/Arnie Zane Dance Company.

**Career:** '40 Under 40', New Jersey Law Journal (2004 and 2003); '40 Under 40', NJBiz (2001, one of two lawyers on the list.); lead counsel in venture capital deal/strategic alliance, which Future Banker Magazine listed as one of the 'Top 10 Technology Deals of 2000,' New Jersey Bar (1992).

**Publications:** By Ed Zimmerman: 'Are Finders Also Broker Dealers?', The National Law Journal; 'The Trouble With Patent Shop Rights (in M&A and Venture Capital Context)', The National Law Journal; 'Shareholder Disputes and Corporate Divorce', New Jersey CPA; 'Five Ways to Ruin Your 'B Round' While Doing Your 'A Round'', NJ Tech News, with Scott Perricelli, LLR Partners; 'Angel Financing: What Entrepreneurs Need to Know', NJ Tech News, with Anthony Marino, Venrock Associates; 'Bridge Financing', National Law Journal; 'Mergers and Acquisitions in Practice', New Jersey Law Journal. About Ed Zimmerman: 'Hoop Dream Nets Thousands for Children's Charity,' The Star Ledger, 'Where Angels Tread', NJBIZ; 'Financially Speaking With Ed Zimmerman & Steve Skolnick,' Corporate Finance Weekly; 'VCs Talk Candidly About Raising Money', NJBIZ.

**Personal:** University of Pennsylvania (JD, 1992); Haverford College (BA, Phi Beta Kappa, 1989).

# ARCHER & GREINER, P.C.

## THE FIRM

**Managing Partners:** James H Carll, Chairman
Gary J Lesneski, President

**Number of partners:** 72
**Number of other lawyers:** 63

**FIRM OVERVIEW:** Established in 1928, Archer & Greiner is a full service law firm with a reputation for providing the highest quality, result-driven legal services to corporate and individual clients. One of the largest law firms in New Jersey, Archer & Greiner serves clients throughout the New Jersey, Pennsylvania and Delaware tri-state region and in an increasing number of other states and jurisdictions. With a network of regional offices, the firm has more than 130 lawyers practicing in all major legal disciplines.

## MAIN AREAS OF PRACTICE:

**Corporate:** The Corporate Department provides advice on general corporate representation and contract negotiation, mergers and acquisitions, the formation and structuring of business entities and joint ventures, securities law representation, and debt and equity financings of both a private and public nature.

**Debtor & Creditors' Rights:** The Debtor and Creditors' Rights Group provides guidance and counsel to business, institutional and individual clients for decades in reorganizing and resolving both their own financial affairs and difficulties as well as dealing with those of their clients and customers.

**Environmental:** The environmental law attorneys handle all facets of environmental practice from litigating major cases to counseling clients on permitting, ISRA, air and water pollution, wetlands, solid and hazardous wastes, contract documentation and litigation involving the remediation of environmental sites, compliance counseling, industrial pretreatment, lender liability, oversight of environmental assessments in land sales, and land use/environmental approvals.

**Intellectual Property:** The Intellectual Property Practice includes the full range of patent, trademark, copyright, trade secret, and computer and internet law experience in the areas of litigation, licensing and transfer, registration and counseling.

**Labor & Employment:** The labor and employment law attorneys represent management and defendants in employment litigation; discrimination litigation; non-competition disputes; and traditional labor law, including drafting and negotiating collective bargaining agreements, rendering advice concerning strike planning. They also counsel nonunion employers facing union boycotts, organizational campaigns and other union activity.

**Land Use:** The Land Use and Environmental Permitting and Compliance Group regularly obtains permits, approvals and certifications from local planning and zoning boards, county boards, special regional agencies, and State and Federal agencies concerning every aspect of land use, land development and regulatory compliance.

**Litigation:** The firm's Litigation Department is its largest, with over 50 lawyers and several formal practice groups, covering labor and employment, environmental litigation, personal injury litigation, bankruptcy and creditors' rights, and commercial litigation. Litigation department attorneys are also members of interdepartmental practice groups in computer and high technology law, education law, environmental law, estates law, healthcare law, intellectual property, and media and communications law.

**Real Estate:** Archer & Greiner's real estate attorneys handle matters involving every facet of the sale, leasing, development, financing and acquisition of real property. They regularly handle complex multi-state sales, acquisitions and financings, as well as simple real estate transactions.

**Estates & Trusts:** The Estates and Trusts Department provides estate, business continuity, charitable giving and elder care planning, estate and trust administration and litigation services, as well as tax services to individuals, professionals and institutions.

## HEAD OFFICE

**NEW JERSEY**
One Centennial Square, 33 East Euclid Avenue, **Haddonfield**, NJ 08540
**Tel:** 856 795 2121  **Fax:** 856 795 0574
**Website:** www.archerlaw.com

## BRANCH OFFICES

**DELAWARE**
300 Delaware Avenue, Suite 1370, **Wilmington**, DE 19801
**Tel:** 302 777 4350  **Fax:** 302 777 4352

**NEW JERSEY**
Plaza One, 1 State Route 12, Suite 201, **Flemington**, NJ 08822
**Tel:** 908 788 9700  **Fax:** 908 788 7854

700 Alexander Park, Suite 102, **Princeton**, NJ 08540
**Tel:** 609 580 3700

**PENNSYLVANIA**
One South Broad Street, Suite 1620, **Philadelphia**, PA 19107
**Tel:** 215 963 3300  **Fax:** 215 963 9999

ARCHER & GREINER, P.C.
ATTORNEYS AT LAW

# GIBBONS, DEL DEO, DOLAN, GRIFFINGER & VECCHIONE, P.C.

## THE FIRM

**Managing Director:** Patrick C Dunican, Jr

**Number of directors:** 89
**Number of other lawyers:** 111

**FIRM OVERVIEW:** Gibbons is one of the region's premier law firms established in 1926, and ranked among the nation's top 250 firms by The National Law Journal. The firm provides transactional, litigation and counseling services to leading businesses throughout the Metropolitan New York region and nationally. The firm's attorneys are recognized among the nation's leading business attorneys in the Chambers USA Guide to America's Leading Business Lawyers, The Best Lawyers in America and Super Lawyers.

## MAIN AREAS OF PRACTICE:

**Business & Commercial Litigation:** Handling sophisticated and complex commercial litigation including securities class actions, regulatory and administrative law, Lanham Act and unfair competition, restrictive covenants and all manner of contractual disputes.

**Corporate:** Advising leading corporations and financial institutions on corporate law matters, including mergers, acquisitions, divestitures, restructurings, joint ventures, licensing, corporate finance, commercial lending, capital raising, regulatory compliance, corporate governance and tax planning, as well as serving as outside general counsel.

**Criminal Defense:** Investigating and defending against allegations of business, accounting, securities, bank, insurance, tax, healthcare and government contract fraud. The department attorneys have been involved in many high-profile investigations and prosecutions of alleged political corruption and business crime, particularly in the pharmaceutical and communications industries.

**Employment Law:** Representing employers in Federal and state court, in litigation involving discrimination, harassment, retaliation, wage and hour, employment contract, restrictive covenant, wrongful discharge, employee benefits and ERISA claims. Providing the full range of preventive and compliance counseling and training with an emphasis on discipline and discharge, harassment, disability-related leaves and accommodations, work-force restructurings, restrictive covenants and executive compensation; as well as workplace investigations and audits of employment practices.

**Financial Restructuring & Creditors' Rights:** Representing creditors, debtors and various fiduciaries in all aspects of complex business insolvency issues and proceedings, including federal bankruptcy proceedings, state court litigation involving receiverships, attachments, replevins and foreclosures, out of court 'workouts' and related debtor and creditor relations counseling to resolve insolvency issues and disputes outside a formal proceeding.

**Government Affairs:** Comprehensive State and Federal government relations counseling for entities in the public, private and nonprofit sectors including legislative lobbying, regulatory counseling and interaction with state agencies. Intellectual Property: Full range of patent, trademark, copyright, unfair competition, e-commerce, trade secret, and computer and internet law experience in the areas of litigation, strategic licensing and transactional work, patent prosecution, trademark and copyright registrations, corporate due diligence, intellectual property audits and general intellectual property counseling.

**Products Liability:** Defending and advising manufacturers of ethical pharmaceuticals and medical/surgical devices, as well as diagnostic laboratories, in complex matters involving issues such as purported adverse effects, design, warnings and/or manufacturing defects, and results of laboratory analyses. A team of attorneys is also dedicated to the defense of manufacturers of a diverse array of products such as industrial equipment, automotives and consumer products.

## HEAD OFFICE

**NEW JERSEY**
One Riverfront Plaza, **Newark**, NJ 07102
**Tel:** 973 596 4500  **Fax:** 973 596 0545
**Email:** firm@gibbonslaw.com
**Website:** www.gibbonslaw.com

## BRANCH OFFICES

**NEW JERSEY**
224 West State Street, **Trenton**, NJ 08608
**Tel:** 609 394 5300  **Fax:** 609 394 5301

**NEW YORK**
One Pennsylvania Plaza, **New York**, NY 10119
**Tel:** 212 649 4700  **Fax:** 212 333 5980

**PENNSYLVANIA**
1700 Two Logan Square, **Philadelphia**, PA 19103
**Tel:** 215 665 0400  **Fax:** 215 636 0366

## CONTACTS

**Business & Commercial Litigation** .........................Brian J McMahon
**Corporate** ................................................................Frank T Cannone
**Criminal Defense** ..................................................Lawrence S Lustberg
**Employment Law** ...................................................Christine A Amalfe
**Financial Restructuring & Creditors' Rights** ...........Karen A Giannelli
**Government Affairs** ..................................................David J Pascrell
**Intellectual Property** .............................................David E De Lorenzi
**Products Liability** .........................................................Kim M Catullo
**Real Property & Environmental**..........................Russell B Bershad

**Real Property & Environmental:** Extensive Real Property Practice handling sales, purchases and development of all types of properties, including office buildings, industrial and flex buildings, retail centers, apartment buildings and hotels. Environmental Team is comprised of attorneys with both public and private sector experience who are capable of supporting clients' litigation, regulatory and transactional needs.

**INTERNATIONAL WORK:** Gibbons is the North American law firm member of the Geneva Group International/Lawspan, a network of independent professional service firms offering a full range of legal, accounting and other services worldwide.

# GREENBAUM ROWE SMITH & DAVIS LLP

## THE FIRM

**Managing Partner:** Paul A Rowe

**Number of partners:** 50
**Number of other lawyers:** 52

**FIRM OVERVIEW:** Greenbaum, Rowe, Smith & Davis LLP is recognized throughout New Jersey as one of its most respected and distinguished law firms. Established in 1914, the firm's tradition and reputation have been based upon an unfailing commitment to the highest professional standards and a keen personal interest in its clients. The firm's approach to practicing law is cutting edge with its talented attorneys possessing the knowledge and skills necessary to meet the sophisticated demands and challenges that the modern world places upon its clients.

## MAIN AREAS OF PRACTICE:

**Litigation:** The firm's Litigation Department is one of the largest and most comprehensive in New Jersey, providing a full complement of commercial and civil litigation services in a broad range of practice areas. The firm is distinguished in its ability to handle complex matters and manages some of the largest and most sophisticated business litigation in the State. The firm has a notable reputation for handling 'sensitive', high profile matters that include the defense of white collar criminal charges, matrimonial matters and professional malpractice.

**Corporate:** The firm's Corporate Department provides a broad range of general business representation necessary to respond to the diverse needs of today's demanding business climate. Its Corporate Practice encompasses all aspects of acquisitions, mergers and sales, initial formation of the business entity, business dissolutions, contract preparation and negotiation, state and federal securities law, general counseling and business planning, sophisticated estate and tax planning and dispute resolution.

**Real Estate:** The firm's Real Estate Department has been prominently associated with New Jersey's real estate development, financing and brokerage industries for many decades, and is one of the largest practices within the State. Appropriate to New Jersey, the firm has a Redevelopment Practice Group within the department. Representation includes all aspects of New Jersey real property law including acquisition and sales of residential and commercial real estate, registration of planned real estate developments, condominium and community association law, commercial leasing, construction and permanent financing, land use approvals, prerogative writ actions, environmental matters, condemnation and tax appeals.

**Tax, Trusts & Estates:** The firm's Tax, Trusts and Estates Department renders complete tax services for its commercial clients, which encompasses all phases of federal and state tax matters. The firm's attorneys practice in the areas of audits, appeals, tax planning and structuring for all business formats and transactions. The attorneys practice before all courts, including the New Jersey and United States Tax Courts. The firm also provides counseling in the areas of employee benefits and executive compensation. In addition to counseling corporate clients in their tax matters, its attorneys also provide services to individuals in their personal tax, trust and estate planning, estate administration, elder law concerns and business succession goals.

**CLIENTS:** The firm represents clients from major public corporations and Fortune 500 companies to established medium and small publicly- and privately-held businesses, as well as general and limited partnerships on both large and modest scales.

## HEAD OFFICE

**NEW JERSEY**
P.O. Box 5600, **Woodbridge**, NJ 07095
**Tel:** 732 549 5600   **Fax:** 732 549 1881
**Email:** info@greenbaumlaw.com
**Website:** www.greenbaumlaw.com

## BRANCH OFFICE

**NEW JERSEY**
6 Becker Farm Rd., **Roseland**, NJ 07068
**Tel:** 973 535 1600   **Fax:** 973 535 1698

## CONTACTS

| | |
|---|---|
| Litigation | Paul A Rowe |
| Corporate, M&A, Securities | Alan E Davis |
| Real Estate | Robert C Schachter |
| Tax, Trusts & Estates | Michael A Backer, Martin L Lepelstat |

# LERNER DAVID LITTENBERG KRUMHOLZ & MENTLIK, LLP

## THE FIRM

**Managing Partner:** William L Mentlik

**Number of Partners:** 21
**Number of other lawyers:** 40

## AREAS OF PRACTICE:

Intellectual Property . . . . . . . . . . . . . . . . . . . . . . . . . . . . . . . . . 100%

**FIRM OVERVIEW:** Established in 1969, Lerner David has focused exclusively on intellectual property law for more than 35 years. With over 60 lawyers, the firm's attorneys focus solely on patent, trademark, unfair competition and copyright litigation, patent, trademark, and copyright prosecution, trade secret matters, licensing, corporate advising on all facets, and other forms of intellectual property. The firm provides intellectual property advice based on asset growth as an integral part of the clients' business goals and strategies. Nearly all of Lerner David's attorneys hold a scientific or technical undergraduate degree and many have significant work experience in various areas of technology. Extending beyond the traditional claim-based attorney-client relationship, Lerner David serves clients as counselors, providing sound, practical advice to help them make intelligent choices about the legal and business benefits associated with intellectual property. This is a role they are proud to serve their clients. To learn more about how Lerner David can help your business, please visit www.ldlkm.com.

**MAIN AREAS OF PRACTICE:** Full service intellectual property law firm.

**CLIENTS:** Lerner David proudly represents clients both nationally and internationally. Their client base includes some of the leading corporations in the world in the areas of medical devices, pharmaceuticals, footwear and apparel manufacturers, biotechnology products, chemicals, electrical arts, retailers, computers, food and beverages, toys, marketing and advertising.

**INTERNATIONAL WORK:** Lerner David possesses exemplary skill and experience in protecting intellectual property assets throughout the world both by representing US corporations in foreign jurisdictions, and foreign corporations in the United States. Through this experience, Lerner David has achieved a breadth and depth of understanding respecting the coordination of the laws of many jurisdictions permitting effective representation across the spectrum of intellectual property. Consequently, the firm's clients have been able to greatly leverage their intellectual property assets through licensing and litigation on virtually every continent.

## HEAD OFFICE

**NEW JERSEY**
600 South Avenue West, **Westfield**, NJ 07090-1497
**Tel:** 908 654 5000   **Fax:** 908 654 7866
**Email:** rjaneczek@ldlkm.com
**Website:** www.ldlkm.com

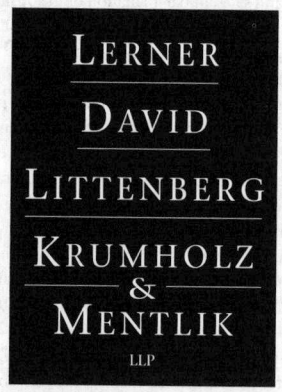

# LOWENSTEIN SANDLER PC

## THE FIRM

**Managing Partner:** Michael L Rodburg

**Number of partners:** 76
**Number of other lawyers:** 161

**FIRM OVERVIEW:** Lowenstein Sandler is a nationally recognized law firm with more than 235 attorneys who provide a full range of legal services to the corporate, financial, industrial and governmental communities. Ranked among the Am Law 200 largest law firms in the nation, the firm assists clients ranging from small public and privately held companies to Fortune 500 corporations in a variety of sophisticated business and legal issues. Additionally, Lowenstein Sandler ranked number 20 in the 2005 'Top100 Law Firms for Diversity' by Multicultural Law magazine, and is well-known for its commitment to pro bono service and use of technology. The firm's main areas of practice include corporate, business litigation, bankruptcy, employment, environmental, insurance, real estate, technology, trusts and estates, and white collar criminal defense. One of Lowenstein Sandler's recent achievements was its successful bid to represent the creditors committee in the $1.6 billion bankruptcy filing of Kansas City-based Interstate Bakeries, the manufacturer of Twinkies and Wonder Bread. Lowenstein Sandler's subsidiary, Issues Management, is consistently ranked as the number one lawyer-lobbying consulting firm in New Jersey.

## MAIN AREAS OF PRACTICE:

**Corporate:** Lowenstein Sandler has extensive experience in corporate counseling and transactional work, as well as business reorganizations. The Corporate Department provides a full range of services to clients in connection with: organization and structuring of business entities; initial public offerings and subsequent offerings; general business counseling; mergers and acquisitions; financing transactions; and investment management. Lowenstein Sandler also provides a full range of tax services to the business community, as well as tax and estate planning for individuals.

**Business Litigation:** The firm's Litigation Department represents clients in all stages of litigation (both trial and appellate) in both state and federal courts, as well as before administrative and governmental agencies. Lowenstein Sandler is the law firm of choice for out-of-state clients embroiled in complex litigation in New Jersey and has developed several prominent, nationally recognized niche practices in areas such as environmental litigation and toxic tort defense, insurance coverage litigation, securities litigation, and white collar criminal defense.

**Bankruptcy, Financial Reorganization and Creditors' Rights:** Lowenstein Sandler's Bankruptcy, Financial Reorganization and Creditors' Rights Practice Group has extensive experience representing debtors, trustees, secured and unsecured creditors, and investors in high-profile Chapter 11 reorganizations, out-of-court workouts, financial restructurings, and litigation. The group also frequently provides bankruptcy advice on corporate and structured finance matters, and on the acquisition of assets out of bankruptcy.

**Employment:** With attorneys drawn from the corporate, securities, litigation, tax, insurance, and environmental practices, Lowenstein Sandler's Employment Law Practice Group counsels clients on a wide range of matters including managing workplace risks, compliance and documentation, and corporate transactions. The firm's ability to assist in strategic planning and follow-through affords clients the benefit of dealing with human resource and benefits issues as part of their overall integrated business plans.

**Environmental:** Lowenstein Sandler's Environmental Department assists clients with virtually every type of lawsuit involving environmental matters in federal and state courts throughout the country. The firm counsels clients on a variety of matters including compliance and auditing; acquisitions and divestitures; site remediation; natural resource damages; toxic tort cases; occupational health and safety; and insurance coverage.

### HEAD OFFICE

**NEW JERSEY**
65 Livingston Avenue, **Roseland** NJ 07068
**Tel:** 973 597 2500   **Fax:** 973 597 2400
**Website:** www.lowenstein.com

### BRANCH OFFICES

**NEW YORK**
1251 Avenue of the Americas, **New York** NY 10020
**Tel:** 212 262 6700   **Fax:** 212 262 7402

**NEW JERSEY**
Post Office Plaza, Suite 504, 50 Division Street, **Somerville** NJ 08876
**Tel:** 908 526 3300   **Fax:** 908 725 5124

**Insurance:** Lowenstein Sandler is one of a handful of nationally known firms who pioneered the development of insurance coverage litigation. The Insurance Law Practice Group has litigated coverage cases in more than 20 states, has appeared for the policyholder in more than 30 reported decisions, and has collected more than $500 million in settlements and judgments.

**Real Estate & Real Estate Finance:** Lowenstein Sandler's Real Estate and Real Estate Finance Group assists a wide range of clients in all phases of real estate transactions, including acquisitions, financings, leasing, construction, land use planning and environmental issues, as well as tax counseling and litigation. The firm also boasts an experienced mortgage banking practice that represents various participants in the primary and secondary mortgage markets in all aspects of the acquisition, disposition, financing and securitization of loans secured by real property.

**Technology, IP & Venture Capital:** The Tech Group at Lowenstein Sandler counsels technology-driven businesses and their investors at all stages of growth and has earned a reputation for excellence in venture capital and other financing transactions. The group has closed hundreds of private company financing transactions including angel rounds, complex venture financings, bridge fundings and IPOs. Members of the Tech Group also include intellectual property attorneys, registered patent lawyers and practitioners who counsel clients on matters pertaining to intellectual property, technology and privacy law.

**Trusts & Estates:** Lowenstein Sandler's Trusts & Estates Practice Group helps clients preserve and pass on their families' wealth, while minimizing taxes and assisting fiduciaries in fulfilling their duties. The group's attorneys are skilled in fiduciary litigation, business counseling, and domestic and international business tax planning, all of which enhance both its planning and administration practices.

**White Collar Criminal Defense:** Lowenstein Sandler's White Collar Criminal Defense Practice Group has decades of experience defending corporate and individual clients in state and federal prosecutions, as well as conducting internal investigations for private and public corporations. The group regularly defends clients in all phases of criminal proceedings, including grand jury investigations, trials and appeals.

**LOWENSTEIN SANDLER** PC
*Attorneys at Law*

*www.lowenstein.com*

# LUM, DANZIS, DRASCO & POSITAN LLC

## THE FIRM

**Managing Director:** Wayne J Positan

**Number of attorneys:** 30
**Number of firm members:** 16

**FIRM OVERVIEW:** The firm traces its roots back to 1870. Throughout its history, the firm has remained focused on the dynamic needs of the business community in New Jersey, and those doing business or engaged in litigation in New Jersey. The firm is regularly employed by corporate counsel or through national and international law firms to represent businesses and individuals in labor and employment, litigation, and general business counseling matters.

## MAIN AREAS OF PRACTICE:

**Labor & Employment:** The firm represents management and defendants in employment litigation; discrimination litigation; non-competition disputes; traditional labor law, including collective bargaining negotiations, arbitration and NLRB practice, administrative law; appellate practice; human resources counseling and training; and ADR/mediation processes.

**Litigation:** The firm represents a broad range of clients in the areas of commercial litigation, construction law, condemnation, life and health insurance law, professional liability litigation, environmental and toxic tort law, personal injury litigation, arbitration, mediation, and appellate practice.

**Business Law:** The firm assists clients in the areas of finance, taxation, mergers and acquisitions, banking, estate planning, estate and trust administration, real property, zoning, loan workouts, and other commercial transactions.

**Mediation:** The firm has eight members who are New Jersey Court Approved Mediators. It has successfully mediated matters in a variety of areas, including employment matters, commercial disputes and internal entity disputes. For example, Wayne Positan successfully mediated a discrimination matter which had resulted in a seven-million dollar award against a UK company through voluntary mediation while the matter was on appeal.

**CLIENTS:** The firm represents a variety of clients from closely held corporations to Fortune 500 companies, as well as public entities, such as the State of New Jersey, various county governments, and individuals. Recent matters have included settlement of the largest wage and hour case in the history of the NJ Department of Labor representing Pepsi Bottling Group; resolution of two major design defect cases involving condominium construction in Atlantic City and Jersey City; NJ Supreme Court decisions on anti-harassment law and administrative law; handling condemnation aspects of redevelopment projects, and direct representation of the New Jersey Attorney General in employment discrimination litigation. The firm has also negotiated collective bargaining agreements in the areas of compressed gas and dry ice distribution, warehousing, moving, manufacturing, and car processing at the port, among others. The firm was also involved in a number of major non-competition litigated matters involving payroll/software; pharmaceuticals; placement/temporary staffing; and telecommunications businesses.

## HEAD OFFICE

**NEW JERSEY**
103 Eisenhower Parkway, **Roseland** NJ 07068-1049
**Tel:** 973 403 9000  **Fax:** 973 403 9021
**Email:** wpositan@lumlaw.com
**Website:** www.lumlaw.com

## BRANCH OFFICE

**NEW YORK**
325 Broadway, **New York** NY 10007
**Tel:** 212 775 9002

## CONTACTS

Administrative Law ................................................Richard A West
Banking Law ...............................................Edward R McMahon
Business Law ......................................................Philip Chapman
Condemnation Law ..............................................Dennis J Drasco
Commercial Litigation ..........................................Dennis J Drasco
Construction Litigation...........................................Paul A Sandars
Employment Law.................................................Wayne J Positan
................................................................................Richard A West
Estate Planning ...................................................Kevin F Murphy
HR Counseling/Training ...................................Christina Silva Lee
Labor Law .........................................................Wayne J Positan
................................................................................Anthony R Sica
Life & Health Insurance Law ...............................Kevin J O'Connor
Mediation...........................................................Wayne J Positan
................................................................................Dennis J Drasco
................................................................................Paul A Sandars
................................................................................Edward R McMahon
Non-Compete Disputes .......................................Wayne J Positan
................................................................................Richard A West
Professional Liability ...............................................Jane S Kelsey
Tax Appeals ...................................................Steven J Eisenstein

# McELROY, DEUTSCH, MULVANEY & CARPENTER LLP

## THE FIRM

**Managing Partner:** Edward B Deutsch
**Number of partners:** 69
**Number of other lawyers:** 146

**FIRM OVERVIEW:** In May 2004, a major new law firm, McElroy, Deutsch, Mulvaney & Carpenter, LLP, came into being. MDM&C is a combination of McElroy, Deutsch & Mulvaney, LLP, one of New Jersey's fastest-growing law firms, with Carpenter, Bennett & Morrissey, one of New Jersey's oldest and most respected law firms. The two firms share many cultural values and ethical standards and have a well developed philosophy of placing the client first. MDM&C takes advantage of the talents and strengths of both firms to produce a unique legal and business synergy to create a result greater than the sum of their individual strengths and capabilities. Together they form a legal powerhouse – one of the largest firms in New Jersey, with over 200 lawyers and five offices in three states. The firm offers a full range of legal services, and its attorneys have significant trial experience in both state and federal courts and substantial appellate experience.

## MAIN AREAS OF PRACTICE:

**Litigation:** MDM&C's Litigation Practice includes both trial and appellate work in the following areas: commercial disputes and business torts, insurance defense, insurance coverage, environmental, fidelity and surety, product liability and toxic tort, malpractice, errors and omissions, directors and officers, construction, private and public contract disputes, workers' compensation, labor and employment, trade regulation, antitrust, intellectual property, franchise, real estate, banking, pension, probate, and white-collar criminal defense. Although the firm is pleased to be recognized nationally for its efforts in complex litigation, it is also equipped to handle smaller litigated matters with equal efficiency and zeal. The firm's collective experience has consistently allowed it to develop winning case strategies both in and out of the courtroom.

**Labor & Employment:** MDM&C lawyers defend employers against discrimination, retaliation and other claims arising out of the employment relationship. Its cases range from nationwide class actions to single plaintiff suits, and often include novel constitutional, statutory, and public policy issues, and encompass federal, state and administrative forums. Clients regularly seek advice to minimize the risk of litigation and to assist in compliance with the various employment statutes and regulations. Employers turn to MDM&C for representation in labor contract disputes, arbitration, picketing, strikes, organizing campaigns, plant closings, and reductions in force. Clients employ the firm as principal spokespersons in collective bargaining negotiations – or to act as behind-the-scenes legal and tactical advisors. The firm's labor attorneys also represent employers in unfair practice proceedings before the National Labor Relations Board and the New Jersey Public Employee Relations Commission.

**Insurance:** MDM&C's comprehensive service to the insurance industry involves both corporate and regulatory matters. It represents insurers and reinsurers in the property, casualty, life, and health insurance areas. The firm's lawyers frequently address issues of policy drafting, insurance practices, policy interpretation, claims administration, and government regulations. The firm has also counseled insurers and reinsurers on mergers and acquisitions, startups, captive companies, licensing, regulatory compliance, and product development. The talents and experience of the lawyers at MDM&C have attracted the attention of an array of the world's largest insurance companies.

**Fidelity & Surety:** The firm enjoys an excellent nationwide reputation in the handling of all aspects of fidelity, surety, and related reinsurance matters. It has represented and counseled surety companies in handling some of the industry's largest bonded contractor defaults. The firm has negotiated and implemented financing agreements, inter-creditor arrangements, tender arrangements, takeover agreements, and replacement contractor performance agreements. It has procured replacement contractors with the assistance of consultants through competitive bidding and negotiations. The firm has regularly participated in

## HEAD OFFICE

**NEW JERSEY**
1300 Mount Kemble Avenue, PO Box 2075, **Morristown**, NJ 07962-2075
**Tel:** 973 993 8100  **Fax:** 973 425 0161
**Email:** info@mdmc-law.com
**Website:** www.mdmc-law.com

## BRANCH OFFICE

**COLORADO**
Mile High Center, 1700 Broadway, Suite 1900, **Denver**, CO 80290-1901
**Tel:** 303 293 8800  **Fax:** 303 839 0036

**NEW JERSEY**
Three Gateway Center, 100 Mulberry Street, **Newark**, NJ 07102-4079
**Tel:** 973 622 7711  **Fax:** 973 622 5314

40 West Ridgewood Avenue, **Ridgewood**, NJ 07450
**Tel:** 201 445 6722  **Fax:** 201 445 5376

**NEW YORK**
88 Pine Street, 24th Floor, **New York**, NY 10005
**Tel:** 212 483 9490  **Fax:** 212 483 9129

## CONTACTS

| | |
|---|---|
| Litigation | Edward B Deutsch |
| Labor & Employment | Francis X Dee |
| Insurance | Edward J DePascale |
| | Anthony M Carlino |
| Fidelity & Surety | James M Mulvaney |
| Corporate | Joseph P LaSala |

bankruptcy proceedings and adversary proceedings arising from debtor transactions, and has structured, on behalf of its surety clients, pre-packaged bankruptcy arrangements involving debtor contractors. The firm has prosecuted and defended complex construction claims for its surety clients.

**Corporate:** The firm's corporate lawyers counsel its business clients in all the traditional areas of corporate practice. The firm prepares and negotiates commercial contracts, including buy-sell agreements, shareholder agreements, employee agreements, intellectual property contracts, as well as many other transactional matters. The firm has extensive experience in the areas of the organization, purchase, sale, and merger of businesses, including leveraged buyouts. In addition, the firm has counseled clients on joint ventures, including the formation of an off-shore captive insurance company. The firm's business clients cover the entire spectrum of industry, ranging from entrepreneurial start-up businesses to large publicly-held and privately-held companies and banks. The firm regularly provides strategic advice and practical solutions on the planning, organization, recapitalization, and restructuring of new or existing businesses, guiding its clients through the applicable legal landscape, assuring compliance with laws and regulations, and assuming responsibility for managing all issues in connection with the undertaking – all with the aim of best meeting clients' business objectives.

**INTERNATIONAL WORK:** The firm's international practice in representing both domestic and international corporations is significant and growing. The firm's knowledge of international law directly benefits clients seeking advice on: joint ventures; mergers and acquisitions and other globally-strategic alliances; lending/structured finance; labor; environmental, regulatory compliance, auditing, and site remediation; aircraft financing and leasing; ship financing and leasing; distribution – dealership arrangements; and automotive and hotel representation.

*McElroy, Deutsch, Mulvaney & Carpenter,* LLP

ATTORNEYS AT LAW

# PITNEY HARDIN LLP

## THE FIRM

**Managing Partner:** Dennis R LaFiura, Esq

**Number of partners:** 61
**Number of other lawyers:** 111

**FIRM OVERVIEW:** Founded in 1902, Pitney Hardin is a full-service firm with offices in Morristown (New Jersey) and New York City. The firm is the exclusive member firm for New Jersey of Lex Mundi, the world's leading association of independent law firms.

## MAIN AREAS OF PRACTICE:

**Litigation:** Clients have built Pitney Hardin's Litigation Practice into a national powerhouse by entrusting the firm's top litigators with their most challenging cases including those involving commercial contracts, toxic torts, products liability, white collar crime defense, and employee-related suits.

**Labor & Employment:** Pitney Hardin provides clients with services that cover every aspect of the labor and employment relationship, including: counseling and training; strategic planning to help them optimize opportunities in connection with mergers and other business change; representation in the litigation, negotiation, and arbitration/ADR of employment disputes; and counsel with respect to wage and hour compliance, union labor relations, and workplace safety and health (OSHA).

**Employee Benefits & Executive Compensation:** Intricate laws govern benefits and compensation plans. By leveraging in-depth knowledge of them—and of the tax and securities issues often involved—the firm helps each client structure, fund, and administer their plans in ways ideally suited to their situation and goals.

**Mergers & Acquisitions:** With a full scope of expertise, including in SEC compliance, tax, employee benefits, and environmental law, the Mergers and Acquisitions Group helps ensure the success of clients' transactions. Of the 30 largest M&A transactions announced in 2005 that involved a New Jersey-based target or acquiror, Pitney Hardin represented principals in two of the largest, both billion-dollar-plus deals. The firm was the only New Jersey-based law firm to have done deals of that magnitude.

**Corporate & Securities:** The firm's corporate and securities lawyers guide public company clients through SEC compliance issues, and help to ensure the smooth execution of their corporate financing strategies.

**Bankruptcy & Workouts:** The practice focuses on all facets of bankruptcy practice/creditors' rights and related commercial litigation, including post-petition financing and cash collateral matters, plan negotiation and confirmation issues, asset sales, representation of creditors' committees and Chapter 11 trustees, and negotiating and drafting commercial loan documents, including those related to asset-based transactions. Pitney Hardin has represented clients in many out-of-court restructurings and Chapter 11 proceedings.

**Banking:** The firm represents financial institutions in all types of credit transactions, from uncomplicated secured commercial loans to multi-million-dollar syndicated facilities. In addition, Pitney Hardin advises clients about their risks and rights under the myriad of laws and regulations that govern their operations.

**Intellectual Property & Technology:** The firm provides a full range of services including prosecution of patents, trademarks, and copyrights and litigation encompassing all aspects of IP law involving patents, trademarks, copyrights, marketing law, technology, and transactions.

**Real Estate:** Pitney Hardin's attorneys structure acquisitions, sales, exchanges, and leases of real property with keen attention to tax implications, environmental issues, and land use and planning considerations.

**Environmental:** Pitney Hardin was among the first law firms in the United States to establish a practice to serve the comprehensive environmental needs of its clients. Today, the firm's Environmental Group represents clients nationwide.

**Trusts & Estates:** Pitney Hardin's Trusts and Estates Group provides expert personalized advice and assistance to clients in implementing estate plans, establishing trusts, and administering estates and trusts.

## HEAD OFFICE

**NEW JERSEY**
200 Campus Drive, **Florham Park**, NJ 07932 (Deliveries)
PO Box 1945, **Morristown**, NJ 07962-1945 (Mail)
**Tel:** 973 966 6300  **Fax:** 973 966 1015
**Email:** info@pitneyhardin.com
**Website:** www.pitneyhardin.com

## BRANCH OFFICE

**NEW YORK**
7 Times Square, **New York**, NY 10036-7311
**Tel:** 212 297 5800  **Fax:** 212 916 2940

## CONTACTS

| | |
|---|---|
| Litigation | Anthony J Marchetta, Esq |
| | Elizabeth J Sher, Esq |
| Labor & Employment | Patrick J McCarthy, Esq |
| | Gregory C Parliman, Esq |
| Employee Benefits & Executive Compensation | Kathy A Lawler, Esq |
| Mergers & Acquisitions | Warren J Casey, Esq |
| | Ronald H Janis, Esq |
| Corporate & Securities | Warren J Casey, Esq |
| Bankruptcy & Workouts | Peter A Forgosh, Esq |
| Banking | Peter A Forgosh, Esq |
| Intellectual Property & Technology | Gerald E Levy, Esq |
| Real Estate | Colleen R Donovan, Esq |
| | Glenn C Geiger, Esq |
| Environmental | Gail H Allyn, Esq |
| Trusts & Estates | Richard Kahn, Esq |
| Tax | Michael J Guerriero, Esq |
| Franchise Law | Dennis R LaFiura, Esq |

**Tax:** In practical and cost-effective ways, Pitney Hardin helps clients solve tax issues and controversies. The firm's expertise covers a full spectrum of complex federal, state, and local tax matters involving choice of entity, structures for transactions, taxable and tax-free re-organizations, and specialized tax incentives, credits and deferrals.

**Franchise Law:** Pitney Hardin has represented national franchisors in hundreds of disputes involving terminations, trademark infringement, and enforcing system standards, and the firm's efforts have resulted in scores of written opinions upholding forum selection provisions, enforcing liquidated damages, enjoining infringement, and defeating fraud claims.

**CLIENTS:** Clients in a wide range of industries including Alpharma Inc., Cendant Corporation, CIT Group, Inc., Dendrite International, Inc., Hunter Douglas, Inc., JA Apparel Corp., The LEGO Group A/S, New Jersey Resources Corp., Ryan Beck & Co., Inc., Schering-Plough Corporation, The Talbots Inc., United Parcel Service, Inc., and W.R. Grace & Co.

# PORZIO, BROMBERG & NEWMAN, P.C.

## THE FIRM

**Managing Partner:** D Jeffrey Campbell

**Number of partners:** 27
**Number of other lawyers:** 55

**FIRM OVERVIEW:** Since its founding in the early 1960s, Porzio, Bromberg & Newman has steadily built on its founders' strengths as litigators and trial attorneys, expanding its range of services to support its clients' evolving needs. As the firm continues to expand and diversify its portfolio of services, its singular devotion to serving the best interests of its clients creates the energy and passion that form the foundation for its growth.

## MAIN AREAS OF PRACTICE:

**Bankruptcy & Financial Restructuring:** Porzio specializes in providing legal counsel to troubled companies, boards of directors, creditors, lenders, investors and other stakeholders with a financial interest in a distressed business or its assets.

**Business Disputes & Counseling:** The firm litigates disputes arising under the Uniform Commercial Code, securities statutes, intellectual property laws, Internet legislation, and many other federal and state statutes and regulations that affect business and commerce.

**Corporate Law/Mergers & Acquisitions/Securities Law:** Attorneys in Porzio's Corporate Department are experienced legal and business advisors, who offer valuable insight into what it takes to establish, run and grow a company. The firm's mergers and acquisitions team is committed to helping clients implement successful business strategies and providing advice that is focused on achieving client goals. The firm's attorneys have handled the acquisition of numerous companies while working as both outside lawyers and in-house counsel. Porzio's securities lawyers offer practical advice to expedite the efficient completion of transactions and counsel clients on how to avoid unnecessary disclosure problems and compliance roadblocks.

**Dispute Resolution:** The Dispute Resolution Department is comprised of highly respected and experienced former judges, who are skilled at providing third-party services in the resolution of complex legal matters. The team includes former New Jersey Supreme Court Justice James H Coleman, Jr, former Appellate Division Judge Robert Muir, Jr, former Essex County Assignment Judge Alvin Weiss and former Trial Court Judge John M Newman.

**Employment & Labor:** Porzio's Employment and Labor Department has over 25 years experience representing corporate and public sector clients, including Fortune 500 companies such as Wyeth and Pfizer, and smaller entities such as NSI Software and Fabcon, Inc. The firm counsels clients on the effective avoidance of employment-related claims and provides early recommendations on which cases to defend vigorously and which cases to settle.

**Environmental Law & Litigation:** Porzio's environmental lawyers focus on matters of environmental compliance, permitting, property and Brownfields development, OSHA issues, property transfer litigation, defense and settlement of environmental violations, and environmental issues that arise in the context of commercial and industrial transactions.

**Governmental Affairs:** The Governmental Affairs Department assists clients with legislative and regulatory matters pending in Trenton, NJ and Washington, DC. On behalf of clients, the firm raises critical issues with regulators and legislators on a wide-range of industry-specific matters.

**Insurance Coverage Law:** Porzio's Insurance Coverage Department handles matters involving complex insurance claims. Porzio's experience includes claims for environmental clean-up, property and business income losses, product coverage, errors and omissions, employment matters and more.

## HEAD OFFICE

**NEW JERSEY**
100 Southgate Parkway, **Morristown** NJ 07962-1997
**Tel:** 973 538 4006  **Fax:** 973 538 5146
**Website:** www.pbnlaw.com

## BRANCH OFFICES

**NEW JERSEY**
263 Drum Point Road, **Brick** NJ 08723-6399
**Tel:** 732 262 9248  **Fax:** 732 262 9267

**NEW YORK**
156 West 56th Street, **New York** NY 10019-3800
**Tel:** 212 265 6888  **Fax:** 212 957 3983

**Intellectual Property:** This team's work includes copyright and trademark infringement, royalty agreements and licensing, trademark and copyright clearance, regulation and enforcement, telecom initial applications and tariff filings, trade secrets, arts and entertainment, new media, unfair competition, computers and high technology.

**Land Use, Real Estate & Construction Law:** Attorneys in Porzio's Land Use, Real Estate and Construction Department help clients navigate through the maze of required governmental approvals related to local, state and federal land use requirements and environmental restrictions, as well as represent their interests in complex commercial development matters. The firm's clients include buyers and sellers, real property developers, public and private owners, contractors, subcontractors, suppliers, construction managers and design professionals.

**Pharmaceutical & Medical Device:** Porzio has a long history of representing pharmaceutical and medical device manufacturers, from global drug makers to small specialty equipment companies, in complex product liability cases. More recently, the firm has gained recognition as the nation's premier law firm in the areas of state sample distribution laws, PDMA compliance and managing risk associated with state marketing disclosure and prohibition laws.

**Product Liability & Mass Tort:** For more than 25 years, Porzio has received national, regional and state-wide recognition for representing major corporations as coordinating and/or trial counsel in numerous product liability, toxic tort and mass tort litigations.

**Transportation & Motor Carrier:** Attorneys in Porzio's Transportation and Motor Carrier Department are widely recognized as trucking company counsel in New Jersey and New York, and are highly visible in the industry's legal defense. The firm regularly manages the full range of practical, safety, risk management, investigation, claims, insurance and litigation issues surrounding truck accidents.

PORZIO
BROMBERG & NEWMAN P.C.
ATTORNEYS AT LAW

# RIKER DANZIG SCHERER HYLAND & PERRETTI LLP

## THE FIRM

**Managing Partner:** Glenn A Clark

**Number of partners:** 47
**Number of other attorneys:** 116

**FIRM OVERVIEW:** Riker Danzig Scherer Hyland and Perretti LLP is proud to have served the New Jersey business community for over 120 years. Riker Danzig has earned a national reputation as being the firm to go to in New Jersey for practical, innovative and cost-effective legal solutions. The reputation of the firm and its lawyers provides inherent credibility in the capital markets, courts, and government hallways of New Jersey. Among the firm's attorneys and alumni are many distinguished New Jersey leaders, including former US Congressman and Ambassador to Panama William J Hughes, former New Jersey Attorneys General William F Hyland, Peter N Perretti, Jr, and Peter C Harvey, former New Jersey Supreme Court Justices Sidney M Schreiber and Stewart G Pollock, former New Jersey Commissioner of Transportation John P Sheridan, Jr, and former Chairman of the New Jersey State Bar Examiners Edward A Zunz, as well as federal and state judges.

## MAIN AREAS OF PRACTICE:

**Litigation:** Riker Danzig's seasoned trial and appellate attorneys, numbering over 100 strong, have earned the firm a national reputation as zealous courtroom advocates. The group litigates complex civil cases, and is a leader in banking, securities arbitrations, fraud claims and class actions, insurance, reinsurance (national and international), product liability, construction and intellectual property litigation. The firm also has active school law and family law practices.

**Real Estate:** Riker Danzig's Real Estate Practice includes all aspects of real estate law, transactions and litigation, including substantial property acquisitions, complex sales and exchanges, sale-leasebacks and build-to-suits, commercial, retail and industrial leasing, joint-venture projects, zoning and planning, mortgage lending and financing, construction contracts, title litigation and real property tax appeals.

**Employment:** The employment law attorneys at Riker Danzig counsel clients on various issues, including employee relations, wage and hour and contract issues. They also defend management in federal and state courts in New Jersey and elsewhere on all employment related claims, including discrimination, wrongful termination, whistleblower, restrictive covenants, unfair competition and employee fidelity bonds. They also conduct internal investigations.

**Corporate:** A diverse client base seeks counsel and solutions from Riker Danzig's corporate attorneys, from start-up entrepreneurial enterprises to established public companies. The group counsels clients in the full spectrum of corporate matters, including mergers, acquisitions and divestitures, corporate finance, technology licensing, international transactions, regulatory matters, and logistics and distribution, as well as the issues unique to non-profit and tax-exempt corporations.

**Environmental:** In a state noted for its strict and pace-setting environmental legislation, Riker Danzig's Environmental Group is among the largest and most diverse practices of its kind. The experienced environmental lawyers have in-depth knowledge of federal, state and local law. The firm handles litigation, regulatory, permitting and counseling, and real estate development matters addressing all environmental areas, including hazardous substances, air, water and noise pollution, and solid waste.

**Insurance:** Riker Danzig's Insurance Group draws on the combined resources of experienced litigators, governmental affairs attorneys and corporate attorneys to bring comprehensive understanding to matters on behalf of the insurance industry. They represent their clients in a variety of insurance matters, including coverage, reinsurance, bad faith litigation, insurance defense, insolvencies, intermediary and agency disputes and legislative and regulatory matters.

## HEAD OFFICE

**NEW JERSEY**
Headquarters Plaza, One Speedwell Avenue, **Morristown**, NJ 07962-1981
**Tel:** 973 538 0800   **Fax:** 973 538 1984
**Email:** info@riker.com
**Website:** www.riker.com

## BRANCH OFFICES

**NEW JERSEY**
50 West State Street, Suite 1010, **Trenton**, NJ 08608-1220
**Tel:** 609 396 2121   **Fax:** 609 396 4578

**NEW YORK**
500 Fifth Avenue, Suite 4920, **New York**, NY 10110
**Tel:** 212 302 6574   **Fax:** 212 302 6628

## CONTACTS

| | |
|---|---|
| Litigation | Gerald A Liloia |
| Real Estate | Victoria A Morrison |
| Employment | Michael K Furey |
| Corporate | Andrew J Stamelman |
| Insurance | Shawn L Kelly |
| Environmental | Dennis J Krumholz |

**CLIENTS:** American Centennial Insurance Co., AT&T, AXA Versicherungs AG, Bank of America, Carrier Clinic, Central Garden & Pet Co., CIGNA Corp., Crum & Forster Corp., Ecko.Complex, L.L.C., Gerling Global Reinsurance Corporation of America, Harleysville Insurance Co., The Hertz Corp., Hoechst Corp., IBM, Johnson & Johnson, JPMorgan Chase, Lucent Technologies, Inc., McNeil Pharmaceuticals, Merrill Lynch, National Starch and Chemical Co., New Jersey Bankers Association, Prudential Insurance Company of America, R.J. Reynolds Tobacco Co., Schering-Plough, UBS, Unilever Ltd., Wachovia Bank, N.A., Wakefern Food Corp., Wal-Mart Stores, Inc.

**INTERNATIONAL WORK:** Riker Danzig handles the needs of its clients around the world. In the area of reinsurance, for example, Riker Danzig has been successful in arbitrating and litigating reinsurance claims worldwide. In one case in which the firm represented Gerling Global Reinsurance Corporation of America and other insurance companies, the United States Supreme Court struck down a California law intended to force European insurers to disclose detailed information regarding all policies sold in Europe before and during the Second World War.

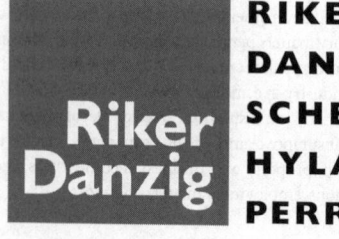

**RIKER**
**DANZIG**
**SCHERER**
**HYLAND**
**PERRETTI** LLP

# SILLS CUMMIS EPSTEIN & GROSS P.C.

## THE FIRM

**Managing Partner:** Steven E Gross
**Number of Partners:** 65
**Number of other lawyers:** 100

**FIRM OVERVIEW:** Sills Cummis Epstein & Gross P.C., a full-service law firm, has developed an outstanding reputation for excellence and service on both a national and international level. Nationally, the firm's attorneys are known for successfully handling precedent-setting issues for clients, ranging from Fortune 500 to emerging growth, in corporate transactions, complex litigation/class actions, real estate, employment and labor, healthcare and regulatory work. On an international level, the firm is frequently called upon and has been focusing on cross-border transactions with foreign-based public and private companies doing business in the United States. The firm's work is diversified among industries such as banking and finance, pharmaceutical/medical device, retail and commercial real estate, healthcare, life sciences, manufacturing and technology.

## MAIN AREAS OF PRACTICE:

**Complex Litigation/Class Action Defense:** The Litigation Practice Group has a broad spectrum of expertise reflecting the diversity of its clients. Working in tandem with its transactional attorneys, the firm's litigators regularly assist companies in the litigation of business matters such as commercial transactions, securities, contracts, technology, intellectual property, banking, construction, toxic torts, real estate, insurance, administrative law, antitrust, healthcare, employment, unfair competition, public contracting, environmental cleanup and compliance, and business crimes.

**Corporate Internal Investigations & Business Crimes:** Drawing from backgrounds that include a former Justice of the New Jersey Supreme Court, several former Assistant United States attorneys, former Justice Department attorneys and former Internal Revenue Service attorneys, the firm's principal areas of expertise include federal grand jury investigations, United States Attorney's Office investigations, criminal IRS investigations, securities fraud investigations, criminal antitrust investigations, government contracting fraud, bank fraud, political corruption, criminal environmental investigations, States of New York and New Jersey tax investigations and state grand jury investigations.

**Corporate/M&A:** Mergers and acquisitions account for a large part of the firm's transactional practice. Its M&A attorneys handle complex strategic alliances, negotiated and contested acquisitions and mergers, divestitures, proxy contests, tender offers, joint ventures, managed sale auctions, corporate partnering relationships and leveraged buyouts. The firm represents buyers, sellers, investors, shareholder groups, boards of directors, special committees of boards and financial advisors in structuring, negotiating and consummating complex domestic and international business combinations and other commercial transactions.

**Employment & Labor:** The firm has one of the largest employment and labor practices in a full-service firm in the metropolitan region and is counsel to some of the region's largest employers. Its attorneys counsel and litigate matters relating to age, gender, pregnancy, family leave, whistle-blowing, equal pay, collective bargaining and unfair labor practice charges to name a few. The firm also provides diversity and other training and drafts employee handbooks, employment agreements and human resources policies for employers. Its attorneys have developed working relations with officials of many labor organizations throughout the country.

**Healthcare:** The firm's Health and Hospital Law Practice Group represents hospitals, nursing homes, medical groups, independent practice associations, physicians and other healthcare professionals, and management companies, among others, in a broad range of matters. The group's experience includes mergers and acquisitions, joint ventures and affiliations, compliance programs, financings, state and federal regulatory compliance issues, Medicare and Medicaid reimbursement issues, government investigations, administrative and civil litigation, managed care and commercial contracting, employment counseling and litigation, licensure issues and non-profit organization issues.

### HEAD OFFICE

**NEW JERSEY**
The Legal Center, One Riverfront Plaza, **Newark**, NJ 07102
**Tel:** 973 643 7000   **Fax:** 973 643 6500
**Email:** sillsmail@sillscummis.com
**Website:** www.sillscummis.com

### BRANCH OFFICES

**NEW YORK**
30 Rockefeller Plaza, **New York**, NY 10112
**Tel:** 212 643 7000   **Fax:** 212 643 6500

**Intellectual Property:** The firm offers a wide range of integrated services designed to help its clients protect and exploit their valuable intellectual property. The firm's Intellectual Property Practice Group is experienced in patents, trademarks and copyrights; litigation and dispute resolution; FDA, FTC, ITC practice and proceedings; opinions; licensing and other transactions; IP due diligence; unfair trade practices; software development and outsourcing transactions; trade secrets; IP portfolio analysis; strategic IP planning; and trademark portfolio management.

**Life Sciences:** The firm has become a major player in the life sciences industry, handling complex transactions on a national and international platform. Given the complexities of these transactions, the firm's interdisciplinary team provides a full range of legal services focusing on all aspects of these transactions, including mergers and acquisitions; public and private financing; strategic alliances, collaborations and joint ventures; research and development; technology transfers; licensing, development, supply and distribution arrangements; intellectual property; regulatory matters; corporate governance; national and international corporate counseling; and litigation.

**Pharmaceutical/Medical Device:** For the last two decades, the firm has represented pharmaceutical companies and medical device companies in transactional matters, as well as acting as national, regional and special counsel in thousands of cases involving allegations of product liability. The firm has represented clients in acquisitions of medical device companies involving cardiovascular systems and other instrumentation in transactions throughout the United States. The firm has the distinction of trying the first pharmaceutical Lanham Act case in which false and misleading advertising was ordered corrected in medical journals. The Pharmaceutical/Medical Device Litigation Team has defended manufacturers in both individual and class actions alleging personal injury, property damage or economic loss.

**Product Liability:** Sills Cummis has earned a reputation as a 'go-to' firm for complex product liability cases and mass tort litigation. The firm's Product Liability Practice Group includes a number of related areas, including toxic tort, mass tort liability, mechanical and scientific-based litigation, catastrophic injury, environmental and federal multi-district litigation. Engagements have included national, regional and local counsel handling virtually all details of individual cases to counseling on strategic issues for thousands of cases.

**Real Estate:** Sills Cummis provides a full range of legal and related services to participants in all aspects of the real estate industry on a national level. The Real Estate Practice Group is segmented into various disciplines: landlord representation (with subspecialties in all elements of retail and non-retail leasing); tenant representation (retail and non-retail); acquisitions, development and investment; zoning and land use; conventional and capital markets financing (including securitized and mezzanine financings); and construction.

**Sills Cummis Epstein & Gross**
A Professional Corporation

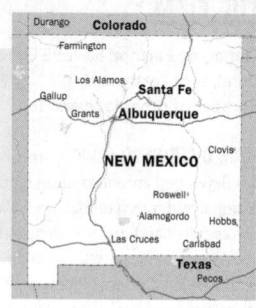

## How lawyers are ranked

Every year we carry out thousands of in-depth interviews with clients and lawyers in order to assess the reputations and expertise of business lawyers across the USA. Chambers rankings and editorial are referred to extensively by General Counsel and other purchasers of legal services who look to our recommendations when choosing their lawyers.

# CORPORATE/COMMERCIAL

### Corporate/Commercial
### Leading Firms

1. **BROWNSTEIN HYATT & FARBER PC** *Albuquerque*
   **MODRALL, SPERLING, ROEHL** *Albuquerque*
   **RODEY, DICKASON, SLOAN, AKIN** *Albuquerque*
2. **KELEHER & MCLEOD, PA** *Albuquerque*
   **SUTIN, THAYER & BROWNE** *Albuquerque*
3. **BETZER ROYBAL & EISENBERG PC** *Albuquerque*
   **LEWIS AND ROCA JONTZ DAWE** *Albuquerque*

### Leading Individuals

1. **BROWN Duane** *Modrall, Sperling*
   **BUCHHOLTZ David** *Brownstein Hyatt & Farber*
   **HALL Alan** *Rodey*
2. **APODACA Patrick** *Keleher & McLeod, PA*
   **BENDICKSEN Perry** *Brownstein Hyatt & Farber*
   **HEYMAN Robert** *Sutin, Thayer & Browne*
   **MONNHEIMER Donald** *Rodey*
   **PAISLEY Bonnie** *Brownstein Hyatt & Farber*
   **PARKER James** *Modrall, Sperling*
   **ROSENBLUM Jay** *Sutin, Thayer & Browne*
3. **BARLOW Richard** *Barlow & Wilcox PA*
   **BETZER Stan** *Betzer Roybal & Eisenberg*
   **JONTZ Dennis** *Lewis and Roca Jontz Dawe*
   **MCDONALD Randall** *Miller Stratvert PA*
   **SCHULER Alison** *Schuler, Messersmith*
   **SWEENEY Jill** *Brownstein Hyatt & Farber*

## Band 1

### Brownstein Hyatt & Farber PC
See firm details p.368

**The Firm:** This respected firm has continued to grow through recent hires to its corporate practice group and has firmly secured its place at the forefront of the market. It advises clients on general corporate and finance issues such as M&A, securities and matters relating to emerging technologies. One area of particular activity is work arising out of the real estate sector, especially from out-of-state investors mainly located in Texas and California. The municipal finance arena has also provided a significant level of cases, where, for instance, it represents the City of Albuquerque. As part of a large nationwide firm, its New Mexico-based attorneys can pull specialists in from other offices and benefit from the firm's broad expertise in different areas of law, such as litigation, tax and real estate.

**The Lawyers:** **David Buchholtz** (see p.1328) acts as bond counsel for the City of Albuquerque and Intel. He focuses on public finance work, tax issues and corporate matters. Interviewees praised his *"thoughtfulness and insight into solving problems."* **Perry Bendicksen** (see p.1328) is *"one of the best technical lawyers."* He is an expert in M&A, private equity, venture capital and corporate finance. Recently he represented the New Mexico State Investment Council in more than $300 million worth in private equity fund investments. *"Very commercial and trusted"* **Bonnie Paisley** (see p.1329) is very active in the municipal finance arena, where she advises issuers, trustees and underwriters in government securities issues. Additionally, she represents small businesses and startups in their corporate and venture capital work. What clients appreciate about **Jill Sweeney** (see p.1330) is that *"she walks in, does the job and walks out with the minimum of fuss."* This *"very thorough and detailed lawyer"* concentrates on public finance and economic development. She also serves as bond counsel for the City of Albuquerque and University of New Mexico.

**Clients/Work Highlights:** The firm's client roster includes government agencies; technology companies; public and private corporations; private equity investors and investment partnerships.

### Modrall, Sperling, Roehl, Harris & Sisk, PA

**The Firm:** This top full-service law firm is one of the largest in New Mexico and according to clients, *"it has a great brand name for corporate work."* It provides advice on various business transactions, employment, tax and securities issues to local venture capitalists, large corporations and partnerships. The team earned particular praise for bond work in the government finance arena, where it recently picked up a number of new school district clients. In addition, the group has witnessed renewed activity in the energy field, where lawyers advise on renewable energy projects such as windmills and wind farms. The firm holds offices in Santa Fe, Albuquerque, Las Cruces and Roswell.

**The Lawyers:** Clients had *"nothing but praise and respect"* for **Duane Brown**. He is a leader in municipal bond issues, where he acts for the New Mexico Finance Authority and the New Mexico Hospital Equipment Loan Council. Additionally, he worked as underwriter's counsel and disclosure counsel on a number of New Mexico public finance projects. **James Parker's** broad commercial practice encompasses corporate, federal taxation, healthcare and employee benefits work. He is a *"superb practitioner with a lot of enthusiasm to get things done."*

**Clients/Work Highlights:** Clients include Bank of America and New Mexico State University.

### Rodey, Dickason, Sloan, Akin & Robb, PA

**The Firm:** This *"top-notch firm gives zero-risk advice"* in a variety of fields such as municipal bonds, securities, metropolitan redevelopment bonds and industrial revenue bonds. Lately the team has been engaged in a number of energy-related industrial bond matters connected to nuclear power plants, coal-fired power plants and wind farms. According to clients, the group is *"really efficient and puts lots of effort into providing excellent work."* Clients include insurers, banks, utilities and healthcare providers. Recently the group acted in a $31.5 million hospital revenue bond issue in connection with a New Mexico medical center's $55 million expansion and renovation.

**The Lawyers:** Experienced **Alan Hall** advises clients on general corporate, municipal bonds, industrial revenue bonds, securities and M&A matters. *"He is a very smart, hands-on lawyer,"* who also has a wealth of knowledge on taxation and projects issues. Head of the bonds and securities practice group **Donald Monnheimer** is an authority on activity in the public finance arena. Additionally, his workload includes the issuance of taxable and tax-exempt industrial revenue bonds, securities offerings and real estate transactions.

**Clients/Work Highlights:** Presbyterian Healthcare Services; Bank of America; Bank of the West and San Juan Regional Medical Center.

## Band 2

### Keleher & McLeod, PA

**The Firm:** Despite the departure of Charles Moore this firm has attracted loyal clients, especially in the utilities field, where it represents public service companies among others. Along with Keleher's business growth in general goes an expansion of the group's corporate and M&A practice. The team continues to advise on a substantial level of commercial and residential real estate development. It has also witnessed a boom in the oil and gas and banking arenas. Further areas of expertise include tax, securities, employment and antitrust issues.

**The Lawyers:** **Patrick Apodaca**'s practice encompasses commercial advice to utilities as well as his M&A and real estate caseload. According to interviewees, "*he is incredibly personable, which is infectious and makes the deals go smoothly. He is a skilled attorney and has a proactive work ethos.*" Patrick represents clients in regional and international transactions.

**Clients/Work Highlights:** PNM Resources, Public Service Company of New Mexico and Ever Ready Oil are among the firm's client base.

### Sutin, Thayer & Browne

**The Firm:** This "*switched-on*" business firm has expanded its corporate group considerably over the past year. Its broad expertise means that attorneys advise clients on a range of M&A, securities, structured and commercial financings and environmental law. The 18-strong team advises venture capitalists, partnerships and private and public corporations from its offices in Albuquerque, Santa Fe and Farmington. The attorneys draw additional expertise from lawyers in other departments, such as employment, real estate, banking and finance and commercial litigation.

**The Lawyers:** Deemed a "*superior adviser for high-level work,*" **Robert Heyman** combines his corporate practice with a specialty in municipal bond work, where he "*knows the business environment and is very sharp and smart.*" He also advises banks and other financial institutions on transactional and regulatory matters. President and CEO of the firm **Jay Rosenblum** is experienced in the corporate and tax arena. He also advises extensively on employee benefits matters.

**Clients/Work Highlights:** Clients include City of Albuquerque, University of New Mexico Hospital and New Mexico State Board of Finance.

## Band 3

### Betzer Roybal & Eisenberg PC

**The Firm:** This "*small but highly skilled*" outfit is respected for its advice on corporate and M&A work, where it has attracted an enviable client base. The firm advises a range of New Mexico companies, such as the Santa Fe Natural Tobacco Company.

**The Lawyers:** Name partner **Stan Betzer** is "*known and respected across New Mexico*" for his expertise in M&A and partnership matters.

### Lewis and Roca Jontz Dawe

**The Firm:** With additional capabilities in the Southwest, this respected team can advise on a range of M&A, securities and fund formations. Public finance and real estate finance fields have been particular areas of activity recently, where the team advises a number of out-of-state companies as well as regional businesses. It has represented the purchaser of a big shopping center in its real estate refinance transactions and advised federal contractors in their government relations.

**The Lawyers:** According to sources, **Dennis Jontz** is "*very well connected and respected in New Mexico.*" He focuses on M&A and real estate matters in the region and also provides advice on government contracts law and commercial litigation issues. Additionally, he is experienced in IP such as trademark registration and software licensing.

**Clients/Work Highlights:** Clients include Compass Bank; Phillips National; The Bell Group and Sandia National Laboratories.

### Other Notable Practitioners

Experienced **Richard Barlow** of Barlow & Wilcox PA is an "*extremely thorough and methodical*" adviser on corporate, estate planning and complex tax matters. **Alison Schuler** of Schuler, Messersmith, Daly & Lansdowne is an expert in private placements and securities. **Randall McDonald**, now at Miller Stratvert PA, has carved out a strong reputation as "*a decent lawyer who rolls up his sleeves and gets the job done.*" Further areas of expertise include technology and science law as well as IP.

# EMPLOYMENT

| Employment: Mainly Defendant |
|---|
| Leading Firms |
| [1] GILKEY & STEPHENSON PA *Albuquerque* |
| TINNIN LAW FIRM *Albuquerque* |
| [2] CONKLIN, JENKE & WOODCOCK PC *Albuquerque* |
| MOODY & WARNER PC *Albuquerque* |
| RODEY, DICKASON, SLOAN, AKIN *Albuquerque* |

| Leading Individuals |
|---|
| [1] CONKLIN Robert *Conklin, Jenke & Woodcock* |
| GILKEY Duane *Gilkey & Stephenson PA* |
| [2] GORDON Scott *Rodey* |
| MOODY Christopher *Moody & Warner PC* |
| STEPHENSON Barbara *Gilkey & Stephenson PA* |
| TINNIN JR Robert *Tinnin Law Firm* |
| WARNER Whitney *Moody & Warner PC* |
| [3] KOTOVSKY Stanley *Tinnin Law Firm* |
| PARRISH Theresa *Rodey* |
| RANDALL Ryan *Tinnin Law Firm* |

## Band 1

### Gilkey & Stephenson PA

See firm details p.1331

**The Firm:** This "*tremendous*" boutique firm has earned a "*well-deserved reputation as one of the best in New Mexico for employment matters.*" Its attorneys provide a "*top-notch service and an excellent quality of work,*" agree clients. The team advises employers across a range of employment issues including sexual harassment, employee benefits and whistle-blower cases. The team has experienced a growth of discrimination cases during the past year. In the labor law field, attorneys have advised employers moving to New Mexico on union activities, such as collective bargaining, wage and hour law and the management of pension funds. Additionally, the group is expert in dispute resolution – mediation and arbitration – in order to help clients avoid trial.

**The Lawyers:** Managing partner **Duane Gilkey** is "*certainly one of the best and as good as it gets.*" His caseload includes discrimination, wrongful discharge, collective bargaining and labor arbitration matters. He enjoys an outstanding reputation with judges and clients, as one put it: "*He is an excellent old-style lawyer, who is very experienced, skilled and personable.*" **Barbara Stephenson** devotes much of her time to employment litigation. She is a "*no-nonsense lawyer*" and is "*detail-oriented and most effective.*"

**Clients/Work Highlights:** American Gypsum; Delta Air Lines; Philips; Intel; CUNA Mutual Group and Citigroup.

### Tinnin Law Firm

**The Firm:** This widely commended group of three attorneys advises employers in labor relations, insurance, contractual disputes and discrimination litigation. Arbitration and preventive counseling are key platforms for the group in its attempts to keep clients out of court. Interviewees agree that, despite its size, the firm is a force in the market because of its "*good quality of work and wealth of experience.*" Clients range from public to private employers and managements in a variety of areas, such as manufacturing, retailing, hospitality, construction and utilities.

**The Lawyers:** Well-connected **Robert Tinnin** is highly experienced in union relations, collective bargaining and wage and hour matters. He is "*one of the best in the state*" because of his practical, solutions-focused advice. **Stanley Kotovsky** concentrates on employment litigation, where he defends public and corporate entities before federal and state courts in disability, discrimination and breach of contract disputes. According to sources, **Ryan Randall** "*is a very bright and capable lawyer.*" Skilled in both litigation and arbitration, he represents private and public employers in harassment, unfair labor practice, and contractual disputes.

Clients/Work Highlights: Clients include St. James Healthcare; First National Bank of Santa Fe; City of Albuquerque; University of New Mexico; Bueno Foods; Yates Petroleum and Halliburton Energy Services.

## Band 2

## Conklin, Jenke & Woodcock PC

The Firm: This five-attorney team is a spin-off from Keleher & McLeod. Established in May 2005, it specializes in employment law counseling and litigation and utilities law. It serves a range of large clients, who appreciate the "*intense commitment and high service standards*" of its attorneys. Recently, the team has been engaged in age discrimination and disability cases.

The Lawyers: Clients describe **Robert Conklin** as an outstanding employment litigator, respected across the region for his "*immense courtroom presence.*" Among his specialties are insurance defence

work and age discrimination.

Clients/Work Highlights: The firm represents a number of public and private utilities.

## Moody & Warner PC

The Firm: This excellent boutique firm is well equipped to advise clients on all aspects of labor and employment law, including at the trial stage. The attorneys here have witnessed an acceleration of employment termination lawsuits due to employees' rising awareness of their rights. In addition to this recent caseload, the team provides preventive counseling and contract negotiation.

The Lawyers: **Christopher Moody** is a "*very amenable character on top of his abundance of skills.*" His practice covers a wide range of matters, such as employment counseling, collective bargaining, labor relations and litigation, where he "*has seen every trick in the book.*" Sources also recommended **Whitney Warner** as a "*very sharp lawyer, who gets to the heart of the matter quickly.*" She is an expert in labor and employment law and litigation, where she "*delivers a great performance, comforts the client and is able to find solutions.*"

Clients/Work Highlights: Otero County Electric Cooperative; Coca-Cola Enterprises; Central New Mexico Electric Cooperative; Comcast; Southwest Cheese and SYSCO Corporation.

## Rodey, Dickason, Sloan, Akin & Robb, PA

The Firm: One of the largest in the state and "*great in all areas of practice.*" The eight-strong employment law group handles all facets of employment and

labor law. "*High standards of expertise*" are displayed in such areas as discrimination, OSHA, pension and employee benefits and wrongful discharge matters. Recently the team represented a large national retailer in claims of breach of a collective bargaining agreement from the largest union in New Mexico. The arbitration took place before an arbitrator from the Federal Mediation and Conciliation Service. It also acted for one of the state's largest employers in a lawsuit in federal court, brought from a surgeon alleging national origin and age discrimination.

The Lawyers: A "*hands-on attorney,*" **Scott Gordon** is a skilled litigator who handles employment and labor law cases as well as civil trials. In addition, he advises clients through teaching seminars and policy training. "*Reliable and well respected in the community,*" **Theresa Parrish** represents employers in individual and class actions before state and federal courts. She also advises on employee discipline and discharge and provides preventive counseling.

Clients/Work Highlights: The firm's client roster includes Smith's Food and Drug Centers; IBM; Basic Contracting Services and Santa Fe Natural Tobacco.

## Other Notable Practitioners

**James Parker** of Modrall, Sperling, Roehl, Harris & Sisk, PA is an employee benefits specialist. Interviewees regard him as "*one of the top players in this area*" and commend his experience in healthcare law, estate planning and federal taxation.

---

# ENVIRONMENT, NATURAL RESOURCES & REGULATED INDUSTRIES

## Band 1

## Hinkle Hensley Shanor & Martin LLP

See firm details p.1332

The Firm: "*Oil and gas is the area in which this firm truly stands out,*" say clients. The 11-strong team covers all aspects of this field, including regulatory issues. The increase of oil prices and greater interest from out-of-state oil and gas companies have ensured that this remains a busy field for the group, and one where its "*high competence and great judgment*" stand out. Contracts, financing, title examination and disputes arising from the sector are all on

the agenda here. In addition, the group provides expertise in environmental and water law as well as advice on the mining sector.

The Lawyers: "*Excellent all-rounder for oil and gas*" **Gregory Nibert** (see p.1329) was named as a "*powerful figure in the industry – experienced and reliable.*" He advises clients on acquisitions and divestitures, title examinations, and oil and gas administrative agency matters. Sources also singled out **Andrew Cloutier** (see p.1328) as a "*very smart and clued-up oil and gas litigator.*" He represents industry associations and corporate entities before state and federal courts. Another key strand to his practice is advice on post-production cost and royalty valuation litigation, where he displays "*logical thinking and clearly presented arguments.*" **Harold Hensley** (see p.1329) resides in the firm's Midland office and has carved out a reputation as "*the dean of natural resources litigation*" through his wealth of experience.

Clients/Work Highlights: Pogo Producing Company; ExxonMobil; Yates Petroleum; Conoco Phillips; BP and Energen Resources.

## Modrall, Sperling, Roehl, Harris & Sisk, PA

The Firm: This talented group of lawyers has pooled together a broad set of skills and, according to clients, "*they communicate well and complement each other's experience.*" It handles a broad range of environmental litigation, regulation and compliance matters. In the dispute resolution sphere, the caseload has included such areas as water, air, oil and gas, hazardous waste and mining. In addition, the team advises clients on land use and permitting and the protection of endangered species. Commentators were "*impressed with the quality of work, expertise and professionalism displayed by this organisation.*" As part of the all-around service, the attorneys also provide environmental law support to banks and other lenders involved in real estate transactions.

The Lawyers: An experienced regulatory attorney, **Larry Ausherman** is well-equipped to advise on environmental matters arising out of the mining sector as well as the more specialist areas such as royalties disputes. He has also secured an excellent statewide profile for his oil and gas expertise. The "*very skilled and experienced*" **John Cooney** is also a key adviser in the oil and gas sector. His caseload also includes natural resources and antitrust disputes. **William Scott** has a broad natural resources practice that features a significant number of water law issues. He *"settles into the cases with a quick and effective manner,"* agreed sources. **Lynn Slade** focuses on utilities work with a Native American law slant. He provides advice in natural resources matters, such as mining and coal, as well as energy law. Another further area of expertise is complex environmental litigation and arbitration, where he is said to be *"a man who can think out of the box and structure arguments to his clients' advantage."* **Walter Stern** handles a variety of cases in connection with Native American tribes, which include land use as well as all facets of natural resources and environmental law. *"He is a remarkable gentleman, and one can always rely upon him to produce the best results."* **Maria O'Brien** has a very strong reputation as *"the go-to person"* in water supply litigation. She acts for an impressive list of clients in water quality and supply issues, as well as permitting.

**Clients/Work Highlights:** El Paso Natural Gas; BP; ConocoPhillips; Oklahoma Department of Environmental Quality; Transwestern Pipeline; BHP Billiton and Navajo Refining are among the firm's clients.

## Montgomery & Andrews, PA

See firm details p.1333

**The Firm:** This respected team resides in Santa Fe and handles a variety of environmental and natural resources matters arising out of the oil, gas and mining sector. Water law is the group's forte and sources endorsed its *"highly valued advice in litigation, where it has a long history of success."* With 22 lawyers, the firm is the largest in Santa Fe and serves clients across the state.

**The Lawyers:** *"The smartest water attorney in town,"* **John Draper** has carved out a national profile for his skill in handling water litigation. He is active on a regional and national basis, including proceedings before the US Supreme Court, where his *"wealth of experience, intelligence and thoughtfulness"* is prized. He represented the State of Kansas in a lawsuit before the US Supreme Court involving Kansas, Nebraska and Colorado regarding the Republican River. **Sarah Singleton** has *"decades of experience in oil and gas litigation under her belt"* and was described as a superb choice for this field. She also stands out for her work on water supply issues, where she is *"outstanding in the detail of her preparation, strategies and memory."* **Edmund Kendrick** is an environmental law expert and represents clients in oil, gas and water litigation as well as regulatory compliance. Additionally, he has obtained air, hazardous and solid waste permits from the New Mexico Environment Department.

**Clients/Work Highlights:** State of Kansas; Burlington Resources; Devon Energy; Marathon Oil and El Paso Natural Gas.

## Band 2

## Rodey, Dickason, Sloan, Akin & Robb, PA

**The Firm:** This *"effective, professional and exceptionally well-organized"* firm covers a wide range of environmental law and natural resources issues, including hazardous waste and air quality management, oil and gas, permitting and mining. Recently, the team represented a pro-mining citizens' group in two closure permitting actions for major open-pit copper mines in southwest New Mexico. With water law becoming increasingly important in the region, the group continues to dedicate resources to this sector. It provides advice on water rights, water quality management, stormwater regulation and groundwater discharge plans. For instance, attorneys acted in a major toxic tort lawsuit arising out of a claim of groundwater contamination involving geology, hydrology and medical causation issues. The environmental aspects of real estate transactions and land use are also handled by the group.

**The Lawyers:** Practice group leader **Mark Adams** has experience in a broad spectrum of environmental and natural resources matters. However, his focus is on water law and water supply litigation, where he impresses as an *"intelligent attorney and a hard worker who sets high standards of client service."* **Sunny Nixon** earned praise from commentators for her expertise in natural resources, environment and water litigation. She handles cases before authorities and courts in New Mexico, where her performances are viewed as *"very thoughtful and creative."*

**Clients/Work Highlights:** Clients include Citizens for Economic Growth & Environmental Protection; Eljer Plumbingware; Wells Fargo; Intrepid Mining; Palm Desert National Bank; Lafarge North America; City of Santa Fe and Peabody Engineering.

## Band 3

## Gallegos Law Firm PC

**The Firm:** This small boutique concentrates on oil and gas work, where its *"high-caliber skills and experience"* are widely recognized. Its attorneys are expert in regulatory and contract issues as well as antitrust and royalty disputes.

**The Lawyers:** **J E Gallegos** was applauded for his *"great knowledge in oil and gas law."* Clients described him as a *"tremendous litigator with an abundance of style and flair."*

**Clients/Work Highlights:** Doyle Hartman; Whiting Petroleum; Maralex Resources; BNP Paribas and Ramah Navajo Chapter.

## Holland & Hart LLP

See firm details p.369

**The Firm:** This national firm is a leader across the oil and gas field; however, its hallmark rests on its advice on royalty disputes. Recently, the team has been engaged in natural resources work, especially in the western USA, where there has been increased oil, gas and coal exploration. It also experienced a growth in the renewables sector, such as wind and solar energy. Its litigation caseload features Native American water rights claims as well as water quality and compliance issues.

**The Lawyers:** A skilled litigator, **Michael Campbell** (see p.1328) represents large oil and gas companies in the federal and state courts and advises clients on environmental and antitrust matters. **William Carr** (see p.1328) has an extensive practice in oil and gas matters, including conservation and environmental compliance.

**Clients/Work Highlights:** Clients include large oil and gas companies.

## Other Notable Practitioners

The *"smart and practical"* **Michelle Henrie** (see p.1329) has joined Brownstein Hyatt & Farber PC from Rodey, Dickason, Sloan, Akin & Robb where she was head of the water law practice group. She acts for clients before administrative bodies throughout New Mexico as well as in state and federal court. In addition, she advises on land use and real estate development work.

# LITIGATION

## GENERAL COMMERCIAL

## Band 1

### Keleher & McLeod, PA

**The Firm:** This "*strong and efficient litigation team*" represents private and public companies and banks and financial institutions in complex commercial litigation matters. Clients appreciate its breadth of experience and the group provides assistance in contracts and securities disputes, insurance, medical malpractice and products liability matters. In addition, the group is experienced in alternative dispute resolution and other tools utilized to avoid trial.

**The Lawyers:** **Charles Pharris** is the "*go-to guy*" for complex cases because of his "*extremely capable and knowledgeable approach.*" His complex commercial litigation caseload also features medical malpractice and insurance defense. A "*timely and effective lawyer,*" **Spencer Reid** concentrates on complex commercial disputes, where his "*advice and counseling are very highly valued,*" reported clients.

**Clients/Work Highlights:** Bank of America; The University of New Mexico; Public Service Company of New Mexico; Albuquerque Public Schools; Home Insurance; Presbyterian Healthcare Services; Bridgestone; Wells Fargo; Archdiocese of Santa Fe and First American Title Insurance.

### Modrall, Sperling, Roehl, Harris & Sisk, PA

**The Firm:** This sizable litigation group has earned "*high marks for its responsive and effective service,*" said clients. It acts for clients in state, federal and tribal courts in complex commercial and tort litigations as well as in medical malpractice and insurance lawsuits. A further area of expertise is alternative dispute resolution, such as mediation and arbitration.

**The Lawyers:** **Kenneth Harrigan** "*is the real deal and a spectacular lawyer who really stands out.*" His focus is on complex business and tort litigation, malpractice and insurance. His "*thorough, driven and intelligent*" approach to the courtroom has made him a popular choice for products liability cases. Sources characterized **Douglas Schneebeck** as a "*talented lawyer with a lot of flair.*" He is the chair of the firm's litigation department and his practice includes class actions, drug liability and medical devices litigation. **Douglas Baker** litigates in commercial, civil, tort and liability lawsuits and was recognized as a "*very methodical, logical and meticulous litigator with a calm demeanor.*" He also acts as arbitrator in the Court-Annexed Arbitration Program for the Second Judicial District Court of New Mexico.

**Clients/Work Highlights:** Wal-Mart; BP; New York Life; Johnson & Johnson; Walgreen; GlaxoSmithKline; Progressive Insurance and 3M are all found on the firm's client roster.

### Rodey, Dickason, Sloan, Akin & Robb, PA

**The Firm:** This "*number-one competitor*" is one of the preeminent defense firms in the state. It covers a variety of complex litigation issues including banking, environmental, insurance and IP law. A growing area of the team's practice is drug and medical device liability as well as professional liability claims. Employment lawsuits have also become more significant and have resulted in an increase in class actions undertaken by the group. Recently, it represented a local electrical subcontractor in wrongful termination and stockholder oppression claims brought by one of the closely held corporation's owner-managers. The firm also defended several life insurance companies in nationwide class actions for failing to adequately disclose to policyholders the differences between paying premiums on an annual basis and more frequently. In addition, the "*well-organized and highly regarded group*" provides expertise in alternative dispute resolution, like arbitration and mediation, as well as preventive counseling.

**The Lawyers:** The "*dean of litigation,*" **Bruce Hall**, takes on a broad range of complex litigation – including environmental and liability cases – for clients of the caliber of University of California. He is "*well respected, honest, hard working and very skilled.*" Sources also commended **Robert Lasater** for his ability to "*gain the confidence of the jury – he's a commanding presence in the courtroom.*" He primarily litigates medical malpractice cases, where he represents hospitals, physicians and other healthcare providers. He also earned respect for his products liability practice and his "*very thorough and highly ethical*" approach to cases. **Nelson Franse**'s practice is "*a great success story.*" His focus lies on professional liability and medical malpractice defense, where "*clients just love him because of his great personality and trial skills.*" He is also involved in products liability and PI litigation. President and managing partner of the firm **Andrew Schultz** was characterized as a tough litigator, respected by both the jury and the bench. He handles national cases in class action and civil rights litigations and appeals before state and federal courts. "*Gentlemanly*" **Rex Throckmorton** has a broad litigation experience including business torts and class actions, as well as a specialism in natural resources and real estate work. He is "*smart, reliable and skillful in the courtroom.*"

**Clients/Work Highlights:** Prudential Insurance; The Williams Companies; Farmers; State Farm and Fidelity National Title.

## Band 2

### Freedman Boyd Daniels Hollander Goldberg & Cline PA

**The Firm:** Clients endorsed the "*excellent trial skills*" displayed by this group of ten lawyers. It handles a wide range of complex commercial litigation such as antitrust, securities, civil rights and PI cases. The firm's workload also includes white-collar criminal defense and support on procedural and appellate levels.

**The Lawyers:** A large part of **Joseph Goldberg**'s

work originates from outside New Mexico, and alongside his general commercial caseload is a significant strand of antitrust. A "*great thinker and strategist,*" he possesses a "*great courtroom performance and holds everyone spellbound.*"

Clients/Work Highlights: Clients include regional and national businesses and corporations.

### Hinkle Hensley Shanor & Martin LLP

See firm details p.1332

The Firm: This Roswell-based firm received acclaim from clients for its strong statewide public utilities, oil, gas and energy litigation practice. This forms a major part of its workload, alongside employment defense and complex commercial lawsuits. Furthermore, the team represents clients in civil rights, liability, and insurance matters. The firm's sizable resources ensure a breadth of expertise is available to clients.

The Lawyers: Commercial litigation takes up most of "*skillful, wise and incredibly friendly practitioner*" **Stuart Shanor**'s (see p.1329) time. He is in charge of the Roswell office and has experience in banking, corporate and real estate litigation.

Clients/Work Highlights: Devon Energy; New Mexico Self Insurers' Fund; Liberty Mutual; Chevron; Pogo Producing Company; National General Insurance; ConocoPhillips; EOG Resources; BP; ExxonMobil and Texaco.

### Sutin, Thayer & Browne

The Firm: This firm recently bolstered its litigation department through the recruitment of attorneys from Eaves, Bardacke, Baugh, Kierst & Larson. With an emphasis on commercial litigation, the team is also engaged in antitrust, employment, securities and IP matters. The attorneys here can also draw on the additional expertise of other departments such as insurance defense, corporate and business; and bankruptcy and creditors' rights. Arbitration and mediation expertise ensures a rounded service to clients.

The Lawyers: **Paul Bardacke**, former name partner of Eaves, Bardacke, Baugh, Kierst & Larson has a wide-ranging experience of litigation. According to interviewees; "*he is a very smart and skillful lawyer who enjoys the highest reputation among peers and the bench; and he has a great personality.*"

Clients/Work Highlights: The State of New Mexico and The Office of the State Engineer are found on the firm's client roster.

## Band 3

### Carpenter & Stout Ltd

The Firm: This Albuquerque-based team is best known for its expertise in toxic tort law. Although smaller than some rivals, it is widely recognized as "*an excellent trial law firm.*" Its workload includes products liability, PI and insurance litigation on both trial and appellate level.

The Lawyers: **David Stout** has carved out a reputation as "*a great lawyer with great skills, who will do his best to represent clients' interests,*" agreed sources. He focuses on PI, products liability and insurance

matters. Firm founder **Bill Carpenter** is a "*larger-than-life trial lawyer, who is widely admired.*" He is a specialist and preeminent in PI and products liability cases. In addition, he handles insurance, toxic torts and commercial litigation. Interviewees singled him out because "*he is very careful and effective with judge and jury.*"

Clients/Work Highlights: Insurers, businesses and individuals are among the firm's clients.

### Eaves & Mendenhall PA

The Firm: This team of nine lawyers is well equipped to advise on a range of disputes, such as professional liability, real estate, employment and environmental law matters. **John Eaves** "*is well known for his ability to get things moving, and is a very successful lawyer.*" This highly experienced litigator focuses on tobacco and oil and gas disputes, as well as antitrust litigation.

### Gallegos Law Firm PC

The Firm: The hallmark of this boutique firm is its expertise in oil and gas litigation. The four-strong group represents clients in contract, ownership, royalty, regulatory and antitrust matters as well as domain proceedings. The group is also able to advise clients on the impact of Native American law in this sector.

The Lawyers: Name partner **J E Gallegos** is regarded as a "*fine lawyer who knows how to achieve results.*" He specializes in oil and gas law, business litigation, class actions and antitrust matters.

Clients/Work Highlights: Maralex Resources; Whiting Petroleum; BNP Paribas; Doyle Hartman and Ramah Navajo Chapter.

### Madison Harbour Mroz & Brennan PA

The Firm: The 16-strong team provides support to clients, such as large businesses and insurance companies, in all sorts of general commercial litigation. However, it stands out in the field of medical malpractice, insurance and products liability defense litigation. It has attracted a respected client base of pharmaceutical companies, doctors and nursing homes.

The Lawyers: "*Well respected and very smart,*" **William Madison** is a respected litigator in the field of medical malpractice and insurance defense. He also acts for numerous industries in mediation cases.

Clients/Work Highlights: Baxter; Houston General Insurance; Bank of America; Fireman's Fund; American National Insurance; Pfizer and Trinity Universal Insurance.

### Miller Stratvert PA

The Firm: This large firm has captured a significant statewide presence through its expertise in medical malpractice and insurance cases. Support is provided to all sorts of professionals, institutions and professional organizations in the healthcare, architectural and engineering sectors. The team also handles commercial litigation such as banking, real estate and oil and gas matters.

The Lawyers: A tough litigator, **Gary Gordon** is respected for his medical malpractice and insurance litigation skills. He represents mainly physicians and

was described as "*very exciting and flamboyant in the courtroom.*" **Stephan Vidmar** focuses on medical and legal malpractice, insurance and products liability. He is a "*very straightforward, organized and effective cross-examiner, who is very sincere and trustworthy,*" agree sources. **Ranne Miller** is the firm's founder and managing director. He is especially well respected for his medical malpractice work, where commentators rated him an "*exceptionally fine and effective lawyer who is as good as it gets in this field.*" A senior figure in the market, he is also the go-to guy for advice on mediation and alternative dispute resolution.

Clients/Work Highlights: The firm acts for individuals, professional organizations and businesses, which are regional, national and local in nature.

### Montgomery & Andrews, PA

See firm details p.1333

The Firm: This well-established Santa Fe firm covers a variety of litigation matters including general commercial, employment and environmental law suits. The group of 20 lawyers serves both regional and national clients, such as American Insurance Association; Burlington Resources; City of Santa Fe and DaimlerChrysler. **Andrew Montgomery** is "*a good litigator with a good sense of direction*" who represents clients in civil and criminal matters on trial and at appellate level. According to sources, "*he is clearly a safe pair of hands.*"

### Peifer, Hanson & Mullins PA

The Firm: This litigation firm handles proceedings before federal and state courts on a regional and national basis. Areas of expertise include complex commercial, class action, white-collar crime and partnership cases. The team acts for large corporations, such as Wal-Mart, and also represents public institutions, such as the New Mexico Taxation and Revenue Department. Commercial litigation and class actions expert **Charles Peifer** stands out as "*a smart, careful, hard-working attorney – he's a good choice for complex cases.*" He acts before the New Mexico and Arizona District Courts as well as the US Court of Appeal for the Ninth and Tenth Circuits.

### Other Notable Practitioners

Former physician **Carl Bettinger** of Shapiro Bettinger Chase LLP has established a strong reputation through his work in nursing home liability matters. According to interviewees, he "*enjoys a high level of respect*" because he is "*very thorough and ethical and strategic.*" Sources described **Terry Word** of Word & Bogardus as a "*tremendous lawyer of a very high caliber with an outstanding track record at trial.*" He devotes his time to medical malpractice litigation as well as PI, insurance and products liability cases. **Ben Allen** of Hatch, Allen & Shepherd P.A. specializes in medical malpractice, insurance and products liability litigation. He is "*confident, careful in his preparation and has an effective approach to the jury.*" **Wayne Wolf** of Wolf Taylor & McCaleb, PA is a skilled mediator, and well versed in insurance defense litigation.

# NATIVE AMERICAN LAW

## Band 1

### Modrall, Sperling, Roehl, Harris & Sisk, PA

**The Firm:** This full-service firm provides expertise in various areas of Native American law, including environmental, construction, oil and gas matters as well as employment and finance issues. The team of six lawyers has a "*great all-around reputation*" representing clients across the USA on disputes under Native American jurisdictions. For example, the group advised Astaris in a lawsuit regarding a tribal employment rights ordinance requiring a preference for local Native Americans. The firm also represented BNSF Railway as tribal court counsel on appeal concerning the right of way within a reservation.

**The Lawyers:** **William Scott** is a water law expert who "*resolves issues in a quick and efficient manner.*" He has a broad experience of the regulatory and transactional matters arising out of this market. "*Thoughtful and smart*" **Lynn Slade** advises companies and individuals on development and environmental issues on Indian land. He also acts as counsel in arbitrations and mediations. Sources said: "*He is as good as it gets and consistently provides high-caliber advice.*" Much of **Walter Stern**'s practice relates to energy, natural resources and environmental law. A "*very reliable, thoughtful and methodical character,*" he is respected for his litigation prowess.

**Clients/Work Highlights:** The firm's client list includes businesses; financial institutions; utilities and natural resource developers.

## Band 2

### Holland & Hart LLP

See firm details p.369

**The Firm:** This respected firm houses attorneys in offices across the region and in Washington, DC, who come together to advise on natural resources and business issues that relate to Native American law. Well equipped to act at trial and appellate level, the group also provides clients with preventive counseling. The recent caseload has included matters relating to gaming, land acquisition, taxation and tribal sovereignty.

**The Lawyers:** **Mark Sheridan** (see p.1329) possesses vast experience in oil, gas and water litigation before trial and appellate courts. For example, he represented a diversified energy company in a number of federal appeals regarding royalty accounting for oil and gas production on Native American reservation land.

### Sutin, Thayer & Browne

**The Firm:** The eight-strong team advises on real estate development, natural resources, gaming and tribal sovereignty. Its attorneys are entitled to practice before numerous tribal courts and advise on obligations relating to tribes as well as federal and tribal law.

**The Lawyers:** **Christopher Holland** is a highly experienced litigator who impresses as being "*knowledgeable beyond his years.*" Litigation practice group leader **Andrew Simons** is very active at the Navajo Bar and is licensed to practice before various tribes and tribal courts. His wealth of experience is a major drawing card for clients.

# REAL ESTATE

## Band 1

### Myers Oliver & Price

**The Firm:** This firm is the "*first choice for many,*" with its broad service to residential and national developers. Its expertise spans development and leasing, financing and land use issues. Interviewees praised the team for its "*good knowledge of the market,*" its professionalism and its consistently high-quality advice. Additional expertise is provided in the farm and ranch sector, as well as business formation.

**The Lawyers:** "*First-class lawyer*" **John Myers** advises corporations across the USA on land development and home-building projects. A "*smooth and well-respected lawyer,*" he "*gets the job done and has an easygoing attitude.*" He recently advised on a large mixed-use community development project, Mesa Del Sol. **Charles Price** is an "*excellent, no-nonsense and straightforward attorney.*" He focuses on real estate transactional and development work as well as on mortgage finance and commercial workouts.

**Clients/Work Highlights:** Albuquerque Academy; Bank of America; Columbia Mutual Life Insurance; Crescent Real Estate Funding; Forest City Enterprises; High Desert Investment; International Council of Shopping Centers; Siemens and Sun Life of Canada.

### Rodey, Dickason, Sloan, Akin & Robb, PA

**The Firm:** Real estate transactions, development and leasing are key strands to this practice. The "*hardworking and thoroughly competent team*" advises regional and national clients on project financing, construction and zoning issues. Recently, it represented The University of New Mexico in a case where the City of Albuquerque sought to acquire additional land for airport expansion. The group also acted for Diamond Tail Estates in zoning, subdividing and developing a residential community near Placitas, New Mexico.

**The Lawyers:** **John Salazar** was named by sources as a primary contact for real estate matters because he is "*able to visualize the bigger picture.*" He represented key client The University of New Mexico in the acquisition of land in connection with the Mesa Del Sol project. The "*very hands-on*" **Catherine Goldberg** is "*best known for her technical skills and careful analysis,*" reported sources. She acts for buyers and sellers in real estate transactions and also advises on title and zoning matters.

**Clients/Work Highlights:** Albuquerque Technical Vocational Institute; Angel Fire Resort; Prudential Insurance Company of America and Albertson's are among the firm's clients.

## Band 2

### Hurley Toevs Styles Hamblin & Panter PA

**The Firm:** This "*very skilled and experienced*" firm has secured long-term relationships with developers, buyers and sellers on a regional and nationwide level. It provides advice on commercial real estate development, as well as complex workouts and related litigation. Clients endorsed the team's attorneys as "*thorough, well prepared and knowledgeable.*"

**The Lawyers:** According to interviewees, **Patrick**

## Real Estate
### Leading Individuals

#### Senior Statesman
KELEHER William *Keleher & McLeod, PA*
[1] HURLEY Patrick *Hurley Toevs Styles*
MYERS John *Myers Oliver & Price*
PRICE Charles *Myers Oliver & Price*
SALAZAR John *Rodey*
[2] EK Dale *Modrall, Sperling*
GOLDBERG Catherine *Rodey*
PATTERSON John *Scheuer Yost & Patterson*
STYLES Mark *Hurley Toevs Styles*
[3] AHERN Janice *Sommer, Udall, Hardwick*
JONTZ Dennis *Lewis and Roca Jontz Dawe*
SCHIFANI Ruth *Modrall, Sperling*
WELLS Lawrence *Campbell and Wells PA*

#### Up-and-coming individuals
MEISTER Margaret *Modrall, Sperling*

## Real Estate: Zoning/Land Use
### Leading Individuals
[1] CAMPBELL David *Vogel Campbell & Blueher*
MYERS John *Myers Oliver & Price*
SALAZAR John *Rodey*

---

**Hurley** *"is known as one of the best, and is sought after due to his skills and networks."* He devotes much of his time to real estate financing where he often represents landowners and developers. *"Outstanding deal-doer"* **Mark Styles** is *"just brilliant, very precise and knows the market like the back of his hand."* He acts for lenders and borrowers in real estate sales, acquisitions and financings.

## Modrall, Sperling, Roehl, Harris & Sisk, PA
**The Firm:** This excellent group handles a wide range of real estate development and financings. In the zoning and land use arena, it acts for clients in connection with approvals and changes before boards and commissions as well as courts on trial and appellate level. Recently, the group experienced an increasing demand for its advice on the development of wind farms and the purchase of agricultural land. Accordingly, this group is able to draw additional support from the firm's public lands department.
**The Lawyers:** Financing expert **Dale Ek** represents a broad spread of clients including out-of-state investors, developers and financial institutions. Commentators described him as *"a tremendous player in the market who is credible in every respect."* **Ruth Schifani** is *"a meticulous and technically skilled finance specialist who has a very good business sense and is sensitive to clients' needs."* She focuses on transactional matters related to commercial and residential real estate. Up-and-coming **Margaret Meister** covers various real estate matters, such as sales, tax-free exchanges, leases and land use. A *"talented negotiator,"* she also advises on environmental and Native American law issues.
**Clients/Work Highlights:** The firm's client roster includes purchasers and sellers of ranches, conservations and commercial, residential and mineral properties.

## Band 3

## Keleher & McLeod, PA
**The Firm:** *"A great firm with a good track record in real estate,"* its team of six lawyers covers financings, developments and leasing issues for clients both in the state and beyond.
**The Lawyers:** A senior figure in the market, **William Keleher** enjoys a *"great reputation as a vastly experienced real estate attorney,"* said commentators.

## Lewis and Roca Jontz Dawe
**The Firm:** With offices in Albuquerque as well as Phoenix, Tucson and Las Vegas, this sizable firm serves clients in New Mexico, the Southwest and across the USA. It represents investors and developers in a diversity of transactions and leasing arrangements. Additional expertise is drawn from the firm's environmental, tax and bankruptcy practice groups, while a dedicated group of zoning and land use specialists resides in the Tucson office.
**The Lawyers:** *"Soft-spoken and hard-working"* **Dennis Jontz** is a *"diligent attorney with excellent communication skills."* He concentrates on advising clients on large real estate transactions and land developments. One client commented: *"He is an exceptional individual. If all lawyers were like him, life would be easier."*

**Clients/Work Highlights:** The firm's client roster includes financial institutions; insurance companies; pension funds; retailers; restaurants and other private and public entities.

## Scheuer Yost & Patterson PC
**The Firm:** This Santa Fe-based group of nine lawyers has established an *"excellent real estate practice with a firm lock on the market and good local clients."* The team fields experience in an array of real estate issues, such as development and land conservations, tax and estate planning. Real estate litigation is also a forte, in which it adopts a *"realistic approach to work."*
**The Lawyers:** **John Patterson** is a *"very strong, knowledgeable and bright attorney."* His focus lies on real estate property and condominium law.
**Clients/Work Highlights:** Tri-State Generation and Transmission Association; Commonwealth Land Title Insurance; Union Carbide; GE Capital and The County of Los Alamos.

## Sommer, Udall, Hardwick, Ahern & Hyatt LLP
**The Firm:** This local player's workload contains a variety of commercial and residential real estate subjects, for example condominiums, titles, transactions, developments, exchanges and litigation. Advice is provided to developers and small businesses. Real estate expert **Janice Ahern** has experience in real estate and condominium law as well as in land use matters.

## Vogel Campbell & Blueher PC
**The Firm:** Located in Albuquerque, this small outfit advises local clients on real estate transactions, titles matters, zoning and land use. Commentators recommended the group's strongest real estate practitioner, **David Campbell**, as a *"well-recognized and very skilled land use expert."*

## Other Notable Practitioners
**Lawrence Wells** of Campbell and Wells PA resides in Albuquerque and was commended for his expertise in transactions related to retail and industrial property.

# Leaders in New Mexico

**ADAMS, Mark**
Rodey, Dickason, Sloan, Akin & Robb, PA,
Santa Fe 505 984 0100
*Recommended in Environment*

**AHERN, Janice**
Sommer, Udall, Hardwick, Ahern & Hyatt
LLP, Santa Fe 505 982 4676
*Recommended in Real Estate*

**ALLEN, Ben**
Hatch, Allen & Shepherd PA, Albuquerque
505 341 0110
*Recommended in Litigation*

**APODACA, Patrick**
Keleher & McLeod, PA, Albuquerque
505 346 4646
*Recommended in
Corporate/Commercial*

**AUSHERMAN, Larry**
Modrall, Sperling, Roehl, Harris & Sisk, PA,
Albuquerque 505 848 1800
*Recommended in Environment*

**BAKER, Douglas**
Modrall, Sperling, Roehl, Harris & Sisk, PA,
Albuquerque 505 848 1800
*Recommended in Litigation*

**BARDACKE, Paul**
Sutin, Thayer & Browne, Albuquerque
505 883 2500
*Recommended in Litigation*

**BARLOW, Richard**
Barlow & Wilcox PA, Albuquerque
505 248 1300
*Recommended in
Corporate/Commercial*

**BENDICKSEN, Perry**
Brownstein Hyatt & Farber PC, Albuquerque
505 724 9564
pbendicksen@bhf-law.com
*Recommended in
Corporate/Commercial*
**Practice Areas:** Shareholder in Brown-
stein Hyatt & Farber's Corporate Finance
Group. Focuses on private equity, venture
capital, corporate finance, and mergers
and acquisitions. Clients include private
equity and venture capital funds and
their investors, investment banking firms,
and emerging technology companies.
**Prof. Memberships:** American Bar
Association; New Mexico Bar Assocation;
National Association of Bond Lawyers.
**Personal:** Harvard Law School
(JD,1982); Amherst College (BA, 1978).

**BETTINGER, Carl**
Shapiro Bettinger Chase LLP, Albuquerque
505 888 6463
*Recommended in Litigation*

**BETZER, Stan**
Betzer Roybal & Eisenberg PC, Albuquerque
505 797 0105
*Recommended in
Corporate/Commercial*

**BROWN, Duane**
Modrall, Sperling, Roehl, Harris & Sisk,
PA, Albuquerque 505 848 1800
*Recommended in
Corporate/Commercial*

**BUCHHOLTZ, David**
Brownstein Hyatt & Farber PC, Albuquerque
505 724 9565
dbuchholtz@bhf-law.com
*Recommended in
Corporate/Commercial*
**Practice Areas:** Shareholder in Brownstein Hyatt & Farber's Corporate and
Securities, Corporate Finance, Mergers
and Acquisitions, and Public Finance
groups. Focuses on government finance
law, economic development and state tax
incentive law, financial institutions law,
securities law, and corporate matters.
Additionally, he represents issuers, under-
writers, and trustees in connection with
the issuance of government securities.
**Prof. Memberships:** American Bar
Association; Albuquerque Bar Association; National Association of Bond
Lawyers.
**Personal:** Georgetown University Law
Center (JD,1976); State University of
New York at Binghamton (BA,1973).

**CAMPBELL, David**
Vogel Campbell & Blueher PC, Albuquerque
505 884 8444
*Recommended in Real Estate*

**CAMPBELL, Michael**
Holland & Hart LLP, Santa Fe
505 954 7282
mcampbell@hollandhart.com
*Recommended in Environment*
**Practice Areas:** Mr Campbell's practice
concentrates on oil and gas and environmental litigation, with over 30 years experience in the state and federal courts of
New Mexico. He has represented large,
integrated oil and gas companies, as well
as independent operators, in a wide variety of oil and gas disputes, several of
which were putative class actions. His
jury experience has included surface use
disputes, tort claims, and royalty controversies with both private and governmental entities. He has tried to verdict
antitrust claims in the oil and gas arena,
including a price fixing claim brought
pursuant to Section 1 of the Sherman
Act.
**Prof. Memberships:** Member, State Bar
of New Mexico; the Federalist Society.
**Career:** Admitted to State Bar of New
Mexico (1975); US District Court, District of New Mexico; US Court of
Appeals, Tenth Circuit; and the US
Supreme Court.
**Personal:** Received a JD (1975) and a BA
(1971) from the University of New Mexico.

**CARPENTER, William**
Carpenter & Stout Ltd, Albuquerque
505 243 1336
*Recommended in Litigation*

**CARR, William F**
Holland & Hart LLP, Santa Fe
505 988 4421
wcarr@hollandhart.com
*Recommended in Environment*
**Practice Areas:** US federal and State of
New Mexico oil and gas regulation, with
focus on development and environmental issues and the unitization of reservoirs
for primary and enhanced recovery operations. He represents major and independent operators and oil and gas trade associations before the New Mexico legislature, Oil Conservation Division/Com-
mission, New Mexico State Land Office
and state and federal courts.
**Prof. Memberships:** New Mexico State
Bar (Member Natural Resources Committee of the Board of Legal Specialization); New Mexico Oil and Gas Association (Chairman, Regulatory Practices
Committee); Independent Petroleum
Association of New Mexico (Legal Counsel). He also served on the Governor's
Energy Policy Advisory Board and the
State Land Office Advisory Board.
**Career:** Partner at Holland & Hart LLP
since 2001.
**Publications:** Author on oil and gas top-
ics, including articles in the Natural
Resources Journal, and Special Institutes
and Annual Meetings of the Rocky
Mountain Mineral Law Foundation. He
is a frequent speaker on topics related to
the regulation of oil and gas development
and the unitization of oil and gas fields.
**Personal:** University of New Mexico
School of Law (JD, 1972); University of
New Mexico (BA. 1968).

**CLOUTIER, Andrew J**
Hinkle Hensley Shanor & Martin LLP,
Roswell 505 622 6510
dcloutier@hinklelawfirm.com
*Recommended in Environment*
**Practice Areas:** Oil and gas litigation;
complex commercial litigation; class
action litigation.
**Prof. Memberships:** New Mexico Bar
Association; Texas Bar Association; New
Mexico Oil and Gas Association; Rocky
Mountain Mineral Law Foundation;
Chaves County Bar Association
**Career:** Partner since 1994.
**Personal:** University of Texas (JD 1987);
University of Dallas (BA 1984).

**CONKLIN, Robert**
Conklin, Jenke & Woodcock PC, Albuquerque
505 224 9160
*Recommended in Employment*

**COONEY, John**
Modrall, Sperling, Roehl, Harris & Sisk, PA,
Albuquerque 505 848 1800
*Recommended in Environment*

**DRAPER, John**
Montgomery & Andrews, PA, Santa Fe
505 982 3873
*Recommended in Environment*

**EAVES, John**
Eaves & Mendenhall PA, Albuquerque
505 888 4300
*Recommended in Litigation*

**EK, Dale**
Modrall, Sperling, Roehl, Harris & Sisk, PA,
Albuquerque 505 848 1800
*Recommended in Real Estate*

**FRANSE, Nelson**
Rodey, Dickason, Sloan, Akin & Robb, PA,
Albuquerque 505 765 5900
*Recommended in Litigation*

**GALLEGOS, J E**
Gallegos Law Firm PC, Santa Fe
505 983 6686
*Recommended in Environment,
Litigation*

**GILKEY, Duane**
Gilkey & Stephenson PA, Albuquerque
505 242 4466
*Recommended in Employment*

**GOLDBERG, Catherine**
Rodey, Dickason, Sloan, Akin & Robb, PA,
Albuquerque 505 765 5900
*Recommended in Real Estate*

**GOLDBERG, Joseph**
Freedman Boyd Daniels Hollander Goldberg & Cline PA, Albuquerque
505 842 9960
*Recommended in Litigation*

**GORDON, Gary**
Miller Stratvert PA, Albuquerque
505 842 1950
*Recommended in Litigation*

**GORDON, Scott**
Rodey, Dickason, Sloan, Akin & Robb, PA,
Albuquerque 505 765 5900
*Recommended in Employment*

**HALL, Alan**
Rodey, Dickason, Sloan, Akin & Robb, PA,
Albuquerque 505 765 5900
*Recommended in
Corporate/Commercial*

**HALL, Bruce**
Rodey, Dickason, Sloan, Akin & Robb, PA,
Albuquerque 505 765 5900
*Recommended in Litigation*

**HARRIGAN, Kenneth**
Modrall, Sperling, Roehl, Harris & Sisk, PA,
Albuquerque 505 848 1800
*Recommended in Litigation*

**HENRIE, Michelle**
Brownstein Hyatt & Farber PC, Albuquerque
505 724 9582
mhenrie@bhf-law.com
*Recommended in Environment*
**Practice Areas:** Associate in Brownstein Hyatt & Farber's Real Estate, Land Use, Water & Public Lands, and Environment & Natural Resources groups. Focuses on real estate development, water law, land use, planning and zoning, appeals, administrative law and local government, and environmental law and natural resources.
**Personal:** Vermont Law School (JD, 1999); The University of Chicago (PhD studies, no degree awarded, 1991-96); The University of Chicago (AM, 1991); Hebrew University of Jerusalem, (1989-90); Utah State University (BA, 1989).

**HENSLEY, Harold**
Hinkle Hensley Shanor & Martin LLP, Midland 432 683 4691
*Recommended in Environment*
**Practice Areas:** Complex litigation primarily in the fields of oil and gas, commercial law and condemnation. He has been involved in extended litigation in many states including New Mexico, Texas, Oklahoma, Kansas and Wyoming.
**Prof. Memberships:** American College of Trial Lawyers, Roehl Circle of Honor for New Mexico Trial Lawyers.
**Career:** Partner since 1963.
**Personal:** University of Texas (LLB 1960), Rice Institute (BBA, 1956).

**HEYMAN, Robert**
Sutin, Thayer & Browne, Albuquerque
505 883 2500
*Recommended in Corporate/Commercial*

**HOLLAND, Christopher**
Sutin, Thayer & Browne, Albuquerque
505 883 2500
*Recommended in Native American Law*

**HURLEY, Patrick**
Hurley Toevs Styles Hamblin & Panter PA, Albuquerque 505 888 1188
*Recommended in Real Estate*

**JONTZ, Dennis**
Lewis and Roca Jontz Dawe, Albuquerque
505 764 5400
*Recommended in Corporate/Commercial, Real Estate*

**KELEHER, William**
Keleher & McLeod, PA, Albuquerque
505 346 4646
*Recommended in Real Estate*

**KENDRICK, Edmund**
Montgomery & Andrews, PA, Santa Fe
505 982 3873
*Recommended in Environment*

**KOTOVSKY, Stanley**
Tinnin Law Firm, Albuquerque
505 768 1500
*Recommended in Employment*

**LASATER, Robert**
Rodey, Dickason, Sloan, Akin & Robb, PA, Albuquerque 505 765 5900
*Recommended in Litigation*

**MADISON, William**
Madison Harbour Mroz & Brennan PA, Albuquerque 505 242 2177
*Recommended in Litigation*

**MCDONALD, Randall**
Miller Stratvert PA, Albuquerque
505 842 1950
*Recommended in Corporate/Commercial*

**MEISTER, Margaret**
Modrall, Sperling, Roehl, Harris & Sisk, PA, Albuquerque 505 848 1800
*Recommended in Real Estate*

**MILLER, Ranne**
Miller Stratvert PA, Albuquerque
505 842 1950
*Recommended in Litigation*

**MONNHEIMER, Donald**
Rodey, Dickason, Sloan, Akin & Robb, PA, Albuquerque 505 765 5900
*Recommended in Corporate/Commercial*

**MONTGOMERY, Andrew**
Montgomery & Andrews, PA, Santa Fe
505 982 3873
*Recommended in Litigation*

**MOODY, Christopher**
Moody & Warner PC, Albuquerque
505 944 0033
*Recommended in Employment*

**MYERS, John**
Myers Oliver & Price, Albuquerque
505 247 9080
*Recommended in Real Estate*

**NIBERT, Gregory J**
Hinkle Hensley Shanor & Martin LLP, Roswell 505 622 6510
gnibert@hinklelawfirm.com
*Recommended in Environment*
**Practice Areas:** Oil and gas law, including title examination, financing, contract preparation, acquisitions and divestitures, division orders, oil and gas administrative agency matters.
**Prof. Memberships:** State Bar of New Mexico (Member: Natural Resources, Energy and Environmental Law; Chair, 1990-91); Independent Petroleum Association of New Mexico (Board Member 2000-present); Rocky Mountain Mineral Law Foundation (Trustee, 2002-present).
**Career:** Partner since 1989.
**Personal:** Pepperdine University School of Law, JD, cum laude, 1983. Recognized by the NM Board of Specialization as a specialist in oil and gas natural resources law.

**NIXON, Sunny**
Rodey, Dickason, Sloan, Akin & Robb, PA, Albuquerque 505 765 5900
*Recommended in Environment*

**O'BRIEN, Maria**
Modrall, Sperling, Roehl, Harris & Sisk, PA, Albuquerque 505 848 1800
*Recommended in Environment*

**PAISLEY, Bonnie**
Brownstein Hyatt & Farber PC, Albuquerque
505 724 9573
bpaisley@bhf-law.com
*Recommended in Corporate/Commercial*
**Practice Areas:** Shareholder in Brownstein Hyatt & Farber's Public Finance and Corporate & Securities groups. Concentrates on corporate and securities law, general business transactions, and municipal finance. Represents small businesses, primarily technology companies, in various stages of development. Works with clients on many aspects of their businesses, including choice of entity, securities matters, contracts, and various types of transactions, including acquisitions and mergers. Also represents issuers, underwriters, and trustees in connection with the issuance of government securities.
**Personal:** Harvard Law School (JD,1985); Salem State College (BA,1983).

**PARKER, James**
Modrall, Sperling, Roehl, Harris & Sisk, PA, Albuquerque 505 848 1800
*Recommended in Corporate/Commercial, Employment*

**PARRISH, Theresa**
Rodey, Dickason, Sloan, Akin & Robb, PA, Albuquerque 505 765 5900
*Recommended in Employment*

**PATTERSON, John**
Scheuer Yost & Patterson PC, Santa Fe
505 982 9911
*Recommended in Real Estate*

**PEIFER, Charles**
Peifer, Hanson & Mullins PA, Albuquerque
505 247 4800
*Recommended in Litigation*

**PHARRIS, Charles**
Keleher & McLeod, PA, Albuquerque
505 346 4646
*Recommended in Litigation*

**PRICE, Charles**
Myers Oliver & Price, Albuquerque
505 247 9080
*Recommended in Real Estate*

**RANDALL, Ryan**
Tinnin Law Firm, Albuquerque
505 768 1500
*Recommended in Employment*

**REID, Spencer**
Keleher & McLeod, PA, Albuquerque
505 346 4646
*Recommended in Litigation*

**ROSENBLUM, Jay**
Sutin, Thayer & Browne, Albuquerque
505 883 2500
*Recommended in Corporate/Commercial*

**SALAZAR, John**
Rodey, Dickason, Sloan, Akin & Robb, PA, Albuquerque 505 765 5900
*Recommended in Real Estate*

**SCHIFANI, Ruth**
Modrall, Sperling, Roehl, Harris & Sisk, PA, Albuquerque 505 848 1800
*Recommended in Real Estate*

**SCHNEEBECK, Douglas**
Modrall, Sperling, Roehl, Harris & Sisk, PA, Albuquerque 505 848 1800
*Recommended in Litigation*

**SCHULER, Alison**
Schuler, Messersmith, Daly & Lansdowne, Albuquerque 505 872 0800
*Recommended in Corporate/Commercial*

**SCHULTZ, Andrew**
Rodey, Dickason, Sloan, Akin & Robb, PA, Albuquerque 505 765 5900
*Recommended in Litigation*

**SCOTT, William**
Modrall, Sperling, Roehl, Harris & Sisk, PA, Albuquerque 505 848 1800
*Recommended in Environment, Native American Law*

**SHANOR, Stuart D**
Hinkle Hensley Shanor & Martin LLP, Roswell 505 622 6510
sshanor@hinklelawfirm.com
*Recommended in Litigation*
**Practice Areas:** Complex commercial litigation.
**Prof. Memberships:** American College of Trial Lawyers (President 2001-02), American Bar Foundation, Recipient - New Mexico Bar Professionalism Award, ABA, American Judicature Society, American Inns of Court, Chaves County Bar Association.
**Career:** Partner since 1969.
**Personal:** University of Michigan (LLB 1962), Wittenberg College (AB 1959).

**SHERIDAN, Mark F**
Holland & Hart LLP, Santa Fe
505 988 4421
msheridan@hollandhart.com
*Recommended in Native American Law*
**Practice Areas:** Complex civil matters in federal and state trial and appellate courts, particularly in commercial, antitrust and natural resources litigation, including extensive experience in contract, business tort, real property, land use, oil and gas, water rights and Indian law matters and litigation arising out of administrative agency regulation of business and industry.
**Prof. Memberships:** State Bar of New Mexico; American Bar Association
**Career:** Partner at Holland & Hart since

2001.

**Publications:** Has spoken on a number of Indian law and water law issues at CLE conferences.

**Personal:** London School of Economics and Political Science (LLM 1975); University of Illinois (JD 1974); Benedictine College (AB 1970, magna cum laude)

### SIMONS, Andrew
Sutin, Thayer & Browne, Albuquerque
505 883 2500
*Recommended in Native American Law*

### SINGLETON, Sarah
Montgomery & Andrews, PA, Santa Fe
505 982 3873
*Recommended in Environment*

### SLADE, Lynn
Modrall, Sperling, Roehl, Harris & Sisk, PA, Albuquerque 505 848 1800
*Recommended in Environment, Native American Law*

### STEPHENSON, Barbara
Gilkey & Stephenson PA, Albuquerque
505 242 4466
*Recommended in Employment*

### STERN, Walter
Modrall, Sperling, Roehl, Harris & Sisk, PA, Albuquerque 505 848 1800
*Recommended in Environment, Native American Law*

### STOUT, David
Carpenter & Stout Ltd, Albuquerque
505 243 1336
*Recommended in Litigation*

### STYLES, Mark
Hurley Toevs Styles Hamblin & Panter PA, Albuquerque 505 888 1188
*Recommended in Real Estate*

### SWEENEY, Jill K
Brownstein Hyatt & Farber PC, Albuquerque
505 724 9567
jsweeney@bhf-law.com
*Recommended in Corporate/Commercial*

**Practice Areas:** Shareholder in Brownstein Hyatt & Farber's Public Finance, Government Relations, and Corporate & Securities groups. She focuses on public finance and economic development.

**Personal:** Wake Forest University Babcock Graduate School of Management (MBA, 1992); Wake Forest University School of Law (JD, 1992); University of New Mexico (BBA, 1986).

### THROCKMORTON, Rex
Rodey, Dickason, Sloan, Akin & Robb, PA, Albuquerque 505 765 5900
*Recommended in Litigation*

### TINNIN, Robert
Tinnin Law Firm, Albuquerque
505 768 1500
*Recommended in Employment*

### VIDMAR, Stephan
Miller Stratvert PA, Albuquerque
505 842 1950
*Recommended in Litigation*

### WARNER, Whitney
Moody & Warner PC, Albuquerque
505 944 0033
*Recommended in Employment*

### WELLS, Lawrence
Campbell and Wells PA, Albuquerque
505 830 9213
*Recommended in Real Estate*

### WOLF, Wayne
Wolf Taylor & McCaleb, Albuquerque
505 888 6600
*Recommended in Litigation*

### WORD, Terry
Word & Bogardus, Albuquerque
505 842 1905
*Recommended in Litigation*

# GILKEY & STEPHENSON, P.A.

## THE FIRM

**Managing Partner:** Duane C Gilkey
**Senior Partners:** Duane C Gilkey, Barbara G Stephenson

**Number of partners:** 4
**Number of other lawyers:** 1

## AREAS OF PRACTICE:

Employment & Labor Litigation . . . . . . . . . . . . . . . . . . . . . . . . . . . . . 90%
Employment & Labor Counseling . . . . . . . . . . . . . . . . . . . . . . . . . . 10%

**FIRM OVERVIEW:** Gilkey & Stephenson, P.A. offers employers specialized representation in employment and labor law matters. From its founding in 1995, the firm's mission has been to offer the high-quality representation of a big firm with the personalized and cost-effective touch of a small firm. More than 90% of the firm's work is defending lawsuits brought against national and local clients. The firm's litigation practice is enhanced by the firm's active practice in counseling and training employers to prevent disputes from turning into administrative charges or litigation.

**MAIN AREAS OF PRACTICE:** The firm provides effective representation in the following areas:

**Employment/Discrimination Matters:** Race, sex, disability, and age discrimination; sexual harassment and hostile work environment claims; whistleblower claims; and retaliation claims, under state and federal law.

**Employment Contracts:** Confidentiality agreements; non-compete agreements; compensation agreements; executive compensation; and state common law claims.

**Employee Benefits:** ERISA litigation; FLSA litigation; FMLA litigation; workplace safety (and violence claims); employee privacy; and contract claims.

**Labor Law:** Claims under the NLRA; union organization, union certification, union elections, and related litigation; administration of labor contracts, including grievance procedures; renegotiation of collective bargaining agreements; strikes, picketing, lockouts, and injunctions; and federal court litigation and appeals.

**Employment Law Counseling:** Wage and hour issues; leaves of absence; trade secrets; wrongful termination; sexual harassment investigations; principal independent contractor relationships; litigation avoidance; policy audits; policy manual development; employee training.

**Alternative Dispute Resolution:** Mediation and arbitration.

**Reported Cases:** Some reported cases handled by the firm's attorneys include: Brillhart v Philips Electronics North America Corp., 179 F.3d 1271 (10th Cir. 1999) (reinstating jury verdict in favor of employer in retaliation claim); Armijo v Prudential Ins. Co. of America, 72 F.3d 793 (10th Cir. 1995) (decision compelling arbitration); Carr v Stryker Corp., 28 F.3d 112 (10th Cir. 1994) (affirming summary judgment for employer in breach of contract case); Jackson v City of Bloomfield, 731 F.2d 652 (10th Cir. 1984) (wrongful termination claim under 42 U.S.C. § 1983); Sheet Metal Workers Intern. Ass'n Local Union No. 49, AFL-CIO v Los Alamos Constructors, Inc., 550 F.2d 1258 (10th Cir. 1977) (holding in favor of contractor on forum selection clause); Chicano Police Officer's Ass'n v Stover, 552 F.2d 918 (10th Cir. 1977) (suit challenging allegedly race-motivated hiring procedures); Salazar v Furr's Inc., 629 F. Supp. 1403 (D.N.M. 1986) (dismissing pregnancy discrimination and related claims); Zuniga v Sears, Roebuck & Co., 671 P.2d 662 (N.M. App. 1983) (affirming summary judgment for employer in wrongful discharge and slander action).

## HEAD OFFICE

**NEW MEXICO**
500 Marquette Avenue NW, Suite 505, **Albuquerque,** NM 87102
**Tel:** 505 242 4466    **Fax:** 505 242 3145
**Website:** www.gilkeylaw.com

**CLIENTS:** Gilkey & Stephenson, P.A. represents a variety of employers ranging from local to international, as well as local and state-wide public entities. Some of the clients the firm has represented include: Intel Corporation; Washington TRU Solutions LLC; Philips Semiconductors; Southwest Airlines Co.; Raley's of New Mexico; Business Environments; Citigroup Inc.; CUNA Mutual Insurance Group; Dillard Store Services, Inc.; Risk Management Division, State of New Mexico; New Mexico Association of Counties; the University of New Mexico; American Gypsum Company; Lovelace Respiratory Research Institute; Bowlin Travel Centers, Inc.; and Delta Air Lines.

**INTERNATIONAL WORK:** The firm has represented a number of non-US clients in litigation within the United States.

# HINKLE, HENSLEY, SHANOR & MARTIN L.L.P.

## THE FIRM

**Managing Partner:** C D Martin, Midland, TX office

**Number of partners:** 27
**Number of other lawyers:** 7

**FIRM OVERVIEW:** Hinkle, Hensley, Shanor & Martin, L.L.P. is one of the oldest and largest law firms in New Mexico and West Texas. Tracing its history to 1888 when its founder, Granville A Richardson, opened the first law office in Roswell in the Territory of New Mexico, the firm now has offices in Roswell and Santa Fe, New Mexico, and in Midland and Austin, Texas. The firm's geographical diversity has contributed to its growth and stability. The Roswell and Midland offices are located on or adjacent to large on-shore oil and gas reserves. The Santa Fe office is located at the commercial, financial, and governmental centers of New Mexico. Offices and lawyers communicate and work together as if they were in a single location. The educational and specialty diversities of the firm's lawyers provide the highest quality of services.

## MAIN AREAS OF PRACTICE:

**Natural Resources:** The Hinkle law firm's natural resources practice area represents the largest area of expertise in the firm. The group conducts all types of title examinations in NM and Texas including fee, state, federal and Indian lands, and land grants. The firm's attorneys also have an extensive practice in all areas of natural resources contract law, including purchase and sale agreements, oil and gas leases, oil field accidents, exploration and joint venture agreements, and Indian development contracts. An extensive litigation practice relating to natural resources also has developed within the firm. Litigators have considerable experience in specific areas of natural resources such as titles, contracts, royalty issues, operations, and taxation, as well as general knowledge and expertise in oil, gas and other natural resources and environmental operations. Oil, gas and other natural resources attorneys are continually involved in matters relating to due diligence and the preparation of instruments necessary to finance natural resources transactions, such as mortgages, deeds of trust, loan agreements, financing opinions and documentation in both Texas and New Mexico. They also practice regularly before various federal and state agencies relating to industry matters. These agencies include the New Mexico Oil Conservation Division, the Texas Railroad Commission, the Bureau of Land Management, the Forest Service, the Interior Board of Land Appeals, the Bureau of Indian Affairs, FERC, the Minerals Management Service, the New Mexico State Engineer, and various Texas, New Mexico and federal environmental agencies.

**Water Law:** The firm's attorneys have extensive experience in the area of water law and represent clients before state administrative agencies and state and federal courts concerning all aspects of water rights law, including permitting, acquisitions, transfers, adjudications and other litigation.

**Environmental Law:** Environmental attorneys have broad expertise in environmental compliance and litigation. They regularly assist with the performance of environmental audits and assessments in real estate transactions. They also analyze natural resource business activities to ensure compliance with state and federal environmental regulations, including the New Mexico Oil and Gas Act, the New Mexico Hazardous Water Act and Clean Water Act, Texas Clean Water Act, Texas Solid Waste Disposal Act, CECLA, RCRA, NEPA, and a variety of other environmental laws.

**Litigation:** In addition to its natural resources litigation practice the firm also has extensive litigation experience in other litigation including bankruptcy, banking, contracts, construction, corporations, environmental, general commercial, government contracts, insurance, employment, land use and zoning, personal injury and wrongful death, products liability, professional negligence, public utility, real estate, tax and torts.

## HEAD OFFICE

**NEW MEXICO**
400 Penn Plaza, Suite 700, **Roswell**, NM 88201
**Tel:** 505 622 6510   **Fax:** 505 623 9332
**Website:** www.hinklelawfirm.com

## BRANCH OFFICES

**NEW MEXICO**
218 Montezuma Ave, **Santa Fe**, NM 87501
**Tel:** 505 982 4554   **Fax:** 505 982 8623

**TEXAS**
550 W Texas Ave, Suite 1200, **Midland**, TX 79701
**Tel:** 432 683 4691   **Fax:** 432 683 6518

919 Congress Ave, Suite 1150, **Austin**, TX 78701
**Tel:** 512 476 7137   **Fax:** 512 476 7146

## CONTACTS

| | |
|---|---|
| **Natural Resources Litigation** | Harold Hensley (Midland) |
| **Natural Resources other** | Douglas Lunsford (Roswell) |
| **General Litigation** | Stuart D Shanor (Roswell) |
| **Environmental** | Tom Hnasko (Santa Fe) |
| **Public Utilities** | Richard Wilfong (Austin) |

**Public Utilities:** Hinkle, Hensley, Shanor & Martin's longtime representation of a large electric utility operating in Texas, New Mexico, Oklahoma, and Kansas has enabled the firm to acquire the skills and experience needed for effective representation of clients before the various regulatory commissions in the four states including the Public Utility Commission of Texas and the New Mexico Public Regulation Commission.

**General Business Practice:** The firm maintains a broad general business practice including bankruptcy, federal and state taxation, estate planning, probate, contract, employment law, banking, real estate, and general corporate counsel.

**CLIENTS:** Hinkle, Hensley, Shanor & Martin, L.L.P. represents a broad range of regional and national clients including ExxonMobil, ChevronTexaco, Conoco Phillips, Pogo Producing, Bass Enterprises, Devon Energy, The Goodyear Tire and Rubber Company, Wells Fargo Bank, Southwestern Public Service Company, and Xcel Energy.

# MONTGOMERY & ANDREWS, PA

## THE FIRM

**Managing Shareholders:** Gary Kilpatric, Thomas W Olson, Randy Bartell
**Senior Shareholder:** Victor R Ortega

**Number of shareholders:** 13
**Number of other lawyers:** 6

**FIRM OVERVIEW:** Montgomery & Andrews, PA, is a full-service law firm in Santa Fe, New Mexico. Founded in 1937, M&A is known for the breadth and depth of its experience in legal and regulatory matters and its familiarity with how the executive and legislative branches of the New Mexico state government function. Firm members have served as state legislators during the firm's history, and former members have gone on to serve as a Chief Judge of the United States Court of Appeals for the Tenth Circuit, as Chief Justices of the New Mexico Supreme Court, and as Chief United States District Judge for the District of New Mexico. William R Federici, who is now counsel emeritus to the firm, is a former Chief Justice of the New Mexico Supreme Court. The firm also has a strong background in natural resources, employment, utility regulation, insurance defense, products liability, medical malpractice defense and commercial and real estate transactions.

## MAIN AREAS OF PRACTICE:

**Environmental Law:** Regulatory compliance and legislative services for mining, oil and gas, municipal and other clients.
**Insurance Defense & Regulation, Products Liability Defense & Commercial Litigation:** General commercial litigation, litigation on behalf of insurance companies and their policyholders against all types of claims in federal and state courts, and in regulatory matters before the Insurance Division of the Public Regulation Commission, and defense of litigation against pharmaceutical companies, vehicle manuacturers, and healthcare providers.
**Legislative Services:** Lobbying and legislation drafting for a great many corporate, business, and trade association clients. Complex commercial litigation.
**Utility Regulation & Commercial Transactions:** Administrative and litigation services in a wide range of utility areas, and contractual and other business and real estate transactions.
**Water Law:** Litigation, legislative, administrative and transactional services in interstate water disputes, water right acquisition and transfer, and water right adjudication and administration.

**CLIENTS:** Representative clients include Allstate Insurance Co.; American Express; American Insurance Association; Anheuser-Busch Companies, Inc.; Bayer Corporation; Burlington Resources Oil and Gas Co.; City of Santa Fe; Community Health Systems; DaimlerChrysler Corporation; Delta Dental Plan of New Mexico; Devon Energy Corporation; Duke Energy Field Services, L.P.; El Paso Corporation; General Motors Corporation; Giant Industries, Inc.; Harland Financial Solutions; Home Depot U.S.A., Inc.; Intel Corporation; IronStone Bank; LAC Minerals (USA), Inc.; Louisiana Energy Services; Marathon Oil Company; Massachusetts Mutual Life Insurance Co.; Michelin North America, Inc.; Molycorp, Inc.; New Mexico Oil and Gas Association; New Mexico-American Water Co.; New Mexico Association of Counties; New Mexico Lodging Association; New Mexico Utilities, Inc.; Oglebay-Norton, Inc.; Pfizer Inc.; Phelps-Dodge Corporation; Protection Technology Los Alamos, Inc.; Qwest Corporation; Realtors Association of New Mexico; Regents of University of California (Los Alamos National Laboratory); Schlumberger, Ltd.; St. Vincent Hospital; State of Kansas; State of Montana; State of New Mexico; The New Mexican; St. Paul/Travelers Insurance Co.; University of New Mexico; Wyeth; XTO Energy.

## HEAD OFFICE

**NEW MEXICO**
325 Paseo de Peralta, **Santa Fe**, NM 87501
**Tel:** 505 982 3873   **Fax:** 505 982 4289
**Website:** www.montand.com

## CONTACTS

| | |
|---|---|
| Environmental Law | Louis W Rose |
| Insurance Defense & Regulation, Products Liability Defense & Commercial Litigation | Walter J Melendres |
| Legislative Services | Gary Kilpatric |
| Oil & Gas, Mining & Employment Litigation | Sarah M Singleton |
| Utility Regulation & Commercial Transactions | Thomas W Olson |
| Water Law | John B Draper |

## How lawyers are ranked

Every year we carry out thousands of in-depth interviews with clients and lawyers in order to assess the reputations and expertise of business lawyers across the USA. Chambers rankings and editorial are referred to extensively by General Counsel and other purchasers of legal services who look to our recommendations when choosing their lawyers.

# ANTITRUST

**Antitrust**

**Leading Firms**

1. CRAVATH, SWAINE & MOORE LLP *New York*
   DAVIS POLK & WARDWELL *New York*
   SIMPSON THACHER & BARTLETT LLP *New York*
   SKADDEN, ARPS *New York*
   WEIL, GOTSHAL & MANGES LLP *New York*
2. SHEARMAN & STERLING LLP *New York*
   WACHTELL, LIPTON, ROSEN & KATZ *New York*
3. PAUL, WEISS *New York*
   SULLIVAN & CROMWELL LLP *New York*
4. AXINN, VELTROP & HARKRIDER LLP *New York*
   BOIES, SCHILLER & FLEXNER LLP *Armonk*
   DEBEVOISE & PLIMPTON LLP *New York*
   DEWEY BALLANTINE LLP *New York*
   FRIED, FRANK *New York*
   KAYE SCHOLER LLP *New York*
   MAYER, BROWN, ROWE & MAW LLP *New York*
   WHITE & CASE LLP *New York*
   WILLKIE FARR & GALLAGHER LLP *New York*

## Band 1

### Cravath, Swaine & Moore LLP

See firm details p.1527

**The Firm:** Competitors agree that this firm's illustrious heritage in the litigation arena has placed it in pole position for attracting complex and high-profile antitrust matters. While much praise is reserved for its transactional practice, which contains "*great negotiators who know how to get a deal done,*" Cravath is best known for the experience and expertise it leverages when circumstances become contentious. The litigation team is a familiar presence before the FTC and DOJ, representing clients in a variety of merger and unfair practice investigations. Commentators approve of a group ethos that recognizes that "*the goal is not simply to attack but to seek creative and long-lasting solutions.*" Attorneys are currently defending Bristol-Myers Squibb before the California Superior Court in an action alleging that a number of major drug companies have formed a cartel, the effect of which is to charge artificially higher prices for their drugs in the USA than abroad. **The Lawyers: Robert Joffe** (see p.1468) is "*an*

*absolutely fantastic litigator, who achieves his aims without ruffling any feathers.*" He deploys these skills in a range of antitrust matters, most recently obtaining unconditional clearance for the Sprint-Nextel merger. **Evan Chesler** (see p.1444) has "*one of the best courtroom and boardroom presences,*" according to peers. In a broad practice that includes securities and IP-related litigation expertise, antitrust is a particular strength, with observers confirming: "*He excels at leading a large team of lawyers in addressing complex issues.*" Along with Elizabeth Grayer, Chesler is defending American Express in class action litigation arising from claims that merchants who accept American Express charge cards have been compelled to accept the company's credit and debit cards as well. **Ronald Rolfe** (see p.1493) is widely renowned as a "*hard-driving and tenacious litigator.*" Antitrust, securities, SEC and grand jury investigations all fall within his considerable remit. **Katherine Forrest** (see p.1456) regularly provides companies with advice on the antitrust and competition law implications of structuring business ventures. Onlookers applaud her "*analytical and organizational aptitude*" and her prominence in the media industry. She is assisting major client Time Warner with assorted issues relating to next-generation DVD formats.

**Clients/Work Highlights:** The team successfully defended IBM against accusations by Compuware that it had violated antitrust laws by tying the sale of goods to the sale of mainframe software that competed with Compuware products. Other clients include RDI, QUALCOMM and Ripplewood Holdings.

### Davis Polk & Wardwell

See firm details p.1528

**The Firm:** Davis Polk's "*first-tier*" antitrust group is integrated into its "*powerhouse*" litigation department and represents corporations and individuals allegedly involved in marketing and sales conspiracies. In the last twelve months the team has consolidated its market-leading position. For example, it has defended one of the largest defendants embroiled in a series of vitamins price-fixing claims; such claims have been tried in federal and state jurisdictions all over the USA. On behalf of F. Hoffmann-La Roche, the firm was victorious in both the Supreme Court and the Court of Appeals for the DC circuit in a case

pertaining to the international compass of federal antitrust laws. The group also represents clients facing tying, monopolization and patent misuse allegations. In light of this track record, it is unsurprising that the firm's profile in the antitrust arena has been dominated by litigation. Peers also note that the firm has recently capitalized on its prestigious corporate practice to boost its transactional output. As such, it advised manufacturer Gillette on the antitrust aspects of its $57 billion acquisition by Procter & Gamble, "*one of the most significant deals*" of 2005. **The Lawyers: Ronan Harty** (see p.1464) brings "*intelligence and great judgment*" to a practice that encompasses representing clients in enforcement agency investigations, domestic and cross-border acquisitions and related litigation. **Arthur Golden** (see p.1460) earns the respect of peers for an impressive performance as lead counsel in the Gillette-Procter merger. He provides advice on corporate governance matters and acts in civil and criminal disputes. Experienced in domestic and international acquisitions, and joint ventures with dual US and EC antitrust considerations, **Paul Bartel** (see p.1436) "*always gets to the bottom line of a deal and keeps things streamlined.*" **Joel Cohen** (see p.1446) applies a "*common-sense and pragmatic touch*" to antitrust litigation arising from alleged patent misuse.

**Clients/Work Highlights:** The firm is national counsel to AstraZeneca and lead coordinating counsel for all the manufacturers involved in myriad federal and state governmental actions, challenging the role of 'average wholesale price' as an appropriate reimbursement standard for the pharmaceutical industry. Other clients include Cargill; CNOOC; Comcast; DLJ Merchant Banking Partners III; Allmerica Financial; Imagistics; Olympus; Jacuzzi Brands; VF and Mueller Water Products.

### Simpson Thacher & Bartlett LLP

See firm details p.1555

**The Firm:** Matching a strong and deep bench with star turns by some of the market's most venerated practitioners, Simpson Thacher is flying high at the moment. The antitrust practice is booming on the transactional side, with attorneys supervising adidas' $4.3 billion acquisition of Reebok, and Kmart's $11 billion purchase of Sears. The group is equally active in major litigation, representing Lehman Brothers

## Antitrust
### Leading Individuals

#### Senior Statesman

HAWK Barry *Skadden, Arps*

★ ARQUIT Kevin *Simpson Thacher & Bartlett*

[1] GOTTS Ilene *Wachtell*

HARTY Ronan *Davis Polk & Wardwell*

JOFFE Robert *Cravath, Swaine & Moore*

[2] AXINN Stephen *Axinn, Veltrop & Harkrider*

BOIES David *Boies, Schiller & Flexner*

CONSTANTINE Lloyd *Constantine Cannon PC*

LOGAN Kenneth *Simpson Thacher & Bartlett*

SCHER Irving *Weil, Gotshal & Manges*

[3] ANGLAND Joseph *Heller Ehrman LLP*

BYOWITZ Michael *Wachtell, Lipton, Rosen & Katz*

CHESLER Evan *Cravath, Swaine & Moore*

COLLINS W Dale *Shearman & Sterling LLP*

GOLDEN Arthur *Davis Polk & Wardwell*

GOLDFEIN Shepard *Skadden, Arps*

JOHNSTON M Elaine *White & Case LLP*

KOOB Charles *Simpson Thacher & Bartlett*

PEARLSTEIN Debra *Weil, Gotshal & Manges LLP*

PRINCE Kenneth *Shearman & Sterling LLP*

ROLFE Ronald *Cravath, Swaine & Moore*

ROONEY William *Willkie Farr & Gallagher LLP*

STEUER Richard *Mayer, Brown*

WARDEN John *Sullivan & Cromwell LLP*

WEINER Michael *Skadden, Arps*

[4] ALBERT Lauren *Axinn, Veltrop & Harkrider*

ARONSON Clifford *Skadden, Arps*

BARTEL II Paul *Davis Polk & Wardwell*

BOAST Molly *Debevoise & Plimpton LLP*

COHEN Joel *Davis Polk & Wardwell*

COLLINS John *Dewey Ballantine LLP*

CROSS Wayne *White & Case LLP*

FASTOW Jay *Weil, Gotshal & Manges*

FORREST Katherine *Cravath, Swaine & Moore*

JAFFE Helene *Weil, Gotshal & Manges*

KESSLER Jeffrey *Dewey Ballantine LLP*

KRAMER Kenneth *Shearman & Sterling LLP*

MORGENSTERN Saul *Kaye Scholer LLP*

NEILL David *Wachtell*

ORR Dennis *Mayer, Brown*

QUINN Yvonne *Sullivan & Cromwell LLP*

SILVERMAN Moses *Paul, Weiss*

STOLL Neal *Skadden, Arps*

SYNNOTT Aidan *Paul, Weiss*

TRINGALI Joseph *Simpson Thacher & Bartlett*

UROWSKY Richard *Sullivan & Cromwell LLP*

VICTOR A Paul *Weil, Gotshal & Manges*

#### Up-and-coming individuals

HARKRIDER John *Axinn, Veltrop & Harkrider*

LARSON Joseph *Wachtell*

MARTIN Scott *Weil, Gotshal & Manges*

SCHAEFFER Fiona *Weil, Gotshal & Manges*

and JPMorgan Chase in a class action alleging that underwriter fees in public offerings were fixed at 7% as a result of underwriter conspiracy. It also defended

M-real in federal and state investigations and private class action litigations relating to price-fixing allegations in the publication paper industry.

**The Lawyers:** Formerly head of the Bureau of Competition at the FTC, **Kevin Arquit**'s (see p.1434) "*tremendous command of antitrust law*" combines profound knowledge of merger clearance issues with a "*wonderful*" – and much envied – rapport with government agencies. Peers draw attention to his substantial regulatory expertise, for which "*he is on everybody's shortlist.*" He represents clients drawn from the airline, pharmaceutical, electronic, chemical and healthcare sectors in a variety of transactions and class actions. "*One of the best antitrust attorneys in the country,*" **Kenneth Logan** (see p.1476) "*remains calm under pressure. He is a great conciliator.*" These attributes are at the center of a highly successful merger practice that focuses on the entertainment, telecom and pharmaceutical industries. Co-head of the litigation department, **Charles Koob** (see p.1472) is an established figure at the antitrust Bar. Koob received plaudits for his trial skills, with clients praising the quality of his counsel in matters ranging from FTC and DOJ merger investigations, to criminal and civil injunction hearings and jury trials. **Joseph Tringali** (see p.1509) specializes in litigating civil antitrust actions under the Sherman, Robinson-Patman and Hart-Scott-Rodino acts. Tringali has acquired a reputation as a "*formidable and aggressive*" attorney, who is devoted to his clients.

**Clients/Work Highlights:** The firm is representing Weyerhaeuser in five monopolization cases challenging Weyerhaeuser's purchases of logs in the Pacific Northwest. Other clients include Express Scripts; Mastercard; Galen Holdings and M-real.

### Skadden, Arps, Slate, Meagher & Flom LLP & Affiliates
See firm details p.1557

**The Firm:** Skadden is indubitably one of the largest firms in the country, and peers decree that it is also "*one of the most formidable presences*" in the New York antitrust marketplace. The team's proficiency in a multitude of sectors, including healthcare, technology and investment banking, extends to comprehensive experience in the sports arena. It acted for the National Hockey League in a player dispute relating to the negotiation of national and global broadcasting contracts. Elsewhere, team members work on a myriad of criminal and civil cases in federal and state courts. It has also represented a host of other entertainment, beverage and chemical companies before the FTC. Sources applaud a "*rapid response time*" that enables the firm to handle the most complex cases with skill and assurance. The firm also boasts a reputation for excellence in transactional matters, with antitrust attorneys working closely with M&A colleagues to offer clients comprehensive regulatory assistance and agency advice. For example, the group recently advised Guidant on a $25 billion acquisition offer.

**The Lawyers:** "*Street smart*" **Shepard Goldfein** (see p.1460) handles a wide range of complex antitrust actions, fielding particular expertise in high-stakes

sports litigation, cultivated through representation of the National Hockey League. Elsewhere, he advises clients on business practices as they fall within the sphere of price-fixing regulations. Goldfein is involved in a unique monopolization case on behalf of International Paper. **Michael Weiner**'s (see p.1512) practice is evenly split between federal and state litigation and merger work arising from the technology and insurance markets. He "*gets the job done in an efficient way*" and demonstrates a "*great understanding of the way in which the agencies operate.*" The charismatic **Clifford Aronson** (see p.1434) combines technical finesse with an "*acute awareness of the potential risks of a transaction.*" He acts for a range of major pharmaceutical and energy companies. **Neal Stoll** (see p.1505) is a beacon for clients seeking representation in connection with FTC investigations stemming from the bureaus of competition and consumer protection. He took a leading role in the Guidant transaction. One of the first attorneys to explore domestic antitrust law in an international context, **Barry Hawk** (see p.1464) has a "*well-deserved reputation*" for excellence when it comes to "*identifying the intersections*" of global merger control laws.

**Clients/Work Highlights:** National Basketball Association; NFL; IBC; CEMEX; Coastal; Warner-Lambert; Citigroup; DaimlerChrysler and UnitedHealth Group.

### Weil, Gotshal & Manges LLP
See firm details p.1565

**The Firm:** Sources agree that this firm's New York office continues to provide unsurpassed "*depth of experience and breadth of expertise.*" The team has recently grown, bolstering its ranks in the last couple of years with three new partners, while the firm's expansion into DC has caused ripples throughout the market. In addition to providing businesses with counseling and representation before government agencies, the team offers specialist advice on advertising, distribution and consumer protection issues to retailers such as Wal-Mart. A long history in the financial services arena has also seen the firm representing clients such as MasterCard in multidistrict litigation involving seven leading US financial organizations. In the health sector the group is overseeing the UnitedHealthcare-PacifiCare merger, and defending the former against class actions brought by doctors and a range of other healthcare professionals. A "*wonderful practice, populated by talented practitioners,*" the firm regularly represents its clientele before grand jury investigations.

**The Lawyers:** "*Dean of the Bar*" **Irving Scher** (see p.1497) focuses on issues arising from distribution practices. Boasting wide-ranging experience of litigation at a national coordination level, he "*always comes up with the goods*" during trial. Recently, **Debra Pearlstein** (see p.1487) has turned her "*incredible mastery of the law*" toward cases with overlapping antitrust and IP concerns. She receives countless marketplace panegyrics as a "*extremely talented attorney*" and "*wonderful human being.*" Clients flock to **Jay Fastow** (see p.1453) for his insight into their businesses, and praise him for being "*thorough and responsive – he has a low-key style that plays well with judges.*" Fastow continues to immerse himself in the financial services sector, winning a reversal for MasterCard in a matter arising from fraudulent practice allegations. **Helene Jaffe** (see p.1468) employs her "*formidable skill set*" in competitor suing and marketing-related litigation. Following three years with the DOJ's antitrust division, **Paul Victor** (see p.1509) is frequently lead trial lawyer in criminal and civil international cartel cases. Peers credit him with raising the firm's profile in Asia. "*Zealous advocate*" **Scott Martin** (see p.1477) also specializes in litigation connected with alleged cartel activity. He "*really knows his stuff,*" assisting a variety of heavy-manufacturing clients. **Fiona Schaeffer** (see p.1497) is deeply involved in UnitedHealthcare's acquisition of PacifiCare and undertakes a range of work on behalf of MasterCard. Peers relish the fact that she is "*always on the same page*" during difficult cases and envy her knowledge of EU competition law.

## Band 2

### Shearman & Sterling LLP
See firm details p.1554

**The Firm:** Originating in the firm's corporate department, the antitrust group's unrivaled expertise in econometrics and its acute understanding of the nuances of complex transactions ensure that it is a potent advocate before government authorities. In the past year it has effected a swift conclusion to DeVita's purchase of Gambro's dialysis technology, overseen Novartis's absorption of Eon Labs, and advised Mittal Steel on its acquisition of SIG Steel. Although, as peers are quick to point out, much of the firm's dispute work is generated in a merger context, team members regularly collaborate with colleagues in the litigation department to tackle cartel investigations and enforcement claims. As an illustration, the group is representing two leading elevator contractors in a class action relating to alleged EU and US price fixing and bid rigging. It is also acting for Syngenta in its suit against Monsanto. **The Lawyers:** **Dale Collins** (see p.1446) cuts a distinctive figure against the backdrop of the New York antitrust scene. A "*practical and savvy practitioner in this arena,*" Collins boasts a PhD in economics, melded with technical skills gained during his time at Caltech, and provides clients with spirited and sophisticated defense during federal and state merger investigations. Peers concur that **Kenneth Prince** (see p.1490) knows statutory policy and interpretation "*forward and backward.*" He divides his practice between M&A matters, cartel investigations and general litigation where he receives praise for being "*good on his feet in court.*" **Kenneth Kramer** (see p.1472) is a senior partner and former chair of the litigation practice. Combining shrewd judgment with a long experience of the marketplace, he represents a raft of domestic and international corporations in antitrust disputes.

**Clients/Work Highlights:** The firm represented Thomson Scientific & Healthcare in its acquisition of IHI. Other clients include Barclays Bank; Norske Skog; Merck; Blockbuster; Schindler Holding and Schindler Elevator.

### Wachtell, Lipton, Rosen & Katz
See firm details p.1561

**The Firm:** Wachtell's reputation as an "*absolutely fantastic*" corporate law firm has led to the antitrust team founding its "*powerhouse*" reputation on M&A work, as opposed to enforcement and unfair practice cases. It assists clients with the development of strategies intended to circumvent potential government agency objections during the merger process. As such, its members boast considerable insight into the mechanisms of the FTC, the Federal Reserve Board and foreign antitrust enforcement authorities.

**The Lawyers:** The "*fabulous*" **Ilene Gotts** (see p.1461) directs her myriad talents toward M&A work, specializing in telecom and hi-tech-related acquisitions. She continues to represent AT&T, advising on filings in foreign jurisdictions such as the UK. Spearheading the antitrust practice, **Michael Byowitz** (see p.1442) devotes his time to guiding multinational corporations through significant domestic and global mergers and corporate takeovers. Financial services expert **David Neill** (see p.1482) is regarded as adept at counseling on bank acquisitions. He is advising on NYSE's merger with Archipelago Holdings. **Joseph Larson** (see p.1473) textures his experience of US antitrust law with a deep understanding of EU, South American, Canadian and Asian antitrust standards. "*Just so smart,*" he is applauded by clients for the aptitude and proficiency he demonstrates throughout transactions.

## Band 3

### Paul, Weiss, Rifkind, Wharton & Garrison LLP
See firm details p.1548

**The Firm:** Paul Weiss operates a "*sophisticated, broad-based litigation practice,*" according to interviewees, and with a caseload that includes representing AIG in the high-profile investigation of the insurance industry launched by Attorney General Eliot Spitzer, it is not difficult to understand why. The firm's "*highly accomplished bunch*" of attorneys also acts for MasterCard in all its US litigation, winning dismissals of numerous separate state indirect purchaser suits. The group also assists with obtaining antitrust approval of major transactions and handles FTC and DOJ investigations. One source asserts: "*From a public company standpoint, the team is flawless with its advice, prediction and execution.*" In the past year, the group advised Intelsat on its acquisition of PanAmSat, and continues to represent a plethora of clients from the food and beverage, motion picture, petrochemical, pharmaceutical and automobile sectors.

**The Lawyers:** **Moses Silverman** (see p.1502) "*has a deep understanding of business fundamentals,*"

observed peers. He has successfully defeated class certification in antitrust and securities cases, representing clients in litigation as well as mergers and second request matters. "*One of the best at communicating articulately with business people and setting realistic objectives,*" **Aidan Synnott** (see p.1506) undertakes a combination of litigation and M&A work. He has been handling work for major client ACNielsen, winning on motion an important case before it went to trial.

**Clients/Work Highlights:** ACNielsen; Dun & Bradstreet; IMS Health; Siemens and Becton Dickinson.

### Sullivan & Cromwell LLP
See firm details p.1558

**The Firm:** Sullivan & Cromwell's "*trademark style*" in litigation, characterized by one observer as "*aggressive and energetic,*" may divide opinion among peers, but results in a market visibility, case volume and rate of success envied by many. Boasting a "*well-organized*" antitrust team that "*thinks outside the box,*" the firm represents US and non-US companies before regulatory bodies and courts across the country. Interviewees also noted the strength of its affiliation with the investment banking quarter. As well as defending Microsoft in a milestone action brought by the DOJ in 19 states, it advises clients on mergers, joint ventures, asset sales, licensing, distribution and marketing strategies.

**The Lawyers:** "*Terrific trial lawyer*" **John Warden** (see p.1511) was lead counsel in the Microsoft litigation and represents clients such as Goldman Sachs and British Airways on board-level antitrust disputes. Warden displays a "*great ability to cross-examine witnesses.*" While many attorneys "*glide along the surface of a deal,*" **Yvonne Quinn** (see p.1490) "*is not afraid to get her hands dirty and immerse herself in the nitty-gritty details.*" She represents financial institutions, newspapers, television operators and book publishers, inter alia, in a full range of matters. Peers admire the way in which Quinn "*keeps her cool in the most difficult circumstances.*" **Richard Urowsky** (see p.1509) is "*superb*" in complex litigation, honing his skills with extensive experience of competition issues, as well as M&A, joint venture and pricing concerns.

**Clients/Work Highlights:** Avon Products; Computer Associates International; Diageo; MBNA and BP.

## Band 4

### Axinn, Veltrop & Harkrider LLP
See firm details p.1518

**The Firm:** Attorneys at this respected boutique are "*always available, diligent and work extremely hard.*" For observers, the team's strength lies in its healthy relationships with government agencies and its corresponding depth of expertise in the realm of M&A. Adept at all elements of state, federal and international antitrust and trade regulation compliance, attorneys were successful in obtaining clearance for GameStop's acquisition of Electronics Boutique without the need for a second request. The firm also represented one of Cingular's parent companies during its purchase by AT&T. While its litigation practice does not receive as much press, it is no stranger to grand jury investigations. In the past twelve months, the team was counsel to the plaintiff in a case arising from a suit brought against leading US motion picture distributors by an exhibitor alleging a boycott. The firm is also retained by the enforcement agencies, which instruct it to investigate mergers on their behalf.

**The Lawyers:** Remaining at the cutting edge of legal theory as a consequence of his *"tenacious, client-focused and hard-working"* attitude, **Stephen Axinn** (see p.1434) is regarded by many as *"the main show."* In a career that includes heading the antitrust and trade regulation department at Skadden Arps, Axinn has represented major corporate and plaintiff clients in countless significant trial and appellate matters, and also counsels on the agency nuances of merger clearance. Peers opine that **Lauren Albert** (see p.1432) is *"a great counselor and knows the government merger review market better than anyone."* As well as a pivotal role in the Cingular transaction, she acted for GameStop and MovieGallery in their respective acquisitions of Electronics Boutique and Hollywood Video. Albert is said to be *"good at getting critical papers filed and pulling together massive documentation."* *"Intelligent and accessible,"* **John Harkrider** (see p.1463) is characterized by peers as someone who *"brings to the table impressive economic knowledge – an important dimension that you don't always find elsewhere."* His client base includes MasterCard International's board of directors.

**Clients/Work Highlights:** The firm represented Omnicare in its successful acquisition of NeighborCare, and acted for SunGard in its acquisition of numerous private equity firms. The team also concluded litigation against CSFB on behalf of Prisma Energy.

## Boies, Schiller & Flexner LLP
See firm details p.1520

**The Firm:** To separate this firm from its progenitor, David Boies, is an impossible task. By virtue of this, it has cast-iron credibility in the litigation arena, boasting extensive experience defending and prosecuting high-stakes matters throughout the USA. In recent times, these have included United States v Microsoft, and the current vitamins price-fixing proceedings. The team also undertakes merger counseling, representing clients before the FTC and DOJ, and coordinating between offices in New York, DC, California, Florida, New Hampshire and New Jersey.

**The Lawyers:** **David Boies** (see p.1440) is chairman of the firm and undoubtedly its *"drawing card."* Omnipresent in the upper echelons of the antitrust market, he is *"a wonderful advocate"* and one of the premier litigators in the country, whose volume of work testifies to his superlative courtroom abilities.

**Clients/Work Highlights:** Philip Morris; DuPont; FEMSA Cerveza; Tyco International and SBC.

## Debevoise & Plimpton LLP
See firm details p.1529

**The Firm:** *"Respected leaders around the negotiation table,"* attorneys at this litigation-oriented practice bring *"exceptional clarity"* to a constellation of issues affecting clients from a range of industries, including those in the pharmaceutical, energy, chemical and aviation sectors. The team's expertise covers all areas of competition law, ranging from civil and criminal investigations brought by federal and state authorities, to private litigation relating to antitrust statutes. Attorneys applied this expertise on a novel dispute arising from United Airlines' bankruptcy, in which the airline claimed that its creditors, by working together to reclaim their money, had formed a price-fixing cartel. The team won for the creditors. Attorneys also assist clients with obtaining governmental approval for domestic and international mergers, and provide multifaceted advice on joint ventures and licensing agreements.

**The Lawyers:** Partner in the litigation department, **Molly Boast**'s diverse practice encompasses civil and criminal investigations and actions, private litigation, and US and foreign agency review of potential domestic and international acquisitions. She is currently advising the Associated Press on a raft of antitrust issues connected with its member newspapers.

## Dewey Ballantine LLP
See firm details p.1530

**The Firm:** This New York group represents a variety of industry clients in antitrust and trade regulation, boasting particular prominence in matters arising within the electronics industry. The departure in recent times of esteemed figures such as Joseph Angland has undoubtedly had an impact on Dewey's market profile, altering perceptions of its focus and areas of strength. However, interviewees agree that the firm's general aptitude for private litigation provides it with a momentum that shows no sign of lessening. For example, it defended Panasonic against a major monopolization claim brought by Tallis, relating to in-flight entertainment equipment. The firm also obtained a favorable settlement on behalf of five schools involved in a dispute with the National Collegiate Athletic Association. Attorneys are equally proficient assisting with the development of business strategies and advising clients on all aspects of competition and IP law.

**The Lawyers:** Peers have *"great affection"* for **John Collins** (see p.1446), who *"brings together immense knowledge of the law and a deep understanding of why businesses do what they do."* An impressive breadth of experience includes representing clients before the FTC and DOJ in relation to premerger notification proceedings and defending them in litigation. Litigation department cochair **Jeffrey Kessler**'s (see p.1470) expertise in sports law makes him a crucial element in the composition of Dewey's antitrust practice. Observers are full of praise for the *"capability and assuredness"* he demonstrates on behalf of heavyweights such as the National Football League Players' Association, the National Hockey League

Players' Association and adidas. Additional experience representing international companies in domestic criminal and civil investigations cements his value to the firm.

**Clients/Work Highlights:** The firm's clientele spans the automotive, chemical, energy and entertainment industries, and includes Matsushita and JVC.

## Fried, Frank, Harris, Shriver & Jacobson LLP
See firm details p.1532

**The Firm:** Although this firm's excellent DC practice attracts the lion's share of praise, the New York group continues to offer skilled and reliable advocacy in antitrust counseling and litigation. Team members also collaborate with colleagues fielding IP, technology and white-collar expertise in matters relating to trademark and patent issues. Experience defending clients against unfair competition, consumer protection and false advertising claims adds depth and variety to an already impressive array of services.

**The Lawyers:** **Allen Kezsbom**, a senior partner in the litigation department, offers a range of expertise, including in antitrust and unfair competition issues. Colleague **Linda Blumkin**, a respected presence in this market, became of counsel in 2005.

**Clients/Work Highlights:** Scotts; BellSouth; CIGNA; Columbia TriStar Motion Picture Group; El Paso; GKN; McKesson; National Services Industries and Rio Tinto.

## Kaye Scholer LLP
See firm details p.1536

**The Firm:** *"Great for raw brain power,"* this group's forte has always been litigation. Attorneys undertake a significant amount of biotech and pharmaceutical work, focusing on the cross-fertilization between the two industries and demonstrating an *"excellent"* degree of knowledge. The practice is currently in the final stages of brand-name prescription drug litigation, for Pfizer, in the Eastern District Court of New York. It is also no stranger to the complexities of multiple class actions connected with chemicals such as sorbates. Regular coordination with members of the firm's IP and e-commerce groups ensures that the team is ideally equipped to assist clients with every permutation of a problem, including alleged anticompetitive conduct.

**The Lawyers:** *"In conference calls, consisting of many lawyers clamoring for attention, one voice emerges as the voice of reason,"* and it belongs to **Saul Morgenstern** (see p.1481). Interviewees were unbounded in their plaudits, asserting that as a consequence of an *"astute and well-versed"* approach to complex matters, *"his presence embellishes the practice's standing."* A stellar caseload includes representing Novartis before the Californian courts in a horizontal price-fixing claim.

**Clients/Work Highlights:** Other clients include RJ Reynolds and Infineon.

## Mayer, Brown, Rowe & Maw LLP

See firm details p.876

**The Firm:** Boasting extensive global integration, this is "*one of the leading firms in the country*" for transatlantic work, and the New York offering is also bolstered by "*outstanding DC credentials.*" The four-partner team specializes in advising international chemical and pharmaceutical clients who are unaccustomed to US law and jurisdictional differences, particularly where distribution proposals are concerned. It is currently involved in an ongoing grand jury investigation pertaining to regulatory actions on several continents, including Asia. In the domestic arena, the firm advised Crompton on its merger with Great Lakes Chemical.

**The Lawyers:** Peers greatly admire **Richard Steuer**'s (see p.1505) ability to "*walk clients through every aspect*" of complex mergers. He "*gives advice instinctively and understands problems intuitively.*" He combines a counseling role with defending clients in private suits and against government organizations at all levels of federal and state court. **Dennis Orr** (see p.1485) offers clients "*good judgment, a sense of strategy and a wonderful rapport with business people,*" all of which more than validates his reputation as a "*stupendous attorney*" who is greatly in demand in this market. Orr has been retained to represent a major Swiss chemical company in an Illinois-based grand jury investigation into alleged price-fixing, relating to the marketing of certain chemicals. He is also representing Unilever in case pending in New Jersey, arising from the marketing of ice cream.

**Clients/Work Highlights:** Novartis; Lonza; Cadbury Schweppes and Pepsi Bottling Group.

## White & Case LLP

See firm details p.1566

**The Firm:** Few firms can match White & Case for global presence, making it the first port of call for international organizations seeking representation on US soil. Market commentators note that, in recent years, its corporate practice has been enhanced by a sophisticated and highly coordinated litigation team. Its representation of major Slovakian pharmaceutical company, Lek Pharmaceutical, in a case relating to alleged monopolization by GlaxoSmithKline, is indicative of the firm's global profile for contentious antitrust work. The firm's reputation for government and cartel investigations is also particularly well established: the team continues to represent Novartis before the FTC and various state enforcement agencies in complex, multidistrict antitrust litigation, arising from challenges to pricing practices under the Sherman and Robinson-Patman Acts. Clients were deeply impressed by attorneys' dedication to getting under the skin of their operations. One interviewee noted: "*They spend a lot of time learning about us, which warms my heart because not everyone does. They give excellent advice, couched in terms we understand.*" The firm also undertakes a substantial amount of merger counseling for clients appearing before the FTC and DOJ.

**The Lawyers:** The "*impressive*" **Elaine Johnston** (see p.1468) was praised for her "*competency and intelligence*" displayed during trade regulation, licensing arrangement and M&A reviews. Johnston was one of two lead partners who obtained clearance for Smiths Group in connection with the sale of Smiths Heimann Biometrics to Cross Match Technologies. Her role in the sale of pool cleaner manufacturer, Polaris Pool Holdings, to Zodiac is further testimony to her success before the scrutiny of the FTC. Practice cochair **Wayne Cross** (see p.1447) is "*a fine trial attorney: he doesn't irritate judges and has an impeccable sense of timing.*" He specializes in representing clients from the pharmaceutical industry, and in the past year he has acted for Sandoz (formerly Geneva Pharmaceuticals Technology), a manufacturer of generic drugs, in a challenge to a restrictive supply agreement, which Sandoz alleges was used by a competitor attempting to block its market access. Following a victory at the US Court of Appeals, which saw the reversal of an earlier dismissal of the company's claims, the case is set to go to trial shortly.

**Clients/Work Highlights:** Agfa-Gevaert; Banca di Roma; Experian; First American; Saudi Refining; Syngenta Seeds; Syngenta Crop Protection; T-NETIX; Takeda Chemical Industries; Triton; Tyco and Visa USA.

## Willkie Farr & Gallagher LLP

See firm details p.1567

**The Firm:** Although Willkie Farr may not be best known for its antitrust practice, its sterling reputation for litigation – historically one of the firm's defining features – guarantees it a place in the market. The group, which is integrated into the litigation department, handles domestic and international merger filings and cartel investigations before the DOJ, FTC and foreign enforcement agencies. The pharmaceutical and credit card industries are particular beneficiaries of team members' expertise. In the past year, the group represented USAA Federal Savings Bank in two major pieces of litigation, and was involved in a large suit brought by AMX against Visa and MasterCard. It also obtained clearance in the USA and the EU for Teva Pharmaceutical in its $7.4 billion merger with IVAX.

**The Lawyers:** **William Rooney**'s (see p.1493) broad knowledge base grants him an "*absolutely encyclopedic knowledge of case law.*" His antitrust experience includes matters falling within the remit of the Sherman Act, state antitrust laws and deceptive trade practice laws. Peers highlight his work in the copper tubing litigation and praise his dynamism: "*If the case came out at 5 pm yesterday, he's read it by the morning.*"

## Other Notable Practitioners

**Lloyd Constantine**, chair of the eponymous Constantine Cannon PC, is a favourite with clients enlisting his aid on complex, multistate antitrust cases. He has litigated for major corporations in federal and state courts. **Joseph Angland**'s (see p.1433) appointment has significantly boosted Heller Ehrman LLP's visibility in the high-stakes New York market. "*Extremely knowledgeable in law and procedure,*" he is also considered "*adept in politically sensitive situations.*" This alchemic union of skill and diplomacy is admired by peers and will come in useful when he takes the chair of the ABA's section of antitrust law in August 2006. Clients from the automobile, communications, petroleum and pharmaceutical industries benefit from his "*talents as a litigator.*"

# BANKING & FINANCE

## Band 1

## Cravath, Swaine & Moore LLP

See firm details p.1527

**The Firm:** Market observers unanimously concede that this vibrant finance practice is "*by far and away among the most talented groups out there.*" Committed to banking and finance since the turn of the 19th century, the firm has allocated the best of its resources to this practice area and, as a result, has a "*depth of experience that only a few can match.*" It boasts a small team of "*exceptionally skilled*" lawyers, who are often referred to as "*the special forces of banking – the elite of lender representation.*" The team is also able to tackle highly leveraged acquisitions and the most complex syndicated credits. Observers also noted that Cravath's outstanding high-yield finance practice is another trump card, allowing it to assist clients in state of the art structured financings. The quality of advice provided by this team has won it the loyal following of clients such as JPMorgan, CSFB and Goldman Sachs. Key transactions for 2005 include representing JPMorgan, Citigroup and Deutsche Bank in connection with a $5 billion credit facility used to finance the acquisition of SunGard Data Systems by a consortium of private equity firms. The group also acted for CSFB in connection with a $2.5 billion credit facility provided for Targa Resources to finance the acquisition of Dynegy's mainstream gas businesses.

**The Lawyers:** Clients appreciate a team of partners who "*truly deliver hands-on work to tailor personalized structures.*" Among them is **Jim Cooper** (see p.1447), a "*top-flight partner, who understands that lenders have their own clients to satisfy, and works relentlessly at getting the deal done smoothly.*" Cooper advised JPMorgan and Bank of America in connection with a $1 billion facility made available to Expedia for its spin-off from IAC/InterActive. "*I would recommend him above all other banking lawyers,*" said clients of **Rob Kiessling** (see p.1470). In addition to leading the team advising the lenders in the SunGard matter, he also represented JPMorgan as agent in a $950 million facility that was connected to the acquisition of Verizon Hawaii by The Carlyle Group. An "*extremely smart partner leading a team of fantastic associates,*" **Allen Parker** (see p.1486) has resumed his focus on transactional banking work after a four-year tenure as managing partner of the firm. He recently advised JPMorgan and Citigroup on a $1.1 billion refinancing for Burger King. The highly regarded **James Vardell** (see p.1509) led the team advising CSFB on the $2.5 billion facility provided to Targa Resources, while colleague **Michael Goldman** (see p.1460) continues to impress. He works prolifically with CSFB, which he represented, together with Barclays Capital, on a $6 billion facility for Fortune Brands that was used by the company to finance its acquisition of certain branded spirits from Allied Domecq. Entering the tables for the first time is **George Zobitz** (see p.1515), who caught the market's attention advising JPMorgan on a $770 million facility for Hexion Specialty Chemicals.

**Clients/Work Highlights:** Key clients include CSFB, Goldman Sachs and JPMorgan Chase. The team also acts regularly for Deutsche Bank; Citigroup; Leonard Green Partners; Golden Gate Capital and The Blackstone Group.

## Davis Polk & Wardwell
See firm details p.1528

**The Firm:** A smaller offering than its direct competitors, this firm continues to impress with "*the phenomenal quality*" of its attorneys. The credit group is widely considered to be "*among the preeminent banking practices in the USA.*" The group enjoys strong ties with large financial institutions, such as JPMorgan, Morgan Stanley and CSFB, advising them on "*complex and esoteric*" acquisition financings, bridge loans and recapitalizations. Thanks to its leading reputation for capital markets, the group is also perceived as "*an excellent choice to undertake transactions involving highly leveraged and structured financings.*" Recent noteworthy transactions include providing credit and capital markets advice to Banc of America Securities, CSFB and Wachovia, in connection with a high-yield financing for the acquisition of American Tire Distributors by an investment group sponsored by Investcorp. The group is equally active representing the market's most dynamic borrowers such as AT&T, E*TRADE FINANCIAL, Verizon and many other of its corporate clients. It also has significant experience advising lenders and borrowers extending or receiving credit through project finance.

**The Lawyers:** "*A superstar of the banking profession,*" senior partner **Brad Smith** (see p.1503) offers years of experience acting as preferred adviser to institutions such as JPMorgan. This, in turn, has given him a "*distinctive flair for steering clear of the pitfalls and focusing on core matters.*" The highly respected **Peter Levin** (see p.1474) routinely represents JPMorgan, Bank of America and Morgan Stanley in acquisition financings and restructurings secured by collateral located in North America, South America, Europe and Asia. Market sources praised **Larry Wieman** (see p.1513) for his "*elegant negotiation skills.*" He specializes in advising lenders and financially distressed borrowers on workouts and debt restructurings, as well as representing various clients, as lenders and borrowers, on senior and subordinated financings. **James Florack** (see p.1456) is "*an amazingly resourceful lawyer,*" able to advise clients on a range of lending transactions, as well as structured financings, high-yield debt offerings and other capital markets transactions.

**Clients/Work Highlights:** The firm's clients include lenders such as Bank of America; CSFB; JPMorgan Chase; BNP Paribas and Morgan Stanley. Borrower clients include Comcast; CSG Systems; Emerson Electric; Honeywell; International Paper and Limited Brands.

## Simpson Thacher & Bartlett LLP
See firm details p.1555

**The Firm:** According to market observers, this firm's banking and credit practice continues to stand "*head and shoulders above all other firms in the banking arena.*" Clients choose the team not only because it has a deep bench and the "*ability to staff any transaction thrown at it,*" but also because this "*well-oiled machine*" brings to bear so many decades of experience that it is now "*effortlessly good for syndicated lending and leveraged finance transactions.*" The group enjoys a colossal market share, acting for major lenders as well as the most active borrowers. It is this ability to act on both sides of the table that is thought to give it "*a significant edge over its competitors.*" The principal focus of the group is syndicated lending. A recent highlight was representing JPMorgan, Bear Stearns and Lehman Brothers in connection with the financing of the acquisition of Telcordia Technologies by Warburg Pincus and Providence Equity Partners for approximately $1.35 billion in cash. This financing included a $570 million senior credit facility. The team is also benefiting from the fact that a large portion of the current market is revolving around leveraged finance transactions for private equity sponsors. As the team is renowned for its huge client base of private equity houses and hedge funds, it is "*beautifully set up to dominate the borrower segment of the market.*" A highlight was counselling KKR, The Blackstone Group and Texas Pacific Group on the financing for their acquisition of Texas Genco. The team subsequently represented Texas Genco in the sale of its outstanding equity interests to NRG Energy for $5.825 billion. The highest profile transaction of late, however, was the group's representation of Ford and Hertz in connection with the $5.6 billion sale of the latter to a consortium of private equity firms as part of a $15 billion LBO transaction. Other areas of expertise include project and energy finance, sports financing and media and entertainment financing.

**The Lawyers:** Observers remain impressed by the "*incredible concentration of talent in this group.*" The key name here remains **Frank Huck** (see p.1466), an "*inspiring practitioner, adept at reaching creative yet practical solutions.*" He has been especially active recently in acquisition financings by private equity groups and public companies, and in restructuring financings. One of the "*greatest lawyers on the borrower side,*" **James Knight** (see p.1471) focuses on acquisition finance. His principal clients include KKR, The Blackstone Group and their portfolio companies. **Jim Buresh** (see p.1441) was highly recommended for displaying a "*tremendous combination of expertise in syndicated lending and high-yield financings,*" while colleague **James Cross** (see p.1447) has extensive experience representing leading financial institutions and private equity firms in significant financing transactions. His recent transactions include representing KKR in the $1.27 billion acquisition of Accelent, a medical device manufacturer. **Marissa Wesely** (see p.1513) continues to attract praise from the market. Wesely specializes in domestic and international bank finance transactions, with an emphasis on leveraged acquisition finance, principally advising equity sponsors and corporate borrowers.

**Clients/Work Highlights:** Banking practice clients include JPMorgan; Lehman Brothers; CIBC; Bear Stearns and UBS Warburg. There is also an exceptional client base of private equity sponsors, their portfolio companies and other corporate borrowers.

## Band 2

### Latham & Watkins LLP

**The Firm:** Portrayed emphatically as "*the clear success story of the industry,*" this firm's banking group has "*grown tremendously and made great client wins.*" According to observers, the team "*has got exactly what it takes to break into the current market,*" including a group of "*extremely talented lawyers*" and a balanced client base. The latter includes major lenders, borrowers and private equity sponsors such as The Carlyle Group and Apollo Management. Experienced on both sides of financing deals, the lawyers here are renowned for their ability to "*reach business sensitive solutions, and manage both parties' expectations.*" Members of the group are also praised for "*the uncompromising quality of the product they deliver.*" The team handles a variety of sophisticated financing transactions and, while it initially relied on its fantastic high-yield and capital markets reputation to source banking work, the firm now boasts an independently strong leveraged and bank lending practice. Highlights include acting for Deutsche Bank and Lehman Brothers in a $3.85 billion bank financing, part of the $15 billion LBO of Hertz by a consortium of private equity sponsors. Commentators also spoke admiringly of the firm's premier aircraft finance practice and cross-border abilities.

**The Lawyers:** "*Latham is the place to look to find the next generation of leading banking lawyers,*" said one observer. Already firmly established as a "*preeminent*

leveraged and acquisition finance expert,*" **Marc Hanrahan**, who joined from Skadden, Arps in 2004, is largely credited for having turned the spotlight on the firm's banking group. The "*knowledgeable and responsive*" **Chris Plaut** led the team in the $3.85 billion financing that was connected with the Hertz LBO. He also counts UBS among his most loyal clients, and recently represented them in the $2.9 billion financing for Omnicare that was used for the acquisition of NeighborCare. Initially focused on project finance, **Michèle Penzer** now boasts a "*robust and busy leveraged finance practice.*" She acts extensively for Bear Stearns, and recently represented the bank in a bridge loan financing for the acquisition of Elvis Presley Enterprises.

**Clients/Work Highlights:** Bear Stearns; RBS; HSBC; Goldman Sachs; CSFB; Barclays Capital; JPMorgan; CIBC; Merrill Lynch; Wachovia; SunTrust; UBS; The Carlyle Group and Apollo Management.

### Shearman & Sterling LLP

See firm details p.1554

**The Firm:** The firm maintains its reputation as a "*strong and highly visible player in the leveraged lending and investment grade finance fields.*" Admired for its "*clever one-stop shop approach,*" the banking team works closely with the firm's renowned capital markets and high-yield finance experts to provide "*integrated first-class advice on the most complex financing structures.*" Shearman recently combined its bank finance, structured finance and project finance teams into a single practice group in an effort to improve communication between the teams and better answer clients' needs. The team continues to act extensively for Citigroup, and recently represented it as lender of a $2.25 billion unsecured revolving credit facility for Disney. Commentators also noted that, "*far from relying on an exclusive institutional relationship,*" the firm has built strong relationships with other major financial institutions. One such institution is CSFB, which the group represented in a $3 billion financing for Oracle. On the borrower side, the group acted for Eddie Bauer Holdings in a $300 million syndicated secured term loan facility arranged by JPMorgan. In addition, the firm's network of practices in the UK, France and Germany provide a distinct advantage to clients in cross-border financings.

**The Lawyers:** Head of the firm's banking practice, **Bill Hirschberg** (see p.1465) is prominent in the thoughts of peers and clients. A "*pioneer and rain-maker in the profession,*" he is routinely involved in the most sophisticated transactions. For example, he recently advised SunGard Data Systems on the financing aspects of its $11.3 billion acquisition by a consortium of private equity firms.

**Clients/Work Highlights:** Banc of America Securities; Citicorp; JPMorgan Chase; Morgan Stanley; Royal Bank of Canada and Wachovia are among the firm's most important clients.

### Skadden, Arps, Slate, Meagher & Flom LLP & Affiliates

See firm details p.1557

**The Firm:** Skadden maintains its reputation as a "*big name around town for banking and finance.*" According to market players, the banking and institutional investing team did not suffer a major setback when several lawyers left for Latham & Watkins, and the firm remains highly recommendable for handling complex acquisition and structured financings, workouts and restructurings. As a renowned M&A powerhouse, the firm enjoys a huge corporate client base, which the banking team routinely represents on the borrower side of financing transactions. Highlights include acting for NASDAQ in obtaining $1 billion of bank and bridge financing for its acquisition of Instinet Group, and assisting Affiliated Computer Services in securing a $9 billion financing to support a potential acquisition. The team also undertakes significant transactions involving private equity sponsors, as well as maintaining a high profile for lender representation. It is also regularly instructed by major Wall Street institutions. Recently, the team represented Morgan Stanley in a $2 billion financing made available to E*TRADE FINANCIAL for its acquisition of Brown & Co from JPMorgan. In addition, clients regard the firm's related expertise in high-yield offerings as a distinctive advantage.

**The Lawyers:** Co-head of the practice group, **Jim Douglas** (see p.1450) is consistently described as "*a great lawyer, extremely well versed in leveraged finance.*" His practice also concentrates on the areas of acquisition financings, bridge financings and restructurings. A "*clever and practical counselor,*" **Joe Halliday** (see p.1463) is said to be a "*pleasure to work with.*" Chair of the firm's opinion committee, and less involved in transactional matters than previously, Halliday continues to provide "*exceptional guidance on complex structures*" and to draft legal opinions. **Peter Neckles** (see p.1482) is strongly recommended for his expertise in workouts and corporate restructuring financings. Recent highlights include advising Interstate Bakeries and Winn-Dixie in their debtor-in-possession financings. A new entrant to the tables, **Rob Copen** (see p.1447) is endorsed as "*an effective counselor who combines commercial awareness with detailed technical knowledge.*" His practice includes lenders' and borrowers' representation, and he recently represented Morgan Stanley in providing $3 billion of leveraged and bridge financing to E*TRADE FINANCIAL for its proposed acquisition of Ameritrade. The group also recently recruited highly regarded acquisition finance lawyer **Sal Guerrera** (see p.1462) from Mayer, Brown, Rowe & Maw.

**Clients/Work Highlights:** Borrower clients include Allegheny Energy; AXIS Capital; PacifiCare; Doughty Hanson; Fortress Investment Group; DRS Technologies; Rite Aid; Amerigroup and Wasserstein. The lender client base includes JPMorgan Chase; Bear Stearns; Merrill Lynch; Citigroup and Société Générale.

## White & Case LLP

See firm details p.1566

**The Firm:** According to commentators, this firm has *"a vast history of excellence in the banking field."* The New York bank finance team is regularly associated with the most sophisticated acquisition and leveraged finance transactions, as well as long-standing relationships with top-pedigree financial institutions such as Deutsche Bank, JPMorgan and UBS, which supply a healthy deal flow. Headline deals include advising Deutsche Bank and Citigroup, as arrangers, in providing $2.05 billion of senior secured financing to Graham Packaging for the acquisition of Owens-Brockway Plastic Products' stock. Given its size and geographical reach, the firm also continues to win plaudits for its *"impressive multijurisdictional and global finance capabilities,"* aided by *"strong European offices."* A major cross-border assignment was the representation of BNP Paribas and RBS, as arrangers of the $2.9 billion international fleet bridge loan facilities, financing part of the $15 billion LBO of Hertz. Clients particularly rated attorneys for their ability to *"work efficiently together,"* and because *"they are extremely commercial and never get caught up in the legalese."* In addition, the firm is active in the field of project finance and has represented lenders in many infrastructure and other developments. Finally, the firm boasts one of the most highly regarded Islamic finance practices.

**The Lawyers:** Global head of the bank finance group **Eric Berg** (see p.1438) is strongly endorsed by market commentators as *"a superior banking lawyer, who is never intimidated by innovative structures."* Clients appreciate the fact that *"he gets personally involved in structuring the financings."* In addition to advising on the $2.05 billion Graham Packaging financing, Berg also represented Bank of America, Deutsche Bank and Bank of Nova Scotia in arranging credit facilities of $1.05 billion for Dole Food. **David Bilkis** (see p.1439) is an *"efficient young partner, productive and precise in his drafting."* He recently acted for Deutsche Bank in a $1.55 billion acquisition financing of Pulitzer by Lee Enterprises. **David Koschik** (see p.1472) is another respected member of the team, who recently caught the market's attention acting for Deutsche Bank on a $650 million financing for the acquisition of PanAmSat by Intelsat. Koschik also specializes in representing lenders extending credit to insurance and reinsurance companies. Although he now works in the Milan office, Sean Geary is still recognized as a *"driving force of the practice."*

**Clients/Work Highlights:** Citigroup; Lehman Brothers; BNP Paribas; Gleacher Partners; Briscoe Capital Management; Calyon; Bank of Montreal; JPMorgan; CSFB; Bank of America; HSBC and UBS.

## Band 3

## Debevoise & Plimpton LLP

See firm details p.1529

**The Firm:** This increasingly popular banking and finance group has clearly established itself as *"the prime destination for borrowers' representation."* The team is widely renowned for advising an impressive pool of dynamic private equity houses and their portfolio companies, as well as other corporate clients, in all aspects of their domestic and international leveraged finance transactions, including syndicated loans, high-yield offerings and mezzanine investments. Attorneys here are particularly rated for the high level of client service they deliver: *"They always marshal adequate resources and work around the clock to provide us with excellent results,"* clients said. According to observers, this group has also been *"the most influential in reshaping the balance of power to create a more borrower-favorable market."* Accordingly, the group is regularly retained to advise borrowers in epic transactions, and was notably instructed by Clayton Dubilier & Rice, The Carlyle Group and Merrill Lynch Private Equity to negotiate several billion dollars' worth of high-yield financing and credit facilities used towards the acquisition of Hertz. Other noteworthy transactions include representing New York Life in its $1.5 billion revolving credit facility with JPMorgan. The group also occasionally handles lenders' representation.

**The Lawyers:** **David Brittenham** is highly recommended by clients for his *"versatility, creativity and appetite for complex products."* This *"well-regarded, high-yield finance expert"* recently represented Rexel in obtaining $2.4 billion of credit facilities from a syndicate of banks led by JPMorgan.

**Clients/Work Highlights:** American Airlines; The Carlyle Group; Citigroup Private Equity; Clayton, Dubilier & Rice; CSFB; Deutsche Bank; Kelso; Merrill Lynch; North Castle; Providence Equity Partners; Rexel and Zurich Capital Markets.

## Mayer, Brown, Rowe & Maw LLP

See firm details p.876

**The Firm:** This firm's New York banking and finance group is now recognized as an active player in the acquisition and syndicated finance field, and it is winning market-wide plaudits for its *"highly commercial approach to the transactions."* The team's lawyers are said to display an *"effective give-and-take approach in negotiations."* Established teams deal with syndicated lending, acquisition and project finance, working closely with the firm's internationally renowned securitization and capital markets experts. Lender representation and cross-border transactions form a substantial portion of the work handled by the team, often originating from the gaming, energy and LBO sectors. Recent significant transactions include representing Bank of Nova Scotia, Deutsche Bank and UBS in a $2.3 billion acquisition financing to a Canadian borrower controlled by KKR, for the going private transaction of Masonite. Another highlight involved counseling Bank of America in a $3 billion senior secured financing to Reliant Energy. On the borrower side, the team represented a collection of funds in a $600 million credit facility, secured by each fund's right to receive equity contributions from limited partners.

**The Lawyers:** Clients strongly recommended **Andrew Mattei** (see p.1478) as a *"practical deal facil-* itator, who understands that the perfect legal answer is not always the right one for our business."* Clients also value his flexible and consensual methods, but added: *"He can be hard hitting when defending his clients' interests."* Market sources also endorsed **Mark Wojciechowski** (see p.1513), global co-head of the practice, as a *"hands-on, smart and helpful banking lawyer."* He has been instrumental in strengthening the firm's relationship with major financial institutions such as Morgan Stanley, CSFB and RBS.

**Clients/Work Highlights:** Barclays Capital; DrKW; Banc of America Securities; Merrill Lynch and Jefferies Babson Finance.

## Milbank, Tweed, Hadley & McCloy LLP

**The Firm:** The firm maintains a preeminent position in the project finance arena, in addition to performing strongly in the syndicated and leveraged finance spheres. In the latter arena, the banking and institutional investment teams represent a wide array of clients, including leading financial sponsors, and senior and mezzanine lenders and borrowers. For example, it recently represented key client JPMorgan in a $1.8 billion senior secured credit facility for Motorola, and a $1.4 billion financing for Mediacom Broadband. The team also made its mark representing Macquarie Bank and Cintra as acquirers in the Chicago Skyway transaction, and recently represented the underwriters in the partial refinancing of debt and floated bonds. Observers noted that the team is also highly recommendable to advise on cross-border transactions, particularly in Latin America and Asia. In Brazil, the team completed a complex refinancing of the $571 million debt of Light Serviços de Electricidade.

**The Lawyers:** **Richard Wight**'s practice concentrates on representing banks and other investors in complex financing transactions, particularly in the media and telecom sectors.

**Clients/Work Highlights:** Loan Syndication and Trading Association; CSFB; ABN AMRO and JPMorgan.

## Weil, Gotshal & Manges LLP

See firm details p.1565

**The Firm:** This *"excellent"* firm continues to go from strength to strength in the acquisition and leveraged finance markets. A substantial part of the team's caseload originates from its vast client base of private equity sponsors and investors, for which it assumes borrower representation. However, competitors noted that commercial and investment banks increasingly retain the team to act as lender's counsel on the most complex financing transactions. Particularly visible are the strong relationships built with Citigroup and GE Capital. Among its headline deals, the team acted for Citicorp North America and Citigroup Global Markets in a $13.2 billion financing for the acquisition of Georgia-Pacific by Koch Industries. Historically associated with the firm's leading insolvency practice, the banking team also continues to act in tandem with the firm's bankruptcy and restructuring lawyers, successfully closing debt restructurings and corporate reorganizations.

**The Lawyers:** The "*sharp and creative*" **Daniel Dokos** (see p.1450) maintains a strong reputation in the market, particularly for his "*ability to create a good working environment*." Observers also consistently endorsed the "*outstanding*" **Warren Buhle** (see p.1441), who concentrates on aircraft and maritime finance, bank credit facilities, equipment-leveraged leasing and healthcare finance. **Marsha Simms** (see p.1502) is another key player in the team. This "*top lawyer*" is particularly recommended for providing "*well-structured advice*" to lenders on workouts, debtor-in-possession financing and exit financing.

**Clients/Work Highlights:** Citibank; Lehman Brothers; GE Capital and Goldman Sachs.

## Band 4

### Cahill Gordon & Reindel LLP

**The Firm:** Smaller than most of its competitors, this firm manages to maintain its momentum and is generally perceived as a serious player in the banking market. Key to the group's success is its reputation as a "*top high-yield practice.*" The group has found itself ideally positioned to advise the most dynamic lenders in high-yield issues launched in connection with LBOs. For example, it recently advised Deutsche Bank, Citigroup and JPMorgan in relation to the LBO financing of SunGard Data Systems, including the issuance of $3 billion of high-yield debt. The group also represents investment banks in highly leveraged finance transactions, as well as mainstream bank financings and mezzanine loans.

**The Lawyers:** William Hartnett and Jonathan Schaffzin are the key contact partners of the high-yield finance practice.

**Clients/Work Highlights:** The firm represents many of the largest investment and commercial banks including Banc of America Securities; CSFB; Deutsche Bank; Goldman Sachs; JPMorgan Chase; Merrill Lynch; Citigroup; UBS and Wachovia.

### Fried, Frank, Harris, Shriver & Jacobson LLP

See firm details p.1532

**The Firm:** Market participants traditionally regard the firm's banking and financing group as a "*busy borrower-focused practice.*" A significant part of the team's work consists of representing large LBO and private equity investor clients on acquisition financings involving high-yield offerings. However, the grouping has also established a serious presence on the lender side, and regularly represents commercial and investment banks in syndicated senior financings for leveraged transactions. For example, it acted for Merrill Lynch and JPMorgan in connection with a $265 million first and second credit facility for the acquisition of AxleTech by The Carlyle Group. Clients noted that the firm's expertise in high-yield, mezzanine and senior finance "*gives it an excellent perspective of all levels of the financings,*" and a distinct advantage for the negotiation and structuring of complex transactions. The team demonstrated such a combination of talents when representing Merrill Lynch, as lead arranger in a $1.7 billion senior secured credit facility and a related high-yield offering for the Jean Coutu Group, which was used in connection with the Eckerd drugstores acquisition.

**The Lawyers:** Arthur Kaufman, William Reindel and Brian Murphy are the key contact partners.

**Clients/Work Highlights:** Bank of America; Deutsche Bank; Goldman Sachs Mezzanine Partners; AEA Mezzanine Fund; Apollo Investment and National Bank of Canada.

### Kirkland & Ellis LLP

See firm details p.875

**The Firm:** This firm has "*seriously raised its profile in the New York banking market,*" according to rivals. As one of the most active private equity and LBO practices, the firm is ideally positioned to act as borrowers' counsel for equity investors and buyout sponsors. The team's experience includes the negotiation and documentation of acquisition loans, LBO and mezzanine financings and other bank

facilities. The team also represents domestic and foreign lenders.

**The Lawyers:** Ashley Gregory is the key contact partner in New York.

**Clients/Work Highlights:** Borrower clients range from Fortune 50 corporations to private equity houses and their portfolio companies, as well as emerging growth companies. Lender clients include banks; pension funds; mezzanine lenders and private equity funds.

### Sullivan & Cromwell LLP

See firm details p.1558

**The Firm:** This firm boasts a well-established banking finance team, supported by an "*outstanding banking regulatory practice*". Lawyers in the commercial lending group are particularly commended for their representation of borrowers, LBO firms and project sponsors in a variety of credit facilities, including secured and unsecured senior, term and revolving loans. The team has been involved in the establishment of several significant credit facilities, such as the $1.8 billion senior secured facility provided by Citibank, Morgan Stanley and UBS to Novelis. The team also routinely acts for single lenders.

**The Lawyers:** The "*absolutely brilliant*" **Erik Lindauer** (see p.1475) is a prominent figure in the transactional banking group. He specializes in transactional banking, secured lending and bankruptcy, while his financing experience includes advising clients in a broad range of complex secured and unsecured financings, including acquisition, project, cable television and media financings.

**Clients/Work Highlights:** The firm represents the full range of participants in commercial financings, including syndicates; single lenders; funds; loan insurers and a diverse client base of borrowers.

# BANKRUPTCY/RESTRUCTURING

## Band 1

### Weil, Gotshal & Manges LLP

See firm details p.1565

**The Firm:** With "*more bodies working on more matters than any other firm in the field,*" Weil Gotshal "*still has a breadth of coverage nobody else can match.*" The team has an "*army of lawyers*" familiar with bankruptcy proceedings, ranging from out-of-court restructurings to Chapter 11 filings and distressed M&A transactions. The bankruptcy practice is augmented by financial services and derivatives expertise, with one client noting that it is "*in a class of its own on matters relating to CDOs and complex financial transactions.*" Traditionally driven by debtor cases, the current market has led to more creditor

representations for large institutional clients in the past year. For example, the group is representing GM as a creditor in the Delphi Automotive bankruptcy. It is also acting for GE in its position in both the Delta Air Lines and Northwest Airlines Chapter 11 proceedings. The team continues to attract significant debtor cases and, according to clients, its vast experience means that it enjoys a level of influence in the legal community that sets it apart from rivals. It recently navigated both Atkins Nutritionals and New World Pasta through bankruptcy proceedings to emerge from protection in late 2005, and successfully negotiated a $350 million DIP loan for Saint Vincent Catholic Medical Centers. The group is supported by a litigation team famous for its zealous advocacy and take no prisoners attitude. On the other side of the

spectrum, clients also value the group's corporate counseling skills, and it often works with companies and their boards on risk management strategies.

**The Lawyers:** This team of "*enormously talented and effective lawyers*" is cochaired by **Martin Bienenstock** (see p.1439) and **Marcia Goldstein** (see p.1460). Sources consider Bienenstock to be "*brilliant – one of the smartest lawyers in the field.*" He represented CSFB as agent for a 43-bank consortium in the Owens Corning litigation, and is currently navigating Footstar through the final stages of its Chapter 11 proceedings. He also advises companies and their boards on risk management strategies, where clients appreciate his clear communication skills and "*ability to assist in making intelligent business choices.*" Marcia Goldstein's practice has a strong international flavor, and she is currently involved in a major restructuring affecting companies in the USA and Hungary. She also leads the debtor representation of Atkins Nutritionals, and is involved in the ongoing litigation arising from the Parmalat and Eurotunnel cases. Clients put her success down to her ability to know exactly what is important: "*She gets to the point and gets it right.*" Another partner with extensive cross-border restructuring experience is **Steve Karotkin** (see p.1469), whose "*assertive, hands-on manner*" is a draw for clients. He was debtor counsel to New World Pasta and, together with **Lori Fife** (see p.1454), recently confirmed a plan of reorganization for Loral Space & Communications. Clients describe Fife as a keen and constructive force in negotiations, while the "*intelligent and personable*" **George Davis** (see p.1448) stands out due to his success in building consensus among groups with extremely different viewpoints. Senior partner **Richard Krasnow** (see p.1473) has extensive experience in the aircraft industry, and currently acts for GE in connection with the Delta Air Lines bankruptcy. **John Rapisardi**'s (see p.1490) star continues to rise in the healthcare industry. Interviewees value his integrity, calling him "*as honest as the day is long,*" while those who have worked with **Jeffrey**

Tanenbaum (see p.1507) would do so again "*in a heartbeat.*" Both he and his colleague **Michael Walsh** (see p.1511) are described as "*completely focused on their clients' needs.*" Walsh founded the firm's telecom and healthcare restructuring practices, while Tanenbaum is known for his experience in the retail industry. Up-and-coming **Paul Basta** (see p.1436) is recommended for his keen intellect and loyal client following.

**Clients/Work Highlights:** In addition to representing companies and financial institutions, the group acts for an increasing number of hedge funds and other investors. It currently acts for equity holders in USG and Federal-Mogul, as well as Thomas H Lee Partners as the major shareholder in REFCO.

## Band 2

### Akin Gump Strauss Hauer & Feld LLP
See firm details p.559

**The Firm:** One of the firms to have truly focused on creditor committee representations, Akin Gump has become a "*go-to creditors' rights firm,*" particularly for bondholders. Because of this specialization, the firm has drawn criticism for being too narrowly focused, most notably in the recent FiberMark examiners report. However, the group remains a favorite among clients for its forceful creditors' rights advocacy, and it has most recently been enlisted to represent the high-profile Delta Air Lines Creditor Committee. This mix of negotiation and advocacy skills has built the firm a loyal client following. As one client explains: "*They are incredibly good at understanding exactly what it is that we want, and then preparing both the documents and arguments to get us there.*" Other high-profile representations include the Official Committees of Unsecured Creditors in ATA Holdings, Solutia, Collins & Aikman and Tower Automotive. The group also acts for a growing number of private equity and hedge fund clients in distressed M&A transactions and their associated financing.

**The Lawyers:** "*A name consistently seen in committee representations,*" **Daniel Golden** (see p.1460) is often enlisted by clients for his ability to present them with the big picture. Such clients also appreciate his "*confident but relaxed*" approach to negotiations. His recent appointment as head of the New York office adds administrative duties to his current work with the committees in the Delta Air Lines, Tower Automotive and Solutia bankruptcies. **Fred Hodara** (see p.1465) has a strong international practice involving US companies in cross-border proceedings, as well as clients based in both Norway and Russia. An eloquent communicator, clients value his clarity, explaining:"*He did an excellent job laying out the various paths we could take.*" Clients also think highly of the hard work and dedication of **Lisa Beckerman** (see p.1437). She currently handles the committee representations for the firm's steel company clients, alongside her involvement in the Delta Air Lines and ATA Holdings cases. Michael Stamer heads the representation of the Collins & Aikman committee.

**Clients/Work Highlights:** Primarily known to act for bondholders, clients include private equity funds, hedge funds and insurance companies. The team also represents individual creditors in restructurings, for example acting for the Russian hedge fund VR Capital as one of the major creditors in the REFCO Chapter 11.

## Davis Polk & Wardwell
See firm details p.1528

**The Firm:** Primarily known for its representation of banks, this relatively small team of eight partners and 25 associates has picked up one of the largest debtor cases to be filed of late. In addition to acting as debtor counsel to Delta Air Lines in its Chapter 11 proceedings, this "*intellectual powerhouse*" maintains a premier creditor practice. Clients appreciate its "*high-quality work in complex and difficult situations;*" while peers enjoy acting both with and against the group, as they "*thoroughly understand the entire process.*" Creditor clients also spoke of the firm's general financial depth and well-crafted loan documentation. The team represents the senior agent bank in the REFCO bankruptcy, and has put together a $2 billion DIP loan for Delphi Automotive on behalf of JPMorgan Chase and Citigroup.

**The Lawyers:** Quality is a word repeatedly employed to describe this group of "*intelligent and decent people who never resort to scorched-earth tactics.*" **Donald Bernstein** (see p.1438) is judged "*completely outstanding*" by both clients and peers, and focuses on creditor representations for major clients JPMorgan Chase, Citigroup and Bank of America. He is also chair of the National Bankruptcy Conference, a group of lawyers, law professors and judges convened to advise Congress on bankruptcy legislation. The "*extremely intelligent and hard-working*" **Marshall Huebner** (see p.1466) leads the debtor representation of Delta Air Lines. He possesses "*a wonderful even temperament that makes him both an effective lawyer and a pleasure to deal with.*"

**Clients/Work Highlights:** The team acts for both groups and individual banks as creditors, including JPMorgan Chase, Citigroup and Bank of America. It also advises Goldman Sachs, UBS and Deutsche Bank as part of its credit risk management practice. It is currently debtor counsel for Delta Air Lines and has cross-border restructuring cases underway in both Argentina and Spain.

## Kirkland & Ellis LLP
See firm details p.875

**The Firm:** "*A Chicago-centric firm that has developed a truly national practice,*" this group commands a lot of respect, especially in debtor circles where its advice is valued in both strategic and crisis filings. The New York team, supported by its Midwest counterparts, is now one of the premier debtor groups "*giving Weil Gotshal a real run for its money.*" It recently filed a string of high-profile Chapter 11 proceedings including Tower Automotive, Collins & Aikman and Solutia, but it also comes recommended for its out-of-court and counseling skills. According to clients, the team not only has the ability to make the

## Bankruptcy/Restructuring
### Leading Individuals

### Senior Statesman

**TREPPER Myron** *Willkie Farr & Gallagher*

| | |
|---|---|
| [1] **ABRAMS Marc** *Willkie Farr & Gallagher* | **BAKER D** *Skadden, Arps* |
| **BERNSTEIN Donald** *Davis Polk & Wardwell* | **BIENENSTOCK Martin** *Weil, Gotshal & Manges* |
| **CIERI Richard** *Kirkland & Ellis LLP* | **DESPINS Luc** *Milbank, Tweed* |
| **GOLDEN Daniel** *Akin Gump* | **GOLDSTEIN Marcia** *Weil, Gotshal & Manges* |
| **MILMOE J Gregory** *Skadden, Arps* | **NOVIKOFF Harold** *Wachtell* |
| **PANTALEO Peter** *Simpson Thacher & Bartlett* | |
| [2] **BALL Corinne** *Jones Day* | **BARTNER Douglas** *Shearman & Sterling LLP* |
| **DUNNE Dennis** *Milbank, Tweed* | **FRIEDMAN David** *Kasowitz* |
| **FUHRMAN Steven** *Simpson Thacher & Bartlett* | **HUEBNER Marshall** *Davis Polk & Wardwell* |
| **KAROTKIN Stephen** *Weil, Gotshal & Manges* | **KORNBERG Alan** *Paul, Weiss* |
| **ROSENBERG Robert** *Latham & Watkins LLP* | **SCHELER Brad Eric** *Fried, Frank* |
| **SCHONHOLTZ Margot** *Kaye Scholer LLP* | **TODER Richard** *Morgan, Lewis* |
| **ZIRINSKY Bruce** *Cadwalader, Wickersham & Taft* | |
| [3] **BOROWITZ Peter** *Debevoise & Plimpton LLP* | **BROZMAN Tina** *Bingham McCutchen LLP* |
| **CANTOR Matthew** *Kirkland & Ellis LLP* | **CHARLES Scott** *Wachtell* |
| **ECKSTEIN Kenneth** *Kramer Levin* | **FELDMAN Matthew** *Willkie Farr & Gallagher* |
| **FIFE Lori** *Weil, Gotshal & Manges* | **GROSS Steven** *Debevoise & Plimpton LLP* |
| **HAHN Richard** *Debevoise & Plimpton LLP* | **HANDELSMAN Lawrence** *Stroock & Stroock* |
| **HAZAN Scott** *Otterbourg* | **HODARA Fred** *Akin Gump* |
| **HYMAN Alan** *Proskauer Rose LLP* | **LEAKE Paul** *Jones Day* |
| **MASON Richard** *Wachtell* | **MAYER Thomas** *Kramer Levin* |
| **MINDLIN Philip** *Wachtell* | **SAGE Michael** *Stroock* |
| **SHIMSHAK Stephen** *Paul, Weiss* | **ZIMAN Kenneth** *Simpson Thacher & Bartlett* |
| [4] **BECKERMAN Lisa** *Akin Gump* | **BELTZER Howard** *White & Case LLP* |
| **BROMLEY James** *Cleary Gottlieb* | **BROUDE Mark** *Latham & Watkins LLP* |
| **COOK Michael** *Schulte Roth & Zabel LLP* | **DAVIS George** *Weil, Gotshal & Manges* |
| **FLICS Martin** *Linklaters* | **FRATIANNI Constance** *Shearman & Sterling LLP* |
| **FREEDMAN Theodore** *Kirkland & Ellis LLP* | **GARRITY James** *Shearman & Sterling LLP* |
| **GRANFIELD Lindsee** *Cleary Gottlieb* | **HARRIS Adam** *O'Melveny & Myers LLP* |
| **KELLY Michael** *Willkie Farr & Gallagher* | **KIRPALANI Susheel** *Milbank, Tweed* |
| **KRASNOW Richard** *Weil, Gotshal & Manges* | **LISCIO Mark** *Kaye Scholer LLP* |
| **LUSKIN Michael** *Luskin, Stern & Eisler LLP* | **RAPISARDI John** *Weil, Gotshal & Manges* |
| **REISMAN Steven** *Curtis* | **RICE Glenn** *Otterbourg* |
| **ROSNER David** *Kasowitz* | **SAFERSTEIN Jeffrey** *Paul, Weiss* |
| **SCHEIBE Robert** *Morgan, Lewis* | **SEIDER Mitchell** *Latham & Watkins LLP* |
| **SOSNICK Fredric** *Shearman & Sterling LLP* | **STEINBERG Arthur** *Kaye Scholer LLP* |
| **STERN Richard** *Luskin, Stern & Eisler LLP* | **TANENBAUM Jeffrey** *Weil, Gotshal & Manges* |
| **THOMPSON Mark** *Simpson Thacher & Bartlett* | **TOGUT Albert** *Togut Segal & Segal LLP* |
| **WALSH Michael** *Weil, Gotshal & Manges LLP* | **WEISFELNER Edward** *Brown Rudnick* |
| **WOLFSON Peter** *Sonnenschein* | |

### Up-and-coming individuals

| | |
|---|---|
| **BASTA Paul** *Weil, Gotshal & Manges* | **MELWANI Vivek** *Fried, Frank* |
| **SHIFF Adam** *Kasowitz* | |

advises private equity and hedge funds on their investment management issues. He is both "*intelligent and practical*," traits he shares with his colleague **Ted Freedman** (see p.1456). As a further resource for the team, Chicago-based Jamie Sprayregen also spends two days a week in the New York office.

**Clients/Work Highlights:** The firm is known for its company-side debtor representations, as well as acting for public and private companies in distressed M&A transactions. It also acts for many private equity and hedge funds as both creditors in restructurings and acquirers of distressed assets, for example it represented JC Flowers it its recent bid for the REFCO assets.

## Milbank, Tweed, Hadley & McCloy LLP

**The Firm:** "*As aggressive on the creditor side as the leading debtor firms are for companies,*" Milbank enjoys a reputation for its robust representation of clients. "*Without doubt a lead-line bondholder firm,*" the team boasts an impressive list of creditor committee representations including the official committees in the REFCO, Winn-Dixie and EaglePicher proceedings. On behalf of the REFCO committee, the group successfully negotiated the sale of the debtor's futures merchant to Man Group for $1.2 billion. The team's "*well-rounded general creditor practice*" includes both groups of banks and large individual creditors, such as acting for first-lien lenders in Meridian Automotive Systems, and a group of secured creditors in Adelphia Communications. The support of a strong finance group is an additional attraction for clients, who report the bankruptcy team is particularly adept in situations that require a combination of new financing alongside the reorganization of existing loans.

**The Lawyers:** "*Confident, smart and effective,*" **Luc Despins**' confrontational approach can rub some up the wrong way, but a long record of high-profile cases attests to his skills in representing committees. He continues to be involved in the winding up of Enron, and he is currently lead counsel for the REFCO committee. "*The kind of guy you always like to see on the other side of a deal,*" peers admire **Dennis Dunne**'s constructive approach to negotiations; while clients appreciate his hard work and close attention to their individual business needs. He is currently representing the Winn-Dixie creditor committee alongside colleague **Susheel Kirpalani**, who is "*incredibly poised and softly spoken, yet terribly effective.*"

**Clients/Work Highlights:** The group regularly represents committees of secured and unsecured creditors, bondholders and noteholders as well as leading financial institutions Citigroup; JPMorgan Chase; Merrill Lynch and Deutsche Bank.

tough calls, but also possesses the "*softer boardroom skills*" necessary to guide a company through the bankruptcy process. Adversaries also admired this combined approach, reporting that they "*like working with Kirkland: they are tough, but they know how to get a deal done.*" The team benefits from being able to draw on the firmwide network of litigators at its disposal, while the expertise of its strong corporate and private equity practices means the group is well positioned to act for clients in the distressed M&A arena.

**The Lawyers:** Clients have made it clear that the strong personality of **Richard Cieri** (see p.1445) is one of the major drawing cards in New York. "*An incredibly good listener,*" Cieri has the ability to "*distill information into meaningful advice*" and keep a cool head in negotiations. He acts for Solutia and Collins & Aikman in their bankruptcy proceedings, as well as regularly providing restructuring and financial advice to boards of directors. **Matthew Cantor** (see p.1442) represents high-profile debtors such as Tower Automotive and Boyds Collectables, and

## Paul, Weiss, Rifkind, Wharton & Garrison LLP

See firm details p.1548

**The Firm:** Clients were impressed by the "*extraordinary advice and support*" they received from this "*innovative and forward-thinking team.*" Its wide-ranging practice effectively bridges the divide between debtor and creditor representations, and is characterized by "*an in-depth understanding of the financial world.*" The group has the resources to undertake substantial debtor cases, and it most recently filed Chapter 11 proceedings for Foamex, North America's largest manufacturer of polyurethane foam. On the creditor side, it has a healthy committee practice, representing the official creditor committee in Armstrong World Industries, and represents large financial institutions, such as the steering committee of banks in Pegasus Communications. The third arm of the practice is distressed M&A transactions, where the group advises on the acquisition of distressed companies for clients such as Time Warner and the KPS funds. Clients also highlighted the deep pool of litigation talent available at the firm as a major attraction as it is "*superbly coordinated*" with the team's bankruptcy advice. One client stated: "*I cannot speak highly enough of the services provided by Paul Weiss; I am basically in awe of their abilities.*"

**The Lawyers:** "*A consummate professional,*" **Alan Kornberg** (see p.1472) has the ability to handle the political and legal intricacies of business with "*complete finesse.*" His practice neatly straddles both creditor and debtor cases, as he leads the representation of both Foamex and several of the creditor committees, as well as acting for Time Warner in its bid for Adelphia Communications' assets. **Steve Shimshak** (see p.1501) acts for the creditor committee in Armstrong World Industries and is an accomplished litigator. **Jeffrey Saferstein** (see p.1495) has been newly appointed as deputy chair of the practice. He divides his time between committee representations and distressed M&A for Time Warner.

**Clients/Work Highlights:** On the company side, the group continues to advise the debtor Cone Mills and recently guided Penn Traffic through the final stages of its bankruptcy proceedings to emerge from Chapter 11 protection. It also advises Time Warner, Calvin Klein, Major League Baseball and Lehman Brothers in relation to investments and financial restructurings. The team represents large financial institutions such as Citigroup and Morgan Stanley, as well as groups and committees of creditors such as the noteholders of IWO Holdings.

## Simpson Thacher & Bartlett LLP

See firm details p.1555

**The Firm:** Long considered one of the premier bank firms in the city, commentators believe this group has "*practically cornered the market*" for senior secured lenders. Catering for creditors, the firm packages its core bankruptcy group with capital markets, litigation and credit lawyers. Clients appreciate that the group's involvement in the initial financing of complex loans means that it is ideally placed to deal with distressed credit when it arises. Because of its reputation for "*quality work for leading creditors,*" the group is involved in the lion's share of the market's restructurings. It represents Wachovia as agents in the Adelphia Communications bankruptcy, and in its interests in the recent automotive industry filings, as well as acting as lead counsel to JPMorgan Chase in the Delphi Chapter 11 proceedings. DIP financing forms a large part of the team's caseload and it most recently represented joint arrangers Deutsche Bank and CSFB in creating a $2 billion DIP loan facility for Calpine. Distressed M&A transactions round out the practice, the largest example of which was the representation of Toys 'R' Us in the proposed sale of the entirety of its $6.6 billion worth of assets.

**The Lawyers:** Practice head **Peter Pantaleo** (see p.1486) combines intelligence with a practical, business-savvy approach, which means "*it's hard not to like him.*" He has been dividing his time between acting for Wachovia and organizing a DIP loan for JPMorgan Chase. "*One of the true stars at the firm,*" **Steve Fuhrman** (see p.1457) is high on clients' lists of go-to lawyers for complex matters. He concentrates on restructuring large syndicated credit facilities for banks. **Kenneth Ziman** (see p.1515) is an excellent younger lawyer making inroads into the banking and investment world. He regularly represents both senior secured lenders and distressed investors, including Toys 'R' Us, while **Mark Thompson** (see p.1508) comes from a litigation background and has strong ties to many of the firm's hedge fund clients.

**Clients/Work Highlights:** ABN AMRO; CSFB; Deutsche Bank; JPMorgan Chase and Wachovia feature on the client list. In addition to major financial institutions, the team also represents investors Evercore Partners; GE Capital; Lehman Brothers; Quadrangle Group; Perry Capital and private equity fund The Blackstone Group.

## Skadden, Arps, Slate, Meagher & Flom LLP & Affiliates

See firm details p.1557

**The Firm:** Described as "*monolithic,*" the firm's penetration into corporate America means it is "*fantastically positioned*" to represent companies in distress. As testament to that, the team has filed a string of recent high-profile Chapter 11 proceedings both for REFCO and Delphi Automotive in the automotive industry, and for retail supermarket chain Winn-Dixie. The group was also debtor counsel in the acrimonious FiberMark case, and continues its representation of Interstate Bakeries. Out-of-court restructurings also feature prominently on the agenda, and clients report the team can just as easily turn its hand to creditor representations, most prominently in the area of creditor committees and DIP financing. The group put together the DIP financing for the secured lenders in the Levitz Home Furnishings bankruptcy, and regularly brings its "*awesome M&A capabilities*" into play representing purchasers of distressed companies and in negotiating sales of company debt.

**The Lawyers:** Not only "*one of the smartest lawyers around,*" but also "*one of the classiest guys on the planet,*" **Jan Baker** (see p.1435) is a major draw for clients. Interviewees describe him as one of the premier debtor lawyers in the country, a feat that he achieves with "*less of a meat-eating mentality than some, which gets good results for his clients.*" He currently has primary responsibility for the Winn-Dixie, FiberMark and DELACO bankruptcies. Best known for his out-of-court restructurings, **Greg Milmoe** (see p.1480) is nevertheless enjoying a high profile in the area with a number of recent headline engagements. Commentators remark: "*He seems to be everywhere.*" A "*cool, calm and collected attorney,*" he heads up the REFCO case and also acts for ITC DeltaCom in their restructuring. Clients appreciate that the team "*has a lot of people they can bring to bear on a case,*" and Rick Levin's recent move from the Los Angeles office can only strengthen the New York bench.

**Clients/Work Highlights:** With its huge corporate client base, the firm is best known for its company-side representations. The team represents an impressively large proportion of the market's recent Chapter 11 debtors, mainly in the automotive and communications areas, as well as numerous out-of-court restructurings for companies such as Health-South and ITC DeltaCom. Creditor clients include Goldman Sachs, CSFB and Deutsche Bank.

## Wachtell, Lipton, Rosen & Katz

See firm details p.1561

**The Firm:** The success of this "*staggeringly good firm*" is attributed to the combination of "*brilliant creditors' rights attorneys and phenomenal litigation support.*" The team's sophisticated practice is built on a strong foundation of bank representations, bondholder work and distressed M&A, in addition to financing the firm's entire range of corporate transactions. Typical engagements include acting for JPMorgan Chase in the Collins & Aikman and Northwest Airlines filings, and arranging the DIP financing for CSFB in the Meridian Automotive Systems bankruptcy. It also acted for JPMorgan in the debt restructuring of Blockbuster Video. Clients explain that the "*phenomenal caliber of work*" from the group means it often "*gets the nod on the most complex cases;*" a highlight was representing the Man Group in its successful acquisition of REFCO's assets. The group also excels at coordinating litigation and clients appreciate this seamless interaction between practice areas, praising the communication as "*effective, efficient and impressive.*"

**The Lawyers:** "*A typical Wachtell lawyer is very, very smart,*" agree interviewees, and "*there are few people with as much expertise*" as **Hal Novikoff** (see p.1484). Clients say he is possessed of "*extraordinarily sound judgment*" that is based on in-depth knowledge of the bankruptcy code and considerate assessment of each company's circumstances. He uses these skills to great effect when representing both individual creditors, as well as lender groups, and is currently handling a number of matters for both JPMorgan Chase and CSFB. "*A major factor in the Kmart success story,*" **Scott Charles** (see p.1443) continues to represent what is now named ESL as the company's largest stockholder, most recently navigating it through its lengthy litigation with Chapter 11 debtor Footstar. In addition to being both smart and creative, clients believe: "*It's his command of the details that gives him the advantage over his counterparts.*" The "*personable and intelligent*" **Richard Mason**'s (see p.1477) no-nonsense approach to deals wins praise from all quarters of the market. Clients testify that he can "*adapt effectively to any situation,*" and has a diverse creditor practice that includes acting for a major bondholder in Delphi Automotive, and leading the representation of the Bank of Nova Scotia in the Intermet case. **Philip Mindlin** (see p.1480), hailed as "*a genius,*" provides creative out-of-court solutions and was integral in perhaps the largest distressed M&A transaction of the year, acting for Man Group in its successful bid for REFCO's assets.

**Clients/Work Highlights:** A cross-section of the firm's clients include CSFB; Bank of Nova Scotia; Man Group; Bank of America and JPMorgan Chase.

## Willkie Farr & Gallagher LLP

See firm details p.1567

**The Firm:** Best known for its representation of large debtors, this team of "*fair, reasonable and experienced lawyers*" is a constructive force in the bankruptcy process as they "*always approach work in a collaborative way.*" Strong both domestically and on cross-border issues, the US bankruptcy practice is concentrated in the New York office, and complemented by a European contingent in Paris. Representing Adelphia Communications continues to dominate the team's workload, and they have won praise from industry sources for their skilled handling of this difficult case. At the time of print, the group was past the disclosure stage and was constructing a formal plan of reorganization. Other ongoing matters include advising Monsanto on their investment in Solutia and acting for Telmex in issues arising out of WorldCom (now MCI). The group is also heavily involved in confirming a plan of liquidation in order to distribute the capital of Verestar. Company counseling and distressed M&A for a growing number of hedge fund clients are the team's other main concerns.

**The Lawyers:** One of the leading debtor lawyers in New York, **Marc Abrams** (see p.1431) leads the representation of Adelphia Communications, and is currently involved in structuring the asset purchase agreement to sell all of the debtor's cable systems. "*An outstanding lawyer who works well with both adversaries and clients,*" his style is "*smart, diligent and effective.*" Working closely with Abrams on the Verestar case, **Matthew Feldman** (see p.1453) possesses both intelligence and sound judgment. He has the ability to be nonconfrontational but "*is never afraid of litigating when necessary.*" **Michael Kelly** (see p.1470) has close ties to the firm's hedge fund clients, and handles the bulk of work for Quadrangle Group, most recently representing them as creditors in the REFCO case. A senior member of the practice and of the market, **Myron Trepper** (see p.1508) spends the bulk of his time counseling

companies on liability and mass tort issues. A lawyer who can "*reach back to the founding principles to create innovative new law,*" his knowledge and experience is invaluable to both clients and the wider bankruptcy community.

**Clients/Work Highlights:** In addition to acting for companies such as Air Canada, ATX Communications and Adelphia Communications, the team has made a particular effort to expand its representation of hedge funds, particularly in distressed M&A transactions. Among these are Davidson Kempner Partners, DE Shaw and Quadrangle Group.

## Bingham McCutchen LLP

See firm details p.1110

**The Firm:** Primarily a bondholder firm, the group has built up a strong creditor practice through its "*deep involvement in both new and distressed investments.*" This is partly due to the financing depth in the Hartford office, which works hand in hand with the New York team. Following its role in the Italian-US restructuring of Parmalat, the team's international practice is going from strength to strength. It is currently involved in restructurings involving Mexican, Argentinian and Norwegian companies, all on behalf of bondholders. The domestic practice is also gathering momentum, as the group is heavily involved in the Mirant bankruptcy in Texas and has just been retained by Delta Air lines, in both instances on behalf of the Equipment & Engine Training Council (EETC) holders. In addition to its related corporate and securities strengths, clients appreciate that the team also has the ability to deal with "*the most heated and ugly litigation,*" when necessary.

**The Lawyers:** A former bankruptcy judge, **Tina Brozman** (see p.1441) brings "*intellect and vast experience*" to her practice. In addition to having a great deal of success in the courtroom, she represents the bondholders in Corporation Durango, which was filed in both Mexico and New York, and Deutsche Bank in the Ponderosa Pine Energy bankruptcy.

**Clients/Work Highlights:** Bond groups and institutional investors such as insurance companies, particularly in privately placed debt securities. Also private equity funds and high-yield bank loan groups.

## Cadwalader, Wickersham & Taft LLP

See firm details p.1522

**The Firm:** Fielding a large group of dedicated bankruptcy lawyers, this outstanding team straddles the divide between creditor and debtor cases with remarkable success. It represents an array of debtors from the healthcare, retail and steel industries, but it is the recent filing of the Northwest Airlines Chapter 11 case that grabbed commentators' attention. Creditor highlights include representing Morgan Stanley in its position in other airline bankruptcies, and acting for the Official Committee of Unsecured Creditors in Mirant. The group often acts for bank

syndicates in loan restructurings, and wins praise for skillfully integrating aspects of both its structured finance and capital markets practice into its bankruptcy advice.

**The Lawyers:** The financial restructuring department now numbers around 55 lawyers across its US and UK offices, and is chaired from New York by **Bruce Zirinsky** (see p.1515). "*An elegant negotiator,*" his diverse practice mirrors that of the firm's, encompassing debtor, creditor committee and bondholder work. He is lead counsel for Northwest Airlines, and his ability to "*pull together diverse groups and personalities*" is just as valued by creditors.

**Clients/Work Highlights:** Company representations include Northwest Airlines and Enron, as well as financial institutions such as BNP Paribas; Morgan Stanley Senior Funding; Barclays Capital; Barclays Bank; Merrill Lynch and CSFB. The team also represents hedge funds, state insurance commissioners and municipal bond insurers.

## Cleary Gottlieb Steen & Hamilton LLP

See firm details p.1525

**The Firm:** With its impressive financial services clout, clients elected this firm one of the best at dealing with "*the most technical and esoteric of bankruptcy issues.*" Supported by derivatives, benefits and corporate expertise, the group handles the full spectrum of creditor and debtor cases and also offers credit risk management advice. The group currently acts for ten of the leading investment banks in the Delta Air Lines, Northwest Airlines and Delphi Automotive bankruptcies, and its representation of a syndicate of banks in the Adelphia Communications litigation won it considerable market acclaim. Internationally, leading matters include acting for a major Mexican auto parts manufacturer in the Delphi Automotive proceedings, and the ad hoc creditors committee in the $3.3 billion debt restructuring of Telecom Argentina. The group also advises a number of foreign governments, most notably the Republic of Argentina in the restructuring of approximately $85 billion of its public debt.

**The Lawyers:** With "*a high level of experience and excellent business acumen,*" **Jim Bromley**'s (see p.1441) gift for technical planning is well respected by clients. He leads the firm's representation of Lehman Brothers, and is currently advising the labor union United Automobile Workers of America in negotiations with GM over the restructuring of healthcare benefits. **Lindsee Granfield** (see p.1461) acted for the syndicate of banks in the Adelphia litigation.

**Clients/Work Highlights:** The team represented a consortium of Warburg Pincus, Merrill Lynch and Susquehanna International Group in their bid for REFCO's commodities assets. Investment banks Bear Stearns; CSFB; JPMorgan Chase; Lehman Brothers; Merrill Lynch; Morgan Stanley and UBS were all part of the syndicate in the Adelphia litigation. In the ongoing Enron litigation the group again represented Lehman Brothers, this time with Goldman Sachs, in swaps and commercial paper issues.

## Debevoise & Plimpton LLP

See firm details p.1529

**The Firm:** Best known for its prowess in handling restructurings arising out of the insurance market, this relatively small group caters to a rather larger clientele, including debtors, creditors and other institutional investors. It also spans a range of proceedings; commentators see the group in a high number of out-of-court restructurings, and clients testify to its excellent litigation capacity when in bankruptcy court. Restructurings for creditors include acting for Oaktree Capital Management in relation to Eurotunnel's debt, and on the other side of the table, it advised South American debtor Globopar in its $1.3 billion reorganization. The group handles a number of pre-negotiated Chapter 11 cases for debtors in the healthcare and food industries and having represented Delta Air lines out of court, it continues to act as special aircraft counsel to the debtor in its Chapter 11 proceedings.

**The Lawyers:** This interdisciplinary group is comprised of *"talented people who do excellent work for their clients."* According to clients, *"the name to go to when a file needs serious attention"* is **Peter Borowitz**. His practice focused on institutional lending, with a particular emphasis on US insurance companies and hedge funds. Practice chair **Steven Gross** has a hearty international and cross-border workload, particularly in South America. He acted for Globopar in its reorganization, and sources rate him a *"big contributor to the firm's out-of-court expertise."* The *"smart, sensible and sophisticated,"* **Richard Hahn** is a member of both the bankruptcy and corporate groups. He focuses primarily on in-court debtor work, most recently for Delta Air lines.

**Clients/Work Highlights:** Globo Comunicações e Participações SA; Delta Air lines; American Airlines; Oaktree Capital management, and insurance clients Prudential Insurance Company of America, Teachers Insurance and Annuity Association of America and XL Capital Assurance.

## Fried, Frank, Harris, Shriver & Jacobson LLP

See firm details p.1532

**The Firm:** A *"small, talented group working on highly complex matters for very big clients,"* reported sources. This team handles both sides of bankruptcy cases but is most often employed by creditors. Recent highlights include representing WR Huff Asset Management as one of the major creditors in the Adelphia Communications bankruptcy, and it continues to act for both the bondholders in the Oxford Automotive bankruptcy, as well as the Official Committee of Unsecured Creditors in the New World Pasta Chapter 11 proceedings. The team does a lot of work for private equity portfolios, and its track record representing aggressive investors and *"tough litigation skills"* earn it a reputation for having *"tenacious advocates for its clients."* The New York team gained a new partner through internal promotion, and the Paris office has enlisted two new insolvency practitioners further boosting the firm's international resources.

**The Lawyers:** *"Intelligent and incisive,"* **Brad**

Scheler (see p.1497) heads the practice and focuses on strategic planning and corporate advice. Clients are particularly impressed with his high level of personal involvement in their business and his knowledge of the industry players, reporting: *"The tentacles of his influence spread far and wide."* **Vivek Melwani**'s (see p.1479) practice spans the range of creditor, debtor and distressed M&A transactions. He represents the committee in the Oxford Automotive proceedings, and is described as a constructive and able adversary by those across the table from him.

**Clients/Work Highlights:** In addition to its substantial creditor practice, the team also represents debtors AAIPharma and apparel company Donnkenny in their Chapter 11 proceedings. It also acts for a range of acquisitive investors in distressed M&A transactions.

## Jones Day

See firm details p.570

**The Firm:** The New York team at this national firm impresses both clients and adversaries with its combination of strong individuals and vast resources. The practice is powered by the twin engines of debtor work and distressed M&A, which it complements with corporate governance advice for its large investor clientele. On the debtor side, the group navigated WHX Corporation through filing Chapter 11 proceedings to emerging from bankruptcy protection in less than four months. In the airline industry it handles the bankruptcy-related labor negotiations for Continental Airlines, and represents FLYi in its recent filing. Commentators agree the firm *"really draws efficiently on its other offices,"* and the New York team, together with the London office, acts for major investor WL Ross & Co on a vast array of distressed M&A transactions. These included the company's bids to acquire the Horizon Natural Resources Company out of bankruptcy, and its attempts to acquire the assets of both REFCO and WestPoint Stevens. This integrated approach means the team offers an excellent full service to clients.

**The Lawyers:** *"Flat out smarter than most other lawyers,"* **Corinne Ball**'s (see p.1435) aptitude for bridging law and business is a hit with clients. She is the architect of many of the team's most complex distressed M&A transactions for MBIA Insuranceand WL Ross & Co and recently represented Citibank in its DIP loan proposals for Delta Air Lines. Described as *"one of those rare lawyers who has the complete package,"* commentators praise **Paul Leake** (see p.1474) as smart, professional and ethical. He is renowned as a *"talented and effective lawyer who does both creditor and debtor cases, and does them well."*

**Clients/Work Highlights:** MBIA Insurance; WHX Corporation; Levitz Home Furnishings and Citibank.

## Kasowitz Benson Torres & Friedman

**The Firm:** Housed in a firm that specializes in complex civil litigation, the bankruptcy group has a superb plaintiff-side practice for creditor committees, equity and security holders. Since its inception in 1993, the firm has *"done a tremendous job building up a niche bankruptcy practice for bondholders,"* and to date is best known for representing the Committee of Unsecured Creditors in the Adelphia Communications proceedings. The lack of a corporate M&A department means it has relatively fewer conflicts than other firms, and is not afraid of suing financial institutions. As well as intercreditor disputes, the team represents debtors and investors in distressed companies, and also undertakes corporate control disputes in the bankruptcy court.

**The Lawyers:** *"Smart and to the point,"* **David Friedman** leads the creditors' rights and bankruptcy practice. Commentators report that *"he has bruised some shins in his time,"* but his forceful approach serves his clients well. **David Rosner** also enjoys a high profile in the area, and his wide-ranging practice sees him involved in an impressive number of cases, as is the *"very bright and promising"* **Adam Shiff**.

**Clients/Work Highlights:** The firm made its name with roles in WorldCom, Enron and Global Crossing (through its subsidiary Asia Global Crossing). It also represented Silver Point Capital as one of the three main bondholders in the FiberMark case.

## Kramer Levin Naftalis & Frankel LLP

See firm details p.1539

**The Firm:** A well-established team with *"a great historical resume,"* this group is respected for its experience across a wide range of bankruptcy matters. Its workload is varied and, while bondholder engagements make up a significant proportion of the practice, it also represents agent lenders, debtors and acquirers. Highlights include acting for bondholders in the Mirant, WestPoint Stevens and WCI Steel bankruptcies and, on the debtor side, it has confirmed a plan of reorganization for Elite Model Management. The team also showed its litigation mettle in the ongoing Owens Corning bankruptcy litigation, where it acted as co-counsel to agent bank CSFB in its successful bid to overthrow a mass tort consolidation claim.

**The Lawyers:** Bankruptcy chair **Kenneth Eckstein** (see p.1451) is *"deeply experienced – he has been around and seen everything."* He represents debtors, bondholders and led the team on the Owens Corning litigation. Both *"academic and strategic,"* **Thomas Mayer** (see p.1478) is the lead on WestPoint Stevens and has a particular specialty acting for distressed investors.

**Clients/Work Highlights:** In addition to banks and other more traditional financial institutions, the group acts for a wide array of special investors in their capacities as both lenders and acquirers. It is currently advising Harbert Distressed Investment Master Fund in relation to bonds it holds in the struggling energy producer Calpine. It also represents Farallon Capital Management, Bear Stearns and Angelo, Gordon & Co.

## Latham & Watkins LLP

**The Firm:** Part of the matrix of resources provided by this leading international firm, this group of *"tough, business-minded attorneys"* enjoys a level of support that few other firms can match. Creditor representations dominate the practice, and the team's headline engagement this past year was acting for the official creditors' committee of Delphi Auotomotive. It also has roles in many of the other high-profile bankruptcies on behalf of financial institutions. The group acts for CSFB as agent on $310 million in first-lien debt in Meridian Automotive Systems, and for the Bank of New York as an indentured trustee with $3.5 billion in unsecured bonds in Delta Air Lines. Also rated as *"effective and efficient debtor lawyers,"* clients appreciate the speed with which they handle both prepackaged and crisis filings. The group has just completed the reorganization of casinos and investment facilities for Trump Hotels, and currently represents Southaven Power in its Chapter 11 proceedings.

**The Lawyers:** According to clients, senior partner **Bob Rosenberg** *"is one of the smartest people you will ever come across."* He is described as someone who *"lives and breathes the law,"* and has the ability to convert that knowledge into intelligent business advice for clients. **Mark Broude** acts primarily for debtors and was the lead on both the Trump Hotels and Southaven Power Chapter 11 proceedings. Clients value his intimate knowledge of the bankruptcy code, and his *"strategy and business sense."* **Mitchell Seider** is hailed as *"confident and hardworking."* He concentrates on lender representations and currently acts for the Delphi Automotive creditors' committee.

**Clients/Work Highlights:** In addition to acting for Bank of New York and CSFB, the group also represents Wells Fargo of Minnesota as indentured trustee in Tower Automotive proceedings. Other clients include MBIA Insurance and Wilmington Trust.

## Morgan, Lewis & Bockius LLP

See firm details p.1758

**The Firm:** This team's practice is primarily focused on financial institutions. It has a long and successful track record representing banks as major creditors of troubled companies, and is involved in an increasing amount of DIP lending work. For example, it currently acts for core client JPMorgan Chase in the structuring of DIP lending facilities for both Tower Automotive and Iridium Satellite. Having handled the DIP finance for United Airlines, the team is now organizing the company's exit financing on behalf of co-agents JPMorgan Chase and Citigroup. While banks remain central to the firm's practice, the team does undertake debtor cases when able, and research has indicated that large lenders are more inclined to waive conflicts than in the past. The team has just confirmed a plan of reorganization for Century/ML Cable Venture and is currently working on the sale of its assets to another entity.

**The Lawyers:** The collaborative nature of the team sees **Richard Toder** (see p.1508) and **Robert Scheibe** (see p.1497) complementing each other's skills on the biggest representations. Interviewees praised Toder's intelligence and dubbed him *"one of the best bankruptcy lawyers around."* He is currently working on the litigation side of the Tower Automotive and Iridium Satellite deals, while *"superb DIP lawyer"* Robert Scheibe draws on his finance background and takes charge of the transactional side.

**Clients/Work Highlights:** The team enjoys a particularly close relationship with JPMorgan Chase and, in addition to arranging DIP loans, it also represents the bank as the largest lender in the liquidation of Coudert Brothers. Distressed investing is another growth area, and the team often acts for developers, landlords and other real estate clients in Section 363 sales.

## Otterbourg, Steindler, Houston & Rosen

**The Firm:** Commentators respect this team as having *"worked hard and built up a high-end committee practice."* While still viewed as specialized, it has broadened out its representation of trade committees, and now regularly competes for top creditor matters. As testament to this, the group recently landed the representation of the official creditors' committee in the high-profile Northwest Airlines Chapter 11 proceedings. In other airline industry bankruptcies, the team has successfully negotiated reorganization plans for the creditor committees in both US Airways and Hawaiian Airlines. Interviewees note: *"With its tremendous contacts it can really pull in the business,"* and the group numbers the creditors' committees in the Friedman's, Buehler Food and Brooklyn Hospital Center bankruptcies in its sizable caseload.

**The Lawyers:** A client favorite, **Scott Hazan** has the *"intangible skill set required to bring a group around to a consensus in a commercially reasonable way."* He currently leads the representation of the Northwest Airlines committee, while **Glenn Rice** acts for the committees in the Friedman's and Brooklyn Hospital Center bankruptcies. Competitors are impressed with Rice's intimate knowledge of committee workings, while clients appreciate that he is always focused on getting the best results in each different situation.

**Clients/Work Highlights:** The team represents creditors' committees, major financial institutions, commercial banks, insurance companies and asset-based lenders.

## Shearman & Sterling LLP

See firm details p.1554

**The Firm:** With great strengths in tax, M&A and capital markets, the bankruptcy team operates against a backdrop of financial and corporate expertise. The group has a diverse practice, with debtor cases making up around half of its workload. On the company side, the team recently acted as co-counsel to Delphi Automotive, negotiating the $2 billion DIP loan for the debtor, and managed the prepackaged Chapter 11 bankruptcy proceedings for Smarte Carte. On the creditor side, acting as co-counsel to the Official Committee of Unsecured Creditors in Mirant continued to absorb a substantial amount of the team's time. A network of offices around the globe means the group has an impressive geographical reach, and is often involved in some of the largest international bankruptcies. It acts for the combined steering committee of creditors in Asia Pulp and Paper, South-East Asia's largest bankruptcy to date, and on the other side of the table, represents debtor AOL Latin America in its Chapter 11 proceedings.

**The Lawyers:** Heading the department, **Douglas Bartner** (see p.1436) is *"a level-headed attorney who thinks ahead and anticipates problems."* Peers consider him *"a good adviser and great competitor,"* while clients appreciate his in-depth understanding of the complex financial matters that underlie bankruptcy transactions. **Constance Fratianni** (see p.1456) is a well-rounded lawyer with a solid corporate grounding and particular skills in acquisition financing; while ex-judge **James Garrity** (see p.1458) is *"low key, thoughtful and works hard to bring people together."* Garrity focuses on international insolvencies, while generalist **Fredric Sosnick**'s (see p.1504) most recent engagement is for the Official Committee of Unsecured Creditors in Mirant.

**Clients/Work Highlights:** The team represents leading financial institutions Citigroup; CSFB; JPMorgan Chase and Bank of America as well as committees of both secured and unsecured lenders. Recent engagements for Smarte Carte and AOL Latin America top the list of a multijurisdictional debtor practice.

## Stroock & Stroock & Lavan LLP

**The Firm:** The group's practice is based on the three pillars of creditor committee, debtor and distressed investment work, and interviewees particularly noted its success representing bondholders. *"Traditionally the creditor committee counsel of choice,"* the team maintains a significant practice in the area, most recently representing the official creditors' committee in the WestPoint Stevens bankruptcy. It is also acting for the ad hoc bondholder committee in the REFCO Chapter 11 proceedings, and for large individual bondholders in both the Adelphia Communications and Loral Space & Communications cases. The team's other significant engagements for the past year have been on the debtor side. The group represented Brooklyn Hospital Center in its recent filing, and has a specialized role as corporate counsel to Delta Air Lines, having previously negotiated its acquisition of substantial assets from Eastern Airlines. It acts for a range of investors in distressed companies, notably a large number of energy traders and financiers in the acquisition of troubled energy groups. The integration of financing and corporate securities expertise means the group also offers both creditor and debtor clients regular advice on claims trading.

**The Lawyers:** The team's equanimity is widely recognized: its lawyers are *"always reasonable and strive to get deals done."* Cochair of the practice, **Larry Handelsman** leads by example, as sources praised him as a constructive lawyer who is *"excellent at mediating and brokering deals."* He has a mixed debtor and creditor practice, while another of the team's cochairs, **Michael Sage** primarily focuses on bondholders. He acted for the major bondholders in the REFCO and Loral Space & Communications cases, and his experience in the area means he is a go-to for investment clients.

Clients/Work Highlights: The team represents Wilmington Trust, an indentured trustee in the US/Canadian cross-border case, Calpine. Bondholder and investment clients include WL Ross & Co; Perry Capital; Lehman Brothers; Merrill Lynch; Conseco Services and Barclays.

## White & Case LLP
See firm details p.1566

The Firm: The bankruptcy team at this international firm has built a substantial New York practice featuring both domestic and cross-border cases. The group benefits from its connection to a network of other teams, and currently works closely with the Miami office on the headline representation of Mirant in restructuring $10 billion in debt. The same resources contribute to the team's success in cross-border insolvencies; it is negotiating a plan of conciliation with US creditors for Satmex, a satellite communications company part-owned by the Mexican government. On the creditor side, attorneys continue to represent banks and other financial institutions in the Adelphia bankruptcy, and offer specialized insurance insolvency expertise.

The Lawyers: Clients praised the caliber of junior team members supporting the four partners, and five new associates have been added in recent months. Leading the team is **Howard Beltzer** (see p.1437), who is also the co-head of the global bankruptcy group. His practice is an even split between creditor and debtor work, as he divides his time between the Mirant and Adelphia Communications cases.

Clients/Work Highlights: The firm has ties to many major international financial institutions including ANZ; Commerzbank; Royal Bank of Canada; Bank of Nova Scotia and Société Générale, as well as US banks JPMorgan Chase, Bank of America and Bank of New York. It also acts for Wilmington Trust, United Pan-Europe Communications and GE Corporate Financial Services.

## Band 4

## Brown Rudnick Berlack Israels LLP

The Firm: Best known for its representation of unsecured creditors and its aggressive litigation style, this group *"will fight until its clients get results."* The team represents existing bond and equity holders in bankruptcies, as well as clients who buy into distressed debt, leading to roles in most of the industries high-profile cases. Examples of current engagements are for the indentured trustees in Delphi Automotive, and the ad hoc committee of bondholders in the Tower Automotive Chapter 11. The group is also expanding its resources, adding an ex-Akin Gump partner to its London office in an effort to bolster its international reach.

The Lawyers: While his aggressive approach is not to everyone's taste, **Edward Weisfelner** is viewed as *"a talented lawyer who gets results for people in difficult situations."* He leads the firm's bankruptcy and corporate restructuring group, and is an *"incredibly creative courtroom performer."*

Clients/Work Highlights: Secured and unsecured creditors including high-yield investors and fund managers feature on the list of clients.

## Gibson, Dunn & Crutcher LLP
See firm details p.328

The Firm: This small group may have a lower profile than some, but it has long-standing relationships with many financial institutions and maintains a healthy creditor practice. It represented Merrill Lynch in its role in the Adelphia Communications litigation, and continues to represent it in much of its Enron-related business. *"Much more than just attack-dogs,"* the lawyers are also respected business advisers, and are praised for their politic handling of sensitive situations. They represent Citigroup in a number of loans made to other law firms, including the Brobeck, Phleger & Harrison liquidation.

The Lawyers: The business restructuring and reorganization group has a core of two bankruptcy specialists, and includes lawyers with corporate, financial and litigation backgrounds. Jon Landers heads the New York group.

Clients/Work Highlights: Among the firm's clients are committees and individual creditors in bankruptcies and out-of-court restructurings, as well as acquirers of distressed companies.

## Kaye Scholer LLP
See firm details p.1536

The Firm: Since the integration of an experienced team of creditors' rights lawyers from Clifford Chance, the group has developed a balanced practice. Headline matters of late included arranging the Bank of America's DIP loans to both Foamex and Saint Vincent's Catholic Medical Center and coordinating the defense of core banking clients in the Adelphia Communications and Enron litigation. The group also represents trustees and examiners in relation to their fiduciary roles in restructurings, and handles debtor matters for a growing roster of private equity and hedge fund clients.

The Lawyers: *"Results-oriented"* **Margot Schonholtz** (see p.1498) has cultivated long-standing relationships with many key financial institutions. A *"smart and aggressive workout lawyer,"* clients appreciate her ability to pick up on the more subtle business and personal nuances in difficult situations. **Mark Liscio** (see p.1476) also possesses *"an incredibly good manner with business people and opposing counsel."* He has devoted a portion of his practice to advising private equity funds buying in the distressed debt market. Clients describe him as *"a practical lawyer who makes an effort to understand our business."* **Arthur Steinberg** (see p.1504), cochair of the business reorganization and creditors' rights team, is no stranger to complex bankruptcy matters having taken a role in both the Worldcom and Enron North America sagas. His recent caseload has included an

appointment in the Wood River Capital Management et al proceedings.

Clients/Work Highlights: The team has a strong following among senior lenders, such as Bank of America, ABN AMRO and Citigroup, and has a growing number of private equity and hedge fund clients.

## Luskin, Stern & Eisler LLP

The Firm: This firm was established in 1989 to cater solely to creditors in debt restructurings and Chapter 11 bankruptcy proceedings. The group of ten lawyers offers a comprehensive range of financial and litigation services, and particularly excels in the redocumentation of troubled loans. Because of this strength, it often acts for banks, either as individual creditors or as agents for larger groups of financial institutions. Recent matters include representing the Bank of Nova Scotia as agent for 30 other banks in the Adelphia Communications bankruptcy, and Deutsche Bank in various restructurings and syndicated financing deals. Despite its small size, the team is regularly involved in international bankruptcies, often coordinating with local counsel in Brazil, Mexico and the UK.

The Lawyers: Clients appreciate the good working combination of **Michael Luskin** and **Richard Stern** and praise both as *"gifted technical lawyers"* in their differing areas of expertise. Luskin is a *"great litigator and very user-friendly bankruptcy adviser,"* while Stern is recommended for his DIP financing where his low-key approach serves him well in negotiations.

Clients/Work Highlights: The group has built its practice around representing financial institutions such as Deutsche Bank; ABN AMRO; Bank of America and Citibank. It also represents Bear Stearns and John A Levin & Co in the distressed debt market.

## Mayer, Brown, Rowe & Maw LLP
See firm details p.876

The Firm: The New York team at this premier transactional firm has made an impact on the New York market on the strength of its creditors' rights practice. Its focus is primarily on representing banks and other senior lenders, who testify to the group's proficiency in creating new DIP loan arrangements, as well as managing existing debt. The bankruptcy team benefits particularly from its close relationship with the Chicago office, but also enjoys the support of an international network, which is also a major draw for clients.

The Lawyers: Clients were impressed with the intellectual horsepower of the New York lawyers and recommended them as savvy business people. Michael Richman is the contact partner for the team.

Clients/Work Highlights: While the group gained the most market recognition for its bank work, it caters to a full range of creditor clients, including creditor committees, bondholders and institutional investors.

## Proskauer Rose LLP

See firm details p.1551

**The Firm:** This "*small but talented team*" of six bankruptcy partners continues to gain recognition for debtor work, particularly in the retail and telecom sector. The group has also expanded its creditor-side practice, particularly in the area of DIP financing for banks, and it currently acts for a group of creditors in the REFCO bankruptcy. The bankruptcy team is housed in the corporate department, and readily draws on the firm's tax and litigation capabilities to complement its practice.

**The Lawyers:** Head of the bankruptcy and reorganization practice group, **Alan Hyman**'s (see p.1467) depth of experience, particularly in debtor matters, stands out and clients recommend him as a constructive force in negotiations.

## Schulte Roth & Zabel LLP

See firm details p.1552

**The Firm:** This bankruptcy group has developed particular expertise in acquisition financing and litigation through catering to large distressed investors, and commentators judge it "*light years ahead of almost everyone in its representation of hedge funds.*" It is also a consistent performer in the creditors' rights arena, as many of the group's investor clients buy significant equity positions in troubled companies, such as Cerberus Capital Management, which now owns a controlling interest in the debtor Anchor Glass. The team also acts for real estate developers

when commercial tenants go into Chapter 11, and has a good track record of asbestos debtor cases.

**The Lawyers:** **Michael Cook**'s experience in financial and litigation matters is said to have "*given the firm a good lift.*"

**Clients/Work Highlights:** The group acts for funds that have acquired large equity positions in both Solutia and Armstrong World Industries, and is currently representing a subsidiary of Pfizer in an asbestos-related Chapter 11 case.

## Sonnenschein Nath & Rosenthal LLP

See firm details p.884

**The Firm:** Peers "*take their hats off*" to this group for making a name for itself in the equity committee world. Vociferous advocates for their clients, this group of "*long-time New York practitioners*" often operates in concert with the Chicago bankruptcy team, recently combining to represent the United Airlines creditors' committee. The group's current headline representation is for the creditors' committee in the Federal-Mogul Chapter 11 proceedings, but it also turns its hand to debtor representations.

**The Lawyers:** The team is strengthening its ranks with both new associates and a lateral hire, and now stands at 12 lawyers. Commentators regard the combination of senior partners **Peter Wolfson** (see p.1514) and **Carole Neville** as the key driver of the firm's New York practice.

**Clients/Work Highlights:** The group made its name with equity committee representations for the

likes of Loral Space & Communications and Interstate Bakeries, but has a wider committee practice that encompasses bondholders and general creditors.

## Other Notable Practitioners

**Martin Flics** (see p.1455) joined Linklaters in 2003 from Latham & Watkins, and while already a notable presence in US/European and other cross-border cases, commentators view him as a valuable resource for developing the firm's New York bankruptcy practice. **Adam Harris** (see p.1464) is singled out as the key player for O'Melveny & Myers LLP, and an effective complement to the firm's strong West Coast practice. Best known for representing financial institutions and insurance companies, he is "*a very practical lawyer, he does not waste time with posturing but gets right to what's important.*" While also a respected creditor lawyer, **Steven Reisman** (see p.1492) of Curtis, Mallet-Prevost, Colt & Mosle LLP is best known for his role as conflict counsel for major debtors, most recently working with Cadwalader, Wickersham & Taft in Northwest Airlines matters. He is recommended as one of the premier lawyers in this niche area as he is "*highly regarded by the courts and works well with everyone involved.*" **Albert Togut** of bankruptcy specialists Togut Segal & Segal LLP has also carved out a formidable practice in conflict counsel engagements, most recently working with Skadden Arps in the Delphi Automotive proceedings. He is described as "*intelligent, hardworking and fair, the perfect conflict counsel.*"

# CONSTRUCTION

### Construction
#### Leading Firms

| 1 | PECKAR & ABRAMSON PC *New York* |
|---|---|
| 2 | BROWN RAYSMAN *New York* |
| | SACKS MONTGOMERY PC *New York* |
| | THELEN REID & PRIEST LLP *New York* |
| | ZETLIN & DE CHIARA LLP *New York* |
| 3 | ARENT FOX PLLC *New York* |
| | GOETZ FITZPATRICK LLP *New York* |
| | LEPATNER & ASSOCIATES LLP *New York* |
| | MAZUR, CARP & RUBIN PC *New York* |

## Band 1

## Peckar & Abramson PC

See firm details p.1549

**The Firm:** Standing "*head and shoulders above the others,*" this firm has consolidated its position at the forefront of the New York construction market through a merger with DC firm Bastianelli, Brown & Kelley. In particular, this move has added depth to the firm's government contracts practice. Already regarded as "*an excellent firm with significant depth of talent,*" the addition of respected lawyer Adrian Bastianelli to the roster ensures Peckar & Abramson a strong DC presence. Headquartered in New Jersey,

but with offices in New York, this integrated team advises contractors and construction managers on matters such as risk management, dispute resolution and contractual matters. It is currently involved in the prosecution of an arbitration involving a major municipal transit system with more than $150 million in claims and counterclaims. It is also engaged in an ongoing trial against a federal agency with regard to a claim for equitable adjustment.

**The Lawyers:** Founding partner and "*face of the firm*" **Robert Peckar** (see p.1487) is an outstanding lawyer. Clients endorse him as "*super-intelligent, creative and business-oriented,*" and he is widely respected for his mediation skills and is "*on everyone's shortlist*" for dispute resolution. As well as handling general construction work, fellow founding partner **Richard Abramson** (see p.1431) is a specialist in the energy industry, and can count GE among his clientele. He spent much of the past year on an arbitration concerning a power plant in Saudi Arabia. **Steven Charney** (see p.1444) is a talented advocate and "*incredibly knowledgeable about the workings of the construction industry.*" In the wake of Hurricane Katrina, he is currently working with the Associated General Contractors (AGC) of America regarding legislative approaches to obtain government protection for contractors in the aftermath of such disasters. George Pierson has recently left the

firm, taking his practical, level headed approach to Parsons Brinckerhoff.

**Clients/Work Highlights:** The firm represents some of the country's largest and most well-known construction management firms and general contractors. It is also active with industry bodies and works for the general contractors of the New York Building Congress and the Building Trades Employers' Association.

## Band 2

## Brown Raysman Millstein Felder & Steiner LLP

See firm details p.1521

**The Firm:** Formerly known as Ross & Cohen LLP, it is too early to gauge the impact of the merger with full-service Brown Raysman Millstein Felder & Steiner LLP on this respected New York practice, but the extra resources and broader reach should stand the construction department in good stead. The team is best known for its transactional strength and experience of representing owners but also has considerable expertise in arbitrations and mediations. The group acts as construction counsel in the redevelopment of the Mayflower Hotel site on Central Park West into a residential complex, and is involved in both the Moynihan Station redevelopment and the Bronx Terminal Market redevelopment.

**The Lawyers: Allen Ross** (see p.1494) is *"very respected as a senior player in the construction Bar."* A *"guru of mediation,"* he has devoted a significant portion of his practice to arbitration and mediation work, and won high praise for his *"ability to bring things to a conclusion."*

**Clients/Work Highlights:** The firm's clientele includes owners, managers and contractors.

## Sacks Montgomery PC

**The Firm:** This relatively small but *"highly respected team of top-notch lawyers"* has carved out a broad practice covering transactional work, litigation, arbitration and mediation for clients across the USA. Recent highlights include representing a large West Coast manufacturing company in a $60 million construction dispute involving plants in Minnesota, and representing the surety in a construction lawsuit in Ohio involving a power plant in Indonesia. The team also provided project structure advice and drafted contracts for a major museum's renovation projects. Clients praised this outstanding team for being *"knowledgeable, innovative and responsive."*

**The Lawyers:** The litigation skills of **David Montgomery** have led peers to describe him as *"extremely capable and a very worthy adversary."* He is *"a lawyer's lawyer,"* who adopts an *"aggressive and firm approach but with a style of open communication."* Clients also appreciate that *"his total commitment to his client stands out."* Clients like **Frederick Rohn** because he is *"efficient and value conscious; he will not spend unnecessary money."* His common-sense and rational approach is popular: *"Unlike a lot of lawyers, he doesn't become unnecessarily adversarial."* **Scott St Marie** is another respected partner. *"Straightforward, bright and*

*hard-working,"* he impresses with his litigation skills.

**Clients/Work Highlights:** The client base is split between large owners and construction companies. Examples include the Dormitory Authority of the State of New York; MeadWestvaco; Museum of Modern Art; Verizon; AMEC; Metropolitan Steel Industries and Chubb Group. It continues to handle matters such as contract drafting for New York University.

## Thelen Reid & Priest LLP

See firm details p.342

**The Firm:** The New York office of this strong national group handles projects throughout the USA. Its international practice is also thriving, with the firm reaping the benefits of its joint venture with respected British construction firm Pinsent Masons. As well as handling mediation and arbitration, the team also undertakes transactional work. Recent highlights include settling a claim of more than $1 million against the New York City Housing Authority and advising a general contractor completing a $30 million nursing home for the surety of a defaulted contractor. It has also been engaged on the construction of a number of new high rises in the New York area.

**The Lawyers: Barry Grove** (see p.1462) is a fine litigator who splits his practice between contentious work and project structuring, contract formation and consulting on ongoing projects. He is highly regarded for his expertise in dispute resolution and his international experience. While also a skilled litigator, **Richard Dyer** (see p.1451) is currently focusing on domestic transactions. For example, he has worked with the Lincoln Center for the Performing Arts on its revitalization program. **Robert MacPherson** (see p.1476) is a new addition to the firm's roster, having come from the now defunct Postner & Rubin. *"Levelheaded and easy to talk to,"* he is respected for his negotiation skills.

**Clients/Work Highlights:** The firm represents both owners and contractors. Examples of clients include New York City Opera; Ceebraid-Signal; Liddell Brothers; Sherwood Equities; LBL Skysystems; Heller Group and the Lincoln Center for the Performing Arts.

## Zetlin & De Chiara LLP

**The Firm:** This fine firm continues to dominate the market when it comes to representing the design community. Clients highlighted the *"quality of work, attention and intelligence"* provided by these attorneys, who advise architects and engineers on a broad range of matters. The caseload includes dispute resolution, construction contracts, employment issues and organizing company structures. Insurance defense work is also a forte, and the group is seen as *"developing a prominent leading practice."* Examples of recent work include representing the development team for the construction of a large mixed-use project on Manhattan's West Side, and representing an engineering firm in defense of claims of around $50 million relating to the alleged flaws in the design of a bridge.

**The Lawyers: Michael Zetlin** is *"extraordinarily capable, knowledgeable and an upright guy."* He is a skilled litigator and mediator with a *"commanding yet personable presence,"* said clients. **Michael De Chiara** impresses clients with his *"devotion to the protection of design professionals' practices."* *"A tough character"* when he needs to be, he is widely respected for his litigation expertise. He acts as outside counsel to the General Services Administration for construction litigation.

**Clients/Work Highlights:** The firm's client list includes some of the most prominent names in architecture, including Richard Meier and Polshek Partnership. As well as acting for a number of owners, the firm is also outside counsel to a number of industry bodies including the American Institute of Architects New York State and the New York Building Congress.

## Band 3

## Arent Fox PLLC

**The Firm:** This firm has increased its profile in the New York market with the arrival of two attorneys from LePatner & Associates. The team represents owners, developers and design professionals in a broad range of matters including project planning, dispute resolution and contract preparation. It also has transactional and litigation experience. It recently represented a major university in connection with the expansion of its research and academic facilities.

**The Lawyers:** Formerly of LePatner & Associates, **Aaron Abraham** (see p.1431) and **David Pfeffer** (see p.1487) are starting to build profiles in the sector. According to sources, Abraham is *"honest, hard-working and makes sound decisions,"* while Pfeffer commands loyalty through his *"energy and a real gift for keeping people focused."* Examples of Pfeffer's work include representing artist Julian Schnabel in the project construction and financing matters related to the development of a residential condominium, and representing Brack Capital regarding contract negotiations and project management on a $300 million construction project.

**Clients/Work Highlights:** The clientele includes Brack Capital, Sleepy's and Millennium Partners, as well as owners, developers and design professionals.

## Goetz Fitzpatrick LLP

**The Firm:** This boutique construction firm has expertise in litigation, arbitration and mediation as well as drafting and reviewing construction contracts. It also regularly deals with real estate, environmental, insurance, risk management and banking matters.

**The Lawyers:** Founding partner **Peter Goetz** is recognized as a senior figure in the construction arena. An experienced litigator and negotiator, he is particularly known for his arbitration work.

**Clients/Work Highlights:** The firm's clientele includes owners, developers, design professionals, insurance companies and general contractors.

## LePatner & Associates LLP

See firm details p.1541

**The Firm:** The bulk of this firm's practice consists of representing corporate, institutional and real estate developer clients, for whom it regularly acts as business and legal advisers on major construction projects as well as handling their dispute resolution needs. It also acts for major engineering and architectural firms, including Richard Rogers Partnership and Frank Gehry. Recent work highlights include representing the owner in the construction of the Core Club in Manhattan and representing Andalex Group LLC in a $100 million residential conversion in Long Island City. It also negotiated design contracts for Frank Gehry Architects regarding a $400 million performing arts center at the Ground Zero site. On the litigation side, the firm acted for Wimberly Allison Tong & Goo in the Tropicana Atlantic City garage collapse case in New Jersey.

**The Lawyers:** The firm's founder **Barry LePatner** continues to be a prominent figure in the sector. As well as being very active in the practice, he is a well-known speaker at industry events.

**Clients/Work Highlights:** The firm represents owners, developers institutional organizations and design-related companies. JPMorgan Chase, Andalex Group LLC and Richard Rogers Partnership are among the firm's clients.

## Mazur, Carp & Rubin PC

**The Firm:** This *"fantastic team of seasoned construction lawyers"* handles transactional matters and disputes for developers, owners and contractors, primarily in the New York state and metropolitan area. Further afield, the firm recently concluded construction management, architectural services and trade contracts for a $1 billion development in Chicago. Other examples of work include helping a major New York city landlord and its landlord-tenant counsel organize a case to eject a commercial tenant for violating the terms of the lease. It also instituted a suit against a municipality and one of its prime contractors on a pollution control facility with regard to the flooding of a companion project. Attorneys here also conduct educational seminars and create training materials for clients.

**The Lawyers:** *"A straight shooter who inspires confidence,"* **Sayward Mazur** has the ability to *"get what he needs to get done for the client without ego,"* said one interviewee. A *"charismatic, smart and honorable"* attorney, he grasps the issues quickly by *"accessing the most important information and articulating his arguments effectively."* **Ira Schulman** is an excellent advocate who takes a *"smart and aggressive"* approach to the presentation of his cases. He also handles transactional work.

**Clients/Work Highlights:** The firm works with contractors, developers, and public and private owners.

## Other Notable Practitioners

**Robert Rubin** has joined Seyfarth Shaw LLP following the dissolution of Postner & Rubin. He is highly rated for his excellent construction disputes practice, which includes a strong international component. His *"tremendous experience"* and engineering qualifications gain him the respect of clients, and he is also an esteemed mediator. **William Postner** can't fail to attract respect at his new firm Schiff Hardin LLP, where he is of counsel.

# CORPORATE/M&A

**OVERVIEW:** As part of our research for the 2006 edition of *Chambers USA*, we had considered introducing a chapter on Corporate Governance issues, an area of increasing specialization and of major importance to those doing business in the USA. However, our interviews with clients and key industry specialists have indicated that corporate governance issues have now become ingrained into daily life. Any lawyers worth their salt (both corporate deal-doers and litigators) are providing corporate governance and Sarbanes-Oxley Act advice as part of their day-to-day client service. There are, of course, certain attorneys whose advice to the boards of Fortune 500 corporates and major financial institutions and whose work with the key regulatory bodies deserves especial recognition. Our hats, therefore, are tipped in New York to Ira Millstein of Weil, Gotshal & Manges; Marty Lipton and David Katz of Wachtell, Lipton, Rosen & Katz; Dick Beattie, George Krouse and Casey Cogut of Simpson Thacher & Bartlett; Roger Aaron and Peter Atkins of Skadden, Arps, Slate, Meagher & Flom; John White and John Gaffney of Cravath, Swaine & Moore; while in DC, former SEC man Jim Doty now at Baker Botts, and John Olson, Brian Lane and Amy Goodman at Gibson, Dunn & Crutcher, were all the subject of commendation during our research.

## Band 1

### Simpson Thacher & Bartlett LLP

See firm details p.1555

**The Firm:** One cannot underestimate the importance of this firm's impact on the corporate market. Firstly, and most importantly, it has cemented close relationships with key clients: *"It has expertise in all the important areas and made a commitment to provide outstanding people who are easy to work with and responsive."* Clients also refer to a *"business-oriented firm with high ethical standards"* whose teams *"take things personally and care about the business perspective – it is more than just a job for them."* The firm also had the foresight in the 1980's to recognize the growing importance of private equity and has skillfully combined its public company M&A expertise with what is arguably the world's leading private equity practice. Long-standing relationships with leading buyout sponsors such as KKR and The Blackstone Group have paid dividends in this buoyant market and an increase in consortia deals has followed. Simpson Thacher has taken its place on the highest profile deals of the year. It represented adidas-Salomon in its acquisition of Reebok International for $3.8 billion, the Neiman Marcus Group in its $5.1 billion acquisition by TPG and Warburg Pincus and The Blackstone Group in its $3.24 billion purchase of Wyndham. The group is also representing Goldman Sachs, the financial adviser to ConocoPhillips in its proposed acquisition of Burlington Resources. The firm also has an impressive financial institutions practice. As one interviewee summed up: *"Simpson is a fantastic firm with depth, great practitioners and a great client base. It offers a full-service package to clients."* This firm also adopts a conservative global model focused on offices in London, Hong Kong and Tokyo and offering a global reach.

**The Lawyers:** Client service and a commitment to the completion of a deal are common traits among the Simpson Thacher lawyers. Firm chairman **Dick Beattie** (see p.1436) has a vast wealth of M&A experience that has led many to describe him as a luminary in the market. Although still involved in the thick of complex deals, much of his time of late has been devoted to the increasingly important area of corporate governance and advisory matters. **Casey Cogut** (see p.1445) attracts high-profile work and clients through his ability to *"diffuse issues and make them workable."* He acted in the adidas-Salomon deal and represented the special committee of Fox Entertainment Group in the acquisition by News Corporation of the shares of Fox it did not already own. Cogut combines duties as the global head of M&A and a key client relationship partner for a number of big names, including KKR, with a busy M&A practice. **John Finley** (see p.1454) *"provides clear concise advice on the business issues and can explain things to the board in an easy to understand way that sounds logical,"* said clients. He has enjoyed a formidable year acting on a series of billion-dollar deals, including the auctions of Toys 'R' Us and the Neiman Marcus Group, and advice to VNU in the $2.55 billion sale of its Yellow Pages directories. **Pete Ruegger** (see p.1495) is *"easy-going yet professional; he certainly has an incredible breadth of experience,"* according to clients. As chairman of the firm's executive committee and head of the corporate department, Ruegger spends up to half of his time on M&A matters. He represented Travelers in its merger with St. Paul. He also oversees the firm's relationship with The Blackstone Group. **Robert Spatt** (see p.1504) is often chosen for "*those special event transactions.*" He "*gets stuff done and you can work with him effectively. He's not a time waster,*" mused one source. **Lee Meyerson** (see p.1479) is a "*pleasure to work with and represents clients effectively.*" He acted for Washington Mutual in its $6.6 billion acquisition of Providian Financial and assisted Independence Community Bank in its sale to Sovereign Bancorp for $3.6 billion. Pragmatic and solution-focused **David Sorkin** (see p.1504) advised Hertz and Ford in Hertz's sale to a consortium of private equity firms in a deal valued at $15 billion. **William Curbow** (see p.1448) is a partner to watch. Admired by competitors, he is "*technically superb and has a great table manner when it comes to negotiation style. He is a complete lawyer.*"

**Clients/Work Highlights:** JPMorgan Chase; The Blackstone Group; KKR; St. Paul Travelers; Lehman Brothers; MasterCard; Silver Lake Partners; Hellman & Friedman; Hertz; Toys 'R' Us; Evercore Partners; UBS; Accenture; adidas; Deutsche Bank; Apax Partners; Neiman Marcus Group and Virgin Mobile.

### Skadden, Arps, Slate, Meagher & Flom LLP & Affiliates

See firm details p.1557

**The Firm:** A behemoth of the legal world, the firm continues to dominate the M&A market, playing a prominent role in the largest US and international matters: "*You can bet that Skadden is involved on one side or another in almost any major transaction.*" This deal exposure has subsequently spawned a team of lawyers who are "*probably the most experienced and creative in the States for complex M&A.*" Recent highlights include representing Apax Partners in its acquisition of Tommy Hilfiger, via an auction, in a

deal reportedly valued at $1.6 billion. The team has also represented News Corporation in a number of matters, including its $6 billion acquisition of the outstanding shares of Fox Entertainment Group that it did not already own. Billion-dollar deals aside, the team also supports midmarket and emerging companies, handling a range of midsized transactions. Accordingly, clients highlighted the "*wide range of expertise for diverse situations*" and impeccable service levels as a major attraction. The firm is "*incredibly consistent, no matter which office is used,*" and has a "*tremendous infrastructure.*" This is no mean feat when one considers that the firm offers services from more than 20 offices across the globe. Its recent cross-border expertise has been displayed in counsel to the Australian government for its $19 billion sale of its remaining stake in telecom giant Telstra.

**The Lawyers:** Internationally renowned, **Joe Flom** (see p.1455) is a legend in M&A circles. His "*fantastic business judgment combines with superb legal advice and a devotion to his clients.*" He recently acted for The May Department Stores Company in its acquisition by Federated Department Stores. **Kenneth Bialkin** (see p.1439) has a broad practice, which includes domestic and international M&A, corporate finance transactions and SEC enforcement matters. His powerful relationships with institutional clients and his extensive deal experience are valuable tools in the continued success of the firm. A "*terrific and trusted business adviser,*" **Roger Aaron** (see p.1431) heads Skadden's corporate practice areas. His long track record in the multibillion-dollar deals has led many to describe him as a consummate dealdoer: "*He knows how to manage deals, will not waste time or permit egos to get in the way.*" **Peter Atkins'** (see p.1434) broad range of experience includes M&A, corporate governance and securities work. He is a great board adviser as his authoritative advice and sound, practical judgment are respected at the highest levels. **Morris Kramer's** (see p.1472) creative thought and ability to see the big picture have made him a favorite for a range of friendly and hostile transactions, as well as strategic M&A. Similarly, **Lou Kling** (see p.1471) is "*someone whose word you can trust in transactions – he wants to see the deal succeed and quickly gets to the point.*" The "*cool, calm and collected*" **David Fox** (see p.1456) impresses clients with his solution-oriented approach to matters. He represented the board of directors of Toys 'R' Us in its strategic review and the subsequent $6.6 billion acquisition by an investment group. Head of the M&A practice, **Franklin Gittes** (see p.1459) represented MacAndrews & Forbes Holdings in its $750 million acquisition of Deluxe Film from The Rank Group. He is a business-savvy attorney and shares with **Thomas Kennedy** (see p.1470) a strategic, 360-degree view of the market. Kennedy "*listens to clients and works their interests into the deal.*" He represented Penn National Gaming in its $2.2 billion acquisition of Argosy Gaming. **Eric Cochran's** (see p.1445) practice focuses on M&A, securities and general corporate law. He represented Merrill Lynch as financial adviser to Ventas in its acquisition of Prov-

ident Senior Living Trust. He also acted for Merrill Lynch as financial adviser to the special committee of the board of directors of Eon Labs, which was established to consider an acquisition by Novartis. During transactions, **Eric Friedman** (see p.1457) "*has an eye on the big picture.*" He keeps "*negotiations moving, has a good technical ability and is excellent at project managing a complicated deal.*" **Eileen Nugent** (see p.1484) is co-head of the firm's private equity department, and a "*business and solution-oriented lawyer*" with strong technical skills. Her public company M&A work is combined with private equity matters, and she handles both elements with aplomb: "*She is not over-burdened by ego.*" **Paul Schnell** (see p.1498) brings a "*degree of sure-footedness*" to his negotiations. Clients also praised his ability to marshal resources in major deals such as his advice to PacifiCare in its proposed $8.1 billion sale to UnitedHealth Group. In the summer of 2005, Michael Schell left the firm to join Citigroup.

**Clients/Work Highlights:** Penn National Gaming; Apax Partners; Haier; News Corporation; PacifiCare; Honeywell; Hewlett-Packard; VHA; Cendant; Bear Stearns; Deutsche Bank; Telefónica; JPMorgan Chase and CIGNA.

### Wachtell, Lipton, Rosen & Katz

See firm details p.1561

**The Firm:** This select corporate group regularly attracts headline deals through its provision of "*the greatest uniformity in the quality of its practice.*" Over the years, the firm has established a dominant position as leading counsel for the targets of hostile takeovers, and continues to act on the market's choicest deals. Such is Wachtell's stellar reputation, it operates on a different model to many rivals, preferring to carefully select the deals it works on for the best strategic and cultural fit. This approach seems to work well for clients who praise the quality and consistency of the group; advice is "*seamless from one attorney to another and the talent is there at every level.*" Peers ascribe "*a tremendous amount of credibility and respect*" to the practice, and its decision not to expand through overseas offices has not hindered its ability to handle high-profile, cross-border transactions. In the Asia-Pacific region, the firm's role advising Unocal on its proposed acquisition by China National Offshore Oil Corp (CNOOC) for $20.4 billion is widely endorsed. Closer to home, recent highlights include representing Tommy Hilfiger in its acquisition by Apax Partners and acting for Lazard, financial adviser to WellChoice, in WellPoint's proposed acquisition of WellChoice. The firm also advised AT&T in its acquisition by SBC Communications for $22.5 billion.

**The Lawyers:** **Marty Lipton** (see p.1476) is "*the biggest name in the business.*" A guru in the defense of hostile takeovers, he is "*extremely smart, assertive, aggressive and knowledgeable and is right at the top of his game.*" He represented ConocoPhillips in its proposed acquisition of Burlington Resources for $35.6 billion. A "*wonderful legal and business adviser,*" **Edward Herlihy** (see p.1465) is a prime choice for bank-related M&As as "*he has mastered the bank*

## Corporate/M&A
### Leading Individuals

#### Senior Statesmen

| | |
|---|---|
| BEATTIE Richard *Simpson Thacher & Bartlett* | BIALKIN Kenneth *Skadden, Arps* |
| FLEISCHER JR Arthur *Fried, Frank* | FLOM Joseph *Skadden, Arps* |
| LIPTON Martin *Wachtell* | NUSBAUM Jack *Willkie Farr & Gallagher* |

[1]

| | |
|---|---|
| AARON Roger *Skadden, Arps* | ATKINS Peter *Skadden, Arps* |
| BLOCK Dennis *Cadwalader* | COGUT Charles *Simpson Thacher & Bartlett* |
| COHEN H Rodgin *Sullivan & Cromwell LLP* | FINKELSON Allen *Cravath, Swaine & Moore* |
| HERLIHY Edward *Wachtell* | KATCHER Richard *Wachtell* |
| KRAMER Morris *Skadden, Arps* | LEWKOW Victor *Cleary Gottlieb* |
| MORPHY James *Sullivan & Cromwell LLP* | |

[2]

| | |
|---|---|
| AQUILA Francis *Sullivan & Cromwell LLP* | BROWNSTEIN Andrew *Wachtell* |
| CONDON Creighton *Shearman & Sterling LLP* | FINLEY John *Simpson Thacher & Bartlett* |
| KATZ David *Wachtell* | KLING Lou *Skadden, Arps* |
| LYONS Peter *Shearman & Sterling LLP* | MADDEN John *Shearman & Sterling LLP* |
| PIERCE Morton *Dewey Ballantine LLP* | RUEGGER Philip *Simpson Thacher & Bartlett* |
| SAEED Faiza *Cravath, Swaine & Moore* | SCHUMER Robert *Paul, Weiss* |
| SPATT Robert *Simpson Thacher & Bartlett* | STAPLETON Benjamin *Sullivan & Cromwell LLP* |
| STEPHENSON Alan *Cravath, Swaine & Moore* | WASSERMAN Craig *Wachtell* |

[3]

| | |
|---|---|
| BARSHAY Scott *Cravath, Swaine & Moore* | BASON JR George *Davis Polk & Wardwell* |
| BIRD Paul *Debevoise & Plimpton LLP* | EMMERICH Adam *Wachtell* |
| FOX David *Skadden, Arps* | FRAIDIN Stephen *Kirkland & Ellis LLP* |
| GELSTON Philip *Cravath, Swaine & Moore* | GITTES Franklin *Skadden, Arps* |
| HALL Richard *Cravath, Swaine & Moore* | KENNEDY Thomas *Skadden, Arps* |
| NATHAN Charles *Latham & Watkins LLP* | NEFF Daniel *Wachtell* |
| O'BRIEN Clare *Shearman & Sterling LLP* | PROFUSEK Robert *Jones Day* |
| ROBERTS Thomas *Weil, Gotshal & Manges* | ROSEN Jeffrey *Debevoise & Plimpton LLP* |
| ROSENBLUM Steve *Wachtell* | RYAN Michael *Cleary Gottlieb* |
| SEYMON Pamela *Wachtell* | |

[4]

| | |
|---|---|
| BEVILACQUA Louis *Cadwalader* | CAPLAN David *Davis Polk & Wardwell* |
| CERABINO Thomas *Willkie Farr & Gallagher* | CHATZINOFF Howard *Weil, Gotshal & Manges* |
| COCHRAN Eric *Skadden, Arps* | DE WIED Warren *Fried, Frank* |
| FRIEDMAN Dennis *Gibson, Dunn & Crutcher* | FRIEDMAN Eric *Skadden, Arps* |
| FRUMKIN Joseph *Sullivan & Cromwell LLP* | GREEN Frederick *Weil, Gotshal & Manges* |
| KISLIN Scott *Gibson, Dunn & Crutcher* | MEYERSON Lee *Simpson Thacher & Bartlett* |
| MILLS Phillip *Davis Polk & Wardwell* | MYERSON Toby *Paul, Weiss* |
| NUGENT Eileen *Skadden, Arps* | PALEY Alan *Debevoise & Plimpton LLP* |
| REISS John *White & Case LLP* | SCHNELL Paul *Skadden, Arps* |
| SEIDMAN Steven *Willkie Farr & Gallagher* | SHIM Paul *Cleary Gottlieb* |
| SORKIN David *Simpson Thacher & Bartlett* | STERNBERG Daniel *Cleary Gottlieb* |
| THOYER Judith *Paul, Weiss* | TOWNSEND Robert *Cravath, Swaine & Moore* |
| VLAHAKIS Patricia *Wachtell* | |

#### Up-and-coming individuals

| | |
|---|---|
| AIELLO Michael *Dewey Ballantine LLP* | ASLANI-FAR Adel *Dewey Ballantine LLP* |
| CURBOW William *Simpson Thacher & Bartlett* | KOTRAN Stephen *Sullivan & Cromwell LLP* |
| SHOEMATE Steven *Gibson, Dunn & Crutcher* | |

*regulatory merger environment.*" He specializes in complex bank and financial institution M&A and recapitalizations, as does **Craig Wasserman** (see p.1512). He cuts a powerful figure in the financial institutions sector with his practical understanding of the impact of such deals. **Richard Katcher** (see p.1469) is an "*absolute gem.*" His recent caseload has included the representation of Maytag in its acquisition by Whirlpool in a deal valued at $2.7 billion. He "*manages transactions extremely effectively and he knows what's important and what's not.*" The impres-

sive **Andrew Brownstein** (see p.1441) "*is there to get the deal done.*" He has broad experience of M&A and corporate governance matters. Although one of the younger partners of this deeply talented group, interviewees sense that the "*extraordinarily bright* **David Katz** (see p.1469) *is going to be a superstar.*" He employs his "*tireless work ethic*" within a practice that has included US and cross-border M&A and corporate governance issues. The "*talented, thoughtful and intelligent*" **Adam Emmerich** (see p.1452) focuses on M&A and securities law matters. Clients also appre-

ciate the extensive deal experience of **Daniel Neff** (see p.1482), the managing partner of the firm. **Steve Rosenblum** (see p.1494) is "*one of the smartest guys around*" and has a deep well of experience in corporate reorganization and M&A, while **Pamela Seymon** (see p.1500) is praised for her dedication to her clients' interests. She is "*extremely bright, hardworking and a real problem solver.*" **Patricia Vlahakis** (see p.1510) impresses with her shrewd judgment. Her practice concentrates on transactional matters including M&A, cross-border deals, hostile takeovers and corporate governance.

**Clients/Work Highlights:** Tommy Hilfiger; Apollo Advisors; Kraft; JPMorgan Chase; ConocoPhillips; Novartis; Hellman & Friedman; Constellation Brands; Compass Bancshares; Intelsat; York International; MBNA; Cinergy; Unocal and Seminis.

### Band 2

## Cravath, Swaine & Moore LLP
See firm details p.1527

**The Firm:** This elite New York firm offers clients an "*incredibly high level of consistency in terms of talent,*" and has cultivated a host of "*no-nonsense, to-the-point deal-doers.*" Despite external pressures to change its famously conservative approach (the firm recently made its first lateral hire in more than 60 years), Cravath retains its treasured US law focus. It concentrates its resources in New York and London, and is smaller in size than some of its competitors with a group of 20 M&A partners in the New York office. A clear focus on organic growth goes some way to explain the collegiate atmosphere valued by clients. The technical skills and high service levels of the team's younger partners and associates are also the subject of praise. Although it would be hard to maintain the success of 2004 (the firm landed $100 billion worth of deals in December alone), Cravath's "*terrific lawyers*" have continued to attract the key market deals. For example, the team acted for DreamWorks SKG and the seller group in the sale of DreamWorks SKG to Paramount Pictures for approximately $1.6 billion. It also acted for FPL Group in its $28 billion merger with Constellation Energy, and BAE Systems in its $4.2 billion acquisition of United Defense Industries.

**The Lawyers:** Cravath is home to a "*uniform set of high-quality partners.*" Among these, "*lawyer's lawyer*" **Allen Finkelson** (see p.1454) is a "*great technician,*" said clients, who enthused that he is "*one of the preeminent lawyers for megadeals. He has just the skill set to keep extraordinarily large transactions on track and to solve the most difficult negotiation issues.*" Finkelson was part of the team that represented Chevron in the takeover battle between Chevron and CNOOC to acquire Unocal. Sources see "*brilliant*" **Faiza Saeed** (see p.1495) as a "*leading light*" at the firm. She is a "*real productive deal-doer*" and acted in the DreamWorks SKG sale. "*Hard-working*" **Alan Stephenson** (see p.1505) possesses a "*fabulous base of experience,*" which he employs to good effect on the most complex of corporate transactions. He acted with **Scott Barshay** (see p.1436) in the Chevron matter. Barshay, a talented and trusted adviser, also acted for IBM in its $865 million acquisition of Micromuse. A tough negotiator, **Philip Gelston** (see p.1458) is committed to his clients and adopts a business-savvy approach to deals. He represented FPL Group in its merger with Constellation Energy and BAE Systems in its acquisition of United Defense Industries. Clients and competitors rate **Richard Hall** (see p.1463) highly. "*He brings extremely creative ideas to the table.*" He is one of several relationship partners for Time Warner and recently acted for them in an agreement with Google to expand their current strategic alliance. **Robert Townsend** (see p.1508) is "*extremely good at getting clients to focus on the important things.*" He represented Johnson & Johnson in its acquisition of Animas for approximately $518 million. He also acted for The Brink's Company in the sale of its BAX Global operating unit to Deutsche Bahn for approximately $1.1 billion.

**Clients/Work Highlights:** Ashland; AXA; Barrick; Bristol-Myers Squibb; DreamWorks SKG; IBM; Johnson & Johnson; Lucent Technologies; Nestlé; PwC; Royal Dutch Shell; Sprint Nextel; Time Warner and Unilever.

## Davis Polk & Wardwell
See firm details p.1528

**The Firm:** The strength of this heavyweight firm lies in the consistency of quality among its attorneys, its high-caliber advice and the respect it commands from peers for not pulling punches. The firm boasts an old-line client base and can count many of the market's largest financial institutions among its roster. It is therefore no surprise that 2005 saw highly respected Dennis Hersch move to JPMorgan. The jury is still out as to how this departure will affect the firm's M&A practice. The team has a strong base of more than 20 dedicated M&A partners in the New York office, complemented by highly rated capital markets and banking and finance specialists as well as one of the largest and most imposing litigation offerings in the city. This expertise has led to what peers concede to be "*a fantastic couple of years*" dealwise for the firm, including securing a key role advising Gillette on its $57 billion acquisition by Procter & Gamble. Other highlights include representing Oracle in its successful $10.3 billion hostile takeover of PeopleSoft, and acting for Comcast in its $17.6 billion proposed joint acquisition with Time Warner Cable of the assets of Adelphia Communications. Internationally, the firm has traditionally benefited from a complementary best-friends relationship with leading independent firms abroad such as Hengeler Mueller (Germany) and Slaughter and May (UK). It also offers US corporate advice from offices in Tokyo, Madrid, Frankfurt, Hong Kong and Paris, and recently scored a coup by launching its first non-US law practice by hiring former Freshfields Bruckhaus Deringer head of M&A in Paris, Arnaud Pérès. This represents a significant change in the firm's international strategy.

**The Lawyers:** Co-head of Davis Polk's M&A practice, **Gar Bason** (see p.1436) is a larger-than-life character, who displays great enthusiasm in deal negotiations. Lead counsel for Gillette in the merger with Procter & Gamble, his practice is a mixture of straightforward M&A, public transactions and private equity work. **David Caplan** (see p.1442) is a "*terrific guy – extremely thoughtful and intelligent.*" He represents corporate and investment banking clients in M&A, joint ventures, corporate governance issues and related matters. The "*straight-talking*" **Phillip Mills** (see p.1480) is also well regarded by interviewees. He co-leads the corporate team's representation of MCI on its $8.5 billion acquisition by Verizon.

**Clients/Work Highlights:** Comcast; Gillette; MCI; Oracle; Telefónica; BBVA and ntl.

## Sullivan & Cromwell LLP
See firm details p.1558

**The Firm:** A firm that is less vocal than some of its rivals in shouting about its talents, it has a long pedigree and inherent talent, agree market commentators. Providing "*universal quality*" and an "*outstanding team with strength in depth,*" the firm earns the highest acclaim for its preeminent financial institutions practice. Clients here view it as a go-to firm, especially within the M&A arena where it has acted as counsel in most major bank mergers in recent years. The firm was also one of the first to focus on international expansion and today boasts a roster of 12 offices located in leading financial centers across Asia, Australia, Europe and the USA. It subsequently attracts non-US clients who retain the firm to act on US aspects of cross-border transactions. For example, the team recently won a role to act for Bank of China on the US aspects of the bank's $8 billion IPO. The firm also boasts a reputation for homegrown talent, with a group of more than 60 M&A lawyers in New York alone. An impressive deal list for 2005 includes representing Adelphia Communications in its $17.6 billion sale to Time Warner and Comcast; Archipelago Holdings in its $2.5 billion merger with the NYSE; and SBC Communications in its acquisition of AT&T. Although securities work forms the engine of the practice, litigation and capital markets are also notoriously strong areas for the firm.

**The Lawyers:** Despite the inevitable constraints on his time as chairman of the firm, **Rodgin Cohen** (see p.1446) maintains a "*tremendous reputation and a huge book of business in the banking area.*" A specialist in M&A banking deals and financial services work, he was part of the team representing Mitsubishi Tokyo Financial Group in its $29 billion merger with UFJ Holdings – creating the world's largest financial group. The outstanding **James Morphy** (see p.1481) heads the M&A practice and is noted for his no-nonsense approach to the deal table, bringing "*substance, style and status*" to proceedings. Clients praised **Frank Aquila** (see p.1433) for his "*purposeful, service-oriented approach,*" deeming him a "*deal-closer;*" a particularly useful trait on the large cross-border transactions that form a significant part of his practice. Aquila recently acted for Amgen in its $2.2 billion acquisition of Abgenix. A long-standing figure on the corporate scene, **Ben Stapleton** (see p.1504) wins applause for his hard work and depth of expertise. He advised Medco Health Solutions in its $2.2 billion acquisition of Accredo Health. **Joe Frumkin** (see p.1457) "*knows how to get a deal done.*" Recent examples of this talent include advising Telewest Global in its $11.4 billion merger with ntl. **Stephen Kotran** (see p.1472) impresses commentators as "*definitely a rising star – his clients are sophisticated and he is extremely efficient in handling demanding clients' needs.*"

**Clients/Work Highlights:** Adelphia Communications; Amgen; Occidental Petroleum; Wachovia; Telewest Global; Intelsat; INEOS; SBC Communications; Archipelago Holdings; Cingular Wireless and Vornado Realty.

## Band 3

### Cadwalader, Wickersham & Taft LLP
See firm details p.1522

**The Firm:** Clients agree that this team is "*exceptional in its proactiveness, commercial skills and general ability to get down and do deals.*" The arrival of Dennis Block in 1998 has propelled the practice, and his success in attracting megadeals to the practice has been matched by the firm's increased corporate profile. Clients also attest to the bench strength of the group: a growing team of high-quality lawyers specializing in M&A where "*the work of the team is excellent.*" Admittedly, market sources find it hard to see past the profile of Block. Domestically, the firm has three offices in the USA, while internationally, bases in London and the opening of an office in Beijing in 2005 further assist the cross-border needs of clients. The firm scored a major coup by landing a role representing Procter & Gamble in its acquisition of Gillette. Other high-profile transactions the firm has worked on include the sale of StorageTek to Sun Microsystems for $4.1 billion and the acquisition by Pfizer of Vicuron Pharmaceuticals for $1.8 billion. The firm can also offer expertise in other areas of law to complement its M&A practice; it is one of the biggest names in structured finance while its skills within the antitrust, restructuring and tax sectors attract special praise.

**The Lawyers:** A "*tiger*" in the corporate jungle, **Dennis Block** (see p.1440) has built himself a tremendous book of business over the years. He is "*prolific, bombastic and effective,*" and his clients love him because he "*hits a stunning home run every time.*" He represented Procter & Gamble in its acquisition of Gillette. The "*resourceful*" **Lou Bevilacqua** (see p.1439) is also a big hit with clients: "*You look for added value – and he gives it! His knowledge of people beyond just the legal sphere is of exceptional use.*"

**Clients/Work Highlights:** Bear Stearns; Procter & Gamble; Pfizer; Merrill Lynch; MassMutual; Dayton Power & Light; Banc of America Securities; Morgan Stanley; CSFB; Six Flags; Mack-Cali Realty and American Home Mortgage.

## Cleary Gottlieb Steen & Hamilton LLP

See firm details p.1525

**The Firm:** *"Quality and consistency with outstanding client care"* exudes from this team. Cleary is a powerful global player with strong local law practices across its ten offices overseas, soon to be bolstered by a planned launch in China. Peers pointed to the firm's consummate cross-border presence, espying a *"wonderful depth of capacity in the international arena."* This international presence secures the firm's place at some of the largest cross-border deals in the market, such as the representation of Mittal Steel in an unsolicited bid for Acelor, a deal worth €18.6 billion. The takeover will encompass six national regulatory regimes. Its M&A group is supported by one of the largest financial products practices in the country, placing the firm at the vanguard of the capital markets industry due to enduring relationships with key clients in the sector. A hugely respected tax and employee benefits practice also underscores the client-focused nature of this firm. In the past year, the M&A group has handled a number of high-value transactions. These include representing the founder/controlling stockholder of Linsco/Private Ledger in its sale to Hellman & Friedman and Texas Pacific Group for $2.5 billion, and acting for Home Depot in its acquisition of Hughes Supply for $3.5 billion. Cleary also represented Goldman Sachs as financial adviser to New Skies Satellites in its pending all-cash merger with SES Global. The enterprise value of the deal is $1.16 billion.

**The Lawyers:** A senior figure in the wider market, **Victor Lewkow** (see p.1475) is *"extremely capable at getting right to the key issue of a deal. He's pragmatic and comes up with good business solutions,"* agree clients. Lewkow represented Capital One Financial in its acquisition of Hibernia. **Michael Ryan** (see p.1495) is *"a superb lawyer from the technical and practical perspective and knows how to get things done."* His broad practice focuses on financial and corporate matters, from M&A to securities offerings, while **Paul Shim** (see p.1501) focuses on private and public M&A. Shim is *"extremely quick on his feet. He can mobilize teams of people in a productive way and is really client savvy."* **Daniel Sternberg** (see p.1505) has a great track record in cross-border M&A deals. He represented UCB, a Belgian pharmaceutical company, in the sale of its chemicals division to Cytec Industries.

**Clients/Work Highlights:** American Express; Bank of America; Texas Pacific Group; Hewlett-Packard; Suntory International and ON Semiconductor.

## Debevoise & Plimpton LLP

See firm details p.1529

**The Firm:** *"Quite simply terrific corporate deal-doers"* was the consensus among clients. Although it is typically the private equity practice that attracts the lion's share of praise, the strong overlap between the buyouts practice and M&A per se ensures that the firm appears on some of the market's choicest deals. As an illustration, the team acted for Clayton, Dubilier & Rice, The Carlyle Group and Merrill Lynch Global Private Equity in their acquisition of Hertz from Ford in a transaction valued at $15 billion. The New York M&A team has 20 partners offering a *"deep reservoir of experience"* and ensuring that matters are staffed with *"a consistent, excellent product focus on getting the right people on the job."* Such jobs include representing Pernod Ricard in its $2.4 billion sale of Dunkin' Brands to the consortium of BainCapital, The Carlyle Group and Thomas H Lee Partners. The M&A lawyers also receive strong support from the firm's lawyers in the antitrust, tax, finance, real estate, IP and bankruptcy groups. The core New York office is further strengthened by an international network, which includes a burgeoning London office and bases in Paris, Frankfurt, Moscow, Hong Kong and Shanghai.

**The Lawyers:** Clients extol the negotiation skills of **Paul Bird**, cochair of the firm's M&A group: *"He manages to be tough without being overly adversarial. He also has terrific judgment on what's worth fighting for."* He represented Pernod Ricard in its $14 billion acquisition of Allied Domecq and the related $5.4 billion sale of certain Allied Domecq brands and assets to Fortune Brands. An impressive deal negotiator, **Jeff Rosen** is *"always there in the thick of things."* He has an *"extremely strong tax background, is exceedingly smart and imaginative, and is a great communicator."* He cochairs the group with Bird, and represented Verizon in its acquisition of MCI. **Alan Paley** is well noted for his experience in securities matters and his smooth handling of M&A transactions.

**Clients/Work Highlights:** The M&A group has also represented the Dolan family in its bid to take private Cablevision Systems, and the special committee of UnitedGlobalCom's board of directors in its $3.5 billion acquisition by Liberty International to form Liberty Global. Other clients include Phelps Dodge and Verizon.

## Fried, Frank, Harris, Shriver & Jacobson LLP

See firm details p.1532

**The Firm:** This top-notch M&A practice with its *"skilled and constructive"* attorneys wins praise for its fantastic client care: *"Nothing is too much trouble for them,"* recalled one impressed client. A fruitful year for the practice has seen it advise on M&A transactions with an aggregate value of $175 billion, including advice to ConocoPhillips on its acquisition of Burlington Resources. The firm also sustains valuable relationships with investment banks such as Goldman Sachs and Merrill Lynch. For example, the team represented Goldman Sachs as financial adviser to Veritas Software in its acquisition by Symantec in a $13.5 billion transaction. The private equity practice is also undergoing a renaissance: it recently represented a consortium of investors, including Goldman Sachs Capital Partners and Cerberus Capital Management, in its bid to acquire Toys 'R' Us and acted for Dow Jones & Co in its acquisition of MarketWatch for $519 million. The firm also offers clients the advantage of offices in Paris, London and Frankfurt.

**The Lawyers:** The *"marvelous"* **Art Fleischer** (see p.1455) *"is a legendary and important figure"* at Fried Frank. The firm's senior partner, he represented Goldman Sachs as financial adviser to Federated Department Stores in its $17 billion acquisition of The May Department Stores Company. *"Poised and professional,"* **Warren de Wied** (see p.1449) wins praise from clients for his spot-on legal and business judgment as well as his wealth of experience. He represented Merrill Lynch, financial adviser to Eyetech Pharmaceuticals, in the acquisition of Eyetech by OSI Pharmaceuticals. The deal was worth approximately $935 million. He co-heads the M&A practice group with Fleischer.

**Clients/Work Highlights:** The firm advised SPX in the sale of its fire detection systems business to GE for $1.4 billion. Other clients include Burlington Resources; Boeing; Merck; Brookfield Financial Properties; SAIC; ntl; Rouse Company and WPP.

## Weil, Gotshal & Manges LLP

See firm details p.1565

**The Firm:** A *"terrific team doing a terrific job,"* it is growing both nationally and internationally and remains a popular choice for M&A work. The New York offering is bolstered by corporate partners in more than 18 offices worldwide, providing what clients described as a seamless, coordinated service. These offices stretch across Europe to Shanghai and Singapore, while recent lateral hires to the London and Paris offices demonstrate that this firm has its sights set firmly on global expansion. Its broad approach to the transactional market encompasses a real strength in private equity. The firm also possesses the premier bankruptcy practice in the USA, which works closely with the M&A partners on high-caliber matters. Recent deals include acting for Merrill Lynch as the financial adviser to Procter & Gamble in the Gillette deal, and advising GE in its $8.5 billion pending sale of its insurance portfolio, including Employers Reinsurance, to Swiss Re.

**The Lawyers:** An excellent deal-doer, **Tom Roberts** (see p.1493) is *"extremely hands-on and client-oriented."* He is cochair of the firm's corporate department and recently represented UnitedHealth Group in its $9.2 billion acquisition of PacifiCare. **Howard Chatzinoff** (see p.1444) is well regarded in M&A circles. He represented CBS Corporation in the separation of Viacom into two separate public companies, CBS and the new Viacom. He also acted for Molson Breweries in its $6 billion merger with Adolph Coors. **Frederick Green** (see p.1461) co-heads the firm's domestic M&A practice as well as chairing the firm's Latin American practice. His strengths are in public mergers and private transactions work, joint ventures and corporate governance.

**Clients/Work Highlights:** Highlight deals include representing Bear Stearns as the financial adviser to Goldcorp in its $2 billion bid for Wheaton River Minerals. Other clients include CBS; GM; Hughes Supply; Macquarie Bank; UnitedHealth Group; Vivendi Universal and Whirlpool.

## Band 4

### Latham & Watkins LLP

**The Firm:** *"On the upswing,"* this is a firm that is providing a textbook guide on how to crack the notoriously difficult New York market. Firstly, the firm has leveraged its premier finance expertise and subsequent relationships with key investment banks to secure a steady flow of deals. Secondly, it has hired senior attorneys who are able to bring added value to the team, such as former Fried, Frank partner Chuck Nathan. The firm also recently surprised the market by recruiting corporate partner Barry Bryer from rivals Wachtell, an almost unheard of lateral hire. Clients were impressed by the depth of the firm: *"It is just fabulous through and through; and everybody from the most junior to the most senior attorney is super bright and capable."* Recent work highlights include representing Beverly Enterprises in its acquisition by North American Senior Care for $1.9 billion and The Carlyle Group's acquisition of Verizon Hawaii from Verizon Communications for $1.65 billion. This firm also possesses a strong global footprint, with more than ten overseas offices. It has recently ramped up international operations with the launching of a local office in Munich.

**The Lawyers:** Despite his relatively recent arrival, to many **Chuck Nathan** embodies the M&A practice at Latham. Global cochair of the firm's M&A group, he attracts a loyal client following, in part because *"he has a way of making you feel taken care of."* In addition, he is *"incredibly effective in negotiations and pragmatic. He is well known in the field and has an extremely high stature among investment bankers and practitioners."*

**Clients/Work Highlights:** AMC Entertainment; The Carlyle Group; Goldman Sachs; Merrill Lynch; UBS; The Pritzker Organization; National Semiconductor and Symbol Technologies.

### Paul, Weiss, Rifkind, Wharton & Garrison LLP

See firm details p.1548

**The Firm:** A popular team that is increasing its profile in the corporate arena thanks to attorneys who are viewed favorably by the market for their *"credibility and expertise."* Clients spoke of its *"client-focused, smart and responsive"* approach to deal negotiations. Although the firm's preeminent litigation group may enjoy a higher profile in the market, it is now the corporate offering that is proving to be a major drawing card for clients. For example, a year of stellar deals includes the representation of Spectra-Site in its $11.3 billion merger with American Tower. It also advised Intelsat regarding its $6.4 billion acquisition of PanAmSat Holding and assisted Nextel Communications in its stock and cash merger with Sprint.

**The Lawyers:** The *"superbly effective"* **Bob Schumer** (see p.1498) has won a loyal following among clients because *"he just gives good, common-sense, sanguine advice in a thoughtful manner."* Schumer represented Time Warner in its $17.6 billion acquisition of Adelphia Communications, and acted for Wyndham in

its sale to The Blackstone Group in a transaction valued at $3.24 billion. **Judith Thoyer** (see p.1508) is *"engaging, smart and responsive: she's unflappable in a crisis situation,"* observed clients. She represented Sun Chemical in the sale of its 50% stake in Kodak Polychrome Graphics to Kodak. She also represented the special committee of Weight Watchers International in the company's acquisition, in a two-step transaction, of the 80% of WeightWatchers.com that it did not already own. **Toby Myerson** (see p.1481) is a *"cerebral and tenacious"* attorney who commands respect, particularly within the investment banking fraternity, for his knowledge of Asian markets. He brings to the deal table his experience as managing director of Wasserstein Perella & Co in Tokyo, and is a *"very senior lawyer with quality work and a great reputation."*

**Clients/Work Highlights:** Mitsubishi Tokyo Financial Group; Time Warner; Intelsat; Terasen; Citigroup; PetroKazakhstan; General Atlantic; Sun Chemical and International Institute for Research.

### Shearman & Sterling LLP

See firm details p.1554

**The Firm:** Clients applaud the *"first-rate, effective and efficient job"* delivered by this team, highlighting its timely service, broad expertise and understanding of the global nature of the M&A markets. While market commentators wait to see how the practice regroups following the departure of senior partner David Heleniak to Morgan Stanley, one should not ignore the cadre of talented attorneys. Domestically, the team has recently secured roles on some of the largest deals in the marketplace, such as advising Viacom on the $50 billion division of its businesses into separate publicly traded companies – CBS Corporation and the new Viacom – in the largest transaction of its type. The firm also bagged the lead role advising Boston Scientific on its $27 billion bid for Guidant, outmaneuvering Johnson & Johnson in the process. This firm was one of the first to push toward international expansion and now boasts an established network of offices across Europe, Asia and the Middle East. It is therefore unsurprising to see the firm on a wealth of cross-border deals such as the representation of E.ON and its subsidiary, E.ON Ruhrgas, in its $1.8 billion sale of Ruhrgas Industries to an affiliate of CVC Capital Partners. It also recently landed the lead role in BASF's $4.9 billion hostile bid for Engelhard.

**The Lawyers:** **Creighton Condon** (see p.1446) is *"super-smart. He develops creative and practical solutions and is extremely careful."* Condon represented Viacom in a number of transactions, including its $2 billion sale of its 81.5% interest in Blockbuster via a split-off exchange offer. Clients also commended the advice of **Peter Lyons** (see p.1476), an *"extremely responsive attorney – he knows his stuff."* Co-head of the firm's M&A group, he is noted for his expertise in cross-border transactions. He led the BASF deal and advised National Bank of Greece in its $400 million sale of Atlantic Bank of New York to New York Community Bancorp. **John Madden** (see p.1477) is co-managing partner of the firm. Despite his management responsibilities, he also maintains a

busy M&A practice. He represented BOC in the sale of its packaged gas business to Airgas and acted for Merrill Lynch in its acquisition of Advest. Popular attorney **Clare O'Brien** (see p.1484) is *"persistent and meticulous without being obnoxious. Clients feel comfortable having her deal with difficult matters as she would not let anything slip through the cracks."* O'Brien is acting on the Boston Scientific bid for Guidant.

**Clients/Work Highlights:** BASF; Boston Scientific; CIT Group; Citigroup; CSFB; Deutsche Bank; GlaxoSmithKline; Merrill Lynch; Mittal Steel; Morgan Stanley; SunGard Data Systems and The Thompson Corporation.

## Band 5

### Dewey Ballantine LLP

See firm details p.1530

**The Firm:** When it comes to M&A capabilities, *"what differentiates Dewey from a lot of the other firms is that they are extremely responsive to us as a client."* This sentiment was echoed throughout interviews with clients who also described the M&A lawyers as having great business judgment and being *"just remarkably hands-on and deal-doers."* Dewey enjoys a strong reputation when it comes to financial advisory, capital markets and project finance work, and has developed long-standing relationships with several leading investment banks such as Lehman Brothers, Goldman Sachs and CSFB. Recent deals include representing CSFB as financial adviser to SunGard Data Systems in its $10.8 billion acquisition by a consortium of private equity investors. Dewey's New York office is part of an international network that extends to cities such as Beijing, London and Warsaw.

**The Lawyers:** Chairman of the firm's management and executive committee, **Mort Pierce** (see p.1488) has *"fabulous judgment; nothing fazes him,"* said clients, who also lauded his *"ability to help the other side see our position and get a resolution quickly."* Pierce represented CSFB in the SunGard Data Systems transactions. **Michael Aiello** (see p.1432) is *"someone who keeps his eye on the prize and focuses on getting the deal done."* Not only is he *"extraordinarily diligent,"* he also has *"great technical skills and amazing tenacity."* He and Pierce worked on the TBC and Sumitomo deal. **Adel Aslani-Far** (see p.1434) is a rising star: according to clients, he is *"creative in trying to solve problems,"* and particularly effective when *"you need an aggressive lawyer because the other side is being especially difficult."*

**Clients/Work Highlights:** The M&A group represented JPMorgan, the financial adviser to Guidant in the proposed acquisition of Guidant by Johnson & Johnson, and advised Sumitomo in its $1.1 billion acquisition of TBC. It also acted for Actavis Group in its $600 million acquisition of Amide Holdings.

### Gibson, Dunn & Crutcher LLP

See firm details p.328

**The Firm:** Clients note that *"probably more than just about any other firm, they have the ability to focus on* *what's important, putting together compelling arguments for the critical issues."* Focusing on the mid to high-end market, clients point to the *"same quality of service across different deal sizes."* This is a West Coast native continuing to make inroads into the East Coast market: Gibson offers clients a highly developed domestic and international network spanning 13 locations worldwide, and clients appreciate the additional resources available. The firm has also cultivated strong relationships with investment banks such as Lazard Frères and Goldman Sachs. For instance, the firm acted for Goldman Sachs as financial adviser to Target in its $1.65 billion sale of Mervyn's. It also acted for UBS as financial adviser to Gas Natural in its $28.8 billion unsolicited offer for Indesa SA.

**The Lawyers:** Offering clients *"great common sense, knowledge, access to resources, judgment and understanding of our business needs,"* the pragmatic **Dennis Friedman** (see p.1457) cochairs the firm's corporate transactions practice group. Clients welcome his industry experience born from his time as an investment banker at several Wall Street firms. Friedman acted for Ask Jeeves in its $2.3 billion sale of Interactive. The dedicated **Scott Kislin** (see p.1470) *"brings to the table the right balance of business sense, getting the deal done and covering all the bases."* Clients also note that he is *"even-keeled and creative."* He represented the special committee of Hollywood Entertainment Corporation in response to a $900 million unsolicited acquisition proposal from Blockbuster. **Steven Shoemate** (see p.1501) is *"a great attorney and a great businessman."* He has an *"extremely analytical brain and has a personal style which is particularly effective and disarming."* He represented Baker Capital in its acquisition of RiverOne.

**Clients/Work Highlights:** Ask Jeeves; Lazard Frères; UBS; Lehman Brothers; Catterton Partners; Baker Capital; Oldcastle; Investcorp; WellChoice and Morgan Stanley.

## Jones Day
See firm details p.570

**The Firm:** *"In terms of being able to call on expertise from around the globe,"* this is the firm to go to. For clients, Jones Day offers size and cross-jurisdictional capability fielded by lawyers who are of the highest caliber and are *"extremely user-friendly."* A national and international multioffice approach is entrenched into the firm's attorneys – no surprise considering that the firm has over 2,200 lawyers in 30 offices around the world. It was originally a Midwestern operation and one client mused that its non-New York roots led to the firm being greater value for money than native rivals. Recent high-profile deals include Nextel Communications' merger with Sprint, and the group also advised Federated Department Stores in its $17 billion acquisition of The May Department Stores Company and France Télécom in its $10.7 billion acquisition of Amena.

**The Lawyers:** A lawyer committed to client service, **Bob Profusek** (see p.1490) co-heads the firm's M&A practice. He has *"seen just about everything"* and clients extol both his business sense and his judg-

ment: *"He knows when to be tough and when not to."* He has been advising UICI in its acquisition by a consortium led by The Blackstone Group in a going-private transaction valued at $1.8 billion. He also acted for Wasserstein & Co in its $385 million acquisition of the Business Information unit of PRIMEDIA.

**Clients/Work Highlights:** WL Ross & Co; AEP; Procter & Gamble; GM; Reynolds American and R H Donnelley.

## Kirkland & Ellis LLP
See firm details p.875

**The Firm:** This seven-office, Chicago-headquartered firm continues its march into New York with a steadily growing profile due to the volume and high caliber of attorneys and deals undertaken. Offering a *"quality service,"* clients point to an incredibly responsive group that *"will do whatever necessary to accommodate our needs in terms of timing."* A powerful global private equity practice is an additional trump card for the firm. Recent work highlights include advising Merrill Lynch, financial adviser to Constellation Brands, in Constellation's $1.36 billion cash-and-debt buyout of Robert Mondavi. The firm also represented Coors Brewing in its $6.7 billion merger with Molson and acted for Bain Capital in its bid with KKR and Vornado Realty Trust for Toys 'R' Us.

**The Lawyers:** Clients find **Stephen Fraidin** (see p.1456) *"an invaluable source of advice – you can rely on his word and he is also forthright."* He represented the special committee of Net2Phone in a buyout bid from its largest shareholder, IDT. He also acted for Forstmann Little & Co in its $750 million acquisition of International Management Group and $1.6 billion acquisition of 24 Hour Fitness Worldwide.

**Clients/Work Highlights:** Belden CDT; Coors Brewing; Dow Chemical; Forstmann Little & Co; GenCorp; Houlihan Lokey; Merrill Lynch; Net2Phone; Solutia and Peter J Solomon Company.

## White & Case LLP
See firm details p.1566

**The Firm:** International clients seeking an international corporate and commercial service would be hard-pressed to find better than White & Case. The firm has a network of just under 40 offices worldwide, and is renowned for its banking and finance practice in addition to its international reach. When it comes to M&A matters, clients are attracted by the firm's *"breadth of resources, multidisciplinary capability and size. It is a large enough firm to handle major transactions."* The New York office has over 50 M&A lawyers who are *"extremely innovative and flexible."* Recent deals the team has worked on include WellPoint's $6.5 billion acquisition of WellChoice and Liberty's $2 billion acquisition of Cablecom.

**The Lawyers:** Clients highlighted **John Reiss'** (see p.1492) *"outstanding intellect,"* adding that such is his level of service that he is *"always on call."* Reiss is global co-head of the firm's M&A group and was involved in the Warner Chilcott deal. He also represented WellPoint in its acquisition of WellChoice.

**Clients/Work Highlights:** The group has also advised on Aviation Capital Group's $2.65 billion acquisition of Boullioun Aviation Services from WestLB, and represented the management of Warner Chilcott in its acquisition by investment group, Waren Acquisition. Other clients include Agfa-Gevaert; Consorcio Comex; Deutsche Bank; EchoStar Communications; Mohawk Paper Mills; Pitney Bowes; Quintiles Transnational; Royal Ahold; Stolt-Nielsen and Tyco International.

## Willkie Farr & Gallagher LLP
See firm details p.1567

**The Firm:** Clients applaud the *"impeccable service"* they receive from the M&A attorneys: *"When we call, they really drop everything to service our needs,"* reported one. This full-service firm has over 600 attorneys working in eight offices in the USA and Europe. Clients add that Willkie Farr is *"broad and strong across all the service areas, and that's a distinguishing feature of the firm."* For instance, the firm boasts a strong private equity practice, as well as its thriving business reorganization and restructuring group, both of which feed into the work of the M&A team. Recent highlights include representing Monsanto in its acquisition of Seminis for $1.4 billion and advising Zurich Financial Services in its agreement to sell its wholly-owned subsidiary, Universal Underwriters Group, to a consortium led by Hellman & Friedman for approximately $1.1 billion.

**The Lawyers:** Firm chairman **Jack Nusbaum** (see p.1484) is admired for his authoritative judgment and effective negotiation skills. Furthermore, he is *"good at managing people and getting the right person for the right issues."* He represented Titan Corporation in its acquisition by L-3 Communications for $2.65 billion, including the assumption of Titan's debt. **Thomas Cerabino** (see p.1443) has worked on a number of significant transactions including representing Colony Capital in its acquisition of the Raffles hotel business. The deal was valued in excess of $1 billion. He also acted for Ventas in its acquisition of Provident Senior Living Trust for $1.1 billion. **Steve Seidman** (see p.1499) acted for Eon Labs in its joint sale with Hexal AG to Novartis in an $8.4 billion transaction. He also represented Shurgard Self Storage in its defense against an unsolicited takeover by Public Storage. Both Seidman and Cerabino are noted for their technical skills and their practical approach to deal negotiations.

**Clients/Work Highlights:** The group also advised Lehman Brothers, financial adviser to Engineered Support Systems, in ESS's $1.97 billion merger with DRS Technologies, and acted for UBS, financial adviser to Extra Space Storage and Prudential Real Estate Investors, in their acquisition of GE's Storage USA. Other clients include Colony Capital; Fortress Investment Group; MidAmerican Energy Holdings Company; Simon Property Group; Teléfonos de México; Teva Pharmaceutical Industries; Warburg Pincus and Zurich Financial Services.

# CORPORATE/M&A

### Corporate/M&A: Mid-Tier Firms

**Leading Firms**

**1** DECHERT LLP *New York*

HUGHES HUBBARD & REED LLP *New York*

KAYE SCHOLER LLP *New York*

KING & SPALDING LLP *New York*

KRAMER LEVIN NAFTALIS & FRANKEL *New York*

MAYER, BROWN, ROWE & MAW LLP *New York*

MCDERMOTT WILL & EMERY *New York*

PROSKAUER ROSE LLP *New York*

ROPES & GRAY LLP *New York*

**2** AKIN GUMP STRAUSS HAUER & FELD *New York*

BRYAN CAVE LLP *New York*

MORGAN, LEWIS & BOCKIUS LLP *New York*

O'MELVENY & MYERS LLP *New York*

PAUL, HASTINGS, JANOFSKY & WALKER *New York*

### Leading Individuals

**1** GREENBERG Joel *Kaye Scholer LLP*

JEWELL Ronald *Dechert LLP*

KRUGMAN BEINECKE Candace *Hughes Hubbard*

LEFKOWITZ Ken *Hughes Hubbard & Reed*

LOBO Glyndwr *Dechert LLP*

SUYDAM John *O'Melveny & Myers LLP*

WOJCIECHOWSKI Mark *Mayer, Brown*

**2** BERCHEM Kerry *Akin Gump*

NUSSBAUM Martin *Dechert LLP*

PAPA Ronald *Proskauer Rose LLP*

SAUERMILCH Thomas *McDermott Will & Emery*

SHUBE Eric *Allen & Overy LLP*

SMITH Scott *Covington & Burling*

## Band 1

### Dechert LLP

See firm details p.1752

**The Firm:** Clients repeatedly stress the importance of having a firm that understands a company's business objectives and is responsive to their needs. Dechert's New York office fits the bill perfectly in both of these respects. Clients are impressed with the firm's depth of expertise and high service levels: "*The lawyers have been extremely accessible whatever the time of day or night; we've had things happen at 3am.*" Clients also say that the lawyers are good to bounce strategic ideas off. The New York M&A attorneys are part of an extensive firmwide corporate/M&A practice that has 127 lawyers in offices on both sides of the Atlantic, including Brussels, London, Paris, Philadelphia and Princeton. Recent transactions include representing Wyeth in the sale of its Solgar Vitamin and Herb business to NBTY, and acting for Goody's Family Clothing in its acquisition by Sun Capital Partners.

**The Lawyers:** **Ron Jewell** (see p.1468) is applauded for his technical proficiency and his ability to control the progress of complex transactions. **Glyn Lobo** (see p.1476) is a "*man of many talents,*" reported

clients, who appreciated his "*collaborative spirit. He gives us the best legal advice and helps us to evaluate what's a real risk and what's a practical risk.*" He is equally effective in a lead or background role on matters. With the opposition, "*he can play the bad cop if you need him to. I certainly never feel that he hasn't carried my card.*" **Martin Nussbaum** (see p.1484) possesses a "*trusted business insight.*" Clients appreciate his creativity and his negotiating style. "*He makes extremely rational arguments in a way that does not cause the other side to be defensive.*"

**Clients/Work Highlights:** Wyeth; Pfizer; B&G Foods; Campbell Soup; Rothschild; Merrill Lynch and Goody's Family Clothing.

### Hughes Hubbard & Reed LLP

See firm details p.1535

**The Firm:** Time and again clients talk about the practice's excellent client focus. One said that although "*they are a smaller firm than many others in New York, the attention they offer you is exceptional.*" Clients also point to the caliber of the service; the lawyers provide "*high-quality answers very quickly.*" Its efficient staffing of matters has also won the firm many fans; clients appreciate that when they hire the firm, they get the top partners and "*don't tend to have just the junior people*" in cases. The group recently represented a dissident stockholder in a successful proxy fight for Cenveo. It also represented British-based First Choice Holidays in its acquisition of Grand Expeditions from the private equity firm North Castle Partners for $94.8 million. The 25 M&A partners in the New York office can also call upon the firm's national and international resources, particularly in cross-border transactions. Its network of offices extends to Los Angeles, DC, Miami, New Jersey, Paris and Tokyo.

**The Lawyers:** The "*superb*" **Candace Beinecke** (see p.1473) chairs the firm. She is a "*really exceptional solutions-orientated lawyer and client advocate*" with a "*firm but not obnoxious*" negotiation style. Clients also add that she is someone "*who really understands business and brings the skills of the firm and herself to bear on matters.*" The "*smart, unfussy and extremely professional*" **Ken Lefkowitz** (see p.1474) is another highly respected figure in the firm. "*He knows and understands his clients' business objective.*"

**Clients/Work Highlights:** Viacom; ALSTOM; Burlington Coat Factory; Sun Capital Partners; Greenbriar Partners; Northwest Airlines; PwC; Media News Group; Rockwood Specialties; National Home healthcare and Cenveo.

### Kaye Scholer LLP

See firm details p.1536

**The Firm:** M&A work is at the core of this full-service firm's corporate practice. Although based in New York, the firm is part of an international network fielding eight offices in cities such as Washington DC, Los Angeles, London and Shanghai. This international reach assists the firm's capability in cross-border deals and in-bound work from foreign

investors attracted to the US market. Matters with an international element comprise about half of the New York office's M&A workload. The attorneys are committed to the needs of their clients and, as such, are equally adept in handling deals in the tens of millions of dollars as well as the billion-dollar transactions. The group has acted for Onex Corporation and Onex Partners in several M&A transactions including the acquisition of American Medical Response and EmCare Holdings. The purchase price was approximately $1 billion.

**The Lawyers:** Clients have complete confidence in **Joel Greenberg** (see p.1462) and point to his availability to them, "*no matter how busy he is.*" He co-chairs the corporate and finance department. Greenberg has acted for Onex, and represented Russ Berrie in its acquisition of KidsLine.

**Clients/Work Highlights:** Clients include several private equity clients and major international and domestic companies.

### King & Spalding LLP

See firm details p.1538

**The Firm:** Interviewees described this Atlanta-headquartered firm as having "*a good sense of corporate America,*" and endorsed the wealth of resources provided by its international network of offices. However, the firm is continuing to make inroads into the New York market through the depth of expertise and quality of service its attorneys offer. The advice is "*extremely timely and to a high standard.*" The New York lawyers often work seamlessly with their Atlanta counterparts and are rewarded for their efforts with the quality of the deals they have attracted. The Sprint Nextel $35 billion merger is a case in point, as is the recently announced $7.5 billion merger of equals of Jefferson-Pilot with Lincoln National.

**The Lawyers:** William Bates is the senior M&A partner in the firm's New York office. He was one of the lead lawyers in the recent Sprint Nextel and Jefferson-Pilot deals.

**Clients/Work Highlights:** The team represented American Tower in its May 2005 merger with SpectraSite in an $11 billion stock-for-stock transaction. It also acted for Sprint Nextel in its $4.3 billion acquisition of Alamosa Holdings. Other clients include BioScrip; Consolidated Communications; GE; ING Clarion Partners; Jefferson-Pilot and Rock-Tenn.

### Kramer Levin Naftalis & Frankel LLP

See firm details p.1539

**The Firm:** This diverse New York firm has a robust practice in midmarket M&A work. Its deal roster includes joint ventures, cross-border transactions, leverage buyouts and auction transactions of public and private companies. A broad client base includes startups right through to multinational corporations. This full-service firm has offices in New York and Paris and benefits from an alliance with Berwin Leighton Paisner LLP in London and Brussels.

**The Lawyers:** Scott Rosenblum stands out in the practice for his M&A work.

**Clients/Work Highlights:** Fortune 500 companies are among the firm's clients. Named clients include Vishay Technology and Scientific Games.

## Mayer, Brown, Rowe & Maw LLP
See firm details p.876

**The Firm:** Mayer Brown is one of the ten largest firms in the world, home to over 230 M&A lawyers practicing out of its 13 international offices. Consequently, the resources at this full-service firm's disposal ensure it can draw on a vast pool of specialist lawyers across the firm as and when needed. The firm's international reach is also an advantage in cross-border transactions. A broad spectrum of clients, including private equity and leveraged buyout firms, joint ventures and institutional investors, are attracted by the coverage and business-savvy approach of the group. Work highlights include representing ProLogis in its $4.9 billion enterprise value acquisition of Catellus Development. It also represented Starwood Capital Group Global in its $365 million acquisition of a controlling interest in Mammoth Mountain Ski Area.

**The Lawyers: Mark Wojciechowski** (see p.1513) is a particularly *"practical deal lawyer. He understands the business side as well as the legalities of deals."* His work is an even mix of representing the private equity shops and strategic M&A.

**Clients/Work Highlights:** Other clients include BellSouth; Odyssey Pharmaceuticals; Celtic Pharmaceutical Holdings; Unilever; Chemtura and Vue Entertainment Holdings.

## McDermott Will & Emery
See firm details p.878

**The Firm:** *"Their work is brilliant and they are always accessible,"* enthuse clients of the firm's New York M&A practice. Almost 40 lawyers make up the New York M&A team. The work they do is varied and includes domestic and cross-border mergers, acquisitions, divestitures and joint ventures. Clients looking for a one-stop shop for their M&A matters are satisfied with the service they receive, particularly as the M&A team can tap into the resources of the other practices across the firm. Furthermore, the M&A practice is run as one team on an integrated, worldwide basis. Its overseas offices include Dusseldorf, Rome and London and a new office was recently opened in Brussels in 2005.

**The Lawyers: Thomas Sauermilch** (see p.1496) is *"extremely creative when it comes to a transaction's design."* Clients also said that he is *"keen on not billing you to death but on getting the transaction done."* His practice concentrates on cross-border transactional and commercial matters with a particular emphasis on cross-border German/US deals. Sauermilch represented Aixtron AG, a German publicly listed company, in its stock-for-stock cross-border acquisition of Genus, an American publicly listed company.

**Clients/Work Highlights:** Degussa; DaVita; Merrill Lynch and JW Childs Associates.

## Proskauer Rose LLP
See firm details p.1551

**The Firm:** Proskauer Rose is one of the oldest firms in New York, having been in the city for over 125 years. While its media and entertainment practice has gained national recognition, its M&A practice is also increasingly a force to be reckoned with. Clients rate the practice's *"forward-thinking, first-class lawyers,"* and while their workload is national and international in scope, the core strength resides in New York. All areas of M&A work are catered for and the group can draw on other practices to form interdisciplinary teams to support transactions. A good proportion of the M&A work completed out of the New York office involves non-US clients, such as French and German corporations. Recent work highlights include representing Alcatel in its $300 million acquisition of Spatial Communications Technologies. The group also represented Kramont Realty Trust and its controlled operating partnership subsidiaries in their acquisition by affiliates of Australian-based Centro Properties. That deal was worth $1.2 billion.

**The Lawyers:** Cochair of the corporate department, **Ron Papa** (see p.1486) is *"intelligent, balanced and solid in his opinions."* Clients appreciate his business-oriented approach to matters. He has a significant expertise in cross-border transactions, often those arising out of industries such as telecommunications, office technology and services, and pharmaceuticals.

**Clients/Work Highlights:** The Dress Barn; ML Media Partners; Pitney Bowes and Charterhouse Group.

## Ropes & Gray LLP
See firm details p.1117

**The Firm:** A national law firm with offices in Boston, New York, Palo Alto, San Francisco and DC, Ropes & Gray has the depth of resources to serve both national and international clients. Private equity forms the backbone of the practice alongside the firm's public company M&A and securities law caseload.

**The Lawyers:** Othon Prounis co-heads the firm's private equity transactions practice. He concentrates on M&A, securities and transactional work, primarily for private equity funds and their portfolio companies.

## Band 2

## Akin Gump Strauss Hauer & Feld LLP
See firm details p.559

**The Firm:** The attorneys at Akin Gump are *"knowledgeable, personable and consistently understand our language,"* reported clients. A strong energy practice, an excellent restructuring group and leading private equity specialists provide support to the firm's M&A capability. The team in New York has counseled buyers, sellers, controlling stockholders and boards of directors. Work is varied and includes auction processes, LBOs and cross-border deals. For exam-

ple, it advised Louis Dreyfus on the sale of its forestry, wood products and chemical businesses in Brazil and Argentina to Celulosa Arauco y Constitución. Clients comment on the firm's *"breadth of expertise and its international reach,"* and with almost 1,000 lawyers in 16 offices worldwide it has the support to advise on a range of deals.

**The Lawyers:** Clients trust **Kerry Berchem** (see p.1437) implicitly. She is a pleasure to work with and has a *"good business head."* She focuses principally on corporate restructuring transactions and representation of restructured issuers.

**Clients/Work Highlights:** Recent work highlights include representing Horizon PCS, a Sprint PCS affiliate, in its stock-for-stock merger with iPCS. Other clients include Bush Industries; DDJ Capital Management; FirstEnergy; Getty Petroleum Marketing; Greenlight Capital and Medicis Pharmaceutical.

## Bryan Cave LLP

**The Firm:** This national firm takes its M&A work extremely seriously as transactional matters are a core practice of the firm. Although the size of the deal may vary – from smaller matters to the multibillion-dollar level – the quality of the practice does not. Multidisciplinary teams including IP, environmental and financing lawyers work on transactions depending on the nature of the deal. The New York office of this St Louis-based firm fields 30 M&A lawyers. However, the practice operates on a 'one firm' approach, uniting its national and international offices into one practice group. A busy year has seen the lawyers representing Gamestop in its acquisition of Electronics Boutique Holdings in a transaction worth $1.5 billion.

**The Lawyers:** Ken Henderson heads the New York office corporate group.

**Clients/Work Highlights:** Other work highlights include representing Palmer & Cay, a Georgia-based insurance brokerage, in its sale to Wachovia. The team also acted in the sale of Manchester Technologies for $56 million and the sale of NextCycle by Lincolnshire in a $135 million deal. Other clients include Barnes & Noble; Terex; Lincolnshire Management and its various private equity funds; Activision and Ampal-American Israel.

## Morgan, Lewis & Bockius LLP
See firm details p.1758

**The Firm:** Clients repeatedly praise the excellent service and *"practical, timely advice"* they receive from this firm. Over 20 M&A lawyers work in the New York office of this international firm. They provide advice on a variety of M&A transactions including tender offers, restructuring and negotiated purchases and divestitures. The New York office has a sweet spot for the more sophisticated, midmarket sized transactions, although it can also handle billion-dollar deals. The SunGard deal is a case in point. The team represented the management in SunGard Data Systems' $11.3 billion acquisition by a consortium of seven private equity houses.

**The Lawyers:** Charles Engros is managing partner

of the New York office and co-heads the firm's M&A practice.

**Clients/Work Highlights:** Other deals the team has worked on include acting for The New York Times in its $410 million acquisition of About.com and representing AmeriTrade in its $2.9 billion acquisition of TD Waterhouse.

### O'Melveny & Myers LLP

See firm details p.336

**The Firm:** This 900-attorney international firm is considered "*the 'A Team' for high-quality work*" by clients. Private equity work feeds into the corporate group and the public company M&A practice remains robust. Moreover, the recent arrivals of Spencer Klein, Gregory Puff and Paul Scrivano from McDermott Will & Emery should help to bolster the strength of the growing New York M&A team, which has been involved in some impressive deals. The firm recently represented Apollo Management in its $1.8 billion acquisition of Cendant Corporation's marketing services division.

**The Lawyers: John Suydam** is an "*extremely accomplished M&A lawyer*" and is recognized for his work in the private equity sector. He heads the firm's private equity practice while Spencer Klein heads the M&A group.

**Clients/Work Highlights:** Other work highlights include representing DaVita in its $3.1 billion acquisition of Gambro Healthcare and acting for Merrill Lynch in its acquisition of the energy trading business of Entergy-Koch. The firm also acts for JPMorgan Partners; DHL and Specialty Laboratories.

### Paul, Hastings, Janofsky & Walker LLP

See firm details p.339

**The Firm:** This is an international firm with 17 offices and 1,000 attorneys worldwide. Its M&A practice in New York delivers a "*high quality and responsive service*," agreed clients. Although much of the firm's profile rests in the middle market, clients appreciate that the practice is capable of handling any deal sizes "*from five to ten million to billions of*

dollars." This is because its lawyers are "*absolutely top-flight legal professionals and highly skilled*." The group undertakes domestic, cross-border and international transactions with experience both in the developed and emerging markets.

**The Lawyers:** Barry Brooks chairs the New York office of the firm and advises on a variety of public and private M&A and corporate finance transactions.

### Other Notable Practitioners

"*Commercial*" **Eric Shube** (see p.1501) of Allen & Overy LLP "*is one of the best technical lawyers on the street.*" Clients note his deep experience in M&A matters and appreciate that "*he would try to work problems out before they arose.*" **Scott Smith** (see p.1503) of Covington & Burling also impresses interviewees with his technical proficiency and business-savvy approach to M&A matters.

# EMPLOYEE BENEFITS & EXECUTIVE COMPENSATION

| Employee Benefits & Executive Compensation Leading Firms |
| --- |
| [1] CLEARY GOTTLIEB STEEN & HAMILTON *New York* |
| PILLSBURY WINTHROP SHAW PITTMAN *New York* |
| SIMPSON THACHER & BARTLETT LLP *New York* |
| WACHTELL, LIPTON, ROSEN & KATZ *New York* |
| [2] DAVIS POLK & WARDWELL *New York* |
| DEBEVOISE & PLIMPTON LLP *New York* |
| SHEARMAN & STERLING LLP *New York* |
| SULLIVAN & CROMWELL LLP *New York* |
| [3] FRIED, FRANK *New York* |
| MILBANK, TWEED, HADLEY & MCCLOY *New York* |
| PAUL, WEISS *New York* |
| PROSKAUER ROSE LLP *New York* |
| SKADDEN, ARPS *New York* |
| WHITE & CASE LLP *New York* |

## Band 1

### Cleary Gottlieb Steen & Hamilton LLP

See firm details p.1525

**The Firm:** This "*terrific*" three-partner team is considered by clients to be "*as good as it gets.*" It has enjoyed a busy year, not least due to the government's addition of section 409A to the Internal Revenue Code, which has revolutionized the treatment of deferred compensation in the USA. An integrated practice, it offers advice that spans securities, tax, corporate governance, proxy disclosure and NYSE rules. Particular strengths include representing financial institutions in relation to investment vehicles, and the team acts for a glittering cast of investment banks on ERISA matters, including

Goldman Sachs, Morgan Stanley and Barclays. The group has also advised investment banks holding derivative positions with bankrupt sponsor companies that are looking at pension plan terminations. In the executive compensation field, the firm has recently acted for Abercrombie & Fitch, Under Armour and United Technologies.

**The Lawyers:** The "*outstanding*" **Brick Susko** (see p.1471) operates at the top of his field, according to clients who view him as "*someone who understands financial products better than the people who do it for a living!*" An experienced fiduciary lawyer, he was called on to represent the United Auto Workers (UAW) in their negotiations to restructure the $70 billion retiree medical program for the 1.1 million UAW retirees of GM. **Arthur Kohn** (see p.1471) won client praise as a "*responsive and highly intelligent*" adviser who is "*skilled at balancing business considerations with technical requirements.*" He recently worked with key client Citibank, designing stock option products. His repertoire encompasses executive compensation, pension investment, tax, securities and M&A. **Robert Raymond** (see p.1491) is a "*smart negotiator*" who focuses his practice on transactions. He advised Warburg Pincus and Texas Pacific in connection with the $5.1 billion buyout of Neiman Marcus in March 2005. Additional expertise includes alternative investment arrangements, and SEC and securities-law reporting requirements.

**Clients/Work Highlights:** The firm acts for major investment banks as well as commanding instructions from Fortune 500 companies.

### Pillsbury Winthrop Shaw Pittman LLP

See firm details p.1550

**The Firm:** A firm which is expanding its broad-based executive compensation and benefits practice, it demonstrates both national and international capabilities in this discipline. Clients consider the "*forward-thinking*" team to be "*up-to-date with cutting-edge developments in the market.*" For example, it handles high-level corporate and plan governance issues for clients who sponsor pension plans. It is also equipped to carry out plan audits in line with government regulations. The team is increasingly busy in terms of M&A, and recently acted for Chevron on the employee benefit aspects of the company's $18.1 billion stock and cash merger with Unocal. It also advises clients on the new nonqualified stock rules and on stock option issues. Clients add that this excellent unit has "*significant bench strength,*" with notable "*soup-to-nuts attorneys putting in the ground work.*"

**The Lawyers:** Described by one client as "*the best resource there is,*" **Susan Serota** (see p.1500) is an experienced practitioner who combines a "*big-picture strategy with a detail-oriented approach.*" She chairs the executive compensation and benefits team and is a member of the ERISA litigation group. Clients add that she is "*able to translate particularly complex ERISA law into understandable terms.*" **Peter Hunt** (see p.1467) "*gets the job done*" and works with sponsors of broad-based pension, equity-based and 401k plans. He has been reviewing nonqualified plan arrangements for clients in the light of the recent changes to deferred compensation. Transactional matters also form a consistent part of his practice.

**Clients/Work Highlights:** Bank of New York; Bristol-Myers Squibb; Gen Re; Charles Schwab; Sony BMG Music Entertainment; The New York Times and Morgan Crucible.

## Simpson Thacher & Bartlett LLP

See firm details p.1555

**The Firm:** This "*excellent*" team is especially prevalent in the transactional arena and finds favor with clients for its high level of professionalism and expertise. Headline-grabbing deals are typical fodder for this M&A giant, which has recently acted on a series of LBOs for marquee clients such as The Blackstone Group and KKR. Recent deals include the $15 billion LBO of Hertz to a private equity group led by Clayton, Dubilier & Rice, where the team acted for the target company and the selling shareholders. The firm also represented the seller in the Neiman Marcus LBO. The firm counsels compensation committees and corporates on a variety of complex compliance issues, on replacing CEOs and on plan divestitures.

**The Lawyers:** Ken Edgar (see p.1451) is a popular figure in the marketplace and is best known for his "*sharp mind*." He heads the firm's executive compensation and employee benefits practice and is "*one of the top*" players when it comes to transactional work. Other experience includes working with clients on compensation-related corporate governance issues and matters pertaining to Sarbanes-Oxley.

**Clients/Work Highlights:** Time Warner; Sears Holdings; VNU; Lehman Brothers; Accenture; ARAMARK; JPMorgan Chase and Wachovia.

## Wachtell, Lipton, Rosen & Katz

See firm details p.1561

**The Firm:** Described by market sources as "*first rate*," this practice is principally M&A-oriented. The firm recognizes that employee benefits and executive compensation issues are pivotal to the success of business transactions and accordingly devotes considerable resources to this practice area. The three-partner team actively counsels clients on section 409A issues and other compliance matters. It also advises management on team moves and employment arrangements for CEOs in transition. Recent highlights include representing Providian in its $6.54 billion acquisition by Washington Mutual, and working for MBNA in its $32.4 billion acquisition by Bank of America.

**The Lawyers:** An experienced lawyer known by peers for his "*aggressive negotiating style*," **Adam Chinn** (see p.1445) enjoys a strong reputation in the field. He works closely with high-profile financial institutions, especially in relation to tax and executive compensation considerations. **Michael Katzke** (see p.1469) is a valuable resource for clients undertaking major transactions. A highly skilled attorney, he advises on employment, pension and fiduciary issues, as well as executive compensation matters related to SEC filings. Peers and clients alike endorse the talented Karen Krueger and lament her withdrawal from full-time practice.

**Clients/Work Highlights:** AT&T and Morgan Stanley are among the firm's notable clients.

## Band 2

## Davis Polk & Wardwell

See firm details p.1528

**The Firm:** This practice is held in high esteem by market observers, who highlight the firm's prowess when it comes to transactional work and executive compensation. It is increasingly prevalent in major cross-border transactions, and its high-profile engagements include acting for China's CNOOC in its controversial proposed acquisition of Unocal. This "*fine*" team has recently counseled clients on new regulatory developments in relation to disclosure rules and deferred compensation. Additional expertise lies in the ERISA fiduciary arena, where the team operates in conjunction with the trusts and estates unit, and is praised for its cutting-edge work with investment vehicles.

**The Lawyers:** Barbara Nims (see p.1483) is a well-regarded practitioner who splits her time between transactional affairs, and advisory and regulatory work. Her expertise extends to securities law and she has a niche addressing the reporting requirements of large shareholders entering into derivative transactions. Described by one client as a "*go-to guy for ERISA issues*," **Ed FitzGerald** (see p.1454) is increasingly recognized by the market as a "*rising star who is able to put a deal together*." He advises private funds, hedge funds and investment managers on structuring compensation and ERISA issues.

**Clients/Work Highlights:** The firm acts for funds offered by leading financial institutions such as CSFB, Morgan Stanley, JPMorgan Chase and Bank of America. Other clients include Welsh, Carson, Anderson & Stowe; Francisco Partners; Thomas Weisel Partners and Lindsay Goldberg & Bessemer.

## Debevoise & Plimpton LLP

See firm details p.1529

**The Firm:** This "*knowledgeable and responsive*" team focuses on four areas of practice: transactions, executive compensation, fiduciary matters and employee benefits. This wide perspective means that clients can benefit from corporate, securities, ERISA, tax and financial accounting advice, all under one roof. The group has witnessed an increase in its work as special counsel for compensation committees, particularly as it becomes increasingly popular for compensation boards to seek independent counsel from the company management. For example, the team acted as special compensation consultant to both First Reserve and Dresser-Rand, creating and restructuring the companies' ownership and investment arrangements. Other advice centers on dealing with underfunded pension plans in an M&A context.

**The Lawyers:** Chair of the executive compensation and employee benefits group, **Lawrence Cagney** is commended for his "*extremely good substantive knowledge and practical approach*." Clients say: "*He is remarkably responsive to our questions and concerns*." He recently acted for Disney's compensation committee in a matter regarding senior executive employment agreements. **David Mason** frequently advises board compensation committees and proves another popular choice with clients. Highlights include advising Clayton Dubilier & Rice, The Carlyle Group and Merrill Lynch Global Private Equity in their $15 billion acquisition of Hertz from Ford. **Beth Pagel Serebransky** brings a corporate background to bear on a wide range of securities and executive compensation matters. She has been advising clients on the ramifications of section 409A.

**Clients/Work Highlights:** NBC Universal; AXA Financial; UBS; Verizon and Dean Foods.

## Shearman & Sterling LLP

See firm details p.1554

**The Firm:** This sophisticated firm boasts a "*first-rate*" executive compensation and employee benefits practice. The "*thorough and experienced*" team has enjoyed a busy year, advising clients on their executive compensation arrangements and the wide-ranging ramifications of section 409A. In line with the government's high level of scrutiny, it is increasingly counseling management boards and compensation committees on corporate governance issues. The executive compensation and employee benefits unit complements the firm's stellar corporate practice, and recent deals include acting for Georgia-Pacific in its $13.2 billion acquisition by family-owned Koch Industries. The firm is expanding its international capabilities in this area to better serve cross-border clients, and has members in New York, California, Germany, Paris and London.

**The Lawyers:** Clients praised **Linda Rappaport**

(see p.1491) as "*pragmatic, knowledgeable and attentive,*" observing that "*she brings extensive experience to the table and is a skilled deal-maker.*" Master of a broad practice, she represents individuals as well as companies and boards of directors. She recently advised NBC in relation to the employee issues inextricably linked to the broadcast giant's buyout of Paxson Communications.

**Clients/Work Highlights:** Viacom; UBS; Wyeth; Campbells; Con Edison; CSFB; Merrill Lynch; Morgan Stanley and Citigroup.

## Sullivan & Cromwell LLP
See firm details p.1558

**The Firm:** This "*highly responsive*" practice keeps clients abreast of the latest changes in tax, securities and labor law affecting executive compensation and employee benefit plans. As well as operating a high-level counseling arm, the group plays an integral part in sophisticated M&A transactions such as acting for SCB Communications in its $16 billion merger with AT&T. The team has also seen an increase in its work as special counsel to compensation committees as a result of the enhanced environment of corporate governance in the USA. For example, it represented the compensation committee of Payless ShoeSource on the retirement of the company's CEO and the hiring of a new executive.

**The Lawyers:** An important member of the tax section of the ABA, the "*fabulous*" **Max Schwartz** (see p.1493) was praised by market sources as "*smart, creative and plugged in*" to industry developments. He leads the firm's executive compensation and benefits practice.

**Clients/Work Highlights:** CSFB; UBS; NYSE and Anthem.

## Band 3

## Fried, Frank, Harris, Shriver & Jacobson LLP
See firm details p.1532

**The Firm:** This "*extremely service-oriented group is always forthcoming with reliable and practical answers,*" according to clients. The practice focuses its attentions on three principal areas: M&A, CEO employment arrangements and working for investment funds. The group is active in the hedge fund and private equity arena, structuring funds and advising marquee clients on ERISA issues. Clients have also called on the team for executive compensation advice, especially in relation to the recent changes in accounting and tax rules. The unit has acted as special counsel to compensation committees in instances where CEOs have allegedly been over-compensated.

**The Lawyers:** The practice is split into two complementary departments that are run in turn by **Don Carleen** (see p.1443) and **Laraine Rothenberg** (see p.1443).

## Milbank, Tweed, Hadley & McCloy LLP

**The Firm:** Clients recommended this small but experienced group for its comprehensive service in the executive compensation and employee benefits arena. The team is singled out for its structured finance work, assisting clients with plan investment products and prohibited transaction issues to create deals. Expertise in this area encompasses advice on fiduciary responsibility and ERISA, and the team has also been involved in the development of widely used investment structures. The burgeoning executive compensation practice centers on advice to individual executives and compensation committees, and the team recently acted for the CEO of a prestigious Fortune 100 company. It has also represented several management teams in an M&A context.

**The Lawyers:** "*Refined and thoughtful*" **Frederick Kneip** heads the employee benefits group within the tax department, while colleague **Scott Price** can be relied on to "*get the job done.*" Both attorneys are well versed in all aspects of executive compensation and employee benefits and are increasingly working with clients to tackle issues arising from Sarbanes-Oxley.

## Paul, Weiss, Rifkind, Wharton & Garrison LLP
See firm details p.1548

**The Firm:** The market views this outfit as a strong contender for all types of ERISA, executive compensation and employee benefit matters. The group attracts clients on a stand-alone basis, as well as providing valuable support to the corporate arm on M&A transactions and to the litigation department in connection with significant ERISA-related claims. It also works in conjunction with the investment funds group in the structuring, implementation and operation of funds, typically for plan sponsors. ESOP transactions form an additional part of the group's portfolio.

**The Lawyers:** Co-chair of the employee benefits and executive compensation practice, **Michael Segal** (see p.1499) is a prominent industry figure. A "*skilled negotiator,*" he represents executives and employers in high-level employment relationships. "*At the top in terms of technical competence,*" **Robert Fleder** (see p.1455) has 30 years of experience handling ERISA, employee benefits and executive compensation matters.

**Clients/Work Highlights:** Clarion Capital Partners, Polo Ralph Lauren and Malaysia International Shipping are some of the clients.

## Proskauer Rose LLP
See firm details p.1551

**The Firm:** The firm's well-recognized employee benefits and executive compensation group complements its prowess in related areas such as employment, tax and ERISA litigation. This broad-based practice spans a range of advice on golden parachutes, deferred compensation plans, employment agreements, incentive compensation and retirement arrangements. The team represents tax-exempt employers dealing with the application of benefits

and compensation law to this unique area. It also has a niche advising 'troubled' multiemployer benefit plans. Renowned for working with individuals, the team represented Jim McNerney, Boeing's new CEO, in executive compensation matters.

**The Lawyers:** Well respected by peers and winning a lot of referral work, **Mike Sirkin** (see p.1502) has built an excellent reputation representing individuals in executive compensation matters and hiring-and-exit deals. He also advises a range of clients on nonqualified arrangements and the design and implementation of plans.

**Clients/Work Highlights:** Alliance Capital Management; Amerada Hess; American Standard; Bear Stearns; Foot Locker; Mount Sinai Medical Center and the Metropolitan Museum of Art.

## Skadden, Arps, Slate, Meagher & Flom LLP & Affiliates
See firm details p.1557

**The Firm:** Market observers regard this prominent practice as principally deal-oriented. Major highlights include representing May Department Stores in employee benefit and executive compensation matters in connection with the retail company's $17 billion acquisition by Federated Department Stores. The nationwide team also operates an extensive counseling arm, advising on deferred compensation, employee benefits and related securities and tax issues. It is deeply involved in corporate governance matters, enabling clients to comply with disclosure rules by putting together proxy statements and advising on best practice.

**The Lawyers:** **Stuart Alperin** (see p.1432) is an "*excellent*" adviser, well versed in ERISA and executive compensation and employee benefits issues. His practice takes in M&A, including ESOP-related transactions, as well as extensive advisory work. He is skilled in negotiating employment contracts for senior executives.

**Clients/Work Highlights:** Dana and Stanley Works are among the firm's reputable client list.

## White & Case LLP
See firm details p.1566

**The Firm:** Clients are quick to praise this "*terrific*" team for its "*fast and accurate advice.*" The group tackles a broad range of matters as part of a growing executive compensation, benefits and employment law practice (ECBEL) that provides clients with a comprehensive service across the board. Strengths lie in ERISA, benefit plans (including medical and dental), qualified and nonqualified pension plans, and executive compensation. Highlights include advising Newmont Mining on securities and tax issues relating to the preparation and implementation of the company's new stock incentive plan on a worldwide basis. The team is also involved in benefits litigation and defended Amerada Hess in a class action lawsuit alleging breaches of fiduciary duty in violation of ERISA.

**The Lawyers:** Clients agree that the global head of the ECBEL practice, **Ken Raskin** (see p.1491), is an "*excellent communicator who finds solutions to poten-*

tially complex problems." His particular expertise lies in fiduciary issues as well as wider benefits and compensation matters. An active member of the employee benefits committee of the New York state Bar, he has written reports about section 409A. **Clients/Work Highlights:** Profit Sharing/401k Council of America; Corporación Durango; ABN AMRO; UBS; BSCH and Mohawk Paper Mills.

## Other Notable Practitioners

*"Thoughtful and reliable"* **Richard Gilbert** (see p.1459) divides his time between Orrick, Herrington & Sutcliffe LLP's New York and San Fransisco offices. He is an authority on the fiduciary responsibility

provisions of ERISA and public pension law, and has won ERISA exemptions for many clients to permit special investments. He advises leading financial institutions on fiduciary investment issues. Another oracle on investment matters, **Broni Grala** (see p.1461) of Cadwalader, Wickersham & Taft LLP, is billed as one of the best fiduciary lawyers in the country. Clients say: *"He is smart, creative and responsive – he is involved in almost anything new that happens in the financial services industry."* He represents investment bankers, broker-dealers and plan management, and obtained several important exemptions from the DOL in the last year. At Clifford Chance LLP, **Andrew Oringer**'s reputation is on the

up and up. An *"intelligent, thoughtful and extremely capable"* lawyer, he leads the firm's ERISA, employee benefits and executive compensation group in the Americas. Clients describe **Bradd Williamson** of Latham & Watkins LLP as a *"business adviser – he understands what we are trying to do and provides valuable advice."* He represents clients in executive compensation matters, especially pertaining to private equity transactions and corporate M&A. He recently acted for Dex Media with respect to employee benefits and executive compensation matters in the context of the company's merger with RH Donnelley.

# EMPLOYMENT

# MAINLY DEFENDANT

| Employment: Mainly Defendant |
| --- |
| Leading Firms |
| 1. PROSKAUER ROSE LLP *New York* |
| 2. MORGAN, LEWIS & BOCKIUS LLP *New York* |
| 3. BOND, SCHOENECK & KING, PLLC *New York* |
|    KAYE SCHOLER LLP *New York* |
|    ORRICK, HERRINGTON & SUTCLIFFE *New York* |
|    SULLIVAN & CROMWELL LLP *New York* |
| 4. EPSTEIN BECKER & GREEN PC *New York* |
|    HOGAN & HARTSON LLP *New York* |
|    JACKSON LEWIS *New York* |
|    MAYER, BROWN, ROWE & MAW LLP *New York* |
|    NIXON PEABODY LLP *New York* |
|    O'MELVENY & MYERS LLP *New York* |
|    PAUL, HASTINGS, JANOFSKY & WALKER *New York* |
|    WEIL, GOTSHAL & MANGES LLP *New York* |

## Band 1

## Proskauer Rose LLP

See firm details p.1551

**The Firm:** Ardent admirers view this *"top-quality"* employment practice as the *"500lb gorilla in New York City."* Its long association with the labor and employment movement leaves it well placed to act on matters for an extensive and high-end client list. The firm's commitment to this area of law is further demonstrated by the fact that it fields the largest single team of labor and employment lawyers in the state. Following new regulations issued by the DOL in 2005, the team has acted on numerous litigations under the FLSA. In particular it has witnessed an increase in wage and hour and whistle-blower cases. The firm is also well regarded for its traditional labor practice, where it is active in collective bargaining, arbitrations and negotiations between employers and their unions. Industries in which the team excels include publishing, entertainment, education and finance.

**The Lawyers:** Chairman of Proskauer Rose and former co-chair of the labor and employment law department, **Allen Fagin** (see p.1453) enjoys a strong

reputation in the sector. He recently acted on a wage and hour class action for AIG, in which the court granted summary judgment to the insurance company on the basis that the plaintiffs involved were administratively exempt employees and not entitled to overtime. Well-respected and widely known for her work with the New York City Bar Association, **Bettina Plevan** (see p.1488) is a lawyer who demonstrates *"good experience and judgment."* Recent highlights include defending a nationwide insurance brokerage company in a discrimination class action, and acting for AFTRA Health and Retirement Funds in an ERISA class action. Clients describe **Howard Ganz** (see p.1458) as a *"smart and highly articulate individual who knows the industry extremely well."* The co-chair of the group, he is closely associated with professional sports and represents prestigious clients such as the Women's National Basketball Association and Major League Baseball. Major projects include negotiating a new collective bargaining agreement between the National Basketball Association and National Basketball Players Association to succeed the agreement that expired in June 2005. **Paul Salvatore** (see p.1496) is representing the NYSE in several employment litigations, as well as its collective bargaining negotiations with the union representing its clerical and facilities employees. His practice encompasses traditional labor relations work as well as employment litigation. Co-chair of the department, **Bernard Plum** (see p.1489) represents clients in the newspaper and entertainment sector in complex collective bargaining arrangements. He recently stepped in to enforce emergency labor injunctions against the Pressmen's Union for breaching its agreement with The New York Times.

**Clients/Work Highlights:** JPMorgan Chase; Bristol-Myers Squibb; Dow Jones; Citigroup; Bear Sterns; MetLife; League of American Theatres and Producers; Coca-Cola Enterprises and The New York Times.

## Band 2

## Morgan, Lewis & Bockius LLP

See firm details p.1758

**The Firm:** This *"knowledgeable and responsive"* firm has taken a proactive approach in addressing the current proliferation of overtime cases, most notably those affecting the stockbroker industry. It has pulled together a team of lawyers who combine expertise of the sector with experience of wage and hour matters in a way that meets the needs of a demanding clientele. Clients praise the lawyers as skilled in *"presenting issues in a way that highlights their importance and points out creative solutions."* The New York band can additionally leverage support from a *"terrific national practice,"* while the firm is also expanding its capabilities on the international playing field with the recent addition of an employment team to its London office. The firm also runs Morgan Lewis Resources, a venture that provides high-level training to employers.

**The Lawyers:** The *"outstanding"* **Mike Curley** (see p.1448) is a *"highly regarded and proficient"* lawyer who leads the charge in New York. This practice group manager is well versed in traditional labor law and is particularly active in negotiations with the recording, motion picture and entertainment industries. *"Practical and pragmatic,"* **Christopher Reynolds** (see p.1492) is experienced in Title VII employment litigation as well as human resources-related counseling. In particular, he has assisted employers in implementing cutting-edge diversity programs. His clients emanate from the transportation, retail, entertainment and financial services sectors. Another serious contender in the financial services industry, **Andrew Schaffran** (see p.1497) continues to represent Merrill Lynch in arbitrating the claims of high-profile members of a major class action. He has also defended clients in gender discrimination and whistle-blowing claims. *"Accessible and responsive,"* **Ken Turnbull** (see p.1509) has made impressive headway at the firm. He provides ongoing advice to financial services companies trying to revamp and remodel their compensation policies.

| Employment: Mainly Defendant |
| --- |
| Leading Individuals |

**[1]** CURLEY Michael *Morgan, Lewis*

DELIKAT Michael *Orrick*

FAGIN Allen *Proskauer Rose LLP*

PLEVAN Bettina *Proskauer Rose LLP*

ROGERS JR Theodore *Sullivan & Cromwell LLP*

WAKS Jay *Kaye Scholer LLP*

**[2]** BERNSTEIN Michael *Bond, Schoeneck & King*

DILORENZO Louis *Bond, Schoeneck & King*

GANZ Howard *Proskauer Rose LLP*

REYNOLDS Christopher *Morgan, Lewis*

SALVATORE Paul *Proskauer Rose LLP*

SCHAFFRAN Andrew *Morgan, Lewis*

**[3]** BERKOWITZ Philip *Nixon Peabody LLP*

CANONI John *Nixon Peabody LLP*

COHEN Joel *McDermott Will & Emery*

FASMAN Zachary *Paul, Hastings*

FRIEDMAN Gary *Mayer, Brown*

GREEN Ronald *Epstein Becker & Green*

KLEIN Jeffrey *Weil, Gotshal & Manges*

KOHN Jeffrey *O'Melveny & Myers LLP*

O'NEIL Terry *Bond, Schoeneck & King*

PLUM Bernard *Proskauer Rose LLP*

STARR Michael *Hogan & Hartson LLP*

TURNBULL Kenneth *Morgan, Lewis*

**Clients/Work Highlights:** Morgan Stanley; AG Edwards; Prudential Financial; MetLife; Merrill Lynch; NBC; American Airlines; JPMorgan Chase; UBS Financial Services and Colgate-Palmolive.

## Band 3

### Bond, Schoeneck & King, PLLC

**The Firm:** This *"strong regional player"* boasts offices throughout the state, including its New York City base which opened in 2004. The firm fields a large group of dedicated attorneys whom clients say provide *"prompt and top-quality service."* The team handles traditional labor matters, including negotiations and arbitrations, and a wide range of employment issues. It also represents prominent clients such as the NLRB and is particularly well known for its union avoidance work. In the employment litigation sphere, the band has been active on restrictive covenant and wage and hour cases. Additional resources include an OSHA practice and an employee benefits group.

**The Lawyers:** **Louis DiLorenzo** (see p.1449) is singled out by market sources for his impressive communication skills and *"tremendous labor relations knowledge in terms of law and experience."* A lawyer who *"inspires confidence,"* he is well practiced in negotiating contracts between employers and their unions. *"Lawyer's lawyer"* **Michael Bernstein** (see p.1438) enjoys a strong reputation and is admired for his broad practice. He represents numerous law firms in New York. **Terry O'Neil** (see p.1485) is especially well known for his work with universities and

colleges. This year he was retained by Pace University to handle the institution's union negotiations, among other matters.

**Clients/Work Highlights:** Carrier; Colgate University; Bechtel Construction; Otis Elevator; Syracuse University; Clarkson University and Hamilton College.

### Kaye Scholer LLP

See firm details p.1536

**The Firm:** This *"highly regarded"* group has scored some decisive victories in 2005. Foremost among these was winning over $700 million in pay for the police officers of the City of New York in long-running arbitration proceedings. This award was the largest of its kind to date. Other highlights include carrying out corporate board investigations for a major regional energy company, and successfully defending a national financial services company in arbitration against a collective action. The practice focus is on employment litigation and counseling.

**The Lawyers:** *"Knowledgeable, responsive and practical,"* **Jay Waks** (see p.1510) chairs the employment and labor law practice. He has been retained by national law firms to assist in defending corporate clients and has testified as an expert witness in a highly sensitive discrimination suit.

**Clients/Work Highlights:** Celestica; Ameriquest Mortgage; Bear Stearns; Anheuser-Busch; Metallgesellschaft; Sidney Frank Importing; Morgan Stanley and American Kennel Club.

### Orrick, Herrington & Sutcliffe LLP

See firm details p.337

**The Firm:** This *"top-notch"* employment group commands a particularly strong following in the financial services sector, based on its expertise and reputation for high quality. In an environment where Sarbanes-Oxley is the pervading force, it has built up an impressive practice relating to the investigation and trial of whistle-blowing cases. For example, the team recently handled a high-profile Sarbanes-Oxley whistle-blower charge on behalf of a major financial services firm. Other recent successes include the dismissal of EEOC v Carrols Corporation (a case relating to claims of sexual harassment) after seven years of litigation. Following notable wins, this was the first loss for the EEOC in its efforts to expand the application of pattern and practice theory to such cases.

**The Lawyers:** Well-known industry figure and chair of the employment law practice group, **Mike Delikat** (see p.1449) *"gets to the heart of the matter quickly."* He recently handled a Sarbanes-Oxley whistle-blower federal court litigation on behalf of a major pharmaceutical company. Other highlights include the dismissal of an incentive compensation case brought in New York Supreme Court by a former trader of JPMorgan Chase.

**Clients/Work Highlights:** Citibank; CSFB; PG&E; Prudential Financial and Primedia.

### Sullivan & Cromwell LLP

See firm details p.1558

**The Firm:** This *"first-class"* firm operates a *"sophisticated and high-level"* employment practice. The team has been occupied with arbitrations on behalf of a large securities firm concerning the company's equity plans and claims by former employees that they should not have been divested of stock upon leaving. Additional highlights include representing a major sports organization in an arbitration that resulted in a favorable conclusion for the employer concerning the classification of former personnel. A relatively small unit, it is looking to expand and has recently recruited expert in labor union law, John Fullerton, from Proskauer Rose.

**The Lawyers:** *"Practical and patient,"* **Ted Rogers** (see p.1493) *"figures out how to solve problems and how to avoid them."* Clients also appreciate his creative bent and his high levels of commercial understanding. The coordinator of the labor and employment law group, he is an experienced litigator and mediator.

**Clients/Work Highlights:** AIG; Barclays; Microsoft; Nomura and UBS Warburg.

## Band 4

### Epstein Becker & Green PC

**The Firm:** This boutique firm is known for its strong labor and employment practice, which is divided into specialized practice groups such as disability, OSHA, public sector and international. The group frequently handles employment discrimination and civil rights claims, and is experienced in jury and bench trials at both federal and state level. It also runs a comprehensive seminar series and provides training and educational programs to clients. Home to one of the largest labor and employment teams worldwide, the firm's capabilities are further enhanced by its association with the International Lawyers Network, a federation of independent law firms.

**The Lawyers:** Cofounder of the firm, **Ronald Green** (see p.1461) drives forward the firm's national labor and employment law practice.

**Clients/Work Highlights:** Clients range from Fortune 500 multinationals to startup companies.

### Hogan & Hartson LLP

See firm details p.568

**The Firm:** A firm that *"leaves no stone unturned,"* this team enters the ranking tables through strong client feedback. Sources say that they can rely on attorneys for advice on *"complex and esoteric issues"* relating to employment and labor law. Notable matters include winning Second Circuit affirmation of summary judgment on behalf of WWOR-TV, Fox Television Stations and News Corporation in an age discrimination case. In the traditional labor sphere, the team represented Lifespire in defense of a union's corporate campaign to force recognition. It also acted for the New York Post in a case against the Newspaper and Mail Deliverers' Union, which was alleged to have violated federal labor law. In addition, the team advises executives in the termination of employment agreements.

**The Lawyers:** Clients view **Michael Starr** (see p.1504) as "*an extremely intelligent and well-versed lawyer, whose visceral reactions are spot-on.*" His practice spans all areas of labor and employment law including noncompete matters and trade secrets. He recently settled a claim on behalf of Wyeth.

**Clients/Work Highlights:** Clients stem from a broad range of industries, including financial services, communications, media, publishing and management consulting, as well as in retail, manufacturing and construction.

## Jackson Lewis

**The Firm:** This well-known boutique can devote considerable resources to workplace law, fielding lawyers based in 21 locations across the USA. The firm has 45 years of experience under its belt in areas ranging from alternative dispute resolution, litigation, immigration and labor relations. With 397 attorneys at hand to advise on a multitude of employment-related matters, it can provide a high turnover of work at competitive rates. Market sources note that the firm is home to some excellent lawyers.

**The Lawyers:** Greg Rasin is a key contact for this group.

## Mayer, Brown, Rowe & Maw LLP
See firm details p.876

**The Firm:** This team of "*extremely thorough and bright lawyers*" wins promotion to the tables this year through a mix of strong client feedback and an impressive work roster. One of the group's attractions is its ability to handle "*employment-related issues that cross international boundaries*" for both domestic and internationally based clients. Particular experience includes covenants not to compete, trade secrets and restrictive covenant cases, which the firm has litigated in over 30 states. For example, it represented TIAA-CREF in a trade secret violation case and a National Association of Securities Dealers arbitration. It has also acted on numerous other arbitrations, particularly on behalf of securities industry clients. Wage and hour matters and whistle-blower cases also feature highly.

**The Lawyers:** Spearheading the firm's New York initiative, **Gary Friedman** (see p.1457) is a "*good strategic thinker and an effective communicator.*" Clients describe him as a "*proactive adviser who pays close attention to detail.*" He is currently handling a gender discrimination and equal pay claim for a financial services company.

**Clients/Work Highlights:** CIBC; Geico; Wal-Mart; Bank of Montreal and Marsh & McLennan.

## Nixon Peabody LLP
See firm details p.1546

**The Firm:** This firm runs a well-respected labor and employment department, fielding some 50 attorneys nationwide. The team handles a broad range of matters relating to employment law on the manage-

ment side, such as litigation, workplace training and labor relations. It also places emphasis on alternative dispute resolutions and advising clients on implementing mediation systems. Recent highlights include representing a US-based environmental company in the closing of a unionized facility and in the resulting arbitrations. The firm operates an international practice and represented a foreign bank doing business in New York in a National Association of Securities Dealers arbitration, pertaining to sexual harassment and denial of bonus claims.

**The Lawyers:** A figurehead of the New York employment Bar, **John Canoni** (see p.1442) enjoys a broad management practice. He recently acted for a multinational, US-based travel company relating to the dismissal of a senior executive alleging race and age discrimination. "*Thorough, diligent and responsive,*" **Philip Berkowitz** (see p.1438) has a good head for strategy, according to clients. He has built up an impressive international practice and represents multinationals in litigation.

**Clients/Work Highlights:** KeyBank; Xerox; Kodak; Corning; John Hancock and Gannett.

## O'Melveny & Myers LLP
See firm details p.336

**The Firm:** Clients refer to the "*high quality of service and consistent level of responsiveness*" delivered by the team. Although market commentators feel that the firm's profile has been on the wane since the departure of key labor and employment partners, Ken Turnbull and Mike Curley, to rival practice Morgan Lewis, clients point to its strength in depth, with seamless interaction between partners and associates. The department also continues to attract high-end clients particularly in the airline, financial services and entertainment industries. The team has been especially active in the traditional labor field and recently advised cargo carriers, Atlas Air and Polar Air Cargo, on union relations and litigation during a major strike carried out by airline pilots. Additional highlights include representing US Airways and America West in disputes arising out of the former airline's bankruptcy proceedings, which involved the termination of pilot's pension plans, among other matters.

**The Lawyers:** **Jeffrey Kohn** (see p.1472) spearheads the firm's New York-based labor and employment efforts, and is well respected by peers and clients alike. He recently represented Cintas, the world's largest uniform supplier, in a union organization drive by Unite for national recognition.

**Clients/Work Highlights:** UBS; Sotheby's; New York Mets; Bear Sterns and Korn/Ferry International.

## Paul, Hastings, Janofsky & Walker LLP
See firm details p.339

**The Firm:** This "*high-quality*" firm boasts a strong national presence and continues to expand its New York-based employment law department. Particular attention is paid to developing international labor and employment capabilities for an increasingly global client base (the firm has eight offices across

Europe and Asia). For example, the team advised a biotech firm on employee transitions in Europe following the company's acquisition and subsequent reorganization. The employment team also has an impressive track record when it comes to handling class actions, and is frequently involved in high-level litigation. Recent highlights include Iliadis v Wal-Mart Stores, a major wage and hour case that was denied class certification at hearing.

**The Lawyers:** "*Highly regarded*" **Zachary Fasman** (see p.1453) chairs the employment law department in New York. He was recently appointed by IBM to act as lead trial counsel in the discrimination case Torrico v IBM, after the company and its previous outside counsel lost at summary judgment. The case resulted in a complete defense victory.

**Clients/Work Highlights:** Airborne Freight; Agence France-Presse; Metropolitan Transport Authority; Bell Atlantic; Philip Morris and Cendant.

## Weil, Gotshal & Manges LLP
See firm details p.1565

**The Firm:** Market observers view this firm as a "*niche player that offers high-quality advice*" when it comes to employment law. The team scored a decisive victory in a recent race discrimination case, Rowe v William Morris, in which it won summary judgment for its client, the Creative Artists Agency. Other highlights include representing UnitedHealth in the implementation of a restraining order against several employees who were poached by a rival managed care company, and negotiating favorable terms for their departures. The practice is well known for representing Enron in connection with the company's bankruptcy and it is currently handling a vast array of related employment litigation.

**The Lawyers:** The "*terrific*" **Jeffrey Klein** (see p.1471) heads the employment litigation practice. Well-respected by peers and clients alike, he is identified as a strong litigator, whose portfolio includes significant ERISA litigation matters. He is well versed in disability cases and is currently acting for Master-Card and Avon in a case filed by the EEOC alleging mental health disorders and disabilities.

**Clients/Work Highlights:** MasterCard; Avon; Brooks Brothers; UnitedHealth; Reader's Digest and Enron.

## Other Notable Practitioners

"*Practical and goal-oriented,*" **Joel Cohen** (see p.1446) leads the New York employment team at McDermott Will & Emery LLP. He has been particularly active handling overtime claims under the FLSA. With a wealth of experience in jury trials, he recently represented Travelers in a case concerning employment fraud. Clients describe him as an "*excellent advocate and a determined competitor.*"

# ENERGY & NATURAL RESOURCES

## Band 1

### LeBoeuf, Lamb, Greene & MacRae LLP

See firm details p.1540

**The Firm:** Few firms boast the regulatory and transactional capability that LeBoeuf offers clients in the energy sector. Energy and insurance are the twin pillars of the firm's practice. It has developed its expertise, from its origins as a utility counsel, to encompass all power, oil and gas entities. The firm has secured a role on almost all the headline deals in the industry, such as advising Cinergy in its merger with Duke Energy and Mid-American in its acquisi-

tion of Pacificorp. The firm has prudently turned its attention to the renewables sector where it is attracting significant instructions from clients such as Puget Sound Energy, which it advised on two major deals. Clients report: *"the reason we continue to use LeBoeuf is because it's the best – at no other firm can we access the same level of regulatory and transactional expertise nor the in-depth industry knowledge the lawyers possess."* Commentators predict that the firm is incredibly well positioned to take advantage of the anticipated upswing in merger activity following the repeal of the Public Utility Holding Company Act.

**The Lawyers:** **William Lamb** (see p.1473) is lauded for his transactional skills in M&A and financing as well as his regulatory knowledge. A significant industry figure, clients happily retain him because he is *"competent and inside counsel love him."* Managing partner **Steven Davis** (see p.1448) is dubbed *"the great facilitator"* by clients due to his particular flair for bringing parties to the table. **John Klauberg** (see p.1470) enters the table due to overwhelming client feedback. Researchers were told: *"He is by far the most knowledgeable and diverse energy transactional lawyer in the country; he provides great legal advice and is an even-tempered and strategic thinker."*

**Clients/Work Highlights:** The team represented China National Petroleum in its acquisition of a 35% stake in a gas field in northwest Kazakhstan from Nimir Petroleum. JPMorgan and Citigroup are further evidence of the firm's broad client base, while other clients include AGL Resources; Enron; Energy East; CSFB; Aquila and Macquarie Infrastructure.

### Skadden, Arps, Slate, Meagher & Flom LLP & Affiliates

See firm details p.1557

**The Firm:** A *"world-class firm boasting a world-class energy practice,"* no other firm attracted such high praise from both clients and peers, who point to the winning combination of the firm's transactional reputation and almost unparalleled regulatory expertise provided by the DC office. The team has recently been involved in more than its fair share of headline deals, advising Duke Energy in its Cinergy merger and Exelon on its acquisition of Public Service Electric and Gas. Clients say: *"Its transactional capability is so strong and the team so deep – we know we've got all our bases covered when it's on the deal."*

**The Lawyers:** **Sheldon Adler** (see p.1432) is *"a leading light,"* according to sources. Clients enjoy his affable manner as much as his attention to detail and technical skills: *"He has a heart and really wants to do what is right by his clients."*

**Clients/Work Highlights:** TECO Energy, Northeast Utilities and CMS Energy are among the firm's clients.

## Band 2

### Dewey Ballantine LLP

See firm details p.1530

**The Firm:** This firm climbs up the table due to the growing profile of its energy practice. Grounded in the capital markets sector, the team specializes in high-yield, tax-exempt transactions. Advising designated underwriters has become the group's signature, with a roster of financial houses crowding its client list. According to clients: *"Its problem-solving skills are unique – the attorneys use their minds creatively to get the deal closed."* A recent highlight was representing Merrill Lynch and Lehman Brothers as dealer-managers of Sierra Pacific Resources in a series of transactions designed to improve the capital structure and credit quality of SPR and its subsidiaries.

**The Lawyers:** **Emmett Ellis** (see p.1452) *"is a slick operator"* and noted for his underwriter expertise while **Michael Fitzpatrick** (see p.1455) and **Peter O'Brien** (see p.1484) are new to the tables, recommended by impressed commentators for being *"capable and good, rising stars."* Colleague **Anthony Terrell** (see p.1507) is *"first rate,"* say clients.

**Clients/Work Highlights:** The team counseled two underwriting syndicates in the refinancing of Ohio Power's structured lease financing. Other clients include Southern California Edison; AEP; TXU; CenterPoint Energy; Consolidated Edison; Banc of America Securities; Barclays Capital; Citigroup Global Markets; Goldman Sachs; Unisource; Duquesne Light Holdings; UBS Securities and GE.

### Jones Day

See firm details p.570

**The Firm:** This international powerhouse covers all the bases in the energy chain, from upstream and transportation to the extreme downstream of energy trading. FERC regulatory work, finance and corporate matters are also handled by the team. It recently counseled AEP on the sale by its subsidiary of its stake in the 2,500 MW south Texas project nuclear plant. On the finance side, Morgan Stanley is a key client to which the team gave advice as underwriter in the refinancing of Dayton Power and Light's CDO. Sources were impressed by *"the firm's ability to field such a comprehensive team."*

**The Lawyers:** **William Henze**'s (see p.1464) client base is drawn from the oil, gas and power sectors. A *"sharp and savvy"* attorney, he is increasingly involved in advising hedge funds moving into the sector. **Michael Cusick** (see p.1448) is *"good on transactions,"* adopting *"a dynamic approach"* to deals.

**Clients/Work Highlights:** BP; FirstEnergy; International Coal Group; OGE Energy; SCANA Corporation and The Williams Companies.

## Pillsbury Winthrop Shaw Pittman LLP

See firm details p.1550

**The Firm:** This firm continues to win market approval, securing roles on a series of significant transactions. *"Big on power,"* the firm counts some major players in the utilities sector among its roster of clients. A recent standout deal includes advising Public Service Enterprise Group (PSEG) on the transactional issues in its merger with Exelon. In addition to this corporate capability, the firm is ramping up its capital markets offering at the electric and gas end of the spectrum, representing a healthy cross section of banks and finance houses.

**The Lawyers:** **David Falck** (see p.1453) offers skills across a number of practice areas in the energy sector with clients noting: *"He is one of the best I've worked with,"* while peers point to *"an excellent securities lawyer."*

**Clients/Work Highlights:** The team is noted for its underwriting advice, representing syndicates led by Citigroup, JPMorgan, Merrill Lynch, Deutsche Bank and Wachovia in two common stock offerings and a CDO for CMS Energy. Other clients include Banc of America Securities; Lehman Brothers; CSFB; PNM Resources; Pinnacle West; Northeast Utilities; American Transmission; Marubeni; Mitsui; PPL Global; Tenaska and Trans-Elect.

## Simpson Thacher & Bartlett LLP

See firm details p.1555

**The Firm:** This firm is synonymous with high-end, top-quality transactional work in both the private equity and M&A arenas, a reputation that has served as an entrée into the energy sector. Recent highlights include representing Texas Genco in connection with the sale of its outstanding equity interests to NRG, while private equity houses such as First Reserve are regular clients of the firm. Well-positioned to take advantage of the increasing interest among private equity and finance players in the energy market, the team was praised by clients for being *"high-quality attorneys – all you would expect from a firm of that caliber."* The team additionally boasts expertise in a diversified energy market, advising on deals in the coal, power, oil and gas sectors.

**The Lawyers:** Ken Wyman, David Lieberman and James Cotter are the key contacts for energy-related transactions.

**Clients/Work Highlights:** KKR; The Blackstone Group; JPMorgan; British Energy; Duke Energy; KeySpan Energy; PPL; GE; Lehman Brothers; RBS; Foundation Coal Holdings and Peabody Energy.

## Sullivan & Cromwell LLP

See firm details p.1558

**The Firm:** A Wall Street thoroughbred, Sullivan & Cromwell boasts one of the finest utility and public company M&A practices on the market. It is this corporate expertise that has given the firm leverage into the energy arena and secured industry heavyweights such as BP as regular clients. Recent highlight matters include counseling Danielson Holding on its acquisition of American Ref-Fuel Holdings. Unsurprisingly, capital markets is also a strong suit

for the firm, and it advises clients including Constellation Energy in this sector.

**The Lawyers:** An M&A specialist across a number of sectors including energy, **Joseph Frumkin** (see p.1457) is described as being *"on the aggressive end of the spectrum and super smart; he certainly knows what he is doing."*

**Clients/Work Highlights:** Allegheny Energy; TXU; Sempra Energy and EON.

## Band 3

## Cravath, Swaine & Moore LLP

See firm details p.1527

**The Firm:** This firm prides itself on its prestigious corporate practice, providing advice on some of the most complex transactions across a range of industries, including energy. While the firm does not have a discrete energy practice, the caliber and quality of the lawyers is such that they are regularly retained on some of the biggest deals in the industry. The team has a strong brand in utilities work and distinguishes itself from some of its New York peers with its particular expertise in advising oil and gas companies on corporate and antitrust matters. Illustrating its top-tier work, the team advised Chevron in its acquisition of Unocal as well as Ashland in connection with the transfer of interests to Marathon Oil. In the utilities sector, the firm represented FPL Group in its $28 billion merger with Constellation Energy.

**The Lawyers:** Richard Hall is the key contact for energy matters.

**Clients/Work Highlights:** Shell; Ashland; ConocoPhillips; EnCana; Florida Power & Light; WPS Resources; RWE and Crown Castle International.

## Debevoise & Plimpton LLP

See firm details p.1529

**The Firm:** Providing a *"truly exceptional standard of advice"* say clients, this is another high-end firm staking its claim on the energy sector. Work stems from its transactional, project finance and litigation practices while multijurisdictional matters are an added specialty. Key deals include advising Kelso & Company in its equity investment in the buyer of an oil refinery in Kansas and counseling Sithe Energies in its sale to Dynergy. Mitsui is also an important client, with the team recently advised it in its acquisition of Gas Participacoes.

**The Lawyers:** Jack Allen chairs the energy practice.

**Clients/Work Highlights:** The firm continues to advise Shell in relation to governmental investigations. Other clients include Cogentrix Energy; Culligan; Deutsche Bank; Drax Holdings; Inter-American Development Bank; K Road Power; Powerco and SG Barr Devlin.

## King & Spalding LLP

See firm details p.1538

**The Firm:** Combining the firm's historic roots in the oil and gas sector with the New York office's recently enhanced utilities capability, this team continues to impress commentators. Providing a soup to nuts

service for clients, the group acts on deals and projects from the early stages, such as gaining regulatory approval, through to commercial execution and construction where needed. The firm's solid litigation and arbitration reputation is well played out in the energy sector too. Recent highlights include acting for Rothschild and Citigroup as financial adviser, and Citigroup as underwriter, on their bid for NorthWestern Corporation. The team's natural gas and, more especially, LNG regulatory capability is reflected in its recent work for the Freeport LNG development and for Cheniere Energy in the development of several Gulf Coast LNG terminals.

**The Lawyers:** Working predominantly on transactions, **Tia Barancik** (see p.1435) is highly regarded by the market, particularly for her burgeoning hedge fund work: *"She has a good gut sense of how laws will impact our business, and is good at anticipating what investors want,"* say clients. **Lisa Tonery** (see p.1508) is a recognized expert in gas regulatory matters and is particularly lauded for her FERC work in LNG.

**Clients/Work Highlights:** CSFB; Lehman Brothers; Colonial Pipeline and Financial Guaranty Insurance (FGIC).

## Milbank, Tweed, Hadley & McCloy LLP

**The Firm:** A major force in the energy projects arena, the firm's capability in this area is complemented by its M&A and capital markets know-how, having essentially cultivated a great reputation for representing sources of capital. Fielding *"a fantastic team with an amazingly quick turnaround,"* the firm is a popular choice among banks and finance houses and is picking up more than its fair share of private equity work as a result. Highlights include counseling the private equity group in PNM Resources' $1 billion acquisition of TNP Enterprises, which comprises a regulated utility and non-regulated subsidiary in Texas. The M&A team also posted a stellar year representing Scottish Power in its sale of Pacificorp.

**The Lawyers:** **Douglas Dunn** chairs the firm's energy and power practice. Boasting significant experience in the utility sector, Dunn *"has regulatory roots but is very good at translating his advice into the commercial context,"* according to sources.

**Clients/Work Highlights:** KKR; Trimaran Capital Partners; JPMorgan Partners; Wachovia Capital Partners and the Enron creditors' committee.

## Thelen Reid & Priest LLP

See firm details p.342

**The Firm:** This firm enjoys a distinguished pedigree as *"a quintessential energy firm"* due to its historical roots in utilities, which stretch back to the earliest days of the market. Having developed with the industry, the firm has adapted to the ebb and flow of the market to accomodate its clients needs. Recognized as a Public Utility Holding Company Act specialist, the energy team also taps into the firm's respected corporate and securities practice, harnessing the increasing interest in the sector from private equity investors. Clients praise the team-oriented approach the firm takes with such comments as: "*I know that when I deal with the firm I am tapping into the resources of the entire group – there is definitely no silo approach to the work there.*"

**The Lawyers:** **William Baker** (see p.1435) is invariably described as the "*dean of the Holding Company Act,*" and his expertise in the industry has led him to contribute to the development of the Energy Policy Act. **Thomas Giblin** (see p.1459) is "*one of the brightest lawyers in New York,*" say sources. He lends his corporate and securities skills to the energy sector. **Robert Reger** (see p.1491) is a corporate lawyer who is well respected in the energy field. Researchers were told: "*You can always count on his papers being well prepared.*"

**Clients/Work Highlights:** Entergy; NiSource; Ameren; FPL Group; Unisource Energy and TXU.

## Vinson & Elkins LLP
See firm details p.1938

**The Firm:** Clients report that this is a team providing "*the highest quality legal advice.*" With a worldwide reputation for its oil and gas work, this firm needs no introduction. While the bulk of its matters are driven from Houston, the New York office provides expert transactional advice across the M&A, project finance and capital markets fields. The team has developed a particular niche for advising partnerships such as client Buckeye Partners, the owner and operator of refined products pipelines and terminals. It counseled the company in three public offerings of late. Clients praised the team because "*importantly, it knows that legal issues are only part of our problem – they understand the business context too.*"

**The Lawyers:** **Michael Rosenwasser** (see p.1494) is a corporate and securities lawyer who clients lauded as "*one of the most respected energy lawyers in the USA.*"

**Clients/Work Highlights:** The team advised Seaspan on its IPO, the largest shipping IPO in US history; and Teekay LNG Partners in its recent IPO. Other clients include Goldman Sachs; Citigroup; CSFB; AG Edwards & Sons; Pacific Energy Partners; Forest Oil; Penn Virginia Resource Partners and US Shipping Partners.

## Band 4

## Chadbourne & Parke LLP
See firm details p.1524

**The Firm:** The energy practice here is grounded in the firm's phenomenal projects offering, which boasts significant lender and developer expertise across all energy industries. The firm has been a major player in the power sector but its oil and gas work, particularly LNG, continues to attract the lion's share of praise. Renewables work is also coming to the fore. In addition to the project finance offering, the energy team is showing strength in the corporate field, advising on both M&As and offerings.

**The Lawyers:** Chaim Wachsberger and Richard Sonkin are the key energy contacts.

**Clients/Work Highlights:** Dexia Credit; AES Eastern Energy; EIF Group; El Paso; AES; CSFB; Citibank; Union Bank of California; Duke Energy and Tractebel.

## Davis Polk & Wardwell
See firm details p.1528

**The Firm:** Clients point to the firm's innovative approach to financing, particularly in project and leveraged finance, as a key draw. Although the firm is a corporate powerhouse that does not field a specialist energy team, its capabilities across finance, including project finance, and derivatives is such that it advises some of the most prominent clients in the market. The standout instruction of late was advising CNOOC on its $18.5 billion attempted merger with Unocal.

**Clients/Work Highlights:** The firm is advising JPMorgan Securities as financial adviser to Burlington Resources in connection with ConocoPhillips' acquisition of Burlington. Other clients include ExxonMobil; Emerson Electric; Con Edison; Constellation Energy; KeyBanc Capital Markets and Cantera Resources Holdings.

## Latham & Watkins LLP

**The Firm:** The footprint of this firm's international project practice is firmly planted in the energy sector. As the financing arrangements become ever more complex, this team is becoming increasingly involved in a range of energy-related transactions. "*True industry specialists,*" according to the market, this firm offers a deep team with real breadth to its stellar client roster. It has been involved in some of the

largest recent deals in the international arena, such as the Qatargas II and RASGas II/3 LNG developments. Domestically it has advised banking clients on a range of deals, making significant inroads into the renewables sector. For example, the firm represented Citigroup Global Markets in the refinancing of the Caithness Coso geothermal facilities in California.

**The Lawyers:** Project finance stars William Voge and Dave Gordon are the key energy contacts.

**Clients/Work Highlights:** Lehman Brothers; ABN AMRO; Morgan Stanley; Société Générale; Nigerian National Petroleum and ExxonMobil.

## Wachtell, Lipton, Rosen & Katz
See firm details p.1561

**The Firm:** This firm is recommended on the strength of its renowned transactional practice. While there is no formal energy group, the company's deal list establishes it firmly as a significant player in the market. Recently the team advised Cinergy in its merger with Duke Energy, and was counsel to ConocoPhillips on its $35.6 billion acquisition of Burlington Resources.

**The Lawyers:** Andrew Brownstein is the highly respected contact for energy matters.

**Clients/Work Highlights:** Financial institutions and energy corporates are among the firm's clients.

## White & Case LLP
See firm details p.1566

**The Firm:** Clients say: "*There is a very good level of expertise and understanding of the sector*" housed at this firm. Although it has already displayed its energy credentials in the project finance sphere, the firm is additionally making a concerted push to bolster its corporate transaction capability. As an illustration, the team has recently acted on the Exelon-PSEG merger, advising ICF Consulting on behalf of the New Jersey Board of Public Utilities in connection with its review of the merger. Another key client is Amerada Hess, which the firm is advising on a range of matters including its joint venture to construct and operate an LNG facility in Massachusetts.

**The Lawyers:** **Stuart Caplan** (see p.1442) brings significant regulatory expertise to the table and is, say clients, "*a smart guy who knows his FERC stuff.*"

**Clients/Work Highlights:** The firm is general counsel to MACH Gen. Other clients include Shell Trading, Abu Dhabi Water and Electricity Authority and Lehman Brothers.

# ENERGY

# UPSTATE NEW YORK

| Energy: Upstate New York |
| --- |
| **Leading Firms** |
| [1] **LEBOEUF, LAMB, GREENE & MACRAE** *Albany* |
| **NIXON PEABODY LLP** *Albany* |
| [2] **COUCH WHITE, LLP** *Albany* |
| **READ AND LANIADO** *Albany* |

| Leading Individuals |
| --- |
| [1] **DAX John** *Cohen Dax and Koening* |
| **FITZGERALD Brian** *LeBoeuf, Lamb* |
| **GANSBERG Andrew** *Nixon Peabody LLP* |
| **LANIADO Sam** *Read and Laniado* |
| **SINGER Leonard** *Couch White, LLP* |
| **WHITE Algird** *Couch White, LLP* |

## Band 1

### LeBoeuf, Lamb, Greene & MacRae LLP

See firm details p.1540

**The Firm:** The Albany office of this international powerhouse advises clients on regulatory issues as well as appearing regularly at the New York State Public Service Commission. The team benefits from the ability to tap into the resources provided by its city headquarters. The group has impressed commentators with its work in the renewables sector, attracting clients such as AES. In electricity, the team advises across the regulatory spectrum, counseling on rate cases, transmission and independent system operator issues. Market sources praised the team for its proactive approach in representing its clients.

**The Lawyers:** The *"incredibly thorough"* **Brian FitzGerald** (see p.1454) was applauded for his regulatory knowledge in both the energy and telecom sectors: *"He provides clear advice in plain English and is always on the other end of the phone line if I have a question,"* report clients.

**Clients/Work Highlights:** Energy East subsidiaries and Fortuna Energy are among the firm's clients.

### Nixon Peabody LLP

See firm details p.1546

**The Firm:** *"A quality team,"* say sources of a firm whose energy offering is concentrated on regulatory matters. State proceedings and approvals take up the bulk of its work, while the firm is strongly recommended by the market for its facility-siting expertise. Developers of generation and transmission facilities are the core of the firm's client base.

**The Lawyers:** **Andrew Gansberg** (see p.1458) manages the firm's Albany office and is the key energy contact here.

**Clients/Work Highlights:** TransÉnergie US and Athens Generating are among the team's clients.

## Band 2

### Couch White, LLP

**The Firm:** Recommended for its work representing large power users, this firm was praised by market sources for its dedication to clients' interests. Peers admire its work on large projects and the dynamic approach to handling regulatory proceedings.

**The Lawyers:** **Leonard Singer** is a name recommended by peers for his understanding of the workings of Fortune 500 companies. Colleague **Algird White** possesses deep industry knowledge and was lauded by peers as a fine attorney.

### Read and Laniado

**The Firm:** This niche practice specializes in environmental and energy work, with the latter being concentrated in the electric sector. Regulatory work is the mainstay of the practice with the team representing clients at all relevant state and federal bodies. The concentrated team has garnered a reputation for advising independent power producers and counts the Independent Power Producers of New York as a key client. Siting work for electric production facilities has been a focus of the group, as has gas and renewable projects. A recent highlight includes counseling Florida Power & Light in relation to an offshore wind project.

**The Lawyers:** **Sam Laniado** is *"technically excellent and takes a strategic approach to matters,"* report clients.

### Other Notable Practitioners

**John Dax** of Cohen and Dax PC represents power marketers and developer companies and is well regarded by peers for his strategic approach.

# ENVIRONMENT

| Environment |
| --- |
| **Leading Firms** |
| [1] **SIVE PAGET & RIESEL PC** *New York* |
| [2] **ARNOLD & PORTER LLP** *New York* |
| **BRYAN CAVE LLP** *New York* |
| **NIXON PEABODY LLP** *Albany* |
| **WHITEMAN OSTERMAN & HANNA LLP** *Albany* |
| [3] **BEVERIDGE & DIAMOND PC** *New York* |
| **CARTER LEDYARD & MILBURN LLP** *New York* |
| **PROSKAUER ROSE LLP** *New York* |
| **YOUNG, SOMMER** *Albany* |

### Sive Paget & Riesel PC

See firm details p.1556

**The Firm:** *"The Sive Paget guys are leaders in their field,"* say market commentators. This boutique has a long history of environmental work in New York. Its team of 20 specialist lawyers covers the environmental landscape, from litigation in toxic tort and New York State Environmental Quality Review Act (SEQRA) cases, to issues concerning hazardous waste. Land use is also a big part of the practice, and its prowess in Superfund matters is widely recognized. The practice represents clients all over the country, although the majority of the office's work is in the greater metropolitan area.

**The Lawyers:** **Daniel Riesel** (see p.1492) is *"a terrific adviser and a pitbull when defending his clients."* A strong litigator with experience in enforcement defense, white-collar crime and toxic torts, he also provides counseling to industrial entities. Of late, his practice has also featured land use advice for developers. **Mark Chertok** (see p.1444) is well respected for his work on land use matters and environmental impact statements. An all-rounder, he is an impressive figure in the courtroom. **David Paget** (see p.1486) possesses extensive experience of environmental law and related litigation matters. This includes preparing and processing environmental impact statements and permits under the CAA, the CWA and the NEPA.

**Clients/Work Highlights:** Kraft; The Trump Organization; Empire State Development; Domino Sugar; City of New York; World Kitchen; USG and Toll Brothers.

### Arnold & Porter LLP

See firm details p.560

**The Firm:** Clients love the *"extraordinary level of ownership"* that these *"wonderfully talented lawyers"* take of matters. A team of five attorneys represents corporations, developers, utilities and public agencies in environmental litigation, regulatory and transactional matters. Recent highlights include advising Honeywell on a broad range of environmental matters around the world. The team also represented PPL in several pieces of litigation concerning air and water pollution. This New York-based practice works closely with its counterparts in Washington DC, particularly utilizing their strength in regulatory matters.

**The Lawyers:** **Mike Gerrard**'s (see p.1458) name is synonymous with environmental work at Arnold & Porter. *"He is everything that's advertised,"* and was described by interviewees as an *"omnipresent guy: he is here, there and everywhere; he mustn't sleep."* As well as being a prolific writer and speaker on environmental issues, Gerrard maintains a busy regional development practice. He continues to act for Silverstein Properties in the environmental permitting work for the reconstruction of the World Trade

Center site. He also represented Madison Square Garden in litigation opposing the construction of a proposed football stadium in Manhattan. He heads the New York office's environment group.

**Clients/Work Highlights:** Silverstein Properties; Metropolitan Museum of Art; Madison Square Garden; Honeywell; PPL and GE.

## Bryan Cave LLP

**The Firm:** This national firm has carved out a name for its environmental work. With 12 "*top-flight environment specialists*," this is one of the largest practices in New York City. It has a strong air practice that utility clients take full advantage of. Clients also like the fact that they can use the firm for both transactional matters and for a range of more substantive environmental issues, including Superfund work, litigation and general counseling. The practice can also help clients with environmental matters outside the USA due to its international expertise in this area.

**The Lawyers:** **Kevin Healy** is an expert in air quality issues. "*Talented and exceptionally bright,*" he is well equipped to advise on environmental impact review matters and has a strong regulatory practice. His client list includes major New York utilities, public authorities and industrial and commercial corporations. **Chuck Warren**'s practice encompasses transactional work and the major environmental statutes, such as CWA, CAA and Toxic Substances Control Act (TOSCA). His time as a former EPA regional administrator goes some way to explain his skill in dealing with regulatory agencies on a federal and state level. As one interviewee remarked: "*He understands government. He is also a decent, honest person who wins the trust of the people he negotiates with.*" "*Diligent and articulate,*" **Philip Karmel** is well known for his litigation skills. Environmental litigation and toxic tort defense comprise a large part of

his practice. However, he also undertakes environmental counseling, CAA, Superfund, permitting and enforcement work. Karmel recently represented Monsanto in several Superfund-related matters, and acted for the New York City Transit Authority in a CAA litigation case. **Roberta Gordon** is "*extremely thorough and careful,*" and stands out for her transactional expertise and her negotiation skills. Her practice focuses on managing environmental risks in domestic and international corporate and real estate transactions and on environmental insurance.

**Clients/Work Highlights:** The firm represents numerous major companies in manufacturing, energy utilities and transport. It also acts for city agencies, authorities and municipalities.

## Nixon Peabody LLP

See firm details p.1546

**The Firm:** With three major offices in the New York area (Rochester, Albany and Long Island), this firm attracts major clients through its geographical reach in the area and its impressive local profile. Four experienced environment technicians (specialists in geology, engineering and health) reside in the Rochester office, bolstering the service the firm offers to its loyal clientele. A diverse client base, which includes academic institutions, pharmaceutical and electronics manufacturers, ensures a steady flow of matters. Wetlands, brownfield redevelopment, clean air, power generation matters and energy sector disputes are all covered in this comprehensive practice.

**The Lawyers:** **John Greenthal** (see p.1462) is highly respected for his experience in this area. He was a previous head of enforcement in the New York State Department of Environmental Conservation. He brings this experience to bear in his practice, where he represents clients in enforcement defense proceedings, Superfund issues, brownfield redevelopments and hazardous waste matters. **Scott Turner** (see p.1509) is "*down to earth and pleasant to work with,*" according to clients. He specializes in helping clients obtain permits that are required to build large facilities. The bulk of his work is in the electric energy and solid waste arena. Clients also commend his strength in air matters. He has counseled Covanta Energy on air permit issues at facilities in Minnesota, Virginia, Massachusetts and New York.

**Clients/Work Highlights:** Pfizer; NRG Energy; AstraZeneca; Puerto Rico Industrial Development; Indiana Municipal Power Agency; DuPont; KeySpan; Sherwin-Williams; Constellation Energy Group and Kodak.

## Whiteman Osterman & Hanna LLP

**The Firm:** This highly respected Albany firm has evolved over the years to become a leader in environmental matters in upstate New York. It represents clients in a comprehensive range of matters, from compliance, permitting and SEQRA issues to conducting environmental due diligence reviews for businesses and financial institutions. The group is often found on state cleanup and land development matters and works closely with the firm's government relations practice. This enables the group to

update clients on developments at the federal and state level and to help provide input into the legislative and regulatory processes.

**The Lawyers:** Senior partner **Daniel Ruzow** "*is practical and reasonable. He is also extremely knowledgeable about the state and State Environmental Quality Review Act,*" agreed sources. His areas of expertise include environmental impact assessment and environmental and land use permitting and compliance. The "*skilled and effective*" **Scott Fein** impresses with his litigation skills. "*He is a leader when it comes to handling particularly difficult enforcement and criminal matters.*"

**Clients/Work Highlights:** Clients include Fortune 500 and smaller companies, land developers, government and quasi-government agencies.

## Beveridge & Diamond PC

See firm details p.562

**The Firm:** Clients praise the efficiency of this New York environmental boutique. One said: "*In an hour, Beveridge & Diamond accomplish what other firms may take two hours to do.*" Although smaller than its well-established sister office in DC, the 15 attorneys in the New York office have the resources to handle any environmental issue thrown at them. The firm has three main practice groups: environmental law, land use and litigation. The lawyers draw from a deep well of experience and work together with the firm's other offices around the country. Clients appreciate this and find the offices "*well placed around the USA to service our needs.*" Offices in California, Massachusetts, Maryland and New Jersey now extend to Texas, following the opening of a new branch in Austin in late 2005.

**The Lawyers:** Stephen Gordon manages the New York office. He practices in almost all areas of environmental law including regulatory and brownfield work.

**Clients/Work Highlights:** Caithness Energy; Silverstein Properties; Goldman Sachs; Aquacalma and Cogentrix Energy.

## Carter Ledyard & Milburn LLP

See firm details p.1523

**The Firm:** Sources endorsed Carter Ledyard & Milburn for its skills in land use, development projects and environmental impact statements. The team of ten full-time environment lawyers provides consistently high-quality advice, and stands out for its litigation capabilities and its understanding of energy projects. It works for a number of public authorities in the power generation field. The group is also involved in complex air emissions permitting, transmission line permitting and clean energy projects. The remediation of hazardous sites is a further string to this firm's bow. On the international front, the group has represented European, Canadian, Latin American, Japanese and Israeli businesses and individuals in corporate transactions, property acquisitions, environmental reviews and litigation.

**The Lawyers:** **Stephen Kass** is well known for his advice on New York Power Authority, as well as redevelopment work and land use projects, particularly

## Environment: Mainly Transactional

### Leading Firms

[1] **CRAVATH, SWAINE & MOORE LLP** *New York*
    **DAVIS POLK & WARDWELL** *New York*

[2] **SIMPSON THACHER & BARTLETT LLP** *New York*
    **SULLIVAN & CROMWELL LLP** *New York*

[3] **CAHILL GORDON & REINDEL LLP** *New York*
    **DEBEVOISE & PLIMPTON LLP** *New York*
    **PROSKAUER ROSE LLP** *New York*
    **SIDLEY AUSTIN LLP** *New York*
    **WHITE & CASE LLP** *New York*

### Leading Individuals

[1] **FLESHER Gail** *Davis Polk & Wardwell*
    **SMITH Jeffrey** *Cravath, Swaine & Moore*

[2] **BATTISTA Gregory** *Cravath, Swaine & Moore*
    **BRENNAN Matthew** *Sullivan & Cromwell LLP*
    **FADIL Adeeb** *Simpson Thacher & Bartlett*
    **HALLMAN Robert** *Cahill Gordon & Reindel LLP*
    **HAMMER Stuart** *Debevoise & Plimpton LLP*
    **KAFIN Robert** *Proskauer Rose LLP*
    **PORT Gail** *Proskauer Rose LLP*

[3] **CHENG Loyti** *Davis Polk & Wardwell*
    **CROUGH Maureen** *Sidley Austin LLP*
    **GORDON Roberta** *Bryan Cave LLP*
    **HORSCH Richard** *White & Case LLP*
    **MILMED Paul** *White & Case LLP*
    **ROSENBERG Mark** *Sullivan & Cromwell LLP*
    **STEVER Donald** *Kirkpatrick & Lockhart*

large and complex ones in and around urban areas. He founded the environment practice group and is its co-director.

**Clients/Work Highlights:** United Water New Rochelle; Metropolitan Transportation Authority issues; Empire State Development; Ferry Point Partners; Roosevelt Island Operating Corporation; Comprehensive Care Management; New York City Council; Natural Resources Defense Council and Environmental Integrity Project.

## Proskauer Rose LLP

See firm details p.1551

**The Firm:** A "*first choice*" for clients, a core team of seven environment lawyers work from the New York office of Proskauer Rose. As part of the firm's nationwide environmental practice group, the lawyers can call on the resources of the firm's other departments and offices, as need be, to serve their clients' needs. The practice is comprehensive and the team offers expertise in environmental insurance, licensing and permitting, litigation, and cleanup of contaminated properties. However, market commentators all agree that it is the group's transactional work that really gets it noticed. Recent work includes representing CSFB on several transactional matters, and acting for Kramont Realty Trust in its $1.2 billion acquisition by affiliates of Centro Properties Group. On the environmental litigation side, the group represented the New York Jets football team and handled the envi-

ronmental work on the proposed West Side stadium for the Jets.

**The Lawyers:** The lawyers in the group are "*forward-thinking and results and closure-oriented.*" The "*skilled and effective*" **Robert Kafin** (see p.1469) maintains a steady balance between his management responsibilities as chief operating partner of the firm and his busy environmental practice. His varied workload includes general environmental counseling, brownfield work and contaminated sites. However, he works predominantly on corporate transactions and environmental risks and liabilities. Although a large component of her practice is transactional, **Gail Port** (see p.1489) is also well equipped to handle the full range of environmental matters. She has worked on large-scale Superfund cases, such as the Lower Passaic River cleanup, and high-profile brownfield matters such as the Con Edison power plant decommissioning. According to clients, she is "*knowledgeable and well plugged in*" and can put "*a practical business perspective on issues.*"

**Clients/Work Highlights:** CSFB; CharterMac; Henry Schein; Teva Pharmaceuticals; The Laird Group; TRC Companies and Total.

## Young, Sommer, Ward, Ritzenberg, Wooley, Baker & Moore LLC

**The Firm:** Interviewees remarked that Young Sommer has captured the upstate New York market and is now expanding into New York. A growing practice of 14 attorneys offers clients "*fantastic advocacy and an extremely responsive and solution-oriented*" service. The firm's development of a model to keep legal fees affordable while providing quality service appears to be working. Clients frequently referred to the firm's reasonable costs and effective service. The practice's environmental expertise is right across the board, covering air, bulk storage, power generation, Superfund and permitting issues to name but a few. However, its work for municipalities and public interest cases involving environmental issues also distinguishes it from the crowd.

**The Lawyers:** **Dean Sommer** is an illustrious litigator with experience of both defendant and plaintiff litigation. He also has a fine Superfund practice and wide experience of brownfield matters. He recently served as counsel to Union College and several private developers to redevelop brownfield properties in areas of Schenectady, New York. "*Pragmatic and efficient,*" **Kevin Young** has an excellent reputation as a regulatory lawyer. Clients note that he excels in strategizing and has "*excellent contacts with the regulatory agencies.*" Work highlights include representing a coalition of 36 towns and three counties in a controversial Department of Environmental Conservation adjudicatory permit proceeding regarding New York City's discharge from the Shandaken Tunnel.

**Clients/Work Highlights:** National Grid; GE; Union College; Remington Arms; Keymark and Delaware Engineering.

## Cravath, Swaine & Moore LLP

See firm details p.1527

**The Firm:** The small environmental practice of this powerful corporate firm has developed a strong reputation for its expertise in matters related to the transactional market. The environmental group primarily works with the firm's esteemed corporate practice and attracts a mixture of cross referrals and stand-alone work. The lawyers are extremely "*sharp, responsive and high quality.*" Recently, the team represented Unilever United States in the sale of its global fragrance business to Coty for approximately $800 million. The group also acted for BAE Systems North America in its acquisition of United Defense Industries for approximately $4 billion. The group also supports the firm's litigation teams, handling matters with environmental implications such as mass tort actions and stockholder litigation, regarding the adequacy of environmental disclosure under SEC regulations.

**The Lawyers:** **Jeffrey Smith** (see p.1503) has "*top-flight lawyering skills*" and is praised for being a "*bigger picture thinker.*" He secured a profile for his effective handling of huge deals and the top end of transactional work. Peers also add that he is "*in the Cravath mold of being very thorough and precise.*" The "*excellent and trusted adviser*" **Gregory Battista** (see p.1436) assists clients on environmental liability and regulatory matters in connection with M&A, securities offerings and finance arrangements. A hit with clients, they point out that he is "*extremely responsive and his counsel is always on point.*"

**Clients/Work Highlights:** Bristol-Myers Squibb; IBM; CSFB; BAE Systems North America and Unilever.

## Davis Polk & Wardwell

See firm details p.1528

**The Firm:** The environmental group at Davis Polk sits as part of the firm's corporate department. It is therefore unsurprising that the practice is focused heavily on transactional work. However, the lawyers in the group also advise on a broad range of advisory matters. These include corporate policy and environmental controversy. Litigators in the group work closely with their corporate colleagues in tort, contract and indemnification disputes.

**The Lawyers:** Of the "*high-caliber*" attorneys fielded by this group, **Gail Flesher** (see p.1455) stands out for her transactional expertise. She is "*tough when she needs to be*" and alongside her conscientiousness and thoroughness "*she still tries to be flexible and practical.*" **Loyti Cheng** (see p.1444) enters the tables and is seen as a "*great lieutenant*" to Flesher on transactional matters.

**Clients/Work Highlights:** Emerson Electric; Kraft; Morgan Stanley; Lindsay Goldberg & Bessemer; Carl Zeiss; Canadian National Railway and Comcast.

## Simpson Thacher & Bartlett LLP

See firm details p.1555

**The Firm:** The environment law group at Simpson Thacher is essentially anchored in the firm's litigation department; however, it is the transactional work of the team that gets it noticed. "*Simpson Thacher has all the extra pieces they need to support the transactions, be it IP lawyers, bankruptcy people or insurance people*," said clients. The environment group has supported the firm in a number of significant transactions. One example of this is the firm's representation of adidas-Salomon in its acquisition of Reebok International in a deal worth $3.8 billion. It also represented KKR in its $1.27 billion acquisition of Accellent, a medical device manufacturer.

**The Lawyers:** **Adeeb Fadil** (see p.1453) attracts a loyal client following. His excellent client care skills, as well as his astuteness as a lawyer, have something to do with this. According to clients: "*Doing a deal without him is a bit like going cave diving without a light.*" He has the ability "*not to over-lawyer a matter or run up the outside consultant's fees*" and he is "*always looking for workable solutions to problems.*" Fadil's practice is primarily transactional support. However, he also handles some environmental litigation matters.

**Clients/Work Highlights:** KKR; Genesee & Wyoming; Texas Genco; adidas-Salomon; Sears Holdings; Citigroup and JPMorgan.

## Sullivan & Cromwell LLP

See firm details p.1558

**The Firm:** Sullivan & Cromwell is a "*highly professional firm offering a quick and seamless service across various practice areas,*" reported clients. The New York environmental practice wins plaudits for its transactional strength, in line with the firm's sterling corporate practice. Clients appreciated the attorneys' "*commercial acumen in addition to their in-depth knowledge of environmental law.*" Recent transactions include representing Cytec Industries in its purchase of UCB, a Belgian biopharmaceutical and specialty chemicals company. The group also acted for Medco Health Solutions in its acquisition of Accredo Health for more than $2 billion. Attorneys also assist clients in the structuring of transactions and their relationships with corporate affiliates to avoid alter ego and successor liability. Litigation expertise has been illustrated by work in the asbestos, chemical exposures and Superfund work arena. Restructuring and insolvency remain important areas for the practice group.

**The Lawyers:** **Matthew Brennan's** (see p.1441) busy year has included representing Telewest Global in its agreement with ntl to combine the companies in a transaction valued at approximately $11.4 billion. He also acted for Adelphia Communications in its sale of substantially all of its assets to Time Warner Cable and Comcast for $12.7 billion and a 16% equity interest in Time Warner Cable. **Mark Rosenberg** (see p.1494) combines his transactional workload with intricate environmental litigation cases. He advises clients on complex alter ego, successor liability, fraudulent conveyance, insurance coverage and bankruptcy issues. He coordinates the firm's

environmental law and insurance groups.

**Clients/Work Highlights:** AT&T; Adelphia Communications; Telewest Global; Vornado Realty Trust; Occidental Petroleum and Cytec Industries.

## Cahill Gordon & Reindel LLP

**The Firm:** Cahill Gordon has developed a strong specialist environmental practice over the years. Its team of four attorneys works closely with members of the firm's litigation department to assist on matters as and when required. Clients note the firm's strong capabilities in transactional matters, particularly in complex financing deals, and say that the lawyers do a "*first-rate job in the toughest of situations.*" The practice handles all areas of environmental law, including its international aspects.

**The Lawyers:** **Robert Hallman** "*knows how to get a deal done.*" Clients observed that he is "*highly analytical and is someone you can trust.*" He has been a stalwart on the environment scene for many years and has served three times in governmental positions. He heads the environment group. An all-rounder, Hallman's focus is on transactional matters; however, he also wins praise for his regulatory work.

**Clients/Work Highlights:** Investment banks, private equity houses and underwriters are among the firm's clientele.

## Debevoise & Plimpton LLP

See firm details p.1529

**The Firm:** You will find, within Debevoise & Plimpton's litigation and corporate departments, extremely capable environment lawyers busying themselves in their work. However, it is the transactional side of the environmental practice that especially steals the limelight. The firm's key strengths are "*having a consistent, excellent product focus and getting the right people on the job.*" Five attorneys devote their time exclusively to environmental due diligence and work on the environmental aspects of major corporate deals. Recent highlights include representing NBC and GE in the $14 billion merger of NBC and Vivendi Universal.

**The Lawyers:** Transactional specialist **Stuart Hammer** is extremely "*detail-oriented but knows when to cut to the chase.*" He "*shoots straight and has a wonderful practical approach.*" He represented Clayton, Dubilier & Rice, The Carlyle Group and Merrill Lynch Global Private Equity in their agreement with Ford to acquire Hertz in a $15 billion deal.

**Clients/Work Highlights:** Clayton, Dubilier & Rice; DaimlerChrysler; Kelso & Company; Mitsui; North Castle Partners; Oaktree Capital Management and Phelps Dodge.

## Sidley Austin LLP

See firm details p.883

**The Firm:** The New York branch of the Sidley Austin environmental group is perhaps in the shadow of its sizable and highly regarded DC counterpart. Nevertheless, the New York office has carved a strong profile through the hard work of its dedicated environment lawyers, particularly in the transactional arena. Attorneys also accommodate the other envi-

ronmental needs clients may have. This is because the team functions as part of the firm's national environmental practice group, and therefore has access to more than 40 other environment lawyers and extra resources firmwide to meet whichever challenges are presented by the case in hand.

**The Lawyers:** **Maureen Crough** (see p.1447) is highly thought of for her experience in transactional matters, and built a broad-reaching practice that includes regulatory compliance counseling, insurance coverage work and Superfund matters.

## White & Case LLP

See firm details p.1566

**The Firm:** Clients testified to the excellent service levels and quality of advice provided by this group. This broad-based practice is renowned for its transactional work. Recent matters include representing Quiport, the developer of the proposed new international airport in Quito, on environmental issues. International and cross-border work also plays to the firm's advantage with a network of offices enabling the New York practice to handle complex environmental transactional matters with an international element. For example, White & Case represented Saudi Aramco in the formation of a joint venture with Sumitomo Chemical to build and operate a petrochemical facility in Saudi Arabia.

**The Lawyers:** "*It's the level of detail he gets into and his business understanding*" that makes **Richard Horsch** (see p.1466) a popular figure with clients. His practice has an emphasis on international environmental transactional matters and litigation and he is the practice head of White & Case's global international environmental group. **Paul Milmed** (see p.1480) has a strong presence in New York, no doubt helped by the fact that he was formerly chief of the Environmental Protection Unit in the US attorney's office for the Southern District of New York. He "*really puts his clients first*" and is extremely "*bright and effective.*" Superfund and brownfield work are key parts of his practice.

**Clients/Work Highlights:** Amerada Hess; Ciba Specialty Chemicals; Deutsche Bank/Bankers Trust; Estée Lauder; FiberMark; Foster Wheeler; Inter-American Development Bank; Newmont Mining; Novartis; Starwood Capital and Volvo International.

## Other Notable Practitioners

**Donald Stever** (see p.1505) of Kirkpatrick & Lockhart Nicholson Graham LLP is a "*bright, knowledgeable and experienced attorney, particularly in Superfund matters.*" He is also "*easy to work with and can make the law easy to understand*" for clients. Stever's practice is a blend of transactional, regulatory and environmental litigation work. **David Freeman** (see p.1456) chairs the New York environmental practice group of Paul, Hastings, Janofsky & Walker LLP and has a wealth of experience in brownfield development matters. He is also commended for his advice on hazardous waste, Superfund, environmental insurance and transactional work. Clients trust his judgment and say that he is "*always working for our best interests – he is an* *absolute joy to work with.*" **Sharyl Reisman** (see p.1492) of Jones Day does a tremendous job for her clients. "*Efficient, smart and creative,*" she is admired for her experience in mass tort litigation and health and safety issues. She also has a niche in vapor intrusion work. She has defended Dole Food against multijurisdictional mass tort suits brought by foreign agricultural workers. She has also counseled IBM in various environmental and health and safety issues. Clients have the highest regard for **Peter Sacripanti** (see p.1495) of McDermott Will & Emery. First and foremost a trial litigator, his practice in the environmental area includes mass toxic tort matters, and his clients include ExxonMobil and Honeywell.

# HEALTHCARE

## Healthcare
### Leading Firms

1. **EPSTEIN BECKER & GREEN PC** *New York*
   **GARFUNKEL, WILD & TRAVIS PC** *Great Neck*
   **MANATT PHELPS & PHILLIPS LLP** *New York*
   **NIXON PEABODY LLP** *New York*
   **PROSKAUER ROSE LLP** *New York*
   **ROPES & GRAY LLP** *New York*
2. **CADWALADER, WICKERSHAM & TAFT** *New York*
   **HOGAN & HARTSON LLP** *New York*
   **KATTEN MUCHIN ROSENMAN LLP** *New York*
   **MCDERMOTT WILL & EMERY** *New York*
3. **ARENT FOX PLLC** *New York*
   **HODGSON RUSS LLP** *Buffalo*
   **ISEMAN CUNNINGHAM RIESTER & HYDE** *Albany*

### Leading Individuals

1. **BARNES Mark** *Ropes & Gray LLP*
   **BECKER Jeffrey** *Epstein Becker & Green*
   **BERGMANN Peter** *Cadwalader*
   **KALKINES George** *Manatt Phelps & Phillips LLP*
   **KORNREICH Edward** *Proskauer Rose LLP*
   **NADEL Peter** *Katten Muchin Rosenman*
   **WILD Robert** *Garfunkel, Wild & Travis PC*
2. **BERNSTEIN William** *Manatt Phelps & Phillips LLP*
   **ROBFOGEL Susan** *Nixon Peabody LLP*
   **ROTH Andrew** *McDermott Will & Emery*
   **WARNKE Stephen** *Ropes & Gray LLP*
   **WEISSMAN Ellen** *Hodgson Russ LLP*
3. **BLASS Michael** *Arent Fox PLLC*
   **ISEMAN Robert** *Iseman Cunningham Riester*
   **MILLOCK Peter** *Nixon Peabody LLP*
   **SCHNEIDER Jeffrey** *Hogan & Hartson LLP*
   **SCHNELL Paul** *Skadden, Arps*
   **SERBAROLI Francis** *Cadwalader*
   **TRAVIS Norton** *Garfunkel, Wild & Travis PC*
   **ZALL Richard** *Proskauer Rose LLP*

## Band 1

### Epstein Becker & Green PC

**The Firm:** "*Epstein Becker & Green has a fantastic team of highly professional lawyers who display stellar knowledge of healthcare law.*" So said one client, echoing the views of many. The firm's popularity is no doubt connected to its national experience in all areas of healthcare transactions and regulatory matters.

**The Lawyers: Jeffrey Becker** is "*one of the big names – the select few who really know the market and land the important clients.*" He is a cofounder of the firm and advises commercial, voluntary and governmental entities on healthcare compliance and corporate issues. His practice also assists clients with antitrust, medical reimbursement and third party payment issues.

### Garfunkel, Wild & Travis PC

**The Firm:** This renowned firm takes its place in the top tier of the tables on the strength of its excellent nationwide reputation and long-standing dedication to general healthcare law. Clients attribute its success to "*business acumen and a team of responsive lawyers who provide a good value for money service.*" These high standards mean the firm is counsel to leading hospitals in the state. According to one in-house counsel at a major New York hospital "*Garfunkel, Wild & Travis is as good as it gets when it comes to medical defense work.*"

**The Lawyers: Bob Wild** serves as the firm's chairman. Clients appreciate him for "*leadership that reflects the ethos of the practice – he is a well-rounded adviser who listens, asks pertinent questions and gives answers in a concise manner.*" He represents national and regional healthcare institutions, companies, practitioners, and nonprofit groups. His work focuses on advising healthcare providers on regulatory compliance, M&A, real estate, antitrust and reimbursements. Professional conduct and patient care issues also form a significant portion of his work. **Norton Travis** commands market respect for his healthcare corporate finance expertise. He notably represents regional and national diagnostic testing and managed care facilities in M&A and joint ventures.

### Manatt Phelps & Phillips LLP

**The Firm:** Manatt Phelps & Phillips benefits from its ties to an enviable platform of healthcare clients who value its M&A and restructurings experience. Interviewees were impressed with the firm's track record on government investigations: "*It is tops for lobbying in Albany and offers plenty of insight. The group has potent industry knowledge and takes a candid and accurate approach to healthcare regulatory matters.*" Further bolstered by a presence in Washington, DC, the practice clearly thrives in assisting healthcare entities with both federal and state compliance.

**The Lawyers: George Kalkines** receives high praise from both peers and clients. His defining quality is "*his astute and efficient handling of hospital corporate finance and restructurings.*" Hospitals, in particular, expressed gratitude for "*Kalkines' cool and thorough negotiation style.*" He is a past member of the special mayoral task group connected with the restructuring of New York City's public hospital system. **William Bernstein** is best known for advising clients in the healthcare industry on business strategy and state and federal legislation. Alongside George Kalkines, he founded Kalkines, Arky, Zall & Bernstein LLP, which merged with Manatt in January 2003.

### Nixon Peabody LLP

See firm details p.1546

**The Firm:** The firm enjoys prominence within the healthcare community. In the words of one client: "*Their lawyers are of a high caliber, charge reasonable rates and know how to get the job done without any hassle.*" Many interviewees attribute its success to partner Susan Robfogel's venerable employment-related healthcare practice, as well as the firm's established network of offices across the state.

**The Lawyers: Susan Robfogel** (see p.1480) delivers "*fantastic advice in plain English – she is very clever and knows her stuff.*" Splitting her time between the firm's Buffalo and Manhattan offices, she has a niche advising healthcare clients on labor-related collective bargaining matters. Albany-based partner **Peter Millock** (see p.1480) specializes in emerging healthcare issues, such as Health Insurance Portability and Accountability Act (HIPAA) compliance work, while also advising on general healthcare transactions, regulatory issues and lobbying work.

## Proskauer Rose LLP

See firm details p.1551

**The Firm:** Undoubtedly one of the success stories of 2004-5, Proskauer Rose is pursuing a strategy of growth in the New York healthcare market. The firm is particularly popular with hospitals involved in litigation and finance entities investing in medical and nursing home facilities. This high profile clearly results from Ed Kornreich's sterling reputation as an outstanding lead counsel. As one enthusiastic client put it: "*I have a strong regard for Proskauer Rose because of him – there are few healthcare lawyers in New York with his breadth of experience and few firms with the depth of Proskauer Rose.*"

**The Lawyers:** **Ed Kornreich** (see p.1472) is indisputably known as the "*group's driving force and a brilliant strategist.*" He is a constant presence in the front line of his team's healthcare transactions. Clients agree that "*he knows everyone in the industry, is a terrific problem solver and is always aware of new regulatory developments.*" **Richard Zall** (see p.1472) makes his debut in the healthcare rankings this year, having recently arrived from Mintz Levin Cohn Ferris Glovsky and Popeo PC. Clients report him to be "*a great draftsman who knows key regulators and has a wealth of finance experience.*" His practice centers on corporate and regulatory representation of academic medical institutions, hospitals and physician organizations. He also advises private equity funds looking to invest in medical device companies and managed care facilities.

**Clients/Work Highlights:** The firm represents a variety of entities regarding ongoing healthcare regulatory analysis and advice. These include Celgene; Mount Sinai Medical Center; Beth Israel Medical Center; New York Organ Donor Network; ImClone; Hospital for Special Surgery; Planned Parenthood Federation of America and Jewish Guild for the Blind.

## Ropes & Gray LLP

See firm details p.1117

**The Firm:** This firm is making a remarkable impact on the market, having made notable progress in *Chambers'* healthcare rankings this year. Its lawyers are "*smart, highly ethical and increasingly present in high-profile cases,*" asserted one rival. Thanks to a broad-based practice and a premium client base, this team offers a depth of resources in all areas of healthcare law.

**The Lawyers:** **Mark Barnes** (see p.1435) is renowned as "*a very solid advocate who is highly respected for his top-notch regulatory compliance skills.*" He has long-standing experience advising on government programs in the healthcare field and is especially noted for his HIPAA expertise. **Steve Warnke** (see p.1435) is admired unequivocally for his "*integrity and brains*" in advising clients on healthcare fraud compliance and investigations. He has comprehensive experience acting for clients before the New York State Legislature and state and federal regulatory agencies.

## Band 2

## Cadwalader, Wickersham & Taft LLP

See firm details p.1522

**The Firm:** The market consensus is that "*Cadwalader is always a contender for high-level healthcare advocacy and regulatory work.*" Although disputes remain at the heart of the practice, lawyers also advise on corporate, real estate, tax and restructuring-related healthcare matters. Attorneys also provide expertise on Medicare and Medicaid compliance and reimbursement issues.

**The Lawyers:** For many interviewees, **Peter Bergmann** (see p.1438) is viewed as "*a marvelous litigator who is top of the totem pole.*" He is general counsel to the New York Association of Homes and Services for the Aging, and also acts for the New York State Association of Counties on Medicaid reimbursement matters. **Frank Serbaroli** (see p.1438) is recognized as a leading luminary on healthcare law and has first-class experience of regulatory issues. He is currently serving a six-year appointment as a member of the New York State Public Health Council.

**Clients/Work Highlights:** The team is representing Elderplan, a health maintenance organization that serves senior citizens, in a dispute relating to a Medicaid contract it entered into with the City and State of New York in 1990. Another highlight includes advising Amsterdam Nursing Home in connection with the development of a new $250 million continuing care retirement community in Long Island. It is also acting for The Osborn, a continuing care retirement community in Westchester County, in a major real estate tax dispute.

## Hogan & Hartson LLP

See firm details p.568

**The Firm:** The firm continues to be recognized as a premier outfit for regulatory litigation work. Clients commend the team's "*practical and relaxed approach*" to advising on healthcare law matters, adding that "*their presence is growing on a national scale – they truly stand out in terms of exemplary service.*" Its expanding blue-chip client base includes Bristol-Myers Squibb, which it has advised on several regulatory disputes.

**The Lawyers:** **Jeff Schneider** (see p.1498) is admired by clients as "*a genuinely nice person who is always available and has great knowledge of healthcare law.*" He has acted for several long-term healthcare providers on corporate compliance issues, coverage and reimbursement matters, and the negotiation of contracts with vendors and payors.

**Clients/Work Highlights:** The group regularly assists the State University of New York with restructurings, renegotiations of hospital affiliations, and potential joint ventures. Other representative clients include AMDeC Foundation; American Board of Neurological Surgery; Blue Cross of North Carolina; Lutheran Medical Center; Patient Care Associates; Rockefeller University; Columbia University; Continuing Care Leadership Coalition; Gurwin Jewish Geriatric Center and Kinderhook Industries.

## Katten Muchin Rosenman LLP

See firm details p.874

**The Firm:** Katten Muchin Rosenman benefits from a prominent standing in the New York healthcare market. It is especially famed for its disputes work, but is also active representing healthcare institutions, academic medical centers, managed care entities and physician groups on M&A, antitrust, tax and regulatory compliance.

**The Lawyers:** **Peter Nadel** (see p.1482) is "*a very talented and successful healthcare litigation specialist who is truly making his mark.*" He received particular endorsement for his reimbursement expertise.

## McDermott Will & Emery

See firm details p.878

**The Firm:** The firm is winning praise as a national practice with a small but preeminent presence in New York. The team advises healthcare networks, hospitals, managed care institutions and physicians on the full spectrum of mainstream transactions and regulatory matters.

**The Lawyers:** **Andrew Roth** (see p.1495) is the group's charismatic figurehead. In the words of one client: "*He works very hard and is very involved in our growth. His familiarity with our business provides us with so much comfort that we would not think of going elsewhere.*" His highly commended corporate and regulatory healthcare practice also sees him advising on the accreditation of graduate medical programs.

**Clients/Work Highlights:** The team, led by Andrew Roth, notably advised Margaret Tietz Nursing and Rehabilitation Center on both an affiliation with Beth Abraham Health Services, and on the acquisition of a facility on the campus of Queens Hospital Center from the City of New York. The lawyers also advised Fidelis Care on its successful acquisition of another tax-exempt HMO, CenterCare. Other clients include Prison Health Services; Bronx-Lebanon Hospital Center; Long Beach Medical Center; Lenox Hill Hospital; Buena Vida Continuing Care and Rehabilitation Center and St Barnabas Hospital.

## Band 3

## Arent Fox PLLC

**The Firm:** Following enthusiastic endorsements from clients, Arent Fox debuts in *Chambers'* healthcare tables. The firm has prominent experience advising on corporate M&A in the healthcare industry and was involved in Integrated Health Services's $1.25 billion acquisition of Horizon Healthcare.

**The Lawyers:** Interviewees highlighted **Michael Blass** (see p.1439) as the firm leader in the area of healthcare transactions. Clients report that he "*successfully combines legal knowledge with business acumen – he does not fight to score points and remains calm and analytical under pressure.*"

## Hodgson Russ LLP

**The Firm:** The lawyers here have a forte in advising hospitals and nursing facilities on reimbursement and compliance matters. The firm is especially appreciated by sources as a leading choice thanks to partner Ellen Weissman's high-quality practice in this field.

**The Lawyers:** **Ellen Weissman** is viewed by many as *"a real pro who knows her stuff"* when it comes to healthcare regulatory matters.

## Iseman Cunningham Riester & Hyde LLP

**The Firm:** This firm is a highly respected name in Albany. In addition to its quality tax transactional practice, the group is particularly strong in the area of third party disputes. In this domain, attorneys represent both integrated delivery systems and third party payers in litigation.

**The Lawyers:** **Robert Iseman** is an established figure in the market and is highly respected for his acuity when it comes to healthcare law. He advises multiprovider healthcare systems, hospitals and health maintenance organizations in all areas of healthcare counsel, including corporate matters, risk management and provider reimbursements.

## Other Notable Practitioners

Clients distinguish **Paul Schnell** of Skadden, Arps, Slate, Meagher & Flom LLP & Affiliates as *"very meticulous, a superb draftsman and a real expert in advising on healthcare M&A."* In recent matters of note, he advised in two of the market's top healthcare transactions: AdvancePCS in its $14 billion merger with Caremark Rx, and UnitedHealth Group in connection with its acquisition of Oxford Health Plans.

# IMMIGRATION

## Immigration
### Leading Firms

1. FRAGOMEN *New York*
   KRAMER LEVIN NAFTALIS & FRANKEL *New York*
2. BARST & MUKAMAL LLP *New York*
   WILDES & WEINBERG PC *New York*
3. CYRUS D MEHTA & ASSOCIATES PLLC *New York*
   MCDERMOTT WILL & EMERY *New York*
   SATTERLEE STEPHENS BURKE & BURKE *New York*
   WORMSER, KIELY, GALEF & JACOBS LLP *New York*

### Leading Individuals

#### Senior Statesmen

FRAGOMEN JR Austin *Fragomen*
MAILMAN Stanley *Satterlee Stephens Burke*
WILDES Leon *Wildes & Weinberg PC*

1. RUTHIZER Theodore *Kramer Levin*
   YALE-LOEHR Stephen *True Walsh & Miller LLP*
2. GRUNBLATT David *Proskauer Rose LLP*
   NOTKIN Deborah *Barst & Mukamal LLP*
   PATRICK Michael *Fragomen*
   SCHORR Naomi *Kramer Levin*
3. ADLERSTEIN Jo *Brown Raysman*
   CARPENTIER Joan-Elisse *McDermott Will & Emery*
   CATILLAZ Margaret *Harter, Secrest & Emery LLP*
   CHIAPPARI Ted *Satterlee Stephens Burke*
   KOESTLER Mark *Kramer Levin*
   MEHTA Cyrus *Cyrus D Mehta*
   REICH William *Serotte, Reich & Wilson LLP*
   WANG Annie *Wormser, Kiely, Galef*

#### Up-and-coming individuals

DUNN Matthew *Kramer Levin*

## Band 1

### Fragomen, Del Rey, Bernsen & Loewy, LLP

**The Firm:** With offices across the USA, this immigration heavyweight was described by clients and peers as *"the first stop for any immigration matter."* It boasts lawyers who *"consistently produce high-quality work and have ample experience of every immigration issue under the sun."* Undeniably respected, its group of 12 partners, 35 associates and three counsel focus primarily on prime business categories such as the H-1B, E-1 and L-1 visas. Additionally, they regularly file green card applications for clients and advise on strategic ways of obtaining O visas for 'aliens of extraordinary abilities'. Recently, the team has experienced an increasing demand for advice from business visa applicants whose applications have been put on hold due to the limited numbers of visas currently made available by Congress.

**The Lawyers:** *"A lawyer who makes the law work for him,"* **Michael Patrick** received plaudits for his *"highly engaging personality and exemplary knowledge of the field."* Peers and clients asserted that they *"like to listen to what he has to say because he always manages to get to the bottom of things."* Patrick is best known for representing a large number of companies that are subject to government audits and investigations, and he is frequently invited to speak on immigration topics before Bar associations, international trade organizations and human rights NGOs. **Austin Fragomen** *"has been in the immigration market since day one."* Credited with having been able to foresee the large demand that would one day be created in the USA for immigration law, he is praised for his *"fantastic business acumen and far-seeing outlook."* Among his main achievements is the implementation of an increasingly global strategy that has seen a large number of international clients flock to the practice in recent years.

**Clients/Work Highlights:** The firm acts for large corporates drawn from a broad range of industries and is noted for its niche practice in sports franchises where it regularly advises individual athletes and sports teams on obtaining P visas, which are designed for entertainers and athletes. Another specialty of the practice is the representation of scholars and academics in their visa applications. It also received acclaim for its global immigration services division, established in 1991. This provides information and guidance to clients on global work authorization procedures and policies, in order to ensure compliance with local regulations worldwide.

### Kramer Levin Naftalis & Frankel LLP
See firm details p.1539

**The Firm:** Clients and peers were unanimous in their praise for this New York City-based, full-service group, ranking it *"firmly among the elite of all immigration firms."* The team's *"high ethical standards"* found particular favor among interviewees, who pointed to its *"impeccable record"* in obtaining business visas for its clients. With a team of six full-time lawyers, of whom two are partners, it handles the entire range of immigration visa petitions, ranging from H-1B and L-1 visas to O visas and J-1 visas. In line with its success rate in processing business visas, the team has also handled subsequent green card applications for its clients. Recently, due to the federal backlog in processing business immigration petitions, the team has advised an increasing number of applicants on obtaining O-1 visas and J-1 visas.

**The Lawyers:** *"Wonderful lawyer"* **Ted Ruthizer** (see p.1495) received overwhelming praise from interviewees, who commended him for being *"fantastically speedy, responsive and incredibly knowledgeable."* *"Taking it all in his stride,"* he boasts *"high energy levels"* and is also a respected professor of immigration law at Columbia Law School. Ruthizer specializes in every aspect of immigration law and has recently handled a disproportionately high amount of O-1 visas. *"Driving force"* **Naomi Schorr** (see p.1498) was emphatically endorsed for her *"careful and deep thinking, qualities that allow her to approach issues with a lot of insight."* Market sources also commented on the *"first-rate attention she gives to clients"* and her *"outstanding articles on the law, with which she continues to dazzle the world of immigration law."* As special counsel at the firm, she principally advises multinational organizations and frequently speaks on immigration matters at regional and national conferences. The *"highly knowledgeable and dynamic"* **Mark Koestler** (see p.1471) is popular among clients and peers for his skill in handling immigration matters in the areas of advertising, theater and film. Clients said that up-and-comer **Matt Dunn** (see p.1450) "*knows exactly what he is talking about.*"

**Clients/Work Highlights:** The team has a niche practice advising Canadian, Mexican and Singaporean citizens who all have special preference for business visas due to free trade agreements entered into with the USA. In addition to representing employers with regard to business visa applications for their employees, the lawyers also represent clients at all stages of administrative proceedings, including at appellate level and in immigration-related federal court litigation. Additionally, attorneys advise clients from the entertainment industry and regularly advise individuals from the medical profession.

## Band 2

### Barst & Mukamal LLP

**The Firm:** Interviewees portrayed the firm as "*one of the most established and renowned practices around.*" In existence since the mid-1930's, it boasts a particularly strong Chinese clientele. Offering the full range of business visas, the team regularly advises clients ranging from multinational executives to researchers and scientists, treaty investors, NAFTA professionals, as well as fashion models, artists and entertainers. In this respect, lawyers regularly file applications for L-1, H-1B, E-1, TN and O visas. Additionally, they obtain visas for spouses or other family members of applicants who have been granted business visas. Increasingly, the firm also advises Australian citizens on obtaining E-3 visas for certain professional occupations, under a category recently approved by Congress.

**The Lawyers:** Regarded as a well-respected name in the field, **Deborah Notkin** was elected to the position of national president of the American Immigration Lawyers Association for 2005-6, a development that is likely to further raise the profile of the firm. Described as "*a terrific lawyer who comes across as forceful, dynamic and on top of it all, and knows her stuff inside-out,*" she regularly advises clients on a broad range of visa options.

### Wildes & Weinberg PC

**The Firm:** This New York City-based firm is a bastion of immigration law in the state. Known for its "*involvement in some of the most spectacular cases one can think of in the field,*" this power player first opened its doors in 1960 when it was founded by name partner Leon Wildes. Originally launched as a practice that focused on obtaining immigration visas for individuals rather than corporations, it has steadily expanded the range of its services to cater to the needs of large and midsized companies. It now offers advice on H-1B, L, O and E visa categories, for example. Additionally, the lawyers regularly file labor certificates for their clients, a complex procedure that typically involves a prolonged wait. The firm boasts 11 attorneys who all have expertise in a range of aspects of immigration law, with several professionals having significant experience representing enter-

tainers and people from the world of show business. **The Lawyers:** Boasting "*a formidable reputation that is hard to beat,*" the legendary **Leon Wildes** is still involved in a wide range of both family and business-related immigration petitions, but probably remains best known for his representation of John Lennon and Yoko Ono in the 1960's, when he successfully secured permanent residence for both despite much controversy.

## Band 3

### Cyrus D Mehta & Associates PLLC

**The Firm:** Described as a practice that "*consistently manages to do a tremendous job,*" this New York City-based boutique is also known as "*an interesting, relative newcomer in the field.*" Praised for having lawyers who are "*very prompt and considerate in their responses,*" the firm has had an active year representing clients in their petitions for business visas. Due to the current cap imposed on H-1B visas, the firm has been regularly advising clients on temporary visa options. It has also worked intensively on several applications for labor certificates. A large proportion of the work consists of drafting and filing L visas for intracompany managers and executives and, increasingly, the lawyers are also concentrating on advising their clients on O visas for people of extraordinary merit. The one-partner, three-associate firm also regularly handles pro bono work such as applications for asylum.

**The Lawyers:** The "*highly professional*" **Cyrus Mehta** drew applause from clients who praised his "*ability to turn around cases in the span of 48 hours.*" Also described as "*precise and strategic in his advice,*" he is considered "*an expert at consulate matters and at dealing with the relevant authorities.*" A frequent speaker at immigration seminars, Mehta was further applauded for his "*ability to always keep abreast of the latest developments in the field.*"

### McDermott Will & Emery

See firm details p.878

**The Firm:** The compact immigration department at this international full-service firm advises clients on a range of business visa options, from the classical categories such as the H, E and L visas, to the relatively novel O and E visas. The one-partner team operating out of New York City prides itself on attracting a range of clients from the entertainment industry, but also has a successful track record obtaining visas for students in US universities under the D category. It boasts long-standing relationships with government entities.

**The Lawyers:** The "*extremely knowledgeable, fast and accurate*" **Joan-Elisse Carpentier** (see p.1443) heads the New York City immigration department of the firm. "*Always up to date with the knowledge of the law and informative on all occasions,*" she typically advises large corporates and is fast accumulating a vibrant entertainment clientele.

### Satterlee Stephens Burke & Burke LLP

**The Firm:** Known as an "*outstanding firm,*" this traditional immigration powerhouse has a long-standing reputation for offering clients temporary work-based visas, and for successfully securing permanent residence for many of its clients. Additionally, the lawyers frequently advise Canadian and Mexican citizens on visa options under NAFTA. The lawyers here are also expert in securing entertainment and arts-based visas, and further advise clients on health-related visas, having acquired extensive experience acting for hospitals and their staff.

**The Lawyers:** Known as "*the dean of immigration law and an ace among lawyers,*" **Stanley Mailman** has been one of the foremost authorities of US immigration law for the past few decades. A highly respected scholar and prolific writer, he coauthored the most authoritative immigration treatise to date and is also a regular contributor to the New York Law Journal. He received emphatic praise from peers and clients in equal measure for his "*sharp, thoughtful and highly ethical approach to any case he touches.*" Described as "*very astute and efficient in his dealings,*" **Ted Chiappari** has a "*formidable knowledge of international taxation.*" He focuses on counseling companies in their attempts to obtain temporary work visas for their employees, and regularly advises on the tax aspects of the international transfer of personnel.

### Wormser, Kiely, Galef & Jacobs LLP

**The Firm:** The immigration practice of this New York City-based firm is a "*smooth-running operation.*" The team advises clients from a range of industries, including the restaurant and hospitality sector, the entertainment community, foreign investors and athletes, on all aspects of their business-based visas. It also counsels law firms, the financial industry and journalists on all their immigration needs. In addition, lawyers provide regular advice to individuals petitioning for family-based visas and permanent residence in the USA.

**The Lawyers:** Praised for having "*a high level of integrity and impeccable ethical standards,*" **Annie Wang** was also described "*as a joy to work with*" by interviewees. She is known for providing clients with "*careful, well thought-out advice*" and boasts a large clientele in the financial industry.

### Other Notable Practitioners

The "*absolutely brilliant*" **Stephen Yale-Loehr** of Ithaca-based boutique True Walsh & Miller LLP could not receive high enough praise from enthusiastic commentators. They expressed "*complete admiration for his formidable intellect, his outstanding academic track record*" and the "*fantastic advocacy skills that he regularly employs on behalf of his clients.*" Known as "*the man in the state for all immigration matters,*" peers also described him as "*a great asset to the Bar.*" Described as "*a terrific lawyer who drives the work forward and gets the case done,*" **David Grunblatt** was emphatically endorsed by peers and clients. He has recently relocated from the firm that bore his name, Wildes & Weinberg, to Proskauer Rose LLP in

Newark, where it is assured his *"incredible insider knowledge of the field"* will continue to impress. Hailed as *"a first-rate lawyer, especially in complex situations,"* **Jo Anne Adlerstein** (see p.1432) of New York City-based Brown Raysman Millstein Felder & Steiner LLP enjoys a long-standing following among medical professionals in particular. She frequently advises clients on obtaining J-1 visas for exchange

visitors and on their subsequent H-1B options. Additionally, she regularly advises clients on E and L-1 visas, and provides expertise on green card applications. **Margaret Catillaz** of the Rochester-based firm Harter, Secrest & Emery LLP was praised for her *"rock solid knowledge of immigration law"* and for her work acting as president of the American Immigration Association. In addition to handling the whole

gamut of business visa applications, she also counts a substantial number of medical personnel among her clients, regularly obtaining J-1 visas for them. **Bill Reich**, of Buffalo-based firm Serotte, Reich & Wilson LLP, was recommended for his *"outstanding"* border control immigration work.

# INSURANCE

## Insurance: Dispute Resolution
### Leading Firms

1. **ANDERSON KILL & OLICK P.C.** *New York*
   **LEBOEUF, LAMB, GREENE & MACRAE** *New York*
   **SIMPSON THACHER & BARTLETT LLP** *New York*
2. **CADWALADER, WICKERSHAM & TAFT LLP** *New York*
   **CLIFFORD CHANCE US LLP** *New York*
   **PROSKAUER ROSE LLP** *New York*
   **STROOCK & STROOCK & LAVAN LLP** *New York*
3. **CAHILL GORDON & REINDEL LLP** *New York*
   **DEBEVOISE & PLIMPTON LLP** *New York*
   **DEWEY BALLANTINE LLP** *New York*
   **MOUND COTTON WOLLAN & GREENGRASS** *New York*
   **SKADDEN, ARPS** *New York*
   **SONNENSCHEIN NATH & ROSENTHAL** *New York*
4. **DICKSTEIN SHAPIRO MORIN & OSHINSKY** *New York*
   **DUANE MORRIS LLP** *New York*
   **EDWARDS ANGELL PALMER & DODGE** *New York*
   **MENDES & MOUNT LLP** *New York*
   **SULLIVAN & CROMWELL LLP** *New York*
   **WACHTELL, LIPTON, ROSEN & KATZ** *New York*
   **WILLKIE FARR & GALLAGHER LLP** *New York*
   **WILSON, ELSER** *New York*

## Anderson Kill & Olick P.C.
See firm details p.1517

**The Firm:** This insurance litigation heavyweight is a leading choice for policyholders. Clients hail it as *"one of the best firms out there for policyholders, as the lawyers achieve results without the fuss. They are tenacious and dedicated."* Andersen Kill & Olick's success as a national practice was particularly on display in the past year as it enjoyed leading roles in prominent insurance disputes. In a major victory for policyholders, the firm successfully represented Times-Picayune Publishing in the Fifth Circuit Court of Appeals. In this case, the company won entitlement to recover the entire amount of long-term embezzlement losses against the excess insurer Swiss Re.

**The Lawyers:** Firm founder **Gene Anderson** is widely acknowledged as *"a pioneer in policy dispute work and a senior statesman of the field."* According to peers: *"Gene is a role model to the policyholder dispute resolution community."* Clients are delighted with **Bob Horkovich** who is recognized as *"a litigator who truly believes in what he does and knows how to lead a legal team to victory."* He recently won a landmark verdict for the State of California against

CNA, Wausau, Yosemite, Horace Mann (ACE) and Stonebridge Life Insurance in relation to coverage for the cleanup of the Stringfellow Acid Pits. New entrant **William Passannante** was described by clients as *"a tremendous tactician and an incredible trial lawyer."*

## LeBoeuf, Lamb, Greene & MacRae LLP
See firm details p.1540

**The Firm:** Clients and peers unequivocally hailed this firm as *"the premier regulatory practice in the country."* In the words of one in-house counsel: *"It is the practice of choice as a result of its team of highly responsive lawyers who cover the full gamut of insurance transactions and disputes – it is a juggernaut of the insurance world."* The firm's strength and depth were also affirmed as reasons behind its success: *"What I like about LeBoeuf is that it has appropriate practitioners who can handle anything from run of the mill matters to more complex insurance M&A and securitizations."* The practice has advised on the crème de la crème of insurance transactions, notably acting for MetLife in its $11.8 billion acquisition of Travelers Life and Annuity from Citigroup.

**The Lawyers:** Clients describe **Alexander Dye** (see p.1434) as *"a lawyer to have on a dream team of top insurance counsel thanks to his sheer brain power."* He is perceived as being *"very much in demand"* for his extensive M&A insurance expertise, handling hostile and negotiated takeovers, sponsored demutualizations, and asset sales structured as reinsurance transactions. **Michael Groll** (see p.1434) is *"really superb at understanding insurance finance and has had a brilliant year."* He advised St. Paul on the merger with Travelers. **Donald Henderson** (see p.1434) is widely admired as *"one of the finest insurance and reinsurance specialists around."* He advised AEGON USA on its acquisitions of Transamerica and Providian. **Scott Avitabile** (see p.1434) *"combines the right mix of insurance regulatory acumen with finance know-how – he is the embodiment of the LeBoeuf ethos."* **Jane Boisseau** (see p.1434) is highly esteemed by clients as *"great value for money – she is one smart cookie when it comes to finance and regulatory issues."* Her contribution to the practice includes advising on some of the firm's most prominent capital markets and M&A insurance transactions. **Stephen Rooney** (see p.1434) is another new entry to the tables. Clients and peers concur that he is among the *"leading names for insurance regulatory compliance – he is*

*really great at negotiating corporate finance insurance deals and knows all the regulators."* **John Schwolsky** (see p.1434) achieves market recognition as *"an innovative thinker who is clearly loved by his clients."* His practice revolves around advising insurance carriers on securities offerings and recapitalizations, and representing insurance issuers and underwriters in IPOs of financial service companies. **Cynthia Shoss** (see p.1434) focuses her practice on regulatory matters relating to demutualizations, mergers, conversions and other restructurings and acquisitions of insurance companies. The firm's market-leading profile in insurance disputes is closely tied to that of **John Nonna** (see p.1434) who received widespread praise from clients. According to one in-house counsel: *"John is invaluable to me as a strategist and I would follow him anywhere. His technical expertise is unparalleled and he leads us straight to the solution without having to write a book about it. He truly makes our business goals happen."* Another client enthused: *"He is such a fabulous trial lawyer because of his tenacious yet effective style."* **Larry Schiffer** (see p.1434) is *"super when it comes to defending clients in tricky insurance and reinsurance disputes."*

**Clients/Work Highlights:** The team's highlights include acting for Lincoln National regarding its $7.5 million merger with Jefferson-Pilot, and advising Hillenbrand Industries on the $280 million sale of its subsidiary, Forethought Financial Services, to FFS Holdings. Other clients include Allstate; Aspen; AXA; Fidelity National Financial; Genworth; General Re; Liberty Mutual Insurance; Nationwide Insurance; New York Life; Prudential Financial and Sun Life of Canada.

## Simpson Thacher & Bartlett LLP
See firm details p.1555

**The Firm:** The firm is a *"class act"* that stands out, first and foremost, for its insurance dispute resolution track record and corporate finance breadth. In the opinion of clients: *"Simpson Thacher is one of the leading firms, providing an amazing level of service from partner to associate level. It has marvelously talented lawyers."* Amply illustrating this fact, it has an enviable client base of leading global insurance groups such as AIG and St. Paul Travelers. Its luster has been further enhanced thanks to its landmark victory for key client Swiss Re in the multibillion-dollar World Trade Center insurance litigation case.

**The Lawyers:** **Barry Ostrager** (see p.1433) is *"one of the top insurance litigators in the country. He is very*

*smart, tactical in approach and very results-oriented for his clients.*" Peers would "*refer work to him, anytime*" and admire his "*ability to get along with both opponents and judges.*" There was also widespread praise for **Mary Kay Vyskocil** (see p.1433) who was described as "*on the ball and leaving no stone unturned when it comes to convincing a jury in a courtroom.*" Her partner, **Andrew Amer** (see p.1433), received enthusiastic compliments from interviewees. "*He continues to grow in prominence*" and acts for insurers in several direct insurance coverage actions involving asbestos, pollution and other mass tort claims. **Gary Horowitz** (see p.1433) is a new entry to the transactional and regulatory tables. He is reported to be "*very visible in transactions*" and "*superb at getting to the heart of the matter in order to clarify the consequences for business.*"
Clients/Work Highlights: Indicative of the firm's strength in private equity-related insurance work, Gary Horowitz notably advised KKR in connection with its acquisition of Rhine Reinsurance and its purchase of stock and assets of Bristol West Insurance Group. On the litigation front, Barry Ostrager led the team in successfully representing JPMorgan Chase in obtaining a $370 million positive verdict in a guarantee contract action against Motorola. Other clients include AXA; CNA Financial; Genworth Financial and Hannover Re.

## Cadwalader, Wickersham & Taft LLP

See firm details p.1522
The Firm: Cadwalader, Wickersham & Taft has lawyers working on the most prominent national trials and boasts a reputation for fielding high-quality trial attorneys in the mold of Dennis Block. Its strong position in reinsurance disputes owes much to its talent pool of premium specialists in the field. In the opinion of many, "*this group is hugely admired for its tough yet effective style in convincing umpires, judges and juries.*"
The Lawyers: Group leader **Larry Brandes** (see p.1440) has put this practice on the reinsurance industry radar. "*I like Cadwalader's team because of Larry, who can really outperform his opponents in a dispute proceeding,*" opined one enthusiastic in-house counsel at a large insurance company. His experience as a reinsurance litigator includes acting as counsel and arbitrator in several reinsurance arbitrations and litigations. **Cliff Schoenberg** (see p.1440) is also held in esteem for his insurance disputes practice. He led the team in representing Sompo Japan in obtaining a $1 billion compensatory damage award and a $100 million punitive damage award in arbitration against Fortress Re. **Harry Cohen** (see p.1440) is admired as "*a Brandes protégé*" who is increasingly making his mark in reinsurance litigations and arbitration. Joining him as a new entry in the tables is **Ken Pierce** (see p.1440). Clients acclaim him for a diverse practice that consists of insurance and reinsurance dispute experience and transactions. He has particular knowledge of structuring capital markets and corporate finance deals.
Clients/Work Highlights: Lawyers advised an English global trading company in RICO litigation against the president of its US subsidiary for losses connected to insurance frauds relating to the theft and disappearance of $50 million in gold. The team also assists Allstate, XL America, Transamerica Reinsurance and Trenwick America Reinsurance.

## Clifford Chance US LLP

See firm details p.1526
The Firm: "*Clifford Chance's insurance practice is growing in stature,*" said sources. Clients attribute its New York success to "*superior value for money service, high standards of professionalism and a meticulous approach to insurance and reinsurance matters.*" The firm displays particular vitality in reinsurance disputes and can rely upon a sizable international network of excellent insurance and reinsurance lawyers.
The Lawyers: Commentators acclaim **Paul Meyer**'s "*common-sense approach*" to insurance transactions. His practice is active in advising insurance companies on investments and regulatory issues. **Nick Williams**' move to Clifford Chance from White & Case was hailed as a veritable coup for the firm. He has already enhanced the team's activity in life settlement transactions, insurance-linked securities and Triple X-related financial guarantee transactions. **Peter Chaffetz** is the global head of the firm's litigation practice. He received plaudits for his "*tactfulness and commercial acuity*" in arriving at solutions to disputes. His partner **Steve Schwartz** is involved in representing insurance and reinsurance companies in property, casualty, life and health insurance matters, and reinsurance insolvency matters.
Clients/Work Highlights: The team represented Swiss Re in the Crystal Credit insurance-linked securities transaction, and AMBAC in the Banner Life Triple X transaction, a matter that involved contingent capital security and financial guarantee insurance. The team also represents AIG; Deutsche Bank; Merrill Lynch; Nomura Securities; UBS; IXIS Asset Management; BNP Paribas; Centre Reinsurance and New York Life.

## Proskauer Rose LLP

See firm details p.1551
The Firm: "*Proskauer Rose is the best of the best when it comes to representing policyholders in disputes,*" confirm market observers. The practice's strong suit is in insurance coverage work and the lawyers notably acted as trial counsel to Silverstein Properties in its 9/11 multibillion-dollar property damage claim.
The Lawyers: **John Gross** (see p.1462) is regularly cited by clients and rivals as "*a premier insurance litigator who knows everyone in the industry.*" He is a civil trial specialist who reaps rich rewards for the clients from his insurance coverage claims successes.
Clients/Work Highlights: A Fortune 500 client base characterizes the firm. It notably acts for JPMorgan Chase and Lucent Technologies in significant policyholder insurance coverage claims disputes. Other key clients of the group include AT&T; Bear Stearns; Brunswick; Champion; DuPont; Georgia-Pacific; Home Depot and Omnicom.

## Stroock & Stroock & Lavan LLP

The Firm: The firm is at the forefront of the insurance market in the opinion of many clients. It has successfully pursued a strategy of growth and an increased focus on quality, and provides "*good service and dynamic people who are well connected in the insurance industry.*" Insurance carriers are particularly impressed by how attorneys "*are always timely and their fees are always reasonable.*" Many interviewees also attribute the firm's success to partner William Rosenblatt's arrival from Dewey Ballantine.
The Lawyers: Clients and peers agree that **William Rosenblatt** is developing a "*rock solid transactional team at Stroock.*" Sources paint a compelling picture of Rosenblatt's talent: "*He is very practical and has the business acumen and wealth of finance experience to back him up.*" Complementing him on the regulatory side is his "*highly esteemed*" partner, **Donald Gabay**. He leads the firm's insurance group and is a seasoned

## Insurance: Transactional & Regulatory
### Leading Firms

1 **DEBEVOISE & PLIMPTON LLP** *New York*
  **DEWEY BALLANTINE LLP** *New York*
  **LEBOEUF, LAMB, GREENE & MACRAE** *New York*
  **STROOCK & STROOCK & LAVAN LLP** *New York*

2 **SIMPSON THACHER & BARTLETT LLP** *New York*
  **SKADDEN, ARPS** *New York*
  **SULLIVAN & CROMWELL LLP** *New York*

3 **CLIFFORD CHANCE US LLP** *New York*
  **EDWARDS ANGELL PALMER & DODGE LLP** *New York*
  **FRIED, FRANK** *New York*
  **LOVELLS** *New York*
  **MOUND COTTON WOLLAN & GREENGRASS** *New York*
  **WACHTELL, LIPTON, ROSEN & KATZ** *New York*
  **WILLKIE FARR & GALLAGHER LLP** *New York*

### Leading Individuals

★ **DUNHAM JR** Wolcott *Debevoise & Plimpton LLP*

1 **DYE** Alexander *LeBoeuf, Lamb*
  **LIEBMANN** Jeff *Dewey Ballantine LLP*
  **ROSENBLATT** William *Stroock*
  **SULLIVAN** Robert *Skadden, Arps*

2 **COTTON** Stuart *Mound Cotton*
  **GABAY** Donald *Stroock*
  **GROLL** Michael *LeBoeuf, Lamb*
  **HENDERSON JR** Donald *LeBoeuf, Lamb*
  **KELLY** Thomas *Debevoise & Plimpton LLP*
  **POTTER** Nicholas *Debevoise & Plimpton LLP*
  **ROWEN** Andrew *Sullivan & Cromwell LLP*

3 **ALBERTS** David *Lovells*
  **AVITABILE** Scott *LeBoeuf, Lamb*
  **BOISSEAU** Jane *LeBoeuf, Lamb*
  **FITZPATRICK JR** James *Dewey Ballantine LLP*
  **FREEDMAN** Jonathan *Dewey Ballantine LLP*
  **GREENGRASS** Lawrence *Mound Cotton*
  **HERZECA** Lois *Fried, Frank*
  **HOROWITZ** Gary *Simpson Thacher & Bartlett*
  **LATZA** William *Stroock*
  **MEYER** Paul *Clifford Chance US LLP*
  **PEARSON** Nick *Edwards Angell Palmer*
  **ROONEY** Stephen *LeBoeuf, Lamb*
  **SARCHIO** John *Chadbourne & Parke LLP*
  **SCHWOLSKY** John *LeBoeuf, Lamb*
  **SHOSS** Cynthia *LeBoeuf, Lamb*
  **SUTHERLAND** Susan *Skadden, Arps*
  **WILLIAMS** Nicholas *Clifford Chance US LLP*

player in the New York insurance scene. **Bill Latza** is highly regarded as *"a first-class regulatory specialist."* The team is rounded off by insurance dispute resolution specialists **Michele Jacobson** and **Robert Lewin**. They won client recognition for being *"very thorough and quick to identify the Achilles heels of their foes in the courtroom."* The duo notably represented Continental Casualty in a dispute brought against certain underwriters of Lloyd's in the US District Court.

**Clients/Work Highlights:** Recent successes include advising MBIA as the financial guarantor of the River Lake structured finance Triple X transaction, and representing Health Insurance Plan of Greater New York in its proposed merger with Group Health Insurance. Other clients include Arch Insurance; Financial Guaranty Insurance; Goldman Sachs; CNA Financial; Royal & SunAlliance; Zurich Financial Services and Lehman Brothers.

### Cahill Gordon & Reindel LLP

**The Firm:** This well-established name is a consistent presence in the most prominent insurance disputes, inevitably making it *"a leading choice for counsel."* Interviewees attribute its success to a highly enviable roster of clients that includes leading insurance provider AIG and the exceptional dispute resolution talents of Ed Krugman.

**The Lawyers:** **Ed Krugman** is viewed as *"a top referral because he is so capable and has a lot of integrity,"* according to competitors. Clients praise him as *"thoughtful and creative in his approach to preparing for trials."*

### Debevoise & Plimpton LLP

See firm details p.1529

**The Firm:** This New York blue blood maintains a long-standing tradition of acting for insurance and reinsurance companies, and fields a *"fantastic team of knowledgeable, responsive and pragmatic lawyers."* Clients particularly acclaim a *"strength and depth that comes from being a practice staffed with outstanding M&A and capital markets experts who have close ties to state and federal insurance regulators."* Although strong on transactional and regulatory matters, the lawyers here have also acted as lead counsel for insurers in many of the industry's most complex disputes. These include asbestos and environmental claims, and New York attorney general and SEC investigations.

**The Lawyers:** Clients regard **Wolcott Dunham** as *"a wonderful lawyer with sterling finance insight who is just extraordinary on regulatory matters."* He wins special recognition for his *"stellar technical expertise"* and *"calm, cool and collected demeanor"* when structuring big-ticket M&A insurance transactions. In this context, he notably assisted the team in representing AXA Financial in its $1.5 billion acquisition of MONY Group. **Thomas Kelly** is *"a talented negotiator"* advising insurance companies on a full range of capital markets and M&A transactions. His areas of particular interest include IPOs and demutualizations. Key highlights include advising Principal Financial Group on its $550 million offering of noncumulative perpetual preferred stock. **Nicholas Potter** received glowing praise from interviewees for his *"terrific aplomb"* when handling corporate finance-related insurance transactions. Peers consider him *"great at getting deals done because he always applies logic without the histrionics and never raises his voice."* **Robert Goodman** makes his debut in the insurance dispute rankings this year. Clients characterize him as *"bright and hard-working with great analytical abilities."* He leads the team acting for St. Paul Travelers and several commercial liability insurers in negotiations surrounding proposed federal legislation aimed at the establishment of a $140 billion national asbestos trust fund.

**Clients/Work Highlights:** The team advised Swiss Re subsidiary, Reassure America Life Insurance, in securitizing its future profits from a portfolio of US life insurance companies acquired through its M&A activities. It further acted for Stone Point Capital on the $1.5 billion capital formation of Harbor Point, a global reinsurance company based in Bermuda. In another significant highlight, lawyers advised private equity fund, JC Flowers, on its acquisition from Marsh of its wholesale broking operation, Crump Group. The team's impressive client roster also includes ACE; Allstate; Hartford Group; MetLife; OPIC; Prudential Financial and Zurich.

### Dewey Ballantine LLP

See firm details p.1530

**The Firm:** *"Dewey Ballantine provides consistent quality in both insurance litigation and transactions. Lawyers are really savvy and work in a truly collaborative style with in-house counsel – you can really trust their judgment."* So said one in-house counsel at a major insurance carrier. As another client noted: *"The team consists of practitioners who really know the insurance business, have a terrific rapport with regulators and are adept at advising on both federal and state regulations."* The firm's popularity is no doubt connected to its *"superlative track record"* in M&A and capital markets work, as well as reinsurance arbitrations.

**The Lawyers:** The *"intelligent and resourceful"* **Jeff Liebmann** (see p.1452) is famed for his prominence in insurance transactions. He regularly advises MetLife on M&A, restructurings and securitizations. **James FitzPatrick** (see p.1452) is global chairman of the firm's corporate group and acts for several leading insurance carriers on M&A and regulatory matters. New entrant to the tables **Jonathan Freedman** (see p.1452) wins widespread acclaim in insurance circles as an *"emerging talent"* on corporate finance deals. Clients endorse dispute specialist **David Grais** (see p.1452) as *"very well versed in reinsurance law and a highly effective advocate, as he is levelheaded and presents issues in a precise manner."* He notably represents Royal & SunAlliance on several reinsurance arbitrations. **Harvey Kurzweil** (see p.1452) cochairs the firm's litigation group, and wins peer recognition as *"a smart thinker who is quick on his feet."* He is the lead counsel for MONY Group in a class action involving the alleged marketing of vanishing premium life insurance policies. Clients describe **Kathryn Ellsworth** (see p.1452) as *"a bright spark who can really liven up a courtroom."* She specializes in insurance and reinsurance arbitrations and litigations and is currently representing American Re in a $1 billion asbestos liabilities dispute.

**Clients/Work Highlights:** The firm represented CNA Financial in the sale of its block of specialty group medical and dental insurance businesses to Aetna. Other highlights include advising Platinum Underwriters Holdings and its subsidiaries in a series of capital markets-related transactions. The group also acts for Beazley Group; Scottish Re (Dublin); Scottish Annuity & Life Insurance (Cayman); Scottish Re (USA) and Trenwick Group.

## Mound Cotton Wollan & Greengrass

See firm details p.1545

**The Firm:** The *"very effective"* Mound Cotton Wollan & Greengrass advises on all areas of insurance and reinsurance law. It also has a historic presence in dispute resolution, with an impressive track record in the defense of first and third-party insurance claims. One client described it as *"a truly specialist outfit with high-caliber expertise in insurance regulatory matters."*

**The Lawyers:** Clients and peers endorse **Stuart Cotton** (see p.1447) as *"a talented insurance defense litigator"* with long-established experience in this field. He is especially noted for his work in relation to the World Trade Center. **Larry Greengrass** (see p.1447) is also a respected insurance dispute specialist with an important niche in reinsurance matters.

## Skadden, Arps, Slate, Meagher & Flom LLP & Affiliates

See firm details p.1557

**The Firm:** Skadden Arps is *"in a league of its own among M&A and litigation powerhouses in New York,"* commented one client, echoing the opinion of many interviewees. There was a similar consensus over the reasons for the firm's robustness in insurance transactions and litigation. *"Lawyers understand the unique regulatory framework of insurance finance and can fight your corner when it comes to corporate and coverage disputes. The team provides reliable and clear advice, and truly believes in building close relationships with clients."*

**The Lawyers:** In insurance transactions, the driving force of the practice is **Bob Sullivan** (see p.1439). He impresses clients with his *"unbelievable familiarity of insurance and reinsurance regulatory matters."* In the view of one in-house counsel: *"He knows his stuff and delivers the information in a style that business people can understand."* He acts for insurance and reinsurance companies and their financial advisers and underwriters in a variety of M&A, public and private financings and restructurings. Joining him in the tables is capital markets insurance specialist **Susan Sutherland** (see p.1439). Clients recommended her as *"wonderful for insurance finance compliance issues. She truly probes, asks the right questions and will outline the pros and cons without getting too technical."* She represents issuers and underwriters in a diversity of public offerings and private placements of debt and equity securities. **Sheila Birnbaum** (see p.1439) is regarded as *"a dynamic presence"* on mass torts and complex insurance coverage disputes. She successfully acted for State Farm when the US Supreme Court reversed a $145 million punitive damages award against the company on the grounds that it was unconstitutionally excessive. **Tim Reynolds** (see p.1439) focuses on insurance and reinsurance coverage litigation and arbitration. His practice has been active advising clients in matters involving innovative alternative risk transfer and finite risk insurance products.

**Clients/Work Highlights:** The team represented Travelers Life and Annuity, a subsidiary of Citigroup, in its $11.5 million sale to MetLife. Other notable deals include advising PacifiCare Health Systems on its $8.1 million sale to UnitedHealth Group, and acting for financial adviser Lazard Frères in the $7.5 million Lincoln National merger with Jefferson-Pilot. The group also assists Skandia Insurance, St. Paul Travelers and JPMorgan Chase.

## Sonnenschein Nath & Rosenthal LLP

See firm details p.884

**The Firm:** The firm enjoys superb growth and is winning acclaim for its coverage-related insurance disputes work. Lawyers do *"a phenomenal job for clients in achieving courtroom victories,"* asserted one in-house counsel at a major insurance carrier. The firm appears in high-profile cases across the country and has successfully defended Prudential Financial in a series of class actions.

**The Lawyers:** Clients sing the praises of **Reid Ashinoff** (see p.1434) for *"combining brains and tenacity and being concise and articulate in presenting his arguments to a judge and jury."* He chairs the firm's New York office litigation department and has represented Swiss Re America in a significant reinsurance dispute with a financial institution claiming more than $400 million in damages. **Michael Barr** (see p.1434) is in demand for his *"primo advocacy skills and sharp mind – he is a real pro to see in action."* He is acting for Royal & SunAlliance in the World Trade Center property coverage litigation, having obtained summary judgment for the company on a significant portion of its coverage. In addition, he serves as national coordinating counsel for Royal & SunAlliance in defending a series of class actions relating to retrospective premium workers' compensation issues.

**Clients/Work Highlights:** The firm also represents Allstate, GE and Freeman Fund.

## Dickstein Shapiro Morin & Oshinsky LLP

See firm details p.565

**The Firm:** *"The insurance disputes practice is really taking off on a national level."* Much of the practice's accolades in New York are linked to the considerable domestic and international alternative dispute resolution talents of lead partner Richard Fields, who was previously based in the firm's Washington, DC office.

**The Lawyers:** **Richard Fields** (see p.1454) is widely revered as *"a leading light on complex insurance disputes."* He additionally benefits from an extensive international practice that spans products liability, professional indemnity, environmental, asbestos, and insurance matters. His coverage client base numbers Amtrak, GM and CSFB, among others. Clients also value **Robin Cohen**'s (see p.1446) technical skills and her high service levels. She *"can be aggressive in litigation but is always strategic and very thorough in her approach – she is someone you can trust for the truly large matters."*

## Duane Morris LLP

See firm details p.1753

**The Firm:** Duane Morris is emerging as a leading contender for high-level insurance disputes work as its lawyers are regularly involved in leading national and international liability claims. The group is also distinguished for its insurance and reinsurance arbitrations work thanks to the outstanding reputation of Tom Newman in this field.

**The Lawyers:** **Joseph Monteleone** (see p.1480) makes a first-time appearance in the rankings. Insurance companies commend him for *"successfully combining legal wisdom with business practicality."* **Tom Newman** (see p.1480) is rated as *"top of the heap"* when it comes to his performance on reinsurance arbitrations. He is frequently called upon as an expert witness in insurance cases in the USA and the UK.

## Edwards Angell Palmer & Dodge LLP

See firm details p.1112

**The Firm:** The firm has had a successful year both in reinsurance disputes and general insurance transactions and regulatory matters. Its lawyers are *"well connected and have excellent reputations,"* confirmed interviewees. A growing roster of US and international insurance carriers are increasingly turning to the firm for significant insurance and reinsurance work.

**The Lawyers:** **Nick Pearson** (see p.1487) is perceived as the driver of the insurance regulatory and transactional practice. His practice emphasizes reinsurance agreements, fraud investigations, insolvency and surplus line issues. **James Shanman** (see p.1500) is an impressive new entrant to the tables. He is distinguished by clients as *"user-friendly"* and *"very knowledgeable about the insurance industry."* Shanman splits his time between the firm's New York and Connecticut offices. His dispute resolution practice is centered on property and casualty and life and health insurance litigation. **Vince Vitkowsky** (see p.1487) is highly regarded for his insurance arbitration work. He is active in insurance claims litigation, not least in matters relating to 9/11 and Enron.

**Clients/Work Highlights:** AIG; French Insurance Association; MassMutual and QBE International.

## Mendes & Mount LLP

**The Firm:** Mendes & Mount maintains a fabulous reputation as home to 150 first-class insurance lawyers. It scores highly with interviewees because it provides clients with expertise across the full range of insurance disputes. Areas of specialty include PI, marine and pollution coverage, and healthcare. The firm is also noted for its quality reinsurance practice. John Larkin is a contact partner.

## Sullivan & Cromwell LLP

See firm details p.1558

**The Firm:** *"Outstanding at capital markets and M&A,"* this firm is also recognized as having the regulatory expertise to handle leading insurance finance work. The practice is especially renowned for advising on SEC disclosure issues and assessment of insurance risks. Additionally, lawyers have extensive transactional skills in the areas of life and property and casualty and health insurance. In the context of insurance defense work, the group is involved in significant policy coverage issues relating to environmental and products liability litigation.

**The Lawyers:** The firm's accomplishments in insurance transactions owe a lot to **Andy Rowen** (see p.1495). Clients acknowledge him to be *"remarkable in structuring corporate insurance deals. He is clever and has top-notch technical expertise."*

**Clients/Work Highlights:** The firm represented Goldman Sachs in its $345 million acquisition of the life insurance and annuity businesses of Allmerica Financial. In another highlight, the group acted as US counsel to ING Groep and ING Canada in a CAD1.04 billion common stock IPO.

## Wachtell, Lipton, Rosen & Katz
See firm details p.1561

**The Firm:** This firm is a market leader in both litigation and M&A. Unsurprisingly, given its stature in both these practice areas, a number of major clients describe the firm as *"an important port of call"* for insurance disputes and transactions. It is especially famed for its role acting for Silverstein Properties against insurance companies seeking property damage claims arising out of 9/11, and for advising MetLife on various acquisitions.

## Willkie Farr & Gallagher LLP
See firm details p.1567

**The Firm:** The firm has made a remarkable impact on the insurance market. Its lawyers are accomplished in the areas of insurance-related capital markets, M&A and disputes. Headline-grabbing work includes advising Swiss Re and its affiliates on a range of investments, acquisitions and dispositions made by its Alternative Assets Group. It also acted as counsel to RenaissanceRe Holdings in relation to the sale of its stake in Platinum Underwriters Holdings by way of a public offering. John D'Alimonte and Richard Mancino are among the firm's insurance contact partners.

## Wilson, Elser, Moskowitz, Edelman & Dicker LLP

**The Firm:** The firm has a national standing in insurance disputes. Clients regard it as *"a go-to operation thanks to its formidable presence in the courts,"* while also appreciating it for its well-integrated national network of insurance specialists. Thomas Wilson is chairman of the executive committee of the firm and is respected industry-wide for his insurance defense claims work.

## Fried, Frank, Harris, Shriver & Jacobson LLP
See firm details p.1532

**The Firm:** According to clients and peers, the firm's renowned corporate finance and regulatory profile provides it with an established depth in insurance transactions. Ever popular with investment banks, this outfit is increasingly involved in leading insurance-related capital markets deals. Lawyers notably represented Goldman Sachs and Merrill Lynch in connection with offerings of common shares and mandatory convertible preferred shares in Platinum Underwriters Holdings. The net aggregate proceeds of this transaction are valued at approximately $300 million.

**The Lawyers:** **Lois Herzeca** (see p.1465) is viewed by many as the *"cornerstone of the insurance transactions practice."* Her work focuses on capital markets and M&A insurance deals and she led the team in advising Transatlantic Holdings in connection with a $750 million high-yield notes offering.

**Clients/Work Highlights:** Highlights include acting as counsel to Goldman Sachs and financial advisers to MetLife in the acquisition of Travelers Life & Annuity from Citigroup. On the disputes front, it represented underwriters at Lloyd's in relation to 17 arbitration demands issued by affiliates of ACE regarding asbestos-related reinsurance claims. The client roster also includes Dow Jones; Liberty Mutual; Fortress Re and Equitas.

## Lovells
See firm details p.1543

**The Firm:** This preeminent UK firm is making a highly favorable impression among clients. According to one in-house counsel: *"We are incredibly happy with Lovells, in terms of quality, responsiveness and*

breadth of transactional, dispute and regulatory coverage. We give them the highest recommendation without any hesitation whatsoever."* Another affirmed: *"They have an excellent record of performance when it comes to reinsurance arbitrations."* In addition to its successful London and constantly expanding New York insurance and reinsurance practices, it is also building a substantial presence in Chicago. Lawyers act as counsel in arbitration and dispute proceedings in the USA, Bermuda, the UK and continental Europe.

**The Lawyers:** **Dave Alberts** (see p.1432) *"displays formidable skill in making complex insurance matters simple and applicable to commercial situations."* His finance and regulatory insurance practice encompasses the areas of alternative risk transfer, liability-based restructuring, reinsurance matters and portfolio transfers.

**Clients/Work Highlights:** Recent work includes representing ACE Group in liquidation proceedings relating to the Home Insurance Group. In another highlight, the team is acting for Randall & Quilter Group, a leading run-off specialist company, on a series of reinsurance company acquisitions in the USA, UK and Belgium. These are being acquired from the ACE Group and total $1 billion in value. Other clients include Max Re; Hannover Life Re; Munich American Re; Berkshire Hathaway; American Council of Life Insurers and Equitas.

## Other Notable Practitioners

**Edward Joyce** (see p.1468) of Heller Ehrman LLP is an established name acting for policyholders in disputes. He is a former Andersen Kill & Olick PC partner and, according to clients, *"can really take charge of a negotiation and assemble an excellent team of lawyers who provide a high level of service."* One highlight of his year came with his representation of the Rank Group in international litigation regarding its business interruption claims for the New York and DC Hard Rock Cafe restaurants following the 9/11 terrorist attacks. **John Sarchio** (see p.1496) has recently left White & Case LLP and has now joined Chadbourne & Parke LLP. He is co-head of the firm's insurance and reinsurance practice group and is highly respected for his instrumental role in developing the firm's finance regulatory expertise in these areas.

# INTELLECTUAL PROPERTY

<table>
<tr><td colspan="2">Intellectual Property: Patent<br>Leading Firms</td></tr>
<tr><td>1</td><td>FITZPATRICK, CELLA, HARPER & SCINTO New York<br>KIRKLAND & ELLIS LLP New York<br>ROPES & GRAY LLP New York</td></tr>
<tr><td>2</td><td>JONES DAY New York<br>KAYE SCHOLER LLP New York<br>KENYON & KENYON LLP New York<br>PATTERSON, BELKNAP, WEBB & TYLER New York<br>WEIL, GOTSHAL & MANGES LLP New York<br>WHITE & CASE LLP New York</td></tr>
<tr><td>3</td><td>BAKER BOTTS LLP New York<br>CRAVATH, SWAINE & MOORE LLP New York<br>FISH & RICHARDSON P.C. New York<br>GOODWIN PROCTER LLP New York<br>MORGAN & FINNEGAN, LLP New York<br>SKADDEN, ARPS New York<br>WILMERHALE New York</td></tr>
<tr><td>4</td><td>FRIED, FRANK New York<br>ORRICK, HERRINGTON & SUTCLIFFE LLP New York<br>SIDLEY AUSTIN LLP New York</td></tr>
</table>

## Fitzpatrick, Cella, Harper & Scinto

See firm details p.1531

**The Firm:** Commentators remarked that there is *"no doubt as to the supremacy of this firm."* It has forged a *"stellar practice"* that encompasses a range of IP issues, particularly capturing the limelight in its representation of proprietary drug companies against generics. The intellectual capability of its attorneys stands out, and the presence of *"some of the best patent lawyers in the business"* allows the firm to attract an impressive volume of international work. The large team also devotes a significant portion of its time to defensive litigation for clients such as IBM and Canon, alongside its patent prosecution and trademark work. Of late, it has obtained a preliminary injunction blocking generics with respect to Pfizer's Accupril drug.

**The Lawyers:** **Bob Baechtold** (see p.1435) is the pivotal player at the firm and viewed by many as *"one of the best in the country"* for pharmaceutical work, due to his experience and excellent courtroom skills. He is in tremendous demand and has recently been defending Bristol-Myers Squibb and sanofi-aventis against generic companies, challenging the validity of their anticlotting drug patents. While his profile shines bright, there are a number of attorneys securing a high profile in the market. One example is **Joseph O'Malley** (see p.1435), a *"thorough litigator"* who is extremely able when it comes to complex matters. He acts largely in the patent litigation sphere.

**Clients/Work Highlights:** Merck; Bristol-Myers Squibb; sanofi-aventis; Novartis; GlaxoSmithKline; AstraZeneca; Canon; PepsiCo and Mars.

## Kirkland & Ellis LLP

See firm details p.875

**The Firm:** *"At the top of the IP tree,"* this 55-attorney team of lawyers has attracted a sizable chunk of the market. Proficient in patent litigation, it works for a number of clients in the electronics and pharmaceuticals area. A *"nucleus of talented litigators"* enables the firm to attract both able young associates and high-profile work. Many return to the firm as a result of its client-oriented service and competitive billing rates. Recently, its lawyers won a summary judgment for Infineon Technologies against MOSAID, declaring that their client had not infringed MOSAID's patents. The firm also undertakes trademark work.

**The Lawyers:** Clients applauded **John Desmarais** (see p.1449) as a renowned and talented patent litigator, who *"wins cases he might not at first seem to deserve to."* He is *"a natural in court, intelligent and incisive in manner,"* and recently represented Boston Scientific in its attempts to countersue Johnson & Johnson over coronary stent technology.

**Clients/Work Highlights:** Hermes International; Honeywell Aerospace; Siemens; Boston Scientific; Infineon Technologies; Lucent Technologies; Forest Labs and Schering-Plough.

## Ropes & Gray LLP

See firm details p.1117

**The Firm:** Since absorbing IP boutique Fish & Neave, Ropes & Gray has boosted its prosecution, counseling and transactional work while retaining a traditional strength in litigation. The approximately 150-strong group does a great job catering to the broad needs of its clients, who in turn appreciate the *"highly inventive and industrious"* attorneys and their high service levels. Boasting one of the finest reputations in patent litigation, the team recently won AstraZeneca's Abbreviated New Drug Application (ANDA) litigation against Mayne Pharmaceuticals. Clients say they have developed a relationship of trust with this *"top-flight practice"* and value its multilevel approach.

**The Lawyers:** The firm is home to a number of the market heavyweights. **Herb Schwartz** (see p.1499) is a *"master of his craft,"* whom clients say *"exceeds all expectations."* A skilled patent litigator with a national reputation, he *"deserves every accolade available"* and is an *"excellent field general"* at the firm. He was the driving force behind AstraZeneca's ANDA success against Mayne Pharmaceuticals regarding its Diprivan drug patents. **Jesse Jenner** (see p.1468) is the *"full package and a real star"* when it comes to patent litigation. *"Credible and charismatic,"* he can connect with the court. One peer said: *"When he talks you just find yourself nodding."* He recently handled the famous billion-dollar Lemelson patent case, defeating the inventor's machine vision and barcode patents. **Robert Morgan** (see p.1481) is a first-class attorney who has developed a great reputation, particularly in the field of electrical circuits and chip cases. Biotech is more the domain of **James Haley** (see p.1463), an attorney who *"definitely knows his*

*trade."* His interests lie largely in patent procurement, enforcement and defense work.

**Clients/Work Highlights:** Motorola; Yale University; Cognex; Praxair; Ford; Emerson Electric; AstraZeneca; Lucent Technologies; Saifun Semiconductors and Nestlé.

## Jones Day

See firm details p.570

**The Firm:** Since acquiring the IP group of Pennie & Edmonds, this national firm's New York-based group has dramatically increased its stature in the market. More than 100 attorneys conduct the full range of IP work, from litigation and licensing to general counseling on day-to-day matters. As a team, it is one of the deepest around and was described by clients as *"tremendous in terms of both quality and bench strength."* The firm has recently advised on the Martek Biosciences infringement case, which concerned the development of alpha omega oils technology.

**The Lawyers:** **Laura Coruzzi** (see p.1447), formerly of Pennies, is a renowned patent prosecutor working in the life sciences, biotech and pharmaceutical sectors. A *"smart, hard-working and intelligent"* attorney, she commands the respect of clients who feel that *"she always does justice to the matter in hand."* She is currently defending Herbalife against an alleged patent infringement of amino acid dietary supplements. **Theresa Gillis** (see p.1459) is a *"dedicated and accomplished litigator,"* respected for her hard work and commitment to clients. She is involved in a host of IP issues, including patent and copyright infringement and validity.

**Clients/Work Highlights:** The firm represents national and international clients from the biotech, pharmaceutical, chemical, electrical and mechanical industries, among others.

## Kaye Scholer LLP

See firm details p.1536

**The Firm:** The IP team of this firm has reinvigorated its practice with the addition of several attorneys to its ranks. Effort is largely concentrated on patent litigation and licensing, although trademark and unfair competition work is well to the fore. Clients have nothing but praise for the lawyers here, stating that they *"always have the exact answer you're looking for."* Commentators were also impressed with the high-caliber skills of the younger associates at the firm.

**The Lawyers:** The tenacious **Leora Ben-Ami** (see p.1437) devotes much of her practice to patent litigation and advises a number of firms in the biotech, chemical and medical industries. With an *"ability to do what a lot of attorneys can't,"* she has established a great client base for herself. She is currently representing Pfizer in its billion-dollar Celebrex drug patent case against Teva Pharmaceuticals. Clients refer to **Gerald Sobel** (see p.1503) as their *"secret weapon."* He is a cerebral advocate who *"can handle any uncertainty that comes along"* and always *"insists that his team achieves excellent results."*

**Clients/Work Highlights:** DuPont; Siemens;

Chiron; ARIAD Pharmaceuticals; Pfizer; Roche Pharmaceuticals and Wyeth.

## Kenyon & Kenyon LLP

See firm details p.1537

**The Firm:** This IP boutique continues to be successful despite shunning the path taken by many of its ilk in refusing to be swallowed up by a larger firm. A full-service practice of 150 attorneys, it is a formidable competitor that handles all facets of IP for clients in the electrical, mechanical and life sciences areas. Clients remain tremendously loyal to it and respect the know-how provided by its talented and highly practical attorneys.

**The Lawyers:** **Richard DeLucia**'s (see p.1449) contemporaries applaud his persistent and tenacious approach to patent litigation. He is a "*confident and strategic*" player who "*simply wins a lot.*" Of late, he has successfully represented Boston Scientific in an allegation of stent implant patent infringement by Johnson & Johnson. The "*highly focused*" **Steven Lee** (see p.1474) is a respected biotech and chemical industry litigator. "*Never less than on an even keel,*" he has represented Teva Pharmaceuticals against Pfizer in its ANDA over the Neuriton drug, successfully keeping his client's product on the market.

**Clients/Work Highlights:** Teva Pharmaceuticals; Impax; Housey; KV Pharmaceutical; GE Healthcare; Sony; Mattel; Fisher-Price; Enzo Biochem; Memorial Sloan-Kettering Cancer Center; Columbia University; Amersham and Toyota.

## Patterson, Belknap, Webb & Tyler LLP

See firm details p.1547

**The Firm:** The IP team of this midtown New York firm is respected for its client service skills. The team has a history of medical and pharmaceutical work and is renowned for its long-term work with Johnson & Johnson. A large preponderance of the caseload is patent and trademark litigation, although the team does some trade secrets and licensing matters. Clients say they appreciate the "*collaborative nature*" of the firm, which has recently represented TAP (the Takeda and Abbott Pharmaceuticals joint venture) against a generic company that is challenging its products.

**The Lawyers:** The "*unflappable*" **Greg Diskant** (see p.1450) is an experienced trial lawyer: "*You have to do a good job when you are up against him,*" said peers. Chair of the group, clients say he is "*one of the smartest lawyers*" in the courtroom. In the past year, he has continued his long-standing role enforcing Johnson & Johnson's stent patents, winning cases against Medtronic and Boston Scientific.

**Clients/Work Highlights:** Johnson & Johnson; Abbott Pharmaceuticals; Siemens; Schering-Plough; GE and Splenda.

## Weil, Gotshal & Manges LLP

See firm details p.1565

**The Firm:** This dedicated IP group undertakes a large amount of patent litigation, as well as some trademark and copyright work. Its lawyers have something of a reputation as "*aggressive litigators who come into the courtroom guns ablazing.*" The offices in New York and California work closely together tackling a raft of serious matters. Recently, the team has handled prominent electronics work and has an ongoing case for Applera against Stratagene and Bio-Rad Laboratories regarding PCR technology.

**The Lawyers:** The "*wonderful trial attorney*" **Steven Glazer** (see p.1459) is cochair of the patent litigation and counseling practice. Clients say he is an astute adviser and brings "*a good mix of legal and technical expertise.*" He defended BPB America in its patent litigation against Georgia-Pacific.

**Clients/Work Highlights:** Applera; Yahoo!; Microsoft; American Airlines; Applied Materials; BMW; Bristol-Myers Squibb; Cisco Systems; Exxon-Mobil; Matsushita Electric Industrial; Pirelli; Reuters and GlaxoSmithKline.

## White & Case LLP

See firm details p.1566

**The Firm:** Truly a full-service firm, this 60-strong team is renowned in both the patent and trademark areas, but also has a niche interest in the antitrust aspects of patent law. Its excellence in trademark matters was recently evidenced by its representation of the NFL over the copyright of its Washington Redskins and Baltimore Ravens merchandise. On the patent side, it has represented Syngenta in its patent infringement litigation. Clients value the quality of both the attorneys and the advice rendered, with one saying: "*They achieve amazing results.*"

**The Lawyers:** **Dimitrios Drivas** (see p.1450) is a respected patent trial attorney who is co-head of the global IP practice. A "*strategic legal thinker,*" his contemporaries say he "*can apply multiple strategies without losing momentum.*" He possesses polished courtroom skills and has a commanding presence during oral argument. Clients say **Fred Koenigsberg** (see p.1471) is "*everything that you'd want*" in a copyright lawyer. A sophisticated attorney with a broad set of skills and knowledge, he has undertaken copyright work for IBM, for a successful children's book author and for several music publishers. He additionally serves as general counsel of the American Society of Composers, Authors and Publishers, and has advised Congress on its copyright legislation.

**Clients/Work Highlights:** Novartis; Disney; Syngenta; AstraZeneca; Verizon; BMG Music Publishing; Garth Brooks; American Society of Composers, Authors and Publishers; IBM and Bristol-Myers Squibb.

## Baker Botts LLP

See firm details p.1922

**The Firm:** The firm's 35 specialist attorneys have come together to form "*one of the finest groups in an increasingly competitive IP market.*" Work ranges from patent litigation and copyright to licensing and trade secrets. The team represents MasterCard in all of its patent litigation.

**The Lawyers:** **Robert Neuner** (see p.1483) is an "*excellent litigator who really knows his law.*" With his "*clear, prepared and honest*" approach, he has a terrific courtroom presence. Recently, he defended FindWhat against Overture's claims of search engine technology patent infringement. The "*highly personable*" **Robert Scheinfeld** (see p.1497) possesses the "*ability to reduce the complex to the simple,*" which clients value greatly.

**Clients/Work Highlights:** Columbia University; Infineon Technologies; MasterCard; Fuji Photo Film; Siemens; Hitachi; Dell and Samsung.

## Cravath, Swaine & Moore LLP

See firm details p.1527

**The Firm:** Despite not possessing a discrete IP team, the firm is well known for both its patent and copyright work. The firm is home to *"extremely bright attorneys of a high caliber,"* who are *"dedicated in their approach."* Clients feel that they *"take things on with the attitude that they are going to make them work."* Of late, they have negotiated a settlement for IBM in the Compuware case, a matter regarding the copyright of software code.

**The Lawyers:** **Evan Chesler** (see p.1444) is *"one of the most intelligent trial lawyers in the country."* He possesses *"keen lawyerly instincts"* and has an *"almost photographic memory"* of the facts. A skilled trial lawyer, he now combines his practice with duties as presiding partner of the firm. **Thomas Rafferty** is a litigator with *"instant insight into the complexities of a case."* This *"sharp and aggressive"* lawyer is respected above all for *"courtroom skills that have confounded many an opponent."* **Katherine Forrest** (see p.1456) is a superb copyright attorney with a *"clear focus on the task in hand."* Recently, she acted for the Martha Graham Center in a case concerning the copyright of certain dances.

**Clients/Work Highlights:** Warner Music Group; QUALCOMM; Medinol; GlaxoSmithKline; IBM; Time Warner and Alcoa.

## Fish & Richardson P.C.

See firm details p.1113

**The Firm:** The key distinguishing features of this firm are its broad geographic reach and national reputation for patent litigation. The New York office comprises 30 lawyers, who are well equipped to handle complex litigation: *"They really know how to try cases,"* peers said. The team recently represented Bose against Stevco Group in a case relating to distribution rights.

**The Lawyers:** Head of the firm's IP practice, **David Francescani** (see p.1456) is a *"personable attorney with highly polished trial skills."* He has recently represented semiconductor manufacturer, Atmel, over an alleged patent infringement of the company's programmable electronic circuits.

**Clients/Work Highlights:** LSI Logic; Nokia; Bose; Lehman Brothers and Mars.

## Goodwin Procter LLP

See firm details p.1114

**The Firm:** Cited as *"one to watch,"* this firm is a growing presence in the area. The team performs a large amount of pharmaceutical work and has a strong chemicals group.

**The Lawyers:** Much of **Thomas Creel's** (see p.1447) practice is devoted to patent litigation, but he also undertakes trademark work and general counseling. He is chair of the firm's IP litigation practice and has *"many successful years of experience"* under his belt. This effective attorney is representing Cytec in its upcoming trial concerning chemicals used for paper making. He is also renowned for his work as an arbitrator. **Ethan Horwitz** (see p.1466) is a talented copyright and trademark lawyer whom peers say *"knows the law like the back of his hand."* He is *"highly diligent and very attentive to his client's needs,"* agreed sources.

**Clients/Work Highlights:** Teva Pharmaceuticals; JPMorgan Chase; Cytec; PepsiCo; Cablevision; Cisco Systems; Campbells; Colgate-Palmolive and Avon.

## Morgan & Finnegan, LLP

See firm details p.1544

**The Firm:** This respected boutique firm adopts a customer-oriented approach to cases, fielding 105 attorneys with a broad set of skills. Together they formed a team that recently co-counseled IBM in the Compuware case.

**The Lawyers:** **John Sweeney** (see p.1506) is a patent litigator who peers deem to be *"the real deal."* With his strong communication skills, he is a *"quality attorney who gets results."* He recently successfully defended Bombardier against Boss Control's claim of patent infringement. **Chris Hughes** (see p.1466) is a skilled patent attorney who commands respect in court. His recent highlights have included acting on behalf of Medinol against Medtronic in a patent infringement matter. Also recommended, **Mark Abate** (see p.1431) tries a number of patent infringement cases in the computer and medical devices industries.

**Clients/Work Highlights:** Medinol; United Technologies; Canon; Bombardier; ChevronTexaco; Hoffmann-La Roche; Toyota; IBM; Rolex; Procter & Gamble; Tyco; Gerber Scientific; Rheem; Sephora and Lorillard Tobacco.

## Skadden, Arps, Slate, Meagher & Flom LLP & Affiliates

See firm details p.1557

**The Firm:** Clients appreciate that this *"fabulous, talented firm"* has a 65-strong team providing *"balanced legal and business advice."* Its attorneys display a *"marvelous gift for solving legal quandaries."* A formidable competitor to all, it attracts the blue-chip clients.

**The Lawyers:** **Edward Filardi** (see p.1454) is a *"first-rate patent litigator with an excellent courtroom demeanor."* He *"inspires confidence with his persuasive style,"* and is currently representing Endo Pharmaceuticals in a challenge against Purdue Pharmaceuticals' patent of the OxyCotin drug.

**Clients/Work Highlights:** Intel; McKesson; JPMorgan Chase; Bank One; Applied Materials; Yahoo! and eBay.

## WilmerHale

See firm details p.580

**The Firm:** This firm *"has perfected the art of putting the client's mind at ease."* It does so by combining the twin virtues of *"excellent preparation and superb strategy"* to produce an excellent job time after time. Although perhaps better known in the Boston arena, commentators feel it does much of its best patent work in New York.

**The Lawyers:** The dedicated **William DiSalvatore** is a patent attorney who stands out for his *"encyclopedic knowledge and superlative communication skills."* Both of these qualities were demonstrated recently in his successful defense of Kodak and Altek in ITC proceedings against Ampex, regarding thumbnail imaging technology. **Calvin Walden** (see p.1511) is another valuable member of the team who *"can always be relied on to give it his all in any situation."*

**Clients/Work Highlights:** Kodak; Pfizer; Syngenta; Taro Pharmaceuticals; Broadcom and Creo.

## Fried, Frank, Harris, Shriver & Jacobson LLP

See firm details p.1532

**The Firm:** Having taken on several lawyers from Pennie & Edmonds, the firm's 15-attorney team continues to forge ahead in the IP sphere. Recently, the group represented Herbalife against Unither Pharmaceuticals, which alleged that Herbalife had breached several of their patents.

**The Lawyers:** **Jim Dabney** (see p.1448) is a patent, trademark and copyright attorney who is a *"born trial lawyer."* His tactical skills are well known to clients, with one noting: *"Everything turned out the way he said!"* He is currently representing KSR International against Teleflex before the US Supreme Court, regarding alleged infringement of vehicle control system patents. Originally at Pennie & Edmonds, **Stephen Rabinowitz** (see p.1490) is a respected patent litigator. He obtained summary judgment for Hoffmann-La Roche against Carnegie Mellon University, showing that their patented enzyme technology had not been infringed.

**Clients/Work Highlights:** Virgin; Hoffmann-La Roche; ICAP; White Consolidated Industries; KSR International; EMI; LabCorp and Herbalife.

## Orrick, Herrington & Sutcliffe LLP

See firm details p.337

**The Firm:** This 20-attorney team performs a great deal of technology and financial services work, focusing particularly on major cases in the patents arena. In the earlier part of 2005, the team represented ELA Medical and Sorin Group on a cross-license negotiation with Medtronic over their pacemaker technology.

**The Lawyers: Daniel Thomasch** (see p.1507) is one of a rare breed of patent attorneys with an ability to simplify things and convey clear messages in court. **Robert Isackson** (see p.1467) is a patent attorney who clients say "*plays to win.*" Described as "*the Colin Powell of the courtroom,*" he succeeds by employing his thoughtful and persuasive manner. Recently, he has obtained a verdict of willful infringement for Nikko Materials, which alleged a third party had infringed its patent.

**Clients/Work Highlights:** Dow AgroSciences; Nikko Materials; Charles Schwab; Universal Instruments; Alcon Laboratories; Applied Biosystems; Bayer; Wyeth; Protus IP Solutions and TCL Communications.

## Sidley Austin LLP

See firm details p.883

**The Firm:** The firm's IP group provides a range of services, from patent to copyright, although its forte lies in major patent litigation. The group's patent team has grown recently and the firm is very effective in utilizing its network of resources to serve its clients' needs.

**The Lawyers:** Trained under the guidance of Bob Baechtold at Fitzpatrick, **Thomas Beck** (see p.1436) is a "*thorough and effective*" patent attorney working largely in the chemical and pharmaceutical area. Clients described him as a highly intelligent lawyer, who "*delivers great results.*" The accomplished **Jennifer Gordon** (see p.1461) undertakes patent work in the biotech area.

**Clients/Work Highlights:** The team represents clients from a range of industries including software; consumer products; biotech; healthcare and pharmaceuticals.

## Cowan, Liebowitz & Latman

**The Firm:** With a "*deep knowledge*" of trademark and copyright law, peers say that this is one firm "*you can't knock.*" The group fields smart and business-savvy attorneys, who are the first choice for many peers when referring work. This well-rounded copyright and trademark group "*produces great work and achieves great results*" and has developed an impressive counterfeiting team.

**The Lawyers:** Moving within computer copyright circles, **Morton Goldberg** is an "*absolutely brilliant copyright attorney.*" During his extensive 45 years of practice, he has performed a variety of work for clients from the music and computer industries. **Christopher Jensen** is chair of the firm and an excellent copyright litigator. His adversaries say he "*knows how to handle himself in court.*"

**Clients/Work Highlights:** Donna Karan; Warner Chappell Music; EMI; AT&T; QVC; Coca-Cola and Universal Studios.

## Fross Zelnick Lehrman & Zissu PC

**The Firm:** This firm specializes in trademark and copyright work and does an extremely good job of it too. Clients say they were impressed with the firm's "*shrewd legal abilities*" and great courtroom skills. The firm attracts a large volume of work from clients in the entertainment industry, some of which is international in scale.

**The Lawyers: Roger Zissu** is a major player at the copyright Bar. He is famed within the area due to his long and successful practice, and has litigated for clients on a range of copyright issues including infringements of literary and graphic characters, music and artwork.

**Clients/Work Highlights:** DC Comics; Bristol-Myers Squibb; Chanel; Jim Henson Company; Miramax Film; Parfums Christian Dior; Sony BMG Music Entertainment and Yum! Brands.

## Debevoise & Plimpton LLP

See firm details p.1529

**The Firm:** This 36-attorney team is a force in the copyright arena. This "*terrifically effective*" practice is handling a large case for Pernod Ricard whose subsidiary, Allied Domecq, faces having the trademark of its Stolichnaya vodka taken away by the Russian government. The team's workload also encompasses a range of domain and Internet-based cases.

**The Lawyers:** A renowned trademarks lawyer, **Bruce Keller** is a "*litigation star; he wins – and that's what matters,*" said clients. He is currently working for several publishers that have filed a lawsuit against Google regarding its plans to copy books and create an online library. **David Bernstein** adopts an aggressive approach in the courtroom, where he is a popular choice for high-stakes trademark litigation.

**Clients/Work Highlights:** Yahoo!; NFL; GE; Sony Pictures; Sony BMG Music Entertainment; Kraft; Pernod Ricard; American Express; Novartis; Shell and Pfizer.

## O'Melveny & Myers LLP

See firm details p.336

**The Firm:** A respected firm, the 15-attorney copyright group has attracted high praise from clients, particularly for its timeliness and high service levels. It is currently representing Cryptic Studios against Marvel Entertainment with respect to the copyright of their City of Heroes computer game.

**The Lawyers:** The "*superb*" **Dale Cendali** (see p.1443) is a talented litigator, who has recently attained a successful judgment for Twentieth Century Fox before the Ninth Circuit Court of Appeals in its case against Dastar.

**Clients/Work Highlights:** The Upper Deck Company; HBO; MGA Entertainment; News Corporation; Twentieth Century Fox; Le Tigre; Cryptic Studios; Sony BMG Music Entertainment and Honeywell.

## Brown Raysman Millstein Felder & Steiner LLP

See firm details p.1521

**The Firm:** With a forte in computer and media copyright issues, the 20-attorney team at this firm attracts a lot of interesting cases. The team also performs a range of patent work including patent litigation, prosecution, mining and auditing. The firm recently represented Micromuse against a third party that alleged Micromuse had infringed their computer networking technology.

**The Lawyers: Frank DeRosa** (see p.1449) has been involved in the past year in establishing patents and counseling clients on their technologies. He has recently been advising Axa Equitable Life Insurance with respect to litigation avoidance.

**Clients/Work Highlights:** Bloomberg, Quest Diagnostics and AXA Equitable Life Insurance are some of the clients represented by this firm.

## Paul, Hastings, Janofsky & Walker LLP

See firm details p.339

**The Firm:** The team at Paul Hastings is renowned primarily for its work in the trademark sphere. The 17-attorney group of IP lawyers performs registration, due diligence, litigation and licensing of trademarks.

**The Lawyers:** An "*excellent communicator,*" **Robert Sherman** (see p.1501) has an ability to counsel clearly and effectively, say clients. A talented copyright and trademark lawyer, he has represented clients across a range of industries, and is defending L'Oréal against Juicy Couture with respect to their Juicy Tube lipsticks. **Victoria Cundiff** (see p.1447) is a renowned copyright attorney who gives her clients her full attention. She undertakes a large amount of trade secrets work and is "*always on the ball.*"

**Clients/Work Highlights:** BMG Direct; Nestlé Purina PetCare; SMIC; Jennifer Lopez; Masco; Toni&Guy; Jones Apparel Group; L'Oréal and Colgate-Palmolive.

## Other Notable Practitioners

**Paul Gupta** (see p.1463) from Mayer, Brown, Rowe & Maw LLP is "*academic in his style, but extraordinarily accessible.*" He is renowned for his work in the technology arena and is lead counsel for NCR in its patent litigation. From Morgan, Lewis & Bockius LLP, **Stephen Judlowe** (see p.1468) is a "*brilliant, bright and aggressive*" patent attorney. **Salem Katsh** from Kasowitz Benson Torres & Friedman continues to be rated as a major player in patent litigation. **Rochelle Seide** (see p.1499) at Arent Fox PLLC is a scholarly patent counselor and prosecutor who has worked for a number of well-known biotech clients. At Willkie Farr & Gallagher LLP, **John DiMatteo** (see p.1450) is a respected patent attorney who peers say is "*always thoroughly well-prepared.*" Recently, he achieved an en banc judgment victory for Philips defeating allegations of electric shaver technology patent infringement.

# LITIGATION

## Cravath, Swaine & Moore LLP

See firm details p.1527
**The Firm:** A "*formidable powerhouse*" of an adversary in both securities litigation and corporate disputes, this excellent practice consistently produces a high-quality work product. With 43 litigators in its New York office the firm has the capability to deliver a broad range of services to a wonderful stable of clients, who admire these "*impressive, hard-working, thoughtful lawyers.*" Clients expect and receive high-value representation: "*Cravath lawyers are excellent at what they do, providing the right results and leverage cost effectively.*" This is partly due to the team's excellent use of associates and junior partners. One highlight includes the defense of IBM in litigation involving copyright issues, trade secret misappropriation and antitrust claims, ending with a favorable resolution for IBM in the eighth week of the trial. Cravath has also been retained to defend Merck and its directors in all of its Vioxx-related securities, derivative and ERISA litigation in state and federal courts.
**The Lawyers:** Lauded as a terrific lawyer, deputy presiding partner of the firm and member of the litigation department **Evan Chesler** (see p.1444) is "*extraordinarily smart and one of the best courtroom presences*" in the city. His superb preparation skills

and aggressive approach are well suited to arguing tough cases in both federal and state courts throughout the USA. He frequently acts as lead counsel in antitrust, securities, intellectual property and general commercial cases, leading the charge in the IBM defense and representing Time Warner in securities litigation connected with AOL's advertising revenue after the companies' merger. As lead counsel for CSFB in all its Enron-related civil litigation, **Richard Clary** (see p.1445) also sits at the forefront of the market. Alongside securities, antitrust, bankruptcy and patent litigation he handles both international and domestic arbitrations. JPMorgan Chase and Schering AG also feature in his impressive list of clients. The fabulous **Robert Baron** (see p.1435) is highly regarded for being articulate, humorous and "*understanding the complexities of dealing with a client in a crisis.*" A pragmatic litigator, he "*sees the forest for the trees, cutting through all the detail of a case.*" Clients say he is "*a passionate advocate, but one who doesn't get carried away.*" He takes on a range of commercial cases, acting for domestic and international carriers and financial entities in securities-related litigation.
**Clients/Work Highlights:** The firm, led by Robert Baron, represented Deutsche Telekom AG in class action litigation instigated by purchasers of the company's stock in June 2000, who alleged material misstatements and omissions relating to merger discussions and real estate holdings. The case was settled in 2005 without Deutsche Telekom suffering any material impact. In other matters, the firm represented Medinol in claims that Boston Scientific breached contract in relation to the manufacturing and sale of stents – medical devices employed to support arteries after clearing. The matter culminated with Boston Scientific agreeing to pay out $750 million and surrender the shares it held in Medinol.

## Davis Polk & Wardwell

See firm details p.1528
**The Firm:** Clients find this preeminent litigation firm "*responsive and respectful*" and spoke of a mature team with a cross-departmental work ethic. The firm represents a sophisticated clientele, including financial institutions and overseas clients who hire the firm in high-stakes and time-sensitive litigation – often when senior management is under investigation. These intelligent advocates are "*bright and extremely effective*" in securities cases. The team represented Oracle in its $10.3 billion acquisition of PeopleSoft in a well-publicized, hostile transaction, litigated to conclusion in Delaware, ending an 18-month struggle between the two companies. The firm has built an outstanding white-collar and investigations practice with lawyers who "*truly understand the intricacies of the legal environment, know how the regulators operate and are effective in a tough marketplace.*" The firm is involved in almost every headlining investigation, including representing Marsh & McLennan in an industry-wide inquiry into bid-rigging activities in the insurance market. One

distinguishing feature is this firm's involvement in parallel proceedings, where it excels at the defense of companies facing competing actions in multiple forums.
**The Lawyers:** "*Sensational – the best mind in the business,*" senior statesman **Robert Fiske** (see p.1454) is a lawyer with "*terrific talent and wisdom*" and clients appreciate his sound advice. Dean of the white-collar criminal Bar, he was involved in the Kumar case, in which the firm is representing two former Computer Associates executives caught up in an accounting scandal. **Michael Carroll** (see p.1443) is described as "*the legitimate heir to the Robert Fiske throne.*" He does a great deal of work for KPMG and was the lead trial lawyer in the Oracle takeover of PeopleSoft. **Dennis Glazer** (see p.1459) splits his practice between M&A work and general commercial and securities litigation, while the experienced **Daniel Kolb** (see p.1472) is one of the go-to securities attorneys in New York; clients find him to be an "*extremely smart, collegial, hands-on and thorough defense lawyer*" who is great at working with witnesses. Kolb excels in accounting securities matters and representation of financial heavyweights. The "*extremely talented*" **Lawrence Portnoy** (see p.1489) impressed interviewees with his manner and "*great analytical abilities.*" Sources highlight the skill he displays when representing financial institutions such as Bank of America in SEC enforcement matters, grand jury investigations and in relation to regulator inquiries. **Carey Dunne** (see p.1450) is "*smart, savvy and knows how to protect his client – he is great at managing the aspects of an institutional representation.*" He spearheaded the Marsh & McLennan matter and successfully represented ImClone Systems in cases connected with insider trading, and the obstruction of justice and securities fraud trial of Martha Stewart. Currently, Dunne is counseling a panoply of clients under investigation by Attorney General Eliot Spitzer, the SEC and various other agencies. Commentators from all quarters respect his ability to "*quickly connect with management and figure out how a company ticks.*" **Denis McInerney** (see p.1478) is one of the firm's "*personable stars,*" who impresses with his thoroughness: "*He works hard and is always thoroughly prepared.*" He is playing a pivotal role in the Kumar case.
**Clients/Work Highlights:** The team acted for Gillette in litigation stemming from its $57 billion acquisition by Procter & Gamble. It also represented CSFB in the dismissal of a securities class action filed on behalf of shareholders in Agilent Technologies, based in California. Deloitte & Touche; Citibank; Ernst & Young; JPMorgan Chase and Pfizer all feature in the firm's elite client list.

## Paul, Weiss, Rifkind, Wharton & Garrison LLP

See firm details p.1548
**The Firm:** A dominant force in the market, this firm has a cadre of "*tremendous litigators*" – numbering more than 200 – who continue to produce top-qual-

## Litigation: General Commercial
### Leading Individuals

#### Senior Statesmen
FISKE Robert *Davis Polk & Wardwell*
LONDON Martin *Paul, Weiss*
REARDON Roy *Simpson Thacher & Bartlett*
WACHTELL Herbert *Wachtell*

[1] BOIES David *Boies, Schiller & Flexner LLP*
CHESLER Evan *Cravath, Swaine & Moore*
NUSSBAUM Bernard *Wachtell*
OSTRAGER Barry *Simpson Thacher & Bartlett*
WELLS JR Theodore *Paul, Weiss*
WHITE Mary Jo *Debevoise & Plimpton LLP*

[2] JOSEPH Gregory *Gregory P Joseph*
KOOB Charles *Simpson Thacher & Bartlett*
LERNER Jonathan *Skadden, Arps*
LEVINE Alan *Kronish Lieb*
MASTRO Randy *Gibson, Dunn & Crutcher*
NAFTALIS Gary *Kramer Levin*

[3] ARCHER Judith *Fulbright & Jaworski L.L.P.*
BELLER Daniel *Paul, Weiss*
BYRNE Lawrence *White & Case LLP*
CARROLL Michael *Davis Polk & Wardwell*
CLARY Richard *Cravath, Swaine & Moore*
CYR Joseph *Lovells*
FAGEN Leslie *Paul, Weiss*
FELDBERG Michael *Allen & Overy LLP*
FITZPATRICK JR Vincent *White & Case LLP*
FLAUM Douglas *Fried, Frank*
FLUMENBAUM Martin *Paul, Weiss*
GITTER Max *Cleary Gottlieb*
GLAZER Dennis *Davis Polk & Wardwell*
ICHEL David *Simpson Thacher & Bartlett*
KAVALER Thomas *Cahill Gordon & Reindel LLP*
KIERNAN John *Debevoise & Plimpton LLP*
KURZWEIL Harvey *Dewey Ballantine LLP*
MCSHERRY JR William *Arent Fox PLLC*
ORR Dennis *Mayer, Brown*
PLATT Charles *WilmerHale*
POLKES Jonathan *Weil, Gotshal & Manges*
PULTMAN Jacob *Allen & Overy LLP*
QUINN James *Weil, Gotshal & Manges*
ROGERS CHEPIGA Pamela *Allen & Overy LLP*
SALTZSTEIN Susan *Skadden, Arps*
SHUSTER Michael *White & Case LLP*
SNYDER Orin *Gibson, Dunn & Crutcher*
WOLOWITZ Steven *Mayer, Brown*

#### Up-and-coming individuals
ESPOSITO Grant *Mayer, Brown*

ity work covering all the bases in general commercial, securities and white-collar litigation. Outstanding, particularly in the latter two areas, the robust New York team has a reputation for being tough, with a strong stable of experts in the field and a reservoir of government experience. "*They truly understand how to try cases*" in the financial sector. No stranger to bet-the-company situations, the group has defended major client Citigroup in lawsuits and regulatory inquiries arising from its connections with Enron and WorldCom. It made headlines in June 2005 by entering into a preemptive $2 billion settlement in the nationwide Enron class action 15 months before trial was set to begin. In the WorldCom litigation, the firm settled underwriting claims for about $1.4 billion. The group's enviable reputation for being a force in the securities litigation field is further bolstered by its representation of AIG in the insurance company's publicity-grabbing exchanges with the SEC, DOJ and Attorney General Spitzer. The firm's hiring by Frank Quattrone to handle his appeal against conviction of obstruction of justice and witness tampering confirms its lofty position in the pantheon of New York firms.

**The Lawyers:** Cochair of the litigation department **Theodore Wells** (see p.1512) is recognized by many as "*the greatest trial lawyer of our generation.*" Known for impeccable judgment, his ability to relate to a jury is regarded as second to none. His practice handles some of the highest-profile matters currently in the court system. In addition to directing the team co-leading Philip Morris's defense against the DOJ's huge civil RICO action, he has been retained to defend Lewis 'Scooter' Libby against five counts of perjury, obstruction of justice and lying to the FBI relating to the exposure of a CIA operative's identity. Also cochairing the litigation department is **Brad Karp** (see p.1469), appreciated by clients for his "*experience, judgment and pure talent.*" A "*tiger*" of the courtroom, he leads on Citigroup-Enron and WorldCom litigation as well as doing a significant amount of work for JPMorgan, the NFL and McAndrews & Forbes. Interviewees characterize him as an "*indefatigable worker, always on top of everything.*" **Daniel Beller** (see p.1437) attracts the accolades "*wonderful and smart*" for the high-quality work he produces in general commercial, government enforcement and white-collar defense litigation. **Leslie Fagen** (see p.1453) is "*calm and unflappable – a great tactician*" in large-scale commercial matters. A highly experienced trial lawyer, **Martin London** (see p.1476) is "*a formidable force in the courtroom.*" He combines a "*commanding presence*" with an "*assured and strategic approach.*" Commentators hugely respect white-collar and appellate attorney **Mark Pomerantz** (see p.1489). Combining "*raw intelligence*" and nuanced legal analysis, his fortitude before prosecutors is legendary – unsurprising given his background as a former Supreme Court clerk. Sources greatly appreciate his attention to detail: "*It's the difference between a contractor who leverages himself by having a lot of foremen who actually do the hard work, versus a craftsman who does one job at a time, does the carpentry and is polishing the brass right before the client moves in.*" He handles a substantial amount of work on behalf of AIG and represented Frank Quattrone in his appeal. **Richard Rosen** (see p.1494) is thoroughly versed in every aspect of securities law, deploying his "*keen analytic and writing skills*" for clients such as Morgan Stanley and Citigroup. **Daniel Kramer**'s (see p.1472) specialty, too, is in the securities arena. He represented Merck in its Vioxx-related dealings with the SEC and is lead attorney for AIG and Hollinger in their various litigations. "*Fabulous at dealing with people, you can go to him with the toughest problems and he will solve them.*" He has turned his hand to internal investigations in recent times. **Martin Flumenbaum** (see p.1456) applies a "*veneer of toughness*" to his hugely intelligent and strategic approach to litigation. His emphasis on complex securities issues, playing a pivotal role in AIG's defense.

**Clients/Work Highlights:** On behalf of Adecco SA, Paul Weiss concluded in March 2005 an 18-month SEC investigation into the company's finances without recourse to regulatory action. At the request of Fannie Mae's board of directors and its special review committee, the group is conducting an internal investigation into accounting practices deemed to be improper by the SEC. The firm continues to act for leading investment bank Lehman Brothers in litigation arising from investigations by the SEC, the New York attorney general and the NYSE. Other clients include ACNielsen; Gillette; Music Publishers' Association; Time Warner Cable; Hollinger International and MasterCard.

## Simpson Thacher & Bartlett LLP
See firm details p.1555

**The Firm:** Perennially top of the heap for general commercial and securities matters, this "*no-nonsense litigation firm is one of the best in the country.*" It has a wide-ranging and diversified practice, with expertise encompassing complex products liability and antitrust actions. Clients are particularly impressed with the way in which Simpson Thacher leverages its corporate and transactional clout in securities litigation, achieving "*an enormous depth of resource*" in the process. "*Their recruitment is fantastic and they have strong associates and support.*" Much work is also generated by the firm's private equity clientele, coordinated by a specialized public investment fund team that offers assistance beyond the usual federal securities counseling and representation. The New York team, comprising more than 45 attorneys, has been involved in corporate scandals ranging from Enron to WorldCom and is representing AIG's special committee in the Spitzer investigation. Profound knowledge of insurance law also contributed to the group's achievement on behalf of Swiss Re of a decision that the 9/11 terrorist attack on the World Trade Center (WTC) constituted a single insurable event – saving the client in the region of $900 million. The group is equally proficient in the international arbitration arena, representing Bechtel and GE in a power plant dispute that culminated in the recovery of hundreds of millions of dollars from the political risk insurer and the Indian government. In light of the firm's successes this year, one interviewee's assertion that "*these lawyers move mountains*" does not appear to be an exaggeration.

**The Lawyers:** Co-head of the litigation department **Barry Ostrager** (see p.1485) is on clients' shortlists for sensitive and important matters, as demonstrated by his pole position in the WTC litigation. A great strategist and a robust litigator, he is a "*bulldog in court and good at handling the cold cross-examina-*

*tion,*" said clients. His competitors grant him equal praise for coordinating "*an extremely collegial group.*" **Charles Koob** (see p.1472) has a well-deserved reputation as an "*experienced and talented business litigator,*" known for his work on securities and antitrust litigation. Commercial and securities lawyer **David Ichel** (see p.1467), who also handles major products liability litigation, has had a stellar year. He obtained a favorable settlement for JPMorgan in an IPO allocation securities case comprising 309 separate actions brought against a group of underwriters. Currently, he is lead counsel to Heineken in a class action arising from the alleged targeting of underage drinkers in alcohol advertisements. Interviewees find him "*thorough and experienced – he brings balance and perspective to the most difficult cases.*" Revered throughout the country for his knowledge of commercial, antitrust and securities law, **Roy Reardon** (see p.1491) is "*without doubt, one of the most outstanding members of the litigation Bar in New York;*" while **Michael Chepiga** (see p.1444) impresses as "*at the top of his game.*" Focusing on corporate securities litigation (ranging from derivative actions to corporate control matters), he synthesizes "*litigious tenacity with a nice business demeanor.*" He was instrumental in obtaining the dismissal of all the claims asserted against five of the six underwriters of a 2001 global offering of shares of Royal Ahold NV, which pivoted on subtle jurisdictional issues. AIG and Northwest Airlines are also clients. Co-head of the securities practice, **Bruce Angiolillo** (see p.1433) is "*just terrific, smart, savvy – a classy litigator and wonderful person.*" For the last three years he has been coordinating JPMorgan Chase's global defense in the aftermath of the Enron crisis, overseeing class actions, bankruptcy claims and lawsuits brought by institutional investors. A similarly high standard of expertise in the securities

arena earns former assistant US attorney **Paul Curnin** (see p.1448) praise as a "*consummate professional.*" Clients feel comfortable around him, asserting that "*he is superb at separating the wheat from the chaff in complex cases.*" His adept representation of WorldCom adds further luster to a glowing professional image. Peers congratulate Simpson Thacher on an excellent choice in its appointment from Fried Frank in early 2005 of **Mark Stein** (see p.1504). Admirable legal skills and a "*winning personality*" make him one to watch.

**Clients/Work Highlights:** The group represented Goldman Sachs, CSFB, Deutsche Bank and others in a class action arising out of the 2000 IPO of 96 million American depository shares of Turkcell Iletisim Hizmetleri, the leading Turkish mobile communications provider. It also achieved a favorable result for Daiichi Pharmaceutical in a major patent infringement case. Most recently, the firm has been retained to represent the underwriters of offerings of Italian debt since 2005 in a putative class action filed in the US District Court for the Southern District of New York at the end of 2005. Additional clients range from The Blackstone Group, Viacom and American Electric Power to BAT and Teleglobe.

## Skadden, Arps, Slate, Meagher & Flom LLP & Affiliates
See firm details p.1557

**The Firm:** Skadden's superlative transactional practice provides a wonderful platform for the litigation department, generating an abundant amount of work as a consequence of this legal behemoth's extensive corporate clientele. "*Outstanding talent, a high level of service and a willingness to learn*" ensures, however, that the 25-strong team can stand on its own achievements. While it has secured national recognition for its products liability capability, commercial and securities-related litigation is the backbone of its success. Major victories this year include obtaining on behalf of DaimlerChrysler a complete dismissal of all federal securities and common law fraud claims brought by Tracinda. The firm is also representing toy manufacturer Jakks Pacific against a 14-count complaint by World Wrestling Entertainment alleging RICO and Robinson-Patman Act violations. Although smaller, the firm's discrete white-collar group – an offshoot of the litigation department and consisting of a number of former federal prosecutors – has a no less active portfolio. It has been heavily involved in accounting fraud cases and a number of internal investigations, including the defense of a former head of sales at Computer Associates. The team also represented Merrill Lynch during Attorney General Spitzer's multistate investigation into investment banking practice.

**The Lawyers:** "*Tremendously talented, articulate, gracious, bare-knuckled and tough,*" securities expert **Jay Kasner** (see p.1469) is a distinctive presence in the market, perfectly suited to the maelstrom of the WorldCom litigation. He is a "*strong presence in court*" and, as peers freely acknowledge, preeminent

in the investment banking arena, representing Merrill Lynch in its analyst-related suits. "*Tenacious, with a good grasp of the issues,*" **Jonathan Lerner** (see p.1474) is an "*excellent litigator and business lawyer,*" with long experience of general commercial litigation tethered to securities class actions. He was lead trial counsel for DaimlerChrysler. **Susan Saltzstein** (see p.1496) has a strong track record and "*a real staying power in the field – she has a long run ahead of her*" in the world of complex commercial litigation. As well as a comprehensive familiarity with corporate and partnership matters, she has represented clients in federal, state and international environments. **Samuel Kadet** (see p.1469), like Jonathan Lerner, is a commercial litigator with a reputation for securities matters. He handled the successful dismissal of a class action arising out of AES' acquisition of IPALCO – a local utility in Indianapolis – sued by former stockholders of the utility. Clients describe **Edward Yodowitz** (see p.1514) as "*bright and insightful, capable of seeing the bigger picture and moving between the litigation and regulatory worlds with ease.*" He focuses on securities and financial fraud investigations, including class, derivative and SEC enforcement actions. "*An extremely smart lawyer,*" **David Zornow** (see p.1515) acts in the financial institutions area, immersing himself in money laundering investigations.

**Clients/Work Highlights:** The firm counseled a major airport screening company that sued the US government for not paying reasonable compensation following the passing of legislation which effectively nationalized the industry. The government has lost two appeals. Other clients include CIBC World Markets; JPMorgan Chase; Cendant; Honeywell; Nextel; Thomson and Anheuser-Busch.

## Sullivan & Cromwell LLP
See firm details p.1558

**The Firm:** This firm engenders a "*high level of trust*" in its clientele; for "*polished professionalism*" textured with an "*easy to deal with*" approach, it is unbeatable. Expert in all areas of complex litigation, much kudos is awarded to the group's securities practice, which runs the gamut of stockholder derivative and fraud cases. At present, it represents Goldman Sachs in matters including the government's investigation into research analyst conflicts, and acts as liaison counsel to a raft of underwriters embroiled in hundreds of cases arising from the purchase of IPOs. The team continues to be extremely active in litigation affecting its broker-dealer and investment banking clients, advising Barclays and UBS in their respective Enron and HealthSouth class actions. Thriving in the fertile climates of products liability and antitrust, it is firing on all cylinders in the context of white-collar criminal defense, where it acts for both corporate and individual clients in a variety of matters, ranging from securities fraud to money laundering and bribery. In contrast to the bombast of some of its rivals, team members employ "*concise and razor-sharp*" tactics in court that command enduring client loyalty.

**The Lawyers:** Reigning over the securities market,

## Litigation: Securities
### Leading Individuals

[1] **CHEPIGA Michael** *Simpson Thacher & Bartlett*
**DIBLASI Gandolfo** *Sullivan & Cromwell LLP*
**KASNER Jay** *Skadden, Arps*
**MCCAW Robert** *WilmerHale*

[2] **ANGIOLILLO Bruce** *Simpson Thacher & Bartlett*
**BARON Robert** *Cravath, Swaine & Moore*
**BASKIN Stuart** *Shearman & Sterling LLP*
**BENEDICT James** *Milbank, Tweed*
**CURNIN Paul** *Simpson Thacher & Bartlett*
**KARP Brad** *Paul, Weiss*
**KOLB Daniel** *Davis Polk & Wardwell*
**LERNER Jonathan** *Skadden, Arps*
**LOWENTHAL Mitchell** *Cleary Gottlieb*
**MARKEL Gregory** *Cadwalader*
**MIRVIS Theodore** *Wachtell*
**ROSEN Richard** *Paul, Weiss*
**SMITH Jeffrey** *King & Spalding LLP*
**YOUNG Michael** *Willkie Farr & Gallagher*

[3] **ALLERHAND Joseph** *Weil, Gotshal & Manges*
**AUSPITZ Jack** *Morrison & Foerster LLP*
**BRODSKY David** *Latham & Watkins LLP*
**DICICCO Susan** *King & Spalding LLP*
**ECKAS Scott** *King & Spalding LLP*
**GITTER Max** *Cleary Gottlieb*
**GIUFFRA JR Robert** *Sullivan & Cromwell LLP*
**HOLLAND Mark** *Clifford Chance US LLP*
**KADET Samuel** *Skadden, Arps*
**KRAMER Daniel** *Paul, Weiss*
**MAGUIRE William** *Hughes Hubbard & Reed LLP*
**MURPHY Sean** *Milbank, Tweed*
**PIETRZAK Robert** *Sidley Austin LLP*
**PORTNOY Lawrence** *Davis Polk & Wardwell*
**POSEN Richard** *Willkie Farr & Gallagher*
**PRITCHARD John** *Pillsbury Winthrop*
**SHAPIRO Stuart** *Shapiro Forman Allen Sava*
**VIZCARRONDO JR Paul** *Wachtell*
**YODOWITZ Edward** *Skadden, Arps*

## Litigation: Securities Mainly Plaintiff
### Leading Firms

[1] **BERNSTEIN LITOWITZ BERGER** *New York*
**MILBERG WEISS BERSHAD & SCHULMAN** *New York*

### Leading Individuals

[1] **BERGER Max** *Bernstein Litowitz Berger*
**BERSHAD David** *Milberg Weiss*
**COFFEY John** *Bernstein Litowitz Berger*
**WEISS Melvyn** *Milberg Weiss*

---

"*talented, top-notch*" practitioner **Vince DiBlasi** (see p.1449) crowns his position with his work for Goldman Sachs. Interviewees praise his "*homespun style*" as a useful communication tool: "*He can make difficult law understandable for judges and juries – and speaks with a combination of intellectual acuity and toughness that makes him a fearsome adversary.*" "*Extremely smart and very busy,*" **Robert Giuffra** (see

p.1459) brings similar verve and passion to his work. One client declared him "*an absolute delight to work with; he is always willing to brainstorm and looks at every angle of every decision.*" His background in criminal, government and civil matters has played a crucial role in his defense of clients such as UBS Financial Services, for whom, in 2005, he successfuly resolved a National Association of Securities Dealers (NASD) arbitration arising from a claim seeking recission of a large reinsurance contract. This was connected with Enron and Oxford Health Plans. Commentators agree that **Karen Patton Seymour**'s (see p.1500) return to the firm from the US attorney's office, where she served as chief of the criminal division, is a "*big shot in the arm*" for the litigation practice. Head of the criminal defense and investigation group, she dedicates her brand of "*terrific, smart levelheadedness*" to representing clients subject to allegations of securities fraud, money laundering, insider trading and obstruction of justice. Demonstrating "*superb judgment,*" **Samuel Seymour** (see p.1500) is applauded for his personable approach and aptitude for "*sizing up a case and identifying the risks.*" He has participated in internal investigations for public companies under government scrutiny, including Computer Associates.

**Clients/Work Highlights:** AmSouth; Entergy-Koch Trading; Riggs National; Strong Financial; Thomas Weisel Partners; Van der Moolen Holding; CSFB; Bank of New York; Bankers Trust; Microsoft; Mattel; Vodafone; BP; Diageo and Glaxo Wellcome.

## Wachtell, Lipton, Rosen & Katz
See firm details p.1561

**The Firm:** One of the finest firms around, its fabulous credentials derive from bedrock corporate expertise and "*uniformly spectacularly smart, talented people,*" who it is able to recruit, train and keep. These roots, coupled with an "*aggressive, deeply effective*" litigation ethos, has guaranteed the firm preeminence in the realm of hostile takeovers; it has, however, developed a substantial presence in commercial disputes, major securities matters, white-collar litigation and a constellation of class actions. One of the most important characteristics of the New York office – noted with approbation by market commentators – is its choice of "*a different paradigm*" to many of its rivals. Small, it replaces sheer number of attorneys with an economy of approach that prioritizes "*exceedingly good preparation of strategic issues*" and affords clients the advantage of a partner-to-associate ratio close to one-to-one. The firm continued its representation of the leaseholder of the WTC, Silverstein Properties, in insurance litigation, and defended PNC Financial in a combined fiduciary/appraisal action in the Delaware Court of Chancery stemming from a squeeze-out merger. The group cemented its importance by overseeing NYSE's headline-making union with Archipelago Holdings. Its strength in securities matters is highlighted by a central role in litigation connected with NYSE's IPO allocation.

**The Lawyers:** "*The quintessential New York lawyer,*" **Bernard Nussbaum** (see p.1484) earns his stripes

for a string of exemplary performances in corporate and securities litigation. His "*brilliant insights and ability to get to the core of an issue*" leave rivals uneasy, while his intelligence and disarming sense of humor endear him to clients and ensure that cases progress smoothly. He was crucial to the WTC litigation; as was **Herbert Wachtell** (see p.1510), foundation stone of the firm and a "*spectacular business lawyer.*" He has shaped both the litigation group and the market itself. Observers characterize him as a "*gifted speaker and analyst*" – a description equally applicable to **Paul Vizcarrondo** (see p.1510), "*the man*" when it comes to civil securities litigation. The litigation arising from the IPO of the NYSE Group rested in his capable hands. Possessing "*an encyclopedic knowledge of Delaware law,*" few attorneys would have been better placed to handle the defense of PNC in the Delaware Court of Chancery than deal litigator **Theodore Mirvis** (see p.1480). A "*brilliant writer and thinker,*" he avoids the potential pitfall of arcane academia by throwing himself into a diverse range of matters, from defending Disney and its directors in litigation brought by major stockholders connected with the CEO selection process to advocacy on behalf of Invemed Associates in a full three-week evidentiary hearing that concluded in February 2005. A former chief of the criminal division, **Lawrence Pedowitz** (see p.1487) receives enormous respect for his white-collar work, evincing the "*perfect demeanor and intellect*" for representing boards of directors involved in complicated and large-scale investigations. He is renowned for the creativity of his legal defenses: "*He walks on water, he really does – exploring every logical avenue and case pattern. An excellent tactician, he is also a fantastic human being,*" exclaimed one source. **John Savarese** (see p.1496) is described in similar superlatives by interviewees, who identify him as "*one of the leading lights of this generation – charming, with excellent analytic ability and strategic judgment.*"

**Clients/Work Highlights:** The firm was involved in all aspects of the Sprint Nextel merger, including connected litigation. Other clients include Kimco Realty; Refco; Citigroup; Lazard Freres; Bank of America; Sears and Comerica.

## Cleary Gottlieb Steen & Hamilton LLP
See firm details p.1525

**The Firm:** Although traditionally Cleary's forte has been its unparalleled global corporate practice, the signs are that the firm is translating its expertise in this area into formidable litigation capability. The litigation team has seen dramatic growth recently both in terms of workload and resources, with more than 100 attorneys in New York regularly liaising with colleagues worldwide. This network of contacts has not gone unnoticed by clients, who appreciate a "*one-firm approach; it doesn't matter where their expert resides, they will be able to get them to help us.*" A highflier in both international arbitration and securities litigation, Cleary also has tremendous general commercial litigators. It is counsel to the Argentine Republic in litigation in New York, Italy and Germany, outwitting holdout creditor attempts to block the restructuring of more than $60 billion of the Republic's debt. Clients also praise the team's consistency, and its ability to negotiate in a "*prompt and professional*" manner. It has a strong securities litigation practice, representing many of the major investment banks in the Wall Street community. This dovetails neatly with the firm's deep corporate bench, enabling the litigation team to draw on a number of experts experienced in underwriting. By means of illustration, attorneys succeeded in obtaining the complete dismissal of all claims against Smith Barney, relating to the $2 billion IPO of Genuity – the largest Internet IPO in history. The evolution of a "*strong, cohesive culture*" ensures that the firm's more understated white-collar crime and enforcement profile benefits from this deep grounding in securities and corporate governance issues. Team members represented Bear Stearns in both state and federal investigations and class actions connected with allegations of improper mutual fund trading. **The Lawyers:** Playing a substantial role in Enron-related litigation, **Max Gitter** (see p.1459) is admired for his protean aptitude; a generalist who is equally proficient in complex securities matters, he is a "*strong advocate with great judgment.*" He takes few prisoners in court, adopting a "*hard-nosed approach*" that unseats his opposition. Clients deem him a "*pleasure to work with, open-minded and extremely responsive.*" The quality of his appellate work also wins him fans. Securities expert **Mitchell Lowenthal** (see p.1476) impresses as "*sensitive and intellectual, empowered by humor and great negotiation skills.*" Seasoned market authorities predict a bright future for this talented litigator. He led a team representing more than 20 investment banks, including Citigroup, ABN AMRO and Bank of New York, who underwrote Adelphia – the cable company undergoing bankruptcy. He succeeded in obtaining the dismissal of a series of claims brought by class action plaintiffs, eliminating billions of dollars of exposure. **Lewis**

**Liman** (see p.1475), a smart lawyer and former assistant US attorney, achieves market approval for his adroit handling of investigations relating to violations of federal securities laws – particularly those that affect broker-dealers and accounting firms. Clients/Work Highlights: Among the firm's busy caseload, a notable highlight was the group's representation of the board of directors of Citigroup in derivative claims arising from Citigroup's business dealings with Enron, WorldCom and Dynegy. In a similar vein, it is counsel to Goldman Sachs in an action pending in the Manhattan bankruptcy court in which Enron seeks to void $300 million in payments for commercial paper repurchase. It is also acting for the investment bank in securities litigation based in the Southern District of Texas. Other clients include Barclays; Bank of Nova Scotia; Crédit Lyonnais; Deutsche Bank; JPMorgan Chase; Morgan Stanley; Société Générale; SunTrust Bank; Toronto-Dominion Bank; The Shinnecock Indian Nation; Merrill Lynch; Fresh Del Monte Produce and Fleet Bank.

## Debevoise & Plimpton LLP
See firm details p.1529

**The Firm:** This terrific firm is "*going great guns*" at the moment, building on the momentum provided by its inimitable white-collar practice to entrench itself, with equal aplomb, in the securities litigation arena. Interviewees unhesitatingly attribute this "*explosion in profile*" to the appointment, three years ago, of Mary Jo White and a host of prosecutors fresh from the government. With more than 200 attorneys in New York dedicated to litigation, the firm is equipped to handle a broad range of matters, including mutual fund and securities fraud. It is particularly adept at overseeing proceedings concerning the insurance industry, representing a panoply of companies in Attorney General Spitzer's investigation. Much of the firm's high-stakes caseload originates in SEC investigations that contain a criminal or class action element, often relating to generalized challenges to industry-wide conduct. Most recently, the firm has been retained by HCA – one of the largest hospital providers in the USA – in connection with the SEC's investigation of alleged insider trading. "*Sophisticated, easy to work with and producing amazing work,*" the team has enjoyed a wave of successes this year. In a typically tour de force move, it negotiated a deferred prosecution agreement for Bristol-Myers Squibb in an investigation by the New Jersey US attorney's office into the company's accounting inventory practices. Triumphs also include securing a favorable outcome for a special committee of the Tommy Hilfiger Corporation in an internal and DOJ investigation pivoting on accounting fraud and disclosure issues – a matter that garnered considerable press coverage. Elsewhere, the team has busied itself with high-profile litigation arising from cutting-edge technological advancements, representing Sony in a number of consumer class actions and government investigations relating to a computer program installed on CDs to prevent piracy.

**The Lawyers:** **Mary Jo White**'s influence on the dramatic growth of Debevoise's litigation practice is undeniable; clients assert that, in light of her nine years as the US attorney for the Southern District of New York, she "*stands alone*" for her "*phenomenal talent*" in white-collar and commercial defense matters. "*She's it,*" one awestruck peer exclaims, "*I'll tell you, right now, she's in the first rank – by universal acclaim.*" Her recent caseload includes the ongoing representation of ACE Bermuda Insurance in a New York attorney general antitrust investigation. It would distort the strengths of the practice, however, to assume that one individual is solely responsible for its stellar reputation. "*Great litigator*" **John Kiernan** is cochair of the department and undertakes a broad range of commercial litigation and arbitration, including contract disputes, international treaty claims, securities actions and suits relating to the purchase and sale of businesses. He successfully recovered more than $400 million from the Czech Republic over its mistreatment of a client's insurance company and obtained the dismissal of a £1.8 billion creditors' claim against directors of a failed telecom company. "*Smart, thoughtful and strong,*" **Matthew Fishbein** is another white-collar expert, with profound experience at trial and appellate levels of all facets of securities and contract fraud and money laundering. Well-respected practitioner Fred Davis has recently joined Debevoise's Paris office, where he is expected to continue to make an impact on the litigation market. Clients/Work Highlights: The firm is assisting a special committee of the board of major pharmaceutical Merck to review the company's actions before the withdrawal of Vioxx in 2004. It is also representing a special committee of independent directors of Alliance Capital Management to investigate matters connected with market timing transactions in Alliance-managed mutual funds. Additional clients range from Amvescap; Forest Labs; Global Crossing and MetLife to Teleglobe; MedQuist; Royal Dutch/Shell and Westar Energy.

## Weil, Gotshal & Manges LLP
See firm details p.1565

**The Firm:** Although the view persists that Weil Gotshal's litigation practice is predominantly located in the domain of bankruptcy, this paints an incomplete picture of its scope and depth. Demonstrating "*outstanding talent and offering a high level of client service,*" the firm's 300 New York litigators are divided into 11 specialist groups designed to cater for potential claims and lawsuits in fields ranging from media and entertainment to sport. Clients highlight the proficiency with which the department coordinates this vast pool of expertise, lauding "*focus and commitment*" as the lubricant that oils the wheels of the firm's litigation machine. Peers draw attention to attorneys' significant insurance and financial services experience, which has won clients such as the NYSE. Alleged advertising impropriety provides another wellspring for the group; following the successful defense of Procter & Gamble against a multimillion-dollar claim by Colgate-Palmolive of false advertising, it has been retained by Gillette in a similar case relating to the promotion of razors. Other major litigation includes representing Bertelsmann in a $17 billion suit arising from its connections with Napster, and settling a $400 million case on behalf of AT&T. **The Lawyers:** Jonathan Polkes (see p.1489), previously at Cadwalader, Wickersham & Taft, is a lucrative catch for the firm. Sources characterize him as a *"star both in and out of the courtroom, exhibiting great common sense – he is a terrific communicator."* He works closely with a number of prominent invest-

ment banks and has achieved great results in complex securities regulatory investigations and related class actions. **James Quinn**'s (see p.1490) responsibilities as chair of the global litigation/regulatory practice have not prevented him from acquiring a reputation for being *"smart and hands-on"* in complex commercial disputes and matters arising in the IP, insurance, antitrust and products liability markets. Observers agree that he excels in jury trials. In addition to approaching his work with *"great creativity and persistence,"* co-head of the securities/corporate governance practice **Joseph Allerhand** (see p.1432) has a gift for *"commanding control in the biggest cases."* This ability is invaluable in a practice that frequently involves counseling boards of directors and special committees in disputes arising from major SEC and bankruptcy proceedings.

**Clients/Work Highlights:** Lehman Brothers; CIBC; NASDAQ; Parmalat; GE; American Airlines; ExxonMobil; Citigroup; MasterCard; Enron; CSFB and Merrill Lynch.

## Boies, Schiller & Flexner LLP
See firm details p.1520

**The Firm:** It is easy, when discussing a firm that features an attorney of such public distinction as David Boies, to overlook the strong foundations of the litigation practice from which he operates. While some interviewees maintain that the group is powered by Boies, others point to a stable of *"wonderful lawyers,"* highly active in corporate management and accounting fraud investigations, as evidence to the contrary. In the past year, the team has conducted an internal investigation on behalf of Tyco International and Qwest and defended the former chair of AIG, Hank Greenberg, in domestic and foreign regulatory investigations into the insurance and reinsurance industries. The latter suit is symptomatic of the firm's egalitarian approach to litigation; observers admire the group's adeptness at representing both plaintiffs and defendants – a situation that is particularly true in securities-related cases. Elsewhere, the practice is dedicated to increasing its international profile, adding several foreign firms to its expansive client base.

**The Lawyers:** David Boies (see p.1440) is indubitably *"one of the most in-demand lawyers in America,"* with a reputation stretching back to his involvement in the Gore v Bush case. Clients venerate him as *"the one and only"* for commercial litigation, while another market commentator expressed awe at his *"omnipotence"* in the current legal scene. He successfully represented Lloyd's of London in the WTC insurance litigation and is, among other things, acting for Hank Greenberg in the AIG matter.

**Clients/Work Highlights:** Additional clients include Adelphia Communications; American Express; Monsanto; Northwest Airlines; New York Yankees and Viacom.

## Cadwalader, Wickersham & Taft LLP
See firm details p.1522

**The Firm:** Reinsurance and securities are the mainstays of this sturdy litigation department, consisting of more than 80 attorneys. Although much of Cadwalader's expansion in recent times has taken place in DC, clear lines of communication and regular collaboration have ensured that the effects resound throughout the New York office. Taking full advantage of an expanded antitrust capability, split between the two states, the firm is representing Pfizer in multidistrict securities and derivatives litigation relating to the anti-inflammatory drug Celebrex. Involvement in high-profile matters defined a large proportion of 2005, with attorneys echoing their successful representation of Bank of America in the Enron scandal by acting for it in connection with WorldCom. The firm attracts many of Wall Street's most important financial entities, with investment banks such as Bear Stearns benefiting greatly from the team's expertise. Although some perceive Jonathan Polkes' departure to Weil Gotshal & Manges to be a setback, Bruce Hiler's appointment to the securities group in DC is expected to be a significant boon to the firm.

**The Lawyers:** According to interviewees, head of department **Gregory Markel** (see p.1477) is *"the main show,"* known throughout the USA and credited with building the firm's securities practice into a force to be reckoned with. An *"extremely knowledgeable and sophisticated lawyer, with great judgment, he never shies away from difficult issues and always finds a way to resolve them."* He represents a diverse range of clients, including Tyco International, HealthSouth and Adelphia.

**Clients/Work Highlights:** Additional highlights in the client roster include Bank of New York; ABN AMRO; HSBC; Lehman Brothers; Merrill Lynch; Morgan Stanley; GM and Park Place Entertainment.

## Cahill Gordon & Reindel LLP

**The Firm:** An esteemed presence in the New York litigation landscape, this top-flight practice harvests a high-yield of business due to its *"tough, no-nonsense"* disposition. The group handles a vast array of work in the fertile territories of antitrust, products liability, commercial and corporate disputes, but market authorities assert that complex investment banking-related securities actions are where its cadre of experienced litigators truly distinguish themselves. Interviewees were quick to praise strong performances in court and the excellent strategic skills on display in every conceivable environment – from national and international arbitrations to government and agency investigations. Clients turn to Cahill when they need a firm that can draw from a deep pool of knowledge in difficult circumstances to come out *"with all guns blazing."*

**The Lawyers:** Client favorite **Thomas Kavaler** brings an *"amazing mind"* and full-blooded flair for delivery to the courtroom. *"Flashy and effective,"* he argues his cases with a combination of personality, erudition and preparation that, according to sources, frequently outstrips his opposition.

**Clients/Work Highlights:** Clients include Sony Music; Time Warner; Deutsche Bank; AIG; CBS Broadcasting and CNN.

## Fried, Frank, Harris, Shriver & Jacobson LLP
See firm details p.1532

**The Firm:** Clients are thrilled with the service they receive from this firm, particularly highlighting the litigation team's prowess in court. It fully exploits the benefits of a prestigious corporate department and central position in the capital markets world to attract some of the most important cases around. Adopting *"an extremely honest approach to litigation in terms of evaluation of exposure and strategy,"* the group is also notable for *"not over-lawyering a case"* – a testament to the firm's watertight organization and application of more than 120 attorneys practicing in this arena. The team thrives on civil litigation flowing from corporations in distress. Its representation of Delta & Pine Land, a publicly traded international leader in transgenic and standard cotton seed, in suing Monsanto for a $1 billion breach of contract is emblematic of its high standing in this febrile environment. Observers hold out as talismanic the group's expertise in securities litigation, where it immerses itself in accounting frauds and government investigations. The firm has had a busy couple of years in these areas, representing the NYSE in class action litigation and CIT Group in a suit arising from the aftermath of its 2002 IPO and subsequent announcement of increased loan loss reserves. The team was successful in having dismissed the claim that CIT's prospectus was false and misleading. It is currently representing regular client Goldman Sachs in major litigation. A recent dedication to discovery law as a specialty, coupled with a first-rate IP practice and premier white-collar group, which defends broker dealers, insurance companies and hedge funds in criminal and regulatory investigations, completes a highly appealing package.

**The Lawyers: Douglas Flaum** (see p.1455) is lauded by clients as an *"outstanding attorney – bright and personable; a great strategist, always prepared, and a wonderful team player."* He splits his practice evenly between securities and general commercial litigation, devoting much of his time to representing committees and boards of directors during investigations. His work this year has included defending CIT and a selection of its officers and directors in a securities class action, and representing three Goldman Sachs managing directors in a suit alleging tortious interference and breach of duty resulting in dismissal. On the commercial side, he defeated a motion for summary judgment in a case involving breach of license agreement for medical products. **Audrey Strauss** (see p.1505) *"has just the right qualities to go into a room and take charge – she's understated but extremely powerful."* Clients look to her for assistance with the most serious white-collar criminal defense matters, confident that her acute intelligence, experience and devotion to their cause will *"navigate the rockiest shores."* With insight into the inner workings of the SEC, she represents a range of investment

banks and other financial entities. William McGuinness is the chair of the New York office's litigation department while Carmen Lawrence co-heads the securities regulation and enforcement practice.

**Clients/Work Highlights:** The firm plays pivotal roles in actions connected with Enron and Adelphia, and successfully represented Martha Stewart Living Omnimedia and its board of directors in stockholder derivative litigation. Other clients include State Bank of Long Island; Shamrock Holdings; Kindred Healthcare; PDI; Soros Fund Management; Ameritrade Holdings; Datek and Merrill Lynch.

## Kirkland & Ellis LLP
See firm details p.875

**The Firm:** A *"formidable operation,"* this group's exemplary trial preparation and trademark toughness draw in those clients that want attorneys who are *"unafraid to litigate the most difficult cases."* Although smaller in scale than the firm's Chicago headquarters, the New York office is far from being the weaker sibling. Among its numerous victories this year, the team successfully defended Morgan Stanley against accusations that its sales of proprietary and partner funds contravened provisions in the Massachusetts Uniform Securities Act. In a separate matter, the group achieved the dismissal of a claim alleging that the investment bank had breached its fiduciary duty of loyalty to its online brokerage customers as a consequence of the sale of its online brokerage accounts. The firm's coverage of the market is strengthened by its commitment to training attorneys *"from top to bottom"* to a high standard of advocacy, and bolstered by the sizable resources of the DC office. As well as a strong showing in the general commercial market, where Kirkland deploys more than 50 lawyers, insurance and IP litigation are fundamental tenets of the practice. The group handles work in the latter regard for clients such as Honeywell, for which it obtained a defense verdict in a case originating in the closure of a microturbine division and relating to breach of contract, IP conversion and fraudulent misrepresentation. A healthy stream of work in the products liability and securities arenas completes the picture, exemplified by Kirkland's emphatic defense of the independent directors of a major mutual fund against a barrage of federal securities and common law claims.

**The Lawyers:** One of the founding partners of the New York office, William Pratt undertakes a substantial amount of work for Verizon, including securing the successful dismissal of a large class action case claiming improper conduct in relation to Verizon's prior ownership of Genuity. His comprehensive realm of experience spans antitrust, IP and tort matters.

**Clients/Work Highlights:** Again on behalf of Verizon, the group won a motion to compel arbitration between it and its insurance carrier. Additional work this year included obtaining injunctive relief against the FDA for Teva Pharmaceuticals in a patent-related dispute, and representing Kmart in its breach of

contract litigation with Capital One. Further clients include Lucent Technologies; GM; American Skandia and News Corporation.

## Kramer Levin Naftalis & Frankel LLP
See firm details p.1539

**The Firm:** The *"utterly excellent and very smart people"* comprising this tight group of predominantly New York-based litigators are commonly perceived to be involved in *"everything under the sun."* The practice's reach encompasses real estate, employment, ERISA and bankruptcy disputes – a breadth that leaves competitors deeply impressed – but most of the plaudits are reserved for its complex securities and white-collar litigation expertise. The team is well known for its polished performance on behalf of major public companies and individuals under investigation for alleged insurance and accounting fraud and financial irregularities. It won much positive press for its work for AIG, handling the antitrust aspects of the government's investigation into insurance industry procedure, and represented Kenneth Langone, the founder of Home Depot, in a lawsuit relating to the compensation of NYSE head Richard Grasso. Other market-rippling representations include defending Deloitte Touche Tohmatsu in litigation stemming from the Parmalat bankruptcy, and advising Canary Capital Partners in investigations connected with the mutual fund industry, achieving a $40 million settlement with regard to accusations of improper trading.

**The Lawyers: Gary Naftalis** (see p.1482) is a great all-rounder, an extremely skilled general commercial litigator and a *"big-league white-collar defense"* lawyer. His responsibilities as head of the litigation department and cochair of the firm are matched only by the magnitude of his caseload, the centerpieces of which include his victorious defense of Disney CEO, Michael Eisner, in the stockholders' derivative suit relating to Michael Ovitz's hiring and contract termination. Lead partner in the Canary Capital Partners suit and currently acting for the former chief executive of REFCO, he is *"at the top of his game."*

**Clients/Work Highlights:** Other work for the group, and spearheaded by Naftalis, includes successfully representing Gary Winnick, former chair and founder of Global Crossing, in various SEC and regulatory inquiries. Clients range from Johnson & Johnson; Procter & Gamble; Bear Stearns and Vishay Intertechnology to CIBC World Markets and Lehman Brothers.

## Shearman & Sterling LLP
See firm details p.1554

**The Firm:** With more than 100 litigators worldwide, Shearman & Sterling has undisputed international presence, which equips it for an array of multijurisdictional matters. Flying high in banking and finance circles, it is unsurprising that a large proportion of the firm's ever-expanding litigation caseload is devoted to representing corporations and financial entities involved in the most sensitive business disputes. Following a bench trial in July 2005, the group successfully concluded Merrill Lynch's long-standing breach of contract claim against Allegheny, obtaining damages in excess of $115 million on behalf of the bank. Commentators argue that the firm's assured entrance into the Enron litigation – representing Merrill Lynch – has elevated the firm's securities practice onto a greater stage. In addition to two dozen ongoing SEC investigations, attorneys have acted for Ford in class action litigation connected with the nationwide recall of Firestone tires on Ford Explorers. There is also a rich seam of white-collar defense work, which the firm treats as commensurate with the criminal elements of securities litigation. The group achieved the dismissal of a putative class action instigated by mutual fund shareholders and directed at its independent executives. It has also overseen a variety of internal investigations relating to the Foreign Corrupt Practices Act and represented company CEOs facing criminal charges. Preferring a flexible structure as opposed to division into rigid practice groups, the litigation department operates with *class and subtlety*."

**The Lawyers:** "*Terrific attorney and extremely smart*" **Stuart Baskin** (see p.1436) is a securities expert. Leading the charge in the Merrill Lynch and Enron litigations, his achievements in 2005 also include securing a billion-dollar conclusion for Con Edison to a case arising from a terminated merger with Northeast Utilities, and handling major litigation on behalf of Elan Pharmaceuticals. A formidable enforcement attorney, SEC investigations are frequently the meat of his practice.

**Clients/Work Highlights:** The firm made the most of its global prowess to represent the Slovak Republic in a lengthy arbitration, concluded in 2005, arising from the dissolution of Czechoslovakia and involving hearings in DC, London and Prague. Other clients include NBC Universal; Delphi; BCE (Bell Canada); Boston Scientific; Flag Telecom; Viacom; Deloitte & Touche; KPMG; Nokia and Royal Group.

## White & Case LLP
See firm details p.1566

**The Firm:** White & Case continues to move into the New York limelight, adding to the brilliance of its illumination with six lateral hires during 2005. These join a deep litigation bench, applauded for containing "*extremely smart partners and excellent junior members, who are aggressive but not to the point of being counterproductive.*" While some peers were uncertain about the firm's visibility in this market, client admiration was voluble, ranging from praise leveled at the group's expeditious handling of complex commercial litigation to its "*amazing written product*" and performance in IP, products liability and antitrust matters. A unit of attorneys led the charge in defense of Syngenta Seeds in a putative class action originating in allegations that several manufacturers had conspired to fix the price of genetically modified corn. The firm is also highly active in the securities arena, having obtained a precedent-setting conclusion to a sprawling SEC investigation of major client Royal Ahold that

resulted in no monetary penalties. A well-fashioned defense of Deutsche Bank against various actions lurking in the murky waters of the Enron litigation, which saw the most serious securities claims dismissed in early 2005, adds further sheen to a polished reputation.

**The Lawyers:** Head of commercial litigation **Michael Shuster** (see p.1501) is "*aggressive and creative*," focused on the endgame and employing "*excellent courtroom abilities and tactical judgment*" to achieve the best possible results. He successfully represented Comcast in obtaining the dismissal of one of the biggest claims ever brought within the orbit of the Securities Exchange Act. His work in the securities area extends to the energy sector, where Saudi Aramco and Amerada Hess are notable client examples. "*Great in situations where finesse is essential,*" chair of the New York corporate defense group **Lawrence Byrne** (see p.1442) was one of the flag bearers in the Ahold litigation and is currently representing Ian Norris, the former CEO of Morgan Crucible, in a Pennsylvania-based criminal antitrust action marking the first time the USA has sought to extradite a UK executive on price-fixing charges. Tasked with coordinating the firm's global dispute work, **Vince FitzPatrick** (see p.1455) receives hearty commendation as "*a harmonizer, a wonderful strategist.*" Quality work behind the scenes is not, however, his only strength: "*He has a winning manner in the courtroom, coming across as eminently fair and reasonable, with a style that appeals to both judge and jury.*" In a practice that, inevitably, takes him all over the world, his caseload includes involvement in the investigation into the UN's oil-for-food program in Iraq. Closer to home, he played an important role in bringing the Sygenta case to a close.

**Clients/Work Highlights:** British Airways; Citigroup; JPMorgan Chase; Mirant; Moody's Investors Service; Novartis; Republic of Poland; Royal Bank of Canada; Sandoz and Takeda Chemical Industries.

## Dewey Ballantine LLP
See firm details p.1530

**The Firm:** Engaging in work across the board, including IP, antitrust, securities and corporate fraud matters, this accomplished firm demonstrates a particular panache for bondholder disputes and litigation connected with insurance claims. As well as continuing its defense of Travelers Indemnity Company and its subsidiary, Gulf Insurance, in the multibillion-dollar insurance coverage-related lawsuit precipitated by 9/11 and the WTC's destruction, Dewey triumphed in obtaining the dismissal of the first of several massive nationwide actions leveled at the MONY Group's sales practices. Attorneys at the firm are also representing the US lumber industry in a mammoth trade dispute with Canada concerning unfair dumping practices. This has involved appearances before numerous courts, administrative agencies and international tribunals. Dewey has made its presence felt, too, in the lucrative arena of sports antitrust, acting for the Metropolitan Intercollegiate Basketball Association in an action against the National Collegiate Athletic Asso-

ciation. Interviewees have a healthy respect for the firm's distinctive brand of "*hard-nosed pragmatism*" and highlight its winning combination of expertise and competitive billing.

**The Lawyers:** Cochair of the litigation department **Harvey Kurzweil** (see p.1473) has stamped his mark on many of the firm's most significant cases since joining in 1969. Although his practice encompasses major commercial disputes of every hue, peers reserve their most glowing accolades for his work in antitrust and insurance litigation. He is pivotal in both the WTC and MONY Group matters.

**Clients/Work Highlights:** Additional clients include AXA Financial; Coalition for Fair Lumber Imports; Deutsche Bank AG New York and Matsushita Electric.

## Gibson, Dunn & Crutcher LLP
See firm details p.328

**The Firm:** Historically a legal juggernaut on the West Coast, the firm's New York office sustains a Californian mentality which clients find refreshing; the team is "*not at all stuck up*" and pursues work with vigor. To this end, it has greatly expanded its litigation practice. Consisting of 16 partners, the group undertakes the full spectrum of complex commercial and securities-related disputes. Leading the charge in opposition to the West Side Stadium project, which attracted more press coverage than almost any other public policy issue in New York in the last couple of years, it is no stranger to highly visible and demanding cases. The team – led by Randy Mastro – figures prominently in a myriad of Wall Street controversies, and is representing Bear Stearns in consolidated federal securities class actions involving several underwriters and relating to the allocation of hi-tech IPOs. A sizable tranche of the practice is devoted to accountancy fraud, with a heavyweight clientele that includes Deloitte & Touche, and dealing with insurance coverage issues for the likes of Empire Blue-Cross BlueShield and AIG.

**The Lawyers:** An alumnus of the Giuliani administration, **Randy Mastro's** (see p.1478) experience, which included coordinating efforts to clear the streets of organized crime, serves him well in a practice centered on white-collar matters as they overlap and emanate from commercial disputes. Respected by clients for his integrity and honesty, he has created a name for himself as one of the few litigators in New York willing to bring a law suit against the state. In an echo of his past, he successfully challenged the Bloomberg administration's plan to move Manhattan's Fulton Fish Market to the Bronx excluding his client (the unloading firm Laro Service Systems), arguing that its absence would leave the fish-selling business vulnerable to corruption. "*Great on his feet,*" he also won a major appellate victory establishing the legality of Indian casino gaming in New York State and spearheaded the West Side Stadium litigation. Cochair of the media and entertainment practice, **Orin Snyder's** (see p.1503) "*terrific instincts*" and excellence as a cross-examiner give the firm a razor-sharp edge in the cut-throat environment of music and film-related litigation.

He is equally adept in white-collar matters and internal corporate investigations.

**Clients/Work Highlights:** The firm's impressive clientele also includes Peerless Importers; Madison Square Garden; Cablevision; Newsday; Edison Schools; Dow Jones; Verizon; Edison Properties and UBS Financial Services.

## Jones Day

See firm details p.570

**The Firm:** This New York office of this international giant comprises 18 partners and 55 other lawyers, and demonstrates an ability to acquire respected market players and new strands of expertise that makes it a powerful force. Its experience stretches from IP and general corporate criminal investigations to securities fraud and products liability and it is a familiar presence to its peers. A host of significant actions include obtaining a ruling following a two and a half week bench trial in the Southern District that awarded American Electric Power $123 million in relation to a breach of contract dispute with TEMI. The well-established securities litigation practice, accustomed to heavy-duty matters, has come to particular eminence in the Enron litigation, acting for Lehman Brothers and RBS in more than 100 actions consolidated in the Southern District of Texas.

**The Lawyers:** Richard Werder coordinates the New York office's litigation department while David Carden co-heads the firm's securities litigation practice, focusing on derivates and shareholder matters. He represented Lehman Brothers in the Enron litigation.

**Clients/Work Highlights:** In September 2005, the team successfully defended Nextel Communications in an action brought by Nextel Partners that sought to enjoin the rollout of the new Sprint Nextel brand. Additional clients include Air Products; Cablevision; Bear Stearns; Chevron; Deutsche Bank; Federated Department Stores; GM; IBM; International Paper; Pfizer; RJ Reynolds; Symbol Technologies and Textron.

## Kaye Scholer LLP

See firm details p.1536

**The Firm:** Kaye Scholer has been a celebrated feature of New York's litigation landscape for decades with a 190-strong team that raises the bar for much of the market, with manifest expertise in antitrust and IP matters. The firm's specialist products liability and mass tort practice group, in particular, is showered with plaudits for its performance as national coordinating counsel in trials throughout the country. In addition, the firm has also been busy in general commercial disputes – often with an international dimension. By way of illustration, the team represented the Government of China in major derivatives litigation in an eight-week trial in the Southern District of New York. Nor has it neglected the securities arena, undertaking a variety of SEC investigations and favorably concluding complex, tax-related litigation for National Energy Group.

**The Lawyers:** Aaron Rubinstein specializes in securities and derivatives issues, heading the firm's titular practice group. He acts for Pappas Telecasting Companies in numerous disputes and is representing a former director of an international telecom company.

**Clients/Work Highlights:** Clients in the pharmaceutical, tobacco and other industries include Pfizer; Boston Scientific; Novartis; sanofi-aventis; RJ Reynolds; Minmetals and Sony.

## Latham & Watkins LLP

**The Firm:** As one branch of a global outfit, the New York office's horizons are far reaching; the firm's international overview enables members of the securities litigation and professional liability practice to keep abreast of developments in EU securities law, ensuring it is an attractive proposition to both foreign and domestic clients embroiled in class actions before US courts. Deemed a *"real player"* in this environment by seasoned commentators, the group achieved a total defense victory for CIBC in an NYSE arbitration, which involved negotiating the intricacies of ERISA law and dealing with allegations of breach of fiduciary duty. In other matters, attorneys continued their winning representation of John Cassese by having the quashing of his conviction for insider trading affirmed by the Second Circuit Court of Appeals.

**The Lawyers:** The appointment in 2002 of the *"smart, high-energy"* **David Brodsky** has contributed greatly to the invigoration of Latham's litigation group. In his role as chair, he has cultivated a name for himself as someone who can *"sort out all manner of problems,"* utilizing his experience as general counsel at CSFB in such a deft way that one observer exclaimed: *"Boy, is he good in a tight spot."* He has a global litigation docket that also covers financial service claims and internal investigations. As well as defending John Cassese and representing CIBC, he is spearheading Latham's involvement, following an extensive selection process, in REFCO's investigation into the circumstances surrounding a previously undisclosed transaction involving a former CEO.

**Clients/Work Highlights:** Other victories this year include persuading the plaintiffs to drop a securities class action against Ernst & Young without having to file a motion to dismiss, and obtaining summary judgment for Koch Investment Group in a shareholder derivative lawsuit arising from allegations of unlawful trading. Elsewhere, the firm has been retained by Deloitte & Touche to represent it in a $12 billion securities class action arising from a multibillion-dollar stock drop connected with Attorney General Spitzer's investigation into alleged bid rigging by Marsh & McLennan brokers. Further clients include MetLife, Ameriprise Financial; Cambrex and Willbros.

## Proskauer Rose LLP

See firm details p.1551

**The Firm:** Sewn into the fabric of the New York legal world since its formation in the Big Apple in 1875, Proskauer's excellent litigation and dispute resolution department operates along classical lines; it offers *"fierce, no holds barred"* advocacy and a case-winning ease in court born of years of trial experience. The practice contains more than 300 litigators with no fewer than 18 subgroups, focusing on corporate finance, insurance, securities, antitrust and IP-related litigation. Its clientele includes issuers, directors, officers, broker-dealers, accountants and law firms. Recently, the firm has played a pivotal role in several matters at the heart of the city. As well as representing the New York Jets in the West Side Stadium dispute, a team working alongside Wachtell, Lipton, Rosen & Katz in the WTC litigation won $2 billion worth of insurance coverage for leaseholder Silverstein Properties.

**The Lawyers:** Experienced trial lawyer Louis Solomon took over as co-head of the practice in early 2005. He has tried multiple complex commercial cases in federal and state courts across the country and fields expertise in government investigations that cuts across numerous industry lines.

**Clients/Work Highlights:** The firm's appearances on the international stage include winning litigation arising from the billion-dollars restructuring of Multicanal. Bristol-Myers Squibb also features in the group's client roster.

## Willkie Farr & Gallagher LLP

See firm details p.1567

**The Firm:** A strong general litigation presence, the group's real strength lies in securities, with an emphasis on financial reporting and accounting problems. In the wake of Enron and the subsequent explosion of auditing-related lawsuits and class actions, clients have recognized the huge advantages of this firm's expertise in this arena. Accordingly, the group has had a busy year. In addition to representing KPMG and BDO Seidman in litigation connected with the marketing of tax shelter strategies, attorneys are involved in an investigation into alleged pension-related financial irregularities connected with the City of San Diego. The firm is also handling insurance, IP and FCPA cases, frequently appearing before the SEC and supervising internal investigations. A rapidly growing presence in the antitrust arena completes a practice built on broad foundations.

**The Lawyers:** **Michael Young** (see p.1514) is *"wonderful – there is no one better at accounting firm issues,"* agreed sources. Gifted in the vocabulary of financial litigation, he is, in the estimation of sources, one of the few attorneys to regularly try cases in this field. **Richard Posen** (see p.1489) is described as *"a strong litigator with great judgment."* He is known for representing boards of directors in corporate securities litigation and was hired by Goldman Sachs and Lehman Brothers in the WorldCom litigation.

**Clients/Work Highlights:** Further clients include Deloitte & Touche; American Institute of Certified Public Accountants; Philips and Johnson & Johnson.

## Allen & Overy LLP

See firm details p.1516

**The Firm:** Although the firm's New York office may be relatively small, with a total of 23 lawyers, it fosters "*positive relationships*" with clients, drawing on its global powerhouse reputation for dispute resolution to complement its nascent litigation practice. Boasting a clutch of federal prosecutors, the team undertakes a fair amount of white-collar defense work, acting as liaison counsel for 12 directors of World-Com in securities litigation in the Southern District. In other big-name work, the firm is representing Barclays Bank in bankruptcy court litigation arising from Enron's implosion and counseling CSFB in the Parmalat securities litigation.

**The Lawyers:** Former assistant US attorney for the Southern District of New York, **Michael Feldberg** (see p.1453) is lauded by clients as a creative adviser who is "*great to bounce ideas off – thoughtful, responsive, diligent, enthusiastic and focused.*" **Jacob Pultman** (see p.1490) creates a wonderful rapport with clients, who praised his pragmatism and skill in simplifying complex litigation issues: "*He is incredible at details and at looking at the whole picture – he sees the forest and the bark on the tree at the same time.*" Sources "*wouldn't hesitate to hire*" **Pamela Rogers Chepiga** (see p.1493), depicting her as "*able, focused, effective and strong.*" She served as chief of the securities and commodities fraud task force for the Southern District of New York.

**Clients/Work Highlights:** Barclays Bank; CSFB; RBS and former directors of WorldCom.

## Mayer, Brown, Rowe & Maw LLP
See firm details p.876

**The Firm:** Clients are impressed by Mayer Brown's corporate culture of flexibility and sincerity, and its ability to handle litigation fought in multiple jurisdictions. With 400 attorneys worldwide and 70 based in New York, the group can "*bring 18-inch guns to bear, with great effect,*" in a broad sweep of a practice that takes in products liability, environmental, insurance, securities and general commercial disputes. In addition to a fearsome appellate practice, the firm has a reputation for fighting off complex class actions. The team successfully extracted Crédit Lyonnais from a series of federal suits arising from conspiracy allegations relating to the global copper futures market. The firm also hits the mark in the securities and SEC enforcement arena, where centerpiece matters this year include representing 11 current and former officers and directors of AIG in headline-grabbing fraud and shareholder derivative suits in New York and Delaware, filed in the aftermath of Hank Greenberg's departure. Observers relish the group's pragmatism and lack of courtroom posturing and spotlight the strong communication between senior and junior members.

**The Lawyers:** Clients view **Dennis Orr** (see p.1485) as "*an innovator, a thinker who does his homework, comes up with the goods and doesn't holler in court.*" A veteran of more than 30 state and federal court trials, he acted for AIG's former executives in securities litigation and continues to be a member of the issuer defendants committee in the IPO allocation fraud case pending in New York's Southern District. He is also a figure of considerable stature in major antitrust, IP and related patent litigation. Commen-

tators are in awe of **Steven Wolowitz** (see p.1514) breadth of vision in the preparation and execution of cases: "*He is telescopic when identifying problems on the horizon, wide-angled in his ability to see who is coming at us sideways and microscopic when picking up on trial-winning details.*" His niche is complex commercial and financial services litigation, where he is currently defending Bank of America in a case brought by Allied Irish Banks, arising from the loss of $700 million by AIB's US subsidiary Allfirst Bank. Younger than his colleagues in this list, **Grant Esposito** (see p.1452) is fast becoming a lightning rod for praise, with interviewees applauding his work in commercial litigation, accountants' liability and general securities matters as "*practical, timely and effective.*" According to one client; "*he understands from the beginning your strengths and weaknesses and is not afraid to tell you.*"

**Clients/Work Highlights:** Other clients include Société Générale, CIBC World Markets and TIAA-CREF.

## Morrison & Foerster LLP
See firm details p.335

**The Firm:** Clients are not shy in their praise of this firm, with one awarding the litigation practice "*a big fat ten out of ten*" for its general commercial and securities capability, often weighted on the technology side. While it may lack the profile of some its immediate competition, the New York group is rapidly ascending to reach the lofty standing of its colleagues on the West Coast, garnering attention for a "*smart, detail-oriented*" approach that prioritizes running that extra mile in complex cases: "*They care about problems and make timely, unsolicited recommendations.*" The firm has been heavily involved in the government's expansive investigation of the insurance industry, representing The Hartford in securities, derivative and ERISA cases and persuading the plaintiffs in the latter to dismiss their action before a motion to dismiss had to be filed. Increasingly, the firm has also been recognized for its "*global amenity,*" undertaking internal investigations on behalf of Asian companies with a US presence.

**The Lawyers:** Cochair of the securities and white-collar defense group, **Jack Auspitz** (see p.1434) is commended for a terrific performance in the IPO allocation litigation. Adopting a more understated approach than a number of his rivals, "*he gets along well with people on all sides.*" In keeping with the firm's focus on international matters, he has begun acting for a Chinese manufacturer against its US distributor for $450 million worth of products delivered but not paid for. His busy caseload also includes representing two of four individual defendants in a large consolidated securities class action connected with Metromedia Fiber Network.

**Clients/Work Highlights:** Other clients include Sichuan Changhong Electric; deCODE Genetics; Barnes & Noble and Bank of America.

## WilmerHale
See firm details p.580

**The Firm:** A relatively young firm in the history of New York litigation, WilmerHale has permeated the securities market with alacrity; as one attorney observes: "*They're in everything.*" The 18-partner group has entrenched itself in Wall Street, representing a variety of the city's leading financial institutions. Peers were particularly impressed by its commanding role in the infamous IPO allocation litigation, where it acted for CSFB and Citigroup Global Markets in connection with more than 300 filed complaints. "*Knowledgeable and extremely responsive, producing an extraordinarily high quality of work,*" the team has attracted a high-caliber caseload that also includes acting for the underwriting consortium in the 2005 IPO of REFCO in shareholder actions relating to alleged accounting fraud. While the firm's distinctive footprint in securities litigation attracts most attention, the group is no slouch when it comes to complex commercial matters and white-collar criminal defense. Performing on a national stage, lawyers are representing Daimler-Chrysler in multijurisdictional litigation and arbitration of an international dispute that encompasses Korea and Germany.

**The Lawyers:** Partner in the litigation, financial institutions and securities departments, **Charles Platt** (see p.1488), formerly of LeBoeuf, Lamb, Greene & MacRae, has done a superb job for clients, being "*extremely knowledgeable in the insurance sales practice area, extraordinarily responsive, practical and creative. He is also exceptionally well-informed about the latest trends and developments.*" **Robert McCaw** (see p.1478) brings "*tremendous brainpower*" to a broad-based practice that sees him act for heavyweight brokerage firms, corporations and accounting entities in virtually any matter. A steady hand with the regulators, he has "*impeccable judgment and perspective, exuding a confidence that really stands out.*" His facility in IPO cases is legendary. Clients bask in the order and discipline **Paul Engelmayer** (see p.1452) brings to the most difficult white-collar disputes, while peers respect him as a "*clear and forceful*" advocate and counselor. He is involved in the defense of The Hartford in the putative class actions looming over the insurance industry.

**Clients/Work Highlights:** Additional clients include Bayer; HSBC; Capital One; Citigroup; JPMorgan Chase; Bear Stearns and Merrill Lynch.

## Clifford Chance US LLP
See firm details p.1526

**The Firm:** Clifford Chance remains a key part of the New York landscape, despite the inevitable effect of losing several major figures in the last couple of years. It also has cachet as the only magic circle firm to have made a significant impact on the US market, challenging preconceptions about the culture shock associated with such a migration. With more than 300 IPO allocation cases pending in the Southern District, the litigation practice is certainly not short of work; housing a specialist securities group, its forte is white-collar criminal defense as it overlaps with securities disputes. As well as ongoing representation of enduring client Merrill Lynch, the firm triumphed on behalf of Alliance Capital in a jury trial arising from the Enron catastrophe and regularly defends public companies facing accounting fraud actions. It has profound experience of helping clients navigate the rocky terrain of SEC investigations, enforcement proceedings and – benefiting from its international purview – the Foreign Corrupt Practices Act. Other successes include winning a full acquittal for the division CFO of a major banking institution, who had been indicted in connection with conspiracy and mail fraud.

**The Lawyers:** With decades-long experience, **Mark Holland** is closely and warmly identified with litigating major securities class actions and derivatives suits. He is admired in court and viewed as a "*steady and understated leader*" in IPO allocation matters, garnering considerable market exposure. **John Carroll**, a former chief of the securities and commodities fraud task force in the US attorney's office, has a "*great bedside manner: calm and informed in fiendishly difficult circumstances.*" A large proportion of his time is spent representing financial institutions and senior officers in accounting fraud-related investigations.

**Clients/Work Highlights:** Clifford Chance's extensive clientele includes ABN AMRO; AXA Advisors; Charles Schwab; Instinet; Merck; Morgan Stanley and Sakura Global Capital.

## King & Spalding LLP
See firm details p.1538

**The Firm:** King & Spalding's importation of a raft of high-quality attorneys from Cadwalader has had an immensely successful outcome, with the firm drawing praise from clients for a "*deeply impressive*," ever-expanding team of litigators in New York, well versed in commercial, antitrust and securities matters. It differentiates itself from much of the market by virtue of its expertise in cases connected with complex financial instruments such as collateral, fixed income and derivatives transactions. Observers applaud the group's aptitude in the latter area while drawing equal attention to its profound knowledge of capital markets-related disputes and ability to unravel complicated trading claims. United under the direction of Jeffrey Smith, this cohesive unit of attorneys represents a panoply of investment banks in SEC investigations. The team is currently acting for CSFB in a number of consolidated cases pending in Arizona, New Jersey, New York and Ohio – arising from the collapse of National Century Financial Enterprises – and does a substantial amount of work for Lehman Brothers.

**The Lawyers:** Senior partner **Jeffrey Smith** (see p.1503) is a beacon for clients seeking assistance with complex securities and commercial cases. "*Low-key but effective,*" he is a "*person of high integrity and a market-savvy, versatile negotiator.*" Antitrust is another arena in which he is renowned. **Scott Eckas** (see p.1451) "*takes a more analytical approach than most,*" excelling at representing clients in the bankruptcy court. He shines in cases of "*manifest*

complexity," said clients. **Susan DiCicco**'s (see p.1449) experience of commercial and securities litigation ranges from breach of contract and fiduciary duty matters to business torts, but she is "*absolutely spectacular*" in the trading structure space, sources report.

**Clients/Work Highlights:** Clients also include Freddie Mac; Brown & Williamson Tobacco; Coca-Cola; Dow Chemical; GSK; KPMG; Merrill Lynch; Purdue Pharma and UCB.

## Milbank, Tweed, Hadley & McCloy LLP

**The Firm:** Doing great work in major disputes, this is the firm's largest practice area, with securities-related litigation being a real strength. For the past 30 years the team has specialized in defending class actions and derivatives suits, boasting enduring relationships with NYSE and JPMorgan Chase, among others. It advises all limbs of Citigroup, handling a multimillion-dollar IPO dispute arising from Citibank's underwriting of a major telecom company currently going through bankruptcy proceedings. The team is also heavily involved in mutual funds litigation and represents Fidelity Investments in alleged securities and antitrust law violations. Attorneys continue to act in one of the largest claims ever brought under the Investment Company Act of 1940, following the demise of Bennett Funding Group. The firm's liberal sprinkling of expertise also covers insurance and white-collar disputes, where clients benefit from the presence of five former federal prosecutors and a number of SEC specialists.

**The Lawyers:** Since joining the firm in October 2004, the "*highly talented*" **James Benedict** has employed his intellect and experience gained at Clifford Chance to drive forward the defense of major securities class actions and derivative suits. Another Clifford Chance alumnus, **Sean Murphy** "*does a fantastic job, speaking in a language everyone understands.*" He was one of three principal lawyers who tried a $3 billion case for Alliance Capital and is currently involved in the defense of Fidelity Investments. **Scott Edelman** has cultivated a gilt-edged reputation effortlessly melding white-collar and civil litigation. In addition to representing financial titans UBS and JPMorgan Chase, he has acted for senior executives from the world's leading pharmaceutical, brokerage and telecom companies.

## Bernstein Litowitz Berger & Grossmann LLP
See firm details p.1519

**The Firm:** Clients are unanimous in their opinion that Bernstein Litowitz gives "*the best advice in the field.*" Wall Street, meanwhile, has been left shaken by the firm's decimation of its defenses in the WorldCom litigation. It has always had a strong reputation for prosecuting class and private actions on behalf of individual and institutional clients, but, as commentators observe and recent headlines confirm, the team has "*really stepped up to the game on this one.*" It applied specialized securities expertise and

resources to devastating effect, recovering more than $6 billion from the 17 investment banks that underwrote the sale of WorldCom bonds. Arthur Andersen, the only defendant in the class action trial before Judge Cote, contributed $65 million to this immense cash pool, shortly before closing arguments. The firm's sterling track record also includes securing an almost unprecedented class action verdict in favor of investors in the Clarent securities fraud trial, and obtaining corporate governance reforms on a wide scale. Deemed "*ethical, honorable and not just out to get a large fee*" by market authorities, Bernstein Litowitz's role as the Robin Hood of New York law firms seems assured for years to come.

**The Lawyers:** The "*tough and passionate*" **Sean Coffey** (see p.1445) spearheaded the team prosecuting the WorldCom securities class action, earning the respect – and fear – of the financial world. Prior to his appointment to the firm, he was a litigation partner at Latham & Watkins. Founding member **Max Berger** (see p.1438) has a similarly weighty profile, having obtained a $3.2 billion settlement in the Cendant securities litigation. Interviewees laud him as "*one of the best fraud litigators out there.*" Together, he and Coffey attract praise for keeping clients fully informed: "*They never make a decision without consultation.*"

**Clients/Work Highlights:** The firm regularly represents investors, share and bondholders in a variety of securities fraud class actions.

## Milberg Weiss Bershad & Schulman LLP

**The Firm:** This firm is a lighthouse for institutional investors sailing into the stormy waters of individual and class action securities litigation relating to corporate fraud and breaches of fiduciary duty. Intense media scrutiny following its 2004 split, which saw William Lerach lead the charge in San Diego and Melvyn Weiss assume sole responsibility for the New York office, has not dented its allure as one of the most prominent plaintiff firms in the country. "*People looking at this book are going to be looking for Milberg,*" agreed sources. With more than 120 attorneys in the securities practice and additional offices in Florida, Delaware and DC, the "*600 lb gorilla*" team's focus has grown since its inception in 1965 to accommodate insurance, antitrust and products liability litigation. A multilayered SEC, accounting and federal prosecution background adds further muscle to this aggressive opponent of major corporations and financial institutions.

**The Lawyers:** Senior and founding partner of the firm **Mel Weiss** is, competitors agree, "*in a league of his own.*" A well-known figure in the New York business world, he is a regular participant in public forums and debates concerning the evolution of securities law; a fearsome adversary in court, he prosecutes the full gamut of class, derivative, and mass actions and significant private claims. **David Bershad**, like Weiss, is a familiar market presence, engaged in prosecutions connected with federal securities, antitrust and consumer law issues – topics on which he is also a prolific writer.

**Clients/Work Highlights:** The firm represents a host of stockholders and investors in mutual fund, telecom and investment banking organizations.

## Covington & Burling

See firm details p.563

**The Firm:** Covington & Burlington is *"developing strongly"* in the New York white-collar and securities environment, agreed commentators. The 50-strong team dedicates 20 partners (13 of whom are former district attorneys) to the defense of corporate and individual clients before the SEC, NYSE and various government enforcement and regulatory agencies. Exploiting a deep well of products liability knowledge and focusing on the litigation hotbed that is the city's Southern District, the firm specializes in representing pharmaceutical companies undergoing government investigation. To this end, clients find its substantial FDA practice hugely advantageous. Attorneys are representing Pfizer in relation to criminal and regulatory litigation at both state and federal level, arising from the sale, marketing and alleged health effects of the anti-inflammatory drugs Bextra and Celebrex. The team is also deeply involved in the SEC's investigation of alleged accounting irregularities at Goodyear, following its retention by the manufacturer to conduct an internal audit in 2003.

**The Lawyers:** Co-chair of the white-collar practice **Aaron Marcu** (see p.1477) focuses primarily on criminal matters relating to securities fraud. Years spent as a federal prosecutor and chief of the major crimes unit have prepared him for disputes of considerable magnitude; involvement in the Enron and Tyco crises has given way to pivotal roles in Pfizer's Celebrex litigation and a range of securities-related matters. He is a tonic to clients, who find that *"amidst extraordinary stress and turmoil, he keeps his head, fights hard and is not afraid to stand up to the government and demand fair treatment."* A comprehensive background, including several positions at the US attorney's office, and a name for displaying great judgment more than equip **Alan Vinegrad** (see p.1509) for a caseload that encompasses representing Adelphia Communications in defense of a criminal investigation, and conducting an extensive review of any and all forms of potential misconduct for the special committee of Tyco's board of directors.

**Clients/Work Highlights:** The team has acted for SG Cowen Securities and Société Générale in a range of federal and state grand jury investigations, SEC and NYSE enforcement actions and a host of subsequent civil lawsuits. Other clients include Freddie Mac; Bank One; UBS; Computer Associates; EP MedSystems and Ernst & Young.

## Kronish Lieb Weiner & Hellman LLP

**The Firm:** At the heart of Kronish Lieb's ten-partner litigation team is a hub of six former federal prosecutors, who focus on white-collar crime and regulatory defense. The group covers a broad range of criminal matters, stretching from insider trading, bank fraud and price fixing to public corruption and foreign corrupt practices. It has garnered considerable international press attention for its representation in the Southern District of a merchant banker who was the principal negotiator in the sale of the Republic of Kazakhstan's oil rights. The US government has accused him of contravening the Foreign Corrupt Practices Act and related trading offenses. Corollary expertise in IP-related disputes enables the firm to undertake a range of cutting-edge cases; most recently, the group successfully defended an Internet pop-up company against accusations of copyright laws.

**The Lawyers:** Former prosecutor and excellent trial lawyer **Alan Levine** is *"aggressive, smart and thinks outside the box."* He channels trademark *"pugnacity and resourcefulness"* towards white-collar criminal litigation. **William Schwartz**, who chairs the litigation group, is admired for his talent, and his experience in a matrix of high-profile disputes. He is coordinating the team handling the oil-trading offenses case.

**Clients/Work Highlights:** The firm acts for a vast array of pharmaceutical, investment banking, electronic and energy clients.

## Morvillo, Abramowitz, Grand, Iason & Silberberg, PC

**The Firm:** Few would claim to be able to match this veteran white-collar boutique, acclaimed for its prowess in court and sensible, forceful representation of its clientele. Comprising approximately 40 *"outstanding, deeply savvy"* attorneys, who *"live and breathe this work,"* the practice trains its blistering arsenal of expertise on cases arising from allegations of bank fraud and bribery to claims of antitrust, securities and tax violations. It handles cases for individuals and corporations at all levels of federal and state courts, with high-profile performances this year including acting for the former CFO of Adelphia Communications in alleged accounting irregularities, and representing a major insurance broker charged with money laundering and tax offenses linked to a change of insurance programs. As these examples illustrate, the firm is no stranger to government investigations and enforcement proceedings conducted by the SEC, the IRS and the Office of Thrift Supervision, among others. A deep-rooted appellate presence also came into play when the firm won a unanimous affirmation by the New York Appellate Division of a judgment dismissing all claims leveled at a law firm by a client's former business partner.

**The Lawyers:** **Robert Morvillo** continues to be one of the leading figures in white-collar criminal litigation, an arena he has influenced and shaped since his days as chief of the criminal division at the US attorney's office. *"He knows his way around the block"* and his commanding presence demands respect from all interviewees: *"Absolutely terrific, he is one of the best in the country. The end."* A potent combination of *"experience, intelligence and composure"* defines **Elkan Abramowitz**, another unquestioned dean of the field. He excels at being *"street-smart, incredibly persuasive and personable"* in state and federal courts. **Barry Bohrer** combines know-how of complex civil and criminal matters, including corporate internal investigations, with a thriving trial and appellate practice. In all things, he is *"scholarly, deep thinking and commonsensical."*

**Clients/Work Highlights:** High-profile individuals and corporations account for much of the firm's client base.

## Lankler Siffert & Wohl LLP

**The Firm:** This excellent litigation and dispute outfit continues to move onward and upward, according to interviewees, who draw attention to a youthful team and a recent lateral hire as evidence of its commitment to the future. The 22 lawyers at the firm represent corporations, financial entities and individuals across the globe in a broad spectrum of matters, particularly issues connected with securities, commodities, banking and antitrust laws. As well as defending banks and bankers against claims of fraud, money laundering, RICO violations and lender liability, the eight partners – six of whom are former prosecutors – represent law firms, attorneys and accountants in scenarios ranging from SEC investigations to suits stemming from law firm dissolutions. Clients embroiled in IP, entertainment or employment disputes are also in safe hands with Lankler Siffert.

**The Lawyers:** Time spent in the US attorney's office and as co-head of the litigation department of a national law firm has granted **John Siffert** a *"business-savvy"* outlook responsible for the assured course of his firm and the high esteem in which he is held. Sources find his *"wonderfully low-key manner"* a great relief in high-pressure situations. The appointment of **Rusty Wing** in January 2006 is a winning move by a firm recognized for its strategic aptitude. Formerly a partner at Weil Gotshal & Manges, he achieves market approbation as a trial lawyer of enormous distinction. He represents clients under investigation for violations of securities, tax, antitrust, fraud, money laundering and RICO laws. **Frank Wohl** is another experienced litigator, a leader, best known for representing individuals in high-stakes matters. Observers attest to his *"greatness in court."*

**Clients/Work Highlights:** Individuals and other corporate and banking organizations receive representation in civil, regulatory and white-collar criminal actions.

## Stillman & Friedman

**The Firm:** Possessing a wide and varied pool of expertise drawn from major New York law firms and the US attorney's office, Stillman's accumulation of some of the state's finest litigators throughout its 29-year history guarantees it a high standing in the eyes of the market. The team immerses itself in complex litigation, civil and criminal, for political figures, businesses and various accountants, lawyers and doctors. An expansive caseload takes in matters affecting the financial services industry, where it defends employees charged with breaches of federal securities, real estate and telecom laws. The readiness with which other firms turn to the group for assistance with sensitive internal investigations is testament to its credentials in the white-collar arena.

**The Lawyers:** **Charles Stillman** continues to be recognized as one of the most skilled attorneys in

New York in a career that has spanned more than 40 years. He is renowned for his advocacy of individuals and corporations before the SEC, NASD and other securities regulators. His glittering list of representations include a former US defense secretary, the mayor of New York and a myriad of other civic and political personalities. **Paul Schechtman** has moved from one elevated position to another in government organizations ranging from the US attorney's office to the office of the governor of New York state. He has established an equally top-drawer litigation practice, and is noted for his "*brilliant trial presence*" and winning style with juries.

**Clients/Work Highlights:** The firm acts for corporations, partnerships and individuals across the business community.

### Other Notable Practitioners

**Gregory Joseph** is an excellent attorney, who represents individuals as well as companies. Since establishing his own litigation outfit, Gregory P Joseph Law Offices LLC, he has deployed his skills in areas ranging from securities fraud and corporate governance to fiduciary duty and federal taxation. "*Extremely smart, calm and confident, he strives to find the best solution for his client.*" **Judith Archer** (see p.1434) brings to Fulbright & Jaworski L.L.P. an industry insight born of her years in AT&T's department of law and government affairs. She is a talented litigator, whose merits include the ability to "*handle the opposition with ease*" in complex commercial matters – particularly those arising within the telecom industry. "*Excellent communicator*" **Joe Cyr** (see p.1448), a senior partner at Lovells, inscribes his "*intelligent and meticulous*" mark on commercial class action proceedings at state and federal level. Clients respect his "*commanding presence*" in court – a demeanor informed by 25 years of experience. A similar level of trust is awarded to Pillsbury Winthrop LLP's **John Pritchard** (see p.1490), whom sources value for the "*wisdom, expe-*rience and pragmatism*" he applies to mutual fund litigation and highly sensitive internal investigations. Heading up Shapiro Forman Allen Sava & McPherson LLP, the eponymous **Stuart Shapiro** adopts a "*smart, savvy and serious*" approach to his work that explains his meteoric rise through the ranks of Skadden Arps (his former firm) and his continuing success in litigation veering towards securities and white-collar defense work. Sole practitioner **Stephen Kaufman** remains "*the man to see*" if clients – often former chief executives of major corporations – have problems with the DA's office. Smith Barney and Fidelity are two heavyweight examples of an impressive roll call. **Howard Heiss** (see p.1464) operates a practice burnished with "*excellence in legal advice and business strategy.*" Formerly of Morrison & Foerster, his residency at O'Melveny & Myers LLP affords him ample opportunity to demonstrate his skills in white-collar, regulatory and SEC investigations. **Andrew Levander** (see p.1474), a partner at Dechert LLP, is venerated as "*one of the brightest, most effective lawyers in New York.*" In addition to obtaining the acquittal of Michael Rigas on counts of conspiracy and fraud in the Adelphia case (which saw John and Timothy Rigas convicted in June 2005) – a success that has put Levander's name in lights – he persuaded the government not to indict Symbol Technologies after a two-year internal investigation. **Lee Richards** of Richards Spears Kibbe & Orbe is an experienced white-collar crime practitioner, whom clients admire for his securities banking and commercial litigation trial work. "*A calming influence in fraught circumstances,*" his famously "*excellent writing*" sustains a career-long winning streak in court. Chair of Goodwin Procter LLP's litigation group, **Richard Strassberg** (see p.1505) is no stranger to cases illuminated by the glare of the public spotlight – with the outcome of Peter Bacanovic's appeal pending in litigation connected with the Martha Stewart case, and the defense of former Bristol-Myers Squibb executive Richard Lane against charges of accounting fraud – he is at the pinnacle of the market. **Robert Pietrzak** (see p.1488) of Sidley Austin LLP receives warm recommendation for his superlative writing skills and polished representation of broker-dealers and other financial institutions. Cochair of Arent Fox PLLC's litigation department alongside Barbara Wahl, **William McSherry** (see p.1479) impresses clients with his "*brilliant mind*" and ability to distill complex facts into lucid points. He is lauded as a "*marvelous communicator*" with "*tremendous judgment and a memory like an elephant.*" **Peter Fleming** (see p.1455) of Curtis, Mallet-Prevost, Colt & Mosle LLP moves with prestige into the senior statesman category, enjoying a reputation as a "*sterling trial lawyer*" and leaving in his wake countless major victories. **William Maguire**, partner in Hughes Hubbard & Reed LLP's litigation practice, is indubitably "*the guy on the biggest things.*" He handles business disputes and professional liability claims as they impact in the securities arena. "*An intelligent oral advocate,*" his litany of talents includes keen business instincts and a singular rapport with juries. Recently making the transition from the warm climes of White & Case in Florida to Quinn Emanuel Urquhart Oliver & Hedges LLP's New York office, former federal prosecutor **Faith Gay** (see p.1458) is "*a skilled courtroom performer,*" with well-honed instincts and a "*bright, practical and hard-working*" approach to her white-collar criminal cases. Gay is also recommended for her work in the commercial litigation field. **Fred Hafetz** (see p.154063), of the eponymous Hafetz & Necheles, is "*one of the most active*" lawyers in the city. A "*tenacious and dogged*" advocate in court, this hands-on quality guarantees that "*he should be on any list*" Boasting a similar pedigree, **Andrew Lawler** (see p.154037) at Andrew M Lawler PC translates his bountiful trial experience into continuing demand and high visibility in cases of considerable magnitude.

# MEDIA & ENTERTAINMENT

# ADVERTISING

| Media & Entertainment: Advertising |
| --- |
| Leading Firms |
| 1 DAVIS & GILBERT New York |
| KRAMER LEVIN NAFTALIS & FRANKEL New York |
| PATTERSON, BELKNAP, WEBB & TYLER New York |
| PROSKAUER ROSE LLP New York |
| 2 FRANKFURT KURNIT KLEIN & SELZ New York |
| LOEB & LOEB LLP New York |
| MANATT PHELPS & PHILLIPS LLP New York |
| REED SMITH LLP New York |
| SKADDEN, ARPS New York |

## Band 1

### Davis & Gilbert

**The Firm:** This "*excellent, expert group*" is perceived by commentators to be "*the number-one firm for advertising agency work.*" It has extensive experience of all aspects of agency-related matters and is undoubtedly one of the busiest firms in the field. The team is regarded as extremely strong on advertising agreements and clearance matters, and is one of the first ports of call for regulatory issues. It has recently been active in a multistate investigation of the wireless carrier industry and the marketing practices of those businesses, specifically in relation to how the products present themselves.

**The Lawyers:** The firm boasts a large advertising, marketing and promotions group that was recommended as having "*across the board, the highest caliber of lawyers.*" Cochair **Ron Urbach** is "*one of the smartest lawyers around and knows this area better than the back of his hand.*" Fellow co-head **Gerald Schwartz** is recognized as a busy, experienced lawyer with excellent skills in dealing with talent.

**Clients/Work Highlights:** The group works with major marketers in their advertising and marketing issues relating to the automobile, retail and package goods industries. It has recently been looking at advertising matters in relation to the ongoing development of new media.

### Kramer Levin Naftalis & Frankel LLP

See firm details p.1539

**The Firm:** "*One of the leaders in the market,*" this group wins praise for its skills and experience in advertising disputes. The team represents a range of companies in litigation relating to false advertising, acting on both expressly made and implied claims. The lawyers are seen as particularly strong at making complex scientific research palatable in a courtroom setting.

**The Lawyers:** *"Top-flight advertising lawyer"* **Harold Weinberger** (see p.1512) is *"a man who understands the industry and knows the law cold."* Clients praise him for offering *"an impeccable legal service with a great commercial focus – he is master of the courtroom."* A highlight of his past year was representing McNeil-PPC – the manufacturer of Reach dental floss – in a case against Pfizer. Pfizer claimed their product Listerine was as effective as dental floss, a claim that Weinberger was able to disprove.

**Clients/Work Highlights:** The group has a strong following in the pharmaceutical industry and receives regular instructions from Procter & Gamble and Johnson & Johnson. However, the team of nine partners does not concentrate on one sector and has received instructions for a range of different businesses – including food companies and manufacturers.

## Patterson, Belknap, Webb & Tyler LLP
See firm details p.1547

**The Firm:** This well thought-of advertising group has grown out of the firm's IP practice and is felt to be *"one of the best firms, with a team of extremely clued-up lawyers."* Its attorneys are active on false advertising matters and have represented corporations in a number of large trials. They are also busy in the preparation of campaigns, counseling clients on the appropriate substantiation for advertising campaigns, as well as on television network clearance processes.

**The Lawyers:** The *"phenomenal litigator"* **Thomas Morrison** (see p.1481) is *"one of the most experienced lawyers in the field. He has seen and done it all and you know nothing will surprise him."* The *"highly involved"* **Steven Zalesin** (see p.1515) is *"a great courtroom lawyer, who writes well and really knows the law."* One competitor said: *"We've had a number of good, friendly battles. He's a great litigator and pleasant with it."* He has been acting for McNeil Nutritionals in federal court actions charging false advertising of Splenda no-calorie sweetener.

**Clients/Work Highlights:** The group has handled cases for pharmaceuticals, consumer products companies, food and drink manufacturers and car rental operators.

## Proskauer Rose LLP
See firm details p.1551

**The Firm:** This quality outfit is hailed for its expertise in false advertising matters and proves *"knowledgeable and tenacious in disputes."* A focused litigation practice, it primarily acts for manufacturers and advertisers in contentious matters while also examining proposed campaigns for potential disputes. The group has a strong following in the pharmaceutical industry and is endorsed for its skills in the evaluation of scientific testing. It also helps clients with the statistical analysis of their own testing.

**The Lawyers:** Litigator **Lawrence Weinstein** (see p.1512) has a wide media practice, but is hailed as *"one of the major advertising lawyers – what he doesn't know isn't worth knowing."* He recently acted for SC Johnson in a National Advertising Division (NAD) proceeding against Reckitt Benckiser precluding it from using certain television commercials. **Brendan O'Rourke** (see p.1485) is *"a great false advertising lawyer – forthright, dedicated and good on his feet."* A recent highlight was defending Bausch & Lomb in an NAD proceeding brought by Alcon relating to a television advertisement for contact lenses.

**Clients/Work Highlights:** Colgate-Palmolive; Bristol-Myers Squibb; Diageo; Mead Johnson; Church & Dwight and Kraft.

## Band 2

## Frankfurt Kurnit Klein & Selz
**The Firm:** This well-known media and entertainment practice has a sizable presence in the advertising market, with particularly strong experience in the representation of agencies. The group acts on a range of commercial and regulatory matters and also handles challenges before the FTC and NAD. The group's expertise in entertainment issues is felt to give it a great edge in the acquiring of talent for campaigns.

**The Lawyers:** The *"sharp as a blade"* **Rick Kurnit** (see p.1473) is said by commentators to be *"highly experienced in every aspect of copyright and trademark; he knows how it works in the advertising world."* A strong litigator, he wins kudos for his skills in comparative advertising cases.

**Clients/Work Highlights:** The firm's substantial client base includes large consumer products, travel, leisure, media and entertainment companies.

## Loeb & Loeb LLP
See firm details p.334

**The Firm:** This *"experienced and versatile"* team receives great backing from both large advertisers and advertising agencies. It acts on contract arrangements, copy review and disputes arising from campaigns, and is particularly busy handling the advertising needs of the entertainment industry. The group has a niche in acting for promotions agencies and is also expert on sweepstakes.

**The Lawyers:** **James Taylor** (see p.1507) is head of the firm's advertising and promotions law group, and is recommended as *"an excellent lawyer who it's always great to deal with."*

**Clients/Work Highlights:** The team advises on sophisticated branding campaigns for global clients and has acted for clients in the financial services, cosmetic, fast food, automotive and soft drinks industries.

## Manatt Phelps & Phillips LLP
**The Firm:** Skilled in both contentious and noncontentious issues, this group's clear specialty lies in examining claims being made through advertising, both stated and implied, and it is also seen as one of the most active at NAD. It has been involved in a number of high-profile matters including Schick Manufacturing v Gillette, a case concerning claims made about razor blades.

**The Lawyers:** **Linda Goldstein** is recommended for her skills in marketing across new media and has expertise in both regulatory issues and legal risks involved in advertising online. She has a particular niche in representing marketers in the structuring of sweepstakes.

**Clients/Work Highlights:** The group's clients include both advertisers and advertising agencies.

## Reed Smith LLP
See firm details p.1762

**The Firm:** This team's strengths lie in representing advertisers and advertising agencies on the full range of issues from comparative advertising to government regulations. It is particularly active in issues arising from telemarketing and the Internet, as well as matters relating to promotions. Celebrity endorsements are regarded as another string to the firm's bow.

**The Lawyers:** **Douglas Wood** (see p.1514) is chair of the advertising and marketing law group. He is general counsel to the Association of National Advertisers and the Advertising Research Foundation and is recommended as *"a good fount of knowledge – he has a lot of experience both domestically and globally."*

**Clients/Work Highlights:** The group represents advertisers and advertising agencies.

## Skadden, Arps, Slate, Meagher & Flom LLP & Affiliates
See firm details p.1557

**The Firm:** Although a smaller practice than some of its competitors, this group wins plaudits as *"a good team that can rival virtually anyone else."* The group is based within the IP practice and handles both contentious and noncontentious matters – both in trademarks and advertising. The advertising client base is rated as particularly strong and the team is seen as adept in disputes, NAD hearings and campaign advice. It has been acting for Anheuser-Busch in the so-called Beer Wars dispute with SAB Miller.

**The Lawyers:** The lodestone of the group is **Kenneth Plevan** (see p.1489) who is recommended as "*a key player. He's always good to deal with as he* knows exactly what he's doing and doesn't give you any nonsense." Primarily known for his litigation work, he is representing GlaxoSmithKline in an ongoing dispute with Merix Pharmaceutical.
**Clients/Work Highlights:** Other clients include Estée Lauder, Virgin Mobile and Verizon.

# MEDIA & ENTERTAINMENT　　COMMERCIAL

| Media & Entertainment: Commercial |
| --- |
| **Leading Firms** |
| [1] FRANKFURT KURNIT KLEIN & SELZ *New York* |
| FRANKLIN, WEINRIB, RUDELL *New York* |
| GRUBMAN, INDURSKY & SHIRE, PC *New York* |
| LOEB & LOEB LLP *New York* |
| [2] GREENBERG TRAURIG LLP *New York* |
| PAUL, WEISS *New York* |
| PRYOR CASHMAN SHERMAN & FLYNN *New York* |

| Leading Individuals |
| --- |
| [1] BREGLIO John *Paul, Weiss* |
| BROWN Elliot *Franklin, Weinrib, Rudell* |
| GELBLUM Seth *Loeb & Loeb LLP* |
| GRUBMAN Allen *Grubman, Indursky & Shire* |
| HELLER Richard *Frankfurt Kurnit Klein & Selz* |
| INDURSKY Arthur *Grubman, Indursky & Shire* |
| KRESS Alan *Alan H Kress* |
| RUDELL Michael *Franklin, Weinrib, Rudell* |
| SUKIN Michael *Sukin Law Group* |
| [2] ANDERSON Kenneth *Loeb & Loeb LLP* |
| ARAR Roger *Loeb & Loeb LLP* |
| BEER Steven *Greenberg Traurig LLP* |
| CHAMLIN Marc *Loeb & Loeb LLP* |
| GOOGE JR Charles *Paul, Weiss* |
| GORDON Nicholas *Franklin, Weinrib, Rudell* |
| HOFSTETTER Richard *Frankfurt Kurnit Klein & Selz* |
| JACOBSON Marc *Greenberg Traurig LLP* |
| LAZARUS Scott *Lazarus & Harris LLP* |
| ROSINI Neil *Franklin, Weinrib, Rudell* |
| SCHINDLER Paul *Greenberg Traurig LLP* |
| SLOSS John *Sloss Law Office* |

## Band 1

### Frankfurt Kurnit Klein & Selz

**The Firm:** Clients recommend this group as "*a superb, dedicated team which has a full appreciation of the media and entertainment business. It knows how to operate in an intelligent, businesslike way.*" Its versatility is a key asset. Especially skilled in film and TV production, it is also supremely adept at publishing, theater work and media across new technology matters. The group boasts a strong client base of individuals and companies and is increasingly active in representing international producers selling programs within the USA.
**The Lawyers:** Although highly rated for his movie-making work, **Richard Heller** (see p.1464) is hailed as "*a genuine Renaissance man in the entertainment field. He has the smarts and experience to take on anything.*" In the past year he has acted for best-sell-

ing authors, on a play staged in London's West End and on branding matters for celebrities. One highlight was acting for 'West Wing' creator Aaron Sorkin on a new television show. **Richard Hofstetter** (see p.1465) is a "*fantastic lawyer to deal with, a friendly presence in the marketplace and an attorney with a great grasp on the industry.*" His practice is primarily television-oriented and he has been active in methods to exploit programming beyond traditional television.
**Clients/Work Highlights:** The firm's clients include television and film producers, as well as financing companies and high-profile individuals. The group is particularly active in the independent film sector.

### Franklin, Weinrib, Rudell & Vassallo

**The Firm:** "*One of the finest media practices not just in the city, but in the country,*" according to commentators. The firm is active on a broad spectrum of matters across the television, film, book publishing and theater sectors. It also has substantial involvement in the exploitation and development of new media content. One observer commented: "*The firm has experienced lawyers for every conceivable matter.*"
**The Lawyers:** **Elliot Brown** is "*without a doubt one of the top theater lawyers – magnificently knowledgeable and commercial.*" He is endorsed for his work with producers and writers, but also represents actors, directors and rights holders. Highlights of his past year include representing the writers on the hit Broadway musical 'Spamalot', as well as acting for Frankie Valli on the musical 'Jersey Boys'. **Michael Rudell** is recommended as "*one of the best transactional lawyers in New York.*" A corporate and commercial expert, he has recently been busy on book publishing matters. **Nicholas Gordon** is praised by peers as "*a great lawyer to go to in conflict situations. You know that his work will be exemplary.*" He has great experience of the music industry and has been active in online access issues. **Neil Rosini** continues to have a following for his expertise in new media matters.
**Clients/Work Highlights:** The group's media clients run the full gamut of actors, writers, producers, publishers, financiers and corporations.

### Grubman, Indursky & Shire, PC

**The Firm:** This "*top-class*" practice is regarded as unbeatable on music industry issues. Its highly experienced team has great strength in depth, with one commentator remarking: "*Every lawyer I would think of as excellent in music is at that firm.*" The group's skills include advising on all issues that arise for both record companies and artists. It further wins plaudits for handling the media aspects of large transactions.

**The Lawyers:** The legendary **Allen Grubman** is "*an extremely smart guy who knows the music industry better than anyone else.*" He is recommended for his skills on the media side of substantial corporate deals and is "*great at putting a relationship together. He'll get two sides talking so a deal can take place.*" **Arthur Indursky** is hailed as "*a superb legal brain. I like dealing with him a lot; he's always sharp and picks out points other lawyers might miss.*"
**Clients/Work Highlights:** The group represents record companies and major recording artists.

### Loeb & Loeb LLP
See firm details p.334
**The Firm:** Positioned on both coasts (and also handling some music matters in Nashville), the firm continues to impress as "*an incredible group for acquisition and deal management advice.*" Clients say: "*The guys there are always looking at creative ways to do things and don't indulge in the hysterical gamesmanship of some of their rivals.*" The depth and versatility of the group are frequently praised by the market and the firm can truly be said to have clients across the full spectrum of entertainment law.
**The Lawyers:** Theater specialist **Seth Gelblum** (see p.1458) is "*highly knowledgeable in the field and a great people person. He gets the deal done swiftly, efficiently and as pleasantly as possible.*" He acts for a mix of producers, actors and writers and has been involved in a number of large musical productions over the past year. **Kenneth Anderson** (see p.1433) is "*an excellent talent lawyer with a superb client base.*" He is primarily involved in the music industry and tackles both traditional matters and issues involving the exploitation of new media. **Roger Arar** (see p.1433) is "*a top-class television lawyer – he is expert right from high-end transactions down to the nitty-gritty.*" He has been handling negotiations for reality, documentary and scripted television. Clients recommend **Marc Chamlin** (see p.1443) as "*smart, pragmatic and great at getting a deal done.*" Boasting a diverse practice, he handles television, film and publishing matters for a range of individuals and corporate entities.
**Clients/Work Highlights:** BMG Music; Disney; Lions Gate Entertainment; Nickelodeon Networks; Paramount Pictures; Beastie Boys; Dixie Chicks and William Shatner.

## Band 2

### Greenberg Traurig LLP
See firm details p.664
**The Firm:** This highly regarded commercial firm continues to be a growing presence in the media

market and demonstrates particular expertise within the music industry. The group represents a range of record companies, producers, songwriters and artists. It handles both large commercial deals and the smaller aspects of contract negotiation, touring, merchandising and sponsorship. It is seen as particularly strong in IP matters related to music.

**The Lawyers:** The "*dynamic*" **Steven Beer** (see p.1437) has a practice that includes film, television, book publishing and music. He is "*precise and diligent and has a great client rapport, which means that even the most arduous transaction won't seem that much of a chore.*" He has just put together a high-profile prepay broadcasting deal for a media company in relation to a concert by a major artist. **Marc Jacobson** (see p.1468) has skills in publishing, primarily in the music business but also in book deals. He acts for both publishers and songwriters in various matters and has handled the purchase of a number of catalogs in the past year. The recruitment of **Paul Schindler** (see p.1497) from Grubman, Indursky & Schindler is seen as a great boon for the practice. A highly experienced practitioner, he is seen as "*a music lawyer par excellence.*"

**Clients/Work Highlights:** Although best known for its music industry work (where the group represents everyone from individual artists to record companies), this firm also acts for broadcasters, television and film production companies and high-profile individuals.

## Paul, Weiss, Rifkind, Wharton & Garrison LLP

See firm details p.1548

**The Firm:** A strong commercial media practice sits side by side with a highly recommended corporate team. It handles nuts-and-bolts entertainment matters, as well as sizable transactions, and is active for clients in the film, music, publishing and theater industries. Talent work is seen as a great area of expertise for a group that represents both individuals and companies. It has acted for Spike Lee in matters relating to a film and has further advised a major figure in television entertainment.

**The Lawyers:** **John Breglio** (see p.1441) chairs the practice and is regarded as "*an excellent competitor in music matters.*" He does much of his best work representing the estates of songwriters but is generally endorsed for his skills on IP issues within the media. **Charles Googe**'s (see p.1460) practice mixes both corporate and commercial aspects. "*A smart-as-a-whip lawyer who has done some good work on international matters,*" according to clients, he has recently been active on a number of live entertainment matters.

**Clients/Work Highlights:** The group's clients include film-makers, authors and musicians, as well as world-famous live acts. It also represents large entities in commercial/media matters.

## Pryor Cashman Sherman & Flynn

**The Firm:** This substantial practice wins kudos for its movie and music work. It is seen as an excellent resource in film matters, representing both production companies and banks on film financing. Other areas of success include the television and publishing sectors.

**The Lawyers:** Stephen Rodner handles film and theater matters.

**Clients/Work Highlights:** The group acts for broadcasters, music companies, film production companies and financing bodies.

## Other Notable Practitioners

The "*intelligent and straightforward*" sole practitioner **Alan Kress** is said by clients to give "*absolutely phenomenal advice. You never get a bad surprise when dealing with him.*" In the past year, he has represented record companies, music publishers and sponsors and acted for Cirque du Soleil in their music work. **Michael Sukin** of Sukin Law Group has a distinctly music-focused practice. Representing estates, banks and artists, he is "*a lawyer who understands the music industry backward, inside out and upside down.*" Currently, he is acting on matters concerning protection of copyright, both domestic and international. **Scott Lazarus** of Lazarus & Harris LLP is "*an incredible theater lawyer*" who has a strong practice among producers, while **John Sloss** of Sloss Law Office is rated as "*superb in representing film producers.*"

---

# MEDIA & ENTERTAINMENT

# CORPORATE

## Media & Entertainment: Corporate
**Leading Firms**

[1] **CRAVATH, SWAINE & MOORE LLP** *New York*
**DEBEVOISE & PLIMPTON LLP** *New York*
**HOGAN & HARTSON LLP** *New York*

[2] **MORGAN, LEWIS & BOCKIUS LLP** *New York*
**PAUL, WEISS** *New York*
**SKADDEN, ARPS** *New York*

[3] **DAVIS POLK & WARDWELL** *New York*
**DEWEY BALLANTINE LLP** *New York*
**FRIED, FRANK** *New York*
**SHEARMAN & STERLING LLP** *New York*

## Band 1

### Cravath, Swaine & Moore LLP

See firm details p.1527

**The Firm:** "*A strong and solid transactional practice,*" this group is recommended for its experience and nuanced skill in high-end corporate matters. It is best known for its representation of Time Warner, with the attorneys handling a range of issues for the parent company and its subsidiaries, such as HBO and Time Warner Cable. It has recently represented publisher Time Inc on the purchase of a large, rival

publisher in Mexico. The team is also increasingly busy in matters relating to the ongoing development of digital media.

**The Lawyers:** "*Dedicated and detailed lawyer*" **John Gaffney** (see p.1457) has skill in securities offers, joint ventures and M&A. "*Able to swiftly build up a rapport with the client,*" he has forged strong links with Time Warner. **Faiza Saeed** (see p.1495) is also known for her work for Time Warner and is hailed as "*busy and incredibly bright. She is particularly good on dealing with bankers in the M&A arena.*" She has also acted for DreamWorks SKG in the past year.

**Clients/Work Highlights:** Other clients include Clear Channel Communications, Comcast and The Washington Post.

### Debevoise & Plimpton LLP

See firm details p.1529

**The Firm:** Always a strong presence, this firm has been careful not to sit on its laurels. Through good management of its all too evident resources, it has attracted some of the biggest deals of recent years and can now be truly described as "*a stellar practice.*" One definite highlight has been its representation of NBC who it acted for in relation to its acquisition of Vivendi Universal Entertainment. This created Vivendi-Universal, an entity valued at $43 billion. The group is particularly rated for its television work,

an area that ties in closely with the firm's well-regarded telecom practice.

**The Lawyers:** The "*competitive but likeable*" **Richard Bohm** gets "*the mix between legal and commercial advice just right.*" His M&A practice is distinctly media-focused and he has recently acted for the Dolan family in taking Cablevision private. This involved the spin-off of Cablevision's programming, sports and entertainments businesses in a deal valued at $18.6 billion. **Michael Gillespie** is rated for his skills in broadcasting and for his experience in international transactions. He has worked closely with Latin American media giant Globo Organization.

**Clients/Work Highlights:** The Associated Press; The Carlyle Group; Greater Media; Hasbro; The Jim Henson Company; Oxygen Media; Sony and Verizon.

### Hogan & Hartson LLP

See firm details p.568

**The Firm:** Primarily known for its work for News Corporation, this group is "*highly focused in the broadcasting sector. It knows the structures and how to get deals done within them.*" Boasting a strong global presence, the team is well versed in the complexities of international transactions. It recently acted for News Corporation and its affiliate DIRECTV in the consolidation of its Direct-to-Home satellite entertainment distribution platforms in Mexico and Brazil. Another highlight was acting for News Corporation in its acquisition of $6.2 billion worth of stock from Fox Entertainment Group that it did not already own.

**The Lawyers:** Clients speak of head of team **Mark Weinstein** (see p.1512) as "*an intelligent, knowledgeable and fun lawyer to deal with.*" Although traditionally a tax specialist, he is felt by clients to be "*such a broad-gauge lawyer that we always think of him for deals.*" **Mitchell Ames** (see p.1433) is "*a great merger lawyer who navigates his way through deals with aplomb.*" He acts as counsel for the joint development group formed by Gemstar-TV Guide International and Comcast.

**Clients/Work Highlights:** The group's work for News Corporation includes acting for subsidiaries Fox Entertainment Group, FOX News Network and HarperCollins Publishers. It has other clients in the broadcasting and music sectors.

## Band 2

### Morgan, Lewis & Bockius LLP

See firm details p.1758

**The Firm:** A well-regarded group that wins plaudits for its corporate skills and media knowledge. Although a smaller practice than some of its competitors, it is recognized as possessing a strong client base – particularly in the publishing and information sectors. The group continues to be active for The New York Times which it represented in a $500 million offering of senior notes, as well as in the $400 million acquisition of online consumer information provider About.com. The team is also strong in the representation of strategic companies looking to invest in the media sector.

**The Lawyers:** The "*fantastic*" **Charles Engros** (see p.1452) is "*a sharp lawyer who doesn't miss the wood for the trees.*" One interviewee stated: "*He's truly meticulous and we like that in a lawyer as it means we can afford to be less meticulous.*" He is active in the Internet market and has also done a number of transactions involving educational publications.

**Clients/Work Highlights:** The New York Times; Pearson; Time Out and United Business Media feature on the client list. The group has an international profile and does a lot of work with UK-based publishers.

## Paul, Weiss, Rifkind, Wharton & Garrison LLP

See firm details p.1548

**The Firm:** The firm boasts experience in both entertainment and corporate matters for media corporations. It was recommended to researchers as "*a solid corporate competitor that has built up years of experience through some very good deals.*" Its broad-based practice involves representing film companies, broadcasters and publishers and it has been especially active in music deals over the past year. Key matters for the group include acting in the merger of two major music entities and representing the US subsidiary of a worldwide media company in the purchase of a UK-based music company.

**The Lawyers:** **Robert Schumer** (see p.1498) is co-head of the M&A group and is "*a top-dollar lawyer who is really astute on media matters.*" **Peter Felcher** (see p.1453) is acclaimed for his representation of media and entertainment entities in merger matters. He has particular expertise in financings and is praised as "*a great guy to get an opinion from.*"

**Clients/Work Highlights:** The group's clients include broadcasters, record companies and publishers.

## Skadden, Arps, Slate, Meagher & Flom LLP & Affiliates

See firm details p.1557

**The Firm:** "*They're Skadden Arps, so they have skills in everything*" was the verdict of one commentator. Based within the M&A department, the team represents a number of high-end media companies. In the past year, it has acted for News Corporation in taking the Fox Entertainment Group private in a deal worth $6 billion. It has also represented private equity funds with sizable interests in the media sector. Although the firm lacks the focused team of some of its competitors, peers say: "*It has built up great knowledge and experience and, of course, its M&A skills are second to none.*"

**The Lawyers:** Howard Ellin is active in this sector.

**Clients/Work Highlights:** The firm represents News Corporation, Goldman Sachs and Wasserstein & Co. It is acting for Disney in its proposed acquisition of Pixar. The deal is reported to be valued at approximately $7.4 billion.

## Band 3

### Davis Polk & Wardwell

See firm details p.1528

**The Firm:** The practice is recognized by peers for its transactional skills, especially in dealing with IP companies and financial organizations. It frequently represents cable broadcasters and has handled a number of high-profile mergers and transactions in recent times. The departure of the highly regarded Dennis Hersch at the end of 2005 is regarded as a great blow to the team but one that it can absorb.

**The Lawyers:** John Bick is the contact partner here.

**Clients/Work Highlights:** The group represents major cable companies and investment banks.

## Dewey Ballantine LLP

See firm details p.1530

**The Firm:** This "*forward-thinking*" practice has "*a substantial knowledge bank*" and "*really understands how M&A works within content and distribution.*" Disney is a major client and has furnished the firm with a range of media, M&A and capital markets work. By way of example, it recently acted for Disney and ESPN on a major licensing agreement with EA Sports. In other matters, it represented a major consortium in a $15.5 billion acquisition of a European content provider.

**The Lawyers:** Michael Aiello is active in the area.

**Clients/Work Highlights:** Disney and Sony are the group's two major clients. It has also been involved in sizable deals in the publishing sector.

## Fried, Frank, Harris, Shriver & Jacobson LLP

See firm details p.1532

**The Firm:** This small but experienced group is busy advising major corporates, investment banks and private equity funds on a range of media M&A work. A versatile practice, it has recently handled transactions concerning film, publishing and advertising companies. One highlight was acting for Tracinda and Kirk Kerkorian, the controlling stockholders of MGM, in connection with the sale of MGM to a consortium including Sony.

**The Lawyers:** Warren de Wied makes a significant contribution to the practice's efforts in this sector.

**Clients/Work Highlights:** The group's client base includes major investors and private equity funds.

## Shearman & Sterling LLP

See firm details p.1554

**The Firm:** This "*hard-working team, sharp and efficient in deals*" is best known for its work for Viacom. It is currently representing the company in its pending split into two separate companies – a deal estimated to be worth $80 billion. Commentators have speculated as to what the post-split relationship will be between client and law firm but accept that, currently, the deal represents a major piece of business for the practice. Elsewhere, the group is primarily active in M&A and capital markets matters and has handled a number of media transactions for Morgan Stanley.

**The Lawyers:** Creighton Condon is a partner in this field.

**Clients/Work Highlights:** The group also acts for Canadian information company Thomson, and receives regular instructions from Blockbuster.

# MEDIA & ENTERTAINMENT

# LITIGATION

## Band 1

### Cahill Gordon & Reindel LLP

**The Firm:** The top firm for First Amendment matters, this outfit has *"a forthright and battling litigation practice that can surpass anyone else when it comes to knowledge of the sector."* The presence of Floyd Abrams undoubtedly contributes to the group's prominence to the extent that there is a slight suspicion that more junior members of the team find it hard to climb out from his shadow. However, not one market commentator quibbled with the quality of the group's lawyers, client base and workload. Strong and confident to take on anything, it has acted in some of the major cases of recent times. These have included one case where the firm represented broadcasters in a dispute relating to exit polls in the 2004 presidential election.

**The Lawyers:** The legendary **Floyd Abrams** is *"absolutely the dean of the First Amendment Bar. He wrote the book, so there is nobody who knows as much as he does."* Clients view him as *"a fantastic resource who has never given us less than perfect quality work."* The highlight for him in the past year was representing Judith Miller in the case arising from the leaking of Valerie Plame's name. At one point in this complex and extremely high-profile case, he was acting for Judith Miller, Matt Cooper, The New York Times and Time magazine. **Dean Ringel** is recommended as *"an astute and quick-thinking lawyer – he is amazingly swift in seeking out the correct solution."* In recent times, he has been active in matters relating to libel and prior restraint.

**Clients/Work Highlights:** The group represents all the broadcast networks – NBC; ABC; CNN – as well as CBA; The New York Times; Time Magazine; Time Warner and King World Productions.

### Davis Wright Tremaine LLP

**The Firm:** This *"talented and versatile firm"* is felt to have one of the strongest and deepest teams in New York. Closely linked with the California and DC offices, it is seen as offering top-quality service in First Amendment, copyright, contract, IP, libel and technology disputes. The presence of Victor Kovner is seen as raising the firm to the highest level but the quality around him is recognized.

**The Lawyers:** The *"heavyweight"* **Victor Kovner** is *"an undeniably superb lawyer. He and Floyd Abrams are the two totems of First Amendment law."* Commentators admire him as *"a tenacious litigator who knows his area backward and is never stuck for an idea."* He has been acting for McGraw-Hill subsidiary Platts in relation to a publication that covers the oil, natural gas and electricity industries. Proceedings have centered around an attempt to get access to the privilege file of Platts' journalists. **Elizabeth McNamara** wins her spurs for her copyright and IP expertise, as well as her skills in libel. Clients rate her as *"a truly gifted lawyer whose professionalism and dedication are a joy to behold."* She recently obtained a dismissal for Dan Brown and Random House in a copyright infringement case relating to 'The Da Vinci Code'. She has also acted for author James Patterson in a number of matters. **Marcia Paul** is *"a smart media litigator,"* highly rated for her copyright skills. She has acted for BBC Worldwide on a dispute involving the release of archive performances recorded for British radio program 'The John Peel Show'.

**Clients/Work Highlights:** MTV; CNN: CBS; NBC; Showtime; HBO; Warner Books; Paramount Pictures and Simon & Schuster.

### Debevoise & Plimpton LLP

See firm details p.1529

**The Firm:** This *"focused and hard-fighting firm"* is primarily known for its skills in copyright litigation but is active across a range of media disputes. Its team is comprised of *"extremely business-savvy advocates who offer advice that makes sense in a business setting."* The expense of hiring the firm is noted, but clients comment: *"It is worth every penny you pay."* The versatility of the firm allows it to tackle matters of infinite variety. In the past year, lawyers have acted on a case regarding the transmission of cable broadcasting to Brazil and defended a radio station over claims that a DJ had offended a listener on air.

**The Lawyers:** **Bruce Keller** was described by commentators as *"the best copyright lawyer in the world."* He has *"tremendous experience, creativity and imagination"* and *"the quality of his advice is impeccable."* His varied practice sees him act for publishers, broadcasters and sporting teams. He recently acted for a major Hollywood studio in a copyright dispute concerning a superhero franchise. Although best known for his copyright work, **Lorin Reisner** also enjoys a substantial practice in First Amendment matters. Clients describe him as *"sharp as a knife. If you need to get a succinct answer to a difficult question right there and then, he's the guy you call."* Of late, he has been involved in a substantial case for The American Lawyer.

**Clients/Work Highlights:** The group's clients include publishers, broadcasters, film companies, sporting teams and Internet entities.

## Band 2

### Cowan, Liebowitz & Latman

**The Firm:** This highly regarded, copyright-focused practice is recognized as having a good and experienced team of copyright, trademark and IP lawyers. Litigation defense in the publishing sector provides much of the team's caseload but it is also active for clients in the music and new media sectors. Commentators warm to it due to the fact that *"with these lawyers you always have a chance of getting a home run."*

**The Lawyers:** **Richard Dannay** is *"absolutely in the top echelon of US copyright lawyers."* His skills in publishing matters are highly regarded, with peers noting: *"He has phenomenal knowledge of the law and is also quite subtle as a litigator – he won't use a sledgehammer to crack a nut."* He is endorsed for his work for publishers and was recently successful in defending a publisher in a case concerning the reproduction of 1960's rock concert posters. He has also handled a number of interesting matters for Universal Studios.

**Clients/Work Highlights:** The team's client base includes publishers, record companies, music publishers, film companies and new technology clients.

## Gibson, Dunn & Crutcher LLP

See firm details p.328

**The Firm:** This *"brilliantly insightful"* team is *"superb in complex matters, offering advice that goes far beyond the normal cookie-cutter fare."* Primarily known for its First Amendment skills, the group has close links with Dow Jones and its subsidiaries. It is currently representing Dow Jones in matters arising from the Valerie Plume case, as it seeks to unseal eight blank pages in the DC court's ruling. Its work in copyright and contract matters continues to grow and it has acted for Sony BMG, EMI and Atlantic Records in a variety of cases.

**The Lawyers:** Clients recommend **Jack Weiss** (see p.1512) as *"one of the shrewdest lawyers in New York and personally charming, which makes a difference in dealing with judges."* He is hailed for his creativity, with one client saying: *"Part of the problem with media law is that it's all self-reverential, they all quote each other and do the same thing. Jack goes beyond that and comes up with genuinely innovative and imaginative ideas."* His practice encompasses First Amendment issues, IP and libel. He has been active in Umar v Dow Jones, a case concerning a libel arising from a front-page story in The Wall Street Journal.

**Clients/Work Highlights:** Clients include the Associated Press and Penguin, and it has also handled copyright matters for such artists as Mariah Carey, Bob Dylan and The Osbournes.

## Hogan & Hartson LLP

See firm details p.568

**The Firm:** Although regarded as a small litigation team, the group is felt to punch above its weight thanks to its top-end client base and unbeatable experience. Slade Metcalf is the most recognized member of the group and has an *"outstanding reputation"* that others at the firm struggle to match. However, as a unit the team is very solid and handles matters in the film, broadcasting and publishing arenas for the likes of News Corporation.

**The Lawyers:** The *"savvy"* **Slade Metcalf** (see p.1479) *"brings an intelligence and attention to detail to the table that marks him out from his peers."* He has been particularly active for HarperCollins in recent times, successfully representing the company and two of its authors, Michael Corbitt and Sam Giancana, in the Illinois Court of Appeal. This matter concerned a privacy suit brought by a Chicago criminal defense attorney.

**Clients/Work Highlights:** As well as its work for News Corporation and its subsidiaries, the group is active for Disney, TV Guide, Inside TV and Hollywood Reporter. It also acts for insurance companies active in the media field.

## Levine Sullivan Koch & Schulz LLP

**The Firm:** This firm has an ever-growing presence in the New York marketplace despite being primarily known as a DC-based practice. Its team does well on First Amendment, libel, defamation and privacy issues, and is rated as *"a fast and knowledgeable group that produces a phenomenal end product."* Although the highly regarded David Schulz is the best-known

individual, clients speak of a deep bench strength and the excellent value for money provided by the attorneys here.

**The Lawyers:** Clients regard **David Schulz** as *"one of the leading people. He is a walking encyclopedia of New York state media law and is incredibly skilled at identifying the strengths and weaknesses of any case."* He is particularly endorsed for his abilities as a strategist and recently advised the Associated Press in an invasion of privacy and copyright infringement case. This concerned the publication of photos of Navy SEALs guarding Iraqi prisoners. He works closely with his DC-based partners.

**Clients/Work Highlights:** The Associated Press; Hearst Communications; New York Press Association; The New York Times; Tribune and Viacom/CBS.

## O'Melveny & Myers LLP

See firm details p.336

**The Firm:** This strong firm enjoys enthusiastic market support on both coasts. Recommended to researchers as *"a team just as good on the big points as the nitty-gritty of a case,"* it is hailed for its skills in copyright and in contract litigation. The group has a wide client base and is recognized for the versatility of its work in the music, film, television, publishing and video games industries.

**The Lawyers:** The *"fantastic"* **Dale Cendali** (see p.1443) is *"absolutely top dollar on copyright matters. Her knowledge is impeccable and she applies it with great precision."* She is known as *"a tenacious courtroom presence who is definitely one to pick for the big cases."* In the past year, she has successfully defended a case brought by a liberal group that claimed FOX News' slogan 'A Fair And Balanced View' was inaccurate. She has also represented MGA Entertainment – the manufacturers of the Bratz dolls – in a number of disputes with Mattel.

**Clients/Work Highlights:** The group acts for News Corporation, HBO and Cryptic Studios. It has also handled a range of matters for JK Rowling.

## Proskauer Rose LLP

See firm details p.1551

**The Firm:** This national presence has a wide-ranging practice and an enviable client base. The group handles production and finance matters for motion picture companies, as well as the full gamut of copyright, contractual, libel, defamation, privacy and infringement cases for individuals and companies across the entertainment industry. With professionals on both coasts, the practice has close links with the firm's IP group and presents as *"a really bright team that gives commercially sound advice."*

**The Lawyers:** *"One of the top people to go to for music matters,"* **Charles Ortner** (see p.1485) has *"a wonderful combination of knowledge, enthusiasm and dedication to the cause."* He is skilled at contract, copyright, trademark, IP and libel disputes and represents both industry bodies and individual artists. Clients say that **Charles Sims** (see p.1502) is *"always worth giving a call as, when you can get him, he's worth his weight in gold."* In the past year, he has

been acting for The New York Times on a contract dispute case arising out of the television production 'Trauma: Life In The ER'.

**Clients/Work Highlights:** Clients include record companies, songwriters and high-profile recording artists. The group acts for publishers involved in the newspaper, book, database and scientific areas. It also acts for Tribune and Reed Elsevier.

## Weil, Gotshal & Manges LLP

See firm details p.1565

**The Firm:** This *"fantastic"* team is said to *"understand copyright issues in the way few others do; they almost breathe it."* Busy and versatile, it handles trademark, licensing and First Amendment issues in music, publishing, advertising and television. It is particularly active in technology work and is seen as having a good bench of smart lawyers in this area. A national presence, the group enjoys support from partners in DC and on the West Coast.

**The Lawyers:** The *"absolutely magnificent"* **Bruce Rich** (see p.1492) is *"one of the best copyright lawyers in the world – there is seriously no one better than him."* He is rated as *"a superb brief writer and excellent litigator"* and is effective in both IP and copyright matters. Recent matters he has handled include acting for eBay in defense of a claim by Tiffany & Co alleging that there was a fake Tiffany product being auctioned on eBay and that it was eBay's job to monitor it. This high-profile matter is ongoing. Colleague **Robert Sugarman** (see p.1506) has *"an excellent courtroom presence"* and displays skills in IP and copyright litigation. He is particularly active in the music industry and has represented both recording artists and record companies. The well-regarded Kenneth Steinthal is now based in California.

**Clients/Work Highlights:** National Geographic Society; Copyright Clearance Center; Association of American Publishers; Television Music Licensing Committee; McGraw-Hill and Disney/ABC.

## Band 3

## Cravath, Swaine & Moore LLP

See firm details p.1527

**The Firm:** Although best known for its corporate work within the media sector, the group does retain a small and experienced team in media litigation. Like its corporate counterparts, the group enjoys a strong relationship with Time Warner and has handled a range of IP and copyright disputes with both national and global aspects. A highlight of the past year was acting for Time Warner Cable in a contract dispute with American Movie Classics. The firm also successfully represented the Martha Graham Dance Company in a trademark and copyright dispute.

**The Lawyers:** Senior attorney Robert Joffe is the principal lawyer in litigation.

**Clients/Work Highlights:** Time Warner and its subsidiaries remain the firm's best-known clients.

## Loeb & Loeb LLP

See firm details p.334

**The Firm:** The highly regarded transactional group of this practice sits beside a litigation practice that has a growing reputation on the East Coast. Although best known for its work in music, it is also active in film and television cases, as well as matters relating to content across new technology. Copyright is a key component of the team's work and it has handled a number of matters with hi-tech and international aspects.

**The Lawyers:** Barry Slotnick (see p.1502) is "*a clued-up lawyer who knows what he's doing.*" He is especially busy for music industry clients and recently acted for peer music and Broadcast Music in a large copyright infringement case (involving more than 450 copyrights) against Latin American Music Company.

**Clients/Work Highlights:** The group acts for BMG and Rainbow Media. It also handles a range of matters for the JRR Tolkien estate.

## Patterson, Belknap, Webb & Tyler LLP

See firm details p.1547

**The Firm:** Clients recommend this group as "*excellent in the courtroom, a great choice for big cases.*" The team's strategic skills are picked out and the lawyers have been involved in major matters including acting for Sony BMG in Eliot Spitzer's investigation into payola. Although skilled in First Amendment and copyright issues, the group is known for acting on the full range of commercial litigation matters for media companies. It has handled fraud, libel and securities cases for clients in recent times and has also undertaken a number of internal investigations for media companies.

**The Lawyers:** Gregory Diskant and Saul Shapiro are active in this arena.

**Clients/Work Highlights:** The group represents the full gamut of media companies including publishers, record companies and television networks.

## Paul, Weiss, Rifkind, Wharton & Garrison LLP

See firm details p.1548

**The Firm:** Market sources say that "*although this isn't a firm you'd immediately associate with this type of work, it does have some hard-fighting lawyers who know their stuff.*" Technology and music are seen as the team's core areas of strength but it has also handled complex IP cases for publishing clients.

**The Lawyers:** The "*fantastic music lawyer*" Carey Ramos (see p.1490) is picked out by peers for his work in copyright and IP. Technology disputes make up a substantial part of his practice as he handles international cases with regard to the Internet and other new media developments. He also has a strong hardware practice and acts on litigation, counseling and licensing matters for clients in the DVD field (he is outside counsel to the DVD Forum). The music industry seeks him out too, and he has advised numerous music publishers in Grokster-related litigation.

**Clients/Work Highlights:** The group represents industry bodies and corporates as well as a selection of noteworthy individuals.

## Sheppard, Mullin, Richter & Hampton LLP

**The Firm:** A new entry to the tables this year thanks to the arrival of Kevin Goering from Coudert Brothers, this firm has a small but growing team. The group has a reputation in film work, representing studios and independent producers in a range of disputes. It is also active in matters arising from broadcasting, technology and advertising.

**The Lawyers:** Kevin Goering is "*a genuinely excellent lawyer with a really good practice.*" He is praised for his skills in First Amendment and libel matters and has a particular following among publishing clients.

**Clients/Work Highlights:** Grove/Atlantic, The Perseus Books Group and Condé Nast Publications feature on the list of clients.

## Other Notable Practitioners

The "*enthusiastic and proactive*" Robert Raskopf (see p.1491) recently moved from White & Case to Quinn Emanuel Urquhart Oliver & Hedges, LLP. He is recommended for his courtroom skills and his expertise in copyright and trademark matters. He is experienced in acting for both entertainment and sports bodies, undertaking a range of libel and licensing dispute work.

---

# PRIVATE EQUITY

# BUYOUTS & VENTURE CAPITAL INVESTMENT

| Private Equity: Buyouts & Venture Capital Investment Leading Firms | |
|---|---|
| **1** | DEBEVOISE & PLIMPTON LLP *New York* |
| | SIMPSON THACHER & BARTLETT LLP *New York* |
| **2** | DAVIS POLK & WARDWELL *New York* |
| | FRIED, FRANK *New York* |
| | KIRKLAND & ELLIS LLP *New York* |
| | LATHAM & WATKINS LLP *New York* |
| | ROPES & GRAY LLP *New York* |
| | WEIL, GOTSHAL & MANGES LLP *New York* |
| **3** | GIBSON, DUNN & CRUTCHER LLP *New York* |
| | KING & SPALDING LLP *New York* |
| | MORGAN, LEWIS & BOCKIUS LLP *New York* |
| | WHITE & CASE LLP *New York* |
| | WILLKIE FARR & GALLAGHER LLP *New York* |

## Band 1

### Debevoise & Plimpton LLP

See firm details p.1529

**The Firm:** Clients love this firm because "*it consistently delivers a super service,*" through a talent base which is "*deep in all areas; the associates are strong and the partners are client-focused.*" Committed to the private equity market since its inception – unlike some larger rivals – this firm's depth of expertise and appreciation of the finer points in buyout transactions and venture capital financing has earned it a stellar reputation. Clients also pointed to a modern business-savvy and practical approach employed in negotiations and the advantage of the firm's international offices in cross-border matters; although some felt it would be useful if this could be developed further. Clients range from LBO giants to market newcomers. Among recent highlights, the team acted for investors including Apax Partners, Goldman Sachs Capital Partners and Providence Equity Partners on the €1.73 billion acquisition of Deutsche Telekom.

**The Lawyers:** According to clients, Franci Blassberg is "*a master of all skills used in M&A nego-*

tiation; she's effective, and can be hard-nosed when necessary and subtle where it is more appropriate.*" Blassberg acts for key clients such as Clayton Dubilier & Rice (CD&R), recently advising it as part of a consortium including Eurazeo and Merrill Lynch Global Private Equity in the acquisition of Hertz from Ford – a transaction valued at $15 billion and the second largest LBO to date. Peggy Davenport is a "*bright attorney – she doesn't miss a thing and keeps everyone's egos in check.*" Her established client relationships include Teachers' Private Capital and Kelso & Company. Davenport recently acted for a consortium of private equity investors in the $1.6 billion purchase of the private equity portfolio of Deutsche Bank by MidOcean Partners. A "*smart, dogged, tireless and practical attorney,*" Paul Bird adopts a client-oriented approach. The media and telecommunications industry knowledge of Richard Bohm is widely commended. A strategic business adviser, he is "*genuinely concerned about putting the client's best foot forward.*" He has advised Kelso & Company on its interests in media companies such as Ellis Communications and King Broadcasting. Kevin Schmidt is "*pragmatic, smart and has the ability to see the complex issues and simplify them.*" He is currently acting on the Hertz acquisition.

Clients/Work Highlights: The firm's client roster reads like a Who's Who of the private equity industry and includes Providence Equity Partners, The Blackstone Group and Morgan Stanley Capital Partners to name but a few.

### Simpson Thacher & Bartlett LLP
See firm details p.1555

**The Firm:** "*First-rate and exceptional in every respect,*" the firm is focused on the completion of the deal, which makes it easy to work with. "*There is talent through the firm's ranks,*" agreed clients, who also pointed to the breadth of expertise available. Although renowned as a premier private equity practice, the firm's engagements for targets have hit the headlines recently. For example, it represented Ford and Hertz in the sale of Hertz in a $15 billion LBO by way of a private equity consortium. A powerful finance practice – recently bolstered by the addition of leveraged finance specialist Tony Keal from Allen & Overy to the London office – also adds value for clients. No stranger to cross-border transactions, the group recently advised a consortium of

investors in the $12 billion acquisition of TDC, Denmark's largest telecom company, by Nordic Telephone Company, one of the largest private equity takeovers in Europe.

**The Lawyers:** Head of the firm's global M&A practice, **Casey Cogut** (see p.1445) offers clients the benefit of his "*heavyweight intellect,*" cushioned by a user-friendly manner. Cogut is the relationship partner for clients such as KKR, JC Flowers & Co and Silver Lake Partners. Chairman of the firm's executive committee, **Pete Ruegger** (see p.1495) brings to the deal table "*a wealth of experience and an easygoing manner.*" He has a long track record of deals for high-caliber clients such as The Blackstone Group. **Alan Schwartz** (see p.1498) has already "*done a million deals*" in his legal career. The resulting experience has made him "*a smart negotiator – he will cut through the crap and is a reasonable, to-the-point kind of guy.*" Firm chairman **Dick Beattie** (see p.1436), "*the man to go to for tough deals,*" is respected as a luminary in the field. His recent caseload has included the representation of the consortium of seven private equity firms that has agreed to acquire SunGard.

Clients/Work Highlights: KKR; The Cypress Group; Silver Lake Partners; Ripplewood Holdings; Apax Partners and Cinven.

### Band 2

### Davis Polk & Wardwell
See firm details p.1528

**The Firm:** "*The number one for breadth,*" say clients, who applaud this team's overall capability and quality. Although the firm is perceived as more hierarchical and old line than some rivals, "*it is the one I admire the most; every time I work with a lawyer there they are terrific,*" observers agreed. "*There is a nice style about them, they deal with people in a tough but fair manner.*" The M&A and private equity groups work as one and benefit from the support of a respected fund formation team. A recent series of M&A megadeals has included the firm's advice to Morgan Stanley on the sale of AWAS, its aircraft leasing business, to Terra Firma Capital Partners for $2.5 billion in cash plus the assumption of liabilities. The team is also adept at turning its hand to cross-jurisdictional matters: it is advising the EQT IV fund on its acquisition of German engine manufacturer MTU Friedrichshafen from DaimlerChrysler.

**The Lawyers:** Head of the firm's M&A practice, **George Bason** (see p.1436) is "*just a great lawyer,*" clients reported. He possesses a wealth of experience and a strategic view of the private equity sphere. **John Bick** (see p.1439) is "*cool, calm and collected*" in his work with clients such as Morgan Stanley Private Equity and Metalmark Capital. Esteemed **Louis Goldberg** (see p.1460) counseled Morgan Stanley in its strategic acquisition of the real estate equity investment management business of Lend Lease, and acted in the conversion of Prime Property Fund from an insurance company separate account sponsored by Equitable to a private REIT. Managing part-

ner of the firm, **John Ettinger** (see p.1452) remains an eminent figure in the marketplace.

Clients/Work Highlights: Lehman Brothers; JPMorgan; Merrill Lynch and Morgan Stanley.

### Fried, Frank, Harris, Shriver & Jacobson LLP
See firm details p.1532

**The Firm:** Many in the market feel that this is a firm undergoing a resurgence, particularly through its close working relationships with the likes of Morgan Stanley and Goldman Sachs Capital Partners. Clients use the firm because "*it is current and commercial in its advice. Attorneys cut to the chase, have good judgment and deliver thoughtful, smart and savvy business advice.*" Highlight matters include counseling Goldman Sachs Capital Partners in its joint bid with Ripplewood Holdings to acquire Maytag. The firm also acted for the investor group led by Formation Capital, Appaloosa Management and Franklin Mutual Advisers in its proposed acquisition of nursing facility operator Beverly Enterprises.

**The Lawyers:** Chair of the firm's corporate department, **Bob Schwenkel** (see p.1499) is "*a client's dream because he speaks in straight business terms and will not waste your time.*"

Clients/Work Highlights: A growing client roster includes Permira Advisers, New Mountain Capital and AEA Investors.

### Kirkland & Ellis LLP
See firm details p.875

**The Firm:** That the market is no longer focusing purely on the Chicago office when discussing this firm is surely indicative of its success in establishing a prominent and respected New York group. Private equity has always been a focus for K&E, and a substantial number of its attorneys are involved in private equity activities. Peers are perhaps right to consider it "*a significant and real threat,*" while clients point to its "*cost-effective, capable and tough negotiators.*" Although this tough stance is not to the taste of all, clients appreciate the high service levels and results-driven approach of this seamless international group.

**The Lawyers:** **Stephen Fraidin** (see p.1456) remains a major figure in the industry. He recently acted for key client Forstmann Little on its $750 million acquisition of IMG and its $1.6 billion acquisition of 24 Hour Fitness. Clients say that **Kirk Radke** (see p.1490) is a rare beast: a complete deal lawyer. "*He can do everything, soup to nuts, has the ability to step away from the immediate legal issues and focus on the business concerns.*" Radke acted for BainCapital in the $550 million acquisition of Innophos from Rhodia.

Clients/Work Highlights: The firm acts for both marquee names (such as Forstmann Little and AIG Capital Partners) as well as smaller clients, an approach that results in greater diversity and exposure to the marketplace.

## Latham & Watkins LLP

**The Firm:** A breath of fresh air in the marketplace, sources agree. This firm manages to combine a young, dynamic feel with a burgeoning international network, all the while delivering high-quality advice to clients. The private equity team has successfully leveraged off Latham's stellar reputation in leveraged finance, essential in a climate where clients look to this element for breaking or making a deal. For example, it acted for KKR on its acquisition along with BainCapital and Vornado Realty Trust of Toys 'R' Us for $6.6 billion. The team also counseled The Carlyle Group on its acquisition of Verizon Hawaii from Verizon Communications. The firm's sizable resources enable it to provide clients with sector specialists in support of its transactions – for example, the DC office houses a team of over 50 telecom specialists.

**The Lawyers:** **Ron Hopkinson** impresses clients with his *"practical business sense"* in deals, said clients. He led the team acting for a consortium formed by The Carlyle Group and Welsh, Carson, Anderson & Stowe in the $7.05 billion acquisition of QwestDex. **Robert Kennedy** continues to impress market commentators as an attorney whose star is on the rise.

**Clients/Work Highlights:** Although market feedback typically centres on the firm's relationship with blockbuster client The Carlyle Group, it is interesting to note the volume and quality of other clients such as JPMorgan; Welsh, Carson, Anderson & Stowe; KKR and Leonard Green & Partners. Clients such as the Goldman Sachs power group echo the firm's traditional strength in the energy and project finance arenas.

## Ropes & Gray LLP

See firm details p.1117

**The Firm:** This firm seamlessly operates out of its Boston, Washington and New York offices and can also draw on the support of offices on the West Coast. Its increasing resources have allowed this firm to make its presence felt on some of the choicest recent consortium deals, such as counseling SunGard, Neiman Marcus, Hertz and Dunkin' Donuts. Clients range from large fund players such as BainCapital, Thomas H Lee Partners and Welsh, Carson, Anderson & Stowe to middle-market players such as AIG Altaris Health Partners and J.W. Childs Associates.

**The Lawyers:** The deal and client-focused **Othon Prounis** (see p.1490) is co-head of the firm's private equity practice.

**Clients/Work Highlights:** Silver Lake Partners; Goldman Sachs Capital Partners; The Carlyle Group and Fenway Partners.

## Weil, Gotshal & Manges LLP

See firm details p.1565

**The Firm:** *"A terrific team, which does a terrific job."* This is a firm whose buyouts and funds practices act as one, offering clients a full-cycle service. Weil also offers clients one of the few truly established international practices in this area with high-profile prac-

tices in London, Paris and Munich. Operations in London were recently ramped up by the acquisition of a team from Lovells, sending a clear message out to the market that the firm is set on becoming the world leader in the private equity market. And specialists in France and Germany ensure that the firm is well placed to capitalize on the buoyant European markets. Further cross-border highlights include acting for Thomas H Lee Partners, Quadrangle, JPMorgan and Provident Financial in an investment in a Spanish company.

**The Lawyers:** **Tom Roberts** (see p.1493) commands a great deal of respect in the industry for both his M&A and private equity expertise. Clients described him as a *"fabulous, client-oriented"* attorney. They also *"trust the judgment and common-sense approach"* employed by **Doug Warner** (see p.1511). He is particularly skilled in cross-border deals. **David Blittner** (see p.1439) has impressed clients as a *"smart, experienced, commercial and practical attorney."* He acts for various sponsors such as Apax Partners.

**Clients/Work Highlights:** Thomas H Lee Partners; KKR; Summit Partners and Texas Pacific Group.

## Band 3

## Gibson, Dunn & Crutcher LLP

See firm details p.328

**The Firm:** Clients benefit from an expanding network of offices, both nationally and internationally, to service their cross-border needs. The team has successfully leveraged off the growing success of its New York M&A practice and relationships with investment banks to secure its place on a steady flow of deals.

**The Lawyers:** **John Herbert** (see p.1464) won client plaudits as *"a deal-maker not a deal-breaker."*

**Clients/Work Highlights:** Morgan Stanley Capital Partners, Metalmark Capital and Rhône Capital are among the clients.

## King & Spalding LLP

See firm details p.1538

**The Firm:** The firm is growing in stature in this sector, particularly in the booming midmarket buyout sector. Its recent workload has included LBOs for a client base that includes Apollo Management LP and JPMorgan Partners. The buyouts practice can call upon the support of offices in Atlanta, Houston, Washington and London in its provision of specialist advice in the real estate and venture capital arenas. The firm recently demonstrated its commitment to the private equity sector as a whole through the addition to the funds practice of Stephen Culhane, former vice president and in-house counsel of Goldman Sachs.

**The Lawyers:** Dominick DeChiara co-heads the private equity practice. Lawrence Graev although still active in the sector, is now largely involved with The GlenRock Group.

**Clients/Work Highlights:** AEA Investors; First Atlantic Capital; The GlenRock Group; Warburg

Pincus; SAIC Venture Capital and Flinn Asset Management.

## Morgan, Lewis & Bockius LLP

See firm details p.1758

**The Firm:** The attorneys – *"hard-working, smart, creative, personable and pleasant to deal with"* – have attracted clients through their sensible approach to deals and *"good value for the dollar,"* clients reported. The cross-jurisdictional needs of clients are serviced by offices throughout the USA, as well as London, Paris, Brussels and Frankfurt. The expanding Asian market is also an area of focus, and the firm has established a new joint venture with TMI Associates, the sixth largest law firm in Japan. The transactional private equity offering is supported by industry-specific skills for investors targeting such areas as technology, life sciences, energy and retail. The recent lateral hires of key fund formation attorneys Jedd Wider and Louis Singer is also a boost to the practice.

**The Lawyers:** **Philip Werner** (see p.1513) and **Ira White** (see p.1513) were praised by clients for their *"good business sense and smart, dynamic approach"* to transactions.

**Clients/Work Highlights:** Its client list includes One Equity Partners; HIG Capital; Wellspring Capital Management; Apollo Management LP and Sun Capital Partners. Unlike many in the sector, the firm also enjoys a strong venture capital offering.

## White & Case LLP

See firm details p.1566

**The Firm:** The firm is a popular choice because of its strengths in the finance sector and, naturally given its extensive office network, its cross-border prowess. The firm counseled property investment firm Starwood Capital Group in its $3.1 billion acquisition of Groupe Taittinger and Société du Louvre. Further highlights include advising Lehman Brothers Merchant Banking portfolio company Phoenix Brands in its purchase of Colgate-Palmolive's North American laundry detergent business.

**The Lawyers:** Much of the firm's profile in the private equity arena rests with **John Reiss** (see p.1492). He led on the Starwood Capital Group deal.

**Clients/Work Highlights:** An impressive and extensive roster of clients includes The Blackstone Group, Advent International and 3i as well as Deutsche Bank; Lehman Brothers; Investcorp and HIG Capital.

## Willkie Farr & Gallagher LLP

See firm details p.1567

**The Firm:** An international private equity presence – the USA, France and Germany for example – has allowed this firm to carve out a strong reputation. Although many market commentators focus on the firm's relationship with Warburg Pincus, new clients such as Fortress Investment Group and Insight Capital are testament to its broad reach and commitment to client service. Attorneys from the New York and Frankfurt office represented Warburg Pincus in its acquisition of Multikabel from German cable group

PrimaCom for $616 million. The firm also acted for Warburg Pincus when it and Texas Pacific Group bought Neiman Marcus for $5.1 billion.

**The Lawyers:** **Steve Gartner** (see p.1458) spearheads the team. He was praised by clients as a *"very smart deal lawyer, yet with an easygoing personality that makes him popular with all parties."*

**Clients/Work Highlights:** Highlight matters include acting for Providence Equity Partners and Warburg Pincus in the acquisition of Telcordia Technologies from SAIC for $1.35 billion. The firm also

represented Colony Capital in its $1 billion agreement to purchase all of the hotel interests of Singapore-based Raffles Holdings.

### Other Notable Practitioners

**Doug Cifu** (see p.1445) of Paul, Weiss, Rifkind, Wharton & Garrison LLP enters our tables following strong client commendation for his deal-focused approach and *"excellent client service."* He acts for clients such as General Atlantic, Sandler Capital Management and Invemed Catalyst Fund.

**Paul Jacobs** (see p.1468) of Fulbright & Jaworski L.L.P. is co-head of the firm's corporation, business and banking department. He possesses a wealth of experience across a broad range of sectors and gained the respect of the market for his wise counsel. **Bob Schwed** (see p.1499) of WilmerHale impresses clients as an *"exceptionally good lawyer – he is intuitive and responsive."* Clients also felt that the years of experience he brings to bear on proceedings makes them feel *"entirely confident and comfortable"* with his advice.

# PRIVATE FUND FORMATION

| Private Fund Formation | |
|---|---|
| Leading Firms | |
| [1] | DEBEVOISE & PLIMPTON LLP *New York* |
| | SIMPSON THACHER & BARTLETT LLP *New York* |
| [2] | DAVIS POLK & WARDWELL *New York* |
| | ROPES & GRAY LLP *New York* |
| | WEIL, GOTSHAL & MANGES LLP *New York* |
| [3] | AKIN GUMP STRAUSS HAUER & FELD *New York* |
| | CLEARY GOTTLIEB STEEN & HAMILTON *New York* |
| | KIRKLAND & ELLIS LLP *New York* |
| | MORGAN, LEWIS & BOCKIUS LLP *New York* |
| | SCHULTE ROTH & ZABEL LLP *New York* |
| [4] | DEWEY BALLANTINE LLP *New York* |
| | GIBSON, DUNN & CRUTCHER LLP *New York* |
| | MAYER, BROWN, ROWE & MAW LLP *New York* |
| | SEWARD & KISSEL LLP *New York* |

## Band 1

### Debevoise & Plimpton LLP
See firm details p.1529

**The Firm:** A pioneer in the sector for many years, this firm has taken its place at the top of the market because of its *"deep pool of talent"* combined with an ability to *"understand the business side of what is going on as well as, if not better than, anyone,"* agree clients. The firm also fields cross-border expertise with six international offices, of which London and Paris drew special praise. In 2005, half of the funds that the firm worked on pursued either a global or primarily non-US investment strategy. For example, the firm's rapidly developing Hong Kong office recently acted for Morgan Stanley in its $515 million private equity fund dedicated to investing in Asia. The team has also acted on its fair share of spinouts, which have recently hit the market place, such as acting for the Morgan Stanley private equity team which left to form Metalmark Capital.

**The Lawyers:** One of the early specialists in the area, **Mike Harrell** brings *"a disarmingly charming demeanor"* to negotiations, demonstrated in his experience and tone, which is *"reassuring, balanced and fair."* Clients also appreciate that he is *"quick to point out where the market is and describe the relative merits on both sides."* **Jennifer Burleigh** *"serves her*

clients to get the best terms possible with an understanding of the ramifications"* while **Adele Karig** delivers sound strategic advice. She is *"adept at working under circumstances of extreme uncertainty,"* said clients. Many sources pointed to **Rebecca Silberstein** as the best of the next generation in the private equity market. *"Chairman of the whole industry"* **Woody Campbell** remains a preeminent presence and sage counsel for the team while **David Schwartz** is a new entrant to the tables following strong client commendation for his practical and pragmatic approach: *"He doesn't pull any punches and is not just a yes man, which is just what we need."*

**Clients/Work Highlights:** AIG; Oaktree Capital Management; North Castle Partners; Kelso & Company; Prudential; Clayton, Dubilier & Rice; Morgan Stanley and Merrill Lynch.

### Simpson Thacher & Bartlett LLP
See firm details p.1555

**The Firm:** A set of superior advisers with a terrific reputation, this team has enjoyed a formidable year by anyone's standards. For example, it closed Carlyle Europe and represented Lexington Fund on its secondary fund of over $2 billion. Clients point to the high level of service and a *"creative, solutions-rather than issues-oriented approach"* as distinguishing features of this firm. Key to much of the firm's success in the area is its attention to quality, not quantity, fielding a small but deeply experienced team able to focus closely on the needs of clients. An expanding international network and stellar client list ensures that the firm inevitably appears on the markets' choicest formations.

**The Lawyers:** A senior figure and hugely popular, **Thomas Bell** (see p.1437) is *"the Michael Jordan of the fund formation world."* He recently represented The Carlyle Group in the issuance of over $10 billion in limited partnership interests in two buyout funds. Carlyle Partners IV, Carlyle's principal LBO fund in North America, closed on $7.85 billion of capital commitments, while Carlyle Europe Partners II, focused on Western Europe, closed on nearly €1.8 billion of commitments. Clients concluded that Bell is *"professional, knowledgeable and provides extremely good advice."* **Michael Wolitzer** (see p.1514) is *"one of the smoothest first closers going,"* report sources, who also note his tight and effective running of

matters. Wolitzer closed Cyprus Graw, a spin-out of Soros, and recently closed a second mezzanine fund for The Blackstone Group. Clients choose **Glenn Sarno** (see p.1496) because he is *"responsive, understands all the issues and is very decisive"* and looks at things from a commercial point of view.

**Clients/Work Highlights:** Ripplewood Holdings; The Carlyle Group; The Blackstone Group; Evercore Partners.

## Band 2

### Davis Polk & Wardwell
See firm details p.1528

**The Firm:** The firm is renowned for its relationship with investment banks and for its strong regulatory practice. In the fund formation field, much of the firm's profile rests on the shoulders of the much-respected Yukako Kawata. The team advises on the formation and operation of private investment funds including private equity, hedge, venture capital, real estate and fund of funds. It also benefits from a steady flow of work from its much vaunted finance practice and international offices in Hong Kong and Tokyo, well placed to serve the burgeoning Asian market.

**The Lawyers:** One of the key players in the market, **Yukako Kawata** (see p.1470) is *"The brand"* that attracts clients to the firm. She is a no-nonsense adviser, respected for her wealth of knowledge and authoritative judgment. Similarly **Leor Landa** (see p.1473) adopts a straightforward and pragmatic manner that makes her an effective negotiator.

**Clients/Work Highlights:** Chilton Investments, Mercantile Bankshares and Farallon Capital Management are among the clientele.

### Ropes & Gray LLP
See firm details p.1117

**The Firm:** This firm has successfully combined its powerful investor and private equity capabilities with a commitment for fund formation that ensures it a place at the forefront of the market for all-around expertise. Adding to this the recent merger with IP heavyweight Fish & Neave, the market now has a firm which has doubled in size and can count the likes of Morgan Stanley among its roster of clients.

Transactional deals, such as the $11.3 billion SunGard Data Systems buyout for the consortium of private equity houses, show that the firm is a serious national and international contender in private equity and venture capital structuring and related transactions.

**The Lawyers:** *"A real gentleman and a wonderful guy, whom everyone respects,"* **William Hewitt** (see p.1465) is a mentor to the industry. His practical stance in negotiations makes him a popular sight at the deal table. **William McCormack** (see p.1478) offers substantial expertise on non-US funds; he is also endowed with *"the ability to see things from a high level and not get bogged down by the detail."* Sources proclaimed their *"deep respect"* for **John MacMurray** (see p.1476) while clients value his *"good judgment on what are acceptable terms with certain kinds of investors and management teams."*

Clients/Work Highlights: Bain Capital; KKR; Welsh, Carson, Anderson & Stowe and Fenway.

## Weil, Gotshal & Manges LLP

See firm details p.1565

**The Firm:** Clients praised this firm for its ability to *"identify the key issues and see things from our perspective,"* a service delivered by a team that can *"get the deal done in a first-class manner."* Private equity and the formation of funds is a thriving market for this firm: *"It has developed a terrific practice and provides a soup-to-nuts service,"* agree sources. The team is also benefiting from an upward swing in hedge fund work, and is setting up a private equity fund to do deals in China, pooling support from both the Shanghai and New York offices. Further highlights include the closing of a third fund for Wilbur Ross and PAI.

**The Lawyers:** Head of the firm's global private equity practice, **Barry Wolf** (see p.1513) brings to the table his terrific understanding of the tax structuring essential to this market. *"Tax lawyers tend to be smart and he typifies this rule,"* observed one interviewee. Clients also pointed to his *"business-minded and practical approach to lawyering."* Wolf looks after key clients such as Lindsay Goldberg & Bessemer and is acting on a new fund called Snow, Phipps & Guggenheim. A well-respected figure in the industry, **Jeffrey Tabak** (see p.1507) is noted for his deep knowledge of the area.

Clients/Work Highlights: Capital Z; Vestar Capital Partners; Oak Investment Partners; CSFB Private Equity and Thomas H Lee Partners.

## Band 3

## Akin Gump Strauss Hauer & Feld LLP

See firm details p.559

**The Firm:** Perhaps best known for its work in the hedge funds sector, this firm has enjoyed a busy year acting on one of the largest funds to date as well as a number of spin-out transactions. Clients spoke of the firm's *"knowledgeable, creative and responsive lawyers, who are up to speed on the law and on business issues."* The group combines its hedge funds workload with private equity, venture capital and fund of funds matters, and has recently witnessed an increasingly international flavor to the workload. Its European and US clients are currently setting their sights on India and China. An office in London furthers the cross-border needs of clients, while closer to home, the Washington, DC office provides the regulatory know-how for complex fund structuring.

**The Lawyers:** Head of department **Stephen Vine** (see p.1509) is renowned as a leader in the field. Clients described him as an *"incredibly intelligent and creative attorney,"* blessed with problem-solving skills.

Clients/Work Highlights: The firm recently represented Sandler Capital Management in its private equity investment in the $1.1 billion leveraged acquisition of Mobiltel, the largest telecom operator in Bulgaria.

## Cleary Gottlieb Steen & Hamilton LLP

See firm details p.1525

**The Firm:** This firm has won a loyal following among clients because of its *"quality lawyers who take a personal interest and give attention to our matters."* Its advice is *"practical, responsive and timely."* Although the firm is perhaps best known for its work with key client Texas Pacific Group (TPG), its ability to attract clients of the caliber of Silver Point and Dune Capital Management testifies to its broad appeal. Work for CSFB on multi-strategy hedge fund launches is also coming to the fore. There is a strong international network with offices in ten overseas locations ranging from London to Tokyo, soon to be bolstered by the opening of an office in Beijing. This reflects client demand for funds in Asia; for example, the firm is acting for MBK Partners in the formation of a Pan-Asian private equity fund with commitments in excess of $1 billion.

**The Lawyers:** An attorney who *"gives practical solutions to complex problems,"* **Michael Gerstenzang** (see p.1459) impresses clients with his *"experience and understanding of the underlying business issues and concerns."*

Clients/Work Highlights: CSFB; Silver Point; Dune Capital Management; Goldman Sachs; Citibank and Deutsche Bank.

## Kirkland & Ellis LLP

See firm details p.875

**The Firm:** A Chicago giant that has made not just a substantial impact on the New York market but has also created an international footprint in the private equity market. The firm has adopted a slow and steady approach to geographical expansion; an approach which appears to be reaping dividends. The firm's seven offices include bases in the key markets of London and Munich. This cross-border capability has enabled the firm to act on the representation of UK buyout house CVC Equity Partners on its formation of CVC Capital partners IV, a fund worth $7.3 billion, the largest buyout fund outside the US to date. It also advised this client on the formation of CVC Capital Partners Asia Pacific II LP.

**The Lawyers:** An impressive and dynamic attorney, **Kirk Radke** (see p.1490) is the driving force of the New York private equity team. He acted for former members of DLJ Merchant Banking Partners on the formation of Avista Capital Partners.

Clients/Work Highlights: Other clients include AIG Private Equity; Merrill Lynch Private Equity; Welsh, Carson, Anderson & Stowe and Warburg Pincus.

## Morgan, Lewis & Bockius LLP

See firm details p.1758

**The Firm:** The recent addition of fund formation specialists from Orrick, Herrington & Sutcliffe LLP has married well with the firm's growing presence in the equity buyouts arena. Clients point to its *"diplomatic and constructive"* attorneys and value the responsive and business-oriented advice that ensure *"a real comfort blanket"* when using the firm.

**The Lawyers: Louis Singer** (see p.1502) is blessed with *"great people skills and integrity"* which he brings to bear on proceedings. Clients spoke of his ability *to "make a measured decision based on an in-depth view of law."* The *"accomplished, efficient and direct"* **Jedd Wider** (see p.1513) has a long track record in the hedge funds arena. *"He knows where to put the pressure on; what are the big points to achieve and what's second priority: he doesn't lose his time or our money."*

**Clients/Work Highlights:** New clients include New Jersey State Pension Fund, Washington DC Pension and LA County Pensions.

### Schulte Roth & Zabel LLP

See firm details p.1552

**The Firm:** The *"premier practice for hedge funds,"* agree sources. The firm is also increasingly making its presence felt in the private equity arena and many pointed to a broadening of the group's expertise, particularly in the REITS and venture capital market. The firm is strategically well placed to benefit from the buoyant market in private fund formation and clients are drawing benefit from the specialist attorneys based in the firm's London office.

**The Lawyers: Stephanie Breslow** is an expert in the field, whose depth of experience means she is *a pure delight to work with,"* said clients.

**Clients/Work Highlights:** Cerberus Capital Management Bear Stearns Asset Management and Merrill Lynch Asset Management are are among the clientele, while venture capital clients include Wasserstein & Co and TL Ventures.

## Band 4

### Dewey Ballantine LLP

See firm details p.1530

**The Firm:** Clients point to this team's *"excellent client service and team orientation"* adding: *"You always get someone of quality with a high work ethic."* The firm is successfully leveraging off its reputation in the capital markets, projects and corporate arenas to build a practice in this area. Its international network of offices across London, Frankfurt, Milan and Rome also provide a clear advantage in cross-border matters. The firm recently advised The Praedium Group on the formation of and interests in The Praedium Fund VI, a $700 million private equity fund formed to invest in real estate and related assets.

**The Lawyers:** Head of department **Sanford Morhouse** (see p.1481) provides clients with a clear strategy as well as technical legal advice. *"He is a*

*'makes deals happen' kind of guy and has the right contacts and industry knowledge."* Clients also singled out **Joseph Smith** (see p.1503) as *"industrious, professional, intelligent and personable,"* and appreciated his consistently high service levels.

**Clients/Work Highlights:** The firm advised GE Asset Management on the establishment of the GEAM International Private Equity Fund. Other clients include Morgan Stanley Investment Management, Coller Capital and ARCIS Finance SA.

### Gibson, Dunn & Crutcher LLP

See firm details p.328

**The Firm:** The private equity practice at this firm is run on a cross-office operation with partners across the US working in conjunction with specialists in London and Munich. The firm has captured a significant share of the secondary market while also undertaking a sizable workload for the likes of CSFB and Lehman Brothers. Highlight matters include advising CSFB in the organization of the $2 billion CSFB Strategic Partners III, and assisting Investcorp in the organization of Investcorp Co-investment Partners LP. The team also advised New York Life in the organization of New York Life Capital Partners III.

**The Lawyers:** Key to much of the firm's success in this area is **Ed Sopher** (see p.1503), who enjoys a strong following of clients.

**Clients/Work Highlights:** The team further acted for Lehman Brothers in the organization of Lehman Brothers Secondary Opportunities Fund and Marsh & McLennan Companies in the spinoff of MMC Capital and the Trident Funds.

### Mayer, Brown, Rowe & Maw LLP

See firm details p.876

**The Firm:** Although the team has a lower profile in the market than some direct competitors, its accomplished attorneys have forged strong relationships in the industry that have allowed this practice to develop. Highlight matters include representing LS Power Group on the formation of its first private equity fund, LS Power Equity Partners. The team acted for The Jordan Company in the formation of The Resolute Fund, and is advising on its successor fund, The Resolute Fund II, which is seeking commitments of $2 billion.

**The Lawyers: Kathy Walsh** (see p.1511) is head of the corporate and securities practice in the New York office. She advises on a range of fund formation issues and recently represented Onex Corporation in the formation of its first private equity fund, Onex Partners LP. Clients praised her ability to deliver *"a*

*superior level of service."*

**Clients/Work Highlights:** Further highlights include acting for Carousel Capital, a private equity firm based in Charlotte, North Carolina, in the formation of Carousel Capital Partners III, LP.

### Seward & Kissel LLP

See firm details p.1553

**The Firm:** A sizable presence in the hedge funds arena, this practice of *"highly skilled and pragmatic attorneys"* is thriving in the buoyant market. Investment management has always been a major drawing card for this New York-based operation and it has attracted over 200 fund managers to its client roster. The focus here includes arbitrage funds, distressed debt and crossover funds.

**The Lawyers:** A popular figure in the market, **John Tavss** (see p.1507) advises clients on securities, tax and business law matters relating to the investment management sector.

**Clients/Work Highlights:** The Blackstone Group; Alda Capital Management; Wellington Management Company and Kingdon Capital Management.

### Other Notable Practitioners

**Howard Bergtraum** (see p.1438) of O'Melveny & Myers advises investors and sponsors on the formation and operation of venture capital, mezzanine, private equity and hedge funds. Now firmly ensconced at Linklaters, **Scott Bowie** (see p.1440), formerly of Latham & Watkins, attracted plaudits for his great experience. *"He has been through a lot of battles and has a great manner about him,"* said clients. **Stephen Culhane** (see p.1447) is charged with building up the practice at King & Spalding. Former head of the private equity group at Goldman Sachs, he has already acted on such high-profile matters as closing the Macquarie Global Property Fund. The *"exceptionally talented"* **Robert Insolia** (see p.1467) of Goodwin Procter LLP is *"one of the smartest lawyers around on complex structuring – he has the ability to translate it into layman's terms"* said clients. He spearheads the firm's activity in this sector, and has acted for Colony Capital on a REIT. Other clients include Deacon Capital, Prudential and Five Mile Capital Partners. **Charles Jacobs** (see p.1467) of Nixon Peabody LLP is a *"deal-maker, not a deal-breaker,"* and able to bring great judgment, gleaned by years of experience, to bear on proceedings. At Paul, Weiss, Rifkind, Wharton & Garrison LLP, **Marco Masotti** is best known for his high quality fund structuring advice which takes in a range of private investment funds, including buyout and hedge funds.

# PROJECTS

## Band 1

### Latham & Watkins LLP

**The Firm:** *"Breadth and depth"* is a phrase many firms use to describe their practice, but few, if any, have as legitimate a claim to it as Latham & Watkins. Client feedback confirms that the projects team offers a host of stars among its partners and a quality of associates which is second to none. Whichever direction the projects market has moved in, this team has been ready to pounce, with clients reporting that *"as a team it's just much more proactive and focused on getting things done than some other firms."* The expertise this group has in M&A, leveraged finance and capital markets is also a big draw for clients. Oil and gas, and naturally LNG, have dominated the firm's deal list, and its historic involvement in the power sector has allowed it to make the most of the increasing transactional activity in the domestic electricity and renewables market. The New York office has been involved in some of the banner deals of the year, advising the project borrowers and sponsors on RasGas II/III and advising the US Ex-Im Bank on Qatargas II. In the power sector, the team advised the joint arrangers on the acquisition of the La Paloma Generating facility in California. As in other years, clients mentioned a particular 'brand' of Latham lawyer emerging, commenting that *"every attorney is top-notch and easy to deal with."*

**The Lawyers:** While the departure of Andy Singer was noted by commentators, clients observed that he has left a strong and capable team as his legacy. **David Gordon** is managing partner of the New York office and was praised for his ability to *"make tricky deals as easy as possible." "Superb attorney"* **William Voge** is co-head of the global projects practice and was said to have done *"phenomenal"* work on RasGas II/III. **Jonathan Rod** was praised by clients and peers alike for his *"amazingly strategic mind"* which he put

to good effect as the lead on Qatargas II. Colleague **Warren Lilien** is recommended as *"an outstanding lawyer and destined for even greater stuff"* while **Jeffrey Greenberg** is applauded for his lender work. Greenberg was heavily involved on the La Paloma deal. **Michèle Penzer** is *"an extremely professional attorney with excellent drafting skills,"* and was noted for her work representing investment and commercial banks. **Jennifer Massouh** attracted high praise from peers and clients who observed that *"for bond work she's better than anyone for strong execution and is able to manage many clients at once."*

**Clients/Work Highlights:** ABN AMRO; Lehman Brothers; JPMorgan Chase; Morgan Stanley; WestLB; Deutsche Bank Securities; Mobil Producing Nigeria; Nigerian National Petroleum; Cogentrix Energy; Citigroup Global Markets; CSFB and Goldman Sachs.

## Band 2

### Milbank, Tweed, Hadley & McCloy LLP

**The Firm:** A true *"powerhouse"* in the projects sector, few firms offer such truly global expertise across the power and transport sectors. Known for its superb lenders practice, the firm boasts most of the key financial movers and shakers among its clients, advising them on some of the standout deals of the year. The firm has always enjoyed strong relationships with banks and commercial lenders, and this has positioned it favorably to take advantage of the increased activity among private equity and hedge funds. For example, the team acted for Energy Investors Funds on its acquisition of a majority interest in Tierra Energy. Internationally, few firms have the profile of Milbank in Latin America, and its reach into other markets has been bolstered by its phenomenal mining projects expertise. A further highlight for the team was acting for key client CSFB on its $1.3 billion recapitalization of Boston Generating.

**The Lawyers:** Renowned for his capital markets expertise **Jonathan Green** is *"extremely bright, always ahead of the game and gets the deal done no matter what,"* according to clients. **Douglas Harris** was lauded for his *"excellent business-minded"* approach to matters while **Richard Brach** *"brings significant experience to a deal; he is pragmatic and capable."* Head of the group, **Eric Silverman**, is a highly visible player on the market. Colleague **Daniel Bartfeld** attracted comment from observers for his *"pragmatic and capable approach to deals."*

**Clients/Work Highlights:** The team recently closed an $850 million financing for the Cerro Verde project in Peru. Other clients include WestLB; ANZ; Fortis Bank; Dexia; BayernLB; BNP Paribas; Matlin Patterson; Oak Tree Investors; Citigroup; JBIC; Mitsubishi; Diamond Energy; Cap Rock Energy; Leucadia National; Total and Tractebel.

### Skadden, Arps, Slate, Meagher & Flom LLP & Affiliates
See firm details p.1557

**The Firm:** *"One of the slickest outfits in the country,"* this is a firm whose transactional capability is a key draw for clients. Gas, and particularly LNG, has come to the fore recently. As illustrations, the team's representation of the underwriters on the $3 billion Ras Laffan project in Qatar, and the lenders on the Qatargas II expansion project, underlines the firm's ability to handle huge, complex deals. The Middle East is also a key focus for the team; it advised Egyptian General Petroleum in a Rule 144A financing of floating-rate notes. With a focus on borrower and lender work, this office was praised by commentators for its transactional ability, with researchers being told: *"The turnaround time is amazing – I don't know how they come back to us so quickly."* The deep financial expertise of the firm also gives clients great confidence to entrust them with high-stakes deals.

**The Lawyers:** *"Clearly the backbone of the practice,"* said clients of **Harold Moore** (see p.1481). He enjoys a fine reputation in the market as a *"spectacular"* attorney and is credited with driving the projects capability at the firm. **Sarah Ward** (see p.1511) is highly regarded for her leveraged finance ability and is said to possess *"an amazing ability to understand all the issues quickly as well as the commercial implications of legal advice."* The *"diligent and dynamic,"* **Julia Czarniak** (see p.1448) is rated for her advice to borrowers and has recently been focusing on the bank side of transactions.

**Clients/Work Highlights:** Edison Mission Energy is a major client of the group. It has also advised CSFB on three ethanol projects. Other clients include RBS; NRG; Mirant and Goldman Sachs.

### Sullivan & Cromwell LLP
See firm details p.1558

**The Firm:** Clients report that the consistency of the team here is outstanding: *"From senior partners to associates, I trust them all."* This offering has become synonymous with international big-ticket deals. While others boast about the size of their teams, this one doesn't have to; the lean offering here punches well above its weight and its deal list confirms the success of its *"quality, not quantity"* approach to projects. The firm's transactional capabilities are well known and researchers were told that the team *"wins significant transactions from people anxious to maintain a good reputation on Wall Street."* The projects practice is grounded in the natural resources sector. The New York office has a string of complex financings in the mining sector in Latin America to its name. While the legal expertise of the team is beyond doubt, its commercial and business acumen is also a real draw to clients, who conclude: *"I find them to be the best project finance attorneys – they're business-focused, pragmatic, and don't get bogged down in lawyering a deal – they get it done."*

**The Lawyers:** **Frederic Rich** (see p.1492) is *"brilliant on the legal side, but very much part of the deal,"* and enjoys a prominent presence in the market. **Sergio Galvis** (see p.1458) coordinates the Spanish and Latin American practice and is respected for his *"no-nonsense approach."* **Christopher Mann** (see p.1477) manages to combine a calm and good-natured manner with a proactive approach to deals. **Clients/Work Highlights:** Illustrating the firm's preeminence in the Latin American natural resources sector, the team was counsel to Sumitomo Metal Mining and Sumitomo Corporation in connection with the Cerro Verde II copper mine in Peru. Other clients include Palabora Mining; Escondida Project; Tengizchevroil and BP Exploration.

## White & Case LLP
See firm details p.1566

**The Firm:** *"Definitely one of the best"* is how commentators described this firm. The New York office is responsible for driving the lender-leaning practice both domestically and internationally. In the energy sector the team has a string of gas and power projects under its belt; however, it really stands out in the market for its involvement in the transportation sector. In Latin America the firm advised a consortium in connection to two new airports in Quito, Ecuador. The Middle East has also proved to be a healthy source of work, with the group securing advisory roles on the Rabigh, Taweelah B IWPP and Q-Chem II petrochemical projects. The team has positioned itself nicely to profit from the upswing in the power and renewables sectors, and recently advised the underwriters, led by CSFB, in their senior-secured bond offering of FPL Energy National Wind. Clients conclude that *"the team is dynamic – it puts a lot of thought into how it can best serve its clients."*

**The Lawyers:** According to one client, **Arthur Scavone** (see p.1497) *"is the best lawyer in New York,"* a sentiment echoed throughout the market with another client observing that: *"Even though he has many clients, when we deal with him we feel like we're the only ones."* **Troy Alexander** (see p.1432) has attracted attention for his work in Latin American markets and for his advice to multilaterals: *"He knows the issues inside out and knows how to explain them to nonlawyers,"* said sources.

**Clients/Work Highlights:** Abu Dhabi Water and Electricity Authority; Deutsche Bank; US Ex-Im Bank; Inter-American Development Bank; IFC; JBIC; MACH Gen; Qatar Petroleum; Skyway Concessions and Société Générale.

## Band 3

## Chadbourne & Parke LLP
See firm details p.1524

**The Firm:** Offering the expertise that comes with being a long-term player in the projects market, this firm maintains a strong presence in the sector. Although power has historically been the focus of the group, oil and gas and, more particularly, LNG are becoming increasingly prominent. While the Washington, DC office is renowned for its advice to multilaterals, the New York office complements this capability with a string of sponsors and finance sources on its books. The team has impressed the market with its push into emerging markets, and this office works with colleagues across the globe, most notably in London and Moscow. The firm has turned its attention to renewable energy and is advising clients, including a healthy slice of private equity players, on financing in this sector.

**The Lawyers:** *"Great for complex and sensitive deals,"* **John Baecher** (see p.1435) concentrates his practice in the power sector, advising a large global developer of power projects. **Chaim Wachsberger** (see p.1510) is a *"luminary"* according to clients, and commands

much respect from the industry. He primarily represents sponsors in the energy industry.

**Clients/Work Highlights:** CSFB; AES; Carlyle Riverstone; GE Commercial Finance; Citibank; Union Bank of California; Duke Energy and Tractebel.

## Davis Polk & Wardwell
See firm details p.1528

**The Firm:** This firm concentrates on offering clients a high level of service on complex and ground-breaking deals. Rather than building up a projects-dedicated team, the firm has chosen to hone the skills of its attorneys in the securities and leveraged finance acquisition arenas, so that these generalists can essentially act for any party in any sector. Developers, underwriters and commercial and lending agencies have all engaged the firm on projects spanning telecoms, toll roads and energy. The firm has established a strong reputation in Latin America and is currently undertaking a number of significant projects in Venezuela. Clients report that this is *"the one to go to when novel transactions and novel structures are required."* The concentration of talent in this lean team also impresses the market, with one peer conceding: *"I was surprised when I found out the actual size of the team – it is a huge compliment to them."*

**The Lawyers:** Corporate partner **Joseph Hadley** (see p.1463) *"can do anything,"* say clients. He was praised as being especially strong on international projects and for his ability to manage multiparty transactions. **Waide Warner** (see p.1511) heads the project finance group and was lauded by market sources as *"incredibly thorough and always ahead of the game."*

**Clients/Work Highlights:** The team has advised significant client Digicel on a number of projects in the Caribbean. Other clients include AES; Morgan Stanley; NatWest and OPIC.

## Dewey Ballantine LLP
See firm details p.1530

**The Firm:** Dewey Ballantine maintains a strong profile in the projects sector, largely due to its expertise in energy. Representing all players in the market, the group receives particular recognition for its lender work where the finance group operates closely with its energy colleagues. The team's work over the last year reflects the uptake in renewable projects, with an increased flow of nuclear work. *"A solid team with strong corporate credentials,"* according to sources, its profile still appears to be pegged to the presence of Rich Shutran. The group has acted on a number of renewable projects in the southwestern states, while internationally the firm's footprint is firmly placed in Latin America with a number of transport, particularly toll road, deals to its credit. Building a reputation for its ability to handle deals in complex international markets, Dewey recently represented Phoenix Park Gas Processors, as borrower, to finance the increasing capacity of its facility in Trinidad and Tobago. Domestically, the firm represented the private placement investors in connection with the Cross-country Pipeline financing.

The Lawyers: The *"tremendously capable"* **Richard Shutran** (see p.1501) *"has a great sense of humor and is very easy to work with,"* say clients. Shutran has a wealth of experience in advising all parties and a great understanding of the Latin American market. **Junaid Chida** (see p.1444) has developed a solid profile for his tax-advantaged project finance work, particularly in the power sector. He is said to be *"a thorough lawyer, able to anticipate potential issues very early on."* Clients/Work Highlights: Calpine; CSFB; HypoVereinsbank and UBS.

## Shearman & Sterling LLP

See firm details p.1554

The Firm: With deep roots in the Latin American market, this firm has built a reputation for advising on complex and difficult projects in the region, displaying a special knack for restructurings and limited recourse financings. Energy, and particularly natural resources and mining, is a strong suit of the team, with a solid toll road and transportation expertise rounding out the practice. Shearman has long been a major player in the corporate finance arena. This has fed into the group's reputation as a premier lender's counsel, with a string of key banking players on its client list, which includes an impressive showing of Japanese banks. Commentators agreed that the group *"is a smaller player in terms of the size of its team, but everything it does is quality."* Recent highlights include advising the lead arrangers on the Mexico City Airport expansion financing. Also of note is the firm's Latin American experience, which has allowed it to foster an *"exceptionally impressive"* political risk insurance capability.

The Lawyers: *"A good person to have on your side when things get ugly,"* **Cynthia Urda Kassis** (see p.1509) is *"competent, precise and understands not just the legal but also the cultural and political context of the deals,"* say clients. Other lawyers appreciate the fact that *"she is incredibly easy to work with and the standard of her work is always impressive."* **Jeanne Olivier** (see p.1484) enjoys a formidable reputation for her work representing banks in domestic and international projects. Her risk insurance work is *"market-leading,"* say sources, and clients report she *"always has her eye on the ball."*

Clients/Work Highlights: Mizuho Bank; Japanese Ventures Investment Club; Mitsui; Marubeni; CSFB; Citigroup; ABN AMRO; Barclays; Crédit Lyonnais; Central American Bank for Economic Integration (CABEI); Deutsche Investitions-und Entwicklungsgesellschaft (DEG); BNP Paribas; PSEG Global and Placer Dome.

## Band 4

## Debevoise & Plimpton LLP

See firm details p.1529

The Firm: Established as a Wall Street thoroughbred, this firm adheres to the quality-not-quantity mantra in terms of the instructions it takes on. The projects team here has a broad mandate advising lenders and sponsors, although it is its financial guarantor work

that really attracts attention. One of the few players in the monoline insurance market, Debevoise is in pole position to be a major player in the emerging US PPP market. The team recently counseled Financial Security Assurance as financial guarantor in the $1.4 billion project bond financing for the Chicago Skyway. The projects team reflects the consistency and quality across the firm, with clients noting that *"the depth and experience offered is incredible, every single attorney is outstanding."* The team's involvement in airport projects demonstrates its ability to advise sponsors and lenders in domestic and international markets; it is counseling the developer for the proposed South Suburban Airport in Illinois, the project company in the restructuring of the privatised international terminal at JFK and an Aeroflot subsidiary in the development of the new terminal at Sheremetyevo Airport in Moscow.

The Lawyers: **Robert Gibbons** has deep experience in public and private sector development across all sectors. He is *"relaxed in his manner but incredibly thorough in the execution of his work,"* say clients. **Ivan Mattei** joins the *Chambers* table this year thanks to him *"basically inventing the legal technology in the guarantor market,"* according to sources. He led on the Chicago Skyway project.

Clients/Work Highlights: The team represented Phelps Dodge as sponsor in the debt financing for the expansion of the Cerro Verde copper mine in Peru. MBIA is a longstanding client, and the team advised it as financial guarantor on several projects. Other clients include XL Capital; Inter-American Development Bank; Teachers Insurance and Annuity Association; MetLife; Prudential Finance; American Airlines; Cogentrix Energy; Drax Power; John Hancock; Powerco and Sithe Energies.

## Freshfields Bruckhaus Deringer LLP

The Firm: This UK magic circle firm has a projects practice concentrated in the energy sector, the team is renowned for its work in the power arena, with coal, oil and gas deals also coming to the fore. The team is respected for its work for export credit agencies and private equity funds. Clients report that they are drawn to the depth of experience the firm offers. Cross-border and portfolio transactions are a specialty of this group, and it recently advised a private equity fund in the acquisition and project financing of various power assets in France.

The Lawyers: **Ted Burke** recently returned to London to become CEO of the firm. **Melissa Raciti-Knapp** was applauded for her knowledge and experience in Latin American markets.

Clients/Work Highlights: The firm enjoys a long-standing relationship with the US Ex-Im Bank. Other clients include BNP Paribas; ArcLight Capital Partners; JPMorgan; WestLB; IFC and OPIC.

## Orrick, Herrington & Sutcliffe LLP

See firm details p.337

The Firm: Working closely with its California office, the New York team of this firm has acted on a healthy share of matters in the domestic, renewable energy market. Power has been a focus area for the group

recently, with transportation and telecoms also within its remit. Offering a broad practice, the team represents developers, offtakers and lenders, and has developed a niche for its municipal finance work. Sources say that this specialization places it favorably to take advantage of the increasing interest in the PPP model. AES is a key client, and the team advised it on its acquisition of SeaWest Holdings, a wind generation, operation and development company. The team also counseled Solar Integrated Technologies as sponsor/lessee in connection with the manufacture of a solar roofing product.

The Lawyers: **Michael Meyers** (see p.1479) enjoys a significant profile in the market and is *"commercially and technically excellent."* The recommendation for **Carl Lyon** (see p.1476) is based on his work undertaking financings for public and private utility projects. He is *"really making his mark in the area,"* according to sources.

Clients/Work Highlights: The team represents Osaka Gas Energy America in its acquisition of nine IPP project assets from ArcLight Energy Partners Fund I. Other clients include CIT Power Energy and Infrastructure; Atlantic Power Holdings; UPC Wind and Eurus Energy America.

## Simpson Thacher & Bartlett LLP

See firm details p.1555

The Firm: The projects practice at this firm is heavily intertwined with its energy group, and advises clients such as sponsors and lenders on a range of projects across the sector. Representing the sponsors of Texas Genco was a highlight, as was advising CSFB on the financing of an ethanol project. The team is recognized for its stellar work in acquisitions and is accumulating an enviable list of private equity groups as clients, leveraging off the firm's preeminent reputation in the private equity arena. Coal is a particular niche for this group, which is advising Calyon on the development of a project in this field.

The Lawyers: *"A sharp operator,"* according to clients, **Martin Jacobson** (see p.1468) has a broad range of experience representing sponsors, lenders and underwriters. Colleague **David Lieberman** (see p.1475) is *"the one you want for complicated structured finance and tax issues,"* clients say. **Kenneth Wyman** (see p.1514) is *"incredibly good"* and was nominated as a top lawyer in the coal sector; while newcomer to the *Chambers* table, **George Miller** (see p.1479), *"is smart and effective,"* with clients appreciating his understated yet effective manner.

Clients/Work Highlights: RBS; CSFB; The Blackstone Group; JPMorgan and Lehman Brothers.

## Band 5

## Allen & Overy LLP

See firm details p.1516

The Firm: This streamlined team benefits from the huge international platform of the firm's global network. The projects practice is grounded in the firm's work for multilaterals, and has grown to encompass developers, banks and export credit

agencies, operating across the full panoply of the transport and energy sectors. The team is currently representing four ECAs and multilaterals as lenders to the Quito airport in Ecuador. In the waste sector, the team is counseling GE Infrastructure, Water & Process Technologies in connection with the Hamma seawater desalination plant in Algeria.
**The Lawyers:** David Slade leads the New York project finance group and Robert Kartheiser is co-head of the firm's Latin American practice group
**Clients/Work Highlights:** OPIC; US Ex-Im Bank; Inter-American Development Bank; Export Development Canada; EBRD; GE Infrastructure, Water & Process Technologies; Marubeni; AES; Grupo México; Government Development Bank for Puerto Rico; BSCH and Calyon.

### Bingham McCutchen LLP
See firm details p.1110
**The Firm:** Leveraging off its strong relationships with banks and lenders, this firm enters the *Chambers* table because of the strength of a projects practice which is focused on the energy sector. This practice has expanded to offer advice to multilaterals and sponsors. Key deals this year include advising on the refinancing of the Astoria Energy project. Commentators pointed to the burgeoning wind practice at the firm and its solid work in emerging markets.

**The Lawyers: Marc Reardon** (see p.1491) cochairs the firm's projects and structured finance practice and was reported to be *"thorough and great to work with."*
**Clients/Work Highlights:** GE Energy Financial Services; AIG; OPIC; CS Energy; ING; Prudential Finance; Deutsche Bank and ArcLight Capital Partners.

### Clifford Chance US LLP
See firm details p.1526
**The Firm:** While the US projects team at Clifford Chance is headquartered in Washington DC, the New York office provides an important link in the chain. Mandated to advise the firm's enviable banking client roster, the New York grouping is admired by peers for its *"lean but tremendous"* offering. The group is advising Citigroup and a variety of commercial and multilateral lenders in relation to a $2 billion alumina mining and refining project in Guinea.
**The Lawyers:** Evan Cohen is the key contact at the New York office.
**Clients/Work Highlights:** The team boasts a number of key banks and financial institutions in its client base.

### Paul, Hastings, Janofsky & Walker LLP
See firm details p.339
**The Firm:** This firm enters the tables this year due to its recent firmwide push to ramp-up its projects practice, evidenced by a key lateral hire to this local office. Robert Vitale has joined from Cadwalader, Wickersham & Taft LLP. He brings with him extensive international experience, particularly in Latin American markets, melded with broad experience across the energy, transport and telecoms sectors. Commentators commend the firm's push in the market and are confident that it is drafting in quality attorneys which should serve the firm well. Recent instructions include advising the Trust Company of the West (TCW) in its acquisition financing of oil and gas assets in Peru, and on a North Sea project. The team also recently advised the lender on a Mexican toll road.
**The Lawyers:** *"Well equipped to drive the practice forward,"* **Robert Vitale** (see p.1509) is *"respectful and listens to what clients and other lawyers have to say,"* market sources say.
**Clients/Work Highlights:** The team serves the full range of project clients including sponsors, multilaterals, export credit agencies and lenders.

## REAL ESTATE

### Band 1

### Fried, Frank, Harris, Shriver & Jacobson LLP
See firm details p.1532
**The Firm:** This vibrant firm is an indisputable market leader, with an excellent range of sales, acquisitions and development work. The group has been involved in many of the highlight deals in New York, several involving trophy properties key to the city's landscape. The group has cultivated a powerful leasing practice, with the firm's foremost personalities driving this side of the firm forward. Clients appreciated the *"tremendously effective advice of this first-class team,"* which has a deep bench of talented lawyers throughout the ranks. Indeed, when it comes to *"top dirt lawyering,"* in the sense of handling real estate transactions from the ground up, this firm takes much of the limelight. A national practice, its work in capital markets transactions and complex financings illustrates the lawyers' flexibility.
**The Lawyers:** The *"inexhaustible"* **Jonathan Mechanic** (see p.1479) *"has the publicity and the force of personality"* to succeed on any transaction, said sources. He is the chair of the group, and *"the perennial standout guy."* Lauded for his encyclopedic knowledge of the New York market, his vigorous yet personable negotiation style is welcomed by the market. **Stephen Lefkowitz** (see p.1474) forms the

vanguard of the firm's land use and zoning practice. Sources applaud him as an *"unbelievably intelligent"* specialist who commands great respect. His achievements in New York's complex administrative landscape include work on the Atlantic Yards project and the proposed Yankee stadium. **Joshua Mermelstein** (see p.1479) is a top transactional player, acting for developers, owners, financial institutions and investors. *"As smart a lawyer as there is in the city,"* he is praised for his *"tactful yet effective"* negotiating style. **Robert Sorin** (see p.1503) is a transactional lawyer whose high-level work on development, financing, leasing and joint ventures gives him a growing presence across the market.
**Clients/Work Highlights:** The group's leading work for Tishman Speyer Properties has continued, with the $1.72 billion acquisition of the MetLife Building being a clear high point. Other highlights include the acquisition and financing of office buildings at One Court Square in Long Island City, and for the Anti-Defamation League Foundation, the lawyers worked on the sale of the League's New York City headquarters at 823 United Nations Plaza. Leasing highlights include acting for Macklowe Properties on a lease to McDermott Will & Emery LLP of space at 340 Madison Avenue, and acting for Brookfield Financial Properties on a lease to the SEC of space at Three World Financial Center. A top mixed-use development is the Atlantic Yards project in

Brooklyn, a proposed project which will include a sporting arena for the Nets basketball team. The group is also active on portfolio transactions, and it was counsel to Wachovia on the $1 billion acquisition of the Westfield portfolio by Beacon Properties.

### Paul, Hastings, Janofsky & Walker LLP
See firm details p.339
**The Firm:** A leading outfit for general real estate, this group also forges ahead in the increasingly important capital markets arena. The team is *"one of the most credible real estate practices in the city,"* say peers, yet the reach of this firm is comprehensively international, with many of the firm's highlight portfolio transactions occurring across several major cities. The focus of work has been on major deals involving portfolio properties, and acquisitions of corporate entities in real estate. The group is also a tremendous presence for major New York developments, and here its powerhouse reputation allies well with its excellent level of resources. The firm's high-profile work on the James A. Farley Post Office Building for The Related Companies and Vornado Realty Trust has ensured the group long-term work and excellent market visibility. This is a significant Manhattan project involving a major historic property and will involve retail, postal facilities and a new transport system.

**The Lawyers: Marty Edelman** (see p.1451) is a premier lawyer and a linchpin of the group. He is an *"extraordinary force in the market,"* combining as he does, excellent business acumen with very deep real estate knowledge. As a *"top rainmaker and power-broker,"* he remains a drawing card for clients. **Robert Wertheimer** (see p.1513) is co-vice chair of the group. This outstanding transactional lawyer has been busy with developments, hotel leases, and capital markets transactions. Clients praised his *"hands-on style"* and calm approach to negotiations. **Ann Shipley** (see p.1501) has proven herself to be a *"terrific, versatile and capable"* lawyer across a range of transactions. She is client-focused in her approach and *"is tenacious and really digs in – she does a great job for her client."* She is best known for her representation of The Related Companies.

**Clients/Work Highlights:** The team represented Millennium Partners in a $260 million refinancing of six Ritz-Carlton hotels throughout the country. It also represented Talisker Corporation on the negotiation of a 999-year ground lease to Montage Hotels & Resorts, for the development of a five-star resort in Utah. A corporate highlight has been the representation of Marathon Asset Management on the acquisition of a majority share interest in a company developing a 1000-room hotel near the San Antonio Convention Center. The firm is also making progress with foreign clients and related issues, with one highlight being its representation of Reckson New York Property Trust on due diligence and financing of an Australian property trust investing in the New York Tri-State area.

## Skadden, Arps, Slate, Meagher & Flom LLP & Affiliates
See firm details p.1557

**The Firm:** Clearly a leading player for securitized finance, this global firm has a tremendous profile for its skills in handling the most complex transactions. The group is best known for its work with Deutsche Bank, for which the group engages in major loan origination and securitization. For example, it advised Deutsche Bank Securities on a refinancing of $1.2 billion of debt secured on the GM Building. It also represented Deutsche Bank on the origination of an $800 million CMBS loan facility to part finance the acquisition of Toys 'R' Us, as well as on the origination and securitization of a $1.5 billion floating rate loan to refinance a portfolio of hotels. The team's market-leading reputation gives it a broad platform, allowing it to pioneer cutting-edge sophisticated finance structures. Furthermore, the group has a growing profile in development work and general real estate, allowing clients to capitalize on the full-service offering of the firm.

**The Lawyers:** The *"vast experience"* and tremendous legal acumen of **Benjamin Needell** (see p.1482) puts him in the front line for all areas of real estate. He heads the group and is as adept on financing as he is on leasing matters: *"You need him in the room for the hard issues – he has an excellent background negotiating deals."* He is key contact for blue-chip clients and leading market names, such as Larry Silverstein. **Harvey Uris** (see p.1509) is a key contact for capital markets-related real estate matters, with his work for Deutsche Bank grabbing the most attention. *"Definitely a member of the A-team,"* he receives enthusiastic commendations for his superb finance proficiency, and his particular CMBS, loan origination and securitization background. The creative style of **Martha Feltenstein** (see p.1454) wins plaudits, and she advises top lending clients alongside her work in global real estate development. **Neil Rock** (see p.1493) has been busy with financing from the borrower side, and his highlights include helping The Trump Group on the financing and development of a project in California, as well as acting for Empire State Development Corporation on the development of the New York Sports and Convention Center.

**Clients/Work Highlights:** The group acted for Bank of America on a $650 million offering of Liberty bonds for its new headquarters in New York. It also advised Empire State Development on a proposed basketball arena in Brooklyn, and acted for The May Department Stores Company in the acquisition of 62 Marshall Field's retail outlets. Other clients include Wyndham International; ING Real Estate; Fortress Credit and Brascan Real Estate Financial Partners.

## Band 2

## Shearman & Sterling LLP
See firm details p.1554

**The Firm:** Building on its long-standing market strength, this group has continued to play a key role in the real estate sector. It is active in assisting private equity funds on acquisitions and financing. With foreign-based entities forming a large part of the team's client base, the group is also credited with bringing a significant portion of international investment into the New York market and beyond. Peers state that the team is strong on lender side financing, and *"the lawyers have excellent drafting skills."* It is no surprise to see this powerful transactional firm acting on the borrower and lender side in complex financing transactions, and the forward-looking team is witnessing a growth in the construction and mezzanine lending fields too.

**The Lawyers: Chris Smith** (see p.1503) is a deal-oriented generalist, who has an excellent footprint in transactions across the country. His booming finance practice is balanced by significant acquisitions and sales in major cities. This experienced attorney certainly has the respect of clients: *"He has all the skills that a lawyer needs – he is tough, subtle and wickedly smart."* **Malcolm Montgomery** (see p.1481) has a burgeoning practice covering domestic and cross-border real estate. His clients include Deutsche Bank and Eurohypo.

**Clients/Work Highlights:** The group represented Deutsche Bank in a $415 million syndicated construction financing of a Las Vegas resort. It also acted for Shorenstein Realty Investors Six in the recapitalization of the joint venture ownership of the Starrett-Lehigh Building, as well as on the sale of 450 Lexington Avenue. The team has continued to act for Battery Park City Authority on issues relating to the ground lease of Site 26, Battery Park, to Goldman Sachs. For CSFB the group assisted on the sale of 575 Fifth Avenue.

## Stroock & Stroock & Lavan LLP

**The Firm:** This group has succeeded in bridging its long-standing, classic New York real estate reputation with many new engagements across a variety of areas. The group is predominantly involved in major city developments, acquisitions and mortgage financings. Also, the lawyers have become increasingly active working on investment vehicles from the formation stage onwards. Peers relate how this firm has gone from an *"old-line New York real estate practice to an extremely visible force vying for the big-ticket matters."* At 11 partners in the New York office, the midsized team is well positioned to take on a variety of issues, with condominiums proving a particularly important niche. Clients enthused about the *"large bullpen of talented and sensitive lawyers who can do the heavy lifting,"* and the firm's New York-centric reputation.

**The Lawyers:** The *"legendary"* **Leonard Boxer** chairs the practice group, and he is key to its identity. One of the most senior and well-respected attorneys in the market, his wealth of relationships throughout the city places him as a vital contact. Clients appreciate that his finance and funds expertise is matched by his skill in arbitration. **Brian Diamond** is recommended for his high-quality funds work. Clients count him as a *"pleasure to work with"* for his *"knowledgeable and incredibly strong"* practice.

## Real Estate
### Leading Individuals

#### Senior Statesman
BOXER Leonard *Stroock*

[1] EDELMAN Marty *Paul, Hastings*
MECHANIC Jonathan *Fried, Frank*
NEEDELL Benjamin *Skadden, Arps*
SHENKER Joseph *Sullivan & Cromwell LLP*

[2] ADLER Arthur *Sullivan & Cromwell LLP*
LIPSON Lawrence *Proskauer Rose LLP*
MERMELSTEIN Joshua *Fried, Frank*
PINOVER Eugene *Willkie Farr & Gallagher*
SIMKIN Steven *Paul, Weiss*
SMITH Chris *Shearman & Sterling LLP*
URIS Harvey *Skadden, Arps*
WHITE W Christopher *Cadwalader*

[3] DIAMOND Brian *Stroock*
FELTENSTEIN Martha *Skadden, Arps*
FORTE Joseph *Alston & Bird LLP*
HOROWITZ Steven *Cleary Gottlieb*
NEVELOFF Jay *Kramer Levin*
ROSEN J Philip *Weil, Gotshal & Manges*
STEIN Joshua *Latham & Watkins LLP*
WEINBERGER Michael *Cleary Gottlieb*
WERTHEIMER Robert *Paul, Hastings*

[4] ALDEN Steven *Debevoise & Plimpton LLP*
ALTSCHULER Fredric *Cadwalader*
COLLETTA Anthony *Sullivan & Cromwell LLP*
IVANHOE Robert *Greenberg Traurig LLP*
KANE Meredith *Paul, Weiss*
KLEIN Steven *Willkie Farr & Gallagher*
LASCHER Alan *Weil, Gotshal & Manges*
MILLER Peter *Akin Gump*
PANOVKA Robin *Wachtell*
ROSS Barry *Bryan Cave LLP*
SHIPLEY Ann *Paul, Hastings*

[5] BENNER Michael *Wachtell*
BOND W Michael *Weil, Gotshal & Manges*
CHADAKOFF Richard *Latham & Watkins LLP*
CIABARRA Laura *Dechert LLP*
EDELSTEIN Mark *Morrison & Foerster LLP*
EVANUSA Michel *Stroock*
FODOR Susanna *Jones Day*
FREIDUS Harris *Paul, Weiss*
GLIATTA Stephen *Kaye Scholer LLP*
GOLDEN Matthew *Debevoise & Plimpton LLP*
KOBAK Scott *Simpson Thacher & Bartlett*
MONTGOMERY Malcolm *Shearman & Sterling LLP*
MOSKOWITZ Steven *Stroock*
POLEVOY Martin *DLA Piper*
RESSA Gregory *Simpson Thacher & Bartlett*
ROCK Neil *Skadden, Arps*
SANSEVERINO Raymond *Brown Raysman*
SERNAU Ronald *Proskauer Rose LLP*
SORIN Robert *Fried, Frank*
STEINER Jeffrey *Brown Raysman*
WEINBERGER David *Proskauer Rose LLP*

#### Up-and-coming individuals
IRWIN Peter *Debevoise & Plimpton LLP*

**Michel Evanusa** has a well-defined niche in co-ops and condominiums, while the *"very politically savvy"* **Steven Moskowitz** has gained recognition for his attention to detail and fortitude. Clients say he is *"a relentless worker,"* and a strong point is his *"pitbull-like, tough negotiation style."* Pension funds, REITs and other institutional investors are among his clients.

**Clients/Work Highlights:** The team represents the owner of the New York Mets in its development of a new stadium adjacent to Shea Stadium. In this project the lawyers have been busy in negotiations with city and state authorities. For Alexandria Real Estate Equities the group is acting on the development of the East River Science Park, a $700 million project. Recently, it assisted JPMorgan Investment Management on the purchase of a 70% interest in One Court Square, Long Island City. Also, the group acted for The Lefrak Organization in its privatization of the Hudson Towers Housing Company. Other clients include Apollo Real Estate Advisors; The Carlyle Group; AXA Equitable Life; Lehman Brothers; Millennium Partners and Vornado Realty Trust.

### Sullivan & Cromwell LLP
See firm details p.1558

**The Firm:** This *"highly evolved"* group has an excellent reputation for its breadth of work and the quality of its client base. Its representation of institutional investors and corporate real estate is an important part of this high-end practice. The team's excellent profile is in no small part due to the work it undertakes for Whitehall Street Real Estate Funds. However, this is but one client, and the team has an extensive track record in the fund formation and REIT market too. The firm's achievements are comprehensive throughout New York – where it works on several trophy assets including sports stadiums – as well as the rest of the USA. With hotel and resort transactions across the country, the *"very savvy and extremely capable"* lawyers have an excellent grasp of the market.

**The Lawyers:** **Joseph Shenker** (see p.1500) *"flies the flag"* for the firm, reported sources. He is an *"impressive, knowledgeable and polished"* practitioner and has a tremendous range of influential contacts. His high-end fund work is balanced by the profile of clients like the Tisch, Pritzker and Mara families. **Arthur Adler** (see p.1431) is a leading light for his high-profile development and borrower financing work. In 2005, he continued to act for Goldman Sachs on Site 26, Battery Park, the location of its new headquarters development. This involved a significant bond financing. Sources rate his *"civil, smart and responsive"* approach and his *"ability to cut to the chase and recognize the bottom line."* **Anthony Colletta** (see p.1446) is a bright attorney who is praised for his phenomenal workload. His private equity, finance and development work has been dominated by nationwide hotel transactions, and his *"very pragmatic and business-oriented"* style makes him very popular among clients.

**Clients/Work Highlights:** Acting for Vornado Realty Trust, the team has a key role on continuing issues relating to the acquisition of Toys 'R' Us. Lawyers acted for Whitehall Street Real Estate Funds and Highgate Hotels on leveraged recapitalizations of the Lexington Radisson Hotel and the New York Doubletree. An ongoing instruction includes acting for an owner consortium that includes the Zeckendorfs and Whitehall Street Real Estate Funds on the $950 million construction financing of the Mayflower development site at 15 Central Park West in Manhattan. In the corporate real estate arena, the team acted for bidding parties attempting to acquire several major hotel groups with significant US and international real estate assets. Other clients include Aetos Capital; CIM Group; Sunstone Hotel Properties; Goldman Sachs; Lazard Freres Real Estate Investors and Zeckendorf Realty.

### Weil, Gotshal & Manges LLP
See firm details p.1565

**The Firm:** This firm's overall successes are best viewed from an international standpoint, as many of the leading transactions have taken place on a global canvas. Here, the team's finance expertise, especially on mezzanine and construction loans, shines. Its skill on the debts side is balanced by close synergy with the corporate lawyers, and the firm's *"deserved reputation"* internationally keeps it in the eyes of the market. One development in the New York office has been the retirement of legendary Alan Pomerantz, whom peers characterized as *"synonymous with New York real estate."*

**The Lawyers:** **Philip Rosen** (see p.1494) *"makes deals happen,"* according to clients. Co-head of the team and a skilled corporate lawyer, his *"excellent negotiation style"* and *"smart and intelligent"* outlook wins him plaudits. **Alan Lascher** (see p.1474) is a seasoned attorney who has a national real estate practice consisting of finance, development, tax and leasing. Sources acknowledged his excellent standing: *"His experience spans real estate from A to Z."* **Michael Bond** (see p.1440) is well equipped to handle corporate transactions relating to real estate, and financing of entities involved in real estate. He is best noted for his work with leading financial institutions, including Lehman Brothers.

**Clients/Work Highlights:** The team represented Hypo Real Estate on a $537 million construction loan to the Trump Organization for the construction of a condominium complex in Las Vegas. The group represented Lehman Brothers on the provision of bridge equity for the $1.7 billion acquisition of 200 Park Avenue (the Met Life Building). For Fortress Credit, the firm acted on various bridge loans and mezzanine construction loans. Other clients include CSFB; Starwood Hotels and Resorts Worldwide; Morgan Stanley; Fisher Island Holdings and Macquarie Bank.

### Willkie Farr & Gallagher LLP
See firm details p.1567

**The Firm:** This firm has witnessed a growing synergy between its corporate and real estate lawyers. Staffed with *"extremely friendly and capable"* lawyers, the team has the depth of experience to handle complex transactions in capital markets while retaining a rounded general real estate capability. Working with REITs and opportunity funds, the group has managed to capture a good share of national work. It also has a particularly strong name in the shopping malls sector, where it has some of its top portfolio transactions.

**The Lawyers:** Chair of the department **Eugene Pinover** (see p.1488) attracts widespread market praise for his *"calm but powerful negotiating style."* *"He has clearly got the smarts,"* and his work encompasses transactions for opportunity funds and REITs. He is also a member of the International Council of Shopping Centers. **Steven Klein** (see p.1471) has a broad practice, but is particularly well regarded for his New York leasing and development work.

**Clients/Work Highlights:** For New Plan Excel Realty Trust, the team sold a portfolio of 69 community and neighborhood shopping centers at a value of more than $900 million in cash and equity. The team advised The Mills Corporation on its $452 million purchase of a portfolio of two shopping malls, one in Minneapolis, the other in Milwaukee. The team also assisted the Paramount Group on the creation of an opportunity fund for German investors to acquire US properties and advised Ventas, a healthcare REIT, on the $1.2 billion acquisition of Provident Senior Living Trust. A leasing highlight includes representing Apollo Real Estate Advisors on a lease of 450,000 sq ft of space in Lake Success, New York. Other clients include Wal-Mart; McKinsey & Company; Goldman Sachs; Hudson Development and UBS.

## Band 3

## Cadwalader, Wickersham & Taft LLP
See firm details p.1522

**The Firm:** *"Going great guns on the CMBS side,"* this firm cements its position as a dominant market leader for real estate finance. The ten-partner group is simply one of the leading national teams for CMBS work, and an evident powerhouse for all types of lender side financing. Attorneys have also advised on acquisitions in the sector, such as an office building in Chicago and several hotels across the country.

**The Lawyers:** Chair of the real estate team, **Christopher White** (see p.1513) is a true pioneer in guiding his group to its current market position. He has a bold market presence, his dominance and authority attracting the commendation of clients who say: *"He is top of my list."* He is confidently expanding his team's focus, and his own practice features a significant level of development work in

addition to CMBS transactions. **Fredric Altschuler** (see p.1432) is a dynamic and flexible lawyer who has excelled on several key refinancings in the shopping mall and office building sectors. *"Just a great guy, and a long-standing, bright member of the community,"* he continues to attract the acclamation of peers.

**Clients/Work Highlights:** A highlight transaction was representing The Blackstone Group on the $5.2 billion refinancing of 650 Extended Stay hotels across the country. This is one of the single largest loans originated for CMBS execution. Elsewhere, the team worked on a $1 billion mortgage loan origination and three mezzanine loans for the Hancock Tower, Brown Building and Berkeley Building in Boston, Massachusetts. Attorneys here played a central role on the $540 million refinancing of the Short Hills Mall in New Jersey, as well as on the $205 million mortgage and mezzanine financing of 260 Madison Avenue, New York. Other leading finance transactions include the $820 million refinancing of the Houston Galleria shopping complex, and $1.5 billion in refinancings of shopping malls owned by General Growth Properties.

## Cleary Gottlieb Steen & Hamilton LLP
See firm details p.1525

**The Firm:** With its widespread market appeal and an international reach, this firm makes its mark particularly in the field of real estate finance. The efficient and relatively compact group has a distinguished name for its work with Goldman Sachs. It acted for this client on the origination and securitization of a $1.7 billion loan secured on New York's Rockefeller Center and advised it on a $450 million construction loan secured on the Del Amo Fashion Center in Torrance, California. Peers see the firm as *"excellent for capital markets and blessed with huge and significant clients."* However, the group covers all the flourishing areas of real estate, and to this end it has acted on sales of landmark buildings, joint venture acquisitions, significant corporate acquisitions and sale and leaseback transactions. Also, the firm's success in attracting international private equity and investment houses is worthy of note.

**The Lawyers:** **Steven Horowitz** (see p.1465) has established a superb reputation acting for investors in corporate transactions, as well as on the financing and acquisition of actual real estate. His highlights have included acting for Texas Pacific and Warburg Pincus on their $5.1 billion acquisition of the Neiman Marcus Group. **Michael Weinberger** (see p.1512) is a much sought-after lawyer for his skill in securitized mortgage financings. He has been central to the firm's headline work for Goldman Sachs, and is *"one of the finest lawyers around"* for complex and novel financing structures.

**Clients/Work Highlights:** In the international sphere, the team has assisted key client Goldman Sachs on its mezzanine financing of the Canary Wharf complex in London. Tapping into the booming Dubai market, the firm represented an Emirati development firm and finance company on a $350 million securitization of Dubai real estate contracts.

A highlight New York sale is that of 230 Park Avenue, which was a transaction valued at $705 million. Separately, the firm was also retained by the investment group purchasing 230 Park Avenue to act on financing aspects. Other clients include Home Depot; Kindred Healthcare; Standard & Poor's; Warburg Pincus and Texas Pacific.

## Paul, Weiss, Rifkind, Wharton & Garrison LLP
See firm details p.1548

**The Firm:** An excellent choice for many clients due to its experience of high-end work on acquisitions, financings and development. This team has *"the talent and the high profile"* to handle long-term international projects. The group has a good name with key lenders and has acted on several large construction loans. On the development front, it has participated on some of the best-known hotel and resort projects across the world. Internationally, the group acted for the Government of Hong Kong on the development of Hong Kong Disneyland. A highlight financing transaction was the representation of GMAC Commercial Mortgage on a $1.4 billion construction and mezzanine financing for Time Warner Center. The thrust of this firm's work with owners and developers reflects the healthy state of the industry, particularly in the hospitality and gaming sector, and the firm's high-quality lawyers are well placed to capitalize on this.

**The Lawyers:** **Steven Simkin** (see p.1502) chairs the department, and is key to many of the firm's successes. He is well versed in development work, has built a strong focus in mezzanine finance, and is universally praised as a *"fine deal-doer."* **Meredith Kane** (see p.1469) has a background in city government, and is well positioned to advise on development issues. Clients appreciate that she *"really does know everyone in the city."* She is a key figure for the firm's work on the redevelopment and historic restoration of Grand Central Terminal, acting for the Metropolitan Transit Authority. **Harris Freidus** (see p.1457) attracts attention for his work on casinos and hotels. *"A real mover and shaker,"* his profile with top lending clients is also notable.

**Clients/Work Highlights:** An example of a New York office acquisition is the firm's representation of the purchaser of 660 Madison Avenue. The team also represented an investor in a complex Section 1031 exchange to acquire tenancy-in-common ownership of 1370 Avenue of the Americas. International resort developments include representation of the Municipal Government of Shanghai on Universal Studios Shanghai, and acting for the City of Osaka on Universal Studios Japan. The team continued to represent the owner-developer of The Venetian in Las Vegas, with further development and finance work for resorts in Macau.

## Proskauer Rose LLP
See firm details p.1551

**The Firm:** Progressing steadily in the market, this firm has built a growing name for its lending, leasing and development practice. The eight-partner,

18-associate team is prominent in major New York office leasings, acting for landlords and tenants. While the firm's New York focus has always been a core strength of the group, its geographic reach is illustrated by transactions in Connecticut and New Jersey. Also, burgeoning capital markets work with private real estate funds and REITs ensures this team's growing peer recognition as a *"strong competitor."*

**The Lawyers: Lawrence Lipson** (see p.1475) is *"just an excellent lawyer – period."* He wins plaudits for his mature practice and his tenacious style of negotiation. Chair of the department, he is very active on leasing and development, as well as finance and fund formation. His flexibility in combination with his *"extraordinary business focus"* certainly pleases clients. **Ronald Sernau** (see p.1500) is gaining the respect for his focus on leasing innovations. Sources appreciated his smart and efficient style, and his long-term work on innovative leasing software. **David Weinberger** (see p.1512) has cultivated a respected finance practice, working with top lender clients such as Wachovia and Morgan Stanley.

**Clients/Work Highlights:** The team represented Hines Interests on leasing transactions at 499 Park Avenue and 600 Lexington Avenue, and acted for Lincoln Property on two major residential developments in Manhattan. For The Pegasus Group, the team worked on a major urban renewal project in Harrison, New Jersey. Other clients include DLJ Real Estate Capital Partners, Babcock & Brown and Vornado Realty Trust.

## Band 4

### Brown Raysman Millstein Felder & Steiner LLP
See firm details p.1521

**The Firm:** This *"phenomenally talented"* practice of over 50 lawyers is recognized for its national flair in handling the more intricate real estate transactions for clients of the caliber of Charles Schwab. It has carved out a particular reputation in real estate lending, having *"seen every structure in NYC."* These *"dogged and business-focused"* attorneys possess vast experience in mortgage securitizations, mezzanine loans and condominium conversion deals. It also has a national span in multifamily and affordable housing work from the lender side. Commercial lease work also remains a forte; building headquarters, retail and sports leases featuring heavily in the team's diet. With a team *"steeped in a strong work ethic,"* it gains high accolades from clients who confirm the group's responsive service-oriented reputation – as one source remarked, the lawyers go *"above and beyond, the loyalty is extraordinary."*

**The Lawyers:** Chairing the business and finance department, **Jeffrey Steiner**'s (see p.1505) focus resides in structured finance and capital markets work. Clients assert: *"He is fantastic, there's no deal he doesn't know about!"* Meanwhile **Raymond Sanseverino** (see p.1496), chair of the commercial real estate leasing group, is well regarded for his mastery of the leasing world. He earns credence for

his diligence and *"artful negotiation style"* and his ability to be a *"tenacious warrior"* when needed. Indeed, his pragmatism attracts clients who regard him as a *"very gifted businessman who just happens to have tremendous lawyerly skills."* This year, highlights on the tenant side include the recent negotiation of a 30,000 sq ft office lease at 340 Madison Avenue for Massachusetts Mutual Life Insurance Company.

**Clients/Work Highlights:** The group has advised on leasing matters in San Francisco, representing a New York City law firm in a 233,000 sq ft office lease for its headquarters, and acted for an investment bank on $450 million worth of loans to a New York developer-owner to acquire and refinance office properties in the Grand Central district. Further highlights include working for an investor in a $155 million acquisition, the leaseback and disposition of a multistate supermarket chain's assets, and acting for Thomson Learning as tenant, on a 1,300,000 sq ft net lease of build-to-suit office and warehouse space. Other clients include CSFB; UBS Real Estate Investments; Citibank; GMAC Commercial Mortgage and the Community Preservation Corporation.

### Bryan Cave LLP

**The Firm:** A substantial team of 43 attorneys delivers adroit performances in a variety of midmarket real estate issues, both nationally and internationally. Sources endorsed the team's *"thorough, responsive and creative"* style, apparent in its increased workload. The firm retains its core strengths in development, funds, financings and leases, while areas such as multifamily and residential projects, mixed-use and condominium projects have been particularly active. A major highlight was representing Global Holdings in the acquisition of the Mayflower Hotel development site at 15 Central Park West.

**The Lawyers:** With a *"tough, no-nonsense"* style, **Barry Ross** is an effective real estate lawyer and *"the real deal"* for many in the sector. One of his recent triumphs consists of acting on the $1.8 billion sale of the property known as Riverside South, one of the largest ever single sales of residential real estate in New York City. He has also proved key in matters such as the redevelopment of the Farley Post Office Building, a $2 billion project, on behalf of the State of New York, and has helped on ground lease negotiations and residential developments for The Cathedral Church of Saint John the Divine.

**Clients/Work Highlights:** The group regularly counsels National Cooperative Bank on mortgage securitizations and loans, totaling more than $4.5 billion in the past year. It also worked on the $230 million sale of the mixed-use building, Pennmark, acting on behalf of a joint venture between Feinberg Properties and JD Carlisle Development. Other clients include Colonnade Properties; Aimco; Asbury Partners; Eastgate Realty; Barnes & Noble; Merrill Lynch; and Edward J. Minskoff Equities.

### Debevoise & Plimpton LLP
See firm details p.1529

**The Firm:** *"Tenacious at pushing deals forward,"* this *"impressive, high-quality"* team is experienced in

acquisition, dispositions and financings of office, retail and trophy buildings. Its prowess has also proved popular in the realms of funds, REITs and mortgage work. For example, a strong relationship with JPMorgan Investment Management has seen the group acting on numerous joint venture transactions, including the acquisition of the Barlow Building in Chevy Chase, Maryland, and of Union Square in Washington, DC. Prized for its full-service capabilities, sources commended the group for its practicality: *"The lawyers fully appreciate the big picture but can get into the detail when needed."*

**The Lawyers:** *"Smart, savvy and incredibly timely in his advice,"* **Steven Alden** heads the practice. In a year heavily focusing on office building acquisitions and counseling, his versatile style makes him a client favorite. His highlights include acting for Prudential Financial in the merger of its retail broker business with Wachovia, subsequently producing the third largest brokerage firm in the USA, and representing Actus Lend Lease on the $2.6 billion financing of a military housing project in Hawaii. The *"unflappable problem solver"* **Matthew Golden** is best known for his acquisitions and funds work. Clients credit him for his *"very reasoned"* demeanor, and a *"tough but gentlemanly"* style. Of late, his skills have been utilized on matters such as the acquisition of five Mervyn department stores on behalf of Westfield America, and acting for Beacon Capital Partners in the $620 million financing of its acquisition of the John Hancock complex, Boston. Up-and-comer **Peter Irwin** is considered a *"creative, personable counselor"* with a particular efficiency in the securitized mortgages arena.

**Clients/Work Highlights:** Other clients include AXA Equitable; Carmel Partners; Cherokee Investment Partners; Clayton, Dubilier & Rice; Daimler-Chrysler; Deutsche Bank Real Estate; Equitable Life Assurance Society; Domtar; Donau Immobilien Gruppe; Edison Schools; Kelso & Company; NLI Properties; Oaktree Capital; Talcott Realty and Teachers Insurance and Annuity Association.

### DLA Piper Rudnick Gray Cary US LLP
See firm details p.870

**The Firm:** Weaving together core competencies such as a general real estate transactional and development expertise, this group is well placed to advise clients across the range of real estate matters. This year has seen an expansion of the firm's REITs and funds coverage following significant new recruits, bringing the national team to over 240 members. The firm's international offices provide it an even greater geographic reach. These *"trusted advisers"* continue to deliver quality advice to the Port Authority of New York and New Jersey in the redevelopment of the World Trade Center site, and they supported Citigroup in its real estate and asset-based financing.

**The Lawyers: Martin Polevoy** (see p.1489) is a business-savvy lawyer, who acts as real estate counsel to Cornerstone Real Estate Advisers and The New York Times. In addition, he has acted for Commerz Grundbesitz on the purchase and sale of office buildings in Texas and Virginia, totaling in excess of $500 million.

**Clients/Work Highlights:** Clients include Cornerstone Real Estate Advisers; Lehman Brothers; Wachovia Securities; Citicorp; CIT and Berkshire Capital.

## Kramer Levin Naftalis & Frankel LLP

See firm details p.1539

**The Firm:** This comprehensive practice's drawing cards are its particular fluidity navigating large development work and its expertise in land use matters. Prized for its multistate and international workload, much of this consists of representing borrowers in acquisitions and development financing. The arrival of land use lawyers from Paul Hastings adds to the pool of talent, bolstering the firm's status as a zoning and land use powerhouse. "*Not only do the lawyers have excellent responsiveness, they get around the smoke and mirrors,*" clients reported. Recent highlights include the redevelopment and the preparation of condominium offering plans of The Plaza Hotel, and the substantial sale of trophy property Manhattan House for New York Life.

**The Lawyers:** The "*pragmatic*" **Jay Neveloff** (see p.1483) is acclaimed as a development and condominiums man, with acquisitions and sales also featuring prominently in his workload. "*A quality guy who doesn't over-lawyer things,*" his negotiating strengths have brought success. He recently advised on the purchase of the landmark Helmsley Building, 230 Park Avenue for Istithmar. Peers acknowledge **Samuel Lindenbaum**'s (see p.1475) forte in the land use sphere. Of late, his skills have been effectively utilized redeveloping the Con Edison properties at First Avenue and East 40th Street, and the renovations of the GM Building, the Rockefeller Center and the Chrysler Building. A recent arrival from Paul Hastings, the "*thoughtful and intellectual*" **Paul Selver** (see p.1499) has a flair in dovetailing the zoning and environment worlds which propels him to great acclaim. Cochairing the land use group, he demonstrated his dexterity in the acquisition of development rights and building development projects in Manhattan for Extell Development Company. He also represented New Jersey Transit in what is one of the largest New York City infrastructure projects in 50 years, comprising a rail tunnel development and a new terminal under West 34th Street in Manhattan.

**Clients/Work Highlights:** The group represented a mortgage lender on its $138 million construction loan to a developer of luxury condominiums in Manhattan. For Columbia University, the team worked on land use and environmental approvals regarding a new 17-acre campus in West Harlem. Dia Art Foundation is another client.

## Latham & Watkins LLP

**The Firm:** This "*sophisticated and experienced*" group thrives on a practice dominated by complex multiproperty financings – both from the lender and more recently, borrower side – but its focus also spans mixed-use development work where it has advised on a host of projects in the hospitality and

gaming field. The firm continues to work for Morgan Stanley on work pertaining to mortgage loan portfolios. The lawyers have also represented Citigroup Global Markets and are counseling long-term client GE Capital on acquisition work. Clients were impressed not only by the group's "*responsive, thoughtful and considerate*" approach but also by its "*absolute strength in support.*"

**The Lawyers:** With a practice increasingly tilted towards developments work, the "*smart and knowledgeable*" **Joshua Stein** is regarded as a guru on ground leases and complex leaseholds. His "*extremely personable but steadfast*" approach extends to other areas, especially financings and acquisitions. Lately, he successfully acted for AvalonBay Communities in negotiating a 70,000 sq ft supermarket lease in Manhattan. Heading the global real estate practice group, **Richard Chadakoff** is "*an extremely sophisticated and deal-oriented*" attorney held in high esteem. Though best known as a lender side lawyer on high-end financings, this year has seen development matters taking up a sizable portion of his workload.

**Clients/Work Highlights:** Recent highlights include acting as primary outside counsel for Black-Rock Financial Management on more than $1 billion of loans purchased, originated or financed in 2005. The group's skills were also utilized by Meristar Hospitality Corporation in a refinancing involving a 17-property multijurisdictional CMBS loan. Other clients include Apollo Real Estate Advisors, health care Property Investors and Flagstone Development Company.

## Simpson Thacher & Bartlett LLP

See firm details p.1555

**The Firm:** With its foundations of "*tactical skill and sound business judgment,*" this team has become a strong contender especially in work relating to funds. Large opportunity funds, condominium conversions, developments and hospitality and hotel acquisitions have provided a broad palette of work here. Attorneys have displayed an "*ability to wade through all the nuances*" and their involvment in major transactions has boosted the firm's profile. Among its highlights, the firm acted for Baha Mar Resorts on the $1.6 billion acquisition and development of what is one of the largest single-phase resorts in the Caribbean.

**The Lawyers:** Sources note that **Scott Kobak** (see p.1471) mixes "*pragmatism with a gentle firmness.*" This "*gifted deal-maker*" represents The Carlyle Group on its headline $1.76 billion purchase of the Riverside South Project/Trump Place. **Gregory Ressa** (see p.1492) has an excellent reputation for a range of real estate matters, particularly his funds expertise. He has a close relationship with The Blackstone Group and advised it on the $5.5 billion refinancing of Extended Stay/Homestead Village, two companies which own in total more than 650 properties.

**Clients/Work Highlights:** The group advised key client The Blackstone Group in its $3.2 billion acquisition of Wyndham Hotel Company, and the $3.4 billion purchase of La Quinta Corporation. Other

clients include The Carlyle Group; K. Hovnanian; Wyndham International; Marsh & McLennan Companies and Och-Ziff Real Estate.

## Akin Gump Strauss Hauer & Feld LLP

See firm details p.559

**The Firm:** With an expanding practice, this eight-strong group has a particular strength in private equity transactions and opportunity funds work originating from the real estate sector. The past year has seen the group's workload increase with respect to discrete leasing for New York landlords and also national undertakings, where clients such as The Feil Organization provide the group with extra visibility.

**The Lawyers:** The "*personable*" **Peter Miller** (see p.1480) is the real estate and finance group head, whose practice features expertise in the owner, developer and borrower side. His client base also includes real estate investment funds.

**Clients/Work Highlights:** The team continues to represent Bear Sterns on financing matters regarding its headquarters. The firm recently represented a real estate developer on an acquisition and $500 million development project involving retail, residential and condominium components. Other clients include Oaktree Capital Management and Zev Wolfson.

## Dechert LLP

See firm details p.1752

**The Firm:** The departure of Joseph Forte to Alston & Bird, in November 2005, is a setback for this well-regarded firm, but with more than 40 dedicated real estate lawyers in the New York office, its presence in the market remains assured. Sources highlighted the success of the lender-focused practice and the attorneys, effective handling of large mortgage loan originations. Condominium conversions, Islamic finance, resort development and equity work are also found on the agenda here. The group services clients across the USA and Europe, as well as the Middle East. Attorneys are also able to advise on Shari'a compliant financings, a field where the firm has long-term client contacts. Indeed, interviewees agreed: "*They've created a global brand and have made great strides in CMBS.*"

**The Lawyers:** Splitting time between both the New York and Hartford offices, **Laura Ciabarra** (see p.1445) is well versed in structured finance, and particularly noted for her work in mezzanine lending and subordinate debt. Her "*prominence on the radar screen*" coupled with an ability to "*take directions and run with it*" have produced favorable results. She has acted for Deutsche Bank's Real Estate Equity Fund, one highlight being the joint venture acquisition of the Aston Waikiki Hotel in Hawaii.

**Clients/Work Highlights:** The team acted on the lender side on both a $4.8 million mortgage and mezzanine financing secured on 650 Extended Stay hotels, and a $2.8 million financing secured on 32 Wyndham hotels. In both cases The Blackstone Group was the borrower. It also counseled a real estate fund working on the $913 million financing of The Plaza Hotel, New York. Other representative clients include PB Capital Corporation; JPMorgan Chase; Wells Fargo; Gulf Investment House; New York State Teachers' Retirement System; Morgan Stanley; Calyon Securities (USA); Siemens; Gramercy Capital; BlackRock; Zara USA and Helaba Bank.

## Gibson, Dunn & Crutcher LLP
See firm details p.328

**The Firm:** A "*commercial sensibility*" matched with "*consummate knowledge*" has brought this group significant attention in real estate capital markets as well as development and acquisition work. With its work increasingly taking on a national flavor, the team regularly acts on joint ventures, office and hotel property acquisitions, land developments and condominium projects. Clients praised this "*tremendously deep firm*" for its "*consistent delivery — the lawyers work very hard and turn things around very quickly.*"

**The Lawyers:** Cochair of the real estate group, Andrew Levy leads a contingent of "*capable and conscientious*" attorneys. He focuses on capital markets, regularly working with joint ventures, REITs and real estate opportunity funds.

**Clients/Work Highlights:** The team led Madison Square Garden in a bid to acquire the Metropolitan Transportation Authority's West Side Railyard, which involved mixed-use residential development and financing. Other clients include Investcorp International; RFR Realty; Apollo Real Estate; JPMorgan Investment Management and HSBC Securities.

## Greenberg Traurig LLP
See firm details p.664

**The Firm:** Regarded as a "*versatile, full-service real estate and capital markets*" group, the team has a strong track record in real estate developments, acquisitions and sales, commercial leasing and financing transactions. Work on opportunity funds this year has been coupled with a buoyant market for structured finance and particular activity in the hospitality and multifamily sectors. A "*wonderful, results-oriented team approach*" ensures the effective representation of a host of developers, investors and institutions.

**The Lawyers:** Head of the national real estate group, **Robert Ivanhoe**'s (see p.1467) focus spans high-end real estate acquisitions, joint ventures and financings. Sources commended him as a "*fine development-side lawyer who is smart on opportunity funds.*" Delivering a "*calm, relaxed*" demeanor in negotiations, he wins many fans for his user-friendliness.

**Clients/Work Highlights:** Recent highlights include representing Column Financial, in a joint venture with SL Green Realty, in the $918 million acquisition of One Madison Avenue. As primary outside acquisitions counsel, the team also helped Westbrook Partners purchase 450 Madison Avenue for $450 million. Other notable clients include World Market Center; The Related Companies; Blackacre Capital Group; Boston Properties; Glenwood Management; Greenfield Partners; the Kushner Family; Lefrak Organization; Max Capital Manage-

ment; RFR Holdings; Starwood Capital Group; Starwood Hotels and Resorts Worldwide and Taconic Investment Partners.

## Jones Day
See firm details p.570

**The Firm:** This "*diligent, client-centric*" team's driving force is a compelling finance capability, with a particular acuity in real estate secured mortgage loans, sophisticated joint ventures and global investment funds. The group's "*value and sound judgment*" is also evident in high-end resort developments and commercial leasing. It recently represented Morgan Stanley Real Estate in its $287 million acquisition of The New York Marriott East Side hotel, and acts for Sotheby's on acquisitions, sales, leasing, design and construction projects throughout North America.

**The Lawyers:** A "*commercially savvy*" approach makes **Susanna Fodor** (see p.1456) highly recommended in development deals. She is also involved in large-scale tenant work, including build-to-suit leasing transactions both nationally and globally. Her efficiency and effective lawyering was on display in the five-year renovation, redevelopment and refurbishment of Madison Square Garden in New York City. She has also acted on a 2,000,000 sq ft mixed-use waterfront development project for Flagstone Island Gardens. As one client noted: "*She really gets to the heart of things.*"

**Clients/Work Highlights:** The group regularly counsels The Estée Lauder Companies and subsidiaries on leasing transactions around the USA. It acted for Blue Capital, in a joint venture with JBG Companies, on a portfolio acquisition of 758,000 sq ft of office buildings. Other active clients include Citigroup; Greenpoint Landing Associates; MetroNexus; The Sapir Organization; Westbrook Partners; Lexin AmTrust Real Estate Partners; JPMorgan Chase; Simon Property Group; Jones Lang LaSalle; R. Squared; Ciba Specialty Chemicals; DP Partners; Levitz Furniture; District of Columbia Retirement Board and Merrill Lynch.

## Katten Muchin Rosenman LLP
See firm details p.874

**The Firm:** The group's 32 "*well-rounded and hard-working*" lawyers exercise an excellent proficiency in real estate acquisitions and capital markets. The lion's share of the work is from a lender viewpoint, with the team handling loans and complex mezzanine financings across multifamily, office, hotel, retail and construction developments. The launch of a London office (Katten Muchin Rosenman Cornish LLP) in June 2005 has also increased the firm's international profile.

**The Lawyers:** Marc Shapiro chairs the New York real estate practice and has a niche advising institutional owners and lenders on complex debt and equity matters. The practice dovetails with the hospitality group, headed by KC McDaniel, who frequently works on major hotel property developments around the USA.

**Clients/Work Highlights:** On behalf of Lehman Brothers Holdings, the group worked on a 7,000-acre property development in South Carolina, a

project involving 4,500 homes and a Jack Nicklaus Signature Golf Course. In a similar transaction, it acted for Property Markets Group on an 800-acre development on the island of Anguilla. It also advised on the development, recapitalization and expansion of a New York City hotel. Murray Hill Properties is another client.

## Wachtell, Lipton, Rosen & Katz
See firm details p.1561

**The Firm:** Viewed as an excellent real estate M&A practice, this group focuses on the complex real estate transactions, with a particular forte in matters on behalf of REITs and institutional investors. The team's "*smart and practical*" style has assured success on issues encompassing development work as well as financing, real estate opportunity fund formation and representation. As an example of the group's breadth, the lawyers acted for Universal Studios on resort developments.

**The Lawyers:** The talented **Robin Panovka** (see p.1486) is well known for his REITs and M&A expertise. He has acted on transactional aspects of the redevelopment of the World Trade Center for Silverstein Properties. He has also been busy working for Tishman Speyer Properties on the recapitalization of Rockefeller Center, 666 Fifth Avenue and the Chrysler Building, in addition to trophy building and portfolio acquisitions and restructurings. The "*smart and capable*" **Michael Benner** (see p.1437) is also a go-to guy for REITs advice.

**Clients/Work Highlights:** Security Capital Group used the firm on REIT acquisitions and its sale to GE Capital. The team also successfully represented and sold National Golf Properties to the joint venture between Goldman Sachs and Starwood Capital Group. The team was also active on the disposition of Reckson Associates Realty's industrial portfolio. Other clients include Apollo Real Estate Advisors; UBS PaineWebber; AvalonBay Communities; New Plan Excel Realty Trust and Boston Properties.

## Other Notable Practitioners
**Joseph Forte** (see p.1456) left Dechert LLP in November 2005 to join Alston & Bird LLP. His renowned expertise and flair in real estate securitization work is appreciated by the market: "*He is the known name; he holds the flag in that area.*" The past year's work has encompassed several CMBS loans, work for REITs and trophy building acquisitions. **Mark Edelstein** (see p.1451) of Morrison & Foerster LLP has a terrific reputation for finance. His detailed representation of lenders and his "*solutions-oriented approach*" attract strong praise, and he is especially knowledgeable on syndicated and participated loan arrangements. Lauded by clients for his "*ability to see the big picture,*" **Stephen Gliatta** (see p.1459) of Kaye Scholer LLP is a "*user-friendly and pragmatic*" real estate finance and capital markets lawyer. Key clients of his include RBS Greenwich Capital and UBS Real Estate Investments, and he is highly regarded for his work on the origination and securitization of first mortgages, mezzanine loans and preferred equity investments.

# TAX

## Band 1

### Cleary Gottlieb Steen & Hamilton LLP

See firm details p.1525

**The Firm:** This firm's *"magnificent"* tax group fields *"some of the most brilliant scholarly minds"* in the tax field, according to clients. The department's great strength is its vast familiarity with current tax developments in the financial products field, a fact that allows it to advise high-profile banks on cutting-edge structures. In a recent matter it represented Bank of America in its estimated $35 billion acquisition of MBNA, a deal which united the USA's largest domestic bank with a foremost provider of credit card and payment products. Clients feel the *"assiduous and reliable"* 30-attorney group *"runs the gamut."* It is celebrated for national and multinational M&A, joint venture and startup issues and offers *"a brilliant understanding of intricate international planning matters."* Its other key matters included the representation of Texas Pacific Group in the $11.3 billion purchase of computer software provider SunGard Data Systems by an investment consortium of seven private equity firms, including Texas Pacific Group, The Blackstone Group, Goldman Sachs, Providence and others.

**The Lawyers:** *"Intellectual heavyweight"* **Leslie Samuels** (see p.1496) offers a *"simply terrific technical awareness."* *"This gentleman is extremely personable but should never be underestimated,"* clients note. Interviewees agree that *"clients and competitors alike will consult him on judgment calls."* He impresses with his international tax planning, cross-border M&A and joint ventures for large corporate clients and financial institutions including Bank of America and

American Express. **Yaron Reich** (see p.1491) enjoys a diverse transactional practice and focuses on M&A and corporate international restructurings. Clients admire this *"thoughtful and creative"* advocate and peers find it *"comforting to have such an intelligent planner on the same side."* He advises international banks on their US tax issues and provides international and cross-border expertise to clients like Texas Pacific Group and HSBC. *"Genius"* **Edward Kleinbard** (see p.1471) spends a fair amount of time on controversy, corporate and international tax but continues to impress clients in the field of financial products, where he is considered *"the daddy."* On the same wavelength is financial institutions *"superstar"* **James Peaslee** (see p.1487), who clients rave possesses *"an off-the-chart IQ level with a brain the size of a planet."* *"Brilliant tactician"* **Erika Nijenhuis** (see p.1483) *"oozes creativity"* and is, according to clients, *"authoritative in her conclusions"* and *"one of the bright stars"* in financial products. A new entry to the tables is *"diligent"* **Jason Factor** (see p.1452), who impressed clients with his *"careful and smart approach."*

**Clients/Work Highlights:** Bank of America; Capital One; Warburg Pincus; 3M; American Express; Citigroup; Morgan Stanley and Henkel KGaA.

### Cravath, Swaine & Moore LLP

See firm details p.1527

**The Firm:** *"They've got the whole package,"* enthused clients of this *"fantastic firm."* Accolades piled up for the strength and skill deployed by the tax team in intricate M&A transactions, aptly demonstrated by its recent representation of Ashland. This deal involved a tax-free spin-off and merger of Ashland's 38% interest in the MAP joint venture into Marathon Oil, valued at $3.7 billion. Depth of expertise is a renowned feature of the firm. Clients are confident that *"once Cravath are there, they will argue the case very effectively,"* and hail the *"very thorough"* resources available. The team is valued for its experience in both domestic and global transactions. Morgan Stanley utilized these skills in a recent organization and offering of a series of international real estate investment funds.

**The Lawyers:** Interviewers were deluged with plaudits for the *"absolutely brilliant"* **Michael Schler** (see p.1498). The *"energy and fathomless knowledge"* of this *"known power"* impressed clients and peers alike. *"He is able to instantly penetrate to the heart of any complex issue; it's amazing how he does it,"* remarked one satisfied source. Sprint recently retained Schler to handle its $35 billion merger with Nextel and planned spin-off of certain businesses. He also conducted the $4 billion sale of the Renal Care Group to Fresenius Medical Care. Applauded for his *"fair-minded, result-oriented"* approach, **Stephen Gordon** (see p.1461) is *"top of the list"* for clients. Having practiced or 25 years ensures this *"superb lawyer"* possesses *"loads of M&A experience."* This year, Gordon represented Royal Dutch Shell in the unification of Netherlands-based Royal Dutch Petro-

leum and Shell Transport and Trading (UK) under a new parent company, Royal Dutch Shell. The transaction is valued at $81 billion. Gordon's practice also includes public offerings and syndicated bank loans. Long-term client DreamWorks SKG retained him recently to handle a $930 million IPO of its computer animation business. **William Brannan** (see p.1440) is renowned for his investment partnership and real estate expertise, notably in REITs. He acted as counsel to Ripplewood Holdings in the conversion of its Japanese private equity fund into RHJ International, and in an IPO of RHJ International. The combined value of the transactions was $400 million. Sources described Brannan as *"focused, bright and meticulous."* The *"extremely talented"* **Patricia Geoghegan** (see p.1458) boasts an excellent reputation in the leasing tax area and leads the employee benefits practice of the firm's tax department.

**Clients/Work Highlights:** Citigroup; DreamWorks SKG; IBM; Johnson & Johnson; JPMorgan Chase; Morgan Stanley; Lucent Technologies; Royal Dutch Shell; Sprint Nextel; Time Warner and Weyerhaeuser.

### Davis Polk & Wardwell

See firm details p.1528

**The Firm:** *"A force in the market,"* this New York office houses 80% of the firm's lawyers and commands most of the tax work. Creating unique equity derivatives and convertible debt offerings is a specialty for the *"amazing team."* In the tax controversy sphere, a stable of esteemed clients receives advice on the formation and operation of private funds. The attorneys' skill in domestic and international transactions and proficiency in financial products guarantees *"the big players in the field look to them."* Bank of America, Morgan Stanley and JPMorgan provide evidence of this as the firm's most prominent clients.

**The Lawyers:** According to sources, **Dana Trier** (see p.1508) is *"simply a genius."* Though partnerships absorb much of this *"creative"* attorney's time, he also applies his wide knowledge of tax to M&A and financial products. Trier's talents have enabled him to attract *"an enormous client following"* from the likes of Merrill Lynch and Citigroup. Head of the tax department **Avishai Shachar** (see p.1500) impressed clients with his *"fantastic"* ability in M&A. His *"sharp and practical"* talent also covers financial products and spin-offs; Shachar was responsible for the spin-off of Yum! Brands from PepsiCo. The *"terrific integrity"* of **Michael Mollerus** (see p.1480) attracts clients, who seek out his advice on major corporate transactions including structured financings. When financial products issues are on the table, clients look to **Samuel Dimon** (see p.1450). He is not only *"highly qualified and knowledgeable"* but is *"able to speak off the top of his head authoritatively."* His strength lies in advising clients on federal income tax issues in domestic and international contexts. Cut from the same cloth is **Po Sit** (see p.1502), *"a thoughtful person who can look at all angles and give*

## Tax
### Leading Individuals

#### Senior Statesmen

| | |
|---|---|
| **TAYLOR** Willard *Sullivan & Cromwell LLP* | **YOUNGWOOD** Alfred *Paul, Weiss* |

[1]

| | |
|---|---|
| **BLESSING** Peter *Shearman & Sterling LLP* | **CANELLOS** Peter *Wachtell* |
| **HEITNER** Kenneth *Weil, Gotshal & Manges* | **ROSEN** Matthew *Skadden, Arps* |
| **SCHLER** Michael *Cravath, Swaine & Moore* | **TODRYS** Steven *Simpson Thacher & Bartlett* |
| **TRIER** Dana *Davis Polk & Wardwell* | |

[2]

| | |
|---|---|
| **COHEN** Ben *Cahill Gordon & Reindel LLP* | **FRIEDMAN** Gary *Debevoise & Plimpton LLP* |
| **GORDON** Stephen *Cravath, Swaine & Moore* | **LEE** Carolyn *Roberts & Holland LLP* |
| **REINHOLD** Richard *Willkie Farr & Gallagher* | **SAMUELS** Leslie *Cleary Gottlieb* |
| **SCHWARTZ** Jodi *Wachtell* | **SHACHAR** Avishai *Davis Polk & Wardwell* |

[3]

| | |
|---|---|
| **BERG** Andrew *Debevoise & Plimpton LLP* | **BLANCHARD** Kimberly *Weil, Gotshal & Manges* |
| **BRANNAN** William *Cravath, Swaine & Moore* | **GALLAGHER** Patrick *Kirkland & Ellis LLP* |
| **GOLDRING** Stuart *Weil, Gotshal & Manges* | **HAIMS** Bruce *Debevoise & Plimpton LLP* |
| **HART** John *Simpson Thacher & Bartlett* | **MASON** Andrew *Sullivan & Cromwell LLP* |
| **MAYO** David *Paul, Weiss* | **PHILLIPS** Greer *Kirkland & Ellis LLP* |
| **PHILLIPS IV** Barnet *Skadden, Arps* | **POLLACK** Martin *Weil, Gotshal & Manges* |
| **REICH** Yaron *Cleary Gottlieb* | **ROSEN** Burt *Debevoise & Plimpton LLP* |
| **SALEM** Irving *Latham & Watkins LLP* | **SCHARFSTEIN** Joel *Fried, Frank* |
| **SICULAR** David *Paul, Weiss* | **STAFFARONI** Robert *Debevoise & Plimpton LLP* |
| **SWARTZ** Linda *Cadwalader* | **WOLLMAN** Diana *Sullivan & Cromwell LLP* |

[4]

| | |
|---|---|
| **AMDUR** Martin *Weil, Gotshal & Manges* | **ANDERSEN** Richard *Arnold & Porter LLP* |
| **CASSANOS** Robert *Fried, Frank* | **CREAMER JR** Ronald *Sullivan & Cromwell LLP* |
| **DREYFUS** James *Fulbright & Jaworski L.L.P.* | **EINHORN** David *Wachtell* |
| **FINKELSTEIN** Stuart *Skadden, Arps* | **GEOGHEGAN** Patricia *Cravath, Swaine & Moore* |
| **GONZALEZ** Edward *Skadden, Arps* | **INDOE** William *Sullivan & Cromwell LLP* |
| **KARIG** Adele *Debevoise & Plimpton LLP* | **LEVY** Lisa *Fried, Frank* |
| **MANDEL** Gary *Simpson Thacher & Bartlett* | **MOLLERUS** Michael *Davis Polk & Wardwell* |
| **PAUL** Deborah *Wachtell* | **PONIKVAR** Dale *Milbank, Tweed* |
| **RAAB** David *Latham & Watkins LLP* | **ROSEN** Arthur *McDermott Will & Emery* |
| **ROSEN** Seth *Debevoise & Plimpton LLP* | **RUSMAN** Jared *Wachtell* |
| **SAMUELS** Jeffrey *Paul, Weiss* | **SCHNABEL** David *Debevoise & Plimpton LLP* |
| **SHORT** Andrew *Paul, Hastings* | **SILBERBERG** Marc *Weil, Gotshal & Manges* |
| **THURSTON** Sally *Skadden, Arps* | **TREESH** Kevin *Kirkland & Ellis LLP* |

#### Up-and-coming individuals

| | |
|---|---|
| **CLEMENS** Steven *Kirkland & Ellis LLP* | **FACTOR** Jason *Cleary Gottlieb* |
| **FURCI** Peter *Debevoise & Plimpton LLP* | **GALL** Phillip *Kronish Lieb* |

*full evaluations."* Throughout his career Sit has represented financial institutions in derivatives and other transactions. Also valued for financial products expertise is up-and-comer **Michael Farber** (see p.1453), an attorney who is *"totally bright and really knows his stuff."* Investment banks and other financial institutions regularly take advantage of his copious knowledge of financial and capital markets activities.

**Clients/Work Highlights:** Morgan Stanley; JPMorgan Chase; Citigroup and Bank of America are some of the firm's most prominent clients.

### Sullivan & Cromwell LLP
See firm details p.1558

**The Firm:** Clients of this *"exceptional group"* enjoy *"round the clock service from a firm at the top of their game."* The team's expertise in the US tax aspects of creating new financial products and structures ensures it stays *"at the cutting edge of financial transactions."* It was instrumental in forming the rules

relating to the issuance of securities in the Eurobond market. Another forte for the group is tax controversy, where the firm *"goes the extra step"* in providing efficient client service by encouraging close collaboration between the tax and litigation departments. The immense depth of talent available was consistently praised. Commentators agreed the assortment of *"brilliant lawyers"* makes Sullivan & Cromwell *"one of the best New York firms for tax."*

**The Lawyers:** A leading name for handling the tax issues of real estate transactions is **Andrew Mason** (see p.1477). This *"quick thinker satisfies client needs at all times,"* according to commentators. Partnerships and international transactions form a large portion of Mason's practice. *"Making a big splash"* in the tax pond is *"firecracker"* **Diana Wollman** (see p.1514). She advises clients on tax litigation and controversies but mainly counsels on transactional and planning issues for a booming client roster. **Willard Taylor** (see p.1507) remains *"one of the acknowledged giants in the field."* His *"great breadth of*

*expertise in multiple areas of tax"* and *"business-savvy"* approach make him essential in any global transaction. Taylor has represented international corporations in disputes with the IRS and has worked with the Treasury Department on tax legislation. **Ronald Creamer** (see p.1447) and **William Indoe** (see p.1467) are cultivating thriving practices; peers remarked they are *"opposite me all the time."* Creamer focuses on tax-efficient structuring in cross-border corporate M&A deals and is an established author in the field. Indoe is a specialist in structuring complex financial transactions, notably M&A, divestitures and spin-offs. In the financial products arena, *"tax genius"* **David Hariton** (see p.1463) springs to the mind of interviewees. Clients celebrate this *"absolutely brilliant"* lawyer as *"a very deep thinker who can get to the bottom of things."* Hariton is a renowned expert and prolific writer on financial instruments and cross-border investment. Up-and-coming **Jeffrey Hochberg** (see p.1465) continues to impress peers and clients alike with his robust practice in cross-border structured investment and finance.

**Clients/Work Highlights:** Allianz; Bank of New York; Philips; Barclays Capital; Morgan Stanley; Diageo; Securities Industry Association and UBS.

### Wachtell, Lipton, Rosen & Katz
See firm details p.1561

**The Firm:** *"A terrific firm"* comprised of *"top-notch people who really know their tax law"* is the market opinion of this noted New York firm. It sails into the top band following a fine year in which the tax crew has directed a flood of highflying deals including Sears' merger with Kmart. Day-to-day, crucial transactions for industry titans are handled by the team; it is currently acting as counsel to the NYSE in its demutualization and combination with the Archipelago Exchange. Though private equity investments and divestments comprise a large chunk of the practice, it is M&A where the *"phenomenal individuals"* truly shine. Transactional highlights include acting for Unocal in its acquisition by Chevron and representing Maytag in its acquisition of Whirlpool.

**The Lawyers:** Head of the tax department **Peter Canellos** (see p.1442) is responsible for advising on all transactions handled by the team. He wins acclaim from both peers and clients for his enormous intellect and balanced and perceptive approach. AT&T took advantage of **Jodi Schwartz's** (see p.1499) mastery of M&A in their recent merger with SBC. She also represented Hellman & Friedman LLC and Texas Pacific Group in their purchase of a majority stake in Linsco/Private Ledger. Her *"hardworking and dynamic approach"* to the area of tax won plaudits from clients and peers alike. **David Einhorn** (see p.1452) is *"excellent at making his way through the intricacies of tax law."* Although M&A accounts for a substantial portion of his work, Einhorn's true strength lies in REITs. Tishman Speyer Properties recently hired him to handle an initial public offering for Tishman Speyer Office Fund, an Australian land property trust, and also the formation of a US REIT in which the Government of Singapore holds a 49% interest. "*Dynamic and passionate,*" **Deborah Paul** (see p.1487) is always "*insightful and persuasive in her views,*" according to market sources. These qualities inspired Intelsat to retain her to conduct their acquisition of PanAmSat. Paul also directed the subsequent acquisition of Intelsat by Apax, Apollo, Madison Dearborn and Permira and led the team managing the Sears merger. **Jared Rusman**'s (see p.1495) "*practical, effective and thoughtful*" manner impresses commentators. Transactional beacons for him this year include representing InterActiveCorp in its acquisition of Ask Jeeves and advising St. Paul Travelers on the disposition of its stake in Nuveen Investments.

**Clients/Work Highlights:** Sears; Lazard; St. Paul Travelers; AT&T; Novartis; Tishman Speyer Properties; Reckson Associates Realty and Texas Pacific Group.

## Band 2

## Debevoise & Plimpton LLP

See firm details p.1529

**The Firm:** For "*exemplary service,*" Debevoise is a popular choice for clients. These tenacious advocates "*will go to the nth degree to defend their position,*" and "*will roll their sleeves up and dig in,*" according to sources. One observer enthused: "*They never miss a deadline and have never got the wrong result.*" The firm is hailed as "*a driving force*" in fund formation, as illustrated by its recent representation of Providence Equity Partners in the closure of its $4.25 billion private equity fund. Another centerpiece deal for the group was representing the official committee of unsecured creditors in the restructuring of Aurora Foods. This was effected through a prearranged Chapter 11 plan under which Aurora was merged with Pinnacle Foods. The combined entity is valued at over $1.7 billion, and evidences the boundless

experience that enables the team to provide a "*top-drawer*" service.

**The Lawyers:** "*Phenomenally gifted,*" according to clients, M&A specialist **Gary Friedman** is "*tremendously quick*" and "*subtle and pragmatic*" in his approach. He is currently advising Verizon in its pending acquisition of MCI, a deal with an equity value of $8.5 billion. Clients value his aptitude for "*structuring complex matters quickly and communicating issues succinctly.*" The tax practice of creative thinker **Andrew Berg** focuses on M&A, debt restructurings and joint ventures. According to sources, Berg "*has tremendous judgment; he always tries to interpret agreements in a manner that makes sense.*" Long-standing client Kelso retained Berg to organize a $2 billion private equity fund and handle corporate acquisitions by the fund. He is also serving as sole arbitrator in a commercial dispute between two Fortune 100 companies involving partnership taxation. "*A real star*" of the team is **Bruce Haims**, whose "*extraordinary attention to detail and high level of integrity*" are noted by clients and peers alike. One interviewee enthused that "*his dedicated service allows a client to sleep at night.*" Haims was recently involved in unwinding a multibillion-dollar tax shelter for several individuals, and also advised Charles Dolan on behalf of the Dolan Family Group on the proposed spin-off of Cablevision's satellite and national programming services. With his "*phenomenal intellectual ability,*" **Burt Rosen** "*never misses a trick.*" Clients celebrate him not only for his legal acumen but also for his "*calm and collected*" manner and sense of humor. Rosen is chair of the firm's tax department and is representing DaimlerChrysler in connection with the sale of its subsidiary, New Venture Gear, to Magna International. His practice focuses on the tax aspects of complex financing transactions. **Robert Staffaroni** is the man clients look to for "*expert representation in international and financial markets.*" He is especially renowned for derivatives and partnerships work. Sources acclaim him as "*a superb guy with an excellent brain.*" For fund formation work, **Adele Karig** is "*top of the heap.*" Clients praised her ability to be "*technical and analytical, yet easy to talk to and work with.*" Karig recently represented HarbourVest in the formation of a $4 billion private equity fund of funds which will invest in US venture and buyout partnership interests. **Seth Rosen** works predominantly in the insurance industry dealing with M&A refining issues, tax planning and product development. "*Completely professional*" in his approach, Rosen assisted Prudential Financial in its agreement with Wachovia to combine retail brokerage businesses, leading to combined client assets of $537 billion. The "*amazingly creative*" **David Schnabel** "*understands how to unravel a complicated tax situation to find an effective solution.*" His practice centers on M&A and forming private equity funds and he frequently handles transactional work for Kelso. Rising star **Peter Furci** has been actively involved in the design and development of Income Deposit Security offerings for numerous issuers. He assisted Verizon in the MCI acquisition.

**Clients/Work Highlights:** Air Liquide; American

Airlines; DaimlerChrysler; GE; Merrill Lynch; L'Oréal; Phelps Dodge; Providence Equity; Verizon and Westpac Bank.

## Simpson Thacher & Bartlett LLP

See firm details p.1555

**The Firm:** Active for well over a century, this prominent firm boasts torrents of tax expertise and has achieved a global reputation for handling critical tax issues in M&A and LBOs. Indicative of the team's ability, it had a role in the merger of Colorado brewery Coors Brewing Co, with Montreal-based Molson Canada. The resulting company will become the world's fifth-largest brewer with $6 billion in sales. Organizing private equity funds is another area of specialty for the group. Principal clients in this area are KKR and The Blackstone Group, which retained the team in its recent acquisition of Extended StayAmerica. Advice on both domestic and foreign investments is offered to the market and the firm has advised Blackstone Capital Partners in offshore investments in Europe and Latin America.

**The Lawyers:** The "*spectacular*" **Steven Todrys** (see p.1508) continues to act as principal tax counsel to KKR. In addition, he is representing adidas in its pending acquisition of Reebok and also advising Toys 'R' Us in its sale to a consortium of private equity funds. Ford is further reaping the benefit of Todrys' M&A expertise in its pending sale of Hertz. According to clients, his "*practical commercial sense*" and "*ability to communicate tax concepts to business-people*" make him "*the number-one name.*" "*Top-quality lawyer*" **John Hart** (see p.1464) is highly sought after by loyal clients for his experience in forming private investment funds. This year, he acted as principal tax counsel to The Blackstone Group in connection with the formation of Blackstone Capital Partners V, a private investment fund. At the first closing the fund raised $10.5 billion, making it one of the largest private funds ever raised. Also invaluable to the firm's private equity clients is the "*creative and unstoppable*" **Gary Mandel** (see p.1477). He advised on the spin-off of several businesses of HJ Heinz and the company's merger with Del Monte Foods. In the financial products arena, **Dickson Brown** (see p.1441) "*has a wealth of experience.*" He continues to advise bankers and issuers on variations of convertible debt securities and also does restructuring work.

**Clients/Work Highlights:** The Blackstone Group; Lexington Partners; KKR; CIBC; Citigroup; Leeds Weld; Ripplewood Holdings; Silver Lake and Soros.

## Skadden, Arps, Slate, Meagher & Flom LLP & Affiliates

See firm details p.1557

**The Firm:** This "*terrific group*" handles business and technical issues with flair. Clients are confident of its ability to resolve "*the most complicated and most risky transactions*" and to "*always look at the big picture.*" Market luminaries rely on the firm for advice on the effects of the latest tax reform on their businesses and for tenacious representation in tax controversies. Peers agreed that Skadden is one of the most visible firms in the state. The team also enjoys an enviable reputation in the M&A sphere and is currently representing the NASDAQ Stock Market in its acquisition of shareholder.com. The value of the transaction is undisclosed. "*Fantastic resources*" are offered through the enormous international network built by the firm, ensuring that "*for cases with unique tax dimensions, Skadden is first choice*" for clients.

**The Lawyers:** "*The man is a genius,*" said commentators of tax department cochair **Matthew Rosen** (see p.1494). Sources dubbed Rosen "*top of the top*" for acquisitions and divestitures, due to his "*fantastic expertise.*" **Barnet Phillips** (see p.1488) is prominent for M&A and REIT-related tax issues. Centro Properties Group benefited from his expertise in its $1.3 billion acquisition of Kramont Realty Trust, a publicly traded REIT. Phillips also acted for NorthStar Realty Finance in its $750 million IPO. Outside of the corporate sphere, Phillips counsels a number of charitable organizations on a pro bono basis. The "*incisive and innovative*" **Stuart Finkelstein** (see p.1454) has advised Citigroup on several multibillion-dollar transactions, including its acquisition of Golden State Bancorp. This provides just one example of the "*terrific M&A work*" for which he is renowned. Divestiture transactions and matters relating to executive compensation also feature strongly in his practice. Clients celebrate "*a brilliant attorney who explains technical issues with great clarity.*" **Edward Gonzalez**'s (see p.1460) "*smart and helpful*" style "*makes it easy to get issues resolved.*" In recent years, his practice has focused on financial product development and representing major financial institutions in cross-border transactions. He has also worked with several investment bankers in the development of trust-preferred securities and other regulatory capital products. **Sally Thurston** (see p.1508) is "*practical and personable*" and an expert in M&A, divestitures and spin-offs. She counts several household names among her clients, including Mead Corporation. Exhibiting panache in financial products is the "*very bright*" **Charles Morgan** (see p.1481). Interviewees complimented Morgan's "*great client manner; he is interested in things working out well.*" He is currently assisting financial institutions in developing financial instruments and continues to advise on hedge funds and private equity transactions. A combination of "*high intellect and excellent judgment*" ensures **Kirk Wallace** (see p.1511) gains "*tremendous respect*" from market commentators. He has represented a range of underwriters and collateral managers in structured finance transactions.

**Clients/Work Highlights:** Dell; Deloitte & Touche; IBM; Intel; International Paper; KPMG; Royal Dutch/Shell Group and Schering-Plough.

### Weil, Gotshal & Manges LLP
See firm details p.1565

**The Firm:** Weil Gotshal enjoys a prolific practice, as evidenced by its commanding client roster and participation in a plethora of highflying deals. Using the firm as M&A counsel is "*always a positive experience,*" according to clients, and its attorneys are always busy on this front. A significant recent example of its work has seen it advising on the pending acquisition of Whirlpool by Maytag. However, it is the "*top-notch bankruptcy practice*" that steals the limelight for commentators. As part of this, the "*tremendous team*" advises both debtors and creditors of financially troubled businesses including financial institutions and insurance companies. By way of example, it recently handled the bankruptcy of Loral Satellite. The international prominence of the firm is a great asset as it allows its attorneys to gain knowledge of tax matters in manifold jurisidictions. The team boasts knowledge of tax law in the UK, France, Germany and Poland and can bring a global perspective to any transaction.

**The Lawyers:** "*Superstar*" **Kenneth Heitner** (see p.1464) is not only "*an exceptional lawyer*" but also "*a sheer pleasure to work with, a prince of a person.*" He possesses an "*outstanding reputation*" for "*finding solutions to complicated situations.*" The centerpiece transaction of his year so far is handling the acquisition of Maytag by Whirlpool. **Kimberly Blanchard** (see p.1439) is "*a well-respected legal thinker able to provide real-world-oriented opinions.*" Her practice comprises mostly international M&A and joint ventures and she recently managed Comverse's acquisition of the GSS Division of CSG. The firm's "*bankruptcy guru*" is **Stuart Goldring** (see p.1460). Plaudits flooded in for Goldring's wealth of knowledge; some sources are convinced he "*knows everything – he really does specialize.*" Goldring has advised debtors, creditors and potential investors of financially distressed companies and handled the bankruptcy of Loral Satellite. For "*rock-solid, practical*" tax advice, clients seek out the "*incredible*" **Martin Pollack** (see p.1489). The acquisition of Great Lakes Chemical by Crompton was his most significant transaction this year. Pollack has nurtured a booming practice in structuring private equity and M&A transactions and is a chairman of the firm's global tax department. Also providing "*quality*" work to the firm's clientele is **Martin Amdur** (see p.1433). He conducted the sale of NextWave to Verizon and has advised on complex real estate investments, executive compensation and bankruptcy restructuring. **Marc Silberberg** (see p.1501) is another "*terrific lawyer*" at the firm. He was retained to handle the investment in Grupo Corporative Ono by Thomas H Lee Partners, Providence Equity Partners, JPMorgan Partners and Quadrangle Capital Partners. Commentators applauded his "*pleasant, smart and hard-working*" approach. "*Exceptional for financial products,*" **Karl Walli** (see p.1511) regularly advises on tax-advantaged methods for structuring and using financial instruments, particularly cross-border financial arbitrage transactions and hedging strategies.

**Clients/Work Highlights:** GE; Merrill Lynch; Leucadia; DLJ Merchant Banking Partners; Enron; Lehman Brothers; Viacom; Providence Equity Partners; UnitedHealth Group; Great Lakes Chemical and Seacor.

### Cadwalader, Wickersham & Taft LLP
See firm details p.1522

**The Firm:** Noted by the market for its sophisticated tax practice, this firm is seen as "*a leader for structured finance work.*" The tax team plays an instrumental role in the firm's premier M&A and corporate finance deals and has closed numerous domestic and international transactions. Examples include the group's representation of Pfizer in its $1.9 billion acquisition of Vicuron Pharmaceuticals and its $60 billion acquisition of Pharmacia. Van der Moolen USA took advantage of the firm's expertise in financial products to secure a tax refund in respect of a loss of more than $43 million. This year, the team also acted as counsel to various participants in over 45 collateralized debt and collateralized loan obligation transactions in both the USA and the UK.

**The Lawyers:** **Linda Swartz** (see p.1506) is cochair of the firm's tax department. She routinely advises an illustrious client roster on the tax aspects of global M&A, spin-offs, restructurings and bankruptcies. This year Swartz has devoted her time to a number of stunning deals. She acted for Procter & Gamble in its $57 billion acquisition of Gillette and also represented Storage Technology in its $4.1 billion acquisition by Sun Microsystems. "*Solution-oriented and personable,*" **David Miller** (see p.1479) has garnered a horde of similarly impressive transactions, including representing a major European money manager in the establishment of a $23 billion medium-term note commercial paper and capital note program. Miller's expertise lies in the financial products field, particularly the taxation of financial instruments and derivatives. He is also experienced in the taxation of public charities and private foundations and has undertaken pro bono representation of numerous charitable organizations in establishing nonprofit status.

**Clients/Work Highlights:** Pfizer; Banc of America Securities; Bear Stearns; Barclays Bank; UBS Securities; Lehman Brothers; TIAA-CREF; Northwest Airlines; Burger King; American Home Mortgage; Skandia Insurance and Klesch & Company.

### Cahill Gordon & Reindel LLP

**The Firm:** Breadth of knowledge is paramount at this venerable firm. Attorneys are encouraged to become skilled tax generalists in order to ensure clients can be counseled on a diverse range of tax issues by any lawyer. The tax team is also responsible for litigating its own cases, giving it crucial experience representing clients in administrative appeals and controversies. The firm boasts a distinguished history of precedent-setting trial victories and an international presence that cannot be overlooked. Lately, it has played a significant role in the formation of offshore investment vehicles and handled several cross-border acquisitions for its multinational clients. Peers covet the firm's renowned relationship with GE and endorse its "*absolutely tremendous reputation.*"

**The Lawyers:** "*Clearly a star,*" **Ben Cohen** utilizes his "*wonderful mastery of the tax code*" to assist an impressive clientele who "*think the world of him.*" To the envy of peers, he continues to act as counsel to GE.

**Clients/Work Highlights:** The team advises national clients on a broad range of tax matters.

## Fried, Frank, Harris, Shriver & Jacobson LLP

See firm details p.1532

**The Firm:** The New York branch is the oldest and largest of the firm's offices, housing 345 attorneys. This huge team has been further strengthened by the addition of a London-based European tax group, which collaborates closely with the New York attorneys. This European dimension also manifestly enhances the firm's notable global presence. Worldwide transactional and litigious matters are undertaken for clients and the alliance with Canadian firm McCarthy Tétrault produces efficient service on cross-border issues. Goldman Sachs continues to be an eminent client, with the firm recently counseling the company in the formation of Goldman Sachs Capital Partners V and affiliated funds. The result was an $8.5 billion private equity fund, at the time the largest ever raised. Another recent highlight was representing Berry Plastics in acquiring Kerr Group for $445 million in cash.

**The Lawyers: Robert Cassanos** (see p.1443) devotes his time to Canadian and US cross-border transactions. This "*knowledgeable and easy to work with*" attorney brings "*a sense of flair*" to any transaction, according to sources. Cassanos recently represented Kirk Kerkorian and Tracinda on the $5 billion acquisition of MGM by Sony and acts as tax counsel to Goldman Sachs, JPMorgan Chase, and TransCanada. The "*talented, straightforward*" **Joel Scharfstein** (see p.1497) continues his work for New Mountain Capital. He assisted the company in its investment in MailSouth, the largest provider of shared mail advertising to the US rural and suburban markets. Investment partnerships, divestitures and partnerships form most of his practice. ONEOK sought the expertise of "*super*" **Lisa Levy** (see p.1474) this year. She represented the company in the issuance of 4.20% notes due 2015 and 6% notes due 2035 for $800 million.

**Clients/Work Highlights:** Goldman Sachs; Procter & Gamble; Merck; New Mountain Capital; Merrill Lynch; Methanex and KeyBank.

## Kirkland & Ellis LLP

See firm details p.875

**The Firm:** Champions of complex litigation and tax controversy, this firm has obtained favorable rulings from the IRS for a host of clients including United Airlines, Conseco and GM. It has also tried numerous tax cases before the US Supreme Court. Its prowess in court is equalled by its transactional strength. CVC Capital Partners enlisted the team's assistance in its creation of CVC European Equity Partners IV. Experienced attorneys raised $7.2 billion from institutional investors across the USA, Middle East and Europe. The team also acted as lead counsel on the closing of CVC Capital Partners Asia Pacific

II (Fund II), a joint venture with Citigroup. The fund closed at $2 billion and is reportedly the largest private equity fund in the Asia-Pacific Region.

**The Lawyers:** Described as "*methodical and thoughtful,*" **Patrick Gallagher** (see p.1457) is recognized for his substantial private equity fund formation practice. He is equally schooled in bankruptcy restructurings and workouts. "*Intensely knowledgeable*" **Greer Phillips** (see p.1487) "*always comes up with brilliant solutions.*" He is "*superexperienced*" in both domestic and cross-border transactions and advises clients in Europe, Asia and Latin America, as well as US investors. **Kevin Treesh** (see p.1508) focuses on planning and structuring both domestic and international acquisitions and dispositions. He enters the rankings following glowing market feedback. Also garnering plaudits for his thriving M&A practice is rising star **Steven Clemens** (see p.1445), an attorney equally experienced in the formation of private equity funds.

**Clients/Work Highlights:** Clients of the firm hail from the USA, Europe, Asia and Latin America.

## Latham & Watkins LLP

**The Firm:** With a colossal 1,600 lawyers worldwide, this firm is able to offer geographic breadth as well as historical strength in tax law. A whirlwind of high-profile deals ensured this "*extremely capable*" firm put its "*real-world experience*" to good use this year. The team represented The Carlyle Group in its $2.1 billion purchase of Japanese wireless company DDI Pocket and also acted as counsel to Beverly Enterprises in the $2.1 billion sale of the company to North American Senior Care. According to clients, the group "*shines in high-dollar transactions where there is money at stake,*" but is also indispensable "*as a sounding-board when we are not comfortable with a transaction.*"

**The Lawyers: Irving Salem** is "*a distinguished gentleman and a guru of consolidated returns.*" Clients appreciate his "*pragmatic and sensible approach.*" Salem commands expertise in planning corporate acquisitions and restructuring and has further experience handling controversies. **David Raab** recently represented MGM in its $5 billion acquisition by a group of investors, among them Sony, Providence Equity Partners and Texas Pacific Group. He was also counsel to Trump Hotels and Casino Resorts in connection with its $2 billion Chapter 11 bankruptcy reorganization. Commentators described Raab as "*a talented, technical lawyer.*"

**Clients/Work Highlights:** The Carlyle Group; Trump Hotels and Casino Resorts; Hilton Hotels; Citibank and Allianz.

## Milbank, Tweed, Hadley & McCloy LLP

**The Firm:** This firm succeeds in combining a small firm personality with large firm transactional might. An integrated team that includes New York attorneys advised Apax Partners and Goldman Sachs Capital Partners in the recent sale of their stockholdings in Kabel Deutschland, Europe's largest cable company. Comprehensive tax experience is offered in asset

securitization, M&A and structured finance.

**The Lawyers: Bruce Kayle**'s finesse in asset securitization and derivatives and "*readiness to really roll up his sleeves*" makes him "*a name to fear*" in the financial products field. He chairs the firm's tax department and wins applause from market sources for his commitment to pro bono work. Also praised at the firm is the "*terrifically insightful*" **Dale Ponikvar**. Ponikvar boasts extensive M&A cross-border experience, having handled tax matters for British, Japanese, Canadian and Saudi investors.

**Clients/Work Highlights:** Domestic and foreign clients and wealthy individuals feature on the client roster.

## Paul, Weiss, Rifkind, Wharton & Garrison LLP

See firm details p.1548

**The Firm:** This "*brilliant*" firm has been bombarded with high-profile deals lately. It advised Viacom on its split into two separate companies and counseled Triarc on its acquisition of Deerfield and Arby's. It also represents many companies in the entertainment industry. The team's "*client-oriented*" service and reputation for being "*excellent at what they do*" inspires confidence in clients and peers alike.

**The Lawyers:** "*Spectacular and supersmart,*" **Alfred Youngwood** (see p.1515) is celebrated for balancing his role as managing partner of the firm with an industrious tax practice. One of his most significant transactions this year was advising Time Warner Cable on its acquisition of the assets of Adelphia and the separation of Comcast from Time Warner. **David Sicular** (see p.1501) represented Oak Hill and General Atlantic in their acquisition of a majority interest in GE's worldwide outsourcing businesses. His energetic yet "*even-tempered*" style reaped compliments from interviewees. Clients hiring "*super*" **David Mayo** (see p.1478), until recently of Gibson, Dunn & Crutcher, are guaranteed "*creative yet non-flamboyant*" service. This "*terrific*" attorney possesses "*extremely strong technical knowledge*" and a practice that encompasses corporate and partnership taxation and M&A. "*Talented*" **Jeffrey Samuels** (see p.1496) devotes his practice to counseling leading entertainment companies and financial institutions on the tax issues of M&A and real estate transactions. The Sprint Nextel merger occupied much of his time this year.

**Clients/Work Highlights:** Carnival Cruise Lines; Citigroup; General Atlantic; Oak Hill; Sprint Nextel; Time Warner; Triarc and Viacom.

## Roberts & Holland LLP

**The Firm:** Acclaimed as "*a great tax boutique,*" Roberts & Holland offers concentrated tax expertise that few can match. Its 40-strong team is fluent in the minutiae of state and city tax laws (particularly their effect on New York property), making it invaluable in loan workouts and bankruptcy. "*One of the giants of real estate taxation,*" the firm counsels a distinguished client roster on a miscellany of transactions including sale-leasebacks and multiparty and delayed exchanges. The group also undertakes international deals for corporate clients including Fortune 500 companies.

**The Lawyers:** Researchers were besieged with praise for the *"fantastic"* **Carolyn Joy Lee**. A virtuoso of state and local tax, Lee enjoys a *"spectacular reputation"* for her representation of clients in real estate deals. Her expertise is enhanced by a federal tax background that allows Lee to provide unique insights into handling controversies. Peers called her *"the most respected female lawyer in town,"* while clients described *"an incredibly modest person and an exceptional attorney."*

## Shearman & Sterling LLP

See firm details p.1554

**The Firm:** These *"excellent lawyers"* counsel clients on the effects of global tax law and specialize in representing multinational companies in cross-border transactions and financial offerings. A feast of deals is provided through the group's representation of financial institutions and investment banks in the financial products arena. Controversies are also a forte and the firm is reputed to have cultivated one of the strongest tax litigation teams in the state. Its attorneys have handled disputes with tax authorities in the USA and Europe and have argued cases before the IRS and US Federal Claims Court.

**The Lawyers:** **Peter Blessing** (see p.1439) is *"one of the best international guys around."* This *"legend"* heads the international tax practice of the firm, a role which involves managing the European tax department. However, this has not prevented him from developing an *"outstanding"* practice. Commentators found it *"remarkable that he can do so many things at the same time."* Blessing is best known for his work in the field of cross-border financial transactions.

**Clients/Work Highlights:** Wyeth; Credit Suisse First Boston; Merrill Lynch; CIT Financial; Groupe DANONE; Linde; Thomson Corporation; Citigroup; Raytheon; Lehman Brothers; ABB; Vivendi Unviersal; Société Générale and Husky Energy.

## Band 4

## McDermott Will & Emery

See firm details p.878

**The Firm:** With more than 70 years of tax experience and 1,000 lawyers worldwide, McDermott offers true breadth and depth of tax expertise. A highly trained team is poised to handle complex global deals as well as intricate state and local tax matters. It counts over half of the Fortune 100 list among its clients. Though the firm offers zealous representation in litigation, it is also experienced in alternative dispute resolution strategies. A strong legislative tax group in Washington, DC further enhances the group's ability to succeed in tax controversies.

**The Lawyers:** **Art Rosen** (see p.1494) was described to researchers as *"a very polished attorney"* who is *"very quick and available."* He is renowned as *"top of the league"* for state and local tax issues. His expertise in state and local telecom and IP matters has enabled Rosen to become a pioneer of Internet and e-commerce tax issues. He dispenses guidance on e-commerce questions arising under current tax law and is actively involved in molding future legislation.

**Clients/Work Highlights:** Barclays Group; drugstore.com; Bayer; Prudential and GE Capital.

## Paul, Hastings, Janofsky & Walker LLP

See firm details p.339

**The Firm:** This international giant has focused its activities on foreign capital markets and real estate. It recently handled several major deals for GE Capital including its bid to acquire Gables Residential Trust, a publicly traded REIT. GE also sought the team's advice in the sale-leaseback of $17 million in solar equipment which will provide electricity to the San Diego school system. However, the firm is easily able to reach beyond the real estate sector. CKx hired these *"quality lawyers"* in relation to its acquisition of an 85% stake in Elvis Presley Enterprises and its acquisition of 19 Entertainment, producer of 'American Idol.'

**The Lawyers:** Real estate tax maestro **Andrew Short** (see p.1501) has been occupied with a flurry of deals this year. One significant matter was his representation of a consortium of buyers in the $1.3 billion acquisition of the real estate commercial mortgage subsidiaries of GM. Short was also engaged by Lexington Corporate Properties as tax counsel in its $750 million acquisition of 27 properties from Wells Real Estate Funds.

**Clients/Work Highlights:** Walker Digital Management; SBC; Hyperion Capital Management; Atrium Companies; Capital Trust; Fisher Brothers and Strategic Hotels.

## Other Notable Practitioners

The *"extremely astute"* **Richard Reinhold** (see p.1491) chairs the tax department of Willkie Farr & Gallagher LLP. Described as a *"luminary,"* Reinhold recently advised longtime client Zurich Financial Services in its $1.3 billion offering of enhanced capital advantaged preferred securities. This unique hybrid security will provide Zurich with long-term finance and significant equity credit. Reinhold also collaborated closely with the firm's M&A team on the $7.4 billion acquisition of Ivax (US) by Teva Pharmaceutical Industries (Israel). **Richard Andersen** (see p.1433) of Arnold & Porter LLP boasts a predominantly international practice. He advised CSX on the international tax aspects, particularly foreign tax credit ramifications, of its disposition of its international terminal business to Dubai Ports International. Inbound investment is his specialty, with Andersen being recently hired by a consortium of international investors to handle their acquisition of a controlling interest in Citco Group. He has also advised the Government of Turkey on sovereign debt financings and reopenings. As well as handling major cases before the IRS, **James Dreyfus** (see p.1450) of Fulbright & Jaworski L.L.P. continues to build a mighty transactional practice. He has been closely involved in organizing the financial structuring for a recent cross-border acquisition by Petro-Canada and advises prominent charitable organizations on a variety of tax and non-tax matters. Dreyfus is currently counseling a group of US individuals in the distribution of proceeds from the sale of assets of a large offshore gas and oil company. Praised for his *"encyclopedic knowledge,"* **Phillip Gall** of Kronish Lieb Weiner & Hellman LLP is renowned as a partnership expert. He has represented multinational corporations and private businesses as well as wealthy individuals in disputes at all levels. Clients predict a bright future for Gall, with one source enthusing: *"He is a future megastar in the tax field."* *"Intellectually courageous,"* **David Nirenberg** (see p.1483) of Orrick, Herrington & Sutcliffe LLP is *"absolutely top-notch,"* according to commentators. He has achieved a national reputation as an authority on the tax aspects of securitizations and derivative products and has written and lectured extensively on the subject. **Thomas Hood** (see p.1465) of Mayer, Brown, Rowe & Maw LLP primarily practices in the field of corporate M&A. In the past year, he has provided comprehensive domestic and international corporate tax advice to Devon Energy including counseling the company on the restructuring of $5 billion of Canadian operations. Hood also developed a tax opinion on a unique US limited liability company structure for a $300 million oil facility financing for ABN AMRO. Sources described a *"professional, dignified and extremely personable"* attorney. Clients are also impressed with the *"technical and analytical knowledge"* of **Robert Scarborough** of Freshfields Bruckhaus Deringer. An *"extremely smart"* lawyer, Scarborough's broad practice encompasses capital markets transactions and complex financings.

# TECHNOLOGY & IT OUTSOURCING

## Band 1

### Mayer, Brown, Rowe & Maw LLP
See firm details p.876

**The Firm:** With a *"truly global vision,"* this *"top-class"* practice was praised by peers for being a powerhouse in the outsourcing field in particular. *"Constantly pitching and eating up market share,"* it is noted for the fact that it *"walks both sides of the street"* in repre-senting customers and vendors alike in both outsourcing and technology transactional work. In addition, its long-term relationship with consulting firm TPI is seen to contribute to a heavy deal flow on the ITO side in particular.

**The Lawyers:** Rated equally by interviewees for both his general technology and outsourcing expertise, **Nigel Howard** (see p.1466) benefits from a *"cool, calm demeanor"* and *"achieves mutually accept-able resolutions."* His recent work includes advising digital rights management company Trymedia Systems in relation to a number of stand-alone IT projects including distribution and sales arrange-ments. The *"personable"* **David Hudanish** (see p.1466) is the New York office's outsourcing practice head. He won accolades from clients for his *"incred-ibly current knowledge of operations, suppliers and investment processes"* in the outsourcing arena. His recent work includes representing TXU Corporation (including subsidiaries TXU Energy and TXU Gas) in a ten-year $3.5 billion outsourcing transaction with Capgemini. He also represented National Asso-ciation of Security Dealers in a series of IT outsourc-ing transactions with OM Technologies.

**Clients/Work Highlights:** Clients include TXU Corporation; National Association of Security Deal-ers; Scripps Networks; Trymedia Systems; Merrill Lynch; Procter & Gamble; Fifth Third Bank; Aon; Sun Microsystems and Gillette.

### Milbank, Tweed, Hadley & McCloy LLP

**The Firm:** This practice's lawyers were described by competitors as *"seasoned campaigners"* in the outsourcing field who benefit from the fact that *"everyone who's anyone or thinking of becoming anyone in this business knows their brand name."* Clients commented that *"if you have an ugly deal, they are the ones you want to help you through it."* In recent times, the firm has been especially active in relation to HRO work, with practice head John Halvey leading the team on matters for clients such as PepsiCo, Omnicom, DuPont and VNU. Other work has included BPO matters for clients such as Home Depot and TXU.

**The Lawyers:** *"One of the deans of the outsourcing Bar,"* according to both competitors and clients, **John Halvey** also *"manages a huge magnitude of complex deals"* and is *"so far ahead of the curve in the area that there's no need to shop around. He creates an atmos-phere at the table where vendors know he's the sheriff."* Described by peers as the *"dean of satellite finance within the legal profession,"* space and satellite special-ist **Peter Nesgos** won plaudits from clients for being *"always prepared, proactive and consensus-based"* in negotiations. *"He understands how the industry works from both the legal and the business perspective."* *"Great at working a room,"* **Rob Finkel** is also *"acces-sible"* and has *"top business judgment around the edges."* He recently advised Tyco in an outsourcing transaction with Automatic Data Processing, involv-ing employer-related functions. Another of his matters involved advising MasterCard on a call center transaction with Convergis. A recently appointed partner, **Steve Nordahl** won plaudits from peers for being *"a quick learner"* who *"drafts excellently"* and is *"great at strategy and document turnaround."* Associate **Janet Parkhurst** won praise from clients for being similar to *"John Halvey in approach and style."* She is *"a good leader and works phenomenally hard."*

**Clients/Work Highlights:** Clients include General Atlantic; Prudential Financial; Home Depot; AT&T; DuPont; Cendant; Pepsi Bottling Group; Master-Card and Tyco International.

## Band 2

### Brown Raysman Millstein Felder & Steiner LLP
See firm details p.1521

**The Firm:** When it comes to technology and outsourcing deals, this practice has *"been doing it as long as anyone,"* for both vendors and customers. Its expertise includes advising in relation to agreements for technology development, procurement, licensing, distribution and transfer of software, hardware, and telecom products and services.

**The Lawyers:** Clients believe that **Julian Millstein** (see p.1480) *"commands respect, is practical and makes the deal more businesslike than adversarial."* Particularly noted by peers for his vendor-side work, especially for AT&T Solutions, his expertise includes negotiating and litigating outsourcing matters, in addition to computer-related, e-commerce and IP matters. The *"technically expert"* **Richard Raysman** (see p.1491) has recently been active in relation to offshore outsourcing work and co-location agree-ments, with his practice also including computer law and IP issues. **Ken Adler**'s clients come predomi-nantly from the insurance, financial services and healthcare sectors. His practice encompasses advis-ing on ITO, BPO and HRO agreements. He also counsels on issues relating to e-commerce and computer and telecom products and services.

**Clients/Work Highlights:** Clients include Wall Street investment banks; Fortune 50 entertainment and media companies; leading financial services and insurance firms; top-tier software and technology infrastructure vendors and well-known e-commerce concerns.

### Morgan, Lewis & Bockius LLP
See firm details p.1758

**The Firm:** Commentators believe that this practice's New York office is *"clearly moving ahead,"* a year after the arrival of outsourcing experts Akiba Stern and Ed Hansen from Pillsbury Winthrop Shaw Pittman. Its recent activity includes advising clients in the life sciences and pharmaceutical industries and the insurance and financial services sectors on a variety of outsourcing and general technology transactions.

**The Lawyers:** *"Well-known and respected"* for his

ITO work in particular, the *"smart and savvy"* **Akiba Stern** (see p.1505) is *"one hell of a marketeer,"* according to competitors. He recently advised an international confectionery and beverages company in relation to finance and accounting and HR outsourcing. Particularly noted by our interviewees for his telecom outsourcing work, **Ed Hansen**'s (see p.1463) practice also encompasses negotiating system acquisitions, telecom service agreements, custom software development and software distribution agreements. His recent work has included advising on a facilties management outsourcing in the healthcare field and an HR outsourcing in the entertainment field.

**Clients/Work Highlights:** Clients include insurance and financial services companies, in addition to biotech firms; large multinational pharmaceutical companies; research hospitals and scientific institutions.

## Pillsbury Winthrop Shaw Pittman LLP
See firm details p.1550

**The Firm:** This practice's New York office is now a year on from both its merger with Pillsbury Winthrop and the departures of leading practitioners Akiba Stern and Ed Hansen to Morgan, Lewis & Bockius. While the prevailing market comment is that the proverbial dust is yet to settle following both these events, the practice nevertheless continues to undertake a range of BPO and ITO transactions. Other work includes systems integration, software transactions and licensing, technology transfer and distribution and privacy and data protection. Its clients come from sectors including financial services, retail, manufacturing and healthcare. The workload in recent times has included offshoring work such as call centers and back office sales.

**The Lawyers:** Joshua Konvisser and Vipul Nishawala have recently been appointed partners in the global sourcing group's New York office.

**Clients/Work Highlights:** Recent highlights for the practice include advising JPMorgan Chase on the outsourcing of its global IT infrastructure (except desktop) to IBM. The practice also represented Capital One in a fast track facilities management outsourcing of its data center to IBM, and in the outsourcing of its print, embossing and remittance processing functions to First Data. Clients include; Dun & Bradstreet; Bank of New York; Arrow Electronics; Gap; Nike; Lehman Brothers; American Express and GE Consumer Finance.

## Skadden, Arps, Slate, Meagher & Flom LLP & Affiliates
See firm details p.1557

**The Firm:** *"Because they're Skadden, they'll always get good work in the sector,"* was one competitor's complimentary assessment of this practice. It represents a range of both users and providers in matters including outsourcing transactions, strategic alliances, joint ventures, technology transfers, marketing agreements and licensing arrangements.

**The Lawyers:** IT and e-commerce practice head **Stu Levi** (see p.1474) has been particularly active in relation to outsourcing transactions in recent times. His

caseload also includes technology and IP licensing, technology transfers, strategic alliances and joint ventures. Also noted by peers for her outsourcing expertise, **Rita Rodin**'s (see p.1493) recent highlight matters include representing Skype in its $2.6 billion upfront acquisition by eBay, plus potential performance-based consideration. She also represented Capgemini in its agreements with TXU Energy and ONCOR Electronic Delivery to form a joint venture for the provision of IT and other business processing outsourcing services to TXU.

**Clients/Work Highlights:** Other recent work for the practice includes advising in relation to an insourcing for a major US insurance company and representing a major US retailer in outsourcing a number of different aspects of its back office financial infrastructure to another party. Provider clients include software developers; outsourcers; content providers; domain name registries and registrars, infrastructure and network providers. Its user clients come from the financial services, transportation, manufacturing, publishing, entertainment and retail sectors.

## Weil, Gotshal & Manges LLP
See firm details p.1565

**The Firm:** With a *"massive IT department"* and strong institutional clients, this practice is seen by commentators as having *"always had a fair amount of work in the area."* It has recently acted on a number of ITOs, as well as various outsourcings of title insurance, a fulfillment service outsourcing, and an outsourcing of point-of-sale and back office operations.

**The Lawyers:** **Jeff Osterman**'s (see p.1485) practice encompasses IT and technology with an emphasis on sourcing. He recently advised GE in its sale of a majority interest in its captive offshore outsourcing business, GE Capital International Services (GECIS), with an ancillary agreement for GE to continue acquiring services from GECIS for eight years. The *"bright"* **Michael Epstein** (see p.1452) was praised by peers for being an *"excellent and high-profile technology litigator"* in the New York market. His practice takes in a broad subject matter that includes outsourcing, patents, copyright, trade secrets and trademarks. He recently represented Lenovo in its acquisition of a PC business from IBM. He has also been representing CBS in the splitting of Viacom into its two component parts, namely Paramount and CBS.

**Clients/Work Highlights:** Clients include GE; MGM; Fidelity National Information Services; Intel; Microsoft; Cisco Systems; BMG; Pirelli; Weitzman Institute; Telecom Italia; Olivetti and Merrill Lynch.

## Willkie Farr & Gallagher LLP
See firm details p.1567

**The Firm:** This practice's lawyers are *"good at finding common ground in deals,"* according to commentators. One particularly appreciative client noted: *"They make sure things get done and if they're involved I don't have to worry that I'll get a call from the other side saying we've hit a brick wall."* Its recent work

includes software acquisitions in addition to software licensing and development agreements.

**The Lawyers:** *"Good negotiator"* **Gordon Caplan** (see p.1442) has *"an infinite capacity to work like crazy,"* and is *"not shy in laying out the pros and cons to his clients so they can make the decision as to how they'd like a transaction structured or negotiated."* His practice focuses on private equity and M&A transactions, in addition to commercial licensing and distribution agreements for IT software, technology and telecom companies. His recent work includes advising Sprint on technology integration issues in relation to the Sprint Nextel merger. He has also been representing Insight Venture Partners in the leverage buyout of GFI Software. With a background in M&A and corporate finance, **Bruce Kraus** (see p.1473) has undertaken a significant number of telecom-oriented deals, according to our interviewees. His recent work includes telecom workouts, M&A and venture transactions and financings. His clients include XO Communications, Loral Space & Communications and ICOM.

**Clients/Work Highlights:** Clients include Insight Venture Partners; Sprint; Liberty Associated Partners; Movida Communications and Kanoodle.com.

## Band 3

## Bierce & Kenerson, P.C.

**The Firm:** This New York-based, midmarket boutique advises a range of domestic and international clients in the business, technology and finance sectors. Its expertise includes outsourcing, shared services and strategic alliances, in addition to data protection, computers, and software development and licensing matters.

**The Lawyers:** Peers believe that **Bill Bierce** is an accomplished outsourcing lawyer who has been especially active in relation to HRO transactions in recent times. His work includes representing foreign service providers coming to the USA and US companies setting up offshore.

**Clients/Work Highlights:** Clients emanate from the financial services, insurance, real estate, manufacturing, mining, pharmaceuticals and healthcare, IT and e-commerce sectors.

## Kaye Scholer LLP
See firm details p.1536

**The Firm:** This practice's recent work has included IP protection work in relation to outsourcing matters. Its expertise encompasses handling transactional, litigation and IP protection matters, with a focus on institutional customers of IT.

**The Lawyers:** Noted for his presence on the outsourcing conference circuit, **Bill Tanenbaum** (see p.1507) is the international chair of the firm's technology, IP and outsourcing group. He has built on his IP and patent background and won plaudits from commentators for having *"one of New York City's most outstanding transactional IT law practices."* He has handled *"a wide variety of complex matters, often at the leading edge of technology."*

**Clients/Work Highlights:** Clients include Fortune 100 companies and large institutional IT and outsourcing customers.

## Morrison & Foerster LLP

See firm details p.335

**The Firm:** Despite the recent departure of John Kennedy to LeBoeuf, Lamb, Greene & MacRae's New York office, this practice continues to be lauded due to the presence of its "*tech-savvy attorneys*," who act as "*zealous advocates for their clients.*" The team continues to undertake outsourcing work including both ITO and BPO matters. It is also well-known for its technology expertise, advising on matters such as software development, software licensing and licensing of content for online distribution. Its clients include a range of media and entertainment companies.

**The Lawyers:** The "*sharp*" John Delaney (see p.1449) is "*excellent both in his skills and how he thinks about things,*" according to interviewees.

**Clients/Work Highlights:** Clients include A&E Television Networks; The Harry Fox Agency; Hertz; Time Warner Cable; Yahoo! HotJobs and EMI Music Publishing.

## White & Case LLP

See firm details p.1566

**The Firm:** The firm's New York office is the hub of its global technology practice group. The bulk of the work undertaken involves advising on IT issues and various BPO, HRO and finance and accounting outsourcings for clients in the financial services industry. The team does a lot of work with Deutsche Bank and also has a number of key contacts in the pharmaceutical industry.

**The Lawyers:** An expert when it comes to "*nuts and bolts technology agreements,*" global IT practice head Steve Betensky (see p.1438) recently represented Deutsche Bank in connection with outsourcing certain managed IT and level three support services. He also advised United Business Media (UBM) on a number of outsourcing and IT-related transactions including the negotiation of a 'multi-entry visa' master services agreement for IT services. He also represented the company in relation to the $11.3 million acquisition of ICMI by UBM's subsidiary CMP Media.

**Clients/Work Highlights:** Clients include Agfa-Gevaert; Comcast; Deutsche Bank; EchoStar; First American; HJ Heinz; Royal Ahold; Saudi Aramco; UBM and Verizon.

## Other Notable Practitioners

John Kennedy (see p.1470) has recently joined LeBoeuf, Lamb, Greene & MacRae LLP's New York office from Morrison & Foerster and has been advising a number of the firm's insurance clients. His practice involves technology transactions, with his primary focus being on advising customers in relation to offshoring and outsourcing agreements both of the ITO and BPO variety. Commentators noted his "*calm demeanor*" and "*good negotiating skills.*" They further alluded to the fact that "*he is completely conversant with his field to the point that he can engage in highly technical discussions with vendors.*"

# Leaders in New York

## AARON, Roger S
Skadden, Arps, Slate, Meagher & Flom LLP & Affiliates, New York
212 735 3300
raaron@skadden.com
*Recommended in Corporate/M&A*

**Practice Areas:** Senior Partner in charge of all corporate practice areas, including mergers and acquisitions, finance, banking and institutional investing, tax, employee benefits, investment companies, and restructuring and bankruptcy reorganization. Is a frequent lecturer at various seminars and symposiums on M&A, corporate and securities law matters.
**Career:** LLB, JD, Yale Law School, 1968; MBA, Amos Tuck School of Business Administration, Dartmouth College, 1965 (with high distinction); AB, Dartmouth College, 1964 (magna cum laude).

## ABATE, Mark J
Morgan & Finnegan, LLP, New York
212 415 8723
mjabate@morganfinnegan.com
*Recommended in Intellectual Property*

**Practice Areas:** Intellectual property, including patent litigation, intellectual property litigation, appeals, counseling and opinions and due diligence.
**Prof. Memberships:** Mr Abate has chaired numerous committees and sub-committees for state, local and national Bar associations, including the American Bar Association, American Intellectual Property Law Association, New York Intellectual Property Law Association and Federal Circuit Bar Association. He currently serves as Secretary of the NYIPLA and on the Board of Governors of the Federal Circuit Bar Association.
**Career:** Mr Abate's practice focuses on trials and appeals of patent infringement cases. He has been involved in complex high technology patent litigation and has particular expertise in electronics, computers and computer software, financial systems, chemical compositions and processes and medical devices. He has successfully handled trials in the US District Courts and appeals before the US Court of Appeals for the Federal Circuit. He successfully argued in what was then a case of first impression, that a district court ruling on claim construction was entitled to collateral estoppel in the case of TM Patents v IBM. He authored the amicus brief of IBM, Ford and Kodak that was followed and cited by the Federal Circuit in the landmark en banc case of Festo v Shoketsu. In two other appeals before the Federal Circuit, Mr Abate's arguments created new law regarding patent infringement damages. Although litigation has been Mr Abate's focus, he also counsels clients on a wide range of intellectual property matters. He has written counsel opinions successfully used by his clients to defend against allegations of willful infringement. Prior to joining Morgan & Finnegan, Mr Abate was a law clerk for Chief Judge Howard T Markey of the US Court of Appeals for the Federal Circuit from 1988-90. He also was a patent examiner at the US Patent and Trademark Office from 1984-85.
**Publications:** 'Experience With Markman Proceedings In Patent Litigation', NYSBA Bright Ideas, vol 14, no 3, at 5-10 (Winter 2005). 'Intellectual Property Law Cases In The New York Federal Courts', NYIPLA Bulletin Columnist (2002-present). 'The Disclosed But Unclaimed Limitation On The Doctrine Of Equivalents', NYIPLA Bulletin (September 2003). 'Patentability Of Computer Software Under U.S. Law', The Journal of World Intellectual Property, Vol. 3, No. 5 (Sept. 2000). 'Patent Law – Protecting Software', National Law Journal (July 19, 1999). 'Software Patents Go Back To The Future', Mealey's Litigation Report Intellectual Property (December 21, 1998). 'State Street Bank: An Unremarkable Ruling For Remarkable Technology', Computer Litigation Journal, vol 5, no 7 (October 1998). 'Experience With Markman In Patent Litigation: A Practicum For Trial Attorneys', Mealey's Litigation Report Intellectual Property (August 3, 1998). 'Design Patent Infringement Put To Sea Without Guiding Charts', American Intellectual Property Law Association Quarterly Journal, 22 AIPLAQJ 135 (Spring 1994). 'Practical Tips For Using The Federal Circuit Rules Of Practice When Filing Patent Appeals From The PTO', Federal Circuit Bar Journal, 4 Fed Cir Bar J 389 (Winter 1994). 'Supreme Court Review Of The United States Court Of Appeals For The Federal Circuit 1982-92', Federal Circuit Bar Journal, 2 Fed Cir Bar J 307 (Fall 1992).
**Personal:** Mark Abate is a Partner of Morgan & Finnegan, and is a member of the firm's Executive Committee. He has been selected as one of the country's foremost intellectual property lawyers by Chambers USA; voted by his peers as one of the World's Leading Patent Law Experts (Guide to the World's Leading Patent Law Experts, Managing Intellectual Property, 2005); named in 'Who's Who in American Law' and is a Fellow of the American Bar Foundation.

## ABRAHAM, Aaron N
Arent Fox PLLC, New York
212 484 3977
abraham.aaron@arentfox.com
*Recommended in Construction*

**Practice Areas:** Represents developers and corporate and institutional owners, design professionals, and contractors on major construction projects nationally, negotiating all construction-related agreements and resolving complex fee, financing, budget, design, indemnification, insurance, surety, dispute resolution, and distressed project issues. Litigates complex construction and design related disputes, including those related to project delay, design errors and omissions, structural failures and collapse, mold and water infiltration, insurance coverage disputes, and surety bond and lien claims.
**Personal:** Temple University School of Law, JD 1995; New York University, BS 1992.

## ABRAMOWITZ, Elkan
Morvillo, Abramowitz, Grand, Iason & Silberberg, PC, New York
212 856 9600
*Recommended in Litigation*

## ABRAMS, Floyd
Cahill Gordon & Reindel LLP, New York
212 701 3900
*Recommended in Media & Entertainment*

## ABRAMS, Marc
Willkie Farr & Gallagher LLP, New York
212 728 8200
mabrams@willkie.com
*Recommended in Bankruptcy*

**Practice Areas:** Partner in the Business Reorganization and Restructuring Department and a Member of the firm's Executive Committee. Has been instrumental, principally on behalf of debtors, in several complex Chapter 11 cases and non-judicial restructurings. Frequently represents clients in the telecommunications, retail, construction, manufacturing, entertainment/recreation, automotive, healthcare, hospitality, and hi-tech industries. International experience includes matters involving the insolvency laws of Argentina, Australia, Bermuda, Canada, France, Germany, Russia, Spain, Switzerland, and the UK, among other nations. Recent significant matters include serving as debtors counsel in the following complex Chapter 11 cases: Adelphia Communications Corp., AMF Bowling Worldwide, Inc., ATX Communications, Inc., Mosler Inc., Schwinn Cycling & Fitness, Inc., Sunterra Corporation, and The Multicare Companies. Actively involved on behalf of creditors in the W.R. Grace and Enron Corporation Chapter 11 cases. Extensive experience representing official and unofficial creditors' committees, hedge funds and sophisticated investors, individual creditors, landlords, DIP lenders, general partners, and other parties in interest.
**Prof. Memberships:** Former Chair of the Committee on Bankruptcy and Corporate Reorganization of the Association of the Bar of the City of New York (2002-04), and has served as the Head of its Subcommittee on DIP Financing Guidelines. Fellow of the American College of Bankruptcy. Has also been active in a number of additional reorganization-related groups, including the American Bar Association (Business Reorganization Committee), the American Bankruptcy Institute, the International Bar Association (Committee J) and the New York Chapter of the Turnaround Management Association. Certified mediator for the US Bankruptcy Courts for the Southern District of New York and the District of Delaware.
**Career:** Admitted to the Delaware Bar (1978), Pennsylvania Bar (1981) and New York Bar (1985); the United States Courts of Appeal for the Second and Third Circuits; and the US District Courts of Delaware and the Southern and Eastern Districts of New York.
**Personal:** Received a JD (cum laude) from Widener University in 1978 and a BA (cum laude) from Villanova University in 1975.

## ABRAMSON, Richard
Peckar & Abramson PC, New York
212 382 0909
rabramson@pecklaw.com
*Recommended in Construction*

**Practice Areas:** Mr Abramson has enjoyed a distinguished career with substantial success in highly complex litigations and arbitrations, particularly in the area of major construction industry disputes. He has also resolved several complex multi-party disputes through negotiation, mediation and other alternative dispute resolution mechanisms.
**Prof. Memberships:** Mr Abramson is admitted to practice before the United States Supreme Court, the United States Court of Appeals for the Third Circuit, the United States Court of Federal Claims, the United States District Court for the Eastern and Southern Districts of New York and the District of New Jersey as well as the courts of the State of New York and the State of New Jersey. He is a certified mediator for the United States District Court of New Jersey. Mr Abramson is a Member of the Bergen County and the New Jersey State Bar Association.
**Career:** Founding Partner.
**Personal:** He is a graduate of the University of Wisconsin at Madison and Brooklyn Law School, where he was editor of the Brooklyn Law Review.

## ADLER, Arthur S
Sullivan & Cromwell LLP, New York
212 558 4000
adlera@sullcrom.com

*Recommended in Real Estate*

**Practice Areas**: Commercial real-estate expertise, including mortgage and mezzanine loans and preferred equity transactions; securitizations and other public/private investment vehicles; sale-lease-backs and lease-backed financings; development and investment joint ventures; acquisitions and dispositions of improved and unimproved properties; construction contracting; insurance; and commercial leasing. Clients include Goldman, Sachs; Toys 'R' Us; UBS; Vornado Realty Trust; Computer Associates; Brinker International; Prudential Financial; General Growth and Tisch Family Interests.

**Prof. Memberships**: ABA; NYSBA; ABCNY.

**Career**: Partner since 1990.

**Personal**: Columbia University (AB, 1979); Columbia Law School (JD, 1982).

## ADLER, Kenneth

Brown Raysman Millstein Felder & Steiner LLP, New York 212 895 2000
*Recommended in Technology*

## ADLER, Sheldon S

Skadden, Arps, Slate, Meagher & Flom LLP & Affiliates, New York
212 735 2136
sadler@skadden.com
*Recommended in Energy*

**Practice Areas**: Primarily responsible for development of the firm's Utility Merger and Acquisition Practice, a subgroup of the Corporate Practice that handles utility acquisition transactions. Represents a wide variety of clients in merger and other acquisition transactions. Involved in many recent public utility merger transactions. Has also been involved in many recent generation assets divestiture transactions. Clients include Duke Energy Corporation, Exelon Corporation, National Grid plc, Sierra Pacific Resources, CMS Energy Corporation, and Northeast Utilities.

**Career**: JD, Yale Law School, 1979 (editor, Yale Law Journal); BA, City College of New York, 1976.

## ADLERSTEIN, Jo Anne

Brown Raysman Millstein Felder & S teiner LLP, New York 212 895 2507
jadlerstein@brownraysman.com
*Recommended in Immigration*

**Practice Areas**: Jo Anne Adlerstein heads the firm's immigration practice. She specializes in business visas, extraordinary alien cases, J-1 residence requirement waivers, physician transfers and political asylum cases. A former assistant US attorney, Ms Adlerstein handles white-collar criminal defense and federal agency compliance issues. She provides immigration law due diligence for mergers and acquisitions, and conducts in-house immigration audits. She also prepares clients for consular processing and entry issues, and is fluent in French and Spanish.

**Personal**: BA, Brandeis University 1969, magna cum laude; MA, NDEA Teaching Fellow, Columbia University Teachers College 1970; JD, Columbia University Law School 1976.

## AIELLO, Michael

Dewey Ballantine LLP, New York
212 259 8554
maiello@deweyballantine.com
*Recommended in Corporate/M&A*

**Practice Areas**: Mr Aiello regularly represents acquirors, targets, board of directors, special committees and investment banks in complex domestic and international negotiated and unsolicited transactions. Mr Aiello also regularly counsels clients on a broad range of corporate and securities law. In 2005, Mr Aiello was named one of The National Law Journal's '40 under 40' for his work in the mergers and acquisitions area.

**Career**: Partner, Dewey Ballantine LLP. Admitted to practice 1995. Clerkship, US Court of Appeals for the 3rd Circuit (1994-95).

**Personal**: Born June 1, 1969. BA, New York University, 1991. JD, Widener University School of Law, 1994.

## ALBERT, Lauren S

Axinn, Veltrop & Harkrider LLP, New York
212 728 2230
lsa@avhlaw.com
*Recommended in Antitrust*

**Practice Areas**: Commercial litigation, antitrust and trade regulation.

**Prof. Memberships**: New York Women Antitrust Lawyers Group, Founder and Chair; American Bar Association, Member Antitrust Section, Vice-Chair of the Intellectual Property Committee; Executive Committee of the NY State Bar Association Antitrust Law Section.

**Career**: Lauren Albert's practice ranges from merger reviews to antitrust and complex commercial litigation, government investigations and counseling. Recent mergers include representing GameStop Corp. in its acquisition of Electronics Boutique, MovieGallery in its acquisition of Hollywood Video, and BellSouth and Cingular in their acquisition of AT&T Wireless. Ms Albert has an active practice counseling clients in distribution, pricing and other Sherman and Robinson-Patman Act issues as well as Hart-Scott-Rodino compliance. She also advises trade associations on compliance with the Sherman Act.

**Publications**: 'Rethinking Second Requests', The Deal, September 26, 2005; co-editor, 'Handbook on the Antitrust Aspects of Standards Setting', American Bar Association, Antitrust Section 2004; 'Non-Reportable Smaller Deals May Present Greater Risks, Costs Than Big Ticket Deals That Must Be Reported to FTC, DOJ', 18 BNA Corp. Couns. Wkly. 280 (2003); 'Antitrust Law – Women Seek Power in Numbers', 88 Women Law. J. 11, 2003; 'US Supreme Court Again Clarifies the Power of Arbitrators', 229 NYLJ 4, 2003; contributor, 'Antitrust Law Developments' (Second, Third and update to Third), American Bar Association's Antitrust Law Section; contributor to Mergers and Acquisitions: The Monthly Tax Journal.

**Personal**: Ms Albert graduated magna cum laude from Brown University with a BA in 1985 and proceeded on to receive her JD in 1988 from George Washington University, National Law Center.

## ALBERTS, David

Lovells, New York
212 909 0612
dave.alberts@lovells.com
*Recommended in Insurance*

**Practice Areas**: Insurance and reinsurance.

**Career**: Dave's practice focuses on insurance, reinsurance and alternative risk transfer matters (ART). His financial solutions and ART advisory services and transactional practice includes credit enhancements, new product development, evaluation and management of run-off liabilities, and development and implementation of exit strategies such as liability-based restructuring, financial reinsurance and portfolio transfers. He also has a wide range of experience in other types of insurance and reinsurance matters, including dispute resolution. In addition, David has authored several articles for industry publications.

**Personal**: College of Law, University of Iowa (JD, 1991); Georgetown University (BSFS, 1986).

## ALDEN, Steven

Debevoise & Plimpton LLP, New York
212 909 6000
*Recommended in Real Estate*

## ALEXANDER, Troy

White & Case LLP, New York
212 819 8532
talexander@whitecase.com
*Recommended in Projects*

**Practice Areas**: Co-Head of the firm's Energy, Infrastructure and Project Finance Group. Concentrates on international project finance and banking in power, oil and gas, telecommunications and mining industries. Clients include sponsors, sovereigns, commercial banks, multilateral financial institutions and export credit agencies. Also involved in construction projects, joint ventures, leasing, acquisitions, public securities offerings, domestic and international loan transactions, privatizations and debt restructurings.

**Career**: Admitted to New York Bar 1988; became Partner January 1996.

**Personal**: Princeton University, Woodrow Wilson School of Public and International Affairs, MPA, 1987; New York University School of Law, JD, 1987.

## ALLERHAND, Joseph

Weil, Gotshal & Manges LLP, New York
212 310 8725
joseph.allerhand@weil.com
*Recommended in Litigation*

**Practice Areas**: Joseph Allerhand is a nationally recognized litigator with extensive experience in securities litigation, SEC investigations, busted deal litigation, arbitrations and contested bankruptcy proceedings. Mr Allerhand regularly counsels boards of directors and special committees on a variety of corporate disputes and in connection with internal investigations. Mr Allerhand advises during the pre-dispute stage, and will then litigate the dispute through trial if necessary. He is equally adept representing plaintiffs and defendants, and has argued and tried numerous high profile cases in state and federal courts, and before arbitration panels.

**Personal**: Columbia University, BA, 1975; Georgetown University Law Center, JD, 1978.

## ALPERIN, Stuart N

Skadden, Arps, Slate, Meagher & Flom LLP & Affiliates, New York
212 735 3920
salperin@skadden.com
*Recommended in Employee Benefits*

**Practice Areas**: Emphasizes ERISA and other employee benefits and executive compensation matters, particularly the treatment of employee benefits in M&A and other corporate restructurings; the uses of employee stock ownership plans (ESOPs); executive compensation issues such as golden parachutes, deferred compensation tax rules and the non-deductibility of annual compensation in excess of $1 million; and issues arising under the short-swing profit and compensation disclosure provisions of the Securities Exchange Act of 1934.

**Career**: LLM, Taxation, New York University, 1980; JD, Syracuse University, 1976 (survey editor, 1975 Survey of New York Law; Order of the Coif); AB, SUNY Binghamton, 1973.

## ALTSCHULER, Fredric L

Cadwalader, Wickersham & Taft LLP, New York 212 504 6525
fredric.altschuler@cwt.com
*Recommended in Real Estate*

**Practice Areas**: Represents numerous clients with respect to the acquisition, financing, mortgage securitization, disposition and leasing of commercial real estate. Has represented institutional lenders and investment banks in connection with construction, interim and permanent financings of real estate (land assemblages, hotels, regional shopping centers, office buildings, industrial parks, mixed-use projects, residential and commercial condominiums and cooperatives), workouts of nonperforming loans, foreclosures and acceptances of deeds in lieu of foreclosure and dispositions of properties acquired in workouts and foreclosures. Has represented institutional lenders and investment banks in connection with the origination and securitization of commercial mortgage loans (both single asset and pools), including the establishment of numerous commercial conduit programs. Has represented investors acquiring performing and non-performing loans and properties, including the financing of such purchases and restructuring and disposition of the purchased assets.

**Personal:** JD, St John's University (1972); BA, Syracuse University (1968).

## AMDUR, Martin
Weil, Gotshal & Manges LLP, New York
212 310 8224
martin.amdur@weil.com
*Recommended in Tax*

**Practice Areas:** Martin Amdur has a broad-based Tax Practice, representing private investment partnerships and public investment funds in the structuring of their investments in the equity, debt and/or partnership interests of private companies and advising public domestic and multinational corporations on tax-free reorganizations, taxable acquisitions and dispositions and a multiplicity of forms of senior and junior debt financing. He frequently represents taxpayers at various levels within the Internal Revenue Service.

**Personal:** Cornell University, BA, 1964; Yale Law School, JD, 1967; New York University School of Law, LLM, 1968.

## AMER, Andrew S
Simpson Thacher & Bartlett LLP, New York 212 455 2953
aamer@stblaw.com
*Recommended in Insurance*

**Practice Areas:** Litigation Partner at Simpson Thacher & Bartlett LLP. Represents clients in a wide range of commercial litigation, with particular emphasis on reinsurance and insurance-related coverage disputes.

**Prof. Memberships:** American Bar Association, AIDA-Reinsurance & Insurance Arbitration Society (ARIAS-US).

**Career:** Has served in the role of national coordinating counsel for various insurers with respect to insurance and reinsurance issues. Has represented insurers in a number of direct insurance coverage actions involving asbestos, pollution and other mass tort claims, and has represented both ceding insurers and reinsurers in a number of significant reinsurance coverage arbitrations and lawsuits, including Cigna Re (52 F.3d 1194) and Unigard (79 N.Y.2d 576; 4 F.3d 1049).

**Personal:** Received his undergraduate Degree in Engineering from Cornell University and his Law Degree from the University of Pennsylvania, where he was an editor of the Law Review.

## AMES, Mitchell
Hogan & Hartson LLP, New York
212 918 8423
msames@hhlaw.com
*Recommended in Media & Entertainment*

**Practice Areas:** International mergers and acquisitions, joint ventures and joint development groups, private equity and venture capital transactions, restructurings, intellectual property licensing and private and public finance, with a special focus on media and communications and healthcare industry transactions.

**Prof. Memberships:** ABA; NYS Bar Association.

**Career:** Mitchell has been a Partner at Hogan & Hartson since March 2002. Prior to joining Hogan & Hartson, he was a Partner from 2000-02 at Squadron Ellenoff Plesent & Sheinfeld LLP (which merged with Hogan & Hartson in 2002). Mitchell represents clients in traditional and new media, telecommunications, financial and investment services, healthcare, manufacturing, and high technology.

**Publications:** Co-author, 'Attorney Standards of Conduct', SEC Update, Hogan & Hartson L.L.P. (November 2002).

**Personal:** New York University (JD, magna cum laude, contributing editor of The Journal of International Law and Politics, AmJur Scholar); State University of New York at Buffalo (BA, magna cum laude). Admitted to practice before the US District Courts for the Southern and Eastern Districts of New York.

## ANDERSEN, Richard
Arnold & Porter LLP, New York
212 715 1095
Richard.Andersen@aporter.com
*Recommended in Tax*

**Practice Areas:** Practices international tax law, primarily for foreign enterprises investing and doing business in the United States in such areas as cross-border acquisitions and joint ventures; international real estate investment in the United States; licensing; financial products; global investment funds; and transfer pricing.

**Prof. Memberships:** He belongs to numerous professional associations, including the USA Branch Council of the International Fiscal Association.

**Publications:** He writes and speaks often on such topics as tax treaties, withholding taxes and investment in US real estate.

**Personal:** He is an Adjunct Professor of Law at New York University and advises numerous professional journals, including the Journal of International Taxation and Tax Management.

## ANDERSON, Eugene
Anderson Kill & Olick P.C., New York
212 278 1000
*Recommended in Insurance*

## ANDERSON, Kenneth B
Loeb & Loeb LLP, New York
212 407 4856
kanderson@loeb.com
*Recommended in Media & Entertainment*

**Practice Areas:** Representation of premier talent and progressive independent companies and investors in music and entertainment industries. Ken is general counsel and supervises litigation for recording/touring artists, composers, producers, actors and others. Builds and maximizes careers from negotiation of first agreements for gifted new talent, to renegotiations and restructuring of business relationships for superstars.

**Prof. Memberships:** National Academy of Recording Arts and Sciences.

**Career:** Partner since 1991.

**Publications:** Frequent speaker on music industry, talent development and new technologies.

**Personal:** Rutgers University Law School (JD, research editor, Rutgers Computer & Technology Law Journal); Rutgers University (BA in Music, cum laude).

## ANGIOLILLO, Bruce
Simpson Thacher & Bartlett LLP, New York 212 455 3735
bangiolillo@stblaw.com
*Recommended in Litigation*

**Practice Areas:** Senior litigation Partner at Simpson Thacher & Bartlett LLP. His areas of expertise are in securities litigation, including class actions, derivative actions and contests for corporate control, and complex commercial, bankruptcy and real estate litigation. Representative cases in the securities area include: Enron, Westar Energy, Sirius Satellite Radio, Winstar, DOV Pharmaceutical, Bre-X, Prison Realty/CCA, Teleglobe, Synthetic Industries, Smith's Foods, Computervision, Starter and WPPSS. Regularly represents Blackstone, KKR and Vestar in matters arising from their investment activities. The Best Lawyers in America (2005-07) awarded him its highest Bet-the-Company Litigation ranking and Lawdragon 500 selected him as one of the 500 leading lawyers in America (2005-07).

**Prof. Memberships:** American Bar Association, the New York State Bar Association, the Federal Bar Council and Association of the Bar of the City of New York. He is a Member of the Mediation Panel of the US District Court for the Southern District of New York.

**Career:** Joined Simpson Thacher in 1980 and became Partner in 1985. Currently a Member of the Board of Directors of Common Ground Community, which provides innovative solutions to homelessness in New York City.

**Publications:** Frequent contributor to legal publications on securities and other litigation topics. For many years, he has been a featured panelist at PLI's annual

Securities Litigation Conference.

**Personal:** Received his BA magna cum laude from Amherst (1974) and his JD from Columbia Law School (1977). He was a Member of the Presidential Search Committee for Amherst College in 1994, received its Medal for Eminent Service in 1996, and served as President of the College's Society of Alumni in 2004.

## ANGLAND, Joseph
Heller Ehrman LLP, New York
212 847 8730
joseph.angland@hellerehrman.com
*Recommended in Antitrust*

**Practice Areas:** Antitrust and trade regulation, tax.

**Prof. Memberships:** ABA; Fellow, American Bar Foundation; Legal Aid Society; New York State Bar Association; Association of the Bar of the City of New York.

**Career:** Mr Angland has represented clients in the automobile, banking, communications, computer software, medical equipment, mortgage, petroleum, pharmaceutical and semiconductor industries. He has litigated jury and non-jury cases before federal and state courts and has handled matters before the FTC. Mr Angland has also litigated in the US Tax Court, the US Court of Federal Claims and district courts.

**Personal:** Harvard University Law School (JD, 1975).

## AQUILA, Francis J
Sullivan & Cromwell LLP, New York
212 558 4048
aquilaf@sullcrom.com
*Recommended in Corporate/M&A*

**Practice Areas:** Advises on acquisitions and divestitures, including Amgen in acquisition of Abgenix, Diageo in sales of Burger King and Pillsbury and acquisitions of Chalone and Seagram, Sainsbury in sale of US businesses, EchoStar in proposed acquisition of Hughes Electronics, British Airways in proposed alliance with American Airlines, Medtronic in MiniMed and MRG acquisitions, and SITA Foundation in sale of interest in Equant.

**Career:** Partner since 1992.

**Publications:** Recipient, 2005 Burton Award for Legal Achievement.

**Personal:** Columbia University (AB, 1979); Brooklyn Law School (JD, 1983).

## ARAR, Roger M
Loeb & Loeb LLP, New York
212 407 4906
rarar@loeb.com
*Recommended in Media & Entertainment*

**Practice Areas:** Concentrates on motion picture and television finance, production, distribution and talent. Principal clients include television networks, motion picture and television production and distribution companies and producers, actors, writers, directors and investors.

**Prof. Memberships:** New York Media/Entertainment Roundtable; UCLA Entertainment Symposium Advisory Committee (also former Co-Chair); ABA – Entertainment ADR Committee.
**Career:** Partner since 1990.
**Publications:** Author, A Rational Approach to Trademark Parody (Unpublished).
**Personal:** Columbia University Law School (JD, 1982); Yale University (BA, 1977).

## ARCHER, Judith A
Fulbright & Jaworski L.L.P., New York
212 318 3342
jarcher@fulbright.com
*Recommended in Litigation*
**Practice Areas:** Litigation.
**Prof. Memberships:** Association of the Bar of the City of New York; American Bar Association – Litigation Section.
**Career:** Judi brings a diverse amount of experience to Fulbright, having worked both as outside and in-house counsel on a wide variety of cases in state and federal courts across the United States at the trial and appellate level, as well as arbitrations and regulatory proceedings. She specializes in complex commercial matters, including contract disputes, telecommunications, securities and entertainment.
**Publications:** Prior Consistent Statements: Temporal Admissibility Standard under Federal Rule of Evidence 801(d)(1)(B), 55 Fordham L Rev 759, 1987.
**Personal:** JD, Fordham Law School (1988); BA, cum laude, Fordham University (1985).

## ARONSON, Clifford H
Skadden, Arps, Slate, Meagher & Flom LLP & Affiliates, New York
212 735 2644
caronson@skadden.com
*Recommended in Antitrust*
**Practice Areas:** Represents clients in antitrust matters relating to mergers and acquisitions. Has experience advising clients on other types of antitrust matters and representing them before federal and state antitrust agencies as well as grand juries.
**Prof. Memberships:** Previous Vice-Chair, Mergers and Acquisitions Committee of the Antitrust Section of the American Bar Association.
**Career:** JD, Georgetown University Law Center, 1980; BS, Wharton School, University of Pennsylvania, 1977 (cum laude).
**Publications:** Co-editor, 'Mergers and Acquisitions – Understanding the Antitrust Laws', American Bar Association.

## ARQUIT, Kevin J
Simpson Thacher & Bartlett LLP, New York 212 455 2000
karquit@stblaw.com
*Recommended in Antitrust*

**Practice Areas:** Has represented clients in major antitrust class actions, involving the healthcare, telecommunications, financial service and insurance areas. Has obtained merger clearance from the US Federal Trade Commission (FTC) or Department of Justice (DOJ) for dozens of transactions in the airline, pharmaceutical, computer hardware and software, chemical, healthcare, optics, food and various consumer product industries. Has extensive experience dealing with international antitrust issues. Current matters in which he is involved include: defending MasterCard in two related actions brought by American Express and Discover that were filed after the conclusion of a previous lawsuit brought by the Department of Justice; representing Automatic Data Processing in a putative class action filed in November 2005 in the District of Western Missouri and representing Weyerhaeuser Company in a series of monopolization cases concerning its purchases of logs in the Pacific Northwest.
**Prof. Memberships:** Member, BNA Advisory Board on Trade Regulation; Member, Board of Advisors to The Antitrust Counsellor; Member, Executive Committee of the Antitrust Law Section of the New York State Bar Association. Member, Board of Directors for The Appleseed Foundation, a non-profit network of public interest law centers located throughout North America.
**Career:** Prior to joining private practice, was General Counsel of the Federal Trade Commission, and then Director of its Bureau of Competition, responsible for the FTC's antitrust enforcement program.
**Personal:** St Lawrence University (BA cum laude 1975), Cornell Law School (JD cum laude 1978).

## ASHINOFF, Reid
Sonnenschein Nath & Rosenthal LLP, New York 212 768 6730
rashinoff@sonnenschein.com
*Recommended in Insurance*
**Practice Areas:** Chair, Litigation Department, New York. Member, firm Management Committee (Policy & Planning). Focuses on commercial crises, multi-jurisdiction matters, class actions, consumer fraud, contractual disputes, real estate, securities litigation and counseling, and complex commercial challenges to products and services. Counsels and represents companies, corporate boards, and executives in trial and appellate courts and before regulatory agencies throughout the US. Served as National Co-ordinating Counsel and Chief Trial Counsel for The Prudential Insurance Company of America, 1995-2003. Created a training program on litigation strategy, tactics and management presented to clients throughout the US, including McDonalds Corporation, Prudential and

The Equitable Life Assurance Society of the United States.
**Prof. Memberships:** ABA; New York City Bar Association, US Supreme Court Bar; National Board of Directors, Tourette Syndrome Association.
**Personal:** Harvard Law School, JD, cum laude; City College of New York, BA, summa cum laude, Phi Beta Kappa.

## ASLANI-FAR, Adel
Dewey Ballantine LLP, New York
212 259 7606
aaslanifar@deweyballantine.com
*Recommended in Corporate/M&A*
**Practice Areas:** Mergers and acquisitions.
**Career:** Represents acquirors, targets, significant stockholders and investment banks in complex domestic and cross-border negotiated and unsolicited mergers, tender offers, stock and asset acquisitions, recapitalizations and joint ventures. Counsels clients with respect to corporate governance and defensive matters. Speaks regularly on M&A developments. Recent representative transactions include advising The Walt Disney Company in the combination of its ABC Radio business with Citadel Broadcasting Corporation in a reverse Morris Trust structure, and Sony Corporation of America in the consortium acquisition of Metro-Goldwyn-Mayer Inc.
**Personal:** Born December 20, 1968. AB, Columbia University, 1990. JD, Georgetown University, 1993.

## ATKINS, Peter Allan
Skadden, Arps, Slate, Meagher & Flom LLP & Affiliates, New York
212 735 3700
patkins@skadden.com
*Recommended in Corporate/M&A*
**Practice Areas:** Senior Partner in Skadden's M&A, Corporate, Securities, Restructuring and Financial Practices. Represents acquirors, targets, special committees and investment banks in mergers, acquisitions, takeovers, leveraged buyouts and joint ventures. Involved in all phases, including planning, negotiating and implementing. Counsels on other corporate, securities and business-related matters, including corporate governance, directors' duties and responsibilities, disclosure and investigations. Transactional involvement includes airline, defense and aerospace, energy, financial institutions, forest products, healthcare, information technology, insurance, media and telecommunications, retail and utilities industries. Member of firm's senior management.
**Career:** LLB, Harvard University, 1968; AB, Brooklyn College, 1965.

## AUSPITZ, Jack
Morrison & Foerster LLP, New York
212 468 8046
jauspitz@mofo.com
*Recommended in Litigation*

**Practice Areas:** Commercial litigator focused on securities, banking and other complex civil litigation. Has litigated numerous private and class action securities and banking cases. Represents China-based companies in US litigation. Has been a court-appointed Special Counsel and Special Escrow Agent in various SEC cases.
**Career:** Admitted to practice in New York.
**Publications:** Co-author, 'Settling a Class Action', Settlement Agreements in Commercial Disputes (Aspen, 2000): 'A Litigator's View of Due Diligence' (PLI, annually); 'Dealing with Damages: Private Actions for Securities Fraud' (PLI, annually).
**Personal:** AB, Columbia University, 1964; JD, magna cum laude, Harvard Law School, 1968; editor, Harvard Law Review; law clerk, Honorable Irving R Kaufman, US Court of Appeals, Second Circuit.

## AVITABILE, Scott D
LeBoeuf, Lamb, Greene & MacRae LLP, New York 212 424 8491
scott.avitabile@llgm.com
*Recommended in Insurance*
**Practice Areas:** Mr Avitabile specializes in securities offerings, alternative risk transfer transactions and mergers and acquisitions in the insurance and banking industries. He advises issuers, underwriters and financial guarantors in a variety of structured finance transactions, with an emphasis on securitizations of insurance products. Mr Avitabile also advises insurance companies and investment banks in structured derivative and insurance risk transfer transactions. Mr Avitabile has extensive experience in mergers and acquisitions in the insurance industry.
**Career:** Joined LeBoeuf Lamb in 1996; Cuddy & Feder (1994-96).
**Personal:** Fordham University (JD) 1994; Berklee College of Music (BM) 1980.

## AXINN, Stephen
Axinn, Veltrop & Harkrider LLP, New York
212 728 2200
sma@avhlaw.com
*Recommended in Antitrust*
**Practice Areas:** Antitrust and trade regulation, complex litigation.
**Prof. Memberships:** American Bar Association, Antitrust Section, 1980-83; Chair, Committee on Section 7 of the Clayton Act; New York State Bar Association, Antitrust Section, 1982-85; Chair, Practicing Law Institute, 1991; Co-Chair, White-Collar Crime and the Federal Sentencing Guidelines.
**Career:** Steve Axinn has represented many of this country's leading corporate and individual clients in a wide variety of precedent-setting cases in trial and appellate courts throughout the nation. He

represented BellSouth and Cingular in Cingular's acquisition of AT&T Wireless, the largest all-cash merger in history. Mr Axinn has also represented parties in a number of antitrust and commercial litigations including the merger of MCI-WorldCom and Sprint, where he was retained as lead counsel to the Antitrust Division of the US Department of Justice and the landmark case of United States v SunGard, where Mr Axinn was lead trial counsel for SunGard. He is currently antitrust counsel to the Mastercard International Board of Directors.

**Publications:** Milton Handler Annual Antitrust Review 2002: 'In Search of Congruence Between Legislative Purpose and Administrative Policy', 2003 Colum. Bus. L. Rev. 431 (2003). 'Merger Review and Litigation Involving the Acquisition of Bankrupt Companies', ANTITRUST, Summer 2002, a publication of ABA Section of Antitrust Law.

**Personal:** Mr Axinn graduated from Syracuse University with a BS in 1959 and proceeded on to receive his LLB in 1962 from Columbia Law School.

### BAECHER, John
Chadbourne & Parke LLP, New York
212 408 5100
jbaecher@chadbourne.com
*Recommended in Projects*

**Practice Areas:** Partner John Baecher advises sponsors, lenders and investors on the development and financing of privately financed independent power projects and on project restructurings, corporate financings and asset acquisitions and divestitures. He has assisted several of the largest global independent power companies in the expansion of their US holdings and in their international development and acquisition activities throughout Latin America and the UK. He also advises sponsors and lenders on responding to RFPs relating to the acquisition or development of power plants and associated facilities, and transmission and distribution systems.

### BAECHTOLD, Robert
Fitzpatrick, Cella, Harper & Scinto, New York 212 218 2213
rbaechtold@fchs.com
*Recommended in Intellectual Property*

**Practice Areas:** Lead Counsel in litigation for major corporate clients, including Bristol-Myers Squibb, Warner-Lambert, Merck, Astellas Pharma, Eisai, Wyeth, Altana Pharma AG, GD Searle, Novartis, AstraZeneca, Bausch & Lomb, Pharmacia, Pfizer, Hoffman La Roche, American Cyanamid, SC Johnson & Son, Hoechst Celanese, Hoechst-Roussel, American-Maize Products, EI du Pont, and Union Carbide. Recent cases include: successfully defending Pharmacia in inventorship challenges by the University of Rochester regarding its sale of blockbuster products Celebrex and Bextra;

successfully defending Bristol-Myers Squibb in inventorship challenges by the University of Michigan and Repligen Corporation concerning biotechnology patents related to therapeutic fusion proteins important in the regulation of the immune system, successfully asserting AstraZeneca patents against validity challenges to its $5 billion per year Prilosec product and successfully defending a multi-billion dollar infringement claim and receiving an award of over $32 million in attorneys fees for client Bristol-Myers Squibb. Mr Baechtold was selected as a top intellectual property law practitioner in the 2005-06 edition of the Best Lawyers in America and for Euromoney Magazine's 'Guide to the World's Leading Patent Law Experts' and 'Guide to the World's Leading Trademark Law Practitioners'. He was selected as one of the 10 best patent lawyers in the world, and the highest rated in the United States, in Euromoney's Best of the Best surveys in 2000, 2002 and 2004. In the 2005 edition of Chambers USA: America's Leading Lawyers for Business, Bob was named as the star player whose 'first name rolls off everyone's lips, the standard by which others are judged'.

**Prof. Memberships:** Former President, Federal Circuit Bar Association; Founding Fellow, American Intellectual Property Law Association; Member of the Bars of New York, New Jersey and Pennsylvania and of several Federal District Courts and Courts of Appeal. Previously served as: Member, Advisory Committee of the Court of Appeals for the Federal Circuit; Board of Directors, American Intellectual Property Law Association and New York Intellectual Property Law Association; President, New Jersey Patent Law Association.

**Career:** Research chemist, American Cyanamid Co. (1958-62); patent agent, M&T Chemicals (1962-65); Ward, McElhannon, Brooks and Fitzpatrick, joined 1965, Partner 1969; Fitzpatrick, Cella, Harper & Scinto, Founding Partner, 1971.

**Personal:** Rutgers University (BS Chemistry); Seton Hall University School of Law (JD magna cum laude). Married with three children, five grandchildren. Enjoys music, golf, tennis, sailing and travel.

### BAKER, D J (Jan)
Skadden, Arps, Slate, Meagher & Flom LLP & Affiliates, New York
212 735 2150
djbaker@skadden.com
*Recommended in Bankruptcy*

**Practice Areas:** Represents public companies in restructurings. Advises officers and directors on duties and governance. Has had primary responsibility in numerous Chapter 11 cases and out-of-court restructurings. Companies represented include: American Pad & Paper; CIRCLE K; Delaco; FiberMark; FoxMey-

er Drug Company; Gen-Tek; Global Marine; HealthSouth; MCorp.; MicroAge; Owens Corning; RCN; Safety-Kleen; Sterling Chemicals; and Winn-Dixie.

**Career:** JD, University of Houston Law School (Editor-in-Chief, Houston Law Review); AB, Harvard University (cum laude). Fellow, American College of Bankruptcy.

### BAKER JR, William T
Thelen Reid & Priest LLP, New York
212 603 2106
wbaker@thelenreid.com
*Recommended in Energy*

**Practice Areas:** Mr Baker is Chair of his firm's Energy Policy and Regulatory Group. He advises energy and public utility clients, both electric and gas, and specializes in corporate matters with emphasis in the corporate area on financing and restructuring. He also specializes in regulatory matters, chiefly under the Public Utility Holding Company Act of 1935.

**Prof. Memberships:** American Bar Association, Member: Section on Business Law, Subcommittee on the Public Utility Holding Company Act of 1935, 1986 (Chairman, 1994); Section on Public Utility, Transportation and Communications Law (1987), Vice-Chair, Subcommittee on Corporate Finance (2004); The Association of the Bar of the City of New York; Edison Electric Institute Legal Committee (Chairman, 1997-2000); Public Utility Holding Company Act of 1935 Counsel Group, 1984 (Chairman, 1994).

**Career:** Partner of Thelen Reid & Priest LLP's New York office. Admitted to practice in New York and Southern and Eastern Districts of New York; United States Supreme Court; United States Court of Appeals for the DC Circuit.

**Personal:** Received his JD from the University of Virginia (1968). Graduate of Yale University, BA, cum laude (1965).

### BALL, Corinne
Jones Day, New York
212 326 7844
cball@jonesday.com
*Recommended in Bankruptcy*

**Practice Areas:** Co-heads the New York office's Restructuring and Reorganization Practice and organizes the firm's Global Restructuring Practice. Significant experience in business finance and restructuring with a focus on complex corporate reorganizations and distress acquisitions. Recognized as a leading bankruptcy attorney in publications such as 'Who's Who in International Insolvency', 'Global Counsel 3000', and the 'K&A Restructuring Register'. Official observer to the Drafting Committee on Business Trust Act of the National Conference of Commissioners on Uniform State Laws.

**Prof. Memberships:** American College of Bankruptcy; American Bankruptcy

Institute.

**Publications:** Authors a column on distress M&A for the New York Law Journal.

### BARANCIK, Tia
King & Spalding LLP, New York
212 827 4081
tbarancik@kslaw.com
*Recommended in Energy*

**Practice Areas:** Corporate with extensive experience structuring and implementing strategic corporate and credit transactions in regulated industries, with a particular emphasis on energy companies.

**Prof. Memberships:** American Bar Association, Section of Business Law and Section of Public Utility, Communications and Transportation.

**Personal:** AB, Princeton University, 1983; JD, Vanderbilt University, 1986.

### BARNES, Mark
Ropes & Gray LLP, New York
212 497 3635
mark.barnes@ropesgray.com
*Recommended in Healthcare*

**Practice Areas:** Has practiced and taught law and administered governmental programs in the healthcare field for the past 20 years. Recognized as a leading lawyer in research compliance, HIPAA, and other privacy regulations. Represents hospitals, medical schools, physicians, social service agencies and related organizations in regulatory, reimbursement, research, HIPAA compliance and litigation matters. Member of the Advisory Committee for Human Research Protections of the Secretary of the United States Department of Health and Human Services.

**Career:** Connecticut Bar (1985); New York Bar (1986); Partner, Ropes & Gray (2001).

**Personal:** LLM, Columbia Law School (1991); JD, Yale Law School (1984).

### BARON, Robert
Cravath, Swaine & Moore LLP, New York
212 474 1422
rbaron@cravath.com
*Recommended in Litigation*

**Practice Areas:** Commercial litigation and arbitration, including representation of major domestic and foreign issuers, financial institutions, private equity firms and hedge funds in securities, contract, fraud, intellectual property, ERISA, shareholder derivative, M&A and antitrust cases in federal and state courts and arbitration of purchase price and employment disputes.

**Prof. Memberships:** Admitted in New York, US Supreme Court, US Courts of Appeals for Second, Third, Ninth and Federal Circuits, and Southern District of New York.

**Career:** Partner since 1988.

**Personal:** Harvard Law School (JD, cum laude, 1981); Princeton University (AB, cum laude, 1978).

## BARR, Michael H
Sonnenschein Nath & Rosenthal LLP,
New York 212 768 6788
mbarr@sonnenschein.com
*Recommended in Insurance*
**Practice Areas:** Concentrates on commercial, class action, consumer fraud, professional liability, insurance coverage and securities litigation and related counseling. Litigates before trial and appellate courts and administrative forums throughout the US. Experience includes securities, workers compensation, consumer fraud, environmental, insurance coverage, trade regulation, real estate, professional liability and contractual disputes.
**Career:** National Litigation and Business Regulation Practice Vice-Chair, Managing Partner, New York.
**Personal:** Harvard University, JD, cum laude; Oberlin College, AB, with highest honors.

## BARSHAY, Scott
Cravath, Swaine & Moore LLP, New York
212 474 1009
sbarshay@cravath.com
*Recommended in Corporate/M&A*
**Practice Areas:** Mergers and acquisitions, hostile takeovers, corporate governance, general representation of corporate clients. In 2005 he represented Chevron in its successful takeover battle to acquire Unocal ($18 billion); the Board of MCI in the takeover battle between Verizon and Qwest ($7.5 billion); and IBM in substantially all of its US mergers and acquisitions.
**Prof. Memberships:** ABA; ABCNY; NYSBA.
**Career:** Joined Cravath in 1991.
**Personal:** Columbia Law School (JD, 1991; Stone Scholar; associate editor of the Journal of Transnational Law); Colgate University (BA, magna cum laude, 1988; Phi Beta Kappa).

## BARTEL II, Paul W
Davis Polk & Wardwell, New York
212 450 4000
paul.bartel@dpw.com
*Recommended in Antitrust*
**Practice Areas:** Member of Davis Polk & Wardwell's Litigation Department. Represents US and non-US companies in antitrust litigation and enforcement agency investigations. Is active in domestic and cross-border acquisitions and joint ventures involving US and European Community antitrust considerations. Representations include The St. Paul Companies in its combination with Travelers; Royal Caribbean Cruises in its proposed combination with P&O Princess Cruises; EMI in its proposed combination with Warner Music; Bertelsmann in its acquisition of Random House; Compaq Computer in its acquisition of Digital Equipment; Texas Instruments in the sale of its defense business to

Raytheon; Hudson Foods in the sale of its business to Tyson Foods; and Borg Warner in the creation of a joint venture combining the businesses of Wells Fargo and Loomis.

## BARTFELD, Daniel
Milbank, Tweed, Hadley & McCloy LLP,
New York 212 530 5000
*Recommended in Projects*

## BARTNER, Douglas
Shearman & Sterling LLP, New York
212 848 8190
dbartner@shearman.com
*Recommended in Bankruptcy*
**Practice Areas:** Practice Group Leader of Bankruptcy and Reorganization Group. Regularly represents debtors and creditors and acquirors of assets in Chapter 11 bankruptcies and out-of-court restructurings. Recent representations include Delphi Corporation, Applied Extrusion Technologies, America Online Latin America, CSFB in multi-billion dollar DIP loan to Calpine Corporation and Oneida Ltd in its out-of-court restructuring.
**Prof. Memberships:** New York and California Bar. Committee on Commercial Bankruptcy, New York County Lawyers' Association. INSOL International. American Bankruptcy Institute.
**Career:** Joined Shearman & Sterling in 1982. Elected to partnership in 1991.
**Personal:** George Washington University, National Law Center, JD, 1982; Lehigh University, BS, 1979.

## BASKIN, Stuart
Shearman & Sterling LLP, New York
212 848 4974
sbaskin@shearman.com
*Recommended in Litigation*
**Practice Areas:** Head of Shearman & Sterling's Litigation Group. Experience in securities litigation, M&A litigation, class action litigation, criminal defense and antitrust matters.
**Career:** Assistant US Attorney in the Southern District of New York (1978-82); Special Assistant to Director, Office for Civil Rights, Department of Health, Education and Welfare (1977-78); clerk to Justice William J Brennan, Jr of the US Supreme Court (1976-77) and to Judge Walter R Mansfield of the US Court of Appeals (1975-76).
**Publications:** Articles in American Bar Association, Federal Bar Council and Practicing Law Institute publications.
**Personal:** BA, Stanford University (1972); JD, Stanford University (1975).

## BASON JR, George R
Davis Polk & Wardwell, New York
212 450 4000
george.bason@dpw.com
*Recommended in Corporate/M&A, Private Equity*
**Practice Areas:** Member of Davis Polk & Wardwell's Corporate Department,

and Head of the firm's M&A Department. Concentrates primarily in mergers, acquisitions and joint ventures, with a special focus on merchant banking. Has experience in cross-border transactions, restructurings, takeover defenses and corporate governance issues, as well as in providing general corporate and securities law advice. Transactions he has worked on include Gillette's acquisition by Procter & Gamble, JPMorgan's $38.6 billion merger with Chase; DLJ's acquisition by Credit Suisse First Boston; Exxon's $81 billion merger with Mobil; Ford's acquisition of Volvo Cars; Procter & Gamble's acquisition of Iams; and management's attempted leveraged buyout of RJR Nabisco.

## BASTA, Paul M
Weil, Gotshal & Manges LLP, New York
212 310 8772
paul.basta@weil.com
*Recommended in Bankruptcy*
**Practice Areas:** Paul Basta's practice consists of representing creditors, debtors and investors in restructuring distressed companies. He has represented Global Crossing, Rhythms Netconnections, Acterna, Footstar and NextWave as well as numerous other debtors. On the creditor side, he has represented Citigroup in Criimi Mae, Inc., Service Merchandise, and Friedman's Jewelers. Mr Basta also represented the bondholders of Excite.
**Personal:** University of Michigan, BA, 1988; George Washington University Law School, JD, 1992. Crain's New York Business named Mr Basta one of the 40 Young Rising Stars in New York.

## BATTISTA, Gregory J
Cravath, Swaine & Moore LLP, New York
212 474 1948
gbattista@cravath.com
*Recommended in Environment*
**Practice Areas:** Specializes in environmental law. Acquisition, divestiture and financing transactions where environmental issues must be identified, quantified and properly managed. Industries represented include heavy manufacturing, mining, forestry, energy, pharmaceuticals, real estate and telecommunications. Counsels clients in remediation and regulatory matters, disputes over environmental claims.
**Prof. Memberships:** ABA (Section of Environment, Energy and Resources).
**Career:** Senior Attorney since 2004. Hannoch Weisman P.C., New Jersey 1986-93. Adjunct Professor of Environmental Law at Stevens Institute of Technology since 1992. New Jersey Department of Environmental Protection 1980-83.
**Personal:** Seton Hall University (JD, 1986); Rider University (MBA, 1983); Boston College (BA, 1980).

## BEATTIE, Richard I
Simpson Thacher & Bartlett LLP,
New York 212 455 2000
rbeattie@stblaw.com
*Recommended in Corporate/M&A, Private Equity*
**Practice Areas:** Chairman of Simpson Thacher & Bartlett LLP specialising in mergers and acquisitions, leveraged buyouts and corporate law and finance. Has participated in some of the larger and more complex transactions, including the merger of America Online with Time Warner, the merger of Wellpoint Health Networks with Anthem, Inc. and JPMorgan Chase & Co.'s $58 billion acquisition of Bank One Corporation.
**Career:** Has a long record of public service. During the Carter Administration, served as General Counsel of the Department of Health, Education and Welfare, and in 1980, was Director of the Transition and Counsel to the Secretary of Education. During the 1980s, served on the New York City Board of Education. Has served as a special advisor to the Secretary of State and during 1996-97 was President Clinton's Emissary for Cyprus.
**Personal:** Chairman of the board and founder of New Visions for Public Schools, a not-for-profit organization that develops and implements programs to affect system-wide improvements in public education in New York City. Is a member of the Board of Directors of Harley-Davidson, Inc, Heidrick & Struggles and the National Women's Law Center, as well as a member of the Council on Foreign Relations and Vice Chairman of the Boards of Overseers and Managers of Memorial Sloan-Kettering Cancer Center and Chairman of the Board of Managers of Memorial Hospital for Cancer and Allied Diseases. Has served on the Board of Directors of the Institute for International Education, the Board of Trustees of WNET/Channel Thirteen and as a trustee for the Carnegie Corporation. Joined Simpson Thacher in 1968 after graduating from the University of Pennsylvania Law School. Prior to law school, served four years in the Marine Corps as a jet pilot, after graduating from Dartmouth College in 1961.

## BECK, Thomas H
Sidley Austin LLP, New York
212 839 5940
tbeck@sidley.com
*Recommended in Intellectual Property*
**Practice Areas:** Focuses on complex chemical and pharmaceutical litigation matters. Leading roles, including as lead counsel, in chemical and pharmaceutical litigation at both the trial and appellate levels for leading pharmaceutical, chemical and biotechnology companies. Counseled clients in connection with drug analogs, fusion proteins, recombinant DNA techniques, and analytical methods involving viral DNA mutations.

Appeared as lead counsel in litigation for major corporate clients, including Bristol-Myers Squibb and GlaxoSmithKline. Notable decisions include successfully defending a multi-billion dollar infringement claim in a six year litigation and obtaining an award of $32 million in attorney fees and other expenses for client Bristol-Myers Squibb. Recognized as a top intellectual property law practitioner in the Global Counsel Handbook: Intellectual Property 2004/05 and the Global Counsel Handbook: Life Sciences 2004/05.

**Prof. Memberships:** Member of the Board of Directors and served as Chairman of the Committee on Litigation Practice and Procedure for the New York Intellectual Property Law Association. Member of AIPLA, ABA. New York State Bar, Federal Circuit, numerous Federal District Courts.

**Personal:** Harvard Law School, JD 1979; North Dakota State University, BS (Chemistry and Mathematics) 1975.

## BECKER, Jeffrey H
Epstein Becker & Green PC, New York
212 351 4747
jbecker@ebglaw.com
*Recommended in Healthcare*

**Practice Areas:** Represents healthcare-related entities in mergers, acquisitions, joint ventures, governance issues, complex contractual arrangements and other affiliations and collaborative efforts. Provides clients with a full range of legal advice and services, including antitrust law; Medicare reimbursement and other third party payment issues; Stark, fraud and abuse, and other healthcare compliance issues; tax and tax-exempt counseling; privacy law; bankruptcy and restructuring; labor and employment law; and liability and litigation matters.

**Prof. Memberships:** American Bar Association, American Health Lawyers Association, New York Business Group on Health, Director, New York State Bar Association, The Association of the Bar of the City of New York.

**Career:** Co-founder of the firm.

**Personal:** JD, New York University School of Law, with distinction, editor, New York University. Law Review, 1969. BA, Brown University, 1966

## BECKERMAN, Lisa G
Akin Gump Strauss Hauer & Feld LLP, New York 212 872 8012
lbeckerman@akingump.com
*Recommended in Bankruptcy*

**Practice Areas:** Lisa Beckerman is a Partner in the Financial Restructuring Group, focusing on corporate insolvency. She has represented official and unofficial unsecured creditors' committees and bondholder committees, debtors, unofficial committees of secured noteholders and acquirers of distressed businesses and assets. Recent matters include Delta Air-

lines, Kaiser Aluminum Corporation, ATA Holdings, Inc., Weirton Steel Corporation, Hawaiian Airlines, National Steel Corporation, Florsheim Shoe and LTV Steel Corporation.

**Personal:** BA, University of Chicago (1984); MBA, University of Texas (1986); JD, Boston University (1989).

## BEER, Steven C
Greenberg Traurig LLP, New York
212 801 9294
beers@gtlaw.com
*Recommended in Media & Entertainment*

**Practice Areas:** Entertainment.

**Prof. Memberships:** President, Executive Board and Member of the National Board, Independent Feature Project, New York; co-founder, The Center for the Protection of Athletes Rights (CPAR); Executive Committee, Young Media Professionals; Member, American Bar Association, Sports and Entertainment Law Forum; Member, National Academy of Television Arts and Sciences.

**Publications:** Author, 'Relief Effort: Tax Incentives for Film Producers', Filmmaker magazine, 2005.

**Personal:** JD, Villanova University School of Law, 1986; BA, summa cum laude, Washington University, 1981.

## BELL, Thomas
Simpson Thacher & Bartlett LLP, New York 212 455 2000
tbell@stblaw.com
*Recommended in Private Fund Formation*

**Practice Areas:** Corporate Partner at Simpson Thacher & Bartlett LLP. Specialises in investment management matters and oversees the firm's practice in the area of private investments funds, where the firm has a pre-eminent international presence. Advises clients globally on a wide range of buyout funds, real estate funds and other kinds of private equity funds, as well as hedge funds, and other kinds of funds for 'alternative asset' categories. Responsible for representative private equity clients, such as: The Carlyle Group, Evercore Partners, The J.E. Robert Companies, J.C. Flowers & Co., New Mountain Capital, Candover, Moorfield, Terra Firma, Altor, Brait, Ferrer Freeman, Sterling and Fremont funds. Representative hedge fund clients include JWM Partners (and its predecessor firm, Long-Term Capital Management), ESL Investments, Brummer & Partners and Watershed Capital Management.

**Prof. Memberships:** Founder and past Co-Chair of the annual International Conference on Private Investment Funds.

**Career:** Joined firm 1983; became Partner 1992. Past Chair of the Subcommittee on Specialised Investment Vehicles of the International Bar Association and member of the Subcommittee on Private Investment Entities of the American Bar

Association.

**Personal:** Dartmouth College, BA, summa cum laude, 1978; MA, with honors, New College, Oxford University,1980; JD, Yale Law School, 1983.

## BELLER, Daniel J
Paul, Weiss, Rifkind, Wharton & Garrison LLP, New York 212 373 3312
dbeller@paulweiss.com
*Recommended in Litigation*

**Practice Areas:** Senior Partner in the Litigation Department. Leading trial lawyer and litigator with extensive experience handling complex civil and criminal matters, including antitrust, securities, real estate and general commercial litigation, government enforcement matters, internal corporate investigations and compliance, and white-collar criminal defense. Has litigated and tried significant cases for major institutional and individual clients in federal and state courts and arbitrations throughout the US. Former Chief of the Major Crimes Unit in the US Attorney's Office for the Southern District of New York. Fellow, American College of Trial Lawyers. Selected for 2006 edition of The Best Lawyers in America.

## BELTZER, Howard S
White & Case LLP, New York
212 819 8306
hbeltzer@whitecase.com
*Recommended in Bankruptcy*

**Practice Areas:** Co-Head of White & Case LLP's Worldwide Financial Restructuring and Insolvency Practice Group and Head of its New York Banking Section. Focuses on major Chapter 11 proceedings and multinational bankruptcy cases.

## BEN-AMI, Leora
Kaye Scholer LLP, New York
212 836 7203
lbenami@kayescholer.com
*Recommended in Intellectual Property*

**Practice Areas:** Partner, Patent Litigation. Concentration in intellectual property and patent litigation. Her practice covers all areas of technology, including biotechnology, pharmaceutical and chemistry, medical devices, mechanical devices and electronics. She also has extensive appellate experience, having argued before the United States Court of Appeals for the Federal Circuit several times and having clerked there. Ms Ben-Ami has handled approximately 10 cases for Genentech in courts throughout the United States in the field of biotechnology. The verdict she won in Glaxo v Genentech was cited by the National Law Journal as 'defense verdict of the year'. She also has been counsel to DuPont in several areas, including genetically modified plants, contrast agents, polymers and paints. Ms Ben-Ami has litigated approximately 10 cases for Pfizer Inc. in the medical device area. She is lead counsel to Hoffman LaRoche in the Amgen v. Roche

patent case featured in The New York Times and represents several pharmaceutical companies, including Pfizer and Wyeth, in patent cases where generics seek to enter the market by copying patented medicines.

**Prof. Memberships:** Admitted to practice in New York and before the Federal Circuit. Memberships include: New York State Bar Association; Federal Circuit Bar Association; New York Patent, Trademark and Copyright Law Association; American Intellectual Property Law Association.

**Career:** Formerly Partner and Chair of the Americas Intellectual Property Group at Clifford Chance. Ms Ben-Ami was recently named to the 'American Lawyer's 45 under 45', a selection, based on peer review, of the most accomplished Members of the Private Bar. JD (cum laude), SUNY Buffalo; BS, SUNY Stony Brook; law clerk to Senior Circuit Judge Philip Nichols, Jr, US Court of Appeals for the Federal Circuit, 1984-85.

**Publications:** 'Incomplete DNA Sequences Patented; Action Under New Guidelines Raises Questions, Concerns', New York Law Journal, March 15, 1999 (co-author); 'Unpredictability Factor Narrows Biotech Patents', The National Law Journal, June 16, 1997 (co-author).

## BENEDICT, James
Milbank, Tweed, Hadley & McCloy LLP, New York 212 530 5000
*Recommended in Litigation*

## BENNER, Michael B
Wachtell, Lipton, Rosen & Katz, New York 212 403 1253
mbbenner@wlrk.com
*Recommended in Real Estate*

**Practice Areas:** Specializes in real estate.

**Prof. Memberships:** The Association of the Bar of the City of New York; American Bar Association.

**Career:** Partner at Wachtell, Lipton, Rosen & Katz.

**Personal:** Graduated summa cum laude from Dartmouth College in 1977 (BA) and cum laude from Harvard Law School in 1980 (JD).

## BERCHEM, Kerry E
Akin Gump Strauss Hauer & Feld LLP, New York 212 872 1095
kberchem@akingump.com
*Recommended in Corporate/M&A*

**Practice Areas:** Acts as corporate advisory and transactional counsel to official and informal creditors' committees, typically comprised of hedge funds, insurance companies and institutional investors, as well as US and offshore companies, with an emphasis on out-of-court and Chapter 11 corporate restructurings. Advises companies and boards of directors in a variety of industries on mergers and acquisitions, securities, general corporate governance, corporate finance and Sarbanes-Oxley matters.

**Prof. Memberships:** New York Bar Association; Connecticut Bar Association; American College of Investment Counsel; Yale Alumni School Committee
**Personal:** BA, Yale University (1988); JD (cum laude), Tulane University (1991).

## BERG, Andrew
Debevoise & Plimpton LLP, New York
212 909 6000
*Recommended in Tax*

## BERG, Eric L
White & Case LLP, New York
212 819 8253
eberg@whitecase.com
*Recommended in Banking & Finance*
**Practice Areas:** Member of the firm's Management Board and Head of its Global Bank Finance Practice. Represents leading commercial and investment banks in a broad range of matters, including representing lead agents and underwriters in leveraged finance transactions. Extensive experience includes hostile takeovers as well as negotiated public and private acquisitions. Numerous and varied representations of banks in Chapter 11 proceedings, restructurings of leveraged financings and other reorganization and workout matters.
**Career:** BA, cum laude, Muhlenberg College, 1978; JD, magna cum laude, Cornell Law School, 1981, Order of the Coif.

## BERGER, Max
Bernstein Litowitz Berger & Grossmann LLP, New York 212 554 1403
mwb@blbglaw.com
*Recommended in Litigation*
**Practice Areas:** Complex litigation; securities fraud litigation; derivative actions; accounting malpractice; directors and officers liability; employment discrimination; civil rights.
**Prof. Memberships:** Advisor, American Law Institute, Restatement Third of Torts; Member, Dean's Council and the Board of Visitors, Columbia Law School; Member, Board of Trustees, Baruch College; 2006 Distinguished Alumnus, Baruch College; Member, Advisory Board, Columbia Law School Center on Corporate Governance; past Chairman, Commercial Litigation Section of the Association of Trial Lawyers of America.
**Career:** Litigation counsel to many public and private institutional investors. Lead counsel in many of the largest and most significant securities cases in history including $6.15 billion recovery of WorldCom securities litigation, $3.2 billion recovery in Cendant securities litigation, and $960 million partial settlement of McKesson HBOC securities litigation. Honored for outstanding contribution to public interest by Trial Lawyers For Public Justice as 1997 Trial Lawyer of the Year Finalist for work as lead counsel in precedent-setting discrimination case Roberts, et al v Texaco, on behalf of Texaco's African-American employees.
**Publications:** Has written and lectured extensively on securities fraud, shareholder rights and corporate governance trends.
**Personal:** Baruch College, 1968; Columbia University Law School, 1971; editor, Columbia Survey of Human Rights Law

## BERGMANN, Peter G
Cadwalader, Wickersham & Taft LLP, New York 212 504 6595
peter.bergmann@cwt.com
*Recommended in Healthcare*
**Practice Areas:** Concentrates on healthcare litigation; general counsel to the New York Association of Homes and Services for the Aging and counsel to the New York State Association of Counties on Medicaid reimbursement matters.
**Personal:** JD, George Washington University Law School (1973). Law clerk, Chief Judge of the United States District Court for the Northern District of New York. Member, American Bar Association (former Chairman, Regional Forum on Health Law); the Federal Bar Council; and the New York County Lawyers' Association.

## BERGTRAUM, Howard M
O'Melveny & Myers LLP, New York
212 408 2408
hbergtraum@omm.com
*Recommended in Private Fund Formation*
**Practice Areas:** Howard Bergtraum, Co-Head of O'Melveny & Myers' Private Equity Fund Practice, counsels fund sponsors in matters related to the formation and operation of venture capital funds, mezzanine funds, buyout funds, hedge funds, fund of funds and secondary funds. He also represents institutional investors in connection with their investments in private equity funds and in the formation of feeder funds and parallel investment vehicles to suit the needs of both institutional and high net worth individual investors. Howard advises a number of major financial institutions on the creation of equity participation plans for their executives. These funds cover a broad range of sectors and geographic areas. Howard is representing the Private Equity 754 Coalition with respect to mandatory Section 754 elections under the Internal Revenue Code in connection with legislation before Congress. Prior to focusing in matters related to private equity funds, Howard's practice included extensive experience in mergers and acquisitions, securities laws and tax, giving an indepth understanding of the needs of a private equity fund in relation to its investments. He has also served as an attorney-advisor at the United States Securities and Exchange Commission.

## BERKOWITZ, Philip M
Nixon Peabody LLP, New York
212 940 3128
pberkowitz@nixonpeabody.com
*Recommended in Employment*
**Practice Areas:** Represents corporate clients: alleged discrimination; harassment; wrongful dismissal; Sarbanes-Oxley whistle-blowing and retaliation claims; ERISA fiduciary breach, denial of benefits claims; employment contracts; restrictive covenants. Litigates trade secret, non-compete cases. Cases: federal and state courts, arbitrations in domestic and international forums. Chair Nixon Peabody International Labor and Employment Team.
**Prof. Memberships:** Chair, American Bar Association, International Labour & Employment Law Committee, International Law and Practice Section (1998-2002); Co-Chair, NYS Bar Association, International Labour and Employment Law Committee (2003-present); Member, Japan Society Corporate Council Advisory Board (2004-present).
**Career:** Partner: Nixon Peabody LLP. Previously: Seyfarth Shaw; Salans; Epstein Becker & Green. Associate, Epstein Becker & Green, P.C.
**Publications:** Columnist, 'Employment Law Issues', New York Law Journal (1999-present); co-editor, 'International Labor and Employment Law: A Practical Guide', American Bar Ass'n (2006); author, 'Sarbanes-Oxley Act – Whistleblower Regulations', National Law Journal (Sept 20, 2004); 'Arbitration of Employment Disputes in the Securities Industry' Int'l Bar Ass'n Journal (April 1999); 'The Volkswagen-General Motors Trade Secrets Lawsuit, Its Settlement: Avoiding the Lopez Effect', Int'l HR Journal (Sept 1997).
**Personal:** Education: Cornell Law School, visiting student, 1977-78; Northwestern School of Law, JD 1978; State University of New York College at New Paltz, BA English and Journalism 1975.

## BERNSTEIN, David
Debevoise & Plimpton LLP, New York
212 909 6000
*Recommended in Intellectual Property*

## BERNSTEIN, Donald S
Davis Polk & Wardwell, New York
212 450 4000
donald.bernstein@dpw.com
*Recommended in Bankruptcy*
**Practice Areas:** Partner, Davis Polk & Wardwell, concentrating in insolvency. Represents creditors, debtors, liquidators, receivers, indenture trustees and acquirers in major corporate restructurings and insolvencies. Recent matters include Delphi, Refco, Enron, Conseco, Adelphia, Bethlehem Steel, Polaroid, McLeodUSA, Dow Corning, Memorex Telex, R.H. Macy, Morrison-Knudsen, Drexel Burnham Lambert, Crown Paper, U.S. Office Products and Toshoku America. Also advises financial institutions and other clients regarding credit risks involved in derivatives, securities transactions, and other domestic and international financial transactions.
**Prof. Memberships:** Chairman, National Bankruptcy Conference. Director, American College of Bankruptcy, International Insolvency Institute. Past Chairman, New York City Bar Association Committee on Corporate Reorganization. Board of Editors, 'Collier on Bankruptcy'. Member, US delegation to UNCITRAL Insolvency Working Group.
**Personal:** Princeton (AB) and University of Chicago (JD).

## BERNSTEIN, Michael
Bond, Schoeneck & King, PLLC, New York 646 253 2310
mbernstein@bsk.com
*Recommended in Employment*
**Practice Areas:** Represents management in every facet of labor and employment law; served as Chair of the Labor and Employment Law Section of New York State Bar Association, the Labor Committee of the New York City Bar Association and the Federal Labor Standards Legislation Committee of the American Bar Association; appointed to Task Forces of Governor and Lieutenant Governor of New York; elected Fellow to College of Labor and Employment Lawyers and to New York Bar Foundation; active lecturer and author.
**Personal:** University of Michigan (BA, Economics, 1959); Columbia University Law School (1962).

## BERNSTEIN, William
Manatt Phelps & Phillips LLP, New York
212 790 4500
*Recommended in Healthcare*

## BERSHAD, David
Milberg Weiss Bershad & Schulman LLP, New York 212 594 5300
*Recommended in Litigation*

## BETENSKY, Steven
White & Case LLP, New York
212 819 8497
SBetensky@whitecase.com
*Recommended in Technology*
**Practice Areas:** Chair of the firm's Global Technology Practice Group. Concentrates in patent, trademark and technology licenses, technology transfers, IT-related acquisitions, outsourcing arrangements, technology development agreements and collaborations, and technology diligence reviews, particularly in connection with cross-border transactions. Also litigates IP-related disputes. Clients include those in the pharmaceutical, electronic, computer software, petrochemical and finance industries.
**Prof. Memberships:** New York State Bar; US District Court for the Southern District of New York; US Courts of Appeals for the Federal Circuit; American Intel-

lectual Property Law Association.
**Personal:** Oberlin College (BA, honors, 1986); University of Chicago Law School (JD, honors, 1989).

### BEVILACQUA, Louis
Cadwalader, Wickersham & Taft LLP, New York 212 504 6057
louis.bevilacqua@cwt.com
*Recommended in Corporate/M&A*
**Practice Areas:** Chairman, Corporate/Mergers and Acquisitions Department. Concentrates in corporate transactions, securities law, mergers and acquisitions. Represents clients in public offerings, tender offers, mergers, leveraged buyouts, proxy contests, joint ventures, exchange offers, private placements of debt and equity securities. Significant experience in international transactions, including acquisitions and securities matters. Provides legal advice for public and private companies in variety of areas, including contractual negotiation, financial structuring, corporate governance, other general legal matters. Served as special counsel to Independent Directors Committees in complex international mergers, contested going-private transactions, leveraged buyouts. Frequently lectures on domestic and international corporate and securities law.
**Prof. Memberships:** New York State Bar; New York County Lawyers Association; American Bar Association.
**Publications:** 'Have Corporate Reforms Gone Too Far? The Hidden Costs of Tighter Controls', Chief Executive, June 2004; 'The New SEC Disclosure Rules', The Corporate Board, May 1, 2004; 'Disclosure Under Sarbanes-Oxley: an Assessment and a Look Forward', Directorship, December 1, 2003.
**Personal:** JD, Fordham University School of Law (1977); MBA, New York University (1977); BA, Holy Cross College (1970).

### BIALKIN, Kenneth J
Skadden, Arps, Slate, Meagher & Flom LLP & Affiliates, New York
212 735 2130
kbialkin@skadden.com
*Recommended in Corporate/M&A*
**Practice Areas:** Extensive experience in representing insurance companies, broker-dealers, investment banks and other financial institutions. Has represented US and non-US companies invovled in US public and private offerings, and government and regulatory investigations by such agencies as the SEC and the Department of Justice.
**Prof. Memberships:** Legal Advisory Committee (or subcommittees thereof) of the Board of Directors of the New York Stock Exchange, Inc. (1981-present); Chair, Ad Hoc Committee on Insider Trading Legislation, Business Law Section, American Bar Association (1987-present).

**Career:** JD, Harvard Law School, 1953; Certificate of Attendance, London School of Economics, 1952; AB, University of Michigan, 1950.

### BICK, John
Davis Polk & Wardwell, New York
212 450 4000
john.bick@dpw.com
*Recommended in Private Equity*
**Practice Areas:** Member of Davis Polk & Wardwell's Corporate Department and advises clients in mergers and acquisitions, private equity transactions, joint ventures, partnerships, takeover defenses, and corporate governance issues. Also represents clients in general corporate and securities law matters. Works extensively in the area of private equity, regularly representing Morgan Stanley Capital Partners, Morgan Stanley Venture Partners, Metalmark Capital Partners and Tailwind Capital Partners. Also regularly represents Morgan Stanley in their strategic private equity investments and other private equity clients of the firm.

### BIENENSTOCK, Martin
Weil, Gotshal & Manges LLP, New York
212 310 8530
martin.bienenstock@weil.com
*Recommended in Bankruptcy*
**Practice Areas:** Martin J Bienenstock is Co-Chair of the Business Finance and Restructuring Department and teaches reorganization at Harvard Law School. His practice incorporates providing legal and strategic advice to directors and management in the conference room, leading complex courtroom battles to win successful reorganizations of companies, and developing and arguing legal theories to win appeals in high courts. Mr Bienenstock specializes in governance advice for healthy and troubled companies, crisis management and restructuring, and in international restructuring, including composing the initial draft of Ireland's reorganization statute.
**Personal:** University of Pennsylvania, BS, 1974; University of Michigan Law School, JD, 1977.

### BIERCE, William
Bierce & Kenerson, P.C., New York
212 840 0080
*Recommended in Business Process Outsourcing, Technology*

### BILKIS, David
White & Case LLP, New York
212 819 8413
dbilkis@whitecase.com
*Recommended in Banking & Finance*
**Practice Areas:** The New York Banking Section's Administrative Partner whose practice focuses on representing leading commercial and investment banks as lead agent and arranger in a variety of lending transactions, with an emphasis on acquisition and leveraged financings. Extensive experience includes negotiated public and

private acquisitions as well as hostile takeovers and exit financings and other restructurings involving borrowers in an array of industries, including manufacturing, gaming, hotel, investment funds, real estate and media and communications.
**Personal:** BA, magna cum laude, Phi Beta Kappa, Brandeis University, 1985; JD, cum laude, with honors, Fordham University School of Law, 1988.

### BIRD, Paul
Debevoise & Plimpton LLP, New York
212 909 6000
*Recommended in Corporate/M&A, Private Equity*

### BIRNBAUM, Sheila L
Skadden, Arps, Slate, Meagher & Flom LLP & Affiliates, New York
212 735 2450
sbirnbau@skadden.com
*Recommended in Insurance, Products Liability*
**Practice Areas:** Head of Skadden's Products Liability Department. Practices primarily in the areas of products liability, toxic torts and insurance coverage litigation. Represents corporations in complex mass tort and insurance litigation.
**Career:** Associate Dean of the Graduate Division (1982-84), Professor of Law (1978-84) and Adjunct Professor of Law (1984-Present), New York University School of Law; Professor of Law, Fordham University School of Law (1972-78).
**Publications:** Co-author, 'Practitioner's Guide to Litigating Insurance Coverage Actions'.
**Personal:** LLB, New York University School of Law, 1965; MA, Hunter College, 1962; BA, Hunter College, 1960 (cum laude; Phi Beta Kappa).

### BLANCHARD, Kimberly S
Weil, Gotshal & Manges LLP, New York
212 310 8799
kim.blanchard@weil.com
*Recommended in Tax*
**Practice Areas:** Kimberly Blanchard's practice encompasses a variety of international transactions involving mergers and acquisitions, private equity investments and joint ventures. She has lectured and published extensively on topics ranging from international tax planning for US businesses to the special tax issues facing foreign persons, pension plans and other exempt investors who invest in US private equity partnerships and in US real estate. Ms Blanchard is the Chair of the Tax Section of the New York State Bar Association.
**Personal:** Dartmouth College, BA, 1976; University of Wisconsin, MS, 1978; New York University School of Law, JD, 1981.

### BLASS, Michael S
Arent Fox PLLC, New York
212 484 3902
blass.michael@arentfox.com
*Recommended in Healthcare*

**Practice Areas:** Concentrates in corporate, transactional, regulatory and other aspects of healthcare law, including acquisitions and divestitures of healthcare facilities and businesses, joint ventures and financing transactions. Has represented some of the nation's largest healthcare companies in hundreds of multi-state acquisitions and divestitures, including the purchase of the nation's largest privately owned home health and home respiratory companies.
**Prof. Memberships:** Member: the American Health Lawyers Association; the Association of the Bar of the City of New York.
**Personal:** Fordham University School of Law, JD 1979; Georgetown University, AB 1976.

### BLASSBERG, Franci
Debevoise & Plimpton LLP, New York
212 909 6000
*Recommended in Private Equity*

### BLESSING, Peter H
Shearman & Sterling LLP, New York
212 848 4106
pblessing@shearman.com
*Recommended in Tax*
**Practice Areas:** Head of firm's International Tax Group, focusing on tax aspects of major business transactions. Also represents clients in transfer pricing matters, ruling requests and controversies.
**Prof. Memberships:** American College of Tax Counsel; ABA Tax Section's Committee on Foreign Activities of US Taxpayers (Chair); International Tax Institute (President); NY State Bar Association Tax Section (Executive Committee); International Fiscal Association (Council Member, USA Branch).
**Publications:** Author of treatise on US tax treaties and numerous other international tax publications.
**Personal:** BA, Princeton University (1973); JD, Columbia University Law School (1977); LLM in Taxation, New York University School of Law (1981).

### BLITTNER, David
Weil, Gotshal & Manges LLP, New York
212 310 8329
david.blittner@weil.com
*Recommended in Private Equity*
**Practice Areas:** David Blittner represents private equity sponsors in connection with acquisitions, dispositions and financings. He has extensive experience with leveraged buyouts and dispositions of public and private companies, as well as with minority investments, public recapitalizations and restructurings. He also counsels clients on general corporate matters, including governance and securities law compliance matters with respect to portfolio company investments, proposed acquisitions and equity capital markets liquidity events.
**Personal:** SUNY Binghamton, BA, 1988; Columbia University School of Law, JD, 1991.

## BLOCK, Dennis

Cadwalader, Wickersham & Taft LLP,
New York 212 504 5555
dennis.block@cwt.com
*Recommended in Corporate/M&A*

**Practice Areas:** Specializes in mergers
and acquisitions, other corporate transactions, corporate governance, securities
law. Handles M&A transactions, hostile
and friendly, for acquirers and targets,
joint ventures, self-tender offers, spin-
offs, other corporate restructurings.
Highly visible transactions include Procter & Gamble's acquisition of Gillette,
Pfizer Inc.'s acquisition of Pharmacia,
Vivendi Universal's acquisition of
Houghton Mifflin Co., Pepsi-Cola's
acquisition of Quaker Oats, Pfizer Inc.'s
acquisition of Warner-Lambert, AT&T's
acquisition of Media One, US West's
merger with Qwest. Represents boards
and board committees in corporate
transactions, public companies, investment and commercial banks, entrepreneurs in connection with major issues,
including the Business Roundtable (corporate governance issues), Texaco (discrimination matters), Cendant directors,
and Merrill Lynch (lead negotiator, $1
billion industry settlement, Nasdaq trading).

**Publications:** 'The Business Judgment
Rule: Fiduciary Duties of Corporate
Directors' (co-author); 'The Corporate
Counsellor's Deskbook' (co-editor);
monthly column, New York Law Journal;
Member, editorial boards of several legal
publications.

**Personal:** JD, Brooklyn Law School;
Adjunct Professor, Advanced Corporate
Law, Brooklyn Law School; Former
Branch Chief of Enforcement, New York
Regional Office of the Securities and
Exchange Commission.

## BOAST, Molly

Debevoise & Plimpton LLP, New York
212 909 6000
*Recommended in Antitrust*

## BOHM, Richard

Debevoise & Plimpton LLP, New York
212 909 6000
*Recommended in Media &
Entertainment, Private Equity*

## BOHRER, Barry

Morvillo, Abramowitz, Grand, Iason &
Silberberg, PC, New York
212 856 9600
*Recommended in Litigation*

## BOIES, David

Boies, Schiller & Flexner LLP, Armonk
914 749 8200
dboies@bsfllp.com
*Recommended in Antitrust, Litigation*

**Practice Areas:** David Boies is Chairman of the law firm of Boies, Schiller &
Flexner LLP, and widely regarded as one
of the nation's preeminent trial lawyers.
As the citation for the Milton Gould

Award for Outstanding Oral Advocacy
said, "No lawyer in America has tried and
argued on appeal as many landmark
cases in as many different areas as Mr
Boies". Mr Boies' notable matters include:
counsel to the Federal Deposit Insurance
Corporation in litigation to recover losses
for failed savings and loan associations;
Special Trial Counsel for the US Department of Justice in its antitrust suit against
Microsoft; lead counsel for former Vice
President Al Gore in the 2000 election litigation; lead trial counsel for Lloyd's of
London in a successful 11 week trial con-
cerning property insurance coverage for
destruction of the World Trade Center on
September 11, 2001; lead counsel for
Maurice R 'Hank' Greenberg, former
Chairman and Chief Executive Officer of
American International Group in exten-
sive investigations, regulatory and civil
proceedings; and, most recently, lead
counsel for the Alaska Gasline Port
Authority in its antitrust lawsuit against
ExxonMobil and BP for colluding to pre-
vent the sale of natural gas from the
North Slope of Alaska.

**Prof. Memberships:** Member, New York
State Bar; Phi Beta Kappa; Fellow of the
American College of Trial Lawyers; Fel-
low of the International Academy of Trial
Lawyers; Trustee of St. Luke's/Roosevelt
Hospital Medical Center; Trustee of Con-
tinuum Health Partners, Inc.

**Career:** Founder and Chairman, Boies,
Schiller & Flexner LLP (1997-present);
Cravath, Swaine & Moore (1966-77,
1980-97); Chief Counsel and Staff Director, US Senate Antitrust Subcommittee
(1978); Chief Counsel and Staff Director,
US Senate Judiciary Committee (1979).

**Publications:** Courting Justice (2004);
Public Control of Business (1977).

**Personal:** BS (1964) Northwestern; LLB
magna cum laude (1966) Yale; LLM
(1967) New York University; LLD, University of Redlands; William Brennan
Award from the University of Virginia
and numerous professional and charitable awards.

## BOISSEAU, Jane

LeBoeuf, Lamb, Greene & MacRae LLP,
New York 212 424 8644
jane.boisseau@llgm.com
*Recommended in Insurance*

**Practice Areas:** Co-Chair of the firm's
insurance regulatory practice and a
member of the executive committee, with
substantial experience in insurance regulatory and transactional matters, many of
which involve cross-border dimensions.
Ms Boisseau advises US and international
clients in the insurance and reinsurance
industries on regulatory aspects of various transactions, including M&A, securitizations, securities offerings and reinsurance transactions. She also counsels
clients regarding regulatory examinations
and government investigations.

**Career:** Joined LeBoeuf Lamb in 1985.

**Publications:** 'Liability of Brokers,
Agents, and Intermediaries in Insurer
Insolvency', Insurance Company Solven-
cy (1991).

**Personal:** New York University (JD)
1985; University of New Orleans (BA)
1967.

## BOND, W Michael

Weil, Gotshal & Manges LLP, New York
212 310 8035
michael.bond@weil.com
*Recommended in Real Estate*

**Practice Areas:** Michael Bond co-heads
the Real Estate Transaction and Finance
Practice. He represents financial institutions in diverse transactional matters,
helps create joint ventures and has extensive experience in restructurings, bankruptcy and related issues. He advises
clients such as investment banks, money
center banks and insurance companies
on general corporate issues, mortgage-
backed securitizations, commercial lending transactions, company and asset
portfolio acquisitions, and private equity
and real estate transactions. He represents
capital sources and providers of products
or services in forming joint ventures and
strategic alliances for new businesses.

**Personal:** University of South Carolina,
BS, 1977; University of Virginia, JD, 1980.

## BOROWITZ, Peter

Debevoise & Plimpton LLP, New York
212 909 6000
*Recommended in Bankruptcy*

## BOWIE, Scott O

Linklaters, New York
212 903 9161
scott.bowie@linklaters.com
*Recommended in Private Fund
Formation*

**Practice Areas:** Practice leader in private equity and investment management
and represents a broad array of private
equity fund managers, debt and other
investment fund sponsors/managers and
has raised funds, including buyout, venture capital, real estate, debt and hedge
funds, which range from $100 million to
$6 billion of committed capital.

**Prof. Memberships:** New York and California Bar Associations.

**Personal:** Received his JD from the University of California, Los Angeles in 1988
and received his AB from Occidental College in 1984.

## BOXER, Leonard

Stroock & Stroock & Lavan LLP,
New York 212 806 5400
*Recommended in Real Estate*

## BRACH, Richard

Milbank, Tweed, Hadley & McCloy LLP,
New York 212 530 5000
*Recommended in Projects*

## BRANDES, Lawrence

Cadwalader, Wickersham & Taft LLP,
New York 212 504 6946
larry.brandes@cwt.com
*Recommended in Insurance*

**Practice Areas:** Experienced reinsurance litigator who has acted as counsel,
arbitrator or umpire in over 500 reinsurance arbitrations and litigations, a number of which have established industry
precedents. A frequent lecturer on reinsurance arbitration and litigation, he has
addressed the Independent Reinsurance
Underwriters, the Society of CPCU, the
American Bar Association, the British
Commercial Bar Association, Executive
Enterprises, Inc., and numerous Mealey's
conferences. Served as Co-Chair of
Mealey's 2003 Insurance Insolvency and
Reinsurance Roundtable.

**Prof. Memberships:** Member, New York
State Bar Association; American Bar
Association – Tort and Insurance Practice
Section; Association of the Bar of the City
of New York (served as a Member of the
Insurance Law Committee and Chair-
man of the Reinsurance Subcommittee);
British Commercial Bar Association
(Honorary Overseas Member).

**Personal:** JD, New York University
School of Law (Member of the New York
University Law Review, 1974). BA, University of Virginia (with distinction,
1971); Former Executive Vice President
of APP-CAP Reinsurance Company, Ltd.,
Hamilton, Bermuda; former Chairman
of the Board of Directors of National
Consulting Services, Inc., a professional
reinsurance auditing company.

## BRANNAN, William

Cravath, Swaine & Moore LLP, New York
212 474 1600
wbrannan@cravath.com
*Recommended in Tax*

**Practice Areas:** Wide variety of domestic and international transactions, including securities offerings, mergers and
acquisitions, investment partnerships and
real estate (including REIT) transactions.

**Prof. Memberships:** NYSBA (member
of the Executive Committee of the Tax
Section; Co-Chair of Committee on Real
Property); ABA; ABCNY; NAREIT; Pen-
sion Real Estate Association; Tax Club of
New York City.

**Career:** Joined firm in 1983; Partner
since 1991.

**Publications:** Has written numerous
tax-related papers and Bar Association
reports and is a frequent speaker at tax-
related seminars and professional programs.

**Personal:** Harvard Law School (JD,
magna cum laude, 1983); Vanderbilt University (BS, summa cum laude, 1980).

## BREGLIO, John F
Paul, Weiss, Rifkind, Wharton & Garrison LLP, New York 212 373 3391
jbreglio@paulweiss.com
*Recommended in Media & Entertainment*
**Practice Areas:** Chair of Entertainment Department. Member of Intellectual Property Group. Represents companies and individuals involved in all aspects of the entertainment industry, including legitimate theater, motion picture, publishing and music businesses, and intellectual property matters. Has been instrumental in assisting his clients develop, finance and produce hundreds of plays, musicals and films for more than 30 years. Has extensive experience ranging from advising film, television, and video companies develop, finance and distribute entertainment products to advising Broadway producers and theater owners on producing and presenting plays and musicals. Selected for 2006 edition of The Best Lawyers in America.

## BRENNAN, Matthew J
Sullivan & Cromwell LLP, New York 212 558 4000
brennanm@sullcrom.com
*Recommended in Environment*
**Practice Areas:** Advises on environmental issues in commercial transactions for the firm's corporate, M&A, project finance, real estate, securities and finance groups. Evaluates environmental liabilities and risks, structures transactions to minimize risk and negotiates environmental risk allocation among parties in commercial transactions. 20 years' experience providing environmental advice to a diverse clientele, including corporations, lenders and governments.
**Prof. Memberships:** ABA; ABCNY.
**Career:** Special counsel since 1998.
**Personal:** State University of New York at New Paltz (BA, 1979); University of Pennsylvania Law School (JD, 1986).

## BRESLOW, Stephanie
Schulte Roth & Zabel LLP, New York 212 756 2542
stephanie.breslow@srz.com
*Recommended in Private Fund Formation*
**Practice Areas:** Investment management, partnerships and securities.
**Prof. Memberships:** Association of the Bar of the City of New York, including Corporation Law Committee (1993-96), Chair, Subcommittee on Business Trusts (1995-96); Member, Committee on the Revised Uniform Partnership Act (1993-96); founding Member and Steering Committee, Wall Street Hedge Fund Forum; founding Member and past Chair, Private Investment Fund Forum; Committee of Hearts 2003-04, Hedge Funds Care; and Member of the Board of Trustees, The Joyce Theater, New York.
**Career:** Partner since 1996.

**Publications:** Has lectured and written extensively on matters related to investment management, partnerships and securities law.
**Personal:** Recognized in 'Who's Who Legal, The International Who's Who of Business Lawyers' 2002, 2003, 2004, 2005; Chambers Global – The World's Leading Lawyers, 2002, 2003, 2004 and 2005; 'America's Leading Lawyers 2005'

## BRITTENHAM, David
Debevoise & Plimpton LLP, New York 212 909 6000
*Recommended in Banking & Finance, Capital Markets*

## BRODSKY, David
Latham & Watkins LLP, New York 212 906 1200
*Recommended in Litigation*

## BROMLEY, James L
Cleary Gottlieb Steen & Hamilton LLP, New York 212 225 2264
jbromley@cgsh.com
*Recommended in Bankruptcy*
**Practice Areas:** Bankruptcy, workout and acquisition advice to debtors, creditors and strategic investors, and commercial litigation involving bankruptcy and insolvency matters. He has substantial experience in international restructurings with complex cross-border issues that have involved the US, Canada, Mexico, EU, Japan, Korea and Hong Kong. He has particular expertise in M&A in the insolvency context. Notable transactions: Covanta Energy's successful reorganization, SK Networks' $7 billion debt restructuring, Daewoo Motors' sale of its Korean automotive business to a joint venture controlled by General Motors, and representation of Lehman Brothers, Goldman Sachs and other major investment banks relating to NOL trading orders.

## BROUDE, Mark
Latham & Watkins LLP, New York 212 906 1200
*Recommended in Bankruptcy*

## BROWN, Dickson G
Simpson Thacher & Bartlett LLP, New York 212 455 2850
dbrown@stblaw.com
*Recommended in Tax*
**Practice Areas:** A senior member of the firm's Tax Department. Areas of concentration are federal income tax with an emphasis on financial instruments, domestic and foreign joint ventures, mergers and acquisitions and financial institutions. Advises on various financial products such as hybrid debt instruments, tracking stock, trust preferred securities and investment units, cross-border and domestic joint ventures, and structuring of foreign operations.
**Prof. Memberships:** Member of the Bar Association of the City of New York, the New York and American Bar Associations.

**Career:** Joined Simpson Thacher in 1971 and became a Partner in 1978.
**Personal:** Received BA (1968) from the University of Michigan and was elected Phi Beta Kappa; received JD (1971) from University of Michigan School of Law and also elected Order of the Coif. Earned an LLM in 1975 from New York University.

## BROWN, Elliot
Franklin, Weinrib, Rudell & Vassallo, New York 212 935 5500
*Recommended in Media & Entertainment*

## BROWNSTEIN, Andrew R
Wachtell, Lipton, Rosen & Katz, New York 212 403 1233
arbrownstein@wlrk.com
*Recommended in Corporate/M&A*
**Practice Areas:** Specializes in mergers and acquisitions, takeovers, leveraged buyouts, corporate governance and securities law matters. Has been a leading participant in numerous landmark and precedent setting transactions, including: the takeover defenses of Household International, Inc., Phillips Petroleum Company, and Revlon, Inc.; the complex restructurings of W.R. Grace & Co.'s medical services and packaging divisions in successive Morris Trust transactions with Fresenius AG and Sealed Air Corporation; Sears' merger with Kmart; the merger of Conoco and Phillips Petroleum; Amoco Corporation's merger with British Petroleum Company p.l.c. and Reynolds Metals Company's merger with Alcoa Inc. More recently represented ConocoPhillips in its acquisition of Burlington Resources; Novartis in its acquisitions of Hexal and Eon Labs and SuperValu in its acquisition of Albertson's, Inc. Also represents several leading private equity investors, including Apollo Advisors, L.P., Merrill Lynch and Warburg Pincus LLC.
**Prof. Memberships:** Has been an Adjunct Professor of Securities Law at Rutgers University Law School; is past Chairman of the Ray Garrett Jr Corporate and Securities Law Institute at Northwestern University School of Law and is on the Executive Planning Committee of that institute; and is Chairman of the Annual M&A Lawyers Institute held in New York City.
**Career:** Partner at Wachtell, Lipton, Rosen & Katz since 1985, Member of the Management Group of the firm and responsible for the day to day operations of the firm's Corporate Group. Clerked for the Honorable Leonard Garth of the US Court of Appeals for the Third Circuit.
**Publications:** Frequent author and lecturer on legal subjects.
**Personal:** Graduated from the University of Pennsylvania in 1975 (BA, English, BS, Economics), from the Wharton School of the University of Pennsylvania in 1976

(MBA) and from Harvard Law School in 1979 (JD), where he was articles editor of the Harvard Law Review.

## BROZMAN, Tina L
Bingham McCutchen LLP, New York 212 705 7756
tina.brozman@bingham.com
*Recommended in Bankruptcy*
**Practice Areas:** Serves as co-leader of firm's Financial Restructuring Group and Deputy Chair of the firm's Finance Area. Focuses on US and international financial restructuring issues, serving clients around the world.
**Career:** Served nearly four years as Chief Judge of the Southern District of New York Bankruptcy Court and as a Member of the Second Circuit Bankruptcy Appellate Panel. Issued more than 150 published decisions on a wide range of bankruptcy issues.
**Personal:** Fordham University School of Law, JD, 1976; New York University, BA, 1973.

## BUHLE, Warren
Weil, Gotshal & Manges LLP, New York 212 310 8898
warren.buhle@weil.com
*Recommended in Banking & Finance*
**Practice Areas:** Warren T Buhle is a Member of the firm's Corporate Department specializing in representing lenders and borrowers in a wide variety of financial transactions, such as secured and unsecured credit facilities, leveraged leases, healthcare financings, restructurings, acquisition financings, letter of credit facilities, inventory and receivables borrowing base financings, tax-exempt revenue bond transactions and commercial paper facilities. Mr Buhle's areas of particular concentration include aircraft and maritime finance, bank credit facilities, equipment leveraged leasing and healthcare finance.
**Personal:** Johns Hopkins University, BA, 1973; Columbia University School of Law, JD, 1976.

## BURESH, James
Simpson Thacher & Bartlett LLP, New York 212 455 7221
jburesh@stblaw.com
*Recommended in Banking & Finance*
**Practice Areas:** Corporate Partner advising clients in banking and credit and capital markets and securities matters.
**Prof. Memberships:** Admitted to practice in New York (1989). Member, American Bar Association.
**Career:** Joined Simpson Thacher in 1987; became Partner in 1997.
**Personal:** Received JD, 1986, Yale Law School; notes editor, Yale Law Journal. Received AB, with honors, 1983, The University of Chicago.

## BURKE, Ted
Freshfields Bruckhaus Deringer LLP, New York 212 277 4000
*Recommended in Projects*

## BURLEIGH, Jennifer
Debevoise & Plimpton LLP, New York
212 909 6000
*Recommended in Private Fund Formation*

## BYOWITZ, Michael H
Wachtell, Lipton, Rosen & Katz,
New York 212 403 1268
mhbyowitz@wlrk.com
*Recommended in Antitrust*
**Practice Areas:** Specializes in antitrust law and policy, principally advising multinational corporations on major domestic and international mergers, acquisitions, joint ventures and corporate takeovers. Represents many clients at the Department of Justice, the Federal Trade Commission, and State Attorneys General in the United States and consults on investigations by foreign antitrust authorities in the European Union, Australia, Canada, Mexico, South America, the United Kingdom and many other jurisdictions.
**Prof. Memberships:** A leader of the American Bar Association's Section of International Law and Practice; Chair of the Section and the former Chair of its Business Regulation Division, its General Division, its Public International Law Division and its International Antitrust Law Committee. Former Chair of the Antitrust and Trade Regulation Committee of the Association of the Bar of the City of New York.
**Career:** Partner at Wachtell, Lipton, Rosen & Katz, where he heads the Antitrust Department. Served as Senior Trial Attorney and Trial Attorney with the Department of Justice's Antitrust Division from 1979-83.
**Publications:** Writes articles on antitrust issues and is a contributor to legal publications, including the international antitrust law chapter of the ABA's 'The International Lawyer's Deskbook'. Frequent speaker on International Antitrust Law and Compliance in the United States and abroad.
**Personal:** Graduated from Columbia University in 1973 (AB) and from New York University School of Law in 1976 (JD), where he was awarded the Order of the Coif and served as an editor of the Law Review.

## BYRNE, Lawrence
White & Case LLP, New York
212 819 8336
lbyrne@whitecase.com
*Recommended in Litigation*
**Practice Areas:** Handles complex white-collar criminal, government regulatory and civil litigation matters. Has particular experience in antitrust, securities, class action defense, commercial, bankruptcy, and First Amendment and media litigation, as well as representation of clients involved in government and internal investigations and related trial

and appellate matters.
**Prof. Memberships:** Securities Industry Association; Federal Bar Council; ABCNY; ABA.
**Career:** White & Case since 2002.
**Publications:** Extensive writings on securities law.
**Personal:** Hofstra University (BA 1981); New York University School of Law (JD 1984).

## CAGNEY, Lawrence
Debevoise & Plimpton LLP, New York
212 909 6000
*Recommended in Employee Benefits*

## CAMPBELL, Woodrow
Debevoise & Plimpton LLP, New York
212 909 6000
*Recommended in Private Fund Formation*

## CANELLOS, Peter C
Wachtell, Lipton, Rosen & Katz,
New York 212 403 1000
pcanellos@wlrk.com
*Recommended in Tax*
**Practice Areas:** Specializes in the tax aspects of the corporate acquisitions, dispositions and financings that constitute Wachtell, Lipton, Rosen & Katz's major practice areas, whose large and complex transactions frequently involve multinational tax considerations.
**Prof. Memberships:** Served as Chairman of the New York State Bar Association Tax Section.
**Career:** Partner at Wachtell, Lipton, Rosen & Katz. Clerked for the Honorable Judge Charles D Breitel of the New York Court of Appeals and was a Fulbright Scholar at the University of Amsterdam in the Netherlands.
**Publications:** Frequent writer and lecturer on tax matters. General Reporter, International Fiscal Association, International Mergers and Acquisitions (2005). Published articles include: 'Contingency and the Debt/Equity Continuum' (with Deborah Paul, in the Journal of Financial Products, 2002); 'A Tax Practitioner's Perspective on Substance, Form and Business Purpose in Structuring Business Transactions and in Tax Shelters' (in SMU Law Review, 2001); 'Reasonable Expectations and the Taxation of Contingencies' (in Tax Lawyer, 1997); 'Dividend Access Shares' (49th IFA Congress, Cannes, 1995); and 'Corporate Inversions and Similar Transactions' (in the 54th NYU Annual Institute on Federal Taxation, 1995).
**Personal:** Graduated summa cum laude from Columbia University (BA), where he was elected to Phi Beta Kappa, and magna cum laude from Columbia Law School in 1967 (LLB), where he was Editor-in-Chief of Columbia Law Review.

## CANONI, John
Nixon Peabody LLP, New York
212 940 3169
jcanoni@nixonpeabody.com
*Recommended in Employment*
**Practice Areas:** Mr Canoni handles a wide range of labor and employment matters including: NLRB, contract negotiations, arbitrations, employment discrimination, FMLA and ADA. He represents major media, insurance, utility, and construction companies.
**Prof. Memberships:** Admitted to practice: New York, the US Supreme Court, and the First, Second, Third, Fourth, Fifth, Seventh, and DC Circuit Courts. Member of the CPR Institute for Dispute Resolution's Employment Law Mediator Panel. Listed in 'The Best Lawyers in America' since 1991. Served as Chair of the NYS Bar Association's Labor and Employment Law Section.
**Personal:** Yale Law School, LLB; Amherst College, BA, cum laude.

## CANTOR, Matthew
Kirkland & Ellis LLP, New York
212 446 4846
mcantor@kirkland.com
*Recommended in Bankruptcy*
**Practice Areas:** Mr Cantor focuses his practice on strategic counseling in financial and operational corporate reorganizations. Notable representations include NRG Energy; Allegiance Telecom; Wellman, Inc.; the ad hoc committee of the MAGI bondholders in the Mirant Corporation case; Limbach Facility Services LLC; KMC Telecom; Quality Stores, Inc.; American Commercial Lines, LLC; Ziff-Davis Media; and CornerStone Propane Partners LP. Additionally, Mr Cantor advises buyout, private equity and hedge funds in the management of investments in distressed situations and developing control acquisition strategies.
**Personal:** State University of New York at Binghamton, BA, 1986. New York University School of Law, JD, 1989.

## CAPLAN, David L
Davis Polk & Wardwell, New York
212 450 4000
david.caplan@dpw.com
*Recommended in Corporate/M&A*
**Practice Areas:** Member of Davis Polk & Wardwell's Corporate Department. Advises corporate and investment banking clients in mergers and acquisitions, joint ventures, corporate governance issues and related matters. Regularly represents a number of clients, including Aetna, Canadian National Railway, Comcast, Harvard University, Limited Brands, Lockheed Martin and the New York Mets, in a range of transactions and other matters. Also represents a number of leading investment banking firms in connection with merger and acquisition transactions.

## CAPLAN, Gordon
Willkie Farr & Gallagher LLP, New York
212 728 8266
gcaplan@willkie.com
*Recommended in Technology*
**Practice Areas:** Partner in the Corporate and Financial Services Department, specializing in technology and telecommunications-related corporate matters, buy-outs, venture capital, and recapitalizations. He has extensive experience representing private equity firms as well as public and private companies on a spectrum of corporate matters, including private equity financing, securities offerings, exchange offers, privatizations, mergers and acquisitions, banking, commercial contracts, licensing, and employment issues. He has also been responsible for the structuring, drafting and negotiation of significant technology licensing, procurement, and outsourcing transactions for a number of major telecommunications and technology companies over the last several years. Recent significant matters include representation of Insight Capital Partners and Bain Capital in connection with their joint acquisitions and recapitalizations of Solanoids.net, as well as Insight Capital Partners' leveraged buyout of GFI Software Ltd, a Malta-based software developer. He also represented Sprint Corporation in connection with technology and network integration matters and contracts relating to the Sprint Nextel merger.
**Career:** Admitted to the Bar of the State of New York.
**Publications:** Has published on the subject of high-technology transactions, has lectured on venture capital transactions at Columbia University Graduate School of Business, and has lectured on representing technology and communications clients at Fordham Law School.
**Personal:** Received a JD from Fordham Law School in 1991, where he was an editor of the Fordham Law Review, and a BA from Cornell University College of Arts and Sciences in 1988.

## CAPLAN, Stuart A
White & Case LLP, New York
212 819 8868
scaplan@whitecase.com
*Recommended in Energy*
**Practice Areas:** Draws on over 20 years of experience with state and federal regulation and energy markets to provide strategic counseling. As part of White & Case's energy initiative, he provides regulatory and market expertise to support M&A, securities, project finance, leasing and banking transactions in the energy sector. As lead regulatory counsel to energy companies he advises clients on FERC and state PUC electric and gas proceedings, energy supply and transportation and the evolution of competitive energy markets.
**Prof. Memberships:** Serves on the Ener-

gy Bar Association Board of Directors and speaks regularly on legal and industry issues.

### CARLEEN, Donald P
Fried, Frank, Harris, Shriver & Jacobson LLP, New York 212 859 8202
Donald.Carleen@FriedFrank.com
*Recommended in Employee Benefits*

**Practice Areas:** Chairman of Executive Compensation and Employee Benefits Department. Regularly advises corporations, boards of directors, compensation committees and senior executives on all aspects of executive compensation, ERISA, employee benefits. Advises on these matters in complex mergers and acquisitions, leveraged buyouts, private equity, hedge fund, other investment partnerships, bankruptcy and restructuring transactions.
**Career:** Joined Fried Frank in 1983. Became a Partner in 1987.
**Personal:** JD (1983), summa cum laude, Brooklyn Law School. BA (1977), St. Johns School of Risk Management (formerly The College of Insurance).

### CARPENTIER, Joan-Elisse
McDermott Will & Emery, New York 212 547 5544
jcarpentier@mwe.com
*Recommended in Immigration*

**Practice Areas:** Practices all areas of immigration and nationality law affecting corporations and other businesses in a wide range of industries. Represents artists, entertainers, authors and others in the arts in their immigration matters. Works on behalf of United States citizens and foreign nationals to obtain visas for other countries. Represents clients with respect to immigration compliance issues, including government audits.
**Prof. Memberships:** Member, Massachusetts, New York and California Bars. Member of American Immigration Lawyers Association.
**Personal:** Boston University School of Law (JD); St Lawrence University (BA, cum laude)

### CARROLL, John
Clifford Chance US LLP, New York 212 878 8596
john.carroll@cliffordchance.com
*Recommended in Litigation*

**Practice Areas:** Represents institutional and individual clients in criminal, regulatory and complex commercial disputes. Has represented clients in matters involving federal and state prosecutors, the SEC and other regulators, and the New York Attorney General's Office, including securities fraud and accounting fraud prosecutions and international price-fixing prosecutions. Has represented clients in complex commercial disputes relating to financial products. Has tried numerous jury cases, criminal and civil, and has argued numerous appeals.
**Career:** Partner since 1992. Chief, Secu-

rities and Commodities Fraud Task Force 1991-92. Yale University (BA, English). New York University School of Law (JD, Law Review).

### CARROLL, Michael P
Davis Polk & Wardwell, New York 212 450 4000
michael.carroll@dpw.com
*Recommended in Litigation*

**Practice Areas:** Member of Davis Polk & Wardwell's Litigation Department. He has represented a wide range of clients in federal and state jury trials, and in government investigations and administrative trials. He also defends corporations and boards of directors in federal and state class-action litigation. His most recent trial was the Oracle vs PeopleSoft M&A litigation in Delaware Chancery Court. His work also includes confidential internal investigations on behalf of corporations facing potential criminal and regulatory exposure.

### CASSANOS, Robert
Fried, Frank, Harris, Shriver & Jacobson LLP, New York 212 859 8278
Robert.Cassanos@FriedFrank.com
*Recommended in Tax*

**Practice Areas:** Chairman of the New York Tax Department of Fried Frank. Concentrates his practice in the areas of domestic mergers and acquisitions, cross-border M&A and joint ventures, going-public transactions, international taxation, real estate, hedge funds and investment funds, and structured finance and financial transactions.
**Career:** Joined Fried Frank in 1981. Became a Partner in 1988.
**Publications:** 'Single Taxation of Publicly Traded Entities', 99 Tax Notes 1663, June 16, 2003.
**Personal:** JD (1981), Rutgers University. AB (1974), Cornell University.

### CATILLAZ, Margaret
Harter, Secrest & Emery LLP, Rochester 585 232 6500
*Recommended in Immigration*

### CENDALI, Dale
O'Melveny & Myers LLP, New York 212 326 2051
dcendali@omm.com
*Recommended in Intellectual Property, Media & Entertainment*

**Practice Areas:** Dale Cendali was named by theNational Law Journal as one of America's Top 50 Women Litigators, by IP Worldwide Magazine as one of the Magnificent Seven – IP's Best Young Trial Lawyers and by the Harvard Law Bulletin as one of the Nifty 50, celebrating 50 of Harvard Law's 7,200 women alumnae who have made a name for themselves. Dale is a Partner at O'Melveny & Myers, heads the New York Intellectual Property Department, and is Chair of the Copyright, Trademark and Internet Group. She argued Dastar v Twenti-

eth Century Fox before the US Supreme Court. Dale has successfully handled numerous high profile cases involving such properties as Harry Potter, the X-Men, the X-Files, Gallo Wine, Bratz dolls, Lionel Trains, The City of Heroes video game and individuals such as Martha Graham and O J Simpson. She lectures and writes prolifically and has been the Chair of various committees of the INTA, ABA Litigation Section and the Association of the Bar of the City of New York.

### CERABINO, Thomas M
Willkie Farr & Gallagher LLP, New York 212 728 8208
tcerabino@willkie.com
*Recommended in Corporate/M&A*

**Practice Areas:** Partner in the Corporate and Financial Services Department, Chair of the Mergers & Acquisitions Practice Group, and a Member of the firm's Executive Committee. Specializes in mergers and acquisitions, debt restructurings, debt and equity financings, and general corporate and securities law matters. Recent significant matters include representation of Colony Capital in its $5.5 billion agreement to acquire (with Kingdom Hotels International) Fairmont Hotels & Resorts Inc., and in its $1 billion acquisition of the Raffles hotel business. He also recently advised Ventas, Inc. in its $1.2 billion acquisition of all the outstanding common shares of Provident Senior Living Trust, and an affiliate of Fortress Investment Group LLC in its $530 million agreement to acquire Liberty Group Publishing. Has represented various public and private companies, private equity funds, and investment banking firms in a wide range of domestic and cross-border transactions, including business combinations, divestitures, leveraged buyouts, public and private offerings of securities, and change-of-control matters. Has advised boards of directors and board committees on a variety of governance and other issues.
**Prof. Memberships:** Serves as counsel and a Director of United Neighborhood Houses of New York, Inc., a not-for-profit organization, which is the umbrella organization for the New York City settlement house system, and is a Member of the Board of Regents of Georgetown University. Member of the Association of the Bar of the City of New York, and previously served on its Committee on Securities Regulation (1990-92).
**Career:** Admitted to the Bar of the State of New York.
**Personal:** Received a JD from St John's University School of Law (cum laude) in 1981, where he served as notes and comments editor of the St John's Law Review, and a BSFS from Georgetown University in 1978.

### CHADAKOFF, Richard
Latham & Watkins LLP, New York 212 906 1200
*Recommended in Real Estate*

### CHAFFETZ, Peter
Clifford Chance US LLP, New York 212 878 4910
peter.chaffetz@cliffordchance.com
*Recommended in Insurance*

**Practice Areas:** Serves as global practice leader for litigation and dispute resolution for Clifford Chance. In nearly 20 years as a reinsurance specialist he has led a succession of prominent cases, involving such issues as finite risk covers, the collapse of the workers comp 'carve out' market, pollution and asbestos coverage disputes, disputes arising from managing general agencies, surety reinsurance, the enforceability of cut-through endorsements, insurance insolvency and the destruction of the World Trade Center. Regularly speaks and publishes in the field and has been US legal correspondent for Reinsurance Magazine.

### CHAMLIN, Marc
Loeb & Loeb LLP, New York 212 407 4855
mchamlin@loeb.com
*Recommended in Media & Entertainment*

**Practice Areas:** Represents cable networks, production companies, branded content companies, producers, actors, directors, television series/screenplay writers, book authors, newscasters and advertising/promotion/public relation agencies. Transactional work includes non-scripted and scripted television series development, production and distribution; advertiser-financed television series and television motion picture production; animation and live action television production and distribution; documentary film production; merchandising and licensing; book publishing and co-author agreements; television commercials production; product endorsements; sports tour, event sponsorship and athlete service contracts; infomercials; executive employment contracts.
**Career:** Partner since 1988.
**Personal:** NYU Law School (JD, 1980); Princeton University (AB, 1977, magna cum laude).

### CHARLES, Scott K
Wachtell, Lipton, Rosen & Katz, New York 212 403 1202
skcharles@wlrk.com
*Recommended in Bankruptcy*

**Practice Areas:** Specializes in the areas of commercial transactions, distressed mergers and acquisitions and bankruptcy and has represented many institutional lenders, creditors' committees and distressed securities investors in various troubled debt situations. His recent cases have included Kmart Corporation, Enron Corporation, NRG Corporation, Avianca

Airlines, Calpine Corporation, Footstar, Inc., Frank's Nursery & Crafts, Inc., PSINet, Inc., Spalding Holdings Corporation and Exide Technologies.

**Career:** Partner in the Creditors' Rights Department of Wachtell, Lipton, Rosen & Katz in 1991. Frequently lectures at various seminars conducted by the Practicing Law Institute, the Commercial Finance Association, Turnaround and Management Association and the Continuing Legal Education.

**Publications:** Has authored and co-authored several articles and outlines involving distressed mergers and acquisitions, prepackaged plans of reorganization, debtor-in-possession financing, the rights of secured and unsecured creditors both inside and outside of bankruptcy, and various aspects of the Chapter 11 process.

**Personal:** Graduated from the Wharton School of Business, University of Pennsylvania in 1981 (BS in Economics) and from Harvard Law School in 1984 (JD); Member of Beta Alpha Psi, Beta Gamma Sigma and Phi Beta Kappa.

## CHARNEY, Steven M
Peckar & Abramson PC, New York
212 382 0909
scharney@pecklaw.com
*Recommended in Construction*

**Practice Areas:** Mr Charney's practice includes extensive ongoing representation of the largest contractors in the country as well as developers. Mr Charney's background couples extensive academic and hands-on experience as a contractor prior to entering the practice of law.

**Prof. Memberships:** Mr Charney is a Member of Associated General Contractors of America (AGC) and serves on both the Contract Documents and Risk Management Committees of this leading national organization. He is a Member of the Association of the Bar of the City of New York and served on the Construction Law Subcommittee of that prestigious association. He is also a Member of the American Bar Association and the New York State Bar Association. He is admitted to practice in New York and New Jersey.

**Career:** Managing Partner of the New York office and a member of the firm's Executive Committee. Former Eastern Division Counsel, Assistant Superintendent, Field Engineer and Costs and Scheduling Engineer for Turner Construction Company.

**Publications:** Mr Charney lectures nationally regarding matters related to construction contracting, and frequently presents private lectures and training to the nation's leading contractors. He presented a three-part program before the prestigious Association of the Bar of the City of New York entitled Truly Understanding Construction Contracts. He is a

frequent lecturer before the General Building Contractors of the State of New York, the Construction Financial Managers Association, the New Jersey Building Contractors Association, the American Concrete Institute, Associated General Contractors of America (AGC), National Association of Surety Bond Producers, the Building Trades Employers Association of New York, Risk Management Committee of the AGC, Surety and Bonding Committee of the AGC, the South Florida Chapter of the Associated General Contractors, Associated Minority Enterprises of New York, Insurance Risk Management Institute (IRMI) and the Construction Industry Super Conference and other construction-related organizations. He has also published commentary regarding issues applicable to the construction and developmental industries, including commentary in New York Construction.

**Personal:** Mr Charney is a graduate of Syracuse University, the School of Civil Engineering at New Jersey Institute of Technology, and Seton Hall University School of Law.

## CHATZINOFF, Howard
Weil, Gotshal & Manges LLP, New York
212 310 8340
howard.chatzinoff@weil.com
*Recommended in Corporate/M&A*

**Practice Areas:** Howard Chatzinoff, Co-Chair of the firm's M&A Practice, has a wide-ranging Corporate and Securities Law Practice, with emphasis on public and private M&A transactions, divestitures, spin-offs and joint ventures. In the media sector, he advised CBS in its separation from Viacom and in its acquisitions of College Sports Television and King World Productions. He also counseled GE in its pending sale of GE Insurance Solutions to Swiss Re and its acquisitions of Ionics and InVision Technologies. He also advised Molson in its merger with Coors.

**Personal:** Princeton University, BSE, 1974; University of Virginia, JD, 1977.

## CHENG, Loyti
Davis Polk & Wardwell, New York
212 450 4000
loyti.cheng@dpw.com
*Recommended in Environment*

**Practice Areas:** Counsel in Davis Polk & Wardwell's Corporate Department. Specializes in providing advice on environmental matters to domestic and international companies and financial institutions involved in a variety of transactions, including mergers and acquisitions, real estate investments, securities offerings and bank lending transactions and assisting clients in thoroughly understanding potential environmental liabilities and on allocating or disclosing those liabilities in the context of the transaction. Has experience with environmental issues arising

in various types of industries, including oil and gas and power generation.

## CHEPIGA, Michael J
Simpson Thacher & Bartlett LLP, New York 212 455 2000
mchepiga@stblaw.com
*Recommended in Litigation*

**Practice Areas:** Represents clients in securities litigation, class actions, derivative actions and corporate control litigation. Representative securities cases include litigation involving Royal Ahold, Dynegy, St. Paul-Travelers, Deutsche Telekom, HealthSouth, American Electric Power, Celera Genomics, Express Scripts and KeySpan. M&A litigations include Reuters/Instinet Litigation, Wachovia/First Union/SunTrust Litigation, Telecorp Shareholders Litigation and many others.

**Prof. Memberships:** Fellow, American Bar Foundation (1998-); The Association of the Bar of the City of New York (Federal Courts Committee, 1992-95); American Bar Association; NY State Bar Association (Federal Courts Committee, 1986-88); Federal Bar Council; Legal Aid Society of New York (Director 1986-98, President 1996-98, Presidents Council 1998-present. Volunteers of Legal Services (Director, 2000-present).

**Career:** Joined Simpson Thacher 1981 and became Partner 1986. Law clerk to the Honorable Milton Pollack (SDNY) 1979-80 and to the Honorable Amalya Kearse (Second Circuit) 1980-81.

**Publications:** 'Commercial Litigation in New York State Courts', second edition, Chapter on Mergers and Acquisitions; Play, 'Getting and Spending' (produced on Broadway, NYC, 1998). Numerous articles and lectures on federal civil litigation and federal securities law.

**Personal:** Yale University, JD, 1979; Fordham University, BA 1970, cum laude; New York University, PhD, 1976 (English Literature).

## CHERTOK, Mark
Sive Paget & Riesel PC, New York
212 421 2150
mchertok@sprlaw.com
*Recommended in Environment*

**Practice Areas:** Mark A Chertok is a Partner in Sive, Paget & Riesel, P.C., with offices in New York City and White Plains, New York. Mr Chertok, a graduate of Harvard Law School (JD 1970, cum laude) and the State University of New York at Buffalo (AB 1967, magna cum laude), has been active in environmental and land use counseling, permitting, enforcement and litigation for more than 25 years.

**Prof. Memberships:** He is a member of the Executive Committee of the New York State Bar Association, Environmental Law Section, and Co-Chair of its Committee on Environmental Impact Assessment. He has served on the faculty of numerous institutions. He was an

organizer of the March 2001 SEQRA 25th Anniversary Conference, co-chaired the October 2001 SEQRA 25th Anniversary Conference Symposium, and lectured at each.

**Career:** His experience spans a broad spectrum of substantive areas and his clients include state, regional and local governmental bodies, private industrial, commercial and financial entities, and national and regional environmental and civic organizations.

**Publications:** Mr Chertok is a contributing author in 'The Treatise on New York Environmental Law', New York State Bar Association (1992) and 'Supplement' (1995), as well as in Environmental Impact Review in New York, Gerrard, Ruzow and Weinberg (1999).

**Personal:** Mr Chertok was an Adjunct Professor at the Benjamin N Cardozo School of Law, where he taught Environmental Litigation. He also formerly taught Environmental Litigation as an Adjunct Professor at the Pace University School of Law and Development Law as an Adjunct Associate Professor at the Columbia University Graduate School of Architecture, Planning and Historic Preservation. Mr Chertok served, or currently serves, as principal counsel for project proponents in both governmental approval processes and litigation.

## CHESLER, Evan
Cravath, Swaine & Moore LLP, New York
212 474 1243
echesler@cravath.com
*Recommended in Antitrust, Intellectual Property, Litigation*

**Practice Areas:** Deputy Presiding Partner. Antitrust, securities, intellectual property, general commercial cases.

**Prof. Memberships:** ABA; NYSBA; ABCNY; Institute for Judicial Administration (President); American College of Trial Lawyers (Fellow).

**Career:** Partner since 1982. Clerkship: Hon Inzer B Wyatt (US District Court for the Southern District of New York).

**Publications:** Numerous articles on legal topics. Chapter in 'Inside the Minds of Leading Litigators'. Editor, 'The Russian Jewry Reader'. Adjunct Assistant Professor of History, NYU.

**Personal:** New York University School of Law (JD, cum laude, 1975; Order of the Coif); Hunter College (MA, 1973); New York University (AB, highest honors, 1970).

## CHIAPPARI, Ted
Satterlee Stephens Burke & Burke LLP, New York 212 818 9200
*Recommended in Immigration*

## CHIDA, Junaid H
Dewey Ballantine LLP, New York
212 259 6308
jchida@deweyballantine.com
*Recommended in Projects*

**Practice Areas:** Project finance and

leasing. In particular, Mr Chida's practice focuses on infrastructure projects in the United States and internationally, utilizing highly structured non-recourse vehicles and tax-advantaged financing. Current and recent transactions include several wind, geothermal and solar projects in the United States, oil and gas projects in Brazil and a metro/subway system expansion in Chile.

**Prof. Memberships:** California Bar Association.

**Career:** Admitted to practice New York, California, Wisconsin. Partner, Dewey Ballantine LLP.

**Personal:** Born June 23, 1956. BBA, University of Wisconsin-Eau Claire, 1978. JD, University of Wisconsin, 1983.

### CHINN, Adam D
Wachtell, Lipton, Rosen & Katz, New York 212 403 1000
adchinn@wlrk.com
*Recommended in Employee Benefits*

**Practice Areas:** Specializes in both merger and acquisition tax practice and its transaction-related executive compensation practice, with a particular emphasis on transactions involving financial services institutions. Has been involved in many major financial institution mergers, both bank and non-bank, including Wells Fargo/Norwest, Fleet/BankBoston, GE/Heller Financial, Credit Suisse/DLJ and AIG/American General, FleetBoston Financial Corp./Bank of America Corporation, Dresdner/Wasserstein Perella, Household International, Inc./HSBC Holdings plc and National Golf Properties Inc/Goldman Sachs Group Inc.

**Career:** Partner in the New York law firm of Wachtell, Lipton, Rosen & Katz.

**Publications:** Has written and spoken frequently on tax and executive compensation issues. Is the author of the chapter on Change of Control Arrangements in 'Executive Compensation' (Law Journal Seminars-Press 1996) and 'Bank Mergers: Change of Control Employment Arrangements and Employee Benefit Aspects of Merger Agreements', 15 Bank and Corporate Governance Law Reporter at 8 (Sept. 1995).

**Personal:** Graduated from Oxford University, England in 1982 (BA), from the College of Law, England in 1983 (CPE) and cum laude from New York University in 1987 (JD) where he was Order of the Coif and editor, New York University Law Review and author: Note 'Attacking Tax Shelters 183 Leaves the Farm and Goes to the Movies', 61, New York University Law Review, 89, 1986. Was chosen by 'The American Lawyer' as one of the 45 highest performing Members of the Private Bar under the age of 45.

### CIABARRA, Laura G
Dechert LLP, Hartford
860 524 3926
laura.ciabarra@dechert.com
*Recommended in Real Estate*

**Practice Areas:** Ms Ciabarra is a Partner in the Finance and Real Estate Group. Ms Ciabarra focuses her structured finance and real estate practice on mezzanine real estate finance and equity joint ventures, with an emphasis on loan securitization and intercreditor agreements. She has also represented major financial institutions on large-scale financing transactions.

**Prof. Memberships:** Member, Connecticut and New York Bar; admitted to practice before the United States District Court for the District of Connecticut.

**Personal:** Yale University, BA and JD; Completed graduate studies at both the University of Cambridge and the London School of Economics.

### CIERI, Richard
Kirkland & Ellis LLP, New York
212 446 4770
rcieri@kirkland.com
*Recommended in Bankruptcy*

**Practice Areas:** Mr Cieri's practice involves represents debtors, creditors' committees and creditors in out-of-court and in-court restructurings; advising the boards of directors of financially troubled companies; providing advice in connection with legacy liability and environmental, retiree, pension tort and product liability claims facing a debtor, and technology and intellectual property issues; structuring of secured and commercial transactions (including advice related to fraudulent conveyance, corporate spin-offs, and related securities issues); and the acquisition of and lending to financially troubled companies.

**Personal:** JD, University of Michigan, cum laude, 1981.

### CIFU, Douglas A
Paul, Weiss, Rifkind, Wharton & Garrison LLP, New York 212 373 3436
dcifu@paulweiss.com
*Recommended in Private Equity*

**Practice Areas:** Douglas Cifu represents private equity sponsors and corporate clients in acquisitions, dispositions and financings, and serves as Deputy Chair of the Corporate Department and Co-Head of the Private Equity Group. Mr Cifu has extensive experience with leveraged buy-outs and dispositions of public and private companies as well as minority investments, joint ventures and financing transactions. Mr Cifu has represented various private equity sponsors and corporate clients including General Atlantic LLC, Sandler Capital, Pegasus Partners, Halyard Capital Partners, Angelo Gordon & Co., Automatic Data Processing, Inc, Pitney Bowes Inc. and Polo Ralph Lauren.

### CLARY, Richard W
Cravath, Swaine & Moore LLP, New York
212 474 1227
rclary@cravath.com
*Recommended in Litigation*

**Practice Areas:** Head of Litigation Department. Securities, antitrust, patent, trade secret, trademark, bankruptcy and commercial litigation (trials and appeals). International and domestic arbitrations.

**Prof. Memberships:** ABA (Intellectual Property and Litigation sections); NYSBA; ABCNY; London Court of International Arbitration; Federal Bar Council.

**Career:** Partner since 1985. Clerkships: Hon Thurgood Marshall (US Supreme Court), Hon Walter R Mansfield (US Court of Appeals for the Second Circuit).

**Personal:** Harvard Law School (JD, magna cum laude, 1978; Developments Officer of the Law Review; Sears Prize); Amherst College (BA, magna cum laude, 1975; Phi Beta Kappa). Legal Aid Society: Vice-Chair, Executive Committee.

### CLEMENS, Steven E
Kirkland & Ellis LLP, New York
212 446 4787
sclemens@kirkland.com
*Recommended in Tax*

**Practice Areas:** Steven Clemens focuses his practice primarily on tax matters that arise from complex mergers and acquisitions, both domestic and cross-border, involving both strategic and financial clients. He also advises clients on the formation of investment funds such as private equity funds, and has represented both fund sponsors and significant investors in newly formed investment funds. Additionally, Mr Clemens has represented numerous issuers of various securities and has advised them on the tax implications of such issuances.

**Personal:** Eastern University, BA (magna cum laude), 1991; Harvard Law School, JD (magna cum laude), 1994.

### COCHRAN, Eric L
Skadden, Arps, Slate, Meagher & Flom LLP & Affiliates, New York
212 735 2596
ecochran@skadden.com
*Recommended in Corporate/M&A*

**Practice Areas:** Concentrates in mergers and acquisitions, securities law and general corporate law. Has advised clients on a wide variety of friendly and hostile transactions. Recent transactions have included negotiated acquisitions and divestitures, hostile defenses, proxy fights, restructurings, leveraged buyouts, private equity investments and minority buy-outs. Also has advised clients on corporate governance matters. Has been on the faculty of Practising Law Institute seminars, speaking on corporate and securities topics.

**Career:** JD, New York University School of Law, 1986; MS, New York University,

1984; BA, Williams College, 1982.

### COFFEY, John
Bernstein Litowitz Berger & Grossmann LLP, New York 212 554 1409
sean@blbglaw.com
*Recommended in Litigation*

**Practice Areas:** Commercial litigation; employment litigation.

**Prof. Memberships:** Member, Association of the Bar of the City of New York; Member, American Bar Association.

**Career:** Litigation counsel to many public and private institutional investors. Lead trial counsel in many of largest and most significant US securities cases in history including $6.15 billion recovery of WorldCom securities litigation (2005), and $217 million recovery in BFA Liquidation Trust v. Arthur Andersen LLP (2002). Captain, United States Naval Reserves (Ret) – 1978-86 active duty, 1986-2004 US Naval Reserves. Assistant United States Attorney, Southern District of New York, (1991-95).

**Publications:** Has written and lectured extensively on securities fraud, shareholder rights and corporate governance trends and is frequent legal commentator for major news media including The Wall Street Journal, The New York Times, NBC and PBS, among others.

**Personal:** United States Naval Academy (BS, Ocean Engineering, with merit, 1978); Georgetown University (JD, magna cum laude, 1987) – Order of the Coif; articles editor, Georgetown Law Journal; Recipient, Charles A Keigwin Award (academic excellence).

### COGUT, Charles 'Casey'
Simpson Thacher & Bartlett LLP, New York 212 455 2550
ccogut@stblaw.com
*Recommended in Corporate/M&A, Private Equity*

**Practice Areas:** Head of Simpson Thacher's global Mergers and Acquisitions Group, specializing in domestic and international mergers and acquisitions, and transactions involving private equity firms. Currently oversees the firm's relationships with Kohlberg Kravis Roberts & Co., Silver Lake Partners, Ripplewood Holdings, JC Flowers & Co., JLL Partners, adidas-Salomon AG, Aramark Corporation, Becton Dickinson & Company, Nets Sports & Entertainment LLC, Shinsei Bank and Wyeth. In addition, throughout his career he has advised boards of directors with respect to corporate governance matters and responsibilities of directors. In 2005, among other transactions, he represented (i) adidas in its acquisition of Reebok; (ii) a consortium of seven private equity firms led by Silver Lake Partners in its $11.3 billion acquisition of SunGuard Data Systems, Inc., and (iii) KKR in its $1.3 billion acquisition of Accellent Inc.

**Prof. Memberships:** Member, Association of the Bar of the City of New York, International Bar Association.

**Career:** Joined firm in 1973; Partner since 1980. Senior Resident Partner in firm's London office (1990-93); in this capacity participated in many cross-border transactions. Current Member of firm's Executive Committee.

**Personal:** Received JD (1973) from the University of Pennsylvania Law School after graduating summa cum laude from Lehigh University (1969). Member, Board of Overseers of the University of Pennsylvania Law School and the Board of Advisors of the University's Institute for Law and Economics.

## COHEN, Ben
Cahill Gordon & Reindel LLP, New York
212 701 3900
*Recommended in Tax*

## COHEN, H Rodgin
Sullivan & Cromwell LLP, New York
212 558 4000
cohenhr@sullcrom.com
*Recommended in Corporate/M&A, Financial Services*

**Practice Areas:** Regulatory, acquisitions, corporate governance and securities laws matters for domestic and foreign financial institutions and The Clearing House. Regulatory matters include anti-money laundering, OFAC, powers and enforcement. Involved in most major US bank acquisitions as well as numerous major cross-border and other financial services acquisitions. Has been a Member of Group of 30 Studies and participated in bank negotiations to free the Iranian hostages.

**Career:** Partner since 1977; Chairman since 2000.

**Personal:** Harvard College (AB, 1965); Harvard Law School (LLB, 1968).

## COHEN, Harry P
Cadwalader, Wickersham & Taft LLP, New York 212 504 6262
harry.cohen@cwt.com
*Recommended in Insurance*

**Practice Areas:** Handles multi-million dollar reinsurance arbitrations, litigations and mediations covering the full range of procedural and substantive reinsurance issues, including carve-out and buy-down covers, novations and commutations, contract interpretation and coverage disputes, fronting arrangements, spirals and arbitrage, agency, broker and underwriting manager disputes, captive insurance and reinsurance arrangements, environmental and other reinsurance allocations, set-off, extracontractual obligations, follow the fortunes and follow the settlements, IBNR recoverability, late notice, London Market business and brokers, punitive damages, recovery of declaratory judgment expenses, direct and reinsurance pooling arrangements, security requirements, service of process upon and enforcement of judgments

against alien companies, and all issues arising under the Federal Arbitration Act and state arbitration schemes.

**Prof. Memberships:** New York and Massachusetts Bars; United States District Courts for the Southern, Eastern, Northern Districts of New York, District of Connecticut; United States Courts of Appeals for the Second, Third, Fifth, Sixth and Seventh Circuits.

**Personal:** JD, Boston University School of Law (1981); BA, State University of New York at Stony Brook (1978).

## COHEN, Joel
McDermott Will & Emery, New York
212 547 5566
jcohen@mwe.com
*Recommended in Employment*

**Practice Areas:** Practices exclusively in the representation of management in employment law litigation and counseling. Experience includes work on employment discrimination lawsuits and administrative proceedings, National Labor Relations Board (NLRB) matters, unionization campaigns, collective bargaining and employment contracts. Represents clients in the manufacturing, service, financial and healthcare industries.

**Career:** Won eight jury trials in employment cases involving race, age, national origin and disability discrimination, whistle-blowing claims and employment fraud for clients such as Union Carbide, Travelers Insurance, Reader's Digest, Pitney Bowes and Memorial Sloan-Kettering Cancer Center.

**Personal:** Fordham University School of Law (JD); Queens College (BA).

## COHEN, Joel M
Davis Polk & Wardwell, New York
212 450 4000
joel.cohen@dpw.com
*Recommended in Antitrust*

**Practice Areas:** Member of Davis Polk & Wardwell's Litigation Department. Represents clients in a variety of antitrust and general civil litigation and arbitration matters. Also represents clients in merger investigations, joint ventures, and/or antitrust counseling and litigation. Representations include civil litigation, international arbitration and governmental investigations in the areas of professional malpractice, M&A, securities law enforcement, commercial contracts and others. Has advised numerous clients regarding licensing strategies and the permissible uses of intellectual property, and has represented clients in patent and antitrust litigation concerning the alleged misuse of patents.

## COHEN, Robin L
Dickstein Shapiro Morin & Oshinsky LLP, New York 212 277 6777
CohenR@dsmo.com
*Recommended in Insurance*

**Practice Areas:** Represents insureds in complex insurance coverage matters in

federal and state courts throughout the country. Over the course of her career, she has recovered more than one billion dollars for Fortune 500 clients whose insurance claims have been disputed by carriers.

**Career:** Managing Partner of the New York office. Previously a Partner at Anderson Kill Olick and Oshinsky LLP in New York. Lectures on insurance coverage issues.

**Personal:** University of Pennsylvania Law School (JD, 1986); University of Pennsylvania (BA, 1983).

## COLLETTA, Anthony J
Sullivan & Cromwell LLP, New York
212 558 4000
collettaa@sullcrom.com
*Recommended in Real Estate*

**Practice Areas:** Commercial real estate, senior/mezzanine financings, JVs, and corporate matters. Extensive experience with the formation of and investment and financing activities for real estate funds. Clients: Whitehall Funds since inception in 1991; Aetos Capital and Broadreach Capital Partners in forming real estate funds; Strategic Hotel Capital and Sunstone Hotels in financings; investors in acquiring/financing $1.5 billion mixed-use development; GS affiliates in $2.5 billion+ hotel acquisitions and leveraged recapitalisations; and Safeguard Self Storage in $400 million recapitalisation.

**Prof. Memberships:** ABA.

**Career:** Partner since 1997.

**Personal:** Fordham University (BA, 1985); St. John's University Law School (JD, 1988).

## COLLINS, John
Dewey Ballantine LLP, New York
212 259 7080
jcollins@deweyballantine.com
*Recommended in Antitrust*

**Practice Areas:** Antitrust and trade regulation, international arbitration and ADR, insurance/reinsurance litigation and arbitration, M&A, securities, corporate governance, white-collar crime and government investigations.

**Career:** Mr Collins has over 30 years of experience representing plaintiffs and defendants in jury and non-jury civil commercial litigations in federal and state courts throughout the United States and represented clients in administrative proceedings before the FTC, the ITC, the Antitrust Division of the Department of Justice and the SEC. He has represented clients, and served as arbitrator, in American Arbitration Association sanctioned proceedings.

**Personal:** BA, Fordham University, 1970. JD, University of Chicago Law School, 1973.

## COLLINS, W Dale
Shearman & Sterling LLP, New York
212 848 4127
wcollins@shearman.com
*Recommended in Antitrust*

**Practice Areas:** Partner in Shearman & Sterling's Antitrust Group. Represents clients in merger investigations by federal and state antitrust enforcement agencies. Co-ordinates multi-jurisdictional antitrust defense of numerous transactions throughout the world.

**Career:** Joined Shearman in 1978. Resigned in 1981 to work in Reagan Administration as White House Fellow, serving as Special Assistant to Vice President George Bush. Served as Deputy Assistant Attorney General, Department of Justice Antitrust Division. Returned to Shearman, 1983.

**Personal:** BS with Honors, California Institute of Technology (1973); MS, California Institute of Technology (1974); JD, University of Chicago Law School (1978); PhD candidate, University of Minnesota (1979).

## CONDON, Creighton
Shearman & Sterling LLP, New York
212 848 7628
ccondon@shearman.com
*Recommended in Corporate/M&A*

**Practice Areas:** Partner in Shearman & Sterling's M&A Group and Head of the firm's Sports Group. Member of the firm's Policy Committee. Represents United States and multinational corporations in acquisitions and sales of public and private companies and in joint ventures. Also represents the M&A groups of investment banks. Advises on issues regarding corporate governance and control.

**Prof. Memberships:** American Bar Association; New York State Bar Association; California State Bar Association.

**Personal:** BA, University of Pennsylvania (1978); JD, Columbia Law School (1982).

## CONSTANTINE, Lloyd
Constantine Cannon PC, New York
212 350 2700
*Recommended in Antitrust*

## COOK, Michael L
Schulte Roth & Zabel LLP, New York
212 756 2150
michael.cook@srz.com
*Recommended in Bankruptcy*

**Practice Areas:** Corporate restructuring, workouts and creditors' rights litigation.

**Prof. Memberships:** Fellow, American College of Bankruptcy; Practising Law Institute Bankruptcy Law Advisory Committee; Chair, Creditors' Rights Litigation Committee, American Bar Association Section of Litigation (1976-81); Bankruptcy Litigation Institute, Chairman, 1980-96; Vice President and Director, Columbia College Alumni Association; past Chairman and Director, Lawyers Alliance for New York; Director, Goddard

Riverside Community Center; Fellow, American Bar Foundation.
**Career:** Schulte Roth & Zabel Partner since 2000; Skadden, Arps, Slate, Meagher & Flom LLP, Partner and Corporate Restructuring Group practice leader, 1980-2000; Weil, Gotshal & Manges LLP, Partner, 1975-80; associate, 1970-75.
**Publications:** Has lectured and written extensively on topics related to business reorganization, workouts and creditors' rights litigation.
**Personal:** Recognized in 'The Best Lawyers In America'; 'Who's Who in American Law' and 'The K&A Restructuring Register'.

### COOPER, James
Cravath, Swaine & Moore LLP, New York
212 474 1326
jcooper@cravath.com
*Recommended in Banking & Finance*
**Practice Areas:** Wide variety of domestic and international financing transactions, including financings of mergers, acquisitions, recapitalizations and spin-offs, working capital financings, restructurings and workouts, and various special-purpose financings. Counsels corporate borrowers negotiating financing arrangements with banks and other financial institutions.
**Career:** Partner since 1986.
**Personal:** Yale Law School (JD, 1979); University of Chicago (AB, summa cum laude, 1976; Phi Beta Kappa).

### COPEN, Robert A
Skadden, Arps, Slate, Meagher & Flom LLP & Affiliates, New York
212 735 3536
rcopen@skadden.com
*Recommended in Banking & Finance*
**Practice Areas:** Represents investment banks, commercial banks and other financial institutions as lenders; and strategic investors, buyout funds and corporations as borrowers in connection with syndicated loans, acquisition financings, leveraged buyouts, bridge loans, asset-based loans, project financings, private placements and other types of complex and traditional transactions. In 2005, negotiated more than $50 billion of fully underwritten bank, bond and bridge commitments in connection with over 60 purchase bids, recapitalizations and acquisitions.
**Prof. Memberships:** Admitted in New York and Connecticut.
**Career:** JD, New York University School of Law, 1989; BA, Tufts University, 1986 (magna cum laude).

### CORUZZI, Laura A
Jones Day, New York
212 326 8383
lacoruzzi@jonesday.com
*Recommended in Intellectual Property*
**Practice Areas:** Chairs the firm's Life Sciences Practice. Her current practice covers all aspects of patent law relating to

the biotechnology and pharmaceutical fields. Her patent procurement practice centers on strategic planning and management of patent portfolios designed to protect emerging technologies, including US prosecution and interferences and corresponding foreign proceedings. She also has an active client counseling, litigation, and appellate practice. She is a frequent invited speaker on patent law issues related to pharmacogenomics, new medical indications, and molecular diagnostics.
**Prof. Memberships:** NY State Bar Association; NYIPLA; AIPLA; AAAS.
**Personal:** Fordham University (JD 1985; PhD in Biology 1979).

### COTTON, Stuart
Mound Cotton Wollan & Greengrass, New York 212 804 4500
scotton@moundcotton.com
*Recommended in Insurance.*

### CREAMER JR, Ronald E
Sullivan & Cromwell LLP, New York
212 558 4000
creamerr@sullcrom.com
*Recommended in Tax*
**Practice Areas:** Tax-efficient structuring of acquisitions and dispositions in cross-border corporate, real estate and utility M&A. Also practices and lectures in the area of tax-advantaged corporate financing techniques and advises investment banking clients in the design of new financial instruments.
**Career:** Partner since 2000.
**Publications:** Co-author (with S&C Partner Emily McMahon) of the textbook 'Tax Planning for Transfers of Business Interests'.
**Personal:** Princeton University (AB, 1987); Yale Law School (JD, 1991); Yale School of Organization and Management (MPPM, 1991).

### CREEL, Thomas L
Goodwin Procter LLP, New York
212 813 8800
tcreel@goodwinprocter.com
*Recommended in Intellectual Property*
**Practice Areas:** Mr Creel's practice involves litigation and counseling in the areas of trade secrets, entertainment, trademarks and copyrights. Recognized for his capabilities in the area of patent litigation, Mr Creel has been appointed by federal district judges to serve as a mediator to attempt to resolve disputes, and as a Special Master to provide proper patent claim construction, supervise all pretrial discovery and recommend rulings on summary judgment motions.
**Personal:** LLB, University of Michigan Law School; BS, University of Kansas.

### CROSS, James
Simpson Thacher & Bartlett LLP, New York 212 455 3386
jcross@stblaw.com
*Recommended in Banking & Finance*
**Practice Areas:** James Cross is a Partner

at Simpson Thacher & Bartlett LLP where he is a Member of the firm's Corporate Department. Mr Cross concentrates on bank finance, with an emphasis on senior credit and subordinated bridge facilities for leveraged acquisitions. He has extensive experience representing leading financial institutions and private equity firms such as JPMorgan Chase Bank and Kolhberg Kravis Roberts & Co. in significant financing transactions. Recent transactions in which he has been involved include representations of Kohlberg Kravis Roberts & Co. and Silver Lake Partners in the acquisition of Avago from Agilent and of a consortium of Silver Lake, Bain Capital, Blackstone, Goldman Sachs, KKR, Providence and Texas Pacific Group in their acquisition of SunGard Data Systems.
**Career:** Mr Cross became a Partner at Simpson Thacher in 1999.
**Personal:** He received his BA from Princeton University in 1986 and his JD from the University of Virginia in 1990.

### CROSS, Wayne A
White & Case LLP, New York
212 819 8797
wcross@whitecase.com
*Recommended in Antitrust*
**Practice Areas:** Has a broad-based Commercial Litigation Practice with special emphasis on antitrust, energy, intellectual property, bankruptcy and international issues. Extensive trial experience with jury and non-jury trials before several state and federal courts as well as before the AAA, the ICC and the Japan Commercial Arbitration Association. Also has extensive appellate experience.
**Prof. Memberships:** ABA; ABCNY.
**Career:** White & Case since 2002.
**Personal:** Columbia College (AB 1967); Columbia Law School (JD 1970).

### CROUGH, Maureen
Sidley Austin LLP, New York
212 839 7323
mcrough@sidley.com
*Recommended in Environment*
**Practice Areas:** Partner in the New York office, representing domestic and non-US purchasers, sellers, lenders, landlords and tenants in the environmental aspects of a broad range of financial transactions. She handles environmental due diligence, evaluation of environmental insurance for use in transactions, negotiation of environmental provisions in acquisition and loan agreements and environmental counseling pertaining to financial transactions and bankruptcy. She also represents clients in buyer/seller environmental dispute resolution, and counsels clients in the requirements of US and NY environmental regulatory compliance. Her practice includes representing clients in the performance of voluntary cleanups in state programs, especially in NY.
**Prof. Memberships:** American Bar

Association (ABA); Program Vice-Chair, Special Committee on Environmental Disclosure of the ABA's Section of Environment, Energy and Resources; New York State Bar Association; The Association of the Bar of the City of New York.
**Publications:** 'Disclosure Requirements for Conditional Asset Retirement Obligations', ABA's Section of Environment, Energy and Resources, Special Committee on Environmental Disclosure Newsletter (Oct 2005).
**Personal:** The University of Michigan Law School, JD, 1986; Princeton University, AB, 1983. Admissions: Illinois, 1986; New York, 1995.

### CULHANE, Stephen
King & Spalding LLP, New York
212 827 4361
sculhane@kslaw.com
*Recommended in Private Fund Formation*
**Practice Areas:** Focuses on a wide range of private investment fund formation and investment, investment management and corporate matters. Substantial experience with alternative investment funds; US, Cayman Islands and Irish-domiciled equity long-short hedge funds; currency trading funds; multi-strategy hedge funds; exchange funds and collateralized bond obligation vehicles. Extensive experience representing the sponsors, managers and distributors of private investment funds.
**Prof. Memberships:** American Bar Association; Association of the Bar of the City of New York; International Bar Association; Securities Industry Association.
**Personal:** BA, Princeton University, 1986; MPhil, Oxford University, England, 1988; JD, New York University 1993.

### CUNDIFF, Victoria
Paul, Hastings, Janofsky & Walker LLP, New York 212 318 6030
*Recommended in Intellectual Property*
**Practice Areas:** Intellectual property litigation, dispute resolution, and preventive counseling, particularly regarding trade secrets, competitive intelligence, unfair competition, software and information technology, and IP licensing. Work often focuses on issues arising at the intersection of intellectual property and employment law, including restrictive covenant, 'inevitable disclosure' and intellectual property ownership disputes. Experienced in developing IP protection programs and contracts and in designing confidential alternative dispute resolution procedures and verification protocols. Has represented clients in financial services, software, pharmaceutical, chemical, consumer product, sales, media and other industries.
**Prof. Memberships:** Intellectual Property Owners Association (Committee on Trade Secrets); New York State Bar Association Section of Intellectual Property

Law (past Chair); American Bar Association; Fellow, American Bar Foundation.
**Career:** Joined Paul Hastings as a Partner 1992.
**Publications:** 'Strategic Planning for Strategic Alliances'; 'Hiring Competitor's Employees: A Trade Secrets Perspective'; 'The New York Law of Trade Secrets: A Practical Guide'; 'How to Put Your Intellectual Property at Risk'; 'What You Need to Know About the Economic Espionage Act'. Frequent invited speaker on IP issues before Practising Law Institute, New York State Bar, and other major professional and academic groups.
**Personal:** JD, Yale Law School; BA, University of Denver, summa cum laude, valedictorian.

### CURBOW, William
Simpson Thacher & Bartlett LLP,
New York 212 455 3160
wcurbow@stblaw.com
*Recommended in Corporate/M&A*
**Practice Areas:** Partner at Simpson Thacher & Bartlett LLP concentrating on mergers and acquisitions. Transactions in which he has been involved include the representation of: L-3 Communications Corporation in connection with numerous acquisitions, including the Aircraft Integration Systems division of Raytheon Company, Northrop Grumman's Electron Devices and Displays-Navigation Systems businesses, the Goodrich Avionics Systems division of Goodrich Corp. and The Titan Corporation; The Cypress Group in connection with the purchases of Meow Mix Holdings, Inc., the automotive aftermarket group of Dana Corporation, the automotive business segment of Cooper Tire & Rubber Company and the sale of Meow Mix Holdings, Inc.; Brooklyn Basketball, LLC in connection with the purchase of the New Jersey Nets; Reuters Limited with respect to the acquisition by its subsidiary, Instinet Group Incorporated of Island ECN and the subsequent sale of Instinet Group Incorporated; New Skies Satellites Holdings Ltd. in the sale thereof to SES Global S.A.; and Abbott Laboratories in connection with the purchase of the vascular intervention and endovascular solutions businesses of Guidant Corporation.
**Career:** Joined Simpson Thacher in 1989; became Partner in 1996.
**Personal:** Received BA, summa cum laude, University of Connecticut (1984); JD, Harvard Law School (1987).

### CURLEY, Michael
Morgan, Lewis & Bockius LLP, New York 212 309 6711
mcurley@morganlewis.com
*Recommended in Employment*
**Practice Areas:** Michael Curley is a Partner in the Labor and Employment Practice. Mr Curley has represented clients in numerous proceedings before the National Labor Relations Board, both

in union representation and unfair labor practice cases. He has also had extensive experience in state and federal courts, defending clients in employment discrimination, whistleblower and wrongful discharge cases. In recent years, Mr Curley has tried and won a high profile whistleblower arbitration in the securities trading industry and he also tried and won a high profile case before the National Labor Relations Board in the entertainment industry.
**Prof. Memberships:** American Bar Association (Labor and Employment Law Section); New York State Bar Association (Labor and Employment Law Section and Committee on Alternative Dispute Resolution).

### CURNIN, Paul C
Simpson Thacher & Bartlett LLP,
New York 212 455 2000
pcurnin@stblaw.com
*Recommended in Litigation*
**Practice Areas:** Paul Curnin is a Partner in the firm's Litigation Department. He frequently represents clients in corporate and securities matters including class and derivative actions, takeover litigations, as well as government investigations and enforcement actions (particularly by the SEC), internal investigations and other matters. Selected representations include WorldCom Inc., JPMorgan Chase, as well as numerous directors, officers and other individuals.
**Prof. Memberships:** American Bar Association, Association of the Bar of the City of New York (Faculty, Effective Trial Advocacy Workshop, 1998-2000; secretary, Committee on Criminal Law, 1992-95; Legal Aid Society (Member, Board of Directors).
**Career:** Joined Simpson Thacher in 1990, became a Partner in 1995. Prior to joining the firm, Mr Curnin was a Trial Attorney in the Federal Defenders Services Unit for the Southern District of New York, served as a law clerk to the Hon Roger Wollman of the Eighth Circuit Court of Appeals and to the late Hon Lloyd F MacMahon of the Southern District of New York. In 2003, he was named one of the country's top 45 Lawyers Under 45 in the United States by American Lawyer magazine.
**Personal:** Received BA from Dartmouth College, 1983; JD from Fordham University School of Law, 1987.

### CUSICK, Michael
Jones Day, New York
212 326 7830
mcusick@jonesday.com
*Recommended in Energy*
**Practice Areas:** Advises issuers and underwriters on public and private US and international offerings of securities, particularly in the public utility industry where he has gained national recognition. He also counsels on restructuring and

acquisition-related matters for regulated and unregulated companies. His representations have included: advising the acquiring company in the successful combination of two Midwestern utilities; advising the successful bidder involved in the first contested takeover of an electric utility; the IPO for the Kingdom of Sweden and China Tire Holdings Ltd.; and the initial placement of debt securities in connection with the largest sale and leaseback ever completed.

### CYR, Joseph
Lovells, New York
212 909 0642
joe.cyr@lovells.com
*Recommended in Litigation*
**Practice Areas:** International dispute resolution.
**Career:** Joe's practice focuses on complex commercial litigation, particularly class actions and litigation with an international component. He has served as lead trial counsel in a number of major trials on behalf of corporate clients engaged in international transactions. In addition, Joe has substantial experience in lawsuits and arbitration proceedings involving corporate transactional disputes, commercial banking, the Federal securities laws, human rights, consumer protection laws and product liability.
**Personal:** George Washington University (JD, 1977); Pacific Lutheran University (MA, 1976); George Washington University (Masters in Forensic Studies, 1976); US Military Academy (BS, 1973).

### CZARNIAK, Julia
Skadden, Arps, Slate, Meagher & Flom LLP & Affiliates, New York
212 735 4194
jczarnia@skadden.com
*Recommended in Projects*
**Practice Areas:** Concentrates on banking and institutional investing, representing financial institutions and borrowers in various types of financing transactions with an emphasis on corporate and project finance. Has extensive experience in export credit and mulilateral agency financings as well as in pipeline projects, restructurings and expansions in the United States, Asia and the Middle East.
**Career:** JD, Georgetown University Law Center, 1997; MA, Yale University Graduate School, 1993; BA, Moscow State University, 1990.

### DABNEY, James W
Fried, Frank, Harris, Shriver & Jacobson LLP, New York 212 859 8966
James.Dabney@FriedFrank.com
*Recommended in Intellectual Property*
**Practice Areas:** Litigation Partner. Handles a wide variety of litigation matters with emphasis on patent, trademark, copyright, and related disputes involving intellectual property. Has acted as lead counsel in numerous cases involving questions of validity, enforceability,

infringement, or non-infringement of US patents, copyrights, trade secrets, trademarks, rights of publicity, and neighboring rights
**Career:** Joined Fried Frank in 2004 as Partner.
**Personal:** JD (1979), magna cum laude, Cornell Law School, Order of the Coif and of the Board of Editors of the Cornell Law Review. BA (1976), magna cum laude, from Harvard College.

### DANNAY, Richard
Cowan, Liebowitz & Latman, New York
212 790 9200
*Recommended in Media & Entertainment*

### DAVENPORT, Margaret
Debevoise & Plimpton LLP, New York
212 909 6000
*Recommended in Private Equity*

### DAVIS, George A
Weil, Gotshal & Manges LLP, New York
212 310 8962
george.davis@weil.com
*Recommended in Bankruptcy*
**Practice Areas:** George Davis represents debtors, lenders, creditor groups and investors in restructuring distressed companies. Mr Davis has significant experience in a wide array of industries, including, airline, steel, telecommunications, energy and retail. He has represented debtors in Chapter 11 restructurings, including St. Vincents Catholic Medical Centers, IMPATH Inc., Bethlehem Steel Corporation, Sunbeam Corporation and Carmike Cinemas, Inc. Mr Davis currently represents secured and unsecured creditor groups in the restructurings of Calpine Corporation, Delta Airlines, Independence Air, Kaiser Aluminum & Chemical Corporation, WCI Steel and Eagle Pitcher.
**Personal:** SUNY Binghamton, BS, 1986; Hofstra University School of Law, JD, 1990.

### DAVIS, Steven H
LeBoeuf, Lamb, Greene & MacRae LLP, New York 212 424 8000
sdavis@llgm.com
*Recommended in Energy*
**Practice Areas:** His practice focuses primarily on companies active in the energy industry, including integrated electric and gas companies and independent power producers. He advises US and non-US clients in connection with mergers and acquisitions. He works in bankruptcy proceedings involving energy companies and provides restructuring advice for independent power producers.
**Career:** Joined LeBoeuf Lamb in 1977; Co-Chairman of LeBoeuf Lamb from 1999-2003 and Chairman since 2004.
**Personal:** Yale University (BA) 1977; Yale University (JD) 1977.

**DAX, John**
Cohen Dax and Koening, PC, Albany
518 432 1002
*Recommended in Energy*

**DE CHIARA, Michael**
Zetlin & De Chiara LLP, New York
212 682 6800
*Recommended in Construction*

**DE WIED, Warren**
Fried, Frank, Harris, Shriver & Jacobson
LLP, New York 212 859 8296
Warren.de.Wied@FriedFrank.com
*Recommended in Corporate/M&A*
**Practice Areas:** Co-heads Mergers and
Acquisitions Practice Group. Practice
focuses on mergers and acquisitions,
including negotiated transactions, hostile
takeovers, takeover defense and proxy
contests; leveraged buyouts and private
equity transactions; restructurings, spin-
offs and recapitalizations; joint ventures;
corporate governance; and general corporate counseling.
**Career:** Joined Fried Frank in 1987.
Became a Partner in 1994.
**Personal:** JD (1987), Boalt Hall School
of Law, University of California, Berkeley,
Order of the Coif. BA (1983) and MA
(1987) Trinity College, Cambridge University.

**DELANEY, John**
Morrison & Foerster LLP, New York
212 468 8040
jdelaney@mofo.com
*Recommended in Business Process
Outsourcing, Technology*
**Practice Areas:** Concentrates on high-
technology, outsourcing and IP matters.
Advises clients from Fortune 500 compa-
nies to emerging growth companies on a
range of technology law issues. Repre-
sents clients on copyright, trademark,
and other intellectual property transac-
tions and disputes.
**Prof. Memberships:** Co-Chair, PLI
Annual Conference (The Outsourcing
Revolution); Board Member, Volunteer
Lawyers for the Arts; Board Member,
iMentor.
Career: Bar admission: California and
New York. Co-Chair, Technology Group,
New York office. Recognized as one of the
'Lawyers for the New Economy' by American Lawyer magazine. On Crain's New
York Business Technology 100 list: indi-
viduals 'likely to shape the direction and
growth of New York's economy for years
to come'.
**Personal:** BA, University of Notre Dame,
1986; JD, Columbia Law School, 1989.

**DELIKAT, Michael**
Orrick, Herrington & Sutcliffe LLP,
New York 212 506 5230
mdelikat@orrick.com
*Recommended in Employment*
**Practice Areas:** Represents major cor-
porations in all facets of labor and
employment law, focusing on the finan-

cial services industry. His active trial and
appellate practice encompasses high visibility class actions, trade secret misappropriation litigation and other impact cases.
He maintains an active Sarbanes-Oxley
whistleblower defense practice and
authored the definitive treatise on SOX.
**Prof. Memberships:** Fellow, The College
of Labor and Employment Lawyers;
Board Member, NYU Center for Labor
and Employment Law; ABA and NYBA.
**Career:** Head of Orrick's Employment
Law Department; Managing Director of
all Orrick's Litigation Practices (2005).
**Personal:** JD, Harvard Law School, 1977;
BS, Cornell University, 1974.

**DELUCIA, Richard L**
Kenyon & Kenyon LLP, New York
212 908 6217
rdelucia@kenyon.com
*Recommended in Intellectual Property*
**Practice Areas:** Richard L DeLucia, a
Partner at Kenyon & Kenyon LLP, is a
renowned attorney in the field of intellectual property litigation. He has been chief
trial counsel in over 100 cases. In what is
one of the most important jury verdicts
of 2005, Mr DeLucia prevailed on behalf
of Boston Scientific against Johnson &
Johnson in a trial in which Boston Scientific's patent on the drug-eluting cardiac
stent was found to be infringed by Johnson & Johnson. Other prominent cases he
has conducted include Savient Pharmaceuticals and Teva Pharmaceuticals USA
against Novo Nordisk relating to Human
Growth Hormone, Sony against Sound-
view Technologies in the battle over V-
chip technology, Heidelberg Harris
against Mitsubishi Heavy Industries in a
patent trial involving printing technology
(resulting in infringement damages valued at approximately $900 million), and
RJR Nabisco against Procter & Gamble in
a case known as the 'cookie wars'. Among
other notable clients, he has represented
Fisher-Price/Mattel, GE Healthcare,
BASF Corp., Enzo Life Sciences, and
Sloan-Kettering. Mr DeLucia also counsels clients on the licensing, validity,
enforceability, and infringement of
patents, trademarks and copyrights.
**Prof. Memberships:** Mr DeLucia is past
President of the New York Intellectual
Property Law Association, and has served
as Chairman of the Litigation Committee
of the New Jersey Intellectual Property
Law Association.

**DEROSA, Frank J**
Brown Raysman Millstein Felder &
Steiner LLP, New York 212 895 2010
fderosa@brownraysman.com
*Recommended in Intellectual Property*
**Practice Areas:** Partner and Co-Chair
of the firm's Intellectual Property Practice
Group with over 40 lawyers and technical
specialists. Has over 30 years of IP experience, concentrating on patent law with an
emphasis on counseling, patent procure-

ment, licensing and litigation in computers, software, internet and electronics.
Extensive experience in counseling on
adopting and implementing strategies for
protecting emerging and mature technologies, dealing with patents and portfolios of competitors and patent trolls,
and establishing corporate IP departments. Practiced as an electrical engineer
before law school.
**Personal:** BSEE, Polytechnic University
1963; JD, St John's University Law School
1974 (Member of Law Review).

**DESMARAIS, John M**
Kirkland & Ellis LLP, New York
212 446 4739
jdesmarais@kirkland.com
*Recommended in Intellectual Property*
**Practice Areas:** John Desmarais is a
Partner in the Intellectual Property
Group and since 2004 has been a Mem-
ber of Kirkland's firm Management
Committee.
**Prof. Memberships:** American Bar
Association, New York Bar Association,
Federal Bar Council, New York County
Lawyer's Association, New York Intellec-
tual Property Law Association, Intellectu-
al Property Owners Association, The
Association of the Bar of the City of New
York, International Trademark Associa-
tion (INTA), American Institute of
Chemical Engineers.
**Career:** After practicing intellectual
property litigation and counseling for
several years, Mr Desmarais left private
practice to serve as an Assistant United
States Attorney for the SDNY. During his
three years in this position, he tried crim-
inal jury trials for the federal government,
and later joined Kirkland & Ellis' New
York office. Mr Desmarais is a Member of
the Bars of New York and Washington,
DC, the US Supreme Court, the Federal
Circuit Court of Appeals, and various
other federal courts and courts of appeal.
He is also registered to practice before the
United States Patent and Trademark
Office. Since 1999 he has served on the
Delaware District Court Judges' Intellec-
tual Property Advisory Committee.
**Personal:** Manhattan College, BChE,
1985, New York University School of Law,
JD, 1988.

**DESPINS, Luc**
Milbank, Tweed, Hadley & McCloy LLP,
New York 212 530 5000
*Recommended in Bankruptcy*

**DIAMOND, Brian**
Stroock & Stroock & Lavan LLP, New
York 212 806 5400
*Recommended in Real Estate*

**DIBLASI, Gandolfo V**
Sullivan & Cromwell LLP, New York
212 558 4000
diblasig@sullcrom.com
*Recommended in Litigation*
**Practice Areas:** Represents clients in

securities and commodities class actions
in US federal courts, most recently as liaison counsel for the underwriters in 300
IPO allocation class actions, and counsel
for UnumProvident, Cablevision, and
Iridium directors/officers. Active in
civil/criminal investigations of financial
services industry, with clients in major
federal/state investigations involving
insurance industry, mutual funds,
research analysts, accounting/financial
reporting issues, IPOs, financial derivatives, and criminal cases alleging insider
trading and market manipulation.
**Prof. Memberships:** ABA; ABCNY;
NYSBA; FBC.
**Career:** Partner since 1985.
**Personal:** Yale University (BA, 1975).
Yale Law School (JD, 1978).

**DICICCO, Susan F**
King & Spalding LLP, New York
212 556 2263
sdicicco@kslaw.com
*Recommended in Litigation*
**Practice Areas:** Business litigation
focusing on litigation involving complex
financial instruments and transactions,
including mortgage-backed securities,
asset-backed securities, structured products, CDOs, CLOs, distressed debt trades,
repos, loan participations and the full
range of OTC derivatives.
**Prof. Memberships:** American Bar
Association, Litigation Section, Business
Law Section, Committee on Regulation
of Futures and Derivatives and Federal
Regulation of Securities Committee;
Securities Industry Association, Legal and
Compliance Division.
**Personal:** BA, Binghamton Universi-
ty,1989; JD, magna cum laude, Boston
University, 1992.

**DILORENZO, Louis P**
Bond, Schoeneck & King, PLLC,
New York 646 253 2315
ldilorenzo@bsk.com
*Recommended in Employment*
**Practice Areas:** Mr DiLorenzo represents management in labor and employment law matters. He is Co-Chair of the
firm's Labor & Employment Law Department; former Chair of the NYSBA's
Labor and Employment Law Section; a
Fellow of the American College of Labor
and Employment Lawyers; Adjunct Professor at Syracuse University School of
Management; has written several published articles and books on labor matters; and was selected as the 'Great Negotiator' by Corporate Legal Times, January
2003 issue. Mr DiLorenzo also served as
General Counsel to Agway, Inc. (2002-
04).
**Personal:** Syracuse University (BA,
1973); University of Buffalo Law School
(JD, 1976).

## DIMATTEO, John
Willkie Farr & Gallagher LLP, New York
212 728 8299
jdimatteo@willkie.com
*Recommended in Intellectual Property*
**Practice Areas:** Chair of the Intellectual Property Department and a Partner in the Litigation Department, specializing in patent litigation, trade secret litigation, patent prosecution, trademarks and IP licensing. He is currently representing a leading manufacturer of Automatic External Defibrillators ('AEDs') in asserting its patents against an accused infringer and defending against a counter claim for infringement. The case, involving over 20 patents, is pending in federal district court. He is also currently representing a leading manufacturer of high-pressure mercury-vapor lamps in asserting its patents against a Japanese company accused of infringement, and is defending a leading manufacturer of electric shavers in defense of a claim for patent infringement. He successfully defended a European manufacturer and two of its licenses before the International Trade Commission (ITC) against a claim for infringing three patents, and successfully represented a leading manufacturer of sonic toothbrushes in asserting its patents against an accused infringer.
**Prof. Memberships:** A Member of the American Intellectual Property Law Association, the American Bar Association, the Institute of Electrical and Electronics Engineers, and the Association for Computing Machinery.
**Career:** Admitted to the Bars of New York, New Jersey, and the District of Columbia. He is also admitted to practice before the Supreme Court of the United States; the United States Court of Appeals for the Federal Circuit; the United States Court of Appeals for the Sixth and Seventh Circuits; the United States District Courts for the Southern and Eastern Districts of New York; the District of New Jersey; and the Eastern District of Michigan. He is a Registered Professional Engineer, State of New York (1989) and a Registered Patent Agent, United States Patent and Trademark Office (1987).
**Personal:** Received an LLM in Trial Advocacy from Temple University School of Law in 2001, an MSCS (Computer Science) from the Polytechnic University of New York in 2000, a JD from St John's University School of Law in 1988, and a BSE (Engineering) from Polytechnic Institute of New York in 1984.

## DIMON, Samuel
Davis Polk & Wardwell, New York
212 450 4000
samuel.dimon@dpw.com
*Recommended in Tax*
**Practice Areas:** Member of Davis Polk & Wardwell's Tax Department. Advises clients on federal income tax matters in a variety of contexts, domestic and international, including financial product development and use of derivatives, tax planning for financial institutions, merchant banking and hedge fund organisation and investments, equipment leasings, securities offerings, mergers and acquisitions, joint ventures, bankruptcy reorganisations, workouts and tax audits.

## DISALVATORE, William
WilmerHale, New York
212 230 8800
*Recommended in Intellectual Property*

## DISKANT, Gregory L
Patterson, Belknap, Webb & Tyler LLP, New York 212 336 2710
gldiskant@pbwt.com
*Recommended in Intellectual Property*
**Practice Areas:** Greg Diskant is a Senior Litigation Partner and the Chair of Patterson Belknap. He regularly tries cases in federal and state courts and before arbitration panels, specializing in complex commercial, securities and intellectual property litigation. He has obtained verdicts totaling more than $1 billion, with five separate verdicts greater than $100 million.
**Prof. Memberships:** Fellow, American College of Trial Lawyers.
**Career:** Mr Diskant joined Patterson Belknap as Partner in 1982. Formerly, he was Assistant United States Attorney, Southern District of New York (1976-80), and served as Chief Appellate Attorney in 1980.
**Personal:** Columbia Law School (JD 1974), Kent Scholar, Harlan Fiske Stone Scholar, Editor-in-Chief, Columbia Law Review; Princeton University (AB, Chemistry, 1970).

## DOKOS, Daniel S
Weil, Gotshal & Manges LLP, New York
212 310 8576
daniel.dokos@weil.com
*Recommended in Banking & Finance*
**Practice Areas:** Daniel Dokos, Chair of Weil's Banking and Finance Practice, has extensive experience in bank financing, with a particular focus on leveraged lending and cross-border finance. He has represented both financial institutions and corporate borrowers in leveraged acquisition and recapitalization transactions, syndicated lending, investment grade lending, cash flow lending and asset-based lending, as well as loan restructurings, debtor in possession financings and exit financings. Recently he represented the lead arrangers in connection with senior secured debt financings for Koch/Georgia-Pacific, Affiliated Computer Services, Novelis, JohnsonDiversey, Warnaco, Jarden Corporation and Revlon.
**Personal:** Dartmouth College, BA, 1979; University of Virginia, JD, 1982.

## DOUGLAS, James M
Skadden, Arps, Slate, Meagher & Flom LLP & Affiliates, New York
212 735 2868
jdouglas@skadden.com
*Recommended in Banking & Finance*
**Practice Areas:** Head of Skadden's Banking and Institutional Investing Group. Represents numerous financial institutions, private equity sponsors and corporate clients in all areas of private financings. Concentrates in the areas of acquisition financings, bridge financings and restructurings. Listed in several leading US and international legal publications.
**Career:** JD, Fordham University, 1981 (cum laude; Member, Fordham Law Review); BA, State University of New York at Binghamton, 1978.

## DREYFUS, James K
Fulbright & Jaworski L.L.P., New York
212 318 3248
jdreyfus@fulbright.com
*Recommended in Tax*
**Practice Areas:** Tax.
**Prof. Memberships:** Mr Dreyfus is a Member of the Tax Sections of both the New York State and American Bar Associations.
**Career:** Jim Dreyfus has been a Partner in the New York office since 1981. Mr Dreyfus' practice involves a broad range of transactional matters, including mergers, acquisitions, recapitalizations, buyouts and venture capital transactions. He has also been involved in the formation of private equity funds and hedge funds. Mr Dreyfus' practice is both domestic and international in scope. In addition to his transactional work, Mr Dreyfus has significant experience in tax controversy matters. He also represents various charitable and non-profit organizations.
**Personal:** BA, magna cum laude, Wesleyan University (1969); JD, Harvard Law School (1973).

## DRIVAS, Dimitrios
White & Case LLP, New York
212 819 8286
ddrivas@whitecase.com
*Recommended in Intellectual Property*
**Practice Areas:** Co-Chair of firm's Global Intellectual Property Practice Group. Focuses upon patent infringement litigation for clients including pharmaceutical majors, agribusiness conglomerates, and technology firms. Practice also encompasses counseling and technology transfer, including acquisition, licensing of IP rights, joint development agreements, and strategic alliances. Registered US patent attorney.
**Prof. Memberships:** New York State Bar; US District Courts for the Southern and Eastern Districts of New York; US Court of Appeals for the Federal Circuit; US Patent and Trademark Office.
**Personal:** City College of the City University of New York (BS, Biochemistry, 1977); Fordham University School of Law (JD, 1984).

## DUNHAM JR, Wolcott
Debevoise & Plimpton LLP, New York
212 909 6000
*Recommended in Insurance*

## DUNN, M Douglas
Milbank, Tweed, Hadley & McCloy LLP, New York 212 530 5000
*Recommended in Energy*

## DUNN, Matthew S
Kramer Levin Naftalis & Frankel LLP, New York 212 715 9408
mdunn@kramerlevin.com
*Recommended in Immigration*
**Practice Areas:** Matthew Dunn's Immigration Law Practice focuses on the areas of finance, healthcare and technology. He is Co-Chair of the NY State Bar Association's Immigration and Nationality Law Committee and immediate past Chair of the American Immigration Lawyers Association's NY Chapter. He was a Member of AILA's governing Board of Directors and is a Member of the NY York City Bar Association's Immigration and Nationality Law Committee. Mr Dunn appears on CNN, NBC, FOX and Channel 9 UPN and is quoted regularly in New York dailies. He has been a lecturer on immigration issues for the Practicing Law Institute, ILW.com, AILA's national conference and the Center for Migration Studies.
**Personal:** Received a JD Degree from Brooklyn Law School in 1993 and a BS Degree from Cornell University in 1990.

## DUNNE, Carey R
Davis Polk & Wardwell, New York
212 450 4000
carey.dunne@dpw.com
*Recommended in Litigation*
**Practice Areas:** Member of Davis Polk & Wardwell's Litigation Department. Represents clients in a wide variety of criminal, civil and regulatory matters, including grand jury inquiries, internal investigations, enforcement actions by state and federal agencies, and complex commercial disputes. Most of the cases that he handles involve parallel proceedings: competing actions and investigations that must be defended simultaneously in multiple forums. Recent clients include March & McLennan, Credit Suisse First Boston, ImClone Systems, Federated Investors, Bank of America, Emerson Electric, Deutsche Bank, RTL Television and Consolidated Edison.

## DUNNE, Dennis
Milbank, Tweed, Hadley & McCloy LLP, New York 212 530 5000
*Recommended in Bankruptcy*

## DYE, Alexander M
LeBoeuf, Lamb, Greene & MacRae LLP, New York 212 424 8642
adye@llgm.com
*Recommended in Insurance*
**Practice Areas:** Specializes in corporate transactions involving the insurance

industry. He advises buyers and sellers in hostile and negotiated mergers and acquisitions transactions as well as asset purchases structured as reinsurance. He also advises issuers and underwriters in offerings of equity, debt and hybrid securities by US and non-US insurers. In addition, Mr Dye has considerable experience in restructuring troubled insurers and demutualizing life, health and property-casualty insurers.

**Career:** Joined LeBoeuf Lamb in 1981.

**Personal:** Brown University (AB magna cum laude) 1978; University of Michigan (JD) 1981.

### DYER, Richard
Thelen Reid & Priest LLP, New York
212 603 6533
rpdyer@thelenreid.com
*Recommended in Construction*

**Practice Areas:** Mr Dyer has extensive experience in a broad range of construction transactional and dispute resolution matters, including: preparation and negotiation of construction contracts, turnkey/design-build contracts, EPC contracts, construction management contracts, architect and engineer agreements, and trade contracts/subcontracts; contract administration; EEO and OSHA matters; surety bonding, mechanic's lien and insurance matters. He advises on the resolution of construction, engineering and other commercial disputes through litigation, arbitration (national and international) and mediation. Representative projects include: stadiums, aquariums, waste to energy facilities, power projects, LNG/LPG facilities, infrastructure/transportation facilities, telecom loops, hospitals, institutional buildings, assisted living facilities, museums, hotels, high-rise commercial and residential buildings. Since 1975, Mr Dyer has advised and represented owner/developer, contractors and subcontractors on matters involving the total construction process from the pre-construction phase through the construction phase and beyond, involving matters such as contract formulation, claims, dispute avoidance and resolution, suretyship, liens, insolvency, default and termination. He has been directly involved in some of the most visible construction projects in New York City including: Guggenheim Museum Expansion, Trump Tower; Jacob Javits Convention Center; Trump International Hotel and Tower, Metropolitan Tower; World Wide Plaza; The Grand Hyatt Hotel; Rockefeller University Research Building, Rockefeller University Scholar's Residence, Four Seasons Hotel, Hotel Kitano, Roosevelt Island; Battery Park City residences; Broad Financial Center; Financial Square; 750 Lexington Avenue; 461 Fifth Avenue; 667 Madison Avenue; 535 Madison Avenue; Park Avenue Tower; Shearson Lehman Hutton/American Express Center; 599 Lexington Avenue; 527

Madison Avenue; Rockefeller Research Labs at Memorial Sloan Kettering Hospital; Manufacturers Hanover Trust World Headquarters; ATT World Headquarters completion; 33 Maiden Lane; 40 Broad Street; and 101 Park Avenue.

**Prof. Memberships:** Chairman of the Mechanics' Lienors Creditors Committee, In Re East-West Associates Limited Partnership, US Bankruptcy Court, SDNY; American Bar Association, Section of Litigation, Forum Committee on the Construction Industry; American Society of Civil Engineers, Associate Member; New York Building Congress, Representative Member; General Building Contractors Association of the State of New York, Representative Member.

**Career:** Served as Assistant General Counsel for the George A Fuller Company, Division of Northrop Corporation from 1974-79, and as Vice President, General Counsel of HRH Construction Corporation from 1979-90. Joined Thelen Reid & Priest LLP in 1990. Admitted to practice in Pennsylvania (1974), New Jersey (1975) and New York (1979).

**Publications:** Co-author, Chapter 14, 'Performance Guarantees and Testing; Intellectual Property and Technology Transfer Issues', in 'Design Build Contracting Handbook', 2nd edition, Aspen Law and Business Publishers, 2001. 'New York Reports', a periodic website publication of Thelen Reid & Priest LLP concerning New York decisions of interest to the construction industry.

**Personal:** Received his JD from Villanova University School of Law in 1974. Received his BSCE from Villanova University School of Engineering in 1970 with honors, Tau Beta Pi, National Engineering Honor Society.

### ECKAS, Scott E
King & Spalding LLP, New York
212 556 2273
seckas@kslaw.com
*Recommended in Litigation*

**Practice Areas:** Litigation focusing on a wide range of commercial litigation disputes, with a particular emphasis on banking and securities litigation.

**Prof. Memberships:** State of New York Bar Association.

**Personal:** BA, magna cum laude, Phi Beta Kappa, University of Colorado, Boulder, 1986; JD, Yale Law School, 1989.

### ECKSTEIN, Kenneth H
Kramer Levin Naftalis & Frankel LLP, New York 212 715 9229
keckstein@kramerlevin.com
*Recommended in Bankruptcy*

**Practice Areas:** Partner and Chairman of Kramer Levin Naftalis & Frankel LLP Creditors' Rights and Bankruptcy Department. He has practiced in the area of corporate reorganization and bankruptcy since 1979. Practice includes both in and out-of-court restructurings of

financially distressed businesses on behalf of debtors, creditors' committees, major secured and unsecured creditors, bondholders, trustees, examiners, and third parties seeking to acquire the assets or businesses of financially troubled companies.

**Prof. Memberships:** A frequent lecturer and author in the areas of bankruptcy and corporate reorganization. He is a Member of the Section on Corporation, Banking and Business Law of the American Bar Association. He is also a former Member of the Committee on Bankruptcy and Corporate Reorganization of the Association of the Bar of the City of New York.

**Career:** Chairs a Department of seven Partners, three special counsel and 18 associates and has played a prominent role in many of the largest and most complex Chapter 11 reorganization cases and out-of-court workouts over the past 25 years. Representations include the Adelphia/FrontierVision bondholders, Owens Corning Bank Group, the Dow Corning Claimants Committee and the Official Creditor Committees for Leap Wireless, Big V, SGL Carbon Corp., Cityscape Financial, Olympia & York, Integrated Resources, SLM International, Financial News Network, PSNH, Eastern Airlines and Texaco. Mr Eckstein has also represented the debtors in the bankruptcy of MicroWarehouse, Berry Hill Galleries, Elite Models, Cross Media, and The Wiz, Inc. and has represented bank groups, bondholders, acquirors and other major creditors in Calpine, Northwest Airlines, PTS, Enron, Warnaco, NTL, Twin Lab, Amerco, Mediq, PacCoin, Big City Radio, Jitney Jungle, LTV, New Valley, Herman's Sporting Goods, Tucson Electric and Farley Industries. He has led his firm's representation of the Examiner in Bruno's Inc. and the Independent Restructuring Advisor in Coram Healthcare. He has also represented the Trustee in Island Mortgage and in Sharp International. He regularly represents a wide range of lending and other financial institutions and distressed investors in Chapter 11 cases, workouts and out-of-court restructurings. These institutions include JPMorgan Chase, CSFB, BNP-Paribas, Goldman Sachs, Alliance Capital, Barclays, Elliott Associates, Angelo Gordon, Farrallon and others.

**Personal:** Received a JD Degree from New York University in 1979 and a BA Degree cum laude from the University of Pennsylvania in 1976.

### EDELMAN, Marty
Paul, Hastings, Janofsky & Walker LLP, New York 212 318 6500
martyedelman@paulhastings.com
*Recommended in Real Estate*

**Practice Areas:** Concentrates his practice on large, complex real estate and corporate transactions. He has been involved

in all stages of legal development of pioneering financial structures, including participating mortgages, institutional joint ventures in real estate, and joint ventures between US investors and developers in Mexico, England, France, Japan, China and the Middle East.

**Prof. Memberships:** Board of Directors – Cendant Incorporated, Ashford Hospitality and Capital Trust. Advisory Board – Columbia University Law School and Business School. Advisor – Fisher Brothers, Grove Real Estates Investors Millennium Partners and The Related Companies.

### EDELMAN, Scott
Milbank, Tweed, Hadley & McCloy LLP, New York 212 530 5000
*Recommended in Litigation*

### EDELSTEIN, Mark S
Morrison & Foerster LLP, New York
212 468 8273
medelstein@mofo.com
*Recommended in Real Estate*

**Practice Areas:** Concentrates on real estate finance, acquisition, sale, investment, bankruptcy and workout. Regularly represents lenders and equity sources in a wide variety of transactions and assets, including: office, retail, multi-family, commercial, industrial, hospitality, nursing home, condominium and co-operative. Expert on syndicated, securitized and participated lending, mezzanine finance, debt tranching, subscription, opportunity fund and REIT lines of credit, and construction financing. Has written/lectured extensively on these subjects.

**Prof. Memberships:** Urban Land Institute, Mortgage Bankers Association, Real Estate Board of New York, Real Estate and Construction Council of Lincoln Center, Real Estate Lenders Association.

**Career:** Bar admission: New York.

**Personal:** BA, summa cum laude, City College of New York, 1979; JD, magna cum laude, Cardozo School of Law, Yeshiva University, 1982

### EDGAR, Kenneth C
Simpson Thacher & Bartlett LLP, New York 212 455 2560
kedgar@stblaw.com
*Recommended in Employee Benefits*

**Practice Areas:** Ken Edgar is a Partner and Head of the firm's Executive Compensation and Employee Benefits Practice. With over 30 years' experience in this area, he has advised clients on a wide variety of employee compensation and benefits issues, with emphasis on key executive programs and employment contracts, and compliance with the complex tax and other regulatory provisions associated therewith, as well as compensation and benefits issues raised in connection with complicated merger transactions and leveraged buyouts.

**Prof. Memberships:** Member: New York

State Bar Association (Co-Chairman, Employee Benefits Committee, Tax Section, 1988-98); American Bar Association (Employee Benefits Committee, 1987-present); Association of the Bar of the City of New York.
**Career:** Joined Simpson Thacher in 1976 and was elected Partner in 1980.
**Personal:** Mr Edgar received his JD from New York University School of Law in 1973, where he also received an LLM in Taxation in 1978. He received his BA from Haverford College, with honors in English, in 1969.

## EINHORN, David M
Wachtell, Lipton, Rosen & Katz, New York 212 403 1213
dmeinhorn@wlrk.com
*Recommended in Tax*
**Practice Areas:** Specializes in the tax aspects of the joint ventures, corporate reorganizations, acquisitions, dispositions, financings, and restructurings that constitute Wachtell, Lipton, Rosen & Katz's primary practice, which transactions frequently involve multinational businesses and raise complex multinational tax issues.
**Prof. Memberships:** Tax Sections of the New York State Bar Association; Association of the Bar of the City of New York.
**Career:** Partner at Wachtell, Lipton, Rosen & Katz since 1982. Often lectures on tax matters at professional seminars.
**Personal:** Graduated from Fordham Law School in 1976 (JD) and from New York University Law School in 1979 (LLM).

## ELLIS, Emmett N
Dewey Ballantine LLP, New York 212 259 6150
eellis@deweyballantine.com
*Recommended in Energy*
**Practice Areas:** Mr Ellis works with both regulated and non-regulated entities in the global power markets. He represents energy companies and investment banks in public and private capital markets transactions. Mr Ellis has represented corporate clients in the acquisition and divestiture of energy companies and energy assets in the United States and the United Kingdom.
**Prof. Memberships:** American Bar Association, Vice-Chairman, Infrastructure Finance, Mergers and Acquisitions Committee of the Section of Public Utility, Communications and Transportation Law.
**Career:** Partner, Dewey Ballantine LLP.
**Personal:** Born August 27, 1953. BA, University of Oklahoma, 1975. JD, Yale Law School, 1978.

## ELLSWORTH, Kathryn
Dewey Ballantine LLP, New York 212 259 7128
kelslworth@deweyballantine.com
*Recommended in Insurance*
**Practice Areas:** Insurance/reinsurance

litigation and arbitration, commercial litigation.
**Career:** Ms Ellsworth handles general commercial litigation with concentrations in insurance and reinsurance litigation and arbitration and business tort litigation. Her practice ranges from representing a large reinsurer in litigation over the reinsurance coverage of a billion-dollar settlement of asbestos liabilities to representing the New York State Department of Insurance in an action for breach of fiduciary duty against former officers and directors of an insolvent insurer.
**Personal:** BS, Virginia Polytechnic Institute and State University, 1984. JD, Rutgers University School of Law, 1990.

## EMMERICH, Adam O
Wachtell, Lipton, Rosen & Katz, New York 212 403 1234
aoemmerich@wlrk.com
*Recommended in Corporate/M&A*
**Practice Areas:** Mergers and acquisitions and securities law matters. Practice includes a broad and varied representation of public and private corporations and other entities in a variety of industries throughout the United States and abroad, in connection with mergers and acquisitions, divestitures, spin-offs, joint ventures, and financing transactions. Also has extensive experience in takeover defense and corporate governance issues.
**Prof. Memberships:** Association of the Bar of the City of New York; New York State and American Bar Association; New York County Lawyers Association; Securities Law Committee of the American Society of Corporate Secretaries; and the Corporate Academic Bridge Group of the NYU Center for Law and Business. Member, Board of Directors of the American Friends of the Israel Museum and of the Ramaz School, President of the American Friends of the Israel Antiquities Authority. Previously served on the Visiting Committee of the University of Chicago Law School and currently a Co-Chair of its capital campaign, and as Chair of the Young Lawyers Division of the UJA-Federation in New York. Member of the Board of Directors of the Lawyers Alliance for New York.
**Career:** Joined Wachtell, Lipton, Rosen & Katz in 1986 and named a Partner in 1991. BA, Swarthmore College and JD with honors, University of Chicago. Topics and comments editor of the University of Chicago Law Review; Order of the Coif; Olin Fellow in Law and Economics. Law clerk to Hon Abner J Mikva, United States Court of Appeals for the District of Columbia Circuit. A frequent speaker at Bar and professional conferences on topics relating to mergers and acquisitions.
**Personal:** Born 15 December 1960. Married with three children.

## ENGELMAYER, Paul
WilmerHale, New York 212 230 8820
paul.engelmayer@wilmerhale.com
*Recommended in Litigation*
**Practice Areas:** Co-Chair, Investigations and Criminal Litigation Group. Represents institutional and individual clients in high profile white-collar criminal cases, securities-enforcement investigations; conducts internal investigations; and represents institutions in complex securities and commercial litigation. Has an active appellate practice, in which he represents clients in appellate and Supreme Court litigation. Litigation experience spans federal criminal law, securities law, antitrust law, constitutional law (including First Amendment law), immigration law and consumer-credit law.
**Career:** Assistant US Attorney, Chief of the Major Crimes Unit at the US Attorney's Office for the Southern District of New York. Assistant to the Solicitor General of the United States.
**Personal:** JD, Harvard Law School; BA, Harvard College.

## ENGROS JR, Charles E
Morgan, Lewis & Bockius LLP, New York 212 309 6880
charles.engros@morganlewis.com
*Recommended in Media & Entertainment*
**Practice Areas:** Charles Engros is Head of the firm's Media Practice and also Managing Partner of its New York office and Co-Head of its M&A Practice Group. He represents media and information companies in Europe and the United States in a wide variety of matters including mergers and acquisitions, joint ventures, licensing and financings. He is also active in other industries including, in particular, consumer products, life sciences and the financial services industry.

## EPSTEIN, Michael
Weil, Gotshal & Manges LLP, New York 212 310 8432
michael.epstein@weil.com
*Recommended in Technology*
**Practice Areas:** Michael Epstein has extensive experience litigating and counseling corporations worldwide, and has litigated, negotiated and resolved some of the largest and most complex intellectual property disputes. His practice involves substantial transactional work, including structuring and negotiating technology and intellectual property acquisitions, technology transfer and licensing arrangements, outsourcing transactions and joint ventures and other targeted alliances. He is the author of the treatises 'Epstein on Intellectual Property' and 'Modern Intellectual Property', and a co-author of 'Online – Internet Law, International Intellectual Property'.
**Personal:** Lehigh University, BA, 1975; New York University School of Law, JD,

1979.

## ESPOSITO, Grant J
Mayer, Brown, Rowe & Maw LLP, New York 212 506 2547
gesposito@mayerbrownrowe.com
*Recommended in Litigation*
**Practice Areas:** Complex commercial litigation: accountants' liability; antitrust; ADR; products liability; securities law; electronic discovery and records management. Represents clients in the automotive, pharmaceuticals, and professional services industries in the United States, Germany and Switzerland. Successfully argued an appeal before the Tenth Circuit on behalf of a major pharmaceuticals company on the issue of personal jurisdiction. Responsible for managing national defense of products liability cases.
**Career:** Mayer, Brown, Rowe & Maw LLP, New York, 1997 to date. Shearman & Sterling, New York, 1992-97.
**Publications:** 'Beware These Storm Clouds: How Not to Sink your Chances of Getting that Offer', The New York Law Journal, May 2005. 'E-Discovery and Information Management, Effective Strategies for Avoiding Litigation Disaster', Legal Publishing Group of Strafford Publications, February 22, 2006.
**Personal:** Fordham University School of Law, JD cum laude, 1992; Order of the Coif. Cornell University, BA with distinction in all subjects, 1989; Dean's List.

## ETTINGER, John R
Davis Polk & Wardwell, New York 212 450 4000
john.ettinger@dpw.com
*Recommended in Private Equity*
**Practice Areas:** Managing Partner of Davis Polk & Wardwell. In his own practice, he represents clients in mergers and acquisitions, joint ventures, restructuring, takeover defenses, and corporate governance issues. He represents a number of private equity funds on both transactional and fund management matters.

## EVANUSA, Michel
Stroock & Stroock & Lavan LLP, New York 212 806 5400
*Recommended in Real Estate*

## FACTOR, Jason R
Cleary Gottlieb Steen & Hamilton LLP, New York 212 225 2694
jfactor@cgsh.com
*Recommended in Tax*
**Practice Areas:** Tax matters, particularly formation of investment funds and other partnerships, acquisitions and divestitures, workouts and bankruptcy, partnership tax and compensation of partners.
**Prof. Memberships:** Member of the Bar in New York.
**Career:** Joined firm, 1997; became Partner, 2005. JD, magna cum laude, Order of the Coif, University of Michigan Law

School (1995); BA, magna cum laude with highest honors in History, Phi Beta Kappa, Harvard College (1992).

### FADIL, Adeeb
Simpson Thacher & Bartlett LLP, New York 212 455 7070
afadil@stblaw.com
*Recommended in Environment*
**Practice Areas:** Counsel at Simpson Thacher in the Litigation Department. Specializes in environmental law. Experience includes: advising clients about environmental aspects of transactions, including acquisitions, divestitures, loans, securities offerings, and bankruptcies and restructurings, involving entities with domestic and multinational operations (from extraction of oil/coal/other natural resources, to steel/chemical/paper/other manufacturing, to electrical generation/transmission/distribution, to rail/air/water/other transportation, to commercial real estate and retail businesses); counseling clients in the management of, and in the resolution of disputes over, contractual, statutory and common law environmental liabilities; and litigating environmental matters.
**Prof. Memberships:** American Bar Association, Association of the Bar of the City of New York.
**Career:** Joined the firm in 1989, Counsel since 1994.
**Publications:** 'New EPA Policies: Reforming CERCLA by Administrative Guidance', 10 Toxics Law Reporter 611 (1995).
**Personal:** BA (with highest honors), University of Virginia (1980), Echols Scholar, Phi Beta Kappa; JD, Yale Law School (1984). Clerk to the Hon Robert R Merhige, Jr, US District Judge, Eastern District of Virginia (1984-85). Admitted New York (1986).

### FAGEN, Leslie Gordon
Paul, Weiss, Rifkind, Wharton & Garrison LLP, New York 212 373 3231
lfagen@paulweiss.com
*Recommended in Litigation*
**Practice Areas:** Senior Partner in the Litigation Department and Member of firm's Management Committee. Has extensive experience encompassing product liability, IP, insurance, antitrust, environmental and securities law. Litigated on behalf of plaintiffs and defendants at trial and appellate level in federal and state courts. Secured a victory on behalf of AC Nielsen and other defendants dismissing a nine-year antitrust litigation on motion. Also, achieved a victory for client Polo Ralph Lauren in its trademark dispute with the US Polo Association. Fellow of the American College of Trial Lawyers. Selected for 2006 edition of The Best Lawyers in America.

### FAGIN, Allen
Proskauer Rose LLP, New York
212 969 3030
afagin@proskauer.com
*Recommended in Employment*
**Practice Areas:** Chairman of Proskauer Rose LLP, and the former Co-Chair of Proskauer's Labor and Employment Law Department. He represents employers in all types of employment litigation. His clients are as diverse as his practice, representing fields such as telecommunications, transportation, healthcare, insurance, legal services, utilities, financial services, entertainment and manufacturing.
**Prof. Memberships:** A Member of the American College of Labor and Employment Lawyers. Was chosen by New York Magazine as one of the 100 best lawyers in New York, and was profiled by the National Law Journal as one of the top employment litigators in the country. Was also selected as one of 118 US attorneys in the International Who's Who of Management Labor & Employment Lawyers.
**Publications:** Publishes regularly in the labor and employment field, is a frequent lecturer on employment discrimination matters.
**Personal:** A summa cum laude graduate of Columbia College, graduated with honors from Harvard Law School, holds a Masters Degree in Public Policy from Harvard University's John F Kennedy School of Government.

### FALCK, David
Pillsbury Winthrop Shaw Pittman LLP, New York 212 858 1438
david.falck@pillsburylaw.com
*Recommended in Energy*
**Practice Areas:** Securities offerings, mergers, acquisitions, restructurings, and private equity investments (with particular focus on transactions involving energy companies). Experience includes: advising issuers, their boards of directors and financial advisors on public company mergers and asset and stock acquisitions; public offerings for utility and energy companies; domestic and European Rule 144A offerings of high-yield and project debt; and representing private investors in the acquisition of existing businesses from industrial companies.
**Personal:** JD, Washington and Lee University School of Law, 1978 (summa cum laude; Member, Law Review; Order of the Coif); BA, Colgate University, 1975 (magna cum laude; Phi Beta Kappa).

### FARBER, Michael
Davis Polk & Wardwell, New York
212 450 4000
michael.farber@dpw.com
*Recommended in Tax*
**Practice Areas:** Member of Davis Polk & Wardwell's Tax Department. Has advised clients on a variety of domestic and international transactions, including mergers, acquisitions, joint ventures and securities offerings, and regularly advises investment banks and other financial institutions, including JPMorgan Chase, Goldman Sachs, Deutsche Bank, Lehman Brothers, UBS, Credit Suisse and BNP Paribas, in connection with their financial instruments, derivatives and capital markets activities. Currently Co-Chair of the New York State Bar Association Tax Section's Committee on Financial Instruments.

### FASMAN, Zachary D
Paul, Hastings, Janofsky & Walker LLP, New York 212 318 6315
zacharyfasman@paulhastings.com
*Recommended in Employment*
**Practice Areas:** Chair, Employment Law Department, New York Office. Employment Law Litigation and Advice; Labor Law Litigation and Advice.
**Prof. Memberships:** College of Labor and Employment Lawyers; Best Lawyers in America; Advisory Board, New York University Law School Center for Labor and Employment Law, National Employment Law Institute; Labor Law Committee, United States Chamber of Commerce.
**Career:** Paul, Hastings, Janofsky & Walker, Washington, DC 1988-2000; New York, 2000-present; Crowell & Moring, Washington, 1983-88; Seyfarth, Shaw, Washington and Chicago, 1972-83.
**Personal:** BA Northwestern University, 1969; JD University of Michigan, 1972, with honors, Order of the Coif. Born Chicago, Illinois.

### FASTOW, Jay N
Weil, Gotshal & Manges LLP, New York 212 310 8644
jay.fastow@weil.com
*Recommended in Antitrust*
**Practice Areas:** Jay Fastow heads the firm's Financial Services Practice, is an active member of its Antitrust Practice, and has been lead counsel in litigations from New York to Guam. He has litigated antitrust cases in a variety of industries, played a leading role in co-ordinating multi-defendant litigations, and argued appeals successfully in courts around the country. In the financial services area, he has litigated numerous payment card cases, and has been involved in suits involving auto finance and leasing, consumer credit counseling and other financial services activities.
**Personal:** Brandeis University, BA, 1974; Yale Law School, JD, 1977.

### FEIN, Scott
Whiteman Osterman & Hanna LLP, Albany 518 487 7600
*Recommended in Environment*

### FELCHER, Peter L
Paul, Weiss, Rifkind, Wharton & Garrison LLP, New York 212 373 3390
pfelcher@paulweiss.com
*Recommended in Media & Entertainment*
**Practice Areas:** Partner in the Corporate and Entertainment Departments. Concentrates in mergers and acquisitions, as well as financings, particularly involving companies in the entertainment and media industries. Clients are active in the music publishing, recording, motion picture, theater, book publishing, dance and non-profit areas. Is involved in legislative, regulatory and litigation activity on the industry level in the music business. His practice also involves representation of creative individuals in the entertainment business. Trustee of the Cole Porter Musical and Literary Property Trusts. Selected for 2006 edition of The Best Lawyers in America.

### FELDBERG, Michael
Allen & Overy LLP, New York
212 610 6360
michael.feldberg@allenovery.com
*Recommended in Litigation*
**Practice Areas:** Litigation, with an emphasis on the defense of federal criminal and regulatory cases and federal civil litigation. He has tried over 50 cases, and has represented numerous companies and individuals in matters involving the financial services, retail, healthcare and general corporate industries.
**Career:** Partner at Allen & Overy LLP since 2003. Previously, he was a Partner at Schulte Roth & Zabel LLP (1991-2003); (Chair of Litigation Department, 1999-2003), and served as assistant United States attorney (SDNY) (1981-84).
**Personal:** Harvard Law School (JD, cum laude, 1977); Harvard College (AB, magna cum laude, 1973).

### FELDMAN, Matthew A
Willkie Farr & Gallagher LLP, New York 212 728 8651
mfeldman@willkie.com
*Recommended in Bankruptcy*
**Practice Areas:** Partner in the Business Reorganization and Restructuring Department. Clients include debtors, creditors, lenders, landlords, governmental agencies, and bank committees. Has been significantly involved in numerous complex Chapter 11 cases and non-judicial restructurings, including recent representation of Werner Co., PG&E National Energy Group; Verestar, Inc.; XO Communications, Inc.; Global Crossing, Ltd.; Big V Supermarkets, Inc.; and Golden Books Entertainment. Represented several debtors in cross-border insolvency cases and foreign restructurings including Petroleum Geo-Services ASA; Millicom Cellular SA; ish GmbH & Co. KG and Kabel Baden-Württemberg GmbH & Co. KG, two of the largest German cable television companies; Livent Inc.; Teleglobe, Inc.; Converse Corporation; Alliance Entertainment Corp.; and AIOC Corporation. Regularly represents

investors seeking to acquire assets or businesses from companies operating in Chapter 11.

**Prof. Memberships:** Member of the Connecticut Bar Association, the American Bar Association, and the American Bankruptcy Institute.

**Career:** Honors and Awards: The Best Lawyers in America – 2005 to present; K&A Restructuring Register – 2004 to present; New York Superlawyers – 2006. Admitted to the Bars of New York, Connecticut, and Massachusetts, as well as the Southern and Northern Districts of New York and the District of Massachusetts.

**Personal:** Received a JD from New York University School of Law in 1988 and a BA (magna cum laude) from Tufts University in 1985.

## FELTENSTEIN, Martha
Skadden, Arps, Slate, Meagher & Flom LLP & Affiliates, New York
212 735 2272
mfeltens@skadden.com
*Recommended in Real Estate*

**Practice Areas:** Active in all aspects of Skadden's Real Estate Practice, including bank lending and financial products, real estate development, acquisitions, leasing, joint ventures, financing, public and private offerings of real estate securities, and commercial mortgage securitization. Also represents US and non-US clients in their acquisition and development of hotels, shopping centers, office buildings and residential properties in the United States and abroad.

**Career:** JD, Columbia University, 1981; MPhil, School of Oriental and African Studies, University of London, 1977; BA, Princeton University, 1975.

## FIELDS, Richard
Dickstein Shapiro Morin & Oshinsky LLP, New York 212 277 6755
FieldsR@dsmo.com
*Recommended in Insurance*

**Practice Areas:** State and federal litigation and international arbitration, emphasis on insurance coverage, complex dispute resolution, terrorist financing, and human rights. Resolved some of the largest insurance claims in history involving professional negligence, securities fraud, pollution, asbestos, product liability, directors and officers, and mass torts for Fortune 100 clients in the oil, chemical, utility, banking, and manufacturing sectors.

**Prof. Memberships:** ABA; International Bar Association.

**Career:** Partner, Dickstein Shapiro; Partner, Director, Swidler Berlin.

**Publications:** Published numerous articles on insurance and legal profession.

**Personal:** Indiana University (BA, Phi Beta Kappa, 1977; JD, summa cum laude, 1982); Rose-Hulman Institute of Technology (1974-75).

## FIFE, Lori R
Weil, Gotshal & Manges LLP, New York
212 310 8318
lori.fife@weil.com
*Recommended in Bankruptcy*

**Practice Areas:** Lori Fife's practice covers domestic and international debt restructurings, crisis management and corporate governance. She represents companies, banks, secured and unsecured creditors and committees in Chapter 11 cases and in out-of-court restructurings. Ms Fife co-led the firm's representation of MCI / WorldCom in Chapter 11 and is representing Loral Space & Communications in Chapter 11. She has represented debtors such as Sunbeam, Texaco, Bruno's, Best Products, R.H. Macy, Premium Standard Farms, CHI Energy, and creditors such as CSFB, Prudential and Citibank.

**Personal:** University of Pennsylvania, BA, 1980; Benjamin N. Cardozo School of Law, JD, 1983.

## FILARDI, Edward V
Skadden, Arps, Slate, Meagher & Flom LLP & Affiliates, New York
212 735 3060
efilardi@skadden.com
*Recommended in Intellectual Property*

**Practice Areas:** Has extensive experience in patent, trade secret, unfair competition and antitrust-related matters, specifically regarding litigation and dispute resolution. Registered US patent attorney with extensive jury trial and appellate experience; has litigated patent and trademark cases for both plaintiffs and defendants. Has served as lead trial counsel in matters involving various technologies, including medical devices, chemicals, pharmaceuticals, computers, telecommunications, and mechanics in federal and state courts as well as before the International Trade Commission. Also has significant experience in international litigation related to pharmaceutical, chemical and fabricated materials industries, and has served as advisory lead counsel in coordinating litigation in France, Germany, the Netherlands, the UK, Japan, Denmark and Sweden. Has been an arbitrator and a court-appointed neutral evaluator in intellectual property rights infringement matters.

**Career:** JD, New York Law School, 1968 (articles editor, Law Review); BS, Iona College, 1965.

## FINKEL, Robert
Milbank, Tweed, Hadley & McCloy LLP, New York 212 530 5000
*Recommended in Business Process Outsourcing, Technology*

## FINKELSON, Allen
Cravath, Swaine & Moore LLP, New York
212 474 1262
afinkelson@cravath.com
*Recommended in Corporate/M&A*

**Practice Areas:** Mergers and acquisi-

tions.

**Prof. Memberships:** ABCNY.

**Career:** Partner, 1977-83. Managing Director, Mergers and Acquisitions Group at Lehman Brothers, 1983-85. Partner since 1985.

**Personal:** Columbia Law School (JD, 1971; editor of Columbia Law Review); St. Lawrence University (BA, magna cum laude, 1968; Phi Beta Kappa).

## FINKELSTEIN, Stuart M
Skadden, Arps, Slate, Meagher & Flom LLP & Affiliates, New York
212 735 2841
sfinkels@skadden.com
*Recommended in Tax*

**Practice Areas:** Represents clients on a wide range of tax matters, with particular emphasis on mergers, acquisitions and divestiture transactions, including spin-offs, debt and equity offerings and joint ventures. Also devotes a significant amount of time to advising troubled companies, both in and out of bankruptcy.

**Prof. Memberships:** Admitted in New York and Illinois.

**Career:** JD, The University of Michigan Law School, 1985 (cum laude); BBA, The University of Michigan School of Business Administration, 1982 (with distinction).

**Publications:** Has spoken around the country and published several articles on various corporate tax planning matters.

## FINLEY, John G
Simpson Thacher & Bartlett LLP, New York 212 455 2000
jfinley@stblaw.com
*Recommended in Corporate/M&A*

**Practice Areas:** Senior Member of the Mergers and Acquisitions Group and Chairman of the firm's Corporate Governance Practice Group. Recent transactions include the sale of Neiman Marcus to an investment group consisting of Texas Pacific Group and Warburg Pincus (2005); the sale of Toys R Us to a consortium including Kohlberg Kravis Roberts & Co. (2005), the business combination of Kmart with Sears (2005), the sale of Grey Global to the WPP Group (2005), the sale of VNU's Yellow Pages directories to Apax and Cinven (2004) and the acquisition of Time Warner's Warner Music Group by a consortium led by Thomas H Lee Partners and Edgar Bronfman, Jr (2004).

**Prof. Memberships:** New York State Bar Association (served on Committee on Securities Regulation); International Bar Association (currently Co-Chairman of Committee on Business Organizations).

**Career:** Joined firm 1981; became Partner 1989.

**Publications:** Author and speaker at conferences on mergers and acquisitions sponsored by the Tulane Corporate Law Institure, the UCLA Law First Annual

Institute on Corporate, Securities and Related Aspects of Mergers and Acquisitions, the Center for the Study of Mergers and Acquisitions of the University of Miami School of Law and the International Bar Association.

**Personal:** University of Pennsylvania (BA, College of Arts & Sciences; BS, Wharton School), summa cum laude, 1978); Harvard Law School (JD, cum laude, 1981). Trustee of the Jewish Board of Family and Children's Services.

## FISHBEIN, Matthew
Debevoise & Plimpton LLP, New York
212 909 6000
*Recommended in Litigation*

## FISKE, Robert
Davis Polk & Wardwell, New York
212 450 4000
robert.fiske@dpw.com
*Recommended in Litigation*

**Practice Areas:** Senior Member of Davis Polk & Wardwell's Litigation Department. Among his practice specialties are professional liability, securities, products liability and white-collar crime. Has tried many cases concerning a wide variety of industries and areas of the law in courts across the country. Financial and securities experience includes representation of General Electric, Exxon, Bankers Trust, and other clients in securities actions. Also has significant products liability experience. Experience as a government prosecutor and lawyer is extensive, including as a former US Attorney and Whitewater Independent Counsel.

## FITZGERALD, Brian T
LeBoeuf, Lamb, Greene & MacRae LLP, Albany 202 986 8007
bfitzger@llgm.com
*Recommended in Energy*

**Practice Areas:** Representation of energy and telecommunications clients in federal and state regulatory proceedings and resulting litigation, including financings and asset transfers. Mr FitzGerald also represents VOIP, wireless, cable and utility clients in network security, privacy, site acquisition, pole attachment, rights-of-way, franchising, rate and interconnection matters.

**Prof. Memberships:** New York Bar; Connecticut Bar; District of Columbia Bar; Rhode Island Bar.

**Career:** Joined LeBoeuf Lamb in 1990.

**Publications:** 'Sealed v. Sealed, A Public Court System Secretly Going Private', Journal of Law & Politics 381 (1990).

**Personal:** University of Virginia (JD) 1990; Siena College (BA) 1987.

## FITZGERALD, Edmond
Davis Polk & Wardwell, New York
212 450 4000
edmond.fitzgerald@dpw.com
*Recommended in Employee Benefits*

**Practice Areas:** As a member of Davis Polk & Wardwell's Executive Compensation and Employee Benefits Practice Group, he works closely with the firm's Corporate Department on matters involving executive compensation and employee benefits, both in the ordinary course of clients' business and in the context of mergers and acquisitions, new ventures, and restructurings. He has extensive experience in structuring employment agreements, equity compensation, performance incentives, deferred compensation, change in control protections, and management participation in buyouts and new ventures. He has considerable experience in domestic and international M&A across a variety of sectors. He also works extensively with the firm's Investment Management Group and Derivatives Group in structuring financial products and investment funds to include participation by management personnel and pension plans.

### FITZPATRICK JR, James A
Dewey Ballantine LLP, New York
212 259 6220
jfitzpatrick@deweyballantine.com
*Recommended in Insurance*
**Practice Areas:** Mr FitzPatrick represents public and private insurance and other companies and their boards of directors in transactional matters such as the formation of new business ventures, public and private capital raising, purchase and sale of assets, reinsurance transactions, mergers and acquisitions, insolvencies and reorganizations and restructurings as well as general corporate, insurance regulatory and corporate governance matters.
**Prof. Memberships:** American Bar Association, Torts and Insurance Practice Section.
**Career:** Partner, Dewey Ballantine LLP.
**Personal:** Born July 1, 1949. BA, Dartmouth College, 1971. JD, Albany Law School, Union University, 1974.

### FITZPATRICK JR, Michael F
Dewey Ballantine LLP, New York
212 259 6670
mfitzpatrick@deweyballantine.com
*Recommended in Energy*
**Practice Areas:** Mr Fitzpatrick has extensive experience representing issuers and underwriters in capital markets transactions, principally in the utility and energy area. These transactions involve taxable and tax-exempt securities, including 'hybrid' securities. He represented electric and natural gas utilities in connection with stranded cost securitizations. He advises companies on general corporate and securities law matters, including continuing advice on the Sarbanes-Oxley Act and other aspects of corporate governance.
**Prof. Memberships:** American Bar Association; American Institute of Certified Public Accountants.
**Career:** Energy and corporate finance.

**Personal:** Born April 6, 1961. BS, Villanova University, 1983. JD, Fordham University School of Law, 1990.

### FITZPATRICK JR, Vincent R
White & Case LLP, New York
212 819 8569
vfitzpatrick@whitecase.com
*Recommended in Litigation*
**Practice Areas:** Focuses primarily on complex litigation and arbitration such as SEC enforcement actions, fraud claims, ERISA, securities law, RICO, antitrust, intellectual property, toxic torts, product liability, environmental disputes, insurance coverage (including environmental-related claims), and accountants' liability. Also has extensive experience in compliance and regulatory matters including grand jury investigations and federal and state criminal and regulatory investigations by various government agencies.
**Prof. Memberships:** NYSBA; ABA.
**Career:** White & Case since 2002.
**Personal:** Manhattan College (BA 1966); Columbia University (JD 1969).

### FLAUM, Douglas H
Fried, Frank, Harris, Shriver & Jacobson LLP, New York 212 859 8259
Douglas.Flaum@FriedFrank.com
*Recommended in Litigation*
**Practice Areas:** Litigation Partner. Concentrates practice in securities, corporate governance, fiduciary duty matters and corporate-control contests on behalf of foreign and domestic corporations, boards of directors and their special committees. Also actively litigates all manner of business torts and contract and licensing disputes involving products ranging from, among others, pharmaceutical products to telecommunications satellites to real estate.
**Career:** Joined Fried Frank in 1986. Became a Partner in 1993.
**Personal:** JD (1986), Rutgers School of Law. BA (1982), cum laude, Tufts University.

### FLEDER, Robert C
Paul, Weiss, Rifkind, Wharton & Garrison LLP, New York 212 373 3107
rfleder@paulweiss.com
*Recommended in Employee Benefits*
**Practice Areas:** Co-Chair of Employee Benefits and Executive Compensation Group. Has extensive experience in legal, accounting, actuarial and HR issues connected with implementation and operation of ERISA employee benefit plans (including ESOPs) and executive compensation arrangements. Has extensive experience in M&A transactions, including dealing with stock options, underfunded pensions, retiree health, employment and severance contracts, golden parachutes, and crafting management equity incentives. Defended and resolved serious ERISA fiduciary claims. Significant expertise dealing with PBGC. Member of Taxation Section of New York State

Bar Association; past Co-Chair of its Employee Benefits Committee. Selected for 2006 edition of The Best Lawyers in America.

### FLEISCHER JR, Arthur
Fried, Frank, Harris, Shriver & Jacobson LLP, New York 212 859 8120
Arthur.Fleischer@FriedFrank.com
*Recommended in Corporate/M&A*
**Practice Areas:** Senior Partner. Has led the firm's M&A Practice for over 30 years. Represents corporate clients as acquirers and targets in both negotiated and contested transactions. Advises special committees formed to review buyout proposals, corporate restructurings and litigation possibilities and boards of directors in their governance practices.
**Career:** Joined Fried Frank in 1958. Became a Partner in 1967. Co-author of the seminal textbook on hostile transactions, Takeover Defense. Co-author of Board Games.
**Personal:** LLB (1958). BA (1953), Yale University.

### FLEMING JR, Peter
Curtis, Mallet-Prevost, Colt & Mosle LLP, New York 212 696 6008
pfleming@cm-p.com
*Recommended in Litigation*
**Practice Areas:** Mr Fleming is head of the firm's Litigation Department. He joined the firm in 1970. That same year he served as Special Counsel for the Select Committee on Crime of the House of Representatives. Previously, Mr Fleming was an Assistant and then Executive Assistant to the US attorney, Southern District of New York, Robert Morgenthau. In addition to handling litigation matters for clients of the firm, Mr Fleming has developed an extensive barrister practice in both civil and criminal areas. He has been lead counsel for the defense of several major white-collar criminal prosecutions of individuals and corporations.
**Prof. Memberships:** American College of Trial Lawyers; Association of the Bar of the City of New York; New York County Lawyers' Association; New York State Bar Association; Association of Trial Lawyers of America; Federal Bar Council; New York State Association of Criminal Defense Lawyers; Supreme Court Historical Society.
**Personal:** LLB, Yale Law School, 1958; BA, magna cum laude, Princeton University, 1951.

### FLESHER, Gail
Davis Polk & Wardwell, New York
212 450 4000
gail.flesher@dpw.com
*Recommended in Environment*
**Practice Areas:** Member of Davis Polk & Wardwell's Corporate Department and Co-ordinator of the firm's Environmental Practice Group. Represents national and international companies, investors,

boards of directors and financial institutions on a wide range of environmental matters. In the context of transactions, she primarily focuses on the structuring, diligence, protective devices and contractual commitments involved in complex mergers and acquisitions, real estate acquisitions or other forms of investments, securities offerings, issuance of secured and unsecured debt and bankruptcies and restructurings.

### FLICS, Martin
Linklaters, New York
212 903 9022
martin.flics@linklaters.com
*Recommended in Bankruptcy*
**Practice Areas:** Head of US Restructuring and Insolvency Practice, advises companies, secured and unsecured creditors, and financial advisors in major bankruptcies and restructurings. Significant aspects of his practice include advising purchasers of assets of, and investors in, distressed companies (including providers of debtor-in-possession and exit financing). Broad-based experience is illustrated by transactions such as representing Curative Health Services in its prepackaged plan of reorganization; advising UBS as financial advisor/committed lender in the Nextwave Chapter 11 case; advising Matlin/Patterson in the Ormet Aluminum Chapter 11 case as DIP lender and largest creditor; advising MatlinPatterson in the Varig proceedings; representing CSFB as secured lender in connection with the Premier Cruises proceedings; acting as bankruptcy advisor to the purchaser of Global Crossing in its Chapter 11 case and representing the provisional liquidators of Northern Offshore Limited in their US section 304 ancillary proceedings.
**Personal:** Received his JD from Fordham University in 1979 and his BA from Hampshire College in 1976.

### FLOM, Joseph H
Skadden, Arps, Slate, Meagher & Flom LLP & Affiliates, New York
212 735 3100
jflom@skadden.com
*Recommended in Corporate/M&A*
**Practice Areas:** Leading attorney in M&A area. Credited with pioneering many of the strategies used by bidders, targets and investment bankers. Practice includes all forms of corporate transactions.
**Prof. Memberships:** Director, UrbanAmerica, LLC (1998-present); Advisory Board, RRE Investors, LLC (1999-present); and Trustee, Petrie Stores Liquidating Trust (1996-present).
**Career:** LLB, Harvard Law School, 1948 (cum laude; Editor, Harvard Law Review); College of the City of NY; LHD, Honorary Doctorate in Humane Letters, Queens College, 1984; LLD, Honorary

Doctorate of Law, Fordham University, 1990; Chairman, Woodrow Wilson International Center for Scholars (1994-98).

## FLORACK, James A
Davis Polk & Wardwell, New York
212 450 4000
james.florack@dpw.com
*Recommended in Banking & Finance*
**Practice Areas:** Member of Davis Polk & Wardwell's Corporate Department. Advises clients on a range of lending and other corporate finance transactions, including leveraged lending, structured financings, high-yield debt offerings and other capital markets transactions. Practice includes transactions both in the US and in international markets, particularly Latin America. Clients include a number of financial institutions, including JPMorgan Chase, Morgan Stanley, Bank of America and Credit Suisse First Boston, as well as a number of corporate clients.

## FLUMENBAUM, Martin
Paul, Weiss, Rifkind, Wharton & Garrison LLP, New York 212 373 3191
mflumenbaum@paulweiss.com
*Recommended in Litigation*
**Practice Areas:** Senior Litigation Partner, and former Chair of the department, who advises clients on a broad range of issues with an emphasis on securities, mergers and acquisitions, intellectual property, antitrust and white-collar criminal matters. Serves as trial and litigation counsel on commercial disputes and investigations for numerous clients, including insurance giant AIG, Hollinger International, Weight Watchers, and Fimalac. Fellow of the American College of Trial Lawyers. Noted in the 2006 edition of The Best Lawyers in America as one of the few outstanding lawyers in three categories: 'Bet-the-Company' litigations, Commercial Litigation and White-Collar Criminal Defense.

## FODOR, Susanna Serena
Jones Day, New York
212 326 3476
ssfodor@jonesday.com
*Recommended in Real Estate*
**Practice Areas:** Experienced in all transactional aspects of real property. She is among a handful of attorneys who combines a broad-based real estate practice with an equally strong specialty practice in design, development and construction law. Recognized globally as a leading real estate lawyer.
**Prof. Memberships:** American College of Real Estate Lawyers; American College of Construction Lawyers; CoreNet Global/Master of Corporate Real Estate; founding member of the Editorial Board of the Journal of Corporate Real Estate.
**Publications:** Writes and lectures on real estate law, construction law, and related topics for the Practising Law Institute, American Arbitration Association, and others.

## FORREST, Katherine B
Cravath, Swaine & Moore LLP, New York 212 474 1155
kforrest@cravath.com
*Recommended in Antitrust, Intellectual Property*
**Practice Areas:** Commercial litigation, including antitrust, copyright, trademark, contract and securities. Obtaining regulatory clearance from FTC and DOJ in large transactions.
**Prof. Memberships:** ABA; NYSBA. Admitted to practice before US Supreme Court; US Courts of Appeals for Second, Third and Seventh Circuits; US District Courts for the Northern, Southern and Western Districts of New York and District of Columbia; Courts of the State of New York.
**Career:** Partner since 1998.
**Publications:** Contributing author to The Merger Review Process; frequent lecturer in intellectual property and antitrust law; articles on US/EU merger issues.
**Personal:** NYU (JD, 1990); Wesleyan University (BA, 1986).

## FORTE, Joseph Philip
Alston & Bird LLP, New York
212 210 9400
joseph.forte@alston.com
*Recommended in Real Estate*
**Practice Areas:** Focuses on real estate finance, workouts, capital markets, lending and alternative financing.
**Prof. Memberships:** Member, former Chair, Vice-Chair, and Board Member, Mortgage Bankers Association of America; past President, Commercial Mortgage Securities Association.
**Career:** Developed program documents for first commercial mortgage loan conduit; principal draftsman of Capital Markets Mortgage form published by Capital Consortium; lead draftsman of New York creditor's rights endorsement by American Land Title Association; former real estate Chair, Thacher Proffitt & Wood.
**Personal:** St Francis College (BA, honors, 1969); St John's University School of Law (JD, 1973), Managing Editor of Law Review.

## FOX, David
Skadden, Arps, Slate, Meagher & Flom LLP & Affiliates, New York
212 735 2534
dfox@skadden.com
*Recommended in Corporate/M&A*
**Practice Areas:** Advises leading US and international corporations in planning and structuring complex transactions involving acquisitions, divestitures, restructurings and associated corporate finance matters. Counsels corporations and their boards of directors on corporate governance matters and in connection with crisis situations (eg, accounting restatements and corporate control contests).

**Career:** LLB, Hebrew University, Jerusalem, 1982 (Class Valedictorian; Member of the Editorial Board of Law Review).

## FRAGOMEN JR, Austin
Fragomen, Del Rey, Bernsen & Loewy, LLP, New York 212 688 8555
*Recommended in Immigration*

## FRAIDIN, Stephen
Kirkland & Ellis LLP, New York
212 446 4840
sfraidin@kirkland.com
*Recommended in Corporate/M&A, Private Equity*
**Practice Areas:** General representation of major companies and investment groups, acquisitions and proxy contests. Advised Forstmann Little in the creation of its LBO funds and in a series of negotiated acquisitions, dispositions and restructurings involving over $40 billion; has also represented Alpharma, Dow Chemical, ABB, Pershing Square, JANA Partners, Mason Capital, JPMorgan, Merrill Lynch, Citadel Broadcasting, Peter J. Solomon Co., Lazard Freres and the Special Committees of CSFB, New Valley and Net2Phone.
**Personal:** Tufts University, BA, 1961; Yale University, LLB, 1964.

## FRANCESCANI, David
Fish & Richardson P.C., New York
212 641 2287
francescani@fr.com
*Recommended in Intellectual Property*
**Practice Areas:** Managing Principal of Fish & Richardson's New York office. His practice specializes in intellectual property litigation with particular emphasis in the fields of semiconductors, optics, electronics, computer software, and telecommunications.
**Publications:** Co-author with Maryann V Hayes (1997-2001) and Irene Hudson (2002-04) of the 'Round Up From the Courts' section of Intellectual Property Litigation, a quarterly publication of the ABA's Intellectual Property Litigation Section, reporting on recent trademark and copyright decisions of interest in the Second Circuit.
**Personal:** University of Notre Dame BS Mechanical/Nuclear Engineering 1964; University of Notre Dame Law School LLB 1967.

## FRATIANNI, Constance A
Shearman & Sterling LLP, New York
212 848 8560
cfratianni@shearman.com
*Recommended in Bankruptcy*
**Practice Areas:** Partner in Shearman & Sterling's Bankruptcy & Reorganization Group. Represents debtors and creditors in out-of-court loan workouts and Chapter 11 bankruptcies. Also represents lenders and borrowers in various financings, particularly acquisition financings.
**Prof. Memberships:** Admitted to the

New York Bar and the Southern District of New York Bar.
**Career:** Joined Shearman in 1985 and became a Partner in 2000.
**Personal:** BA, Hofstra University (1982); JD, University of Michigan School of Law (1985).

## FREEDMAN, Jonathan
Dewey Ballantine LLP, New York
212 259 6680
jfreedman@deweyballantine.com
*Recommended in Insurance*
**Practice Areas:** Mr Freedman's practice focuses on corporate finance and mergers and acquisitions in the insurance industry. Recent transactions include the IPOs of insurance companies such as National Atlantic Holding Corporation, National Interstate Corporation, Safety Insurance Group, Inc. and Infinity Property and Casualty Corporation, as well as numerous capital markets transactions for Platinum Underwriters Holdings, Ltd. and Nationwide Financial Services, Inc. He developed a number of innovative financing structures in the insurance industry. In mergers and acquisitions, he concentrates on negotiated transactions.
**Career:** Corporate finance, mergers & acquisitions, insurance.
**Personal:** AB, Columbia University, 1978. JD, Georgetown University Law Center, 1981.

## FREEDMAN, Theodore L
Kirkland & Ellis LLP, New York
212 446 4934
tfreedman@kirkland.com
*Recommended in Bankruptcy*
**Practice Areas:** Represents debtor companies with particular emphasis on all aspects of Chapter 11 counseling and restructuring, debtor-in-possession financing, and use of Chapter 11 to address business issues including mass tort problems. Extensive experience advising private equity and corporate clients regarding options and responsibilities when a portfolio company is in financial distress, the sale and acquisition of assets and companies in a bankruptcy, and structuring transactions where insolvency issues are involved. Significant experience in international insolvency law and is the co-author of Collier International Business Insolvency Guide. Significant experience representing debtors who have filed Chapter 11 to address asbestos claims and other mass tort liabilities.
**Personal:** Lawrence University (BA, 1969); Northwestern University School of Law (JD, 1972).

## FREEMAN, David
Paul, Hastings, Janofsky & Walker LLP, New York 212 318 6555
davidfreeman@paulhastings.com
*Recommended in Environment*
**Practice Areas:** Representation of buyers, sellers and developers of brownfields

and other contaminated properties; representation of parties engaged in hazardous waste cleanups and related litigation; conducting and/or supervising environmental due diligence; and assisting clients in the negotiation for and purchase of environmental insurance.
**Prof. Memberships:** American Bar Association, Section of Environment, Energy and Resources; New York State Bar Association, Environmental Law Section, Co-Chair of Committee on Hazardous Waste/Site Remediation, Co-Chair of Brownfields/Superfund Reform Task Force; Board of Trustees, New York League of Conservation Voters Education Fund; New York City Bar Association; National Brownfields Association; Environmental Business Association of New York State.
**Career:** Partner, Chair of New York Office Environmental Law Practice Group; legislative assistant, Office of Senator Frank E Moss, 1970-72. Trial Attorney, Federal Trade Commission, 1975-77.
**Publications:** Has lectured and written extensively on environmental law matters. Editor-in-Chief, Journal of Environmental Law & Practice (West), 1998-2000; Member of Board of Advisors, Real Estate/Environmental Liability News; contributing author, 'Environmental Aspects of Real Estate and Commercial Transactions' (American Bar Association, 2004).
**Personal:** Harvard Law School (JD, cum laude, 1975); Harvard College (BA, cum laude, 1970).

### FREIDUS, Harris B
Paul, Weiss, Rifkind, Wharton & Garrison LLP, New York 212 373 3064
hfreidus@paulweiss.com
*Recommended in Real Estate*
**Practice Areas:** Partner in the Real Estate Department. Advises developers, entrepreneurial and institutional investors and lenders in all areas of commercial real estate, including developments, mortgage and mezzanine financings, partnerships and joint ventures, sales and acquisitions, construction and leasing. Has significant experience with all real estate asset classes and significant international experience. Major transactions include Time Warner Center, New York Times headquarters building and hotel and gaming developments and financings in Las Vegas and Macau. Representative clients include Las Vegas Sands Corp., Apollo Real Estate Advisors and GMAC Commercial Mortgage Corporation.

### FRIEDMAN, David
Kasowitz Benson Torres & Friedman, New York 212 506 1700
*Recommended in Bankruptcy*

### FRIEDMAN, Dennis J
Gibson, Dunn & Crutcher LLP, New York 212 351 3900
dfriedman@gibsondunn.com
*Recommended in Corporate/M&A*
**Practice Areas:** Co-Chair of the firm's Corporate Transactions Practice, a member of the Executive Committee and the International Management Committee. Widely recognized corporate lawyer with over 30 years in the mergers and acquisitions and capital markets areas.
**Career:** In addition to a 30-year legal career, Mr Friedman was an investment banker at several major Wall Street firms where he was a senior M&A banker and also the head of a merchant banking group.
**Personal:** JD, Georgetown University Law Center, 1969, Articles Editor of the 'Georgetown Law Journal'. BS, economics, University of Pennsylvania, Wharton School of Finance, 1966.

### FRIEDMAN, Eric J
Skadden, Arps, Slate, Meagher & Flom LLP & Affiliates, New York
212 735 2204
efriedma@skadden.com
*Recommended in Corporate/M&A*
**Practice Areas:** Concentrates in mergers and acquisitions, corporate finance and general corporate law. Has been involved in a number of significant transactions in the financial services industry and technology-related transactions. With respect to general corporate matters, has advised many companies on SEC-reporting obligations, board governance and stockholder affairs, and other corporate and securities law matters.
**Career:** JD, University of Pennsylvania, 1989; BBA, University of Michigan, 1986 (High Distinction).

### FRIEDMAN, Gary D
Mayer, Brown, Rowe & Maw LLP, New York 212 506 2574
gfriedman@mayerbrown.com
*Recommended in Employment*
**Practice Areas:** Practice includes all areas of employment law, with particular expertise in defending complex class actions, collective actions and mass actions, and litigating restrictive covenant/trade secret cases. Has tried and argued appeals in numerous employment-related cases in federal and state courts. Has defended numerous employment discrimination and wage and hour class and collective actions nationwide. Has extensive arbitration experience in various arbitral forums, including the New York Stock Exchange, National Association of Securities Dealers, the New York Mercantile Exchange, the American Arbitration Association and JAMS/Endispute. Has handled restrictive covenant/trade secret matters in more than 30 different states nationwide. Also frequently retained to conduct or advise on internal corporate investigations. Frequent presenter and panelist at seminars and forums involving employment law

issues.
**Career:** Mayer, Brown, Rowe & Maw LLP, New York, 1991 to date; Partner, 1997. Simpson Thacher & Bartlett, New York, 1988-91. Judicial law clerk to The Honorable Stanley S Brotman, United States District Court for the District of New Jersey, 1987-88.
**Publications:** Writes and speaks extensively on employment-related topics.
**Personal:** JD, Georgetown University Law Center, 1987; Dean's List; American Jurisprudence Award – Evidence; Associate Editor, The Tax Lawyer. Duke University, BA magna cum laude, 1983.

### FRIEDMAN, Gary
Debevoise & Plimpton LLP, New York 212 909 6000
*Recommended in Tax*

### FRUMKIN, Joseph B
Sullivan & Cromwell LLP, New York 212 558 4000
frumkinj@sullcrom.com
*Recommended in Corporate/M&A, Energy*
**Practice Areas:** Partner, M&A Group. Recent transactions: AT&T Inc. in BellSouth acquisition (pending); Endesa in response to hostile Gas Natural bid (pending); Telewest Global in acquisition by NTL; USF in acquisition by Yellow Roadway; General Growth in Rouse Company acquisition; and SBC and Cingular Wireless in Cingular's acquisition of AT&T Wireless.
**Prof. Memberships:** ABA.
**Career:** Partner since 1994. Investment banker, Merrill Lynch M&A Group (1989-90). Senior aide to US Senator John Heinz.
**Personal:** Georgetown University (BA, 1980); University of Pennsylvania Law School (JD, 1985).

### FUHRMAN, Steven M
Simpson Thacher & Bartlett LLP, New York 212 455 2000
sfuhrman@stblaw.com
*Recommended in Bankruptcy*
**Practice Areas:** Steven Fuhrman is a Partner at Simpson Thacher & Bartlett LLP in the firm's Bankruptcy Department. Mr Fuhrman regularly advises clients in connection with Chapter 11 restructurings, out-of-court workouts, acquisitions of troubled companies and the structuring of corporate and credit transactions. Mr Fuhrman's principal focus since 1985 has been the representation of banks and other financial institutions in the restructuring of large syndicated credit facilities extended to borrowers in a wide variety of businesses and industries. Such work has involved complex out-of-court restructurings and representation prior to, during and after Chapter 11 proceedings, including structuring of DIP and 'exit' financing arrangements, 'pre-packaged' cases, cases involving the sale of substantially all of a

debtor's assets, and structuring of corporate governance arrangements when his clients became owners of reorganized businesses.
**Prof. Memberships:** Association of the Bar of the City of New York and the New York State Bar Association.
**Personal:** BA summa cum laude, from Tufts University in 1982; JD with Honors from New York University School of Law in 1985.

### FURCI, Peter
Debevoise & Plimpton LLP, New York 212 909 6000
*Recommended in Tax*

### GABAY, Donald
Stroock & Stroock & Lavan LLP, New York 212 806 5400
*Recommended in Insurance*

### GAFFNEY, John T
Cravath, Swaine & Moore LLP, New York 212 474 1122
jgaffney@cravath.com
*Recommended in Media & Entertainment*
**Practice Areas:** Mergers and acquisitions, including joint ventures, principally in the media and entertainment, communications and shipping industries. Clients include major US and non-US media and communications companies. Also represents underwriters in all types of capital markets transactions and general corporate representation for a variety of corporate clients.
**Prof. Memberships:** NYSBA; ABCNY.
**Career:** Partner since 1993.
**Personal:** New York University (JD, MBA, 1986); George Washington University (BA, 1982; Phi Beta Kappa).

### GALL, Phillip
Kronish Lieb Weiner & Hellman LLP, New York 212 479 6000
*Recommended in Tax*

### GALLAGHER, Patrick C
Kirkland & Ellis LLP, New York 212 446 4998
pgallagher@kirkland.com
*Recommended in Tax*
**Practice Areas:** Mr Gallagher focuses his practice on federal income tax aspects of complex domestic and cross-border transactions, including mergers, acquisitions, leveraged buyouts, and recapitalizations; formation of domestic and offshore private equity investment partnerships, REITs and other pooled investment vehicles; workouts and bankruptcy restructurings; private equity transactions, and public offerings and other financings (including asset-backed securities and sale-leasebacks).
**Personal:** Pomona College, BA, 1974. University of Chicago, MA, 1977. Harvard Law School, JD, 1985.

### GALVIS, Sergio J
Sullivan & Cromwell LLP, New York

212 558 4740
galviss@sullcrom.com
*Recommended in Projects*
**Practice Areas:** 20 years' experience
handling complex project finance, M&A,
and securities transactions in Asia,
Europe and Latin America. Co-ordinator,
Latin America Practice. Major projects:
Cerro Verde II (Peru) and Panama Canal
expansion. M&A representations: Endesa
regarding Gas Natural's $51.2 billion hostile bid and Camargo Corréa in Loma
Negra acquisition. Securities work: Ternium SA's IPO/NYSE listing and Argentina
debt restructuring.
**Career:** Partner since 1991.
**Publications:** Recipient, 2004 Burton
Award for 'Sovereign Debt Restructurings
– the Market Knows Best' (International
Finance).
**Personal:** William and Mary (BA, 1980);
Harvard Law (JD, 1983). Council of the
Americas and Council on Foreign Relations.

## GANSBERG, Andrew
Nixon Peabody LLP, Albany
518 427 2657
agansberg@nixonpeabody.com
*Recommended in Energy*
**Practice Areas:** Practice concentrates
on public utility matters; has tried proceedings and negotiated settlements
involving electric, gas, and water rates
and regulation before several utility commissions. Mr Gansberg has represented
New York utilities in connection with
mergers, restructuring, asset sales, and
generation and transmission facility siting proceedings. He has advised several
utilities in litigation involving the protection of trade secrets and commercially
sensitive information.
**Prof. Memberships:** Admitted to practice in New York, the Second Circuit
Court of Appeals, and the US District
Courts for the Southern and Eastern Districts of New York.
**Personal:** New York University, JD;
Bucknell University, BA.

## GANZ, Howard
Proskauer Rose LLP, New York
212 969 3035
hganz@proskauer.com
*Recommended in Employment, Sport*
**Practice Areas:** Co-Chair of
Proskauer's Labor and Employment Law
Department, as well as Co-Chair of the
firm's Sports Law Group. When not practicing sports law for clients such as the
National Basketball Association and
Major League Baseball, he has represented a number of the nation's best-known
companies with respect to a wide variety
of labor and employment matters, such
as employment discrimination, sexual
harassment, wrongful discharge, defamation, breach of contract, and large-scale
reductions-in-force. His litigation experience has run the gamut from single plain-

tiff lawsuits to major class actions in federal and state courts in New York and
elsewhere. Howard has been named one
of the 'World's Leading Labor and
Employment Lawyers', one of the '500
Leading Lawyers in America', one of 'The
Best Lawyers in America', and one of the
'100 Best Lawyers in New York'.
**Prof. Memberships:** Previously served
as the Chair of the Sports Law Committee of the Association of the Bar of the
City of New York.
**Publications:** He has lectured widely on
sports law and employment law matters.
**Personal:** A graduate of Colgate University and Columbia Law School, where he
was articles editor of the Columbia Law
Review. Howard spent two years as a law
clerk for a federal district judge in New
York before joining Proskauer Rose LLP.

## GARRITY, James
Shearman & Sterling LLP, New York
212 848 4879
jgarrity@shearman.com
*Recommended in Bankruptcy*
**Practice Areas:** Partner in Shearman &
Sterling's Bankruptcy & Reorganization
Group.
**Prof. Memberships:** Founding Director,
International Insolvency Institute; Fellow,
American College of Bankruptcy;
Adjunct Professor, St John's University
Masters in Bankruptcy Law Program.
**Career:** Joined firm as Partner in 1999.
Served as a Judge in the US Bankruptcy
Court for the Southern District of New
York and as Assistant US Attorney in the
Civil Division of the US Attorney's Office
for SDNY.
**Personal:** BA, College of the Holy Cross
(1977); JD, St John's University School of
Law (1980); LLM in Taxation, New York
University School of Law (1986).

## GARTNER, Steven
Willkie Farr & Gallagher LLP, New York
212 728 8222
sgartner@willkie.com
*Recommended in Private Equity*
**Practice Areas:** Partner in the Corporate and Financial Services Department,
Chair of the Private Equity Group, and a
Member of the firm's Executive Committee. Specializes in private equity (buyout
and venture capital) transactions, as well
as mergers and acquisitions and public
offerings. Actively involved in Willkie's
extensive Private Equity Practice, representing funds controlled by Warburg Pincus and others. Has been involved in over
100 private equity transactions, ranging
from $1 million to over $5 billion. Recent
significant matters include representation
of Warburg Pincus in its agreement (with
Texas Pacific Group) to purchase retail
icon Neiman Marcus for $5.1 billion and
in its $1.6 billion sale of Transkaryotic
Therapies, Inc. (as principal shareholder)
to Shire Pharmaceuticals Group plc. He
also recently represented Warburg in its

$616 million acquisition of Dutch cable
operator NV Multikabel from German
cable group PrimaCom AG, and in its
$645 million acquisition and merger of
medical supply companies Chronic Care
Solutions Inc. and MPTC Holdings Inc.
Has represented clients in Brazil, Hong
Kong, Italy, Sweden, Switzerland, and the
United Kingdom. Mergers and acquisitions experience includes going-private
transactions, stock and asset sales, and
privately negotiated and hostile transactions. Represents both issuers and underwriters in public offerings and private
placements.
**Prof. Memberships:** Member of the
American Bar Association (Section on
Business Law), the New York State Bar
Association, the New York City Bar Association, and the New Jersey Bar Association. A Director of The International
Center in New York, a not-for-profit
organization.
**Career:** Admitted to the Bars of the states
of New York and New Jersey.
**Publications:** Author of 'Corporate
Minutes' (BNA 2004); co-author of
'Doing Business in Europe: Before and
After 1992' (New York State Bar Association 1991).
**Personal:** Received a JD (magna cum
laude) from St John's University School
of Law in 1984, where he served as a
Member of the St John's Law Review, and
a BSBA from Georgetown University in
1981.

## GAY, Faith Elizabeth
Quinn Emanuel Urquhart Oliver &
Hedges, LLP, New York
212 702 8100
faithgay@quinnemanuel.com
*Recommended in Litigation*
**Practice Areas:** Ms Gay concentrates in
white-collar criminal defense and commercial trial and appellate work.
**Career:** Ms Gay has broad courtroom
experience, with more than 25 federal trials and 30 appellate arguments to her
credit. She also represents corporate
clients at every stage of civil, criminal and
administrative proceedings, from newly
filed complaints, corporate internal
investigations and grand jury proceedings through discovery, trial, sentencing
and appeal.
**Personal:** Northwestern University
School of Law (JD, 1986); Duke University (BA, with honors, Public Policy Studies, 1982).

## GELBLUM, Seth D
Loeb & Loeb LLP, New York
212 407 4931
sgelblum@loeb.com
*Recommended in Media &
Entertainment*
**Practice Areas:** Theater and film clients
include producers, theater owners,
motion picture studios, directors, playwrights, composers, performers, music

publishers, designers, investors, not-for-profit theaters and licensing agencies in
Broadway, touring and foreign live stage
productions, as well as directors, writers
and producers in feature film, documentary film and television projects.
**Prof. Memberships:** Chairman of the
Board – New Dramatists; Boards –
Lawyers for Children and Film Forum.
**Career:** Partner since 1998.
**Publications:** Lecturer at Columbia Law
School, Yale University School of Drama,
Commercial Theatre Institute.
**Personal:** Georgetown University Law
Center (JD, 1982); Wesleyan University
(BA, 1975).

## GELSTON, Philip
Cravath, Swaine & Moore LLP, New York
212 474 1548
pgelston@cravath.com
*Recommended in Corporate/M&A*
**Practice Areas:** Mergers and acquisitions, joint ventures and general corporate counseling. His practice encompasses hostile transactions (both offense and
defense), complicated negotiated transactions, cross-border transactions and
advising boards and senior executives.
**Prof. Memberships:** International Bar
Association.
**Career:** Partner since 1984. Clerkship:
Hon John M Wisdom (US Court of
Appeals for the Fifth Circuit).
**Personal:** Harvard Law School (JD,
magna cum laude, 1977; Supreme Court
Note Editor of the Law Review; Sears
Prize); Harvard College (AB, cum laude,
1974; Phi Beta Kappa).

## GEOGHEGAN, Patricia
Cravath, Swaine & Moore LLP, New York
212 474 1584
pgeoghegan@cravath.com
*Recommended in Tax*
**Practice Areas:** Co-Head of Tax
Department. Head of Employee Benefits
Practice. Also practices in the area of
equipment finance representing lessees
and lessors of aircraft, satellite transponders, vessels, power plants, and manufacturing facilities and equipment.
**Prof. Memberships:** ABA; NYSBA;
ABCNY.
**Career:** Partner since 1982.
**Personal:** New York University (LLM,
1982); Yale Law School (JD, 1974); Yale
University (MA, 1972); Michigan State
University (BA, with highest honor, 1969;
Phi Beta Kappa). YWCA of the City of
New York: Former Chair. Academy of the
Holy Angels: Chair. Michigan State University: President's Capital Campaign
Cabinet.

## GERRARD, Michael
Arnold & Porter LLP, New York
212 715 1190
Michael.Gerrard@aporter.com
*Recommended in Environment*
**Practice Areas:** Heads the firm's New
York Environmental Practice.

**Prof. Memberships:** He was the 2004-05 Chair of the American Bar Association's Section of Environment, Energy, and Resources and has chaired the Executive Committee of the Association of the Bar of the City of New York, and the Environmental Law Section of the New York State Bar Association.

**Career:** He has practiced environmental law in New York since 1979. He has been an Adjunct Professor at Columbia Law School and the Yale School of Forestry and Environmental Studies. He has tried numerous cases and argued many appeals. In addition to his domestic practice, Mr Gerrard has advised numerous foreign investors on the environmental aspects of US properties, and he has handled several cases concerning transboundary and marine pollution. He has lectured on environmental law in Great Britain, France, Canada, and China, as well as throughout the United States.

**Publications:** He has written or edited five books, two of which were named Best Law Book of the Year by the Association of American Publishers: the eleven-volume 'Environmental Law Practice Guide' (Matthew Bender, 1992) and the four-volume 'Brownfields Law and Practice: The Cleanup and Redevelopment of Contaminated Land' (Matthew Bender, 1998). His other books concern environmental impact assessment, environmental justice, and facility siting.

### GERSTENZANG, Michael A
Cleary Gottlieb Steen & Hamilton LLP, New York 212 225 2096
mgerstenzang@cgsh.com
*Recommended in Private Fund Formation*
**Practice Areas:** Forming and advising private investment funds including private equity funds, venture capital funds, international funds, hedge funds, and other 'alternative asset' investment vehicles. Regularly represents Texas Pacific Group, Newbridge Asia, CSFB, Goldman Sachs and Knight Vinke.
**Prof. Memberships:** Admitted in New York. Member of the Private Investment Fund Forum and the Committee on Private Investment Funds of the Bar Association of the City of New York.
**Career:** JD, Columbia University (Stone Scholar) (1989); BSFS, magna cum laude, Georgetown University (1986).

### GIBBONS, Robert
Debevoise & Plimpton LLP, New York
212 909 6000
*Recommended in Projects*

### GIBLIN JR, Thomas P
Thelen Reid & Priest LLP, New York
212 603 6568
tgiblin@thelenreid.com
*Recommended in Energy*
**Practice Areas:** As a member of the Business Department, Mr Giblin generally specializes in corporate, finance and

securities matters. He has experience working with the firm's clients on a variety of transactions, including mergers and acquisitions, finance and securities matters as well as general corporate work.
**Prof. Memberships:** American Bar Association, Member.
**Career:** Partner of Thelen Reid & Priest LLP's San Francisco office. Admitted to practice in New York and New Jersey.
**Personal:** Received JD from the University of Virginia School of Law (1997); Executive Editor, Journal of Law & Politics. Graduate of University of Notre Dame; BA, magna cum laude (1993), History, Governmental and International Affairs, graduated Phi Beta Kappa.

### GILBERT, Richard
Orrick, Herrington & Sutcliffe LLP, New York 212 506 5016
rag@orrick.com
*Recommended in Employee Benefits*
**Practice Areas:** Has practiced employee benefits law exclusively for 25 years, advising financial institutions, public pension funds, trustees, and employers on the fiduciary responsibility provisions of ERISA and public pension law, and the establishment of numerous types of 401(k), retirement and deferred compensation plans.
**Prof. Memberships:** Charter Fellow of the American College of Employee Benefits Counsel (2000). American Bar Association: Section of Taxation, Committee on Employee Benefits, Chair of Fiduciary Responsibility Subcommittee (1991-94); California State Bar; State Bar of New York.
**Personal:** JD, cum laude, University of Wisconsin School of Law, 1974; BA, cum laude, Yale University, 1968.

### GILLESPIE, Michael
Debevoise & Plimpton LLP, New York
212 909 6000
*Recommended in Media & Entertainment*

### GILLIS, Theresa
Jones Day, New York
212 326 3679
tmgillis@jonesday.com
*Recommended in Intellectual Property*
**Practice Areas:** Intellectual Property, including patent, trademark and copyright matters. Extensive litigation experience, including conducting jury trials and arguing appeals in the federal courts. Significant transactional experience related to intellectual property in mergers, acquisitions, licenses, research and development arrangements and IPOs. Extensive experience counseling both foreign and domestic clients concerning patent and trademark portfolio enforcement and acquisition strategies.
**Publications:** Intellectual property editor for Defense Research Institute's commercial litigation newsletter; frequent lecturer on patent and antitrust issues for

PLI and local and national Bar Associations.
**Personal:** Georgetown University (JD 1974, Editor: Georgetown Law Journal; Board of Regents: 2000-present)

### GITTER, Max
Cleary Gottlieb Steen & Hamilton LLP, New York 212 225 2610
mgitter@cgsh.com
*Recommended in Litigation*
**Practice Areas:** Corporate and commercial litigation/arbitration, especially involving securities, M&A, intellectual property, governance issues, contracts and lawyers. Clients have included Goldman Sachs, PeopleSoft, Triarc, Bank of America, Time Warner, GAF Corporation, NY State Comptroller, Governance Committee of Starwood Hotels, Texas Pacific Group, major law firms.
**Prof. Memberships:** Member of the City of New York Bar Association and NYSBA. Admitted to practice before US Supreme Court, US Courts of Appeals for the Second, Third, Fourth, District of Columbia, Sixth, Ninth, and Tenth Circuits; US District Courts for Southern and Eastern Districts of New York; and US Tax Court.
**Career:** Joined firm as Partner, 1999. Previously Partner at Paul, Weiss, Rifkind, Wharton & Garrison. Taught at Yale Law School (1985-86) and University of Chicago Law School (1968-69). LLB, Yale Law School (1968); BA, cum laude, Harvard College (1965).

### GITTES, Franklin M
Skadden, Arps, Slate, Meagher & Flom LLP & Affiliates, New York
212 735 3760
fgittes@skadden.com
*Recommended in Corporate/M&A*
**Practice Areas:** Practice Leader, M&A Department. Concentrates in mergers and acquisitions, securities and general corporate law. Advises clients on a wide variety of friendly and contested situations, as well as other corporate, securities and business related matters.
**Prof. Memberships:** American Bar Association; New York State Bar Association; Association of the Bar of the City of New York.
**Career:** JD, Georgetown University, 1973; BSChE, Lehigh University, 1969.

### GIUFFRA JR, Robert J
Sullivan & Cromwell LLP, New York
212 558 3121
giuffrar@sullcrom.com
*Recommended in Litigation*
**Practice Areas:** Complex securities, regulatory, and criminal litigation, including trials, arbitrations and appeals. Has represented BONY, CA, Exxon, GS, ING, Oxford Health Plans, Philips, UBS, Vornado, and David Duncan (lead Arthur Andersen auditor for Enron). Recent matters: settlement of DOJ/SEC investigations for CA, and class actions and government investigations involving Enron,

HealthSouth, and NYSE specialists.
**Career:** Partner since 1998. Commissioner, NY State Ethics Commission, since 1998. Chief Counsel, US Senate Committee on Banking, Housing, and Urban Affairs, 1995-96.
**Personal:** Princeton University (AB, 1983); Yale Law School (JD, 1987).

### GLAZER, Dennis
Davis Polk & Wardwell, New York
212 450 4000
dennis.glazer@dpw.com
*Recommended in Litigation*
**Practice Areas:** Member of Davis Polk & Wardwell's Litigation Department. Represents clients in securities litigation, mergers and acquisitions and related litigation, and bankruptcy, reorganizations and related litigation. Mr Glazer litigates cases throughout the country relating to significant merger and acquisition transactions (both friendly and hostile).

### GLAZER, Steven D
Weil, Gotshal & Manges LLP, New York
212 310 8806
steven.glazer@weil.com
*Recommended in Intellectual Property*
**Practice Areas:** Mr Glazer is Co-Chair of the Patent Litigation and Counseling Practice in the New York office. He has over 25 years' experience litigating patent actions in such diverse technologies as electronics, software, the internet, genetic engineering, sweetener chemistry, semiconductors, petrochemicals and photonics. In addition to appearing in courts throughout the United States and in the International Trade Commission, he has coordinated multinational litigations. Mr Glazer is on the faculty of Rutgers Law School, where he teaches patent litigation and related subjects.
**Personal:** Rutgers University, BA; Rutgers University, BSEE; Fairleigh Dickinson University, MS; Rutgers University School of Law, JD.

### GLIATTA, Stephen
Kaye Scholer LLP, New York
212 836 8618
sgliatta@kayescholer.com
*Recommended in Real Estate*
**Practice Areas:** Partner and Co-Chair, Real Estate Department, member of the firm's Executive Committee. Mr Gliatta's practice is focused on representing investment banks and other institutional lenders in the origination and securitization of first mortgage debt and mezzanine loans. He has worked on many of the largest and most complex securitized mortgage financings completed in the market in recent years and regularly represents opportunity funds in joint ventures with operating partners and in the acquisition and financing of real estate projects.
**Prof. Memberships:** Admitted to practice in New York and is a member of the Commercial Mortgage Securities Associ-

ation (CMSA) and the National Association of Real Estate Investment Trusts.
**Career:** JD, New York University School of Law, 1983; BS, Fordham University, College of Business Administration, 1980.

### GOERING, Kevin
Sheppard, Mullin, Richter & Hampton LLP, New York 212 332 3800
*Recommended in Media & Entertainment*

### GOETZ, Peter
Goetz Fitzpatrick LLP, New York
212 695 8100
*Recommended in Construction*

### GOLDBERG, Louis L
Davis Polk & Wardwell, New York
212 450 4000
louis.goldberg@dpw.com
*Recommended in Private Equity*
**Practice Areas:** Member of Davis Polk & Wardwell's Corporate Department, practicing in the Mergers and Acquisitions Group. Practice focuses on public and private mergers and acquisitions, private equity transactions, board and corporate governance advice, joint ventures, spinoffs, and restructurings and recapitalizations. Also has extensive experience in securities offerings.

### GOLDBERG, Morton
Cowan, Liebowitz & Latman, New York
212 790 9200
*Recommended in Intellectual Property*

### GOLDEN, Arthur F
Davis Polk & Wardwell, New York
212 450 4000
arthur.golden@dpw.com
*Recommended in Antitrust*
**Practice Areas:** Partner in Davis Polk & Wardwell's Litigation Department and a member of the Management Committee for nine years. Leads the firm's practice in competition and antitrust matters, which include domestic and international mergers and acquisitions, antitrust counseling and litigation. Regularly represents large multinational companies with respect to negotiated and contested acquisition-related transactions, criminal antitrust investigations and litigation. Was lead counsel for Gillette in its acquisition by Procter & Gamble, represented Comcast in its acquisition of AT&T Broadband and acted as one of the two lead negotiators for the US tobacco industry in the effort to resolve, through legislation and settlements, the legal issues facing that industry. Represented Freeport in the criminal investigation of the copper concentrate industry and Hoffmann-LaRoche in the vitamin cartel litigation and was counsel of record for the defense group in the Supreme Court. Is currently a Director of Emerson Electric and has been on the board of several other NYSE companies.

### GOLDEN, Daniel H
Akin Gump Strauss Hauer & Feld LLP, New York 212 872 8010
dgolden@akingump.com
*Recommended in Bankruptcy*
**Practice Areas:** Daniel Golden's practice primarily consists of representing creditors' committees and bondholder committees in large, complex out-of-court restructurings and Chapter 11 cases. He served as lead committee counsel in numerous high profile restructurings and Chapter 11 cases, including WorldCom, Delta Airlines, Tower Automotive, XO Communications, Hayes Lemmerz International, Globalstar, Fruit of the Loom, Lernout & Hauspie Speech Products, Loral Space & Communications and Solutia Inc. Additionally, Mr Golden has represented corporate debtors and acquirors of financial distressed businesses and assets. He is also a frequent lecturer on bankruptcy/restructuring issues.
**Personal:** BA, University of Wisconsin-Madison; JD, SUNY at Buffalo Law School.

### GOLDEN, Matthew
Debevoise & Plimpton LLP, New York
212 909 6000
*Recommended in Real Estate*

### GOLDFEIN, Shepard
Skadden, Arps, Slate, Meagher & Flom LLP & Affiliates, New York
212 735 3610
sgoldfei@skadden.com
*Recommended in Antitrust, Sport*
**Practice Areas:** Practice Leader, Antitrust Group. Handles a variety of cases from antitrust litigation to white-collar criminal investigations and mass disaster litigation. Advises on antitrust and sports-related issues (general compliance programs to antitrust patent licensing issues), and professional sports league issues (team ownership, collective bargaining, team location, intellectual property).
**Prof. Memberships:** Chairman, Sports Law Committee, Association of the Bar of the City of NY (1996-99).
**Career:** JD, Rutgers University, 1975 (editor, Rutgers Law Review); MA, Political Science, University of Chicago, 1977; AB, Rutgers University, 1970 (Phi Beta Kappa).
**Publications:** Co-author, monthly trade regulation column, New York Law Journal (1983-present).

### GOLDMAN, Michael
Cravath, Swaine & Moore LLP, New York
212 474 1929
mgoldman@cravath.com
*Recommended in Banking & Finance*
**Practice Areas:** Banking and finance, including complex, multi-currency and multi-jurisdictional syndicated loan transactions, acquisition and leveraged finance and securities offerings for US

and international clients.
**Prof. Memberships:** ABA; NYSBA; ABCNY.
**Career:** Partner since 1995.
**Personal:** Fordham University School of Law (JD, cum laude, 1987); University of Pennsylvania (BA, cum laude, 1984).

### GOLDRING, Stuart
Weil, Gotshal & Manges LLP, New York
212 310 8312
stuart.goldring@weil.com
*Recommended in Tax*
**Practice Areas:** Stuart Goldring's practice focuses on tax. He has nationally recognized experience in federal income tax matters involving financially troubled companies, including extensive experience advising debtors, creditors and potential acquirers and investors in troubled companies. He regularly advises on the structuring of acquisitions, dispositions and other transactions involving corporations and multi-corporate groups. He is a co-author of a tax treatise on troubled corporations and an Adjunct Professor at NYU Law School.
**Personal:** University of Michigan, BBA, 1979; University of Michigan Law School, JD, 1982; New York University School of Law, LLM, 1983.

### GOLDSTEIN, Linda
Manatt Phelps & Phillips LLP, New York
212 790 4500
*Recommended in Media & Entertainment*

### GOLDSTEIN, Marcia
Weil, Gotshal & Manges LLP, New York
212 310 8214
marcia.goldstein@weil.com
*Recommended in Bankruptcy*
**Practice Areas:** As Co-Chair of Weil Gotshal's Business Finance & Restructuring Department, Marcia Goldstein's practice covers all aspects of US and international debt restructurings, crisis management and corporate governance. She leads the firm's representation of MCI, Inc. and Parmalat S.p.A., and is special restructuring counsel to Eurotunnel. Recent representations also include the debtors in Atkins Nutritionals and Galvex Holdings, Inc. and the creditors' committee in Integrated Electrical Services, Inc. She has represented debtors, bank groups, secured and unsecured creditors, statutory creditors' committees, trustees, and DIP penders in numerous debt restructurings and Chapter 11 cases including Regal Cinemas, Inc., Washington Group, Inc., Babcock & Wilcox, Exide, Inc., Oxford Automotive, Inc., Warnaco, Inc., CRIIMI MAE, Inc., and Purina Mills, Inc. She is a member of the National Bankruptcy Conference, American College of Bankruptcy, the International Insolvency Institute, and has been a lecturer at Yale Law School.
**Personal:** Cornell University, BA, 1973; Cornell Law School, JD, 1975.

### GONZALEZ, Edward E
Skadden, Arps, Slate, Meagher & Flom LLP & Affiliates, New York
212 735 3160
EGonzalez@skadden.com
*Recommended in Tax*
**Practice Areas:** US and international tax matters. Handles the tax aspects of a variety of transactions, including mergers and acquisitions, US and non-US financial instruments, leveraged buyouts, private equity investments, cross-border financial transactions, debt restructurings, asset-based financings, derivatives and tax controversies. Has advised both investment banks, corporations, and investment partnerships in the structuring of various acquisitions, financings and refinancings. Has represented Australian, Japanese, Latin American and European corporations in structuring their investments in the United States, and non-US issuers in raising capital in the United States. Has worked in the development of innovative financial products such as tracking stock (General Motors Class E Stock), 100 year debt, trust preferred securities, financial institution regulatory capital products for both US and non-US financial institutions and, most recently, 'basket D' securities. Has also worked extensively with real estate investment trusts (REITs) including the development of the first timber REIT.
**Prof. Memberships:** Admitted in NY and California.
**Career:** JD, Columbia University, 1979; AB, Princeton University, 1976 (summa cum laude; Phi Beta Kappa).

### GOODMAN, Robert
Debevoise & Plimpton LLP, New York
212 909 6000
*Recommended in Insurance*

### GOOGE JR, Charles H
Paul, Weiss, Rifkind, Wharton & Garrison LLP, New York 212 373 3345
cgooge@paulweiss.com
*Recommended in Media & Entertainment*
**Practice Areas:** Partner in Corporate and Entertainment Department. Heads firm's Intellectual Property Group. Has represented individuals and companies involved in all aspects of the entertainment industry, including the film, television, publishing, music, new media and live stage businesses. Has represented producers, production companies, film studios, financiers, distributors, record labels, recording artists, authors, composer/lyricists, designers, directors and choreographers. Has been key player in notable transactions in the magazine publishing industry. Focuses on all aspects of IP and has extensive experience in all forms of transactional work involving IP and technology, including licensing of trademarks, patents, copyrights

and other intellectual property rights.

## GORDON, David
Latham & Watkins LLP, New York
212 906 1200
*Recommended in Projects*

## GORDON, Jennifer
Sidley Austin LLP, New York
212 839 8706
jennifer.gordon@sidley.com
*Recommended in Intellectual Property*
**Practice Areas:** Extensive experience in complex litigation involving biotechnology patents. Also involved in client counseling (including validity, infringement and freedom-to-operate analyses and opinions as well as due diligence investigations) and in various patent office proceedings in the United States and abroad. She has litigated and counseled on a vast array of patented technologies in the life sciences, such as nucleic acid amplification technologies (PCR), recombinant DNA technologies, biological therapeutics (interferons, erythropoietin, human growth hormone, monoclonal antibodies, T-cell receptors and antisense oligonucleotides), enzymes, vaccines, genetically engineered plants, pharmaceutical compounds and medical diagnostics.
**Prof. Memberships:** American Intellectual Property Law Association, The American Chemical Society, The American Association of the Advancement of Science, The New York Academy of Sciences, The New York Intellectual Property Law Association, The New Jersey Intellectual Property Law Association.
**Personal:** Fordham University School of Law, JD, 1985; Massachusetts Institute of Technology, PhD, 1981; Massachusetts Institute of Technology, SB, 1975. Admissions: US Patent & Trademark Office, 1982; US Court of Appeals, 4th Circuit, 2004; US Court of Appeals, Federal Circuit, 1986; US District Court, ND of California, 1994; US District Court, ED of New York, 1986; US District Court, SD of New York, 1986; New York, 1986.

## GORDON, Nicholas
Franklin, Weinrib, Rudell & Vassallo, New York 212 935 5500
*Recommended in Media & Entertainment*

## GORDON, Roberta
Bryan Cave LLP, New York
212 692 1800
*Recommended in Environment*

## GORDON, Stephen
Cravath, Swaine & Moore LLP, New York
212 474 1704
sgordon@cravath.com
*Recommended in Tax*
**Practice Areas:** Co-Head of Tax Department. Advises on tax aspects of mergers and acquisitions, spin-offs and other restructurings, and corporate joint ventures. Also advises on issues related to

corporate finance and domestic and international taxation. Has served as the firm's Hiring Partner and Managing Partner for Administration.
**Prof. Memberships:** ABA; NYSBA; ABCNY; International Fiscal Association; Tax Forum.
**Career:** Associate 1981-87, Partner since 1987.
**Publications:** 'The Taxation of Reinsured Payments' (Tax Forum 2005).
**Personal:** Harvard Law School (JD, cum laude, 1981; editor of the Harvard Law Review); Cornell University (AB, cum laude, 1978).

## GOTTS, Ilene Knable
Wachtell, Lipton, Rosen & Katz, New York 212 403 1247
ikgotts@wlrk.com
*Recommended in Antitrust*
**Practice Areas:** Specializes in antitrust matters, particularly relating to mergers and acquisitions. International transactions in which Mrs Gotts advised include SBC Communications/AT&T Corp., AllTel/Western Wireless, Sanofi-Synthélabo/Aventis, Cingular Wireless Corporation/AT&T Wireless Services, Inc., Apollo Management, L.P./Intelsat Ltd., ConocoPhillips/OAO Lukoil, Nestle S.A./Dreyer's Grand Ice Cream Co., Diageo plc/General Mills, Inc., Deutsche Telekom AG/VoiceStream Wireless Corporation, and Phillips Petroleum Company/Conoco Corp.
**Prof. Memberships:** Has long been an active participant in the Antitrust Section of the American Bar Association; currently serves on the Council and as the International Officer; and previously served as the Chair of the Section's Mergers and Acquisitions Committee. Currently a Member of the American Law Institute, and Chair of the New York State Bar Association's Antitrust Section. In 1995, served as the President of the Washington Council of Lawyers and from 1995-97 as the Chair of the Antitrust and Trade Regulation Section of the Federal Bar Association.
**Career:** Partner at Wachtell, Lipton, Rosen & Katz. Previously worked as a staff attorney in the Bureau of Competition of the Federal Trade Commission in conduct and merger investigations, and in the FTC Bureau of Consumer Protection.
**Publications:** Frequent guest speaker; published approximately 100 articles on antitrust-related topics; editor of the second and third editions of the ABA Merger Review Process Handbook; a Member of the Advisory Board of the Antitrust & Trade Regulation Report; and the editorial board of 'The Antitrust Counselor.'
**Personal:** Graduated magna cum laude from the University of Maryland (BA), where she was elected to membership in Phi Beta Kappa; and cum laude from Georgetown University Law Center in

1984 (JD). Member of Board of Trustees, University of Maryland Foundation; Board of Legal Advisors, Georgetown University Law Center; Board of Legal Advisors, Legal Momentum.

## GRAIS, David J
Dewey Ballantine LLP, New York
212 259 7860
dgrais@deweyballantine.com
*Recommended in Insurance*
**Practice Areas:** Mr Grais has practiced in the arbitration and litigation of reinsurance disputes for over 25 years. He has acted in many of the largest disputes over the reinsurance of large environmental and asbestos claims, workers compensation carveout reinsurance, and various other areas of the insurance and reinsurance business. Most recently, Mr Grais has been active in the governmental investigations of contingent commissions, bidrigging, and finite reinsurance.
**Career:** Partner, Dewey Ballantine LLP. Admitted to practice 1979, New York.
**Personal:** AB, magna cum laude, Princeton University, 1973. MA, Philosophy, Balliol College, University of Oxford, 1975. JD, Yale Law School, 1978.

## GRALA, Bronislaw
Cadwalader, Wickersham & Taft LLP, New York
212 504 6466
bronislaw.grala@cwt.com
*Recommended in Employee Benefits*
**Practice Areas:** Focuses on ERISA and other employee benefit matters, particularly ERISA fiduciary responsibilities and obligations, including the ERISA and tax implications of various plan investments and investment formats. Serves as ERISA counsel to plan asset managers, but also advises broker-dealers, investment bankers and others seeking to provide services, or develop and sell investment products, to ERISA plans. Extensive experience in dealings with the Employee Benefits Security Administration in the US Department of Labor.
**Personal:** JD, New York University School of Law (cum laude, 1972), editor, NYU Law Review; Member, the Order of the Coif, and Founder's Day Scholar; BA, Fordham College (cum laude, 1968). Selected as Charter Fellow in the American College of Employee Benefits Counsel. Member, New York State Bar Association (Section on Taxation) and the Association of the Bar of the City of New York.

## GRANFIELD, Lindsee P
Cleary Gottlieb Steen & Hamilton LLP, New York 212 225 2738
lgranfield@cgsh.com
*Recommended in Bankruptcy*
**Practice Areas:** Restructuring, insolvency, bankruptcy, and commercial litigation. She represents debtors, creditors' committees, individual creditors and equity holders in major bankruptcy and

insolvency cases throughout the United States and in international cross-border restructurings involving many industries including healthcare, financial services, heavy equipment manufacturing, telecommunications, broadcasting, retail, mining, energy generation, oil services and steel production. Clients include Bank of America; Citigroup; Goldman Sachs & Co; Morgan Stanley; Multicanal, SA; Kindred Healthcare, Inc.
**Prof. Memberships:** Member of the Committee on Bankruptcy and Corporate Reorganization of the Bar of the City of New York; American Bankruptcy Institute.
**Career:** Joined firm, 1985; became Partner, 1998. Admitted to practice: NY, CA, SDNY, EDNY, Second Circuit, Third Circuit. JD, University of California, Berkeley School of Law (Boalt Hall) (1985); AB, UCLA (1982).

## GREEN, Frederick
Weil, Gotshal & Manges LLP, New York
212 310 8524
frederick.green@weil.com
*Recommended in Corporate/M&A*
**Practice Areas:** As Co-Chair of Weil Gotshal's M&A Practice, Frederick Green's practice focuses on business combinations, including mergers, acquisitions, private equity and spin-offs. He also advises on corporate governance matters, restructurings and joint ventures. He is counsel to the Board of General Motors, and has been involved in a number of recent prominent transactions, including the sale of Hylsamex to Grupo Techint, the representation of Macquarie in proposed acquisitions of Sprint's cell tower operations and of New Skies, and the acquisition of PanAmSat by KKR.
**Personal:** University of Pennsylvania, Wharton School, BS, 1976; Fordham University, JD, 1979.

## GREEN, Jonathan
Milbank, Tweed, Hadley & McCloy LLP, New York 212 530 5000
*Recommended in Projects*

## GREEN, Ronald
Epstein Becker & Green PC, New York
212 351 4646
rgreen@ebglaw.com
*Recommended in Employment*
**Practice Areas:** Ronald M Green is a co-founder of EBG and a member of the firm in the New York office. He manages the firm's national Labor and Employment Law Practice. An accomplished trial attorney of national reputation, Mr Green represents multinational and domestic corporations on a wide variety of labor and employment matters.
**Career:** Prior to co-founding Epstein Becker & Green, Mr Green gained substantial labor regulatory expertise while working for the US Department of Labor. As counsel for the Department's Office of

Contract Compliance, and thereafter head of the Civil Rights Division, Mr Green helped author many of the agency's regulations. He also played integral roles in the litigation and settlement of the landmark AT&T case and the Steel Industry Consent Decree.

## GREENBERG, Jeffrey
Latham & Watkins LLP, Los Angeles
213 485 1234
*Recommended in Projects*

## GREENBERG, Joel I
Kaye Scholer LLP, New York
212 836 8201
jigreenberg@kayescholer.com
*Recommended in Corporate/M&A*
**Practice Areas:** Partner in New York City office and Co-Chair of the firm-wide Corporate and Finance Department. Concentrates in domestic and cross-border mergers and acquisitions of public and private companies, representation of financial sponsors, joint ventures, and public and private securities offerings. Also advises publicly held and private companies on a wide variety of general corporate governance and corporate matters, as well as transactional matters.
**Prof. Memberships:** Member, American Bar Association (Vice-Chair of Committee on Negotiated Acquisitions and Member of the Federal Regulation of Securities and Legal Opinion Committees); Association of the Bar of the City of New York (Member of the Committee on Corporation Law, 1983-87); New York County Lawyers' Association; Tribar Opinion Committee, 1987-91; Admissions: New York.
**Career:** JD, Yale University, 1974; BS, New York University, 1967.
**Publications:** 'The Impact of Sarbanes-Oxley on Merger & Acquisition Practices', The M&A Lawyer, June 2003 (with Leigh Walton); 'Negotiating Acquisitions of Public Companies', University of Miami Business Law Review, Winter/Spring 2002 (with Richard E Climan, Lou R Kling and the Honorable E Norman Veasey); 'The Material Adverse Change Clause', New York Law Journal, April 23, 2001 (with A Julia Haddad); 'Forward-Looking Statements; Safe Harbor Provisions of Federal Act Create Controversy', New York Law Journal, October 17, 1997 (with Nancy E Fuchs and Anne M Lane); 'Third Party Legal Opinions Under ABA Accord', New York Law Journal, August 16, 1993. Frequent lecturer on mergers and acquisitions topics, including at programs sponsored by the American Bar Association, the Association of Corporate Counsel, the Association of the Bar of the City of New York, the Center for International Legal Studies, Columbia Law School, The Inter-Pacific Bar Association, International Financial Law Review, Law Journal Seminars, Stanford Law School, UCLA School of Law, the University of

Miami Law School and the University of Texas Law School.

## GREENGRASS, Lawrence
Mound Cotton Wollan & Greengrass, New York 212 804 4237
lgreengrass@moundcotton.com
*Recommended in Insurance*

## GREENTHAL, John
Nixon Peabody LLP, Albany
518 427 2670
jgreenthal@nixonpeabody.com
*Recommended in Environment*
**Practice Areas:** Environmental enforcement, hazardous waste, state/federal Superfund matters. Judicial/administrative proceedings brought by governmental authorities, private cost-recovery actions; negotiating with regulatory agencies regarding noncompliance.
**Prof. Memberships:** Admitted to practice in NY. NY State Bar Association (Former Chair, Environmental Law Section); Business Council of NY State; NY League of Conservation Voters (Board of Directors).
**Career:** Through 1987: Regional Counsel, NY State Department of Environmental Conservation (DEC); Compliance Counsel in DEC's General Counsel's Office; Director of DEC's Division of Environmental Enforcement. Chair, 11-State Northeast Hazardous Waste Project.
**Personal:** Harvard University, JD; Amherst College, BA, cum laude.

## GROLL, Michael
LeBoeuf, Lamb, Greene & MacRae LLP, New York 212 424 8616
mgroll@llgm.com
*Recommended in Insurance*
**Practice Areas:** He has expertise in the area of corporate and securities law, specifically public and private securities offerings, merger and acquisitions, and other transactions in the insurance industry. He has represented underwriters, insurance companies and lenders in such transactions. He has also represented investors, companies and investment banks in the formation, private financing and acquisition of insurance companies as well as many insurers and investment banks in connection with structured financial product transactions and credit derivative transactions involving both domestic and offshore insurance and reinsurance companies.
**Personal:** Columbia University (JD) 1978; Boston University (BA) 1975.

## GROSS, John
Proskauer Rose LLP, New York
212 969 3145
jgross@proskauer.com
*Recommended in Insurance*
**Practice Areas:** Has been lead counsel in civil litigations for many major US corporations including the holders of The World Trade Center leases in their litigation involving their insurance claims for property damage and business interrup-

tion resulting from the September 11, 2001 terrorist attacks. He also advised the City of New York on legal issues arising from the September 11 events.
**Career:** Served as an Assistant United States Attorney for the Southern District of New York, where he was assistant Chief of the Criminal Division. He also taught Trial Advocacy as an Adjunct Associate Professor at New York University Law School and has been a faculty member on trial advocacy programs sponsored by the United States Department of Justice, the Association of the Bar of the City of New York, and Harvard Law School.
**Personal:** A graduate of The Wharton School of Finance and Commerce of the University of Pennsylvania, and George Washington University Law School, where he was a Member of the Law Review.

## GROSS, Steven
Debevoise & Plimpton LLP, New York
212 909 6000
*Recommended in Bankruptcy*

## GROVE, Barry
Thelen Reid & Priest LLP, New York
212 603 6540
barrygrove@thelenreid.com
*Recommended in Construction*
**Practice Areas:** Mr Grove is a trial lawyer with substantial litigation, mediation, dispute review board and arbitration experience in all phases of construction claims on major projects such as dams, tunnels, pipelines, powerhouses, wastewater treatment plants, waste to energy projects, cement plants, highways, bridges, mass transit, telecommunications and municipal, industrial and high-rise buildings; insurance disputes including builder's risk claims; and contract formation, contract administration and project structuring advice to owners and contractors.
**Prof. Memberships:** American Bar Association, Litigation Section and Construction Law Committee; American College of Construction Lawyers, Charter Member, 1989; Secretary, 1992; Treasurer, 2001; President Elect, 2002; President 2003; Consultant to the Government of the Special Administrative Region of Hong Kong, 1998; Center for Public Resources, Construction Panel; Member, London Court of International Arbitration; Member, The Chartered Institute of Arbitrators; American Arbitration Association, Construction Panel.
**Career:** Partner with Thelen Reid & Priest LLP. Admitted to practice in California (1966), New York (1993) and the District of Columbia (1994) and US District Court, Northern District of California; US District Court, Southern District of California; US District Court, Southern District of New York Ninth Circuit Court of Appeals; US Court of Claims; US Supreme Court; Pro hac vice admis-

sions: Mississippi, Connecticut, Nevada, Alaska, Michigan, Utah, Wyoming and New Jersey. His speaking engagements include: Practicing Law Institute construction law courses, 1980-90, 1993 and 1998-2005; Construction Law Superconference, 1985-98 and 2001-02; Forbes Conference on Project Financing and Construction in the 1990's, 1992; Forbes Conference on Rebuilding America, 1993, 1994; Forbes Conference on Worldwide Infrastructure Partnerships, 1998; and Forbes Conference on International Energy/Power Projects, 2002; and The Global Construction Superconference London, 2001-04. He was Chairman of World Conference on Construction Risk, Paris, Singapore, 1994-96.
**Publications:** Contributing author, 'Construction Law Treatise', Matthew Bender, 1987; contributing author, 'Construction Failures', Wiley, 1989; contributing author, 'Construction Subcontracting', Wiley, 1990; contributing author, 'Proving and Pricing Construction Claims', Wiley, 1990; contributing author, 'Construction Subcontracting', Wiley, 1991; contributing author, 'Construction Litigation: Representing the Contractor', 2nd ed, Wiley, 1992; contributing author, 'Lien and Bond Laws', Wiley, 1992; contributing author, 'Design-Build Construction Workbook', Wiley, 1992; contributing author, 'Construction Law', Wiley, 1992; Contributing author, 'Design-Build Contracting Handbook', 2nd ed, Aspen, 2001; 'The Grove Report for the Government of the Special Administrative Region of Hong Kong', 1998. He has been on the Editorial Board of The International Construction Law Review since 2001.
**Personal:** Received his JD in 1966 from the University of Virginia Law School and his BA in French in 1963 from the Washington and Lee University. Selected for The International Who's Who of Construction Lawyers, 2005 and for The Best Lawyers in America, 2005. Recognized as the leading construction attorney in New York in the 2003 and 2004 Chambers USA Guide to America's Leading Business Lawyers.

## GRUBMAN, Allen
Grubman, Indursky & Shire, PC, New York 212 554 0400
*Recommended in Media & Entertainment*

## GRUNBLATT, David
Proskauer Rose LLP, Newark
973 274 3200
*Recommended in Immigration*

## GUERRERA, Sal
Skadden, Arps, Slate, Meagher & Flom LLP & Affiliates, New York
212 735 3910
sal.guerrera@skadden.com
*Recommended in Banking & Finance*
**Practice Areas:** Represents banks and

other financial institutions in domestic and international financings, including financings of tender offers, mergers and acquisitions generally; financings of recapitalizations and spin-offs; first lien/second lien financings; working capital and asset-based financings; subordinated debt, bridge and mezzanine financings; restructurings and workouts; and special-purpose financings. While primarily representing financial institutions, including Credit Suisse, Toronto-Dominion Bank, Merrill Lynch, Jefferies Babson Finance and AEA Investors, Mr Guerrera also represents borrowers and issuers, including Devon Energy Corporation. **Career:** JD, University of Pennsylvania School of Law, 1987; BA, Fairfield University, 1984 (summa cum laude).

### GUPTA, Paul R
Mayer, Brown, Rowe & Maw LLP, New York 212 506 2670
pgupta@mayerbrownrowe.com
*Recommended in Intellectual Property*
**Practice Areas:** Intellectual property. Information technology. Antitrust. Other complex litigation. Represents Fortune 500 and other clients in the following industries: computer, e-commerce, and outsourcing; telecommunications; financial services; and scientific, photographic and control equipment.
**Prof. Memberships:** Advisory Boards of four technology law publications; BNA's Computer Technology Law Report, Electronic Commerce & Law Report, E-Commerce Law and Strategy, and the Electronic Banking Law and Commerce Report; Correspondent, European Intellectual Property Review. Member, Special Committee on Cyberspace Law of the New York State Bar Association.
**Career:** Mayer, Brown, Rowe & Maw LLP (IP Practice Leader). Sullivan & Worcester LLP. Cravath, Swaine & Moore.
**Publications:** Writings: 'The Changing Landscape of Business Method Patents', New York Law Journal. 'Implementing the Recent Developments in Information Security, Business Continuity and Corporate Governance', Electronic Banking Law and Commerce Report. 'Strategic Alliances', The Deal. 'Lessons Learned from Three Generations of Technology Contracts', Electronic Banking Law & Commerce Report. Conferences: Frequent speaker on IP and IT issues before Practicing Law Institute (New York and San Francisco), New York City Bar Association, Georgetown University Law Center Annual Advanced E-Commerce Institute, and other major groups.
**Personal:** JD, Harvard Law School; BA, Yale College, Phi Beta Kappa.

### HADLEY, Joseph P
Davis Polk & Wardwell, New York
212 450 4000
joseph.hadley@dpw.com
*Recommended in Projects*
**Practice Areas:** Member of Davis Polk & Wardwell's Corporate Department. Advises corporations, financial institutions and governmental agencies on a wide variety of corporate and financing matters, with special emphasis on international joint venture and project and leveraged financings. Has extensive experience advising clients raising financing in the telecommunications, power and oil and gas sectors from the debt capital markets, syndicated loan market and governmental and multi-lateral financing sources.

### HAFETZ, Fred
Hafetz & Necheles, New York
212 997 7595
*Recommended in Litigation*

### HAHN, Richard
Debevoise & Plimpton LLP, New York
212 909 6000
*Recommended in Bankruptcy*

### HAIMS, Bruce
Debevoise & Plimpton LLP, New York
212 909 6000
*Recommended in Tax*

### HALEY JR, James F
Ropes & Gray LLP, New York
212 596 9034
james.haley@ropesgray.com
*Recommended in Intellectual Property*
**Practice Areas:** Focuses on worldwide procurement, defense, and enforcement of patents in the biotechnology, pharmaceutical, and chemical industries. Drafted and prosecuted some of the basic patents in rDNA technology. Handles numerous US and foreign patent litigations, European and other oppositions. Secured more than $4 billion in royalties for clients.
**Career:** Massachusetts Bar (1975); New York Bar (1977); USPTO; Partner, Fish & Neave (1983); Partner, Ropes & Gray (2005); Co-Head, Fish & Neave IP Group of Ropes & Gray.
**Personal:** JD, magna cum laude, Suffolk University Law School (1975); PhD, Brandeis University (1975).

### HALL, Richard
Cravath, Swaine & Moore LLP, New York
212 474 1293
rhall@cravath.com
*Recommended in Corporate/M&A*
**Practice Areas:** Mergers and acquisitions (particularly in the natural resources sector), cross-border transactions, hostile takeovers; corporate governance and general corporate advice.
**Prof. Memberships:** ABA; International Bar Association.
**Career:** Partner since 1996.
**Publications:** Frequent speaker and

author on the topics of mergers and acquisitions and corporate governance.
**Personal:** Harvard University (LLM, 1988); University of Melbourne (LLB, with honors, 1986; BComm, with honors, 1984).

### HALLIDAY, Joseph W
Skadden, Arps, Slate, Meagher & Flom LLP & Affiliates, New York
212 735 3260
j a@skadden.com
*Recommended in Banking & Finance*
**Practice Areas:** Founder, Skadden's Banking and Institutional Investing Group, represents commercial banks, investment banks, insurance companies, finance companies and leveraged buyout funds, as well as borrowers from, and equity participants with, such institutions. Practice involves international banking and financing, project financing, aircraft financing, equipment leasing, workouts and restructurings, creditors' rights, leveraged buyouts, oil and gas transactions and public utility financings.
**Prof. Memberships:** Member, Banking Law Committee, NY State Bar Association; Member, TriBar Legal Opinion Committee.
**Career:** LLB, Fordham University, 1963 (cum laude; Editor-in-Chief, Fordham Law Review); AB, Fordham University, 1960 (egregia cum laude).

### HALLMAN, Robert
Cahill Gordon & Reindel LLP, New York
212 701 3900
*Recommended in Environment*

### HALVEY, John
Milbank, Tweed, Hadley & McCloy LLP, New York 212 530 5000
*Recommended in Business Process Outsourcing, Technology*

### HAMMER, Stuart
Debevoise & Plimpton LLP, New York
212 909 6000
*Recommended in Environment*

### HANDELSMAN, Lawrence
Stroock & Stroock & Lavan LLP, New York 212 806 5400
*Recommended in Bankruptcy*

### HANRAHAN, Marc
Latham & Watkins LLP, New York
212 906 1200
*Recommended in Banking & Finance*

### HANSEN, Edward J
Morgan, Lewis & Bockius LLP, New York
212 309 6035
ehansen@morganlewis.com
*Recommended in Business Process Outsourcing, Technology*
**Practice Areas:** Edward Hansen is a Partner in the Outsourcing Practice. Mr Hansen's practice is devoted solely to representing clients in technology transactions, with an emphasis in representing clients in complex information technology and business process outsourcing

transactions. Mr Hansen frequently works with clients from the initial stages of a transaction, working from the project definition phase and assisting clients apply a 'best practices' approach to the business and legal negotiation process.
**Prof. Memberships:** Member, Computer Law Association; Member, American Bar Association.

### HARITON, David P
Sullivan & Cromwell LLP, New York
212 558 4000
haritond@sullcrom.com
*Recommended in Tax*
**Practice Areas:** Focuses on the US federal income taxation of financial instruments and transactions and on cross-border investment. Has represented the securities industry in Washington, chaired the New York State Bar Association Tax Section, and advised the government on the taxation of financial transactions.
**Career:** Partner since 1994.
**Publications:** Has published more than 50 articles on the taxation of financial instruments and transactions.
**Personal:** Stanford University (BA, 1981); Stanford Law School (JD, 1985; Order of the Coif).

### HARKRIDER, John D
Axinn, Veltrop & Harkrider LLP, New York
212 728 2210
jdh@avhlaw.com
*Recommended in Antitrust*
**Practice Areas:** Antitrust and trade regulation, commercial litigation.
**Prof. Memberships:** American Bar Association, Vice-Chair, Economics Committee of Antitrust Section, 2003-present; New York State Bar Association; New York City Bar Association.
**Career:** John Harkrider chairs the AVH Antitrust Practice. He represented BellSouth and Cingular in their acquisition of AT&T Wireless and the Department of Justice in its investigation of WorldCom's attempted acquisition of Sprint, culminating in a decision to seek a preliminary injunction blocking what would have been the largest merger in history. Other significant mergers include Harcourt in its sale to Reed Elsevier and Omnicare's acquisition of Neighborcare. Mr Harkrider represented SunGard against the US DOJ's attempt to enjoin SunGard's acquisition of Comdisco's Business Recovery division, represented IBP in a billion dollar class action brought by cattle producers in the Middle District of Alabama, represented Bar/Bri in the Ninth and Tenth Circuit on Sherman Act claims, successfully represented Vantico in preventing a hostile takeover of Vantico by Apollo Management, and currently represents MasterCard International Board of Directors in connection with their announced public offering. Mr Harkrider gave the Milton Handler lec-

ture in 2004.

**Publications:** Econometrics in Antitrust, ABA Section of Antitrust Law (J Harkrider and D Rubinfeld, ed) (2005); 'Exporting Antitrust Law to China', Global Competition Review (2006); 'Sophistication Snag', The Deal, January 17, 2005; 'Proving Anticompetitive Impact: Moving Past Merger Guidelines Presumptions', 2004 Milton Handler Antitrust Review, 2005 Colum Bus L Rev 317 (2005); 'Resolving Complex Antitrust Cases Promptly', Icarus, Summer/Fall 2002, a publication of ABA Section of Antitrust Law; 'Risk Shifting Provisions and Antitrust Risk: An Empirical Examination', Fall 2005.

**Personal:** Mr Harkrider received a BA from the University of Michigan in 1988 (highest honors) and a JD in 1991 from the University of California, Hastings College of the Law (Order of the Coif).

### HARRELL, Michael
Debevoise & Plimpton LLP, New York
212 909 6000
*Recommended in Private Fund Formation*

### HARRIS, Adam
O'Melveny & Myers LLP, New York
212 326 2182
aharris@omm.com
*Recommended in Bankruptcy*

**Practice Areas:** Adam Harris's practice covers a wide spectrum of representations in both Chapter 11 cases and out-of-court workouts and restructurings. Principally, Adam represents financial institutions (including both traditional and non-traditional lenders) in connection with loans and other financial accommodations made to companies experiencing financial difficulties. These representations have involved the restructuring of existing loans, debt for equity swaps, and new extensions of credit (including debtor-in-possession financing facilities).

### HARRIS, L Douglas
Milbank, Tweed, Hadley & McCloy LLP, New York 212 530 5000
*Recommended in Projects*

### HART, John
Simpson Thacher & Bartlett LLP, New York 212 455 2830
jhart@stblaw.com
*Recommended in Tax*

**Practice Areas:** Tax Partner at Simpson Thacher & Bartlett LLP. Active on a variety of tax matters, including formation of private investment funds; real estate transactions, real estate company mergers and acquisitions; bankruptcy and insolvency matters and international matters. Fund formation experience includes real estate opportunity funds, private equity funds, mezzanine funds and other asset categories. Regularly represents leading fund sponsors, including Blackstone, Carlyle, Hellman & Friedman, Joseph E

Robert, KKR, Lexington, Platinum, Ripplewood and Silver Lake. Also represents institutional investors in private funds, such as Howard Hughes Medical Institute.

**Prof. Memberships:** Member, New York City Tax Club (President, 2003-04). Member, Private Investment Fund Forum (independent group of New York-based practitioners specializing in private funds), International Fiscal Association and the New York State Bar Association (serves on the Tax Section's Committee on Partnerships and Committee on US Activities of Foreigners).

**Publications:** 'Restructuring the Bankrupt Corporation', 2004 Annual Survey of Bankruptcy Law (West Services, Inc.), also in PLI Course Handbook 'Tax Strategies for Corporate Acquisitions, Dispositions, Spin-Offs, Joint Ventures, Reorganizations & Restructurings 2005'.

**Personal:** JD, cum laude, Harvard Law School,1979; AB, High Distinction, Highest Honors in English Literature, University of Michigan, 1976, Phi Beta Kappa.

### HARTY, Ronan
Davis Polk & Wardwell, New York
212 450 4000
ronan.harty@dpw.com
*Recommended in Antitrust*

**Practice Areas:** Member of Davis Polk & Wardwell's Litigation Department, provides general antitrust counseling to US and non-US companies and represents clients in enforcement agency investigations, domestic and cross-border acquisitions and joint ventures, and litigations. Recent matters include representation of parties in antitrust lawsuits and before the US federal antitrust enforcement agencies in a variety of transactions, including mergers, joint ventures and other matters in the telecommunications, electronics, paper, agricultural biotechnology, chemicals, pharmaceutical, publishing and banking industries.

### HAWK, Barry E
Skadden, Arps, Slate, Meagher & Flom LLP & Affiliates, New York
212 735 3892
bhawk@skadden.com
*Recommended in Antitrust*

**Practice Areas:** Partner, New York and Brussels. Advises clients primarily in the areas of European Union and national antitrust laws and merger controls, European Union regulatory law, US antitrust law and merger control laws throughout the world. Has advised on EU and European Law in connection with M&A, joint ventures, privatizations, distribution and licensing, enforcement actions and litigation, public procurement, project financing, state aids or government subsidies, and various regulatory matters.

**Career:** LLB, University of Virginia School of Law, 1965; AB, Fordham College, 1962.

### HAZAN, Scott
Otterbourg, Steindler, Houston & Rosen, New York 212 661 9100
*Recommended in Bankruptcy*

### HEALY, Kevin
Bryan Cave LLP, New York
212 541 2000
*Recommended in Environment*

### HEISS, Howard E
O'Melveny & Myers LLP, New York
212 326 2116
hheiss@omm.com
*Recommended in Litigation*

**Practice Areas:** Howard Heiss focuses on white-collar criminal defense, SEC enforcement, internal investigations, and trial practice. He represents clients in criminal securities and SEC enforcement matters involving allegations of accounting fraud, offering fraud, sales practice fraud, insider trading, and other securities offenses. He handles criminal matters involving mail, wire and bank fraud and tax, bribery and customs offenses. Previously, Howard served as an Assistant US Attorney in the US Attorney's Office for the Southern District of New York for more than 11 years and was Head of the office's Securities and Commodities Fraud Task Force immediately before entering private practice.

### HEITNER, Kenneth H
Weil, Gotshal & Manges LLP, New York
212 310 8288
kenneth.heitner@weil.com
*Recommended in Tax*

**Practice Areas:** Kenneth Heitner is Co-Head of Weil Gotshal's Tax Department. He is a Member of the American Bar Association's Tax Section, Association of the Bar of the City of New York, and was formerly an Executive Committee member of the New York State Bar Association's Tax Section and the Chairman of committees on reorganizations, corporations, practice and procedure and net operating losses. Mr Heitner is an Adjunct Professor at New York University School of Law.

**Personal:** Rutgers University, BA, 1969; New York University School of Law, JD, 1973; New York University School of Law, LLM, 1977.

### HELLER, Richard B
Frankfurt Kurnit Klein & Selz, New York
212 826 5533
rheller@fkks.com
*Recommended in Media & Entertainment*

**Practice Areas:** Co-Head of the firm's Entertainment and Sports Group. Practice focuses on motion pictures and television, new media, publishing, celebrity branding and intellectual property. Clients include actors, writers, individual producers, directors, production companies and distributors in the motion picture and television fields. Handles film

clients from acquisition of rights through financing, production and exploitation of project. Actively counsels prominent best-selling authors, fashion models, designers and other celebrity clients in managing their valuable intellectual property rights and implementing fully coordinated branding strategies for exploiting motion picture, television, print, audio, electronic new media, merchandising/licensing and other rights.

### HENDERSON JR, Donald B
LeBoeuf, Lamb, Greene & MacRae LLP, New York 212 424 8694
dhenders@llgm.com
*Recommended in Insurance*

**Practice Areas:** Corporate lawyer with extensive experience in insurance M&A, financing, and related insurance regulatory matters. Experience includes purchases and sales of businesses, including stock and asset transactions, and purchases and sales of specific blocks of business. Regularly advises on life settlement and premium finance matters.

**Prof. Memberships:** New York Bar; Alabama Bar.

**Publications:** A frequent public speaker, he has written on insurance and corporate issues for publications including 'Best's Review', 'Business Insurance', 'National Underwriter', 'International Insurance Law Review', 'Reactions' and 'Reinsurance'.

**Personal:** New York University (LLM) 1976; University of Alabama Law Center (JD) 1974; University of Alabama (BS) 1971.

### HENZE II, William F
Jones Day, New York
212 326 3603
wfhenze@jonesday.com
*Recommended in Energy*

**Practice Areas:** Represents energy sector clients, including integrated oil and gas companies, pipelines, local distribution companies, electric utilities, nonregulated electricity producers, and lenders to and investors in energy-related businesses and assets. A frequent speaker and author of numerous articles, he is listed in Who's Who in America and Who's Who in American Law. Recognized for his capability to provide superior client service by BTI Consulting Group.

**Prof. Memberships:** Member of the drafting committee for the EEI Master Power Purchase & Sale Agreement. Advisory Board Member of the Institute for Energy Law. Energy Bar Association. State Bars of Texas and Arizona.

### HERBERT, John S
Gibson, Dunn & Crutcher LLP, New York
212 351 2424
jherbert@gibsondunn.com
*Recommended in Private Equity*

**Practice Areas:** Mr Herbert has over 25 years of experience in representing US and international financial buyers in the private equity, leveraged buyout and venture capital areas and a wide variety of other clients in complex M&A transactions. He advises funds in connection with their portfolio investments, including initial acquisitions or start-ups, divestitures, add-on acquisitions, bank financings and high-yield offerings, and various exit transactions, including dispositions, initial public offerings and recapitalizations.

**Personal:** JD, magna cum laude, George Washington University Law School, 1978, Order of the Coif. MBA, Harvard Business School, 1976. BA, University of Pennsylvania, 1970.

### HERLIHY, Edward D
Wachtell, Lipton, Rosen & Katz, New York 212 403 1207
edherlihy@wlrk.com
*Recommended in Corporate/M&A, Financial Services*

**Practice Areas:** Specializes in the largest and most complex bank and financial institution mergers and acquisitions and recapitalizations throughout the United States and is often called upon to represent companies involved in takeover battles and proxy contests, including investment banking firms in connection with a wide variety of financial institution matters.

**Career:** Partner at Wachtell, Lipton, Rosen & Katz. Serves as Co-Chairman of the firm's Executive Committee.

**Publications:** Writes and lectures regularly on issues involving banking and financial matters.

### HERZECA, Lois F
Fried, Frank, Harris, Shriver & Jacobson LLP, New York 212 859 8076
Lois.Herzeca@FriedFrank.com
*Recommended in Insurance*

**Practice Areas:** Corporate Partner. Practice includes representation of corporate clients and investment banks in complex transactions including securities offerings, mergers and acquisitions, spin-offs, restructurings and joint ventures, particularly involving insurance and reinsurance companies. Counsels corporations on corporate governance and securities matters.

**Career:** Joined Fried Frank in 1980. Became a Partner in 1986.

**Personal:** JD (1979), cum laude, Boston University Law School. BA (1976), with honors, State University of New York at Binghamton.

### HEWITT, William J
Ropes & Gray LLP, New York 212 841 5709
bill.hewitt@ropesgray.com
*Recommended in Private Fund Formation*

**Practice Areas:** Specializes in private equity and mergers and acquisitions. Represents several buyout and venture capital firms, including Welsh, Carson,

Anderson & Stowe, in fund formation and transactions by the funds and their portfolio companies. Member of the American Bar Association, Association of the Bar of the City of New York, and the New York State Bar Association.

**Career:** New York Bar (1965); Partner, Reboul, MacMurray, Hewitt & Maynard; Partner, Ropes & Gray (2003).

**Personal:** LLB, Harvard Law School (1964); AB, Harvard College (1961).

### HIRSCHBERG, William E
Shearman & Sterling LLP, New York 212 848 7097
whirschberg@shearman.com
*Recommended in Banking & Finance*

**Practice Areas:** Head of Shearman & Sterling's Banking Practice for the Americas with extensive experience in all areas of bank financing, including acquisition and leveraged buyout financing, workouts, restructurings, structured financing, project financing and inter-creditor issues.

**Prof. Memberships:** Member, American Bar Association Commercial Financial Services Committee; Chairman, Acquisition Financing Subcommittee (1987-91).

**Career:** Attorney in the Office of the General Counsel of the Federal Deposit Insurance Corporation in Washington, DC, 1972-76. Joined Shearman in 1976 and became a Partner in 1981.

**Personal:** AB, Indiana University (1969); JD, Loyola University of Chicago School of Law (1972).

### HOCHBERG, Jeffrey D
Sullivan & Cromwell LLP, New York 212 558 4000
hochbergj@sullcrom.com
*Recommended in Tax*

**Practice Areas:** Primarily focused on the taxation of financial instruments and products, private equity and real estate transactions, partnership transactions, real estate investment trusts and structured finance transactions. Also has extensive experience advising clients on the tax consequences of domestic and cross-border mergers, acquisitions and restructurings and has worked on numerous debt exchanges and refinancings.

**Prof. Memberships:** NYSBA (Member, Executive Committee, Tax Section; Co-Chair, Tax Accounting Committee).

**Career:** Partner since 2004.

**Personal:** Yeshiva University (BA, 1992); Columbia Law School (JD, 1995).

### HODARA, Fred S
Akin Gump Strauss Hauer & Feld LLP, New York 212 872 8040
fhodara@akingump.com
*Recommended in Bankruptcy*

**Practice Areas:** Chair, firmwide Financial Restructuring Practice Group. Represents creditors' committees in Chapter 11 cases and out-of-court and cross-border restructurings, with emphasis on com-

mittees comprised of diverse creditor constituencies. Represents insurance companies and other institutional investors, high-yield and distressed investors, trade creditors and committees of creditors, and corporate debtors. Cross-border insolvency work has included companies based in the United Kingdom, France, Germany, Norway, Canada, Korea and Australia.

**Prof. Memberships:** INSOL International; American College of Investment Counsel; Turnaround Management Association.

**Personal:** BA, State University of New York at Binghamton; JD, New York University. Named among 'America's Top 100 Restructuring Professionals'.

### HOFSTETTER, Richard
Frankfurt Kurnit Klein & Selz, New York 212 826 5537
Rhofstetter@fkks.com
*Recommended in Media & Entertainment*

**Practice Areas:** Co-Head of firm's Entertainment and Sports Group. Particular emphasis in all forms of television development, production and ancillary platforms, including licensing, merchandising and advertiser supported and branded entertainment. Represents performers, producers, writers and production companies for scripted and dramatic programs; news and reality-based programming; distribution companies and television networks; programming/distribution for network, syndication, cable, public television, children's programming, international production/distribution and format sales; advertising sponsorships. Counsels international producers in licensing formats, producing and distributing their programming in the US.

**Prof. Memberships:** Voting Member, Academy of Television Arts and Sciences; International Television Academy; BAFTA; Board of Advisors, New York Television Festival.

### HOLLAND, Mark
Clifford Chance US LLP, New York 212 878 8000
*Recommended in Litigation*

### HOOD, Thomas R
Mayer, Brown, Rowe & Maw LLP, New York 212 506 2595
thood@mayerbrown.com
*Recommended in Tax*

**Practice Areas:** Tax law, with emphasis on domestic corporate matters and multi-jurisdictional corporate planning; mergers, acquisitions, and spin-offs; partnerships; domestic and international transactions, and structured finance (including securitization and financial products); IRS letter rulings.

**Prof. Memberships:** Admitted to practice: New York, District of Columbia, Minnesota, and Nebraska. American Bar

Association Tax Section: Corporate Tax Committee, Financial Transactions Committee, and Committee on Legislative Recommendations.

**Career:** Mayer, Brown, Rowe & Maw LLP, New York, Partner, 1993. Counselor to the IRS Commissioner, Washington, DC, 1990-93. Kutak Rock & Campbell, Partner, Omaha and New York, pre-1990.

**Publications:** Note, 'Federal Income Tax Treatment of Business and Employment Investigatory Expenses', 56 Minn L Rev 1157.

**Personal:** BA, Yale University, 1969; JD (cum laude), University of Minnesota School of Law, 1973; primary editor, Minnesota Law Review, 1972-73; LLM in Taxation, New York University School of Law, 1974.

### HOPKINSON, R Ronald
Latham & Watkins LLP, New York 212 906 1200
*Recommended in Private Equity*

### HORKOVICH, Robert
Anderson Kill & Olick P.C., New York 212 278 1000
*Recommended in Insurance*

### HOROWITZ, Gary I
Simpson Thacher & Bartlett LLP, New York 212 455 7113
ghorowitz@stblaw.com
*Recommended in Insurance*

**Practice Areas:** Partner at Simpson Thacher & Bartlett in the firm's Corporate Department. Concentrates on mergers and acquisitions, joint ventures and corporate finance matters, with an emphasis on insurance and healthcare. Recent deals include representing Swiss Re in its acquisition of Employers Re from General Electric, WellPoint Health Systems in its sale to Anthem, Assurant Inc. in its IPO and Manulife Financial Corporation in its acquisition of John Hancock.

**Prof. Memberships:** President, Miracle House; Counsel to the Board of Directors of Common Cents.

**Career:** Joined Simpson Thacher in 1982 and became Partner in 1989. Currently a member of the firm's Executive Committee and Co-Administrative Partner of the firm; former Chairman of the firm's Personnel Committee (2000-03).

**Personal:** BS, Cornell University (1978); JD, Columbia University School of Law (1981), Editor, Columbia Law Review, Harlan Fiske Stone Scholar. Law clerk, The Honorable Edward N Cahn in the United States District Court for the Eastern District of Pennsylvania (1981-82).

### HOROWITZ, Steven G
Cleary Gottlieb Steen & Hamilton LLP, New York 212 225 2580
shorowitz@cgsh.com
*Recommended in Real Estate*

**Practice Areas:** Real estate finance, joint ventures, capital markets, sale-leasebacks and mortgage finance. Clients include Citigroup, Goldman Sachs, Genting Group, Home Depot, Istithmar, Kindred Healthcare, McDonald's, Neiman Marcus, Open Space Institute, Shinnecock Indian Nation, Starwood Hotels, Targa Resources, Texas Pacific Group, Tom Ford.

**Prof. Memberships:** American College of Real Estate Lawyers; Anglo-American Real Property Institute; Legal Aid Society, Director.

**Career:** Joined firm, 1987; became Partner, 1989. Lecturer in Law, Columbia Law School, (2003-present). Hill & Barlow (1981-87); US District Court Monitor (1979-81); Judicial clerk to Joseph L Tauro (1978-79). JD, cum laude, Harvard Law School (1978); MPP, cum laude, Kennedy School of Government, Harvard University (1978); BA, magna cum laude, Yale University (1972).

**Publications:** Frequent lecturer and author for continuing legal education seminars.

## HORSCH, Richard
White & Case LLP, New York
212 819 8866
rhorsch@whitecase.com
*Recommended in Environment*

**Practice Areas:** Chairs firm's International Environmental Practice. Advises on all aspects of environmental law. Counsels clients on environmental issues in all types of transactions across a broad range of industries, domestically and internationally. Represents clients in environmental and toxic tort litigation. Has represented chemical company, multinational oil company, multilateral development bank, and homeowner class in major environmental disputes.

**Prof. Memberships:** NY Bar; New Jersey Bar; ABA.

**Publications:** NYU 'Journal of International Law and Politics' (managing editor).

**Personal:** University of New Hampshire (BA, magna cum laude, Phi Beta Kappa, 1974); New York University School of Law (JD, 1980).

## HORWITZ, Ethan
Goodwin Procter LLP, New York
212 813 8800
ehorwitz@goodwinprocter.com
*Recommended in Intellectual Property*

**Practice Areas:** Mr Horwitz maintains a diverse practice and has over 25 years of experience in the full range of intellectual property law. Mr Horwitz has advised clients and has litigated patent, trademark, trade dress, copyright and false advertising cases in the United States and internationally. His practice includes worldwide acquisition and enforcement of intellectual property and advising clients on the enforcement of their intellectual property. Mr Horwitz has represented a variety of clients in various electronic, chemical and mechanical patent litigations.

**Prof. Memberships:** International Association for the Protection of Intellectual Property: Member; Federation Internationale Des Conseils En Propriete Industrielle-Commision d'Etude et de Travail (FICPI): Member; United States Trademark Association: Member; American Intellectual Property Law Association: Member.

**Personal:** JD, St John's University School of Law; MS, New York University, Courant Institute; BA, Polytechnic Institute.

## HOWARD, Nigel L
Mayer, Brown, Rowe & Maw LLP,
New York 212 506 2121
nhoward@mayerbrownrowe.com
*Recommended in Business Process Outsourcing, Technology*

**Practice Areas:** Complex and mission-critical technology transactions: outsourcing, licensing, joint venture, and strategic alliance transactions. Represents clients in intellectual property purchases and sales and in reviews of IP portfolios in relation to corporate financing and M&A transactions. Advises on cross-border technology transfer. Advises on development and testing arrangements, distribution channels, technology deployment and electronic commerce and internet strategies. Expert on privacy laws as they relate to electronic databases and online services.

**Prof. Memberships:** Admitted to practice in England and Wales, 1990; New York, 1993.

**Career:** Joined Mayer, Brown, Rowe & Maw LLP, New York, as Partner, 2003. Brobeck, Phleger & Harrison LLP, New York, 1993-2003; Partner, 1998; Head of Technology Group, 2000. Boodle Hatfield, London, 1988-92.

**Publications:** 'Exploring the 'virtual' company strategy through outsourcing in the Biotech industry', SRI, 2003; 'Living with the FTC Safeguard Rules: Industry Tips and Experiences', The Investment Lawyer, October, 2003; 'Outsourcing and ASP Arrangements', PLI Publications, 2002; 'New Developments in Outsourced Manufacturing Arrangements', University of Texas, 2002.

**Personal:** London University, Masters Degree, intellectual property law (pass with merit), 1991. Lancaster University, Bachelors Degree in Law (with honors), 1987; Veronica Cowan prize for law.

## HUCK, L Francis
Simpson Thacher & Bartlett LLP, New York 212 455 2000
lfhuck@stblaw.com
*Recommended in Banking & Finance*

**Practice Areas:** Frank Huck is a Partner in the firm's Corporate Department where he specializes in syndicated commercial lending. Over the past 20 years, Mr Huck has represented domestic and foreign banks in a variety of bank financing transactions. In recent years, he has been especially active in financing of acquisitions by private equity groups and public companies and in restructuring financings. Typical recent matters include the representation of the arranging bank in financings for Lucent Technologies, GE Capital, AT&T/Comcast, Time Warner and Standard Aero. He has also represented the bank lenders to the former Yugoslavia through four debt restructurings beginning in 1998 and the division of the external bank indebtedness among the five successor republics in 1996-98.

**Prof. Memberships:** An active Member of the American Bar Association and the Bar Association of the City of New York.

**Career:** Joined Simpson Thacher in 1972 and became a Partner in 1980.

**Personal:** Received an AB in 1969 from Harvard University and a JD in 1972 from Stanford Law School.

## HUDANISH, David M
Mayer, Brown, Rowe & Maw LLP,
New York 212 506 2524
dhudanish@mayerbrownrowe.com
*Recommended in Business Process Outsourcing, Technology*

**Practice Areas:** Partner in Outsourcing Practice and Technology Practice. Represents companies in structuring and negotiating complex information technology and business process outsourcing agreements, development agreements, licensing agreements, royalty agreements and strategic alliance and joint venture agreements. Advises companies in connection with all aspects of their technology development, procurement, licensing and protection. Advises clients on a variety of internet and e-commerce initiatives. Frequent author and speaker on outsourcing and technology topics.

**Prof. Memberships:** Admitted to practice in New York, New Jersey, and District of Columbia.

**Career:** Joined Mayer, Brown, Rowe & Maw LLP in 2003. Previously, Head of Outsourcing Practice at Brobeck, Phleger & Harrison LLP.

**Publications:** Recent presentations: Outsourcing in a Regulated Environment (NASD Annual Members Conference, February 2006); Software Licensing (PLI, November 2005); Multi-Process Outsourcing (Mayer, Brown, Rowe & Maw LLP Quarterly International IT and Outsourcing Newsletter, Fall 2004); Outsourcing – Managing the Unique Risks (Executive Roundtable, Mayer, Brown, Rowe & Maw LLP and PA Consulting, November 2004); Compliance and Risk Management Issues in Outsourcing (The Evolution of Globalization: Strategy, Execution, Results for Insurance and Banking Industry, SRI, September 2004).

**Personal:** Georgetown University Law Center, JD cum laude, 1991; Georgetown University, BA magna cum laude, 1987.

## HUEBNER, Marshall S
Davis Polk & Wardwell, New York
212 450 4000
marshall.huebner@dpw.com
*Recommended in Bankruptcy*

**Practice Areas:** Member of Davis Polk & Wardwell's Corporate Department, concentrating in corporate restructuring and insolvency. Represents financial institutions, preeminent corporations and agent banks in large and complex domestic and international restructurings and bankruptcies, including major roles in Enron, Adelphia, Loral, Polaroid and Magellan. Currently lead restructuring counsel to Delta Air Lines. Also provides advice on insolvency issues relating to complex financial products and on M&A transactions involving troubled companies.

**Personal:** Attended Princeton University (awarded Fulbright Scholarship) and Yale Law School (awarded Ford Foundation Fellowship). Publishes and lectures frequently on insolvency topics, including DIP lending, silent second liens, and pension and ERISA issues in bankruptcy.

## HUGHES, Christopher
Morgan & Finnegan, LLP, New York
212 415 8524
cahughes@morganfinnegan.com
*Recommended in Intellectual Property*

**Practice Areas:** For more than 30 years, Christopher A Hughes has concentrated his practice on complex patent, trade secret and trademark litigation, as well as licensing and intellectual property counseling. He joined Morgan & Finnegan immediately after law school and has been a Partner since 1983.

**Prof. Memberships:** Mr Hughes is a Member of the New York Intellectual Property Law Association, where he has served on the Board of Directors since 2001 – Board of Directors (2001-04), Second Vice President (2004-05), First Vice President (2005 to date); District of Delaware Intellectual Property Advisory Committee (2004 to date); American Intellectual Property Law Association; Licensing Executives Society; American Judicature Society; Intellectual Property Owners; New York State Bar Association, where he is a Member of the Litigation and Intellectual Property Sections; and American Bar Association, where he is also a Member of the Litigation and Intellectual Property Sections. He is a founding Board Member of the New York University Lawyer Alumni Mentoring Program ('LAMP'), and serves on the Executive Advisory Board (1998 to date), and was elected a Fellow of the American Bar Association.

**Career:** Since the early 1990s, Mr Hughes has headed the Morgan & Finnegan teams representing IBM in several patent litigations involving a variety of computer software and hardware technologies and in many different District Courts. He also represented Priceline.com in litigations involving the famous 'Priceline Patent'. He has also headed the Morgan & Finnegan teams representing such European companies as Heidelberger Druckmaschinen and Robert Bosch GMBH. He is also currently handling patent infringement actions in the District of Delaware and the Southern District of New York dealing with cardiovascular stent technologies on behalf of Medinol Ltd. Mr Hughes has spent several years directing patent infringement trials and hearings throughout Europe (including trials seeking preliminary relief and cross-border injunctions). He has also participated in various nullity, cancellation and opposition proceedings on important patent rights in European Courts and Patent Offices. In these matters, he has coordinated the corresponding activities in the United States with respect to the US counterpart patents and litigations. Mr Hughes has been appointed Special Master by the US District Court for the District of Rhode Island for the purpose of assisting the Court in Arendi U.S.A., Inc. v Microsoft Corporation, Civil Action No 02-CV-343 (ECT). As Special Master, he dealt with several complex discovery issues and motions in limine for the court.

**Publications:** Mr Hughes has lectured extensively throughout the United States, Japan and Korea on such topics as attorney-client privilege, contributory and induced infringement, means-plus-function claim elements, various aspects of Markman claim construction proceedings, the doctrine of equivalents including the impact of the Federal Circuit and Supreme Court decisions in the 'Festo' case, and US trade secret law. In addition, he has had several articles published on those topics. Mr Hughes was recently featured in several Lawcast presentations discussing 'New Patent Litigation Tactics for the Post-Festo World'. He also discussed 'Strategies For Litigating Against Patent Holding Companies', at the AIPLA 2004 Spring Meeting in Dallas, and participated on two panels, 'Securing Ownership of Employee Innovations' and 'Protecting and Embracing Your IP', at the 2004 IP Strategies in Deals Conference, sponsored by Findlaw Corporate Counsel Center.

**Personal:** Mr Hughes has been featured in The Best Lawyers in America; 'Chambers USA Leaders in Their Field; Chambers USA America's Leading Lawyers for Busines's – recommended in Intellectual Property; Best Lawyers, Intellectual Property: The Year in IP Almanac, published by IP Law and Business; and Guide to the World's Leading Patent Law Experts (Legal Media Group).

### HUNT, Peter J
Pillsbury Winthrop Shaw Pittman LLP, New York 212 858 1139
peter.hunt@pillsburylaw.com
*Recommended in Employee Benefits*
**Practice Areas:** Mr Hunt advises employers, financial institutions and investment funds on fiduciary and compliance issues under ERISA, the Internal Revenue Code and securities laws. He regularly advises on the employee benefits and executive compensation aspects of corporate acquisitions and dispositions. Recent experience also includes designing and drafting equity-based compensation plans, deferred compensation plans, and complex employer pension and profit-sharing plans.
**Prof. Memberships:** American College of Employee Benefits Counsel; American Bar Association; New York State Bar Association.
**Personal:** JD, New York University, 1984; BS, University of Virginia, 1978.

### HYMAN, Alan
Proskauer Rose LLP, New York
212 969 3275
ahyman@proskauer.com
*Recommended in Bankruptcy*
**Practice Areas:** A leading Member of the Bankruptcy and Corporate Reorganization Bar, heads Proskauer's Bankruptcy and Reorganization Practice Group. For 30 years he has been actively involved in a wide spectrum of the nation's largest corporate reorganization proceedings.
**Prof. Memberships:** A Member of the American College of Bankruptcy Lawyers.
**Publications:** Has lectured extensively in the Bankruptcy and Reorganization Field. Has been a guest lecturer at the Turnaround Industry Conference, the United States Trustee Symposium and at programs sponsored by the American Bankruptcy Institute and the Institute for International Research.
**Personal:** A graduate of New York University and New York University Law School.

### ICHEL, David
Simpson Thacher & Bartlett LLP, New York 212 455 2563
dichel@stb.com
*Recommended in Litigation*
**Practice Areas:** Partner at Simpson Thacher & Bartlett LLP in the Litigation Department. Specializes in complex litigation, including product liability, securities, distributor termination, intellectual property, insurance, banking, and mergers and acquisitions disputes.
**Prof. Memberships:** American Law Institute, Product Liability Advisory Council, Duke Law School Board of Visitors, Federal Bar Council; Chair, Product Liability Committee, Association of the Bar of the City of New York.
**Career:** Joined the firm in 1978 and

elected Partner in 1985.
**Publications:** Author of numerous publications on litigation and commercial insurance issues.
**Personal:** Duke University, BA 1975 (summa cum laude, Phi Beta Kappa), and JD 1978 (Duke Law Journal). Admitted in NY, NJ, DC District, US Supreme Court and numerous federal Circuit Courts of Appeals and district courts.

### INDOE, William F
Sullivan & Cromwell LLP, New York
212 558 4000
indoew@sullcrom.com
*Recommended in Tax*
**Practice Areas:** Focuses on tax structuring of complex financial transactions, including: tax-free mergers; cross-border acquisitions; conversions of 'C corps' into REITs; privately owned business sales; divestitures via joint ventures; and transactions involving asset managers. Tax advisor in: securities offerings; preparation and negotiation of employment/severance arrangements, stock option and other incentive compensation plans; and resolution of employee benefit issues in ordinary course and change of control situations.
**Prof. Memberships:** ABA; ABCNY; NYSBA.
**Career:** Partner since 1976.
**Personal:** Lehigh University (BA, 1964); University of Virginia Law School (LLB, 1968).

### INDURSKY, Arthur
Grubman, Indursky & Shire, PC, New York 212 554 0400
*Recommended in Media & Entertainment*

### INSOLIA, Robert S
Goodwin Procter LLP, New York
212 813 8800
rinsolia@goodwinprocter.com
*Recommended in Private Fund Formation*
**Practice Areas:** Mr Insolia represents and advises a wide range of clients involved in the capitalization of real estate through public and private capital markets. Mr Insolia has assisted clients with complex real estate financings (including senior and subordinate debt structures), and preferred equity and mezzanine financings; portfolio acquisitions and dispositions of real estate and loans secured by real estate; REIT IPOs and follow-on public equity and debt offerings; and mergers and acquisitions of real estate operating companies.
**Personal:** JD, Fordham University School of Law, 1984; BA, New York State University College at New Paltz, 1979.

### IRWIN, Peter
Debevoise & Plimpton LLP, New York
212 909 6000
*Recommended in Real Estate*

### ISACKSON, Robert M
Orrick, Herrington & Sutcliffe LLP, New York 212 506 5280
rmisackson@orrick.com
*Recommended in Intellectual Property*
**Practice Areas:** Represents plaintiffs and defendants in patent litigation and strategy relating to numerous core technical disciplines, including: biotechnology, electronics, financial services, medical devices, pharmaceuticals, data encryption, and software systems and simulations. He also handles trade secret and commercial disputes involving technology and software, and counsels clients in procuring, protecting, and enforcing patent, trademark, copyright, and trade secret rights.
**Prof. Memberships:** NY IP Law Association; Intellectual Property Owners.
**Career:** Leader, Orrick's East Coast IP Practice; Leader, Global IP Integration.
**Personal:** JD, University of Michigan Law School, 1982; BSE, Electrical Engineering, magna cum laude, University of Michigan College of Engineering, 1978.

### ISEMAN, Robert
Iseman Cunningham Riester & Hyde LLP, Albany 518 462 3000
*Recommended in Healthcare*

### IVANHOE, Robert
Greenberg Traurig LLP, New York
212 801 9333
ivanhoer@gtlaw.com
*Recommended in Real Estate*
**Practice Areas:** Real estate.
**Prof. Memberships:** Board Member, American Friends of Rabin Medical Center; Executive Committee, Albert Einstein College of Medicine; Executive Committee, Real Estate Lawyers Division of the UJA Federation.
**Career:** Listed, Who's Who Legal: The International Who's Who of Business Lawyers, 2006; listed, Best Lawyers in America, 2006; listed, Chambers & Partners USA Guide, 2003-06.
**Publications:** Author, 'Real Estate Overview and Trends', Who's Who Legal: The International Who's Who of Business Lawyers, 2006.
**Personal:** JD, American University Washington College of Law, 1978; BA, Johns Hopkins University, 1975.

### JACOBS, Charles P
Nixon Peabody LLP, New York
212 940 3170
cjacobs@nixonpeabody.com
*Recommended in Private Fund Formation*
**Practice Areas:** Leader, Private Equity Practice. Focus: venture capital and private equity fund formation, related matters. Represents private equity funds and investors, including funds of funds, public pension systems and endowments, in connection with the formation of private equity funds.
**Prof. Memberships:** Admitted to prac-

tice in New York. Member of the International Bar Association, American Bar Association, and New York State Bar Association.

**Career:** Partner since 1989. Chair: Business and Finance Department, 1999 to 2004.

**Publications:** Advisory Board, Private Equity Analyst Terms and Conditions Study, 4th edition.

**Personal:** University of Pennsylvania (BA); State University of New York at Buffalo (JD).

## JACOBS, Paul
Fulbright & Jaworski L.L.P., New York
212 318 3348
pjacobs@fulbright.com
*Recommended in Private Equity*

**Practice Areas:** Private equity; business, commercial, corporate, international, and securities law; and mergers and acquisitions.

**Prof. Memberships:** Mr Jacobs is a member of the American Bar Association, the Association of the Bar of the City of New York, and the New York State Bar Association.

**Career:** Partner in Fulbright's New York office since 1978, Mr Jacobs is Co-Head of the firm's Corporation, Business and Banking Section and a member of the firm's Policy Committee. He has been recognized by 'Who's Who in American Law', 'Who's Who in America', and 'Who's Who in the World'.

**Personal:** BA, Colgate University (1967); JD, Columbia University Law School (1971). Admitted to practice in New York in 1971.

## JACOBSON, Marc
Greenberg Traurig LLP, New York
212 801 9200
jacobsonm@gtlaw.com
*Recommended in Media & Entertainment*

**Practice Areas:** Entertainment; technology, media and telecommunications.

**Prof. Memberships:** Founding Chairman, New York State Bar Association Section on Entertainment, Arts and Sports Law; Chairman of the Board of Advisors, The Internet Alliance; Board of Directors, Long Island Film and Television Foundation; Advisory Board Member, New York e-Commerce Group, Business Development Network; Adjunct Professor, Fordham University Law School, Entertainment Law.

**Career:** Listed, Chambers & Partners USA Guide, 2005-06.

**Personal:** JD, New York University School of Law; BA, magna cum laude, State University of New York at Buffalo.

## JACOBSON, Martin D
Simpson Thacher & Bartlett LLP,
New York 212 455 7023
mjacobson@stblaw.com
*Recommended in Projects, Transportation*

**Practice Areas:** A Partner at Simpson Thacher & Bartlett LLP and a Member of the Corporate Department. Advises clients in project and infrastructure financing as well as structured equipment financing. Has represented sponsors, lenders, underwriters and other credit providers. Has a broad range of experience involving the financing of infrastructure, industrial property, aircraft and other transportation equipment.

**Prof. Memberships:** American Bar Association and Association of the Bar of the City of New York and founding Chair of its committee on project finance.

**Career:** Joined Simpson Thacher in 1979 and became a Partner in 1984. Received BS summa cum laude from the University of Pennsylvania in 1969. MBA from New York University Stern School of Business in 1973 and a JD from the University of Chicago Law School in 1976.

## JACOBSON, Michele
Stroock & Stroock & Lavan LLP,
New York 212 806 5400
*Recommended in Insurance*

## JAFFE, Helene D
Weil, Gotshal & Manges LLP, New York
212 310 8572
helene.jaffe@weil.com
*Recommended in Antitrust*

**Practice Areas:** Helene Jaffe is Co-Head of Weil Gotshal's Antitrust/Competition Practice and regularly represents clients buying or selling companies in the US or abroad, or whose pricing, promotional or marketing practices are under investigation. She has also been involved in numerous Lanham Act advertising, trademark and trade dress cases. The mergers/joint ventures she has handled include CBS's joint venture with Warner Brothers to form the CW Network and United HealthCare's purchase of PacifiCare. She has also been lead trial counsel for some of American Airlines' largest antitrust cases.

**Personal:** Barnard College, BA, 1976; Columbia University School of Law, JD, 1976.

## JENNER, Jesse J
Ropes & Gray LLP, New York
212 596 9019
jesse.jenner@ropesgray.com
*Recommended in Intellectual Property*

**Practice Areas:** Litigates in all technological areas; trial practice has focused particularly in electronics and electronic products, semiconductor technology and manufacturing, medical products, telecommunications and the internet. Has argued numerous appeals before the Court of Appeals for the Federal Circuit. Best known for successful decision holding 16 Lemelson patents not infringed, invalid and unenforceable.

**Career:** New York Bar (1973); USPTO; Partner, Fish & Neave (1981); Partner, Ropes & Gray (2005); Fellow, American

College of Trial Lawyers.

**Personal:** JD, Harvard Law School (1972); BSEE, Cornell University (1969); Rotary Foundation Fellow, University of Warwick, UK (1972-73).

## JENSEN, J Christopher
Cowan, Liebowitz & Latman, New York
212 790 9200
*Recommended in Intellectual Property*

## JEWELL, Ronald R
Dechert LLP, New York
212 698 3589
ronald.jewell@dechert.com
*Recommended in Corporate/M&A*

**Practice Areas:** Mr Jewell is a Partner in the Mergers and Acquisitions, Private Equity, and Corporate and Securities Groups. He focuses on acquisitions, dispositions, joint ventures, debt restructurings, secured financings, public offerings, and private placements.

**Prof. Memberships:** Member, New York and Maryland Bars.

**Career:** Attorney, US Department of Treasury (Office of General Counsel, Office of Foreign Assets Control); attorney, US Securities and Exchange Commission (Division of Corporate Finance).

**Personal:** Loyola College, BA, 1971; University of Baltimore School of Law, JD, cum laude, 1975, editor of University of Baltimore Law Review; Georgetown University Law Center, LLM in Taxation, 1977.

## JOFFE, Robert D
Cravath, Swaine & Moore LLP, New York
212 474 1440
rjoffe@cravath.com
*Recommended in Antitrust*

**Practice Areas:** Presiding Partner. Extensive litigation and counseling experience in the areas of antitrust, securities, contract and corporate governance.

**Prof. Memberships:** ABA (Litigation and Antitrust Practice Sections); NYSBA (Antitrust Section); ABCNY (previously Trade Regulation including Chair; Vice President 2003-04).

**Career:** Partner since 1975. Ministry of Justice, Government of Malawi, 1967-69.

**Publications:** Author of numerous articles on antitrust issues.

**Personal:** Harvard Law School (JD, cum laude, 1967); Harvard College (AB, cum laude, 1964). Human Rights First: Board of Directors. Board of Directors, Franklin Resources and Fiduciary Trust. Member of the Council of Foreign Relations.

## JOHNSTON, M Elaine
White & Case LLP, New York
212 819 8736
mejohnston@whitecase.com
*Recommended in Antitrust*

**Practice Areas:** Antitrust, including antitrust aspects of mergers, acquisitions, joint ventures. Co-ordinating US, European, other antitrust clearances on complex cross-border deals. Handling government non-merger investigations. Advising

on distribution, licensing, other business conduct, trade association activities.

**Prof. Memberships:** New York State Bar; United States District Court for the Southern District of New York; United States District Court for the Eastern District of New York; American Bar Association (Antitrust Section); New York State Bar Association (Antitrust Section, Executive Committee); 'Antitrust Law Journal' (former associate editor).

**Personal:** Cambridge University (BA (hons), 1980, MA, 1984); University of Michigan Law School (LLM, 1987), Fulbright Scholar.

## JOSEPH, Gregory
Gregory P Joseph Law Offices LLC, New York 212 407 1200
*Recommended in Litigation*

## JOYCE, Edward M
Heller Ehrman LLP, New York
212 847 8765
edward.joyce@hellerehrman.com
*Recommended in Insurance*

**Practice Areas:** Insurance recovery, real estate and finance, international arbitration and ADR.

**Prof. Memberships:** New York State Bar Association; Association of the Bar of the City of New York; ABA.

**Career:** Mr Joyce has experience in professional liability, employee dishonesty, directors/officers' liability, business interruption, all risk, construction defect, intellectual property, advertising injury, business torts, products liability, employment liability and environmental liability matters. He has represented policyholders and clients in a variety of industries: food and beverage, industrial, textile, retail, real estate services and construction, entertainment, pharmaceutical, telecommunications, energy, financial institutions and municipalities.

**Personal:** Fordham University School of Law (JD, 1986).

## JUDLOWE, Stephen B
Morgan, Lewis & Bockius LLP, New York
212 309 2101
sjudlowe@morganlewis.com
*Recommended in Intellectual Property*

**Practice Areas:** Stephen B Judlowe leads the firm's Intellectual Property Litigation Practice. He has been lead trial attorney litigating intellectual property rights for domestic and international interests for more than 30 years in federal district courts across the United States, the Court of Appeals for the Federal Circuit and the US International Trade Commission. He has been responsible for patent matters involving all substantial areas of technology including electronics, pharmaceuticals and medical devices, chemistry, software and financial services and consumer goods.

**Prof. Memberships:** Member, American Bar, New York State Bar and New Jersey State Bar Associations.

## KADET, Samuel
Skadden, Arps, Slate, Meagher & Flom
LLP & Affiliates, New York
212 735 2570
skadet@skadden.com
*Recommended in Litigation*

**Practice Areas:** Represents corporations and individuals in complex litigation, including securities, takeover and other commercial matters. Represented Cendant Corporation in proceedings arising out of the widely reported accounting irregularities at CUC International Inc., one of the companies that merged to form Cendant.
**Career:** JD, St John's University, 1977 (cum laude; editor, St John's Law Review); BA, State University of New York at Binghamton, 1971 (magna cum laude, Phi Beta Kappa).

## KAFIN, Robert
Proskauer Rose LLP, New York
212 969 3280
rkafin@proskauer.com
*Recommended in Environment*

**Practice Areas:** He is Proskauer's General Counsel. Concentrates his practice in the area of environmental law where he regularly provides compliance counseling advice to businesses facing regulation under all of the major federal environmental laws and state analogues. In recent years, he has been called upon in major transactions involving almost every type of industry to review and evaluate environmental compliance and liabilities.
**Prof. Memberships:** He is the past Chair of the Environmental Law Section of the New York State Bar Association. He also served as Chair of Parks and Trails NY and sits on the Boards of the Council on the Environment of NYC and The Adirondack Council.
**Personal:** Harvard Law School, JD, magna cum laude, 1966. Franklin & Marshall College, AB, magna cum laude, 1963 Phi Beta Kappa.

## KALKINES, George
Manatt Phelps & Phillips LLP, New York
212 790 4500
*Recommended in Healthcare*

## KANE, Meredith J
Paul, Weiss, Rifkind, Wharton & Garrison LLP, New York
212 373 3065
mjkane@paulweiss.com
*Recommended in Real Estate*

**Practice Areas:** Partner in the Real Estate Department. Represents developers, equity investors, institutional and entrepreneurial owners and government agencies in all aspects of development, finance, acquisitions and sales, leasing and securitization of real estate. Experienced in complex joint ventures, large-scale mixed-use and multi-investor development projects. Named one of the Top 50 Women in Real Estate and one of 25 Current Leaders in the Industry by Real

Estate Weekly and the Association of Real Estate Women; one of Top 10 Women in Real Estate Development by Grid Magazine. Mayoral and gubernatorial appointee to several NY City and State boards and commissions.

## KARIG, Adele
Debevoise & Plimpton LLP, New York
212 909 6000
*Recommended in Private Fund Formation, Tax*

## KARMEL, Philip
Bryan Cave LLP, New York
212 541 2000
*Recommended in Environment*

## KAROTKIN, Stephen
Weil, Gotshal & Manges LLP, New York
212 310 8350
stephen.karotkin@weil.com
*Recommended in Bankruptcy*

**Practice Areas:** Stephen Karotkin concentrates his practice in the area of corporate reorganizations, out-of-court debt restructurings, debtors' and creditors' rights and financing transactions. He represents corporations and lenders in reorganization cases under Chapter 11, and he represents both lenders and companies in connection with out-of-court financial restructurings. Mr Karotkin is a Fellow of The American College of Bankruptcy, a Member of the American Bar Association, and a Member of the New York State Bar Association.
**Personal:** Union College, BS, 1973; New York University School of Law, JD, 1976.

## KARP, Brad S
Paul, Weiss, Rifkind, Wharton & Garrison LLP, New York
212 373 3316
bkarp@paulweiss.com
*Recommended in Litigation*

**Practice Areas:** Co-Chair of Litigation Department. Member of Management Committee. Profiled in The American Lawyer (2003) as one of the 45 leading lawyers in the US under the age of 45, and (2006) for handling of 'bet-the-company' litigations. Achieved national prominence as a trial lawyer and corporate advisor. In 2005 and 2006, named one of the leading lawyers in the US handling 'Bet-The-Company' litigations by The Best Lawyers in America. Extensive experience handling and trying a broad range of matters, with particular emphasis on defending complex securities and commercial matters and representing financial institutions and other clients before regulatory authorities.

## KASNER, Jay B
Skadden, Arps, Slate, Meagher & Flom LLP & Affiliates, New York
212 735 2628
jkasner@skadden.com
*Recommended in Litigation*

**Practice Areas:** Experience in federal and state court litigation, including secu-

rities, corporate and takeover litigation and general commercial matters. Represents numerous public companies in their defense of actions arising under federal and state securities and corporate laws. Handles litigation arising from corporate control contests, which traditionally require expedited litigation.
**Prof. Memberships:** Co-Chair, Practising Law Institute Securities Litigation Conference (1996-2004).
**Career:** JD, Boston University, 1980 (cum laude; Editor, Boston University Law Review; author, 'Minimizing Minimization: Scott v United States', Boston University Law Review); BA, Union College, 1977 (magna cum laude).

## KASS, Stephen
Carter Ledyard & Milburn LLP, New York
212 732 3200
*Recommended in Environment*

## KATCHER, Richard D
Wachtell, Lipton, Rosen & Katz, New York 212 403 1222
rdkatcher@wlrk.com
*Recommended in Corporate/M&A*

**Practice Areas:** Specializes in mergers and acquisitions and corporate and securities law and governance. Has participated in numerous mergers and acquisitions and related matters, representing both acquirers and targets as well as investment bankers. Transactions include AT&T Corp's merger with SBC, Cole National's acquisition by Luxottica, IBP's acquisition by Tyson, Monsanto's merger with Pharmacia, Warner Lambert's merger with Pfizer, AT&T Corp's acquisitions of MediaOne Group and Tele-Communications, Inc, the break-up of AT&T Corp, including the AT&T Broadband/Comcast transaction, Lilly Industries, Inc's sale to The Valspar Corporation, Hussmann International, Inc's sale to Ingersoll-Rand Company, American Stores' sale to Albertson's, Browning Ferris' sale to Allied Waste Industries, AT&T Corp's acquisition of McCaw Cellular, AT&T's disposition of Lucent Technologies and NCR Corp, and Monsanto's disposition of Solutia Inc. Cross-border transactions include the sale of Pet Incorporated to Grand Metropolitan and the sale of a greater than majority interest in Genentech Inc to Hoffman-LaRoche. Also represented clients in joint ventures and recapitalizations and has counseled boards and non-management directors on governance issues and investigations and on other crisis situations.
**Prof. Memberships:** Member of the Board of Trustees of New York University; former Chairman of the Special Committee on Mergers, Acquisitions and Corporate Control Contests of the Association of the Bar of the City of New York; Member of the Securities Regulation Committee of the New York State Bar Association and the Association of the

Bar of the City of New York.
**Career:** Partner at Wachtell, Lipton, Rosen & Katz since 1971; Chairman of Wachtell Lipton's management committee from 1997-2003.
**Publications:** Frequent lecturer on continuing legal education programs.
**Personal:** Graduated from Lafayette College in 1963 (BA) and from New York University School of Law in 1966 (LLB). A Member of the New York University Law Review, a Member of the Order of the Coif and a John Norton Pomeroy Scholar.

## KATSH, Salem
Kasowitz Benson Torres & Friedman, New York 212 506 1700
*Recommended in Intellectual Property*

## KATZ, David A
Wachtell, Lipton, Rosen & Katz, New York 212 403 1309
dakatz@wlrk.com
*Recommended in Corporate/M&A*

**Practice Areas:** Specializes in the areas of mergers and acquisitions, complex securities transactions, corporate governance matters and board crisis management, and has been involved in many major international and domestic corporate transactions.
**Prof. Memberships:** Member of the American Bar Association (Section on Business Law); Member of the Committee on Negotiated Acquisitions Task Force on Public Company Acquisitions; Chairman of the American Bar Association Task Force on Dictionary of M&A Terms; Member of the Federal Securities Laws Committee, the New York State Bar Association (Section on Business Law); and the Association of the Bar of the City of New York. Member, American Society for Corporate Secretaries, Corporate Practice Committee.
**Career:** Partner at Wachtell, Lipton, Rosen & Katz since 1996. Adjunct Professor at New York University School of Law, Senior Professional Fellow at New York University Center for Law and Business and Adjunct Professor at the Owens Graduate School of Management at Vanderbilt University.
**Publications:** Has written extensively.
**Personal:** Graduated from Brandeis University and from New York University School of Law.

## KATZKE, Michael S
Wachtell, Lipton, Rosen & Katz, New York 212 403 1345
mskatzke@wlrk.com
*Recommended in Employee Benefits*

**Practice Areas:** Specializes in executive compensation and employee benefits.
**Career:** Partner at Wachtell, Lipton, Rosen & Katz.
**Publications:** Author: 'Executive Compensation, Board Liability and Corporate Governance in a Post-Disney World', The Corporate Governance Advisor (Novem-

ber/December 2005); 'Change-of-Control Employment Arrangements – What Directors Are Asking Today', The M&A Lawyer (2004); 'Post-Merger Employment Changes Insufficient to Trigger 'Chute' Benefits', The M&A Lawyer (2003); 'Importance of Administration Provisions in Change in Control Severance Plans', The M&A Lawyer (2003); 'Employee Benefit Change of Control Protections: Recent Trends and Development', The M&A Lawyer, vol 2, no 3, June 1998; 'Executive Compensation Practices May Inadvertently Limit Change of Control Severance Benefits', INSIGHTS, vol 12, no 2, February 1998; 'Shareholder Approval of Equity Plans', INSIGHTS, vol 11, no 2, February 1997; '1995 Developments in Change in Control Related Employee Benefits', INSIGHTS, Vol 10, no 3, March 1996.
**Personal:** Graduated from State University of New York at Stony Brook in 1980 (BA) and from New York University School of Law (JD, 1984; LLM, 1988).

### KAUFMAN, Stephen
Stephen E Kaufman, PC, New York
212 826 0820
*Recommended in Litigation*

### KAVALER, Thomas
Cahill Gordon & Reindel LLP, New York
212 701 3900
*Recommended in Litigation*

### KAWATA, Yukako
Davis Polk & Wardwell, New York
212 450 4000
yukako.kawata@dpw.com
*Recommended in Private Fund Formation*
**Practice Areas:** Member of Davis Polk & Wardwell's Investment Management Group. Advises clients on the formation and operation of private investment funds and other investment vehicles exempt under the US Investment Company Act, including private equity funds, venture capital funds, hedge funds, fund of funds and funds investing in particular sectors or countries. Also advises clients on the formation and operation of various types of carried interest plans and employee investment arrangements. Advises funds and fund sponsors on the regulatory aspects implicated by their operations, including considerations under the US Investment Advisers Act and other US securities laws.

### KAYLE, Bruce
Milbank, Tweed, Hadley & McCloy LLP, New York 212 530 5000
*Recommended in Tax*

### KELLER, Bruce
Debevoise & Plimpton LLP, New York
212 909 6000
*Recommended in Intellectual Property, Media & Entertainment*

### KELLY, Michael J
Willkie Farr & Gallagher LLP, New York
212 728 8686
mkelly@willkie.com
*Recommended in Bankruptcy*
**Practice Areas:** Partner in the Business Reorganization and Restructuring Department, representing debtors in large, complex, Chapter 11 cases. Clients in this area have included AMF Bowling Worldwide, Maxxim Medical, Classic Communications, Converse, G&G Shops, The Grand Union Company, Integrated Resources, Petrie Retail, Inc., Starter Corporation, Sunterra Corp. and Winkelman. He has also represented creditors and investors in Chapter 11 cases, including Quadrangle (REFCO), Foodtown (Twin County Chapter 11 and Chapter 7 cases), Warburg Pincus (Proxim, Centennial, Phycor, Presspoint, Hookt, Alliant and Evolve bankruptcy cases), Crown Management (Gruntal), Ventas, Inc. (Vencor, Sun, Integrated Health, Lenox, and Texas Health Chapter 11 cases), Merit Health (DVI). He also represented financial and other consultants in Chapter 11 cases, including KPMG, NERA, Mercer and FTI Consulting, and has represented the Trustee in the Granite cases and the examiner in the Caribbean Petroleum cases. His practice also includes representing debtors, creditors, investors and board members in out-of-court restructurings.
**Prof. Memberships:** A Member of the New York State Bar Association.
**Career:** Admitted to the Bar of the State of New York. He is also admitted to the United States Court of Appeals for the Third Circuit and the United States District Courts for the Eastern and Southern Districts of New York.
**Personal:** Received a JD from New York University in 1988, where he was elected to the Order of the Coif, and a BA from the State University of New York at Albany in 1985. Serves as a lecturer at the New York University School of Continuing and Professional Studies, Center for Finance, Law and Taxation, where he teaches the Bankruptcy, Workouts and Reorganization course.

### KELLY, Thomas
Debevoise & Plimpton LLP, New York
212 909 6000
*Recommended in Insurance*

### KENNEDY, John B
LeBoeuf, Lamb, Greene & MacRae LLP,
New York 212 424 8505
jkennedy@llgm.com
*Recommended in Technology*
**Practice Areas:** Transactions, litigation, and counseling in intellectual property, outsourcing and offshoring, licensing, technology transfer, information privacy, information security, and electronic commerce. Clients include Fortune 500 companies as well as emerging compa-

nies in widely varying industries. Has negotiated cross-border and domestic outsourcing and licensing transactions, complex licenses and joint ventures, and settlements involving contested intellectual property, licenses and services agreements.
**Prof. Memberships:** Sedona Institute, Sourcing Interests Group, INTA.
**Career:** Morrison & Foerster, Co-Chair, Technology Transactions Group, New Media Group.
**Personal:** Columbia University School of Law (JD) 1985; University of Chicago (MA with honors) 1976; Carleton College (BA magna cum laude) 1970.

### KENNEDY, Robert
Latham & Watkins LLP, New York
212 906 1200
*Recommended in Private Equity*

### KENNEDY, Thomas H
Skadden, Arps, Slate, Meagher & Flom LLP & Affiliates, New York
212 735 2526
tkennedy@skadden.com
*Recommended in Corporate/M&A*
**Practice Areas:** Focuses on M&A, corporate finance, and other transactions with an emphasis on the telecommunications and information technology industries. Deputy Head of firm's global Corporate Practice; Co-ordinator of the firm's Corporate Technology Practice. Experience in many hostile transactions, leveraged buyouts, proxy fights and other governance matters.
**Career:** JD, Georgetown University Law Center, 1981; BA, University of Virginia, 1978.

### KESSLER, Jeffrey L
Dewey Ballantine LLP, New York
212 259 8050
jkessler@deweyballantine.com
*Recommended in Antitrust, Sport*
**Practice Areas:** Mr Kessler has extensive experience in all aspects of antitrust law, sports law, intellectual property litigation and other complex litigation. He has been lead counsel in some of the most complex antitrust, sports law and IP law cases in the country including major jury trials and has represented a number of US and international companies in criminal and civil investigations in the antitrust and trade areas.
**Career:** Partner, Dewey Ballantine LLP. Co-Chair, Litigation Department. Member of the firm's Executive Committee.
**Personal:** BA, summa cum laude, Columbia University, 1975. JD, Kent Scholar, Columbia Law School, 1977.

### KIERNAN, John
Debevoise & Plimpton LLP, New York
212 909 6000
*Recommended in Litigation*

### KIESSLING, B Robbins
Cravath, Swaine & Moore LLP, New York
212 474 1500
bkiessling@cravath.com
*Recommended in Banking & Finance*
**Practice Areas:** Broad range of finance, banking, financial institution and related matters, including syndicated bank financings, structured finance, capital markets transactions and mergers and acquisitions.
**Prof. Memberships:** NYSBA; ABCNY; TriBar Opinions Committee.
**Career:** Partner since 1983. Clerkship: Hon Edward Weinfeld (US District Court for the Southern District of New York).
**Personal:** New York University School of Law (JD, cum laude, 1976; articles editor, Law Review; Order of the Coif); Yale University (BA, cum laude, 1973).

### KIRPALANI, Susheel
Milbank, Tweed, Hadley & McCloy LLP, New York 212 530 5000
*Recommended in Bankruptcy*

### KISLIN, Scott A
Gibson, Dunn & Crutcher LLP, New York
212 351 4078
skislin@gibsondunn.com
*Recommended in Corporate/M&A*
**Practice Areas:** Mr Kislin has been involved in all aspects of M&A transactions, representing both buyers and sellers in public and private deals, private equity and hostile takeover transactions. He has particular experience in public company M&A, including hostile takeover transactions and proxy contests.
**Personal:** JD, Columbia University School of Law, 1992; Harlan Fiske Stone scholar.

### KLAUBERG, John G
LeBoeuf, Lamb, Greene & MacRae LLP, New York 212 424 8125
jklauber@llgm.com
*Recommended in Energy*
**Practice Areas:** Co-Head of LeBoeuf Lamb's Energy and Utilities Practice, with extensive experience in electric power and gas industry transactions, including mergers and restructurings of regulated utilities; acquisitions and dispositions of power plants, including large wind generating facilities; leases of generating and transmission facilities and similar utility assets; and large-scale and complex structured wholesale and retail power transactions. Advises on transactions involving both regulated utilities and unregulated companies in the electric and gas markets.
**Prof. Memberships:** ABA, NYSBA, DCBA.
**Career:** Joined LeBoeuf Lamb in 1985.
**Personal:** Georgetown University Law Center (JD) 1981; New York University (LLM, Taxation)1984; Hamilton College (AB) 1978.

## KLEIN, Jeffrey
Weil, Gotshal & Manges LLP, New York
212 310 8790
jeffrey.klein@weil.com
*Recommended in Employment*
**Practice Areas:** Jeffrey Klein chairs Weil Gotshal's Employment Litigation Practice. He has defended employers around the country in all aspects of labor and employment litigation in both individual and class action claims, with particular emphasis on employment discrimination, trade secrets, ERISA and wage and hour litigation. Representative clients include Avon Products, ExxonMobil, MasterCard, Merrill Lynch, Reader's Digest, and UnitedHealth Group.
**Publications:** Co-author, bi-monthly Employment Law column, New York Law Journal (1998-present).
**Personal:** Amherst College, BA, magna cum laude, 1978; Columbia University School of Law, JD, 1981. Frequent lecturer at CLE courses.

## KLEIN, Steven D
Willkie Farr & Gallagher LLP, New York
212 728 8221
sklein@willkie.com
*Recommended in Real Estate*
**Practice Areas:** Partner in the Real Estate Department, specializing in REITs, joint ventures, acquisition and disposition, financing, and leasing transactions. Represents clients in all types of estate transactions, and drafting and negotiating agreements in connection therewith, including REIT and securitized financing agreements, construction and permanent loan agreements and mortgages, loan restructuring agreements, partnership and limited liability company agreements, property management agreements, construction and development agreements, contracts of sale, retail and office leases, and regional shopping center agreements. Represented Bloomberg L.P. in the lease for its 700,000 square-foot new world headquarters in New York City, and in numerous other acquisitions and leases, nationally and internationally. Has also represented Lehman Brothers, McKinsey & Company and Apollo Real Estate in major leasing transactions. Represented DiamondRock Hospitality Company in numerous acquisitions and financings with respect to hotel properties, and CBL Properties, The Mills Corporation and Simon Property Group in numerous acquisitions, joint ventures and financings with respect to regional mall centers and portfolios.
**Prof. Memberships:** Member of the Commercial Leasing Committee of the American Bar Association, the Real Estate Development Committee of the New York State Bar Association, the Real Property Law Committee of the New York City Bar Association, and the International Council of Shopping Centers.
**Career:** Admitted to the Bar of the State

of New York.
**Publications:** Has published and spoken on a variety of real estate topics for the New York Law Journal, the Practising Law Institute, the Association of the Bar of the City of New York and the International Council of Shopping Centers, among others.
**Personal:** Received a JD from Rutgers University in 1986 and a BA from Queens College in 1983.

## KLEINBARD, Edward D
Cleary Gottlieb Steen & Hamilton LLP, New York 212 225 2480
ekleinbard@cgsh.com
*Recommended in Tax*
**Practice Areas:** Federal income tax matters, including taxation of new financial products, financial institutions, and international mergers and acquisitions.
**Prof. Memberships:** Member of the American College of Tax Counsel, International Fiscal Association.
**Career:** Joined firm, 1977; became Partner, 1984. JD, Yale Law School (1976); MA and BA, magna cum laude, Brown University (1973).
**Publications:** 'Designing an Income Tax on Capital' (paper presented at a Brookings Institution Conference). 'Proposed Treasury Regulation Offer Dealers and Traders Safe Harbor for Section 475 Mark-to-Market Valuations', Journal of Taxation and Regulation of Financial Institutions. 'The Business Enterprise Income Tax: A Prospectus', Tax Notes. 'Competitive Convergence in the Financial Services Markets', Taxes. 'Taxing Convertible Debt: A Layman's Perspective', SMU Law Review. 'Contingent Interest Convertible Bonds and the Economic Accrual Regime' (co-author), Tax Notes. 'Disclosing Book – Tax Differences' (co-author), Tax Notes. 'The US Taxation of Equity Derivative Instruments', Handbook of Equity Derivatives. 'Corporate Tax Shelters and Corporate Tax Management', The Tax Executive. 'Risky and Riskless Positions in Securities', Taxes.

## KLING, Lou R
Skadden, Arps, Slate, Meagher & Flom LLP & Affiliates, New York
212 735 2770
lkling@skadden.com
*Recommended in Corporate/M&A*
**Practice Areas:** Has extensive experience in mergers and acquisitions of public and private companies, subsidiaries and divisions, including negotiated and contested acquisitions, leveraged buyouts and recapitalizations. Represents borrowers, issuers and underwriters in a broad spectrum of financing transactions. Serves on firm's Policy Committee, its top governing committee. Currently Co-Chairman of the firm's Opinion Committee, and Chairman of the Financial Oversight Audit Committee.
**Career:** JD, New York University, 1977

(Order of the Coif; Law Review); MA, Mathematics, University of Illinois, 1974; BA, New York University, 1973 (magna cum laude; Phi Beta Kappa). Co-author, 'Negotiated Acquisitions', a treatise.

## KNEIP, Frederick
Milbank, Tweed, Hadley & McCloy LLP, New York 212 530 5000
*Recommended in Employee Benefits*

## KNIGHT, James T
Simpson Thacher & Bartlett LLP, New York 212 455 2000
jknight@stblaw.com
*Recommended in Banking & Finance*
**Practice Areas:** James T Knight is a Partner in the firm's Corporate Department. Mr Knight's practice focuses on banking matters and the representation of lenders and borrowers in acquisitions and other leveraged transactions. His principal clients include JPMorgan Securities Inc., JPMorgan Chase Bank, N.A. and The Blackstone Group and its portfolio companies.
**Career:** Joined Simpson Thacher in 1979 and became a Partner in 1986.
**Personal:** He received his BA summa cum laude from Dartmouth College in 1976 where he was a member of Phi Beta Kappa and earned his JD cum laude from Harvard Law School in 1979.

## KOBAK, Scott M
Simpson Thacher & Bartlett LLP, New York 212 455 7210
skobak@stblaw.com
*Recommended in Real Estate*
**Practice Areas:** Real Estate Partner at Simpson Thacher & Bartlett LLP. Main area of concentration has been representing institutional investors in complex domestic and international commercial real estate, real estate company acquisitions and developments, joint ventures and financings, including involvement with many of the most prominent real estate private equity funds. Recent transactions completed include Carlyle Realty Fund's $1.76 billion acquisition and financing of the Riverside South project in Manhattan (reported as largest New York City real estate deal for 2005), Carlyle's $800 million sale of three Manhattan residential towers sale to Equity Residential, Blackstone Real Estate Fund's $3.2 billion acquisition and financing of Extended Stay America, Hovnanian Enterprise's acquisition of Town & Country Homes in the largest private homebuilder acquisition to date, the $475 million mortgage financing of Marsh & McLennan's headquarters in NYC and Carlyle's acquisition and development of several New York City condominium projects, including the Orion, a 500-unit luxury condominium project in the Times Square area of New York City and Ariel East and West on the Upper West Side of Manhattan.
**Career:** Joined firm 1993; elected to

membership 2000.
**Personal:** JD, Boston University Law School, magna cum laude. Associate Editor, Boston University Law Review.

## KOENIGSBERG, I Fred
White & Case LLP, New York
212 819 8806
fkoenigsberg@whitecase.com
*Recommended in Intellectual Property*
**Practice Areas:** Copyright law, including counseling, litigation. Negotiates, drafts license agreements. Counsels on copyright issues. Litigates infringement claims. Conducts administrative proceedings before the US Copyright Office and Copyright Royalty Judges. Participates in legislative efforts in US Congress.
**Prof. Memberships:** New York State Bar, admitted 1973; United States Supreme Court; various Federal Courts of Appeal and District Courts; American Bar Association Section of Intellectual Property Law (past Chair); American Intellectual Property Law Association (past President); Columbia University (Adjunct Professor).
**Personal:** Cornell University (BA, 1967); Annenberg School of Communications, University of Pennsylvania (MA, 1969); Columbia University School of Law (JD, 1972).

## KOESTLER, Mark D
Kramer Levin Naftalis & Frankel LLP, New York 212 715 9385
mkoestler@kramerlevin.com
*Recommended in Immigration*
**Practice Areas:** Mr Koestler has developed a national reputation in the handling of immigration law matters in the areas of advertising, theater and film (including representing numerous Tony and Academy Award winners). He served as the 2003-04 Chair of the 1,000-member American Immigration Lawyers Association's NY Chapter. He has lectured on a number of different business immigration topics at regional and national conferences of the American Immigration Lawyers Association. Mr Koestler is listed in The Best Lawyers in America and The International Who's Who of Corporate Immigration Lawyers, and has authored a number of articles in the field of business immigration.
**Personal:** Received a JD Degree cum laude from Brooklyn Law School in 1991 and an AB Degree from Hamilton College in 1988.

## KOHN, Arthur H
Cleary Gottlieb Steen & Hamilton LLP, New York 212 225 2920
akohn@cgsh.com
*Recommended in Employee Benefits*
**Practice Areas:** Compensation and benefit matters, including executive compensation, corporate governance, pension compliance and investment, employment law and related matters.
**Prof. Memberships:** Member of the Bar

of New York.

**Career:** Joined firm, 1986; became Partner, 1995. JD, Columbia University School of Law (1986); BA, Columbia University (1986).

## KOHN, Jeffrey

O'Melveny & Myers LLP, New York
212 326 2067
jkohn@omm.com
*Recommended in Employment*

**Practice Areas:** Jeff Kohn's practice focuses on the litigation and arbitration of a broad range of employment and traditional labor law matters, including employment discrimination, sexual harassment, wage and hour class actions, labor disputes, executive contracts, and trade secret litigation. Jeff has significant experience in executive compensation and bankruptcy matters (including 1113 motions). Jeff represents clients in a variety of industries including the airline industry; entertainment industry; financial and professional services; construction; manufacturing; technology; and telecommunications. He is the former Co-Chair of the Employment Law Committee of the American Bar Association and a frequent lecturer on labor and employment law.

## KOLB, Daniel

Davis Polk & Wardwell, New York
212 450 4000
daniel.kolb@dpw.com
*Recommended in Litigation*

**Practice Areas:** Member of Davis Polk's Litigation Department. A practicing litigator and trial lawyer in both federal and state trial and appellate courts throughout the United States for more than 38 years. His practice has included a wide range of professional liability, securities litigation, general litigation, and antitrust matters for various clients, including major accounting firms, industrial corporations, and financial institutions.

## KOOB, Charles E

Simpson Thacher & Bartlett LLP, New York 212 455 2000
ckoob@stblaw.com
*Recommended in Antitrust, Litigation*

**Practice Areas:** Partner at the firm and Co-Head of the Litigation Department. Specializes in competition and antitrust law. Experience includes counseling clients on antitrust issues affecting mergers, acquisitions, joint ventures and distribution practices. Has represented clients before the Federal Trade Commission, the Antitrust Division of the Department of Justice and state and foreign competition authorities; defended corporate clients in both criminal and civil antitrust litigation; represented individuals in grand jury investigations and corporate plaintiffs in major private antitrust litigation. Recent experience includes: the successful defense of Appleton Papers Inc. in a criminal price-fixing trial; the represen-

tation of Virgin Atlantic Airways in a private treble action against British Airways; and the representation of the special committee of the Board of Directors of Archer Daniels Midland in a federal grand jury investigation of price-fixing. Has also tried both large commercial and product liability actions to verdict.

**Prof. Memberships:** Trustee of the Natural Resources Defense Council; Chairman of Stanford Law School's Board of Visitors.

**Career:** Joined the firm 1969; became Partner 1977.

**Publications:** Co-author, 'Private Antitrust Remedies Under U.S. Law', PLC Competition Law Handbook, 2003-04.

**Personal:** BA, 1966, Rockhurst College and JD, 1969, Stanford Law School.

## KORNBERG, Alan W

Paul, Weiss, Rifkind, Wharton & Garrison LLP, New York 212 373 3209
akornberg@paulweiss.com
*Recommended in Bankruptcy*

**Practice Areas:** Chair of the Bankruptcy and Corporate Reorganization Department. Member of the firm's Management Committee. Handles Chapter 11 cases, transnational insolvency matters, out-of-court restructurings, bankruptcy-related acquisitions, bankruptcy-related litigation and insolvency-sensitive transactions. Clients include debtors, official and unofficial creditors' committees, court-appointed fiduciaries and investors focusing on distressed situations. Is representing Time Warner in its acquisition, together with Comcast, of Adelphia Communications through a Chapter 11 plan and represented the California Public Utilities Commission in the Pacific Gas & Electric Company Chapter 11 case. Chairs the Bankruptcy and Corporate Reorganization Committee of the City Bar Association of New York.

## KORNREICH, Edward S

Proskauer Rose LLP, New York
212 969 3395
ekornreich@proskauer.com
*Recommended in Healthcare*

**Practice Areas:** Co-Chair of Proskauer Rose LLP's Health Care Law Department. A recognized authority on the legal, regulatory and business issues related to healthcare services, he works primarily on healthcare transactions, regulatory compliance and healthcare payment issues for varied providers (both for-profit and not-for-profit), HMOs, pharmaceutical companies, medical device companies, pharmacy benefit management companies and entrepreneurs. He also counsels providers on issues related to research, technology transfer and governance.

**Prof. Memberships:** A past Chair of the Health Law Committee of the Association of the Bar of the City of New York and a past Chair of the Providers' Com-

mittee, and now Treasurer, of the Health Law Section of the New York State Bar Association. He was named one of the '40 Health Care Lawyers Who Have Made Their Mark' by the National Law Journal, was recognized as one of the 'Outstanding Fraud and Compliance Lawyers of 2004' in Nightingale's Healthcare News, and has received many other honors.

**Publications:** Frequently writes and lectures on Medicare and Medicaid reimbursement, healthcare integration, not-for-profit law and corporate governance issues.

**Personal:** Harvard Law School, JD, 1977. Columbia University, Columbia College, BA, magna cum laude, 1974, Phi Beta Kappa.

## KOSCHIK, David N

White & Case LLP, New York
212 819 8241
dkoschik@whitecase.com
*Recommended in Banking & Finance*

**Practice Areas:** The firm's New York Executive Partner whose practice focuses on representing major commercial and investment banks in lending transactions, particularly in acquisition and highly leveraged financings, and in various types of financings for insurance companies. Served as senior bank lenders' counsel in connection with many notable such matters. Also represents institutions in other types of financings, including letter of credit facilities and commercial paper back-up facilities.

**Personal:** BA, cum laude, Miami University, 1979; MSFS, Georgetown University, 1984; JD, magna cum laude, Georgetown University Law Center, 1984.

## KOTRAN, Stephen M

Sullivan & Cromwell LLP, New York
212 558 4000
kotrans@sullcrom.com
*Recommended in Corporate/M&A*

**Practice Areas:** Partner, M&A Group. Recent clients include: American Express, AIG, Anthem, Cytec, Eastman Kodak, Goldman, Sachs & Co., Prudential Financial, Swift Transportation and Wachovia Securities.

**Prof. Memberships:** ABA (Member, Committee on Negotiated Acquisitions); ABCNY (Member, Special Committee on Mergers, Acquisitions & Corporate Control Contests).

**Career:** Partner since 1999.

**Personal:** Harvard University (AB, 1985); University of Virginia Law School (JD, 1990; Law Review, Order of the Coif).

## KOVNER, Victor

Davis Wright Tremaine LLP, New York
212 489 8230
*Recommended in Media & Entertainment*

## KRAMER, Daniel J

Paul, Weiss, Rifkind, Wharton & Garrison LLP, New York 212 373 3020
dkramer@paulweiss.com
*Recommended in Litigation*

**Practice Areas:** Leading trial lawyer and litigator with extensive experience in securities litigation and internal investigations. Has handled complex litigations for some of the largest companies in the US. Has significant experience representing boards of directors on corporate governance issues and special committees in internal investigations. Recent matters include representation of AIG, Hollinger International and Merck in securities matters and special committees of Adecco and Fannie Mae in internal investigations. Lectures and writes on securities litigation, regulatory issues and ethical issues for securities lawyers. Identified as one of the leading litigators in 2006 edition of The Best Lawyers in America.

## KRAMER, Kenneth M

Shearman & Sterling LLP, New York
212 848 4172
kkramer@shearman.com
*Recommended in Antitrust*

**Practice Areas:** Senior Partner and former Chair of the Litigation Group at Shearman & Sterling. Represents a wide range of domestic and international clients in complex commercial litigation and specializes in antitrust, securities law and corporate governance litigations.

**Prof. Memberships:** Director, International House; New York Lawyers for the Public Interest; Episcopal Social Services; Juvenile Diabetes Research Foundation International.

**Career:** Clerk for Orrin G Judd, United States District Court for the Eastern District of New York, 1972-73.

**Personal:** AB, Colgate University (1965); JD, Albany Law School/Union University, Editor-in-Chief of the Law Review (1972).

## KRAMER, Morris J

Skadden, Arps, Slate, Meagher & Flom LLP & Affiliates, New York
212 735 2700
mkramer@skadden.com
*Recommended in Corporate/M&A*

**Practice Areas:** Practice includes friendly and hostile transactions and has involved many of the largest and most publicized deals. Counsels bidders, targets and their financial advisors in non-negotiated acquisition situations. Extensive experience in strategic and negotiation issues involving public and private company mergers, acquisitions and dispositions. Advises shareholders, boards of directors and managements in leveraged and management buyouts, proxy fights and other corporate control transactions. Represents parties from around the globe in transactions into and from North America, as well as cross-border intra-

European deals.
**Career:** LLB, Harvard University, 1966; AB, Dartmouth College, 1963.

### KRASNOW, Richard P
Weil, Gotshal & Manges LLP, New York
212 310 8493
richard.krasnow@weil.com
*Recommended in Bankruptcy*
**Practice Areas:** Extensive experience representing borrowers, creditors, asset purchasers, committees and trustees. Mr Krasnow's matters have covered almost every segment of the business landscape, including retailing; real estate; offshore oil servicing, steel, financial services; entertainment, telecommunications; transportation and airlines. Representative matters include Macy's, Edison Brothers Stores, Factor Card Outlet, Drexel Burnham, Lion Capital, Lombard Wall, National Steel, LTV, Daewoo Motors, Fruit of the Loom, U.S. Home, Johns-Manville, DirecTV Latin America, Pegasus Satellite, Eastern, Pan Am, United, U.S. Airways, Delta and Northwest.
**Personal:** University of Chicago, AB, 1968; New York University School of Law, JD, 1972.

### KRAUS, Bruce R
Willkie Farr & Gallagher LLP, New York
212 728 8237
bkraus@willkie.com
*Recommended in Technology*
**Practice Areas:** Partner in both the Corporate and Financial Services and Telecommunications Departments, specializing in corporate finance, mergers and acquisitions and general corporate advice for telecommunications and other corporate clients. Mergers and acquisitions experience includes public company takeovers, private company and subsidiary acquisitions, spin-offs, domestic and international joint ventures, and strategic equity investments. Considerable experience in corporate finance, including registered public offerings, pre-IPO convertible debt and 144A placements of debt securities and preferred stock. Represents telecom, industrial and private equity clients in venture capital financings, initial and subsequent offerings of common stock, placements of partnership and LLC interests. Telecom industry experience includes undersea cable companies, competitive local exchange carriers (CLECs), long distance and internet backbone networks, fixed and mobile wireless networks and satellite telecommunications. Recently represented XO Communications, Inc. in the pending sale of its CLEC business and Hong Kong's Techtronic Industries Co. Ltd. in its acquisition of the Milwaukee Electric Tool and AEG power tool businesses from Sweden's Atlas Copco AB.
**Career:** Admitted to the Bar of the State of New York. Law clerk (1979-80) to the Chief Judge of the Second Circuit Court

of Appeals.
**Publications:** Authored 'Structuring Global Satellite Systems', Space Finance, 1998 and 'Pyrrhic Victory in Spectrum Auction', The National Law Journal, August 25, 1997 among others.
**Personal:** Received a JD from Yale Law School in 1979, where he was an Editor of the Yale Law Journal and the winner of the 1979 Harlan Fiske Stone Moot Court Competition, and a BA (magna cum laude) in economics from Harvard College in 1975.

### KRESS, Alan
Alan H Kress, New York
212 944 6622
*Recommended in Media & Entertainment*

### KRUGMAN, Edward
Cahill Gordon & Reindel LLP, New York
212 701 3900
*Recommended in Insurance*

### KRUGMAN BEINECKE, Candace
Hughes Hubbard & Reed LLP, New York
212 837 6040
beinecke@hugheshubbard.com
*Recommended in Corporate/M&A*
**Practice Areas:** Mrs Beinecke is the Chair of Hughes Hubbard and a Member of its Corporate Department. She represents US and multinational companies and partnerships on transactional matters, corporate governance issues and internal investigations.
**Prof. Memberships:** Director and Member of the Executive Committee, The Partnership for New York City; Member, Women's Forum; Member, Board of Advisors, Yale Law School Center for the Study of Corporate Law.
**Career:** Chair, Hughes Hubbard & Reed LLP since 1999. Chair First Eagle Funds (public mutual fund family); Director, Rockefeller and Co.; Director, Alstom.
**Personal:** New York University (BA, 1967); Rutgers University (JD, 1970).

### KURNIT, Rick
Frankfurt Kurnit Klein & Selz, New York
212 826 5531
rkurnit@fkks.com
*Recommended in Media & Entertainment*
**Practice Areas:** Has 30 years' experience in the advertising, marketing, and publishing industries, representing advertisers, advertising agencies, public relations, promotion, and publishing companies, and executives and talent in these industries. Has handled some of the leading cases defining the application of intellectual property law to advertising and marketing communications, including representing the defendants in the Vanna White, Woody Allen and Jackie Onassis look-alike cases; representing Viking Press, Terry McMillan, and other authors and publishers in libel cases; Prodigy in the Stratton Oakmont case and other

cases defining online liability; John Deere in defining use of trademarks in comparative advertising; the maker of a smaller copy of the necklace from Titanic in defining the scope of parallel marketing; and 'Gone With The Wind' in defining parody and copyright infringement. Advises on M&A, succession plans, employment agreements, partnership agreements, stock option and phantom equity plans. Teaches advertising and intellectual property law and lectures regularly for the American Association of Advertising Agencies, the Promotion Marketing Association, and other groups. Has been a featured speaker at Beijing University, Harvard, Columbia, University of Pennsylvania, and other institutions. Member of the Board of Directors of the Art Directors Club and the Entertainment, Media & Technology Dean's Advisory Board at NYU's Stern School of Business.

### KURZWEIL, Harvey
Dewey Ballantine LLP, New York
212 259 8300
hkurzweil@deweyballantine.com
*Recommended in Insurance, Litigation*
**Practice Areas:** Antitrust and trade regulation, complex commercial litigation, intellectual property.
**Prof. Memberships:** International Academy of Trial Lawyers, American Bar Foundation, Federal Bar Council, New York State Bar Association, Columbia Law School: Board of Visitors (2000-present) and Menniger Foundation: Board of Trustees (1997-present).
**Career:** Partner, Dewey Ballantine LLP. Co-Chair, Litigation Department.
**Personal:** AB, Columbia College, 1966. JD, Columbia University School of Law, 1969.

### LAMB, William S
LeBoeuf, Lamb, Greene & MacRae LLP, New York 212 424 8170
blamb@llgm.com
*Recommended in Energy*
**Practice Areas:** Advises energy companies on a wide variety of structural and corporate matters. Represents clients in a broad range of corporate transactions, including bidders and targets in both negotiated and unsolicited mergers and acquisitions and underwriters and issuers in financing and corporate governance matters. Has also written extensively on utility and securities law, including articles and papers discussing corporate governance, accounting, and disclosure issues.
**Prof. Memberships:** Committee on Business Law, ABA; AICPA.
**Career:** Joined LeBoeuf Lamb in 1983, Partner in 1991.
**Personal:** New York University (BS magna cum laude) 1978; New York University (JD, Law Review Executive Editor) 1983.

### LANDA, Leor
Davis Polk & Wardwell, New York
212 450 4000
leor.landa@dpw.com
*Recommended in Private Fund Formation*
**Practice Areas:** Partner in Davis Polk & Wardwell's Investment Management Group. Advises clients on structuring, marketing and operating private investment funds, including private equity funds, hedge funds, real estate funds and funds of funds. Advises private fund managers in connection with their formation and operation and in connection with employee compensation and investment arrangements. Represents clients in structuring and executing private equity investments and in acquisitions of investment advisors. Advises private fund clients on various regulatory and compliance matters arising under the US Investment Advisers Act, US Investment Company Act and other US securities laws. Also represents clients investing in private funds.

### LANIADO, Sam
Read and Laniado, Albany
518 465 9313
*Recommended in Energy*

### LARSON, Joseph D
Wachtell, Lipton, Rosen & Katz, New York 212 403 1360
JDLarson@wlrk.com
*Recommended in Antitrust*
**Practice Areas:** Specializes in antitrust advice in mergers & acquisitions.
**Prof. Memberships:** American Bar Association.
**Career:** Joseph D Larson became a Partner at Wachtell, Lipton, Rosen & Katz in 2002 as a member of the Antitrust Department. He provides critical assessment and counsel to merger and acquisition clients with respect to United States antitrust matters. Mr Larson is also familiar with European, South American, Canadian and Asian antitrust standards. He regularly counsels corporations through a wide range of matters, covering pre-merger filings through antitrust challenges, and represents clients before the Department of Justice Antitrust Division, the Federal Trade Commission, the Federal Reserve Board, the Federal Energy Regulatory Commission, and the Department of Defense. His expertise spans diverse industries, including electric and gas utilities, software, internet, consumer products, defense, petroleum, and banking. As a panelist at the Workshop on Best Practices for Merger Investigations, Mr Larson advised the Federal Trade Commission about policy standards that would streamline the antitrust review process. Mr Larson was a featured panelist at the International Dimensions of Competition Law of 2002 in Toronto and provided the annual antitrust review for

the Southeastern Corporate Law Institute in 2001.

**Personal:** Graduated from St Johns College (BA, 1990) and magna cum laude from Harvard Law School (JD, 1994).

## LASCHER, Alan

Weil, Gotshal & Manges LLP, New York
212 310 8144
alan.lascher@weil.com
*Recommended in Real Estate*

**Practice Areas:** Alan Lascher has a national real estate acquisition and finance practice, and advises institutional investors and lenders, real estate developers, investment bankers and retailers in a variety of transactional areas, including portfolio acquisitions and financings. Mr Lascher has worked for lenders and borrowers in connection with loan and workout transactions and has handled leasing transactions for department stores, specialty retail stores and multi-floor office spaces. He has handled the largest leasing transactions in New York City for three of the last four years.

**Personal:** Union College, BS, 1963; Brooklyn Law School, JD, 1967.

## LATZA, William

Stroock & Stroock & Lavan LLP,
New York  212 806 5400
*Recommended in Insurance*

## LAWLER, Andrew

Andrew M Lawler PC, New York
212 832 3160
*Recommended in Litigation*

## LAZARUS, Scott

Lazarus & Harris LLP, New York
212 302 5252
*Recommended in Media & Entertainment*

## LEAKE, Paul

Jones Day, New York
212 326 3482
pdleake@jonesday.com
*Recommended in Bankruptcy*

**Practice Areas:** Co-Head of the firmwide Business Restructuring and Reorganization Practice and co-ordinator of the New York office's Corporate Practice. His practice is focused on US and transnational business reorganizations, including Chapter 11 reorganizations and liquidations, out-of-court restructurings, refinancings, distressed acquisitions, and investments in troubled companies. He has represented all of the major constituencies in restructurings, including debtors, bank groups, bondholder committees, official creditors' committees, unsecured creditors, and distressed investors. Principal debtor representations include Independence Air, Globalstar, Olympia & York, Drexel Burnham Lambert and Marvel Entertainment.

**Personal:** Columbia University School of Law (JD, 1988); Amherst College (BA, 1985).

## LEE, Carolyn

Roberts & Holland LLP, New York
212 903 8700
*Recommended in Tax*

## LEE, Steven J

Kenyon & Kenyon LLP, New York
212 908 6305
slee@kenyon.com
*Recommended in Intellectual Property*

**Practice Areas:** Dr Lee's current practice covers all areas of pharmaceutical patents: litigation, interferences, counseling, prosecution. He has been involved in generic drug litigations from A to Z, involving generic versions of Allegra, Augmentin, Claritin, Hytrin, Oxycontin, Paxil, Procardia, Relafen, Sarafem, Seldane, Ticlid, Zantac and Zithromax; other pharmaceutical litigations involving Duracef, Kadian, Lovenox, Ortho-Cyclen and Xalatan; monoclonal antibodies for septic shock and against stem cells, machines for the synthesis of DNA, and transdermal drug delivery systems; as well as other chemical-related litigations ranging from coatings for aluminum cans, paints for automobiles, and striped toothpaste. He also prosecutes patent applications in these areas, counsels inventors and patent owners on the scope and validity of their intellectual properties and advises clients introducing new products and services as to any potential for infringement of the patent rights of others. Typical clients include pharmaceutical companies, both generic and brand-name, and other chemical-related industries.

**Career:** Dr Lee had been practicing chemistry for 11 years when, in 1984, he exchanged a position of Associate Professor of Chemistry at Fordham University for a position as associate attorney at Cahill Gordon & Reindel in New York City, specializing in commercial litigation. In 1986 he joined Kenyon & Kenyon where he now co-chairs the Chemical/Life Sciences Practice Group.

**Publications:** Recent publications include a chapter in the ABA's Patent Litigation Strategies Handbook on 'Waxman-Hatch Litigation From the Perspective of the Generic Pharmaceutical Industry' (2005) and a chapter in BNA's International Pharmceutical Law and Practice, 2nd ed (2005) on US patent law.

## LEFKOWITZ, Ken

Hughes Hubbard & Reed LLP, New York
212 837 6557
lefkowitz@hugheshubbard.com
*Recommended in Corporate/M&A*

**Practice Areas:** Partner, New York since 1993. Co-Chair of Corporate Department. Concentrates on mergers and acquisitions, joint ventures, public and private financings, corporate governance, proxy contests, venture capital and private equity.

**Career:** Hughes Hubbard & Reed since

1983. Member of firm's Executive Committee and Co-Chair of its Mergers, Acquisitions and Joint Ventures Practice Group.

**Personal:** Born February 4, 1958. Tufts University BA 1980 (summa cum laude, Phi Beta Kappa); Cornell Law School JD (cum laude) 1983.

## LEFKOWITZ, Stephen

Fried, Frank, Harris, Shriver & Jacobson LLP, New York 212 859 8780
Stephen.Lefkowitz@FriedFrank.com
*Recommended in Real Estate*

**Practice Areas:** Real Estate Partner. Primary practice is real estate development, emphasis on financing, planning, land use and zoning and large-scale, complex projects involving public/private developments. Clients: Durst Organization, Forest City Ratner Companies, New York City Economic Development Corporation, New York Mercantile Exchange, New York Yankees, New York Stock Exchange, Time Warner, Tishman Speyer, Verizon.

**Career:** Joined firm in 2003 as Partner.

**Personal:** LLB(1962), magna cum laude, Harvard Law School, Harvard Law Review. BA(1959), Yale College, summa cum laude.

## LEPATNER, Barry

LePatner & Associates LLP, New York
212 935 4400
*Recommended in Construction*

## LERNER, Jonathan J

Skadden, Arps, Slate, Meagher & Flom LLP & Affiliates, New York
212 735 2550
jlerner@skadden.com
*Recommended in Litigation*

**Practice Areas:** Federal litigation, emphasizing securities, corporate and commercial litigation, and commercial arbitration. Lead trial counsel for DaimlerChrysler, AG in victory over Kirk Kerkorian's multi-billion dollar securities action; defended Cendant Corporation in its multi-billion dollar securities litigation; represented McKesson HBOC's Audit Committee in internal investigation and Company in related class action securities litigation; and CTF Hotels & Resorts, Inc. in highly-publicized arbitration and litigation against Marriott International, Inc.

**Career:** JD, St John's University, 1973 (magna cum laude); BA, Binghamton University, 1970. Adjunct Professor, Brooklyn Law School.

## LEVANDER, Andrew J

Dechert LLP, New York
212 698 3683
andrew.levander@dechert.com
*Recommended in Litigation*

**Practice Areas:** Mr Levander, Partner, focuses on complex commercial and securities litigation and white-collar defense and has an extensive state and

federal appellate practice.

**Prof. Memberships:** Member, New York and District of Columbia Bars; admitted to practice before numerous federal courts; former Chair, American Bar Association Committee on Securities Litigation Professional Issues Subcommittee.

**Career:** Assistant to Solicitor General; Assistant US Attorney, Southern District of New York (Securities and Commodities Fraud Unit); Associate Independent Counsel in Michael Deaver investigation.

**Personal:** Tufts University (BA summa cum laude, 1973); Columbia University Law School (JD, 1977) notes and c omments editor, Columbia Law Review.

## LEVI, Stuart D

Skadden, Arps, Slate, Meagher & Flom LLP & Affiliates, New York
212 735 2750
slevi@skadden.com
*Recommended in Business Process Outsourcing, Technology*

**Practice Areas:** Head of Skadden's Information Technology and E-commerce Practice. Represents a broad spectrum of clients, ranging from early stage start-ups to global corporations seeking to use information technologies to enhance current business models and create new opportunities. Counsels on a variety of issues, including outsourcing agreements, software licensing, joint ventures, strategic alliances, website policies, IP matters, privacy issues, and mergers and acquisitions.

**Career:** JD, Harvard Law School, 1986 (cum laude); BA, Computer Science and Political Science, Columbia University, Columbia College, 1983 (magna cum laude).

## LEVIN, Peter

Davis Polk & Wardwell, New York
212 450 4000
peter.levin@dpw.com
*Recommended in Banking & Finance*

**Practice Areas:** Practice co-ordinator of Davis Polk & Wardwell's Credit Group. Has broad experience in secured financing and debt restructuring transactions, including complex international syndicated lending transactions. Also advises both dealers and end users of derivatives on management controls and management and board responsibilities, documentation, issues relating to new products and new kinds of counterparties, and problems arising from the bankruptcy or insolvency of counterparties.

## LEVINE, Alan

Kronish Lieb Weiner & Hellman LLP,
New York 212 479 6000
*Recommended in Litigation*

## LEVY, Lisa

Fried, Frank, Harris, Shriver & Jacobson LLP, New York 212 859 8228
Lisa.Levy@FriedFrank.com
*Recommended in Tax*

**Practice Areas:** Tax Partner. Specializes in the taxation of mergers and acquisitions, international and cross-border transactions and financial instruments, including debt and equity offerings, asset securitizations and derivatives.
**Career:** Joined Fried Frank in 1993. Became a Partner in 1998.
**Personal:** JD (1990), Columbia Law School, Kent Scholar, Stone Scholar and a member of the Journal of Law & Social Problems. LLM (1994), New York University. BS (1985), with distinction, McIntire School of Commerce at University of Virginia. Received Virginia Society of CPAs' Award of Achievement.

### LEWIN, Robert
Stroock & Stroock & Lavan LLP, New York 212 806 5400
*Recommended in Insurance*

### LEWKOW, Victor I
Cleary Gottlieb Steen & Hamilton LLP, New York 212 225 2370
vlewkow@cgsh.com
*Recommended in Corporate/M&A*
**Practice Areas:** Domestic and international merger and acquisitions, including public and private acquisitions, negotiated and hostile bids, proxy contests, leverage buyouts and advising Boards and Special Committees. Represented Capital One Financial (Hibernia acquisition), GlaxoSmithKline (Corixa acquisition), PeopleSoft (takeover defense resulting in sale to Oracle at 65% price increase), HSBC (Household International acquisition), Kroll (sale to Marsh & McLennan), South African Breweries (Miller Brewing acquisition to form SABMiller), Synopsys (Avant! acquisition), Deutsche Bank (Bankers Trust acquisition). Adjunct Professor, NYU Law School.
**Personal:** BA, State University of New York at Binghamton (1970); JD, magna cum laude, University of Pennsylvania Law School (1973).

### LIEBERMAN, David
Simpson Thacher & Bartlett LLP, New York 212 455 2000
dlieberman@stblaw.com
*Recommended in Projects*
**Practice Areas:** Corporate Partner specializing in international and domestic transactions involving energy, infrastructure and transportation assets. Advised Blackstone in connection with its acquisition of and ongoing investment in Sithe Global, an independent power project developer; Blackstone and First Reserve Corp. in their $1 billion acquisition of Foundation Coal Corporation; Virgin America in its purchase and lease acquisition of up to 105 Airbus A319 and A320 aircraft; CSFB in its $760 million construction/lease financing of Tri-State Generation's Springerville coal-fired power project; the underwriters in the $1.8 billion, 1,884 MW Homer City bond financing of EME; Elektrizitäts der Stadt

Zürich as a lessee in a $1.2 billion leveraged lease financing of hydro-electric facilities in Switzerland. Representative clients include Blackstone, Credit Suisse First Boston, Lehman Brothers, Virgin America, Elektrizitäts der Stadt Zürich, HypoVereinsbank and The State of Berlin.
**Prof. Memberships:** New York State Bar Association.
**Career:** Joined the firm in 1989 and became a Partner in 1998.
**Personal:** BA, Columbia University, magna cum laude, Phi Beta Kappa (1986). JD with High Honors, Duke Law School, Order of the Coif (1989).

### LIEBMANN, Jeff S
Dewey Ballantine LLP, New York 212 259 6230
jliebmann@deweyballantine.com
*Recommended in Insurance*
**Practice Areas:** Jeff Liebmann has 25 years of experience in the corporate and insurance areas. He has served as counsel for: Nationwide Mutual Insurance Company in its deaffiliation from Employers of Wausau; New England Mutual Life Insurance Company in its merger with Metropolitan Life Insurance Company; Metropolitan Life Insurance Company in its acquisition of GenAmerica Corporation; and MONY Group in its closed block securitization. He is active in the field of insurance securitizations, representing insurers, underwriters and commercial banks.
**Prof. Memberships:** New York State Bar Association; American Bar Association; Society of Actuaries.
**Personal:** JD, Harvard University, 1978. AB, Princeton University, 1971.

### LILIEN, Warren
Latham & Watkins LLP, New York 212 906 1200
*Recommended in Projects*

### LIMAN, Lewis J
Cleary Gottlieb Steen & Hamilton LLP, New York 212 225 2550
lliman@cgsh.com
*Recommended in Litigation*
**Practice Areas:** Focuses on the defense of white-collar, SEC and regulatory enforcement matters and parallel civil litigation for institutions and executives. Experienced in securities litigation, derivative actions, commercial litigation and internal investigations.
**Prof. Memberships:** Trustee, Federal Bar Council; Director, NY Council of Defense Lawyers; Task Force on the Role of Lawyers in Corporate Governance, Association of the Bar of the City of New York; Member, United States Court of Appeals for the Second Circuit Advisory Committee on the Local Rules of Appellate Procedure; EDNY Committee on Civil Litigation; Trustee, Lawyer's Committee for Civil Rights Under Law; American Bar Association; selected as New

York Super Lawyer.
**Career:** Before joining the firm as Partner, Mr Liman was a Partner at Wilmer Cutler & Pickering and an Assistant US Attorney in the Southern District of New York, where he served as Deputy Chief Appellate Attorney. He clerked for the US District Court, Southern District of New York and the US Supreme Court. JD, Yale Law School (1987); MSc, Economics with distinction, London School of Economics (1984); AB, Harvard University (1983).
**Publications:** Mr Liman has lectured and published articles and materials on internal investigations, white-collar criminal defense and sentencing, and securities class actions.

### LINDAUER, Erik D
Sullivan & Cromwell LLP, New York 212 558 4000
lindauere@sullcrom.com
*Recommended in Banking & Finance*
**Practice Areas:** Transactional banking, secured lending, commercial law (UCC), corporate reorganisations and bankruptcy. Complex secured and unsecured financings experience. Represented General Growth Properties, Inc. in negotiation of bank lines for its acquisition of the Rouse companies; Allegheny Energy in renegotiating and securing unsecured bank lines; Intelsat, Ltd. in Loral satellites acquisition; and AIG Financial Products in various structured investments.
**Prof. Memberships:** ABA; ABCNY; NYSBA.
**Career:** Partner since 1989.
**Personal:** SUNY Albany (BA, 1978); SUNY Buffalo Law School (JD, 1981).

### LINDENBAUM, Samuel H
Kramer Levin Naftalis & Frankel LLP, New York 212 715 7840
slindenbaum@kramerlevin.com
*Recommended in Real Estate*
**Practice Areas:** Is of Counsel to Kramer Levin Naftalis & Frankel LLP and a Member of the Land Use Department. For more than 30 years, his extensive experience in land use and zoning has been utilized in handling special permits, zoning changes, variances, landmark proceedings, air rights transfers, tax abatements and economic development incentives for many of the city's most prominent commercial and residential developments and for the expansion programs of many of the city's leading non-profit institutions.
**Prof. Memberships:** He is an Honorary Trustee of the Metropolitan Museum of Art, Honorary Chairman of the Executive Committee of the Board of Directors of the American Friends of the Israel Museum, and a member of the Advisory Board of the Peggy Guggenheim Collection in Venice. He is Chair of the Executive Committee of the Jewish Association for Services for the Aged, a member of the Board of Trustees of the Real Estate

Institute of Baruch College, and a Member of the Board of the Real Estate Committee of UJA-Federation. He is Vice-President and a Member of the Executive Committee of the Board of Governors of the Real Estate Board of New York, and a founder, Director and Vice-President of the Association for a Better New York. He is a former Member of the New York State Council on the Arts (1976-86 and 1994-99), and a past Member of the Board of Overseers of the Albert Einstein College of Medicine.
**Career:** Represents major commercial and residential developers, corporations, financial institutions and non-profit organizations such as Carnegie Hall, The Whitney Museum, Columbia University, the Guggenheim Museum, the Archdiocese of New York, Yeshiva University, Weill Cornell Medical College, Bear Stearns, Tishman Speyer Properties, Vornado Realty Trust, Glenwood Management, Millennium Partners, and the Resnick, Silverstein and Solow Organizations. Current projects for which he acts as counsel include the expansion of the Museum of Modern Art, a new tower atop the Hearst headquarters building on Eighth Avenue, redevelopment of the former Alexander's site on Lexington Avenue and East 59th Street by Vornado, redevelopment of the Con Edison properties at First Avenue and East 40th Street, Sheldon Solow's new residential towers on York Avenue and 60th Street, and renovation of the General Motors Building. Recent approvals include renovations of Rockefeller Center and the Chrysler Building, and the new Penn Center Special Signage District. Other major approvals in recent years include Trump's Riverside South development and New York Hospital's expansion over the FDR Drive.
**Personal:** Earned a BA Degree cum laude from Harvard College in 1956 and a JD Degree cum laude from Harvard Law School in 1959. After graduating from law school, he was awarded a Fulbright Fellowship.

### LIPSON, Lawrence
Proskauer Rose LLP, New York 212 969 3760
llipson@proskauer.com
*Recommended in Real Estate*
**Practice Areas:** Mr Lipson is the Chair of Proskauer Rose LLP's Real Estate Department and a Member of Proskauer's nationally recognized Hospitality Practice Group. He has three decades of diverse experience crafting major real estate deals and representing all sides to the real estate transaction including lenders and borrowers, landlords and tenants, and investors and developers. Mr Lipson's clients include a cross section of the many types of investors in and users of real estate, including individual developer entrepre-

neurs, large corporate tenants, equity investors, real estate investment trusts and real estate opportunity funds. He is also a key and influential player in Proskauer's Hospitality Practice Group and has closed on a substantial number of major domestic and international hotel and resort chain acquisitions.

**Career:** Mr Lipson was involved in the design of the first major office building real estate investment trust (REIT) in New York, which has become the model for future office building REIT transactions in the New York metropolitan area.

**Personal:** Mr Lipson attended Columbia University School of Law, JD, magna cum laude, 1970. Scholar: Harlan Fiske Stone Scholar. Brooklyn College of the City University of New York, BA, magna cum laude, 1967.

### LIPTON, Martin
Wachtell, Lipton, Rosen & Katz, New York 212 403 1200
mlipton@wlrk.com
*Recommended in Corporate/M&A*

**Practice Areas:** Specializes in corporate law, corporate governance and mergers and acquisitions.

### LISCIO, Mark F
Kaye Scholer LLP, New York
212 836 7550
mliscio@kayescholer.com
*Recommended in Bankruptcy*

**Practice Areas:** Partner, Business Reorganization and Creditors' Rights Group. Focuses his practice on creditors' rights and insolvency law on behalf of lenders. He has more than 22 years' experience representing syndicate agents and major financial institutions in debt restructurings and insolvency proceedings. He has structured and negotiated a wide variety of complex insolvency financings throughout his career, for which he has developed a reputation as a firm and fair advocate and pragmatic deal maker.

**Prof. Memberships:** Member of the American Bar Association, American Bankruptcy Institute and Insol International.

**Career:** JD, Pace University School of Law, Editor of the Law Review; BBA, Pace University.

### LOBO, Glyndwr P
Dechert LLP, New York
212 698 3567
glyndwr.lobo@dechert.com
*Recommended in Corporate/M&A*

**Practice Areas:** Mr Lobo, a Partner in the Corporate Finance, Private Equity, and Mergers and Acquisitions Groups, concentrates on cross-border and domestic transactions and corporate finance, including mergers, acquisitions, capital markets, venture capital, and international joint venture and collaboration transactions. He has significant experience in life sciences and pharmaceutical transactions.

**Prof. Memberships:** Member, New York Bar; Member, Board of Advisors of the Corporate Counsel Institute of Georgetown University Law Center and the Association of Corporate Counsel; member, Georgetown University National Law Alumni Board.

**Personal:** The Wharton School of the University of Pennsylvania (BS, 1985); Georgetown University Law Center (JD, 1988).

### LOGAN, Kenneth
Simpson Thacher & Bartlett LLP, New York 212 455 2000
klogan@stblaw.com
*Recommended in Antitrust*

**Practice Areas:** Kenneth R Logan has been a litigator and antitrust practitioner for over 33 years at Simpson Thacher & Bartlett. He has tried jury and non-jury antitrust cases to judgment and handled merger and non-merger proceedings before the US enforcement agencies and the European Commission. Mr Logan has also conducted a range of antitrust and other complex matters for Viacom, Paramount, MTV Networks, NBC Universal, Seagram, American Electric Power, ITT Industries, Kohlberg Kravis & Roberts, Wyeth, Express Scripts and others. He has developed substantial background in issues affecting, among other industries, healthcare, financial services, entertainment, telecommunications and pharmaceuticals. He frequently writes and speaks on US and international antitrust issues.

**Personal:** Mr Logan graduated from Princeton University in 1967 and from the University of Pennsylvania Law School in 1972.

### LONDON, Martin
Paul, Weiss, Rifkind, Wharton & Garrison LLP, New York
212 373 3197
mlondon@paulweiss.com
*Recommended in Litigation*

**Practice Areas:** Recently retired litigation Partner who remains of Counsel to the firm. Has extensive experience encompassing broad litigation issues both domestically and internationally, involving both criminal and civil matters. Civil experience includes trials and litigation of commercial cases involving antitrust, breach of contract, tortious interference, real estate, product liability, securities, environmental laws, insurance, administrative law and miscellaneous torts. Fellow of the American College of Trial Lawyers. Received the Award for Outstanding Oral Advocacy, presented by the Office of the Appellate Defender. Appointed Special Trial Counsel twice by special New York judicial tribunals to prosecute judicial misconduct cases. Selected for the 2006 edition of 'The Best Lawyers in America'.

### LOWENTHAL, Mitchell A
Cleary Gottlieb Steen & Hamilton LLP, New York 212 225 2760
mlowenthal@cgsh.com
*Recommended in Litigation*

**Practice Areas:** Corporate and securities litigation. Has represented issuers, directors and officers, underwriters, lending institutions and professional advisors in complex civil litigation primarily involving the capital formation process, mergers and acquisitions, and derivative and shareholder disputes.

**Prof. Memberships:** Member of the Bar in New York. Admitted to practice before the US Supreme Court, US District Courts (Southern and Eastern Districts of New York and Eastern District of Wisconsin) and US Court of Appeals (Second and Ninth Circuits).

**Career:** Cornell University (JD, 1981; AB, 1978). Law clerk, Hon Edward Weinfeld (SDNY, 1982-83). Chair, Urban Justice Center.

### LUSKIN, Michael
Luskin, Stern & Eisler LLP, New York 212 293 2700
*Recommended in Bankruptcy*

### LYON JR, Carl
Orrick, Herrington & Sutcliffe LLP, New York 212 506 5180
cflyon@orrick.com
*Recommended in Projects*

**Practice Areas:** All areas of finance and contractual negotiations for rural electric cooperatives, public power issuers, federal power agencies, and investor-owned utilities and their affiliates. Experienced in taxable, tax-exempt, and tax-advantaged financings for electric, gas, water, and waste water projects. Worked on three financings that were named 'Deals of the Year' by Institutional Investor.

**Prof. Memberships:** Member, American Public Power Association and G&T Cooperative Lawyers Association; Former Co-Chairman, American Bar Association Special Committee on Energy Financing.

**Career:** Chair, Orrick's Public Power Practice.

**Personal:** JD, with distinction, Order of the Coif, Duke University School of Law, 1968; AB, Duke University, 1965.

### LYONS, Peter D
Shearman & Sterling LLP, New York 212 848 7666
plyons@shearman.com
*Recommended in Corporate/M&A*

**Practice Areas:** Co-head of the firm's Mergers & Acquisitions Group. Advises on acquisitions and sales of public and private companies, asset acquisition and disposition transactions and joint ventures. Also regularly represents the mergers and acquisitions group of the firm's investment banking clients, and provides general securities law advice.

**Prof. Memberships:** Member, Board of Editors, The M&A Lawyer.

**Career:** Joined the firm in 1980, practiced in the Bay Area office from 1983-85. Became a Partner in 1989. Headed the firm's Bay Area offices during 2000 and 2001.

**Personal:** BA, University of Virginia (1977); JD, Georgetown University Law Center (1980).

### MACMURRAY, John C
Ropes & Gray LLP, New York
212 841 5711
john.macmurray@ropesgray.com
*Recommended in Private Fund Formation*

**Practice Areas:** Corporate law with a practice that principally includes representation of domestic and international private investment funds. Client responsibilities principally involve representation of private equity sponsor groups in their fundraising projects and investment programs.

**Career:** New York Bar (1965); Partner, Reboul, MacMurray, Hewitt & Maynard (1973); Partner, Ropes & Gray (2003).

**Personal:** LLB, Columbia Law School (1965); AB, Princeton University (1961).

### MACPHERSON, Robert J
Thelen Reid & Priest LLP, New York 212 603 8988
rmacpherson@thelenreid.com
*Recommended in Construction*

**Practice Areas:** Mr MacPherson's practice is focused on construction matters; primarily the prevention and resolution of disputes arising out of construction projects. Mr MacPherson is a court appointed and privately-designated arbitrator and mediator. He has been involved in developing and conducting mediation education and training programs presented by the New Jersey State Bar Association, Justice Marie L Garibaldi American Inn of Court for Alternative Dispute Resolution and the NJ Institute for Continuing Legal Education.

**Prof. Memberships:** Fellow of the American College of Construction Lawyers; American Bar Association: Forum on the Construction Industry; Governing Committee (2002-05); Chair of Division 1, which focuses on dispute avoidance and resolution (2000-02); New Jersey Bar Association, Chair of the Dispute Resolution Section (1994-95); Original member of the Garibaldi ADR Inn of Court (the first Inn of Court in the United States devoted to ADR); Committee on Complementary Dispute Resolution of the New Jersey Supreme Court (1994-96); Member of the General Building Contractors of New York State, Associated General Contractors of America, and a member of the AGC task force that produced AGC Document 800, the Standard Form of Program Management Agreement and General Conditions.

**Career:** Partner of Thelen Reid & Priest LLP's New York office. Admitted to prac-

tice in New York and New Jersey, US District Court, Southern and Eastern Districts of New York; US District Court, District of New Jersey; United States Supreme Court; Court appointed mediator for the Federal District Court of New Jersey, the Southern District of New York, the Superior Court of New Jersey and Supreme Court of New York, New York County. Has spoken before: New Jersey Judicial College; American Bar Association; American Arbitration Association; New Jersey Institute of Continuing Legal Education; New Jersey Bar Association; Associated General Contracts of America; General Building Contracts of New York; Pratt University, New York; Pace University, New York.
**Publications:** Executive editor, 'Discovery Desk Book for Construction Disputes', ABA Publishing, 2005; co-editor, 'Sticks and Bricks, A Practical Guide to Construction Technology', Forum on the Construction Industry, ABA Publishing, 2001; co-author, 'New York Construction Law Manual', Shepard's/McGraw-Hill, 1992, republished by West Publishing 1998, Supplement, 2004; co-editor, and Chapter co-author, Partnering in Design and Construction, 'Alternative Dispute Resolution as a Partnering Tool', McGraw Hill, 1996; co-author, New York chapter of the State Public Construction Law Source Book, CCH Incorporated, 2002. Mr MacPherson is also the author of several articles on construction contracting and dispute resolution.
**Personal:** Graduate of Seton Hall University School of Law, JD (1980) and Monmouth University, BA(1976); Practitioner of the Year, 2001, Dispute Resolution Section of the New Jersey Bar Association, James B. Boskey ADR; Best Lawyers in America (Construction Law); Chambers, USA Guide to America's Leading Business Lawyers (Leading Construction Lawyer, New York, NY).

### MADDEN, John J
Shearman & Sterling LLP, New York
212 848 7055
jmadden@shearman.com
*Recommended in Corporate/M&A*
**Practice Areas:** Co-Managing Partner of Shearman & Sterling and a Partner in the Mergers & Acquisitions Group. His practice involves assisting corporate and other clients with various M&A transactions, both negotiated and unsolicited, including tender and exchange offers, leveraged buyouts, takeover defense strategies, joint ventures, divestitures and cross-border transactions. Also advises corporate clients on other matters, including corporate governance issues.
**Career:** Head of the firm's M&A Group from 1995-2001; Co-Head of the group from 1987-91; Managing Partner of the firm's European offices 1991-95.
**Personal:** BA, University of Pennsylvania (1968); JD, Fordham Law School (1975).

### MAGUIRE, William
Hughes Hubbard & Reed LLP, New York
212 837 6000
*Recommended in Litigation*

### MAILMAN, Stanley
Satterlee Stephens Burke & Burke LLP, New York 212 818 9200
*Recommended in Immigration*

### MANDEL, Gary B
Simpson Thacher & Bartlett LLP, New York 212 455 7963
gmandel@stblaw.com
*Recommended in Tax*
**Practice Areas:** Partner in the firm's Tax Department. His areas of concentration are federal income tax with a particular emphasis on corporate mergers and acquisitions, joint ventures, restructurings and spin-offs. Mr Mandel advises on tax matters for, among others, several of the firm's private equity fund clients. He advised on the spin-off of several businesses of H.J. Heinz and its merger with Del Monte, Swiss Re's acquisition of GE Insurance Solutions, the Toronto Dominion Bank in connection with its sale of TD Waterhouse Group to Ameritrade and numerous buyout transactions by the Blackstone Group and the firm's other private equity fund clients including a consortium of private equity funds in the acquisition of TDC A/S, Denmark's largest telecom company. He also has advised on multiple acquisitions and initial public offerings in the insurance industry.
**Prof. Memberships:** Association of the Bar of the City of New York; New York State Bar Association, Member, Tax Section, Executive Committee (2001-05), Committee on Pass-Through Entities (2002-present); American Bar Association, Tax Section (1997-present).
**Career:** Joined Simpson Thacher in 1997 as an associate and became Partner in 2003.
**Personal:** BS, from Brooklyn College (1985), MBA Pace University (1990); JD cum laude, Saint John's School of Law (1994); LLM with distinction Georgetown University School of Law (1996).

### MANN, Christopher L
Sullivan & Cromwell LLP, New York
212 558 4625
mannc@sullcrom.com
*Recommended in Projects*
**Practice Areas:** Acts for sponsor and lending clients in oil and gas, mining and power in the US, Latin America, southern Africa and elsewhere. Key projects include Sincor extra heavy oil project (Venezuela), Camisea gas pipeline (Peru) and Coega LNG project (South Africa).
**Prof. Memberships:** ABCNY (former Chair, Project Finance Committee); ABA.
**Career:** Partner since 1998. Judicial clerk, Hon Ralph K Winter, US Court of Appeals, 2nd Circuit, 1989-90.
**Personal:** Harvard College (AB, 1985);

Cambridge University (MPhil, 1987); Harvard Law School (JD, 1989).

### MARCU, Aaron R
Covington & Burling, New York
212 841 1078
amarcu@cov.com
*Recommended in Litigation*
**Practice Areas:** Chair, Covington's White Collar Group. Focusing on defense of criminal and SEC enforcement cases and parallel civil litigation. Representative clients: Pfizer, Philip Morris, Goodyear, Pitney Bowes, NBC, and Société Générale, and executives in the Enron, Tyco, research analyst, mutual fund, Daiwa, Bankers Trust, Salomon, and Lloyd's of London investigations.
**Career:** US Attorney's Office, Southern District of New York (1983-89): Associate US Attorney (1989), Chief, Major Crimes Unit (1988-89); Chief Appellate Attorney (1987-88). Commissioner, NY Civilian Complaint Review Board (1995-98).
**Personal:** Harvard University (JD 1980); Northwestern University (BSJ 1977). Law clerk, Hon Richard Owen, US District Judge, SDNY (1980-82).

### MARKEL, Gregory
Cadwalader, Wickersham & Taft LLP, New York 212 504 6112
gregory.markel@cwt.com
*Recommended in Litigation*
**Practice Areas:** Chairman, Litigation Department. Focuses on securities, antitrust, and other complex commercial and financial litigation. Extensive experience and expertise in securities litigation, including class action defense, derivative actions, private securities litigation, antitrust, accountants' defense, banking, financial products litigation.
**Publications:** Frequently speaker and author on securities law, class actions, directors' and officers' liability, director and officer market trends, financial institutions' liability developments, litigation against financial institutions, including: 2005 D&O Market Trends Seminar Series, February 2005; Pleading Loss Causation in Securities Litigation, October 18, 2004; Derivative Litigation chapter in Treatise on Litigation in New York Courts, 2004; Commentary and Instruction to Banks and Investment Banks on Interagency Statement on Sound Practices Concerning Complex Structured Finance Activities, July, August 2004; Financial Institution's Liability Developments, June 2004; Commentator on legal issues for CNBC, Bloomberg TV, Bloomberg Radio, New York Times, Time, Newsweek and Associated Press.
**Personal:** JD, Yale Law School (1972); MBA, Finance and Accounting, University of Michigan (1968); BA, Economics, Columbia College (1967); Member, American Bar Association: Litigation, Antitrust Sections; Member, Federal Bar Council.

### MARTIN, Scott
Weil, Gotshal & Manges LLP, New York
212 310 8481
scott.martin@weil.com
*Recommended in Antitrust*
**Practice Areas:** Scott Martin is a Partner in Weil Gotshal's Litigation/Regulatory Department, and focuses in the areas of antitrust and complex commercial litigation. Mr Martin has extensive experience in complex litigation and class actions, including bench and jury trials in federal and state courts. He has been involved in many of the most significant antitrust class action litigation and civil and criminal international cartel cases in recent years, and also frequently counsels clients on price discrimination, exclusive dealing, and other distribution issues.
**Personal:** Stanford University, AB, 1987; Stanford Law School, JD, 1990.

### MASON, Andrew S
Sullivan & Cromwell LLP, New York
212 558 4000
masona@sullcrom.com
*Recommended in Tax*
**Practice Areas:** Provides tax advice for a wide range of transactions, including real estate, project finance, leveraged lease, mergers, acquisitions and international transactions, and matters involving the firm's individual clients.
**Prof. Memberships:** American Bar Association; Association of the Bar of the City of New York (former Chair, Committee on Taxation of Partnerships and Other Pass-Throughs); New York State Bar Association.
**Career:** Partner since 1989.
**Publications:** Has lectured at a number of tax conferences.
**Personal:** Yale College (BA, 1978); Yale Law School (JD, 1981).

### MASON, David
Debevoise & Plimpton LLP, New York
212 909 6000
*Recommended in Employee Benefits*

### MASON, Richard G
Wachtell, Lipton, Rosen & Katz, New York 212 403 1252
rgmason@wlrk.com
*Recommended in Bankruptcy*
**Practice Areas:** Specializes in Wachtell, Lipton, Rosen & Katz's insolvency and corporate finance practice, representing significant creditors, as well as bank and bondholder groups and creditors' committees, in many large Chapter 11 cases and out-of-court restructurings, including the Delphi Corporation, Calpine Corporation, Intermet Corporation, Cone Mills, Pacific Gas & Electric Company, Rand McNally & Company, Allegheny Energy Supply, Inc., Viatel, Integrated Health and LTV Corp. matters, and borrowers in private equity transactions, leveraged buyouts, mergers and other complex financing arrangements.

**Prof. Memberships:** Active member of the Association of the Bar of the City of New York (recently serving on its Committee on Bankruptcy & Corporate Reorganization), the New York State Bar and the American Bar Association. Recently became a Fellow in the American College of Bankruptcy.
**Career:** Partner at Wachtell, Lipton, Rosen & Katz since 1994. Recently named one of the 'Outstanding Young Bankruptcy Lawyers of the Year' by the 'Turnarounds & Workouts' magazine. Has given numerous seminars on bankruptcy subjects for the Practicing Law Institute and other prominent organizations.
**Publications:** Co-author of 'Collier's Bankruptcy Practice Guide'.
**Personal:** Graduated magna cum laude from Virginia Commonwealth University in 1983 (BS, Economics) where he was inducted into the Phi Kappa Phi honor fraternity; and cum laude from New York University in 1987 (JD) where became a Member of the Order of the Coif and was on the staff of the 'Annual Survey of American Law'.

## MASOTTI, Marco
Paul, Weiss, Rifkind, Wharton & Garrison LLP, New York 212 373 3034
mmasotti@paulweiss.com
*Recommended in Private Fund Formation*
**Practice Areas:** Marco Masotti is a Partner in the Investment Funds Group and serves as Co-Head of the firm's Private Equity Group. He focuses on the organization and operation of a wide variety of private investment funds, including buyout funds, venture capital funds, hybrid funds, hedge funds, distressed funds, mezzanine funds, sponsorship funds, co-investment funds and funds of funds. Mr Masotti has represented a diverse group of sponsors of private investment funds and has significant experience with profit participation arrangements of investment professionals. He is Chair of the Committee on Private Investment Funds of the New York City Bar.

## MASSOUH, Jennifer
Latham & Watkins LLP, New York
212 906 1200
*Recommended in Projects*

## MASTRO, Randy
Gibson, Dunn & Crutcher LLP, New York
212 351 3825
rmastro@gibsondunn.com
*Recommended in Litigation*
**Practice Areas:** Co-Chair of Litigation Practice and Crisis Management Groups, Executive and Management Committees, former Co-Partner-in-Charge of New York Office. Prominent litigator who handles complex civil cases, securities litigation and white-collar criminal matters.
**Career:** Mr Mastro led the litigation to defeat the controversial West Side Stadium project. Before rejoining Gibson

Dunn in 1998, Mr Mastro served as Deputy Mayor in the Giuliani administration, where he spearheaded the City's initiatives to remove organized crime from the Fulton Fish Market and private carting industry.
**Personal:** JD, University of Pennsylvania Law School, 1981, Moot Court Champion. BA, cum laude, Yale, 1978.

## MATTEI, Andrew
Mayer, Brown, Rowe & Maw LLP, New York 212 506 2572
amattei@mayerbrownrowe.com
*Recommended in Banking & Finance*
**Practice Areas:** Corporate finance. Represents both domestic and foreign banks and other financial institutions. Areas of expertise: highly leveraged, syndicated lending transactions, including acquisition financing and tender offer financings, and corporate recapitalisations. Also, focuses on subordinated debt financings (including bridge financings). Many cross-border transactions - for example, representing the Agents (Scotia Capital, Deutsche Bank and UBS Securities LLC) in KKR's 2005 $2.35 billion (debt) acquisition of Masonite by KKR. Also representing Royal Bank of Scotland as agent and lead arranger in its $5 billion underwriting of SuperValue to purchase Albertsons. Routinely represents lenders in workouts and restructurings of troubled credits.
**Prof. Memberships:** Admitted in New York, 1988.
**Career:** Joined Mayer, Brown, Rowe & Maw LLP, New York, 1987; became Partner, 1996.
**Publications:** Contributing author: 'How to Buy a U.S. Business: A Guide to Negotiated and Hostile Acquisitions'. Chapter 5: 'Senior and Subordinated Acquisition Financing'. 'Advising Illinois Financial Institutions', Chapter 11, Multi-Bank Credit Facilities, 1997 and 2001.
**Personal:** JD, Fordham University School of Law, 1987; 'Fordham Urban Law Journal'. BS (honors), State University of New York, Cortland, 1979.

## MATTEI, Ivan
Debevoise & Plimpton LLP, New York
212 909 6000
*Recommended in Projects*

## MAYER, Thomas Moers
Kramer Levin Naftalis & Frankel LLP, New York 212 715 9169
tmayer@kramerlevin.com
*Recommended in Bankruptcy*
**Practice Areas:** Mr Mayer specializes in representing investors in claims against, and interests in, financially distressed businesses. He has represented investors who purchased claims as a way to acquire controlling or substantial equity interests in, among other reorganizations, WCI Steel, Inc., Venture Holdings Corporation (n/k/a Cadence Precision, Inc.), Northwestern Corporation, General Chemicals,

Pinnacle Towers, Key 3 Media and Wheeling-Pittsburgh Steel Corporation, and also represented investors who have bought claims against or securities issued by distressed companies to take profits in cash and debt instead of equity, such as Solutia, Jitney Jungle, Levitz Industries, Grand Union and Reeves Industries, the majority holders of $560 million in FrontierVision Bonds in Adelphia's chapter 11, the majority holders of $970 million Choctaw/Zephyrus bank debt in Enron's chapter 11, the holders of $750 million in MCI Qualified Income Debt Securities, Washington Group and Iridium bank debt, Finova Trust Offered Preferred Certificates, and bonds and bank debt issued by Macy's, Woodward & Lothrop, Insilco, Revco, National Gypsum and Todd Shipyards. Mr Mayer is the leading scholar on the law of trading claims and taking control of corporations in chapter 11 and on the ethical, civil and criminal exposure of lawyers who aid and abet fraudulent transfers by setting up off-shore asset protection trusts.
**Personal:** Received a JD Degree magna cum laude from Harvard University in 1981, where he was on the Harvard Law Review, and an AB Degree summa cum laude, Phi Beta Kappa from Dartmouth College in 1977.

## MAYO, David W
Paul, Weiss, Rifkind, Wharton & Garrison LLP, New York 212 373 3324
dmayo@paulweiss.com
*Recommended in Tax*
**Practice Areas:** Partner in the Tax Department whose practice focuses on corporate and partnership taxation, taxable and tax-free mergers and acquisitions, restructurings and cross-border transactions.
**Prof. Memberships:** Member of the Executive Committee of the Tax Section of the New York State Bar Association; Co-Chair of the Committee on Tax Policy.
**Career:** Law clerk to the Honorable Theodore Tannenwald Jr, of the United States Tax Court from 1987-88.
**Publications:** 'Restricted Stock Notes', 57 Tax Lawyer 61 (2003); numerous Bar Reports.
**Personal:** JD, Harvard Law School, cum laude, 1987, Editor-in-Chief of the Harvard Journal of Law & Public Policy.

## MAZUR, Sayward
Mazur, Carp & Rubin PC, New York
212 686 7700
*Recommended in Construction*

## MCCAW, Robert M
WilmerHale, New York
212 230 8810
robert.mccaw@wilmerhale.com
*Recommended in Litigation*
**Practice Areas:** Senior Partner and Co-Chair of firm's Securities Department, represents brokerage firms, investment

advisors, corporations, accounting firms, lawyers and law firms in criminal proceedings, regulatory investigations, enforcement proceedings, and litigation, including that involving securities fraud, insider trading, manipulation, improper sales practices, trading irregularities, failure to supervise, financial misconduct, breach of fiduciary duty, negligent misrepresentation, malpractice, rule violations, and other allegations.
**Prof. Memberships:** Professional lecturer in Law (Securities Regulation) at The George Washington University School of Law, 1980-83.
**Personal:** Georgetown University (BS 1965); University of Virginia (JD 1970). Clerked for Justice Hugo L Black of the US Supreme Court (1970-71).

## MCCORMACK, William F
Ropes & Gray LLP, New York
212 841 0627
william.mccormack@ropesgray.com
*Recommended in Private Fund Formation*
**Practice Areas:** Represents numerous domestic and international private investment funds, including buyout, venture capital, mezzanine funds and fund of funds. Concentrates on tax planning for corporations, partnerships and joint ventures, focusing on mergers and acquisitions, public and private financings, international transactions, and executive compensation matters. Focuses on tax matters in connection with the formation, operation and investment activities of both domestic and offshore private equity investment funds.
**Career:** Virginia Bar (1971); New York Bar (1973); Partner, Ropes & Gray (2003); Co-Chairman, Private Equity Group of Ropes & Gray.
**Personal:** LLM, University of Virginia (1972); JD, Catholic University (1971).

## MCINERNEY, Denis
Davis Polk & Wardwell, New York
212 450 4000
denis.mcinerney@dpw.com
*Recommended in Litigation*
**Practice Areas:** Member of Davis Polk & Wardwell's Litigation Department. Represents corporate and individual clients in grand jury and regulatory investigations, criminal trials, internal investigations, and civil litigation.
**Career:** From 1989-94, was an Assistant US Attorney in the Southern District of New York, serving as a Deputy Chief of the Criminal Division from 1993-94. In 1994, worked with Robert B Fiske Jr as an Associate Independent Counsel in the Whitewater Investigation.

## MCNAMARA, Elizabeth
Davis Wright Tremaine LLP, New York
212 489 8230
*Recommended in Media & Entertainment*

## MCSHERRY JR, William J
Arent Fox PLLC, New York
212 484 3944
mcsherry.william@arentfox.com
*Recommended in Litigation*

**Practice Areas:** Partner-In-Charge of the New York office and Co-Chair of the Litigation Department. Experienced litigator in the areas of securities, derivatives, financial institutions, insurance, life sciences, real estate, product liability and trademark law. Conducted scores of trials and arbitrations throughout the US. Represents banks, investment banks, broker dealers and consumer product companies in civil litigation. Represents individuals, corporations and partnerships in civil trials, class and derivative actions. Represents various financial industry participants in actions involving complex financial instruments, and derivatives. Also represents developers, lenders and investors in real estate and real estate securities disputes. Represents consumer product companies in litigation involving product recalls, insurance, reinsurance coverage, insurance fraud, trademark and anti-counterfeiting litigation. Extensive experience in mediations, arbitrations and other forms of alternative dispute resolution.

**Personal:** Harvard Law School, JD (cum laude) 1973; Fordham College, BA 1969 (cum laude, Phi Beta Kappa).

## MECHANIC, Jonathan
Fried, Frank, Harris, Shriver & Jacobson LLP, New York 212 859 8222
Jonathan.Mechanic@FriedFrank.com
*Recommended in Real Estate*

**Practice Areas:** Chairman of Real Estate Department. Practice includes acquisitions, dispositions, financings, joint ventures, restructurings, REIT transactions and commercial leasing. Representations have included Conde Nast Publications Inc., Jack Resnick & Sons, Lehman Brothers, RFR Holdings, Tishman Hotel & Realty, Tishman Speyer Properties, UBS, Vornado Realty.

**Career:** Joined Fried Frank as a Partner 1987. Rated Leading Individual by Chambers USA past three years. Lecturer, Harvard Law School (2006).

**Personal:** JD(1977), New York University, Member Law Review, Order of the Coif. BA(1974), magna cum laude, Brandeis University.

## MEHTA, Cyrus
Cyrus D Mehta & Associates PLLC, New York 212 425 0555
*Recommended in Immigration*

## MELWANI, Vivek
Fried, Frank, Harris, Shriver & Jacobson LLP, New York 212 859 8208
Vivek.Melwani@FriedFrank.com
*Recommended in Bankruptcy*

**Practice Areas:** Bankruptcy Partner. Practice involves all aspects of in, and out-of-court restructurings of financially distressed businesses. Active in the representation of corporate debtors, official and unofficial creditors' committees, lenders and purchasers of distressed businesses.

**Career:** Joined Fried Frank in 1995. Became a Partner in 2003. Admitted to practice before the United States District Court for the Southern District of New York.

**Personal:** JD(1995), with distinction. BBA(1992), Hofstra University. Member of the Law Review and the Labor Law Journal.

## MERMELSTEIN, Joshua
Fried, Frank, Harris, Shriver & Jacobson LLP, New York 212 859 8137
Joshua.Mermelstein@FriedFrank.com
*Recommended in Real Estate*

**Practice Areas:** Real Estate Partner. Practice includes representation of financial institutions, owners, developers, opportunity funds and offshore investors. Clients include Millenium & Copthorne Hotels plc; Brookfield Financial Properties, Inc. Reckson Associates Realty Corp.; Lazard Freres & Co's Real Estate Funds; Credit Suisse First Boston Corporation.

**Career:** Joined Fried Frank in 1980. Became a Partner in 1986. Board of Overseers of UJA Federation of New York

**Personal:** JD(1980), Columbia University Law School, where he was a Harlan Fiske Stone Scholar. AB(1977), Columbia University.

## METCALF, Slade R
Hogan & Hartson LLP, New York 212 918 3637
srmetcalf@hhlaw.com
*Recommended in Media & Entertainment*

**Practice Areas:** Media law and litigation for various media and entertainment companies. Counsels newspapers, television stations, magazines and book publishers on pre-publication and pre-broadcast issues; assists motion picture studios on issues relating to film production; represents media companies, reporters, authors, and photographers in litigations regarding issues of libel, invasion of privacy, copyright, and trademark.

**Prof. Memberships:** Forum on Communications Law of the ABA; Committee on Media Law of the NYSBA (Member, former Chair); ABCNY; Copyright Society of the U.S.A. (Member, former Trustee).

**Career:** Slade has been a Partner at Hogan & Hartson since March 2002. Prior to joining Hogan & Hartson, he was a Partner from 1981-2002 at Squadron Ellenoff Plesent & Sheinfeld LLP (which merged with Hogan & Hartson in 2002). Slade is a former Chairman of the Legal Affairs Committee of the Magazine Publishers of America, Inc., and has participated in numerous Bar Association committees regarding media, communications, art, copyright, and literary property. He has lectured extensively on media law at forums including conferences of the Media Law Resource Center, the American Bar Association, the International Trademark Association, International Municipal Lawyers Association, Practicing Law Institute, the Magazine Publishers of America, Inc., and the American Society of Magazine Editors.

**Publications:** 'Rights and Liabilities of Publishers, Broadcasters and Reporters', a leading media law resource book since 1981; Media Law Update, Hogan & Hartson L.L.P. (quarterly).

**Personal:** New York University School of Law (JD); Princeton University (AB). Admitted to the New York Bar, the Bar of the Supreme Court of the United States, as well as the Bars of several circuits of the US Courts of Appeals.

## MEYER, Paul
Clifford Chance US LLP, New York 212 878 8000
*Recommended in Insurance*

## MEYERS, Michael
Orrick, Herrington & Sutcliffe LLP, New York 212 506 5270
mmeyers@orrick.com
*Recommended in Projects*

**Practice Areas:** Expert in infrastructure project development and finance, representing developers, lenders, and equity investors in power, telecommunications, industrial, and other US and international infrastructure projects. Recent projects: representation of participants in US and international electric industry workouts; a multinational corporation in restructuring power generation business worldwide; sellers of power projects in Latin America; insolvency workouts of failed telecommunications and power projects; and development of power projects in Spain and Greece.

**Career:** Chair, Global Finance Group (1993-2005); Orrick Partner since 1993; Graham & James (1979-93).

**Personal:** JD, Stanford Law School, 1979; BS, summa cum laude, Florida State University, 1976.

## MEYERSON, Lee
Simpson Thacher & Bartlett LLP, New York 212 455 2000
lmeyerson@stblaw.com
*Recommended in Corporate/M&A, Financial Services*

**Practice Areas:** Senior member of the Mergers and Acquisitions Group, specialising in M&A as well as capital markets transactions for financial institutions. Has participated in many of the largest financial services mergers of the past decade, including representing JPMorgan Chase & Co. in its $58 billion merger with Bank One Corporation. During 2005 he represented Washington Mutual in its $6.6 billion acquisition of Providian Financial, The Toronto-Dominion Bank in its $3.8 billion acquisition of a 51% interest in Banknorth, and the merger of its Waterhouse subsidiary with Ameritrade ($3 billion), Federated Dept. Stores in the sale of its credit card portfolio to Citibank ($7.4 billion), Independence Community Bank in its sale to Sovereign Bancorp ($3.6 billion) and JPMorgan Chase in the sale of its discount broker subsidiary, Brown & Co. to E*Trade ($1.6 billion). Capital markets practice includes IPOs and a broad range of debt, equity and innovative capital securities offerings for financial institutions.

**Career:** Joined Simpson Thacher in 1981 and became a Partner in 1989.

**Personal:** Received a BA from Duke University, magna cum laude in 1977 and JD from NYU Law School in 1981, where he was an editor of The Law Review.

## MILLER, David S
Cadwalader, Wickersham & Taft LLP, New York 212 504 6318
david.miller@cwt.com
*Recommended in Tax*

**Practice Areas:** Concentrates on matters relating to the taxation of financial instruments and derivatives, cross-border lending transactions and other financings, international and domestic mergers and acquisitions, multinational corporate groups and partnerships, bankruptcy and workouts, high net worth individuals and families, and public charities and private foundations. Speaks regularly at conferences and universities. Author of numerous articles for legal publications.

**Personal:** JD, Columbia Law School (1989; Notes and Comments editor, Columbia Law Review); LLM, New York University School of Law (1994); BA, University of Pennsylvania (summa cum laude, 1986); clerk to the Honorable Mary M Schroeder of the Ninth Circuit Court of Appeals (1989-90); Awarded Burton Award for Legal Achievement (recognizing exceptional legal writing); Member, New York State Bar Association, Tax Section (Second Vice-Chair; will chair the section in 2008); and the Tax Forum.

## MILLER, George
Simpson Thacher & Bartlett LLP, New York 212 455 2000
gmiller@stblaw.com
*Recommended in Projects*

**Practice Areas:** Partner in the firm's Corporate Department, concentrating in domestic and international project finance and leasing. Represents financing parties and sponsors in power, energy, telecommunications and transportation projects in the US, Asia and Latin America. Represented principals in the privatization of six airports in the Dominican Republic and of Sangster International Airport in Montego Bay, Jamaica, the Dabhol power project in India, the Shandong Zhonghua power project in China and the Paiton I and the MGTI telecommunications project in Indonesia. Represents US and non-US parties (including Airbus Industrie, The Royal Bank of Scotland, the Brazilian Economic and Social Development Bank and Korea Development Bank) in domestic and cross-border lease financings of aircraft and other equipment and facilities, including structured financings in the capital markets.

**Prof. Memberships:** Association of the Bar of the City of New York, Project Finance Committee; American Bar Association; International Bar Association; New York State Bar Association, Editorial Board, Committee on Publications

**Career:** Partner at the firm since 1989 and resident Partner in the firm's Asian offices, 1991-98.

**Personal:** BA Yale University magna cum laude (1975); JD Harvard Law School (1979) and MPA John F Kennedy School of Government (1979).

## MILLER, Peter A
Akin Gump Strauss Hauer & Feld LLP, New York 212 872 1004
pamiller@akingump.com
*Recommended in Real Estate*
**Practice Areas:** Heads the New York Real Estate and Finance Practice Group. Experienced in real estate finance, with an emphasis on acquisitions, development, joint ventures and financings. Represents owners and developers of investment properties, including private equity funds and other emerging titleholders in the real estate market.
**Prof. Memberships:** New York State Bar Association.
**Career:** Prior to joining Akin Gump, was a Partner at Stroock & Stroock & Lavan LLP.
**Personal:** BS, accounting and finance, University of Pennsylvania's Wharton School of Business (1980); JD, New York University School of Law (1984).

## MILLOCK, Peter J
Nixon Peabody LLP, Albany
518 427 2651
pmillock@nixonpeabody.com
*Recommended in Healthcare*
**Practice Areas:** Affiliations and networks of physicians, hospitals and other health and mental health providers, regulatory and enforcement matters before state agencies, legislative lobbying on healthcare issues.
**Prof. Memberships:** Admitted to practice in New York; New York City Bar Association.
**Career:** Between 1980-95 served as General Counsel, New York State Department of Health. He was chief legal advisor to the Commissioner of Health and provided advice to state policy makers on all health related matters.
**Personal:** Harvard University, JD cum

laude; Harvard College, BA, Economics, magna cum laude.

## MILLS, Phillip R
Davis Polk & Wardwell, New York
212 450 4000
phillip.mills@dpw.com
*Recommended in Corporate/M&A*
**Practice Areas:** Member of Davis Polk & Wardwell's Mergers and Acquisitions Group. Advises companies on US and cross-border strategic transactions. Advised MCI on its acquisition by Verizon; EMI on its proposed business combination with AOL Time Warner; Alliance Capital on its acquisition of Sanford Bernstein; Imclone on its strategic relationship with Bristol-Myers; Emerson Electric on a variety of M&A transactions; Roche on its acquisition of Tastemaker; Tycom on its going private with Tyco; Keebler Foods' acquisition by Kellogg; and Kawasaki Steel on its proposed merger with NKK.

## MILLSTEIN, Julian
Brown Raysman Millstein Felder & Steiner LLP, New York
212 895 2420
jmillstein@brownraysman.com
*Recommended in Business Process Outsourcing, Technology*
**Practice Areas:** Julian Millstein concentrates on negotiating and litigating complex outsourcing and computer-related, e-commerce, and intellectual property matters. Before entering the practice of law, he had an extensive career as a computer programmer, systems analyst and information technology consultant. He is co-author of the book 'Doing Business on the Internet: Forms and Analysis.' Mr Millstein co-chairs the firm's outsourcing practice and has been a thought leader on outsourcing, presenting since 1993 at the Sourcing Interests Group, Outsourcing Institute, Conference Board, Outsourcing World Summit and the Gartner Outsourcing Summit.
**Personal:** BA, Brandeis University 1965; JD, Fordham University Law School 1978.

## MILMED, Paul K
White & Case LLP, New York
212 819 8751
pmilmed@whitecase.com
*Recommended in Environment*
**Practice Areas:** Environmental law including litigation; domestic/international M&A transactions.
**Prof. Memberships:** New York State Bar, 1976; New Jersey State Bar, 1975; US Court of Appeals for the Second Circuit; US District Courts for the Southern and Eastern Districts of New York and the District of New Jersey; ABCNY.
**Career:** Assistant US Attorney, SDNY (1983-93), Chief, Environmental Protection Unit (1990-93); US District Court for the Southern District of New York appointed mediator.

**Personal:** Amherst College (AB, 1966); London School of Economics and Political Science, University of London (MSc, 1968); Harvard University (EdM, 1969); New York University School of Law (JD, 1975).

## MILMOE, J Gregory
Skadden, Arps, Slate, Meagher & Flom LLP & Affiliates, New York
212 735 3770
jmilmoe@skadden.com
*Recommended in Bankruptcy*
**Practice Areas:** Co-Head, Corporate Restructuring Group. Experience includes in-court and out-of-court restructurings, hostile and negotiated mergers and acquisitions, leveraged buyouts, and corporate financings (including IPOs). Draws on experience from various legal disciplines to develop pragmatic, sometimes novel solutions to complex problems.
**Career:** JD, Fordham University, 1975 (articles editor, Fordham Law Review); AB, Cornell University, 1970.

## MINDLIN, Philip
Wachtell, Lipton, Rosen & Katz, New York 212 403 1217
pmindlin@wlrk.com
*Recommended in Bankruptcy*
**Practice Areas:** Specializes in bankruptcy and finance law.
**Career:** Partner at Wachtell, Lipton, Rosen & Katz since 1991. Represents buyers and sellers of distressed assets, creditors in Chapter 11 cases and out-of-court workouts, lenders and borrowers in leveraged acquisitions and other mergers and acquisitions matters. Experience includes representation of key parties in distress transactions involving Refco Group, Cable and Wireless plc's US subsidiaries, Olympia & York, FINOVA Capital, Adelphia Communications, At Home Corp, National Golf Properties, Safelite Glass, NorthPoint Communications, American Commercial Lines, Kingston Square Associates and PA Bergner & Co. Frequent lecturer on insolvency law and is listed in the K&A Restructuring Register of America's top 100 bankruptcy lawyers and financial advisors.
**Personal:** Graduated from the University of Pennsylvania (BA) and magna cum laude from Fordham University (JD), where he was a member of the Fordham Law Review and was a recipient of the Stillman Memorial Prize, the Chapin Prize and the Constitutional Law Medal.

## MIRVIS, Theodore N
Wachtell, Lipton, Rosen & Katz, New York 212 403 1204
tnmirvis@wlrk.com
*Recommended in Litigation*
**Practice Areas:** Specializes in litigation involving corporate governance and complex securities matters, and directors' fiduciary duties in mergers and acquisitions.

**Prof. Memberships:** American Law Institute and Planning Committee, Tulane Corporate Law Institute.
**Career:** Partner at Wachtell, Lipton, Rosen & Katz since 1982; law clerk, Honorable Henry J Friendly, United States Court of Appeals for the Second Circuit, 1976 term.
**Publications:** Author of numerous articles on corporate governance; and co-author, Wachtell & Mirvis, New York Practice under the CPLR.
**Personal:** Graduated summa cum laude from Yeshiva College in 1973 (BA) and magna cum laude from Harvard Law School in 1976 (JD). While at Harvard Law School, he was editor of Harvard Law Review, vol 88, and case editor of Harvard Law Review, vol 89.

## MOLLERUS, Michael
Davis Polk & Wardwell, New York
212 450 4000
michael.mollerus@dpw.com
*Recommended in Tax*
**Practice Areas:** Member of Davis Polk & Wardwell's Tax Department. His practice centers on advice to corporate and private equity fund clients on mergers, acquisitions, spinoffs and other major transactions, including structured financings.

## MONTELEONE, Joseph P
Duane Morris LLP, New York
212 692 1048
jpmonteleone@duanemorris.com
*Recommended in Insurance*
**Practice Areas:** Joseph P Monteleone practices primarily in the area of financial products and professional liability insurance coverage. The former Vice President and Claims Counsel for investment and insurance company The Hartford Financial Services Group, Inc., Mr Monteleone has nearly 25 years of experience in the insurance industry and has managed insurance coverage disputes and underlying litigation in many types of liability claims, internationally and domestically, including directors and officers, professional liability, employment practices liability, intellectual property, errors and omissions, fidelity, fiduciary, kidnap and ransom and environmental risks.
**Prof. Memberships:** American Bar Association; Professional Liability Underwriters Society - Trustee and Education Committee (Chair); Mealey Publications Insurance Advisory Council; USLAW NETWORK Professional Liability Practice Group - Client Advisor.
**Career:** Admitted to practice in New York and New Jersey; US District Courts for the Eastern and Southern Districts of New York; US District Court for the District of New Jersey.
**Publications:** 'A Look at the Future in Asia through the Looking Glass of the US Scene', 2nd Asian Conference on Corporate Governance and Directors' & Offi-

cers' Liability Insurance, Singapore, January 24, 2006.
**Personal:** New York Law School, JD, cum laude, 1980; Hunter College, MA, 1975; St John's University, BA, cum laude, 1972.

### MONTGOMERY, David
Sacks Montgomery PC, New York
212 355 4660
*Recommended in Construction*

### MONTGOMERY, Malcolm K
Shearman & Sterling LLP, New York
212 848 7587
mmontgomery@shearman.com
*Recommended in Real Estate*
**Practice Areas:** Partner, Real Estate Group. Practice spans domestic and cross-border real estate investment and finance as well as leveraged lending and bank finance for real estate investment trusts and other major companies.
**Prof. Memberships:** Association of the Bar of the City of New York; New York State Bar Association, Real Estate Financing Committee; Real Estate Board of New York; Association of Foreign Investors in Real Estate; Fellow, American College of Mortgage Attorneys.
**Publications:** Regularly contributes to leading industry publications covering legal aspects of real estate finance and investment.
**Personal:** BA, Princeton University (1986); JD, New York University (1989).

### MOORE, Harold F
Skadden, Arps, Slate, Meagher & Flom LLP & Affiliates, New York
212 735 3252
hmoore@skadden.com
*Recommended in Projects*
**Practice Areas:** General corporate and bank finance lawyer with a concentration in project finance. Has been the lead lawyer in over 110 domestic and international project financings, representing underwriters, banks and issuers in some of the most complex projects financed in recent years.
**Career:** JD, Notre Dame, 1980 (summa cum laude; articles editor, Notre Dame Law Review; Thomas J White Scholarship; Peters Scholarship; Farabaugh Prize for High Scholarship in Law); PhD, Fordham University, 1971; MA, Fordham University, 1970; BS, Fordham University, 1968.

### MORGAN, Charles
Skadden, Arps, Slate, Meagher & Flom LLP & Affiliates, New York
212 735 2470
cmorgan@skadden.com
*Recommended in Tax*
**Practice Areas:** Practice emphasizes tax law relating to financial products, hedge funds, private equity and international matters. Advises clients in connection with design, operation and/or tax consequences associated with financial prod-

ucts and transactions; establishment of hedge fund and private equity fund structures and tax consequences associated with international transactions and legal structures.
**Prof. Memberships:** Executive Committee Member, NY State Bar Association Tax Section (1986-present). Mr Morgan is the Secretary of the NYSBA's Tax Section, and will Chair the Tax Section in 2009.
**Career:** LLM, New York University, 1981; JD, Pepperdine University, 1977; BS, Wharton School, University of Pennsylvania, 1972.

### MORGAN, Robert C
Ropes & Gray LLP, New York
212 596 9133
robert.morgan@ropesgray.com
*Recommended in Intellectual Property*
**Practice Areas:** IP litigation in the fields of telecommunications, electronics, semiconductor technology, medical instruments and products. Lead counsel or co-counsel in more than 25 trials and has argued numerous appeals before the Court of Appeals for the Federal Circuit. Also specializes in IP asset management, licensing, patent validity and infringement issues.
**Career:** Fellow, American College of Trial Lawyers; California Bar (1970); New York Bar (1970); USPTO; Partner, Fish & Neave (1978); Partner, Ropes & Gray (2005).
**Personal:** JD, Harvard Law School (1969); MSEE, California Institute of Technology (1966); BS, University of California, Los Angeles (1965).

### MORGENSTERN, Saul P
Kaye Scholer LLP, New York
212 836 7210
smorgenstern@kayescholer.com
*Recommended in Antitrust*
**Practice Areas:** Partner, Litigation Group. Vice-Chair of the Antitrust and Trade Regulation Practice. Focuses his practice on the preparation and trial of complex cases, principally in the areas of antitrust (civil and criminal) and trade regulation, intellectual property and technology, as well as the representation of companies and individuals in connection with Department of Justice and Federal Trade Commission investigations. He has litigated jury and non-jury cases before federal and state courts throughout the United States, the Federal Trade Commission, the US International Trade Commission, and international and domestic arbitral tribunals. Has particular experience in defending multi-jurisdictional antitrust class actions in federal and state courts, in cases involving the alleged abuse of intellectual property rights and in price and promotional discrimination cases. He has counseled and represented clients in a variety of industries, including the chemical (agricultur-

al, petrochemical and specialty), computer hardware and software, energy, entertainment, insurance, investment banking, leasing, leisure, real estate, pharmaceutical, publishing, telecommunications and toy industries.
**Prof. Memberships:** American Bar Association: Section of Antitrust; Internet Committee, Trade Associations Committee, Vice Chair 2002-05; Section of Intellectual Property; Section of Litigation. New York State Bar Association: Antitrust Law Section; Vice Chair 2006, Executive Committee 2001-present. Federal Bar Council: Public Service Committee 2002-present. Association of the Bar of the City of New York.
**Career:** JD with Distinction, Hofstra University School of Law; BS, Boston University.
**Publications:** 'Antitrust Enforcement in High Technology Industries: Keeping Cyberspace Safe for Innovators or Just Another Speed Trap on the Information Superhighway?' with Eamon O'Kelly, 19th Annual Institute on Computer Law (Practising Law Institute (547) 1999); 'Antitrust Issues Affecting the Publishing Industry', Print and Electronic Publishing (Practising Law Institute (516) 1998 and (480) 1997).

### MORHOUSE, Sanford W
Dewey Ballantine LLP, New York
212 259 8400
smorhouse@deweyballantine.com
*Recommended in Private Fund Formation*
**Practice Areas:** Mr Morhouse focuses primarily in the areas of corporate and real estate finance. His principal clients include major pension funds, investment advisors and fund sponsors. His practice involves the creation of, and investments in, private and public investment vehicles, as well as representing the portfolio companies and properties acquired thereby.
**Career:** Partner, Dewey Ballantine LLP. Member of Management Committee and Chairman of firm's Private Equity and Real Estate Groups. Former Co-Chairman of the firm's Management and Executive Committees. Admitted to practice 1969, New York.
**Personal:** Born December 13, 1944. BA, Williams College, 1966. JD, Columbia Law School, 1969.

### MORPHY, James C
Sullivan & Cromwell LLP, New York
212 558 4000
morphyj@sullcrom.com
*Recommended in Corporate/M&A*
**Practice Areas:** M&A Managing Partner. Advisor on friendly mergers, proxy contests and hostile acquisitions. Recent transactions: Board Directors of Albertson's in private equity consortium buyout; Special Committee of Wrigley; Inco-Falconbridge merger; Computer Associ-

ates' Netegrity, Concord Communications and Niku acquisitions; KKR-Masonite; Special Committee of Abercrombie & Fitch; John Hancock-Manulife cross border merger; and various Hershey Foods acquisitions.
**Career:** Partner since 1986.
**Publications:** Contributing author: Transactional Lawyer's Deskbook (West).
**Personal:** Harvard College (BA, Phi Beta Kappa, 1976); Harvard Law School (JD, 1979).

### MORRISON, Thomas
Patterson, Belknap, Webb & Tyler LLP, New York 212 336 2650
tcmorrison@pbwt.com
*Recommended in Media & Entertainment*
**Practice Areas:** Thomas Morrison is nationally renowned as a trial and appellate attorney, author and lecturer in the field of trademarks, false advertising and unfair competition. He has tried more than 60 cases and argued more than 30 appeals in federal courts throughout the United States and has represented a wide range of pharmaceutical, media and consumer products companies.
**Prof. Memberships:** Chairman of the Board of Trustees, Otterbein College (Ohio).
**Career:** Mr Morrison joined Patterson Belknap as Partner in 1977. He began his legal career with the Judge Advocate General's Corps of the US Air Force (1967-70).
**Personal:** New York University School of Law (LLB 1966), Order of the Coif, Moot Court Board; Otterbein College (BA 1963).

### MORVILLO, Robert
Morvillo, Abramowitz, Grand, Iason & Silberberg, PC, New York 212 856 9600
*Recommended in Litigation*

### MOSKOWITZ, Steven
Stroock & Stroock & Lavan LLP, New York 212 806 5400
*Recommended in Real Estate*

### MURPHY, Sean
Milbank, Tweed, Hadley & McCloy LLP, New York 212 530 5000
*Recommended in Litigation*

### MYERSON, Toby S
Paul, Weiss, Rifkind, Wharton & Garrison LLP, New York
212 373 3033
tmyerson@paulweiss.com
*Recommended in Corporate/M&A*
**Practice Areas:** Toby Myerson is a Partner in the Corporate Department, member of the firm's Management Committee and Co-Head of the firm's Mergers and Acquisitions Group. He devotes most of his practice to mergers and acquisitions of public and private companies, leveraged buyouts, corporate governance, corporate finance and advice to boards of directors. He has advised major US and

international corporations, financial institutions, buyout groups and other institutions on merger and acquisition, tender offer, investment banking and financial transactions. Mr Myerson also counsels boards of directors on strategic issues and corporate governance matters.

### NADEL, Peter F
Katten Muchin Rosenman LLP,
New York 212 940 7010
peter.nadel@kattenlaw.com
*Recommended in Healthcare*
**Practice Areas:** Partner, represents a wide variety of local and national healthcare providers and hospital associations in both transactional and contested matters. Has negotiated dozens of contracts, each in excess of $100 million, and has recovered more than $1 billion in reimbursement litigations against federal and state governments for clients in New York and nationally.
**Personal:** Columbia University (LLB 1964); Columbia Law Review; Harlan Fiske Stone Scholar; Cornell University (BA 1961) With Distinction.

### NAFTALIS, Gary P
Kramer Levin Naftalis & Frankel LLP,
New York 212 715 9253
gnaftalis@kramerlevin.com
*Recommended in Litigation*
**Practice Areas:** One of the nation's leading trial lawyers, Co-Chair of Kramer Levin Naftalis and Frankel LLP and Head of the firm's Litigation Practice. For more than 30 years, he has represented individuals and corporations in all phases of complex civil, criminal, and regulatory matters including those involving allegations of insider trading, market manipulation, accounting irregularities and other financial fraud.
**Prof. Memberships:** He is a Fellow of the American College of Trial Lawyers and a member of the Trial Attorney Advisory Board of the Litigation Section of the American Bar Association. He is also a director of the Legal Aid Society.
**Career:** During his 30+ year career, he has successfully represented numerous securities industry clients, including Salomon Brothers in the investigation of US Treasury auction bidding practices, Kidder, Peabody in the Wall Street insider trading probe, and Canary Capital Partners in the mutual fund inquiries. He recently successfully defended Michael Eisner, the CEO of The Walt Disney Company, in the shareholders derivative lawsuit relating to the hiring and termination of Michael Ovitz. After a 37-day trial in the Delaware Chancery Court, Mr Eisner and the other Disney Directors prevailed on all counts. He is currently counsel to Kenneth Langone in the litigation relating to the compensation of New York Stock Exchange Chairman Richard Grasso. He is counsel for significant figures and entities in the current inquiries

and related civil litigation concerning corporate accounting irregularities including the recent successful representation of the Chairman and Founder of Global Crossing. He also represents the CFOs of Cendant and Bristol-Myers Squibb; the CEO of Refco; and the investment banking firm of CIBC in the Enron investigation. He also represents a director and senior officer of Tyco in securities class action and ERISA litigation and the former CEO of Arthur Andersen in the Enron civil litigation. He also serves as counsel to audit and special committees of a number of major public companies in connection with regulatory inquiries. He formerly served as an Assistant US Attorney in the Southern District of New York, holding the title of Deputy Chief of the Criminal Division. He also served as special counsel to the US Senate Subcommittee investigating abuses in the nursing home industry. He has been a Member of the faculty at Columbia and Harvard Law Schools.
**Publications:** He is the author or coauthor of numerous books and articles including the leading work on the grand jury system: The Grand Jury: An Institution on Trial (with Judge Marvin E Frankel).
**Personal:** Received his AB Degree from Rutgers University in 1963, his MA from Brown University in 1965, and his LLB from Columbia Law School in 1967.

### NATHAN, Charles
Latham & Watkins LLP, New York
212 906 1200
*Recommended in Corporate/M&A*

### NECKLES, Peter J
Skadden, Arps, Slate, Meagher & Flom LLP & Affiliates, New York
212 735 2466
pneckles@skadden.com
*Recommended in Banking & Finance*
**Practice Areas:** Represents corporate borrowers and institutional lenders in bank loan transactions, with an emphasis on corporate restructurings, workouts, debtor-in-possession loans, bankruptcy reorganizations, acquisition financings and other highly leveraged financings.
**Career:** JD, Fordham University School of Law, (cum laude; editor, Fordham Law Review); BS, Rensselaer Polytechnic Institute.

### NEEDELL, Benjamin F
Skadden, Arps, Slate, Meagher & Flom LLP & Affiliates, New York
212 735 2600
bneedell@skadden.com
*Recommended in Real Estate*
**Practice Areas:** Head of Skadden's Real Estate Department. Practice emphasizes purchase and sale transactions, financings, securitized real estate loans, real estate development, partnership law, real estate investment trusts, syndications, major headquarters leases, hotel opera-

tion, development and financing, and matters relating to pension fund investments in real estate.
**Prof. Memberships:** Member, Board of Directors, Rock and Roll Hall of Fame (1986-present); Wenner Media, Inc. (1978-present); Stratton Mountain School (1980-present); New York Restoration Project (2002-present), Chairman (2002-present); Westchester Land Trust (2001-present).
**Career:** LLB, St John's University, 1966 (Editorial Board, St John's Law Review); BA, Rutgers University, 1963.

### NEFF, Daniel A
Wachtell, Lipton, Rosen & Katz,
New York 212 403 1218
daneff@wlrk.com
*Recommended in Corporate/M&A*
**Practice Areas:** Specializes in mergers and acquisitions. During more than 25 years of practice has been extensively involved in negotiated as well as hostile acquisitions, and has represented bidders and targets, public and private companies, private equity firms and special committees of directors. Has represented companies in divestitures, cross-border transactions and proxy contests and has counselled managements and boards of directors concerning acquisition matters, conflict transactions and other significant issues. Among other matters, he has represented Goldman Sachs Capital Partners and Apollo Advisors LP in their acquisition of Nalco Chemical Company; Apollo Advisors LP in its acquisition of AMC Entertainment Inc; Western Wireless Corporation in its merger with ALLTEL Corporation; VoiceStream Wireless Corporation in its merger with Deutsche Telekom AG; Kellogg Company in its acquisition of Keebler Foods Company; Litton Industries Inc in its merger with Northrop Grumman Corporation; Orion Power Holdings Inc in its sale to Reliant Resources, Inc; Mirage Resorts Incorporated in its merger with MGM Grand Inc; Anadarko Petroleum Corporation in its acquisition of Union Pacific Resources Group Inc; Vivendi Universal SA in its acquisitions of United States Filter Corporation and Cendant Software Corporation; Transamerica Corporation in its merger with Aegon NV and its acquisition of Whirlpool Financial Corporation; Newmont Mining Corporation in its acquisitions of Franco-Nevada Mining Corporation Limited, Normandy Mining Limited and Santa Fe Pacific Gold Corporation; Western Atlas Inc. in its merger with Baker Hughes Incorporated; and Vons Companies in its merger with Safeway Inc; and has represented special board committees of Wausau Insurance, Hayes Wheels International and Enron Oil & Gas Company (now EOG Resources Inc).
**Prof. Memberships:** Member of the Law Review at Columbia University School of

Law.
**Career:** Partner at Wachtell, Lipton, Rosen & Katz since 1984. Serves as Co-Chairman of the firm's Executive Committee.
**Personal:** Graduated magna cum laude from Brown University and from the Columbia University School of Law.

### NEILL, David S
Wachtell, Lipton, Rosen & Katz, New York 212 403 1263
dsneill@wlrk.com
*Recommended in Antitrust*
**Practice Areas:** Specializes in antitrust. Has handled the antitrust aspects of mergers affecting a broad variety of industries, including most recently the Sears-Kmart, Unocal-Chevron, and New York Stock Exchange-Archipelago mergers. Has represented the buyer or the seller in most of the largest bank mergers in US history.
**Prof. Memberships:** The Association of the Bar of the City of New York (Antitrust and Trade Regulation Committee, 1997-98); New York State and American (Section on Antitrust, Vice-Chairman of Financial Market and Institutions Committee, 1997-2001) Bar Associations.
**Career:** Partner at Wachtell, Lipton, Rosen & Katz.
**Publications:** Co-author: 'Antitrust Standards for Bank Holding Company Mergers and Acquisitions', Bank and Corporate Governance Law Reporter, Vol VIII, Nos 4 & 5, p 812 (June/July 1992); 'Justice's Review of Bank Acquisitions Continues to Reflect Uncertainty', Banking Policy Report, Vol 11, No 23, p 3 (December 7, 1992); 'FDICIA Taxes Justice Department's Antitrust Analysis of Bank Mergers', Banking Policy Report, Vol 12, No 1, p 1 (January 4, 1993); 'Relevant Product and Geographic Markets in Bank Mergers: A Comparison of the Methodologies Used by the Justice Department and the Federal Reserve Board', Special Report published by BNA (1994); 'Bank Merger Impact on Small Business Services Is Changing', Banking Policy Report, Vol 15, No 8 (April 15, 1996); 'Documentary Evidence and Antitrust Merger Enforcement', ALI-ABA's Practice Checklist Manual on Advising Business Clients, p21 (1997); 'Proposed 'Streamlining' of Bank Merger Antitrust Review by House Banking Bill May Have Unintended Consequences', BNA's Banking Report, Vol 69, No 2, p93 (July 14, 1997); 'Antitrust Considerations in Mergers and Acquisitions of Financial Institution', Bank and Corporate Governance Law Reporter, Vol 19, No 5, p762 (January 1998); 'Acquisitions of Non-Bank Operations in Financial Holding Company Mergers', The Review of Banking and Financial Services, Vol 20, No 3 (March 2004). Co-editor: Bank Merger Practice Manual, American Bar Associa-

tion (forthcoming). Author: 'Lending to Small and Medium-Sized Businesses and the Antitrust Analysis of Bank Mergers', BNA's Banking Report, Vol 60, p 814 (May 31, 1993); 'Fed Antitrust Change Could Boost Thrift Acquisitions by Banks', Banking Policy Report, Vol 12, No 17, p 1 (September 6, 1993); 'Antitrust Divestiture Policies Can Impact Bank Merger Planning', Banking Policy Report, Vol 14, No 23, p1 (December 4, 1995); 'New Antitrust Policies Add Complexity and Uncertainty to Bank Mergers', Bank and Corporate Governance Law Reporter, Vol 17, No 2, p 196 (Oct. 1996); 'New Safe Harbor or Not? Fed Clarifies Antitrust Thresholds for Bank Deals', Banking Policy Report, Vol 16, No 13, p1 (July 7, 1997); 'M & A Review Role for the FTC on Banking Deals: A Flawed Idea', Banking Policy Report, Vol 16, No 18, p1 (Sept 15, 1997); 'The ATM Surcharge Debate: Logical Fallacies and Antitrust Reality', BNA's Banking Report, Vol 71, No 5, p233 (August 3, 1998); 'Antitrust Lessons from Recent Bank Megamergers', Banking Policy Report, Vol 17, No 21, p1 (November 2, 1998); 'U.S. Antitrust Considerations in Mergers and Acquisitions of Bank Holding Companies', Antitrust Report, p4 (February 1999). 'Antitrust Merger Review Will Be More Complicated After Financial Modernization', Banking Policy Report, Vol 18, No 17, p 1 (September 7, 1999); 'New Banking Act Complicates Merger Review', International Financial Law Review, p 13(February 2000); 'A Guide to the Policies and Procedures Affecting Antitrust Divestitures in Bank Mergers', The Banking Law Journal, Vol. 118, No 7, p 603 (July/August 2001); 'Geographic Market Definition in the Antitrust Analysis of Bank Mergers', The Banking Law Journal (forthcoming). **Personal:** Graduated cum laude from Yale University in 1979 (BA); from Goldman School of Public Policy, University of California, Berkeley in 1983 (MPP); and from Columbia Law School in 1984 (JD).

## NESGOS, Peter
Milbank, Tweed, Hadley & McCloy LLP, New York 212 530 5000
*Recommended in Technology*

## NEUNER, Robert
Baker Botts LLP, New York
212 408 2552
robert.neuner@bakerbotts.com
*Recommended in Intellectual Property*
**Practice Areas:** The trial and appeal of complex cases with emphasis on intellectual property. Cases tried nationwide, mostly to juries, have involved all important areas of technology. Has also functioned as a court-appointed special master.
**Prof. Memberships:** American Intellectual Property Law Association; Federal Bar Council; New York Intellectual Prop-

erty Law Association, past President.
**Career:** New York State Bar (1965); USPTO (1968).
**Publications:** Written and lectured on trial and appeal of intellectual property cases, including a regular column in the New York Law Journal.
**Personal:** JD, Fordham University School of Law, 1965; BS, electrical engineering, Manhattan College, 1960.

## NEVELOFF, Jay A
Kramer Levin Naftalis & Frankel LLP, New York 212 715 9290
jneveloff@kramerlevin.com
*Recommended in Real Estate*
**Practice Areas:** Mr Neveloff represents numerous nationally recognized real estate developers and owners in the development, operation and financing of real estate projects, institutional and other ventures in the acquisition of property (including portfolios of properties), and joint ventures involving a broad variety of assets, as well as major international funds and financial institutions, in commercial lending transactions, loan restructurings and workouts.
**Prof. Memberships:** Served for several years as the Vice-Chair of the American Bar Association Committee on Partnerships, Joint Ventures and Other Investment Vehicles. He is an active Member of both The American College of Real Estate Lawyers and American Law Institute, and is a Member of the Practicing Law Institute Real Estate Advisory Committee. He also served as the Vice-Chair of the International Health Network Society.
**Career:** Mr Neveloff has represented developers of numerous mixed-use, commercial, retail and residential projects, including Time Warner Center (a joint development among The Related Companies, Apollo Investments, Time Warner and Mandarin Hotels), the conversion of Trump Park Avenue, the former Delmonico Hotel, and Trump International Hotel and Tower (the former Gulf + Western Building and a joint venture of General Electric Investment Trust, Donald Trump and The Galbreath Organization), as well as numerous regional and local shopping centers, and other commercial projects throughout the country. Recently, Mr Neveloff represented New York Life Insurance Company in the sale of Manhattan House, a residential complex comprising an entire block on the upper east side of Manhattan and Istithmar in the purchase of the Helmsley Building, 230 Park Avenue, New York City. Mr Neveloff regularly assists clients actively involved in numerous hotel transactions including the acquisition of numerous hotels, the development of hotels, and loan restructurings relating to numerous hotels including The Plaza Hotel in New York. He also represents opportunity funds in the acquisition and joint venturing of projects throughout

the United States. Mr Neveloff is also a leading practitioner of innovative hotel condominium projects, including The Plaza Hotel and the St. Regis in New York City and successfully obtained a critical SEC no-action letter involving a hotel condominium structure.
**Personal:** Received a JD Degree from New York University in 1974 and a BA Degree from Brooklyn College in 1971.

## NEWMAN, Thomas R
Duane Morris LLP, New York
212 692 1028
trnewman@duanemorris.com
*Recommended in Insurance*
**Practice Areas:** Thomas R Newman practices in the areas of insurance and reinsurance law, including coverage, claims handling, contract drafting and arbitration and litigation. He has served as lead counsel in more than 50 reinsurance arbitrations, representing both cedents and reinsurers. He has handled hundreds of appeals in both state and federal courts, including 80 in the New York Court of Appeals and 30 in the US Court of Appeals for the Second Circuit.
**Prof. Memberships:** American Bar Association; New York State Bar Association; The Association of the Bar of the City of New York; American Law Institute; Federation of Insurance and Corporate Counsel; American Academy of Appellate Lawyers; AIDA Reinsurance and Insurance Arbitration Society.
**Career:** Admitted to practice in New York, Supreme Court of the United States, United States Court of Appeals for the Second Circuit, United States District Courts for the Southern and Eastern Districts of New York. Duane Morris LLP, Of Counsel, 2003-present; Luce, Forward, Hamilton & Scripps LLP, Of Counsel, 1999-2003; Newman & Company, PC - President, 1991-99; Bower & Gardner - Partner, 1971-91; Siff & Newman - Partner, 1971-87; Sabin, Bermant & Blau - associate/Partner, 1963-70.
**Personal:** New York University School of Law, LLB, 1960.

## NIJENHUIS, Erika W
Cleary Gottlieb Steen & Hamilton LLP, New York 212 225 2980
enijenhuis@cgsh.com
*Recommended in Tax*
**Practice Areas:** US income tax, especially financial products and international tax planning. Clients include Citigroup, Goldman Sachs, Lehman, Merrill Lynch, Morgan Stanley.
**Prof. Memberships:** NYSBA Tax Section Executive Committee, Co-Chair financial instruments subcommittee; ABA Tax Section, Co-Chair debt instruments subcommittee.
**Career:** Became Partner, 1997. LLM in Taxation, NYU (1996). JD, cum laude (1987); BA, summa cum laude (1982), University of Pennsylvania. Included in

Best Lawyers in America 2006.
**Publications:** Articles on wash sales, tax shelter disclosure rules, contingent interest convertible bonds, securities futures, off-shore 'trading in securities', global dealing operations, mandatory convertible debt instruments, swaps and other financial instruments.

## NIMS, Barbara
Davis Polk & Wardwell, New York
212 450 4000
barbara.nims@dpw.com
*Recommended in Employee Benefits*
**Practice Areas:** Member of Davis Polk & Wardwell's Corporate Department. Advises clients on executive compensation, stock-based incentive, deferred compensation and pension plans and other employee benefit arrangements, with particular emphasis on issues arising in the contexts of merger, acquisition, corporate reorganization and bankruptcy and workout transactions. Also advises on pension investment and fiduciary considerations, employment and consulting arrangements, the applicability of federal securities and tax laws to executives and employees, and on general employment-related matters.

## NIRENBERG, David Z
Orrick, Herrington & Sutcliffe LLP, New York 212 506 5085
dnirenberg@orrick.com
*Recommended in Tax*
**Practice Areas:** Nationally recognized for his tax work in the areas of securitization and derivative products. He has played a significant role in the structuring of a wide variety of innovative, domestic and cross border financial products in both the structured finance and derivative products markets.
**Career:** Leader, Orrick's New York Corporate Tax Group.
**Publications:** Co-author, Federal Income Taxation Of Securitization Transactions (2001); Federal Income Taxation of Mortgage-Backed Securities (Probus Publishing, 1989, revised 1994).
**Personal:** JD, Columbia University School of Law, 1985; Harlan Fiske Stone Scholar; MBA, with honors, Boston University Graduate School of Management, 1985; BS, Cornell University, 1981.

## NONNA, John M
LeBoeuf, Lamb, Greene & MacRae LLP, New York 212 424 8311
jnonna@llgm.com
*Recommended in Insurance*
**Practice Areas:** His practice in commercial litigation and arbitration includes insurance and reinsurance disputes. Has conducted arbitrations and bench and jury trials on a variety of claims including accounting malpractice, breach of fiduciary duty, fraud, sales and distributorship contracts, insurance and reinsurance coverage, and employment discrimination. Has lectured at numer-

ous conferences on trial practice, arbitration, mediation, and insurance and reinsurance coverage.

**Publications:** Co-editor, Insurance Law Practice, NY State Bar Association (2001); contributing author, Commercial Litigation in New York State Courts (1995).

**Personal:** Has served as Mayor of Pleasantville, NY. Was a member of the 1972 and 1980 US Olympic Teams.

## NORDAHL, Stephen
Milbank, Tweed, Hadley & McCloy LLP, New York 212 530 5000
*Recommended in Technology*

## NOTKIN, Deborah
Barst & Mukamal LLP, New York
212 686 3838
*Recommended in Immigration*

## NOVIKOFF, Harold S
Wachtell, Lipton, Rosen & Katz, New York 212 403 1249
hsnovikoff@wlrk.com
*Recommended in Bankruptcy*

**Practice Areas:** Specializes in creditors' rights, bankruptcy, debt restructurings, and derivative and financial markets transactions. During the past year, has represented major creditors of Collins & Aikman, Northwest Airlines, Blockbuster, Meridian Automotive, HealthSouth, 360 networks, Independent Wireless One, Looking Glass Networks, National Century Financial Enterprises, American Business Financial Services and Navigator Gas.

**Prof. Memberships:** Member of the Executive Committee of the National Bankruptcy Conference and Co-Chair of the Chapter 11 Committee and Capital Markets Committee of the National Bankruptcy Conference; Fellow of the American College of Bankruptcy; former Chair of the Committee on Bankruptcy and Corporate Reorganization of the Association of the Bar of the City of New York.

**Career:** Partner at Wachtell, Lipton, Rosen & Katz since 1981.

**Publications:** Contributing author to 'Collier on Bankruptcy'.

**Personal:** Graduated with distinction from Cornell University in 1972 (BS) and from Columbia University Law School in 1975 (JD) (Member of Law Review); Board of Visitors of the Columbia Law School; Board of Advisors of the Mailman School of Public Health at Columbia University.

## NUGENT, Eileen T
Skadden, Arps, Slate, Meagher & Flom LLP & Affiliates, New York
212 735 3176
enugent@skadden.com
*Recommended in Corporate/M&A*

**Practice Areas:** Co-Head, Private Equity Group. Concentrates in mergers and acquisitions, particularly leveraged buy-

out transactions. Has worked on a wide variety of acquisitions and dispositions of companies, subsidiaries and divisions, both public and private, hostile and negotiated, both in the United States and around the world, representing a wide variety of parties. The breadth of her experience has resulted in her being increasingly regarded as a senior legal, business and strategic advisor to her clients, particularly in the areas of corporate governance and conflict-of-interest situations.

**Career:** JD, Brooklyn Law School, 1978; AB, Cornell University, 1975

## NUSBAUM, Jack H
Willkie Farr & Gallagher LLP, New York
212 728 8060
jnusbaum@willkie.com
*Recommended in Corporate/M&A*

**Practice Areas:** Chairman of the firm, specializing in mergers and acquisitions, corporate governance and fiduciary duties, and internal investigations. Regularly advises boards of directors of public companies on issues of fiduciary duty and corporate governance, particularly in the context of change-in-control transactions. Continues to be involved in many of the most notable US and cross-border transactions. In 2005, he advised The Titan Corporation in its $2.65 billion acquisition by L-3 Communications, and Monsanto Company in its $1.4 billion acquisition of Seminis, Inc. He also recently advised the Management Team of PanAmSat Corp. in its $4.3 billion acquisition by Kohlberg Kravis Roberts & Co. from DirecTV Group Inc., and Neuberger Berman Inc. in its $2.63 billion acquisition by Lehman Brothers Holdings, Inc. Noted for his significant involvement in: the historic merger of NASDAQ with the American Stock Exchange, the leveraged buyout of R.J.R. Nabisco, the acquisition of McCaw Cellular Communications by AT&T, the acquisition of Magma Copper by Broken Hill Proprietary Limited, and various going-private transactions and restructurings on behalf of Donald Trump and his related entities. Headed the team responsible for the 1998 Cendant Report, the internal investigation of Cendant Corporation on behalf of its Audit Committee, which The New York Times called a definitive case study for accountants in the area of accounting irregularities and fraud.

**Prof. Memberships:** Member of the New York State and American Bar Associations. Serves as a Director of publicly held corporations including W.R. Berkley Corporation, Strategic Distribution, Inc. and The Topps Company, Inc. Serves on the Board of Visitors of Columbia University Law School and is a trustee of Prep for Prep and The Joseph Collins Foundation. Serves as a Member of the Legal Advisory Committee to the Board of Directors of the New York Stock

Exchange and is a member of the Board of Advisors of the New York University Center for Law & Business.

**Career:** Admitted to the Bar of the State of New York.

**Personal:** Received a JD from Columbia Law School in 1965 and a BS from the Wharton School of the University of Pennsylvania in 1962.

## NUSSBAUM, Bernard W
Wachtell, Lipton, Rosen & Katz, New York 212 403 1266
bwnussbaum@wlrk.com
*Recommended in Litigation*

**Practice Areas:** Specializes in corporate and securities litigation.

**Prof. Memberships:** Admitted to practice in the United States District Courts for the Southern and Eastern Districts of New York, the United States Court of Appeals for the Second Circuit, and the United States Supreme Court; and Member of the Association of the Bar of the City of New York (Vice President from 1984-85), the New York State Bar Association, the American Bar Association, and the Federal Bar Council (President from 1990-92).

**Career:** Partner at Wachtell, Lipton, Rosen & Katz since 1968. Has served in both the public and private sectors throughout his career, working as an assistant attorney in the United States Attorney's Office for the Southern District of New York after graduating from law school, as Senior Associate Counsel to the United States House of Representatives Judiciary Committee's impeachment inquiry in 1974 regarding President Richard Nixon and as Counsel to the President during the Clinton Administration in 1993 and 1994. Has been a lecturer at Columbia University Law School.

**Personal:** Graduated from Columbia University in 1958 (BA), where he was a Member of Phi Beta Kappa, from Harvard Law School in 1961 (LLB), where he was notes editor of Harvard Law Review, and awarded a Harvard University Sheldon Travelling Fellowship, and was awarded an honorary LLD from George Washington University National Law Center in 1993.

## NUSSBAUM, Martin
Dechert LLP, New York
212 698 3596
martin.nussbaum@dechert.com
*Recommended in Corporate/M&A*

**Practice Areas:** Mr Nussbaum is a Partner in the Corporate and Securities and Mergers and Acquisitions Groups. He represents industrial companies and financial institutions in both the public and private sectors. He also advises clients on transactions involving changes in control, proxy contests, mergers, and acquisitions.

**Prof. Memberships:** Member, New York Bar and several federal.

**Publications:** Mr Nussbaum has chaired many panels on M&A issues for the Practising Law Institute and is frequently a guest speaker on topics on M&A, restructuring matters, and the securities industry.

**Personal:** Columbia College, AB, 1967; Columbia Law School, JD, 1970.

## O'BRIEN, Clare
Shearman & Sterling LLP, New York
212 848 8966
cobrien@shearman.com
*Recommended in Corporate/M&A*

**Practice Areas:** Partner at Shearman & Sterling specializing in mergers and acquisitions. Advises on a large variety of public and private transactions, including public company restructurings, joint ventures and large public transactions.

**Prof. Memberships:** Member of the New York Bar; Member of the Irish Roll of Solicitors.

**Career:** Joined Shearman in 1988 and became Partner in 1995.

**Personal:** Educated at the Incorporated Law Society of Ireland, and Trinity College (Dublin), BA Legal Science; Member of the Board of Directors of the American Association of the International Commission of Jurists.

## O'BRIEN, Peter
Dewey Ballantine LLP, New York
212 259 6186
pobrien@deweyballantine.com
*Recommended in Energy*

**Practice Areas:** Mr O'Brien has extensive experience in all aspects of domestic and international capital markets transactions, with a particular emphasis on financing by energy and utility companies. He acts as designated underwriters counsel to several large US utility companies and acted as company counsel for electric distribution and supply companies in Australia and the UK in various US securities offerings.

**Career:** Partner, Dewey Ballantine LLP. Energy, corporate finance, tax exempt finance. Admitted to practice, 1992, New York.

**Personal:** Born June 17, 1966. BA, The College of Holy Cross, 1988. JD, Washington & Lee University School of Law, 1991.

## OLIVIER, Jeanne C
Shearman & Sterling LLP, New York
212 848 8593
jolivier@shearman.com
*Recommended in Projects*

**Practice Areas:** Partner in Shearman & Sterling's Project Development and Finance Group. Has broad experience in both international and domestic financings, including acquisition financings, asset-based financings, lease financings, project financings, privatisations and sovereign and corporate restructurings. Advises sponsors and lenders in complex political risk insurance matters. Also has extensive experience in financings and restructurings in Latin America.

**Prof. Memberships:** Bars of the State of New York and the State of Louisiana.
**Career:** Joined Shearman in 1980 and became a Partner in 1988.
**Personal:** BA, Newcomb College of Tulane University (1975); JD, University of Pennsylvania Law School (1979).

## O'MALLEY JR, Joseph M
Fitzpatrick, Cella, Harper & Scinto, New York 212 218 2260
jomalley@fchs.com
*Recommended in Intellectual Property*

**Practice Areas:** Lead trial counsel for various clients, including Pfizer, Bristol-Myers Squibb, Eisai and Kos Pharmaceuticals, through all phases of pharmaceutical patent litigation. In 2004, Mr O'Malley served as lead trial counsel for plaintiffs Pfizer and Warner-Lambert in a successful patent litigation involving their $700 million per year cardiovascular drug Accupril. Mr O'Malley also successfully argued the appeal of those trial rulings. In 2005, Mr O'Malley was lead counsel for Pfizer in obtaining what was reported to be the first preliminary injunction to succeed in enjoining a generic product that had already entered the market. Mr O'Malley also successfully argued the appeal of that preliminary injunction. Mr O'Malley was ranked as one of the top intellectual property attorneys in New York in the 2005 edition of Chambers USA: America's Leading Lawyers for Business and was listed as a 'recommended' attorney in both the 2005/2006 edition of PLC Which Lawyer and PLC's Which Lawyer Yearbook 2006. Mr O'Malley will be profiled in the PLC Cross-Border Intellectual Property Handbook 2006/2007. Mr O'Malley is also a winner of the 2004 Burton Award for Legal Achievement.

**Prof. Memberships:** American Bar Association; New York Intellectual Property Law Association; New Jersey Intellectual Property Law Association (Litigation Committee); Member of the Bar of the State of New York, US Court of Appeals for the Federal Circuit, and US District Courts for the Southern and Eastern Districts of New York.
**Career:** Chemical Engineer, DuPont. Supervised the design and construction of new chemical and pharmaceutical processing facilities.
**Personal:** Rutgers College of Engineering (BS chemical engineering, highest honors); Rutgers-Camden School of Law (JD, honors). Father of three children. Enjoys sports, travel and reading.

## O'NEIL, Terry
Bond, Schoeneck & King, PLLC, New York 516 267 6310
toneil@bsk.com
*Recommended in Employment*

**Practice Areas:** Mr O'Neil's practice

includes collective bargaining, arbitration, employment discrimination and litigation, wage-hour matters, ERISA, and OSHA. He has represented some of the largest municipalities in New York. He has represented numerous school districts, and regularly handles 'high profile' disciplinary proceedings, including an Education Law 'a73020-a case with the highest fine ($100,000) in the history of the State. He has represented private sector clients in negotiations and litigation throughout the US, and has extensive experience in the printing, service and restaurant industries.

**Personal:** St John's University (BA, cum laude, 1967) and St John's University School of Law (JD, 1970).

## ORINGER, Andrew
Clifford Chance US LLP, New York 212 878 8171
andrew.oringer@cliffordchance.com
*Recommended in Employee Benefits*

**Practice Areas:** Serves as Head of US ERISA and Executive Compensation practice. Counsels clients regarding their benefit programs, and fiduciary issues arising in connection with the investment of benefit plan assets. Works closely with Corporate attorneys to advise clients on benefits strategies in respect of corporate transactions. Published articles include articles on such topics as executive compensation, ERISA implications of structuring investment funds, tax-qualification issues and the treatment of benefits in bankruptcy. Serves as Co-Chairperson of the Employee Benefits Committee of the Tax Section of the NY State Bar Association, lectures regularly and is quoted frequently in major publications.

## O'ROURKE, Brendan
Proskauer Rose LLP, New York 212 969 3240
borourke@proskauer.com
*Recommended in Media & Entertainment*

**Practice Areas:** False advertising, trademarks, unfair competition, copyright, IP, entertainment, commercial litigation.
**Career:** Brendan concentrates in false advertising, trademark and unfair competition law. A first-rate litigator, having successfully tried numerous IP cases, including Colgate v P&G, Guinness v Anheuser-Busch; Extreme Color v Clairol; TT Sounds Good v Tommy Lee; EMI v Hill Holiday; Emergency One v AFE; RIAA v Napster; Parisi v Madonna; Platypus v Bad Boy/Sean John; SC Johnson v Clorox; Phillip Morris v Allen; Elk v GAF; Fabrications v Hygenic; Bristol-Myers v McNeil. His expertise includes complex issues involving consumer survey research and claim substantiation He is a frequent lecturer, has had numerous articles published, and has appeared on national television to discuss important cases. He has been an active member of

INTA, AIPLA, and NYIPLA. Mr O'Rourke has significant experience in arbitration and mediation through the federal courts, NAD, and the INTA panel of neutrals for clients such as Kraft, Estee Lauder, Madonna, Bristol-Myers Squibb, Federal Signal, and EMI. Mr O'Rourke received his BA in English and Philosophy from Boston College, cum laude, in 1981 and his JD in 1984 from Fordham, where he captained the Fordham National Trial Advocacy Team. He is admitted to practice in all courts in the State of New York and numerous United States District Courts and Federal Courts of Appeals, including the Second, Fourth, Ninth, and Federal Circuits.

## ORR, Dennis P
Mayer, Brown, Rowe & Maw LLP, New York 212 506 2690
dorr@mayerbrownrowe.com
*Recommended in Antitrust, Litigation*

**Practice Areas:** Litigation. Primary focus on antitrust; securities; products liability; environmental; general commercial litigation; insurance litigation.
**Notable cases:** In re American International Group Securities Litigation; In re Vitamins Antitrust Litigation; The Topps Company v Cadbury Stani, s.a.i.c.; Wilmington Trust v Q Capital; Great Northern Nekoosa v Georgia-Pacific; In re IPO Allocation Litigation; In re Beverly Hills Supperclub Fire Litigation; Orthofix S.r.l., et al. v EBI Medical Systems, Inc.; In re: Pay 'N Pak: The Official Unsecured Creditors Committee v Court Square Capital, Ltd.; Alesayi Beverage Corporation v Canada Dry Corporation; Arthur D Little v Ernst & Young.
**Career:** Mayer, Brown, Rowe & Maw LLP, New York, 1997 to date; Partner, 1997. Shearman & Sterling, 1978-97; Partner, 1986.
**Publications:** Several articles on securities and commercial litigation.
**Personal:** JD, St John's University (editor of law review), 1978. BA, Boston College, 1975. Nation's Top Ten Trial Lawyers 1997 (National Law Journal). 'Who's Who in American Law'. 'Best Lawyers in America'. Faculty member in ABA 'Business Litigation' video series, Practising Law Institute and the National Institute of Trial Advocacy. Faculty member in numerous seminars and programs sponsored by the Practising Law Institute on trial practice and procedures and negotiation techniques.

## ORTNER, Charles B
Proskauer Rose LLP, New York 212 969 3990
cortner@proskauer.com
*Recommended in Media & Entertainment*

**Practice Areas:** Represents many of the leading institutions and creative and business leaders of the music industry in virtually every area, including copyright,

trademark, enforcement of personal services contracts, rights of privacy and publicity, libel, unfair competition, personal matters, employment disputes, contract and royalty disputes and general corporate and commercial matters. He also serves as advisor on business and strategic planning for owners and senior executives of leading music industry institutions. Among the recording artists, record producers and songwriters he has represented in litigation and related matters are Madonna, Michael Jackson, Shania Twain, Lauryn Hill, Whitney Houston, Jon Bon Jovi, Kenny 'Babyface' Edmonds, Sean 'P Diddy' Combs, Trent Reznor and Nine Inch Nails, Sting, Cyndi Lauper, Collective Soul, Bonnie Raitt, Matchbox 20, Rob Thomas, Phil Ramone and Rick Rubin. Among the music industry entrepreneurs Mr Ortner has represented are Chris Blackwell, Clive Calder, Jimmy Iovine, and Antonio 'L.A.' Reid. He represents many music companies and labels, including Sony BMG, EMI and Wind-up Records.
**Career:** He also represents The National Academy of Recording Arts and Sciences (the GRAMMY® organization), and serves as its National Legal Counsel.
**Personal:** Brooklyn Law School, JD, 1971. Washington University, AB, 1967.

## OSTERMAN, Jeffrey D
Weil, Gotshal & Manges LLP, New York 212 310 8155
jeffrey.osterman@weil.com
*Recommended in Technology*

**Practice Areas:** Jeffrey D Osterman is a Partner in Weil Gotshal's Litigation/Regulatory Department and concentrates in the area of intellectual property, with a particular focus on complex transactions. He has extensive experience with technology development and licensing agreements, professional services agreements, life sciences agreements and outsourcing arrangements (such as the landmark services agreement between General Electric Company and its formerly captive offshore outsourcing business, Genpact). He also led a variety of intellectual property matters on behalf of Vivendi in the merger between Vivendi Universal Entertainment and NBC.
**Personal:** Cornell University, BA, 1992; Harvard Law School, JD, 1995.

## OSTRAGER, Barry R
Simpson Thacher & Bartlett LLP, New York 212 455 2655
bostrager@stblaw.com
*Recommended in Insurance, Litigation*

**Practice Areas:** Barry R Ostrager is a senior litigation Partner and Co-Head of the Litigation Department. He has tried dozens of cases and argued scores of appeals throughout the country and has been prominently involved in many high-profile cases. He successfully represented Travelers in a $5 billion arbitration with ACandS, J.P. Morgan Chase in a breach of guarantee contract action against Motorola in which JPMorgan Chase obtained a $370 million verdict against Motorola, and Andersen Consulting against a $14 billion claim by Arthur Andersen in connection with Andersen Consulting's successful bid to win a separation without cost from the Andersen Worldwide organization in the largest ICC arbitration in history. He was lead trial counsel for Swiss Re in the highly publicized insurance coverage dispute involving the World Trade Center tragedy, which resulted in a unanimous jury verdict in favor of Swiss Re.

**Prof. Memberships:** Association of the Bar of the City of New York, American Bar Association, American Law Institute. **Career:** Member of the firm since 1979. He is a Member of the firm's Executive Committee.

**Publications:** Co-author: 'Handbook on Insurance Coverage Disputes' (Aspen Publications, 13th ed 2006); co-author: 'Modern Reinsurance Law and Practice' (Glasser Publications, 2nd Ed, 2000). **Personal:** BA (1968) and MA (1973), City College of the City University of New York. JD (1972) New York University School of Law.

### PAGEL SEREBRANSKY, Elizabeth
Debevoise & Plimpton LLP, New York
212 909 6000
*Recommended in Employee Benefits*

### PAGET, David
Sive Paget & Riesel PC, New York
212 421 2150
dpaget@sprlaw.com
*Recommended in Environment*

**Practice Areas:** David Paget is a 1964 honors graduate of New York University Law School and editor of the Law Review. He has extensive experience in environmental law and related litigation, particularly in preparing and processing environmental impact statements and permits pursuant to the Clear Air Act, the Clean Water Act, the National Environmental Policy Act, and the Natural Historic Preservation Act. David began litigating environmental cases in the early 1970s, following his service as an Assistant United States Attorney for the Southern District of New York.

**Career:** Among the many projects for which David has been a central participant in the preparation of environmental impact statements and in obtaining related permits and approvals, and for which he has successfully defended legal challenges, are: the Hudson River Park, the expansion of the United States Tennis Association facilities in New York City; major residential and mixed use developments, including Battery Park City, Donald Trump's Riverside South, the Davids Island project, and the Tuxedo Reserve project. Currently, he is working on the

expansion of the Javits Convention Center, the Brooklyn Bridge Park, the Tappan Zee Bridge replacement, the New York Yankees and the Forest City Arena project.

### PALEY, Alan
Debevoise & Plimpton LLP, New York
212 909 6000
*Recommended in Capital Markets, Corporate/M&A*

### PANOVKA, Robin
Wachtell, Lipton, Rosen & Katz, New York 212 403 1352
rpanovka@wlrk.com
*Recommended in Real Estate*

**Practice Areas:** Specializes in mergers and acquisitions, strategic transactions and corporate governance principally in the real estate, REIT and hospitality industries. Active in a wide variety of M&A transactions (both negotiated and contested), restructurings, divestitures, buyouts and other transactions involving both publicly traded and privately held companies, the formation and investment activity of private equity real estate opportunity funds, and strategic joint ventures, acquisitions, dispositions and development of significant properties and portfolios, both in the United States and in cross-border transactions. Examples of recent or ongoing representations include advising the Silverstein Properties group in the redevelopment of the World Trade Center; representation of a Morgan Stanley/Onex venture in the pending acquisition of the Town & Country REIT; representation of Taubman Centers, Inc. in connection with Simon Property Group's unsolicited offer and Taubman UPREIT's prior restructuring; representation of Public Storage in its proposed acquisition of the Shurgard REIT; representation of Lend Lease in the sale of its US businesses; representation of Hometown in the acquisition of the Chateau REIT; and representation of Apollo Real Estate Advisors in connection with the formation and structuring of its opportunity funds.

**Prof. Memberships:** Co-Chair, Advisory Board, The REIT Center of New York University; Member of the Board of Visitors, Duke University School of Law; Member, Advisory Board, New York University Real Estate Institute; Member, Board of Directors, Harlem Educational Activities Fund; Member of the State Bar of Georgia, New York State and American Bar Associations.

**Career:** Partner at Wachtell, Lipton, Rosen & Katz.

**Publications:** Author or Co-author, 'REIT Takeovers and Governance', Real Estate Securities Weekly, December 1, 2003; 'Taking REITs Private: A Potential Win-Win for all Parties', Real Estate Securities Daily, December 2, 2003; 'Criticism of REITs goes too far - Selling Out or

Merging Isn't Always Best for Shareholders', 'Real Estate Issues', Winter 2000/01; 'Taking REITs Private', 'Real Estate Issues', Summer 2000; and 'Public Real Estate Companies Advantages Will Overpower the REIT Bear Market', 'Real Estate Issues', Winter 1999. Co-author, 'REIT M&A Transactions - Peculiarities and Complications', 'The Business Lawyer', February 2000; 'REITs and Rights Plans', 'Property', Winter 2000; 'The 'UP' Factor in UPREIT Change of Control Transactions', 'The REIT Report', Spring 1998; 'REIT Takeovers — Novel Issues Raised by Excess Share Provisions and UPREIT Structures', 'The M&A Lawyer', October 1997; 'Will REIT Takeovers Take Off?', 'CPN's Real Estate Financial Review', Summer 1997; 'REIT Mergers and Acquisitions and Takeover Preparedness: Poison Pills and Excess Shares', 'The REIT Report', Autumn 1995; and 'REIT Mergers and Acquisitions: Structuring Transactions, Protecting Deals and Responding to Unsolicited Offers', 'The REIT Report', Spring 1996; senior editor, Alaska Law Review 1984-86; Member, Duke Moot Court Board, 1984-86.

**Personal:** Graduated cum laude from Cornell University (Bachelor's Degree) and with honors from Duke University (JD).

### PANTALEO, Peter
Simpson Thacher & Bartlett LLP, New York 212 455 2000
ppantaleo@stblaw.com
*Recommended in Bankruptcy*

**Practice Areas:** Partner at Simpson Thacher & Bartlett LLP specialising in bankruptcy and restructuring. Has been lead lawyer on behalf of bank syndicates and other major investors in some of the largest most complex bankruptcies, including NRG Energy, Inc., Adelphia Communications Inc., Sunbeam, Inc., Dade Behring, Inc., LTV Corporation, Lomas Financial Corporation, Mariner Health Group, Burlington Industries, Acterna Communications, RCN Communications Inc., New World Pasta, Inc., Calpine Corporation and in and out of court workouts in a variety of industries, including telecommunications, energy, textile and retail. Clients include most major financial institutions in the restructuring community, including JP Morgan Chase, Deutsche Bank, Wachovia Securities, Credit Suiss First Boston and ABN Amro.

**Career:** Joined Simpson Thacher as a Partner in October, 2001. Formerly a member of O'Melveny & Myers LLP.

**Publications:** Recent articles include 'Unexpired Real and Personal Property Leases in Bankruptcy', Practising Law Institute (2001); 'Reorganization Value', The Business Lawyer, Vol. 51, No.2 (1996); 'Rethinking the Role of Recourse in the Sale of Financial Assets', The Business Lawyer, Vol. 52, No.1 (1996). Guest

lecturer on Bankruptcy Topics at Duke Law School and Cornell Business School. **Personal:** BA, Columbia College, 1978; JD, NYU School of Law, 1982.

### PAPA, Ronald
Proskauer Rose LLP, New York
212 969 3325
rpapa@proskauer.com
*Recommended in Corporate/M&A*

**Practice Areas:** He is Co-Chair of Proskauer's Corporate Department and a member of its Mergers and Acquisitions Group. He is a former Member of the firm's Executive Committee. His practice is concentrated on domestic and international transactions, mergers and acquisitions, securities offerings, joint ventures and other business combinations. For a diverse range of French and other foreign and domestic and public and private clients, he handles various transactions, including acquisitions and divestitures, public and private offerings of debt and equity, as well as matters ranging from licensing to supply, distribution, guest-host and other commercial agreements. **Career:** He clerked for Hon Stewart Pollock of the Supreme Court of New Jersey (1979-80), and joined Proskauer in 1987. **Personal:** He holds Degrees in mathematics and physics from Rensselaer Polytechnic Institute. He is a cum laude graduate of Cornell Law School.

### PARKER, C Allen
Cravath, Swaine & Moore LLP, New York
212 474 1765
aparker@cravath.com
*Recommended in Banking & Finance*

**Practice Areas:** Extensive experience in syndicated loan transactions, primarily in the context of acquisition financings and leveraged recapitalizations. Has served as the firm's Managing Partner, Corporate. **Prof. Memberships:** NYSBA; ABCNY. Clerkship: Hon Amalya Kearse (US Court of Appeals for the Second Circuit). **Career:** Partner since 1990. **Personal:** Columbia Law School (JD, magna cum laude, 1983); University of Chicago (MA, 1980); Duke University (BA, magna cum laude, 1977).

### PARKHURST, Janet
Milbank, Tweed, Hadley & McCloy LLP, New York 212 530 5000
*Recommended in Technology*

### PASSANNANTE, William
Anderson Kill & Olick P.C., New York
212 278 1000
*Recommended in Insurance*

### PATRICK, Michael
Fragomen, Del Rey, Bernsen & Loewy, LLP, New York 212 688 8555
*Recommended in Immigration*

## PAUL, Deborah L

Wachtell, Lipton, Rosen & Katz, New York 212 403 1300
dlpaul@wlrk.com
*Recommended in Tax*

**Practice Areas:** Specializes in the tax aspects of corporate transactions, including mergers and acquisitions, joint ventures, spin-offs and financial instruments; has been the principal tax lawyer on numerous domestic and cross-border transactions in a wide array of industries, including telecommunications, oil and gas, food, defense and energy.
**Prof. Memberships:** Active Member of the Executive Committee of the Tax Section of the New York State Bar Association (principal co-author of 2005 Circular 230 report and principal author of 2004 continuity of proprietary interest reports).
**Career:** Partner at Wachtell, Lipton, Rosen & Katz since 2001. Prior to joining the firm in 1997, was an Assistant Professor at the Benjamin N Cardozo School of Law (1995-97) and an Acting Assistant Professor at New York University School of Law (1994-95). Clerked for Chancellor William T Allen of the Court of Chancery of the State of Delaware (1989-90).
**Publications:** 'The Use of Disregarded Entities and Pass-Throughs in Corporate Transactions' (with Richard Gipstein) (in USC 56th Institute on Federal Taxation 2004); 'Tax-Free M&A Transactions' (with Lewis Steinberg) (in NYU 62nd Institute on Federal Taxation 2004); 'Triple Taxation' (in The Tax Lawyer 2003); 'Contingency and the Debt/Equity Continuum' (with Peter Canellos) (in the Journal of Taxation of Financial Products 2002); 'United Dominion: Implications for Attribute Reduction' (in Tax Notes 2002); 'The Sources of Tax Complexity: How Much Simplicity Can Fundamental Tax Reform Achieve?' (in the North Carolina Law Review 1997).
**Personal:** Graduated from Harvard University in 1986 (AB), from Harvard Law School in 1989 (JD) and from New York University School of Law in 1994 (LLM in taxation).

## PAUL, Marcia

Davis Wright Tremaine LLP, New York 212 489 8230
*Recommended in Media & Entertainment*

## PEARLSTEIN, Debra J

Weil, Gotshal & Manges LLP, New York 212 310 8686
debra.pearlstein@weil.com
*Recommended in Antitrust*

**Practice Areas:** Debra Pearlstein specializes in antitrust litigation and counseling and has extensive experience in complex private antitrust litigation, lawsuits brought by the federal antitrust agencies and merger investigations. Ms Pearlstein's counseling practice covers joint ventures and other collaborations with competitors, trade associations, Hart-Scott-Rodino regulations, gun jumping concerns, relations with distributors and customers and the antitrust aspects of patent licensing. Understanding her clients' business needs and making practical assessments of litigation and enforcement risks are key strengths of Ms Pearlstein's practice.
**Personal:** Williams College, BA, 1981; New York University School of Law, JD, 1985; Princeton University, MPAFF, 1985.

## PEARSON, Nick

Edwards Angell Palmer & Dodge LLP, New York 212 912 2798
npearson@eapdlaw.com
*Recommended in Insurance*

**Practice Areas:** Nick Pearson is a Partner in the firm's Insurance and Reinsurance Department. He represents US and foreign insurers, reinsurers and producers and has served as outside General Counsel to admitted and nonadmitted insurers. He has broad insurance regulatory and transactional experience and has successfully represented cedents and reinsurers before industry arbitration panels.
**Prof. Memberships:** Trustee - Insurance Federation of New York, Business Council for the United Nations.
**Publications:** Nick has authored numerous articles on insurance law and has lectured and moderated many national conferences.
**Personal:** Duke University, BA, 1976; Duke University School of Law, JD 1973.

## PEASLEE, James M

Cleary Gottlieb Steen & Hamilton LLP, New York 212 225 2440
jpeaslee@cgsh.com
*Recommended in Tax*

**Practice Areas:** US tax matters, with an emphasis on financial products and structured finance.
**Prof. Memberships:** Member of the Executive Committee of the New York State Bar Association's Tax Section and Chair of the Tax Section from 1991-92.
**Career:** Joined firm, 1976; became Partner, 1984. LLM, New York University School of Law (1979); JD, cum laude, Harvard Law School (1976); MA, BA economics, magna cum laude, Yale University (1973).
**Publications:** Co-author of 'Federal Income Taxation of Securitization Transactions' (third edition - www.securitizationtax.com) and author of many articles on tax subjects.

## PECKAR, Robert S

Peckar & Abramson PC, New York 212 382 0909
rpeckar@pecklaw.com
*Recommended in Construction*

**Practice Areas:** Is a recognized Leader among the Construction Bar. While he has obtained very substantial recoveries in litigation and arbitration, he has gained recognition for formulating creative, multimillion dollar settlements in the litigation of complex multiparty construction disputes and the implementation of alternative dispute resolution mechanisms to achieve expeditious solutions to complicated construction disputes. Is one of the nation's leading advocates for the appropriate use of Alternative Dispute Resolution (ADR) procedures and serves as an arbitrator in complex international arbitrations.
**Prof. Memberships:** Is a Fellow of the American College of Construction Lawyers; Member of the New Jersey State Bar Association (Chairman, Public Contract Law Section, 1979-81; Chairman, Effective Dispute Resolution Committee, 1990-91; Member, New Jersey Supreme Court Committee on Dispute Resolution, 1991-95) as well as a Member of the American Bar Association (New Jersey State Chairman, Section on Public Contract Law, Litigation Section, 1979-83; Region II Chairman 1984-88). Admitted to practice in New York and New Jersey.
**Career:** Founding Partner. Serves as General Counsel Emeritus to the New York Building Congress, where he was general counsel for over 15 years. He also serves as General Counsel to the Building Contractors Association of New Jersey, the New York City Building Trades Employers Association and the National Construction Financial Management Association (CFMA).
**Publications:** Throughout his career in construction law, has participated as a guest lecturer to local and national construction industry groups as well as in continuing legal education programs and has otherwise devoted substantial time and effort in service to the construction industry. An author of many articles on construction law topics, he is also a contributing author in several construction law textbooks and the author of 'New Jersey Practice: Construction Law'.
**Personal:** Is a graduate of Rutgers University in New Jersey and Columbia University Law School in New York.

## PEDOWITZ, Lawrence B

Wachtell, Lipton, Rosen & Katz, New York 212 403 1231
lbpedowitz@wlrk.com
*Recommended in Litigation*

**Practice Areas:** Specializes in corporate litigation, regulatory and white-collar criminal matters.
**Prof. Memberships:** Has served on several committees of the Association of the Bar of the City of New York, including: the Criminal Law, Federal Legislation and Federal Courts Committees. In addition, is a Vice Chairman and Director of the Legal Aid Society, a Director and Executive Committee Member of the Brennan Center at New York University Law School, and a co-founder of New York Law Firms for the Homeless, which is the financial support organization for the New York Coalition for the Homeless.
**Career:** Partner at Wachtell, Lipton, Rosen & Katz for over 20 years. Prior to joining the firm, had significant experience as law clerk to Second Circuit Court of Appeals Chief Judge Henry J Friendly (1972-73) and to United States Supreme Court Justice William J Brennan (1973-74). Also served as Chief Appellate Attorney (1976-78) and Chief of the Criminal Division (1982-84) in the United States Attorney's Office for the Southern District of New York.
**Publications:** Has lectured for numerous continuing education programs, including programs sponsored by the American Bar Association, New York Law Journal, Practicing Law Institute, Federal Bar Council, Securities Industry Association and Hofstra Trial Advocacy Program. Has also taught Trial Practice at New York University Law School.
**Personal:** Graduated summa cum laude from Union College in 1969 (BA) and from New York University Law School in 1972 (JD), where he served as Editor-in-Chief of the Law Review and was a Root-Tilden Scholar for the Second Circuit.

## PENZER, Michèle

Latham & Watkins LLP, New York 212 906 1200
*Recommended in Banking & Finance, Projects*

## PFEFFER, David J

Arent Fox PLLC, New York 212 484 3948
pfeffer.david@arentfox.com
*Recommended in Construction*

**Practice Areas:** Serves the construction industry in the private, public and non-profit sectors. Represents owners, design professionals and developers in matters ranging from project planning and contract preparation to dispute resolution. Also concentrates his practice in contract law and commercial litigation. Prosecutes and defends construction and real estate related disputes, including design errors, mold and water infiltration claims, building failures, delay, acceleration and consequential damage claims, surety bond claims, insurance coverage disputes, lien and trust fund issues, bid protests, lease and ownership disputes and copyright claims.
**Personal:** Hofstra University School of Law, JD; John Jay College of Criminal Justice, BS.

## PHILLIPS, Greer L

Kirkland & Ellis LLP, New York 212 446 4955
gphillips@kirkland.com
*Recommended in Tax*

**Practice Areas:** Mr Phillips plans and structures the tax aspects of complex domestic and cross-border transactions, including private and public mergers,

acquisitions and buyouts, spinoffs and spin-merge transactions, joint ventures, bankruptcy and workout transactions and financial instruments. He has structured a wide variety of domestic and cross-border acquisitions, spinoffs, joint ventures and recapitalizations, involving strategic and financial buyers, for European, Asian and Latin American clients and for United States clients in cross-border or other complex transactions.
**Personal:** Princeton University, AB, 1979. Harvard Law School, JD, 1982.

## PHILLIPS IV, Barnet
Skadden, Arps, Slate, Meagher & Flom LLP & Affiliates, New York
212 735 2220
bphillip@skadden.com
*Recommended in Tax*
**Practice Areas:** Specialises in tax aspects of corporate mergers, acquisitions, divestitures, leveraged buyouts, restructuring and recapitalisations and the structuring of business organisations and investment vehicles, including REITs, Regulated Investment Companies, investment partnerships and exchange funds.
**Career:** LLM, New York University, 1977 (graduate editor, Tax Law Review); JD, Fordham Law School, 1973 (associate editor, Fordham Law Review); BA, Yale University 1970.
**Publications:** Co-author, 'Structuring Corporate Acquisitions-Tax Aspects', Tax Management Inc., (2005).

## PIERCE, Kenneth R
Cadwalader, Wickersham & Taft LLP, New York 212 504 6813
kpierce@cwt.com
*Recommended in Insurance*
**Practice Areas:** Concentrates in dispute resolution and transactions in the insurance and reinsurance area. Has handled all facets of large reinsurance cases for insurers and reinsurers, including property and casualty, surety, finite, life and annuity matters. Has substantial experience in regulatory investigations of finite and financial reinsurance. Experienced in capital markets and corporate finance, uses transactional, regulatory, and litigation skills to serve the legal needs of reinsurers, banks, investment banks, hedge funds, and private equity funds facing issues connected with risk transfer and reinsurance. Advises, negotiates and structures complex reinsurance transactions, including life, annuity and property catastrophe transactions, advises on regulatory matters, including life settlements, premium finance, and other insurance/capital markets products, and evaluates portfolios of insurance and reinsurance receivables.
**Personal:** JD, Harvard Law School; AB, Brown University (magna cum laude), Phi Beta Kappa. Clerk, United States District Court Judge Sidney M Aronovitz of the Southern District of Florida; former

Senior Vice President, Lehman Brothers Inc., Insurance Products Group; former Executive Claim Officer, Lehman Re Ltd.

## PIERCE, Morton A
Dewey Ballantine LLP, New York
212 259 6640
mpierce@deweyballantine.com
*Recommended in Corporate/M&A*
**Practice Areas:** Morton Pierce is Chairman of the firm's Management and Executive Committees and Chairman of the Mergers and Acquisitions Group since 1991. The group consists of more than 60 lawyers based in New York, Washington DC, Los Angeles, East Palo Alto, Houston, Austin, London, Frankfurt, Milan, Rome and Central Europe. He has participated in numerous merger and acquisition matters and related financings. He has represented acquirers, targets, investment bankers and investors in numerous acquisitions, including the Omnicare acquisition of NCS Healthcare, the Fortis acquisition of American Bankers, the Starwood acquisition of ITT, The Walt Disney Company acquisition of Capital Cities/ABC, the Wells Fargo acquisition of First Interstate Bank and the HCA acquisition of Healthtrust. Mr Pierce also has extensive experience in cross-border merger and acquisition transactions. These include the Zimmer Holdings acquisition of Centerpulse AG, the Burns Philp acquisition of Goodman Fielder, the Guinness/GrandMet merger, the Luxottica Group S.p.A. acquisition of The United States Shoe Corporation, the Eridania Beghin-Say S.A. acquisition of American Maize-Products Company and the Cable & Wireless acquisition of NYNEX CableComms.
**Prof. Memberships:** American Bar Association; Association of the Bar of the City of New York.
**Career:** Partner, Dewey Ballantine since 1986.
**Personal:** Born June 25, 1948. Oxford University, 1974-75; JD, University of Pennsylvania Law School, 1974; BA, Yale University, 1970.

## PIETRZAK, Robert
Sidley Austin LLP, New York
212 839 5537
rpietrzak@sidley.com
*Recommended in Litigation*
**Practice Areas:** Partner and Co-Head of the Litigation Group in the New York office, a Member of the firm's Executive Committee, as well as Co-Head of the firm's Office of General Counsel and Committee on Professional Responsibility. His practice primarily involves the litigation in US courts of commercial and governmental disputes for domestic and overseas financial institutions, including the defense of securities class actions and large contract actions. He has been counsel in regulatory proceedings and civil actions involving bonds, public offerings,

investment companies, antitrust claims and other major commercial and governmental disputes. He has represented defendants in some of the largest litigations in the US.
**Prof. Memberships:** American Bar Association; American Law Institute; Association of the Bar of the City of New York; Securities Regulation Committee; Futures Regulation Committee; Fordham International Law Journal, Editorial Advisory Board; Futures Industry Association; The Bond Market Association; Securities Industry Association.
**Publications:** 'Securities Litigation', in Commercial Litigation in New York State Courts; 'Standard Form Agreements in the Securities Field', published in The Review of Securities & Commodities Regulation (with A Stern).
**Personal:** Columbia Law School (JD, 1974); Fordham University (BA, 1971). Admission: New York, 1975.

## PINOVER, Eugene
Willkie Farr & Gallagher LLP, New York
212 728 8254
epinover@willkie.com
*Recommended in Real Estate*
**Practice Areas:** Partner and Chair of the Real Estate Department, specializing in representing domestic and foreign real estate developers and institutional clients in acquisitions, sales, restructuring and sophisticated financings and development projects throughout the United States. Practice also includes representing public real investment trusts, underwriters and investors in equity offerings and debt securitizations. In 2005, he represented New Plan Excel Realty Trust in the $968 million sale of 69 community and neighborhood shopping centers to Galileo America LLC; Westfield Realty Inc. Properties in the $1 billion sale of a 12-building property portfolio to Beacon Capital Partners; and Lyme Properties in the $531 million sale of its portfolio of life science/biomed properties to BioMed Realty Trust Inc. He also recently represented Simon Property Group in its $3.5 billion acquisition of Chelsea Property Group.
**Prof. Memberships:** Member of the Real Estate Advisory Board of Dartmouth College and Associate Member of the Association of Foreign Investors in Real Estate (AFIRE). Member of the Association of the Bar of the City of New York, the American Bar Association, the International Council of Shopping Centers, and the New York Advisory Board of Chicago Title Insurance Company. Serves as a Director of Trinity School, Cardigan Mountain School, Ballet Hispanico and was elected Fellow of the American College of Real Estate Lawyers.
**Career:** Admitted to the Bar of the State of New York.
**Publications:** Writings have been published extensively in the New York Law

Journal, the Real Estate Finance Journal, and AFIRE News.
**Personal:** Received a JD (cum laude) from New York University School of Law in 1973 and a BA (cum laude) from Dartmouth College in 1969.

## PLATT, Charles C
WilmerHale, New York
212 230 8860
charles.platt@wilmerhale.com
*Recommended in Litigation*
**Practice Areas:** Leading commercial litigator, recognized nationally for defense work in class action matters for large financial services institutions and insurance companies.
**Prof. Memberships:** 1992, appointed Special Assistant United States Attorney for the Banco Nazionale Del Lavoro ('Iraqgate') Investigation by the US Department of Justice. Current Member Board of Trustees of the Federal Bar Council and Board of Trustees of Saint David's School in New York; Board of Trustees of the Brooklyn Law School from 1986 to 1988. Admitted to practice in New York and United States Supreme Court.
**Personal:** JD, Brooklyn Law School, 1979; BA, University of Virginia, 1975.

## PLAUT, Christopher
Latham & Watkins LLP, New York
212 906 1200
*Recommended in Banking & Finance*

## PLEVAN, Bettina
Proskauer Rose LLP, New York
212 969 3065
bplevan@proskauer.com
*Recommended in Employment*
**Practice Areas:** Represents a wide range of industries handling both single plaintiff and class action lawsuits involving issues of discrimination, harassment, wage and hour and benefits. She has extensive experience counseling employers on litigation avoidance and investigations. Has successfully tried many jury and non-jury cases in New York and elsewhere in the US.
**Prof. Memberships:** President of the New York City Bar. Former President of the Federal Bar Council. Member of the American Law Institute. Former Chair of the Second Circuit Judicial Conference.
**Career:** Fellow of the American College of Trial Lawyers. Has argued more than 50 appeals in state and federal courts and is a Member of the American Academy of Appellate Lawyers. Member of the College of Labor and Employment Lawyers.
**Publications:** Named by New York Magazine as one of the '100 Best Lawyers in New York' and by the National Law Journal as one of the best Labor and Employment Lawyers in the country. Writes and lectures frequently on litigation and employment law issues.
**Personal:** Graduated from Wellesley College and is a magna cum laude gradu-

ate of Boston University Law School where she was an editor of the Law Review.

## PLEVAN, Kenneth A
Skadden, Arps, Slate, Meagher & Flom LLP & Affiliates, New York
212 735 3410
kplevan@skadden.com
*Recommended in Media & Entertainment*
**Practice Areas:** Co-Head of Skadden's Intellectual Property and Technology Group. Has practiced in the area for more than 20 years. His principal areas of concentration include counseling and litigation involving advertising substantiation, trademark infringement, dilution, copyright infringement, domain name disputes and intellectual property licensing, and e-commerce issues.
**Career:** JD, Harvard Law School, 1969 (cum laude); BA, Harvard College, 1966 (cum laude); Member, Federal Bar Council (1983-present).

## PLUM, Bernard
Proskauer Rose LLP, New York
212 969 3070
bplum@proskauer.com
*Recommended in Employment*
**Practice Areas:** Co-Chair Proskauer Labor and Employment Department, concentrates on collective bargaining, arbitration, and labor litigation in newspaper, entertainment, theater and utilities industries. Chief spokesperson in many collective bargaining situations, and litigates in state and federal courts.
**Career:** Represents New York Times Co, Dow Jones, American Lawyer, League of American Theaters & Producers, New York City Ballet, Nederlander and PPL. Represented Metro-North and LIRR in precedent-setting suit to enjoin sympathy strikes and many other employers faced with work stoppages.
**Personal:** Columbia Law, JD, 1979; notes editor, Columbia Law Review; Columbia University, MPHIL, 1976; MA, 1974; NYU, BA, cum laude, 1973.

## POLEVOY, Martin D
DLA Piper Rudnick Gray Cary US LLP, New York 212 835 6100
martin.polevoy@dlapiper.com
*Recommended in Real Estate*
**Practice Areas:** Real estate; acquisitions, development, leasing, financing, joint ventures.
**Career:** Practice includes representation of well known New York, national and international owners, developers, investors, and institutions. Currently acting as counsel in many high profile transactions, including redevelopment of the World Trade Center site in New York. A frequent participant as Program Chair and speaker in continuing legal education programs and has written extensively on various aspects of real estate law. He is a past Governor of the American College of

Real Estate Lawyers and member of the Anglo-American Real Property Institute.
**Personal:** LLB, University of Pennsylvania; AB, Colgate University.

## POLKES, Jonathan
Weil, Gotshal & Manges LLP, New York
212 310 8881
jonathan.polkes@weil.com
*Recommended in Litigation*
**Practice Areas:** Jonathan Polkes is a former federal prosecutor who has conducted over 25 jury trials and argued 12 times before the US Court of Appeals. He handles regulatory, criminal and civil matters for clients in the financial services industry. He has represented prominent institutional clients and executives in virtually every major legal event to have affected Wall Street in recent memory, including: market timing and late trading investigations, IPO laddering cases, allegations of conflicts of interest between investment banking and research departments, and the Enron bankruptcy.
**Personal:** Haverford College, BA, 1981; New York University School of Law, JD, 1984.

## POLLACK, Martin
Weil, Gotshal & Manges LLP, New York
212 310 8461
martin.pollack@weil.com
*Recommended in Tax*
**Practice Areas:** Martin Pollack is Co-Head of Weil Gotshal's Global Tax Department and advises his clients on the tax aspects of private equity and M&A transactions, the formation and operation of private equity funds and other ventures, bankruptcy and insolvency, leasing transactions and technology intensive enterprises. He lectures at tax seminars, chairs an American Bar Association Tax Section subcommittee and is a co-author of a treatise on tax considerations pertaining to partnership buy/sell agreements.
**Personal:** Johns Hopkins University, BA, 1973; Johns Hopkins University, MA, 1973; University of Pennsylvania Law School, JD, 1976; New York University School of Law, LLM, 1979.

## POMERANTZ, Mark F
Paul, Weiss, Rifkind, Wharton & Garrison LLP, New York
212 373 3010
mpomerantz@paulweiss.com
*Recommended in Litigation*
**Practice Areas:** Partner in the Litigation Department. Nationally known trial lawyer and senior litigator with extensive public and private experience in criminal and regulatory matters. Has represented prominent corporations and individuals with regard to many sensitive and high-profile matters. Has represented some of the largest companies in the US in investigations undertaken by the US Department of Justice, the Securities and Exchange Commission, and various state

and local prosecutors. Has substantial appellate experience, arguing dozens of appeals before courts throughout the country. Fellow of the American College of Trial Lawyers. Selected for 2006 edition of 'The Best Lawyers in America'.

## PONIKVAR, Dale L
Milbank, Tweed, Hadley & McCloy LLP, New York 212 530 5000
*Recommended in Tax*

## PORT, Gail
Proskauer Rose LLP, New York
212 969 3243
gport@proskauer.com
*Recommended in Environment*
**Practice Areas:** Heads the interdepartmental national and international Proskauer Rose LLP Environmental Practice Group, based in the New York office. She has been practicing environmental law, land use and environmental litigation for 30 years. Her practice at Proskauer is extremely diverse, covering most aspects of environmental law and is concentrated in counseling clients in mergers and acquisitions and real estate transactions and financings, environmental compliance under federal and state environmental programs and remediation, including several high-visibility brownfield remediation projects. She also handles environmetal issues in land use and redevelopment projects and environmental litigation and administrative proceedings, including complex Superfund cases.
**Prof. Memberships:** A past Chair of the New York State Bar Association's Environmental Law Section, the former Chair of the Environmental Law Committee of the Association of the Bar of the City of New York, and a Member of the Boards of Directors of the prestigious not-for-profit organizations Environmental Advocates and the New York League of Conservation Voters Education Fund. She is also a citizen member of the New York State Environmental Board, having been appointed by Governor Cuomo in 1992 and reappointed twice by Governor Pataki.
**Career:** Prior to joining the firm she served as Deputy General Counsel (and Acting General Counsel) and the chief environmental advisor to the New York State Urban Development Corporation, where she was involved in the environmental law aspects of high visibility large-scale land use and development projects and related financing transactions. Before that, she practiced environmental law and litigation at a well respected NYC environmental boutique firm, handling the environmental aspects of large scale land use projects and cutting edge environmental litigations. She has written and lectured widely on diverse environmental topics and has taught law school environmental law courses. She is also

listed in 'The Best Lawyers of America' (2005-06 and 2006-07).
**Personal:** New York Law School, JD, magna cum laude, 1976 articles editor, New York Law School Law Review, 1974-76. State University of New York at Cortland, BS, 1973.

## PORTNOY, Lawrence
Davis Polk & Wardwell, New York
212 450 4000
lawrence.portnoy@dpw.com
*Recommended in Litigation*
**Practice Areas:** Member of Davis Polk & Wardwell's Litigation Department. Represents clients in a wide range of securities and commercial matters in federal and state courts and before regulatory agencies. Has also represented clients in NASD, New York Stock Exchange and American Arbitration Association arbitrations. Has represented investment banks and other financial institutions as well as industrial and manufacturing companies in class action litigations in federal district courts in New York, Massachusetts, New Jersey, Pennsylvania, Connecticut, Texas, California, Florida and the District of Columbia. Has also represented clients in state court matters in New York, Delaware, California and South Carolina and in SEC enforcement matters.

## POSEN, Richard
Willkie Farr & Gallagher LLP, New York
212 728 8255
rposen@willkie.com
*Recommended in Litigation*
**Practice Areas:** Partner in the Litigation Department and a Member of the firm's Executive Committee. Specializes in securities litigation and mergers and acquisitions. Has significant experience representing boards of directors on corporate governance issues and special committees in internal investigations. Recent significant matters include representation of Shurgard Storage Centers, Inc. in its $5 billion acquisition by Public Storage, Inc. He represented Lehman Brothers, Goldman Sachs, UBS and CSFB in the Worldcom securities litigation, and represents the independent directors of Merck. Representation of Morgan Stanley, MetLife and H&R Block in a variety of securities matters.
**Prof. Memberships:** Member of the Association of the Bar of the City of New York and the Federal Bar Council. Former Director of Ralphs Supermarkets and Ralphs Grocery Company (1992-94).
**Career:** Admitted to the New York State Bar; various district courts including the United States District Court for the Southern District of New York; the United States Courts of Appeal for the First, Second, Third, Fifth, Ninth, and Eleventh Circuits; and the United States Supreme Court. Currently serves as Mediator in the US District Court for the Southern

District of New York Mediation Program (since 1993).
**Personal:** Received a JD from New York University School of Law in 1975 and a BA from Johns Hopkins University in 1972.

### POSTNER, William
Schiff Hardin LLP, New York
212 753 5000
*Recommended in Construction*

### POTTER, Nicholas
Debevoise & Plimpton LLP, New York
212 909 6000
*Recommended in Insurance*

### PRICE, Scott D
Milbank, Tweed, Hadley & McCloy LLP, New York 212 530 5000
*Recommended in Employee Benefits*

### PRINCE, Kenneth S
Shearman & Sterling LLP, New York
212 848 4139
kprince@shearman.com
*Recommended in Antitrust*
**Practice Areas:** Practice Group Leader of Shearman & Sterling's Global Antitrust Group. Advises clients on the antitrust implications of mergers and acquisitions, joint ventures, horizontal arrangements among competitors, dominant firm conduct, intellectual property licensing agreements and pricing arrangements. Maintains an active criminal grand jury defense practice. Regularly appears before the United States Department of Justice and the Federal Trade Commission.
**Career:** Joined Shearman in 1975 and became Partner in 1983. Antitrust Practice Leader 1992-2003 and 2005-present.
**Personal:** AB, University of Pennsylvania (1972); JD, magna cum laude, Order of the Coif, Boston College Law School (1975); editor, Boston College Law Review.

### PRITCHARD, John F
Pillsbury Winthrop Shaw Pittman LLP, New York 212 858 1620
john.pritchard@pillsburylaw.com
*Recommended in Litigation*
**Practice Areas:** Department Leader, Pillsbury's Litigation & IP Department. Mr Pritchard has concentrated on representing domestic and foreign financial institutions in cases involving the federal securities laws and complex commercial disputes of all kinds. He has been particularly active in representing these institutions in investigations by the SEC and other financial regulators and has conducted numerous internal investigations for companies and their boards arising from regulatory or other allegations of wrongdoing by corporate officers and directors.
**Personal:** JD, University of California at Berkeley, Boalt Hall, 1968 (articles editor, California Law Review; Order of the Coif); BA, Yale College, 1965.

### PROFUSEK, Robert A
Jones Day, New York
212 326 3800
raprofusek@jonesday.com
*Recommended in Corporate/M&A*
**Practice Areas:** Co-chairs the firm's M&A Practice. He is an advisor to substantial businesses, focusing on M&A/takeovers, restructurings, and corporate governance matters, including compensation. He is a frequent speaker regarding corporate takeovers and corporate governance, has authored or co-authored numerous articles, and has testified before Congress and the SEC about takeover and compensation-related matters. Recognized globally as a leading M&A lawyer, he has been featured in numerous North American and European legal publications, including being selected in 2005 as Dealmaker of the Year by The American Lawyer for his representation of Nextel Communications in its merger of equals with Sprint.

### PROUNIS, Othon A
Ropes & Gray LLP, New York
212 841 5785
othon.prounis@ropesgray.com
*Recommended in Private Equity*
**Practice Areas:** Concentrates in mergers and acquisitions, securities and transactional work, primarily for private equity funds and their portfolio companies. Has extensive experience working in the healthcare, life sciences, and technology sectors, and has represented underwriters, issuers and investors in public and private securities offerings.
**Career:** New York Bar (1987); Partner, Ropes & Gray (2003); Co-Head, Private Equity Transactions Practice of Ropes & Gray.
**Personal:** JD, Columbia Law School (1986); AB, Columbia College (1983).

### PULTMAN, Jacob
Allen & Overy LLP, New York
212 610 6340
jacob.pultman@allenovery.com
*Recommended in Litigation*
**Practice Areas:** Broad-based general commercial litigation experience, representing leading investment and commercial banks, multinational corporations, insurance companies and individual directors and officers. He specializes in securities, product liability, insurance coverage, class action, corporate governance, internal investigations, regulatory and general commercial litigation.
**Career:** Joined Allen & Overy LLP in 2003 as senior counsel. Partner since 2005. Previously, he was at Simpson Thacher & Bartlett (1995-2003).
**Personal:** Yale Law School (JD, 1990); Brooklyn College (BA, summa cum laude, 1987).

### QUINN, James W
Weil, Gotshal & Manges LLP, New York
212 310 8385
james.quinn@weil.com
*Recommended in Litigation, Sport*
**Practice Areas:** James Quinn chairs Weil Gotshal's Global Litigation/Regulatory Department. He specializes in high-stakes commercial disputes, and practices in all areas of complex litigation and alternative dispute resolution, with emphasis on antitrust, products liability, insurance, entertainment, patent and intellectual property law. Mr Quinn has earned a reputation for his unmatched experience in sports and entertainment litigation, and is the most successful litigator of sports antitrust cases in the quarter-century that these cases have been played out in the national arena.
**Personal:** University of Notre Dame, AB, 1967; Fordham University, LLB, 1971.

### QUINN, Yvonne S
Sullivan & Cromwell LLP, New York
212 558 4000
quinny@sullcrom.com
*Recommended in Antitrust*
**Practice Areas:** Co-ordinator, Antitrust Practice. Handles a variety of antitrust and commercial litigations. Regular antitrust counsel in proposed acquisitions, such as Cerberus-Bayer blood plasma business, Medco-Accredo, John Hancock-Manulife and various acquisitions by Goldman Sachs, among others, and in litigations.
**Prof. Memberships:** ABA; ABCNY (former Chair, Antitrust and Trade Regulation Committee); Federal Bar Council; NYSBA (Executive Committee, Antitrust Section).
**Career:** Partner since 1984.
**Personal:** University of Illinois (BA, 1973); University of Michigan Law School (JD, 1976); University of Michigan (MA, economics, 1977).

### RAAB, David S
Latham & Watkins LLP, New York
212 906 1200
*Recommended in Tax*

### RABINOWITZ, Stephen S
Fried, Frank, Harris, Shriver & Jacobson LLP, New York 212 859 8973
Stephen.Rabinowitz@FriedFrank.com
*Recommended in Intellectual Property*
**Practice Areas:** Litigation Partner. Concentrates practice in field of patent litigation, with emphasis on the fields of medicine and biotechnology. Has litigated patent cases concerning recombinant DNA technology, nucleic acid amplification, biochemical reagents such as enzymes, medical diagnostics, pharmaceuticals, and dietary supplements. Intellectual property practice includes validity, infringement, patentability and freedom-to-operate opinions, patent prosecution, and portfolio management.
**Career:** Joined Fried Frank in 2004 as a

Partner.
**Personal:** JD(1994), cum laude, Harvard Law School. DPhil in Immunology (1990), University of Oxford. MB, ChB(1981) with honours, University of Cape Town.

### RACITI-KNAPP, Melissa
Freshfields Bruckhaus Deringer LLP, New York 212 277 4000
*Recommended in Projects*

### RADKE, Kirk
Kirkland & Ellis LLP, New York
212 446 4940
kradke@kirkland.com
*Recommended in Private Fund Formation*
**Practice Areas:** Concentrates on representing private equity sponsors in all aspects of private equity investment activity including leveraged acquisitions and recapitalisations, growth equity investments in public and private companies, start-up investments, and formation of private equity funds.
**Personal:** Stanford University, BA, 1980, Phi Beta Kappa awarded 1979. University of Virginia, JD/MBA, 1984, Editorial Board, Virginia Law Review; Order of the Coif; William Michael Shermet Award (MBA).

### RAFFERTY, Thomas G
Cravath, Swaine & Moore LLP, New York
212 474 1000
*Recommended in Intellectual Property*

### RAMOS, Carey R
Paul, Weiss, Rifkind, Wharton & Garrison LLP, New York 212 373 3240
cramos@paulweiss.com
*Recommended in Media & Entertainment*
**Practice Areas:** Partner in the Litigation Department. Co-Chair of the Communications and Technology Group and the Intellectual Property/Litigation Group. Has a broad practice that concentrates on intellectual property and technology litigation. Has represented prominent clients in widely publicized copyright, patent and trademark actions involving music, motion pictures, computer and internet technology, telecommunications, media and the fashion industry. Also has extensive experience in licensing and other transactions involving intellectual property rights in technology and entertainment media. Serves as outside general counsel to The DVD Forum, the international standards body for the DVD formats.

### RAPISARDI, John
Weil, Gotshal & Manges LLP, New York
212 310 8840
john.rapisardi@weil.com
*Recommended in Bankruptcy*
**Practice Areas:** John Rapisardi's business finance and restructuring practice entails the representation of debtors, creditors' and bondholders' committees,

secured creditors, financial institutions, investment bankers and distressed investment funds in restructurings and bankruptcy cases. He currently represents St Vincents Catholic Medical Centers in their Chapter 11 cases. He has been the bankruptcy columnist for the New York Law Journal for the last eight years.
**Personal:** Fordham University, BS, 1979; Pace University School of Law, JD, 1982; New York University School of Law, LLM, 1985.

### RAPPAPORT, Linda E
Shearman & Sterling LLP, New York
212 848 7004
lrappaport@shearman.com
*Recommended in Employee Benefits*
**Practice Areas:** Partner and Head of Shearman's Global Executive Compensation and Employee Benefits Group. Specializes in all aspects of executive compensation and benefits, including corporate, securities, employment and tax laws, and ERISA.
**Prof. Memberships:** Member, Shearman Executive Group; Advisory Director, New York Women's Foundation; Member, Advisory Committee, Practicing Law Institute; Fellow, American College of Employee Benefits Counsel, Inc.; Member, Board of Governors, Mannes College of Music; Member, Board of Directors, Legal Aid Society
**Career:** Joined Shearman in 1979 and became Partner in 1986.
**Personal:** BA, magna cum laude, Wesleyan University (1974); JD, New York University School of Law (1977).

### RASKIN, Kenneth A
White & Case LLP, New York
212 819 8508
kraskin@whitecase.com
*Recommended in Employee Benefits*
**Practice Areas:** Heads the firm's Executive Compensation, Benefits and Employment Law Practice; provides counsel to corporations and individuals on the entire spectrum of employee benefit concerns, concentrating on executive compensation and employment law.
**Prof. Memberships:** New York State Bar Association; American Bar Association.
**Publications:** Author of numerous articles and frequent lecturer on executive compensation and benefits-related topics.
**Personal:** JD, St John's University School of Law; MBA, SUNY Binghamton; BA, University of Vermont.

### RASKOPF, Robert
Quinn Emanuel Urquhart Oliver & Hedges, LLP, New York
212 702 8100
robertraskopf@quinnemanuel.com
*Recommended in Media & Entertainment*
**Practice Areas:** An experienced trial lawyer across many subject areas, his regular clients include media, sports, enter-

tainment and consumer products companies. His practice combines the complete range of IP and media subject areas, and includes long time representation of sports giants such as NFL and ESPN. He also represents AIG, retail giant Wal-Mart and consumer product giant Coca-Cola among many others. He has an extensive libel/First Amendment and privacy practice. Raskopf is an experienced trial and appellate lawyer and has been lead counsel of record in over 60 reported decisions.
**Personal:** Boston College (BS 1973, magna cum laude; JD 1976).

### RAYMOND, Robert J
Cleary Gottlieb Steen & Hamilton LLP, New York 212 225 2994
rraymond@cgsh.com
*Recommended in Employee Benefits*
**Practice Areas:** Executive compensation and employee benefits matters, including: executive employment agreements; equity and non-equity based compensation; carried interest and co-investment plans, particularly in M&A and private equity; and general advice regarding federal and state statutes and regulations governing fiduciary relationships, tax and securities laws, and the terms and conditions of employment. Recent matters include advising TPG and Warburg Pincus on executive compensation arrangements related to the Neiman Marcus acquisition; Home Depot in its acquisition of Hughes Supply; Citigroup and Deutsche Bank on deferred compensation, carried interest and co-investment plans.
**Career:** JD, summa cum laude, New York Law School (1994).

### RAYSMAN, Richard
Brown Raysman Millstein Felder & Steiner LLP, New York
212 895 2360
rraysman@brownraysman.com
*Recommended in Business Process Outsourcing, Technology*
**Practice Areas:** Focuses on computer law, outsourcing and intellectual property issues, including the structuring of technology transactions. He has also litigated reported cases for the New York State and Federal Courts, and he has had over one dozen titles.
**Publications:** Co-author: 'Emerging Technologies and the Law: Forms and Analysis', 'Computer Law: Drafting and Negotiating Forms and Agreements' and 'Intellectual Property Licensing: Forms and Analysis'. He also writes a monthly computer law column for the New York Law Journal.
**Personal:** BS, Massachusetts Institute of Technology 1968; JD, Brooklyn Law School 1973; Systems engineer for IBM Corporation for six years.

### REARDON, Marc A
Bingham McCutchen LLP, Boston

617 951 8297
marc.reardon@bingham.com
*Recommended in Projects*
**Practice Areas:** Serves as Co-Chair of the firm's Project and Structured Finance Practice. Focuses on development, construction, financing and transfer of electric generating facilities and other infrastructure, including industrial, transportation, recycling and waste disposal and water and wastewater treatment facilities. Has been actively involved in the independent power sector since its inception in the early 1980s. Represented the sponsors of Astoria Energy, named North American Deal of the Year by Project Finance International Magazine.
**Personal:** Georgetown University Law Center, JD, 1979; Harvard College, BA, 1972.

### REARDON, Roy
Simpson Thacher & Bartlett LLP, New York 212 455 2000
rreardon@stblaw.com
*Recommended in Litigation, Products Liability*
**Practice Areas:** Roy L Reardon is a member of the firm's Litigation Department. His trial and litigation experience covers a wide gamut of areas, including conducting many jury trials in state and federal trial courts around the country and arguing numerous appeals, including arguments in the US Supreme Court. His areas of particular specialty include commercial law, antitrust, product liability, professional responsibility, and securities law.
**Prof. Memberships:** Fellow, American College of Trial Lawyers; Association of the Bar of the City of New York; New York State Bar Association; American Bar Association; Nassau County Bar Association; First Department, Disciplinary Committee, Appellate Division, Special Counsel.
**Career:** Mr Reardon joined Simpson Thacher in 1954. He has been a Member of the firm's Executive Committee for many years, as well as Chairman of the Litigation Department.
**Personal:** Received his JD in 1954 from St John's University Law School, and his BA in 1951 from St Francis College.

### REGER, Robert
Thelen Reid & Priest LLP, New York
212 603 2204
rreger@thelenreid.com
*Recommended in Energy*
**Practice Areas:** Mr Reger's practice focuses on the representation of utility clients in the area of corporate finance, general corporate law and Securities and Exchange Commission-related matters. As a corporate finance expert, Mr Reger also represents investor-owned utilities and underwriting firms in the public and private issuances of first mortgage bonds, collateral trust bonds, secured facility

bonds, debentures, preferred stock, preference stock and common stock. He has also spearheaded the restructuring of several investor-owned utilities, and represents several foreign clients with investments in the United States as well as several risk arbitrage/hedge fund limited partnerships.
**Prof. Memberships:** American Bar Association.
**Career:** Partner of Thelen Reid & Priest LLP. Member of the firm's Partnership Council.
**Personal:** Received his JD from the University of Virginia in 1973, where he graduated Phi Beta Kappa. Received his BA, summa cum laude, from Fordham University in 1970.

### REICH, William
Serotte, Reich & Wilson LLP, Buffalo
716 854 7525
*Recommended in Immigration*

### REICH, Yaron Z
Cleary Gottlieb Steen & Hamilton LLP, New York 212 225 2540
yreich@cgsh.com
*Recommended in Tax*
**Practice Areas:** Taxation including tax aspects of corporate acquisitions, restructurings, financings and international transactions; financial institution taxation; and tax controversies.
**Prof. Memberships:** Member of the Bar in New York. Admitted to practice before US District Court (SDNY), US Claims Court and Tax Court.
**Career:** Joined firm, 1979; became Partner, 1986. LLM in Taxation, New York University School of Law (1984); JD (Kent and Stone Scholar), special issue editor of Columbia Law Review, Columbia University School of Law (1978); BA, summa cum laude, Columbia College (1975).
**Publications:** Mr Reich has published several significant articles on international tax issues.

### REINHOLD, Richard L
Willkie Farr & Gallagher LLP, New York
212 728 8292
rreinhold@willkie.com
*Recommended in Tax*
**Practice Areas:** Partner and Chair of the Tax Department, specializing in domestic and international business tax matters relative to mergers and acquisitions, joint ventures, new financial products, corporate restructurings, and financing transactions. Significant matters in 2005 include handling the tax aspects of Teva Pharmaceutical's $8.5 billion acquisition of IVAX Corp., and Carlos Slim's and affiliated entities $1.1 billion sale of a 13% block of MCI Corp. to Verizon Corporation. He also handled the tax aspects of National Energy & Gas Transmission Inc.'s $1.7 billion sale of its Canadian pipeline unit to Trans-Canada Corp., and the restructuring of Zurich

Re's reinsurance operations into Converium AG in conjunction with an IPO by that company.

**Prof. Memberships:** Former Chair of the New York State Bar Association (Tax Section) and has been a Member of its Executive Committee since 1985. Fellow of the American College of Tax Counsel, Member of the American Bar Association (Corporate Tax Committee), Member of the New York University Tax LLM Advisory Group, and member of the Tax Forum and Tax Club.

**Career:** Admitted to the New York and Florida Bars.

**Publications:** Has lectured and written widely on federal income tax matters.

**Personal:** Received a JD from the State University of New York at Buffalo School of Law in 1976 and an AB from Cornell University in 1973.

### REISMAN, Sharyl A
Jones Day, New York
212 326 3405
sareisman@jonesday.com
*Recommended in Environment*

**Practice Areas:** She has represented and counseled clients on virtually all aspects of environmental law, with emphasis on occupational safety and health counseling and toxic tort litigation. She has significant experience, during pretrial and trial phases, in cases involving reproductive issues, birth defects, and cancer, and specifically in working with experts on the clinical, epidemiology and toxicology aspects of those cases. She also has substantial experience in counseling clients on environmental regulatory matters, recently emerging issues of vapor intrusion, as well as safety and health-related issues, including media relations, employee communications, medical monitoring programs, and document retention requirements.

### REISMAN, Steven J
Curtis, Mallet-Prevost, Colt & Mosle LLP, New York 212 696 6065
sreisman@cm-p.com
*Recommended in Bankruptcy*

**Practice Areas:** Mr Reisman is Co-Chair of the firm's Bankruptcy and Creditors' Rights Department. He participates in a wide range of domestic and international matters involving bankruptcy, restructuring and creditors' rights on behalf of governmental, public company and private clients. Mr Reisman has represented clients of the firm in all facets of bankruptcy cases as well as insolvency issues in business transactions, out-of-court restructurings, Chapter 11 filings, Creditors' Committee engagements and as Conflicts' Counsel in large Chapter 11 cases. Representations include: Calpine Corp, as Conflicts' Counsel; Musicland Holdings, as Conflicts' Counsel; North-Western Energy, as special counsel; the Air Transportation Stabilization Board, as

senior secured lender in the US Airways, Aloha Airlines and ATA Holdings cases.

**Prof. Memberships:** Association of the Bar of the City of New York; Bankruptcy and Corporate Reorganization Committee of the Association of the Bar of the City of New York; American Bar Association, Litigation Section and Business Law Section, New York State Bar Association; Bankruptcy Law Committee, New Jersey State Bar Association; Turnaround Management Association; American Bankruptcy Institute; Commercial Law League of America.

**Personal:** JD, with Honors, St John's University School of Law, 1990; BS, magna cum laude, State University of New York at Oneonta, 1987.

### REISNER, Lorin
Debevoise & Plimpton LLP, New York
212 909 6000
*Recommended in Media & Entertainment*

### REISS, John
White & Case LLP, New York
212 819 8200
jreiss@whitecase.com
*Recommended in Corporate/M&A, Private Equity*

**Practice Areas:** Global Co-Head of M&A Practice Group. Represents parties in mergers and acquisitions, private equity transactions, restructurings, and boards of directors in corporate governance matters.

**Prof. Memberships:** New York State Bar Association.

**Career:** Partner since 1992. Co-Head of Global M&A Practice Group since 2000.

**Publications:** Recipient of the Burton Award for Legal Achievement; regularly contributes to, and is often quoted in, leading business and legal publications covering the M&A and private equity markets.

**Personal:** JD, University of Pennsylvania Law School, 1984; MBA, University of Pennsylvania (Wharton School), 1984; BS, summa cum laude, University of Pennsylvania (Wharton School),1981.

### RESSA, Gregory J
Simpson Thacher & Bartlett LLP, New York 212 455 7430
gressa@stblaw.com
*Recommended in Real Estate*

**Practice Areas:** Head of the Real Estate Department at Simpson Thacher & Bartlett LLP. Practice involves all aspects of the real estate industry with particular emphasis on representation of real estate opportunity funds, real estate mergers and acquisitions and real estate finance.

**Prof. Memberships:** Association of the Bar of the City of New York.

**Career:** Recent transactions on which Mr Ressa has advised include: the $3.4 billion acquisition of La Quinta Corporation (NYSE: LQI) by The Blackstone Group; $3.2 billion acquisition of Wyndham International Inc. (AMEX: WBR) by

The Blackstone Group; $5.5 billion securitized mortgage and mezzanine financing for Extended Stay Inc. and Homestead Village L.L.C.; $3.2 billion acquisition of Extended Stay America (NYSE: ESA) by The Blackstone Group; $1.4 billion sale of The Savoy Group, owner of four of London's most famous hotels; Claridges, The Berkely, The Connaught and The Savoy; and $1.25 billion acquisition of Boca Resorts Inc. (NYSE: RST) by The Blackstone Group

**Personal:** Joined Simpson Thacher 1987; Partner, 1995. BA, Tufts University (1984); JD Fordham University School of Law (1987); associate editor, Fordham Law Review.

### REYNOLDS, Christopher
Morgan, Lewis & Bockius LLP, New York
212 309 6807
creynolds@morganlewis.com
*Recommended in Employment*

**Practice Areas:** Christopher Reynolds is a Partner in the Labor and Employment Law Practice Group. Mr Reynolds's practice includes the litigation of single plaintiff, multi-plaintiff and class action employment matters in federal, state and administrative fora. His practice also involves the counseling of employers in a broad range of matters, including those involving issues of discrimination, equal employment opportunity, global workforce diversity, regulatory compliance and workforce restructuring.

**Prof. Memberships:** National Employment Law Council; American Employment Law Council; American Bar Association (Labor and Employment Law and Litigation Sections); Association of the Bar of the City of New York.

### REYNOLDS, Timothy G
Skadden, Arps, Slate, Meagher & Flom LLP & Affiliates, New York
212 735 2316
treynold@skadden.com
*Recommended in Insurance*

**Practice Areas:** Concentrates in matters involving insurance and reinsurance as well as insurance coverage litigation and arbitration. Represents clients in matters involving innovative alternative risk transfer and finite risk insurance products. Extensively represents directors and officers of various corporations with respect to obtaining D&O insurance coverage for a variety of alleged security class actions, and consults frequently with firm clients with respect to D&O placements and renewals and property insurance issues.

**Career:** JD, Fordham University School of Law, 1980; BA, Fordham College, 1976; law clerk, Hon William Hughes Mulligan, United States Court of Appeals, 2d Cir.

### RICE, Glenn
Otterbourg, Steindler, Houston & Rosen, New York 212 661 9100
*Recommended in Bankruptcy*

### RICH, Frederic C
Sullivan & Cromwell LLP, New York
212 558 4000
richf@sullcrom.com
*Recommended in Projects*

**Practice Areas:** Head, Global Project Finance Group. Has more than 20 years experience representing sponsors and lenders in major projects, including landmark oil and gas, metals and mining, and infrastructure transactions in countries as diverse as Argentina, Australia, Azerbaijan, China, Indonesia, Kazakhstan, Kyrgyzstan, Papua New Guinea, Russia, Tanzania, Turkey and Zimbabwe. Has extensive experience in global capital markets and international privatisation transactions.

**Prof. Memberships:** ABA (former Chair, Committee on Privatisation); ASIL; IBA.

**Career:** Partner since 1989.

**Personal:** Princeton University (AB, 1977); King's College, Cambridge (Keasby Fellow, 1978); University of Virginia Law School (JD, 1981).

### RICH, R Bruce
Weil, Gotshal & Manges LLP, New York
212 310 8170
r.bruce.rich@weil.com
*Recommended in Media & Entertainment*

**Practice Areas:** R Bruce Rich Co-Heads Weil Gotshal's Intellectual Property and Media Practice, and is a nationally recognized expert in intellectual property law, focusing on communications industry clients, including book, magazine and newspaper publishers, broadcasters, cable television entities, and trade associations of these entities. His areas of concentration include copyright, music licensing, First Amendment, trademark and antitrust law. Mr Rich has served as lead trial counsel in significant cases for clients including Random House, Warner Books, The Walt Disney Company, ABC, CBS, The New York Post and Reuters.

**Personal:** Dartmouth College, BA, 1970; University of Pennsylvania Law School, JD, 1973.

### RICHARDS III, Lee
Richards Spears Kibbe & Orbe, New York 212 530 1840
*Recommended in Litigation*

### RIESEL, Daniel
Sive Paget & Riesel PC, New York
212 421 2150
driesel@sprlaw.com
*Recommended in Environment*

**Practice Areas:** Daniel Riesel is a member of Sive, Paget & Riesel, P.C., a firm with offices in New York City and White Plains, New York. The firm maintains a national practice concentrating on environmental law and litigation.

**Prof. Memberships:** He is a lecturer in Law at the Columbia University School of Law, and has been an Adjunct Professor at the Benjamin Cardoza School of Law. For the Annual American Law Institute-American Bar Association, Mr Riesel chairs the Annual Environmental Litigation Course, and is Co-Chair of the annual course in Environmental Law. He served as Chair of the Committee on Environmental Law for the Bar of the City of New York from 1984-87, and chaired the Section on Environmental Law for the New York Bar Association in 1999-2000.

**Career:** Although Mr Riesel's practice involves all aspects of environmental law, he specializes in litigating environmental issues before State and Federal courts and representing clients before administrative agencies in enforcement, permitting and siting matters. His work includes defense of toxic tort cases, litigation over failed commercial transactions, CERCLA cost recovery matters, and the defense of alleged environmental criminal defendants. Mr Riesel has also been engaged in numerous contested developmental projects assisting developers in land use and environmental matters.

**Publications:** He has authored numerous articles on litigation and environmental law, including his recent book: 'Environmental Enforcement: Civil and Criminal'.

**Personal:** Mr Riesel is a 1961 graduate of Columbia Law School and has been engaged in litigation and environmental law since 1970. He served as an Assistant United States Attorney in the Southern District of New York, where he was a founder of the first Environmental Protection Unit in any US Attorney's office. Mr Riesel's clients include numerous Fortune 500 corporations as well as governmental entities that have ranged from the City of New York to the Commonwealth of Puerto Rico.

**RINGEL, Dean**
Cahill Gordon & Reindel LLP, New York
212 701 3900
*Recommended in Media & Entertainment*

**ROBERTS, Thomas A**
Weil, Gotshal & Manges LLP, New York
212 310 8479
thomas.roberts@weil.com
*Recommended in Corporate/M&A, Private Equity*

**Practice Areas:** Thomas Roberts is Co-Head of Weil Gotshal's Corporate Department. Mr Roberts' practice primarily involves M&A, divestitures, contested takeovers, and private equity. He is active in the representation of major public and private companies, several of the leading private equity funds and a number of leading investment banks. Recent significant transactions include representing CSFB in its $1.8 billion acquisition of Nycomed, Great Lakes Chemical Corporation in its $1.8 billion merger

with Crompton Corporation, General Electric with respect to various corporate matters and in numerous acquisition and divestiture situations; Hughes Supply in its $3.47 billion sale to the Home Depot; Microsoft in its proposed joint venture with AOL; Huntsman Corporation (Special Committee) in consideration of an unsolicited $11 billion acquisition proposal; Six Flags in its defense against a consent solicitation and tender offer; UnitedHealth in its $9.2 billion merger with PacifiCare; and Whirlpool in its $1.7 billion proposed acquisition of Maytag.

**Personal:** Georgetown University, BA, 1969; Georgetown University Law Center, JD, 1972.

**ROBFOGEL, Susan S**
Nixon Peabody LLP, New York
212 940 3116
srobfogel@nixonpeabody.com
*Recommended in Healthcare*

**Practice Areas:** Practice includes extensive experience in preventive labor relations, labor negotiations, employee/executive recruitment and retention policies, substance abuse, supervisory training and human rights matters. Has wide and varied corporate experience in the health care industry in general. Has lectured widely on employment/healthcare topics across the country.

**Prof. Memberships:** Mrs Robfogel has handled cases before all New York State courts, in various federal district courts, the Second Circuit Court of Appeals and the US Supreme Court. Fellow of the College of Labor and Employment Lawyers.

**Personal:** Cornell Law School, JD; Smith College, BA, cum laude.

**ROCK, Neil L**
Skadden, Arps, Slate, Meagher & Flom LLP & Affiliates, New York
212 735 3787
nrock@skadden.com
*Recommended in Real Estate*

**Practice Areas:** Active in all areas of Skadden's real estate practice, including acquisitions, developments, shopping centers and hotels, leasings, financings, securitized real estate loans, partnerships and joint ventures, workouts and corporate retention projects.

**Career:** JD, Fordham University School of Law, 1988 (cum laude, Member, Fordham Law Review); BA, Brandeis University, 1985 (cum laude).

**ROD, Jonathan**
Latham & Watkins LLP, New York
212 906 1200
*Recommended in Projects*

**RODIN, Rita A**
Skadden, Arps, Slate, Meagher & Flom LLP & Affiliates, New York
212 735 3774
rrodin@skadden.com
*Recommended in Business Process*

*Outsourcing, Technology*

**Practice Areas:** Partner in Skadden's Intellectual Property and Technology and Internet and E-Commerce practices. She represents clients in structuring and negotiating domestic and international information technology and business process outsourcing agreements, strategic alliances, joint ventures, development and distribution agreements, trademark and technology licensing agreements and marketing and co-branding agreements. She also advises companies on internet and e-commerce business and compliance issues, open source issues, privacy matters, branding issues and intellectual property and technology issues that arise in connection with mergers and acquisitions, project finance matters, and initial public offerings. She is a frequent author and speaker on various outsourcing and intellectual property topics.

**Career:** JD, St John's University School of Law, 1993; BS, Finance, Boston College, 1990 (magna cum laude, Beta Gamma Sigma).

**ROGERS CHEPIGA, Pamela**
Allen & Overy LLP, New York
212 756 1125
pamela.chepiga@allenovery.com
*Recommended in Litigation*

**Practice Areas:** Specializes in criminal, civil and regulatory securities litigation.

**Career:** Joined Allen & Overy LLP in 2003 as senior litigation counsel. Partner since 2004. Previously, she was the founding Director of the Securities Arbitration Clinic at Fordham University School of Law (1998-2003); a Partner at Cadwalader, Wickersham & Taft (1984-93); and the Chief of Securities and Commodities Frauds Unit in the United States Attorney's Office (SDNY) (1982-84).

**Personal:** Fordham University (JD, cum laude, 1973; BA, cum laude, 1970).

**ROGERS JR, Theodore O**
Sullivan & Cromwell LLP, New York
212 558 4000
rogerst@sullcrom.com
*Recommended in Employment*

**Practice Areas:** Recognized litigator specializing in labor and employment law and estates litigation. Represents employers in all manner of labor and employment issues; was lead counsel in one of two consolidated cases where NY State's highest court upheld arbitrability of employment discrimination claims. Has successfully represented clients in complex will contests, trust accountings and fiduciary responsibility matters.

**Prof. Memberships:** Fellow, College of Labor and Employment Lawyers; Executive Committee, NYSBA; ABCNY; DCBA.

**Publications:** Co-author: Employment Litigation in New York (West Group, 1996); Employment Law Deskbook for Human Resources Professionals (West

Group, 2001).

**Personal:** Harvard University (AB, 1976); Harvard Law (JD, 1979).

**ROHN, Frederick**
Sacks Montgomery PC, New York
212 355 4660
*Recommended in Construction*

**ROLFE, Ronald**
Cravath, Swaine & Moore LLP, New York
212 474 1714
rrolfe@cravath.com
*Recommended in Antitrust*

**Practice Areas:** Major antitrust and securities cases, SEC and grand jury investigations and a wide range of commercial litigation and arbitrations for US and international clients.

**Prof. Memberships:** ABA; NYSBA; ABCNY; American Law Institute; Federal Bar Council.

**Career:** Partner since 1977. Clerkship: Hon Marvin E Frankel (US District Court, Southern District of New York).

**Personal:** Columbia Law School (JD, magna cum laude, 1969; editor, Columbia Law Review); Harvard College (BA, cum laude, 1966). Columbia Law School Dean's Council. President, The Allen-Stevenson School Board of Trustees. Lawrenceville School Board of Trustees. De La Salle Academy Board of Trustees.

**ROONEY, Stephen G**
LeBoeuf, Lamb, Greene & MacRae LLP, New York
212 424 8013
sgrooney@llgm.com
*Recommended in Insurance*

**Practice Areas:** Specializes in securities offerings, mergers and acquisitions, and securitization transactions. He advises buyers and sellers in negotiated mergers and acquisitions, as well as issuers, underwriters and investors in public and private offerings of equity, debt, hybrid and structured securities in the US and international markets. He also advises US and non-US insurance and reinsurance companies on corporate governance matters.

**Prof. Memberships:** Structured Finance Committee of the NYC Bar Association.

**Career:** Joined LeBoeuf Lamb in 1986; Simpson Thacher & Bartlett (1982-86); law clerk to federal judge (1980-82).

**Personal:** Fordham University (JD) 1980; University of Pennsylvania, Wharton School (BS) 1977.

**ROONEY, William H**
Willkie Farr & Gallagher LLP, New York
212 728 8259
wrooney@willkie.com
*Recommended in Antitrust*

**Practice Areas:** Partner in the Litigation Department, specializing in complex antitrust litigation, mergers and acquisitions, and civil and criminal antitrust investigations. Antitrust experience includes litigation and counseling in matters under the Sherman Act (contracts in

restraint of trade and monopolization), the Clayton Act (mergers and acquisitions), and the Robinson-Patman Act (price discrimination). Appears regularly in federal courts and before the Antitrust Division of the Department of Justice and the Federal Trade Commission. Selected significant matters include: In re Interchange Fee Antitrust Litigation; American Express v Visa U.S.A. Inc., et al.; In Re Copper Tubing Litigation; Teva v FDA; In Re Nabumetone Antitrust Litigation; Stock Exchange Antitrust Litigation; Coalition for Level Playing Robinson-Patman litigation; Toys 'R' Us antitrust litigation; Teva/Ivax; Teva/Sicor; Teva/Novopharm; CompUSA/Computer City; Mattel/The Pleasant Co.; Loral/Orion; Loral/Skynet; Loral/Lockheed Martin; Mattel/Tyco; Mattel/Fisher Price.
**Prof. Memberships:** Association of the Bar of the City of New York (immediate past chair, Committee on Antitrust and Trade Regulation), NYSBA (Executive Committee Section of Antitrust Law), and the American Bar Association (Section on Antitrust Law).
**Career:** Admitted to the New York, New Jersey and the District of Columbia Bars.
**Personal:** Received a Postgraduate Diploma in Law from Oxford University (Magdalen College) in 1987; a JD from Yale Law School in 1983, where he was a senior editor of the Yale Law Journal; and a BA (summa cum laude) from the University of Notre Dame in 1980, where he was elected to Phi Beta Kappa.

### ROSEN, Arthur R
McDermott Will & Emery, New York
212 547 5596
arosen@mwe.com
*Recommended in Tax*
**Practice Areas:** Practice focuses on state and local tax planning and litigation for businesses. Chairs firm's nationwide State and Local Tax Practice. Formerly deputy counsel of New York State Department of Taxation and Finance, as well as counsel to Governor's Temporary Sales Tax Commission and tax counsel to New York State Senate Tax Committee, held executive tax management positions at Xerox Corporation and AT&T. Deeply involved in nationwide corporate income/franchise and sales tax issues that arise in the context of remote commerce.
**Personal:** St John's University School of Law (JD); Rensselaer Polytechnic Institute (MBA); New York University (APC, BA)

### ROSEN, Burt
Debevoise & Plimpton LLP, New York
212 909 6000
*Recommended in Tax*

### ROSEN, J Philip
Weil, Gotshal & Manges LLP, New York
212 310 8604
philip.rosen@weil.com

*Recommended in Real Estate*
**Practice Areas:** Philip Rosen is Head of Weil's Real Estate Transactions and Finance Practice. He specializes in the origination, structuring, and restructuring of property debt, M&A involving real estate and real estate companies, and is the top private equity lawyer in the property arena. Mr Rosen also practices in a range of other areas, including joint ventures and real estate investment trusts. He is also one of the country's leading authorities on doing business in Israel and the Middle East, and represents numerous clients with interests in that region.
**Personal:** Yeshiva University, BA, 1978; Georgetown University Law Center, JD, 1981.

### ROSEN, Jeffrey
Debevoise & Plimpton LLP, New York
212 909 6000
*Recommended in Corporate/M&A*

### ROSEN, Matthew A
Skadden, Arps, Slate, Meagher & Flom LLP & Affiliates, New York
212 735 2230
mrosen@skadden.com
*Recommended in Tax*
**Practice Areas:** Co-Head, Skadden's Tax Group. Represents clients in every aspect of tax work, with particular emphasis on acquisitions, divestitures and restructurings, both domestic and cross-border. Also handles matters involving partnerships of every type, joint ventures and executive compensation. In addition, practice includes the development of financial instruments and financial products. Clients include many significant public and private companies, investment banks and investment funds. Regularly highly placed in professional rankings. Frequent lecturer on a broad variety of topics.
**Career:** LLM, New York University, 1979 (Memorial Award for Distinction); JD, Boston University, 1976 (cum laude); BA, Swarthmore College, 1973.

### ROSEN, Richard
Paul, Weiss, Rifkind, Wharton & Garrison LLP, New York 212 373 3305
rrosen@paulweiss.com
*Recommended in Litigation*
**Practice Areas:** Litigation Partner. Has extensive experience in civil litigation in state and federal courts, involving securities, derivatives, banking, M&A and other complex business disputes. Has represented major financial institutions and public companies in class action litigations and SEC investigations. Has authored numerous articles on corporate and securities law issues. Frequently speaks at Bar Association and securities industry conferences. Selected for 2006 edition of 'The Best Lawyers in America'.

### ROSEN, Seth
Debevoise & Plimpton LLP, New York
212 909 6000
*Recommended in Tax*

### ROSENBERG, Mark F
Sullivan & Cromwell LLP, New York
212 558 4000
rosenbergm@sullcrom.com
*Recommended in Environment*
**Practice Areas:** Co-ordinator, Environmental Law and Insurance Groups. Extensive litigation/transactional experience in insurance, reinsurance, asbestos, environmental and toxic tort matters, including related alter ego, successor liability, fraudulent conveyance, insolvency and bankruptcy issues. Broad arbitration/litigation expertise in spearheading foreign sovereign debt recoveries. Acted as international lead counsel in debt recovery and political risk insurance litigation, and as national counsel in domestic environmental and toxic tort matters.
**Prof. Memberships:** ABA; NYSBA (Co-Chair, Environmental Committee, International Section).
**Career:** Partner since 1993.
**Personal:** Michigan State University (BA, 1977); George Washington Law School (JD, 1980).

### ROSENBERG, Robert
Latham & Watkins LLP, New York
212 906 1200
*Recommended in Bankruptcy*

### ROSENBLATT, William
Stroock & Stroock & Lavan LLP, New York 212 806 5400
*Recommended in Insurance*

### ROSENBLUM, Steve A
Wachtell, Lipton, Rosen & Katz, New York 212 403 1221
sarosenblum@wlrk.com
*Recommended in Corporate/M&A*
**Practice Areas:** Specializes in mergers and acquisitions, buyouts, takeover defense, joint ventures, restructurings, corporate governance and securities law.
**Prof. Memberships:** The Association of the Bar of the City of New York; New York State and American Bar Associations.
**Career:** Partner at Wachtell, Lipton, Rosen & Katz since 1989. Prior to joining the firm in 1983, was a law clerk to the Honorable Joseph L Tauro, United States District Court Judge for the District of Massachusetts. Has extensive experience representing major telecommunications companies from creation and initial public offerings, through spin-offs, mergers and acquisitions. His clients include high profile companies in the communications, media, technology, energy, consumer foods, insurance and hospitality industries. Has also written and participated in panels on a number of topics, including mergers and acquisitions, corporate disclosure, proxy reform and cor-

porate governance.
**Personal:** Graduated magna cum laude from Harvard College in 1978 (BA) and from Yale Law School in 1982 (JD). While at Harvard, he was a Member of Phi Beta Kappa.

### ROSENWASSER, Michael
Vinson & Elkins LLP, New York
1 (212) 237 0019
mrosenwasser@velaw.com
*Recommended in Energy*
**Practice Areas:** Corporate Finance & Securities and Mergers and Acquisitions; Co-Section Head of the Corporate Finance & Securities Practice; Co-Chair of the Private Equity Practice.
**Prof. Memberships:** American Bar Association.
**Career:** Practicing over 30 years, he has worked on over 150 public financings and 100 M&A transactions. He has participated in developing several unique financing techniques including the development of master limited partnerships. He has worked on several gas pipeline projects in the United States and South America.
**Personal:** Graduated from The University of Texas, BBA, summa cum laude, 1968; The University of Texas, JD, magna cum laude, 1971.

### ROSINI, Neil
Franklin, Weinrib, Rudell & Vassallo, New York 212 935 5500
*Recommended in Media & Entertainment*

### ROSNER, David
Kasowitz Benson Torres & Friedman, New York 212 506 1700
*Recommended in Bankruptcy*

### ROSS, Allen
Brown Raysman Millstein Felder & Steiner LLP, New York
212 895 2810
aross@brownraysman.com
*Recommended in Construction*
**Practice Areas:** Allen Ross is Co-Chair of the firm's Construction Practice Group and has over 40 years of experience practicing law. He is highly regarded for his work in construction law, litigation and real estate. In addition to traditional legal work, he has also developed a career in alternative dispute resolution in the construction industry, earning success as an arbitrator, mediator and dispute review board Chair.
**Personal:** JD, New York University School of Law; BA, Cornell University.

### ROSS, Barry
Bryan Cave LLP, New York
212 541 2000
*Recommended in Real Estate*

## ROTH, Andrew B
McDermott Will & Emery, New York
212 547 5543
aroth@mwe.com
*Recommended in Healthcare*
**Practice Areas:** Represents health clients on transactional and regulatory matters, including healthcare networks, integrated delivery systems, hospitals, managed care companies and physicians. Practice includes M&As, fraud and abuse, corporate compliance, corporate and medical staff bylaws, and long term healthcare facility representation. National practice involving accreditation of graduate medical education programs in academic medical centers and teaching hospitals and Accreditation Council for Graduate Medical Education (ACGME), and accreditation of medical schools by Liaison Committee on Medical Education (LCME).
**Personal:** Hofstra University School of Law (JD); State University of New York-Stony Brook (BA, cum laude)

## ROTHENBERG, Laraine S
Fried, Frank, Harris, Shriver & Jacobson LLP, New York 212 859 8745
Laraine.Rothenberg@FriedFrank.com
*Recommended in Employee Benefits*
**Practice Areas:** Chair of Employee Benefits and Plans, Executive Compensation and Exempt Organizations Department. Tax Partner. Advises compensation committees, corporations and chief executive officers on employment agreements, governance issues, severance protection agreements, stock options, other compensatory equity participation agreements, benefit plans, the related requirements of the securities and tax laws. Advises clients in connection with corporate transactions and investment vehicles used by ERISA.
**Career:** Joined Fried Frank as a Partner in 1994.
**Personal:** JD(1971), Columbia University. BA(1967), University of Pennsylvania.

## ROWEN, Andrew S
Sullivan & Cromwell LLP, New York
212 558 4000
rowena@sullcrom.com
*Recommended in Insurance*
**Practice Areas:** Co-ordinator, Insurance Group. Focuses on acquisition, finance and corporate matters involving insurance companies. Practice includes: acquisitions/divestitures and other change of control transactions, including insurance regulatory approvals and antitrust advice; securities offerings and advice regarding SEC disclosure issues and investigations; SOX and corporate governance; demutualizations; reinsurance; offshore companies; private equity investments in and by insurers; securitization of insurance risks; and regulatory matters.
**Prof. Memberships:** ABA; NYSBA; ABCNY (Committee on Insurance Law and Co-Chair, Legislation Sub-Committee).
**Career:** Partner since 1987.
**Publications:** Speaker at various industry conferences.
**Personal:** University of California, Berkeley (AB, 1976); Harvard Law (JD, 1979).

## RUBIN, Robert
Seyfarth Shaw LLP, New York
212 218 5500
*Recommended in Construction*

## RUDELL, Michael
Franklin, Weinrib, Rudell & Vassallo, New York 212 935 5500
*Recommended in Media & Entertainment*

## RUEGGER, Philip T
Simpson Thacher & Bartlett LLP, New York 212 455 3220
pruegger@stblaw.com
*Recommended in Corporate/M&A, Private Equity*
**Practice Areas:** Partner at Simpson Thacher & Bartlett LLP, Chairman of the Executive Committee and Head of the firm's Corporate Department. Advises clients on mergers and acquisitions, leveraged buyouts, corporate governance, corporate finance, and general corporate and securities law matters. Represented Travelers in its merger with St Paul and AOL in its merger with Time Warner. Regular clients include Blackstone, St. Paul Travelers, Accenture and Vestar.
**Career:** Joined Simpson Thacher in 1974 and became a Partner in 1981. Became Head of the Corporate Department in 2002, has been a Member of the firm's Executive Committee since 1993 and became Chairman of the Executive Committee in 2004.
**Publications:** Articles/Presentations include: 'Private Equity and LBOs-Trends in Financing and Exit Structures', PLI 37th Annual Institute on Securities Regulation, Nov 2005; 'M&A of High Technology Companies', Stanford Law School Directors' College 2000; 'Structuring International Acquisition Transactions', for the Third Annual Institute on Mergers and Acquisitions in February 1999; and 'Going Global, How to Do an International Deal', The M&A Journal, Vl 1, No 6.
**Personal:** AB, Dartmouth College, magna cum laude (1971), elected to Phi Beta Kappa. JD, University of Virginia School of Law (1974).

## RUSMAN, Jared M
Wachtell, Lipton, Rosen & Katz, New York 212 403 1322
JMRusman@wlrk.com
*Recommended in Tax*
**Practice Areas:** Specializes in United States federal income taxation with emphasis on mergers, acquisitions and spin-offs.
**Career:** Partner at Wachtell, Lipton, Rosen & Katz since 2002.
**Publications:** Author: 'Equity Swaps and Post-Transaction Continuity of Interest', 72 Tax Notes 113. Contributing author: Financial Institutions Mergers and Acquisitions, An Annual Review of Leading Developments.
**Personal:** Graduated from Georgetown University in 1991 (BSBA), summa cum laude, and from New York University School of Law in 1994 (JD), where he was notes and comment editor of the New York University Law Review and Order of the Coif.

## RUTHIZER, Theodore (Ted)
Kramer Levin Naftalis & Frankel LLP, New York 212 715 9421
truthizer@kramerlevin.com
*Recommended in Immigration*
**Practice Areas:** Ted Ruthizer is recognized as one of the country's leading immigration lawyers, and has more than 25 years of experience in the field. He is the Partner in charge of Kramer Levin's Business Immigration Group, as well as a past President and General Counsel of the American Immigration Lawyers Association. Mr Ruthizer is a lecturer in Law at Columbia Law School, where he teaches an advanced seminar in immigration law and policy. Mr Ruthizer, a graduate of the Columbia Law School, is a frequent lecturer on business immigration law and has authored many publications in the field.
**Personal:** Received a JD Degree from Columbia Law School in 1972 and a BA Degree with honors from Lafayette College in 1969.

## RUZOW, Daniel
Whiteman Osterman & Hanna LLP, Albany 518 487 7600
*Recommended in Environment*

## RYAN, Michael L
Cleary Gottlieb Steen & Hamilton LLP, New York 212 225 2520
mryan@cgsh.com
*Recommended in Corporate/M&A, Financial Services*
**Practice Areas:** Involved since 1978 in Cleary's Corporate, M&A, Capital Markets and Restructuring Practices. Represents acquirors, targets and corporate boards. Early in his career, he had broad experience in the development of financial products (including the first collateralized mortgage obligation) and financial institution restructuring. Since 1990, he has focused on private equity (as long-time counsel to Texas Pacific Group) and counseling senior executives and corporate boards.
**Personal:** BA, Harvard College (1973); JD, New York University School of Law (1978).

## SACRIPANTI, Peter
McDermott Will & Emery, New York
212 547 5583
psacripanti@mwe.com
*Recommended in Environment*
**Practice Areas:** Partner-in-Charge of New York Office, member of Trial Department. Focuses practice on complex litigations matters including mass tort, products liability and class action litigation. Currently serves as lead trial lawyer for ExxonMobil in all of its products liability litigation concerning the gasoline additive MTBE. Acts on behalf of petroleum industry as defense Liaison Counsel in MDL 1358 II Products Liability Litigation. Serves as senior trial lawyer for Honeywell International regarding involvement in NARCO Bankruptcy and the company's Bendix litigation. One client recently quoted saying, "if you're going to have a fight, you want him on your team".

## SAEED, Faiza
Cravath, Swaine & Moore LLP, New York
212 474 1454
fsaeed@cravath.com
*Recommended in Corporate/M&A, Media & Entertainment*
**Practice Areas:** Mergers and acquisitions, both domestic and cross-border. Takeover defense and corporate governance matters.
**Prof. Memberships:** ABA; NYSBA; ABCNY; CSBA.
**Career:** Partner since 1999.
**Publications:** Editorial Board Member, M&A Lawyer; Planning Committee member, Tulane Corporate Law Institute.
**Personal:** Harvard Law School (JD, magna cum laude, 1991); University of California at Berkeley (BA, with highest distinction, 1987; Phi Beta Kappa). Named a Young Global Leader by World Economic Forum, 2006 and a Dealmaker of the Year by The American Lawyer, 2005. Member of Harvard Law School Visiting Committee.

## SAFERSTEIN, Jeffrey D
Paul, Weiss, Rifkind, Wharton & Garrison LLP, New York 212 373 3347
jsaferstein@paulweiss.com
*Recommended in Bankruptcy*
**Practice Areas:** Partner and Deputy Chair of the Bankruptcy and Corporate Reorganization Department. Practices exclusively in the areas of corporate restructurings and workouts, bankruptcy and specialized financings. Has been involved in major domestic and international restructurings and bankruptcies, including Worldcom, Adelphia Communications, Maxwell Communication Corporation plc., Macmillan, Inc., Drexel Burham Lambert, Canadian Airlines, The Penn Traffic Company, Loehmann's Inc., United Pan-Europe Communications N.V. and Asia Global Crossing Ltd. Has written and lectured on numerous bankruptcy topics.

## SAGE, Michael
Stroock & Stroock & Lavan LLP, New York 212 806 5400
*Recommended in Bankruptcy*

## SALEM, Irving
Latham & Watkins LLP, New York 212 906 1200
*Recommended in Tax*

## SALTZSTEIN, Susan L
Skadden, Arps, Slate, Meagher & Flom LLP & Affiliates, New York 212 735 4132
ssaltzst@skadden.com
*Recommended in Litigation*
**Practice Areas:** Has represented clients in complex commercial litigation spanning corporate, partnership and commercial matters. Her experience extends to federal and state court litigation and arbitration before international and domestic arbitrators. Has also represented numerous public companies in their defense of actions arising under state and federal laws and has been involved in a number of precedent setting litigations.
**Career:** JD, Columbia University School of Law, 1991; BA, University of Pennsylvania, 1987.

## SALVATORE, Paul
Proskauer Rose LLP, New York 212 969 3022
psalvatore@proskauer.com
*Recommended in Employment*
**Practice Areas:** Represents employers in employment law and litigation, as well as union/ management relations and collective bargaining. Handles all types of employment litigation, arbitration and mediation. He also provides advice and guidance to clients, counseling employers on how to avoid litigation and achieve their employee relations objectives through such techniques as proactive human resources policies and alternative dispute resolution. Negotiates major collective bargaining agreements in several industries, including real estate and construction, and tries arbitrations and litigations arising from the collective bargaining relationship.
**Publications:** An active speaker and writer on labor and employment law issues. He has been quoted in, among other publications, The New York Times, The Wall Street Journal, USA Today and The National Law Journal, and he has appeared on CNN, Fox News and other business television news programs. Among other groups he works with, he serves as a speaker for the Society for Human Resource Management (SHRM), and on its National Labor Relations Panel. He is noted in 'The Best Lawyers in America', 'Super Lawyers' and other definitive attorney guidebooks.
**Personal:** An honors graduate of Cornell University's School of Industrial and Labor Relations (ILR) and The Cornell Law School.

## SAMUELS, Jeffrey B
Paul, Weiss, Rifkind, Wharton & Garrison LLP, New York 212 373 3112
jsamuels@paulweiss.com
*Recommended in Tax*
**Practice Areas:** Partner and Co-Chair of Tax Department whose practice covers a broad range of international and domestic transactions, including public and private M&A, organization of investment funds, partnership and joint venture transactions, and structuring of complex real estate transactions including formation of REITs. Clients include leading entertainment and communications companies, major investment banks and other financial institutions, major hotel owners and operators, and a number of private equity funds. Member of the New York State and City Bar Associations. Selected for 2006 edition of 'The Best Lawyers in America' and 'Guide to The World's Leading Tax Advisors'.

## SAMUELS, Leslie B
Cleary Gottlieb Steen & Hamilton LLP, New York 212 225 2250
lsamuels@cgsh.com
*Recommended in Tax*
**Practice Areas:** International and domestic taxation, including mergers and acquisitions, joint ventures, spin-offs, foreign investment in the US, financial products, capital markets activities and tax controversies.
**Prof. Memberships:** Association of the Bar of the City of New York and the NYSBA.
**Career:** Joined firm, 1968; became Partner, 1975. Assistant Secretary for Tax Policy of the US Treasury Department (1993-96). Vice-Chair, Committee of Fiscal Affairs, OECD (1994-96). LLB, magna cum laude, Harvard Law School (1966); BS, Economics, Wharton School of Finance and Commerce, University of Pennsylvania (1963). Fulbright Scholar, London School of Economics and Political Science (1967-68). Certified public accountant.

## SANSEVERINO, Raymond
Brown Raysman Millstein Felder & Steiner LLP, New York 212 895 2910
rsanseverino@brownraysman.com
*Recommended in Real Estate*
**Practice Areas:** Raymond A Sanseverino is Chair of the firm's Commercial Real Estate Leasing Group. Mr Sanseverino concentrates on commercial real estate law, with an emphasis in leasing, brokerage and conveyancing transactions. He represents both landlords and tenants in the leasing of all types of commercial real estate, including office, industrial and retail space. He also represents sellers and purchasers of real estate, real estate brokers, and owners and tenants in connection with real estate brokerage commission and agency agreements and commission claims.

**Personal:** AB, Franklin & Marshall College 1968; JD, cum laude, Fordham University School of Law 1972.

## SARCHIO, John J
Chadbourne & Parke LLP, New York 212 408 5225
jsarchio@chadbourne.com
*Recommended in Insurance*
**Practice Areas:** Head of Insurance Industry Practice Group. Experience in domestic and cross-border property/casualty and life mergers, acquisitions, demutualizations, financings and regulatory matters; insurer reorganizations and insolvencies; reinsurance transactions; securitizations; captive insurance; bank-insurer affiliations.
**Prof. Memberships:** Admitted New York (1980). Member: American Bar Association; New York State Bar Association; New York City Bar Association; International Bar Association.
**Publications:** Contributing author: 'New York Insurance Law & Practice' (Matthew Bender treatise); numerous speeches, seminars and trade publication articles.
**Personal:** Born 2 February 1954. JD, University of Pennsylvania, 1979; BS, Bucknell University, 1976; LLM (International Law), London School of Economics, 1986.

## SARNO, Glenn R
Simpson Thacher & Bartlett LLP, New York 212 455 2706
gsarno@stblaw.com
*Recommended in Private Fund Formation*
**Practice Areas:** Corporate Partner, focusing on private investment funds and other facets of 'alternative asset management'. Represents sponsors of domestic and international private funds, such as The Carlyle Group, Lehman Brothers, The Cypress Group, Leeds Weld & Co. and Cherokee Investment Partners, in a variety of asset classes including merchant banking, real estate, venture capital, healthcare, CDO, mezzanine debt, education, telecommunications, co-investment, secondary and fund-of-funds. Advises on the creation of employee securities companies, represents various hedge fund sponsors, including Credit Suisse Asset Management, Endeavour, Pendragon and Horizon, and reviews private fund investments on behalf of investors.
**Prof. Memberships:** Private Investment Fund Forum; Advisory Board of the Private Equity CFO Association.
**Career:** Joined firm in 1993, practiced in London from 1996-98, became a Partner in 2001; judicial clerk, Supreme Court of the State of New Jersey 1992-93 term.
**Publications:** 'Fund Formation - United States' in 'Getting the Deal Through - Private Equity, Law Business Research Limited', 2006.
**Personal:** University of Connecticut, BA,

summa cum laude, 1989 (University Scholar; Phi Beta Kappa); Duke Law School, JD, with honors, 1992 (winner Hardt Cup Moot Court Competition; Best Judge Award Dean's Cup Competition).

## SAUERMILCH, Thomas
McDermott Will & Emery, New York 212 547 5532
tsauermilch@mwe.com
*Recommended in Corporate/M&A*
**Practice Areas:** Practices cross-border M&A, joint ventures and related antitrust matters. Represents publicly listed companies, large family-owned businesses and portfolio companies of large private equity funds. Experience includes several cross-border acquisitions and divestitures for world's largest specialty chemicals company, contested acquisition of pharmaceutical supply company by portfolio company of large private equity fund, acquisition of large family-owned manufacturing company and the sale of a worldwide packaging business by portfolio company of large European private equity group.
**Personal:** Fordham University School of Law (JD); Fletcher School of Law and Diplomacy (MALD); Indiana University School of Law (LLM); University of Kiel-Germany (Staatsexamen).

## SAVARESE, John F
Wachtell, Lipton, Rosen & Katz, New York 212 403 1235
jfsavarese@wlrk.com
*Recommended in Litigation*
**Practice Areas:** Specializes in the representation of investment banking and financial service firms, as well as Fortune 500 companies, in connection with the defense of regulatory, white-collar criminal and complex civil litigation. Also advises clients on the design of compliance policies and systems, and on the conduct of internal investigations.
**Prof. Memberships:** The Association of the Bar of the City of New York (Secretary-Treasurer, Criminal Law Committee, 1989-92); American Bar Association.
**Career:** Joined Wachtell, Lipton, Rosen & Katz in 1988, after working for the United States Attorney's Office for the Southern District of New York for four years. Received the Attorney General's John Marshall Award for Outstanding Legal Achievement in connection with his work on United States v Salerno, in which the heads of New York's La Cosa Nostra families were prosecuted. Also served as the Chief Appellate Attorney in the US Attorney's Office. Prior to his work with the US Attorney's Office, served as a law clerk to the Honorable Louis H Pollak of the United States District Court for the Eastern District of Pennsylvania and to Justice William J Brennan of the United States Supreme Court. Frequent lecturer and panelist for the American Bar Associ-

ation, the Practicing Law Institute, the Securities Industry Association, and Stanford Law School's Director's College program. He also has been a lecturer at Harvard Law School, teaching a course on advanced criminal procedure.
**Personal:** Graduated magna cum laude from Harvard University in 1977 (AB) and cum laude from Harvard Law School in 1981 (JD), where he served as articles editor of the Harvard Law Review and as a Teaching Fellow in European Intellectual History.

### SCARBOROUGH, Robert
Freshfields Bruckhaus Deringer LLP, New York 212 277 4000
*Recommended in Tax*

### SCAVONE, Arthur A
White & Case LLP, New York
212 819 8710
ascavone@whitecase.com
*Recommended in Projects*
**Practice Areas:** Co-Head of the firm's Global Energy, Infrastructure and Project Finance Group, with extensive experience in international and domestic projects. Represents sponsors, commercial banks, underwriters and export credit agencies in projects involving power plants, petrochemical facilities, mines, pipelines, LNG facilities, and other industrial facilities.
**Prof. Memberships:** Association of the Bar of the City of New York, project finance subcommittee.
**Career:** New Jersey Bar, 1984; New York Bar, 1986; White & Case Tokyo office 1987-88.
**Personal:** Muhlenberg College, magna cum laude, 1981. Fordham University School of Law, cum laude, Fordham Law Review.

### SCHAEFFER, Fiona A
Weil, Gotshal & Manges LLP, New York
212 310 8919
fiona.schaeffer@weil.com
*Recommended in Antitrust*
**Practice Areas:** Fiona Schaeffer has expertise in a broad range of antitrust counseling, litigation and transactional matters. She represents major corporations in multi-district class actions and private suits in federal and state courts around the country. She advises corporate and private equity clients on antitrust-related aspects of mergers, acquisitions and joint ventures/strategic alliances, and coordinates worldwide antitrust approvals for multinational transactions. Representative transactions include: UnitedHealth Group's acquisitions of PacifiCare Health Systems and Mid-Atlantic Medical Services, Rayovac's purchase of Tetra, Wal-Mart Stores' acquisition of Supermercados Amigo, Hughes Satellite Systems' sale to Boeing and the mergers of Unum/Provident, Coltec/BF Goodrich and Guinness/Grand Metropolitan. She also has expertise in EU competition law, and

has represented clients in investigations and proceedings before the European courts, the EC Commission and national regulators.
**Prof. Memberships:** She is a Vice-Chair of the International Antitrust Committee of the ABA's Section of International Law and a past Member of the Antitrust and Trade Regulation Committee of the Association of the City Bar of New York, where she also served as committee liaison to the International Competition Network (ICN).
**Personal:** University of Adelaide, B.Economics, 1992; University of Adelaide, Law School, LLB, 1992; Oxford University, BCL, 1994.

### SCHAFFRAN, Andrew
Morgan, Lewis & Bockius LLP, New York
212 309 6380
aschaffran@morganlewis.com
*Recommended in Employment*
**Practice Areas:** Andrew Schaffran is a Partner in the Labor and Employment Practice and is nationally recognized in the employment law field, particularly in the financial securities industry. Mr Schaffran regularly counsels and represents securities firms and other financial services companies in all aspects of employment law, including complex as well as single plaintiff employment litigation, arbitration before NASD and NYSE panels, Sarbanes-Oxley whistleblower complaints and corporate diversity and ADR programs.
**Prof. Memberships:** American Bar Association (Labor and Employment Law Section and Co-Chair of Securities Employment Litigation Subcommittee of Litigation Section); SIA Compliance and Legal Division; New York State Bar Association (Labor and Employment Law Section).

### SCHARFSTEIN, Joel
Fried, Frank, Harris, Shriver & Jacobson LLP, New York 212 859 8172
Joel.Scharfstein@FriedFrank.com
*Recommended in Tax*
**Practice Areas:** Tax Partner. Practice focuses on corporate acquisitions and divestitures, partnerships, real estate transactions, investment partnerships and restructurings. Member of the Executive Committee of the Tax Section of the New York State Bar Association and has served as Co-Chair of its committees on partnerships, bankruptcy, consolidated returns, reorganizations, and basis and cost recovery.
**Career:** Joined Fried Frank in 1977. Became a Partner in 1984.
**Personal:** JD(1977), University of Michigan Law School. AB(1969), Columbia College. AM(1972), Harvard University.

### SCHECHTMAN, Paul
Stillman & Friedman, New York
212 223 0200
*Recommended in Litigation*

### SCHEIBE, Robert H
Morgan, Lewis & Bockius LLP, New York
212 309 6083
rscheibe@morganlewis.com
*Recommended in Bankruptcy*
**Practice Areas:** Robert Scheibe is a Partner in the Business and Finance Practice. Mr Scheibe has represented financial institutions in restructuring and bankruptcy matters for more than 30 years and has frequently acted as counsel for major financial institutions as debtor-in-possession lender (including in the Chapter 11 cases of major airlines, retailers, manufacturers, technology firms and entertainment industry companies).
**Prof. Memberships:** American College of Bankruptcy (Fellow); Member, American Bar Association; Member, The Association of the Bar of The City of New York.

### SCHEINFELD, Robert
Baker Botts LLP, New York
212 408 2512
robert.scheinfeld@bakerbotts.com
*Recommended in Intellectual Property*
**Practice Areas:** Head of New York office's Intellectual Property Department. For 20 years, practiced IP law and litigation, representing companies in patent, copyright, and trade secret misappropriation disputes and lawsuits, resulting in favorable district court and Federal Circuit decisions. Technical expertise is diverse and representations involve a broad range of fields in the high technology industry, including electronics, data processing and management software, telecommunications, smart cards, electronic commerce, and flash memory.
**Career:** Bimonthly 'New York Law Journal' patent and trademark columnist (1995-present). Adjunct professor, Patent Law (1991-97). NYIPLA, Board of Directors (2005-present), Patent Law and Practice Committee, Chair (present), Trade Secret Practice Chair (1996-2003).

### SCHELER, Brad Eric
Fried, Frank, Harris, Shriver & Jacobson LLP, New York 212 859 8019
Brad.Scheler@FriedFrank.com
*Recommended in Bankruptcy*
**Practice Areas:** Senior Partner and Chairman of the Bankruptcy and Restructuring Department. Practice includes both in and out-of-court restructurings and the rehabilitation of financially distressed businesses. Represents corporate debtors, creditors' committees, bondholders' committees, trustees, financial institutions that are lenders to and investors in financially troubled companies, buyers and sellers of distressed securities and businesses, and third parties seeking to invest in and/or acquire the assets and businesses of financially troubled companies.
**Career:** Joined Fried Frank in 1981. Became a Partner in 1984. Contributing author to Collier on Bankruptcy, 15th

Edition Revised, and Norton Annual Survey of Bankruptcy Law.
**Personal:** JD(1977), Hofstra University School of Law. BA(1974), with high honors, Lehigh University.

### SCHER, Irving
Weil, Gotshal & Manges LLP, New York
212 310 8120
irving.scher@weil.com
*Recommended in Antitrust*
**Practice Areas:** Irving Scher's practice focuses on antitrust law and advertising and marketing litigation and counseling. He has extensive experience in such matters with respect to a broad spectrum of products and services, involving all phases of litigation, including national coordination of cases, trial and appellate work. Mr Scher is an antitrust Adjunct Professor at New York University Law School, and is a former Chair of the Antitrust Law Sections of both the American Bar Association and New York Bar Associations.
**Personal:** City University of New York, BA; Columbia University, JD.

### SCHIFFER, Larry P
LeBoeuf, Lamb, Greene & MacRae LLP, New York 212 424 8086
larry.schiffer@llgm.com
*Recommended in Insurance*
**Practice Areas:** Practices in the areas of commercial, insurance, and reinsurance litigation, arbitration, and mediation. Also serves as a mediator for the Southern District of New York and the New York Supreme Court, Commercial Division.
**Prof. Memberships:** ABA, NYSBA, FDCC, ARIAS-US.
**Career:** Joined LeBoeuf Lamb in 1999; Werner & Kennedy and predecessors (1982-99); law assistant, New York Appellate Division, Second Department (1979-81).
**Publications:** Expert Commentator, Reinsurance, IRMI.com; co-author, Reinsurance, Insurance Law Practice (NYSBA).
**Personal:** Albany Law School, Union University (JD) 1979; Brooklyn College, City University of New York (BA) 1976.

### SCHINDLER, Paul D
Greenberg Traurig LLP, New York
212 801 6785
schindlerp@gtlaw.com
*Recommended in Media & Entertainment*
**Practice Areas:** Entertainment.
**Prof. Memberships:** Executive Committee, NARAS/Grammys Entertainment Law Initiative; Executive Committee, Lifebeat; Executive Committee, TJ Martell Foundation; Executive Committee, Nordoff Robbins; Executive Committee, City of Hope; Member, New York State Bar Association.
**Career:** Listed, 'Who's Who in Entertainment'.
**Personal:** JD, Brooklyn Law School, 1971; BA, Syracuse University, 1968.

**SCHLER, Michael**
Cravath, Swaine & Moore LLP, New York
212 474 1588
mschler@cravath.com
*Recommended in Tax*

**Practice Areas:** Corporate tax, corporate finance (including structured finance and securitizations), mergers and acquisitions, international transactions.
**Prof. Memberships:** ABA (Section of Taxation); NYSBA (former Chair, Tax Section; Member of Tax Section Executive Committee); American College of Tax Counsel; New York Tax Forum (Chair); American Tax Policy Institute (Trustee); American Law Institute (Consultant).
**Career:** Partner since 1982. Clerkship: Hon Max Rosenn (US Court of Appeals, Third Circuit).
**Publications:** Author of numerous articles on taxation. Frequent speaker at tax conferences.
Personal: New York University (LLM in Taxation, 1979); Yale Law School (JD, 1973); Harvard University (BA, magna cum laude, 1970).

**SCHMIDT, Kevin**
Debevoise & Plimpton LLP,
New York 212 909 6000
*Recommended in Private Equity*

**SCHNABEL, David**
Debevoise & Plimpton LLP, New York
212 909 6000
*Recommended in Tax*

**SCHNEIDER, Jeffrey G**
Hogan & Hartson LLP, New York
212 918 3503
jgschneider@hhlaw.com
*Recommended in Healthcare*

**Practice Areas:** Regulatory compliance, transactions, litigation and general counseling for healthcare organizations.
**Prof. Memberships:** Hospice Care of DC (Officer and Director, Board of Directors; 1992-97); American Health Lawyers Association.
**Career:** Jeff joined Hogan & Hartson following law school in 1986. His practice focuses on healthcare provider entities, including hospitals, academic medical centers, nursing homes, home health agencies, hospices, physician groups, and mental health practitioners. He provides assistance to these clients in the areas of regulatory compliance and counseling, joint ventures, mergers, acquisitions and other transactions, and reimbursement and other litigation. He also represents a number of professional and trade associations.
**Publications:** 'Dispelling Myths About Employer Health Plans Under The HIPAA Privacy Rules', HIPAA Update, Hogan & Hartson L.L.P. (1/30/2003); numerous legal updates published through the National Register of Health Service Providers in Psychology, including 'Legal Issues Involving Repressed Memory of Child Sexual Abuse' (August 1994); 'Joining Battle With Your State

Over Medicaid', Nursing Homes Long Term Management (August 1992).
**Personal:** Stanford Law School (JD); University of Michigan (BA, with highest honors). Admitted to the Bars of New York, the District of Columbia and Illinois.

**SCHNELL, Paul T**
Skadden, Arps, Slate, Meagher & Flom LLP & Affiliates, New York
212 735 2322
pschnell@skadden.com
*Recommended in Corporate/M&A, Healthcare*

**Practice Areas:** Represents many of the world's leading companies and financial firms in some of the most significant corporate transactions. Practices in M&A, private equity, governance, finance and restructuring. In last two years, advised on over 40 announced M&A and financing transactions, including 13 deals valued at over $1 billion, in US, Latin America, Asia and Europe. Active in broad range of industries. Coordinates Skadden's worldwide Healthcare Practice Group. Co-heads Latin America practice. Chairs leading M&A publication; chairs leading annual program on negotiating acquisitions; and lectures and writes frequently on governance, M&A, finance and other topics. Active in firm management.

**SCHOENBERG, Clifford H**
Cadwalader, Wickersham & Taft LLP,
New York 212 504 6992
cliff.schoenberg@cwt.com
*Recommended in Insurance*

**Practice Areas:** Handles large, complex reinsurance arbitrations, litigations, disputes between insurance companies and agents. Principal responsibility for and lead trial counsel in: arbitration Sompo Japan against Fortress Re obtaining $1 billion compensatory and $100 million punitive damage awards; fraud and malpractice litigation against Fortress Re's auditors. Leads team of attorneys in company and individual representations relating to governmental investigations of insurance industry focusing on finite reinsurance. Has litigated direct insurance coverage actions, been retained as arbitrator and expert in reinsurance arbitrations, represented insurance companies in regulatory matters before NY State Insurance Department. Acted as co-ordinating and supervising counsel for federal and state class action lawsuits against insurers, including a large number in Alabama involving significant punitive damage claims. Has served as lead counsel on insurance company mergers, acquisitions and divestitures totalling over $1 billion.
**Personal:** JD, Boston University School of Law (magna cum laude, 1975); BA, Dickinson College (summa cum laude, 1972). Served on Board of Directors of Zurich Life Insurance Company of New York; former Assistant General Counsel

of The Home Insurance Company.

**SCHONHOLTZ, Margot**
Kaye Scholer LLP, New York
212 836 7064
mschonholtz@kayescholer.com
*Recommended in Bankruptcy*

**Practice Areas:** Partner and Co-Chair, Business Reorganization and Creditors' Rights Group. Focuses her practice on bankruptcy, restructuring matters and complex litigation. She has more than 27 years' experience representing leading institutional creditors, agents to syndicated lending groups, large lender groups, official and unofficial creditors' committees and commercial lenders in out-of-court debt restructurings, loan workouts, creditors' rights litigation, asset sale transactions and bankruptcy matters. She also has extensive cross-border experience in restructuring and insolvency proceedings in the UK, Europe, Latin America, Canada and Asia.
**Prof. Memberships:** Member of the Bars of the State of New York, Southern and Eastern Districts of New York and admitted to practice before the Second Circuit Court of Appeals and the US Supreme Court.
**Career:** JD (magna cum laude), American University Washington College of Law, Law Review, Honor Society, International Academy of Trial Lawyers' Award for Distinguished Advocacy; BA, Smith College.

**SCHORR, Naomi**
Kramer Levin Naftalis & Frankel LLP,
New York 212 715 9339
nschorr@kramerlevin.com
*Recommended in Immigration*

**Practice Areas:** Naomi Schorr's practice area focuses primarily on employment-based immigration, principally for large, multinational organizations. Ms Schorr is a frequent speaker on business immigration matters at regional and national conferences of the American Immigration Lawyers Association. She is listed in The International Who's Who of Corporate Immigration Lawyers, where she is referred to as 'one of the leading NY-based immigration lawyers.'
**Personal:** Received a JD Degree from Fordham University School of Law in 1983, an MA Degree from New York University in 1979 and a BA Degree from Queens College of the City University of New York in 1974.

**SCHULMAN, Ira**
Mazur, Carp & Rubin PC, New York
212 686 7700
*Recommended in Construction*

**SCHULZ, David**
Levine Sullivan Koch & Schulz LLP, New York 212 850 6100
*Recommended in Media & Entertainment*

**SCHUMER, Robert B**
Paul, Weiss, Rifkind, Wharton & Garrison LLP, New York 212 373 3097
rschumer@paulweiss.com
*Recommended in Corporate/M&A, Media & Entertainment*

**Practice Areas:** Co-Head of M&A Group focusing on mergers and acquisitions and joint ventures. Has represented clients in significant merger and acquisition transactions, many involving multi-billion-dollar acquisitions or dispositions, including contested takeovers. Representative transactions include Time Warner Cable Inc.'s bid to acquire the cable properties of Adelphia Communications for approximately $17.4 billion, sale of Wyndham Hotels to an affiliate of Blackstone for $3.24 billion, King World Productions $2.5 billion merger with CBS, Time Warner's $58 billion bid for AT&T Broadband and $9 billion restructuring of Time Warner Entertainment with Comcast and AT&T, and Telemundo's $2.7 billion merger with NBC. Has been involved in numerous international and domestic multibillion-dollar joint ventures including Time Warner Inc.'s creation of Time Warner Entertainment, a $20 billion joint venture with Itochu and Toshiba. Also represents special committees of boards of directors and leading investment banking firms in mergers and acquisitions context. Selected for 2006 edition of The Best Lawyers in America, Law Business Research's Who's Who of Merger and Acquisitions Lawyers, and one of The American Lawyer's 'Dealmakers of the Year'. Clients include Time Warner Inc., AIG, Liz Claiborne, Inc., Lazard Freres and Airgas, Inc.

**SCHWARTZ, Alan**
Simpson Thacher & Bartlett LLP,
New York 212 455 3629
aschwartz@stblaw.com
*Recommended in Private Equity*

**Practice Areas:** Partner in the firm's Corporate Department, where he concentrates primarily in mergers and acquisitions and leveraged buyouts. Mr Schwartz maintains strong ties with many of the firm's private equity clients, including Kohlberg Kravis Roberts & Co., First Reserve Corporation, Ripplewood Holdings L.L.C. and Evercore Capital Partners. Represented Ripplewood in its disposition of Kraton Polymers to the Texas Pacific Group and Evercore in restructuring its investment in a Belgium cable venture. Also recently represented Evercore in its investment in Fidelity National Information Services, Inc., Doshi Diagnostics and Fidelity Sedgwick Holdings, Inc.
**Career:** Mr Schwartz has been a member of the firm since 1998.
**Personal:** He received his BS from the University of New Hampshire in 1983 and his JD from Fordham Law School in 1989.

## SCHWARTZ, David
Debevoise & Plimpton LLP, New York
212 909 6000
*Recommended in Private Fund Formation*

## SCHWARTZ, Gerald
Davis & Gilbert, New York
212 468 4800
*Recommended in Media & Entertainment*

## SCHWARTZ, Herbert F
Ropes & Gray LLP, New York
212 596 9010
herbert.schwartz@ropesgray.com
*Recommended in Intellectual Property*
**Practice Areas:** IP litigator best known for work on behalf of pharmaceutical companies such as AstraZeneca and Purdue Pharmaceutical in ANDA litigation as well as Polaroid Corporation action against Eastman Kodak Company. Represents numerous clients in the pharmaceutical, technology, and consumer product sectors in significant patent, trademark, copyright, trade secret, and licensing litigation and appeals.
**Career:** New York Bar (1964); USPTO; Partner, Fish & Neave (1971); Partner, Ropes & Gray (2005); Member, American College of Trial Lawyers.
**Personal:** LLB, cum laude, University of Pennsylvania Law School (1964); MA, University of Pennsylvania, Wharton School (1964); BSEE, Massachusetts Institute of Technology (1957).

## SCHWARTZ, Jodi J
Wachtell, Lipton, Rosen & Katz, New York 212 403 1212
jjschwartz@wlrk.com
*Recommended in Tax*
**Practice Areas:** Specializes in the tax aspects of the joint ventures, corporate reorganizations, acquisitions, dispositions, financings, and restructurings that constitute Wachtell, Lipton, Rosen & Katz's primary practice, which transactions frequently involve multinational businesses and raise complex multinational tax issues.
**Prof. Memberships:** Member of the New York State Bar Association Tax Section Executive Committee.
**Career:** Partner at Wachtell, Lipton, Rosen & Katz since 1991.
**Personal:** Graduated magna cum laude from the University of Pennsylvania in 1981 (BS, economics), from the University of Pennsylvania (Wharton School) in 1984 (MBA), magna cum laude from the University of Pennsylvania Law School in 1984 (JD), and from New York University Law School in 1987 (LLM, taxation).

## SCHWARTZ, Max J
Sullivan & Cromwell LLP, New York
212 558 4000
schwartzma@sullcrom.com
*Recommended in Employee Benefits*
**Practice Areas:** Head, Executive Com-

pensation and Benefits Practice Group. Broad experience in securities, tax and labor laws affecting executive compensation and employee benefits, advising both on a regular basis and in context of corporate transactions and IPOs.
**Prof. Memberships:** ABA (Tax and Business Law Sections); NYSBA (Executive Committee, Tax Section and Co-Chair, Employee Benefits Committee).
**Career:** Joined firm in 1998 as Of Counsel. Partner since 2000.
**Publications:** Employee Benefits Advisory Committee, PLI.
**Personal:** Institut d'Etudes Politiques (BA, 1970); University of Michigan Law School (JD, 1973).

## SCHWARTZ, Steven
Clifford Chance US LLP, New York
212 878 8000
*Recommended in Insurance*

## SCHWARTZ, William
Kronish Lieb Weiner & Hellman LLP, New York 212 479 6000
*Recommended in Litigation*

## SCHWED, Robert
WilmerHale, New York
212 937 7276
robert.schwed@wilmerhale.com
*Recommended in Private Equity*
**Practice Areas:** Represents private equity firms and portfolio companies in corporate finance transactions including intial public offerings, venture capital and buyout firms and other institutional investors in equity and debt investments, public and private buyout transactions, recapitalizations and other restructurings. Leveraged buyout experience includes the acquisition of business units from major industrial, financial services, healthcare, retailing, media and communications companies, and the acquisition of public companies in the computer, data processing, healthcare and communications industries.
**Prof. Memberships:** Board of Directors at Project Reach Youth (Brooklyn, NY).
**Personal:** Harvard Law School (JD 1974); Williams College (BA 1971).

## SCHWENKEL, Robert C
Fried, Frank, Harris, Shriver & Jacobson LLP, New York 212 859 8167
Robert.Schwenkel@FriedFrank.com
*Recommended in Private Equity*
**Practice Areas:** Chairman of Corporate Department and Head of Private Equity Group. Has diverse transactional corporate practice concentrating in private equity and mergers and acquisitions. He is also actively involved in advising clients regarding activist shareholder strategies.
**Career:** Joined Fried Frank in 1982. Became a Partner in 1989, Chairman of Corporate Department in 2003. Co-chairs annual seminar sponsored by Practising Law Institute, 'Advanced Doing Deals'.

## SCHWOLSKY, John
LeBoeuf, Lamb, Greene & MacRae LLP, New York 212 424 8667
jschwols@llgm.com
*Recommended in Insurance*
**Practice Areas:** He has expertise in the area of corporate and securities law, specifically public and private securities offerings, mergers and acquisitions, recapitalizations, and other transactions involving the insurance industry. He has represented insurance companies and underwriters of their securities in these transactions. He has also represented insurers and investment banks in connection with structured financial product transactions involving both domestic and off-shore insurance and reinsurance facilities.
**Personal:** Cornell University (JD) 1985; Yale University (BA magna cum laude) 1982.

## SEGAL, Michael J
Paul, Weiss, Rifkind, Wharton & Garrison LLP, New York 212 373 3364
msegal@paulweiss.com
*Recommended in Employee Benefits*
**Practice Areas:** Co-Chair of Employee Benefits and Executive Compensation Group. Counsels clients with respect to compensation and benefits programs. Advises executives and employers with regard to entering and exiting CEO and other senior-level employment relationships. Practice involves the creation and maintenance of public and private company equity-based compensation arrangements. Has extensive experience advising corporations, trustees, lenders and advisors in the establishment and termination of employee stock ownership plans. Has counseled clients on compensation and benefits aspects of buying and selling businesses. Regularly speaks and writes on benefits and compensation topics. Selected for 2006 edition of The Best Lawyers in America.

## SEIDE, Rochelle
Arent Fox PLLC, New York
212 484 3945
seide.rochelle@arentfox.com
*Recommended in Intellectual Property*
**Practice Areas:** Concentrates in patent law, particularly in the life sciences, including obtaining licensing and enforcing patents in biotechnology, chemistry and pharmaceuticals. Counsels clients on legal issues, including patent enforcement, validity and infringement, licensing and collaborations. Transactional experience in IP due diligence and audits and structuring deals and collaborations. Experienced in patent litigation before the federal courts, and in inter partes patent interferences in the US Patent and Trademark Office, in biotechnology,

pharmaceutical, and medical device technologies. Frequent speaker and author on biotechnology issues.
**Personal:** University of Akron School of Law, JD 1984 (Akron Law Review); City University of New York, Mount Sinai School of Medicine, PhD 1977 (Human Genetics); Long Island University, MS 1974 (Immunology); Syracuse University, BS 1968 (Sigma Ki).

## SEIDER, Mitchell
Latham & Watkins LLP, Los Angeles
213 485 1234
*Recommended in Bankruptcy*

## SEIDMAN, Steven
Willkie Farr & Gallagher LLP, New York
212 728 8763
sseidman@willkie.com
*Recommended in Corporate/M&A*
**Practice Areas:** Partner in the Corporate and Financial Services Department, mergers and acquisitions, corporate governance advice, private equity and venture capital investments, public offerings, and general corporate and securities law. Recent transactions include the bid by Oriole Partnership (comprised of Essex Property Trust, UBS Wealth Management and AEW) to acquire The Town and Country Trust; the proposed sale of StorageMart Partners by Warburg Pincus; the acquisition of Eon Labs, Inc. and Hexal AG by Novartis AG; the investment into Fortunoff by Trimaran Capital Partners/K Group; the acquisition of GovPX, Inc. by ICAP plc; MatlinPatterson's acquisition of Southeast Generation Portfolio from Duke Energy; General Investment & Development Co. in connection with Post Properties proxy contest; Simon Property Group's proposed acquisition of Taubman Centers, Inc.; and the sale of Warburg Pincus' stake in Price Enterprises, Inc. Recent representations of financial advisors in transactions include: Merrill Lynch & Co. in connection with Boston Scientific's proposed acquisition of Guidant, Inc., Special Committee of the Sports Authority, Inc. in connection with its sale, Neoforma's proposed sale to Global Healthcare Exchange, LLC., and ALLTEL's acquisition of Western Wireless. He also recently advised UBS in connection with the purchase by Extra Space Storage and Prudential Financial of Storage USA, and Fairmont Hotels in connection with its sale; as well as Peter J. Solomon Company Limited in connection with The J. Jill Group's proposed sale to Talbot's Inc.
**Career:** Judicial clerk, Delaware Court of Chancery (1990-91).
**Personal:** Yale University (BA, 1987); University of Virginia Law School (JD, 1990).

## SELVER, Paul D
Kramer Levin Naftalis & Frankel LLP, New York 212 715 9199
pselver@kramerlevin.com

*Recommended in Real Estate*

**Practice Areas:** Practice encompasses all aspects of land use and development law, with a special emphasis on environmental, zoning and historic preservation. Over the past 15 years, he has successfully co-ordinated the public approval and environmental review process for more than 8,000,000 square feet of office space, more than 7,500 apartments, hundreds of thousands of square feet of retail and entertainment space, hundreds of hotel rooms, and numerous institutional buildings.
**Publications:** Co-author, New York Practice Guide: Real Estate, Volume II: Land Use Regulation (1986).
**Personal:** Received a JD Degree from Harvard University Law School in 1972 and a BA Degree magna cum laude from Harvard College in 1969.

## SERBAROLI, Francis J
Cadwalader, Wickersham & Taft LLP, New York 212 504 6001
francis.serbaroli@cwt.com
*Recommended in Healthcare*
**Practice Areas:** Clients have included numerous teaching and community hospitals, ambulatory care centers and clinics; clinical laboratories; home health agencies; imaging service providers; individual physicians and group practices; and numerous other healthcare-related entities, as well as health insurers and managed care organizations. Served as counsel to and represented hospital governing boards, administrators and medical staffs.
**Publications:** Authors Health Law column for the New York Law Journal; author of 'The Corporate Practice of Medicine Prohibition in the Modern Era of Health Care', (BNA). Numerous articles published in health, pharmaceutical and insurance publications.
**Personal:** JD, Fordham University School of Law (1977); BA, Fordham University (1973). Former Assistant Attorney General of New York and general counsel at two prominent teaching hospitals. Appointed by Governor Pataki to NY State Public Health Council 1995, reappointed 2001, presently serve as Vice-Chairman. Member of the Governor's NYPHRM task force. Chaired a special task force of the Public Health Council on the confidentiality of medical information.

## SERNAU, Ronald D
Proskauer Rose LLP, New York
212 969 3785
rsernau@proskauer.com
*Recommended in Real Estate*
**Practice Areas:** Mr Sernau has significant experience in real estate law, representing sophisticated real estate developers and investors in virtually all areas of real estate practice in New York City.
**Publications:** Mr Sernau's articles have appeared in law journals and in publications of the American Bar Association.

He also speaks frequently, including at events sponsored by the Real Estate Board of New York, the Bar Association of the City of New York and the New York State Bar Association.
**Personal:** Cornell Law School, JD, magna cum laude; Order of the Coif; Editor, Cornell Law Review.

## SEROTA, Susan P
Pillsbury Winthrop Shaw Pittman LLP, New York 212 858 1125
Susan.Serota@pillsburylaw.com
*Recommended in Employee Benefits*
**Practice Areas:** Ms Serota is the Chair of Pillsbury's Executive Compensation and Benefits Practice, and has experience in all areas of pensions, employee benefits (health, life and severance plans), non-qualified deferred compensation, executive compensation and stock options and in fiduciary matters relating to ERISA. Ms Serota advises both foreign and domestic governments regarding pensions and privatization.
**Prof. Memberships:** ABA - Section on Taxation, Chair-elect 2005-06; immediate past president, American College of Employee Benefits Counsel.
**Career:** Admitted to practice in New York, Illinois, and District of Columbia.
**Personal:** JD, New York University School of Law, 1971; AB, University of Michigan, 1967.

## SEYMON, Pamela S
Wachtell, Lipton, Rosen & Katz, New York 212 403 1205
psseymon@wlrk.com
*Recommended in Corporate/M&A*
**Practice Areas:** Specializes in corporate law; mergers and acquisitions; securities; corporate governance. Has represented corporations on offense as well as defense, in both friendly and unsolicited transactions; and clients engaged in some of the most notable transactions over the years, including MCA INC. in its sale to Matsushita Electric Industrial Co., Ltd., QVC Inc. in its unsolicited bid for Paramount Communications Inc., HSN, Inc. (which then became USA Networks, Inc.) in the acquisition of USA Networks and the domestic television business of Universal Studios and, thereafter, USA Networks, Inc. (which then became USA Interactive) in the contribution of its entertainment assets to Vivendi Universal Entertainment; also represented CSX Corporation in its acquisition of Conrail, the Special Committee of the Board of Directors of Delhaize America in the sale to Delhaize Group and, most recently, USA Interactive in its purchases of Ticketmaster, Expedia and Hotels.com.
**Prof. Memberships:** Has served on the Committee on Securities Regulation of the New York City Bar Association and as a member of the Board of Trustees for New York University School of Law.
**Career:** Partner at Wachtell, Lipton,

Rosen & Katz, where she has practiced since 1982.
**Personal:** Graduated as a Wellesley Scholar from Wellesley College in 1977 (AB) and from New York University School of Law in 1982 (JD).

## SEYMOUR, Karen Patton
Sullivan & Cromwell LLP, New York
212 558 3196
seymourk@sullcrom.com
*Recommended in Litigation*
**Practice Areas:** Head, Criminal Defense and Investigations Group. White-collar criminal defense and government investigations involving securities fraud, money laundering, obstruction of justice, insider trading, FCPA violations, healthcare fraud and criminal antitrust violations. Numerous jury/bench trials in federal court and appeals before US Court of Appeals, 2nd Circuit. Public service in US Attorney's Office, SDNY: Chief, Criminal Division (2002-04), overseeing World-Com, Adelphia, and ImClone investigations and leading Martha Stewart and Peter Bacanovic prosecution; Asst. US Attorney, SDNY (1990-96).
**Career:** Partner since 2000.
**Personal:** Southern Methodist University (BA/BS, 1983); University of Texas Law School (JD, 1986); University of London (LLM, 1987).

## SEYMOUR, Samuel W
Sullivan & Cromwell LLP, New York
212 558 3156
seymours@sullcrom.com
*Recommended in Litigation*
**Practice Areas:** Specialises in white-collar criminal defense, regulatory enforcement matters and internal investigations. Has represented clients in numerous high profile investigations involving allegations of securities fraud, foreign bribery, OFAC violations, price fixing, money laundering and obstruction of justice.
**Prof. Memberships:** ABA; ABCNY (former VP and Chair, Executive Committee); New York Council of Defense Lawyers.
**Career:** Partner since 1994. Assistant US Attorney, Southern District of New York, 1988-91.
**Publications:** Lecturer on trial advocacy, Columbia Law School.
**Personal:** Dartmouth College (AB, 1979); Columbia Law School (JD, 1982).

## SHACHAR, Avishai
Davis Polk & Wardwell, New York
212 450 4000
avishai.shachar@dpw.com
*Recommended in Tax*
**Practice Areas:** Member of Davis Polk & Wardwell's Tax Department. Advises clients primarily in the areas of US and cross-border mergers and acquisitions, leveraged buyouts, spinoffs and financial products. Designed the capital structure of SmithKline Beecham and played a leading role in the merger of SmithKline

with Beecham and Comcast with AT&T Broadband, the spinoffs of YUM! Brands from Pepsi, of Visteon from Ford, and the split-off by way of an exchange offer of Abercrombie & Fitch from The Limited. Also advised Burlington Northern on tax matters relating to its acquisition of Santa Fee Pacific, Texaco on tax matters relating to its merger with Chevron, as well as Comcast on a variety of matters including the sale of its stake in QVC, the restructuring of Time Warner Entertainment, the acquisition of cable assets from Adelphia and numerous other cable systems acquisitions.

## SHANMAN, James A
Edwards Angell Palmer & Dodge LLP, Stamford 212 756 0273
JShanman@eapdlaw.com
*Recommended in Insurance*
**Practice Areas:** Jim represents national and international clients in major insurance and reinsurance litigation and arbitration matters. He is an accomplished trial lawyer and has tried jury and non-jury cases in federal and state courts, administrative proceedings and arbitrations throughout the United States. His practice includes representation and counseling in property and casualty, life and health reinsurance, insolvencies and a large variety of other insurance matters, as well as work with complex commercial litigation.
**Publications:** Jim has authored many articles about reinsurance issues and has spoken at numerous conferences.
**Personal:** University of Pennsylvania, BS,1963; Yale Law School, JD,1966.

## SHAPIRO, Stuart
Shapiro Forman Allen Sava & McPherson LLP, New York 212 972 4900
*Recommended in Litigation*

## SHENKER, Joseph C
Sullivan & Cromwell LLP, New York
212 558 4000
shenkerj@sullcrom.com
*Recommended in Real Estate*
**Practice Areas:** Co-ordinator, Commercial Real Estate Group. Broad experience in: M&A; joint ventures; private equity investments; family investment offices; securities offerings; private/public financings; property development; and related tax/estate planning, primarily in real estate industry. Representations: NY Giants and Tisch and Mara families regarding new football stadium and entertainment/retail complex; GS concerning worldwide headquarters in Lower Manhattan; General Growth in $12.6 billion Rouse acquisition (the largest REIT merger ever); Vornado in Toys 'R' Us acquisition; and Pritzker Family in its restructurings.
**Career:** Partner since 1986. Management Committee since 1996. Vice-Chairman since 2006.
**Personal:** CUNY (BS, 1977); Columbia

University (JD, 1980).

### SHERMAN, Robert L
Paul, Hastings, Janofsky & Walker LLP,
New York 212 318 6037
robertsherman@paulhastings.com
*Recommended in Intellectual Property*
**Practice Areas:** Has advised clients on
trademark protection and risk avoidance.
Has litigated cases for trademark
infringement, trade dress, false advertising, dilution, counterfeiting, cybersquat-
ting and under ICANN. Has represented
clients in trademark prosecution, opposi-
tion and cancellation proceedings.
**Prof. Memberships:** INTA; NYSBA.
**Career:** Came to firm as Partner in 1992.
**Publications:** Adjunct Professor, Medill
(graduate school), Northwestern Univer-
sity, Evanston, IL; teaches seminar on the
Law of Direct and Ineractive Marketing;
frequent industry speaker on direct marketing.
**Personal:** American University Law
School (JD 1971), member of Law
Review; George Washington University
Law School; University of Rhode Island
(BSIE 1967).

### SHIFF, Adam
Kasowitz Benson Torres & Friedman,
New York 212 506 1700
*Recommended in Bankruptcy*

### SHIM, Paul J
Cleary Gottlieb Steen & Hamilton LLP,
New York 212 225 2930
pshim@cgsh.com
*Recommended in Corporate/M&A*
**Practice Areas:** M&A and leveraged
buyouts. Represented American Express
(spin-off of Ameriprise Financial), Bank
of America (investment in China Con-
struction Bank), TPG (numerous invest-
ments), Suntory Limited (sale of bottled
water business to Groupe Danone).
**Career:** Joined firm, 1987; became Part-
ner, 1996. JD, cum laude, NYU, 1987. BS,
MS (Chem E), MIT, 1984.
**Publications:** 'You Don't Say: Informa-
tion Disclaimers in M&A Contracts', by P.
Shim and D Leinwand, New York Law
Journal, July 23, 2003. 'IBP v. Tyson Foods
- Acquiror Must Consummate Merger
When Court Finds No 'Material Adverse
Effect', by V Lewkow and P Shim, M&A
Lawyer, June 2001.

### SHIMSHAK, Stephen J
Paul, Weiss, Rifkind, Wharton & Garrison LLP, New York 212 373 3133
sshimshak@paulweiss.com
*Recommended in Bankruptcy*
**Practice Areas:** Partner in the Bankruptcy and Corporate Reorganization
Department with a diverse practice that
includes US and foreign insolvency proceedings, as well as restructurings and
workouts involving debtors, creditors
(including banks and other lenders),
court-appointed liquidators, trustees,
asset purchasers and investors. Has writ-

ten on various bankruptcy issues. Member of the Bar of the State of New York
and admitted to various federal courts
throughout the country. Recognized as
one of the leading bankruptcy and corporate restructuring lawyers in New York
by a number of peer review organizations
including The Best Lawyers in America
and SuperLawyers.

### SHIPLEY, Ann
Paul, Hastings, Janofsky & Walker LLP,
New York 212 318 6870
annshipley@paulhastings.com
*Recommended in Real Estate*
**Practice Areas:** All areas of real estate
development and finance, with a speciality
in representing developers in acquisition
and development of complex multi-use
projects as well as borrowers in so-called
'80-20 and other bond financings. She represented the developers of the new Time
Warner Center in New York City from
inception to completion of the project.
**Prof. Memberships:** New York City Bar
Association - Real Property Committee.
**Career:** Partner since 2000; prior thereto,
Partner at Battle, Fowler LLP from 1987-
2000.
**Personal:** Columbia Law School (LLB,
1966); University of Illinois (BA 1963).

### SHOEMATE, Steven R
Gibson, Dunn & Crutcher LLP, New York
212 351 3879
sshoemate@gibsondunn.com
*Recommended in Corporate/M&A*
**Practice Areas:** Public and private
mergers and acquisitions with an emphasis on private equity, joint ventures, venture capital financings and general corporate counseling. He has extensive experience in the various types of public and
private mergers and acquisitions transactions including private company stock
and asset sales, public mergers, tender
offers, exchange offers stock and cash ten-
ders and cross-border transactions.
**Career:** Co-Partner-in-Charge of the
New York office.
**Personal:** JD, Duke University, 1988,
Member of the Duke Law Journal and the
Duke chapter of the Order of the Coif.

### SHORT, Andrew
Paul, Hastings, Janofsky & Walker LLP,
New York 212 318 6018
andrewshort@paulhastings.com
*Recommended in Tax*
**Practice Areas:** Partner in tax whose
practice includes a broad range of
domestic and international transactions,
including mergers and acquisitions, joint
ventures, equipment and project finance,
real estate, funds and capital markets.
**Career:** Partner since 1993.
**Personal:** The Johns Hopkins University
(BA with honors, 1982). Cornell Law
School (JD, cum laude, 1985).

### SHOSS, Cynthia R
LeBoeuf, Lamb, Greene & MacRae LLP,

New York 212 424 8129
cshoss@llgm.com
*Recommended in Insurance*
**Practice Areas:** Senior insurance regulatory attorney, concentrating in demutualizations and mutual holding company
conversions, complex restructurings,
mergers and acquisitions, and debt and
equity offerings. Advises life, health and
property/casualty insurers and state
insurance regulators on same and on policy, strategy, legislation and regulations.
Provides insurance regulatory counsel on
product launches, corporate governance,
examinations and internal investigations.
Certified IMSA assessor.
**Prof. Memberships:** Admitted to practice in New York, Illinois, Missouri and
Louisiana.
**Career:** Joined LeBoeuf Lamb in 1982;
Managing Partner, London Office (1987-
89).
**Personal:** New York University (LLM,
Taxation) 1980; Tulane University (JD)
1974; Newcomb College (BA cum laude)
1971.

### SHUBE, Eric
Allen & Overy LLP, New York
212 610 6366
eric.shube@allenovery.com
*Recommended in Corporate/M&A*
**Practice Areas:** Focuses on M&A, representing principals on negotiated and
hostile acquisitions and dispositions, private equity firms in investments in public
and private companies, and investment
banking firms in their activities as financial advisor in acquisition transactions.
He regularly advises on cross-border
transactions.
**Career:** Partner at Allen & Overy LLP
since 2001. Previously, he was a Partner at
Vinson & Elkins, and, prior to that, he
was an associate at Cravath, Swaine &
Moore.
**Personal:** Harvard Law School (JD, cum
laude, 1984); Brown University (AB,
magna cum laude, 1981).

### SHUSTER, Michael
White & Case LLP, New York
212 819 8528
mshuster@whitecase.com
*Recommended in Litigation*
**Practice Areas:** Head of firm's worldwide Commercial Litigation Practice
Group. Particular experience in complex
financial matters, antitrust matters, class
actions. Has tried cross-border arbitration matters under rules of ICC and
other arbitral bodies, and matters in US
Federal Courts and New York State
Courts. Extensive alternative
dispute/mediation proceedings experience. Clients include major financial
institutions, insurers, multinational conglomerates.
**Prof. Memberships:** New York State Bar,
1987; US District Courts for the Southern
and Eastern Districts; ABA (litigation,

antitrust, entertainment and sports law
sections).
**Personal:** York University (BA, 1982);
McGill University Law School (LLB, BCL,
1986).

### SHUTRAN, Richard
Dewey Ballantine LLP, New York
212 259 6710
rshutran@deweyballantine.com
*Recommended in Projects*
**Practice Areas:** Richard Shutran is
Chairman of the firm's Project Finance
Group. Mr Shutran's practice involves the
representation of developers, investors
and lenders in relation to the development, financing, construction and operation of a wide range of capital-intensive
projects in the energy, industrial, mining
and public infrastructure sectors both in
the United States and abroad. Mr
Shutran has counseled clients in all phases of projects, including structuring, contract negotiation, regulatory compliance,
financing and post-financing matters,
including restructuring and acquisitions.
Mr Shutran has extensive experience in
the use of both 144A and registered capital markets offerings to finance domestic
US and international projects. Mr
Shutran is fluent in Spanish and has participated extensively in transactions in
Latin America.
**Career:** Partner, Dewey Ballantine LLP.
**Personal:** Born March 27, 1952. JD, New
York University, 1978. BA, Trinity Col-
lege, 1974.

### SICULAR, David R
Paul, Weiss, Rifkind, Wharton & Garrison LLP, New York 212 373 3082
dsicular@paulweiss.com
*Recommended in Tax*
**Practice Areas:** Tax Partner with broad
practice in corporate, partnership and
international transactions, including
public and private mergers and acquisitions, financings, restructurings, financial
products and general tax planning.
Clients include public and private companies in the United States and abroad,
private equity and other investment
funds, private investors and individual
entrepreneurs. Member of Executive
Committee of the New York State Bar
Association's Tax Section and Co-Chair
of its Committee on 'Inbound' US Activities of Foreign Taxpayers; Member, Tax
Forum. Selected for the 2006 edition of
The Best Lawyers of America.

### SIFFERT, John
Lankler Siffert & Wohl LLP, New York
212 921 8399
*Recommended in Litigation*

### SILBERBERG, Marc L
Weil, Gotshal & Manges LLP, New York
212 310 8261
marc.silberberg@weil.com
*Recommended in Tax*
**Practice Areas:** Tax aspects of mergers,

acquisitions, spin-offs and other restructurings; domestic and cross-border transactions for private equity funds and their portfolio companies; securities offerings; transactions involving REITs; and executive compensation.

**Career:** Recent representative transactions include acquisitions of Warner Chilcott plc and Grohe AG by private equity funds, the split-off of Hughes Electronics from GM, and the sale of PanAmSat Corporation. Member of the Executive Committee of the New York State Bar Association Tax Section; has served as Co-Chair of Committees on Pass-Through Entities and Tax Accounting.

**Personal:** Northwestern University, BA; New York University, JD, LLM.

## SILBERSTEIN, Rebecca
Debevoise & Plimpton LLP, New York
212 909 6000
*Recommended in Private Fund Formation*

## SILVERMAN, Eric
Milbank, Tweed, Hadley & McCloy LLP, New York 212 530 5000
*Recommended in Projects*

## SILVERMAN, Moses
Paul, Weiss, Rifkind, Wharton & Garrison LLP, New York 212 373 3355
msilverman@paulweiss.com
*Recommended in Antitrust*
**Practice Areas:** Litigation Partner with significant experience in antitrust litigation, securities litigation, corporate and derivative litigation, commercial litigation and international and domestic arbitration. Has tried cases involving complex commercial disputes, antitrust law, copyright law and employment issues and has argued appeals involving antitrust, securities, patent and corporate law. Has defended clients in civil and criminal investigations involving antitrust and securities law; represented clients in international arbitration and litigation in Europe, South American and North America; and counseled clients on antitrust matters and negotiated mergers and acquisitions with the Federal Trade Commission and Department of Justice.

## SIMKIN, Steven
Paul, Weiss, Rifkind, Wharton & Garrison LLP, New York 212 373 3073
ssimkin@paulweiss.com
*Recommended in Real Estate*
**Practice Areas:** Chair of Real Estate Department. Maintains an active practice in major financings, acquisitions and development projects, representing both lenders and developers. Has been involved in multi-state mortgage financings, real estate-related litigations and disputes, and complex joint ventures, partnership agreements and ground leases. Has extensive shopping centre experience, having been involved in the purchase, sale or financing of several hundred regional malls. Has broad experience in commercial office leasing. Selected by Real Estate Weekly as one of the 'Current Leaders' in the industry and by The Best Lawyers of America as one of the top real estate lawyers.

## SIMMS, Marsha E
Weil, Gotshal & Manges LLP, New York
212 310 8116
marsha.simms@weil.com
*Recommended in Banking & Finance*
**Practice Areas:** Marsha Simms is a Partner in Weil Gotshal's Corporate Department, and practices primarily in the areas of debt financing and restructuring. She has extensive experience negotiating financing and restructuring documentation, and has represented major lenders providing debtor-in-possession financing and exit financing. Ms Simms lectures at PLI and ALI/ABA seminars and is a Member of the American Law Institute.
**Personal:** Barnard College, BS, 1974; Stanford Law School, JD, 1977.

## SIMS, Charles
Proskauer Rose LLP, New York
212 969 3950
csims@proskauer.com
*Recommended in Media & Entertainment*
**Practice Areas:** Concentrates on copyright, First Amendment, and defamation law, as well as appellate practice and constitutional law generally.
**Career:** Argued twice in the US Supreme Court, and second-chaired more than a dozen cases. He has represented the motion picture studios in their groundbreaking and successful litigation, under the Digital Millenium Copyright Act, against hackers who were publicly providing illegal software for decrypting DVDs, and Lexis-Nexis in its victory against an internet start-up which had attempted to steal the entire Lexis database for uploading onto the Web. He has also represented the League of American Theatres and Producers in an arbitration over the ownership of the Tony Award programs, and England's Royal Court Theatre in connection with a copyright infringement lawsuit based on David Hare's play Via Dolorosa. Counsel for Reed Elsevier Inc., and lead counsel for the defense group generally, in the class action In re Literary Works in Electronic Database Copyright Litigation, settlement of which afforded databases and publishers continuing rights to almost all previously published freelance articles. In the First Amendment field, he represents The New York Times and Discovery in connection with invasion of privacy claims lodged against a documentary they produce and cablecast, and has litigated challenges to content-based federal restrictions of cable television programming, which the Supreme Court largely invalidated in Denver Area Educational Television Consortium v FCC, and joined in handling, a facial First Amendment challenge to New York's Son of Sam law for Simon & Schuster, which the Supreme Court unanimously invalidated.
**Personal:** Yale Law School, JD, 1976; Amherst College, BA, magna cum laude, 1971 Phi Beta Kappa.

## SINGER, Leonard
Couch White, LLP, Albany
518 426 4600
*Recommended in Energy*

## SINGER, Louis H
Morgan, Lewis & Bockius LLP, New York
212 309 6603
lsinger@morganlweis.com
*Recommended in Private Fund Formation*
**Practice Areas:** Head of the firm's Private Investment Funds Practice. He represents leading pension funds, life insurance companies, asset managers, private funds, universities and family offices. His practice covers virtually every type of private investment fund, including buyout, venture capital, hedge, real estate opportunity, corporate governance, distressed asset and mezzanine funds. He has broad experience in the formation of funds-of-funds and co-investment funds and in their investment activities.
**Prof. Memberships:** Trustee and former President, American College of Investment Counsel; Board of Governors, the Association of Life Insurance Counsel; Member of the Committee on Private Investment Funds of the Association of the Bar of the City of New York, the Private Investment Funds Forum, and the National Association of Public Pension Attorneys.
**Publications:** Numerous articles in various publications. Speaking engagements include meetings of the International Bar Association, the Institute for Private Investors, the National Association of Public Pension Attorneys, the American College of Investment Counsel and SuperReturn USA.

## SIRKIN, Michael
Proskauer Rose LLP, New York
212 969 3840
msirkin@proskauer.com
*Recommended in Employee Benefits*
**Practice Areas:** Michael practices primarily in the areas of executive compensation and employee benefits. He frequently represents companies, compensation committees, senior executives and management teams in connection with executive employment and severance agreements, mergers and acquisitions and other compensation and equity arrangements. He also advises on all types of equity, pension and benefit plans and issues. He also has extensive experience with benefits and compensation for tax exempt entities and their executives.
**Career:** He has represented corporations and executives in a diverse assortment of businesses, including Fortune 500 industrial companies, financial-service companies, high-tech start-ups, dot.coms, REITs, tax-exempt organizations and privately held companies.
**Publications:** He is co-editor and co-lead author of the treatise Executive Compensation published by Law Journal Seminar-Press, and the co-author of the Chapter on ERISA in the 403(b) Answer Book. He is serving as one of only six members in the employee benefits area of the Advisory Committee to the Tax Exempt/Governmental Entity Division of the IRS. He has served as an Adjunct Assistant Professor at the New York University Law School tax program. Michael serves on the Advisory Board of a number of publications and is a frequent writer and speaker.
**Personal:** Columbia University School of Law, JD, 1972. Rutgers University, New Brunswick, BS, 1969.

## SIT, Po
Davis Polk & Wardwell, New York
212 450 4000
po.sit@dpw.com
*Recommended in Tax*
**Practice Areas:** Member of Davis Polk & Wardwell's Tax Department. Works principally in the areas of derivative products, partnerships, mergers and acquisitions. Has been representing financial institutions primarily in the areas of financial products and derivatives for years.

## SLOSS, John
Sloss Law Office, New York
212 627 9898
*Recommended in Media & Entertainment*

## SLOTNICK, Barry I
Loeb & Loeb LLP, New York
212 407 4162
bslotnick@loeb.com
*Recommended in Media & Entertainment*
**Practice Areas:** Concentrates on copyright and trademark infringement cases and matters in entertainment industry addressing the respective rights of owners and users, including cases on rights of privacy and publicity. Represents clients in entertainment, advertising, licensing and merchandising industries in courts nationwide.
**Prof. Memberships:** President - USA Copyright Society; Board of Directors - Association of Independent Music Publishers; International Trademark Association; ABA.
**Career:** Partner since 2001.
**Publications:** Lectures and writes extensively for the Practicing Law Institute and other industry and professional groups.
**Personal:** Syracuse University College of Law (JD 1972); Queens College (BA 1968).

**SMITH, Bradley Y**
Davis Polk & Wardwell, New York
212 450 4000
bradley.smith@dpw.com
*Recommended in Banking & Finance*
**Practice Areas:** Senior Partner in Davis Polk & Wardwell's Credit Group and advises senior and subordinated lenders, as well as borrowers, in corporate finance transactions. Areas of concentration include secured financing; structured finance; receivables and lease purchase transactions; oil, gas and other mineral-based financing; project and other limited-recourse financing; and acquisition and other leveraged financing transactions. Has been a principal advisor to JP Morgan for many years, and has represented the Morgan interests in many US and international financing transactions, as well as in restructurings and recapitalisations.

**SMITH, Chris M**
Shearman & Sterling LLP, New York
212 848 8238
csmith@shearman.com
*Recommended in Real Estate*
**Practice Areas:** Partner in Shearman & Sterling's Real Estate Group. Represents clients on developments, financings, investment funds, acquisitions, dispositions, real estate workouts, foreclosures and bankruptcies.
**Prof. Memberships:** Member, Association of the Bar of the City of New York and New York State Bar Association; Member, Association of Foreign Investors in Real Estate; Member, Real Estate Board of New York.
**Career:** Joined Shearman in 1976 and became a Partner in 1984.
**Personal:** BS, Rutgers University (1973); JD, Columbia University School of Law (1976).

**SMITH, Jeffrey**
Cravath, Swaine & Moore LLP, New York
212 474 1514
jsmith@cravath.com
*Recommended in Environment*
**Practice Areas:** Environmental issues in financings, underwritings and mergers and acquisitions. Counseling on environmental compliance issues and advice on complex environmental litigation, including toxic torts, asbestos and insurance.
**Prof. Memberships:** ABA (Chair, Committee for Environmental Disclosure).
**Career:** Massachusetts Executive Office of Environmental Affairs, 1976-78. Private practice, Philadelphia, 1981-91. Joined Cravath 1992, Partner since 1998. Managing Partner, Administration, 2000-05.
**Publications:** 'Environmental Disclosure Requirements under Securities Laws' (ABA). 'Implications of the Kyoto Protocol and the Global Warming Debate in Business Transactions' (NYU Journal of Law & Business).
**Personal:** University of Pennsylvania (JD, 1981); Harvard University (AB,

1974). The Urban Assembly: Board Member.

**SMITH, Jeffrey Q**
King & Spalding LLP, New York
212 556 2283
jqsmith@kslaw.com
*Recommended in Litigation*
**Practice Areas:** National Litigation Practice with particular concentration in antitrust/trade regulation, securities, and other complex commercial cases. Experienced in the supervision and management of large cases. Well versed in various forms of alternative dispute resolution, including arbitration and mediation, and maintains an active counseling practice designed to help clients avoid and/or minimize litigation risks.
**Prof. Memberships:** American Bar Association (Member, Sections on: Antitrust and Litigation).
**Personal:** Yale University; JD, New York University, Order of the Coif, 1977.

**SMITH, Joseph A**
Dewey Ballantine LLP, New York
212 259 7268
jsmith@deweyballantine.com
*Recommended in Private Fund Formationl*
**Practice Areas:** Mr Smith is a Partner in the firm's Private Equity Group, where he represents fund sponsors, investment advisors, pension funds and endowments in connection with the formation of investment partnerships and the acquisition of portfolio investments. He has extensive experience with all alternative asset classes, including LBO, secondaries, real estate and hedge funds, as well as US and international corporate acquisitions, venture capital and later-stage equity investments, and real estate ventures.
**Career:** Partner, Dewey Ballantine LLP. Private Equity. Admitted to Practice, 1990, New York.
**Personal:** Born October 14, 1960. AB, Columbia University, 1983. JD, New York University, 1988.

**SMITH, Scott**
Covington & Burling, New York
212 841 1056
ssmith@cov.com
*Recommended in Corporate/M&A*
**Practice Areas:** Mr Smith is Co-Chair of the firm's Corporate Practice and Chair of the firm's M&A Group. His practice includes advising clients on public and private mergers and acquisitions, hostile takeovers, proxy contests and leveraged buyouts. He also advises corporate boards and audit committees on corporate governance and general securities law matters.
**Personal:** JD, with high honors, The University of Texas (1980), member of the Order of the Coif; AB, magna cum laude, Harvard University (1976).

**SNYDER, Orin**
Gibson, Dunn & Crutcher LLP, New York
212 351 2400
OSnyder@gibsondunn.com
*Recommended in Litigation*
**Practice Areas:** Mr Snyder has a national civil and criminal litigation practice, including complex commercial, intellectual property and media litigation, internal corporate investigations and other white-collar matters. He recently led the defense of Warner Music Group in connection with the NY Attorney General's well-publicized 'payola' investigation.
**Career:** Previously, name Partner of the well-known boutique, Parcher Hayes & Snyder. Served as Assistant US Attorney for the Southern District of NY, Securities Fraud and Organized Crime Units, and Chief of the Narcotics Unit.
**Personal:** JD, University of Pennsylvania Law School, cum laude, 1986; BA, Wesleyan University, Phi Beta Kappa, High Honors.

**SOBEL, Gerald**
Kaye Scholer LLP, New York
212 836 8515
gsobel@kayescholer.com
*Recommended in Intellectual Property*
**Practice Areas:** Senior Partner, Chair, Patent Litigation Group. Focuses on patent, antitrust, trade secret and licensing cases, including appeals. Mr Sobel recently prevailed against the University of Rochester in the Celebrex patent infringement case for Pfizer on appeal at the Federal Circuit and earlier on summary judgment at the District Court level. His trials include two landmark jury wins. He represented Xerox in its win in the patent-antitrust litigation involving office copier and electromechanical technology in the District of Connecticut, the longest federal civil jury trial. He was lead counsel for Xoma in its win on patent infringement against Centocor before a San Francisco jury in the longest biotech trial to date.
**Prof. Memberships:** Member of the New York Bar and admitted to practice before the US District Courts for the Southern, Eastern and Northern Districts of New York, the US Courts of Appeals for the Second, Third and Federal Circuits, the United States Supreme Court and the US Patent Office. He is on the Advisory Committee for Patent Litigation of the District Court in Delaware. Teaching and Lecturing: Mr Sobel is a member of the Advisory Committee of the Engelberg Intellectual Property Institute at the New York University School of Law and taught as an Adjunct Associate Professor there. He recently testified at the Innovation and Competition hearings conducted by the Federal Trade Commission and has delivered lectures at Columbia, Stanford, Cardozo, Washington University, Case Western and Brooklyn Law Schools. Mr Sobel has delivered

over 100 lectures at CLE programs.
**Career:** JD, New York University School of Law, 1963, Law Review, Hays Fellow; BEE, Electrical Engineering, City College of New York, 1960; law clerk to Hon Richard H Levet (SDNY) (1964-65).
**Publications:** Mr Sobel has also published widely. A recent publication is 'Competition Policy in Patent Cases and Antitrust' in Perspectives on Properties of The Human Genome Project (Elsevier, 2003).

**SOMMER, Dean**
Young, Sommer, Ward, Ritzenberg, Wooley, Baker & Moore LLC, Albany
518 438 9907
*Recommended in Environment*

**SOPHER, Edward D**
Gibson, Dunn & Crutcher LLP, New York
212 351 3918
esopher@gibsondunn.com
*Recommended in Private Fund Formation*
**Practice Areas:** Establishment and operation of private investment funds, including private equity, hedge, real estate and distressed investment funds, and funds of funds. Represents investment managers and sponsors of these funds, institutional and seed investors, placement agents and joint venture partners. Also active in secondary transactions involving fund interests, and M&A, financing and other transactions involving investment management firms and portfolio companies.
**Prof. Memberships:** New York Bar; Solicitor, England & Wales; Association of the Bar of the City of New York; New York Private Investment Funds Forum.
**Personal:** BA, Cambridge University, 1982; MA, Cambridge University, 1985.

**SORIN, Robert J**
Fried, Frank, Harris, Shriver & Jacobson LLP, New York 212 859 8487
Robert.Sorin@FriedFrank.com
*Recommended in Real Estate*
**Practice Areas:** Real Estate Partner. Practice covers a broad range of commercial real estate transactions, including development of mixed-use buildings, commercial mortgage, construction and mezzanine financing, leasing, sale and acquisition of office, shopping center and industrial properties, joint ventures and debt restructurings. Clients include: Macklowe Properties, Swig Equities, The Moinian Group and The New York Presbyterian Hospital/Weill Cornell Medical Center.
**Career:** Joined Fried Frank as a Partner in 1997.
**Personal:** JD(1982), cum laude, Georgetown University. BA(1979), magna cum laude, Washington University.

## SORKIN, David
Simpson Thacher & Bartlett LLP, New York 212 455 2000
dsorkin@stblaw.com
*Recommended in Corporate/M&A*
**Practice Areas:** A Partner at Simpson Thacher & Bartlett practising in the firm's Corporate Department. Advises clients in merger and acquisition transactions, securities law matters, corporate governance and other corporate law matters. Regularly advises the investment firm Kohlberg Kravis Roberts & Co. and its portfolio companies, as well as other major private equity firms and consortiums of private equity firms, including in the recent Texas Genco and SunGard acquisitions. Among other clients, represents Ford Motor Company, including in connection with its sale of The Hertz Corporation and numerous other acquisitions, divestitures and joint ventures, and Time Warner Inc., and represented America Online Inc. in connection with is US$165 billion merger with Time Warner. Also represented Associates First Capital Corporation in numerous matters, including its US$31 billion merger with Citigroup Inc.
**Career:** Joined the firm in 1985 and became a Partner in 1993. From 1984-85 clerked for Hon Charles M Merrill of the US Court of Appeals for the Ninth Circuit in San Francisco.
**Personal:** Received a BA, summa cum laude in 1981 from Williams College and a JD, cum laude in 1984 from Harvard University.

## SOSNICK, Fredric
Shearman & Sterling LLP, New York 212 848 8571
fsosnick@shearman.com
*Recommended in Bankruptcy*
**Practice Areas:** Partner in the Bankruptcy and Reorganization Group at Shearman & Sterling. Has extensive experience representing debtors, official creditors' committees, lender groups, creditors and acquirors of assets in large and complex domestic and international out-of-court restructurings and US Chapter 11 cases.
**Prof. Memberships:** Member, New York State Bar Association; Admitted in US District Courts, Southern District of New York and Eastern District of New York.
**Career:** Joined Shearman in 1997, became Partner in 2001.
**Personal:** BS, cum laude, State University of New York at Albany (1987); JD, magna cum laude, American University, Washington College of Law (1990).

## SPATT, Robert E
Simpson Thacher & Bartlett LLP, New York 212 455 2000
rspatt@stblaw.com
*Recommended in Corporate/M&A*
**Practice Areas:** Partner specializing in corporate and governance advice to boards, and M&A and restructurings for

companies, their financial advisors, control stockholders, LBO firms and special committees.
**Prof. Memberships:** Co-Chairman, M&A Tulane Corporate Law Institute; Professional Fellow of the NYU Center for Law and Business.
**Career:** Recent transactions include representing the Special Committee of Lafarge North America in the buyout offer by its controlling stockholder Lafarge S.A., Placer Dome in its response to the unsolicited bid by, and sale to, Barrick Gold, Seagate in its acquisition of Maxtor, the Special Committee of Sotheby's in its buyout of its controlling stockholder, the Special Committee of Eon Labs in its sale to Novartis, UFJ in its merger with MTFG, Citizens Communications in its evaluation and implementation of financial and strategic alternatives, CSL Limited in its acquisition of Aventis' worldwide blood plasma business, H.J. Heinz in its spin/merge transaction with Del Monte Foods, and Artal International in its acquisitions of Weight Watchers, Keebler and Sunshine. Also has an extensive practice in representing financial advisors in M&A transactions, including the financial advisors for Conoco Phillips in its pending acquisition of Burlington Resources, for MCI in its acquisition by Verizon, for Gillette in its acquisition by P&G, for Nextel in its merger with Sprint, for Comcast in its acquisition of ATT Broadband and its bid for Disney and for Compaq in its merger with H-P.
**Personal:** Brown University, AB (1977), University of Michigan Law School, JD, magna cum laude, Order of the Coif (1980).

## ST MARIE, Scott
Sacks Montgomery PC, New York 212 355 4660
*Recommended in Construction*

## STAFFARONI, Robert
Debevoise & Plimpton LLP, New York 212 909 6000
*Recommended in Tax*

## STAPLETON, Benjamin F
Sullivan & Cromwell LLP, New York 212 558 4000
stapletonb@sullcrom.com
*Recommended in Corporate/M&A*
**Practice Areas:** Senior Partner, M&A Group. Has participated in hundreds of M&A transactions over 30 years, representing bidders, targets, independent Board committees and financial advisors in both friendly and contested situations.
**Career:** Partner since 1977.
**Personal:** Harvard College (AB, 1965); Yale Law School (JD, 1969).

## STARR, Michael
Hogan & Hartson LLP, New York 212 918 3638
mstarr@hhlaw.com
*Recommended in Employment*

**Practice Areas:** Employment and labor relations law, focusing on employment discrimination; employee non-competition; theft of trade secrets and disloyalty litigation; executive employment; class-action litigation; labor-management relations and collective-bargaining; mediation and arbitration of both employment and labor disputes; and international employment law.
**Prof. Memberships:** Labor and Employment Section and International Employment Law Committee, ABA; ABCNY; Federal Bar Council; International Society for Labor Law; Board of Directors of the Court Appointed Special Advocates (CASA) (Founding Board Member; 1983-2000); Human Resources Committee for the New York City Partnership and Chamber of Commerce (1990-98).
**Career:** In his 25 year career as a labor and employment lawyer, Michael has represented clients in matters before the National Labor Relations Board, the Equal Employment Opportunity Commission and other administrative agencies and arbitration tribunals; defended employers in discrimination, employment contract, executive compensation, wage-hour and other matters, and represented management in injunction and other litigation against labor unions. He regularly advises global companies on preventive employment-law practices, and currently serves as a court-appointed mediator for the federal district court in New York.
**Publications:** In The National Law Journal: 'Promissory Estoppel' (1/9/06); 'Retaliation Claims' (10/3/05); 'Appearance Bias' (6/20/05); 'Non-competition By Employee Choice' (1/5/2004); 'Deconstructing "Constructive Discharge"' (4/19/2004); 'Mental Disabilities' (11/1/2004); 'Harassment by Consensual Sex' (8/1/2004); 'The New Law of Continuing Violations' (1/25/2003); 'Spoliation by Oversight' (11/12/2001); 'Restrictive Covenants' (9/6/1999); 'Investigating Harassment' (6/21/1999). In The Corporate Counselor: 'Hands Across the Water: Sexual Harassment and the Global Company' (1/1997); 'Deja Vu All Over Again: Automatic Renewal of Employment Contracts' (11/1/1996). 'Whistleblower Protections and the Sarbanes-Oxley Act', New York Law Journal (4/4/05); 'A Witness-Friendly Guide to Surviving a Deposition', ALI-ABA's Practice Checklist Manual on Trial Preparation II (1999). 'Who's the Boss? The Globalization of United States Employment Law', Business Lawyer (5/1996); 'Americans With Disabilities Act of 1990: Employer Responsibilities', Employment Law Handbook 44 (1993); 'The 'Sexual Shakedown' in Perspective: Sexual Harassment in Its Social and Legal Contexts', Employment Relations Law Journal (1982); 'Accommodation and Accountability: A Strategy for Judicial Enforcement of Institutional

Reform Decrees', Alabama Law Review (1981); 'The Mental Hospitalization of Children and the Limits of Parental Authority', Yale Law Journal (1979).
**Personal:** Yale Law School (JD, editor of the Yale Law Journal); University of Michigan (PhD in Philosophy, Woodrow Wilson Fellow); State University of New York, Binghamton University (BA, summa cum laude). Michael served as law clerk to The Honorable Abner J Mikva, Circuit Judge for the US Court of Appeals in Washington, DC. Admitted in New York and the US Supreme Court and several other federal trial and appellate courts.

## STEIN, Joshua
Latham & Watkins LLP, New York 212 906 1200
*Recommended in Real Estate*

## STEIN, Mark
Simpson Thacher & Bartlett LLP, New York 212 455 2310
mstein@stblaw.com
*Recommended in Litigation*
**Practice Areas:** Represents companies and individuals involved in investigations conducted by the US Department of Justice, US Attorney's Offices around the country, the New York State Attorney General's Office, the SEC, and other federal, state and self-regulatory bodies. Also conducted numerous internal investigations for companies confronting potential misconduct by its officers and employees. Has reviewed compliance programs and policies of many companies and made recommendations for improvement. As a member of the Criminal Justice Act panel, he has extensive trial experience as defense counsel in federal criminal cases and has achieved a high percentage of acquittals over the past few years. Also handles a broad range of civil litigation, including cases that are parallel to governmental investigations.
**Career:** Assistant United States Attorney in the Southern District of New York (1989-94), ending his tenure there as Deputy Chief of the Criminal Division. In 1994, served as an assistant in the Office of the Independent Counsel for the Whitewater investigation involving allegations concerning the Madison Guaranty Savings & Loan in Arkansas and members of the Clinton administration.
**Personal:** Received JD in 1983 from University of Michigan and BA 1980 from State University of New York at Albany.

## STEINBERG, Arthur
Kaye Scholer LLP, New York 212 836 8564
asteinberg@kayescholer.com
*Recommended in Bankruptcy*
**Practice Areas:** Partner and Co-Chair, Business Reorganization and Creditors' Rights Group. Represents troubled companies, and business entities seeking to protect their interests as creditors, equity hold-

ers and/or acquirers with respect to troubled companies in and out of bankruptcy. He is acting as a trustee and/or receiver for failed hedge funds at the recommendation of the Securities and Exchange Commission. Has multiple experiences as lead counsel for secured and unsecured lender groups, creditors' committees, and corporate and individual debtors.
**Prof. Memberships:** Member of the Bar of the State of New York; American Bar Association; American Bankruptcy Institute; Turnaround Managers Association.
**Career:** JD, New York University School of Law, Order of the Coif; BA, Columbia University, Economics (cum laude).

### STEINER, Jeffrey
Brown Rayman Millstein Felder & Steiner LLP, New York 212 895 2260
jsteiner@brownrayman.com
*Recommended in Real Estate*
**Practice Areas:** Jeffrey B Steiner is Chairman of the Business and Finance Department and also heads the firm's Real Estate Finance Group. He regularly represents Wall Street investment banks and institutional lenders in complex structured finance transactions, including construction, conduit, floating and fixed rate financings, forward loan commitments, mezzanine loans, loan participations, low-income housing tax credit, preferred equity and mortgage-backed securities transactions. Mr Steiner has written extensively on real estate, banking and structured finance issues. He co-authors the Real Estate Finance column of the New York Law Journal.
**Personal:** BA, McGill University 1977; JD, Fordham University 1980.

### STEPHENSON, Alan
Cravath, Swaine & Moore LLP, New York 212 474 1400
astephenson@cravath.com
*Recommended in Corporate/M&A*
**Practice Areas:** Mergers and acquisitions, joint ventures.
**Prof. Memberships:** NYSBA; ABCNY.
**Career:** Partner, 1978-88. Managing Director, Wasserstein Perella & Co., Inc., 1988-92. Partner since 1992.
**Personal:** University of Virginia School of Law (JD, 1970); University of North Carolina at Chapel Hill (AB, 1967; Phi Beta Kappa). University of North Carolina at Chapel Hill: External Advisory Board, Undergraduate Honors Program. Board of Trustees, Cold Spring Harbor Laboratory.

### STERN, Akiba
Morgan, Lewis & Bockius LLP, New York 212 309 6037
astern@morganlewis.com
*Recommended in Business Process Outsourcing, Technology*
**Practice Areas:** Akiba Stern concentrates his practice on complex, long-term sourcing and services arrangements including outsourcing transactions,

information technology-enabled business transactions, electronic commerce, technology transfers, licensing, intellectual property, joint ventures, and strategic alliances. He helps his clients structure, negotiate, and implement commercial strategies, alliance structures, pricing models, governance arrangements, change management protocols, contract administration, and supplier compliance strategies. Chambers USA and Chambers Global Leading Lawyers Guides note his 'long track record' in the outsourcing field and cite him as 'the one to go to' for information technology and corporate transactions, and for 'his facility for closing enormous deals'. HRO Today Magazine listed him among its 2006 HRO Superstars. Mr Stern is on the Board of Directors of the Human Resources Outsourcing Association (HROA) along with a small group of other industry leaders. He lectures widely and publishes frequently.
**Prof. Memberships:** Member, Computer Law Association; Member, Licensing Executives Society; Member, American Bar Association.

### STERN, Richard
Luskin, Stern & Eisler LLP, New York 212 293 2700
*Recommended in Bankruptcy*

### STERNBERG, Daniel S
Cleary Gottlieb Steen & Hamilton LLP, New York 212 225 2630
dsternberg@cgsh.com
*Recommended in Corporate/M&A*
**Practice Areas:** Domestic and international M&A transactions with a particular focus on cross-border transactions and the representation of international clients. Counseling on corporate governance matters, including duties of corporate officers and directors. Representation of institutional shareholders in their relations with public issuers, including election contests.
**Prof. Memberships:** Chairman of the New York City Bar Association's Special Committee on Mergers, Acquisitions and Corporate Control Contests.
**Career:** Joined firm, 1980; became Partner, 1988. Resident Partner in firm's Paris office, 1991-96. JD, Columbia University Law School (1979), Kent Scholar, editor - Law Review. BA, cum laude, Yale University (1976).

### STEUER, Richard M
Mayer, Brown, Rowe & Maw LLP, New York 212 506 2530
rsteuer@mayerbrownrowe.com
*Recommended in Antitrust*
**Practice Areas:** Litigates at all levels of federal and state courts, on behalf of defendants and plaintiffs, in private suits and against government entities. Represents clients in government investigations, both civil and criminal, including agency review of mergers, acquisitions

and joint ventures. Regularly advises leading companies on structuring their business practices, including distribution arrangements and licensing programs.
**Career:** Joined Mayer, Brown, Rowe & Maw LLP, New York, as Partner, 2002. Kaye Scholer LLP, 1973-2002 (Chair, Antitrust Practice Group).
**Publications:** Recent writings: 'Bidding for a Rational Robinson-Patman Act', Antitrust, Vol. 20 No. 2 (2006). 'Dysfunctional Discounts', Antitrust, Vol. 19 No. 2 (2005). [With Peter A Barile III] 'Antitrust in Wartime', Antitrust, Vol. 16 No. 2 (2002). 'Customer-Instigated Exclusive Dealing', 68 Antitrust Law Journal 239 (2000).
**Personal:** Columbia Law School, JD, 1973. Hofstra University, BA, 1970. Adjunct Associate Professor, New York University School of Law, 1985. Adjunct Professor, St John's University School of Law, 2003. Chair, Antitrust Committee, Association of the Bar of the City of New York 1995-98. Antitrust Section Delegate to American Bar Association House of Delegates, 2005-present.

### STEVER, Donald W
Kirkpatrick & Lockhart Nicholson Graham LLP, New York 212 536 4861
dstever@klng.com
*Recommended in Environment*
**Practice Areas:** Civil and criminal environmental litigation and counseling experience (all areas); transactional environmental law, domestic and international.
**Prof. Memberships:** Bars of NY, CT, NH, DC, US Supreme Court, numerous federal courts, Environmental Law Institute, ABA, NYS Bar Association.
**Career:** Kirkpatrick & Lockhart Nicholson Graham LLP (Partner); Dewey Ballantine LLP (Partner); Sidley & Austin (Partner); Pace University School of Law (Professor of Law); Day, Berry & Howard (Special Counsel); United States Department of Justice (Section Chief, Pollution Control & Environmental Defense Sections); Dartmouth College (Visiting Professor); State of New Hampshire Office of Attorney General, Environmental Protection Divison; Aetna Life and Casualty, Hartford, CT.
**Publications:** The Law of Chemical Regulation and Hazardous Waste, West Group; Environmental Law & Practice - Compliance Litigation Forms, West Group (co-author); Seabrook and the Nuclear Regulatory Commission: The Licensing of a Nuclear Power Plant, University Press of New England; Several Treatise Chapters and Numerous Articles and Lectures.
**Personal:** JD, University of Pennsylvania Law School; BA, Lehigh University.

### STILLMAN, Charles
Stillman & Friedman, New York 212 223 0200
*Recommended in Litigation*

### STOLL, Neal R
Skadden, Arps, Slate, Meagher & Flom LLP & Affiliates, New York 212 735 3660
nstoll@skadden.com
*Recommended in Antitrust*
**Practice Areas:** Represents clients involved in investigations conducted by the staff of the Department of Justice, Antitrust Division; Part 2 investigations conducted by the staffs of the Federal Trade Commission's Bureau of Competition and Bureau of Consumer Protection; Part 3 administrative proceedings and appeals; and Federal trial and appellate experience in cases involving monopolization, distribution practices, the Robinson-Patman Act and acquisitions. Counsels clients on antitrust issues regarding mergers and acquisitions, as well as antitrust and consumer protection matters, including compliance programs and proposed business plans.
**Career:** JD, Fordham University, 1973 (Member, Fordham Law Review); BA, Pennsylvania State University, 1970.

### STRASSBERG, Richard M
Goodwin Procter LLP, New York 212 813 8800
rstrassberg@goodwinprocter.com
*Recommended in Litigation*
**Practice Areas:** Mr Strassberg specializes in white-collar criminal defense, corporate internal investigations, corporate regulatory practice, and complex business and financial litigation. In addition to his work in the white-collar and regulatory arenas, Mr Strassberg represents clients in complex civil litigation, including representations involving securities class action defense, minority shareholder rights, ERISA class action defense, healthcare and insurance litigation, and employment issues.
**Prof. Memberships:** Federal Bar Council: Member.
**Personal:** JD, Harvard Law School, 1988 (cum laude); BS, Cornell University, 1985 (with distinction).

### STRAUSS, Audrey
Fried, Frank, Harris, Shriver & Jacobson LLP, New York 212 859 8544
Audrey.Strauss@FriedFrank.com
*Recommended in Litigation*
**Practice Areas:** Litigation Partner. Represents institutions and individuals in white-collar criminal defense and regulatory matters. Handles internal investigations and a broad range of civil litigation, including matters that run parallel to grand jury and Securities and Exchange Commission matters.
**Career:** Joined Fried Frank as a Partner in 1990. Served in US Attorney's Office for Southern District of New York from 1975-82. Fellow of the American College of Trial Lawyers. Writes regular column on corporate criminal issues for New York Law Journal.

**Personal:** JD(1971), Columbia University, Kent Scholar. BA(1968), Barnard College, cum laude.

## SUGARMAN, Robert G
Weil, Gotshal & Manges LLP, New York
212 310 8184
robert.sugarman@weil.com
*Recommended in Media & Entertainment*
**Practice Areas:** Robert Sugarman is a nationally recognized trial lawyer who specializes in intellectual property and First Amendment matters. He is a Fellow of the American College of Trial Lawyers who has litigated significant cases in the libel, privacy, copyright, trademark, trade dress, unfair competition and false advertising areas. He has also had extensive experience in arbitration under the rules of the American Arbitration Association. Mr Sugarman has also represented publishers, as well as individuals in intellectual property, counseling and licensing matters.
**Personal:** Yale University, BA, 1960; Yale Law School, JD, 1963.

## SUKIN, Michael
Sukin Law Group, New York
212 302 5800
*Recommended in Media & Entertainment*

## SULLIVAN, Robert J
Skadden, Arps, Slate, Meagher & Flom LLP & Affiliates, New York
212 735 2930
rsulliva@skadden.com
*Recommended in Insurance*
**Practice Areas:** Over 30 years of experience representing insurance and reinsurance companies and extensive experience with corporate transactions, insurance regulatory matters, reinsurance and complex restructurings.
**Career:** JD, New York Law School, 1974 (research editor, New York Law Review); BA, Fordham University, 1971.

## SUSKO, A Richard
Cleary Gottlieb Steen & Hamilton LLP, New York 212 225 2410
bsusko@cgsh.com
*Recommended in Employee Benefits*
**Practice Areas:** Employee benefits and executive compensation, including fiduciary and tax aspects of pension fund investments, golden parachutes, stock options, and other executive incentive compensation plans. Extensive experience in benefits aspect of mergers and acquisitions, ESOPs, plan terminations, and bankruptcy. He is an Adjunct Professor of Executive Compensation at New York University School of Law.
**Prof. Memberships:** Member of the Bar in New York; Charter Member, American College of Employee Benefits Counsel.
**Career:** Joined firm, 1974; became Partner, 1982. LLM in taxation, New York University School of Law (1980); JD and MBA, Stanford University (1974); BS

(Mathematics), Union College (1969).

## SUTHERLAND, Susan J
Skadden, Arps, Slate, Meagher & Flom LLP & Affiliates, New York
212 735 2388
ssutherl@skadden.com
*Recommended in Insurance*
**Practice Areas:** Practice focuses on transactions involving US and international insurance and reinsurance companies in all lines of business. Has over 20 years of experience representing US and international issuers and underwriters in a wide variety of capital markets transactions, including public offerings and private placements of debt and equity securities. Has also worked on merger and acquisition transactions, leveraged buyouts, exchange offers and restructurings, and corporate governance and securities law disclosure matters.
**Career:** JD, New York University School of Law, 1982 (Root-Tilden Scholar; Member, Review of Law and Social Change); BA, Denison University, 1979 (highest honors; Phi Beta Kappa).

## SUYDAM, John
O'Melveny & Myers LLP, New York
212 326 2000
*Recommended in Corporate/M&A*

## SWARTZ, Linda Z
Cadwalader, Wickersham & Taft LLP, New York 212 504 6062
linda.swartz@cwt.com
*Recommended in Tax*
**Practice Areas:** Co-Chair, Tax Department. Specializes in the tax and business issues of global mergers and acquisitions, spin-offs, joint ventures, restructurings and bankruptcies. Routinely advises clients with respect to international tax planning issues, executive compensation, new financial products, and other financings. Frequent speaker and writer on a wide range of transactional tax issues.
**Personal:** JD, Pennsylvania Law School; BA, Bucknell University (Phi Beta Kappa). Member, New York State Bar Association Tax Section (Executive Committee); American Bar Association, New York City Tax Club. Authors chapters on Securities Lending Transactions in Taxation of Financial Institutions (Clark Boardman Callaghan) and Debt Exchanges in Collier on Bankruptcy Taxation (Matthew Bender). Other significant publications include: Global Tax-Free Deals: Mergers, Acquisitions and Spins at Home and Abroad; Circular 230 and Tax Shelters in 2005; ABCs of Cross-Border Derivatives.

## SWEENEY, John
Morgan & Finnegan, LLP, New York
212 415 8525
JFSweeney@morganfinnegan.com
*Recommended in Intellectual Property*
**Practice Areas:** Trials and appeals, alternative dispute resolution, interference

practice, patent, licensing, antitrust, trademark and trade dress in the consumer product, medical device, pharmaceutical and computer technology industries.
**Prof. Memberships:** Mr Sweeney is a Member of the American Bar Association (1975), New York County Lawyers Association (1981), Association of the Bar of the City of New York (1981), American Intellectual Property Law Association (1990) and New York Intellectual Property Law Association. He was a Member of the Board of Directors of the New York Intellectual Property Law Association from 1992-95, served as Secretary of the NYIPLA from 1996-98 and was President of The New York Intellectual Property Law Association in 2000.
**Career:** Mr Sweeney has been involved in patent, trade secret and trademark litigation since 1973. His litigation experience includes patent, antitrust, trademark and trade dress bench and jury trials and appeals. He has acted as lead trial counsel for The Procter & Gamble Company, Boehringer Ingelheim Corporation, Sankyo, Bombardier, Inc., C.R. Bard, Inc., Dot Hill Systems Corporation, Finisar Corporation, Tile Council of America and Arthur D. Little, Inc. in numerous cases. He acted as co-counsel for Digital Equipment Corporation in the Digital/Intel litigation involving microprocessor technology. He has had extensive jury trial practice and has argued many times in the United States Court of Appeals for the Federal Circuit. Before entering legal practice, Mr Sweeney worked as a mathematician and computer analyst for the US Army Strategy and Tactics Analysis Group. His work involved mathematical modeling, including war games.
**Publications:** Sweeney, John F, author of Chapter 10, 'Injunctions' in Patent Litigation, edited by Laurence H Pretty, published 2001 by The Practising Law Institute. Sweeney, John F, 'What Is the Zurko Case And What Does It Mean?' American Conference Institute Seminar on 'Tactical Considerations And Strategies For Success In Litigating Patent Disputes', March 9-10, 2000, Washington, DC. Sweeney, John F, 'Trying A Patent Case To a Jury And the Federal Circuit At the Same Time', The IP Litigator, 2000. Sweeney, John F, and Bush, James F, 'The Doctrines of Equivalents And Prosecution History Estoppel: What Has Warner-Jenkinson Changed?', The Practising Law Institute, 1999. Sweeney, John F and Sanders, Charles H, 'The On-Sale Bar To Patentability: Understanding The Doctrine's Past, Present, And Future', The Practising Law Institute, 1998. Sweeney, John F, and Pomerance, Brenda, 'Significant Developments in Patent Litigation in 1995', The IP Litigator, March 28, 1996. Sweeney, John F, and Kaman, Elaine J, 'nequitable Conduct Developments', The

Practising Law Institute, 1995. Sweeney, John F, Hyman, Midge M, Greenberg, Scott D, and Bitler, Margaret A, 'Using U.S. Courts And International Treaties To Protect Against Infringement Abroad And At Home', The Practising Law Institute, 1994. Sweeney, John F, and Connolly, Kim D, 'The Rocky Road to Harmonization: Complications Raised by the Impending United States Transition to a First-To-File Patent System', 1993. Sweeney, John F, Greenberg, Scott D, and Bitler, Margaret A., 'Heading Them Off At The Pass — Can Counterfeit Goods of Foreign Origin be Stopped at the Counterfeiter's Border?', The Trademark Reporter, 1993. Sweeney, John F, and Manbeck, Alexandra T, 'Antitrust Law: The Year In Review', 1993 NYIPLA Intellectual Property Annual, 1993. Sweeney, John F, and Connolly, Kim D, 'How To Handle Litigation Of A Patent: Defenses', The Licensing Journal, 3 volumes, December 1992, January 1993, and February 1993, Stamford, CT 06704-1311. Lee, Jerome G, Sweeney, John F, Kaman, Elaine J, and Snow, Jeffrey L, 'Equitable Defenses In Patent Litigation', The Practising Law Institute, 1991.
**Personal:** Mr Sweeney is listed in the 2001-05 editions of The Best Lawyers in America. He also was named one of the best intellectual property lawyers in the United States by IP Law and Business in 2003 and 2004, as well as one of the 'Leaders in the Their Field', by Chambers USA 2005 and 2006. In addition, he has been named by Chambers & Partners as one of the Leading Lawyers for Business in the Chambers Global Clients' Guide for 2004-05. Mr Sweeney also has been ranked as one of the country's top-tier lawyers by Chambers Global 2006, A Client's Guide to the World's Leading Lawyers for Business.

## SYNNOTT, Aidan
Paul, Weiss, Rifkind, Wharton & Garrison LLP, New York 212 373 3213
asynnott@paulweiss.com
*Recommended in Antitrust*
**Practice Areas:** Partner in the Litigation Department. Focuses on antitrust litigation and compliance, intellectual property litigation, securities litigation and complex commercial litigation. Has extensive trial experience in state and federal courts as well as in alternative dispute resolution forums such as the American Arbitration Association. Frequently represents clients in antitrust investigations by the governmental agencies of the United States and the European Union. Has published in the areas of antitrust, trade regulation and intellectual property law, and serves as an associate editor of the Antitrust Law Journal. Member of the Leadership of the Antitrust Section of the American Bar Association.

## TABAK, Jeffrey E
Weil, Gotshal & Manges LLP, New York
212 310 8343
jeffrey.tabak@weil.com
*Recommended in Private Fund Formation*

**Practice Areas:** Jeffrey Tabak is Co-Head of Weil Gotshal's Private Equity Fund Formation Practice. He represents a number of private investment funds and their sponsors with regard to their organization and the acquisition and disposition of their investments. Mr Tabak counsels institutional investors and represents a number of money management firms, and has been involved in the acquisitions of several money managers. He also advises clients on the formation and representation of basic business structures, particularly limited and general partnerships and limited liability companies.
**Personal:** Duke University, BA, 1979; Duke University School of Law, JD, 1982.

## TANENBAUM, Jeffrey L
Weil, Gotshal & Manges LLP, New York
212 310 8276
jeff.tanenbaum@weil.com
*Recommended in Bankruptcy*

**Practice Areas:** Jeffrey Tanenbaum has experience in all aspects of debtors' and creditors' rights, and has represented borrowers, lenders and investors in out-of-court restructurings and Chapter 11 cases throughout the US. He also has experience handling real estate-related workouts and bankruptcies. His clients have included creditors such as G.E. Capital and Bank of Montreal, investors Odyssey Partners and Centre Partners and debtors such as The Grand Union Company and Bethlehem Steel Corporation.
**Personal:** SUNY Binghamton, BA, 1973; SUNY Buffalo, JD, 1976.

## TANENBAUM, William A
Kaye Scholer LLP, New York
212 836 7661
wtanenbaum@kayescholer.com
*Recommended in Business Process Outsourcing, Technology*

**Practice Areas:** Chair, Technology, Intellectual Property and Outsourcing Group. Mr Tanenbaum is an internationally recognized intellectual property, technology and outsourcing lawyer. He represents clients in transactional, litigation and intellectual property matters. He advises companies in the US and around the world in the development, acquisition, licensing, protection, use, sale, marketing and litigation of technology products and services. He has long-standing experience in outsourcing and in complex computer and technology agreements. Chambers noted that he 'commands the respect of his peers for his ability and success, and of clients for his efficiency and responsiveness'. He is frequently retained to represent technology and non-technology companies in

resolving competing patent rights in technology and outsourcing arrangements, and to obtain, enforce, defend and license intellectual property rights generally. He handles patent and technology litigations for clients in a wide range of industries. Mr Tanenbaum is a past President of the Computer Law Association and the founder and Co-Chair of a leading annual outsourcing conference. His expertise and leadership in technology law was also recognized when he was selected to serve as the neutral arbitrator in a $30 million outsourcing dispute. His speeches in a series entitled 'Tanenbaum on Technology Law' are sponsored by Westlaw and Celesq. He has advised NASA and the New York County Lawyers' Association on IP matters and is the only lawyer to have received the annual award of achievement from the New York Society of Architects (for his work on the intellectual property protection of functional works). Other areas of his practice include assisting companies in establishing privacy and data protection policies and practices; establishing technology infrastructures; developing corporate policies for the use of open source software; information technology agreements for healthcare businesses e-commerce; and the information technology and intellectual property aspects of Homeland Security legislation. Mr Tanenbaum has been selected as Outside Technology Counsel by members of the Fortune 500 and leading technology companies.
**Prof. Memberships:** Admitted to practice in New York. Memberships include: past President and current advisory Board Member, The Computer Law Association; past Chair, Internet and Electronic Commerce Task Force of the Computer Law Association; Board of Editors, Journal of Internet Law, Multimedia Law Strategist and Multimedia Law Report; Chair of annual legal conferences.
**Career:** JD, Cornell Law School, 1979; BA, Brown University (highest honors and Phi Beta Kappa), 1976.
**Publications:** 'A Guide to the European Data Protection and Privacy Laws for US Companies' (co-author); a chapter on 'Intellectual Property Aspects of Outsourcing' in Technology and Offshore Outsourcing Strategies; 'Revisiting Key Provision in Software and Outsourcing Agreements' Vol. 6 No. 9 Journal of Internal Law; and 'Land Mines and Gold Mines in Intellectual Property Aspects of Outsourcing Agreements'.

## TAVSS, John
Seward & Kissel LLP, New York
212 574 1261
tavss@sewkis.com
*Recommended in Private Fund Formation*
**Practice Areas:** Investment management.

**Prof. Memberships:** New York State Bar Association (Tax Division).
**Career:** Mr Tavss advises clients on a wide variety of securities, tax and business law matters, relating to private investment funds and the investment management business. He has significant expertise in the investment management area including the representation of 'hedge funds', other private investment vehicles (both onshore and offshore) and private equity funds. Seward & Kissel is one of the leading law firms in the hedge fund area dating back to the early 1950s, having represented A.W. Jones & Company, which purports to be the first 'hedge fund'. The Investment Management Group represents both registered and unregistered funds, as well as investment advisors, underwriters, sponsors and directors to those funds. Seward & Kissel, with offices in both New York and in Washington DC, offers sophisticated legal advice emphasizing business, financial and commercial law and related litigation.
**Personal:** Mr Tavss received a BA Degree (with honors) from University of Virginia in 1976, a JD Degree from Vanderbilt University School of Law in 1979, and a LLM Degree in Taxation from New York University School of Law. He has practiced at Seward & Kissel since 1979, and has been a Partner since 1988.

## TAYLOR, James D
Loeb & Loeb LLP, New York
212 407 4895
jtaylor@loeb.com
*Recommended in Media & Entertainment*
**Practice Areas:** Counsels advertisers, advertising and promotion agencies, entertainment and media companies on regulatory compliance/investigations and varied transactional matters from strategic partnerships and sponsorships/branded content agreements to agency and vendor contracts, talent and music agreements and content licenses. Counseling also includes intellectual property protection, rights of publicity/privacy, data collection, sweepstakes, contests and other promotions.
**Prof. Memberships:** Government and Legal Affairs Committee, Promotion Marketing Association.
**Career:** Partner since 1995.
**Publications:** Frequent speaker on advertising and promotions, branded entertainment, intellectual property and media topics.
**Personal:** Brooklyn Law School (JD, 1987); University of Illinois, Urbana-Champaign (BS, 1979).

## TAYLOR, Willard B
Sullivan & Cromwell LLP, New York
33 1 44 50 60 60
taylorw@sullcrom.com
*Recommended in Tax*
**Practice Areas:** US federal/state tax mat-

ters, including advice regarding taxation of US corporations' foreign operations, foreign companies' US operations, M&A and diverse international transactions. Represents domestic and foreign corporations before IRS and in tax litigation; has worked with Treasury Department and Congressional staffs on tax legislation.
**Prof. Memberships:** ABA; ABCNY; NYSBA (former Chairman, Tax Section); ALI (Tax Advisory Group, Federal Income Tax Project); IFA (US Council); Adjunct Faculty, NYU Law School.
**Career:** Partner since 1973.
**Publications:** Extensive writings on US tax matters; regular PLI, IFA, and IBA speaker.
**Personal:** Yale Law School (LLB); Yale University (BA).

## TERRELL, Anthony
Dewey Ballantine LLP, New York
212 259 7070
jterrell@deweyballantine.com
*Recommended in Energy*
**Practice Areas:** Mr Terrell represents issuers and underwriters in public and private offerings of equity, debt and hybrid securities, which are secured and unsecured, taxable and tax-exempt. He has also worked on lease transactions involving generating stations and other energy-related assets. Mr Terrell advises energy companies on corporate, financial, and other aspects of business combinations and corporate restructurings, including reorganizations, divestitures and financial restructurings.
**Career:** Partner, Dewey Ballantine LLP. Corporate finance, bank and institutional finance, energy, and mergers and acquisitions.
**Personal:** Born September 20, 1943. BA, New York University, 1965. JD, Villanova University, 1968. LLM, Taxation, New York University, 1975.

## THOMASCH, Daniel J
Orrick, Herrington & Sutcliffe LLP, New York 212 506 3755
dthomasch@orrick.com
*Recommended in Intellectual Property*
**Practice Areas:** Defends companies in pharmaceutical, biotechnology, chemical, and medical device industries in patent infringement and product liability actions. Experience litigating and trying cases involving organic chemistry, recombinant DNA technology, microbiology, statistics, epidemiology, drugs/vaccines, and medical devices. Appellate argument experience: US Courts of Appeal (Second, Third, Sixth, Eleventh, and Federal Circuits; Court of Appeals of the State of New York; New York and New Jersey Appellate Divisions.
**Career:** Member, Orrick's Executive Committee; Former Managing Director, Litigation (2002-04); Donovan Leisure Newton & Irvine (1982-98); clerk, Thomas Griesa, US District Judge, SDNY

(1981-82).
**Personal:** JD, Columbia University, 1981; BA, Northwestern University, 1978.

## THOMPSON, Mark
Simpson Thacher & Bartlett LLP, New York 212 455 7355
mthompson@stblaw.com
*Recommended in Bankruptcy*
**Practice Areas:** Mark Thompson is a Partner in the firm's Bankruptcy Practice, where he concentrates on business reorganizations, acquisitions of troubled companies, creditors' rights and structured financing.
**Prof. Memberships:** American Bankruptcy Institute.
**Career:** Mr Thompson joined Simpson Thacher in 1982 and became Partner in 1991. He has practiced in the Bankruptcy Department since 1986.
**Personal:** He received his BA summa cum laude from Columbia University in 1979 and JD cum laude from Harvard Law School in 1982.

## THOYER, Judith R
Paul, Weiss, Rifkind, Wharton & Garrison LLP, New York 212 373 3002
jthoyer@paulweiss.com
*Recommended in Corporate/M&A*
**Practice Areas:** Former Co-Head of the Mergers and Acquisitions Group of the firm's Corporate Department. Has extensive experience in the area of acquisitions and dispositions of public and private companies, covering negotiated transactions, contested takeovers and acquisitions, and dispositions of companies in connection with chapter 11 proceedings. Advises public company boards of directors and special committees. Recently, represented Hollinger International Inc. in its 'Strategic Process' to sell significant assets and a Special Committee of Weight Watchers International in connection with a purchase of a related business. Member of the Committee on Mergers, Acquisitions and Corporate Control Contests of the Association of the Bar of the City of New York. Selected for the 2006 edition of The Best Lawyers in America.

## THURSTON, Sally A
Skadden, Arps, Slate, Meagher & Flom LLP & Affiliates, New York
212 735 4140
sthursto@skadden.com
*Recommended in Tax*
**Practice Areas:** Advises US and international clients on a wide range of tax matters, including tax aspects of mergers and acquisitions, joint ventures, restructurings, divestitures and spin-offs. Advises multinational clients regarding the US tax aspects of cross-border merger and acquisition transactions and tax minimization structures. The former includes utilization of dual-listed company and exchangeable share structures. In US, regularly advises clients on taxable and tax-

free acquisitions and divestitures and has significant experience in the partnership taxation area.
**Career:** JD, Harvard Law School, 1986 (cum laude); BS, Chemical Engineering, Cornell University, 1983 (with distinction).

## TODER, Richard
Morgan, Lewis & Bockius LLP, New York
212 309 6052
rtoder@morganlewis.com
*Recommended in Bankruptcy*
**Practice Areas:** Richard Toder is the leader of the firm's Bankruptcy and Restructuring Practice. Mr Toder represents major institutional creditors and committees in bankruptcy in restructuring cases throughout the nation and in cross-border situations. Mr Toder served as an Assistant United States Attorney in the Southern District of New York. Mr Toder is a certified mediator in the Southern District of New York Bankruptcy Court and is often appointed by the Court and parties to serve in that capacity.
**Prof. Memberships:** American College of Bankruptcy (Director and Fellow); National Bankruptcy Conference (Executive Committee and Conferee).

## TODRYS, Steven C
Simpson Thacher & Bartlett LLP, New York 212 455 2000
stodrys@stblaw.com
*Recommended in Tax*
**Practice Areas:** A Partner at Simpson Thacher & Bartlett LLP and the Head of the firm's Tax Department. Specialises in federal income taxation, with a particular emphasis on corporate mergers and acquisitions, joint ventures and restructurings. Recent experience includes the acquisition of Reebok International by adidas-Salomon, the sale of Toys R Us, the merger of Kmart and Sears Roebuck, the acquisition of Warner Music Group and the numerous buyout transactions of Kohlberg Kravis Roberts & Co.
**Career:** Served as Chair of the Tax Section of the New York State Bar Association in 1998 and also served as a Co-Chair of the Committee on Corporations and Committee on Foreign Activities of US Taxpayers. Admitted to practice in New York, the US Tax Court and the US Supreme Court.
**Personal:** Graduated from the University of Rochester in 1975 and obtained a JD, in 1978 with honors from the University of Chicago.

## TOGUT, Albert
Togut Segal & Segal LLP, New York
212 594 5000
*Recommended in Bankruptcy*

## TONERY, Lisa
King & Spalding LLP, New York
212 556 2307
ltonery@kslaw.com
*Recommended in Energy*
**Practice Areas:** Federal and state regu-

latory law, litigation and transactions involving the energy industry focusing on gas, electric, oil and transactional matters on behalf of natural gas companies, natural gas marketers and end-users, oil pipelines and shippers, independent power producers and power marketers. Regulatory advice and strategy on a transactional basis and representation in proceedings before the Federal Energy Regulatory Commission and state regulatory agencies.
**Prof. Memberships:** District of Columbia Bar; New York Bar; Energy Bar Association.
**Personal:** BA, Catholic University,1984; JD, Catholic University,1989.

## TOWNSEND, Robert
Cravath, Swaine & Moore LLP, New York
212 474 1964
rtownsend@cravath.com
*Recommended in Corporate/M&A*
**Practice Areas:** Mergers and acquisitions, including public and private negotiated transactions; corporate governance and general corporate advice. Managing Partner, Corporate.
**Prof. Memberships:** ABA; NYSBA; ABCNY (Special Committee on Mergers, Acquisitions and Corporate Control Contests).
**Career:** Partner since 1998.
**Personal:** Harvard Law School (JD, magna cum laude, 1990; executive editor, Harvard Law Review); Harvard College (AB, magna cum laude, 1987).

## TRAVIS, Norton L
Garfunkel, Wild & Travis PC, Great Neck
516 393 2200
*Recommended in Healthcare*

## TREESH, Kevin
Kirkland & Ellis LLP, New York
212 446 4959
ktreesh@kirkland.com
*Recommended in Tax*
**Practice Areas:** Mr Treesh's Tax Practice primarily involves planning and structuring domestic and international business acquisitions and dispositions. He has been active in advising both domestic and foreign clients with respect to their US investments and operations, ranging from start-ups and joint ventures to more mature private and public equity investments. He has also advised both sponsors and investors in domestic and international buyout, private equity and mezzanine funds ranging in size from tens of millions to over one billion dollars in capital commitments.
**Personal:** Indiana University (BA, 1983); Yale University (JD, 1991).

## TREPPER, Myron
Willkie Farr & Gallagher LLP, New York
212 728 8276
mtrepper@willkie.com
*Recommended in Bankruptcy*
**Practice Areas:** Partner and Chair of the Business Reorganization and Restruc-

turing Department and serves as Co-Chairman of the firm. Specializes in all areas of debtor and creditor representation and in the transactional aspects of business reorganizations. Recent significant matters include representation of Adelphia Communications Corp. and Maxxim Medical Group in complex chapter 11 proceedings, and Teléfonos de México SA de CV in its $206.7 million acquisition of bankrupt AT&T Latin America Corp. and in its $400 million acquisition of Embratel Participacoes Ltda from MCI. He is also representing the interests of Monsanto Company in the chapter 11 case of Solutia Inc. Has practiced continuously in this area for more than 30 years and has been counsel to Petrie Retail, Inc., Heilig Meyers Company, Livent, Inc., Paragon Trade Brands, Inc., Alliance Entertainment, Corp., Harvard Industries, Inc., Woodward & Lothrop Holdings, Inc., The Grand Union Company, Orion Pictures, and Maxwell Communications, among others.
**Prof. Memberships:** Member of the Association of the Bar of the City of New York and the American Bankruptcy Institute; Fellow of the American College of Bankruptcy; and Member of the Board of Directors of the Legal Aid Society of New York.
**Career:** Admitted to the Bar of the State of New York.
**Publications:** Has authored numerous articles and materials for legal and other publications, including: the American Bankruptcy Institute, Protecting Foreign Assets in a United States Bankruptcy Filing (Commentator); New York University School of Law, Annual Survey of American Law (contributing author); and Turnarounds and Workouts, Richard D. Irwin, Inc., 1991, 'The Lawyer's Role in Representing the Distressed Company'.
**Personal:** Received a JD from Brooklyn Law School in 1968 and a BA from Hunter College in 1965. Lectures on bankruptcy-related matters for seminars and panels sponsored by the ALI-ABA, the American Bankruptcy Institute, New York University School of Law, University of Pennsylvania Institute for Law and Economics, and other professional organizations.

## TRIER, Dana L
Davis Polk & Wardwell, New York
212 450 4000
dana.trier@dpw.com
*Recommended in Tax*
**Practice Areas:** Member of Davis Polk & Wardwell's Tax Department. Principal expertise is in business taxation, including particularly domestic and international tax planning for corporate mergers, acquisitions, joint ventures, spinoffs and other major corporate transactions. Also has extensive experience in structured finance, investment partnerships and derivatives, and has done a significant amount of work involving novel executive compensation and employee

benefits arrangements. In addition to his tax planning practice, has represented clients on ruling and legislative matters and in tax controversies.

## TRINGALI, Joseph
Simpson Thacher & Bartlett LLP, New York 212 455 2000
jtringali@stblaw.com
*Recommended in Antitrust*

**Practice Areas:** A Partner at Simpson Thacher & Bartlett LLP and a member of the firm's Litigation Department representing clients on antitrust and general commercial litigation. Has handled jury and bench trials and argued appeals in diverse areas, including antitrust, breach of contract, copyright and patent infringement and employment discrimination. Primarily, has litigated civil antitrust actions on behalf of both plaintiffs and defendants and counsels clients under the Sherman, Clayton, Robinson-Patman and Hart-Scott-Rodino Acts. Has handled merger transactions before the Department of Justice, the Federal Trade Commission and various state antitrust enforcement agencies as well as coordinating competition law filings on a global basis. Work includes acting for Master-Card, J.P. Morgan Chase, Lehman Brothers, Kohlberg Kravis Roberts, The Blackstone Group, KMart, Owens-Illinois, Veritas, Viacom, and Weyerhaeuser.
**Career:** Joined the firm in 1983 and became a Partner in 1989.
**Personal:** Received a BA from Wesleyan University in 1977 and a JD from the New York University School of Law in 1980.

## TURNBULL, Kenneth J
Morgan, Lewis & Bockius LLP, New York 212 309 6055
kturnbull@morganlewis.com
*Recommended in Employment*

**Practice Areas:** Kenneth J Turnbull is a Partner in the Labor and Employment Law Practice Group. Mr Turnbull represents employers in a wide range of employment litigation matters before state and federal courts in cases, including class actions, involving discrimination and wage and hour issues, as well as restrictive covenants and trade secret litigation and corporate planning and restructuring. Mr Turnbull also works extensively in traditional labor matters and represents clients before the National Labor Relations Board in collective bargaining, union representation elections, labor arbitrations and unfair labor practice charges.
**Prof. Memberships:** American Bar Association.

## TURNER, Scott M
Nixon Peabody LLP, Rochester 585 263 1612
sturner@nixonpeabody.com
*Recommended in Environment*

**Practice Areas:** Permitting/regulation

of electric generating and other industrial facilities throughout the US. Air/water pollution permit, enforcement, rulemaking proceedings regarding power plants, waste-to-energy facilities, and landfills. Clean Air Act citizen suit defense. Prevention of significant deterioration and nonattainment new source review regulations. Clean Water Act permitting issues.
**Prof. Memberships:** Admitted to practice in NY, DC, US District Court (Western District of NY), US Courts of Appeals (Second, Third Circuits). Air/Waste Management Association; American Society of Mechanical Engineers.
**Career:** Chaired Environmental Practice Group for 14 years.
**Personal:** Washington & Lee University, JD, magna cum laude; Colgate University, BA, with honors.

## URBACH, Ronald
Davis & Gilbert, New York 212 468 4800
*Recommended in Media & Entertainment*

## URDA KASSIS, Cynthia
Shearman & Sterling LLP, New York 212 848 7969
curdakassis@shearman.com
*Recommended in Projects*

**Practice Areas:** Co-Head, Project Development & Finance Group with significant experience representing sponsors and lenders in a wide variety of project and structured financing transactions, and joint venture arrangements. Significant experience in multi-source project financings involving export credit agencies and local financing sources. Considerable expertise in the mining and energy sectors on a broad range of transactions around the globe, most recently in the US, Latin America and Asia.
**Career:** Joined the firm in 1984. Became a Partner in 1992.
**Personal:** BA, University of Virginia (1980); MA, University of Notre Dame (1981); JD, American University, Washington College of Law (1984).

## URIS, Harvey R
Skadden, Arps, Slate, Meagher & Flom LLP & Affiliates, New York 212 735 2212
huris@skadden.com
*Recommended in Real Estate*

**Practice Areas:** Specializes in capital markets-related real estate transactions; commercial mortgage-backed loan origination and securitization transactions; private equity funds and private placements; bondable and other credit tenant lease transactions; sale-leasebacks; off balance sheet synthetic lease transactions; the acquisition, financing, sale, exchange and other disposition of office buildings, shopping centers, hotels, multi-family and other property types; multi-property and multi-state mortgage financing; mezzanine, preferred equity and so-called bifur-

cated secured financing transactions; partnerships; limited liability companies; and US and non-US joint ventures.
**Career:** Boston University: JD, 1979 (cum laude); BA, 1976 (cum laude).

## UROWSKY, Richard J
Sullivan & Cromwell LLP, New York 212 558 5000
urowskyr@sullcrom.com
*Recommended in Antitrust*

**Practice Areas:** Specialises in antitrust, securities and tax litigation, as well as other forms of complex litigation. Extensive experience in advising clients on competition issues, including mergers, acquisitions, joint ventures and pricing policy. Representative clients: Goldman, Sachs & Co., Microsoft, Avon Products, Computer Associates, Diageo, MBNA, BP, and RR Donnelley.
**Prof. Memberships:** ABA; ABCNY; FBC; NYCLA.
**Career:** Partner since 1980. Law clerk to Hon Stanley F Reed (US Supreme Court, 1972-73).
**Personal:** Yale University (BA, 1967); Oxford (BPhil, 1970); Yale Law School (JD, 1972).

## VARDELL, James C
Cravath, Swaine & Moore LLP, New York 212 474 1900
jvardell@cravath.com
*Recommended in Banking & Finance*

**Practice Areas:** Broad range of corporate finance transactions; primarily representing banks in complex syndicated financings, both domestic and international. Extensive experience in acquisition financings and other leveraged financings. Also experienced in equipment financings, project financings, leveraged-lease financings and vendor financings.
**Career:** Partner since 1987.
**Personal:** Yale Law School (JD, 1980); Washington and Lee University (BA, 1977).

## VICTOR, A Paul
Weil, Gotshal & Manges LLP, New York 212 310 8110
paul.victor@weil.com
*Recommended in Antitrust*

**Practice Areas:** Paul Victor is an internationally known expert in antitrust and competition law. Mr Victor has been involved in many criminal and civil international cartel cases, representing major corporations with respect to such products as lysine, nucleotides, carbon fiber, MCAA, impact modifiers, and vitamins. In addition, he has handled transactions and litigated cases in the merger control area, and represented Matsushita in the famous Matsushita case and in the Go-Video case tried successfully to a verdict. He has also focused on cross-border and other international antitrust issues.
**Personal:** BBA, 1960; JD, with distinction, 1963; University of Michigan.

## VINE, Stephen M
Akin Gump Strauss Hauer & Feld LLP, New York 212 872 1030
svine@akingump.com
*Recommended in Private Fund Formation*

**Practice Areas:** For the past 25 years, Steve Vine has advised some of the largest and most prominent private investment funds and fund managers in connection with their fund formation and capital raising activities in investment disciplines including global macro, distressed investments, private equity, domestic and foreign real estate, arbitrage, financial services and country funds. In addition, he provides advice on planning and execution of investment and financing transactions, and on formation and operation of investment management firms and related service companies, including broker-dealers. He also assists fund managers in registration and regulatory compliance.
**Personal:** AB, JD, Harvard University.

## VINEGRAD, Alan
Covington & Burling, New York 212 841 1000
avinegrad@cov.com
*Recommended in Litigation*

**Practice Areas:** Partner, White Collar and Trial Groups. Focusing on defense of criminal and regulatory enforcement, and representing clients in complex civil litigation. Clients include: Adelphia Communications; Special Committee, Board of Tyco; SG Cowen; Morgan Stanley; Ernst & Young; and, executives in mutual fund and reinsurance investigations.
**Career:** US Attorney, Eastern District of NY; Chief Assistant US Attorney, Chief, Criminal Division, Deputy Chief, Criminal Division, Chief, Civil Rights Litigation and Chief, General Crimes. Argued over 20 cases before US Court of Appeals.
**Personal:** Wharton School of Business (1980). NYU School of Law (1984). Clerk, Honorable Leonard B Sand (1984-85).

## VITALE, Robert L
Paul, Hastings, Janofsky & Walker LLP, New York 212 318 6086
robertvitale@paulhastings.com
*Recommended in Projects*

**Practice Areas:** Member of the firm's Global Projects Group. Sector expertise includes energy, telecommunications, water, oil and gas, pipelines, transportation and industrial facilities. Mandated for work in more than 20 countries. Privatization practice includes counseling governments and private parties on bid and tender programs, BOT contracts, management contracts, construction contracts, and asset sales. Advises clients on private/public M&A transactions in indicated sectors. Clients include private equity funds, monoline insurers, institutional investors, commercial and investment banks, governments, and industrial companies.

**Prof. Memberships:** Chair of New York City Bar Association's Committee on Project Finance.

## VITKOWSKY, Vincent J
Edwards Angell Palmer & Dodge LLP, New York 212 912 2828
Vvitkowsky@eapdlaw.com
*Recommended in Insurance*
**Practice Areas:** Vince represents insurance and reinsurance industry clients in significant disputes. He serves as lead counsel in arbitration and litigation arising from property and casualty, life and health, finite, aviation, specific and aggregate stop loss, contingency, and fidelity and surety business.
**Prof. Memberships:** International Bar Association, Association Internationale de Droit des Assurances, British Commercial Bar Association - Honorary Overseas Member.
**Publications:** Vince has written dozens of articles on reinsurance and arbitration subjects.
**Personal:** Northwestern University, BA, 1977; Cornell University School of Law, JD, 1980.

## VIZCARRONDO JR, Paul
Wachtell, Lipton, Rosen & Katz, New York 212 403 1208
pvizcarrondo@wlrk.com
*Recommended in Litigation*
**Practice Areas:** Specializes in corporate and securities litigation and regulatory and white-collar criminal matters.
**Prof. Memberships:** Served on several committees of the Association of the Bar of the City of New York, including the Criminal Law Committee and the Federal Courts Committee, has been a Master of the Federal Bar Council's Inn of Court, is a Member of the Columbia Law School Board of Visitors, and a Fellow of The New York Bar Foundation.
**Career:** Partner at Wachtell, Lipton, Rosen & Katz since 1981. Has tried significant cases in courts throughout the United States. Worked as law clerk to the Honorable Edward Weinfeld, United States District Judge for the Southern District of New York (1973-74) and as an Assistant United States Attorney in the Southern District of New York (1974-78). Awarded the Department of Justice's Special Achievement Award for his work in the Securities and Commodities Fraud Unit of the United States Attorney's Office. Has taught Trial Practice as an Adjunct Assistant Professor of Law at New York University School of Law and as a faculty member at the National Institute for Trial Advocacy; has lectured on United States federal securities laws for the Practicing Law Institute; and has lectured on litigation issues as a member of numerous continuing legal education panels.
**Publications:** Wrote the chapter on 'RICO' in Obermaier & Morvillo's 'White Collar Crime; Business and Regulatory

Offenses'.
**Personal:** Graduated from Cornell University in 1970 (BS) and from Columbia University School of Law in 1973 (JD) where he was a Harlan Fiske Stone Scholar and Articles and Book Reviews editor of Columbia Law Review.

## VLAHAKIS, Patricia A
Wachtell, Lipton, Rosen & Katz, New York 212 403 1206
pavlahakis@wlrk.com
*Recommended in Corporate/M&A*
**Practice Areas:** Specializes in corporate and securities law, concentrating on transactional matters, mergers and acquisitions, hostile takeovers, cross-border transactions and private equity investments, as well as corporate governance. Represented Hellman & Friedman and Warburg Pincus in their investment in Arch Capital, Computer Associates in its proxy fight with Ranger Governance, Fort James in its merger with Georgia-Pacific, Young & Rubicam in its merger with WPP Group, Polygram in its acquisition by Seagrams and Motorola in a number of acquisitions, investments and divestitures.
**Prof. Memberships:** Member of the American Bar Association; served for five years as Co-Chair of the Practicing Law Institute's Annual Institute on Securities Regulation; is a Member of the Advisory Board for the Annual Securities Regulation Institute; is a Member of the Board of Directors of Phoenix House Foundation, Inc, a not-for-profit organization for the treatment and prevention of drug addiction.
**Career:** Partner at Wachtell, Lipton, Rosen & Katz.
**Publications:** Lectured extensively and published numerous articles in the areas of mergers and acquisitions and securities law.
**Personal:** Graduated summa cum laude from Bryn Mawr College in 1978 (BA) and from Columbia University School of Law in 1981 (JD).

## VOGE, William
Latham & Watkins LLP, New York 212 906 1200
*Recommended in Projects*

## VYSKOCIL, Mary Kay
Simpson Thacher & Bartlett LLP, New York 212 455 3093
mvyskocil@stblaw.com
*Recommended in Insurance*
**Practice Areas:** Litigation Partner handling complex commercial cases, concentrated in the insurance, reinsurance, securities and financial services sectors. Represents major domestic and foreign insurers in complex coverage litigations (including numerous jury trials) throughout the US in a wide variety of contexts, including environmental, asbestos, breast implants and other mass tort claims. Currently representing the lead property insurer in connection with

coverage issues arising out of the September 11 World Trade Center attack, including the successful jury trial in the Silverstein case on one versus two occurences. Active in the representation of ceding insurers in reinsurance litigations and arbitrations in the US, the UK and Bermuda. Outside the insurance area, she was involved in a bench trial which resulted in a $365 million verdict on behalf of the firm's client, JPMorganChase, against Motorola. Also involved in the representation of Paramount Communications in the Paramount-Viacom-QVC takeover litigation and represented Matsushita Electrical Industries in MCA v Epstein, which was successfully argued in the US Supreme Court. Has served as outside counsel to the Archdiocese of New York.
**Prof. Memberships:** American Law Institute and Federal Bar Council; co-Chair of the Annual Meeting and of the Reinsurance Subcommittee of the American Bar Association's Insurance Coverage Committee; Association of the Bar of the City of New York (past Chair, Insurance Committee); Trustee, St Joseph's Seminary; Treasurer, Alumni Board of Directors of St John's University School of Law; Subcommittee Co-Chair, Second Circuit (US Court of Appeals) Study on Racial, Ethnic & Gender Fairness (1994-97).
**Career:** Joined firm 1983; elected Partner 1990. Cited in the National Law Journal's '40 Under 40' (November 1995), and Euromoney's 'Guide to World Leading Insurance and Reinsurance Lawyers' (International Financial L Rev 2003). Named one of 'America's Top 50 Women Litigators' by the National Law Journal (Dec. 2001). Currently serves on the firm's New Partners Committee.
**Publications:** B Ostrager and M Vyskocil, 'Modern Reinsurance Law & Practice', 2nd ed (Glasser LegalWorks, 2000). Frequent lecturer on insurance, reinsurance and trial skills.
**Personal:** JD, 1983, St John's University School of Law (Member, National Moot Court Team).

## WACHSBERGER, Chaim
Chadbourne & Parke LLP, New York 212 408 5100
cwachsberger@chadbourne.com
*Recommended in Projects*
**Practice Areas:** Heads Global Project Finance Practice. Represents sponsors, commercial and agency lenders, and underwriters on development and project financing of greenfield industrial, energy, infrastructure and transportation projects in the US and abroad. Work includes mergers and acquisitions, portfolio financings and financings involving complex structures, multilateral and export credit agency participation, and political risk insurance projects
**Prof. Memberships:** New York State Bar Association; American Bar Association (Section on Corporation, Banking and

Business Law).

## WACHTELL, Herbert M
Wachtell, Lipton, Rosen & Katz, New York 212 403 1216
hmwachtell@wlrk.com
*Recommended in Litigation*
**Practice Areas:** Specializes in major, complex case litigation.
**Prof. Memberships:** Fellow, American College of Trial Lawyers, American Bar Association; Member, American Law Institute, American Bar Association, Association of the Bar of the City of New York, New York County Lawyers.
**Career:** Partner at Wachtell, Lipton, Rosen & Katz and predecessor, 1958 to date; Assistant US Attorney, Southern District of New York, 1955-57.
**Publications:** Author: 'New York Practice under the CPLR', First Edition, 1963, Second Edition, 1966, Third Edition, 1970, Fourth Edition, 1973, Fifth Edition, 1976, Sixth Edition, 1986; Practicing Law Institute.
**Personal:** Graduated from New York University in 1952 (BS), from New York University in 1954 (LLB) where he was decisions editor, New York University Law Review, Order of the Coif and Root-Tilden Scholar, and from Harvard University in 1955 (LLM).

## WAKS, Jay W
Kaye Scholer LLP, New York 212 836 8558
jwaks@kayescholer.com
*Recommended in Employment*
**Practice Areas:** Partner, Litigation Department and Chair, Employment and Labor Law Practice. Mr Waks has over 30 years experience representing major US and international companies in employment and labor relations litigations (especially class and collective actions) and related matters. He concentrates on litigation of fair labor standards, employment rights, discrimination and benefits claims, formulation of employment policies and dispute resolution procedures (including sexual harassment avoidance and Glass Ceiling, family leave, ADA, substance abuse, workplace surveillance and privacy matters), executive employment, termination, restrictive covenant and forfeiture matters, resolution of employment law and benefits problems arising from corporate reorganizations and workforce reductions, alternatives to litigation of employment and other business disputes, preventive employee relations programs, matters before the NLRB, EEOC and securities exchanges, and international labor and employment matters. His US and overseas clients span virtually every industrial sector.
**Prof. Memberships:** Mr Waks is admitted to practice in New York State, and before the US Supreme Court, US Court of Appeals for Second, Third and DC Circuits, and US District Courts in

Northern, Southern and Eastern Districts of New York. He is past Chair of the Work in America Institute and the former Chair of the Committee on Labor & Employment Law of the Association of the Bar of the City of New York. He is a Member of the Board of Directors and serves as General Counsel to Legal Momentum (new name of the NOW Legal Defense and Education Fund) and is a Member of the Executive Committee of the CPR Institute for Dispute Resolution. He is long-time Chair of CPR's Employment Disputes Committee. He also is a sustaining Member of the Federal Bar Council, where he serves on the Executive Committee and on the Board of the Federal Bar Council Foundation. He is a Member of the ABA and the Bar Associations of New York State and City and California (assoc. member). He is a frequent speaker at ABA and other national CLE programs, a Member of the Cornell University Council and its Admin. Board and the Advisory Council of Cornell's ILR School. Mr Waks is Chair of the Advisory Council of the Cornell Law School and past National Chair, CLS Annual Fund. He has authored numerous articles on employment law subjects published in various professional journals.
**Career:** JD, 1971, Cornell Law School, editor and officer of Cornell Law Review; BS, 1968, Cornell University (School of Industrial & Labor Relations), Co-Editor-in-Chief of ILR Forum; law clerk to Hon Inzer B Wyatt, USDJ, SDNY 1971-72.

### WALDEN, S Calvin
WilmerHale, New York
212 937 7215
calvin.walden@wilmerhale.com
*Recommended in Intellectual Property*
**Practice Areas:** Practice focuses on intellectual property advice and litigation, with an emphasis on patent litigation and licensing disputes, and on advising clients concerning intellectual property asset management, new products and licensing issues. Counsel for a broad range of clients, including public companies, private high technology and medical technology companies, and companies in the graphic arts.
**Prof. Memberships:** American Bar Association, New York State Bar Association, and New York City Bar Association.
**Personal:** Yeshiva University, Benjamin N Cardozo School of Law (JD 1996); State University of New York at Stony Brook (MA 1994); University of North Carolina (BA 1989).

### WALLACE, W Kirk
Skadden, Arps, Slate, Meagher & Flom LLP & Affiliates, New York
212 735 2933
kwallace@skadden.com
*Recommended in Tax*
**Practice Areas:** Practice covers a broad

range of federal income tax matters - including M&A transactions, international financings and investment fund offerings - with a particular focus on financial product development and structured finance transactions. Represents underwriters and issuers in the development of a variety of publicly and privately offered debt and equity derivatives and other financial products, as well as underwriters and issuers in connection with a variety of asset-backed securitization transactions.
**Career:** LLM, New York University School of Law, 1991; JD, The University of Chicago Law School, 1986 (Law Review Member); BA, Yale University, 1983.

### WALLI, Karl T
Weil, Gotshal & Manges LLP, Washington, DC 202 682 7177
karl.walli@weil.com
*Recommended in Tax*
**Practice Areas:** Karl Walli has worked on a variety of transactions, including structured debt instruments, convertible debt and equity, and derivative financial instruments. He has advised financial service entities and end users on tax-advantaged methods for structuring and employing financial instruments, with an emphasis on cross-border tax arbitrage transactions and tax-efficient hedging strategies. His practice also includes the taxation of foreign entities and investments in the US. Prior to joining Weil Gotshal, Mr Walli spent 10 years with the IRS and the US Treasury Department.
**Personal:** University of Tennessee, BA, 1979; University of North Carolina School of Law, JD, 1984.

### WALSH, Kathleen A
Mayer, Brown, Rowe & Maw LLP, New York 212 506 2553
kwalsh@mayerbrown.com
*Recommended in Private Fund Formation*
**Practice Areas:** Corporate and Securities Department practice leader, New York. Focuses on representation of private equity funds and their sponsors. Regularly advises private equity fund sponsors in connection with fund structuring and formation, including the representation of buyout funds, industry focused funds and venture capital funds, as well as the secondary purchase of private equity portfolios and the spin out of private equity managers from financial institution private equity funds. Advises private equity funds and their portfolio companies in connection with mergers, acquisitions, leveraged buy-outs and early- and late-stage equity and mezzanine financings, as well as dispositions and spin-offs.
**Career:** Mayer, Brown, Rowe & Maw LLP, New York, 1991 to date; Partner, 1998. Willkie Farr & Gallagher, New York, 1989-91.
**Personal:** JD, Fordham University

School of Law, 1989; Dean's List; Fordham Law Review. BA, Fordham University, 1984.

### WALSH, Michael F
Weil, Gotshal & Manges LLP, New York 212 310 8197
michael.walsh@weil.com
*Recommended in Bankruptcy*
**Practice Areas:** Michael Walsh concentrates his practice in business reorganizations, corporate finance, and secured transactions. He has represented both creditors and debtors in a variety of restructuring and bankruptcy matters, and has experience advising boards of directors in situations involving financial distress. Mr Walsh handles restructuring matters for companies involved in the telecommunications and healthcare sectors. He served as lead bankruptcy counsel for Global Crossing, and has also represented Genesis Health Ventures, Inc. and Sun Healthcare Group, Inc.
**Personal:** Hamilton College, BA, 1972; University of San Diego School of Law, JD, 1977; New York University School of Law, LLM, 1979.

### WANG, Annie
Wormser, Kiely, Galef & Jacobs LLP, New York 212 687 4900
*Recommended in Immigration*

### WARD, Sarah M
Skadden, Arps, Slate, Meagher & Flom LLP & Affiliates, New York
212 735 2126
sward@skadden.com
*Recommended in Projects*
**Practice Areas:** Corporate and bank finance lawyer with a concentration in project finance. Represents commercial banks, investment banks, institutional investors and corporate borrowers in some of the most complex power, oil and gas, telecommunications and infrastructure project financings in recent years. Has extensive experience in export credit and multilateral agency financings. Has handled major transactions in the US as well as Asia, Europe and Latin America.
**Career:** JD, Fordham University School of Law, 1986; AB, Princeton University, 1981.

### WARDEN, John L
Sullivan & Cromwell LLP, New York
212 558 4000
wardenj@sullcrom.com
*Recommended in Antitrust*
**Practice Areas:** Active Litigation Practice covering antitrust, banking, contract, corporate and securities areas. Antitrust defenses include: Berkey Photo v Eastman Kodak; Union Carbide/GAF and BONY/Irving Trust takeover litigations; FMC v Goldman Sachs; Virgin Atlantic Airways v British Airways; United States v Microsoft; and United States v Amax, et al. Extensive appellate practice, including constitutional cases and victory in United States v D'Amato. Amicus curiae for The

New York Clearing House.
**Prof. Memberships:** US Antitrust Modernization Commission; Fellow, ACTL; Member, ALI.
**Career:** Partner since 1973.
**Personal:** Harvard College (AB); University of Virginia Law School (LLB; Editor-in-Chief, Virginia Law Review).

### WARNER, Douglas
Weil, Gotshal & Manges LLP, New York 212 310 8751
doug.warner@weil.com
*Recommended in Private Equity*
**Practice Areas:** Douglas Warner has represented private equity sponsors in connection with acquisitions, dispositions and financings for more than 10 years. He has extensive experience in leveraged buyouts and dispositions of both public and private US and European companies, as well as minority investments and restructurings. Mr Warner also has significant experience in 'going private' transactions, acquisitions and dispositions of bankrupt companies and corporate governance matters.
**Personal:** University of Puget Sound, BA, 1981; Boston University School of Law, JD, 1986.

### WARNER, E Waide
Davis Polk & Wardwell, New York
212 450 4000
waide.warner@dpw.com
*Recommended in Projects*
**Practice Areas:** Member of Davis Polk & Wardwell's Corporate Department, heads the firm's Project Finance Group and is active in biotechnology and healthcare practice. Has been involved for more than 25 years in a wide range of US and international financings, debt and equity capital markets transactions and joint ventures, including biotechnology research and development financings and a number of project financings in the oil and gas, petrochemical, mining, power and telecommunications sectors.

### WARNKE, Stephen A
Ropes & Gray LLP, New York
212 841 0681
stephen.warnke@ropesgray.com
*Recommended in Healthcare*
**Practice Areas:** Focus on healthcare fraud and abuse, compliance and investigations, third-party reimbursement, capital financing, managed care representations. Represents clients before the NY State Legislature and state and federal regulatory agencies. Counsels healthcare providers, managed care organizations, pharmaceutical companies on Medicaid drug formulary and drug rebate questions, and state supplemental rebate initiatives.
**Career:** California Bar; New York Bar; District of Columbia Bar; Partner, Ropes & Gray (2003). Principal author, 'Health Care Fraud and Abuse', White Collar Crime: Business and Regulatory Offenses (Law Journal Press, 1990-).

**Personal:** JD, Yale Law School (1985); BA, magna cum laude, Harvard University (1981).

## WARREN, Charles
Bryan Cave LLP, New York
212 541 2000
*Recommended in Environment*

## WASSERMAN, Craig M
Wachtell, Lipton, Rosen & Katz,
New York 212 403 1232
cmwasserman@wlrk.com
*Recommended in Corporate/M&A,
Financial Services*

**Practice Areas:** Specializes in mergers and acquisitions, banking and securities law matters.

**Prof. Memberships:** Member of the New York State Bar and various Bar Associations.

**Career:** Partner at Wachtell, Lipton, Rosen & Katz since 1993. Law clerk to Chief Judge Wilfred Feinberg, United States Court of Appeals, Second Circuit. Member of the Board of Advisors of the Yale Law School Center for the Study of Corporate Law. Extensive experience in the field of banking and financial institution mergers and acquisitions transactions and has worked on numerous public company acquisitions, corporate control contests, corporate governance and compliance matters and private equity and joint venture transactions both in and outside the financial services sector.

**Publications:** Frequent speaker and author on corporate governance, banking, mergers and acquisitions, financial services and securities law topics. Editor and co-author of 'Partnerships, Joint Ventures & Strategic Alliances'.

**Personal:** Graduated summa cum laude from Yale University in 1982 (BA/MA, economics) and from Yale Law School in 1986 (JD) where he was editor, 'Yale Law Journal', editor and senior articles editor, 1985-86, 'Yale Journal in Regulation'.

## WEINBERGER, David J
Proskauer Rose LLP, New York
212 969 3405
djweinberger@proskauer.com
*Recommended in Real Estate*

**Practice Areas:** Real estate, real estate finance.

**Prof. Memberships:** Commercial Mortgage Securities Association.

**Career:** David J Weinberger, a Partner in the Real Estate Department, has represented real estate lenders, investors and owners in connection with financings, acquisitions, sales and public offerings of equity and debt. He has developed special expertise in the origination and securitization of complex mortgage loans. David regularly represents investment banking clients, such as Wachovia Bank and Morgan Stanley, and high yield debt funds with respect to the origination of mortgage loans which are to be securitized in the CMBS markets. These loans, which

involve properties across the United States, often include preferred equity, mezzanine and/or participation components. David also has extensive experience in the structuring of 'A/B' loans. He often represents clients in connection with the origination of revolving and term credit facilities. David has been involved in the origination of numerous large loans which were securitized in single-borrower transactions, as well as thousands of conduit loans ranging in size from $5 Million to over $1 Billion.

**Personal:** Boston University School of Law (JD), 1986 (editor of the Probate Law Journal), University of Michigan (BA), 1983.

## WEINBERGER, Harold P
Kramer Levin Naftalis & Frankel LLP,
New York 212 715 9132
hweinberger@kramerlevin.com
*Recommended in Media &
Entertainment*

**Practice Areas:** Harold Weinberger is recognized as one of the country's leading lawyers in the litigation of false advertising cases under the Lanham Act. Over the last several decades he has been lead counsel in many of the most significant cases in the field. Mr Weinberger is also a Lecturer in Law at Columbia Law School, from which he graduated in 1970 and where he teaches a Seminar in False Advertising Law. Mr Weinberger has spoken at many conferences on various aspects of false advertising law and has authored numerous published articles in the field.

**Personal:** Received a JD Degree, magna cum laude, from Columbia Law School in 1970 and a BA Degree from City College of the City University of New York in 1967.

## WEINBERGER, Michael
Cleary Gottlieb Steen & Hamilton LLP,
New York 212 225 2092
mweinberger@cgsh.com
*Recommended in Real Estate*

**Practice Areas:** Real estate finance, commercial mortgage securitizations. Recent transactions include origination and securitization of $1.7 billion financing of Rockefeller Center; $700 million financing of multistate portfolio of 34 hotels; $320 million financing of multistate portfolio of 36 industrial properties; and $450 million construction loan to expand a regional mall.

**Career:** Partner since 2000. Judicial clerk, Hon Leonard Garth, US Court of Appeals, Third Circuit (1991-92).

**Personal:** JD, magna cum laude, Law Review, Harvard Law School (1991); BA, summa cum laude, Phi Beta Kappa, Yale University (1988).

## WEINER, Michael L
Skadden, Arps, Slate, Meagher & Flom
LLP & Affiliates, New York
212 735 2632
mweiner@skadden.com
*Recommended in Antitrust*

**Practice Areas:** Represents clients in antitrust investigations of merger and acquisition transactions, and in antitrust class action and other complex litigations.

**Career:** JD, Georgetown University Law Center, 1980 (magna cum laude); BA, University of Pennsylvania, 1976 (cum laude).

## WEINSTEIN, Lawrence I
Proskauer Rose LLP, New York
212 969 3240
lweinstein@proskauer.com
*Recommended in Media &
Entertainment*

**Practice Areas:** False advertising litigation and counseling, including Lanham Act litigation, state law consumer class action litigation and NAD proceedings; trademark litigation; trade secret litigation; copyright litigation; entertainment litigation; art litigation.

**Prof. Memberships:** Co-Chair, Proskauer Rose Trademark and False Advertising Practice Group; former Chair, Intellectual Property Subcommittee of the ABA Committee on Corporate Counsel; Member, International Trademark Association.

**Career:** Partner, Proskauer Rose, since 1999; Partner at other law firms from 1986-99.

**Publications:** Frequent lecturer and writer in the field of intellectual property law. Articles in 2005-06 have included 'False Advertising Law: Consumer Class Action Suits', published in the National Law Journal; 'Developments in Advertising Law in 2005'; 'Recent Developments in US Federal Trademark Dilution Law'. Lectured in 2006 to the Association of National Advertisers, the National Intellectual Property CLE Course co-sponsored by the ABA and INTA, and the British Institute of Trade Mark Attorneys.

**Personal:** Johns Hopkins University, BA 1974, MA 1975; New York University School of Law, JD 1978, Order of the Coif, John Norton Pomeroy Scholar, articles editor, NYU Law Review; law clerk to the Honorable James Hunter, US Court of Appeals for the Third Circuit, 1978-79.

## WEINSTEIN, Mark
Hogan & Hartson LLP, New York
212 918 8269
mjweinstein@hhlaw.com
*Recommended in Media &
Entertainment*

**Practice Areas:** Mark Weinstein has over 25 years of experience providing sophisticated tactical solutions to businesses in the media, entertainment, sports and technology areas.

**Prof. Memberships:** ABA; NYSBA.

**Career:** Mark is highly regarded as a valued advisor to the world's largest communications and media conglomerates. He often advises his clients on cross-border investment, licensing and finance. For example, he has been the lead advisor for

a global media company in restructuring its co-ownership of programming, sports and entertainment assets.

**Publications:** Mark has authored several articles for US and international publications and is frequently quoted in the press.

**Personal:** New York University (LLM); The State University of New York, University of Buffalo Law School (JD, cum laude); New York University (BS, magna cum laude).

## WEISFELNER, Edward
Brown Rudnick Berlack Israels LLP,
New York 212 704 0100
*Recommended in Bankruptcy*

## WEISS, Jack M
Gibson, Dunn & Crutcher LLP, New York
212 351 3890
jmweiss@gibsondunn.com
*Recommended in Media &
Entertainment*

**Practice Areas:** Serves as principal outside publication counsel to Dow Jones & Company. Has more than 25 years hands-on courtroom experience defending the rights of the nation's leading media. Has defended many high-profile libel cases, including (recently) Umar v Dow Jones, Cuomo v Plume, and Iqbal v AP.

**Prof. Memberships:** Lecturer in law, Columbia Law School (media law).

**Career:** Law clerk, Judge John Minor Wisdom and Chief Justice Warren Burger.

**Publications:** 'It Depends on the Meaning of "Ex Parte"', Litigation Magazine, Winter 2003.

**Personal:** JD, Harvard Law School, 1971, magna cum laude; Treasurer and Managing Editor, Harvard Law Review.

## WEISS, Melvyn
Milberg Weiss Bershad & Schulman LLP,
New York 212 594 5300
*Recommended in Litigation*

## WEISSMAN, Ellen
Hodgson Russ LLP, Buffalo
716 856 4000
*Recommended in Healthcare*

## WELLS, JR, Theodore V
Paul, Weiss, Rifkind, Wharton & Garrison LLP, New York
212 373 3089
twells@paulweiss.com
*Recommended in Litigation*

**Practice Areas:** Co-Chair of Litigation Department. Has extensive experience in white-collar criminal defense, complex civil and corporate litigation, SEC regulatory work and class action litigation. Selected repeatedly by The National Law Journal as one of the 100 most influential lawyers in America and one of America's top white-collar criminal defense lawyers. Has defended political figures, corporate executives and corporations in jury trials, grand jury investigations and before the SEC. Fellow of American College of Trial Lawyers. Served as Co-Chair of White-

Collar Criminal Section of National Association of Criminal Defense Lawyers. Selected for 2006 edition of The Best Lawyers in America.

### WERNER, Philip
Morgan, Lewis & Bockius LLP, New York
212 309 6080
pwerner@morganlewis.com
*Recommended in Private Equity*
**Practice Areas:** Mr Werner is a Partner in the Business and Finance Practice. His practice focuses on mergers and acquisitions and corporate finance. Mr Werner is involved in a wide range of acquisition and corporate finance transactions representing private equity funds, institutional investors and strategic acquirers. He is a leader in the areas of leveraged acquisitions, strategic equity and corporate partnering investments, recapitalizations and restructurings involving various industries.
**Prof. Memberships:** Member, American Bar Association, International Section.

### WERTHEIMER, Robert J
Paul, Hastings, Janofsky & Walker LLP, New York 212 318 6550
robertwertheimer@paulhastings.com
*Recommended in Real Estate*
**Practice Areas:** Co-Vice-Chair of firm's Real Estate Practice Group. Commercial real estate purchase/sale transactions, joint ventures, development and finance matters. Represents entrepreneurial investors, prominent real estate individuals/families, institutional/investment fund clients, not-for-profits and public agencies. Has international/domestic experience.
**Prof. Memberships:** New York State and American Bar Associations; active in Association of the Bar of the City of New York (served on Committee on Corrections).
**Career:** Donovan Leisure Newton & Irvine (1979-82); Battle Fowler (1982-2000); Paul, Hastings, Janofsky & Walker LLP (2000 to date).
**Personal:** Columbia University School of Law (JD, 1979); Cornell University (BA, distinction in all subjects, 1976).

### WESELY, Marissa C
Simpson Thacher & Bartlett LLP, New York 212 455 7173
mwesely@stblaw.com
*Recommended in Banking & Finance*
**Practice Areas:** Partner in the firm's Corporate Department. Specialises in domestic and international bank finance transactions, with an emphasis on leveraged acquisition finance, advising equity sponsors, corporate borrowers and lenders in connection with senior lending facilities and bridge loans. Recent experience includes: representation of Blackstone in the financing of its acquisition of Team Health, Hellman & Friedman and TPG in their acquisition of LPL Financial, Cypress in its acquisition of Cooper Standard and Affinia, and Express Scripts

in its acquisition of Priority Healthcare, as well as representation of L-3 Communications and St. John Knits in recent refinancings of their senior debt. Also active in financing transactions in Latin America, including the representation of JPMorgan and other bank lenders in the restructuring of the debt of Sanluis Corporacion and of Banco Hipotecario in the restructuring of its bank debt.
**Prof. Memberships:** International Bar Association, New York State and New York City Bar Associations, Women's Bar Association.
**Career:** Member of the firm since 1989.
**Publications:** 'Securitization Techniques in International Trade and Project Financing', The Review of Banking and Financial Services, Vol. 12, No. 7, 1996.
**Personal:** Williams College, BA 1976, magna cum laude, Harvard Law School, JD 1980, cum laude.

### WHITE, Algird
Couch White, LLP, Albany
518 426 4600
*Recommended in Energy*

### WHITE, Ira
Morgan, Lewis & Bockius LLP, New York
212 309 6115
iwhite@morganlewis.com
*Recommended in Private Equity*
**Practice Areas:** Mr White is a Partner in the Business and Finance Practice and Co-Chair of the firm's Private Equity Practice. Mr White's practice focuses on mergers and acquisitions, private equity and venture capital matters. Mr White has been involved in a wide range of transactions representing private equity funds; venture capital funds; corporations, limited liability companies and partnerships; and management.

### WHITE, Mary Jo
Debevoise & Plimpton LLP, New York
212 909 6000
*Recommended in Litigation*

### WHITE, W Christopher
Cadwalader, Wickersham & Taft LLP, New York 212 504 6633
christopher.white@cwt.com
*Recommended in Real Estate*
**Practice Areas:** Chairman, Global Finance Department. Specializes in commercial real estate with emphasis on debt and equity financing. Represents many of the largest US and foreign institutional investors in the full spectrum of their real estate investment activity. Spearheads Cadwalader's representation of investment banks and institutional lenders in public and private securitizations and other secondary market transactions. Structured acquisition and financing for commercial properties in Europe and Latin America. Represented institutional investors in joint ventures and other investment vehicles for the acquisition and development of hotels, office build-

ings, shopping centers and internet datacenters. Experienced with hotel and property management agreements and leasing agreements. Structured acquisitions of interests in companies owning and operating hotels, shopping centers, entertainment complexes and office buildings. Experienced in the workout of troubled assets, including restructurings, foreclosures and bankruptcies. Devised procedures for foreclosure by power of sale in New York.
**Personal:** JD, University of Michigan Law School (1977); BA, University of Notre Dame (1973).

### WIDER, Jedd
Morgan, Lewis & Bockius LLP, New York
212 309 6605
jwider@morganlewis.com
*Recommended in Private Fund Formation*
**Practice Areas:** Jedd H Wider is a Partner in the Business and Finance Practice and a member of the firm's Private Investment Funds Practice. Mr Wider concentrates his practice in the structuring and formation of and investment in international and domestic private investment funds, particularly global private equity funds, hedge funds, real estate funds, venture capital funds and funds-of-funds and in the subsequent representation of these funds in their investment activities.
**Prof. Memberships:** Member, American Bar Association; Member, Association of the Bar of the City of New York; Member, Order of the Coif.

### WIEMAN, Lawrence E
Davis Polk & Wardwell, New York
212 450 4000
lawrence.wieman@dpw.com
*Recommended in Banking & Finance*
**Practice Areas:** Member of Davis Polk & Wardwell's Credit Group. Represents borrowers and lenders in secured and unsecured financings for US and non-US transactions. Advises lenders and financially distressed borrowers on workouts and debt restructurings, various lender, borrower and acquirer or clients on senior and subordinated financing for contested and friendly acquisitions, and financial institutions and other clients regarding credit risks involved in domestic and cross-border securities and derivatives transactions and related collateral arrangements.

### WIGHT, Richard
Milbank, Tweed, Hadley & McCloy LLP, New York 212 530 5000
*Recommended in Banking & Finance*

### WILD, Robert Andrew
Garfunkel, Wild & Travis PC, Great Neck
516 393 2200
*Recommended in Healthcare*

### WILDES, Leon
Wildes & Weinberg PC, New York
212 753 3468
*Recommended in Immigration*

### WILLIAMS, Nicholas
Clifford Chance US LLP, New York
212 878 8000
*Recommended in Insurance*

### WILLIAMSON, Bradd
Latham & Watkins LLP, New York
212 906 1200
*Recommended in Employee Benefits*

### WING, John
Lankler Siffert & Wohl LLP, New York
212 921 8399
*Recommended in Litigation*

### WOHL, Frank
Lankler Siffert & Wohl LLP, New York
212 921 8399
*Recommended in Litigation*

### WOJCIECHOWSKI, Mark S
Mayer, Brown, Rowe & Maw LLP, New York 212 506 2525
mwojciechowski@mayerbrownrowe.com
*Recommended in Banking & Finance, Corporate/M&A*
**Practice Areas:** Banking and finance, corporate, corporate finance, and private equity. Has extensive experience not only in banking and finance but also mergers and acquisitions, joint ventures (domestic and international), and private equity investment.
**Prof. Memberships:** Admitted to practice in New York (1982). Member of International Law Advisory Committee of the Practising Law Institute; American Bar Association, Section on Corporation, Banking, and Business Law; the New York State Bar Association, Section of International Law and Practice; and the Association of the Bar of the City of New York. Appointments: Immediate past Chairman, Corporation Law Committee, Association of the Bar of the City of New York; Member, Mergers & Acquisitions Committee, Association of the Bar of the City of New York.
**Career:** Joined Mayer, Brown, Rowe & Maw LLP, 1986; became Partner, 1988. Member, Mayer, Brown, Rowe & Maw Executive Committee (Policy and Planning Committee).
**Publications:** Co-author, 'How to Buy a US Business: A Guide to Negotiated and Hostile Acquisitions' (1999).
**Personal:** JD (cum laude), Indiana University (Bloomington), 1981; AB, Columbia College, 1976.

### WOLF, Barry M
Weil, Gotshal & Manges LLP, New York
212 310 8209
barry.wolf@weil.com
*Recommended in Private Fund Formation*
**Practice Areas:** Barry Wolf is Co-Chair of Weil Gotshal's Corporate Department.

He regularly represents private investment funds and their sponsors in their organization and operation. Mr Wolf also has extensive experience representing institutional investors in investing in private equity funds, providing both commercial advice as well as tax advice. His clients include American Securities, Centre Partners, Genstar Capital, Gores Technology Group and Lindsay Goldberg & Bessemer.

**Personal:** SUNY Albany, BS, 1981; University of Michigan Law School, JD, 1984; New York University School of Law, LLM, 1989.

## WOLFSON, Peter D
Sonnenschein Nath & Rosenthal LLP, New York 212 768 6840
pwolfson@sonnenschein.com
*Recommended in Bankruptcy*

**Practice Areas:** Represents debtors, creditor committees, equity committees, bondholder committees, plan sponsors and purchasers of assets in large, complex out-of-court restructurings and chapter 11 cases, including cross-border and asbestos related cases. Served as lead committee counsel in high-profile restructurings and chapter 11 cases including Federal Mogul, WHX, Hexcel, USG, Gillette Holdings, Loral Space & Communications, Interstate Bakeries, Grand Union, Community Newspapers, Wilson Foods, New Valley Corporation (Western Union), LTV Steel, and At Home Corp. He was retained as special litigation counsel for committees in Exide and Hayes Lemmerz. He served as lead debtor counsel in cases such as Philip Services, Maxicare Health Plans, Hayes Microcomputer, ICH Corp. and Gibson Discount Stores. He lectures on bankruptcy/restructuring issues.
**Prof. Memberships:** American Bar Association, New York State Bar Association, American Bankruptcy Institute.
**Personal:** State University of New York at Buffalo, JD, State University of New York at Fredonia, BA.

## WOLITZER, Michael
Simpson Thacher & Bartlett LLP, New York 212 455 2000
mwolitzer@stblaw.com
*Recommended in Private Fund Formation*

**Practice Areas:** Corporate Partner at Simpson Thacher & Bartlett LLP. His practice focuses on private investing and other facets of 'alternative asset management'. Represents some of the largest and well known sponsors of private equity funds, such as Blackstone, Citigroup, Lexington Partners, Quadrangle and Silver Lake Partners. Involved in many acquisitions of, and investments in, private investment firms.
**Prof. Memberships:** Former Chairman and Member of the Executive Committee of the 'Private Investment Fund Forum',

Member of the City Bar Association's Subcommittee on Private Investment Funds and Co-Chairman of the Private Investment Funds Subcommittee of the International Bar Association. Member of the Advisory Boards of the Private Equity Analyst's Survey of Fund Terms and Conditions, and and the Private Equity Investment Guidelines Group. Served on many panels at private equity industry conferences.
**Career:** A Partner at the firm since 1998.
**Personal:** JD, 1989, Columbia University School of Law (James Kent Scholar and a Harlan Fiske Stone Scholar).

## WOLLMAN, Diana L
Sullivan & Cromwell LLP, New York 212 558 4000
wollmand@sullcrom.com
*Recommended in Tax*

**Practice Areas:** US federal tax matters, including broad range of domestic and international planning and transactional matters, for domestic and foreign clients.
**Prof. Memberships:** NYSBA (Co-Chair, Committee on Tax Policy); ABA (Tax Section); ITI Board Member.
**Career:** Partner since 2000. Adjunct Professor, Columbia Law School ('International Taxation' and 'Tax Ethics').
**Publications:** Published author on a variety of issues. Frequent speaker: NYSBA, ABA, ITI, PLI, UCLA Annual M&A Tax Institute, Institute of International Bankers, NYU Tax Planning Institute, and USC Major Tax Planning Institute.
**Personal:** Harvard University (AB, 1986); UCLA Law School (JD, 1991).

## WOLOWITZ, Steven
Mayer, Brown, Rowe & Maw LLP, New York 212 506 2535
swolowitz@mayerbrownrowe.com
*Recommended in Litigation*

**Practice Areas:** Represent investment banks, commercial banks, broker-dealers and issuers in securities litigation. Represent FCMs, broker-dealers, banks and institutional users of the markets in complex cases involving derivatives, futures, foreign exchange, securitizations, hedge funds, insurance, mutual funds, asset management and fixed income instruments. Represent financial institutions in claims of lender liability, equitable subordination, letters of credit and operational matters (eg, wire transfers). Represent financial institutions, corporations and individuals in regulatory investigations by the SEC, NASD and state attorneys general. Conduct internal investigations and report to boards of directors and audit committees. Defend US and foreign companies and financial institutions in antitrust cases. Represent corporate and individual clients in the federal and state courts and in arbitral tribunals.
**Career:** Mayer, Brown, Rowe & Maw LLP, New York, 1988 to date. Rosenman & Colin, New York, 1977-88.

**Publications:** Co-author: 'Serving Two Masters: When is Joint Representation of a Corporation and its Employees Permissible?' New York Law Journal, July, 18, 2005. 'Contesting Price-Fixing Class Action Claims in Commodities Futures Markets', The Journal of Investment Compliance (Summer 2001).
**Personal:** George Washington University, JD (honors), 1977. George Washington University, BA with distinction, 1974; Phi Beta Kappa; Phi Eta Sigma Honor Society.

## WOOD, Douglas J
Reed Smith LLP, New York 212 549 0377
dwood@reedsmith.com
*Recommended in Media & Entertainment*

**Practice Areas:** Represents national and multinational companies in advertising, marketing, promotions, unfair competition, intellectual property, e-commerce. Legal advisor to several worldwide advertising industry trade organizations, general counsel to the Association of National Advertisers and the Advertising Research Foundation.
**Prof. Memberships:** Founder and Chairman of Global Advertising Lawyers Alliance, a network of law firms in more than 50 countries that have expertise in advertising and marketing.
**Career:** Hall Dickler, combined with Reed Smith in 2004.
**Publications:** Author of 'Please Be AdVised' and numerous articles.
**Personal:** Franklin Pierce Law Center (JD, 1976); New York University School of Law (LLM, 1977).

## WYMAN, Kenneth
Simpson Thacher & Bartlett LLP, New York 212 455 7435
kwyman@stblaw.com
*Recommended in Projects*

**Practice Areas:** Corporate Partner at Simpson Thacher & Bartlett LLP. Specializes in international and domestic finance with an emphasis on project finance and leasing. Recent transactions include representation of KeySpan Energy Corp. and subsidiaries as lessee in connection with the leveraged lease financing of its 250 MW expansion to the Ravenswood generating facility located in New York City; representation of Credit Suisse First Boston as sole underwriter in connection with the $940 million construction and leveraged lease project financing of the 400 MW Springville Unit 3 coal-fired electric generating facility leased by Tri-State Generation and Transmission Association, awarded Euromoney's Asset Finance International/US Power Deal of the Year 2003; representation of Credit Lyonnais, BNP Paribas, Bank of America, Australia and New Zealand Bank and other project finance lenders in connection with numerous project financings of electric generating facilities sponsored by Cogen-

trix Energy, Inc., including its Southaven, Green Country, Rathdrum, Ouachita, Richmond and Indiantown facilities.
**Prof. Memberships:** Member, American Bar Association; New York State Bar Association.
**Career:** Joined the firm in 1987 and became a Partner in 1997.
**Personal:** Received BS, Wharton School of the University of Pennsylvania, 1984; JD, University of Pennsylvania School of Law, 1987.

## YALE-LOEHR, Stephen
True Walsh & Miller LLP, Ithaca 607 273 4200
*Recommended in Immigration*

## YODOWITZ, Edward J
Skadden, Arps, Slate, Meagher & Flom LLP & Affiliates, New York 212 735 3450
eyodowit@skadden.com
*Recommended in Litigation*

**Practice Areas:** Focuses on complex securities and financial fraud investigations and related litigation, including appeals. Handles accounting litigation and securities litigation relating to the 1933 and 1934 Acts, including class and derivative actions. Represents clients in SEC enforcement actions as well as banking, professional malpractice and insurance litigation. Experienced in the management of long-term, complex and document-intensive cases. Frequent lecturer on securities litigation for the Practising Law Institute and the Securities Industry Association.
**Career:** JD, University of Baltimore, 1969; BS, Long Island University, 1965.

## YOUNG, Kevin
Young, Sommer, Ward, Ritzenberg, Wooley, Baker & Moore LLC, Albany 518 438 9907
*Recommended in Environment*

## YOUNG, Michael
Willkie Farr & Gallagher LLP, New York 212 728 8280
Myoung@willkie.com
*Recommended in Litigation*

**Practice Areas:** Litigation Partner specializing in securities and financial reporting with a particular emphasis in accounting irregularities. Practice focuses upon the representation of officers, directors, audit committees, accounting firms, outside professionals, and companies in securities class actions, SEC proceedings, and special investigations. Named by Accounting Today as one of the 'top 100 most influential people in accounting'. Trial work includes financial reporting matters in courts throughout the United States, including the first class action tried to a jury pursuant to the Private Securities Litigation Reform Act of 1995.
**Prof. Memberships:** Member of the American Bar Association's Committee on Law and Accounting, and Member of

the Financial Accounting Standards Advisory Council to the Financial Accounting Standards Board.
**Career:** Admitted to the New York State Bar; the US District Courts for the Eastern and Southern Districts of New York; the United States Courts of Appeal for the Second, Ninth, and Eleventh Circuits; and the United States Supreme Court. Has submitted testimony at the request of both the SEC and the Public Oversight Board on financial reporting and corporate governance issues, and has testified before the United States Senate Banking Committee on important developments in financial reporting.
**Publications:** Writes and lectures frequently on financial reporting and liability issues. Publications include Accounting Irregularities and Financial Fraud and The Financial Reporting Handbook.
**Personal:** Received a JD from Duke University School of Law in 1981, where he served as research and managing editor of the Duke Law Journal, and a BA (magna cum laude) from Allegheny College in 1978, where he was elected to Phi Beta Kappa.

### YOUNGWOOD, Alfred D
Paul, Weiss, Rifkind, Wharton & Garrison LLP, New York 212 373 3080
ayoungwood@paulweiss.com
*Recommended in Tax*
**Practice Areas:** Chair of the firm and its Management Committee. Tax Partner who concentrates on acquisitions, reorganizations and financings involving American and foreign businesses. Tax representations include advising clients in the creation of major joint ventures in media and cable television, the proposed acquisition of substantial cable television properties, the disposition of a major soft drink business and the split into two public companies of a major publicly-traded media company. Selected for the 2006 edition of The Best Lawyers in America.

### ZALESIN, Steven A
Patterson, Belknap, Webb & Tyler LLP, New York 212 336 2110
sazalesin@pbwt.com
*Recommended in Media & Entertainment*
**Practice Areas:** Steven Zalesin is a noted trial attorney with substantial, first-chair experience in intellectual property, false advertising and complex commercial litigation. Mr Zalesin has represented clients in a variety of arbitration and appellate proceedings. He has represented several major record labels in music industry disputes and has also represented television networks and a major magazine.
**Prof. Memberships:** Member, Editorial Advisory Board, Advertising Compliance Service; American Bar Association (Sections on Litigation and Patent, Trademark and Copyright Law); New York

State Bar Association.
**Career:** Mr Zalesin joined Patterson Belknap in 1985 (Partner since 1994).
**Personal:** University of Pennsylvania Law School (JD 1985), cum laude, editor, University of Pennsylvania Law Review; Syracuse University, SI Newhouse School of Public Communications (BS in Journalism, 1982), magna cum laude.

### ZALL, Richard J
Proskauer Rose LLP, New York
212 969 3945
rzall@proskauer.com
*Recommended in Healthcare*
**Practice Areas:** Mr Zall's practice is focused on corporate and regulatory representation of a wide array of healthcare clients, including academic medical centers, hospitals, and physician organizations; information technology and medical device companies; managed care and health benefit management companies; and private equity firms. He also advises healthcare clients and health sector investors on business strategy, product and service development, mergers and acquisitions, and new venture implementation. Mr Zall provides clients with legal and business counsel in the planning and execution of healthcare-related corporate transactions, including M&A and equity and debt financings; the structuring of joint ventures and other contractual relationships among various health industry parties; and compliance with federal and state healthcare regulations.
**Prof. Memberships:** Member, Board of Directors, NPower New York, Inc. (www.npowerny.org) (2004-present); Member, Dean's Strategic Advisory Council, NYU School of Law (2004-05); Member, Board of Trustees, WNYC Foundation (1992-95); Member, American Health Lawyers Association; Member, Association of the Bar of the City of New York; Member, American Bar Association.
**Career:** Prior to joining Proskauer, Mr Zall was a Partner at Mintz Levin Cohn Ferris Glovsky and Popeo, PC from January 2003 until December 2005. Before that, Mr Zall served in a number of healthcare related legal and business positions. Most notably, from 1988 to 1996, he was a Founding Partner of Kalkines, Arky, Zall & Bernstein LLP, a 50-person New York-based law firm that specialized in healthcare. From 1996 through 1999, Mr Zall served as Co-Chairman and CEO of Telesis Medical Management, Inc., a venture-backed medical management company.
**Publications:** 'Venturing Forward', Health Executive (January 2006); 'Implementing Pay-for-Performance: Overcoming Policy, Legal Challenges', BNA Health Plan & Provider Reporter (15 June 2005), BNA Medicare Report (10 June 2005), BNA Health Law Reporter (9 June 2005); 'Tax-Exempt Hospitals Face Class Action Lawsuits Challenging Charity Care and

Billing Practices', Mintz Levin Health Law Advisory (1 July 2004); 'The Truth About Managed Care: The Silent Provider Discount', Managed Care Quarterly (Winter 2004); 'New Medicare Provisions to Promote Improvements in the Management of Chronically Ill Patients', Mintz Levin Health Law Advisory (10 December 2003); 'Building Bridges Across the Chasm', Health Leaders (26 March 2003); Note, 'Maintaining Health Care in the Inner City: Title VI and Hospital Relocations', 55 NYU Law Review 271 (1980).
**Personal:** 2006 New York Super Lawyer; New York Magazine Best Health Care Lawyers in New York (July 2005); 2005-06 Best Lawyers in America; NYU School of Law, Member NYU Law Review (1979-80); Arthur Garfield Hays Fellow (1980).

### ZETLIN, Michae
Zetlin & De Chiara LLP, New York
212 682 6800
*Recommended in Construction*

### ZIMAN, Kenneth S
Simpson Thacher & Bartlett LLP, New York 212 455 2000
kziman@stblaw.com
*Recommended in Bankruptcy*
**Practice Areas:** Ken Ziman is a Partner in the Bankruptcy and Restructuring Practice Group of the firm's Corporate Department. He regularly represents clients in connection with out-of-court restructurings and chapter 11 cases. His work has focused primarily on advising financial institutions in connection with their loans to troubled companies through all stages of the restructuring process. He also represents acquirers of financially distressed companies and significant individual creditors in chapter 11 cases and provides advice regarding the structuring of corporate transactions.
**Prof. Memberships:** American Bar Association, Business Section; The Bar Association of the City of New York.
**Personal:** He received his BA magna cum laude from Colgate University in 1987 and his JD from the University of Pennsylvania in 1990.

### ZIRINSKY, Bruce R
Cadwalader, Wickersham & Taft LLP, New York 212 504 6404
bruce.zirinsky@cwt.com
*Recommended in Bankruptcy*
**Practice Areas:** Chairman, Financial Restructuring Department. Counsels debtors, secured and unsecured creditors, creditors committees, public bondholders, shareholders, and investors, in large, complex US and international reorganizations, restructurings, financial transactions, litigation, mergers and acquisitions, involving businesses in numerous industries. Significant representations: Northwest Airlines Corporation's chapter 11 cases (lead debtor's counsel); Pfizer Inc. (Quigley Company, Inc. chapter 11 case);

Pharmacia Corporation (Solutia Inc. chapter 11 cases); creditors' committees in Mirant Americas Generation, LLC and Grove Worldwide LLC cases; Barclays Capital and Barclays Bank plc, as lender, agent and arranger, in the Reliant Resources Inc. debt restructuring; Senior Secured Lenders of Flag Telecom; also clients in Adelphia, Air Canada, Arch Wireless, Breed Technologies, Cadillac Fairview, Chase REIT, Continental Airlines, Dictaphone Corporation, Dow Corning, Eurotunnel, Florida Coast Paper, FNN, Glencore Nickel, Golden Ocean Group, Harrah's Jazz, Huntsman Corp., Jitney Jungle, North American Refractories, Olympia & York, Parmalat, Pathmark Stores, Resorts International, Tucson Electric, US Air, US Gypsum, Winstar Communications, World Access, and Wright Medical Technology reorganizations.
**Career:** JD, New York University School of Law (1972); BS, Cornell University (1969).

### ZISSU, Roger
Fross Zelnick Lehrman & Zissu PC, New York 212 813 5900
*Recommended in Intellectual Property*

### ZOBITZ, George E
Cravath, Swaine & Moore LLP, New York 212 474 1996
gzobitz@cravath.com
*Recommended in Banking & Finance*
**Practice Areas:** Extensive experience in syndicated loan transactions, primarily in the context of multijurisdictional acquisition financings and leveraged recapitalizations.
**Career:** Partner since 2003.
**Personal:** New York University (JD, 1995); Franklin Marshall College (BA, 1991).

### ZORNOW, David M
Skadden, Arps, Slate, Meagher & Flom LLP & Affiliates, New York
212 735 2890
dzornow@skadden.com
*Recommended in Litigation*
**Practice Areas:** Head of firm's New York office White Collar Crime Practice. Represents corporations and individuals in connection with federal and state grand jury investigations and at trial. Also works on civil enforcement actions, including matters before the Securities and Exchange Commission, as well as internal investigations on behalf of corporate boards of directors.
**Career:** JD, Yale Law School, 1980; BA, Harvard College, 1976 (summa cum laude; Phi Beta Kappa).

# ALLEN & OVERY LLP

## THE FIRM

**Managing Partners:** Michael Feldberg, Ian Shrank
**Senior Partner:** Daniel Cunningham

**Number of Partners in the United States:** 26

**FIRM OVERVIEW:** Allen & Overy LLP is a premier international legal practice with more than 4,850 staff, including approximately 420 partners, working in 25 major centers worldwide. Allen & Overy's New York office has more than 110 lawyers providing comprehensive legal services to organizations around the world. What distinguishes Allen & Overy in New York is its ability to bring together lawyers and staff who focus as a team on each client's needs to provide effective, efficient and tailored service in the United States and across borders. In the New York office, Allen & Overy has lawyers who are fluent in Arabic, Cantonese, Dutch, English, French, German, Greek, Italian, Japanese, Korean, Mandarin, Portuguese, Russian, Spanish and Yiddish.

## MAIN AREAS OF PRACTICE:

**Banking and Finance:** Allen & Overy has a leading international finance practice acting for banks, financial institutions and corporations. The practice advises on complex cross-border and domestic transactions in all major financial centers worldwide. In New York, the practice focuses on the US, English and Dutch law aspects of international and domestic finance transactions. Specialty areas in the banking and finance practice include asset finance and leasing, project finance, global loans, regulation, leveraged finance, and real estate finance.

**Corporate/M&A:** The US Corporate Team consists of dedicated M&A and securities lawyers, complemented by antitrust, employment/benefits, tax, environmental, regulatory, litigation and intellectual property specialists. Combined, they have experience advising on a broad range of public and private M&A transactions across many different industries and jurisdictions. Clients benefit from Allen & Overy's experienced US-qualified corporate lawyers working throughout the United States, Europe and Asia.

**International Capital Markets:** Allen & Overy's International Capital Markets Practice includes a top-tier US securities law practice. The team is involved in all aspects of international capital markets transactions, regularly advising issuers, corporations, sovereigns, financial institutions, underwriters and arrangers in all types of offerings of bonds and other debt securities, including project bonds, high yield bonds and investment grade bonds; SEC-registered and Rule 144A/Regulation S offerings; equity offerings, including ADR/GDR offerings, convertible bonds and equity warrants; securitizations, structured finance transactions and repackagings; and derivatives transactions, including index- and commodity-linked bonds and warrants.

**Litigation:** Allen & Overy's US Litigation Practice represents clients in many of the major litigations in the country, with a focus on financial service institutions, governmental regulation, complex commercial litigation and professional liability. The US Litigation Practice has successfully represented clients in controversies involving all forms of business activity, including financial services, retail, healthcare, entertainment, manufacturing and professional services. The team also has substantial experience in arbitrations, mediations and other forms of alternative dispute resolution.

**Restructuring:** The US Restructuring Team has many years of experience in US-based restructurings, both in bankruptcy proceedings and out-of-court restructurings. As part of the market leading global restructuring practice, the US team offers the highest level of expertise for multi-jurisdictional restructurings and is at the forefront of the evolving international restructuring environment. The team represents issuers, financial institutions, holders of public debt and debtors, as well as acquirers of the business or assets of financially distressed companies.

**Tax:** Allen & Overy has senior US tax professionals in New York and London, and complements this team with tax specialists in every major jurisdiction around the globe. The team's expertise includes strategic tax planning and tax minimization analysis; cross-border finance, funds, capital markets, derivatives and structured finance; mergers, acquisitions, divestitures, outsourcing and joint ventures; restructurings and insolvencies; real estate; employee incentive planning; tax investigations and litigation; and legislative and regulatory developments.

**China:** Allen & Overy established a China group in the New York office in 2005, positioning it to build on its recognized expertise representing China-based corporations and financial institutions investing abroad, and US-based corporations and financial institutions investing in China. Lawyers in Allen & Overy's Beijing, Shanghai, Hong Kong and New York offices work closely together to form a strong, dynamic China team.

**Latin America:** Allen & Overy's Latin America team has a proven track record assisting regional clients with US and other jurisdictional legal advice when doing business in international markets. Its efforts are led from the New York office, although the team frequently works with colleagues in Amsterdam, London, Madrid, Milan, Paris and Tokyo.

## HEAD OFFICE

**NEW YORK**
Allen & Overy LLP
1221 Avenue of the Americas, **New York**, NY 10020
**Tel:** 212 610 6300   **Fax:** 212 610 6399
**Website:** www.allenovery.com

## INTERNATIONAL OFFICES

Amsterdam, Antwerp, Bangkok, Beijing, Bratislava, Brussels, Budapest, Dubai, Frankfurt, Hamburg, Hong Kong, London, Luxembourg, Madrid, Milan, Moscow, Paris, Prague, Rome, Shanghai, Singapore, Tokyo, Turin and Warsaw.

## CONTACTS

| | |
|---|---|
| Antitrust | Michael Jahnke |
| Asset Finance | Barry Biggar, Ian Shrank |
| Banking | Thomas Abbondante, Carl Sheldon |
| Corporate/M&A | Daniel Cunningham |
| | Peter Harwich, Eric Shube |
| China Practice | Mitchell Silk |
| Derivatives | Joshua Cohn |
| | Daniel Cunningham, David Wainer |
| Dutch and Netherlands Antilles | Helena Sprenger |
| Employee Benefits & Executive Compensation | Henry Morgenbesser |
| Environmental and Regulatory | Kenneth Rivlin |
| International Capital Markets | Joshua Cohn, Daniel Cunningham |
| | Cathleen McLaughlin, David Wainer |
| Latin America Practice | Robert Kartheiser |
| | Cathleen McLaughlin |
| Leveraged Finance | Thomas Abbondante |
| Litigation | Pamela Rogers Chepiga |
| | Michael Feldberg, Jacob Pultman |
| Project Finance | Ernest Chung, Robert Kartheiser |
| | Mitchell Silk, David Slade |
| Real Estate | Kevin O'Shea |
| Restructuring | Ken Coleman |
| | Carolyn Conner, Hugh McDonald |
| Tax | Jack Heinberg |

*'Allen & Overy' means Allen & Overy LLP and/or its affiliated undertakings. Any reference to a partner in relation to Allen & Overy LLP means a member, consultant or employee of Allen & Overy LLP.*

# ALLEN & OVERY

# ANDERSON KILL & OLICK P.C.

## THE FIRM

**Managing Partner:** Jeffrey L Glatzer
**Number of lawyers:** 120-150

**FIRM OVERVIEW:** Anderson Kill & Olick, P.C., founded in 1969 has offices in New York, Chicago, Greenwich, Newark, Philadelphia and Washington, DC. Anderson Kill has a reputation for combining corporate polish with pugnacity. This reputation is built upon the firm's central philosophy of aggressively representing clients. Too often, the typical law firm approach to legal services ignores that attorneys are service professionals who provide solutions. Clients come to a law firm for solutions to their problems. The firm takes advantage of the wealth of experience of Anderson Kill's attorneys and avoids 'reinventing the wheel'. This approach results in creative and cost-effective resolutions of its clients' problems. Many of Anderson Kill's attorneys are recognized experts in their practice areas, leaders and active participants in professional associations, and are frequently invited to speak to business organizations. Anderson Kill prides itself on attracting and retaining smart, personable and well-rounded attorneys. The effect of Anderson Kill's experience, background, and unique approach to practice is better results for its clients. That is the Anderson Kill difference.

## MAIN AREAS OF PRACTICE:

**Bankruptcy & Restructuring:** Anderson Kill has a pre-eminent Bankruptcy and Financial Restructuring Practice. The group represents business clients in debt restructurings, bankruptcy cases, creditors' rights matters, litigation and related finance, mergers and acquisitions and other corporate transactions throughout the United States and in Europe. In addition, Anderson Kill has a premier reputation in the representation of creditors, with engagements on behalf of committees, lending groups and holders of control positions.

**Business Law:** Anderson Kill's Corporate Practice includes expertise in mergers and acquisitions, securities, international transactions, business immigration, venture capital issues, reorganization, partnership law, as well as general corporate representation. The Real Estate Group is engaged in a broad range of commercial real estate transactions, with particular emphasis on real estate finance, development, conveyancing, commercial leasing, land use and dispute resolution. The Finance Group is actively engaged on behalf of institutional lenders as well as borrowers in all manners of commercial lending. In addition, the Tax Practice is broadly diversified, with experience in both domestic and international tax planning.

**Corporate & Commercial Litigation:** Anderson Kill is nationally recognized for its ability to deliver practical, efficient and innovative solutions to the variety of litigation and alternative dispute resolution issues confronting businesses today. The group offers a broad range of services and is experienced in all aspects of corporate and commercial litigation. Specific areas of focus include antitrust litigation and advice, class action, bankruptcy and financial services, consumer fraud defense, real estate and construction dispute resolution, securities and unfair competition.

**Employment & Labor Law:** Anderson Kill counsels and represents management in every phase of employment and labor law while focusing on two primary goals in the workplace: to provide accurate and practical preventive advice and counseling on a full range of issues which may arise and, if litigation ensues, Anderson Kill provides cost-effective, and result-oriented representation. In addition, Anderson Kill has represented employers in many union negotiations and arbitrations and has guided employers in successful efforts to maintain a union-free workplace.

**Insurance Recovery:** Anderson Kill attorneys are recognized as the most prominent insurance recovery attorneys in the country, successfully representing policyholders in a variety of disputes with insurance companies. Anderson Kill has recovered billions of dollars for policyholders. Its attorneys have more insurance recovery trial experience than any other firm, along with a reputation for securing favorable settlements. With an unparalleled wealth of resources including an unrivaled computerized bank of insurance materials, Anderson Kill's

## HEAD OFFICE

**NEW YORK**
1251 Avenue of the Americas, **New York**, 10020
**Tel:** 212 278 1000　**Fax:** 212 278 1733
**Website:** www.andersonkill.com

## BRANCH OFFICES

**CONNECTICUT**
Two Sound View Drive, Suite 100, **Greenwich**, 06830
**Tel:** 203 622 7668　**Fax:** 203 622 0321

**DISTRICT OF COLUMBIA**
2100 M Street N.W., Suite 650, **Washington**, 20037
**Tel:** 202 218 0040　**Fax:** 202 218 0055

**ILLINOIS**
230 West Monroe St., Suite 2540, **Chicago**, 60606
**Tel:** 847 925 5430　**Fax:** 847 925 5431

**NEW JERSEY**
One Gateway Center, Suite 1510, **Newark**, 07102
**Tel:** 973 642 5858　**Fax:** 973 621 6361

**PENNSYLVANIA**
1600 Market Street, Suite 2500, **Philadelphia**, 19103
**Tel:** 215 568 4202　**Fax:** 215 568 4573

## CONTACTS

| | |
|---|---|
| **Insurance Recovery** | Robert M Horkovich |
| | William G Passannante |
| **Bankruptcy & Restructuring** | J Andrew Rahl Jr |
| | Andrea J Pincus |
| **Business Law** | Arnold L Bartfeld |
| **Corporate & Commercial** | Steven Cooper |
| **Employment & Labor Law** | Bennett Pine |
| **Products Liability** | Judith A Yavitz |
| **Intellectual Property** | David A Einhorn |
| **Trusts & Estates** | James G Clements |

Insurance Recovery Practice makes a difference where it counts – in the results obtained for clients.

**Intellectual Property:** Anderson Kill regularly works with the full range of intellectual property issues and problems for a broad cross-section of domestic and international clients. Its expertise includes all aspects of intellectual property law relating to patents, trademarks, domain names, copyrights and mask works, and unfair competition.

**Products Liability:** Anderson Kill is well known for its supervisory expertise as national defense counsel in product liability actions that include thousands of asbestos and hundreds of DES personal injury. Having tried cases involving complex design, trade, and manufacturing issues, Anderson Kill coordinates the settlement of claims, provides analysis of verdict trends, and assesses group settlements.

**Trusts & Estates:** Anderson Kill regards giving advice to individuals concerning personal tax, financial planning, and trusts and estates as a significant aspect of its practice. Anderson Kill advises clients on methods of accumulating, managing, and preserving wealth, as well as its disposition during life and upon death. Specifically, Anderson Kill assists clients in building their estates and planning for the transfer of property to family members and other beneficiaries in ways that minimize income, gift, and estate taxes.

**CLIENTS:** Anderson Kill clients include the nation's largest corporate and industrial companies as well as utilities, municipalities, state governments, charities, major religious and not-for-profit organizations, small companies and individuals.

# AXINN, VELTROP & HARKRIDER LLP

## THE FIRM

**Senior Partner:** Stephen M Axinn
**Managing Partner:** William M Rubenstein
**Chair of Antitrust Practice:** John D Harkrider
**Chair of IP & Patent Practice:** James D Veltrop

**Number of partners:** 8
**Number of other lawyers:** 22

**FIRM OVERVIEW:** Axinn, Veltrop & Harkrider LLP offers its clients a unique range of legal counseling and litigation services in the areas of antitrust and trade regulation, intellectual property and complex litigation. AV&H is focused on providing its clients with the highest possible level of professionalism and skills and is led by a team of attorneys who have represented many leading corporate clients in a wide variety of precedent-setting cases before the Federal Trade Commission, Antitrust Division, and European competition authorities, as well as in federal courts throughout the nation.

## MAIN AREAS OF PRACTICE:

**Antitrust & Trade regulation:** AV&H has earned an unsurpassed reputation in the antitrust field and regularly litigates claims and advises clients regarding antitrust matters. The firm has substantial experience in all aspects of state, federal and international antitrust and trade regulation compliance, including mergers, joint ventures, restraints of trade, monopolization, price discrimination, Hart-Scott-Rodino and international filing requirements, and civil and criminal investigations. AV&H has represented clients in antitrust matters before federal and state agencies, as well as the federal courts.

**Intellectual Property:** The firm represents clients seeking to effectively enforce intellectual property rights and to avoid and defend against charges of infringement and misappropriation. AV&H litigates intellectual property cases in federal and state courts across the country, as well as in arbitration proceedings. The firm devotes a significant portion of its practice to pharmaceutical-related patent and FDA litigation, and is active in numerous other industries as well. AV&H has an active counseling practice in the areas of patent, trademark and trade secret law and provides ongoing advice and services to clients regarding the acquisition, management and enforcement of intellectual property portfolios. The firm also evaluates patent and trademark infringement claims in a variety of other industries, including industrial equipment, medical devices, consumer goods, chemicals and computer software and hardware.

**Complex Litigation:** The cases handled by the firm typically involve complex factual or legal issues and often are of tremendous significance to the client either from a damages or operational perspective. The firm has litigated cases involving deceptive advertising, unfair competition, ERISA, Lanham Act claims, contract issues, and numerous consumer protection issues.

**CLIENTS:** AV&H represents Global 1000 companies in the following fields: aerospace, accounting services, consumer retail, financial services, healthcare, industrial technologies, publishing, software, tools, metals, and telecommunications.

**INTERNATIONAL WORK:** AV&H has represented numerous clients before the European Commission, the UK Office of Fair Trading and Competition Commission, and other competition authorities for transactions in a broad range of industries.

## HEAD OFFICE

**NEW YORK**
1370 Avenue of the Americas, **New York**, NY 10019
**Tel:** 212 728 2200   **Fax:** 212 728 2201
**Website:** www.avhlaw.com

## BRANCH OFFICES

**CONNECTICUT**
90 State House Square, **Hartford**, CT 06103
**Tel:** 860 275 8100   **Fax:** 860 275 8101

**DISTRICT OF COLUMBIA**
1801 K Street NW,  Suite 411, **Washington**, DC 20006
**Tel:** 202 912 4700   **Fax:** 202 912 4701

## CONTACTS

**Antitrust & Trade Regulation** ....................Stephen Axinn (New York)
**Intellectual Property** .............................James Veltrop (Connecticut)
**Complex Litigation** .................................Richard Order (Connecticut)
.................................................................Lauren Albert (New York)

AXINN,
VELTROP &
HARKRIDER LLP

# BERNSTEIN LITOWITZ BERGER & GROSSMANN LLP

## THE FIRM

**Managing Partners:** Max Berger, John (Sean) Coffey, Douglas McKeige, Alan Schulman

**Number of partners:** 14
**Number of other lawyers:** 36

**FIRM OVERVIEW:** Bernstein Litowitz Berger & Grossmann LLP (BLB&G) is a premier litigation boutique representing individual and institutional clients worldwide. Since its founding in 1983, BLB&G has obtained nearly $20 billion in recoveries for investors and achieved precedent-setting corporate governance reforms on behalf of its institutional investor clients. The firm has also prosecuted some of the most significant employment discrimination, civil rights and consumer protection cases on record. Equally important, the firm has advanced novel and beneficial principles by developing important new law in the areas in which it litigates. As a result of its accomplishments, the firm and its attorneys have been the subject of numerous feature articles in major media publications in the United States and abroad. A distinguished group of trial-tested litigators, BLB&G has repeatedly and consistently earned high praise from the courts in which it practices, as well as the respect of the defense firms and insurance carriers whom it faces in court and across the negotiating table.

## MAIN AREAS OF PRACTICE:

**Securities Litigation:** BLB&G specializes in the litigation of securities fraud claims. Regularly appointed by the courts as lead counsel in US securities class actions, BLB&G has distinguished itself by focusing on the representation of respected institutional investors in meritorious cases. The firm is extremely selective in its prosecutions, only taking cases where its clients have significant holdings. While BLB&G does not file a high volume of actions, it is well known for "consistently bringing high-impact cases"" (*Institutional Shareholder Services*) Unique among its peers, BLB&G has obtained six of the ten largest securities fraud recoveries in history. The firm's reputation for trial readiness is well established – it has successfully tried several of the largest and most high-profile civil fraud cases in history, most recently in representing the investors victimized by the massive accounting fraud and subsequent bankruptcy of WorldCom, Inc.

**General Commercial Litigation:** The firm handles general complex commercial litigation – often on a contingency basis - involving allegations of breach of contract, accountants' liability, breach of fiduciary duty, fraud and negligence. BLB&G represents institutions and individuals in disputes arising from a variety of commercial transactions, including private placements, derivatives and other specialty financial instruments, distressed debt and bankruptcy claims, as well as patent infringement and intellectual property rights. With the firm's practice focused mainly on the representation of plaintiffs, unlike the corporate defense bar, BLB&G does not have conflict issues that prevent it from taking positions helpful to its institutional clients.

**Corporate Governance & Shareholder Rights:** One of the first law firms to demonstrate that litigation can be an effective tool for stimulating positive change in failing corporate management settings, BLB&G is an acknowledged leader in corporate governance reform. The firm's partners speak frequently on developing trends at events for the financial, insurance and legal communities and have written extensively on these subjects. Through the cases which the firm has prosecuted, BLB&G has confronted discriminatory management, sought to make corporate boards effective and independent, expanded accountability to the corporate boardroom, and improved the quality of 'due diligence' performed by investment banks, changing 'Wall Street' practices for the better.

## MAIN OFFICE

### NEW YORK
1285 Avenue of the Americas New York, NY 10019
**Tel:** 212 554 1400   **Fax:** 212 554 1444
**Email:** blbg@blbglaw.com
**Website:** www.blbglaw.com

## BRANCH OFFICES

### CALIFORNIA
12481 High Bluff Drive, Suite 300, **San Diego**, CA 92130
**Tel:** 858 793 0070   **Fax:** 858 793 0323

### LOUISIANA
2727 Prytania Street, Suite 14, **New Orleans**, LA 70130
**Tel:** 504 899 2339   **Fax:** 504 899 2342

### NEW JERSEY
220 St. Paul Street, **Westfield**, NJ 07090
**Tel:** 908 928 1700   **Fax:** 908 301 9008

## CONTACTS

**Firm Contact** ..........................................Douglas McKeige (New York)

**Asset Protection, Fraud Monitoring & Claims Administration:** BLB&G is the trusted securities fraud monitoring counsel for hundreds of public pension funds and institutional investors worldwide. The firm monitors financial and business media, as well as all securities and shareholder derivative litigation to provide our institutional clients with comprehensive reporting on potential claims that may impact their holdings. Additionally, the firm assists its clients in the filing and administration of securities claims.

**CLIENTS:** BLB&G's client base include some of the world's largest institutional investors including public pension funds, Taft-Hartley funds, fund managers and foreign investment managers.

**INTERNATIONAL WORK:** The firm represents international and non-US based institutional investors in numerous commercial matters.

BERNSTEIN LITOWITZ BERGER & GROSSMANN LLP

# BOIES, SCHILLER & FLEXNER LLP

## THE FIRM

**Managing Partners:** David Boies, Jonathan D Schiller, Donald L Flexner

**Number of partners:** 79
**Number of other lawyers:** 154

**FIRM OVERVIEW:** Less than a decade after its founding, Boies, Schiller & Flexner has grown to 233 lawyers in 11 offices located across the United States. The firm's partners, who have tried more than 300 cases before juries and judges in federal and state courts throughout the United States, include the former lead trial attorney for the United States in United States v Microsoft, a former Deputy Assistant Attorney General in charge of the Antitrust Division, a former lead attorney for the United States in United States v AT&T, and the former US Attorney who created the securities fraud branch of that office in San Francisco. The Wall Street Journal describes the firm as a 'litigation powerhouse,' (April 6, 2000), and the National Law Journal as 'unafraid to venture into controversial' and 'high risk' matters. (February 12, 2001).

**MAIN AREAS OF PRACTICE:** Complex commercial trials and litigation, including antitrust, securities and insurance, and international arbitration are the centerpieces of the firm's practice. Boies, Schiller & Flexner also enjoys one of the most selective and successful class action practices in the country, representing both plaintiffs and defendants in cases involving the widest range of subject matters. The firm also represents corporate clients and financial institutions in significant merger and acquisition and project financing transactions.

**CLIENTS:** In 2005, the firm's partners have been involved in (i) significant antitrust matters, including the prosecution of American Express' claims against Visa, MasterCard and several banks concerning rules that unlawfully prevented banks from issuing American Express cards, and representing an agency of the State of Alaska in a lawsuit alleging that BP and ExxonMobil are conspiring to withhold natural gas from US markets to artificially inflate natural gas prices and to control Alaskan gas fields; (ii) securities defenses of Qwest Communications International and Tyco International; (iii) representing the Board of Directors of RenaissanceRe Holdings, Ltd. in connection with ongoing federal and state governmental investigations of securities law matters in the insurance industry; and (iv) most recently, the defense of Maurice R ('Hank') Greenberg, former Chairman and Chief Executive Officer of American International Group Inc. and the C.V. Starr companies, in connection with criminal, civil and regulatory proceedings concerning the insurance industry. The firm's clients include some of the largest and most sophisticated companies in the world: Aetna, American Express, AT&T, CBS, Columbia University, DuPont, Ernst & Young, FPL Group, Goldman Sachs, Guardsmark, Monsanto, Northwest Airlines, Philip Morris, Public Broadcasting System, Qwest Communications, Siemens, The New York Yankees, The Republic of France, Tyco International, Unisys, Viacom, Inc., Yankees Entertainment & Sports Network and Zurich Capital Markets Inc.

**INTERNATIONAL WORK:** Partners at Boies, Schiller & Flexner have practiced arbitration and international arbitration for more than 25 years, including ICC, LCIA, UNCITRAL, ICSID, AAA, NASD and ad hoc arbitration. The firm's partners have represented client's in arbitral proceedings before tribunals in Paris, Geneva, London, Zurich, Stockholm, and Hong Kong, and throughout the United States. The practice is headed by Managing Partner Jonathan Schiller, who is a member of the Milan Chamber of National and International Arbitration Club of Arbitrators, and has served both as an advocate and arbitrator in international arbitration.

## HEAD OFFICE

### NEW YORK
333 Main Street, **Armonk**, NY 10504
**Tel:** 914 749 8200   **Fax:** 914 749 8300
**Website:** www.bsfllp.com

## BRANCH OFFICES

### CALIFORNIA
1999 Harrison Street, Suite 900, **Oakland**, CA 94612
**Tel:** 510 874 1000   **Fax:** 510 874 1460

### DISTRICT OF COLUMBIA
5301 Wisconsin Avenue, NW, **Washington**, DC 20015
**Tel:** 202 237 2727   **Fax:** 202 237 6131

### FLORIDA
100 Southeast 2nd St, Suite 2800, **Miami**, FL 33131
**Tel:** 305 539 8400   **Fax:** 305 539 1307

401 East Las Olas Blvd, Suite 1200, **Fort Lauderdale**, FL 33301
**Tel:** 954 356 0011   **Fax:** 954 356 0022

255 South Orange Avenue, Suite 905, **Orlando**, FL 32801
**Tel:** 407 425 7118   **Fax:** 407 425 7047

### NEVADA
777 North Rainbow Blvd, Suite 350, **Las Vegas**, NV 89107
**Tel:** 702 464 2800   **Fax:** 702 464 2897

### NEW HAMPSHIRE
26 South Main Street, **Hanover**, NH 03755
**Tel:** 603 643 9090   **Fax:** 603 643 9009

### NEW JERSEY
150 JFK Parkway, Suite 100, **Short Hills**, NJ 07078
**Tel:** 973 218 1111   **Fax:** 973 218 1106

### NEW YORK
570 Lexington Avenue, 16th Fl, **New York**, NY 10022
**Tel:** 212 446 2300   **Fax:** 212 446 2350

10 North Pearl Street, 4th Floor, **Albany**, NY 12207
**Tel:** 518 434 0600   **Fax:** 518 434 0665

# BROWN RAYSMAN MILLSTEIN FELDER & STEINER LLP

## THE FIRM

**Managing Partners:** Peter Brown, Richard Raysman and Julian Millstein
**Number of partners:** 90
**Number of other lawyers:** 164

**FIRM OVERVIEW:** Brown Raysman Millstein Felder & Steiner LLP has built on its international reputation as a leader in the area of technology and intellectual property law to emerge in the new millennium as a renowned multi-disciplinary law firm. Today, the focus of the firm extends from technology and intellectual property law to real estate finance and leasing and corporate transactional work, as well as securities, mergers and acquisitions, commercial and IP litigation, construction, bankruptcy, media, life sciences, healthcare, trusts and estates, tax, and employment law.

## MAIN AREAS OF PRACTICE:

**Technology, Media & Communications:** As a leader in technology, media and communications law for over 25 years, Brown Raysman is uniquely qualified to handle transactions and disputes for its clients and does so on a regular basis in areas such as voice and data communications, cable (including interactive and other enhanced services) and broadcast television, internet and mass media, enterprise solutions, privacy and security, licensing, mobile and wireless, networking infrastructure and management, video conferencing, technology transfers and new media.

**Intellectual Property:** As a pioneer of technology law, Brown Raysman offers unparalleled services in the global clearance, acquisition, maintenance and enforcement of patents, trademarks, service marks, copyrights, trade secrets and related intellectual property such as internet domain names. In particular, Brown Raysman has a premier high-technology and life sciences patent prosecution and litigation practice. Many of the firm's patent attorneys are former electrical or bio-medical engineers, with prior experience in their respective fields, a number of whom have PhD's in various scientific areas.

**Outsourcing:** Brown Raysman is one of a handful of law firms internationally known for its outsourcing practice and has negotiated complex IT and BPO deals on both the vendor and customer sides of a transaction. The firm has also negotiated numerous offshore outsourcing deals with companies based in India, Europe, Asia and the Caribbean.

**Real Estate & Commercial Finance:** The firm's Real Estate Finance Practice is nationally recognized for its capital markets and structured finance practice, representing premier Wall Street companies. It provides representation of both lenders and borrowers in complex real estate financing transactions, including construction, conduit, interim and permanent financings, forward loan commitments, lines of credit, mezzanine loans, low-income housing tax credit transactions, loan participations and mortgage-backed bond credit enhancement transactions. The firm's commercial finance attorneys have expertise in equipment finance, commercial and asset-based lending, factoring, franchise finance and other corporate and transactional matters. Brown Raysman provides counsel to a wide range of financial institutions and other lenders and borrowers on business issues including capital equipment acquisitions and sales, asset-based finance transactions, and tax-advantaged leasing activities. In addition, the firm has represented issuers, servicers, credit enhancers and investors in the mortgage-backed and asset-backed securities markets.

**Commercial Leasing:** Brown Raysman is one of the premier law firms in commercial leasing transactions. The firm's attorneys regularly represent both landlords and tenants in complex leasing transactions, including net leasing, ground leasing and subleasing, commercial office leasing, and retail leasing. They also have extensive experience with a myriad of real estate brokerage issues and regularly have served as counsel to real estate brokerage companies.

**Corporate & Securities:** Brown Raysman's corporate attorneys have extensive experience counseling issuers, underwriters, placement agents and selling shareholders in private placements, initial and secondary public offerings of equity and debt securities, Rule 144A offerings and other financings for domestic and foreign companies. Brown Raysman renders general securities law and regulatory compliance advice to its public company clients regarding such matters as Sarbanes-Oxley, proxy solicitations, executive compensation disclosure, Section 16 planning and reporting, and exchange listing rules. The firm advises funds and other private equity investors in their portfolio investments, from the

## HEAD OFFICE

### NEW YORK
900 Third Avenue, **New York**, NY 10022
**Tel:** 212 895 2000 **Fax:** 212 895 2900
**Email:** info@brownraysman.com
**Website:** www.brownraysman.com

## BRANCH OFFICES

### CALIFORNIA
303 Twin Dolphin Drive, **Redwood Shores**, CA 94065
**Tel:** 650 632 4324 **Fax:** 650 632 4328

1880 Century Park East, **Los Angeles**, CA 90067
**Tel:** 310 712 8300 **Fax:** 310 712 8383

### CONNECTICUT
Cityplace II, 185 Asylum Street, **Hartford**, CT 06103
**Tel:** 860 275 6400 **Fax:** 860 275 6410

### NEW JERSEY
163 Madison Avenue, PO Box 1989, **Morristown**, NJ 07962-1989
**Tel:** 973 775 8900 **Fax:** 973 775 8901

term sheet through due diligence and closing, and in connection with the management of their assets. The firm is experienced in organizing both domestic and offshore private equity funds.

**Labor & Employment:** Brown Raysman's highly skilled and experienced labor and employment attorneys are capable of expertly handling any employment-related issue. The firm has a proven track record of successfully representing *Fortune* 100s and smaller companies in connection with virtually every type of labor and employment matter, and has counseled senior management on the most sensitive and complex employee relations topics.

**Commercial & IP Litigation & Arbitration:** Brown Raysman's diverse and international litigation and arbitration practice encompasses both established and emerging areas of the law and is closely aligned with the firm's core expertise in the areas of intellectual property, high-technology and the internet, as well as the more traditional areas of employment, banking, bankruptcy, real estate, construction, securities (including NASD and NYSE arbitrations), antitrust and finance.

**Creditors' Rights & Bankruptcy:** The firm regularly represents a broad range of debtors, creditors and other stakeholders in a wide range of business restructuring and insolvency matters, including bankruptcy cases, creditors' rights, litigations, and out-of-court restructurings.

**Construction & Surety & Fidelity:** The firm has one of the leading national construction litigation practices. It counsels owners, developers, lenders, contractors and others on building technology, bidding, construction agreements and complex litigation matters. On surety and fidelity matters, the firm assists clients with underwriting claims investigations and issues involving all manner of bonds vehicles.

**Trusts & Estates & Tax:** Brown Raysman's Trusts and Estates Group advises clients in a broad range of estate planning and related tax matters. Brown Raysman's tax attorneys provide sophisticated and strategic tax planning and advice regarding a wide range of complex domestic and international corporate and non-corporate commercial, real estate and other business transactions.

**CLIENTS:** Brown Raysman has a wide range of domestic and international clients represented in numerous industries, including: technology, real estate, internet, financial services, media and entertainment, sports, communications, satellite, direct marketing, life sciences, healthcare, timeshare finance, construction, automotive, insurance, manufacturing, government entities and public utilities.

BROWN RAYSMAN MILLSTEIN FELDER & STEINER LLP

# CADWALADER, WICKERSHAM & TAFT LLP

## THE FIRM

**Chairman & Managing Partner:** Robert O Link Jr

**Number of partners worldwide:** 113
**Number of other lawyers worldwide:** 469

**FIRM OVERVIEW:** Established in New York in 1792, Cadwalader, Wickersham & Taft LLP, a premier international law firm with over 600 attorneys in five offices, offers clients innovative solutions to legal and financial issues. With strategically placed offices, the firm is superbly positioned to offer top-flight legal services to internationally-based clients conducting transactions all over the world.

## MAIN AREAS OF PRACTICE:

**Antitrust:** With market-leading practitioners, Cadwalader's Antitrust Team represent foreign and domestic clients in merger, monopolization, price-fixing, patent infringement, unfair competition and leveraging cases against the US Department of Justice, the Federal Trade Commission, state attorneys general and private parties in state and federal courts. The group is one of the most knowledgeable in the US in advising on merger review, the intricacies of Hart-Scott-Rodino, and the implications of all forms of commercial arrangements. The attorneys also work with clients in establishing antitrust compliance programs and offer counsel on distribution, pricing, standard-setting, joint purchasing, research and development, and intellectual property.

**Business Fraud:** Staffed by internationally recognized leaders in the field, the Business Fraud and Complex Litigation Group has extensive expertise in the areas of corporate compliance and governance. On behalf of major international corporations, banks, brokerage firms and investment banks, the group has drafted, implemented and audited licensing compliance programs covering all areas of the law (including Sarbanes-Oxley), conducted internal investigations and audits of US and foreign operations of businesses, advised on and defended a large number of enforcement actions before all federal and many state agencies and regulatory bodies, and handled related criminal and civil fraud litigation.

**Capital Markets:** This preeminent practice includes traditional fixed-income and equity capital markets, structured finance, synthetic products, hybrid products, and derivatives. In recognition of the firm's excellence in securitization, Cadwalader perennially ranks at or near the top of annual rankings in issuer and underwriter representations in both commercial mortgage-backed and asset-backed securitization transactions. The firm also has a broad asset-backed commercial paper practice counseling sponsors and placement agents regarding asset-backed commercial paper conduits.

**Corporate/Mergers & Acquisitions:** Representing issuers, purchasers and underwriters of securities in the domestic and foreign public and private capital markets, the firm's corporate attorneys participate in the full range of securities transactions, including initial public offerings, exchange and secondary offerings, private placements and workouts of senior and subordinated debt, convertible debt and equity securities, venture capital and start-up financing and commercial paper in the US and Eurodollar markets. Lawyers in the firm have represented US and multinational clients in many of the most complex and noteworthy mergers, acquisitions, recapitalizations, spin-offs, and split-offs in recent years.

**Financial Restructuring:** Possessing significant cross-border expertise, this group represents secured and unsecured lenders, bondholders, creditors' committees, borrowers, asset purchasers and other entities involved in financial restructuring transactions or reorganization cases. The firm's attorneys have been at the forefront of many of the largest and most complex recent US and international insolvencies and routinely advise clients with interests in Europe, Asia, Latin America and Africa.

## HEAD OFFICE

**NEW YORK**
One World Financial Center, **New York**, NY 10281
**Tel:** +1 212 504 6000
**Email:** cwtinfo@cwt.com
**Website:** www.cadwalader.com

## BRANCH OFFICES

**DISTRICT OF COLUMBIA**
1201 F Street, NW, **Washington**, DC 20004
**Tel:** +1 202 862 2200   **Fax:** +1 202 862 2400

**NORTH CAROLINA**
227 West Trade Street, **Charlotte**, NC 28202
**Tel:** +1 704 348 5100   **Fax:** +1 704 348 5200

## INTERNATIONAL OFFICE

The firm also has offices in London and Beijing.

**Global Finance:** This team advises on all aspects of finance transactions throughout the world, including commercial lending, bank regulatory needs, mortgage banking, real estate finance, warehouse lending, and domestic and cross-border leasing. The industry leading real estate finance team handles financings, securitizations, acquisitions, sales and exchanges, development, construction, joint ventures, real estate investment funds, loan syndications, management, leasing, workouts, land use, government-assisted projects and environmental matters.

**Healthcare/Not-for-Profit:** Cadwalader is a leader in the diverse areas affecting the healthcare industry, including corporate governance, corporate finance, government regulation, Medicare and Medicaid, insolvency and restructuring, labor relations, litigation, risk management, securities, capital markets, and tax.

**Insurance and Reinsurance:** Cadwalader's attorneys perform the full range of work related to the insurance and reinsurance industry, from business transactions to litigation to regulatory compliance, representing some of the largest insurance and reinsurance companies, domestic and international industrial and service corporations, pension funds, investment and commercial banks, thrift institutions, and stock and commodity exchanges.

**Litigation:** Cadwalader's renowned litigators handle significant disputes for a broad spectrum of financial institutions, major commercial, industrial and service corporations and high net worth individuals in state and federal courts throughout the US and in England, as well as proceedings before administrative and regulatory agencies and international tribunals. The practice focuses on corporate and securities; complex financial products, derivatives and commodities; environmental; and real estate disputes.

**Private Client:** Providing effective and creative personal, financial, charitable and tax planning to individual clients and closely-held family companies, this department places particular emphasis on the preservation of wealth and the minimization of wealth transfer and income taxation.

**Securities & Financial Institutions Regulation:** This group works closely with many of the world's major broker-dealers and investment banks, developing strategy, advising on planning, compliance and supervisory procedures, and as needed, conducting full-scale reviews to identify potential violations.

**Tax:** While playing a crucial role in the firm's leading securitization, mergers and acquisitions, insolvency, structured products, and corporate finance practices, this sophisticated and diverse group also pioneers innovative tax structures, many of which involve cross-border components. The firm also maintains a significant tax controversy practice for US and non-US corporations and financial institutions.

# CADWALADER

# CARTER LEDYARD & MILBURN LLP

## THE FIRM

**Managing Partner:** Judith A Lockhart

**Number of partners:** 42
**Number of other lawyers:** 72

**FIRM OVERVIEW:** Founded in 1854, Carter Ledyard & Milburn LLP is a full service law firm serving corporations, financial institutions, government agencies and individuals. The Corporate Practice focuses on international mergers and acquisitions, joint ventures, IPOs and other public offerings, private equity, asset management and investment funds, antitrust, telecommunications and other government regulation. The Litigation and Arbitration Practice concentrates on commercial, securities, employment, environmental, intellectual property, criminal defense, maritime, insurance defense and reinsurance disputes. Other practice areas include intellectual property, bankruptcy and reorganization, real estate, trusts and estates, corporate investigations, employment, tax, employee benefits, tax exempt organizations and immigration.

## MAIN AREAS OF PRACTICE:

**Corporate/M&A/Securities:** Mergers and acquisitions, joint ventures and strategic alliances, public and private securities offerings, venture capital and private equity investments, bank lending, securitizations, antitrust, telecommunications, broker-dealer and other regulatory compliance and investigations.

**Litigation/Arbitration:** Complex litigations, arbitrations and alternative dispute resolution proceedings to resolve commercial contract, securities, employment, environmental, intellectual property, insurance defense, reinsurance, criminal, first amendment and construction disputes.

**Investment Management:** Advice on the formation, registration, operation and regulation of exchange-traded funds, mutual funds, unit investment trusts, hedge funds, private equity funds, investment advisors, broker-dealers and other financial institutions.

**Media & Technology:** Representing technology-based business in media, e-commerce, telecommunications, software and biotechnology industries based in the US and overseas in financing, mergers and acquisitions, licensing transactions and general representation. The firm has helped more than 50 Israeli technology clients start and develop operations in the US.

**Telecommunications:** Representing television cable and radio broadcasters, programming companies, telephone system operators and telecom equipment manufacturers in all regulatory and licensing matters, mergers and acquisitions, carriage and distribution agreements and related litigation.

**Real Estate:** Representing property owners, lenders, tenants and government agencies in commercial and residential property sales, leases, financings, and development contracts.

**Intellectual Property:** Advice on protecting and commercialising technology and intellectual property assets. Filing and prosecution of patents, trademarks, copyrights and domain names, protection of trade secrets, software and technology licensing, e-commerce contracts and handling of litigation and administrative proceedings.

**Maritime/Shipping:** Ship finance transactions, charter parties, cross-border leasing, regulatory advice, environmental advice, bankruptcy and workouts, attachments and arrests, insurance coverage and claims, capital markets transactions, maritime litigation and arbitration.

**Personal Representation:** Representing US and offshore individuals in all aspects of their personal affairs requiring legal counsel, including estate and income tax planning and structuring, will and trust instrument drafting and estate administration, real estate, criminal defense and immigration work.

**Bankruptcy/Reorganization:** Representing creditors, debtors and asset acquirers in Chapter 11 and other bankruptcy cases and in non-bankruptcy workouts and enforcement actions.

**Environmental:** Environmental regulatory advice, litigation and administrative proceedings, land use planning, environmental impact assessment and disclosure, compliance and environmental audits.

**Employment:** Counseling concerning employment and immigration laws, regulations and claims. Litigation and arbitration of employment termination, discrimination, harassment and employee non-competition, confidentiality and trade secret claims.

**Tax/Employee Benefits:** Tax planning advice, transaction structuring advice, and IRS representation. Planning, documentation, IRS qualification and regulation of employee benefit and incentive plans, executive compensation plans, stock option plans, and other benefits.

**CLIENTS:** Clients include American Stock Exchange, Bank of New York, Bristol-Myers Squibb, Costco, Danisco A/S, Deutsche Bank, Empire State Development Corporation, Fox Sportsnet, Goldman Sachs, Globus-Gateway Tours Ltd., Honeywell, Kaneka Ltd., Liberty Media, Liberty Mutual, Lower Manhattan Development Corporation, Marvel Characters Inc., Metropolitan Transportation Authority, Pall Corporation, Playtex Products, Trinity Biotech plc, Tullett & Tokyo Liberty plc.

**INTERNATIONAL WORK:** Recent cross-border transactions include representing Orient-Express Hotels Ltd. (Bermuda) in its IPO and NYSE listing; United Business Media plc (UK) in US acquisitions including CMP Media Inc. and Allison-Fisher International Inc. and the sales of Visual Communications Group and United Advertising Publications; Cultor Corporation (Finland) in its acquisition of the food science group of Pfizer Inc. and in its merger with Danisco A/S (Denmark) and Danisco in connection with its pending tender offer to acquire Genencor (US); Sea Containers Ltd. (Bermuda) in its joint venture with GE Capital (US) to form shipping container lessor GE SeaCo SRL (Barbados); Bowater Incorporated (US) in its acquisition of Alliance Forest Products Inc. (Canada); Garban plc (UK) and Intercapital plc (UK) in their merger to create Garban-Intercapital plc (now ICAP plc); ICAP plc (UK) in its acquisitions of APB Energy, Inc. and First Brokers Securities, Inc.; and Pengrowth Energy Trust (Canada) in its acquisition of Calpine Corporation and in its U.S. public securities offering and New York Stock Exchange Listing.

## HEAD OFFICE

**NEW YORK**
Two Wall Street, **New York**, NY 10005
**Tel:** 212 732 3200   **Fax:** 212 732 3232
**Email:** info@clm.com
**Website:** www.clm.com

## BRANCH OFFICES

**DISTRICT OF COLUMBIA**
1401 Eye Street, NW, Suite 300, **Washington**, DC 20005
**Tel:** 202 898 1515   **Fax:** 202 898 1521

**NEW YORK**
570 Lexington Avenue, 41st Floor, **New York**, NY 10022
**Tel:** 212 371 2720   **Fax:** 212 371 4234

# CHADBOURNE & PARKE LLP

## THE FIRM

**Managing Partner:** Charles K O'Neill
**Number of partners:** 129
**Number of other lawyers:** 281

**FIRM OVERVIEW:** Founded in 1902, Chadbourne & Parke LLP has evolved into an international law firm with 11 offices in key markets around the world. The firm provides an array of legal services, both in the United States and internationally. The firm's diversity of practices enables attorneys from different practices to work together to meet its clients' full range of legal needs.

**MAIN AREAS OF PRACTICE:** Chadbourne provides a diverse portfolio of legal services, including mergers and acquisitions, securities, project finance, corporate finance, private equity, energy, telecommunications, commercial and products liability litigation, intellectual property, antitrust, domestic and international tax, reinsurance and insurance, environmental, real estate, bankruptcy and financial restructuring, employment law and ERISA, trusts and estates and government contract matters.

**CLIENTS:** The firm's clients include leading international and US corporations, financial institutions, trade associations and foundations, start-up businesses, partnerships and individuals.

**INTERNATIONAL WORK:** With its global network of approximately 410 attorneys, the firm is positioned to analyze market, institutional and regulatory trends as they evolve, and offer its clients a full range of legal services on virtually all matters affecting them. In addition to its European work, the firm has established substantial practices in the Commonwealth of Independent States (CIS), Central Asia and Latin America. The firm's knowledge and experience is enhanced through its long-term working relationships with law firms in other key markets around the world.

## HEAD OFFICE

### NEW YORK

30 Rockefeller Plaza, New York, NY 10112

**Number of lawyers:** 229
**Office Profile:** As the hub of Chadbourne's international network of offices, the New York office draws on the expertise of its other offices, both within and outside the United States, to represent clients both nationally and internationally.
**Main Areas of Practice:** Attorneys in the New York office represent all of the firm's practice areas, including bankruptcy and financial restructuring, corporate, employment, intellectual property, commercial and products liability litigation, securities litigation and regulatory enforcement, special investigations and litigation, project finance, reinsurance and insurance, real estate, tax, and trusts and estates.

## BRANCH OFFICES

### CALIFORNIA

350 South Grand Avenue, Suite 3300, Los Angeles, CA 90071

**Number of lawyers:** 7
**Office Profile:** Chadbourne attorneys in Los Angeles represent clients on a range of matters and litigation both national and international in scope.
**Main Areas of Practice:** Attorneys in the Los Angeles office specialize in complex business litigation, involving commercial and securities fraud and government contract matters; products liability counseling and litigation; and reinsurance/insurance.

## HEAD OFFICE

**NEW YORK**
30 Rockefeller Plaza, **New York**, NY 10112
**Tel:** 212 408 5100   **Fax:** 212 541 5369
**Website:** www.chadbourne.com

## BRANCH OFFICES

**CALIFORNIA**
350 South Grand Avenue, Suite 3300, **Los Angeles**, CA 90071
**Tel:** 213 892 1000   **Fax:** 213 622 9865

**DISTRICT OF COLUMBIA**
1200 New Hampshire Avenue, NW, **Washington**, DC 20036
**Tel:** 202 974 5600   **Fax:** 202 974 5602

**TEXAS**
1100 Louisiana Street, Suite 3500, **Houston**, TX 77002
**Tel:** 713 571 5900   **Fax:** 713 571 5970

## INTERNATIONAL OFFICES

The firm also has offices in London, United Kingdom; Moscow and St Petersburg, Russian Federation; Warsaw, Poland; Kiev, Ukraine; Almaty, Kazakhstan; Tashkent, Uzbekistan; and Beijing, China.

## DISTRICT OF COLUMBIA

1200 New Hampshire Avenue, NW, Washington, DC 20036

**Number of lawyers:** 57
**Office Profile:** Attorneys in the Washington office handle a wide variety of sophisticated international and domestic transactions, as well as complex litigation.
**Main Areas of Practice:** Attorneys in the Washington office represent the firm's project finance and energy, corporate, antitrust, reinsurance/insurance, litigation, telecom, international arbitration, securities litigation and regulatory enforcement, special investigations and litigation, tax, environmental law and lobbying practices.

## TEXAS

1100 Louisiana Street, Suite 3500, Houston, TX 77002

**Number of lawyers:** 6
**Office Profile:** Lawyers in the Houston office advise clients on all aspects of energy transactions, including acquisitions and divestitures, general corporate transactions, restructurings and refinancings, project development and bank and capital markets financings. The Houston office is also one of the hubs of Chadbourne's liquefied natural gas (LNG) and natural gas practice, with special expertise in the structuring, development and financing of production, pipeline and marine transportation and receiving facilities, and commodity sale, purchase, storage and transportation arrangements.
**Main Areas of Practice:** Attorneys in the Houston office focus primarily on corporate, project finance, energy and oil and gas matters. They are also active in the development and financing of renewable fuels projects, including ethanol and biofuel production facilities.

CHADBOURNE
& PARKE LLP

# CLEARY GOTTLIEB STEEN & HAMILTON LLP

## THE FIRM

**Managing Partner:** Mark A Walker

**Number of partners worldwide:** 180
**Number of lawyers worldwide:** 854

**FIRM OVERVIEW:** Cleary Gottlieb is a leading international law firm widely recognized for its expertise in finance, mergers and acquisitions, tax, regulatory issues, employee benefits, real estate, and litigation. The firm represents corporations, banks and other financial institutions engaged in US and international business. The firm also represents sovereign governments and international organizations, as well as individuals, trusts, and nonprofit institutions. For 60 years, clients have relied on the firm for its vast legal expertise, quick responsiveness and business acumen, a combination providing unparalleled value. The firm's New York and Washington offices were established in 1946 and approximately two-thirds of the firm's lawyers practice in the United States. Recent accolades include US Tax Firm of the Year in Chambers and Partners (2003); Western Europe Competition/Antitrust Law Firm of the Year in Chambers and Partners (2004); French Tax Firm of the Year in International Tax Review (2005); German Law Firm of the Year in Juve (2005); Best International Securities Law Firm in LatinFinance (2005); number one Global Financial Industry M&A Legal Advisor in Bloomberg (2005); number one Lead Advisor on European M&A in Legal Week (US-based law firms, announced 2005); number two in Asian M&A in Thomson Financial (US-based law firms, announced 2005); Top Five Firm in Worldwide M&A in Thomson Financial (Based on deal value, announced 2005); number three underwriters' counsel in US High Grade Corporate Debt and US Convertibles in Thomson Financial (2004); Top Latin America Legal Advisor from 1988-2002 in LatinFinance; counsel in five deals of the year in LatinFinance (2004); counsel in eight deals of the year in Euromoney (2004); counsel in Equity Deal of the Year and Restructuring Deal of the Year in International Financial Law Review (2004); and counsel in Latin American Oil and Gas Deal of the Year in Project Finance (2004).

**MAIN AREAS OF PRACTICE:** Antitrust and competition; banking and financial institutions; bankruptcy; corporate governance; derivatives and structured products; employee benefits and ERISA; environmental; global capital markets; individual clients and charitable organizations; intellectual property and technology; international trade; Latin America; litigation and arbitration; mergers, acquisitions and joint ventures; project development and infrastructure; real estate; restructuring; sovereigns; tax; and white-collar defense.

**INTERNATIONAL WORK:** For 60 years, Cleary Gottlieb has been preeminent in shaping the globalization of the legal profession. The firm's worldwide practice has a proven track record for innovation and providing work of the highest quality to meet the domestic and international needs of the clients. Cleary Gottlieb's clients include multinational corporations and international financial institutions, sovereign governments and their agencies, as well as domestic corporations and financial institutions in the countries where the firm's offices are located. Although each of the 12 offices has its own practice, Cleary Gottlieb's 'one firm' approach offers clients the ability to access the full resources of all of the firm's offices and lawyers worldwide to the extent their matters so require. More than 850 lawyers work at Cleary Gottlieb worldwide.

## HEAD OFFICE

**NEW YORK**
One Liberty Plaza, **New York**, NY 10006
**Tel:** 212 225 2000   **Fax:** 212 225 3999
**Website:** www.clearygottlieb.com

## BRANCH OFFICE

**DISTRICT OF COLUMBIA**
2000 Pennsylvania Avenue, NW, **Washington**, DC 20006
**Tel:** 202 974 1500   **Fax:** 202 974 1999

## INTERNATIONAL OFFICES

**EUROPE:** Brussels, Cologne, Frankfurt, London, Milan, Moscow, Paris and Rome.
**ASIA:** Hong Kong and Beijing.

## BRANCH OFFICES

### NEW YORK

One Liberty Plaza, New York, NY 10006

**Office Profile:** The New York office handles corporate, securities and structured finance matters; mergers, acquisitions and joint ventures; litigation; banking and financial institutions; bankruptcy and restructuring; representation of sovereign governments in financial matters; taxation; employee benefits; real estate; and work for individual clients and charitable organizations. Clients range from the top investment banking firms and corporate entities to sovereign governments throughout Latin America and high net worth individuals. The New York office has more than 400 lawyers.

### WASHINGTON

2000 Pennsylvania Avenue, NW, Washington, DC 20006

**Office Profile:** The Washington office focuses on banking and financial institutions regulations; corporate and securities law; environmental, public and administrative law; structured finance; litigation; antitrust and international trade; taxation; and legislative counseling. The office serves as the focal point for the firm's US regulatory practice and, in particular, its counsel on corporate governance issues. Clients range from government loan agencies to Fortune 500 corporations. More than 90 lawyers work in the Washington office.

CLEARY GOTTLIEB STEEN & HAMILTON LLP

# CLIFFORD CHANCE US LLP

## THE FIRM

**Regional Managing Partner:** Craig Medwick
**Number of partners:** 75
**Number of other lawyers:** 292

**FIRM OVERVIEW:** US and global organizations require the highest quality US legal capability coupled with seamless international service. Clifford Chance offers a comprehensive and nationally recognized practice, backed by top-ranked practices in 28 of the world's major financial and business centers. Through a single, worldwide partnership and a client-focused approach, the firm delivers consistent, commercially-oriented advice wherever its clients do business. In the US, Clifford Chance's practice is dedicated to complex corporate and financial transactions and high-stakes dispute resolution. The firm regularly advises the leading international financial institutions and US and international corporations, as well as governments and multilateral agencies.

## MAIN AREAS OF PRACTICE:

**M&A & Private Equity:** Clifford Chance has a long history of advising in landmark US and cross-border transactions. The firm represents publicly and privately held buyers and sellers, joint venture partners, venture capitalists, fund sponsors and financial advisors. It offers a team of investment fund, tax, ERISA and regulatory specialists that act for leading private equity groups. Clifford Chance also has an interdisciplinary practice in corporate technology, bringing commercial and intellectual property expertise to the structuring of complex IT-driven ventures.

**Corporate Finance:** Clifford Chance leverages its industry and product knowledge to raise capital in the most strategic way for each client. The firm has a track record of successful domestic and cross-border transactions on behalf of a wide range of issuers and virtually every Wall Street underwriter. Product coverage includes: IPOs, secondary equity, ADRs, private placements, preferred equity, equity-linked products, REITs, debt and high yield offerings.

**Financial Products:** Clifford Chance's team has been at the forefront of developing and issuing hybrid and synthetic products and transactions, including, among others, specialized derivatives and SEC-registered cross-border securitizations. This experience has led the firm to advise regulators rating and responding to CBO, CDO, CLO, SIVs, bank solvency and other specialized regulatory matters.

**Finance & Restructuring:** The firm's Finance and Restructuring Practice focuses on the representation of financial institutions in complex national and multinational insolvency and restructuring proceedings. In addition, sophisticated lenders and borrowers call on the firm for acquisition finance, bank lending, asset finance, equipment leasing, debt trading and financial regulatory advice. The firm is among the most active in the world in project finance, representing lenders, sponsors and developers, particularly in the oil and gas, telecom and petrochemical sectors.

**Litigation:** Clifford Chance offers a preeminent national Litigation Practice, combining market leading local capability in the US with a unique ability to work efficiently with firm colleagues across its global network. The firm helps clients resolve complex disputes in a manner that promotes their business objectives and develop compliance programs to assist in minimizing future risks. The firm has trial expertise in all manners of civil and criminal cases before juries and judges in multiple juristictions, and in appellate practice before national and interntional courts and tribunals. Cifford Chance offers one of the most experienced teams of securities litigators in the US, with excellence in public company defense and in underwriter and investment company representation, combined with a prestigious white collar capability. Its Intellectual Property Team has extensive experience in complex patent litigation and also provides full IP service in the areas of patents, trademarks, copyright, design, trade secrets and unfair competition. The International Arbitration

## HEAD OFFICE

**NEW YORK**
31 W 52nd Street, **New York**, NY 10019
**Tel:** 212 878 8000   **Fax:** 212 878 8375
Email: info@cliffordchance.com
**Website:** www.cliffordchance.com

## BRANCH OFFICES

**CALIFORNIA**
990 Marsh Road, **Menlo Park**, CA 94025-1949
**Tel:** 650 566 4300   **Fax:** 650 566 4399

**DISTRICT OF COLUMBIA**
2001 K Street NW, **Washington**, DC 20006 1001
**Tel:** 202 912 5000   **Fax:** 202 912 6000

## CONTACTS

| | |
|---|---|
| **New York** | Craig Medwick |
| **California** | Daniel Harris |
| **Washington, DC** | Leiv Blad |
| **M&A & Private Equity** | John Healy |
| | Brian Hoffmann |
| **Corporate Finance** | Jay Bernstein |
| | Alex Camacho |
| **Financial Products** | Steve Kolyer |
| **Finance & Restructuring** | Evan Cohen |
| **Litigation** | Peter Chaffetz |
| | Mark Kirsch |
| **Intellectual Property** | Daniel Harris |
| **Real Estate** | David Djaha |
| | Howard Peskoe |
| **Tax & ERISA** | David Moldenhauer |

Practice has substantial experience handling cross-border, commercial and trade-investment disputes, including those under ICC, ICSID and UNCITRAL rules. The Reinsurance Team represents insurers, reinsurers, brokers and their financial advisors, offering a comprehensive range of services including reinsurance litigation and arbitration, class actions, run-off and insurance insolvency commutations, product development and policy review. Clifford Chance has a sophisticated Products Liability Practice in the United States representing leaders in science, engineering, and high technology. The firm's Antitrust Practice has been involved in many of the most significant antitrust and fair trade cases before the courts in the US. Clifford Chance's approach emphasizes practical understanding of its clients' business problems with experience across every segment of the corporate and financial world.

**Real Estate:** Clifford Chance helps clients execute real estate dispositions, acquisitions, leasing transactions and development arrangements. The firm offers sophisticated real estate finance expertise and is a leader in both real estate securities and private equity real estate investment funds transactions.

**Tax & ERISA:** The firm's Tax Group provides advice on US and international taxation, covering financing, investment, corporate and commercial transactions, the design of tax-efficient structured deals, transfer pricing and the resolution of tax disputes. The firm offers an in-depth understanding of US rules, combined with the knowledge of international tax systems and how the systems interlink. It also provides ERISA and executive compensation advice.

# CRAVATH, SWAINE & MOORE LLP

## THE FIRM

**Presiding Partner:** Robert D Joffe
**Deputy Presiding Partner:** Evan R Chesler
**Number of partners in US:** 86
**Number of other lawyers in US:** 363

**FIRM OVERVIEW:** Cravath, Swaine & Moore LLP is widely recognized as one of the preeminent law firms in the world, with an unparalleled reputation for superior legal work. In a survey of partners that recently appeared in the 2006 edition of the "Vault Guide to the Top 100 Law Firms", Cravath was voted the most prestigious law firm in the United States. The Corporate, Tax and Litigation Departments were recognized as among the finest, both in the practice of US law and for work on international transactions. Cravath was founded in 1819 and maintains offices in New York and London.

## MAIN AREAS OF PRACTICE

**Corporate:** Clients repeatedly choose Cravath when they need the highest quality skills and experience in large and complex matters, particularly with respect to cross-border transactions. The firm's corporate lawyers advise large and small businesses in a diverse range of merger and acquisition transactions, including divestitures, spin-offs and joint ventures. Cravath often advises corporate clients on antitrust matters that may arise in connection with these transactions, whether at the initial steps or in the process of securing regulatory clearance. The firm's record of success in both making hostile bids and defending against takeover attempts is a measure of the combined strength of its Corporate and Litigation Departments. Cravath has one of the most highly regarded US and international securities practices, with lawyers representing issuers and underwriters in all types of US and global offerings. The firm's banking lawyers are among the most prominent and accomplished in the US, and the firm serves as one of the primary outside counsels for JPMorgan Chase, Credit Suisse First Boston, and other major financial institutions and borrowers. Cravath's experience in M&A, banking and securities is a significant advantage to the firm's private equity clients, whose business concerns may involve one or more of these areas. Cravath's environmental lawyers work with the firm's clients on matters related to acquisition and disposition strategies, financings and regulatory compliance with respect to a broad range of environmental issues.

**Tax:** Clients bring their most complex tax challenges to Cravath. The firm's tax lawyers are at the center of structuring and negotiating all types of transactions, including mergers, spin-offs, joint ventures, securities offerings, and intricate private equity acquisitions and financings. Cravath's Tax Department is well-known for designing efficient tax structures for complex domestic and international transactions, having pioneered the development of innovative types of financing structures in both the US and international markets. Working with tax advisors in other countries, the firm's tax lawyers design sophisticated structures that capture the benefits of differences in the tax law in different countries. Further, Cravath's Benefits Group, a part of the firm's Tax Department, works on employee benefits and compensation matters, which are often central concerns in acquisitions, dispositions, and other transactions.

**Litigation:** Few firms can match the breadth or depth of Cravath's litigation experience or record of successes in such diverse areas of the law as antitrust, securities, contracts and commercial disputes, business torts, intellectual property, mergers and acquisitions, real estate and tax. Cravath's litigators are called upon for work involving contested merger and acquisition transactions, while boards of directors and special committees depend on the firm's lawyers to guide them through the intricacies of shareholder litigation and government investigations. Cravath's antitrust experience encompasses a broad range of industries, from mining to telecommunications. Although much of the firm's litigation work focuses on US law, many cases have an international component and draw upon Cravath's experience in international courts and tribunals. In the area of intellectual property, the firm handles a broad range of complex and challenging matters across all industries. A significant portion of the firm's litigation work relates to contracts and commercial disputes, often in the form of business torts as well as other areas of general business litigation. In the area of securities litigation, Cravath is widely recognized for its success in handling complex and often precedent-setting cases.

**Trusts & Estates:** Cravath's trusts and estates lawyers have served as advisors and trustees to several generations of the families that built many of the most important businesses in the world. The firm's discretion, insight and sound judgment have earned the respect and trust of these highly successful private clients in their trusts and estates matters. The firm continues to represent many leading entrepreneurs, senior executives and private corporations and partnerships. The firm's lawyers work closely with private clients and their families to protect and distribute assets by creating and endowing trusts, estates, and charitable foundations.

**CLIENTS:** Cravath has served some of the world's best known companies and financial institutions, including: Alcoa, Ambac Assurance, American Express, Ashland, BAE Systems, Bristol-Myers Squibb, British American Tobacco, Chevron, Citigroup, Credit Suisse First Boston, DreamWorks Animation, DuPont, FPL Group, Goldman Sachs, Hertz, IBM, Johnson & Johnson, JPMorgan Chase, Lazard, Lehman Brothers, Lucent Technologies, Martha Graham Center of Contemporary Dance, Medinol, Merck, Morgan Stanley, Nestlé, Overseas Shipholding, Rogers Communications, Royal Dutch Shell, RWE AG, Schering AG, Sprint, Technomar Shipping, Thales, The Washington Post Company, Time Warner, Vitro America and Xerox.

**INTERNATIONAL WORK:** Cravath has had an office in the heart of London's financial district since 1973. Lawyers here work on a diverse range of matters and regularly advise corporate and financial institution clients—in Europe and other parts of the world, including India and South Africa—on a variety of capital markets, mergers and acquisitions, general corporate and SEC compliance matters. They also work closely with leading law firms in Europe and elsewhere, providing advice on complex transactions that require extensive knowledge of, and experience in, the laws of multiple jurisdictions.

## HEAD OFFICE

**NEW YORK**
Worldwide Plaza, 825 Eighth Avenue, **New York**, NY 10019
**Tel:** 212 474 1000   **Fax:** 212 474 3700
**Website:** www.cravath.com

## INTERNATIONAL OFFICE

**LONDON**
CityPoint, One Ropemaker Street, **London,** EC2Y 9HR, England
**Tel:** +44 20 7453 1000   **Fax:** +44 20 7860 1150

## CONTACTS

| | |
|---|---|
| **Antitrust** | Robert D Joffe |
| **Commercial Banking** | C Allen Parker |
| **Corporate** | Kris F Heinzelman |
| **Environmental** | Jeffrey A Smith |
| **International (London)** | William P Rogers, Jr |
| **Litigation** | Richard W Clary |
| **Mergers & Acquisitions** | Allen Finkelson |
| **Securities Offerings** | Kris F Heinzelman |
| **Tax** | Stephen L Gordon |
| **Trusts & Estates** | Daniel L Mosley |

# DAVIS POLK & WARDWELL

## THE FIRM

**Managing Partner:** John R Ettinger

**Number of partners worldwide:** 144
**Number of other lawyers worldwide:** 459

**FIRM OVERVIEW:** Davis Polk & Wardwell is a global law firm based in New York City. Founded in 1849, the firm maintains a preeminent practice across a wide range of areas, including corporate finance, mergers and acquisitions, credit, litigation, insolvency and restructuring, investment management and tax. With more than 600 lawyers, Davis Polk has offices in New York, Menlo Park, CA, Washington, DC, London, Paris, Frankfurt, Madrid, Hong Kong and Tokyo.

## MAIN AREAS OF PRACTICE:

**Corporate:** Davis Polk's Global Corporate Practice is comprised of almost 400 lawyers, including 95 partners, in a range of practice areas, including capital markets, mergers and acquisitions, credit, private equity, investment management, insolvency and restructuring, executive compensation and employee benefits, equipment finance, environmental and real estate. The firm maintains a leadership position across all of these areas, and our corporate lawyers are frequently involved in the largest and most complex matters of the day. For example, in 2005 we advised on the largest IPO (the $9.2 billion IPO by China Construction Bank), the largest M&A transaction (the $57 billion acquisition of Gillette by Procter & Gamble) and the largest bankruptcy filing (by Delta). In 2005, the firm's corporate lawyers also worked on the largest-ever takeover attempt by a Chinese company (CNOOC/Unocal) and one of the year's most complex contested matters (MCI/Verizon).

**Litigation:** Litigation has been a cornerstone of Davis Polk's practice since the firm's inception. Companies from around the world in every industry, as well as their executives and directors, retain Davis Polk lawyers for their most significant litigation matters. The firm's 173 litigators, based in its New York and Menlo Park offices, routinely represent clients in trials, criminal and regulatory investigations, congressional inquiries, arbitrations, hearings, appeals and crisis management situations. This broad-based practice encompasses matters involving securities litigation, antitrust, white collar crime, mass tort and products liability, acquisition-related litigation, banking litigation, insolvency and restructuring, directors' and officers' liability, professional liability, commercial arbitration, tax controversy and intellectual property. Recent litigation matters include obtaining a dismissal of an antitrust class action filed against AstraZeneca relating to a patent infringement case, and the successful defense of Sterling Mets L.P. in litigation, which enabled the N.Y. Mets to proceed in forming a Mets-anchored cable sports network in partnership with Time Warner and Comcast.

**Tax:** Davis Polk has long been a leader in US and international tax law. Today, the firm's 38 tax lawyers remain at the leading edge of innovation, working closely with clients on complex transaction and corporate structures, as well as first-of-their-kind derivatives and other financial products. Davis Polk's Tax Controversy Group has prevailed in a number of significant tax matters and is frequently sought out by companies that are not regular clients to handle their most sensitive tax disputes.

## HEAD OFFICE

**NEW YORK**
450 Lexington Avenue, **New York**, NY 10017
**Tel:** 212 450 4000   **Fax:** 212 450 3800
**Website:** www.davispolk.com

## BRANCH OFFICES

**CALIFORNIA**
1600 El Camino Real, **Menlo Park**, CA 94025
**Tel:** 650 752 2000   **Fax:** 650 752 2111

**DISTRICT OF COLUMBIA**
1300 I Street NW, Suite 1000 East, **Washington**, DC 20005
**Tel:** 202 962 7000   **Fax:** 202 962 7111

## INTERNATIONAL OFFICES

London, Paris, Frankfurt, Madrid, Hong Kong, Tokyo.

**CLIENTS:** The firm's clients include ABN AMRO, Aetna, Altria, AstraZeneca, Bank of America, BBVA, Bertelsmann, Citigroup, Comcast, Credit Suisse First Boston, CVS, Delta Air Lines, Deutsche Bank, E*Trade, ExxonMobil, FedEx, Ford, Honeywell, JPMorganChase, KPMG, Lloyds TSB, LVMH, Morgan Stanley, Oracle, Pepsi, Pfizer, Roche, The Royal Bank of Scotland, Shell, Banco Santander Central Hispano, Siemens, Sodexho, Suez, Telefónica, Texas Instruments, Verizon Wireless and Yahoo!

# DEBEVOISE & PLIMPTON LLP

## THE FIRM

**Presiding Partner:** Martin Frederic Evans
**Number of partners worldwide:** 137
**Number of other lawyers worldwide:** 518

**FIRM OVERVIEW:** Debevoise & Plimpton LLP, founded in 1931, has approximately 650 lawyers practicing in key financial centers of the world, including New York, Washington DC, London, Paris, Frankfurt, Moscow, Hong Kong and Shanghai. The firm's lawyers represent clients in all principal practice areas, including complex acquisition and financing transactions, litigation and arbitration, tax, employee benefits, and trusts and estates.

## MAIN AREAS OF PRACTICE:

**Corporate:** The Corporate Department is the firm's largest practice group. Its work spans the full range of general corporate, transactional and regulatory representations in the United States and throughout the world. Major corporate practice areas include mergers and acquisitions, private equity, capital markets, insurance industry transactions, banking, bankruptcy and restructuring, derivatives, structured finance, project finance, equipment and leveraged finance, real estate, investment fund and asset management, intellectual property, media and technology, energy, and environmental law. The firm has a proven track record of handling innovative and complex US, international and cross-border transactions. Lawyers from the firm's offices around the world cooperate to provide integrated, seamless legal services to meet the needs of the firm's clients. Debevoise represents multinational, US and non-US industrial and commercial companies, and financial institutions including insurance companies, investment companies, banks and broker-dealers, individuals and non-profit organizations in a comprehensive range of assignments.

**Litigation:** The Litigation Department handles a broad range of complex matters in federal and state courts nationwide, and before agencies, administrative bodies and arbitration tribunals worldwide. Mary Jo White, the former US Attorney for the Southern District of New York, heads the Litigation Practice. The firm's litigators include another former US Attorney, eight former Assistant US Attorneys, a former Director of the Federal Trade Commission's Bureau of Competition, a former Chief Assistant US Attorney in both the Southern and Eastern Districts of New York, and a former Assistant to the US Treasury for Enforcement. Areas of concentration include securities litigation and enforcement proceedings, white collar crime, investigations, antitrust, bankruptcy, general commercial litigation, international dispute resolution, insurance industry disputes, intellectual property and media, and products liability.

**Tax & Employee Benefits:** The Tax Department works closely with the firm's corporate lawyers in structuring complex transactions. The department also focuses on tax planning and advice for business entities, high net worth individuals and exempt organizations and includes an active executive compensation and employee benefits practice.

**Trusts & Estates:** The firm's diverse and highly sophisticated Trusts and Estates Practice combines a significant tax orientation with frequent interdisciplinary projects involving the litigation and corporate areas.

**INTERNATIONAL WORK:** Debevoise's global partnership combines local insight and accessibility with firm-wide skills to handle its clients' assignments seamlessly across international boundaries and time zones. The firm's highly competitive, multicultural offices and multilingual teams of lawyers have established a compelling track record in both major and emerging markets, representing US, European, Asian, and Latin American clients.

## HEAD OFFICE

**NEW YORK**
919 Third Avenue, **New York,** NY 10022
**Tel:** 212 909 6000  **Fax:** 212 909 6836
**Email**: mailbox@debevoise.com
**Website:** www.debevoise.com

## BRANCH OFFICE

**DISTRICT OF COLUMBIA**
555 13th Street, NW, **Washington,** DC 20004
**Tel:** 202 383 8000  **Fax:** 202 383 8118
**Email**: mailbox@debevoise.com

## INTERNATIONAL OFFICES

Debevoise has offices in London, Paris, Frankfurt, Moscow, Hong Kong and Shanghai.

## CONTACTS

| | |
|---|---|
| Corporate | Michael W Blair |
| Mergers & Acquisitions | Paul S Bird, Jeffrey J Rosen |
| Private Equity/Fund Formation | Woodrow W Campbell, Jr |
| | Michael P Harrell |
| Private Equity/M&A | Franci J Blassberg, Margaret Andrews Davenport |
| Insurance Industry | Wolcott B Dunham, Jr |
| Capital Markets | Alan H Paley |
| | Peter J Loughran |
| Litigation | Mary Jo White |
| Media & Technology | Richard D Bohm |
| | Michael J Gillespie, Jeffrey P Cunard |
| Securities Litigation | Jonathan Tuttle |
| Products Liability | Roger E Podesta |
| Intellectual Property/Litigation | Bruce P Keller |
| Intellectual Property/Corporate | Jeffrey P Cunard |
| International Arbitration | David W Rivkin |
| White Collar Crime | Mary Jo White |
| Tax | Burt Rosen |
| Trusts & Estates | Jonathan J Rikoon |

DEBEVOISE & PLIMPTON LLP

# DEWEY BALLANTINE LLP

## THE FIRM

**Chairman:** Morton A Pierce
**Co-Managing Partners:** Richard Shutran, Gordon E Warnke

**Number of partners worldwide:** 145
**Number of other lawyers worldwide:** 424

**FIRM OVERVIEW:** Dewey Ballantine LLP, founded in 1909, is an international law firm with more than 550 attorneys. Through its network of offices, the firm handles some of the largest, most complex corporate transactions, litigation and tax matters in areas such as M&A, private equity, project finance, corporate finance, corporate reorganization and bankruptcy, antitrust, intellectual property, sports law, structured finance and international trade. Industry specializations include energy and utilities, healthcare, insurance, financial services, media, consumer and industrial goods, consumer electronics, technology, telecommunications and transportation.

**MAIN AREAS OF PRACTICE:** Antitrust and trade regulation; arbitration and alternative dispute resolution; bank and institutional finance; banking and financial institutions litigation; bankruptcy litigation; compensation and benefits; corporate finance; corporate reorganization and bankruptcy; derivatives; emerging markets; employment law; energy; insurance; insurance/reinsurance litigation; intellectual property litigation; intellectual property transactions and technology; international arbitration; international transactional and foreign tax advice; international litigation; international trade; Latin America; leasing and tax-advantaged financing; legislative; life sciences and healthcare, litigation; mergers and acquisitions; private clients; private equity; project finance; public policy: legislative and executive branch; real estate; securities, M&A and corporate governance; sports law litigation; structured finance; tax; tax controversy and litigation; tax exempt financing; taxation of financial products; tax planning and transactional tax advice; white collar crime and government investigations.
**Corporate Finance:** Dewey Ballantine's leading Corporate Finance Group handles transactions throughout the world. Clients include a broad range of issuers and borrowers, from major international corporations to early-stage private companies. The firm advises leading investment banks, commercial banks and other financial institutions acting as principals or intermediaries in corporate finance transactions.
**Litigation:** Dewey Ballantine has one of the most highly regarded litigation departments in the country - representing clients in complex litigation in federal and state trial and appellate courts, before government agencies, prosecutors and administrative bodies, and in arbitrations, mediations and other forms of alternative dispute resolution, around the world.
**M&A:** Dewey Ballantine's Mergers and Acquisitions Group consists of experienced attorneys around the world. The Mergers and Acquisitions Group represents acquirers, targets, financial advisors, leveraged buy-out groups, independent board committees, shareholder groups, equity investors, subordinated and senior lenders and arbitrageurs. The firm's attorneys are involved in both domestic and cross-border acquisition transactions, in negotiated transactions and in hostile takeovers. The group has been active in the full range of acquisition transactions, such as mergers, assets and stock sales, leveraged buyouts, restructurings and work outs, tender offers, spin-offs and proxy contests.
**Private Equity:** Dewey Ballantine's Private Equity Group works in three primary areas: fund formation, private equity and venture capital investment and private company corporate and securities representation. The firm's fund formation work includes representation of (i) sponsors raising private equity funds (including domestic and international vehicles, funds-of-funds, buyout and venture capital funds and funds primarily focused on real estate investments) and (ii) institutional investors in connection with their potential investments in blind pooled investment vehicles. The firm's private equity/venture capital investment work includes representation of pooled investment vehicles

## HEAD OFFICE

**NEW YORK**
1301 Avenue of the Americas, **New York**, NY 10019-6092
**Tel:** 212 259 8000 **Fax:** 212 259 6333
**Email:** marketing@deweyballantine.com
**Website:** www.deweyballantine.com

## BRANCH OFFICES

**CALIFORNIA**
333 South Grand Avenue, Suite 2600, **Los Angeles**, CA 90071-1530
**Tel:** 213 621 6000 **Fax:** 213 621 6100

1950 University Avenue, Suite 500, **East Palo Alto**, CA 94303-2225
**Tel:** 650 845 7000 **Fax:** 650 845 7333

**DISTRICT OF COLUMBIA**
1775 Pennsylvania Avenue, NW, **Washington**, DC 20006-4605
**Tel:** 202 862 1000 **Fax:** 202 862 1093

**TEXAS**
401 Congress Avenue, Suite 3200, **Austin**, TX 78701-3788
**Tel:** 512 226 0300 **Fax:** 512 226 0333

700 Louisiana, Suite 2050, **Houston**, TX 77002-2725
**Tel:** 713 445 1500 **Fax:** 713 445 1533

## INTERNATIONAL OFFICES

Dewey Ballantine LLP also has offices in London, Warsaw, Frankfurt, Milan, Rome, and Beijing.

and institutional investors in connection with their investments in portfolio companies and other investment vehicles. Private company corporate and securities work includes advice on most legal aspects of forming and running a business, including corporate, securities, tax, intellectual property, employment and benefits and real estate.
**Project Finance:** Dewey Ballantine's Project Finance Group is widely acknowledged as one of the leading project finance practices in the world. The firm's project finance attorneys routinely coordinate with their energy regulatory and project finance colleagues worldwide to execute global transactions. Dewey Ballantine's project finance teams represent developers, investors, underwriters, lenders, financial advisors, multilateral institutions, contractors and governments in the development, financing, construction and operation of a wide range of capital intensive projects and facilities throughout the world. Financings handled by the firm have been implemented through a variety of structures, including traditional offtaker-based project financings, so-called 'merchant' structures, traditional leveraged leases, cross-border leases, joint ventures and partnership arrangements, project leases and 'genco' financings, corporate finance offerings, and various combinations of the above.
**Structured Finance:** Dewey Ballantine's Structured Finance Group represents issuers, underwriters, placement agents, credit enhancers, investors, trustees, warehouse lenders and borrowers, sponsors of commercial paper conduits and swap participants in all types of structured finance transactions. These include securitizations of traditional and exotic assets in the United States; structured financial products (commercial paper programs, including cash flow and market value extendible programs) and cross-border structured financings involving assets originated in a wide variety of countries in Latin America, Europe, the Middle East and Asia.
**Tax:** Dewey Ballantine has one of the largest tax departments among general practice law firms; with attorneys practicing a full spectrum of corporate tax work in their global offices. The principal areas of its tax practice include transactional tax, international tax, lease financing, financial products, tax controversy and litigation, legislative and employee benefits.

# FITZPATRICK, CELLA, HARPER & SCINTO

## THE FIRM

**Managing Partner:** Dominick A Conde

**Number of partners:** 55
**Number of other lawyers:** 95

## AREAS OF PRACTICE:
Intellectual Property . . . . . . . . . . . . . . . . . . . . . . . . . . . . . . . . . . . 100%

**FIRM OVERVIEW:** Founded in 1971, Fitzpatrick, Cella, Harper & Scinto is one of the leading intellectual property law firms in the United States, with over 150 attorneys, and offices in New York, Washington, DC, and Costa Mesa, California. The firm's practice covers the spectrum of intellectual property services, including applying for protection, litigation, appeals, interferences, alternative dispute resolution, licensing, opinions, corporate transactions and due diligence. The firm provides these services to clients from virtually every industry, including pharmaceuticals, chemicals, automotive, energy, biotechnology, medical products, consumer products, computers, electronics, transportation, telecommunications, financial services, food products, and e-commerce. As new technologies emerge, the firm is at the forefront in developing strategies for their intellectual property protection. Over 95 percent of the firm's attorneys hold scientific or technical degrees and most have substantial industry experience in various fields of technology including chemistry, biotechnology, pharmaceuticals, electronics, physics, software, computers and the mechanical arts.

**MAIN AREAS OF PRACTICE:** Patent, trademark, copyright, trade secret, unfair competition, computer law, licensing, antitrust and international trade law. Trials and appeals in federal and state courts and administrative agencies.

**Patent & Trademark Litigation:** In the past year, the firm's clients prevailed in several major intellectual property litigations. The Federal Circuit affirmed a decision by Chief Judge Baker of the Southern District of Indiana that Eli Lilly's patent claiming a method of using fluoxetine to treat PMS was infringed and valid. This case involved Lilly's highly successful product Sarafem, which is used to treat Premenstrual Dysphoric Disorder (PMDD), a severe form of PMS. Fitzpatrick obtained a preliminary injunction on behalf of their clients Pfizer and Warner Lambert, halting sales of a generic quinapril product marketed by Teva Pharmaceuticals USA Inc., and Ranbaxy Laboratories Limited. In a case brought against 17 defendants, including several leaders in the electronics industry, Fitzpatrick successfully obtained summary judgment of non-infringement for its client IBM Corporation. The Court, which liberally cited IBM's motion papers, adopted the claim contstruction urgd by the defendants and found that the accused products did not infringe the asserted patent, either literally or under the docrtine of equivalents.

**Patent & Trademark Prosecution:** The firm has an extensive practice in the prosecution of patent and trademark applications, trademark oppositions and cancellations, due diligence studies, patent and trademark opinions, technology transfers and licensing. In addition, the firm is experienced in specialized and sophisticated areas such as patent interference procedures and prosecuting applications under the Patent Cooperation Treaty. The firm has prosecuted over 15,000 patents to issuance in the past 10 years, and is responsible for obtaining more than 1500 patents in 2005 alone.

## HEAD OFFICE

**NEW YORK**
30 Rockefeller Plaza, **New York**, NY 10112
**Tel:** 212 218 2100   **Fax:** 212 218 2200
**Website:** www.fitzpatrickcella.com

## BRANCH OFFICES

**CALIFORNIA**
650 Town Center Drive, Suite 1600, **Costa Mesa**, CA 92626
**Tel:** 714 540 8700   **Fax:** 714 540 9823

**DISTRICT OF COLUMBIA**
1900 K Street, NW, **Washington**, DC 20006
**Tel:** 202 530 1010   **Fax:** 202 530 1055

**INTERNATIONAL WORK:** The firm's clients include some of the world's largest multinational corporations in the United States, Asia, Europe, Australia and South America. The firm counsels clients on global intellectual property strategies, coordinates international litigation strategies and works closely with co-counsel throughout the world. The firm also assists in worldwide filing for patent, TM and copyright protection, and maintains worldwide TM portfolios.

**CLIENTS:** American Express, Altana Pharma, AstraZeneca, Astellas Pharma Inc., Bausch & Lomb, Bear USA, Bristol-Myers Squibb, Canon, Conde Nast, Dixon Ticonderoga Co., Eisai, Essilor International S.A., Frederick Warne & Co. Inc, GlaxoSmithKline, Hughes Network Systems, IBM, Instinet, Kyowa Hakko Kogyo, Merck, New York Clearing House, Novartis and Pfizer.

# Fitzpatrick

**FITZPATRICK, CELLA, HARPER & SCINTO**

# FRIED, FRANK, HARRIS, SHRIVER & JACOBSON LLP

## THE FIRM

**Chairperson:** Valerie Ford Jacob
**Managing Partner:** Justin Spendlove
**Total number of partners worldwide:** 139
**Total number of lawyers worldwide:** 525

**FIRM OVERVIEW:** Fried, Frank, Harris, Shriver & Jacobson LLP is a leading international law firm with more than 500 lawyers located in offices in New York, Washington, DC, London, Paris and Frankfurt. Fried Frank is best known for its ability to craft sophisticated and imaginative solutions for complex issues and intricate business transactions, frequently creating the precedents that others follow. Its lawyers work on some of the largest and most high profile transactions in financial centers around the world. The firm works closely with clients to gain a practical understanding of their business needs, while providing the tools necessary for the client to make well-informed decisions suitable to its own risk and tolerance and the marketplace.

**MAIN AREAS OF PRACTICE:** Antitrust; banking and finance; bankruptcy and restructuring; benefits and compensation; corporate; health care; international trade; litigation; real estate; securities regulation, compliance and enforcement; tax and trusts and estates.

**Antitrust:** Provides state-of-the art counsel on a wide variety of matters in connection with trade competition law in the United States and abroad. It works closely with the Corporate Practice on major transactions, the Intellectual Property Group on matters relating to trademark and patent litigation issues and with the firm's white-collar defense lawyers on matters relating to fraud and corrupt practices.

**Bankruptcy & Restructuring:** Provides sophisticated representation, in both in-court and out-of-court restructurings, of a wide range of clients, including corporate debtors, creditors' committees, bondholders' committees, trustees, financial institutions, buyers and sellers of distressed securities and businesses and parties seeking to invest in and/or acquire the assets and businesses of financially troubled companies.

**Benefits & Compensation:** Offers counsel to privately and publicly held corporations, their boards of directors and their compensation committees, as well as to commercial banks, investment banks, trust companies and other entities, with respect to the structuring and implementation of a wide range of benefit plans and programs for executives and other employees.

**Corporate:** Represents major corporations and investment banks in asset management, capital markets, corporate governance, financings, international/cross-border transactions, private acquisitions and private equity and public mergers and acquisitions. The firm's Mergers and Acquisitions Practice advises clients in the most complex situations, including negotiated mergers, hostile takeovers and takeover defense, leveraged buyouts, proxy contests and restructuring transactions. The Private Equity Practice is actively engaged in matters with many of the most prestigious private equity fund sponsors, structuring acquisitions and dispositions, as well as structuring and organizing private investment funds. The firm's Capital Markets Practice provides counsel in private and United States Securities and Exchange Commission-registered debt and equity offerings, including initial public offerings, high-yield debt and Rule 144A financings, structured finance and securitizations, real estate investment trusts and leveraged buyout financings, as well as investment-grade issuances. The firm's Financings Practice represents lenders and borrowers in a full range of financings, including merger and acquisition financing, mezzanine financing and leveraged lease and project financing. The firm's Asset Management Practice serves the needs of the investment management industry by providing a full range of legal services to a diverse group of clients, including US and international asset management and private equity firms, broker-dealers, hedge funds and their managers (exempt or registered), family offices, high-net-worth individuals and institutional investors.

**Intellectual Property & Technology:** The firm's Intellectual Property Lawyers defend clients accused of copyright, trademark and patent infringement in United States courts. The firm provides qualitative assessments of intellectual property

## OFFICES

**NEW YORK - HEAD OFFICE**
One New York Plaza, **New York**, NY 10004
**Tel:** 212 859 8000  **Fax:** 212 859 4000
**Website:** www.friedfrank.com

**DISTRICT OF COLUMBIA**
1001 Pennsylvania Avenue, NW, **Washington**, DC 20004
**Tel:** 202 639 7000  **Fax:** 202 639 7003

## INTERNATIONAL OFFICES

The firm also has offices in Frankfurt, London an d Paris

and intellectual property claims in the context of mergers and acquisitions, private equity investments, secured financing and other business transactions and prosecutes applications for patents and United States registrations of trademarks.

**International Trade:** Offers strategic consulting, international negotiation and transnational government procurement for both multinational corporations and governmental organizations. The firm represents clients in antidumping and countervailing duty and safeguards proceedings, as well as other market access disputes related to regulation of exports, protection of intellectual property and foreign investment restrictions.

**Litigation:** Active in trial and appellate matters in state and federal courts throughout the country, as well as alternative dispute forums. With its history on Wall Street, the Litigation Practice and its White-Collar Criminal Defense and Civil Litigation Team is on the forefront of cutting edge developments in the financial and commercial markets, having played a substantial role in public and non-public litigations and investigations arising out of Enron, Global Crossing, Adelphia, Computer Associates International, Martha Stewart Omnimedia and others. Fried Frank litigation attorneys are also actively involved in environmental, government contracts, and health care fraud litigation.

**Real Estate:** Encompasses a broad range of transactions, including capital markets and financings, acquisitions and dispositions, joint ventures, construction and development projects, leasing, portfolio transactions and real estate investment trusts. Its Active Land Use Practice represents developers and institutional clients before various administrative and regulatory agencies. The firm's clients are developers, owners, institutional investors, lenders, tenants, real estate advisors and underwriters and the transactions involve every type of property, including office, retail, industrial, residences and hotels.

**Securities Regulation, Compliance & Enforcement:** Serves public companies and their directors, officers and employees, as well as broker-dealers, investment advisors, accounting and legal professionals and other participants in the securities markets. Working closely with the Litigation Team, the practice represents companies and individuals in connection with government investigations involving securities and corporate law issues, counsels public companies and regulated entities on complex securities law and other regulatory issues and conducts, often in a crisis setting, independent internal investigations for companies, including regulated entities.

**Tax:** Encompasses all principal forms of corporate transactions, including mergers, acquisitions and dispositions, as well as joint ventures. Working closely with the firm's other practices it works on financings in both private equity offerings and public capital markets, participates in real estate transactions, bankruptcy and restructuring matters, international tax planning matters, tax controversies and individual tax planning.

# HEALY & BAILLIE, LLP

## THE FIRM

**Executive Committee:** John D Kimball, Jack A Greenbaum, LeRoy Lambert
**Number of partners:** 16
**Number of other lawyers:** 15

**FIRM OVERVIEW:** Founded in 1948 to serve the maritime industry, Healy & Baillie continues its leading position as a provider of legal services to that industry but has also expanded into an international general commercial law firm practicing in New York, Connecticut, New Jersey and Hong Kong. The firm regularly handles complex, multi-jurisdictional and international maritime and commercial litigation matters. As of the end of 2004, they have been counsel of record in more than 620 New York arbitration awards reported by the Society of Maritime Arbitrators in New York, more than any other firm. They have a strong and active bankruptcy practice and have also represented clients in several multi-million dollar corporate veil piercing and fraud cases. They have handled more than 200 personal injury jury trials over the years. The firm has also been involved in large insurance and reinsurance matters, both maritime and non-maritime in nature. The firm has an oil-spill response team ready to respond to a major casualty, and are well equipped to handle not only the civil consequences of such an incident but also the potential criminal implications that are more and more a fact of life in such matters.

Complementing the firm's strength in litigation and arbitration is a robust Ship Finance and Corporate Law Practice. In 2005, the firm added public securites law to its practice areas and increased its ability to handle private equity transactions and mergers and acquisitions. The firm regularly handles corporate transactions such as ship mortgage loan financing; leasing of vessels, oil rigs and other equipment; debt and equity placements; joint ventures; commercial and residential real estate transactions; and other similar matters.

The firm's pool of talent encompasses a wide variety of backgrounds and experience. John Kimball, Chairman of the firm, is consistently ranked as the leading shipping lawyer in the United States and is referenced as "an outstanding name in the marketplace". Other attorneys include former naval and coast guard officers as well as a naval architect and marine engineer who is also a licensed professional engineer. Some have served as law clerks to state or federal judges before joining the firm. Mr Kimball teaches admiralty law at New York University School of Law, and several of the firm's partners are authors or editors of leading maritime treatises and textbooks, including *Time Charters, Voyage Charters, The Law Of Marine Collision*, the *Benedict on Admiralty* volumes relating to Salvage, Carriage of Goods by Sea, Charter Parties, and Marinas and Recreational Boating, and the law school case book *Admiralty*. Over the years, the firm's partners have served terms as president of the United States Maritime Law Association and the Connecticut Maritime Association. They have also served as Titulary Members of the Comite Maritime International. One partner recently concluded a term as MLA delegate to the BIMCO documentary committee, and another served as part of the United States delegation to the UNESCO meetings relating to the development of the Convention on the Protection of Underwater Cultural Heritage. Members of the firm have often been called upon to serve as arbitrators, and its partners have also served as expert witnesses in foreign litigation on numerous occasions, testifying in foreign courts on issues of American law. One recent case involved a major reinsurance dispute before the High Court of Justice in London arising out of the 1989 *Exxon Valdez* oil spill.

**MAIN AREAS OF PRACTICE:** Maritime, shipping and transportation law; commercial and general litigation; corporate/finance including ship and asset financing, private equity and M&A, public securities law; bankruptcy and debtor/creditor law; personal injury; insurance and reinsurance; environmental; criminal defense; employment; real estate.

## HEAD OFFICE

**NEW YORK/NEW JERSEY**
61 Broadway, **New York**, NY 10006-2834
**Tel:** 212 943 3980   **Fax:** 212 425 0131
**Email:** reception@healy.com
**Website:** www.healy.com

## BRANCH OFFICES

**CONNECTICUT**
The Lock Building, 20 Marshall Street, Suite 104,
**South Norwalk**, CT 06854
**Tel:** 203 354 1360   **Fax:** 203 354 1363

## INTERNATIONAL OFFICES

The firm also has an office in Hong Kong.

**CLIENTS:** Since its inception, the firm has represented clients in all areas of the shipping industry, including: shipowners, operators and charterers; governments and government-owned carriers; marine insurers and reinsurers including P&I insurers, FD&D associations, hull and machinery underwriters and war risk insurers; NVOCC's, freight forwarders and other shipping agents; cargo interests; lending banks and other financing institutions; and debtors and creditors in bankruptcy proceedings.

**Performance:** Maritime casualties (Kariba, APL China, Barge Texas, Amphion, Achille Lauro hijacking, Atlantic Empress/Aegean Captain and Seiryu/Stena Freighter collisions, Estonia and Scandinavian Star ferry disasters, Marine Electric sinking, Amoco Cadiz and Torrey Canyon pollution incidents); hundreds of maritime arbitrations; over 200  personal injury trials; Norwegian Guarantee Institute v. Hambros Bank, Lexmar, Premier Products Tankers and Westbond litigations; US Lines, Hellenic Lines, Regency Lines, Premier Cruise Lines and Millenuim bankruptcies; and the Marathon Ashland Petroleum charterparty dispute.

**INTERNATIONAL WORK:** Healy & Baillie has a long history of representing international clients in the United States and in assisting domestic clients in protecting their interests abroad. The firm is well equipped to support its clients in the global arena. Many of the firm's attorneys are fluent or conversant in other languages, including Greek, Norwegian, Spanish, French, German, Mandarin, and Cantonese. The firm has a partner admitted to practice in Greece and two who are authorized to practice law in England and provide advice on English law. The firm's Hong Kong office, which celebrated its 10th Anniversary in 2004, offers a full service Maritime Practice in that jurisdiction. Healy & Baillie is the only US-based maritime law firm with a local license to practice Hong Kong law, and the firm regularly appears before the Hong Kong courts. That office is also well positioned to assist clients in China and throughout Asia and Oceania.

1533

# HOLLAND & KNIGHT LLP

## THE FIRM

**Managing Partner:** Howell W Melton, Jr

**Number of partners:** 697
**Number of other lawyers:** 563

**FIRM OVERVIEW:** At Holland & Knight the talents and resources of the entire firm are leveraged to deliver effective advocacy and comprehensive, integrated solutions in virtually all areas of the law, across the US, and around the world. To address clients' needs as effectively and efficiently as possible, the firm works collaboratively, drawing upon its depth and breadth of legal experience and industry knowledge. Holland & Knight's clients' businesses range in scope from local to global and span a wide range of industries. Their 'one-firm' structure positions them to support the most complex matters at all levels, with comprehensive and integrated service. The firm is organized into four Practice Sections – Litigation, Government, Business and Real Estate. Through integrated practice groups and industry-based teams, the firm provides efficient and responsive legal representation anywhere in the world. The firm serves clients on the basis of need, not merely location. Their interdisciplinary approach assures that clients have access to the lawyers with the most appropriate experience.

**Diversity:** At Holland & Knight, they believe their clients receive the highest quality service when their legal teams are drawn from an experienced pool of professionals reflective of the marketplace in which they do business. They have a diverse workforce of lawyers and staff from across racial, gender, age, ethnic, national, sexual orientation and religious lines. For the past five years, Holland & Knight has ranked as one of the top two law firms nationally for the total number of minority partners, as well as in the top five for the highest number of African-American and Hispanic attorneys (Minority Law Journal, Summer 2005). Holland & Knight is dedicated to diversity and has created several initiatives to promote diversity within the firm, in the legal profession and their communities.

## MAIN AREAS OF PRACTICE:

**Litigation:** Holland & Knight's Litigation Section is one of the nation's largest and most powerful with more than 500 lawyers. This highly regarded group includes more than 20 former federal prosecutors, and several former federal and state regulatory officials. Sophisticated investigative and forensic services provided by experienced former federal investigators enhance the representation of the firm's clients. Their clients include many Fortune 500 companies, regional corporations, government entities and nonprofit organizations in a broad range of venues. Holland & Knight's lawyers appear in state and federal courts across the US and in tribunals around the world. The firm's infrastructure and resources support large, complex cases and the docket includes numerous multimillion-dollar class actions, securities litigation, intellectual property, product liability and mass tort cases.

**Business:** Holland & Knight's Corporate Practice Group consists of more than 250 attorneys who regularly advise clients in a wide variety of corporate transactions, corporate financings, and securities law compliance matters. From complex public company acquisitions to early stage business considerations, the firm takes a proactive approach to identify key issues, develop sophisticated solutions, and adhere to clients' objectives as they help guide the matter to a successful conclusion consistent with clients' business strategy. Holland & Knight represents businesses and financial institutions of every size in all matters relating to banking and finance;

syndication; mergers and acquisitions; corporate and securities law and corporate governance. Holland & Knight is nationally recognized in fields as diverse as estate, gift and generation-skipping transfer tax planning, probate litigation, IRS litigation, life insurance planning, business succession planning, asset protection, international taxation, charitable foundations and matrimonial law.

**Real Estate:** Holland & Knight's Real Estate Section represents one of the most accomplished legal resources in the United States. With more than 200 lawyers, the firm's real estate practice is also the largest of any law firm in the country. Clients rely on the lawyer's abilities in the acquisition, development, disposition, leasing and financing of commercial, retail, residential, resort, industrial, mixed-use, and public housing projects. Clients include regional and national developers, builders, investors, lenders, asset and property managers, syndicators, pension funds, tax-exempt organizations, broker-dealers, municipalities, real estate investment trusts and life insurance companies.

**Government:** Holland & Knight's Government Section is one of the most experienced and respected in the US. They have extensive knowledge of local, tribal, state and federal issues and a thorough understanding of the legislative and regulatory processes affecting business and governmental entities. They draw on the experience of their lawyers, lobbyists and public relations advisors to achieve clients' goals. Holland & Knight's bipartisan team of professionals, some of whom are former members of Congress and the executive branch, have relationships in the state capitals, the White House and Congress. They are on-site in many state capitals in major cities across the US.

## HEAD OFFICE

**NEW YORK**
195 Broadway, 24th Floor, **New York**, NY 10007
**Tel:** 212 513 3200
**Website:** www.hklaw.com

## US OFFICES

The firm's United States offices are located in California, Florida, Georgia, Illinois, Maryland, Massachusetts, New York, Oregon, Rhode Island, Texas, Virginia, Washington state and Washington DC.

## INTERNATIONAL OFFICES

Internationally, the firm's offices are located in Mexico City, Tokyo and Beijing, with representative offices in Helsinki, Caracas and Tel Aviv.

# Holland+Knight

# HUGHES HUBBARD & REED LLP

## THE FIRM

**Chair:** Candace Krugman Beinecke
**Managing Director:** Charles Scherer

**Number of partners and counsel:** 108
**Number of attorneys:** 332

**FIRM OVERVIEW:** Founded over 100 years ago, Hughes Hubbard & Reed is among those law firms that have been designated by *The American Lawyer* as an A-List firm, which the magazine calls "the profession's top tier", "the best law firms in the land" and "the new elite". The firm's namesake was the legendary Chief Justice of the United States, Charles Evans Hughes, and the firm takes pride in the fact that it has retained many of its clients for more than half a century. Hughes Hubbard has also been a leader in diversity. It was the first New York firm to make an African-American woman a partner and the first major New York firm to be chaired by a woman.

## MAIN AREAS OF PRACTICE:

**LITIGATION:** In a survey by *International Commercial Litigation*, Hughes Hubbard was recognized as a leading US firm for litigation. A substantial portion of the firm's practice is devoted to litigation. A number of the firm's litigators are members of the American College of Trial Lawyers and many are particularly skilled in handling complex and transnational litigation, as well as hard-to-try scientific, technical and engineering cases.

**Product Liability & Toxic Tort:** More than 75 attorneys in all offices have extensive product liability experience. The firm has successfully defended major product liability litigation in pharmaceuticals, aircraft, trains and automobiles, specialty chemicals, fire and other disasters, large machinery, blood and biologics, and toxic workplace exposure.

**Insurance Coverage Litigation:** The firm was lead counsel in large and complex insurance coverage and mass tort cases including those involving breast implants, tainted blood, dental implants, asbestos, and alleged radio frequency radiation from cellular phones.

**Securities Litigation:** The firm has an extensive practice in representing issuers, accounting firms, and corporate directors and executives in securities class actions and regulatory and white collar criminal investigations relating to alleged securities fraud or other business misconduct. The team includes lawyers with prosecutorial and agency backgrounds and has experience in all phases of the work, from internal investigations to civil and criminal trials and appeals.

**International Arbitration:** More than 50 Hughes Hubbard lawyers, located in all offices, are engaged in arbitration. Many are multi-lingual and qualified to practice in both common and civil law jurisdictions. The firm is consistently ranked among the top firms for International Arbitration.

**CORPORATE:** Hughes Hubbard's corporate clients include some of the world's largest multinational companies. The firm has a strong M&A Practice which includes hostile takeovers and proxy fights as well as joint ventures and other strategic alliances, including those involving multi-country cross border transactions. Attorneys involved in capital markets transactions represent issuers and underwriters in public and private equity and debt offerings, private equity transactions, initial public offerings and equipment financings.

**OTHER:**

**Antitrust:** This group advises on mergers, acquisitions, joint ventures and other business combinations, alliances and patent pools, and pricing, distribution and licensing strategies.

**Corporate Reorganization:** This practice is international and multidisciplinary integrating traditional bankruptcy expertise with banking, litigation, corporate and other specialties to provide maximum return for the client.

**Environmental:** Attorneys regularly counsel clients about the laws governing air pollution, water quality, soil contamination, and indoor environmental quality, including criminal as well as civil matters.

**Financial Services:** Attorneys represent banks, credit card companies and insurance companies, in matters as diverse as syndicated lending, regulatory matters, derivatives, commercial paper programs and asset dispositions.

## HEAD OFFICE

**NEW YORK**
One Battery Park Plaza, **New York**, NY 10004-1482
**Tel:** 212 837 6000   **Fax:** 212 422 4726
**Website:** www.hugheshubbard.com

## BRANCH OFFICES

**DISTRICT OF COLUMBIA**
1775 I Street NW, **Washington**, DC 20006-2401
**Tel:** 202 721 4600   **Fax:** 202 721 4646

**CALIFORNIA**
350 South Grand Avenue, **Los Angeles**, CA 90071-3442
**Tel:** 213 613 2800   **Fax:** 213 613 2950

**FLORIDA**
201 South Biscayne Boulevard, **Miami**, FL 33131-4332
**Tel:** 305 358 1666   **Fax:** 305 371 8759

**NEW JERSEY**
101 Hudson Street, **Jersey City**, NJ 07302
**Tel:** 201 536 9220   **Fax:** 201 536 0799

## INTERNATIONAL OFFICES

The firm also has offices in Paris and Tokyo.

**Intellectual Property:** Global practice includes trademarks, patents, licenses, copyrights, technology and, increasingly, trade secrets and unfair competition.

**International Trade:** Hughes Hubbard's Washington office advises clients on US export controls, economic sanctions, customs matters and trade policy.

**Labor:** Attorneys are well-versed in the full range of employment law issues, including collective bargaining, discrimination, harassment, wrongful discharge, and non-competition agreements.

**Real Estate:** Global practice covers every aspect of real estate across a wide variety of industries including construction and hospitality.

**Tax & Employee Benefits:** Attorneys in this area provide solutions that both comply with the labyrinth of governmental rules and regulations and achieve their clients' business objectives. Employee Benefits attorneys handle all aspects of employee pensions, executive compensation and ERISA work.

**CLIENTS:** PricewaterhouseCoopers in several important divestitures. Burlington Coat Factory Warehouse Corporation in its agreement to be acquired by Bain Capital for $2.06 billion dollars; JPMorgan Chase Bank and Citibank in a $12.25 billion financing in connection with the separation of Viacom into two publicly traded companies; Burlington Capital Management and Goodwood Funds, Inc in two of the most innovative and high-profile proxy fights of the year: Creo Inc and Cenveo Inc. Merck in litigation coming out of the withdrawal of Vioxx; American Bureau of Shipping in a suit brought by the Kingdom of Spain arising out of the sinking of the oil tanker Prestige.

**INTERNATIONAL WORK:** With lawyers from over 20 countries who speak more than two dozen languages, Hughes Hubbard has a truly international perspective. The firm's Paris office has conducted an extensive practice throughout Europe since 1968. Hughes Hubbard also has a significant Pacific Basin practice with an office in Tokyo and a Latin America practice, located in the firm's Miami and New York offices, that is bi-lingual and bi-cultural.

Critical matters. Critical thinking.

# KAYE SCHOLER LLP

## THE FIRM

**Managing Partner:** Barry Willner
**Number of partners:** 144
**Number of other lawyers:** 354

**FIRM OVERVIEW:** Kaye Scholer has represented many of the world's largest corporations in some of their most significant business transactions and difficult complex litigations. The firm's ability to handle sophisticated representation has consistently attracted clients who depend on the highest standard of legal counsel. Founded in 1917 in New York City, today the firm counts some 500 lawyers in eight offices: New York, Chicago, Los Angeles, Washington, DC, West Palm Beach, Frankfurt, London and Shanghai.

## MAIN AREAS OF PRACTICE:

**Litigation:** Kaye Scholer is widely recognized as one of the leading litigation firms in the United States. With more than 230 lawyers in its Litigation Department, the firm handles some of the highest-profile cases in the country. The firm's team of experienced trial and appellate lawyers, supported in some cases by a cadre of in-house, PhD-level scientists, makes the firm one of the preeminent firms in product liability, intellectual property (patent, trademark and copyright), antitrust, white collar, employment and complex commercial and securities litigation. The firm's litigators are in court often and have a strong record of big wins for clients in jury trials. The firm collaborates with its clients, considering fresh interpretations of legal issues, developing bold strategies and balancing risk on all fronts. Kaye Scholer succeed through a deep understanding of its clients' short- and long-range business objectives and its ability to develop cost-effective legal strategies to achieve them.

**Corporate:** Kaye Scholer offers talent, experience and exceptional service to its corporate and finance clients. The firm's lawyers are based in business centers around the world, enabling the firm to provide clients with an understanding of the markets and trends that affect their businesses and to extend the web of legal communications globally. The firm has the flexibility to manage all types of transactions, from the middle market to high profile, multibillon dollar deals. The firm works daily with financial institutions, financial sponsors and their portfolio companies, public corporations and foreign entities expanding into US markets. The firm's clients trust Kaye Scholer to know its business and theirs, eliminate problems quickly and provide dependable results.

**Real Estate:** Kaye Scholer's real estate group has one of the premier practices in the country. The firm applies its expertise to the representation of clients who are in the business of owning, developing, investing, financing and trading in real property and real property assets. The firm's real estate attorneys are well known throughout the industry for the excellence of its work, the experience and judgment the firm brings to each transaction and the efficient execution it provides.

**Bankruptcy:** Kaye Scholer has one of the largest and most experienced groups of attorneys in the country dedicated exclusively to restructurings and bankruptcy work. The firm offers clients a comprehensive, nationwide restructuring and insolvency practice based in its offices in New York, Chicago and Los Angeles. The firm excels at resolving complex issues whether in the context of an out-of-court restructuring or a bankruptcy proceeding in addition to working through complicated structures, many of which involve cross-border issues.

**Tax:** Kaye Scholer's tax lawyers work to ensure that the tax implications or its clients' business and investment transactions are addressed in the most practical and efficient manner. The firm also has a significant practice in counseling clients in tax controversies with federal, state and local tax attorneys.

**Wills & Estates:** The wills and estates lawyers service clients in all related tax and legal matters, but are also involved with the very human and personal side of wills and estates law, helping clients make sound decisions about important family matters and providing comfort and reassurance to individuals in trying times.

**CLIENTS:** The firm's client base includes national, foreign and multinational corporations, as well as private equity funds and government entities.

## HEAD OFFICE

### NEW YORK
Kaye Scholer LLP, 425 Park Avenue, **New York**, NY10022-3598
**Tel:** 212 836 8000   **Fax:** 212 836 8689
**Website:** www.kayescholer.com
**Email:** webmaster@kayescholer.com

## BRANCH OFFICES

### CALIFORNIA
1999 Avenue of the Stars, Suite 1700, **Los Angeles**, CA 90067-6048
**Tel:** 310 788 1000   **Fax:** 310 788 1200

### DISTRICT OF COLUMBIA
The McPherson Building, 901 Fifteenth Street, N.W., Suite 1100, **Washington**, DC 20005-2327
**Tel:** 202 682 3500   **Fax:** 202 682 3580

### FLORIDA
Phillips Point, West Tower, Suite 900, 777 South Flagler Drive, **West Palm Beach**, FL 33401-6163
**Tel:** 561 802 3230   **Fax:** 561 802 3217

### ILLINOIS
3 First National Plaza, Suite 4100, 70 West Madison Street, **Chicago**, IL 60602-4231
**Tel:** 312 583 2300   **Fax:** 312 583 2360

### INTERNATIONAL OFFICES
The firm has international offices in Frankfurt, Germany; Shanghai, People's Republic of China; and London, United Kingdom

**INTERNATIONAL WORK:** Kaye Scholer attorneys manage cross-border deals from offices in London, Frankfurt, Shanghai and the US. Clients run businesses in Europe, North America, Asia, Australia and Latin America and expect Kaye Scholer to create a seamless and efficient transaction process, regardless of the direction their investments and profits travel. The firm's international trade attorneys represent multinational corporations, industry coalitions and foreign governments in proceedings in numerous trade fora throughout the world.

KAYE SCHOLER

# KENYON & KENYON LLP

## THE FIRM

**Managing Partner:** Robert T Tobin
**Executive Committee:** Richard L DeLucia, James E Rosini,
Stuart J Sinder, Robert T Tobin

**Number of partners:** 58
**Number of other lawyers:** 151

## AREAS OF PRACTICE:

Intellectual Property . . . . . . . . . . . . . . . . . . . . . . . . . . . . . . . . . . . 100%

**FIRM OVERVIEW:** Kenyon & Kenyon LLP is one of the largest full-service intellectual property law firms in the United States, with offices in New York, Washington DC, and Silicon Valley. For its global and domestic clients, the firm provides litigation, prosecution, licensing and counseling services relating to patents, trademarks, copyrights, trade secrets and related matters, such as unfair business and unfair trade practices.

The firm includes one of the preeminent intellectual property litigation groups in the country, which has won some of the most important decisions of the past decade. The firm's proficiency in and out of the courtroom allows it efficiently and effectively to handle all the details and issues that may arise during the course of litigation. The key to any successful trial is preparation. Assembling the right team, collecting and reviewing documentation, and organizing mock trials and preparing witnesses are all part of representing the firm's clients in courtrooms across the country. The litigation group includes many lawyers with trial experience, including several with extensive 'first-chair' jury and non-jury trial experience.

More than 95 per cent of the firm's 200-plus lawyers have undergraduate or advanced degrees in technical disciplines such as electrical engineering, computer science, chemistry, chemical engineering, biology, mechanical engineering, aerospace engineering and materials sciences.

The firm's reputation and position in the profession has been confirmed by some recent survey rankings: by IP Law & Business as one of the top three firms to represent defendants in patent cases, one of the top three firms to bring patent cases for plaintiffs, and as one of the top five firms for most patent cases filed in 2004; by Managing Intellectual Property as one of the top firms for IP in both contentious and non-contentious patent and trademark representation; and in 2003 and 2004 by IP Today's Top Trademark survey as one of the top 15 for number of trademarks issued.

The firm strives to provide the best client representation through its experience, technological expertise, anticipation of client needs, clear and open communication, and an understanding of the vital role played by a comprehensive intellectual property protection and enforcement strategy. The firm is committed to comprehending its clients' products, processes and services in the context of their industries. The legal ability, training, technical expertise and experience of the firm's lawyers enable them to design and implement legal strategies to protect innovation essential to the health of their clients' businesses, to protect those assets in court and at the United States International Trade Commission, and to defend against claims by others. A number of our attorneys also wrote and maintain the authoritative work on the subject, Unfair Competition and the ITC, Actions before the International Trade Commission under Section 337 of the Tariff Act of 1930.

## HEAD OFFICE

### NEW YORK
One Broadway, **New York**, NY 10004
**Tel:** 212 425 7200   **Fax:** 212 425 5288
**Email:** info@kenyon.com
**Website:** www.kenyon.com

## BRANCH OFFICES

### DISTRICT OF COLUMBIA
1500 K Street, NW, **Washington**, DC 20005
**Tel:** 202 220 4200   **Fax:** 202 220 4201

### CALIFORNIA
333 W. San Carlos Street, Suite 600, **San Jose**, CA 95110
**Tel:** 408 975 7500   **Fax:** 408 975 7501

**CLIENTS:** The firm's experience spans the business spectrum. It represents clients in such technological areas as computers (both hardware and software), biotechnology products and processes, machinery, pharmaceuticals, and plastics. Additionally, the firm provides services to clients in aerospace, photography, medical devices, metallurgy, basic chemicals and petrochemicals, environmental processes, financial services, food and beverages, transportation vehicles, agribio products, robotics, and telecommunications. It also represents clients in entertainment and the arts, toys, publishing, interactive entertainment, travel, sports, marketing, and advertising.

**INTERNATIONAL WORK:** Kenyon & Kenyon has a worldwide clientele. The firm represents not only American companies, but also European, Asian and multinational firms. It coordinates multinational disputes in a number of instances, both to ensure that the US litigation, which is its primary responsibility, is not compromised by events in other countries and to assist counsel in those countries to present the most effective claims and defenses. The firm also develops and maintains international IP portfolios for its worldwide clients and has garnered great relationships with foreign associates in every major industrial country.

1537

# KING & SPALDING LLP

## THE FIRM

**Chairman:** Robert D Hays
**Managing Partner, Atlanta:** Mason W Stephenson
**Managing Partner, Houston:** Robert E Meadows
**Managing Partner, London:** John L Keffer
**Managing Partner, New York:** Michael J O'Brien
**Managing Partner, Washington:** J Sedwick Sollers

**Number of partners:** 240
**Number of other lawyers:** 560

**FIRM OVERVIEW:** King & Spalding LLP is an international law firm with more than 800 lawyers in Atlanta, Houston, London, New York, and Washington, DC. The firm represents more than 250 public companies, including over half of the *Fortune* 100.

## MAIN AREAS OF PRACTICE:

**Antitrust:** King & Spalding's antitrust lawyers are trial lawyers who know how to litigate in 'bet the company' situations. The firm has been counsel for clients in numerous antitrust litigation settings, ranging from class actions and multi-district litigation to disputes between particular suppliers and their customers or competitors.

**Financial Transactions:** The practice group provides legal services for domestic and non-US banks and other financial institutions. It handles all aspects of credit-facilities and financial products.

**Construction:** Today, the Construction and Procurement Practice Group represents some of the world's largest organizations involved in global construction projects. King & Spalding was one of the first large, general practice firms in the nation to establish a practice devoted to construction and procurement law.

**Corporate/M&A:** Consistently ranks among the leading M&A practices in the United States in terms of aggregate deal value and total number of transactions handled.

**Corporate Finance:** The firm represents issuers, underwriters, investors, and other corporate finance participants, and provides corporate advice to public and private companies.

**Employment & Labor Law:** The firm defends *Fortune* 500 corporate defendants against complex claims of unlawful employment policies and conduct involving allegations of discrimination under federal and state non-discrimination statutes.

**Energy:** The firm's energy attorneys have been involved in transactions throughout the world related to energy and natural resources. King & Spalding's experience includes developing project structures as well as the drafting and negotiating of project agreements, contracts and documentation. Additionally, King & Spalding lawyers have been active advisors to the Liquefied Natural Gas (LNG) marketplace for the last 30 years. As pioneers on this legal scene, the internationally recognized group of lawyers have been key participants in LNG export, transport, and import projects . Today, King & Spalding's team is sought after by LNG players worldwide owing to depth of experience, knowledge, skill, and determination.

**Environment:** King & Spalding is recognized as one of the leading environmental firms and combines substantive expertise, technical knowledge and litigation experience on numerous environmental issues.

**Insolvency/Corporate Recovery:** The Financial Restructuring Group at King & Spalding provides valuable knowledge and experience in the areas of corporate reorganizations, commercial debt restructuring, workouts, bankruptcy, and insolvency litigation.

**Intellectual Property:** The firm's IP lawyers concentrate on acquiring, creating, licensing, protecting, and litigating intellectual property rights, both domestically and internationally.

## HEAD OFFICE

**GEORGIA**
1180 Peachtree Street, **Atlanta**, GA 30309-3521
**Tel:** 404 572 4600 **Fax:** 404 572 5100
**Email:** kingspalding@kslaw.com
**Website:** www.kslaw.com

## BRANCH OFFICES

**NEW YORK**
1185 Avenue of the Americas, **New York**, NY 10036-4003
**Tel:** 212 556 2100 **Fax:** 212 556 2222
**Email:** kingspalding@kslaw.com

**TEXAS**
1100 Louisiana, Suite 4000, **Houston**, TX 77002-5213
**Tel:** 713 751 3200 **Fax:** 713 751 3290
**Email:** kingspalding@kslaw.com

**DISTRICT OF COLUMBIA**
1700 Pennsylvania Avenue, N.W., **Washington,** DC 200006-4706
**Tel:** 202 737 0500 **Fax:** 202 626 3737
**Email:** kingspalding@kslaw.com

## INTERNATIONAL OFFICES

King & Spalding International LLP, London.

**Litigation & Arbitration:** The firm provides litigation services in the areas of antitrust, appellate, class action, commercial disputes, product liability, shareholder and securities litigation, trade and customs, and toxic tort. The firm also has a substantial international arbitration practice.

**Real Estate:** The firm's real estate practice includes acquisition, development, financing and leasing of commercial real estate primarily for nationally recognized developers, and non-US institutional and private investors.

**Tax:** The firm works with clients on the planning and execution of business transactions of all sizes and types arising in domestic and cross border settings, including acquisitions, disposition, joint ventures, and financing transactions.

**CLIENTS:** 3M, Brown & Williamson Tobacco Corporation, Chevron Corporation, The Coca-Cola Company, Credit Suisse First Boston LLC, The Dow Chemical Company, Ernst & Young LLP, ExxonMobil Corporation, General Electric Company, General Motors Corporation, Georgia-Pacific Corporation, GlaxoSmithKline, Goldman Sachs & Company, The Home Depot, Inc., Honeywell International Inc., KPMG LLP, Lehman Brothers Inc., Lockheed Martin Corporation, Merrill Lynch & Co., Inc., Morgan Stanley Capital Group, Inc., Purdue Pharma L.P., Scientific-Atlanta, Inc., Shell Oil Company, Sprint Nextel Corporation, SunTrust Banks Inc., Turner Broadcasting System, Inc., UCB Inc., UPS.

# KING & SPALDING

# KRAMER LEVIN NAFTALIS & FRANKEL LLP

## THE FIRM

**Managing Partner:** Paul S Pearlman

**Number of partners:** 100
**Number of other lawyers:** 224

**FIRM OVERVIEW:** Kramer Levin Naftalis & Frankel LLP is a premier, full-service law firm with offices in New York and Paris and an alliance with UK-based Berwin Leighton Paisner. With more than 300 attorneys, they have the deep knowledge and expertise to provide a full range of innovative legal solutions. The firm's strong focus on client service and commitment to excellence have enabled it to build long-term relationships with major domestic and international corporations, institutions and individuals that look to it for innovative and practical solutions for both everyday and complex matters. The firm guides Global 1000 companies and emerging growth entities to help them fully realize their business goals.

## MAIN AREAS OF PRACTICE:

**Corporate:** Handles virtually every type of complex corporate and securities transaction from public offerings and private placements to mergers, acquisitions, dispositions and joint ventures, while also providing the full range of general corporate law services from contract preparation to strategic counseling. The department regularly represents companies large and small, domestic and foreign, public and private, mature and entrepreneurial in cutting-edge as well as conventional transactions.

**Corporate Restructuring & Bankruptcy:** The Corporate Restructuring and Bankruptcy Practice, one of the nation's foremost, has played a central role in many of the country's largest and most complex reorganizations. Working closely with the firm's other departments, this diverse practice includes representation of creditors' committees, debtors, banks, bondholders, trade creditors, landlords, investors, debtor-in-possession lenders and acquirors as well as investors in the purchase and sale of securities and assets of troubled companies.

**Intellectual Property:** Handles all aspects of intellectual property law - patents, trademarks, copyrights, trade secrets, technology transfer, unfair competition and false advertising, internet and new media. Attorneys in this full-service department provide litigation, prosecution and registration, counseling and transactional services to their clients to help them acquire, value, maintain, protect and exploit all forms of intellectual property.

**Litigation:** From its beginning in 1968, Kramer Levin has specialized in the litigation of high profile, high-stakes commercial cases. The firm's White Collar Defense and SEC Regulatory Group is one of the nation's most prominent. The Litigation Department is chaired by Gary P Naftalis, one of the country's leading trial lawyers, and numbers over 75 lawyers. Litigation Department attorneys work in virtually every area of commercial litigation. Such expertise spans the following practice areas: antitrust; appellate and constitutional; bankruptcy; commercial; employment law; ERISA; false advertising; insurance; intellectual property (patent, trademark and copyright); international dispute resolution; real estate; securities and shareholder; and white collar defense.

**Real Estate:** The Real Estate Department's attorneys have extensive experience analyzing and applying all the relevant law - real estate, corporate, environmental, land use, restructuring and tax - to deliver creative, cost-effective and practical legal and business solutions. The department has the size, knowledge, experience and dedication to assist on the full array of real property matters including office, residential, industrial, hotel and retail property development, acquisitions and sales; financings and refinancings; workouts and restructuring transactions for lenders, borrowers, and equity participants; retail and office and industrial leasing; joint ventures; structured finance sales/leasebacks; the conversion of new and existing commercial and residential properties to condominium and cooperatives uses; and zoning.

**Employment Law, Benefits & Business Immigration:** Employers turn to the firm for assistance in the areas of employment law, business immigration, and

## HEAD OFFICE

**NEW YORK**
1177 Avenue of the Americas, **New York**, NY 10036
**Tel:** 212 715 9100 **Fax:** 212 715 8000
**Website:** www.kramerlevin.com

## CONTACTS

| | |
|---|---|
| **Business Immigration** | Theodore (Ted) Ruthizer |
| **Corporate** | Scott S Rosenblum |
| **Corporate Restructuring & Bankruptcy** | Kenneth H Eckstein |
| **Employee Benefits** | Michael J Nassau |
| **Employment Law** | Kevin B Leblang |
| **Environmental** | Richard G Leland |
| **Individual Clients** | John C Novogrod |
| **Intellectual Property** | Nicholas L Coch |
| **Land Use** | Paul D Selver/ |
| | Michael T Sillerman |
| **Litigation** | Gary P Naftalis |
| **Outsourcing & Technology Transactions** | Randy Lipsitz |
| | Howard T Spilko |
| **Paris Office** | Alexander Marquardt |
| **Real Estate** | Jay A Neveloff |
| **Tax** | Howard J Rothman |

benefits and executive compensation. The firm provides practical, proactive counsel to employers to guide them through the myriad of statutes, regulations, and judge-made rules governing employmenet matters. If a dispute arises, the firm's clients draw on their expertise to provide the best and fastest solution possible, whether through negotiation, arbitration, mediation or litigation. In the business immigration area, the firm is counsel to leading US and international companies, to whom they provide expert business immigration services inovlving the hiring and transfer of foreign national executives, managers, professionals, and performing artists for both temporary and permanent visa statuses.

**CLIENTS:** Today, many of Kramer Levin's clients range from Global 1000 to emerging growth companies that look to the firm for creative solutions for their rapidly changing needs. KL has also played key roles in developing entrepreneurial successes in industries as diverse as fashion and cosmetics, telecommunications and financial services.

**INTERNATIONAL WORK:** Through its Paris office, Kramer Levin offers clients the benefits of a full-service legal practice based in Europe. The firm's Paris-based attorneys assist domestic and foreign clients with a wide variety of corporate matters, including mergers and acquisitions, corporate securities and finance, banking law, structured financings and securitizations, reorganizations and bankruptcies, complex real estate matters, employment law and foreign investment. The firm also represents clients in all types of business litigation before French courts and in international arbitrations. Kramer Levin's alliance with UK-based Berwin Leighton Paisner further strengthens its ability to provide truly superior global representation. The UK-based alliance focuses on cross-border corporate and finance matters, and on some of the firm's other highly regarded practice areas including real estate, litigation, intellectual property and technology, bankruptcy and tax.

## KRAMER LEVIN NAFTALIS & FRANKEL LLP

# LEBOEUF, LAMB, GREENE & MACRAE LLP

## THE FIRM

**Chairman:** Steven H Davis
**Number of partners:** 195
**Number of other lawyers:** 463

**FIRM OVERVIEW:** LeBoeuf, Lamb, Greene & MacRae LLP is a full-service, global law firm with more than 650 lawyers practicing in 19 offices worldwide. Well known as one of the preeminent legal services providers to the insurance/financial services and energy and utilities industries, the firm has built upon these strengths to gain prominence in corporate, litigation, bankruptcy, international, environmental, taxation, information technology/intellectual property, real estate, trust and estates, antitrust, corporate governance and compliance, and white-collar criminal defense practice. LeBoeuf Lamb's multinational network of strategically located offices and broad range practice areas serves clients' local interests as well as ensures clients' access to, and ease of doing business in, major international markets.

## MAIN AREAS OF PRACTICE:

**Insurance:** LeBoeuf Lamb has been widely recognized as a leading legal advisor to the insurance industry for the past four decades. Its practice covers every segment of the insurance industry, with an impressive depth of resources and experience. This depth has enabled the firm to develop strong working relationships with major insurers, brokers, investment bankers, commercial bankers, regulators, legislators, actuaries, and other service providers to the insurance industry.

**Energy:** LeBoeuf Lamb represents energy and utility suppliers in all aspects of their business. More than 100 LeBoeuf Lamb attorneys devote the bulk of their time to providing services that touch upon the energy, telecommunications and water industries, making LeBoeuf Lamb a recognized leader in the energy and utilities legal practice worldwide.

**Corporate:** The Corporate Group regularly handles some of the world's largest and most challenging transactions, including mergers and acquisitions; public and private securities offerings; private equity and venture capital transactions; securitizations; privatizations; and transactions relating to public finance, project finance, investment management, and derivatives. The firm consistently ranks among leading advisors in mergers and acquisitions for announced transactions.

**Litigation:** LeBoeuf Lamb's Litigation Department specializes in multibillion-dollar complex and multinational cases. For decades, the firm has been recognized as one of the world's leading firms in energy and insurance litigation and arbitration. Its expertise has expanded to include white-collar crime, corporate governance, securities litigation, and international litigation and mediation. The firm's lawyers are among the world's preeminent experts in each of these fields, and represent clients in some of the world's largest investigations and disputes.

**Bankruptcy & Restructuring:** The Bankruptcy and Debt Restructuring Group has played a significant role in numerous complex, high-profile restructurings. LeBoeuf Lamb has represented clients in significant bankruptcy and debt restructuring cases in virtually every major city and region of the United States. With more than 20 highly experienced lawyers, the firm offers top-quality service in this specialized field of law.

**Technology & Intellectual Property:** LeBoeuf Lamb combines its expertise in intellectual property law with a multidisciplinary approach to devise creative and efficient methods of acquiring, protecting and exploiting intellectual property rights on a global basis. The attorneys in the LeBoeuf Lamb Technology and Intellectual Property Group counsel clients on a wide range of matters relating to information technology, intellectual property, privacy, information security, and document retention.

**Tax:** LeBoeuf Lamb's Tax Practice is broad-based, reflecting the diversified nature of the firm's practice and experience in many subspecialty areas. The firm counsels clients on a variety of sophisticated tax issues.

**Executive Compensation, Employee Benefits & ERISA:** LeBoeuf Lamb has developed a comprehensive practice in employee benefits and executive compensation, reaching a clientele with the same broad scope and range as that of the firm as a whole.

## HEAD OFFICE

**NEW YORK**
125 West 55th Street, **New York**, NY 10019
**Tel:** 212 424 8000   **Fax:** 212 424 8500
**Email:** info@llgm.com   **Website:** www.llgm.com

## BRANCH OFFICES

**CALIFORNIA**
725 South Figueroa Street, Suite 3100, **Los Angeles**, CA 90017-5404
**Tel:** 213 955 7300   **Fax:** 213 955 7399

One Embarcadero Center, Suite 400, **San Francisco**, CA 94111-3619
**Tel:** 415 951 1100   **Fax:** 415 951 1180

**CONNECTICUT**
Goodwin Square, 225 Asylum Street, 13th Floor, **Hartford**, CT 06103
**Tel:** 860 293 3500   **Fax:** 860 293 3555

**DISTRICT OF COLUMBIA**
1875 Connecticut Ave., N.W., Suite 1200, **Washington**, DC 20009-5728
**Tel:** 202 986 8000   **Fax:** 202 986 8102

**FLORIDA**
50 North Laura Street, Suite 2800, **Jacksonville**, FL 32202-3650
**Tel:** 904 354 8000   **Fax:** 904 353 1673

**ILLINOIS**
Two Prudential Plaza, 180 North Stetson Avenue, Suite 3700, **Chicago**, IL 60601
**Tel:** 312 794 8000   **Fax:** 312 794 8100

**MASSACHUSETTS**
260 Franklin Street, **Boston**, MA 02110-3173
**Tel:** 617 748 6800   **Fax:** 617 439 0341

**NEW YORK**
One Commerce Plaza, 99 Washington Avenue, Suite 2020
**Albany**, NY 12210-2820
**Tel:** 518 626 9000   **Fax:** 518 626 9010

**PENNSYLVANIA**
One Gateway Center, 420 Fort Duquesne Boulevard, Suite 1600
**Pittsburgh**, PA 15222-1437
**Tel:** 412 594 2300   **Fax:** 412 594 5237

**TEXAS**
Reliant Energy Plaza, 1000 Main Street, Suite 2550,
**Houston**, TX 77002
**Tel:** 713 287 2000   **Fax:** 713 287 2100

## INTERNATIONAL OFFICES

The firm also has offices in Almaty, Beijing, Brussels, Johannesburg, London, Moscow, Paris and Riyadh.

**Environmental, Health & Safety:** LeBoeuf Lamb has developed a substantial Environmental, Health and Safety Practice. Environmental attorneys represent clients before federal, state, and local courts and governmental agencies on a wide variety of regulatory, legislative, and civil and criminal litigation matters.

**Telecommunications:** Since the 1970s, LeBoeuf Lamb has been engaged in representing clients in the telecommunications field. Its telecommunications work is truly national and international in character, often crossing borders as its clients expand and their legal needs grow, to combine its telecommunications expertise with local insight in numerous markets.

The firm also has significant practices in project finance, international, real estate, trusts and estates, antitrust, corporate governance and compliance, and white-collar criminal defense. For additional information, please visit the firm online at www.llgm.com.

# LePATNER & ASSOCIATES LLP

## THE FIRM

**Managing Partner:** Barry B LePatner

**Number of partners:** 5
**Number of other lawyers:** 3
**Number of design consultants:** 1

## AREAS OF PRACTICE:

| | |
|---|---|
| Commercial Litigation & Claims Representation | 35% |
| Construction Contracts | 35% |
| Business Advisory Services | 30% |

**FIRM OVERVIEW:** Founded by Barry LePatner in 1980, LePatner & Associates LLP is widely recognized as one of the nation's leading law firms providing business and legal advice affecting the real estate, design and construction industries. On behalf of its many corporate, institutional and commercial real estate clients, the firm provides sophisticated project planning, state-of-the-art contracts and respected advisory services at all levels of today's complex real estate projects.

## MAIN AREAS OF PRACTICE:

**Construction Contracts:** For more than 25 years, the firm has been instrumental in protecting owners' capital investments from pre-construction to lease negotiations and through post-construction claims handling. Seamlessly coordinated construction agreements are specifically tailored to address the business imperatives of each project. The firm's dedicated contract law team provides negotiation services including due diligence of all team members, structuring agreements, contract negotiation with project teams, insurance and bonding compliance and coordination of design/construction scheduling. The firm has outstanding expertise in the area of coordinated construction contracts.

**Business Advisory Services:** The firm offers business advisory and consulting services for the design and construction industry from site selection, due diligence and selection of the construction team, project management, applicability of industry laws, regulations and codes, through claims management and handling of warranty issues. The practice specializes in addressing complexities faced by projects that are subject to the mandates of multiple governmental jurisdictions.

**Commercial Litigation & Claims:** The firm is widely recognised for its expertise in litigation and arbitration, dispute resolution alternatives, claims analysis and negotiation and claims avoidance strategies.

## HEAD OFFICE

**NEW YORK**
600 Lexington Ave, 21st Floor, **New York**, NY 10022
**Tel:** 212 935 4400   **Fax:** 212 935 4404
**Email:** blepatner@lepatner.com
**Website:** www.lepatner.com

## CONTACTS

**Contracts & Business Advisory Services**....................Barry B LePatner

**CLIENTS:** The firm's clients represent a spectrum of major commercial and residential property owners, corporations, institutions of higher education, and real estate developers, and includes: Starwood Resorts and Hotels, the Government of Spain, Thirteen.wnet, United Nations Mission in Kosovo, Rosewood Hotels and Resorts, Barnard College, DaimlerChrysler, the Osborn Retirement Community, Asprey Ltd.

**INTERNATIONAL WORK:** The firm has advised international corporations and foreign government entities operating within the US with regard to their construction projects. In addition to protecting their construction investment, LePatner & Associates guides these clients through the complex maze of government building codes and regulations.

# LINKLATERS

## THE FIRM

**US Managing Partner:** R Paul Wickes
**Global Managing Partner:** Tony Angel
**Number of partners in US:** 20
**Number of lawyers worldwide:** 2000

**FIRM OVERVIEW:** Linklaters' New York team practices across the legal spectrum, offering the highest quality advice on a wide range of domestic and cross-border deals and cases. In addition to its on-the-ground strength in New York, the firm's integrated international network gives its clients access to a US lawyer team based in 13 major financial centers throughout the globe, as well as its first-class, 2000-lawyer global practice. This unparalleled reach enables Linklaters to provide outstanding service not only within the United States but across the world.

## MAIN AREAS OF PRACTICE:

**Corporate:** Linklaters' US Capital Markets Team advises corporate, financial institution and government clients, as issuers and underwriters, on domestic and international, primary and secondary, public, Rule 144A/Reg S and private offerings of equity, equity-linked and debt securities. Products include high yield debt, convertible and exchangeable debt, structured debt, securitizations, subordinated debt, hybrid securities and other complex securities. The team also regularly advises on liability management transactions, including exchange offers, tender offers and consent solicitations.

The M&A and Private Equity Team represents domestic and international clients on US-based transactions and on cross-border and non-US transactions, advising on acquisitions, dispositions, and general corporate and governance issues. Representations include mergers, stock or asset purchases, joint ventures, going-private transactions, and exchange and tender offers.

The Corporate Restructuring Team advises leading corporate and financial institutions and private investment funds on recapitalizations and restructurings (including spin-offs and divestitures), with an emphasis on 'special situation' investment funds making investments and acquisitions or executing control strategies in distressed companies.

**Antitrust:** The firm's US Antitrust Team provides counsel on a broad range of matters, particularly advising on the antitrust implications of mergers and acquisitions, including under the Hart-Scott-Rodino Act, and representing clients in civil litigation and criminal grand jury investigations.

**Executive Compensation:** Linklaters advises on all aspects of securities and tax/ERISA law issues affecting executive compensation and employee benefits matters.

**Investment Management:** The US Investment Management Team represents private equity, hedge fund and other alternative investment sponsors, including those operating within global financial institutions. The group advises sponsors of management buyout, growth capital, venture capital, mezzanine and special situation funds, single strategy hedge funds and funds of hedge funds, as well as more esoteric funds and fund-linked products.

**Banking:** Linklaters' US Banking Team represents financial institutions, equity sponsors, companies and other investors and issuers in a range of domestic and international loan and bank finance products and structures at all rating and leverage levels, including leveraged buyouts, acquisition financings; sponsor based and general corporate financings; multi-priority secured financings; mezzanine financings, loan workouts; out-of-court restructurings; debtor-in-possession financings; asset-based loans; leveraged leasing transactions; structured financings; trade financings, portfolio acquisitions and other complex bank and loan market transactions and vehicles.

**Restructuring & Insolvency:** The US Restructuring and Insolvency Team represents investment funds, lending institutions, financial advisors and global companies. In all phases of in-court and out-of-court restructurings and workouts, specifically: private funds investing in distressed capital structures, including on capital structure arbitrage and on transactions such as public/private exchanges, recapitalizations, and section 363 acquisitions; providers of debt and equity financing to distressed companies, including debtor-in-possession and exit financing, rights offerings and 'plan fundings', advising lenders on enforcing and defending their senior debt positions in distressed or insolvent companies; advising financial advisors to creditors and debtors during restructurings and recapitalizations of distressed companies and debtors in both US domestic and cross-border bankruptcy proceedings.

**Structured Finance & Derivatives:** The US Structured Finance and Derivatives Team advises on cash collateralized debt obligations (CDOs); structured investment vehicles; synthetic CDOs; cash/synthetic hybrid CDOs and CDO/investment fund hybrids; credit-linked notes; hedge fund, hedge fund basket and hedge fund-linked products; hedge fund finance products; future flow and other asset securitizations; pure derivatives work (both advisory and transactional); securitized derivatives and repackagings of varying complexity using special purpose vehicles or trusts.

**Tax:** The US Tax Team provide planning and structuring advice on all aspects of the firm's practice. The Team has considerable experience in cross-border acquisitions and financings, including blending competing US and foreign jurisdiction tax considerations, identifying and structuring to resolve tax issues, advising on ERISA and negotiating tax related matters.

**Litigation & Arbitration:** The US Litigation Team has extensive trial and appellate experience before federal and state courts, bankruptcy courts, governmental agencies, and other tribunals. The Team is trial-ready and has extensive experience handling substantively and procedurally complex commercial litigation matters from inception through bench or jury trial and appeal. The Team also represents clients in mediations and arbitrations of both domestic and international disputes in numerous jurisdictions, and under the governing rules of various public and private tribunals, and provides strategic and research-based advice on transactional matters.

**CLIENTS:** Linklaters specializes in advising the world's leading companies, financial institutions and governments on their most challenging transactions and assignments.

## HEAD OFFICE

**NEW YORK**
1345 Avenue of the Americas, **New York**, NY 10105
**Tel:** 212 903 9000 **Fax:** 212 903 9100

## INTERNATIONAL OFFICES

Linklaters has offices in 30 cities: Amsterdam, Antwerp, Bangkok, Beijing, Berlin, Bratislava, Brussels, Bucharest, Budapest, Cologne, Dubai, Frankfurt, Hong Kong, Lisbon, London, Luxembourg, Madrid, Milan, Moscow, Munich, New York, Paris, Prague, Rome, São Paulo, Shanghai, Singapore, Stockholm, Tokyo, Warsaw.

## CONTACTS

| | |
|---|---|
| Antitrust | Thomas McGrath |
| Banking/Restructuring & Insolvency | Marty Flics |
| Capital Markets | Peter E Ruhlin |
| Executive Compensation | Bindu Culas |
| Investment Management | Scott Bowie |
| Litigation & Arbitration | R Paul Wickes |
| M&A and Private Equity | Mark Palmer |
| Structured Finance & Derivatives | Adam Glass |
| Tax | Stephen Land |

# Linklaters

# LOVELLS

## THE FIRM

**Managing Partner:** David Harris
**Senior Partner:** John Young

**Number of Partners in US offices:** 15
**Number of other lawyers in US offices:** 52
**Number of Partners worldwide:** 333
**Number of other lawyers worldwide:** 1221

**FIRM OVERVIEW:** With over 3000 people operating from 26 offices in Asia, Europe and the United States, Lovells is a truly international law firm. Its history can be traced back to 1899 with its inception in the UK, and, since then, the firm's significant growth has been driven by its ambition to provide clients with a broad range of legal services in key jurisdictions around the world.

**MAIN AREAS OF PRACTICE:** The US region focuses its practice in the following areas.

**Banking:** Lovells' US Banking Team represents prominent banks, corporate entities and other financial institutions in connection with their financing activities, including, secured and unsecured credit facilities, acquisition finance, project finance, asset-based lending, letters of credit and other trade financing arrangements, credit enhancement for public and private debt issuance, securitization and other sales of financial assets, derivatives, and non-judicial restructurings.

**Business Restructuring & Insolvency:** Lovells is consistently regarded as a top tier firm for legal advice on business restructuring and insolvency matters. They regularly assist banks, insurance companies, trade creditors and other financial stakeholders, directors, and acquirors of distressed assets in formulating and implementing strategic solutions to maximize business objectives.

**Dispute Resolution:** The US team is an integral part of Lovells' international Dispute Resolution Practice which covers all areas of dispute resolution, including litigation, arbitration and mediation. Many of the US dispute resolution attorneys are former federal prosecutors and have served as both arbitrators and mediators with significant experience in complex litigation, conducting trials and briefing and arguing appeals. A core strength of the firm's practice is international arbitration, including conducting arbitrations before the ICC, ICSID, and LCIA and the AAA. In addition, they have extensive experience in antitrust, commercial, cross-border, human-rights, securities, and financial litigation as well as in commercial fraud and asset-tracing. Lovells' dispute resolution experience extends to more than 100 countries and is consistently ranked in the top tiers of all the legal directories.

**Insurance & Reinsurance:** Lovells' US Insurance and Reinsurance Practice is part of one of the world's leading international teams. Their clients include many of the world's primary insurance and reinsurance companies, as well as financial institutions, investment advisors, corporations, brokers, other intermediaries and trade associations. They have successfully handled numerous insurance and reinsurance arbitrations and litigations involving billions of dollars of exposure and have extensive experience advising clients on a full range of domestic and cross-border transactions and complex disputes.

**Securities/Capital Markets:** Lovells' Securities Practice focuses on cross-border financings involving the firm's international client base. They represent issuers, underwriters and corporate trustees on a broad range of debt and equity offerings and have substantial experience both with public offerings registered with the SEC, as well as private placements to institutional investors.

**Tax:** Lovells' US Tax Practice represents numerous prominent companies and banks around the globe, engaged in cross-border transactions. The team has experience on a broad range of international transactions, including cross-border public and private securities offerings, mergers and acquisitions, financial transactions, investment funds, as well as inbound and outbound tax planning.

## US OFFICES

### ILLINOIS
One IBM Plaza, 330 N. Wabash Avenue, Suite 1900, **Chicago**, IL 60611
**Tel:** 312 832 4400 **Fax:** 312 832 4444 0660
**Website:** www.lovells.com

### NEW YORK
590 Madison Avenue, **New York**, NY 10022
**Tel:** 212 909 0600 **Fax:** 212 909 0660

## INTERNATIONAL OFFICES

The firm also has offices in Alicante, Amsterdam, Beijing, Berlin, Brussels, Budapest (Associated Office), Dusseldorf, Frankfurt, Hamburg, Ho Chi Minh City, Hong Kong, London, Madrid, Milan, Moscow, Munich, Paris, Prague, Rome, Shanghai, Singapore, Tokyo, Warsaw, and Zagreb (Associated Office).

## CONTACTS

| | |
|---|---|
| Banking | Russell DaSilva |
| Business Restructuring & Insolvency | Gary Lee |
| Dispute Resolution | Joe Cyr, Marc Gottridge, Tom Bush |
| Insurance & Reinsurance | Joe McCullough |
| Securities/Capital Markets | Robert Ripin |
| Tax | David Alberts |

**INTERNATIONAL WORK:** Advising many of the world's largest corporations, financial institutions and governmental organizations, Lovells regularly acts on complex, multi-jurisdictional transactions as well as some of the most high-profile commercial disputes. The firm is recognized for its formidable dispute resolution practice as well as its banking and capital markets and insurance and reinsurance practices. In addition, they offer clients an unusually rich and well-balanced range of legal experience in other fields of corporate law. These include Commercial, Competition, EU and Trade, Employment, Employee Share Incentives, Energy, Engineering and Construction, Intellectual Property, Media and Telecommunications, Outsourcing and Tax, Pensions, Technology and Financial Services.

## Lovells

# MORGAN & FINNEGAN, LLP

## THE FIRM

**Number of partners:** 41
**Number of other lawyers:** 64

## AREAS OF PRACTICE:

Intellectual Property ..................................... 100%

**FIRM OVERVIEW:** Morgan & Finnegan is one of the largest and most experienced law firms specializing in litigating, protecting and securing intellectual property rights. For more than a century, the firm has represented a wide variety of clients in all aspects of intellectual property law including patents, trademarks, copyrights, trade secrets, unfair competition and antitrust matters. Morgan & Finnegan has compiled a distinguished record in patent and other complex intellectual property litigation. Several of the patent cases litigated by the firm have achieved landmark status. In addition, two inventions based on patents prosecuted by Morgan & Finnegan attorneys, one for a portable computer navigational system and the other for synthetic diamonds, are part of the permanent collection of the Smithsonian Institution in Washington. Morgan & Finnegan has amassed an impressive record of successful Markman determinations based on its intimate familiarity with the claim construction issues of patent law. In cases in which Morgan & Finnegan has defended against an infringement claim, it has used these Markman results to great advantage in obtaining successful summary judgment dispositions, avoiding the expense and uncertainty of trial for clients. Today, in an era of increasingly complex science and technology, the necessity for protecting innovation is more important than ever. As boundaries expand, and as new industries grow, the vision of the firm's founders is reflected in the high standards of service and value that the firm provides and in the spectrum of clients that it represents.

**MAIN AREAS OF PRACTICE:** The firm's partners, associates, counsel and PhD scientific advisors serve the following industry groups: banking and financial services; chemical; computers and software; consumer and industrial electronics; consumer products and industrial equipment; e-commerce and financial systems; life sciences and biotechnology; mechanical and medical devices; nanotechnology and MEMS; and pharmaceuticals. All attorneys are devoted entirely to intellectual property work and related unfair competition and antitrust matters.

**INTERNATIONAL WORK:** Morgan & Finnegan is at the forefront of international intellectual property developments. The firm's expertise enables it to understand more precisely the problems and concerns of Asian and European companies doing business both in the United States and abroad, and brings benefits to its multinational clients. The firm also has first-hand, in-depth experience directing counter-part activities in Europe, including directing patent infringement actions (such as requests for preliminary relief and cross-border relief) as well as nullity actions and patent office oppositions.

## HEAD OFFICE

**NEW YORK**
3 World Financial Center, **New York**, NY 10281-2101
**Tel:** 212 415 8700 **Fax:** 212 415 8701
**Website:** www.morganfinnegan.com

## BRANCH OFFICES

**CALIFORNIA**
44 Montgomery Street, Suite 2550, **San Francisco**, CA 94104
**Tel:** 415 318 8800 **Fax:** 415 676 5816

**CONNECTICUT**
100 First Stamford Place, **Stamford**, CT 06902
**Tel:** 203 391 2100 **Fax:** 203 391 2101

**DISTRICT OF COLUMBIA**
1775 Eye Street, NW, Suite 400, **Washington**, DC 20006
**Tel:** 202 857 7887 **Fax:** 202 857 7929

## INTERNATIONAL OFFICES

The firm also has an office in Shanghai.

# Morgan & Finnegan

Intellectual Property Law

# MOUND COTTON WOLLAN & GREENGRASS

## THE FIRM

**Number of partners:** 38
**Number of other lawyers:** 57

**FIRM OVERVIEW:** Founded in 1933 and based in New York's financial district with approximately 90 attorneys at that location, Mound Cotton Wollan & Greengrass is primarily engaged in insurance, reinsurance, and commercial litigation and arbitration. Although still best known for its insurance and reinsurance practices, the firm also has a corporate, commercial, securities, and commodities practice.

## MAIN AREAS OF PRACTICE:

**Insurance & Reinsurance:** For over 70 years, the firm has represented companies in the insurance industry in a wide variety of matters respecting virtually all aspects of the business. Mound Cotton's focus throughout its history has been to provide counsel to insurers, reinsurers and other companies in the insurance world on major commercial issues involving contract interpretation, coverage and the various other types of questions that arise in the context of the business of insurance and reinsurance. A major portion of the firms work has been acting for insurers and reinsurers in complex litigation and in arbitrations. The firm also represents clients before administrative agencies, and in other regulatory proceedings.

On reinsurance matters, Mound Cotton, represents reinsureds, reinsurers, intermediaries, pool managers, managing general agencies, underwriters, liquidators, and others with interests in the reinsurance market. Clients are based in the United States, Great Britain, Europe, Japan, Australia, and a number of other foreign jurisdictions. The firm is knowledgeable concerning the nature and operations of insurance markets throughout the world, and has considerable experience dealing with insurer and reinsurer insolvencies, as well as specialized classes of business such as environmental, business interruption and other time element, terrorism and war risk, professional indemnity/errors and omissions, and residual value, efficacy, performance guaranty and other financial guaranty. Mound Cotton's corporate attorneys are well grounded in statutory and regulatory law and procedure, and thoroughly familiar with the agencies that oversee the activities of insurers, reinsurers, agents, and intermediaries. Their expertise is available to the firm's reinsurance attorneys and is regularly utilized in a wide variety of litigated and arbitrated matters.

**Litigation:** Mound Cotton's attorneys have significant and extensive trial experience in federal and state courts and before arbitration panels and administrative agencies throughout the United States and the United Kingdom as well as in various other foreign jurisdictions. The work includes: trials, appeals, arbitration, bankruptcy/creditors' rights proceedings, and mediation/alternative dispute resolution.

**Corporate/Insurance Regulatory:** Mound Cotton is involved in the formation, domestication, and redomestication of insurance and reinsurance companies operating in the property and casualty as well as life, health and accident arenas, both for its own clients and as counsel to other law firms. The firm represents individuals and companies in hearings before state insurance and other administrative and regulatory agencies and exchanges. Mound Cotton is also experienced in both the P & C and life arena in ART transactions, securitization of risk, and other financial vehicles currently utilized by insurers and reinsurers to manage their liabilities/risk portfolios and reserves.

## HEAD OFFICE

**NEW YORK**
One Battery Park Plaza, **New York**, NY 10004
**Tel:** 212 804 4200   **Fax:** 212 344 8066

## BRANCH OFFICES

**NEW JERSEY**
60 Park Place, **Newark**, NJ 07102
**Tel:** 973 494 0600   **Fax:** 973 242 4244

**NEW YORK**
855 Franklin Avenue, **Garden City**, NY 11530
**Tel:** 516 417 5700   **Fax:** 516 741 6831

## INTERNATIONAL OFFICES

The firm also has an office in London.

**Corporate/Business:** Mound Cotton work includes counseling clients in corporate matters, both domestic and foreign, including corporate formation, shareholders' agreements, contract negotiations, employment agreements, distributorships, regulatory and compliance issues, licensing, mergers and acquisitions, managed buyouts, tender offers, restructurings, joint ventures and partnerships, and intellectual property. Clients include telecommunications firms, computer software companies, healthcare providers, venture capital organizations, Internet technology providers, private investment companies, hedge funds, commodities exchanges and clearing organizations, securities and commodities brokerages, broker/dealers, floor brokers and floor traders, investment advisory firms, commodity pool operators, commodity trading advisors, and labor organizations.

**INTERNATIONAL WORK:** The firm represents insurers, reinsurers, intermediaries, managing agents, pools, and other insurance-related concerns throughout the world in matters litigated in various foreign jurisdictions, as well as in international arbitrations. In conjunction with local counsel, the firm has acted for its clients in the United Kingdom, Bermuda, Canada, Germany, Spain, Italy, Greece, Australia, and Trinidad.

# NIXON PEABODY LLP

## THE FIRM

**Chairman, CEO & Co-Managing Partner:** Harry P Trueheart, III
**Co-managing Partner:** Nestor M Nicholas
**Number of lawyers:** 680

**FIRM OVERVIEW:** Nixon Peabody attorneys provide comprehensive legal services for a range of businesses, from major US and international companies to publicly- and privately-held businesses, financial institutions, universities, entrepreneurs and non-profit organizations. A fully integrated organizational structure along with state-of-the-art technology provides clients with superior service and access through any Nixon Peabody office.

## MAIN AREAS OF PRACTICE:

**Business:** The firm serves a broad range of business clients in the areas of securities, private equity and venture capital, M&A, tax, bank regulatory, international trade and many other matters. While clients represent a range of technologies and services, the firm possesses specific experience in: energy, life sciences, telecommunictions, pharmaceutical, software and digital technologies, healthcare, beverages and alcohol and transportation industries.

**Business Litigation:** The firm litigates a wide array of business matters concerning: government investigations, financial services and securities litigation issues, franchise disputes, international arbitrations, antitrust matters, and general commercial and contract litigation issues. The firm's emphasis is on providing litigation services as well as mediation, early case assessment and risk analysis services as part of a full-service, strategic approach to dispute resolution.

**Financial Services & Specialty Finance:** Services include: corporate trust, cash-flow-based lending, loan syndication, securitization and structured finance, equipment leasing and other aspects of business finance. The group structures, negotiates, documents, and manages to completion all types of financial transactions.

**Technology & Intellectual Property:** A full range of patent prosecution, litigation and interference services, as well as trademark, licensing, copyright, brand management and trade secret services.

**Real Estate:** The firm serves institutional owners and investors, developers, landlords, tenants, lenders, and others concerning a variety of commercial, industrial and multi-family real estate projects.

**Public Finance:** One of the largest public finance practices in the US, regularly ranked among the 10 most active bond and underwriter counsels nationally in dollar value of bonds issued. Experience extends from the financing of arenas and stadiums to power generation facilities and housing projects.

**Labor & Employment:** 50 labor and employment lawyers counsel on wage/hour law, Title VII class action defense, ERISA, OSHA, non-compete/trade secret litigation, diversity and preventive strategies.

**Products Liability:** Nixon Peabody attorneys have repeatedly proven their abilities in high stakes cases involving products liability and complex tort litigation across many industries and sectors including: aviation, automotive, medical devices and life sciences, pharmaceutical and environmental.

**Energy & Environment:** The firm, with an in-house staff of engineers and scientists, has an international reputation with large-scale energy and infrastructure projects, and an array of environmental regulatory and litigation issues.

**Health Services:** Service to healthcare providers including: corporate, regulatory, licensing and certificates of need, reimbursement counseling, development and financing of capital projects, strategic planning, graduate medical education and residency training accreditation matters, physician/ hospital and medical staff issues, patient care issues, physician practice issues and managed care contracting.

**Insurance:** Emphasis on international reinsurance, corporate, regulatory, litigation and pre-litigation strategic counseling. The group tries coverage disputes throughout the US in all major industries.

**Corporate Restructuring & Bankruptcy:** The firm is skilled in addressing a wide spectrum of insolvency issues, from debt restructuring and reorganization planning to asset acquisitions and collateral liquidations.

**Private Clients:** Services include income, estate and gift tax planning and compli-

## US OFFICES

### CALIFORNIA
2040 Main Street, Suite 850, **Irvine**, CA 92614
**Tel:** 949 475 6900
Gas Company Tower, 555 West Fifth St, **Los Angeles,** CA 90013
**Tel:** 213 533 1050
Two Embarcadero Center, **San Francisco**, CA 94111
**Tel:** 415 984 8200

### CONNECTICUT
185 Asylum Street, **Hartford**, CT 06103
**Tel:** 860 275 6820

### DISTRICT OF COLUMBIA
401 9th Street, N.W., Ste. 900 **Washington**, DC 20004
**Tel:** 202 585 8000

### FLORIDA
4400 PGA Boulevard, Suite 900, **Palm Beach Gardens**, FL 33410
**Tel:** 561 626 3011

### MASSACHUSETTS
100 Summer Street, **Boston**, MA 02110
**Tel:** 617 345 1000

### NEW HAMPSHIRE
900 Elm Street, **Manchester**, NH 03101
**Tel:** 603 628 4000

### NEW YORK
30 South Pearl Street, **Albany**, NY 12207
**Tel:** 518 427 2650
Key Towers at Fountain Plaza, 40 Fountain Plaza, Ste 500 **Buffalo**, NY 14202
**Tel:** 716 853 8100
437 Madison Avenue, **New York**, NY 10022
**Tel:** 212 940 3000
Clinton Square, PO Box 31051, **Rochester**, NY 14603
**Tel:** 585 263 1000
990 Stewart Avenue, **Garden City**, NY 11530
**Tel:** 516 832 7500

### PENNSYLVANIA
1818 Market Street, 11th floor, **Philadelphia**, PA 19103
**Tel:** 215 246 3520

### RHODE ISLAND
One Citizens Plaza, Ste 500, **Providence**, RI 02903
**Tel:** 401 454 1000

**Website:** www.nixonpeabody.com

ance, financial planning, estate administration, retirement planning and investment advice and management.

**Affordable Housing:** Decades of experience in private practice and government service. These leading practitioners have a comprehensive understanding of federally assisted housing issues.

**Syndication:** The firm's syndication attorneys are among the foremost authorities on transactions involving low income housing, new markets and other tax credits. Nixon Peabody's Syndication practice is the largest such practice in the US.

**INTERNATIONAL WORK:** Clients include international and multinational corporations in a wide range of industries including: financial services, insurance, aviation, telecommunications, life sciences, digital and computer technologies and more. We have significant experience in international arbitration proceedings. Languages of their attorneys include: Afrikaans, Chinese, Danish, Dutch, French, German, Italian, Norwegian, Portuguese, Russian, Spanish, Swedish and many more.

# PATTERSON BELKNAP WEBB & TYLER LLP

## THE FIRM

**Chair of the firm:** Gregory L Diskant
**Managing Partner:** Rochelle Korman
**Executive Director:** Marvin J Brittman

**Number of partners:** 60
**Number of other lawyers:** 129

**FIRM OVERVIEW:** Patterson Belknap is a law firm of nearly 200 lawyers committed to maintaining its independence, its diversity, and its focus of providing superior legal advice and service to clients. The firm makes its clients' business issues its own. At the same time, it cares about its attorneys and staff and the community it is privileged to serve. As a result of the firm's performance and values, it has earned the number two ranking on *The American Lawyer*'s 2005 'A-List' of elite US firms and has ranked in the top 10 each year since the list's inception. A dedication to public service is at the heart of Patterson Belknap's pro bono work. Patterson Belknap is also ranked in the top 10 of *The American Lawyer*'s 2005 pro bono survey and has been in the top 10 since 1999.

**MAIN AREAS OF PRACTICE:** Patterson Belknap's practice combines experience in litigation, including intellectual property, trademark, patent, securities, antitrust, false advertising, media, products liability, law firm defense and white-collar criminal defense, with experience in such transactional and counseling areas as corporate, real estate, personal planning, employee benefits, intellectual property and tax. In addition, the firm has the leading tax-exempt organizations practice in New York City.

**Litigation:** More than half of Patterson Belknap's attorneys are devoted to litigation. The litigating partners at Patterson Belknap have tried hundreds of cases, including many of the most complex in their fields. One client has described its lawyers as 'courtroom artisans'. Its attorneys are not afraid to go to trial, and clients – and the firm's adversaries – know it. In many situations, of course, settlement may be the best option. In those instances, the firm's reputation and track record should enhance its clients' chances for a favorable settlement.

**Intellectual Property:** Patterson Belknap recognizes the importance and impact of intellectual property. Clients can feel confident knowing that the firm's approach to representation is based upon an understanding of their legal needs and underlying business objectives. The attorneys in the IP Practice Group are well-rounded, handling litigation as well as transactions; for instance, generalists and registered patent attorneys often work side by side on the most complex patent matters. A distinguishing feature of the Patterson Belknap IP Practice is the frequency with which the firm's litigators take complex cases to trial.

**Corporate:** As outside counsel to multinational and Fortune 500 corporations and small and mid-sized companies, Patterson Belknap advises on the full range of business activities. Understanding that every client's needs are different, the firm adjusts its approach to the representation as appropriate in each case. For some clients, it functions as sole legal counsel, providing critical advice on day-to-day issues and operations, as well as transactional representation. In other cases, the firm works together with in-house legal departments, teaming up to address highly specialized areas of the law, often with respect to major transactions. Regardless of the scope or context of representation, though, the firm's goal is always to assist its client in achieving its business objectives in the most advantageous and efficient manner possible.

**HEAD OFFICE**

**NEW YORK**
1133 Avenue of the Americas, **New York** NY 10036
**Tel:** 212 336 2000  **Fax:** 212 336 2222
**Email:** info@pbwt.com
**Website:** www.pbwt.com

**CLIENTS:** The firm's clients include Fortune 500 corporations, such as multi-national pharmaceutical manufacturers, media conglomerates, and financial services institutions. In addition, it represents foreign governments, state-owned enterprises, major banks, national accounting firms, brokerage firms, pension funds, insurance companies, individual officers and directors of large companies, major investors, entrepreneurs, and closely held corporations. The firm has in-depth experience in a number of industries, including pharmaceuticals, medical devices, consumer products, media and entertainment, financial instruments, securities and derivatives, manufacturing, technology and communications, commercial real estate, and others.

**INTERNATIONAL WORK:** Patterson Belknap provides a unique combination of cross-border corporate finance and cross-border mergers and acquisitions practices. Its lawyers have established an international reputation in the depositary receipts arena, and have been instrumental in developing such novel cross-border instruments as American depositary notes and depositary receipts eligible for trading and settlement in multiple jurisdictions. In an increasingly fast-paced transactional environment, the firm's combined experience in these areas affords its clients the benefit of cutting-edge and efficient multi-jurisdictional transaction structuring and implementation. A well-developed network of foreign counsel complements Patterson Belknap's presence in the cross-border arena, so that clients are assured of seamless representation of transaction-appropriate counsel in all jurisdictions.

**Patterson Belknap Webb & Tyler** LLP

# PAUL, WEISS, RIFKIND, WHARTON & GARRISON LLP

## THE FIRM

**Managing Partner:** Alfred D Youngwood

**Number of partners:** 110
**Number of other lawyers:** 409

**FIRM OVERVIEW:** Paul, Weiss, Rifkind, Wharton & Garrison LLP is a world-class law firm whose influence spans the globe and whose lawyers have left their imprint on the landscape of modern jurisprudence. Few firms can match the breadth and depth of skill provided by its leading corporate and litigation practices. The firm is equally recognized for its capabilities in the areas of bankruptcy and corporate reorganization, intellectual property, real estate and tax law. Engaged in a diverse international practice serving clients throughout the world, Paul, Weiss has played key roles in many of the major deals and cases that grabbed headlines over the past few years. The firm has negotiated transactions on behalf of clients on virtually every continent, handling several of the largest registered global equity offerings. Internationally recognized for its representation of clients in prosecuting and defending litigation and arbitration throughout the world, the firm also successfully represents clients in connection with investigations and proceedings by US governmental and regulatory agencies. With offices in New York, Washington, DC, London, Hong Kong, Beijing and Tokyo, and an extensive international network of 'relationship' firms, the firm combines knowledge and skills with local expertise to provide efficient and comprehensive services to clients across a broad spectrum, anywhere in the world.

## MAIN AREAS OF PRACTICE:

**Antitrust:** Paul, Weiss lawyers have played an important part in shaping antitrust law in the United States. The firm has represented many of the world's largest companies in resolving antitrust issues and has handled the full range of antitrust matters in federal and state courts. The firm's cases range from large corporate transactions investigated by the Federal Trade Commission and Department of Justice to private litigation, involving monopolization, vertical restraints and price fixing

**Bankruptcy & Corporate Reorganization:** The Paul, Weiss Bankruptcy Department has wide experience in transnational and cross-border insolvency matters and represents debtors, official and unofficial committees of creditors and shareholders, secured and unsecured creditors, and shareholders in chapter 11 cases, corporate reorganizations and workouts, non-bankruptcy insolvency proceedings, and other matters involving litigation or transactional advice relating to financially distressed companies. The firm also has extensive experience representing purchasers of the assets, debt and securities of distressed companies.

**Communications & Technology:** Paul, Weiss has a world-renowned Communications and Technology Group. Its lawyers are knowledgeable about US and international regulation of communications and broadcasting, and are active in matters before the FCC, other US agencies, and non-US regulatory bodies. They advise clients about the complex interplay between the regulatory environment and the fast-changing business of technology.

**Corporate:** Paul, Weiss consistently ranks among the world's leading practices and has been involved in some of the most highly publicized merger, acquisition, divestiture and takeover transactions. Clients rely on Paul, Weiss lawyers for their versatility and ability to help navigate the legal complexities of novel and complex matters involving mergers and acquisitions, capital markets and securities, finance, private equity, investment fund management and corporate governance. The firm provides clients comprehensive global corporate services that help them complete sophisticated transactions in a rapidly changing competitive environment, both at home and abroad.

**Employee Benefits & Executive Compensation:** The Paul, Weiss Employee Benefits Department is comprised of lawyers who work full time on all types of ERISA, executive compensation and employee benefit matters. It has the experi-

ence and resources to handle special projects involving complex and financially important ERISA and related tax and securities laws issues. One of the department's greatest strengths is its deep knowledge of the more technical aspects of benefit plan administration.

**Entertainment:** The lawyers in the Paul, Weiss Entertainment Department handle an extensive range of corporate and litigation matters on behalf of clients engaged in legitimate theater, motion pictures, music, radio and television broadcasting, and book and magazine publishing. The firm is active in counseling many of its corporate and individual entertainment clients on a broad range of copyright, trademark, and related intellectual property issues.

**Intellectual Property:** Paul, Weiss lawyers are at the cusp of developments in the field of intellectual property and have established a strong record of supporting clients in intellectual property litigation, intellectual property transactions, and patent litigation. It advises a number of the world's largest corporations from media, communications, software and biotechnology companies to industrial and manufacturing firms whose businesses are remarkably diverse and global in scope. The firm's capacity to respond to client needs, particularly in today's digital age of global and instantaneous information dissemination, demonstrates a unique ability to provide comprehensive services across a broad international spectrum.

**Litigation:** The Paul, Weiss Litigation Department is involved in nearly every high-profile US litigation today and has achieved an international reputation for excellence. Its lawyers focus on a number of areas including antitrust, arbitration, commercial litigation, criminal and regulatory enforcement, intellectual property litigation, patent litigation, securities litigation, and tax litigation, among others. They handle disputes in every forum, from traditional court cases to domestic and international arbitrations, and from alternative dispute resolution processes to administrative tribunals of all kinds.

**Personal Representation:** Attorneys in the Paul, Weiss Personal Representation Department provide services to clients ranging from estate planning and administration and representation of private foundations and public charitable organizations, to matrimonial matters, litigated Surrogate's Court cases and the tax issues affecting such matters.

**Real Estate:** The Paul, Weiss Real Estate Department has extensive experience in real estate transactions, representing developers, entrepreneurial and institutional investors, REITs and equity funds, lenders, public-private partnerships, governmental entities and other major players in the real estate industry. The lawyers provide a full range of services, from organizing and structuring the largest, most complex transactions throughout the country and around the globe, to advising clients on their daily portfolio management issues.

**Tax:** Paul, Weiss fields a very prominent team of tax lawyers with vast experience in international representations. Members of the Tax Department have played a critical role in devising structures that involve the interplay of the US tax system with the tax systems of virtually every major financial center in Europe and Asia.

## HEAD OFFICE

**NEW YORK**
1285 Avenue of the Americas, **New York** NY 10019-6064
**Tel:** 212 373 3000  **Fax:** 212 757 3990
**Email:** mailbox@paulweiss.com  **Website:** www.paulweiss.com

## BRANCH OFFICES

**DISTRICT OF COLUMBIA**
1615 L Street, NW, Suite 1300, **Washington** DC 20036-5694
**Tel:** 202 223 7300  **Fax:** 202 223 7420

## INTERNATIONAL OFFICES

The firm also has offices in London, Tokyo, Hong Kong and Beijing.

# PECKAR & ABRAMSON, P.C.

## THE FIRM

**Managing Partner:** Robert S Peckar

**Number of partners:** 38
**Number of other lawyers:** 47

**FIRM OVERVIEW:** Peckar & Abramson has been serving the construction industry for almost 30 years, having achieved national recognition for its successes in the representation of members of the construction industry, both domestically and internationally. The firm combines its unique problem-solving expertise and litigation/arbitration experience with its substantial experience in providing counsel to clients regarding the management of transactional risks inherent in their contracts and in the industry. In the area of government contracts, the firm's depth of experience includes counseling clients on issues ranging from dispute avoidance to corporate integrity and then litigating on behalf of government contractors in the resolution of all manner of claims, including many that involve very substantial sums and complex legal issues. Having represented clients in every category of construction, Peckar & Abramson has successfully resolved disputes at all levels of complexity arising from a wide range of construction projects, from moderately sized projects to mega-projects in both the public and private sectors. The firm has particular expertise in projects such as airports, government buildings, highways and bridges, power generation facilities, environmental clean-ups, sports arenas, manufacturing facilities, hotels and other hospitality industry projects and residential communities.

**INTERNATIONAL WORK:** The firm focuses its practice on the representation of general contractors and construction managers, but also represents other construction industry participants with matters throughout the US, Asia, the Middle East, the Caribbean, Latin and South America and Europe. In addition to and complementing its construction industry practice, the firm offers the full services of its complementary Employment and Labor Law Group, as well as its Corporate and Real Estate Transactional Practice.

**CLIENTS:** Peckar & Abramson serves the needs of its clients from its offices in New York, New Jersey, Florida California and Washington, DC and offers its international clients the benefits of its joint venture with a British construction law firm and its relationship with other allied international firms through its membership in the International Construction Law Alliance (ICLA), including members in the Americas, Europe and Asia.

## HEAD OFFICE

**NEW YORK**
546 Fifth Avenue, 17th Floor, **New York**, NY 10036
**Tel:** 212 382 0909   **Fax:** 212 382 3456
**Email:** rpeckar@pecklaw.com
**Website:** www.pecklaw.com

## BRANCH OFFICES

**CALIFORNIA**
550 South Hope Street, Suite 1655, **Los Angeles**, CA 90071
**Tel:** 213 489 9220   **Fax:** 213 489 9215

250 Montgomery Street, 16th Floor, **San Francisco**, CA 94104
**Tel:** 415 8371968   **Fax:** 415 837 1320

**DISTRICT OF COLUMBIA**
Two Lafayette Centre, 1133 21st Street, NW, Suite 500,
**Washington**, DC 20036
**Tel:** 202 293 8815   **Fax:** 202 293 7994

**FLORIDA**
One Southeast Third Avenue, Suite 3050, **Miami**, FL 33131
**Tel:** 305 358 2600   **Fax:** 305 375 0328

401 East Las Olas Boulevard, Suite 1600, **Fort Lauderdale**, FL 33301
**Tel:** 954 764 5222   **Fax:**  954 764 5228

**NEW JERSEY**
70 Grand Avenue, **River Edge**, NJ 07661
**Tel:** 201 343 3434   **Fax:** 201 343 6306

# PILLSBURY WINTHROP SHAW PITTMAN LLP

## THE FIRM

**Chair:** Mary B Cranston
**Vice-Chair:** Stephen B Huttler
**Managing Partner:** Marina H Park

**FIRM OVERVIEW:** Pillsbury Winthrop Shaw Pittman LLP is an international law firm offering legal services for more than 130 years. The firm has over 900 lawyers in 16 locations.

## MAIN AREAS OF PRACTICE:

**Aviation:** Pillsbury represents many of the world's largest aerospace companies, top cities and airports, major air carriers, new entrants, charter operators, cargo carriers, large repair stations, international banks, and leasing companies and brokers. The firm's lawyers advise on complex accident investigations and litigation, regulatory and enforcement matters, finance and insurance matters, securities offerings, financial restructuring, bond issuances, international trade and licensing, and tax policies.

**Corporate & Securities:** Pillsbury represents clients in securities, private equity and venture capital, mergers and acquisitions and real estate investment trusts throughout the US. The firm handles diverse legal matters, from startup funding and formation for emerging companies, to IPOs, acquisitions and divestitures, and corporate governance and compliance issues for seasoned public companies.

**Executive Compensation & Benefits:** Pillsbury's practice, headed by Susan P Serota, 2005-06 Chair-Elect of the ABA Section on Taxation, advises on employee compensation packages, benefit plans, equity programs, federal tax, ERISA, securities, labor laws and regulations, and applicable state laws.

**Finance:** Pillsbury represents domestic and international clients in regulatory matters and financial transactions, including capital formation, commercial lending, derivatives, equipment finance, leveraged finance, project finance, trade finance, structured finance, and debt restructuring. Clients include investment companies, foreign and domestic banks, insurance companies, private funds, and other financial institutions.

**Global Energy:** Pillsbury's Global Energy Practice handles mergers and acquisitions, corporate and project finance, regulatory and industry restructuring, environmental, alternative dispute resolution, litigation and IP/IT licensing. The 2005 merger with Shaw Pittman added a first-tier Washington, DC energy practice, and significant strength in nuclear energy, real estate capital markets and technology sourcing. Clients include industry leaders in oil and gas, petrochemicals, nuclear power, independent power, public utilities, and water.

**Global Sourcing:** Pillsbury's top-ranked Global Sourcing Practice is one of the largest sourcing practices in any law firm. It is uniquely composed of both lawyers and technical and business consultants working seamlessly on the full range of complex global sourcing initiatives, including information technology and business process outsourcing transactions.

**Insolvency & Restructuring:** Pillsbury's Insolvency and Restructuring Group works on complex, sophisticated and distressed financial situations. Clients include banks, financial institutions, creditors, debtors, agents and participants in syndicated loan transactions, indenture trustees and bondholders, landlords, official and unofficial committees, equipment lessors, investment funds, venture capital funds and other interested parties.

**Litigation:** Pillsbury attorneys work closely with clients to develop aggressive yet practical strategies for varied business goals and needs. With more than 30 practice specialty teams, the firm's litigation, trial and arbitration experience crosses a wide range of industries – including financial institutions, energy and technology – and includes securities litigation, corporate investigations and white-collar defense, appellate, arbitration and ADR, and intellectual property.

**Real Estate:** Pillsbury's market-leading, 125-attorney Real Estate Group represents developers, investors, institutional clients, and others in the acquisition and disposition of commercial, retail, and multifamily properties; foreign and domestic banks and other lenders in the financing and restructuring of real estate investments of all types; participants in complex public sector financings and large scale public/private partnerships throughout the US; and corporate clients and not-for-profit entities in the development of real estate assets, including the leasing of office space and other institutional facilities. Pillsbury is one of the nation's leaders in REIT and public finance law.

**Tax & Tax Controversy:** Pillsbury's Tax and Tax Controversy Practices bring a full-service, interdisciplinary and experienced approach to the resolution of diverse tax-related issues and tax disputes. They are trusted advisors to an extensive client base in a wide range of international, domestic and state and local tax matters.

**Technology & Intellectual Property:** Pillsbury's Intellectual Property Practice has been at the cutting edge of IP for over 100 years. The firm's attorneys advise clients on developing successful and comprehensive IP strategies by protecting, managing, asserting, defending and leveraging their IP assets.

## HEAD OFFICES

### DISTRICT OF COLUMBIA
2300 N Street, NW, **Washington**, DC 20037
**Tel:** 202 663 8000   **Fax:** 202 663 8007

### CALIFORNIA
50 Fremont Street, **San Francisco**, CA 94105
**Tel:** 415 983 1000   **Fax:** 415 983 1200

### NEW YORK
1540 Broadway, **New York**, NY 10036
**Tel:** 212 858 1000   **Fax:** 212 858 1500

**Email:** info@pillsburylaw.com
**Website:** www.pillsburylaw.com

## BRANCH OFFICES

### CALIFORNIA
650 Town Center Drive, 7th Floor, **Costa Mesa**, CA 92626
**Tel:** 714 436 6800   **Fax:** 714 436 2800

MGM Tower, 10250 Constellation Blvd, 21st Floor, **Los Angeles**, CA 90067
**Tel:** 310 203 1100   **Fax:** 310 286 6672

725 South Figueroa Street, Suite 2800, **Los Angeles**, CA 90017
**Tel:** 213 488 7100   **Fax:** 213 629 1033

2475 Hanover Street, **Palo Alto**, CA 94304
**Tel:** 650 233 4500   **Fax:** 650 233 4545

400 Capitol Mall, Suite 1700, **Sacramento**, CA 95814
**Tel:** 916 329 4700   **Fax:** 916 441 3583

SBC Building, 101 West Broadway, Suite 1800, **San Diego**, CA 92101
**Tel:** 619 234 5000   **Fax:** 619 236 1995

11682 El Camino Real, Suite 200, **San Diego**, CA 92130
**Tel:** 619 234 5000   **Fax:** 858 509 4010

### TEXAS
2 Houston Center, 909 Fannin, 22nd Floor, **Houston**, TX 77010
**Tel:** 713 425 7300   **Fax:** 713 425 7373

### VIRGINIA
1650 Tysons Blvd, **McLean**, VA 22102
**Tel:** 703 770 7900   **Fax:** 703 770 7901

## INTERNATIONAL OFFICES

The firm has offices in Australia, Japan, Taiwan and the United Kingdom.

Pillsbury
Winthrop
Shaw
Pittman LLP

# PROSKAUER ROSE LLP

## THE FIRM

**Chairman:** Allen I Fagin

**Number of partners:** 185

**FIRM OVERVIEW:** Proskauer Rose LLP is one of the nation's largest law firms, providing a wide variety of legal services to major corporations and other clients throughout the United States and around the world. Headquartered in New York City since 1875, the firm also has offices in Los Angeles, Washington DC, Boston, Boca Raton, Newark, New Orleans and Paris. During its history Proskauer has been distinguished by its dedication to client service, technical excellence and high integrity. It also has adapted rapidly to changes in the needs of businesses, whether it be for expertise in emerging areas of law, employing new methods of communicating, or deploying the latest information technology.

**MAIN AREAS OF PRACTICE:** The firm's practice areas provide traditional services to corporations and other business entities such as corporate finance and securities, tax, litigation, real estate, and labor and employment advice. It also has leading practices in the areas of arbitration and other forms of alternative dispute resolution, bankruptcy and reorganizations, broker-dealer regulation, employee benefits and executive compensation, entertainment, environmental law, healthcare and pharmaceuticals, high technology and the internet, intellectual property, private equity financing, sports, trade secrets and non-competition, and white-collar crime. Representing the publishing, motion picture and recording industries as they confront new challenges, Proskauer recently has been at the leading edge of the law, as the dramatic emergence of a freer flow of information and knowledge over the global networks of servers and computers tests and strains established principles protecting intellectual property. As its litigators handle disputes arising in this arena, Proskauer's corporate and tax lawyers have been working on the business and financial structures and contractual licensing needs of the entrepreneurs building new companies, established corporations adjusting to new technologies, and financial services firms developing new financing products. Trained at leading law schools, Proskauer lawyers are civic and philanthropic leaders as well as highly skilled practitioners. In addition to service in the wider community, lawyers in the firm have recently held the presidencies of legal organizations such as the Association of the Bar of the City of New York, the New York State Bar Association, New York Woman's Bar Association, the American College of Trial Lawyers, the Federal Bar Council, the Fund for Modern Courts, the New York County Lawyers Association and the American Judicature Society.

**INTERNATIONAL WORK:** Proskauer's international practice has its roots in the representation early last century of various French industrialists. Since that time the firm has developed a recognized stature in international transactions and an understanding of and commitment to the global markets and the transnational needs of its clients. The firm's international practice includes the representation of foreign clients doing business in the United States and American clients abroad. It is also called on by foreign clients for transactions based abroad to which the firm brings its particular skill and experience in international transactions. The representation of international clients encompasses all aspects of the practice and involves lawyers in each of the firm's seven departments: corporate, tax, labor, real estate, litigation and dispute resolution, healthcare and personal planning. The firm regularly assists its international clients in mergers and acquisitions, joint ventures, licensing, international aspects of litigation, arbitration, tax planning, labor relations, antitrust, intellectual property and immigration.

## HEAD OFFICE

**NEW YORK**
1585 Broadway, **New York**, NY 10036-8299
**Tel:** 212 969 3000

## BRANCH OFFICES

**CALIFORNIA**
2049 Century Park East, 32nd Floor, **Los Angeles**, CA 90067-3206
**Tel:** 310 557 2900

**DISTRICT OF COLUMBIA**
1001 Pennsylvania Avenue NW, Suite 400 South,
**Washington**, DC 20004-2533
**Tel:** 202 416 6800

**MASSACHUSETTS**
One International Place, 14th Floor, **Boston**, MA 02110-2600
**Tel:** 617 526 9600

**FLORIDA**
One Boca Place, 2255 Glades Road, Suite 340 West,
**Boca Raton**, FL 33431-7383
**Tel:** 561 241 7400

**NEW JERSEY**
One Newark Center, 18th Floor, **Newark**, NJ 07102-5211
**Tel:** 973 274 3200

**LOUISIANA**
909 Poydras Street, Suite 1100, **New Orleans**, LA 70112-4017
**Tel:** 504 310 4088

## INTERNATIONAL OFFICES

The firm also has an international office in Paris.

**PROSKAUER ROSE LLP®**

# SCHULTE ROTH & ZABEL LLP

## THE FIRM

**Firm Management:** Executive Commitee
**Senior Partner:** Paul N Roth

**Number of partners:** 77
**Number of other lawyers:** 319

**FIRM OVERVIEW:** Founded in 1969, Schulte Roth & Zabel has grown to nearly 400 attorneys practicing a broad variety of disciplines. The firm focuses on client service and has a deep appreciation of the importance of building and maintaining long-term relationships. Its clients include major corporations, institutional and individual clients.

## MAIN AREAS OF PRACTICE:

**Investment Management:** SRZ has occupied the fund formation space for over 30 years and has a premier practice in the area. The firm represents over 400 investment management firms with equity capital estimated in excess of $300 billion. These include global investment banking and advisory firms, hedge fund firms, mutual fund complexes and private equity firms.

**Business Transactions:** SRZ is one of the preeminent law firms in the areas of mergers and acquisitions, special opportunity investments, proxy fights, leveraged buyouts and venture capital funds, initial public offerings, high-yield debt and PIPEs transactions.

**Business Reorganization:** The firm provides counsel to key participants in debt restructurings (workouts and reorganizations) acquisition of troubled companies, financing (debtor-in possession and reorganization plans), and bankruptcy litigation (including fraudulent transfers, preferences and contract disputes).

**Finance:** SRZ's Finance Group represents clients in the asset-based lending community, including asset-based loans, leveraged acquisitions, financing and restructurings, debtor-in-possession and exit financings, unsecured corporate borrowings, and private placements by investment-grade companies.

**Structured Products:** SRZ's Structured Products Practice has been involved in some of the most innovative structured finance transactions, including CDOs, CLOs, and CFOs, asset and mortgage securitizations and asset-backed commercial paper programs.

**Litigation:** More than 100 litigators counsel clients in matters including securities litigation, defense of white collar criminal cases, anti-money laundering, antitrust, defense of derivative actions, general commercial litigation and arbitrations.

**Employment & Employee Benefits:** SRZ's Employment Practice includes litigation and ongoing guidance, counsel and prevention of employment disputes. The firm represents employers in all aspects of labor relations and collective bargaining. The Employee Benefits Practice encompasses every aspect of benefits law and ERISA.

**Intellectual Property:** SRZ has expertise in all aspects of intellectual property and information technology law, including patents, trademarks, copyrights, unfair competition, trade secrets and information technology licensing, development and outsourcing.

**Real Estate:** The firm represents a diverse group of clients in the sale and acquisition of commercial property, securitized mortgage loans and mezzanine financings, leasing of commercial property, construction and architectural agreements, all aspects of the development process and real estate equity funds.

## HEAD OFFICE

**NEW YORK**
919 Third Avenue, **New York**, NY 10022
**Tel:** 212 756 2000   **Fax:** 212 593 5955

**Website:** www.srz.com

## INTERNATIONAL OFFICES

The firm also has an office in London.

## CONTACTS

| | |
|---|---|
| **Investment Management** | Stephanie R Breslow |
| **Business Transactions** | Marc Weingarten |
| **Business Reorganization** | Michael L Cook |
| **Finance** | Frederic L Ragucci |
| **Structured Products** | Paul N Watterson |
| **Litigation** | Robert M Abrahams |
| **Employment** | Mark E Brossman |
| **Intellectual Property** | Joel E Lutzker |
| **Real Estate** | Jeffrey A Lenobel |
| **Environmental Law** | Howard B Epstein |
| **Tax** | Alan S Waldenberg |
| **Individual Clients** | William D Zabel |

**Environmental:** SRZ counsels major institutions and Fortune 500 companies on a wide range of national and international environmental issues. The firm advises on preventive methods, offering the technical knowledge and legal experience to provide the best advocacy. The firm represents clients before local, state and federal agencies and in the courtroom.

**Tax:** The SRZ Tax Group provides tax planning for mergers, sales and other dispositions, acquisitions and leveraged buyout arrangements, including analysis of cross-border financing and transfer pricing issues. The group structures sophisticated financing transactions, advises on special tax issues confronting foreign investors making corporate, portfolio securities and real estate investments in the US. SRZ also provides tax advice to managers of domestic and foreign private investment, private equity and mutual funds.

**Individual Clients:** SRZ's Client Services Department is one of the most sophisticated, extensive and diverse of any major law firm. The firm represents many of the wealthiest individuals in the country on tax planning, successor planning, charitable giving, will contests and family law matters, including mediation of large divorce matters.

**SCHULTE ROTH & ZABEL LLP**

# SEWARD & KISSEL LLP

## THE FIRM

**Managing Partner**: John E Tavss

**Number of partners:** 33
**Number of other lawyers:** 99

### AREAS OF PRACTICE:

Investment Management . . . . . . . . . . . . . . . . . . . . . . . . . . . . . . . . . . . . . . 25%
Corporate Finance & Capital Markets . . . . . . . . . . . . . . . . . . . . . . . . . 20%
Litigation . . . . . . . . . . . . . . . . . . . . . . . . . . . . . . . . . . . . . . . . . . . . . . . . . . 20%
Structured Finance & Asset Securitization . . . . . . . . . . . . . . . . . . . . 15%
Maritime . . . . . . . . . . . . . . . . . . . . . . . . . . . . . . . . . . . . . . . . . . . . . . . . . . . . 10%
Real Estate . . . . . . . . . . . . . . . . . . . . . . . . . . . . . . . . . . . . . . . . . . . . . . . . . . . 5%
Tax, Employee Benefits, Trusts & Estates . . . . . . . . . . . . . . . . . . . . . . . 5%

**FIRM OVERVIEW:** Seward & Kissel is a New York based law firm (with an office in Washington, DC) that offers sophisticated legal advice in the areas of business, financial and commercial law and litigation, as well as a number of specialized fields of law. Originally established in 1890, the firm combines its tradition of superior service with innovative and creative approaches that help clients achieve their goals.

## MAIN AREAS OF PRACTICE:

**Investment Management:** Regularly cited as one of the leading legal advisers to the private investment fund industry, Seward & Kissel is recognized both nationally and internationally for its work in the hedge fund area. The firm also is well known for its work representing a wide range of registered investment companies and their advisers.

**Corporate Finance & Capital Markets:** Attorneys in Seward & Kissel's Corporate Finance and Capital Markets Group combine their skills as transactional lawyers with a comprehensive knowledge of relevant regulatory and business issues affecting clients to address a broad range of matters, including: equity and debt offerings; workouts, restructurings and distressed debt transactions; mergers and acquisitions; and new product and financial derivative transactions.

**Structured Finance & Asset Securitization:** The firm's Corporate Finance and Securitization Group has considerable experience representing clients in connection with a full range of financings, including both secured and unsecured, committed and discretionary commercial credit facilities, and asset-based and cash flow transactions. The firm represents many types of financial institutions, including domestic and international banks, trust companies, insurance companies, broker-dealers and investment banks.

**Maritime:** Internationally recognized as the leading legal advisors to the shipping industry, the firm advises many of the world's most prominent ship finance institutions, including international commercial banks, investment banks, and providers of subordinated and equity financing. The firm is involved in all aspects of the financing of ships, offshore oil rigs, barges, shipping containers and other marine equipment. In addition, the firm offers guidance in secured lending, equipment leasing, public and private debt and equity offerings, acquisition financing, debt for equity swaps and the issuance of securities backed by maritime assets representing major public and private shipping companies, lenders and investors.

**Litigation:** The firm represents major domestic and foreign financial institutions (including banks, broker-dealers and investment management firms) and individual clients in courts, administrative tribunals and arbitrations throughout the world, specializing in the following areas: securities related litigation; commercial disputes; employment matters; insurance; maritime; trademark; and bankruptcy and workout matters. The firm is particularly well known for its work advising clients on employment related matters and securities related litigation.

### HEAD OFFICE

**NEW YORK**
One Battery Park Plaza, **New York**, NY 10004
**Tel:** 212 574 1200   **Fax:** 212 480 8421
**Email:** sknyc@sewkis.com
**Website:** www.sewkis.com

### BRANCH OFFICE

**DISTRICT OF COLUMBIA**
1200 G Street, NW, Suite 350, **Washington,** DC 20005
**Tel:** 202 737 8833   **Fax:** 202 737 5184
**Email:** sknyc@sewkis.com

### CONTACTS

| | |
|---|---|
| **Corporate Finance & Capital Markets** | James H Hancock |
| **Employee Benefits** | S John Ryan |
| **Investment Management** | John E Tavss |
| **Structured Finance & Asset Securitization** | Kalyan Das |
| **Litigation** | M.William Munno |
| **Maritime** | Lawrence Rutkowski, Gary Wolfe |
| **Real Estate** | Mark A Brody |
| **Tax & Employee Benefits** | Peter E Pront |
| **Trusts & Estates** | Hume R Steyer |
| **Washington DC Office** | Paul T Clark |
| **Bankruptcy** | Ronald L Cohen |

**Real Estate:** Seward & Kissel advises real estate owners, developers, lenders and institutional investors involved with commercial and residential facilities and mixed-use projects throughout the United States. Helping major public pension funds and other institutions to structure and implement their real estate investments is a particular strength for the Real Estate Group.

**Tax, Employee Benefits, & Trusts & Estates:** The firm's Tax and Employee Benefit Group counsels clients from a broad range of industries on a variety of issues including tax and employee considerations relevant to structuring complex securities and financing transactions, issues relating to financial products including pooled investment funds and with regard to real estate matters. The firm also advises individual clients with planning to preserve and build wealth for future generations and achieve philanthropic objectives.

# SHEARMAN & STERLING LLP

## THE FIRM

**Senior Partner:** Rohan S Weerasinghe
**Co-Managing Partners:** John J Madden and Georg F Thoma

**Numbers of partners worldwide:** 212
**Number of lawyers worldwide:** 1,013

**FIRM OVERVIEW:** Founded in 1873, Shearman & Sterling LLP is one of the few genuinely global firms providing legal expertise that is integrated across jurisdictions, industries and legal disciplines. The firm's international network comprises approximately 1,000 attorneys in 19 financial centers throughout the Americas, Europe and Asia. The firm delivers expertise and resources aligned to meet clients' needs wherever they arise. More than one-third of the firm's attorneys practice outside the United States, and their lawyers are fluent in more than 30 languages. The firm's lawyers practice US, English, French, Italian, German and EU law.

**MAIN AREAS OF PRACTICE:** Antitrust/competition, bank finance, bankruptcy and reorganization, capital markets, corporate governance, executive compensation and employee benefits/private client, intellectual property, international arbitration, international trade and government relations, investment funds and asset management, litigation, mergers and acquisitions, privatization, project development and finance, property, structured finance, and tax.

**Antitrust/Competition:** Shearman & Sterling has a strong global antitrust practice with a proven track record in securing clearance in both the US and Europe for complex cross-border mergers, acquisitions and joint ventures. The practice uses a multi-disciplinary approach, working with the M&A, capital markets and litigation teams, to provide legal expertise across jurisdictions.

**Bank Finance:** Shearman & Sterling has substantial capabilities in global bank finance and represents a wide range of clients in leveraged buyouts and recapitalizations; "jumbo" acquisition, high-yield bridge, mezzanine, letter of credit and debtor-in-possession financings; complex debt restructurings; and secured lending and investment grade loans. The firm recently represented Citigroup Global Markets Inc. as sole lead arranger and sole book runner of a $24 billion financing for Procter & Gamble S.a.r.l., a wholly owned subsidiary of The Procter & Gamble Company.

**Bankruptcy/Restructuring:** The firm has a long history of involvement in US and international restructurings and bankruptcies, advising many of the world's leading financial institutions, corporations and individuals. The firm has played a prominent role in restructurings and insolvencies in both the traditional and emerging commercial centers around the world.

**Capital Markets:** Shearman & Sterling has a formidable global capital markets practice, which includes former directors and other senior officials of the SEC's Division of Corporation Finance. The firm has extensive experience in representing issuers and underwriters in a wide range of transactions, including public and private securities offerings, liability management transactions, structured products and hybrid securities, and securities law and corporate governance.

**Executive Compensation & Employee Benefits/Private Client:** The firm regularly advises clients in employee-related aspects of domestic and cross-border merger and acquisition transactions. The firm's expertise in corporate, tax, securities, employment law and ERISA issues affecting ECEB is supplemented by top-tier attorneys who negotiate and implement sophisticated equity-based incentive plans, advise on issues raised in initial public offerings and design investment partnerships and co-investment vehicles for venture capital and other entities.

**International Arbitration:** Shearman & Sterling has one of the world's finest international arbitration teams. The group has represented hundreds of clients in proceedings throughout the world under the rules of all major international arbitral institutions. The team also regularly appears before national courts in arbitration-related proceedings.

**Investment Funds & Asset Management:** The firm represents both US and foreign investment companies, their sponsors, advisors, underwriters and administrators in all regulatory aspects of fund and investment advisory operations as well as new product development.

**Litigation:** Shearman & Sterling represents clients in major commercial, regulatory and enforcement disputes and in sensitive internal and external investigations.

**Mergers & Acquisitions:** The firm is consistently ranked as a global leader in M&A in an array of transactions, including financial advisories, acquisitions, divestitures, joint ventures, strategic alliances and minority investments. The firm recently advised Viacom Inc. on the $50 billion division of its businesses into separate publicly traded companies, CBS Corp. and 'new' Viacom Inc., the largest transaction of its type ever completed.

**Project Development & Finance:** The PD&F Group is recognized as one of the world's leading practices and has attorneys located throughout the firm's worldwide network. The firm's project attorneys have solid backgrounds in sovereign and project restructurings, political risk insurance and other novel split-risk arrangements, as well as experience with export credit agencies and multilateral lending institutions.

**Property:** Shearman & Sterling's Property Group includes one of the most experienced full-service real estate practices in the world and a multinational group of attorneys dedicated to environmental counseling and litigation. The firm is active in areas such as financings, acquisitions, dispositions, development, joint ventures and leasing representing lenders, borrowers, sellers, buyers, developers, investors, general partners and limited partners.

**Tax:** The Tax Group plays an integral role in the firm's Cross-Border Practice. The firm provides international strategic tax planning advice and representation on a diverse variety of complex transactions including cross-border mergers and acquisitions, spin-offs and mergers, equity and debt financings of domestic and foreign issuers, restructurings and public and private real estate transactions.

## US OFFICES

**NEW YORK**
599 Lexington Avenue, **New York**, NY 10022-6069
**Tel:** 212 848 4000  **Fax:** 212 848 7179

**CALIFORNIA**
1080 Marsh Road, **Menlo Park**, CA 94025-1022
**Tel:** 650 838 3600  **Fax:** 650 838 3699

525 Market Street, Suite 2000, **San Francisco**, CA 94104-1522
**Tel:** 415 616 1100  **Fax:** 415 616 1199

**DISTRICT OF COLUMBIA**
801 Pennsylvania Avenue, N.W., **Washington**, DC 20004-2604
**Tel:** 202 508 8000  **Fax:** 202 508 8100

## INTERNATIONAL OFFICES

Abu Dhabi, Beijing, Brussels, Düsseldorf, Frankfurt, Hong Kong, London, Mannheim, Munich, Paris, Rome, São Paulo, Singapore, Tokyo and Toronto.

# SIMPSON THACHER & BARTLETT LLP

## THE FIRM

**Chairman, Executive Committee:** Phillip T Ruegger
**Administrative Partners:** George R Krouse, Gary I Horowitz

**Number of partners in US:** 149
**Number of other lawyers in US:** 550

**FIRM OVERVIEW:** The firm was established in 1884 and currently has approximately 700 lawyers worldwide, including 165 partners. Through its New York City headquarters, the firm provides coordinated legal advice and transactional capability in the world's principal international financial centers, including London, Hong Kong and Tokyo. The firm also maintains offices in Los Angeles, Palo Alto, and Washington, DC.

## MAIN AREAS OF PRACTICE:

**Banking & Finance:** The practice has particular experience in syndicated lending and acquisition finance, with JPMorgan and its affiliates among its principal clients. The practice also represents representing borrowers throughout the US, Europe, Latin America and Asia. The firm is involved in financial institution mergers and acquisitions, as well as in the interpretation and application of laws and regulations governing consolidation and convergence in the financial sector. In 2005, they were ranked number one for "All Top Tier Roles" in the LPC banking survey.

**M&A:** The firm acts for purchasers, sellers, lenders and financial advisors and is experienced in LBOs, stock and asset purchases, mergers, restructurings, spin-offs, joint ventures and contested transactions. Recent notable work includes representation of: Ford Motor Company in the $15 billion sale of Hertz Corporation to a private equity consortium; a consortium of 7 private equity firms in the $11 billion acquisition of SunGard Data; Swiss Re in its $6.8 billion acquisition of GE Insurance Solutions; Toys R Us in its $6.6 billion sale to a consortium and adidas-Salomon in its $3.9 billion acquisition of Reebok International.

**Capital Markets & Securities:** The firm advises issuers and underwriters in IPOs, high yield debt offerings and derivative and complex instruments for both domestic and international clients, with Lehman Brothers among its principal clients. In 2005, the firm was ranked number one as issuer's counsel for common stock, US IPOs and high yield debt offerings. They represented the issuers in a number of IPOs, including Warner Music Group, PanAmSat Holdings, Celanese, New Skies Satellites and Dresser-Rand; and the underwriters, led by China International Capital Corporation Ltd, in China Shenhua Energy's $3.3 billion IPO, the underwriters in the $4.3 billion follow on common stock offering by Google, and the underwriters in the $4 billion common stock offering by Hudson City Bancorp.

**Litigation:** The Litigation Practice encompasses every type of complex litigation nationwide - trials and appeals- including antitrust, securities, insurance and reinsurance, intellectual property matters, product liability/mass tort, mergers and acquisitions, labor and employment, and other commercial litigation for US and non-US clients. The firm is well known for successfully taking cases to trial, including in recent years, the highly publicized jury verdict for Swiss Re in the multi-billion dollar World Trade Center insurance litigation, a judgment in favor of Daiichi Pharceuticals on a multi-billion dollar patent, a several hundred million dollar judgment in favor of JP Morgan Chase, a dismissal following trial of a mjaor antitrust case against Viacom amd Blockbuster and international and domestic arbitration awards for G.E., Accenture and numerous insurer clients worth many billions of dollars.

**Real Estate:** The firm has one of the most sophisticated real estate practices among major US law firms. STB's practice is international in scope and spans all areas of the real estate industry, including real estate finance, sales and acquisitions, mergers and acquisitions, real estate development, leasing, joint ventures and partnerships.

**Tax:** The firm's Tax Practice is expert and diverse; principal tax clients are corporations and financial services institutions. STB's tax lawyers play a major role in the structuring and tax planning aspects of mergers and acquisitions, financing and capital markets transactions.

## HEAD OFFICE

**NEW YORK**
425 Lexington Avenue, **New York**, NY 10017
**Tel:** 212 455 2000   **Fax:** 212 455 2502
**Website:** www.simpsonthacher.com

## BRANCH OFFICES

**CALIFORNIA**
1999 Avenue of the Stars, 29th Floor, **Los Angeles**, CA 90067
**Tel:** 310 407 7500   **Fax:** 310 407 7502

2550 Hanover Street, **Palo Alto**, CA 94304-1204
**Tel:** 650 251 5000   **Fax:** 650 251 5002

**DISTRICT OF COLUMBIA**
555 11th Street, NW, 7th Floor, **Washington**, DC 20004
**Tel:** 202 220 7700   **Fax:** 202 220 7702

## INTERNATIONAL OFFICES

The firm also has offices in London, Hong Kong and Tokyo.

## CONTACTS

| | |
|---|---|
| Corporate | Philip T Ruegger |
| Banking | L Francis Huck |
| Capital Markets | George R Krouse, Vince Pagano, John Tehan |
| M&A | Charles "Casey" Cogut |
| Litigation | Barry R Ostrager, Charles E Koob |
| Insurance | Barry R Ostrager, MaryKay Vyskocil |
| Intellectual Property | Hank Gutman |
| Tax | Steven C Todrys |
| Executive Compensation | Kenneth C Edgar |
| Real Estate | Gregory J Ressa |
| Exempt Organizations | Victoria B Bjorklund |
| Personal Planning | Mildred Kalik |

**Executive Compensation:** This practice group specializes in the planning, drafting, negotiation and compliance aspects of compensation of employees at all income levels, with emphasis on handling complex executive compensation plans and employment contracts; and all types of employee benefit plans, including retirement, profit-sharing, medical, severance and disability arrangements.

**Personal Planning:** The firm counsels clients regarding gift, estate, and generation-skipping transfer taxes; complex estate and trust planning and administration; wealth preservation across generations.

**CLIENTS:** Accenture, ACE, adidas-Salomon, American Electric Power, AIG, The Blackstone Group, Doctors Without Borders, Deutsche Bank, Ford Motor Company, GE Capital, Heineken, H.J. Heinz, JPMorgan Chase & Co. and its affiliates, Kmart Corporation, Kohlberg Kravis Roberts & Co., Lehman Brothers, Northwest Airlines, St. Paul Travelers, Swiss Re, Virgin, Wachovia, Warner Music Group, Washington Mutual, Wyeth.

**INTERNATIONAL WORK:** International finance and capital markets, mergers and acquisitions, banking, sovereign finance and privatization, asset based and specialized financing, litigation and arbitration, tax and real estate are important aspects of the firm's international practice. The firm's three foreign offices coordinate with one another to provide a truly global capability for local clients as well as clients of the firm based elsewhere in the world.

## SIMPSON THACHER & BARTLETT LLP

# SIVE, PAGET & RIESEL, P.C.

## THE FIRM

**Founding Partner:** David Sive

**Number of partners:** 9
**Number of other lawyers:** 10

**FIRM OVERVIEW:** Since its inception in 1962, Sive, Paget & Riesel, P.C. has focused on environmental law and litigation. It has been instrumental in the formulation of many important precedents now comprising the body of environmental law. Today, the firm's extensive experience allows it to bring comprehensive cost effective solutions to emerging development, business, real estate, and litigation problems that involve almost all aspects of environmental law.

**Environmental Law Network:** The firm is a member of the Environmental Law Network, consisting of 18 affiliated environmental law firms throughout the United States.

## MAIN AREAS OF PRACTICE:

**General Environmental:** Sive, Paget & Riesel, P.C. solves environmental problems in a broad array of different economic and enforcement situations. Its professional work ranges from advice on future development to the defense of criminal enforcement actions. A significant aspect of the firm's practice involves facilitating financial and real estate transactions, including the performance of due diligence, negotiation of environmental provisions in contractual documents, and obtaining appropriate insurance coverage. The firm is engaged in Superfund and Brownfield remediations, development of commercial, residential and industrial projects, electrical generating facilities, and public infrastructure. The firm also represents industrial facilities seeking to obtain or renew air, water and hazardous waste permits. The firm provides advice to its institutional clients on their environmental compliance programs, analysing the company's ability to meet present and ongoing environmental regulations. The firm's Environmental Litigation Practice involves all of the above described aspects of environmental law.

**Development & Land Use:** Large-scale development now faces a myriad of regulatory hurdles, which range from complex environmental impact studies to the remediation of hazardous waste. Often these issues become enmeshed in political disputes that further obstruct development. The firm evaluates the requirements for development and guides clients through this process by utilizing its knowledge to formulate a time sensitive course of action, assuring that the project successfully emerges from the process in the minimum period of time with a record that will withstand litigation.

**Environmental Litigation:** The firm is engaged in extensive environmental litigation, which ranges from cost recovery actions under CERCLA to the defense of Toxic Tort actions. The firm is often called upon to litigate contract disputes involving environmental liabilities. The firm has been active in litigating decisions made by state and federal regulatory agencies. The firm is also frequently called upon to defend local governments' land use and environmental actions. Usually, the attorney handling the administrative process is the attorney that is fully prepared to litigate any judicial challenge.

**Hazardous & Solid Waste:** The firm's practice involves development and enforcement problems arising from hazardous and solid waste. The firm has developed approaches and techniques to minimize the costs and time involved in the remediation of hazardous substance sites. It has also been active in the reduction, transfer and treatment of solid waste, often representing municipalities as well as private parties.

**General Litigation:** The firm has a robust Civil Litigation Practice and represents clients in matters ranging from employment issues to construction disputes. It has also developed a speciality in representing not-for-profit organizations and academic institutions.

## HEAD OFFICE

**NEW YORK**
460 Park Avenue, 10th Floor, **New York**, NY 10022
**Tel:** 212 421 2150  **Fax:** 212 421 1891
**Email:** sprlaw@sprlaw.com
**Website:** www.sprlaw.com

## CONTACTS

| | |
|---|---|
| Project Development | David Paget |
| Environmental Enforcement & Litigation | Daniel Riesel |
| Brownfield Remeidation | Mark Chertok |

**CLIENTS:** Sive, Paget & Riesel, P.C. represents a unique range of clients. In addition to a broad array of corporate, development and manufacturing clients, it has and continues to represent government agencies ranging from small townships to state agencies and the Commonwealth of Puerto Rico. It represents domestic and international clients in environmental litigation and in administrative matters involving large-scale development, particularly within the New York Metropolitan area.

**INTERNATIONAL WORK:** Sive, Paget & Riesel, P.C.'s extensive experience in representing the interest of the regulated community allows the firm to represent both domestic and international clients with respect to environmental problems in the United States.

SPR
SIVE · PAGET · RIESEL

# SKADDEN, ARPS, SLATE, MEAGHER & FLOM LLP & AFFILIATES

## THE FIRM

**Executive Partner:** Robert C Sheehan
**Senior Partner:** Joseph H Flom

**Number of US partners:** 344
**Number of other US lawyers:** 1,200

**FIRM OVERVIEW:** With approximately 1,750 attorneys in 22 offices, Skadden, Arps, Slate, Meagher & Flom LLP and Affiliates is one of the largest and most highly respected law firms in the world. The firm provides a wide array of legal services globally to the corporate, financial, industrial and governmental communities.

## MAIN AREAS OF PRACTICE

**Corporate/M&A:** Skadden has consistently ranked first among law firms in the US for handling the greatest number of the largest M&A transactions announced annually, and has been involved in many of the largest transactions ever. The firm's clients range from start-ups and middle-market companies to the largest of the *Fortune* 250. Transactions include recapitalizations and restructurings, including spin-offs, divestitures and other techniques for maximizing value for the client.

**Corporate Restructuring:** The firm's Corporate Restructuring Group serves corporations and their principal creditors and investors by providing upper margin, value-added legal solutions to troubled company merger and acquisition, financial and restructuring situations. The firm has advised on some of the most widely publicized corporate restructurings recently announced or pending, including several of the largest Chapter 11 cases in US history. The firm also has a substantial practice in advising clients on non-judicial restructurings.

**Litigation:** Skadden represents clients in federal and state trial and appellate courts nationwide, and has developed a premier securities class action defense practice. The firm's work on antitrust matters includes counseling and litigating for clients in connection with mergers, acquisitions and joint ventures. The firm assists clients in resolving disputes without litigation by using various alternative dispute resolution procedures, including arbitration, mediation, conciliation, and mini-trials, and has represented US and non-US clients in arbitrations under all major rules systems and before every major arbitral institution worldwide.

**Banking & Finance:** Skadden advises underwriters, issuers and purchasers in public and private financings. It advises on all types of debt and equity instruments; structured finance; public finance; lease and project financings; and commodities, futures and derivative products. The firm's clients include investment companies; advisors and broker-dealers; and private investment funds.

**Industry-related Practices:** The firm has a number of industry-related practice areas, including banking and financial services, communications, energy, healthcare, information technology, insurance, real estate and utilities.

**CLIENTS:** The firm represents a broad spectrum of clients, from small high-technology start-up companies to nearly half of the *Fortune* 250 industrial and service corporations in the US.

**INTERNATIONAL WORK:** Skadden's offices in Beijing, Brussels, Frankfurt, Hong Kong, London, Moscow, Munich, Paris, Singapore, Sydney, Tokyo, Toronto and Vienna, in addition to substantial practices in Latin America, the Middle East and Africa, enable the firm to offer clients an integrated cross-border service. Main international practices include corporate transactions such as mergers and acquisitions, privatizations, joint ventures, project financings, international trade matters, litigation, capital markets, banking and finance transactions, and tax matters. The firm also has an alliance with Chiomenti Studio Legale, one of the premier corporate firms in Italy.

## HEAD OFFICE

**NEW YORK**
Four Times Square, **New York**, NY 10036
**Tel:** 212 735 3000   **Fax:** 212 735 2000
**Website:** www.skadden.com

## BRANCH OFFICES

**CALIFORNIA**
300 South Grand Avenue, Suite 3400, **Los Angeles**, CA 90071
**Tel:** 213 687 5000   **Fax:** 213 687 5600

525 University Avenue, Suite 1100, **Palo Alto**, CA 94301
**Tel:** 650 470 4500   **Fax:** 650 470 4570

Four Embarcadero Center, Suite 3800, **San Francisco**, CA 94111
**Tel:** 415 984 6400   **Fax:** 415 984 2698

**DELAWARE**
One Rodney Square, **Wilmington**, DE 19801
**Tel:** 302 651 3000   **Fax:** 302 651 3001

**DISTRICT OF COLUMBIA**
1440 New York Avenue, NW, **Washington**, DC 20005
**Tel:** 202 371 7000   **Fax:** 202 393 5760

**ILLINOIS**
333 West Wacker Drive, **Chicago**, IL 60606
**Tel:** 312 407 0700   **Fax:** 312 407 0411

**MASSACHUSETTS**
One Beacon Street, **Boston**, MA 02108
**Tel:** 617 573 4800   **Fax:** 617 573 4822

**TEXAS**
1000 Louisiana Street, Suite 6800, **Houston**, TX 77002
**Tel:** 713 655 5100   **Fax:** 713 655 5200

**Skadden, Arps, Slate, Meagher & Flom LLP & Affiliates**

# SULLIVAN & CROMWELL LLP

## THE FIRM

**Chairman:** H Rodgin Cohen
**Vice Chairman:** Joseph C Shenker

**Number of partners worldwide:** 163
**Number of other lawyers worldwide:** 435

**FIRM OVERVIEW:** Founded in New York in 1879, Sullivan & Cromwell LLP comprises approximately 600 lawyers conducting a global practice through 12 offices on four continents. The firm's organization as a single, unified partnership worldwide, combined with its reliance primarily on internally generated growth, has contributed to its reputation for providing consistently high quality legal services.

During the past several decades, Sullivan & Cromwell has grown in response to the increasing volume and complexity of its clients' affairs. The expansion of the scope and nature of its practice has led the firm to have lawyers in leading financial centers around the world, with offices in Washington, DC, Los Angeles and Palo Alto in the United States; in Paris, London and Frankfurt in Europe; in Tokyo, Hong Kong and Beijing in Asia; and in Melbourne and Sydney in Australia. Also, Sullivan & Cromwell has developed select capabilities in English, French, German and Japanese law.

**GLOBAL STRATEGY:** Sullivan & Cromwell provides the highest quality legal advice and representation to clients around the world. The results achieved on behalf of those clients have set the firm apart for more than 125 years, and Sullivan & Cromwell is today a leader in each of its core practice areas and geographic regions.

Sullivan & Cromwell's success derives from the quality of its lawyers, who are the most broadly and deeply trained attorneys in the world. The firm hires the very best law school graduates and trains them to be generalists within broad practice areas. Sullivan & Cromwell elects its partners almost entirely from among its own associates. The resulting partnership offers clients a unique diversity of experience, exceptional professional judgment and a demonstrated history of innovation. Chambers most recently has recognized the quality of Sullivan & Cromwell's work in more than 40 different practice areas and jurisdictions, and more than 50 S&C partners as leading practitioners.

## MAIN AREAS OF PRACTICE:

**Capital Markets:** Sullivan & Cromwell has had an internationally prominent securities practice for nearly a century. The firm's reputation for the highest quality securities work is based on both the volume and value of offerings in which it is involved and on its ability to structure novel and effective transactions to address its clients' needs, in representations of issuers, underwriters, selling and controlling shareholders and other market participants from all over the world. Sullivan & Cromwell's capital markets work in 2005 included acting in four of the Wall Street Journal's top 10 global stock issues and in four of the Financial Times' top 10 global IPOs. The strength of the firm's international Capital Markets Practice is underscored by its work in "deal of the year" transactions from the US, Asia, Australia, Europe and Latin America, as recognized by leading financial publications.

Recent representative work includes award-winning deals for 2005, such as Lehman Brothers' US$300 million ECAPs issue, named FIG Innovation of the Year by Euromoney; the US$4.6 billion equity offering by Mizuho Financial Group in Japan, recognized by Asiamoney and FinanceAsia; the US$3.3 billion IPO of China Shenhua Energy (Best IPO, Asiamoney) and the US$2.2 billion IPO of Bank of Communications (Equity Deal of the Year, CFO Asia) in China; the £1.08 billion capital increase by Standard Chartered in the UK (European Equity Issue of the Year, IFR); the €539 million IPO by TomTom NV in the Netherlands (European IPO of the Year, IFR); and the US$81.8 billion debt restructuring by the Republic of Argentina (LatinLawyer, The Banker) and Mexico's US$2.5 billion debt exchange warrant offering (Euromoney, The Banker). Other notable transactions are the US$7.5 billion partial privatization

## HEAD OFFICE

**NEW YORK**
125 Broad Street, **New York** NY 10004-2498
**Tel:** 212 558 4000  **Fax:** 212 558 3588
**Email:** fergusc@sullcrom.com
**Website:** www.sullcrom.com

## BRANCH OFFICES

**CALIFORNIA**
1888 Century Park East, **Los Angeles** CA 90067-1725
**Tel:** 310 712 6600  **Fax:** 310 712 8800
**Email:** sacksr@sullcrom.com

1870 Embarcadero Road, **Palo Alto** CA 94303-3308
**Tel:** 650 461 5600  **Fax:** 650 461 5700
**Email:** millersc@sullcrom.com

**DISTRICT OF COLUMBIA**
1701 Pennsylvania Avenue, NW, **Washington** DC 20006-5805
**Tel:** 202 956 7500 **Fax:** 202 293 6330
**Email:** craftr@sullcrom.com

## INTERNATIONAL OFFICES

London, Paris, Frankfurt am Main, Tokyo, Hong Kong, Beijing, Melbourne, Sydney.

of France's EDF, for which Sullivan & Cromwell provided US and French law advice; the US$1.5 billion and US$800 million high-yield debt offerings, respectively, by EchoStar DBS (2006) and Tenet Healthcare; and IPOs by American Reprographics, Dollar Financial, OptionsXpress, IHS Group, IntercontinentalExchange, VeriFone Holdings, and Under Armour.

**Litigation:** Sullivan & Cromwell's Litigation Group regularly represents leading international industrial corporations, financial institutions and individuals before federal and state courts throughout the US and before US regulatory agencies, including the Department of Justice and Securities and Exchange Commission. With an experienced team in the US and London, the firm offers specialized expertise in international commercial arbitration. Major recent representations included: Computer Associates in the government investigation of its accounting practices and subsequent deferred prosecution agreement; Goldman Sachs in 310 securities class actions arising out of IPO allocations practices and service as liaison counsel to all 55 underwriter defendants in those litigations; Barclays in connection with Enron-related claims; UBS in a securities class action/government investigation regarding its role as lead investment bank for HealthSouth; Riggs National Bank in resolving investigations by a number of federal agencies; Omnicom Group in securities class action litigation; dismissals in numerous class actions against Diageo, the largest spirits manufacturer in the world, in litigation over advertising practices; CSR Limited in insurance coverage litigation; Oxford Health Plans in customer and provider class actions; Willis, the third largest US insurance broker, in an investigation by the New York Attorney General and in class action litigation; Morgan Stanley in litigation arising out of the merger of Time Warner and America Online; and Van der Moolen, the New York Stock Exchange specialist firm, in class actions and regulatory investigations.

**Mergers & Acquisitions:** Sullivan & Cromwell regularly advises on some of the largest cross-border merger and acquisition transactions, as well as on domestic transactions in the United States and major markets in Europe and Asia. In 2005, the firm was the leading counsel to principals in M&A deals announced worldwide by value (Bloomberg and Dealogic), the leading counsel to all parties in M&A deals announced worldwide by value (Bloomberg and Dealogic) and the leading counsel in deals completed worldwide by value

# SULLIVAN & CROMWELL LLP CONT'D

(Thomson). Sullivan & Cromwell also was the top legal advisor in announced Latin American M&A deals by value in 2005. The firm was involved in six of the Wall Street Journal's 10 largest M&A deals announced worldwide in 2005, including Procter & Gamble (US) - Gillette Co. (US); Mitsubishi Tokyo Financial Group (Japan) - UFJ Holdings (Japan); Telefónica (Spain) - O2 (UK); Gas Natural (Spain) - Endesa (Spain); UniCredito Italiano (Italy) - HypoVereinsbank (Germany); and Time Warner/Comcast (US) - Adelphia Communications (US). These include the largest deal each in Asia (MTFG-UFJ), Europe (Telefónica-O2) and the United States (P&G-Gillette).

**Antitrust & EC Competition Law:** Sullivan & Cromwell has one of the most diverse practices of any US firm in successfully litigating contested antitrust cases and representing clients before competition law enforcement agencies around the world. Over the last seven years, the firm has represented Microsoft in private antitrust litigation brought in numerous jurisdictions by competitors and classes of end-users of Microsoft software. Sullivan & Cromwell has obtained dismissals on the merits of dozens of these cases, including victories in the Supreme Courts of five states, five significant victories in the US Court of Appeals for the Fourth Circuit, many additional dismissals in an MDL proceeding, and a victory in a jury trial in federal court in Connecticut. The firm also has litigated successfully and obtained dismissal on summary judgment of a US$ 1 billion antitrust claim brought against client Philips Electronics. The dismissed claims included allegations of tying, monopolisation, and price fixing, among others. Sullivan & Cromwell has cleared a number of mergers through antitrust authorities in the United States and Europe, and its practice extends to numerous successful efforts both in court and before enforcement agencies with regard to competition law-based challenges to the assertion of intellectual property. In addition to Microsoft and Philips, the firm recently has been involved in antitrust-related work for Thomson, Sony, Mitsubishi, and IntercontinentalExchange.

**Financial Institutions:** Sullivan & Cromwell's Financial Institutions Practice encompasses M&A, the development of new products and services, regulatory matters, credit activities and litigation and enforcement matters for international banks, insurance companies and investment management firms.

**Intellectual Property & Technology:** The firm's Intellectual Property and Technology Group draws from all aspects of its practice to respond to clients' needs across the full spectrum of IP and technology issues, including enforcing patents and trademarks against infringers, technology transfer and licensing arrangements, evaluating the desirability of federal intellectual property protection, obtaining security interests in IP, and conducting adequate intellectual property due diligence in IP transactions.

**Real Estate:** Sullivan & Cromwell advises on the purchase, sale, construction, financing, and securitisation of real estate assets worldwide. Clients include investors, developers, lenders and investment bankers. Recent representations have included General Growth in its US$ 12.6 billion acquisition of The Rouse Company (the largest ever REIT merger), the NY Football Giants and their owners in the US$ 1+ billion joint venture development with the NY Jets of a new football stadium, and Goldman Sachs in the development of its new 2.2 million square foot world headquarters in Lower Manhattan.

**Project Finance:** Sullivan & Cromwell is counsel to sponsors of, and lenders to, world-class projects in developed and emerging markets. The practice is well diversified by industry, including oil and gas, mining, infrastructure development, telecommunications and power. Notable representations in 2005 included the Sumitomo companies in connection with the Cerro Verde Sulfide Project in Peru, named Latin American Mining Deal of the Year by ProjectFinance, China Minmetals in its copper joint venture with Corporación Nacional del Cobre de Chile, and continuing work on behalf of the sponsors and the borrowers for the BTC pipeline in the Caspian region, winner of multiple project finance awards in 2004.

**Tax:** Sullivan & Cromwell's Tax Group plays a leading role in structuring new, tax-advantaged financial instruments and complex M&A transactions, and represents prominent industrial and commercial enterprises worldwide in US, French and cross-border tax matters.

**Private Equity:** Drawing on the strength of its leading finance and M&A practices, Sullivan & Cromwell's Private Equity Group advises clients on private equity M&A and strategic investments and on M&A and capital markets exits from those investments.

**Employment/Executive Compensation & Benefits:** Sullivan & Cromwell provides comprehensive employment law services, including litigation and advice to clients on all manner of labor and employment law issues, including resolution of allegations of harassment and other employee wrongdoing, and implementation of workforce changes. The firm also has a dedicated group that advises on the planning, drafting and implementation of executive compensation arrangements and employee benefit plans.

**CLIENTS:** Clients of Sullivan & Cromwell are nearly evenly divided between US and non-US entities. They include leading industrial and commercial companies, financial institutions, private funds, educational, charitable and cultural institutions; governments; and a select group of individuals, estates and trusts. The firm's client base is exceptionally diverse by industry and geography, a result of Sullivan & Cromwell's capacity to tailor its experience to specific client needs.

**INTERNATIONAL WORK:** Sullivan & Cromwell has long played a leading role in the expanding access by non-US enterprises to US capital markets, global privatisation transactions, cross-border mergers and acquisitions, the integration of financial services, cross-border litigation, antitrust/competition law matters, intellectual property and technology, and project and structured finance for developed and emerging markets. The firm's work in cross-border capital flows has continued and includes substantial experience in foreign direct investment and project finance, in the Euro and other global capital markets, and in the financial flows to Asia and Latin America.

# SULLIVAN & CROMWELL LLP

# THACHER PROFFITT & WOOD LLP

## THE FIRM

**Managing Partner:** Paul D Tvetenstrand
**Executive Committee:** Thomas M Leslie, Robert E McCarthy, Douglas J McClintock, Richard A Schaberg, and Anthony S Cassino (Executive Director)

**Number of US partners, as of 11.30.05:** 63
**Number of other US lawyers, as of 11.30.05:** 188

**FIRM OVERVIEW:** For more than 150 years, Thacher Proffitt has led the way in creating and implementing innovative, workable solutions that bring finance and business together. The firm's strong focus and deep experience, combined with its relationships with major financial institutions help investors and principals worldwide put capital to work. Thacher Proffitt represents financial institutions, investors and corporations throughout the US, Latin America and Europe. While the firm has experience in numerous industries, it is known for its strength and expertise in financial services, structured finance, banking, insurance, maritime, automotive, aviation, construction, government, real estate, technology, telecommunications, and transportation. According to The National Law Journal, Thacher Proffitt is the fastest growing law firm in the US, based on a 31% increase in lawyers for 2004 to 2005. According to Thomson Financial, Thacher Proffitt is counsel to the largest volume of US debt, equity and equity-related structured finance transactions year after year. Recently Latin Lawyer named Thacher Proffitt as one of "Latin America's Leading Business Law Firms."

## MAIN AREAS OF PRACTICE:

**Corporate & Financial Institutions:** Banking, corporate finance, securities, investment funds and investment advisors including '40 Act, regulatory compliance, mergers and acquisitions, employment, compensation and benefits, and ERISA.

**Litigation & Dispute Resolution:** Alternative dispute resolution, arbitration, bankruptcy and creditors' rights, complex commercial litigation, insurance and reinsurance, maritime and admiralty, real estate litigation, and technology and intellectual property.

**Real Estate:** Commercial real estate finance/asset backed finance; federal and state regulation of real estate; leasing; loan sales, syndication and servicing; mezzanine financing; and mortgage securitization.

**Structured Finance:** Asset backed securitization; financing of financial assets; global securitization and finance; leasing and lease securitization; purchase, sale and servicing of financial assets; regulatory compliance; and residential and commercial mortgage securitization.

**Tax:** Public and private offerings of debt and equity, including financial instruments issued by REMICs, FASITs, REITs, qualified REIT subsidiaries, domestic special purpose entities and offshore special purpose entities; mergers and acquisitions; partnerships and limited liability companies, real estate transactions, bankruptcy and creditors' rights, cross-border leasing, equipment finance, state, local and international taxation.

**Trusts & Estates:** Estate planning and administration, charitable giving planning, gift and estate tax, trust administration, and will and trust preparation.

**Technology & Intellectual Property:** Intellectual property registration, licensing and protection; Internet domain names; trademark and service mark registration, licensing and protection.

**INTERNATIONAL WORK:** Thacher Proffitt has counseled clients in virtually every business center worldwide, and are one of a very few law firms with a significant presence in one of Latin America's principal financial centers—Mexico City. From Brazil to The Netherlands, Germany to Australia, China to Mexico, and Japan to Kazakhstan, Thacher Proffitt can complete the most complex deals and resolve the most difficult commercial disputes. International clients call upon the firm to handle the structural, regulatory and tax aspects of their transactions, as well as to negotiate and implement joint ventures, mergers and acquisitions, equity and debt offerings, securitized financings, project finance, government procurement bid processes, privatizations, commercial real estate financings, cross-border financing, leasing transactions and shipping matters. Thacher Proffitt is lead counsel on precedent-setting commercial arbitration and litigation throughout the world. The firm is known for its ability to offer practical and creative business solutions no matter where an issue arises.

**Latin America Practice Focus:** Bankruptcy and workouts; corporate and securities; energy; labor and employment; litigation and arbitration; securitization; and tax.

## HEAD OFFICE

**NEW YORK**
Two World Financial Center, **New York** NY 10281
**Tel:** 212 912 7400 **Fax:** 212 912 7751
**Website:** www.tpw.com

## BRANCH OFFICES

**NEW JERSEY**
25 DeForest Avenue, **Summit**, NJ 07901
**Tel:** 908 598 5700 **Fax:** 908 598 5710

**NEW YORK**
50 Main Street, **White Plains**, NY 10606
**Tel:** 914 421 4100 **Fax:** 914 421 4150

**DISTRICT OF COLUMBIA**
1700 Pennsylvania Avenue, NW, Suite 800
**Washington** DC 20006
**Tel:** 202 347 8400 **Fax:** 202 626 1930

## INTERNATIONAL OFFICES

**MEXICO**
Paseo de Tamarindos, No. 400-B Piso 22, Col. Bosques de las Lomas, 05120, **Mexico DF**
**Tel:** +52 (55) 3000 0600 **Fax:** +52 (55) 3000 0698/0699

# WACHTELL, LIPTON, ROSEN & KATZ

## THE FIRM

**Co-Chairman of the Executive Committee:** Edward D Herlihy, Daniel A Neff
**Number of partners worldwide:** 78
**Number of other lawyers worldwide:** 125

## HEAD OFFICE

**NEW YORK**
51 West 52nd Street, **New York**, NY 10019
**Tel:** 212 403 1000   **Fax:** 212 403 2000
**Email:** info@wlrk.com   **Website:** www.wlrk.com

**FIRM OVERVIEW:** Founded in 1965, Wachtell, Lipton, Rosen & Katz is one of the most prominent business law firms in the US. The firm specializes in merger and acquisition transactions, sensitive litigation matters, advice on corporate governance and related matters, and corporate restructurings. With approximately 200 lawyers, the leanly staffed firm handles demanding, high profile transactions and advisory matters on an extremely personalized basis. The relatively concentrated nature of the practice, together with the absence of repetitive, standardized transactions, means that the firm's lawyers each have a broad range of skills and experience. Matters undertaken by the firm are at all times afforded the direct personal attention of partners having expertise and sophistication with respect to the issues involved, and staffing is designed to provide the highest quality representation. Clients include enterprises of virtually every nature, including industrial firms, financial institutions, securities firms, healthcare and pharmaceutical providers, technology companies, real estate companies, and media and information systems companies, including many *Fortune* 500 companies and other leading enterprises.

Wachtell Lipton is consistently in the very top rank of legal advisors by transaction dollar volume, notwithstanding that all of its major competitors are significantly larger. Since the beginning of the year 2000, Wachtell Lipton has been the legal advisor on six of the top 10 transactions in the United States and four of the top 10 transactions globally, as well as numerous other acquisition and restructuring transactions across many industries.

Wachtell Lipton originated the so-called 'poison pill'; represented the issuer in the US$10.6 billion initial public offering of AT&T Wireless (the largest US IPO in history); structured the first cross-border 'Morris Trust' transaction, between SmithKline Beckman and Beecham, including the related spin-offs of Beckman and Allergan; and has been involved in the transactions resulting in most of the landmark corporate governance decisions in Delaware, including the Household, Revlon, Newmont Mining, Macmillan, Interco, Time Warner, QVC and Omnicare cases.

Wachtell Lipton has recently represented, among others, ConocoPhillips in its US$35.0 billion acquisition of Burlington Resources; MBNA in its US$35.0 billion acquisition by Bank of America; Unocal in its US$19.0 billion sale to ChevronTexaco, and in responding to the US$20.0 billion overbid by CNOOC Limited; AT&T Wireless in its US$40.7 billion acquisition by Cingular (the largest cash acquisition in history); The Walt Disney Company in its response to Comcast's US$54.1 billion hostile acquisition proposal; Bank One in its US$58.0 billion merger with JPMorgan Chase; Sanofi-Synthelabo in its US$60.2 billion hostile exchange offer for Aventis; FleetBoston in its US$47.0 billion acquisition by Bank of America; the New York Stock Exchange in its pending merger with Archipelago; Instinet in its sale to NASDAQ; the divestiture by Sears of its credit card portfolio for US$32.0 billion and its US$13.0 billion merger with Kmart; Dana Corporation in its successful defense against a hostile bid by ArvinMeritor; and Taubman Centers in its successful defense against a hostile bid by Simon Property Group and Westfield.

## MAIN AREAS OF PRACTICE:

**Corporate:** Wachtell Lipton has handled some of the largest and most complex US and international transactions. It advises on a range of corporate matters, including mergers and acquisitions, spin-offs and split-ups, public offerings, financial products and financing transactions. Wachtell Lipton also counsels companies, and their boards of directors, on corporate disclosure, governance and policy issues.

**Litigation:** Wachtell Lipton handles a wide variety of high profile, complex litigation for major corporations and leading financial institutions. The firm's Litigation Practice is national in scope, and involves appearances in state and federal courts at both the trial and appellate levels. The firm also represents clients in arbitrations and mediations, and in regulatory and criminal investigations. Many of the firm's litigators served as law clerks on federal or state courts, and several distinguished themselves as trial lawyers in United States Attorneys' Offices. Work undertaken includes precedent-setting securities and corporate governance litigation, representation of major corporations in highly sensitive criminal and regulatory investigations, and libel and First Amendment cases. The firm has been involved in landmark corporate governance litigation cases in Delaware, including the Household, Revlon, Macmillan, Interco, Time Warner and Paramount cases. The firm often handles extremely high-stakes civil litigation. For example, the firm is representing affiliates of Silverstein Properties, the 99-year lessees of the World Trade Center, in connection with the September 11, 2001 collapses of the Twin Towers and the redevelopment of the World Trade Center. Following a jury trial in 2004, the firm obtained a verdict in Silverstein's favor that what happened on September 11 constituted two 'occurrences' for property insurance purposes with respect to US$1.1 billion of Silverstein's coverage. The firm also recently successfully defended Campbell Soup Company and affiliates in the trial of a fraudulent conveyance and breach of fiduciary duty lawsuit brought by unpaid creditors of a former Campbell subsidiary, in which the plaintiff had sought to recover more than US$500 million in damages. Other major recent representations include Bank of America and various of its subsidiaries in connection with regulatory matters and civil litigation arising out of alleged market timing in mutual funds; Nextel Partners in a Delaware Chancery Court trial relating to the terms of the buyout of its public shareholders by Sprint Nextel; the New York Stock Exchange in litigation concerning its merger with Archipelago; The Walt Disney Company in litigation brought by Roy E Disney to invalidate the results of the 2005 Disney annual meeting and board election, and the resulting settlement of that litigation; and IAC/InterActiveCorp in litigation leading to the recovery of significant tax distributions in connection with the 2002 transaction that created Vivendi Universal Entertainment. Having achieved dismissal of all allegations in a securities fraud class action against Chubb, the firm recently won affirmance of that dismissal in the Third Circuit. The firm also represents insurance companies and defendants faced with mass tort liabilities. In those matters, the firm has distinguished itself by structuring complex and creative settlements involving numerous parties and claimants on a national scale as well as major questions of public policy. The firm has defended major securities firms, financial institutions, retailers, software manufacturers, healthcare providers, news and information systems companies, and a variety of other companies in enforcement proceedings and class actions. These matters typically involve questions of corporate governance, complex accounting issues, sensitive public and investor relations problems, and significant interaction with senior state and federal law enforcement officials.

**Bankruptcy & Creditors' Rights:** The firm's Bankruptcy and Creditors' Rights Practice represents buyers, investors, lenders, and creditors in national and multinational bankruptcy cases and out-of-court debt restructurings. Its lawyers regularly work with the firm's Corporate Group in handling complicated acquisitions and divestitures of businesses in financial distress, highly leveraged transactions, and major transactions involving significant creditors' rights issues. Recent restructuring work has included representing AT&T and Cable and Wireless in connection with troubled subsidiaries; representing the acquirers of bankrupt retailer Kmart, bankrupt brokerage firm Refco and the Colombian-based airline Avianca; representing the official creditors committee of PSINet; and representing bank and bondholder groups (or other significant creditors) in the restructurings of Collins & Aikman, Delphi, Intermet, Calpine, Blockbuster, Northwest Airlines, Footstar, Inc., HealthSouth, Rand McNally, Trump Hotels & Casino Resorts, Spalding/Top-Flite, Allegheny Energy, Pacific Gas and Electric,

# WACHTELL, LIPTON, ROSEN & KATZ cont'd

Budget Rent-a-Car, World Kitchen, National Century Financial Enterprises, Independent Wireless One, Sunbeam, Exide Technologies, 360networks, Fruit of the Loom, Regal Cinemas, and many other companies. The group's lawyers also have significant expertise in asbestos matters, D&O liability issues, and in the defense of bankruptcy-related litigation, such as fraudulent transfer litigation and litigation against control persons of bankrupt entities.

**Antitrust:** Wachtell Lipton's Antitrust Practice focuses on mergers and acquisitions, government investigations, international antitrust and banking antitrust issues. Wachtell Lipton analyzes transactions to determine whether they raise antitrust issues, develops strategies to address those issues, and represents clients before enforcement officials in the United States, including the US Department of Justice, the Federal Trade Commission, the Board of Governors of the Federal Reserve System and state attorneys general, and in antitrust litigation challenging transactions. Wachtell Lipton is active on matters involving foreign antitrust enforcement authorities, frequently serving as worldwide lead antitrust counsel and participating with local counsel in proceedings and investigations in the European Union, Canada, Australia, Mexico, and many other jurisdictions. The firm has represented many of the world's leading companies in important transactions, including Wal-Mart, Cardinal Health, Novartis, ConocoPhillips, and Valero. Recent transactions handled by Wachtell Lipton include Maytag in its pending sale to Whirlpool; Instinet Group in its merger with Nasdaq; Cinergy in its merger with Duke Energy; Sears in its merger with Kmart; Unocal in its merger with Chevron; the New York Stock Exchange in its merger with Archipelago; Air Canada in its investment in the merger of US Airways/America West; AT&T Corp. in its sale to SBC; Sanofi in its merger with Aventis; Novartis in its pending acquisition of Chiron; ConocoPhillips in its pending acquisition of Burlington Resources; Vulcan Materials Company in the sale of its chemicals division to Occidental Petroleum; Valero LLP in its purchase of Kaneb Partners; and Valero Energy in its purchase of Premcor. In addition, Wachtell Lipton has represented the buyer or the seller in nearly every one of the largest bank mergers in US history, including Bank One in its acquisition by JPMorgan Chase and FleetBoston in its acquisition by Bank of America.

**Tax:** Wachtell Lipton's tax lawyers regularly advise clients on the tax aspects of corporate reorganizations, acquisitions, spin-offs and other dispositions, joint ventures, financings and restructurings. These transactions frequently involve large multinational businesses and raise complex domestic and multinational tax issues. Indeed, tax considerations often determine the form, and occasionally the viability, of contemplated transactions. Examples of major transactions in which the firm's tax expertise has played a formative role include: the restructuring and initial public offering of Lazard (using a non-US entity taxed as a partnership); the merger of Sears and Kmart; the acquisition of Intelsat by Apax, Apollo, Madison Dearborn, and Permira; IAC/InterActiveCorp's acquisition of Ask Jeeves, spin-off of Expedia and sale of its interest in Vivendi Universal Entertainment; the unsolicited offer by Public Storage, Inc. for Shurgard Storage Centers, Inc.; the conversion of the New York Stock Exchange into a for profit public company and its simultaneous acquisition of Archipelago Holdings; and the acquisition of Albertson's by SUPERVALU, Cerberus and CVS. The tax group is also actively involved in new financial products and innovative real estate transactions.

**Employment & Benefits:** The firm's Executive Compensation and Employee Benefits Practice focuses primarily on compensation and benefit issues in connection with mergers and acquisitions and other corporate transactions, including management and equity arrangements in the private equity context, and for executive officers of major corporations and financial institutions. Wachtell Lipton also advises clients about a wide variety of ongoing executive compensation issues, including key executive employment contracts, equity compensation plans, deferred compensation arrangements and compliance with evolving corporate governance standards. The executive compensation and employee benefits group will often advise clients on pre-change in control planning, including adoption and modification of existing change in control severance arrangements.

**Real Estate:** Wachtell Lipton has a preeminent Real Estate M&A Practice, focusing on strategic real estate transactions, mergers and acquisitions of REITs and other real estate companies, major development projects and joint ventures, structuring real estate opportunity funds, acquisitions and dispositions of significant assets and asset portfolios, innovative capital markets transactions, and restructurings. Recent or ongoing matters include the representation of Silverstein Properties in connection with the redevelopment of the World Trade Center; Tishman Speyer Properties in connection with the recapitalization of Rockefeller Center, 666 Fifth Avenue and the Chrysler Building, an initial public offering in Australia and acquisitions or restructurings of numerous trophy office buildings and portfolios; a Morgan Stanley/Onex vehicle in the pending acquisition of the Town & Country REIT; Taubman Centers in its successful defense against Simon Property Group's unsolicited offer; Public Storage in its unsolicited offer for Shurgard; Lend Lease in the sale of the bulk of its US businesses; Hometown America in its acquisition of the Chateau REIT; Security Capital Group in various REIT acquisitions and its ultimate sale to General Electric Capital; the Seymour Milstein Family in the restructuring of the Milstein Family portfolio of office, residential, and hotel properties; Reckson Associates Realty in the disposition of its industrial portfolio; Kmart in the sale of numerous retail properties to Home Depot and Sears; National Golf Properties in its sale to a Goldman Sachs/Starwood Capital Group joint venture; Four Seasons Hotels in the sale of its interest in the Pierre Hotel in New York City to Taj Hotels; and the restructuring of Morgans Hotel Group and the company's joint venture with Boyd Gaming to build hotels in Las Vegas. The firm has also been involved in real estate M&A transactions involving AvalonBay Communities, Kimco, New Plan Excel Realty Trust, Boston Properties, and various hotel companies, among others; significant hotel and resort developments for Universal Studios and various financial institutions; and the formation or strategic representation of the Apollo Real Estate Advisors, UBS/PaineWebber, NorthStar and Lazard real estate opportunity funds.

**CLIENTS:** In addition to the matters noted above, Wachtell Lipton currently is representing or has recently represented the following clients in the matters listed below:

**Cross-border Strategic Combinations & Acquisitions:** Household International in its US$14.2 billion transaction with HSBC Holdings; USA Networks in its US$11.7 billion joint venture with Vivendi Universal; Newmont Mining in its US$4.4 billion acquisitions of Normandy Mining of Australia and Franco-Nevada Mining of Canada, and its US$986.0 million equity offering; Jefferson Smurfit Group in its US$3.5 billion acquisition by Madison Dearborn Partners; Publicis Groupe in its US$3.3 billion transaction with Bcom3Group; Wal-Mart in its US$1.9 billion investment in The Seiyu, Ltd., its US$225.0 million acquisition of Supermercados Amigo, its US$300.0 million acquisition from Ahold of Bompreco in Brazil, and its attempted US$5.5 billion acquisition of Safeway plc; VoiceStream Wireless in its US$55.0 billion transaction with Deutsche Telekom; Novartis in its US$8.2 billion acquisition of Hexal AG and Eon Labs and its pending US$4.5 billion acquisition proposal for the shares of Chiron it does not own; Amoco in its US$55.0 billion acquisition by BP; AT&T Wireless Services in the US$9.8 billion investment by NTT DoCoMo; The Furukawa Electric Co. in its US$2.3 billion acquisition of Lucent Technologies' optical fibre business; Pinault-Printemps-Redoute in its strategic investment in and acquisition of majority control of Gucci Group, including the settlement among Pinault-Printemps-Redoute, Gucci Group and LVMH Moët Hennessy Louis Vuitton, as well as in a number of other group acquisitions and dispositions; Monsanto in its US$26.9 billion combination with Pharmacia & Upjohn; Tommy Hilfiger Corporation in its pending US$1.6 billion sale to Apax Partners; Colgate in its US$830.0 million acquisition of GABA Holding; Cole National in its US$401.0 million merger with Luxottica Group; and Cardinal Health in its US$530.0 million acquisition of The Intercare Group.

**Other Strategic Combinations & Acquisitions:** AT&T (AT&T Broadband & Internet Services) in its US$72.0 billion transaction with Comcast and the split-

# WACHTELL, LIPTON, ROSEN & KATZ cont'd

up of the US$9 billion Time Warner Entertainment partnership; Sears in its US$13.0 billion merger with Kmart; Union Planters in its US$14.0 billion merger of equals with Regions Financial; GreenPoint Financial in its US$6.3 billion acquisition by North Fork Bancorp; Warner-Lambert in its US$89.7 billion acquisition by Pfizer; Phillips Petroleum in its US$35.0 billion combination with Conoco and its US$9.4 billion acquisition of Tosco; a consortium of investors led by SUPERVALU in its US$17.4 billion pending acquisition of Albertson's; Western Wireless in its US$6.0 billion sale to ALLTEL; Constellation Brands in its successful US$1.3 billion hostile acquisition of the Robert Mondavi Corporation; Cinergy in its US$9.1 billion merger with Duke Energy; Valero Energy in its US$8.0 billion merger with Premcor; American International Group in its US$24.6 billion acquisition of American General; Wachovia in its US$13.6 billion transaction with First Union; General Mills in its US$10.5 billion acquisition of The Pillsbury Company; IBP in its US$6.0 billion transaction with Tyson Foods; Heller Financial in its US$6.0 billion transaction with General Electric Capital; InterActiveCorp (formerly USA Interactive) in its US$1.85 billion acquisition of Ask Jeeves, its US$1.1 billion acquisition of Hotels.com, its US$3.3 billion acquisition of Expedia, and its US$684.0 million acquisition of Ticketmaster; Kellogg in its US$4.5 billion acquisition of Keebler Foods; Litton Industries in its US$5.2 billion transaction with Northrop Grumman; Cardinal Health in its US$802.0 million acquisition of Syncor International; State Street Bank & Trust in its US$1.5 billion acquisition of Deutsche Bank's worldwide custody business; Maytag in its pending US$2.7 billion sale to Whirlpool; HotJobs.com in its US$436.0 million acquisition by Yahoo!; and Trigon Healthcare in its US$4.0 billion transaction with Anthem.

**Divestitures & Sales:** Sears Roebuck in the US$32.0 billion sale of its credit card portfolio to Citigroup; Altria (formerly Philip Morris Companies) in its US$5.6 billion sale of Miller Brewing to South African Breweries; Hercules in its US$1.8 billion sale of its BetzDearborn water treatment business to General Electric Capital; and Allied Irish Banks in the US$3.1 billion sale of Allfirst Financial to M&T Bank.

**Takeover Defenses:** The Walt Disney Company in its response to Comcast's US$54.1 billion hostile acquisition proposal; Taubman Centers in responding to the US$4.0 billion hostile tender offer by Simon Property Group and Westfield, which was withdrawn; Dana in responding to the US$4.8 billion hostile tender offer by ArvinMeritor, which also was withdrawn; Circuit City Stores in its successful defense to a US$3.3 acquisition proposed by Highfields Capital Management; Payless ShoeSource in its successful defense of a hostile proxy fight by Barington Capital and the Ramius Group; and Hercules in its successful defense of acquisition proposals from and proxy fight by Sam Heyman.

**Private Equity Transactions:** A consortium of leading private equity firms, including Apax, Apollo, Goldman Sachs and Permira, in its US$5.0 billion acquisition of Intelsat; Intelsat in its pending US$6.4 billion merger with PanAmSat Holding; Goldman Sachs in its US$11.3 leveraged buyout (with Bain Capital, the Blackstone Group, Kohlberg Kravis Roberts & Co., Silver Lake Partners and Texas Pacific Group) of SunGuard Data Systems; Apollo Management and Goldman Sachs Capital Partners in their US$4.2 billion acquisition (with the Blackstone Group) of Ondeo Nalco; a consortium, consisting of Apollo, Goldman Sachs and Soros, in its US$1.5 billion acquisition of Cablecom GmbH; the US$3.7 billion sale of Cablecom Holdings to an affiliate of Liberty Media; Hellman & Friedman and Texas Pacific Group in their $2.5 billion acquisition of Linsco/Private Ledger Corp.; and Apollo Management in its US$975.0 million

acquisition of Tyco International's plastics and adhesives business.

**IPOs & Spin-offs:** Lazard in its initial public offering; InterActiveCorp in its US$16.0 billion spin-off of Expedia; FMC Technologies in its initial public offering; AT&T Wireless in its US$10.6 billion IPO (the largest US IPO in history), and subsequent US$26.8 billion exchange offers and spin-off to AT&T shareholders; Lucent in its US$3.0 billion IPO (then the largest US IPO); Piper Jaffray's US$804.0 million spin-off from USBancorp; and Motorola in its US$5.0 billion spin-off of its semiconductor business to shareholders.

**Corporate Governance:** Wachtell Lipton represents the New York Stock Exchange in connection with the Exchange's listing standards and corporate governance initiatives for listed companies. The firm is representing a number of major corporations, such as Citigroup, in connection with corporate governance and related matters, and has advised special committees of boards of directors, including PNC Financial Services Group and National Australia Bank, in connection with various corporate governance investigations and related matters.

# WATSON, FARLEY & WILLIAMS

## THE FIRM

**Chairman:** Frank Dunne
**Managing Partner:** Michael Greville
**New York Office Head:** Alfred Yudes

**Number of partners worldwide:** 62
**Number of other lawyers worldwide:** 211

**FIRM OVERVIEW:** Opened in 1990, the New York office originally serviced ship finance, tax and litigation markets, but quickly expanded to include asset finance and leasing and bank finance. The firm's presence in New York acknowledges the significance of New York and US federal law to international financial and corporate transactions and the significance of New York as a global business centre. The New York office advises on US federal law and New York law. The firm works aggressively to find innovative, quality answers to meet the rapidly changing needs of clients. By using its resource of international lawyers, the firm can deliver global solutions. Particular expertise includes: structured finance, asset finance, real estate, ship finance, shipping, oil and gas; litigation and arbitration; bank finance and regulation; bankruptcy and workouts; and taxation.

## MAIN AREAS OF PRACTICE:

**Structured Finance, Asset Finance & Real Estate:** Watson, Farley & Williams has a substantial cross-border finance practice focused on structured lending transactions, equipment finance and real estate finance using innovative structures. The practice is involved in a wide range of industries, but particularly in energy, real estate, equipment leasing, ship finance, film and television finance, and secured lending. The firm's specialists have extensive experience in the financing of aircraft, vessels, rolling stock, satellites, computerized equipment, power generation facilities, manufacturing equipment and other industrial equipment. This aspect of the practice complements the firm's international reputation in ship finance. In addition, the group advises on sophisticated real estate transactions, including acquisitions, disposals and financings. The Tax Group also provides structural tax advice in real estate transactions in relation to US taxes and tax credits and coordination of US tax planning with the tax rules of other countries.

**Ship Finance, Shipping & Oil & Gas:** Watson, Farley & Williams has one of the largest shipping practices in the world. The firm acts for owners seeking finance and for banks and other financial institutions providing it. The firm advises on all legal aspects of the shipping business in all its offices. Watson, Farley & Williams experience encompasses newbuilding and secondhand ship acquisitions and financings, cross-border leasing, bareboat charters, operating leases and other off-balance sheet financings, credit enhancement structures, syndication and securitization and advice on environmental laws and all major ship registries.

**Litigation & Arbitration:** The Litigation Group handles all varieties of commercial litigation in US and UK courts and before all major international arbitration tribunals. The firm's litigators are admitted to practice before all state and federal courts in New York and have appeared in courts and tribunals throughout the country. Several have been appointed as commercial arbitrators in recognition of their expertise in matters relating to international finance and trade, transportation, insurance, securities and EC law. In New York, the firm advises shipping and energy clients on US environmental laws, including the Oil Pollution Act 1990.

**Bankruptcy & Workouts:** The Bankruptcy and Workout Practice in New York has developed in conjunction with the firm's general asset finance practice with particular expertise in shipping, aviation, offshore drilling and other cross-border transactions. The firm represents various banking interests as secured creditors in Chapter 11 bankruptcy proceedings. The firm represents secured and unsecured creditors in major cases involving US bankruptcy proceedings and has also represented creditors in tandem with its London, Paris and Singapore partners in cross-border administration proceedings.

## HEAD OFFICE

**NEW YORK**
Watson, Farley & Williams (New York) LLP
100 Park Avenue, **New York**, NY 10017
**Tel:** 212 922 2200  **Fax:** 212 922 1512
**Email:** ayudes@wfw.com
**Website:** www.wfw.com

## INTERNATIONAL OFFICES

Watson, Farley & Williams (New York) LLP or an affiliated undertaking also has offices in Paris, Piraeus, Hamburg, Rome, Singapore, Bangkok and London.

**Taxation:** The tax specialists both advise clients directly and work closely with the firm's banking, asset finance, shipping and corporate teams. The firm has particular expertise in the US taxation of international financings and corporate transactions. The firm represents taxpayers in controversies with the Internal Revenue Service and state and local taxing authorities. The firm's international offices and contacts allow us to address the worldwide tax issues that arise in cross-border financings and other international business transactions. Watson, Farley & Williams tax lawyers are frequently involved in developing tax efficient structures for their clients.

## Watson, Farley & Williams

# WEIL, GOTSHAL & MANGES LLP

## THE FIRM

**Chairman:** Stephen J Dannhauser
**Number of partners worldwide:** 307
**Number of other lawyers worldwide:** 912

**FIRM OVERVIEW:** Weil, Gotshal & Manges LLP advises many of the world's most successful organizations on matters as complex and interconnected as the businesses themselves. With more than 1,200 lawyers in 20 offices across the US, Europe and Asia, the firm is a leader in the marketplace for sophisticated, international legal services. An important part of the firm's philosophy is the team approach. Weil, Gotshal & Manges LLP is "one-firm" that provides seamless service no matter the location or area of expertise. The firm's goal is to understand and work toward achieving clients' key objectives, providing their best judgment on close calls and tough issues. In addition to professional excellence, Weil Gotshal is committed to being a model in providing pro bono legal assistance that impacts global and local organizations in the communities it serves.

## MAIN AREAS OF PRACTICE:

**Business Finance & Restructuring:** As one of the largest, most broadly based restructuring/insolvency practices in the world, the firm has been involved in virtually every major Chapter 11 reorganization case in the US and in major international out-of-court debt restructurings. For instance, the firm was at the epicenter of the massive and historic Enron and WorldCom restructurings. Rated as the premier bankruptcy and restructuring practice in the US, the department's services encompass crisis management, domestic and international restructuring, corporate governance and acquisition strategies in distressed situations.

**Corporate:** With more than 500 corporate lawyers across the US, Europe and Asia, Weil Gotshal is regularly involved in the largest and most complex transactions in the world. The global corporate practices offer unrivaled depth and quality across borders and legal service areas. The corporate practices span complex mergers and acquisitions, joint ventures, private equity transactions, securities offerings, financings, debt restructurings, real estate transactions and other commercial transactions. The practice handles an array of general corporate matters, including SEC and regulatory compliance, corporate governance practices and proxy solicitations.

**Litigation/Regulatory:** The Litigation/Regulatory Practice has earned a reputation for representing clients facing complex legal issues - efficiently and successfully. The practice has an impressive record for winning extremely large and difficult cases. With more than 500 litigation and regulatory lawyers worldwide, the firm helps clients solve their toughest problems in any forum, from jury trials and appeals before the US Supreme Court to complex international arbitrations and all forms of alternate dispute resolution. Additionally, the practice handles not only class actions, "mass actions", bankruptcies and other private litigation, but also civil regulatory and criminal proceedings, shareholder derivative actions, fiduciary duty disputes and litigation involving complex corporate transactions. When the stakes are high and a successful result must be obtained, the world's leading corporations regularly turn to the firm's litigators to handle complex commercial litigations and arbitrations of virtually every type. These disputes include breach of contract, fraud, tortious interference, unfair competition and other business tort claims, class actions, and litigations arising under RICO and numerous other statutes. The firm's Patent Litigation Practice, one of the world's most respected, understands, protects and defends the critical products, information and services of businesses operating internationally across a range of industries. The Antitrust/Competition Practice, one of the largest, most diversified and highly respected in the legal and business community, provides integrated global counseling, litigation, regulatory and transactional services to a wide range of industries. The firm handles major antitrust/competition litigation for corporations and other entities, representing both plaintiffs and defendants before US and European courts and regulatory authorities.

**Public Company Advisory Group:** The Public Company Advisory Group advises corporate boards and officers, individuals, specific committees, investors and auditors concerning virtually every area of corporate governance including such matters as periodic or special securities law filings, restatements, and extraordinary transactions involving related parties or corporate control. The attorneys counsel corporate clients at each point of a company's development and cover initial and "follow-on" financing activities, deal-making, public reporting, disclosure obligations, change-of-corporate control scenarios, restructurings, investigations and potential enforcement actions. The group coordinates with the firm's corporate governance, securities law, corporate M&A and litigation specialists to enable clients to see the whole picture and not just the small pieces of a large, complex regulatory environment.

**Tax:** Weil Gotshal's Tax lawyers engage in a sophisticated practice that mirrors the breadth of the firm's transactional practices. The firm's team approach to multidisciplinary representations enables the firm to devise innovative solutions to problems that present a multitude of competing considerations. Weil Gotshal lawyers are well-versed in the tax and employee benefit laws of the US, the UK, France, Germany and Poland. The firm brings combined experience together to deliver coordinated tax advice in all types of regional and cross-border transactions.

## HEAD OFFICE

**NEW YORK**
767 Fifth Avenue, **New York** NY 10153, USA
**Tel:** 212 310 8000   **Fax:** 212 310 8007
**Website:** www.weil.com

## BRANCH OFFICES

**CALIFORNIA**
201 Redwood Shores Parkway, Silicon Valley, **Redwood Shores** CA 94065
**Tel:** 650 802 3000   **Fax:** 650 802 3100

**DELAWARE**
1201 N Market Street, 14th Floor, **Wilmington** DE 19801
**Tel:** 302 656 1410   **Fax:** 302 656 1405

**DISTRICT OF COLUMBIA**
1300 Eye Street NW, Suite 900, **Washington** DC 20005
**Tel:** 202 682 7000   **Fax:** 202 857 0940

**FLORIDA**
1395 Brickell Avenue, Suite 1200, **Miami** FL 33131
**Tel:** 305 577 3100   **Fax:** 305 374 7159

**MASSACHUSETTS**
100 Federal Street, 34th Floor, **Boston** MA 02110
**Tel:** 617 772 8300   **Fax:** 617 772 8333

**RHODE ISLAND**
50 Kennedy Plaza, **Providence**, RI 02903
**Tel:** 401 278 4700   **Fax:** 401 278 4701

**TEXAS**
8911 Capital of Texas Highway, Suite 1350, **Austin** TX 78759
**Tel:** 512 349 1930   **Fax:** 512 527 0798

200 Crescent Court, Suite 300, **Dallas** TX 75201-6950
**Tel:** 214 746 7700   **Fax:** 214 746 7777

700 Louisiana, Suite 1600, **Houston** TX 77002
**Tel:** 713 546 5000   **Fax:** 713 224 9511

## INTERNATIONAL OFFICES

The firm has offices in Brussels, Budapest, Frankfurt, London, Munich, Paris, Prague, Shanghai, Singapore and Warsaw.

# WHITE & CASE LLP

## THE FIRM

**Managing Partner:** Duane D Wall

**Number of US partners:** 188
**Number of other US lawyers:** 590

**FIRM OVERVIEW:** White & Case LLP is a leading global law firm with nearly 2,000 lawyers in 25 countries. Among the first US-based law firms to establish a truly global presence, the firm provides counsel and representation in virtually every area of law that affects cross-border business. The firm's clients value both the breadth of the network and depth of US, English and local law capability in each of its offices and rely on the firm for their complex cross-border commercial and financial transactions and for cross-border arbitration and litigation. Whether in established or emerging markets, the hallmark of White & Case is complete dedication to the business priorities and legal needs of its clients. The firm's approach is based on taking the time to understand its clients' business and responding with effective strategies and solutions, no matter how big the opportunity or formidable the challenge.

**MAIN AREAS OF PRACTICE:** Antitrust, appellate, arbitration, banking, bankruptcy and workouts, capital markets, construction and engineering, corporate, corporate defense and special litigation, employee benefits and compensation, environmental, European Union, global equity-based compensation, insurance, intellectual property, international trade, internet, media and technology, investment funds, labor and employment, leasing and equipment finance, legislative/law reform, litigation, mergers and acquisitions, private clients, private equity, privatization, project and infrastructure finance, public finance, public international law, real estate, securities, securitization, sovereign, tax, telecommunications, trade and commodity finance.

**CLIENTS:** The firm's clients are public and privately held businesses and financial institutions involved in sophisticated transactions and complex dispute resolution proceedings. The firm works with the world's most established and respected companies, including 75 percent of the Global *Fortune* 100 and 25 percent of the Fortune 500, as well as with start-up visionaries, governments and state-owned entities. With new technologies, globalization, consolidation and other forces continuously changing how business gets done, the firm helps its clients evaluate the risks and rewards of ventures designed to advance their interests.

**INTERNATIONAL WORK:** The firm's ability to handle complex, cross-border matters truly distinguishes White & Case from other firms – even those who call themselves global. Located in the world's major business and financial centers and key emerging markets, the firm's 2000 lawyers are adept at working within myriad legal systems, distinguishing subtle, cultural nuances and identifying local concerns while simultaneously managing the larger multi-jurisdictional issues. As a result, White & Case is better able to detect and address the countless factors, both common and unusual, that make or break deals or win or lose cases.

## US OFFICES

**NEW YORK**
1155 Avenue of the Americas, **New York**, NY 10036-2787
**Tel:** 212 819 8200   **Fax:** 212 354 8113
**Website:** www.whitecase.com

**CALIFORNIA**
633 West Fifth Street, Suite 1900, **Los Angeles**, CA 90071-2007
**Tel:** 213 620 7700   **Fax**: 213 687 0758

Five Palo Alto Square, 10th Floor, 3000 El Camino Real,
**Palo Alto**, CA 94306
**Tel:** 650 213 0300   **Fax:** 650 213 8158

**DISTRICT OF COLUMBIA**
701 Thirteenth Street, NW, **Washington**, DC 20005-3807
**Tel:** 202 626 3600   **Fax:** 202 639 9355

**FLORIDA**
Wachovia Financial Center, Suite 4900, 200 South Biscayne Boulevard,
**Miami**, FL 33131-2352
**Tel:** 305 371 2700   **Fax:** 305 358 5744

## INTERNATIONAL OFFICES

The firm also has offices in Almaty, Ankara, Bangkok, Beijing, Berlin, Bratislava, Brussels, Budapest, Dresden, Düsseldorf, Frankfurt, Hamburg, Helsinki, Ho Chi Minh City, Hong Kong, Istanbul, Johannesburg, London, Mexico City, Milan, Moscow, Mumbai, Munich, Paris, Prague, Riyadh, São Paulo, Shanghai, Singapore, Stockholm, Tokyo and Warsaw.

## CONTACTS

| | |
|---|---|
| **Los Angeles** | Richard Smith Jr |
| **Miami** | Victor Alvarez |
| **New York** | David Koschik |
| **Palo Alto** | William Coats |
| **Washington DC** | Victor DeSantis |

WHITE & CASE

# WILLKIE FARR & GALLAGHER LLP

## THE FIRM

**Chairman, Executive Committee:** Jack H Nusbaum
**Co-Chairman:** Myron Trepper, Richard DeScherer

**Partners in US offices:** 117
**Number of other lawyers in US:** 349

**FIRM OVERVIEW:** Established in 1888, Willkie Farr & Gallagher LLP is a full-service international law firm renowned for its expertise in corporate and securities law, litigation, business reorganization and restructuring, real estate, intellectual property, and a number of specialized fields of law, including compliance and enforcement, environmental, executive compensation and employee benefits, government relations, insurance, international trade, investment management, private clients, tax, and telecommunications. With approximately 600 attorneys in offices in New York, Washington, Paris, London, Milan, Rome, Frankfurt, and Brussels, the firm's clients rely on it for its creativity and skill in structuring and implementing complex transactions and providing counsel on critical business and legal issues in virtually all areas of business law.

## MAIN AREAS OF PRACTICE:

**Corporate & Financial Services:** The firm's Corporate and Financial Services Department offers corporations and financial institutions broad expertise in all types of commercial transactions. Its extensive Corporate Practice includes mergers and acquisitions, private equity/venture capital, investment management, public finance, insurance, broker-dealer regulation, private placement and banking, institutional lending, structured finance, and capital markets. The firm is internationally renowned for handling complex, cross-border M&A transactions, and for advising on the complete spectrum of corporate governance and accounting irregularities matters. Additionally, Willkie has built one of the top investment management teams in country.

**Litigation:** The firm represents clients in every type of forum, including federal and state court actions, government regulatory and administrative proceedings, and arbitration, mediation and other alternative dispute resolution proceedings. It is well known for its expertise in all of the major areas of business and corporate litigation, including securities and transactional litigation, class-action lawsuits, battles for corporate control, antitrust issues, white-collar crime and compliance and enforcement, First Amendment and media litigation, intellectual property, accountants' and other professional liability actions, insurance brokerage and coverage actions, environmental litigation, and employee benefits and employment litigation.

**Business Reorganization & Restructuring:** The firm represents debtors, lenders, secured and unsecured creditors, creditors' and shareholders' committees, shareholders, governmental units, investment advisors, investors, landlords and tenants, and entities seeking investment opportunities in Chapter 11 cases. The firm's practice also includes deal structuring with respect to potential insolvency and bankruptcy issues.

**Real Estate:** The firm is regularly involved in major domestic and international real estate transactions, including REIT mergers and debt and equity offerings, pooled and stand-alone securitized financings, development projects, commercial leases, sales and acquisitions, construction and permanent financings, restructurings, joint ventures, private placements of domestic and foreign real estate funds, and real estate aspects of corporate and bankruptcy transactions.

**Intellectual Property:** The firm represents foreign and domestic clients in litigation, transactions, counseling, prosecution, licensing and lobbying involving patents, trademarks, copyrights, domain names and trade secrets, spanning most industries and technologies.

**CLIENTS:** The firm represents a roster of significant corporate clients on a wide variety of legal matters across many borders.

## HEAD OFFICE

**NEW YORK**
787 Seventh Ave, **New York**, NY 10019-6099
**Tel:** 212 728 8000   Fax: 212 728 8111
**Website:** www.willkie.com

## BRANCH OFFICES

**DISTRICT OF COLUMBIA**
1875 K Street, NW, **Washington** DC 20006-1238
**Tel:** 202 303 1000   **Fax:** 202 303 2000

## INTERNATIONAL OFFICES

The firm also has offices in Paris, London, Milan, Rome, Frankfurt and Brussels.

## CONTACTS

| | |
|---|---|
| **Business Reorganization & Restructuring** | Myron Trepper |
| **Corporate & Financial Services** | Jack H Nusbaum |
| **Environmental** | E Donald Elliott |
| **Executive Compensation & Employee Benefits** | Stephen T Lindo |
| **Government Relations** | Russell L Smith |
| **Insurance** | John S D'Alimonte |
| | Mitchell J Auslander |
| **Intellectual Property** | John DiMatteo |
| **International Trade** | William H Barringer |
| **Litigation** | Richard L Posen |
| **Real Estate** | Eugene A Pinover |
| **Tax** | Richard L Reinhold |
| **Telecommunications** | Philip L Verveer |
| | Bruce R Kraus |
| **Private Clients Group** | David J McCabe |

## INTERNATIONAL WORK:

**M&A:** The firm regularly represents clients that buy and sell companies in complex cross-border transactions. It also represents a large number of issuers and underwriters in relation to debt and equity offerings in the United States.

**Private Equity:** The firm has extensive experience in virtually every type of private equity transaction ranging from cross-border multibillion-dollar leveraged buyouts to early stage venture capital financings. The firm represents private equity investors, issuers and financial advisors in all aspects of domestic and international private equity transactions. Willkie attorneys routinely work on sophisticated transactions such as leveraged buyouts, management buyouts, spin-offs, venture capital financings, going-private transactions, recapitalizations and dispositions.

**Capital Markets:** The firm regularly advises clients on initial public offerings, including those with dual listings on European and US stock exchanges and offerings that combine one or more European listings with a Rule 144A private placement in the US. The firm represents clients in global equity offerings, private placements of securities, and debt offerings (including high-yield debt offerings and medium-term note programs).

**International Trade:** The firm advises many foreign manufacturers and foreign governmental bodies on issues arising from regulations governing the importation of goods from the United States.

**Business Reorganization & Restructuring:** The firm has extensive experience in business reorganization and restructuring, advising companies across various industries as well as investment funds.

**Telecommunications:** The firm has significant expertise advising on regulatory issues and commercial transactions involving all types of telecommunications, information technology and outsourcing, e-commerce, media and entertainment matters.

## WILLKIE FARR & GALLAGHER LLP

**CONTENTS:** Antitrust p.1568;  Banking & Finance p.1569;  Bankruptcy/Restructuring p.1570; Corporate/M&A p.1571; Employment p.1573;  Environment p.1574;  Litigation p.1577;  Real Estate p.1579; Individuals' Profiles p.1580;  Firm' Profiles p.1587.

## How lawyers are ranked

Every year we carry out thousands of in-depth interviews with clients and lawyers in order to assess the reputations and expertise of business lawyers across the USA. Chambers rankings and editorial are referred to extensively by General Counsel and other purchasers of legal services who look to our recommendations when choosing their lawyers.

# ANTITRUST

| Antitrust |
| --- |
| **Leading Firms** |
| [1] BROOKS, PIERCE, MCLENDON, *Greensboro* |
| ELLIS & WINTERS LLP *Cary* |
| ROBINSON, BRADSHAW & HINSON PA *Charlotte* |
| WOMBLE CARLYLE SANDRIDGE *Winston-Salem* |

| Leading Individuals |
| --- |
| [1] BOWMAN Everett *Robinson, Bradshaw & Hinson* |
| COPENHAVER W Andrew *Womble Carlyle Sandridge* |
| ENNS Rodrick *Enns & Archer LLP* |
| HOROSCHAK Mark *Womble Carlyle Sandridge* |
| KENYON Douglas *Hunton & Williams LLP* |
| MERRITT Mark *Robinson, Bradshaw & Hinson* |
| MURCHISON John *Kennedy Covington Lobdell* |
| OLEYNIK Jeffrey *Brooks, Pierce, McLendon* |
| SAWCHAK Matthew *Ellis & Winters LLP* |

## Band 1

### Brooks, Pierce, McLendon, Humphrey & Leonard LLP

**The Firm:** This "*respectable, highly regarded*" team comprises ten lawyers who offer advisory counsel as well as litigation expertise. The group has extensive experience counseling companies on compliance with antitrust regulations and also provides a skilled bench of litigators who have acted before both state and federal courts. It has long represented trade associations and automobile dealerships throughout the state, and further draws on its outstanding Raleigh-based media practice to advise sundry ABC affiliates on communications and media-related antitrust matters. Recent highlights include acting for national tobacco companies against tobacco growers in price-fixing disputes. The team has also undertaken extensive advisory work in the healthcare sector.

**The Lawyers:** **Jeffrey Oleynik** is "*one of the best attorneys I've ever seen*," according to one interviewee. He maintains a wide antitrust practice in addition to his corporate and bankruptcy litigation work, and most recently advised on a number of class actions in the textile industry. These cases alleged price-fixing and unfair business practices.

**Clients/Work Highlights:** Clients include national corporations, manufacturing companies, automo-bile dealers, media companies and healthcare providers.

### Ellis & Winters LLP

**The Firm:** This compact litigation boutique is highly regarded across the market for its antitrust work. One client commented: "*They are outstanding lawyers and our first choice for representation.*" A group of five focuses on a wide range of antitrust work at federal and state level, both in an advisory and litigious capacity. A busy unit, the team acts before business tribunals as well as the courts and has a foot firmly in the textile industry. Recently, it handled two multijurisdictional matters concerning cotton yarn manufacturing disputes.

**The Lawyers:** Market sources sang the praises of **Matthew Sawchak**, describing him as "*one of the leading individuals for antitrust.*" In addition to litigating on a wide variety of unfair trade practices, he also maintains a commercial litigation practice, representing civil and corporate clients throughout the region.

**Clients/Work Highlights:** The firm represents corporate and industrial clients based in the Southeast.

### Robinson, Bradshaw & Hinson PA

**The Firm:** Clients and peers enthusiastically endorsed this team of "*superb attorneys capable of handling every shade of antitrust work.*" A five-strong group focuses on civil antitrust and business compliance for a wide range of corporate clients. Experienced and well regarded, these litigators have also worked as government counsel on complex antitrust matters and appeared as general counsel to a slew of prominent healthcare organizations. Practice highlights of late include acting as counsel to the federal government in a matter involving an international animal vitamin supplement company. The team is also currently fielding a series of multidistrict claims made by textile companies relating to the manufacture of polyester.

**The Lawyers:** **Everett Bowman** is "*a first-choice, downright excellent attorney,*" according to clients, many of whom commended him for his advisory work in the field. Colleague **Mark Merritt** currently chairs the antitrust section of the North Carolina Bar Association and "*has a brilliant mind.*" He recently represented the Southeastern Conference in a case alleging antitrust law violation brought by a former University of Kentucky football coach.

**Clients/Work Highlights:** CommScope; Mission Hospitals; Springs Industries; Southeastern Conference and other regional and national companies.

### Womble Carlyle Sandridge & Rice, PLLC

See firm details p.1589

**The Firm:** This outfit's antitrust advisory group is supplemented by attorneys from the firm's litigation department to produce a team of 17 antitrust specialists. As a group, it advises on the general range of antitrust matters while also attending to niche areas such as IP-related work. It is particularly renowned for its expertise in healthcare antitrust matters and represents companies and healthcare providers across the country. Recent highlights include the representation of RJ Reynolds in a major class action case that was successfully resolved in appeal to the Fourth Circuit Court of Appeals. The team has also acted for a national producer of office printers in multifaceted patent litigation against competitors in the market.

**The Lawyers:** **Andrew Copenhaver** (see p.1581) is "*a fine attorney,*" according to market sources. He advises on antitrust and unfair trading matters while acting for clients in general commercial matters. **Mark Horoschak** (see p.1583) heads up the team's niche healthcare group and represents national companies in joint ventures and distributional matters.

**Clients/Work Highlights:** The client base includes regional and national corporations, tobacco companies, manufacturers and healthcare providers.

### Other Notable Practitioners

**Rodrick Enns** of Enns & Archer LLP is "*accessible, knowledgeable and thorough.*" He has recently been involved with motor fuel cost-pricing issues and antitrust matters in the IP industry. Interviewees described **Douglas Kenyon** (see p.1584) of Hunton & Williams LLP as "*extremely conversant with antitrust law.*" His practice portfolio includes representation of national and multinational corporations in complex antitrust matters. **John Murchison** of Kennedy Covington Lobdell & Hickman LLP is recommended for his counsel on antitrust compliance and regulation.

# BANKING & FINANCE

## Banking & Finance
### Leading Firms

1. **MOORE & VAN ALLEN, PLLC** *Charlotte*
2. **HELMS MULLISS & WICKER PLLC** *Charlotte*
   **KENNEDY COVINGTON LOBDELL** *Charlotte*
   **ROBINSON, BRADSHAW & HINSON PA** *Charlotte*
   **WOMBLE CARLYLE SANDRIDGE** *Winston-Salem*
3. **PARKER, POE, ADAMS & BERNSTEIN LLP** *Charlotte*

### Leading Individuals

1. **HAZLETT Richard** *Helms Mulliss & Wicker PLLC*
   **HOVIS James** *Moore & Van Allen, PLLC*
   **KUPEC Christopher** *Mayer, Brown, Rowe & Maw*
2. **BUCK Peter** *Robinson, Bradshaw & Hinson*
   **FULLER III William** *Moore & Van Allen, PLLC*
   **GREENE Kenneth** *Carruthers & Roth PA*
   **LUCAS Edwin** *Robinson, Bradshaw & Hinson*
   **MOSER Kenneth** *Womble Carlyle Sandridge*
3. **CALDWELL Stokely** *Robinson, Bradshaw & Hinson*
   **CAMPBELL JR Boyd** *Helms Mulliss & Wicker PLLC*
   **DUNN JR J Thomas** *Moore & Van Allen, PLLC*
   **KLUTTZ Joseph** *Kennedy Covington Lobdell*
   **LAMPE Donald** *Womble Carlyle Sandridge*
   **LASSITER Donnell** *Kennedy Covington Lobdell*
   **LEON Christopher** *Womble Carlyle Sandridge*
   **ROBERTSON Allen** *Robinson, Bradshaw & Hinson*
   **SINGER Robert** *Brooks, Pierce, McLendon*
   **UBELL Donald** *Parker, Poe, Adams & Bernstein*
   **WINSLOW III Edward** *Brooks, Pierce, McLendon*

## Band 1

### Moore & Van Allen, PLLC

**The Firm:** Market sources agreed that this "*gold-standard firm*" has maintained its reputation as "*the most outstanding group in the state,*" despite some recent significant departures from its financial team. The 60-strong group retains its strong lending practice and continues to win praise for its representation of major state-based financial institutions which it advises on venture capital and private equity investments, as well as various debt transactions. The team also offers a full and sophisticated finance service for corporate clients in all sectors. It has particular expertise in leveraged finance and credit matters, securitizations and borrowing-related transactions. The firm continues its ongoing relationship with Bank of America and Wachovia and also acts for other national financial institutions.

**The Lawyers:** **James Hovis** maintains his reputation as "*the dean of banking law*" and acts as head of the finance group, as well as managing partner of the firm. He primarily advises leading financial institutions and is noted for being "*savvy when it comes to securities.*" **William Fuller** is highly recommended as an expert in complex lending transactions and has acted for large financial institutions, as well as for corporate clients, in acquisition financings and debt

matters. **Thomas Dunn** was described as a "*smart and resourceful attorney.*" He acts as Wachovia's ongoing counsel and specializes in capital markets, commercial lending and insolvency matters.

**Clients/Work Highlights:** Bank of America and Wachovia are the firm's major clients but it also acts for a host of other regional and national financial institutions and investors.

## Band 2

### Helms Mulliss & Wicker PLLC

**The Firm:** This team of 25 "*first-rate attorneys*" continues to draw plaudits as a "*strong and responsive financial unit*" with a particular focus on debt and public bond finance. Among the many strings to its bow, it excels at capital expenditure financings for a range of private and public entities, including colleges and hospitals. It has arranged significant syndicated loan transactions for governmental bodies and acts as bond counsel for the State of North Carolina. Other practice strengths include tax-exempt financing, as well as a nationwide syndicated loan practice.

**The Lawyers:** Especially skilled at tax bond matters, **Richard Hazlett** impressed clients and peers alike as a "*superb transactional lawyer.*" Well acquainted with every aspect of corporate lending, he has acted in aggregate financings of $230 million for educational and healthcare providers across the Southeast. Colleague **Boyd Campbell** has an enviable corporate securities practice but is also acclaimed for his debt financing and his work on a significant tranche of euro MTN programs.

**Clients/Work Highlights:** Bank of America; BB&T; SunTrust; First Charter Bank; Wachovia; Merrill Lynch and the State of North Carolina.

### Kennedy Covington Lobdell & Hickman LLP

**The Firm:** Market sources were impressed with the depth and range of this team, noting that "*these guys are really strong in syndicated finance and private equity.*" The group of 22 attorneys focuses on lender and borrower representation in all manner of secured and unsecured transactions, and also has significant cross-border financing and multicurrency experience. Other areas of interest include investment and merchant banking, financial institution regulatory work and structured finance. The team also advises Bank of America and Wachovia among other major national financial institutions.

**The Lawyers:** **Donnell Lassiter** continues to draw praise as a "*superb, on-the-ball attorney*" who is an especially skilled adviser on sophisticated credit transactions for single institution and multibank clients. Department chair **Joseph Kluttz** is recognized for his financial restructuring expertise. Highlights of his practice include advising banking institutions in the restructuring and insolvency management of large credit transactions.

**Clients/Work Highlights:** Bank of America; Wachovia; Wells Fargo; Capital Investment Companies and Academy Funds.

### Robinson, Bradshaw & Hinson PA

**The Firm:** This team won praise for its "*wonderful all-around expertise*" and "*thorough versatility*" in a wide variety of deals. The banking group works within the corporate umbrella of the firm, an arrangement which one client described as providing "*excellent healthy interaction between attorneys and areas of expertise.*" Twenty-five attorneys handle complex financial transactions, representing both lenders and borrowers in senior and mezzanine loan deals, asset securitizations, acquisition financing, loan workouts and restructurings. Recently, the firm acted on behalf of Allied Capital in a variety of M&A transactions and represented Wachovia Securities in a series of credit facilities totaling $1.75 billion.

**The Lawyers:** **Peter Buck** was praised by banking and corporate clients alike as "*one of the most skilled and well-regarded financial attorneys in the state.*" Highly rated for his investment banking expertise, he works alongside **Stokely Caldwell**, who impressed interviewees with his expertise in syndicated leasings and debt financings. His practice further includes a specialization in senior and mezzanine loan transactions for national financial institutions, and he represents NASCAR teams on an ongoing basis. **Edwin Lucas** is rated as a public finance and bonds specialist. He recently acted as bond counsel for a major power company in multiple waste recovery transactions. **Allen Robertson** co-heads the public finance team of the group and focuses on healthcare financings.

**Clients/Work Highlights:** Allied Capital; BB&T; Wachovia; Bank of America; Mecklenburg County and State of North Carolina.

### Womble Carlyle Sandridge & Rice, PLLC

See firm details p.1589

**The Firm:** Clients felt that "*these attorneys are well versed in the field, reliable, timely and just all-around excellent.*" They are particularly highly rated for their expertise in capital markets, lending and tax work but have recently broadened their caseload to include environmental, IP and benefits work. The team of 35 attorneys has also expanded its representation of leading financial institutions in the state and now boasts a truly excellent client list that includes Wachovia, Bank of America and Regions Bank. The group also offers a broad public finance and real estate finance practice, advising on a wide variety of securities and lending matters. Practice highlights include acting for Wachovia in the recapitalization of an international parent company. The firm has further advised on the development of Piedmont Triad Research Park and acted as general counsel to the Piedmont Federal Savings and Loan Association.

**The Lawyers:** According to market sources, **Christopher Leon** (see p.1584) is "*the guy to call for* large and complex loan agreements." His practice area focuses on corporate finance and he has advised on a number of complex acquisitions by private entities in the manufacturing, retail and consumer service industries. He recently acted for National Textiles in the sale of a 90% equity interest to Sara Lee. **Ken Moser** (see p.1585) was praised as a real estate finance expert with "*decades of experience*" advising financial institutions and corporations. Highlights of his practice include representing a furniture showroom facility in a $90 million development sale. **Donald Lampe** (see p.1584) is highly recommended for his capital markets expertise. He has advised clients on compliance regulations, product development and complex financial transactions.

**Clients/Work Highlights:** Wachovia; Bank of America; Regions Bank; BB&T and Assemblies of God Financial Services.

## Band 3

### Parker, Poe, Adams & Bernstein LLP

**The Firm:** Deemed "*a quality practice*" by clients and peers, Parker Poe's banking work is the preserve of ten impressive attorneys. These form into a team with an excellent breadth of representation across the lending, borrowing and investment markets. Attorneys have advised foreign and domestic entities in real estate, securitized and structured financings, and also enjoy a solid reputation in the public finance sector. In this last respect, the firm has traditionally done well and to this day continues to prosper, representing an aggregate of 36 municipal bodies in a range of sophisticated public finance transactions. Members of the team have additionally acted as bond counsel and underwriter's counsel in jurisdictions all over the Southeast.

**The Lawyers:** **Donald Ubell** was hailed as "*one of the premier bond counsels in the state.*" He heads the public finance practice group and has extensive experience in general governmental, higher education and healthcare finance.

**Clients/Work Highlights:** The client base includes regional banks and lenders as well as municipalities across the state.

## Other Notable Practitioners

**Christopher Kupec** (see p.1584) moved to Mayer, Brown, Rowe & Maw LLP from Moore & Van Allen this year and continues to be widely praised as "*a smart, excellent and sophisticated lawyer.*" **Kenneth Greene** at Carruthers & Roth PA drew plaudits as "*a great finance attorney*" who acts primarily as counsel for lending institutions and banks. He also practices bankruptcy and insolvency law. Highlights of his practice include assisting on a recent $100 million syndicated asset-based loan to a domestic textile company. The "*outstanding*" **Robert Singer** of Brooks, Pierce, McLendon, Humphrey & Leonard LLP was noted for his expertise in M&A activity relating to financial institutions. He has recently advised on the establishment of a number of new banks and is also very active in financial regulatory matters. **Edward Winslow** is managing partner of Brooks Pierce and is celebrated for his work in community banking. His team represents the North Carolina Bankers Association, among other financial institutions, investors and public and private clients.

# BANKRUPTCY/RESTRUCTURING

### Bankruptcy/Restructuring
#### Leading Firms

| | |
|---|---|
| 1 | **HELMS MULLISS & WICKER PLLC** *Charlotte* |
| | **KENNEDY COVINGTON LOBDELL** *Charlotte* |
| | **MOORE & VAN ALLEN, PLLC** *Charlotte* |
| | **ROBINSON, BRADSHAW & HINSON PA** *Charlotte* |

#### Leading Individuals

| | |
|---|---|
| 1 | **BOOE Mike** *Kennedy Covington Lobdell* |
| | **EADES David** *Moore & Van Allen, PLLC* |
| | **KLUTTZ Joseph** *Kennedy Covington Lobdell* |
| | **PRYOR Robert** *Helms Mulliss & Wicker PLLC* |
| | **SCHILLI David** *Robinson, Bradshaw & Hinson PA* |
| | **VAUGHN Scott** *Helms Mulliss & Wicker PLLC* |

## Band 1

### Helms Mulliss & Wicker PLLC

**The Firm:** This "*fundamentally sound*" team of nine lawyers impressed commentators with its "*execution-oriented*" approach and strong banking background. "*They're responsive, knowledgeable and they understand my business propositions,*" according to one interviewee. The group advises on all aspects of bankruptcy and debt-related law, including workouts, debt restructuring, insolvency and syndicated loan proceedings. It is particularly active at present in the distressed debt market, as well as in real estate defaults. The team recently acted for various Miami and New York-based money centers in loan sourcing matters.

**The Lawyers:** **Robert Pryor** won praise from clients and peers as "*a superb and very experienced attorney,*" whose decades of expertise particularly evident in matters of commercial bankruptcy law. He is also a highly skilled litigator and has represented clients in bankruptcy courts throughout the Southeast. "*First-choice bankruptcy lawyer*" **Scott Vaughn** focuses on the representation of financial institutions in workouts and refinancings. His recent highlights include the representation of various institutions regarding loans to significant food franchises along the eastern seaboard.

**Clients/Work Highlights:** Bank of America; BB&T; Citibank; First Charter; Wachovia and SunTrust.

### Kennedy Covington Lobdell & Hickman LLP

**The Firm:** The team comprises 12 highly regarded attorneys, whose depth and breadth of expertise is boosted by close links with the banking and commercial litigation teams within the firm. Interviewees drew attention to the group's experience with large and sophisticated proceedings: "*These guys offer a really extensive practice and are the ones we always call for volatile, large-dollar matters.*" Significant areas of representation include restructuring large senior credit facilities, the negotiation of workout and Chapter 11 plans, and all aspects of bankruptcy litigation. The firm's attorneys have acted in bankruptcy courts throughout the region.

**The Lawyers:** Certified bankruptcy specialist **Mike Booe** enjoys a stellar reputation among clients and

peers as an "*experienced and knowledgeable attorney*" who focuses on single lender and syndicated financing transcations. He heads the financial restructuring practice group and is a frequent speaker on bankruptcy and insolvency proceedings for the North Carolina Bar Association. **Joseph Kluttz** is chair of the financial services department and has represented creditors and debtors in large banking restructuring transactions. He is particularly experienced at Chapter 11 proceedings and has recently represented a debtor in one of the largest trucking bankruptcies in the country.

**Clients/Work Highlights:** Clients include banks, lending institutions and corporate entities.

### Moore & Van Allen, PLLC

**The Firm:** Clients strongly endorsed this "*sophisticated, finance-savvy team*" of 16 attorneys as one of the premier bankruptcy groups in the state. Although it maintains a strong financial focus, it also offers an extensive range of expertise as debtor's counsel in corporate bankruptcies and has acted for syndicated lending groups in distressed corporate credit proceedings. Recent highlights include advising a lending agent in negotiations for a stability loan for a national airline. The team has also won a $130 million solvency arbitration and clearance of $500 million of debt in a consensual agreement between a national timber company and the lender.

**The Lawyers:** Group head **David Eades** drew plaudits across the market for his "*confidence and professionalism.*" Clients felt that he "*offers brains and guts to get deals done and is an excellent and very pleasant *adversary.*" Eades most frequently acts for financial institutions in bankruptcy matters and recently advised on workouts for both a national theater chain and a western grocery store chain.

### Robinson, Bradshaw & Hinson PA

**The Firm:** "*These guys take the ball and run with it,*" according to one client. Six attorneys band together to form a tight-knit unit that is "*always absolutely engaged: they take the case to heart and really care*

*about the client's business values.*" Drawing on the corporate and real estate strengths of the firm, the group offers a diverse practice that represents both debtors and creditors. Areas of particular expertise include asbestos-related bankruptcies as well as sophisticated Chapter 11 representations in judicial districts throughout the region.

**The Lawyers: David Schilli** impressed clients with "*his responsiveness, terrific knowledge of the subject matter and excellent understanding of business.*" Head

of the bankruptcy group, Schilli most recently represented a national insurance company in a restructuring matter relating to automobile insurance policies. He also regularly advises the corporate team within the firm.

**Clients/Work Highlights:** Assurant Solutions; Caraustar; CommScope; LaSalle Bank; ORIX Capital Markets and Comporium.

# CORPORATE/M&A

| Corporate/M&A |
|---|
| **Leading Firms** |
| [1] ROBINSON, BRADSHAW & HINSON PA *Charlotte* |
| [2] BROOKS, PIERCE, MCLENDON *Greensboro* |
| HELMS MULLISS & WICKER PLLC *Charlotte* |
| KENNEDY COVINGTON LOBDELL *Charlotte* |
| MOORE & VAN ALLEN, PLLC *Charlotte* |
| SMITH, ANDERSON, BLOUNT *Raleigh* |
| [3] HUNTON & WILLIAMS *Charlotte* |
| KILPATRICK STOCKTON LLP *Charlotte* |
| WOMBLE CARLYLE SANDRIDGE *Winston-Salem* |

| Leading Individuals |
|---|
| **Senior Statesmen** |
| DAGENHART Larry *Helms Mulliss & Wicker PLLC* |
| HINSON Robin *Robinson, Bradshaw & Hinson* |
| ROBINSON Russell *Robinson, Bradshaw & Hinson* |
| WALKER Clarence *Kennedy Covington Lobdell* |
| [1] BUCK Peter *Robinson, Bradshaw & Hinson* |
| JERNIGAN John *Smith, Anderson, Blount, Dorsett* |
| PRUDEN Norfleet *Kennedy Covington Lobdell* |
| [2] BALDWIN Garza *Womble Carlyle Sandridge* |
| CAMPBELL Boyd *Helms Mulliss & Wicker PLLC* |
| KIRKLAND Byron *Smith, Anderson, Blount* |
| ROACH Gerald *Smith, Anderson, Blount* |
| [3] CAPEL Christopher *Smith, Anderson, Blount, Dorsett* |
| HAZLETT Richard *Helms Mulliss & Wicker PLLC* |
| HOPE Stephen *Moore & Van Allen, PLLC* |
| LYNCH Stephen *Robinson, Bradshaw & Hinson* |
| SINGER Robert *Brooks, Pierce, McLendon* |
| WINSLOW Edward *Brooks, Pierce, McLendon* |
| WREN Elizabeth *Kilpatrick Stockton LLP* |

## Band 1

### Robinson, Bradshaw & Hinson PA

**The Firm:** Clients and peers alike praised this longtime market leader as the "*preeminent firm for sophisticated corporate matters.*" Blessed with "*the best client base in the market*" and "*an excellent understanding of business objectives,*" the group "*combines outstanding legal minds with good heads for business and works tirelessly to get the deal done.*" The team's expertise takes in Sarbanes-Oxley Act compliance advice, domestic and international M&A, leveraged finance

and securities work among others. Interviewees were particularly impressed with the "*Renaissance-like*" flexibility and client focus of the group: "*No matter how senior the partner, the sole priority is the client's objective. They always make you feel as if they were waiting for your call.*"

**The Lawyers:** The inimitable **Russell Robinson** was lauded as "*the standard-bearer of corporate law in the state.*" A man of "*tremendous knowledge and wisdom,*" his treatise 'Robinson On North Carolina Corporation Law' continues to be the authoritative text in the field. Interviewees described **Peter Buck** as "*a brilliant client's lawyer,*" and he garnered particular praise for the quality and flexibility of his joint corporate and banking practice. He continues to act for Duke Energy and other corporate boards in an independent advisory capacity and recently closed a multifaceted merger and division deal for Venturi Staffing Partners. **Robin Hinson** also enjoys an outstanding reputation as a corporate and banking multitasker. He is currently engaged in a $300 million corporate reorganization of a New York company. **Stephen Lynch** won particular plaudits for his securities expertise but focuses primarily on M&A and compliance work, as well as some Chapter 11 proceedings.

**Clients/Work Highlights:** The Cato Corporation; Duke Energy; EnPro Industries; Goodrich; Martin Marietta Materials; National Gypsum; SPX and Wachovia.

## Band 2

### Brooks, Pierce, McLendon, Humphrey & Leonard LLP

**The Firm:** This group of "*outstanding attorneys*" is headquartered in Greensboro and impresses with its "*team approach, gentlemanly attitude and great counsel.*" The team offers a full range of corporate services, proving particularly adept at corporate governance and venture capital financings. Recent highlights include the representation of Unilin in the sale of its US holdings to Mohawk Industries, a deal estimated to be worth €2.2 billion. The firm also has an excellent media and communications corporate group based in Raleigh, which has acted for Hearst-Argyle Television and other national media corporations.

**The Lawyers: Robert Singer** was singled out for his

securities and advisory work for a variety of publicly traded corporations. **Edward Winslow** is a managing partner who displays particular acumen in financial and banking matters. Interviewees stated that he was "*an absolute professional and justifiably well regarded.*"

### Helms Mulliss & Wicker PLLC

**The Firm:** This "*all-star team*" was hailed across the market as one of the preeminent corporate groups in the state. "*I really respect their opinion and enjoy working with them,*" was one interviewee's verdict. The team of 25 lawyers handles a varied regimen of work. Securities law proves a particularly rich seam of work, with a large volume of matters being undertaken for Bank of America and other financial institutions. However, the group shines in other areas as well, with its corporate governance expertise and general transactional work across a host of national and international industries being justly celebrated. Recently, the firm acted in a series of arbitrations involving the consequences to the tobacco industry of some $400 million worth of payments made to tobacco growers.

**The Lawyers: Larry Dagenhart** is "*one of the figureheads of North Carolina corporate law.*" He is particularly active in corporate governance and as a fount of knowledge is regularly consulted by other attorneys at the firm. **Boyd Campbell** won praise for his "*first-rate M&A knowledge*" and efforts in the financial regulatory field. He is also an experienced securities lawyer for a variety of public and private companies. **Richard Hazlett** maintains both a banking and a corporate practice and earned plaudits as a "*responsive, quality attorney.*" In the past year, he has worked on several large transactions with an aggregate value of some $400 million.

**Clients/Work Highlights:** Bank of America; Compass Group; Ruddick Corporation and BB&T.

### Kennedy Covington Lobdell & Hickman LLP

**The Firm:** This highly rated and well-established group of some 30 "*excellent and very bright*" attorneys impressed clients with the breadth and depth of their "*well-balanced practice.*" Interviewees, many of whom were particularly effusive about the group's securities capability, remarked that "*the large size of the group means that they can be both general and* *specialized at the same time."* Other practice areas include corporate formation, company reorganizations and general M&A advisory work. Recent highlights include extensive work in the formation and restructuring of several corporations across the Southeast, as well as ongoing advisory work to a wide range of business entities.

**The Lawyers: Norfleet Pruden** was esteemed among peers and clients as an *"outstanding transactional lawyer – the top of the lot."* He won particular praise for his expertise in the private equity sector. Pruden recently represented a national Internet company in a $700 million acquisition and serves as special counsel to a variety of independent business entities. **Clarence Walker** has manifest expertise in the utilities sector and dispute resolution skills commensurate with his decades of experience. He is *"one of the standard-setters for corporate law in North Carolina."*

**Clients/Work Highlights:** Beacon Industrial Group; Charlotte Pipe and Foundry Company; Coca-Cola Bottling Co. Consolidated; Glenayre Technologies; Lance; McRae Industries; SELEE Corporation and Soliant.

## Moore & Van Allen, PLLC

**The Firm:** Part of an *"excellent firm providing exceptional service,"* the corporate team here comprises 50 attorneys who divide their time between transactional M&A and niche areas such as securities, real estate, tax and employee benefits. A wide range of industries is catered to and most commentators were quick to highlight the protean nature of the attorneys' caseloads. Recent transactions include representing Rexam in a $150 million product offering expansion, and assisting in the sale of two North Carolina power plants.

**The Lawyers: Stephen Hope** impressed clients and peers with his *"incredible precision and experience."* Head of the business law department, he is a *"gifted negotiator"* who specializes in complex M&A as well as corporate finance transactions. Notable cases include a significant sale transaction for a national grocery chain. Hope is currently engaged on a series of bids for a major air-conditioning manufacturer.

**Clients/Work Highlights:** Alcatel; Cogentrix Energy; MedCath; Watsco; Nucor and Rexam.

## Smith, Anderson, Blount, Dorsett, Mitchell & Jernigan, LLP

See firm details p.1588

**The Firm:** Smith Anderson is blessed with having one of the largest and most respected teams in the market. *"Extremely pleasant Southern gentlemen with resolves of steel,"* they are *"known for bringing as much to the transaction as possible."* The group offers a full portfolio of corporate services, with particular focus on the more complex and sophisticated transactions of both public and private science and biotech entities. Its highlights include a series of substantial transactions for Quintiles Transnational involving the issuance of $150 million in secured notes and a $125 million reorganization and assets sale. It continues to act as primary counsel for Progress Energy, The Pantry and GlaxoSmithKline, as well as many other major national and international corporate bodies.

**The Lawyers:** Managing partner **John Jernigan** (see p.1583) continues to impress clients for having *"an iron fist in a velvet glove."* Commentators drew particular attention to his *"vast knowledge and experience as a corporate relationship adviser."* His recent highlights include advising PepsiCo on a range of matters and acting for a client of The Shircliff & Sisisky Company in a significant merger transaction. **Gerald Roach** (see p.1586) was praised as a *"beyond excellent business attorney who always anticipates the client's needs."* He is head of the corporate group and has represented Quintiles Transnational in some of the most sophisticated transactions in the market. He was also recently responsible for a $200 million exchange offering at Pharma Services Holdings. **Byron Kirkland** (see p.1584) is *"as good as it gets,"* according to market sources excited about his expertise in venture capital financings and public companies corporate work. He acted as lead counsel for TriVirix in two recent domestic and international acquisitions. **Christopher Capel** (see p.1581) appears in the tables for the first time and was recommended as *"a diligent attorney whose absolute goal is to get the deal done."* Highlights of his workload include acquisitions of publicly traded pharmaceutical assets for GlaxoSmithKline and a stock sale of $65 million for Triangle Ice.

**Clients/Work Highlights:** Pharma Services Holdings; Bioglan Pharmaceuticals; PepsiCo; Cree; The Pantry; TriVirix and Progress Energy.

## Band 3

## Hunton & Williams LLP

See firm details p.1959

**The Firm:** This relatively compact group of 12 attorneys is based at the Raleigh office and was highly praised for its *"excellent judgment and responsiveness."* One commentator noted: *"These guys have consistently exceeded my expectations in everything they do."* The team offers especially highly rated experience in M&A, debt financings and securities and is fully integrated firmwide, working on major transactions all over the Southeast. Recent highlights include acting for a subsidiary of Progress Energy in a $400 million deal relating to the rail industry.

**The Lawyers:** Tim Goettel specializes in transactional M&A in the energy industry.

**Clients/Work Highlights:** Clients include Progress Energy and Blue Cross and Blue Shield Association.

## Kilpatrick Stockton LLP

See firm details p.735

**The Firm:** Commentators agreed that although the group is *"part of one of the better firms in the country,"* its visibility in North Carolina has been down on previous years. That said, the Raleigh office was nonetheless praised as a *"strong contender"* in the corporate market, specializing in securities compliance work, public offerings financing and investments.

**The Lawyers: Elizabeth Wren** (see p.1586) was widely praised by clients and peers as *"the kind of attorney you'd want on your team."* She specializes in public offerings and securities and is an experienced counsel on Sarbanes-Oxley compliance.

**Clients/Work Highlights:** The client base includes midsized North Carolina entities as well as large international manufacturing, media and telecommunications corporations.

## Womble Carlyle Sandridge & Rice, PLLC

See firm details p.1589

**The Firm:** This 15-strong team impressed clients as being a *"well-regarded and forthright group"* that is *"always prepared and gets the job done with the minimum of fuss."* The group won particular praise for its advisory and securities expertise, and recently expanded to include a niche team of fund formation attorneys as well as a specialized private equity practice group. It represents Wachovia on a variety of deals and also advises National Textiles, DashAmerica and BB&T.

**The Lawyers: Garza Baldwin** (see p.1580) was highly praised by clients and peers alike as an *"outstanding and very well-informed M&A specialist."* His practice includes advising large public companies, securities representation and debt-related transactions. Baldwin recently counseled Old Dominion Freight Line on a $70 million follow-on offering of common stock.

**Clients/Work Highlights:** Wachovia Securities; BB&T; RF Micro Devices; Targacept; DashAmerica; National Textiles; Old Dominion Freight Line and GlaxoSmithKline.

# EMPLOYMENT

# MAINLY DEFENDANT

## Band 1

## Constangy, Brooks & Smith, LLC

**The Firm:** This national labor and employment boutique has 11 "*fine and accomplished attorneys*" working at its Winston-Salem office. "*Consistent and with a great depth of experience,*" its attorneys tackle employment litigation, labor relations, benefits matters, OSHA and affirmative action proceedings. They also have extensive experience defending alleged class action and FLSA violations, and recently successfully defended a multimillion-dollar class action alleging off-the-clock work and falsified time records by former employees. Other team highlights include winning the first wrongful discharge case ever put to jury in North Carolina.
**The Lawyers:** Managing partner **John Doyle** is a "*tremendous, enthusiastic attorney*" who has over 30 years' experience in all aspects of labor and employment law. He shares top billing at the firm with fellow managing partner **Randolph Loftis**. "*Conscientious and business-oriented,*" he heads the firm's litigation group but also has a niche specialism in agricultural labor law. The presence of **Penni Bradshaw** is "*a coup for any team,*" according to interviewees. "*Diligent and energetic,*" her practice focuses on

employment litigation and immigration counsel.
**Clients/Work Highlights:** Branch Banking & Trust; Chubb Group; Duke Energy; GE; Hertz; High Point Regional Hospital; RJ Reynolds and Randolph Hospital.

## Ogletree, Deakins, Nash, Smoak & Stewart, PC

See firm details p.738
**The Firm:** This nationwide labor and employment firm operates from three offices in North Carolina, with the largest group of 22 attorneys based in Raleigh. Interviewees were "*extremely pleased*" with the team, with one commenting: "*They're responsive and cost-effective – I'd give them an A-plus.*" A full service is proffered, embracing employer defense work, labor law and employee benefits matters. A specialist immigration group also features and the team has a growing caseload in ERISA proceedings. Practice highlights include ongoing advisory work for national corporations and assisting an employer on a significant workforce reduction involving thousands of employees.
**The Lawyers:** **Thomas Farr** (see p.1582) is "*one of the best employment lawyers in the state,*" according to interviewees. He focuses on workplace law, and assists employers in contract management and union arbitrations. **Matthew Keen** (see p.1584) was praised as "*a thorough and excellent attorney.*" He divides his time between advisory and litigation work.
**Clients/Work Highlights:** GE; IBM; Duke Energy; GlaxoSmithKline and American Airlines.

## Smith Moore LLP

See firm details p.1587
**The Firm:** Praise was uniform for this 20-strong group of "*responsive and all-around excellent*" attorneys who work from three offices across the state. The practice encompasses a wide range of employment law including labor relations, workers' compensation, immigration and OSHA matters. The attorneys have vast state and federal litigation experience, in addition to a significant advisory portfolio, and successfully represented a national employer in federal court regarding a sexual harassment matter alleged by a female employee.
**The Lawyers:** **Martin Erwin** (see p.1582) is "*the best trial lawyer in the region,*" according to more than a few observers. An experienced litigator and mediator, he has recently expanded his practice to take in an increasing amount of ERISA litigation. **Julianna Theall** (see p.1586) joins him in the rankings following effusive recommendations across the market. She has litigated in state and federal courts and is also a certified mediator.
**Clients/Work Highlights:** The client base includes multinational corporations as well as regional employers.

## Band 2

## Brooks, Pierce, McLendon, Humphrey & Leonard LLP

**The Firm:** Market sources held this Greensboro-based outfit in high regard, saying that it is "*an extremely high-quality firm with some of the finest attorneys in the state.*" "*Responsiveness and a genial demeanor*" prove the overriding characteristics of the 11 lawyers who make up its team. Together, they cover a full range of employment law including litigation matters arising from labor unions, race and gender discrimination cases, FLSA compliance work and a significant amount of mediation matters. Recent group highlights include acting for employers on several race discrimination cases, as well as representing a national franchise association in an alleged sexual harassment matter.
**The Lawyers:** **Daniel McGinn** is "*an outstanding lawyer who always behaves with urbanity even in heated litigations.*" He has vast experience of employment litigation and labor law, and recently acted as defense counsel in a lengthy sexual harassment case. **William Cary** "*is an expert on the state of the law*" who was also praised for his "*all-around excellence.*" He focuses on mediation and class action work relating to the FLSA.
**Clients/Work Highlights:** AT&T; Battleground Restaurants; Citicorp; Crown Motors; Guilford County Schools; LaSalle Bank; Lorillard Tobacco; Moses Cone Health System and Wachovia.

## Maupin Taylor, PA

**The Firm:** This team of nine drew effusive praise from clients and peers. Interviewees considered them "*sharp and responsive*" and were especially impressed with "*the excellent interfirm communication: they always take the time to find the appropriate expert.*" The practice focuses largely on employment discrimination matters, as well as labor relations, union activity, ERISA litigation, and wage and hour issues. The group has further experience with immigration law and employee benefits matters. In the past year it has represented a trucking contractor in an interstate commerce wage and hour dispute, and handled a significant number of alleged disability discrimination cases.
**The Lawyers:** **Frank Ward** is "*a first-class defense attorney*" with experience in EEOC and DOL hearings. He recently acted for an employer in a discrimination dispute involving the issue of the religious observance of an employee. The "*incredibly professional*" **Mike Lord** focuses on noncompetition litigation and OSHA matters, as well as general management representation in state and federal courts.
**Clients/Work Highlights:** Alcoa; Blue Cross and Blue Shield Association; Caterpillar; City of Raleigh; DaimlerChrysler; Kerr Drug; SpectraSite and Waste Industries USA.

## Van Hoy Reutlinger Adams & Dunn

**The Firm:** Clients were adamant that this Charlotte-based employment boutique "*has an unimpeachable reputation.*" The group covers a wide range of employment expertise with particular emphasis on employment discrimination defense, OSHA work, wage and hour claims, and disability matters. Additional areas of expertise include healthcare matters, contracts and noncompetition agreements. Recent practice highlights include a series of EEOC-related cases for a large education authority.

**The Lawyers:** **Philip Van Hoy** was praised as "*a dean of labor management*" who "*never fails to instill the client with anything less than total trust.*" He focuses on extensive employment discrimination matters and litigation proceedings.

**Clients/Work Highlights:** Cape Fear Valley Medical Center; City of Charlotte; Corporate Health International; Employers Association; Pfeiffer University; Sanger Clinic and Mecklenburg County.

## Band 3

## Robinson, Bradshaw & Hinson PA

**The Firm:** Market sources highly recommended this team of nine attorneys, drawing particular attention to its management advisory work on a wide range of disputes. Painting on a wide canvas, the group focuses on disability and workers' leave disputes, healthcare matters and some noncompetition contract work, in addition to the general run of employment issues. Recent practice highlights include representing Wal-Mart in a misappropriated trade secrets case against two former employees, and the defense of PCA International in a class action in Florida. The team also acted for a regional healthcare

provider in a case of alleged racial discrimination brought by a former employee before a federal court.

**The Lawyers:** **Charles Johnson** was praised as an "*outstanding trial attorney*" who maintains a strong management defense practice. Colleague **John Wester** is a highly regarded litigator who is renowned for his broad employment expertise before state and federal courts.

**Clients/Work Highlights:** The client base includes employers from small and midsize state-based companies as well as larger national corporations.

## Smith, Anderson, Blount, Dorsett, Mitchell & Jernigan, LLP

See firm details p.1588

**The Firm:** This "*responsive team of fine lawyers*" was commended for its business-oriented practice. Clients said that "*they speak a tremendously straightforward language and maintain a wonderful corporate focus.*" The group comprises eight lawyers who negotiate a full-service employment practice, with particular expertise in executive compensation and benefits matters, immigration and OSHA proceedings. Attorneys have also been involved in a series of whistle-blower cases for a wide range of companies, including significant pharmaceutical corporations. Other practice highlights include defending a company in a complex series of class actions involving alleged wage and hour and FLSA violations.

**The Lawyers:** **Kimberly Korando** (see p.1584) heads the group and was praised across the board as "*a diligent, top-tier attorney.*" She focuses on compliance matters, advising on and developing workplace policies and contracts.

**Clients/Work Highlights:** GlaxoSmithKline; Cree; Buckeye Technologies; Progress Energy; Quintiles Transnational and The Pantry.

## Womble Carlyle Sandridge & Rice, PLLC

See firm details p.1589

**The Firm:** This "*prominent and impressive labor group*" works from five North Carolina offices and makes effective use of the firm's strong presence across the region. Fifteen attorneys constitute a group offering counsel on all manner of traditional labor and employment practices, as well as trade protection expertise and wage and hour matters. Litigation forms a major part of the practice and attorneys have acted in state and federal courts, as well as before the EEOC, OSHA and DOL. Headline cases of late include successfully defending a poultry producer being sued for wrongful death, and acting in a multiplaintiff wage and hour matter against Wal-Mart.

**The Lawyers:** **Richard Rainey** (see p.1585) is a skilled litigator who also advises employers from various sectors on employment law liability.

**Clients/Work Highlights:** Enterprise Rent-A-Car; Wal-Mart; Microsoft; Patterson Dental; ALLTEL; INVISTA; Republic Mortgage Insurance; VF and AT&T.

## Other Notable Practitioners

**Albert Bell** of Ward and Smith PA heads the firm's employment group and is a "*very knowledgeable big-hitter.*" He focuses on wage and hour matters as well as general civil rights discrimination. **Keith Weddington** of Parker, Poe, Adams & Bernstein LLP is recommended for his "*impressive range of expertise.*" His practice features extensive litigation on behalf of employers embroiled in defense suits.

# ENVIRONMENT

| Environment |
| --- |
| Leading Firms |
| [1] HUNTON & WILLIAMS LLP *Raleigh* |
| [2] BROOKS, PIERCE, MCLENDON, *Greensboro* |
| HELMS MULLISS & WICKER PLLC *Charlotte* |
| KENNEDY COVINGTON LOBDELL *Charlotte* |
| KILPATRICK STOCKTON LLP *Raleigh* |
| MAUPIN TAYLOR, PA *Raleigh* |
| POYNER & SPRUILL LLP *Raleigh* |
| SMITH MOORE LLP *Greensboro* |
| WOMBLE CARLYLE SANDRIDGE & RICE *Charlotte* |
| [3] HAMILTON FAY MOON STEPHENS *Charlotte* |
| PARKER, POE, ADAMS & BERNSTEIN *Charlotte* |
| ROBINSON, BRADSHAW & HINSON PA *Charlotte* |

## Band 1

## Hunton & Williams LLP

See firm details p.1959

**The Firm:** The Raleigh office of this international

firm maintains its stellar reputation as "*best in the state*" for environmental law. Clients were impressed with the breadth of the team, observing that its 75 attorneys "*work hard to be familiar with many fields of expertise and never lose sight of our business objectives.*" Niche areas of particular note include advising on clean air and water regulations, waste management and a general agricultural business focus. The group has latterly expanded to include an FDA practice that deals with matters relating to prescription drugs and animal feeds. Recently, the team advised on a waterfront development on the East Coast, a matter that involved the relocation of a large shipping firm and the simultaneous planning of a convention center and hotel complex. It has also been involved in the development of former textile mills, automobile factories and other brownfield sites.

**The Lawyers:** **Charles Case** (see p.1581) is "*an undoubted maven of environmental law,*" celebrated for his "*sound business judgment and prompt, practical advice*". Head of the practice group, his area of expertise includes health and safety law, toxic and hazardous

waste regulation, and brownfield development. Matters he has handled include actions for developers on several proposed sites on the East Coast. Case also advises and assists in strategic energy planning.

**Clients/Work Highlights:** Ingersoll Rand; North Carolina Pork Council; Raleigh-Durham Airport Authority and Waste Management.

## Band 2

## Brooks, Pierce, McLendon, Humphrey & Leonard LLP

**The Firm:** Interviewees warmly praised this "*established environmental group*" and were especially impressed with its "*superb land and transactions work.*" The team comprises seven attorneys whose practice centers on general environmental work including air, water and waste matters, RCRA and CERCLA advisory work, and general construction issues. The group enjoys a strong science background and offers an experienced litigation group, in addition to a general advisory team. It has represented the City of Greensboro in various permitting matters and acted for a major copper fabricator in an insurance company contestation in Tennessee. At present, the group is litigating in nine lawsuits relating to an airport expansion in Wake County.

**The Lawyers:** **George House** was unequivocally praised as *"one of the best environmental litigators in the state."* He focuses largely on litigating and negotiating a full range of environmental matters for manufacturing companies, raw materials developers and government municipalities.

**Clients/Work Highlights:** Caldwell County; City of Salisbury; ECOFLO; Guilford Mills; PCS Phosphate; Piedmont Triad Airport Authority and Village of Bald Head Island.

## Helms Mulliss & Wicker PLLC

**The Firm:** This group of three attorneys was praised across the market for its quality and *"impressive business focus."* Its workload embraces a full range of environmental services including permitting proceedings, contamination cleanups and developments, regulatory work, business litigation and administrative litigation. The team is also experienced with air and water quality matters, as well as waste issues. Recent proceedings have included acting for a major waste disposal company challenging a municipal monopoly on waste disposal within city limits. Another highlight saw the firm representing various developers in seven brownfield projects totalling $200 million investments.

**The Lawyers:** **Benne Hutson** heads the group and is *"an excellent regulatory lawyer"* highly skilled in the environmental aspects of real estate matters. His activities as lead negotiator for North Carolina's Brownfields Agreement caught the eye of the market recently.

**Clients/Work Highlights:** Rexam; Ruddick; Radiator Speciality; Allied Waste; Siemens Westinghouse and City of Charlotte.

## Kennedy Covington Lobdell & Hickman LLP

**The Firm:** Interviewees enthusiastically recommended this *"all-around excellent team of experienced lawyers,"* drawing attention to their strong links with the firm's highly rated real estate group. The group is made up of four attorneys based in Charlotte and Raleigh whose practice expertise covers all aspects of corporate and real estate environmental law. Particular matters of interest include permitting and regulatory advice, air and water quality, cleanup assessment, toxic tort defense and Superfund litigation. Matters of note include an appearance in a vapor intrusion and air quality case relating to a new shopping mall development. The team has also advised on a wetlands stream fill permit for a home improvement store.

**The Lawyers:** **Carolyn Jones Van Buren** focuses on environmental risk and compliance issues in real estate and corporate matters. She impressed clients with her *"outstanding business focus, wonderful contact network and fee-conscious approach."* She is currently involved in several land use litigation matters and is regularly advising on regulatory compliance. **David Franchina** heads the environmental department and is *"extremely capable and very well respected in the field."* He is particularly regarded for his expertise in environmental remediation and wetlands reclamation work.

**Clients/Work Highlights:** Key clients of the firm include real estate developers, financial institutions, manufacturers and other corporate entities.

## Kilpatrick Stockton LLP

See firm details p.735

**The Firm:** This Atlanta-based firm has more than 20 years' experience of practicing in the state. Its nine attorneys work across three offices and are seen as *"smart attorneys who understand the lie of the land and the need to move with the market."* The breadth of their practice is notable. Expert advice is available on matters pertaining to clean air and water acts, permitting work, waste disposal, brownfields and regulatory compliance. Other niche areas include real estate development, endangered species regulations and toxic waste matters. The team recently acted on a 1,000-acre groundwater contamination matter in Raleigh involving a complex regulatory process, and has engaged itself in a multitude of cases arising from the Superfund hazardous waste program.

**The Lawyers:** **Alan McConnell** (see p.1585) focuses on compliance and regulatory work and was acknowledged to be *"the best air regulation attorney in the Southeast."* *"One of the most efficient attorneys around,"* he is also active in the Superfund market and recently represented a client charged under Federal Insecticide, Fungicide and Rodenticide Act (FIFRA) regulations. **Stephen Berlin** (see p.1581) heads the environmental team in the firm's Winston-Salem office and handles some of the largest and most sophisticated brownfield projects in the state. Although much of his practice is transactional and regulatory, he has also litigated in several toxic tort

actions, as well as in matters arising under CERCLA and RCRA regulations. **Steven Levitas** (see p.1584) is *"an outstanding litigator"* who impressed clients with his handling of complex waste disposal matters in new areas of development throughout the state. His other highlights include representing the City of Raleigh in a number of civil violations of waste regulations, and also acting as strategic counsel for several investing institutions.

**Clients/Work Highlights:** The client base includes manufacturers, developers, investors and municipalities across the Southeast.

## Maupin Taylor, PA

**The Firm:** The team offers a broad spectrum of expertise in environmental issues, focusing primarily on transactional matters and administrative litigation proceedings. It comprises two *"good, strong attorneys"* who were noted by peers for their permitting and appeals expertise, as well as the wide range of their real estate-related practice. They recently worked on some permit work for a coastal area development project, and are involved in an ongoing hazardous waste matter for the SeaBoard Group in High Point. The team's other activities have included working as counsel for large manufacturing clients and assisting the firm's real estate group in lending and developing matters.

**The Lawyers:** **Amos Dawson** is an *"outstanding litigator"* and an experienced mediator, assisting in matters in both state and federal courts. In addition, he focuses on permitting matters for environmental groups throughout the state and has represented a number of developments in RCRA proceedings.

**Clients/Work Highlights:** Developers, large corporations, coastal management groups and municipalities are among the firm's clientele.

## Poyner & Spruill LLP

**The Firm:** This *"solid and effective"* group of four attorneys works from the firm's Raleigh office and has garnered an outstanding reputation for environmental regulation and liabilities work. It further has extensive experience of the state's Coastal Area Management Program and a keen familiarity with redevelopment projects and state brownfield programs. In addition, the team has successfully represented clients charged in alleged violations of the wetlands protection laws and has provided expert counsel on CAA compliance, among other environmental statutes.

**The Lawyers:** **Glenn Dunn** is the group head and an expert in coastal area matters. He also represents municipalities and industrial clients in wastewater treatment and landfill proceedings.

**Clients/Work Highlights:** Clients include municipalities, corporate and industrial entities, coastal management bodies and developers.

## Smith Moore LLP

See firm details p.1587

**The Firm:** The five environmental attorneys here coalesce into a *"responsive, professional group that can handle everything given it."* The team is heavily involved in a large volume of contaminated property cleanups, among other land use matters, and is also very experienced in permitting and general compliance work. Clients praised its strong business focus and pointed to its healthy interaction with the firm's rapidly expanding real estate group as a reason for its success. This has resulted in a significant amount of recent work in property acquisition and brownfield developments, matters totaling tens of millions of dollars. In addition to transactional expertise, the firm also offers vast litigation experience and has acted for clients in all manner of RCRA, CERCLA and CAA legal disputes.

**The Lawyers:** **Stephen Earp** (see p.1582) is *"an excellent attorney"* who heads the group. He handles a wide range of land dispute and corporate acquisition work, and also acts for national as well as regional companies in regulatory and compliance matters. He is something of a maven when it comes to dealing with cleanups and related issues at contaminated sites.

**Clients/Work Highlights:** The group acts for state and community environmental bodies, corporate and industrial clients, and developers.

## Womble Carlyle Sandridge & Rice PLLC

See firm details p.1589

**The Firm:** The six-person team here forms the bedrock of the firm's environmental presence in the Southeast, impressing commentators as *"a strong regional practice with an unwavering business focus."* In addition to its wide range of regulatory work, it tackles general environmental litigation and liability matters, and has a particularly strong focus on the compliance and enforcement needs of large industrial entities. It further involves itself with Superfund matters and recently acted to resolve proceedings arising from contaminated transformer sites in South Carolina. Other practice highlights include litigating in relation to potential chemical exposures and acting for a number of large petrochemical companies.

**The Lawyers:** **Howard Grubbs** (see p.1583) divides his time between the North and South Carolina branches of the firm. He focuses on CERCLA and RCRA compliance work as well as Superfund matters for clients all over the country. **Bradford de Vore** (see p.1582) was praised as a *"good, experienced litigator."* Recent highlights of his practice include successfully defending cases of alleged contamination of groundwater by petroleum.

**Clients/Work Highlights:** Regional and national industrial entities, corporate bodies and major utility companies are among the firm's key clients.

## Band 3

## Hamilton Fay Moon Stephens Steele & Martin, PLLC

**The Firm:** Formerly Hamilton Gaskins Fay & Moon, the firm suffered some turmoil in the past year as Richard Gaskins moved to Moore & Van Allen PLLC and Richard Fay was called for active duty in Iraq. (Fay has since returned to the practice.) Clients remain phlegmatic about these developments, however, noting that *"they're a small outfit but still one of the highest-quality and most cost-efficient groups in the state."* Maintaining a reputation for being *"really excellent litigators,"* its attorneys were praised for their regulatory and compliance work on a wide range of environmental issues, as well as their advice in class action, toxic tort and Superfund matters.

**The Lawyers:** **Richard Fay** heads the environmental group and is a highly regarded toxic tort and environmental litigator.

**Clients/Work Highlights:** The group represents a broad client base of manufacturing, retail, corporate and governmental entities.

## Parker, Poe, Adams & Bernstein LLP

**The Firm:** This *"very capable environmental practice"* can rely on five talented attorneys to offer a consistently high service. The team directs transactional matters for industries and real estate developers and further advises counties, municipalities and corporate bodies. Brownfield proceedings are a distinct specialism and the team is a deft exponent of

every facet of compliance and regulatory advice. On the litigation front, it handles matters generally, but particularly defends clients in both Superfund and toxic tort actions.

**The Lawyers:** **Thomas Griffin** acts as a litigator for clients in wetlands protection and waste-permitting matters. An attorney with *"an excellent demeanor,"* he also represents environmental engineers in claims and regulations work.

**Clients/Work Highlights:** The group acts for clients from the manufacturing, industrial, real estate and agribusiness sectors.

## Robinson, Bradshaw & Hinson PA

**The Firm:** The group here, comprising five attorneys, impressed clients and peers alike with its skill in environmental litigation. Representing industrial and corporate clients in various cleanup and regulatory matters, it also provides environmental counsel in real estate and development issues. The team adopts an intensely interactive approach and works closely with a first-rate corporate team to provide environmental expertise in complex corporate transactions. This allows it to garner a number of matters of signal importance. By way of example, it recently advised several financial institutions on a site lease and acted as common counsel to a group of 40 responsible for the clean up of a bankrupt hazardous waste incinerator in South Carolina.

**The Lawyers:** **William Toole** was recommended by interviewees as *"an attorney with really good experience and a bright future."* He is a respected compliance attorney as well as an experienced litigator and he recently acted for a financial institution in a potential environmental liability matter.

**Clients/Work Highlights:** CommScope; National Gypsum; Carastaur Industries and May Department Stores.

## Other Notable Practitioners

**Richard Gaskins** moved to Moore & Van Allen PLLC this year and continues to win praise as *"an excellent litigator and all-around attorney."* He is particularly experienced in air, water and zoning disputes, as well as matters relating to electrical generation facilities.

# LITIGATION

# GENERAL COMMERCIAL

## Band 1

### Robinson, Bradshaw & Hinson PA

**The Firm:** This "*absolutely top-tier outfit*" was identified by clients and peers alike as "*the go-to firm for sophisticated litigation matters.*" "*Responsive and extremely cost-efficient,*" the group "*takes the time to get to know the client and always invests itself fully in*" any cases." There are 45 attorneys on hand offering a collective expertise that covers the full range of commercial litigation matters. Particular focus lies on actions arising in the healthcare and energy sectors, and the team is often to be seen working on ERISA and securities actions. Other areas of expertise include white-collar crime, bankruptcy and real estate matters. Recent practice highlights include successfully defending Medex in an alleged wage and hour violation, and acting for the Carolina Panthers in a complex arbitration matter brought by a former player.

**The Lawyers:** Interviewees praised **John Wester** to the hilt, saying that he is "*a bright, fun and kick-ass smart litigator who inspires a lot of confidence.*" Ever active, he recently successfully defended Novant Health in an alleged suit of unfair dismissal. **Ward McKeithen** is "*one of the most experienced attorneys on the block,*" with decades of trial experience. He works alongside **Mark Merritt**, an antitrust specialist and a "*thorough and experienced attorney who knows his way around the courtroom.*" Highlights of his practice include acting for the Carolina Panthers in connection with a lawsuit by former NFL player Patrick Jeffers. **Robert Fuller** joins the tables for the first time following strong market endorsement. He maintains a broad commercial practice and represents corporate clients in commercial and government agency disputes.

**Clients/Work Highlights:** Charlotte-Mecklenburg Hospital Authority; Duke Energy; McDevitt Street Bovis; Wachovia; Duke Endowment; Belk; National Gypsum; CommScope; Carolinas Medical Center; Mission Hospitals and Springs Industries.

### Womble Carlyle Sandridge & Rice, PLLC

See firm details p.1589

**The Firm:** This large firm is home to "*an outstanding team of responsive, talented attorneys*" and is noted for "*the sheer volume and scope of its business litigation.*" As many as 160 lawyers divide their time between general commercial litigation, products liability matters, environmental and toxic tort actions, and insurance defense proceedings. Recent practice highlights include acting in a federal civil rights case before a North Carolina District Court and handling a significant volume of work for various insurance companies in the state. Attorneys also continue to litigate on behalf of a number of major tobacco and pharmaceutical companies.

**The Lawyers:** **Keith Vaughan** (see p.1586) is the managing partner of the firm and was praised as "*a creative and enterprising attorney*" who continues to act as products liability and class action counsel to large corporate entities. Another senior member of the group is the "*hard-nosed and inventive*" **William Raper** (see p.1585), an attorney noted for his expertise in sophisticated commercial litigation. **James Cooney** (see p.1581) continues to impress commentators as "*an extraordinary lawyer and certainly one of the best in the state.*" **Andrew Copenhaver** (see p.1581) maintains an impressive commercial litigation practice in addition to his antitrust portfolio. Recent highlights of his practice include acting for a national printer manufacturer in a complex patent matter. **Pressly Millen** (see p.1585) maintains an excellent litigation practice along with his extensive antitrust work, while **Jeffrey Furr** (see p.1583) is "*tough and confident*" when focusing on products liability and toxic tort cases. Also rated are **Timothy Barber** (see p.1580), a technology and securities expert, and former chief justice of the North Carolina Supreme Court **Burley Mitchell** (see p.1585). Mitchell's practice focuses on appellate advocacy and government relations.

**Clients/Work Highlights:** The client base includes regional, national and international corporations and financial institutions as well as governmental and other public bodies.

## Band 2

### Brooks, Pierce, McLendon, Humphrey & Leonard LLP

**The Firm:** Warm praise emanated from all quarters for this "*diligent, top-quality team of 27 lawyers,*" with more than a few clients insisting that it "*is undoubtedly one of the best firms in the state and it is a pleasure to work with them.*" The ligitation expertise of the group spans the full gamut, but it does its best work in plaintiff class actions, securities and accounting litigation proceedings. Securities fraud constitutes a significant proportion of its caseload. Of late, the firm has acted for financial institutions in a range of innovative and unprecedented banking reorganizations.

**The Lawyers:** **Jim Williams** enjoys an outstanding reputation throughout the market as "*one of the most sophisticated and well-respected litigators in the state.*" He represents clients across the country, as well in the Carolinas, and is active in a wide range of commercial disputes. **Jim Phillips** is "*a top-notch attorney*" who focuses on professional malpractice and securities fraud cases, while **Jeffrey Oleynik** is an experienced general litigator and antitrust expert with "*an encyclopedic knowledge of the law.*"

**Clients/Work Highlights:** The group represents financial institutions, professional organizations, and regional and national corporate clients.

### Kennedy Covington Lobdell & Hickman LLP

**The Firm:** Clients offered effusive feedback for a "*strong, solid team*" that numbers 35 attorneys working in four offices across the state. It was described as "*really broad-based in its approach and excellent at volatile, large-dollar matters.*" Litigation work is largely centered on securities, real estate, ERISA and general commercial matters, but the firm also acts extensively in employment, financial and land use cases. Strong relationships with major financial institutions in Charlotte and the presence of a raft of other clients mean that the firm is never short of work. This situation allows it to undertake a telling proportion of work on a pro bono basis. Recent case highlights include a multidistrict ERISA litigation in Maryland where the firm acted for Bank of America. **The Lawyers: George Covington** maintains his reputation as a "*top-notch litigator*" for financial services and securities work. He is also a skilled employment and IP litigator working in a team that includes **Kiran Mehta**, who enters the tables for the first time following strong client and peer recommendation. His practice focus is environmental law and he recently acted on a major pro bono case against the US Navy. This related to the Navy's proposed construction of a landing strip on a state wildlife refuge.

**Clients/Work Highlights:** AAC Real Estate Services; Bank of America; Coca-Cola and Duke Energy.

## Band 3

### Ellis & Winters LLP

**The Firm:** This litigation boutique operates from offices in Raleigh and Greensboro and is rated as being "*small but outstanding.*" Practice areas offered include general business litigation as well as construction and commercial real estate matters. The team also has experience in products liability and medical malpractice suits. Headline projects include acting for a distributing trustee responsible for providing compensation to tobacco farmers in its settlement negotiations with a national tobacco company.

**The Lawyers:** According to clients, the "*thorough and professional*" **Richard Ellis** is "*the go-to attorney for tort and complex litigation matters.*" His wide-ranging practice also takes in product liability work.

**Clients/Work Highlights:** The team's client base comprises regional and national companies. It includes corporations, manufacturers, investors, real estate developers and public bodies.

### Helms Mulliss & Wicker PLLC

**The Firm:** Clients felt that the 40 attorneys here were "*good, solid business lawyers with a strong financial focus.*" Prominent areas of practice include insurance coverage, labor and employment, and general commercial litigation. The firm recently expanded the Raleigh team, which continues to work closely with Bank of America and other large financial entities. Recent practice highlights include advising on a healthcare company dispute in Birmingham, Alabama, as well as providing extensive counsel to various IT and technology firms.

**The Lawyers:** Firm chairman **Peter Covington** is "*smart, hard-working and constantly on the ball.*" Commentators remarked on his financial services expertise and frequent representation of broker-dealer clients. **Douglas Ey** is head of the litigation group and acts primarily for regional and national corporate clients.

**Clients/Work Highlights:** The client base includes

financial institutions, insurance companies, brokers, healthcare bodies and corporate entities.

### Hunton & Williams LLP

See firm details p.1959

**The Firm:** This international firm has two offices in the state, both of which have a pronounced litigation capability. Commentators told researchers that "*they regularly prove worthy opponents to the finest opposing counsel.*" The growing North Carolina team offers a wide range of commercial litigation expertise and also specializes in IP and ERISA arbitration matters. It benefits from the national presence of the firm as a whole and is building a rapidly expanding client base in the state. Matters undertaken in the past year include the representation of a national financial institution in a business method patent infringement case.

**The Lawyers:** The "*precise and impressive*" **Frank Emory** (see p.1582) represents clients across the corporate market and recently acted in a medical malpractice matter for a leading Southeastern university.

**Clients/Work Highlights:** The client base includes medical companies, large manufacturers, corporate entities and leading financial institutions.

### Moore & Van Allen, PLLC

**The Firm:** This well-established team of 30 attorneys has a reputation as an "*outstanding group of financial litigators.*" That is not to detract, however, from its efforts on a wider canvas. Happy to tackle disputes of differing natures, the group is highly adept at general commercial arbitration, employment, construction, environmental, securities and ERISA litigation. The team further handles a lot of pretrial mediation, corporate governance cases and a significant amount of pro bono work. Recent matters of note include a class action ERISA matter in the Sixth Circuit Court of Appeals.

**The Lawyers: Jeffrey Davis** was praised as being "*excellent and always cool under pressure.*" He has vast experience in general litigation matters and is a major force behind the firm's mediation prowess. **George Hanna** brings decades of experience to each case and is also a certified trial court mediator. Interviewees also strongly recommended **James McLoughlin**, saying that he was a "*well-respected and incredibly smart lawyer.*" He is currently involved in pro bono proceedings for detainees at Guantanamo Bay.

**Clients/Work Highlights:** Financial institutions; telecom companies; healthcare providers; national retailers and construction industries.

### Parker, Poe, Adams & Bernstein LLP

**The Firm:** This is a group of 30 "*experienced and knowledgeable*" attorneys who represent clients right across the market. The team practices across a wide range of areas including antitrust, IP and contract tort law in state as well as federal courts. It was particularly noted for its strong insurance defense and medical malpractice expertise, and for an appellate practice rated as above average.

**The Lawyers: William Rikard** was lauded "*a top*

*litigator*" who specializes in sophisticated commercial disputes. He also practices in antitrust and trade dispute matters.

**Clients/Work Highlights:** The client base includes national corporations, pharmaceutical companies and governmental bodies.

### Smith Moore LLP

See firm details p.1587

**The Firm:** "*This group is thorough, professional and responsive and an excellent choice for commercial litigation,*" according to clients. A broad range of practice areas is covered by 20 attorneys, including commercial fraud and professional liability, and they have extensive experience in class action proceedings. The client base includes regional and national clients as well as local corporate, industrial, manufacturing and pharmaceutical entities. The team has acted in a number of medical malpractice matters and has represented a national financial institution in its attempts to recover settlement amounts made as a result of the Enron litigation.

**The Lawyers: Donald Cowan** (see p.1582) is considered "*one of the best guys in the state for products liability.*" He was also highly rated as an outstanding general commercial litigator. **Larry Sitton** (see p.1586) is an experienced commercial litigator who also works in antitrust proceedings. He represents financial institutions and large corporations. **Alan Duncan** (see p.1582) is ranked for the first time following strong peer and client recommendation. He is particularly experienced at medical malpractice work.

**Clients/Work Highlights:** Atlantic Coast Conference; Eli Lilly; GE; Miller Brewing Company; Solutia; Stockhausen; Procter & Gamble; Philip Morris; Tradewinds Airlines and Honeywell.

### Smith, Anderson, Blount, Dorsett, Mitchell & Jernigan, LLP

See firm details p.1588

**The Firm:** Clients pointed to the "*excellent interaction*" between departments at this highly regarded corporate firm. Such interplay affords the 40 litigators here the opportunity to shine in a myriad of areas. Of particular note are its efforts in securities, commercial contracts, construction matters and employment disputes. Recent practice highlights include acting in a public bid procurement involving a $200 million Medicaid program and representing the plaintiffs in a royalties dispute brought against a nonprofit think tank. The team has also acted for a security company in a case brought following the death of an employee in Iraq.

**The Lawyers: Carl Patterson** (see p.1585) heads the litigation team and specializes in contract disputes and commercial litigation. He recently represented Cree in a series of class actions and alleged securities fraud matters.

**Clients/Work Highlights:** Cree; Krispy Kreme Doughnuts; Quintiles Transnational and Wachovia.

## Other Notable Practitioners

**William Davis** of Bell, Davis & Pitt, PA continues to draw praise as "*one of the best in the state*" for his securities and banking litigation. **Daniel Taylor** (see p.1586) of Kilpatrick Stockton LLP is "*smart and capable.*" His practice focuses on complex commercial litigation, as does that of **William Diehl** of James McElroy & Diehl, who is said by interviewees to be "*one of the finest and most interesting lawyers around.*" **Keith Merritt** of Hamilton Fay Moon Stephens Steele & Martin, PLLC is also recommended for being "*a strong, all-around litigator.*"

# REAL ESTATE

## Real Estate
### Leading Firms

1. **KENNEDY COVINGTON LOBDELL** *Charlotte*
   **ROBINSON, BRADSHAW & HINSON PA** *Charlotte*
2. **MANNING FULTON & SKINNER PA** *Raleigh*
   **WOMBLE CARLYLE SANDRIDGE** *Winston-Salem*
3. **HELMS MULLISS & WICKER PLLC** *Charlotte*
   **MAUPIN TAYLOR, PA** *Raleigh*
   **MOORE & VAN ALLEN, PLLC** *Charlotte*
   **SMITH MOORE LLP** *Greensboro*
   **SMITH, ANDERSON, BLOUNT, DORSETT** *Raleigh*

### Leading Individuals

#### Senior Statesman
**FULTON Charles** *Manning Fulton*

1. **ADAMS Alfred** *Womble Carlyle Sandridge*
   **OLIVER JR Samuel** *Manning Fulton*
   **TORSTRICK Brent** *Robinson, Bradshaw*
2. **DONADIO Donald** *Womble Carlyle Sandridge*
   **EVANS Brian** *Kennedy Covington Lobdell*
   **OATES J Christopher** *Moore & Van Allen, PLLC*
   **PRICHARD Allen** *Kennedy Covington Lobdell*
3. **CLARK Reuben** *Maupin Taylor, PA*
   **DORTON David** *Maupin Taylor, PA*
   **HARDYMON Glen** *Kennedy Covington Lobdell*
   **HINSON Bobby** *Womble Carlyle Sandridge*
   **LOEB Christopher** *Robinson, Bradshaw*
   **MASON C Steven** *Smith, Anderson, Blount*
   **TIPPS Maynard** *Kennedy Covington Lobdell*

## Band 1

### Kennedy Covington Lobdell & Hickman LLP

**The Firm:** Market sources could not have been more positive about this "*very strong and prominent*" group of 50 attorneys spread across four offices statewide. The team was described as "*the undoubted leader in North Carolina, with a sizable practice and a really deep bench.*" It focuses on mixed-use practice, leasing, zoning, land use and environmental matters within North Carolina but has also carved a niche handling a number of large, regional and national high-rise and infrastructure issues. The firm received particular praise for its zoning and land use group, and has recently expanded and developed its mixed-use practice to accommodate market trends. Transactional highlights include acting for Kimco Realty on a number of retail development projects across the country and a high-end resort residential project on Gulf Shores, Alabama.

**The Lawyers:** **Brian Evans** is co-chair of the mixed-use and planned development group and is widely regarded as "*a superstar market leader.*" He is a well-respected authority on condominium development and recently acted for a developer in a 1,700-acre mixed-use development in the Research Triangle Park. **Allen Prichard** is a commercial real estate specialist who focuses on development and lending. "*An exceptional team leader,*" he is part of a group that includes real estate finance expert **Glen Hardymon**. Hardymon has acted for the City of Charlotte in a significant sporting arena development and has advised regional and national clients in sophisticated developments and investments. **Maynard Tipps** was praised as a "*strong player*" who has decades of experience on complex commercial real estate transactions.

**Clients/Work Highlights:** Mills Corporation; Spectrum Properties; City of Charlotte; Kimco Realty; Crescent Resources and Crosland.

### Robinson, Bradshaw & Hinson PA

**The Firm:** This group houses "*very proactive, timely and intelligent lawyers who work tirelessly for the client's objective.*" One client noted that the collegial-style interaction of attorneys from various practice areas created "*really good cooperation across the board, such that one can always be confident that one's business objectives are being met.*" A team of ten concentrates on developer representation and offers expertise in all aspects of office, residential and mixed-use development. It also acts for a number of significant industrial clients and excels at resolving environmental issues within a construction context. Recent highlights for the firm include advising Mecklenburg Hospital Authority in the development of new medical complexes throughout North and South Carolina. The team has also acted for Crescent Resources as general counsel and represented affiliates of Faison Enterprises in negotiating a multimillion-dollar credit facility for a mixed-use development in Washington, DC.

**The Lawyers:** **Brent Torstrick** was enthusiastically recommended for his "*intelligent, personable and efficient approach to problem solving.*" Interviewees pointed to his particular skills in estate-based lending and large retail projects. Torstrick most recently led a team for affiliates of Crescent Resources in a mixed-use development of Piedmont Town Center. Impressed interviewees highlighted **Christopher Loeb**'s skills in environmental law as well as in commercial real estate. Highlights of his practice include acting for Faison Enterprises affiliates in a one million sq ft office disposition in Richmond, Virginia.

**Clients/Work Highlights:** Other clients include Mecklenburg Hospital Authority and Collett & Associates.

## Band 2

### Manning Fulton & Skinner PA

**The Firm:** This Raleigh-based outfit was widely praised as "*an excellent real estate group with strong local ties.*" Its well-established team comprises ten attorneys, whose practice area covers all aspects of real estate law. The group involves itself in a significant number of retail development transactions and offers particular expertise in residential housing complexes. It has acted for buyers, lenders and sellers across the Southeast and has represented a number of leading title insurance brokers. The firm continues to counsel major Research Triangle Park developers, including Highwoods Properties and Carolantic Realty.

**The Lawyers:** **Charles Fulton** was praised to the hilt as "*one of the foremost authorities on real estate in North Carolina.*" Interviewees drew attention to his decades of experience in retail, office and residential matters, as well as his ongoing pro bono work. **Samuel Oliver** drew plaudits as "*an awfully good attorney who appreciates the complexities of a deal.*" His practice centers on real estate acquisitions and financing matters, and he also advises on REITs.

**Clients/Work Highlights:** Highwoods Properties; General Parts; Carolantic Realty; Southern Equipment and Fonville Morisey Realty.

### Womble Carlyle Sandridge & Rice, PLLC

See firm details p.1589

**The Firm:** Clients were absolutely delighted with the performance of this group, with one interviewee stating: "*I would consider them national players in the real estate market.*" The team of 40 offers the full range of commercial development services including extensive financing, leasing and tax expertise. It is noted for its strengths in the office and retail sectors and is busy on behalf of international biomedical and manufacturing clients. The group recently assisted Dell in the acquisition and opening of its newest facility in Winston-Salem and the negotiation of a significant incentive package. It also continues to act as adjunct counsel for Lowe's Home Centers.

**The Lawyers:** **Alfred Adams** (see p.1580) is "*always impressive and just a pleasure to work with.*" He focuses on transactional and acquisition work and works closely with Lowe's Home Centers. Recently, he advised them on a $100 million multijurisdictional investment. **Donald Donadio** (see p.1582) was praised as "*experienced, committed and extremely trustworthy.*" He is particularly knowledgeable on matters of economic development incentives and shares a reputation with **Bobby Hinson** (see p.1583) of being "*an extraordinary professional.*" Hinson's strengths include acting for both developers and lenders in large commercial transactions.

Clients/Work Highlights: Other clients include Dell, Thomasville Furniture Industries and Natuzzi Americas.

## Band 3

### Helms Mulliss & Wicker PLLC

The Firm: This relatively diminutive team of "*experienced, pragmatic and very bright attorneys*" has impressed with the quality of its response to the North Carolina real estate boom of the last few years. Commentators found that "*these guys do great real estate for corporate bodies,*" observing that its client base has expanded to include some significant developers. The group is also frequently involved in servicing the real estate needs of educational institutions throughout the state and recently acted in the financing of two out-of-state sports complexes. Additional highlights include lender representation in a $1.8 billion acquisition by Walter Industries.

The Lawyers: Robert Simmons heads a group that is expected to expand even further in the next year.

Clients/Work Highlights: Corporate entities; developers; educational bodies and other property bodies.

### Maupin Taylor, PA

The Firm: Interviewees were extremely impressed with this "*superior-grade, compact group,*" in which the attorneys are "*personable and really good problem solvers with a fantastic ability to adapt to each project.*" The Raleigh-based team focuses largely on commercial development and is particularly skilled at dispute resolution, loan programs and other complex real estate financings. Its attorneys further display great construction expertise and have acted for a number of shopping complex developers across the state. Practice highlights include advising Coastal Federal Credit Union on the establishment of a $30 million commercial loan program.

The Lawyers: **David Dorton** is a "*reactive, thorough and just real estate attorney.*" His portfolio features a significant amount of retail development and he recently oversaw the completion of a new shopping mall in Durham. **Reuben Clark** focuses on financings as well as development and has a substantial out-of-state practice. He has acted in the development and construction of office space in the Research Triangle Park area.

Clients/Work Highlights: Kerr Drug; Kodak; Coastal Federal Credit Union; Midland Atlantic Development; Southport Business Park; New Plan Excel and Weingarten Realty Investors.

### Moore & Van Allen, PLLC

The Firm: Interviewees concur that this "*formidable team*" punches well above its weight, noting its "*ability to look beyond the law to make a deal.*" Three offices statewide house 22 attorneys, offering a general service and niche banking expertise relating to permanent financing, loan fixtures and other collateral financing matters. The bulk of the group's caseload centers on retail and urban mixed-use development projects, while many of its number are highly regarded for their tax-related expertise. Recent highlights include advising on a significant hotel and convention center development in Charlotte.

The Lawyers: **Christopher Oates** heads the real estate group and was praised for his "*steady and professional demeanor.*" He specializes in zoning and land use law and also acts for construction and permanent lenders in a variety of financing matters.

Clients/Work Highlights: State and regional developers; financial institutions; insurance companies and other investors.

### Smith Moore LLP

See firm details p.1587

The Firm: This team of 15 "*excellent, efficient lawyers*" bands together to offer a real estate practice described by interviewees as being of a national standard. It is currently engaged in significant expansion, having opened a new office in Wilmington and made new additions to the Raleigh and Greensboro offices. The group continues to focus on land use and residential development work and has a large client base for complex real estate financings. Recent highlights include representing a UK-based public entity in a series of residential developments on the North Carolina shoreline.

The Lawyers: Charlie Melvin is the practice group head.

Clients/Work Highlights: The firm acts for developers, lenders and businesses with property portfolios.

### Smith, Anderson, Blount, Dorsett, Mitchell & Jernigan, LLP

See firm details p.1588

The Firm: Covering many areas of expertise, this team is "*very thorough and professional in all its dealings.*" Eight attorneys focus primarily on real estate finance work and have substantial tax and environmental expertise. A significant amount of the team's real estate practice has centered on large mixed-use developments in the Raleigh area and the servicing of the real estate needs of regional and national corporate clients. The attorneys have also acted in large construction lending projects for Bank of America and advised The Pantry on a series of acquisitions throughout the region.

The Lawyers: **Steven Mason** (see p.1584) is a "*reasonable and experienced lawyer*" who does a lot of work with Bank of America.

Clients/Work Highlights: Other clients include Progress Energy, The Pantry and other corporate entities.

# Leaders in North Carolina

### ADAMS, Alfred G
Womble Carlyle Sandridge & Rice, PLLC, Winston-Salem 336 721 3642
aadams@wcsr.com
*Recommended in Real Estate*
Practice Areas: Mr Adams practices in the areas of commercial real estate transactions and real estate lending.
Prof. Memberships: North Carolina Bar Association, Board of Governors and Chair, Real Property Section; American College of Mortgage Attorneys; American College of Real Estate Attorneys. Certified Specialist, North Carolina State Bar Board of Legal Specialization in Real Property Transactions: Business, Commercial, Industrial and Residential.
Career: Adjunct Professor of Law, 1995-

present, Wake Forest University School of Law; JD, 1973, Wake Forest University School of Law, associate editor, Wake Forest Law Review, Moot Court Board; BA, 1968, Wake Forest University.

### BALDWIN III, Garza
Womble Carlyle Sandridge & Rice, PLLC, Charlotte 704 331 4907
gbaldwin@wcsr.com
*Recommended in Corporate/M&A*
Practice Areas: Garza Baldwin has over 25 years' experience as securities and M&A counsel for public companies, helping them raise capital, structure and negotiate M&A transactions and comply with the federal securities laws. He also provides corporate governance advice to

public companies and their directors and officers and represents special committees and their financial advisors in connection with change in control transactions.
Prof. Memberships: American Bar Association and North Carolina Bar Association, Business Law Sections.
Personal: JD, 1978, Wake Forest University School of Law, managing editor of the Law Review; AB, 1973, University of North Carolina at Chapel Hill.

### BARBER, Timothy G
Womble Carlyle Sandridge & Rice, PLLC, Charlotte 704 331 4937
tim.barber@wcsr.com
*Recommended in Litigation*

Practice Areas: Mr Barber has a broad-based business litigation practice, with emphasis on securities issues and technology.
Prof. Memberships: North Carolina Bar Association and American Bar Association, Litigation Sections. Admitted to practice before the US Supreme Court; US District Courts for the Eastern, Middle and Western Districts of North Carolina; US Court of Appeals for the Federal Circuit; US Court of Appeals for the Fourth Circuit.
Career: Practice Group Leader, Business Litigation, 1998-present. JD, 1985, Wake Forest University School of Law, cum laude, Editor-in-Chief, Law Review; BA, 1977, Kenyon College.

**BELL, Albert**
Ward and Smith PA, Raleigh
919 836 4260
*Recommended in Employment*

**BERLIN, Stephen R**
Kilpatrick Stockton LLP, Charlotte
336 607 7304
SBerlin@KilpatrickStockton.com
*Recommended in Environment*
**Practice Areas:** Environmental law,
including environmental litigation, busi-
ness transactions involving environmen-
tal issues (including brownfields) and
environmental compliance matters, pri-
vate environmental costs recovery actions
and representations of potentially
responsible parties at Superfund sites and
RCRA issues.
**Prof. Memberships:** Forsyth County Bar
Association (President), North Carolina
Bar Association, Master of Bench, Joseph
Branch Inn of Court.
**Career:** Head of the firm Environmental
Team; Adjunct Professor, Wake Forest
University.
**Publications:** Has published papers and
made presentations on various environ-
mental topics.
**Personal:** BA, Wake Forest University,
magna cum laude; JD, Wake Forest Uni-
versity, cum laude, 1984; law clerk to
Chief Judge Hiram H Ward.

**BOOE, Mike**
Kennedy Covington Lobdell & Hickman LLP,
Charlotte 704 331 7400
*Recommended in Bankruptcy*

**BOWMAN, Everett**
Robinson, Bradshaw & Hinson PA,
Charlotte 704 377 2536
*Recommended in Antitrust*

**BRADSHAW, Penni Pearson**
Constangy, Brooks & Smith, LLC,
Winston-Salem 336 721 1001
*Recommended in Employment*

**BRADY, Christopher J**
Mayer, Brown, Rowe & Maw LLP,
Charlotte 704 444 3511
cbrady@mayerbrownrowe.com
*Recommended in Capital Markets*
**Practice Areas:** Specializes in securitization and other structured finance products. Represents issuers, underwriters,
placement agents, servicers and trustees
in private and public executions in term
securitizations of a range of asset types,
including commercial mortgages, residential mortgages, auto loans, aircraft
loans and student loans. Also represents
two of the largest servicers of commercial
mortgage-backed securities, including in
connection with acquisitions of servicing
rights. Represent program sponsor in
connection with the establishment of
commercial paper program and mortgage originator in connection with warehouse facility.
**Career:** Mayer, Brown, Rowe & Maw
LLP, Charlotte, 1999 to date; Partner,

2002. Kilpatrick Stockton LLP, 1993-99.
**Personal:** JD, University of North Car-
olina School of Law, 1993; Order of the
Coif, Dean's List; North Carolina Law
Review. BS (cum laude), University of
North Carolina at Charlotte, 1983.

**BUCK, Peter**
Robinson, Bradshaw & Hinson PA,
Charlotte 704 377 2536
*Recommended in Banking & Finance,
Corporate/M&A*

**BUCKLEY, Kevin J**
Hunton & Williams LLP, Richmond
804 788 8616 kbuckley@hunton.com
*Recommended in Capital Markets,
Corporate/M&A*
**Practice Areas:** Mr Buckley is Co-Head
of Hunton & Williams' nationally-prominent Asset Securitization Practice. His
practice focuses on mortgage and asset-
backed securitizations, structured financings, and other capital markets transactions. He represents issuers, underwriters,
trustees, master servicers, insurers, and
other participants in securitizations and
other capital markets transactions. Mr
Buckley has served as issuer's counsel in
connection with the design and implementation of securitization programs
involving unique asset types and innovative securities structures, including the
first REMIC program backed by a full
faith and credit guarantee of the US and
the first public securitization of reperforming government-guaranteed loans.

**CALDWELL, Stokely**
Robinson, Bradshaw & Hinson PA,
Charlotte 704 377 2536
*Recommended in Banking & Finance*

**CAMPBELL, Boyd**
Helms Mulliss & Wicker PLLC, Charlotte
704 343 2000
*Recommended in Banking & Finance,
Corporate/M&A*

**CAPEL, Christopher**
Smith, Anderson, Blount, Dorsett,
Mitchell & Jernigan, LLP, Raleigh
919 821 6759
ccapel@smithlaw.com
*Recommended in Corporate/M&A*
**Practice Areas:** Has extensive experience in domestic and international mergers and acquisitions, corporate finance
(including public offerings and private
placements of securities), strategic
alliances and joint ventures, intellectual
property licensing, venture capital, public
company reporting and compliance, corporate governance, and general corporate
and business law matters.
**Prof. Memberships:** Admitted to practice in North Carolina (1985) and New
York (1987). Member of American Bar
Association, North Carolina Bar Association, Wake County Bar Association. Past
member of governing Council of Business Law Section of North Carolina Bar
Association.

**Career:** 1990: Joined Smith, Anderson,
Blount, Dorsett, Mitchell & Jernigan, LLP,
1986-90: White & Case, LLP, New York,
New York. 1985-86: Federal judicial clerk
to Sam J Ervin III, United States Court of
Appeals, Fourth Circuit.
**Personal:** JD (with honors), University
of North Carolina at Chapel Hill School
of Law, 1985; BA, University of North
Carolina at Chapel Hill, 1979.

**CARROLL, James P**
Cadwalader, Wickersham & Taft LLP,
Charlotte 704 348 5116
james.carroll@cwt.com
*Recommended in Capital Markets*
**Practice Areas:** Managing Partner, Cadwalader's Charlotte office. Member, firm's
Management Committee. Concentrates
in the areas of real estate finance and
securitization. Represents national, international, and regional financial institutions, investment banks, pension funds,
and investors in the financing, acquisition, disposition and leasing of commercial office buildings, shopping centers,
hotels, industrial warehouses, merchandise marts, multifamily housing, residential and planned unit developments,
including golf course developments. Has
an active capital markets practice in
mortgage loan conduit programs, mortgage pool purchases and sales as well as
multiple property and single asset real
estate securitizations.
**Prof. Memberships:** Chairman of the
Real Estate Securitization Section of the
American Bar Association's Real Property
Division (2003-04), and Vice Chairman
(2001-02).
**Personal:** JD, The Catholic University of
America (with honors); BA, Georgetown
University (with honors); Adjunct Pro-
fessor of Law, Real Estate Finance, George
Washington University (1985-96).

**CARY, William**
Brooks, Pierce, McLendon, Humphrey &
Leonard LLP, Greensboro
336 373 8850
*Recommended in Employment*

**CASE, Charles D**
Hunton & Williams, Raleigh
919 899 3045
ccase@hunton.com
*Recommended in Environment*
**Practice Areas:** Charles Case's practice
focuses on state and federal environmental, health and safety regulation, as well as
administrative law and lobbying, with
particular emphasis on the regulation of
air quality, toxic and hazardous materials
and wastes, land and water resource
usage, and contaminated site remediation. He was named in 2004 by Business
North Carolina to the Legal Elite Hall of
Fame (ranked as the state's top practitioner in environmental law for the first
three years of the Legal Elite ranking).

**CLARK, Reuben**
Maupin Taylor, PA, Raleigh
919 981 4000
*Recommended in Real Estate*

**COHEN, Steven N**
Cadwalader, Wickersham & Taft LLP,
Charlotte 704 348 5176
steven.cohen@cwt.com
*Recommended in Capital Markets*
**Practice Areas:** Represents domestic
and foreign commercial banks, investment banks and other financial institutions in a wide variety of financing transactions, including leveraged finance and
other syndicated bank loan transactions,
the financing of financial assets, structured finance transactions, cross-border
financings, commodity finance transactions, hedge fund financings, credit
enhancement transactions, workouts and
debtor-in-possession financings, the
trading of distressed debt, and various
innovative financing transactions. Serves
as a member of Cadwalader's Legal Opinions Committee.
**Prof. Memberships:** American Bar
Association, Business Law Section.
**Personal:** JD, New York University
School of Law (note and comment editor,
New York University Law Review,1981);
BA, Wesleyan University (magna cum
laude, 1976); Baccalauréat, Lycée Clas-
sique Mixte, Saintes, France, (high honors - mention bien, 1971). Law clerk,
Honorable Max Rosenn, Senior Circuit
Judge, United States Court of Appeals for
the Third Circuit.

**COONEY III, James P**
Womble Carlyle Sandridge & Rice, PLLC,
Charlotte 704 331 4980
jcooney@wcsr.com
*Recommended in Litigation*
**Practice Areas:** Mr Cooney practices in
the areas of business litigation, medical
malpractice defense, criminal defense,
commercial litigation, catastrophic torts
and appellate law.
**Prof. Memberships:** Mecklenburg
County Bar Association and North Car-
olina Bar Association; Permanent Mem-
ber, Fourth Circuit Judicial Conference;
Fellow, American College of Trial
Lawyers.
**Career:** Associate and Member, 1983-
2000, Kennedy Covington Lobdell &
Hickman, LLP, Charlotte, NC. Law clerk,
the Honorable John D Butzer Jr, US
Court of Appeals, Fourth Circuit. JD,
1982, University of Virginia School of
Law, Order of the Coif, Virginia Law
Review. AB, 1979, Duke University,
summa cum laude, Phi Beta Kappa.

**COPENHAVER, W Andrew**
Womble Carlyle Sandridge & Rice, PLLC,
Winston-Salem
336 721 3633
acopenhaver@wcsr.com
*Recommended in Antitrust, Litigation*
**Practice Areas:** Andy Copenhaver's

diverse litigation practice includes a range of antitrust, trade regulation and business litigation matters in state and federal courts throughout the United States.
**Prof. Memberships:** Forsyth County Bar Association; North Carolina Bar Association, Antitrust (Member, Executive Council), Litigation and Intellectual Property Sections; American Bar Association, Antitrust and Litigation Sections; Member, Fourth Circuit Judicial Conference; Fellow, American College of Trial Lawyers; Member and Chairman, North Carolina Federal Bar Advisory Council.
**Career:** JD, 1972, University of North Carolina School of Law; City College, 1971, University of London Certificate in International Law, with honors; AB, 1969, Duke University.

## COVINGTON, George
Kennedy Covington Lobdell & Hickman LLP, Charlotte 704 331 7400
*Recommended in Litigation*

## COVINGTON, Peter
Helms Mulliss & Wicker PLLC, Charlotte 704 343 2000
*Recommended in Litigation*

## COWAN JR, J Donald
Smith Moore LLP, Greensboro
336 378 5329
don.cowan@smithmoorelaw.com
*Recommended in Litigation*
**Practice Areas:** Litigation, product liability, antitrust, appellate, intellectual property litigation, class action.
**Prof. Memberships:** Fellow, American College of Trial Lawyers; PLAC; Fellow, American Academy of Appellate Lawyers; Fellow, International Society of Barristers; American Board of Trial Advocates; Member, Fourth Circuit Judicial Conference.
**Career:** JD, with honors, Wake Forest University, 1968; BA, Wake Forest University, 1965; 1968-73: US Army JAGC; 1973-present: Smith Moore LLP.
**Personal:** Duke University Law School Adjunct Professor, Trial Practice; 'Best Lawyers in America' (10 consecutive years): Personal Injury Litigation, Antitrust Law; Business NC's Legal Elite: Antitrust, Litigation, Patents; NC Super Lawyers (Top 10).

## DAGENHART, Larry
Helms Mulliss & Wicker PLLC, Charlotte 704 343 2000
*Recommended in Corporate/M&A*

## DAVIS, Jeffrey
Moore & Van Allen, PLLC, Charlotte 704 331 1000
*Recommended in Litigation*

## DAVIS, William
Bell, Davis & Pitt, P.A., Winston-Salem 336 722 3700
*Recommended in Litigation*

## DAWSON, Amos
Maupin Taylor, PA, Raleigh
919 981 4000
*Recommended in Environment*

## DE VORE, Bradford A
Womble Carlyle Sandridge & Rice, PLLC, Charlotte 704 331 4941
bdevore@wcsr.com
*Recommended in Environment*
**Practice Areas:** For nearly 20 years, Brad De Vore has represented energy, chemical, pharmaceutical and manufacturing companies in environmental and toxic tort litigation throughout the United States. His experience with the fate and transport of chemicals and their impact on human health and the environment has allowed for successful results in various complicated environmental and toxic tort litigation matters.
**Personal:** JD, 1986, University of South Carolina School of Law; Order of the Wig and Robe, International Moot Court Team; BA, 1983, Michigan State University, cum laude, National Honor Society of Historians.

## DIEHL, William
James McElroy & Diehl, Charlotte
704 372 9870
*Recommended in Litigation*

## DONADIO, Donald A
Womble Carlyle Sandridge & Rice, PLLC, Raleigh 919 755 2102
ddonadio@wcsr.com
*Recommended in Real Estate*
**Practice Areas:** Don Donadio represents issuers, owners, lenders and underwriters in taxable and tax exempt financing of capital projects. He also represents companies in site selection and incentives negotiations.
**Prof. Memberships:** North Carolina Bar Association and American Bar Association, Business Sections; National Association of Bond Lawyers; listed in the Directory of Municipal Bond Attorneys of the US; American College of Real Estate Lawyers.
**Career:** Raleigh Office Managing Member, 1982-present; Captain, Judge Advocate Generals Corps, 1967-72, US Army; JD, 1967, Wake Forest University, cum laude; BA, 1965, Wake Forest University, cum laude.

## DORTON, David
Maupin Taylor, PA, Raleigh
919 981 4000
*Recommended in Real Estate*

## DOYLE, John
Constangy, Brooks & Smith, LLC, Winston-Salem 336 721 1001
*Recommended in Employment*

## DUNCAN, Alan W
Smith Moore LLP, Greensboro
336 378 5315
alan.duncan@smithmoorelaw.com
*Recommended in Litigation*

**Practice Areas:** Products liability, first amendment, intellectual property, insurance, antitrust, healthcare, professional liability.
**Prof. Memberships:** Board of Governors, NC Bar Association; past President, NC Association of Defense Attorneys; past Chair, NC Bar Association's Litigation Section; American Bar Association's Intellectual Property Law/ Antitrust Law Sections.
**Career:** JD, Vanderbilt University, 1979; Executive Editor, Law Review; AB, Davidson College, 1976; Phi Beta Kappa; 1979-present: Smith Moore LLP.
**Personal:** Fellow, American College of Trial Lawyers; Chairman, Guilford County Board of Education; 'Best Lawyers in America': Business, First Amendment (13 consecutive years), Personal Injury Litigation; Business NC's Legal Elite; NC Super Lawyers (Top 100).

## DUNN, Glenn
Poyner & Spruill L.L.P., Charlotte
704 342 5250
*Recommended in Environment*

## DUNN, Thomas
Moore & Van Allen, PLLC, Charlotte
704 331 1000
*Recommended in Banking & Finance*

## EADES, David
Moore & Van Allen, PLLC, Charlotte
704 331 1000
*Recommended in Bankruptcy*

## EARP, Stephen W
Smith Moore LLP, Greensboro
336 378 5314
steve.earp@smithmoorelaw.com
*Recommended in Environment*
**Practice Areas:** Environmental and OSHA, real estate development, brownfield, mergers and acquisitions.
**Prof. Memberships:** Past Chair, NC Bar Association's Environmental Law Section; former President, NC Beautiful; legal advisor, Guilford County Local Emergency Planning Committee; Board Member, Piedmont Land Conservancy.
**Career:** JD, University of Virginia, 1977; BA, cum laude, Davidson College, 1974; 1977-present: Smith Moore LLP, Chair of Smith Moore's Management Committee.
**Personal:** 'Best Lawyers in America': Environmental; Business NC's Legal Elite: Environmental.

## ELLIS, Richard
Ellis & Winters LLP, Cary
919 865 7000
*Recommended in Litigation*

## EMORY JR, Frank E
Hunton & Williams, Charlotte
704 378 4708
femory@hunton.com
*Recommended in Litigation*
**Practice Areas:** Co-Head, Complex Commercial Litigation Practice. Practice focuses on litigation representing busi-

ness entities and principals in jury trials, bench trials, class actions and alternative dispute resolution proceedings in cases involving intellectual property, complex contract disputes, business torts, consumer finance issues, and covenants against competition. Mr Emory has tried more than 50 cases in state and federal courts and before arbitration panels and administrative agencies.
**Prof. Memberships:** American Bar Association, Section of Litigation, Co-Chair, Trial Evidence Committee; North Carolina Bar; North Carolina Bar Association; Mecklenburg County Bar (President, 2002-03); American Law Institute; Certified Instructor, National Institute of Trial Advocacy.

## ENNS, Rodrick
Enns & Archer LLP, Winston-Salem
336 723 5180
*Recommended in Antitrust*

## ERWIN, Martin N
Smith Moore LLP, Greensboro
336 378 5327
martin.erwin@smithmoorelaw.com
*Recommended in Employment*
**Practice Areas:** Labor and employment, employment litigation, human resources counseling and training, labor relations, litigation.
**Prof. Memberships:** American Bar Association; NC Bar Association; Greensboro Bar Association.
**Career:** JD, University of North Carolina, 1967; MA, University of North Carolina, 1965; BA, Wake Forest University, 1959; 1967-68: clerk, Hon J Braxton Craven, Jr, US Court of Appeals for the Fourth Circuit; 1968-present: Smith Moore LLP.
**Personal:** 'Best Lawyers in America': Employment; Business NC's Legal Elite: Labor and Employment; NC Super Lawyers (Top 100).

## EVANS, Brian
Kennedy Covington Lobdell & Hickman LLP, Charlotte 704 331 7400
*Recommended in Real Estate*

## EY JR, Douglas
Helms Mulliss & Wicker PLLC, Charlotte
910 254 3800
*Recommended in Litigation*

## FARR, Thomas A
Ogletree, Deakins, Nash, Smoak & Stewart, PC, Raleigh
919 787 9700
thomas.farr@ogletreedeakins.com
*Recommended in Employment*
**Practice Areas:** Class action defense, complex litigation/non-competes, constitutional law.
**Prof. Memberships:** North Carolina Bar Association, American Bar Association, Fourth Circuit Judicial Conference, Campbell University (Adjunct Professor of Employment Law, 1990-95).
**Career:** Admitted in North Carolina,

Virginia and Georgia. Named in 'The Best Lawyers in America' and the 2002-06 editions of Business North Carolina's Legal Elite.
**Publications:** Mr Farr is the co-author of the 'NCCBI Employment Law Guide' and has written articles for the Campbell Law Observer and the Triangle Business Journal.
**Personal:** Hillsdale College (BLS, summa cum laude, 1976), Emory University (JD, 1979), Georgetown University (LLM, labor law, 1983).

### FAY, Richard
Hamilton Fay Moon Stephens Steele & Martin, PLLC, Charlotte
704 344 1117
*Recommended in Environment*

### FRANCHINA, David
Kennedy Covington Lobdell & Hickman LLP, Charlotte 704 331 7400
*Recommended in Environment*

### FULLER, Robert
Robinson, Bradshaw & Hinson PA, Charlotte 704 377 2536
*Recommended in Litigation*

### FULLER, William
Moore & Van Allen, PLLC, Charlotte
704 331 1000
*Recommended in Banking & Finance*

### FULTON, Charles
Manning Fulton & Skinner PA, Raleigh
919 787 8880
*Recommended in Real Estate*

### FURR, Jeffrey L
Womble Carlyle Sandridge & Rice, PLLC, Winston-Salem 336 721 3532
jfurr@wcsr.com
*Recommended in Litigation*
**Practice Areas:** Jeff Furr has been litigating toxic tort and product liability cases for over 15 years. He has tried high profile cases, including class actions in West Virginia, Mississippi, California, Florida, Missouri, Indiana and North Carolina. Jeff serves as national coordinating counsel for the R. J. Reynolds Tobacco Company.
**Prof. Memberships:** Bar Associations: Forsyth County Bar Association; North Carolina Bar Association, Litigation Section; American Bar Association.
**Personal:** BS Pharmacy, 1981, West Virginia University, cum laude; residency in Clinical Pharmacy, 1981-82, Rush-Presbyterian-St. Luke's Medical Center; JD, 1987, Wake Forest University School of Law, cum laude, Editor-in-Chief, Wake Forest Law Review.

### GASKINS JR, Richard
Moore & Van Allen, PLLC, Charlotte
704 331 1000
*Recommended in Environment*

### GOLDSTEIN, Stuart N
Cadwalader, Wickersham & Taft LLP, Charlotte 704 348 5258

stuart.goldstein@cwt.com
*Recommended in Capital Markets*
**Practice Areas:** Concentrates on structured finance, structured products and the federal securities laws. Practices primarily in the areas of commercial mortgage and asset securitization, representing issuers, underwriters, institutional investors, servicers and trustees in both public and private transactions. Has extensive experience analyzing and structuring securities, collateralized debt obligations and other instruments and products, as well as structuring transactions involving interest rate swaps, caps, floors and other derivative instruments. Also represents clients in the purchase and sale of commercial and multifamily mortgage loans, mezzanine debt, subordinate debt and residential first and second mortgage loans (including FHA, VA, conventional and manufactured housing) in whole loan and participation structures. Has additional extensive experience in secured lending and represents lenders in structuring and negotiating finance facilities.
**Prof. Memberships:** Member of the New York State Bar Association.
**Personal:** JD, Boalt Hall School of Law, University of California at Berkeley; BS, Cornell University.

### GREENE, Kenneth
Carruthers & Roth PA, Greensboro
336 273 8651
*Recommended in Banking & Finance*

### GRIFFIN III, Thomas
Parker, Poe, Adams & Bernstein LLP, Charlotte 704 372 9000
*Recommended in Environment*

### GRUBBS, R Howard
Womble Carlyle Sandridge & Rice, PLLC, Winston-Salem 864 255 5413
hgrubbs@wcsr.com
*Recommended in Environment*
**Practice Areas:** Howard Grubbs represents industry in complex multi-party CERCLA and RCRA litigation and counseling matters nationwide. He also counsels both buyers and sellers of contaminated real estate on issues ranging from brownfields to underground storage tanks.
**Prof. Memberships:** North Carolina and South Carolina Bar Association; Woodward and White's 'Best Lawyers in America', 1994-2005; Business North Carolina quotes 'Legal Elite' for Environmental Law, 2004.
**Career:** Practice Group Leader, Environmental/Toxic Tort, 1992-present; JD, 1977, University of South Carolina School of Law, with honors; BA, 1968, Dennison University.

### HAHN, Robert J
Hunton & Williams, Charlotte
704 378 4764
rhahn@hunton.com

*Recommended in Capital Markets*
**Practice Areas:** Practice focuses on asset securitization, primarily in non-mortgage assets, including synthetic securitizations. Represents financial institutions, issuers, underwriters, credit enhancers, liquidity providers, asset-backed commercial paper conduits and other securitization participants in issuing, administering, servicing and underwriting asset-backed securities. Extensive experience in structuring securitizations, including public and 144A/Reg S offerings, asset-backed commercial paper conduits and synthetic structures. Active in structuring transactions involving a wide variety of financial assets, including vehicle loans, credit card receivables, trade receivables, HELOCs, home equity loans, iquipement leases, aircraft and charged-off loans and receivables. Member of Hunton & Williams' pro bono committee.

### HANNA III, George
Moore & Van Allen, PLLC, Charlotte
704 331 1000
*Recommended in Litigation*

### HARDYMON, Glen
Kennedy Covington Lobdell & Hickman LLP, Charlotte 704 331 7400
*Recommended in Real Estate*

### HAZLETT, Richard
Helms Mulliss & Wicker PLLC, Charlotte
704 343 2000
*Recommended in Banking & Finance, Corporate/M&A*

### HINSON, Bobby D
Womble Carlyle Sandridge & Rice, PLLC, Charlotte 704 331 4918
bhinson@wcsr.com
*Recommended in Real Estate*
**Practice Areas:** Bobby Hinson has 18 years of experience in commercial real estate development and finance, including acquisitions, development and leasing of office, retail and flex projects. He has extensive experience in condominium and mixed-use, urban in-fill developments.
**Prof. Memberships:** Mecklenburg County Bar Association; North Carolina State Bar; North Carolina Bar Association, Real Property Section; South Carolina State Bar, Real Property Section. Practice Group Leader, Real Estate Development Practice Group; Member, Firm Budget Committee.
**Career:** Associate Member, Urban Land Institute; Board of Directors, Jackson Park Ministries.
**Personal:** JD, 1987, University of Virginia; AB, 1984, Duke University, magna cum laude.

### HINSON, Robin
Robinson, Bradshaw & Hinson PA, Charlotte 704 377 2536
*Recommended in Corporate/M&A*

### HOPE, Stephen
Moore & Van Allen, PLLC, Charlotte
704 331 1000
*Recommended in Corporate/M&A*

### HOROSCHAK, Mark J
Womble Carlyle Sandridge & Rice, PLLC, Charlotte 704 331 4928
mhoroschak@wcsr.com
*Recommended in Antitrust*
**Practice Areas:** Mr Horoschak has a national antitrust practice, with emphasis on the healthcare industry. He represents business clients before federal and state antitrust agencies, and has a broad-based litigation practice.
**Prof. Memberships:** American Bar Association and North Carolina Bar Association, Antitrust Sections; North Carolina State Bar; South Carolina Bar.
**Career:** From 1989-95, Mr Horoschak served as Assistant Director of the Bureau of Competition of the Federal Trade Commission. He currently serves as the Antitrust Practice Group Leader. JD, 1976, College of William and Mary, articles editor for Law Review; BA, 1973, American University, cum laude.

### HOUSE, George
Brooks, Pierce, McLendon, Humphrey & Leonard LLP, Greensboro
336 373 8850
*Recommended in Environment*

### HOVIS, James
Moore & Van Allen, PLLC, Charlotte
704 331 1000
*Recommended in Banking & Finance*

### HUTSON, Benne
Helms Mulliss & Wicker PLLC, Charlotte
704 343 2000
*Recommended in Environment*

### JERNIGAN, John L
Smith, Anderson, Blount, Dorsett, Mitchell & Jernigan, LLP, Raleigh
919 821 6611
jjernigan@smithlaw.com
*Recommended in Corporate/M&A*
**Practice Areas:** Managing Partner of Smith, Anderson, Blount, Dorsett, Mitchell & Jernigan, LLP. Practices in the areas of mergers and acquisitions, banking, and corporate law. Has over 25 years' experience structuring, negotiating, and closing mergers and acquisitions involving public companies and large privately-owned companies. He has advised public company boards on special committees, audit committees and corporate governance.
**Prof. Memberships:** Admitted to North Carolina Bar (1967). Past President of the North Carolina Bar Association. Served as a Member of the Board of Governors of the North Carolina Bar Association from 1989-92, and two terms as Chair of the North Carolina Bar Association's Business Law Section. Member of the Wake County Bar Association, North Carolina Bar Association, and American

Bar Association, the American Judicature Society, American College of Mortgage Attorneys, and American Counsel Association. Fellow of the American Bar Foundation.

**Career:** He is listed in a leading legal US publication, and the Business North Carolina Legal Elite.

**Personal:** JD, University of North Carolina, 1967; AB, Davidson College, 1964.

## JOHNSON, Charles
Robinson, Bradshaw & Hinson PA, Charlotte 704 377 2536
*Recommended in Employment*

## JONES VAN BUREN, Carolyn
Kennedy Covington Lobdell & Hickman LLP, Charlotte 704 331 7400
*Recommended in Environment*

## KEEN, C Matthew
Ogletree, Deakins, Nash, Smoak & Stewart, PC, Raleigh 919 789 3162
matt.keen@ogletreedeakins.com
*Recommended in Employment*

**Practice Areas:** Labor and employment. Represents employers in employment litigation, including discrimination, wage and hour and ERISA matters. Advises companies on a national basis regarding employment law compliance.

**Prof. Memberships:** American Bar Association (Committee on WARN), North Carolina Bar Association (Labor and Employment and Litigation Sections), and American Employment Law Council. Selected by 'Best Lawyers in America', Business North Carolina's Legal Elite and SuperLawyers for employment law.

**Career:** Practiced with Ogletree Deakins since 1987; Partner since 1994.

**Publications:** North Carolina Employers' Desk Manual' (editor).

**Personal:** North Carolina State University (BS, 1983), University of North Carolina at Chapel Hill (JD, 1987).

## KENYON, Douglas W
Hunton & Williams, Raleigh
919 899 3076
dkenyon@hunton.com
*Recommended in Antitrust*

**Practice Areas:** Doug Kenyon is Administrative Head of Hunton & Williams' Raleigh Litigation Practice Group, Co-Head of the firm's Carolina's Litigation Practice Group and of the Copyright and Trademark component of the Intellectual Property Group. His practice focuses on antitrust, trade regulation and intellectual property law. Kenyon is a frequent speaker and author in these areas and is recognized for his expertise in antitrust law in 'The Best Lawyers in America'.

## KIRKLAND, Byron B
Smith, Anderson, Blount, Dorsett, Mitchell & Jernigan, LLP, Raleigh
919 821 6682
bkirkland@smithlaw.com
*Recommended in Corporate/M&A*

**Practice Areas:** Practices in the areas of securities law, corporate law, venture capital, mergers and acquisitions, and technology law. Extensive experience in public offerings; venture capital transactions; and structuring, negotiating and closing mergers and acquisitions for both public and private companies.

**Prof. Memberships:** Admitted to practice in North Carolina (1987). Member of the American Bar Association, Section of Business Law, North Carolina Bar Association, Wake County Bar Association and American Counsel Association; Member of the Board of Directors of the Council for Entrepreneurial Development; past Chair of the North Carolina Bar Association Young Lawyers Division.

**Career:** Smith, Anderson, Blount, Dorsett, Mitchell & Jernigan, LLP, 1987-present.

**Personal:** JD (with honors), University of North Carolina, 1987; MBA, University of North Carolina, 1987; BA, University of North Carolina, 1983.

## KLUTTZ, Joseph
Kennedy Covington Lobdell & Hickman LLP, Charlotte 704 331 7400
*Recommended in Banking & Finance, Bankruptcy*

## KORANDO, Kimberly J
Smith, Anderson, Blount, Dorsett, Mitchell & Jernigan, LLP, Raleigh
919 821 6671
kkorando@smithlaw.com
*Recommended in Employment*

**Practice Areas:** Heads Employment, Labor and Human Resources Practice Group. Has extensive experience with federal and state employment law compliance, HR best practices and prevention of employee lawsuits; conducting internal harassment and employee misconduct investigations; representing employers in federal and state compliance audits and investigations; and defending employers in state and federal civil actions, including multi-plaintiff and class actions.

**Prof. Memberships:** Admitted to practice in North Carolina (1986); US Court of Appeals, Fourth Circuit (1989), US Supreme Court (1991). ABA EEO Committee.

**Career:** Partner since 1993. Co-founder, Institute for Human Resources Training.

**Publications:** Chapter editor, 'Litigation Procedure' (2002, cum supp), 'Sexual Orientation' (4th edition in progress), 'BNA Employment Discrimination Law'. Author, 'Model Employee Policies and Forms for North Carolina Employers' (NCCBI 2005).

**Personal:** JD (with honors), University of Oklahoma, 1986; BS, in Psychology, University of Oklahoma, 1980.

## KUPEC, Christopher C
Mayer, Brown, Rowe & Maw LLP, Charlotte 704 444 3561
ckupec@mayerbrownrowe.com

*Recommended in Banking & Finance*

**Practice Areas:** Banking and finance.

**Prof. Memberships:** Admitted: North Carolina, 1980.

**Career:** Mayer, Brown, Rowe & Maw LLP, Charlotte, 2005 to date. Moore & Van Allen, PLLC, Charlotte, 1980-2005.

**Personal:** University of North Carolina at Chapel Hill, JD, with high honors, 1980; Order of the Coif; North Carolina Law Review. University of North Carolina at Chapel Hill, BA, 1975; Phi Beta Kappa.

## LAMPE, Donald C
Womble Carlyle Sandridge & Rice, PLLC, Charlotte 336 574 8057
dlampe@wcsr.com
*Recommended in Banking & Finance*

**Practice Areas:** Compliance counseling, administrative and legislative matters, product development, litigation and dispute resolution, and complex financial transactions for financial services providers, technology companies and industry organizations.

**Prof. Memberships:** American Bar Association, Vice Chair, Consumer Financial Service Committee; Fellow, The American College of Consumer Financial Services Lawyers; Governing Committee, The Conference on Consumer Finance Law; Advisory Board, UNC Center for Banking and Finance; Mortgage Bankers Association State and Local Regulatory Steering Committee; Best Lawyers in America.

**Personal:** Duke University School of Law, JD, 1982, Duke Law Journal, Administrative Law editor; Massachusetts Institute of Technology, BS, 1978, Phi Beta Kappa.

## LASSITER, Donnell
Kennedy Covington Lobdell & Hickman LLP, Charlotte 704 331 7400
*Recommended in Banking & Finance*

## LEON, Christopher E
Womble Carlyle Sandridge & Rice, PLLC, Winston-Salem 336 721 3518
cleon@wcsr.com

*Recommended in Banking & Finance*

**Practice Areas:** Chris Leon practices primarily in corporate and real estate finance and mergers and acquisitions. He has extensive experience advising public and private businesses in connection with structuring, negotiating and documenting all aspects of acquisitions, divestitures, complex financings and third party credit arrangements.

**Prof. Memberships:** North Carolina Bar Association; Georgia Bar Association, Corporate and Banking Law Section; Member, Loan Syndications and Trading Association, Inc.

**Career:** JD, 1983, Wake Forest University School of Law, cum laude, editorial staff, Wake Forest Law Review; American Society of International Law Proceedings; Moot Court Board; BS Industrial Engineering, 1980, Northwestern University, with distinction.

## LEVITAS, Steven J
Kilpatrick Stockton LLP, Raleigh
919 420 1707
SLevitas@KilpatrickStockton.com
*Recommended in Environment*

**Practice Areas:** Represents a wide range of corporate and governmental clients on environmental regulatory matters, with an emphasis on wastewater permitting and compliance, waste remediation, and real estate development.

**Career:** Deputy Secretary, North Carolina Department of Environment, Health and Natural Resources (1993-96); Director and senior attorney, North Carolina Environmental Defense Fund (1987-92); Law clerk to Hon James B McMillan (WDNC).

**Personal:** BA, University of North Carolina at Chapel Hill, Phi Beta Kappa, 1976; JD, Harvard Law School, cum laude, 1982. Member, North Carolina Progress Board, Carolina Environmental Program Board of Visitors, and Triangle Land Conservancy Board of Trustees.

## LOEB, Christopher
Robinson, Bradshaw & Hinson PA, Charlotte 704 377 2536
*Recommended in Real Estate*

## LOFTIS, Randolph
Constangy, Brooks & Smith, LLC, Winston-Salem 336 721 1001
*Recommended in Employment*

## LORD, Michael
Maupin Taylor, PA, Raleigh
919 981 4000
*Recommended in Employment*

## LUCAS, Edwin
Robinson, Bradshaw & Hinson PA, Charlotte 704 377 2536
*Recommended in Banking & Finance*

## LYNCH, Stephen
Robinson, Bradshaw & Hinson PA, Charlotte 704 377 2536
*Recommended in Corporate/M&A*

## MASON, C Steven
Smith, Anderson, Blount, Dorsett, Mitchell & Jernigan, LLP, Raleigh
919 821 6642
smason@smithlaw.com
*Recommended in Real Estate*

**Practice Areas:** Practices in the areas of commercial real estate, lending transactions, and corporate law.

**Prof. Memberships:** Admitted to practice in North Carolina (1981). Member of Wake County Bar Association, North Carolina Bar Association and American Bar Association.

**Career:** Joined Smith, Anderson, Blount, Dorsett, Mitchell & Jernigan, LLP, 1999. Moore & Van Allen PLLC, 1981-99.

**Personal:** JD, University of Virginia, 1981; BA, University of North Carolina, 1978.

## MCCONNELL, Alan
Kilpatrick Stockton LLP, Raleigh
919 420 1798
AMcConnell@KilpatrickStockton.com
*Recommended in Environment*
**Practice Areas:** Provides environmental representation, counseling and litigation services on a wide range of legislative, administrative and regulatory matters, with a particular emphasis on federal and state implementation of the Clean Air Act. Other areas of experience include solid and hazardous waste regulation, the Federal Insecticide, Fungicide and Rodenticide Act, the Clean Water Act, occupational safety and health issues, land use issues, and environmental liabilities attendant to corporate transactions.
**Prof. Memberships:** Carolinas Air Pollution Control Association. Admitted in North Carolina, Virginia and the District of Columbia.
**Personal:** BS Forest Resources, University of Georgia, 1982; JD, George Washington University, 1988.

## MCGINN, Daniel
Brooks, Pierce, McLendon, Humphrey & Leonard LLP, Greensboro
336 373 8850
*Recommended in Employment*

## MCKEITHEN, Ward
Robinson, Bradshaw & Hinson PA, Charlotte 704 377 2536
*Recommended in Litigation*

## MCLOUGHLIN JR, James
Moore & Van Allen, PLLC, Charlotte
704 331 1000
*Recommended in Litigation*

## MEHTA, Kiran
Kennedy Covington Lobdell & Hickman LLP, Charlotte 704 331 7400
*Recommended in Litigation*

## MERRITT, Keith
Hamilton Fay Moon Stephens Steele & Martin, PLLC, Charlotte 704 344 1117
*Recommended in Litigation*

## MERRITT, Mark
Robinson, Bradshaw & Hinson PA, Charlotte 704 377 2536
*Recommended in Antitrust, Litigation*

## MILLEN, Pressly M
Womble Carlyle Sandridge & Rice, PLLC, Raleigh 919 755 2135
pmillen@wcsr.com
*Recommended in Litigation*
**Practice Areas:** Press Millen is a trial attorney who has litigated a wide variety of antitrust and other complex business cases, including class actions, in federal and state courts throughout the United States. Press has represented both defendants and plaintiffs in antitrust cases tried to verdict in federal courts. Press has also litigated a wide variety of other business disputes including civil RICO, securities fraud and tax.
**Prof. Memberships:** ABA, Antitrust and

Litigation Sections; NC Bar Association.
**Career:** JD, 1985, Duke University School of Law, with high honors, note editor, Duke Law Review; AB 1982, Yale University, magna cum laude.

## MITCHELL JR, Burley B
Womble Carlyle Sandridge & Rice, PLLC, Raleigh 919 755 8166
bmitchell@wcsr.com
*Recommended in Litigation*
**Practice Areas:** A Former Chief Justice of the North Carolina Supreme Court, Justice Mitchell now heads Womble Carlyle's Appellate Advocacy and Government Relations Groups. He has served both as an advocate and judge in handling landmark cases in the United States for more than 30 years, authoring 484 appellate decisions.
**Prof. Memberships:** American Bar Association; North Carolina Bar Association; ABA Presidential Task Force on Corporate Responsibility, 2002; Board of Trustees, North Carolina State University; National Conference of Chief Justices' Committee on Professionalism, 1996-99; Institute of Judicial Administration.
**Personal:** JD, 1969, University of North Carolina; BA, 1966, North Carolina State University.

## MOSER, Kenneth A
Womble Carlyle Sandridge & Rice, PLLC, Winston-Salem 336 721 3504
kmoser@wcsr.com
*Recommended in Banking & Finance*
**Practice Areas:** Ken Moser has structured, documented, negotiated and closed numerous commercial real estate transactions and commercial, corporate, asset-based and real estate finance transactions. He advises banks, other financial institutions and corporations on all forms of financing and commercial real estate transactions.
**Prof. Memberships:** American College of Real Estate Lawyers; American College of Mortgage Attorneys; American, North Carolina and Forsyth County Bar Associations; American Counsel Association.
**Career:** JD, 1968, Wake Forest University School of Law, cum laude, associate editor, Law Review; Phi Delta Phi Magister (President); BA, 1965, Wake Forest University, President, Senior Class; Omicron Delta Kappa Honorary Leadership Fraternity.

## MURCHISON, John
Kennedy Covington Lobdell & Hickman LLP, Charlotte 704 331 7400
*Recommended in Antitrust*

## MURPHY, Paul
Moore & Van Allen, PLLC, Charlotte
704 331 1000
*Recommended in Capital Markets*

## NEDZBALA, Michael
Hunton & Williams, Charlotte
704 378 4703
mnedzbala@hunton.com

*Recommended in Capital Markets*
**Practice Areas:** Mr Nedzbala's practice focuses on structured finance, securitization and other capital markets transactions. He is Co-Head of the firm's Asset Securitization Group and a member of the Global Capital Markets Team.

## OATES, J Christopher
Moore & Van Allen, PLLC, Charlotte
704 331 1000
*Recommended in Real Estate*

## OBERKFELL, Keith F
Mayer, Brown, Rowe & Maw LLP, Charlotte 704 444 3549
koberkfell@mayerbrownrowe.com
*Recommended in Capital Markets*
**Practice Areas:** Specializes in securitization and other structured finance products, including CDOs, CLOs and derivatives. Advises foreign and domestic financial institutions, underwriters, placement agents, liquidity providers and issuers in private, public and Rule 144A/Regulation S executions in securitizations of a wide range of asset types, including trade receivables; aircraft, container and other equipment loan and lease portfolios; student loans; credit card receivables; automobile loans and other financial assets. Represents program sponsors with respect to the development of novel multi-seller commercial paper and medium term note conduit structures.
**Prof. Memberships:** Admitted: North Carolina, 2000; Illinois, 1993.
**Career:** Mayer, Brown, Rowe & Maw LLP, Charlotte, 1999 to date; Chicago, 1996-99; Partner, 2002. Vedder Price Kaufman and Kammholz, Chicago, 1994-96. Chapman and Cutler, Chicago, 1993-94.
**Personal:** Harvard Law School, JD cum laude, 1993. University of Virginia, BA with highest distinction, 1990; Phi Beta Kappa, Dean's List.

## OLEYNIK, Jeffrey
Brooks, Pierce, McLendon, Humphrey & Leonard LLP, Greensboro
336 373 8850
*Recommended in Antitrust, Litigation*

## OLIVER JR, Samuel
Manning Fulton & Skinner PA, Raleigh
919 787 8880
*Recommended in Real Estate*

## PATTERSON, Carl N
Smith, Anderson, Blount, Dorsett, Mitchell & Jernigan, LLP, Raleigh
919 821 6647
cpatterson@smithlaw.com
*Recommended in Litigation*
**Practice Areas:** Firm Practice Group Leader in commercial litigation. Practices in the areas of contract disputes and commercial litigation and corporate and securities litigation.
**Prof. Memberships:** Admitted to practice in North Carolina (1976). Member of the Wake County Bar Association; North Carolina Bar Association, Litigation,

Business Law and Law Practice Management Sections; American Bar Association; and the American Judicature Society. Past Chairman of the Young Lawyers Division of the North Carolina Bar Association.
**Career:** Became Partner Smith, Anderson, Blount, Dorsett, Mitchell & Jernigan, LLP, 1981. Member, Smith, Anderson, Blount, Dorsett, Mitchell & Jernigan Policy, Planning and Compensation Committees.
**Personal:** JD (with honors), University of North Carolina, 1976; BA, Davidson College, 1973.

## PHILLIPS, Jim
Brooks, Pierce, McLendon, Humphrey & Leonard LLP, Greensboro
336 373 8850
*Recommended in Litigation*

## PRICHARD, Allen
Kennedy Covington Lobdell & Hickman LLP, Charlotte 704 331 7400
*Recommended in Real Estate*

## PRUDEN, J Norfleet
Kennedy Covington Lobdell & Hickman LLP, Charlotte 704 331 7400
*Recommended in Corporate/M&A*

## PRYOR, Robert
Helms Mulliss & Wicker PLLC, Charlotte
704 343 2000
*Recommended in Bankruptcy*

## RAINEY, Richard L
Womble Carlyle Sandridge & Rice, PLLC, Charlotte 704 331 4967
rrainey@wcsr.com
*Recommended in Employment*
**Practice Areas:** Richard's labor and employment law experience includes representation of management regarding claims of race, age, sex, religion and disability discrimination, wrongful discharge and unlawful harassment and retaliation; unfair competition and misappropriation of trade secrets; wage and hour and FMLA compliance.
**Prof. Memberships:** ABA and North Carolina Bar Association, Labor and Employment Law Sections; admitted to practice before the North Carolina Supreme Court, the Fourth Circuit Court of Appeals and all US District Courts for North Carolina.
**Personal:** JD, 1987, University of North Carolina School of Law, Order of the Coif; BA, 1984, University of Delaware, summa cum laude.

## RAPER, William C
Womble Carlyle Sandridge & Rice, PLLC, Charlotte 704 331 4935
braper@wcsr.com
*Recommended in Litigation*
**Practice Areas:** Bill Raper's litigation practice involves commercial, corporate and shareholder transactions and professional negligence defense.
**Prof. Memberships:** North Carolina and

American Bar Associations, Litigation Sections; CPR Institute for Dispute Resolution; North Carolina Association of Defense Attorneys; loss prevention Partner for all North Carolina and South Carolina Member law firms of Attorneys Liability Assurance Society; Fellow, American College of Trial Lawyers.

**Career:** Judicial clerk, Judge J Braxton Craven, US Court of Appeals for the Fourth Circuit, 1972-73; JD, 1972, Vanderbilt University School of Law, editor, Law Review; legal assistant to Senator Sam Ervin, 1970; AB, 1968, University of North Carolina.

## RIKARD, William
Parker, Poe, Adams & Bernstein LLP, Charlotte 704 372 9000
*Recommended in Litigation*

## ROACH, Gerald F
Smith, Anderson, Blount, Dorsett, Mitchell & Jernigan, LLP, Raleigh
919 821 6668
groach@smithlaw.com
*Recommended in Corporate/M&A*

**Practice Areas:** Head of firm Corporate Team. Firm Practice Leader in Securities Practice Group. Has extensive experience with public offerings, domestic and international mergers and acquisitions, joint ventures, general corporate matters, private financings, technology law, and advising boards of directors and special committees.

**Prof. Memberships:** Admitted to practice in North Carolina (1982). Member of the American Bar Association, North Carolina Bar Association, Wake County Bar Association, American Counsel Association and the North Carolina Commission on Business Laws and the Economy. Past Chair of the Business Law Section of the North Carolina Bar.

**Career:** Joined Smith, Anderson, Blount, Dorsett, Mitchell & Jernigan, LLP, 1982. Chairman, Smith, Anderson, Blount, Mitchell & Jernigan Policy and Planning Committee. Included in a leading US legal publication. Also, he has been named one of 'Ten to Watch: Attorneys That Have an Impact on North Carolina Business' by the Triangle Business Journal and as a member of the 'Legal Elite' in two categories by Business North Carolina.

**Personal:** JD (cum laude), Wake Forest University School of Law, 1982; BA (cum laude), Wake Forest University, 1980.

## ROBERTSON, Allen
Robinson, Bradshaw & Hinson PA, Charlotte 704 377 2536
*Recommended in Banking & Finance*

## ROBINSON, Russell
Robinson, Bradshaw & Hinson PA, Charlotte 704 377 2536
*Recommended in Corporate/M&A*

## SAWCHAK, Matthew
Ellis & Winters LLP, Cary
919 865 7000
*Recommended in Antitrust*

## SCHILLI, David
Robinson, Bradshaw & Hinson PA, Charlotte 704 377 2536
*Recommended in Bankruptcy*

## SINGER, Robert
Brooks, Pierce, McLendon, Humphrey & Leonard LLP, Greensboro
336 373 8850
*Recommended in Banking & Finance, Corporate/M&A*

## SITTON, Larry B
Smith Moore LLP, Greensboro
336 378 5208
larry.sitton@smithmoorelaw.com
*Recommended in Litigation*

**Practice Areas:** Commercial litigation, insurance coverage litigation, financial services litigation, antitrust, class action.

**Prof. Memberships:** Past President, NC Bar Association; Permanent Member, Judicial Conference for the Fourth Circuit of Appeals; Master of the Bench, Chief Justice Joseph Branch Inn of Court; Fellow, American College of Trial Lawyers.

**Career:** LLB, cum laude, Wake Forest University, 1964; BA, cum laude, Wake Forest University, 1961; 1966-67: clerk, Hon Eugene A Gordon, US District Court for Middle District of NC; 1967-present: Smith Moore LLP.

**Personal:** 'Best Lawyers in America' (10 Consecutive Years); Business NC's Legal Elite (Hall of Fame); NC Super Lawyers (Top 100).

## TAYLOR, Daniel
Kilpatrick Stockton LLP, Winston-Salem
336 607 7330
DanTaylor@KilpatrickStockton.com
*Recommended in Litigation*

**Practice Areas:** Trial, appellate and arbitration experience representing plaintiffs and defendants in a broad range of business litigation matters involving corporate governance, corporate dissolution, securities, business tort, shareholder rights, intellectual property, and complex contracts.

**Prof. Memberships:** Fourth Circuit Judicial Conference; Chief Justice Joseph Branch Inn of Court (barrister).

**Career:** Army Airborne and Ranger School graduate, Vietnam veteran, resigned Commission, Captain, 1973.

**Personal:** BS Engineering, United States Military Academy, 1968; George Washington University, 1973 (Graduate School of Government and Business Administration); JD, Wake Forest University, cum laude, 1976; law clerk for Judge Hiram H Ward, USDC, MDNC; instrument rated private pilot.

## THEALL, Julianna C
Smith Moore LLP, Greensboro
336 378 5256
julie.theall@smithmoorelaw.com
*Recommended in Employment*

**Practice Areas:** Labor and employment, employment litigation, human resources counseling and training, litigation, education.

**Prof. Memberships:** Master, Guilford Inn of Court.

**Career:** JD, magna cum laude, University of Georgia, 1986; BBA, summa cum laude, University of Georgia, 1983; 1986-present: Smith Moore LLP.

**Personal:** Chair, Federal Bar Advisory Council (1999); BTI Client Service All-Star Team (2005); 'Best Lawyers in America': Labor and Employment (2003-06); Business NC's Legal Elite: Employment (2003-06); NC Super Lawyers (Top 50 Women, 2006).

## TIPPS, Maynard
Kennedy Covington Lobdell & Hickman LLP, Charlotte 704 331 7400
*Recommended in Real Estate*

## TOOLE, William
Robinson, Bradshaw & Hinson PA, Charlotte 704 377 2536
*Recommended in Environment*

## TORSTRICK, Brent
Robinson, Bradshaw & Hinson PA, Charlotte 704 377 2536
*Recommended in Real Estate*

## UBELL, Donald
Parker, Poe, Adams & Bernstein LLP, Charlotte 704 372 9000
*Recommended in Banking & Finance*

## VAN HOY, Philip
Van Hoy Reutlinger Adams & Dunn, Charlotte 704 375 6022
*Recommended in Employment*

## VAUGHAN, Keith W
Womble Carlyle Sandridge & Rice, PLLC, Winston-Salem
336 721 3540
kvaughan@wcsr.com
*Recommended in Litigation*

**Practice Areas:** Keith Vaughan has extensive litigation experience involving business, product liability, toxic tort and environmental issues. During his 30-year career, he has tried jury and bench trials, handled administrative proceedings and argued a wide range of matters in appellate courts.

**Prof. Memberships:** Georgia Bar Association; North Carolina Bar Association and American Bar Association, Litigation Sections; Master of the Bench, Chief Justice Joseph Branch Chapter, American Inns of Court.

**Career:** Chair of the firm Management Committee and firm Managing Member, 2002-present; JD, 1975, University of Georgia, cum laude, Editor-in-Chief, Georgia Law Review; BA, 1972, Wake Forest University, cum laude.

## VAUGHN, Scott
Helms Mulliss & Wicker PLLC, Charlotte
704 343 2000
*Recommended in Bankruptcy*

## WALKER, Clarence
Kennedy Covington Lobdell & Hickman LLP, Charlotte 704 331 7400
*Recommended in Corporate/M&A*

## WARD JR, Frank
Maupin Taylor, PA, Raleigh
919 981 4000
*Recommended in Employment*

## WEDDINGTON, Keith
Parker, Poe, Adams & Bernstein LLP, Charlotte 704 372 9000
*Recommended in Employment*

## WESTER, John
Robinson, Bradshaw & Hinson PA, Charlotte 704 377 2536
*Recommended in Employment, Litigation*

## WILLIAMS, Jim
Brooks, Pierce, McLendon, Humphrey & Leonard LLP, Greensboro
336 373 8850
*Recommended in Litigation*

## WINSLOW III, Edward
Brooks, Pierce, McLendon, Humphrey & Leonard LLP, Greensboro
336 373 8850
*Recommended in Banking & Finance, Corporate/M&A*

## WREN, Elizabeth
Kilpatrick Stockton LLP, Charlotte
704 338 5123
BWren@KilpatrickStockton.com
*Recommended in Corporate/M&A*

**Practice Areas:** Securities matters and corporate finance transactions in connection with initial and secondary public offerings, Rule 144A offerings and shelf offerings. Transactions related to investment grade and high grade debt, trust preferred securities and medium term note programs, as well as common and preferred equity. Public and private merger and acquisition transactions, including tender and exchange offers, corporate governance issues and SEC reporting and compliance issues.

**Personal:** BA English, Emory University; JD, with honors, University of North Carolina School of Law, 1980.

# SMITH MOORE LLP

## THE FIRM

**Managing Partner:** Stephen W Earp

**Number of partners:** 56
**Number of other lawyers:** 58

**FIRM OVERVIEW:** Smith Moore LLP serves clients in North Carolina, Georgia, the Southeast, the nation, and abroad through attorneys who are committed to excellence, teamwork, and innovation. Each attorney is personally invested in solving the firm's clients' complex legal issues. This commitment to client success has distinguished the firm since Julius C Smith began his practice in 1919. Smith Moore's offices are located in Atlanta, Georgia, and in Greensboro, Raleigh, and Wilmington, North Carolina. The firm has nearly 120 attorneys who concentrate in a wide range of substantive areas. The attorneys of Smith Moore have earned reputations for excellence in four core areas: litigation, business, health care, and labor and employment. Smith Moore uses its knowledge and experience to develop creative legal solutions to complicated problems.

## MAIN AREAS OF PRACTICE:

**Litigation:** Smith Moore's Litigation Group tries and litigates cases in state and federal trial courts throughout the United States. The firm regularly serves as both trial counsel and coordinating counsel in complex litigation matters. The firm's Appellate Team also has handled appeals of sophisticated matters throughout the Southeast. Smith Moore's Litigation Practice and trial experience cover a broad range, including: antitrust, commercial and business torts, product liability, toxic tort, financial services, construction, and catastrophic injuries. To best serve its clients, the firm is also very experienced in alternative dispute resolution methods, which are often more efficient and cost-effective. Smith Moore's Litigation Group takes pride in teamwork and on understanding its clients' businesses, working with them to achieve their goals in complex legal situations. Smith Moore exemplifies confidence through experience.

**Business:** Smith Moore's Business Group is comprised of experienced attorneys who handle a wide variety of issues on a daily basis for businesses ranging from small, entrepreneurial start-ups to large, publicly-owned companies. The firm's experience covers all forms of business enterprises, including corporations, limited liability companies, partnerships, and professional corporations. Smith Moore's Business Group is skilled in representing buyers, sellers, and equity investors with mergers, acquisitions, and other transactions involving business combinations. The firm offers tax services, advice on start-up issues and regulatory compliance, and regularly assist with contract issues involving corporate documents such as shareholder agreements, employment contracts, licensing agreements, supply contracts, consulting agreements, purchase and sale forms, and warranty agreements.

**Healthcare:** The firm's Healthcare Group is one of the largest in the Southeast and has helped healthcare providers in over 21 states. The firm is currently the counsel of record for more than 50 hospitals and hospital systems and 50 long-term care facilities, as well as a number of physician groups. The Health Care Group focuses on the following areas: Certificate of Need and licensure, corporate compliance, bioethical issues, financial and business transactions, fraud and abuse, HIPAA, managed care, management counselling, medical staff matters, provider defense litigation, regulatory compliance, and risk management.

**Labor & Employment:** Smith Moore's Labor and Employment Group counsels and advises employers on a full range of employment issues and litigates in state and federal courts, in arbitration and before governmental agencies. The group restricts its practice exclusively to the representation of management. The Labor and Employment Group emphasizes the following areas: employee benefits, employment litigation, human resource counseling and training, immigration, labor relations, as well as workers' compensation.

## OFFICES

**NORTH CAROLINA**
300 N. Greene Street, Suite 1400, **Greensboro**, NC 27401
**Tel:** 336 378 5200   **Fax:** 336 378 5400
**Website:** www.smithmoorelaw.com

2800 Two Hannover Square, **Raleigh**, NC 27601
**Tel:** 919 755 8700   **Fax:** 919 755 8800

300 N. 3rd Street, Suite 301, **Wilmington**, NC 28401
**Tel:** 910 251 7001   **Fax:** 910 251 7007

**GEORGIA**
One Atlantic Center, Suite 3700, 1201 West Peachtree Street,
**Atlanta**, GA 30309
**Tel:** 404 962 1000   **Fax:** 404 962 1200

**CLIENTS:** Smith Moore serves clients in the Southeast, the nation, and abroad. The firm represents insurance carriers, financial institutions, consumer products companies, manufacturing companies, educational institutions, hospitals, pharmaceutical companies, trade associations, and real estate developers, among many others.

**INTERNATIONAL WORK:** The firm's international practice includes a wide range of services sought by entities involved in international business. The firm's attorneys and staff integrate a thorough understanding of foreign cultures, high-quality legal skills, and ability to work effectively in such languages as German, French, and Spanish. Many of the attorneys have lived in the countries where the firm represents international clients. The firm has extensive international experience with both foreign and domestic companies and the legal issues that concern them.

# SMITH, ANDERSON, BLOUNT, DORSETT, MITCHELL & JERNIGAN, LLP

## THE FIRM

**Managing Partner:** John L Jernigan

**Number of partners:** 55
**Number of other lawyers:** 41

**FIRM OVERVIEW:** Since the firm's founding in 1912, it has grown to be the largest law firm in Raleigh and the Research Triangle region of North Carolina, and one of the largest in the state. The firm provides a full range of legal services and is dedicated to the principles of professionalism, excellence, and service to its clients and the community. The firm has a broad business practice representing large and medium size public and private companies and venture funds nationally and internationally in sectors that include financial services, pharmaceuticals, energy, healthcare, manufacturing, technology, service and retail, and government. The firm represents clients in litigation at every level of the judicial system, including the state and federal trial and appellate courts. It also appears regularly before state and federal agencies and in other forums to advance the interests of its clients and is experienced in all forms of alternative dispute resolution.

## MAIN AREAS OF PRACTICE:

**Commercial Transactions:** The firm has been a leader in assisting North Carolina businesses and individuals with commercial transactions, and has the legal and business skills needed for dynamic businesses today, including bank and other private finance, access to capital markets, mergers and acquisitions, environmental compliance, commercial real estate, bankruptcy, and international transactions. The firm has significant experience in secured and unsecured bank lending, joint ventures and strategic alliances, venture and mezzanine investments, leveraged buyouts and acquisition financing, letters of credit, mergers and acquisitions, commercial paper, derivatives, workouts and reorganizations, commercial real estate, employment, environmental compliance, conduit financing, securitizations and other asset-based financings, divestitures, licensing, international trade and transactions, and franchising. The firm has an extensive tax practice providing planning and advice, as well as representation of clients in tax controversies.

**Commercial Litigation:** The firm's Commercial Litigation Practice Group has substantial trial experience, and is adept at handling complex, document-intensive cases. The firm offers expertise in all forms of alternative dispute resolution. Some members of the Commercial Litigation Practice Group are certified mediators or arbitrators. The Commercial Litigation Practice Group includes members of the American College of Trial Lawyers, the International Society of Barristers, the International Association of Defense Counsel, the American Board of Trial Advocates, the American Judicature Society, and the Judicial Conference of the Fourth Circuit Court of Appeals. The firm has extensive experience in counseling and representing clients in banking litigation, disputes between buyers and sellers of goods and services, commercial real estate disputes, insurance matters and shareholder actions.

**Corporate, Securities & Technology:** The firm has one of the state's leading public company practices as measured by number and size of transactions and public company clients. The firm provides a broad range of general corporate, mergers and acquisitions, corporate finance, securities, joint venture, venture capital, employee benefits, intellectual property and technology advice to clients ranging from established public companies to venture capital backed start-ups and venture funds, many involving technology fields. The firm also regularly advises boards of directors or committees, including special committees.

**Regulatory - Government Relations, Healthcare, Public Utilities:** The firm has a long history of working on behalf of its business clients with local, state and federal government and represents a broad array of clients before the North Carolina General Assembly. The firm's Healthcare Practice provides business and regulatory counsel to a wide variety of healthcare clients across the Southeast, from physicians and physician organizations to other providers to informatics companies and e-health entities. Primary services and typical transactions include antitrust, business/contract disputes, certificate of need, covenants not to compete, employment agreements, HIPAA and other federal and state confidentiality and privacy laws, fraud and abuse, including Stark, healthcare financing, licensing board issues, managed care, medical staff issues, Medicare compliance, mergers and acquisitions/joint ventures, negotiations with insurers, physician organizations, PSOs and insurance, and quality assurance. The firm regularly represents clients engaged in the energy and telecommunications industries. Services include negotiation with and litigation before state regulatory agencies and drafting, management and representation of clients in connection with energy and telecommunications issues before the North Carolina General Assembly.

**General Litigation:** The firm's Medical Malpractice Practice Group defends physicians, hospitals, and other healthcare providers with a philosophy that combines an aggressive and efficient approach to litigation with an in-depth understanding of relevant medical issues. It is experienced in assisting health care providers through every stage of malpractice actions, including risk management prelitigation claims, discovery, depositions, trial, and appellate advocacy. The firm's Products Liability Group regularly represents large manufacturers in the automotive, chemical and other industries providing services ranging from risk management advice to litigation defense.

**CLIENTS:** The firm's clients include some of the largest financial institutions, insurance companies, public utilities, retailers, manufacturing, pharmaceutical, and biotechnology companies in its region and the nation, as well as emerging growth and technology companies. The firm also represents smaller businesses and individuals, as well as trade and professional associations and their members.

**INTERNATIONAL WORK:** The firm represents a number of international companies that have ongoing business interests in its market, including companies based in the United Kingdom, France, Japan, Germany, Holland, and Israel, as well as numerous companies located in the United States with foreign subsidiaries or interests.

## HEAD OFFICE

**NORTH CAROLINA**
2500 Wachovia Capitol Center, **Raleigh**, NC 27601
**Tel:** 919 821 1220   **Fax:** 919 821 6800
**Website:** www.smithlaw.com

## CONTACTS

| | |
|---|---|
| **Commercial** | John L Jernigan |
| **Corporate/Securities** | Gerald F Roach |
| **Commercial Litigation** | Carl N Patterson |
| **General Litigation** | Samuel G Thompson |
| **Regulatory** | Julian D Bobbitt, Jr |

SMITH ANDERSON

# WOMBLE CARLYLE SANDRIDGE & RICE, PLLC

## THE FIRM

**Managing Member:** Keith W Vaughan

**Number of partners:** 230
**Number of other lawyers:** 301

**FIRM OVERVIEW:** Womble Carlyle Sandridge & Rice, PLLC, which traces its history to 1876, is one of the largest law firms in the Southeast and mid-Atlantic, with over 530 lawyers in nine offices from Atlanta to Washington, DC. Womble Carlyle is a full-service business law firm providing legal advice to a wide spectrum of regional, national and international clients in sectors that include financial services, manufacturing, transportation, telecommunications, energy, health care, life sciences, government, education and technology.

## MAIN AREAS OF PRACTICE:

**Capital Markets:** The firm provides legal services – including regulatory compliance and the structuring, negotiating and closing of capital markets transactions – to participants in the capital markets, including capital providers (such as commercial banks, investment banks and investment funds), entities accessing the capital markets to obtain capital (from startups to Fortune 500 companies) and intermediaries acting in the capital markets to mitigate risk related to movement in the values of currencies, commodities, equities and interest rate indices.

**Corporate & Securities:** Lawyers in the Corporate and Securities Practice provide representation in the areas of general corporate law, mergers and acquisitions, venture capital, securities offerings and securities regulation, fiduciary obligations and rights of directors and officers, partnership and limited liability company formation and syndication and business contract negotiations.

**Tax:** The firm provides creative tax planning and advice on mergers and acquisitions, corporate reorganizations, real estate development, tax controversies before the Internal Revenue Service and state taxing authorities, and tax-sensitive and tax-enhanced financings.

**Real Estate Development:** Members of the group represent clients in the acquisition, financing, development, and sale of all types of unimproved land and improved properties for residential and commercial use, including large land assemblages, major office buildings and office parks, shopping malls and centers, luxury hotels and resorts, condominiums and multifamily housing projects throughout the region.

**Intellectual Property:** Representation includes all aspects of domestic and foreign intellectual property law, including patent investigations and analyses, procurement of US and foreign patents and general client counseling regarding license agreements, corporate-sponsored research contracts, development agreements, technology transfer agreements and software protection.

**Litigation & Arbitration:** The firm has a litigation practice of national scope, encompassing business litigation; intellectual property litigation; environmental and toxic tort litigation; insurance, governmental and tort litigation; and product liability litigation. Attorneys have handled matters from trials of national class actions, to coordination of litigation nationally, to defense of clients in mediation and arbitration in many states throughout the country, including potentially high verdict jurisdictions.

**Employee Benefits:** Lawyers in this group provide all facets of employee benefits representation, including design, drafting and implementation of tax-qualified retirement and welfare benefit plans, non-qualified retirement arrangements, and executive compensation programs. The group also counsels clients regarding ERISA compliance and related federal and state legislation affecting employee benefit programs.

**Government Affairs:** Womble Carlyle bridges the gap between law practice and public policy by delivering expert advice and assistance in dealing effectively with all levels and branches of government – local, state and federal. Members of this group combine years of on-the-job experience in government with legal training and the resources of an established law firm to engage the legislative and regulatory system expertly and persistently.

## HEAD OFFICE

**NORTH CAROLINA**
One West Fourth Street, **Winston-Salem** NC 27101
**Tel:** 336 721 3600   **Fax:** 336 721 3660
**Email:** kmoser@wcsr.com
**Website:** www.wcsr.com

## BRANCH OFFICES

The firm has offices in Atlanta, Georgia; Charlotte, Durham, Greensboro and Raleigh in North Carolina; Greenville, South Carolina; Tysons Corner, Virginia; and Washington, DC. Please see firm's website for further details.

## CONTACTS

| | |
|---|---|
| **Antitrust, Distribution & Franchise** | Mark N Poovey |
| **Bankruptcy & Creditor's Rights** | William B Sullivan |
| **Business Litigation** | Timothy G Barber |
| **Capital Markets** | James E Lilly |
| **Corporate & Securities** | Jeffrey C Howland |
| **Employee Benefits** | Michael D Gunter |
| **Environmental** | R Howard Grubbs |
| **Government Affairs** | Burley B Mitchell, Jr |
| **Insurance, Governmental & Tort Litigation** | Reid C Adams, Jr |
| **Labor & Employment** | Charles A Edwards |
| **Product Liability Litigation** | Keith A Clinard |
| **Real Estate Development** | Bobby D Hinson |
| **Tax** | Howard N Solodky |
| **Trust & Estates** | George A Ragland |

**Labor & Employment:** The firm represents management in every aspect of the employer-employee relationship, including employment-related litigation before federal and state courts, agencies and arbitration panels, as well as providing advice on how to avoid litigation and minimize legal liabilities.

**CLIENTS:** Representative clients include: ALLTEL Carolina, Inc.; American International Group, Inc.; Armstrong World Industries, Inc.; BB&T Corporation; Bank of America; Centex Homes; Collins & Aikman Floorcoverings, Inc.; GlaxoSmithKline; INVISTA; Dell Inc., Lowes Companies, Inc.; Medigital, Inc.; NCR Corporation; Novartis Pharmaceuticals Corporation; ReynoldsAmerican, Inc.; Remington Arms Company, Inc.; Sealy Corp.; Thomas Built Buses, Inc.; Thomasville Furniture Industries, Inc.; The Travelers; Unicomp, Inc.; Universal Tax Systems, Inc.; UnumProvident Corporation; Wachovia Bank and Wake Forest University.

**INTERNATIONAL WORK:** The firm's lawyers advise on business acquisitions, joint ventures, the protection and licensing of intellectual property, commercial leasing, sales and distribution arrangements, US export controls, customs and immigration in the context of inbound and outbound international transactions and operations. The firm defends the interests of its clients, including patent and trademark rights, in dispute resolution involving litigation, mediation and international arbitration throughout the world.

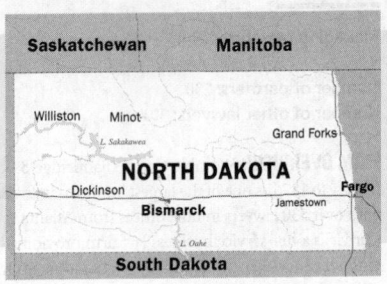

## How lawyers are ranked

Every year we carry out thousands of in-depth interviews with clients and lawyers in order to assess the reputations and expertise of business lawyers across the USA. Chambers rankings and editorial are referred to extensively by General Counsel and other purchasers of legal services who look to our recommendations when choosing their lawyers.

# CORPORATE/COMMERCIAL

### Corporate/Commercial
### Leading Firms

1. VOGEL LAW FIRM *Fargo*
2. ANDERSON & BOTTRELL *Fargo*
   CONMY FESTE LTD *Fargo*
   DORSEY & WHITNEY LLP *Fargo*
   SERKLAND LAW FIRM, PC *Fargo*
   ZIMNEY FOSTER PC *Grand Forks*
3. MCNAIR, LARSON & CARLSON LTD *Fargo*
   NILLES, HANSEN & DAVIES LTD *Fargo*
   OLSON BURNS LEE PC *Minot*
   PEARSON CHRISTENSEN CAHILL *Grand Forks*
   TSCHIDER & SMITH *Bismarck*

### Leading Individuals

1. JOHNSON Steven *Vogel Law Firm*
   SMITH Sean *Tschider & Smith*
   THOMAS Michael *Conmy Feste Ltd*
2. CHRISTENSEN Douglas *Pearson Christensen Cahill*
   FOSS Marilyn - *Sole Practitioner*
   SCHLOSSMAN William *Vogel Law Firm*
   SELBO Gregory *Nilles, Hansen & Davies Ltd*
   STRINDEN Jon *Dorsey & Whitney LLP*

### Corporate/Commercial: Bankruptcy
### Leading Individuals

1. BOTTRELL Lowell *Anderson & Bottrell*
   BRAKKE Jon *Vogel Law Firm*
   DEMARS David *DeMars & Turman Ltd*
   FOSTER John *Zimney Foster PC*
   JOHNSON David *McNair, Larson & Carlson Ltd*
   MINCH Roger *Serkland Law Firm, PC*
   OLSON Richard *Olson Burns Lee PC*

## Band 1

### Vogel Law Firm

**The Firm:** Market commentators declare this eight-lawyer corporate team to be the state's *"leader for corporate law."* Its unrivaled size means it is able to offer a *"first-class"* depth of expertise across the spectrum of corporate and commercial law from its network of offices in Fargo, Bismarck and Moorhead. Its workload encompasses advice on the creation and dissolution of corporate entities, M&A and taxation. The firm regularly represents high-profile clients drawn from within and beyond the state's borders, especially those in the healthcare industry. Bankruptcy matters also feature prominently, particularly related to the agricultural sector; these usually involve the representation of creditors in collection claims. For example, the firm was representing an unsecured creditors' committee in the reorganization of a company involved in the processing of bison meat in 2005.

**The Lawyers:** Interviewees applaud **Jon Brakke's** *"statewide reputation for debtor-creditor work,"* particularly on behalf of clients in the agricultural sector, and also note his expertise in real estate and litigation. Peers acknowledge: *"There is no one smarter nor more persistent for his clients."* Sources praise the *"business-minded approach"* of leading corporate law practitioner **Steven Johnson.** He is renowned for advising large and small businesses on sales and purchases, reorganizations and stockholder disputes. Market sources warmly recommended the *"bright"* **William Schlossman** for his *"quality corporate advice"* on a broad range of commercial transactions. He also features prominently on commercial real estate matters.

**Clients/Work Highlights:** Acceptance Corporation; Forum Communications; Agribank; Ag Services of America; First International Bank & Trust; MeritCare Health System; State Bank of Fargo and Western State Bank.

## Band 2

### Anderson & Bottrell

**The Firm:** This corporate team comprises six attorneys experienced in the full spectrum of business matters. Key areas of strength include advising on the structuring of business transactions and handling a steady stream of loan collections. Its client base consists of local businesses, banks, dealerships and farming organizations, which it assists in matters such as the licensing of a hog confinement operation.

**The Lawyers:** At the *"top of the North Dakota corporate tree,"* **Lowell Bottrell** is warmly praised by clients for his *"incredible command of commercial matters, responsiveness and high level of client service."* He handles a diverse corporate and commercial practice and maintains a particular niche in bankruptcy-related representations of creditors in commercial collections. He advised North Dakota State University on various licenses and agreements entered into with large technology corporations in 2005.

**Clients/Work Highlights:** North Dakota State University; Western State Bank; Northern State Bank; Centennial National Bank and RDO Equipment.

### Conmy Feste Ltd

**The Firm:** This three-lawyer corporate group has built a stellar reputation for *"first-class"* advice on midsized M&A and banking matters. It services a healthy stable of clients from the agricultural, manufacturing and banking industries.

**The Lawyers:** The *"gentlemanly"* **Michael Thomas** divides his practice between banking, corporate transactions and estate planning. Market sources enthuse: *"He stands out for his understanding of the business goals behind a transaction – he is reasonable enough to compromise when the situation calls for it."* In 2005 he devoted much of his time to advising on company acquisitions and complex bank lending work.

**Clients/Work Highlights:** Wells Fargo; Bremer Bank; Brandt Holdings and Border States Electric.

### Dorsey & Whitney LLP

See firm details p.1169

**The Firm:** Market sources observe that the three-lawyer corporate team based at this international firm *"has established a deep footprint in Fargo."* Indeed, a prominent rival acknowledged the firm to be its *"primary competitor"* based on its *"wide range of expertise and the excellent backup available from its Minnesota office."* The practice is renowned for its excellence in handling corporate M&A transactions, as well as advising emerging companies on venture capital deals and structuring alternative finance. Additionally, the firm has further developed its real estate projects practice over the past year; for example, it has been advising on a $50 million hotel and water park complex and a $12 million historic federal and state tax credit project. The firm attracts a broad client base, encompassing companies from the technological, manufacturing, agriculture and hospitality industries.

**The Lawyers:** Qualified accountant **Jon Strinden** (see p.1597) is singled out as the cornerstone of the corporate team. He is well versed in advising private companies on new ventures, sales and purchases, tax planning and general corporate matters. Highlights of his 2005 caseload included assisting a number of North Dakota companies in raising capital through the preparation of private placement memorandums and filings with the federal and state securities offices.

**Clients/Work Highlights:** On the M&A front, lawyers handled a cross-border transaction wherein a North Dakota client acquired a controlling interest in a Canadian company. Key clients include Otter Tail; AgCountry Farm Credit Services; Renaissance Ventures; Flint Communications and Packet Digital.

## Serkland Law Firm, PC

**The Firm:** Clients enthuse that *"you get a lot of a bang for your buck"* from this impressive four-lawyer corporate team. Lawyers are experienced in representing a predominantly banking client base on bankruptcy proceedings and restructurings, as well as handling foreclosure documentation and regulatory compliance. Advice on corporate matters such as sale and purchase transactions and stockholder agreements is another key area of focus.

**The Lawyers:** **Roger Minch** receives hearty praise for his *"outstanding"* expertise in representing banks and agricultural lenders, particularly as creditors in bankruptcy cases. His practice has recently broadened to encompass a greater volume of state court commercial litigation. For example, in a major trial in July 2005 he successfully established the misrepresentation of rents by the seller of a shopping center on behalf of his client, the buyer.

**Clients/Work Highlights:** American Federal Bank; Bremer Bank; State Bank & Trust; First State Bank of LaMoure; CoBank; ACB; Citizens State Bank; Citizens State Bank of Finley and Union State Bank Fargo.

## Zimney Foster PC

**The Firm:** This Grand Forks-based corporate team is recognized as a key player in the corporate and banking market. Its expertise in devising loan documentation for commercial ventures and handling distress management attracts a host of prominent local and national financial institution clients. The group also handles a broad spectrum of company law matters, including incorporations, partnership law and stock transfers.

**The Lawyers:** Interviewees identify **John Foster** as the *"dean of banking and creditors' rights."* *"A well-rounded practitioner who knows commercial law inside out,"* he advises banks and financial institutions on

structuring finance packages and liquidations.

**Clients/Work Highlights:** Wells Fargo; Bremer Bank; Farm Credit Services and US Bank.

## Band 3

### McNair, Larson & Carlson Ltd

**The Firm:** This compact outfit maintains a strong reputation for its expert advice in the corporate and bankruptcy arenas. Its client base includes banks, agricultural lenders and commercial clients.

**The Lawyers:** Interviewees recommend **David Johnson** for being *"top choice for bankruptcy debtors,"* and marvel at his noncontentious, commercial abilities.

**Clients/Work Highlights:** First State Bank of Munich, Security State Bank Wishek and Union State Bank of Hazen.

### Nilles, Hansen & Davies Ltd

**The Firm:** This full-service firm houses a quality corporate practice well versed in advising corporations, partnerships and nonprofit organizations on M&A, contractual matters and taxation. It services a diverse client base drawn from across the healthcare, manufacturing and financial industries.

**The Lawyers:** The *"highly knowledgeable and detail-oriented"* **Gregory Selbo** handles a wide-ranging corporate, real estate and probate caseload. According to his peers, *"his word is his bond and he can be counted on to look for solutions, not problems."*

### Olson Burns Lee PC

**The Firm:** This Minot-based practice is a well-established player in the corporate and banking market. It represents an impressive array of North Dakota banks and financial institutions in bankruptcy and transactional and regulatory matters.

**The Lawyers:** The *"top-flight"* **Richard Olson** wins the admiration of the market for his *"tough representation of creditors' rights."* Notwithstanding his bankruptcy experience, he also handles a busy caseload of corporate matters, particularly those involving M&A.

**Clients/Work Highlights:** Security State Bank of North Dakota, Farm Credit Services of North Dakota and First International Bank & Trust.

### Pearson Christensen Cahill & Clapp, PLLP

**The Firm:** Clients praise this *"highly professional"* three-lawyer corporate group for the scope and quality of its expertise. Lawyers based in Grand Forks and in Moorhead, Minnesota benefit from extensive tax experience to offer *"unique expertise in tax,"* according to sources. In 2005 the team was involved in structuring corporate M&A transactions, financing

projects and advising on complex commercial disputes.

**The Lawyers:** Satisfied clients applaud the *"brilliant"* **Douglas Christensen** for being a *"great communicator who you can rely on for his responsiveness and focused commercial knowledge."* He boasts a wealth of experience in handling business formation and succession planning matters and also devotes a significant portion of his practice to commercial litigation.

**Clients/Work Highlights:** Rydell; Acme Electrical Tool Crib of the North; Alerus Financial and Milestone Investments.

## Tschider & Smith

**The Firm:** This four-lawyer team is a source of quality advice on the full gamut of corporate law, including incorporation, business development and taxation. Banking and finance matters also feature heavily in its workload, as does an increasing volume of commercial real estate development transactions. Over 2005, the team was particularly active in advising numerous large retail clients on setting up outlets in North Dakota. Accordingly, lawyers recently assisted Wal-Mart as local counsel to its operations in Bismarck.

**The Lawyers:** Commentators hail the *"logical and straightforward"* **Sean Smith** as a leading light for corporate and commercial advice. Indeed, peers acknowledge, *"we would unhesitatingly recommend him,"* explaining that *"his background as a qualified accountant has helped him to develop a profound understanding of corporate and real estate transactions."* He advised on numerous business acquisitions and regulatory compliance issues in 2005. He also maintains a visible profile in healthcare matters, including a position as corporate counsel to St. Alexius Medical Center.

**Clients/Work Highlights:** AgriBank FCB, Farm Credit Services of Mandan and St. Alexius Medical Center.

## Other Notable Practitioners

Clients applaud the *"bulldog"* **David DeMars** of DeMars & Turman Ltd for being *"a real veteran of the bankruptcy court."* He handles a mixed caseload of debtor-creditor, commercial and real estate law, and represents high-profile clients such as Community First National Bank and First Financial Bank. Sole practitioner **Marilyn Foss** is based in Bismarck and is renowned for her expertise in bank regulatory issues. Sources praise her for her work as general counsel to the North Dakota Bankers Association, and note her assistance to individual banks and financial institutions regarding lobbying and day-to-day operational matters.

# EMPLOYMENT

# MAINLY DEFENDANT

---

**Employment: Mainly Defendant**

**Leading Firms**

1. **DORSEY & WHITNEY LLP** *Fargo*
2. **ANDERSON & BOTTRELL** *Fargo*
   **VOGEL LAW FIRM** *Fargo*
3. **CONMY FESTE LTD** *Fargo*
   **PAGE LAW FIRM LLC** *Fargo*
   **WOLD JOHNSON PC** *Fargo*
   **ZUGER KIRMIS & SMITH** *Bismarck*

**Leading Individuals**

★ **HERMAN Sarah** *Dorsey & Whitney LLP*
1. **ALBRECHT Kristy** *Dorsey & Whitney LLP*
   **DONARSKI Michelle** *Anderson & Bottrell*
   **EDISON-SMITH Lisa** *Vogel Law Firm*
   **PAGE Adele** *Page Law Firm LLC*
   **SCHULTZ Robert** *Conmy Feste Ltd*
   **THOMAS Benjamin** *Wold Johnson PC*
   **WARD Patrick** *Zuger Kirmis & Smith*

---

## Band 1

### Dorsey & Whitney LLP

See firm details p.1169

**The Firm:** This three-lawyer labor and employment group benefits from unrivaled access to resources drawn from its national network of offices to offer timely and strategic advice on employment law. Areas of expertise include the defense of employers facing discrimination claims, workers' compensation and the negotiation of collective bargaining agreements. Wage and hour litigation featured significantly in the firm's workload in 2005, as did a series of labor disputes affecting its stable of prominent local and national clients.

**The Lawyers:** The *"fantastic"* **Sarah Herman** (see p.1596) *"commands the utmost respect"* for the unsurpassed depth and breadth of her labor and employment experience. Clients applaud her for being *"simply the best employment law practitioner in North Dakota for clear, concise advice, which always keeps us out of trouble."* Herman handles a mixed caseload of labor, employment and commercial litigation. Interviewees have *"only good things to say"* about employment lawyer **Kristy Albrecht** (see p.1596).

**Clients/Work Highlights:** Blue Cross and Blue Shield Association of North Dakota; Dakota Medical Foundation; Microsoft Business Solutions; MDU Resources Group and Otter Tail.

## Band 2

### Anderson & Bottrell

**The Firm:** This two-member employment team complements the firm's busy corporate practice by acting for an impressive stable of local and national clients. In 2005 lawyers were particularly active in employment law cyber-liability claims, concerning an employee's purchase of their employer's domain name and related allegations of Internet defamation. Other areas of expertise include advice on the breach of noncompete provisions in employment contracts and overtime litigation.

**The Lawyers:** **Michelle Donarski** is an *"aggressive litigator,"* whom clients recommend for her *"ethical, upfront and professional manner. She is easy to talk to and successfully explains complex situations without ever talking down to us."* A significant portion of her practice is devoted to providing preventive employment counseling to employers. She also handles a busy caseload of employment defense litigation, responding to claims before the EEOC and the DOL.

**Clients/Work Highlights:** Global Electric Motorcars; Advantage Credit Bureau; Triad Broadcasting; PRACS Institute; North Dakota State University; Buffalo Wild Wings Bar and Grill and AgriPro Wheat.

### Vogel Law Firm

**The Firm:** This stellar employment group draws upon the strengths of the firm's superlative commercial litigation practice and high-profile client base. Seven attorneys advise on a broad spectrum of labor and employment matters, such as immigration and employee benefits work. Particular areas of expertise include advising on OSHA compliance, defending discrimination litigation and handling labor disputes for a varied roster of clients, a healthy share of which are in the healthcare sector. Ongoing work includes the defense of a small software company against a pending state disability discrimination claim brought by an employee.

**The Lawyers:** Head of the labor and employment department **Lisa Edison-Smith** is praised for her *"excellent and detailed analytical skills."* Her practice consists of an even mixture of employment counseling and defense litigation; she has recently been handling an increased volume of disability and age discrimination claims, alongside a steady stream of wage and hour litigation. In 2005 highlights included obtaining a dismissal with no probable cause on an alleged disability discrimination claim brought against MeritCare Health System.

**Clients/Work Highlights:** Cass County Electric Cooperative; Prairie St. John's; Gate City Bank; Western State Bank and Integrity Windows.

## Band 3

### Conmy Feste Ltd

**The Firm:** This full-service firm continues to provide quality advice on employment and workers' compensation matters.

**The Lawyers:** The *"gentlemanly"* **Robert Schultz** attracts the plaudits of peers for his *"straight-up and ethical approach."* He is well versed in workers' compensation matters and also features in a steady stream of domestic relations cases.

### Page Law Firm LLC

**The Firm:** This unique two-lawyer outfit is dedicated to advising companies on employment law consulting and litigation. In 2005 lawyers represented North American Bison Cooperative in an employment contract dispute, and acted for Rotech Medical Corporation in an appeal before the North Dakota Supreme Court regarding a retaliatory discharge claim. Clients are drawn mainly from the banking, manufacturing and healthcare sectors.

**The Lawyers:** Clients enthuse that **Adele Page** *"has a direct and confident style, but you can always sense the compassion; she keeps in mind the people elements of a case alongside the legal issues."* Page is *"highly qualified in all facets of employment law,"* with a practice that encompasses expertise on the FMLA, the FLSA and employment discrimination in the form of day-to-day counseling and representation in litigation. Satisfied clients describe her as *"exceptionally bright, hard-working and responsive."* The firm has doubled in size in 2005 with the addition of associate Matthew Greenley, who has a special focus on ERISA and employee benefits issues.

**Clients/Work Highlights:** American Federal Bank; Trinity Hospital; Riverwood Healthcare Center and Tecton Products.

### Wold Johnson PC

**The Firm:** The firm is highly experienced in handling state and federal employment law matters on behalf of plaintiffs and defendants. This involves lawyers in advice on employment discrimination, executive compensation, employment termination and employee benefits.

**The Lawyers:** The *"strategic"* **Benjamin Thomas** has a *"knack for figuring out what the important issues are and focusing on them,"* according to market sources. Peers endorse him as a *"highly ethical and bright"* employment law practitioner with *"plenty of common sense."* He also features in a significant volume of civil litigation.

**Clients/Work Highlights:** Moorhead Public Service; Community First Bank; Union State Bank and US Bank.

### Zuger Kirmis & Smith

**The Firm:** This Bismarck-based firm is renowned for its capabilities in handling employment litigation. Lawyers offer expert advice on discrimination and relation claims, alongside an active labor law practice involving contract negotiations.

**The Lawyers:** **Patrick Ward** enjoys an excellent reputation for employment law litigation, a focus he combines with a caseload of commercial dispute resolution. He is particularly adept at defending unions against members' claims.

**Clients/Work Highlights:** Montana-Dakota Utilities; BNI Coal; Bridgestone/Firestone; Microsoft; Coventry healthcare and the City of Medora.

# LITIGATION

## Litigation: General Commercial
### Leading Firms

**1** NILLES, HANSEN & DAVIES LTD *Fargo*
 VOGEL LAW FIRM *Fargo*
 ZUGER KIRMIS & SMITH *Bismarck*

**2** DORSEY & WHITNEY LLP *Fargo*
 MARING WILLIAMS LAW OFFICE PC *Fargo*
 SERKLAND LAW FIRM, PC *Fargo*

**3** FLECK, MATHER & STRUTZ, LTD *Bismarck*
 MCGEE HANKLA BACKES & DOBROVOLNY *Minot*
 MCNAIR, LARSON & CARLSON LTD *Fargo*
 PEARCE & DURICK *Bismarck*
 PEARSON CHRISTENSEN CAHILL *Grand Forks*
 SMITH BAKKE OPPEGARD PORSBORG *Bismarck*

### Leading Individuals

#### Senior Statesman
 KLINGER Edward *Vogel Law Firm*

**1** CARLSON Bruce *McNair, Larson & Carlson Ltd*
 FISCHER Ronald *Pearson Christensen Cahill*
 HILL James *Zuger Kirmis & Smith*
 MARING David *Maring Williams Law Office PC*
 MCLEAN Ronald *Serkland Law Firm, PC*
 STORSLEE Steven *Storslee Law Firm*
 THIEM Rebecca *Zuger Kirmis & Smith*

**2** BAKKE Randall *Smith Bakke Oppegard Porsborg*
 DUNN Daniel *Maring Williams Law Office PC*
 DURICK Patrick *Pearce & Durick*
 HAGGART Todd *Vogel Law Firm*
 HANSON Mark *Nilles, Hansen & Davies Ltd*
 ILVEDSON Duane *Nilles, Hansen & Davies Ltd*
 KIRMIS Lyle *Zuger Kirmis & Smith*
 MCGEE II Richard *McGee Hankla Backes*
 MORLEY Patrick *Morley Law Firm Ltd*
 PLAMBECK Stephen *Nilles, Hansen & Davies Ltd*
 SINCLAIR Brad *Serkland Law Firm, PC*
 ZIMMERMAN Todd *Dorsey & Whitney LLP*

## Band 1

### Nilles, Hansen & Davies Ltd

**The Firm:** Rivals rate this impressive outfit as a "*real competitor*" in the disputes field. A 15-strong team covers all aspects of commercial litigation, with particular emphasis on defense of insurance claims and construction litigation. Lawyers also command respect for their handling of PI and products liability claims. The firm operates throughout the upper Midwest in federal and state courts and maintains a healthy profile in alternative dispute resolution processes, including arbitration and mediation. Peers note that the lawyers "*realistically evaluate the situation and make timely recommendations to the client.*"
**The Lawyers:** As head of both the litigation and insurance teams, **Duane Ilvedson** undertakes insurance defense and coverage cases, alongside a raft of PI work. Peers affirm that they have an "*enormous*

amount of respect*" for his depth of experience, and say that they "*would feel totally comfortable calling him as an expert witness.*" **Mark Hanson** stands out in the field for being "*extremely diligent and down to earth.*" Sources recommend him for his management of case law, and appreciate his "*common-sense approach to the law.*" He focuses predominantly on commercial litigation, insurance policy interpretation and railroad defense. **Stephen Plambeck**'s practice also covers railroad law, as well as construction litigation, professional liability and products liability. Recognized by his peers as a "*hard-working*" and "*real solid litigator,*" he is known for his considerable tenacity when defending the validity of a case.
**Clients/Work Highlights:** The firm recently obtained a temporary restraining order, permitting the closure of two limited liability companies accused of defrauding investors and mismanaging corporate funds. Major clients include CNA Insurance Companies; Farmers; Northern Santa Fe Railway and State Farm.

### Vogel Law Firm

**The Firm:** Three offices across the state service North Dakota, South Dakota, northwestern Minnesota and Montana-based disputes. The firm continues to benefit from its merger with Gunhus, Grinnell, Klinger, Swenson & Guy, to offer a "*broad array of specialists*" and a "*highly professional level of client care,*" say interviewees. "*They understand our needs, and know how to help us achieve them,*" one client reports. The team handles products liability, lender liability, warranty claims, and federal and state tax issues.
**The Lawyers:** **Edward Klinger**'s vast experience spans finance-related work, including debtor-creditor relations, contracts and bankruptcy litigation, as well as legal malpractice. Sources recognize that his reduced involvement in day-to-day transactions means that he is able to offer seasoned advice on a broad range of issues. Clients marvel at **Todd Haggart**'s ability to "*turn a jury around.*" He engages in business and IP litigation and products defense, while also offering niche expertise in medical malpractice cases. In 2005 he featured in complex contractual disputes related to a municipal waste energy project. Clients state: "*If we ask him he'll hit us a home run out of the park.*" The "*bright, approachable and energetic*" **Wayne Carlson** is popular among clients for the "*excellent rapport he develops with us*" and his "*extremely timely reporting.*" He devotes a substantial amount of his practice to medical malpractice defense, although risk management consulting and the representation of healthcare providers in medical board disciplinary proceedings also keep him busy. He successfully defended two physicians at MeritCare Health System against allegations of recommending unnecessary surgery in 2005. **Patrick Weir** also has many years' medical malpractice experience. Clients highlight his particularly strong communication skills, and also note his positive influence on younger partners, "*teaching them all the tricks of the trade.*" He is also regularly

involved in corporate and banking matters.
**Clients/Work Highlights:** Lawyers represented a local government body in connection with a dispute concerning the demolition of old county buildings. Altru Health System is another major client.

### Zuger Kirmis & Smith

**The Firm:** This Bismarck-based outfit covers the gamut of commercial litigation, from PI defense to professional malpractice and products liability. It also commands respect for its defense of banks in lender liability claims. The 15-strong team is currently seeing an upswing in the volume of employment litigation and legal malpractice cases. Administrative law and Native American law round off this "*responsive and professional*" firm's caseload.
**The Lawyers:** Clients admire **James Hill** for his "*straightforward, no-nonsense personality.*" He brings an "*objective and complete*" approach to the defense of legal and medical professional malpractice claims. In 2005, he was involved in commercial appellate litigation on behalf of the City of Fargo, and contract-based litigation on behalf of a construction firm in the federal court. Interviewees praise **Rebecca Thiem** for her "*strong academic approach and communication skills.*" Her caseload is dominated by employment disputes, including the representation of both North Dakota and out-of-state insurance agents. She also remains heavily involved in general commercial litigation, and is currently undertaking a large commercial case for Williston Basin Interstate Pipeline. **Lyle Kirmis** divides his time between corporate transactional work, and commercial and construction litigation. He successfully resolved a construction dispute for Dakota Community Bank, gaining a dismissal without prejudice in 2005. Clients continue to go to him for PI claims. **Lance Schreiner**'s esteemed reputation attracts clients from across North Dakota and Minnesota, including larger medical facilities in Bismarck, and healthcare entities involved in medical negligence cases in Minneapolis. He knows how to "*keep the cases moving*" and can "*bring in the right experts*" to bolster the defense, according to commentators.
**Clients/Work Highlights:** Key clients include Canadian Pacific Railway; Aetna; Great West Casualty; KEM Electric and Lonesome Dove Petroleum.

## Band 2

### Dorsey & Whitney LLP
See firm details p.1169
**The Firm:** The firm focuses on high-stakes commercial and business litigation on behalf of prominent local and regional clients. Lawyers are well equipped to handle intricate technology issues, especially from a well-regarded Fargo office.
**The Lawyers:** **Todd Zimmerman** (see p.1597) acts for banks, insurance agents, real estate firms and brokerage companies in a range of commercial disputes. He impresses peers with his "*articulate*

*nature"* and an impressive record of favorable judgments. In 2005, he was involved in a breach of fiduciary duties charge against a bank, and a high-profile wrongful discharge case brought against a large local corporation.

Clients/Work Highlights: The team is currently assisting a publicly held company in a major contract dispute and defending a brokerage company in a class action. It also successfully enforced nonsolicitation provisions against a group of financial advisers in 2005. Notable clients include Berthel Fisher; Noridian Mutual Insurance; Otter Tail; RBC Dain Rauscher; US Bank and Wells Fargo.

## Maring Williams Law Office PC

The Firm: This *"upfront and honest"* litigation boutique specializes in business disputes, malpractice defense and extensive PI and domestic relations cases. The team's six attorneys are *"distinguished by their thoroughness and outstanding work,"* say clients. Lawyers carried out arbitration work for an insurance company in 2005.

The Lawyers: The *"exceptionally professional and polished"* **David Maring** devotes his time to business disputes, professional liability defense and PI litigation. Peers are *"glad to have him on the other side of the courtroom"* because of his *"inscrutable sense of fair play."* He acted for defendants in three medical malpractice jury trials, including a complex failure-to-diagnose case in 2005. In the commercial sphere, he continues to represent a railroad car manufacturer in a toxic spill case, and also takes on a high volume of construction disputes. **Daniel Dunn** brings a *"dogged and meticulously prepared"* approach to a blend of corporate, plaintiff PI and insurance defense work. He appeared in an inheritance dispute that reached the Supreme Court and a regulation compliance case on behalf of a crop insurance company.

Clients/Work Highlights: In 2005 the team was involved in a wrongful termination case and the defense of a PI lawsuit filed against a shop, concerning shop floor hazards and employee conduct. Major clients include Attorneys' Liability Protection Society; Menards; Midwest Industrial Metal and Zurich American Insurance Company.

## Serkland Law Firm, PC

The Firm: Interviewees are impressed with a *"top-notch"* team operating statewide and across Minnesota. The business and commercial litigation practice groups offer a full range of services and handle complex cases for pharmaceutical companies, lenders, insurance companies and multinational corporations.

The Lawyers: Sources applaud **Ronald McLean**'s *"strong communication skills"* and personable approach to a varied commercial litigation caseload. In 2005, he was involved on behalf of the plaintiff in the sizable settlement of a nine-year-long commercial class action. He also settled a multimillion-dollar class action on behalf of farmers and oil companies, and is currently the managing attorney supervising some 300 diet drug lawsuits in the state. The *"seasoned"* **Jack Marcil** specializes in medical malpractice suits, undertaking wrongful death and other medical negligence claims, as well as PI charges. Aside from regular disputes, he also features in arbitration and mediations. Commercial litigator **Brad Sinclair** frequently represents banks and credit unions, as well as numerous corporations in litigation and enforcement cases. His *"detailed and principled"* approach recently benefited a bank trustee in a $1 million claim. He also boasts niche expertise in transportation law.

Clients/Work Highlights: The firm won a large settlement from an insurance company for bad faith against a lumberyard. It is also currently involved in bringing a $300,000 claim against a bridge construction firm. Additional clients include Bremer Bank and Country Credit Union.

## Band 3

## Fleck, Mather & Strutz, Ltd

The Firm: The firm's lawyers frequently appear in a number of state and federal courts in North Dakota, Montana, Minnesota, Iowa and Wyoming, as well as the US Supreme Court. Sources recommend the team for its polished insurance and medical malpractice defense and its natural resources capabilities.

The Lawyers: Much of **John Morrison**'s caseload is dominated by the representation of oil and gas companies in state and federal administrative matters. He regularly appears before the Bureau of Land Management, the North Dakota Public Service Commission and the North Dakota Tax Department. The *"gentlemanly"* **Michael Waller** is highly regarded in the medical malpractice arena. Peers praise him for being *"a real professional with a methodical and civil approach to his work."* He focuses on the defense of medical and dental malpractice claims.

Clients/Work Highlights: Major clients include Burlington Resources Oil & Gas, ExxonMobil and Koch Industries.

## McGee Hankla Backes & Dobrovolny P.C.

The Firm: The Minot-based team of *"top-notch litigators"* operates in several areas of litigation, from insurance defense and professional negligence, to commercial and PI work. Operating throughout northwestern Dakota, the firm's attorneys are licensed in state, federal and tribal courts.

The Lawyers: **Richard McGee** commands the respect of the market for his commercial litigation, medical malpractice and products liability capabilities. He is popular with both clients and peers for his *"targeted aggression"* and *"thorough, comprehensive"* approach.

Clients/Work Highlights: Major clients include Attorneys' Liability Protection Society; CIGNA; CNA Insurance Companies; Dakota Fire Insurance; Horace Mann Insurance and State Farm.

## McNair, Larson & Carlson Ltd

The Firm: This Fargo-based litigation team is known for a level of flexibility that enables lawyers to act on a range of disputes. Corporate litigation prowess is allied with insurance defense, contractual and stockholder disputes and the resolution of agricultural disputes.

The Lawyers: **Bruce Carlson** is cited for his *"excellent judgment"* in insurance defense and corporate disputes. A *"nuts-and-bolts litigator,"* clients appreciate the time and energy he invests in their cases.

## Pearce & Durick

The Firm: A well-respected commercial litigation group here deals with a broad array of matters, from business torts to commercial banking and financial transactions. In the PI sector, lawyers are capable of handling insurance defense, products liability, premises liability and motor vehicle accident claims.

The Lawyers: Interviewees recommend the *"resoundingly honest and trustworthy"* **Patrick Durick** for his experience in insurance defense and products liability. He has served on the Gender Fairness Implementation Committee of the North Dakota Supreme Court since 1997. **Lawrence Bender** advises on all oil, gas, coal and environmental regulations and liabilities issues in North Dakota and Minnesota. His profound trial experience is the foundation of the firm's widely respected natural resources and environmental law group, which tackles issues connected to both state and federal resources.

Clients/Work Highlights: Notable clients include BNC National Bank; GM; MDU Resources; Meyer Broadcasting; Millers First Insurance; Montana Power; Chevron and US Bank.

## Pearson Christensen Cahill & Clapp, PLLP

The Firm: This full-service firm benefits from its Grand Forks location to operate in both North Dakota and across the border in Minnesota. Originally a tax litigation boutique, clients recognize that the team has successfully expanded to cover all areas of litigation. Attorneys draw on significant trial and appellate experience, as well as arbitration and mediation capabilities.

The Lawyers: The *"articulate and super-intelligent"* **Ronald Fischer** undertakes a wide variety of civil rights litigation. He was heavily involved in employment cases in 2005, as well as appearing in a steady stream of commercial contract lawsuits and water district representations. Clients commend his "*excellent judgment, poise and exceptionally well-prepared approach.*"

Clients/Work Highlights: Cass County Electric Cooperative features in a varied client roster.

### Smith Bakke Oppegard Porsborg & Wolf

The Firm: Lawyers based in Moorhead and Fargo cover insurance defense, products liability defense, civil and tort litigation, professional liability and PI claims. Clients range from small local businesses to larger regional corporations and insurance firms.

The Lawyers: **Randall Bakke** has developed a reputation for bad faith claims and plaintiff work. His

workload also includes environmental and toxic tort litigation, alongside insurance coverage, PI and construction cases.

Clients/Work Highlights: Major clients include Chubb Group; Deere & Company; North Dakota Insurance Reserve Fund and the City of Bismarck.

### Other Notable Practitioners

The "*extremely skilled*" **Steven Storslee** of Storslee Law Firm is well known for both insurance defense and coverage work, and products and professional liability cases. He also participates in some family mediation work. Peers respect the "*tremendous job*" he does on complex asbestos cases. Morley Law Firm Ltd's **Patrick Morley** is renowned for his "*unconventional but extremely successful style.*" He remains active in commercial and construction litigation, and

handles medical and legal malpractice claims. A "*polite and respectful*" approach belies an ability to "*really cut to the heart of a matter,*" say sources. Peers rate **Patrick Maddock** of Camrud, Maddock, Olson & Larson, Ltd for his "*unique and wonderful view of the law.*" Key areas of expertise include medical malpractice and professional negligence defense, PI, products liability and other tort litigation. His colleague **Randall Hanson** is an "*astute, aggressive lawyer with an extremely effective courtroom manner,*" according to interviewees. Aside from medical malpractice defense, he also handles health law and serious PI litigation. His educational positions include lecturing at the College of St Francis and the University of North Dakota School of Medicine.

# REAL ESTATE

| Real Estate |
|---|
| Leading Firms |
| [1] CONMY FESTE LTD *Fargo* |
| NILLES, HANSEN & DAVIES LTD *Fargo* |
| VOGEL LAW FIRM *Fargo* |
| [2] MCCONN & RINDY *Fargo* |
| OHNSTAD TWICHELL PC *Fargo* |
| SHAFT, REIS & SHAFT LTD *Grand Forks* |
| WOLD JOHNSON PC *Fargo* |

| Leading Individuals |
|---|
| Senior Statesman |
| JOHNSON Philip *Wold Johnson PC* |
| [1] BUEIDE Daniel *Vogel Law Firm* |
| HUBBARD Paul *Conmy Feste Ltd* |
| STROUP Robert *Nilles, Hansen & Davies Ltd* |
| [2] RINDY Dean *McConn & Rindy* |
| SHAFT Grant *Shaft, Reis & Shaft Ltd* |
| WANNER David *Ohnstad Twichell PC* |

## Band 1

### Conmy Feste Ltd

The Firm: This two-lawyer team is widely admired for the "*sophisticated level of its advice*" to real estate developers and commercial lenders. Loan foreclosure work continues to be a key area of focus for the group, as do tax-deferred real estate transactions and title insurance issues. Highlights of 2005 include advising a prominent North Dakota developer on the financing of a shopping center.

The Lawyers: The "*tremendously thorough*" **Paul Hubbard** is recognized as a leading real estate expert. He boasts considerable experience in real estate foreclosures and is accustomed to working closely with banks and financial institutions.

Clients/Work Highlights: Key clients include Wells Fargo, Bremer Bank and Western State Bank.

### Nilles, Hansen & Davies Ltd

The Firm: Considered by interviewees to be a mainstay in the market, this group is proficient in the full gamut of both residential and commercial real estate matters. Lawyers frequently advise on sales and purchases, leases, loan documentation and title correction. Clients also benefit from the firm's Northern Title sister division, which is dedicated to providing a range of real estate services to commercial lenders, individuals and companies.

The Lawyers: Market sources declare that the "*tried and true real estate expert*" **Robert Stroup** has "*been at the game long enough to know it inside out.*" His considerable experience spans title insurance and advice on complex commercial real estate developments.

Clients/Work Highlights: Major clients include Travellers/Aetna; Prudential; Bank of America; US Bank and Olaf Anderson & Son Construction.

### Vogel Law Firm

The Firm: This six-strong real estate practice has expanded to be able to handle a healthy flow of commercial real estate transactions, loan foreclosures and land use matters. The firm is also active in the representation of property owners in numerous eminent domain disputes and negotiations. Other key areas of expertise include handling a steady stream of leasing transactions for recently completed high-profile retail developments.

The Lawyers: Sources recommend **Daniel Bueide** for his work on behalf of a loyal client base of developers related to the development and leasing of commercial real estate. He also advises on financings and land use.

Clients/Work Highlights: Notable clients include MeritCare Medical Group; Northern Improvement; Dakota Clinic; Forum Communications; Borg Properties and Butler Properties.

## Band 2

### McConn & Rindy

The Firm: This two-lawyer outfit has won the respect of the market for its expert handling of commercial and residential real estate developments, sales and purchase, and financings. In 2005 the team carried out title examination work for a large local healthcare facility.

The Lawyers: Clients applaud **Dean Rindy** for the high quality of his advice and his consistently "*excellent responsiveness and client service.*" He handles a broad spectrum of real estate matters but is particularly renowned for his proficiency in title insurance.

Clients/Work Highlights: Key clients include Alerus Financial; Union State Bank; Blue Cross and Blue Shield Association; Midwest Bank and Trust and Vision Bank.

### Ohnstad Twichell PC

The Firm: This full-service outfit is widely recognized as housing an eminently capable real estate division. Lawyers advise on the sale and purchase of land, title opinions and easements for both commercial and residential clientele. Loan foreclosures and real estate development also feature prominently in the team's workload.

The Lawyers: **David Wanner** wins plaudits for being a "*thorough and reasonable attorney, whose even temperament makes him easy to work with.*" Commentators speak highly of the balance he strikes between real estate-related advice, estate planning and banking assistance.

### Shaft, Reis & Shaft Ltd

The Firm: This compact firm enjoys an impressive reputation for the quality of its advice on real estate development, foreclosures, title insurance and leasehold transactions. The group attracts a diverse residential and commercial client base, encompassing prominent banks and financial institutions and developers.

The Lawyers: Interviewees rate **Grant Shaft** as "*the*

best real estate attorney in Grand Forks." He is particularly respected for his depth of expertise in title insurance matters.

Clients/Work Highlights: Major clients include Alerus Financial; Choice Financial; First State Bank; Gate City Bank and Wells Fargo.

## Wold Johnson PC

The Firm: A steady stream of real estate transactions and developments for both local and national clients ensures that the firm continues to attract positive feedback from sources. Lawyers are also well versed in title work and financing transactions.

The Lawyers: The "sharp" Philip Johnson is "the

condominium guru," according to peers. Alongside the development of condominiums and town houses, he is also regarded as a seasoned adviser on commercial real estate, probate and banking matters.

Clients/Work Highlights: Major clients include Gate City Bank; Bank of America; Bank One; Red River Commodities; CIGNA and Union State Bank.

# Leaders in North Dakota

**ALBRECHT, Kristy L**
Dorsey & Whitney LLP, Fargo
701 271 8888
albrecht.kristy@dorsey.com
*Recommended in Employment*
**Practice Areas:** Employment law. Civil litigation.
**Prof. Memberships:** Member, American Bar Association. Member, Minnesota State Bar Association. Member, State Bar Association of North Dakota. Member, Iowa State Bar Association. Member, Cass County Bar Association.
**Personal:** University of Iowa College of Law, JD, 1995, High honors, Order of the Coif. Jamestown College, BA, Music Education/Piano Performance, 1983, summa cum laude.

**BAKKE, Randall**
Smith Bakke Oppegard Porsborg & Wolf, Bismarck 701 258 0630
*Recommended in Litigation*

**BENDER, Lawrence**
Pearce & Durick, Bismarck
701 223 2890
*Recommended in Litigation*

**BOTTRELL, Lowell**
Anderson & Bottrell, Fargo
701 235 3300
*Recommended in Corporate/Commercial*

**BRAKKE, Jon**
Vogel Law Firm, Fargo 701 237 6983
*Recommended in Corporate/Commercial*

**BUEIDE, Daniel**
Vogel Law Firm, Fargo 701 237 6983
*Recommended in Real Estate*

**CARLSON, Bruce**
McNair, Larson & Carlson Ltd, Fargo
701 293 9190
*Recommended in Litigation*

**CARLSON, Wayne**
Vogel Law Firm, Fargo 701 237 6983
*Recommended in Litigation*

**CHRISTENSEN, Douglas**
Pearson Christensen Cahill & Clapp, PLLP, Grand Forks 701 775 0521
*Recommended in Corporate/Commercial*

**DEMARS, David**
DeMars & Turman Ltd, Fargo
701 293 5592
*Recommended in Corporate/Commercial*

**DONARSKI, Michelle**
Anderson & Bottrell, Fargo
701 235 3300
*Recommended in Employment*

**DUNN , Daniel**
Maring Williams Law Office PC, Fargo
701 241 4141
*Recommended in Litigation*

**DURICK, Patrick**
Pearce & Durick, Bismarck
701 223 2890
*Recommended in Litigation*

**EDISON-SMITH, Lisa**
Vogel Law Firm, Fargo 701 237 6983
*Recommended in Employment*

**FISCHER, Ronald**
Pearson Christensen Cahill & Clapp, PLLP, Grand Forks 701 775 0521
*Recommended in Litigation*

**FOSS, Marilyn**
Marilyn Foss - Sole Practitioner, Bismarck
701 355 4538
*Recommended in Corporate/Commercial*

**FOSTER, John**
Zimney Foster PC, Grand Forks
701 772 8111
*Recommended in Corporate/Commercial*

**HAGGART, Todd**
Vogel Law Firm, Fargo 701 237 6983
*Recommended in Litigation*

**HANSON, Mark**
Nilles, Hansen & Davies Ltd, Fargo
701 237 5544
*Recommended in Litigation*

**HANSON, Randall**
Camrud, Maddock, Olson & Larson, Ltd., Grand Forks 701 775 5595
*Recommended in Litigation*

**HERMAN, Sarah Andrews**
Dorsey & Whitney LLP, Fargo
701 271 8883

herman.sarah@dorsey.com
*Recommended in Employment*
**Practice Areas:** Civil and commercial litigation, concentrating in employment and labor law, transportation law, product liability, medical products defense, and health care. Assists corporate clients in North Dakota with complex regulatory obligations under OFCCP, OSHA, NLRB, and FLSA rules, and more.
**Prof. Memberships:** Member, Federal Practice Committee Joint Procedures, Committee/Study Commission on Ethics. Member, American Bar Association, Litigation Section. Member, Cass County Bar Association. Member, State Bar Association of North Dakota's Board of Governors. Member, The Fellows, American Bar Association.
**Personal:** University of Michigan Law School, JD, 1977. University of North Dakota, BA, French and English, 1974, Phi Beta Kappa.

**HILL, James**
Zuger Kirmis & Smith, Bismarck
701 223 2711
*Recommended in Litigation*

**HUBBARD, Paul**
Conmy Feste Ltd, Fargo
701 293 9911
*Recommended in Real Estate*

**ILVEDSON, Duane**
Nilles, Hansen & Davies Ltd, Fargo
701 237 5544
*Recommended in Litigation*

**JOHNSON, David**
McNair, Larson & Carlson Ltd, Fargo
701 293 9190
*Recommended in Corporate/Commercial*

**JOHNSON, Philip**
Wold Johnson PC, Fargo 701 235 5515
*Recommended in Real Estate*

**JOHNSON, Steven**
Vogel Law Firm, Fargo 701 237 6983
*Recommended in Corporate/Commercial*

**KIRMIS, Lyle**
Zuger Kirmis & Smith, Bismarck
701 223 2711
*Recommended in Litigation*

**KLINGER, Edward**
Vogel Law Firm, Fargo 701 237 6983
*Recommended in Litigation*

**MADDOCK, Patrick**
Camrud, Maddock, Olson & Larson, Ltd., Grand Forks 701 775 5595
*Recommended in Litigation*

**MARCIL, Jack**
Serkland Law Firm, PC, Fargo
701 232 8957
*Recommended in Litigation*

**MARING, David**
Maring Williams Law Office PC, Fargo
701 241 4141
*Recommended in Litigation*

**MCGEE, Richard**
McGee Hankla Backes & Dobrovolny P.C., Minot 701 852 2544
*Recommended in Litigation*

**MCLEAN, Ronald**
Serkland Law Firm, PC, Fargo
701 232 8957
*Recommended in Litigation*

**MINCH, Roger**
Serkland Law Firm, PC, Fargo
701 232 8957
*Recommended in Corporate/Commercial*

**MORLEY, Patrick**
Morley Law Firm Ltd, Grand Forks
701 772 7266
*Recommended in Litigation*

**MORRISON, John**
Fleck, Mather & Strutz, Ltd., Bismarck
701 223 6585
*Recommended in Litigation*

**OLSON, Richard**
Olson Burns Lee PC, Minot
701 839 1740
*Recommended in Corporate/Commercial*

**PAGE, Adele**
Page Law Firm LLC, Fargo
701 237 3423
*Recommended in Employment*

**PLAMBECK, Stephen**
Nilles, Hansen & Davies Ltd, Fargo
701 237 5544
*Recommended in Litigation*

**RINDY, Dean**
McConn & Rindy, Fargo 701 271 8500
*Recommended in Real Estate*

**SCHLOSSMAN, William**
Vogel Law Firm, Fargo 701 237 6983
*Recommended in
Corporate/Commercial*

**SCHREINER, Lance**
Zuger Kirmis & Smith, Bismarck
701 223 2711
*Recommended in Litigation*

**SCHULTZ, Robert**
Conmy Feste Ltd, Fargo 701 293 9911
*Recommended in Employment*

**SELBO, Gregory**
Nilles, Hansen & Davies Ltd, Fargo
701 237 5544
*Recommended in
Corporate/Commercial*

**SHAFT, Grant**
Shaft, Reis & Shaft Ltd, Grand Forks
701 772 8156
*Recommended in Real Estate*

**SINCLAIR, Brad**
Serkland Law Firm, PC, Fargo
701 232 8957
*Recommended in Litigation*

**SMITH, Sean**
Tschider & Smith, Bismarck
701 258 4000
*Recommended in
Corporate/Commercial*

**STORSLEE, Steven**
Storslee Law Firm, Bismarck
701 222 1315
*Recommended in Litigation*

**STRINDEN, Jon E**
Dorsey & Whitney LLP, Fargo
701 271 8896
strinden.jon@dorsey.com
*Recommended in
Corporate/Commercial*
**Practice Areas:** Counsels privately held
companies, including providing services
in the acquisition and disposition of busi-
nesses; representing business start-ups;
business and tax planning; and advising
businesses on general corporate issues.
**Prof. Memberships:** Clay County Bar
Association. Cass County Bar Associa-
tion. American Bar Association, Member
Tax and Business Law Sections. State Bar
Association of North Dakota. Member:
Drafting Committee, North Dakota Lim-
ited Liability Company Act; North Dako-
ta Limited Liability Partnership Act;
North Dakota Nonprofit Corporate Act.
**Personal:** University of North Dakota
School of Law, JD, 1982. University of
North Dakota, BSBA, Accounting, 1979.

**STROUP, Robert**
Nilles, Hansen & Davies Ltd, Fargo
701 237 5544
*Recommended in Real Estate*

**THIEM, Rebecca**
Zuger Kirmis & Smith, Bismarck
701 223 2711
*Recommended in Litigation*

**THOMAS, Benjamin**
Wold Johnson PC, Fargo 701 235 5515
*Recommended in Employment*

**THOMAS, Michael**
Conmy Feste Ltd, Fargo 701 293 9911
*Recommended in
Corporate/Commercial*

**WALLER, Michael**
Fleck, Mather & Strutz, Ltd., Bismarck
701 223 6585
*Recommended in Litigation*

**WANNER, David**
Ohnstad Twichell PC, Fargo
701 282 3249
*Recommended in Real Estate*

**WARD, Patrick**
Zuger Kirmis & Smith, Bismarck
701 223 2711
*Recommended in Employment*

**WEIR, H Patrick**
Vogel Law Firm, Fargo 701 237 6983
*Recommended in Litigation*

**ZIMMERMAN, Todd E**
Dorsey & Whitney LLP, Fargo
701 271 8881
zimmerman.todd@dorsey.com
*Recommended in Litigation*
**Practice Areas:** Commercial litigation
matters and related business transactions.
Contract litigation, corporate governance
and shareholder disputes, securities liti-
gation and broker/dealer claims, real
estate litigation, and other business dis-
putes. Products liability matters and
accounting malpractice claims.
**Prof. Memberships:** Member, North
Dakota State Bar Association. Member,
Cass County Bar Association. Member,
Minnesota State Bar Association. Mem-
ber, American Bar Association, Litigation
Section.
**Career:** Certified Public Accountant,
North Dakota, 1987 (inactive status).
**Personal:** University of Minnesota Law
School, J.D., 1990, magna cum laude.
University of North Dakota, BBA,
Accounting, 1987, summa cum laude.

## How lawyers are ranked

Every year we carry out thousands of in-depth interviews with clients and lawyers in order to assess the reputations and expertise of business lawyers across the USA. Chambers rankings and editorial are referred to extensively by General Counsel and other purchasers of legal services who look to our recommendations when choosing their lawyers.

# BANKING & FINANCE

| Banking & Finance |
| --- |
| Leading Firms |
| **1** JONES DAY *Cleveland* |
| **2** CALFEE, HALTER & GRISWOLD LLP *Cleveland* |
| SQUIRE, SANDERS & DEMPSEY LLP *Cleveland* |
| THOMPSON HINE LLP *Cleveland* |
| **3** FROST BROWN TODD LLC *Cincinnati* |
| PORTER WRIGHT MORRIS & ARTHUR *Columbus* |
| TAFT, STETTINIUS & HOLLISTER LLP *Cincinnati* |
| VORYS, SATER, SEYMOUR AND PEASE *Columbus* |
| **4** BENESCH, FRIEDLANDER, COPLAN *Cleveland* |
| DINSMORE & SHOHL LLP *Cincinnati* |
| MCDONALD HOPKINS CO *Cleveland* |

| Leading Individuals |
| --- |
| **1** GUINN Guy *Calfee, Halter & Griswold* |
| MILLS JR Osborne *Squire, Sanders* |
| MIRALDI Leslee *Thompson Hine* |
| RAWSON Rachel *Jones Day* |
| **2** BEDREE Melvin *Vorys, Sater, Seymour* |
| CICARELLA Thomas *Calfee, Halter & Griswold* |
| GATES Martin *Buchanan Ingersoll PC* |
| GRADY Timothy *Porter Wright Morris* |
| KALLAS Hani *Vorys, Sater, Seymour* |
| RUSH Jeffery *Frost Brown Todd LLC* |
| SCHLOEMER Jeffrey *Taft, Stettinius* |
| TEPLITZKY Ronald *Benesch, Friedlander* |
| Up-and-coming individuals |
| BARRAGATE Brett *Jones Day* |

## Band 1

### Jones Day

See firm details p.570

**The Firm:** The combination of a "*seamless*" global network with impressive Cleveland-based expertise ensures that "*you just have to pick Jones Day for nationally syndicated deals*," commentators report. Sources especially recommend the team for its leveraged finance capabilities, and recognize its experience in acquisitions, private equity, equity-sponsored loans and real estate financing on behalf of both borrowers and lenders.

**The Lawyers:** The "*pragmatic and professional*" **Rachel Rawson** (see p.1636) impresses interviewees with her private equity and LBO-oriented practice. She represented Sprint Nextel in its $9.2 billion grade-one investment financing and represented Riverside in financings for 15 acquisitions. **Brett Barragate** (see p.1623) brings a "*levelheaded and business-focused*" approach to corporate and nonacquisition-related matters. Clients "*wonder whether he ever actually sleeps,*" stating: "*When he gets on a deal he is 110% behind it.*" He represented Cleveland-Cliffs on a $350 million acquisition facility with Fifth Third Bank.

**Clients/Work Highlights:** Lawyers represented National City Bank in a $150 million revolving credit facility for OM Group and assisted Oglebay Norton with a $320 million exit facility. Other key clients include KeyBank, JPMorgan Chase and Industrial Growth Partners.

## Band 2

### Calfee, Halter & Griswold LLP

See firm details p.1644

**The Firm:** The commercial finance group here "*really understands what it takes to get a deal done,*" according to peers. The Cleveland-based attorneys act mainly for banks and funds in a broad spectrum of lending transactions, including syndicated loans, securitizations and real estate financings. The team also coordinates with its bankruptcy counterpart to assist upper-middle market clients with workouts and restructurings. Noting the quality of the senior partners, expectant clients look forward to a deepening of the bench.

**The Lawyers:** The "*absolutely first-class*" **Guy Guinn**'s (see p.1628) "*superb work ethic, creative thinking and substantive knowledge of international legal issues*" impresses clients. Interviewees single out his experience in syndications for particular praise. **Tom Cicarella** (see p.1625) maintains a varied practice encompassing asset securitizations, bank-based financings and bankruptcies. Enthusiastic commentators aver: "*He is a pleasure to deal with, never antagonistic and always working to get the deal done.*"

**Clients/Work Highlights:** Major clients include ABN AMRO; JPMorgan Chase; Bank of America; Citizens Bank; Huntington National Bank; KeyBank; LaSalle Bank; National City Bank and US Bank.

### Squire, Sanders & Dempsey L.L.P.

See firm details p.1650

**The Firm:** As part of the firm's extensive international network, a trio of Ohio offices combine to offer comprehensive guidance on traditional commercial lending, bank M&A, capital markets, regulatory matters and bankruptcy. A thriving lenders practice operates out of the Cleveland office, where lawyers represented KeyBank in two syndicated credit facilities, aggregating $400 million, for a domestic insurance holding company. Cincinnati houses a wealth of capital markets and derivatives expertise, and lawyers here were recently involved in representing US Bancorp in a $900 million debt tender offer for trust preferred securities and subordinated debt. Clients appreciate the firm's attitude to fees, reporting: "*They don't 'nickel and dime' us for five-minute phone calls and the like – that's really important to us.*"

**The Lawyers:** "*The dean of commercial lending in Cleveland,*" **Osborne Mills** (see p.1634) is widely admired for his "*seasoned, knowledgeable and thorough*" approach. Peers extol his "*easygoing and patient*" presence at the negotiating table, relating that "*he never negotiates for sport.*"

**Clients/Work Highlights:** On the financing side, lawyers acted for National City Bank in $180 million syndicated credit and loan facilities, and assisted LaSalle Bank in a $55 million credit facility for a multinational manufacturer. On the capital markets side, the Cincinnati team represented US Bank in the formation of an evergreen commercial paper program totaling CAD2 billion. Other notable clients include Mercantile Financial; Mercantile Savings Bank; Huntington National Bank; Sky Bank; First Citizens Banc; Bank of Kentucky; United Commercial Bank; JPMorgan Chase; Bank of Ireland and Citizens & Northern Bank.

### Thompson Hine LLP

See firm details p.1651

**The Firm:** The group works with offices in New York and Washington, DC and achieves a high-profile presence on major transactions. A steady stream of commercial loan representations on behalf of borrowers and lending instructions in syndicated credit transactions kept the team busy in 2005. Public finance representations of utilities and energy entities also formed a major part of the firm's workload. Clients praise the depth of the firm's resources, stating: "*The lawyers over there have guided us through complex transactions and preempted issues that would have surprised or discomforted us.*"

**The Lawyers:** **Leslee Miraldi** (see p.1634) "*defuses egos by cutting through all the chest puffing to the real issues,*" according to clients. Sources claim that she possesses "*a unique combination of assets – she's a great manager, practical, energetic and creative.*" Her work on behalf of lenders, including cross-border transactions, technology-related deals and asset-based facilities, benefits from her experience at a predecessor of KeyBank. Dividing her time between New York and Cleveland, Kathie Brandt heads the firm's commercial and public finance group.

**Clients/Work Highlights:** Key clients include Lubrizol; American Greetings; PolyOne; Goodyear; KeyBank; National City Bank; JPMorgan Chase; Charter One; Jo-Ann Stores; Parker Hannifin; Nordson; STERIS; Verizon; Avery Dennison; NetJets; Formica; Eaton; MeadWestvaco and LaSalle Bank.

## Band 3

### Frost Brown Todd LLC
See firm details p.954

**The Firm:** This group is a leading player in southern Ohio's lending work. Lawyers are involved in a significant volume of commercial real estate construction lending, structured finance, securitizations and M&A financing.

**The Lawyers:** **Jeffery Rush** (see p.1637) "*works with you on a practical level to resolve issues and never lets egos get in the way of a deal,*" sources relate. His Cincinnati-based practice encompasses construction-flavored real estate lending, corporate lending and asset-based lending.

**Clients/Work Highlights:** Notable clients include Cheviot Building & Loan; Cincinnati Bell; Convergys; First Clermont Bank; First Financial Bancorp; Huntington National Bank; KeyBank; LaSalle Bank; Midland Atlantic Properties; National City Bank; PNC Bank; Rockwood Properties; US Bank and Fifth Third Bank.

### Porter Wright Morris & Arthur LLP
See firm details p.1648

**The Firm:** This Columbus-centered outfit "*brings everything we need to the table,*" clients report. The team acts for both lenders and borrowers on midmarket acquisition financings, including a $150 million purchase on behalf of Rocky Shoes & Boots, as well as asset-based lending matters.

**The Lawyers:** **Timothy Grady** (see p.1628) "*uses his vast experience to visualize the overall ramifications of issues key to a transaction,*" according to clients. He

was involved in several acquisition financings on behalf of JPMorgan Chase in 2005.

**Clients/Work Highlights:** Lawyers assisted JPMorgan Chase with the $20 million acquisition of Northern Contours, and assisted Huntington National Bank on significant refinancing work.

### Taft, Stettinius & Hollister LLP

**The Firm:** This multifaceted group is adept at both traditional domestic-based transactions on behalf of lenders and borrowers, and international corporate financing and exchange agreements. Clients appreciate the team's "*highly knowledgeable and timely approach*" to its caseload.

**The Lawyers:** Known for his lender work for major Ohio-based financial institutions, **Jeffrey Schloemer** "*clearly separates the business and legal aspects of the negotiation process, leaving both sides of the transaction happy,*" clients claim. He is also active on the borrower side, assisting Chiquita Brands with two major financings in 2005.

**Clients/Work Highlights:** Major banking clients include Fifth Third Bank and US Bank.

### Vorys, Sater, Seymour and Pease LLP
See firm details p.1652

**The Firm:** With experience acting for both borrowers and lenders, this group impresses commentators with the depth and sophistication of its banking and finance offering. Lawyers act regularly on Ohio-based lending work, asset-based financings and lease transactions, and have a reach that extends to Canada and Europe. Clients highlight the team's cohesion: "*If one of the attorneys is unavailable for any reason, another takes up the reins with the minimum of fuss.*"

**The Lawyers:** "*What differentiates* **Melvin Bedree** (see p.1624) *from the crowd is that he really listens to the client and cares about the transaction,*" according to interviewees. In 2005, he was involved in a raft of midmarket asset-based lending transactions, including acting for two major steel manufacturers, several contracting firms and service-related businesses. Partner **Hani Kallas** (see p.1631) maintains a similar practice, with a particular focus on representing lenders in loans and workouts. Clients recognize the pair as "*a well-balanced team that does a fantastic job of taking care of their clients.*"

## Band 4

### Benesch, Friedlander, Coplan & Aronoff LLP
See firm details p.1643

**The Firm:** Attorneys based in Cleveland and Columbus focus on representing banks and senior lenders in acquisition financings. Clients value the team's "*phenomenal responsiveness and fair pricing – you can trust them implicitly.*" The firm maintains a representative office in China, which enables it to advise

its impressive raft of banking clients on lending to the country. On the borrower side, the team is often found acting for clients in the polymer industry.

**The Lawyers:** **Ronald Teplitzky** (see p.1640) "*understands how best to represent his client while always striving to get the deal done,*" peers remark. His "*business-friendly*" approach finds favor with interviewees.

**Clients/Work Highlights:** The firm was involved in a large volume of private equity deals on behalf of banks, including National City, KeyBank and Fifth Third, in 2005. Other key clients include PNC Business Credit and Huntington National Bank.

### Dinsmore & Shohl LLP
See firm details p.1645

**The Firm:** The firm has made a name for itself representing Midwestern community banks. Lawyers assist the banks in M&A, securities and regulatory matters, as well as offering strategic and formation advice to an industry sector in the process of consolidation.

**The Lawyers:** Susan Zaunbrecher heads the team. She advised United Bancshares on all aspects of corporate, securities and banking law.

**Clients/Work Highlights:** The team worked on aspects of Exchange Bank's sale to Rurban Financial. Other major clients include First National Bank of New Holland; Fifth Third Bank; Community National Bank; LCNB; Ripley National Bank; Citizens Bank; First Safety Bank and Commodore Bank.

### McDonald Hopkins Co

**The Firm:** Known primarily for its work for financial institutions and service providers, the firm's lender practice is experienced in secured and unsecured financings and a range of debt transactions. Clients praise the "*competent and reasonably priced*" service offered by a team that often works in conjunction with the firm's restructuring group on distressed loans.

**The Lawyers:** Anne Corrigan is a key contact for banking finance matters.

**Clients/Work Highlights:** Major banking clients include JPMorgan Chase; US Bank; National City Bank; KeyBank; Fifth Third Bank; Provident Bank; PNC Business Credit; Huntington National Bank; Charter One Bank and Roynat Capital.

### Other Notable Practitioners

**Martin Gates** (see p.1627) of Buchanan Ingersoll PC is recommended for his "*knowledgeable and astute*" loan work in the northern Ohio market. In 2005, he was particularly involved in lending work for key client JPMorgan Chase, including acting on a $123 million syndicated, multiborrower, multicurrency senior secured credit facility given to a US and Canada-based manufacturer of building supplies.

# BANKRUPTCY/RESTRUCTURING

## Bankruptcy/Restructuring

### Leading Firms

1. **JONES DAY** *Cleveland*
   **SQUIRE, SANDERS & DEMPSEY LLP** *Cleveland*
2. **THOMPSON HINE LLP** *Cleveland*
3. **DINSMORE & SHOHL LLP** *Cincinnati*
   **FROST BROWN TODD LLC** *Cincinnati*
   **HAHN LOESER & PARKS LLP** *Cleveland*
   **VORYS, SATER, SEYMOUR AND PEASE** *Columbus*
4. **BAILEY CAVALIERI** *Columbus*
   **MCDONALD HOPKINS CO** *Cleveland*
   **TAFT, STETTINIUS & HOLLISTER LLP** *Cincinnati*
5. **BAKER & HOSTETLER LLP** *Cleveland*
   **CALFEE, HALTER & GRISWOLD LLP** *Cleveland*
   **KEATING, MUETHING & KLEKAMP, PLL** *Cincinnati*
   **PORTER WRIGHT MORRIS & ARTHUR** *Columbus*
   **SCHOTTENSTEIN, ZOX & DUNN** *Columbus*

### Leading Individuals

1. **HEIMAN David** *Jones Day*
   **LEPENE Alan** *Thompson Hine LLP*
   **LERNER Stephen** *Squire, Sanders & Dempsey*
   **MEYER G Christopher** *Squire, Sanders & Dempsey*
2. **GOLD Ronald** *Frost Brown Todd LLC*
   **LEWIS Kim Martin** *Dinsmore & Shohl LLP*
   **OSCAR Lawrence** *Hahn Loeser & Parks LLP*
   **RILEY Shawn** *McDonald Hopkins Co*
   **SIDMAN Robert** *Vorys, Sater, Seymour*
3. **BASH Brian** *Baker & Hostetler LLP*
   **CAVALIERI Nick** *Bailey Cavalieri*
   **DEMARCO Daniel** *Hahn Loeser & Parks LLP*
   **GIBBONS Colette** *Schottenstein, Zox & Dunn*
   **GOLDMAN Matthew** *Baker & Hostetler LLP*
   **HURLEY Timothy** *Taft, Stettinius & Hollister LLP*
   **HUTCHINSON JR Joseph** *Baker & Hostetler LLP*
   **IRWIN Kevin** *Keating, Muething & Klekamp, PLL*
   **JACKSON Reginald** *Vorys, Sater, Seymour*
   **LATOUR Randall** *Vorys, Sater, Seymour*
   **LAWNICZAK James** *Calfee, Halter & Griswold LLP*
   **LENNOX Heather** *Jones Day*
   **MARKS Jeffrey** *Squire, Sanders & Dempsey LLP*
   **OELLERMANN Charles** *Jones Day*
   **PAROBEK Drew** *Vorys, Sater, Seymour*
   **PIGMAN Jack** *Porter Wright Morris*
   **POWAR Lee** *Hahn Loeser & Parks LLP*
   **POWERS Victoria** *Schottenstein, Zox & Dunn*
   **ROBERTSON Jean** *McDonald Hopkins Co*
   **SANKER Robert** *Keating, Muething*
   **SOLIMINE Louis** *Thompson Hine LLP*

### Up-and-coming individuals

**MILLER W Timothy** *Taft, Stettinius & Hollister LLP*

## Band 1

### Jones Day
See firm details p.570

**The Firm:** This firm is widely recognized in Ohio and beyond as a leader in all aspects of bankruptcy work. Clients tell of "*massive bench strength allied to a team ethic that makes them hard to beat.*" The experienced group offers expertise in debtors' committee, creditors' committee and acquisition matters to clients that are largely concentrated in the airline, healthcare and automotive industries. The firm's traditional strength in debtor matters is undiminished, as evidenced by its continued work for Oglebay Norton in Chapter 11 proceedings totaling $560 million.

**The Lawyers:** **David Heiman**'s (see p.1629) "*judgment, instincts and advice are as good as those of any lawyer I have ever worked with,*" according to one major client. His presence on large debtor cases, as well as his work for secured lenders, is recognized far beyond state boundaries. He is the firm's senior figure on the Oglebay Norton case and maintains a close relationship with Wilbur Ross, advising the investor on the potential $650 million acquisition of assets in WestPoint Stevens. The "*polite, thoughtful and practical*" **Heather Lennox** (see p.1632) acts primarily as a debtors' counsel. She is able to "*stake out her client's position well and hold on to that position when necessary,*" according to peers. In 2005, she was heavily involved in LTV Steel's ongoing $5 billion Chapter 11 proceedings. Commentators recommend Columbus-based **Charles Oellermann** (see p.1635) for his "*hugely thoughtful and considered*" debtor-oriented work. He remains involved in National Century Financial Enterprises' high-profile Chapter 11 cases totaling $4 billion.

**Clients/Work Highlights:** Key clients include USG; Wachovia; National City Bank; International Coal; HQ Global Holdings and Alderwoods.

### Squire, Sanders & Dempsey LLP
See firm details p.1650

**The Firm:** This well-regarded outfit climbs the table in recognition of its growing national presence. Clients report: "*Every time we've needed technical assistance Squire, Sanders has been superb – we would, and indeed have, recommended the firm to anybody.*" The team's workload is a balanced mix of debtor and creditor committee representation, although in 2005 it devoted considerable resources to assisting WCI Steel in its Chapter 11 case. The attorneys' experience also encompasses secured lender and acquisition instructions.

**The Lawyers:** "*There is no one close to* **Stephen Lerner** (see p.1632) *anymore*" for debtor and creditor committee work in Ohio, interviewees claim. His "*smart, straightforward and creative*" approach impresses commentators, who recognize him as "*a man of his word and a pleasure to work with.*" His high-profile involvement on behalf of the creditors' committee in the Enron case and his representation of EaglePicher Holdings in its reorganization are testament to the nationwide reach of his practice. **Chris Meyer** (see p.1634) "*brings a realistic approach to the table and knows that there is no need to throw good money after bad.*" Sensitive to both sides' needs, "*he realizes that there is a middle ground to be reached,*" according to clients. The "*gravitas and poise*" he brings to both debtor and creditor representations impress sources. He played a leading role in the WCI Steel Chapter 11 proceedings in 2005. Based in Cincinnati and working closely with Lerner, of counsel **Jeff Marks** (see p.1633) focuses on creditor work, specifically representing institutional lenders. Peers identify him as a "*solid, thorough and calm guy who, in his own quiet way, is immensely skilled.*"

**Clients/Work Highlights:** Major clients include Organized Living; WorldCom; National Century Financial Enterprises; Adelphia Communications and the creditors' committee of SHC.

## Band 2

### Thompson Hine LLP
See firm details p.1651

**The Firm:** Already recognized for stellar secured lender work, this "*outstanding team*" is increasingly representing debtors involved in complex restructurings. Instructions from KeyBank and JPMorgan Chase epitomize the firm's long-standing strength acting for major financial institutions. The team also assisted Amcast International in its $175 million Chapter 11 reorganization, which proves its credentials on the debtor side. Clients identify a "*seamless network nationwide and extraordinary depth in Cleveland*" as the twin foundations of the firm's success in recent years.

**The Lawyers:** **Alan Lepene** (see p.1632) demonstrates "*the ability to marry the law with practical business decisions,*" clients state. His reputation is based on a consistent track record acting for lenders, though 2005 saw him involved in increased volumes of debtor transactions. As well as taking a leading role in the Amcast case, he represents the trustee of NEBS Financial Services in liquidation proceedings. Based in Cincinnati, **Louis Solimine** (see p.1639) "*takes a genuine concern for his client's position and is willing to drop what he's doing to help you out,*" say clients. He successfully defended Contech Construction Products against claims filed by the trustee of Computrex alleging preferential payments. He is also the national bankruptcy counsel for Duke Realty.

**Clients/Work Highlights:** The team assisted GEO Specialty Chemicals with its successful $200 million Chapter 11 reorganization. Lawyers also represented JPMorgan Chase in the Deaconess Hospital bankruptcy. Other key clients include KeyBank; Sight Resource; ParkStone Medical; Cincinnati Gear; Pak-Mor Manufacturing and Regional Diagnostics.

## Band 3

### Dinsmore & Shohl LLP
See firm details p.1645

**The Firm:** The team offers *"truly significant expertise"* to an impressive raft of corporate debtor clients. While it has a strong record acting for creditors and committees, the firm is mainly known for assisting midmarket clients from the food and retail sectors involved in Chapter 11 proceedings or nonbankruptcy restructurings. As such, 2005 saw lawyers advising Huffy on its bankruptcy process.

**The Lawyers:** The *"hands-on and creative"* **Kim Martin Lewis** is recommended for her *"technical strength allied with real business acumen."* In 2005 she appeared in the Supreme Court on behalf of Bernard Katz, the liquidating supervisor for Wallace's Bookstores.

**Clients/Work Highlights:** The team is regularly involved in creditor work on behalf of Procter & Gamble. Other key clients include rue21 and Chiquita Brands.

### Frost Brown Todd LLC
See firm details p.954

**The Firm:** This regional player maintains its traditionally strong presence in southwest Ohio and Kentucky. The team represents regional manufacturing and corporate debtors, including clients in the retail and telecom sectors, as well as creditors' committees. Clients have *"total confidence"* in the team and compliment its professionalism and depth of experience within the region.

**The Lawyers:** Interviewees praise **Ronald Gold** (see p.1628) for his *"comprehensive coverage"* of bankruptcy law. Clients enthuse: *"It's so rare that you find someone who will make themselves available 24/7 and update you on everything – you feel like you're really kept on top of every part of the case with Ron."* He was co-counsel with Milbank Tweed in Los Angeles for the creditors' committee in the EaglePicher Industries Chapter 11 cases and is similarly co-counsel with Pachulski Stang for the creditors' committee in the Organized Living Chapter 11 case.

**Clients/Work Highlights:** Attorneys have been assisting HealthEssentials Solutions and its affiliates in Chapter 11 cases pending in the Western District of Kentucky. Other notable cases include creditors'-committee instructions for RMA Management, Buehler Foods and Cook & Sons.

### Hahn Loeser & Parks LLP

**The Firm:** This experienced group has the resources to assist creditor and debtor clients involved in long-term distressed sectors, including remnants of the steel industry and newer areas such as automotive, airline and healthcare. Clients state that the team *"really hits it out of the park,"* especially for creditor work, where lawyers act as regional counsel to Johnson Controls, assisting it in Chapter 11 proceedings involving Northwest and Delta Airlines.

**The Lawyers:** *"If* **Lawrence Oscar** *has something to say, it's always worth listening to,"* say clients. His *"rational, reasonable and analytical"* approach was applied in the Johnson Controls matter, and to Cleveland-Cliffs on over $2 billion worth of insolvencies among its steel industry customers. The *"reliability and dedication"* of creditor-oriented **Dan DeMarco** wins high praise from sources. He took the lead for the creditors' committee of Regional Diagnostics' recent Chapter 11 filing. **Lee Powar** is *"a great guy to bounce ideas off"* thanks to his *"tremendous experience"* in steel and metal cases, clients report. The creditors' committee of DeVlieg Bullard II engaged him in the machine tool manufacturer's Chapter 11 case.

**Clients/Work Highlights:** Other major clients include Nucor; Enprotech Mechanical Services; Deaconess Hospital; Delphi; St. Paul Travelers; Laich Industries; Ormet; Corrpro; Hi-Rise Recycling; Malrite Communications; Heritage Bank; CoBank; Arter & Hadden; Nippon Electric Glass America and Ohio State University.

### Vorys, Sater, Seymour and Pease LLP
See firm details p.1652

**The Firm:** This *"creative and tenacious"* Columbus-based team is admired for its creditor-oriented work. *"The firm truly has the client's best interests at heart,"* say clients, who add that they would not hesitate to recommend the attorneys here for their *"profound experience in Chapter 7 and 11 cases."*

**The Lawyers:** Former bankruptcy judge **Robert Sidman** (see p.1638) is *"the dean of the bankruptcy Bar in Columbus,"* according to commentators. His *"thoughtful, analytical and gentlemanly"* manner has played well in creditor representations over the years. The *"businesslike"* **Reggie Jackson** (see p.1630) is *"a sound strategic thinker and is comprehensively knowledgeable on the practical aspects of case management and the US court system,"* according to clients. He splits his time between debtor and creditor matters and worked with **Randall LaTour** (see p.1632) assisting United Producers in Chapter 11 proceedings in 2005. Interviewees value LaTour's *"business acumen and deep experience."* The Cleveland-based **Drew Parobek** (see p.1635) is a *"fine negotiator and a great guy"* with a sound record representing creditors.

**Clients/Work Highlights:** Clients are typically drawn from the local business community and include both debtors and creditors.

## Band 4

### Bailey Cavalieri

**The Firm:** The firm's bankruptcy offering covers debtor and creditor committees and a significant volume of lender work. Sources recommend the ten-strong Columbus-based team for its *"experienced and thorough"* work on behalf of debtor clients from industries including manufacturing and retail, as well as for its expert representation of major lenders, including Bank of America and PNC Bank.

**The Lawyers:** The *"bright and articulate"* **Nick Cavalieri** is particularly well regarded for his Ohio-centered creditors' expertise.

**Clients/Work Highlights:** Recent debtor clients include Baja Boats; Colfor Manufacturing; Genesis Worldwide and Nationwise Automotive. The team has acted for creditors' committees in cases involving Cook United; Horizon PCS; National Petroleum; Southern Air Transport and Ormet.

### McDonald Hopkins Co

**The Firm:** Having steadily extended the scope of its debtor and creditor committee capabilities, this team is able to act effectively for midmarket entities across the Great Lakes region. Clients from the automotive, steel, retail and telecom sectors benefit from the ten-lawyer team's *"upfront and communicative"* approach.

**The Lawyers:** **Shawn Riley** is *"a real go-getter who has built an extremely strong practice"* in Ohio, according to sources. He focuses on debtor work, such as helping RMA Management to find a buyer for its distressed business, but also acts for private equity groups in acquisitions. *"Good on her feet and exceptionally smart,"* **Jean Robertson** is best known for her creditors' committee work in the automotive sector. She acted for the committee in Amcast International's $185 million Chapter 11 case.

**Clients/Work Highlights:** Lawyers represented the creditors' committee in the $220 million Huffy bankruptcy case.

### Taft, Stettinius & Hollister LLP

**The Firm:** Traditionally a creditor-oriented group, this team continues to bolster its expertise in debtor representations across the state. Although the group is centered in Cincinnati, the firm has developed a healthy presence in Cleveland and maintains a thriving niche representing insurers in asbestos-related matters.

**The Lawyers:** **Tim Hurley** *"has the valuable ability to explain complex aspects of the bankruptcy code in layman's terms,"* say clients. Apart from several debtor and creditor matters, he was prominent in asbestos-related cases and acquisitions of distressed businesses in 2005. He acted for Steelox in the manufacturer's bankruptcy proceedings. Up-and-comer **Tim Miller** *"has all the qualities necessary to reach the top,"* according to peers. He worked on the reorganization of Kennedy Manufacturing in 2005.

**Clients/Work Highlights:** Major clients include Cincinnati Insurance; United States Steel; Baldwin Piano; Intrenet and David J Joseph Company.

## Band 5

### Baker & Hostetler LLP

**The Firm:** A strong bench and an even balance between debtor, creditor, committee and acquisition-based work distinguish this *"talented and successful"* outfit. Its national network enables the team to act for national entities in Chapter 11 proceedings in the manufacturing, retail and energy sectors.

**The Lawyers:** Sources recommend the *"exceptional and ever-improving"* **Brian Bash** for his Cleveland-based bankruptcy practice. **Matthew Goldman** co-manages the team and offers "*vast experience and a sure touch*" in both debtor and creditor matters. Arriving recently from Brouse McDowell's Cleveland office, the "*creative and tenacious*" **Joseph Hutchinson** strengthens an already deep pool of talent at the firm.

**Clients/Work Highlights:** Lawyers assisted Regional Diagnostics with its Chapter 11 case and the subsequent sale of the company. The team is also representing the administrative claimants' committee in LTV Steel's bankruptcy. Other key clients include Scripps Network; Universal Automobile Industries; Global Photon; FirstEnergy and Pinnacle Airlines.

## Calfee, Halter & Griswold LLP

See firm details p.1644

**The Firm:** This firm mainly represents midmarket debtors but also turns its hand to creditor and committee work. It also acts for potential acquirers of distressed businesses. Clients laud an effective team "*with an excellent handle on all key issues and points of law.*"

**The Lawyers:** The "*user-friendly and flexible*" **James Lawniczak** (see p.1632) has been heavily involved in corporate bankruptcy sales over the past year; for example, he acted for AECOM in the sale of Austin in Cleveland. He acts for both creditors and debtors.

**Clients/Work Highlights:** Lawyers assisted Linsalata Capital Partners in several acquisitions in 2005. Additionally, the team advised RPM International on the creditor side, and represented the creditors' committee in the Cleveland bankruptcy of Gliatech.

## Keating, Muething & Klekamp, PLL

**The Firm:** This specialized outfit concentrates its efforts in a two-pronged approach to bankruptcy work. On the one hand, a focus on creditors' rights involves lawyers in representing major regional banks and insurers, while on the other, a national mass tort practice continues to represent trusts in asbestos and silica claims.

**The Lawyers:** **Kevin Irwin**'s nationally respected mass tort practice goes from strength to strength, according to sources. "*He is one of the brightest guys around: detail-oriented, thoughtful and doesn't shoot from the hip,*" claim observers. In 2005 he became involved in several new matters, including advising Keene Creditors Trust and Raytech Trust. On the creditors' rights side, **Robert Sanker** "*is a delight to deal with,*" say interviewees, who add: "*He understands what needs to be done and doesn't play games.*"

**Clients/Work Highlights:** The firm continues to act for Armstrong World Industries Asbestos Personal Injury Settlement Trust; A-Best Asbestos Settlement Trust; DII Industries Silica PI Trust; Celotex Asbestos Settlement Trust and UNR Asbestos Disease Claims Trust.

## Porter Wright Morris & Arthur LLP

See firm details p.1648

**The Firm:** This regional player is best known for its work on behalf of creditors and financial institutions. The firm has enjoyed a long association with Huntington National Bank, although it can also be seen acting for debtors involved in Chapter 11 proceedings. Attorneys advise clients of all kinds on their interests in nationwide bankruptcy cases.

**The Lawyers:** **Jack Pigman** (see p.1636) "*has a keen business sense and can easily differentiate when it's time to fight or time to settle,*" say peers. As well as his work for creditors and committees, he gets involved in commercial mediation on a voluntary basis.

**Clients/Work Highlights:** Lawyers advised a direct marketing firm on the restructuring of revolving debt totaling $100 million. Other major clients include LMS Contracting, Bank of New York and National City Bank.

## Schottenstein, Zox & Dunn

See firm details p.1649

**The Firm:** The firm enjoys a solid reputation for lower midmarket deals and has experience acting for debtors, creditors, committees and trustees. Lawyers act for clients from the retail, construction, agricultural, industrial and manufacturing sectors.

**The Lawyers:** **Colette Gibbons** (see p.1628) is "*immensely talented at figuring out what needs to be done in a practical way without spending a ton of money doing it,*" according to commentators. She often represents debtors and committees in bankruptcy matters. Interviewees remark that partner **Victoria Powers** (see p.1636) "*pays attention to details and is a fearless trial lawyer.*" She is more often involved in creditor and committee work.

**Clients/Work Highlights:** Notable clients include Metatec; Genesis Worldwide; Cooker Restaurant; Horizon PCS; LTV Steel and Bush Leasing.

# CONSTRUCTION

## Construction
### Leading Firms

1. **THOMPSON HINE LLP** *Cleveland*
2. **BRICKER & ECKLER LLP** *Columbus*
   **FRANTZ WARD LLP** *Cleveland*
   **SCHOTTENSTEIN, ZOX & DUNN** *Columbus*
3. **BENESCH, FRIEDLANDER, COPLAN** *Cleveland*
   **BUCKINGHAM DOOLITTLE & BURROUGHS** *Columbus*
   **FROST BROWN TODD LLC** *Cincinnati*
   **KEGLER, BROWN, HILL & RITTER** *Columbus*
   **SQUIRE, SANDERS & DEMPSEY LLP** *Columbus*
   **ULMER & BERNE LLP** *Columbus*

## Band 1

## Thompson Hine LLP

See firm details p.1651

**The Firm:** This firm enjoys a leading position in Ohio and inspires universal admiration; indeed, it is widely regarded as "*one of the best in the country*" for construction depth and capability. The team's experience and talent ensure that it continually impresses its broad clientele. The firm handles a large number of high-profile transactional projects, as well as litigious issues, and continues its drive to expand nationally. Its consultancy arm is flourishing. Recent accomplishments include handling the $350 million new ballpark for the St. Louis Cardinals, and The San Francisco 49ers' NFL Stadium.

**The Lawyers:** **Jeffrey Appelbaum** (see p.1623) has "*one of the strongest names in the business*" and is a prolific partnering facilitator. He was invited to act for the Ohio School Facilities Commission on a multibillion-dollar project. Other triumphs include the Ohio State University football stadium expansion and the Ohio State University Larkins Hall project. He also undertakes mediation, arbitration and litigation roles. The "*personable, savvy and assertive*" **Michael Currie** (see p.1626) consolidates the firm's preeminent position. He has an enviable practice handling high-end work for big contractor clients and was notable recently in Corporex v Shook Building Company. **Peter Welin**'s (see p.1641) "*pragmatism and industriousness*" command respect. His recent work includes multimillion-dollar claims resolution proceedings for a privately held electric power generator. **James Robenalt**'s (see p.1637) litigation practice is powerful and broad, and he is a landmark figure in the construction sector. By all accounts, he is "*a pleasure to work with or against.*"

**Clients/Work Highlights:** URS Corporation; Gilbane Building Company; Pittsburgh Pirates; Florida Marlins; Ohio School Facilities Commission; Kokosing Construction; Dugan & Meyers Construction; Rudolph/Libbe Companies; Boykin Lodging Company; XL Design Professional; The Musical Arts Association; Ruscilli Construction; CJ Mahan Construction; Forrest City; Hammes Sports Development; Trucco Construction and Danis Building Construction.

## Band 2

## Bricker & Eckler LLP

**The Firm:** The team is packed with attorneys with engineering degrees and commentators agree that it has developed an imposing depth. The group concentrates on owners, particularly public owners, and selected contractors, construction managers and design professionals. It recently represented a port authority against a contractor accused of installing a faulty roofing system.

| Construction |
| --- |
| Leading Individuals |

**1** APPELBAUM Jeffrey *Thompson Hine LLP*
PETRO John *Williams & Petro Co. LLC*

**2** CURRIE Michael *Thompson Hine LLP*
GREGORY Donald *Kegler, Brown, Hill*
HOLMAN Michael *Bricker & Eckler LLP*
LEACH Donald *Buckingham Doolittle*
MILLER Barry *Benesch, Friedlander*
NATALE Andrew *Frantz Ward LLP*
ROSATI Jack *Bricker & Eckler LLP*
TARULLO Michael *Schottenstein, Zox*
WELIN Peter *Thompson Hine LLP*

**3** FRIEDMAN Steven *Squire, Sanders*
GURNEY Scott *Frost Brown Todd LLC*
REMINGTON Royce *Hahn Loeser*
ROBENALT James *Thompson Hine LLP*
ROSENBERG Thomas *Roetzel & Andress, LPA*
VICKERS F Thomas *Ulmer & Berne LLP*
WAMPLER Samuel *Bricker & Eckler LLP*

**4** BISSINGER Mark *Dinsmore & Shohl LLP*
LIGGETT Luther *Bricker & Eckler LLP*
REDER Henry *Buckingham Doolittle*
SABO Roger *Schottenstein, Zox*
WALLACE David *Taft, Stettinius*

| Up-and-coming individuals |
| --- |
| CRIST Thomas *Benesch, Friedlander* |
| FRANK Ian *Frantz Ward LLP* |

The Lawyers: The "*phenomenally knowledgeable*" department head, **Michael Holman**, "*cuts an impressive figure*," according to commentators. **Jack Rosati** is an "*incredibly strong litigator*," as is **Samuel Wampler**. **Luther Liggett** is acknowledged as an effective lobbyist.

Clients/Work Highlights: Miller Brothers Construction; Clark County Board of Commissioners; Sandusky Library; Medina City School District; Westerville City School District; City of Grove City; Memorial Hospital of Union County; Dayton Public Schools; City of Upper Arlington and Turner Construction.

### Frantz Ward LLP

The Firm: This industrious and well-respected group concentrates on managing construction claims and delivering claims avoidance counsel. General contractors, specialty trades, designers and owners make up the bulk of the client base. Attorneys offer polished litigation and alternative dispute resolution services, and have recently got more involved in insurance coverage and general liability risk matters. The team recently handled a case concerning the interplay of Ohio's anti-indemnification statute and contractual insurance requirements. The Lawyers: The "*capable and dependable*" **Andrew Natale** "*rules the roost*" here, say commentators. He is a "*diligent, top-notch*" lawyer who "*always looks for the reasonable approach first*." **Ian Frank** is a bright young newcomer to the tables, having caught the eye of commentators who fully

expect him to feature more prominently in the market over the coming years.

Clients/Work Highlights: Whitacre Engineering; Great Lakes Construction; GEM Industrial; Tremco; Havens Steel; The Shelly Company; Mole Constructors; Independence Excavating; Hensel Phelps Construction; Precision Environmental and Cleveland Marble Mosaic.

### Schottenstein, Zox & Dunn

See firm details p.1649

The Firm: Contractors and subcontractors dominate the client list of a team that engages in both regional and national practice. It acts for numerous trade associations, such as the Builders Exchange and Associated General Contractors, and is acknowledged widely as the industry's choice. The team recently handled a number of significant projects for a large developer as part of a healthy transactional workflow.

The Lawyers: Group head **Michael Tarullo**'s (see p.1640) long experience and background in engineering gives him an insight and the ability to anticipate the developments that is gold dust for clients. **Roger Sabo** (see p.1637) undertakes construction and labor issues and serves as general counsel to the Ohio Contractors Association and the Associated General Contractors of Ohio.

Clients/Work Highlights: Corna/Kokosing Construction; Performance Site Management; Steiner + Associates; Continental Building Systems; Nielsons Skanska; Sauer Industries; HR Gray & Associates; Miles McClellan Construction & Development; PRO-TERRA Environmental Contracting; Robertson Construction; ConTrak and Mid City Electric.

### Band 3

### Benesch, Friedlander, Coplan & Aronoff LLP

See firm details p.1643

The Firm: This team offers a "*solid and reliable*" service that covers all aspects of the industry. It is has an excellent track record settling disputes, and recently represented a property owner in a case concerning a construction defect. On the transactional side, it has a good track record in negotiating agreements and advising on architectural services.

The Lawyers: The "*experienced, energetic and responsive*" **Barry Miller** (see p.1634) is the firm's leading light in the field. He has been busy recently settling disputes. He is expert in construction claims, arbitration and litigation, and also advises on transactions. **Thomas Crist** (see p.1625) is a "*highly skilled and reassuringly competent*" settler of disputes, whose stock among commentators is rising steadily.

Clients/Work Highlights: The Albert M. Higley Company; Applied Industrial Technologies; Cleveland Construction; Construction One; Crittenden Court Apartment Associates; Donley's; high-tech pools; Highland County Board of Education; Industrial Power Systems; Marous Brothers Construction;

Moser Construction; National Engineering & Contracting; Ohio State University; Prestress Service Industries and The Ruhlin Company.

### Buckingham Doolittle & Burroughs LLP

The Firm: The construction attorneys here work in tandem with their real estate counterparts to offer services to industry and developer clients. Many come from backgrounds in architecture and engineering, adding real depth to the offering. The team acts as project counsel on an ongoing $15 billion renovation scheme. Other recent highlights include the negotiation of a $100 million hospital contract and the prosecution of a multimillion-dollar claim concerning the refurbishment of a power plant.

The Lawyers: The "*ever-reliable*" **Donald Leach** represents contractors and owners in the private sector, dealing predominantly with contracting and dispute matters. He is recommended as a "*comfortable and very professional communicator*." **Henry Reder** has more than a decade of experience at architectural firms under his belt and focuses on architectural and construction law.

Clients/Work Highlights: Columbus Regional Airport Authority; Smoot Construction; Danis Building Construction; Columbus Public Schools; Miller Pavement Maintenance; Moran Construction and Tetra Tech.

### Frost Brown Todd LLC

See firm details p.954

The Firm: This "*exceptionally proactive*" team acts for general contractors and subcontractors, and key client Turner Construction dominates the practice. Matters for this company are handled on a regional basis by offices in Kentucky and Tennessee, as well as from the team's main base in Cincinnati. Recent highlights include the ongoing representation of a national general contractor involving claims of more than $20 million, and the representation of a site development subcontractor in recovering $1.5 million in insurance proceeds relating to damage caused by fire.

The Lawyers: **Scott Gurney** (see p.1628) is an "*incredibly active, conscientious and knowledgeable*" lawyer who is "*able to bring people together*" to resolve conflicts, say sources. He has been active over the past year representing general contractors and subcontractors in disputes.

Clients/Work Highlights: Turner Construction; The Nelson Stark Company; Ben Hur Construction; Kelchner; Allied Construction Industries and The Weitz Company.

### Kegler, Brown, Hill & Ritter

The Firm: This group is a popular choice among subcontractors and trade associations, and also represents owners. Commentators commend the team's contract and dispute capability within the state. It recently represented the Subcontractors' Legal Defense Fund of the American Subcontractors Association in the Ohio Supreme Court. The team also successfully represented a design professional in a jury trial involving architectural assessments for the schools building program.

**The Lawyers:** Interviewees recommend **Donald Gregory** as *"exceptionally experienced, knowledgeable and accomplished."*

**Clients/Work Highlights:** The team acts for national trade associations including the American Subcontractors Association, the Ceilings & Interior Systems Construction Association, and the National Ground Water Association. It also represents institutional owners such as the Catholic Diocese of Columbus; the Butler County Transportation Improvement District; Montgomery County and school districts around the state. Subcontractor and supplier clients include George J. Igel, Fishel and Jess Howard Electric.

## Squire, Sanders & Dempsey LLP

See firm details p.1650

**The Firm:** This group serves a variety of clients, although owners predominate; public bodies such as school districts feature prominently. The team has been acting as project counsel for the Cleveland Municipal School District's $1.6 billion schools construction program, and as construction counsel on several projects for The Cleveland Clinic. In a recent highlight, it represented Perrysburg Village School District in construction defect and cost over-

run claims relating to a $36 million high school project.

**The Lawyers:** **Steven Friedman** (see p.1627) attracts recommendations as *"an experienced and incredibly reasonable"* lawyer. He is described as professionally adroit and a *"terrific representative for his clients."*

**Clients/Work Highlights:** The Cleveland Clinic; Cleveland Municipal School District; City of Elyria; Avon Lake City School District; Rocky River City School District; Solon City School District; Perry Local School District; Garfield Heights City School District; Perrysburg Village School District; Bedford City School District; Cleveland Heights-University Heights City School District and Nordonia Hills City School District.

## Ulmer & Berne LLP

**The Firm:** Clients extol this *"thorough and impressive"* group for its flair and dedication. It acts for owners and contractors, but is best known for its niche strength representing the interests of design professionals. Attorneys are experienced in disputes, as one should expect, and have a good track record in settling cases before trial.

**The Lawyers:** The versatile **Thomas Vickers** is a *"wily and charismatic, but always sensible and realistic lawyer,"* say commentators. He focuses on the

defense of construction claims and can be counted on to throw his all into his client's cause.

**Clients/Work Highlights:** The team recently resolved a $1.5 million claim against a geotechnical engineer, securing summary judgment in favor of its architectural client in federal court proceedings. The team also represents one of Cleveland's largest architectural firms in vapor migration issues.

## Other Notable Practitioners

*"Undoubted surety expert"* **John Petro** is counsel to Williams & Petro Co. and primarily represents bond companies. While his is a decided niche, commentators agree that there is *"nothing he doesn't know about the industry."* Commercial litigator **Royce Remington** of Hahn Loeser & Parks LLP has a good deal of experience in the construction industry and brings *"terrific skill and business sense"* to the table. **Thomas Rosenberg** flies the standard at Roetzel & Andress, LPA, and clients extol the consistency and thoroughness of his work. Dinsmore & Shohl LLP's **Mark Bissinger** (see p.1624) advises in diverse matters ranging from contract preparation to litigation; by all accounts he *"always does a terrific job."* Interviewees were also impressed with **David Wallace**, who provides a varied service to a wide spectrum of clients at Taft, Stettinius & Hollister LLP.

# CORPORATE/M&A

| Corporate/M&A |
|---|
| **Leading Firms** |
| [1] JONES DAY *Cleveland* |
| [2] BAKER & HOSTETLER LLP *Cleveland* |
| SQUIRE, SANDERS & DEMPSEY LLP *Cleveland* |
| THOMPSON HINE LLP *Cleveland* |
| [3] CALFEE, HALTER & GRISWOLD LLP *Cleveland* |
| DINSMORE & SHOHL LLP *Cincinnati* |
| FROST BROWN TODD LLC *Cincinnati* |
| KATZ, TELLER, BRANT & HILD *Cincinnati* |
| KEATING, MUETHING & KLEKAMP, PLL *Cincinnati* |
| TAFT, STETTINIUS & HOLLISTER LLP *Cincinnati* |
| VORYS, SATER, SEYMOUR AND PEASE *Columbus* |

## Band 1

### Jones Day

See firm details p.570

**The Firm:** A far-reaching global network backs up Ohio's seasoned local experts, impressing sources who *"can't say enough good things about the firm."* Offices in Cleveland, Columbus and Cincinnati are *"packed with quality attorneys"* proficient in public M&A, private equity, securities and capital markets matters. From major multijurisdictional deals to smaller local transactions, lawyers act for clients ranging from industrials to life science and telecom companies.

**The Lawyers:** Global corporate/M&A head **Lyle**

Ganske (see p.1627) is *"the only lawyer who can get into a room of investment bankers and lock them into whatever he says,"* clients enthuse. *"Extraordinarily up to speed on what's going on in the M&A world,"* his transactional practice sees him involved in huge regional and international deals, including acting for Federated Department Stores in its $17 billion acquisition of The May Department Stores Company. The *"exceptionally bright and focused"* **David Porter** (see p.1636) is a key man for capital markets and securities work. His *"technical and substantial"* approach wins praise from peers. **Christopher Kelly** (see p.1631) oversees the firm's capital markets practice and brings *"a first-rate professionalism to everything he does,"* say sources. He represented KeyBanc Capital Markets as underwriter in the $73 million IPO of common stock by Superior Well Services. **Christopher Hewitt** (see p.1629) *"knows deals backward and forward,"* clients claim. Commentators tip his *"rock-solid"* Cleveland-based public M&A practice for great things.

**Clients/Work Highlights:** Key corporate clients include Nextel Communications; Albertson's; International Steel Group; Argo-Tech; Transtar Industries; Abbott Laboratories; CTS and Axsys Technologies. On the private equity side, lawyers act for Kirtland Capital Partners; Questor Management; Industrial Growth Partners; Morgenthaler; Edgewater Capital Partners and Riverside.

## Band 2

### Baker & Hostetler LLP

**The Firm:** This full-service provider acts for an impressive roster of midmarket clients in public M&A and private equity transactions. Clients are impressed by the firm's *"expansive network,"* regarding the team as *"holding all the keys"* to a successful transaction. Lawyers have expertise in securities and a niche in REITs, in which *"they can't be bettered,"* according to observers.

**The Lawyers:** **Albert Adams** enjoys a fine reputation in M&A, private equity and REITs. He assisted SeverCorr in the financing of a steel mill in Mississippi. The *"absolutely unflappable"* **John Gherlein** *"thinks two or three moves ahead on the chessboard in deals,"* clients report. In 2005, he was active as general counsel to Cardinal Health and was responsible for securities and M&A matters. He acted for Lincoln Electric Holdings in its purchase of $70 million worth of stock in Harris Companies. Executive partner **Steve Kestner** is recommended for his experience in securities and M&A matters. Clients agree that he *"can accomplish negotiations that satisfy our objectives while maintaining a positive relationship with the other side."* He enjoys close ties with key client Aleris International. **Robert Weible** receives top marks from interviewees for his M&A, securities and corporate governance expertise.

**Clients/Work Highlights:** Lawyers assisted EW Scripps in the $525 million acquisition of Shopzilla, as well as the $184 million acquisition of Summit America Television. The team also advised Developers Diversified Realty on the $2.3 billion acquisition of assets from Benderson Development. Other major clients include Neovest; Lincoln Electric Holdings; TransDigm; Fisher Scientific; GE; International Power; Stonehenge Partners and PPI Holdings.

## Squire, Sanders & Dempsey LLP
See firm details p.1650

**The Firm:** This respected outfit offers a transactional and corporate governance practice that is national and cross-border in scope. Sources praise a team that is *"really on top of its game – that knows the finer points of the law and is methodical in everything it does."* The firm offers key expertise in project finance matters around the world, recently acting on the Belgrade Airport upgrade.

**The Lawyers:** Her reputation for securities and M&A work notwithstanding, **Mary Ann Jorgenson** (see p.1631) has been most heavily involved in corporate governance matters recently. Peers respect her *"unfailingly comprehensive"* approach. Widely respected for his seasoned approach and long-term relationship with Eaton, **Gordon Kaiser** (see p.1631) handles a mixed caseload of transactional work, corporate governance and compliance matters. In 2005, he assisted Cedar Fair with transactions and governance issues. Another key member of this

dynamic team is the *"first-class"* **David Zagore** (see p.1642). He is active in general M&A and financings, and advised Green Briar on several transactions in 2005.

**Clients/Work Highlights:** Major clients include GE; Compass Group; Goodyear; AEP; FirstEnergy; Fortress America; Medical Mutual; The Cleveland Clinic; Continental Global and United Commercial Bank.

## Thompson Hine LLP
See firm details p.1651

**The Firm:** This team of *"ultra-responsive"* attorneys is *"totally geared towards solving practical problems,"* according to clients. The firm's transactional capabilities extend beyond its traditional Cleveland base, with international coalitions boosting its overseas reach. M&A expertise is allied with corporate governance, private equity, joint venture and a degree of capital markets experience. Clients are full of praise for the firm's senior lawyers.

**The Lawyers:** **James Carlson** (see p.1625) *"has the ability to straighten out complex issues,"* say clients. His experience representing strategic buyers aided KeyCorp in the $2 billion disposal of its auto loan business. M&A and securities expert **Thomas Aldrich** (see p.1623) *"takes issues by the scruff of the neck and deals with them intelligently."* He assisted Eaton with several transactions. Dayton-based **Joseph Rigot** (see p.1637) was involved in the restructuring of Robbins & Myers in 2005 and handled the $2.3 billion sale of MeadWestvaco's coated paper business to a private equity firm. **April Boise's** (see p.1624) *"bright and analytical"* approach impresses interviewees, who regard her as a rising star at the firm. She is involved in M&A, capital markets and private equity work, and clients assert that she *"understands the ins and outs of the structure of agreements, as well as the business and economic risks."* She was lead counsel in an IPO for National Interstate.

**Clients/Work Highlights:** The team represented Noranda Aluminum in the sale of its subsidiary, American Racing Equipment. Lawyers also acted for Goodyear in the $65 million sale of its Wingtack resins business to Sartomer. Other notable clients include Convergys; LexisNexis; Lion Apparel; Lubrizol; Luxottica Retail; Michelman; PolyOne; Richard E Jacobs; SENCO Products; Solvay Pharmaceuticals; Standard Textile; STERIS; TBC and Walther Engineering & Manufacturing.

## Band 3

## Calfee, Halter & Griswold LLP
See firm details p.1644

**The Firm:** This regional powerhouse serves a solid roster of lower and midmarket clients. Commentators praise the team's M&A transactional strength and its experience in securities, IP, venture capital and capital markets. Interviewees report: *"Calfee is a notch above your average Ohio group thanks to serious bench strength and active clients."*

**The Lawyers:** Sources recommend capital markets expert **John Jenkins** (see p.1630) for his *"smart, practical and business-oriented"* approach. Dale LaPorte has moved to an in-house role.

**Clients/Work Highlights:** Key clients include Invacare; RPM International; Agilysys; TravelCenters of America and Linsalata Capital.

## Dinsmore & Shohl LLP
See firm details p.1645

**The Firm:** This long-standing Cincinnati group built its reputation by offering *"solid, intellectual, creative and dynamic"* advice to a host of midmarket clients. The firm's marquee client remains Procter & Gamble. Attorneys also act for developers such as Jeffrey R Anderson Real Estate, which benefit from the lawyers' niche experience in real estate M&A. Clients extol the firm's community-oriented approach, highlighting its historical assistance to nonprofit organizations in the area.

**The Lawyers:** Managing partner **Clifford Roe** (see p.1637) is involved in M&A and securities and offers niche strength in healthcare-related matters. According to sources, *"you can't help but like George Vincent* (see p.1640)." He *"mixes wit and humor with insight into the core issues of a deal, and he puts people at ease,"* enthuse clients. He worked on the high-profile $160 million acquisition of the Cincinnati Reds and continues to assist Huffy in its reorganization.

**Clients/Work Highlights:** Key clients include Eagle Hospitality; Cincinnati Financial; Standard Register; Burke; Community Bankers Association; Xanodyne Pharmaceuticals; Castellini and Chiquita Brands.

## Frost Brown Todd LLC
See firm details p.954

**The Firm:** Sources rate this southern Ohio firm for its broad experience advising both public companies and a raft of privately held businesses. The firm's regional expertise is particularly pronounced in joint ventures and healthcare: the team represented Group Health Associates in its acquisition by TriHealth, and worked on the $15 million acquisition of a Texas hospital.

**The Lawyers:** Attorneys are particularly adept at tricky litigious assignments, according to sources. Tom Anthony is a key contact for transactions and maintains a niche in healthcare work. He was lead counsel in both the Group Health Associates and TriHealth transactions.

**Clients/Work Highlights:** Major clients include Cincinnati Bell; Convergys; AK Steel; ZAR Fund and Anthem.

## Katz, Teller, Brant & Hild

**The Firm:** This six-lawyer team focuses its energies on midmarket, privately owned companies in the $10 million to $50 million range. Clients relate: *"All our business needs are met in a responsive, punctual and helpful way – it really is a pleasure to work with them."*

**The Lawyers:** Many private clients *"would not buy or sell anything without consulting* **Mark Jahnke** *first."*

His "*practical, thorough and meticulously organized*" approach is brought to bear on behalf of medical practices, as well as privately held businesses. He assisted Ampac Packaging in the acquisition of Kapak in Minneapolis.

**Clients/Work Highlights:** Attorneys handled the purchase of Fund Evaluation from Old National Bank by the company's management team. Other notable clients include Lion Apparel and Marketing Research Services.

### Keating, Muething & Klekamp, PLL

**The Firm:** This Cincinnati-centered group is best known for its M&A and securities work. Its association with Carl Lindner helps to reinforce its reputation among publicly held corporations, and the team also acts for private clients from the service, insurance and biotech sectors.

**The Lawyers:** "*The dean of securities law*," senior figure **Gary Kreider** displays "*business sense and fundamental solidity*," say peers. Co-leader of the firm's business representation and transactions group, **Edward Steiner** "*is one of the brightest guys in the state*" for M&A and pure securities work, according to commentators. He brought a "*hard-working approach and a quick mind*" to numerous transactions on behalf of American Financial in 2005, including the acquisition of Cintas. **Robert Coletti**

debuts in the tables, thanks to praise for his "*extraordinarily able legal mind*." He is involved in M&A and securities work and is "*a joy to work with*," say peers. The "*excellent and personable*" **Mark Weiss** continues to cut a dash in the federal securities market. Many commentators see him as Kreider's natural successor.

### Taft, Stettinius & Hollister LLP

**The Firm:** The firm's Cincinnati office impresses sources with the scope of its expertise in the corporate arena. While best known for work in the public securities market and assisting IPO issuers and venture capital groups such as Blue Chip Venture, the team has developed niches in sophisticated corporate real estate transactions and the representation of Japanese clients on inbound deals.

**The Lawyers:** "*A total and complete gentleman*," **Tim Hoberg** is admired by commentators for his "*sophisticated understanding of the interplay between legal and business issues.*" An experienced securities attorney, "*he is great at pointing clients in the right direction*," according to clients. He acted for Cornerstone Brands in its $700 million sale to IAC/InterActive.

**Clients/Work Highlights:** The firm acts for a significant roster of e-commerce businesses. Other

notable clients include LCA-Vision, Chiquita Brands and Federal Home Loan Bank of Cincinnati.

### Vorys, Sater, Seymour and Pease LLP

See firm details p.1652

**The Firm:** Sources admire the firm's "*enviable connections*" in the Columbus business community. The team deals with a wide spectrum of corporate issues, including M&A, securities and venture capital transactions.

**The Lawyers:** George Jenkins is the firm's most recognizable face for M&A. He specializes in financing for startup or emerging companies.

### Other Notable Practitioners

The "*no-nonsense*" approach of Porter Wright Morris & Arthur LLP's **Ted Grosser** (see p.1628) is endorsed by peers. His "*high ethical standards and his understanding of how to effectively represent a client and get the deal done*" explain the success of his M&A practice. **Michael Hirschfeld** of Graydon Head & Ritchey LLP has made a name for himself representing closely held businesses. In 2005 he was active in venture capital and pure M&A work, in which he displays "*real commitment and intellect*," according to clients. His clientele includes Fifth Third Bank; Clear Channel; First Watch Restaurants; Hilltop Basic Resources and OfficeWare.

## EMPLOYEE BENEFITS & EXECUTIVE COMPENSATION

## Band 1

### Jones Day

See firm details p.570

**The Firm:** This firm brings unparalleled breadth of expertise to the Ohio market, and the impressive client roster is packed with household names. The team assists institutional fiduciaries in ESOP-based financings and acquisitions, and counsels on the tax incentives available. Attorneys are adept in the benefits and compensation aspects of M&A transactions, and at integrating the plans of acquired companies into clients' existing employee programs. The group recently acted for Federated Department Stores on the benefits and compensation aspects of its $17

billion acquisition of The May Department Stores Company. Another forte is representing public pension plans and their governmental sponsors, and clients in the healthcare industry. The combination of "*awesome people*" with a global reach ensures that the group is regarded as "*one of the best in the state, the country, perhaps the world.*"

**The Lawyers:** **Daniel Hagen** (see p.1629) manages the benefits and compensation aspects of M&A transactions. He led the team handling the Federated Department Stores acquisition and offers niche expertise in the employee benefits issues in professional sports law. Cleveland's **Jeffrey Leavitt** (see p.1632) leads compliance reviews of employee benefit plans and their administration, and is well versed in the fiduciary aspects of pension administration and investment.

**Clients/Work Highlights:** Clients of the firm range from multinational companies to family-owned businesses, nonprofit organizations and public employers.

### Thompson Hine LLP

See firm details p.1651

**The Firm:** Clients heartily praise this "*attentive*" team, with one declaring it "*the best firm I've ever used.*" The lawyers' commitment to understanding clients' business needs is famous, and clients agree: "*They know our history, so their guidance reflects our culture.*" Several members of the team are former employees of federal agencies such as the IRS, giving

them useful insight into regulatory issues. Based in Ohio, the team has cultivated a strong national practice. This year it acted for Lubrizol in its $1.8 billion acquisition of Noveon International.

**The Lawyers:** The "*detail-oriented*" **Tim Brown** (see p.1624) offers a wealth of knowledge and the ability to make his clients feel they are his topmost priority. Clients applaud the fact that he is "*aware of issues before we are.*" He recently obtained a prohibited transaction exemption from the DOL for Milacron. ERISA and litigation expert **Jack Fuchs** (see p.1627) focuses on defined benefit and defined contribution plans. He recently successfully defended a claim under ERISA filed by retirees of Formica. When tax issues are on the table, the "*intuitive*" **Shane Starkey** (see p.1639) is the man clients look to. Interviewees applaud his "*complete understanding*" of executive compensation issues. He is expert in the executive compensation aspects of M&A, especially the tax penalties imposed on golden parachute payments.

**Clients/Work Highlights:** ALLTEL; Cinergy; Formica; Kelly Services; Lubrizol; Milacron; Newell Rubbermaid and STERIS.

## Band 2

### Baker & Hostetler LLP

**The Firm:** Backed by polished litigation and tax attorneys, the dedicated benefits and compensation

specialists here provide a comprehensive service to clients. The group's representation of REITs and emerging businesses is renowned, and attorneys also handle negotiations with individual executives. Commentators praise them as "*a wonderful team who keep their skills up to date.*"
**The Lawyers: Raymond Malone** is "*a luminary*" of benefits and compensation law. In more than 20 years of practice, he has handled all manner of benefits and compensation issues for a range of clients, including several Fortune 100 companies. Commentators believe **John McGowan** "*has memorized practically every ruling under ERISA.*" Controversies, ownership of trust assets and dealing with benefits in bankruptcy are matters in which he has significant experience. He represented the defendants in a punitive class action involving a dispute over the value of an ESOP created with $500 million of securities.
**Clients/Work Highlights:** Emerging businesses, private companies and large, multinational clients from the public and private sectors.

## Dinsmore & Shohl LLP
See firm details p.1645
**The Firm:** Clients see the smaller size of this Cincinnati-based team as an advantage, and applaud its cost-efficient and responsive service. It has amassed a wealth of benefits and compensation expertise and is quite at home on large transactions. It recently represented Huffy on the employee benefits implications of a Chapter 11 filing, including terminating and consolidating retirement plans, and negotiating with creditors. In another matter, the team assisted The Kroger Company to consolidate the defined benefit plans of three divisions into a single one and convert it into a cash balance plan.
**The Lawyers:** "*He is one of the most knowledgeable people in the region,*" observe clients of **Ben Wells** (see p.1641). He chairs the practice group and advises on

the design, implementation and operation of nonqualified retirement plans, stock option and deferred compensation plans. ESOPs are his specialty, and he recently handled the recapitalization of Burke using a leveraged employee stock ownership plan.
**Clients/Work Highlights:** The Kroger Company; Burke; Cracker Barrel Old Country Store; United Retail Group and Beverly Enterprises.

## Porter Wright Morris & Arthur LLP
See firm details p.1648
**The Firm:** This seven-strong team handles a diverse benefits and compensation workload, including health, life insurance and long-term disability plans. Advising clients on the design and implementation of new defined contribution structures that are ERISA and tax compliant has been a major plank of the year's workload. Interviewees celebrate the "*insightful and knowledgeable*" lawyers, with one commentator remarking: "*I can't think of many times where I have called them and they haven't been able to give me an answer over the phone.*"
**The Lawyers:** "*If he gives you an answer, you can take it to the bank,*" say clients of **Rich Helmreich** (see p.1629). He is "*open, honest and engenders a sense of confidence in what he is doing,*" according to sources, and he possesses the useful ability to break down complex subjects into simple language.
**Clients/Work Highlights:** The client roster includes companies in the manufacturing, finance and construction sectors.

## Squire, Sanders & Dempsey L.L.P.
See firm details p.1650
**The Firm:** Clients can rely on this international firm for astute advice on the benefits and compensation aspects of any case. The team is regarded as "*excellent across the board,*" and has litigated in state and federal courts. Attorneys offer technical experience in drafting employee plans, and are said to have an edge in advising clients on cutting-edge issues.
**The Lawyers: Carl Draucker** (see p.1626) offers expertise in tax-qualified retirement plans and executive compensation. He is also experienced in issues arising from corporate and real estate transactions. **Greg Viviani** (see p.1640) specializes in matters relating to governmental bodies and tax-exempt organizations.
**Clients/Work Highlights:** A global client base includes governmental bodies, hospital systems, universities and clients in the aviation and pharmaceutical sectors.

## Band 3

## Frost Brown Todd LLC
See firm details p.954
**The Firm:** From retirement, health and welfare plans to ESOPs, life insurance plans and COBRA compliance, Frost Brown Todd's experienced and dedicated attorneys offer "*the works.*" On the executive compensation side, they use their deep knowledge of

corporate control issues, securities and tax laws to develop stock-based compensation plans.
**The Lawyers: John Appel** (see p.1623) is "*a lawyer of the highest quality*" and represents clients of all sizes. He is the principal employee benefits counsel to several large public corporations.
**Clients/Work Highlights:** The firm represents clients across a broad range of industries including construction; healthcare; automotive; financial services and sport.

## Ulmer & Berne LLP
**The Firm:** Commentators extol this group's "*great strength in this arena.*" The team really shines in pension and welfare benefit plans work, and clients seek it out for advice on plan design, mergers, forfeiture allocations and compliance. It has assisted clients in disputes before the IRS and defended Fortune 500 companies in pension fund litigation.
**The Lawyers:** More than 30 years of legal experience ensures that **Ronald Kahn** always provides "*expeditious and satisfactory*" service to his clients. As well as the usual benefits and compensation advice, he is experienced in ERISA litigation. His recent workload has included advising businesses on the design and maintenance of pension and welfare benefit programs.
**Clients/Work Highlights:** Financial institutions; pharmaceutical companies; family businesses; investor groups; local and regional government and nonprofit organizations.

## Vorys, Sater, Seymour and Pease LLP
See firm details p.1652
**The Firm:** A key feature of this venerable firm is its substantial litigation experience in defending employers and insurers who provide funding to benefit plans. The team is equally skilled in advising clients on regulatory issues. Household names such as Honda use the firm as regional counsel in benefits and compensation matters.
**The Lawyers: Anthony Ciriaco** (see p.1625) practices predominantly on the regulatory side of employee benefits and counsels clients on income tax consequences and the effects of ERISA on their benefit programs.
**Clients/Work Highlights:** Worthington Industries, Bob Evans Farms and Eaton all feature on the client roster.

## Other Notable Practitioners
**Thomas Jorgensen** (see p.1631) of Calfee, Halter & Griswold LLP "*has done so many victory laps people have lost count,*" according to commentators. He advises publicly held companies on developing qualified and nonqualified employee benefit, health benefit and incentive plans. He also assists clients with tax issues arising from ESOPs and restricted stock plans. **Russell Shaw** chairs the employee benefits team of Cleveland's Walter & Haverfield LLP. His broad practice includes creating ESOPs and representing the boards of directors of multiemployer organizations.

# EMPLOYMENT

# MAINLY DEFENDANT

| Employment: Mainly Defendant |
| --- |
| Leading Firms |
| [1] **BAKER & HOSTETLER LLP** Cleveland |
| **DUVIN, CAHN & HUTTON** Cleveland |
| **FRANTZ WARD LLP** Cleveland |
| **JONES DAY** Cleveland |
| [2] **DENLINGER, ROSENTHAL** Cincinnati |
| **FROST BROWN TODD LLC** Cincinnati |
| **MILLISOR & NOBIL CO LPA** Cleveland |
| **PORTER WRIGHT MORRIS & ARTHUR** Columbus |
| **SQUIRE, SANDERS & DEMPSEY LLP** Cleveland |
| **TAFT, STETTINIUS & HOLLISTER LLP** Cincinnati |
| [3] **DINSMORE & SHOHL LLP** Cincinnati |
| **KEGLER, BROWN, HILL & RITTER** Columbus |
| **SPIETH BELL MCCURDY & NEWELL** Cleveland |
| **ULMER & BERNE LLP** Cleveland |
| **VORYS, SATER, SEYMOUR AND PEASE** Columbus |

## Band 1

### Baker & Hostetler LLP

**The Firm:** This venerable firm is ready to handle anything, say commentators, "*from gargantuan union-organizing drives to employment litigation.*" Its legion of employment lawyers has defended several race discrimination class actions recently. The team is nationally recognized and has a sterling reputation in labor-related arbitration. It has secured a niche representing employers in the railroad and airline industries, and possesses a thriving stable of clients in media.

**The Lawyers: John Lewis** chairs the group and is hailed as an "*outstanding practitioner.*" He has handled arbitration proceedings before the AAA for a nationwide retailer, and appeared in court on class actions relating to the Railway Labor Act. **Greg Mersol** is "*a subtle litigator who quickly understands complex issues.*" He is an expert in discrimination litigation and recently closed several complex race discrimination class actions in southern Ohio. **Elliot Azoff**'s representation of newspapers in various forms of dispute resolution is the bedrock of his practice. In this he has a national reputation and acts for household-name publications. He is also experienced in steel industry matters. **Richard Leukart** is "*one of the most experienced there is*" when it comes to counseling clients on day-to-day labor issues and managing the employment aspects of corporate transactions. Media is **Victor Strimbu**'s field of expertise, and he is regarded as a masterful negotiator in dealings with unions.

**Clients/Work Highlights:** The firm's clients are drawn from various industries, including newspapers; publishing; steel; construction; retail and insurance.

### Duvin, Cahn & Hutton

See firm details p.1646

**The Firm:** Clients praise this group of tenacious advocates for its problem-solving zeal and its dynamic willingness to go to trial. Labor relations work is the historical cornerstone of the firm; attorneys excel in collective bargaining, contract arbitration, and union-related litigation. The team is felt to be "*especially solid on the public sector side,*" where it represents government agencies. It is active in discrimination, privacy and wage and hour class actions. It acts as national employment counsel to Delaware North.

**The Lawyers: Bob Duvin** (see p.1626) is "*a legend round here – a force to be reckoned with*" on litigation and labor matters. He acts for national companies in diverse industries including retail, music and finance, appearing in high-stakes cases before state and federal courts. **Frank Buck** (see p.1624) is a collective bargaining expert, and also advises on wrongful termination, discrimination and restructuring issues. **Andrew Meyer**'s (see p.1634) traditional labor practice encompasses union avoidance, collective bargaining, arbitrations and FLSA issues. **Robert Wolff** (see p.1641) has been acting for the City of Cleveland to defend against a class action brought by Caucasian applicants to the police force. He is also defending a hospital before the Ohio Supreme Court in a case centering on the interpretation of the Fair Practices Act.

**Clients/Work Highlights:** City of Cleveland; Dominion East Ohio; Ohio Gas; The Cleveland Clinic Foundation; Electrolux and Hawk.

### Frantz Ward LLP

**The Firm:** This firm delivers big-firm expertise in the context of small-firm entrepreneurialism and, according to respondents, delivers genuine "*value for money.*" The "*talented and seasoned lawyers*" have won the admiration of clients and peers alike. The recent workload has included advising healthcare and transportation clients on union-organizing activity. The team offers a broad service that covers union law, labor arbitration and general employment law.

**The Lawyers: Michael Frantz** attracts praise for his "*skillful judgment and excellent client skills.*" Clients value his "*easygoing demeanor,*" which is an asset in the collective bargaining that is the heart of his practice. He recently acted for a Pennsylvania manufacturing client in a contentious collective bargaining process. Also applauded for his "*fantastic client skills*" is founding partner **Daniel Ward**, "*a tireless and aggressive hard worker who quickly becomes indispensable.*" **Keith Ashmus** has an eclectic practice that includes OSHA litigation and mediating in commercial employment cases. He recently resolved a class action for a client in the haulage business. **Merritt Bumpass** counsels clients on matters including sexual harassment and assault cases for clients in healthcare and aviation. He has represented employers in arbitrations and proceedings in state and federal courts, and before state and federal administrative agencies.

**Clients/Work Highlights:** Yellow Roadway is a major client of the firm. Others include Oberlin College and businesses in manufacturing, finance and the arts.

### Jones Day

See firm details p.570

**The Firm:** "*Absolutely on the top rung*" for "*intellectual capability and trial experience,*" this firm impresses clients with its "*overwhelming resources*" and preparedness to "*go the extra mile.*" Its international network equips the team to handle large-scale class actions for employers just about anywhere in the world. It offers the usual employment and labor services and also counsels on the employment aspects of transactions, including employee practices of target companies, drug testing issues and federal contract compliance matters.

**The Lawyers: Roger King** (see p.1631) is an "*exceptionally bright and strategic*" lawyer with an impressive national healthcare practice. He has been advising a Los Angeles medical center on avoiding the unionization of registered nurses. He also recently defended GM in a class action resulting from a plant closing in New Jersey. The "*exceptional*" **Barbara Leukart**'s (see p.1632) clients applaud her "*no-nonsense approach*" and steadfastness: "*She does not cave in – she really holds her own.*" She defends management in Title VII, age discrimination, employment contract and intentional tort matters at trial and appellate level. She also advises in Taft-Hartley Act, Equal Pay Act and FLSA cases. The "*intellectually rigorous and aggressive*" **Matt Lampe** (see p.1632) was lead defense counsel in Bailey v Wal-Mart Stores, obtaining reversal and remand of the class certification. **Jim Rydzel** (see p.1637) is "*not only knowledgeable, but will roll up his sleeves and do the work,*" according to clients. He has handled class action litigation for Crown Cork & Seal and has negotiated contracts with steel workers for Bridgestone/Firestone.

**Clients/Work Highlights:** Verizon; GE; Sterling Commerce; The Scotts Company; Bridgestone/Firestone; ProMedica Health System and Thomson multimedia.

## Band 2

### Denlinger, Rosenthal & Greenberg LPA

**The Firm:** This boutique outfit offers "*a level of talent and quality that belies its size.*" Acting exclusively for management, the team counsels across the board on labor and employment law, including union contracts, arbitrations, unfair competition and regulatory compliance. Highlights for the team this year include asset purchases of unionized plants in different parts of the country, and completing several pieces of trade secret and noncompete litigation.

**The Lawyers:** Founding partner **Daniel Rosenthal** is "*intellectual, and also possesses good sense and judg-*

ment." **Gary Greenberg** is a "*smart and passionate*" lawyer with decades of experience as a labor law specialist under his belt.

Clients/Work Highlights: Clients include small and large companies in a range of industries including manufacturing; hospitality; construction; retail; healthcare and professional firms. The firm also represents municipalities and governmental entities.

## Frost Brown Todd LLC

See firm details p.954

The Firm: The key to this team is the "*knowledgeable and helpful attorneys, who provide realistic business solutions,*" say clients. Litigation and arbitration are areas of expertise, but observers emphasize the team's track record in avoiding trial. It offers business-critical and day-to-day advice to clients on all manner of labor and employment topics, and provides them with thorough training in legal developments and statutory and common-law principles.

The Lawyers: **Deborah Adams** (see p.1623) has a "*great presence in front of a jury*" and a high profile representing management in sexual harassment cases. **James Lawrence** (see p.1632) is a noted mediation specialist, and clients are particularly taken with his training work and "*great critical analysis.*" **George Yund** (see p.1642) is a "*firm, experienced and thoughtful lawyer*" to whom sports leagues and teams turn to avoid employment liability. **Robert Dimling** (see p.1626) has "*a knack for clarifying issues.*" OSHA features strongly in his practice and he recently had a case involving a workplace fatality vacated.

Clients/Work Highlights: Cincinnati Bell; Cincinnati Insurance; Kinder Morgan; Littleford Day; Mazak and Smurfit-Stone Container.

## Millisor & Nobil Co LPA

The Firm: This boutique aims to prevent labor and employment problems before they begin, and to this end, it offers an active human resources practice. Clients declare: "*Their legal analysis is excellent and they give down-to-earth, practical advice.*" This year the team has been involved in negotiating a union contract covering the faculty at a major state university.

The Lawyers: To his clients, **Ken Millisor** is "*an outstanding resource.*" His practice centers on labor law and negotiation. He recently advised on the relocation of unionized workplaces to new nonunionized facilities. **Steve Nobil** focuses on maintaining union-free environments for clients who are drawn to his "*thoroughness and deep research.*" He achieved labor cost reductions in contract negotiations for a waste hauling company. **David Hiller** is applauded for his "*perfect combination of expertise and creativity.*"

Clients/Work Highlights: ThyssenKrupp; The May Department Stores Company; PolyOne; Sekely Industries and Case Farms.

## Porter Wright Morris & Arthur LLP

See firm details p.1648

The Firm: The Columbus office is part of a nationwide network of offices and home to "*sensational, terrific attorneys.*" Employment litigation is the busiest part of the practice, and the team has seen an increase in multiple plaintiff discrimination cases. Clients appreciate the "*effective and creative*" lawyers' dedication, saying: "*They will defend us to the last dollar.*"

The Lawyers: **Bradd Siegel** (see p.1638) is "*a master of the law,*" say sources, who note that he "*always anticipates cutting-edge topics.*" The "*professional and smart*" **Charles Warner** (see p.1641) recently obtained summary judgment in a notable sexual harassment case. The down-to-earth **John Stephen** (see p.1639) "*wrote the book on employment and labor law – literally and figuratively.*" He recently succeeded in getting the EEOC to dismiss a case involving a plaintiff alleging he was sacked for being too effeminate.

Clients/Work Highlights: Morgan Lewis; SBC; UPS; Ohio State University and ArvinMeritor.

## Squire, Sanders & Dempsey LLP

See firm details p.1650

The Firm: This practice is booming at home and internationally. The team was recently retained by the Kingdom of Bahrain to advise on the reform of labor and employment legislation. It has also been handling cutting-edge issues at home, such as card check neutrality. The practice focuses on employment issues and has instructed in an increasing number of FLSA and wage and hour cases. Clients are impressed with the attorneys' "*willingness to stand on principle and stick to their guns on something that is precedent-setting.*"

The Lawyers: Group leader **Susan Hastings** (see p.1629) impresses clients with her "*creative, bright and effective manner in the courtroom.*" She defends private employers throughout the USA and specializes in sex and disability discrimination cases. **David Millstone** (see p.1634) is acknowledged as "*an excellent technician.*" He headed the group working with the economic investment board of Bahrain, and generally works for international companies. **William Nolan** (see p.1635) has a robust employment counseling practice. He was recently involved in an interesting matter centering on the rights and obligations of an employer in relation to the privacy of employee data. **Tim Sheeran** (see p.1638) represents Ohio school districts in contract negotiations, grievance arbitrations and employment litigation. **Lewis Clark**'s (see p.1625) "*wonderful ability to convince senior leadership to do what is right for the company*" wins him kudos among clients. He too was involved in the Kingdom of Bahrain work. **Susan DiMickele** (see p.1626) catches the eye with her "*outstanding trial talents*" and assured way with juries.

Clients/Work Highlights: The team acts for public and private clients, including Prayon.

## Taft, Stettinius & Hollister LLP

The Firm: Loyal clients avow: "*There is no one better in Cincinnati.*" The team is noted for its work in the steel industry, and during the past year it has handled major arbitrations for AK Steel. Its broad offering includes labor relations, antidiscrimination law and administrative labor law. Particular specialty areas include NLRB, the Taft-Hartley Act, trade secret and OSHA. Observers admire the team's "*intellect, quality and ethics,*" and describe the attorneys as "*dignified – not cut-throat, but strong.*" The team acted recently for Freudenberg-NOK at all of its Ohio facilities, including representing the company in collective bargaining agreements.

**The Lawyers: Mark Stepaniak** is *"great in negotiations and good on his feet,"* according to commentators. He recently represented Cincinnati Public Schools in civil litigation and also acted for the Cincinnati Symphony Orchestra to negotiate a collective bargaining agreement with the American Federation of Musicians. Trial lawyer **Doreen Canton** *"does a nice job"* eliciting information and admissions in court, and clients value her *"nonconfrontational manner."* **Roger Weber**'s clients recommend his deft touch, avowing: *"He has handled every issue we have ever taken to him masterfully."* He is especially experienced in wrongful discrimination and whistle-blower cases, and strikes.

**Clients/Work Highlights:** University of Cincinnati; AK Steel; Freudenberg-NOK; Cincinnati Symphony Orchestra and Cincinnati Public Schools.

## Band 3

### Dinsmore & Shohl LLP
See firm details p.1645

**The Firm:** This regional player has a healthy practice representing multinational companies in litigation. The team was recently designated national employment counsel for Beverly Enterprises, and over the past year has litigated in nearly 30 states for them. It is also preferred regional counsel to GE, and has been for the past ten years; it acts nationally for them on labor, employment and benefit class action cases.

**The Lawyers: Michael Hawkins** (see p.1629) is well versed in all aspects of labor and employment law, and he stands out for his litigation.

**Clients/Work Highlights:** Private employers including Fortune 500 companies.

### Kegler, Brown, Hill & Ritter
**The Firm:** Clients view this group as *"a vital business partner"* and value its *"smart, useful and practical advice."* It represents management interests across a broad spectrum of expertise. Recent work includes several cases involving questions on employee mobility and the protection of confidential information.

**The Lawyers:** Clients single out the *"wonderful"* **Larry Feheley** for his ability *"to find safe ways through any minefield."* He has been working recently on two major age discrimination cases involving a reduction in force at a Fortune 500 company.

### Spieth Bell McCurdy & Newell Co LPA
**The Firm:** This Cleveland firm represents employer businesses and nonprofit organizations in collective bargaining, restructuring and work systems matters. It has been active in assisting the buyers of failed companies in matters such as restructuring work systems. Collective bargaining agreements in the aerospace industry have been key for the group this year.

**The Lawyers:** Commentators declare **Dan Pace** *"an excellent collective bargaining negotiator."* Much of his practice centers on advising businesses on their employment policies.

**Clients/Work Highlights:** Parker Hannifin; Brush Engineered Materials; Rolls-Royce; Ferro; MTD Products; Crane and Goodrich.

### Ulmer & Berne LLP
**The Firm:** Specializing in employment litigation, the firm offers a statewide capability out of Cleveland. The team is home to dedicated experts who cover the gamut of labor and employment matters between them, including OSHA and collective bargaining.

**The Lawyers: Tom Barnard** is *"a superb lawyer and*

*a true man of integrity,"* say sources, and he offers *"the best trial experience in the state."* Clients appreciate his *"common-sense approach"* and popularity with juries. He recently handled a race discrimination case for a prominent testing company, and was involved in the first labor contract negotiations for a public library.

**Clients/Work Highlights:** Clients include CNF, Sisters of Charity Health System and Marathon Ashland Petroleum.

### Vorys, Sater, Seymour and Pease LLP
See firm details p.1652

**The Firm:** This *"large and seasoned group of attorneys"* regularly represents clients on a national or regional basis in NLRB and OSHA matters. Commentators identify the implementation of union-free maintenance programs, collective bargaining and defending against wrongful discharge claims as areas of strength.

**The Lawyers:** Jonathan Norman chairs the labor and employment group.

**Clients/Work Highlights:** Worthington Industries; AirNet Systems; ABX Air; Liquibox and The Scotts Company.

### Other Notable Practitioners
**Steven Moss** (see p.1635) chairs Kahn Kleinman, LPA's labor and employment group and is a respected negotiator. He recently helped a client to defeat a union-organizing attempt at a plant in Indianapolis. **Keith Spiller** (see p.1639) of Thompson Hine is a *"client-first lawyer who provides quick and accurate answers."* Labor work forms the bulk of his practice and he is much engaged in aiding clients to counter union-organizing activity and advising employers on OFCCP compliance.

# ENVIRONMENT

| Environment Leading Firms | |
|---|---|
| **1** | PORTER WRIGHT MORRIS & ARTHUR *Columbus* |
| | SQUIRE, SANDERS & DEMPSEY LLP *Cleveland* |
| | THOMPSON HINE LLP *Cleveland* |
| | VORYS, SATER, SEYMOUR AND PEASE *Columbus* |
| **2** | FROST BROWN TODD LLC *Cincinnati* |
| | JONES DAY *Cleveland* |
| | MCMAHON DEGULIS LLP *Cleveland* |
| | SHUMAKER LOOP & KENDRICK LLP *Toledo* |
| **3** | BAKER & HOSTETLER LLP *Columbus* |
| | BRICKER & ECKLER LLP *Columbus* |
| | EASTMAN & SMITH LTD *Toledo* |
| | ROETZEL & ANDRESS, LPA *Akron* |
| | SCHOTTENSTEIN, ZOX & DUNN *Columbus* |
| | TAFT, STETTINIUS & HOLLISTER LLP *Cincinnati* |
| | VAN KLEY & WALKER *Columbus* |
| | WALTER & HAVERFIELD LLP *Cleveland* |

## Band 1

### Porter Wright Morris & Arthur LLP
See firm details p.1648

**The Firm:** This is a broad-based team and one of the best established in the state; commentators agree that it dominates the utility market and air purity law. Clients know that they are in capable hands, citing as reasons for their confidence the *"methodical, steady and highly competent"* partners, *"effectively backed up by fantastic associates."* *"It's all in the attitude,"* observe sources, who report that the lawyers *"make things happen and report regularly."* The environmental capability is complemented by the attorneys' substantial experience in real estate, public finance, developments and incentive tax programs. Lawyers also enjoy close ties with officials at state and federal agencies. Recent highlights include the successful representation of a major steel producer to force the US EPA to revise treatment standards it had sought to apply to the company's wastewaters.

**The Lawyers: Jeffrey McNealey** (see p.1633) is *"huge in this area,"* say observers, and he concentrates on avoiding litigation for his clients, who are drawn to his *"creative and innovative approach and fantastic experience."* His focus is on water purity and brownfield issues, including enforcement and permitting matters. **Robert Brubaker** (see p.1624) is the king of air pollution, in the opinion of sources. He has worked on many of the landmark cases that established Ohio law in this area and is closely linked to agency authorities. Recent activity has included representing a client in its successful appeal against the Ohio EPA's imposition of operational restrictions in Title V operating permits. *"Heavyweight"* **Christopher Schraff** (see p.1638) inspires the *"utmost respect"* for his *"unbeatably deep"* water pollution, power siting and hazardous waste practice. Recent highlights include the successful representation of individual employees in RCRA enforcement actions and the defense of two clients in a CERCLA contribution action. **Martin Seltzer** (see p.1638) has every reason to be *"extremely confident:"* his background in chemical engineering and hazardous water, together with his sound relationships with authorities, places him in a *"strong"* position, say commentators. **Katerina Milenkovski** (see p.1634) works primarily on CAA permitting and enforcement cases. Other areas of experience include cost recovery and regulation.

Clients/Work Highlights: The firm's client list includes household names such as AEP and FirstEnergy.

### Squire, Sanders & Dempsey LLP

See firm details p.1650

The Firm: Clients declare that *"nobody has deeper roots"* than this 32-lawyer, Cleveland-based team. Its history runs deep, and the firm has been active in this area for clients such as steelmakers since before the US EPA was even thought of. It is generally to be found in significant, precedent-setting cases, and in the past year it has worked on several fallout and contamination cases, an increasing number of toxic cases and mass tort actions. It is growing beyond its historical industrial client base by representing more municipalities, and has added partners to offices in the USA and China. The group is also a traditional leader in litigation.

The Lawyers: To his clients, **Van Carson** (see p.1625) is the *"fountain of knowledge,"* an experienced veteran who knows how to *"keep it low-key in order to resolve issues in a nonheated way."* He is one of the few experts in the emerging area of environmental equity. **Geoffrey Barnes** (see p.1623) has a quarter of a century's experience in the field and is an authority on workplace exposure standards and toxic tort claims. **Douglas McWilliams** (see p.1633) is *"technically as sound as they come and on the front end of emerging issues,"* according to clients. He is an air expert with particular experience in the generation, use and trading of emission reduction credits and allowances, complex permitting and rule development. *"Excellent communicator"* **Karen Winters** (see p.1641) deals with all aspects of environmental law and general litigation. She is described as *"intellectually sharp."* **Wendlene Lavey** (see p.1632) is *"fast becoming a leader,"* according to commentators, and is particularly active litigating mass tort cases. The iron and steel industry, and related concerns such as foundries and coke manufacturing plants, are a notable part of her practice. **Craig Sturtz** (see p.1639) has *"made a great impression"* with his balanced environmental and litigation practice.

Clients/Work Highlights: Association of Metropolitan Sewerage Agencies; Cooper Industries; Electrolux Home Products; International Steel Group; MeadWestvaco; Northeast Ohio Regional Sewer District; Republic Engineered Products; US Steel and WCI Steel.

### Thompson Hine LLP

See firm details p.1651

The Firm: This team is a *"familiar and secure presence"* in the field and undertakes large volumes of work in the air, water and brownfield sectors. It is

national counsel to a number of large companies. Clients praise the team for its consistent high quality in complex matters and its cost-effectiveness: *"Every person we have worked with is excellent,"* and the team *"uses younger folk when a senior guy isn't necessary, keeping costs low."* Despite the departure of David Nash, it is *"business as usual"* for the firm, which has added several strong associates to its team this year. Recent highlights include settling in the remedy phase of the Ohio Edison Sammis NSR case. The team also represented a consultant who was sued by homeowners after they discovered lead contamination on property that had previously been used as a skeet range.

The Lawyers: Part of the *"original crew"* and partner-in-charge of the Cleveland practice, **Michael Hardy** (see p.1629) is considered an *"outstanding, technically skilled lawyer with excellent judgment."* Commentators praised his *"calm temperament and unflappable demeanor."* Rivals acknowledge that the *"personable"* **Wray Blattner** (see p.1624) *"inspires confidence,"* and is *"biting at the heels"* of those in the top tier. He is a well-known transactional lawyer with particular specialty in air and real estate matters. A rival concedes that the *"dedicated"* **Andrew Kolesar** (see p.1631) is *"one of the few I would refer a client to, especially for litigation issues."* His work covers regulatory matters, brownfield, litigation and transactional work. **Louis McMahon** (see p.1633) *"thinks terrifically clearly"* and is expert in clearwater rights and legislation.

Clients/Work Highlights: The firm acts for leading clients such as FirstEnergy; Goodrich; Mead-Westvaco and Whirlpool.

### Vorys, Sater, Seymour and Pease LLP

See firm details p.1652

The Firm: This sizable team offers services across the gamut of environmental law out of offices in Cincinnati, Columbus and Washington, DC. It has a knack for keeping clients happy and competitors on their toes. It has a sterling reputation in Superfund work, and is noted for financing, PI and real estate-related work. By maintaining *"a solid base of people for a long time,"* the team has a mature capability and has developed solid relationships with regulatory personnel. It acts for large corporations, small businesses and local governments.

The Lawyers: **Scott Doran** (see p.1626) has *"tremendous expertise, especially in land law,"* observe sources, adding that he is an *"authority on wetland law and regulation."* His practice also covers Superfund, RCRA and toxic tort issues. **Richard Fahey** (see p.1626) *"knows everything,"* according to sources. He advises clients on compliance issues, storage tanks, groundwater management and water rights, Superfund and property redevelopment. Commentators unanimously laud **William Hayes** (see p.1629) as a *"stunning air lawyer."* He provides regulatory and litigation advice to clients from a variety of industries, including automobile manufacturing, mineral processing, printing, coating and wood processing. *"Dedicated and thorough,"* **Mark Norman** (see p.1635) is a *"true environmental gener-*

*alist,"* which is *"particularly important for compliance counseling type deals,"* say peers. He has dealt with many multiparty cleanup actions and brownfield developments in Ohio, and is a leader in transactional and administrative work.

Clients/Work Highlights: The firm represents lenders; individuals and classes; operating facilities; owners and operators of underground storage tanks; petroleum marketers' associations; operators of solid waste facilities and employers and companies in a range of sectors. It counts Honda and the Port of Greater Cincinnati Development Authority among its clients.

## Band 2

### Frost Brown Todd LLC

See firm details p.954

The Firm: This team fields several lawyers with scientific or industry-related backgrounds, and loyal clients assert: *"For a comprehensive, tricky job, they're fantastic."* The team provides *"meticulously thorough and analytic"* advice that is *"first-rate, cost-effective and timely,"* say clients. Authoritative in both transactional and litigation work, with *a "particularly strong defense team,"* clients value the team's ability to work together to produce work that is always of the highest quality. The group recently acted for Mahoning County in the successful termination of a consent order relating to a water pollution settlement.

The Lawyers: The *"charismatic and motivational"* **Paul Casper** (see p.1625) bowls over his clients with his *"incredibly impressive demeanor."* He is a *"hands-on and methodical"* lawyer whose *"aggressive and analytic style and tremendous perseverance"* constitute a winning formula for his mainly litigation practice. He focuses on high-profile, high-stake cases and counsels on the CAA. **Terrence Fay** (see p.1627) is primarily an environmental litigator, and he works closely with waste management clients. He has represented many Fortune 500 companies in litigation proceedings relating to all manner of environmental concerns. **Stephen Haughey** (see p.1629) is experienced in environmental litigation, the CWA and Superfund work. The *"extremely effective"* **Kevin McMurray** (see p.1633) provides transactional advice and a broad counseling service to clients engaged in brownfield redevelopment. **Christopher Habel** (see p.1629) is a *"bright and pragmatic guy, with the ability to focus on what is important,"* report clients. He offers advice in transactional and brownfield matters, as well as litigation.

Clients/Work Highlights: AK Steel; Bay West Paper; Butler County; Cincinnati Bell; Cinergy; Convergys; Flowserve; Givaudan; Global Home Products; Kinder Morgan; Louisville Gas & Electric; Milacron; Ryland Homes; Smurfit-Stone Container; Titanium Metals and Waste Management.

## Environment
### Leading Individuals

### Senior Statesman

MCNEALEY J Jeffrey *Porter Wright Morris & Arthur*

[1] BRUBAKER Robert *Porter Wright Morris & Arthur LLP*
CARSON Van *Squire, Sanders & Dempsey LLP*
CASPER JR Paul *Frost Brown Todd LLC*
HARDY Michael *Thompson Hine LLP*
SCHRAFF Christopher *Porter Wright Morris & Arthur*
TOSI Louis *Shumaker Loop & Kendrick LLP*

[2] BARNES Geoffrey *Squire, Sanders & Dempsey LLP*
BLATTNER J Wray *Thompson Hine LLP*
BURKE Kim *Taft, Stettinius & Hollister LLP*
DORAN Scott *Vorys, Sater, Seymour and Pease*
FAHEY Richard *Vorys, Sater, Seymour and Pease*
FAROLINO Shane *Roetzel & Andress, LPA*
GUNSETT Daniel *Baker & Hostetler LLP*
HAYES William *Vorys, Sater, Seymour and Pease*
JANKE Ronald *Jones Day*
MCMAHON Michael *McMahon DeGulis LLP*
NASH David *McMahon DeGulis LLP*
SARGEANT Richard *Eastman & Smith Ltd*
SELTZER Martin *Porter Wright Morris & Arthur*
VAN KLEY Jack *Van Kley & Walker*

[3] CYPHERT Michael *Walter & Haverfield LLP*
HAYNAM Douglas *Shumaker Loop & Kendrick LLP*
KOLESAR Andrew *Thompson Hine LLP*
MCMAHON Louis *Thompson Hine LLP*
MERRILL Frank *Bricker & Eckler LLP*
NORMAN Mark *Vorys, Sater, Seymour and Pease*
PATBERG William *Shumaker Loop & Kendrick LLP*
PFEFFERLE Ben *Baker & Hostetler LLP*
SAMUELS Stephen *Schottenstein, Zox & Dunn*
STAMP Vincent *Dinsmore & Shohl LLP*
TERP Thomas *Taft, Stettinius & Hollister LLP*
WALKER Christopher *Van Kley & Walker*

[4] BRENNAN Maureen *Baker & Hostetler LLP*
CASCARILLA Ralph *Walter & Haverfield LLP*
FAY Terrence *Frost Brown Todd LLC*
FINN Terrence *Roetzel & Andress, LPA*
GREGG Joseph *Eastman & Smith Ltd*
HAUGHEY Stephen *Frost Brown Todd LLC*
JONES Christopher *Calfee, Halter & Griswold LLP*
MCMURRAY Kevin *Frost Brown Todd LLC*
MCWILLIAMS Douglas *Squire, Sanders & Dempsey*
MILENKOVSKI Katerina *Porter Wright Morris & Arthur*
REIDY Joseph *Schottenstein, Zox & Dunn*
WINTERS Karen *Squire, Sanders & Dempsey LLP*

### Up-and-coming individuals

HABEL Christopher *Frost Brown Todd LLC*
LAVEY Wendlene *Squire, Sanders & Dempsey LLP*
STURTZ Craig *Squire, Sanders & Dempsey LLP*

## Jones Day

See firm details p.570

**The Firm:** This *"refreshingly direct"* team works closely with its Washington, DC office to provide a well-rounded, litigation-focused service. The firm's clients declare: *"They can handle anything – from cita-* tions to advising on mediation strategies."* Clients identify the team's key strengths as *"weeding through problems and getting to the point."* It recently defended Eramet Marietta against allegations that a wastewater treatment facility violated the CWA. Compliance advice is an important aspect of the practice, and attorneys handle regulatory work worldwide for clients such as Brush Wellman. Recent highlights include the representation of Sumitomo Bakelite in its $119.6 million acquisition of Vyncolit and Vyncolit North America from Sydsvenska Kemi, and acting for International Coal Group in its planned $300 million IPO.

**The Lawyers:** **Ronald Janke** (see p.1630) is *"easy to talk to, easy to work with and efficient,"* according to commentators. He is *"clued-up"* and makes a point of *"learning about the company inside out,"* say appreciative clients. He has broad experience in regulatory work, transactional advice and litigation. Jack Van Kley has left to cofound a new environmental boutique in the state.

**Clients/Work Highlights:** Cargill; Cooper Tire & Rubber; Diebold; Gould Electronics; Ohio Farm Bureau Federation; Stony Point Group; The Riverside Company; Timken; Transpro; WL Ross and Yellow Roadway.

## McMahon DeGulis LLP

**The Firm:** Clients rate this *"superior"* boutique highly because it is *"first and foremost responsive as well as extremely knowledgeable."* The team of 12 is dedicated to environmental and toxic tort matters. Work includes brownfield developments such as Steelyard Commons, and the team has had great successes in asbestos, silica and benzene-related litigation. It successfully defended a mesothelioma case for a gasket manufacturer, giving rise to an opinion that has significantly impacted asbestos cases since. The group also offers expertise in the CAA, enforcement, insurance, products liability and underground storage issues. It plays a crucial role as the environmental department of several midsized firms, and was recently selected by two Cleveland real estate firms to serve in this capacity.

**The Lawyers:** **Michael McMahon** is universally hailed as a first-class brownfield development lawyer. His practice covers a broad spectrum and benefits from the readiness of peers to refer conflicts to him. Recently joined from Thompson Hine, **David Nash** is another brownfield and sustainability expert.

**Clients/Work Highlights:** Sears; Norfolk Southern; John Crane; KraftMaid; Sherwin-Williams; YSI and First Interstate Properties.

## Shumaker Loop & Kendrick LLP

**The Firm:** Clients confirm that *"this extraordinarily talented environmental team can handle anything we throw at it."* The lawyers combine comprehensive technical skills with experience-based common sense: after all, as clients observe, *"it's no good being bright if you can't stand in court or relate to business."* Add to the mix exceptional service values and versatility, and the result is a loyal and dedicated repeat clientele. Over the past year, lawyers have been active in the refining industry, primarily on clean air matters, and representing utilities on everything from regulations and enforcement to the occasional criminal case. They have also handled landfill work and volumes of transactional counseling.

**The Lawyers:** The *"animated and energetic"* **Louis Tosi's** clients applaud him for being an *"animated and energetic lawyer who articulates and understands everything."* He is *"great fun to watch in court,"* agree sources, and one client observes: *"He blew me away – I couldn't believe how he got the judge to let in some things."* He performs his magic before federal and state courts and administrative tribunals, as well as counseling on multimillion-dollar transactions. The *"terrific"* **Douglas Haynam** handles litigation, consultation and administrative matters, while **William Patberg** practices principally in air and water pollution control matters.

**Clients/Work Highlights:** The firm represents a large number of electrical utilities, Fortune 500 industrial companies and small local corporations. GM is a key client.

## Band 3

## Baker & Hostetler LLP

**The Firm:** Clients come here for the *"seamless relationship between the environmental practice and the rest of the team."* The firm offers a broad energy and environmental practice that provides *"an unsurpassed level of service"* nationwide, according to sources. Clients commend the *"enthusiastic, extremely competent, friendly, timely and practical"* attorneys, whose core practice areas are transaction management, regulatory advice, Superfund and dispute resolution. The team has handled heightened levels of labeling and disclosure work over the past year.

**The Lawyers:** **Daniel Gunsett's** clients commend his impeccable follow-up and describe him as *"incredibly able on technical issues."* His clients include electric cooperatives, port authorities, multinational oil companies and chemical plants. He has been involved recently in the brownfield redevelopment of a contaminated school property, and litigation in Texas concerning the sale of a contaminated industrial site. The *"creative"* **Ben Pfefferle** provides an all-around service to clients. He is well connected and *"can avoid conflict – though he is an able advocate and aggressive as needed."* He represents the Solid Waste Authority of Central Ohio on landfill expansion, construction and operational issues. **Maureen Brennan** *"doesn't get hung up on whether agency people like her and can be quite pushy, which is great,"* say sources. She enters the tables on the strength of admiration for her wetlands work.

**Clients/Work Highlights:** Clients come from the industrial, energy and services sectors and include petroleum and utility companies and a core of Fortune 150 businesses.

## Bricker & Eckler LLP

**The Firm:** Clients appreciate this group's *"well thought-out legal and political advice."* The small, polished team is particularly recommended for land use issues and litigation. It serves as general environmental counsel to the Ohio Manufacturers' Association and has close day-to-day links to regulatory and administrative agents. Attorneys have been working on high-profile litigation concerning sewers, and giving ongoing counsel to manufacturing clients on the revision of Ohio's residual waste rules.

**The Lawyers: Frank Merrill** is *"consistent, coolheaded and composed"* in the line of fire, say clients, and holds his ground admirably. He focuses on solid waste and real estate transactions that involve wetlands and water-related issues.

**Clients/Work Highlights:** Verizon Wireless; Ohio Manufacturers' Association; Von Roll America; CEMEX; Allied Waste Industries; Dayton Power & Light; Marion Steel; Mineral Processing; Ohio Cast Products; City of Columbus; Pike Sanitation; City of Delaware and The Belden Brick Company.

## Eastman & Smith Ltd

**The Firm:** This team is divided into two areas: the first covers landfills, brownfield development and solid waste, while the second deals with liabilities. It *"works hard to avoid litigation"* but can field heavyweight litigators if needed. Clients aver that the team is *"beyond excellent – the comfort level for me is at the top of my chart."* Over the past two years' it has carried out extensive litigation in the field of competition in public water services.

**The Lawyers:** *"Just saying* **Richard Sargeant**'s *name calms people down,"* according to sources. With his scientific training he can *"solve the impossible"* on the most complex transactions, and *"listens extraordinarily well."* He is expert in hazardous waste, landfill and solid waste regulatory matters, and has represented the County Court Authority in the wetlands arena. The *"exceptionally experienced"* **Joseph Gregg** enters *Chambers'* tables this year for his work in regulatory, funding and insurance matters.

**Clients/Work Highlights:** Clients include The Toledo-Lucas County Port Authority, The Solid Waste Authority of Central Ohio and Defiance County. The firm also acts for Fortune 500 companies and major RCRA hazardous waste treatment, storage and disposal facilities.

## Roetzel & Andress, LPA

**The Firm:** Clients explain that they come here because it is a *"cost-effective and well-supported"* group that enjoys *"superb contacts in major state agencies."* Home to accomplished litigators and corporate lawyers, the team offers a *"smooth and rounded service."* Specialties include brownfield redevelopment work, the resolution of historic problems at old manufacturing sites and toxic tort litigation defense. Lawyers provided pathfinding advice on the construction of a shopping center on former municipal landfill facilities. It also represents an Ohio municipality in its efforts to comply with requirements under the federal CWA, particularly in rela-

tion to combined sewer systems.

**The Lawyers: Shane Farolino** has *"excellent people and trial skills – just top-notch,"* say commentators, who characterize him as the archetypal *"aggressive and analytical leader."* He is a respected all-rounder, and acted in the shopping center matter mentioned above. **Terrence Finn** is *"a people person,"* according to clients, and complements Farolino perfectly. He combines *"first-rate legal analysis and practicality"* with personal experience of working for the government.

**Clients/Work Highlights:** Marathon Ashland Petroleum; City of Akron; Lowe's; PPG Industries; Easton; Pentair; GenCorp; FirstEnergy; TravelCenters of America; Zaremba Group and Duke Realty.

## Schottenstein, Zox & Dunn

See firm details p.1649

**The Firm:** This *"well-coordinated team"* has *"brilliant depth,"* say clients. The bulk of the workload is transactional, but the team also has a healthy flow of litigation-based work. It has been active recently on brownfield development projects and there has been an increase in water rights work. It has been representing the City of Toledo in its plans to convert a former landfill site into a vehicle storage area.

**The Lawyers:** The *"straightforward, no-nonsense"* **Stephen Samuels** (see p.1638) is the attorney to go to if you need a *"nonconfrontational and matter-of-fact"* attorney. His clients value his negotiating skills and sensitivity with delicate issues. He is a *"tenacious and effective"* generalist with substantial experience in hazardous waste matters. He recently defended the City of Lima against CWA claims by the US EPA. **Joseph Reidy** (see p.1636) is *"painstaking and lucid"* and has an understanding of the mysteries of the EPA that is *"second to none."* He represented Harry Thomas Jr and Lexington Manor in a CERCLA contribution case involving lead contamination in a housing development. Both lawyers are expert in brownfield redevelopment projects and are experienced in water rights and real estate matters.

**Clients/Work Highlights:** Kraft; Benjamin Steel; Campus Apartments; Civil & Environmental Consultants; Clermont County; Continental Real Estate; Decker, Vonau, Seguin, Lackey & Viets; ESAB Group; Fairfield County; Hall China; Lexington Manor; McArthur Lumber & Post; Penn-Ohio Coal; City of Toledo and Wagenbrenner Realty.

## Taft, Stettinius & Hollister LLP

**The Firm:** Clients use this Cincinnati-based team for its *"unbeatable responsiveness, cost-effectiveness and ability to get results – which is what matters."* The practice has a strong litigation flavor and covers air, water and hazardous waste matters for a cosmopolitan clientele. The team has been involved in the protection of the water supplies of several municipalities in Ohio and West Virginia. It also offers transactional advice.

**The Lawyers:** Once **Kim Burke** *"gets his teeth into you it is going to hurt for a while,"* admit sources. This *"tough, smart and detail-oriented guy is hands-on and keeps the costs down,"* report delighted clients. He

recently persuaded the South Carolina Supreme Court that environmental cleanup costs count as damages within the meaning of comprehensive general liability. **Thomas Terp** chairs the group and clients recommend him as a *"no-nonsense, results-focused"* lawyer and powerful litigator. His broad practice includes a niche in Superfund work, and he recently acted for Brilliant National Services to coordinate Superfund matters around the country. He has acted for Cintas on transactions throughout the USA.

**Clients/Work Highlights:** The Danis Companies; Morton International; EaglePicher and Teflon.

## Van Kley & Walker

**The Firm:** Recently formed, this boutique was founded by *"two environmental stalwarts"* who together offer long and deep experience across the board, including brownfield redevelopment and site remediation, real estate and business transactions, air and water matters and conservation. The niche area of agriculture and farming is an important speciality. Observers avow: *"These two are naturally made for each other,"* and peers predict great things for the firm.

**The Lawyers:** The *"smart and aggressive"* **Jack Van Kley** quit Jones Day to help establish this team and is acknowledged to be *"a superb litigator and negotiator."* He enjoys a high profile and is well acquainted with both the law and the regulators; he is also an agricultural specialist. Clients admire the way *"he sits, listens and processes, then advises; he is thorough and complete and truly understands how the rules should be interpreted."* He is the key environmental adviser to the Ohio Livestock Coalition. Former assistant attorney general **Christopher Walker** has five years' experience of running his own legal practice and has done a great deal of agricultural and industrial-related work. He acted for Community Mercy Health Partners on the environmental aspects of a brownfield redevelopment to construct a regional medical center in Springfield.

**Clients/Work Highlights:** Broadway Sand & Gravel; Cargill; Charter Steel; City of Kent; City of Miamisburg; Community Mercy Health Partners; Cornett Trucking Company; Miamisburg Mound Community Improvement; Ohio Farm Bureau Federation; DaimlerChrysler; Vreba-Hoff Dairy Development and West Central Ohio Port Authority.

## Walter & Haverfield LLP

**The Firm:** This compact team handles environmental and toxic torts work, counseling clients on how to avoid environmental liability as well as offering representation in court. It acts for national and regional corporations, and recently represented a group of PRPs, including Fortune 500 companies, with regard to the Tremont Barrel Fill Superfund site.

**The Lawyers:** Wherever *"thorough and knowledgeable"* **Michael Cyphert** goes *"he wins respect for being a straight shooter."* He has a thriving practice organizing and handling PRP committees in Superfund matters. He was recently appointed to a committee set up to review Ohio's laws and regulations on the disposal of C&DD waste, and advises Ohio's legislature on environmental protection. **Ralph Cascarilla** is known for his work in both Superfund and white-collar cases. He is an *"outstanding trial lawyer and effortlessly capable handler of issues in the courtroom."*

Clients/Work Highlights: The practice attracts government bodies; manufacturers; waste operators; contractors and industrial and commercial property owners. The clientele includes Total Waste Logistics; Construction & Demolition Association of Ohio; Harvard Refuse; Annaco; World Kitchen and Kurtz Bros.

## Other Notable Practitioners

The *"effective and accomplished"* **Vincent Stamp** (see p.1639) of Dinsmore & Shohl specializes in environmental litigation, particularly Superfund work and toxic torts. Clients value his *"humor and thoroughness."* He represented nine companies in the Valleycrest Superfund cost recovery litigation. Former head of the EPA, **Christopher Jones** (see p.1630) is rated as *"an immensely smart guy"* who is tipped to achieve great things at Calfee, Halter & Griswold.

# INTELLECTUAL PROPERTY

## Intellectual Property
### Leading Firms

1. JONES DAY *Cleveland*
2. CALFEE, HALTER & GRISWOLD LLP *Cleveland*
   FROST BROWN TODD LLC *Cincinnati*
   WOOD, HERRON & EVANS, LLP *Cincinnati*
3. DINSMORE & SHOHL LLP *Dayton*
   FAY SHARPE FAGAN MINNICH & MCKEE *Cleveland*
4. GREENEBAUM DOLL & MCDONALD PLLC *Cincinnati*
   TAROLLI, SUNDHEIM, COVELL *Cleveland*
   THOMPSON HINE LLP *Cleveland*

### Leading Individuals

#### Senior Statesmen

FAGAN Christopher *Fay Sharpe Fagan Minnich*
KILLWORTH Richard *Dinsmore & Shohl LLP*
TAROLLI Thomas *Tarolli, Sundheim, Covell*

1. ADAMO Ken *Jones Day*
   DREITLER Joseph *Frost Brown Todd LLC*
   GERMAIN Kenneth *Thompson Hine LLP*
   GOLDSTEIN Steven *Frost Brown Todd LLC*
   LYON Charles *Calfee, Halter*
   SCHMIT David *Frost Brown Todd LLC*
2. ALBAINY-JENEI Stephen *Frost Brown Todd LLC*
   BRINKMAN David *Wood, Herron & Evans, LLP*
   EBLING Louis *Greenebaum Doll*
   FREI Donald *Wood, Herron*
   SCHNAPP Karlyn *Frost Brown Todd LLC*
   WAMSLEY James *Jones Day*
3. BAUMGARTNER Bruce *Baker & Hostetler LLP*
   GILLEN Stephen *Greenebaum Doll*
   HOGAN Patricia *Keating, Muething*
   KOZLOWSKI Holly *Dinsmore & Shohl LLP*
   LEVY Mark *Thompson Hine LLP*
   LUNN Gregory *Wood, Herron*
   LYMAN Beverly *Wood, Herron*
   ROESCH Lynda *Dinsmore & Shohl LLP*
   SZABO Paul *Calfee, Halter*

#### Up-and-coming individuals

GAUNT Karen Kreider *Keating, Muething*
KRAFTE Lori *Greenebaum Doll*

## Band 1

### Jones Day
See firm details p.570

**The Firm:** This international giant towers over the market, and with 275 IP lawyers worldwide, it is *"able to bring in whatever skills are needed."* The team is adept in complex patent litigation and the IP aspects of corporate transactions. With global tendrils running as far as China and Taiwan, the team smoothly handles cross-border transactions for major US clients. It recently advised MOSAID in patent litigation against Infineon Technologies. Since the assimilation of Pennie & Edmonds, the practice has been growing beyond its historical patent litigation roots, and patent prosecution and trademark work now feature increasingly on the menu. Most of the team have specialist training in technical and scientific fields, and niche talents include semiconductors and medical devices. Younger companies working in niche areas seek out the firm for its software expertise and *"unbeatable analysis on tricky points of law."* A stunning client roster of household names only adds to the impression that Jones Day *"is in a league of its own in Ohio."*

**The Lawyers:** **Ken Adamo** (see p.1623) *"has a statesmanlike quality about him, and gravitas and credibility when he speaks"* – a winning formula in court for clients. He *"is a master of the arcane nature of patent law,"* according to sources, and recently defended Texas Instruments in a patent infringement investigation involving digital signal processors. He has also been heavily involved in ITC 337 proceedings. Patent litigation is the bread and butter of **James Wamsley**'s (see p.1640) practice. He is an expert in hi-tech electronics and software cases, and has been acting for Kodak in a series of patent infringement cases.

Clients/Work Highlights: Procter & Gamble; Kodak; Nestlé; Tennessee Eastman; MOSAID; RAM and GE.

## Band 2

### Calfee, Halter & Griswold LLP
See firm details p.1644

**The Firm:** Clients are quick to acclaim this group as *"professional and of the highest integrity,"* and peers are happy to refer clients there. The team covers the complete spectrum of IP. Ongoing opinion work for Procter & Gamble is a significant pillar of the practice, and the team has represented Invacare in patent litigation relating to treatment for obstructive sleep apnea.

**The Lawyers:** **Chuck Lyon** (see p.1633) *"puts every fiber of himself into his work,"* say sources. His practice combines litigation, strategic advice and opinion writing. **Paul Szabo** (see p.1640) concentrates on patent preparation and prosecution. He has handled applications in the mechanical and electro-mechanical industries technologies.

Clients/Work Highlights: The clientele includes financial institutions, healthcare organizations and research and educational institutions.

### Frost Brown Todd LLC
See firm details p.954

**The Firm:** This team *"understands academic culture and speaks the language of the scientist-inventor."* The firm is hoping to build on its strengths in patent litigation and the biomedical sector with a concerted push in trademark and copyright matters; this was boosted by the arrival of IP lawyers from Jones Day. The team has a healthy line in advising startups and managing cutting-edge issues for institutional clients like Ethicon. It eclipses the competition in the area of medical devices and recently handled several matters relating to spinal implants. Attorneys are active for hospitals and universities. Clients declare: *"They do an excellent job of protecting and managing our creative assets."* They also *"prompt us and let nothing fall through the cracks."* In a recent highlight the team has been representing iPix in a patent infringement lawsuit concerning imaging technology on real estate Web sites.

**The Lawyers:** The arrival of **Joseph Dreitler** (see p.1626) from Jones Day is a triumph for the team. His trademark and copyright expertise will undoubtedly rejuvenate the firm's IP roots. He recently successfully defended Joel Hyatt and former Vice President Al Gore against a trademark lawsuit attempting to scupper the launch of a new cable channel, CurrentTV. Chair of IP **Steven Goldstein** (see p.1628) has over 30 years' experience of patent prosecution under his belt and the useful experience of being former in-house counsel at Procter & Gamble. His background in biochemistry is invaluable to his pharmaceuticals-focused practice. The centerpiece of his year was succeeding in an EPO opposition proceeding involving a patent on the *H. pylori* assay. **David Schmit** (see p.1638) concentrates on IP litigation and recently completed a case involving trade dress, trademark and unfair competition issues for toy companies making magnetic games. With his biotechnology background, **Stephen Albainy-Jenei** (see p.1623) *"speaks the language of scientists and communicates extremely well with them."* He has been busy developing a substantial patent portfolio for a pharmaceutical company's treatment for inflammatory ailments. **Karlyn Schnapp** (see p.1638) *"always does an excellent job,"* in part thanks to her PhD in organic chemistry. She does opinion work for pharmaceutical companies and her clientele ranges from corporate and university researchers to entrepreneurial startups. Nicole Vickroy Hickey is now in-house counsel for Abbott Laboratories.

Clients/Work Highlights: University of Cincinnati; Chiquita Brands International; Medennium; National Association of Professional Baseball Leagues; Senco; Meridian Bioscience; Mylan Laboratories; Cincinnati Bell; Convergys and totes.

## Wood, Herron & Evans, LLP

The Firm: This is *"certainly the best boutique in the state,"* according to commentators. The team combines experienced senior lawyers with a vibrant wave of younger blood to handle a demanding client base. The attorneys offer diverse technical expertise and the team counsels on the IP aspects of topics as intricate and varied as CGI scripts, nucleotide and peptide therapeutics, polymer compositions, metallurgy and musical instruments. Cases handled by the firm include patent work concerning devices for sports-related injuries and trauma.

The Lawyers: Experienced in all facets of IP, **David Brinkman** is sought out particularly for his electronics and mechanics expertise. Patent prosecution constitutes the bulk of his work, and he handles applications for clients in the healthcare industry. **Donald Frei** is a *"truly excellent trademark practitioner,"* say sources. He has long experience of domestic and international IP issues and enforcement strategies, and a niche representing clothing companies. **Gregory Lunn** has *"a great head for patents"* and focuses on chemical patent prosecution and infringement evaluation, as well as handling trademark and copyright matters. His knowledge of mechanics and willingness to *"take time to understand what the client needs"* are attractive to clients. Biochemistry expert **Beverly Lyman** impresses commentators with her *"razor-sharp"* lawyering skills.

Clients/Work Highlights: IBM; Sony; Procter & Gamble; Cincinnati Children's Research Foundation; Tyco Healthcare/Mallinckrodt and Givaudan Schweiz.

## Band 3

## Dinsmore & Shohl LLP

See firm details p.1645

The Firm: This team offers a broad and polished IP service, but its *"outstanding trademark work"* still steals the limelight. Operating out of Cincinnati and Dayton, it fields patent and trademark specialists backed up by specialist litigators. As well as advising local companies, the firm counsels national and international clients based outside Ohio. Working closely with colleagues in other practice areas, the group provides clients with *"flexible, efficient and responsive"* service.

The Lawyers: *"Absolute star"* **Richard Killworth** (see p.1631) is known as a chemical patents specialist, and he is in demand as both a prosecutor and an expert witness. He is a key opinion writer for GE, and recently provided expert witness for Dell in defense against a $10 billion suit filed by MicroUnity. **Holly Kozlowski** (see p.1631) provides inventor and corporate counseling on patent-related issues. Clients describe her as *"responsive and efficient,"* and most importantly, *"she doesn't try to scam you with mumbo-jumbo."* Copyright and trademark expert **Lynda Roesch** (see p.1637) *"keeps her eye on the ball."* Valued for her *"ability to go directly to the heart of a problem,"* she is experienced in trademark, copyright and unfair competition litigation across the country.

Clients/Work Highlights: Sovereign Bank; Procter & Gamble; Standard Register; Battelle Memorial Institute and Dow Corning Foundation.

## Fay Sharpe Fagan Minnich & McKee LLP

See firm details p.1647

The Firm: With over 40 dedicated IP lawyers, this venerable boutique is one of the largest IP practices in the Midwest. Attorneys prepare and prosecute patents, and counsel clients on product design. They also represent plaintiffs and defendants in litigation. The team handles national and international patent issues for a diverse clientele that includes Fortune 500 companies.

The Lawyers: The market identifies **Christopher Fagan** (see p.1626) as the leading litigator at the firm. He counsels in all kinds of IP law, including copyright, trademark and patents.

Clients/Work Highlights: Canadian Meter; Xerox; Spalding and Evenflo are among the clients of the firm.

## Band 4

## Greenebaum Doll & McDonald PLLC

See firm details p.955

The Firm: This blossoming Cincinnati practice combines local work with international transactions advice. The key client here is Hillenbrand Industries, which provides a steady and interesting workflow. The team advises local industries on patent issues, particularly in the mechanical and electrical sectors, and also handles trademark and copyright matters.

The Lawyers: If there is a way to get a trademark through, the *"smart, friendly and fiercely determined"* **Lou Ebling** will find it, according to sources. His practice has an international flavor, generally handling inbound transactions for corporations and law firms. He represents several Mexican tequila companies and is expert in the use of trademark assets as loan collateral. **Stephen Gillen** is a *"stellar copyright and computer guy"* whose clients extol his *"immensely deep"* knowledge of the publishing industry; his clients include legal and music publishers. The *"bright and capable"* **Lori Krafte** is an admired trademark and copyright scholar, and her reputation grows day by day. She has represented sports leagues and teams in prosecution, enforcement and licensing issues.

Clients/Work Highlights: Hillenbrand Industries, Tetris and Batesville Casket all feature on the client roster.

## Tarolli, Sundheim, Covell, & Tummino LLP

The Firm: The work of this smaller Cleveland team cuts across the chemical, electrical and mechanical areas, and the team has garnered a compelling roster of multinational clients. Patent prosecution makes up the backbone of the practice. The team also counsels on the infringement and validity of patents in the USA and abroad. Trademark work is also covered.

The Lawyers: Renowned patent prosecution specialist **Thomas Tarolli** concentrates on patent law and trademarks, primarily in the mechanical sector.

Clients/Work Highlights: TRW Automotive US is the firm's biggest client. Others include The Cleveland Clinic; Texas Instruments; Hewlett-Packard; Lockheed Martin and Northrop Grumman.

## Thompson Hine LLP

See firm details p.1651

The Firm: This noted national firm offers a balanced IP service that includes patent preparation and prosecution work, licensing and opinions. Several of the attorneys have chemistry-related degrees, which attracts clients from that sector. With the corporate group at its back, the team is adept on the finance and business aspects of patent work and has *"the resources to deal with issues no matter how complicated they get."* Attorneys' *"exemplary interpersonal skills"* also come in for praise. The team has been advising a manufacturer on the proposed sale of its engineered products division.

The Lawyers: **Ken Germain**'s (see p.1628) outstanding national reputation makes him a hot property as an expert witness on a wide range of IP issues. Pampered Chef used him in a product design trade dress jury trial involving the client's Cut-N-Seal tart maker. Clients celebrate **Mark Levy**'s (see p.1632) *"excellent business sense,"* observing that he *"really understands how to relate IP to commercial objectives."* With a background in science and chemistry, he frequently carries out licensing and opinion work for the pharmaceutical industry. He has been representing Intertape Polymer in a trademark infringement action brought by 3M.

**Clients/Work Highlights:** MeadWestvaco; Ethicon Endo-Surgery; Eurand; Illinois Tool Works; KeyCorp; Goodrich; Solvay America and International Specialty Products.

## Other Notable Practitioners

For the past ten years, **Bruce Baumgartner** of Baker & Hostetler LLP's Cleveland office has been managing the IP interests of clients in more than 60 countries. He also acts as a consultant on the revision of IP laws in other countries. **Patty Hogan** of Keating, Muething and Klekamp PLL is applauded for her

work in trademarks, copyright and unfair competition matters. From the same firm, **Karen Kreider Gaunt** is *"extraordinarily hard-working and dedicated to the client's cause."* She represents both plaintiffs and defendants in trademark and copyright cases, and counts household names in the beauty, music and healthcare industries among her clients.

# LITIGATION

### Litigation: General Commercial
#### Leading Firms

1. **JONES DAY** *Cleveland*

2. **SQUIRE, SANDERS & DEMPSEY LLP** *Cleveland*
   **THOMPSON HINE LLP** *Cleveland*
   **VORYS, SATER, SEYMOUR AND PEASE** *Cleveland*

3. **BAKER & HOSTETLER LLP** *Cleveland*
   **CALFEE, HALTER & GRISWOLD LLP** *Cleveland*
   **FARUKI IRELAND & COX PLL** *Dayton*
   **PORTER WRIGHT MORRIS & ARTHUR** *Columbus*
   **TAFT, STETTINIUS & HOLLISTER LLP** *Cincinnati*
   **ZEIGER, TIGGES, LITTLE & LINDSMITH** *Columbus*

4. **CARPENTER & LIPPS LLP** *Columbus*
   **CHESTER, WILLCOX & SAXBE LLP** *Columbus*
   **HAHN LOESER & PARKS LLP** *Cleveland*
   **KATZ, TELLER, BRANT & HILD** *Cincinnati*
   **KEATING, MUETHING & KLEKAMP** *Cincinnati*
   **KEGLER, BROWN, HILL & RITTER** *Columbus*
   **MCLAUGHLIN & MCCAFFREY, LLP** *Cleveland*
   **SCHOTTENSTEIN, ZOX & DUNN** *Columbus*
   **TUCKER ELLIS & WEST LLP** *Cleveland*
   **ULMER & BERNE LLP** *Cleveland*

## Band 1

### Jones Day
See firm details p.570
**The Firm:** Clients declare this litigation powerhouse to be *"far and away the best in the state for performance."* It offers *"incredible strength and depth,"* and serves an imposing client list that includes more than half the Fortune 500 companies. Quite apart from its global reach, the firm provides national coverage in the USA. Experts are brought in from around the country on an as-needed basis, and the team has the resources to deal with the largest multidistrict litigation.
**The Lawyers:** Described as *"quite simply one of the best ever,"* **Patrick McCartan** (see p.1633) occupies a senior role advising on appellate and Supreme Court arguments. **John Newman** (see p.1635) is *"absolutely A-plus,"* according to interviewees. He handles a wide range of general commercial matters and has particular expertise in stockholder actions and fiduciary and governance claims. **John Strauch** (see p.1639) brings a *"cachet"* to his nationwide cases. **Theodore Grossman** (see p.1628) has a powerful reputation in tobacco litigation and tries cases and argues appeals across the country. He argued for all defendants against class certification in Schwab v

Philip Morris in district court for the Eastern District of New York. Partner-in-charge in Columbus, **Fordham Huffman** (see p.1630) was a key figure in the recent win in Crowley v Chait, resulting in approximately $183 million in damages and prejudgment interest for the receiver of the defunct Ambassador Insurance. **Kevin Cogan** (see p.1625) has extensive trial experience in complex litigation across the board, and recently acted on two major bankruptcy and insolvency litigation cases. **Steve Sozio** (see p.1639) is a member of the firm's corporate criminal investigations practice, and commentators acknowledge him to be *"a giant"* for white-collar litigation. **George Moscarino** (see p.1634) counsels corporate organizations in white-collar crime issues and takes the litigation of sophisticated cases in his stride.
**Clients/Work Highlights:** OGE Energy; FirstEnergy; GM; RJ Reynolds; Parker Hannifin; Wyeth; IBM; Nextel Communications; The Cleveland Clinic; Kodak; Scott Fetzer; Nestlé and Procter & Gamble.

## Band 2

### Squire, Sanders & Dempsey LLP
See firm details p.1650
**The Firm:** This is one of the state's leading forces in commercial litigation, as well as being recognized worldwide. It litigates throughout the USA for a client roster that includes local, national and international entities. In a major development, the firm combined with Steel Hector & Davis, increasing the number of trial lawyers available nationally. Recent highlights include winning a trade secrets case in federal court in Columbus on behalf of a major producer of paper products from recycled materials. The group also won a unanimous jury trial verdict for a manufacturer of asbestos-containing wire and cable.
**The Lawyers:** **Thomas Kilbane** (see p.1631) heads the worldwide litigation practice and is experienced in litigating highly technical multiparty commercial disputes with particular emphasis on antitrust, contract, construction and securities cases. His *"aggressive but thoughtful approach"* makes him effective and pleasant to work with, say commentators. **David Young** (see p.1642) is known for *"terrific work"* in the healthcare sector. **John Gall** (see p.1627) has an extensive trial and appellate practice that covers a range of commercial issues, including busi-

ness contract disputes, IP rights, professional liability claims, corporate control contests and public sector contract and financial matters. Despite **Damond Mace**'s (see p.1633) relative youth, he attracts fulsome praise for his work on commercial contract disputes, UCC, construction, products liability, torts and class actions.
**Clients/Work Highlights:** The Newark Group; Nationwide Insurance; Glimcher Realty Trust; Medical Mutual of Ohio; Catholic Conference of Ohio and the City of Cincinnati.

### Thompson Hine LLP
See firm details p.1651
**The Firm:** The rise and rise of this national heavyweight continues apace, and it has made great strides in the international and litigation arenas. The litigation group in Ohio caters to businesses and individuals in all manner of commercial disputes, and is renowned for its representation of financial institutions and companies involved in tax controversies. Clients sing the praises of the *"highly responsive lawyers,"* singling out the sheer quality of the work and the attorneys' *"ability to think outside the box."*
**The Lawyers:** The *"thoughtful, thorough and tenacious"* **William Wilkinson**'s (see p.1641) clients are delighted that he *"obtains results that far exceed our expectations."* He regularly acts for clients in the financial services industry and successfully represented JPMorgan recently in litigation concerning its involvement in automobile loan securitizations. Amid a hectic and diverse caseload, he also handled a series of criminal investigations at state and federal levels concerning Republican Party fund-raising. Managing partner **David Hooker** (see p.1630) is expert in complex business litigation and he is a key link to some of the firm's most prominent clients. Group chair **Steven Kaufman** (see p.1631) enters the tables on the strength of high praise for his *"stunning contacts"* and his *"deft handling of major issues."* He recently represented AT Kearney in a $20 million dispute with OfficeMax regarding the terms of their consulting agreement. **Earle Maiman** (see p.1633) focuses on commercial litigation, including all forms of contract and tort claims, products liability, legal malpractice defense, insurance defense and disputes involving health insurance and employment law. According to sources, **James Robenalt** (see p.1637) is a *"skillful and experienced"* lawyer who handles emerging technology business disputes and complex litigation, including economic espionage and trade secret cases, international disputes, investment tax

credit cases and construction-related matters.
**Clients/Work Highlights:** KeyBank; Charter 1; KPMG; Highlands Insurance Group; Clear Channel; PolyOne; PPG Industries and American Chemistry Council.

## Vorys, Sater, Seymour and Pease LLP
See firm details p.1652

**The Firm:** This firm has a national presence and a strong showing in Ohio. Approximately one third of its lawyers are dedicated to litigation, and it is well equipped to handle large and complex disputes. The team takes on a varied caseload in which general corporate and commercial litigation predominates. Work includes the prosecution or defense of breach of contract cases, enforcement of contractual covenants, employment disputes and securities litigation.

**The Lawyers:** Commentators heap praise on the "*incredibly talented*" **David Cupps** (see p.1626), with one interviewee reporting: "*He is absolutely top of my list – I cannot think of a better commercial litigator in the state.*" He has more than 30 years of experience in matters including antitrust, IP and securities disputes. According to sources, **Sandra Anderson** (see p.1623) is an "*incredibly intelligent*" litigator. Her workload stems from a general litigation practice that includes employment, commercial, business and products liability law. Peers view **Daniel Buckley** (see p.1624) as a "*fantastic advocate, who doesn't waste time or make things personal.*" Based in Cincinnati, he focuses on business and healthcare litigation. Cleveland chief **Anthony O'Malley** (see p.1635) is endorsed by commentators as an "*extremely impressive presence in the courtroom.*" He is heavily involved in hospital law. Senior litigator **Thomas Ridgley** (see p.1636) is similarly revered for his ability to handle himself in court. His diverse litigation practice has evolved over the years and he is now concentrating increasingly on class action defense in areas such as labor law, and on securities cases. **James Phillips** (see p.1636) is admired for his "*unfaltering determination*" in the white-collar arena, while **Glenn Whitaker** (see p.1641) is adept in complex criminal litigation and government procurement cases.

**Clients/Work Highlights:** The group is defending Abercrombie & Fitch in six related federal securities class action cases and two derivative cases, all pending in federal court in Ohio. Highlights also include representing several large national retailers in defense against employment and wage and hour class action throughout the USA. Other clients include Honda; Scotts Miracle-Gro; Lockheed Martin; Goodyear and Boehringer Ingelheim.

## Band 3

### Baker & Hostetler LLP

**The Firm:** This firm has a strong national presence and three offices across Ohio, all of which offer expertise in litigation. The group handles a diverse array of cases for prominent clients and has continued to expand its litigation capability.

**The Lawyers:** **Randall Solomon** splits his time between commercial litigation and the defense of mass toxic injury cases. Much of his time of late has been consumed by a major arbitration between two large manufacturing clients. His Cleveland-based colleague **Daniel Warren** is a newcomer to the table, following endorsements from clients. His complex business liti-

gation practice emphasizes the representation of banks, and he acts for clients at trial and on appeal. **James Wooley** is described as an "*extraordinarily competent, fair and honorable practitioner.*" He offers the full package when it comes to commercial litigation, and is particularly fêted for his white-collar work.

**Clients/Work Highlights:** An impressive client roster includes financial institutions and energy companies.

## Calfee, Halter & Griswold LLP
See firm details p.1644

**The Firm:** This Ohio stalwart has offices in Cleveland and Columbus and offers approximately 40 lawyers dedicated to commercial litigation. The team has particular expertise in plaintiff business cases, class action defense, securities litigation and IP. The firm continues to develop a niche in insurance coverage and has an expanding stand-alone group dedicated to the representation of corporate policyholders. The recent workload has included the representation in coverage matters of a number of public companies and large privately held companies such as RPM; Applied Industrial; Park-Ohio; OMNOVA Solutions and KeyBank.

**The Lawyers:** **Mitchell Blair** (see p.1624) is popular with clients, who highlight his "*incredible analytical skills and thoughtfulness*" and his "*thoroughly prepared and unflappable*" approach in the courtroom. He cochairs the litigation group with **Mark Wallach** (see p.1640), who is described as a "*worthy adversary and an aggressive litigator.*" Sources report that he is "*extremely smart, fast on his feet and shoots from the hip.*" He acted as lead counsel for Cleveland State University in a fraud case against PeopleSoft in relation to the sale and installation of enterprise computer software.

**Clients/Work Highlights:** Family Heritage; Fifth Third Bank; FirstEnergy; Regal Cinemas; Agilysys and Cingular Wireless.

## Faruki Ireland & Cox PLL

**The Firm:** This highly specialized trial firm focuses on complex business litigation and fields approximately 40 dedicated lawyers. Based in Dayton, there is a distinctly national flavor to the practice. The group's relatively new media practice is thriving, while lawyers concentrating on IP, and in particular patent infringement litigation, have been kept particularly busy. Class action work also takes up a significant amount of the attorneys' time.

**The Lawyers:** **Charles Faruki** (see p.1627) is an "*enormously successful litigator, capable of handling an incredible breadth of matters.*" Sources also point out that in addition to being an "*excellent, thorough lawyer, he is a lot of fun to work with.*" He has been advising Procter & Gamble on two claims of patent infringement against Coca-Cola. **Jeffrey Ireland** (see p.1630) focuses increasingly on competition matters, and he recently represented Crown Equipment in a series of lawsuits with Toyota Material Handling.

**Clients/Work Highlights:** Reed Elsevier; Cargill; NCR; Premier Health Partners; Iams; Dayton Newspapers and Dayton Power and Light.

## Porter Wright Morris & Arthur LLP

See firm details p.1648

**The Firm:** This national player has the resources and expertise to handle the most substantial and complex multiparty disputes. The team of accomplished trial lawyers litigates business and commercial disputes across a huge range of areas and regularly represents Fortune 500 companies.

**The Lawyers:** Managing partner **Robert Trafford** (see p.1640) commands a high level of respect for his *"thoughtful, thorough and effective"* work. He focuses on complex business litigation. **Kathleen Trafford** (see p.1640) makes her first appearance in the tables because of resounding recommendations: *"She does a fantastic job and, to top it all off, she's a delight to work with."* Her broad practice includes particular expertise in governmental and regulatory litigation and constitutional law.

## Taft, Stettinius & Hollister LLP

**The Firm:** The *"talented"* lawyers here attract praise from clients for their *"judgment and responsiveness."* The firm has four offices in Ohio and another in Kentucky, and offers more than 70 dedicated litigation attorneys. General commercial and financial litigation makes up the bulk of the workload, and the team offers specialty expertise in IP, antitrust and environmental matters. The firm has also been heavily involved in international disputes recently, particularly arbitrations.

**The Lawyers:** Clients describe **Clifford Craig** as a *"low-key but firm and incredibly impressive lawyer."* Commentators praise his *"articulate, passionate and diligent approach."* He chairs the litigation practice and focuses on complex commercial and financial litigation, with an emphasis on federal and state securities litigation.

**Clients/Work Highlights:** Cinergy; Georgia Power; Gibson Greetings; Firstar and Celina Financial Services.

## Zeiger, Tigges, Little & Lindsmith LLP

**The Firm:** This specialist commercial litigation boutique owes its reputation to *"an all-star cast"* of 11 attorneys. It acts for an impressive client roster that includes leading international banks and some of the state's most prominent law firms. Much of the workload consists of corporate litigation defense, professional liability and media cases. Recent highlights include the defense of a legal malpractice action involving claims of more than $50 million, and the defense of a class action involving alleged industrywide price-fixing of foundry resins.

**The Lawyers:** **John Zeiger** is admired as a *"ferocious, hard-working litigator who combines creative thinking with excellent writing skills."* The backbone of his practice is complex litigation, primarily representing corporations, high net worth individuals and legal professionals. He is an experienced trial lawyer and is well versed in class action defense.

**Clients/Work Highlights:** Abercrombie & Fitch; The Columbus Dispatch; eFunds; Fifth Third Bank; Hexion Specialty Chemicals; JPMorgan Chase; Nationwide Insurance; The New Albany Company; OhioHealth; Scotts Miracle-Gro; State Automobile Mutual Insurance and UnitedHealth Group. The group also represented seven major law firms in professional liability contexts.

## Band 4

## Carpenter & Lipps LLP

**The Firm:** This Columbus-based group offers 16 lawyers and focuses on class action and complex litigation on a national scale. It represents clients in business and banking, particularly in the automotive industry. It has been expanding its healthcare litigation potential and recently added white-collar capability. The team fields specialists in products liability and IP litigation. Satisfied clients highlight the group's sense of camaraderie and cost-effectiveness: *"The work is the same quality as that of larger firms but at a much more reasonable rate."*

**The Lawyers:** Cofounder **Michael Carpenter** impresses clients with his pragmatism and *"constant striving for perfection."* His expertise lies in commercial litigation, products liability, class actions and multidistrict litigation.

**Clients/Work Highlights:** The firm represented Evenflo as plaintiff in a multimillion-dollar commercial dispute that was favorably resolved at mediation. Other highlights include acting for Crest Cadillac in a statutory appraisal trial regarding valuation of the shares of one of its minority stockholders. Clients include Daewoo Motor America; Developer Finance; Honda; Isuzu Motors America; New United Motor Manufacturing; Nissan; GM and Toyota.

## Chester, Willcox & Saxbe LLP

**The Firm:** A traditional player in litigation, this Columbus-based group handles everything from routine commercial and business litigation to complex class actions. The firm offers trial experi-ence in a variety of areas including banking, contract, fraud and RICO violations.

**The Lawyers:** Peers happily refer clients to group chair **Stephen Fitch**, a *"low-key but astonishingly good lawyer."* He focuses on civil trial and appellate work, alternative dispute resolution and professional responsibility, and he regularly represents other law firms in malpractice cases. **Charles Saxbe** is regarded as a *"well-connected, politically oriented lawyer with a fantastic knowledge of how things work at a state level."*

## Hahn Loeser & Parks LLP

**The Firm:** Representing clients in every major type of dispute, the *"knowledgeable and diligent"* attorneys in this practice group attract special recognition for their expertise in complex commercial litigation, employment/noncompetition agreements, IP and tort litigation. Clients feel comfortable handing anything to them: *"They fully understand our business and our expectations and provide a prompt, effective service."* The workload has most recently centered on cases in the healthcare, antitrust, insurance coverage, construction, securities and fraud areas.

**The Lawyers:** *"Heavyweight litigator"* **Robert Fogarty** recently defended Aetna in two separately filed class action lawsuits, and represented Lawyers Title in a suit against First American. He has also argued cases before the Ohio Supreme Court and the Sixth Circuit Court of Appeals.

**Clients/Work Highlights:** The year's highlights include the successful representation of JCI in a matter against a just-in-time supplier threatening to discontinue supplying parts. The group also won $43 million in a unanimous jury verdict for Chicago Title, in a case that centered on the enforcement of business ethics and liability arising from improper recruiting tactics. Other clients include ExxonMobil; Cendant; The Cleveland Clinic; Bechtel Power; Cleveland Museum of Art and The Ohio State University.

## Katz, Teller, Brant & Hild

**The Firm:** This seven-attorney litigation group represents clients from individuals to Fortune 100 companies in all areas of civil litigation. It has been particularly busy recently with cases relating to antitrust, breach of contract, employment, patents and insurance coverage. Recent highlights include acting as trial counsel for the University of Cincinnati Surgeons and the Medical Center Fund of Cincinnati in a suit alleging fraud and breach of an employment contract.

**The Lawyers:** Group chair **Robert Pitcairn** *"handles incredibly complex cases with aplomb."* His extensive experience in business litigation includes defending various types of class actions, stockholder derivative suits, commercial disputes and employment discrimination cases. He recently defended the Cincinnati Bengals in relation to allegations of antitrust violations.

**Clients/Work Highlights:** Jeff Wyler Dealer Group; Pharmacia; RMS Realty; the Estate of Austin E. Knowlton; Tyco Healthcare; Hebrew Union

College; Medical Center Fund of Cincinnati and Washing Systems.

## Keating, Muething & Klekamp, PLL

**The Firm:** The litigators here act for both plaintiffs and defendants. The lawyers are well versed in all areas of commercial litigation and the group has an impressive track record in court. Interviewees praise the "*tremendous results*" achieved, and clients are pleased with the lawyers' involvement of them in all strategic and tactical decisions. Recent notable victories include a verdict against US Bank, a victory in the United States Appeals Court and a directed verdict in the General Tool case. The firm has also filed a class action lawsuit on behalf of individuals and businesses damaged by a styrene leak incident.

**The Lawyers:** The "*extremely hard-working and conscientious*" **James Burke** focuses on business litigation, securities and commercial and financial disputes.

**Clients/Work Highlights:** AK Steel; American Financial Group; Cincinnati Reds; Cincom Systems; Cintas; Fifth Third Bank; Great American Financial Resources; Great American Insurance and National City Bank.

## Kegler, Brown, Hill & Ritter

**The Firm:** This skilled team of 25 litigators provides an impressive depth of experience and an undeniable capacity to deal with high-profile cases, whether in court or through alternative resolution. The firm serves an impressive client roster that includes Fortune 500 companies.

**The Lawyers:** Sources commend **Thomas Hill** (see p.1630) as an eminent business litigation attorney. He has experience of litigating before the US Supreme Court and a "*strong understanding of the intricate relationship between law and business*."

**Clients/Work Highlights:** Virginia Homes and Thrifty Car Rental are two of the team's main clients.

## McLaughlin & McCaffrey, LLP

**The Firm:** This boutique counsels plaintiffs and defendants in a range of cases. Peers rate the firm's work as "*notably superior*," which they attribute to a strong team of practitioners supported by high-quality junior staff. The group prides itself on a combination of white-collar and civil litigation work from products liability matters to major federal criminal investigations.

**The Lawyers:** **Patrick McLaughlin** is widely regarded as "*one of the best names in white-collar criminal defense.*" He has plentiful trial experience and clients commend his responsive and positive attitude. **John McCaffrey** attracts praise for his "*keen intelligence and calm demeanor.*" He enjoys long-standing political connections, and clients applaud his "*candid*" nature.

**Clients/Work Highlights:** Cingular Wireless; Electrolizing Corporation of Ohio; Lorillard Tobacco; Miller Brewing; RE Kramig & Co; Safeco Insurance and URS.

## Schottenstein, Zox & Dunn

See firm details p.1649

**The Firm:** This group of "*quick-thinking and aggressive attorneys*" counsels a full spectrum of business clients. The "*up to the minute*" trial lawyers are making a push into corporate governance and securities matters. Recent highlights include successfully acting for a manufacturer of electronic voting equipment against the Ohio Secretary of State, and a dispute over ownership rights to leased pallets recovered by a recycling company.

**The Lawyers:** **John McDonald** (see p.1633) is an "*exceptional practitioner,*" according to interviewees. He recently prevailed in a high-profile Ohio Supreme Court case in which petitions seeking to overturn a recently passed school levy were ruled invalid.

**Clients/Work Highlights:** Central Funding; Welsh Ohio; Ohio Company; G Siempelkamp; The Frank Gates Companies; Equinox Fund; Chemical Abstracts; Ashland and North American Securities Administrators Association.

## Tucker Ellis & West LLP

**The Firm:** This firm houses a team of "*thorough yet practical, tough yet reasonable*" attorneys offering business litigation trial experience in state and federal courts. The clientele ranges from established corporate businesses to smaller companies.

**The Lawyers:** **Hugh Stanley**'s clients depict him as "*practical and highly effective in court.*" His litigation and trial practice extends across a number of states. **Robert Tucker** offers extensive trial expertise.

**Clients/Work Highlights:** Pharmed Group, Ohio Savings Bank and Aon are three of the firm's major clients.

## Ulmer & Berne LLP

**The Firm:** This large team specializes in counseling financial institutions in all areas of banking litigation. The "*driven*" attorneys are credited with "*a superior knowledge level*" and sensitivity to clients' needs. Highlights of 2005 include the successful defense of PNC/Hilliard Lyons in a prospective stockholder class action in the Federal District Court of Denver.

**The Lawyers:** **Marvin Karp** is an experienced commercial litigator who frequently acts for high-profile corporate enterprises in multibillion-dollar deals. Sources commend his "*sharp legal mind*" and "*unfaltering counsel.*" **John Haggerty** handles complex products liability cases and is at home in federal and state courts across the USA. Recent highlights include securing dismissals for Avery Dennison and Solvay Chemicals of separate class action antitrust cases brought by indirect purchasers. He also successfully defended NCR in a $40 million matter in federal court in Utah.

**Clients/Work Highlights:** Altria Group; AT&T; Cleveland-Cliffs; Barr Laboratories; IMG Worldwide; JPMorgan Chase; Linde Gas; Morgan Stanley; NCR; PNC Bank; Procter & Gamble; Rexall Sundown; Twin Laboratories and Wachovia.

## Other Notable Practitioners

Sources describe **David Greer** of Dayton's Bieser, Greer & Landis LLP as a "*fantastic lawyer, versatile and hugely able.*" He has been occupied recently with trial work in business and IP disputes, and a number of professional ethics cases. **Neil Freund** of specialist litigation boutique Freund, Freeze & Arnold focuses on business litigation and recently tried a number of legal and medical malpractice suits, winning them all. According to sources, it is "*terrific to see him in action.*" IP suits and professional liability cases for doctors, engineers and architects round off his practice. **Roger Fry** of Rendings, Fry, Kiely & Dennis LLP attracts praise for his diverse litigation practice and, in particular, his work in the area of insurance coverage. **James Arnold** of the Law Office of James S. Arnold is a "*polite bulldog.*" Managing partner of White, Getgey & Meyer Co. LPA **David Kamp** is a "*no-nonsense lawyer with a great deal of common sense.*" His practice covers commercial litigation, medical and professional malpractice, PI, domestic relations and products liability. **Richard Kerger**, cofounder of Toledo-based Kerger & Kerger, specializes in trials and appeals as well as complex employment law issues. Conflicted peers, all of whom eagerly endorse his work, refer a large portion of his caseload. Sole practitioner **William Meeks** focuses on criminal defense and sources commend the depth of his expertise in the area. **Niki Schwartz** of Schwartz, Downey & Co, LPA handles a mixture of civil and criminal litigation and has developed "*finely polished skills.*" He earns particular respect for his mediation work and involvement in white-collar criminal cases. **Ralph Cascarilla**, chair of the firm's litigation group, is a "*splendid*" attorney who specializes in federal criminal defense and white-collar work. Managing partner **Robert Rotatori** of Rotatori, Bender, Gragel, Stoper & Alexander Co LPA, has more than 30 years' experience in criminal litigation, principally in the federal court, and is an authority in white-collar crime. **Terry Sherman** of Terry K Sherman in Columbus is a confident courtroom performer with more than three decades of experience in criminal defense. Sources recommend him as "*a fearless lawyer with well-honed trial preparation skills and 100% commitment to his clients.*" Interviewees praise **Roger Synenberg** of Synenberg & Associates LCC for his "*versatility and friendly attitude.*" He is "*politically aware*" and offers broad white-collar expertise. **Samuel Weiner** of Samuel B Weiner Co LPA is an old hand at criminal trials and has a thriving white-collar practice. Recently moved to Boucher & Boucher Co. LPA, **Roger Makley** is a general commercial litigator with a white-collar niche.

# REAL ESTATE

| Real Estate |
| --- |
| Leading Firms |
| [1] **BRICKER & ECKLER LLP** *Columbus* |
| **JONES DAY** *Cleveland* |
| **THOMPSON HINE LLP** *Cleveland* |
| **VORYS, SATER, SEYMOUR AND PEASE** *Columbus* |
| [2] **BAKER & HOSTETLER LLP** *Cleveland* |
| **KAHN KLEINMAN, LPA** *Cleveland* |
| **PORTER WRIGHT MORRIS & ARTHUR** *Columbus* |
| **SQUIRE, SANDERS & DEMPSEY LLP** *Cleveland* |
| [3] **BENESCH, FRIEDLANDER, COPLAN** *Cleveland* |
| **CALFEE, HALTER & GRISWOLD LLP** *Cleveland* |
| **FROST BROWN TODD LLC** *Cincinnati* |
| **SCHOTTENSTEIN, ZOX & DUNN** *Columbus* |
| **ULMER & BERNE LLP** *Cleveland* |

## Bricker & Eckler LLP

**The Firm:** Sources commend this firm's *"creative and business-driven approach."* Operating out of offices in Cleveland, Columbus and now Cincinnati, the team is a dominant player in the region. Clients value the lawyers' deep understanding of their businesses, and the fact that they *"clearly understand the difference between the business and legal sides."* The team offers expertise in lifestyle centers and recently acted for a bank providing $210 million permanent financing for a mixed-use lifestyle center. As part of a thriving development practice the team acted for the developer in the acquisition and rehabilitation of 600 low-income housing units at 13 project sites.

**The Lawyers:** **David Baker** has a glowing reputation for finance, telecom and real estate work. His easygoing nature and realistic attitude earn him an avalanche of praise. The *"remarkably intelligent"* **David Conrad** focuses on real estate transactions. **Charles McCreary** is a *"creative"* lawyer and a renowned lender representative. Commentators report that **Steve Intihar** is becoming every bit the star he promised to be. His deep understanding of the issues surrounding CAP developments has gained him immense respect, and clients declare him the *"leading lender counsel in Ohio."*

**Clients/Work Highlights:** McGraw-Hill; National City Bank; North Star Realty; Continental Real Estate; Casto; Lifestyle Communities; JPMorgan Chase; Fifth Third Bank; KeyBank; Huntington National Bank; the City of Cincinnati and Whirlpool.

## Jones Day

See firm details p.570

**The Firm:** The *"kings of Cleveland"* handle a robust national and international projects practice, largely geared to supporting the firm's glittering corporate clientele. One satisfied customer vows that they produce *"the best work I have ever seen."* The team recently acted for Micron on the real estate aspects of its $2.4 billion joint venture with Intel. In another recent highlight, it represented Developers Diversified Realty in its $1.145 billion acquisition of 15 shopping centers in Puerto Rico from the Caribbean Property Group.

**The Lawyers:** **Richard Reppert** (see p.1636) wows developer clients with the skillful way he services their financing needs. *"Rainmaker"* **Zachary Paris** (see p.1635) is an esteemed transactional lawyer who is active in corporate real estate deals. **Stephen Mixter** (see p.1634) acts for institutional clients. **Michael Ording** (see p.1635) has a strong reputation among clients, and one commentator reports: *"He is the most professional and competent real estate attorney I know."* **Michael Owendoff** (see p.1635) has come into his own, proving himself to be the kind of lawyer that *"you could throw in the trenches."*

**Clients/Work Highlights:** Forest City Enterprises; Ray Fogg Building Methods; Robert L. Stark Enterprises; CalEast Industrial Investors; Continental Airlines; KeyCorp; Fedex Ground; Mittal Steel USA ISG; ProCare Automotice Service Solutions; Alderwoods Group; Arctic Glacier; The Riverside Company; Marine Mechanical and Micron.

## Thompson Hine LLP

See firm details p.1651

**The Firm:** This firm attracts *"profound admiration"* from competitors and clients, and enjoys an unbeatable profile in Ohio for development, corporate, financing and capital markets work. The workload has an increasingly strong international and capital markets flavor. The team's center of gravity is in Cleveland, but it has a national reach and attorneys frequently act across the USA. Recent highlights include two developer representations in joint venture acquisitions of $100 million and $319 million respectively.

**The Lawyers:** **Linda Striefsky** (see p.1639) lives up to her reputation for technical excellence. Sources trust her and commend her professional and traditional approach. **Thomas Coyne** (see p.1625) heads up the team and is acclaimed as not only *"an incredibly strong and pragmatic lawyer"* but also *"an excellent manager."* **James Aronoff** (see p.1623) chairs the capital markets team and interviewees recommend him as a *"deals lawyer."*

## Vorys, Sater, Seymour and Pease LLP

See firm details p.1652

**The Firm:** This is an *"extremely active,"* statewide player with its deepest roots in Columbus. Observers regard it as a *"key participant in the market"* and are especially warm in praise of its tax and finance advice. The bulk of the work lies in the development area, though attorneys can and do *"turn their hands to just about anything."* Highlights from the past year include representing the borrower in the $300 million refinancing of the Easton Town Center mixed-use project. The group also acted as lead counselor for the purchaser group of a residential development with a golf course. Zoning and land use matters are a particular niche for the firm, and it fields six lawyers that cover it all, including building regulation and litigation advice.

**The Lawyers:** Clients declare **Stephen Buchenroth** (see p.1624) their *"number one"* in conflict disputes, and the market is unanimous in praise of his *"personal and professional"* approach. Practice head **John Wellner** (see p.1641) has a great many strings to his bow and is best known in real estate for his development work. According to peers, *"he's fun to work with and you know it's going to be good if you see him on the other side."* **Ted Smith** (see p.1639) is a senior associate with particular experience in condominium law. **Daniel Schoedinger** (see p.1638) is a zoning and land use expert, and sources report that *"he has a fantastic understanding of the process."*

**Clients/Work Highlights:** Schottenstein Stores; Pizzuti; M/I Homes; The Limited; The Don M Casto Organization and Arshot Investment.

## Baker & Hostetler LLP

**The Firm:** This team represents a diverse set of clients from large corporations to individuals, and takes on a varied portfolio of projects. It is renowned for advising on the finance and tax elements of transactions. Already a strong regional contender, the firm overall has consolidated its international aspirations by affiliating with practices in Central and South America. Recent highlights include two large redevelopment projects, one of which involves the rehabilitation of an entire downtown neighborhood.

**The Lawyers:** **Lawrence Lindberg** is *"a major force in the team"* and concentrates on development, leasing, construction and financing. **Patricia O'Donnell**'s clients value her as a talented deal-maker with extensive knowledge of all aspects of development, especially the structuring and negotiation of complex transactions. Similarly, clients praise **David Strauss** as *"outstanding when it comes to creative structures."* His specialties are partnerships and tax planning.

**Clients/Work Highlights:** Advance Auto; American Standard; Cardinal Health; Citigroup; The E.W. Scripps Company; Hyatt and OfficeMax.

## Kahn Kleinman LPA

**The Firm:** Commentators agree that this smart and credible group is *"large enough to get what is needed done, yet small enough to be personable"* and clients happily announce: *"We do not feel like we are just a number."* It has taken on some high-profile projects over the past year, including acting on a major retail development and representing Cleveland State University in the development of a $2 million biotech center.

**The Lawyers:** **Richard Rosner** (see p.1637) is experienced in residential developments, particularly condominiums. Clients praise his results-oriented approach and pro bono work. Group chair **Bruce Gaynor** (see p.1627) has a mainly managerial role and is described as *"a good quarterback – he knows how to get the team together."* Clients rest easy in the knowledge that he *"knows the law like the back of his hand."* Commentators recommend *"responsive"* retail leasing expert **Bill Phillips** (see p.1636) for his shopping center and retail development expertise. He has recently joined the firm from Calfee, Halter & Griswold.

**Clients/Work Highlights:** City of Cleveland; City of Shaker Heights; Case Western Reserve University; Cleveland State University; Chase Properties; First Interstate Properties; Fifth Third Bank; LaSalle Bank; National City Bank and St. Vincent's Charity Hospital.

## Porter Wright Morris & Arthur LLP

See firm details p.1648

**The Firm:** This nationwide firm takes on an array of projects from affordable housing to commercial leasing and agriculture. Representing lenders is at the heart of the practice, though the workload has included an increasing amount of development work recently. In an active year, the team has been involved in transactions in the $5 million to $75 million range, including condominium conversions, refinancing, brownfield redevelopment and the acquisition and leasing of restaurants. The firm's extensive zoning and land use capability includes industrial, commercial, residential and recreational developments, and the team has taken on some sizable projects of late.

**The Lawyers:** **John Rohyans** (see p.1637) *"does it all"* and has a thriving lender-based practice. Clients know **Bill Weir** (see p.1641) as *"an accommodator who understands the complexities of transactions."* He is popular with banks, which frequently insist on his presence on a transaction. **Jeffrey McNealey**'s (see p.1633) practice centers on zoning and environmental crossover work. He was recently involved in a $20 million development on a brownfield site. **Robert Meyer** (see p.1634) is an *"outstanding zoning lawyer"* with more than a quarter of a century's experience in the field. He represents Dominion Homes on their land development matters.

**Clients/Work Highlights:** AEP; Bayview Financial; Citicorp; Dominion Homes; the Don M Casto Organization; Fifth Third Bank; Huntington National Bank; JPMorgan; Max & Erma's Restaurants; National Church Residences; Nationwide; State Farm and Value City Department Stores.

## Squire, Sanders & Dempsey L.L.P.

See firm details p.1650

**The Firm:** The vigorous public finance practice here drives a dynamic real estate workflow. Attorneys act nationally and globally in a variety of sectors, including hotels, resorts and leisure, affordable housing and development projects. An eventful year has seen growth in the firm's hospitality, transactional and finance practices. Lawyers specialize in complex deals, bringing real estate, tax and environmental expertise to the table.

**The Lawyers:** **Samuel Pearlman**'s (see p.1636) extensive practice has been broadened to include litigation, and sources commend his *"tenacity and dedication."* **Michael Saad**'s (see p.1637) varied portfolio includes Islamic financing. He acts as a firmwide coordinator for real estate matters. **Bryan Venesy**'s (see p.1640) practice continues to grow, and clients are attracted to his courteous manner and wide experience.

**Clients/Work Highlights:** The firm's clients include Mid-America Management and Schottenstein Stores.

## Benesch, Friedlander, Coplan & Aronoff LLP

See firm details p.1643

**The Firm:** This traditional regional player offers an extensive real estate and land use service to commercial clients, notably retail developers, and charities. Its environmental and development capabilities have been quietly strengthened through internal expansion. Recent work includes ongoing representation of the Greater Cleveland Regional Transit Authority in connection with the $168 million Euclid Corridor Transportation Project. Other highlights include handling the real estate aspects of the $190 million acquisition and leasing by United Rehab of nursing facilities and rehabilitation hospitals in three states.

**The Lawyers:** **Howard Steindler** (see p.1639) is a veteran lawyer with specialist experience in shopping malls and mixed-use developments. **Norman Gutmacher** (see p.1629) is recommended for his commercial real estate work on a national level.

**Clients/Work Highlights:** Clients include Cuyahoga Board of County Commissioners, House of Blues and Frisch's.

## Calfee, Halter & Griswold LLP

See firm details p.1644

**The Firm:** Clients highlight this team's leasing work, and it is an acknowledged specialist in shopping center and mixed-use developments, especially multisite and multilocation projects. Recent highlights include advising First Interstate Properties on the public finance, land acquisition and leasing aspects of the Steelyard Commons shopping center.

**The Lawyers:** **Mara Cushwa** specializes in the development and environmental aspects of real estate transactions.

**Clients/Work Highlights:** The Richard E. Jacobs Group; Robert L. Stark Enterprises; Visconsi Companies; Snavely Development; Hudson Village Finance; Fairmount Properties; TravelCenters of America and RPM International.

## Frost Brown Todd LLC

See firm details p.954

**The Firm:** This team receives abundant praise from clients, who observe: *"All our needs are met – it's just not necessary to look elsewhere."* The *"practical, timely and cost-effective"* lawyers are a byword for client care. Recent highlights include land acquisition, site development and financing advice for a national bakery café chain, a national retail chain, lifestyle centers and a hotel chain. The team has also been litigating in a tribal land claim.

**The Lawyers:** Clients value **John Cadwallader** (see p.1625) for his combination of technical skill and *"personal integrity."* **Richard Oberschmidt** (see p.1635) achieves recognition for his *"high-quality product"* in commercial lending and office development matters. Clients describe **Russell Wilson** (see p.1641) as *"one of the brightest lawyers you'll ever meet,"* and recommend him for complex commercial developments.

**Clients/Work Highlights:** AK Steel; Anchor Properties; Bunnell Hill Development; Convergys; Guar-

| Real Estate: Zoning/Land Use |
| --- |
| Leading Firms |
| [1] SMITH & HALE |
| [2] PLANK & BRAHM |
| PORTER WRIGHT MORRIS & ARTHUR LLP |
| VORYS, SATER, SEYMOUR AND PEASE LLP |

| Leading Individuals |
| --- |
| [1] BRAHM Richard *Plank & Brahm* |
| HALE Ben *Smith & Hale* |
| MCNEALEY J Jeffrey *Porter Wright Morris* |
| SCHOEDINGER Daniel *Vorys, Sater, Seymour* |
| SMITH Harrison *Smith & Hale* |
| [2] BROWN Jeffrey *Smith & Hale* |
| MEYER JR Robert *Porter Wright Morris* |
| MILLER Craig *Ulmer & Berne LLP* |
| PLANK Don *Plank & Brahm* |
| SHANNON Michael *Crabbe, Brown, James LLP* |

antee Title & Trust Company; Koll Development; Midland Atlantic Development; Mercy Health Partners; North American Properties; Rookwood Properties; Ryland Homes and ServiceMaster.

## Schottenstein, Zox & Dunn
See firm details p.1649
**The Firm:** The *"practical and dependable"* real estate team here continues its rapid growth and acts for a clientele that ranges from large corporations to small entrepreneurial businesses. Retailers and investors yield a significant proportion of the workload. Recent highlights include handling the $7.5 million sale of undeveloped land, and representing landlords with their leasing and commercial developments.
**The Lawyers:** **Randall Arndt** (see p.1623) chairs the group and clients have *"deep admiration and affection"* for him. He represents a diverse clientele of developers and landlords in national and local

matters. **Herbert Godby**'s (see p.1628) practice also focuses on retail. He was recently involved in a $175 million financing deal for a consortium of banks.
**Clients/Work Highlights:** DSW; City of Dublin; Skilken Company; The Limited and Consolidated Stores.

## Ulmer & Berne LLP
**The Firm:** Clients sing the praises of this team, which fields lawyers that are *"talented and always respond on a timely basis."* The national and regional client base includes retail developers and lenders. The team takes on diverse projects, such as the recent development of low-income housing across 12 states, and acts for Yum! Brands in restaurant sales across the country.
**The Lawyers:** Clients declare **Bill Gagliano** a *"bright and energetic lawyer with good business judgment."* He recently represented the developer of affordable housing projects in seven states. **Craig Miller** chairs the public law group and handles zoning and land use issues at a local and regional level.
**Clients/Work Highlights:** KFC; Pizza Hut; Taco Bell; NVR; Jo-Ann Stores; Office Depot and Steiner + Associates.

## Smith & Hale
**The Firm:** This zoning and land use boutique is unanimously declared the *"outright number one"* in the state. It offers a number of lawyers who are dedicated to this field, and clients commend them on their *"surefooted and comprehensive"* advice.
**The Lawyers:** Senior partner **Ben Hale** is a fixture of the local zoning scene. **Harrison Smith** and **Jeffrey Brown** are also experienced practitioners in this area.
**Clients/Work Highlights:** Clients include University Gateway Center, The Limited and The New Albany Company.

## Plank & Brahm
**The Firm:** This developer-oriented team counsels clients in the private and public sectors on zoning and land use matters, and acts for a great many housing developers. Clients praise the *"well-informed and very effective"* lawyers.
**The Lawyers:** The *"systematic and determined"* **Dick Brahm** is *"always well prepared,"* say sources. **Don Plank** is also recommended for his deep knowledge in this area.
**Clients/Work Highlights:** Central Ohio Contractors; CV Perry; Donald W. Kelley & Associates; Dominion Homes; DiYanni Homes; Rockford Homes; Triangle Properties; Homewood; The Edwards Land Company; FW Sloter; Hamilton Parker; Huntington National Bank; Mid-City Electric; Personal Service Insurance; S.G. Loewendick & Sons; The Computer Group and Creative Child Care.

## Other Notable Practitioners
*"Class-act"* **Ed Diller** chairs Taft, Stettinius & Hollister LLP's business and finance department and is praised as a *"smart, thorough and professional"* practitioner. Allen, Kuehnle & Stovall, LLP's **Kenton Kuehnle** has carved a niche in the condominium development sector, and sources declare: *"He knows more about condos than anyone."* The *"authoritative"* **Herbert Weiss** of Keating, Muething & Klekamp, LLP is enormously experienced in the real estate sector, and clients acclaim the *"wonderful"* **Stephen Hunt** of Aronoff, Rosen & Hunt as *"the guy you need at the top."* Transactional specialist **Joanne Schreiner** (see p.1638) of Dinsmore & Shohl LLP is described by clients as *"outstandingly bright and professional."* **Michael Shannon** of Crabbe, Brown & James LLP has more than 12 years' experience in zoning, land development and government relations, and is strongly recommended by peers.

# Leaders in Ohio

## ADAMO, Ken
Jones Day, Cleveland
216 586 7120
kradamo@jonesday.com
*Recommended in Intellectual Property*
**Practice Areas:** Complex IP litigation
matters. He has extensive lead trial counsel experience in jury and nonjury matters before state and federal courts and
before the International Trade Commission, as well as ex parte and inter partes
experience in the US Patent and Trademark Office. He also has extensive appellate experience before the US Court of
Appeals for the Federal Circuit, having
appeared in 30 appeals, most of which he
has argued himself.
**Publications:** Written and lectured
extensively on intellectual property law
and trial advocacy for US and non-US
publications and organizations.

## ADAMS, Albert
Baker & Hostetler LLP, Cleveland
216 621 0200
*Recommended in Corporate/M&A*

## ADAMS, Deborah
Frost Brown Todd LLC, Cincinnati
513 651 6705
dadams@fbtlaw.com
*Recommended in Employment*
**Practice Areas:** Represents employers
in areas of employment discrimination
and wrongful discharge through litigation defense, as well as advice and coun-
sel. Experienced in class and collective
action defense. Developed national
recognition as trainer on human-
resources topics.
**Prof. Memberships:** Admitted to prac-
tice in Ohio (1982) and Kentucky (1983).
Member of Cincinnati and Ohio Bar
Associations and Ohio Management
Lawyers Association.
**Career:** Joined Frost & Jacobs, 1982;
Partner 1989.
**Publications:** 'Sexual Harassment Myths
and Realities - A Kentucky Employer's
Guide', Kentucky Labor Letter.
**Personal:** Born 17 May 1955. JD, Har-
vard Law School (1982); MA, Harvard
University (1979); BA, University of
Cincinnati (1977).

## ALBAINY-JENEI, Stephen R
Frost Brown Todd LLC, Cincinnati
513 651 6839
salbainyjenei@fbtlaw.com
*Recommended in Intellectual Property*
**Practice Areas:** Intellectual property
law, particularly patent counseling and
prosecution, licensing, infringement and
validity opinions, portfolio management.
As a member of Frost Brown Todd LLC,
works closely with biotechnology and
emerging growth companies, as well as
universities and research institutions, to

develop successful business models,
strategic intellectual property protection
and complex technology transactions.
**Career:** Prior to joining Frost Brown
Todd in 2000, was Assistant General
Counsel for the University of Cincinnati,
ultimately serving as the Acting Director
of Intellectual Property. (1995-2000).
**Personal:** Born 7 November 1964; JD,
University of Cincinnati, 1995; MS, University of Dayton, 1988.

## ALDRICH, Thomas A
Thompson Hine LLP, Cleveland
216 566 5500
Thomas.Aldrich@ThompsonHine.com
*Recommended in Corporate/M&A*
**Career:** Tom is a Partner in Thompson
Hine's Corporate Transactions and Securities Practice Group and was practice
Group Leader from 1999 to 2004. He
focuses on domestic and international
mergers and acquisitions and joint ventures, securities law compliance and
reporting (including Sarbanes-Oxley
issues) and corporate governance.
**Personal:** Harvard Law School, JD, 1982,
cum laude. The Ohio State University,
1978-79, University Fellow, Graduate
School. Ohio University, AB, 1978,
summa cum laude, Phi Beta Kappa.

## ANDERSON, Sandra J
Vorys, Sater, Seymour and Pease LLP,
Columbus 614 464 6405
sjanderson@vssp.com
*Recommended in Litigation*
**Practice Areas:** Partner focusing on
General Litigation Practice which
includes employment, commercial, busi-
ness and product liability law.
**Prof. Memberships:** Fellow, American
College of Trial Lawyers; Columbus,
Ohio State, and American Bar Associa-
tions; Columbus Bar Foundation; Advi-
sory Committee on Local Rules for the
US District Court for the Southern Dis-
trict of Ohio; Board of Commissioners
on Grievances and Discipline for the
Supreme Court of Ohio.
**Career:** Admitted Ohio Bar (1976).
**Personal:** Northwestern University
School of Law, JD, magna cum laude,
Order of the Coif, 1976; Ohio University,
BSC; summa cum laude, 1973.

## APPEL, John H
Frost Brown Todd LLC, Cincinnati
513 651 6830
jappel@fbtlaw.com
*Recommended in Employee Benefits*
**Practice Areas:** Employee benefits and
executive compensation.
**Prof. Memberships:** Member of the
Ohio, Cincinnati, and American Bar
Associations, Cincinnati Bar Association
Taxation Committee, Midwest Benefits
Conference.

**Personal:** JD, Harvard University 1974,
magna cum laude; BA, University of
Cincinnati, 1971.

## APPELBAUM, Jeffrey
Thompson Hine LLP, Cleveland
216 566 5500
jeff.Appelbaum@ThompsonHine.com
*Recommended in Construction*
**Career:** For over 25 years, Jeff has served
the construction industry as trial and
transactional attorney, project counsel,
project management consultant, mediator and partnering facilitator. Jeff provides distinguished service to public and
private owners, design professionals, construction managers and contractors on
important projects throughout the United States and Canada. He has served as
lead trial lawyer for dozens of cases
involving hundreds of millions of dollars
of disputed claims. He has served as project counsel for over 50 projects involving
billions of dollars of construction. Jeff has
facilitated over 150 partnering sessions
and has conducted dozens of complex
construction mediations.

## ARNDT, Randall
Schottenstein, Zox & Dunn, Columbus
614 462 2235
rarndt@szd.com
*Recommended in Real Estate*
**Practice Areas:** Mr Arndt chairs the
firm's Real Estate Practice. He has broad
experience in real property law, including
residential, commercial, retail, mixed-use
and warehouse properties. He represents
national, regional and local landlords,
tenants, developers, buyers, sellers and
others in the commercial real estate arena
in the acquisition and development of
undeveloped and developed land, sales,
leasing, real estate title matters, including
the overlay of easements, conditions,
restrictions and various frameworks for
mixed-use, shopping center and real
estate developments. He practices extensively in the retail and shopping center
leasing and development areas.

## ARNOLD, James
Law Office of James S Arnold, Cincinnati
513 984 8313
*Recommended in Litigation*

## ARONOFF, James
Thompson Hine LLP, Cleveland
216 566 5500
*Recommended in Real Estate*
**Career:** Jim is a Partner in the Real Estate
Group and chairs the Real Estate Capital
Markets Practice. He represents real
estate investment trusts (REIT's) and real
estate equity funds both transactionally,
and in evaluating internal structures to
maximize value. He also focuses on structuring partnerships, joint ventures, LLC's

and other pass-through entities; commercial real estate financing, including
representation of REMICs and others in
securitized offerings; shopping center
development and construction; as well as
acquisitions and divestitures of resort and
other lodging properties. A frequent lecturer, Jim is a Member of the Board of
Governors of Ohio's Real Property Bar.

## ASHMUS, Keith
Frantz Ward LLP, Cleveland
216 515 1660
*Recommended in Employment*

## AZOFF, Elliot
Baker & Hostetler LLP, Cleveland
216 621 0200
*Recommended in Employment*

## BAKER, David
Bricker & Eckler LLP, Columbus
614 227 2300
*Recommended in Real Estate*

## BARNARD, Thomas
Ulmer & Berne LLP, Cleveland
216 583 7000
*Recommended in Employment*

## BARNES, Geoffrey K
Squire, Sanders & Dempsey LLP,
Cleveland 216 479 8646
gbarnes@ssd.com
*Recommended in Environment*
**Practice Areas:** Partner with more than
25 years of experience in environmental
law and related issues involving workplace exposure standards and toxic tort
claims. Named in 'The Best Lawyers in
America.' Practice involves corporate
counseling, trade association representation and litigation before state and federal
courts and agencies. Handles matters
under federal and state air, water, solid
and hazardous waste laws enforcement
claims; private party claims for cost
recovery or diminution in property value;
insurance claims for recovery of environmental cleanup costs; environmental
criminal proceedings; employee exposure
claims; and disputes over environmental
indemnities.

## BARRAGATE, Brett
Jones Day, Cleveland 216 586 7205
bpbarragate@jonesday.com
*Recommended in Banking & Finance*
**Practice Areas:** Involved in all aspects
of commercial financing, including the
representation of banks, financial institutions, and public and private companies
in senior and subordinated debt facilities,
and the representation of creditors and
debtors in loan workouts, loan restructurings, and chapter 11 proceedings.
Extensive experience with syndicated,
multibank senior credit facilities; asset-
based and structured finance facilities;

asset securitizations; acquisition financing; letter of credit facilities; foreign currency facilities; debtor-in-possession financing; and real estate financing.

**Prof. Memberships:** Ohio State Bar Association (Chair of the Loan Documentation and Legal Opinion Subcommittee of the Banking, Commercial and Bankruptcy Law Committee); Cleveland Bar Association.

### BASH, Brian
Baker & Hostetler LLP, Cleveland
216 621 0200
*Recommended in Bankruptcy*

### BAUMGARTNER, Bruce
Baker & Hostetler LLP, Cleveland
216 621 0200
*Recommended in Intellectual Property*

### BEDREE, Melvin
Vorys, Sater, Seymour and Pease LLP, Cincinnati 513 723 4023
mabedree@vssp.com
*Recommended in Banking & Finance*
**Practice Areas:** Partner who practices in the area of commercial finance, including asset based financing. Represented national and regional asset based and structured finance lenders. Practice includes multi-borrower, multijurisdiction transactions, acquisition financing, asset sales out of bankruptcy, multi-lender (club) deals, capital expenditure financing, negotiating subordinated debt and preferred stock arrangements with institutional providers of mezzanine capital.
**Prof. Memberships:** Ohio State and American Bar Associations.
**Career:** Admitted to Ohio Bar, 1984; and US District Court, Southern District of Ohio, 1984.
**Personal:** University of Cincinnati, JD, 1984; Depauw University, BA, magna cum laude, 1981.

### BISSINGER, Mark C
Dinsmore & Shohl LLP, Cincinnati
513 977 8118
mark.bissinger@dinslaw.com
*Recommended in Construction*
**Practice Areas:** Chairperson of the firm's Construction Law Practice. Practice involves all aspects of public and private projects.
**Prof. Memberships:** Selected to The Best Lawyers in America since 1995; Co-Chair, Cincinnati Bar Association Construction Law Committee; Order of the Coif; Commissioner, Anderson Park District; Trustee, Center for Chemical Addictions and Treatments.
**Career:** BSCE from Purdue University (1979); JD from University of Cincinnati School of Law (1983); Elected to partnership in 1990; Has served on numerous firm committees including the General Management Committee.

### BLAIR, Mitchell G
Calfee, Halter & Griswold LLP, Cleveland
216 622 8361
mblair@calfee.com
*Recommended in Litigation*
**Practice Areas:** Business, corporate and commercial litigation; securities litigation; insurance coverage litigation; alternative dispute resolution proceedings.
**Prof. Memberships:** American, Ohio State and Cleveland Bar Associations.
**Career:** Co-Chair of the firm's Litigation Group, heads the Securities Litigation Practice, and is a member of the Executive Committee. He litigates and tries complex disputes, with special emphasis on securities litigation and enforcement and corporate investigations.
**Personal:** Marshall-Wythe School of Law of the College of William and Mary, JD, 1982; Union College, BA, magna cum laude, 1979.

### BLATTNER, J Wray
Thompson Hine LLP, Dayton
937 443 6539
Wray.Blattner@ThompsonHine.com
*Recommended in Environment*
**Career:** Wray is a Partner in Thompson Hine's Environmental Practice Group. His practice includes defense of federal, state and local government enforcement actions and private party environmental litigation, environmental permitting, site remediations, regulatory compliance counseling and environmental management systems, environmental audits, commenting on rulemakings, and counsel in connection with business and real estate acquisitions and sales. Wray received his Undergraduate Degree from Denison University and his Law Degree from Georgetown University Law Center.

### BOISE, April V
Thompson Hine LLP, Cleveland
216 566 5785
April.Boise@ThompsonHine.com
*Recommended in Corporate/M&A*
**Career:** April is a Partner in Thompson Hine's Corporate Transactions and Securities Practice Group. She focuses her practice on mergers, acquisitions and joint ventures; securities offerings for public and private companies; corporate governance including Sarbanes-Oxley and private equity transactions and the formation of venture and buyout funds.
**Personal:** The University of Chicago Law School, JD, 1994. University of Michigan, BBA, 1990, magna cum laude.

### BRAHM, Richard
Plank & Brahm, Columbus
614 228 4546
*Recommended in Real Estate*

### BRENNAN, Maureen
Baker & Hostetler LLP, Cleveland
216 621 0200
*Recommended in Environment*

### BRINKMAN, David
Wood, Herron & Evans, LLP, Cincinnati
513 241 2324
*Recommended in Intellectual Property*

### BROWN, Jeffrey
Smith & Hale, Columbus
614 221 4255
*Recommended in Real Estate*

### BROWN, Timothy R
Thompson Hine LLP, Cincinnati
513 352 6800
tim.brown@thompsonhine.com
*Recommended in Employee Benefits*
**Career:** Tim is the leader for the firm's Employee Benefits and Executive Compensation Practice Group. He focuses his practice on employee benefits, executive compensation and ERISA, including benefit issues and liabilities in corporate mergers and acquisitions; creation, maintenance and termination of tax-qualified retirement plans and master trusts; development and maintenance of non-qualified executive compensation arrangements and compliance with IRC 409A; welfare plan administration and documentation; compliance with SEC rules affecting benefit plans; IRS and DOL audits; ERISA litigation; COBRA; HIPAA; multi-employer plans and withdrawal liability; governmental reporting obligations; and compliance with ERISA fiduciary and prohibited transaction rules.

### BRUBAKER, Robert
Porter Wright Morris & Arthur LLP, Columbus 614 227 2033
rbrubaker@porterwright.com
*Recommended in Environment*
**Practice Areas:** Represents manufacturers, utilities, small businesses, trade associations, and public sector clients with regard to the Clean Air Act and other environmental matters. Practice includes permitting (especially Title V and New Source Review), administrative rulemaking and federal and state court appeals.
**Prof. Memberships:** ABA Standing Committee on Environmental Law; Environmental Committee of Public Utility, Communications and Transportation Section, Chair; National Coal Council.
**Career:** Admitted in Ohio; US District Court, Southern District of Ohio; US Court of Appeals, District of Columbia, Third, Fourth, Sixth, Seventh Circuits; US Supreme Court.
**Personal:** JD, University of Chicago, 1972; BA, Earlham College, 1969.

### BUCHENROTH, Stephen
Vorys, Sater, Seymour and Pease LLP, Columbus 614 464 6366
srbuchenroth@vssp.com
*Recommended in Real Estate*
**Practice Areas:** Real estate law; franchising.
**Prof. Memberships:** Columbus (Board

of Governors, 1986-94; President, 1992-93), Ohio State (Council of Delegates, 1986-88, 1991; Real Property Section, Board of Governors, 1990; Chair, 2003-05) and American (Sections on: Antitrust Law; Business Law, Chairman, Franchising Subcommittee of Small Business Committee, 1991-92; Real Property, Probate and Trust Law; Forum Committee on Franchising) Bar Associations; American College of Real Estate Lawyers; Ohio Supreme Court Commission on Continuing Legal Education, 1994-2000, Chairman, 2000; Board of Trustees Ohio Legal Assistance Foundation, 2006.
**Career:** Ohio Bar (1974).
**Personal:** University of Chicago, JD, 1974; Wittenberg University, AB, cum laude, 1970.

### BUCK, Frank W
Duvin, Cahn & Hutton, Cleveland
216 696 7600
fbuck@duvin.com
*Recommended in Employment*
**Practice Areas:** Practice includes labor relations for both private and public sector clients. For over 26 years, he has served as the chief negotiator for employers in their negotiations with unions. He has handled negotiations for numerous industries including food, steel, aluminum, appliances, heavy manufacturing, wholesale distribution and public sector. He provides day to day counsel on problems arising under collective bargaining agreements, and matters relating to employment discrimination, wrongful termination, business restructuring, and sales and acquisitions. He regularly represents clients before the National Labor Relations Board and other state and federal agencies, and appears before all levels of federal and state courts on a variety of matters.
**Prof. Memberships:** Member of the Cleveland and American Bar Associations.
**Career:** Partner since 1987.
**Publications:** He has lectured on various labor law topics including effective management and discipline, wage and hour laws, employment terminations, and successorship issues.
**Personal:** University of Michigan (JD, 1979; BA, with distinction, 1976). Serves on the Board of Trustees of the Achievement Centers for Children. Member, 1998 Class of Leadership Cleveland.

### BUCKLEY, Daniel J
Vorys, Sater, Seymour and Pease LLP, Cincinnati 513 723 4002
djbuckley@vssp.com
*Recommended in Litigation*
**Practice Areas:** Partner in Litigation Group with extensive experience in business and healthcare litigation, representing financial institutions, venture capital firms, accounting firms, software companies, inside and outside directors, phar-

maceutical companies and hospitals in complex litigation.

**Prof. Memberships:** American, Ohio State and Cincinnati Bar Associations. **Career:** Admitted to Ohio Bar (1974), US Federal Court (1974), US Supreme Court (1982).

**Personal:** Fellow, American College of Trial Lawyers. Adjunct Professor, University of Cincinnati College of Law. Listed in legal publication under business litigation and personal injury. Ohio Wesleyan University, BA, Pi Sigma Alpha, 1971. University of Cincinnati College of Law, JD, 1974.

## BUMPASS, T Merritt
Frantz Ward LLP, Cleveland
216 515 1660
*Recommended in Employment*

## BURKE, James
Keating, Muething & Klekamp, PLL, Cincinnati 513 579 6400
*Recommended in Litigation*

## BURKE, Kim
Taft, Stettinius & Hollister LLP, Cincinnati 513 381 2838
*Recommended in Environment*

## CADWALLADER, John I
Frost Brown Todd LLC, Columbus
614 464 1211
jcadwallader@fbtlaw.com
*Recommended in Real Estate*
**Practice Areas:** Partner in Retail Development Group serving as lead counsel for developers of shopping centers, and industrial, hotel and commercial properties.
**Prof. Memberships:** American College of Real Estate Lawyers; International Council of Shopping Centers; American, Ohio State (Member, Real Property Section Board of Governors; Chair, Legislative Review Committee) and Columbus Bar Associations.
**Career:** Admitted in Ohio and Florida.
**Publications:** Frequent speaker and author on real estate development and leasing topics.
**Personal:** JD, The Ohio State University, 1978; MA, University of Chicago, 1975 (Rockefeller Foundation Fellow); BA, Denison University, 1974 (cum laude).

## CANTON, Doreen
Taft, Stettinius & Hollister LLP, Cincinnati 513 381 2838
*Recommended in Employment*

## CARLSON, James
Thompson Hine LLP, Cleveland
216 566 5556
Jim.Carlson@ThompsonHine.com
*Recommended in Corporate/M&A*
**Career:** Jim is a Partner in Thompson Hine's Corporate Transactions and Securities Practice Group. He focuses his practice on takeover preparedness programs, including shareholder rights plans, and takeover defense; acquisitions and dispositions, including high tech transactions;

mergers, including mergers of publicly held companies; leveraged recaps and buyouts; representation of special Board committees; SEC registration statements, proxy statements, other filings, and compliance; joint ventures, including e-commerce alliances; and financing, including senior, mezzanine, and junior lending and venture capital.
**Personal:** Harvard Law School, JD, 1975. Oberlin College, BA, 1969, magna cum laude, Phi Beta Kappa.

## CARPENTER, Michael
Carpenter & Lipps LLP, Columbus
614 365 4100
*Recommended in Litigation*

## CARSON, Van
Squire, Sanders & Dempsey LLP, Cleveland 216 479 8559
vcarson@ssd.com
*Recommended in Environment*
**Practice Areas:** Partner with more than 30 years experience representing the interests of industrial and public clients in environmental matters. Co-ordinates the firm's Environmental, Health and Safety Practice. Particular expertise dealing with Clean Water Act, Clean Air Act and Superfund matters. Represents companies from the manufacturing, refining, steel, mining and chemical industries, as well as numerous public sector clients. Selected by his peers for inclusion in 'The Best Lawyers in America.'
**Prof. Memberships:** Ohio Chamber of Commerce, Executive Committee, Board of Directors, Vice-Chairman.

## CASCARILLA, Ralph
Walter & Haverfield LLP, Cleveland
216 781 1212
*Recommended in Environment, Litigation*

## CASPER JR, Paul W
Frost Brown Todd LLC, Cincinnati
513 651 6490
pcasper@fbtlaw.com
*Recommended in Environment*
**Practice Areas:** Chair, Environmental Department; 25 years experience in virtually all areas of environmental law, with emphasis on defense of enforcement actions brought by the United States, its state brethren and/or citizens groups such as the Sierra Club, the NRDC, and Ohio Citizen Action; longstanding representation of the steel, chemical, paper, foundry and metal finishing industries.
**Career:** Joined Frost, Brown Todd, 1989, as a Partner. Frost Brown Todd LLC Governance Committee, Chairman of Environmental Department.
**Personal:** Chemical Engineer, US Steel (1968); US Army 18th Airborne Corp. (1969-72); MS Biology (emphasis in Environmental Physiology); designated Ohio Super Lawyer.

## CAVALIERI, Nick
Bailey Cavalieri, Columbus
614 221 3155
*Recommended in Bankruptcy*

## CICARELLA, Thomas
Calfee, Halter & Griswold LLP, Cleveland
216 622 8378
tcicarella@calfee.com
*Recommended in Banking & Finance*
**Practice Areas:** Commercial business and finance; bankruptcy and creditors' rights.
**Prof. Memberships:** American and Ohio State Bar Associations.
**Career:** Co-Chair of the firm's Commercial Business and Finance Group and a Member of the Executive and Management Committees. He has more than 30 years of experience counseling clients through the complexities of leveraged buyouts, and domestic and international financing.
**Personal:** Indiana University, JD, magna cum laude, 1974; Indiana University, BA, 1971.

## CIRIACO, Anthony C
Vorys, Sater, Seymour and Pease LLP, Columbus 614 464 6429
acciriaco@vssp.com
*Recommended in Employee Benefits*
**Practice Areas:** Partner focusing predominantly on the regulatory side of the Employee Benefits Practice where he has counseled clients in qualified retirement plan areas, including both defined benefit and defined contribution plans, as well as, non-qualified deferred compensation, other forms of executive compensation and welfare plan areas. Focus on Employee Retirement Income Security Act (ERISA) and tax related aspects of employee benefit programs.
**Prof. Memberships:** Columbus and Ohio State Bar Associations.
**Career:** Ohio Bar 1983.
**Personal:** University of North Carolina School of Law, JD, 1983; University of Virginia, BS, with distinction in accounting, Beta Gamma Sigma, Beta Alpha Psi, 1980.

## CLARK JR, D Lewis
Squire, Sanders & Dempsey L.L.P., Columbus 614 365 2703
lclark@ssd.com
*Recommended in Employment*
**Practice Areas:** Partner with expertise in counseling and advocacy for private and public sector employers in labor and employment matters. Trial lawyer who represents employers in employment litigation, administrative matters and provides counsel on compliance with all federal and state labor and employment laws. Performs comprehensive reviews of clients' employment policies and practices and trains supervisors and other employees. Listed in 'The Best Lawyers in America'.
**Prof. Memberships:** Mediator, US Dis-

trict Court, Southern District of Ohio; Labor Committees of the Ohio State and Columbus Bar Associations; Labor and Employment Section of the New York State Bar Association.

## COGAN, J Kevin
Jones Day, Columbus 614 281 3825
jcogan@jonesday.com
*Recommended in Litigation*
**Practice Areas:** Extensive experience trying complex cases, including corporate control contests, class actions, securities fraud, environmental enforcement actions and insurance coverage disputes, to courts and juries in state and federal courts. Current representations include a (i) Fortune 50 corporation in a securities class action and derivative action, (ii) financial institution in a dispute with its former CEO, (iii) global real estate investment joint venture in a commercial lease dispute, and (iv) major metropolitan hospital system in a dispute with an insurer involving the scope of prompt pay legislation.

## COLETTI, Robert
Keating, Muething & Klekamp, PLL, Cincinnati 513 579 6400
*Recommended in Corporate/M&A*

## CONRAD, David
Bricker & Eckler LLP, Columbus
614 227 2300
*Recommended in Real Estate*

## COYNE, Thomas
Thompson Hine LLP, Cleveland
216 566 5500
Thomas.Coyne@ThompsonHine.com
*Recommended in Real Estate*
**Career:** Tom is the Group Leader of the firm's 35 member, national Real Estate Practice Group. Tom concentrates on commercial development, planning and strategy on properties throughout the United States and foreign countries. Principal types of transactions include: corporate and international real estate; government incentives; plant and headquarters siting and relocation; construction; real estate joint ventures; REIT transactions; shopping centers and mixed use; complex easement agreements; acquisitions, development, leasing and financing; office, hotel and industrial; arena, stadium and other special use; brownfields; asset management; real estate entity formation; real estate tax abatement and valuation reductions; and commercial real estate disputes.

## CRAIG, Clifford
Taft, Stettinius & Hollister LLP, Cincinnati
513 381 2838
*Recommended in Litigation*

## CRIST, Thomas
Benesch, Friedlander, Coplan & Aronoff LLP, Cleveland 216 363 6108
tcrist@bfca.com
*Recommended in Construction*

**Practice Areas:** Public and private construction law. Annually provides interim project counseling on projects exceeding $300,000,000 in contracts. Litigates in state and federal courts, and is a certified mediator/arbitrator.
**Career:** Co-Chair of the Construction Law practice. Represents the gamut of participants on substantial projects, including sports stadiums and arenas, hospitals, marquee structures for one of the country's largest public universities, power plants, dams, bridges and highways. Representation includes every form and type of claim on most types of commercial, industrial and infrastructure improvements.
**Personal:** Capital University (JD, Order of the Curia, 1994); The Ohio State University (BA Cum Laude, 1992).

## CUPPS, David
Vorys, Sater, Seymour and Pease LLP, Columbus 614 464 6318
dscupps@vssp.com
*Recommended in Litigation*
**Practice Areas:** Partner in the Litigation Group. Practices in the areas of complex and multi-district litigation; antitrust, intellectual property, securities litigation, and professional malpractice litigation.
**Prof. Memberships:** American, Columbus, District of Columbia, and Ohio State Bar Associations.
**Career:** Admitted to New York Bar (1966), Ohio Bar (1972), District of Columbia Bar (1979), US Supreme Court (1971).
**Personal:** Harvard College, AB, 1958. The Ohio State University, JD, summa cum laude, 1965. Order of the Coif. Mershon Fellowship, 1964-65. Editor, Ohio State Law Journal, 1964-65; Fellow, American College of Trial Lawyers and Regent, 1997-2001.

## CURRIE, Michael
Thompson Hine LLP, Columbus
614 469 3200
Mike.Currie@ThompsonHine.com
*Recommended in Construction*
**Career:** Mike is a Partner in the firm's Construction Practice Group concentrating on public/private construction law, real estate law, complex construction and commercial litigation. His focus is representing contractors and owners in all aspects of construction, including project structure, finance, project delivery and claims litigation. Negotiating experience is wide ranging involving numerous construction projects including Olympic and stadium construction, corporate headquarters and power/industrial ventures. He has litigated complex claims ranging to $40 million dollars. Mike has extensive trial and appellate experience, including five appearances before the Ohio and Indiana Supreme Courts. He is a member of the firm's Executive Committee.

## CYPHERT, Michael
Walter & Haverfield LLP, Cleveland
216 781 1212
*Recommended in Environment*

## DEMARCO, Daniel
Hahn Loeser & Parks LLP, Cleveland
216 621 0150
*Recommended in Bankruptcy*

## DILLER, Edward
Taft, Stettinius & Hollister LLP, Cincinnati
513 381 2838
*Recommended in Real Estate*

## DIMICKELE, Susan M
Squire, Sanders & Dempsey L.L.P., Columbus 614 365 2842
sdimickele@ssd.com
*Recommended in Employment*
**Practice Areas:** Partner focused on counseling and advocacy for private and public sector employers in labor, employment, dispute resolution and education matters with significant jury trial experience in employment discrimination and breach of contract cases. Represents employers in state and federal court in matters involving wrongful termination, wage and disability discrimination, unfair labor practices, trade secrets, personal injury and restrictive covenants. Named a 2004 Ohio Super Lawyer and a 2005 Rising Star in Ohio.
**Prof. Memberships:** Ohio State Bar Association; Labor and Employment Section of the Columbus Bar Association; Mock Trial Case Committee of the Ohio Center for Law-Related Education.

## DIMLING, Robert A
Frost Brown Todd LLC, Cincinnati
513 651 6821
rdimling@fbtlaw.com
*Recommended in Employment*
**Practice Areas:** OSHA and employment discrimination.
**Prof. Memberships:** Admitted to practice in Ohio (1966). Member of Ohio State Bar Association, Section on Labor and Employment Law, and the Cincinnati Bar Association, Labor Law Committee.
**Career:** Joined Frost & Jacobs, 1966; became Partner, 1975. Co-Chair Labor and Employment Department, Frost Brown Todd, LLC.
**Publications:** Author, 'Asbestos and the Insurer as Lender, Employer and Property Owner', Tax & Insurance Law Journal, Fall 1988.
**Personal:** Born 14 August 1941. JD, University of Michigan, 1966; BA, Bowling Green State University, 1963.

## DORAN, Scott
Vorys, Sater, Seymour and Pease LLP, Columbus 614 464 8248
smdoran@vssp.com
*Recommended in Environment*
**Practice Areas:** Partner and Chairman of Environmental Law Group. Focuses on Superfund, RCRA, toxic tort, and variety

of environmental issues raised by industrial, commercial, and residential real estate developments. Authority on wetland law and regulation; regularly appears before the Army Corps of Engineers, US and Ohio EPA on permit issues and appeals. Participated in formation of the Ohio Wetlands Foundation.
**Prof. Memberships:** Columbus and Ohio State Bar Associations.
**Career:** Admitted to Ohio (1986), US District Court, Southern District of Ohio (1986), US Federal Court (1986).
**Personal:** University of Cincinnati, JD, 1986. Miami University, BA, 1979; Miami University, MS, 1983.

## DRAUCKER, Carl A
Squire, Sanders & Dempsey LLP, Cleveland 216 479 8766
cdraucker@ssd.com
*Recommended in Employee Benefits*
**Practice Areas:** Partner focused on tax-qualified retirement plans, deferred compensation plans and executive compensation. Practices before the Internal Revenue Service and the US Tax Court. Extensive experience in the employee benefits aspects of corporate and real estate transactions, including acquisitions, dispositions and mergers, and employee stock ownership plans. Listed in 'The Best Lawyers in America.'
**Prof. Memberships:** Section of Taxation of the American Bar Association; Akron Bar Association; ESOP Association; a trustee and secretary of Hiram College.

## DREITLER, Joseph R
Frost Brown Todd LLC, Columbus
614 559 7280
jdreitler@fbtlaw.com
*Recommended in Intellectual Property*
**Practice Areas:** Extensive experience in global trademark clearance, brand development, prosecution and portfolio management, advertising review, and client counseling. Practice includes the trademark, copyright, and domain name aspects of global business transactions; also trademark, trade dress, unfair competition, copyright, and domain name litigation in the courts and Trademark Trial and Appeal Board. Recent speaking engagements include the International Trademark Association (INTA) 2004 meeting on ethics in trademark practice and 2005 on Fair Use; and Practicing Law Institute seminars on non-traditional trademarks, 2004 and 2005.
**Prof. Memberships:** Chair, Ohio State Bar Association Intellectual Property Section. Served on the board of INTA.

## DUVIN, Robert P
Duvin, Cahn & Hutton, Cleveland
216 696 7600
rduvin@duvinlaw.com
*Recommended in Employment*
**Practice Areas:** Represents national corporations in the retail, food, musical arts, healthcare, sports, industrial, and

financial industries. He also represents many large public sector clients. He provides day to day advice and counsel on questions concerning contract interpretation and problems arising from collective baegaining agreements, and matters relating to employment discrimination, wrongful termination, and business restructuring. As a chief negotiator, he has successfully produced contracts which have included company saving concessions. Represents clients in commercial and high-stakes litigation matters. He has appeared before all levels of federal and state courts.
**Prof. Memberships:** Member of the Ohio State Bar and Cleveland Bar Associaitons.
**Career:** Founded the firm in 1972.
**Publications:** Frequent lecturer on labor relations.
**Personal:** Columbia University (LLM, with high honors, 1964); Indiana University (JD, with honors, 1961; BA, with honors, 1958). He has been profiled numerous times by national media including The American Lawyer. Firm has been selected as one of the top six management labor law firms in the USA by The American Lawyer.

## EBLING, Louis
Greeenbaum Doll & McDonald PLLC, Cincinnati 513 455 7600
*Recommended in Intellectual Property*

## FAGAN, Christopher
Fay Sharpe Fagan Minnich & McKee LLP, Cleveland 216 861 5582
cfagan@faysharpe.com
*Recommended in Intellectual Property*
**Practice Areas:** Patent, trademark and copyright litigation.
**Prof. Memberships:** Cleveland and Ohio Bar Associations. Cleveland and American Intellectual Property Law Associations.
**Career:** University of Notre Dame, BSME, 1959. Lieutenant US Navy 1959-63. Georgetown University, JD, 1965. Examiner, USPTO, 1963-65. Patent Attorney, Eaton Corporation, 1965-67. Associate, Partner & Of Counsel, Fay Sharpe, 1967-present.
**Publications:** 'Proprietary aspects of Names & Titles', Cleveland Bar Journal, Volume 47, No. 4.
**Personal:** Adjunct Professor of Law, Cleveland-Marshall School of Law.

## FAHEY, Richard
Vorys, Sater, Seymour and Pease LLP, Columbus 614 464 5601
rpfahey@vssp.com
*Recommended in Environment*
**Practice Areas:** Partner, Environmental Group.
**Prof. Memberships:** Columbus, Ohio State, New Mexico State and American Bar Associations.
**Career:** Admitted New Mexico and US District Court, District of New Mexico

(1971); US Court of Appeals, Tenth Circuit (1972); Ohio and US District Court, Northern and Southern Districts of Ohio (1973); US Supreme Court (1975).
**Personal:** Northwestern University, JD, 1971. San Francisco State University, BA, 1966.

### FAROLINO, Shane
Roetzel & Andress, LPA, Akron
330 376 2700
*Recommended in Environment*

### FARUKI, Charles
Faruki Ireland & Cox PLL, Dayton
937 227 3705
cfaruki@ficlaw.com
*Recommended in Litigation*
**Practice Areas:** Business litigation, including intellectual property; antitrust; class actions.
**Prof. Memberships:** Fellow, American College of Trial Lawyers; Member, American Board of Trial Advocates; Fellow, American Bar Foundation; Past President, Dayton Bar Association; Past President, Dayton Chapter, Federal Bar Association; member Dayton, Ohio State, Federal, American, and Federal Circuit Bar Associations.
**Career:** 1974-89, Smith & Schnacke (Partner, 1979-89); Founder and Managing Partner, Faruki Ireland & Cox PLL, 1989-present. One of Top 10 Lawyers in Ohio in SuperLawyers poll of all Ohio attorneys. Selected as both 'Best of the Bar' and repeatedly as one of only three lawyers in Dayton Business Journal's 'Power List: Most Influential People' in Dayton area.
**Publications:** Numerous publications in law journals and legal press.

### FAY, Terrence M
Frost Brown Todd LLC, Columbus
614 559 7213
tfay@fbtlaw.com
*Recommended in Environment*
**Practice Areas:** Environmental law and litigation, administrative law, and public contract law.
**Prof. Memberships:** Bar Admissions State of Ohio (1978); US District Court, ND Ohio (1980); US District of Ohio, SD Ohio (1986); US District Court, ND Indiana (1987); US Court of Appeals, Sixth Circuit (1986). Member, American Bar, Ohio State Bar, and Columbus Bar associations.
**Career:** Frost Brown Todd LLC (2002-present); Benesch Friedlander Coplan & Aronoff LLP (1989-2002); Smith & Schnacke (1988-89); Assistant Attorney General of Ohio (1978-88).
**Personal:** Born 25 February 1953. JD Ohio State University, 1978; BS Baldwin Wallace College, 1976; BA Baldwin Wallace College 1975.

### FEHELEY, Lawrence
Kegler, Brown, Hill & Ritter, Columbus
614 462 5400
*Recommended in Employment*

### FINN, Terrence
Roetzel & Andress, LPA, Akron
330 376 2700
*Recommended in Environment*

### FITCH, Stephen
Chester, Willcox & Saxbe LLP, Columbus
614 221 4000
*Recommended in Litigation*

### FOGARTY, Robert
Hahn Loeser & Parks LLP, Cleveland
216 621 0150
*Recommended in Litigation*

### FRANK, Ian
Frantz Ward LLP, Cleveland
216 515 1660
*Recommended in Construction*

### FRANTZ, Michael
Frantz Ward LLP, Cleveland
216 515 1660
*Recommended in Employment*

### FREI, Donald
Wood, Herron & Evans, LLP, Cincinnati
513 241 2324
*Recommended in Intellectual Property*

### FREUND, Neil
Freund, Freeze & Arnold, Dayton
937 222 2424
*Recommended in Litigation*

### FRIEDMAN, Steven
Squire, Sanders & Dempsey LLP, Cleveland 216 479 8327
sfriedman@ssd.com
*Recommended in Construction*
**Practice Areas:** Partner and trial lawyer with extensive experience in commercial litigation areas including antitrust, contract, banking and trade secret matters. Represents owners in all aspects of construction projects including dispute resolution and trial work, and numerous Ohio public entities in municipal and constitutional lawsuits. Substantial experience representing a local television station in a First Amendment matter. Listed in 'The Best Lawyers in America.'
**Prof. Memberships:** Anthony J Celebrezze Inn of Court, barrister; Cleveland MetroKicks, co-founder and Co-Chair of the board; Cleveland State University's Cleveland-Marshall College of Law, member, Visiting Committee

### FRY, Roger
Rendings, Fry & Dennis, LLP, Cincinnati
513 381 9200
*Recommended in Litigation*

### FUCHS, Jack F
Thompson Hine LLP, Cincinnati
513 352 6741
Jack.Fuchs@ThompsonHine.com
*Recommended in Employee Benefits*
**Career:** Jack Fuchs, a Thompson Hine

LLP Partner, focuses his practice on employee benefits litigation. Jack has handled numerous class actions involving a wide range of disputes, including employee stock and other 401(k) investments, the modification and termination of retiree health benefits in both the union and non-union contexts, the termination of pension plans, cash balance whipsaw and age discrimination issues, alleged interference with benefits under ERISA 510, and breach of fiduciary duties claims. Jack also litigates claims involving the Department of Labor, third-party administrators, and service providers, as well as participants or beneficiaries claiming benefits.

### GAGLIANO, Bill
Ulmer & Berne LLP, Cleveland
216 583 7000
*Recommended in Real Estate*

### GALL, John R
Squire, Sanders & Dempsey L.L.P., Columbus 614 365 2806
jgall@ssd.com
*Recommended in Litigation*
**Practice Areas:** Partner who leads the litigation activities for the firm's Columbus office. Extensive trial and appellate practice involves commercial issues including business contract disputes, intellectual property rights, professional liability claims, corporate control contests and public sector contract and financial matters. Experience in protecting trade secret information from theft; defending securities fraud and malpractice claims involving a 'final four' accounting firm; defending corporate takeover, governance and control suits; and enforcing and defending substantial contract rights involving business acquisitions, asset sales and purchases, and government projects subject to public bid. Recognized in 'The Best Lawyers in America'.

### GANSKE, Lyle
Jones Day, Cleveland 216 586 7264
lgganske@jonesday.com
*Recommended in Corporate/M&A*
**Practice Areas:** Co-chairs Jones Day's global Mergers & Acquisitions Practice. He is an advisor to significant companies, focusing primarily on M&A, takeovers, takeover preparedness, corporate governance, executive compensation, and general corporate counseling. He has extensive experience in transactions involving regulated industries, including telecom and energy. He is a frequent speaker on M&A, takeover preparedness, and corporate governance issues and has co-authored articles that have appeared in publications such as 'The Business Lawyer,' 'Director's Monthly,' and the 'New York Law Journal.' He has submitted comments to the Securities and Exchange Commission on various proposed rules.

### GATES, Martin S
Buchanan Ingersoll PC, Cleveland
216 363 0984
gatesms@bipc.com
*Recommended in Banking & Finance*
**Practice Areas:** Focuses his practice on representing lending institutions, publicly and privately held companies and private equity groups in all types of secured and unsecured financing transactions, syndications, venture financings including SBIC financings, mezzanine debt financings, asset securitization transactions, commercial transactions, mergers, acquisitions, divestitures, leveraged buyouts, restructurings, debtor-in-possession financings, workouts, multi-currency financings and reorganizations.
**Prof. Memberships:** Cleveland Bar Association; Ohio State Bar Association; American Bar Association.
**Personal:** JD University of Pittsburgh, School of Law, 1988; AB Princeton University, 1984.

### GAUNT, Karen Kreider
Keating, Muething & Klekamp, PLL, Cincinnati 513 579 6400
*Recommended in Intellectual Property*

### GAYNOR, Bruce
Kahn Kleinman, LPA, Cleveland
216 696 3311
bgaynor@kahnkleinman.com
*Recommended in Real Estate*
**Practice Areas:** Real estate law.
**Prof. Memberships:** Member of the Cleveland and Ohio State Bar Associations; Member, International Council of Shopping Centers; Member of the Advisory Board, Chicago Title Insurance Company.
**Career:** Bruce Gaynor, Partner at Kahn Kleinman and Chair of its Real Estate Practice Group, dedicates his practice to real estate developers, REITs, commercial property owners, private investors, financial institutions, public bodies and non-profit institutions. He has extensive experience representing clients on both sides of the table: purchasers and sellers, landlords and tenants, lenders and borrowers, owners and contractors. In 'public/private partnership' transactions, he has represented governmental bodies in their cooperative real estate ventures with private developers, and private developers in their cooperative real estate ventures with governmental bodies.
**Publications:** Mr Gaynor has spoken on construction law, limited-liability companies and other real estate entities, real property sales and acquisitions, and construction law.
**Personal:** A former Assistant Dean at Syracuse University Law School, he has devoted the last 25 years of his legal career to the practice of commercial real estate law, first as in-house counsel for a major national shopping center developer and then for over 22 years as a practi-

tioner with Kahn Kleinman.

## GERMAIN, Kenneth
Thompson Hine LLP, Cincinnati
513 352 6527
Ken.Germain@ThompsonHine.com
*Recommended in Intellectual Property*
**Career:** Ken is a Partner in the Intellectual Property Practice Group. He focuses his practice on trademark and trade dress counseling, consulting and litigation. Ken is retained as an expert witness on issues relating to trademarks and unfair competition, often working on cases involving some of the largest companies in high stakes, cutting-edge cases. As a consultant, Ken worked with winning counsel on the landmark trademark dilution case, Moseley v V Secret Catalogue (US Supreme Court, 2003). New York University School of Law, JD, 1969, associate editor, NYU Law Review. Rutgers University, AB, 1966, magna cum laude, Phi Beta Kappa.

## GHERLEIN, John
Baker & Hostetler LLP, Cleveland
216 621 0200
*Recommended in Corporate/M&A*

## GIBBONS, Colette
Schottenstein, Zox & Dunn, Cleveland
216 394 5063
cgibbons@szd.com
*Recommended in Bankruptcy*
**Practice Areas:** Ms Gibbons is the Partner-in-Charge of SZD's Cleveland office and a member of the bankrutpcy and litigation practice areas. She focuses her practice on insolvency related issues, including representation of debtors, debtors-in-possession, creditors, lending institutions, trustees, and creditors' committees. Recent notable engagements include Official Committee of Unsecured Creditors of Giant Eagle Companies v Asea Brown Boveri, et al 2004 313 BR 219 (ND Ohio), in which she acheived a wide ranging ruling established limit on ability of creditors' committees to maintain derivative actions against former shareholders of the debtor, resulting in dismissal of Committee action against former shareholders.

## GILLEN, Stephen
Greenebaum Doll & McDonald PLLC, Cincinnati 513 455 7600
*Recommended in Intellectual Property*

## GODBY, Herbert R
Schottenstein, Zox & Dunn, Columbus
614 462 2240
hgodby@szd.com
*Recommended in Real Estate*
**Practice Areas:** Mr Godby has extensive experience in all real estate related transactions, including all types of real estate financing (traditional construction and permanent financing, as well as industrial revenue bond financing and other forms of tax-exempt and taxable bond financing), office and commercial retail leasing and the purchase and sale of real estate. He has lectured on leases and general business issues, is listed as a municipal bond attorney in The Bond Buyer's Municipal Marketplace, is a licensed title insurance agent, and is an active Member of the federal, state and local bar associations.

## GOLD, Ronald
Frost Brown Todd LLC, Cincinnati
513 651 6156
rgold@fbtlaw.com
*Recommended in Bankruptcy*
**Practice Areas:** Co-Chair of firm's national Financial Restructuring Group. Extensive experience in Chapter 11 restructurings representing corporate debtors, debtor-in-possession lenders, secured lenders, landlords, official committees and purchasers of businesses and business segments.
**Prof. Memberships:** Admitted to practice in Illinois (1989) and Ohio (1993). Listed in Bankruptcy Section of recent leading leading publication.
**Career:** Katten Muchin & Zavis (Chicago), 1989; Frost & Jacobs LLP (Cincinnati), 1992, became Partner, 1996; member Frost Brown Todd LLC, 2000-present.
**Personal:** Born Erie, Pennsylvania, 1964. The University of Michigan, AB, 1986; University of Pittsburgh School of Law, JD (magna cum laude, Order of the Coif), 1989.

## GOLDMAN, Matthew
Baker & Hostetler LLP, Cleveland
216 621 0200
*Recommended in Bankruptcy*

## GOLDSTEIN, Steven
Frost Brown Todd LLC, Cincinnati
513 651 6131
sgoldstein@fbtlaw.com
*Recommended in Intellectual Property*
**Practice Areas:** Intellectual property law, particularly US and international patent counseling, prosecution (pharmaceutical, chemical technologies), licensing, trade secrets, infringement and validity opinions, portfolio management.
**Prof. Memberships:** Admitted to practice in Ohio (1975); US Patent and Trademark Office (1976). Member - American Intellectual Property Law Association, Cincinnati Bar Association.
**Career:** Chairman, Intellectual Property Department. Joined Frost Brown Todd (Frost & Jacobs) 1994 as a Partner and Department Chair. Prior was Associate General Counsel-Patents, Procter & Gamble (1975-94). Adjunct Professor of Law, University of Cincinnati (1986-present).
**Personal:** Born 1 September 1951; JD, Boston University, 1975; SB (Chemistry), Massachusetts Institute of Technology, 1972.

## GRADY, Timothy
Porter Wright Morris & Arthur LLP, Columbus 614 227 2105
tgrady@porterwright.com
*Recommended in Banking & Finance*
**Practice Areas:** Represents senior lenders, note purchasers, and corporate borrowers in asset-based lending and leveraged financings, recapitalizations, syndicated lending, acquisition financing, loan workouts and restructuring. Recently, he has led financings in such diverse industries as managed care, tier 2 automobile supplier, manufacturers of wood products, grocery store chain, shoes, boots and outdoor gear, optical equipment, home building, chemicals, information storage, trucking, electric coil, 'off-price' apparel and footwear.
**Career:** Admitted in Ohio.
**Personal:** JD (cum laude), University of Illinois, 1979; MA, Northern Arizona University, 1973; BA (magna cum laude), Bradley University, 1972.

## GREENBERG, Gary
Denlinger, Rosenthal & Greenberg LPA, Cincinnati 513 621 3440
*Recommended in Employment*

## GREER, David
Bieser, Greer, & Landis LLP, Dayton
937 223 3277
*Recommended in Litigation*

## GREGG, Joseph
Eastman & Smith Ltd, Toledo
419 241 6000
*Recommended in Environment*

## GREGORY, Donald
Kegler, Brown, Hill & Ritter, Columbus
614 462 5400
*Recommended in Construction*

## GROSSER, Theodore D
Porter Wright Morris & Arthur LLP, Cincinnati 513 369 4280
tgrosser@porterwright.com
*Recommended in Corporate/M&A*
**Practice Areas:** Practices corporate and commercial law, representing a diversified mix of clients - large public and closely held companies to start-ups. Represents private and public companies in mergers, acquisitions, divestitures, joint ventures and other complex transactions, ranging from a few million to hundreds of millions of dollars. Primary legal counsel for many corporate clients and closely held business entities. Significant experience in construction law and construction dispute resolution.
**Prof. Memberships:** Kentucky Bar Association; Ohio State Bar Association.
**Career:** Admitted in Ohio; Kentucky.
**Personal:** JD (cum laude), Washington and Lee University, 1977; BA (summa cum laude), University of Cincinnati, 1974.

## GROSSMAN, Theodore
Jones Day, Cleveland 216 586 7268
tgrossman@jonesday.com
*Recommended in Litigation*
**Practice Areas:** Repeatedly cited as 'one of the nation's top litigators' by 'The National Law Journal,' and other leading publications, he has tried landmark cases and argued appeals in every section of the country. He has broad experience in product liability, commercial, constitutional, and regulatory litigation and has served as lead counsel in cases brought by or against virtually every federal department. He has lectured extensively on cross-examination, deposition techniques, oral advocacy, and trial tactics at professional seminars. Also guest lectured at Georgetown University Law Center and Case Western Reserve University.
**Prof. Memberships:** Fellow, American College of Trial Lawyers.

## GUINN, Guy
Calfee, Halter & Griswold LLP, Cleveland
216 622 8453
gguinn@calfee.com
*Recommended in Banking & Finance*
**Practice Areas:** Commercial business and finance; bankruptcy and creditors' rights; international; real estate.
**Prof. Memberships:** American and Ohio State Bar Associations; former Chair of American Bar Association Business Law Section's Joint Subcommittee on Domestic and International Business Transactions, and Ohio State Bar Association's Opinion and Loan Documentation Subcommittee.
**Career:** Co-Chair of the Commercial Business and Finance Group. Handles all forms of commercial and real estate financings and syndications, securitizations, domestic and international commercial business arrangements, capital formation and restructurings.
**Personal:** University of Michigan Law School, JD, cum laude, 1975; Duke University, BA, summa cum laude, Phi Beta Kappa, 1971.

## GUNSETT, Daniel
Baker & Hostetler LLP, Columbus
614 228 1541
*Recommended in Environment*

## GURNEY, Scott
Frost Brown Todd LLC, Cincinnati
513 651 6841
sgurney@fbtlaw.com
*Recommended in Construction*
**Practice Areas:** Chairman of firrm's Construction Law Group. Represents construction managers, general contractors, trade/specialty contractors, suppliers, sureties, and project owners in contract drafting, bid and contract disputes, mechanics' liens, delay, disruption, and defect claims, and mediation, arbitration, and litigation of construction disputes.
**Prof. Memberships:** Member ABA Forum on the Construction Industry.

Member ABA Committee on Construction Litigation. Past Chairman of Cincinnati Bar Association Construction Law Committee.
**Career:** Admitted to practice in Ohio (1986). Elected member of Frost & Jacobs (predecessor firm) in 1997.
**Personal:** Born 28 April 1961. JD Indiana University (Bloomington) 1986; BA Indiana University (Bloomington) 1983.

### GUTMACHER, Norman
Benesch, Friedlander, Coplan & Aronoff LLP, Cleveland 216 363 4591
ngutmacher@bfca.com
*Recommended in Real Estate*
**Practice Areas:** Commercial real estate, particularly commercial leasing, development and financing, and AIA contract matters.
**Career:** Often represents national restaurant chains and franchisees in leasing or purchasing locations. Represents borrowers and in construction and permanent loans and refinancings ranging in size from $1 million to more than $100 million. Advised a multinational company on the sale of 50+ parcels of land in two counties, including coordinating title and survey requirements. Often advises on leasing, purchase and/or sale of shopping centers ranging in size from $1 million to $17 million.
**Personal:** University of Cincinnati (JD, 1971); Ohio State University (BS, 1968).

### HABEL, Christopher S
Frost Brown Todd LLC, Cincinnati 513 651 6993
chabel@fbtlaw.com
*Recommended in Environment*
**Practice Areas:** Environmental, construction and DOT hazardous materials transportation law.
**Prof. Memberships:** 1995, Ohio; 1999, US District Court, Northern and Southern Districts of Ohio; US Court of Appeals, Sixth Circuit.
**Personal:** The Ohio State University College of Law, JD, 1995, University of Cincinnati College of Engineering, BS Civil and Environmental Engineering, 1992

### HAGEN, Daniel C
Jones Day, Cleveland 216 586 7159
dchagen@jonesday.com
*Recommended in Employee Benefits*
**Practice Areas:** Chairs Jones Day's Employee Benefits and Executive Compensation Practice. He advises clients on all aspects of their executive compensation and employee benefits programs and in managing those programs through business and regulatory change. He handles senior level executives' employment agreements and severance arrangements, supplemental deferred compensation and retirement plans, and equity and other cash-based long-term incentive programs. Routinely handles benefits and compensation issues that arise in transac-

tions including company mergers, tender offers, sales of large divisions, private equity fund leverage buyouts, and joint ventures. Experienced in the personnel and employee benefits aspects of professional sports law as well.

### HAGGERTY, John
Ulmer & Berne LLP, Cleveland 216 583 7000
*Recommended in Litigation*

### HALE, Ben
Smith & Hale, Columbus 614 221 4255
*Recommended in Real Estate*

### HARDY, Michael
Thompson Hine LLP, Cleveland 216 566 5500
Mike.Hardy@ThompsonHine.com
*Recommended in Environment*
**Career:** Mike is a Partner in Thompson Hine's Environmental Practice Group. His focus on environmental law began over 30 years ago. While his primary work lies in environmental litigation, he also works extensively with clients in the development of business and strategic solutions to environmental problems arising from business transactions.
**Personal:** Received a JD (cum laude) from the University of Michigan, an AB (magna cum laude) from John Carroll University.

### HASTINGS, Susan C
Squire, Sanders & Dempsey LLP, Cleveland 216 479 8723
shastings@ssd.com
*Recommended in Employment*
**Practice Areas:** Leads the firm's Labor and Employment Practice Group. Represents private and public sector employers in all facets of labor and employment matters including collective bargaining, arbitration and federal and state agency proceedings. Significant experience in employment counseling and compliance training. Trial experience in federal and state courts. Represents boards of education in education law. Adjunct Professor, Kent State University. Listed in 'The Best Lawyers in America' and 'Ohio Super Lawyers'.
**Prof. Memberships:** American Bar Association and Ohio State Bar Association, Labor and Employment Law Sections; Ohio Council of School Board Attorneys; National School Boards Association.

### HAUGHEY, Stephen N
Frost Brown Todd LLC, Cincinnati 513 651 6127
shaughey@fbtlaw.com
*Recommended in Environment*
**Practice Areas:** Member Environmental Department. Emphasis in public and private enforcement defense litigation with particular emphasis in wastewater enforcement, counseling, criminal and civil defense, and appellate practice.

**Prof. Memberships:** Ohio (1984), Northern (1999) and Southern (1984) Ohio Federal District Courts, and Federal Sixth Circuit (1994). Member Ohio and Cincinnati Bar Associations and Environmental Law Committees, Water Environment Federation, and Ohio Water Environment Association.
**Career:** Member of Frost Brown Todd since 1992.
**Publications:** Numerous articles and presentations on Clean Water Act issues and Superfund defense.
**Personal:** Born 8 April 1955, BS Wright State University (1978), JD University of Dayton (1984).

### HAWKINS, Michael
Dinsmore & Shohl LLP, Cincinnati 513 977 8270
michael.hawkins@dinslaw.com
*Recommended in Employment*
**Practice Areas:** Represents private and public employers in all phases of employment law and labor relations matters including litigation in state and federal court, wrongful discharge, collective bargaining negotiations, and representation before various agencies. Successfully argued NLRB v KRCC before the United States Supreme Court.
**Prof. Memberships:** American Arbitration Association; American National Red Cross, Board of Governors; Refugees International, Board Member.
**Career:** Listed in The Best Lawyers in America in labor and employment law; Named Ohio Super Lawyer by Law & Politics Media; Received Leadership Cincinnati Distinguished Alumni Award.
**Personal:** JD and BA University of Kentucky.

### HAYES, William D
Vorys, Sater, Seymour and Pease LLP, Cincinnati 513 723 4024
wdhayes@vssp.com
*Recommended in Environment*
**Practice Areas:** Partner, Environmental Group with focus on air quality issues.
**Prof. Memberships:** Cincinnati (Chair, Environmental Committee) and Ohio State (Member, Environmental Committee) Bar Associations; Air and Waste Management Association; Cincinnati Chamber of Commerce (Member, Air Quality Committee); Ohio Small Business Clean Air Act Stationary Source Compliance Advisory Panel (appointed Chair); Southwest Ohio Air Quality Advisory Committee; Ohio EPA Permit Processing Efficiency Committee (Co-Chair); Ohio EPA Advisory Committee.
**Career:** Admitted to Ohio and US District Court, Southern District of Ohio (1986). Managing Attorney, Air and Water Divisions, Ohio EPA (1986-91).
**Personal:** Capital University, JD, 1986; Denison University, BA, 1983.

### HAYNAM, Douglas
Shumaker Loop & Kendrick LLP, Toledo 419 241 9000
*Recommended in Environment*

### HEIMAN, David G
Jones Day, Cleveland 216 586 7175
dgheiman@jonesday.com
*Recommended in Bankruptcy*
**Practice Areas:** Represents debtors, financial institutions, creditors, and asset purchasers in restructuring matters, chapter 11 cases and distressed M&A. He has played a key role in many of the country's largest chapter 11 and business restructuring matters, including, among others, Federated Department Stores, Marcy's, USG Corporation, Pillowtex Corporation, Burlington Industries, and LTV Corporation.
**Prof. Memberships:** Director, American College of Bankruptcy; American College of Commercial Finance Lawyers; Member of the Board of Advisers of the Banking Law Review; Member of the editorial advisory board of the Journal of Bankruptcy Law and Practice.

### HELMREICH, Richard J
Porter Wright Morris & Arthur LLP, Columbus 614 227 2088
rhelmreich@porterwright.com
*Recommended in Employee Benefits*
**Practice Areas:** Employee benefits - compliance and audits; deferred compensation plans; ERISA litigation; qualified plan correction; retirement plans; welfare plans.
**Prof. Memberships:** Columbus Bar Association, Employee Benefits Committee, Chair 1999-2001; Vice-Chair 1997-99; Certified Employee Benefit Specialist Program; Ohio State Bar Association.
**Career:** Admitted in Ohio.
**Publications:** 'New Pre-tax Savings Opportunity Created for Certain Small Business Executives', The Daily Reporter, February, 27, 2002.
**Personal:** The Ohio State University College of Law, JD, 1989; Oxford University, Oxford, England, Summer Law Program, 1987; Bowling Green State University, BS, Business/Accounting, 1986; Ecole Superior de Commerce, Nantes, France, Summer Economics Program, 1985.

### HEWITT, Christopher J
Jones Day, Cleveland 216 586 7254
cjhewitt@jonesday.com
*Recommended in Corporate/M&A*
**Practice Areas:** Corporate and securities law, with a primary focus on mergers and acquisitions, takeovers, takeover preparedness, corporate governance, general corporate counseling, and SEC compliance. He represents buyers and sellers in public and private transactions, as well as financial advisors in public transactions. In addition, he has worked on financing transactions, including spin-offs, primary and secondary equity offerings, and pri-

vate placements of preferred stock. Recognized by The National Law Journal in 2005 as one of the country's leading young attorneys in its annual '40 Under 40' feature, one of only eight attorneys in the 40 who practice corporate law.

## HILL, Thomas
Kegler, Brown, Hill & Ritter, Columbus
614 462 5403
thill@keglerbrown.com
*Recommended in Litigation*
**Practice Areas:** Trial lawyer with over 30 years experience in complex business litigation.
**Prof. Memberships:** Fellow of the American College of Trial Lawyers; American Bar Association; Columbus Bar Association; Ohio State Bar Association.
**Career:** Representative cases include: successful defense of a Fortune 100 company in a $500m fraud claim tried to a jury in federal court in Texas; representation of a publicly-traded company in litigation in federal court in Ohio arising out of a hostile takeover attempt that produced a $20m settlement for the client; representation of the American Cancer Society in litigation arising out of a $7-million dollar embezzlement of Cancer Society funds; lead trial counsel in Donatos Pizza's successful prosecution of trademark infringement claim involving Donatos 'Edge to Edge' trademark; successful defense of a local university in wrongful discharge litigation brought by discharged faculty members; successful defense of a publicly traded company in federal court litigation alleging defectively manufactured products; defense of a Catholic Diocese in litigation alleging sexual abuse; successful defense of a national pension fund in claims over rights to participate in the fund. Profiled in leading American publications.
**Publications:** Federal Civil Procedure and Evidence During Trial - 6th Circuit - a two-volume treatise on trial practice in the federal courts in the Sixth Circuit.
**Personal:** Juris Doctorate, Cornell University Law School, Ithaca, New York, 1970; Bachelor of Arts, Political Science, Grinnell College, Grinnell, Iowa, 1967.

## HILLER, David
Millisor & Nobil Co LPA, Columbus
614 221 2234
*Recommended in Employment*

## HIRSCHFELD, Michael
Graydon Head & Ritchey LLP, Cincinnati
513 621 6464
*Recommended in Corporate/M&A*

## HOBERG, Timothy
Taft, Stettinius & Hollister LLP,
Cincinnati 513 381 2838
*Recommended in Corporate/M&A*

## HOGAN, Patricia
Keating, Muething & Klekamp, PLL,
Cincinnati 513 579 6400
*Recommended in Intellectual Property*

## HOLMAN, Michael
Bricker & Eckler LLP, Columbus
614 227 2300
*Recommended in Construction*

## HOOKER, David J
Thompson Hine LLP, Cleveland
216 566 5500
David.Hooker@ThompsonHine.com
*Recommended in Litigation*
**Career:** David is the Managing Partner of Thompson Hine LLP. He previously served as Chair of the Litigation area where he has practiced since joining the firm following his law school graduation. David focuses his practice on complex business litigation. He has experience in securities litigation, cases about corporate and partnership control, breach of contract actions, and construction disputes. He also has defended public accountants and consultants in malpractice claims.
**Personal:** Received his JD from Stanford Law School (Member, 'Stanford Law Review') and his BS (with highest honors, Phi Beta Kappa) from Denison University.

## HUFFMAN, Fordham
Jones Day, Columbus 614 281 3934
fehuffman@jonesday.com
*Recommended in Litigation*
**Practice Areas:** Partner-in-Charge of the Columbus office. General litigation practice with extensive experience in insurance, product liability, and bankruptcy litigation. With Richard Whitney (Cleveland), served as counsel to the liquidator of Ambassador Insurance Company, in litigation against the company's former management and auditors, resulting in a jury verdict of $119.9 million. Served as lead litigation counsel to the court-appointed trustee for Cardinal Industries, Inc., as well as bankruptcy litigation counsel for Rax Restaurants and Loewen International, Inc. He regularly represents clients in commercial and employment litigation and has served as nationwide product liability defense counsel for a building products manufacturer.

## HUNT, Stephen
Aronoff Rosen & Hunt, Cincinnati
513 241 0400
*Recommended in Real Estate*

## HURLEY, Timothy
Taft, Stettinius & Hollister LLP,
Cincinnati 513 381 2838
*Recommended in Bankruptcy*

## HUTCHINSON, Joseph
Baker & Hostetler LLP, Cleveland
216 621 0200
*Recommended in Bankruptcy*

## INTIHAR, Steve
Bricker & Eckler LLP, Columbus
614 227 2300
*Recommended in Real Estate*

## IRELAND, D Jeffrey
Faruki Ireland & Cox PLL, Dayton
937 227 3710
djireland@ficlaw.com
*Recommended in Litigation*
**Practice Areas:** Competitive litigation, including false advertising, trademarks and trade secrets; antitrust; employment; class actions and general commercial.
**Prof. Memberships:** American Bar Association; Ohio State Bar Association (Board of Governors, Antitrust Section); Dayton Bar Association.
**Career:** 1980-89, Smith & Schnacke (Partner, 1987-89); founding Partner, Faruki Ireland & Cox P.L.L., 1989-present; selected as Ohio Super Lawyer 2004-05 in poll of all Ohio lawyers and 'Best of the Bar' in poll of Dayton lawyers.
**Publications:** Has lectured and written on all aspects of commercial litigation.
**Personal:** University of Dayton, College of Law (1980); Denison University (1976).

## IRWIN, Kevin
Keating, Muething & Klekamp, PLL,
Cincinnati 513 579 6400
*Recommended in Bankruptcy*

## JACKSON, Reginald W
Vorys, Sater, Seymour and Pease LLP,
Columbus 614 464 5621
rwjackson@vssp.com
*Recommended in Bankruptcy*
**Practice Areas:** Partner in the bankruptcy, workout and restructuring areas with emphasis on representing secured creditors, creditors' committees and debtors in Chapter 11 reorganization proceedings and workouts.
**Prof. Memberships:** Columbus (former Chair, Bankruptcy Committee), American (Chapter 11 and Executory Contracts Subcommittee, former Chair of Conference of Minority Partners in Corporate/Majority Law Firms), and Ohio State (Member, Board of Governors) Bar Associations, Ohio State Bar Foundation (former President), American Bankruptcy Institute (Member, Board of Trustees, Executive Committee and editor of the 'ABI Journal').
**Career:** Admitted to Ohio (1980).
**Personal:** Cornell University, BA, 1977; University of Pennsylvania Law School, JD, 1980.

## JAHNKE, Mark
Katz, Teller, Brant & Hild, Cincinnati
513 721 4532
*Recommended in Corporate/M&A*

## JANKE, Ronald R
Jones Day, Cleveland
216 586 7279
rrjanke@jonesday.com
*Recommended in Environment*
**Practice Areas:** Broad experience with the application of state and federal environmental laws to numerous industries. He has litigated state and federal enforce-

ment actions, citizen suits and permit appeals. He has represented clients at more than 100 National Priority List sites remediated under federal and state laws. Lectures extensively on environmental compliance and litigation.
**Prof. Memberships:** Chairman of the Ohio Water Resources Council Advisory Group; Ohio State Bar Association; Environmental Law Institute; Great Lakes Regional Collaboration.
**Publications:** 'Preserving CERCLA Defenses: Reasonable Steps'.

## JENKINS, John
Calfee, Halter & Griswold LLP, Cleveland
216 622 8507
jjenkins@calfee.com
*Recommended in Corporate/M&A*
**Practice Areas:** Securities; corporate; mergers and acquisitions.
**Prof. Memberships:** American and Cleveland Bar Associations; former Chair of the Cleveland Bar Association's Securities Law Section.
**Career:** Partner in Securities and Capital Markets Group and Member of the firm's Operating Committee. He represents issuers and underwriters in securities offerings and has extensive experience in corporate governance, mergers and acquisitions and representation of investment bankers. Also represents corporations and individuals in SEC investigations. He teaches mergers and acquisitions law at Cleveland-Marshall College of Law.
**Personal:** The University of Virginia School of Law, JD, 1986; Canisius College, BA, magna cum laude, 1983.

## JONES, Christopher
Calfee, Halter & Griswold LLP, Columbus
614 621 7004
cjones@calfee.com
*Recommended in Environment*
**Practice Areas:** Environmental, government relations and legislation.
**Prof. Memberships:** Former: President of Environmental Council of the States, Board of Directors of Environmental Research Institute of the States, Chairman of Lake Erie Commission, Great Lakes Commission, Ohio's Security Task Force; Ohio and Columbus Bar Associations.
**Career:** Senior counsel in Environmental and Government Groups. He has six years experience as Director of the Ohio Environmental Protection Agency, four years as Chief of the Ohio Attorney General's Environmental Enforcement Section and five years as an environmental attorney in the private sector.
**Personal:** Georgetown University Law Center, JD, 1990; Ohio Wesleyan University, BA, 1979.

## JORGENSEN, Thomas A
Calfee, Halter & Griswold LLP, Cleveland
216 622 8443
tjorgens@calfee.com
*Recommended in Employee Benefits*
**Practice Areas:** Employee benefits; executive compensation; ERISA; pensions.
**Prof. Memberships:** American and International Bar Associations; American College of Employee Benefits Counsel; International Pension and Employee Benefits Lawyers Association.
**Career:** The Senior Partner in firm's Employee Benefits and Executive Compensation Group. He has been involved in all aspects of employee benefits and executive compensation plans from inception to termination. Has written and spoken extensively on many aspects of employee benefit matters. He is Chair of several ABA committees, the first president of ACEBC, and a Member of the ABA Tax Section Council, ACEBC's Board of Governors, and IPEBLA's Steering Committee.

## JORGENSON, Mary Ann
Squire, Sanders & Dempsey LLP, Cleveland 216 479 8654
mjorgenson@ssd.com
*Recommended in Corporate/M&A*
**Practice Areas:** Partner who represents public and private companies in securities matters, corporate governance, mergers and acquisitions, tender offers and contests for corporate control, venture capital and other financing, and executive compensation. Experienced in corporate growth strategies. Counsels and advises CEOs and boards of large and growing businesses as well as director or secretary of several public and private companies and charitable organizations. Served on firm's management committee. Listed in 'The Best Lawyers in America'. Frequent speaker at national securities law and corporate governance seminars.
**Prof. Memberships:** Immediate past Chair, Committee on Corporate Laws, American Bar Association.

## KAHN, Ronald
Ulmer & Berne LLP, Cleveland
216 583 7000
*Recommended in Employee Benefits*

## KAISER JR, Gordon S
Squire, Sanders & Dempsey LLP, Cleveland 216 479 8681
gkaiser@ssd.com
*Recommended in Corporate/M&A*
**Practice Areas:** Partner and leader of the firm's Corporate Practice. Extensive experience in domestic and international mergers and acquisitions, public utility law, complex finance, corporate governance and US securities law. Lead counsel in one of the largest electric utility mergers in the United States. International experience includes structuring transactions with Japanese companies and repre-

senting the Czech electric utility in the first public bond offering in the Czech Republic since the 1989 change in government.
**Prof. Memberships:** American Bar Association, Co-Chair, Infrastructure Finance, Mergers and Acquisitions Committee; Vice-Chair, Corporate Governance Committee of Public Utility, Communications and Transportation Law Section.

## KALLAS, Hani R
Vorys, Sater, Seymour and Pease LLP, Cincinnati 513 723-4615
hrkallas@vssp.com
*Recommended in Banking & Finance*
**Practice Areas:** Partner in the Commercial and Real Estate Group that practices in the areas of banking law, commercial law, general business law, and real estate law. Concentrates in the representation of lenders and small businesses, with an emphasis on representing lenders in loan transactions and workouts.
**Career:** Admitted in Ohio (1994).
**Personal:** University of Cincinnati College of Law, JD, Order of the Coif, 1994. Miami University, BA, cum laude, 1991.

## KAMP, David
White, Getgey & Meyer Co LPA, Cincinnati 513 241 3685
*Recommended in Litigation*

## KARP, Marvin
Ulmer & Berne LLP, Cleveland
216 583 7000
*Recommended in Litigation*

## KAUFMAN, Steven S
Thompson Hine LLP, Cleveland
216 566 5528
Steve.Kaufman@ThompsonHine.com
*Recommended in Litigation*
**Career:** Steve is on the firm's Executive Committee and the immediate past Chair of the Business Litigation Practice Group. He is lead trial counsel for some of the firm's largest clients in complex litigation matters. His areas of focus include fiduciary duty, real estate, land use and eminent domain litigation for publicly held and private commercial developers, airport authorities, and commercial and professional liability litigation. He is a Past President of the Cleveland Bar Association and the City of Shaker Heights Board of Education. Steve has been listed in Ohio Super Lawyers and Best Lawyers in America for Business Litigation.

## KELLY, Christopher
Jones Day, Cleveland 216 586 1238
ckelly@jonesday.com
*Recommended in Corporate/M&A*
**Practice Areas:** Chairs the firm's Capital Markets Practice and heads the firm's Sarbanes-Oxley Act team. His practice is concentrated in the areas of capital markets, securities, and corporate governance matters. He represents clients ranging from Fortune 500 companies to venture-

backed companies in a variety of transactions, including public offerings, Rule 144A offerings and regulatory compliance matters. He commonly advises on securities matters in reorganization and acquisition transactions. He represents financial institutions, investment firms, and many New York-based institutions in a wide range of capital markets transactions. Recognized by publications for his high level of skill and integrity.

## KERGER, Richard
Kerger & Kerger, Toledo 419 255 5990
*Recommended in Litigation*

## KESTNER, Steven
Baker & Hostetler LLP, Cleveland
216 621 0200
*Recommended in Corporate/M&A*

## KILBANE, Thomas S
Squire, Sanders & Dempsey LLP, Cleveland 216 479 8564
tkilbane@ssd.com
*Recommended in Litigation*
**Practice Areas:** Leads the firm's Litigation Practice Group, comprising more than 200 trial lawyers worldwide. Extensive trial experience in litigating highly technical, multiparty commercial disputes with expertise in antitrust, contract, construction and securities. Listed in 'International Who's Who of Professionals', 'The Best Lawyers in America', 'Who's Who in American Law', 'Who's Who in the World', 'The Guide to the Leading US Litigation Lawyers' and 'PLC Cross-border Dispute Resolution Handbook' and is a Top 100 Super Lawyer in 'Ohio Super Lawyers'.
**Prof. Memberships:** Fellow of the International Academy of Trial Lawyers, the American College of Trial Lawyers and American Bar Association.

## KILLWORTH, Richard
Dinsmore & Shohl LLP, Dayton
937 449 6424
richard.killworth@dinslaw.com
*Recommended in Intellectual Property*
**Practice Areas:** Practices in areas of intellectual property, patent, licensing, and litigation. Has been in the private practice of patent law for over 30 years, working on chemical patent matters.
**Prof. Memberships:** Admitted in Ohio and Virginia. Member of American Bar Association, American Intellectual Property Law Association, Ohio State Bar Association, Dayton Bar Association, Sixth Circuit Judicial Conference, American Law Institute, Dayton Lawyer's Club, and Licensing Executives Society.
**Career:** Joined Dinsmore & Shohl in 2003 as Partner. Former Senior Partner of Killworth, Gottman, Hagan and Schaeff.
**Personal:** LLM (1972); JD (1970) George Washington University; MA (1966); BS (1965) Purdue University.

## KING, G Roger
Jones Day, Columbus 614 281 3874
gking@jonesday.com
*Recommended in Employment*
**Practice Areas:** Labor and employment relations practice, representing management in the National Labor Relations Act, state and federal equal employment statutes, the Americans with Disabilities Act, the Family and Medical Leave Act, the Fair Labor Standards Act, and Office of Federal Contract Compliance and covenant-not-to-compete matters. Represents employers in collective bargaining negotiations, grievance and arbitration matters, and labor-related litigation in state and federal trial and appellate courts.
**Prof. Memberships:** Fellow of The College of Labor and Employment Lawyers.
**Publications:** Editor of 'The Developing Labor Law' and contributing editor to HR Advisor.

## KOLESAR, Andrew
Thompson Hine LLP, Cincinnati
513 352 6545
Andrew.Kolesar@ThompsonHine.com
*Recommended in Environment*
**Career:** Andrew is a Partner and leader of Thompson Hine's Environmental Practice Group. His practice includes permitting, litigation and administrative practice concerning environmental, health and safety matters; assisting in all stages of cleanups under state and federal programs; counseling on environmental aspects of corporate and real estate transactions; and developing pro-active environmental compliance programs. Andrew received his Law Degree from Georgetown University, where he was cum laude, an Olin Fellow in law and economics and an associate editor of the Georgetown Law Journal. Prior to becoming a lawyer, Andrew worked as an environmental engineer in manufacturing and as a consultant.

## KOZLOWSKI, Holly D
Dinsmore & Shohl LLP, Cincinnati
513 977 8568
holly.kozlowski@dinslaw.com
*Recommended in Intellectual Property*
**Practice Areas:** Ms Kozlowski's practice is focused in the areas of patent application preparation and prosecution, including reissue, reexamination, interference and patent term extension proceedings in the United States and opposition proceedings abroad, and corporate counseling in intellectual property protection, infringement, validity, licensing and related litigation matters. Ms Kozlowski also provides counseling in patent matters related to new drug applications and abbreviated new drug applications, and Orange Book-related strategies. Her technical experience includes organic chemistry, including pharmaceuticals, inorganic chemistry, polymer

chemistry, chemical engineering and processing, and semiconductor fabrication and structures.

### KRAFTE, Lori
Greenebaum Doll & McDonald PLLC, Cincinnati 513 455 7600
*Recommended in Intellectual Property*

### KREIDER, Gary
Keating, Muething & Klekamp, PLL, Cincinnati 513 579 6400
*Recommended in Corporate/M&A*

### KUEHNLE, Kenton
Allen, Kuehnle & Stovall LLP, Columbus 614 221 8500
*Recommended in Real Estate*

### LAMPE, Matthew W
Jones Day, Columbus 614 281 3863
mwlampe@jonesday.com
*Recommended in Employment*
**Practice Areas:** Employment class action and other complex litigation, with particularly broad experience in FLSA, ERISA, Title VII, and ADEA cases. He has litigated numerous class and collective actions to successful conclusions for employers across the country. Among his successes is the denial of certification in one of the largest employment class actions reported in Ohio. He also advises management on wage and hour compliance, work force restructuring, and litigation avoidance. He lectures widely on class action topics.
**Personal:** Cornell University (JD magna cum laude 1989; Order of the Coif); Kenyon College (BA magna cum laude 1986; Phi Beta Kappa).

### LATOUR, Randall D
Vorys, Sater, Seymour and Pease LLP, Columbus 614 464 8290
rdlatour@vssp.com
*Recommended in Bankruptcy*
**Practice Areas:** Partner focusing on bankruptcy, debtor/creditor, collection, commercial, secured lending, real estate and commercial litigation with emphasis on bankruptcy proceedings and workouts.
**Prof. Memberships:** Columbus Bar Association.
**Career:** Admitted in Ohio (1987); US Court of Appeals 4th Circuit (1990); US Court of Appeals 6th Circuit (1994); US District Court for the Northern (1997) and Southern Districts of Ohio (1988).
**Personal:** The Ohio State University College of Law, JD, with honors, 1987; The Ohio State University, BA, with honors, 1977.

### LAVEY, Wendlene M
Squire, Sanders & Dempsey LLP, Cleveland 216 479 8545
wlavey@ssd.com
*Recommended in Environment*
**Practice Areas:** Partner experienced in environmental counseling and litigation under major regulatory programs with emphasis on compliance counseling, per-

mitting, enforcement defense and site investigation/remediation. Focus on iron and steel industry, ranging from Title V and new source permitting under the Clean Air Act to RCRA corrective action and defense of enforcement actions under the Clean Air Act, Clean Water Act and RCRA. Represents private and public sector clients in CERCLA litigation, toxic tort defense, environmental aspects of corporate transactions and financial reporting, insurance coverage and European Community environmental regulation.

### LAWNICZAK, James
Calfee, Halter & Griswold LLP, Cleveland 216 622 8364
jlawniczak@calfee.com
*Recommended in Bankruptcy*
**Practice Areas:** Bankruptcy and creditors' rights; commercial business and finance.
**Prof. Memberships:** Member and trustee of the Cleveland Bar Association, and 2003-04 Chair of its Bankruptcy and Commercial Law Section. Member and former trustee and committee Chair of the Northern Ohio chapter of the Turnaround Management Association.
**Career:** Partner in the Commercial Business and Finance Group. He handles all aspects of corporate bankruptcy and workout proceedings. Represents secured and unsecured creditors, debtors and unsecured creditors committees.
**Personal:** University of Michigan School of Law, magna cum laude, JD, 1977; University of Michigan, magna cum laude, BA, 1974.

### LAWRENCE, James K L
Frost Brown Todd LLC, Cincinnati 513 651 6822
jlawrence@fbtlaw.com
*Recommended in Employment*
**Practice Areas:** Firm Practice Leader in labor, employment, and negotiation. Has extensive experience in defending employment discrimination matters and unfair labor practices before the National Labor Relations Board; collective bargaining negotiations and grievance administration and arbitration; and in negotiation and mediation of disputes.
**Prof. Memberships:** Admitted to practice in Ohio (1965). Member of the CPR Institute for Dispute Resolution; Fellow of the College of Labor and Employment Lawyers; Member of the Dispute Resolution Committee and the Labor and Employment Law Section of the Ohio State Bar Association; Member of the Section of Dispute Resolution of the American Bar Association.

### LEACH, Donald
Buckingham Doolittle & Burroughs LLP, Columbus 614 221 8448
*Recommended in Construction*

### LEAVITT, Jeffrey S
Jones Day, Cleveland 216 586 7188
jleavitt@jonesday.com
*Recommended in Employee Benefits*
**Practice Areas:** With respect to ERISA plan asset issues, represents venture capital, private equity and hedge fund clients in connection with the design and operation of investment funds and investment banking clients in structured finance transactions employing special purpose vehicles and involving securitizations and swaps. Also represents corporate employers, governmental employers and plans and institutional fiduciaries with respect to employee benefits, including compliance reviews of plans and their administration, benefit aspects of acquisitions, cash balance plan conversions, and the insulation of individuals from fiduciary liability through the design of plans and their governance.
**Prof. Memberships:** ABA; Cleveland Bar Association

### LENNOX, Heather
Jones Day, Cleveland 216 586 7111
hlennox@jonesday.com
*Recommended in Bankruptcy*
**Practice Areas:** Plays an active and leading role in Jones Day's representations of debtors and potential debtors, creditors' committees, prepetition secured lenders, bank groups, DIP lenders, credit card processors, and other significant creditors in many of the nation's largest corporate restructurings. Has substantial experience counseling clients in fraudulent conveyance, illegal dividend, preferential transfer, fiduciary duty, and piercing the corporate veil issues. She has represented clients in out-of-court restructuring transactions and has extensive experience in bankruptcy-related litigation.
**Prof. Memberships:** American Bankruptcy Institute.
**Publications:** Co-authored bankruptcy-related articles published in The Business Lawyer and the Journal of Bankruptcy Law and Practice.

### LEPENE, Alan
Thompson Hine LLP, Cleveland 216 566 5520
Alan.Lepene@ThompsonHine.com
*Recommended in Bankruptcy*
**Career:** Alan is the leader of the firm's Bankruptcy Practice Group and a former member of the firm's Executive Committee. Alan focuses his practice on bankruptcy (primarily chapter 11 reorganizations), workouts and commercial litigation. Alan has had significant experience representing senior lenders in major bankruptcy cases and workouts. He also has had considerable experience in the representation of creditors' committees and debtors in numerous cases under chapter 11 of the Bankruptcy Code.

### LERNER, Stephen D
Squire, Sanders & Dempsey L.L.P., Cincinnati 513 361 1220
slerner@ssd.com
*Recommended in Bankruptcy*
**Practice Areas:** Partner with extensive national bankruptcy and restructuring practice. Regularly represents debtors, creditors committees, secured lenders, acquirers of troubled businesses and other parties in Chapter 11 reorganization cases and out-of-court restructurings. Lead bankruptcy counsel in connection with the firm's representation of the Enron Creditors Committee, co-counsel to WorldCom and lead counsel to EaglePicher Holdings. Fellow of the American College of Bankruptcy. Recognized in 'The Best Lawyers in America' each year since 1997. Frequent speaker on bankruptcy and restructuring issues.
**Prof. Memberships:** American Bankruptcy Institute; Tri-State Association for Corporate Renewal, founder and board member; Midwest Regional Bankruptcy Seminar, Executive Committee.

### LEUKART, Barbara
Jones Day, Cleveland 216 586 7190
bjleukart@jonesday.com
*Recommended in Employment*
**Practice Areas:** Represents management and counsels companies in all areas of labor and employment relations. Defends numerous cases at the administrative, trial, and appellate levels, including class and individual claims regarding sex, race, and age discrimination, ERISA, pay equity, wage and hour violations, and employment torts. Advises companies on union representation campaigns, contract negotiations, and the creation of employment policies. Appointed by the US Court of Appeals for the Sixth Circuit to serve on that court's Advisory Committee on Rules. Serves as a Mediator for the US District Court, Northern District of Ohio.
**Prof. Memberships:** Celebrezze Inn of Court; ABA.

### LEUKART II, Richard
Baker & Hostetler LLP, Cleveland 216 621 0200
*Recommended in Employment*

### LEVY, Mark P
Thompson Hine LLP, Dayton 937 443 6600
*Recommended in Intellectual Property*
**Career:** Mark is a registered patent attorney and practice group leader of Thompson Hine's Intellectual Property Practice Group. He specializes in the management, prosecution and enforcement of all aspects of intellectual property, including technology transfer licensing and joint venture agreements; patent and trademark validity and infringement opinions; intellectual property audits; patent application preparation; intellectual property

litigation; foreign patents; and trade secrets. Mark is admitted to practice in Ohio, the District of Columbia and before the United States Patent and Trademark Office. Mark has negotiated pharmaceutical development and license agreements and participated in significant and successful patent litigations.

**LEWIS, John**
Baker & Hostetler LLP, Cleveland
216 621 0200
*Recommended in Employment*

**LEWIS, Kim Martin**
Dinsmore & Shohl LLP, Cincinnati
513 977 8200
*Recommended in Bankruptcy*

**LIGGETT, Luther**
Bricker & Eckler LLP, Columbus
614 227 2300
*Recommended in Construction*

**LINDBERG, Lawrence**
Baker & Hostetler LLP, Cleveland
216 621 0200
*Recommended in Real Estate*

**LUNN, Gregory**
Wood, Herron & Evans, LLP, Cincinnati
513 241 2324
*Recommended in Intellectual Property*

**LYMAN, Beverly**
Wood, Herron & Evans, LLP, Cincinnati
513 241 2324
*Recommended in Intellectual Property*

**LYON, Charles**
Calfee, Halter & Griswold LLP, Cleveland
216 622 8510
clyon@calfee.com
*Recommended in Intellectual Property*
**Practice Areas:** Intellectual property; intellectual property litigation.
**Prof. Memberships:** Active Member of Northern District of Ohio Alternative Dispute Resolution Panel; acted as a mediator or special master in many intellectual property disputes; former Director of Cleveland Patent Law Association.
**Career:** Chair of the Intellectual Property Group. Handles patent and trademark matters and litigates intellectual property cases. Has been involved in the full scope of intellectual property practice, including negotiating employment and licensing contracts, technology transfers and lawsuit settlements.
**Personal:** George Washington University Law School, JD, with honors, 1970; University of Oklahoma, BS in Mechanical Engineering, 1967.

**MACE, Damond R**
Squire, Sanders & Dempsey LLP, Cleveland 216 479 8764
dmace@ssd.com
*Recommended in Litigation*
**Practice Areas:** Partner and trial lawyer with extensive experience representing clients in commercial contract disputes, UCC, product liability and tort actions.

Broad litigation experience also includes royalty disputes, environmental/pollution, construction, wrongful death, banking, premises liability, real estate, trademark/trade secrets, wrongful discharge and antitrust. Successfully handled many jury trials and appeals as well as numerous arbitration, mediation and other ADR proceedings.

**MAIMAN, Earle Jay**
Thompson Hine LLP, Cincinnati
513 352 6747
Earle.Maiman@ThompsonHine.com
*Recommended in Litigation*
**Career:** For more than 25 years, Earle has been trying cases in courtrooms throughout the country. His success at trial has involved a variety of complex commercial disputes, product liability actions, employment cases and even a high-profile murder defense which ended in a 'not guilty' verdict with national media attention. Earle is a Vice-Chair in Thompson Hine's Business Litigation Practice Group. He represents both plaintiffs and defendants. Earle's distinguished service has included considerable experience and success whether it be in the courtroom, arbitration, at appeals or complex negotiations.

**MAKLEY, Roger**
Boucher & Boucher Co LPA, Dayton
937 223 0122
*Recommended in Litigation*

**MALONE, Raymond**
Baker & Hostetler LLP, Cleveland
216 621 0200
*Recommended in Employee Benefits*

**MARKS, Jeffrey A**
Squire, Sanders & Dempsey L.L.P., Cincinnati 513 361 1242
jemarks@ssd.com
*Recommended in Bankruptcy*
**Practice Areas:** Of counsel focusing in the areas of bankruptcy, Chapter 11 reorganizations, debtors' and creditors' rights and debt restructurings, representing secured lenders, creditors' committees, debtors, equity holders, lessors, contract counterparties and business acquirers.
**Prof. Memberships:** Cincinnati Bar Association, Bankruptcy Law Committee, past Chair; American Bankruptcy Institute; Tri-State Association for Corporate Renewal; Advisory Committee for Local Rules of the US Bankruptcy Court, Southern District of Ohio, past Member.

**MCCAFFREY, John**
McLaughlin & McCaffrey, LLP, Cleveland
216 623 0900
*Recommended in Litigation*

**MCCARTAN, Patrick F**
Jones Day, Cleveland 216 586 7272
pmccartan@jonesday.com
*Recommended in Litigation*
**Practice Areas:** Currently serves as a Senior Partner concentrating on appellate litigation and corporate governance

matters. Has extensive complex case experience in antitrust, taxation, takeovers, officer and director liability, and securities and shareholder litigation matters. Featured in The Wall Street Journal, Institutional Investor, and The American Lawyer and cited in every survey conducted by The National Law Journal as one of America's most respected lawyers. He is also a subject of 'America's Top Trial Lawyers: Who They Are & Why They Win.'
**Prof. Memberships:** Fellow of the American College of Trial Lawyers and the International Academy of Trial Lawyers.

**MCCREARY, Charles**
Bricker & Eckler LLP, Columbus
614 227 2300
*Recommended in Real Estate*

**MCDONALD, John**
Schottenstein, Zox & Dunn, Columbus
614 462 2201
jmcdonald@szd.com
*Recommended in Litigation*
**Practice Areas:** Mr McDonald focuses his practice on complex litigation, patent litigation, commercial litigation and arbitration and construction law. He has tried over 160 cases in State and Federal courts throughout the United States during the past 35 years. Additionally, Mr McDonald provides alternative dispute resolution services as a consultant with SZD's ancillary service, Alternative Litigation Resources, Inc.

**MCGOWAN JR, John**
Baker & Hostetler LLP, Cleveland
216 621 0200
*Recommended in Employee Benefits*

**MCLAUGHLIN, Patrick**
McLaughlin & McCaffrey, LLP, Cleveland
216 623 0900
*Recommended in Litigation*

**MCMAHON, Louis L**
Thompson Hine LLP, Cleveland
216 566 5639
Louis.McMahon@ThompsonHine.com
*Recommended in Environment*
**Career:** Lou is a Partner in Thompson Hine's Environmental Practice Group. He focuses his practice on environmental and water rights litigation, environmental regulatory and legislative matters, Great Lakes and public trust issues and brownfields redevelopment. In addition, he is the Vice-Chair of the Ohio State Bar Association Environmental Law Committee. Lou received his Law Degree from Cleveland-Marshall College of Law, where he graduated summa cum laude and received the HG Fuerst Award for Highest First Year Average.

**MCMAHON, Michael**
McMahon DeGulis LLP, Cleveland
216 621 1312
*Recommended in Environment*

**MCMURRAY, Kevin N**
Frost Brown Todd LLC, Cincinnati
513 651 6160
kmcmurray@fbtlaw.com
*Recommended in Environment*
**Practice Areas:** Environmental litigation, defense of environmental enforcement actions, and counseling on environmental and regulatory issues arising in business and transactions (real estate, financing, and corporate acquisitions/divestitures). Significant experience in acquisition and redevelopment of 'brownfield' properties.
**Prof. Memberships:** Admitted to practice in Ohio (1989), Southern District of Ohio, and Sixth Circuit Court of Appeals. Member of American, Ohio State and Cincinnati Bar Associations.
**Career:** Joined Frost Brown Todd (Frost & Jacobs), 1989; became Partner, 1996. Chair, Client Relations Committee, Member, Executive Committee (1998-2003).
**Personal:** Born 7 January 1963. JD University of Cincinnati, 1989; BS ChE University of Cincinnati, 1986.

**MCNEALEY, J Jeffrey**
Porter Wright Morris & Arthur LLP, Columbus 614 227 2074
jmcnealey@porterwright.com
*Recommended in Environment, Real Estate*
**Practice Areas:** Practice areas include, business formation, business transactions, Brownfields redevelopment, environmental law including Clean Air Act and Clean Water Act, real estate acquisition and development, and zoning and land use planning.
**Career:** Admitted in Ohio; US Supreme Court; US Court of Appeals, District of Columbia, Fourth, Sixth, Seventh, and Eighth Circuits; US District Court, District of Columbia; US District Court, Northern and Southern Districts of Ohio; US District Court, Western District of Missouri; US District Court, Western District of North Carolina.
**Personal:** JD, The Ohio State University College of Law, 1969; BA, Cornell University, 1966.

**MCWILLIAMS, Douglas A**
Squire, Sanders & Dempsey LLP, Cleveland 216 479 8332
dmcwilliams@ssd.com
*Recommended in Environment*
**Practice Areas:** Practice encompasses environmental counseling with emphasis on air permitting, enforcement and administrative procedure. Experienced in the generation, use and trading of emission reduction credits and allowances, complex major source permitting and rule development. Counsels and represents clients in hazardous waste litigation and environmental enforcement cases. Listed in 'The Best Lawyers in America'.
**Prof. Memberships:** Section of Environ-

ment, Energy and Resources, American Bar Association; Ohio Bar Association; Clean Air Act Information Network; Ozone Task Force of the Greater Cleveland Growth Association; Permit Process Efficiency Committee sponsored by the Ohio Chamber of Commerce and the Ohio EPA.

## MEEKS, William
R. William Meeks - Sole Practitioner, Columbus 614 228 4141
*Recommended in Litigation*

## MERRILL, Frank
Bricker & Eckler LLP, Columbus 614 227 2300
*Recommended in Environment*

## MERSOL, Gregory
Baker & Hostetler LLP, Cleveland 216 621 0200
*Recommended in Employment*

## MEYER, Andrew C
Duvin, Cahn & Hutton, Cleveland 216 696 7600
ameyer@duvin.com
*Recommended in Employment*
**Practice Areas:** Represents private and public sector clients in all aspects of labor relations, including counsel and advice on union avoidance issues, serving as chief negotiator in numerous collective bargaining negotiations, advocate in arbitrations, employment and discrimination matters, and handling various issues under the Fair Labor Standards Act. Represents numerous clients before the National Labor Relations Board on issues including union representation and unfair labor practices.
**Career:** Partner since 1981.
**Publications:** Frequent lecturer on labor relations topics.
**Personal:** Case Western Reserve University (JD 1976), Heiss Labor Award for outstanding third year student; National Championship Labor Moot Court Team Member; Ohio University (AB, MA, 1973, Phi Beta Kappa); Pi Gamma Mu, Omicron Delta Epsilon.

## MEYER, G Christopher
Squire, Sanders & Dempsey LLP, Cleveland 216 479 8692
cmeyer@ssd.com
*Recommended in Bankruptcy*
**Practice Areas:** Partner with significant experience in workouts, restructurings and bankruptcy reorganizations, including representing debtors, creditors, committees in commercial cases; additional experience in general real estate and commercial lending and troubled loan issues. Listed in 'The Best Lawyers in America'.
**Prof. Memberships:** American Bar Association; Cleveland Bar Association; American College of Bankruptcy, fellow; American Bankruptcy Institute; Turnaround Management Association, past chapter trustee and President.

## MEYER JR, Robert A
Porter Wright Morris & Arthur LLP, Columbus 614 227 2096
rmeyer@porterwright.com
*Recommended in Real Estate*
**Practice Areas:** Environmental Law - Clean Air Act; Governmental Affairs - Lobbying and Regulatory representation; Real Estate - Acquisition and development, Zoning and land use planning.
**Prof. Memberships:** American Bar Association; Ohio State Bar Association; Kentucky Bar Association; Columbus Bar Association; Building Industry Association of Central Ohio.
**Career:** Admitted in Ohio and in the Commonwealth of Kentucky; US District Court for the Southern District of Ohio; US Court of Appeals for the Sixth and District of Columbia Circuits.
**Personal:** The Ohio State University College of Law, JD, 1978; Indiana University, BS, Public Affairs, 1975.

## MILENKOVSKI, Katerina Eftimoff
Porter Wright Morris & Arthur LLP, Columbus 614 227 2035
kmilenkovski@porterwright.com
*Recommended in Environment*
**Practice Areas:** Practices environmental law, particularly Clean Air Act permitting and enforcement under Title V, major, and minor New Source Review programs. Experienced with regulation under Emergency Planning and Community Right to Know Act (EPCRA). Chairs Air Subcommittee of Environmental Litigation Committee of ABA Section of Litigation and is assistant editor of the Litigation Section's 'Litigation News' magazine. Formerly appointed to ABA Standing Committee on Environmental Law.
**Career:** Admitted in Ohio; US Court of Appeals, Sixth Circuit; US District Court, Southern District of Ohio.
**Personal:** JD (summa cum laude), Capital University, 1994; BS (Chemical Engineering), The Ohio State University, 1989.

## MILLER, Barry
Benesch, Friedlander, Coplan & Aronoff LLP, Cleveland 216 363 4454
bmiller@bfca.com
*Recommended in Construction*
**Practice Areas:** Public and private construction law, real estate law and commercial litigation. Represents owners, general contractors, subcontractors, developers, public agencies, design professionals and sureties in every form of construction dispute including: bid protests, extra work disputes, delay and disruptions claims, lost productivity disputes, and post-acceptance building failures.
**Career:** Chairman of the Construction Practice Group. Serves as project counsel on public and private projects with values to approximately $800 million; serves as

an arbitrator and mediator in over 100 construction cases.
**Personal:** Case Western Reserve University (JD, 1983); Kent State University (MArch., 1979); Miami University (BED, 1977).

## MILLER, Craig
Ulmer & Berne LLP, Cleveland 216 583 7000
*Recommended in Real Estate*

## MILLER, W Timothy
Taft, Stettinius & Hollister LLP, Cincinnati 513 381 2838
*Recommended in Bankruptcy*

## MILLISOR, Kenneth
Millisor & Nobil Co LPA, Cleveland 440 838 8000
*Recommended in Employment*

## MILLS JR, Osborne
Squire, Sanders & Dempsey LLP, Cleveland 216 479 8343
omills@ssd.com
*Recommended in Banking & Finance*
**Practice Areas:** Partner with broad experience in all aspects of commercial and real estate lending, loan workouts, debtor-creditor issues and real estate law. Represents financial institutions in secured and unsecured loan transactions, complex debt and mortgage financings, mezzanine debt transactions, venture capital transactions, loan restructurings, workouts and bankruptcy proceedings. Represents purchasers, sellers, lessors and lessees in multifamily, commercial and industrial real estate transactions. Listed in 'The Best Lawyers in America'.
**Prof. Memberships:** Ohio State Bar Association and Cleveland Bar Association, Corporation, Banking and Business Law Section, Bankruptcy and Commercial Law Section and Real Estate Section.

## MILLSTONE, David J
Squire, Sanders & Dempsey LLP, Cleveland 216 479 8574
dmillstone@ssd.com
*Recommended in Employment*
**Practice Areas:** Partner, firm's Labor and Employment Practice co-ordinator for 15 years. Significant experience in all aspects of private and public sector employment law including general employment counseling, employment litigation, international labor and employment issues, FLSA litigation, union avoidance, collective bargaining, arbitration, employment discrimination, employment termination, labor and employment issues, executive contracts, executive terminations and merger and acquisition issues. Listed in 'The Best Lawyers in America'.
**Prof. Memberships:** American Bar Association, Ohio State Bar Association, Cleveland Bar Association, Labor and Employment Law Sections.

## MIRALDI, Leslee
Thompson Hine LLP, Cleveland 216 566 5500
Leslee.Miraldi@ThompsonHine.com
*Recommended in Banking & Finance*
**Career:** Leslee is a Partner in the Commercial and Public Finance Practice Group. She focuses on commercial lending, representing banks, financial institutions and public and private companies in connection with senior and subordinated debt facilities. She has extensive experience with syndicated, multi-bank senior credit facilities, asset based and structured finance facilities, cross-border transactions (involving foreign borrowers and foreign collateral), acquisition financing, letter of credit facilities, foreign currency transactions, second lien lending and real estate financing. Leslee also has extensive experience in the area of secured transactions, including both personal and real property. Her representation includes loan restructuring and workouts.

## MIXTER, Stephen
Jones Day, Cleveland 216 586 1085
smixter@jonesday.com
*Recommended in Real Estate*
**Practice Areas:** General real estate practice, with a particular emphasis on providing corporate real estate services to companies not primarily in the real estate industry but who occupy real estate as a necessary support function for their core businesses. His practice includes the acquisition, disposition, financing, development, leasing, subleasing, and exchanging of commercial and industrial real estate. He has significant experience in dealing with the real estate aspects of corporate acquisitions, dispositions, mergers, financings, and bankruptcies and has been involved in numerous multi-asset transactions for Fortune 500 companies.
**Publications:** Authored articles published in the Journal of Corporate Real Estate.

## MOSCARINO, George
Jones Day, Cleveland 216 586 7203
gmoscarino@jonesday.com
*Recommended in Litigation*
**Practice Areas:** International criminal defense and white-collar practice involves complex criminal litigation and government and grand jury investigations. Has extensive experience representing corporations, their management, boards of directors, and employees in criminal matters, and has represented clients in many high-profile criminal investigations and cases.
**Prof. Memberships:** Fellow of the American College of Trial Lawyers; International Bar Association. Charter and life member of the Ohio Eighth District Judicial Conference.
**Publications:** An active international

lecturer on civil and criminal litigation techniques and white-collar crimes and has published articles on those subjects in the US, Canada, England, and Japan.

## MOSS, Steven M
Kahn Kleinman, LPA, Cleveland
216 479 6417
smoss@kahnkleinman.com
*Recommended in Employment*
**Practice Areas:** Labor and employment.
**Prof. Memberships:** Member, American, Ohio State and Cleveland Bar Associations; Member of the Labor and Employment Law sections of the Cleveland, Ohio State and American Bar Associations; Epilepsy Foundation of Northeast Ohio, Board of Trustees.
**Career:** Steve Moss counsels and represents employers in all aspects of traditional labor relations and employment law, including negotiating and administrating collective bargaining agreements, labor contract arbitrations, union representation and decertification campaigns and proceedings, and related National Labor Relations Board litigation. He has litigated cases before the Board all over the country and regularly provides counsel to management clients on all issues affecting their workplace.
**Publications:** As a recognized leader on labor and employment law issues, Mr Moss has lectured at numerous conferences across America and has been quoted in several publications, including The Wall Street Journal, The New York Times, and USA Today.

## NASH, David
McMahon DeGulis LLP, Cleveland
216 621 1312
*Recommended in Environment*

## NATALE, Andrew
Frantz Ward LLP, Cleveland
216 515 1660
*Recommended in Construction*

## NEWMAN JR, John (Jack) M
Jones Day, Cleveland 216 586 7207
jmnewman@jonesday.com
*Recommended in Litigation*
**Practice Areas:** Oversees the Trial Practice in the Cleveland office. His practice encompasses a variety of general business matters, with a focus on shareholder actions and fiduciary and governance claims, and also includes banking services, employee benefits, bankruptcy, tax and accounting-related litigation, and other commercial controversies. Admitted to practice before the US Tax and Supreme Court and numerous federal district courts and courts of appeals.
**Prof. Memberships:** Fellow of the American College of Trial Lawyers; ABA; Los Angeles County Bar Association; Cleveland Bar Association.

## NOBIL, Steven
Millisor & Nobil Co LPA, Cleveland
440 838 8000
*Recommended in Employment*

## NOLAN, William A
Squire, Sanders & Dempsey L.L.P.,
Columbus 614 365 2784
wnolan@ssd.com
*Recommended in Employment*
**Practice Areas:** Partner representing private and public sector employers in labor and employment disputes; counsels clients on proactively minimizing the cost and business disruption of such disputes including litigation of numerous covenant not to compete and trade secret cases in federal and state courts. Defends employers in age, disability, sex, race and military discrimination lawsuits and works with clients to minimize employee-related liability.
**Prof. Memberships:** Columbus Bar Association, Labor and Employment Law Committee, Member and past Chair; former two-term Councilman and Mayor of Powell, Ohio; United Way of Delaware County, Chair-Elect of the Board of Trustees.

## NORMAN, Mark A
Vorys, Sater, Seymour and Pease LLP,
Cincinnati 513 723-4006
manorman@vssp.com
*Recommended in Environment*
**Practice Areas:** Partner. Represents business in environmental compliance, business transactions, enforcement and litigation. Prosecutes and defends private cost-recovery actions, and defends toxic tort litigation and government enforcement actions in state and federal courts. Has a substantial 'brownfields' redevelopment practice (including Ohio EPA Voluntary Action and Clean Ohio programs) and a government organizations practice. Elected by peers as an 'Ohio Super Lawyer'.
**Prof. Memberships:** Ohio State and Cincinnati Bar Associations.
**Career:** Admitted to Ohio Bar (1983).
**Publications:** Co-author 'RCRA and Superfund', Shepards/McGraw-Hill.
**Personal:** Georgetown University Law Center, JD, cum laude, 1983. George Washington University, BA, with honors 1977.

## OBERSCHMIDT, E Richard
Frost Brown Todd LLC, Cincinnati
513 651 6887
roberschmidt@fbtlaw.com
*Recommended in Real Estate*
**Practice Areas:** Real Estate Law and Mortgage Financing.
**Prof. Memberships:** 1978, Ohio Bar; Chair, Commercial Transactions and Real Estate Department. Member, Ohio Land Title Association. Member, Board of Zoning Appeals, Anderson Township, Ohio.
**Career:** Member of Cincinnati, Ohio State and American Bar Associations.
**Personal:** University of Virginia, JD, 1978, Miami University, BA, 1975, Phi Beta Kappa.

## O'DONNELL, Patricia
Baker & Hostetler LLP, Cleveland
216 621 0200
*Recommended in Real Estate*

## OELLERMANN, Charles M
Jones Day, Columbus 614 281 3948
coellermann@jonesday.com
*Recommended in Bankruptcy*
**Practice Areas:** Oversees the Business Restructuring and Reorganization Practice in the Columbus Office. His practice focuses primarily on corporate bankruptcy, restructuring, and other insolvency-related matters. He has represented debtors, creditors' committees, and other parties in large corporate restructurings nationwide and has provided insolvency-related advice to clients in litigation and transactional contexts. Regularly counsels clients on fraudulent conveyance, illegal dividend, preferential transfer, fiduciary duty, and corporate veil piercing issues as well as the structuring and consummation of spin-offs, secured financings, distressed mergers and acquisitions, and other transactions.
**Prof. Memberships:** American Bankruptcy Institute; Ohio State Bar Association; Columbus Bar Association.

## O'MALLEY, Anthony
Vorys, Sater, Seymour and Pease LLP,
Cleveland 216 479 6159
ajomalley@vssp.com
*Recommended in Litigation*
**Practice Areas:** Managing Partner of the Vorys Cleveland office. His practice focuses on complex business litigation, with particular expertise in class actions, corporate and banking law. Elected by peers as 'Ohio Super Lawyer' and listed in 'The Best Lawyers in America'.
**Prof. Memberships:** Anthony J Celebrezze Inn of Court (Master Bencher); Life Member, Judicial Conference for Ohio's Eighth Appellate Judicial District.
**Career:** Admitted to Ohio Bar 1984.
**Personal:** John Carroll University, BA, cum laude, (1980); Case Western Reserve University Law School, JD, (1984); Law Review: Case Western Law Review, articles editor, (1984).

## ORDING, Michael K
Jones Day, Columbus 614 281 3839
mkording@jonesday.com
*Recommended in Real Estate*
**Practice Areas:** Real estate and real estate finance. Extensive experience with joint ventures, real estate-related securities and tax-exempt finance. Has represented several clients on large portfolio acquisitions and dispositions. Also extensive experience in workouts.
**Career:** Partner since 1987.
**Personal:** Ohio Northern University (BA 1977), The Ohio State University (JD summa cum laude, 1980).

## OSCAR, Lawrence
Hahn Loeser & Parks LLP, Cleveland
216 621 0150
*Recommended in Bankruptcy*

## OWENDOFF, Michael
Jones Day, Cleveland 216 586 7183
msowendoff@jonesday.com
*Recommended in Real Estate*
**Practice Areas:** Practice encompasses all aspects of the development, financing, leasing, exchanging, purchasing, and selling of commercial real estate throughout the US. He represents national and regional developers and provides real estate advice relating to the ownership, operation, and finance of real estate to nondeveloper clients. He represents landlords and tenants in ground, retail, office, and industrial leases and advises borrowers and lenders in commercial real estate loan transactions.
**Prof. Memberships:** ABA; Cleveland Bar Association.
**Publications:** Co-authored articles published in the Journal of Corporate Real Estate and has been a moderator and speaker on real estate issues at various seminars.

## PACE, Stanley Dan
Spieth Bell McCurdy & Newell Co LPA,
Cleveland 216 696 4700
*Recommended in Employment*

## PARIS, Zachary
Jones Day, Cleveland
216 586 7275
ztparis@jonesday.com
*Recommended in Real Estate*
**Practice Areas:** Practice focuses on real estate development, corporate real estate services, and the hospitality industry. Represented developers in commercial and industrial ownership and development, including the acquisition of land, the installation of improvements, the construction and leasing of buildings, the negotiation of easement agreements, and the acquisition of existing buildings. His corporate real estate services work includes corporate headquarters development projects, ground leases for large industrial properties, and leases and financings for airport expansion projects. As co-leader of the firm's Hospitality Practice, he has been involved in the acquisition, sale, and/or financing of individual hotels and hotel portfolios.

## PAROBEK, Drew
Vorys, Sater, Seymour and Pease LLP,
Cleveland 216 479 6100
dtparobek@vssp.com
*Recommended in Bankruptcy*
**Practice Areas:** Partner in the Commercial Group with emphasis on bankruptcy, commercial law and banking.
**Prof. Memberships:** Cleveland (Executive Committee; Trustee; Member, Bankruptcy and Commercial Law Section; Chair, Continuing Legal Education Com-

mittee), Lorain County and Ohio State Bar Associations; Turnaround Management Association.
**Career:** Admitted to Ohio (1984); US District Court, Northern and Southern Districts of Ohio; US Court of Appeals, Sixth Circuit.
**Personal:** Vanderbilt University School of Law, JD, 1984; Vanderbilt University, BA, summa cum laude, 1980. Trustee, Cleveland Zoological Society; Contemporary Youth Orchestra; Bay Soccer Club.

## PATBERG, William
Shumaker Loop & Kendrick LLP, Toledo
419 241 9000
*Recommended in Environment*

## PEARLMAN, Samuel
Squire, Sanders & Dempsey LLP, Cleveland 216 479 8025
spearlman@ssd.com
*Recommended in Real Estate*
**Practice Areas:** Partner with broad experience in real estate, general corporate and securities law matters; focuses on commercial real estate transactions, real estate and other business loans from both a borrower's and a lender's perspective, business mergers, acquisitions and divestitures and negotiation of joint venture and limited liability company agreements. Represents and counsels publicly held and private corporations, partnerships, joint ventures, limited liability companies and real estate investment trusts in sophisticated corporate and real estate transactions.
**Prof. Memberships:** American Bar Association, Business Law Section; Cleveland Bar Association, Real Estate Law and Corporation and Business Law Sections; Ohio State Bar Association.

## PETRO, John
Williams & Petro Co. LLC, Columbus
614 224 0531
*Recommended in Construction*

## PFEFFERLE, Ben
Baker & Hostetler LLP, Columbus
614 228 1541
*Recommended in Environment*

## PHILLIPS, James E
Vorys, Sater, Seymour and Pease LLP, Columbus 614 464 5610
jephillips@vssp.com
*Recommended in Litigation*
**Practice Areas:** Partner in the Litigation Group with emphasis on white-collar criminal defense.
**Prof. Memberships:** Columbus (Professional Ethics Committee, 2002-; Committee on the Judiciary, 2003-), Ohio State and American (Criminal Justice Section, White Collar Crime Committee) Bar Associations; Ohio Association of Criminal Defense Lawyers (Board of Trustees, 2000-, Trsr, 2003-); National Association of Criminal Defense Lawyers, Sixth Circuit Judicial Conference Life Member (1893-).

**Career:** Admitted to Ohio (1975); US District Court, Southern District of Ohio and US Supreme Court (1979); US Court of Appeals, Fourth, Sixth, Tenth Circuits and US District Court, Southern and Northern Districts of Ohio, Western District of Michigan. Adjunct Prof of Law, Moritz Colllege of Law (Ohio State University), (2004-present).
**Personal:** Case Western Reserve University, JD, 1975; Boston University, BA, cum laude, 1971.

## PHILLIPS, William M
Kahn Kleinman, LPA, Cleveland
216 696 3311
wphillips@kahnkleinman.com
*Recommended in Real Estate*
**Practice Areas:** Real estate law.
**Prof. Memberships:** He is a founding Member of the Ohio International Council of Shopping Center Law Symposium, member of the International Council of Shopping Centers, and of the American, California, Ohio State, and Cleveland Bar Associations.
**Career:** William Phillips, Partner in Kahn Kleinman's Real Estate Practice, represents a significant number of national and regional shopping center developers, including national and regional chain tenants, and is fully conversant with issues regarding the development of retail projects in partnership with major anchor tenants.
**Personal:** The Ohio State University Law School, JD, with honors, 1983; Miami University, BS, cum laude, 1979.

## PIGMAN, Jack R
Porter Wright Morris & Arthur LLP, Columbus 614 227 2119
jpigman@porterwright.com
*Recommended in Bankruptcy*
**Practice Areas:** Represents debtors, committees, banks and other financial institutions in significant Chapter 11 bankruptcy cases, receiverships, business reorganizations, workouts and loan restructurings. Often assists clients in the purchase and sale of businesses.
**Career:** Admitted in Ohio; US Court of Appeals, Sixth Circuit; US District Court, Eastern District of Michigan; US District Court, Northern and Southern Districts of Ohio.
**Personal:** JD (cum laude), The Ohio State University, 1969; BA, University of Notre Dame, 1966.

## PITCAIRN JR, Robert
Katz, Teller, Brant & Hild, Cincinnati
513 721 4532
*Recommended in Litigation*

## PLANK, Don
Plank & Brahm, Columbus
614 228 4546
*Recommended in Real Estate*

## PORTER, David
Jones Day, Cleveland 216 586 7215
dporter@jonesday.com

*Recommended in Corporate/M&A*
**Practice Areas:** Practices principally securities and corporate governance law, with extensive experience in corporate restructurings.
**Prof. Memberships:** ABA; Cleveland Bar Association. Currently serves as Vice-Chair of the Corporation Law Committee of the Ohio State Bar Association and actively participates in drafting revisions to Ohio's corporate statutes.
**Publications:** Regularly writes and lectures on securities, corporate governance, and corporate structuring subjects. He has served as an Adjunct Professor at Case Western Reserve University's School of Law teaching advanced securities regulation.

## POWAR, Lee
Hahn Loeser & Parks LLP, Cleveland
216 621 0150
*Recommended in Bankruptcy*

## POWERS, Victoria E
Schottenstein, Zox & Dunn, Columbus
614 462 5010
vpowers@szd.com
*Recommended in Bankruptcy*
**Practice Areas:** Ms Powers concentrates her practice in the areas of complex Chapter 11 reorganization, bankruptcy court litigation and out-of-court workouts, with an emphasis on creditor and indenture trustee representations.
**Prof. Memberships:** American Bankruptcy Institute; Commercial Law League of America; International Women's Insolvency and Restructuring Confederation, Central Ohio Chapter; listed in Bankruptcy Law Section of The Best Lawyers in America, 2005-2006.

## RAWSON, Rachel
Jones Day, Cleveland
216 586 7276
rlrawson@jonesday.com
*Recommended in Banking & Finance*
**Practice Areas:** Oversees Jones Day's Lending/Structured Finance Practice in the Cleveland office. Represents lenders and corporate clients, with an emphasis on portfolio companies of private equity funds, in commercial financing transactions, including asset-based secured loans, complex leveraged buyout financings, investment grade loans, private placements of debt securities, and subordinated debt facilities. Frequently advises financial institution clients on intercreditor issues, helping them structure and negotiate transactions. Represents capital providers and users in cross-border secured and unsecured transactions, including multijurisdictional and multicurrency facilities.
**Prof. Memberships:** ABA; Cleveland Bar Association.
**Publications:** Author and lecturer on commercial financing topics.

## REDER, Henry
Buckingham Doolittle & Burroughs LLP, Cleveland 216 621 5300
*Recommended in Construction*

## REIDY, Joseph M
Schottenstein, Zox & Dunn, Columbus
614 462 2207
jreidy@szd.com
*Recommended in Environment*
**Practice Areas:** Mr Reidy provides counsel and representation for environmental and natural resource permits, compliance and enforcement to state and local government, agriculture and industry, including litigation in state and federal courts and administrative agencies. As the Head of the firm's Brownfield Practice Group, he assists buyers, sellers and developers of real estate with the resolution of environmental issues, including hazardous waste, lead-based paint, asbestos and wetlands. He also has extensive experience in securing state, federal and private funding for the remediation of air and water pollution and hazardous materials, including brownfield and greenspace grants from the Clean Ohio Fund.

## REMINGTON, Royce
Hahn Loeser & Parks LLP, Cleveland
216 621 0150
*Recommended in Construction*

## REPPERT, Richard L
Jones Day, Cleveland
216 586 7235
rreppert@jonesday.com
*Recommended in Real Estate*
**Practice Areas:** His practice is primarily transaction-oriented, typically pertaining to real estate or financing matters. He represents real estate developers in transactions involving land acquisition, development, construction financing, and permanent financing. He also represents banks and other financial institutions making loans secured, at least in part, by real estate. Experience in syndicated loans, secured credit lines, and loans that are or will be securitized. He is familiar with capital markets requirements and is involved in the formation of special purpose entities required by rating agencies in securitized transactions.
**Prof. Memberships:** American College of Real Estate Lawyers.

## RIDGLEY, Thomas
Vorys, Sater, Seymour and Pease LLP, Columbus 614 464 6229
tbridgley@vssp.com
*Recommended in Litigation*
**Practice Areas:** Litigator with experience in all areas of civil litigation including commercial, business, takeover, securities, labor, insurance, environmental, and products liability litigation.
**Prof. Memberships:** Columbus, Cincinnati, Ohio State, and American Bar Associations.

**Career:** Admitted in Ohio (1968); United States District Courts for the Northern and Southern Districts of Ohio; United States Courts of Appeals, Third, Sixth and Tenth Circuits; US Supreme Court.
**Personal:** University of Michigan, JD, with distinction, 1965; Princeton University, AB, magna cum laude, 1962. Fellow, American College of Trial Lawyers. Listed in a leading legal publication for commercial and toxic tort litigation and product liability litigation.

### RIGOT, Joseph M
Thompson Hine LLP, Dayton
937 443 6586
Joe.Rigot@ThompsonHine.com
*Recommended in Corporate/M&A*
**Career:** Joe is a member of the firm's Corporate Transactions and Securities Practice Group. He focuses his practice on the representation of public companies, with an emphasis on securities law, merger and acquisition transactions, and strategic alliances. Joe is also general counsel and secretary of Robbins & Myers, Inc. which is listed on the New York Stock Exchange.
**Personal:** Washington University, JD, 1973, Order of the Coif, Law Review. University of Cincinnati, MA, 1969. University of Dayton, BA, 1966, magna cum laude.

### RILEY, Shawn
McDonald Hopkins Co, Cleveland
216 348 5400
*Recommended in Bankruptcy*

### ROBENALT, James
Thompson Hine LLP, Cleveland
216 566 5755
Jim.Robenalt@ThompsonHine.com
*Recommended in Construction, Litigation*
**Career:** Jim is Chairman of the Business Litigation Practice. A trial lawyer his entire career, he handles complex commercial and intellectual property disputes and has tried several major construction cases. Jim was co-lead counsel for a Fortune 500 company in a civil RICO case, resulting in an $81 million jury verdict against Taiwanese defendants that followed the first successful prosecution under the Economic Espionage Act of 1996. In 2004, he was lead counsel in an arbitration among pharmaceutical companies, ending in a $68 million award. He currently heads a team working on a multi-district litigation involving hormone replacement therapy drugs.

### ROBERTSON, Jean
McDonald Hopkins Co, Cleveland
216 348 5400
*Recommended in Bankruptcy*

### ROE JR, Clifford A
Dinsmore & Shohl LLP, Cincinnati
513 977 8227
cliff.roe@dinslaw.com
*Recommended in Corporate/M&A*

**Practice Areas:** Firm Managing Partner and Chairman of the Board of Directors. Practices in the general corporate, health care, transactional and securities law areas, with significant experience in mergers and acquisitions, corporate governance and hospital law.
**Prof. Memberships:** Ohio State and Cincinnati Bar Associations
**Career:** Joined firm in 1967. Managing Partner and Chairman of Management Committee since 1997. Corporate Department Head from 1984-99.
**Publications:** Author, 'The Ohio Corporation', Bureau of Nat'l Affairs Corp. Practice Series, 1998; Author, 'Ohio Corporations Practice Guide', West Group, 1999.
**Personal:** Xavier University (1964); Notre Dame Law School (JD cum laude 1967; note editor, Law Review).

### ROESCH, Lynda E
Dinsmore & Shohl LLP, Cincinnati
513 977 8139
lynda.roesch@dinslaw.com
*Recommended in Intellectual Property*
**Practice Areas:** Practice focuses on litigation involving intellectual property at the trial court and appellate levels. Represented clients in opposition and cancellation proceedings before Trademark Trial and Appeal Board. Tried trademark and copyright infringement and unfair competition actions all over the country.
**Prof. Memberships:** Admitted in Ohio. Member of Cincinnati, Ohio State, and American Bar Associations, International Trademark Association, and Intellectual Property Owners.
**Career:** Chairperson of firm's Trademark and Copyright Practice Group.
**Personal:** JD, University of Toledo College of Law; MS, University of Michigan; BS, University of Notre Dame.

### ROHYANS, John
Porter Wright Morris & Arthur LLP, Columbus 614 227 2055
jrohyans@porterwright.com
*Recommended in Real Estate*
**Practice Areas:** Has worked in the areas of real estate development and finance for more than 30 years. Practice areas include finance and commerce, acquisition and development, commercial leasing, mortgages and sale/leasebacks, and title insurance. Clients include Nationwide Life Insurance Company, State Farm Life Insurance Company, and Jackson National Life Insurance Company. He is the Department Manager of the firm's Real Estate Department and currently serves on the Bexley, Ohio City Council.
**Career:** Admitted in Ohio and US District Court, Southern District of Ohio.
**Personal:** JD, The Ohio State University College of Law, 1969; BS, Miami University, 1966.

### ROSATI, Jack
Bricker & Eckler LLP, Columbus
614 227 2300
*Recommended in Construction*

### ROSENBERG, Thomas
Roetzel & Andress, LPA, Columbus
614 463 9770
*Recommended in Construction*

### ROSENTHAL, Daniel
Denlinger, Rosenthal & Greenberg LPA, Cincinnati 513 621 3440
*Recommended in Employment*

### ROSNER, Richard
Kahn Kleinman, LPA, Cleveland
216 696 3311
rrosner@kahnkleinman.com
*Recommended in Real Estate*
**Practice Areas:** Real estate law.
**Prof. Memberships:** Member of Cleveland Bar Association, past Chairman of Real Estate Section; Chairman of Common Ownership Committee of Cleveland Bar Association; Ohio State Bar Association, Board of Governors, Real Estate Law Section; Vice-Chairman of American Bar Association's Committee H-1 (Development and Financing of Condominiums); Member of the American College of Real Estate Lawyers.
**Career:** Richard Rosner primarily represents developers and builders in buying, financing, developing, leasing and selling residential, commercial and industrial real property. He has substantial experience in condominium developments and conversions, cluster developments, planned unit developments, subdivision developments, easements, restrictive covenants, zoning and other land use issues. Notable clients and matters: Mr Rosner has handled include Pulte Homes (PHM:NYSE) and Kimball Hill Homes (national homebuilders).

### ROTATORI, Robert
Rotatori, Bender, Gragel, Stoper & Alexander Co. L.P.A., Cleveland
216 928 1010
*Recommended in Litigation*

### RUSH, Jeffery
Frost Brown Todd LLC, Cincinnati
513 651 6893
jrush@fbtlaw.com
*Recommended in Banking & Finance*
**Practice Areas:** Banking, commercial law and real estate, including workouts and restructurings.
**Prof. Memberships:** Admitted to practice in Ohio (1975). Member, Banking, Commercial Law and Bankruptcy Subcommittee of the Ohio State Bar Association and the Section of Business Law of the American Bar Association.
**Career:** Joined Frost Brown Todd, 1975; Member, 1982; former Head of Commercial Transactions and Real Estate Department; former Member of the Executive Committee.
**Personal:** Born 18 September 1950. JD,

Vanderbilt University, 1975; BS (Economics), Wharton School of the University of Pennsylvania, 1972.

### RYDZEL, James
Jones Day, Cleveland 216 586 7227
jarydzel@jonesday.com
*Recommended in Employment*
**Practice Areas:** Counsels in the areas of labor and employment matters, with special focus on employment-related litigation, including labor arbitrations and NLRB proceedings. Practice involves all phases of labor relations, including articulation of negotiation goals and strategies, strike preparation, temporary and permanent replacement of strikers, and picket line and Boys Market injunctions. His litigation experience includes ERISA cases, particularly involving retiree medical benefits. He was an adjunct professor of law at Case Western Reserve University, where he taught employment litigation, and has lectured extensively on employment matters.
**Prof. Memberships:** ABA. Member of the Bar of several federal circuits and districts.

### SAAD, Michael D
Squire, Sanders & Dempsey L.L.P., Columbus 614 365 2735
msaad@ssd.com
*Recommended in Real Estate*
**Practice Areas:** Partner and one of the global co-ordinators for real estate issues. Practice focuses on corporate banking, real estate, real estate finance, joint ventures, equity funds, low income housing tax credit, rehabilitation tax credit and government housing law. Served on the firm's management committee. Listed in 'The Best Lawyers in America' and 'Ohio Super Lawyers'.
**Prof. Memberships:** American Bar Association's Forum on Affordable Housing and Community Development; Ohio Housing Council; Columbus Bar Association, Financial Institutions, Bankruptcy and Real Properties Committees.

### SABO, Roger
Schottenstein, Zox & Dunn, Columbus
614 462 5030
rsabo@szd.com
*Recommended in Construction*
**Practice Areas:** Mr Sabo represents trade associations, owners, designers and contractors involved in procurement, bidding, selection processes, alternative dispute resolutions, construction claims that include acceleration, delays defects, changed conditions and termination, affirmative action claims, prevailing wages, labor negotiations and arbitrations, matters involving age, sex, race and disability discrimination and occupational safety and heath law issues. He serves as General Counsel to the Associated General Contractors of Ohio and Ohio Contractors Association; is on the American Arbitration Association Panel for the Construction industry; and speaks for

numerous associations including the National Utility Contractors and Construction Specification Institute annual conventions (2006).

## SAMUELS, Stephen P
Schottenstein, Zox & Dunn, Columbus
614 462 5021
ssamuels@szd.com
*Recommended in Environment*
**Practice Areas:** Mr Samuels chairs SZD's Environmental Practice Group. His practice focuses on water and air pollution permitting and litigation; hazardous, construction and demolition debris, and solid waste regulation; mold claims; and counsel regarding environmental issues associated with mergers and acquisitions, real estate development and other business and property transactions. Previously, Mr Samuels served as Chief of the Court of Claims Defense Section (which defends all claims for money damages brought against the State of Ohio) and Litigation Supervisor of the Environmental Enforcement Section of the Ohio Attorney General's Office, and as in-house counsel at the Ohio Environmental Protection Agency.

## SANKER, Robert
Keating, Muething & Klekamp, PLL, Cincinnati 513 579 6400
*Recommended in Bankruptcy*

## SARGEANT, Richard
Eastman & Smith Ltd, Toledo
419 241 6000
*Recommended in Environment*

## SAXBE, Charles
Chester, Willcox & Saxbe LLP, Columbus
614 221 4000
*Recommended in Litigation*

## SCHLOEMER, Jeffrey
Taft, Stettinius & Hollister LLP, Cincinnati 513 381 2838
*Recommended in Banking & Finance*

## SCHMIT, David E
Frost Brown Todd LLC, Cincinnati
513 651 6985
dschmit@fbtlaw.com
*Recommended in Intellectual Property*
**Practice Areas:** Intellectual property law. Extensive experience in complex patent, trademark, copyright, trade secret, and unfair competition litigation and arbitration.
**Prof. Memberships:** Admitted to practice in Ohio (1975), US Supreme Court, Federal Circuit and Sixth Circuit. Registered patent attorney (1976).
**Career:** Joined Frost & Jacobs (now Frost Brown Todd) 1976, Partner/member since 1982. Lead trial and appellate counsel in Warner Jenkinson, Inc v Hilton Davis Chemical Co; Ethicon v Quigg; Valco Cincinnati, Inc v N&D Machining Co among others.
**Personal:** JD (1975), Salmon P Chase College of Law; BSEE (1969), MSEE

(1976), University of Cincinnati.

## SCHNAPP, Karlyn
Frost Brown Todd LLC, Cincinnati
513 651 6865
kschnapp@fbtlaw.com
*Recommended in Intellectual Property*
**Practice Areas:** Intellectual property law, in particular patent prosecution (chemical/pharma/bio), counseling, infringement, patentability and validity opinions and licensing.
**Prof. Memberships:** Admitted in Ohio, US Patent and Trademark Office, Intellectual Property Law Association, Ohio Bar Association, Cincinnati Bar Association, American Chemical Society.
**Career:** Joined Frost Brown Todd in 2000; prior to joining was a professor of organic chemistry at Northern Kentucky University for nine and a half years.
**Personal:** BS (with honors in Chemistry), University of Cincinnati, 1984; PhD (organic chemistry) 1989, University of Cincinnati; JD 2000, Chase College of Law, Northern Kentucky University.

## SCHOEDINGER, Daniel H
Vorys, Sater, Seymour and Pease LLP, Columbus 614 464 6307
dhschoedinge@vssp.com
*Recommended in Real Estate*
**Practice Areas:** Partner focusing on commercial leasing, commercial real estate, construction law, construction liens, conveyancing, eminent domain, land use and zoning, landlord/tenant, mortgages and foreclosures, municipal corporations, real estate law, residential real estate, state, local and municipal law.
**Prof. Memberships:** Columbus, Ohio State and American Bar Associations.
**Career:** Admitted to Ohio Bar 1969.
**Personal:** University of Denver College of Law, JD, 1969; Order of St Ives, Member, Denver Law Journal (1968-69); Lehigh University, BS in Chemical Engineering, 1966; law clerk to the Honorable C William O'Neill, Chief Justice of the Ohio Supreme Court 1969-71; Columbus City Councilman 1972-79.

## SCHRAFF, Christopher
Porter Wright Morris & Arthur LLP, Columbus 614 227 2097
cschraff@porterwright.com
*Recommended in Environment*
**Practice Areas:** Practices environmental law, with emphasis on the Federal Water Pollution Control Act, CERCLA and RCRA, wetlands regulation, state and local environmental statutes/regulations, and lender and fiduciary liability issues. Lead counsel in Columbus & Franklin County Metropolitan Park District v Shank, 5 Ohio St.3d 86 (1992), the leading decision in Ohio on water pollution control law.
**Career:** Admitted in Ohio; US Supreme Court; US Court of Appeals, Sixth Circuit; and US District Court for Northern and Southern Districts of Ohio.

**Personal:** JD, University of Notre Dame, 1972; AB, John Carroll University, 1969.

## SCHREINER, Joanne M
Dinsmore & Shohl LLP, Cincinnati
513 977 8482
joanne.schreiner@dinslaw.com
*Recommended in Real Estate*
**Practice Areas:** Practice involves commercial and business transactions including acquisitions and mergers, contract negotiation, real estate financing, leasing, sales and acquisitions. Active representation of lenders in commercial lending on a regional counsel (multi-state) basis.
**Prof. Memberships:** Ohio State and Cincinnati Bar Associations; Arizona State Bar Association.
**Career:** Listed in The Best Lawyers in America; named Ohio Super Lawyer by Law & Politics Media (Real Estate and Top 50 Ohio Women Lawyers); Listed as a Cincy Leading Lawyer (Commercial / Contract).
**Personal:** JD, University of Chicago Law School (1979); BA, University of Akron (1976), summa cum laude.

## SCHWARTZ, Niki
Schwartz, Downey & Co LPA, Cleveland
216 696 7100
*Recommended in Litigation*

## SELTZER, Martin S
Porter Wright Morris & Arthur LLP, Columbus 614 227 2050
mseltzer@porterwright.com
*Recommended in Environment*
**Practice Areas:** Practices environmental law, emphasis on hazardous and solid wastes, water issues, and toxic substances. Performed numerous environmental assessments in connection with business and real estate purchases and assisted many clients in obtaining US and Ohio EPA permits. Represented various entities in successful redevelopment of brownfields properties.
**Prof. Memberships:** General Counsel, Ohio Chemistry Technology Council; past Co-Chair, Ohio EPA Public Advisory Group on Solid and Hazardous Waste; past Chair, Environmental Law Committee, Columbus Bar Association.
**Career:** Admitted in Ohio.
**Personal:** JD, The Ohio State University, 1977; PhD, Yale University, 1962; AB, New York University, 1958.

## SHANNON, Michael
Crabbe, Brown, James LLP, Columbus
614 228 5511
*Recommended in Real Estate*

## SHAW, Russell
Walter & Haverfield LLP, Cleveland
216 781 1212
*Recommended in Employee Benefits*

## SHEERAN, Timothy J
Squire, Sanders & Dempsey LLP, Cleveland 216 479 8605
tsheeran@ssd.com

*Recommended in Employment*
**Practice Areas:** Partner representing educational institutions in contract negotiations, grievance arbitration, litigation, education of the disabled and employment discrimination matters. For private sector clients, provides counsel on issues including equal employment opportunity litigation, wage-hour problems, class action litigation, employment of the disabled, private employment agreements, bankruptcy and pension matters. Listed in 'The Best Lawyers in America'.
**Prof. Memberships:** American Bar Association, Labor and Employment Law Section; Ohio State Bar Association, Labor and Employment Law Section; Cleveland Bar Association, Labor and Employment Committee; National Council of School Attorneys; Ohio Council of School Attorneys; Education Law Association.

## SHERMAN, Terry
Terry K Sherman, Columbus
614 444 8800
*Recommended in Litigation*

## SIDMAN, Robert
Vorys, Sater, Seymour and Pease LLP, Columbus 614 464 6422
rjsidman@vssp.com
*Recommended in Bankruptcy*
**Practice Areas:** Partner in the Commercial Group focusing on bankruptcy and debtor creditor law.
**Prof. Memberships:** Columbus, Ohio State and American Bar Associations; Association of Former Bankruptcy Judges; National Conference of Bankruptcy Judges; American Bankruptcy Institute.
**Career:** Admitted to Ohio Bar (1968); US Court of Appeals, Sixth Circuit (1970); US Tax Court and US Supreme Court (1972); US Court of Appeals, Fourth Circuit (1990); US Court of Appeals, Third Circuit (1993).
**Personal:** University of Notre Dame, JD, 1968; Benedictine College, BA, magna cum laude, 1965.

## SIEGEL, Bradd N
Porter Wright Morris & Arthur LLP, Columbus 614 227 2238
bsiegel@porterwright.com
*Recommended in Employment*
**Practice Areas:** Concentrates practice on employment litigation, including defense of individual and class action claims brought under federal and state employment discrimination and labor laws, ERISA, state contract and tort law.
**Prof. Memberships:** Fellow, College of Labor and Employment Lawyers; ABA, Labor and Employment Law Section, EEO Committee, Litigation Section; OSBA, Labor and Employment Law Section .
**Career:** Admitted in Ohio; District of Columbia; Commonwealth of Virginia; Sixth Circuit; US District Courts for Northern and Southern Districts of

Ohio.

**Personal:** LLM, Georgetown University Law Center, 1978; JD (with honors), George Washington University, 1977; AB (with distinction), Cornell University, 1974.

### SMITH, Harrison
Smith & Hale, Columbus
614 221 4255
*Recommended in Real Estate*

### SMITH, J Theodore (Ted)
Vorys, Sater, Seymour and Pease LLP, Columbus 614 464 6232
jtsmith@vssp.com
*Recommended in Real Estate*

**Practice Areas:** Senior associate concentrating his practice on condominium law, real estate acquisition and sales, real estate development, construction contracts, leasing, liens, evictions and real estate secured loans.

**Prof. Memberships:** Columbus and Ohio State (editor, Real Property Section newsletter) Bar Associations.

**Career:** Admitted to Ohio Bar.

**Personal:** University of Illinois College of Law, JD, magna cum laude, 1998. Purdue University, BS Civil Engineering, Chi Epsilon, 1992. Frequent faculty member for condominium-related seminars.

### SOLIMINE, Louis F
Thompson Hine LLP, Cincinnati
513 352 6784
Louis.Solimine@ThompsonHine.com
*Recommended in Bankruptcy*

**Career:** Louis is a Partner and a member of the firm's Bankruptcy and Creditors' Rights Practice Group and has extensive experience in significant Chapter 11 reorganizations, commercial workouts, foreclosure cases and assignments for the benefit of creditors. Louis has represented debtors, creditors' committees, secured lenders, equipment lessors, landlords and tenants, trade creditors, health insurers, prospective acquirers, preference defendants, and other interested parties in numerous major Chapter 11 cases throughout the United States. Louis also focuses his practice on related matters arising under the Uniform Commercial Code including sales, personal property leases, letters of credit, security agreements and secured party sales.

### SOLOMON, Randall
Baker & Hostetler LLP, Cleveland
216 621 0200
*Recommended in Litigation*

### SOZIO, Stephen
Jones Day, Cleveland 216 586 7201
sgsozio@jonesday.com
*Recommended in Litigation*

**Practice Areas:** His practice involves representing businesses and their employees during investigations by federal and local governmental authorities for potential criminal charges; investigating and prosecuting and/or defending civil actions on behalf of clients involved with fraud, false claims, and other business-related wrongdoing; and advising corporate clients regarding compliance issues to avoid governmental sanctions. He has also conducted many internal and external investigations on behalf of boards of directors and senior management. Adjunct Professor at the Cleveland-Marshall College of Law of Cleveland State University where he teaches criminal procedure.

**Prof. Memberships:** American, Federal, and Cleveland Bar Associations.

### SPILLER, Keith P
Thompson Hine LLP, Cincinnati
513 352 6722
Keith.Spiller@ThompsonHine.com
*Recommended in Employment*

**Career:** Keith is a Partner and leader of the firm's Labor and Employment Practice Group. He focuses his practice on the representation of employers in all areas of labor and employment law, including employment discrimination and wrongful discharge litigation; practicing before the National Labor Relations Board, Equal Employment Opportunity Commission, Ohio Civil Rights Commission and Office of Federal Contract Compliance Programs, as well as handling arbitrations, contract administration and negotiations with labor unions. Keith received his Undergraduate Degree from Miami University and his Law Degree from Wake Forest University, where he was a member of the Law Review.

### STAMP, Vincent B
Dinsmore & Shohl LLP, Cincinnati
513 977 8264
stamp@dinslaw.com
*Recommended in Environment*

**Practice Areas:** Environmental Litigation at the federal, state and administrative levels. Chair of the firm's Environmental Practice Group. Served as lead trial counsel for Borden, Inc. in successfully defending a claim brought by Oxy USA, Inc. for indemnification for all response costs incurred by Oxy at the Skinner Landfill. On December 29, 2005, US District Court for the Southern District of Ohio entered judgment in favor of Borden on all claims.

**Career:** 2006 Lifetime Achievement Award for Environmental Law from the Cincinnati Bar Association Environmental Law Committee; named Ohio Super Lawyer by Law & Politics Media.

### STANLEY, Hugh
Tucker Ellis & West LLP, Cleveland
216 696 1100
*Recommended in Litigation*

### STARKEY, J Shane
Thompson Hine LLP, Cincinnati
513 352 6737
Shane.Starkey@ThompsonHine.com
*Recommended in Employee Benefits*

**Career:** Shane advises public companies on the tax, corporate governance and securities law aspects of executive compensation. He designs various executive compensation arrangements such as equity incentive plans, bonus plans, fringe benefit programs, deferred compensation arrangements, employment and severance agreements. He counsels clients on the rules related to the $1 million deduction limit on executive pay and the executive compensation aspects of mergers and acquisitions, including the tax penalties imposed on golden parachute payments. In addition, Shane advises on tax and legal issues related to a wide range of business transactions, such as acquisitions, dispositions, spin-offs and joint ventures.

### STEINDLER, Howard
Benesch, Friedlander, Coplan & Aronoff LLP, Cleveland 216 363 4560
hsteindler@bfca.com
*Recommended in Real Estate*

**Practice Areas:** Commercial leasing, acquisitions and divestitures, development, complex legal structures and multi-use projects, architectural agreements, finance and construction, and general business and commercial law. Extensive experience working with shopping malls, residential developments, shopping centers, mixed use developments, public company real estate representations, public projects, urban projects and commercial buildings.

**Career:** Past Chairman of the Real Estate and Environmental Group. Past Partner-in-Charge of the Cleveland office.

**Personal:** Ohio State University (JD, cum laude, 1967); Miami University (BS, 1964).

### STEINER, Edward
Keating, Muething & Klekamp, PLL, Cincinnati 513 579 6400
*Recommended in Corporate/M&A*

### STEPANIAK, Mark
Taft, Stettinius & Hollister LLP, Cincinnati
513 381 2838
*Recommended in Employment*

### STEPHEN, John M
Porter Wright Morris & Arthur LLP, Columbus 614 227 2193
jstephen@porterwright.com
*Recommended in Employment*

**Practice Areas:** Represents employers in administrative, arbitration, mediation, trial and appellate proceedings in all areas of labor and employment law, including Title VII, NLRA, FLSA, ADA and OFCCP. Provides training and advice on employment policies, and litigation avoidance.

**Career:** Joined firm in 1979; Admitted in Ohio; US Supreme Court; US Courts of Appeals for Second, Third and Sixth Circuits; and US District Courts in Ohio, Michigan, Kentucky, Indiana, and Illinois; Adjunct Professor at Capital Univer-

sity Law and Graduate Center.

**Publications:** 'Ohio Employment Practices Law'.

**Personal:** JD, The Ohio State University, 1979; BA (cum laude), DePauw University, 1976.

### STRAUCH, John L
Jones Day, Cleveland 216 586 7240
jlstrauch@jonesday.com
*Recommended in Litigation*

**Practice Areas:** Former Head of Jones Day's Litigation Practice, with extensive experience in complex litigation matters, including product liability, corporate takeovers, class actions, federal securities, government regulation, commercial litigation, and antitrust. He has been widely quoted in the print media and has appeared on numerous national television programs and has lectured on various aspects of trial practice.

**Prof. Memberships:** American College of Trial Lawyers. Life member, US Sixth Circuit Judicial Conference and Ohio Eighth District Judicial Conference.

**Publications:** Author: featured in 'Inside the Minds: Leading Litigators'; multi-district litigation chapter, 'Business and Commercial Litigation in Federal Courts'.

### STRAUSS, David
Baker & Hostetler LLP, Cleveland
216 621 0200
*Recommended in Real Estate*

### STRIEFSKY, Linda
Thompson Hine LLP, Cleveland
216 566 5500
Linda.Striefsky@ThompsonHine.com
*Recommended in Real Estate*

**Career:** As Chair of the Real Estate Finance Team, Linda represents primarily lenders regarding secured, unsecured, syndicated and portfolio financings, loan workouts and secondary market transactions. She handles sales and purchases, including portfolio deals. She also counsels corporate clients on development, shared services agreements, outsourcing and tax incentives. Linda's leasing and development practice covers ground, credit tenant and other leasing, as well as easements. Recently re-elected to the Board of the American College of Real Estate Lawyers, Linda also is a member of the American College of Mortgage Attorneys, Urban Land Institute and International Council of Shopping Centers.

### STRIMBU, Victor
Baker & Hostetler LLP, Cleveland
216 621 0200
*Recommended in Employment*

### STURTZ, Craig A
Squire, Sanders & Dempsey L.L.P., Columbus 614 365 2761
csturtz@ssd.com
*Recommended in Environment*

**Practice Areas:** Senior attorney in the firm's Environmental Health and Safety Group. Counsels corporations, developers and municipalities on a range of environmental and land-use matters including pursuing permit appeals and defending enforcement actions, compliance with federal and state hazardous and solid waste laws, brownfields redevelopment and voluntary cleanups, and minimizing environmental liability in complex commercial and real estate transactions. Appears before the Ohio EPA, the Environmental Review Appeals Commission and the US EPA regarding compliance and enforcement issues.

**Prof. Memberships:** Columbus Bar Association, Environmental Law Committee, Co-Chair and past secretary; Ohio State Bar Association, Environmental Law Section.

## SYNENBERG, Roger
Synenberg & Associates, Cleveland
216 622 2727
*Recommended in Litigation*

## SZABO, Paul
Calfee, Halter & Griswold LLP, Cleveland
216 622 8578
pszabo@calfee.com
*Recommended in Intellectual Property*
**Practice Areas:** Intellectual property.
**Prof. Memberships:** Member of the American and Cleveland Intellectual Property Law Associations, and Cleveland and Ohio State Bar Associations.
**Career:** Senior attorney in the Intellectual Property Group. He counsels publicly and privately-held clients regarding patent, copyright and trademark matters. Handles preparation and prosecution of patent applications in diverse mechanical and electro-mechanical technologies, including occupant safety devices, medical devices, power transmissions, and vehicle steering and suspension components.
**Personal:** Cleveland-Marshall College of Law, JD, 1979; St. John's College, BA, 1974.

## TAROLLI, Thomas
Tarolli, Sundheim, Covell, & Tummino LLP, Cleveland 216 621 2234
*Recommended in Intellectual Property*

## TARULLO, Michael
Schottenstein, Zox & Dunn, Columbus
614 462 2304
mtarullo@szd.com
*Recommended in Construction*
**Practice Areas:** Both a lawyer and an engineer, Mr Tarullo has almost 20 years of field experience in actual construction, construction-related businesses and field construction claims evaluation and preparation. Mr Tarullo currently services the construction industry through mediation, arbitration and litigation of multiple party disputes, bid protests, quality of work disputes, time impact and productivity claims.

## TEPLITZKY, Ronald J
Benesch, Friedlander, Coplan & Aronoff LLP, Cleveland 216 363 4433
rteplitzky@bfca.com
*Recommended in Banking & Finance*
**Practice Areas:** Bank and lender representation in senior and subordinated debt transactions, borrower representation, mergers and acquisitions, public offerings, and private placements of debt and equity. Loan transactions experience includes asset securitization, collateral issues, loan maintenance and modifications, loan documentation, mezzanine financings, and workouts and recapitalization.
**Career:** Chairman of the Loan Transactions Group and member of the firm's Executive Committee. Represents lenders and borrowers in senior and subordinated debt transactions ranging in size from $1 million to more than $150 million.

## TERP, Thomas
Taft, Stettinius & Hollister LLP, Cincinnati 513 381 2838
*Recommended in Environment*

## TOSI, Louis
Shumaker Loop & Kendrick LLP, Toledo
419 241 9000
*Recommended in Environment*

## TRAFFORD, Kathleen M
Porter Wright Morris & Arthur LLP, Columbus 614 227 1915
ktrafford@porterwright.com
*Recommended in Litigation*
**Practice Areas:** Litigation - appellate; banking and finance; commercial disputes; constitutional claims; healthcare; intellectual property; public utilities.
**Prof. Memberships:** American College of Trial Lawyers, Fellow; Columbus Bar Association, Board of Governors; Equal Justice Foundation, President; Board of Trustees; Federal Bar Association; Ohio State Bar Association.
**Career:** Admitted in Ohio; US Court of Appeals for the Sixth and District of Columbia Circuits; US District Court for Northern and Southern Districts of Ohio; Supreme Court of the United States.
**Personal:** JD (cum laude) Capital University Law School, 1979; Kent State University, MA, 1971; Nazareth College of Rochester, BA, 1970.

## TRAFFORD, Robert W
Porter Wright Morris & Arthur LLP, Columbus 614 227 2149
rtrafford@porterwright.com
*Recommended in Litigation*
**Practice Areas:** Serves as Managing Partner, concentrates practice in complex business litigation - including securities, attorney and accountant malpractice, takeovers, trade secrets, officer and director, constitutional law, public utility and other complex business litigation issues.
**Prof. Memberships:** American College

of Trial Lawyers, Fellow.
**Career:** Admitted in Ohio; US Supreme Court; US Court of Appeals: Fourth, Sixth & Ninth Circuits; US District Court - Northern & Southern Ohio; US District Court - Northern Texas; and US District Court -Eastern District, MI.
**Personal:** JD, The Ohio State University, 1977, Managing Editor, 'Ohio State Law Journal'; BA (distinction in Economics), The Ohio State University, 1974.

## TUCKER, Robert
Tucker Ellis & West LLP, Cleveland
216 696 1100
*Recommended in Litigation*

## VAN KLEY, Jack
Van Kley & Walker, Columbus
614 431 8900
*Recommended in Environment*

## VENESY, Bryan
Squire, Sanders & Dempsey L.L.P., Columbus 614 365 2708
bvenesy@ssd.com
*Recommended in Real Estate*
**Practice Areas:** Partner in the firm's Real Estate Practice with an emphasis on real estate finance, corporate finance, real estate matters, equity funds, low-income housing tax credits, rehabilitation tax credits, partnerships, joint ventures and general business matters. Represents lenders, investors, developers and tenants in regional, national and international transactions.
**Prof. Memberships:** Leadership Columbus, 2000 graduate; American Bar Association; Ohio State Bar Association; Columbus Bar Association.

## VICKERS, Thomas
Ulmer & Berne LLP, Cleveland
216 583 7000
*Recommended in Construction*

## VINCENT, George H
Dinsmore & Shohl LLP, Cincinnati
513 977 8367
george.vincent@dinslaw.com
*Recommended in Corporate/M&A*
**Practice Areas:** Chairs the firm's Corporate Department. Practices in the general corporate, transactional and securities law area, with significant experience in mergers and acquisitions, corporate governance matters and general corporate counseling. Clients include The Procter & Gamble Company, The Cincinnati Reds, Castellini Company, Eagle Hospitality, and The Midland Company Audit Committee.
**Prof. Memberships:** Currently serves as Chairman of the Hamilton County Republican Party and as Chairman of Cincinnati Museum Center.
**Career:** Joined firm in 1982; named Partner in 1988.
**Personal:** JD, University of Michigan Law School (1982); BA, University of Michigan (1979).

## VIVIANI, Gregory J
Squire, Sanders & Dempsey LLP, Cleveland 216 479 8622
gviviani@ssd.com
*Recommended in Employee Benefits*
**Practice Areas:** Partner focused on employee benefits law and related income tax matters including ERISA requirements, tax-qualified retirement plans, nonqualified deferred compensation plans, fringe benefits and employment taxes. Particularly experienced in matters relating to governmental bodies and tax exempt organizations. Listed in 'The Best Lawyers in America.' Frequent speaker at seminars held by the Ohio Association of School Business Officials, the Government Finance Officers Association and other organizations.
**Prof. Memberships:** American Bar Association's Section of Taxation and Worldwide Employee Benefits Network.

## WALKER, Christopher
Van Kley & Walker, Dayton
937 226 9000
*Recommended in Environment*

## WALLACE, David
Taft, Stettinius & Hollister LLP, Cleveland
216 241 2838
*Recommended in Construction*

## WALLACH, Mark
Calfee, Halter & Griswold LLP, Cleveland
216 622 8344
mwallach@calfee.com
*Recommended in Litigation*
**Practice Areas:** Business litigation; municipal litigation; accountants and consultants liability litigation; computer systems litigation; appellate practice; alternative dispute resolution proceedings.
**Prof. Memberships:** American, Ohio State, Federal and Cleveland Bar Associations; Cuyahoga County Law Directors Association; Association of Trial Lawyers of America.
**Career:** Co-Chair of the firm's Litigation Group. He litigates complex business and public sector disputes, and has particular expertise in representing corporations as plaintiffs. Has substantial trial and appellate advocacy experience.
**Personal:** Harvard Law School, JD, cum laude, 1974; Wesleyan University, BA, magna cum laude, Phi Beta Kappa, 1971.

## WAMPLER, Samuel
Bricker & Eckler LLP, Columbus
614 227 2300
*Recommended in Construction*

## WAMSLEY, James
Jones Day, Cleveland 216 586 7251
jlwamsleyiii@jonesday.com
*Recommended in Intellectual Property*
**Practice Areas:** Patent infringement and trade secrets litigation, typically involving electronics, semiconductors and/or software technology. Extensive experience in complex multi-jurisdiction,

multi-party and multi-patent infringement litigation involving parties based in the US, North America, Europe and/or Asia. Has represented clients in litigation matters throughout the US, including in US District Courts in Ohio, New York, New Jersey, Delaware, Michigan, Texas, California and Illinois, and in the US Court of Appeals for the Federal Circuit. Experienced in foreign discovery proceedings.
**Career:** Partner since 1985.
**Personal:** University of Michigan Law School (JD, 1975); University of Virginia (BSEE, 1972).

**WARD, Daniel**
Frantz Ward LLP, Cleveland
216 515 1660
*Recommended in Employment*

**WARNER, Charles**
Porter Wright Morris & Arthur LLP, Columbus 614 227 2013
cwarner@porterwright.com
*Recommended in Employment*
**Practice Areas:** Represents employers in connection with labor arbitrations, discrimination charges, employment contract issues, employment practices, and related tort and benefit claims. Extensive litigation experience includes defense of both opt-out and opt-in class actions.
**Prof. Memberships:** Fellow, College of Labor and Employment Lawyers; Management Chair, ABA EEO Committee, 2000-02; OSBA, Council of Delegates 1993-present; Columbus Bar Association, President 1991-92, Founding Chair, Labor and Employment Law Committee.
**Career:** Admitted in Ohio; Sixth Circuit; US District Court for Northern and Southern Districts of Ohio.
**Personal:** JD (cum laude), The Ohio State University, 1970; BA, Yale University, 1964.

**WARREN , Daniel**
Baker & Hostetler LLP, Cleveland
216 621 0200
*Recommended in Litigation*

**WEBER, Roger**
Taft, Stettinius & Hollister LLP, Cincinnati 513 381 2838
*Recommended in Employment*

**WEIBLE, Robert**
Baker & Hostetler LLP, Cleveland
216 621 0200
*Recommended in Corporate/M&A*

**WEINER, Samuel**
Samuel B Weiner Co. LPA, Columbus
614 443 6581
*Recommended in Litigation*

**WEIR, Bill**
Porter Wright Morris & Arthur LLP, Cleveland 216 443 2540
wweir@porterwright.com
*Recommended in Real Estate*
**Practice Areas:** Concentrates in the

areas of real estate lending, construction and permanent financing, and acquisitions and divestitures. Represents a variety of banks, insurance companies, savings and loans, as well as other financial institutions.
**Career:** Admitted in Ohio.
**Personal:** JD, Case Western Reserve University, 1984; BA, Northwestern University, 1981

**WEISS, Herbert**
Keating, Muething & Klekamp, PLL, Cincinnati 513 579 6400
*Recommended in Real Estate*

**WEISS, Mark**
Keating, Muething & Klekamp, PLL, Cincinnati 513 579 6400
*Recommended in Corporate/M&A*

**WELIN, Peter**
Thompson Hine LLP, Columbus
614 469 3269
Peter.Welin@ThompsonHine.com
*Recommended in Construction*
**Career:** Pete is a Partner in the firm's Construction Practice Group, focusing on public/private construction litigation, construction contracts and government procurement law. He participates in alternative dispute resolution, as a mediator, arbitrator, and as a member of a dispute resolution board involving a high profile public highway project. Pete is a member of Project Management Consultants, an affiliate of Thompson Hine, providing project representation, owner representation and partnering/facilitation services for construction clients and owners around the country. His background in construction engineering and understanding of the nuances of the building process aids immeasurably in the resolution of construction related disputes.

**WELLNER, John P**
Vorys, Sater, Seymour and Pease LLP, Columbus 614 464 5614
jpwellner@vssp.com
*Recommended in Real Estate*
**Practice Areas:** Administrative Partner of the firm's Commercial/Real Estate Group. Concentrates his practice in the general real estate and real estate development areas. Represents developers, ventures, owners, operators, borrowers and lenders in structuring and concluding the acquisition, sale, leasing, financing and development of commercial real estate.
**Prof. Memberships:** Columbus and Ohio State Bar Associations. International Council of Shopping Centers, Urban Land Institute, National Association of Industrial and Office Properties.
**Career:** Admitted to Ohio Bar 1979.
**Personal:** The Ohio State University College of Law, JD, Order of the Coif, with honors, 1979; Indiana University of Pennsylvania, BS in Business Administration, 1973.

**WELLS, Ben F**
Dinsmore & Shohl LLP, Cincinnati
513 977 8108
ben.wells@dinslaw.com
*Recommended in Employee Benefits*
**Practice Areas:** Retirement plans, health and welfare benefits, employee stock ownership plans, executive compensation.
**Prof. Memberships:** Cincinnati Bar Association, ESOP Association, National Center for Employee Ownership, Ohio Employee Ownership Center.
**Publications:** Mr Wells is a frequent author and lecturer on ESOP's and other employee benefits issues.

**WHITAKER, Glenn**
Vorys, Sater, Seymour and Pease LLP, Cincinnati 513 723 4608
gvwhitaker@vssp.com
*Recommended in Litigation*
**Practice Areas:** Partner focusing on complex litigation in areas of qui tam, false claims; environmental issues; construction law; toxic torts; healthcare fraud, abuse; government procurement, antitrust violations.
**Prof. Memberships:** American, Ohio, Cincinnati, Maryland and DC Bar Associations; Fellow, American College of Trial Lawyers; American Board of Trial Advocates; University of Cincinnati College of Law (Adjunct Professor); Potter Stewart American Inn of Court (Emeritus, Master of the Bench).
**Career:** Admitted to Maryland (1972), DC (1973), Ohio (1980).
**Personal:** Denison University, BA, magna cum laude, Phi Beta Kappa, 1969; George Washington University, JD, cum laude, Order of the Coif, 1972.

**WILKINSON, William**
Thompson Hine LLP, Columbus
614 469 3200
william.wilkinson@thompsonhine.com
*Recommended in Litigation*
**Career:** Bill is Vice-Chair of the firm's Business Litigation Practice Group. He handles civil trials, appeals, agency proceedings and investigations , often representing clients in the manufacturing and financial services industries. He also maintains a white-collar criminal defense practice, and has handled several such high-profile cases in Ohio. The subject matter of Bill's cases includes mergers and acquisitions, trade regulation, intellectual property, securities regulation, financial irregularities, election law, failed business relationships, bankruptcies, and fraud/RICO claims. Those cases have resulted in more than 50 published judicial decisions. He lectures frequently on trial practice and is named on numerous 'top lawyer' lists.

**WILSON, W Russell**
Frost Brown Todd LLC, Cincinnati
513 651 6733
rwilson@fbtlaw.com
*Recommended in Real Estate*
**Practice Areas:** Commercial Real Estate and Shopping Center Law.
**Prof. Memberships:** Admitted to practice Ohio 1983.
**Personal:** Born Cincinnati, Ohio, January 23, 1957. University of Cincinnati, JD, 1983, Princeton University, AB, 1980

**WINTERS, Karen A**
Squire, Sanders & Dempsey L.L.P., Columbus 614 365 2750
kwinters@ssd.com
*Recommended in Environment*
**Practice Areas:** Partner who leads the environmental activities in the Columbus office. Focuses on state and federal litigation, administrative law practice before state and federal agencies, corporate and municipal counseling, and government relations and legislative counseling.
**Prof. Memberships:** Ohio State Bar Association, Environmental Law Committee and Board of Governors of the Section on Women in the Profession; Columbus Bar Association, Environmental Law Committee; Ohio Chamber of Commerce, Energy and Environment Committee and Executive Committee.

**WOLFF, Robert M**
Duvin, Cahn & Hutton, Cleveland
216 696 7600
rwolff@duvin.com
*Recommended in Employment*
**Practice Areas:** Represents clients in general litigation, with an emphasis on employment, civil rights, public sector and commercial litigation. He maintains an active trial schedule and has successfully tried wrongful death, age, race, disability, and sex discrimination, trade secret, legal malpractice defense and major civil rights class actions in addition to numerous arbitrations, and has successfully argued many cases before the Ohio Supreme Court and the US Court of Appeals.
**Career:** Partner since 1992. Chairman of firm's Management Committee since 1998. Prior to joining firm, he was the Chief Labor and Employment Counsel, City of Cleveland.
**Personal:** Oberlin College (BA 1977); University of Illinois (JD, cum laude, 1980), editor, Law Review, Harno Scholar, Illinois Governors Fellow. Currently, Trustee and Program Chair, National Conference for Community and Justice; Chair, Northeast Ohio Interfaith Task Force; Vice-Chair and Trustee, Multiple Schlerosis Society of Northeast Ohio; Visiting Committee, Cleveland Marshall College of Law; and Trustee, The Temple Tifereth Israel.

**WOOLEY, James**
Baker & Hostetler LLP, Cleveland
216 621 0200
*Recommended in Litigation*

**YOUNG, David J**
Squire, Sanders & Dempsey L.L.P.,
Columbus 614 365 2826
djyoung@ssd.com
*Recommended in Litigation*
**Practice Areas:** Senior Counsel with
more than 45 years litigation experience.
Focuses on complex health care and class
action litigation, defense of law firms in
malpractice cases and expansive federal
law casework involving litigation before
the US Supreme Court. Listed in 'The
Best Lawyers in America'; named by
'Ohio Lawyer' as one of the Five Best Trial
Lawyers in Ohio. Voted an Ohio top 10
lawyer by 'Cincinnati' magazine.
**Prof. Memberships:** American Arbitration Association, neutral arbitrator; Ohio
Supreme Court Rules Advisory Committee, Chairman; American College of Trial
Lawyers, fellow; former Judge Advocate
and Captain in the US Air Force.

**YUND, George**
Frost Brown Todd LLC, Cincinnati
513 651 6824
gyund@fbtlaw.com
*Recommended in Employment*
**Practice Areas:** Labor and employment
litigation in federal courts and agencies
throughout the country, ERISA litigation,
labor arbitrations and negotiations,
claims against unions for strike-related
misconduct.
**Prof. Memberships:** Ohio and United
States Supreme Court; Courts of Appeals
for the Fourth, Sixth, Ninth, Eleventh and
DC Circuits.
**Career:** Joined Frost Brown Todd's predecessor firm, Frost & Jacobs, in 1977;
Partner 1984; Member, Frost Brown
Todd Compensation Committee.
**Personal:** Born 15 April 1952. JD (cum
laude), University of Michigan School of
Law, 1977; BA, The Ohio State University,
1974, (summa cum laude).

**ZAGORE, David A**
Squire, Sanders & Dempsey LLP,
Cleveland 216 479 8610
dzagore@ssd.com
*Recommended in Corporate/M&A*
**Practice Areas:** Partner who leads the
firm's Midwest offices' Corporate Finance
Practice. Clients include Boards of Direc-
tors of both public and private compa-
nies in connection with mergers, acquisitions and change of control matters. List-
ed in 'The Best Lawyers in America'; one
of 78 lawyers worldwide listed in BTI
Consulting Group's 2001 survey of For-
tune 1000 corporate counsel as providing
superior client service.
**Prof. Memberships:** American Bar
Association, Business Law Section; Ohio
State Bar Association, Corporation Law
Committee; Cleveland Bar Association,
Securities Law Section; Tender Offer Subcommittee, chair; Division of Securities
of the State of Ohio, Takeover Advisory
Committee, Co-Chair.

**ZEIGER, John**
Zeiger, Tigges, Little & Lindsmith LLP,
Columbus 614 365 9900
*Recommended in Litigation*

# BENESCH, FRIEDLANDER, COPLAN & ARONOFF LLP

## THE FIRM

**Managing Partner:** James M Hill
**Chief Operating Officer:** John H Banks II

**Number of partners:** 60
**Number of other lawyers:** 58

**FIRM OVERVIEW:** Benesch, Friedlander, Coplan & Aronoff LLP's national client base includes public, middle market and emerging companies as well as public entities, entrepreneurs, non-profit organizations, trusts and estates.

## MAIN AREAS OF PRACTICE:

**Business Reorganization:** Diligently represent banks and creditors' committees in chapter 11 reorganizations; distressed businesses; trustees for operating bankruptcy estates; equity security holder committees; hedge funds; distressed private equity firms. Attorneys in this group have exceptional knowledge and experience in matters including bankruptcy and restructurings.

**China:** Assist US companies in establishment of China-related strategic alliances and joint ventures for manufacturing, distribution, and business operations in China, and acquire shares or assets of China-based companies, among other services. In 2005, Benesch established a wholly owned subsidiary, Benesch Pacific LLC, which has opened a representative office in Shanghai to better serve clients.

**Construction:** Represent owners, contractors and design professionals in all facets of the industry and work with projects ranging from $.5 million to $1 billion. The practice is comprised of several attorneys who have received AV ratings from Martindale-Hubbell, and who routinely act as arbitrators and mediators for organizations including the American Arbitration Association.

**Corporate & Securities:** Represent business interests in traditional corporate and transactional work including mergers, acquisitions, divestitures, recapitalizations, restructurings, joint ventures, strategic alliances, licensing, and franchise arrangements.

**Employee Benefits & Compensation:** Offer cutting edge counsel on deferred compensation techniques, present clients with highly specialized benefits/tax litigation, design executive compensation arrangements for public and private businesses, focus on sophisticated qualified retirement plan issues and assist in tax advice with an eye towards improved employee relations and corporate risk management.

**Estate Planning & Probate:** Counsel on estate and trust administrations, gift and estate taxation, charitable planned giving, business succession planning, guardianships, and disputes over wills and trusts.

**Healthcare:** Represent healthcare providers, payors, managed care organizations and lenders in a broad range of transactional, financing, regulatory, and reimbursement matters. Represent private equity and venture capital firms in healthcare regulatory and transactional matters.

**Intellectual Property:** A specialized team of attorneys, including engineers and musicians, who secure and enforce patent, trademark, copyright, and trade secret rights. Additionally counsel on matters such as intellectual property validity and infringement, valuations, licensing and technology transfer, and technology-related antitrust issues.

**Labor & Employment; Immigration:** Provide representation in collective bargaining, arbitration, NLRB and SERB hearings, litigation of employment related matters, immigration matters, and workers' compensation defense. Counsel on complying with wage and hour laws, FMLA, ADA, COBRA, OSHA, EEOC, and DOL.

**Loan Transactions:** Represent banks and other financial institutions in commercial loan and financing transactions and provide representation in such matters as loan documentation, senior and subordinated debt, loan workouts, securitizations, letters of credit, and other lending transactions.

**Polymer, Plastics, & Packaging:** Provide access to needed capital, manage human and intellectual property assets, counsel regarding environmental regulations, and represent in complex litigation.

**HEAD OFFICE**

**OHIO**
2300 BP Tower, 200 Public Square, **Cleveland,** OH 44114
**Tel:** 216 363 4500   **Fax:** 216 363 4588
**Website:** www.bfca.com

**BRANCH OFFICE**

**OHIO**
88 East Broad Street, Suite 900, **Columbus,** OH 43215
**Tel:** 614 223 9300   **Fax:** 614 223 9330

**Private Equity:** Significant regional and national experience in representing the unique needs of private equity firms, including leverage buyout firms, mezzanine funds, and venture capital funds, paired with a focus on middle-market companies creates an ideal partnership between the attorneys in this group and private equity firms. Individual specialties of attorneys include corporate finance, securities, and mergers and acquisitions.

**Public Law/Government Relations:** Registered representation on behalf of clients before local, state, and federal legislative bodies and executive branch decision makers, as well as representation before regulatory and administrative agencies and of public entities.

**Real Estate & Environmental:** Represent landlords, tenants, owners, developers, lenders, and borrowers in acquisitions, development, financing, leasing, construction, and management of real property including shopping centers; commercial, industrial, and office developments; hotels; recreational facilities; and condominium and residential developments.

**Tax:** Tax planning and evaluation related to corporate reorganizations and restructurings, acquisitions, dispositions, debt and equity financings, start-up ventures, tax free exchanges and leasing arrangements.

**Transportation & Logistics:** Concentrate on the needs of users and providers of logistics services in areas such as negotiating an operating contract, pursuing or defending a cargo claim, dealing with government regulations, developing a strategic alliance, or financing an acquisition.

**Trial:** Represent clients in courtroom litigation and dispute resolution including business contract disputes, product liability claims, transportation distributorship and franchise, officer and director liability, takeovers and mergers, insurance coverage disputes, building construction and real estate disputes, professional liability, environmental liability, and unfair competition matters.

# CALFEE, HALTER & GRISWOLD LLP

## THE FIRM

**Managing Partner:** Brent D Ballard
**Co-Chairmen:** Thomas F McKee, Thomas E Wagner

**Number of partners:** 85
**Number of other lawyers:** 109

**FIRM OVERVIEW:** Founded in 1903, Calfee is one of the largest law firms in Ohio and provides a full range of legal services in all substantive areas of law through the US and abroad. With over 200 professionals, services encompass the entire spectrum of general business law - from M&A and litigation, to commercial finance and international, to real estate and intellectual property. Lobbying and government relations services are provided by Thomas Green & Associates LLC, a wholly owned subsidiary of the firm. Representing many Fortune 500 companies, Calfee has been named one of the best corporate law firms in America by Corporate Board Member magazine.

## MAIN AREAS OF PRACTICE:

**Antitrust & Trade Regulation:** Represents clients on antitrust matters in every procedural context before the Federal Trade Commission, US Department of Justice, and in state and federal courts on complex civil and criminal litigation.

**Bankruptcy & Creditors' Rights:** Services involve all aspects of bankruptcy, corporate reorganization, workout and creditors' rights matters including complex bankruptcy proceedings, debt restructurings and purchases and sales of financially troubled businesses.

**Commercial Business & Finance:** Counsels financial institutions and borrowers in analyzing, structuring, documenting and negotiating all aspects of finance in private, public, syndicated, international and governmental settings.

**Construction:** Assists in the strategic development of all phases of the project from development, site selection, contract draftmanship and administration, to performance issues, contract completion and disputes. Provides counsel to all levels, from owners, contractors, and subcontractors to design professionals such as engineers and architects.

**Corporate Succession Planning:** Helps privately held companies prepare for and transition to the next generation of owners and managers by offering solutions that increase survival opportunities, ensure estate liquidity, address family issues, and maximize planning flexibility.

**Employee Benefits & Executive Compensation:** Represents clients in all phases of designing and administering employee benefit and retirement programs including design and implementation of sophisticated executive compensation programs, ESOPs and ERISA litigation.

**Environmental:** Represents clients on matters of compliance, proposed rules and changes, business strategies, and objectives for dealing with environmental regulations and agencies.

**Estate & Succession Planning:** Assists clients in developing and implementing comprehensive estate plans, probate and trust administration, litigation services and asset protection planning counsel.

**General Corporate:** Services a variety of public and private businesses at all stages, investors and entrepreneurs on all aspects of entity selection, capital formation, contractual arrangements, and major transactions.

**Government Relations & Legislation:** Represents clients in legislative, lobbying, contract, regulatory and administrative matters before federal, state and local governmental entities in legislative, lobbying, contract, regulatory and administrative matters.

**Health & Long-Term Care/HIPAA:** Represents long-term care providers ranging from multi-level retirement communities, to hospital-based skilled nursing units to non-profit and proprietary nursing home operators.

**Information Technology:** Works with IT clients ranging from start-ups to Fortune 100 companies, vendors and buyers, and from 'bleeding edge' to more traditional enterprises.

### HEAD OFFICE

**OHIO**
1400 McDonald Investment Center, 800 Superior Avenue, **Cleveland,** OH 44114
**Tel:** 216 622 8200  **Fax:** 216 241 0816
**Website:** www.calfee.com

### BRANCH OFFICE

**OHIO**
1100 Fifth Third Center, 21 East State Street, **Columbus,** OH 43215-4243
**Tel:** 614 621 1500  **Fax:** 614 621 0010

**Insurance Coverage:** Assists in obtaining coverage under numerous types of policies. Represents public and private companies, private equity funds, captive insurance programs, and individual policyholders in evaluating and enhancing insurance coverage and in resolving disputes.

**Intellectual Property/BioScience/Technology Transfer:** One of the largest practices in a general firm within the Midwest. Consists of more than 35 attorneys, 30 of whom are registered to practice before the US Patent and Trademark Office. Provides the full range of prosecution, maintenance and litigation services.

**Labor & Employment:** Besides day-to-day employment counseling, handles administrative complaints and litigation concerning state and federal discrimination laws, National Labor Relations Act, Family & Medical Leave Act, Fair Labor Standards Act and state workers' compensation systems.

**Litigation:** Skilled in all areas of complex business litigation including IP litigation and other specialized areas, and works to meet client objectives by developing strategies to resolve business conflicts through the traditional legal process or alternative methods of dispute resolution.

**Mergers & Acquisitions:** Spans the entire spectrum of taxable and non-taxable transfers of private and public companies, as well as the structuring and funding of strategic alliances and other joint ventures.

**Private Investment Funds:** Represents issuers and investors in every type and aspect of a transaction, whether categorized as fund formation, venture capital or other private equity investments, or leveraged-buyout transactions.

**Public Law & Finance:** Assists community development projects from the drawing board to completion and assists clients in developing programs that are models of public and private sector collaboration.

**Real Estate:** Represents a wide range of clients in connection with matters related to the acquisition, disposition, construction, development, leasing and financing of real property assets.

**Securities & Capital Markets:** Nationally recognized as representing issuers and underwriters in more than 75 public offerings raising more than $5 billion over the last 10 years. Assists clients with public and private offerings of securities, regulatory compliance and reporting, proxy solicitations, tender offers and securities litigation.

**Tax:** Provides comprehensive tax law representation and planning for publicly held companies, privately held businesses, not-for-profit corporations, trusts, partnerships, associations and individuals.

**Workers' Compensation & OSHA:** Represents employers facing every conceivable workers' compensation, OSHA and related employer liability concern.

**INTERNATIONAL WORK:** Offers a broad range of services to companies transacting business across the border or overseas and to those venturing into the United States. To enhance the firm's scope of services, Calfee is a founding member of Lex Mundi, a worldwide consortium of more than 160 independent law firms.

# DINSMORE & SHOHL LLP

## THE FIRM

**Managing Partner:** Clifford A Roe, Jr
**Number of partners:** 135
**Total number of attorneys:** 286

**FIRM OVERVIEW:** Dinsmore & Shohl LLP is a full-service law firm with over 280 attorneys practicing in eight offices in four states. For 98 years Dinsmore & Shohl has provided a broad range of integrated services to meet the needs of both large and small businesses as well as institutions, associations, governments, professional firms and individuals. The firm has been named one of the best corporate law firms in America in an annual survey conducted by Corporate Board Member magazine. Dinsmore & Shohl offers counsel in the following areas of law: business and corporate, bankruptcy, employee benefits, environmental, family wealth planning, first amendment and media, general commercial and specialty litigation, intellectual property, international, labor and employment, mass tort and medical litigation, real estate and commercial finance.

## MAIN AREAS OF PRACTICE:

**Corporate/Securities:** Dinsmore & Shohl provides a full range of transactional, regulatory and other advisory services to the firm's regional, national and international business clients. The firm handles business formation and organization; corporate finance; federal and state securities law; federal, state and local tax law; real estate; employee and executive benefits; trust and estate planning; probate; banking; commercial law; mergers and acquisitions; venture capital; partnerships; limited liability companies and joint ventures.

**General Commercial & Specialty Litigation:** Dinsmore & Shohl attorneys practice on a local and regional basis at the trial, appellate and Supreme Court levels in federal and state courts as well as before a wide variety of governmental agencies. The firm also has broad experience in coordinating and defending lawsuits on a national basis. The firm has represented scores of manufacturers in cases filed in various state and federal courts throughout the United States. Attorneys are trained in medicine, nursing, pharmacy, x-ray technology, toxicology and engineering. The firm has represented manufacturers of a wide variety of products in a myriad of markets including automotive, ethical pharmaceutical, household products and appliances, manufacturing/industrial, medical/device, recreational, tobacco, and toxic.

**Labor & Employment:** The firm handles all phases of labor and employment issues including collective bargaining, employment discrimination, sexual harassment, OSHA inspections, workers' compensation, arbitration, alternative dispute resolution, wage and hour, immigration, and class action litigation. The firm represents clients before federal, state, and local administrative agencies, including the EEOC and the NLRB.

**Intellectual Property:** Dinsmore & Shohl's full-service practice group includes a diverse range of technical backgrounds and legal experience to efficiently and effectively respond to client needs. The group's continually expanding worldwide practice includes substantial experience with respect to all areas of intellectual property law including: patents, trademarks, trade names, service marks, copyrights, computer software and hardware, business method and internet-related developments, trade secrets, trade dress, antitrust, unfair trade practices, unfair competition and franchising matters. Dinsmore & Shohl was named one of the top patent and top trademark firms by Intellectual Property Today.

**CLIENTS:** The firm represents clients in the following industries: banking, biotechnology, coal, communications, construction, consumer goods, education, healthcare, high tech, manufacturing, pharmaceuticals, real estate development, retail, software development, telecommunications, transportation and utilities. Representative clients include Arch Coal, Inc.; Allstate; Beverly Enterprises, Inc.; Castellini Company; Chemed Corporation; Cincinnati Children's Hospital Medical Center; Clopay Corporation; Dover Resources Division/OPW Fueling Components; General Electric; General Motors Corp.; Halma PLC; Host Communications, Inc.; Huffy Corporation; International Flavors and Fragrances,

## HEAD OFFICE

**OHIO**
255 East Fifth Street, Suite 1900, **Cincinnati**, OH 45202
**Tel:** 513 977 8200 **Fax:** 513 977 8141
**Email:** info@dinslaw.com
**Website:** www.dinslaw.com

## BRANCH OFFICES

**KENTUCKY**
Lexington Financial Center, 250 West Main Street, Suite 1400, **Lexington**, KY 40507
**Tel:** 859 425 1000 **Fax:** 859 425 1099

1400 PNC Plaza, 500 West Jefferson Street, **Louisville**, KY 40202
**Tel:** 502 540 2300 **Fax:** 502 585 2207

**OHIO**
175 South Third Street, **Columbus**, OH 43215
**Tel:** 614 628 6880 **Fax:** 614 628 6890

One Dayton Centre, One South Main Street, Suite 1300, **Dayton**, OH 45402
**Tel:** 937 449 6400 **Fax:** 937 449 6405

**PENNSYLVANIA**
The Grant Building, 330 Grant Street, Suite 2415, **Pittsburgh**, PA 15219
**Tel:** 412 281 5000 **Fax:** 412 281 50550

**WEST VIRGINIA**
900 Lee Street, Huntington Square, Suite 600, **Charleston**, WV 25301
**Tel:** 304 357 0900 **Fax:** 304 357 0919

2604 Cranberry Square, **Morgantown** WV 26508
**Tel:** 304 594 4125 **Fax:** 304 594 4127

## CONTACTS

| | |
|---|---|
| Bankruptcy | Kim Martin Lewis |
| Corporate/Securities | George H Vincent |
| Employee Benefits | Ben F Wells |
| Environmental | Vincent B Stamp |
| Family Wealth Planning | J Michael Cooney |
| General Commercial & Specialty Litigation | Mark A Vander Laan |
| Intellectual Property | James F Gottman |
| Labor & Employment | Charles M Roesch |
| Mass Tort/Medical Litigation | Frank C Woodside, III |
| Real Estate/Commercial Finance | Thomas J Sherman |
| Workers' Compensation | George B Wilkinson |

Inc.; Jeffrey R. Anderson Real Estate, Inc.; Jewish Hospital Healthcare Services, Inc.; Kentucky Technology, Inc.; Lenscrafters; Liberty Mutual Insurance Co.; Milacron, Inc.; Peabody Energy; Pressley Ridge West Virginia; Progress Energy; Sherwin Williams; The Courier-Journal; The Kroger Co.; The Procter & Gamble Co.; The Standard Register Company; The U.S. Playing Card Co.; United Dairy Farmers; US Bank.

**INTERNATIONAL WORK:** Dinsmore & Shohl represents public and private companies and individuals in a wide range of international transactions and efficiently solves the unique legal, tax and practical issues confronting clients in their foreign dealings. Based on years of repeated collaboration, the firm has also established and maintained close working relationships with several foreign and domestic firms. Dinsmore & Shohl is a founding member of ALFA International, an international network of 120 independently owned law firms.

# DUVIN, CAHN & HUTTON

## THE FIRM

**Managing Partner:** Robert M Wolff
**Senior Partner:** Robert P Duvin

**Number of partners:** 25
**Number of other lawyers:** 24

**FIRM OVERVIEW:** Since the firm's founding in 1972, Duvin, Cahn & Hutton has been recognized as one of the nation's pre-eminent labor and employment law firms. The firm has a nationwide practice in labor relations, employment law and complex commercial litigation.

## MAIN AREAS OF PRACTICE:

**Labor Relations:** The historic foundation of the firm is the Labor Relations Practice which cemented the image of Duvin, Cahn & Hutton as tenacious advocates, securing concessions in collective bargaining. In addition to negotiating major collective bargaining agreements for both private and public sector clients, the firm's attorneys are continuously consulted on the administration of collective bargaining agreements and handle contract arbitrations. The practice also includes extensive union-related litigation before state and Federal courts and administrative agencies. The firm also engages in extensive union organizing counseling and all related litigation.

**Employment Law:** The firm's practice is nationwide including full-service counseling and an active litigation practice in the defense of class actions, employment discrimination, employee privacy issues, wrongful discharge, employment related torts, employee benefits, wage and hour issues, OSHA and workers' compensation.

**Commercial Litigation:** The firm handles complex contract disputes in both private industry and government, securities litigation, anti-trust actions, defense of legal malpractice claims and unfair competition claims.

**CLIENTS:** Duvin, Cahn & Hutton represents both private and public sector clients in the retail, food, industrial, healthcare, musical arts, sports, and financial industries nationwide.

**Representative Firm Clients:** Cleveland Clinic Foundation; Alcan; City of Cleveland; Avery Dennison; Cleveland Browns; Cleveland Orchestra; Continental Airlines; Dominion East Ohio Gas; Electrolux Home Products; Forest City Enterprises; Goldschmidt Chemical; Goodyear Tire & Rubber Company; Lincoln Electric; MBNA; McDonald's; Boise Office Products/OfficeMax; SBC Communications.

## HEAD OFFICE

**OHIO**
Erieview Tower 20th Floor, 1301 E. 9th Street, **Cleveland**, OH 44114
**Tel:** 216 696 7600   **Fax:** 216 696 2038
**Website:** www.duvinlaw.com
**Email:** attorneys@duvin.com

## CONTACTS

| | |
|---|---|
| **Labor** | Robert P Duvin |
| | Frank W Buck |
| **Union Avoidance** | Andrew C Meyer |
| | Stephen J Sferra |
| **Employment** | Lee J Hutton |
| | Sue Marie Douglas |
| **Commercial Litigation** | James F Koehler |
| **OSHA** | Kenneth B Stark |
| **Employee Benefits** | Neal B Wainblat |

# FAY SHARPE FAGAN MINNICH & MCKEE LLP

## THE FIRM

**Management Committee:** Timothy E Nauman, Joseph D Dreher

**Number of Partners:** 20
**Number of other lawyers:** 22
**Number of Registered Patent Agents:** 44

### HEAD OFFICE

**OHIO**
1100 Superior Avenue, 7th Floor, **Cleveland**, OH 44114
**Tel:** 216 861 5582   **Fax:** 216 241 1666
**Email:** fs@faysharpe.com
**Website:** www.faysharpe.com

**FIRM OVERVIEW:** Fay Sharpe has focused on supporting the technology advancements of its clients and safeguarding intellectual property rights since 1884. The firm is one of the largest intellectual property specialty firms in the Midwest with IP attorneys, technical consultants, and a worldwide network of intellectual property resources covering biotechnology, chemistry, engineering, physics, computer science and virtually every technology in between.

## MAIN AREAS OF PRACTICE:

Fay Sharpe offers a complete range of IP legal services and capabilities designed to protect and enhance intellectual property. These services focus on:

**Patents:** To protect a patentable concept or to avoid infringement upon another's patented concept, Fay Sharpe conducts patent searches and studies; renders patentability, patent validity and patent infringement opinions; and prepares, files and prosecutes patent applications (utility and design) before the US Patent and Trademark Office (USPTO), and around the world through their network of foreign associates. For 2004 (the latest year rankings are available) Fay Sharpe was ranked by *IP Today* 46th in the US for utility patents issued.

**Trademarks & Service Marks:** Fay Sharpe helps its clients safeguard their trademarks and service marks through counseling on selection, design and use; rendering opinions concerning trademark infringement and registration of trademarks and service marks; preparing, filing and prosecuting applications for registration of trademarks and service marks before the USPTO, state and foreign administrative offices; and representing clients in trademark opposition and cancellation proceedings in the USPTO and foreign administrative offices. For 2004 (the latest year rankings are available), Fay Sharpe was ranked by Name-Protect 96th in the US and first in Cleveland for trademarks registered.

**Copyrights:** Fay Sharpe counsels its clients on copyright protection for their literary, dramatic, musical, artistic works and computer software; and prepares, files and prosecutes applications to federally register copyright.

**Trade Secrets:** Often trade secret protection is the only viable way of protecting intellectual property, especially where patent or copyright protection is not applicable. In these cases Fay Sharpe counsels clients in protection and commercial exploitation of trade secrets and prepares confidentiality agreements.

**Licensing of Intellectual Property:** Fay Sharpe supports the commercial exploitation of intellectual property by counseling its clients on patent, trademark, copyright and know-how licensing agreements, contracts for high technology enterprises, software licenses, and consulting agreements; and analyzing the antitrust implications of licensing.

**Litigation:** Fay Sharpe's litigators represent both plaintiffs and defendants in state and federal court and before state and federal agencies. Fay Sharpe's litigation services include patent infringement and patent interferences; trademark and service mark infringement; trademark opposition and cancellation proceedings; deceptive business practices; copyright infringement; unfair competition; misappropriation of trade secrets and confidential information; intellectual property related antitrust issues; license agreement disputes; employee contract disputes and actions before the International Trade Commission.

**CLIENTS:** Fay Sharpe clients represent some of the top names in technology and innovation, spanning Fortune 500 and mid-level companies to emerging technology start-ups and individual pacesetters.

**Patents & Technology:** Some representative patents, and their root technology, prepared and prosecuted by Fay Sharpe include:

**Electrical:** GELcore LLC - US6799864 - High power LED power pack for spot module illumination; General Electric Company - US6809477 - Fluorescent lamp electrode for instant start circuits; Koninklijke Philips Electronics, N.V. - US6804546 - Multiple contrast echo-planar imaging for contrast-enhanced imaging; Lincoln Global, Inc. - US6717108 - Electric arc welder and method of designing waveforms therefor; Lucent Technologies Inc. - US6538416 - Border gateway reservation protocol for tree-based aggregation of inter-domain reservations; Xerox Corporation - US6819792 - Automatic detection of colorimetry of unknown CMYK images.

**Mechanical:** Argo-Tech Corporation - US6810674 - Fuel delivery system; Barnes Group Inc. - US6773002 - Compression spring rod; Cloyes Gear and Products, Inc. - US6761657 - Roller chain sprocket with added chordal pitch reduction; Henkel Consumer Adhesives, Inc. - US6579587 - Paint masking for corners; Nu-Kote International, Inc. - US6814433 - Base aperture in ink jet cartridge with irregular edges for breaking surface tension of the ink; Royal Appliance Mfg. Co. - US6735815 - Upright vacuum cleaner with cyclonic air flow; Steris Inc. - US6582654 - Fluid spray system for cleaning and sterilizing medical devices supported on a rack.

**Chemical/Biotech:** BioStratum, Inc. - US6576418 - Method for determining the nucleotide sequence of the gene for the _5(IV) chain of human type IV collagen; Bonne Bell, Inc. - US6723307 - Cosmetic lip product with sour flavor; Case Western Reserve University - US6586561 - Rigid rod ion conducting copolymers; The Clorox Company - US6825158 - Bactericidal cleaning wipe comprising a cationic biocide; Cooper Technology Services, LLC - US6800691 - Blend of EPDM and SBR using an EPDM of different origin as a compatibilizer; Omnova Solutions Inc. - US6793861 - Optimization of in-mold coating injection molded thermoplastic substrates; Spalding Sports Worldwide, Inc. - US6394913 - Multilayer golf ball; Xerox Corporation - US6770904 - Polythiophenes and electronic devices generated therefrom.

**Reported Cases:** Antonious v Spalding & Evenflo Cos., Inc., 281 F.3d 1258 (Fed. Cir. 2002); Microsoft Corp. v Action Software, 136 F.Supp.2d 735 (N.D. Ohio 2001); Dolly, Inc. v Spalding & Evenflo Cos., 16 F.3d 394 (Fed. Cir. 1994); Vanmoor v Wal-Mart Stores, Inc., 201 F.3d 1363 (Fed. Cir 2000); Hoover Co. v Royal Appliance Manufacturing Co., 238 F.3d1357 (Fed. Cir. 2001); Sherwin-Williams Co. v Glidden Co., 49 USPQ2d 1623 (N.D. Ohio 1998).

Fay Sharpe — WE PROTECT YOUR IDEAS.

# PORTER WRIGHT MORRIS & ARTHUR LLP

## THE FIRM

**Managing Partner:** Robert W Trafford

**Number of partners:** 153
**Number of other lawyers:** 160

**FIRM OVERVIEW:** Porter Wright Morris & Arthur LLP is a nationally recognized law firm that traces its origins to 1846 in Ohio. With 313 lawyers, the firm brings together the knowledge, skills, and experience to represent its clients effectively and efficiently with complex legal problems and business opportunities.

## MAIN AREAS OF PRACTICE:

**Antitrust & Trade Regulation:** The firm provides analysis, counseling, litigation, and alternative dispute resolution support on complex antitrust issues.

**Business & Securities:** From business formation to mergers and acquisitions, the firm provides full-service counseling and advice to domestic and international enterprises.

**Construction:** The firm represents clients in construction-related issues ranging from labor disputes to construction contracts and claims.

**Employee Benefits:** Porter Wright provides legal counsel on all aspects of employee benefits, including ERISA, benefits plan design and implementation, audits, and litigation.

**Environmental Law:** Porter Wright works with clients on permitting, compliance, planning, and enforcement matters, including EPCRA, Superfund, and environmental assessment and remediation.

**Finance & Commerce:** The firm represents clients in financing and credit arrangements and related commercial transactions, including bankruptcy, creditors' rights, lease/loan financing, and workouts.

**Financial Institutions:** The firm works with clients on matters from federal/state regulations to M&A, trust administration, real estate acquisitions, and loan/deposit products.

**Government Contracts:** Porter Wright assists clients with government contract matters, including contract negotiations, DCAA audits, debarment/suspension, defective pricing, and protests/claims.

**Governmental Affairs:** Porter Wright represents clients in administrative and legislative matters such as legislation drafting/tracking; lobbying; and legislative, hearing, or regulatory representation.

**Healthcare:** The firm offers comprehensive healthcare-related legal services, in matters relating to licensing; compliance plans/audits; physician practice groups/organizations; hospital and long-term care facilities; financing; and fraud/abuse, Stark, HIPAA, antikickback, and false claims regulations.

**Immigration:** Porter Wright represents clients on immigration matters, including temporary employment visas, national interest waivers, priority worker immigrant visa petitions, and permanent resident applications.

**Insurance & Financial Services:** Porter Wright represents clients in litigation/arbitration, market conduct, M&A, reinsurance, regulatory, and investment matters.

**Intellectual Property:** The firm assists clients in obtaining and preserving/protecting trademark, copyright, and patent protection.

**Labor & Employment:** The firm represents clients in matters regarding executive contracts, OSHA/MSHA, affirmative action, arbitrations, and union contract negotiations, and provides representation in employment litigation ranging from employment discrimination class actions to proceedings before state and federal oversight agencies.

**Litigation:** Porter Wright represents clients at pretrial, trial, and appellate litigation in federal and state courts, before regulatory agencies and arbitration panels, and in alternative dispute resolution.

**Real Estate:** Porter Wright represents clients in commercial real estate, including acquisition/development, fair housing, architect/contractor agreements, and industrial revenue bonds.

**Tax:** The firm provides services in federal, state, local, and international taxation, ranging from business/entity planning and tax disputes to tax credits.

**Technology:** Porter Wright assists clients with technology issues and transactions, including acquisition/licensing, security, Web contracts, and e-business.

**Trusts & Estates:** The firm assists clients with business enterprise transfer of management and control, as well as property interest transfers through wills, trusts, family limited partnerships and LLCs, durable powers of attorney, and charitable remainder trusts.

**Utilities & Energy:** Porter Wright represents utilities clients in areas ranging from competitive complaint cases to market entry or restructuring, power siting, and rulemaking proceedings.

**White Collar Crime/Government Enforcement:** From compliance counseling to grand jury and agency investigations, internal investigations, and victim representation/fraud recovery, Porter Wright represents clients whose operations and activities are placed under government scrutiny or are the subject of governmental enforcement actions.

**INTERNATIONAL WORK:** Porter Wright performs a wide range of international legal services. The firm has gained an international standing and capability before the European Union.

## HEAD OFFICE

**OHIO**
41 South High Street, **Columbus,** OH 43215
**Tel:** 614 227 2000 **Fax:** 614 227 2100
**Email:** columbus@porterwright.com
**Website:** www.porterwright.com

## BRANCH OFFICES

**DISTRICT OF COLUMBIA**
1919 Pennsylvania Avenue N.W., Suite 500, **Washington,** DC 20006
**Tel:** 202 778 3000 **Fax:** 202 778 3063
**Email:** washington@porterwright.com

**FLORIDA**
5801 Pelican Bay Boulevard, Suite 300, **Naples,** FL 34108
**Tel:** 239 593 2900 **Fax:** 239 593 2990
**Email:** naples@porterwright.com

**OHIO**
250 East Fifth Street, Suite 2200, **Cincinnati,** OH 45202
**Tel:** 513 381 4700 **Fax:** 513 421 0991
**Email:** cincinnati@porterwright.com

925 Euclid Avenue, Suite 1700, **Cleveland,** OH 44115
**Tel:** 216 443 9000 **Fax:** 216 443 9011
**Email:** cleveland@porterwright.com

One Dayton Centre, One South Main Street, Suite 1600
**Dayton,** OH 45402
**Tel:** 937 449 6810 **Fax:** 937 449 6820
**Email:** dayton@porterwright.com

**PORTER WRIGHT MORRIS & ARTHUR** LLP
**Attorneys and Counselors at Law**

# SCHOTTENSTEIN ZOX & DUNN

## THE FIRM

**Managing Partner:** James E Davidson
**Number of partners:** 65
**Number of associates:** 46

**FIRM OVERVIEW:** Schottenstein Zox & Dunn prides itself on being an innovative and responsive law firm dedicated to partnering with its clients to ensure the fulfillment of each client's business objectives. An exemplary corporate citizen in the communities it serves, the firm is committed to improving the way law is practiced by leveraging its strong entrepreneurial bias, business experience, superior legal talent, and advanced technologies to enhance the growth and business success of its clients.

## MAIN AREAS OF PRACTICE:

**Banking & Finance:** Provides representation and transaction planning advice to both lenders and borrowers in virtually all types of financing transactions.
**Bankruptcy:** Counsels clients through the complex matters surrounding bankruptcy, debtor/creditor relations, workouts and business reorganizations.
**Construction:** Serves industry clients in a broad range of matters, from bidding awards and contract disputes to labor and employment issues.
**Corporate:** Provides the full range of legal services required by businesses regardless of their form of entity or industry, including corporate governance, mergers and acquisitions and securities.
**E-commerce:** Provides strategic advice and counsel to a dynamic array of clients seeking to increase efficiencies and reach new markets through the internet.
**Employee Benefits:** Provides analysis, advice and documentation for all types of employee benefit programs to provide solutions that mesh with clients' overall business, financial and personal objectives.
**Environmental:** Provides consultation, advice and legal representation to businesses and government entities on compliance with environmental laws and regulations. Specializes in brownfield redevelopment projects and environmental litigation and toxic torts.
**Estate Planning:** Assists families with all phases of the accumulation, preservation and distribution of family wealth; assists closely-held businesses with all aspects of succession planning.
**Government & Regulatory Affairs:** Advises clients on a variety of matters including business regulation, economic development, government contracts, legislative advocacy, telecommunications, e-commerce and zoning to help solve business problems and create opportunities.
**Health Law:** Provides representation and strategic advice to the dynamic healthcare industry, serving hundreds of healthcare organizations across the full spectrum of healthcare delivery and payment systems.
**Intellectual Property & Technology Protection:** Helps clients audit, protect and derive income from their intellectual property, technology and intangible rights.
**Labor & Employment:** Represents clients in a diversified range of industries in all aspects of labor and employment law including business immigration. Provides preventive employee relations to help reduce costly and time consuming litigation.
**Litigation:** Advises clients as to how to take proactive efforts to protect against claims and how to be prepared to aggressively prosecute and defend claims in a manner that advances and protects clients' interests.
**Public Finance:** Provides clients with practical, comprehensive counsel and solutions serving significant government needs and involving some of the region's most valuable public and private projects.
**Public Law:** Provides strategic advice and counsel for addressing legal issues involved in the day to day delivery of government services for municipal clients, industry clients and school districts; works to spur economic growth in response to the needs of various municipalities.

## HEAD OFFICE

**OHIO**
250 West Street, **Columbus** OH 43215
**Tel:** 614 462 2700 **Fax:** 614 462 5135
**Website:** www.szd.com

## BRANCH OFFICES

**OHIO**
US Bank Centre, 1350 Euclid Avenue, Suite 1400, **Cleveland** OH 44115
**Tel:** 216 621 6501 **Fax:** 216 621 6502

8044 Montgomery Road, Suite 630, **Cincinnati** OH 45236-2926
**Tel:** 513 792 0792 **Fax:** 513 792 0803

## CONTACTS

| | |
|---|---|
| **Bankruptcy** | Victoria E Powers |
| **Business Law** | Richard A Barnhart; Robert R Ouellette |
| **E-Commerce, Intellectual Property & Technology Protection** | Susan D Rector |
| **Environmental** | Stephen P Samuels |
| **Government & Regulatory Affairs** | David J Robinson |
| **Health Law** | Peter A Pavarini |
| **Labor & Employment** | Felix C Wade |
| **Litigation** | Kevin R McDermott |
| **Public Law** | Stephen J Smith |
| **Tax/Wealth Preservation Planning** | John Terakedis Jr; Richard Holz |

For specific contact information, please visit **www.szd.com**

**Real Estate:** Represents developers, lenders, investors, tenants, landlords and others in the acquisition, development, financing, selling, leasing and management of properties in all phases of real estate transactions and other property issues.
**Tax:** Assists clients with a myriad of tax-related situations including specific tax issues faced by individuals, small and large closely and widely-held businesses and publicly held companies.
**Workers' Compensation:** Represents self insured and state fund employers in all aspects of the defense of workers' compensation claims in both the administrative and court setting.

**CLIENTS:** Schottenstein Zox & Dunn's clients include national and international corporations as well as regional and local companies in the following industries: construction; financial services; healthcare; hospitality; insurance; manufacturing; non-profit/tax-exempt organizations; professional services; public sector; real estate; retail and consumer products; technology; and telecommunications.

**INTERNATIONAL WORK:** As many of the firm's clients venture into international markets, the firm has extended its legal services to Mexico, Canada, South America, Europe and Asia, with specific emphasis on doing business in China. Services focus on strategic planning, joint ventures, mergers and acquisitions, international financing, international manufacturing, distribution and licensing agreements, export and import, intellectual property, international arbitration and litigation, international tax and business immigration matters.

SCHOTTENSTEIN ZOX & DUNN CO., LPA

# SQUIRE, SANDERS & DEMPSEY L.L.P.

## THE FIRM

**Chairman:** R Thomas Stanton
**Managing Partner:** James J Maiwurm

**Number of partners (US only):** 250
**Number of other lawyers (US only):** 370

**FIRM OVERVIEW:** Founded in 1890, Squire, Sanders & Dempsey L.L.P. is one of the largest international law firms with approximately 800 lawyers practicing in offices in the United States, Latin America, Europe and Asia.

## MAIN AREAS OF PRACTICE:

**Corporate:** Drawing from more than 100 years of experience in corporate law, our lawyers help publicly held and privately owned companies achieve business goals quickly and effectively, while navigating through the ever-changing corporate climate. The firm serves the transactional, counseling and compliance needs of our clients and provide legal advice on a range of complex business situations including mergers, acquisitions and divestitures, joint ventures, industry restructuring and privatization, cross-border deals, SEC compliance, corporate governance, insider trading policies, corporate and legal audits, board and special committee counseling, anti-takeover planning, and executive employment and chain-in-control contracts.

**Environmental:** The practice covers the full range of federal and state regulations, CERCLA, RCRA, the Clean Water Act, the Clean Air Act, OSHA and environmental laws from around the world. Focused on compliance counseling and litigation, the firm represents municipalities and trade associations as well as a broad mix of private sector clients across numerous industries including industrial manufacturing, real estate, steel and utilities.

**Intellectual Property:** The firm represents companies of all sizes in the design, resourcing and implementation of their most valuable assets: patents, trademarks, copyrights and trade secrets. Experience in IP law, combined with the ability to handle the largest of litigation cases, as well as all forms of dispute resolution, enables the firm to help a diverse array of clients (e-commerce, high tech, life sciences, manufacturing, and media and entertainment) protect their intellectual property assets.

**Labor & Employment:** The practice focuses on both general policy concerns and specific legal issues impacting employers, both in the United States and abroad. Areas of significant expertise include affirmative action, employment counseling, litigation including class actions, discrimination/EEO, education/school law, ERISA, executive/employment contracts, immigration, union/labor relations, wage and hour, workplace safety and OSHA. Lawyers also provide counsel on non-US labor and employment issues such as TUPE regulations, employment tribunal claims, and EU directives and regulations.

**Litigation & International Dispute Resolution:** Leveraging a substantial network of more than 200 trial lawyers strategically positioned across the United States, Latin America, Europe and Asia, the firm is ideally positioned to represent clients in complex regional, national and international proceedings. The group combines exceptional problem-solving skills and creative advice to achieve outstanding results for clients whether in a courtroom, arbitration, mediation or negotiation. Areas of significant expertise include antitrust, bankruptcy, business law, construction, ERISA, mass torts, product liability, securities and white-collar crime.

**Public Finance:** Since its earliest days, Squire Sanders has been a nationally recognized bond counsel and is ranked consistently among the top five bond and underwriters' counsel in the United States by The Bond Buyer. The firm has extensive experience developing innovative financing techniques and advising on compliance with state law, federal tax law and federal securities law for governmental bodies, hospital systems, public and private colleges, universities and schools, and cultural institutions. The firm has nationwide expertise in the financing of the entire range of infrastructure, economic development and housing projects.

## HEAD OFFICE

4900 Key Tower, 127 Public Square, Cleveland, **Ohio** 44114-1304
**Tel:** 216 479 8500  **Fax:** 216 479 8780
**Website:** www.ssd.com

## BRANCH OFFICES (US OFFICES ONLY)

Cincinnati, Columbus, Houston, Los Angeles, Miami, New York, Palo Alto, Phoenix, San Francisco, Tallahassee, Tampa, Tysons Corner, Washington DC, West Palm Beach.

## INTERNATIONAL OFFICES

The firm also has offices in Beijing, Bratislava, Brussels, Budapest, Caracas, Hong Kong, London, Moscow, Prague, Rio de Janeiro, Santo Domingo, Shanghai, Tokyo and Warsaw. Associated offices are in Bucharest, Buenos Aires, Dublin, Kyiv, Milan and Santiago.

## CONTACTS

| | |
|---|---|
| Corporate | Gordon S Kaiser |
| Environmental | J Van Carson |
| Intellectual Property | Nathan Lane III |
| Labor & Employment | Susan C Hastings |
| Litigation | Thomas S Kilbane |
| International Dispute Resolution | Mark A Nadeau |
| | George M von Mehren |
| Public Finance | D Bruce Gabriel |
| | David S Goodman |
| Regulatory | Barry A Pupkin |
| Taxation | Terrence G Perris |

**Regulatory:** The firm has considerable experience in providing practical counsel and innovative solutions to challenges stemming from the increasing number and complexity of competition regulations around the world. The firm's expertise extends to issues that are related to antitrust and competition (in the United States, the European Union and other jurisdictions), consumer protection, international trade, export control, customs, government contracts, energy, aviation, telecommunications, intelligent transport services, data information services and EU regulatory matters.

**Taxation:** The practice advises a diverse client base that includes a variety of large US and multinational companies, as well as trade associations, middle-market enterprises, emerging companies and individuals in need of highly sophisticated tax counsel. The lawyers have extensive experience in structuring a broad spectrum of international and US transactions to achieve their clients' business objectives in the most tax-efficient manner.

**CLIENTS:** The firm offers legal services in a broad range of industries including chemicals, communications, construction and engineering, education, energy, financial services, government, healthcare, hospitality and leisure, insurance, life sciences, manufacturing, media and entertainment, pharmaceuticals, real estate, sports, steel, technology and transportation.

# THOMPSON HINE LLP

## THE FIRM

**Managing Partner:** David J Hooker
**Number of partners:** 165
**Number of other lawyers:** 205

**Website:** www.ThompsonHine.com
**Email:** info@ThompsonHine.com

**FIRM OVERVIEW:** Established in 1911, Thompson Hine today is among the largest business law firms in the United States. For the last several years, the firm has been named one of the Best Corporate Law Firms in America (in an annual survey of more than 2,000 corporate directors conducted by Corporate Board Member magazine). With more than 370 lawyers, Thompson Hine serves premier businesses worldwide, including: Ford, Toyota, Goodrich, Goodyear, Parker Hannifin, Solvay Pharmaceuticals, Eaton, Sherwin-Williams, JoAnn Stores, Verizon, and KeyCorp. The firm has offices in Atlanta, Brussels, Cincinnati, Cleveland, Columbus, Dayton, New York, and Washington, D.C. For more information, please visit the firm's website.

## MAIN AREAS OF PRACTICE:

**Admirality & Maritime:** Represents more than 200 carriers and shippers before state and federal courts and agencies.

**Bankruptcy:** Represents lenders, creditors' committees, debtors and other parties in finance transactions, workouts and bankruptcy matters.

**Biotech:** Represents emerging and established biotechnology companies on matters ranging from financing to joint ventures to intellectual property.

**Business Litigation:** Represents clients in a wide variety of business litigation - from corporate control contests and insurance disputes, to class actions, securities fraud, and tax controversies.

**Commercial & Public Finance:** Handle commercial finance transactions, public finance, asset securitizations and general bank regulatory law.

**Competition, Antitrust & White Collar Crime:** Represents clients in trade restraint price discrimination, franchising and distribution, trade secrets, false advertising, and fraud.

**Construction:** Represents owners, design professionals, construction managers, contractors and sureties. Serves in the role of project counsel for billions of dollars of construction at sites across the US.

**Consumer Product Safety:** Represents companies and industry groups before the Consumer Product Safety Commission (CPSC); advises on recalls, civil penalty matters and CPSC safety standards.

**Corporate Transactions & Securities:** Represents both emerging and established businesses in their most important business transactions, from startup through IPOs, joint ventures, mergers, acquisitions and beyond.

**International Trade & Customs:** Represents clients in penalty actions, investigations, and audits before US administrative agencies responsible for regulating imports and exports; advertises clients on issues that affect their global market share, including opportunities under trade agreements and litigation of unfair trade cases.

**E-Business & Emerging Technologies:** Helps businesses realize the opportunities and manage the risks of electronic and technological commerce.

**Employee Benefits & Executive Compensation:** Advises clients regarding benefit plans, ERISA issues, controversies with the IRS, DOL, PBGC and other agencies; incentive and equity-based compensation, and ESOPs.

**Energy & Utilities:** Advises traditional and new business entities participating in the evolving energy markets, with respect to both regulated (at state and federal levels) and non-regulated energy transactions for natural gas, electricity, renewable energy, water and waste energy.

**Environmental:** Advises clients on the environmental aspects on their business transactions, crafting methods of allocating risk and counseling them on their compliance obligations under local, federal and state laws.

**Healthcare:** Represents physician groups, hospitals, clinical laboratories, diagnostic service providers, pharmaceutical manufacturers, medical device manu-

facturers and health insurance providers.

**Intellectual Property:** Assists clients with patents, trademarks, copyrights, trade secrets, computer software, internet-related issues, and IP litigation.

**International:** The firm advises US clients on matters in all regions of the world, as well as foreign clients with interests in the US.

**Labor & Employment:** Represents clients in employment litigation, workers' compensation, immigration, collective bargaining, proceedings before the Department of Labor, OSHA, EEOC, NLRB and various state agencies.

**Life Sciences:** Focuses on creating business solutions and managing critical legal and regulatory issues for companies engaged in all facets of the research, development and delivery of human and animal health products and services.

**Personal & Succession Planning:** Assists clients in the management and transmission of wealth, the succession of businesses and other personal and family concerns.

**Product Liability:** Handles thousands of product liability matters involving mechanical, chemical, electrical, medical, aerospace, automotive and other products.

**Real Estate:** Represents clients in development, corporate real estate, zoning and land use; real estate investment and financing, and REITs.

**Tax:** Advises clients in business transactions and financings, tax controversy litigation, legislative and regulatory activities, international taxation, state and local taxation and foundation and exempt organization matters.

**Telecommunications:** Provides clients with wide-ranging guidance on the regulations and laws affecting telecommunications, broadcasting and other electronic communications companies.

**Transportation:** Represents shippers, third party logistics providers and other intermediaries, as well as other transportation interests in regulatory, commercial, policy, and litigation matters.

## HEAD OFFICE

### OHIO
3900 Key Center, 127 Public Square, **Cleveland,** OH 44114-1291
**Tel:** 216 566 5500  **Fax:** 216 566 5800
**Email:** info@ThompsonHine.com

## BRANCH OFFICES

### DISTRICT OF COLUMBIA
1920 N Street, NW, Suite 800, **Washington,** DC 20036-1600
**Tel:** 202 331 8800  **Fax:** 202 331 8330

### GEORGIA
One Atlantic Center, Suite 1201 West Peachtree Street, Suite 2200, **Atlanta,** GA 30309
**Tel:** 404 541 2900  **Fax:** 404 541 2905

### NEW YORK
One Chase Manhattan Plaza, 58th Floor, **New York,** NY 10005-1401
**Tel:** 212 344 5680  **Fax:** 212 809 6890

### OHIO
312 Walnut Street, 14th Floor, **Cincinnati,** OH 45202-4089
**Tel:** 513 352 6700  **Fax:** 513 241 4771

10 West Broad Street, Suite 700, **Columbus,** OH 43215-3435
**Tel:** 614 469 3200  **Fax:** 614 469 3361

2000 Courthouse Plaza, NE PO Box 8801, **Dayton,** OH 45401-8801
**Tel:** 937 443 6600  **Fax:** 937 443 6635

# VORYS, SATER, SEYMOUR AND PEASE LLP

## THE FIRM

**Managing Partner:** Robert W Werth

**Number of partners:** 172
**Total number of attorneys:** 360

**FIRM OVERVIEW:** Established in 1909, Vorys, Sater, Seymour and Pease LLP has grown to one of the nation's largest law firms through its focus on delivering superior legal versality, experience and depth to its clients. The culture emphasizes self-governing, high ethical standards and a teamwork approach to managing client work. Clients range from some of the world's largest companies to individuals and small businesses. The firm represents them in Ohio, across the country and around the world in litigation, business and personal transactions involving virtually every legal subject. This client and practice diversity is matched by the diversity of the firm's lawyers who come from over 25 states and are graduates of more than 50 law schools. The firm's lawyers also extensively support projects, organizations and affiliations which strengthen their regional communities.

## MAIN AREAS OF PRACTICE:

**Commercial & Real Estate:** Vorys' commercial and real estate attorneys advise financial institutions and large corporate borrowers on sophisticated financing transactions; provide franchising counsel to some of the largest franchisors in the world; advise clients on the full range of real estate matters including acquisitions, sales and exchanges, development, commercial leasing, syndications, equity financing, foreclosures and loan workouts; and provide the full breadth of bankruptcy counsel.

**Corporate & Finance:** Members of the Corporate and Finance Group are legal advisers to Fortune 500 and other public companies, financial institutions, established private businesses and new ventures, communication and technology companies, nonprofit organizations, investment bankers and underwriters, public utilities, individual entrepreneurs and investors.

**Energy & Utilities:** The Energy and Utility Group represents the oil and gas industry, telecommunications companies, broadcasters and cable television operators in a wide variety of legal areas, including contract and general litigation, bankruptcy, environmental matters, and before regulatory bodies.

**Environmental:** Vorys' environmental attorneys have counseled clients on environmental issues since the inception of government regulation, including: regulatory matters, compliance counseling, legislation and rulemaking, PRP groups, cost recovery action, contractual indemnities, toxic tort and environmental litigation, and class action defense.

**Government & Lobbying:** The firm's attorneys in the government and lobbying area are constantly involved in public contracting issues and litigation in all levels of government.

**Healthcare:** Vorys' healthcare lawyers have successfully represented and counseled clients - from independent practitioners to multi-national management systems - on a complete range of legal matters that span from business-related issues such as real estate and insurance to specialized concerns about Medicare reimbursement and HIPAA compliance.

**Intellectual Property:** The firm's intellectual property attorneys have extensive experience in the acquisition, enforcement, and exploitation of patents, trademarks, copyrights, and industrial designs, as well as in unfair competition, trade secrets, computer law, and related matters.

**International Law:** The firm's International Law Practice includes international corporate and commercial transactions, international finance and the regulation of US exports and investment abroad.

**Labor & Employment:** Vorys' labor and employment attorneys represent manufacturers, retailers, transportation service companies, financial institutions, healthcare facilities, colleges and universities, and public employers, many of whom the firm represents on a national or regional basis. In addition, Vorys has unique experience in representing companies, in the area of false claims litigation, who are regulated by the US government's regulatory agencies.

## HEAD OFFICE

**OHIO**
52 East Gay Street, **Columbus**, OH 43215
**Tel:** 614 464 6400  **Fax:** 614 464 6350
**Website:** www.vssp.com

## BRANCH OFFICES

**DISTRICT OF COLUMBIA**
1828 L Street NW, Suite 1111, **Washington**, DC 20036
**Tel:** 202 467 8800  **Fax:** 202 467 8900

**OHIO**
Suite 200, Atrium Two, 221 East Fourth Street, **Cincinnati**, OH 45202
**Tel:** 513 723 4000  **Fax:** 513 723 4056

2100 One Cleveland Center, 1375 East Ninth Street, **Cleveland**, OH 44114
**Tel:** 216 479 6100  **Fax:** 216 479 6060

First National Tower, 106 South Main Street, **Akron**, OH 44308
**Tel:** 330 208 1000  **Fax:** 330 208 1001

**VIRGINIA**
277 South Washington Street, Suite 310, **Alexandria**, VA 22314
**Tel:** 703 837 6999  **Fax:** 703 549 4492

## CONTACTS

| | |
|---|---|
| **Litigation** | Suzanne Richards |
| **Corporate/Finance** | John Vorys |
| **Energy/Utilities** | Scott Doran |
| **Labor/Employment** | Jonathan Norman |
| **Probate/Tax** | Ron Rowland |
| **Commercial/Real Estate** | John Wellner |
| **Technology/IP** | Cory Amron |
| **Marketing Director** | Maureen Conley |

For specific contact information, please see **www.vssp.com**

**Litigation:** About 30% of the firm's lawyers are involved in its Litigation Practice, where it is retained in large, complex and oftentimes sensitive litigation on a regular basis.

**Probate & Estate Planning:** The Probate and Estate Planning Group has extensive expertise in the representation of fiduciaries and beneficiaries of estates, trusts and guardianships, with special emphasis on Ohio and Florida.

**Tax:** The firm's tax lawyers engage in all aspects of federal, state and local tax practice as part of the firm's general representation of clients and as special tax counsel.

**Technology:** Vorys' Technology Group counsels users and vendors on the development, distribution and protection of their technology assets.

**Toxic Tort:** The Toxic Tort Group aggressively represents defendants in matters involving asbestos, silica, mold, mycotoxin, vinyl chloride, MCEs, and radiation.

**VORYS, SATER, SEYMOUR AND PEASE LLP**

**CONTENTS:**

## How lawyers are ranked

Every year we carry out thousands of in-depth interviews with clients and lawyers in order to assess the reputations and expertise of business lawyers across the USA. Chambers rankings and editorial are referred to extensively by General Counsel and other purchasers of legal services who look to our recommendations when choosing their lawyers.

# CORPORATE/COMMERCIAL

### Corporate/Commercial
#### Leading Firms

1. **CONNER & WINTERS, PC** *Tulsa*
   **CROWE & DUNLEVY, PC** *Oklahoma City*
   **MCAFEE & TAFT** *Oklahoma City*
2. **COMMERCIAL LAW GROUP** *Oklahoma City*
   **HARTZOG CONGER CASON & NEVILLE** *Oklahoma City*

#### Leading Individuals

1. **MOORE Lynnwood** *Conner & Winters, PC*
   **STEWART Mike** *Crowe & Dunlevy, PC*
2. **COLEMAN Chris** *McAfee & Taft*
   **DERRICK Gary** *Derrick & Briggs LLP*
   **ELAM Theodore** *McAfee & Taft*
   **SELF Shannon** *Commercial Law Group*
   **STRINGER Martin** *McAfee & Taft*

### Corporate/Commercial: Tax
#### Leading Individuals

##### Senior Statesman
**FULLER Gary** *McAfee & Taft*
1. **DAVIS Steven** *Hartzog Conger Cason*
2. **CASON Len** *Hartzog Conger Cason*
   **CRAIG Richard** *McAfee & Taft*
   **HOLLOMAN JR James** *Crowe & Dunlevy, PC*
   **MOCK Randall** *Mock, Schwabe*
   **RATLIFF Reeder** *Crowe & Dunlevy, PC*

## Band 1

### Conner & Winters, PC

**The Firm:** This Tulsa-based law firm is consistently praised for the depth and breadth of its practice. With offices in Oklahoma City and outside the state, it has the capability to advise a range of clients from small sole proprietorships to NYSE-listed companies. Although the Oklahoma City practice is said to be more limited in its coverage, the firm as a whole advises on all manner of M&A transactions, enterprise financings and corporate governance issues. Recent transaction highlights include several financings for Jameson Inns involving a registration of the Jameson Stock Awards program (an arrangement whereby frequent guests can earn stock by staying at the hotels) and a private placement of a convertible note offering.

**The Lawyers:** Interviewees drew attention to the *"critical mass of outstanding individuals"* in Tulsa. Heading up the firm's corporate and securities practice, leading lawyer **Lynnwood Moore** *"really inspires confidence"* in his clients. In addition to his vast experience in securities law and M&A, sources praised his expert communication skills and ability to *"see the big picture while keeping the transaction moving along."* He represented Pinnacle Packaging and its subsidiary, Oracle Flexible Packaging, in connection with the acquisition of assets from RJ Reynolds.

**Clients/Work Highlights:** WilTel Communications; Vintage Petroleum; Willbros Group; Dover Resources; Jameson Inns; ADDvantage Technology Group; Unit Corporation; Black Hills Corporation; Omni Air International and Global Power Equipment Group.

### Crowe & Dunlevy, PC
See firm details p.1662

**The Firm:** The sheer size and long-term presence of this firm – with offices in Oklahoma City, Tulsa and Norman – give it an edge over its competitors, commentators remarked. Clients note that this preeminent provider of business services has an *"impeccable reputation"* and *"brings more to the table than most."* Fifteen *"high-quality individuals"* advise on a variety of corporate finance issues such as M&A and general securities work relating to offerings and financial institutions. The team has capitalized on the boom in the energy market by getting involved in a startup oil and gas exploration company that is obtaining equity and loan capital from major institutions and individual investors.

**The Lawyers:** Sources were united in their praise for **Mike Stewart** (see p.1660), an attorney who is *"a cut above the rest"* and *"as good as it gets on the corporate side."* His intelligence, diligence and knowledge of the law set him apart from other lawyers. One client remarked: *"He's one of the brightest folks I've ever been privileged to work with."* Competitors acknowledged that he was a tough opponent. *"Technically brilliant"* **Jim Holloman** (see p.1659) chairs the firm's taxation group. Holloman has expertise in tax credits and federal income tax transactions. His colleague **Reeder Ratliff** (see p.1660) was praised for the *"level-*

*headed approach"* he brings to his corporate and tax caseload.

**Clients/Work Highlights:** Pre-Paid Legal Services; GMX Resources; Solara Healthcare and Harold's Stores.

### McAfee & Taft
### A Professional Corporation
See firm details p.1666

**The Firm:** Famed for its business expertise, this firm boasts the largest corporate department in Oklahoma and has grasped a substantial share of the market. The group has branched out from its tax origins into a broad, *"highly creative"* practice that encompasses every type of commercial transaction from private equity investments and the setting up of new companies to securities offerings and public reportings. *"They offer the full service,"* admitted competitors, while clients praised them for having *"top-notch attorneys that can be put on the task at a moment's notice."*

**The Lawyers:** Tax veteran **Gary Fuller** is a favorite among attorneys for having a *"creative yet commonsensical approach"* to deal-making. Best known for his deep knowledge of estate planning, he *"understands how transactions need to be put together to accomplish every objective."* **Chris Coleman** *"gets the deals done,"* according to peers, who credit him with understanding his clients' needs and being a genuine pleasure to work with. Distinguished corporate attorney **Ted Elam** received accolades from a number of sources for being *"a strong leader who is willing to stay with the task until the end."* He has been lead counsel for issuers in public and private offerings of securities. *"Rainmaker"* **Martin Stringer** is a welcome arrival from the law firm McKinney & Stringer. Renowned for his ability to structure transactions creatively and negotiate deals effectively, he has over 40 years of experience in business law. Peers agreed: *"You have to give him his dues – he's one of the best."* **Richard Craig** enters the tables this year in recognition of his achievements in the tax and family wealth arena. He returned to the firm last year from Norman-based law firm Craig & Bauman.

**Clients/Work Highlights:** Devon Energy; The GHK Company; Hiland Partners; Mustang Fuel Corporation; Continental Resources; Nomadics; Ram Energy; American Fidelity Assurance and Tyson Foods.

## Band 2

### Commercial Law Group

**The Firm:** Established in 1991, this Oklahoma City boutique firm specializes in handling complex commercial matters. Sources asserted that *"there should be no adverse bias because of the firm's size: they are all very smart, hard-working lawyers."* The team's varied caseload includes M&A, oil and gas, real estate, venture capital, complex commercial credit workouts and reorganization work.

**The Lawyers:** **Shannon Self** remains *"the major mover and shaker"* in the firm, despite currently being on sabbatical in London. Perhaps best known for his relationship with Chesapeake Energy, Shannon is credited with building up the firm's practice. He is a *"creative guy who never fails to see the big picture."*

**Clients/Work Highlights:** Arvest Bank; Carter Chevrolet Agency; Oklahoma Grocers Association; Chisholm Private Capital Partners; Stillwater National Bank & Trust and SolutionsBank.

## Hartzog Conger Cason & Neville, LLP

See firm details p.1665

**The Firm:** This medium-sized practice is *"definitely on the rise,"* market commentators observed. Having made a name for itself doing high-quality litigation work, it has forged a blossoming reputation on the corporate and securities side thanks to a growing client list. The group serves a range of public and private national corporations, as well as emerging businesses and entrepreneurs. Recent highlights include the sale of a major film company in California to a large private equity firm in the entertainment industry.

**The Lawyers:** Seasoned attorney **Steve Davis** (see p.1659) is *"top of his class,"* conceded peers, who admitted to regularly referring work to him. An accomplished corporate and tax lawyer, he specializes in advising clients on estate and business planning. Founding partner **Len Cason** (see p.1659) is commended for his work in securities and in business purchases and sales. He is said to have a *"a happy facility for keeping the client satisfied."*

**Clients/Work Highlights:** First Commercial Bank;

Horizon Wind Energy; Golf Club Partners; Gaylord Films; STPD/Badlands Golf Club; Great Plains Coca-Cola Bottling; Eastman National Bancshares; MIDCO Fabricators; Hays Trucking and Chem Service.

### Other Notable Practitioners

**Randall Mock** of Mock, Schwabe, Waldo, Elder, Reeves & Bryant continues to impress sources with his tax and estate planning work. Peers reported he was *"extremely bright and knowledgeable"* while clients praised him for his *"even temper and honesty."* **Gary Derrick** of Derrick & Briggs LLP is a *"hardworking, academic individual who is high on ethics and gives solid advice to his clients."* He is responsible for all of the firm's corporate work, and mostly represents businesses in securities offerings, M&A and public reportings. He recently provided local counsel on a $60 million credit facility in the medical field.

# EMPLOYMENT

# MAINLY DEFENDANT

| Employment: Mainly Defendant |
|---|
| **Leading Firms** |
| [1] **CONNER & WINTERS, PC** *Oklahoma City* |
| **CROWE & DUNLEVY, PC** *Oklahoma City* |
| **HALL, ESTILL, HARDWICK, GABLE, GOLDEN** *Tulsa* |
| **MCAFEE & TAFT** *Oklahoma City* |
| [2] **DOERNER, SAUNDERS, DANIEL** *Oklahoma City* |
| **ELDRIDGE COOPER STEICHEN & LEACH** *Tulsa* |
| **NICHOLS, WOLFE, STAMPER, NALLY** *Tulsa* |

| Leading Individuals |
|---|
| ★ **COURT Leonard** *Crowe & Dunlevy, PC* |
| **CREMIN Pat** *Hall, Estill, Hardwick, Gable* |
| [1] **BARRETT Gayle** *Crowe & Dunlevy, PC* |
| **CORDELL David** *Conner & Winters, PC* |
| **NEAL Kathy** *Eldridge Cooper Steichen* |
| **PETRIKIN Ronald** *Conner & Winters, PC* |
| **PLUMB Charles** *Doerner, Saunders, Daniel* |
| **VAN DYKE Peter** *McAfee & Taft* |
| [2] **FULKERSON Sam** *McAfee & Taft* |
| **PUCKETT Tony** *McAfee & Taft* |
| **ROBERTSON Thomas** *Nichols, Wolfe* |
| **STRECKER David** *Strecker & Associates* |
| **WOLFE III Frank** *Nichols, Wolfe* |

## Band 1

### Conner & Winters, PC

**The Firm:** This firm continues to garner respect from all quarters. The bulk of its labor and employment work is carried out in Tulsa where an eight-strong team represents public and private employers in a variety of employment matters. Clients are

advised on traditional labor law issues and on methods of avoiding potential employment disputes. Expert attorneys field claims across the board, from discrimination and wrongful discharge claims to workers' compensation and unfair labor practice. Clients reported: *"They know what we need and when we need it – they're the best and the easiest to work with."*

**The Lawyers:** Highly respected attorney **David Cordell** has specialist knowledge of the Railway Labor Act and is credited with handling the group's biggest cases. Peers admire him for *"working really hard to get results"* and for being *"extremely cognizant of client needs."* Seasoned trial attorney **Ron Petrikin** maintains a diversified practice and cuts an impressive figure on the seminar circuit. *"Aggressive and bright,"* he has extensive experience in union-organizing campaigns and representing management before governmental agencies.

**Clients/Work Highlights:** American Airlines; Wendy's; Avalon Exploration; Sabre; Link America and Dynergy.

### Crowe & Dunlevy, PC

See firm details p.1662

**The Firm:** This market leader fields 16 attorneys in the labor and employment law area across three offices, with the largest team found in Oklahoma City. The firm's national reputation is enhanced by its being a member of the Employment Law Alliance, a worldwide consortium of management side law firms. Attorneys have widespread expertise representing management in the defense of discrimination claims and wrongful discharge actions, as well as advising employers on avoiding unionizations. Interviewees admitted to having no hesitation

in referring work to them. Highlights from the past six months include prevailing for Xerox on a claim for a retaliation under the Family Medical Leave Act. This case took two years to come to trial and just two weeks to close.

**The Lawyers:** Prestigious defense litigator **Leonard Court** (see p.1659) is *"one of the best, if not the best"* and *"at the top of everyone's list – extraordinary"* enthused sources. Heading up the firm's labor and employment group, he is expert in all types of discrimination work and brings over 30 years of experience to the table. Praised for being highly intellectual yet down-to-earth, interviewees were particularly impressed with his *"willingness to do a lot of the leg work himself."* Well-respected attorney **Gayle Barrett** (see p.1658) has established a name for herself as a knowledgeable employment attorney who is heavily involved in client training programs. *"She's a name that we all know,"* observed peers, who endorsed her *"superb presentation skills"* and niche expertise in employee benefits.

**Clients/Work Highlights:** Goodyear; Eagle Corporation; Xerox; Republic Gypsum; Hillco and National Rural Water Association.

### Hall, Estill, Hardwick, Gable, Golden & Nelson, PC

**The Firm:** Sources remarked that the depth of this firm's employment practice makes it a leading competitor in the Oklahoma market. The group extends from Oklahoma to Northwest Arkansas and Washington, DC, representing large employers in the finance and energy sector, as well as a number of family-held companies. In Tulsa, the team handles everything from class actions to large union disputes. A notable highlight came with its recent involvement in litigation regarding the rights of employers across the state to restrict their employees bringing weapons on to company property.

**The Lawyers:** One of the most eminent employment lawyers in the state, **Pat Cremin** is not only *"an extremely dedicated, tough trial attorney"* but also *"one hell of a nice guy,"* proclaimed his supporters. Known for having *"all the right attributes,"* he is well connected locally and with the courts. He has successfully handled litigation for employers in more than 30 states. Peers attributed his success to his strength in the courtroom and a *"wonderful sense of humor"* that makes him popular with clients.

**Clients/Work Highlights:** United States Beef Corporation; The Williams Companies; Sunoco; ConocoPhillips; Doubletree Hotels, Gear Products; Dixon Industries; WilTel Communications; SemGroup; Saint Francis Health System; Blue Cross and Blue Shield of Oklahoma and Chubb Group.

## McAfee & Taft
## A Professional Corporation
See firm details p.1666

**The Firm:** This leading provider of business services can hold its own in the employment defense market, according to sources. In Oklahoma City, 20 skilled attorneys specialize in labor and employment while ten devote themselves to employee benefits. The group represents a mixture of Fortune 500 companies, family-owned businesses and individuals across the Southwest. The firm also represents larger clients, such as Halliburton, on a national level.

**The Lawyers:** **Peter Van Dyke** is *"a real veteran – he's handled it all,"* according to sources, who added that he was *"more reserved than his peers but every bit as good an attorney."* A master of employment litigation with a focus on traditional labor law, he represents private employers on all manner of issues. Chairing the group, **Sam Fulkerson** concentrates on defending employment discrimination claims and has a niche in age and disability. A talented public speaker, he commands respect from his peers for being very pleasant to deal with. *"Capable and smart"* lawyer **Tony Puckett** enters the tables this year in acknowledgment of his work representing municipalities in union negotiations, arbitrations and civil

rights employment actions. Sources affirmed that he was *"very knowledgeable across a broad range of areas."*

**Clients/Work Highlights:** Sysco Food Services of Oklahoma Lopez Foods Dobson Communications; Devon Energy Corporation; Halliburton; Delta Faucet of Oklahoma; Masco; American Cancer Society; The Oklahoma Publishing Company; Trader Publishing Company; MidFirst Bank and Norman Regional Hospital.

## Doerner, Saunders,
## Daniel & Anderson LLP

**The Firm:** Commentators reported that, despite losing several talented attorneys over the years, this firm continues to have a wide-ranging employment practice. Twelve talented attorneys devote their time to litigation and provide guidance and representation on the full spectrum of employment disputes. Training and compliance work are also significant areas of the practice.

**The Lawyers:** Effective trial attorney **Charlie Plumb** has a strong and varied practice and is popular with lawyers and clients alike for being *"personable and intelligent – he's the one I'd call."* An expert in employment litigation, wrongful discharge and statutory violation, he is also a distinguished public speaker. Sources credit him with knowing the industry inside out and being able to *"work from the ground up."*

**Clients/Work Highlights:** The department acts for public and private, unionized and nonunionized clients.

## Eldridge Cooper Steichen
## & Leach PLLC

**The Firm:** This small, Tulsa-based firm is widely respected for its work in employment litigation and products liability. A team of seasoned lawyers spends the bulk of its time on employment matters, representing a number of national giants such as GM. *"They're quick to respond,"* reported clients, who also praised the group for its reasonable rates.

**The Lawyers:** Interviewees described **Kathy Neal** as *"a fabulous lawyer, exceptionally bright and really nice to deal with."* A tenacious litigator with a broad range of expertise, she was celebrated by her peers for her *"ability to get her arms around issues very easily."*

**Clients/Work Highlights:** Clients include Dresser, Inc, Saint Simeon's Episcopal Home and The University of Tulsa.

## Nichols, Wolfe, Stamper,
## Nally, Fallis & Robertson Inc

**The Firm:** This *"well-diversified and easily accessible"* Tulsa labor law firm has a long and distinguished history in the region. Despite a perception from some clients that the firm lacks the depth of some of its rivals, it continues to handle matters to a high standard. Three attorneys focus exclusively on employment, with an emphasis on civil rights and OSHA matters. Clients typically come from the energy and construction sectors.

**The Lawyers:** Heading up the litigation team, **Tom Robertson** is an *"extremely effective oral advocate"* with over 30 years of experience representing management. Peers were won over by his practical judgment skills and easy manner, while clients praised his responsiveness and clarity. *"A veteran of every aspect of labor law,"* **Skip Wolfe** is highly respected in his field. He increasingly concentrates on counseling employers on occupational health and safety matters. Interviewees praised him for being *"courteous and civil, yet aggressive when appropriate."*

**Clients/Work Highlights:** Dober Resources; Paccar; Cust-O-Fab Services; Storey Wrecker Service; Hiland Dairy; Flint Energy Services; Mid-Continent Casualty; City National Bank & Trust; Fintube Technologies; Sportcraft and The Crosby Group.

## Other Notable Practitioners

**David Strecker** of Strecker & Associates is *"the full package"* according to clients, some of whom went as far as to say: *"He is the firm."* With a lengthy track record in employment litigation, he is credited with being a practical advocate for his clients and *"a real honest guy."*

# LITIGATION

## Crowe & Dunlevy, PC
See firm details p.1662

**The Firm:** The largest and oldest firm in the state, this regional heavyweight is *"outstanding from top to bottom,"* agreed sources. It is a full-service firm with a time-honored emphasis on litigation, boasting a department fielding more than 60 *"first-class attorneys"* across offices in Oklahoma City, Tulsa and Norman. Attorneys handle all types of litigation from complex commercial and employment matters

through to construction contract and aircraft disputes. The group is highly respected for an oil and gas practice that has profited from an increase in royalty litigation resulting from the sharp rise in energy prices and increased drilling activity over the past year. Interviewees asserted they *"would not hesitate to refer work to them – they can handle any problem."*

**The Lawyers:** With *"incredible legal talent throughout,"* the firm is brimming with skilled litigators. *"Big hitter"* **Gary Davis** (see p.1659) is widely regarded as one of the masters of oil and gas litigation. A

# GENERAL COMMERCIAL

seasoned trial attorney, he is credited with having *"tremendous jury appeal"* and *"incredible energy in the courtroom."* One lawyer asserted: *"he's one of the cagiest trial lawyers I've ever seen."* Distinguished antitrust lawyer **Kent Meyers** (see p.1660) received warm praise from his peers. *"He's a top-flight professional, deliberate, analytical and very, very thorough. He's all aces in my book."* Renowned in both the courtroom and the classroom, he is also respected for his pro bono work for abused children. Interviewees paid tribute to his *"excellent people skills and composure under pressure."* *"Super smart"* appellate

## Litigation: General Commercial

### Leading Firms

**1** CROWE & DUNLEVY, PC *Oklahoma City*
FELLERS, SNIDER, BLANKENSHIP *Oklahoma City*
GABLE & GOTWALS *Oklahoma City*

**2** HARTZOG CONGER CASON & NEVILLE *Oklahoma City*
MCAFEE & TAFT *Oklahoma City*
RYAN WHALEY COLDIRON *Oklahoma City*

**3** KIRK & CHANEY *Oklahoma City*

### Leading Individuals

#### Senior Statesman

BAILEY Burck *Fellers, Snider, Blankenship, Bailey*

**1** CORBYN George *Corbyn Law Firm*
DAVIS Gary *Crowe & Dunlevy, PC*
HERMES John *McAfee & Taft*
MCKINNEY Kenneth *Tomlinson & O'Connell PC*
MEYERS Kent *Crowe & Dunlevy, PC*
MUCHMORE Clyde *Crowe & Dunlevy, PC*
NEVILLE Drew *Hartzog Conger Cason*
RYAN Patrick *Ryan Whaley Coldiron*
STURDIVANT James *Gable & Gotwals*
TIPPENS Terry *Fellers, Snider, Blankenship, Bailey*

**2** ABOWITZ Murray *Abowitz, Timberlake*
BARGHOLS Steven *Gable & Gotwals*
BURRAGE Michael *Burrage Law Firm*
HAMPTON Joe *Ryan Whaley Coldiron*
KENNEY John *McAfee & Taft*
KIRK James *Kirk & Chaney*
ROBISON Reid *McAfee & Taft*

**3** BICKFORD IV Warren *Fellers, Snider*
DUNAGAN Sidney *Gable & Gotwals*
GEISTER III Charles *Hartzog Conger Cason*
MCCONNELL Laura *Hartzog Conger Cason*
RUPERT Anton *Crowe & Dunlevy, PC*

#### Up-and-coming individuals

EISSENSTAT Eric *Fellers, Snider, Blankenship, Bailey*

---

lawyer **Clyde Muchmore** (see p.1660) has a reputation for being *"the academic lawyer."* Always well prepared, he brings a wealth of knowledge to the table, particularly in constitutional and appellate matters. Commentators were impressed with the determination and optimism he demonstrated in every situation. **Tony Rupert** (see p.1660) is a *"good, steady lawyer"* who is making his mark in the firm. He has expertise in construction litigation and products liability, most recently illustrated by his participation in a $1 million case involving an alleged design defect for C.H. Guernsey and Company, an engineering company in Washington DC.

**Clients/Work Highlights:** The Williams Companies; WilTel Communications; Farmers Group; ExxonMobil; Kerr-McGee; Clear Channel Communications and Cox Communications.

## Fellers, Snider, Blankenship, Bailey & Tippens, A Professional Corporation

See firm details p.1663

**The Firm:** *"Easily top-tier"* was how commentators described this thriving litigation firm. Its reputation has really come on in the past year thanks to a deep pool of skilled individuals. *"They've got top-flight people in all areas,"* sources enthused. Thirty lawyers have expertise in every area of litigation, particularly in intellectual property law, and oil and gas. The team recently achieved a $16 million jury verdict in a patent infringement case and is currently involved in a multi million dollar class action case against several major oil companies. Oklahoma's booming equine industry provides a further source of litigation for the group as it tackles issues of ownership, syndication and the building of racinos: entertainment complexes featuring casino gambling and horse racing.

**The Lawyers:** Widely celebrated as *"the best trial lawyer in the state,"* **Burck Bailey** is *"every bit as good as billed,"* claimed sources. He enjoys a long and distinguished career in complex business litigation and now acts as counsel for the firm. Interviewees described him as *"a real gentleman – when you think of preeminence, he comes to mind."* Hot on his heels is **Terry Tippens**, *"a phenomenal trial lawyer"* who is *"a step behind Burck, but close to reaching his level."* *"Tenacious and forceful,"* he impressed sources with his *"amazing ability to communicate with juries."* One interviewee admitted: *"I really worry when I'm against him!"* **Warren Bickford** is new to the tables this year but is expected to move more and more into the spotlight. Having spent his career working side by side with Burck Bailey, his practice includes the defense of white-collar criminal cases and the prosecution and defense of claims arising under securities, insurance and commercial law. A *"smooth operator,"* he is credited with being an excellent communicator. Also on the rise is **Eric Eissenstat**, identified by sources as *"Burck's protégé,"* and someone who has *"really come on strong in the last five years."* He is respected for having handled a number of high-profile cases for major insurers.

**Clients/Work Highlights:** Enron; Aetna; American Express; Hertz; BancFirst and Wal-Mart.

## Gable & Gotwals, A Professional Corporation

See firm details p.1664

**The Firm:** This *"terrific, confident"* firm has established a name for itself locally and nationwide, largely thanks to an impressive roster of clients that includes major corporations and energy companies. *"Not so much a firm as an institution,"* it is home to a dynamic team of 60 litigators, primarily based in Tulsa but enjoying strong support from Oklahoma City. Half of the group specializes in oil and gas litigation while the rest handles all types of commercial litigation. Recent triumphs include settling six royalty underpayment suits against another client, three of which were class actions in which the total damages sought by plaintiffs amounted to well over $200 million in royalty underpayments and over $5

billion in alleged unjust enrichment profits and punitive damages.

**The Lawyers:** *"A wonderful attorney and a mentor to other lawyers,"* **Jim Sturdivant** (see p.1661) is a favorite among his peers. A skilled and experienced advocate with excellent presence, *"he's not afraid to go into the courtroom and mix things up,"* reported sources. Commentators endorsed his experience in the field of antitrust, praising his ability to make the best of a complex situation. *"Truly exceptional"* attorney **Steve Barghols** (see p.1658) got glowing reports from interviewees who credited him with being *"the finest mediator in the state, hands down."* While he is known for commercial and energy litigation, he has developed a dazzling reputation for complex mediation. One interviewee remarked: *"I could tell you endless stories about complex cases he's taken on and settled in hours rather than weeks."* Prominent trial attorney **Sid Dunagan** (see p.1659) caught the attention of market commentators this year who declared him *"appropriately aggressive, very ethical and easy to get along with."* He was said to perfectly fit the mold of a strong advocate.

**Clients/Work Highlights:** ChevronTexaco; ConocoPhillips; El Paso; Oklahoma Natural Gas Company and The Williams Companies.

### Band 2

## Hartzog Conger Cason & Neville, LLP

See firm details p.1665

**The Firm:** This *"diverse and multitalented"* boutique firm blends complex litigation with a successful transactional practice. A 14-strong team handles a wide variety of cases involving antitrust law, securities litigation, employment, and business litigation. The group represents both plaintiffs and defendants, although there is a tendency towards the defense side."

**The Lawyers:** *"Battle-proven"* litigator **Drew Neville** (see p.1660) is *"head and shoulders above the rest,"* claimed sources. A former legislative assistant in the United Senate and a former Assistant U.S.A. Attorney, he has vast experience handling complex civil cases and white-collar criminal cases across the country. Peers enthusiastically recommended him as *"an extremely hard worker with a tremendous ability to put the jury at ease."* **Charlie Geister** (see p.1659) is widely acknowledged for his work for Enron. Sources remarked that *"he's incredibly talented in terms of written communication skills and really good on his feet."* Acclaimed family law expert **Laura McConnell** (see p.1660) is *"the go-to person for that type of work,"* agreed peers. Clients valued her natural intuition and responsiveness, declaring: *"She has exactly the right personality for the job."* She also handles a mixture of litigation and employment law cases.

**Clients/Work Highlights:** KPMG Peat Marwick; Marriott; American National; Koch Industries; Prudential Securities and The Coca-Cola Bottlers' Association.

## McAfee & Taft
## A Professional Corporation
See firm details p.1666

**The Firm:** Traditionally viewed as a transactional firm, this group has a large litigation group with an emphasis on business disputes. Its diverse practice encompasses everything from oil and gas litigation to securities, construction and trademark cases. Healthcare is also a burgeoning area for the firm with attorneys seeing an increase in drugs liability cases. The team has strong links with the pharmaceutical industry, acting for the likes of Wyeth and appearing in the fen-phen and Vioxx litigations. Clients highlighted responsiveness and value for money as key reasons for choosing the group: *"You get partner-quality service on most matters at very cost effective rates."*

**The Lawyers:** Managing director **John Hermes** is a talented trial attorney whose practice covers all kinds of business-related litigation. A *"true professional"* with a wide range of courtroom experience, he is noted for having superb analytical and judgment skills. *"He comes to good, practical solutions,"* reported sources. **John Kenney** chairs the intellectual property practice group, having carved out a niche for himself in trademarks and technical and scientific litigation; *"ethical, hard-working and always prepared,"* he is best known for acting as lead lawyer for Merck. *"Charismatic"* **Reid Robison** is an effective advocate whose involvement in large white-collar criminal cases has brought him widespread acclaim. *"He understands the issue and is great at trying to simplify it,"* reported clients.

**Clients/Work Highlights:** Dell; Devon Energy; Midwest City Hospital; The GHK Company; American Cancer Society; Medicare and International Steel Group.

## Ryan Whaley Coldiron

**The Firm:** This boutique firm has enjoyed substantial growth over the past year and has benefited from the arrival of a group of environmental specialists. The 18-strong group has expanded its practice beyond complex business litigation to cover all kinds of energy and environmental matters including environmental regulation, litigation, and compliance work. Recent highlights include involvement in several large environmental class actions and complex franchise litigation. Sources applauded the caliber of individuals at the firm: *"They're extremely high-quality lawyers, every one of them."*

**The Lawyers:** *"One of the great lawyers on all counts,"* **Pat Ryan** is a *"professional and principled"* trial attorney who heads up the practice. *"An outstanding courtroom advocate,"* his high-profile cases, such as the prosecution of the Oklahoma City bombers, have brought him national acclaim. One source observed: *"He comes across as a kind, good old boy, but he's actually quite cunning – his mind is always going, he's very clever."* Interviewees admitted they would like to see **Joe Hampton** get more press, given that *"he really is one of the best and brightest young lawyers in the community."* His practice covers complex business and securities-related litigation and, of late, he has tackled an increasing amount of environmental litigation. Sources pointed to his sound and steady judgment: *"You don't see him make a bad step,"* remarked one.

**Clients/Work Highlights:** UBS Financial Services, Oklahoma Tax Commission, Capital West Securities and Sonic.

### Band 3

## Kirk & Chaney

**The Firm:** Commentators endorsed this boutique litigation firm for its high-profile domestic relations work. The practice covers commercial litigation, large divorce cases and a broad range of class action lawsuits involving securities and oil and gas. Because of its size, the nine-person group can offer a personalized service to clients, many of whom cited its *"meticulous case preparation"* as a reason for choosing the firm. Highlights from the year include trying five large family law cases with assets of $1 million to $150 million.

**The Lawyers:** *"Savvy advocate"* **Jim Kirk** is credited with being the driving force of the firm. A specialist in divorce work, he also handles complex litigation and is a much sought-after arbitrator. Sources praised his tactical judgment and sunny disposition, saying *"no matter how hard he works, he'll always keep a pleasant expression on his face."*

**Clients/Work Highlights:** Leading names include Love's Country Stores, Samson Resources and National American Insurance.

## Other Notable Practitioners

Following the reorganization of McKinney & Stringer in November 2005, seasoned trial lawyer **Ken McKinney** has moved to Oklahoma City firm Tomlinson & O'Connell PC. He enjoys a long and illustrious career in litigation and is renowned for a series of high-profile environmental cases. Described as *"absolutely top-notch – an honorable guy who does exactly what he says he'll do,"* he impressed clients with his sincere and subtle style of practice. Tenacious litigator **George Corbyn** of Corbyn Law Firm *"pays attention to every detail,"* agreed peers. With over 33 years of experience as a trial lawyer, he is *"top-notch"* for legal malpractice and breach of contract matters and enjoys a healthy reputation for oil and gas and securities litigation. Interviewees described him as *"hard-working, energetic, and intense."* *"He has such an incredible passion for his work and his clients' cause,"* one said. **Murray Abowitz** of Abowitz, Timberlake & Dahnke PC appears in the tables this year after peers singled him out for *"doing better than most in the last twelve months."* He practices nationally, serving as regional counsel for companies in asbestos and general litigation. Commentators praised his *"diligence, courtroom skill and honesty,"* saying: *"His word is gold."* **Mike Burrage** of Burrage Law Firm can call on his experience as a former US district judge for his practice as a trial attorney and mediator around the state. Peers reported that he had the right personality for mediation: *"He's low-key, unassuming and shows no ego."* He recently defended a case involving the Limitation of Liability Act in which a barge hit an interstate bridge, resulting in 14 deaths and 17 personal injuries.

# REAL ESTATE

### Band 1

## McAfee & Taft
## A Professional Corporation
See firm details p.1666

**The Firm:** This highly respected firm has *"true depth and breadth"* in its real estate practice. Sources observed that these lawyers are *"deal-doers, not deal brokers,"* skilled at fostering a continuum of talented younger lawyers. Fifteen attorneys are adept at handling all types of commercial real estate exchanges and workouts, from complex financing transactions to mortgaging securitizations. The team has a varied client base, representing investors, developers, tenants and owners, as well as banks and other institutional lenders. Over the past year, it has profited from a boom in the healthcare industry by becoming involved in the opening of new hospitals and clinics in the area.

**The Lawyers:** *"High quality and practical"* practitioner **Frank Hill** is *"clearly at the top,"* according to sources. Well respected nationally, he benefits from a heavy tax background, concentrating his practice in the tax and incentive area. He represents a number of tax-exempt organizations such as the University of Oklahoma Foundation with whom he is currently involved in a $500 million, 585-acre, mixed-use development in Norman. *"Thorough"* attorney

| Real Estate |
| --- |
| Leading Individuals |

**Senior Statesman**

> **HASTIE** John *Phillips McFall McCaffrey McVay*

[1] **ELDER** James *Mock, Schwabe, Waldo, Elder, Reeves*

> **HILL** Frank *McAfee & Taft*

[2] **LAIRD** Michael *Crowe & Dunlevy, PC*

> **RIGGS** Richard *McAfee & Taft*

> **SPRADLING** Scott *Spradling, Kennedy & McPhail*

**Richard Riggs** has a broad practice that tends to focus on purchases, sales and leasing. "*He's practical, forthright and looks for ways to make a deal happen,*" enthused commentators who added that he was "*a pleasure to work with.*"
**Clients/Work Highlights:** McBride Clinic Orthopedic Hospital; Sperry Van Ness; Wiggin Properties; Fred Jones Properties.

## Mock, Schwabe, Waldo, Elder, Reeves & Bryant

**The Firm:** This boutique firm has a small but distinguished team of real estate practitioners. Interviewees remarked: that "*they can move quickly as they're a great deal smaller than most.*" Attorneys are dedicated to documenting real estate development projects, acquisitions, and dispositions at a local and national level. In addition to finance-oriented matters, the group also advises on land use and zoning issues.
**The Lawyers:** "*Tenacious and effective*" attorney **James Elder** represents lenders in commercial real estate transactions. Peers found him a delight to work with, describing him as "*totally trustworthy and remarkable for his thoroughness.*"
**Clients/Work Highlights:** BancFirst; Bank of Oklahoma; D.R. Horton; Fidelity Bank; J.M. Huber Corporation; JPMorgan Chase Bank; Lincoln National Life Insurance; Massachusetts Mutual Life Insurance; Metropolitan Life Insurance and Pan-American Life Insurance.

## Band 2

### Crowe & Dunlevy, PC

See firm details p.1662
**The Firm:** This long-established firm has a diverse real estate practice that has undergone some changes of late. Jim Hartmann retired from the group last year while sources continue to lament the loss of Bob Johnson from the firm several years ago. Notwithstanding, the "*highly ethical and responsive*" group benefits from the support of lawyers in cross-disciplinary areas such as taxation and environmental law. Attorneys have expertise across the board from zoning and governmental issues to tax and organizational planning.
**The Lawyers:** "*Flexible and creative*" attorney **Mike Laird** (see p.1660) chairs the group, impressing sources with his ability to find practical solutions to problems. He represents a number of large corporations and real estate developers and has carved a niche for himself in the gaming industry. Highlights from his caseload include the $42 million expansion of Remington Park a racetrack in Oklahoma that is undergoing infrastructural changes to include legal gaming.
**Clients/Work Highlights:** The Williams Companies; Dell; Magna Entertainment; Gardner Tanenbaum Group; Snoddy Properties and BancFirst.

### Phillips McFall McCaffrey McVay & Murrah, P.C.

**The Firm:** This is a young firm renowned for combining its real estate practice with its business practice. Fourteen "*very able*" attorneys are involved in all aspects of complex commercial projects, from their design and construction to management and leasing. Recent highlights include the acquisition and sale of significant out-of-state hotel and resort projects, as well as large track, mixed-use projects with retail and residential components.
**The Lawyers:** "*One of the icons of real estate in the nation,*" and "*a tier unto himself,*" **John Hastie** is stationed in Norman. He has a nationwide reputation as a superb real estate attorney with subset specialties in bankruptcy and other finance matters. Sources admired his deep knowledge and excellent skills as a negotiator.
**Clients/Work Highlights:** Clients include Elgin Development Company, NUCO Investments and Florida Capital Land Corporation.

### Spradling, Kennedy & McPhail LLP

**The Firm:** "*First-class*" was one phrase chosen to describe this compact firm. Three highly skilled attorneys handle a mixture of real estate, financing, litigation and corporate work. They are experienced in advising commercial developers on every aspect of real estate. Clients noted the "*superb quality of workmanship*" demonstrated by practitioners, adding that "*in every deal they identify the potential risks and work towards finding solutions acceptable and fair to all parties.*"
**The Lawyers:** "*One of the less confrontational people you'll want to deal with,*" **Scott Spradling** enjoys the reputation of being a thoughtful, practical lawyer. Clients admire him for always working towards the successful completion of a project. As one said, "*he seems to take that extra step to see that I am satisfied with his performance.*"
**Clients/Work Highlights:** Ackerman McQueen; Anheuser-Busch; Barrick; First American Title & Trust; Prime Time Environments; Lawyers Title of Oklahoma City and American Guaranty Title.

# Leaders in Oklahoma

**ABOWITZ, Murray**
Abowitz, Timberlake & Dahnke PC, Oklahoma City 405 236 4645
*Recommended in Litigation*

**BAILEY, Burck**
Fellers, Snider, Blankenship, Bailey & Tippens, A Professional Corporation, Oklahoma City 405 232 0621
*Recommended in Litigation*

**BARGHOLS, Steven L**
Gable & Gotwals, A Professional Corporation, Oklahoma City
405 235 5500
sbarghols@gablelaw.com
*Recommended in Litigation*
**Practice Areas:** Oil and gas law (litigation and debtor-creditor relations; with transactional-practice background); arbitration and mediation: attorney-fee disputes, business and commercial, eminent domain, construction, contracts, debtor-creditor relations, employment, oil and gas, environmental/pollution, franchising, insurance (coverage and claims), legal and medical malpractice, mold, personal injury, probate/estate administration, products liability, real estate, securities, and trusts.
**Prof. Memberships:** Oklahoma Bar Association; Oklahoma County Bar Association (past President); American Bar Foundation (Oklahoma Fellow); Mediation, arbitration and early-neutral evaluation program panels of the USDC - WD Oklahoma.
**Personal:** University of Oklahoma, BA, 1973 (Phi Beta Kappa); University of Texas School of Law, JD, 1976.

**BARRETT, Gayle**
Crowe & Dunlevy, PC, Oklahoma City
405 235 7700
barrettg@crowedunlevy.com
*Recommended in Employment*
**Practice Areas:** She concentrates her practice in the representation of management in employment litigation in state and federal court. Extensive experience in the representation of management in administrative matters before the US and State Department of Labor, the Oklahoma Human Rights Commission, the EEOC and other administrative agencies. Advises on employment policies and issues.
**Prof. Memberships:** Oklahoma Bar Association's Labor and Employment Law Section (past Secretary and Chairperson). Oklahoma County Bar Association (past Member of the Board of Directors). American Bar Association (Labor and Employment Law Section). Defense Research Institute. General Counsel for Oklahoma City Human Resource Society, 2003 to present.
**Career:** Joined Crowe & Dunlevy in 1982. Member of the firm's Recruiting Committee.
**Publications:** 'Employer's Obligations Under Recent Amendments to The Federal Fair Credit Reporting Act', Lex Mundi World Reports (1998); 'Navagating Through the 'Icebergs' of Employment Law - Pre-Employment Inquiries', The Briefcase (1998); 'Current Status of Employer Liability for Supervisor - Created Sexual Hostile Environment', The Briefcase (1998).
**Personal:** JD, Oklahoma City University, 1982; BS, University of Oklahoma, 1969.

**BICKFORD, Warren**
Fellers, Snider, Blankenship, Bailey &
Tippens, A Professional Corporation,
Oklahoma City 405 232 0621
*Recommended in Litigation*

**BURRAGE, Michael**
Burrage Law Firm, Durant
580 920 0700
*Recommended in Litigation*

**CASON, Len**
Hartzog Conger Cason & Neville, LLP,
Oklahoma City
405 235 7000
lcason@hartzoglaw.com
*Recommended in
Corporate/Commercial*
**Practice Areas:** Tax; trusts and estates;
business and financial transactions. List-
ed in Best Lawyers in America in corpo-
rate law, tax law, and trusts and estates.
**Prof. Memberships:** Fellow, American
College of Trust and Estate Counsel; Fel-
low, American College of Tax Counsel.
Member of Bars of Oklahoma, California
and Texas.
**Career:** Founding Partner, 1979. Adjunct
Professor of Law in Taxation, University
of Oklahoma since 1981. Captain, United
States Air Force JAG, 1972-76.
**Publications:** Various publications in
the Oklahoma Bar Journal, Texas Bar
Journal and Prentice Hall. Most recently,
'Maximizing Funding of Credit Shelter
Trust With Non-Ira Assets' (as published
in the June 2002 edition of Estate Plan-
ning) and The Poorer Spouse Funding
Technique (as published in the May 2004
edition of Estate Planning).
**Personal:** Oklahoma Medical Research
Foundation (Chairman of the Board of
Directors).

**COLEMAN, Chris**
McAfee & Taft A Professional Corporation,
Oklahoma City 405 235 9621
*Recommended in
Corporate/Commercial*

**CORBYN, George**
Corbyn Law Firm, Oklahoma City
405 239 7055
*Recommended in Litigation*

**CORDELL, David**
Conner & Winters, PC, Tulsa
918 586 5711
*Recommended in Employment*

**COURT, Leonard**
Crowe & Dunlevy, PC, Oklahoma City
405 235 7700
courtl@crowedunlevy.com
*Recommended in Employment*
**Practice Areas:** He is the firm Practice
Leader in the representation of management in employment matters in state and
federal court. Extensive experience in the
representation of management in administrative matters before the US and State
Department of Labor, the Oklahoma
Human Rights Commission, the EEOC,
the NLRB, the OGHA and other admin-

istrative agencies. Advises on employment policies and issues.
**Prof. Memberships:** US Chamber of
Commerce (Chairman, Wage, Hour and
Leave Committee, Labor Relations Committee); Center of American and International Law (Member, Planning Committee, Annual Institute on Labor Law);
American Bar Association, Sections on
Labor and Employment Law and Litigation; Oklahoma Bar Association, Section
on Labor Law (former Chairman).
**Career:** Joined Crowe & Dunlevy in
1972; Air Force JAG 1973-77, returned to
firm in 1977; Chairman of firm's Labor
and Employment Law Section; Member
of firm's Risk Management/Loss Prevention Committee.
**Publications:** Co-author, 'Winning Legal
Strategies for Employment Law', Aspatore
Books (2005); 'Closing Argument Tips
for Defending the Employment Case', 13
The Practical Litigator, No 3, p29 (May,
2002); 'Defendant's Motions in Limine -
Winning the Battle That Can Win the
War', 2002 National CLE Conference
Labor and Employment Law, p255 (LEI,
2002); Law Review, Oklahoma City University School of Law.
**Personal:** JD, Harvard University School
of Law, 1972; BA, Oklahoma State Uni-
versity, 1969.

**CRAIG, Richard**
McAfee & Taft A Professional Corporation,
Oklahoma City 405 235 9621
*Recommended in
Corporate/Commercial*

**CREMIN, Pat**
Hall, Estill, Hardwick, Gable, Golden &
Nelson, PC, Tulsa 918 594 0400
*Recommended in Employment*

**DAVIS, Gary**
Crowe & Dunlevy, PC, Oklahoma City
405 235 7798
davisg@crowedunlevy.com
*Recommended in Litigation*
**Practice Areas:** He is the firm Practice
Leader in oil and gas. Extensive experience in the areas of energy, litigation and
trial, and commercial transactions.
**Prof. Memberships:** Admitted to practice in Oklahoma and Kansas (1957).
American Petroleum Institute; Governor's Special Advisory Commission on
oil and gas (1979-82); American Bar
Association; Oklahoma Bar Association.
**Career:** Joined Crowe & Dunlevy in
1982; Chairperson of firm's Oil and Gas
Department.
**Publications:** Chapter: 'Energy Litigation, Business and Commercial Litigation
in Federal Courts', (1998); ''Legal Consideration in the Purchase and Sale of Oil
and Gas Properties', (1983); 'Federal Regulation of the Natural Gas Industry',
(1983).
**Personal:** JD, University of Kansas
School of Law, 1957; BA, University of
Kansas, 1953.

**DAVIS, Steven C**
Hartzog Conger Cason & Neville, LLP,
Oklahoma City 405 235 7000
sdavis@hartzoglaw.com
*Recommended in
Corporate/Commercial*
**Practice Areas:** Tax, business transac-
tions, estates and trusts.
**Prof. Memberships:** ABA; OBA (former
Chairman and officer, Section of Taxa-
tion). Oklahoma Society of Certified
Public Accountants.
**Publications:** Various continuing legal
education articles and materials; articles
in Oklahoma Law Review and Oklahoma
Bar Journal.
**Personal:** American Heart Association
(Past Chairman and Director, Oklahoma
Affiliate). Oklahoma City Community
Foundation (Investment Committee).

**DERRICK, Gary**
Derrick & Briggs LLP, Oklahoma City
405 235 1900
*Recommended in
Corporate/Commercial*

**DUNAGAN, Sidney G**
Gable & Gotwals, A Professional Corporation,
Oklahoma City 405 235 5503
sdunagan@gablelaw.com
*Recommended in Litigation*
**Practice Areas:** Complex business litigation with emphasis in oil and gas disputes, construction issues and profes-
sional and products liability.
**Prof. Memberships:** American Bar
Association, House of Delegates, 1993-
94; Oklahoma Bar Association, President,
1994, Vice President, 1987, Board of Gov-
ernors, 1984-86; Oklahoma County Bar
Association; Tulsa County Bar Associa-
tion, Outstanding Senior Member, 1992,
President, 1990-91; American Bar Foun-
dation - Fellow, State Chairman 1989-
1991; Oklahoma Bar Foundation,
Trustee, 1992-93; Tulsa County Bar
Foundation, Director, 1991-97; American
College of Trial Lawyers.
**Personal:** University of Tulsa, BA, 1965;
University of Tulsa College of Law, JD,
1967.

**EISSENSTAT, Eric**
Fellers, Snider, Blankenship, Bailey &
Tippens, A Professional Corporation,
Oklahoma City 405 232 0621
*Recommended in Litigation*

**ELAM, Theodore**
McAfee & Taft A Professional Corporation,
Oklahoma City 405 235 9621
*Recommended in
Corporate/Commercial*

**ELDER, James**
Mock, Schwabe, Waldo, Elder, Reeves &
Bryant, Oklahoma City 405 235 1110
*Recommended in Real Estate*

**FULKERSON, Sam**
McAfee & Taft A Professional Corporation,
Oklahoma City
405 235 9621
*Recommended in Employment*

**FULLER, Gary**
McAfee & Taft A Professional Corporation,
Oklahoma City 405 235 9621
*Recommended in
Corporate/Commercial*

**GEISTER III, Charles E**
Hartzog Conger Cason & Neville, LLP,
Oklahoma City 405 235 7000
cgeister@hartzoglaw.com
*Recommended in Litigation*
**Prof. Memberships:** ABA; OBA (Civil
Procedure Committee, 1995-2000);
OCBA (Vice President, Continuing Legal
Education and Interprofessional Rela-
tions Committees, former Board of
Directors and Long Range Planning
Committee). US Court of Appeals for the
Tenth Circuit; US District Court for the
Western, Northern and Eastern Districts
of Oklahoma. Luther Bohanon American
Inn of Court (1992-95).
**Career:** Partner since 1998.
**Publications:** Articles on Oklahoma law
regarding statutes of limitation and
repose, liability for off-label use of phar-
maceutical products.
**Personal:** Married, wife Gerry, one child,
Jamie.

**HAMPTON, Joe**
Ryan Whaley Coldiron, Oklahoma City
405 239 6040
*Recommended in Litigation*

**HASTIE, John**
Phillips McFall McCaffrey McVay & Murrah,
P.C., Oklahoma City 405 235 4100
*Recommended in Real Estate*

**HERMES, John**
McAfee & Taft A Professional Corporation,
Oklahoma City 405 235 9621
*Recommended in Litigation*

**HILL, Frank**
McAfee & Taft A Professional Corporation,
Oklahoma City 405 235 9621
*Recommended in Real Estate*

**HOLLOMAN JR, James H**
Crowe & Dunlevy, PC, Oklahoma City
405 235 7725
holloman.james@crowedunlevy.com
*Recommended in
Corporate/Commercial*
**Practice Areas:** Chairperson of firm's
Taxation Practice Group. Has extensive
experience in state taxes, ERISA, trusts,
limited liability entities, M&A and international business.
**Prof. Memberships:** Admitted to practice in Oklahoma (1969); US Tax Court
(1973); American Bar Association; Oklahoma Bar Assocation; New York University School of Law (National Board of
Advisors to Graduate Tax Program).
**Career:** Joined Crowe & Dunlevy, 1972-

81, 1989. Chairperson, firm's 401(k) Profit Sharing Plan.
**Publications:** 'Oklahoma Corporate Forms', (co-author); 'Are Overriding Royalties Unrelated Business Income?', Southwestern Legal Foundation (1975).
**Personal:** LLM, New York University, 1973; JD, University of Oklahoma, 1969; BBA, University of Oklahoma, 1967.

### KENNEY, John
McAfee & Taft A Professional Corporation, Oklahoma City 405 235 9621
*Recommended in Litigation*

### KIRK, James
Kirk & Chaney, Oklahoma City
405 235 1333
*Recommended in Litigation*

### LAIRD, Michael S
Crowe & Dunlevy, PC, Oklahoma City
405 239 6623
lairdm@crowedunlevy.com
*Recommended in Real Estate*
**Practice Areas:** He concentrates his practice in commercial real estate. He also has extensive experience in major construction projects, commercial leasing, energy, healthcare and environmental law.
**Prof. Memberships:** Admitted to practice in Oklahoma (1979). American College of Mortgage Attorneys (Fellow); Oklahoma City Commercial Real Estate Council (Member, Board of Directors, 2004); American Bar Association, Sections on Real Property and Probate and Trust (Chair, Committee H-2); Oklahoma Bar Association.
**Career:** Joined Crowe & Dunlevy in 1985; Chair of Real Estate Practice Group; Vice President of Business Development; past President of Firm (2002-04).
**Publications:** 'Boom Times Can Produce Busted Leases', (February, 2006); 'Water Rights: The Winters Cloud Over the Rockies: Indian Water Rights and the Development of Western Energy Resources', (1979).
**Personal:** JD, University of Oklahoma College of Law, 1979; BA, Harvard University, 1973.

### MCCONNELL, Laura Haag
Hartzog Conger Cason & Neville, LLP, Oklahoma City 405 235 7000
lmcconnell@hartzoglaw.com
*Recommended in Litigation*
**Practice Areas:** Family law, employment law, general and commercial litigation.
**Prof. Memberships:** ABA; OBA, OCBA (Chair, Bench and Bar Committee). American Academy of Matrimonial Lawyers.
**Career:** Listed in Best Lawyers in America (Family Law). WD Oklahoma (Chair Local Rules Committee).
**Publications:** Kerby v Kerby; Smith v Smith; In re CDM; Cysco v Hutchison Hayes International; Robinson v City of Edmond.
**Personal:** Two children, ages 17 and 19.

### MCKINNEY, Kenneth
Tomlinson & O'Connell PC, Oklahoma City
405 606 3350
*Recommended in Litigation*

### MEYERS, Kent
Crowe & Dunlevy, PC, Oklahoma City
405 235 7729
meyersd@crowedunlevy.com
*Recommended in Litigation*
**Practice Areas:** He is the firm Practice Leader in antitrust Law. Has extensive experience in commerical litigation, initiative petition and intellectual property and technology.
**Prof. Memberships:** Admitted to practice in Oklahoma (1964); Member of American College of Trial Lawyers; American Bar Association; Oklahoma Bar Association; Oklahoma County Bar Association (President, 1983).
**Career:** Joined Crowe & Dunlevy in 1964. Chairperson of firm's Litigation Department.
**Publications:** 'Oklahoma's New Antitrust Reform Act', (co-author with Michael Barnett) (1999); 'Private Enforcement of the Antitrust Laws Works Occasionally: The Board of Regents of the Univ of Okla v NCAA, A Case in Point', (co-author with Ira Horowitz) (1995).
**Personal:** LLM, Harvard College of Law, 1976; JD, University of Oklahoma College of Law, 1964; BBA, University of Oklahoma, 1960.

### MOCK, Randall
Mock, Schwabe, Waldo, Elder, Reeves & Bryant, Oklahoma City 405 235 1110
*Recommended in Corporate/Commercial*

### MOORE, Lynnwood
Conner & Winters, PC, Tulsa
918 586 5711
*Recommended in Corporate/Commercial*

### MUCHMORE, Clyde A
Crowe & Dunlevy, PC, Oklahoma City
405 235 7734
Muchmore@crowedunlevy.com
*Recommended in Litigation*
**Practice Areas:** He is a firm leader in litigation with extensive experience in appellate law.
**Prof. Memberships:** Admitted to practice in Oklahoma (1967); American Academy of Appellate Lawyers; American College of Trial Lawyers; Chairman, Oklahoma Bar Association Evidence Code Committee; Luther Bohanon Inn of Court; Oklahoma and American Bar Associations.
**Career:** Joined Crowe & Dunlevy in 1967. President of firm, 1989-91.
**Publications:** 'Oklahoma Appellate Practice' (West Group); 'Oklahoma Civil Procedure Forms - Practice' (Lexis, 2nd edition).
**Personal:** JD with honors, University of

Oklahoma College of Law, 1967; BA, magna cum laude, Phi Beta Kappa, Rice University, 1964.

### NEAL, Kathy
Eldridge Cooper Steichen & Leach PLLC, Tulsa 918 388 5555
*Recommended in Employment*

### NEVILLE, Drew
Hartzog Conger Cason & Neville, LLP, Oklahoma City 405 225 7000
dneville@hartzoglaw.com
*Recommended in Litigation*
**Practice Areas:** Complex litigation in both civil and criminal cases in state and federal court.
**Prof. Memberships:** US Supreme Court; US Court of Appeals for the Fifth, Seventh, Tenth and Eleventh Circuits; US District Court for the Western, Northern and Eastern Districts of Oklahoma, Southern District of New York; Northern and Southern Districts of Texas; Southern District of Florida, District of Colorado; and the Oklahoma Supreme Court. American College of Trial Lawyers. Past President, Federal Bar Association, Oklahoma City. ABA; OBA; OCBA.
**Career:** Director/Shareholder since 2000; Partner, Linn & Neville, 1976-2000.
**Publications:** Written extensively on complex litigation.

### PETRIKIN, Ronald
Conner & Winters, PC, Tulsa
918 586 5711
*Recommended in Employment*

### PLUMB, Charles
Doerner, Saunders, Daniel & Anderson, LLP, Tulsa 918 582 1211
*Recommended in Employment*

### PUCKETT, Tony
McAfee & Taft A Professional Corporation, Oklahoma City 405 235 9621
*Recommended in Employment*

### RATLIFF, Reeder E
Crowe & Dunlevy, PC, Oklahoma City
405 235 7700
ratliffr@crowedunlevy.com
*Recommended in Corporate/Commercial*
**Practice Areas:** While not certified as a specialist under Oklahoma or other applicable law, his field of practice is concentrated in the area of business associations and tax law. He has extensive experience in taxation, mergers and acquisitions, trusts and estates and small business venture capital.
**Prof. Memberships:** Admitted to practice in Oklahoma (1985); Member of the American Bar Association; Oklahoma Bar Association, Section on Business and Corporate Law (Chairman, 2001-02); Certified Public Accountant, Oklahoma (1982-present).
**Career:** Joined Crowe & Dunlevy in 1985. Vice President and Secretary of

firm. Member of Pension and Profit Sharing Committee and Business Acceptance Committee.
**Publications:** Oklahoma Reporter for 'State Limited Partnership Laws', (Aspen, 2001); Oklahoma Reporter for 'State Limited Liability Company & Parntership Laws', (Aspen, 2001).
**Personal:** LLM, New York University School of Law, 1986; JD, University of Oklahoma College of Law, 1985; BA, University of Oklahoma, 1982.

### RIGGS, Richard
McAfee & Taft A Professional Corporation, Oklahoma City 405 235 9621
*Recommended in Real Estate*

### ROBERTSON , Thomas
Nichols, Wolfe, Stamper, Nally, Fallis & Robertson Inc, Tulsa
918 584 5182
*Recommended in Employment*

### ROBISON, Reid
McAfee & Taft A Professional Corporation, Oklahoma City 405 235 9621
*Recommended in Litigation*

### RUPERT, Anton
Crowe & Dunlevy, PC, Oklahoma City
405 235 7790
ruperta@crowedunlevy.com
*Recommended in Litigation*
**Practice Areas:** He concentrates his practice on construction, toxic torts, litigation and trial work, and product liability.
**Prof. Memberships:** Admitted to practice in Oklahoma, 1982; admitted to practice in New York, 1981; American Bar Association, Oklahoma Bar Association; Oklahoma County Bar Association.
**Career:** Joined Crowe & Dunlevy in 1982.
**Personal:** Stanford Law School (JD, 1980); Harvard University (AB, 1977).

### RYAN, Patrick
Ryan Whaley Coldiron, Oklahoma City
405 239 6040
*Recommended in Litigation*

### SELF, Shannon
Commercial Law Group, Oklahoma City
405 232 3001
*Recommended in Corporate/Commercial*

### SPRADLING, Scott
Spradling, Kennedy & McPhail LLP, Oklahoma City 405 418 2700
*Recommended in Real Estate*

### STEWART, Mike
Crowe & Dunlevy, PC, Oklahoma City
405 235 7747
stewartm@crowedunlevy.com
*Recommended in Corporate/Commercial*
**Practice Areas:** He is the firm Practice Leader in the area of business and commercial transactions. Has extensive experience in the areas of financial institu-

tions and finance, business organization, small business and venture capital, mergers and acquisitions and securities.

**Prof. Memberships:** Admitted to practice in Oklahoma (1977); Member of the American Bar Association; Oklahoma Bar Association, Section on Business Association (Vice Chairman, 1979-80).

**Career:** Joined Crowe & Dunlevy in 1977. Past President of the firm. Chairperson of the Business Department. Chairperson of the Technology Committee.

**Publications:** .Potential Immortality of the Old Oklahoma Business Corporation Act' (1994).

**Personal:** JD, University of Oklahoma School of Law, 1976; BA Yale University, 1970. Order of the Coif.

### STRECKER, David
Strecker & Associates, Tulsa
918 582 1716
*Recommended in Employment*

### STRINGER, N Martin
McAfee & Taft A Professional Corporation,
Oklahoma City 405 235 9621
*Recommended in*
*Corporate/Commercial*

### STURDIVANT, James
Gable & Gotwals, Tulsa
918 595 4846
jsturdivant@gablelaw.com
*Recommended in Litigation*

**Practice Areas:** Engaged in private practice since 1964. Has extensive experience as lead trial attorney in complex business disputes with resolution through negotiation, alternate dispute resolution or litigation. Has represented a full spectrum of clients.

**Prof. Memberships:** Member, American (Member, Board of Governors), Oklahoma and Tulsa County Bar Associations. Fellow, American College of Trial Lawyers. American and Oklahoma Bar Foundations. Past Chair, Oklahoma Judicial Nominating Commission.

**Publications:** Lectured and written extensively on litigation related subjects.

Trustee and Research Fellow, Center for American and International Law. Adjunct Professor, University of Tulsa College of Law.

**Personal:** JD, University of Oklahoma, 1964, Order of the Coif, Oklahoma Law Review; BBA, University of Oklahoma, 1959.

### TIPPENS, Terry
Fellers, Snider, Blankenship, Bailey &
Tippens, A Professional Corporation,
Oklahoma City 405 232 0621
*Recommended in Litigation*

### VAN DYKE, Peter
McAfee & Taft A Professional Corporation,
Oklahoma City 405 235 9621
*Recommended in Employment*

### WOLFE, Frank
Nichols, Wolfe, Stamper, Nally, Fallis &
Robertson Inc, Tulsa
918 584 5182
*Recommended in Employment*

# CROWE & DUNLEVY, A PROFESSIONAL CORPORATION

## THE FIRM

**President:** Jimmy Goodman

**Number of attorneys:** 110

**FIRM OVERVIEW:** Crowe & Dunlevy is one of Oklahoma's largest and oldest law firms with offices in the state's three largest cities, Oklahoma City, Tulsa and Norman. The firm was founded in 1902 and represents clients in all aspects of commercial law practice, including complex business transactions, litigation and regulatory practice in both state and federal courts and agencies, energy law, and all types of alternative dispute resolution.

**Legal Alliances:** The firm has 16 attorneys who are members of Employment Law Alliance, the most comprehensive network of employment and labor law attorneys in the world, comprised of 2,000 employment and labor attorneys individually selected from more than 50 nations to form an alliance dedicated to assisting employers. Crowe & Dunlevy is a member of the State Law Resources, a national network of independent law firms – one from each state and two from the District of Columbia – selected for their abilities in handling administrative, regulatory and government relations issues at the state and federal level, helping clients navigate the complex and time-consuming process of managing both legal issues and state government relations. The firm is the sole Oklahoma member of Lex Mundi, a global organization of independent law firms assisting each other in the practice of international business transactions and litigation through consultations, referrals, facility use and often the joint representation of clients, and the World Services Group, an international consortium of professional business providers, including law firms, accountants, financiers and other professional groups.

## MAIN PRACTICE AREAS:

**Aviation/Aircraft:** The firm features a well-known practice group for commercial aviation transactions, including aircraft title examination and aircraft transfers. The attorneys routinely assist major airlines as well as business clients and individuals with importing and exporting aircraft, US registration of foreign-owned aircraft and escrow and documentation needs.

**Commercial Real Estate:** Cowe & Dunlevy represents regional, national and international clients in all areas of commercial real estate, including acquisitions, sales, project development, leasing and financing, title matters, zoning and governmental issues, construction processes, environmental concerns, and tax and organizational planning.

**Corporate & Securities/M&A:** The firm assists a broad and diverse group of business clients, both public and private, in matters ranging from complex transactional work to day-to-day business counseling. Representative transactions include public and private securities offerings, Sarbanes-Oxley and other securities compliance issues, asset and stock sales of large and small businesses and organizational consulting.

**Energy Law:** The firm has more than ten attorneys with broad experience in energy law who provide a wide range of legal services to major energy companies, oil and gas producers, purchasers, contractors and others.

**Financial Institutions/Finance:** Crowe & Dunlevy is well known in the representation of financial institutions of all types for specialized services including loan negotiation and documentation, bank and bank holding company organizations, acquisitions and sales, and regulatory enforcement and compliance matters.

**Healthcare:** The firm has a large and diverse healthcare practice representing hospitals, physicians and physician groups, clinics, HMOs and other managed care groups, long-term care facilities, home health agencies, hospices, academic medical centers and other entities that provide or pay for healthcare services. This practice is comprised of nationally recognized transactional and litigation attorneys.

**Intellectual Property & Technology:** Crowe & Dunlevy's intellectual property and technology attorneys have experience representing national, regional and local companies in patent, trademark, trade secret, copyright and other transactional and litigation intellectual property matters.

**Labor & Employment:** The firm represents management in the rapidly expanding area of labor and employment law. Attorneys have expertise in all facets of labor and employment relationships, including collective bargaining, employment discrimination, wrongful discharge, workers' compensation, employee benefits and administrative practice.

**Litigation & Trial Practice:** Half of the firm's attorneys are regularly involved in representing clients in litigation matters. This includes virtually all aspects of litigation in federal, state and appellate courts, as well as all types of alternative dispute resolution. The firm's litigation clients range from individuals and small businesses, to national and international companies.

## OFFICES

**OKLAHOMA**
20 N. Broadway, Suite 1800, **Oklahoma City,** OK 73102-8273
**Tel:** 405 235 7700   **Fax:** 405 239 6651
**Website:** www.crowedunlevy.com

500 Kennedy Building, 321 South Boston Avenue, **Tulsa,** OK 74103-3313
**Tel:** 918 592 9800   **Fax:** 918 592 9801
**Website:** www.crowedunlevy.com

The Highpoint Office Building, 2500 South McGee Avenue, Suite 140,
**Norman,** OK 73072-6705
**Tel:** 405 321 7317   **Fax:** 405 360 4002
**Website:** www.crowedunlevy.com

## CONTACTS

| | |
|---|---|
| Aviation/Aircraft | Preston G Gaddis II |
| Commercial Real Estate | Michael S Laird |
| Corporate & Securities/M&A | Michael M Stewart |
| Energy Law | Gary W Davis |
| Financial Institutions/Finance | Gary L Betow |
| | Michael M Stewart |
| Healthcare | Karen S Rieger |
| Intellectual Property & Technology | Phillip L. Free, Jr |
| Labor & Employment | Leonard Court |
| Litigation & Trial Practice | Judy Hamilton Morse |

**CROWE&DUNLEVY**
A PROFESSIONAL CORPORATION
Attorneys and Counselors at Law
Founded 1902

# FELLERS, SNIDER, BLANKENSHIP, BAILEY & TIPPENS

## THE FIRM

**President:** Kevin R Donelson
**Number of attorneys:** 54

**FIRM OVERVIEW:** Fellers, Snider, Blankenship, Bailey & Tippens was founded in 1963 and has become one of the major Oklahoma law firms offering broad and diverse legal services to both a local and national clientele. Its founder, James D Fellers served as President of the American Bar Association and the firm has had two presidents of the Oklahoma Bar Association. Its lawyers have developed a strong reputation, both locally and nationally, for providing outstanding legal services.

## MAIN PRACTICE AREAS:

**Banking & Bank Regulations:** Extensive experience representing all categories of banks in virtually all matters, from lender liability, Regulation Z, formation and merger, to all types of regulatory proceedings.

**Bankruptcy:** Active practice in bankruptcy, reorganization, creditors' rights, liquidations, pre-bankruptcy negotiations, and serving as trustees in out-of-court trade arrangements.

**Business, Corporate & Securities:** Comprehensive representation of clients on virtually all facets of business, corporate law, and use of limited liability companies and limited partnerships including choice of entity, financing and structuring sales, mergers and acquisitions, leveraged buyouts, proxy contests and tender offers, buy/sell agreements, asset purchases and sales, stock purchases and sales and executive compensation. It also has substantial experience in the areas of formation, operation, dissolution, liquidation and governance of corporate entities.

**Employment & Labor Law:** Representation of both the public and private employment sectors in all facets of employment litigation and workers' compensation claims. Representation of state, county and local government entities in employment related areas, as well as defending these entities in constitutional and civil rights litigation. Additionally, the firm does extensive pre-litigation resolution of disputes arising in the workplace and formulation of personnel policies and guidelines to address evolving issues in the employment area.

**Energy, Environmental & Natural Resources:** Representation in all aspects of energy transactions, energy marketing and trading, natural gas, energy litigation and administrative/regulatory matters. Negotiation and drafting of agreements in connection with all aspects of the energy industry. Advice and counseling on pre-transaction activities. Development and negotiation of intricate structured transactions. Energy, environmental and toxic tort litigation are handled for the petroleum and petrochemical industry, as well as litigating enforcement actions, natural resource damage claims, citizens suits, common law, and statutory provisions for remediation and cost recovery related to exploration and production, refining, processing, retail, transportation, storage and disposal facilities, to name but a few of the key services provided to the energy industry.

**Intellectual Property:** Handling of intellectual property issues for virtually all technologies. The Domestic Patent Practice is supplemented by considerable experience in procuring international patents. The highly active Trademark Practice is well versed in every element associated with procurement, prosecution and defense of trademarks. The IP Group has valuable experience in obtaining copyright registrations and patents, and structuring acquisition, development and license agreements for innovations. They also advise and counsel clients on all aspects of corporate intellectual property matters. The firm is highly proficient in enforcement of all components of IP law.

**Litigation:** The firm has a national reputation for the quality of its Litigation Practice with a concentration on all facets of commercial litigation on behalf of both plaintiffs and defendants. Its attorneys try cases nationwide, primarily involving complex commercial and business litigation, but also including personal injury and other tort and property damage litigation. In particular, the firm has many attorneys with jury trial experience in oil and gas, insurance,

### OFFICES

**OKLAHOMA**
Chase Tower, 17th Floor, 100 N. Broadway,
**Oklahoma City,** OK 73102-8820
**Tel:** 405 232 0621   **Fax:** 405 232 9659

The Kennedy Building, 321 South Boston Avenue, Suite 800
**Tulsa,** OK 74103-3318
**Tel:** 918 599 0621   **Fax:** 918 583 9659

**Website:** www.fellerssnider.com

intellectual property, antitrust, real estate and banking litigation. The firm also represents both individuals and corporations in a variety of criminal proceedings at all levels of the criminal process. Additionally, the firm is experienced in representing its clients before federal and state administrative agencies. The firm also has an active appellate practice, having presented oral arguments in scores of cases in appellate courts around the country, including the Supreme Court of the United States.

**Real Estate & Commercial Transactions:** The firm serves national and local clients ranging from the most significant real estate transactions in Oklahoma to normal business and personal transactions and mortgage foreclosures. It also represents businesses and individuals in acquiring, financing, selling and leasing real estate. This firm is frequently chosen to serve as local counsel for major national corporations in conjunction with nationwide transactions.

**Regulatory Matters:** The firm has attorneys which have expertise in representing telecommunication and utility companies before the Oklahoma Corporation Commission in all regulatory matters.

**Tax, Trusts, Probate & Estate Planning:** The firm handles numerous estate plans for clients with multi-million dollar estates involving almost every aspect of estate planning. It represents on a regular basis charitable organizations in the handling and administration of charitable gifts, trust departments on numerous matters, beneficiaries in the protection of their interests, creditors and others in estate and trust matters, and handles all aspects of major probates, will contests and other similar litigation. The firm also prepares federal and state estate and gift tax returns for large estates and successfully defends them through the audit process both by the IRS and state agencies.

**CLIENTS:** The unique talents and backgrounds of its lawyers enable the firm to also meet the needs of clients in areas such as aircraft title and financing, agricultural law, and workers compensation. The clients of this firm range from national retail, manufacturing and service organizations whose names are household words, to governmental agencies and entities, to local businesses and individuals. Each client's needs are met and problems solved with the integrity, creativity and dedication upon which the firm's reputation for service and quality has been built.

# GABLE & GOTWALS

## THE FIRM

**Managing Shareholder:** M Benjamin Singletary
**President:** David E Keglovits

**Number of shareholders:** 38
**Number of other lawyers:** 20

**Email:** info@gablelaw.com
**Website:** www.gablelaw.com

**FIRM OVERVIEW:** Gable & Gotwals is a full-service law firm representing a diversified client base in Oklahoma, the southwest and across the nation.

## MAIN AREAS OF PRACTICE:

**Business Litigation:** Gable & Gotwals' trial lawyers represent and counsel major corporations, individuals, businesses and governmental agencies in domestic and international controversies over matters ranging from the simplest to the most complex. This group offers expertise in all aspects of state and federal trial work, state and federal appeals and alternative dispute resolution processes.

**Business Transactions & Securities:** Attorneys in the Business Practice section represent closely held enterprises, publicly traded companies of all sizes, partnerships, limited liability companies and joint ventures in a wide array of business planning opportunities and sophisticated transactions.

**Commercial Law & Bankruptcy:** The firm's Commercial Practice includes business and personal property acquisitions, commercial loan and lease documentation, banking, debtor-creditor relations and consumer law. Gable & Gotwals' vast experience in collections and realization by creditors ranges from the simple replevin, garnishment or attachment to complex federal foreclosures.

**Energy & Regulated Industries:** Gable & Gotwals' energy section offers comprehensive legal services to a wide range of oil and gas concerns, including producers, pipelines, refineries, gas processors, crude oil purchasers, gas storage companies, gas marketers, large independents, and major energy companies. Their transactional work includes acquisitions and sales of large blocks of producing properties in multiple states, preparation of exploration and development agreements, representations of both lenders and borrowers, title examination, marketing contracts, surface damage settlements, gas gathering systems, gas storage facilities, interstate pipelines, and many other oil field, contract and fiscal matters. The firm routinely represents major and independent oil companies in defending litigation throughout the southwestern US and in regulatory matters at the Oklahoma Corporation Commission. The firm successfully prosecutes cases for energy clients and has obtained the largest jury awards, affirmed on appeal, in the states of Oklahoma and Arkansas. Additionally, Gable & Gotwals has obtained defense verdicts for oil and gas companies in cases where claimed damages exceeded $500 million.

**Real Estate & Finance:** The focus of this group encompasses all aspects of real estate, lending and banking law, land and property acquisitions, sales, leasing and development. In lending and banking matters, the firm has a long history of representing national and local financial institutions and insurance companies involved with permanent and construction loans, syndicated credits, project financing, structured financing, sale-leaseback transactions, synthetic leases and other complex financial arrangements.

**Labor & Employment:** Management groups of all sizes and industries count on the attorneys in this group. The firm emphasizes preventative measures to avoid employment-related claims and provide expertise at both the administrative and judicial levels in many specialized areas.

**Environmental Concerns:** Gable & Gotwals routinely handles matters pertaining to environmental concerns. The firm's trial attorneys defend both large and small companies throughout the Southwest. The firm's trial experience in oil field pollution, pipeline spills and toxic waste sites allows it to provide clients with sound evaluation, realistic approaches to case resolution, and the talent needed to present sophisticated environmental issues in state and federal courts.

**Tax, Estate & Business Planning/Trusts & Estates:** From wills to trusts to tax exemption and asset protection, the lawyers of this group have the depth to serve any size client. This practice encompasses business and tax advice, estate planning, employee benefit planning, tax-exempt status, probates and will contests, and guardianship matters.

**Intellectual Property:** Gable & Gotwals provides counsel that inventors, from individuals to corporate research departments, need to protect their ideas from concept to reality. The firm counsels clients with planning and disputes related to patents, trademarks, service marks, copyrights and other intellectual property.

**CLIENTS:** Gable & Gotwals provides efficient, professional and ethical representation for all clients. Featuring a wide range of practice groups, the firm assists an extensive client portfolio with business planning, litigation and arbitration, contract negotiation, and dispute resolution needs. Though Oklahoma-based, the firm's connections are global. Fortune 500 corporations, entrepreneurs, privately owned companies, foundations and individuals entrust the firm every day with the stewardship and strategic management of their legal challenges.

# HARTZOG CONGER CASON & NEVILLE

## THE FIRM

**Managing Partner:** John D Robertson

**Number of partners:** 17
**Number of other lawyers:** 14

**FIRM OVERVIEW:** Hartzog Conger Cason & Neville is known for its results-oriented style of representation and its commitment to unsurpassed client service and responsiveness. The firm has 31 lawyers and is growing in size and capacity to meet the needs of its clientele. The firm expects its lawyers to have strong academic credentials as well as interpersonal skills necessary to communicate effectively with clients and others. Clients include high net worth families and individuals, Section 501(c)(3) organizations, and businesses, some of which conduct business principally in Oklahoma and others that do business on a regional or national level.

## MAIN AREAS OF PRACTICE:

**Business & Financial Transactions, Securities & Business Law:** Hartzog Conger Cason & Neville represents publicly-held corporations, privately-held businesses, entrepreneurs and successful business owners in all aspects of business law, including merger and acquisition transactions, capital formation activities, and securities law matters. This practice area also includes commercial banking and lending transactions, business reorganizations and litigation resulting from these types of commercial transactions.

**Litigation:** Hartzog Conger Cason & Neville has an established Trial and Appellate Practice in state and federal courts. The Litigation Practice includes civil cases involving antitrust law, insurance disputes, professional malpractice, securities litigation, shareholders' derivative actions, products liability, unfair trade practices, agency and licensing board proceeding, general commercial and business litigation, and appeals, as well as white-collar criminal matters. Although the firm represents both plaintiffs and defendants, most of the litigation practice is defense-oriented. During the past five years, the Litigation Practice Group has defended claims in excess of $2 billion. One partner of the firm is a member of the American College of Trial Counsel. Two partners of the firm are individually listed in Chambers among the top business litigators in Oklahoma.

**Employment Law:** The lawyers in this practice group provide legal services and litigation representation in matters concerning all aspects of employment relationships, including employment contracts, personnel policies, employee manuals, drug and alcohol testing, employment termination, sexual harassment, EEOC investigations, executive compensation, hiring and employment of persons with disabilities, wage and hour disputes, health and safety issues, and employee benefits matters.

**Family Law:** The firm handles a variety of family law matters that often have significant financial issues, including divorce trials and appeals, post-decree enforcement and modification, and child support and child custody disputes. The firm has been successful in helping clients reach favorable settlements in family disputes. One of the firm's partners is a Fellow of the American Academy of Matrimonial Lawyers and is listed in 'Best Lawyers in America' in family law.

**Oil & Gas:** This practice group performs oil and gas litigation and handles title matters, property acquisition contracts, operating agreements, environmental matters, and also has an extensive practice before the Oklahoma Corporation Commission.

**Real Estate Law:** The Real Estate Practice Group represents a diverse group of clients in connection with real estate acquisitions and sales, real estate development, multiparty tax-deferred and tenancy-in-common exchanges, environmental law, and a wide variety of complex real estate financing transactions. The firm regularly represents both debtors and creditors in real estate workout transactions and maintains an active practice in the area of real estate disputes and litigation.

### HEAD OFFICE

**OKLAHOMA**
201 Robert S. Kerr Avenue, 1600 Bank of Oklahoma Plaza,
**Oklahoma City**, OK 73102
**Tel:** 405 235 7000   **Fax:** 405 996 3403
**Website:** www.hartzoglaw.com

### CONTACTS

| | |
|---|---|
| **Business & Financial Transactions, Securities & Business Law** | |
| | Len Cason |
| | Armand Paliotta |
| | John D Robertson |
| **Employment Law** | Ryan S Wilson |
| **Family Law** | Laura H McConnell |
| **Litigation** | Drew Neville |
| **Oil & Gas** | David E Pepper |
| **Real Estate Law** | Joseph P Hogsett |
| **Tax Planning & Tax Controversies** | Steven C Davis |
| | Richard B Kells |
| **Wealth Transfer Planning, Trusts & Estates** | Len Cason |
| | Steven C Davis |
| | Susan B Shields |
| | Amy J Sine |

**Tax Planning & Tax Controversies:** Hartzog Conger Cason & Neville's Tax Planning and Tax Controversies Group, which includes three certified public accountants, has a wealth of experience in federal, state and local tax matters, some of which are routine but many of which are unique or special. The firm is regularly involved in ongoing tax planning services for many clients and often is engaged to handle special tax projects, such as criminal tax matters. The firm regularly maintains an extensive tax controversy docket in tax controversies with the state and federal taxing authorities, usually involving business or investment issues. The group regularly assists taxpayer-clients in audits, protest filings, administrative appeals and court proceedings. Two partners of the firm are individually listed in Chambers among the top tax attorneys in Oklahoma.

**Wealth Transfer Planning, Trusts & Estates:** The firm has a significant practice in representing high net worth individuals and families in wealth transfer planning and business succession plans, as well as representing charitable and philanthropic organizations. This practice group is experienced in all aspects of complex estate and trust planning, estate and gift tax, guardianships, estate and trust administration, and in the creation and administration of charitable foundations and trusts. Five partners of the firm are Fellows in the American College of Trust and Estate Counsel (ACTEC); one partner is also a Fellow in the American College of Tax Counsel; and six partners are listed in the 'Best Lawyers in America' in the trusts and estates practice area.

HARTZOG CONGER
CASON & NEVILLE

# MCAFEE & TAFT A PROFESSIONAL CORPORATION

## THE FIRM

**Managing Partner:** John N Hermes

**Number of partners:** 70
**Number of other lawyers:** 46

**FIRM OVERVIEW:** Guided by a client-focused, multi-disciplinary approach, McAfee & Taft has distinguished itself by being an industry leader in developing innovative legal solutions for business. Founded in 1949, the firm has grown to become one of the largest full-service civil practice law firms in the Southwest. The firm is also the sole Oklahoma member of TerraLex®, an international network of independent law firms that serves the business and personal interests of clients whose requirements transcend their state, provincial or national borders.

## MAIN AREAS OF PRACTICE:

**Aviation:** Located just miles from the FAA in Oklahoma City, McAfee & Taft is widely recognized as having one of the largest and most experienced FAA aviation groups in the nation. Its attorneys represent local, national and international clients of all sizes on aviation matters, including the documentation of aircraft transactions, aircraft title and registration matters, aircraft title insurance, escrow closings and closing and post-recordation opinions.

**Business Law:** The firm has significant depth and expertise in representing clients in all aspects of business law, including administrative law, agriculture, antitrust and trade regulations, business immigration, general business and commercial transactions, construction law, energy, environmental, franchising, Native American law and gaming and secured transactions. The firm is also widely regarded for its expertise in handling oil and gas and real estate transactions of all types and sizes.

**Corporate & Securities:** McAfee & Taft has extensive experience advising clients on corporate governance and general corporate matters; partnerships, joint ventures and other business entities; mergers, acquisitions and divestitures; public and private securities offerings; corporate and partnership finance; and venture and private equity capital. The firm also serves the unique legal needs of financial institutions and investment companies, advisors and broker/dealers.

**Employee Benefits:** McAfee & Taft's premier Employee Benefits Practice offers specialized legal solutions in all major areas, including qualified plan design and implementation, multi-employers plans, collectively bargained plans, welfare plans and flexible benefits, executive compensation, plan terminations and surplus assets, plan investments, funding and taxation, plan fiduciary counseling, mergers and acquisitions, legal compliance and ERISA litigation.

**Healthcare:** The firm represents physicians, hospitals and hospital systems, and other healthcare institutions and facilities with respect to managed care contracting, facilities development or expansion, peer review, medical staff issues, medical-legal-ethical issues and affiliation strategies. In its regulatory Healthcare Practice, the firm routinely counsels and advises clients on the fraud and abuse, Stark, tax and antitrust implications related to joint venture arrangements, investment and ownership arrangements, development of outpatient and ancillary facilities, physician practice mergers and acquisitions, corporate affiliations and physician compensation relationship.

**Intellectual Property:** McAfee & Taft represents individuals and businesses in matters involving trademarks, copyrights, patents, domain names, trade secrets, counterfeiting, rights of privacy, Internet liability, unfair competition and false advertising claims, as well as publicity and multimedia rights. The firm's transactional experience includes the registration, licensing, sale and acquisition of complex intellectual property rights and the representation of clients in the entertainment and creative industries. Its dispute practice includes trials, appeals and alternate dispute resolution proceedings.

**Labor & Employment:** McAfee & Taft represents management in all areas of employment-related law. Its practice includes drafting and negotiating labor agreements, resolving labor disputes through arbitration, defending unfair labor practice charges before regulatory agencies, designing and implementing preventive workplace practices, ensuring state and federal compliance, representing management before state and federal administrative agencies, and litigating employment claims in state and federal courts. The firm is actively involved in designing workplace arbitration agreements and arbitrating employment-related cases.

**Litigation:** At its core, this group features senior trial lawyers who have received nationwide recognition from their peers for their experience in handling complex litigation. Firm trial lawyers represent clients in all types of commercial disputes, including litigation and arbitration involving banking, corporations, partnerships and other business entities, franchises, healthcare, insurance, municipal bonds, divorce, oil and gas, products liability, real estate, securities, tax, trusts, telecommunications, trademarks and patents.

**Tax & Family Wealth:** The firm has long been a leader in providing complex tax advice to the business community and individuals. They provide assistance in connection with all forms of family wealth and tax planning, including commercial and private transactions, mergers and acquisitions, oil and gas operations, real estate transactions, deferred compensation arrangements, gift and estate planning, post-mortem planning, foreign transactions and state and local tax issues.

**CLIENTS:** Firm clients are engaged in aviation, banking, communications, construction, employment, energy, wholesale food distribution, franchising, healthcare, insurance, manufacturing, pharmaceuticals, real estate, technology, telecommunications and transportation. The firm also represents non-profit organizations, including universities and foundations, entrepreneurs and individuals.

## MAIN OFFICE

**OKLAHOMA**
Two Leadership Square, 10th Floor, 211 North Robinson
**Oklahoma City**, OK 73102-7103
**Tel:** 405 235 9621  **Fax:** 405 235 0439
Website: www.mcafeetaft.com

## CONTACTS

| | |
|---|---|
| Aircraft | Frank Polk |
| Business Law | Louis Price |
| Corporate & Securities | David Ketelsleger |
| Employee Benefits | Richard Nix |
| Healthcare | Elizabeth Tyrrell |
| Intellectual Property | Michael LaBrie |
| Labor & Employment | Sam Fulkerson |
| Litigation | Henry Hoss |
| Tax & Family Wealth | Steven Cole |

**CONTENTS:** Corporate/M&A p.1667; Employment p.1669; Environment p.1672; Litigation p.1674; Real Estate p.1676; Individuals' Profiles p.1679; Firms' Profiles p.1685.

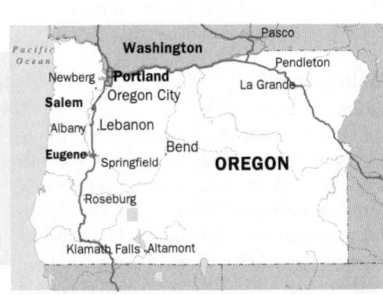

## How lawyers are ranked

Every year we carry out thousands of in-depth interviews with clients and lawyers in order to assess the reputations and expertise of business lawyers across the USA. Chambers rankings and editorial are referred to extensively by General Counsel and other purchasers of legal services who look to our recommendations when choosing their lawyers.

# CORPORATE/M&A

| Corporate/M&A |
| --- |
| Leading Firms |
| 1 STOEL RIVES LLP *Portland* |
| 2 PERKINS COIE LLP *Portland* |
| TONKON TORP LLP *Portland* |
| 3 ATER WYNNE LLP *Portland* |
| MILLER NASH LLP *Portland* |
| 4 DAVIS WRIGHT TREMAINE LLP *Portland* |
| LANE POWELL PC *Portland* |
| PRESTON GATES & ELLIS LLP *Portland* |
| SCHWABE WILLIAMSON & WYATT PC *Portland* |

| Leading Individuals |
| --- |
| **Senior Statesmen** |
| BOOTH Brian *Tonkon Torp LLP* |
| HEWITT Henry *Stoel Rives LLP* |
| 1 CAMPBELL William *Ater Wynne LLP* |
| TUCKER Roy *Perkins Coie LLP* |
| 2 BAUMAN Todd *Stoel Rives LLP* |
| BEYER Ruth *Stoel Rives LLP* |
| CABLE Franklin *Miller Nash LLP* |
| GREENMAN Ronald *Tonkon Torp LLP* |
| MCDONNELL Brendan *Preston Gates* |
| MOORMAN Robert *Stoel Rives LLP* |
| NOTO Margaret *Stoel Rives LLP* |
| SIMPSON Patrick *Perkins Coie LLP* |
| STEPHENS Kenneth *Tonkon Torp LLP* |
| 3 ABRAVANEL Alan *Perkins Coie LLP* |
| BACA David *Davis Wright Tremaine LLP* |
| BULLOCK Brentley *Perkins Coie LLP* |
| CALZACORTA Carmen *Schwabe Williamson* |
| CHESTLER Stuart *Stoel Rives LLP* |
| CORBETT Sherrill *Tonkon Torp LLP* |
| FRANTZ Mary Ann *Miller Nash LLP* |
| HIBBS Carol *Tonkon Torp LLP* |
| PALMER Thomas *Tonkon Torp LLP* |
| STRUXNESS Gregory *Ater Wynne LLP* |
| THOMAS John *Stoel Rives LLP* |
| WOLFSTONE Jeffrey *Lane Powell PC* |
| **Up-and-coming individuals** |
| MATHESON David *Perkins Coie LLP* |

## Band 1

### Stoel Rives LLP

**The Firm:** There is clear blue water between the largest firm in Oregon, which has over 360 lawyers, and its competitors when it comes to corporate/M&A. The team's breadth and depth has led to it being associated with the majority of the high-end work in the state. As commentators remarked, "*its lawyers produce high-quality work and are dedicated to the client and getting the deal done.*"
**The Lawyers:** Firm chair **Henry Hewitt** is widely recognized as "*one of the deans*" of Oregon's corporate Bar. He is commended as an "*outstanding*" representative of the firm, not to mention "*both personable and effective.*" Advising on business strategy and disclosure issues now accounts for much of the time he spends practicing. **Todd Bauman** focuses on deals involving emerging technology sector players and is admired for "*his demeanor and integrity.*" Not only is Bauman "*technically very able,*" but he won praise for his "*very professional approach and treating everyone involved in a transaction with respect.*" Portland office managing partner **Ruth Beyer** primarily provides board-level advice to public and large private companies. She took a lead role in several large M&A transactions in 2005, including Precision Castparts' $185 million stock acquisition of AIC. **Peggy Noto** is "*intelligent, careful, well-informed, and experienced – everything you would expect of a leader in her field.*" Her corporate governance expertise is much in demand, and she is recognized regionally as a securities expert. "*Incredibly able*" head of corporate **Bob Moorman** is frequently seen at the helm when the team advises on more complex transactions involving public company clients. He recently advised on the acquisition of Stormwater Management by CONTECH Construction Products through a reverse triangular merger, with additional payments through earnout. Commentators single out the "*understated but extremely responsive*" **Stuart Chestler** for offering "*the highest level of technical expertise.*" Headline transactions for **John Thomas** include a $210 million senior secured notes offering for VeraSun Energy.
**Clients/Work Highlights:** Electro Scientific Industries; PacifiCorp; PPM Energy; Precision Castparts; Schnitzer Steel Industries; Techtronix and VeraSun Energy.

## Band 2

### Perkins Coie LLP

**The Firm:** The firm is able to provide clients ranging from Fortune 100 companies to startups with a wealth of resources via its 14 offices across the USA and one in China. Though its headquarters in Seattle were most often mentioned as being where the hub of the operation lies, the Portland office is a significant operation in terms of the Oregon market and services a broad spectrum of local and national companies. Public transactions including IPOs and secondary public bonds feature in the workload, in addition to general day-to-day advisory work. One client summarized the firm's approach as follows: "*It always delivers because its lawyers know our business and are probably the most cost-effective counsel we use anywhere in the world.*"
**The Lawyers:** Several market sources consider **Roy Tucker** to be "*in a class of his own.*" A "*lawyer's lawyer,*" he is widely regarded as "*very thorough in his analysis but, more importantly, practical in his counsel*". A principal point of contact both within the firm and in the state as a whole, he is "*one of the smartest guys you'll ever meet and works like a dog.*" Tucker has acted on a number of prominent restructuring transactions and frequently advises on capital and venture capital financings. **Patrick Simpson** has been called "*an extraordinary transactional lawyer with great business sense*" and is well-known for his work in corporate finance and securities law. **Allan Abravanel** focuses on advising both traditional businesses and emerging growth companies in midmarket transactions, sometimes with an international dimension. Seen as a star in the ascendant, **Brentley Bullock** "*is in tune with startup and emerging companies,*" which he advises on corporate finance, securities and M&A. **David Matheson** is a popular choice for leading a team of lawyers and driving a deal forward: "*He just rolls up his sleeves and gets on with it.*" He continues to build on an already impressive profile in the market.
**Clients/Work Highlights:** Teekay Shipping; Merix; Integra Telecom; Innovative Cereal Systems;

PacifiCorp; Qwest; Stockamp & Associates; Tripwire; UPS; Wells Fargo; Weyerhaeuser; Movie Gallery; Endeavour Capital and Corillian.

## Tonkon Torp LLP

See firm details p.1691

**The Firm:** This practice covers all aspects of corporate law on behalf of public and private companies as well as nonprofit entities throughout the Pacific Northwest and beyond. The firm prides itself on its entrepreneurial and creative approach, with particular expertise in M&A, corporate finance and real estate. Privately held midmarket companies based in the Northwest feature heavily in this operation's clientele.

**The Lawyers:** Senior statesman and founding partner **Brian Booth** (see p.1680) is well-connected in Oregon's legal community and has represented the likes of Nike for over 20 years. He is experienced in numerous areas, including corporate governance, representing special committees at board level, M&A and private and public financings. **Ronald Greenman** (see p.1681) is lauded as the "*anchor of the firm's corporate practice*," and is well-known for his technically sophisticated expertise. He specializes in counseling companies undergoing intense periods of growth and advising on associated venture capital financings and later-stage financings, including public offerings. **Kenneth Stephens** (see p.1684) is another of the firm's founding partners and is described in glowing terms by clients as "*a deep thinker who applies his skills to the practice of law with conviction and a huge measure of professionalism.*" He specializes in corporate and securities matters, with a bias in favor of the financial services industry. Clients rate the "*dedicated and energetic*" **Sherrill Corbett** (see p.1680) for her "*responsive and approachable*" manner. One client praised her for paying special attention to "*maintaining an intimate knowledge of our companies' operations, history and goals.*" In addition to her general corporate practice, she offers niche expertise relating to the transportation industry. Clients value **Carol Hibbs** (see p.1681) as "*an exceptionally hard worker who has an incredible mind for detail,*" and for her proactive stance. As one remarked, "*she gets back to us with information before we even ask for it.*" **Thomas Palmer** (see p.1683), chair of the firm's corporate finance group, also won his fair share of praise.

**Clients/Work Highlights:** The Greenbrier Companies; Endeavour Capital; M Financial Group; Nike; Columbia Distributing; Medical Management International; Stimson Lumber; TASER International; Key Technology and DayStar Technologies.

## Band 3

### Ater Wynne LLP

See firm details p.1685

**The Firm:** Advising emerging companies and venture capital funds is the order of the day at this highly respected practice. Technology sector companies feature heavily among its fiercely loyal clientele,

alongside a contingent of sporting brands. In the past year the firm has expanded by adding an office in Menlo Park, Silicon Valley to existing branches in Portland and Seattle. There are now 15 partners in the corporate department, and close cooperation between offices.

**The Lawyers:** Clients describe **William Campbell** as "*an ultrasmart, exceedingly knowledgeable, very committed and hard-working lawyer who focuses on making things happen.*" He came in for further praise for "*throwing everything at a deal, whether it be working all hours to meet deadlines or drawing on the strengths of others when required.*" He is experienced in advising on transactions with an international flavor, especially those involving significant IP issues. Venture funding work has also come to the fore of Campbell's practice recently. Having chaired Ater Wynne's corporate finance group since 2000, **Gregory Struxness** became chairman of the firm in July 2005. His main focus is corporate and securities law. SEC reporting requirements and disclosure obligations all enter into his practice, along with M&A, public offerings, private placements and other finance transactions. Peers respect him as a "*good technical lawyer who represents the interests of public company clients well.*"

**Clients/Work Highlights:** Pixelworks; Planar Systems; TriQuint Semiconductor; FLIR Systems; Golden Valley Electric Association; Oregon Electric Group; Northwest Pipe; Oregon Freeze Dry; Ambric and Avnera.

## Miller Nash LLP

See firm details p.1690

**The Firm:** Miller Nash's clients range from domestic to international operations and include both private and publicly traded companies. It offers expertise in all aspects of business law, whether relating to acquisitions or takeover defense planning. The firm represents acquiring and target companies in a variety of M&A transactions including asset purchases, negotiated stock purchases and tender offers.

**The Lawyers:** Chair of the firm's business department, **Franklin Cable** (see p.1680) made waves, as "*one of a rare breed who has both great breadth of expertise and the ability to draw all the strands of a case together and furnish the client with a global understanding of the issues.*" **Mary Ann Frantz** (see p.1681) is said "*always to provide a timely and thorough response to questions,*" and is renowned for advising on securities matters. Recent highlights for Frantz include advising Blockbuster Video in its attempted takeover of Hollywood Video.

**Clients/Work Highlights:** US Bank; RB Pamplin; Louisiana-Pacific; Pacific Financial and Obsidian Finance Group.

## Band 4

### Davis Wright Tremaine LLP

**The Firm:** This eight-partner team was praised for providing a "*personalized service that takes into consideration the costs involved in a transaction.*" Its

extensive M&A experience largely revolves around advising midmarket companies in traditional industry sectors, although this year two of its big financing deals were for telecom corporations. The fact that several of the team's M&A lawyers have experience as entrepreneurs or of managing their own companies is believed to give them a unique appreciation of the business elements of a deal.

**The Lawyers:** **David Baca** chairs the corporate department and advises small and medium-sized businesses on securities placements as well as M&A. He works closely with underwriters, placement agents and emerging technology companies who appreciate his "*cost consciousness, courtesy and ability to articulate complex ideas.*"

**Clients/Work Highlights:** Advanced Power Technology; Clearwire; Williams Controls; Cascade Bancorp and Banner Bank.

## Lane Powell PC

See firm details p.2009

**The Firm:** Lawyers at the Portland branch of this impressive Pacific Northwest operation work closely with the firm's Seattle office and can "*draw on a wide spectrum of expertise and capabilities to provide an integrated service.*" An M&A team of five represents public and private companies, investors and financial advisors. Acting as tax advisors to foreign governments with regard to US investments helped shape the workload of late, as did advising on venture capital and angel investment matters.

**The Lawyers:** **Jeffrey Wolfstone** is heavily involved in advising startup and midmarket companies as well as national and international businesses with operations in the Pacific Northwest. As one client remarked, "*his professional expertise is of the highest level and his 30 years of experience in the field means he has a skill set perfectly suited to the needs of startup businesses.*" He cochairs the firm's business department.

**Clients/Work Highlights:** Elmer's Restaurants; Nautilus; Theos; EthicsPoint; Norm Thompson Outfitters; Fios; Harry's Fresh Foods; Pendleton Woolen Mills; Epson Portland; Downstream and ERI Acquisition.

## Preston Gates & Ellis LLP

**The Firm:** With over 430 lawyers spread across five western states, not to meniton offices in China, Hong Kong and Taiwan, this firm's up-and-coming Portland office has won a reputation for providing top-quality advice to emerging growth companies, particularly in the areas of life sciences, healthcare and private equity funds. Half of its team focuses on representing government entities and advising on bond issuances. Much of the rest of the practice centers on private equity matters. The firm expects to advise on a growing number of investments and acquisitions involving a heavy debt element.

**The Lawyers:** **Brendan McDonnell** is clearly a hit with clients, who typically commented: "*My preference would be to use Brendan whenever possible.*" Tenacious yet sensitive to "*the different agendas and personalities*" involved in a deal, he shines in listening to his clients and championing his clients' interests. He was billed as a *"phenomenal resource,"* and works primarily with growth companies but also counsels a range of corporations on everyday business issues.

**Clients/Work Highlights:** Columbia Sportswear; QuikTrak; Wells Fargo; Norton Motorcycles; Stelar Tools; Endeavour Capital, Mixx and Empire Pacific Windows.

## Schwabe Williamson & Wyatt PC

**The Firm:** *"Not a firm to be taken lightly,"* its corporate practice has developed an excellent reputation among peers for advising on multistate and interna-

tional transactions, in which it primarily acts for clients based in the Pacific Northwest region. A large part of the corporate finance group's work is real estate-related although its specialists are involved in a range of sectors including agriculture, finance, healthcare, technology, manufacturing and maritime.

**The Lawyers:** Newcomer to this year's tables, **Carmen Calzacorta**, came highly recommended. Her general corporate practice is biased in favor of securities law compliance. Clients say she is *"extremely knowledgeable"* and describe her *"professional yet authoritative demeanor"* as inspiring *"great confidence."* Calzacorta recently advised Columbia

Forest Products on the acquisition of Universal Flooring, a deal involving subsidiaries in Malaysia and Sweden, and also worked with Oregon Steel Mills in relation to the C$22.5 million purchase of the remaining equity in Camrose Pipe.

**Clients/Work Highlights:** Bank of Astoria; Columbia Forest Products; Oregon Steel Mills; Rex Hill Vineyards; Wells Fargo; Washington Federal Savings Bank; NBG Radio Network; Samaritan Health Services; Consonus; Millenium Technology Services; Cammell Laird Pacific and Oremet.

# EMPLOYMENT

# MAINLY DEFENDANT

| Employment: Mainly Defendant |
| --- |
| **Leading Firms** |
| **1** BARRAN LIEBMAN LLP *Portland* |
| **2** BULLARD SMITH JERNSTEDT WILSON *Portland* |
| STOEL RIVES LLP *Portland* |
| **3** AMBURGEY & RUBIN PC *Portland* |
| BULLIVANT HOUSER BAILEY PC *Portland* |
| PERKINS COIE LLP *Portland* |
| WILLIAMS, ZOGRAFOS & PECK *Lake Oswego* |
| **4** DAVIS WRIGHT TREMAINE LLP *Portland* |
| FISHER & PHILLIPS LLP *Portland* |
| MILLER NASH LLP *Portland* |
| SCHWABE WILLIAMSON & WYATT PC *Portland* |

## Band 1

### Barran Liebman LLP

See firm details p.1686

**The Firm:** *"A great firm with great people,"* Barran Liebman is widely regarded as *"the best employment law shop"* in Oregon. The team even represents several of its closest competitor firms in employment matters. The single-office boutique won special praise for its single-plaintiff defense work and has recently been involved in several large public-sector cases. The practice offers employment advice, litigation services and labor relations expertise.

**The Lawyers:** Barran Liebman is home to some of *"the most widely respected and well-known attorneys in town."* As one client commented, *"when you think of employment law in Oregon you think* **Paula Barran**." Described as a *"fabulous practitioner and a fine litigator,"* clients admire her efficiency, competence, thoroughness and quick turnaround on their work. Barran represented the City of Beaverton in a high-profile access to records lawsuit launched by Nike. **Rick Liebman** focuses on traditional labor work and received accolades on all sides as *"a superb lawyer in every respect."* Clients concur that *"his professionalism, substantive knowledge, litigation skills*

and client service are all outstanding." Recent highlights for him include successfully negotiating labor contracts on behalf of Oregon Health & Science University. He is also recognized for the high-quality specialized training he provides to HR professionals. Managing partner **Edwin Harnden** *"provides sound advice that goes straight to the heart of the matter."* He is relied upon for his *"levelheaded"* and *"calming influence"* in strategic planning and advice to management, but when litigation is necessary he *"leaves no stone unturned."* He was also described as *"a forceful and effective advocate."* **Rick VanCleave** specializes in labor relations and collective bargaining. He has recently been working through some complex labor matters with public entity clients.

**Clients/Work Highlights:** Clients include A&I Benefit; City of Beaverton; Don Morissette Homes; Employment Trends; GCR; Lower Umpqua; Mentor Graphics; Oregon Health & Science University; Oregon School District; Port of Portland; TriMet; Unicru and Weyerhaeuser.

## Band 2

### Bullard Smith Jernstedt Wilson

See firm details p.1687

**The Firm:** This 25-attorney Portland-based boutique is well-reputed among competitors and clients alike as Oregon's leading traditional labor law outfit. Competitors praised the breadth of the specialist team's expertise and the balance it strikes between experienced and younger lawyers. The team also offers general employment law advice. Special praise was reserved for its wage and hour work; at the time of going to press the team represented employers in six different class actions. It was recently selected by a large multinational to act as labor and employment counsel for the Northwest region, including Oregon, Washington, Alaska, Montana, Idaho and Wyoming.

**The Lawyers:** Firm president **Kenneth Jernstedt** (see p.1682) is widely recognized as a first-rate traditional labor law expert. Alongside managing the

firm, he recently settled a major contract dispute relating to a processing facility acquired by NORPAC Foods in Quincy, Washington. **David Wilson** (see p.1684) is commended for his *"deep thinking"* and *"critical written work"* while **Richard Alli** (see p.1679) is considered *"an absolutely excellent attorney who can be aggressive when necessary."* He is currently involved in negotiations on behalf of American Steel. **Kenneth Bemis** (see p.1680) focuses on public sector labor law and was recently reselected to represent the City of Tigard in labor negotiations. **Jackie Damm** (see p.1680) enters the main table for the first time this year, thanks to praise from competitors and clients alike for her expertise in traditional labor law and thorough, low-key style. She recently acted as lead spokesperson for Lane Transit District during negotiations relating to an increase in health insurance costs. The team has grown over the past 18 months with a number of lateral hires. **Jathan Janove** (see p.1681) joined in December 2005 from respected Salt Lake City employment boutique Janove Baar Associates. He brings with him considerable litigation expertise and is commended by clients as *"a terrific lawyer of the utmost integrity."* His management training programs are also highly rated. **Thomas Kramer** (see p.1682) runs the firm's employee benefits practice group and is commended for his ERISA work.

**Clients/Work Highlights:** Clients include American Steel; Fred Meyer; NORPAC Foods; Boydstun Metal Works; EC Company; Regis Corp; Rite Aid and Lane Transit District.

### Stoel Rives LLP

**The Firm:** Stoel Rives is currently making bold moves to build its labor and employment team and recently attracted three attorneys from Tonkon Torp, bolstering the team after several recent losses. Now with 15 lawyers in all, the labor and employment practice benefits from the support structure that comes with being part of the largest full-service firm in Portland. The group is particularly well regarded for its contentious capacities. Depending on how the team gels following its growth, competitors concede that recent developments are expected to restore it to being "*one of the strongest and most aggressive*" in Portland, to the extent that it may soon be giving Portland's excellent employment boutiques a run for their money.

**The Lawyers:** Market observers are full of admiration for ex-Tonkon Torp "*star*" **Victor Kisch**, who focuses primarily on labor law. He was praised as being "*very able, personable and gentlemanly*" and "*a great counselor.*" Although heavily involved in the group's lateral hiring strategy, this year **Paul Buchanan** handed in his post as practice group chair to focus more on client matters. HR clients find his employment advice "*invaluable,*" and regard him as "*a teacher as much as an advisor*" in terms of how to respond to difficult situations involving employees. He is also praised for his "*assertive*" yet "*sensitive*" approach as a litigator. "*Top trial attorney*" **Chris Kitchel** recently obtained several complete and partial summary judgments for clients. "*She is experienced, responsive and gets excellent results,*" say sources. Competitors have "*the utmost respect*" for **Amy Pedersen Joseph**, another Tonkon Torp recruit. She was described as a "*straightforward, no-nonsense, smart litigator*" and is renowned as one of

Nike's main external employment lawyers. A number of Oregon-based entities benefit from the "*outstanding consulting skills*" of **Barbara Brainard** in connection with a broad range of employment issues. Clients praise her personable nature and "*thorough, flexible and professional approach.*" **Dan Grinfas** is credited with an "*encyclopedic*" knowledge of the state's labor laws. He is also much in demand for his "*superb*" professional training, regarding which clients say "*he has a terrific sense of humor which helps to engage the audience.*" **Edward Reeves** focuses on employment counseling and collective bargaining, alongside workplace safety and wage and hour issues. Clients appreciate his "*thorough, precise and analytical*" approach, not to mention his "*technical competence and practical nature.*" He is currently working on a broad range of counseling issues for new client Electro Scientific Industries, and cochairs the department with Kisch. Clients say they rely on **Courtney Angeli** for "*top-notch, exemplary work to be done in a timely and cost-efficient manner.*" She enters the table as an up-and-comer and a "*creative thinker who is well humored and sharp.*" Interviewees were also impressed with her "*uniquely persuasive style of communication,*" which makes her equally suited to providing general employment advice as litigation services.

**Clients/Work Highlights:** CH2M HILL; Electro Scientific Industries; Emmis Communications; JELD-WEN; Nike; PCC Structurals; Pope & Talbot; Mentor Graphics; PacifiCorp; Tektronix; Oregon Steel Mills; Advanced Power Technology; HYNI; City of Lake Oswego; Wells Fargo; McCormick & Schmick's Seafood Restaurants; Unified Western Grocers and Graymont.

## Band 3

### Amburgey & Rubin PC

**The Firm:** According to commentators, this small but successful six-attorney employment boutique "*continues to hold its own.*" The firm is well known for its traditional labor law practice but also provides a broad range of employment advice and support in contentious settings, predominantly acting for Pacific Northwest midsized employers.

**The Lawyers:** This team is headed up by eponymous partners **Larry Amburgey** and **Howard Rubin**. The "*charismatic*" Amburgey is "*superb at trial*" and "*one of the best arbitrators in the state.*" Competitors wouldn't hesitate to refer work to him. He is best known for his traditional labor union work and commended for the seminars and in-house training programs he provides. He recently acted as spokesperson for a major communications industry client in successful negotiations with two different union bargaining units, and has also made successful appearances in several labor arbitrations across multiple states. The "*competent, knowledgeable and practical*" Howard Rubin is "*extremely detail-oriented and well versed in the law.*" In addition to core labor expertise his practice covers the gamut of labor and employment work. Clients

consider him "*highly ethical*" and admire his "*concern with regard to delivering the best product and value.*"

**Clients/Work Highlights:** Clients include American Red Cross; Banner Bank; Cascade Steel Rolling Mills; CenturyTel; The Collins Companies; ConAgra Foods; National Frozen Foods; Oregon Bankers Association; OrePac Building Products; Port of Portland; Powells Books; Tri-Cities Laboratory and Willamette Dental Group.

### Bullivant Houser Bailey PC

**The Firm:** The Portland office of this sizable regional player is home to an eight-attorney-strong labor and employment group. The team focuses on employment advice and risk management alongside litigation and employee benefits issues. The past year has seen a major expansion of the firm into California, which has opened the doors to a wider variety of large clients. Indeed, the Portland labor and employment group was recently chosen as preferred multi-state employment counsel for Pfizer.

**The Lawyers:** Practice group chair **Clay Creps** is praised for his "*analytical skills*" and efficiency: "*He is very prepared, very well organized and understands the interrelationships of complex issues,*" said one client. He focuses on employment defense litigation in state and federal courts, and has niche disability law expertise. Partner **Chrys Martin** compliments Creps' practice with further expertise in employment advice and counseling, employee benefits and training for HR and management professionals. Clients describe her as an "*energetic, knowledgeable and approachable*" lawyer with the ability to "*see the big picture, not just the issue at hand.*" It was also remarked that, being a "*skilful strategist,*" "*her methodology instills confidence in the client.*" She benefits from experience as an HR manager.

**Clients/Work Highlights:** Benson Industries; Dr. Martens AirWair USA; Pacific Coast Restaurants; Pfizer; Standard Insurance Company; State Farm and Lewis & Clark College.

### Perkins Coie LLP

**The Firm:** Though its employment practice centers on Seattle rather than the relatively small Portland office, competitors refer work to the latter in cases of conflict. Indeed, the team benefits from being part of the broader network and services a number of major Seattle-based corporate clients. Contentious matters lie at the core of the practice.

**The Lawyers:** **Calvin Keith** heads up the six-attorney Portland employment group, which forms part of the firm's litigation practice. His focus is on high-risk litigation and arbitrations, on which he advises major corporations.

**Clients/Work Highlights:** Most of the firm's clients have national operations and include a number of Fortune 500 companies. Boeing; Boise Cascade; Columbia River Dairy; Gordon Trucking; UPS and Lowe's Home Improvement can all be counted as clients.

## Williams, Zografos & Peck

**The Firm:** The six attorneys at this labor and employment boutique are extremely well-regarded by competitors. The team garners particular praise for the broad range of services it provides to public and quasi-public sector clients and the concern its lawyers show with regard to delivering value for money.

**The Lawyers:** The "*top-notch*" **Kathy Peck** is regarded as an "*outstanding*" lawyer. She won particularly heavy praise for her traditional labor work, in addition to the high-quality specialized training packages she provides.

**Clients/Work Highlights:** Tree Top; City of Lake Oswego; Salem Hospital; GMAC Financial Services; AccuTel; Amcor; Rinker Materials; IDC-CH2M HILL; Concrete Technology; Columbia Distributing; Clackamas County; Clackamas Community College; Southwestern Oregon Community College and Morrow Equipment.

## Band 4

## Davis Wright Tremaine LLP

**The Firm:** This three-partner team is best known for its strength in wage and hour class action defense work, in which it has had a string of successes in recent months at both state and federal levels. The team is also experienced in discrimination, wrongful discharge and breach of contract defense work, and provides employers with extensive advice on preventative employment practices.

**The Lawyers:** Clients describe the "*wonderful*" **Carol Bernick** as "*a tough negotiator*" who "*cuts straight to the chase.*" She represents employers almost exclusively in wage and hour class litigation in state and federal courts. Following her successes at two jury trials last year involving discrimination and breach of contract claims, she recently obtained summary judgment in a case involving allegations of discrimination.

**Clients/Work Highlights:** adidas; Bank of America; GE Capital and Legacy Health System.

## Fisher & Phillips LLP

See firm details p.732

**The Firm:** This Atlanta-based labor and employment powerhouse boasts a national network of 16 offices, providing its Portland operation with a

wealth of resources to draw upon as necessary. The team here merged with the firm in 2003 and, following a number of lateral hires, now comprises seven lawyers in all. It has a broad range of specialists at its disposal, whose areas of expertise include everything from employee benefits to wage and hour issues, whether relating to the healthcare, education or automotive sectors.

**The Lawyers:** Interviewees identify **Corbett Gordon** (see p.1681) as the mainstay of the practice, and she retains a brilliant reputation among competitors and clients alike. She recently acted in a highly publicized investigation for a public body involving over 70 witness interviewees. Her practice covers matters relating to both Oregon and Washington, and she is commended as "*an exceptional practitioner to work with and an insightful strategist.*" Recent new arrival from Stoel Rives, **Clarence Belnavis** (see p.1679), is classed as "*a tireless performer*" and "*excellent litigator.*" He came in for praise for his first-rate customer relations skills. Belnavis covers wage and hour class actions as well as race, gender and religious discrimination defense work. He has also recently taken on managerial duties at the firm.

**Clients/Work Highlights:** Encore Senior Living; Idaho Power; Lee Northwest Publishing and Triumph Composite Systems.

## Miller Nash LLP

See firm details p.1690

**The Firm:** While the Seattle office of this regional firm is heavily involved in employment litigation, the Portland office carries out a great deal of collective bargaining for employers and hospitals in particular. In addition, the 16-strong team covers all aspects of labor and employment law, including labor arbitrations. It is also frequently involved in NLRB proceedings concerning alleged violations of state and federal laws.

**The Lawyers:** In December 2005, "*pillar of the community*" Lou Livingston retired from practice, and both the firm and its competitors concede that his departure is a great loss not only to the team but to "*Oregon labor and employment law in general.*" Nonetheless, clients have the "*highest regard*" for new employment law and labor relations practice group leader **Craig Armstrong** (see p.1679), who is praised for his "*extensive knowledge base, efficiency and interpersonal skills.*" He handles both traditional labor law

and employment law matters. He has taken on a number of Livingston's clients and recently represented Oregon Public Broadcasting in a bargaining agreement, successfully winning major gains for them in cases concerning health insurance contributions.

**Clients/Work Highlights:** healthcare industry clients; Oregon Coast Community College; Oregon Public Broadcasting and Oregon Historical Society.

## Schwabe Williamson & Wyatt PC

**The Firm:** The firm's 12-attorney labor and employment group in Portland covers all aspects of labor and employment law and represent clients in manufacturing, retail and service businesses. Recent highlights for the team include successfully advising the Portland Trail Blazers on issues relating to assistant coaches seeking to move elsewhere that became the subject of proceedings in the federal court. The team was also involved in significant wage and hour litigation for clients. Further highlights include a seven-lawyer team from the firm amicably resolving class proceedings involving 3,000 plaintiffs in Washington and 2,000 in Oregon, relating to allegations of underpayment of overtime and wages.

**The Lawyers:** **Thomas Triplett** "*is able to anticipate reactions from across the other side of the table and diffuse tensions without compromising his client's position on sensitive key issues,*" say sources. Triplett focuses on labor law, and he is described by clients as "*diligent, knowledgeable, creative and likeable.*" The construction industry has been the focus for recent matters which have related to the negotiation of collective bargaining agreements, the arbitration of disputes, Title VII litigation and other wrongful discharge cases. **Mike Garone** carries out both employment and labor work. Wage and hour proceedings take up much of his time and he has recently been involved in a major case relating to the alleged misclassification of an employee's overtime exemption. Following in Triplett's footsteps, Garone has extensive experience in traditional labor law.

**Clients/Work Highlights:** In addition to manufacturers and hospitals, clients include The Trail Blazers/Oregon Arena Corporation; Thompson Metal Fab; Oregon Transfer Company; CLEANPAK International; Columbia Flooring; Alsco-American Linen and Rent-A-Center.

# ENVIRONMENT

## Band 1

### Ater Wynne LLP

See firm details p.1685

**The Firm:** This *"impressive"* Portland outfit is known for its holistic approach to environmental and natural resources law. It combines understanding of such areas as environmental compliance, the Endangered Species Act and air and water quality with experience of environmental permitting and consultation. According to clients, the eight-strong team consistently *"provides high-quality input and a new perspective on complex matters."* Its experience of advising on Superfund matters further defines the practice, and the group is currently involved in the Portland Harbor site cleanup. It is also often retained by Native American tribes to advise on resources issues, often relating to the most remote parts of Oregon.

**The Lawyers:** The *"smart and experienced"* **Claudia Powers** was widely recommended for her strategic skills when handling all manner of environmental liability matters. Interviewees appreciated her ability to *"take a practical approach and work carefully and efficiently for her clients."* Her practice includes assisting businesses with state and federal cleanup and compliance issues. *"When she gets hold of an issue she'll pursue it to the end,"* clients noted. The *"excel-*

*lent"* **Doug MacCourt** works extensively with contaminated brownfield sites and has much experience in their revitalization, sale and redevelopment. His clientele includes manufacturers, transportation companies and local government. MacCourt also offers expertise in endangered species, water and air quality and waste disposal issues.

**Clients/Work Highlights:** Further clients include utility companies, project developers, commercial property owners and businesses such as Cascade General; BP; Advanced Silicon Materials; City of Portland; Northwest Regional Power; Renewable Energy Systems (USA); Weyerhaeuser; Gateway Forest Products; NW Natural and BOC.

### Davis Wright Tremaine LLP

**The Firm:** Interviewees were quick to point out that the firm's general influence in the Pacific Northwest region extends to environmental concerns. Clients praised the environmental team for being *"highly integrated"* in servicing the needs of public and private organizations and companies. Indeed, one of its main drawing cards is the *"joined-up service"* the firm offers, whether it be with regard to litigation or transactional work or both. Recent contentious matters handled by the team include the adjudication of water rights in the Klamath Basin, and defending a fisheries consultancy company against charges involving natural resource damage under the Endangered Species and the Clean Water Acts. Lawyers in the team of 12 also assume regulatory and compliance advisory roles, assisting clients in cleanup actions and steering them through the maze of associated regulation.

**The Lawyers:** *"Formidable environmental litigator"* **Daniel O'Leary** is considered to be *"among the best in the region."* *"His depth of knowledge, outstanding research, thoughtful arguments and timely interventions"* greatly impressed clients. He defended a client in complex commercial environmental litigation involving the EPA and alleged asbestos contamination relating to a housing development, as well as in substantial insurance coverage issues. *"Standout litigator"* **Lawrence Burke** is highly visible. His practice comprises a mixture of air, water and hazardous waste matters along with environmental insurance coverage disputes. *"He's a tough trial lawyer but committed to resolving issues,"* sources stated. In addition, his engineering background affords him a high degree of technical knowledge. **Rick Glick** rounds out the team. He represents local government and developers in water rights adjudications and in hydroelectric power permit proceedings. He also assesses and manages the environmental risk associated with business and real estate transactions.

**Clients/Work Highlights:** The firm represents companies providing agricultural, timber production, real estate development, energy, fishing, maritime and financial services across Oregon and the West Coast.

### Perkins Coie LLP

**The Firm:** This well-structured and *"highly capable"* group of around nine lawyers provides a comprehensive environmental service from its Portland base. Further strengthened by its links with offices across the country, the group handles litigation, permitting and, often in collaboration with real estate and corporate groups, transactional due diligence. Clients assert that these attorneys are *"prompt and easy to reach"* and that they invest in *"developing strong, lasting relationships."* The group acts for a sterling client roster that includes nonprofit agencies, governmental organizations and businesses. Key cases include representing the contractor that built and operates one of the world's largest chemical weapons incinerators in permitting, administrative appeals and litigation.

**The Lawyers:** *"Leading environmental attorney"* **Tom Lindley** is roundly praised by peers and clients alike for the depth and quality of his expertise in such areas as air and water quality, endangered species protection, strategic counseling and litigation. Clients deem him to be *"an expert in his field who enjoys favorable relationships with regulatory agencies."* Others maintain that he *"knows exactly when to jump in and when to stay out of negotiations, ensuring that a successful solution is arrived at."* He represents Owens Corning in contamination cost recovery litigation, site investigations and cleanups. Competitors concede that: *"He doesn't just practice in the field, he has helped develop environmental law and is actively involved in policy development."* **David Bledsoe** stands out on the litigation front, where he acts for a slew of industry clients in environmental and related insurance coverage disputes. Interviewees know him as *"a straight-shooting guy"* whose talent in the courtroom is widely admired.

**Clients/Work Highlights:** Owens Corning; Ross Island Sand & Gravel; GAF; Weyerhaeuser; Washington Group International; Associated Oregon Industries; PG&E Gas Transmission Northwest and Northwest Food Processors Association.

### Schwabe Williamson & Wyatt PC

**The Firm:** The firm has *"done a great job attracting quality lawyers and building the practice"* and now possesses a *"strong environmental offering,"* sources commented. The practice encompasses the full range of environment issues and has an extensive reach across Oregon via its three offices in the state, plus a presence in Washington. The group of five partners works with a substantial number of associates and was enthusiastically praised for its work under the CWA and CAA, and under state and federal regulations as they apply to hazardous waste, real estate transactions and insurance coverage issues. The group has worked on the Portland Harbor Superfund site for a number of clients and taken an active role in ongoing federal litigation over Columbia River flow patterns and the impact on salmon, hydroelectric facilities and navigation.

**The Lawyers: David Bartz** stands out as a *"great litigator with a strong knowledge of environmental issues."* He represents clients in cost recovery and contribution litigation and in administrative proceedings before state and federal agencies. **Patricia Dost** won high marks for her work in environmental cleanup and water quality matters. *"She has developed a strong reputation,"* peers claim, *"as an active, diligent and hard-working attorney."* In addition, she offers niche expertise in endangered species that are potentially affected by contaminated or degraded land or water. Billed as an *"outstanding water lawyer,"* Salem-based **Martha Pagel** manages a large water resources-based practice. Her clients range from regional utilities involved in hydroelectric projects to individuals, government entities, farms and businesses.

**Clients/Work Highlights:** Clients include Boise Cascade; Simpson Timber; NW Natural; Columbia Forest Products; United Airlines; Clean Water Services; West Oregon Electric Cooperative; Port of Vancouver and Kennecott Mining.

## Stoel Rives LLP

**The Firm:** This *"dominant player"* fields a strong environmental and natural resources practice, sustained by what clients and peers describe as *"a large, excellent group that is responsive, accessible and proactive."* It has teams of lawyers dedicated to specific areas such as air quality, timber and forest products, water quality and water rights, and environmental insurance claims. It also handles issues associated with hydroelectric and other power facilities, endangered species and land use, mining projects and paper mills. It has a particularly strong profile in Oregon, though its influence and office network extend throughout the West. The firm's prominence in the corporate and real estate fields further helps to feed the practice.

**The Lawyers:** At the helm of the firm's environmental practice is **Mark Morford**. His clients enthusiastically praised the *"diversity of his practice,"* with many claiming he is *"great across the board, providing a comprehensive service on all environmental matters."* He concentrates on complex regulatory compliance matters and advises companies on air, water and hazardous material issues. Morford represented Clackamas County Development Agency in the acquisition of a Superfund site and, in a separate matter, negotiated the favorable settlement of a CWA citizen suit against a paper mill. *"He was there at the beginning, developing brave new statutes and formulating the shape of environmental law,"* sources maintain, and he continues to be involved in legislative and policy initiatives. **Joan Snyder** works primarily in cleanup matters and environmental compliance and is described by several sources as *"one of the*

*smartest lawyers I ever met."* In addition, she possesses a *"great technical background"* and excellent litigation skills. She represented Oregon Steel Mills in matters relating to the Portland Harbor Superfund site and has specialist expertise in the environmental aspects of real estate transactions. **Michael Campbell** was recommended as a *"real star"* in water quality work, where he represents clients and trade groups. **Thomas Wood** has a national practice and focuses on air quality, along with acting for the wood products industry. He has advised on the permitting of quarries, cement plants, natural gas fields and multiple biofuel power plants in Oregon and Washington.

**Clients/Work Highlights:** TDY Industries; McFarland Cascade; ESCO Corporation; Freightliner; Oregon Steel Mills; Schnitzer Steel Industries; Pacific Realty; Temco and Ash Grove Cement.

## Band 2

## Cable Huston Benedict Haagensen & Lloyd LLP

**The Firm:** The environmental and natural resources department of this midsized Portland firm merits a place in the table for its comprehensive coverage of environmental concerns. It is often retained to act for municipal governments, businesses and individuals in contaminated site compliance and litigation, environmental cost recovery and permitting. Air and water quality as well as waste cleanup and management further contribute to the workload. Several members of the 16-strong team have technical backgrounds in fields such as chemical engineering and biology, and many have representative industry experience.

**The Lawyers:** *"Respected and knowledgeable,"* **James Benedict** stands out for his prominent hazardous waste practice. He advises on waste handling, storage and disposal as well as substance remediation processes. He also represents clients in siting electric generating facilities and issues relating to landfill sites.

**Clients/Work Highlights:** Waste Management; Eugene Water & Electric Board; Bayer CropScience; JH Baxter; Tri-City Service District; City of Albany; Chemical Waste Management of the Northwest; Aventis Agriculture and Rockwood Public Utility District.

## Landye Bennett Blumstein LLP

See firm details p.1689

**The Firm:** This local group is considered a mover and shaker in Oregon on the full gamut of environmental issues. Illustrative projects include the prosecution and defense of numerous Superfund cost

recovery cases in the state and federal courts and the investigation of insurance coverage for pollution claims. Elsewhere, attorneys advise on hazardous waste management regulations, permitting laws and various other kinds of environmental litigation in federal and state courts. The team brings its experience to bear on work throughout Oregon, Alaska and Washington, as well as specific projects across the USA.

**The Lawyers: David Blount** is highly regarded as a litigator but also has significant expertise in environmental regulation and compliance. According to clients, *"he is a tenacious litigator but his greatest strength is to come up with solutions that multiple sides can subscribe to."*

**Clients/Work Highlights:** Clients include public and private entities, individuals, real estate developers, community associations and nonprofit groups.

## Rycewicz & Chenoweth LLP

**The Firm:** The environmental law practice accounts for a weighty proportion of this local firm's civil litigation and transactional output. Water and air quality as well as water rights issues dominate, along with underground storage tank remediation and contaminated site redevelopment. The team of five acts for businesses of all sizes, as well as individuals and nonprofit agencies, in regulatory compliance proceedings, enforcement actions and environmental litigation. Known as *"strong litigators,"* the attorneys here offer specialist expertise in cost recovery actions and insurance coverage for environmental cleanup procedures and disputes.

**The Lawyers:** *"Emerging talent"* **Chris Rich** is increasingly sought after for his ability in environmental compliance matters and litigation.

**Clients/Work Highlights:** The firm's clients include property owners, businesses, industrial facilities, nonprofit organizations, timber organizations and individuals.

## Other Notable Practitioners

**Max Miller** (see p.1682) of Tonkon Torp LLP is characterized as a well-rounded environmental lawyer who covers clean water, clean air and hazardous waste issues, among others. He represents one of the landowners on the Portland Harbor Superfund site, and acts for Stimson Lumber in the cleanup of, and permitting for, current and former mill sites and timberlands in Oregon and across the USA. *"I like him,"* one peer said. *"He is levelheaded and often acts as the calm voice of reason in a room full of upset people."*

# LITIGATION

# GENERAL COMMERCIAL

| Litigation: General Commercial |
|---|
| Leading Firms |

| 1 | MARKOWITZ, HERBOLD, GLADE *Portland* |
|---|---|
| | PERKINS COIE LLP *Portland* |
| | STOEL RIVES LLP *Portland* |
| 2 | BULLIVANT HOUSER BAILEY PC *Portland* |
| | DAVIS WRIGHT TREMAINE LLP *Portland* |
| | MILLER NASH LLP *Portland* |
| | SCHWABE WILLIAMSON & WYATT PC *Portland* |
| | STOLL STOLL BERNE LOKTING *Portland* |
| | TONKON TORP LLP *Portland* |
| 3 | ATER WYNNE LLP *Portland* |
| | DUNN CARNEY ALLEN HIGGINS *Portland* |

| Leading Individuals |
|---|

| Senior Statesman |
|---|
| MARMADUKE Don *Tonkon Torp LLP* |
| ★ ELLIS Barnes *Stoel Rives LLP* |
| MARKOWITZ David *Markowitz, Herbold, Glade* |

| 1 | ENGLISH Stephen *Bullivant Houser Bailey PC* |
|---|---|
| | FORTINO Paul *Perkins Coie LLP* |
| | HOUSER Douglas *Bullivant Houser Bailey PC* |
| | SKERRITT Daniel *Tonkon Torp LLP* |
| | STOLL Robert *Stoll Stoll Berne Lokting* |
| | TONGUE Thomas *Dunn Carney Allen Higgins* |
| 2 | BERNE Gary *Stoll Stoll Berne Lokting* |
| | BLACKHURST Steven *Ater Wynne LLP* |
| | CROW William *Schwabe Williamson* |
| | CROWE Austin *Perkins Coie LLP* |
| | DULCICH Thomas *Schwabe Williamson* |
| | GIDLEY James *Perkins Coie LLP* |
| | GLADE Peter *Markowitz, Herbold, Glade* |
| | MARTSON JR William *Tonkon Torp LLP* |
| | MOWE Gregory *Stoel Rives LLP* |
| | MULLIN Joel *Stoel Rives LLP* |
| | NEWELL Robert *Davis Wright Tremaine LLP* |
| | RAWLINSON Dennis *Miller Nash LLP* |
| | RICHTER Peter *Miller Nash LLP* |
| | ROSENBAUM Lois *Stoel Rives LLP* |
| | SIMON Michael *Perkins Coie LLP* |
| | WALTERS Martha *Walters Romm Chanti* |
| 3 | ARELLANO Joseph *Kennedy, Watts, Arellano* |
| | AXELROD David *Schwabe Williamson* |
| | BANKS Robert *Banks Law Office* |
| | HAGLUND Michael *Haglund Kelley Horngren Jones* |
| | KENT Christopher *Kent & Johnson, LLP* |
| | KILMER Jeffrey *Kilmer Voorhees & Laurick PC* |
| | KNOX Daniel *Schwabe Williamson* |
| | MCGRORY John *Davis Wright Tremaine LLP* |
| | NEUPERT John *Miller Nash LLP* |
| | O'LEARY Daniel *Davis Wright Tremaine LLP* |
| | ROTHAUGE Renée *Bullivant Houser Bailey PC* |
| | SAND Thomas *Miller Nash LLP* |
| | SHLACHTER Robert *Stoll Stoll Berne Lokting* |
| | TURNER Mark *Ater Wynne LLP* |
| | WHITTEMORE Richard *Bullivant Houser Bailey PC* |

## Band 1

### Markowitz, Herbold, Glade & Mehlhaf PC

**The Firm:** The market lavished praise on this *"classy commercial litigation boutique,"* with clients and peers claiming its 13 lawyers *"can do anything."* The firm covers business litigation, arbitration and other methods of dispute resolution, and acts on both plaintiff and defense sides. It is a popular address for referrals, not least because of the *"tremendous job that these highly organized lawyers do on large and complex cases."* Key case highlights include representing local utility companies in disputes over power supply contracts. Professional malpractice and securities litigation are both sustained themes. Clients appreciated the team's ability to *"approach matters calmly and create successful strategies."*

**The Lawyers:** *"Talented, smart and always well-prepared,"* **David Markowitz** is considered a permanent fixture *"on the A-list"* of Oregon trial lawyers. *"He's among the best in the city,"* one client enthused, while others pointed to his communication skills and his ability to do a *"fine job in front of judge and jury"* in the largest cases. Interviewees were *"greatly impressed"* by **Peter Glade**'s work, and one labeled him *"quite excellent as a strategist."* His general commercial litigation practice is complemented by his niche accounting malpractice expertise.

**Clients/Work Highlights:** adidas America; Agassi Enterprises; DR Horton; Georgia-Pacific; Hollywood Entertainment; Lewis & Clark College; Portland General Electric; Sony Pictures Entertainment; Standard Insurance; US Bank; Unified Western Grocers; The Hartford and Oregon Steel Mills.

### Perkins Coie LLP

**The Firm:** Respect in the marketplace remains high for this full-service business law firm and it *"certainly warrants a top-tier ranking for litigation,"* sources agreed. An integrated approach draws on the firm's plentiful resources in Seattle while the Portland group scores highly with interviewees for its *"strong bench"* of highly respected trial lawyers. They are experienced in class actions, products liability, antitrust, patent law and real estate litigation as well as environmental disputes. As such, members of the team appear in federal and state trials as well as appellate courts across the country.

**The Lawyers:** Interviewees described leading light **Paul Fortino** as *"incredibly shrewd in the courtroom."* He tries an array of commercial and fraud cases and is increasingly involved in IP and securities litigation. *"Well-seasoned trial lawyer"* **Austin Crowe** sustains an eclectic caseload and scooped compliments for his ability in products liability, personal injury, toxic tort and construction disputes. Clients describe **Jim Gidley** as a *"natural courtroom performer – he loves being there and does a great job."* His recent portfolio has involved products liability defense and asbestos litigation, but he is also experienced in covering personal injury and mass tort defense cases. **Michael**

**Simon** excels in the areas of antitrust, unfair trade practices and IP litigation. A *"bright, persistent attorney with a practical approach,"* he offers additional expertise in securities and insurance coverage litigation.

**Clients/Work Highlights:** Dex Media; Qwest; PacifiCorp; ScottishPower; Abbott Laboratories; Louisiana-Pacific; Union Carbide; ACL Services; Altec; Deere & Company; UPS; Union Pacific; Hewlett-Packard; Novartis; Genie Industries; Boeing and The Kroger Company.

### Stoel Rives LLP

**The Firm:** The litigation department at this Oregon stalwart is *"definitely one of the best in town,"* clients report. The group acts for a wide range of clients based in the Northwest, including financial companies, utilities, public entities and manufacturers. Several interviewees consider this *"the best firm for major business litigation,"* and its recent highlights include acting for Freightliner in a $500 million civil action to recover damages. Members of the firm also successfully represented PPM Energy in a lawsuit brought by an environmental group seeking to halt construction at the Elk River Wind Farm. Thriving practices in Washington and California, along with firmwide strength in areas such as corporate, real estate and employment, all contribute to its prominence in the field.

**The Lawyers:** Peers and clients alike singled out **Barnes Ellis** as being *"hugely prominent and the destination for many of the major cases in the market."* He boasts *"a fine legal mind and great trial presence,"* not to mention *"a wealth of experience."* He handles a large amount of securities litigation, representing major companies in Oregon and Washington. Recent highlights include his involvement in the criminal trial in Houston of the former CEO of Enron Broadband Services. *"Respected"* **Greg Mowe** affords further scope to the firm on real estate and business litigation fronts. His portfolio includes corporate clients and government bodies. Clients enthusiastically endorse **Joel Mullin** as a *"strategist with great judgment"* who can adapt to the case in hand. He has a strong business litigation practice that involves securities work, corporate governance and contract disputes. Mullin recently represented Nike in an annexation and public records dispute. The *"bright and enthusiastic"* **Lois Rosenbaum** won plaudits for her proven abilities in complex litigation. She has represented public and private companies in class actions, securities litigation and major products liability cases.

**Clients/Work Highlights:** Schnitzer Steel Industries; Farmers; Tektronix; PacifiCorp; NW Natural; Fred Meyer; Safeway; TriMet; The Oregonian; PNGC Power; Freightliner; Precision Castparts and Portland Development Commission.

## Band 2

### Bullivant Houser Bailey PC

**The Firm:** While it has always been renowned for its insurance defense practice, this full-service firm has "*been making a real splash in the last few years*" and has met with significant success in general commercial litigation settings. Clients were impressed by the group's willingness to "*devote resources, time and attention*" to their cause. A deep bench and effective lines of communication between its six large West Coast offices were also noted as counting in the firm's favor. The team frequently handles litigation and other methods of dispute resolution pertaining to complex securities litigation, environmental, real estate, bankruptcy and IP disputes.

**The Lawyers:** **Stephen English** won praise for "*being both detail-oriented and able to keep the big picture in mind at one and the same time.*" This year he appeared in several highly visible business litigation and commercial fraud cases. He also successfully defended an investor in a startup company in a trade secrets claim, and represented Portland Trail Blazers' assistant coach in seeking to be released from a contract with the National Basketball Association. **Doug Houser** was recommended for his "*national reputation in insurance law circles*" along with his work in class actions and appellate hearings. "*Every time he is in the courtroom he reminds me how good he is,*" one interviewee commented. Others added: "*He knows how to pick his fights and the more complex the case, the better he gets.*" "*Highly impressive emerging talent*" **Renée Rothauge** joins the table this year, having come to the attention of peers and clients during a number of large-scale jury trials. Her practice has an IP emphasis, though she handles a wide range of complex business disputes. **Richard Whittemore** is known for his prowess in products liability defense, complex business litigation and estates issues.

**Clients/Work Highlights:** BNSF Railway; Caterpillar; Chubb Group; Deere & Company; Dr Martens; Eli Lilly; Kubota; Louisiana-Pacific; Medline Industries; Sears and Standard Insurance.

### Davis Wright Tremaine LLP

**The Firm:** "*This operation has a significant presence and a substantial pool of talent in the field,*" according to commentators. Its Portland offering can call on the backup of the firm's nationwide network of offices for support as required. This group of "*careful and competent*" lawyers, which is well known for appearing in a range of matters from large class actions to significant alternative dispute resolution proceedings, comfortably retains its position in the table. Antitrust, IP, healthcare, environmental and business torts further define the practice.

**The Lawyers:** A prominent figure in the area, **Robert Newell** is held to be a "*smart lawyer who is reasonable to deal with and a strong advocate.*" Clients appreciate his management ability and aptitude in the courtroom. The "*practical and effective*" **John McGrory** offers expertise in complex antitrust matters, with a recent emphasis on the medical field.

and also covers securities litigation and SEC enforcement work. **Daniel O'Leary** was described as "*truly formidable*" when it comes to environmental and natural resources litigation. In addition, he is experienced in handling employment, insurance coverage and real estate and land use disputes.

**Clients/Work Highlights:** Viacom; XO Communications; Eastern Oregon Public Land Coalition; Oregon Agricultural Legal Foundation; Bank of America; Legacy Health System; adidas America and Dryvit Systems/RPM.

### Miller Nash LLP

See firm details p.1690

**The Firm:** Billed as an "*outstanding law firm with plenty of fine lawyers,*" this Pacific Northwest player is credited with a significant presence in contentious proceedings. According to one client, its practitioners are "*always there when I need them and consistently exercise good judgment.*" The department handles the full range of litigation, arbitration and mediation issues. Disputes relating to employment law, real estate matters, securities and construction all feature in the firm's portfolio. With its "*extensive resources*" and offices in Portland, Seattle and Vancouver, the firm is well positioned in the market.

**The Lawyers:** The "*tireless*" **Dennis Rawlinson** (see p.1683) has a "*great reputation*" both in Bar activities and in the courtroom. Clients describe him as a "*smart, experienced and skillful attorney who effortlessly commands the court's attention when he speaks.*" Clients were unequivocal in their praise for **Peter Richter** (see p.1683), calling him "*simply a darn good trial lawyer.*" His practice includes breach of contract, trade secrets, securities fraud and construction cases, primarily in the federal courts. "*Key litigator*" **John Neupert** (see p.1683) is another of the firm's leaders in the field and is well-known for his work in banking, business, IP and environmental litigation. The firm's managing partner **Thomas Sand** (see p.1684) retains a strong trial practice with an emphasis on securities and employment.

**Clients/Work Highlights:** Abbott Laboratories; GlaxoSmithKline; 3M; Monsanto; City of Portland; Johnson & Johnson; US Bank and Weyerhaeuser.

### Schwabe Williamson & Wyatt PC

**The Firm:** Clients who have dealt with this group of approximately 60 lawyers speak of "*all-around positive experiences.*" While insurance defense has always been a traditional focus area, its "*talented practitioners are well equipped to deal with high-profile matters*" across a range of areas. A strong products liability section is complemented by significant IP, antitrust and pure commercial expertise. A flurry of construction defect claims has contributed heavily to the workload of late. Meanwhile, the firm maintains close relations with top-level clients in the finance, marine, real estate and healthcare arenas.

**The Lawyers:** The universally respected **William Crow** is considered to be a driving force behind the firm's litigation department for, as clients remarked, "*the bottom line is, he gets great results.*" Antitrust is one of his focus areas, where there has been a health-

care flavor to recent matters, along with complex business litigation and products liability disputes at both state and federal levels. **Thomas Dulcich** is frequently associated with high-profile work, his involvement in the Archdiocese litigation being a case in point. This matter involved bankruptcy protection being triggered by claims for damages stemming from allegations of clergy abuse. Discrimination, harassment and defense of injury claims further define his practice. "*Effective courtroom lawyer*" **David Axelrod** has, according to sources, a good range of experience and is "*careful, imaginative and hard-working.*" He focuses on patent law, trade secrets and business litigation. **Daniel Knox** also comes highly recommended as a commercial litigator specializing in the defense of maritime and construction claims.

**Clients/Work Highlights:** Colonial Pacific Leasing; Port of Vancouver; KeyBank; Allied Signal; Dresser Industries; Ford; URS Corporation; Simpson Housing; Volvo Construction Equipment; Wyeth; Rent-A-Center; Wells Fargo/Acordia; Oregon Steel Mills; DuPont; the Primerica Companies and GE.

### Stoll Stoll Berne Lokting & Shlachter

**The Firm:** While this has long been the "*firm of choice*" for plaintiff securities litigation, its focus has broadened of late to include IP and patent cases. Clients and peers point accordingly to its involvement in many high-profile cases on behalf of both plaintiffs and defendants, and credit the team with having developed an "*impressive degree of flexibility.*" Recent highlights include obtaining a $52 million judgment against Farmers in a case involving a dispute over the payment of overtime wages.

**The Lawyers:** Sources claim that "*to work at the firm at all you have to be fairly talented,*" and single out **Robert Stoll** as "*an exceptionally capable trial lawyer.*" "*One of the best practitioners for complex securities class actions,*" he is described as "*a strategic thinker with great courtroom presence.*" Clients agree **Gary Berne** "*sure knows what he is doing,*" especially in terms of complex plaintiff securities work, where he is said to have "*a knack for keeping things simple and understanding how judges like a case to be run.*" **Robert Shlachter** offers a "*likeable, persistent and persuasive*" style. He concentrates on IP, unfair competition and commercial litigation.

**Clients/Work Highlights:** Oregon Public Employees Retirement System; Oregon Health & Science University; Paulson Investment; Waddell & Reed; WM Financial Services; ScanlanKemperBard Companies and Hollywood Entertainment.

### Tonkon Torp LLP

See firm details p.1691

**The Firm:** This Portland powerhouse has successfully leveraged off its strength in the corporate arena to become "*a leader in the field of major business litigation.*" Clients discern a large, diverse team of attorneys with "*strategic vision*" in such areas as trade regulation, securities, real estate and IP disputes. The team has a great deal of trial experience as well as appellate expertise and arbitration know-how. A recent run of energy sector cases included members of the group representing Portland General Electric in a class action relating to its closed nuclear power plant.

**The Lawyers:** "*Grandmaster litigator*" **Don Marmaduke** (see p.1682) specializes in IP and antitrust litigation. Interviewees acknowledged that the fact that he has tried more than 250 cases during his career speaks for itself. **Dan Skerritt** (see p.1684) won plaudits from across the board for his "*low-key, thoughtful and highly persuasive manner.*" Sources describe him as being "*right at the pinnacle of his career*" and, as one client explained: "*He sees the goal and goes after it in a way that is quite remarkable. He is well prepared and never obstructive.*" Clients also recognize a seasoned litigator in **Rick Martson** (see p.1682). He is described as a "*cerebral and demanding attorney who will uncover every weakness in an opponent's case.*" Accountancy sector and high-stakes corporate litigation are the chief subjects of his practice. In a recent significant case he represented a former officer on the Enron board of directors in all Enron-related litigation and governmental investigations.

**Clients/Work Highlights:** Nike; The Greenbrier Companies; Portland General Electric; Pacific Seafood Group; PPM Energy; M Financial Group and Medical Management International.

## Band 3

### Ater Wynne LLP

See firm details p.1685

**The Firm:** The strong, focused group of attorneys that makes up Ater Wynne's litigation group is committed to serving the needs of clients all along the West Coast. From IP to employment litigation,

business torts to construction claims, the group handles a range of disputes. Corporate securities and corporate governance issues are also sustained themes. An increase in telecom regulation work has further defined the workload of late.

**The Lawyers:** Clients rate **Steven Blackhurst** for his "*practical approach to legal problems and canny ability to always bring reason to a case.*" He is much in demand for his securities disputes and corporate governance expertise, but also covers trade secrets, IP and telecom work. **Mark Turner** is another of the firm's most respected litigators. He stands out for his experience in securities litigation settings and recently handled an accounting malpractice suit for plaintiffs.

**Clients/Work Highlights:** Advanced Silicon Materials; Alliance Capital Management; FLIR Systems; Golden Valley Electric Association; Metro One Telecommunications; Northwest Pipe; Oregon Health & Science University and The Schnitzer Group.

### Dunn Carney Allen Higgins & Tongue LLP

See firm details p.1688

**The Firm:** Above all, its sterling insurance defense and securities dispute work distinguishes this full-service firm from competitors. However, sources noted the team's "*visibility in the market at large,*" including with regard to some large-scale cases. It is popular among local and regional clients seeking representation in litigation, appeals, mediation and arbitration. The group is managing a substantial antitrust class action against its client Weyerhaeuser.

**The Lawyers:** Interviewees have only good things to say about **Thomas Tongue** (see p.1684). One interviewee summed him up as "*the cream of the crop at the firm and one of the brightest lawyers in the

state.*" Clients call upon him for assistance with particularly sensitive problems and rely on his "*tactical, strategic advice.*" Many claim that although he is a "*fierce competitor, his first impulse is to avoid unnecessary confrontations.*" This "*practical wisdom*" coupled with "*an encyclopedic knowledge of the law*" means he really stands out to commentators.

**Clients/Work Highlights:** Oregon State Bar Professional Liability Fund; Northwest Physicians Mutual Insurance; Weyerhaeuser; Hollywood Entertainment; North Pacific Group; Safeco Insurance; Allstate; PacificSource Health Plans; Allied Insurance and Farmers.

## Other Notable Practitioners

**Martha Walters** of Walters Romm Chanti & Dickens is warmly recommended as a plaintiff employment litigator. She is based in Eugene and also practices family law. The "*excellent*" **Joseph Arellano** of Kennedy, Watts, Arellano & Ricks LLP concentrates on securities cases along with other complex litigation and professional liability defense. He recently defended a startup company in securities violations. "*He inspires confidence in his clients and is good to work with as co-counsel,*" interviewees stated. The "*highly rated*" plaintiff securities lawyer **Robert Banks** of The Banks Law Office has a practice that is national in scope. He recently handled several arbitrations involving investors and stock brokerage firms. **Michael Haglund** (see p.1681) of Haglund Kelley Horngren Jones & Wilder LLP won his fair share of praise and has been active in the timber industry for many years. **Chris Kent** of boutique firm Kent & Johnson LLP is "*high on many a list when it comes to a conflict,*" while **Jeff Kilmer** of Kilmer Voorhees & Laurick PC is described as "*an excellent, committed lawyer.*"

# REAL ESTATE

| Real Estate | |
|---|---|
| **Leading Firms** | |
| [1] | BALL JANIK LLP *Portland* |
| [2] | PERKINS COIE LLP *Portland* |
| | STOEL RIVES LLP *Portland* |
| [3] | BATEMAN SEIDEL MINER BLOMGREN *Portland* |
| | DUNN CARNEY ALLEN HIGGINS *Portland* |
| | SCHWABE WILLIAMSON & WYATT PC *Portland* |
| | TONKON TORP LLP *Portland* |
| [4] | DAVIS WRIGHT TREMAINE LLP *Portland* |
| | LANDYE BENNETT BLUMSTEIN LLP *Portland* |
| | LANE POWELL PC *Portland* |
| | MCEWEN GISVOLD LLP *Portland* |
| | MILLER NASH LLP *Portland* |

## Band 1

### Ball Janik LLP

**The Firm:** Market observers agreed that this specialist real estate outfit more than deserves its status as clear market leader, with many claiming, "*it's an absolutely stellar real estate and land use firm, a notch above the rest.*" Its name is synonymous with quality and, as one client put it, "*you can look in any direction at that firm and see a highly accomplished real estate lawyer.*" Renowned for its work with "*top-flight*" real estate institutional clients and developers, this "*large, focused*" group is able to provide both "*depth and breadth in its advice.*" This year it worked on a number of high-profile deals including: a mixed-use department store conversion project in downtown Portland; a condominium development in Portland's South Waterfront district; the sale and development of Bridgeport Village shopping and entertainment center, and land use approval for high-rise condominium projects.

**The Lawyers:** Clients were unswerving in their praise of **Stephen Janik**, who many said operates "*on a totally different plane to the rest*" due to his dual strengths in real estate and land use. "*No job is too sophisticated,*" commentators agreed, "*for this extraordinarily creative lawyer.*" He is "*admired for his negotiation skills and political connections*" as well as his "*boundless energy*" and glittering client roster. Managing partner and chair of real estate **Bradley Miller** is credited with excellent transactional skills and an ability to "*close a deal out without appearing to have it all his way.*" All of this gives him an edge over many of his rivals, among whom he is widely regarded as "*intelligent, pragmatic and professional.*" He was involved in the development of Cascade Station as part of the proposed extension to the MAX Light Rail line to Portland International Airport. **Barbara Radler** is distinguished by her speed and technical acumen: "*To be able to rely on a lawyer to produce a first-rate product so rapidly is critical to effective real estate business,*" one commentator

## Real Estate
### Leading Individuals

#### Senior Statesmen

**BALL Robert** *Ball Janik LLP*

**SAMUELS Stanley** *Bateman Seidel Miner Blomgren*

★ **JANIK Stephen** *Ball Janik LLP*

[1] **CANTLIN Richard** *Perkins Coie LLP*

**FEUERSTEIN Howard** *Stoel Rives LLP*

**GREEN David** *Stoel Rives LLP*

**HAUCK Terry** *Schwabe Williamson*

**MILLER Bradley** *Ball Janik LLP*

**PAGE Thomas** *Stoel Rives LLP*

**RADLER Barbara** *Ball Janik LLP*

[2] **BATEMAN Randall** *Bateman Seidel Miner Blomgren*

**BENNETT J David** *Landye Bennett Blumstein LLP*

**GISVOLD Dean** *McEwen Gisvold LLP*

**GOODLING Jonathon** *Miller Nash LLP*

**GRANT Eugene** *Davis Wright Tremaine LLP*

**GUINASSO John** *Schwabe Williamson*

**PARKER Gilbert** *Dunn Carney Allen Higgins*

**VOBORIL Joseph** *Tonkon Torp LLP*

[3] **ANTELL Kenneth** *Dunn Carney Allen Higgins*

**CARTER Don** *McEwen Gisvold LLP*

**JOHNSON Randal** *Ater Wynne LLP*

**KEENEY Jeffrey** *Tonkon Torp LLP*

**MANULIK Mark** *Schwabe Williamson*

**MATTHEWS Christopher** *Perkins Coie LLP*

**PARKS Timothy** *Ball Janik LLP*

**POWELL Bryan** *Lane Powell PC*

**RUSSELL III P Stephen** *Landye Bennett Blumstein*

**STAYER Mark** *Schwabe Williamson*

#### Up-and-coming individuals

**GUSTAFSON Karna** *Landye Bennett Blumstein LLP*

**TOM Rebecca** *Ball Janik LLP*

## Real Estate: Zoning/Land Use
### Leading Individuals

★ **JANIK Stephen** *Ball Janik LLP*

[1] **ABEL Steven** *Stoel Rives LLP*

**PFEIFFER Steven** *Perkins Coie LLP*

**RAMIS Timothy** *Ramis Crew Corrigan LLP*

**ROBINSON Michael** *Perkins Coie LLP*

**SULLIVAN Edward** *Garvey Schubert Barer*

**WHITE Christen** *Ball Janik LLP*

---

opment. She was actively involved in the development of office and condominium towers and major medical buildings in Portland. She is also working on the Portland State University extension plan.

**Clients/Work Highlights:** Williams & Dame; A&B Properties; Melvin Mark; the Goodman Family; Opus Northwest; IKEA and Schnitzer Northwest.

### Band 2

## Perkins Coie LLP

**The Firm:** The firm's "*heavyweight group of acknowledged experts*" stands tall in the Oregon market. The real estate group deals with a spread of transactional work including loans, leases, purchases and sales across a broad range of industry sectors. Residential work makes up a substantial segment of the practice, alongside construction and permitting issues for hospitals, schools and retail outlets. A "*particularly strong land use practice*" works closely with the development group on matters ranging from permitting issues to appeals. The overall team can draw upon the expertise of attorneys in the firm's well-regarded Seattle headquarters for additional input on larger deals.

**The Lawyers:** "*There's nothing he ever misses,*" said one commentator of the "*extraordinarily creative*" **Richard Cantlin**. He has a loyal client following involved in deals that take place across the region and beyond. "*Not only is he capable in terms of knowledge and skill, that much is beyond doubt;* said one client, "*but he also excels at thinking outside the box.*" **Christopher Matthews** has an eclectic practice that has been involved in several innovative projects over the past year, notably the development of Hope VI New Columbia and Cascade Station. "*Top-notch zoning lawyer*" **Steven Pfeiffer** focuses on land use, natural resources law and real estate development. He consistently impresses in matters of the highest profile. "*First chair land use lawyer*" **Michael Robinson** appears regularly before local government bodies and state agencies. "*He's a rock-solid attorney and I would refer work to him in a heartbeat,*" one source asserted.

**Clients/Work Highlights:** Specht Development; PacTrust; West Hills Development; Safeway; Albertson's; Lowe's; Providence Medical Group; Wells Fargo; Ross Island Sand & Gravel; Qwest; Threemile Canyon Farms; PeaceHealth; Bechtel and Kaiser Foundation Hospitals.

## Stoel Rives LLP

**The Firm:** "*This group of strong, bright, professional real estate lawyers is just so good,*" competitors conceded. A full-service firm with a large corporate practice, Stoel Rives represents many leading companies in Oregon. Its strength and depth in real estate, land use and construction guarantees it a place in the upper echelons of practices in the field. Its attorneys are seen to "*understand what matters in real estate transactions*" and they come in for praise among clients for being "*accurate, reliable and customer-focused.*" Condominium developments and various

---

acquisitions, sales and leasing have come to the fore of late. Examples include representing Health Systems Group in the acquisition of the Medical Center Physicians Building in Vancouver, and a transaction for TriMet involving the establishment of a permanent transit center in southeast Portland.

**The Lawyers:** A triumvirate of top-tier practitioners is thought to stand the practice in good stead. "*Amazing lawyer*" **Howard Feuerstein** is "*top of the list*" in high-level transactions, according to clients. He specializes in condominiums, mixed-use development and planned developmental work. "*When it comes to condominiums he knows more than any other lawyer in the state,*" peers claimed, and he ramped up an impressive number of high-end transactions on this front, including in the Pearl District, northwest Portland and downtown Portland. He was also heavily involved in the development of the South Waterfront district. The name **David Green** is associated with "*gigantic transactions*" across the country. His "*unique way of making difficult negotiations go smoothly*" is said to stem from his "*even-tempered manner and the fact that he never ceases being on the lookout for a solution.*" He has worked on several projects for Willamette University, including the construction of Kaneko Commons, a student housing facility. Representing national retailers is another focus area, and he advises Eddie Bauer on new leases at numerous shopping centers and malls across the USA and Canada. Acclaimed as "*a phenomenal technical lawyer whose skill level is unsurpassed,*" **Thomas Page** concentrates on commercial developments, as well as acquisitions, leasings and sales. Clients respect the "*premium he puts on collaboration,*" and those who work with him on a regular basis say he is a "*professional, fast, hard worker.*" Notably, he represented Oregon Clinic in the development of a multi-story medical office, and is currently assisting a large architectural firm with the development of a new mixed-use office and apartment building. The "*strong and professional*" **Steven Abel** affords further scope to the firm on land use and development issues. He represents private and public sector clients in permitting and developing industrial, commercial and residential developments.

**Clients/Work Highlights:** Harsch Investment Properties; Gramor Development; NW Natural; Pacific Realty Associates; PPM Energy; Intel; Trendwest Resorts; Port of Portland; TriMet; Gerding/Edlen Development; Larkspur Hospitality and PacifiCorp.

### Band 3

## Bateman Seidel Miner Blomgren Chellis & Gram, P.C.

**The Firm:** Although the firm was only established in the last year, it is perceived to have been "*incredibly busy*" and is expected to "*really go places.*" It is made up of the real estate practice group and affordable housing team from Preston Gates & Ellis, and deals in the main with real estate financing, secured loans and purchases and sales. The outfit also has a

---

noted. She stands out in the market as an "*ultra-diligent and forthright*" practitioner who has worked on many of the group's most high-profile deals. The prolific **Timothy Parks** handles a high volume of small deals, putting him firmly "*on the radar,*" especially where real estate-related tax issues and the development of hotels and other commercial property is concerned. Commentators branded long-standing real estate expert **Robert Ball** "*a prince,*" adding that "*he has a great track record.*" **Rebecca Tom** is particularly noted for her experience in the field of condominiums and real estate leasing and financing. "*Outstanding practitioner*" **Christen White** concentrates on land use and real estate devel-

reputation for development work. Another area of specialism is low-income housing, where much of the work takes place out-of-state. The 12 "*impressive*" lawyers recently worked on developments for Newland Communities and on the construction, purchase and sale of housing in Oregon.

**The Lawyers: Randall Bateman** is "*definitely an excellent lawyer, no question,*" according to sources. He is heavily involved in lending work and closed a number of large secured loans for life insurance clients last year. He also works for developer clients on the borrower side. Interviewees claim **Stanley Samuels** "*comes from the old school; he is polite, fair and nothing short of a pleasure to work with.*" Peers know him as a "*cut-to-the-chase kind of guy*" and respect his "*organized, logical and straightforward*" style.

**Clients/Work Highlights:** PNC Bank; Newland Communities; Homestead Capital; Oregon Pacific Investment Development; Carla Properties; LSI Logic; New York Life; MassMutual; US Bank; Eastport Plaza Shopping Center and CIGNA.

## Dunn Carney Allen Higgins & Tongue LLP

See firm details p.1688

**The Firm:** Boasting one of Portland's most prominent developers, Gerding/Edlen, as a client, this team of nine lawyers is "*clearly doing something right,*" say competitors. Clients describe the firm's real estate lawyers as "*very knowledgeable and a pleasure to work with,*" and further praise them for "*completing work in a timely manner.*" The team concentrates mainly on real estate development and finance work, where it covers a range of sectors from industrial parks to residential. Construction matters, acquisitions and sales, as well as leasing issues, further shape the workload.

**The Lawyers: Gilbert Parker** (see p.1683) has worked with Gerding/Edlen on the South Waterfront project as well as several other local projects this year. "*He is skilled in preparation and negotiation and outstanding on complex transactions – he can keep several balls in the air at once,*" said one impressed commentator. **Kenneth Antell** (see p.1679) is considered by clients to be an "*even-keeled attorney.*" His care and attention to detail is renowned among peers who claim that "*you wouldn't doubt the job would get done and get done well if Antell was on the case.*" His most significant deal of the past year has been the acquisition, financing and leasing of Keizer Station, a mixed-use site.

**Clients/Work Highlights:** RREEF Management; Bones Construction; CalWest Industrial Holdings; Norris & Stevens; North Pacific Group; Pan Pacific Retail Properties; Hollywood Entertainment; Providence Health System and Powell Development.

## Schwabe Williamson & Wyatt PC

**The Firm:** This "*leading real estate and land use firm*" consists of around 15 lawyers providing a full service to its clients in all aspects of the acquisition, ownership, management and disposition of commercial real estate. The group can call on the support of specialized departments covering environmental and land use issues, and has been active in the strong real estate markets along the West Coast, as well as in Arizona and Idaho. It counts developers, owners and lenders as clients.

**The Lawyers: Terry Hauck**'s "*unassuming manner*" belies his real status "*as one of the deans of the real estate Bar.*" Competitors savor the thought of working with a lawyer "*so clearly at the top of his game.*" Hailed as "*vivacious and smart in equal measure,*" interviewees were united in their praise of Hauck, one of Oregon's "*best-known, most well-rounded lawyers.*" He continues to be active in real estate development and sales and acquisitions. Peers praised "*smart and confident*" lawyer **John Guinasso** for "*his attention to detail and ability to handle huge quantities of information.*" The retail sector and development work are key areas for him, in which he acts for a number of long-term clients such as Harsch Investment Properties. **Mark Manulik** is highly rated for his work on real estate lending. Widely recognized as a "*solid and capable performer,*" he is also president-elect of the American College of Mortgage Attorneys. **Mark Stayer** joins the tables as "*one to watch out for*" where high-value, sophisticated deals are concerned.

**Clients/Work Highlights:** Wells Fargo; Simpson Housing; Bank One; KeyBank; Louis Dreyfus Property Group; Harsch Investment Properties; Morgan Stanley; United Grocers; RBC Mortgage; Bechtel; Office Depot and First Horizon.

## Tonkon Torp LLP

See firm details p.1691

**The Firm:** Real estate transactions and land use are two major focus areas for this "*balanced*" group, though it covers the full range of real estate issues. The presence of several new recruits attests to the firm's growth, and recent work highlights include assisting IKEA Property with the zoning aspects of a new facility near Portland International Airport. The team also advises on the real estate aspects of alternative energy projects and the purchase and construction of distribution warehouses.

**The Lawyers: Joseph Voboril** (see p.1684) is, according to peers, "*always a pleasure to work with.*" He has a "*solid understanding of real estate and how to prepare and negotiate transactions,*" and is well known for his all-round ability. He recently acted for Portland Art Museum on its $40 million renovation project. Known as "*extremely careful and detail-oriented,*" **Jeff Keeney** (see p.1682) has a general real estate practice that emphasizes acquisitions, sales, commercial leasing and land use planning. He represents Costco on all Oregon real estate matters including the development of a new warehouse and fueling station. Clients are impressed by his ability to combine "*attention to detail with timeliness.*"

**Clients/Work Highlights:** Holiday Retirement; Colson & Colson Construction; Costco Wholesale; Nike; Winkler Development; Naito Properties; PPM Energy and Staples.

## Davis Wright Tremaine LLP

**The Firm:** The depth of real estate expertise at this prominent US firm allows it to offer personal attention, cost-effectiveness and efficiency to its clients. These clients include developers, tenants, contractors, lenders, and building and real estate associations throughout the country. In particular, timber, sand, gravel and other resource companies feature heavily. The team works on a mix of leasing, residential and commercial development and condominium sales and is "*particularly strong in transactional settings.*" On the commercial leasing side, the group acted on CH2M HILL's office lease at the Parkside Center and is also frequently involved in the retail sector.

**The Lawyers: Eugene Grant** won commendation for providing "*a fast and thorough reaction in deals.*" He mostly deals with commercial leasing transactions and residential sector work. In the past year he worked on a variety of real estate transactions for Mercy Medical Center in Roseburg and, elsewhere, on numerous mixed-use and residential condominium transactions.

**Clients/Work Highlights:** Government Properties Trust; Mercy Medical Center; Louis Dreyfus Property Group; St Paul Properties; First Technology Credit Union; XO Communications; Evergreen Industrial Park; Citibank; Manufactured Housing Communities of Oregon; PS Business Parks; ScanlanKemperBard and Oregon Rangeland Trust.

## Landye Bennett Blumstein LLP

See firm details p.1689

**The Firm:** Offices in Oregon and Alaska cater for clients in both states as well as in Washington. The firm also represents clients in other parts of the country on specialized matters. Numerous condominium and community associations as well as developers of condominium projects and planned communities feature as clients. Members of the firm also offer niche homeowners' association expertise.

**The Lawyers: David Bennett** is a "*big name*" in the field of homeowners' associations and an "*expert in condominium development,*" say peers. He is a "*very creative thinker, knowledgeable and a joy to see on the other side,*" according to one source. The "*understated*" **Stephen Russell** is perceived as "*excelling when it comes to the business side of real estate transactions*" and is another of the firm's lawyers with specialist expertise relating to homeowner associations. He also acts for community associations and real estate multiple listing services. The "*bright and capable*" **Karna Gustafson** has "*built a great practice for herself,*" which covers several of the firm's specialized focus areas.

**Clients/Work Highlights:** Outside of its niche areas, the firm provides a wide range of services on real estate-related matters to owners, sellers, lenders, borrowers and real estate brokers.

**Lane Powell PC**

See firm details p.2009

**The Firm:** The firm offers a wide range of expertise that covers the purchase and sale of commercial and residential property as well as commercial lending and real estate finance. Leasing, land use and development matters also contribute to the workload along with the real estate aspects of bankruptcies.

**The Lawyers:** Cochair of the real estate and land use group, **Bryan Powell**, works mainly on corporate transactions, particularly those involving affordable housing and commercial and industrial mixed-use projects. He also has broad experience of secured and asset-based lending.

**Clients/Work Highlights:** The firm serves clients throughout the Pacific Northwest as well as national and international corporations. Examples include: Home Depot; Sockeye Development; Oregon Public Employees Retirement System and Portland Development Commission.

**McEwen Gisvold LLP**

**The Firm:** Billed as a *"firm of fine lawyers,"* McEwen Gisvold has a real estate practice that extends to all aspects of real estate transactions and almost every kind of property. It is renowned in the market for its track record in real estate lending, particularly with regard to acting for out-of-town lenders. Local and regional developers account for the majority of its client base.

**The Lawyers:** Sources described the *"widely respected"* **Dean Gisvold** as *"an excellent real estate lawyer, who is enthusiastic and dependable."* He works in general real estate, real estate finance and commercial law. *"Solid and to the point,"* **Don Carter** is primarily a lender's lawyer but also advises on environmental, business and estate planning issues.

**Clients/Work Highlights:** The firm represents mainly developers, investors, lenders and business owners. It has acted for the Oregon Public Employees Retirement Fund on several projects including Plaza Tower One, the California Center, Edgewater Office Park and General Tire Industrial Center.

**Miller Nash LLP**

See firm details p.1690

**The Firm:** This established firm is perceived to thrive on *"good connections, good clients and a high volume of work."* Its lawyers provide a comprehensive real estate service to individuals, partnerships, limited liability companies and corporations. The team is experienced in handling matters relating to residential, commercial and industrial properties, in addition to which it covers associated areas such as tax, land use and environment.

**The Lawyers:** The *"technically excellent"* **Jonathon Goodling** (see p.1681) is known among peers for *"doing what it takes to get the deal done so that everyone walks away happy."* Traditional real estate matters, financing and commercial lending transactions form the bulk of his workload.

**Clients/Work Highlights:** Ashforth Pacific; McMorgan; US Bank National Association (commercial real estate division); Guardian Management and Specht Properties.

**Other Notable Practitioners**

With his *"no-nonsense style,"* **Randal Johnson** of Ater Wynne LLP *"makes negotiating a complex lease simple,"* commented clients. He has substantial experience of representing developers in all aspects of commercial, industrial and residential projects. **Timothy Ramis** of Ramis Crew Corrigan LLP covers land use, transportation planning, local government applications, permitting and legislative drafting. *"He takes a reasonable position and argues his case well,"* enthused peers, with one adding, *"he has a large volume of land use work and is darn good at it."* **Edward Sullivan** of Garvey Schubert Barer *"is one of the first names to trip off the tongue when talking about land use issues in Oregon,"* according to interviewees.

# Leaders in Oregon

**ABEL, Steven**
Stoel Rives LLP, Portland 503 224 3380
*Recommended in Real Estate*

**ABRAVANEL, Alan**
Perkins Coie LLP, Portland
503 727 2000
*Recommended in Corporate/M&A*

**ALLI JR, Richard J**
Bullard Smith Jernstedt Wilson, Portland
503 248 1134
ralli@bullardlaw.com
*Recommended in Employment*
**Practice Areas:** Collective bargaining, private and public sector; labor contract administration; union organizing issues; arbitration; NLRB and Oregon ERB proceedings; grievance and arbitration procedures; personnel policies and practices
**Prof. Memberships:** Oregon State Bar, Labor and Employment Law Sections; American Bar Association, Labor and Employment Law Sections; Multnomah Bar Association.
**Career:** Admitted to Oregon.
**Personal:** JD, Willamette University, 1980; BS, University of Oregon, 1977.

**AMBURGEY, Larry**
Amburgey & Rubin PC, Portland
503 221 0309
*Recommended in Employment*

**ANGELI, Courtney**
Stoel Rives LLP, Portland
503 224 3380
*Recommended in Employment*

**ANTELL, Kenneth S**
Dunn Carney Allen Higgins & Tongue LLP, Portland 503 417 5364
ksa@dunn-carney.com
*Recommended in Real Estate*
**Practice Areas:** Practice focuses on real estate purchase, sale, financing and leasing transactions. Extensive experience in development, construction and environmental issues relating to real property transactions.
**Prof. Memberships:** Admitted to practice in Oregon (1986), Washington (1993) and US District Court, District of Oregon (1988). Member of Oregon State Bar Association, Washington State Bar Association, Multnomah Bar Association. Board of Directors of Building Owners And Managers Association of Portland (BOMA) 2001-present. International Council of Shopping Centers (ICSC), Member (1995-present).
**Career:** Joined Dunn Carney in 1996 as a Partner.
**Publications:** 'Negligent Misrepresentation in Oregon, the Elusive Claim', Oregon State Bar Litigation Journal, Vol 12 No 3, May, 1993; Numerous presentations regarding commercial leasing, real estate purchase and sale agreements and other real estate topics.
**Personal:** JD, University of Oregon School of Law, 1986; BA, University of Michigan, 1981.

**ARELLANO, Joseph**
Kennedy, Watts, Arellano & Ricks LLP, Portland 503 228 6191
*Recommended in Litigation*

**ARMSTRONG, Craig**
Miller Nash LLP, Portland
503 205 2324
craig.armstrong@millernash.com
*Recommended in Employment*
**Practice Areas:** Specializes in employment and labor law, including collective bargaining, union representation matters, employment agreements, noncompetition and confidentiality agreements, personnel policy matters, wage and hour compliance, employee hiring, workforce reductions and reorganizations, employment discrimination, leaves of absence, disability accommodation, and wrongful discharge.
**Prof. Memberships:** Member of the Oregon State Bar and the Washington State Bar Association.
**Career:** Partner, Miller Nash. Chair-Elect of the Oregon State Bar Labor and Employment Law Section.
**Personal:** Received Law Degree from Loyola Law School and was a Member of the Order of the Coif. Earned Undergraduate Degree at the University of California, Berkeley.

**AXELROD, David**
Schwabe Williamson & Wyatt PC, Portland 503 222 9981
*Recommended in Litigation*

**BACA, David**
Davis Wright Tremaine LLP, Portland
503 241 2300
*Recommended in Corporate/M&A*

**BALL, Robert**
Ball Janik LLP, Portland
503 228 2525
*Recommended in Real Estate*

**BANKS, Robert**
Banks Law Office, Portland
503 222 7475
*Recommended in Litigation*

**BARRAN, Paula**
Barran Liebman LLP, Portland
503 228 0500
*Recommended in Employment*

**BARTZ JR, David**
Schwabe Williamson & Wyatt PC, Portland 503 222 9981
*Recommended in Environment*

**BATEMAN, Randall**
Bateman Seidel Miner Blomgren Chellis & Gram, P.C., Portland
503 972 9920
*Recommended in Real Estate*

**BAUMAN, Todd**
Stoel Rives LLP, Portland
503 224 3380
*Recommended in Corporate/M&A*

**BELNAVIS, Clarence**
Fisher & Phillips LLP, Portland
503 242 4262

cbelnavis@laborlawyers.com
*Recommended in Employment*
**Practice Areas:** Clarence Belnavis is a Partner in the Portland office of the national law firm of Fisher & Phillips LLP, practicing exclusively in labor and employment law representing management. He is experienced in handling various types of employment litigation, including disability, racial, and gender discrimination; retaliation; sexual harassment; and wrongful discharge. He also represents employers in wage and hour claims and employment class actions. Belnavis received a JD from Howard University School of Law in Washington, DC and began his legal career as a law clerk in the Office of the General Counsel for the Department of the Navy.

**BEMIS, Kenneth E**
Bullard Smith Jernstedt Wilson, Portland
503 248 1134
kbemis@bullardlaw.com
*Recommended in Employment*
**Practice Areas:** Collective bargaining, private and public sector; labor contract administration; NLRB and Oregon ERB proceedings; union organizing issues; personnel policies and practices; performance and discipline management
**Prof. Memberships:** Oregon State Bar, Labor and Employment Law Sections; Multnomah Bar Association.
**Career:** Admitted to Oregon.
**Personal:** JD, Willamette University, 1989; BA, Principia College, 1986.

**BENEDICT, James**
Cable Huston Benedict Haagensen & Lloyd LLP, Portland 503 224 3092
*Recommended in Environment*

**BENNETT, J David**
Landye Bennett Blumstein LLP, Portland
503 224 4100
*Recommended in Real Estate*

**BERNE, Gary**
Stoll Stoll Berne Lokting & Shlachter, Portland 503 227 1600
*Recommended in Litigation*

**BERNICK, Carol**
Davis Wright Tremaine LLP, Portland
503 241 2300
*Recommended in Employment*

**BEYER, Ruth**
Stoel Rives LLP, Portland
503 224 3380
*Recommended in Corporate/M&A*

**BLACKHURST, Steven**
Ater Wynne LLP, Portland
503 226 1191
skb@aterwynne.com
*Recommended in Litigation*
**Practice Areas:** Litigation; business litigation; employment; alternative dispute resolution
**Prof. Memberships:** Oregon State Bar; Oregon Law Commission, past Commissioner; Oregon Association of Defense

Counsel, past President and past Director; Multnomah Bar Association, Judicial Screening Committee, Chair 2005-06; Ninth Circuit Judicial Conference, past Lawyer Representative; American Bar Association, Litigation Section.
**Career:** Steve Blackhurst represents businesses in commercial disputes. He has extensive experience in both state and federal courts defending a broad variety of statutory and common law claims brought against businesses, directors, officers and shareholders. He joined Ater Wynne in 1978 and has been a Partner since 1981.

**BLEDSOE, David**
Perkins Coie LLP, Portland
503 727 2000
*Recommended in Environment*

**BLOUNT, David**
Landye Bennett Blumstein LLP, Portland
503 224 4100
*Recommended in Environment*

**BOOTH, Brian**
Tonkon Torp LLP, Portland
503 802 2004
brianb@tonkon.com
*Recommended in Corporate/M&A*
**Practice Areas:** Corporate and business matters, including mergers and acquisitions, securities, private and public financings, investment transactions, corporate governance and boaing Boards of Directors.
**Prof. Memberships:** Oregon State Bar: former Chair, Securities Section; Business Law Section, James B Castles Award, 2000; former Chair, Oregon Securities Law Association; American Bar Association; Fellow, American Bar Foundation.
**Personal:** JD, Stanford University School of Law (Order of the Coif, Editor, Stanford Law Review); BS, University of Oregon, Phi Beta Kappa. Corporate lawyer with Stoel Rives LLP until founding Tonkon Torp LLP in 1974. Listed in The Best Lawyers in America for corporate law.

**BRAINARD, Barbara**
Stoel Rives LLP, Portland
503 224 3380
*Recommended in Employment*

**BUCHANAN, Paul**
Stoel Rives LLP, Portland
503 224 3380
*Recommended in Employment*

**BULLOCK, Brentley**
Perkins Coie LLP, Portland
503 727 2000
*Recommended in Corporate/M&A*

**BURKE, Lawrence**
Davis Wright Tremaine LLP, Portland
503 241 2300
*Recommended in Environment*

**CABLE, Franklin**
Miller Nash LLP, Portland
503 205 2508

frank.cable@millernash.com
*Recommended in Corporate/M&A*
**Practice Areas:** Experience includes acting as General Counsel for public and private companies, advising with respect to inbound and outbound international investments, and representing clients in a wide variety of domestic acquisitions, dispositions, joint ventures, and contractual arrangements.
**Prof. Memberships:** Member, American Bar Association. Member, and former member of the executive committees, of the Oregon State Bar Securities and Business Law Sections.
**Career:** Joined Miller Nash in 1967. Partner since 1973.
**Personal:** Received Law Degree from Harvard Law School, and Undergraduate Degree from Stanford University, with distinction, in the honors program in economics.

**CALZACORTA, Carmen**
Schwabe Williamson & Wyatt PC, Portland 503 222 9981
*Recommended in Corporate/M&A*

**CAMPBELL, Michael**
Stoel Rives LLP, Portland
503 224 3380
*Recommended in Environment*

**CAMPBELL, William**
Ater Wynne LLP, Portland
503 226 8462
wcc@aterwynne.com
*Recommended in Corporate/M&A*
**Practice Areas:** Business; emerging business; intellectual property; global trade; corporate finance.
**Prof. Memberships:** Oregon State Bar; Venture Oregon, Organizing Committee; American Electronics Association, Executive Committee, 2005 to present, Oregon Chapter; Oregon Biotechnology Foundation; Pacific Northwest International Trade Association; World Affairs Council of Oregon, President, 1987-88; Board Member, 1984-91; Board of Overseers, 1991-present.
**Career:** Bill Campbell focuses on business solutions to challenges facing growth companies in the Pacific Northwest. He joined Ater Wynne in 1979 and became a Partner in 1985. He served as firm Chair from 2000-05.

**CANTLIN, Richard**
Perkins Coie LLP, Portland
503 727 2000
*Recommended in Real Estate*

**CARTER, Don**
McEwen Gisvold LLP, Portland
503 226 7321
*Recommended in Real Estate*

**CHESTLER, Stuart**
Stoel Rives LLP, Portland
503 224 3380
*Recommended in Corporate/M&A*

**CORBETT, Sherrill A**
Tonkon Torp LLP, Portland
503 802 2049
sherrill@tonkon.com
*Recommended in Corporate/M&A*
**Practice Areas:** Partner at Tonkon Torp LLP. Her practice focuses on mergers and acquisitions, representing public companies and handling public and private securities offerings.
**Prof. Memberships:** Member, Oregon State Bar (Chair-Elect, Securities Regulation Section), State Bar of California, American Bar Association and Oregon Women Lawyers.
**Personal:** JD (magna cum laude) University of California, Hastings College of the Law, 1995; BA (summa cum laude) Saint Mary's College of California, 1992.

**CREPS, Clay**
Bullivant Houser Bailey PC, Portland
503 228 6351
*Recommended in Employment*

**CROW, William**
Schwabe Williamson & Wyatt PC, Portland 503 222 9981
*Recommended in Litigation*

**CROWE, Austin**
Perkins Coie LLP, Portland
503 727 2000
*Recommended in Litigation*

**DAMM, Jacqueline**
Bullard Smith Jernstedt Wilson, Portland
503 248 1134
jdamm@bullardlaw.com
*Recommended in Employment*
**Practice Areas:** Collective bargaining; labor contract administration; NLRB proceedings; labor arbitration; employment discrimination; personnel policies and practices.
**Prof. Memberships:** Oregon State Bar, Civil Rights Section, Corporate Section, Labor and Employment Law Section and Litigation Section; Northwest Equal Employment Opportunity.
**Career:** Admitted in Oregon and Illinois.
**Personal:** JD, University of Minnesota, 1992; BA, University of Wisconsin, 1987.

**DOST, Patricia**
Schwabe Williamson & Wyatt PC, Portland 503 222 9981
*Recommended in Environment*

**DULCICH, Thomas**
Schwabe Williamson & Wyatt PC, Portland 503 222 9981
*Recommended in Litigation*

**ELLIS, Barnes**
Stoel Rives LLP, Portland
503 224 3380
*Recommended in Litigation*

**ENGLISH, Stephen**
Bullivant Houser Bailey PC, Portland
503 228 6351
*Recommended in Litigation*

**FEUERSTEIN, Howard**
Stoel Rives LLP, Portland
503 224 3380
*Recommended in Real Estate*

**FORTINO, Paul**
Perkins Coie LLP, Portland
503 727 2000
*Recommended in Litigation*

**FRANTZ, Mary Ann**
Miller Nash LLP, Portland
503 205 2552
maryann.frantz@millernash.com
*Recommended in Corporate/M&A*
**Practice Areas:** Practice is concentrated
on securities offerings, SEC reporting
compliance, corporate governance issues,
proxy statements, mergers, acquisitions,
and sales of businesses, tender offers,
business transactions, and nonprofit
organizations.
**Prof. Memberships:** Member of Oregon
State Bar and American Bar Association
Committee on Federal Regulation of
Securities.
**Career:** Vice-Chair, 'Annual Review of
Federal Securities Regulation' article published in The Business Lawyer. Contributing Editor to Advising Small Businesses by Steven C Alberty.
**Personal:** Provides pro bono services to
several nonprofit organizations. Currently serves on Board of Directors for Neighborhood House. Earned Bachelor's
Degree, with distinction, and Law Degree
at Stanford University.

**GARONE, Michael**
Schwabe Williamson & Wyatt PC,
Portland 503 222 9981
*Recommended in Employment*

**GIDLEY, James**
Perkins Coie LLP, Portland
503 727 2000
*Recommended in Litigation*

**GISVOLD, Dean**
McEwen Gisvold LLP, Portland
503 226 7321
*Recommended in Real Estate*

**GLADE, Peter**
Markowitz, Herbold, Glade & Mehlhaf PC,
Portland 503 295 3085
*Recommended in Litigation*

**GLICK, Rick**
Davis Wright Tremaine LLP, Seattle
206 622 3150
*Recommended in Environment*

**GOODLING, Jonathon L**
Miller Nash LLP, Portland
503 205 2522
jonathon.goodling@millernash.com
*Recommended in Real Estate*
**Practice Areas:** Handles real property
and commercial-lending transactions,
representing lenders, borrowers, developers, owners, tenants, landlords, purchasers,
and sellers. Has handled numerous real
estate and lending transactions. Prepares

and negotiates documents involving real
property and loan transactions.
**Prof. Memberships:** Partner, Miller
Nash. Former Chair of the Oregon State
Bar Real Estate and Land Use Section and
the Oregon State Bar's Financial Institu-
tions Committee.
**Personal:** Earned Bachelor's Degree in
Political Science and Law Degree at the
University of Oregon and was a Member
of the Order of the Coif.

**GORDON, Corbett**
Fisher & Phillips LLP, Portland
503 242 4262
cgordon@laborlawyers.com
*Recommended in Employment*
**Practice Areas:** Corbett Gordon is the
founding Partner of the Portland office of
the national law firm of Fisher & Phillips
LLP and has practiced exclusively in labor
and employment law representing
employers since 1982. An experienced
jury trial lawyer, she has served as an
Adjunct Professor with Willamette University College of Law. In 1999, Gordon
argued and won a case arising under the
Americans with Disabilities Act (ADA)
before the United States Supreme Court
(Albertsons, Inc. v Kirkingburg, 119 S. Ct.
2162, 527 US 555 (June 22, 1999)). She
received her JD from Harvard University
Law School in 1980.

**GRANT, Eugene**
Davis Wright Tremaine LLP, Portland
503 241 2300
*Recommended in Real Estate*

**GREEN, David**
Stoel Rives LLP, Portland
503 224 3380
*Recommended in Real Estate*

**GREENMAN, Ronald L**
Tonkon Torp LLP, Portland
503 802 2006
ron@tonkon.com
*Recommended in Corporate/M&A*
**Practice Areas:** Partner, Corporate
Finance and Business Transactions. His
practice is focused in the areas of corporate acquisitions, financings for growth-
stage and mature companies, corporate
governance and counseling to Boards of
Directors, and structuring and implementation of management buyouts. He
regularly advises a wide range of both
private and publicly-held clients in the
areas of corporate planning and structure, equity-based compensation plans,
and risk-avoidance techniques.
**Career:** Admitted to practice in Oregon
and California; Brobeck, Phleger & Harrison, San Francisco (1974-78); Tonkon Torp,
LLP, Portland, Oregon (1978 to present).
**Personal:** BS University of Oregon
(1968); Phi Beta Kappa; JD University of
Oregon (1974), Order of the Coif. Listed
in 'The Best Lawyers in America' for corporate law.

**GRINFAS, Dan**
Stoel Rives LLP, Seattle
206 624 0900
*Recommended in Employment*

**GUINASSO, John**
Schwabe Williamson & Wyatt PC,
Portland 503 222 9981
*Recommended in Real Estate*

**GUSTAFSON, Karna**
Landye Bennett Blumstein LLP, Portland
503 224 4100
*Recommended in Real Estate*

**HAGLUND, Michael E**
Haglund Kelley Horngren Jones & Wilder
LLP, Portland 503 225 0777
haglund@hk-law.com
*Recommended in Litigation*
**Practice Areas:** Mr Haglund focuses his
practice in the areas of antitrust, com-
mercial litigation, natural resources and
admiralty law. He served as Lead Counsel
in five cases that generated over $150 mil-
lion in judgments or settlements in the
last three years, including the largest
antitrust verdict in the history of the
Pacific Northwest.
**Prof. Memberships:** Member, Oregon
State Bar, past President, Multnomah Bar
Association.
**Personal:** JD Boston University Law
School, 1977; BA, Western Oregon University, 1973.

**HARNDEN, Edwin**
Barran Liebman LLP, Portland
503 228 0500
*Recommended in Employment*

**HAUCK, Terry**
Schwabe Williamson & Wyatt PC,
Portland 503 222 9981
*Recommended in Real Estate*

**HEWITT, Henry**
Stoel Rives LLP, Portland
503 224 3380
*Recommended in Corporate/M&A*

**HIBBS, Carol Dey**
Tonkon Torp LLP, Portland
503 802 2016
carolh@tonkon.com
*Recommended in Corporate/M&A*
**Practice Areas:** Financial institutions,
mergers and acquisitions, securities and
corporate finance, including private and
public offerings of securities and public
company reporting. Advises clients in many
financial institution industries, including
banks, trust companies, investment advisers, broker-dealers and hedge funds. Substantial experience in forming and maintaining investment vehicles, which include
pooled investment funds, common trust
funds, venture capital funds, limited partnerships and limited liability companies.
**Personal:** JD, Stanford Law School, 1978;
BA, University of Oregon 1970. Listed as
one of Oregon's specialists in financial
institutions and transactions law in The
Best Lawyers in America.

**HOUSER, Douglas**
Bullivant Houser Bailey PC, Portland
503 228 6351
*Recommended in Litigation*

**JANIK, Stephen**
Ball Janik LLP, Portland
503 228 2525
*Recommended in Real Estate*

**JANOVE, Jathan W**
Bullard Smith Jernstedt Wilson, Portland
866 551 6938
jjanove@bullardlaw.com
*Recommended in Employment*
**Practice Areas:** State and federal regula-
tion of employment; employment advice
and litigation; personnel policies and prac-
tices; training; mediation and arbitration.
**Prof. Memberships:** Utah State Bar;
SHRM, SLC-SHRM, PHRMA.
**Career:** Admitted to Utah, Idaho, New
York, Wyoming; admitted to US Court of
Appeals, Ninth Circuit; admitted to US
Court of Appeals, Tenth Circuit.
**Publications:** Jathan's recently published
book 'Managing to Stay Out of Court:
How to Avoid the Eight Deadly Sins of
Mismanagement', (SHRM & Berrett-
Koehler 2005), has been recommended
by Richard Drezen of The Washington
Post as 'an extraordinarily useful book
that will benefit managers and workers.
Strongly recommended.' Jathan's maga-
zine articles since the year 2000 include:
HR Magazine, Sept. 2005: 'The Unkindest
Cut (Pitfalls in Cutting Final Paychecks)';
Association Management Magazine, June
2005: 'Management By Leaning For-
ward'; HR Magazine, June 2005: 'FOB:
Friend of Boss (Managing Personal
Friends)'; HR Magazine, May 2005: 'Keep
'Em At-Will, Treat 'Em for Cause'; HR
Magazine, March 2005: 'A 3,500-Year-Old
Lesson In Delegating (Using the
Pharaoh-Joseph Story to Teach Delega-
tion Skills)'; HR Magazine, Nov. 2004:
'Settle for Less (Early Settlement Strate-
gies)'; HR Magazine, Aug. 2004: 'Con-
clude and Communicate (Concluding an
Internal Investigation)'; HR Magazine,
July 2004: 'Private Eye 101 (Conducting
Investigative Interviews)'; HR Magazine,
April 2004: 'Management By Remote
Control'; HR Magazine, Feb. 2004: 'It's
Not Over – Even When It's Over (The
Employment Litigation Post-Mortem)';
HR Magazine, Sept. 2003: 'The
Faragher/Ellerth Decision Tree (Sexual
Harassment Update)'; HR Magazine,
March 2003: 'Skating Through The
Minefield (the ADA and Job Perfor-
mance)'; HR Magazine, Jan. 2003: 'Speak
Softly And Carry A Big Stick (Manage-
ment Advice From Theodore Roosevelt)';
HR Magazine, May 2002: 'Don't Add
Insult To Injury (Avoiding Litigation
Through Better Communication)'; HR
Magazine, April 2002: 'Use It Or Lose It
(Transfer of Training)'; HR Magazine,
Nov. 2001: 'Sexual Harassment and The

Three Big Surprises'; HR Magazine, May 2001: 'Soothing the EEOC Dragon', and 'Great Expectations (Empathy With Accountability)'; HR News, Nov. 2000: 'Self-Help Techniques In Sexual Harassment Training'.

### JERNSTEDT, Kenneth
Bullard Smith Jernstedt Wilson, Portland
503 248 1134
kjernstedt@bullardlaw.com
*Recommended in Employment*
**Practice Areas:** Collective bargaining; NLRB proceedings; state and federal discrimination law; labor contract negotiations and administration, including grievance and arbitration procedures; personnel policies and practices; employment litigation; union organizing issues.
**Prof. Memberships:** American Bar Association, Labor and Employment Law Sections, Senior Lawyer; Oregon State Bar, Labor and Employment Law Sections; Multnomah Bar Association; Outstanding Lawyers of America; Portland Business Alliance; State Bar of California.
**Career:** Admitted in Oregon, California, United States Supreme Court, United States Ninth Circuit Court of Appeals, United States District Court of Oregon.
**Personal:** JD, University of California at Berkeley, 1969; BA, Stanford University, 1966.

### JOHNSON, Randal A
Ater Wynne LLP, Portland
503 226 8611
raj@aterwynne.com
*Recommended in Real Estate*
**Practice Areas:** Real estate; business; emerging business; land use; Indian law; tax law.
**Prof. Memberships:** American Bar Association, Real Property, Probate and Trust Sections; Oregon State Bar, Title Insurance Committee, Real Estate and Land Use Sections.
**Career:** Randy Johnson's practice emphasizes all aspects of real estate law, including sales and acquisitions, leasing, financing and development. He has particular experience representing developers in the real estate, land use and financing aspects of their commercial, industrial and residential projects, as well as both public and private entities in significant public-private developments. Randy joined Ater Wynne in 1999 and became a Partner in 2000.

### KEENEY, Jeffrey H
Tonkon Torp LLP, Portland
503 802 2025
jeffk@tonkon.com
*Recommended in Real Estate*
**Practice Areas:** Real estate acquisitions, sales and development, commercial financing, commercial leasing and land-use planning. Experience includes representation of wind energy developers in all aspects of the acquisition and development of wind energy projects.

**Prof. Memberships:** Oregon State Bar and Multnomah Bar Association. Member, Executive Committee of the Real Estate and Land Use Section of the Oregon State Bar.
**Career:** Joined Tonkon Torp in 1983. Partner since 1991. Chair of the Real Estate Practice Group.
**Publications:** Author 'Earnest Money Agreements; Letters of Intent', 'Documentation of Real Estate Transactions' (Oregon State Bar).
**Personal:** JD cum laude, Northwestern School of Law at Lewis and Clark College, 1983, BA, University of Vermont, 1980, Phi Beta Kappa.

### KEITH, Calvin
Perkins Coie LLP, Portland
503 727 2000
*Recommended in Employment*

### KENT, Christopher
Kent & Johnson, LLP, Portland
503 220 0717
*Recommended in Litigation*

### KILMER, Jeffrey
Kilmer Voorhees & Laurick PC, Portland
503 224 0055
*Recommended in Litigation*

### KISCH, Victor
Stoel Rives LLP, Portland
503 224 3380
*Recommended in Employment*

### KITCHEL, Chris
Stoel Rives LLP, Portland
503 224 3380
*Recommended in Employment*

### KNOX, Daniel
Schwabe Williamson & Wyatt PC, Portland 503 222 9981
*Recommended in Litigation*

### KRAMER, Thomas
Bullard Smith Jernstedt Wilson, Portland
503 248 1134
tkramer@bullardlaw.com
*Recommended in Employment*
**Practice Areas:** Tax-qualified retirement plans; executive compensation; health and welfare benefits; flexible benefit plans.
**Prof. Memberships:** American Bar Association, Labor and Employment Law Sections; Oregon State Bar, Workers Compensation and Labor and Employment Law Sections.
**Career:** Admitted to practice in Oregon and Ninth Circuit Court of Appeals.
**Publications:** Tom is the co-author of Employee Health Benefits and Health Insurance and Health Plans, for the Oregon State Bar, and Welfare Benefits Under the Tax Reform Act of 1986 for the American Law Institute-American Bar Association.
**Personal:** JD, Yale University; BA, Claremont Men's College, (summa cum laude); University of St Andrews.

### LIEBMAN, Richard
Barran Liebman LLP, Portland
503 228 0500
*Recommended in Employment*

### LINDLEY, Tom
Perkins Coie LLP, Portland
503 727 2000
*Recommended in Environment*

### MACCOURT, Doug
Ater Wynne LLP, Portland
503 226 8672
dcm@aterwynne.com
*Recommended in Environment*
**Practice Areas:** Environmental, land use, natural resources, energy, Indian law, real estate,sustainable practices.
**Prof. Memberships:** US-Germany Bilateral Work Group on Brownfields; National Association of Local Government Environmental Professionals, Co-Chair, Board of Directors; 1000 Friends of Oregon, Cooperating Attorney; Oregon State Bar; American Bar Association
**Career:** Doug MacCourt assists businesses and local governments comply with environmental laws and redevelop urban properties. He has worked extensively with contaminated real property or 'brownfields', including the cleanup, purchase, sale and redevelopment of sites throughout Oregon and other states. Doug joined Ater Wynne in 1999 and became a Partner in 2002.

### MANULIK, Mark
Schwabe Williamson & Wyatt PC, Portland 503 222 9981
*Recommended in Real Estate*

### MARKOWITZ, David
Markowitz, Herbold, Glade & Mehlhaf PC, Portland 503 295 3085
*Recommended in Litigation*

### MARMADUKE, Don H
Tonkon Torp LLP, Portland
503 802 2003
don@tonkon.com
*Recommended in Litigation*
**Practice Areas:** Litigation covering full range of civil actions representing plaintiffs or defendants, more than 250 trials, most before juries, state and federal trial and appellate courts, Oregon and elsewhere.
**Prof. Memberships:** American College of Trial Lawyers, International Society of Barristers, American Board of Trial Advocates, Oregon Association of Defense Counsel, American Bar Foundation, American Bar Association (House of Delegates 1974-8), Multnomah Bar Association (Pres. 1979-80).
**Career:** Admitted in Massachusetts (Inactive) and Oregon; trial lawyer with Stoel Rives LLP's predecessors, Co-Founder of public interest law firm, trial lawyer with Tonkon Torp LLP since 1974. Adjunct instructor of Remedies, Lewis & Clark Law School, State Public Defender Committee Chair (1972-79) appointed

by Oregon Supreme Court.
**Publications:** Co-Editor in Chief, three volume set: Oregon Civil Pleading and Practice, 1964 ed.
**Personal:** Yale University, Harvard Law School. Recipient of Multnomah Bar Association's Professionalism Award (1996), E B McNaughton Civil Liberties Award (1998), American Board of Trial Advocates Trial Lawyer of the Year Award (2000), Oregon Chapter, American Jewish Committee's Judge Learned Hand Lifetime Achievement Award (2001).

### MARTIN, Chrys
Bullivant Houser Bailey PC, Portland
503 228 6351
*Recommended in Employment*

### MARTSON JR, William F
Tonkon Torp LLP, Portland
503 802 2005
rick@tonkon.com
*Recommended in Litigation*
**Practice Areas:** Mr Martson has represented individuals and business entities in a broad range of business, commercial, shareholder, and securities litigation, including defending a former Director of Enron in all of the Enron-related proceedings. He has tried over 200 cases.
**Prof. Memberships:** Fellow and Director of the International Society of Barristers; Fellow of the Center for International Legal Studies; listed in The Best Lawyers in America; Member of the Oregon State Bar, Multnomah Bar Association, American Bar Association, Federal Bar Association, and the Oregon Association of Defense Counsel.
**Personal:** JD University of Michigan, 1972, magna cum laude, Order of the Coif; BA Washington and Jefferson College, 1969, magna cum laude, Phi Beta Kappa.

### MATHESON, David
Perkins Coie LLP, Portland
503 727 2000
*Recommended in Corporate/M&A*

### MATTHEWS, Christopher
Perkins Coie LLP, Portland
503 727 2000
*Recommended in Real Estate*

### MCDONNELL, Brendan
Preston Gates & Ellis LLP, Portland
503 228 3200
*Recommended in Corporate/M&A*

### MCGRORY, John
Davis Wright Tremaine LLP, Portland
503 241 2300
*Recommended in Litigation*

### MILLER, Bradley
Ball Janik LLP, Portland
503 228 2525
*Recommended in Real Estate*

### MILLER JR, Max M
Tonkon Torp LLP, Portland
503 802 2030

max@tonkon.com
*Recommended in Environment*

**Practice Areas:** Acquisitions, sales, leases, and remediation of environmentally impacted or sensitive properties including industrial property, timberlands, and energy facilities; litigation under environmental statutes; federal, state and local agency enforcement and negotiations; land use proceedings.
**Prof. Memberships:** Oregon State Bar (past Chair, Public Service and Information Committee; past Chair, Environmental and Natural Resources Section); and American Bar Association.
**Publications:** Co-editor, 'Environmental and Natural Resources Law' (Oregon State Bar Deskbook 2002); editor 1994-97, Oregon Environmental and Natural Resources Outlook (Oregon State Bar Periodical).
**Personal:** JD, Northwestern School of Law of Lewis and Clark College, 1983; BA, Economics, Pitzer College 1979.

**MOORMAN, Robert**
Stoel Rives LLP, Portland
503 224 3380
*Recommended in Corporate/M&A*

**MORFORD, Mark**
Stoel Rives LLP, Portland
503 224 3380
*Recommended in Environment*

**MOWE, Gregory**
Stoel Rives LLP, Portland
503 224 3380
*Recommended in Litigation*

**MULLIN, Joel**
Stoel Rives LLP, Portland
503 224 3380
*Recommended in Litigation*

**NEUPERT, John**
Miller Nash LLP, Portland
503 205 2461
john.neupert@millernash.com
*Recommended in Litigation*

**Practice Areas:** Practice involves complex commercial litigation, including banking, trade regulation, business torts, intellectual property, and corporate governance.
**Prof. Memberships:** Member of the Oregon State Bar, the American Bar Association, and the Multnomah Bar Association, and participates in their litigation sections' activities. Is admitted to the Oregon federal court and state bar, and has been admitted pro hac vice to many federal and state courts nationwide.
**Career:** Through his professional corporation, is a Partner of Miller Nash LLP.
**Personal:** Earned Law Degree from the University of Oregon and was a Member of the Order of the Coif.

**NEWELL, Robert**
Davis Wright Tremaine LLP, Portland
503 241 2300
*Recommended in Litigation*

**NOTO, Margaret**
Stoel Rives LLP, Portland
503 224 3380
*Recommended in Corporate/M&A*

**O'LEARY, Daniel**
Davis Wright Tremaine LLP, Portland
503 241 2300
*Recommended in Environment, Litigation*

**PAGE, Thomas**
Stoel Rives LLP, Portland
503 224 3380
*Recommended in Real Estate*

**PAGEL, Martha**
Schwabe Williamson & Wyatt, Salem
503 399 7712
*Recommended in Environment*

**PALMER, Thomas**
Tonkon Torp LLP, Portland
503 802 2018
tom@tonkon.com
*Recommended in Corporate/M&A*

**Practice Areas:** Partner and Chair of Corporate Finance Practice Group. Practice focuses on securities and corporate transactions, including mergers and acquisitions, initial public offerings, other equity and debt offerings, and private placements. Mr Palmer also represents special committees of Boards of Directors and advises on corporate governance matters.
**Prof. Memberships:** Oregon State Bar; District of Columbia Bar; New York State Bar; American Bar Association; Association of the Bar of the City of New York.
**Career:** Partner since 1990. Shearman & Sterling, New York, associate, 1979-87.
**Personal:** JD, Cornell Law School, 1976; AB, Hamilton College, 1973.

**PARKER, Gilbert E**
Dunn Carney Allen Higgins & Tongue LLP, Portland 503 306 5315
gep@dunn-carney.com
*Recommended in Real Estate*

**Practice Areas:** Partner in the Real Estate and Land Use Section. His practice focuses on real estate development, real estate finance, business transactions, commercial lending, construction and construction liens, and secured transactions.
**Prof. Memberships:** Admitted to practice in Oregon (1975) and US.District Court, District of Oregon (1976). Member of Oregon State Bar Association and Multnomah Bar Association. Member of American Bar Association Real Property, Probate and Trust Law Sections. Founding Member of Board of Directors for Meritas (formerly known as Commercial Law Affiliates). Board of Directors for Riverbend Youth Center, 1995-2004.
**Career:** Joined Dunn Carney in 1975 and became a Partner in 1981. Served as Managing Partner from 1991-93.
**Personal:** JD, University of California, Hastings College of Law (San Francisco), 1975; BA (with honors), Lewis and Clark College, 1972.

**PARKS, Timothy**
Ball Janik LLP, Portland 503 228 2525
*Recommended in Real Estate*

**PECK, Kathy**
Williams, Zografos & Peck, Lake Oswego
503 699 1300
*Recommended in Employment*

**PEDERSEN JOSEPH, Amy**
Stoel Rives LLP, Portland
503 224 3380
*Recommended in Employment*

**PFEIFFER, Steven**
Perkins Coie LLP, Portland
503 727 2000
*Recommended in Real Estate*

**POWELL, Bryan**
Lane Powell PC, Portland 503 778 2100
*Recommended in Real Estate*

**POWERS, Claudia K**
Ater Wynne LLP, Portland
503 226 8652
ckp@aterwynne.com
*Recommended in Environment*

**Practice Areas:** Environmental, natural resources, land use, energy, public/private ventures, real estate, sustainable practices.
**Prof. Memberships:** Oregon State Bar, Executive Committee, past member, Environmental and Natural Resources Section; American Bar Association; Multnomah Bar Association; Commissioner of first City of Portland Energy and Environment Commission.
**Career:** Claudia Powers' clients include international chemical and industrial gases corporations, light and heavy manufacturing industries, solid and municipal waste companies, a shipyard, forest and agricultural product firms, and utility companies. She joined Ater Wynne in 1987 and became Partner in 1990. Claudia is Chair of the Environmental Practice Group.

**RADLER, Barbara**
Ball Janik LLP, Portland
503 228 2525
*Recommended in Real Estate*

**RAMIS, Timothy**
Ramis Crew Corrigan LLP, Portland
503 222 4402
*Recommended in Real Estate*

**RAWLINSON, Dennis P**
Miller Nash LLP, Portland
503 205 2406
dennis.rawlinson@millernash.com
*Recommended in Litigation*

**Practice Areas:** Has handled numerous cases involving breach of contract, commercial torts, construction and design, shareholder disputes, lender liability, real estate, professional negligence, employment, and trademark disputes.
**Prof. Memberships:** President, Oregon State Bar. Chair, ABA Section of Litigation Trial Evidence Committee. Fellow, American Bar Association.

**Career:** Association of Corporate Counsel (2005). Recommended Commercial Litigation Lawyer, Association of Corporate Counsel (2005). American Board of Trial Advocates (pending). Listed in the Best Lawyers in America, 2006.
**Personal:** Earned Bachelor's Degree, magna cum laude, at University of Notre Dame and Master's Degree in business administration and Law Degree, cum laude, at Cornell University.

**REEVES, Edward**
Stoel Rives LLP, Portland
503 224 3380
*Recommended in Employment*

**RICH, Chris**
Rycewicz & Chenoweth LLP, Portland
503 221 7958
*Recommended in Environment*

**RICHTER, Peter**
Miller Nash LLP, Portland
503 205 2366
peter.richter@millernash.com
*Recommended in Litigation*

**Practice Areas:** Has tried more than 200 jury trials involving numerous legal issues.
**Prof. Memberships:** Member of the American Bar Association, American Board of Trial Advocates, and Oregon Association of Defense Counsel (past Board Member). Fellow of the American Bar Foundation. Admitted to practice in the United States Supreme Court and all Oregon state and federal courts.
**Career:** Adjunct Professor, Trial Advocacy, Lewis and Clark Law School. Cofounder of the Oregon State Bar Trial Advocacy College. Named one of Oregon's ten best litigators by the National Law Journal. Listed in several US publications as leading litigator and trial lawyer.

**ROBINSON, Michael**
Perkins Coie LLP, Portland
503 727 2000
*Recommended in Real Estate*

**ROSENBAUM, Lois**
Stoel Rives LLP, Portland
503 224 3380
*Recommended in Litigation*

**ROTHAUGE, Renée**
Bullivant Houser Bailey PC, Portland
503 228 6351
*Recommended in Litigation*

**RUBIN, Howard**
Amburgey & Rubin PC, Portland
503 221 0309
*Recommended in Employment*

**RUSSELL, Stephen**
Landye Bennett Blumstein LLP, Portland
503 224 4100
*Recommended in Real Estate*

**SAMUELS, Stanley**
Bateman Seidel Miner Blomgren Chellis & Gram, P.C., Portland
503 972 9920
*Recommended in Real Estate*

**SAND, Thomas C**
Miller Nash LLP, Portland
503 205 2475
tom.sand@millernash.com
*Recommended in Litigation*
**Practice Areas:** General trial practice
and civil litigation, with emphasis on
securities, employment, and other com-
mercial matters. Has tried numerous
cases in several state and federal courts,
and has argued appeals in the Ninth Cir-
cuit Court of Appeals, Oregon Supreme
Court, and Oregon Court of Appeals.
**Prof. Memberships:** Member, Securities
Industry Association and Oregon State
Bar.
**Career:** Managing Partner of Miller
Nash. Selected for The Best Lawyers in
America, 2006.
**Personal:** Earned Bachelor's Degree at
University of Oregon and Law Degree at
Lewis and Clark Law School. Received
Distinguished Graduate Award from
Lewis and Clark Law School in 2004.

**SHLACHTER, Robert**
Stoll Stoll Berne Lokting & Shlachter,
Portland 503 227 1600
*Recommended in Litigation*

**SIMON, Michael**
Perkins Coie LLP, Portland
503 727 2000
*Recommended in Litigation*

**SIMPSON, Patrick**
Perkins Coie LLP, Portland
503 727 2000
*Recommended in Corporate/M&A*

**SKERRITT, Daniel**
Tonkon Torp LLP, Portland
503 802 2024
dan@tonkon.com
*Recommended in Litigation*
**Practice Areas:** Practice focuses on
complex commercial litigation and dispute resolution. He represents clients in a
variety of legal specialties, including securities, corporate governance, energy and
general business litigation.
**Prof. Memberships:** Fellow of American
College of Trial Lawyers and International Society of Barristers; Oregon State Bar
(Member, House of Delegates 2003-06;
past Chairman); American Bar Association (Business Tort Committee and Litigation and Labor Sections); Oregon
Association of Defense Counsel.
**Personal:** JD, summa cum laude,
Willamette University College of Law,
1968; LLM, George Washington University, 1972; BA, Willamette University,
1965. Listed in 'The Best Lawyers in
America' for commercial litigation.

**SNYDER, Joan**
Stoel Rives LLP, Portland
503 224 3380
*Recommended in Environment*

**STAYER, Mark**
Schwabe Williamson & Wyatt PC,
Portland 503 222 9981
*Recommended in Real Estate*

**STEPHENS, Kenneth**
Tonkon Torp LLP, Portland
503 802 2008
ken@tonkon.com
*Recommended in Corporate/M&A*
**Practice Areas:** Business associations
and corporate governance; corporate
investigations; securities and financial
transactions; financial institutions; regu-
lation of life insurance and re-insurance.
**Prof. Memberships:** American Bar
Association; American Law Institute;
Society of Corporate Secretaries and
Governance Professionals.
**Personal:** JD University of Oregon
(Order of the Coif), 1967; BS University
of Oregon, 1965. Listed in The Best
Lawyers in America for corporate and
banking law.

**STOLL, Robert**
Stoll Stoll Berne Lokting & Shlachter,
Portland 503 227 1600
*Recommended in Litigation*

**STRUXNESS, Gregory E**
Ater Wynne LLP, Portland
503 226 8449
ges@aterwynne.com
*Recommended in Corporate/M&A*
**Practice Areas:** Corporate finance,
business, emerging business, global trade
and intellectual property, public and private ventures and finance.
**Prof. Memberships:** Association of
Securities and Exchange Commission
Alumni; Oregon State Bar Association,
Securities Regulation Section; American
Bar Association, Corporation, Finance
and Securities Section.
**Career:** Greg Struxness concentrates his
practice on general corporate and securities law, including public and private
offerings of securities under state and
federal securities regulations, mergers
and acquisitions, contests for corporate
control, and corporate reporting and disclosure obligations. He joined Ater
Wynne in 1991, became Partner in 1994
and is currently Chair of the firm.

**SULLIVAN, Edward**
Garvey Schubert Barer, Portland
503 228 3939
*Recommended in Real Estate*

**THOMAS, John**
Stoel Rives LLP, Portland
503 224 3380
*Recommended in Corporate/M&A*

**TOM, Rebecca**
Ball Janik LLP, Portland 503 228 2525
*Recommended in Real Estate*

**TONGUE, Thomas H**
Dunn Carney Allen Higgins & Tongue LLP,
Portland 503 306 5330
tht@dunn-carney.com
*Recommended in Litigation*
**Practice Areas:** A Partner at Dunn Car-
ney since 1973. He specializes in litigation
and appeals, arbitration, mediation and
healthcare law.
**Prof. Memberships:** Present Regent in
the American College of Trial Lawyers;
past President Oregon Association of
Defense Counsel; American Judicature
Society, Member 30+ years; Oregon State
Bar, Chair of multiple committees and
elected delegate; Defense Research Insti-
tute Member; International Association
of Insurance Counsel.
**Career:** Admitted to Oregon, 1968; US
District Court District of Oregon, 1970;
US Court of Appeals 9th Circuit, 1971;
US Supreme Court, 1971.
**Publications:** Awards: The Multnomah
County Bar Association Professionalism
Award; The Oregon State Bar Litigation
Section – Owen M Panner Professional-
ism Award in 2002.
**Personal:** JD, University of Wisconsin,
1968; BA, University of Oregon, 1965.

**TRIPLETT, Thomas**
Schwabe Williamson & Wyatt PC,
Portland 503 222 9981
*Recommended in Employment*

**TUCKER, Roy**
Perkins Coie LLP, Portland
503 727 2000
*Recommended in Corporate/M&A*

**TURNER, Mark A.**
Ater Wynne LLP, Portland
503 226 8463
mat@aterwynne.com
*Recommended in Litigation*
**Practice Areas:** Litigation, alternative
dispute resolution, employment.
**Prof. Memberships:** American Bar
Association; Oregon State Bar; Multnomah Bar Association; Multnomah County
Local Professional Responsibility Committee, 1997-2000 Term; Oregon Association of Defense Counsel, Chair, Commercial Practice Group.
**Career:** Mark Turner has an active trial
practice in the state and federal courts,
emphasizing all types of commercial litigation. He has particular experience in
securities litigation, corporate disputes,
employment matters, intellectual property issues, including trademark and trade
secret infringement, and claims relating
to environmental contamination and
insurance coverage issues. He joined Ater
Wynne in 1986 and became Partner in
1993.

**VANCLEAVE, Richard**
Barran Liebman LLP, Portland
503 228 0500
*Recommended in Employment*

**VOBORIL, Joseph**
Tonkon Torp LLP, Portland
503 802 2009
joe@tonkon.com
*Recommended in Real Estate*
**Practice Areas:** Mr Voboril's practice is
concentrated on complex commercial
real estate transactions and land use matters. Since arriving in Portland in 1973, he
has served on a number of local boards
and commissions. Through his public
service activities, he has developed a solid
reputation with local government officials.
**Prof. Memberships:** Oregon and Washington State Bar Associations; former
Board Member of Portland Public
Schools, Portland City Planning Commission, Portland Area Metropolitan
Boundary Commission.
**Personal:** JD, University of Michigan,
1973; BS University of Nebraska, Phi Beta
Kappa, 1970. Listed in 'The Best Lawyers
in America' for Real Estate law.

**WALTERS, Martha**
Walters Romm Chanti & Dickens,
Eugene 541 683 2506
*Recommended in Litigation*

**WHITE, Christen**
Ball Janik LLP, Portland
503 228 2525
*Recommended in Real Estate*

**WHITTEMORE, Richard**
Bullivant Houser Bailey PC, Portland
503 228 6351
*Recommended in Litigation*

**WILSON, David H**
Bullard Smith Jernstedt Wilson, Portland
503 248 1134
dwilson@bullardlaw.com
*Recommended in Employment*
**Practice Areas:** Labor and employment
litigation in state and federal courts; labor
arbitration; state and federal discrimina-
tion law; appellate proceedings; litigation
before NLRB, ERB and other agencies;
personnel policies and practices.
**Prof. Memberships:** Oregon State Bar,
Labor and Employment Law Section and
Government Law Section.
**Career:** Admitted to Oregon; US District
Court, Western District of Wisconsin; US
District Court, District of Oregon; US
Court of Appeals, Ninth Circuit; US
Supreme Court.
**Personal:** JD, University of Wisconsin-
Madison, 1972; BA, Princeton University,
1967.

**WOLFSTONE, Jeffrey**
Lane Powell PC, Portland
503 778 2100
*Recommended in Corporate/M&A*

**WOOD, Thomas**
Stoel Rives LLP, Portland
503 224 3380
*Recommended in Environment*

# ATER WYNNE LLP

## THE FIRM

**Managing Partner:** Michael W Shackelford
**Firm Chair:** Gregory E Struxness

**Number of Partners:** 33
**Number of other lawyers:** 17

### AREAS OF PRACTICE

Business . . . . . . . . . . . . . . . . . . . . . . . . . . . . . . . . . . . . . . . . . . . . 40%
Litigation . . . . . . . . . . . . . . . . . . . . . . . . . . . . . . . . . . . . . . . . . . . 30%
Regulated Industries . . . . . . . . . . . . . . . . . . . . . . . . . . . . . . . . . 30%

**FIRM OVERVIEW:** Ater Wynne LLP focus their legal services on the strategic needs, business and future of local, national and international companies and organizations. From offices in Portland, Oregon; Seattle, Washington; and Menlo Park, California, they counsel clients in industries ranging from technology, energy, healthcare and telecommunications to construction, real estate, manufacturing and tribal economic development. Their clients benefit from seasoned counsel who grasp issues quickly, apply their skills with a minimum learning curve and bring value in industry knowledge and contacts.Whilst they are serious, tenacious advocates, their clients find them approachable, responsive and easy to work with.

### MAIN AREAS OF PRACTICE:

**Business:** The Business Department of Ater Wynne LLP provides strategic legal advice that helps their clients achieve their business goals. The firm's clients range from closely-held family businesses, to high-growth venture-backed companies, to multinational public corporations. Ater Wynne attorneys are skilled in business, corporate finance, securities, global trade and intellectual property, as well as employment, regulatory, real estate, dispute resolution and other legal issues that may affect expanding companies. Within the Business Department, the firm's Corporate Finance and Securities Practice serves clients at every stage of their development, from formation and initial private financing through the initial public offering and beyond. The firm is involved in venture capital financing, and private offerings, initial and follow-on and secondary public offerings, mergers and acquisitions and leveraged buyouts. They counsel clients on all matters of state and federal securities law compliance. The firm's Real Estate Practice provides clients with innovative, high-quality legal advice designed to bring their clients' real estate transactions to completion. Ater Wynne routinely assist clients in the areas of acquisitions and sales, development, leasing, financing, property management and construction. Their clients include public entities, private developers, national and regional retailers, shopping center owners, banks, telecommunication and cable companies, and large public-private ventures.

**Litigation:** Ater Wynne provides a full range of dispute avoidance and resolution services and represents clients in all phases of litigation in state and federal courts and various alternative dispute resolution venues. The firm represents corporate, commercial and financial clients, and individuals with business interests. Ater Wynne attorneys are often called upon to help clients identify business risks and develop prevention strategies and are skilled at evaluating and resolving cases realistically and effectively – as well as trying them. Ater Wynne is capable of managing complex and multi-district litigation. In addition to having offices along the West Coast, the firm has litigation partners who are experienced in trying cases in forums throughout the country, in supervising litigation in multiple locations for clients, and in working with other local, regional and national coordinating counsel. Representative areas of litigation practice are intellectual property and technology, product liability, toxic torts, securities, environmental and regulatory, construction and lien claims, financial institutions, employment, real estate, energy, insurance, and antitrust.

**Regulated Industries:** For more than 40 years, Ater Wynne has served as counsel to electric utilities as well as users and developers of energy resources throughout the Pacific Northwest, Alaska, Arizona, Nevada and California.

## HEAD OFFICE

**OREGON**
222 SW Columbia, Ste 1800, **Portland**, OR 97201
**Tel:** 503 226 1191   **Fax:** 503 226 0079
**Website:** www.aterwynne.com

## BRANCH OFFICES

**CALIFORNIA**
525 Middlefield Rd, Ste 150, **Menlo Park**, CA 94025
**Tel:** 650 566 1443   **Fax:** 650 325 2340

**WASHINGTON**
Two Union Square, 601 Union St, Ste 5450, **Seattle**, WA 98101
**Tel:** 206 623 4711   **Fax:** 206 467 8406

## CONTACTS

| | |
|---|---|
| Business | Brenda Meltebeke |
| Corporate Finance | Gregory E Struxness |
| Environmental | Claudia K Powers |
| Litigation | Frank V Langfitt |
| Real Estate | Randy Johnson |
| Regulated Industries | Lisa R Rackner |

Within Regulated Industries, the firm's Environmental Group works with clients including utility companies and energy project developers, large commercial property owners, tribal enterprises, municipalities, aluminum and mining companies, chemical manufacturers, forest and agricultural products corporations, paper mills and recycling plants, and advanced technology businesses. The firm represents clients involved in local, state and federal environmental matters, including brownfield and superfund cleanups, environmental compliance, environmental permitting, land and natural resource regulation and development, National Environmental Policy Act/impact statements, Endangered Species Act, and corporate and real estate transactions.

**INTERNATIONAL WORK:** Ater Wynne advises and assists clients in domestic and global transactions involving private parties as well as the US and foreign governments with respect to international trade. In addition to offices along the West Coast and relationships with law firms worldwide, Ater Wynne is a member of Legal Counsel International, a worldwide alliance of law firms with members spread across 13 countries.

**CLIENTS:** Representative clients include: Advanced Silicon Materials LLC; Arkema Inc.; Bank of New York; Bechtel Enterprises, Inc.; BOC Group; Cascade Microtech, Inc.; Crownover Construction Co.; Columbia River People's Utility District; Columbia Ventures Corporation; Coquille Economic Development Corp. (Coquille Tribe); Dine' Power Authority (Navajo Nation); FLIR Systems, Inc.; Golden Valley Electric Association, Inc.; Jack in the Box Inc.; Idaho Power; Mt. Hood Beverage Company; Northwest Pipe Company; ODS Companies; Open Source Development Labs; The Oregon Clinic; Oregon Health & Sciences University; Pacific Northern Inc.; Pixelworks, Inc.; Planar Systems, Inc.; Plum Creek Timber Co.; The Port of Portland; Time Warner Telecom of Oregon; TriQuint SemiConductor, Inc.

# BARRAN LIEBMAN LLP

## THE FIRM

**Managing Partner (Portland, Oregon):** Edwin A Harnden

### AREAS OF PRACTICE:
Litigation. . . . . . . . . . . . . . . . . . . . . . . . . . . . . . . . . . . . . . . . . . . . . . . . . 50%
Labor, Employment . . . . . . . . . . . . . . . . . . . . . . . . . . . . . . . . . . . . . . 50%

**FIRM OVERVIEW:** Barran Liebman LLP formed in 1998, as an Oregon partnership dedicated to representing employers and finding solutions for their labor management and employment law needs. The firm consists of 12 partners, four associates, four paralegals and nine legal secretaries, to offer clients seamless assistance and responsiveness. To assist employers in preventing problems, the firm provides a full range of tools including six "Food for Thought" breakfast seminars, an annual labor and employment seminar for 500 attendees, and customized onsite trainings to meet the individual needs of employers with regards to their industry and experience. As a special service, the firm provides valuable Electronic AlertsSM free of charge. These updates summarize new case law and statutes that impact businesses. Training videotapes and CD-Roms are also available.

**MAIN AREAS OF PRACTICE:** Barran Liebman attorneys specialize in three practice areas: employment law advice, employment litigation and labor relations.
**Employment Law Advice:** The majority of the firm's employment work is in equal employment opportunity, wage and hour, and employment at-will matters. Each year, the firm handles approximately 150 Oregon Civil Rights Division, EEOC, OFCCP and Washington Human Rights Commission charges and defends dozens of court actions in Oregon and Washington. This high volume of work allows them to stay abreast of fast-developing case law, including knowledge of unreported new decisions, an ability which is extraordinarily valuable at a critical time. The attorneys participate in rules development for administrative agencies and in the legislative process, and prepare amicus briefs in employment EEO and employment-at-will cases in state appellate courts. The wide range of employment law issues the firm can address include: discrimination, including ADA, ADEA and Title VII; substance abuse issues in the workplace; compensation issues; employee handbooks and manuals; employee status and clarification; employee theft; employment contracts; equal employment opportunity matters; family medical leave; general employment dispute resolution; policy and procedure reviews; privacy issues in the workplace; retaliation claims; sexual harassment; violence in the workplace; wage and hour issues; workplace investigations; and wrongful termination claims; complex executive disputes over termination; non-competition agreements, misappropriation of trade secrets and other intellectual property, and separation benefits.
**Employment Litigation:** Litigation is a conscious decision that an entity may need to make in individual circumstances. Barran Liebman's goal is to assist in resolving disputes as efficiently as possible. The more successful approach begins with an understanding of what motivates the dispute. The firm frequently evaluates whether there is a benefit to offering counseling, retraining, retirement packages, or other benefits to assist the parties to resolve a matter on mutually beneficial terms.
**Labor Relations:** The firm represents employers in public and private and non-profit sectors offering counsel in both union and non-union environments. Five partners at Barran Liebman LLP maintain a substantial labor relations practice including: Nelson Atkin, Paula Barran, Richard Hunt, Richard Liebman, and Richard VanCleave. Barran Liebman attorneys work together to share ideas and resources.

**CLIENTS:** Barran Liebman attorneys represent clients in the following industries: academic institutions, chemical businesses, civic agencies, communications and media organizations, construction, architectural and engineering firms, energy companies, financial institutions, food and consumer products companies, healthcare organizations, high-tech companies, hospitality businesses, manufacturers, printers, professional sport organizations, real estate developers, retail, trade associations, and transportation companies.

BARRAN LIEBMAN LLP
ATTORNEYS

# BULLARD SMITH JERNSTEDT WILSON

## THE FIRM

**President:** Ken Jernstedt

**Number of partners:** 21
**Number of other lawyers:** 4

### HEAD OFFICE

**OREGON**
1000 SW Broadway, Suite 1900, **Portland**, OR 97205
**Tel:** 503 248 1134   **Fax:** 503 224 8851
**Website:** www.bullardlaw.com

**FIRM OVERVIEW:** Founded in 1977, Bullard has long been regarded as a premier source of labor and employment law representation and advice for employers in both the private and public sectors. Since inception the firm has represented more than 4000 employers, primarily in the Pacific Northwest. The addition of seven attorneys cumulatively through strategic hiring during calendar years 2004-5 brings the current attorney count to 25 and has consolidated Bullard's position as leading a source of experienced management counsel. Five of the seven recent additions involve experienced and highly respected attorneys making lateral transitions from other highly respected firms, bringing with them more than 90 years of legal experience representing employers. This includes the addition of Jathan Janove, a nationally recognized speaker and author who recently was named Employment Attorney of the Year in Utah.

### Affiliation with WORKLAW® network

The firm is pleased to be a member of the Worklaw® Network, a nationwide network of select independent management labor and employment law firms. The Worklaw® Network currently has over 320 attorneys practicing in 26 firms who share helpful information on emerging trends in employment law and union tactics, quality local counsel, as well as maintain a common computer data bank of briefs and research. The Worklaw® Network's website is found at www.worklawnetwork.com.

## MAIN AREAS OF PRACTICE:

**Traditional Labor Law & Litigation Experience:** Traditional labor law work has always been the foundation of the firm. The firm has eleven lawyers with practices focused primarily on traditional labor law, including collective bargaining, labor arbitrations, union avoidance, practice before the NLRB, and day-to-day advice on contract and grievance administration. It is common for the firm's attorneys to be the employer spokesperson in the negotiation of at least 75 separate labor contracts during a calendar year. Although the firm's traditional labor law depth sets it apart, its litigation and employment advice attorneys are equally experienced and effective. The firm is also experienced in defending class actions, including wage and hour class claims.

**HR Advice, Administrative Responses & Training:** When it comes to day-to-day HR advice, union matters, contract administration, and state agency/EEOC issues, Bullard emphasizes preventative strategies to avoid unnecessary and costly litigation or arbitration, wherever possible, or to build a strong company defense or position. Bullard assists clients in developing policies and practices that are proactive and presented to employees or to unions through positive and constructive communication. They support preventative efforts to eliminate employee problems and manage them, rather than merely reacting to issues as they arise. They frequently work with clients, and provide supervisor training, in the following areas, among others: developing effective disciplinary and investigatory follow-up documentation and communications in union and non-union settings; analyzing and managing workplace situations involving the Family and Medical Leave Act (and its state-law equivalents), its interplay with Workers' Compensation and the ADA, and more complex return-to-work, reasonable accommodation issues in both local and multi-jurisdictional settings; developing strategies for addressing workplace harassment, discrimination and retaliation concerns, and related internal investigation and follow-up; assisting with employment policies and contracts, non-compete and confidentiality provisions, compensation and employee status and classification issues; effective management of absences and accommodation, hiring, discipline and firing, wage and hour issues, investigation of employee complaints, alcohol and drug problems, and effective management of union issues and union avoidance strategies.

**Employee Benefits:** Tom Kramer, a recent addition to the firm, leads a group focused on employee benefits law, including retirement and deferred compensation plans, health, life, cafeteria and other fringe benefit plans and funding vehicles of private and public-sector employers. His work includes plan drafting, problem solving and representing employers and others in disputes with regulators. Tom has written and spoken frequently about benefits issues. He is the co-author of Employee Health Benefits and Health Insurance and Health Plans, for the Oregon State Bar, and Welfare Benefits under the Tax Reform Act of 1986 for the American Law Institute–American Bar Association.

**CLIENTS:** State of Oregon; Cities of Tigard, Hillsboro, Beaverton and Pendleton; Counties of Washington, Jackson and Douglas; Fred Meyer Inc.; Holy Rosary Medical Center; JELD-WEN; Jesuit High School; Laidlaw Inc; Lloyd's of London; Goodwill Industries; Nike, Inc.; NW Natural; NORPAC Foods; Standard Insurance; Oregon State Sheriff's Association; Legacy Health System, Portland General Electric; and Rite Aid.

# DUNN CARNEY ALLEN HIGGINS & TONGUE LLP

## THE FIRM

**Managing Partner:** Robert L Allen

**Number of partners:** 28
**Number of other attorneys:** 16

### AREAS OF PRACTICE:
Business Law & Estate Planning . . . . . . . . . . . . . . . . . . . . . . . . . . . . 44%
Litigation . . . . . . . . . . . . . . . . . . . . . . . . . . . . . . . . . . . . . . . . . . . . . . 41%
Real Estate & Land Use . . . . . . . . . . . . . . . . . . . . . . . . . . . . . . . . . . 15%

**FIRM OVERVIEW:** Dunn Carney is a leading client-focused law firm in the Pacific Northwest. Attorneys work with clients to develop and implement solutions designed to avoid the problems that could lead to formal proceedings. In the event of litigation, they have an experienced team of trial attorneys who provide expert counsel and representation in alternative dispute resolution and in the courtroom. Dunn Carney is Oregon's only member of Meritas, a legal service organization that offers high quality worldwide legal services through a closely integrated group of independent law firms.

### MAIN AREAS OF PRACTICE:

**Business Law & Estate Planning:** Many of the lawyers in the firm focus on matters relating to business and corporate law. These lawyers provide counsel for the day-to-day problems and concerns of business owners - including mergers/acquisitions, succession planning, tax, employee benefits, employment law, estate planning and bankruptcy. They serve clients in many industries including manufacturing/distribution, forest products, professional services, banking and finance, auto dealerships, construction and real estate.

**Litigation:** Dunn Carney's litigation attorneys represent clients in a variety of legal areas, including shareholder and partnership disputes, derivative and class actions, contract and warranty issues, trademark, taxation, employment, non-competition, antitrust, securities, banking, foreclosure, construction, international transaction disputes and other types of complex litigation. Dunn Carney is widely recognized for its expertise in insurance law and insurance coverage matters. This experience includes first party claims, employment discrimination, liquor liability, products liability, professional negligence, personal injury, commercial tort and business losses, property damage cases and self-insured defense.

**Real Estate & Land Use:** Dunn Carney's real estate and land use attorneys are recognized as among the Northwest's best at providing efficient, effective real estate services regarding development, acquisition, sale, financing, leasing, construction, land use, environmental issues, exchanges and other real estate tax matters, litigation and dispute resolution. Their work on the nationally recognized Brewery Blocks Development with their client Gerding/Edlen Development involved many complex issues and has led to other significant real estate transactions including the South Waterfront Development on the Willamette River.

**CLIENTS:** North Pacific Group, Pan Pacific Retail Properties, Weyerhaeuser Co., Eastern Western Corporation, Brewery Blocks Investors, Gerding/Edlen Development, OTAK, Inc., Providence Health System-Oregon, R.J. Reynolds Tobacco Company, Microfield Group, U.S. Bancorp, Kuni Enterprises, LbL Windows, Inc., A.W. Chesterton Company, Professional Liability Fund, Allstate Insurance, California Casualty Insurance, Allied Group Insurance, North Pacific Insurance, Orion Speciality, South Park Phase I, LLC, Civic Housing, LLC, Beall Corporation, Oregon Iron Works, Inc., Sunlight Supply, Inc.

### HEAD OFFICE

**OREGON**
851 SW Sixth Ave, Suite 1500, **Portland**, OR 97204 -1357
**Tel:** 503 224 6440   **Fax:** 503 224 7324
**Websites:** www.dunncarney.com

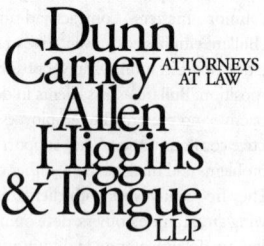

Member
**MERITAS**
LAW FIRMS WORLDWIDE

# LANDYE BENNETT BLUMSTEIN LLP

## THE FIRM

**Managing Partner:** David N Goulder

**Number of partners:** 22
**Number of other attorneys:** 5

## AREAS OF PRACTICE:

| | |
|---|---|
| Administrative Law | 5% |
| Alaska Native & Tribal Law | 20% |
| Business & Personal Injury Litigation | 35% |
| Corporate Business & Tax | 8% |
| Environmental Law | 8% |
| Estate Planning, Trusts, Wills, & Probate | 4% |
| Real Estate | 20% |

## HEAD OFFICE

**OREGON**
1300 S W Fifth Avenue, Suite 3500, **Portland**, OR 97201
**Tel:** 503 224 4100  **Fax:** 503 224 4133
**Website:** www.landye-bennett.com

## BRANCH OFFICES

**ALASKA**
701 West Eighth Avenue, Suite 1200, **Anchorage**, AK 99501
**Tel:** 907 276 5152  **Fax:** 907 276 8433

1981 East Palmer-Wasilla Highway, Suite 220, **Wasilla**, AK 99645
**Tel:** 907 376 5955  **Fax:** 907 376 5979

**FIRM OVERVIEW:** Landye Bennett Blumstein LLP is a regional law firm, founded in 1955. With offices in Anchorage, Alaska, and Portland, Oregon, the firm serves clients throughout the Pacific Northwest. The firm's attorneys devote themselves to delivering results for their clients efficiently and effectively by remaining tuned to their clients' needs throughout the entire legal process. Landye Bennett Blumstein provides personal attention to its clients in order to deliver the best and most courteous professional service possible. The firm's close ties to the communities where it works allows it to interact effectively with businesses, government agencies, and other attorneys. In addition to representing clients throughout the Pacific Northwest, Landye Bennett Blumstein also works with clients located in other parts of the country on specialized matters. Its clients include public and private corporations, real estate developers, condominium and community associations, municipalities, nonprofit groups, and individuals.

## MAIN AREAS OF PRACTICE:

**Administrative Law:** The firm's Administrative Law Practice includes a broad spectrum of clients before federal, state and local government agencies, including in the areas of environmental and natural resources, tax, land use, Native American organizations and gaming. While informal resolution is not always possible, the firm represents its clients at administrative hearings and, as may be required, through the appeals processes.

**Alaska Native & Tribal Law:** Since 1976, the firm has acted as general counsel or special counsel with respect to business and other matters to regional, village, and urban Native corporations organized under the Alaska Native Claims Settlement Act. The firm's attorneys also represent tribal entities, municipalities, and boroughs throughout much of Alaska.

**Litigation, Arbitration & Mediation:** Landye Bennett Blumstein LLP's Litigation Department has successfully represented clients in a wide variety of actions in both state and federal courts throughout the region. The firm represents both plaintiffs and defendants in such practice areas as products liability and toxic torts, aviation, environmental, shareholder and partner matters, including class action, contracts, unfair competition, employment discrimination, and maritime disputes and claims.

**Corporate Business & Tax:** The firm helps companies manage complex business transactions and legal situations its clients may encounter, including corporate finance and securities, mergers and acquisitions, tax planning and business structuring, computer and intellectual property, employment matters, and tax controversies.

**Environmental Law:** The firm's Environmental Practice includes advising a wide range of commercial and industrial clients with the myriad federal, state and local laws and regulations, including compliance with hazardous waste management regulations, regulatory and compliance matters involving the Clean Air Act, the Clean Water Act, the Toxic Substance Control Act, the Resource Conservation and Recovery Act and the Endangered Species Act, among others. Environmental due diligence for lenders and real estate clients is also a key area of the practice. Representing potentially responsible parties at federal and state

Superfund sites, as well as in cost recovery litigation with government agencies and private parties is another critical service provided by the firm's experienced environmental counsel.

**Estate Planning, Trusts, Wills, & Probate:** The firm offers services to its clients in estate planning, including the preparation of wills and trusts, post-mortem tax matters and probate.

**Real Estate:** The firm provides a full range of services for real estate matters. The firm's clients include more than 500 condominium and community associations and developers of more than 600 condominium and planned community projects. The firm assists its clients with acquisitions and dispositions of real estate, tax deferred exchanges, developing condominiums and planned communities, negotiating and documenting financing arrangements for both borrowers and lenders, land and building development, land use planning hearings and appeals, and commercial leases.

**CLIENTS:** Representative clients include A. McGill & Son; Bright Now! Dental, Inc.; Container Properties, LLC; Emerging Markets of North America, Inc.; Gould Electronics, Inc; Herbert Malarkey Roofing Company; Metro Metals Northwest; Pacific Coast Shredding, LLC; National Mortgage Co.; PPG Industries, Inc.; Sealaska Corporation; Sharp Laboratories of America, Inc., United Agri Products, Inc., Vantage Oncology, Inc.

# MILLER NASH LLP

## THE FIRM

**Managing Partner:** Thomas C Sand
**Number of partners:** 65

**FIRM OVERVIEW:** Miller Nash LLP is one of the Pacific Northwest's largest and most respected multi-service law firms offering comprehensive, creative, and innovative services to its business clients. The firm has provided legal services since 1873. Miller Nash has about 117 lawyers serving clients through its offices in Portland, Oregon, and Seattle and Vancouver, Washington. Miller Nash serves a wide range of leading businesses, nonprofit organizations, public entitles, and individuals as well as pro bono activities. The firm's clients work in a variety of significant industries, including banking, biotech, construction, food production, forest products, government, healthcare, high technology, higher education, intellectual property, real estate, and tax. Miller Nash represents the states of Oregon and Washington in the world-wide Employment Law Alliance (http://www.employmentlawalliance.com) and is a member of the Institute for Transnational Arbitration.

## MAIN AREAS OF PRACTICE:

**Business:** Miller Nash serves businesses of all sizes and in all stages of development. The firm's attorneys offer their expertise in multiple specialties, including: emerging business and start-ups; technology protection and acquisition; entity structuring; mergers, acquisitions, and dispositions; public offerings of equity and debt securities; institutional and private placements of debt and equity securities; and corporation law, including director, officer, and shareholder matters.

**Business Litigation:** Miller Nash business litigation attorneys regularly try or arbitrate 'bet the business' disputes as well as claims in the areas of corporate governance, complex insurance coverage, tax, lender liability, securities fraud, real estate, and international transactions.

**Construction Litigation:** Miller Nash provides many construction law services. The firm's primary clients are owners, public entities, prime contractors, and subcontractors. Clients range from national and international contractors doing business in the Northwest to local and regional companies involved in projects in the private and public sectors.

**Employee Benefits:** Individuals, businesses, trusts, and institutions seek Miller Nash's counsel on employee benefits matters. The firm's attorneys work on all types of plans to help clients in all aspects of benefits work and represent them before the Internal Revenue Service, the US Department of Labor, the Pension Benefit Guaranty Corporation, and other federal agencies. Employee benefits attorneys work closely with other attorneys in the firm on related business and litigation needs.

**Employment Law & Labor Relations:** Miller Nash provides complete employment law and labor relations services to private- and public-sector employers, in both union and nonunion environments. The firm partners with clients in proactively solving problems in today's rapidly changing employment environment, and defends employers when disputes arise.

**Healthcare:** Miller Nash represents a broad range of healthcare organizations and providers, including health systems, hospitals, educational institutions, medical technology companies, medical groups, individual healthcare practitioners, payers, healthcare service contractors, nursing homes, and other health-related businesses. The Healthcare Practice Group has extensive experience involving the formation and representation of for-profit and tax-exempt corporations, foundations, professional corporations, partnerships, limited liability companies, and joint ventures.

**Insolvency, Reorganization & Bankruptcy:** Miller Nash's insolvency, reorganization, and bankruptcy attorneys represent creditors, creditors' committees, trustees, and debtors in nonbankruptcy workouts, as well as in reorganization and liquidation bankruptcy cases.

## HEAD OFFICE

**OREGON**
111 SW Fifth Avenue, Suite 3400, **Portland**, OR 97204-3699
**Tel:** 503 224 5858   **Fax:** 503 224 0155
**Website:** www.millernash.com

## BRANCH OFFICES

**WASHINGTON**
4400 Two Union Square, 601 Union Street, **Seattle**
Washington 98101-2352
**Tel:** 206 622 8484   **Fax:** 206 622 7485

500 East Broadway, Suite 400, PO Box 694, **Vancouver**
Washington 98660-3324
**Tel:** 360 699 4771   **Fax:** 360 694 6413

**Intellectual Property:** Intellectual property rights are often the most valuable assets of a company. Safeguarding those rights requires a comprehensive understanding of legal protections. Miller Nash represents clients in intellectual property matters involving patents, copyrights, trademarks, trade dress, and trade secrets.

**Real Estate, Land Use & Environmental:** The firm's real estate, land use, and environmental lawyers assist clients in the buying, selling, financing, development, leasing, and construction of residential, commercial, industrial, and institutional properties. Miller Nash helps individuals and businesses structure, document and obtain government approvals for all types of real estate transactions and developments.

**Regulatory & Government Affairs:** Miller Nash's regulatory, and government affairs attorneys have worked with a variety of clients, including those in the oil, tribal, gaming, telecommunications, cable, broadcasting, computer, financial, construction, transportation, education, medical, and insurance industries. The firm's attorneys have extensive experience interacting with the legislative, judicial, and executive branches of state governments, as well as with federal, state, and local agencies and commissions.

**Securities Litigation:** Miller Nash's Securities Litigation Team regularly represents investment banks, issuers, directors and officers, major wirehouses, and smaller broker-dealers against claims filed by shareholders and investors with the NASD, NYSE, and state and federal courts, including class actions. As a result, Miller Nash has extensive experience with claims under federal and state securities laws as well as suitability, churning, and breach-of-fiduciary-duty claims.

**Tax, Trusts & Estates, and Nonprofit Corporations:** Attorneys in Miller Nash's Tax, Trusts and Estates, and Non-profit Corporations Practice help clients attain their business objectives while minimizing and complying with local, state, and federal tax laws. The Wealth Management Practice combines estate planning, will and trust preparation, and estate and trust administration with a wide range of personal services.

**INTERNATIONAL WORK:** The firm regularly handles litigation in US courts involving transnational issues, as well as international arbitrations before the ICC, AAA, WIPO, Stockholm Chamber of Commerce, London Court of Arbitration, and other international arbitral institutions.

# TONKON TORP LLP

## THE FIRM

**Managing Partner:** Bruce G Berning
**Chief Executive Officer:** Robert E Hirshon
**Number of partners:** 45
**Number of other lawyers:** 23

**FIRM OVERVIEW:** Tonkon Torp LLP is a sophisticated business transaction and litigation firm experienced in the legal areas important to businesses. The firm serves clients throughout the Pacific Northwest and nationally on a wide variety of business law and complex litigation matters. The firm was founded in 1974 by several of Oregon's leading business lawyers, with the objective of providing personalized services to sophisticated business clients. The firm combines a strong entrepreneurial spirit with sophisticated legal knowledge. By concentrating on business clients, Tonkon Torp provides the in-depth legal expertise expected in a much larger firm with the personal service and response associated with smaller firms.

## MAIN AREAS OF PRACTICE:

**Business:** Business services provided by Tonkon Torp to clients include: antitrust and trade regulation; banking and financial services; bankruptcy and reorganizations; commercial; corporate; distribution; emerging growth and technology; energy; environmental; executive compensation and employee benefits; immigration; intellectual property; labor and employment; mergers and acquisitions; natural resources and forest products; real estate; securities; tax; telecommunications; utilities; venture capital; and wealth planning.

**Corporate Finance:** Tonkon Torp has an extensive and varied corporate finance practice. Recognized as a regional leader in corporate finance, firm lawyers combine Wall Street and Silicon Valley business savvy with a personal approach. Tonkon Torp lawyers represent issuers, investors and underwriters in a wide variety of public and private equity and debt transactions. The firm assists publicly-traded clients and private clients in financings and regulatory compliance, and in creation of pooled funds, hedge funds and mutual funds.

**Mergers & Acquisitions:** Firm merger and acquisition attorneys are recognized by peers as among the leaders in the region. Clients have turned to Tonkon Torp for assistance with corporate control transactions including: mergers and acquisitions; leveraged buyouts; joint ventures and strategic alliances; proxy contests; sales and acquisitions of troubled companies; spin-offs and asset sales; and going private transactions. Tonkon Torp represents purchasers, sellers, targets, financial intermediaries, committees of Boards of Directors, and other participants in these transactions.

**Litigation:** The litigation attorneys of Tonkon Torp have a sophisticated commercial practice. The firm routinely handles matters in the following areas: trade regulation; commercial disputes; corporate, shareholder and securities matters; debtor/creditor; employment and labor; regulated industries; environmental and natural resource; financial services; intellectual property; and real estate. Tonkon Torp has pursued its clients' interests in almost every possible forum, from the usual - state and federal trial courts, appellate courts, agency hearings, private arbitrations - to the less common - Indian tribal courts, the US Court of Federal Claims and the US Supreme Court.

**Real Estate:** Tonkon Torp assists clients on real estate acquisitions and sales transactions and related issues. Clients also retain Tonkon Torp for real estate development matters because of the firm's familiarity with Oregon's complex land use laws and experience with government agencies. Firm lawyers help clients comply with environmental issues and regulations to minimize expensive risks and delays.

**Labor & Employment:** Tonkon Torp's relationship-based approach helps the firm provide practical solutions to labor and employment problems for a diverse group of employers. The firm helps its clients promote positive employee relations, protect competitive positions, deal with union activity, and defend employment litigation. Working with clients, firm lawyers pro-actively identify potential problem areas, develop appropriate policies and procedures and train management employees to prevent costly disputes. The firm also helps clients comply with local, state and federal employment laws to minimize exposure to litigation.

## HEAD OFFICE

**OREGON**
888 SW Fifth Avenue, Suite 1600, **Portland**, OR 97204
**Tel:** 503 221 1440  **Fax:** 503 274 8779
**Website:** www.tonkon.com

## CONTACTS

**BUSINESS DEPARTMENT**
| | |
|---|---|
| Banking | Kenneth D Stephens |
| Corporate Finance | Thomas P Palmer |
| Emerging Growth/Technology | Kurt W Ruttum |
| Executive Compensation/Employee Benefits | Darcy M Norville |
| Energy | Michael M Morgan |
| Immigration | Turid L Owren |
| Intellectual Property | Vicki A Ballou |
| Labor & Employment | Lynda J Hartzell |
| Mergers & Acquisitions | Brian G Booth |
| Natural Resources | Max M Miller, Jr |
| Real Estate - Land Development | Joseph S Voboril |
| Tax | Mark F LeRoux |
| Wealth Planning | John H Rosenfeld |

**LITIGATION DEPARTMENT**
| | |
|---|---|
| Antitrust | Scott G Seidman |
| Appellate | Barbee B Lyon |
| Complex Litigation | Daniel H Skerritt |
| Bankruptcy/Reorganizations | Albert N Kennedy |
| Energy & Other Regulatory | Michael M Morgan |
| Insurance Coverage | Frank J Weiss |
| Labor & Employment | Jon P Stride |
| Natural Resources | Steven M Wilker |
| Real Estate & Land Use | Edwin C Perry |
| Shareholders/Securities | William F Martson, Jr |

**CLIENTS:** The firm's client base is as diverse as the economy of the Pacific Northwest and includes regional, national and multinational companies. Corporate clients include: Blount, Inc., Columbia Forest Products, Inc., Costco Wholesale Corporation; Deloitte & Touche LLP, Esco Corporation, The Greenbrier Companies, Key Technology, Inc., M. Financial Holdings Incorporated, Medical Management International, Inc., NIKE, Inc., Northwest Pepsi Cola Bottlers, Oregon Health & Science University, PPM Energy, Inc., Portland General Electric Company, SEH America, Inc., Stimson Lumber Company, Taser International, Inc., Temco Metal Products Company, Tidewater Holdings, Inc., U.S. Trust Company of the Pacific Northwest, Wells Fargo Bank Northwest, N.A., and Weyerhaeuser Company.

## How lawyers are ranked

Every year we carry out thousands of in-depth interviews with clients and lawyers in order to assess the reputations and expertise of business lawyers across the USA. Chambers rankings and editorial are referred to extensively by General Counsel and other purchasers of legal services who look to our recommendations when choosing their lawyers.

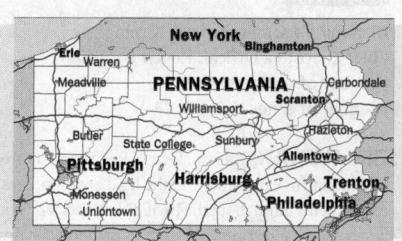

# ANTITRUST

### Antitrust
#### Leading Firms

1. **DECHERT LLP** *Philadelphia*
2. **BERGER & MONTAGUE PC** *Philadelphia*
   **FINE, KAPLAN AND BLACK, RPC** *Philadelphia*
   **PEPPER HAMILTON LLP** *Philadelphia*
3. **DRINKER BIDDLE & REATH LLP** *Philadelphia*
   **KOHN SWIFT & GRAF** *Philadelphia*
   **MONTGOMERY, MCCRACKEN** *Philadelphia*
   **MORGAN, LEWIS & BOCKIUS LLP** *Philadelphia*
   **REED SMITH LLP** *Pittsburgh*
4. **DUANE MORRIS LLP** *Philadelphia*
   **HARKINS CUNNINGHAM LLP** *Philadelphia*

#### Leading Individuals

1. **TATE Joseph** *Dechert LLP*
2. **ARMSTRONG Stephen** *Montgomery, McCracken*
   **BLACK Allen** *Fine, Kaplan and Black*
   **BOOKER Daniel** *Reed Smith LLP*
   **GORDON George** *Dechert LLP*
   **KOHN Joseph** *Kohn Swift & Graf*
   **LIEBENBERG Roberta** *Fine, Kaplan and Black*
   **MATHER Barbara** *Pepper Hamilton LLP*
   **MONTAGUE JR H Laddie** *Berger & Montague*
   **SHIEKMAN Laurence** *Pepper Hamilton LLP*
   **SICALIDES Barbara** *Pepper Hamilton LLP*
   **STACK JR Stephen** *Dechert LLP*
3. **BIZAR Steven** *Buchanan Ingersoll*
   **BROWN Stephen** *Dechert LLP*
   **CRAMER Eric** *Berger & Montague PC*
   **EDWARDS Mark** *Morgan, Lewis & Bockius*
   **KAPLAN Arthur** *Fine, Kaplan and Black*
   **LANGER Howard** *Langer & Grogan PC*
   **LEVIN Christine** *Dechert LLP*
   **NEWELL Francis** *Harkins Cunningham*
   **RODGERS James** *Dilworth Paxson LLP*
   **SAINT-ANTOINE Paul** *Drinker Biddle & Reath*
   **SEDRAN Howard** *Levin Fishbein Sedran*
   **SHADOWEN Steve** *Hangley Aronchick Segal*
   **SITARCHUK Eric** *Ballard Spahr Andrews*
   **SWIRSKY Sherry** *Schnader Harrison Segal*

#### Up-and-coming individuals
**MACK Wayne** *Duane Morris LLP*

## Band 1

### Dechert LLP
See firm details p.1752

**The Firm:** Dechert's antitrust lawyers are famed for their regular presence in *"really big, multijurisdictional cases."* The firm's focus on claims relating to pharmaceutical and chemical patents was sustained by acting for GlaxoSmithKline in the ongoing Paxil antitrust litigation involving sham patent allegations. Other high-profile cases include successfully defending Pfizer against allegations of Sherman Act violations. The team also advised Pfizer on the $1.9 billion acquisition of Vicuron Pharmaceuticals and on the ensuing FTC review. Clients highlighted the *"responsiveness and timeliness"* of a team that *"has the capability to keep a number of top-quality lawyers as backup to the main counsel."* Its practitioners also have a reputation in the market as *"wonderfully smart, articulate, aggressive, creative"* litigators to whom clients keep returning.

**The Lawyers:** *"Unquestionably number one,"* **Joseph Tate** (see p.1744 is hailed by clients and peers alike as *"one of the most experienced, creative and inventive antitrust lawyers currently practicing."* Tate is particularly renowned for his involvement in cases affecting the pharmaceutical and chemical industries. He came in for further praise for his *"intellectual firepower"* and his *"resourcefulness and effectiveness in court."* It is too early to say what impact Jennifer Clarke's departure will have on the practice. She became executive director of The Public Interest Law Center of Philadelphia in February 2006. Interviewees branded young star **George Gordon** (see p.1729) *"the most impressive antitrust lawyer of his generation."* Working closely with Tate, he is seen by many as *"already a leader"* and, given time, *"has the potential to reach Tate's unmatched level of expertise."* Gordon has worked on some of the firm's most significant cases, such as the Paxil litigation and the ongoing Curtis Circulation Company price discrimination litigation. Head of department **Stephen Stack** (see p.1743) is heavily involved in transactional work with potential antitrust ramifications. He oversaw Pfizer's $1.9 billion acquisition of Vicuraon and managed the FTC review of the merger. Though less active in litigation than other members of the team, he is regarded as *"the best for deals"* and received

praise for his *"sound knowledge of the rules and trends in merger situations,"* and for his *"ability to predict issues before they arise and provide solutions accordingly."* **Stephen Brown** (see p.1724) continues to represent FMC with regard to claims of alleged market allocation agreement. Peers underlined his *"outstanding ability"* when it comes to handling criminal antitrust matters. **Christine Levin** (see p.1734) has a solid reputation for her broad antitrust practice, which includes appearing before EU tribunals and grand jury investigations.

**Clients/Work Highlights:** Further highlights include representing a number of truck engine distributing companies in a case related to illegal boycott and price-fixing claims. The client roster features pharmaceutical giants like Pfizer and GlaxoSmithKline. Delta Air Lines, Elan and FMC are also long-standing clients.

## Band 2

### Berger & Montague PC

**The Firm:** As *"the leading plaintiff outfit,"* the firm continues to be active in cases mainly relating to the alleged anticompetitive behavior of manufacturers and pharmaceutical companies. Highlights include representing the direct purchasers of the brand-name drug K-Dur in claiming that Schering-Plough, Upsher-Smith and American Home Products entered anticompetitive agreements. It is also lead co-counsel for US holders of Visa, MasterCard and Diners Club cards in the currency conversion fee antitrust litigation. Card holders claim Visa, MasterCard, Diners Club and seven of the largest credit card issuers, including Citibank and Bank of America, conspired to artificially set and inflate currency conversion fees.

**The Lawyers:** Senior Bar member and firm rainmaker **Laddie Montague** is regarded among peers as *"one of the best antitrust lawyers in the country,"* while **Eric Cramer** is a *"young and extremely smart"* partner with a *"particularly strong grasp of economic analysis."*

**Clients/Work Highlights:** The firm generally represents consumers, businesses, state and local governmental entities. For instance, the team has acted for hundreds of pharmaceutical wholesalers claiming Abbott Laboratories and Geneva Pharmaceuticals agreed to delay the entry onto the market of generic versions of the drug Hytrin (Terazosin). A settlement worth almost $75 million was agreed after five years of litigation. Currently, the group is working on a similar case involving Akzo Nobel and its US subsidiary Organon USA.

### Fine, Kaplan and Black, RPC

**The Firm:** While this litigation boutique traditionally specialized in plaintiff work, it has in recent years forged *"an interesting and enviable niche practice"* that combines both plaintiff and defendant representation. On the defendant side, the firm recently obtained a landmark district court decision enjoining the government from maintaining a criminal prosecution against defendant Stolt-Nielsen. On the plaintiff side, the firm is currently co-lead counsel in the Urethane antitrust litigation in a case alleging conspiracy to fix the price of chemicals used in the manufacture of flexible and rigid foam. Defendants in that case include Bayer, BASF, Dow Chemical, Lyondell and Huntsman.

**The Lawyers:** Competitors respect **Allen Black** as *"a superb litigator with the rare ability to take on both the plaintiff and defendant side."* Interviewees hailed **Roberta Liebenberg** as an *"honorable and knowledgeable lawyer with a thorough grasp of the legal issues, who can therefore put forward good, strong arguments."* **Arthur Kaplan** has been less active lately, leaving his role as partner for a more flexible of counsel position. However, he remains a highly regarded counselor who is regularly called upon for a second opinion.

**Clients/Work Highlights:** Consumer groups, individuals, law firms and healthcare sector companies all feature in the firm's clientele.

### Pepper Hamilton LLP

See firm details p.1760

**The Firm:** Interviewees point to the firm's *"depth of experience"* and *"willingness to please clients with a top-notch service"* as two of its defining characteristics. Its team has a number of long-standing clients for whom it does mainly advisory work on issues relating to the antitrust liability arising from mergers and other transactions. However, members of the firm also have experience of significant antitrust litigation. Overall, the outfit receives unequivocal endorsement for the *"intellect, pragmatism, judgment and interpersonal skills"* of its practitioners.

**The Lawyers:** Cochair of the litigation practice **Barbara Mather** (see p.1735) handles an eclectic range of matters from antitrust to general commercial litigation. Aside from handling Hart-Scott-Rodino filings for a number of acquirers, she defended a leading manufacturer of kitchen and bathroom fixtures in antitrust litigation, and represented the main defendant in the Linerboard antitrust cases. Clients and peers respect her for *"her wide-ranging experience"* and for *"the excellent quality of her work."* Clients regard **Laurence Shiekman** (see p.1742) as *"one of the best litigators in Pennsylvania."* His workload comprises cases relating to the

interface between patents and antitrust, and recently involved litigation arising from allegations of Robinson-Patman Act violations. He also defended a national home builder against price-fixing and monopolization claims. **Barbara Sicalides** (see p.1742) is *"an experienced and insightful antitrust attorney"* renowned for providing *"invaluable guidance and advice"* to businesses on transactional issues. On the litigation side, she defended a major tobacco company facing Robinson-Patman Act infringement and distributor termination claims. Clients praised her *"creative approach"* and *"extensive knowledge,"* which enable her to provide *"immediate and reliable answers."*

**Clients/Work Highlights:** Recent highlights include obtaining a $65 million settlement in LePage's favor in a monopolization claim against 3M. The team also defended a "Big Three" automobile manufacturer against charges of alleged antitrust violations in connection with the sale of branded replacement parts. Pinnacle Health System; Saint-Gobain; Littlejohn & Co and Conrail can also be counted as clients.

## Band 3

### Drinker Biddle & Reath LLP

**The Firm:** Interviewees endorsed the firm's *"array of excellent attorneys"* who are *"hugely knowledgeable, extremely responsive and possess strong analytical skills."* With ten offices across the USA and a 14-attorney antitrust team, the firm has an impressive reach. It has provided ongoing advice to Hoffmann-La Roche in a pharmaceutical antitrust case in California affecting Pfizer. The firm also represented the trade association Building Owners and Managers Association (BOMA) International in a telecom antitrust case filed by IDT.

**The Lawyers:** Commentators underlined the *"high-quality work"* produced by **Paul Saint-Antoine**, and his remarkable *"staffing and budgeting abilities,"* not to mention his willingness to *"liaise closely with clients on everything from general strategy to key aspects of litigation."* Peers also admire him for his *"consensus-building ability."*

**Clients/Work Highlights:** The firm's client roster includes Georgia-Pacific; BOMA International; Hewlett-Packard and Hoffmann-La Roche.

### Kohn Swift & Graf

**The Firm:** This quality boutique outfit is well-known for representing plaintiffs not only in antitrust cases, but also in employment discrimination and consumer class action matters. The firm's recent caseload includes the Compact Disc MAP antitrust litigation, in which five top US distributors of CDs and three large music retailers agreed to a $143 million settlement in the face of allegations of price-fixing. The firm is also involved in the automotive paint refinishing antitrust litigation, which comprises over 60 class action complaints of price-fixing.

**The Lawyers:** Director of the firm **Joseph Kohn** has cemented his reputation for being *"extremely active*

*and effective on the plaintiff side"* of antitrust. The plastic tableware antitrust litigation and the metal building insulation antitrust litigation are among several noteworthy cases handled by Kohn. Other highlights include the graphite electrodes antitrust case filed against Mitsubishi and the Toys 'R' Us antitrust litigation.

**Clients/Work Highlights:** The firm's client portfolio is made up of manufacturers, consumer groups, product representatives and employees.

### Montgomery, McCracken, Walker & Rhoads, LLP

**The Firm:** With eight antitrust partners in its Philadelphia office, the firm has been equally busy on both counseling and litigation fronts. One of the firm's strengths resides in its attorneys' understanding of the nexus between IP and antitrust. A focus on chemical and computer software industries further defines the practice. While the departure of partner Frank Newell to Harkins Cunningham is bound to have an impact, peers still identify Montgomery McCracken as a lean operation that is *"more than capable"* of handling complex antitrust matters.

**The Lawyers:** *"Leading defense lawyer"* **Stephen Armstrong** won plaudits for his *"brilliant work"* in several major cases. He was recently involved in the bath and kitchen fixtures antitrust litigation as defendant's co-counsel and also acted as DRAM's co-counsel in the defense of horizontal price-fixing allegations.

**Clients/Work Highlights:** The team represented Rohm and Haas in the plastics additives antitrust litigation and is acting as counsel to Detroit Diesel in ongoing litigation. The firm's impressive client roster also includes Bayer and Microsoft.

### Morgan, Lewis & Bockius LLP

See firm details p.1758

**The Firm:** The antitrust group specializes in advising corporate entities on antitrust issues relating to M&A, but a considerable part of the team's work is contentious, and involves claims of price-fixing, monopolization and group boycotts. Although the antitrust practice in Pennsylvania is relatively small, the team profits from the backing of both the firm's DC office and a large, first-rate commercial litigation group. As such, lawyers at the firm can be relied upon for *"impressive court performances."*

**The Lawyers:** Partner **Mark Edwards** (see p.1727) is credited with being *"a great counselor and a smart litigator."* Recently, he was successful in having a case brought against Charming Shoppes in Madison County, Illinois, dismissed. He achieved success in defending Armstrong Holdings in an antitrust action brought by distributor Bolick.

**Clients/Work Highlights:** This year the team successfully defended a Sandvik joint venture against claims of price discrimination. Other representative matters include obtaining summary judgment for the Law School Admission Council in an action alleging antitrust violations in the ABA's accreditation process. Further clients include Penn Detroit Diesel; Philips Lighting; Comdata and Integra LifeSciences.

## Reed Smith LLP

See firm details p.1762

**The Firm:** The firm's six-partner team in Pittsburgh handled a significant number of high-profile cases this year, representing a diverse mix of clients including a major financial institution, a European computer manufacturer and a Texas hospital. The group covers both civil and criminal antitrust litigation, and successfully defended a textile manufacturer in a private class action. In addition to contentious matters, members of the firm were busy assisting businesses with minimizing antitrust risks during negotiations and due diligence. Clients value the firm's "*superb work and premium service.*"

**The Lawyers:** **Daniel Booker** (see p.1723) recently won a favorable settlement for Big East American Football League in a sports antitrust claim.

**Clients/Work Highlights:** The firm's client base includes steel manufacturers, health insurers, computer companies and aircraft manufacturers.

## Band 4

## Duane Morris LLP

See firm details p.1753

**The Firm:** The seven-attorney antitrust team at the firm's Philadelphia and Pittsburgh offices has handled a number of antitrust class action cases over the past year. Although the team has an excellent reputation for its healthcare focus, this year it has seen an uptake in the volume of work from manufacturing and dealership sectors.

**The Lawyers:** Healthcare antitrust issues are central to **Wayne Mack**'s (see p.1734) practice. He recently received a verdict in favor of a hospital in an antitrust action brought by a cardiothoracic surgeon who alleged a group of hospitals had conspired to restrict his privileges. Mack is also a member of the firm's dealer services group, which represents automobile and truck dealers in a range of matters.

**Clients/Work Highlights:** The firm defended a Japanese manufacturer against price-fixing allegations, and represented plaintiff Diamond International in the Detroit Diesel litigation. Lehigh Valley Hospital and Lancaster General Hospital can also be counted as clients, among others.

## Harkins Cunningham LLP

**The Firm:** This business and litigation boutique has recently added former Montgomery McCracken partner Francis Newell to its ranks, thus considerably strengthening its antitrust team. Counseling corporations on antitrust compliance has been complemented by defendant and plaintiff action in the courts of late.

**The Lawyers:** **Francis Newell** was cast as "*a very responsive attorney, who devotes a lot of energy to building relationships with us,*" clients said. Nationwide antitrust class action cases are his forte, in which he has represented the likes of Delta Air Lines and Simpson Investment Company.

**Clients/Work Highlights:** Recent examples of the team's work include acting for an industrial products manufacturer in multidistrict proceedings relating to allegations of price-fixing and market allocation. Elsewhere, members of the firm acted for a manufacturer of electronic surveillance technology equipment in an action against a trade association alleged to have engaged in unlawful concerted action that favored a competing manufacturer. The firm has an impressive list of clients, including IBM; 3M; DuPont; Association of American Railroads; Rohm and Haas and CIGNA.

## Other Notable Practitioners

"*Impressive*" Buchanan Ingersoll PC lawyer **Steven Bizar** (see p.1723) is deemed to have achieved significant success relatively early on in his career, and his practice spans everything from antitrust class actions to securities litigation. Bizar's recent highlights include acting in a number of Sherman Act-related class action cases and advising multinational companies affected by EU Commission investigations. Senior attorney **Howard Langer** of Langer & Grogan is highly respected by peers for his expertise and high ethical values. He recently acted as lead counsel for major Italian pharmaceutical company Chemi SpA in a patent antitrust suit filed against GlaxoSmithKline. Although his firm specializes in litigation work for small to midsized businesses, Langer has acted for the likes of International Zinc and the Philadelphia National Bank. **James Rodgers** of Dilworth Paxson LLP makes an entry in the table as a lawyer renowned for both plaintiff and defendant antitrust work. He acted as co-counsel to opt-out plaintiffs in significant multidistrict antitrust litigation, including the Graphite Electrodes antitrust litigation and the Linerboard case. Market sources highlighted his "*varied litigation experience*" and valued his "*highly supportive manner with clients.*" **Howard Sedran** of Levin Fishbein Sedran & Berman is renowned for his "*professionalism, preparedness and diligence*" in pursuing his clients' interests. He was recently involved in the commercial tissue products antitrust litigation. **Steve Shadowen** (see p.1741) at Hangley Aronchick Segal & Pudlin is considered "*an absolute pleasure to work with,*" and mostly acts for plaintiffs in antitrust litigation. He enters the table for the first time this year along with the "*smart and rigorous*" **Eric Sitarchuk** (see p.1742) of Ballard Spahr Andrews & Ingersoll, LLP. Sitarchuk heads up the firm's white-collar crime practice group and has considerable experience of defending federal criminal cases alleging antitrust violations. Judges are said to love the "*capable, smart and aggressive*" **Sherry Swirsky** of Schnader Harrison Segal & Lewis LLP, who comfortably sustains her position in the table.

# BANKING & FINANCE

| Banking & Finance | |
| --- | --- |
| **Leading Firms** | |
| [1] **BLANK ROME LLP** *Philadelphia* | |
| **DUANE MORRIS LLP** *Philadelphia* | |
| [2] **BALLARD SPAHR** *Philadelphia* | |
| **DRINKER BIDDLE & REATH LLP** *Philadelphia* | |
| **KLETT ROONEY LIEBER & SCHORLING** *Pittsburgh* | |
| **MORGAN, LEWIS & BOCKIUS LLP** *Philadelphia* | |
| **REED SMITH LLP** *Pittsburgh* | |
| **STRADLEY RONON** *Philadelphia* | |
| **WOLF, BLOCK** *Philadelphia* | |

## Band 1

## Blank Rome LLP

See firm details p.1747

**The Firm:** This firm's "*powerful, diverse and full-blown*" banking and finance practice attracts praise for its business and consumer finance work, including equipment leasing, securitization, real estate lending, loan workouts, restructurings and regulation. The team is recognized nationally and internationally for its hallmark asset-based lending, mezzanine lending and hedge funds practice. The past year has seen a healthy flow of deals for Merrill Lynch and plenty of acquisition finance work. The client base is studded with financial institutions, which praise the group's "*technical competency and solid business sense.*" The public finance group handles a varied load of capital formation for state and local governments and authorities, such as financings for schools, universities and infrastructure. The firm represents underwriters including investment banks, issuers and insurers in bond issues and letters of credit. Interdisciplinary capability, including tax and litigation, is centered in Pennsylvania and New Jersey.

**The Lawyers:** **Harvey Forman** concentrates on asset-based lending and commercial finance loans. He is rated as "*an outstanding commercial banking lawyer*" who acts mainly for financial institutions such as Wachovia. Public finance supremo **Joan Stern** (see p.1743) focuses on governmental projects and innovative financing programs. She has an active bonds practice and is well-regarded in the tax arena. "*Powerful strategic thinker*" **Lawrence Flick** (see p.1727) is experienced in asset-based finance, hedge funds and private equity. He leads the firm's leasings and securitizations charge. His *"exceptionally creative"* work also includes cash flow lending, senior secured financing and acquisition financing, and he splits his time between Philadelphia and New York. **Mark Rabinowitz** (see p.1738) heads the financial services group, where he runs the administrative side, and is also nationally active in healthcare finance. He is active in commercial lending, asset-based financing, bankruptcy and debt restructuring, and his major clients include Healthcare Business Credit and CIT Group.

**Clients/Work Highlights:** The firm's client roster includes PNC Bank, Commerce Bank and Fleet Capital.

## Duane Morris LLP
See firm details p.1753

**The Firm:** Banking and finance is one of the strongest areas for this team, which is part of an interdisciplinary group that offers commercial finance, corporate finance and tax expertise. The team acquits itself with credit in complex and sophisticated transactions such as asset-based transactions, cash flow, syndicated loans, public securities, tax financing and project financing. The team acted recently as Pennsylvania counsel to the group financing the construction of sports arenas for the Philadelphia Eagles and the Philadelphia Phillies. The firm's merger with San Francisco's Hancock Rothert & Bunshoft increases its footprint nationwide. Lawyers draw on expertise from offices across the USA to advise banks, hedge funds and investment groups, mainly lender-side, on a national and international basis. For example, the team acted for a wholesale and retail lender in transactions in the UK. Clients praise the group's *"excellent commercial and business instincts"* in restructuring and bankruptcy.

**The Lawyers:** **John Horstmann** (see p.1731) heads the corporate group but is equally active on the insolvency and banking and finance sides. Clients appreciate his *"outstanding abilities, combining technical and people skills to great effect."* He handles

lender-side transactions for large insurance companies and banks such as Bank of America, and is praised for his commercial loan documentation and commercial reorganizations. **Dianne Meyer**'s (see p.1736) *"ability to get right to the heart of the matter"* wins her fans. She chairs the commercial finance group and offers a *"significant business background"* as a certified public accountant. She advises lenders such as Wachovia on large loan transactions and asset-based cash flow matters, and is active in healthcare and bond transactions.

**Clients/Work Highlights:** Clients include ABN AMRO; Fifth Third Bank; LaSalle National Bank; Mellon Financial; Northern Trust; Sovereign Bank; Universal American Mortgage; GE Capital and Vauxhall Finance.

## Band 2

### Ballard Spahr Andrews & Ingersoll LLP
See firm details p.1746

**The Firm:** This group is praised particularly for its distinguished bond finance and public finance practice. It advises banks, insurance companies, businesses, investment companies and public utilities. The team draws on strengths in areas such as consumer financial services, real estate finance, tax, project finance and transactional finance. The lawyers impress commentators with their *"interpersonal skills and professionalism."*

**The Lawyers:** The *"well-rounded"* **Carl Fridy** (see p.1728) focuses on bank loans, letters of credit and public and real estate finance. He also handles construction and bankruptcy matters.

**Clients/Work Highlights:** The core of the practice is lender and borrower representation of financial institutions, businesses, investments groups and insurers.

### Drinker Biddle & Reath LLP

**The Firm:** This 17-strong team covers a wide front, including syndicated loans, mezzanine financings, public debt financing, tax-exempt financing and debt securities. It also has a healthy line in corporate transactions and restructurings. The team recently represented a fashion retailer as borrower in a $375 million revolving credit facility, and acted for a charitable organization in the creation of a $100 million asset-backed commercial paper program. Its regionally flavored practice for financial institutions and businesses located in the USA notwithstanding, the team is increasingly active in international transactions.

**The Lawyers:** The *"technically superb"* **Jill Bronson** *"has a firm but velvet touch,"* according to sources. Alongside a vigorous corporate and securities practice, her *"imaginative, energetic and reliable"* banking and finance work centers on the lender-side representation of financial institutions and businesses in senior debt financings and regulatory matters. The *"focused and analytical"* **Judith Reich** advises borrowers and lenders in commercial loan transac-

tions, asset-based lending, syndicated credit facilities, mezzanine lending and bankruptcy matters. She is well-known for representing private equity funds and acquiring companies.

**Clients/Work Highlights:** Bank of America; Citizens Bank; CIT Lending Services; Wachovia and M&T Bank.

### Klett Rooney Lieber & Schorling
See firm details p.1757

**The Firm:** This regional midmarket player has been on the receiving end of an increase in international deals and national syndicated loan transactions. It recently represented a syndicate of banks in a $250 million syndicated acquisition loan facility. The team includes bankruptcy experts as well as banking and finance specialists, acting for financial institutions on the lender side and companies on the borrower side. The *"competent and professional"* lawyers handle loan documentations as well as negotiations.

**The Lawyers:** **Craig Heryford**'s (see p.1730) *"business and legal acumen are wonderful"* and clients praise his *"intellectual approach and ability to build a consensus."* In the banking arena he represents financial institutions in syndicated loan facilities. He acts for several businesses as general corporate counsel and does a fair amount of venture capital work.

**Clients/Work Highlights:** The clientele includes a number of businesses and financial institutions such as Citizens Bank, PNC Bank, Wachovia and LaSalle Business Credit.

### Morgan, Lewis & Bockius LLP
See firm details p.1758

**The Firm:** This *"muscular and far-reaching"* firm impresses clients with its *"breadth of services and expertise in almost every aspect of banking."* The team represents businesses and banks on the borrower side around the country and worldwide, handling large financings, credit facilities and syndicated loans. For example, it acted for FMC on an $850 million credit facility involving US and foreign banks. It also acted for American Financial Realty Trust in several large nonrecourse financings of real property assets. Ancillary expertise is offered in areas such as employment and environmental law.

**The Lawyers:** The *"high-class"* **Lawrence Berger** (see p.1722) focuses on business and corporate finance law. He acts for financial institutions, private and healthcare companies in credit transactions, acquisitions and restructurings, and sources declare him a *"gentleman who handles big deals with integrity, honesty and confidence."* **Michael Pedrick** (see p.1738) is *"a virtuoso negotiator"* who divides his time between private company M&A and finance. In the latter arena he represents corporate borrowers in syndicated loans, structured finance and prebankruptcy workouts.

**Clients/Work Highlights:** Susquehanna Bancshares; IDG Ventures; Church & Dwight; Penn Mutual Life Insurance and Columbia Capital.

## Reed Smith LLP

See firm details p.1762

**The Firm:** Sources recommend this group across the board in this sector, particularly for its *"pace-setting regulatory work."* It has been active on the continued consolidation of banks in Pennsylvania. On the transactional side, it acts for financial institutions in M&A, joint ventures and outsourcings, and recently represented Mellon Financial in the sale of its human resources, consulting and outsourcing business, a transaction with German, UK and Canadian components to it. On the banking side, it provides expertise in secured lending, asset-based lending and securitizations on a national and international level.

**The Lawyers:** Philadelphia-based **Lisa Kabnick** (see p.1731) concentrates on commercial banking transactions and secured lending. Her clients are financial institutions and borrowers and her practice has an international touch. **Leonard Bernstein** (see p.1722) heads up the regulatory group and is a recognized consumer regulations expert. His clients are financial institutions of all kinds as well as mortgage brokers.

**Clients/Work Highlights:** Clients include Bank of America, JPMorgan and Wachovia.

## Stradley Ronon Stevens & Young LLP

**The Firm:** This fine midsize outfit is well-connected in the local area and keeps clients happy with *"competitive and reasonable pricing."* The lawyers in the group tend to have additional expertise in areas such as employment law, and they work closely with specialists in the firm's other offices nationwide. The practice covers banking regulatory and transactional advice, securities, real estate finance and investments. The team recently acted for Harleysville National Bank in its acquisition of Cornerstone. It acts for individuals, businesses, banks and other financial institutions, based principally in Pennsylvania and throughout the mid-Atlantic region.

**The Lawyers:** The core of **Valentino DiGiorgio**'s practice is government relations and banking. He *"gets straight to the point,"* representing banks and other financial institutions in complex financial transactions and commercial lending. He also brings tax and regulatory experience with him to the table.

**Clients/Work Highlights:** Allied Irish Banks; Bank of America; Bank of New York; Citizens Bank of PA; Mellon Financial; Merrill Lynch; Morgan Stanley; Sovereign Bank; Susquehanna Bancshares; The Peoples Bank of Oxford and Wilmington Trust.

## Wolf, Block, Schorr and Solis-Cohen LLP

See firm details p.1764

**The Firm:** This firm is evolving steadily and has offices along the Eastern Seaboard. The group offers expertise in asset-based finance, traditional midmarket lending, subordinate lending and workouts. Clients, who are often drawn from the corporate department, appreciate the team's *"special expertise in financial structuring."* These clients are mainly based in the region and range from financial institutions to borrowers such as closely held businesses and large companies. The team recently represented a bank in a multilender financing for a group of companies engaged in the manufacture and distribution of refrigerant products and machinery throughout the USA and overseas.

**The Lawyers:** **Bruce Lesser** (see p.1734) wins praise as *"an effective lawyer with an intense approach to problems."* He does a great deal of work on the borrower side in large financial transactions and in the asset-based lending area. He also acts as bankruptcy counsel on occasion.

**Clients/Work Highlights:** Wachovia; Congress Financial; PNC Bank; LaSalle Business Credit and Sovereign Bank.

# BANKRUPTCY/RESTRUCTURING

| Bankruptcy/Restructuring Leading Firms | |
|---|---|
| **1** | BLANK ROME LLP *Philadelphia* |
| | DUANE MORRIS LLP *Philadelphia* |
| | REED SMITH LLP *Pittsburgh* |
| **2** | ADELMAN LAVINE GOLD AND LEVIN *Philadelphia* |
| | COZEN O'CONNOR *Philadelphia* |
| | DILWORTH PAXSON LLP *Philadelphia* |
| | HANGLEY ARONCHICK *Philadelphia* |
| | MORGAN, LEWIS & BOCKIUS LLP *Philadelphia* |
| **3** | CAMPBELL & LEVINE *Pittsburgh* |
| | DRINKER BIDDLE & REATH LLP *Philadelphia* |
| | KLEHR HARRISON HARVEY BRANZBERG *Philadelphia* |
| | KLETT ROONEY LIEBER & SCHORLING *Pittsburgh* |
| | PEPPER HAMILTON LLP *Philadelphia* |
| | STEVENS & LEE PC *Philadelphia* |
| | WOLF, BLOCK *Philadelphia* |

## Band 1

## Blank Rome LLP

See firm details p.1747

**The Firm:** This full-service firm continues to win plaudits for the depth and quality of its business restructuring and bankruptcy practice, which is renowned on a national scale. The *"extremely competent and sophisticated"* team of around 30 attorneys is *"probably as talented a group as you will find"* and is spread across offices in Philadelphia, Allentown, New York and Wilmington. The firm's strong New York presence is a particular drawing card for clients, as is the leadership of its key experienced practitioners. The firm excels in creditor representation, but also regularly acts for creditors' committees and is felt to have more debtor capability than some of the other larger firms.

**The Lawyers:** The *"phenomenal"* senior figure **Ray Shapiro** is *"a consummate all-around bankruptcy lawyer who is a great strategist, very skilled at handling clients and well respected by the courts. He displays extraordinary judgment."* Shapiro spends around half of his time in the firm's New York office. **Thomas Biron** (see p.1722) is a bright strategist *"with a great touch in the courtroom."* He impresses with his effective negotiating skills and *"ability to get to the important issues in an organized way."* He represented strategic buyer Hanover Foods in the purchase of assets of distressed businesses, which have been turned around and successfully operated. **Joel Shapiro** (see p.1741) is particularly skilled in the acquisition of real estate interests in bankruptcy situations. Wilmington-based Bonnie Fatell chairs the group.

**Clients/Work Highlights:** Although frequently involved on the creditor side, the past year has seen the firm act for the debtors in the USGen New England, American Business Financial Services, Infrastructure Services and CF Capital Assets d/b/a Convenient Food Mart cases. Creditors' committee representation includes New World Pasta, Datatec Systems, Nobex and Xybernaut. The team has also advised the following asset purchasers and/or creditors: Hewlett-Packard; Hanover Foods; Wells Fargo Business Credit; CIT Group; NCO Group; Metropolitan Airports Commission; Manufacturers and Traders Trust; Big Lots Stores; General Cable; Simply Fashion Stores and Maxell.

## Duane Morris LLP

See firm details p.1753

**The Firm:** A substantial team of over 40 attorneys works on a cross-office basis, from 12 bases right across the country. This broad coverage ensures a national profile. In line with the firm's respected profile in the financial institutions field, this team is especially prominent in secured creditor representation, although the client base has broadened to include debtors, creditors' committees and trustees. The group is known for its ability to achieve early resolution of cases, as one client explained: *"These lawyers are business people who look for practical solutions. They are not just in the business to litigate."* According to clients, the depth of experience of the team's senior figures *"instills a comfort and confidence factor."* The lack of bureaucracy at this firm is another plus point: *"They are always responsive to what I need, and if I need other expertise from within the firm they will call me back in one hour. I like the fact that I don't have to channel everything through one partner."*

**The Lawyers:** Widely respected senior statesman **David Sykes** (see p.1743) *"displays a quality that is often lacking at the bankruptcy Bar – he is not so busy advocating that he forgets to step back and think what it will take to make the deal work. He has brilliant judgment."* Sykes is increasingly called upon to offer expert testimony and frequently represents clients in litigation at trial and appellate level. Head of the firm's corporate practice, *"consensus builder"*

**John Horstmann** (see p.1731) provides the broadest experience and viewpoint, according to clients, who describe him as *"a pragmatic lawyer who knows the right people and gets the job done."* He typically acts for the large financial and lending institutions on a national and international scale. Recent assignments include representing Société Générale in litigation connected to the Adelphia Chapter 11 proceedings. He currently acts for a European-based international bank in secured loans collection and litigation concerning a luxury resort complex in the US Virgin Islands. National practice head **Skip Di Massa** (see p.1726) is *"a superb lawyer with the personality to get the deal done, and a leader who can get a group together to forge an acceptable result."* **Lawrence Kotler** (see p.1732) wins special praise from lender clients, who value his responsiveness and ability to understand both the legal and business issues. **Margery Reed** (see p.1739) is especially well known for her representation of secured lenders, whom she advises on bankruptcy and debt restructuring, secured transactions and credit enhancement issues. She is *"just a practical and smart bankruptcy lawyer – a go-to person for those tricky issues and very responsive to the differing needs of her clients."* Recent assignments on behalf of creditors include Delta Air Lines, Delphi, Allied Holdings and FOAMEX.

**Clients/Work Highlights:** Further highlights include representing GMAC Commercial Mortgage Corporation in the Kmart bankruptcy case and advising Lucent Technologies in the Leap Wireless and Cricket Communications cases.

## Reed Smith LLP
See firm details p.1762
**The Firm:** Considered by many interviewees to be *"the pick of the bunch,"* this firm *"has assembled a practice group of outstanding lawyers, who are respected and active on a national basis."* Clients benefit from the firm's strong presence in both Pittsburgh and Philadelphia, and feel that it offers a truly diverse and versatile practice in terms of industry sector coverage. In addition to representing the debtors in several recent cases, the team has also developed a broad committee and creditor practice, with an emphasis on indenture trustee representation. The firm's European expansion (offices in Munich and Paris were opened this year) has further extended the team's reach. Clients welcome the depth of services available here – *"if you need those extra services in a workout, the firm is certainly very well put together"* – while peers appreciate that these lawyers *"don't feel they have to bang their fists on the table."*
**The Lawyers:** The *"tremendously experienced"* **Paul Singer** (see p.1742) is considered a dean of the Pittsburgh bankruptcy Bar. He is especially experienced in debtor and committee representation in industrial and mass tort Chapter 11 cases. Singer combines outstanding litigation and problem-solving skills with a down-to-earth and pragmatic approach: *"He is capable of really taking on difficult problems without insinuating his own personality into the equation,"* said clients. In his role as creditors' committee counsel in ASARCO he successfully resolved a four-month strike by its unionized workforce. **Claudia Springer** (see p.1743) is based in the firm's Philadelphia office and *"is just doing a great job."* Although traditionally recognized for her secured creditor practice, she also regularly acts for creditors' committees in Chapter 11 cases. For example, she represented the creditors' committee in the USGen New England case, where the unsecured creditors received in excess of 100% of their claims. **Eric Schaffer** (see p.1740) *"knows the bankruptcy code like the back of his hand,"* say clients. He spends over half his time acting for the indenture trustees and counts JPMorgan, Wells Fargo and Bank of New York among his clients. *"Eric has always done extremely well at maximizing recovery for the bondholder while minimizing risk and exposure for the bank – a great combination!"* He has been representing JPMorgan Chase as indenture trustee in the bankruptcy of Solutia in the Southern District of New York. **Peter Clark** (see p.1724) is the firmwide head of the group. His focus is largely on the secured creditor side, representing financial institutions, private equity and hedge funds. He acted for a private equity client in the Chapter 11 case of a national commercial electrical contracting firm, and represented a syndicate of lenders in the restructuring of a publicly traded company in the environmental sector.

**Clients/Work Highlights:** The team also represented the official committees of FastNet, Rouge Industries and WCI Steel, and the creditors' committee in AAIPharma. Additional clients are CIT Group; GE Capital; PNC Bank; Wachovia and Summit Investment Management.

## Band 2

### Adelman Lavine Gold and Levin
**The Firm:** This 19-lawyer boutique is viewed as prime choice when it comes to debtor representation. The firm also fields an extensive creditors' committee practice and benefits from a three-lawyer base in nearby Wilmington, Delaware. The team provides one-stop shopping to clients for insolvency, transactional and litigation issues, and is often selected by other firms on a referral basis.
**The Lawyers:** **Barry Kleban** is a skilled strategist and an outstanding technical lawyer. According to one peer, *"he is particularly well suited to debtor work, as he has the right personality to work through goals that are mutually satisfying to both sides – I always think 'hallelujah' when I see he is on the other side!"* Recent assignments include representing the official creditors' committee in the Chapter 11 bankruptcy of an asbestos manufacturer, which resulted in a 100% dividend to unsecured creditors. Kleban has also counseled businesses from a range of industries in out-of-court restructurings. **Leon Barson** *"just has a wonderful touch when it comes to handling the client, opposing counsel and the court – he understands the situation on a practical level and knows when negotiation needs to take place rather than litigation."* His is a debtor-oriented practice. He recently represented a plastic manufacturer in a successful Chapter 11 proceeding, and represented a national kitchen equipment retailer in a sale and confirmation. **Gary Schildhorn** *"boasts a tremendous sense of humor and the ability to use it productively in this area."* Like many others, his practice is run from Philadelphia and Delaware, and ranges from the out-of-court restructuring of a small family-owned business to advising the debtor or committee in a major national case. He recently represented one of the largest specialty lenders in its Chapter 11 bankruptcy proceedings, resulting in a confirmed plan of reorganization.

### Cozen O'Connor
**The Firm:** This team of 11 attorneys is concentrated primarily across offices in Pennsylvania, Delaware, New York and New Jersey. The firm has built up a fine debtor practice, and its work also extends to representing creditors in some of the larger bankruptcy cases. The team has also been increasingly involved as trustee's counsel in several large Delaware-based cases.

The Lawyers: Experienced senior figure **Neal Colton** is clearly the standout practitioner in this area, and is cochair of the bankruptcy, insolvency and restructuring group. Recent work highlights include representing Charlton Heston in a contract dispute concerning the Chapter 11 of GT Brands, and acting for QVC and Comcast Spectacor in the Adelphia Communications case in New York. He has also served as an expert witness and is certified as a mediator in the Federal Bankruptcy Court in Delaware and Pennsylvania. Peers agree that he is *"one of those lawyers you can reach a commercially reasonable argument with."*

Clients/Work Highlights: Other highlights include representing the Major League Baseball Players Association in the non-bankruptcy liquidation of Fleer/Skybox in New Jersey. The team also continues to be active in the US Airways and Student Finance Corporation bankruptcies.

## Dilworth Paxson LLP

The Firm: This team of 12 full-time insolvency lawyers is spread across offices in Philadelphia and Cherry Hill, New Jersey, with an additional base in Wilmington. The firm has developed an excellent reputation for dealing with entrepreneurial as opposed to institutional clients, and *"houses talented people."* Major clients tend to be large businesses involved in bankruptcy or businesses with some sort of insolvency issue.

The Lawyers: *"Marvelous courtroom lawyer"* **Lawrence McMichael** is easily distinguished from others on the table due to his focus on trial work. His practice divides fairly evenly between bankruptcy and general commercial litigation. It is this multifaceted practice combined with a great business sense that makes him a firm favorite with clients. McMichael recently acted as lead negotiator on behalf of the Rigas Family in the huge $1.6 billion forfeiture settlement with the US government. **Martin Weis** is recognized more as a pure bankruptcy technician and is an up-and-coming figure for both debtor and creditor work.

Clients/Work Highlights: Other assignments include representing the Republic of Uruguay in litigation in New York arising out of the failure of a major Uruguayan bank. Lawyers also continue to act for the debtors in the Field Hotel cases, involving the LaGuardia Crowne Plaza Hotel and the JFK Holiday Inn, with a combined debt exceeding $100 million. Further clients are Dow Chemical; Union Carbide; Merrill Lynch; PNC Bank and Transport International Pool.

## Hangley Aronchick Segal & Pudlin

See firm details p.1756

The Firm: Despite its smaller team of three partners and three associates, this regional practice is considered to have *"as much of a critical mass of senior talent as any in town."* As one peer readily conceded: *"For a small firm it has great depth. If I was looking for someone with good business judgment to represent the insolvent, I would pick a lawyer at the Hangley firm."* Debtor representation is the order of

the day here. The firm acts for a large number of entrepreneurial clients and is heavily engaged in the healthcare industry. Despite a fine reputation for litigated bankruptcy work, the team is also praised for *"trying to work out a deal at an early stage – this is their real strength and produces a win-win situation for everybody."*

The Lawyers: Sources described **Joseph Dworetzky** (see p.1727) as *"a superb, all-around bankruptcy and workout lawyer, plus a great commercial litigator. He is always looking for the solution rather than creating the problem."* He is experienced in debtor work, and has also recently represented governmental institutions in connection with insolvency situations. For example, he acted for the Commonwealth of Pennsylvania through the Department of Education in seeking to put a school district into receivership on the grounds that it was insolvent. He also advised a government entity concerning a whole portfolio of delinquent tax collection. **Myron Bloom** (see p.1723) wins plaudits for his debtor and creditor committee representation. He acts for the creditors' committee in the Field Hotel and LaGuardia Associates cases, and has also been busy representing a director and officer in allegations of breach of fiduciary duty and negligence arising out of the failure of a corporation. **James Matour** (see p.1735) recently represented a manufacturing company that has successfully emerged from bankruptcy and is the cochair of the creditors' committee in a major healthcare case. Much of his recent work has comprised a combination of out-of-court workouts and business sales. One interviewee summed up his strengths: *"He is a trusted lawyer for taking on a discreet assignment that other lawyers may not be comfortable with, and he provides the answers in an efficient and understandable way."*

## Morgan, Lewis & Bockius LLP

See firm details p.1758

The Firm: This firm's renowned New York presence combined with the Philadelphia office's proximity to Delaware makes it especially appealing to clients. The core team has been active in creditors' committee representation, and has also seen a shift toward out-of-court restructurings, refinancings and new financings in the midmarket. In particular, the firm offers expertise in DIP and exit financings. Its representation of music majors and film studios, wholesalers and retailers of film and music distinguishes this group from others. Its experience in the hi-tech and life sciences areas also means it is experienced in advising the parent or fund sponsor in dealing with troubled portfolio companies.

The Lawyers: **Michael Bloom** (see p.1723) is the main name associated with the Philadelphia practice. *"His history of success is key – he knows the players and the law, and has a great ability to bring people together and cut to the bottom line to get things done,"* reported one source. **Rebecca Booth** (see p.1723) picked up commendations for her *"quick grasp of complex situations"* while at Richards, Layton & Finger in Delaware. Described by clients as *"an outstanding young associate,"* she no doubt remains one to watch

for in the future in her new setting.

Clients/Work Highlights: Recent highlights include representing the debtor in the prepackaged bankruptcy of DecisionOne, a District of Delaware filing. Lawyers are currently concluding two large entertainment cases, also in Delaware.

## Band 3

## Campbell & Levine

The Firm: This specialist Pittsburgh firm is widely recognized for its prominence in midsized debtor cases in western Pennsylvania. The firm is also a key competitor for creditors' committee work and is one of the first choices of larger firms from outside the state for local counsel roles: *"These lawyers know their way around and really know what they're talking about,"* report interviewees.

The Lawyers: **Douglas Campbell** is a cofounder of the practice and the individual identified by interviewees as *"very much a leader in the field."*

Clients/Work Highlights: The firm acts for a mix of debtors, creditors and committees, and offers specialist expertise in asbestos reorganization and fraudulent transfer litigation. The team has experience of insolvencies in the retail, healthcare, steel and coal industries.

## Drinker Biddle & Reath LLP

The Firm: This is a successful and growing practice across the mid-Atlantic region. Dedicated bankruptcy attorneys are housed in four of the firm's ten offices, in Pennsylvania, Delaware, New York and New Jersey. This integrated geographical coverage was remarked upon by clients, who also value the fact that *"we get all the New York quality without the New York rates."* As is the case with many of the state's bankruptcy practitioners, a number of the attorneys here divide their time between Philadelphia and the nearby popular filing destination of Wilmington, Delaware. The workload is a real mix of debtor, secured creditor and committee representation, and the team is actively involved in litigated proceedings. It boasts particular experience of matters arising out of the healthcare, retail and automotive sectors.

The Lawyers: Co-head of the finance and restructuring group, **Andrew Kassner** is noted for his versatile and active practice. While clients highlight his hands-on approach and pure technical expertise, peers welcome his calm manner and facilitative skills.

Clients/Work Highlights: Lawyers have been busy representing MIIX Holdings Group (the parent company of one of the largest medical professional responsibility insurance companies in the USA) in a Chapter 11 case. The firm also represented AIM Floating Rate Fund in the Enron bankruptcy case and the official committee of unsecured creditors in the Maxide Chapter 11 case. Additional clients are GE Capital; CIT Communications Finance; Penske Truck Leasing and Burlington Coat Factory Warehouse.

## Klehr Harrison Harvey Branzberg & Ellers LLP

**The Firm:** This young firm wins plaudits for its involvement in a number of major cases and for the strength of its senior bankruptcy attorneys. The practice is one of the original core focuses of the firm, whose *"fine group of lawyers"* is probably best known for its work with secured lenders. Interviewees were keen to stress the group's effective litigation skills and consider this firm a good choice for the midmarket client.

**The Lawyers:** **Morton Branzburg** is a founder of the firm and cochair of its debtor-creditor and insolvency practice group. His experience acting for both creditor and debtor makes him *"versatile, practical, and someone who I think of when I need to refer a challenging case,"* said one source.

## Klett Rooney Lieber & Schorling

See firm details p.1757

**The Firm:** This well-respected player houses a team of seven in its Philadelphia and Pittsburgh offices. A strong secured creditor practice – where it acts for lenders such as PNC Bank, Mellon Financial and Citizens – has taken much of the limelight. One source summed up the team's strengths: *"These lawyers really understand the business side; they know their way around the courtroom and are practical in coming to satisfactory solutions."* The firm is also active in debtor representation, and has additionally acted for the committee and fiduciary in recent cases. Clients benefit from specialist expertise available in connection with the various labor, tax and pension issues surrounding insolvencies.

**The Lawyers:** Senior experienced figure **William Schorling** (see p.1740) is clearly highly regarded in the industry, as *"his practicality and deep knowledge of the bankruptcy code make him a truly effective advocate for his clients."* His many recent assignments include representing the independent fiduciary of the pension plans in the Enron Chapter 11, and counseling the official retirees committee in the Weirton Steel Chapter 11 reorganization. The *"bright and hard-working"* **Jeffrey Carbino** (see p.1724) was one of the lawyers actively involved in the successful Chapter 11 reorganization of large mechanical contractor Voegele Mechanical.

**Clients/Work Highlights:** Lawyers also represented the debtors in the successful Chapter 11 reorganization of PHICO Group and represent the airplane lessors in the US Airways and United Airlines cases. Additional clients are Wells Fargo, National City Bank and Fifth Third Bank.

## Pepper Hamilton LLP

See firm details p.1760

**The Firm:** Many interviewees were keen to stress the strong leadership emanating from the firm's Detroit and Wilmington offices, which form the focus of the firm's national practice in this area. The Philadelphia office houses a ten-strong team of *"excellent, smart and trustworthy"* lawyers with an emphasis on representing creditors and creditors' committees. The three partners offer strong subspecialties in environmental, toxic tort, asbestos, healthcare and construction-related bankruptcy and reorganization matters, and are praised for their effectiveness in achieving their clients' goals.

**The Lawyers:** *"Thorough, smart and hard-working,"* **Francis Lawall** (see p.1733) has a national practice focusing on creditor and creditors' committee representation, with expertise in representing companies in relation to energy and toxic tort matters. Recent assignments include representing three Canadian gas companies in bankruptcy proceedings in Maine, involving the sale of long-term fixed gas contracts. Senior figure **Gregg Miller** (see p.1736) is *"a respected professional, who does a great job for his clients, and does it quietly."* He chairs the Philadelphia group and is generally occupied with creditor representation. Recent highlights include successfully representing the distressed debt lender Greenwich Capital Financial Products as secured creditor in a Chapter 11 case in Philadelphia. In a rare debtor case he also represented RM Shoemaker Company, a large general construction contractor in the Delaware Valley. This involved winding down and negotiating with the creditor on final payment terms and filing for Chapter 7. **Michael Reed** (see p.1739) has historically developed a subspecialty in environment-related issues in the bankruptcy area and has recently combined his practice with a role as president of the Pennsylvania Bar Association. His eclectic workload includes representing all sides of the bankruptcy equation.

**Clients/Work Highlights:** Further clients include the creditors' committees of Interco, Revco DS, Harvard Industries and Wickes. Examples of debtor representation are the Peregrine, Venture Stores, Pacor and Amatex cases. On the trustee side the firm has acted for Maxicare and Allegheny Health, Education and Research Foundation.

## Stevens & Lee PC

**The Firm:** The firm's bankruptcy and workout practice houses around 20 lawyers in the mid-Atlantic region, including 11 in Pennsylvania. A substantial number are based in the firm's Reading office. The

focus of the practice is spread fairly evenly – the firm acts for major institutional creditors such as IBM Credit, Wachovia and Sovereign, and also represents debtors. The geographical coverage is predominantly regional, but the firm does act for a number of acquirer clients based further afield.

**The Lawyers:** **Robert Lapowsky** is clearly the firm's standout lawyer in this area, enjoying a reputation that stretches beyond the local boundaries. Sources consistently pointed to his strong business sense: *"He analyzes the situation not just as it relates to the bankruptcy laws, but he understands the business decisions and takes these into account. He can take the ball and run with it."* Lapowsky handles a mix of debtor and creditor work, in addition to general litigation, for example preference issues.

**Clients/Work Highlights:** Recent engagements include acting for Wachovia in an out-of-court workout for a manufacturing company, and distressed company work in connection with two hospital liquidations.

## Wolf, Block, Schorr and Solis-Cohen LLP

See firm details p.1764

**The Firm:** This team comprises ten attorneys spread across the firm's various East Coast offices, and includes six based in Philadelphia. Areas of focus range from trustee representation to out-of-court work for institutional lender clients. Asset acquisitions and dispositions, debt restructuring, litigation and Chapter 7, 11 and 13 proceedings are all part of the mix here. Attorneys also handle a significant amount of counseling in connection with the firm's real estate transactional practice, concerning the effect of insolvency situations on transactions.

**The Lawyers:** **Mike Temin** (see p.1744) is hugely respected in the community and is *"always well prepared and attracts a lot of business,"* reported sources. He has recently been involved in the representation of preference defendants in Delaware and Alabama.

**Clients/Work Highlights:** Recent highlights include representing the proponent of a reorganization plan for a casino in Louisiana, and involvement in the Chapter 7 liquidation of a hospital in Pennsylvania.

## Other Notable Practitioners

*"Young but terrific star"* **Aris Karalis**, of Ciardi, Maschmeyer & Karalis PC, received numerous recommendations for his local and regional debtor practice. Well respected by the judges, he is *"not afraid to fight if he has to"* and *"is always very fair and honest from the bank's perspective,"* report interviewees.

# CORPORATE/M&A

## Band 1

### Dechert LLP

See firm details p.1752

**The Firm:** *"Dechert is the quintessential businessman's law firm – the lawyers understand our business, they think nothing of working until 3 am, and there are no crazy legal bills. This is the firm of choice for sophisticated, high-level transactions."* This was the consensus of interviewees, who consider the national and international practice a worthy competitor of the New York-based firms. The firm fields 46 corporate and M&A lawyers in Philadelphia alone, a team that integrates well with lawyers across the firm's offices in the USA and in Europe. A broad institutional client base complements the firm's strong investment funds and private equity focus. The team also has a niche expertise in hostile public M&A deals. Recently the group has been involved in a series of major assignments, including the $2.4 billion refinancing of Crown Holdings, and the $2.3 billion sale of Select Medical Corporation to EGL Holding Company. Clients agree: *"The Dechert culture is remarkable – the firm can field a team in any business area you can imagine, there is a refreshing lack of bureaucracy and the extremely focused lawyers won't let the subtleties of a transaction pass them by."*

**The Lawyers:** Firm chairman **Barton Winokur** (see p.1745) typically acts in a special counsel role, advising on the more critical issues in a transaction. He spends around half his time in the New York office, and advises a mix of public and private companies, venture capital and private equity fund sponsors. One client summed up his strengths: *"If I had to make one call, it would be to Bart. He is a businessman's lawyer; smart, articulate, creative, and a patient yet tough negotiator."* M&A practice chair **William Lawlor** (see p.1733) handles a mix of public and private M&A. He was involved in the Crown Holdings refinancing and represented Israel Chemicals in a complex acquisition, one of the first forays into the US market by a major Israeli company. He is *"a super tough negotiator and quick thinker – a lawyer you would follow to any corner of the States."* **Henry Nassau** (see p.1737) has a particular strength in representing Philadelphia-based private equity funds, and also comes recommended for his board of director work. He is cochair of the corporate and securities practice. Recent highlights include representing Captiva Software in its $275 million sale to EMC. Together with Bart Winokur, **Daniel O'Donnell** (see p.1737) is a founder of the private equity practice. Chair of the group, he spends a substantial amount of time in the New York office, typically acting for major clients such as Citigroup Venture Capital Equity Partners. **Carmen Romano** (see p.1739) advises private equity sponsors and their portfolio companies on the range of transactional and corporate matters, for example Jefferies Capital Partners and One Equity Partners. **Geraldine Sinatra**'s (see p.1742) star continues to shine – she is *"as smart as a whip,"* say clients, *"a good all-round legal quarterback for corporate transactions with an incredible understanding of contract issues and negotiations."* She is also noted for her work in the private equity field, representing clients such as Citigroup Venture Capital Equity Partners and Odyssey Investment Partners.

**Clients/Work Highlights:** Further clients include AmerisourceBergen Corporation; Worldspan; Remy International; Church & Dwight; Bruckmann, Rosser, Sherrill & Co; JPMorgan Securities; ValueAct Capital; West Pharmaceutical Services and Graham Partners.

### Morgan, Lewis & Bockius LLP

See firm details p.1758

**The Firm:** With an excellent breadth and depth, this *"wonderful firm of terrific lawyers"* is noted for its capabilities on a national and international scale. With a network of offices across the USA and in Europe, the firm is able to draw expertise from wherever it is needed geographically, and can be involved in the largest, most sophisticated transactions. As one client explained: *"I want great work and I want it done fast. Morgan has that edge – it wants to be a top law firm, whether you compare it with a New York firm or any other for that matter."* In addition to its national platform, the firm takes pride in its regional roots. It has offices in Philadelphia, Pittsburgh and Harrisburg, and maintains strong relationship ties to major regional clients. The firm is no doubt best known for its outstanding emerging companies practice, where it acts for a large number of venture-backed and entrepreneurial clients. Expertise in IPO and corporate governance issues is also a strong feature of this practice.

**The Lawyers:** Cochair of the firm's global technology practice, **Stephen Goodman** (see p.1729) is best known for his venture capital expertise: *"He really has the pulse of the life science and venture capital practice in the city. In addition to possessing great lawyering skills, he has the presence and judgment that make the ultimate difference."* He typically acts as gatekeeper to emerging companies from startup through to public offering or exit. **Marlee Myers** (see p.1737) possesses deep technical knowledge and long experience across the range of corporate matters, from M&A and corporate finance to IPOs, securities compliance and corporate governance issues. She is *"incredibly hard working, very focused on what the client wants to achieve, and does an excellent job of bringing in support as necessary,"* report clients. **Alan Singer** (see p.1742) is *"one of the best in securities law – a veritable dictionary of where it's at and where to find it. He is the first point of contact for a complex disclosure or technical question."* His is a pure securities practice, and includes advising companies on a wide range of matters, from public and private offerings to advice on SEC responsibilities and executive compensation issues. **James McKenzie** (see p.1736) handles a mix of M&A, securities and corporate governance matters, with a focus on public companies and venture capital clients looking to go public. His previous in-house experience means he has *"a deep understanding of the business issues and is tremendously responsive,"* say clients.

**Clients/Work Highlights:** Recent successful exits include the sale of excelleRx to Omnicare for $280 million, and the $65 million sale of drug development software company InnaPhase to Thermo Electron. Further clients are American Financial Realty Trust; Aramark; Buckeye Partners; Pep Boys; Penn Mutual; Church & Dwight; Comcast; GE; Novell; Safeguard Scientifics; Exelon and SEI Investments.

## Band 2

### Ballard Spahr Andrews & Ingersoll LLP

See firm details p.1746

**The Firm:** This firm enjoys a particularly strong reputation for its work with boards of directors and

CEOs on corporate and securities matters. Clients view these lawyers as *"part of the team – excellent legal expertise goes without saying, but what really stands out is their down-to-earth, partnership approach to the client relationship. They are strong team players who can really help the client to accomplish its objectives."* The firm's great bench strength is topped by *"seasoned lawyers with long experience who won't drop the ball."* In addition to its well-documented securities and public company work, the firm also handles general corporate and transactional matters, and maintains strong life science and investment management practices. Recent notable highlights include advising Teleflex on the sale of its automotive pedals division to an affiliate of Sun Capital Partners.

**The Lawyers:** SEC alumnus and *"wonderful counselor"* **Justin Klein** (see p.1732) clearly enjoys a loyal client following. Although best known for his securities law expertise (he chairs the securities practice group), Klein handles the whole spectrum of corporate law: *"He is technically superior, easy to understand and great at communicating with the client."* Sources agree that **Richard Braemer** (see p.1724) *"is just a very intelligent, very well-rounded, general commercial lawyer – someone you can rely on for superb judgment."*

**Clients/Work Highlights:** Additional highlights include representing Janney Montgomery Scott and Edward D. Jones & Co in the public offering of $18.7 million in common stock of Pennichuck, and advising Safeguard Scientifics on its $26 million acquisition of Acsis. Further clients are Aramark; Sunoco; Harleysville Group; Biosyn; Penn National Gaming; Don Rosen Organization; Nature's Sunshine Products; PMA Capital; Saxco International; CompuDyne; Hercules Inc; Triumph Group; Wawa; Vista Exploration; Greka Energy; Neways and LLR Partners.

### Drinker Biddle & Reath LLP

**The Firm:** This sophisticated corporate and securities practice maintains a heavy focus on transactional work, and enjoys a series of long-standing client relationships. The firm has a strong regional presence and is best recognized for advising midmarket companies and private equity funds. Areas of activity include M&A transactions, capital markets and various corporate governance-related assignments. One interviewee summed up what clients most like about this firm: *"There will always be lawyers who have the intellect to do the work, but what's hard to find is the right mix of personality – the ability to be assertive but to relate well to the other side, without speaking down to them or intimidating them."*

**The Lawyers:** **Douglas Raymond** is head of the firm's corporate and securities group. His workload comprises a mix of M&A transactions, public offerings and corporate governance-related matters, predominantly for midcap public companies. Peers and clients acclaim his good sense of judgment and solid boardroom skills, and also find him *"very easy to work with."*

**Clients/Work Highlights:** The firm represented Questor Partners in the $455 million sale of portfolio company GeoLogistics Corporation to Public Warehousing Company. Other highlights include advising Charming Shoppes on the $250 million acquisition of private company Crosstown Traders from JPMorgan Equity Partners. The team also handled a $250 million senior notes public offering for Radion Group. Further clients are Graham Partners; AND 1; Transportation Resources Partners; Cott Beverages and Milestone Partners.

### Kirkpatrick & Lockhart Nicholson Graham LLP

**The Firm:** Around 15 lawyers make up the core corporate practice in Pittsburgh, the transactional center of the firm. They are supported by specialists in ancillary areas such as environment and tax, and form part of a much larger team in offices across the USA and in London. The firm acts for a mix of Fortune 500 and midmarket companies, strategic players and privately owned businesses from core sectors such as manufacturing, energy, media, education, technology, healthcare and financial services. Clients feel the firm *"can play a lot of different roles well, and offers the whole breadth of capability and talent in the M&A field."* In addition to its broad experience in M&A and capital markets, joint ventures, restructuring and general securities matters, the firm boasts a significant national practice centered on the 1940 Act. Recent major highlights include representing Wheeling Pittsburgh Steel Corporation in its complex joint venture with Severstal North America.

**The Lawyers:** **Michael McLean** wins plaudits for his securities expertise and is *"an extremely knowledgeable lawyer with great business instincts."* His practice also encompasses a broad M&A and capital markets workload. **Ronald West** (see p.1745) is also a senior corporate and securities partner at the firm. He represented United Technologies in the $700 million acquisition of the Rocketdyne division of Boeing.

**Clients/Work Highlights:** Eaton Vance; Allegheny Technologies; Philips Electronics North America; PPG Industries; Education Management Corporation; Crane Co; Novartis; State Street Bank & Trust Company and Par Pharmaceutical Companies.

### Pepper Hamilton LLP

See firm details p.1760

**The Firm:** This well-respected firm has established a strong regional presence while operating from a national platform. There are around 100 corporate and securities lawyers firmwide, many of whom are based in one of the firm's four Pennsylvania offices. Like many of the larger players, Pepper Hamilton handles a substantial number of private and public M&A, debt and equity financings. Areas of particular strength include real estate capital markets, life sciences and private equity, as well as the formation of funds and associated transactions.

**The Lawyers:** Market commentators view firm chair **Barry Abelson** (see p.1721) as the counselor of choice for entrepreneurial public companies. He is *"a superb tactician, who is relied on by clients for his great business judgment."* His practice includes M&A,

financing and corporate governance issues. **Michael Friedman** (see p.1728) is *"a terrific corporate governance lawyer, bright and sensitive."* He heads the corporate practice overall and is responsible for the real estate capital markets group. Friedman led the team that represented Brandywine Realty Trust in its $3.3 billion merger with Prentiss Properties Trust, a deal that also included a spin-off of more than $750 million worth of assets to an institutional investor.

**Clients/Work Highlights:** Additional highlights include representing global private equity firm Advent International in a series of transactions worth in excess of $2 billion, and advising Kenexa on its IPO of 5 million shares.

## Band 3

### Blank Rome LLP

See firm details p.1747

**The Firm:** The firm's M&A practice is divided into two main groups that focus on public companies and capital formation, and privately held and emerging companies. These are supported by a number of other practice groups covering areas such as labor and employment, IP and technology. A distinguishing feature of this firm is the Blank Rome Governmental Relations affiliate, which provides specialist input if there is a government relations component to the transaction. In fact, clients highlighted the combination of a very strong securities practice and the notable lobbying capability in the firm's DC office. The team is felt to have a particular understanding of clients in the entrepreneurial market.

**The Lawyers:** Managing partner and CEO of the firm, *"visionary"* **Fred Blume** (see p.1723) continues to win praise for the great judgment he demonstrates in the range of M&A and general corporate matters. **Alan Zeiger** (see p.1723) is head of the emerging companies practice group and is counsel to a variety of emerging companies and funds. Recent highlights include advising NewSpring Mezzanine Capital, in the formation of Fastech Integrated Solutions.

**Clients/Work Highlights:** Lawyers acted as counsel to Compusearch Software Systems in its sale to an affiliate of The Carlyle Group and advised Eyes of the Future, PC on its sale to TLC Vision (USA) for $29 million. Further highlights include acting for Liberty Partners in the sale of iQ NetSolutions to a management-controlled entity and advising Surveillance Data in connection with the sale of its PRtrak business to Video Monitoring Services of America.

### Buchanan Ingersoll PC

See firm details p.1749

**The Firm:** This firm continues to attract a fine reputation in the corporate/M&A field, in particular in its Pittsburgh heartland. There are around 50 attorneys in the team, spread across the firm's offices in Pittsburgh, Philadelphia and Harrisburg. The bulk of the practice is a combination of M&A and securities-related work, ranging from IPOs to ongoing securities counseling and representation. Clients also benefit from strong specialty groups covering areas such as IP, technology and healthcare. One interviewee summed up: *"For corporate/M&A the firm is outstanding – the lawyers have a specialty so they don't dabble in other areas, which means they are always responsive and on target. They come together as a team, which is really instrumental in helping the clients accomplish their goals."* Sources also pointed to the team's ability to tap into other areas: *"They have that specialized philosophy that makes the whole process symbiotic. You don't get billed for a corporate lawyer doing the work of a real estate lawyer; the corporate lawyer just has to call the real estate specialist."*

**The Lawyers:** Sources agree that **Thomas Thompson** (see p.1744) is *"a real gentleman,"* who knows how to deal with the sensitivities of management and brings business acumen to the deal. *"His maturity and calm style means he has the foundations to provide valuable guidance."*

**Clients/Work Highlights:** Recent highlights include assisting Black Box Corporation in the completion of its tender offer acquisition of the entire outstanding stock of Norstan and advising regional investment firm Parker/Hunter on its merger with Janney Montgomery Scott. Additional clients are Aerosonic; CONSOL Energy; Dick's Sporting Goods; Stonepath Group; Kennametal; Kindred Healthcare; RTI International; Tandem healthcare; CNX Gas and II-VI Incorporated.

## Duane Morris LLP
See firm details p.1753

**The Firm:** More than 20 lawyers in Pennsylvania form part of a 100-plus strong team on a national level. Additional lawyers offer specialist expertise in areas such as ERISA, tax, finance, IP, healthcare and bankruptcy – and it is this one-stop shop label that appears most attractive to clients. The team is active across all industry sectors and tends to work with midmarket companies, in addition to some venture and equity funds. The firm's strong insurance focus is an additional drawing card for clients.

**The Lawyers: Kathleen Shay** (see p.1741) has developed a respected emerging businesses, life science and securities practice. Recent successes include advising the developer of antibiotics to combat drug-resistant and life-threatening infections in its $15 million Series B Preferred Stock financing. She also represented a Princeton-based cancer research firm, which raised in excess of $40 million in a deal that included a cross-border restructuring.

**Clients/Work Highlights:** Further clients are Sunoco; Psilos Group; Centocor; Targeted Diagnostics & Therapeutics and Fujirebio Diagnostics.

## Reed Smith LLP
See firm details p.1762

**The Firm:** Traditionally strong in the Pittsburgh area, this respected firm houses around 500 lawyers overall in its business law group. This covers the waterfront of M&A, securities and private equity work, and brings together resources in the firm's offices in the USA and Europe. The firm recently expanded its European presence with the opening of a Paris office. It represents a who's who of blue-chips on a regular basis, in addition to private fund buyers and midcap companies. Industry coverage ranges from manufacturing and healthcare, to pharmaceutical, technology and financial services.

**The Lawyers: David DeNinno** (see p.1726) chairs the business and regulatory department and maintains a versatile corporate and financing practice. Sources describe him as *"a practical, straightforward lawyer, who is easy to deal with and a tough negotiator."*

**Clients/Work Highlights:** Recent deal highlights include representing Océ in a tender offer for the acquisition of all outstanding shares of Imagistics International, with a deal value of $740 million. Lawyers also advised Billing Services Group on its acquisition of EDS Interoperator Services and acted for First Advantage in the acquisition of a credit information group for $600 million. Additional clients are Mellon Financial; World Gaming; Matthews International; National Auto Credit; Wesco International; Eagle Acquisition Partners; Certron Corporation; Respironics; DUSA Pharmaceuticals; Caithness Energy; Altec Lansing Technologies; National Penn Bancshares; GlaxoSmithKline; Almatis Holdings and IVAX.

## Wolf, Block, Schorr and Solis-Cohen LLP
See firm details p.1764

**The Firm:** The corporate and securities practice of around 45 attorneys firmwide handles a good mix of transactional and corporate governance-type work, from significant mergers to 144A and SEC regulatory matters. The firm enjoys a strong regional footprint, with offices in Pennsylvania, New Jersey, Delaware, New York and Massachusetts. Clients range from

startups to large national companies, and come from a range of industry sectors including manufacturing, real estate, gaming, healthcare and technology.

**The Lawyers: Mark Kessler's** (see p.1732) practice ranges from representing public companies to mutual fund and 1940 Act work, and advising independent directors. Recent engagements include advising luxury home builder Toll Brothers on a range of corporate, securities and financing matters, and assisting the boards of Franklin Mutual Series Fund and Franklin Mutual Recovery Fund. **Jason Shargel** (see p.1741) impresses with his deep knowledge, thoughtful approach and nonaggressive style, in particular when dealing with SEC matters.

**Clients/Work Highlights:** Lawyers are currently acting for Bon-Ton in the pending $1.1 billion cash acquisition of the Northern Department Store Group of Saks. The firm also advised Eldorado Resorts on its acquisition of the Hollywood Casino in Shreveport, Louisiana, linked to Chapter 11 bankruptcy proceedings.

## Band 4

## Cozen O'Connor
**The Firm:** This national firm continues to build on its reputation in the corporate arena. Business law is one of its four core areas of focus, with a workload ranging from M&A and corporate planning through to venture capital and securities. Housing a number of former Wolf Block lawyers, the firm is felt to have *"built a strong practice and established a loyal client base."*

**The Lawyers: Richard Busis** chairs the firm's securities offerings and regulations practice group. Peers agree that his business-oriented approach marks him out as a good referral choice in a conflict situation. Michael Heller heads up the emerging business and venture capital side of the practice.

**Clients/Work Highlights:** Lawyers advised a group of physicians, minority shareholders of privately held Kremer Laser Eye Center, in the company's acquisition by TLC Vision, and represented Chester Valley Bancorp in its merger with Willow Grove Bancorp. Additional clients are Pfizer; HSBC; Comcast Spectacor; Aramark; Johnson & Johnson; Taylor Nelson Sofres; Kraft; Morgan Stanley; Trump Entertainment Resorts; CVS; Microsoft; Revlon; Wyeth; Zurich Insurance and Medtronic.

# EMPLOYMENT

## Band 1

## Morgan, Lewis & Bockius LLP
See firm details p.1758

**The Firm:** Few would disagree that this firm is *"the number-one player in Pennsylvania"* for employment law, thanks to the sizable team's substantial depth and level of expertise. Concentrated primarily in Philadelphia, with an additional six lawyers in Pitts-

burgh, this nationally renowned firm provides *"a really excellent work product – they partner well with the client, give practical advice and offer a vast diversity of experience. I know if I go to Morgan I will get the right answer,"* explained one satisfied client. Peers also agree that this firm is a respected competitor *"not just because of sheer size but because of the types of matters the lawyers get the opportunity to work on."* The team handles the full range of work, from tradi-

tional labor and preventative counseling to complex employment and ERISA litigation. The team has seen involvement in national class actions in the wage and hour and sex discrimination areas, and has handled extensive work in connection with corporate campaigns. The firm has also developed an excellent employee benefits practice.

**The Lawyers: Mark Dichter** (see p.1726) is a clear leader in the market: *"For depth of experience and* *pure legal intellect, he is top-drawer."* He maintains a broad labor and employment practice and is counselor to a series of major companies on a national basis. The *"absolutely superb"* **Carole Katz** (see p.1732) heads up the Pittsburgh operation and is skilled in litigation and alternative dispute resolution. Sources describe her as *"just a wonderful lawyer and a tremendous courtroom advocate – she knows the law*

*absolutely cold, and tries the most effective case for her client."* Practice group head **Steven Wall** (see p.1744) *"is just a great relationship partner, and an excellent litigator and negotiator in his own right."* His practice is a mix of union-related counseling and significant employment litigation, for example, class-based lawsuits and executive terminations. He recently won a decision for ARAMARK whereby a retired employee was not entitled to millions in stock value following an IPO of the company. A talented employment litigator, **Michael Ossip** (see p.1738) is a leading authority on the FMLA. Peers appreciate that he *"doesn't try to grab the glory but will move for a quick settlement that is in the client's best interests. He is very courteous and easy to deal with."* He has acted for many hi-tech companies across the Northeast, and recently successfully represented PPL Services in a non-jury ERISA case concerning special separation benefits. **Joseph Costello** (see p.1725) is a leading figure in ERISA litigation and possesses *"excellent substantive knowledge,"* while **Doreen Davis** (see p.1726) wins plaudits for her traditional labor work. She is nationally co-leader of that practice and displays an *"ability to maintain ongoing relationships with the unions through honesty and integrity."* **Timothy O'Reilly** (see p.1738) is also one of the most efficient and experienced labor lawyers around. **Michael Banks** (see p.1721) has impressed many with his jury trial skills. He represents several key clients in litigation across the country. **Judith Harris** (see p.1730) is also a well-known and experienced trial lawyer, counseling and representing clients in a mix of trade secret, discrimination and employee benefits cases. **Robert Lichtenstein** (see p.1734) is a real expert in the executive compensation area, where *"he displays a devotion to client service that is unmatched. He always has a superior grasp of the issues and is extremely conscientious,"* say clients. He was one of the lead lawyers handling the management equity participation and employment agreement matters when a group of major private equity firms agreed to buy Morgan Lewis client SunGard for $11.3 billion. **Robert Abramowitz** (see p.1721) is an innovator when it comes to health and welfare plans and their complex financing arrangements, and is well known for representing a number of the regional healthcare institutions. He headed the team working on benefits matters in connection with Wachovia's acquisition of SouthTrust and Palmer & Cay.

**Clients/Work Highlights:** Weston Foods; Independence Blue Cross; PNC Bank; Church & Dwight; SCA Americas; AtlantiCare Health System; Episcopal Church Pension Fund; Princeton University; Wachovia; SunGard; Unilever and Scotts Company.

## Band 2

### Ballard Spahr Andrews & Ingersoll LLP
See firm details p.1746

**The Firm:** This is a significant practice in the eastern part of the state. A Philadelphia team of more than 30 lawyers works closely with the firm's other offices on a regional and national level. Its sizable traditional

labor law focus marks the firm out and it is widely recognized for its representation of public sector entities and municipalities, for example the City of Philadelphia. The firm's employee benefits practice is also highly regarded.

**The Lawyers:** Senior figure **Thomas Felix** (see p.1727) is typically involved in labor arbitrations and negotiations, for example, representing public employers such as the Commonwealth of Pennsylvania and the City of Philadelphia, in addition to manufacturing and healthcare clients. Trial attorney **John Langel** (see p.1733) is partner-in-charge of the labor, employment and immigration group. His practice comprises an even mix of traditional labor work – for universities and healthcare systems – and employment counseling and litigation. One source said: *"If I ever needed a lawyer I would go to John. He has extraordinary legal skills and a great understanding of the business aspects, and is creative and innovative in approach."* **Kenneth Jarin** (see p.1731) advises on labor contract negotiations with the large state unions, on behalf of public sector clients. His practice also extends beyond the labor and employment field to include government relations and general commercial matters. The firm's reputation in the employee benefits area is topped by **John Bernard** (see p.1722), whom many view as *"a teacher and mentor"* in this field. His practice is concentrated in the traditional areas of retail, healthcare and welfare counseling. **Brian Pinheiro** (see p.1738) has won a following for his ERISA and benefit plan expertise. Clients appreciate the fact that he *"gets the work done on time, with the minimum of upset, and knows how to communicate with the client. He is proactive and really easy to work with."*

**Clients/Work Highlights:** Further clients are Allstate; American Red Cross; Geisinger Health System; DuPont; Philadelphia Housing Authority; Sunoco; University of Pennsylvania; US Womens National Soccer Team; Doylestown Hospital; Agere Systems and C-COR.

### Blank Rome LLP
See firm details p.1747

**The Firm:** A team of around 30 attorneys offers substantial depth in this area, with particular strengths in traditional labor work and employment litigation and civil rights. Although considered to have a strong local practice, the firm also excels in the representation of clients on a national basis, for example in trade secret and noncompete litigation. Clients refer to a team of *"first-rate legal minds"* with the resources at their disposal to do a great job quickly.

**The Lawyers:** Trained as an English barrister, **Anthony Haller** (see p.1729) is an experienced employment litigator who provides high-level strategic counseling and is involved on the traditional labor side. Clients especially value his thoroughness – *"he never misses a trick,"* said one. Clients he has represented nationally in complex litigation include Synthes, Commerce Bank, D&B Receivable Management and Harleysville Insurance. **Michael Hanlon** (see p.1730) chairs the employment, benefits and labor practice group and is *"a negotiator par excel-*

*lence.*" This year saw the culmination of three years of negotiations between the Philadelphia School Reform Commission and the Philadelphia Federation of Teachers, resulting in a $5 billion dollar pact. Hanlon played the role of chief negotiator. **Clients/Work Highlights:** Further clients include Moran Towing, Altec Industries and YWCA of Camden County.

## Klett Rooney Lieber & Schorling
See firm details p.1757
**The Firm:** Clearly one of the strongest contenders in this pool of firms, this firm fields a team of around 40 lawyers, handling the broad range of labor, employment, ERISA, OSHA and immigration law matters. Interviewees point to the firm's great strength in the traditional labor arena, where the lawyers *"understand how fights are fought these days – they are not just ready for a strike but understand the situation in the context of the community."* The firm has made its name in the more complex negotiations, with a client base that extends nationally. Clients point to knowledge base and customer service as the two key strengths of the firm: *"These lawyers are excellent communicators. Despite coming from a big firm, they don't talk down to you and there is no trace of arrogance. They have a great problem-solving mentality and I know they will always find the answer."*
**The Lawyers:** **Thomas Giotto** (see p.1728) is clearly a standout figure on the traditional labor scene. His workload typically involves the negotiation of collective bargaining agreements, union avoidance and grievance arbitration work. Clients especially value his ability to relate well to each party in a negotiation, whether professionals or non-professionals. Philadelphia-based **Alfred D'Angelo** (see p.1725) is also an extremely well-respected labor lawyer who *"serves his clients well,"* attracting a loyal client following. **Mark Foley** (see p.1728) offers broad expertise across the range of local state and federal law issues, and has frequently acted as lead negotiator in collective bargaining negotiations. Practice group cochair **Terrence Murphy** (see p.1737) is especially noted for his handling of equal employment and affirmative action matters and holds a respected position in the Pittsburgh market. **Elizabeth Malloy** (see p.1735) and **James Sullivan** (see p.1743) both win plaudits for their representation of clients in a broad spread of employment litigation matters, while up-and-comer **Alan Pittler**

(see p.1738) enters the tables in recognition of his *"willingness to go above and beyond to secure the right result for the client."*

## Reed Smith LLP
See firm details p.1762
**The Firm:** This is a national practice of 65 lawyers, over half of whom are based in the firm's Pittsburgh and Philadelphia offices. Clients agree that what really stands out about this group is the breadth and depth of experience of its senior practitioners, combined with a strong team of associates and junior partners. The firm has an even balance of employment litigation and traditional labor work, and wins plaudits for its separate burgeoning employee benefits practice. The team acts for a mix of local and national clients in industry sectors such as financial services, manufacturing and higher education.
**The Lawyers:** Trial lawyer **Martha Munsch** (see p.1736) is *"a zealous advocate who fights for her clients"* and is well respected regionally. Her practice includes a heavy emphasis on representing nonprofit organizations and the higher education sector in particular. She provides counseling advice right through to the highest level of appeal, and recently successfully tried a several week jury trial for a higher education client concerning an alleged gender discrimination claim filed by a former faculty member. **William Bevan** (see p.1722) is one of the most knowledgeable NLRB lawyers around. *"His experience and intellect mean he is well equipped to tackle the most difficult issues – Bevan is a first-rate unionized workplace lawyer who knows the law dead cold, communicates effectively and has a lot of credibility."* Similarly, **Eugene Connors** (see p.1725) understands the entire scope of the law and provides clients with practical solutions. According to one client: *"For complex and novel issues, I go to him in a second if I want an immediate definitive answer that I can trust."* **Karl Fritton** (see p.1728) is predominantly involved in union negotiations, arbitrations and NLRB work for various clients across the country. **Cathy Bissoon** (see p.1723) is a further example of the *"great contingent of women trial lawyers at Reed Smith."* She is primarily involved in federal court litigation, in particular race claims. She has recently been involved in a high-profile race harassment class action brought by a variety of employees at a steel company. **John Martini** (see p.1735) is winning acclaim for his developing employee benefits practice.
**Clients/Work Highlights:** Clients include Exelon; Waste Management; UPS and Verizon.

## Band 3

## Buchanan Ingersoll PC
See firm details p.1749
**The Firm:** There are over 20 attorneys spread across the firm's Pittsburgh, Philadelphia and Harrisburg offices, handling a good mix of traditional labor, overall workplace planning matters and the defense of single employee and class action litigation. Clients appreciate the fact that *"these lawyers are specialists –*

*they don't dabble in other areas, so are always responsive and on target."* They also value the lawyers' sensitive approach, which means that issues do not escalate for the client.
**The Lawyers:** Practicality is the key strength consistently attributed to **Mark Hornak** (see p.1731). *"He is very salt-of-the-earth – well equipped from every perspective to deal with litigation and counseling and has great insight into the issues, which he crystallizes and prioritizes for the client."* Hornak was recently appointed special master by the federal and state courts in Pittsburgh to resolve class action employment litigation.
**Clients/Work Highlights:** Lawyers represented a major manufacturing organization in a series of EEOC litigations and investigations, and acted for the City of Philadelphia School District in a major First Amendment retaliation case. Other highlights include defending a major financial service organization in a wage and hour class action case and defending a national satellite broadcasting company in significant NLRB litigation. Lawyers have also been involved in litigation and settlement of a class action consent decree for Allegheny County.

## Cohen & Grigsby PC
**The Firm:** Headquartered in Pittsburgh, this midmarket firm of *"high-quality individuals"* enjoys an established reputation, particularly in the field of traditional labor law. This comprises approximately half of the group's workload, and runs the gamut from representing management in collective bargaining, arbitrations and union-organizing campaigns to counseling and representation before the various government agencies. The expanding group of around 15 includes a number of former NLRB attorneys who are dedicated to this area of work. The past year has also seen the addition of two attorneys in the ERISA area. Employment litigation is another key focus, and the firm is on the panel of one of the major insurance companies in this respect.
**The Lawyers:** **James Brown** predominantly focuses on the range of employment litigation matters, and is also active in mediation and arbitration. Sources describe him as *"a great educator and so knowledgeable – when he talks you always walk away the richer for it."* **Donald Ladov** is a well-respected and seasoned traditional labor lawyer. He handles a significant amount of hands-on supervisory work during campaigns, and is involved in a large number of labor arbitrations, discharge cases and collective bargaining negotiations.
**Clients/Work Highlights:** The firm acts for public and private companies across a broad range of sectors, including healthcare, manufacturing, coal mining, retail and hospitality. Recent highlights include obtaining summary judgment in a significant reverse discrimination case for the Werner Company, and settling a substantial case brought by a group of faculty members against a university, claiming discrimination on the grounds of age and gender.

## Dechert LLP

See firm details p.1752

**The Firm:** The labor and employment team at this first-class corporate firm is predominantly active in class action and individual employment litigation defense work, including high-level executive disputes. General advisory and traditional labor work is also undertaken, in particular for the firm's significant blue-chip clients. The firm enjoys a strong position in ERISA class action defense, and fields a well-regarded employee benefits practice. In addition to numerous US offices, the firm is also able to draw specialist expertise from its London, Paris, Munich and Brussels bases. Clients welcome the depth available here, and are keen to stress the *"extremely high-quality"* junior members of the team working in this area.

**The Lawyers:** *"Practical, easy to deal with, and great at maintaining client relations through addressing honestly the strengths and weaknesses of the client's case"* – this is how one client summed up the advantages of the team here. **Alan Berkowitz** (see p.1722) heads the practice and focuses on complex class action and high-level individual employment litigation. He also enjoys an active counseling role and handles some traditional labor work. *"Quiet and not overly aggressive, he will roll his sleeves up, listen to the client and respond to the pros and cons to come up with an effective solution,"* report clients. He is one of the lawyers currently representing national landscaping company The Brickman Group in a nationwide class action suit brought under the FLSA. A large proportion of **M Frances Ryan**'s (see p.1740) practice involves the counseling and defense of employment discrimination matters, including for major client Boeing. In a recent highlight, the Third Circuit Court of Appeals affirmed a summary judgment in favor of Boeing in a nationwide race class action case. Ryan is also praised for her outstanding skill in non-compete litigation. **David Jones** (see p.1731) chairs the firm's employee benefits and executive compensation group. A significant portion of his practice comprises traditional counseling and M&A support. *"He really has my respect,"* remarked one client, *"I wouldn't give the work to anyone else because it would be an insult to just how good he is."* **Paul Kimbol** (see p.1732) maintains a similar practice and has won a loyal following among clients.

**Clients/Work Highlights:** Lawyers are currently advising Bombardier in a complex class action under the WARN Act. The firm also acted as lead employee benefits and executive compensation counsel to client Crown Holdings in its disposition of a major international business line. Additional clients are Polaroid; The Franklin Mint; Norfolk Southern; GlaxoSmithKline; QVC; Siemens; St. Paul Travelers; Sunoco; York International; FMC; Shire Pharmaceuticals and Constar International.

## Kirkpatrick & Lockhart Nicholson Graham LLP

**The Firm:** Eight full-time lawyers in the firm's well-renowned Pittsburgh office form part of a substantial firmwide group operating across the USA and UK. The employment and labor team handles a good mix of employment counseling, litigation and traditional labor work, for clients ranging from small businesses to large publicly traded corporations. The team has successfully forged long-standing client relationships thanks to a combination of professionalism and sound judgment. Clients value the close interaction between specialists across the firm's various practice groups and find its broad geographical coverage especially helpful.

**The Lawyers:** **Stephen Olson** receives full marks from clients: *"He doesn't just work hard to achieve what the client wants, but is great at assessing when we have reached the limits of what the other party is willing to tolerate. He is polite yet frank, but never arrogant."* His focus includes traditional labor and employment work, in particular counseling, training programs and workplace investigations.

**Clients/Work Highlights:** Lawyers were recently involved in conducting an independent investigation of sex discrimination and sexual harassment charges brought against a high-ranking officer of a publicly traded corporation. In the traditional labor arena, the firm conducted labor negotiations for Harmony Castings and Microbac Laboratories, successfully achieving significant concessions in medical insurance, management rights and work rules. Additional clients are Easter Seals Western Pennsylvania; Partners for Quality Care; dmg world media; WESCO Distribution; Shenango; SeaWest WindPower and Glass & Associates.

## Littler Mendelson, PC

See firm details p.333

**The Firm:** This national boutique occupies a unique position. The team of Pittsburgh and Philadelphia lawyers forms part of a huge nationwide specialist shop of over 400 attorneys. The practice runs the gamut of counseling, traditional labor work and employment litigation, including class-based and individual discrimination claims. Its client base is national in scope and covers the range, from owner-managed businesses to Fortune 500 companies. Clients in the higher education and cultural arena are particularly prominent in this region.

**The Lawyers:** **Sidney Zonn** (see p.1745) is the Pittsburgh office managing stockholder and *"a broad-based player who brings a sense of maturity"* to his cases. Recent highlights include successfully dismissing more than half of the claims in a multiple race discrimination case brought against a large public sector employer, and involvement in union negotia-

tions that resulted in dramatic changes to the employee benefits scheme in favor of the hospital.

**Clients/Work Highlights:** Lawyers also recently resolved a significant wage and hour class action for a large retail client.

## Pepper Hamilton LLP

See firm details p.1760

**The Firm:** This group fields nine partners across four offices, with notable strength in the traditional labor arena and in employment litigation defense. In addition to all types of discrimination claim, the firm is increasingly active in representing clients in wage and hour cases under the FLSA. Day-to-day strategic counseling and training is an important feature, for example advising clients on the prevention of violence in the workplace and on the legal aspects of drug abuse policies. The firm also boasts a highly regarded employee benefits practice.

**The Lawyers:** **Jonathan Kane** (see p.1732) chairs the group and handles a mix of counseling and traditional labor work, including NLRB and arbitration proceedings. Clients described him as *"a very smart lawyer with a real practical sense, who is always fully up to date with what's going on in the field."* **Andrew Rudolph** (see p.1740) is the key figure associated with the employee benefits practice. *"He is exemplary in his dedication and substantive ability, works well with everyone and adds value,"* said clients.

**Clients/Work Highlights:** The team regularly advises clients in the healthcare, manufacturing and service industries. Recent highlights include reaching a very inexpensive settlement on behalf of a large employer in a significant case concerning background checks and hiring procedures. Lawyers advised a major foreign-based corporation on the labor relations issues connected with the client's asset purchase of a facility in the USA and successfully defended an employer in multi-plaintiff age discrimination litigation.

## Other Notable Practitioners

**Tom Servodidio** (see p.1741) chairs the employment and immigration practice groups at Duane Morris LLP. As one client remarked: *"I would put him up against any big New York lawyer in a second; he is a practical and robust advocate for his client and hands-down the person I call for guiding me through the minefield of HR issues."* He handles a mix of short-term and strategic counseling issues, traditional labor issues and employment litigation, including restrictive covenant, defamation, wrongful discharge and retaliation matters.

# ENVIRONMENT

## Band 1

### Babst, Calland, Clements and Zomnir, A Professional Corporation

**The Firm:** Regarded by many as the brightest star in the Pittsburgh firmament, this *"top-notch"* firm's work covers the western part of the state and beyond. *"A well-rounded environmental practice that can handle just about anything,"* it is seen by clients as *"truly a firm that thinks outside the box."* The former boutique has now extended its capabilities to become a full-service firm, but the environmental practice remains its hallmark. Highlights include acting for a chemical company in the petition for Writ of Certiorari in the US Supreme Court in one of the most extensive CERCLA cases ever litigated. This has so far lasted 12 years and concerns disputes over the allocation of environmental responsibilities between the owners of a coking plant in Alabama. As the firm's clients increase their overseas presence, its workflow emanates from increasingly diverse locations. It recently negotiated environmental matters associated with the formation of a European billion-dollar chemical industry joint venture involving seven manufacturing plants in five countries, and undertook similar work in South America and Africa.

**The Lawyers:** Practice head **Chester Babst** is nationally recognized for his pioneering air work and *"sincere dedication to his clients,"* who prize his *"sound technical ability and great integrity."* **Dean Calland** recently led a team in defeating a request to certify a class of thousands of putative plaintiffs for toxic tort and property diminution claims arising out of Pennsylvania's largest Hazardous Sites Cleanup Act (HSCA) site. He is *"skilled and talented, with a deep commitment to finding the right solution for his clients."* With a practice that includes environmental litigation and storm order management, **Kevin Garber** has built up a reputation as a *"wonderful, high-quality attorney."* Clients value his wide-ranging expertise; as one noted: *"He knows all the issues*

and can therefore better understand the things we get involved with."* Recent work includes coalmining, natural gas and other natural resources matters, in addition to acting as lead environment lawyer on one of the largest penalty resolutions to take place in the state. **Donald Bluedorn** is seen by clients as *"a bright individual who will always look at other ways to analyze and resolve situations."* He recently acted as lead counsel in negotiations surrounding environmental risk termination and risk-shifting mechanisms for a Fortune 50 company's portfolio of previously-owned and currently-owned properties. Together with colleagues from across the firm, he also advises clients on mitigating their environmental liabilities. The *"intelligent and practical"* **Lindsay Howard** handles remediation and federal Superfund issues, and regularly counsels clients on how amendments to the law will impact on them. *"Diligent and wise,"* **Joe Reinhart** focuses on natural resource permitting, property remediation and contamination issues. He is currently involved in plans to remediate a site in order to transform it into a racetrack. His strong relationships with the state environmental agencies are said to give him a valuable knowledge of likely regulatory changes.

**Clients/Work Highlights:** In a Florida-based case that is the first of its kind in the state, the firm defended the past owner and indemnitor of a chemical facility from a demand by EPA, state and county officials and the local utility for the removal of all NAPL (Non-Aqueous Phase Liquid)-contaminated soils, which was estimated to cost between $100 million and $500 million. The firm acts for utility companies, chemical companies and manufacturers from across the country and abroad.

### Drinker Biddle & Reath LLP

**The Firm:** Tapping into a national network of resources, the environment team at Drinker Biddle has emerged as *"one of the best practices in town."* It is acknowledged as one of the leaders in the Mid-Atlantic region, impressing clients with its *"ability to understand our business requirements,"* which inspires *"the utmost confidence in the firm's legal know-how."* The team's ability to *"defend clients' positions without being aggressive"* won particular respect from the market. An upswing in brownfield work has allowed it to bolster its expertise in this core area, which also includes environmental litigation and remediation work. Clients appreciate the team's ability to understand the importance of brownfield work as an entrepreneurial venture and a benefit to the environment. Litigation has recently included representing private bodies in challenges to new DEP legislation. Strong ties with government agencies ensure that the firm is at the forefront of regulatory enforcement actions and new developments in legislation.

**The Lawyers:** **Bonnie Barnett** is classed as *"one of the state's brightest stars."* Her Superfund work and litigation experience have attracted a loyal band of clients, who define her as *"energetic, intelligent and seasoned."* She approaches work with an affable yet

assertive manner, which clients find extremely helpful. Recent highlights include negotiating the remediation of a brownfield site for a potential residential development. Her practice complements that of transactional and regulatory expert **David Brooman**, *"an outstanding deal-maker at the top of his profession."* A *"sophisticated and strategic thinker and distinguished individual,"* Brooman moves up the tables in reflection of his impressive track record, which includes assisting ICI Americas with regulatory and transactional issues. Well known for his commercial landfill and waste management expertise, he is *"a stable and careful lawyer with great insight and a meticulous nature."* Clients also value his regulatory knowledge and government contacts. A new addition to this year's rankings, Berwyn-based **David Buzzell** was admired for his expertise in regulatory advice and environmental litigation. A *"highly intelligent and practical"* attorney with a *"rigorous knowledge of the regulatory structure,"* he counsels several publicly and privately owned waste management operations on hazardous, municipal and residual waste regulations. He also defends clients involved in litigation, including Superfund disputes in federal district court.

**Clients/Work Highlights:** Pennsylvania Waste Industries Association; Merck & Co; Millennium Chemicals and ICI Americas.

### Manko, Gold, Katcher & Fox LLP

**The Firm:** This *"truly exceptional"* environment boutique boasts a stable of *"personable and insightful attorneys with a complete knowledge of the law."* Clients see the firm as the premier one of its kind in the state, because *"their advice is always spot-on and falls within our corporate guidelines – so everybody wins."* *"New York or DC firms can't even touch the kind of service we get from Manko, Gold,"* enthused one interviewee. The practice covers all principal areas of environment law, with several of its attorneys having specialist technical knowledge of areas such as chemicals, engineering, water or air. It handles real estate transactions in Pennsylvania, south New Jersey and Delaware, and represents high-profile local environment bodies such as the Philadelphia Industrial Development Corporation, Philadelphia Gas Works and other large industry bodies subject to government regulatory enforcement and compliance. It advises on the environmental aspects of major construction projects in the city, in addition to acting for facilities trying to obtain permits for these constructions and other developments. It recently defended Waste Management in litigation over landfill sites and regularly takes on complex and large-scale brownfield and Superfund work.

**The Lawyers:** Industry *"dignitary"* **Joe Manko** is a *"huge name"* who is credited with being one of the founding fathers of environmental law in the state. Possessing an *"unrivalled depth of knowledge,"* he is particularly recognized for his work in transforming contaminated sites into commercial and profitable properties. Clients say it *"is always a pleasure to deal with him."* Firm founder and water specialist

**Marc Gold** has the *"ability to understand the needs of business and regulators and make things fit together."* He won praise from clients for being able to *"communicate with people at all levels in a way that allows regulatory requirements and company goals to be met simultaneously."* Gold is common counsel to a coalition of dischargers across Pennsylvania, New Jersey and Delaware, advising on TMDL (total maximum daily load) requirements as part of the Clean

Water Act. An expert in brownfield matters having helped write the relevant Pennsylvania statute in 1995, he also represents industrial property sellers in the sale of sites for remediation. **Bart Cassidy** is *"a fabulous and personable lawyer,"* whose regulatory practice centers mainly on air work, which he *"understands back to front."* This includes responding to the government enforcement activity of the EPA and DOJ. He regularly represents refining, chemical and electrical generating companies that have been the subject of national enforcement action and recently obtained a $1 billion consent decree for refineries nationwide. An engineer by trade, he also counsels on regulatory issues and assists facilities in pursuing permits for new constructions. Clients see him as *"a genius – his head is like a filing cabinet. You can ask him any question, no matter how complex, and he'll have the answer."* The *"superb"* **Robert Fox** is *"smart, savvy and a good strategic thinker."* His diverse practice this year allowed him to act in obtaining permits for several major landfill expansions in the state, while also defending class actions and other pieces of litigation, the largest of which involved acting as lead attorney for Waste Management. **Mike Meloy** is *"a practical and constructive problem solver and an avid promoter of clients' interests."* A water resources planning and waste management specialist, he also handles litigation, in which he possesses *"a great talent and creative way of resolving things."* **Jonathan Spergel** enters the rankings this year due to growing admiration for his brownfield work. Clients appreciate his *"energetic and bright approach."* **Clients/Work Highlights:** The firm's client base includes regional government bodies, local entities and Fortune 500 companies.

## Band 2

### Ballard Spahr Andrews & Ingersoll LLP
See firm details p.1746

**The Firm:** This *"vibrant"* ten-strong team *"has a great reputation across the state."* The focus of the practice is gradually shifting from residual Superfund work to more conventional activity in areas such as air, water and waste. Practitioners from three offices acting across the Mid-Atlantic region have taken on an increasing number of waste water discharge matters and air pollution issues. Gas transmission pipeline matters and nuisance claims have also kept the group busy of late. This full-service team is renowned for its strengths in all environment matters, including litigation, and even defends white-collar clients who face criminal prosecution for alleged violations of environment law. It recently successfully defended a company in a major construction project against allegations of permit violation. On the noncontentious side, it handles compliance and regulatory matters for clients in the oil and gas industries, including a growing number of oil refineries.

**The Lawyers:** **David Mandelbaum** (see p.1735) was consistently rated as *"one of the best and smartest lawyers in the state."* A pivotal figure in the practice, he had significant roles in the cases mentioned above and

was also instrumental in rewriting a water usage plan for the state. Clients praised his intellect and environmental knowledge as well as his *"ability to summarize issues and highlight the important points without getting distracted or going off on complicated legal tangents."* Former US Assistant Attorney **Ron Sarachan** (see p.1740) is *"the go-to guy"* for environment-related, white-collar criminal defense work. He focuses on advising clients who face prosecution by the government for environmental crimes. **Brendan Collins** (see p.1725) is *"competent and solution-oriented"* with a wide field of expertise, which covers litigation, real estate and environmental law. He is widely respected for his knowledge of regulatory enforcement issues. **Glenn Unterberger** (see p.1744) enters the tables due to extensive positive feedback. An air quality specialist, he represents the Pennsylvania Chamber of Business and Industry, and is also active in the field of military housing and base reuse. According to clients, he *"has a complicated area mastered."*

**Clients/Work Highlights:** Sunoco; Exelon; Bechtel; BP; Glatfelter and Raytheon.

## Wolf, Block, Schorr and Solis-Cohen LLP
See firm details p.1764

**The Firm:** Operating as valuable support to the firm's respected real estate group, this expanding environmental practice covers not only the environmental aspects of real estate transactions, but a significant amount of litigation and regulatory work. It regularly counsels major companies on environmental issues such as air, water and brownfield redevelopment, and handles the environmental matters relating to the sale of facilities in corporate deals managed elsewhere within the firm.

**The Lawyers:** The *"thoughtful and bright"* **Ken Warren** (see p.1744) is *"one of the most measured and careful lawyers around."* As outside counsel for the Delaware River Basin Commission, he handles issues surrounding river streamflows, discharges and withdrawals. A skilled litigator with a niche specialty in water law expertise, *"he is intellectually one of the top people at the environmental Bar."* Clients appreciated his unsurpassed level of specialist knowledge, remarking *"he is very informed on developments in environmental law."* **Steven Miano's** (see p.1736) reputation has been strengthened by the increasingly high-profile regulatory work he undertakes. A distinguished client base has assured him a steady flow of work centered upon his three main areas of expertise: air, water and brownfield. He recently represented a large energy and transportation company in air matters, reviewing compliance requirements with regulatory agencies. Clients respect his *"excellent judgment and high degree of integrity"* and his *"practical and skilled"* approach. The *"solid and capable"* **Kermit Rader** (see p.1739) handles the environmental aspects of corporate and real estate transactions. This year, he worked on negotiating the approvals and managing the cleanup of a New Jersey site in readiness for the development of a high-rise condominium.

**Clients/Work Highlights:** The firm acts for several corporate clients across a range of industries.

## Band 3

### Dechert LLP

See firm details p.1752

**The Firm:** This relatively small team is nonetheless a *"strong, powerful unit"* that offers *"the quality you would expect to find at Dechert."* Drawing upon the firm's immense national resources, this practice is mainly transaction-led, but also lends its litigation muscle to environmental matters. On the transactional side, it recently represented a client in the divestiture of a business with approximately 30 industrial facilities primarily located throughout Europe, Asia and North America. It also advised the same client on the acquisition of a US chemical facility. Its litigation work involves a significant number of hazardous waste site cleanup cases and it recently acted for Berwind Group in a case brought by Degussa Construction Chemicals Operations over contaminated property, which settled on the second day of trial.

**The Lawyers:** **Hershel Richman** (see p.1739) is widely recognized as one of the pioneers of environmental law in the state. Although his role has now changed to that of special counsel, he remains a true *"éminence grise,"* who is considered *"a very classy guy and one of the originals."* **Abbi Cohen** (see p.1724) undertook over 100 international business, real estate and financial transactions this year, cementing her position as *"an absolutely superb, dedicated lawyer."* She recently completed negotiations with the EPA on behalf of an industrial client, which resulted in an Emergency Removal Settlement Agreement under the federal Superfund program. *"Smart, creative and savvy with a trustworthy, common-sense approach",* she won praise for being *"business-oriented with a good perspective on the issues."* Clients also admired her drafting skills. Litigator **Mike Bogdonoff** (see p.1723) is added to the tables in recognition of his *"in-depth knowledge of his field."* He is *"soft-spoken and effective,"* with the ability to *"solve problems and reach solutions efficiently."* Clients praised his industriousness, remarking that *"he really does his homework and stays up to date on all developments."* Recent work includes successfully representing World Fuel Services Corporation in environmental litigation before the US District Court for the Eastern District of Pennsylvania. The litigation had been brought by a group of potentially responsible parties that had agreed to carry out an EPA-approved remedy at the Malvern Trichloroethylene site in Pennsylvania.

**Clients/Work Highlights:** Clients include Berwind Group; BRS; Crown Holdings; Citicorp Venture Capital; Foster Wheeler and Sensient Technologies Corporation.

### Kirkpatrick & Lockhart Nicholson Graham LLP

**The Firm:** This increasingly prominent team combines the ability to *"understand business requirements and think creatively"* with *"a client-friendly disposition and lack of pretentiousness."* It has built a strong reputation representing a number of distinguished clients in litigation, Superfund, counseling, project and brownfield matters. The firm continues to represent the largest vaccine manufacturer in North America, and this year advised on the environmental and regulatory issues arising from a series of expansions of the client's influenza vaccine-producing facilities.

**The Lawyers:** **Tim Weston** (see p.1745) is *"a real star who is at the top of his game."* A leading light in water resource matters, he elicited acclaim from interviewees across the state for his undisputed prowess in water work and his *"uncommon understanding of both the political and scientific sides to environmental laws."* As the leader of the five-strong team in Harrisburg, he spearheads the diverse range of work that it undertakes and is praised for his ability to *"marshal the firm's human assets effectively."* Clients consider him *"enormously bright and scholarly with a great sense of humor."*

**Clients/Work Highlights:** The firm acts for some high-profile clients in utilities; electrical generating; manufacturing; pharmaceuticals and technology. It recently represented a large specialty steel firm in a clean water enforcement action, obtaining a favorable decision from the Third Circuit Court of Appeals.

### Montgomery, McCracken, Walker & Rhoads, LLP

**The Firm:** Clients like this firm because *"it is always accessible, doesn't overstaff a matter and offers dependable experience and knowledge."* Employing its signature *"straightforward and levelheaded"* approach, the team was prominently involved in the aftermath of the November 2004 oil catastrophe on the Delaware River, one of the largest there in decades. A tear in the hull of the tanker Athos I allowed 30,000 gallons of crude oil to spill into the river. The firm acted on behalf of the vessel owner in the environmental issues that resulted from the spillage, which included five separate pieces of litigation. Its staple work also includes significant brownfield redevelopments, many of which over the past year have been in southeastern Pennsylvania. Its involvement in brownfield projects includes finding appropriate risk transfer mechanisms for parties not willing to assume full liability for a project. Other work includes the successful representation of a foundry owner in a civil penalty proceeding under the RCRA, initiated by the EPA, seeking penalties totaling nearly $1 million.

**The Lawyers:** **Tim Bergère** *"is so good he should be cloned,"* according to clients. Possessing *"great understanding of the issues and excellent communication skills,"* he also has niche expertise in environmental law in an admiralty context, which secured him a significant role in the Delaware River oil spill response. This year he was also involved in the remedial action of a mining operation. The *"terrific and underrated"* **John Judge** won praise for his *"honest and practical nature."* An authority on Superfund and brownfield matters, he handles both transactional and litigation work. He recently acted in the redevelopment of a local steel mill.

**Clients/Work Highlights:** West Pharmaceutical Services; Air Products and Chemicals; Majestic Realty Co. and American Meter Company.

### Morgan, Lewis & Bockius LLP

See firm details p.1758

**The Firm:** Forming part of the firm's influential nationwide environmental practice, the Harrisburg outpost undertakes state environment work in its own right. A strong litigation focus has enabled it to participate in long-running Superfund cases, and the firm also handles transactional work. The group advises on regulatory compliance matters and the environmental aspects of real estate acquisitions, and regularly works with its New York and DC counterparts on larger regional and national transactions.

**The Lawyers:** The *"bright and effective"* **Maxine Woelfling** (see p.1745) is *"one of the most experienced practitioners in the state."* Highly regarded for her *"professionalism and decorum,"* she has held a number of prestigious positions in the state's environmental community over the years, and is known for her strong links with government. Her impressive portfolio includes complex brownfield work and advising a major local power plant affected by the recent Clean Air Interstate ruling. She also represents a trade association of waste coal-fired power plants in the disposal of coal ash. Recently, she handled air litigation over the emissions at a coal plant. Superfund litigation specialist **Glen Stuart** (see p.1743) undertakes an array of regulatory work. An *"energetic, relentless, smart and sensible"* attorney, he is praised by clients as *"a delight to work with."*

**Clients/Work Highlights:** The firm acts on behalf of clients in both the public and private sectors. It recently advised on the remediation responsibilities, permitting and insurance issues relating to the acquisition of a major chemical manufacturing facility.

### Saul Ewing LLP

See firm details p.1763

**The Firm:** This firm is riding high on its reputation for *"good business sense and the capability to help clients reach the best resolution,"* having recently completed an award-winning brownfield transaction for utility company Exelon. This Chester-based project included a brownfield agreement with the Commonwealth of Pennsylvania in the remediation of a contaminated site. The team also acted as outside counsel to Wyeth in a brownfield deal, in which the pharmaceuticals company sold a piece of land to GlaxoSmithKline.

**The Lawyers:** Practice leader and *"top-notch litigator"* **John Stoviak** (see p.1743) focuses on environmental litigation and cost allocation. Clients consider him *"an attorney of the highest integrity and loyalty who is always mindful of costs."* **Carl Everett** (see p.1727) is *"ethical and gentlemanly"* and carries out his work *"with his clients' interests always at heart."* An attorney with a chemical engineering background, he also has extensive Superfund experience. He recently negotiated a set of agreements with the State of Delaware pertaining to the finalization of a new Wilmington-based headquarters for roadside assistance company AAA. **Joseph O'Dea** (see p.1737) is *"a personable and knowledgeable attorney with a sharp intellect."* He is respected for his litigation work, where he has gained the reputation of being *"a thoroughly collegial and effective adversary."* As lead counsel for Waste Management in the Northeast region, he has had significant involvement over the past year in developing alternative environmentally-friendly landfill schemes.

Clients/Work Highlights: The firm acts for a range of companies in heavy industries and pharmaceuticals.

## Band 4

### Fox Rothschild LLP
See firm details p.1755

The Firm: This *"well-rounded"* midsized regional firm inspires *"a lot of confidence"* with its *"conscientious and personable"* approach. Clients also appreciate that *"the firm knows not everyone has an unlimited check-book when they need legal work."* The team advises on the local environmental concerns of national and international companies with Pennsylvania-based operations. It recently negotiated permits for gaming company Harrah's Entertainment in a brownfield project to build a casino in Chester. It also advises homebuilders on due diligence and is heavily engaged in the Waterfront Study that analyses brownfield redevelopment opportunities on the banks of the Delaware River.

The Lawyers: Joel Bolstein is *"an excellent brownfield attorney with a great bedside manner."* A former Pennsylvania deputy secretary of the DEP, he is known for his political connections and policymaking. Clients praised his capacity for *"explaining the issues clearly"* and *"the personable way he takes the time to assist us."* Others commented that *"he is very bright and it is a pleasure dealing with him."* Environmental litigator Philip Hinerman impressed clients with his *"practical and plain-spoken"* manner and his *"ability to understand the bigger picture."* He recently concluded the successful representation of 60 defendants in a large cleanup case. He is also involved with the US Green Building Council, the largest regional trainer of architects in the development of energy-efficient buildings.

Clients/Work Highlights: Ryan Homes; TH Properties; Norfolk Southern Corporation; Berwind Corporation and Harrah's Entertainment.

### Klett Rooney Lieber & Schorling
See firm details p.1757

The Firm: A small but highly respected outfit in the western part of the state, this practice covers environmental litigation, transactional, permitting and regulatory compliance work. In a busy year for brownfield work, it acted in a residential development on a brownfield site under the Pennsylvania industrial recycling program, and elsewhere had significant roles to play in many other pieces of general environmental work. Clients appreciate its strong connections with the DEP, which allows it to keep them up to date on regulatory enforcement issues.

The Lawyers: *"Upstanding and reliable"* practice head Howard Wein (see p.1745) is *"simply one of the finest lawyers in western Pennsylvania."* A *"sharp, talented and ethical"* attorney with a generalist practice, he won praise for his *"gregarious and energetic"* presence.

Clients/Work Highlights: The firm acts for waste management companies; developers; manufacturers and mining companies.

### Reed Smith LLP
See firm details p.1762

The Firm: The work of this *"first-rate and professional"* environment team has had a strong international flavor this year, with the group advising on matters in Europe and South-East Asia. It represented a client in the acquisition of a specialty chemical company with facilities in India, Japan, China and Europe, and advised a packaging company on acquiring brownfield sites in Mexico. Domestically, it advises clients in Arkansas, Mississippi and Washington on enforcement issues, title V permits and the implications of the Clean Air Act. It represented a waste management company in a permit expansion matter before the Pennsylvania DEP, and regularly counsels clients in hazardous waste management matters. The litigation side has continued to be busy, with Superfund and cost recovery cases over a landfill site occupying the team's time.

The Lawyers: Leader Louis Naugle (see p.1737) is *"an outstanding individual."* Clients warmly responded to his aptitude for *"problem solving and reaching a compromise that pleases everyone."*

Clients/Work Highlights: Allied Waste Industries; East Penn Manufacturing Company; Jacuzzi Brands; Valero Energy; Milco Industries and Carmeuse North America.

## Band 5

### Langsam Stevens & Silver LLP

The Firm: As the only full-service environment boutique in central Philadelphia, this niche firm owes its visibility in the marketplace to its strong litigation focus and impressive client roster. The firm acts on AIG's defense panel and it regularly handles insurance-related defense and waste management work.

The Lawyers: A background in environmental engineering has equipped Mark Stevens with *"the technical skills to establish a respectable and eclectic practice."* He is viewed as an authority on site cleanup and brownfield programs and also acts in federal work.

Clients/Work Highlights: The firm represents a variety of chemical companies; contractors; construction companies; engineering firms; financial institutions; hospitals; insurers; manufacturers; municipalities and oil and gas refineries.

### Schnader Harrison Segal & Lewis LLP

The Firm: Working in close conjunction with the firm's DC and New Jersey offices, this regional litigation-based group continues to produce quality work. The Philadelphia team defends clients from a range of industries in government enforcement cleanup actions. It also represents clients in toxic tort and class actions, citizens' suit class actions, compliance on permits, filings, appeals, and land use work.

The Lawyers: Regulatory and litigation guru Robert Collings is widely respected for the *"thoughtful and precise"* qualities he brings to his work. Head of the Philadelphia practice, Collings has been advising on an increasing number of brownfield and other publicly-financed projects, and defending clients in litigation over projects deemed to be environmentally unsound. He is national outside counsel for Exide Technologies, a battery manufacturer. Robert Stoltzfus enters the tables in response to his increasing visibility in the marketplace. The current chair of the Philadelphia Bar Association's Environmental Law Committee, he is known for his work in air and water quality, permitting, remediations, enforcement and Superfund. He earns respect for his *"knowledge and professionalism."*

Clients/Work Highlights: Clients include real estate developers; chemical companies; a major automotive battery manufacturer; waste management companies and waste brokering companies; chemical distributors; trucking companies and railroads.

## Other Notable Practitioners

*"Candid and incredibly knowledgeable,"* Terry Bossert at Post & Schell, PC once again reaped enthusiastic praise as *"probably the best all-around environment lawyer in the state."* He has bolstered the essentially litigation-focused environment practice at Post & Schell since his arrival by adding a regulatory capability to the firm's offering: in response to a ramping-up of the local environment agency's regulation of radiation exposure he recently spearheaded a radiation protection program in local hospitals. Having also served as general counsel for the DEP, Bossert was praised for his broad-based experience, with commentators having *"great admiration for his voice and opinions."* Susan LeGros at Stevens & Lee PC joins the tables this year as a result of positive feedback surrounding her work in water and air quality law. With a background as a Section Chief at the Federal Environment Protection Agency, she is considered *"a master"* of regulatory environment law. Alan Miller is *"an excellent litigator and one of the best appellate advocates in town."* Considered the driving force behind Picadio Sneath Miller & Norton's environmental regulatory and litigation practice, he drew acclaim for the *"care and clarity"* he brings to his work. As part of his role as provider of compliance counseling to his clients, this year he represented a chemical company who unwittingly transported hazardous waste to unsuitable sites for disposal. The *"exact, honest and fair"* Curtis Toll (see p.1744) heads Greenberg Traurig LLP's *"sophisticated"* Philadelphia-based environment unit. His areas of expertise include insured remediation, federal brownfields and the movement of funds. Although the team does not undertake environmental litigation, sources praised its flair for complex transactional work. Jack Ubinger (see p.1744) at Jones Day is an *"outstanding transactional lawyer."* His environmental health and safety practice focuses on strategic planning for clients with long-term environmental liabilities and legacy environmental issues, including those in the chemical and mining sectors. He advises clients such as the Hall Corporation on environmental strategy negotiation – a subject in which he also lectures at Duquesne University.

# INTELLECTUAL PROPERTY

## Band 1

### Drinker Biddle & Reath LLP

**The Firm:** This *"spectacular"* practice continues to build on its reputation as a dynamic unit. Recognized as *"bright, top-notch lawyers who are the best in their field,"* the growing team of heavyweight professionals handles IP matters for a broad range of national and international clients. Litigation work over the past year included several patent infringement cases, and the firm is now seen as *"a genuine presence"* in patent work. One recent highlight in this area was successfully defending flashlight manufacturer Streamlight in a headlamp patent infringement case. The practice has strengthened its technology expertise to keep abreast of its clients' increasingly sophisticated IP needs and has added a biotech specialist to the ten-strong life sciences team in response to the growth of the complex biotech industry.

**The Lawyers:** The linchpin of the practice is the formidable **Arthur Seidel**, who continues to counsel clients on complex matters and is regularly called upon for his wealth of trademark litigation expertise. An icon to many other IP lawyers in the area, his reputation is legendary and he is perceived as *"a terrific lawyer and mentor, godfather and muse to the rest of us."* Practice manager **Greg Lavorgna** impressed clients with his *"intelligence, thoroughness and practical business sense."* Adept in client counseling and litigation, this year he represented a paper manufacturer in defense of patent infringement litigation and negotiated license agreements on behalf of several high-profile clients. His *"straightforward and unfussy"* manner was the subject of unanimous praise by clients, who dubbed him *"a nice guy and very competent lawyer."* The *"impressive"* **John Marshall** is a *"no-nonsense"* litigator who gives *"clear, concise and prompt answers and comes across as credible, honest and knowledgeable."* The past year has seen him heavily involved in technology litigation – such as a case over computer controls – and patent infringement cases, some of which have been at federal level. He regularly advises on clearance and licensing, and has recently been involved in matters relating to stem cell research. **Katherine Doyle's**

expertise in niche biotech work has earned her a loyal client following and a sterling reputation as a leading authority in this area. Handling transactional work and patent prosecution, she also has experience in patent procurement, due diligence, infringement and invalidity opinions and licensing, in addition to strategic counseling and patent portfolio management. **Robert Koons** joined the firm this year from Buchanan Ingersoll, bringing with him new client Sonoco, for whom he undertakes a substantial amount of *"highly impressive"* work. **Harriet Perkins** manages the trademarks portfolios of national and international clients in the health, publishing, insurance, technology, entertainment and banking sectors, with an emphasis on prosecution. Praised by clients for her *"rapid turnaround time,"* she is also considered an asset to the firm thanks to her background at the US PTO, with which she still has strong ties. While Perkins handles the prosecution aspects of incoming workflow, **Nancy Frandsen** handles its accompanying litigation, and the two often work together. A specialist in trademark and copyright litigation, she joins the rankings in response to client acclaim for her experience and *"bright, down-to-earth approach."* **Dan Monaco's** practice focuses on the pharmaceutical and biotech sectors, to which he brings his considerable expertise in biotech patents. The majority of his work is patent-oriented and he regularly handles US and international patent solicitation, due diligence, investigations and litigation.

**Clients/Work Highlights:** The firm represents companies of all sizes, from multinationals to startups, in the pharmaceutical, chemical, biotech and manufacturing sectors, as well as universities and other institutions.

### Woodcock Washburn LLP

See firm details p.1765

**The Firm:** This large and long-established firm is widely acknowledged as *"the biggest patent boutique in town."* Boasting an *"outstanding national reputation"* and a *"gilded client base"* that is the envy of its competitors, it offers in-depth patent and trademark expertise across the fields of chemicals and technology. Following the retirement of several senior partners a few years ago, the firm has been invigorated by a younger generation of *"talented lawyers with great credentials"* and has now reached the critical mass that enables it to compete with full-service firms, as evinced by its inclusion on Microsoft's select list of preferred providers. The team recently successfully represented an online travel company in litigation, as well as representing a plaintiff in litigation regarding trade secrets in the financial services industry.

**The Lawyers:** Described by clients as *"low key and smart,"* **Dale Heist's** (see p.1730) reputation as a premier patent litigator was strengthened this year by his acting in several high-value pieces of litigation. He represented the manufacturer of diagnostic machines in a $50 million settlement and obtained a major

settlement for a beer company. His background in electronic engineering has equipped him with highly prized expertise in IP law as it relates to technology and software, but clients emphasized his communication skills, saying he *"has a great way of explaining complicated things."* Heist is also a member of the American College of Trial Lawyers. Coming from a similar background, **John Donohue** (see p.1726) is *"gentlemanly and charming,"* according to interviewees. He recently represented a software company in a trade secrets case that was resolved via mediation. **Dianne Elderkin's** (see p.1727) area of expertise covers the medical and biotech sectors. This year she handled arbitration for CenterCorp over a drug for rheumatoid arthritis and Crohn's disease, which settled in the client's favor before hearing. She also successfully represented LifeScan in a federal court infringement case over a glucose monitoring device for diabetics. A well-known figure on the local IP circuit, she is a *"high-quality attorney and one bright woman."* **Steven Rocci** (see p.1739) is a *"bright and thorough"* attorney whose experience in telecom, the Internet and electronics secured him admiration from all corners of the market. He handles the bulk of the responsibility for the Microsoft account and his practice covers client counseling, opinion and prosecution work and litigation.

**Clients/Work Highlights:** Johnson & Johnson; Microsoft; Crown Holdings and Bayer.

## Band 2

### Akin Gump Strauss Hauer & Feld LLP

See firm details p.559

**The Firm:** Building on its traditional strengths in patents, this 22-person group has earned a reputation for an *"ethical and detail-oriented"* approach to its work. This year it advised several startup pharmaceutical companies on patent applications, prosecution and due diligence. Another area of its key expertise is in media, and it represents several high-profile clients in the publishing sector on the protection and enforcement of their IP rights in the USA and abroad. The practice can also draw upon a pool of expertise in chemicals, electronics and semiconductors and boasts patent expertise in all these areas. It recently represented the inventor of the Super Soaker in a dispute against toy manufacturers Hasbro, who had bought the rights to the world-famous water pistol.

**The Lawyers:** Rainmaker and head of the transactional IP practice, **Ron Panitch** (see p.1738) is *"a closer who knows how to negotiate."* Exceptionally well regarded by both peers and clients, he is widely known for his *"astute and wise"* business advice. He handles a range of matters including litigation and is currently acting in an ongoing and high-value piece of litigation over patents in the lighting industry. The *"meticulous and patient"* **Alan Nadel** (see p.1737) this year became patent counsel for Erimos Pharmaceuticals, a North Carolina-based company, and adviser to BioNumerik on its entire patent portfolio. He also counseled clients on patent applications and prosecutions relating to pharmaceuticals for the treatment of HIV and some cancers. A *"bright and creative attorney who is always willing to learn more,"* he won praise from clients for his ability to translate complex patent terminology into *"language we can understand."* **Martin Belisario** (see p.1722) oversees the firmwide patent practice and advises clients on how to handle product design in a way that avoids potential litigation. He also undertakes patent clear-

ance work for manufacturing clients. Head of the chemical patent practice, **Bill Schwarze** (see p.1740) is a *"far-range thinker and great communicator."* He joins the rankings this year on the strength of client recommendation. Formerly a chemical engineer by profession, he is recognized for the *"quiet yet brilliant"* way in which he operates. He has a number of prestigious clients, including Matsushita.

**Clients/Work Highlights:** Hamilton Beach/Proctor-Silex; West Pharmaceutical Services; Erimos Pharmaceuticals; BioNumerik Pharmaceuticals; Johnson Research & Development; Matsushita; The New York Times; American Lawyer Media and April Cornell.

## Ballard Spahr Andrews & Ingersoll LLP
See firm details p.1746

**The Firm:** This celebrated Philadelphia practice is home to *"an outstanding collection of lawyers with a great deskside manner."* *"They don't have to remind you how brilliant they are as their work speaks for itself,"* enthused one interviewee. The team handles both national and international work, with recent highlights including a patent infringement suit terminated on summary judgment involving the patent of an auto lock, and the successful settlement of an infringement case relating to a bio trademark on behalf of a biotech company. The firm's highly developed trademark practice continues to win plaudits and it is developing a name for itself in software licensing, domain names and other Internet-related IP law: it has implemented a domain name policing program on behalf of several clients, including Lane Bryant and Fashion Bug.

**The Lawyers:** A celebrated name in IP circles, **Roberta Jacobs-Meadway** (see p.1731) is *"at the top of her game in her practice area."* *"Incredibly organized, bright and pragmatic,"* she is recognized nationally as an authority on trademarks and had significant roles in the work mentioned above. **Jay Meadway** (see p.1736) advises a host of high-profile international clients on protecting their foreign trademark rights, with his practice covering trademark search work, litigation and renewals. Clients view him as *"low-key, placid, yet very effective,"* and value the way he can *"navigate trademark registrations very successfully."* Recently appointed managing partner of the Philadelphia office, **Lynn Rzonca** (see p.1740) is a *"high-quality and dedicated"* attorney who won praise for her IP litigation work. The *"diligent and precise"* **Richard Peirce** (see p.1738) focuses on IP advice and litigation. He undertakes a wealth of Internet-related trademark matters, including domain name disputes. He also handles clearance work and recently advised on a 'phishing' scheme in which a client's mark was being used to elicit fake online charity donations in the wake of the natural disasters of 2004-2005. He is increasingly involved in contextual Internet advertising, such as sponsored links on Google.com and banner advertising.

**Clients/Work Highlights:** Lane Bryant; Fashion Bug; Sexy Hair Concepts; Biogen IDEC; Oki Data; Saint-Gobain Abrasives and Exelon.

## Caesar, Rivise, Bernstein, Cohen & Pokotilow Ltd
See firm details p.1750

**The Firm:** This long-established Philadelphia boutique offers *"the highest standards of civility and ethics."* Peopled by 25 *"senior and experienced sharp cookies,"* the firm has *"a wonderful reputation"* in patent, copyright and trademark prosecution and litigation. Steeped in biochemical and pharmaceutical work, it is heavily involved in an increasing amount of drug litigation. It secured victories for clients in several high-value trials over the past year and is currently defending Canadian drugs giant Apotex in a case against sanofi-aventis over its blood-thinning drug Plavix. In addition, it works on behalf of many research and academic institutions, and is also well known for its computer and IT-related expertise. Several *"bright and accomplished"* new recruits specialize in this growing area of IP law.

**The Lawyers:** *"A formidable opponent and a great guy to work alongside,"* **Manny Pokotilow** (see p.1738) is held in exceptionally high esteem for his *"tireless efforts to maintain the high standards of IP work."* A figure of long-standing renown, he is *"one of the best patent litigation lawyers in the state."* According to clients, he successfully combines *"great charm with encyclopedic knowledge,"* and can *"litigate hard and furious but reasonably too."* *"Smart and experienced,"* **Stan Cohen** (see p.1724) is perceived by his contemporaries to possess *"keen judgment."* He specializes in copyright and trademark law and related counseling, licensing and litigation. **Alan Bernstein**'s (see p.1722) *"mastery of drug litigation"* was felt to be unrivaled. Working particularly with clients in the chemical, pharmaceutical and biotech fields on chemical and pharmaceutical patent application preparation and prosecution, he is widely viewed as the authority on these topics.

**Clients/Work Highlights:** The firm's clientele ranges from individuals and small entrepreneurial organizations to Fortune 500 companies and foreign corporations.

## Kirkpatrick & Lockhart Nicholson Graham LLP

**The Firm:** The Pittsburgh arm of this national IP practice is a firm favorite among clients, because it presents *"flawless courtroom arguments"* and works *"efficiently and cost-consciously."* Interviewees highlighted the practice's aptitude for creating a *"great client rapport"* and fielding lawyers who *"really know the law and understand that losing isn't an option."* The group handles a blend of patent and trademark litigation and advises clients on trademark, patent and copyright issues. The firm is currently acting in litigation for medical device manufacturer INAMED and the maker of a highway de-icer.

**The Lawyers:** A *"gentlemanly and no-nonsense"* practitioner, **Robert Yeager** focuses almost exclusively on patent litigation and was recently involved in a large-scale claim construction to determine the issue of patent infringement and validity. A background in metallurgy has equipped him with specialist technical skills, and he is widely thought of as a *"highly credible and ethical"* attorney. Described as *"bright and scholarly,"* **James Kyper** (see p.1733) undertakes patent litigation and client counseling on a range of IP topics. Clients expressed gratitude for his *"practical, results-oriented approach,"* which he couples with a *"concern for cost-effectiveness."* He recently successfully represented steel framing company Dietrich Industries in a series of patent cases. A new entrant to this year's tables is **Pat McElhinny**, who arrives amid a clamor of recommendations. Portrayed as *"a genius – yet softly-spoken and modest,"* he had significant involvement in some of the cases mentioned above and is currently working closely with his Boston-based counterpart on a patent claims case. With a background in mechanical engineering, he now has a particular focus on IP litigation. He regularly prosecutes and defends patent infringement claims, misappropriation of trade secrets, breaches of noncompetition agreements, trademark and copyright claims and claims for insurance coverage for IP disputes.

**Clients/Work Highlights:** Allegheny Technologies; Dietrich Industries; Cingular Wireless; Student Marketing Group; Axcelis Technologies and Artesyn Technologies.

## Band 3

### Buchanan Ingersoll PC
See firm details p.1749

**The Firm:** Having acquired Virginia-based IP firm Burns, Doane, Swecker & Mathis LLP in June 2005, Buchanan Ingersoll has been boosted by the arrival of 55 new IP professionals and new clients such as Deere & Company and Konica Minolta. The Philadelphia-based practice has carved out a niche in nanotechnology and electronics, while the larger Pittsburgh bureau offers expertise in chemical and pharmaceutical work, with the majority of the trademark and copyright matters being handled there.

**The Lawyers:** **Lynn Alstadt** (see p.1721) is well-known in the Pittsburgh IP community for his *"perceptive and knowledgeable"* demeanor. Over the past year he has represented clients in a range of matters including litigation. Robert Koons has now moved to Drinker Biddle.

**Clients/Work Highlights:** Clients include companies in the toy manufacturing, consumer products, special metals and window coverings industries.

### Duane Morris LLP
See firm details p.1753

**The Firm:** Working as part of a large integrated national practice, this group handles work for clients across the USA. The Philadelphia partners recently successfully represented Internet service providers EarthLink in a Texas-based case, and also handled an injunction proceeding for a New York-based bowling facility that pursued enforcement actions of violations of their mark in the eastern district court of Pennsylvania.

**The Lawyers:** Litigator **Scott Kramer** (see p.1733) represents Tiffany & Co in copyright and trademark

matters in Pennsylvania, New Jersey and Delaware. He also undertakes enforcement proceedings on his clients' behalf. **Peter Cronk** (see p.1725) enters the tables having picked up plaudits for his *"top-notch prosecution and counseling skills."* He assists clients with procuring and litigating patents and is currently representing a client accused of patent infringement for plastic well pipes. He recently represented the manufacturer of styrofoam cups in a case alleging that a lid design infringed a patent.

**Clients/Work Highlights:** The firm acts for clients across a wide range of industries including bioscience; manufacturing; electronics and telecom.

### RatnerPrestia
See firm details p.1761

**The Firm:** This boutique firm has enhanced its well-established reputation for patent prosecution by undertaking an increasing amount of international work. A team of 40 attorneys handles patent prosecutions of applications filed overseas and in the USA, but is also known for its work in counseling and transactions. The group is raising its profile in litigation and biotech work, while maintaining an impressive reputation in consumer electronics, lasers and pharmaceutical patents. Reflecting the fact that clients increasingly wish to integrate IP into business strategy, the firm has become more closely involved with clients in the early stages of planning.

**The Lawyers:** *"A wonderful attorney and a real gentleman,"* **Paul Prestia** (see p.1738) is respected for both his pioneering work within the firm and his extra-curricular IP-related activities in the wider community, particularly for the American Intellectual Property Association. A practitioner with a long-standing reputation in patents, his recent work includes drug patent litigation. **Kenneth Nigon** (see p.1737) is *"continuously impressive"* to both clients and peers. His *"quietly competent"* manner found many fans, while his activity in the PTO and Philadelphia Intellectual Property Law Association has also helped raise his profile. He handles both US and overseas matters, with the majority of his workload consisting of prosecutions. Recent highlights include advising a chemical company on one of its new computer inventions. Making his *Chambers* début, **Benjamin Leace** (see p.1734) has been recognized for his *"high-quality"* trademark and patent litigation practice. With interviewees commenting that it is *"always a pleasure to work with him or against him,"* he is gaining a following in the regional IP community.

**Clients/Work Highlights:** The firm provides patent procurement advice and opinions for a multinational glass manufacturer with an optical semiconductor business; three US laboratories of a large Japanese corporation; an optical semiconductor company and a French automaker.

### Reed Smith LLP
See firm details p.1762

**The Firm:** Working out of offices in Pittsburgh and Philadelphia, this IP practice is a national operation. Its size allows it to provide clients with the full range

of IP services on all trademark, copyright and patent issues. It recently acted in proceedings before the Trade Commission on imported products with alleged patent infringements, and has strong links with pharmaceutical companies, whom it advises on a spectrum of issues. In clients' estimation, the practice repeatedly provides *"sound, personable advice."*

**The Lawyers:** **Frederick Colen** (see p.1724) is *"wonderfully intelligent and practical,"* with the ability to always find *"a simple solution to a messy situation."* Undertaking a mix of litigation, counseling and licensing work, he also focuses on software protection, licensing and enforcement and advising research and development organizations on technology transfer. Philadelphia-based **William McNichol** (see p.1736) is *"a very good attorney and a fine human being."* He handles a variety of patent litigation alongside his counterparts in Reed Smith offices across the country, and over the past year work has included many lawsuits in pharmaceuticals on behalf of organizations such as Medicis Pharmaceutical. He also represents academic research institutes in the USA and abroad, and sits on the advisory board at the Fraunhofer Institute for Molecular Biology. **Gene Tabachnick**'s (see p.1744) strengths lie in his *"straightforward and pragmatic"* attitude. His workload has included a large amount of litigation in the past year; he has represented clients in medical device manufacturing, pharmaceuticals, industrial equipment, healthcare and music publishing in a variety of cases pertaining to copyrights, trademarks and patents. Clients value his *"strategic and accessible"* approach and the fact that *"he looks at everything through the eyes of a litigator."*

**Clients/Work Highlights:** The firm represents companies in a range of industries including technology; pharmaceuticals; telecom; aerospace; medical devices and manufacturing.

### The Webb Law Firm

**The Firm:** Recognized as an expanding practice with *"high integrity,"* this full-service IP firm is now the largest it has ever been, at 30 people. Providing *"a knowledgeable and complete service with reasonable fees,"* it handles all aspects of IP work, including traditional patent and trademarks matters, and boasts an expanding software and Internet transactions dispute practice. It is also developing its international capabilities in protecting clients' rights in foreign patents and trademarks and enforcing those rights abroad.

**The Lawyers:** A highly respected practitioner in the Pittsburgh area, **Richard Byrne** receives acclaim for the *"wonderful practice"* he has built up. His main area of focus is engineering and technology, but he represents patent owners in a variety of transactions and litigation. A growing amount of his time is spent advising clients of the implications of Sarbanes-Oxley compliance as it relates to their IP obligations and business strategy.

**Clients/Work Highlights:** The firm acts for clients ranging from Fortune 100 companies to individual inventors, mainly in chemicals, technology and engineering.

## Other Notable Practitioners

**Kevin Casey** at Stradley Ronon Stevens & Young LLP is *"bright, ambitious and reliable,"* impressing clients with *"understandable and clear communication and a level of service which makes us feel special and important."* Since joining the firm in 2004, this medical devices specialist has been successful in building up the IP practice so that it has added patent prosecution and trademarks work to its existing litigation capabilities. Recent victories include a patent infringement case on behalf of biotech firm Invitrogen. The *"credible and meticulous"* **Paul Beck** of boutique firm Paul A. Beck & Associates, PC is known for the *"quiet and unassuming"* approach he takes to his work. A highly respected name in Pittsburgh IP circles, he handles patent and trademark litigation, copyright and licensing work and has also been appointed to several prestigious posts outside the firm. He is a legal expert on patent matters pending in the federal courts, and advises clients on the legal and administrative issues involved in getting patents through the US PTO. He was assigned by the federal courts in the western district of Pennsylvania to decide motions for summary judgments and patent validity. *"Confident, knowledgeable and cost-effective,"* **Glenn Gundersen** (see p.1729) at Dechert LLP focuses his practice on trademark counseling and transactions for multinational companies, including those in the Fortune 500. An authority on trademark clearance, Gundersen assists companies with in-house IP departments with clearance issues, branding and new trademarks. Widely acknowledged as *"one of the state's best trademark people,"* he impressed clients with his ability to *"get straight to the core issues."* **Robert Lindefjeld** (see p.1734) at Jones Day enjoys a high profile within the state's IP community. His work over the past year includes representing MOSAID Technologies in a dispute over semiconductors against Samsung, and a case pending before the ITC in Washington, DC relating to barcode scanners, in which he is representing Symbol Technologies. At Cohen & Grigsby, PC, **Thomas Wettach** handles substantial IP litigation, while other members of the six-strong team handle patent prosecution and trademark work. A *"smart and competent "* attorney, he recently represented an artist whose work had been infringed by a commercial venture. He also handles overseas matters, with the firm's international scope allowing him to work closely with the European Patent Office. Local clients include Calgon Carbon. Formerly at Woodcock Washburn, newcomer to the tables **Camille Miller** heads up the nascent IP practice at Cozen O'Connor. Forming part of the firm's business law group, the IP practice consists of 15 full-time practitioners and is perceived to be *"growing slowly but surely."* In the past year, Miller represented clients such as Wyeth, Aromark and Celgene in all aspects of trademark and copyright prosecution, opinion and counseling, domain name and privacy rights work and patent litigation. The *"knowledgeable and personable"* **Jordan LaVine** recently joined Flaster Greenberg PC from Akin Gump. He stands out in both prosecution and counseling, and particularly acted for clients in the publishing sector at his previous firm.

# LITIGATION

<table>
<tr><td colspan="2">Litigation: General Commercial</td></tr>
<tr><td colspan="2">Leading Firms</td></tr>
<tr><td>1</td><td>DECHERT LLP Philadelphia</td></tr>
<tr><td>2</td><td>BALLARD SPAHR Philadelphia</td></tr>
<tr><td></td><td>HANGLEY ARONCHICK Philadelphia</td></tr>
<tr><td></td><td>MORGAN, LEWIS & BOCKIUS LLP Philadelphia</td></tr>
<tr><td></td><td>PEPPER HAMILTON LLP Philadelphia</td></tr>
<tr><td>3</td><td>BLANK ROME LLP Philadelphia</td></tr>
<tr><td></td><td>CONRAD O'BRIEN GELLMAN & ROHN Philadelphia</td></tr>
<tr><td></td><td>KIRKPATRICK & LOCKHART Pittsburgh</td></tr>
<tr><td></td><td>REED SMITH LLP Pittsburgh</td></tr>
<tr><td>4</td><td>AKIN GUMP Philadelphia</td></tr>
<tr><td></td><td>BUCHANAN INGERSOLL PC Pittsburgh</td></tr>
<tr><td></td><td>DRINKER BIDDLE & REATH LLP Philadelphia</td></tr>
<tr><td></td><td>DUANE MORRIS LLP Philadelphia</td></tr>
<tr><td></td><td>FOX ROTHSCHILD LLP Philadelphia</td></tr>
<tr><td></td><td>HARKINS CUNNINGHAM LLP Philadelphia</td></tr>
<tr><td></td><td>MONTGOMERY, MCCRACKEN Philadelphia</td></tr>
<tr><td></td><td>SCHNADER HARRISON SEGAL Philadelphia</td></tr>
<tr><td></td><td>THORP REED & ARMSTRONG Pittsburgh</td></tr>
</table>

## Band 1

### Dechert LLP

See firm details p.1752

**The Firm:** Acknowledged to be *"the market leaders,"* the firm received particular recognition from clients for its *"top mass tort and products liability practice."* Recent highlights include the group's representation of Merck in the Vioxx case, and of GlaxoSmithKline in the Baycol litigation. Elsewhere, members of the firm acted as lead trial counsel for Adelphia in a professional negligence and malpractice lawsuit against Deloitte & Touche. Clients were impressed both by the firm's *"amazing resources"* and its array of *"terrific litigators capable of handling highly sophisticated matters."*

**The Lawyers:** *"Top of the profession,"* **Robert Heim** (see p.1730) has a varied practice that includes professional malpractice, antitrust, securities and consumer class action disputes. Known for *"winning lead roles in the big cases,"* he spearheaded the firm's efforts in the Adelphia litigation. Other professional achievements include being recently appointed for a second three-year term to the Judicial Conference of the US Advisory Committee on Civil Rules. **Joseph Tate** (see p.1744) continues to garner the admiration of peers and clients for his combination of *"exceptional technical legal ability and good, aggressive court manner."* Although the bulk of his work is in the antitrust area, he is nonetheless active in commercial litigation. He has recently leapt to the top ranks of white-collar crime specialists through his representation of Lewis Libby in the CIA leak case. The *"superb, thorough and decisive"* **Diane Danoff** (see p.1726) is currently busy representing CSI Industries in the cutting-edge challenge of a judgment rendered in the Dominican Republic, on the grounds that the country's legal system was corrupt at the time. Securities specialist **Steven Feirson** (see p.1727) acted for Safeguard Scientifics in a class action alleging nondisclosure and market manipulation in connection with a senior corporate officer's personal stock trading. He succeeded in obtaining the denial of the plaintiffs' motion for class certification and the award of summary judgment in the defendant's favor. **Fred Magaziner** (see p.1734) has cemented his reputation in the products liability area and is considered *"a delight to work with."* Clients further endorsed his *"wonderfully practical approach"* that *"makes both legal and business sense."* Head of the white-collar department, **David Howard** (see p.1731) represented James Wilson MD PhD in federal, criminal and FDA investigations arising out of the death of a man involved in a clinical experiment. The matter was recently resolved and no charges were filed against Howard's client. Other highlights for him include defending former Bayoil employee Ludmil Dionissiev against allegations that he participated in the scheme to subvert the UN's Oil-for-Food program in Iraq. Fellow white-collar attorney **Stephen Brown** (see p.1724) is also much admired, and recently acted in a criminal case and RICO litigation that settled favorably for his client. Recent arrival from Hangley Aronchick and a newcomer to the rankings, the *"extraordinarily bright"* **Cheryl Krause** (see p.1733) has handled a number of white-collar crime and IP cases in the last year. She was involved in a corruption investigation following the discovery, several years ago, of a wiretap at the mayor of Philadelphia's office.

**Clients/Work Highlights:** The firm represented Phoenix Life Insurance in a case argued before the Pennsylvania Supreme Court involving issues of constitutional importance – namely, whether a case already settled in one state can be retried in a court in another state. Detroit Diesel; Merck; Pfizer; Philadelphia Newspapers; U-Haul International; Pacific Life Insurance and Wyeth are further clients.

## Band 2

### Ballard Spahr Andrews & Ingersoll LLP

See firm details p.1746

**The Firm:** Clients consider this operation *"comparable to the major New York firms,"* and Ballard lawyers have appeared in some of this year's biggest cases, including as co-counsel to Deloitte & Touche in the Adelphia securities litigation. Traditional focus areas include professional malpractice and appellate advocacy, while the demand for preemptive counseling in relation to corporate governance and Sarbanes-Oxley Act issues has grown. The firm further strengthened its already remarkable white-collar crime practice with the addition of former Hangley Aronchick partner Henry Hockeimer. Work highlights include defending private parties and a public official in an investigation of alleged municipal corruption in Philadelphia. Market commentators endorsed the "*smart and vigorous*" courtroom style of the firm's attorneys, coupled with a "*fair and honest approach*," while clients were particularly pleased by Ballard's "*cost-effectiveness*."

**The Lawyers:** Senior statesman **Alan Davis** (see p.1726) is "*everyone's favorite litigator.*" He has focused on securities and appellate matters of late, as well as on counseling. His winning combination of

"*very strong intellectual capabilities, deep experience and nice personal demeanor in court*" is said to seduce clients, opposing counsel and judges. He is also renowned for his white-collar crime practice, although he is currently only working on such issues where they relate to large civil cases. Billed as the "*best criminal defense lawyer in the state,*" **Donald Goldberg** (see p.1729) represents lawyers, doctors, public officials, business persons and prosecutors. This year sees the addition of firm chairman **Arthur Makadon** (see p.1734) to the tables. His practice covers a broad spectrum, including appellate, bankruptcy, corruption, antitrust and securities matters. **Eric Sitarchuk** (see p.1742) has made a name for himself in the field of criminal and white-collar investigations. A former federal prosecutor, he "*knows how to negotiate with government authorities,*" as his success in obtaining immunity for his client in the course of the Enron investigation proves. Another addition to this year's list, the "*extraordinarily talented and thoughtful*" **John Lavelle** (see p.1733) has "*an active and sophisticated products liability practice.*" He is also experienced in mass tort cases, class actions and IP disputes. Sources referred to his "*great analytical mind*" and his "*approachability*" as two defining characteristics. "*Leading white-collar crime defense lawyer*" **Henry Hockeimer** (see p.1730) joined the firm in November 2005. While at his previous firm, Hockeimer represented CACI employee, Steven Stefanowicz, the lead civilian interrogator at the Abu Ghraib prison in Iraq, in a grand jury investigation. No charges were pressed against Stefanowicz. Other major cases include his defense of former senior vice president of Bayer, Martin Petersen, against allegations of price-fixing, and his representation of Robert Feldman, finance chair of John Street's mayoral campaign in Philadelphia, in two federal grand jury investigations.

**Clients/Work Highlights:** Deloitte & Touche; PNC Bank; Jefferson Health System; Hercules and Rite Aid all feature in the firm's client roster.

## Hangley Aronchick Segal & Pudlin

See firm details p.1756

**The Firm:** Clients and competitors continue to view this litigation boutique as a "*preferred choice in many cases.*" Commentators referred to its "*unparalleled ratio of highly talented lawyers,*" who consistently appear in highly sophisticated cases. A diverse range of areas is covered, though healthcare, legal malpractice and pro bono engagements are key focus areas. While the recent departure of Henry Hockeimer and David Wolfsohn to Ballard Spahr is something of a blow, it does not seem to have significantly dented the firm's overall litigation capability.

**The Lawyers:** Competitors respect "*superb litigator and rainmaker*" **William Hangley** (see p.1729) both for his "*strong analytical and strategic abilities*" and for his "*fairness and pleasant personality.*" His recent engagements include representing a major teaching hospital in litigation arising from the breakdown of a joint venture. In a pro bono case, he succeeded in proving that death row inmate Karl Chambers was mentally disabled and therefore should not be

executed. Firm cofounder **Mark Aronchick** (see p.1721) is known as "*a tough litigator.*" Over the past year he has been busy defending companies, both in class actions and grand jury investigations. This year sees the incorporation to *Chambers'* rankings of **Daniel Segal** (see p.1741) and **John Summers** (see p.1743). Segal is currently representing Ron Saphiro, former counsel to the Major League Umpires Association (MLUA), who is facing claims of defamation, tortious interference with the contractual relation between him and the MLUA, and conspiracy. Summers is acting on behalf of Capital Blue Cross in a major civil RICO and breach of contract action filed by over 7,000 doctors and affecting a number of healthcare companies.

**Clients/Work Highlights:** The firm's clientele is varied, ranging from financial institutions to healthcare groups, legal firms and individuals. Among the most significant matters handled by the firm is a case filed against the City of Philadelphia alleging First Amendment violations, in which the team represented a consortium of billboard owners and commercial and noncommercial advertisers. Other highlights include the filing of a $50 million ERISA action against members of Agway's board of directors and other parties.

## Morgan, Lewis & Bockius LLP

See firm details p.1758

**The Firm:** This firm boasts a strong presence in Pennsylvania as well as benefiting from its nationwide reach and approach. Lauded by clients for "*the absolutely top-notch quality*" of its work and for the "*honesty, ethical behavior and class*" of its lawyers, the team acts for a stellar list of corporate clients that includes several major multinational investment banks and financial institutions. Interviewees reserved special praise for the "*unparalleled responsiveness*" of the team.

**The Lawyers:** Clients hailed **Gordon Cooney** (see p.1725) as "*an extremely good communicator with a vast knowledge of law and a creative approach to problems.*" He has successfully led the defense of long-standing client Alcon Laboratories in several matters. Cooney also represented SEI Investments in significant litigation pending in Baltimore concerning late-day trading and market-timing allegations. Interviewees pointed to his ability to "*couch complex issues in terms business people understand*" and to his "*respectful demeanor*" as defining traits. "*Top securities litigator*" **Marc Sonnenfeld** (see p.1742) recently succeeded in obtaining a motion to dismiss all securities claims against three former directors and officers of American Business Financial Services. He successfully argued that the complaint against his client did not satisfy the pleading requirements under the Private Securities Litigation Reform Act (PSLRA). Other engagements include his successful defense of Thermo Lab Systems against claims of false advertising in violation of the Lanham Act. This year sees the entry into the tables of two young white-collar crime attorneys. **John Dodds** (see p.1726) has established a name for himself in the area of white-collar defense, especially in the healthcare and pharmaceutical

sectors. Significant engagements include the representation of AstraZeneca in connection with a federal and state investigation concerning the pricing, marketing and reimbursement of its prostate cancer drug, Zoladex. "*Rising star*" **Michael Holston** (see p.1730) is currently representing two Fortune 50 companies in unrelated criminal investigations by the DOJ and various state attorney generals, relating to allegations of fraud with respect to government contracts.
**Clients/Work Highlights:** Further highlights include representing Pfizer in various average wholesale price litigations. Another case that deserves mention is the nationwide defense of Alcon Laboratories with regard to a product used for Lasik eye surgery. JPMorgan Chase, Lehman Brothers and PwC can also be counted as clients.

## Pepper Hamilton LLP
See firm details p.1760
**The Firm:** The "*business-oriented*" team here is especially well renowned for its counseling work and its ability to settle matters out of court. Clients entrust "*larger, more sophisticated*" issues to the firm because of its "*great trial lawyers.*" The firm's strong securities practice has led to the team advising several clients in SEC investigations. Another of the firm's strengths is in the field of insurance and reinsurance, where the team recently represented a group of policyholders from the automotive industry whose medical insurer went bankrupt. Further areas covered include antitrust and ERISA litigation, along with disputes relating to healthcare services.
**The Lawyers:** Market commentators described **Barbara Mather** (see p.1735) as "*outstanding, insightful and thoughtful,*" and unanimously hailed her as a leader in her field. In addition to offering expansive antitrust experience, she has recently handled a number of professional malpractice cases and defended several companies against securities claims brought by stockholders. Clients appreciate her "*strong analytical skills*" and "*practical approach,*" as well as her ability to "*get to the nub of the matter straight away.*" Securities expert **Robert Hickok** (see p.1730) is "*a terrific lawyer, adept at working alongside government bodies.*" Proof of this is his work on SEC investigations and his involvement in a US Attorney's Office investigation into municipal corruption claims. His broad practice also covers business, insurance, ERISA and criminal litigation. New arrival to the rankings, **Francis Devine** (see p.1726) focuses on insurance disputes but is also active in the areas of professional liability and malpractice, having represented boards of directors in claims brought by stockholders. Sources described Devine as "*a superb strategist*" with "*the ability to conduct very difficult negotiations without creating animosity among his adversaries.*"
**Clients/Work Highlights:** The firm has represented the estate of National American Life Insurance in rehabilitation and insolvency proceedings, with issues relating to reinsurance, asset recovery, commutations, set-off and annuity taxation. On the advisory side, it acted for two Fortune 100 pharmaceutical companies in the restructuring of certain operations, to ensure compliance with fraud and abuse requirements. Other clients include Unisys Savings Plan, Hoechst Celanese and Conrail.

## Band 3

## Blank Rome LLP
See firm details p.1747
**The Firm:** "*Much more litigation-oriented than other big firms,*" Blank Rome is held in high regard for its particularly strong team of insurance litigators. It represented the Insurance Commissioner of the Commonwealth of Pennsylvania as liquidator of Reliance Insurance in all facets of the liquidation process. Other highlights include acting for FMC in a dispute with Solutia in the Southern District Court of New York. At the heart of the dispute is a claim for over $200 million in damages, arising out of the creation of a joint venture concerning the phosphorus businesses of the respective parties. Niche white-collar crime and corporate tax expertise is also on offer.
**The Lawyers:** The "*outstanding*" **Ann Laupheimer** (see p.1733) divides her time between broader complex commercial litigation cases, such as the FMC matter described above, and insurance litigation. She provided ongoing advice to Aetna in its efforts to obtain over $200 million from eight of its insurers.
**Clients/Work Highlights:** The team represents a variety of policyholders in directors' and officers' litigation as well as other professional liability disputes. It also advises both public and private clients on directors' and officers' policy renewals.

## Conrad O'Brien Gellman & Rohn PC
See firm details p.1751
**The Firm:** This prestigious boutique houses "*great lawyers*" with highly specialized practices and a bias in favor of representing law firms in professional malpractice cases. Another strong area of expertise is defamation, where the team has a brilliant track record, and recently became involved in a case affecting Viacom. Clients keep returning to the firm because of its "*extremely smart attorneys,*" who, one source said, "*form a more effective group than any other I ever encountered.*"
**The Lawyers:** **William O'Brien** (see p.1737) is "*famed for his courtroom ability,*" and as a cross-examiner in particular. Defamation cases are considered his true forte, although he also has a solid reputation for general commercial litigation work. His wide-ranging expertise spans environmental and products liability issues. Indeed, he has acted in a swathe of cases concerning asbestos, beryllium, TCE, paint and tobacco. He also offers additional expertise in medical and legal malpractice matters, leaving interviewees in no doubt that, as a senior statesman, O'Brien remains a valuable resource for the firm. **Nancy Gellman**'s (see p.1728) practice is every bit as varied as O'Brien's. She is widely perceived as a "*top name for antitrust,*" but has recently represented a major Philadelphia law firm in a professional malpractice case. Peers admire her "*thoughtfulness*" and her "*poise as an advocate.*" New to this year's list, **James Rohn** (see p.1739) is now an acknowledged leader among Pennsylvania's white-collar crime attorneys, according to sources. He recently acted on behalf of a medical benefits company in highly sensitive matters involving regulatory and enforcement issues. Clients lauded his "*discretion*" and his "*ability to see the big picture,*" qualities that have made him an attorney of choice for companies faced with internal investigations.
**Clients/Work Highlights:** Over the past year, the firm advised a Fortune 100 company on a major internal investigation. It also represented a Fortune 500 chemical company in a case involving claims of natural resources damage. Other typical matters include representing a construction management company seeking over $50 million in an insurance coverage claim, and acting for a chemical sector player in a large antitrust class action.

## Kirkpatrick & Lockhart Nicholson Graham LLP

**The Firm:** This international outfit has a strong presence in Pennsylvania, with more than 150 litigators housed in its Pittsburgh and Harrisburg offices. The team boasts some of the best insurance coverage specialists nationwide, and the firm recently obtained a landmark $1.5 billion insurance coverage settlement in the largest prepackaged bankruptcy case in US history. Lawyers at the firm specializing in this area are likely to sustain heavy workloads in the wake of hurricanes Rita and Katrina. Another significant asset is the firm's strong appellate practice, whose members recently won an appeal on behalf of Ernst & Young, where in excess of $100 million was at stake.

**The Lawyers: David McClenahan** obtained a favorable result on behalf of a healthcare company, claiming its liability insurers should pay a share of a $223 million class action settlement. **Michael Zanic** is regarded by some as "*one of the three or four best insurance coverage lawyers nationwide.*" He was instrumental in obtaining the $1.5 billion insurance coverage settlement described above. On the counseling side, he advised the largest US hospital chain on insurance-related matters.

**Clients/Work Highlights:** The firm represented a group of former partners of one of the largest law firms in Pennsylvania in an arbitration arising from a spin-off operation. Health sector and manufacturing companies make up a significant part of the firm's client roster.

## Reed Smith LLP

See firm details p.1762

**The Firm:** Best known for its mass tort, products liability and white-collar criminal defense practices, this "*leading player*" has recently seen an increase in the volume of work relating to internal investigations in the financial and healthcare sectors. On the products liability front, it successfully defended Wyeth against claims alleging that the laboratory's diet drug had caused heart problems in users. Other highlights include representing Eli Lilly and other manufacturers in a case with more than 100 plaintiffs, who maintained that the pediatric vaccine produced by Eli Lilly had caused their children to become autistic.

**The Lawyers:** "*Excellent trial lawyer*" **Thomas McGough** (see p.1735) has devoted a significant portion of his time over the past year to corporate investigations and white-collar crime defense, where he acted on behalf of mutual funds companies, insurance brokers and healthcare providers. New to this year's tables, **Michael Scott** (see p.1741) acted as the lead lawyer for Wyeth. He is highly regarded for his "*mastery of products liability law*" and for his "*unparalleled skills in the defense of pharmaceutical products.*"

**Clients/Work Highlights:** Further clients include St. Jude Medical; General Dynamics; Volvo Trucks North America; Pharmacia; Pfizer and Medtronic.

## Band 4

### Akin Gump Strauss Hauer & Feld LLP

See firm details p.559

**The Firm:** A "*national powerhouse,*" it is particularly well known in Pennsylvania for its healthcare and securities expertise. The firm continued to represent Independence Blue Cross and Blue Shield in two national class actions centering on RICO claims. On the securities side, the team acted for Deloitte & Touche in a multidistrict proceeding that related to class and derivative claims arising out of the bankruptcy of Fleming Companies. The firm received the endorsement of peers for its "*bright, articulate, persuasive*" attorneys.

**The Lawyers:** The "*extremely sharp and experienced*" **Edward Mannino** (see p.1735) is serving on the defendants' steering committee in the RICO litigation mentioned above. He is also heavily involved in three class actions relating to Allstate. This year sees the incorporation of **David Comerford** (see p.1725) to *Chambers'* tables. He is recognized as a strong securities litigator, and he recently acted for Deloitte & Touche in a securities case resulting from the bankruptcy of finance company, DVI.

**Clients/Work Highlights:** The firm is representing VeriSign with respect to a number of earn-out claims relating to the acquisition of Exault by VeriSign. Other high-profile clients include AmeriHealth HMO; Ross & Hardies; Ernst & Young and Purdue Pharma.

### Buchanan Ingersoll PC

See firm details p.1749

**The Firm:** The firm's three Pennsylvania offices benefit from being part of a substantial nationwide practice. Over the past year, the team has seen a significant increase in high-end work in the areas of antitrust, securities litigation and fraud class actions. A recent highlight is its successful defense of a publicly traded company against breach of contract and fraud claims resulting from an aborted acquisition. Other highlights include representing one of the nation's largest financial institutions in an ongoing RICO action against parties allegedly involved in a scheme to defraud lenders, where in excess of $50 million is at stake.

**The Lawyers:** The "*excellent, smart and tough*" **Howard Scher** (see p.1740) has a broad practice that ranges from antitrust to RICO to securities litigation. Lately, he has been active in a number of securities fraud class actions. New recruit **Bill DeStefano** (see p.1726) has extensive experience dealing with high-profile white-collar cases. During the past year, he won acquittal for investment banker Denis Carlson, after a three-week trial resulting from a two-year FBI investigation into alleged corruption in Philadelphia city government.

**Clients/Work Highlights:** Over the past year, the group succeeded in having a securities class action brought against Stonepath Group dismissed. The firm has also acted for Arkema; BP America; CSX Transportation and Motorola.

### Drinker Biddle & Reath LLP

**The Firm:** With more than 40 commercial litigators in Philadelphia alone, not to mention offices in Washington, Princeton and San Francisco, this firm has the size, reach and experience to attract large clients in high-profile cases. The main areas of work for the team are antitrust, construction, insurance coverage, patents and securities. It also benefits from significant alternative dispute resolution experience.

**The Lawyers: Wilson Brown** is one of the firm's most experienced attorneys.

### Duane Morris LLP

See firm details p.1753

**The Firm:** This national player has a strong presence in Pennsylvania, with around 40 trial lawyers based in Philadelphia. One of the primary focus areas for the team is products liability, where it recently defended the manufacturers of a herbal diet supplement against allegations that the drug had caused health problems in users. Other areas of work include antitrust, insurance coverage, securities and IP disputes. The team is particularly well renowned for its backbone of "*excellent senior lawyers.*"

**The Lawyers: John Soroko** (see p.1742) is chair of the firm's trial practice group and is particularly well regarded as a securities litigator, although he also covers corporate and products liability disputes.

**Clients/Work Highlights:** Wachovia; Delaware Valley Financial Group; Chester County Hospital and Bayer MaterialScience.

### Fox Rothschild LLP

See firm details p.1755

**The Firm:** Fox Rothschild came in for praise for the "*great work ethic*" cultivated by its lawyers, who handle a broad range of business litigation for both plaintiffs and defendants. Over the past year, the team successfully represented Pfizer in the first instance and at appeal, in a suit arising from the acquisition of Pharmacia by Pfizer, and filed by the former employees of the acquired company. Antitrust and libel disputes further contribute to the team's workload.

**The Lawyers:** Highly regarded **Abraham Reich** is a "*terrific*" lawyer who combines his involvement in the Pennsylvania Bar Association with an active and broad-ranging practice.

**Clients/Work Highlights:** Further clients include AAMCO Transmissions; Chubb Insurance; Sallie Mae; JPMorgan Chase and First Data.

### Harkins Cunningham LLP

**The Firm:** This "*quality boutique*" has offices in Washington, DC and New York as well as Philadelphia, and is particularly famed for the ability of its litigators. Its focus on antitrust matters is complemented by involvement in securities class actions, partnerships disputes, mass tort liability cases, trade secrets and RICO civil claims.

**The Lawyers:** "*Superb advocate*" **John Harkins** (see p.1730) continues to elicit the praise of peers and clients alike. The representation of 3M in several antitrust cases has kept him busy over the past year.

**Clients/Work Highlights:** Tyco International;

Aetna; Mitsubishi; Othopedic Associates of Lancaster; IBM; Kodak and Viacom are some of the names on the firm's impressive client portfolio.

## Montgomery, McCracken, Walker & Rhoads, LLP

**The Firm:** Despite a number of defections in recent years, this strong regional player still boasts a robust litigation department, with more than 75 "*savvy*" litigators in its Philadelphia office alone. The team is especially famed for its class action defense work, where it has represented corporations such as Microsoft. Clients appreciate the fact that lawyers at the firm "*take the time to understand the business,*" and that this does not affect the "*reasonable billing,*" as the group is also "*extremely cost-conscious.*"

**The Lawyers:** "*Bright and articulate*" **David Marion** has an excellent reputation for his experience of First Amendment cases and "*great presence*" in the courtroom. White-collar crime specialist **Richard Scheff** enters the tables for the first time this year following consistent market recommendation. Researchers were told that he "*is one of the few white-collar attorneys in town with both the experience and the ability*" to handle tough criminal cases.

## Schnader Harrison Segal & Lewis LLP

**The Firm:** Historically one of the top firms in the area, it continues to deal with complex, high-profile cases. A recent example is the team's involvement as lead trial counsel for the Barnes Foundation, owner of one of the largest private collections of Impressionist paintings in the world, in a case seeking to obtain approval to relocate the foundation's principal gallery. Other highlights include the representation of Conrail in a contractual dispute where $50 million was at stake.

**The Lawyers:** **Dennis Suplee** was recently retained to represent Rohm & Haas in a class action in which employees alleged they developed cancer as a result of being exposed to chemicals in the workplace. Interviewees lauded his "*wonderful skills*" and referred to his experience in handling high-profile cases.

**Clients/Work Highlights:** Additional clients include IFC and Wachovia.

## Thorp Reed & Armstrong

**The Firm:** This midsized outfit with more than 50 litigators in Pennsylvania, the majority of whom are based in Pittsburgh, received particular endorsement for its insurance coverage, securities and bankruptcy practices. The team has also applied its niche professional liability expertise to good effect, and was recently involved in the defense of various legal firms against malpractice allegations.

**The Lawyers:** "*Excellent trial lawyer*" **William Wycoff** is considered "*one of the leading antitrust experts*" in the state. However, his practice is not limited to one field, as proven by his involvement in a growing number of securities and corporate governance matters.

**Clients/Work Highlights:** The group has defended numerous NYSE-listed companies in securities and stockholder class action cases. The firm's client roster is mainly made up of financial institutions, manufacturers, law firms and corporate directive boards.

## Other Notable Practitioners

**Allen Black** of Fine Kaplan & Black RPC was described as a "*wonderful lawyer.*" Although he is best known for his work on behalf of plaintiffs, he is also experienced in acting for defendants, and is "*superbly bright*" to boot. **Albert Bixler** of Eckert Seamans Cherin & Mellott enters the table in recognition of his sterling representation of pharmaceutical corporations in products liability litigation. He is also the member in charge of the firm's Philadelphia office. **Clark Hodgson** of Stradley Ronon Stevens & Young LLP is a highly experienced senior practitioner and, as a leader in the field. Sole practitioner **Creed Black** (see p.1723) is more often than not the first choice among peers for referrals concerning white-collar crime matters. He covers federal court fraud cases relating to securities, banking, tax, government contracts, political corruption and money laundering. These are frequently prosecuted by the DOJ. **Frederick Thieman** of Thieman & Farrell is perceived to excel in white-collar crime contexts, while **William Winning** won his fair share of market commendation, and cochairs the white-collar crime and complex criminal defense practice at Cozen O'Connor. Billed as a "*fine securities lawyer,*" **Michael Coran** of Klehr Harrison Harvey Branzberg Hauer & Ellers LLP is widely recognized for his litigation skills. **Richard Sprague** of Sprague & Sprague is one of the leading trial lawyers in the state with a practice that features both complex civil and criminal matters.

# REAL ESTATE

## Band 1

### Ballard Spahr Andrews & Ingersoll LLP

See firm details p.1746

**The Firm:** Visibility on a national level enhances this firm's reputation for "*all-around, outstanding quality.*" Thanks to the multidisciplinary support on offer, this substantial firm handles real estate work of all types and on any scale. The strengths of key individuals were felt to complement each other well, leading clients to describe the team as a whole as "*strong and formidable in its professionalism.*" It has taken key roles in many of the most significant and high-value real estate and land use transactions in Philadelphia and beyond, and in particular its signature condominium specialty ensures involvement in the major condominium construction and redevelopment projects in downtown Philadelphia. Such projects include the 1,000-unit Waterfront Square, a development of towers along the banks of the Delaware River; a project in the exclusive Rittenhouse neighbourhood; and a luxury high-rise development as part of the Ritz-Carlton project. In the past year, it settled one of the largest tax appeals in the Commonwealth for the Limerick nuclear generating station, and was selected as counsel for a new retail and commercial use town center project in southeastern Pennsylvania. Ongoing work includes the Philadelphia Regional Produce Market, a $150 million public-private joint venture to relocate a distribution facility; the redevelopment of Independence National Historical Park, which includes the controversial development of a new building for the Liberty Bell; and the development of Comcast's new headquarters in Philadelphia. Clients are fervent in their admiration of the firm, not only for its attorneys' legal prowess but also for the firm's involvement in projects that help to shape the community and the city. "*They are lawyers with great vision for their city and pride in its history and future.*" Furthermore, their "*sophisticated*" work is thought by many to be imbued with "*thoughtfulness and care,*" thanks to "*lawyers who can zero in on the issues and aren't afraid to roll up their sleeves and get the job done.*"

**The Lawyers:** At the helm of this "*dream team*" is **Michael Sklaroff** (see p.1742), who is widely credited with being the force behind the practice's "*evolution into a large, terrific department.*" Chair of one of the biggest real estate departments in the country, Sklaroff's management commitments do not appear to be at the expense of his everyday work. He was significantly involved in many of the real estate development projects mentioned above, and is also a key figure in zoning and land use matters, in which he is considered "*the expert.*" Others view him as "*a wonderful lawyer who is well connected and full of integrity.*" **Richard Goldberg's** (see p.1729) expertise in retail and commercial developments has seen him advise on the development of a hotel and convention center in downtown Philadelphia and the fitting of specialist medical buildings in local hospitals and medical centers. In his lending practice he recently represented a mezzanine lender and an apartment owner in financing, acquisition and disposition work. Clients value the fact he can *"think and act like a businessman who understands the business drivers behind a transaction,"* while peers regard him quite simply as *"brilliant."* **Philip Korb**'s (see p.1732) renowned condominium practice was the subject of much praise in this year's research. Recent work includes the high-profile developments mentioned above and he is also involved in the Moravian project, which involves the conversion of Old Original Bookbinder's restaurant, one of Philadelphia's oldest buildings. Market trends such as the influx of so-called 'empty-nesters' into the heart of Philadelphia have boosted Korb's *"accomplished and results-oriented"* practice even further. **Lynn Axelroth** (see p.1721) inspires a great deal of loyalty and confidence among her clients, who regard her as *"gifted in her vision and legal skills and tenacious in her work."* She is advising on an Ohio University project on the public-private development of its main campus, and represents Massachusetts-based HRPT Properties Trust in its leasing work across four states. Much of Axelroth's work involves deal negotiation and she is viewed as *"a dynamo – a spectacular lawyer"* who can *"close deals and find a satisfactory compromise for everyone involved."* Described as *"tremendously skilled technically, and charming in his manner,"* **David Gifford** (see p.1728) represents Comcast on the construction of its new headquarters and has also been involved with the University of Pennsylvania on acquisitions, and luxury home builders Toll Brothers on land acquisitions and joint venture arrangements across the country. *"A true gentleman"* and an *"extremely talented lawyer,"* he is revered for *"the spectacularly good job he does."* Hailed as *"a star of the future"* by clients, *Chambers* newcomer **Tina Makoulian** (see p.1735) debuts in the wake of several recommendations. She has not only *"superb business sense,"* but also a *"practical and detail-oriented"* approach. Makoulian focuses on land use and zoning in addition to mainstream real estate work, and represents a number of developers of hotels, headquarters and other office buildings, and medical, education, and parking facilities.

**Clients/Work Highlights:** SAP; Realen Properties; Korman Commercial Properties; Blue Ridge Real Estate Co; Pitcairn Properties; The Rose Group; The Arden Group; HRPT Properties Trust; Annenberg Center for the Performing Arts; University of Pennsylvania; National Park Service and Independence Visitor Center Corporation.

## Blank Rome LLP

See firm details p.1747

**The Firm:** Strong ties with its New York office enable this firm to take on complex, large-scale work. Collectively a 50-strong, full-service practice, between two of its three offices in the state there is a concentration of *"fine, highly respected lawyers"* in real estate. Increasingly active in residential condominium and conversion projects, it recently put its land use and tax expertise to good effect when assisting a client engaged in using federal US tax credits as a subsidy for the development and conversion of lofts and warehouses into high-end residential units. Last year it represented pension fund and endowment specialist DRA Advisors in acquiring two publicly traded REITs, one of which was valued at $3.5 billion. Other transactions include representing a party in the acquisition of a portion of Philadelphia's Warwick Hotel for condominium conversion, and the representation of a landowner in a sale to Wal-Mart. On the litigation side, it recently represented a client seeking to purchase a $5 million piece of land. A well-established reputation for *"top-end work, great lawyers and an impressive client base"* has assured it a place among the leading firms in Philadelphia. Clients spoke of how they *"come away from working with the firm feeling happy and confident,"* while peer admiration hinged on the fact that *"the lawyers there really do cover the full spectrum of real estate work."*

**The Lawyers:** The venerable and scholarly **Harris Ominsky** (see p.1737) is celebrated not only for his distinguished career as an adviser but also his prolific writing. A well-known figure in the community, his *"keen mind and ability to filter details so that he can solve problems quickly and appropriately"* have impressed clients and contemporaries over a number of years. Former judge **Craig Lord** (see p.1734) represents several REITs, including Pennsylvania Real Estate Investment Trust, on many of their most significant acquisitions. He recently represented an applicant for a gaming license and the acquisition of a piece of ground in Monroe County, and continues to advise the Philadelphia Eagles football team in matters pertaining to its stadium. He is said to have an *"even-tempered and balanced"* manner and *"handles difficult situations with tenacity."* Fellow partner **Julian Rackow** (see p.1739) is portrayed as *"knowledgeable and gentlemanly."* His practice focuses on the booming residential development market, with an emphasis on conversions, condominiums and new constructions. In his clients' estimation, he possesses an ability to *"see the bigger picture"* and *"understands our businesses."* Land use and zoning specialist **Peter Kelsen** (see p.1732) makes an appearance for the first time in this year's tables. Having built a name for himself as an *"effective and knowledgeable"* authority, he advises on the development of offices, shopping centers, hotels, hospitals and other premises.

**Clients/Work Highlights:** The firm acts for REITs, banks and other lending institutions as well as insurers and developers.

## Wolf, Block, Schorr andSolis-Cohen LLP

See firm details p.1764

**The Firm:** A hive of *"bright and brilliant"* people, this firm prompts interviewees to remark on its stellar strengths in all aspects of real estate law. Clients appreciated the lawyers' optimistic disposition: while approaching work with *"responsibility and care,"* *"they really accomplish things rather than making you feel as though there's too much risk involved."* Notable work includes the representation of Liberty Property Trust in its development and lease of the $500 million Comcast Tower. Due for completion in fall 2007, at 700,000 sq ft the tower will be the largest building in Philadelphia and will be leased to five tenants besides Comcast. So-called 'condo-mania' generates substantial work for the team: it has handled the negotiation and documentation for over 20 conversions and constructions in the past year, with no sign of a slowdown forecast. With a head-count of almost 60 lawyers, the real estate department is spread over eight regional offices, with the 35-strong Philadelphia team working alongside its counterparts in New York, New Jersey and Delaware on matters that flow in from across the country. The firm is widely thought of as *"one of the city's finest,"* with a reputation that extends far beyond the city limits.

**The Lawyers:** Clients consistently hail department chair **Herman Fala** (see p.1727) as an outstanding lawyer. Elaborating on his talents, they said he combines *"excellent people skills"* with *"goal and service-oriented enthusiasm."* It is said he is *"never at a loss to find a creative solution,"* that his manner helps to *"expedite resolutions,"* and that an atmosphere of cooperation permeates the whole team as a result. Fala is principal lawyer on the Comcast project, while *"class act"* **Ron Glazer** (see p.1728) represents Liberty Property Trust on the leasing arrangements. The *"preeminent authority in Pennsylvania"* on condominiums, Glazer is said to *"know this area of law better than anyone."* His work over the past year includes a role in the Lanesborough and Locust Walk conversions, both luxury developments. Department cochair and *"fantastic, knowledgeable lawyer"* **James Williams** (see p.1745) is active in negotiating complex financing transactions in addition to his regular real estate transactions. **Henry Miller** (see p.1736) takes a place in *Chambers'* Senior Statesmen category this year as a reflection of the sway he continues to hold over the market. Interviewees repeatedly described him as *"fabulous,"* pointing to his ability to *"guide clients to their business goals and focus on the important issues to achieve the right outcome."*

**Clients/Work Highlights:** Other clients include Deutsche Bank, GE Asset Management and Hilton Hotels.

## Band 2

## Dechert LLP
See firm details p.1752

**The Firm:** Dechert's real estate practice is an adjunct to its corporate and finance practices, for which it has *"a superb national reputation."* It acts for big-name lenders in the area of mezzanine finance, negotiating the finance documents for clients buying subordinated debt in properties, and handles the real estate aspects of the sale and purchase of divisions of various public companies. The Philadelphia real estate group supports not only Dechert's national business, but has handled a selection of international transactions. For instance, it acted recently in Korea on a transaction in which the operations of a semiconductor manufacturer were divided in two, following investment from a private venture capitalist. The firm's well-recognized securitization work has opened up the real estate practice to a wider audience of clients and peers, many of whom believe it to be *"a terrific and substantial group that can handle some of the most complex and sophisticated real estate work around."*

**The Lawyers:** Much of **David Forti**'s (see p.1728) work centers on managing the due diligence and inter-creditor agreement aspects of subordinated debt on behalf of lenders. His approach was described as *"thoughtful and polished,"* and his knowledge was said to be *"encyclopedic."* Clients appreciated the fact he is *"always available and very smart."* As well as running a mortgage and capital markets practice, *"smart and sophisticated"* **Richard Jones** (see p.1731) covers the area of mezzanine debt, acting for clients such as GMAC, and advises clients on securitization and real estate financing at a national level. **Gregory Gosfield**'s (see p.1729) key strengths were felt to be cerebral: he was described as *"one of the most intelligent real estate lawyers around,"* whose talents manifest themselves in *"keen creativity in even the most complex transactions."* Gosfield represents public companies in division purchases and sales and the negotiation and structuring of a variety of real estate activity.

**Clients/Work Highlights:** Standard & Poor's; Ventas; Commerzbank; Pacific Life Insurance; MetLife; Allied Irish Banks; LRP Landesbank Rheinland-Pfalz; LEM Mezzanine; Impact Community Capital and GMAC.

## Morgan, Lewis & Bockius LLP
See firm details p.1758

**The Firm:** Coast-to-coast capability united with *"a tremendous amount of expertise"* allows this 60-lawyer real estate practice to handle a variety of work. It uses its nationwide resources to tackle large-scale, complex matters concerning investment trusts, private equity, corporate development and the general representation of companies in the Fortune 50, 100 and 500. This steady diet of big transactions and its national presence lead to *"great overall continuity and cohesiveness."* Recent work representing sanofi-aventis in the leasing of the pharmaceutical company's North American headquarters has boosted an already sizable life sciences practice, and the firm also works with biotech startups on new facilities and laboratory development deals. The firm's general transactional practice works closely with a number of REITs. Clients approach the Philadelphia practice knowing that it will provide *"the bedrock of the legal advice we seek,"* and are gratified that its lawyers consistently exhibit *"exceptional professional judgment"* that is *"both cost and time-efficient."*

**The Lawyers:** *"True expert"* **JJ Broderick** (see p.1724) undertakes large, complex real estate transactions on a nationwide basis and has a corporate flavor to his work. He recently represented a pharmaceutical company in the sale of 1.4 million sq ft of office space. The perception within the real estate community is that he is *"tremendously customer-responsive"* and *"will do anything he can to make a transaction run as smoothly as possible."* In addition to his role as leader of the firmwide practice group, *"very fine, smart and experienced attorney"* **Eric Stern** (see p.1743) also undertakes complex strategic transactions, a role which has earned him kudos from peers and clients. Recent highlights include a portfolio transfer involving $1 billion of property and real estate, the formation of a new real estate company and the acquisition of a Delaware office campus for a client. As practice manager he is the main point of contact for several clients, many of whom regard him as pivotal to their relationship with the firm, and count upon him to *"coordinate the delivery of response to our real estate needs all over the country."*

Described as a *"real team player,"* **Robert Cooney** (see p.1725) worked extensively on the negotiation agreements for the sanofi-aventis headquarters project, in addition to his regular financing work for real estate startups and joint ventures, and acquisitions for real estate companies. His key skills are his ability to *"see the forest through the trees"* and *"strike the right balance between making decisions on his own and seeking input from others."* His manner combines *"openness and friendliness"* with *"high degrees of integrity and pragmatism."*

**Clients/Work Highlights:** The firm represents corporations such as Cephalon; GMH Communities; Smiths Group; Sunoco and Pfizer, as well as financial institutions and REITs.

## Saul Ewing LLP
See firm details p.1763

**The Firm:** A firm with *"high expectations of itself,"* Saul Ewing's regional mid-Atlantic real estate practice is instilled with an *"honesty and respectability"* that time and again sees it act for prestigious local entities such as the School District of Philadelphia. Alongside the quality of the deals it undertakes, it was the firm's *"philanthropy and community spirit"* that impressed client interviewees. This year the 40-lawyer team represented Philadelphia Shipyard Development in a major site development and construction of several new ships. It worked with Wyeth on the acquisition of over 300 acres of campus and research facilities, and with Pennsylvania Convention Center on the contracting of a $600-$700 million expansion program. Portrayed as *"a firm with a strong local presence and great client appeal,"* the practice is growing steadily and can now count several international companies as clients.

**The Lawyers:** *"A wonderful lawyer and quality human being,"* **Stephen Aichele** (see p.1721) moves up to the top tier in the tables for both mainstream real estate as well as zoning and land use. His work includes a $120 million expansion project for healthcare provider Main Line Health, financing for a new hospital, and working with transportation company CSX on a rail-truck facility in central Pennsylvania. His diverse practice attracts pervasive praise: clients reveal that he is *"smart, articulate and very down-to-earth,"* adding that he is *"technical without coming across too stuffy."* Other commentators say he is *"at the top of his game and is probably one of the most accomplished land use lawyers there is."* Similar praise was likewise accorded to **Frederick Strober** (see p.1743), *"a deal-maker and a gentleman,"* who also ascends *Chambers'* tables this year. His workload consists mainly of construction projects and negotiating contracts for leases, sales and acquisitions. This year he was involved in the construction by the University Hospital of a major new medical facility and the construction by a large school district of its new headquarters in the center of Philadelphia. Clients value his *"straightforwardness and ability to get to the heart of a deal,"* while fellow practitioners are impressed by his client base: *"The fact he represents the School District of Philadelphia is a big responsibility and shows how much respect everyone has for him." Clients consider both Aichele and Strober to be "*a pleasure to do business with.*" Entering the tables for the first time is "*terrifically expert*" **Michael Burg** (see p.1724), who runs the firm's suburban real estate practice out of its Chesterbrook office. He is responsible for securing approvals for office construction, retail property, schools and other suburban establishments, and also handles the concomitant acquisitions, dispositions and leasing. He has been representing UK pharmaceuticals company Shire in its relocation from Kentucky to Philadelphia. Client admiration revolves around his "*sophisticated knowledge and experience on complex projects.*"

**Clients/Work Highlights:** Philadelphia Shipyard Development; Wyeth; AstraZeneca; Shire; Berwind Property Group; CSX; Liberty Property Trust and University of Pennsylvania.

## Band 3

### Drinker Biddle & Reath LLP

**The Firm:** This 50-lawyer real estate team, spread across the region, has close ties with the firm's corporate and finance departments and represents real estate developers and investors in projects of all types and values. It works with clients involved in leveraging finance for real estate projects, whether they are REITs or lenders, and provides advice for businesses on land use issues. The firm is known for its "*conscientious attitude towards helping clients achieve business goals.*"

**The Lawyers:** Cochair of the real estate practice group **Harry Cherken** earns much respect from peers, who say he is "*a marvellous lawyer who understands how to structure a deal.*" His leasing practice in particular drew praise from interviewees impressed by the high profile of his clients. His financing and REIT work also prompted favorable comments. **Rush Haines** enters the tables in recognition of his finance-oriented real estate practice. With experience representing banks on loans and other types of financing, he supervises the foreclosure element of the firm's real estate activities. Haines also represents developers and investors. A new addition to the team, **David Ebby** joins from Hangley Aronchick. His work centers on mortgage financing and leasing, with a recent highlight being the arrangement of a $51 million portfolio loan covering four properties in two states. Observers reported on his "*excellent reputation*" in this area.

**Clients/Work Highlights:** Developers, retailers, investors, banks, landlords and tenants all use the firm's services.

### Hangley Aronchick Segal & Pudlin

See firm details p.1756

**The Firm:** A pool of eight "*very talented people*" makes up this "*small but sophisticated*" real estate practice. It assists clients with acquisitions and developments, financing, leasing, land use and organizational structuring, and has strong connections with state government and local government bodies in the field of urban redevelopment. A well-honed lending practice is also a hallmark. Lawyers were involved in the inception of a plan to build a number of hotels in downtown Philadelphia and have been instrumental in acquiring the land, securing the financing and reaching agreements with franchisers. A reputation for being home to "*high-quality common-sense*" lawyers has helped strengthen the firm's standing within the marketplace this year.

**The Lawyers:** Department chair and **Stuart Ebby** (see p.1727) joins the *Chambers* Senior Statesman category this year, reflecting his long history in the field. Described as "*the quintessential Philadelphia real estate attorney,*" his strengths are those of a "*sensible, practical and reliable*" lawyer who "*understands what's important for business as well as from a legal perspective.*" Ebby serves as expert witness for developers and lenders and also teaches a course in real estate transactions at a local law school. **David Scolnic** (see p.1740) is ranked this year, having established a name for himself as an "*extremely professional and bright*" lawyer whose recent achievements have ensured that he is "*always busy and very popular.*" His two-pronged practice includes the representation of traditional real estate players such as developers, brokers and investors, while also addressing the real estate concerns of companies in various industry sectors. He recently assisted the Oliver Tyrone Pulver Corporation with the leasing of its Conshohocken office space. Well connected politically, Scolnic interacts with state government on urban planning issues – a nexus of which clients approve. Another new addition to the tables is "*talented and efficient*" **Yvonne Clayton** (see p.1724), whose largely finance and lending-oriented practice has attracted a growing fan base. Clayton is much favored for her "*capable and diligent*" demeanor. Senior department member Richard Goldstein also has a significant real estate practice, with work spanning both Pennsylvania and New Jersey.

**Clients/Work Highlights:** United States Cold Storage; Select Medical; Trammell Crow Company; Oliver Tyrone Pulver Corporation; Thomas Properties Group; Thrivent Financial for Lutherans; Jackson National Life Insurance; Subaru of America and Aldi.

### Schnader Harrison Segal & Lewis LLP

**The Firm:** Nine lawyers make up the "*professional yet low-key*" real estate arm of this regional firm. Its true expertise lies in sophisticated financing arrangements for real estate projects, plus sales, leases, lending and workouts on behalf of both publicly and privately held clients. It is representing Internet service providers EarthLink in the Wireless Philadelphia project, a public-private collaboration designed to achieve wireless Internet access across the city by the end of 2006. On the finance side, it represented a syndicate of 15 banks in the negotiation of a $500 million secured credit facility to a publicly held housing developer.

**The Lawyers:** Described by his peers as "*a craftsman and a highly skilled lawyer,*" **Kenneth Rosenberg** masterminds the finance side of the real estate practice and represents banks and other lenders on residential, commercial and retail developments. He undertakes substantial construction financing deals across several states, and for this work he is considered "*a true specialist.*" Rosenberg inspires loyalty among his clients, who appreciate the way "*he just gets things done in a very efficient manner and without a whole lot of bluster.*" As local counsel on the Wireless Philadelphia project, **Marilyn Kutler**'s profile has been strengthened this year. "*A class act,*" she is best known for her ability to "*move complicated matters along effectively.*" Kutler has also worked with local school districts and government units on sales, financing and commercial leasing projects.

**Clients/Work Highlights:** Wachovia; Commerzbank; Firstrust Bank; National City and Liberty Property Trust.

### Other Notable Practitioners

**Carl Primavera** of Klehr Harrison Harvey Branzberg & Ellers LLP has a highly respected zoning and land use practice based in Philadelphia. Alongside regular work such as obtaining permits and approvals for developers in the city, notable work includes representing restaurants and other outlets, such as Starbucks, on zoning and building matters. Primavera is said to be a "*smart and courteous*" attorney who is "*always a pleasure to deal with.*" His network of connections also impressed interviewees, who highlighted his "*close political ties with the city.*" His "*integrity and honesty*" were also held in high esteem.

# Leaders in Pennsylvania

## ABELSON, Barry M
Pepper Hamilton LLP, Philadelphia
215 981 4282
abelsonb@pepperlaw.com
*Recommended in Corporate/M&A*
**Practice Areas:** Partner; Member and Chairman Executive Committee. Experienced in: securities; venture capital; mergers and acquisitions of public and private companies; public and private offerings of equity and debt securities. Represents issuers, underwriters and venture capitalists. Counsels boards of directors, independent board committees and management on governance, disclosure and transactions.
**Prof. Memberships:** Chairman, 2005 Mid-Atlantic Venture Conference; Board of Directors, Greater Philadelphia Venture Group; Children's Crisis Treatment Center; Institute for Law and Economics, University of Pennsylvania; Crohn's & Colitis Foundation, Philadelphia Chapter.
**Career:** JD 1971 University of Pennsylvania Law School; BA 1968 Dartmouth College.

## ABRAMOWITZ, Robert
Morgan, Lewis & Bockius LLP, Philadelphia 215 963 4811
rabramowitz@morganlewis.com
*Recommended in Employment*
**Practice Areas:** Robert L Abramowitz is a Partner in the Employee Benefits and Executive Compensation Practice of Morgan Lewis. His practice involves counseling on all aspects of employee benefits and executive compensation. Mr Abramowitz is a frequent speaker and has published numerous articles. He was a Lecturer in Law in the graduate tax program at Villanova University Law School from 1986-2002.
**Prof. Memberships:** Member, ABA, Tax Section, Employee Benefits Committee. Charter Fellow, American College of Employee Benefits Counsel. Fellow, American College of Tax Counsel.

## AICHELE, Stephen S
Saul Ewing LLP, Philadelphia
215 972 7797
saichele@saul.com
*Recommended in Real Estate*
**Practice Areas:** Mr Aichele has represented developers, property owners and governmental entities in all areas of land use, financing, construction and leasing.
**Prof. Memberships:** Member of the American College of Real Estate Lawyers. Philadelphia Chamber of Commerce's Executive Board and CEO Council for Growth; Adjunct Professor, Temple University School of Law.
**Career:** Past Managing Partner/CEO of Saul Ewing LLP. Over his 25 year career, has represented major developers,

lenders, and governmental entities in land use, zoning, development, financing, construction, and leasing.
**Personal:** JD, Temple University (cum laude), BA, Cornell University.

## ALSTADT, Lynn J
Buchanan Ingersoll PC, Pittsburgh
412 562 1632
alstadtlj@bipc.com
*Recommended in Intellectual Property*
**Practice Areas:** Experienced in all areas of patent, trademark, copyright and unfair competition law including litigation, patent solicitation, licensing, patent interference practice, trademark cancellation and opposition proceedings, International Trade Commission investigations, registration of trademarks and copyrights with the United States Customs Service and related exclusion proceedings. This work involved a wide range of technical subjects including mechanical, electrical, electronic, e-commerce, biotech, chemical, metallurgical and computer fields.
**Prof. Memberships:** Adjunct Professor (Patent Law) University of Pittsburgh, Duquesne University; Practicing Law Institute, Patent Bar Review Course.
**Personal:** BS 1973; JD 1976 University of Pittsburgh.

## ARMSTRONG, Stephen
Montgomery, McCracken, Walker & Rhoads, LLP, Philadelphia 215 772 1500
*Recommended in Antitrust*

## ARONCHICK, Mark Alan
Hangley Aronchick Segal & Pudlin, Philadelphia 215 496 7002
maronchick@hangley.com
*Recommended in Litigation*
**Practice Areas:** Commercial, civil and/or white-collar criminal matters involving intellectual property, healthcare, professional malpractice, banking, financing, accounting, tax, insurance, government fraud, civil rights, unfair trade practices, real estate, and/or regulated industries.
**Prof. Memberships:** Fellow, American College of Trial Lawyers. Member, Judicial Council of the Commonwealth of Pennsylvania. Philadelphia Bar Association: Chancellor, 1998; Member, Board of Governors, 1990-92; Treasurer, 1986-89; Co-Chair, Committee to Elect Qualified Judges, 1993-95; Co-Chair, Trial Advocacy Program, 1987-91; Chair and Member of numerous Bar Association Committees and Task Forces. Philadelphia Bar Foundation: President, 1996; Secretary, 1993; Trustee, 1990; Treasurer, 1986-89. Past Member, House of Delegates, Pennsylvania Bar Association. Member, The Disciplinary Board of the Supreme Court of Pennsylvania. Past Member, Bench Bar

Relations Task Force, United States Court of Appeals for the Third Circuit. Judge Pro Tem, Court of Common Pleas of Philadelphia County. Mediator, United States District Court for the Eastern District of Pennsylvania. Past Chair, Hearing Committee of Disciplinary Board of Supreme Court of Pennsylvania. Member, Civil Rules Committee of Supreme Court of Pennsylvania. Member, Philadelphia Trial Lawyers Association. Member, National Association of Criminal Defense Lawyers.
**Career:** Founder, Shareholder and Board Member, Hangley Aronchick Segal & Pudlin, 1994-present. Shareholder, 1986-94; Executive Committee, 1992-94, Hangley Connolly Epstein Chicco Foxman & Ewing. Partner, 1983-86; associate, 1974-79, Wolf, Block Schorr and Solis-Cohen. City Solicitor, 1983; First Deputy City Solicitor, 1980-82, City of Philadelphia. University of Chicago Law School, JD with highest academic honors, 1974; University of Pennsylvania, BA, cum laude, 1971.

## AXELROTH, Lynn R
Ballard Spahr Andrews & Ingersoll LLP, Philadelphia 215 864 8707
axelroth@ballardspahr.com
*Recommended in Real Estate*
**Practice Areas:** Represents corporate, institutional, developer, individual and public owners, public/private joint venturers, lenders, prime and trade contractors and design professionals, in all aspects of the negotiation and documentation of real estate development, structuring, and implementing complex public/private transactions, construction, turnkey, design and design-build contracts, financing, tax assessment, sale and leasing of real estate, and alternative dispute resolution.
**Prof. Memberships:** Fellow of the American College of Real Estate Lawyer and American College of Construction Lawyers. First Chair and Founding Member of Division of Owners and Lenders of the ABA Forum on the Construction Industry, and Member, Governing Committee. Vice-Chair and then Co-Chair, ABA Real Property Section Committee on Construction Lending (1997-2002). Chair of the Board, Independence Visitor Center Corporation; Member, Executive Committee of The Board of Overseers of the Annenberg Center for the Performing Arts of the University of Pennsylvania; International Association of Attorneys and Executives in Corporate Real Estate; and Women's Leadership Committee of Moore College of Art.
**Career:** Admitted to Pennsylvania Bar (1983); joined firm (1985); Partner (1991); Managing Partner, Philadelphia

office, 1998-2005.
**Publications:** Lectures extensively on and author of publications on development, construction and financing issues, including: editor, Journal of the American College of Construction Lawyers; the chapters on Owners' and Lenders' Issues in the 2005 book for C-Level business executives, 'Inside the Minds: Legal Strategies for the Construction Industry' and the 2001 book 'Fundamentals of Construction Law.' Articles include: 'The Ten Top Issues in Negotiating AIA Contracts' (2005); 'How Construction Lawyers Can Learn to Stop Worrying and Love Public/Private Projects' (2005); 'Understanding the AIA Documents' (2000, 2001, and 2002); 'Construction Owner's Concerns in Construction Loan Agreements' (2000); and 'The New AIA Construction Documents from Owner and Lender Perspectives' (1999).
**Personal:** JD, cum laude, University of Pennsylvania (1983); editor, University of Pennsylvania Law Review; BA, summa cum laude, Temple University (1977); Phi Beta Kappa, President's Scholar.

## BABST, Chester
Babst, Calland, Clements and Zomnir, A Professional Corporation, Pittsburgh
412 394 5400
*Recommended in Environment*

## BANKS, Michael L
Morgan, Lewis & Bockius LLP, Philadelphia 215 963 5387
mbanks@morganlewis.com
*Recommended in Employment*
**Practice Areas:** Michael L Banks is a Partner in the Labor and Employment Practice. Mr Banks has litigated employment and benefits issues in state and federal courts, and has provided representation and advice on wrongful discharge, employment contracts, sexual harassment, discrimination, severance agreements, non-competition and trade secret protections, pension and benefit matters, reductions in force, union activity and a variety of other employment matters.
**Prof. Memberships:** Active in and civic organizations, Mr Banks is a past President of the Board of Directors of the Support Center for Child Advocates, which provides pro bono advocacy on behalf of abused and neglected children, and a Member of the Board of Directors of Need-in-Deed, a service learning organization. Mr Banks was the 2004 recipient of the American Bar Association's Frances Perkins Award for pro bono service, which was given to him based on his successful representation of a death row inmate in Louisiana who was ultimately granted a new trial and exonerated.

## BARNETT, Bonnie Allyn
Drinker Biddle & Reath LLP,
Philadelphia 215 988 2700
*Recommended in Environment*

## BARSON, Leon
Adelman Lavine Gold and Levin,
Philadelphia 215 568 7515
*Recommended in Bankruptcy*

## BECK, Paul
Paul A. Beck & Associates, P.C.,
Pittsburgh 412 343 9700
*Recommended in Intellectual Property*

## BELISARIO, Martin G
Akin Gump Strauss Hauer & Feld LLP,
Philadelphia 215 965 1303
mbelisario@akingump.com
*Recommended in Intellectual Property*
**Practice Areas:** Martin Belisario practices intellectual property and technology law, including representation before the United States Patent and Trademark Office and foreign patent offices, technology licensing, portfolio counseling and litigation. He heads the Patent Prosecution practice at Akin Gump. His practice focuses primarily on the mechanical and electrical arts. His experience includes litigating patent disputes, providing opinions on patent infringement and validity, and supervising prosecution of both US and foreign patents for large high-technology portfolios.
**Prof. Memberships:** Pennsylvania Bar Association; Philadelphia Intellectual Property Law Association; Pennsylvania Bar.
**Personal:** BSME, Drexel University; JD, Widener University School of Law.

## BERGER, Lawrence H
Morgan, Lewis & Bockius LLP,
Philadelphia 215 963 5480
lberger@morganlewis.com
*Recommended in Banking & Finance*
**Practice Areas:** Lawrence Berger is a Partner in the Business and Finance Practice. Mr Berger's practice focuses on representing business organizations, particularly private companies, financial institutions and healthcare companies, in a variety of transactional and regulatory matters involving corporate finance, acquisitions and complex contracts. Mr Berger also frequently advises a number of nonprofit organizations, including museums and educational institutions, in connection with their business affairs and governance matters.
**Prof. Memberships:** Pennsylvania Bar Association (Steering Committee on Legal Opinions and Member of Task Force on Business Corporation Law); American Bar Association (Model Nonprofit Corporation Act Committee); American Bar Foundation (Elected Fellow).

## BERGÈRE, Timothy
Montgomery, McCracken, Walker &
Rhoads, LLP, Philadelphia 215 772 1500
*Recommended in Environment*

## BERKOWITZ, Alan D
Dechert LLP, Philadelphia 215 994 2170
alan.berkowitz@dechert.com
*Recommended in Employment*
**Practice Areas:** Mr Berkowitz, Partner, chairs Dechert's Labor and Employment Group. He represents employers in employment discrimination litigation and has experience with unfair labor practice proceedings before the NLRB.
**Career:** Adjunct Law Professor, University of Pennsylvania Law School, 1982-95; instructor, The Wharton School and Rutgers University School of Law.
**Publications:** Author of treatise on Pennsylvania Employment Law; co-author, 'The Landrum-Griffin Act: Twenty Years of Federal Protection of Union Members' Rights' and 'The NLRB and Secondary Boycotts'.
**Personal:** Cornell University (BS, 1977); University of Pennsylvania Law School (JD, summa cum laude, 1980), first in class, member of Law Review.

## BERNARD, John M
Ballard Spahr Andrews & Ingersoll LLP,
Philadelphia 215 864 8408
bernard@ballardspahr.com
*Recommended in Employment*
**Practice Areas:** Focuses on employee benefits law, including qualified retirement plans, stock option plans, executive and deferred compensation arrangements, and healthcare, severance, and other welfare benefit plans. Extensive background in tax, labor, and securities law. Worked closely with the US Department of Labor (DOL) and Pension Benefit Guaranty Corporation (PBGC) to prepare training materials and conduct training programs for enforcement officers and staff of both agencies.
**Prof. Memberships:** Member, American Bar Association, Pennsylvania Bar Association, and Philadelphia Bar Association, American Bar Association Tax Section, Committee on Employee Benefits. Chair, Employee Benefits Committee of the Philadelphia Bar Association Tax Section. Board of Directors, PENJERDEL Employee Benefits and Compensation Association.
**Career:** Admitted to Pennsylvania Bar (1967); joined as Partner (1986). Teaches and lectures on qualified plans, executive compensation, and welfare benefit programs. Instructor at: University of Pennsylvania, Wharton School MBA Program, Aresty Institute of Executive Education; Temple University LLM Tax Program; Villanova University LLM Tax Program; the Philadelphia Academy for Employee Benefits Training; and the now defunct Institute for Employee Benefits Training.
**Personal:** BA, Swarthmore College (1963); LLB, Harvard University (1967).

## BERNSTEIN, Alan
Caesar, Rivise, Bernstein, Cohen &
Pokotilow Ltd, Philadelphia
215 567 2010
ahbernstein@crbcp.com
*Recommended in Intellectual Property*
**Practice Areas:** Alan has been with the firm since 1959 and is a Partner/shareholder. Prior to joining the firm, he was an examiner in the United States Patent & Trademark Office from 1955-59. Alan's practice consists of all aspects of Intellectual Property law, with particular emphasis in litigation in the chemical, pharmaceutical and biotechnology fields and in chemical and pharmaceutical patent application preparation and prosecution. Alan is Member of the Bars of the US Supreme Court, the Commonwealth of Pennsylvania and the District of Columbia including related federal courts. He is also registered to practice before the United States Patent and Trademark Office.
**Career:** Admitted to practice in 1959, Commonwealth of Pennsylvania; 1960, US Supreme Court; 1962, US Court of Appeals for the Federal Circuit; registered to practice before the US Patent and Trademark Office; Adjunct Professor at Temple Law School teaching patent litigation and Member of Advisory Committee of BNA's weekly Patent, Trademark and Copyright Reports. He has been a co-planner and speaker at continuing legal education seminars sponsored by the Pennsylvania Bar Institute. Alan served as a Member of the Board of Trustees of Pop Warner Little Scholars, Inc. and the Jewish Employment and Vocational Service.
**Personal:** Born November 18, 1932, Drexel University (BchE); George Washington University Law School, Law Review (JD with honors, 1959).

## BERNSTEIN, Leonard A
Reed Smith LLP, Philadelphia
215 851 8143
lbernstein@reedsmith.com
*Recommended in Banking & Finance*
**Practice Areas:** Represents banks, thrifts, mortgage bankers and finance companies, providing consumer credit compliance advice on federal, Pennsylvania and New Jersey laws and regulations. Member of Executive Committee and Management Committee. Founder and Chair of the firm's Financial Services Regulatory Group.
**Prof. Memberships:** Founder, New Jersey State Bar Association's Consumer Finance Committee; past Chair, New Jersey State Bar Association's Banking Law Section
**Publications:** Written numerous articles about consumer finance for the 'New Jersey Lawyer,' the 'New Jersey Law Journal,' and other publications.
**Personal:** Temple University School of Law (JD, 1983); University of Pennsylvania (BA, BS, 1980)

## BEVAN III, William
Reed Smith LLP, Pittsburgh
412 288 3184
wbevan@reedsmith.com
*Recommended in Employment*
**Practice Areas:** Practicing labor law for 35 years, a full range of general labor and employment representation on behalf of employers, emphasizing matters concerning the National Labor Relations Act as administered by NLRB. Provides immigration advice and counsels concerning the hiring, antidiscrimination and verification provisions of US immigration law.
**Prof. Memberships:** Labor and Employment Law Section, ABA; Fellow in the College of Labor and Employment Lawyers.
**Career:** Attorney with the NLRB prior to Reed Smith.
**Publications:** Contributor to 'The Developing Labor Law'.
**Personal:** University of Kansas (JD, 1970); Kansas State University (1967); listed in The Best Lawyers in America.

## BIRON, Thomas E
Blank Rome LLP, Philadelphia
215 569 5562
biron@BlankRome.com
*Recommended in Bankruptcy*
**Practice Areas:** Business reorganization and bankruptcy. Broad experience in restructuring and liquidation matters, strategic transactions and litigation. During the past year has handled and counseled on debt and equity restructurings, deleveraging, fraudulent conveyances, equitable subordination, substantive consolidation, preferences, creditors' rights and remedies, solving mass and toxic tort problems and successor liability, and mergers, acquisitions and combinations. Clients include businesses in distress, creditors' committees, bondholders, indenture trustees, boards of directors, business acquirers and insurers.
**Prof. Memberships:** American Bankruptcy Institute; American Bar Association, Corporation, Banking and Business Law, Litigation and International Sections; Association of Commercial Finance Attorneys; Philadelphia Bar Association, Business Law Section, Bankruptcy and Professional Ethics Committees; The District of Columbia Bar; New Jersey Bar Association.
**Career:** Partner at Blank Rome LLP since 1984; Admitted Pennsylvania, New Jersey and District of Columbia.
**Publications:** Co-author, 'Penn Central Diary,' The Philadelphia Lawyer, Vol. 10, No. 2, July, 1973; contributor, 'Team Loan Handbook,' Committee on Developments in Business Financing of the Section of Corporation, Banking and Business Law, American Bar Association, 1983. He has lectured before and presented educational programs to many industry organizations, including the American Bar

Association and the Turnaround Management Association.
**Personal:** JD, 1972, and BA, 1968, Temple University.

### BISSOON, Cathy
Reed Smith LLP, Pittsburgh
412 288 3268
cbissoon@reedsmith.com
*Recommended in Employment*
**Practice Areas:** Employment discrimination and harassment litigation, counseling and training clients concerning compliance with state and federal laws.
**Career:** Law clerk to the Honorable Gary L Lancaster, US District Court for the Western District of Pennsylvania.
**Publications:** Former editor, Reed Smith's 'Employment Law Review'; authored 'Ten Employment Law Tips for the New and Not-So-New Business', The Practical Lawyer.
**Personal:** Harvard University (JD, 1993); Alfred University (BA, 1990); Reed Smith's Director of Diversity; in 2002, named one of 'Pennsylvania Law Weekly's' top 50 lawyers in Pennsylvania under 40; member of Lawyers Advisory Committee, Judicial Council of the Third Judicial Court.

### BIXLER, Albert
Eckert Seamans Cherin & Mellott,
Philadelphia 215 851 8400
*Recommended in Litigation*

### BIZAR, Steven E
Buchanan Ingersoll PC, Philadelphia
215 665 3826
bizarese@bipc.com
*Recommended in Antitrust*
**Practice Areas:** Handles complex business disputes and trials in federal and state courts and before arbitration panels throughout the country. He represents clients in government antitrust and securities fraud investigations and enforcement proceedings and before administrative agencies and self-regulatory organizations, like the NASD or NYSE. He has broad experience in the defense and trial of multi-district class actions, including alleged cartel cases.
**Prof. Memberships:** Board Member, Anti-Defamation League; Vice-Chair, Federal Courts Committee, Philadelphia Bar Association, Columbia Law School Alumni Association; Lawyers' Club of Philadelphia.
**Personal:** JD Columbia University, 1988; BA, 1984 (summa cum laude); MA, 1987 Brandeis University.

### BLACK, Allen
Fine, Kaplan and Black, RPC,
Philadelphia 215 567 6565
*Recommended in Antitrust, Litigation*

### BLACK, JR, Creed C
Creed C Black Jnr - Sole Practitioner,
Philadelphia 215 564 4060
ccb@creedblack.com
*Recommended in Litigation*
**Practice Areas:** White-collar crime: investigations, grand juries, trials, appeals, ancillary civil and agency proceedings, internal investigations, corporate compliance, SEC enforcement. Defense of antitrust, healthcare fraud, tax evasion, securities fraud, insider trading, RICO, false claims, obstruction of justice, false statements, other fraud (mail, wire, bank, insurance, bankruptcy).
**Prof. Memberships:** National Association of Criminal Defense Lawyers; Pennsylvania Association of Criminal Defense Lawyers; ABA; Philadelphia Bar Association; Federal Bar Association.
**Career:** Federal law clerk (1976-77); US Department of Justice, Criminal Division (1977-82); Ballard Spahr Andrews & Ingersoll (litigation Partner, 1985-96); sole practitioner, 1996-.
**Personal:** University of Pennsylvania (JD, 1976); Yale University (BA, 1973); Order of the Coif.

### BLOOM, Michael
Morgan, Lewis & Bockius LLP,
Philadelphia 215 963 5032
mbloom@morganlewis.com
*Recommended in Bankruptcy*
**Practice Areas:** Michael A Bloom, a Partner in the Business and Finance Practice, has handled major Chapter 11 proceedings and out-of-court restructurings throughout the United States. Mr Bloom has served as counsel to the leading four distributors of pre-packaged music in a variety of significant out-of-court restructurings of music specialty retailers and wholesalers. He also has represented the major film studio distributors of home video products in similar restructurings and Chapter 11 cases.
**Prof. Memberships:** The American College of Bankruptcy (Fellow); American Bankruptcy Institute; Pennsylvania Bar Association (immediate past Chairman, Judicial Evaluation Commission); Eastern District of Pennsylvania Bankruptcy Conference (former Chair).

### BLOOM, Myron A
Hangley Aronchick Segal & Pudlin,
Philadelphia 215 496 7005
mbloom@hangley.com
*Recommended in Bankruptcy*
**Practice Areas:** Corporate reorganization, bankruptcy and creditors' rights. Primarily represents debtors, creditors and committees under chapter 11 of the Bankruptcy Code. Clients include manufacturers, hospitals, nursing homes, retailers, real estate developers, mortgage originators/servicers and all levels of government. Extensive experience in workouts and out-of-court debt restructurings, including asset sales and refinancings.

Founder and Chair of the firm's Bankruptcy Group.
**Prof. Memberships:** Board, Consumer Bankruptcy Assistance Project. Member, American Bankruptcy Institute.
**Career:** Founding Shareholder, Hangley Aronchick Segal & Pudlin, 1994-present. Shareholder, Hangley Connolly Epstein Chicco Foxman & Ewing, 1992-94. Partner and associate, Adelman Lavine Gold and Levin, 1981-92. Associate, Wolf, Block, Schorr and Solis-Cohen, 1978-80. Enforcement Attorney, United States Environmental Protection Agency, 1976-78. Law clerk to the Honorable Daniel J Snyder, Jr, United States District Court, Western District of Pennsylvania, 1974-76. Research assistant, Commission on the Bankruptcy Laws of the United States, 1972-73. JD (with honors), George Washington University, 1974. Notes and comments editor (1973) and senior editor (1974), 'The Journal of International Law and Economics'. BA, Hamilton College, 1970.
**Publications:** Columnist for 'The Legal Intelligencer' and frequent speaker at conferences.

### BLUEDORN II, Donald
Babst, Calland, Clements and Zomnir,
A Professional Corporation, Pittsburgh
412 394 5400
*Recommended in Environment*

### BLUME, Fred
Blank Rome LLP, Philadelphia
215 569 5512
blume@BlankRome.com
*Recommended in Corporate/M&A*
**Practice Areas:** Mr Blume concentrates his practice in the general corporate area, representing companies engaged in mergers, acquisitions, and divestitures. Additionally, he has extensive experience in representing publicly held, family owned, and closely held companies.
**Prof. Memberships:** Admitted in Pennsylvania, Florida, and New York; Member of the Philadelphia Bar Association, Pennsylvania Bar Association, Florida Bar Association, New York Bar Association, and American Bar Association.
**Career:** Managing Partner and CEO of Blank Rome LLP; Member of the Order of the Coif.
**Personal:** Graduated University of Pennsylvania Law School; Board Member of the Greater Philadelphia Chamber of Commerce, Temple University Fox School of Business & Management, City Year, Greater Philadelphia Film Office, and the National Museum of American Jewish History.

### BOGDONOFF, Michael A
Dechert LLP, Philadelphia
215 994 2891
michael.bogdonoff@dechert.com
*Recommended in Environment*
**Practice Areas:** Mr Bogdonoff is a Partner who focuses on environmental and

mass tort litigation. He advises clients in Superfund proceedings, cost-recovery matters, and Clean Water enforcement and appeals. His Tort Practice includes complex liability and medical causation issues, multi-jurisdiction case management, and large-scale electronic and hard copy document production.
**Prof. Memberships:** Member, Pennsylvania and New Jersey Bars; admitted to practice before numerous federal courts.
**Publications:** Frequent lecturer and panelist on environmental issues; Adjunct Professor of environmental litigation, Rutgers School of Law, Camden.
**Personal:** Rutgers College, BA, 1980; Rutgers University School of Law, Camden, JD, with honors, 1983.

### BOLSTEIN, Joel
Fox Rothschild LLP, Warrendale
215 345 7500
*Recommended in Environment*

### BOOKER, Daniel I
Reed Smith LLP, Pittsburgh
412 288 3132
dbooker@reedsmith.com
*Recommended in Antitrust*
**Practice Areas:** Antitrust and trade regulation practice includes counseling and litigation in mergers, acquisitions, price-fixing, distributor relations, advertising, labor/antitrust, consumer banking, monopolization, and franchising. Reed Smith Managing Partner, 1991-2000.
**Prof. Memberships:** Pennsylvania and DC Bars; Member of the Allegheny County Democratic Committee.
**Career:** Trial attorney in the Antitrust Division of the Department of Justice, 1973-77.
**Publications:** Author of articles on trade regulation law, litigation.
**Personal:** University of Chicago Law School (JD, 1971); University of Pittsburgh (1968); listed in The Best Lawyers in America for commercial litigation and corporate law; Chairman of Pittsburgh Regional Alliance.

### BOOTH, Rebecca L
Morgan, Lewis & Bockius LLP,
Philadelphia 215 963 5690
rbooth@morganlewis.com
*Recommended in Bankruptcy*
**Practice Areas:** Rebecca L Booth's practice focuses on corporate bankruptcy, restructuring and other insolvency-related matters. Ms Booth has been involved in the representation of debtors, lenders, formal and informal committees, and other significant parties in large bankruptcy cases.
**Prof. Memberships:** Ms Booth is a Member of the American Bar Association, the Delaware State Bar Association, the American Bankruptcy Institute, the International Women's Insolvency and Restructuring Confederation, and the Delaware Bankruptcy American Inn of Court.

**BOSSERT, Terry**
Post & Schell, P.C., Harrisburg
717 731 1970
*Recommended in Environment*

**BRAEMER, Richard J**
Ballard Spahr Andrews & Ingersoll LLP,
Philadelphia 215 864 8899
braemer@ballardspahr.com
*Recommended in Corporate/M&A*
**Practice Areas:** Focuses on mergers and acquisitions, representing both sellers and buyers, corporate and real estate financings, corporate restructurings, venture capital investments, joint ventures, corporate governance, and executive compensation.
**Prof. Memberships:** Chairman of the Board of a Philadelphia-based, non-profit healthcare network; former President of a childcare agency; oversaw its merger with a family service agency. Director of Toll Brothers, Inc., a NYSE-listed homebuilder; served on the boards of both public and private corporations.
**Career:** Admitted to the Pennsylvania Bar (1966); joined as Partner (1994).
**Personal:** LLB, cum laude, Yale University (1965); BA, magna cum laude, Amherst College (1962).

**BRANZBURG, Morton**
Klehr Harrison Harvey Branzberg & Ellers LLP, Philadelphia 215 568 6060
*Recommended in Bankruptcy*

**BRODERICK, JJ**
Morgan, Lewis & Bockius LLP,
Philadelphia 215 963 5104
jbroderick@morganlewis.com
*Recommended in Real Estate*
**Practice Areas:** JJ Broderick is a Partner in the Real Estate Group. Mr Broderick is also Head of the Corporate Real Estate Practice. He has extensive experience in representing investment banks, commercial banks, insurance companies and other financial institutions in real estate capital markets, senior living real estate, real estate development and real estate workout/bankruptcy. Mr Broderick also has significant experience in representing developers, owners, operators, investors and users in all aspects of real estate including land acquisition, finance, construction, leasing and sales. He has represented real estate lenders and borrowers in complex workouts and real estate creditors and debtors in bankruptcy.

**BRONSON, Jill**
Drinker Biddle & Reath LLP,
Philadelphia 215 988 2700
*Recommended in Banking & Finance*

**BROOMAN, David**
Drinker Biddle & Reath LLP, Berwyn
610 993 2200
*Recommended in Environment*

**BROWN, James**
Cohen & Grigsby PC, Pittsburgh
800 394 4904
*Recommended in Employment*

**BROWN, Stephen D**
Dechert LLP, Philadelphia 215 994 2240
stephen.brown@dechert.com
*Recommended in Antitrust, Litigation*
**Practice Areas:** Mr Brown is an Antitrust Partner and former Chair of the White-Collar Litigation Group. He has experience with internal investigations and criminal and civil antitrust, fraud, RICO, and environmental cases.
**Prof. Memberships:** Member, Pennsylvania Bar; admitted to practice before several federal courts; Co-Chair, Prisoner Civil Rights Panel of the US District Court, Eastern District of Pennsylvania.
**Career:** Law clerk, Hon Daniel H Huyett, III, US District Court, Eastern District of Pennsylvania.
**Personal:** Williams College (BA, 1971); Villanova University School of Law (JD, 1976), Member and Editor-in-Chief of Villanova University Law Review, Member of Order of the Coif.

**BURG, Michael S**
Saul Ewing LLP, Wayne 610 251 5750
mburg@saul.com
*Recommended in Real Estate*
**Practice Areas:** Mr Burg is Vice-Chair of Saul Ewing's Real Estate Department and represents developers, landlords, and tenants in all areas of real estate law, including the development approval process, financing, acquisitions and dispositions, leasing, construction, and tax planning.
**Prof. Memberships:** Former Member, Board of Directors, Independence Blue Cross.
**Career:** Prior to joining Saul Ewing, Mr Burg was the President of a Philadelphia real estate investment firm which acquired and managed properties in the Philadelphia area.
**Personal:** LLM, Villanova University School of Law, JD, Villanova University School of Law (cum laude), BA, Pennsylvania State University.

**BUSIS, Richard**
Cozen O'Connor, Philadelphia
215 665 2000
*Recommended in Corporate/M&A*

**BUZZELL, David**
Drinker Biddle & Reath LLP, Berwyn
610 993 2200
*Recommended in Environment*

**BYRNE, Richard**
The Webb Law Firm, Pittsburgh
412 471 8815
*Recommended in Intellectual Property*

**CALLAND, Dean**
Babst, Calland, Clements and Zomnir,
A Professional Corporation, Pittsburgh
412 394 5400
*Recommended in Environment*

**CAMPBELL, Douglas**
Campbell & Levine, Pittsburgh
412 261 0310
*Recommended in Bankruptcy*

**CARBINO, Jeffrey M**
Klett Rooney Lieber & Schorling,
Philadelphia 215 567 7631
jmcarbino@klettrooney.com
*Recommended in Bankruptcy*
**Practice Areas:** Bankruptcy, insolvency and creditors and debtors' rights.
**Prof. Memberships:** American Bar Association's Business Bankruptcy Committee; Pennsylvania Bar Association's Business Bankruptcy Committee; Eastern District of Pennsylvania Bankruptcy Conference.
**Career:** Admitted to practice in Delaware, New Jersey, Pennsylvania and Tennessee.
**Personal:** BS, State University of New York at Oneonta; JD (cum laude), Widener University School of Law.

**CASEY, Kevin**
Stradley Ronon Stevens & Young LLP,
Philadelphia 215 564 8000
*Recommended in Intellectual Property*

**CASSIDY, Bart**
Manko, Gold, Katcher & Fox LLP, Bala
Cynwyd 484 430 5700
*Recommended in Environment*

**CHERKEN, Harry**
Drinker Biddle & Reath LLP, Philadelphia
215 988 2700
*Recommended in Real Estate*

**CLARK, Peter**
Reed Smith LLP, Philadelphia
215 851 8142
pclark@reedsmith.com
*Recommended in Bankruptcy*
**Practice Areas:** Head of Corporate Restructuring and Bankruptcy Group. Represents lenders, private equity funds, hedge funds, mutual funds, venture capital companies, insurance companies, indenture trustees, investors, and committees of creditors in all aspects of workouts, restructurings, and reorganizations of financially distressed companies.
**Prof. Memberships:** Chair of the Loan Workouts Committee, Business Law Section, ABA; Editorial Advisory Board of the 'Journal of Corporate Renewal'; Turnaround Management Association; American Bankruptcy Institute
**Personal:** Washington University School of Law (JD, 1982); Duke University (1979). Holds AV (highest rating level) by 'Martindale-Hubbell' for skill and integrity. Included in 'Who's Who in American Law.'

**CLAYTON, Yvonne Lee**
Hangley Aronchick Segal & Pudlin,
Philadelphia 215 496 7058
yclayton@hangley.com
*Recommended in Real Estate*
**Practice Areas:** Ms Clayton's practice includes the acquisition, financing and transfer of commercial properties, the leasing of commercial and office properties, and the development of commercial and office buildings.
**Prof. Memberships:** American Bar

Association, Pennsylvania Bar Association, Philadelphia Bar Association.
**Career:** Shareholder, Hangley Aronchick Segal & Pudlin, 2000-present; associate, Hangley Aronchick Segal & Pudlin, 1997-99; associate, Morgan Lewis & Bockius, 1995-97; associate, Stroock & Stroock & Lavan, 1992-95. Columbia Law School, JD, 1992; University of Pennsylvania, BA, 1989.

**COHEN, Abbi L**
Dechert LLP, Philadelphia 215 994 2352
abbi.cohen@dechert.com
*Recommended in Environment*
**Practice Areas:** Ms Cohen, Partner, evaluates environmental liabilities concerning corporate, real estate, and financing transactions. She advises on state and federal permitting and regulatory compliance.
**Prof. Memberships:** Member, Pennsylvania Bar; Chair, Mortgage Bankers Association's Appropriate Inquiry Task Force and Co-Chair of its Environmental Insurance Task Force; Member of environmental advisory boards for 'BNA Due Diligence Guide', Real Estate Roundtable, and national environmental consulting firm; member of various real estate, energy, and environmental organizations; participated in EPA's negotiated rulemaking on All Appropriate Inquiry rule.
**Personal:** Barnard College (BA, high honors, 1980); University of Pennsylvania Law School (JD, 1983).

**COHEN, Stanley H**
Caesar, Rivise, Bernstein, Cohen &
Pokotilow Ltd, Philadelphia
215 567 2010
scohen@crbcp.com
*Recommended in Intellectual Property*
**Practice Areas:** Handles all areas of patent, trademark and copyright litigation, counseling, validity and opinion studies, prosecution and licensing. Has technical expertise in chemical engineering and chemistry. Has litigated over 200 cases in Federal District Courts, with more than 50 reported opinions arising from this litigation.
**Prof. Memberships:** Admitted to practice in 1961, Commonwealth of Pennsylvania; 1966, US Supreme Court; 1982, US Court of Appeals for the Federal Circuit; registered to practice before the US Patent and Trademark Office.
**Personal:** Born February 16, 1935, Drexel University (BS ChE, 1957); George Washington University (JD, with honors 1961).

**COLEN, Frederick**
Reed Smith LLP, Pittsburgh 412 288 4164
fcolen@reedsmith.com
*Recommended in Intellectual Property*
**Practice Areas:** Involved in patent, trademark, copyright and other IP litigation; regularly involved in licensing of proprietary technology and know-how in the United States and abroad.

**Prof. Memberships:** American, Pennsylvania, Allegheny County, and Georgia Bar Associations; American Intellectual Property Law Association; International Trademark Association.
**Career:** Past President and Board Member of The TechLaw Group, an international network of 17 US and foreign law firms having more than 5,000 lawyers.
**Publications:** Author of numerous articles.
**Personal:** Emory University (JD, 1975); Tufts University (BS, Chemical Engineering, 1969); listed in The Best Lawyers in America.

**COLLINGS, Robert**
Schnader Harrison Segal & Lewis LLP, Philadelphia 215 751 2000
*Recommended in Environment*

**COLLINS, Brendan K**
Ballard Spahr Andrews & Ingersoll LLP, Philadelphia 215 864 8106
collins@ballardspahr.com
*Recommended in Environment*
**Practice Areas:** Focuses on litigation of environmental issues in state and federal courts, including actions arising from cleanup cost recovery claims, 'toxic tort' claims alleging personal injury and property damage, indemnity and other contractual claims, and civil and criminal enforcement matters. Maintains an active Counseling and Transactional Practice, advising clients on projects involving contaminated property and operations subject to environmental regulation. Coordinates Petroleum Products Practice.
**Prof. Memberships:** Chair, ABA Section of Environment, Energy and Resources Environmental Litigation and Toxic Tort Committee. Former Co-Chair of the Philadelphia Bar Association's Environmental Law Committee. Member, American Bar Association, Pennsylvania Bar Association, and Montgomery Bar Association. Serves on the Advisory Board of the Environmental Science Program at St Joseph's University and on the Board of Governors, St Thomas More Society of Philadelphia.
**Career:** Admitted to Pennsylvania Bar (1988), and Supreme Court of the United States (1993). Represents clients before United States Supreme Court and Pennsylvania Supreme Court.
**Publications:** Contributing author, Toxic Tort Practitioner's Handbook (2005). Contributing author, 2005/2006 Guidebook on Complying with Pennsylvania Environmental Laws and Regulations (2005). Contributing author to 'Environmental Regulation Essentials', published by John Wiley & Sons, Inc.
**Personal:** JD, magna cum laude, Villanova University (1988), SB (Mathematics), St Joseph's University (1985).

**COLTON, Neal**
Cozen O'Connor, Philadelphia
215 665 2000
*Recommended in Bankruptcy*

**COMERFORD, David L**
Akin Gump Strauss Hauer & Feld LLP, Philadelphia 215 965 1324
dcomerford@akingump.com
*Recommended in Litigation*
**Practice Areas:** David Comerford focuses on complex class actions and other commercial litigation involving business torts, contracts, accountants' liability, lender liability, securities, antitrust, RICO, ERISA, healthcare, products liability and trade secrets. He has lectured on class actions, trade secrets and litigation avoidance.
**Personal:** BA, University of Virginia (1989); JD, Rutgers University (1992). Has been recognized since 2003 in a peer-review survey as a Pennsylvania 'Super Lawyer'. In 2002 he was named by the Legal Intelligencer and Pennsylvania Law Weekly as one of the 50 top Pennsylvania attorneys under age 40.

**CONNORS, Eugene**
Reed Smith LLP, Pittsburgh
412 288 3375
econnors@reedsmith.com
*Recommended in Employment*
**Practice Areas:** Employment and labor law, guides national and international companies on how to balance employer-employee needs to eliminate employment concerns, while maximizing management options.
**Prof. Memberships:** Labor and Employment Sections of the American, Pennsylvania, and Allegheny County Bar Associations.
**Personal:** Columbia University School of Law (JD); College of the Holy Cross (BA). Listed in 'America's Leading Business Lawyers' (1st through latest editions), 'Who's Who in American Law,' and 'Who's Who of Emerging Leaders in America.' Named as 2004 Pennsylvania Super Lawyer by 'Philadelphia Magazine.' Adjunct Professor in St Francis College's Human Resources Master of Arts Program.

**COONEY, J Gordon**
Morgan, Lewis & Bockius LLP, Philadelphia 215 963 4806
jgcooney@morganlewis.com
*Recommended in Litigation*
**Practice Areas:** J Gordon Cooney, Jr is a Partner in the Litigation Practice. Mr Cooney's practice encompasses a variety of commercial and civil litigation, with particular emphasis on class actions in both state and federal courts, including consumer, product liability, deceptive trade practice, toxic tort, RICO and securities class actions. In addition, Mr Cooney's practice has included substantial complex commercial, business and appellate court litigation.

**Prof. Memberships:** Member, American Bar Association, Litigation Section, Class Action and Derivative Suits Committee; Member, Philadelphia Bar Association, Professional Guidance and Federal Courts Committees.

**COONEY JR, Robert L**
Morgan, Lewis & Bockius LLP, Philadelphia 215 963 5806
rcooney@morganlewis.com
*Recommended in Real Estate*
**Practice Areas:** Bob Cooney is a Partner in the Real Estate Group. His practice includes acquisitions and dispositions, commercial leasing, build-to-suit projects, brownfields projects, joint ventures, and financings, including credit tenant and other structured finance transactions. Mr Cooney is also involved in the firm's Zoning Practice, principally in Philadelphia. Mr Cooney's clients include REITs, pension funds and private real estate companies, as well as Fortune 500 companies and non-profit organizations with significant real estate holdings. Mr Cooney has an active practice in Pennsylvania and New Jersey.
**Prof. Memberships:** Member, American Bar Association; Member, Pennsylvania Bar Association; Member, Philadelphia Bar Association.

**CORAN, Michael**
Klehr Harrison Harvey Branzberg & Ellers LLP, Philadelphia
215 568 6060
*Recommended in Litigation*

**COSTELLO, Joseph J**
Morgan, Lewis & Bockius LLP, Philadelphia 215 963 5295
jcostello@morganlewis.com
*Recommended in Employment*
**Practice Areas:** Joseph Costello is a Partner and Deputy Practice Group Leader in the Labor and Employment Law Practice Group. Mr Costello represents employers in a broad range of employment litigation matters and administrative agency proceedings, and provides counseling in connection with strategic and day to day human resources and benefit-related decisions. Mr Costello has extensive experience defending ERISA class actions challenging retirement plan investments in company stock, cash balance plan conversions, changes in retiree medical benefits, and the adequacy of fiduciary disclosures.
**Prof. Memberships:** American Bar Association (Employee Benefits Committee and Committee on the Development of the Law Under the National Labor Relations Act); Philadelphia Bar Association.

**CRAMER, Eric**
Berger & Montague PC, Philadelphia
215 875 3000
*Recommended in Antitrust*

**CRONK, Peter J**
Duane Morris LLP, Philadelphia
215 979 1252
cronk@duanemorris.com
*Recommended in Intellectual Property*
**Practice Areas:** Peter J Cronk assists clients in procuring and litigating patents, trademarks and copyrights. He also practices in the areas of technology transfer and licensing, trade secret protection, trade dress and unfair competition. Mr Cronk provides patent assistance on metallurgy, materials, glass fabrics and medical devices matters. He has worked as a metallurgist for Homet Corporation and has supervised the production of precision cast parts for the aerospace industry.
**Prof. Memberships:** Camden County, New Jersey State, Pennsylvania, and American Bar associations; Intellectual Property Owners, Inc.; American Intellectual Property Law Association; Philadelphia Intellectual Property Law Association; Lehigh University College of Business and Economics - V-Series Professor.
**Career:** Admitted to practice in Pennsylvania and New Jersey; the United States Patent and Trademark Office; United States Court of Appeals for the Federal Circuit; United States District Court for the Eastern District of Pennsylvania; United States District Court for the District of New Jersey; Supreme Court of Pennsylvania; and the Supreme Court of New Jersey.
**Publications:** Co-author, 'From Labs to Riches: Factors to Consider When Negotiating Patent Licenses', Legal Intelligencer, March 1997.
**Personal:** Seton Hall University School of Law, JD, 1986; Lehigh University, BS Materials Engineering, magna cum laude, 1981.

**D'ANGELO JR, Alfred J**
Klett Rooney Lieber & Schorling, Philadelphia 215 567 7703
ajdangelo@klettrooney.com
*Recommended in Employment*
**Practice Areas:** Labor and employment law.
**Career:** Representation of employers in both traditional labor relations and employment litigation, including numerous union prevention campaigns, collective bargaining negotiations and labor contract administration. Also an extensive public sector practice in collective bargaining and employment litigation. Counsels employers on litigation and unionization avoidance; auditing and revising employer practices and procedures; supervisory and management training; and procedures used in promotions and downsizing. In addition, has been counsel to multi-employer pension and welfare plans.
**Personal:** AB, Princeton University; JD (cum laude), Villanova University School of Law.

## DANOFF, Diane S
Dechert LLP, Philadelphia
215 994 2179
diane.danoff@dechert.com
*Recommended in Litigation*
**Practice Areas:** Ms Danoff is a Partner who focuses her practice on intellectual property and employment litigation. She has 20 years of litigation and counseling experience in a range of intellectual property and employment matters, as well as other complex commercial litigation, including those involving highly sophisticated technologies.
**Prof. Memberships:** Member of Pennsylvania Bar; admitted to practice before numerous federal courts.
**Publications:** Featured speaker at many continuing legal education seminars; speaker at the National Conference for Women Litigators.
**Personal:** Harvard University, AB, magna cum laude, Phi Beta Kappa, 1981; University of Chicago Law School, JD, 1984.

## DAVIS, Alan J
Ballard Spahr Andrews & Ingersoll LLP, Philadelphia 215 864 8230
davisa@ballardspahr.com
*Recommended in Litigation*
**Practice Areas:** Focuses on complex and multi-district commercial litigation, securities, criminal law, municipal law and professional liability. Lead counsel on behalf of major accounting firms, corporations and individual directors and officers in the defense of more than 30 securities law class actions, including associated enforcement and investigative proceedings.
**Prof. Memberships:** Vice-Chair, United States Court of Appeals for the Third Circuit Lawyers Advisory Committee, past Chairman and present Member of the Executive Committee of the University of Pennsylvania Law School Inn of Court, Member, American College of Trial Lawyers, Fellow, International Academy of Trial Lawyers. Elected Trustee of The Pew Charitable Trusts. Career: Admitted to the Pennsylvania Bar (1961).
**Career:** Admitted to the Pennsylvania Bar (1961).
**Personal:** LLB, magna cum laude, Harvard University (1960); AB, with honors, University of Pennsylvania (1957).

## DAVIS, Doreen
Morgan, Lewis & Bockius LLP, Philadelphia 215 963 5376
dsdavis@morganlewis.com
*Recommended in Employment*
**Practice Areas:** Doreen Davis is a Partner in the Labor and Employment Law Practice Group. Ms Davis practices nationwide, concentrating in NLRB advice and litigation, union organizational activities and negotiations, and employment litigation. She has served as defense counsel in EEOC nationwide charges involving sex discrimination and in a nationwide class-action lawsuit brought under the provisions of the Fair Labor Standards Act.
**Prof. Memberships:** College of Labor and Employment Lawyers (Fellow).

## DENINNO, David L
Reed Smith LLP, Pittsburgh
412 288 3214
ddeninno@reedsmith.com
*Recommended in Corporate/M&A*
**Practice Areas:** Chairs Business and Regulatory Department. Practice is comprised of general corporate, securities, technology and financing law. Handles wide range of general corporate transactions such as mergers, acquisitions, divestitures and buyouts, and transactions involving various types of financing. Serves as principal outside counsel to a number of publicly traded and privately held business enterprises, including many technology-based businesses.
**Career:** Law clerk to Judge Roger Robb, US Court of Appeals for the District of Columbia.
**Personal:** George Washington University Law School (JD, 1981), editor of 'Law Review'; University of Virginia (BA, 1977).

## DESTEFANO, William
Buchanan Ingersoll PC, Philadelphia
215 665 3887
destefanow@bipc.com
*Recommended in Litigation*
**Practice Areas:** Focuses his practice on defending corporations and individuals against criminal investigations and indictments as well as representing clients in a range of commercial civil cases including antitrust and trade regulation litigation. He has tried more than 100 criminal and civil cases to verdict over the last 30 years, primarily in the federal and state courts of Pennsylvania, New Jersey and Delaware.
**Prof. Memberships:** American Bar Association, Pennsylvania Bar Association, New Jersey State Bar Association, and Philadelphia Bar Association.
**Personal:** JD Duquesne University, 1971; BS Villanova University, 1968.

## DEVINE III, Francis P
Pepper Hamilton LLP, Philadelphia
215 981 4230
devinef@pepperlaw.com
*Recommended in Litigation*
**Practice Areas:** Partner; Chairman, Commercial Litigation Group. Experienced in: complex business and commercial disputes, products liability, insurance coverage, professional liability and malpractice, directors and officers liability, and intellectual property disputes.
**Prof. Memberships:** Past Chancellor, Philadelphia Bar Association. Fellow, American College of Trial Lawyers. Member and past President, Philadelphia Bar Foundation. Member and past President,

Philadelphia Association of Defense Council. Co-founder, Member, Executive Committee, and former Chair, Board of Directors, Philadelphia Volunteers for the Indigent Program. Recipient of Philadelphia Bar Association's Fidelity Award.
**Career:** JD 1973 Villanova University School of Law; BS 1970 University of Pennsylvania.

## DI MASSA JR, Rudolph J
Duane Morris LLP, Philadelphia
215 979 1506
dimassa@duanemorris.com
*Recommended in Bankruptcy*
**Practice Areas:** Rudolph J Di Massa, Jr is Chair of Duane Morris' Business Reorganization and Financial Restructuring Practice Group. He concentrates his practice in the areas of commercial litigation and creditors' rights, representing secured and unsecured lenders and creditors involved in a diverse set of industries. His practice includes domestic clients and international clients doing business in the United States.
**Prof. Memberships:** Philadelphia Bar Association, Business Law Section; American Bar Association, Business Law Section; Pennsylvania Bar Association; American Bankruptcy Institute - Mid-Atlantic Conference (Co-Chair); Eastern District of PA Bankruptcy Conference; Commercial Law League of America.
**Career:** Admitted to practice in Pennsylvania; the United States Court of Appeals for the Third Circuit; United States District Court for the Eastern District of Pennsylvania; United States District Court for the Middle District of Pennsylvania; and the Supreme Court of Pennsylvania.
**Publications:** Staff Writer, The Legal Intelligencer, December 2000 to present - Bankruptcy Update Article.
**Personal:** University of Pennsylvania Law School, JD, 1981; Lehigh University, BA, 1978.

## DICHTER, Mark
Morgan, Lewis & Bockius LLP, Philadelphia 215 963 5291
mdichter@morganlewis.com
*Recommended in Employment*
**Practice Areas:** Mark Dichter is a Partner in the Labor and Employment Law Practice. Mr Dichter has more than 30 years of experience counseling and representing employers in the full spectrum of employment law, including age, gender and race discrimination, sexual harassment, employee benefits and ERISA litigation, employer-employee relations, and labor-management law. Mr Dichter also has extensive experience in dealing with the EEOC, US Department of Labor and OFCCP at the national and regional levels. He is also the Chair of the firm's Labor and Employment Law Practice.
**Prof. Memberships:** College of Labor and Employment Lawyers (Fellow);

American Employment Law Council (Board of Directors); American Bar Association Labor and Employment Section (past Chair and Counsel Member).

## DIGIORGIO, Valentino
Stradley Ronon Stevens & Young LLP, Malvern 610 640 5800
*Recommended in Banking & Finance*

## DODDS, John C
Morgan, Lewis & Bockius LLP, Philadelphia 215 963 4942
jdodds@morganlewis.com
*Recommended in Litigation*
**Practice Areas:** John C Dodds is a Partner in the Litigation Practice and Co-Chair of the Corporate Investigations and White-Collar Practice. Mr Dodds' practice centers on the representation of organizations and individuals in government investigations, internal investigations and litigation involving claims of fraud and abuse. Mr Dodds handles a wide variety of government investigations, white-collar matters and related litigation, including major representations in the pharmaceutical and other healthcare industries, qui tam litigation, securities enforcement and the area of environmental enforcement.
**Prof. Memberships:** Member, American Bar Association; Member, Federal Bar Association, Criminal Law Committee; Member, American Health Lawyers Association.

## DONOHUE, John
Woodcock Washburn LLP, Philadelphia
215 568 3100
donohue@woodcock.com
*Recommended in Intellectual Property*
**Practice Areas:** Litigation and counseling involving computers and computer software, electronics, telecommunications, robotics, medical imaging and automated control systems, and trademarks.
**Prof. Memberships:** Member, Pennsylvania Bar. President, Benjamin Franklin American Inn of Court, 2002-03; Co-Chair, Federal Circuit Bar Association's Jury Instruction Committee, ABA's Litigation Section, AIPLA's Federal Litigation and Electronic and Computer Law Committees.
**Career:** Joined Woodcock Washburn, 1987.
**Publications:** Recognized in Chambers USA 2003, 2004, 2005. Named a Pennsylvania Super Lawyer and in Best Lawyers in America.
**Personal:** LLM in Trial Advocacy, Temple University Law School (1997), JD, New England School of Law (1977); BEE, University of Dayton (1974).

## DOYLE, Katherine
Drinker Biddle & Reath LLP, Philadelphia 215 988 2700
*Recommended in Intellectual Property*

## DWORETZKY, Joseph A

Hangley Aronchick Segal & Pudlin, Philadelphia 215 496 7014
jad@hangley.com
*Recommended in Bankruptcy*

**Practice Areas:** Bankruptcy, creditors rights, commercial litigation, governmental.

**Prof. Memberships:** 3rd Circuit Regent, American College of Bankruptcy; Adjunct Professor, Bankruptcy, Temple Law School (2005-06); Chair, Eastern District of Pennsylvania Bankruptcy Conference (2001); Board, Consumer Bankruptcy Assistance Project (2003); Chair, Bankruptcy Judge Merit Selection Panel of Eastern District of Pennyslvania (2005, 2006).

**Career:** Board Member and Shareholder, Hangley Aronchick Segal & Pudlin, 1997-present. City Solicitor, City of Philadelphia, 1994-96. Managing Partner 1992-93; Partner 1984-93; associate 1978-84, Drinker Biddle & Reath. Law clerk to the Honorable Ellsworth Van Graafeiland, United States Court of Appeals for the Second Circuit, 1977-78. Villanova Law School, 1977 summa cum laude, St Ives Medal (best grades), Pulling Award (best Law Review Article).

**Personal:** A career bankruptcy and workout lawyer, he left private practice for four years in the mid-1990s to work for the then Mayor of Philadelphia, Edward G Rendell, as City Solicitor. As solicitor he was a Member of the Mayor's cabinet and in charge of a 130-lawyer legal department handling all the legal affairs of the country's fourth largest city. He has handled numerous high profile matters both in the bankruptcy and governmental arenas, including serving as trial counsel for Liberty Mutual in JPMorganChase v Liberty Mutual (Enron-related litigation concerning circular gas sale deals); as debtor's counsel in numerous cases involving energy, hospitals, nursing homes, life care facilities and other regulated industries; and as regulatory counsel in connection with the deregulation of the electric, natural gas and local telephone industries in Pennsylvania.

## EBBY, David

Drinker Biddle & Reath LLP, Philadelphia 215 988 2700
*Recommended in Real Estate*

## EBBY, Stuart F

Hangley Aronchick Segal & Pudlin, Philadelphia 215 496 7017
sfe@hangley.com
*Recommended in Real Estate*

**Practice Areas:** Sometimes referred to as the 'Dean of the Real Estate Bar', Mr Ebby has more than 40 years experience representing lending institutions, developers, investors, brokers, title insurers, and others involved in selling, buying, developing, mortgaging, leasing and managing commercial and industrial real estate. Mr Ebby frequently serves as an expert witness in cases involving Pennsylvania real estate law and practice.

**Prof. Memberships:** Member, American College of Real Estate Lawyers; Adjunct Professor of Law, Temple University Law School.

**Career:** Shareholder, Hangley Aronchick Segal & Pudlin, 2001-present. Harvard Law School, LLB, 1961; Harvard College, AB, 1958.

## EDWARDS, Mark

Morgan, Lewis & Bockius LLP, Philadelphia
215 963 5769
medwards@morganlewis.com
*Recommended in Antitrust*

**Practice Areas:** Mark Edwards is a Partner in the Antitrust Practice. Mr Edwards' practice focuses on antitrust litigation, particularly Section 1 and Section 2 Sherman Act claims, price discrimination claims and state law competition claims. He also counsels corporate clients on a broad range of antitrust issues, including distribution and pricing practices, dealer terminations and the licensing of intellectual property.

## ELDERKIN, Dianne

Woodcock Washburn LLP, Philadelphia
215 568 3100
elderkin@woodcock.com
*Recommended in Intellectual Property*

**Practice Areas:** Patent infringement litigation and counseling, especially involving pharmaceuticals, biologics, and medical devices.

**Prof. Memberships:** Member, Pennsylvania Bar, American and Philadelphia Bar Associations, PIPLA, AIPLA, and the Federal Circuit Bar Association. On AAA Panel of Neutrals for Patent Disputes.

**Career:** Member, firm's Policy Committee. Joined Woodcock Washburn, 1987. Previously served nine years as patent counsel at DuPont.

**Publications:** Frequent lecturer and author on IP law. Recognized a Pennsylvania Super Lawyer, to America's Best Lawyers and International Who's Who of Patent Law. Chambers USA 2005.

**Personal:** George Washington University Law School, JD with high honors (1978). Bucknell University, BS (1975).

## EVERETT, Carl B

Saul Ewing LLP, Philadelphia
215 972 7171
ceverett@saul.com
*Recommended in Environment*

**Practice Areas:** Mr Everett has been practicing environmental law for 30 years, focusing on CERCLA, regulatory compliance, enforcement matters brought under federal and state environmental statutes, and tort litigation. Clients have included American Packaging Corp., Beazer East, Celanese, DuPont, Ethyl, Exelon, ChevronTexaco, W.R. Grace and CERCLA groups.

**Prof. Memberships:** American, Delaware, Pennsylvania and Philadelphia Bar Associations; State Bar of Texas.

**Career:** Joined Saul Ewing in 1987. Formerly Senior Counsel in DuPont's Legal Department. Designated a 'Pennsylvania Super Lawyer' by Philadelphia Magazine and Law and Politics Magazine.

**Personal:** JD University of Houston, BS, Chemical Engineering, Massachusetts Institute of Technology.

## FALA, Herman C

Wolf, Block, Schorr and Solis-Cohen LLP, Philadelphia 215 977 2076
hfala@wolfblock.com
*Recommended in Real Estate*

**Practice Areas:** Chairman, Real Estate Department and REIT Practice Group. Has represented banks, pension funds, publicly traded companies, insurance companies, REITs, and real estate developers in many local and national transactions, including complex acquisitions, mergers, financings, joint venture arrangements, leases, project finance transactions, syndications, public and private debt and equity placements, and transactions involving the development and management of hotels, office buildings and other projects. Has extensive experience in management, financing, acquisition, development and franchising of hotels.

**Prof. Memberships:** Member, American College of Real Estate Lawyers. Served as Chairman of Real Property Section of Philadelphia Bar Association (1998) and on numerous other committees of Philadelphia Bar Association, including Professional Responsibility Committee and Executive Committee of Real Property Section.

**Career:** Admitted to Pennsylvania in 1974. Member, Board of Directors of Central Philadelphia Development Corporation, Board of Trustees of Philadelphia's Charter High School for Architecture and Design and Executive Committee of Urban Land Institute, Philadelphia Chapter.

**Personal:** Received BS, summa cum laude, from University of Notre Dame in 1971 and JD, cum laude, from Harvard Law School in 1974.

## FEIRSON, Steven B

Dechert LLP, Philadelphia 215 994 2489
steven.feirson@dechert.com
*Recommended in Litigation*

**Practice Areas:** Mr Feirson is a Litigation Partner who focuses his practice on securities and commercial litigation. During the past 20 years, he has litigated large, complex cases and has spent a significant portion of his career handling appellate matters. Mr Feirson is the firm's Deputy Chair (legal resource acquisition).

**Prof. Memberships:** Member, Pennsyl-

vania Bar; admitted to practice before numerous federal courts; Master of the Inn of Court of the University of Pennsylvania Law School.l

**Personal:** University of Pennsylvania (BA, 1972); University of Chicago Law School (JD, 1975).

## FELIX II, H Thomas

Ballard Spahr Andrews & Ingersoll LLP, Philadelphia 215 864 8136
felixt@ballardspahr.com
*Recommended in Employment*

**Practice Areas:** Focuses on labor and employment law, with emphasis on collective bargaining, arbitration, and employment discrimination issues.

**Prof. Memberships:** Fellow, College of Labor and Employment Lawyers. Past President, Labor Law Section of the Philadelphia and Pennsylvania Bar Associations. Instructor of labor law, collective bargaining, employment discrimination and strikes, picketing and boycotts at Temple University Law School. Listed in every edition of The Best Lawyers in America and every edition of Philadelphia Magazine's Best Lawyers.

**Career:** Admitted to the Pennsylvania Bar (1961); joined as Partner (2002).

**Publications:** Co-author 'Drafting and Revising Employment Contracts' and 'Drafting and Revising Employment Handbooks', and is also a Member of the Editorial Board of the 'Journal of Individual Employment Rights'.

**Personal:** LLB, Temple University James E Beasley School of Law (1961); BA, University of Virginia (1956).

## FLICK II, Lawrence

Blank Rome LLP, Philadelphia
215 569 5556
flick@BlankRome.com
*Recommended in Banking & Finance*

**Practice Areas:** Mr Flick's practice concentrates on general business and corporate law with an emphasis on commercial lending, asset-based financing, secured transactions, securitizations, loan syndications and participations, intercreditor relationships, leasing transactions, lender liability prevention and defense, loan restructuring, debtor-in-possession financing and bankruptcy, reorganizations and workouts.

**Prof. Memberships:** Admitted Pennsylvania and New Jersey; American Bar Association, Section on Corporation, Banking and Business Law, Commercial Financial Services Committee, Vice-Chair, Asset Securitization and Derivatives Sub-Committee, Uniform Commercial Code Committee, former Chair, Personal Property Leasing Subcommittee; College of Commercial Finance Attorneys; Association of Commercial Finance Attorneys; Equipment Leasing Association.

**Career:** Joined Blank Rome, 1984. Named Partner, 1991.

**Publications:** 'Structuring Insider Working Capital Advances', ABF Journal (February 2003); UCC Survey: Leases, The Business Lawyer, (1997-2004); Equipment Leasing, - Matthew Bender (1994) (co-author); 'Portfolio Acquisitions ... Looking Through the Legal Lens', MA Monitor, Portfolio Supplement, September/October 1992) (co-author); 'The Elusive Article 9 First-Lien Security Interest: How Your Lien Position Can Be Eroded and How to Prevent It', 20 Uniform Commercial Code Law Journal, 211 (Winter 1988) (co-author); 'Liability of Banks to their Borrowers: Pitfalls and Protections', Banking Law Journal (1986) (co-author).
**Personal:** Graduated Villanova University School of Law, cum laude.

### FOLEY, Mark
Klett Rooney Lieber & Schorling, Philadelphia 215 567 7719
mjfoley@klettrooney.com
*Recommended in Employment*
**Practice Areas:** Labor and employment law.
**Prof. Memberships:** Board of Governors, Pennsylvania Economy League.
**Career:** Represents employers in all aspects of labor and employment law, and has extensive experience in a broad range of matters under local, state and federal law, including the NLRA, LMRA, PERA and Act 111, Title VII, Section 1983 and the First Amendment, ADEA, ADA, FLSA, whistle-blower laws, restrictive covenants and trade secrets, and employment-at-will principles.
**Personal:** Pennsylvania State University; JD (cum laude), Villanova University School of Law.

### FORMAN, Harvey
Blank Rome LLP, Philadelphia
215 569 5516
forman-hi@BlankRome.com
*Recommended in Banking & Finance*
**Practice Areas:** Mr Forman concentrates his practice on commercial lending, asset-based financing, secured transactions, loan syndications and participations, loan restructurings, intercreditor relationships, loan workouts, lender liability prevention and defense, debtor-in-possession financing, bankruptcy and reorganizations, primarily representing institutional lenders such as banks, commercial finance companies, mortgage companies, and insurance companies.
**Prof. Memberships:** American Bar Association; Philadelphia Bar Association; Association of Commercial Finance Attorneys; Elected Fellow of American College of Commercial Finance Lawyers.
**Career:** Partner, Blank Rome LLP, 1984-present; Wexler, Weisman, Forman & Shapiro, 1970-84 when it merged with Blank Rome; Admitted in Pennsylvania.
**Publications:** Practicing Under the Bankruptcy Reform Act, (contributing

author); Frequent lecturer for clients and professional organizations.
**Personal:** JD, Villanova University School of Law; BA, Brown University.

### FORTI, David W
Dechert LLP, Philadelphia
215 994 2647
david.forti@dechert.com
*Recommended in Real Estate*
**Practice Areas:** Mr Forti is a Partner who focuses his practice on real estate finance and securitization. He represents lenders, issuers, master servicers, and special servicers in transactions involving loan origination, mezzanine financing, CMBS securitization, CMBS/CDOs, post-closing modifications, and workouts. He is lead outside counsel for the Commercial Mortgage Securitization Group of a national rating agency.
**Prof. Memberships:** Member, Pennsylvania Bar; Member, Commercial Mortgage Securities Association (CMSA).
**Personal:** University of Pittsburgh (BA, cum laude, 1992; MBA and JD, magna cum laude 1995), editor of the University of Pittsburgh Law Review and the Journal of Law and Commerce.

### FOX, Robert
Manko, Gold, Katcher & Fox LLP, Bala Cynwyd 484 430 5700
*Recommended in Environment*

### FRANDSEN, Nancy
Drinker Biddle & Reath LLP, Philadelphia 215 988 2700
*Recommended in Intellectual Property*

### FRIDY, Carl H
Ballard Spahr Andrews & Ingersoll LLP, Philadelphia 215 864 8726
fridy@ballardspahr.com
*Recommended in Banking & Finance*
**Practice Areas:** Focuses on secured and unsecured commercial lending, real estate and construction finance, letter of credit-backed and other tax-exempt bond financings, and the workout and restructuring of troubled loans.
**Prof. Memberships:** Member, Commercial Financial Services Sub-Committee of the Section of Business Law of the American Bar Association; Real Property Division of the Section of Real Property, Probate and Trust Law of the American Bar Association. Member, American College of Commercial Finance Lawyers.
**Career:** Admitted to Pennsylvania Bar (1973); joined as associate (1973); Partner (1980).
**Personal:** JD, Duke University (1973); BA, Trinity College (1969).

### FRIEDMAN, Michael H
Pepper Hamilton LLP, Philadelphia
215 981 4563
friedmanm@pepperlaw.com
*Recommended in Corporate/M&A*
**Practice Areas:** Partner; Co-Chairman, Commercial Department; Chairman, Corporate and Securities Practice Group.

Experienced in: mergers and acquisitions; corporate finance; corporate securities; joint ventures and real estate investment trusts (REITs). Counsels boards of directors and senior management of companies on governance, disclosure, regulatory compliance (Sarbanes-Oxley), transactional matters and audit committee issues.
**Prof. Memberships:** Member, Philadelphia Board for Corporate Governance; Board Member, The Council for Relationships. Former Board Member American Red Cross, Southeastern Pennsylvania Chapter.
**Career:** JD 1982 University of Virginia School of Law; MA 1979 University of Chicago; BA 1978 Hamilton College.

### FRITTON, Karl
Reed Smith LLP, Philadelphia
215 241 7956
kfritton@reedsmith.com
*Recommended in Employment*
**Practice Areas:** Employment Law and Benefits Group, Deputy Head; Intellectual Property Practice Group Leader. Represents employers in collective bargaining, labor arbitration, and employment-related litigation before the NLRB and state and federal courts.
**Publications:** Frequent author on labor and employment-related matters
**Personal:** Rutgers University School of Law (JD, 1980); State University of New York at Albany (BS, 1977). Listed in 'The Best Lawyers in America.' Lecturer at Rutgers University Institute of Management and Labor Relations; Adjunct Professor of Labor Law at Rutgers University School of Law. Member, Board of Directors of Philadelphia Volunteer Lawyers for the Arts.

### GARBER, Kevin
Babst, Calland, Clements and Zomnir, A Professional Corporation, Pittsburgh
412 394 5400
*Recommended in Environment*

### GELLMAN, Nancy
Conrad O'Brien Gellman & Rohn PC, Philadelphia 215 864 8065
ngellman@cogr.com
*Recommended in Litigation*
**Practice Areas:** Founding Member, Conrad O'Brien Gellman & Rohn, PC. Practices in area of complex litigation, including commercial cases, class actions, insurance coverage, antitrust, defamation, professional liability, and employment litigation.
**Prof. Memberships:** Fellow, American College of Trial Lawyers; Member, American Law Institute.
**Personal:** AB, Bryn Mawr College; JD, Yale Law School; Fulbright Fellowship, London School of Economics.

### GIFFORD, David
Ballard Spahr Andrews & Ingersoll LLP, Philadelphia 215 864 8703
gifford@ballardspahr.com
*Recommended in Real Estate*
**Practice Areas:** Focuses on real estate and related corporate and general business matters, including commercial, industrial, and residential real estate planning, acquisition, development, construction, leasing and operations; franchise operations and agreements; ground lease and commercial, office and retail lease transactions; partnership and corporate organization and operation; real estate syndication; dispute resolution; construction and permanent loan financing; troubled project workouts; bankruptcy planning; zoning and subdivision; real estate taxation; and real estate and construction litigation.
**Prof. Memberships:** Chair (1994), Vice-Chair (1993), Treasurer (1992), and Secretary (1991), Executive Committee of the Real Property Section of the Philadelphia Bar Association. Chair, Financing of Real Estate Subcommittee 1987-89. Member, American Bar Association, Pennsylvania Bar Association, and Philadelphia Bar Association.
**Career:** Admitted to the Pennsylvania Bar (1980); joined as Partner (1997).
**Personal:** JD, College of William & Mary, Marshall-Wythe School of Law (1979); BA, magna cum laude, Temple University (1975).

### GIOTTO, Thomas
Klett Rooney Lieber & Schorling, Pittsburgh 412 392 2068
tsgiotto@klettrooney.com
*Recommended in Employment*
**Practice Areas:** Labor and employment law.
**Prof. Memberships:** Member of the American Bar Association's Labor and Employment Law Section.
**Career:** Concentrates his entire practice on representing management in all aspects of labor, employment and employment-related litigation. Counsels clients in a wide variety of industries and business sectors. He devotes much of his practice to traditional labor law, which includes representing employers during union organizing campaigns, collective bargaining and grievance arbitrations.
**Publications:** Contributing editor, 'American Bar Association's Developing Labor Law'.
**Personal:** BA, Pennsylvania State University; JD, Duquesne University School of Law.

### GLAZER, Ronald B
Wolf, Block, Schorr and Solis-Cohen LLP, Philadelphia 215 977 2112
rglazer@wolfblock.com
*Recommended in Real Estate*
**Practice Areas:** Partner, Real Estate Practice Group. Concentrates his practice

on shopping centers, office buildings, condominiums, homeowners' associations, cooperatives, structuring mixed-use projects and real estate acquisition, sale, financing, development and operation. Also has extensive experience in representing construction and permanent lenders, REITs and joint venture partners.

**Career:** Chairman, Real Property Law Section of Philadelphia Bar Association (1987) and Member of Association's Board of Governors. Member, American and Pennsylvania Bar Associations Sections on Real Property, Probate and Trust Law, serving on executive committee of the latter (1982-84). Chairman, subcommittees of Pennsylvania Bar Association's Community Association Law Committee that prepared Pennsylvania condominium, cooperative and planned community statutes. Chairman, Pennsylvania Bar Association Common Interest Ownership Committee (1995-96). Member, International Council of Shopping Centers, Community Association Institute's College of Community Association Lawyers and American College of Real Estate Lawyers.

**Publications:** Author, Pennsylvania Condominium Law & Practice, in its third edition but soon to be replaced by new Pennsylvania Community Association Law & Practice.

**Personal:** Received BA, cum laude, from Dickinson College in 1964 and LLB, cum laude, from University of Pennsylvania Law School in 1967.

### GOLD, Marc
Manko, Gold, Katcher & Fox LLP,
Bala Cynwyd 484 430 5700
*Recommended in Environment*

### GOLDBERG, Donald J
Ballard Spahr Andrews & Ingersoll LLP,
Philadelphia 215 864 8345
goldbergd@ballardspahr.com
*Recommended in Litigation*

**Practice Areas:** Focuses on white-collar crime area. Represents organizations ranging from Fortune 500 companies to those more closely held. Representations include: lawyers, doctors, public officials, business persons, prosecutors, and other law enforcement personnel.

**Prof. Memberships:** Member, American College of Trial Lawyers. Appointed in 1999 by Chief Justice Rehnquist to a three-year term on the Federal Judicial Conference's Advisory Committee on the Federal Rules of Criminal Procedure; extended for an additional term to expire on October 1, 2006.

**Career:** Admitted to the Pennsylvania Bar (1955).

**Personal:** LLB, Harvard Law School (1954); BS, University of Pennsylvania (1951).

### GOLDBERG, Richard R
Ballard Spahr Andrews & Ingersoll LLP,
Philadelphia 215 864 8730
goldbergr@ballardspahr.com
*Recommended in Real Estate*

**Practice Areas:** Focuses on areas of real estate including, development, financing, leasing, and acquisition.

**Prof. Memberships:** Past President, American College of Real Estate Lawyers (1991-92); past Chair, Anglo-American Real Property Institute; past Chair, International Council of Shopping Centers Law Conference (1986 and 1987); and Fellow, American College of Mortgage Attorneys. Member, American Law Institute, Adviser, Restatement of Property, Mortgages, Program Advisory Committee of ALI-ABA, and Real Estate Advisory Committees of ALI-ABA and Practising Law Institute. Member, American Bar Association, Section of Real Property, Trust and Probate serving as real property liaison to Drafting Committee for the Revision of Articles 1, and 9 of the Uniform Commercial Code. Served as Chair of Section Committees on Pension Funds; Management of Real Estate; and National Institutes and Satellite Programs.

**Career:** Admitted to the Maryland Bar (1964), New Jersey Bar (1994), Pennsylvania Bar (1994), joined as Partner (1994).

**Publications:** Co-author of a handbook on downtown development for Massachusetts Continuing Legal Education.

**Personal:** LLB University of Maryland (1964); BA Pennsylvania State University (1961).

### GOODMAN, Stephen
Morgan, Lewis & Bockius LLP,
Philadelphia 215 963 5086
sgoodman@morganlewis.com
*Recommended in Corporate/M&A*

**Practice Areas:** Mr Goodman is a Partner in the Business and Finance Practice and Co-Chair of the firm's Global Technology Practice. His practice focuses on representing emerging growth companies in the technology and life sciences sectors. Using the firm's vast resources, he co-ordinates all aspects of the representation of such companies and concentrates his practice on legal aspects of corporate finance and acquisitions. Mr Goodman was also a law clerk for US Supreme Court Justice William J Brennan Jr.

### GORDON, George G
Dechert LLP, Philadelphia 215 994 2382
george.gordon@dechert.com
*Recommended in Antitrust*

**Practice Areas:** Mr Gordon, Partner, focuses his practice on antitrust litigation, counseling, and government investigations. He handles class action matters and antitrust actions involving monopolization, price discrimination, group boycotts, and predatory pricing. He also represents clients in non-public government investigations.

**Prof. Memberships:** Member, Pennsylvania and New Jersey Bars; admitted to practice before numerous federal courts.

**Publications:** Frequent speaker and author on antitrust issues; asked by the Federal Trade Commission to testify in connection with FTC/DOJ intellectual property/antitrust hearings.

**Personal:** Brandeis University, BA, cum laude, 1988; University of Pennsylvania Law School, JD, 1991; London School of Economics, High Commendation, 1987.

### GOSFIELD, Gregory G
Dechert LLP, Philadelphia
215 994 2311
gregory.gosfield@dechert.com
*Recommended in Real Estate*

**Practice Areas:** Mr Gosfield is a Partner and member of the Finance and Real Estate Group. He advises agent banks, general partners, owners, tenants, and institutional investors in matters involving senior and subordinate debt and equity; operation and maintenance of assets and entities; and workouts, insolvencies, and turnarounds.

**Prof. Memberships:** Member, Pennsylvania Bar.

**Publications:** Mr Gosfield's articles have been published in 'The Business Lawyer Today'; 'The Real Property, Probate, and Trust Journal'; and 'The Practical Real Estate Lawyer', among others.

**Personal:** Columbia College (BA, 1972); Temple University School of Law (JD, cum laude, 1979), Member, Temple University Law Review.

### GUNDERSEN, Glenn A
Dechert LLP, Philadelphia
215 994 2183
glenn.gundersen@dechert.com
*Recommended in Intellectual Property*

**Practice Areas:** Mr Gundersen, Co-Chair of the Intellectual Property Group, focuses on trademark, copyright, licensing, internet, advertising, and right of publicity law. He advises on clearance, prosecution, oppositions, fair use, licensing, e-commerce, and infringement disputes.

**Prof. Memberships:** Member, Pennsylvania Bar; Vice-Chair, International Trademark Association; Board of Directors, Philadelphia Volunteer Lawyers for the Arts.

**Publications:** Author, 'Trademark Searching' (1st & 2d. Ed.); co-author, 'Intellectual Property Assets in Mergers & Acquisitions;' speaker, ABA, AIPLA, INTA, PLI, and other programs; founder, Copyright Society of USA, Philadelphia Chapter

**Personal:** College of William and Mary (BA, 1976); University of Virginia (JD, 1980).

### HAINES, Rush
Drinker Biddle & Reath LLP,
Philadelphia 215 988 2700
*Recommended in Real Estate*

### HALLER, Anthony
Blank Rome LLP, Philadelphia
215 569 5690
haller@BlankRome.com
*Recommended in Employment*

**Practice Areas:** All aspects of labor and employment law including preventative counseling, complex litigation, trial and appellate work. Represented clients in cases involving claims of race, age, sex, disability discrimination, wrongful discharge, defamation and sexual harassment. Handled multiple plaintiff, representative, and class actions. Litigated claims involving non-compete agreements and misappropriation of trade secrets. Experience also includes collective bargaining, arbitration, representation and unfair labor practice proceedings, the handling of strikes and picketing activity, federal and state law injunction proceedings, wage and hour claims, and employee benefit litigation.

**Prof. Memberships:** ABA, Labor and Employment and Litigation Sections.

**Career:** Blank Rome LLP - Philadelphia, PA, 2004-present; Pepper Hamilton LLP - Philadelphia, PA, 1982-2004; President, Temple American Inn of Court; frequent lecturer on employment law issues; frequent guest on Law Journal TV, WFMZ-TV (channel 69) discussing employment law issues.

**Publications:** Co-author, Chapter 8, 'An Introduction To The Employment Laws of The United States For The Foreign Investor, Business Opportunities In The United States', (Richard D Irwin, Inc. 1992). Co-author, Chapter 25, 'Labor Law In The Construction Industry, Construction Business Handbook', (Aspen Pub 2003).

**Personal:** St Catharine's College, Cambridge, 1977; LLM, University of Pennsylvania Law School, 1979. Barrister. Attorney.

### HANGLEY, William
Hangley Aronchick Segal & Pudlin,
Philadelphia 215 496 7001
whangley@hangley.com
*Recommended in Litigation*

**Practice Areas:** General business litigation; professional responsibility, legal malpractice and counseling law firms; intellectual property; First Amendment; securities; antitrust.

**Prof. Memberships:** Fellow, American College of Trial Lawyers, 1987- (Chair, Committee on Federal Rules of Evidence, 2001-03; Member, Outreach Committee, 2005-; Member, Communications Committee, 2002-; Member, Pennsylvania State Committee, 1998-2003; Member, Ad Hoc Committee on the Future of the Civil Trial, 2004; Member, Committee on

Federal Rules of Evidence 1999-); Member, PA IOLTA Board, 2005-; Fellow, American Bar Foundation; Member, American Law Institute. University of Pennsylvania Fellow, Salzburg Seminar in American Studies, Law, 1975. Founding Member and Master of the Bench, University of Pennsylvania Inn of Court, 1993-. Judge Pro Tem, Philadelphia Court of Common Pleas, 1990-2000. Member, ABA Section of Litigation (Council, 2005-; Co-Chair, Task Force on the Judiciary, 2004-; Co-Chair, Federal Procedure Committee, 1990-95; Co-Chair, Merit Selection of Judges Task Force, 1995-97; Member, Task Force on Discovery,1997-2000; Member, Task Force on the Judiciary,2000-; Member, Task Force on Training the Trial Lawyer, 2002-03. Member, Philadelphia Bar Association (Member, Special Subcommittee on Proposed Rules of Judicial Conduct, 2005- ). Public Interest Law Center of Philadelphia, Board of Advisors. Member, Legal Club, 1993-present (President 2004-; Vice President 2002-04) Member, Junior Legal Club, 1995-.

**Career:** Founder, Chair, Hangley Aronchick Segal & Pudlin, 1994-present. Founder (Chair 1983-94) Hangley Connolly Epstein Chicco Foxman & Ewing and predecessor firms, 1969-94. Associate, Schnader, Harrison, Segal & Lewis, 1966-69. University of Pennsylvania Law School, Philadelphia, Pennsylvania, 1966 (cum laude, Order of the Coif; comment editor, University of Pennsylvania Law Review). State University of New York College at Fredonia, BS (Music) 1963.

**Publications:** 'Opinions Hidden, Citations Forbidden: Report And Recommendations Of the American College of Trial Lawyers On The Publication And Citation Of Nonbinding Federal Circuit Court Opinions', 208 F.R.D. 645 (2002); 'Teaching Through Experts: Changing the Obscure to the Obvious', Litigation, Spring, 2001; 'Direct and the Director: Writing, Staging and Telling The Story', Litigation, Fall, 1998; 'The Fourth Estate and the Second Front: Winning and Losing in the Press', Litigation, Spring, 1997; 'The Strike Zone, the Trial Judge and Other Moving Targets', California Litigation (California Bar Association, Section of Litigation), Spring, 1995.

## HANLON, Michael J
Blank Rome LLP, Philadelphia
215 569 5652
hanlon@BlankRome.com
*Recommended in Employment*
**Practice Areas:** Mr Hanlon chairs Blank Rome's Employment, Benefits and Labor Practice Group. He has extensive experience in traditional labor law, contract negotiations, and union avoidance as well as representing and counseling employers in employment discrimination, OSHA, and wage-hour matters and negotiating executive contracts. His

clients include large publicly-traded and mid-size corporations in the manufacturing, maritime, and service sectors, as well as large government entities.
**Prof. Memberships:** Admitted to practice in Pennsylvania (1981). Member of the Pennsylvania and Philadelphia Bar Associations, the Industrial Relations Research Association (IRRA) and the National School Boards Association.
**Career:** Mr Hanlon has been a Partner at Blank Rome LLP since 1989. He was Labor Counsel at Ernie Green Industries from 1987-89 and a Partner at Pechner, Dorfman, Wolffe, Rounick & Cabot from 1979-87.
**Personal:** JD, Villanova University, 1981; BS in economics, Wharton School, University of Pennsylvania, 1976.

## HARKINS, John
Harkins Cunningham LLP, Philadelphia
215 851 6701
jharkins@harkinscunningham.com
*Recommended in Litigation*

## HARRIS, Judith E
Morgan, Lewis & Bockius LLP,
Philadelphia 215 963 5028
jeharris@morganlewis.com
*Recommended in Employment*
**Practice Areas:** Judith E Harris is a Partner in the Labor and Employment Law Practice Group. Ms Harris counsels employers in matters involving discrimination, trade secrets, non-compete agreements and employee compensation. Ms Harris represents employers in class action, collective action and single plaintiff litigation, and has successfully tried numerous complex jury and non-jury cases. She has argued in the United State Supreme Court, the United States Court of Appeals Third, Seventh and Eleventh Circuits, Pennsylvania Supreme Court and Pennsylvania intermediate appellate courts.
**Prof. Memberships:** American Bar Association, Pennsylvania Bar Association, Philadelphia Bar Association, former President, Philadelphia Bar Foundation.

## HEIM, Robert C
Dechert LLP, Philadelphia 215 994 2570
robert.heim@dechert.com
*Recommended in Litigation*
**Practice Areas:** Mr Heim, a nationally known trial lawyer, focuses on antitrust, securities, intellectual property, and complex commercial litigation. He has represented major corporations in matters in US state and federal courts.
**Prof. Memberships:** Member, Pennsylvania Bar; admitted to practice before numerous federal courts; member, Judicial Conference Advisory Committee on Civil Rules; Member, Third Judicial Circuit Advisory Committee.
**Career:** Former Chair, Federal Courts Committee; past Chancellor, Philadelphia Bar Association; past President of the National Conference of Bar Presi-

dents.
**Personal:** University of Pennsylvania (BS, 1964); College of William and Mary (MB, 1968); University of Pennsylvania Law School (JD, 1972).

## HEIST, Dale
Woodcock Washburn LLP, Philadelphia
215 568 3100
heist@woodcock.com
*Recommended in Intellectual Property*
**Practice Areas:** Litigated more than 100 patent/IP cases in diverse fields, including robotics, polymers, medical products and computer software.
**Prof. Memberships:** Member, Pennsylvania and New Jersey Bars; Fellow, American College of Trial Lawyers. Member, American, Pennsylvania and Philadelphia Bar Associations; the American, Philadelphia and New York Intellectual Property Law Associations.
**Career:** Joined Woodcock Washburn, 1977.
**Publications:** Recognized in Chambers USA 2003, 2004, 2005. Named a Pennsylvania Super Lawyer and in Best Lawyers in America.
**Personal:** BS (1970) in Electrical Engineering and JD (1976) from Villanova University.

## HERYFORD, Craig
Klett Rooney Lieber & Schorling, Pittsburgh 412 392 2157
csheryford@klettrooney.com
*Recommended in Banking & Finance*
**Practice Areas:** Corporate, finance, technology and international business.
**Career:** Concentrates his practice on the representation of emerging businesses, and venture capital and corporate finance matters. Has extensive experience in a wide variety of commercial transactions, including numerous corporate finance and venture capital funding transactions, merger and acquistion transactions, and private placements of securities. Also has substantial experience representing both emerging and mature businesses in general corporate and business matters.
**Personal:** BS and BFA, Ohio State University; JD (cum laude), Duquesne University School of Law.

## HICKOK, Robert L
Pepper Hamilton LLP, Philadelphia
215 981 4583
hickokr@pepperlaw.com
*Recommended in Litigation*
**Practice Areas:** Partner; Executive Committee Member. Experienced in: antitrust, securities, D and O, white-collar and criminal, and insurance sales practices litigation; corporate investigations; class action defense; application of economic analysis; antitrust cases (product and market definition and product pricing); federal securities law (efficient capital market theory); commercial contract cases (measure of damages); application of technology to information/litigation

management.
**Prof. Memberships:** Member, Executive Committee, Harvard Law School Association of Philadelphia.
**Career:** Former Assistant US Attorney, Eastern District of Pennsylvania (1979-83); JD, 1978, Harvard Law School; AM, 1978, Harvard University; BA, 1974, Lehigh University.

## HINERMAN, Philip
Fox Rothschild LLP, Philadelphia
215 299 2000
*Recommended in Environment*

## HOCKEIMER, Henry
Ballard Spahr Andrews & Ingersoll LLP,
Philadelphia 215 864 8204
hockeimerh@ballardspahr.com
*Recommended in Litigation*
**Practice Areas:** Focuses on white-collar criminal defense, securities fraud and complex civil litigation. Extensive jury trial experience in private practice and as a federal prosecutor.
**Prof. Memberships:** Court-appointed Member, Criminal Justice Act Panel of the United States District Court for the Eastern District of Pennsylvania. Member, American Bar Association, Section on Litigation and ABA's Criminal Justice Section, White Collar Crime Committee and Chair of its Parallel Proceedings Sub-Committee. Board of Directors and Member, Executive Committee, Philadelphia Volunteers for the Indigent Program. Received Philadelphia Bar Association's 2001 Pro Bono Award.
**Career:** Admitted to Virginia Bar (1990), District of Columbia Bar (1991), and Pennsylvania Bar (2001); joined as Partner (2005). Appointed Assistant United States Attorney, Oklahoma City, Oklahoma (1995). Former Member of the FBI's Domestic Terrorism Task Force. Law clerk for the Honorable James C Cacheris of the United States District Court for the Eastern District of Virginia. Adjunct professor in Trial Advocacy, Temple University Beasley School of Law.
**Personal:** JD, with distinction, Catholic University of America, Columbus School of Law (1989); BA, Miami University (1985).

## HODGSON, Clark
Stradley Ronon Stevens & Young LLP,
Philadelphia 215 564 8000

## HOLSTON, Michael J
Morgan, Lewis & Bockius LLP,
Philadelphia 215 963 4885
mholston@morganlewis.com
*Recommended in Litigation*
**Practice Areas:** Michael J Holston is a Partner in the Litigation Practice. His practice is focused on complex civil litigation, primarily defending products liability and consumer fraud class-action lawsuits, and white-collar criminal defense litigation. Mr Holston handles class action lawsuits on a nationwide basis. He

has handled a variety of products liability and consumer fraud class-action lawsuits in more than 15 states in federal and state courts in the past five years. Mr Holston has extensive trial experience and is frequently retained in the latter stages of cases to try jury and non-jury trials.

## HORNAK, Mark
Buchanan Ingersoll PC, Pittsburgh
412 562 8859
hornakmr@bipc.com
*Recommended in Employment*
**Practice Areas:** Represents employers in litigation, fair employment practice and employee privacy issues, negotiates collective bargaining agreements for public and private employers. Mark advises school districts on employment and education law, represents municipalities and government officials in constitutional and civil rights litigation. He represents national broadcasting and publishing clients in litigation and transactional matters. Mark has been appointed Special Master in complex/class action litigation in state and federal courts.
**Prof. Memberships:** Advisory Committee, United States District Court, Western Pennsylvania; Academy of Trial Lawyers; 'Leadership Pittsburgh' Program, American Law Institute; American Bar Foundation.
**Personal:** BS, 1978; JD, 1981 University of Pittsburgh.

## HORSTMANN, John F
Duane Morris LLP, Philadelphia
215 979 1504
horstmann@duanemorris.com
*Recommended in Banking & Finance, Bankruptcy*
**Practice Areas:** John F Horstmann is the Chair of the firm's Corporate Practice Group and practices in the areas of bankruptcy law, corporate reorganization, creditors' rights, out-of-court workouts, bank transactions, complex commercial reorganizations, international finance transactions and commercial loan documentation.
**Prof. Memberships:** American Bar Association - Business Law Section, Business Bankruptcy Committee, Subcommittee on International Bankruptcy; Pennsylvania Bar Association - Corporation, Banking and Business Law Section; Philadelphia Bar Association - Business Law Section, Sub-Committee on Corporate Reorganization and Business Bankruptcy, Sub-Committee on the Uniform Commercial Code (past Chairman); Turnaround Business Management Association - Associate Member.
**Career:** Admitted to practice in Pennsylvania; the United States District Court for the Eastern District of Pennsylvania; United States Bankruptcy Court for the Eastern District of Pennsylvania; and the Supreme Court of Pennsylvania. Duane Morris LLP: Member, Partners Board;

Chairman, Reorganization and Finance Section, 1994-2001; Partner, 1984-present; associate, 1976-84.
**Personal:** Villanova University School of Law, JD, 1976.

## HOWARD, David M
Dechert LLP, Philadelphia
215 994 2218
david.howard@dechert.com
*Recommended in Litigation*
**Practice Areas:** Mr Howard, Chair of the White-Collar Group, concentrates his practice on white-collar criminal defense, corporate investigations, enforcement proceedings, and complex civil litigation.
**Prof. Memberships:** Member, Pennsylvania Bar; admitted to practice before numerous federal courts; Co-Chair, ABA White-Collar Crime Committee's Corporate Internal Investigations Subcommittee.
**Career:** Law clerk, Hon. Marvin Katz (EDPA); Assistant US Attorney, EDPA (1987-94), where he co-ordinated District's Securities and Commodities Fraud Task Force; Office of White House Counsel, Iran/Contra Investigation (1987).
**Personal:** Princeton University (AB, cum laude, 1981); University of Pennsylvania Law School, (JD, cum laude, 1984), Order of the Coif, Law Review.

## HOWARD, Lindsay
Babst, Calland, Clements and Zomnir, A Professional Corporation, Pittsburgh
412 394 5400
*Recommended in Environment*

## JACOBS-MEADWAY, Roberta
Ballard Spahr Andrews & Ingersoll LLP, Philadelphia 215 864 8201
jacobsmeadwayr@ballardspahr.com
*Recommended in Intellectual Property*
**Practice Areas:** Focuses on trademarks, unfair competition issues, including advertising issues, as well as copyrights and licensing of intellectual property, and includes related litigation in the federal courts and before the Trademark Trial and Appeal Board. Serves as mediator in numerous trademark and copyright disputes.
**Prof. Memberships:** Member of the American Law Institute, American Bar Association, Pennsylvania Bar Association, and Philadelphia Bar Association; Philadelphia Intellectual Property Law Association; and International Trademark Association (INTA); selected as a Member of the prestigious Panel of Neutrals (PON) and also serves as a Member of the Alternative Dispute Resolution (ADR) Committee. Member, American Bar Association's Federal Legislation Committee. Civic Activities: Acting Chair of the Board, InterAct Theater Company, chairs the marketing and development committee; Board, Birthright (a non-profit emergency pregnancy counseling service). Lectures and seminars: Planning Co-Chair and lecturer at ALI-ABA pro-

grams on litigating trademark and unfair competition cases; on licensing of intellectual property; and on internet law. Lectures on intellectual property law for PBI, the Iowa Intellectual Property Law Association, the INTA and numerous other organizations.
**Career:** Admitted to the New Jersey Bar (1975); admitted to the Pennsylvania Bar (1975).
**Publications:** Author, numerous articles for business publications and trade periodicals. Contributed chapters to Matthew Bender's treatise, Intellectual Property Counseling and Litigation. Contributing author to World Copyright Law Report.
**Personal:** JD, with honors, Rutgers University School of Law (1975); BA, magna cum laude, Bryn Mawr College (1972).

## JARIN, Kenneth M
Ballard Spahr Andrews & Ingersoll LLP, Philadelphia 215 864 8135
jarink@ballardspahr.com
*Recommended in Employment*
**Practice Areas:** Represents public and private employers in matters relating to labor relations, contract negotiations, interest arbitration, employment discrimination litigation, and wage and hour disputes. Counsels on matters related to Fair Labor Standards Act and Family and Medical Leave Act. Participated in administrative proceedings before National Labor Relations Board and various state agencies. Chief labor negotiator for the Commonwealth of Pennsylvania.
**Prof. Memberships:** Treasurer, Democratic Governors Association; member, ADL's National Executive Committee; Member, Board of Directors of the Recreation Activities Fund for the City of Philadelphia. Chairman of the Board of Directors of the Chamber Orchestra of Philadelphia; member of the Board of Directors for the Kimmel Center for the Performing Arts; Executive Board Member of the Board of Directors for the Penns Landing Corporation; Member, Pennsylvania Interest on Lawyers Trust Account Board (PA IOLTA).
**Career:** Admitted to the Pennsylvania Bar (1975).
**Publications:** Author, 'National League of Cities v. Usery Reversed: What Does It Mean For Municipal Governments?' The Reporter, Pennsylvania League of Cities, 1st Quarter, 1985, and 'Supreme Court Overturns New Cumberland Decision,' The Reporter, Pennsylvania League of Cities, 1st Quarter, 1984.
**Personal:** JD, Temple University James E Beasley School of Law (1975); BA, Duke University (1972).

## JONES, David F
Dechert LLP, Philadelphia 215 994 2822
david.jones@dechert.com
*Recommended in Employment*
**Practice Areas:** Mr Jones, Partner, chairs the Employee Benefits and Execu-

tive Compensation Group. He focuses his practice on qualified and nonqualified retirement plans, equity compensation, executive compensation, and related transactional matters.
**Prof. Memberships:** Member, Pennsylvania Bar; Member, American Bar Association.
**Publications:** Mr Jones lectures at seminars and conferences sponsored by the Association of Corporate Counsel, Practising Law Institute, Pennsylvania-New Jersey-Delaware Employee Benefits Association, and Strategic Research Institute.
**Personal:** Temple University (BBA, cum laude, 1979); Temple University School of Law (JD, cum laude, 1982), business editor of Temple Law Review; New York University School of Law (LLM in Taxation, 1984).

## JONES, Richard D
Dechert LLP, Philadelphia
215 994 2501
richard.jones@dechert.com
*Recommended in Real Estate*
**Practice Areas:** Mr Jones is a Partner and Member of the Executive Committee of Dechert's Finance and Real Estate Group. He focuses his practice on mortgage finance and capital markets.
**Prof. Memberships:** Member, Connecticut and Pennsylvania Bars; former President, Commercial Mortgage Securities Association; founder and officer, Chartered Realty Investors Society; Member and past Governor, American College of Real Estate Lawyers; member, Commercial Mortgage Board of Governors of the Mortgage Bankers Association of America; member, The Real Estate Roundtable.
**Personal:** Washington and Lee University (BA, 1975); University of Virginia School of Law (JD, 1978); Boston University School of Law (LLM, 1981).

## JUDGE, John
Montgomery, McCracken, Walker & Rhoads, LLP, Philadelphia
215 772 1500
*Recommended in Environment*

## KABNICK, Lisa D
Reed Smith LLP, Philadelphia
215 851 8194
lkabnick@reedsmith.com
*Recommended in Banking & Finance*
**Practice Areas:** Represents financial institutions and borrowers in syndicated secured credit transactions, financing companies across industries, and in international transactions and workouts. Served as primary outside counsel to one of the largest US private marine terminal operators and stevedoring companies. Head of Financial Transactions.
**Prof. Memberships:** Former Chair, Philadelphia Bar Association's Banking and Financial Institutions Committee.
**Personal:** University of Pittsburgh (JD, 1980), executive articles editor, 'University of Pittsburgh Law Review'; University

of Pennsylvania (BA, 1976). Selected as one of the 2005 Women of Distinction by 'Real Philly' magazine, and as a 2005 Trailblazer Honoree by 'Philadelphia Magazine.'

## KANE, Jonathan
Pepper Hamilton LLP, Berwyn
610 640 7803
kanej@pepperlaw.com
*Recommended in Employment*
**Practice Areas:** Partner; Chairman, Labor and Employment Group. Experienced in: averting union organizational campaigns, collective bargaining negotiations, labor-related litigation and arbitration; National Labor Relations Board matters; employment litigation; counseling, labor and employment aspects of corporate transactions; prevention of violence in the workplace; legal aspects of drug abuse policies and practice. Provides advice on developing and conducts comprehensive, in-house training programs. Experienced in a wide range of industries, including retail, services and healthcare.
**Prof. Memberships:** Fellow, College of Labor and Employment Lawyers.
**Career:** JD 1973 University of Virginia School of Law; BS 1967 University of Pennsylvania, The Wharton School.

## KAPLAN, Arthur
Fine, Kaplan and Black, RPC, Philadelphia 215 567 6565
*Recommended in Antitrust*

## KARALIS, Aris
Ciardi, Maschmeyer & Karalis PC, Philadelphia 215 546 4500
*Recommended in Bankruptcy*

## KASSNER, Andrew
Drinker Biddle & Reath LLP, Philadelphia 215 988 2700
*Recommended in Bankruptcy*

## KATZ, Carole S
Morgan, Lewis & Bockius LLP, Pittsburgh 412 560 3390
ckatz@morganlewis.com
*Recommended in Employment*
**Practice Areas:** Carole Katz is a Partner in the Labor and Employment Law Practice Group. Ms Katz counsels and represents employers and tries cases in a wide variety of labor and employment law matters, including employment discrimination, harassment, and retaliation issues and cases, wrongful discharge actions, benefits litigation, restrictive covenant/trade secret matters, and all other types of employment-related litigation. Ms Katz also has extensive experience in jury, non-jury, and administrative litigation, and alternative dispute resolution such as mediation and arbitration.
**Prof. Memberships:** American Bar Association (Labor and Employment Law and Litigation Sections); Allegheny County Bar Association.

## KELSEN, Peter Foster
Blank Rome LLP, Philadelphia
215 569 5655
kelsen@blankrome.com
*Recommended in Real Estate*
**Practice Areas:** Mr Kelsen's co-chairs the Institutional Real Estate Department at Blank Rome LLP. His practice is concentrated in the areas of zoning and land use law, real estate development and real estate tax assessment/exemption litigation. He has served as Land Use Counsel in connection with the development of office buildings, shopping centers, telecommunications facilities, hotels, hospitals, research and development facilities and major residential subdivisions. In the real estate tax assessment and Exemption area, he has successfully represented property owners in securing major reductions in Real Estate Taxes in the Philadelphia Metropolitan area. He is a frequent lecturer/author on Land Use matters.
**Prof. Memberships:** Philadelphia Bar Association; Pennsylvania Bar Association; American Bar Association; Board of Directors, Jewish National Fund of the Pennsylvania/New Jersey Region; Member of Building Industry Associations Government Affairs Committee; Chairman of the Zoning Code Drafting Committee.
**Career:** Blank Rome LLP, 1986 - Present, Co-Chair and Partner - Institutional Real Estate Department.
**Publications:** Editor - Philadelphia Zoning Code Publication Project - 1995 to present.
**Personal:** JD, Case Western Reserve, 1981; BA, University of Pennsylvania, 1978.

## KESSLER, Mark K
Wolf, Block, Schorr and Solis-Cohen LLP, Philadelphia 215 977 2576
mkessler@wolfblock.com
*Recommended in Corporate/M&A*
**Practice Areas:** Partner, Corporate/Securities Practice Group. Practice includes corporate and securities counseling with emphasis on mergers, acquisitions and public and private financing, including leveraged financing transactions.
**Prof. Memberships:** Member, American Law Institute, Philadelphia and American Bar Associations. Serves on American Bar Association Committee on Regulation of Securities. Former Chairman, Philadelphia Bar Association Section of Corporation, Banking and Business Law and Committee on Securities Regulation. Named by National Law Journal as leading figure in National Securities Bar.
**Career:** Admitted to Pennsylvania in 1961. Clerked for Pennsylvania Supreme Court Justice and served as Assistant to Commissioner of US Securities and Exchange Commission. Director and Former National President, Big Broth-

ers/Big Sisters of America. Member, Board of Directors of Arcadia University. Member, Board of Trustees of the Albert Einstein Medical Center and Federation of Jewish Agencies of Greater Philadelphia. Member, board of St Peter's School. President, Jewish Family Service of Philadelphia.
**Personal:** Received BA from Brown University in 1957 and JD from University of Pennsylvania Law School in 1960.

## KIMBOL, Paul S
Dechert LLP, Philadelphia
215 994 2603
paul.kimbol@dechert.com
*Recommended in Employment*
**Practice Areas:** Mr Kimbol is a Partner and former Chair of the Employee Benefits and Executive Compensation Group. He advises on the design and operation of qualified and non-qualified plans and executive compensation arrangements. He also works on the employee benefits aspects of mergers, acquisitions, and leveraged buyouts.
**Prof. Memberships:** Member of the Pennsylvania Bar; admitted to practice before several federal courts.
**Publications:** Frequent speaker on employee benefits matters to universities, seminars, and Bar Associations.
**Personal:** University of Pennsylvania, BA, 1967; JD, magna cum laude, 1972, Order of the Coif, Member of the Law Review.

## KLEBAN, Barry
Adelman Lavine Gold and Levin, Philadelphia
215 568 7515
*Recommended in Bankruptcy*

## KLEIN, Justin P
Ballard Spahr Andrews & Ingersoll LLP, Philadelphia 215 864 8606
kleinj@ballardspahr.com
*Recommended in Corporate/M&A*
**Practice Areas:** Focuses on diverse securities matters, including public and private securities offerings, representing boards of directors of public and private companies, and representing parties in regulatory and enforcement proceedings before the Securities and Exchange Commission (SEC), state securities commissions, and securities industry self-regulatory organizations.
**Prof. Memberships:** Chaired, Committee on Securities Regulation and the Executive Committee of the Business Law Section of the Philadelphia Bar Association. Member, Chair, the National Arbitration and Mediation Committee of the National Association of Securities Dealers, Inc. Appointed to Attorney Advisory Committee of The Pennsylvania Securities Commission.
**Career:** Admitted to Maryland Bar (1972); District of Columbia Bar (1973); Pennsylvania Bar (1983); joined Ballard Spahr as Partner (1992). He spent nine

years at the Securities & Exchange Commission (SEC) in Washington DC in various positions including Assistant Director of the Division of Corporation Finance.
**Publications:** Extensive publications in the area of securities law.
**Personal:** JD, with honors, George Washington University National Law Center (1972); BA, University of Pennsylvania (1969).

## KOHN, Joseph
Kohn Swift & Graf, Philadelphia
215 238 1700
*Recommended in Antitrust*

## KOONS, Robert
Drinker Biddle & Reath LLP, Philadelphia 215 988 2700
*Recommended in Intellectual Property*

## KORB, Philip
Ballard Spahr Andrews & Ingersoll LLP, Philadelphia 215 864 8709
korb@ballardspahr.com
*Recommended in Real Estate*
**Practice Areas:** Real estate acquisitions, development, condominiums and planned communities, leasing, taxation, and workouts.
**Prof. Memberships:** Past Chairman, Real Property, Probate and Trust Section of the Pennsylvania Bar Association; past Member of its House of Delegates. Former Chairman, Philadelphia Bar Association's Committee on Condominiums and Cooperatives and Pennsylvania Bar Association's Committee on Taxation of Real Estate. Member, American College of Real Estate Lawyers, served on the Board of Governors.
**Career:** Admitted to the Pennsylvania Bar (1975); joined as Partner (1985).
**Personal:** JD, magna cum laude, Temple University James E Beasley School of Law (1975); BA, Johns Hopkins University (1969).

## KOTLER, Lawrence J
Duane Morris LLP, Philadelphia
215 979 1514
ljkotler@duanemorris.com
*Recommended in Bankruptcy*
**Practice Areas:** Lawrence J Kotler practices in the area of reorganization and finance, representing chapter 11 debtors-in-possession, chapter 11 trustees, creditors' committees, secured creditors and large institutional unsecured creditors in all facets of bankruptcy. Mr Kotler is currently representing a number of unsecured creditors in several high-profile bankruptcy cases.
**Prof. Memberships:** Philadelphia, Delaware, Pennsylvania, New York, and American bar associations; Eastern District of PA Bankruptcy Conference - Pro Bono Committee (Chairman); Consumer Bankruptcy Assistance Project - Board of Directors.
**Career:** Admitted to practice in Pennsyl-

vania, New York, and Delaware; the United States Court of Appeals for the Third Circuit; United States District Courts for the Eastern and Middle Districts of Pennsylvania; and the United States District Court for the Southern District of New York.

**Personal:** Boston University School of Law, JD, 1989; University of Pennsylvania, BA, with honors in the major, 1986.

### KRAMER, J Scott
Duane Morris LLP, Philadelphia
215 979 1122
jskramer@duanemorris.com
*Recommended in Intellectual Property*

**Practice Areas:** J Scott Kramer maintains an active trial practice in the areas of commercial litigation, copyright and trademark litigation and securities litigation, product liability and healthcare related litigation. Mr Kramer has conducted more than 40 civil jury trials and has represented clients before AAA, NASD Regulation, Inc., New York Stock Exchange, American Institute of Architects, the Securities and Exchange Commission, a variety of professional association forums and in the state and federal courts of Pennsylvania, New Jersey, New York and Maryland.

**Prof. Memberships:** American Bar Association; Pennsylvania Bar Association - Corporation, Banking and Business Law Section, Civil Litigation Section, Securities Law Section; Philadelphia Bar Association - Medico-Legal Committee (Co-Chair, 2003); Philadelphia Association of Defense Counsel; Defense Research Institute; Philadelphia Court of Common Pleas - Medical Malpractice Task Force.

**Career:** Admitted to practice in New Jersey and Pennsylvania; the United States District Court for the Eastern District of Pennsylvania; and the Supreme Court of Pennsylvania. Duane Morris LLP, Partner 1988-present, Associate 1980-87.

**Personal:** Temple University School of Law, JD, 1980.

### KRAUSE, Cheryl A
Dechert LLP, Philadelphia
215 994 2139
cheryl.krause@dechert.com
*Recommended in Litigation*

**Practice Areas:** Ms Krause, a Partner in the White-Collar Litigation Group, concentrates her practice on internal investigations and white-collar defense.

**Prof. Memberships:** Member, Pennsylvania, Connecticut, and New York Bars; lecturer, University of Pennsylvania Law School; Member, Federal Bar Council.

**Career:** Former Assistant United States Attorney, Criminal Division, Southern District of New York; Clerkship, Hon Alex Kozinski, US Court of Appeals - Ninth Circuit; Clerkship, Hon Anthony M Kennedy, US Supreme Court.

**Personal:** Stanford Law School, JD, with

distinction, 1993; University of Pennsylvania, BA, summa cum laude, 1989.

### KUTLER, Marilyn
Schnader Harrison Segal & Lewis LLP, Philadelphia 215 751 2000
*Recommended in Real Estate*

### KYPER, James R
Kirkpatrick & Lockhart Nicholson Graham LLP, Pittsburgh 412 355 6542
jkyper@klng.com
*Recommended in Intellectual Property*

**Practice Areas:** IP litigation involving patents, trademarks, trade dress, copyrights and unfair competition. Litigations involving steel framing, thermostatic mixing valves, safety equipment, automobiles, cutting tools, cellular services, medical devices, internet business systems, software and entertainment properties. Litigates non-competes, license and distribution agreements, false advertising and insurance coverage for IP claims.

**Prof. Memberships:** ABA, PBA, ACBA; ABA IP Section; AIPLA, PIPLA, and IPO.

**Career:** K&L since 1976, Partner since 1983. Co-ordinated IP Litigation Group since 1993.

**Publications:** Presented working with experts in patent cases and discovery issues in patent and trademark cases.

**Personal:** JD, Duquesne University, 1976; BS, Penn State, 1967.

### LADOV, Donald
Cohen & Grigsby PC, Pittsburgh
800 394 4904
*Recommended in Employment*

### LANGEL, John B
Ballard Spahr Andrews & Ingersoll LLP, Philadelphia 215 864 8227
langel@ballardspahr.com
*Recommended in Employment*

**Practice Areas:** Chair, Labor, Employment and Immigration Group. Focuses on the representation of management in all phases of labor and employment matters including legal advice, training, policy development concerning labor and personnel issues, collective bargaining, employment litigation, wage and hour investigations, preparation of employment contracts and restrictive covenants, planning of early retirement and reduction in force programs, and implementation and related litigation involving the labor implications in mergers, acquisitions, and asset purchases.

**Prof. Memberships:** Member and past Chairman, Philadelphia Bar Association Labor and Employment Law Committee; Member, American Bar Association Labor and Employment Section; Fellow of The College of Labor and Employment Lawyers. Member of Board of Trustees of Alzheimer's Association-Delaware Valley Chapter and Member of Board of Trustees of Marietta College

**Career:** Admitted to Pennsylvania Bar

(1974); New Jersey Bar (1978); law clerk for the United States Disctict Court for the Eastern District of Pennsylvania (1974); joined the firm (1975); Adjunct Professor of Law, Temple University James E Beasley School of Law.

**Publications:** Contributing editor, Schlei & Grossman, 'Employment Discrimination'.

**Personal:** JD, summa cum laude, Temple University James E Beasley School of Law (1974); case note editor of the Law Review and Member, Editorial Board; Member of the Board of Visitors of Temple University James E Beasley School of Law; BA, Marietta College (1970).

### LANGER, Howard
Langer & Grogan PC, Philadelphia
215 419 6536
*Recommended in Antitrust*

### LAPOWSKY, Robert
Stevens & Lee PC, Philadelphia
215 575 0100
*Recommended in Bankruptcy*

### LAUPHEIMER, Ann Blair
Blank Rome LLP, Philadelphia
215 569 5758
laupheimer@BlankRome.com
*Recommended in Litigation*

**Practice Areas:** Concentrates in insurance coverage, insurance insolvency, business litigation.

**Prof. Memberships:** Philadelphia Bar Association, past Chair of Federal Courts Committee, Advisory Committee of Local Rules of Eastern District of Pennsylvania.

**Career:** Joined Blank Rome, 1986, Partner, 1994, Corporate Litigation Practice Group Leader 2004; law clerk Hon James Hunter III, United States Court of Appeals for the Third Circuit; Admitted in Pennsylvania (1984).

**Publications:** Comment, Sherman Act 'Jurisdiction' in Hospital Staff Exclusion Cases, 132 U Pa L Rev 121 (1983).

**Personal:** Born July 5, 1959, JD, summa cum laude, University of Pennsylvania Law School, 1984; AB, Princeton University, 1979.

### LAVELLE JR, John P
Ballard Spahr Andrews & Ingersoll LLP, Philadelphia 215 864 8603
lavellej@ballardspahr.com
*Recommended in Litigation*

**Practice Areas:** Focuses on product liability, complex commercial, class action, intellectual property litigation and election law.

**Prof. Memberships:** Sustaining Member, Product Liability Advisory Council, Inc. (PLAC); International Association of Defense Counsel (IADC); Defense Research Institute (DRI); American Bar Association; Pennsylvania Bar Association; New Jersey Bar Association; Philadelphia Bar Association, (former Chair, Federal Courts Committee, former

Chair, Business Ligitation Committee).

**Career:** Admitted in: Pennsylvania (1988); New Jersey (1989); US Court of Appeals 3d Circuit (1990); US Court of Appeals 4th Circuit (2002); US District Court Eastern District of Pennsylvania (1988); US District Court District of New Jersey (1989); US District Court Middle District of Pennsylvania (1995); US District Court Western District of Pennsylvania (2003); US Supreme Court (1998). Law clerk to the Honorable Thomas N O'Neill, Jr of the United States District Court for the Eastern District of Pennsylvania (1988-90).

**Publications:** Pharmaceutical and Food Litigation Chapters, Toxic Tort Litigation, (American Bar Association:2006).

**Personal:** JD, cum laude, Harvard Law School (1988); AB, magna cum laude, Princeton University (1985).

### LAVORGNA, Gregory
Drinker Biddle & Reath LLP, Philadelphia 215 988 2700
*Recommended in Intellectual Property*

### LAWALL, Francis J
Pepper Hamilton LLP, Philadelphia
215 981 4481
lawallf@pepperlaw.com
*Recommended in Bankruptcy*

**Practice Areas:** Partner, Bankruptcy and Reorganization Group. Experienced in: national bankruptcy and reorganization matters, including representation of major energy companies and creditors' committees in bankruptcy proceedings throughout the United States; also experienced in reorganization of companies with massive toxic tort liabilities. Represents companies in the petroleum, textile, automotive, clothing and construction materials industries.

**Prof. Memberships:** Board Member, International Energy Credit Association, Inc.

**Career:** JD 1985 Temple University School of Law; MA 1982 Temple University; BA 1981 Temple University.

### LAWLOR, William G
Dechert LLP, Philadelphia 215 994 2823
william.lawlor@dechert.com
*Recommended in Corporate/M&A*

**Practice Areas:** Mr Lawlor chairs the Mergers and Acquisitions Group. He focuses on public and private mergers and acquisitions, securities offerings, strategic investments, and general corporate representation, including governance and compliance. He advises corporate clients, boards of directors, and special committees in negotiated and contested transactions.

**Prof. Memberships:** Member, Pennsylvania and New York Bars; Member of various bar associations and DealLawyers.com Advisory Board.

**Publications:** Frequent lecturer and speaker. Wrote articles featured in publications including 'The Daily Deal', 'Merg-

ers & Acquisitions', 'M&A Lawyer', 'Securities & Commodities Regulation', and 'Corporate Governance Advisor'.
**Personal:** University of Pennsylvania (BA,1977); Stanford Law School (JD, 1980).

## LEACE, Benjamin
RatnerPrestia, Valley Forge 610 407 0700
beleace@ratnerprestia.com
*Recommended in Intellectual Property*
**Practice Areas:** Patent, trademark, copyright and trade secret litigation and internet disputes, alternative dispute resolution, licensing, counseling, and patent procurement
**Prof. Memberships:** Philadelphia Intellectual Property Law Association, Board of Directors (2005-); International Trademark Association, Classification Subcommittee (1997-2001), Emerging Issues Subcommittee (2001-03); Program Committee (2003-05); Philadelphia Local Chapter, Licensing Executives Society (Chair, 1994-97); Benjamin Franklin American Inn of Court; American Intellectual Property Law Association; Institute of Electrical and Electronics Engineers; American Bar Association; Pennsylvania Bar Association; Philadelphia Bar Association.
**Career:** Over 15 years experience in intellectual property law.
**Personal:** Lehigh University (BS, Comp. Engineering, 1988); Temple University School of Law (JD, 1988).

## LEGROS, Susan
Stevens & Lee PC, King of Prussia
610 205 6000
*Recommended in Environment*

## LESSER, Bruce
Wolf, Block, Schorr and Solis-Cohen LLP, Philadelphia 215 977 2450
blesser@wolfblock.com
*Recommended in Banking & Finance*
**Practice Areas:** Co-Chairman, Financial Services Practice Group and Member, Corporate/Securities Practice Group. Concentrates his practice in structuring and documentation of financing transactions and in areas of loan workouts, bankruptcy and business law.
**Prof. Memberships:** Member, Pennsylvania Bar Association, Section on Corporation, Banking and Business Law. Member, American and Philadelphia Bar Associations.
**Career:** Admitted to Pennsylvania in 1973.
**Personal:** Received BA from Pennsylvania State University in 1969 and JD from Villanova University School of Law in 1973.

## LEVIN, Christine C
Dechert LLP, Philadelphia
215 994 4000
christine.levin@dechert.com
*Recommended in Antitrust*
**Practice Areas:** Ms Levin is a Partner in

Dechert's Antitrust and White-Collar Litigation Groups. She has experience in antitrust actions involving baby food, newspapers, chemicals, and pharmaceuticals, and in class actions alleging price-fixing, false advertising, and other product liability claims.
**Prof. Memberships:** Admitted to Pennsylvania Bar, US District Court for the Eastern District of Pennsylvania, US Court of Appeals for the Third Circuit, and US Supreme Court.
**Career:** Law clerk, Hon Clarence C Newcomer, US District Court, Eastern District of Pennsylvania.
**Personal:** Duke University (BA, 1976); University of Pennsylvania Law School (JD, cum laude, 1982), Order of the Coif.

## LICHTENSTEIN, Robert J
Morgan, Lewis & Bockius LLP, Philadelphia 215 963 5726
rlichtenstein@morganlewis.com
*Recommended in Employment*
**Practice Areas:** Robert J Lichtenstein is the Leader of the firm's Employee Benefits and Executive Compensation Practice. He represents executives in negotiating their employment and compensation arrangements and counsels and assists employers in designing executive employment and compensation arrangements, including equity and incentive compensation plan. He also counsels clients on employee benefits issues, including qualified ESOPs, retirement, pension and profit-sharing plans. He has litigated employee benefit claims and disputes, and assists with federal tax law matters and representations before the IRS and DOL. He is an Adjunct Professor at the University of Pennsylvania School of Law and Villanova University Law School.
**Prof. Memberships:** Member, ABA, Tax Section, Employee Benefits Committee.

## LIEBENBERG, Roberta
Fine, Kaplan and Black, RPC, Philadelphia 215 567 6565
*Recommended in Antitrust*

## LINDEFJELD, Robert O
Jones Day, Pittsburgh
412 394 7952
rlindefjeld@jonesday.com
*Recommended in Intellectual Property*
**Practice Areas:** Practices patent, copyright, trademark, trade secrets, and unfair competition law and involved in litigation, transactional, opinion, counseling, or appellate work in these areas. Extensive experience in infringement and trade secret litigation in state and federal courts, including the US International Trade Commission, and business and commercial litigation and appeals. Frequently writes and lectures on IP law.
**Prof. Memberships:** Council Member, ABA IP Section; past President, Pittsburgh IP Law Association; past Chair, Pennsylvania Bar Association IP Section;

Pennsylvania Bar Institute IP Advisory Committee; AIPLA Professional Programs Committee; Chair, Local Patent Rules Committee, USDC for the Western District of Pennsylvania.

## LORD, Craig
Blank Rome LLP, Philadelphia
215 569 5496
lord@BlankRome.com
*Recommended in Real Estate*
**Practice Areas:** Real estate development, real estate lending, real estate sales/acquisitions, commercial litigation, arbitration and mediation.
**Prof. Memberships:** Admitted to practice in Pennsylvania (1972) and Florida (1977). Appointments: Board of Directors/Executive Committee - Philadelphia Industrial Development Corporation; Board of Trustees - Friends Central School; Member, Pennsylvania Judicial Conduct Board.
**Career:** Blank Rome, 1999-present, Partner, Real Estate Department; Department Head, Financial Services/Real Estate Department, 2003-05. Judge, Philadelphia Court of Common Pleas, 1988-97. Raynes, McCarty, 1997-99. Blank Rome, 1972-86.
**Personal:** JD, magna cum laude, University of Pennsylvania Law School, 1971, BA, magna cum laude, Gettysburg College, 1968.

## MACK, Wayne A
Duane Morris LLP, Philadelphia
215 979 1152
wamack@duanemorris.com
*Recommended in Antitrust*
**Practice Areas:** Wayne A Mack represents clients nationally in complex commercial litigation, with particular emphasis on antitrust, franchise, healthcare and securities law and trade regulation. He is a member of the firm's Dealer Services Group, representing automobile and truck dealers in a wide range of legal matters, including contract negotiations, succession issues, regulatory and compliance matters and litigating and mediating disputes. He has represented both plaintiffs and defendants in class action litigation, including cases involving claims of securities fraud, unfair trade practices and violations of the antitrust laws.
**Prof. Memberships:** American Bar Association, Antitrust Law Section, Business Law Section (Business and Corporate Litigation Committee) and Forum Committee on Franchising; Pennsylvania Bar Association, Civil Litigation Section; Philadelphia Bar Association; American Health Lawyers Association.
**Career:** Admitted to practice in Pennsylvania; the Supreme Court of the United States; United States Court of Appeals for the Third and Fourth Circuits; United States District Court for the Eastern District of Pennsylvania; and the Supreme Court of Pennsylvania. Duane Morris

LLP, Partner 1995-present, associate 1986-94. Chair, Franchise Litigation Group; Co-Chair, Antitrust Practice Group; Chair, Professional Standards Committee.
**Personal:** University of Pennsylvania Law School, JD, 1986; Temple University, BS, 1982.

## MAGAZINER, Fred T
Dechert LLP, Philadelphia
215 994 2587
fred.magaziner@dechert.com
*Recommended in Litigation*
**Practice Areas:** Mr Magaziner, Partner, litigates complex product liability cases, including MDL, class action mass torts, commercial matters, and patent cases.
**Prof. Memberships:** Former Chair, Professional Education Committee of the Philadelphia Bar Association; Member, The American Law Institute and advisory board of the Temple University Academy of Advocacy; fellow of the American College of Trial Lawyers.
**Career:** Clerkship, Hon Max Rosenn, US Third Circuit Court of Appeals.
**Publications:** Guest lecturer, Temple University and University of Pennsylvania; author of 'Pennsylvania Civil Trial Guide'.
**Personal:** Columbia University, BA, 1969; Columbia Law School, JD, 1976, notes and comments editor of Columbia Law Review.

## MAKADON, Arthur
Ballard Spahr Andrews & Ingersoll LLP, Philadelphia 215 864 8200
makadon@ballardspahr.com
*Recommended in Litigation*
**Practice Areas:** Chair of the firm. Extensive experience in complex civil and criminal cases. Focuses on white-collar criminal and complex commercial matters. Practice has included the representations of public officials and publicly traded corporations in grand jury matters and other government investigations. He has defended financial institutions for alleged violations under the securities, antitrust and consumer protection laws and ERISA. Defended a major accounting firm for alleged malpractice relating to the collapse of an insurance company. Engaged for appellate work throughout the country and in high profile matters generally. Counseled and represented corporations (and special committees) in connection with corporate governance issues.
**Prof. Memberships:** Engaged in a variety of community efforts. Trustee of the University of Pennsylvania, since 1996. Board of the Pennsylvania Convention Center. Member of the American Bar Association, Pennsylvania Bar Association and Philadelphia Bar Association.
**Career:** Admitted to the Pennsylvania Bar (1968). Law clerk to the Honorable Joseph S Lord, III, Chief Judge for the

United States District Court of the Eastern District of Pennsylvania and was Chief Assistant District Attorney for the City of Philadelphia. Former Adjunct Professor, University of Pennsylvania Law School.
**Personal:** LLB, cum laude, University of Pennsylvania Law School (1967) editor, University of Pennsylvania Law Review, Member, Order of the Coif; BA, Pennsylvania State University (1964).

### MAKOULIAN, Tina R
Ballard Spahr Andrews & Ingersoll LLP, Philadelphia 215 864 8713
makoulian@ballardspahr.com
*Recommended in Real Estate*
**Practice Areas:** Focuses on complex real estate developments, project finance, zoning, subdivisions, and land use. Experienced in developing condominiums, commercial leasing, and the acquisition, development and disposition of commercial properties; represents lenders in loans secured by industrial properties, office parks, and multi-family apartment buildings. Represents land owners to obtain zoning and land development approvals for a variety of developments. Assists hospitals, universities, private clubs, camp owners and operators, residential developers, and telecommunications companies in obtaining all forms of zoning relief, subdivision and land development approvals, and the concomitant municipal agreements.
**Prof. Memberships:** Member of the American Bar Association, Pennsylvania Bar Association, and Philadelphia Bar Association.
**Career:** Admitted to the Pennsylvania Bar (1993).
**Personal:** JD, cum laude, Villanova University School of Law (1993), member of the Villanova Law Review, elected to Order of the Coif; BA, University of Pennsylvania (1990).

### MALLOY, Elizabeth A
Klett Rooney Lieber & Schorling, Philadelphia 215 567 7614
eamalloy@klettrooney.com
*Recommended in Employment*
**Practice Areas:** Labor and employment law.
**Career:** Represents employers in a variety of litigation matters, including sexual harassment, race, national origin, disability and age discrimination cases, wrongful discharge, defamation, and other state law and constitutional claims. She has tried jury and non-jury cases involving sex, race and age discrimination, sexual harassment and breaches of restrictive covenants. Her practice also includes counseling employers of a range of labor and employment matters and is a frequent speaker to employer groups on a variety of topics.
**Personal:** BA (summa cum laude), Catholic University of America; JD (cum

laude), Villanova University School of Law.

### MANDELBAUM, David G
Ballard Spahr Andrews & Ingersoll LLP, Philadelphia 215 864 8102
mandelbaum@ballardspahr.com
*Recommended in Environment*
**Practice Areas:** Focuses on environmental matters including air and water pollution permit disputes, nationally significant contaminated sediment sites, commercial litigation over environmental representations in sale of a manufacturing division, regulation of timber harvesting, regulation of shooting preserves, public trust, wetlands, and 'sprawl' regulation, and complex urban brownfields. Appointed by the Governor to the Pennsylvania Statewide Water Resources Committee.
**Prof. Memberships:** Chair, Special Committee on Smart Growth and Urban Policy of the American Bar Association Section on Environment, Energy and Resources; past Chair, Pennsylvania Bar Association Environmental, Mineral, and Natural Resources Law Section. Member, environmental sections of the Florida Bar and Maryland State Bar Association.
**Career:** Admitted to Pennsylvania Bar (1983); Florida Bar (1984); Maryland Bar (1993); joined the firm (1987). Adjunct professor of Law and Adjunct Associate Professor of Community and Regional Planning at Temple University. Law clerk to Honorable Louis H Pollak.
Publications: 'Cooper Industries v. Aviall Services A Year Later', 51 Chem. Waste Litig. Rep. 320 (Feb 2006)(with M Mooney); 'Kelo v. City of New London: Takings, "Public Use," Urban Waterfront Redevelopment, and the Likely Survival of the Republic,' Comm. Leasing L. & Strat. at 1 (Jan 2006)(with M Fisher); 'Contribution After Cooper Industries v. Aviall Services', 49 Chem. Waste Litig. Rep. 137 (Jan 2005); 'The Timing Provisions of CERCLA for Natural Resource Damage Claims', 19 Toxics L. Rep. (BNA) 22 (Jan 2004); 'Thoughts on the Bush Clean Air 'Strategy' So Far, and a Suggestion for What Might Work', 21 Temple Envtl. L. & Tech. J. 1 (2002).
**Personal:** JD, magna cum laude, Harvard Law School (1983); AB, summa cum laude, Harvard College (1980).

### MANKO, Joseph
Manko, Gold, Katcher & Fox LLP, Bala Cynwyd 484 430 5700
*Recommended in Environment*

### MANNINO, Edward F
Akin Gump Strauss Hauer & Feld LLP, Philadelphia 215 965 1340
emannino@akingump.com
*Recommended in Litigation*
**Practice Areas:** Ed Mannino has tried cases nationwide for 35 years. The National Law Journal named him one of the Nation's Top Litigators and one of the

top 10 Pennsylvania trial lawyers, describing him as a 'stellar litigator who is known for handling high-profile cases'. He has tried to verdict business tort, securities, antitrust, accountant's liability, RICO, ERISA, healthcare, products liability, employment discrimination and intellectual property cases.
**Personal:** BA and JD, University of Pennsylvania.

### MARION, David
Montgomery, McCracken, Walker & Rhoads, LLP, Philadelphia 215 772 1500
*Recommended in Litigation*

### MARSHALL, John
Drinker Biddle & Reath LLP, Berwyn 610 993 2200
*Recommended in Intellectual Property*

### MARTINI, John D
Reed Smith LLP, Philadelphia
215 241 7908
jmartini@reedsmith.com
*Recommended in Employment*
**Practice Areas:** All aspects of employee benefits, focusing on complex executive compensation design, qualified plan compliance, and benefits-related securities issues. A significant portion involves benefit plan audit, design and review work. Frequently represents clients before the Internal Revenue Service and the Department of Labor.
**Career:** Joined Reed Smith in 2003.
**Publications:** 'Employee Plans Compliance Resolution System – The Latest on Plan Compliance,' and 'Addition of Employer Stock as an Investment Option to a 401(k) Plan'.
**Personal:** Villanova University School of Law (JD, 1995), associate editor, 'Villanova Law Review'; Grove City College (BS, 1992).

### MATHER, Barbara W
Pepper Hamilton LLP, Philadelphia
215 981 4895
matherb@pepperlaw.com
*Recommended in Antitrust, Litigation*
**Practice Areas:** Partner; Co-Chair, Litigation and Dispute Resolution Department; past Executive Partner. Experienced in: antitrust, securities, professional malpractice, commercial litigation. Represented: co-counsel for plaintiff LePage's in trial and appeals in monopolization claim that awarded $65 million after trebling, defendant's petition for certiorari before US Supreme Court denied in 2004; bathroom/kitchen fixtures and fittings manufacturer in allegations of price fixing; various entities in shareholder class actions; major law firms in malpractice allegations.
**Prof. Memberships:** Fellow, American College of Trial Lawyers.
**Career:** City Solicitor, Philadelphia, PA (1/84-12/85); JD 1968 University of Chicago Law School; BA 1965 Swarthmore College.

### MATOUR, James M
Hangley Aronchick Segal & Pudlin, Philadelphia 215 496 7016
jmatour@hangley.com
*Recommended in Bankruptcy*
**Practice Areas:** Bankruptcy, creditors rights, mergers and acquisitions, commercial litigation.
**Prof. Memberships:** American Bankruptcy Institute, Healthcare Insolvency Committee; Eastern District of Pennsylvania Bankruptcy Conference; Turnaround Management Association; Founding Board Member, Consumer Bankruptcy Assistance Project; contributing editor, The Bankruptcy Strategist (1983-97); Mediator, Eastern District of Pennsylvania Bankruptcy Court (1988-Present).
**Career:** Hangley Aronchick Segal & Pudlin, Shareholder (2000-present). Middleman & Matour, P.C., Founder & Chairman (1994-2000). Wolf, Block, Schorr & Solis-Cohen, Partner (1991-94), Associate (1986-91). White and Williams, Associate (1980-86). Delaware Law School, 1980 JD cum laude, Law Review, Moot Court Honor Society, and Chairman of the Honor Board.
**Publications:** Various articles in The Bankruptcy Strategist and continuing legal education lectures.

### MCCLENAHAN, David
Kirkpatrick & Lockhart Nicholson Graham LLP, Pittsburgh 412 355 6500
*Recommended in Litigation*

### MCELHINNY, Patrick
Kirkpatrick & Lockhart Nicholson Graham LLP, Pittsburgh 412 355 6500
*Recommended in Intellectual Property*

### MCGOUGH JR, W Thomas
Reed Smith LLP, Pittsburgh
412 288 3088
wmcgough@reedsmith.com
*Recommended in Litigation*
**Practice Areas:** Heads Litigation Department. Represents individuals and corporations in a wide variety of civil and criminal litigation.
**Prof. Memberships:** Former President, Allegheny County Bar Association; American College of Trial Lawyers; American Academy of Appellate Lawyers; Academy of Trial Lawyers of Allegheny County.
**Career:** Law clerk to the late Honorable William H Rehnquist, Chief Justice; assistant counsel to the Senate Select Committee on Secret Military Assistance to Iran and the Nicaraguan Opposition; Staff Liaison to Senator Robert Dole.
**Personal:** University of Virginia School of Law (JD, 1978); Princeton University (1975); listed in 'The Best Lawyers in America'.

**MCKENZIE, James**
Morgan, Lewis & Bockius LLP,
Philadelphia 215 963 5134
jmckenzie@morganlewis.com
*Recommended in Corporate/M&A*
**Practice Areas:** Mr McKenzie is a Partner in the Business and Finance Practice and Co-Chair of the firm's REIT Practice. He advises clients on securities, M&A and corporate law matters. Having been the general counsel of a Nasdaq-listed company, he has extensive experience advising boards of directors on corporate governance and Sarbanes-Oxley compliance. Mr McKenzie's practice includes transactions involving securities laws, such as mergers and acquisitions of publicly and privately held companies, IPOs and other public offerings, 144A offerings and strategic joint ventures.

**MCLEAN, Michael**
Kirkpatrick & Lockhart Nicholson
Graham LLP, Pittsburgh 412 355 6500
*Recommended in Corporate/M&A*

**MCMICHAEL, Lawrence**
Dilworth Paxson LLP, Philadelphia
215 575 7000
*Recommended in Bankruptcy*

**MCNICHOL, William J**
Reed Smith LLP, Philadelphia
215 241 7950
wmcnichol@reedsmith.com
*Recommended in Intellectual Property*
**Practice Areas:** Represents technology-based enterprises in IP matters including the prosecution of patent applications, re-examination and reissues; trademark registration applications, oppositions and cancellation proceedings; and preparation of patent validity and infringement opinions in anticipation of litigation and new product introduction. Extensive background in drug, biotech, and other medical technology IP litigation. In Amgen Inc v US Trade Commission, represented the amicus curiae and presented prevailing arguments in the Court of Appeals. Congress responded by enacting the Biotechnological Process Patents Act of 1995.
**Personal:** Villanova University (JD, 1983; MS in Biochemistry, 1979; BA in Biology, 1977)

**MEADWAY, Jay K**
Ballard Spahr Andrews & Ingersoll LLP,
Philadelphia 215 864 8101
meadwayj@ballardspahr.com
*Recommended in Intellectual Property*
**Practice Areas:** Focuses on foreign trademark protection. Involved in all aspects of trademark protection. Fluent in German, he represents companies and law firms in trademark matters in Europe, Japan, and elsewhere.
**Prof. Memberships:** Member, American Bar Association, Pennsylvania Bar Association, Philadelphia Bar Association, and the International Trademark Association.

**Career:** Admitted to Pennsylvania Bar (1981); District of Columbia Bar (1978); Virginia Bar (1979); New York Bar (1986); joined as Partner (2001). He was a Partner at a large law firm concentrating in international trademark practice and other areas of trademark, copyright, and unfair competition law. He has also been an in-house trademark attorney for Pfizer, Inc., with primary responsibility for the worldwide portfolio of consumer products trademarks.
**Publications:** 'The Community Trademark, A New Registration System For Obtaining Trademark Protection In The European Union' and 'Revised Japanese Trademark Law - An Overview Of Key Changes,' published in the Corporation, Banking and Business Law Newsletter.
**Personal:** JD, George Washington University (1978); BA, University of Pennsylvania (1975).

**MELOY, Michael**
Manko, Gold, Katcher & Fox LLP,
Bala Cynwyd 484 430 5700
*Recommended in Environment*

**MEYER, Dianne A**
Duane Morris LLP, Philadelphia
215 979 1222
dameyer@duanemorris.com
*Recommended in Banking & Finance*
**Practice Areas:** Dianne A Meyer is Chair of the Commercial Finance Practice Group. She practices in the areas of commercial finance, representing lenders and borrowers in secured and unsecured commercial lending transactions. She also practices in the area of municipal finance, acting as bond counsel, counsel to underwriters, borrower's counsel and counsel to credit enhancers on municipal finance transactions. Ms Meyer has extensive experience representing lending institutions in syndicated and other multibank loan transactions both in domestic and international transactions and also specializes in asset-based lending transactions.
**Prof. Memberships:** National Association of Bond Lawyers; Pennsylvania Association of Bond Lawyers - Board of Directors; Pennsylvania Institute of Certified Public Accountants; Philadelphia Bar Association.
**Career:** Admitted to practice in Pennsylvania and the Supreme Court of Pennsylvania.
**Personal:** University of Pennsylvania Law School, JD, 1986; Villanova University, BS, 1978.

**MIANO, Steven T**
Wolf, Block, Schorr and Solis-Cohen LLP,
Philadelphia 215 977 2228
smiano@wolfblock.com
*Recommended in Environment*
**Practice Areas:** Partner, Environmental and Land Use Practice Group. Practicing environmental law since 1985, concentrating in all areas of environmental law

including cases arising under Clean Water Act, Clean Air Act, Resource Conservation and Recovery Act, CERCLA, Toxic Substances Control Act, brownfields redevelopment laws and comparable state laws.
**Prof. Memberships:** Member, American Bar Association Section of Environment, Energy and Resources; Pennsylvania Bar Association Natural Resources Section; and Philadelphia Bar Association Environmental Law Committee, where he served as secretary in 1996. Former Co-Chair, ABA Section Water Quality and Wetlands Committee; current Member of Section Council.
**Career:** Former Assistant Regional Counsel for US Environmental Protection Agency, Region III, Hazardous Waste Branch. Member, Board of Trustees of Support Center for Child Advocates and named Distinguished Child Advocate in 1997. Graduate of Greater Philadelphia Chamber of Commerce Arts & Business Council - Business on Board Program.
**Publications:** Member, editorial board of ABA Section publication, Trends. Co-author, wetlands chapter in Section's Clean Water Act Handbook. Peer reviewer, Section's Basic Practice Series book on RCRA.
**Personal:** Received BS from George Washington University in 1982 and JD from Franklin Pierce Law Center 1985.

**MILLER, Alan**
Picadio Sneath Miller & Norton,
Pittsburgh 412 288 4000
*Recommended in Environment*

**MILLER, Camille**
Cozen O'Connor, Philadelphia
215 665 2000
*Recommended in Intellectual Property*

**MILLER, Henry**
Wolf, Block, Schorr and Solis-Cohen LLP,
Philadelphia 215 977 2182
hmiller@wolfblock.com
*Recommended in Real Estate*
**Practice Areas:** Partner, Real Estate Practice Group. More than 40 years experience in real estate. Represents developers of shopping centers and major high-rise office buildings. Has extensive experience representing real estate brokers, REITs and developers of industrial buildings and industrial parks.
**Prof. Memberships:** Member, American, Pennsylvania and Philadelphia Bar Associations. Former Chairman, Committee on Real Estate Law of Philadelphia Bar Association. Member, American College of Real Estate Lawyers.
**Career:** Admitted to Pennsylvania in 1965. Law clerk to Honorable Edwin D Steel, US District Court of Delaware (1963-65). Joined firm in 1964 and became Partner in 1971. Served as Member of firm's Executive Committee. Board Member and solicitor, Association for Jewish Children of Philadelphia. Former

President and Current Board Member, Jewish Family and Children's Agency of Philadelphia. Board Member, Philadelphia Commercial Development Corporation. Former President and Current Member, Advisory Board of Big Brothers/Big Sisters Association of Philadelphia. Member, Board of Directors of Philadelphia Child Guidance Clinic.
**Personal:** Received AB with honors from Lafayette College in 1959 and LB, cum laude, from the University of Pennsylvania in 1963. First Lieutenant in the US Army Reserve.

**MILLER, J Gregg**
Pepper Hamilton LLP, Philadelphia
215 981 4085
millerj@pepperlaw.com
*Recommended in Bankruptcy*
**Practice Areas:** Partner; Vice-Chair Bankruptcy and Reorganization Group. Experienced in: bankruptcy and reorganization law; represents creditors, groups of creditors and debtors in workouts, mass toxic tort bankruptcies and chapter 11 proceedings. Clients include hospitals; construction contractors, subcontractors, suppliers, sureties and lenders; asbestos products manufacturers and distributors.
**Prof. Memberships:** Co-Chairman, Construction, Surety and Insurance Law Subcommittee, Business Reorganization Committee, American Bankruptcy Institute. President-elect and Director, Board of Directors, Consumer Bankruptcy Assistance Project.
**Career:** LLB 1969 University of Pennsylvania Law School; BA 1966 Yale University.

**MONACO, Daniel**
Drinker Biddle & Reath LLP,
Philadelphia 215 988 2700
*Recommended in Intellectual Property*

**MONTAGUE JR, H Laddie**
Berger & Montague PC, Philadelphia
215 875 3000
*Recommended in Antitrust*

**MUNSCH, Martha Hartle**
Reed Smith LLP, Pittsburgh
412 288 4118
mmunsch@reedsmith.com
*Recommended in Employment*
**Practice Areas:** General labor and employment representation for management clients in private and public sectors, including colleges and universities.
**Prof. Memberships:** National Association of College and University Attorneys; Labor Law Section, Allegheny County Bar Association; Labor Section's Committee on Equal Employment Opportunity Law, ABA.
**Career:** Joined Reed Smith in 1973; joined the faculty of the University of Pittsburgh in 1976 to teach courses in employment discrimination and civil procedures, among others; returned to Reed Smith in 1978.
**Personal:** Yale Law School (JD, 1973);

University of Pittsburgh (1970); listed in The Best Lawyers in America.

### MURPHY, Terrence
Klett Rooney Lieber & Schorling, Pittsburgh 412 392 2044
thmurphy@klettrooney.com
*Recommended in Employment*
**Practice Areas:** Labor and employment law.
**Career:** Represents employers in the entire range of employment law matters, including class and individual employment discrimination actions, wrongful discharge litigation, OFCCP matters and state court claims. Regularly advises on equal employment and affirmative action issues, reductions in force, and FMLA and ADA issues. Also represents employers before the National Labor Relations Board and in collective bargaining and labor arbitration. He has particularly extensive expertise in representing employers in healthcare, higher education and manufacturing.
**Personal:** BA, University of Rochester; MS, Cornell University; JD, University of Pittsburgh School of Law.

### MYERS, Marlee
Morgan, Lewis & Bockius LLP, Pittsburgh 412 560 3310
msmyers@morganlewis.com
*Recommended in Corporate/M&A*
**Practice Areas:** Marlee Myers is a Partner in the Business and Finance Practice and is the Managing Partner of the firm's Pittsburgh office. Her practice focuses on mergers and acquisitions, initial and follow-on public offerings, corporate governance, venture finance, securities compliance, strategic alliances, international business transactions and general corporate counseling. Ms Myers represents companies in growth industries such as information technology, e-commerce, computer networking and life sciences, as well as major domestic and foreign industrial companies with subsidiaries worldwide.
**Prof. Memberships:** Pittsburgh Technology Council (Director).

### NADEL, Alan S
Akin Gump Strauss Hauer & Feld LLP, Philadelphia 215 965 1280
anadel@akingump.com
*Recommended in Intellectual Property*
**Practice Areas:** Represents domestic and foreign corporate clients of all sizes, academic and research institutions, individual physicians and other researchers in all aspects of patent matters involving bioscience, chemical and mechanical inventions, including patent preparation, prosecution, licensing, counseling and litigation. Provides analysis and opinions concerning patent validity, infringement and due diligence. Practice includes negotiating, advising about and preparing licenses, confidentiality, technology transfer, trade secret and consulting

agreements. Devises practical solutions to intellectual property problems.
**Prof. Memberships:** Former President, Philadelphia Intellectual Property Law Association; Director, George Washington University Alumni Association; Pennsylvania Bar.
**Personal:** BS (Chemistry), JD (honors), The George Washington University.

### NASSAU, Henry N
Dechert LLP, Philadelphia
215 994 2138
henry.nassau@dechert.com
*Recommended in Corporate/M&A*
**Practice Areas:** Mr Nassau, Partner, co-chairs Dechert's Corporate and Securities Group. He focuses on mergers, acquisitions, public offerings, private equity, and venture capital. He also advises on capital formation, investments, and acquisitions.
**Prof. Memberships:** Member, Pennsylvania Bar; Board Member of Capital Trust and ICG Commerce.
**Career:** Former Partner and Chair of Dechert's Business Department. Left Dechert in 1999 for Internet Capital Group to serve as chief operating officer, general counsel, and secretary.
**Personal:** Wharton School of the University of Pennsylvania (BS, cum laude, 1976); Dickinson School of Law (JD, magna cum laude, 1979), Managing Editor of the Dickinson Law Review.

### NAUGLE, Louis
Reed Smith LLP, Pittsburgh
412 288 8586
lnaugle@reedsmith.com
*Recommended in Environment*
**Practice Areas:** Head of Environmental Group; litigation and environmental counseling and due diligence; permitting and compliance/ enforcement proceedings.
**Prof. Memberships:** American, Pennsylvania and New York Bar Associations.
**Career:** Formerly in the Litigation Section of the Pennsylvania Department of Environmental Resources, Chief of the Litigation Unit in Harrisburg, 1982-84.
**Publications:** Author of A Practical Guide to Litigation with DER, a chapter in 'Pennsylvania Environmental Law and Practice'.
**Personal:** The Georgetown University Law Center (JD, 1975); Williams College (1972), Phi Beta Kappa; listed in 'The Best Lawyers in America' for natural resources and environmental law.

### NEWELL, Francis
Harkins Cunningham LLP, Philadelphia 215 851 6701
*Recommended in Antitrust*

### NIGON, Kenneth
RatnerPrestia, Valley Forge
610 993 4222
knnigon@ratnerprestia.com
*Recommended in Intellectual Property*
**Practice Areas:** Member of Manage-

ment Committee; Chair of Practice Management.
**Prof. Memberships:** American Bar Association; American Intellectual Property Law Association; Philadelphia Intellectual Property Law Association; Institute of Electrical and Electronics Engineers.
**Career:** 22 years experience in IP law, including five years as Patent Counsel for a major consumer electronics corporation. Nine years as a system programmer prior to entering legal field.
**Publications:** The New Written Description Requirement, 9/2002 issue of the Journal of the Patents & Trademark Office Society; Maintaining Your Competitive Advantage: A Periodic Intellectual Property Audit, 9/2002 issue of The Patent Journal; Chapters 1 and 5 of Electronic and Software Patents, Law and Practice Bureau of National Affairs, Inc. 2000.
**Personal:** University of Notre Dame (BSEE, cum laude, 1973); Stanford University (MSEE, Computer Engineering, 1974); Temple University (JD, 1983).

### O'BRIEN, William
Conrad O'Brien Gellman & Rohn PC, Philadelphia 215 864 8073
wobrien@cogr.com
*Recommended in Litigation*
**Practice Areas:** A leading trial lawyer who has tried high profile cases in state and federal courts. Practice includes product liability and mass tort cases, class actions, defamation, employment discrimination, personal injury, medical malpractice, legal malpractice, insurance coverage, environmental, antitrust, and commercial litigation.
**Prof. Memberships:** Fellow, American College of Trial Lawyers; Fellow, International Academy of Trial Lawyers; Diplomate, American Board of Trial Advocacy.
**Career:** Founding Member, Conrad O'Brien Gellman & Rohn, PC. Listed in legal and non-legal publications recognizing him for his accomplishments as a trial lawyer.
**Personal:** AB, LaSalle University; LLB, Villanova Law School.

### O'DEA, JR, Joseph F
Saul Ewing LLP, Philadelphia
215 972 7109
jodea@saul.com
*Recommended in Environment*
**Practice Areas:** Mr O'Dea represents clients ranging from privately held corporations to one of the nation's largest environmental services companies in environmental litigation matters. He handles complex commercial litigation matters, ranging from commercial contract/business disputes to governmental compliance/enforcement matters. He also represents Fortune 100 clients in the defense industry.
**Prof. Memberships:** Member, Ameri-

can, Pennsylvania, and Philadelphia Bar Associations.
**Career:** Designated a 'Pennsylvania Super Lawyer' by Philadelphia Magazine and Law and Politics Magazine. Litigation Department, Vice-Chair. Co-Chair of White-Collar and Government Enforcement Practice Group, and Diversity Committee.
**Personal:** JD, Villanova University School of Law, BS, Civil Engineering, Princeton University.

### O'DONNELL, G Daniel
Dechert LLP, Philadelphia
215 994 2762
daniel.odonnell@dechert.com
*Recommended in Corporate/M&A*
**Practice Areas:** Mr O'Donnell is a Partner and the Chair of the Private Equity Group. He focuses on mergers, acquisitions, corporate restructurings, and venture capital transactions. He has been involved in some of the major acquisitions of the last 20 years and has been lead adviser to clients in more than 50 leveraged buyout and recapitalization transactions.
**Prof. Memberships:** Member, Pennsylvania Bar; Member, board of advisers of the Penn Wharton Institute for Law and Economics.
**Personal:** University of Notre Dame, BA, summa cum laude, 1973; University of Pennsylvania Law School, JD, 1976, Member of the University of Pennsylvania Law Review.

### OLSON, Stephen
Kirkpatrick & Lockhart Nicholson Graham LLP, Pittsburgh 412 355 6500
*Recommended in Employment*

### OMINSKY, Harris
Blank Rome LLP, Philadelphia
215 569 5668
ominsky@BlankRome.com
*Recommended in Real Estate*
**Practice Areas:** Mr Ominsky is of counsel with Blank Rome LLC. He had co-chaired the firm's Real Estate Department for many years.
**Prof. Memberships:** Admitted in Pennsylvania; former President, Pennsylvania Bar Institute, American College of Real Estate Lawyers; former Board Member and Vice-Chair of Publications, American College of Mortgage Attorneys.
**Career:** Order of the Coif.
**Publications:** Mr Ominsky writes the column, 'Ominsky's Terrain', in the Legal Intelligencer. He has also authored three books and more than 1000 articles and is a frequent lecturer.
**Personal:** Graduated University of Pennsylvania Law School, cum laude.

## O'REILLY, Timothy

Morgan, Lewis & Bockius LLP,
Philadelphia 215 963 5470
to'reilly@morganlewis.com
*Recommended in Employment*

**Practice Areas:** Timothy O'Reilly is a
Partner in the Labor and Employment
Law Practice Group. Mr O'Reilly's practice focuses on all facets of employment
law with a particular emphasis on management labor relations matters. In that
area, he has represented private and public sector employers in a variety of matters. He also has experience with public
employment relations law, arbitration,
pensions and health funds, wage and
hour law issues and sports law.
**Prof. Memberships:** American Bar
Association (Labor and Employment
Law Section, Elected Council Member);
College of Labor and Employment
Lawyers (Fellow).

## OSSIP, Michael

Morgan, Lewis & Bockius LLP,
Philadelphia 215 963 5761
mossip@morganlewis.com
*Recommended in Employment*

**Practice Areas:** Michael Ossip is a Partner in the Labor and Employment Law
Practice Group. Mr Ossip's practice is
devoted exclusively to the representation
of management in all facets of employee
relations, including the litigation of claims
of employment discrimination in federal
and state courts. Mr Ossip has substantial
litigation experience, having tried to verdict many jury and non-jury cases.
**Prof. Memberships:** College of Labor
and Employment Lawyers (Fellow).

## PANITCH, Ronald L

Akin Gump Strauss Hauer & Feld LLP,
Philadelphia 215 965 1300
rpanitch@akingump.com
*Recommended in Intellectual Property*

**Practice Areas:** Co-Chair, firmwide
Intellectual Property Practice. Focuses on
licensing and counseling in both patent
and trademark matters. Has extensive
experience in negotiating and designing
creative settlements for issues that are difficult to resolve in contested proceedings,
and is frequently asked to appear as an
expert witness in such proceedings.
**Prof. Memberships:** Philadelphia, Pennsylvania and American Bar Associations;
Philadelphia Intellectual Property Law
Association; American Intellectual Property Law Association; American Law
Institute (elected); Pennsylvania Bar.
**Personal:** BSME, New Jersey Institute of
Technology; JD, Georgetown University.
Recognized by Philadelphia Magazine as
one of the 'Best Lawyers' in that city.

## PEDRICK, Michael J

Morgan, Lewis & Bockius LLP,
Philadelphia 215 963 4808
mpedrick@morganlewis.com
*Recommended in Banking & Finance*

**Practice Areas:** Michael J Pedrick is a

Partner in the Business and Finance
Group, focusing within the Finance and
Mergers and Acquisitions Practices. Mr
Pedrick's concentration in the finance
area includes the representation of borrowers in financing transactions ranging
from syndicated credits with institutional
lenders to leveraged acquisition and
asset-based financings to senior and mezzanine venture financings. He has significant experience in the use of limited
recourse and bankruptcy-remote financing vehicles, particularly the use of such
arrangements for financings within the
REIT industry, as well as experience
addressing financing issues in restructurings, workouts and bankruptcies.

## PEIRCE, Richard

Ballard Spahr Andrews & Ingersoll LLP,
Philadelphia 215 864 9475
peircer@ballardspahr.com
*Recommended in Intellectual Property*

**Practice Areas:** Focuses on trademarks,
domain names and related internet
issues, and unfair competition issues,
including litigation in federal courts and
before the Trademark Trial and Appeal
Board.
**Prof. Memberships:** Member, American
Bar Association, Pennsylvania Bar Associ-
ation, Philadelphia Bar Association, and
New Jersey State Bar Association. Mem-
ber, American Bar Association's Special
Committee on Online Trademark Issues.
**Career:** Admitted to the Pennsylvania
Bar (2000); joined as associate (2001).
**Personal:** JD, Syracuse University
(2000); BA, Rowan University (1997).

## PERKINS, Harriet

Drinker Biddle & Reath LLP,
Philadelphia 215 988 2700
*Recommended in Intellectual Property*

## PINHEIRO, Brian M

Ballard Spahr Andrews & Ingersoll LLP,
Philadelphia 215 864 8511
pinheiro@ballardspahr.com
*Recommended in Employment*

**Practice Areas:** He represents public,
private, non-profit, government and
church employers on matters relating to
executive compensation arrangements,
tax-qualified retirement plans, including
cash balance pension plans, and health
and welfare benefit plans. He has represented employers before the Internal Revenue Service, the US Department of
Labor, the Pension Benefit Guaranty Corporation and the Centers for Medicare &
Medicaid Services.
**Prof. Memberships:** Member, PENJERDEL
Employee Benefits and Compensation
Association, Program Committee. Member, American Bar Association, Pennsylvania Bar Association, and District of
Columbia Bar Association.
**Career:** Admitted: Pennsylvania Bar
(1995), District of Columbia Bar (1997).
Prior to joining Ballard, he was a tax law
specialist with the Employee Plans Divi-

sion of the Internal Revenue Service
(National Office).
**Publications:** Editor, 'ERISA - A Com-
prehensive Guide' (Aspen Publishers, Inc.
2003); author, 'ERISA Preemption - Cur-
rent Developments', published in ERISA -
A Comprehensive Guide.
**Personal:** LLM, Georgetown University
Law Center (1997); JD, magna cum
laude, Catholic University (1995); BA,
Boston College (1992).

## PITTLER, Alan M

Klett Rooney Lieber & Schorling,
Pittsburgh 412 392 1681
ampittler@klettrooney.com
*Recommended in Employment*

**Practice Areas:** Labor and employment
law.
**Career:** Represents employers in all
aspects of labor and employment law.
Extensive experience in union-related
matters, including organizing efforts, collective bargaining, contract administration and grievance handling, labor arbitrations and proceedings before the
National Labor Relations Board. Has also
defended employers in a wide variety of
employment matters before state and
federal agencies and courts, including
discrimination, wrongful discharge,
harassment and defamation claims.
**Personal:** Cornell University School of
Industrial and Labor Relations; JD
(cum laude), University of Pittsburgh
School of Law.

## POKOTILOW, Manny D

Caesar, Rivise, Bernstein, Cohen &
Pokotilow Ltd, Philadelphia
215 567 2010
mpokotilow@crbcp.com
*Recommended in Intellectual Property*

**Practice Areas:** Handles all areas of
patent, trademark and copyright law
including prosecution, licensing, litigation, validity and infringement studies,
and counseling. Has technical expertise
in the areas of electrical engineering, digital computers, telecommunication and
electronic scanning. Has litigated numerous landmark intellectual property cases.
**Career:** Admitted to practice in 1964,
Commonwealth of Pennsylvania; 1969,
US Supreme Court; 1982, US Court of
Appeals for the Federal Circuit; registered
to practice before the US Patent and
Trademark Office.
**Personal:** Newark College of Engineering (BSEE, 1960); Washington College of
Law of American University (JD, 1964).

## PRESTIA, Paul

RatnerPrestia, Valley Forge
610 993 4204
pprestia@ratnerprestia.com
*Recommended in Intellectual Property*

**Practice Areas:** Chair of firm's Management Committee; IP business management and strategic counseling; litigation
and internet disputes; alternative dispute
resolution; patent procurement; trade

secrets; trademarks.
**Prof. Memberships:** Philadelphia and
American Bar Associations; American
Intellectual Property Law Association;
Philadelphia Intellectual Property Law
Association; Benjamin Franklin Inn of
Court (Founding Member; President,
1996).
**Career:** Began professional career as an
engineer in the air munitions and petro-
leum fields. He then worked as a patent
agent and patent attorney for General
Electric Company before entering private
practice. Co-founded RatnerPrestia in
1981.
**Publications:** 'Tying and Trademark
Franchising: A look at the Developing
Case Law', American Intellectual Property
Law Association Quarterly Journal, Vol.
III, No. 4, 1975; 'Laches and Estoppel: Old
Doctrines Finding Modern Application',
1978 Patent Law Annual, Southwestern
Legal Foundation; 'New Era
Antitrust/Licensing Issues', Selected Legal
Papers, Vol. 5, No. 1 (Page H-1), July
1987, American Intellectual Property Law
Association; 'Decision Tree: Good Tool
for Analysis', Les Nouvelles, Vol. 29, No. 1,
March 1994, Licensing Executive Society;
'Minimizing The Risk of Willfulness In
U.S. Patent Infringement Litigation',
20/20 for The Twenty First Century, A
Special 20th Anniversary Commemora-
tive Issue of I. P. Japan, 1999, Shusaku
Yamamoto Patent Law Offices, Osaka,
Japan.
**Personal:** Lehigh University (BSChE,
1959); Georgetown University (JD, 1967).

## PRIMAVERA, Carl

Klehr Harrison Harvey Branzberg &
Ellers LLP, Philadelphia
215 568 6060
*Recommended in Real Estate*

## RABINOWITZ, Mark I

Blank Rome LLP, Philadelphia
215 569 5629
mrabinowitz@blankrome.com
*Recommended in Banking & Finance*

**Practice Areas:** Mr Rabinowitz concentrates his practice on commercial finance
including commercial lending, asset-
based financing, secured transactions,
mezzanine financing, personal property
leasing, loan syndications and participations, and asset securitization as well as
intercreditor relationships, lender liability
prevention and defense and bankruptcy,
reorganizations and debt restructuring.
**Prof. Memberships:** Equipment Leasing
Association; Eastern Association of
Equipment Lessors; Eastern District of
Pennsylvania Bankruptcy Conference;
Turnaround Management Association;
Pennsylvania Bar Association; New Jersey
Bar Association; Philadelphia Bar Associ-
ation; Florida Bar Association.
**Career:** Mr Rabinowitz is a Partner and
Practice Group Leader of the Financial
Services Group of Blank Rome LLP,

which he joined in 1988.

**Publications:** Co-author: 'Be Careful What You Look For: It Could Be an Authenticated Record', LJN's Equipment Leasing Newsletter, Volume 23, Number 7, August 2004. Contributing author: Update Chapter 23 'Regulation of Bank Leasing Activities' for Matthew Bender's Equipment Leasing Treatise, December 2003. Co-author: 'Golden Books Case Creates New 'Golden Rule' for Lessors', LJN's Equipment Leasing Newsletter, Volume XXI, Number 5, March 2002. Co-author, 'Georgia Upholds the Integrity of Hell or High Water', Equipment Leasing Today, May 1998.

**Personal:** Temple University School of Law (JD, Summa Cum Laude, 1988); Pennsylvania State University (BS, 1981).

### RACKOW, Julian
Blank Rome LLP, Philadelphia
215 569 5671
rackow@BlankRome.com
*Recommended in Real Estate*

**Practice Areas:** Real estate and retail development and finance; emphasis on adaptive reuse of historically-certified properties and development of major mixed-use projects; served as Co-Chair of firm's Real Estate Department and Chair of innovative RetailLaw Group.

**Prof. Memberships:** Admitted to practice in Pennsylvania and in Federal Court for Eastern District of Pennsylvania (1966). Chair, Central Philadelphia Development Corporation; Fellow, American College of Real Estate Lawyers; Board of Directors, Avenue of the Arts, Inc.; Member, National Economic Subcommittee for International Council of Shopping Centers.

**Career:** Joined Blank Rome LLP in 1970; became Partner 1975.

**Publications:** Lectures at the Annual ALI-ABA leasing program.

**Personal:** Born 16 December 1941; JD, Harvard Law School, 1966; AB, Cornell University, 1963.

### RADER, Kermit L
Wolf, Block, Schorr and Solis-Cohen LLP, Philadelphia 215 977 2708
krader@wolfblock.com
*Recommended in Environment*

**Practice Areas:** Partner, Environmental and Land Use Practice Group. His practice focuses on environmental aspects of real estate and corporate transactions, regulatory compliance counseling and remediation issues.

**Prof. Memberships:** Admitted to practice in Pennsylvania and the District of Columbia. Member, Natural Resources Section of American Bar Association and Environmental Section of Pennsylvania Bar Association. Former Co-Chair, Philadelphia Bar Association Environmental Law Committee.

**Career:** Began his legal career as attorney in Office of Environment at US Environ-

mental Protection Agency's headquarters. Became Assistant Regional Counsel and then Associate Regional Counsel and Chief of Superfund Section for Agency's Middle Atlantic Region.

**Publications:** Co-authored chapter, 'A Practical Guide to Litigating with EPA Region III' for 'Pennsylvania Environmental Law & Practice'.

**Personal:** Received BA, magna cum laude, from Duke University in 1975 and JD from George Washington Law School in 1978.

### RAYMOND, Douglas
Drinker Biddle & Reath LLP,
Philadelphia 215 988 2700
*Recommended in Corporate/M&A*

### REED, Margery N
Duane Morris LLP, Philadelphia
215 979 1518
mreed@duanemorris.com
*Recommended in Bankruptcy*

**Practice Areas:** Margery N Reed practices in the areas of business reorganization, bankruptcy law, corporate and commercial finance, syndicated loans, insurance insolvency and secured transactions involving securities and asset-based financing. She represents financial institutions in several capacities, including most recently as agent for a lending group as special servicer and master servicer for securitized mortgage loans and as secured lender.

**Prof. Memberships:** American College of Bankruptcy; American Bar Association - Business Bankruptcy-Business Transactions Subcommittee (Chair); Pennsylvania Bar Association; New Jersey State Bar Association; American Bankruptcy Institute; Eastern District of Pennsylvania Bankruptcy Conference, Chair (1999-2000), Vice-Chairperson (1998-99), Officer (1995-98), Steering Committee (1994-95), Education Committee (Co-Chair, 1993-94); Association of Commercial Finance Attorneys.

**Career:** Admitted to practice in New Jersey and Pennsylvania; the United States District Court for the Eastern District of Pennsylvania; United States District Court for the District of New Jersey; Supreme Court of Pennsylvania; and the Supreme Court of New Jersey. Duane Morris LLP, Member, Partners Board, 2002-present; Partner, 1990-present; Associate, 1982-90.

**Personal:** Villanova University School of Law, JD, 1982; Vassar College, BA, 1976.

### REED, Michael H
Pepper Hamilton LLP, Philadelphia
215 981 4416
reedm@pepperlaw.com
*Recommended in Bankruptcy*

**Practice Areas:** Partner, Bankruptcy and Reorganization Group. Experienced in bankruptcy, creditors' rights and insolvency law. Served as special bankruptcy counsel to Commonwealth of Pennsylva-

nia in LTV bankruptcy and represented amici curiae in litigation that resulted in US Second Circuit landmark decision in environmental and bankruptcy law.

**Prof. Memberships:** Fellow, American College of Bankruptcy. Member, American Law Institute. Board of Trustees, Academy of Natural Sciences. Board of Advisors, Public Interest Law Center of Philadelphia. Member, Pennsylvania Interest on Lawyers Trust Account Board. Former President, Pennsylvania Bar Association.

**Career:** JD 1972 Yale Law School; BA 1969 Temple University.

### REICH, Judith
Drinker Biddle & Reath LLP,
Philadelphia 215 988 2700
*Recommended in Banking & Finance*

### REICH, Abraham
Fox Rothschild LLP, Philadelphia
215 299 2000
*Recommended in Litigation*

### REINHART, Joe
Babst, Calland, Clements and Zomnir,
A Professional Corporation, Pittsburgh
412 394 5400
*Recommended in Environment*

### RICHMAN, Hershel J
Dechert LLP, Philadelphia
215 994 2571
hershel.richman@dechert.com
*Recommended in Environment*

**Practice Areas:** Mr Richman is Special Counsel and a former Partner and Chair of the Environmental Litigation Group. He assists clients in all aspects of environmental law.

**Prof. Memberships:** Former Chair of International Association of Attorneys and Executives in Corporate Real Estate and Pennsylvania Environmental Hearing Board Rules Committee; past President of the Delaware Valley Environmental American Inn of Court.

**Career:** Held key positions in Pennsylvania Department of Environmental Resources and the Bucks County Planning Commission; former Adjunct Professor of Environmental Law at Drexel University.

**Personal:** The Pennsylvania State University (BS, 1964); Villanova University School of Law (JD, 1967).

### ROCCI, Steven
Woodcock Washburn LLP, Philadelphia
215 568 3100
rocci@woodcock.com
*Recommended in Intellectual Property*

**Practice Areas:** Intellectual property litigation and counseling in diverse technology areas, including electronics, computer science, telecommunications and internet technologies, and consumer products. Oversees substantial patent procurement program.

**Prof. Memberships:** Member, Pennsylvania Bar, American, Pennsylvania and

Philadelphia Bar Associations; the PIPLA and the AIPLA.

**Career:** Member, firm's Policy Committee. Adjunct professor, patent law, Temple University Law School. Former engineer of several Fortune 500 companies. Joined Woodcock Washburn, 1986.

**Publications:** Recognized in Chambers USA 2003, 2005. Named a Pennsylvania Super Lawyer. Best Lawyers in America 2005.

**Personal:** Temple University School of Law, JD (1981). Drexel University, BS, cum laude (1977).

### RODGERS, James
Dilworth Paxson LLP, Philadelphia
215 575 7000
*Recommended in Antitrust*

### ROHN, James J
Conrad O'Brien Gellman & Rohn PC,
Philadelphia 215 864 8074
jrohn@cogr.com
*Recommended in Litigation*

**Practice Areas:** Managing Shareholder, Conrad O'Brien Gellman & Rohn, PC. He has tried and been involved as lead counsel in civil RICO cases, class actions, complex commercial litigation, white-collar grand jury investigations, internal corporate investigations and regulatory compliance, antitrust, insurance, securities, asset recovery, environmental, and legal malpractice cases.

**Prof. Memberships:** Fellow, American College of Trial Lawyers.

**Career:** Law clerk, Hon Louis C. Bechtle (EDPa); Assistant United States Attorney (1978-1982), First Assistant United States Attorney (1983-86), Eastern District of Pennsylvania.

**Personal:** BA and JD, Villanova University and Villanova University School of Law, Member of Law Review.

### ROMANO, Carmen J
Dechert LLP, Philadelphia
215 994 2971
carmen.romano@dechert.com
*Recommended in Corporate/M&A*

**Practice Areas:** Mr Romano is a Partner and the former Co-Chair of the Corporate and Securities Group. He focuses his practice on mergers and acquisitions and private equity matters. He executes transactions on behalf of private equity and strategic clients across various industries, including healthcare, education, industrial, and consumer products.

**Prof. Memberships:** Member, Pennsylvania Bar.

**Career:** Clerkship, Honorable Dolores K Sloviter, US Court of Appeals - Third Circuit.

**Personal:** The Wharton School of the University of Pennsylvania, BS, summa cum laude, 1977; Columbia Law School, JD, 1980, note editor of the Columbia University Law Review.

## ROSENBERG, Kenneth
Schnader Harrison Segal & Lewis LLP,
Philadelphia 215 751 2000
*Recommended in Real Estate*

## RUDOLPH, Andrew J
Pepper Hamilton LLP, Philadelphia
215 981 4749
rudolpha@pepperlaw.com
*Recommended in Employment*
**Practice Areas:** Partner; Chair, Employee Benefits Practice Group. Experienced in: employee benefits/ERISA; executive compensation, related tax and corporate law issues for public and private companies. Practice focuses on the development of programs that link compensation and benefits to the employer's performance; qualified and non-qualified retirement plans; executive employment and severance agreements; benefits and compensation aspects of corporate transactions. Represents clients before US Internal Revenue Service and Department of Labor.
**Career:** JD 1982 University of Pennsylvania Law School; 1978 BA University of Pennsylvania.

## RYAN, M Frances
Dechert LLP, Philadelphia
215 994 2438
mfrances.ryan@dechert.com
*Recommended in Employment*
**Practice Areas:** Ms Ryan, a Partner, represents employers in individual and class action employment discrimination suits, trade secrets and non-compete disputes, ERISA claims, and executive compensation disputes. She represents litigants in complex litigation and arbitration matters, including breach of contract, RICO, insurance coverage, and professional malpractice suits.
**Prof. Memberships:** Member, Pennsylvania Bar; admitted to practice before several federal courts.
**Career:** Clerkship, the Honorable Franklin S Van Antwerpen, US District Court, Eastern District of Pennsylvania.
**Personal:** University of Scranton, BA, summa cum laude, 1988; University of Chicago Law School, JD, with honors, 1991, Member of the Law Review.

## RZONCA, Lynn E
Ballard Spahr Andrews & Ingersoll LLP,
Philadelphia 215 864 8109
rzoncal@ballardspahr.com
*Recommended in Intellectual Property*
**Practice Areas:** Managing Partner, Philadelphia office. Specializes in intellectual property litigation and counseling. Participated in a wide range of intellectual property litigation matters in federal courts and before US Trademark Trial and Appeal Board, including patent, trademark, trade secret theft, non-compete agreements, false advertising, counterfeiting, and copyright claims. Prosecuted many trademark applications before the United States Patent and

Trademark Office. Assists clients with clearance of new trademarks and with assessing whether to challenge competitors' use of potentially-infringing trademarks or false or misleading advertising. Reviews clients' advertising material, including websites, for compliance with relevant law.
**Prof. Memberships:** Appointed to Narberth Planning Commission.
**Career:** Admitted in Illinois (1991); Pennsylvania (2001); and United States Patent and Trademark Office (1992). Attorney Advisor to the Honorable Anthony J Scirica, Chief Judge to the United States Court of Appeals for the Third Circuit.
**Personal:** JD, Northwestern University School of Law (1991), Member, International Journal of Law and Business; MA, Loyola University of Chicago (1986); BS, Loyola University of Chicago (with honors, 1984).

## SAINT-ANTOINE, Paul
Drinker Biddle & Reath LLP,
Philadelphia 215 988 2700
*Recommended in Antitrust*

## SARACHAN, Ronald A
Ballard Spahr Andrews & Ingersoll LLP,
Philadelphia 215 864 8333
sarachan@ballardspahr.com
*Recommended in Environment*
**Practice Areas:** Focuses on defending corporations and individuals facing criminal investigation and prosecution, regulatory enforcement action, and related litigation. Represents corporate clients ranging from Fortune 500 companies to closely held corporations in all aspects of complex commercial and criminal litigation, internal investigations, compliance and regulatory matters, and grand jury proceedings.
**Prof. Memberships:** Former Co-Chair, Environmental Crimes Sub-Committee of the ABA White Collar Crime Section. Member, Federal Bar Association Criminal Law Committee and the Pennsylvania Bar Association.
**Career:** Admitted to Pennsylvania Bar (1990); New York Bar (1983); joined as Partner (1997). He was an Assistant United States Attorney and Chief of the Major Crimes Section in the United States Attorney's Office for the Eastern District of Pennsylvania, and served as Chief of the Environmental Crimes Section in the US Department of Justice. Law clerk to the Honorable Edward Weinfeld, United States District Judge for the Southern District of New York.
**Publications:** 'Criminal Negligence Prosecutions under the Federal Clean Water Act', Vol XXXII Environmental Law Reporter, News and Analysis (October, 2002), (co-written with Steven P Solow). Has lectured extensively on criminal and environmental law and testified before the United States Senate Judiciary

Committee and the United States Sentencing Commission.
**Personal:** JD, magna cum laude, The University of Michigan (1981); SCB, in Chemistry, magna cum laude, Brown University (1978).

## SCHAFFER, Eric A
Reed Smith LLP, Pittsburgh
412 288 4202
eschaffer@reedsmith.com
*Recommended in Bankruptcy*
**Practice Areas:** Bankruptcy and commercial litigation; served as Head of the firm's Corporate Restructuring and Bankruptcy Group, 2001-04; represents secured and unsecured creditors in major bankruptcy cases and non-judicial restructurings involving manufacturing enterprises, hospitals, retailers, utilities, airlines, real estate projects, and other businesses.
**Prof. Memberships:** Fellow of the American College of Bankruptcy.
**Publications:** Contributing author of 'Collier Bankruptcy Practice Guide' and 'The Art of Science of Bankruptcy.'
**Personal:** University of Pittsburgh School of Law (JD, 1979); University of Virginia (1976); listed in 'The Best Lawyers in America'; selected as a Pennsylvania Super Lawyer.

## SCHEFF, Richard
Montgomery, McCracken, Walker & Rhoads, LLP, Philadelphia
215 772 1500
*Recommended in Litigation*

## SCHER, Howard
Buchanan Ingersoll PC, Philadelphia
215 665 3920
scherhd@bipc.com
*Recommended in Litigation*
**Practice Areas:** Focuses on complex litigation for business clients and the efficient resolution of complex business problems. He has achieved victories both in the prosecution and the defense of many types of complex and sophisticated business litigation, including antitrust, securities, business torts, RICO, franchise, intellectual property, securities, fraud, tax and accounting, class action and other areas. His experience extends to state and federal court actions, as well as emergency injunctions, jury trials and appeals.
**Prof. Memberships:** International Academy of Trial Lawyers; American College of Trial Lawyers.
**Personal:** JD Rutgers University, 1971; BA Brandeis University, 1967.

## SCHILDHORN, Gary
Adelman Lavine Gold and Levin,
Philadelphia 215 568 7515
*Recommended in Bankruptcy*

## SCHORLING, William H
Klett Rooney Lieber & Schorling,
Pittsburgh 215 567 7508
whschorling@klettrooney.com
*Recommended in Bankruptcy*

**Practice Areas:** Bankruptcy and corporate reorganization.
**Prof. Memberships:** Numerous, including Fellow, American College of Bankruptcy; and Member, Founders' Council of the Commerical Finance Association Education Foundation.
**Career:** Represents debtors, indenture trustees, creditors' committees, secured creditors and unsecured creditors in bankruptcy proceedings. Experience includes the representation of a number of Fortune 500 companies and money center and regional financial institutions. Has also represented lenders in negotiating and documenting secured and unsecured loans and securitized credit facilities and in working out troubled domestic and foreign loans, including multilender loans.
**Personal:** BA (cum laude), Denison University; JD (cum laude), University of Michigan.

## SCHWARZE, William W
Akin Gump Strauss Hauer & Feld LLP,
Philadelphia 215 965 1270
wschwarze@akingump.com
*Recommended in Intellectual Property*
**Practice Areas:** Mr Schwarze chairs the Chemical and Foreign Patent practices in Akin Gump's Philadelphia office. Fluent in German, he counsels many German and Japanese companies in patent matters. He has many clients in the medical arts and focuses his practice on patent prosecution, licensing and opinion work.
**Prof. Memberships:** Pennsylvania Bar; Philadelphia, Pennsylvania and American Bar Associations; Philadelphia Intellectual Property Law Association; US Court of Appeals for the Federal Circuit; United States Patent and Trademark Office.
**Personal:** BChE, Yale University (1965); LLB, University of Pennsylvania (1968).

## SCOLNIC, David
Hangley Aronchick Segal & Pudlin,
Philadelphia 215 496 7046
dscolnic@hangley.com
*Recommended in Real Estate*
**Practice Areas:** Wide variety of local, national and international real estate and corporate matters. Real estate practice includes acquisition, development, construction, financing, investment, leasing and management. Represents developers, investors, lenders, brokers and government as well as companies that do not consider themselves to be "in the real estate business". Corporate practice includes acquisitions, sales, financing, and contracts. Serves as 'outside general counsel' to clients.
**Prof. Memberships:** National Association of Industrial and Office Properties (NAIOP), Member 2004-present, Government Affairs Committee, 2004-05; ABA Section on Real Property, Probate and Trust Law, Member, 1986-present.
**Career:** Hangley Aronchick Segal &

Pudlin, Shareholder, 1997-present, Officer and Director 2002-04; associate, 1995-97. Drinker Biddle & Reath, 1986-95, associate. New York University, School of Law, JD, 1986. University of Pennsylvania, MCP, 1983; BA, 1982.

### SCOTT, Michael T
Reed Smith LLP, Philadelphia
215 851 8248
mscott@reedsmith.com
*Recommended in Litigation, Products Liability*

**Practice Areas:** Complex litigation matters, including antitrust, legal and accounting malpractice, and pharmaceutical and medical device product liability, at the trial court and appellate levels. Extensive experience in the use of arbitration, under the Federal Arbitration Act and the Uniform Arbitration Act, for the resolution of commercial and construction disputes.
**Career:** Civil Division of the Justice Department, where he successfully defended the legality of one of President Reagan's official acts, the decontrol of domestic crude oil and gasoline.
**Personal:** University of Pennsylvania Law School (JD, 1976), editor, 'Penn Law Review'; Penn State University (BS, 1972).

### SEDRAN, Howard
Levin Fishbein Sedran & Berman, Philadelphia
215 592 1500
*Recommended in Antitrust*

### SEGAL, Daniel
Hangley Aronchick Segal & Pudlin, Philadelphia 215 496 7003
dsegal@hangley.com
*Recommended in Litigation*

**Practice Areas:** Civil litigation involving defamation, First Amendment, intellectual property, healthcare, professional ethics, education, civil rights, securities, antitrust, academic research misconduct, employment
**Prof. Memberships:** Juvenile Law Center, President, 2000-02; Philadelphia Bar Association Judicial Selection Commission, Chair, 1997-98; Philadelphia Bar Association Municipal Courts Committee, Co-Chair, 1997-98; University of Pennsylvania Inn of Court, 2001-present; Member, American, Pennsylvania and Philadelphia Bar Associations.
**Career:** Founder Shareholder and Litigation Department Chair, Hangley Aronchick Segal and Pudlin, 1994-present; Shareholder, Hangley Connolly Epstein Chicco Foxman and Ewing, 1979-94; Assistant Professor of Law, University of Pennsylvania Law School, 1976-79; Adjunct Professor of Law, University of Pennsylvania Law School, 1979-94; law clerk to Hon Thurgood Marshall, Associate Justice, United States Supreme Court, 1975-76; law clerk to Hon David L Bazelon, United States Court of Appeals

for the DC Circuit, 1974-75; Harvard Law School, JD, magna cum laude, 1973; Harvard Law Review, executive editor, 1972-73; London School of Economics, MSc, 1969; Yale College, BA, magna cum laude, 1968.
**Publications:** Speaker for professional associations and continuing legal education seminars.
**Personal:** Active in the local and national Jewish community, having served as President of Akiba Hebrew Academy, President of the Auerbach Central Agency for Jewish Education, as Co-Chair of the Philadelphia Soviet Jewry Council, and as a Board Member of the Jewish Educational Services of North America. Currently serving as President of Hillel at the University of Pennsylvania and as a Member of the International Council of the New Israel Fund.

### SEIDEL, Arthur
Drinker Biddle & Reath LLP, Philadelphia 215 988 2700
*Recommended in Intellectual Property*

### SERVODIDIO, Thomas G
Duane Morris LLP, Philadelphia
215 979 1844
tgservodidio@duanemorris.com
*Recommended in Employment*

**Practice Areas:** Thomas G Servodidio practices in the areas of management labor relations and employment law, employment discrimination litigation, restrictive covenant litigation, the Occupational Safety and Health Act, COBRA matters and affirmative action issues. Mr Servodidio also handles arbitrations, collective bargaining negotiations and matters before the National Labor Relations Board.
**Prof. Memberships:** American Bar Association; Pennsylvania Bar Association; Philadelphia Bar Association; The District of Columbia Bar; University of Pennsylvania Law School Inn of the American Inns of Court (1996-98).
**Career:** Admitted to practice in the District of Columbia, New Jersey, and Pennsylvania; the United States Court of Appeals for the Third and Fourth Circuits; United States Court of Appeals for the District of Columbia; United States District Court for the Eastern District of Pennsylvania; United States District Court for the District of New Jersey; Supreme Court of Pennsylvania; and the Supreme Court of New Jersey.
**Publications:** Co-author, Chapter on Labor and Employment Issues, Buying and Selling a Business, Pennsylvania Bar Institute, Fifth Edition (2001); co-author, 'Courts Protect Former Employees Against Retaliation Under Title VII', The Legal Intelligencer, June 11, 1997.
**Personal:** University of Pennsylvania Law School, JD, cum laude, 1987; Bucknell University, BA, magna cum laude, 1984.

### SHADOWEN, Steve
Hangley Aronchick Segal & Pudlin, Harrisburg 717 364 1010
sshadowen@hangley.com
*Recommended in Antitrust*

**Practice Areas:** Commercial and antitrust litigation.
**Prof. Memberships:** American Bar Association, 1985-present; Antitrust section; Vice-Chair, Committee on Trial Evidence, Section of Litigation, 1991-93; Member of the Bar of the United States Courts of Appeals for the First, Second, Third, Sixth, Seventh, and Eleventh Circuits.
**Career:** Shareholder, Hangley Aronchick Segal & Pudlin, 2003-present. Executive Committee, 2002-03; Partner, 1993-2003; associate, 1985-93; Schnader Harrison Segal & Lewis. Law clerk to The Honorable Boyce F Martin, Jr, United States Court of Appeals for the Sixth Circuit, 1984-85. Georgetown Law Center, 1984, cum laude, and editorial board of the Georgetown Law Journal.
**Publications:** Note, Economic and Critical Analyses of the Law of Covenants Not to Compete, 72 Georgetown Law Journal 1425 (1984); Removal of State Law Damage Claims Under the Complete Preemption Doctrine, 60 Transportation Practitioner's Journal 403 (1993); Editor-in-Chief, Trial Evidence, American Bar Association, 1991-93.
**Personal:** For the past 15 years, Mr Shadowen's practice has focused on antitrust litigation, principally on behalf of plaintiffs. He has served as lead counsel on numerous groundbreaking litigations involving the intersection between intellectual property law and antitrust law.

### SHAPIRO, Joel Charles
Blank Rome LLP, Philadelphia
215 569 5746
shapiro-jc@blankrome.com
*Recommended in Bankruptcy*

**Practice Areas:** Mr Shapiro concentrates his practice on bankruptcy, reorganizations and workouts and other banking and commercial lending matters including loan restructuring, debtor-in-possession financing, intercreditor relationships, and lender liability prevention and defense, primarily representing institutional lenders, lender groups, creditors, creditors committees, debtors, plan of reorganization proponents and asset purchasers.
**Prof. Memberships:** Pennsylvania Bar Association, Philadelphia Bar Association, Bankruptcy Committee, Florida Bar Association, New Jersey Bar Association.
**Career:** He joined Blank Rome LLP in 1984 and became a Partner in 1994.
**Publications:** 'The Chapter 11 Process', Pennsylvania Bar Institute Course Materials Journal (1991); 'Advanced Issues in Commercial Bankruptcy', Pennsylvania Bar Institute Course Materials Journal (1993); 'Pennsylvania Uniform Fraudu-

lent Transfer Act: Transfers - What and When', Pennsylvania Bar Institute Course Materials Journal (1995); 'Should The Lessor Care Whether Defaults are Cured?' Leader's Equipment Leasing Newsletter (January 1997); 'Motions for First Day Orders in a Chapter 11 Case', Pennsylvania Bar Institute Course Materials (1999); 'Pre-Bankruptcy Planning Issues', Philadelphia Business Journal (2004)'; 'New Bankruptcy Law Swings Pendulum in Landlords' Favor', Turnaround Management Association - The Journal of Corporate Renewal, July 2005, Vol. 18, No. 7 (2005).
**Personal:** JD, University of Miami Law School, cum laude, 1984; BA, Emory University, 1981.

### SHAPIRO, Raymond
Blank Rome LLP, Philadelphia
215 569 5569
shapiro@BlankRome.com
*Recommended in Bankruptcy*

### SHARGEL, Jason M
Wolf, Block, Schorr and Solis-Cohen LLP, Philadelphia 215 977 2216
jshargel@wolfblock.com
*Recommended in Corporate/M&A*

**Practice Areas:** Partner, Corporate/ Securities Practice Group. Has more than 20 years experience in private practice of corporate and securities law, including public and private merger and acquisition and joint venture transactions as well as representation of issuers and funds in venture capital and growth capital financings. Also actively engaged in general corporate representations of public and private clients.
**Prof. Memberships:** Member, Pennsylvania Bar Association.
**Career:** Began career at US Securities and Exchange Commission Enforcement Division. Served as law clerk to Honorable A Leon Higginbotham, Jr on US Court of Appeals for Third Circuit (1977-79).
**Publications:** Author or co-author of number of articles relating to securities law matters.
**Personal:** Received BA, magna cum laude, from Columbia University in 1974 and JD, magna cum laude, from University of Pennsylvania Law School in 1977.

### SHAY, Kathleen M
Duane Morris LLP, Philadelphia
215 979 1210
kmshay@duanemorris.com
*Recommended in Corporate/M&A*

**Practice Areas:** Kathleen M Shay concentrates her practice in the areas of business law and finance, securities regulation, venture capital financings, mergers and acquisitions, corporations, partnerships and limited liability companies.
**Prof. Memberships:** Greater Philadelphia Venture Group; Women's Investment Network; Technology Council of Eastern Pennsylvania; American Bar

Association - Business Law Section; Pennsylvania Bar Association - Corporation, Banking and Business Law Section; Pennsylvania Biotechnology Association - BIOTECH 2003 and 2002 Symposium Committees; Mid-Atlantic Venture Conference - Coaching Committee (Co-Chair, 2001-03), Steering Committee (1996, 1998, 2000-03); Philadelphia Bar Association - Business Law Section, Executive Committee, Steering Committee on Securities Regulation (Chair, 2001, Vice-Chair, 2000, Secretary, 1999); Order of the Coif.

**Career:** Admitted to practice in Pennsylvania; the United States Court of Appeals for the Third Circuit; United States District Court for the Eastern District of Pennsylvania; and the Supreme Court of Pennsylvania.
**Publications:** Co-author, "Effective Investor Presentations: What the VCs Want to Know", Venture Guide 2003.
**Personal:** Villanova University School of Law, JD, 1977. Villanova Law Review, Editor-in-Chief, 1977, 1976.

### SHIEKMAN, Laurence Z
Pepper Hamilton LLP, Philadelphia
215 981 4347
shiekmanl@pepperlaw.com
*Recommended in Antitrust*

**Practice Areas:** Partner; past Chairman, Commercial Litigation Practice Group. Experienced in antitrust, ERISA, securities, commercial litigation, patent and criminal antitrust. Represented: UK manufacturer in treble damage, class action; truck manufacturer in antitrust and dealer termination; national pizza franchiser in class action alleging monopolization; biomedical manufacturer in patent infringement claims, antitrust counterclaims; a major automotive wholesaler in defense of Robinson-Patman Act 'mass action' by nearly 200 competitors.
**Prof. Memberships:** Board of Directors, Mann Center for Performing Arts.
**Career:** JD 1971 University of Pennsylvania Law School; BSE 1968 University of Pennsylvania.

### SICALIDES, Barbara T
Pepper Hamilton LLP, Philadelphia
215 981 4783
sicalidesb@pepperlaw.com
*Recommended in Antitrust*

**Practice Areas:** Partner; Vice-Chair Commercial Litigation Group, Head of Antitrust Section. Experienced in antitrust counseling and litigation; Hart-Scott-Rodino filings/proceedings. Representing UK flat glass manufacturer in treble-damage class action; tobacco company in Robinson-Patman Act and distributor termination; bathroom/kitchen fixtures/fittings manufacturer in allegations of price fixing; manufacturing companies in acquisitions.
**Prof. Memberships:** Philadelphia Bar

Association, Co-Chair Antitrust Committee. Board of Directors and past President, Philadelphia Volunteers for the Indigent Program. Steering Committee, Philadelphia LawWorks. 2002 recipient of Philadelphia Bar Association's First Union Fidelity Award.
**Career:** JD 1989 Temple University School of Law; BA 1983 Barnard College, Columbia University.

### SINATRA, Geraldine A
Dechert LLP, Philadelphia
215 994 2824
geraldine.sinatra@dechert.com
*Recommended in Corporate/M&A*

**Practice Areas:** Ms Sinatra, Partner, Co-Chairs the firm's Hiring Committee for the Philadelphia office. She focuses on private equity, mergers and acquisitions, securities offerings, debt financings, and public company governance issues. She works with financial sponsors on acquisitions of public and private companies and advises portfolio companies on transactional matters.
**Prof. Memberships:** Member, Pennsylvania and New Jersey Bars.
**Career:** Law clerk, Hon Norma L Shapiro, United States District Court for the Eastern District of Pennsylvania.
**Personal:** Ohio State University (BS, 1988); Ohio State University College of Law (JD, 1991), Order of the Coif, managing editor of Ohio State Law Journal.

### SINGER, Alan
Morgan, Lewis & Bockius LLP,
Philadelphia 215 963 5224
asinger@morganlewis.com
*Recommended in Corporate/M&A*

**Practice Areas:** Alan Singer is a Partner in the Business and Finance Practice. Mr Singer's practice focuses on sophisticated corporate and securities matters, including public and private offerings, annual and periodic Securities and Exchange Commission (SEC) filings, executive compensation disclosures and financial reporting matters. He also provides assistance to public company directors on a variety of corporate governance matters. Before entering private practice, Mr Singer served at the SEC in several positions, including Branch Chief in the Division of Enforcement in Washington, DC.

### SINGER, Paul
Reed Smith LLP, Pittsburgh
412 288 3114
psinger@reedsmith.com
*Recommended in Bankruptcy*

**Practice Areas:** Founder of firm's Bankruptcy Practice, chaired group for more than 20 years. Represents debtors and creditors in bankruptcy and workout matters; involved in industrial cases in the steel, aluminum, railroad, cement, pulp and paper, and natural resource industries. Currently lead counsel in several mass tort chapter 11 cases.
**Prof. Memberships:** American, Pennsyl-

vania, Allegheny Country Bar Associations; former Chair, Bankruptcy and Commercial Law Section, Allegheny County Bar Association.
**Personal:** University of Pittsburgh Law School (JD, 1968), editor of 'Law Review'; Harvard Law School (Masters, 1970); listed in 'The Best Lawyers in America,' 'Who's Who in American Law'.

### SITARCHUK, Eric W
Ballard Spahr Andrews & Ingersoll LLP,
Philadelphia 215 864 8220
sitarchuk@ballardspahr.com
*Recommended in Antitrust, Litigation*

**Practice Areas:** Focuses on white-collar criminal defense and related civil litigation. Defends corporations and individuals in criminal matters including antitrust, securities violations, healthcare and defense contract fraud, federal and state tax violations, official corruption, business fraud and export violations. Counsels clients on internal compliance and ethics programs.
**Career:** Admitted to Pennsylvania Bar (1983). Former Assistant United States Attorney in Philadelphia. Former Special Assistant United States Attorney in the District of Columbia, and deputy prosecutor in charge of the Justice Department's criminal investigation of the conduct of federal law enforcement during and in the aftermath of the 1992 Ruby Ridge standoff.
**Personal:** JD, George Washington University Law School (1983); BA, Franklin & Marshall College (1979).

### SKLAROFF, Michael
Ballard Spahr Andrews & Ingersoll LLP,
Philadelphia 215 864 8700
sklaroff@ballardspahr.com
*Recommended in Real Estate*

**Practice Areas:** Chairman, Real Estate Department. Focuses on real estate development (corporate headquarters, office buildings, industrial facilities, power centers, family entertainment centers, new town centers, condominium and other residential complexes and cultural facilities); real property tax and eminent domain (power generating stations, corporate headquarters, manufacturing facilities, transportation facilities, multifamily housing and shopping centers); zoning and land use (television, radio broadcasting and telecommunications, office, retail, commercial, suburban residential, parking, industrial parks, hospitals, museums, condominiums, and urban mixed-use development); and serving as counsel to cultural institutions (orchestra, museum and medical associations).
**Prof. Memberships:** American College of Real Estate Lawyers; Counselors of Real Estate; Fellow, College of Physicians; Fellow, Royal Institution of Chartered Surveyors; former Member, Philadelphia Planning Commission's Advisory Committee on Center City Zoning; founding

Chairman, Real Property Section, Philadelphia Bar Association and Chair, Committee on Condemnation and Appraisals; Deputy Executive Director, Philadelphia Redevelopment Authority in the early 1970s; chairs the Philadelphia Historical Commission, Member since 1996. Started the movement to save the Dream Garden, the Maxfield Parrish/Louis C Tiffany mural in Philadelphia's Curtis Building. He helped build the Sister Cities relationship between Philadelphia and Nizhny Novgorod, Russia; taught technology transfer, real property and corporate law in Russia under programs sponsored by USIA and USAID; and represented a Russian physics institute in the first licensing agreement to a US company of gyrotron technology used in fusion research.
**Career:** Admitted to the Pennsylvania Bar (1968).
**Personal:** AB, Columbia College (1964); LLB University of Pennsylvania Law School (magna cum laude, 1967). Served as editor of the Law Review and was a Member of the Order of the Coif.

### SONNENFELD, Marc
Morgan, Lewis & Bockius LLP,
Philadelphia 215 963 5572
msonnenfeld@morganlewis.com
*Recommended in Litigation*

**Practice Areas:** Marc Sonnenfeld is a Partner in the Litigation Practice and a Leader of the firm's Securities Litigation Practice. His practice focuses on defending securities and shareholder litigation and the defense of related regulatory enforcement proceedings, as well as counseling directors and officers on corporate governance issues. Mr Sonnenfeld has been recognized as one of the top 10 business litigators in Philadelphia and been named as a top business lawyer in various other publications.
**Prof. Memberships:** American College of Trial Lawyers (Fellow); American Bar Association; Pennsylvania Bar Association; Philadelphia Bar Association.

### SOROKO, John J
Duane Morris LLP, Philadelphia
215 979 1124
soroko@duanemorris.com
*Recommended in Litigation*

**Practice Areas:** John J Soroko is the Vice-Chair of Duane Morris and Chair of the firm's Trial Practice Group. Mr Soroko practices in the area of litigation, with particular emphasis on general business, corporate and securities matters, including the defense of securities and other class actions. He also practices in the areas of professional liability and real estate and probate litigation.
**Prof. Memberships:** Arbitrator, Philadelphia Stock Exchange (Panel Chairman); American Bar Association - Business Law Section, Section of Litigation; Philadelphia Volunteer Lawyers for

the Arts; Pennsylvania Bar Association; Philadelphia Bar Association; Federalist Society for Law & Public Policy Studies - Philadelphia Lawyers' Chapter (Co-Founder, Chairman).
**Career:** Admitted to practice in Pennsylvania; the United States Court of Appeals for the Third and Fourth Circuits; United States District Court for the Eastern District of Pennsylvania; before all federal and state trial and appellate courts; and arbitration hearings before the Commonwealth (Pennsylvania) Board of Claims, American Arbitration Association including Construction Industry arbitrations and various stock exchanges.
**Personal:** New York University School of Law, JD, 1977; Haverford College, AB, 1973.

### SPERGEL, Jonathan
Manko, Gold, Katcher & Fox LLP, Bala Cynwyd 484 430 5700
*Recommended in Environment*

### SPRAGUE, Richard
Sprague & Sprague, Philadelphia
215 561 7681
*Recommended in Litigation*

### SPRINGER, Claudia
Reed Smith LLP, Philadelphia
215 241 7946
cspringer@reedsmith.com
*Recommended in Bankruptcy*
**Practice Areas:** More than 20 years of experience in corporate workouts and bankruptcy, representing every type of constituent in a troubled company situation, including debtors, lenders, creditors' committees
**Prof. Memberships:** American College of Bankruptcy; American Bankruptcy Institute; Bankruptcy Committee, Business Law Section, Pennsylvania and Philadelphia Bar Associations
**Career:** Former judicial clerk to the Honorable William H McCullough, Prince George's County Circuit Court
**Publications:** Court Rulings Erode Collateral Protection, 'ABA Banking Journal'
**Personal:** The National Law Center of The George Washington University (JD, 1980); Trinity College (BA, 1977); named top female bankruptcy attorney in Pennsylvania by 'Pennsylvania Law Weekly'

### STACK JR, Stephen A
Dechert LLP, Philadelphia
215 994 2660
stephen.stack@dechert.com
*Recommended in Antitrust*
**Practice Areas:** Stephen A Stack, Jr, is Co-Chair of Dechert's Antitrust Group. He focuses on litigation, preventive counseling, and practices before US courts and European enforcement agencies. He represents clients in intellectual property/antitrust matters, joint ventures, and mergers.
**Prof. Memberships:** Member, Pennsylvania Bar; admitted to practice before

numerous federal courts; member, American Bar Association Antitrust Section.
**Career:** Mr Stack served on Department of Justice advisory committee of President George W Bush's Transition Team. He has also testified at government agency hearings.
**Personal:** Yale University (BA, cum laude, 1967); University of Pennsylvania School of Law (JD, cum laude, 1970).

### STERN, Eric L
Morgan, Lewis & Bockius LLP, Philadelphia 215 963 5178
estern@morganlewis.com
*Recommended in Real Estate*
**Practice Areas:** Eric L Stern is the Leader of Morgan Lewis' Real Estate Practice. Mr Stern represents real estate investors and owners, including REITs and private equity funds, institutional lenders, retailers and other corporate end-users in the acquisition, financing, restructuring and disposition of office buildings, shopping centers, single-use properties, hotels, development parcels, residential subdivisions and mixed-used projects.
**Prof. Memberships:** American College of Real Estate Lawyers; National Association of Real Estate Investment Trusts; International Council of Shopping Centers; Samuel Zell and Robert Lurie Real Estate Center, The Wharton School, University of Pennsylvania; and Board of Directors, Philadelphia Region, National Association of Industrial and Office Properties.

### STERN, Joan N
Blank Rome LLP, Philadelphia
215 569 5526
stern@BlankRome.com
*Recommended in Banking & Finance*
**Publications:** 'The Role of the Public Finance Attorney', chapter in 'Winning Legal Strategies for Public Finance Lawyers' (2005).
**Personal:** JD, Temple University School of Law; Vice-Chair, Board of Trustees, Moore College of Art and Design; Boards of Trustees, Franklin Institute and Jewish Federation of Greater Philadelphia; Boards of Directors, Police Athletic League and Urban Tree Connection.

### STEVENS, Mark
Langsam Stevens & Silver LLP, Philadelphia 215 732 3255
*Recommended in Environment*

### STOLTZFUS, Robert
Schnader Harrison Segal & Lewis LLP, Philadelphia 215 751 2000
*Recommended in Environment*

### STOVIAK, John F
Saul Ewing LLP, Philadelphia
215 972 1095
jstoviak@saul.com
*Recommended in Environment*
**Practice Areas:** Chair of the Litigation Department. Handles complex commer-

cial, fraud and environmental disputes, business valuation cases, trade secret claims and antitrust claims. Has tried cases in federal and state courts in NY, NJ, IL, PA and DE. He has been the lead lawyer defending various public utilities in Superfund contribution claims.
**Prof. Memberships:** Admitted in Pennsylvania.
**Career:** Former Saul Ewing Managing Partner. Led Saul Ewing in eight continuous years of increasing profitability and growth. Prior to joining Saul Ewing, was a Partner at Dilworth Paxson Kalish & Kauffman.
**Personal:** JD, Dickinson School of Law, BA, Harvard University (cum laude).

### STROBER, Frederick D
Saul Ewing LLP, Philadelphia
215 972 1985
fstrober@saul.com
*Recommended in Real Estate*
**Practice Areas:** Mr Strober is a Partner in Saul Ewing's Real Estate Department and is involved in development, construction, and leasing. Since 1997, he has been involved in the redevelopment of the former Philadelphia Naval Shipyard. He represents several universities and health systems and the School District of Philadelphia in connection with educational reform and development initiatives.
**Prof. Memberships:** Member, American College of Real Estate Lawyers; President, Philadelphia Volunteer Lawyers for the Arts.
**Career:** A former educator, he has practiced at Saul Ewing his entire legal career.
**Personal:** JD, Temple University (with honors), MEd, Temple University, BA, University of Pennsylvania.

### STUART, Glen R
Morgan, Lewis & Bockius LLP, Philadelphia 215 963 5883
gstuart@morganlewis.com
*Recommended in Environment*
**Practice Areas:** Glen Stuart is a Partner in the Litigation Practice and the Hiring Partner of the Philadelphia Office. Mr Stuart's Complex Commercial Litigation Practice focuses primarily on environmental law, toxic torts and energy matters. He has recently been involved in the defense of more than 30 toxic tort conspiracy cases in the federal or state courts of Delaware, Florida, Illinois, Kentucky, Maryland, Massachusetts, Mississippi, New Jersey, Ohio, Texas and West Virginia. In a 2002 survey of more than 185 corporate officers of Fortune 1000 companies, Mr Stuart was one of only 21 lawyers in the country recognized for exceptional client service two years in a row.
**Prof. Memberships:** American Bar Association (Litigation Section); Philadelphia Bar Association.

### SULLIVAN JR, James J
Klett Rooney Lieber & Schorling, Philadelphia 215 567 7739
jsullivan@klettrooney.com
*Recommended in Employment*
**Practice Areas:** Labor and employment law.
**Career:** Devotes his entire practice to counseling employers in all aspects of their labor and employment relations. He has represented employers in federal and state court and before various administrative agencies in virtually all areas of labor, employment, and safety and health-related litigation.
**Personal:** Labor studies (cum laude), Pennsylvania State University; JD, Georgetown University School of Law.

### SUMMERS, John
Hangley Aronchick Segal & Pudlin, Philadelphia 215 496 7007
jsummers@hangley.com
*Recommended in Litigation*
**Practice Areas:** Complex civil and white-collar criminal defense litigation, healthcare, professional malpractice and misconduct, class action and general business cases.
**Prof. Memberships:** American Law Institute, Member; Philadelphia Bar Foundation, Treasurer; The Reinvestment Fund, Vice-Chairman and Executive Committee Member; Disciplinary Board of the Supreme Court of Pennsylvania, former member and past Chair of Hearing Panel
**Career:** Hangley Aronchick Segal & Pudlin, Shareholder, 1994-Present. Hangley Connolly Epstein Chicco Foxman & Ewing, 1986-94. Law clerk to the Honorable Thomas N O'Neill, Jr, United States District Court for the Eastern District of Pennsylvania, 1984-86. University of Pennsylvania Law School, JD, 1984, Editor, Law Review. Wesleyan University, BA, magna cum laude, 1980.
**Publications:** Mr Summers is currently a Lecturer in Law at the University of Pennsylvania Law School where he teaches Appellate Advocacy

### SUPLEE, Dennis
Schnader Harrison Segal & Lewis LLP, Philadelphia 215 751 2000
*Recommended in Litigation*

### SWIRSKY, Sherry
Schnader Harrison Segal & Lewis LLP, Philadelphia 215 751 2000
*Recommended in Antitrust*

### SYKES, David T
Duane Morris LLP, Philadelphia
215 979 1500
sykes@duanemorris.com
*Recommended in Bankruptcy*
**Practice Areas:** David T Sykes practices in the areas of business reorganization and bankruptcy, insurance company rehabilitation, corporate and commercial finance, professional guidance, arbitra-

tion, mediation and commercial trial and appellate work. He directed the firm's representation of creditors and debtors in workouts and bankruptcies throughout the country for over 35 years, and personally led the representation of US Shelter Corporation, the Unsecured Creditors' Committee of The Oxford Finance Companies, Inc., and National Railway Utilization Corporation (one of the earliest pre-arranged chapter 11 cases, completed within 45 days of the chapter 11 filing). He represents major financial institutions in numerous capacities, including as agent for a lending group, as secured lender and letter of credit issuer, and as indenture trustee. He also represents lawyers and law firms charged with legal malpractice and serves as an expert witness in professional liability matters.
**Career:** Admitted to practice in Pennsylvania; the Supreme Court of the United States; US Court of Appeals for the Third Circuit; US District Court for the Eastern District of Pennsylvania; and the Supreme Court of Pennsylvania. Duane Morris LLP - Of Counsel, 2004-present; Vice Chairman, 1998-2004; Member, Partners Board, 1981-present; Partner, 1972-2004.
**Personal:** Temple University School of Law, LLB, 1965; Hamilton College, BA, 1959.

## TABACHNICK, Gene
Reed Smith LLP, Pittsburgh
412 288 3258
gtabachnick@reedsmith.com
*Recommended in Intellectual Property*
**Practice Areas:** Intellectual property involving patents, trademarks, copyrights, and related antitrust and unfair competition matters, emphasizing IP litigation. Counsels clients in a wide variety of technologies. Presents cases to judges and juries, arbitrators, and mediators, and briefs and argues appeals before the Court of Appeals for the Federal Circuit. Handles US and foreign patent prosecution in electrical and mechanical arts, and technology licensing.
**Career:** Worked six years as an electrical engineer in the aerospace industry.
**Personal:** Rutgers Law School (JD, 1988); Fairleigh Dickinson University (MBA, 1984); University of Pittsburgh (BS, 1982); listed in 'Best Lawyers in America'.

## TATE, Joseph A
Dechert LLP, Philadelphia
215 994 2350
joseph.tate@dechert.com
*Recommended in Antitrust, Litigation*
**Practice Areas:** Mr Tate, Partner, defends US and foreign corporations, executives, lawyers, and others against white-collar crime allegations, emphasizing antitrust, patent fraud, and other regulatory issues. His practice also involves civil litigation, class actions, and antitrust

counseling.
**Prof. Memberships:** Member, Pennsylvania and Massachusetts Bars; fellow, American College of Trial Lawyers; faculty member, Philadelphia Bar Association Trial Advocacy Program.
**Career:** Former prosecutor, US Department of Justice, Antitrust Division.
**Publications:** Lecturer on criminal and antitrust issues.
**Personal:** Villanova University (AB, 1963); Villanova University Law School (LLB, 1966), Member of Villanova University Law Review.

## TEMIN, Michael
Wolf, Block, Schorr and Solis-Cohen LLP, Philadelphia 215 977 2000
mtemin@wolfblock.com
*Recommended in Bankruptcy*
**Practice Areas:** Partner, Business Litigation and Financial Services Practice Groups. Deals extensively with business insolvencies, representing debtors, creditors, committees and others participating in restructuring of insolvent businesses.
**Prof. Memberships:** Adjunct Professor, University of Pennsylvania Law School (10+ years). Former Chair, Eastern District of Pennsylvania Bankruptcy Conference. Former Chair, Rules Subcommittee, and Vice-Chair of Chapter 11 Subcommittee of Business Bankruptcy Committee of Business Law Section of American Bar Association. Former Chair, Bankruptcy Committee of the Section of Corporation, Banking and Business Law of both Pennsylvania Bar Association and Philadelphia Bar Association. Former Chair, Section of Corporation, Banking and Business Law of Philadelphia Bar Association. Former Member, Board of Governors of Philadelphia Bar Association. Member, House of Delegates of Pennsylvania Bar Association. Co-Chair, Legal Ethics & Professional Responsibilities Committee. Former Chair, Professional Guidance Committee of Philadelphia Bar Association. Regent, American College of Bankruptcy.
**Career:** Admitted to Pennsylvania and Delaware.
**Personal:** Received BA, magna cum laude, from Yale University in 1954 and LLB, cum laude, from University of Pennsylvania in 1957.

## THIEMAN, Frederick
Thieman & Farrell, Pittsburgh
412 395 1245
*Recommended in Litigation*

## THOMPSON, Thomas M
Buchanan Ingersoll PC, Pittsburgh
412 562 8855
thompsontm@bipc.com
*Recommended in Corporate/M&A*
**Practice Areas:** Works primarily in the areas of corporate acquisitions (both domestic and foreign publicly and privately held companies), corporate governance and private placements and public

offerings of securities. He has represented public companies, family businesses, venture funds, management groups, divesting companies and investors in management buyouts.
**Prof. Memberships:** Adjunct Professor of Law, University of Pittsburgh Law School; Chair, Pennsylvania Bar Association, Business Law Section; Program chair, American Bar Association Committee on Negotiated Acquisitions.
**Personal:** JD Harvard University, 1968 (cum laude); AB Grove City College, 1965.

## TOLL, Curtis
Greenberg Traurig LLP, Philadelphia
215 988 7800
tollc@gtlaw.com
*Recommended in Environment*
**Practice Areas:** Environmental; real estate.
**Prof. Memberships:** Participated in the establishment and structuring of the of the Philadelphia Intergovernmental Cooperation Authority, the board that oversees the finances of the City of Philadelphia.
**Career:** Listed, Chambers & Partners USA Guide, 2005-06.
**Personal:** JD, The Dickinson School of Law; BS, University of Pittsburgh.

## UBINGER JR, John
Jones Day, Pittsburgh
412 394 7908
jwubinger@jonesday.com
*Recommended in Environment*
**Practice Areas:** More than 30 years experience in environmental law matters, including the evaluation of environmental considerations in corporate transactions; the assessment and remediation of contaminated property; structuring of environmental liability transfer transactions; alternative dispute resolution strategies; and the litigation of environmental issues against regulatory agencies and private parties. Teaches a course on environmental conflict resolution and problem solving at Duquesne University. Named among the top 50 environmental/land use lawyers in Pennsylvania.
**Prof. Memberships:** ABA; Pennsylvania Bar Association; Fellow of the Air & Waste Management Association; Association for Conflict Resolution; National Brownfield Association; Director of the Pennsylvania Environmental Council.

## UNTERBERGER, Glenn L
Ballard Spahr Andrews & Ingersoll LLP, Philadelphia 215 864 8210
unterberge@ballardspahr.com
*Recommended in Environment*
**Practice Areas:** Represents clients before federal and state courts and administrative agencies on a full spectrum of environmental issues. Advises on environmental issues arising in permitting, compliance activities, and business and real estate transactions generally, including transactions involving the

reuse of federal facilities. Also actively represents and counsels clients on environmental matters arising in energy and project finance matters.
**Prof. Memberships:** Co-Chair, Pennsylvania Chamber of Business and Industry's Air Quality Work Group, and sits on the Chamber's Environmental Affairs Committee.
**Career:** Admitted to the Pennsylvania Bar (1990), the District of Columbia Bar (1977), and the Maryland Bar (1993) Enforcement attorney, US Environmental Protection Agency in Washington, DC (1977-90). Served as national legal director for the Agency's water enforcement and hazardous waste enforcement programs.
**Publications:** Contributor, American Bar Association's Natural Resources, Energy, and Environmental Law Section publications and environmental reporters and trade journals. Editor-in-Chief of the Chamber's 2005/2006 Guidebook on Complying with Pennsylvania Environmental Laws and Regulations.
**Personal:** JD, Georgetown University (1977); BA, University of Pennsylvania (1974).

## WALL, Steven R
Morgan, Lewis & Bockius LLP, Philadelphia 215 963 4928
swall@moganlewis.com
*Recommended in Employment*
**Practice Areas:** Steven Wall is a Partner in the Labor and Employment Law Practice Group, and the Global Practice Group Leader. Mr Wall's practice focuses on employment litigation matters in federal and state courts, and before several administrative agencies, with an emphasis on class-based discrimination and collective bargaining issues. He has over 22 years experience advising clients on the National Labor Relations Act, the various federal and state discrimination laws, the Fair Labor Standards Act, preventive labor relations, and protection of trade secrets and human capital.
**Prof. Memberships:** American Bar Association - Labor and Employment Law Section.

## WARREN, Kenneth
Wolf, Block, Schorr and Solis-Cohen LLP, Philadelphia 215 977 2276
kwarren@wolfblock.com
*Recommended in Environment*
**Practice Areas:** Partner and Chair, Environmental and Land Use Practice Group. Practice concentrates on regulatory, transactional and litigation matters involving water, waste, hazardous chemicals and compliance. Has handled numerous enforcement actions, citizen suits, environmental criminal prosecutions, insurance recovery cases, appeals of agency decisions, toxic tort actions and other environmental cases in courts and

tribunals throughout US.

**Prof. Memberships:** Former Chair, American Bar Association Section of Environment, Energy and Resources. Previously served on Section's Council and as Section Committee Chair. Chair, American Bar Association Section Officers Conference Task Force on Homeland Security.

**Career:** Admitted to Pennsylvania in 1980. Served as law clerk to Honorable Joseph L McGlynn, Jr in US District Court for Eastern District of Pennsylvania (1979-80). Joined Wolf Block in 1980 and became Partner in 1987. Serves as outside general counsel to Delaware River Basin Commission, federal-interstate compact agency managing the water resources of the Delaware River Basin.

**Publications:** Author of numerous articles on environmental law. Author, chapter in 'The Law of Environmental Justice'.

**Personal:** Received BA, magna cum laude, from Brown University in 1975 and JD, magna cum laude, from University of Pennsylvania Law School in 1979.

### WEIN, Howard
Klett Rooney Lieber & Schorling, Pittsburgh 412 392 2160
hjwein@klettrooney.com
*Recommended in Environment*

**Practice Areas:** Environmental law.
**Career:** Extensive experience before federal and state administrative agencies and courts in a wide variety of environmental matters, including air quality, water quality, water supply, solid and hazardous waste, and federal Superfund and underground storage tank matters. Has successfully handled major environmental litigation in federal court, Pennsylvania Commonwealth Court and Pennsylvania's Environmental Hearing Board. Also has successfully resolved matters with the DER and the US EPA in a wide variety of complex environmental problems by negotiating consent agreements.
**Personal:** BA, George Washington University; JD, University of Pittsburgh School of Law.

### WEIS, Martin
Dilworth Paxson LLP, Philadelphia
215 575 7000
*Recommended in Bankruptcy*

### WEST, Ronald
Kirkpatrick & Lockhart Nicholson Graham LLP, Pittsburgh (412) 355-6752
rwest@klng.com
*Recommended in Corporate/M&A*

**Practice Areas:** Mergers and acquisitions; securities offerings; securities law compliance; joint ventures; general corporate.
**Prof. Memberships:** American Bar Association (Business Law Section); Pennsylvania Bar Association; Allegheny County Bar Association.
**Career:** Partner since 1986.
**Personal:** University of Pittsburgh

School of Law (JD, 1979), Mansfield State College (BA, 1974).

### WESTON, Timothy
Kirkpatrick & Lockhart Nicholson Graham LLP, Harrisburg 717 231 4504
tweston@klng.com
*Recommended in Environment*

**Practice Areas:** Focuses on environmental regulatory counseling and litigation, industrial and energy development projects, environmental issues in transactions, and natural resources management. He is nationally acknowledged in the field of water resources.
**Prof. Memberships:** Admitted to practice in Pennsylvania, the US Supreme Court, the US Courts of Appeal for the Third and Fourth Circuits.
**Career:** Joined Kirkpatrick & Lockhart Nicholson Graham LLP in 1987. Previously served in Pennsylvania Department of Environmental Resources, as Assistant Attorney General (1972-79) and Associate Deputy Secretary for Resources Management (1979-87). Also previously served as Commissioner on the Delaware River Basin Commission, Susquehanna River Basin Commission, Ohio River Basin Commission, and Great Lakes Commission.
**Publications:** Has published numerous articles and treatise chapters in the field of brownfields development, environmental issues in transactions, and water management.
**Personal:** JD (cum laude), Harvard Law School, 1972; BA (cum laude) mathematics, University of California (Santa Barbara), 1969.

### WETTACH, Thomas
Cohen & Grigsby PC, Pittsburgh
800 394 4904
*Recommended in Intellectual Property*

### WILLIAMS, James
Wolf, Block, Schorr and Solis-Cohen LLP, Philadelphia 215 977 2000
jwilliams@wolfblock.com
*Recommended in Real Estate*

**Practice Areas:** Partner, Real Estate Practice Group. Represents financial institutions and developers in real estate transactions, including acquisitions, sales, leasing, development and construction. Has been extensively involved in the negotiation of sophisticated financing transactions.
**Career:** Admitted to Pennsylvania in 1982.
**Personal:** Received BA, magna cum laude, from University of Pennsylvania in 1978 and JD from New York University School of Law in 1982.

### WINNING, William
Cozen O'Connor, Philadelphia
215 665 2000
*Recommended in Litigation*

### WINOKUR, Barton
Dechert LLP, Philadelphia
215 994 2505
barton.winokur@dechert.com
*Recommended in Corporate/M&A*

**Practice Areas:** Mr Winokur, Chairman and CEO of Dechert LLP, is a Corporate Partner and former Chair of the Mergers and Acquisitions and International Law groups. He represents corporations, leveraged buyout sponsor funds, and venture capital firms in complex corporate transactions including mergers, acquisitions, divestitures, joint ventures, and restructurings. He also advises boards of public companies on governance matters.
**Prof. Memberships:** Member of several corporate boards and a Member and former Chair of the Brandeis University board of trustees.
**Career:** Joined Dechert in 1965.
**Personal:** Cornell University (AB, 1961); Harvard Law School (LLB, 1964), editor of the Harvard Law Review.

### WOELFLING, Maxine
Morgan, Lewis & Bockius LLP, Harrisburg 717 237 4065
mwoelfling@morganlewis.com
*Recommended in Environment*

**Practice Areas:** Maxine Woelfling is of counsel in the Litigation Practice. Ms Woelfling concentrates her practice in the area of environmental law. Her practice involves regulatory compliance counseling, negotiation of permit conditions, litigation of permitting and enforcement issues before state and federal administrative and judicial tribunals, and environmental issues in business and financial transactions. She has been extensively involved in counseling clients regarding the remediation and reuse of former brownfields and other contaminated properties under Pennsylvania's innovative Land Recycling Act.
**Prof. Memberships:** Pennsylvania Bar Association, American Bar Association and the James S Bowman American Inn of Court.

### WYCOFF, William
Thorp Reed & Armstrong, Pittsburgh
412 394 7711
*Recommended in Litigation*

### YEAGER, Robert
Kirkpatrick & Lockhart Nicholson Graham LLP, Pittsburgh
412 355 6500
*Recommended in Intellectual Property*

### ZANIC, Michael
Kirkpatrick & Lockhart Nicholson Graham LLP, Pittsburgh 412 355 6500
*Recommended in Litigation*

### ZEIGER, Alan L
Blank Rome LLP, Philadelphia
215 569 5754
zeiger@blankrome.com
*Recommended in Corporate/M&A*

**Practice Areas:** Mr Zeiger chairs Blank Rome LLP's Privately Held & Emerging Companies Practice and represents both public and private companies, as well as entrepreneurs. His frequently counsels clients in the following areas: mergers and acquisitions, general corporate transactions, start-ups, early stage seed capital, private equity/venture capital, securities law, corporate governance, joint venture transactions, tax considerations, antitrust compliance, and capital formation.
**Prof. Memberships:** Philadelphia Bar Association, Corporation, Banking and Business Law Section; Sponsor, Entrepreneurs Organization (Philadelphia Chapter); Greater Philadelphia Venture Group; Board Member and Chair of the Educational Programming, Early Stage East; Board Member, Radnor Valley Country Club
**Career:** Joined Blank Rome in 1985 and became a Partner in 1989. He is Chair of the Privately Held and Emerging Companies Practice and was on the firm's Management Committee from 1997-2001.
**Publications:** Editor, 'Valuing and Selling Your Business'; editor, 'Financing Your Business With Venture Capital'; editor, 'Going Public Handbook'; Management Review, 'Bankruptcy Can Also Mean Smart Investment'.
**Personal:** JD, Brooklyn Law School, 1979. BS Magna Cum Laude, State University of New York at Albany, 1976.

### ZONN, Sidney
Littler Mendelson, PC, Pittsburgh
412 201 7600
szonn@littler.com
*Recommended in Employment*

**Practice Areas:** Focuses on labor and employment law representing management. Investigation and litigation of employment discrimination claims before local, state and federal agencies and courts. Represents employers before NLRB in representation proceedings, unfair labor practice cases. Handles collective bargaining negotiations and arbitrations. Involved in wage/hour investigations with the US Department of Labor, along with unemployment compensation matters.
**Prof. Memberships:** Pittsburgh Human Resources Association; graduate of Greater Pittsburgh Chamber of Commerce's 'Leadership Pittsburgh Program'; currently secretary to Board of Trustees, Robert Morris University.
**Personal:** University of Miami School of Law (JD, with honors, 1978); BA, University of Massachusetts, cum laude, 1972.

# BALLARD SPAHR ANDREWS & INGERSOLL, LLP

## THE FIRM

**Chairman:** Arthur Makadon
**Number of partners:** 196
**Number of other lawyers:** 265

**FIRM OVERVIEW:** Ballard Spahr Andrews & Ingersoll, LLP is an AmLaw 100 firm with over 460 lawyers in seven offices in the mid-Atlantic corridor and the western United States. Ballard combines a national scope of practice with strong local market knowledge to represent companies, individuals, and other entities.

## MAIN AREAS OF PRACTICE:

**Business & Finance:** The firm's Business and Finance Department has a regional, national, and international practice involving public and private companies and nonprofit organizations. Their clients are engaged with wide-ranging and dynamic technology, manufacturing, and service functions; pharmaceutical, energy, telecommunications, and software manufacturing companies; financial institutions; investment companies; sports and other franchises; public utilities; and hospitals and health services. They also represent issuers, underwriters, lenders, and venture capitalists in equity and debt financing for companies large and small, private and public. The firm's business and finance lawyers serve their clients on a national basis in mergers, acquisitions, and other complex transactions and provide legal counseling and compliance for investment companies and advisors, banks, broker/dealers, consumer finance companies, credit card issuers, and public companies and their boards of directors.

**Financial Planning & Management:** Ballard Spahr's Financial Planning and Management Department includes lawyers in the Tax Group, Employee Benefits Group, and Family Wealth Management Group. The firm's Tax Practice involves sophisticated tax planning and handling tax disputes at all levels of government – federal, state, local, and international. The Employee Benefits Group provides clients with legal advice regarding the full range of qualified and nonqualified plans. The Family Wealth Management Group provides a comprehensive range of estate planning services to individuals of means.

**Litigation:** The Litigation Department represents a wide range of local, national, and international clients, including large and small companies in the public, private, and nonprofit sectors. They handle all types of complex litigation and regularly represent clients in local, state, and federal courts, at both the trial and appellate levels, as well as other forums throughout the country.

**Public Finance:** Ballard Spahr has a nationally recognized practice in the field of public finance and federal tax matters relating to the issuance of municipal bonds. The firm has consistently been ranked as one of the leading bond and underwriter counsel firms in the country. The firm's public finance lawyers serve as bond counsel, underwriter's counsel, trustee's counsel, and borrower's counsel for state and local governments and authorities throughout the United States, and have a wide range of experience in many areas of law, including municipal, tax, securities, real estate, housing, environmental, public utilities, energy, healthcare, education, banking, administrative, and corporate.

**Real Estate:** The firm's real estate lawyers provide cutting-edge representation for national and regional clients, including corporate, institutional, entrepreneurial, and public clients in acquisition, development, financing, leasing and sales, and other flagship transactions. In order to serve their clients effectively, the department is organized into discrete service groups: acquisitions and dispositions; complex development; construction; finance; hotel/resort/timeshare; housing; leasing; valuation; workouts; and zoning and land use.

## HEAD OFFICE

**PENNSYLVANIA**
1735 Market Street, 51st Floor, **Philadelphia**, PA 19103-7599
**Tel:** 215 665 8500  **Fax:** 215 864 8999
**Website:** www.ballardspahr.com

## BRANCH OFFICES

**COLORADO**
1225 17th Street, Suite 2300, **Denver**, CO 80202-5596
**Tel:** 303 292 2400  **Fax:** 303 296 3956

**DELAWARE**
919 N. Market Street, 12th Floor, **Wilmington**, DE 19801
**Tel:** 302 252 4465  **Fax:** 302 252 4466

**DISTRICT OF COLUMBIA**
601 13th Street, NW, Suite 1000 South, **Washington**, DC 20005-3807
**Tel:** 202 661 2200  **Fax:** 202 661 2299

**MARYLAND**
300 East Lombard Street, 18th Floor, **Baltimore**, MD 21202-3268
**Tel:** 410 528 5600  **Fax:** 410 528 5650

**NEW JERSEY**
Plaza 1000-Suite 500, Main Street, **Voorhees**, NJ 08043-4636
**Tel:** 856 761 3400  **Fax:** 856 761 1020

**UTAH**
One Utah Center, Suite 600, 201 South Main Street, **Salt Lake City**, UT 84111-2221
**Tel:** 801 531 3000  **Fax:** 801 531 3001

## CONTACTS

| | |
|---|---|
| **Bankruptcy, Reorganization & Capital Recovery** | Tobey M Daluz, Vincent J Marriott III |
| **Biotechnology/Life Sciences** | Richard P Jaffe |
| **Business & Finance** | Brian D Doerner |
| **Construction** | Lynn R Axelroth/Alan S Ritterband |
| **Consumer Financial Services** | Alan S Kaplinsky |
| **Eminent Domain & Valuation** | S David Brandt |
| **Employee Benefits** | John M Bernard |
| **Energy & Project Finance** | C Baird Brown, Charles S Henck |
| **Environmental** | David G Mandelbaum |
| **Family Wealth Management** | Regina O Thomas |
| **Financial Planning & Management** | Frederic L Ballard Jr |
| **Franchise & Distribution** | Benjamin A Levin |
| **Healthcare** | Jean C Hemphill |
| **Housing** | Paul K Casey, Mary Jo George |
| **Insurance** | Douglas Y Christian |
| **Intellectual Property** | Jamie B Bischoff |
| **Investment Management** | William H Rheiner |
| **Labor, Employment & Immigration** | John B Langel |
| **Litigation** | Roger P Thomasch, Stephen J Kastenberg |
| **Mergers & Acquisitions** | Steven B King, Richard J Braemer |
| **Planned Communities & Condiminiums** | Phillip B Korb |
| **Product Liability & Mass Tort** | John P Lavelle Jr |
| **Public Finance** | Blake K Wade |
| **Real Estate** | Michael Sklaroff |
| **Real Estate Development** | David B Gifford |
| **Real Estate Finance** | Beverly J Quail, Thomas A Hauser |
| **Real Estate Leasing** | David L Pollock |
| **Resort & Hotel** | W Michael Clowdus, Steven D Peterson |
| **Securities** | Justin L Klein |
| **Tax** | Wayne R Strasbaugh |
| **Telecommunications** | Jerold G Oldroyd |
| **Transactional Finance** | Carl H Fridy |
| **White Collar Litigation** | Eric W Sitarchuk |
| **Zoning & Land Use** | Joanne Phillips, William F Hyland Jr |

# BLANK ROME LLP

## THE FIRM

**Chairman:** David F Girard-diCarlo
**Managing Partner:** Fred Blume
**Executive Partner:** Carl M Buchholz
**Finance Partner:** Barry H Genkin

**Partners:** 236
**Others:** 250

**FIRM OVERVIEW:** Blank Rome LLP is a full-service firm of nearly 500 attorneys serving clients across the United States and abroad from its principal offices in New York, Philadelphia, Washington, DC and Wilmington, DE, and six additional locations in New Jersey, Pennsylvania, Ohio and Florida. Blank Rome's business-oriented lawyers assist companies from large multi-national corporations to start-up ventures, in a wide range of industries in virtually all aspects of their businesses. The firm has the experience and resources required to handle highly complex transactions and litigation.

Blank Rome's Washington office focuses on transactional, legislative and regulatory matters affecting the marine transportation and shipbuilding industries as well as a wide range of legislative affairs, regulatory and commercial litigation, white-collar defense and investigations, healthcare, international trade, government contracts, securities and environmental law. The Washington office is the center of the firm's extensive patent and intellectual property practices.

Blank Rome's New York office serves public and private companies in mergers and acquisitions in corporate and litigation matters. The firm's New York office represents some of the area's leading real estate, financial services and technology companies. The New York office also has one of the largest and most visible matrimonial and estates and trusts practices in the United States.

The firm's Wilmington, DE office is involved primarily in significant bankruptcy filings and intellectual property litigation in the Delaware courts and in Wilmington. It also focuses on public finance, litigation and dispute resolution and financial services.

**Blank Rome Government Relations LLC:** A wholly-owned subsidiary of Blank Rome LLP, Blank Rome Government Relations LLC, comprised of legal, lobbying and communications professionals, helps clients navigate the complexities of government at the federal, state and local levels. Blank Rome Government Relations LLC establishes and maintains liaisons with federal agencies, officers and elected officials, monitors legislation, pursues potential federal funding sources, arranges meetings with regulatory and congressional representatives, and coordinates lobbying efforts and strategies with government staff. The firm is actively involved in homeland security working, on behalf of clients, with federal, state and local governments on legislation in support of new laws, statutes and procedures.

**MAIN AREAS OF PRACTICE:** Antitrust; aviation; banking; bankruptcy and business restructuring; capital formation; commercial litigation; corporate and securities; environmental law; estate planning; public contracts; health law; insurance; intellectual property and technology; intellectual property litigation; international trade; labor and employment law; maritime law and transportation; matrimonial law; mergers and acquisitions; product liability litigation; public finance; real estate; securities litigation; tax, and white collar defense.

**Pro Bono:** Blank Rome attorneys devote a significant portion of their time and resources to professional and other activities in the public interest and have provided their services, without compensation, to many individuals and causes. The firm's commitment to the local community is illustrated by a 64% increase in pro bono hours in the most recent year. In 2004, the Pennsylvania Bar Association honored partner Peggy McCausland with its Citizens Pro Bono Award for her advocacy work with children.

**Diversity:** Blank Rome LLP and Blank Rome Government Relations LLC recognize that a diversity of ideas, backgrounds, and experiences is crucial to fulfilling its commitment to excellence. Blank Rome endeavors to recruit, hire, promote

## PRINCIPAL OFFICES

**DISTRICT OF COLUMBIA**
600 New Hampshire Avenue, NW, **Washington**, DC 20037
**Tel:** 202 772 5800   **Fax:** 202 772 5858
**Email:** webmaster@BlankRome.com
**Website:** www.BlankRome.com

**NEW YORK**
The Chrysler Building, 405 Lexington Avenue, **New York**, NY 10174-0208
**Tel:** 212 885 5000   **Fax:** 212 885 5001

**PENNSYLVANIA**
One Logan Square, 18th & Cherry Streets,
**Philadelphia**, PA 19103-6998
**Tel:** 215 569 5500   **Fax:** 215 569 5555

**DELAWARE**
Chase Manhatten Centre, 1201 Market Street, Suite 800,
**Wilmington**, DE 19801
**Tel:** 302 425 6400   **Fax:** 302 425 6464

## OTHER OFFICES

**FLORIDA**
1200 North Federal Highway, Suite 417, **Boca Raton**, FL 33432
**Tel:** 561 417 8100   **Fax:** 561 417 8101

**NEW JERSEY**
210 Lake Drive East, Woodland Falls Corporate Park, Suite 200,
**Cherry Hill**, NJ 08002
**Tel:** 856 779 3600   **Fax:** 856 779 7647

200 West State Street, **Trenton**, NJ 08608
**Tel:** 609 278 2320   **Fax:** 609 278 2323

**OHIO**
201 East Fifth Street, 1700 PNC Center, **Cincinnati**, OH 45202
**Tel:** 513 362 8700   **Fax:** 513 362 8787

**PENNSYLVANIA**
1620 Pond Road, Suite 200, **Allentown**, PA 18104
**Tel:** 610 706 4300   **Fax:** 610 706 4343

Rose Tree Corporate Center, 1400 N. Providence Road, Bldg 1, Suite 301,
**Media**, PA 19063
**Tel:** 610 891 7800   **Fax:** 610 891 7804

## CONTACTS

| | |
|---|---|
| **Delaware Office** | Michael D DeBaecke |
| **District of Columbia Office** | Thomas M (Mike) Dyer |
| | Patrick O Cavanaugh |
| | Mark A Holman (Government Relations) |
| **Florida Office** | Michael H Leeds |
| **New Jersey Offices** | Steven D Weinstein |
| **New York Office** | Robert J Mittman |
| | Michael S Mullman |
| **Ohio Office** | Michael L Cioffi |
| **Pennsylvania Offices** | Fred Blume (Philadelphia) |
| | Bernard M Lesavoy (Allentown) |
| | Paul D McNichol (Media) |

and retain, on the basis of demonstrated talent and initiative, individuals throughout the firm representing, among other things, different races, genders, ethnic groups, religions, sexual orientation and national origin. Blank Rome has established a Diversity Committee to recommend specific actions that may be

# BLANK ROME LLP CONT'D

taken in the firm's activities, both internal and external, to achieve these goals.

**CLIENTS:** Blank Rome represents businesses and organizations – from multi-billion dollar international companies to start-up entities. Blank Rome represents companies among the Fortune 500 and the middle market. The firm represents clients in a wide variety of industries including: aviation; banking and insurance; communications; education; energy; entertainment and general services; financial services; health care; leisure; life sciences; manufacturing; professional services; real estate; retail/wholesale trade; technology; transportation, and units of state and local government.

### Representative Transactions:

Represented a joint venture consisting of DRA Advisors LLC and Kimco Realty Corporation in the merger transaction with Price Legacy Corporation, a publicly traded shopping center Real Estate Investment Trust. The merger involved approximately 40 properties having a value in excess of $1 billion.

Representing USGen New England in its chapter 11 bankruptcy case in Greenbelt, Maryland including the sales of its fossil fuel and hydro electric generating assets to two separate acquirers for a combined purchase price in excess of $1.1 billion.

Served as counsel to TransCore Holdings in its $600 million acquisition by Roper Industries from an investor group.

Represented Sunoco, Inc. in lease negotiations for its new corporateheadquarters in the Mellon Bank Center, a transaction recognized as one of the Best Real Estate Deals of 2004 by the Philadelphia Business Journal. Acted as Bond Counsel to The School District of Philadelphia's issuance of $791 million of General Obligation Bonds.

Completed approximately $200 million of financing for Cornerstone Family Services, Inc., the fourth largest cemetery company in the United States.

Represented CapitalSource, Inc. in a $175 million financing for the acquisition of 58 nursing homes in 14 states. The financing included five separate loans secured by fee interest, leasehold interests and accounts receivable.

Reached a four-year $5 billion collective bargaining agreement with the Philadelphia Federation of Teachers on behalf of the School Reform Commission of Philadelphia.

Closed a secondary public offering for Pennsylvania Commerce Bancorp, Inc. ('PA Commerce') of 460,000 shares of its common stock raising $20.8 million. As part of the transaction, Blank Rome assisted PA Commerce in transferring its securities from the Nasdaq SmallCap Market to the Nasdaq National Market.

Closed a private placement transaction in which Commerce Bancorp, Inc. purchased 100,000 shares of PA Commerce's common stock. Commerce Bancorp, Inc. also purchased 50,000 shares of PA Commerce's common stock in the public offering.

### Representative Litigation:

Represented Lyondell Chemical Company as national coordinating counsel for more than 100 lawsuits in 16 states involving the gasoline additive MTBE. Settled the City of Santa Monica case which sought over $500 million in damages for $3.55 million.

Successfully defended L-3 Communications Corp. and Northrop Grumman Corporation in an arbitration proceeding in which a scientist sought damages in excess of $175 million, contending, among other things, that L-3, the company to which he had transferred the rights to certain patents, had failed to exploit his technology, thereby reducing his royalties.

Obtained a $5.6 million judgment for Commercial Federal Bank, F.S.B., following a five-week trial, against the federal government for lost profits caused by the government's breach of contract in a case relating to United States v Winstar Corp. This is the only Winstar case in which the US Court of Federal Claims awarded lost-profits damages to a plaintiff.

Defended Campbell Soup Company in a bench trial that concerned its 1998 spin-off of Vlasic Foods International, Inc., the transaction upon which the successor-in-interest to Vlasic Foods International, Inc., based various claims of fraud and fraudulent transfer.

Successfully prosecuted software patent infringement cases on behalf of Centillion Data Systems, Inc., reaching $25 million in favorable settlements on behalf of Centillion.

In a suit arising from the sale of numerous bank branches by Wachovia Corporation's predecessor-in-interest, caused Wachovia's adversary to abandon its claim and settled Wachovia's counterclaim on terms compelling its adversary to pay Wachovia over $8 million.

In re Genesis Health Ventures, a False Claims Act qui tam action alleging special damages of $325 million for an alleged failure to process credit to the federally-funded Medicaid program for unused and returned medications provided by a national institutional pharmacy provider. The Department of Justice declined intervention in the action. Summary judgment in favor of the pharmacy provider was obtained.

Successfully obtained a summary judgment in a consumer class action in the Superior Court of New Jersey for a national bank and its assignee, a state-licensed mortgage lender, in which the plaintiffs claimed that prepayment penalties and 'points' charged at closing violated New Jersey laws governing second mortgages.

Obtained dismissal of a nationwide consumer lending complaint challenging bankruptcy-related fees in federal bankruptcy court in San Antonio on behalf of prominent national financial institutions.

Defended a manufacturer of products used for military and aerospace applications in a qui tam lawsuit brought under the federal False Claims Act. The lawsuit alleged that the manufacturer had submitted claims to the government that falsely certified that it was in compliance with environmental, health and safety laws, and was settled on terms that were very favorable to the defendant.

Defended a shipyard that had contracted to construct ships for the United States Navy in a qui tam lawsuit brought under the federal False Claims Act. Successfully guided the company and its officials through a Senate investigation and hearing into the contract, and then obtained dismissal of various counts for failure to state a legal claim for relief, dismissal of other counts for lack of jurisdiction, and dismissal of the principal conspiracy count on summary judgment for lack of evidence.

Obtained a favorable ruling in a case of first impression for M&T Bank, holding the force majeure clause in a long-term lease did not excuse a landlord's failure to obtain governmental approvals by the date set in the lease. In so holding, the Bank was able to avoid a commitment to a long-term lease.

Obtained a $26 million award for TransCore Holdings, Inc. on its fraud and breach of contract claims in an arbitration proceeding that concerned the financial condition of a company it had acquired.

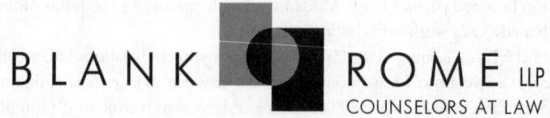

BLANK ROME LLP
COUNSELORS AT LAW

# BUCHANAN INGERSOLL PC

## THE FIRM

**Chief Executive Officer:** Thomas L VanKirk
**Chief Operating Officer:** Francis A Muracca, II

**FIRM OVERVIEW:** Buchanan Ingersoll PC is one of the 100 largest law firms in the United States, with more than 415 attorneys and government relations professionals in its offices throughout the country. The practice covers more than 65 service areas, including banking, corporate finance, government relations, tax, litigation, intellectual property and healthcare.

## MAIN AREAS OF PRACTICE:

**Corporate Finance:** The Corporate Finance Section structures, negotiates, documents and concludes transactions essential to accomplishing both the operations and strategic objectives of its clients. The firm's services in this area include public and private capital formation, merger and acquisition, corporate governance and control and regulatory issues.

**Litigation:** Offering broad trial and appellate experience, the Litigation Section has a long and distinguished record of successful representations that reflects a commitment and determination to achieve its clients' objectives in disputed matters, whether in court or through alternative dispute resolution. The firm's attorneys litigate and provide litigation counseling on behalf of regional, national and international businesses.

**Intellectual Property:** The Intellectual Property Section's experience covers the full scope of intellectual property law and litigation, including patents, trademarks, copyrights, trade secrets, licensing, technology transfer and non-disclosure and non-compete agreements.

**Tax:** The Tax Section's more than 40 attorneys have experience in all aspects of federal tax planning, controversy, legislative and regulatory work. The firm assists clients with business and international tax matters, employee benefits, estates and trusts and real estate tax issues.

**Government Relations:** The Government Relations Section provides its clients with the strongest possible voice in the development of policies, legislation and regulations that affect their businesses. The group also provides comprehensive legislative and regulatory advocacy services.

**Healthcare:** The firm's Healthcare Section provides a wide range of transactional and other legal services. In recent years, the firm's lawyers have been involved in a significant number of mergers, acquisitions and other transactions worth in excess of $14 billion.

**Labor & Employment:** The firm's Labor and Employment Law Section provides legal services for employers on all issues that arise out of the employer-employee relationship. The group addresses workplace issues and helps clients minimize the amount of time, effort and expense required to resolve employment-related problems.

**Financial Institutions:** In representing lenders, the Financial Institutions Section has structured, negotiated, documented and completed hundreds of transactions worth billions of dollars. The group's experience includes syndicated credit, letter of credit, corporate and real estate transactions, as well as workout, restructuring and litigation matters.

**Bankruptcy & Creditors' Rights:** This group represents and counsels debtors and creditors, banks involved in workout situations, creditors' committees and corporations and individuals facing financial difficulty. The group also has experience in insurance insolvency matters.

## OFFICES

**PENNSYLVANIA**
**Pittsburgh** (*founding office*)
One Oxford Centre, 301 Grant Street, 20th Floor, **Pittsburgh**, PA 15219-1410
**Tel:** 412 562 8800   **Fax:** 412 562 1041
**Email:** info@bipc.com
**Website:** www.buchananingersoll.com

1835 Market Street, 14th Floor, **Philadelphia**, PA 19103-2985
**Tel:** 215 665 8700   **Fax:** 215 665 8760

One South Market Square, 213 Market Street, 3rd Floor, **Harrisburg**, PA 17101-2121
**Tel:** 717 237 4800   **Fax:** 717 233 0852

**CALIFORNIA**
12230 El Camino Real, Suite 300, **San Diego**, CA 92130-2090
**Tel:** 858 509 7300   **Fax:** 858 509 7353

Suite 700, 333 Twin Dolphin Drive, **Redwood Shores**, CA 94065-1418
**Tel:** 650 622 2300   **Fax:** 650 622 2499

**DELAWARE**
The Nemours Building, 1007 N Orange Street, Suite 1110, **Wilmington**, DE 19801-1236
**Tel:** 302 428 5500   **Fax:** 302 428 3996

**DISTRICT OF COLUMBIA**
1700 K Street, N.W., Suite 300, **Washington, DC** 20006-3807
**Tel:** 202 452 7900   **Fax:** 202 452 7989

**FLORIDA**
Bank of America Tower, 100 S.E. Second Street, 34th Floor, **Miami**, FL 33131-2158
**Tel:** 305 347 4080   **Fax:** 305 347 4089

SunTrust Financial Centre, 401 East Jackson Street, Suite 2500, **Tampa**, FL 33602-5236
**Tel:** 813 222 8180   **Fax:** 813 222 8189

**NEW YORK**
One Chase Manhattan Plaza, 35th Floor, **New York**, NY 10005-1417
**Tel:** 212 440 4400   **Fax:** 212 440 4401

**NEW JERSEY**
700 Alexander Park, Suite 300, **Princeton**, NJ 08540-6347
**Tel:** 609 987 6800   **Fax:** 609 520 0360

**VIRGINIA**
Suite 500, 1737 King Street, **Alexandria**, VA 22314-2727
**Tel:** 703 836 6620   **Fax:** 703 836 2021

# CAESAR, RIVISE, BERNSTEIN, COHEN & POKOTILOW, LTD.

## THE FIRM

**Managing Shareholder:** Manny D Pokotilow

**Number of partners:** 16
**Number of other lawyers:** 9
**Number of patent agents:** 1

**FIRM OVERVIEW:** Since its founding in 1926 by Abraham D Caesar and Charles Rivise, the firm has focused on patent, trademark, copyright and other intellectual property law. More recently, the firm has expanded its practice to other areas involving high technology law, such as internet, information technology and computer law, in keeping with its goal of protecting and promoting the development of creative ideas and the people who create them. The attorneys of the firm have backgrounds in the fields of chemistry, chemical engineering, pharmaceuticals, biotechnology, nuclear engineering, mechanical engineering, materials science, electrical engineering, computers, the internet and information technology. This combination of varied technical skills among the attorneys creates a synergistic energy that is maximized when fulfilling each client's needs.

## MAIN AREAS OF PRACTICE:

**Patents:** The firm handles all aspects of patent law. This includes the evaluation of inventions for patenting, by conducting patentability searches throughout the world and drafting and prosecuting of patent applications in the United States and internationally. Where appropriate, the firm conducts appeals through the relevant governmental agencies and courts.

**Trademarks:** The firm handles all aspects of trademark law including the evaluation of marks for registration, conducting searches throughout the world and drafting and prosecuting of trademark applications in the United States and internationally. Where appropriate, the firm conducts appeals through the relevant governmental agencies and courts.

**Copyrights:** The firm handles all aspects of copyright law, including drafting and prosecuting applications to register copyrights in the United States.

**Litigation Matters:** The attorneys of Caesar Rivise have 80 years of experience in handling ex parte and inter partes patent and trademark matters in the relevant government agencies of the United States and have been lead counsel in hundreds of cases throughout the United States involving all aspects of intellectual property law.

**Client Counseling & Transactional Matters:** The firm becomes deeply involved in counseling its clients on all matters involving patents, trademarks, copyrights, the internet, information technology and computer law, and in drafting and negotiating agreements for such matters, including, confidentiality agreements, consulting agreements, joint development agreements, clinical research agreements, license agreements, asset purchase and sales agreements, employment agreements and employment policy issues.

**Due Diligence Matters:** The firm conducts right to use and infringement studies, and is frequently involved in the evaluation of intellectual property portfolios for merger, acquisition and asset purchase matters.

**Stability:** Caesar Rivise has been known for its extraordinary stability. Retaining experienced attorneys and staff has resulted in an unrivaled quality of service. Training, mentoring, and advancing each of its attorneys to shareholder or partners positions not only builds an extended legal family and support network, but also serves clients whose needs are ongoing. Clients seeking to obtain and maintain protection over the life of a patent or trademark can count on Caesar Rivise attorneys who know and understand their business, and who can pass that knowledge along to colleagues as necessary.

**CLIENTS:** The firm's client base includes individuals, small entrepreneurial organizations, Fortune 500 companies, international corporations, universities and research hospitals.

**HEAD OFFICE**

**PENNSYLVANIA**
1635 Market Street, 11th Floor, **Philadelphia**, PA 19103-2212
**Tel:** 215 567 2010   **Fax:** 215 751 1142
**Email:** gatekeeper@crbcp.com
**Website:** www.crbcp.com

CAESAR, RIVISE, BERNSTEIN, COHEN & POKOTILOW, LTD.
Intellectual Property, Computer and Information Technology Law

*Intellectual Property Counsel for Visionaries*

# CONRAD O'BRIEN GELLMAN & ROHN P.C.

## THE FIRM

**Managing Shareholder:** James J Rohn

**Number of shareholders:** 12
**Number of other lawyers:** 22

**FIRM OVERVIEW:** Founded over 20 years ago by three prominent litigation partners from a major Philadelphia law firm, Conrad O'Brien has established itself as one of the leading litigation practices in Pennsylvania and around the country. The firm is dedicated to one thing: providing first-rate litigation services to clients involved in complex litigation. The firm achieves that mission by drawing on the extraordinary credentials and experience of its lawyers. Widely recognized for their skills as trial lawyers, one quarter of the firm's shareholders are Fellows of the American College of Trial Lawyers. The firm's roster includes the former Chief Judge of the United States District Court for the Eastern District of Pennsylvania; the former First Assistant US Attorney for that district; a Fellow of the International Academy of Trial Lawyers; faculty members of the National Institute for Trial Advocacy; former Presidents of the Philadelphia Association of Defense Lawyers; a former Chief Assistant Solicitor for the City of Philadelphia; and numerous lawyers with decades of combined experience from practice in some of the largest law firms in the country.

**MAIN AREAS OF PRACTICE:** The firm's attorneys practice regularly in federal and state courts in Pennsylvania, New Jersey and around the country in matters involving commercial litigation, white collar criminal defense, professional liability, products liability, personal injury and mass torts. The firm also provides services in alternative dispute resolution proceedings.

**Commercial Litigation:** The firm's Commercial Litigation Practice covers a broad range of complex matters, including antitrust, unfair business practice claims, class actions, RICO, contract disputes, information technology, employment issues (including employment discrimination litigation), ERISA, defamation, directors and officers liability, copyright, trademark, construction and securities claims. The firm also represents companies in litigation with federal and state governments concerning Superfund sites and natural resource damage claims.

**White Collar Criminal Defense:** Conrad O'Brien attorneys conduct internal corporate investigations, represent both individuals and companies in grand jury investigations, and defend clients in any related criminal, civil, or administrative proceedings. The firm's practice includes defending against prosecutions for alleged violations of antitrust statutes, RICO, the False Claims Act, and state and federal tax and securities laws; representing clients in claims such as false statements, embezzlement, forfeiture, money laundering, insurance fraud, obstruction of justice, and public corruption; and counseling clients on Sarbanes-Oxley compliance issues.

**Professional Liability:** The firm's Professional Liability Practice involves the defense of malpractice claims against hospitals, physicians, law firms and other professionals. Conrad O'Brien attorneys represent physicians, hospitals, nurses, physicians' practices, and other healthcare providers in medical malpractice litigation as well as in actions involving insurance coverage, credentialing and licensing issues. Conrad O'Brien also serves as the firm to which lawyers turn when they need representation for themselves.

**Products Liability, Personal Injury & Mass Torts:** Conrad O'Brien lawyers represent companies in products liability, personal injury, mass tort and class action cases involving products such as pharmaceuticals, lead paint, medical devices and equipment, chemicals and tobacco.

**Alternative Dispute Resolution (ADR):** The firm's lawyers are routinely involved in a wide range of alternative dispute resolution procedures, from arbitrations to mediations. Their experience comes not just from being advocates in these types of cases, but also from serving as the neutrals themselves for state and federal courts and for private organizations such as the American Arbitration Association, the CPR Institute for Dispute Resolution, and the National Association of Securities Dealers.

## HEAD OFFICE

**PENNSYLVANIA**
1515 Market Street, Sixteenth Floor, **Philadelphia**, PA 19102-1916
**Tel:** 215 864 9600  **Fax:** 215 864 9620
**Email:** lawyers@cogr.com
**Website:** www.cogr.com

## BRANCH OFFICES

**PENNSYLVANIA**
17 West Gay Street, Suite 100, **West Chester**, PA 19380-3090
**Tel:** 610 701 9100  **Fax:** 610 701 9195

100 Four Falls Corporate Center, Suite 300,
**West Conshohocken**, PA 19428-2983
**Tel:** 610 940 6045  **Fax:** 610 940 6046

**NEW JERSEY**
1040 Kings Highway North, Suite 600, **Cherry Hill**, NJ 08034
**Tel:** 856 309 3373  **Fax:** 856 309 3375

**CLIENTS:** The firm's clients range from Fortune 500 companies to newer entrepreneurial businesses, who have chosen Conrad O'Brien for its cost-effective litigation, and for its dedication to client interests. Representative clients of the firm include: ACE USA, AEGON USA Inc.; Air Products and Chemicals Inc.; Akzo Nobel Inc.; American Red Cross; Americo Financial Life and Annuity Insurance Company; Broadband & Internet Security Task Force; The Children's Hospital of Philadelphia; Delaware Valley Insurance Trusts; The Medical Protective Company; IBM Corporation; Lorillard Tobacco Company; Motiva Enterprises LLC; Osram Sylvania Products Inc; Motion Picture Association of America; NEC America Inc.; Pennsylvania American Water Company; Polydyne Inc.; Progressive Group of Insurance Companies; Raleigh America Inc.; Rohm and Haas Company; SLM Financial Corporation; Susquehanna Patriot Bank; The Vanguard Group and Viacom International Inc. The firm also represents hospitals, professional organizations, physician groups and law firms.

CONRAD O'BRIEN GELLMAN & ROHN, PC

# DECHERT LLP

## THE FIRM

**Chairman:** Barton J Winokur
**Number of partners:** 277
**Number of other lawyers:** 716
**Website:** www.dechert.com

**FIRM OVERVIEW:** The 900+ lawyers of Dechert LLP work with clients to accomplish their business objectives, minimize risks, resolve challenges, and prevail in litigation. The firm focuses on core transactional and litigation practices, providing world-class, top-ranked services to major corporations, financial institutions, and private funds worldwide.

## MAIN AREAS OF PRACTICE:

### CORPORATE & SECURITIES — Definitive Advice, Practical Guidance

**Mergers & Acquisitions & Private Equity:** Dechert's M&A group, top ranked in the league tables of *Mergerstat, Thomson Financial, Bloomberg*, and *mergermarket*, represents strategic and financial buyers, sellers, investors, and advisers in domestic and international public and private transactions. Ranked one of the most active law firms in private equity based on number of funds structured and deals closed, Dechert forms funds on behalf of private equity sponsors and institutional investors, and advises the portfolio companies of sponsor clients in their subsequent transactions and financings.

**Corporate Finance:** Dechert lawyers advise US and European issuers, underwriters, sponsors, investors, and placement agents in public and private issuances of debt and equity securities, and in major financial restructurings. Dechert's corporate and securities lawyers have a particular focus on working with clients in the life sciences industry, advising on corporate structures, M&A and licensing transactions, financing, intellectual property, and dispute resolution.

### LITIGATION — Powerful Advocacy

**Antitrust:** Dechert focuses on class action defense, government enforcement actions, international cartel investigations, and merger clearance.

**Product Liability:** One of only ten US firms to be named to *The National Law Journal*'s 'Defense Hot List', Dechert handles all aspects of complex cases for companies in the pharmaceutical, tobacco, medical device, consumer product, chemical, and other industries.

**White Collar Criminal Defense:** With one of the largest of such practices, the firm represents clients in government and internal investigations, complex criminal and securities enforcement litigation, and related civil class actions.

**Financial Services & Securities Litigation:** Dechert's trial lawyers defend clients in securities litigation, securities enforcement actions, corporate governance and fiduciary litigation, mergers and acquisitions litigation, and litigation involving banking and financial institutions.

**Intellectual Property Litigation & Counseling:** The firm represents sophisticated technology and life sciences companies in complex patent, trademark, copyright, trade secret, and IP-antitrust disputes.

**Other Litigation:** The firm also litigates insurance, environmental, healthcare, employment, and media cases, and resolves international disputes through litigation and arbitration.

### FINANCE & REAL ESTATE — Complex Deals, Done Efficiently

**Securitization & Structured Finance:** Top ranked in the league tables for mortgage- and asset-backed offerings, Dechert lawyers represent leading issuers, underwriters, and other participants in public and private securitizations. The group closes some of the most significant lease finance transactions in the marketplace on behalf of lenders, equity investors, lessees, and investment banks.

**Real Estate Finance:** The group's lawyers advise on all aspects of mortgage finance, mezzanine lending, syndicated loans, debt/equity financing, portfolio sales, participations, B notes, and high-yield debt. On the lease financing side, the firm represents clients in sale/leasebacks, credit tenant leasing, and net leasing.

## USA OFFICES

Austin, Boston, Charlotte, Harrisburg, Hartford, New York, Newport Beach, Palo Alto, Philadelphia, Princeton, San Francisco, Washington, DC

## INTERNATIONAL OFFICES

Brussels, Frankfurt, London, Luxembourg, Munich, Paris.

For details on these offices, please visit the firm's website at www.dechert.com

## CONTACTS

| | |
|---|---|
| **Mergers & Acquisitions** | William G Lawlor |
| **Private Equity** | G Daniel O'Donnell |
| | Carl A de Brito |
| **Corporate Finance** | Bonnie A Barsamian |
| | Christopher G Karras |
| **Life Sciences** | James A Lebovitz |
| **Antitrust** | Stephen A Stack Jr |
| | Paul Friedman |
| **Product Liability** | Sean P Wajert |
| **White Collar** | David Howard |
| **Securities Litigation** | William K Dodds |
| **IP Litigation & Counseling** | Glenn A Gundersen |
| | Martin J Black |
| | Michael H Kalkstein |
| **Finance & Real Estate** | Malcolm S Dorris |
| | John J Gillies Jr |
| | Richard D Jones |
| **Financial Services** | Joseph R Fleming |
| | Robert W Helm |

**Investment:** The firm's real estate investment funds practice, representing a wide range of investors in the US, Europe, and Middle East, covers fund formation for conventional real estate funds and real estate funds that comply with Islamic *Shari'ah*.

### FINANCIAL SERVICES — Achieve Performance Goals, Strengthen Reputations

**Investment Management:** Top ranked in the league tables for mutual fund representation, Dechert lawyers advise on fund formation and management, transactions, regulatory and compliance matters, investigations by regulatory agencies, and the acquisition and integration of fund groups.

**Hedge Funds:** Dechert's hedge fund practice, top ranked in the industry, represents more than 500 hedge funds and other alternative investment funds, fund sponsors, managers, and service providers. Dechert lawyers use a variety of structures to pool the assets of investors from around the world.

**Insurance Companies:** The firm advises insurance companies on new product development, securitized products, and the securities, tax, and other issues related to product offerings. Dechert lawyers develop innovative insurance products with an investment orientation for the individual, pension, and corporate markets.

**ADDITIONAL AREAS OF PRACTICE:** The firm also has well-established practices in state and federal tax, bankruptcy and reorganization, and environmental law.

# DUANE MORRIS LLP

## THE FIRM

**Chairman:** Sheldon M Bonovitz
**Website:** www.duanemorris.com

**FIRM OVERVIEW:** Duane Morris LLP, among the 100 largest law firms in the United States, is a full-service firm of more than 600 lawyers. In addition to legal services, Duane Morris has independent affiliates employing approximately 100 professionals enaged in other disciplines. With offices in major markets, and as part of an international network of independent law firms, Duane Morris represents clients across the nation and around the world.

## MAIN AREAS OF PRACTICE:

**Litigation & Alternative Dispute Resolution:** Duane Morris attorneys represent clients in every type of litigation, from hard fought, complex commercial disputes to more amicable solution-based mediation. The firm's attorneys have a broad range of experience, including, for example, securities, antitrust, intellectual property, real estate and construction law. All of the attorneys in its Trial Practice Group try cases; some have also devoted themselves to appellate work. Duane Morris attorneys are called upon to represent diverse clients with different needs. Its litigators work closely with the firm's corporate and bankruptcy lawyers in the representation of public and private companies, banks, insurance companies and other financial institutions. Duane Morris attorneys represent all types of business entities and their boards, as well as investors, with regard to breach of fiduciary duty claims, merger-and-acquisition litigation, and all issues involving corporate law and governance. Duane Morris lawyers represent both individuals and corporations facing federal and state allegations of criminal conduct, including fraud, environmental, securities and RICO violations, trade espionage and a variety of business-related offenses. In addition to representing clients in US forums and before international tribunals, the firm also provides counsel on settling disputes using alternative dispute resolution options and advises on methods to anticipate and avoid litigation.

**Corporate, Securities, Mergers & Acquisitions:** Duane Morris corporate attorneys advise early stage and mature companies on a wide variety of corporate and securities matters. The firm represents clients in all aspects of mergers and acquisitions, including negotiated acquisitions and divestitures. Its attorneys are experienced with venture capital and private equity transactions and work with entrepreneurial clients in developing and implementing creative strategies to accomplish their corporate finance and acquisition objectives. Duane Morris lawyers regularly assist closely held companies with equity incentives and succession planning. It represents clients in securities offerings and advises public companies on securities law compliance, ongoing reporting obligations and corporate governance issues.

**Intellectual Property:** Duane Morris' intellectual property lawyers' experience includes trademarks and copyrights, patents and brand protection. Members of the IP Practice Group include highly trained patent attorneys with backgrounds in biosciences, materials, chemicals, polymers, electronics and telecommunications. Duane Morris' IP litigators have substantial trial experience in disputes over patents, trademarks, copyrights, trade secrets and licenses involving such intangible property.

**Business Reorganization & Financial Restructuring:** Lawyers in Duane Morris' Business Reorganization and Financial Restructuring Practice Group represent clients in all aspects of debt restructuring and bankruptcy proceedings. They work closely with debtors, trustees, creditors and other parties in interest to develop and implement successful strategies for achieving clients' goals. The firm has a national team of insolvency lawyers who have been actively involved in the largest and most complex bankruptcy cases in all of the major markets in the United States.

**Healthcare:** Healthcare providers continue to face enormous regulatory and financial pressures, while burdened by soaring costs even as demand for services increases. To meet these challenges, Duane Morris clients rely on its nationally recognized Healthcare Practice Group. Clients benefit from the collective experience of one of the nation's largest healthcare practice groups providing a full

## OFFICES

### CALIFORNIA
633 West Fifth Street, Suite 4600, **Los Angeles,** CA 90071
**Tel:** 213 689 7400   **Fax:** 213 689 7401

101 West Broadway, **San Diego,** CA 92101
**Tel:** 619 744 2200   **Fax:** 619 744 2201

One Market, Spear Tower, **San Francisco,** CA 94105
**Tel:** 415 371 2200   **Fax:** 415 371 2201

850 N. Lake Blvd., Suite 15, PO Box 7199, **Tahoe City,** CA 96145
**Tel:** 530 583 7767   **Fax:** 530 581 3215

### DELAWARE
1100 North Market Street, **Wilmington,** DE 19801
**Tel:** 302 657 4900   **Fax:** 302 657 4901

### DISTRICT OF COLUMBIA
1667 K Street, NW, **Washington,** DC 20006
**Tel:** 202 776 7800   **Fax:** 202 776 7801

### FLORIDA
200 South Biscayne Boulevard, **Miami,** FL 33131
**Tel:** 305 960 2200   **Fax:** 305 960 2201

### GEORGIA
1180 West Peachtree Street, **Atlanta,** GA 30309
**Tel:** 404 253 6900   **Fax:** 404 253 6901

### ILLINOIS
227 West Monroe Street, **Chicago,** IL 60606
**Tel:** 312 499 6700   **Fax:** 312 499 6701

### MASSACHUSETTS
470 Atlantic Avenue, **Boston,** MA 02210
**Tel:** 617 289 9200   **Fax:** 617 289 9201

### NEW JERSEY
744 Broad Street, **Newark,** NJ 07102
**Tel:** 973 424 2000   **Fax:** 973 424 2001

PO Box 5203, **Princeton,** NJ 08543-5203
**Tel:** 609 631 2400   **Fax:** 609 631 2401

### NEW YORK
380 Lexington Avenue, **New York,** NY 10168
**Tel:** 212 692 1000   **Fax:** 212 692 1020

### NEVADA
701 Bridger Avenue, Suite 670, **Las Vegas,** NV 89101
**Tel:** 702 385 1740   **Fax:** 702 385 6862

### PENNSYLVANIA
30 South 17th St, **Philadelphia,** PA 19103
**Tel:** 215 979 1000   **Fax:** 215 979 1020

600 Grant Street, **Pittsburgh,** PA 15219
**Tel:** 412 497 1000   **Fax:** 412 497 1001

968 Postal Road, Suite 200, **Allentown,** PA 18109-0400

### TEXAS
3200 Southwest Freeway, Suite 3150, **Houston,** TX 77027-7534
**Tel:** 713 402 3900   **Fax:** 713 402 3901

### INTERNATIONAL
The firm also has an office in London.

# DUANE MORRIS LLP CONT'D

range of regulatory and transactional services in every major sector of the healthcare industry.

**Insurance:** The changing business climate and shifting regulatory forces affect the insurance industry in unique ways. To meet these unique challenges, Duane Morris' interdisciplinary Insurance & Reinsurance Practice counsels insurer and reinsurer clients on complex litigation and business matters, as well as legislative and ethical issues. Its Insurance & Reinsurance Industry Team brings together lawyers skilled in litigation, regulatory, corporate and transactional matters, as well as lawyers with actuarial, underwriting and policy coverage experience. Duane Morris also has developed proprietary technology tools to help its clients manage their businesses, reduce risk exposure, enhance profitability and efficiently resolve costly litigation.

**Employment & Immigration:** The Duane Morris Employment and Immigration Practice assists clients with the complexities and challenges of the changing workplace. From advising employers on new legislative requirements, unraveling sensitive labor and employment disputes, designing benefit and executive compensation plans, to addressing cross-border employment and visa concerns, Duane Morris attorneys provide a full-range of employment-related services to help clients achieve their business goals in today's borderless global economy.

**Real Estate:** Duane Morris' Real Estate Practice assists clients throughout the US, Europe, Asia and South and Central America. Duane Morris attorneys draw upon their extensive experience to find solutions for complex issues in the following segments of the real estate industry: commercial, retail, hospitality, and housing. The firm represents developers, financial institutions, landowners, corporations, real estate investment trusts, architectural firms, and nonprofit institutions. Duane Morris represents leading developers on projects that range from creating world class sports stadiums, internationally renowned concert halls and high-tech medical facilities to adapting historic properties for new uses.

**Complex Financial Transactions:** Duane Morris has extensive experience with the financing of complex private and public projects, often representing corporations and financial institutions on a regional, national and international level. The firm's attorneys counsel clients in numerous types of transactions covering nearly every aspect of municipal, project and structured finance transactions. Duane Morris public finance attorneys represent national and regional investment banking firms underwriting tax-exempt and taxable state and local government debt, act as bond counsel and special tax counsel for issuers and represent domestic and foreign institutions providing credit enhancement for tax-exempt financing. The firm's project and structured finance attorneys represent clients in acquisition financings, securitized and syndicated loans, and other complex financial transactions. It also has a distinct group of attorneys who focus their practice on affordable housing finance.

**Energy & Environment:** As both advisor and advocate, Duane Morris guides clients through the complex legal, financial, policy and political issues surrounding the basic necessities that power all industries and businesses. Members of Duane Morris' national Energy Practice regularly assist clients with advisory, regulatory and litigation matters involving water, natural resources and environmental issues, often counseling clients in their interactions with federal, state and municipal agencies. In addition, Duane Morris counsels clients concerning their rights and obligations under federal environmental statutes and regulations, as well as similar state and local laws, and represents clients in related enforcement proceedings and litigation.

**Life Sciences:** Duane Morris clients in the life sciences industry traverse new frontiers. From pioneering lifesaving developments to exploring novel technology-sharing agreements, these businesses face a complex range of legal, business and financial challenges. The firm's Life Sciences Practice Group brings together lawyers from several of the firm's practice groups to offer clients a full panoply of legal services – including intellectual property counsel, securities counsel in connection with private and public equity funding, international trade and tax advice, labor and employment guidance, dispute resolution and litigation services – provided within the framework of their business to address each client's specific needs.

## CONTACTS

| | |
|---|---|
| Trial | John J Soroko |
| Corporate | John F Horstmann |
| Intellectual Property | Lewis F Gould |
| Business Reorganization | Rudolph J Di Massa Jr |
| Healthcare | Donald R Auten, David E Loder |
| Insurance | William J Casey |
| Employment & Immigration | Thomas G Servodidio |
| Real Estate | Marc D Brookman |
| Energy & Resources | Stephen L Teichler |
| Environmental | Seth vdH Cooley |
| Estates & Asset Planning | Frank G Cooper |
| | |
| New York | Robert J Hasday |
| Los Angeles | Russell W Roten |
| Chicago | David B Yelin |
| Houston | Richard T Redano |
| San Diego | Christopher Celentino |
| San Francisco | Joseph M Burton |
| Boston | Martin B Shulkin |
| Washington, DC | Douglas Woloshin |
| Las Vegas | Dominica Anderson |
| Atlanta | Charles W Whitney |
| Miami | Charles C Papy, III |
| Pittsburgh | George M Medved |
| Newark | Walter J Greenhalgh |
| Wilmington | Michael R Lastowski |
| Princeton | Frank A Luchak |
| Lake Tahoe | John E Fagan |

**CLIENTS:** Duane Morris' international client base, like its practice, is extremely diverse. Duane Morris represents clients with business and investment interests around the globe. Its clients range from established blue chip companies to start-up entrepreneurs; from publicly traded companies to family-owned businesses; from major institutional investors to governmental authorities to private clients.

**INTERNATIONAL WORK:** Duane Morris' dedicated International Practice Group integrates the services of its senior attorneys in nearly every legal discipline, creating a global infrastructure of international experience and enhanced sensitivity to cultural differences. Services offered by the International Practice Group range from cross-border business transactions to international dispute resolution and enforcement; from customs and international trade to international tax planning; from immigration to international wealth preservation for private clients.

# FOX ROTHSCHILD LLP

## THE FIRM

**Co-Chairmen:** Abraham C Reich, Esq, Phillip Griffin, Esq
**Number of lawyers:** 313

**FIRM OVERVIEW:** Fox Rothschild LLP is a full-service firm providing a range of legal services to public and private business entities; charitable, medical and educational institution; and individuals around the world Founded in 1907, the firm ranks among the top 200 law firms nationally (according to The American Lawyer) and has nine offices throughout the Eastern US to meet the needs of its client base. Its knowledgeable attorneys and skilled staff are supported by industry-leading technologies that link firm offices and promote rapid communication and collaboration among departments and practice groups. Clients have access to the full resources of the firm's attorney network, and to the depth of experience available firmwide. Every matter receives the individualized attention, strategic thinking and cost-effective approach that are Fox Rothschild hallmarks.

## MAIN AREAS OF PRACTICE:

**Civil Litigation:** As the firm's largest department, litigation has effectively represented businesses and individuals in diverse and complex commercial law disputes. Its attorneys have achieved national recognition for their representation of large, publicly held corporations, family-owned businesses and individuals in a broad variety of civil and administrative matters, including contract law, corporate law, securities law, class actions, civil RICO, shareholder disputes, antitrust, banking and finance law, Uniform Commercial Code, franchise law, insurance coverage, defamation, consumer protection law, tax law and probate disputes. Firm attorneys have significant trial and appellate experience before virtually all federal and state courts and administrative agencies. Their record of success as aggressive advocates as well as skilled negotiators on behalf of clients has earned Fox Rothschild a reputation of excellence. They have a group of attorneys who regularly participate in alternate dispute resolution as arbitrators, mediators and advocates for clients.

**Corporate Transactions:** The firm's Corporate Department represents a diverse cross-section of public and privately owned businesses and institutions in all stages of development. Clients include small and large family-owned companies, professional practices, start-up enterprises, and large regional, national and international corporations. The Department also advises (both as attorneys and board members) a rich mix of non-profit organizations, including public charities, hospitals and colleges. Fox Rothschild serves as general counsel to many business clients, providing advice that ranges from dealing with day-to-day employee or regulatory questions to implementing strategies for major transactions. Its transactional experience is deep and varied with a special emphasis on mergers and acquisitions, equity financing, bank and other debt financing, intellectual property, and federal and state regulatory requirements. Members of the Corporate Department work closely with members of the Tax and Estates Department in the structuring of transactions.

**Labor & Employment:** The firm's experience in employment law matters has involved claims of age, handicap, sex and race discrimination. Its attorneys also represent clients in cases involving wrongful discharge, employment at will, whistleblower violations, defamation, fraud, invasion of privacy, public policy employment rights, intentional infliction of emotional distress and a wide variety of other common law and statutory claims arising in the employment context. Fox Rothschild attorneys have successfully handled claims under the Americans with Disabilities Act, Family and Medical Leave Act, Family Leave Act, Older Workers Benefits Protection Act, Age Discrimination in Employment Act, and other employment protection legislation. It also counts experience in employee benefit work, including COBRA and ERISA matters, among its strengths.

**Real Estate:** Combing sound judgment with a practical approach, the firm's Real Estate Department has become one of the largest in the region. Clients as diverse as developers, financial institutions, shopping center owners, retail chain operators, hoteliers, contractors and architects have benefited from its quick, decisive response to their matters involving financing, land planning, acquisi-

tion and development, commercial leasing, syndications, tax credits, condemnation, tax assessment and more. Additionally, Fox Rothschild offers real estate clients a one-stop business partnering solution that is customized to their needs. Its specialized practice groups, such as environmental, construction and finance, can be assembled quickly into a multidisciplinary team of attorneys that responds swiftly and cost-effectively as the client's circumstances require.

**INTERNATIONAL WORK:** Fox Rothschild serves clients in a range of legal situations across the world, including Colombia, Dominican Republic, Peru, Puerto Rico and Uruguay as well as clients in Japan, Korea, and other countries throughout Asia and Europe. Firm attorneys are versed in the intricacies and nuances of international law and are directly involved in the global business community. Services range from assisting companies seeking to establish a presence in the United States to representing corporations involved in worldwide disputes. Its international representation extends to matters of intellectual property rights, including patent, copyright and trademark cases; business litigation; taxation banking; e-commerce; corporate and contract matters; commercial transactions; casino and gaming law; immigration issues and a host of additional legal services. Additionally, as a member of the Great Lakes Law Network, Fox Rothschild is strategically aligned with 12 independent US and Canadian law firms to address the legal needs of clients – not only within their market, but beyond their respective jurisdictions. This consortium provides legal representation for Canadian and US clients, as well as for organizations within Europe and the Pacific Rim.

## OFFICE LOCATIONS

### PENNSYLVANIA
2000 Market Street, Tenth Floor, **Philadelphia**, PA 19103-3291
**Tel:** 215 299 2000  **Fax:** 215 299 2150
**Website:** www.foxrothschild.com

Eagleview Corporate Center, 760 Constitution Drive, PO Box 673, Suite 104, **Exton**, PA 19341-0673
**Tel:** 610 458 7500  **Fax:** 610 458 7337

1250 South Broad Street, PO Box 431, Suite 1000, **Lansdale**, PA 19446-0431
**Tel:** 215 699 6000  **Fax:** 215 699 0231

625 Liberty Avenue, 29th Floor, **Pittsburgh**, PA 15222-3115
**Tel:** 412 391 1334  **Fax:** 412 391 6984

2700 Kelly Road, Suite 300, **Warrington**, PA 18976-3624
**Tel:** 215 345 7500  **Fax:** 215 345 7507

### DELAWARE
Citizens Bank Center, 919 North Market Street, PO Box 2323, Suite 1300, **Wilmington**, DE 19899-2323
**Tel:** 302 654 7444  **Fax:** 302 656 8920

### NEW JERSEY
Midtown Building, 1301 Atlantic Avenue, Suite 400, **Atlantic City**, NJ 08401-7212
**Tel:** 609 348 4515  **Fax:** 609 348 6834

PO Box 5231, **Princeton**, NJ 08543-5231
**Tel:** 609 896 3600  **Fax:** 609 896 1469
(Delivery address: Princeton Pike Corporate Center, 997 Lenox Drive, Building 3, Lawrenceville, NJ 08648-2311)

### NEW YORK
100 Park Avenue, Suite 1500, **New York**, NY 10017
**Tel:** 212 878 7900  **Fax:** 212 692 0940

### FLORIDA
Esperante Building, 222 Lakeview Avenue, Suite 700, **West Palm Beach**, FL 33401
**Tel:** 561 835 9600  **Fax:** 561 835 9602

# HANGLEY ARONCHICK SEGAL & PUDLIN

## THE FIRM

**FIRM OVERVIEW:** Hangley Aronchick Segal & Pudlin is proud that 11 of its 28 members have been singled out by Chambers USA as being among the very best in the fields of antitrust, commercial litigation, bankruptcy and real estate. Founded in 1994, the 50 lawyer firm also maintains robust practices in other areas, including corporate transactions, white collar criminal, and tax and estate planning. Readers are invited to the firm's website, www.hangley.com, for further information on those practice areas and the outstanding lawyers at Hangley Aronchick. The sophistication of matters handled by the firm, the roster of its clients and the quality of its work belie the firm's relatively small size. In the Delaware Valley, the firm is unparalleled in its ability to attract the most highly qualified attorneys, both at the entry level and laterally. The firm includes two former Philadelphia City solicitors, a former United States Supreme Court clerk, several Fellows of the American College of Trial Lawyers, the American College of Bankruptcy, and the American College of Real Estate Lawyers, a former Chancellor of the Philadelphia Bar Association, a member of the Pennsylvania IOLTA Board, members of the American Law Institute and adjunct faculty members at area law schools. The great majority of Hangley Aronchick's trial lawyers have clerked on federal courts of appeals or district courts.

## MAIN AREAS OF PRACTICE:

**LITIGATION:** Clients and referring counsel seek out Hangley Aronchick for cases that will actually have to be tried. The firm has frequently represented some of the country's largest corporations, the Commonwealth of Pennsylvania, the City of Philadelphia, the major universities and healthcare complexes in the Delaware Valley, and the Pennsylvania Bar Association. The firm also regularly represents and counsels local and national law firms when they are drawn into litigation or are seeking to avoid that fate. Lawsuits the firm is currently handling or has recently handled include the following:

**Antitrust:** Representing national pharmacy chains in suits against pharmaceutical manufacturers.

**Appellate:** Representing a wide range of clients in matters before state and federal appellate courts.

**Criminal & Investigative:** Representing subjects and targets in criminal investigations of commercial and financial affairs; assisting in internal investigations for publicly held companies.

**Education Law:** In a matter of first impression, representing the Commonwealth of Pennsylvania Department of Education in an effort to require the Board of a failing school district to comply with provisions of the Public School Code and to ultimately put the district into receivership.

**Finance:** Representing a major writer of surety bonds in litigation with financial institutions arising out of 'circular' gas deals with Enron; defending banks and credit card companies in class and non-class litigation with card holders.

**First Amendment:** Representing city officials in defamation claims against them; representing newspapers in libel matters.

**Healthcare:** Representing leading health maintenance organizations, hospitals, and healthcare service providers in disputes over reimbursement and billing issues, including the defense of class actions, parallel criminal and civil actions, and complex civil disputes.

**Intellectual Property:** Litigating on behalf of patent holders or alleged infringers in fields ranging from securities trading protocols to coloring concrete; representing a major university in a patent royalty dispute with a former faculty member.

**Public Affairs:** Representing the Governor of Pennsylvania and other executive officials in litigation filed by the President Pro Tempore of the Pennsylvania Senate and the Speaker of the Pennsylvania House of Representatives challenging the constitutionality of the Governor's line-item vetoes in connection with enactment of the 2005 General Appropriation Act; representing the Philadelphia Housing Authority in several high profile commercial and employment litigation matters; recovering city tax revenues from the major Philadelphia banks.

### HEAD OFFICE

**PENNSYLVANIA**
One Logan Square, 27th Floor, **Philadelphia**, PA 19103-6933
**Tel:** 215 568 6200   **Fax:** 215 568 0300

**Website:** www.hangley.com

### BRANCH OFFICES

**NEW JERSEY**
20 Brace Road, Suite 201, **Cherry Hill**, NJ 08034-2634
**Tel:** 856 616 2100   **Fax:** 856 616 2170

**PENNSYLVANIA**
30 North Third Street, Suite 700, **Harrisburg**, PA 17101-1701
**Tel:** 717 364 1030   **Fax:** 717 364 1020

**Securities & Corporate Law:** Representing publicly held companies in litigation over mergers and securities offerings; representing individual officers and directors in securities fraud claims involving publicly held companies.

**REAL ESTATE:** The firm's Real Estate Practice covers all aspects of commercial real estate: acquisition, financing, construction, development, leasing, and management of high rise office towers, suburban corporate facilities, hotels, national and regional shopping centers, industrial facilities, apartment complexes and residential subdivisions. The firm specializes in the following areas:

**Finance:** Representing national and regional institutional lenders and borrowers in connection with permanent and construction loans on all types of real estate.

**Leasing:** Representing city and suburban developers and building owners in connection with leases and management agreements.

**Companies & Their Real Estate:** Representing owner and tenant clients, including a national grocery chain, a cold storage company, restaurateurs, communications companies, an owner and operator of physical rehabilitation hospitals, and other large companies in connection with their retail stores, shopping centers, restaurants, headquarters and production facilities.

**Development:** Representing clients in the construction and development of new buildings, including development agreements, construction contracts, architect's contracts, agreements of sale and financing.

**Land Use/Zoning:** Representing clients before zoning and planning boards and other governmental bodies in New Jersey and Pennsylvania.

**BANKRUPTCY & INSOLVENCY:** The effective representation of business debtors and creditors in sensitive restructuring situations demands lawyers who are able to combine business law, negotiation, litigation and problem-solving skills, and who have the sound judgment and counseling skills to help the client navigate the difficult terrain. The firm's Bankruptcy and Insolvency Group has had significant experience in representing clients who must manage their businesses (or collect claims from other businesses) in the crisis atmosphere of insolvency, regularly handling out-of-court liquidations, restructurings and pre-packaged and pre-arranged proceedings as well as cases under Chapters 7 and 11 of the Bankruptcy Code, purchasing and selling assets in distress circumstances, advancing competing or 'hostile' reorganization plans, and prosecuting and defending bankruptcy and non-bankruptcy litigation, including lender liability claims.

HANGLEY
ARONCHICK
SEGAL
& PUDLIN

# KLETT ROONEY LIEBER & SCHORLING, A PROFESSIONAL CORPORATION

## THE FIRM

**Managing Partner:** John A Barbour
**Number of partners:** 70
**Number of other lawyers:** 68

**Email:** info@klettrooney.com
**Website:** www.klettrooney.com

**FIRM OVERVIEW:** Klett Rooney Lieber & Schorling is a full-service, general commercial law firm representing corporations and other business entities through interdisciplinary practice groups that allow sophisticated legal matters to be addressed comprehensively, efficiently and cost effectively.

## MAIN AREAS OF PRACTICE:

**Bankruptcy & Insolvency:** Provides legal advice on matters covering the diversity of issues confronting financially-troubled companies. The firm also represents lending institutions, creditors' committees, secured and unsecured creditors, and other participants in the reorganization of economically-distressed businesses.

**Commercial Litigation:** Provides counsel in resolving commercial disputes prior to the commencement of lawsuits, through mediation and arbitration, and in the courtroom. It represents clients at all levels of the litigation process in a variety of venues, from county, state and federal jurisdictions to arbitration boards and zoning boards and commissions.

**Corporate:** Represents both publicly traded and privately-held business entities in a broad range of corporate and commercial transactions. Specialties include corporate and public finance; healthcare; banking; securities law; educational institutions; emerging business and venture capital; general corporate law; mergers and acquisitions; estate planning and administration; and individual, partnership and corporate taxation.

**Energy & Utilities:** Offers solutions to current regulatory and legislative issues facing the energy and utility industry, specializing in strategic planning and regulatory consultative services for both regulated and non-regulated utilities and suppliers of electricity, gas, water and telecommunications on a national and international basis.

**Government Affairs:** Assists clients in making connections with decision-makers in local, state and federal government to heighten awareness of critical issues, pursue procurement opportunities and develop government solutions to fit their unique needs. The firm has forged a network of public sector relationships with members of both major political parties across all branches of government.

**Labor & Employment:** Exclusively represents management in dealing with virtually every kind of workplace issue confronting employers, including collective bargaining negotiations, employee agreements, workplace restructuring, discrimination and harassment, ADA compliance, OSHA, Railway Labor Act, business immigration, employment litigation and employee benefits matters.

**Real Estate:** Assists developers, financial institutions and property owners in all aspects of commercial real estate transactions, including real property development, lending and leasing transactions. From the establishment of an ownership entity and the purchase of property, to the negotiation of all construction and financing-related documents, involvement continues to the development, operation and disposition of properties.

**CLIENTS:** Klett Rooney's clients range from leading Fortune 500 companies and closely-held businesses to numerous colleges and universities, hospitals and other healthcare institutions, banks and other financial establishments, software and technology companies, minority businesses, charitable and community organizations, and a National Football League team.

**INTERNATIONAL WORK:** The firm offers a diverse range of transactional and litigation services for corporations and other entities, assisting US-based clients in overseas business operations and export of goods and services and foreign-owned businesses seeking to establish, maintain or expand operations in the US.

## HEAD OFFICE

### PENNSYLVANIA
One Oxford Centre, 40th Floor, **Pittsburgh,** PA 15219
**Tel:** 412 392 2000   **Fax:** 412 392 2128

## BRANCH OFFICES

### DELAWARE
1000 West St., Suite 1410, **Wilmington,** DE 19801
**Tel:** 302 552 4200   **Fax:** 302 552 4295

### DISTRICT OF COLUMBIA
600 Pennsylvania Ave., SE, Suite 220, **Washington,** DC 20003
**Tel:** 202 544 4094   **Fax:** 202 544 9497

### NEW JERSEY
550 Broad St., Suite 810, **Newark,** NJ 01702
**Tel:** 973 273 9800   **Fax:** 973 273 9430

### PENNSYLVANIA
Two Logan Square, 12th Floor, **Philadelphia,** PA 19103
**Tel:** 215 567 7500   **Fax:** 215 567 2737

17 N Second St., 15th Floor, **Harrisburg,** PA 17101
**Tel:** 717 231 7700   **Fax:** 717 231 7712

## CONTACTS

| | |
|---|---|
| **Bankruptcy & Insolvency** | William H Schorling |
| **Commercial Litigation** | Christine L Donohue |
| **Corporate** | Robert T Harper |
| **Energy & Utilities** | John M Quain |
| **Government Affairs** | Thomas G Paese |
| **Labor & Employment** | Thomas S Giotto |
| **Real Estate** | Jacqui Fiske Lazo |

## KLETT ROONEY LIEBER & SCHORLING
### A PROFESSIONAL CORPORATION
#### ATTORNEYS AT LAW

www.klettrooney.com

# MORGAN, LEWIS & BOCKIUS LLP

## THE FIRM

**Managing Partner:** Francis M Milone, Chair
**Number of partners:** 440
**Number of other lawyers:** 793

**FIRM OVERVIEW:** With more than 1,200 lawyers and 300 other professionals (including technical specialists, patent agents, and paralegals) in offices worldwide, Morgan Lewis is the only US law firm with more than 250 lawyers in each of its New York, Washington and Philadelphia offices and more than 250 lawyers in California. They have the resources and knowledge to handle the most complex transactional and litigation needs of the world's largest corporations.

**MAIN AREAS OF PRACTICE:** Across practices and offices, the firm represents clients in a wide variety of issues in the energy, life sciences, media and information, securities, and technology industries.

**Antitrust:** The firm's Antitrust Practice offers all the personalized service and attention of a specialty law firm with the resources and global reach of a major international law firm. Their work includes counseling, litigation, representation in government cartel/criminal investigations and prosecutions. Their lawyers, many of whom have previously held senior positions in US antitrust enforcement agencies, advise clients on mergers and acquisitions, trade associations, and consumer protection matters.

**Business & Finance:** The firm's Business and Finance Practice is composed of nearly 300 lawyers located in more than 15 offices—more than 30 of whom are SEC alumni. Their lawyers focus on mergers and acquisitions (including joint ventures, spin-offs and strategic alliances), finance and restructuring, securities (including public and private equity and debt offerings), tax, and emerging business and technology. They service a diverse clientele ranging from Fortune 500 and FTSE 250 companies to investment banks to emerging growth companies.

**Employee Benefits & Executive Compensation:** The firm has more than 80 lawyers and other professionals using their skills as counselors, strategists, problem solvers and trial lawyers to assist clients in finding creative solutions to their employee benefits-related business challenges. This practice is one of the largest in the country and offers a level of substantive knowledge, industry experience and technical skills that makes us a nationwide leader in employee benefits law. It includes plan sponsor consulting, litigation, ESOPs, executive compensation and equity compensation, transactional support, and vendor consulting with regard to financial products intended for tax-favored retirement plans.

**Energy:** The firm's Energy Practice lawyers manage a broad range of domestic and international energy matters, many of which are driven by the restructuring of the US energy industry and the expanding scope of global energy enterprises. Their energy lawyers understand the technical, legal and business needs of clients operating in the industry, and possess sophisticated knowledge and insight into each major market segment: electric, natural gas, oil, nuclear and water. Their integrated teams provide the full range of services on project and structured financing, overseas investment, mergers, acquisitions and divestitures of generation and transmission assets, and restructuring of utilities.

**FDA/Healthcare Regulation:** The firm's FDA/Healthcare Regulation attorneys understand the use of science to support and advance appropriate legal and regulatory positions. No other firm is better positioned to counsel life sciences clients in protecting each product through its full life cycle. Their FDA/Healthcare Practice is a key component of the firm's Life Sciences Interdisciplinary Group, which is composed of more than 200 lawyers and technical specialists and covers all regulatory issues related to research, development, testing, approval, marketing, distribution, pricing, life cycle management, and compliance activities involving pharmaceuticals, biologics, medical devices, food additives/dietary supplements, and other products regulated by the FDA and its international counterparts.

**Intellectual Property:** With more than 200 professionals, including lawyers, patent agents and technical specialists, and a patent litigation practice of more than 100 attorneys, we offer clients business solutions concerning all aspects of intellectual property. The firm's clients include both US and non-US enterprises, and range in size from Fortune 500 companies to small start-ups. Offering

## FIRM OFFICES

### CALIFORNIA
1 Ada, Suite 250, **Irvine**, CA 92618
**Tel:** 949 453 3000   **Fax:** 949 453 3001

300 South Grand Avenue, Twenty Second Floor, **Los Angeles**, CA 90071
**Tel:** 213 612 2500   **Fax:** 213 612 2501

2 Palo Alto Square, 3000 El Camino Real, Suite 900, **Palo Alto**, CA 94306
**Tel:** 650 843 4000   **Fax:** 650 843 4001

One Market, Spear Street Tower, **San Francisco**, CA 94105
**Tel:** 415 442 1000   **Fax:** 415 442 1001

### DISTRICT OF COLUMBIA
1111 Pennsylvania Avenue, NW, **Washington**, DC 20004
**Tel:** 202 739 3000   **Fax:** 202 739 3001

### FLORIDA
5300 Wachovia Financial Center, 200 South Biscayne Boulevard, **Miami**, FL 33131
**Tel:** 305 415 3000   **Fax:** 305 415 3001

### ILLINOIS
77 West Wacker Drive, Sixth Floor, **Chicago**, IL 60601
**Tel:** 617 451 9700   **Fax:** 617 451 9710

### MASSACHUSETTS
225 Franklin Street, Suite 1705, **Boston**, MA 02110
**Tel:** 617 977 2500   **Fax:** 617 977 2560

### NEW JERSEY
502 Carnegie Center, **Princeton**, NJ 08540
**Tel:** 609 919 6600   **Fax:** 609 919 6639

### NEW YORK
101 Park Avenue, **New York**, NY 10178
**Tel:** 212 309 6000   **Fax:** 212 309 6273

### PENNSYLVANIA
One Commerce Square, 417 Walnut Street, **Harrisburg**, PA 17101
**Tel:** 717 237 4000   **Fax:** 717 237 4004

1701 Market Street, **Philadelphia**, PA 19103
**Tel:** 215 963 5000   **Fax:** 215 963 5001

One Oxford Centre, Thirty Second Floor, **Pittsburgh**, PA 15219
**Tel:** 412 560 3300   **Fax:** 412 560 7001

### TEXAS
1717 Main Street, Suit 3400, **Dallas**, TX 75201
**Tel:** 214 438 1550   **Fax:** 214 438 1551

## INTERNATIONAL OFFICES

The firm also has offices in Belgium, China, Germany, England, France and Japan.

boutique-caliber services while providing the resources of a global law firm, their attorneys counsel companies throughout the life cycles of their products and services, including research and development, financing, marketing, licensing and enforcement of relevant rights.

**Investment Management:** The Investment Management Practice is one of the most significant among US law firms, regularly ranked in industry periodicals for representing the most new mutual funds. They represent a broad array of financial services entities, including investment companies, investment advisers, broker-dealers, venture capital and hedge funds, offshore banks and trust compa-

# MORGAN, LEWIS & BOCKIUS LLP CONT'D

nies, insurance companies, pension plans, pension consultants, transfer agents and other industry participants. They provide their clients, who include many of the largest and best known financial services firms in the world, with a full range of legal services.

**Labor & Employment Law:** More than 225 labor and employment law and employee benefits lawyers maintain one of the premier management-side labor and employment practices in the US. Recently recognized by The American Lawyer magazine for its litigation prowess and traditional labor niche, our practice's scope includes employment counseling, complex employment and employee benefits litigation, labor management relations and labor disputes, employee benefits and executive compensation matters, OFCCP/Affirmative Action plans, wage and hour counseling and litigation, non-competition agreements and related obligations, and international labor and employment law counseling and advice.

**Morgan Lewis Resources:** A unique practice informed by the vast intellectual property and up-to-the-minute collective knowledge and skills of the entire firm, MLR provides innovative solutions that help corporate clients across industries and geographic regions meet increasingly demanding federal regulatory requirements. They help clients think and work proactively, by providing them with traditional compliance policy reviews and audits, case management and litigation technology, workplace training, and international executive travel and foreign resident worker visa processing.

**Litigation:** Nearly 600 lawyers throughout the firm combine the highest levels of substantive knowledge, industry experience and courtroom savvy to help meet the litigation needs of global business. They handle the entire range of issues associated with dispute resolution, with a special emphasis on coordination of national litigation, class actions and other complex business and corporate litigation. They represent many of the nation's largest and most prominent companies in high profile 'bet the company' litigation, often as national trial and coordinating counsel. They have handled class action and serial litigation matters in state and federal courts involving the full range of state and federal causes of action, including antitrust, securities, employment, ERISA, product liability and toxic tort/exposure.

**Personal Law:** The Personal Law Practice serves the legal and financial interests of individuals and family-owned businesses, particularly in traditional estate and tax planning, and the administration of estates and trusts.

**Real Estate:** The Real Estate Practice represents major corporations, regional and national developers, institutional lenders, investors, pension funds and advisers, real estate investment trusts, telecommunications providers, technology companies, retailers and agencies of the federal government. Their nationally recognized practice is known for handling large-volume real estate transactions in multiple jurisdictions.

**INTERNATIONAL WORK:** Morgan Lewis has five international offices that focus on a broad range of practice areas. The firm's lawyers work as one worldwide, integrated team, irrespective of location, and are particularly experienced in addressing complex multi-jurisdictional issues.

Morgan Lewis

COUNSELORS AT LAW

# PEPPER HAMILTON LLP

## THE FIRM

**Chairman:** Barry M Abelson
**Executive Partner:** Robert E Heideck

**Number of partners:** 170
**Number of other lawyers:** 265

**FIRM OVERVIEW:** Pepper Hamilton LLP is a multi-practice law firm with more than 400 lawyers in six states and the District of Columbia providing corporate, litigation and regulatory legal services to US and international businesses, governmental entities, nonprofit organizations and individuals. Pepper was founded in 1890.

## MAIN AREAS OF PRACTICE:

**Bankruptcy & Reorganization:** Represents creditors, debtors, trustees, commercial lenders, examiners and other parties in insolvencies.

**Commercial Litigation:** Represents clients in complex contract, corporate governance, securities, ERISA and antitrust litigation and alternative dispute resolution, in the single case, class action and MDL context.

**Construction:** Represents contractors, public and private owners, developers, subcontractors, architects, engineers and sureties in contract negotiations, arbitration, mediation and litigation.

**Corporate & Securities:** Represents public and private companies in M&A activities, corporate governance, disclosure, securities compliance and enforcement, and other business matters; private equity and venture funds in fund formation, investments, buyouts and other transactions.

**Employee Benefits:** Benefits and executive compensation counseling, plan drafting and administration; and benefits/compensation aspects of transactions; ERISA litigation.

**Environmental:** Counsels and defends federal and state lawsuits and administrative proceedings.

**Financial Services:** Represents sophisticated institutional lenders and borrowers in leveraged transactions, secured financings, securitizations and litigation; investment advisory fund formation and regulation.

**Health Effects Litigation:** Risk management, regulatory counseling and litigation related to alleged adverse health effects from pharmaceuticals, medical devices, radiation, chemicals and environmental substances; product liability litigation involving consumer goods and industrial equipment; civil and criminal matters related to clinical trials.

**Insurance & Reinsurance:** Counsels clients on insurance and reinsurance issues and handles litigation and arbitration of complex contract and treaty-based reinsurance claims.

**Intellectual Property:** Procures intellectual property rights and resolves disputes, including patents, copyrights, trademarks, trade secret protection, unfair competition, false advertising, and defamation, publicity and privacy issues.

**Labor & Employment:** Represents employers in all aspects of labor and employment law, from management counseling to complex employment litigation.

**Public Finance:** Represents municipalities, agencies and other bond issuers; underwriter's and special tax counsel for investment banks.

**Real Estate:** Represents major developers in financing, leasing and construction of commercial and residential developments.

**Tax:** Structures businesses and transactions to improve local, state, national and international tax efficiency.

**Trusts & Estates:** Represents individuals and businesses in wealth preservation issues and family-owned businesses.

## OFFICES

**CALIFORNIA**
Suite 500, 5 Park Plaza, **Irvine**, CA 92614-8503
**Tel:** 949 567 3500   **Fax:** 949 863 0151

**DELAWARE**
Hercules Plaza, Suite 5100, 1313 Market Street, PO Box 1709, **Wilmington**, DE 19899-1709
**Tel:** 302 777 6500   **Fax:** 302 421 8390

**DISTRICT OF COLUMBIA**
Hamilton Square, 600 Fourteenth Street, NW, **Washington**, DC 20005-2004
**Tel:** 202 220 1200   **Fax:** 202 220 1665

**MICHIGAN**
36th Floor, 100 Renaissance Center, **Detroit**, MI 48243-1157
**Tel:** 313 259 7110   **Fax:** 313 259 7926

**NEW JERSEY**
300 Alexander Park, CN 5276, **Princeton**, NJ 08543-5276
**Tel:** 609 452 0808   **Fax:** 609 452 1147

**NEW YORK**
14th Floor, 1180 Avenue of the Americas, **New York**, NY 10036-8401
**Tel:** 212 899 5090   **Fax:** 212 899 5091

**PENNSYLVANIA**
400 Berwyn Park, 899 Cassatt Road, **Berwyn**, PA 19312-1183
**Tel:** 610 640 7800   **Fax:** 610 640 7835

200 One Keystone Plaza, North Front and Market Streets, PO Box 1181, **Harrisburg**, PA 17108-1181
**Tel:** 717 255 1155   **Fax:** 717 238 0575

3000 Two Logan Square, Eighteenth and Arch Streets, **Philadelphia**, PA 19103-2799
**Tel:** 215 981 4000   **Fax:** 215 981 4750

50th Floor, 500 Grant Street, **Pittsburgh**, PA 15219-2502
**Tel:** 412 454 5000   **Fax:** 412 281 0717

## CONTACTS

| | |
|---|---|
| Bankruptcy & Reorganization | I William Cohen |
| Commercial Litigation | Francis P Devine III |
| Construction | Bruce W Ficken |
| Corporate & Securities | Michael H Friedman |
| Employee Benefits | Andrew J Rudolph |
| Environmental | John W Carroll |
| HealthCare Services | Henry C Fader |
| Health Effects/Product Liability | Nina M Gussack |
| Insurance & Reinsurance | Deborah F Cohen |
| Intellectual Property | Vincent V Carissimi |
| International | James D Rosener |
| Investment Management | Joseph V Del Raso |
| Labor & Employment | Jonathan Kane |
| Financial Services | Richard P Eckman |
| Real Estate | Norman B Berlin, Dusty Elias Kirk |
| Sports | Charles M Greenberg |
| Tax | Joan C Arnold |
| Trusts & Estates | Robert J Weinberg |

**Pepper Hamilton LLP**
Attorneys at Law

# RATNER PRESTIA

## THE FIRM

**Chair:** Paul F Prestia

**Number of Shareholders:** 14
**Number of other lawyers:** 21
**Number of Patent Agents:** 4

**FIRM OVERVIEW:** Practicing intellectual property law exclusively since its founding in 1981, RatnerPrestia has grown its personnel and resource base deliberately to provide both depth and breadth in legal expertise and in the collective technical and business expertise of its attorneys, patent agents, and technical advisors, all of whom have technical backgrounds and many of whom have advanced degrees and/or industrial, business and research experience. RatnerPrestia's size and its resources enable the firm to serve a wide range of clients on an equally wide range of matters with a rare combination of efficiency and effectiveness.

## MAIN AREAS OF PRACTICE:

**Dispute Resolution, Litigation & ADR:** The firm's practice involves all types of intellectual property and domain name disputes in the federal courts and various administrative agencies, such as the Trademark Trial and Appeal Board and the Board of Patent Appeals and Interferences of the United States Patent and Trademark Office. Because RatnerPrestia takes a business approach when representing clients, alternative dispute resolution (ADR) processes are often pursued because they are less expensive and more efficient and effective than litigation. But when litigation is necessary, RatnerPrestia litigates efficiently and, when appropriate, aggressively. RatnerPrestia's litigators and ADR practitioners are a diverse group of attorneys who have long represented clients as counselors and advocates in various approaches to resolving disputes as both corporate counsel and private practitioners. They are often retained as neutrals in ADR processes not involving RatnerPrestia clients.

**IP Transactions:** IP-based or IP-related licensing, mergers, acquisitions, divestitures, joint ventures, developments, and other inter-corporate transactions typically require sophisticated understanding of the IP involved and the business side of the deal. RatnerPrestia is often called upon to render assistance with such matters. The firm's experience in this area includes that of its attorneys who have held IP-related managerial positions in large corporations and who have handled major transactions around the world.

**IP Counseling:** Strategic guidance, litigation planning, liability assessment (offensive and defensive) and portfolio evaluation are typical counseling objectives. Such counseling often plays a significant role in clients' business plans, due diligence studies and day-to-day risk management.

**Patent Preparation & Prosecution:** RatnerPrestia is well known for its strength in this area across a wide range of technologies, including software, electronics, biotechnology, biomedical devices, pharmaceutical and polymer chemistry, materials science, optics, acoustics and in non-technical areas, such as business methods and designs. Its credentials and experience in patent preparation and prosecution also translate into a strong resource for its litigation, IP business Management and IP Counseling activities.

**Trademarks:** RatnerPrestia handles a wide variety of trademark ex parte and inter parte matters and manages significant trademark portfolios.

**Trade Secrets:** Global competition, the immediate dissemination of information via the Internet, and employee mobility - among other factors - make it more critical than ever for companies to protect their valuable trade secret assets against unauthorized disclosure and misappropriation. RatnerPrestia's trade secrets lawyers stay current on this unique area of IP practice by constantly surveying legal developments in the field.

## OFFICES

### PENNSYLVANIA
Suite 301, 1235 Westlakes Drive, Berwyn,
PO Box 980, **Valley Forge**, PA 19482
**Tel:** 610 407 0700 **Fax:** 610 407 0701
**Website:** www.ratnerprestia.com

Suite 265, Commerce Corporate Center,
5100 Tilghman Street, **Allentown**, PA 18104
**Tel:** 610 530 8100 **Fax:** 610 530 8200

### DELAWARE
Nemours Building, 1007 Orange Street,
Suite 1100, PO Box 1596, **Wilmington**, DE 19899
**Tel:** 302 778 2500 **Fax:** 302 778 2600

## CONTACTS

| | |
|---|---|
| **Litigation & ADR** | Harrie Samaras, Rex Donnelly |
| **Electronic/Software Patents** | Kenneth Nigon, Larry Ashery |
| **Pharma/Bio/Chem Patents** | Christopher Lewis, Jonathan Spadt |
| **Mechanical/BioMed/Design Patents** | Joshua Cohen, Jonathan Spadt |
| **Foreign Patents** | Daniel Calder |
| **Trademarks** | Benjamin Leace, Rex Donnelly |
| **IP Transactions** | Robert Seitter |
| **IP Counseling** | Paul Prestia, Jacques Etkowicz |
| **Copyright** | Jacques Etkowicz |

**CLIENTS:** RatnerPrestia's clients range from start-up companies to multi-billion dollar corporations, both domestic and international, and from private individuals to well-known institutions and universities. RatnerPrestia has also been retained, for opinions and counseling, by venture capital firms and by law firms for opinions and advice in regard to ongoing litigation and for ADR processes.

**Major clients:** Air Products and Chemicals, Ametek, Alcan, Inc., Arkema, Binney and Smith, Boston Scientific, B. Braun, Continental Teves, InTest, ITT Industries, Johnson & Johnson, Johnson Matthey, Kulicke & Soffa, Matsushita, Morton Grove Pharmaceuticals, Multisorb Technologies, Nippon Sheet Glass, Panasonic Technologies, Sarnoff Corp, Tate & Lyle, T-Networks, Unisys, Tyco, V-Span, and various academic institutions including The University of Pennsylvania, The University of Delaware, Rennsalaer Polytechnic Institute, Princeton University, Lehigh University and Drexel University

**INTERNATIONAL WORK:** RatnerPrestia counsels, advises and represents numerous foreign clients in US IP matters and numerous US clients in IP matters in all other major countries and it also participates in World Intellectual Property Organization ADR Procedures.

RatnerPrestia
WE SPECIALIZE IN THE LAW OF CREATIVITY®

# REED SMITH LLP

## THE FIRM

**Managing Partner:** Gregory B Jordan
**Number of partners in US offices:** 420
**Number of other lawyers in US offices:** 547
**Website:** www.reedsmith.com

**FIRM OVERVIEW:** Reed Smith is a leading international law firm with more than 1,000 lawyers in 14 offices in the United States and four in Europe. The firm's geographic and substantive breadth enables Reed Smith to form multidisciplinary teams that serve clients in nearly all types of legal matters throughout the world. Reed Smith has built exceptionally strong areas of focus in financial services and life sciences. The firm distinguishes itself through a commitment to high-quality, individual service.

## MAIN AREAS OF PRACTICE:

**Litigation:** Reed Smith represents clients in all types of litigation. The firm is a national leader in high-stakes class-action, complex and multijurisdictional matters. Firm business trial groups are led by seasoned veterans experienced in every phase of federal and state jury and bench trials. Reed Smith has one of the oldest distinct appellate practices, and firm appellate specialists have succeeded before many of the most influential courts of appeals in the country. The firm has particularly strong substantive litigation capabilities in the areas of antitrust and competition, bankruptcy, construction, environmental law, financial services, fraud, insurance coverage, intellectual property, labor and employment, and product liability. Firm litigators also advise on risk management.
**Business & Regulatory:** Firm transactional lawyers represent clients in industry-leading deals that include mergers, acquisitions, divestitures, joint ventures, licensing arrangements, outsourcing and others. The firm has significant practices in the areas of project and global finance, energy and natural resources development, real estate finance and development, and venture finance. Reed Smith business lawyers assist with securities, corporate restructuring, corporate governance, executive compensation, benefits and business immigration, and provide other corporate advice and services. Firm regulatory and government relations lawyers assist clients in highly regulated sectors with compliance and advocacy in areas such as banking, communications, consumer financial services, energy, food and drug issues, healthcare fraud and abuse, healthcare reimbursement, insurance, investments and pensions.
**Industry Representation:** Reed Smith has multidisciplinary teams devoted to serving all the legal needs of clients operating in industry sectors such as financial services (including banking, consumer specialty finance, investment management, insurance and reinsurance) life sciences (pharmaceutical, medical device and biotechnology), advertising and marketing, construction, energy and natural resources, healthcare, media and entertainment, real estate, technology, higher education, primary and secondary education, nonprofit entities and associations.
**Niche Practices:** Reed Smith has significant capabilities in intellectual property, tax, public finance and government contracts. The firm has built niche practices in debt recovery; private equity; e-commerce; export, customs and trade; homeland security; information technology; infrastructure development and grants; commercial and international arbitration; international distribution; privacy; and record and data management.

**CLIENTS:** Reed Smith represents major corporate clients - including more than half of the Fortune 500 - as well as nonprofit and public sector entities. Firm clients include industry leaders in the financial services, life sciences, manufacturing, energy, healthcare, real estate and other sectors.

**INTERNATIONAL WORK:** Reed Smith has more than 100 lawyers in four offices in Europe and serves clients in all types of legal matters throughout the world. The firm has multilingual French, German and Japanese teams. Reed Smith's internationally recognized global and Project Finance Team has significant experience structuring deals in India and other emerging markets.

## OFFICES

### NEW YORK
599 Lexington Avenue, **New York**, NY 10022
**Tel:** 212 521 5400   **Fax:** 212 521 5450

### CALIFORNIA
355 South Grand Avenue, Suite 2900, **Los Angeles**, LA 90071-1514
**Tel:** 213 457 8000   **Fax:** 213 457 8080

1901 Avenue of the Stars, Suite 700, **Los Angeles**, LA 90067-6078
**Tel:** 310 734 5200   **Fax:** 310 734 5299

Two Embarcadero Center, Suite 2000, **San Francisco**, LA 94111
**Tel:** 415 543 8700   **Fax:** 415 391 8269

1999 Harrison Street, Suite 2400, **Oakland**, LA 94612-3572
**Tel:** 510 763 2000   **Fax:** 510 273 8832

### DISTRICT OF COLUMBIA
1301 K Street, N.W., Suite 1100 - East Tower, **Washington**, DC 20005-3317
**Tel:** 202 414 9200   **Fax:** 202 414 9299

### PENNSYLVANIA
2500 One Liberty Place, 1650 Market Street, **Philadelphia**, PA 19103-7301
**Tel:** 215 851 8100   **Fax:** 215 851 1420

435 Sixth Avenue, **Pittsburgh**, 15219-1886
**Tel:** 412 288 3131   **Fax:** 412 288 3063

### NEW JERSEY
Princeton Forrestal Village, 136 Main Street, Suite 250, **Princeton** NJ 08540
**Tel:** 609 987 0050   **Fax:** 609 951 0824

One Riverfront Plaza, 1st Floor, **Newark**, 07102
**Tel:** 973 621 3200   **Fax:** 973 621 3199

### VIRGINIA
3110 Fairview Park Drive, Suite 1400, **Falls Church**, VA 22042
**Tel:** 703 641 4200   **Fax:** 703 641 4340

44084 Riverside Parkway, Suite 300, **Leesburg**, VA 20176
**Tel:** 703 729 8500   **Fax:** 703 478 8003

Riverfront Plaza - West Tower
901 East Byrd Street, Suite 1700, **Richmond**, VA 23219-4068
**Tel:** 804 344 3400   **Fax:** 804 344 3410

### DELAWARE
1201 Market Street, Suite 1500, **Wilmington**, DE 19801
**Tel:** 302 778 7500   **Fax:** 302 778 7575

### INTERNATIONAL OFFICES:
Reed Smith also has offices in London and the Midlands, UK, Paris, France and Munich, Germany.

## CONTACTS

Litigation ....................................W Thomas McGough, Jr (Pittsburgh)
**Business & Regulatory** ........................David L DeNinno (Pittsburgh)
**Financial Services** ............................Frank T Guadagnino (Pittsburgh)
**Financial Services Litigation** ..................Mary J Hackett (Los Angeles)
**Life Sciences (Regulatory)** ................Kevin R Barry (Washington, DC)
**Life Sciences (Product Liability)** ................Colleen T Davies (Oakland)
**Life Sciences (Transactional)** ..................Diane M Frenier (Princeton)

**Quality Matters.**℠

# SAUL EWING LLP

## THE FIRM

**Managing Partner:** David S Antzis
**Number of partners:** 141
**Number of other lawyers:** 111
**Website:** www.saul.com

**FIRM OVERVIEW:** Founded in 1921, Saul Ewing provides a broad array of legal services to businesses from its offices located throughout the mid-Atlantic region.

## MAIN AREAS OF PRACTICE:

**Bankruptcy:** The firm represents companies in all aspects of cases under the bankruptcy laws, as well as in other matters relating to corporate reorganization, creditors' rights, and insolvency.

**Litigation:** The firm represents corporations and corporate officers and directors in all types of commercial disputes including shareholder derivative actions, securities fraud claims, and other actions to enforce or defend legal or contractual rights. The firm also defends corporations against claims by individuals including mass tort and product liability claims and claims by current or former employees.

**Business:** The firm provides legal services to corporations and corporate officers and directors on all issues related to the operation of their business including corporate formation, corporate governance, business transactions, corporate financings and capitalization, intellectual property rights, and other legal matters that face businesses in today's economy.

**Real Estate:** The firm represents owners, developers, REITs and other investors in the development and construction of new projects, in the acquisition and leasing of existing facilities, and in matters related to the ownership of land generally.

**Public Finance:** Saul Ewing attorneys serve as bond counsel, issuers counsel and underwriters counsel in transactions involving the issuance and sale of tax-exempt state and local government bonds.

**Insurance:** The firm advises corporations in the insurance industry on a wide range of issues related to the operation and regulation of companies in the insurance business including licensing, capitalization and solvency, and the marketing and sale of insurance products. The firm also represents clients in litigation related to the business of insurance including litigation concerning regulatory obligations, insurance insolvencies, agent and other producer terminations, insurance coverage and reinsurance disputes.

**Defense Contracting:** The firm specializes in the representation of defense contractors, from regionally based companies to the nation's leading defense contractors, in all aspects of litigation, including federal investigations, internal compliance investigations, supplier litigation and federal enforcement litigation.

**Construction:** The firm provides services to commercial developers, engineers and contractors on all construction-related legal matters, including initial land acquisition, planning and design, bidding, contract negotiation, and post-construction claims resolution.

**Environmental:** The firm advises clients on matters related to compliance with state and federal environmental regulations and helps to structure real estate and corporate transactions to minimize environmental liability. The firm also represents corporations and corporate officers in litigation related to environmental and regulatory liabilities.

**Personal Wealth, Estates & Trusts:** The firm represents wealthy individuals, trusts and institutions in matters related to wealth preservation and management including tax, estate, and retirement planning, business succession and executive compensation, and charitable giving.

**Labor:** The firm represents clients in areas such as workplace issues, collective bargaining agreements, labor relations, procedures and protocols, employment, pay practices to comply with Federal and State wage and hour laws, and affirmative action plans and programs.

**Utility:** Saul Ewing provides comprehensive advice and representation on energy (electricity, natural gas, liquefied natural gas, steam, and hot and chilled water), water, wastewater, telecommunications and transportation issues. Attorneys represent clients before local, state, and federal regulatory agencies, as well as in state and federal courts.

## US OFFICES

**DELAWARE**
222 Delaware Avenue, Suite 1200, PO Box 1266, **Wilmington**, DE 19899
**Tel:** 302 421 6800  **Fax:** 302 421 6813

**DISTRICT OF COLUMBIA**
1025 Thomas Jefferson Street, NW, Suite 425W, **Washington**, DC 20007
**Tel:** 202 295 6600  **Fax:** 202 295 6700

**MARYLAND**
Lockwood Place, 500 East Pratt Street, Suite 900, **Baltimore**, MD 21202-3171
**Tel:** 410 332 8600  **Fax:** 410 332 8862

**NEW JERSEY**
One Riverfront Plaza, **Newark**, NJ 07102
**Tel:** 973 286 6700  **Fax:** 973 286 6800

750 Colllege Road East, Suite 100 **Princeton**, NJ 08540-6617
**Tel:** 609 452 3100  **Fax:** 609 452 3122

**PENNSYLVANIA**
Penn National Insurance Plaza, 2 North Second Street, 7th Floor, **Harrisburg**, PA 17101
**Tel:** 717 257 7500  **Fax:** 717 238 4622

Centre Square West, 1500 Market Street, 38th Floor, **Philadelphia**, PA 19102-2186
**Tel:** 215 972 7777  **Fax:** 215 972 7725

1200 Liberty Ridge Drive, Suite 200, **Wayne**, PA 19087-5569
**Tel:** 610 251 5050  **Fax:** 610 651 5930

## CONTACTS

**Bankruptcy** .........................................Norman L Pernick (Wilmington)
.........................Jeffrey Hampton (Philadelphia), Irv Walker (Baltimore)
**Litigation**........ Michael Finio (Harrisburg), John F Stoviak (Philadelphia)
............Charles O Monk II (Baltimore), Linda Richenderfer (Wilmington)
..................Michael Lampert (Princeton), Robert Gill (Washington, DC),
......................Henry R Abrams,(Baltimore), Edward J Baines (Baltimore)
**Business** ..................David S Antzis (Wayne), Howard Miller (Baltimore)
....................Howard Slavit (Washington, DC), Barry F Levin (Baltimore)
............Constance B Foster (Harrisburg), Christopher J Pippett (Wayne)
**Real Estate** ....Stephen S Aichele (Philadelphia), John P Pierce (Philadelphia)
................Frederick D Strober (Philadelphia), William Gee (Wilmington)
..................Michael S Burg (Wayne), Wendie C Stabler (Wilmington)
**Public Finance** George T Magnatta (Philadelphia), Timothy A Frey (Wilmington)
**Insurance** ......................................... Michael F Consedine (Harrisburg)
.................................................Constance B Foster (Harrisburg)
......................Paul M Hummer (Philadelphia), Laura L Katz (Baltimore)
**Defense Contracting** ..........................David R Moffitt (Philadelphia),
.................................................Joseph F O'Dea (Philadelphia)
**Construction** ......................................George E Rahn, Jr (Philadelphia)
**Environmental** Jane Kozinski (Princeton), Pamela Goodwin (Princeton)
.........................Joel R Burcat (Harrisburg), Carl B Everett (Philadelphia)
**Personal Wealth, Estates & Trusts** ........Robert H Louis (Philadelphia)
.................................................Sheldon S Satisky (Baltimore)
**Labor** ....Gary B Eidelman (Baltimore), Harriet E Cooperman (Baltimore),
.................................................Christopher J Murphy (Philadelphia)
**Utilities**....................................Stephen B Genzer (Newark),
............William A Mogel (Washington DC), Louise Knight (Harrisburg)

**CLIENTS:** Saul Ewing serves a broad range of regional, national, and international clients from across the business spectrum. The firm's clients include businesses of all sizes, nonprofits, academic institutions, and governments and their agencies. Clients value Saul Ewing for the firm's industry knowledge and the responsiveness of its attorneys.

SAUL
EWING LLP

Thinking ahead.
So you can move ahead.[SM]

# WOLF, BLOCK, SCHORR AND SOLIS-COHEN LLP

## THE FIRM

**Chairman:** Mark L Alderman

**Number of partners:** 150
**Number of other lawyers:** 167

**FIRM OVERVIEW:** WolfBlock is a regional law firm of approximately 300 attorneys representing clients in business and real estate transactions, high-stakes litigation and other legal matters. The firm has offices in New York, NY; Boston, MA; Philadelphia, Harrisburg and Norristown, PA; Cherry Hill and Roseland, NJ; and Wilmington, DE. WolfBlock attorneys provide legal services in a wide range of areas, including real estate, corporate, employment, intellectual property, environmental, healthcare, estate planning, family law, taxation, commercial litigation and more. The firm also provides government relations consulting and lobbying services at the local, state and federal levels of government through WolfBlock Public Strategies, LLC (Boston, MA and Washington, DC) and Wolf-Block Government Relations, LP (Harrisburg, PA). WolfBlock additionally provides a wide range of practical employment-related training to human resource professionals, in-house counsel, benefits administrators and other managers through The WolfInstitute, a division of WolfBlock that features interactive courses taught by WolfBlock employment lawyers.

## MAIN AREAS OF PRACTICE:

**Business Litigation:** The firm's Business Litigation Practice covers a range of commercial disputes, including virtually every substantive area, such as: securities, antitrust, construction, malpractice, civil RICO, products liability, trademark and copyright infringement, real estate, and First Amendment and defamation law. The firm is frequently called upon to represent many of the largest companies in both the United States and throughout the world.

**Corporate/Securities:** The firm has a large, diversified Corporate/Securities Practice Group. Its lawyers are noted for their work in the fields of securities, mergers and acquisitions, venture capital, and emerging business enterprises and represent public and private companies at all stages of development, including family businesses that have been firm clients for decades; start-up and emerging businesses in e-commerce, biotechnology, and other developing areas of commerce; clients going public; clients that are public; and public companies going private.

**Employment Services:** The firm offers preventive employment services, including drafting policies and training methods for employers and providing human resource management and benefit consulting. The Employment Services Group also provides immigration and employee benefits services and defends client interests in courtrooms and before administrative agencies.

**Government Relations:** The Government Relations Group provides comprehensive consulting and lobbying services at the local, state and federal levels of government, including assistance with public policy advocacy and government marketing and procurement as well as promotion of client interests in homeland security matters.

**Health Law:** The firm's Health Law Group provides litigation, corporate, and regulatory services in virtually every aspect of the healthcare delivery system. The Group represents clients in such matters as corporate compliance program development; managed care litigation; structuring practice plans; government audits and investigations; and private and public debt financing.

**Real Estate:** The Real Estate Group's practice is national in scope and encompasses the full range of real estate-related transactions. The group works closely with other firm lawyers skilled in other areas – including securities, tax, and environmental law – on multidisciplinary teams as needed to serve individual client segments or industries.

**Private Client:** The Private Client Services Group provides state-of-the-art planning for clients and their families as well as estate/trust administration. The Group often serves as counsel in situations in which disputes have arisen among family members or business partners.

## HEAD OFFICE

**PENNSYLVANIA**
1650 Arch Street, 22nd Floor, **Philadelphia**, PA 19103
**Tel:** 215 977 2000   **Fax:** 215 977 2334

## BRANCH OFFICES

**DISTRICT OF COLUMBIA**
WolfBlock Public Strategies, LLC, 1401 New York Ave NW, Suite 810, **Washington**, DC 20005
**Tel:** 202 789 4040   **Fax:** 202 789 4242

**DELAWARE**
Wilmington Trust Ctr, 1100 N. Market St, Suite 1001, **Wilmington**, DE19801
**Tel:** 302 777 5860   **Fax:** 302 777 5863

**MASSACHUSETTS**
One Boston Place, **Boston**, MA 02108
**Tel:** 617 226 4000   **Fax:** 617 226 4500

WolfBlock Public Strategies, LLC, One Boston Place, **Boston**, MA 02108
**Tel:** 617 226 4040   **Fax:** 617 226 4500

**NEW JERSEY**
1940 Route 70 East, Suite 200, **Cherry Hill**, NJ 08003
**Tel:** 856 424 8200   **Fax:** 856 424 4446

101 Eisenhower Parkway, **Roseland**, NJ 07068
**Tel:** 973 228 5700   **Fax:** 973 228 7852

**NEW YORK**
250 Park Avenue, **New York**, NY 10177
**Tel:** 212 986 1116   **Fax:** 212 986 0604

**PENNSYLVANIA**
One West Main Street, Fifth Floor, **Norristown**, PA 19401
**Tel:** 610 272 5555   **Fax:** 610 272 6976

213 Market Street, 9th Floor, **Harrisburg,** PA 17101
**Tel:** 717 237 7160   **Fax:** 717 237 7161

WolfBlock Government Relations LP, The Locust Court Building, 212 Locust St, Suite 600, **Harrisburg**, PA 17101
**Tel:** 717 234 8525   Fax: 717 234 8812

## CONTACTS

| | |
|---|---|
| **Business Litigation** | M Norman Goldberger |
| **Corporate/Securities** | David Gitlin |
| **Employment Services** | James Redeker |
| **Environmental Law** | Kenneth Warren |
| **Government Relations (Harrisburg)** | Richard Gmerek |
| **Public Strategies (DC & Boston)** | Robert Crowe |
| **Private Client Services** | Clifford Schlesinger |
| **Family Law** | Lynne Gold-Bikin |
| **Financial Services** | Richard Zucker, Gretchen Santamour |
| **Health Law** | John Fanburg |
| **Intellectual Property & Information Technology** | Martin Raskin |
| **Real Estate** | Herman Fala |
| **Real Estate Structured Finance** | Abby Wenzel |
| **Tax Law** | Thomas Gallagher |
| **Utility Regulation** | Daniel Clearfield |

**CLIENTS:** The firm's clients include large national and international corporations in nearly every industry: banking, financial and insurance institutions, REITs, real estate developers, public utilities, venture capital and private equity investors, healthcare organizations, government entities, technology and biotechnology companies and non-profit organizations, as well as individual entrepreneurs and high net worth individuals.

# WOODCOCK WASHBURN LLP

## THE FIRM

**Policy Committee:** Dianne Elderkin, Dale Heist, Steven Rocci

**FIRM OVERVIEW:** Woodcock Washburn recognizes the importance of intellectual property to business enterprises. As the firm likes to say, "Intellectual property isn't just something we do… it's all we do"®. The firm has built a superb reputation and a wealth of experience in patent, trademark and copyright law, litigation and trade secret protection for more than 60 years.

Its 90-lawyer boutique is one of the largest intellectual property law firms in the United States and the largest in Pennsylvania New Jersey and Delaware. With offices in Atlanta, Philadelphia, and Seattle, the firm is uniquely positioned to serve national and international clients. Woodcock Washburn has achieved outstanding results for clients that have repeatedly sought its counseling and advice on high stake matters. Whether applying for a patent or trademark, advising on a business deal, or litigating in court or in an administrative proceeding, Woodcock Washburn strives to provide high quality, cost effective results that achieve the client's business goals.

Woodcock Washburn has consistently been recognized as a leader in providing intellectual property services. In *Corporate Counsel*, a survey of Fortune 250 companies recognized Woodcock Washburn as one of the 'go to' firms for intellectual property procurement and enforcement. Of the first twelve "Inventor of the Year" awards, three went to Woodcock Washburn clients. Formative work for firm clients became the basis for the first US software patents.

**Legal Expertise:** *IP Law & Business* recognized Woodcock Washburn as one of the top firms nationwide for protecting intellectual property in America. Clients routinely rely on Woodcock Washburn for advice in cases involving damages claims over $100 million.

**Technical Expertise:** Most Woodcock Washburn attorneys have a technical degree in biotechnology, chemistry, chemical, electrical or mechanical engineering, or computer science. Many have advanced degrees, including several PhD's and a DVM. Further, Woodcock Washburn attorneys have nearly 175 combined years of industry experience with companies such as Boeing, DuPont, General Electric, IBM, McNeil Pharmaceuticals, Microsoft, Unisys and Westinghouse.

**In-House Perspective:** Woodcock Washburn attorneys understand its clients' needs since many previously served as in-house counsel for companies including BellSouth, Cingular Wireless, Coca-Cola, DuPont, Hewlett-Packard, Motorola, Nordson, the Recording Industry Association of America, Microsoft, Rohm & Haas, Union Camp, and Unisys.

**Diversity:** The *Vault* recognized the firm as being "very accommodating to women" and "very welcoming to all racial and ethnic minorities." The firm has received an award from the Pennsylvania Bar Association's Women in the Profession Committee for promoting women lawyers to leadership positions within the firm. Woodcock Washburn is a *Gold Sponsor* of the American Intellectual Property Law Education Foundation which promotes diversity in the intellectual property bar.

## MAIN AREAS OF PRACTICE:

**Lawyers as Scientists & Engineers:** Woodcock Washburn lawyers are not just intellectual property lawyers - most are also scientists and engineers, schooled in such demanding disciplines as biotechnology, chemistry, electrical and mechanical engineering, and computer science. As technology specialists, the firm's lawyers possess a unique understanding of the issues faced by clients, and they present those issues in clear and meaningful ways to judges, juries, and government examiners around the world.

**Industry Focused Practice:** The firm has successfully represented clients in diverse biotechnology and chemistry fields that include agricultural chemicals, drug delivery compositions, genetically engineered plants, food additives, monoclonal antibodies, organic chemistry, genomics, nanotechnology, pharmaceuticals, small molecule chemistry and vaccines. The firm also represents clients in mechanical, electrical and computer sciences, offering services in business methods, financial services, computer hardware, digital rights management, encryp-

## HEAD OFFICE

**PENNSYLVANIA**
One Liberty Place, 46th Floor, **Philadelphia**, PA 19103
**Tel:** 215 568 3100
**Website:** www.woodcock.com

## BRANCH OFFICES

**WASHINGTON**
999 Third Avenue, Suite 1606, **Seattle**, WA 98104
**Tel:** 206 332 1380

**GEORGIA**
2002 Summit Blvd., Suite 800, **Atlanta**, GA 30319
**Tel:** 404 459 0050

tion/decryption, medical and dental devices, optics, packaging, robotics, semiconductors, smart cards, telecommunications and wireless technology, among others.

**Effective Litigation Strategies:** The firm aggressively pursues all aspects of litigation, carefully planning discovery and motion practice to optimize a client's position prior to trial. Woodcock Washburn's experience in patent, trademark and copyright law helps it identify the most effective litigation strategies. Woodcock Washburn lawyers have compiled an impressive record of wins before both judges and juries. On the appellate level, they have built an equally enviable chronicle of success. The firm explores alternate strategies to litigation no less aggressively. With court dockets growing more crowded and litigation expenses rising, the percentage of cases that actually make it to trial is shrinking. Often, the firm finds that productive and cost-effective outcomes for its clients are obtained through arbitration, mediation, and settlement - rather than expensively won court decisions.

**CLIENTS:** Woodcock Washburn represents Fortune 100 and 500 companies in diverse, technology-driven industries. The firm's clients have repeatedly sought Woodcock Washburn to handle their complex matters in patent prosecution, patent litigation, trademarks, trade secrets, copyright and licensing. Please view the firm's website at www.woodcock.com to review its client list and patent portfolio.

**INTERNATIONAL WORK:** Woodcock Washburn's experience extends beyond the United States to other countries - an important capability in today's global economy. The firm's lawyers are familiar with the complexities of patent, trademark, copyright, trade secrets and unfair competition laws across jurisdictions worldwide. Guided by its history of practicing intellectual property law and its dedication to quality client service, Woodcock Washburn LLP protects the ideas that will shape the future.

WOODCOCK WASHBURN

INTELLECTUAL PROPERTY LAW
ATLANTA • PHILADELPHIA • SEATTLE

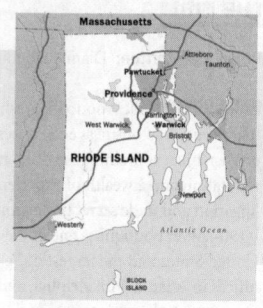

## How lawyers are ranked

Every year we carry out thousands of in-depth interviews with clients and lawyers in order to assess the reputations and expertise of business lawyers across the USA. Chambers rankings and editorial are referred to extensively by General Counsel and other purchasers of legal services who look to our recommendations when choosing their lawyers.

# CORPORATE/COMMERCIAL

### Corporate/Commercial
### Leading Firms

1. **EDWARDS ANGELL PALMER** *Providence*
   **HINCKLEY, ALLEN & SNYDER LLP** *Providence*
2. **ADLER POLLOCK & SHEEHAN PC** *Providence*
3. **DUFFY, SWEENEY & SCOTT LTD** *Providence*
   **PARTRIDGE SNOW & HAHN LLP** *Providence*

### Leading Individuals

1. **CARLOTTI Stephen** *Hinckley, Allen & Snyder LLP*
   **JOHNSON V Duncan** *Edwards Angell Palmer*
2. **FARRELL Margaret** *Hinckley, Allen & Snyder LLP*
   **GRAHAM Christopher** *Edwards Angell Palmer*
   **HAHN James** *Partridge Snow & Hahn LLP*
   **PANNONE Gary** *Pannone Lopes & Devereaux LLC*
   **PARTRIDGE John** *Partridge Snow & Hahn LLP*
   **REED Walter** *Edwards Angell Palmer*
   **SKEFFINGTON James** *Edwards Angell Palmer*
3. **GEANACOPOULOS Steve** *Adler Pollock & Sheehan PC*
   **GILDEN David** *Partridge Snow & Hahn LLP*
   **SWEENEY Michael** *Duffy, Sweeney & Scott Ltd*

### Corporate/Commercial:
### Banking & Finance
### Leading Individuals

1. **CHLEBUS Andrew** *Edwards Angell Palmer*
   **MCCANN Gail** *Edwards Angell Palmer*
2. **FARMER III Malcom** *Hinckley, Allen & Snyder LLP*
3. **MARCELLO III Matthew** *Hinckley, Allen & Snyder LLP*

### Corporate/Commercial:
### Banking & Finance: Mainly Regulatory
### Leading Individuals

1. **JOHNSON V Duncan** *Edwards Angell Palmer*

## Band 1

### Edwards Angell Palmer & Dodge LLP
See firm details p.1112

**The Firm:** *"Top-notch firm"* Edwards Angell, with offices along the East Coast, increased its size through a merger with Boston-based Palmer & Dodge in the fall of 2005. The busy team covers a diversity of corporate and M&A matters, including large private equity and venture capital deals. A noticeable trend is the greater importance of IP in transactions, and in this area the corporate group draws support from experts within the firm. Clients also pointed to other examples of the broad expertise on offer, with tax, employment and financial specialists always ready at hand to assist with transactions. They also praised the lawyers' *"business-like approach."* On the banking and finance side, the firm represents agents and arrangers in syndicated lending and precious metals transactions, as well as in media sector and commercial real estate lending. An impressive client roster includes a number of financial institutions and other lenders from across the state.

**The Lawyers:** Peers considered **Duncan Johnson** (see p.1772) as the firm's *"genius of corporate and banking,"* while clients praised his *"outstanding experience."* His focus is on M&A transactions and bank regulatory matters; large banks and other financial institutions are among his clients. **Christopher Graham** (see p.1772) concentrates on private equity and midmarket corporate transactions nationally, and even internationally. He advises funds and corporations, and these clients respect his *"great business sense."* He also enjoys a good reputation in finance, particularly with regard to early-stage companies. Deputy managing partner **Walter Reed** (see p.1773) divides his time between Rhode Island and New York City, working on corporate and venture capital matters. Sources described **James Skeffington** (see p.1773) as *"absolute dynamite"* and welcomed his *"ability to think outside the box"* and his *"excellent negotiation skills."* He established the firm's bond practice and advises corporations and management teams on a variety of transactional and strategic issues. Skeffington is also proficient in municipal finance. **Andrew Chlebus** (see p.1771) covers a variety of banking and finance areas, including leasing transactions, precious metals and media financings as well as sophisticated lending transactions. Among his recent deals was a $40 million gold, silver, platinum and palladium consignment and loan facility to a corporate family of industrial metals users. Cochair of the firm's finance and capital markets group, **Gail McCann** (see p.1772) is considered *"one of the best lawyers in this field."* She enjoys a particularly good reputation in the areas of commercial real estate financing and midmarket lending.

**Clients/Work Highlights:** The firm represented the seller of a wireless communications business in an auction process that resulted in a $270 million purchase price. Clients include Amtrol; Bank of America; CVS; Dobson Communications; Nautic Partners; Bank of America; CIT Lending Services Corporation; Key Bank; Citizens Bank; Sovereign Bank and Textron Financial.

### Hinckley, Allen & Snyder LLP

**The Firm:** While committed to the local market, this 25-strong practice group also operates outside Rhode Island. It is active in a significant number of public and private finance, real estate and M&A transactions and gives regulatory advice to a broad spread of clients, including national and international corporations. Recently the team represented BLB Investors in its acquisition of the US assets of the UK track-based gaming company Wembley PLC, a deal sporting a value of $600 million. The firm has a commendable international deal tally with a focus on licensing and IP matters. Other specialist departments, such as tax, employment and real estate, support the group. The financing group offers real estate lending experts, who act in large national projects and are corporate lending and business financing specialists. This team also advises on public financing, large syndicated loans and bond issues.

**The Lawyers:** Interviewees applauded *"strategic thinker"* **Stephen Carlotti** for his *"intellect and good business judgment."* He represents clients in M&A deals and security offerings across the USA and internationally. **Margaret Farrell** has expertise in securities matters and advises on cross-border transactions, public offerings and reorganizations; sources *"think very highly of her."* **Malcolm Farmer** is considered *"one of the premier finance attorneys in the state."* He advises lenders and borrowers in Rhode Island and Massachusetts on secured and unsecured corporate financings, some of which are large syndicated loans. He is also active in corporate and M&A transactions. Head of the real estate lending group **Matthew Marcello** is well respected for his sophisticated real estate and banking work.

**Clients/Work Highlights:** The firm represented The Slater Companies in the sale of assets to Duro

Textiles in September 2005. Other clients include Colibri Group; Bank of America; Bank Rhode Island; Sandlapper Fabrics; Rhode Island Economic Development Corporation and Mulberry Child Care.

## Band 2

### Adler Pollock & Sheehan PC
See firm details p.1774

**The Firm:** This sophisticated outfit earned praise for its *"broad range of expertise"* and *"depth and breadth on the M&A side."* Commonly advising on midmarket corporate and M&A transactions, there is also noteworthy activity in joint ventures and the team's work includes public finance, securities and real estate finance. The group additionally has expertise in municipal bonds, trusts, estates and taxation.

**The Lawyers:** Head of department **Stephen Geanacopoulos** (see p.1772) was recommended by clients for his *"nonconfrontational approach"* and *"good personal skills."* He is known to be good at building close relationships with clients, taking on their general corporate and commercial matters, including M&A and securities.

**Clients/Work Highlights:** Clients include universities, colleges, healthcare institutions and governmental entities as well as a variety of corporate entities.

## Band 3

### Duffy, Sweeney & Scott Ltd

**The Firm:** This small boutique firm has impressed clients by providing *"personalized service at cost-efficient prices."* It handles numerous midmarket transactions in Rhode Island, with an emphasis on investor activities and the sale and purchase of companies. Recently it represented Numark Industries in its successful acquisition of AKAI Professional, a leading brand in electronic musical instruments, and the stock of a related Japanese corporation that distributes AKAI products. The team assists manufacturers, financial institutions, technology businesses and distribution companies with their strategy and growth plans, both at home and overseas. In addition, it is active in private equity venture financings, private placements and securities. Colleagues in other specialist groups, including IP, antitrust and trade litigation, support the lawyers.

**The Lawyers:** **Michael Sweeney** is deemed *"a brilliant strategist who has the ability to balance the legal and the business issues successfully for both sides."* This corporate generalist gives advice across the board to a variety of businesses, both locally and around the world. He represented Mar-Lees Seafood in the formation of F/V Holdings, LLC, a new joint venture between Mar-Lees and Síldarvinnslan, and in a simultaneous $8 million acquisition of commercial long-range fishing vessels and a scalloping business.

**Clients/Work Highlights:** Retail Solutions International, Inc.; Paramount Cards Holding; Alesis; Riparian Partners and Business Development Company of Rhode Island.

### Partridge Snow & Hahn LLP

**The Firm:** This team was recommended for its corporate and commercial transactions and its good finance practice. It supports entrepreneurs plus closely held and family-owned businesses in their transactions and expansions, and advice is provided to large regional and international companies in outsourcing and other contracts. Clients, who are predominantly from Rhode Island and southeastern Massachusetts, appreciate the group's face-to-face approach.

**The Lawyers:** **James Hahn** is *"well respected"* by peers for his general corporate and commercial practice. On the banking side, he advises on regulatory and securities issues. **John Partridge** offers expertise in insurance and financial services to large private clients, while *"deal-maker"* **David Gilden** enjoys a good reputation for corporate finance. He mainly represents lenders.

**Clients/Work Highlights:** Clients range from Rhode Island-based individuals and midmarket companies to international enterprises.

### Other Notable Practitioners

Following the closure of Holland & Knight LLP's Providence office, **Gary Pannone** has launched Pannone Lopes & Devereaux LLC which will draw on its founding partners' experience of a national firm to offer services in business, litigation and government relations in a boutique setting. Pannone's own work covers all aspects of corporate law. He has been involved in several transactions and restructurings lately, for example, the restructuring of a $15 million nonprofit corporation, which involved a holding company and six subsidiaries. Interviewees recognized him for his *"good understanding of the business side."*

---

# EMPLOYMENT        MAINLY DEFENDANT

| Employment: Mainly Defendant | |
|---|---|
| Leading Firms | |
| **1** ADLER POLLOCK & SHEEHAN PC *Providence* | |
| HINCKLEY, ALLEN & SNYDER LLP *Providence* | |
| **2** EDWARDS ANGELL PALMER & DODGE *Providence* | |
| LITTLE, MEDEIROS, KINDER, BULMAN *Providence* | |
| PARTRIDGE SNOW & HAHN LLP *Providence* | |
| ST PETER & KASLE *Providence* | |

## Band 1

### Adler Pollock & Sheehan PC
See firm details p.1774

**The Firm:** This five-strong practice group continues to impress with its *"broad range of expertise"* and *"very responsive and cost-effective working."* It gives labor and employment advice to local and national employers, including gas and insurance companies as well as city authorities, such as the City of Pawtucket. The team's work includes labor relations, union contracts, collective bargaining, health and safety, and discrimination matters. Employment and labor litigation is conducted with the assistance of the firm's strong litigation practice group, and there has lately been an increasing focus on arbitration. Lawyers successfully represented C&S Wholesale Grocers in an arbitration regarding the payment of wages alleged to be owed to terminated employees.

**The Lawyers:** **Robert Brooks** (see p.1771) is the team's labor law specialist. His *"number-one strength"* lies in negotiating tough arbitrations and collective bargaining, where he shows *"a good sense of honesty and fairness"* and impresses with his communication skills and proactive approach. According to interviewees, *"he can say no with a smile, and is very adept across the board."* Up-and-comer **Michael Chittick** (see p.1771) handles all kinds of labor and employment matters, among them personnel issues, discrimination, terminations and arbitrations. He was described as *"a very competent and creative practitioner"* who is *"good at getting right to the point."*

**Clients/Work Highlights:** The firm gives ongoing employment law advice to the Providence Washington Insurance Company. Other clients include New England Gas Company; SMG Strategic Management Group; Providence Performing Arts Center and Rhode Island Convention Center Authority.

### Hinckley, Allen & Snyder LLP

**The Firm:** At the Providence office of this New England firm, a busy four-lawyer team spends a significant amount of time representing Rhode Island and national employers plus high-level executives in labor arbitration and union contract negotiations, as well as employee claims and executive disputes. Additionally, it provides specialist advice on immigration issues.

**The Lawyers:** According to sources, **Richard Jocelyn** has *"the memory of an elephant,"* and a background in human resources adds an extra dimension to his legal know-how. He mainly represents large companies and organizations ranging from retailers and manufacturers to municipalities in traditional labor matters. **Joseph Whelan**'s particular interests lie in the manufacturing and healthcare sectors; in the latter he represents regional hospitals and medical centers. He is also an employment law

## Employment: Mainly Defendant

### Leading Individuals

[1] BROOKS Robert *Adler Pollock & Sheehan PC*
GAMBOLI Michael *Partridge Snow & Hahn LLP*
KASLE Jeffrey *St Peter & Kasle*
KINDER Daniel *Little, Medeiros, Kinder*
ST PETER Gary *St Peter & Kasle*
[2] JOCELYN Richard *Hinckley, Allen & Snyder LLP*
MCNAMARA Neal *Nixon Peabody LLP*
POGUE Mark *Edwards Angell Palmer*
WHELAN Joseph *Hinckley, Allen & Snyder LLP*

### Up-and-coming individuals

CHITTICK Michael *Adler Pollock & Sheehan PC*

professor at the local law school.

**Clients/Work Highlights:** The Westerly Hospital; Landmark Medical Center; Brown University; Salter Healthcare Services and Bank Rhode Island.

## Band 2

### Edwards Angell Palmer & Dodge LLP

See firm details p.1112

**The Firm:** The practice group counsels large companies across the state, covering all general employment issues and litigation. Recently the firm handled a discrimination trial for the Rhode Island plant of manufacturer Stanley Fasteners. The team also works on ERISA matters, pensions and benefits for organizations such as Hartford Life Insurance Company. In whichever area they encounter the lawyers, clients appreciate the group's "*capability*" and "*quick response.*"

**The Lawyers:** **Mark Pogue** (see p.1773), who is also a proficient general commercial litigator, devotes much of his time to employment litigation and arbitration. In this field, he is especially expert at discrimination claims. He almost always represents employers, who in turn value his ability to "*do an excellent job in a short amount of time and under great pressure.*" Representing Univar USA, Pogue recently obtained a restraining order in the Rhode Island federal court against a union, some of whose members were conducting a violent strike. The

restraining order was upheld on appeal.

**Clients/Work Highlights:** Clients include large manufacturers and international biotech companies as well as Rhode Island-based banks. Among them are Amgen and GTECH.

### Little, Medeiros, Kinder, Bulman & Whitney PC

**The Firm:** Clients praised the amount of "*partner-level contact*" on offer at this firm, as well as the "*wide range of expertise*" in labor and employment law. The team is adept at handling discrimination matters, employee benefits, labor negotiations and union avoidance campaigns, and it is currently putting resources into audits of clients' employee relations policies. It has an impressive client list of municipal, nonprofit and corporate clients, some of them household-names worldwide.

**The Lawyers:** **Daniel Kinder** is recognized as "*top-notch employment and labor lawyer,*" who represents primarily management in union and labor contract negotiations, as well as termination and other employment disputes.

**Clients/Work Highlights:** Clariant Corporation; Southeastern New England Shipbuilding; Taco; Toray Plastics (America); Scapa Group and Women & Infants Hospital of Rhode Island.

### Partridge Snow & Hahn LLP

**The Firm:** This six-strong Providence group provides regional businesses and international companies with counseling services on various labor and employment law problems, as well as the drafting of employment contracts, business planning and regulatory compliance issues. It also represents them in litigation, arbitration and mediation, with these activities covering collective bargaining, employee benefits, drug testing, discrimination and termination issues. The firm has two additional offices in SouthCoast and Boston, Massachusetts.

**The Lawyers:** Chair of the practice group **Michael Gamboli** was described by clients as a "*responsive and experienced*" employment litigator. He practises in Rhode Island and Massachusetts, mainly representing management in the defense of employment litigation but also giving general advice on human resources matters.

**Clients/Work Highlights:** The firm acts for numerous businesses in Rhode Island and southeast Massachusetts, as well as international companies with operations in the region.

### St Peter & Kasle

**The Firm:** According to clients this small niche firm "*makes a difference by finding a balance between making a living and helping other people.*" Here, two "*perfect gentlemen*" with "*outstanding experience*" support employers in the manufacturing, healthcare and education sectors, predominantly in the southern part of New England. Their employment work encompasses disability and other discrimination cases, while their labor relations practice is closely bound with the nonprofit sector. Although smaller than its competitors, the firm is successful because of the unquestioned "*integrity and expertise*" of its two principals. As one competitor put it: "*If you were looking for a top labor or employment lawyer, you could go to either of them.*"

**The Lawyers:** **Jeffrey Kasle** is "*very much respected in the legal community,*" both for his work in general and as an expert in workers' compensation and other staff issues. This "*showman*" also takes on NLRB cases and related arbitrations. Clients say they can "*count on him to get the job done.*" Partner **Gary St Peter** acts as legal counsel for employers across the board. Illustrating his emphasis on preventive advice, one client said: "*We never end up in court because he always gets us out of it.*" Interviewees ventured beyond legal skills in their assessments of St Peter, referring to him as "*a humanitarian*" with "*an excellent sense of humor.*"

**Clients/Work Highlights:** The firm represents management in both the private and public sectors, and has a number of clients in the nonprofit sector.

### Other Notable Practitioners

Having moved from Holland & Knight, **Neal McNamara** (see p.1772) is now running his employment litigation practice at Nixon Peabody LLP. His work includes sexual harassment, discrimination and disability matters, and a growing number of noncompete cases. McNamara also enjoys a good reputation as a general commercial litigator.

# LITIGATION

## Litigation: General Commercial

### Leading Firms

[1] ADLER POLLOCK & SHEEHAN PC *Providence*
EDWARDS ANGELL PALMER & DODGE *Providence*
HINCKLEY, ALLEN & SNYDER LLP *Providence*
[2] BLISH & CAVANAGH, LLP *Providence*
DUFFY, SWEENEY & SCOTT LTD *Providence*
PARTRIDGE SNOW & HAHN LLP *Providence*
[3] CARROLL, KELLY & MURPHY *Providence*
HIGGINS, CAVANAGH & COONEY LLP *Providence*
LITTLE, MEDEIROS, KINDER, BULMAN *Providence*

## Band 1

### Adler Pollock & Sheehan PC

See firm details p.1774

**The Firm:** This "*first-rate law firm*" with a large bench of 45 full-time litigators "*gets high marks in client service and legal expertise.*" Located exclusively in New England, it covers all types of trial work, representing many national and international clients, among them chemical and pharmaceutical companies, manufacturers, healthcare organizations and insurers. The group has specialists in IP, construction, banking, employment, plus others with notable

# GENERAL COMMERCIAL

sector expertise, for example in healthcare and insurance. During the past year the team was increasingly active in class action and mass tort trials, one involving the defense of a former manufacturer of lead pigment in the public nuisance and toxic tort case State of Rhode Island v Lead Industries Association et al. Arbitration and pre-litigation counseling have an important part in the practice, and here interviewees admired the team's "*creative and intellectual approach.*" Between them, lawyers are admitted to practice in numerous states, thus allowing clients to benefit from the team's ability to provide support in state and federal courts throughout the country.

**The Lawyers:** People "*think the world of* **John Tarantino** (see p.1773)," who also has "*the respect of judges and a great reputation with juries,*" according to interviewees. At the core of his client base are major New England companies, and he has handled a number of large high-profile cases with a focus on mass torts, white-collar crime and class action; in addition to representing clients in arbitrations, he acts as an arbitrator. New chairwoman of the firm **Patricia Rocha** (see p.1773) was described as "*a smart and talented lawyer who fights for her clients.*" Her broad caseload encompasses healthcare, employment, white-collar crime and business disputes as well as commercial arbitration. Clients simply said: "*She is terrific!*" **David Wollin**'s (see p.1773) key interests are torts, public liability and commercial litigation and arbitration. According to sources, "*he is more hard-nosed*" and "*gives a good analysis of the strengths and weaknesses of the case.*" Up-and-comer **Todd White** (see p.1773) represents national and local businesses in IP and commercial litigation and arbitration. Spreading the net wider to take in personal injury defence work, he defended the municipality in MacGregor v City of East Providence, a case brought following the death of a police captain during a SWAT team terrorism training exercise. White is "*highly regarded in town,*" one competitor even admitting to researchers: "*I would send him an offer, if I thought he was available.*"
Clients/Work Highlights: The firm represents local, regional, national and international companies and municipalities.

### Edwards Angell Palmer & Dodge LLP
See firm details p.1112
**The Firm:** This large, recently merged firm has several specialist groups within its Rhode Island liti-

gation department; they cover among other things commercial, employment and tax issues. The team also draws support from other departments, and together these two approaches enable the firm to take on practically any type of case. As one interviewee put it, "*they have a bunch of specialists who can handle any matter we come up with.*" In addition to litigation, the team is well versed in alternative dispute resolution methods. Clients – mainly medium sized regional businesses – appreciate the group's presence right down the East Coast and the spirit of flexibility that is clearly in evidence. One told researchers: "*If I want something done, and done right, I go to them.*" The firm obtained a favourable settlement for Laurelmead Cooperative, a large independent living facility for retired persons, in a \$1.84 million suit against the City of Providence to obtain a refund of overpaid property taxes.
**The Lawyers:** **Mark Freel** (see p.1772) has handled complex cases in IP, mass torts, construction and business litigation. One of his recent highlights was winning a jury verdict for Getty companies in connection with property and contractual rights at a petroleum pier. This "*strong advocate; bright and always well-prepared*" earned interviewees' praise for his "*good relationships with judges*" and "*excellent way of communicating in court.*" **Mark Pogue** (see p.1773) was described as "*a straightforward, fine litigator, who has a calming effect on the jury.*" His activities include general commercial and IP litigation. A "*quick study with a lot of experience,*" he also has an impressive employment law practice.
Clients/Work Highlights: The team acts for a wide range of clients from individuals and closely held businesses to large companies.

### Hinckley, Allen & Snyder LLP
**The Firm:** This 15-strong stable of lawyers covers a wide range of litigation, although the emphasis is on commercial cases. It represents Rhode Island and national corporates in transactional disputes, construction, tax, IP, employment and mass tort cases, and recently obtained a multimillion-dollar recovery in a condemnation claim against a State Highway Department involving damage to adjacent buildings. Clients judged the group to be "*especially good in terms of analysis and communication. In the cases we did with them, they were good in analysing our position and whether we would succeed or fail.*" One client told researchers: "*They are organized and professional, the best business litigators in the state, and they don't have small state mentality.*" Another highlight case was the successful defense of a multinational corporation in a breach of contract claim brought by a former division president who sought three years of pay, stock options and bonuses. The team is also active in alternative dispute resolutions, such as arbitration and negotiated settlements.
**The Lawyers:** Head of the environmental group **Gerald Petros** earned respect from peers as "*someone you have to watch because he is very bright and dangerous, and he presents a beautiful argument.*" Others say "*his greatest strengths are his intelligence, his personal skills and his judgment.*" Petros' practice

has been dominated by the massive tort case, State of Rhode Island v Lead Industries Association et al., in which he has been representing American Cyanamid. Former Supreme Court judge **Robert Flanders** is another key figure within the practice group. This "*fine and talented lawyer*" concentrates on commercial litigation, commonly real estate, contract and stockholder disputes. The market is clearly pleased to see him return to private practice. Clients singled out **William Grimm** for his "*experience and good fighting skills,*" especially in his area of expertise – IP litigation. He is expert at anything within this field, including patents, trademarks and matters related to the Internet. One satisfied client told researchers: "*If it weren't for him I would be on the street. He is smart, aggressive and capable of changing the strategy, if necessary.*"
Clients/Work Highlights: Viacom; Cookson America; Cytec Industries; ExxonMobil and J.T.Baker.

## Band 2

### Blish & Cavanagh, LLP
**The Firm:** Commentators liked this firm's client-focused work ethic. "*They seem to have real concern for their clients. They are compassionate – the client's problems come first and the financial aspect of the whole relationship is secondary,*" they told researchers. The seven-partner firm was originally set up 20 years ago as a trial boutique but has over time broadened the range of services on offer. In the contentious sphere it concentrates on commercial and business litigation, including cases dealing with insurance, employment, the environment, securities, construction and the media. Additionally, the lawyers take on arbitration and mediation. Larger competitor firms confirmed their willingness to refer clients and work to the team.
**The Lawyers:** Cofounder and current managing partner, "*trustworthy*" **Joseph Cavanagh** is "*a great lawyer who can build a sophisticated argument.*" He covers corporate, antitrust, employment, medical, patent and media law, representing both plaintiffs and defendants, be they businesses, local or state government entities, or professional individuals. First Amendment cases for newspaper clients are a forte. **Karen Pelczarski** conducts business litigation and constitutional work, often dealing with stockholder disputes. She has a strong appellate practice and is also active in arbitration and mediation. "*She is knowledgeable and researches thoroughly, and she remains very professional with her counterpart,*" clients reported.
Clients/Work Highlights: The firm represents local and national businesses as well as individuals and governmental bodies.

### Duffy, Sweeney & Scott Ltd
**The Firm:** According to clients of this Providence and Boston firm, "*it offers the quality of a New York law firm, but at Rhode Island fees.*" The four-partner litigation team covers a wide range of complex

commercial litigation, including securities, trade, franchise disputes, antitrust, insurance, employment and environmental cases. It is perhaps best known for its IP litigation, however, and presently has four lawyers devoting most of their time to cases in ten different states. Clients were certain of their views on the firm: "*There's very little bureaucracy,*" said one, while another remarked: "*They are fantastic because they are very strategic in their approach, very professional, easy to work with and ensure a minimum of disruption to our business.*" Researchers even heard from one client: "*They defended us against a suit, and now they are our plaintiff's attorney!*"

**The Lawyers: Robert Duffy** specializes in commercial litigation with a focus on stockholder, trade regulation, securities and broker-dealer disputes. Interviewees remarked favorably on his way of "*getting right to the heart of the matter and quickly eliminating the risks.*" **Craig Scott** is the IP expert within the firm. Researchers were told: "*He has a self-confidence that is very reassuring to a client, and he is very strategic – he has a vision of how he'll defend something.*" Also specializing in IP litigation, up-and-comer **Christine Bush** is "*as sharp as a tack – she digs into a business to understand it.*" Clients additionally admire her efficiency.

**Clients/Work Highlights:** The practice group acts for pharmaceutical and financial businesses as well as manufacturers and numerous Fortune 500 companies.

### Partridge Snow & Hahn LLP

**The Firm:** This small practice group of eight partners and five associates represents businesses, banks, universities, hospitals and individuals in Rhode Island and Massachusetts. As well as handling complex business litigation, real estate disputes, antitrust, IP, healthcare and class action consumer defense, the firm also conducts public hearings before various municipalities, official boards and administrative agencies.

**The Lawyers:** The leading name here is **Stephen Snow**, an established figure who earned praise as "*a true gentleman who does a good job for his clients.*" His

core clients are Rhode Island businesses, some of which have a national presence. The firm has recently recruited business, insurance, products liability and media litigator Howard Merten to the ranks.

**Clients/Work Highlights:** The firm's client base comprises insurance companies, hospitals, universities, governmental agencies, financial institutions and state-based corporates.

## Band 3

### Carroll, Kelly & Murphy

**The Firm:** This 12-lawyer firm celebrates its 40th year in 2006. Its litigation practice centers on insurance defense, medical malpractice and personal injury. Although far smaller than the biggest players in the market, it still enjoys a good reputation in the state.

**The Lawyers:** Senior statesman **Joseph Kelly** was described by one commentator as "*the most beloved attorney in New England,*" and by another as an "*inspiration for many litigation lawyers.*" The heart of the firm's litigation capability, one commentator remarked: "*Nobody talks to a jury better than he does.*"

### Higgins, Cavanagh & Cooney LLP

**The Firm:** This 15-lawyer civil and commercial litigation practice group is best known for its insurance defense work; other activities include products liability, healthcare, environmental, construction and labor disputes. In addition to its insurance clients, the firm acts for numerous companies based in, or running operations from, Rhode Island. Higgins is the state's representative within the global legal network, ALFA International.

**The Lawyers:** According to interviewees, **Gerald DeMaria** is "*the top guy for liability defence.*" His practice focus is on products liability and commercial cases, and he also undertakes personal injury and insurance work. He is the cofounder of the DCRI, the Defense Counsel of Rhode Island.

**Clients/Work Highlights:** The firm's client roster includes manufacturers, owners and developers of

commercial and residential real estate, software and insurance companies, banks and other financial institutions.

### Little, Medeiros, Kinder, Bulman & Whitney PC

**The Firm:** In addition to its excellent employment and labor practice, this firm – the product of a 2003 merger – has a genuine focus on commercial litigation. Exhibiting a noticeable shift towards business clients, the eight-strong litigation practice is split into two areas: one team tackles business-to-business disputes, including unfair competition, breach of contract, IP, securities, banking and fraud; the second handles construction and related disputes, including land use and other problems with municipalities. Clients appreciate the lawyers' practical approach. As one interviewee put it: "*They don't just tell me what I want to hear; they give me realistic advice.*"

**The Lawyers:** Smart, aggressive and respected **John Bulman** is "*a master of construction law.*" He has a satisfied clientele of Rhode Island and Massachusetts-based construction companies, municipalities and individuals and was recently elected as a fellow of The American College of Construction Lawyers. Bulman is also active in business and employment disputes and from time to time provides a service as an arbitrator or mediator. Clients say, "*he has patience to do thorough research, is very calm and collected and is quick to respond.*" Business litigator **Christopher Little** has carved a good reputation for himself and recently obtained a $5.8 million settlement against a local bank in an embezzlement case. Like Bulman, he is an experienced environment and construction litigator. Clients like the way "*he always asks the right questions and really goes into the detail of your matters.*"

**Clients/Work Highlights:** A.F. Lusi Construction; Baltimore Gas and Electric Company; Hasbro; Rhode Island Hospital; USI New England; General Motors; Massachusetts Turnpike Authority and Siemens Building Technologies.

---

# REAL ESTATE

| Real Estate |
|---|
| Leading Firms |
| [1] HINCKLEY, ALLEN & SNYDER LLP *Providence* |
| [2] ADLER POLLOCK & SHEEHAN PC *Providence* |

| Leading Individuals |
|---|
| [1] TRACY David *Hinckley, Allen & Snyder LLP* |
| [2] BATTY Jerome *Hinckley, Allen & Snyder LLP* |
| DISTEFANO Joseph *Adler Pollock & Sheehan PC* |
| KANTER Stanley *Adler Pollock & Sheehan PC* |
| NOONAN Elizabeth *Adler Pollock & Sheehan PC* |
| RUBIN David *Hinckley, Allen & Snyder LLP* |
| STOLZMAN Robert *Adler Pollock & Sheehan PC* |

## Band 1

### Hinckley, Allen & Snyder LLP

**The Firm:** According to clients, this good all-rounder of a firm is "*ethical, reliable and competent, with a good business sense.*" It supports Rhode Island and US developers on a swathe of projects – residential, retail, office and industrial – as well as straightforward acquisitions, joint venture and leasing transactions. For example, it advises a Fortune 100 retailer in the leasing, acquisition, development, financing and secondary market disposition of its portfolio of several hundred properties. The team also handles regulatory and environmental matters with all levels of authorities. It has experience in

zoning and land use as well as all aspects of construction permitting and entitlements. It is this full coverage that most impresses clients; as one of them put it, "*we are loyal and expect to be so for ever.*" Recently the group became general counsel to Quonset Development Corporation, which manages a 3,000-acre industrial park in Rhode Island and is a new subsidiary of the Economics Development Corporation. The firm has built a niche in advising financial services organizations, such as banks and pension funds, on a regional and national level. For these clients it advises on financings and loans for apartments, condominiums, hotels, offices, shopping centers, hotels and industrial parks.

**The Lawyers: David Tracy** has returned to the firm

following the closure of the Providence office of Holland & Knight. He enjoys a reputation as *"one of the best real estate lawyers in the region"* and was described by one commentator as *"a great businessman who knows how to marry the legal and the business sides."* Concentrating on development and retail work, he recently acted for KGI Properties in the renovation of a mall in New Hampshire and its conversion to mixed-use. Of **Jerome Batty** it is said *"you can't go wrong with this man."* He mainly represents Rhode Island developers and recently acted for Aspen River Bend Apartments in a 252-unit condominium project, advising on all aspects of its formation and development. Another of his key areas is real estate finance. Of **David Rubin**, people say, *"his greatest attribute is his business sense."* The chair of the practice group concentrates on real estate finance, for example representing Picerne Development Corporation across the USA in the acquisition, development, financing and exchange of four apartment complexes with an aggregate value in excess of $100 million.

**Clients/Work Highlights:** The firm recently represented Citizens Financial Group in the $60.2 million sale of its 224,000 sq ft headquarters in Providence to American Financial Realty Trust of Jenkintown, Pennsylvania. Other clients include major national, regional and local developers as well as banks and other financial institutions, insurance companies and pension funds.

## Band 2

### Adler Pollock & Sheehan PC
See firm details p.1774

**The Firm:** This firm handles a diversity of real estate work, covering both governmental estate and private sector properties. Recently it represented the purchaser of land in southern Rhode Island, where the project involved local and state permitting, financing and development into a 60-unit, high-end, age-restricted, residential condominium and an assisted living facility. The firm has taken advantage of a boom in development, acting for a number of those investing in condominium projects. Clients appreciate the level of personal attention they receive from attorneys – one happy customer asserted: *"This law firm is the best."* The contribution of the firm's litigators must not be left out of any analysis of the real estate practice, particularly in construction matters.

**The Lawyers:** **Joseph DiStefano** (see p.1771) is familiar with sophisticated real estate issues, such as the concept of condominium ownership on leased land and the conversion of apartments into condominiums. Unsurprisingly, he earned praise from clients for his *"vast experience and knowledge."* In the past year he advised a group of developers in a 102-unit condominium development in a Providence suburb, and acted for another client in a $13 million transaction. Head of the group **Stanley Kanter** (see p.1772) is a popular choice for development, financing and leasing. He is involved in major transactions for golf courses, shopping centers, hotels, condominiums and residential developments. Recently he represented the real estate holding company of a major international and East Coast retailer in its acquisition of properties in East Greenwich, including dealing with the permitting and construction aspects. Broadly talented **Elizabeth Noonan** (see p.1772) excels at development, construction, permitting and other regulatory matters, as well as real estate tax. Much of her work includes zoning and land use advice, and she is also a capable real estate litigator, widely recognized for her *"skills before the local authorities."* Noonan is heavily involved with a major retail client operating throughout the eastern part of the USA. Completing the picture for the firm is **Robert Stolzman** (see p.1773), who advises various government agencies plus local and out-of-state companies in complicated real estate transactions, developments, zoning and land use.

**Clients/Work Highlights:** Clients include major corporations such as Dow Chemical and Brooks Pharmacy, and the firm recently advised a charitable corporation in its purchase of a Deed of Conservation Easement and Restrictions plus Development Rights over shorefront property in southern Rhode Island.

# Leaders in Rhode Island

### BATTY, Jerome
Hinckley, Allen & Snyder LLP, Providence
401 274 2000
*Recommended in Real Estate*

### BROOKS, Robert
Adler Pollock & Sheehan PC, Providence
401 274 7200
rbrooks@apslaw.com
*Recommended in Employment*
**Practice Areas:** Labor and employment, alternative dispute resolution, construction, governmental and legislative.
**Prof. Memberships:** Rhode Island Bar Association, Labor Law Committee.
**Career:** Partner and Chairman of the firm's Labor and Employment Law Group, he represents management in all facets of labor relations and employment law in the public and private sectors. He has successfully represented employers in employment discrimination matters, and counsels employers on complex administrative law issues. He regularly handles collective bargaining negotiations and the defense of union organizing campaigns.
**Personal:** Former Deputy Chief of Staff to the Mayor of Providence.

### BULMAN, John
Little, Medeiros, Kinder, Bulman & Whitney PC, Providence 401 272 8080
*Recommended in Litigation*

### BUSH, Christine
Duffy, Sweeney & Scott Ltd, Providence
401 455 0700
*Recommended in Litigation*

### CARLOTTI, Stephen
Hinckley, Allen & Snyder LLP, Providence
401 274 2000
*Recommended in Corporate/Commercial*

### CAVANAGH JR, Joseph
Blish & Cavanagh, LLP, Providence
401 831 8900
*Recommended in Litigation*

### CHITTICK, Michael D
Adler Pollock & Sheehan PC, Providence
401 274 7200
mchittick@apslaw.com
*Recommended in Employment*
**Practice Areas:** Labor and employment, alternative dispute resolution.
**Prof. Memberships:** Rhode Island Bar Association, Labor Law Committee.
**Career:** Partner in the Labor and Employment Law Group, handling all facets of labor and employment law and related litigation in both the public and private sectors. He has successfully represented employers in both federal and state courts on matters including collective bargaining negotiations, alleged unfair labor practices, wage-hour laws, medical leave, reductions-in-force, OSHA compliance, employment discrimination, and termination issues.
**Publications:** Contributing editor, 7th edition of BNA publication, How to Take a Case Before the NLRB, and the 2005 cumulative supplement to it.

### CHLEBUS, Andrew J
Edwards Angell Palmer & Dodge LLP, Providence 401 276 6473
achlebus@eapdlaw.com
*Recommended in Corporate/Commercial*
**Practice Areas:** During the past 25 years, Andy has represented at least ten different banks and commercial finance companies in structuring and closing loans to customers in the radio, television, cable television, billboard, publishing and related media industries. In addition to traditional secured loan transactions, Andy has experience in non-traditional areas of finance including consignments of gold and other precious metals to manufacturers, equipment leasing and ESOP loans.
**Prof. Memberships:** American Bar Association, Business Law Section; Rhode Island Bar Association.
**Personal:** Brown University, AB, magna cum laude, Phi Beta Kappa, 1971; Harvard Law School, JD, 1974.

### DEMARIA, Gerald
Higgins, Cavanagh & Cooney LLP, Providence 401 272 3500
*Recommended in Litigation*

### DISTEFANO, Joseph R
Adler Pollock & Sheehan PC, Providence
401 274 7200
jdistefano@apslaw.com
*Recommended in Real Estate*
**Practice Areas:** Business and corporate, governmental and legislative, real estate.
**Career:** Partner who handles major commercial real estate transactions. He was instrumental in the redevelopment of Downtown Providence, and as one of the originators of the Capital Center Project, he spearheaded the development of several major downtown office buildings.
**Personal:** Previous State Senator and President of the Senate. Chair of the

Board of Trustees of Salve Regina University, Chair of the RI Board of Elections for over 15 years, former Chair of the RI Convention Center Authority. Serves on the New England Advisory Board of Sovereign Bank.

**DUFFY, Robert**
Duffy, Sweeney & Scott Ltd, Providence
401 455 0700
*Recommended in Litigation*

**FARMER III, Malcom**
Hinckley, Allen & Snyder LLP, Providence
401 274 2000
*Recommended in Corporate/Commercial*

**FARRELL, Margaret**
Hinckley, Allen & Snyder LLP, Providence
401 274 2000
*Recommended in Corporate/Commercial*

**FLANDERS JR, Robert**
Hinckley, Allen & Snyder LLP, Providence
401 274 2000
*Recommended in Litigation*

**FREEL, Mark**
Edwards Angell Palmer & Dodge LLP, Providence 401 276 6681
Mfreel@eapdlaw.com
*Recommended in Litigation*
**Practice Areas:** Mark frequently handles matters involving unfair competition, construction and real estate disputes, non-disclosure agreements, covenants not to compete, and shareholder and business disputes. He frequently represents manufacturers in a variety of commercial and product liability matters, and handles disputes between and among shareholders in the closely held corporate context.
**Prof. Memberships:** Defense Research Institute, RI Manufacturers' Association.
**Publications:** Mark frequently writes for such publications as For the Defense, DRI, and the Rhode Island Bar Journal.
**Personal:** University of Connecticut School of Law, JD, 1987; highest honors; University of New Hampshire, MA, 1981; University of New Hampshire, BA, 1975.

**GAMBOLI, Michael**
Partridge Snow & Hahn LLP, Providence
401 861 8200
*Recommended in Employment*

**GEANACOPOULOS, Steve**
Adler Pollock & Sheehan PC, Providence
401 274 7200
sgeanacopoulos@apslaw.com
*Recommended in Corporate/Commercial*
**Practice Areas:** Business and corporate, governmental and legislative, real estate.
**Prof. Memberships:** Rhode Island Bar Association and American Bar Association, Business Law Section.
**Career:** Chair of the Corporate Department, whose practice focuses on mergers and acquisitions and securities. He repre-

sents the firm's largest and most sophisticated corporate clients including foreign-based multinationals, US-based public companies, and emerging companies. He has extensive experience with the needs of closely-held companies and family businesses, including resolution of shareholder disputes.
**Publications:** Author of 'Resales of Securities', Amerercian Bar Association's Business Law Today, Vol. 7, No. 2, Nov.Dec. 1997.

**GILDEN, David**
Partridge Snow & Hahn LLP, Providence
401 861 8200
*Recommended in Corporate/Commercial*

**GRAHAM, Christopher**
Edwards Angell Palmer & Dodge LLP, Providence 401 276 6579
CGraham@eapdlaw.com
*Recommended in Corporate/Commercial*
**Practice Areas:** Chris, Co-Partner-In-Charge of the firm's Providence office, negotiates acquisitions, dispositions and management buyouts for corporate buyers and sellers, private equity funds and management teams. He represents borrowers in financing transactions, including highly leveraged financings that are integral parts of private equity buyouts. He also counsels start-up enterprises and assists in their capital formation, represents emerging companies and private equity investors in their equity financings, and advises companies at all stages on matters of corporate and business law.
**Prof. Memberships:** Rhode Island Bar Association.
**Personal:** University of Pennsylvania Law School, JD, 1981; Brown University, BA, magna cum laude, 1976.

**GRIMM, William**
Hinckley, Allen & Snyder LLP, Providence
401 274 2000
*Recommended in Litigation*

**HAHN, James**
Partridge Snow & Hahn LLP, Providence
401 861 8200
*Recommended in Corporate/Commercial*

**JOCELYN, Richard**
Hinckley, Allen & Snyder LLP, Providence
401 274 2000
*Recommended in Employment*

**JOHNSON, V Duncan**
Edwards Angell Palmer & Dodge LLP, Providence 401 276 6477
djohnson@eapdlaw.com
*Recommended in Corporate/Commercial*
**Practice Areas:** Duncan's practice has been in the general corporate area with a specific focus on the financial services industry. He has led the firm's Bank Regulatory and Mergers and Acquisitions

Practice for a number of years. He served as principal outside counsel for Fleet-Boston Financial Corporation in substantially all of its acquisitions. He has, in addition, represented a variety of other regional financial services firms in corporate and regulatory matters.
**Prof. Memberships:** Rhode Island Bar Association.
**Personal:** Harvard Law School, LLB, 1963; Harvard University, AB, cum laude, 1960.

**KANTER, Stanley**
Adler Pollock & Sheehan PC, Providence
401.274.7200
skanter@apslaw.com
*Recommended in Real Estate*
**Practice Areas:** Real estate, financial & estate planning.
**Prof. Memberships:** American Bar Association, Rhode Island Bar Association, Title Standards Committee.
**Career:** Chair of the Real Estate Group, representing clients in both domestic and international matters in all aspects of purchase, development, leasing, financing and sale of real estate. Represented builders in all phases of project development. Well-versed in the intricacies of title insurance policies, including the analysis and resolution of complicated transactions.
**Personal:** Fellow, American College of Trust and Estate Counsel; Real Estate Council of Cornell University; Chicago Title Insurance Company Advisory Council; International Council of Shopping Centers.

**KASLE, Jeffrey**
St Peter & Kasle, Providence
401 453 4330
*Recommended in Employment*

**KELLY, Joseph**
Carroll, Kelly & Murphy, Providence
401 331 7272
*Recommended in Litigation*

**KINDER, Daniel**
Little, Medeiros, Kinder, Bulman & Whitney PC, Providence 401 272 8080
*Recommended in Employment*

**LITTLE, Christopher**
Little, Medeiros, Kinder, Bulman & Whitney PC, Providence 401 272 8080
*Recommended in Litigation*

**MARCELLO III, Matthew**
Hinckley, Allen & Snyder LLP, Providence
401 274 2000
*Recommended in Corporate/Commercial*

**MCCANN, Gail E**
Edwards Angell Palmer & Dodge LLP, Providence 401.276.6527
gmccann@eapdlaw.com
*Recommended in Corporate/Commercial*
**Practice Areas:** Gail is a Co-Chair of the firm's Real Estate Department and

has particular knowledge in construction, project and mezzanine financing, including apartments, hotels, power retail centers, office and industrial space, healthcare facilities, and affordable housing projects throughout the US.
**Prof. Memberships:** American College of Mortgage Attorneys, New England Legal Foundation, Rhode Island Bar Association.
**Publications:** Gail speaks frequently at seminars, and has served as Faculty Presenter for many years at the RI Bar Association's seminar on Basic Commercial and Real Estate Loan Documentation.
**Personal:** University of Pennsylvania Law School, JD, 1978; Brown University, AB, magna cum laude, 1975.

**MCNAMARA, Neal**
Nixon Peabody LLP, Providence
401 454 1019
nmcnamara@nixonpeabody.com
*Recommended in Employment*
**Practice Areas:** Partner in the firm's Litigation Section, focusing on employment law. His practice focuses on both litigation and counseling. He has successfully handled matters involving all major employment related statutes, including Title VII, ADEA, the ADA, FMLA, and ERISA, as well as state law employment issues and non-compete and confidentiality agreements. A major portion of his practice is devoted to counseling clients on a wide range of employee issues in order to prevent matters from reaching litigation. He has developed employment handbooks and policies, conducted internal investigations and regularly conducts seminars on employment law topics.
**Prof. Memberships:** ABA; Rhode Island Bar Association.
**Career:** Partner since 2006; previously a Partner with Holland & Knight.
**Personal:** University of Pennsylvania, BA, 1977; Columbia University, MA, 1979; New York University, JD, 1982.

**NOONAN, Elizabeth**
Adler Pollock & Sheehan PC, Providence
401 274 7200
bnoonan@apslaw.com
*Recommended in Real Estate*
**Practice Areas:** Real estate, environmental, governmental and legislative, litigation.
**Prof. Memberships:** RI Trial Lawyers Association.
**Career:** Partner who represents developers of commercial and residential properties in all phases of development, from acquisition to permitting and construction. She has been involved in several significant property rights cases. She also handles commercial, tax and construction litigation, and has represented national and local clients in successfully challenging state and local tax levies. Major clients include Dow Chemical Company and Brooks Pharmacy.

**Personal:** Past President of RI Women's Bar Association; former delegate to the Democratic National Convention.

## PANNONE, Gary
Pannone Lopes & Devereaux LLC, Providence 401 824 5115
*Recommended in Corporate/Commercial*

## PARTRIDGE, John
Partridge Snow & Hahn LLP, Providence 401 861 8200
*Recommended in Corporate/Commercial*

## PELCZARSKI, Karen
Blish & Cavanagh, LLP, Providence 401 831 8900
*Recommended in Litigation*

## PETROS, Gerald
Hinckley, Allen & Snyder LLP, Providence 401 274 2000
*Recommended in Litigation*

## POGUE, Mark
Edwards Angell Palmer & Dodge LLP, Providence 401.276.6491
Mpogue@eapdlaw.com
*Recommended in Employment, Litigation*
**Practice Areas:** Mark's practice is focused on employment law, insurance litigation, and intellectual property matters. His clients include corporations with large payrolls and diverse employment law issues; companies seeking to register or protect trademarks or copyrights; insurance companies; and companies with substantial real estate holdings seeking to reduce their property taxes.
**Prof. Memberships:** Rhode Island Bar Association, Massachusetts Bar Association.
**Publications:** 'Property Taxation In Rhode Island', Gannet Publications, 2002.; 'Procedures For Appealing Your Tax Assessment', Newport, Rhode Island.
**Personal:** Harvard Law School, JD, cum laude, 1983; Williams College, BA, summa cum laude, 1978.

## REED, Walter G D
Edwards Angell Palmer & Dodge LLP, Providence 401 276 6647
wreed@eapdlaw.com
*Recommended in Corporate/Commercial*
**Practice Areas:** With nearly 30 years of experience as a corporate lawyer, Walter serves as outside general counsel to a number of major business clients and specializes in corporate transactions including mergers and acquisitions, joint ventures, partnerships and private equity investments. Walter is a Co-Chair of the firm's M&A Practice Group, and is also the Chairman of the firm's Executive Committee.
**Prof. Memberships:** Rhode Island Bar Association, Past Chairman, Committee on Corporations and Partnerships.

**Personal:** Columbia University School of Law, JD, 1977; Chancellor Kent Scholar and Harlan Stone Scholar; Harvard University, BA, magna cum laude, 1974.

## ROCHA, Patricia
Adler Pollock & Sheehan PC, Providence 401 274 7200
procha@apslaw.com
*Recommended in Litigation*
**Practice Areas:** Litigation, labor and employment, criminal/white-collar defense, healthcare.
**Prof. Memberships:** Rhode Island Bar Foundation Board; Defense Counsel of Rhode Island Board; Association of Trial Lawyers of America; RI Trial Lawyers Association.
**Career:** Partner and Chair of the firm's Litigation Group. She has tried and defended cases ranging from product liability and toxic tort, employment discrimination, redistricting legislation, to bribery, wire fraud, honest services and conspiracy. She has also successfully represented healthcare providers in acquiring regulatory approvals. Co-authored an important national text on trial advocacy and produced a collection of model closing arguments for defense attorneys.

## RUBIN, David
Hinckley, Allen & Snyder LLP, Providence 401 274 2000
*Recommended in Real Estate*

## SCOTT, Craig
Duffy, Sweeney & Scott Ltd, Providence 401 455 0700
*Recommended in Litigation*

## SKEFFINGTON, James
Edwards Angell Palmer & Dodge LLP, Providence 401 276 6560
Jskeffington@eapdlaw.com
*Recommended in Corporate/Commercial*
**Practice Areas:** James Skeffington concentrates his practice in the areas of development, financing, syndication, leasing projects for governmental and private enterprise and management of civil and employment litigation for large multi-state corporations.
**Prof. Memberships:** American Bar Association; National Association of Bond Lawyers; American College of Bond Counsel.
**Publications:** Jim frequently lectures at national conferences on revenue bond financings for public and private projects as well as state/local legislative initiatives to stimulate economic development.
**Personal:** Boston University School of Law, LLM, 1967; Taxation; Georgetown University Law Center, JD, 1969; Boston College, BS, 1964.

## SNOW, Stephen
Partridge Snow & Hahn LLP, Providence 401 861 8200
*Recommended in Litigation*

## ST PETER, Gary
St Peter & Kasle, Providence 401 453 4330
*Recommended in Employment*

## STOLZMAN, Robert
Adler Pollock & Sheehan PC, Providence 401 274 7200
rstolzman@apslaw.com
*Recommended in Real Estate*
**Practice Areas:** Real estate, business and corporate, governmental and legislative, public finance.
**Prof. Memberships:** Fellow, American College of Real Estate Attorneys.
**Career:** As Partner, he focuses his practice in land use, real estate transactions, small business and governmental relations. He has shepherded projects for national and local clients through regulatory and governmental agencies. A registered lobbyist for trade associations and private businesses, he has also drafted and assisted with the passage of a wide range of business legislation. Serves as counsel to, and Secretary of, the Board of Directors of the RI Economic Development Corporation.

## SWEENEY, Michael
Duffy, Sweeney & Scott Ltd, Providence 401 455 0700
*Recommended in Corporate/Commercial*

## TARANTINO, John
Adler Pollock & Sheehan PC, Providence 401 274 7200
jtarantino@apslaw.com
*Recommended in Litigation*
**Practice Areas:** Litigation, alternative dispute resolution, products liability/toxic tort, white-collar defense, insurance, appellate.
**Prof. Memberships:** Defense Research Institute, American Judicature Society, National Association of Bar Presidents, American College of Trial Lawyers, International Academy of Trial Lawyers.
**Career:** Firm President, Partner in the Litigation Group. Counsel in numerous high profile cases, successfully representing local, national and international clients in sophisticated litigation matters, including constitutional law for state government. Successful defense of manufacturer in precedent-setting RI lead paint trial.
**Personal:** 2005 Lawyer of the Year by RI Lawyers Weekly, 2005 Top 500 Lawyers in the country by Lawdragon Magazine.

## TRACY, David
Hinckley, Allen & Snyder LLP, Providence 401 274 2000
*Recommended in Real Estate*

## WHELAN, Joseph
Hinckley, Allen & Snyder LLP, Providence 401 274 2000
*Recommended in Employment*

## WHITE, Todd
Adler Pollock & Sheehan PC, Providence 401 274 7200
twhite@apslaw.com
*Recommended in Litigation*
**Practice Areas:** Appellate, construction, litigation, products liability/toxic tort, insurance.
**Prof. Memberships:** RI Trial Lawyers Association; Association of Trial Lawyers of America.
**Career:** Partner in the Litigation Group, focusing on personal injury, product liability, toxic tort, medical malpractice, complex commercial litigation, securities litigation, insurance defense and insurance coverage issues. Clients include Rhode Island municipalities, real estate developers, national insurance carriers and a variety of mid-size local businesses as well as individuals. Has secured plaintiff's verdicts of $500,000, $1,500,000 and $3,100,000 in personal injury and minority shareholder disputes.

## WOLLIN, David A
Adler Pollock & Sheehan PC, Providence 401 274 7200
dwollin@apslaw.com
*Recommended in Litigation*
**Practice Areas:** Litigation, appellate, products liability/toxic tort, insurance, environmental.
**Prof. Memberships:** International Association of Defense Counsel; Regional Roster of Neutrals, American Arbitration Association; RI Bar Association, Supreme Court Bench/Bar Committee.
**Career:** Partner, Vice President of the firm, handling all aspects of civil litigation, including mediations, arbitrations, trials and appellate proceedings in federal and state courts. Successfully represented a major cigarette manufacturer in a series of cases brought by smokers seeking damages resulting from smoking-related injuries. He obtained one of the largest jury awards in RI Superior Court in 2002.
**Publications:** Co-author, Rhode Island Civil and Appellate Procedure.

# ADLER POLLOCK & SHEEHAN P.C.

## THE FIRM

**Founding Partners:** Walter Adler (1896-1991)
Bernard R Pollock (1926-1984)
William J Sheehan (1917-1999)
**Managing Partner:** Mark O Denehy

**Number of attorneys:** 65

**FIRM OVERVIEW:** For the past 45 years, Adler Pollock & Sheehan P.C. has delivered client-focused, business law services designed to achieve cost-effective solutions for today's complex challenges. AP&S successfully combines the depth and breadth of expertise of a large law firm with the advantages of responsive and direct personal service by partners found in smaller firms. Adler Pollock & Sheehan is a full service law firm featuring a sophisticated Corporate Practice and a nationally- renowned Litigation Practice. AP&S services clients in 43 jurisdictions throughout New England, across the country, and around the world.
**Network:** AP&S is the Rhode Island member of the State Capital Global Law Firm Group, an organization of independent law firms in every capital city and commercial center in the United States and abroad. Membership is significant since it is by invitation only to firms who have demonstrated the highest quality service and industry leadership. (Member firms practice independently and not in a relationship for the joint practice of law).

## MAIN AREAS OF PRACTICE:

**Litigation:** Among the largest and most experienced in New England, the AP&S Litigation Department is recognized nationally for its high quality and cost effectiveness. With over 30 litigators and a dozen para-professionals, AP&S has assembled the largest litigators group in Rhode Island, which includes a diverse and broad-based civil and white-collar criminal practice. AP&S serves as national coordinating counsel in mass-tort litigation. Recent high profile cases include the landmark lead paint lawsuit brought by the State of Rhode Island Attorney General in which the firm successfully defended the paint manufacturers. Additionally, the firm defended a major tobacco company in the first New England case brought by the family of a deceased smoker. AP&S was selected as one of 18 firms internationally to be listed as Dow Chemical's selected trial firms.
**Labor & Employment:** The Labor and Employment Group represents and counsels public and private sector employers in connection with virtually every aspect of the employment relationship, including discrimination and wrongful discharge matters, labor-management relations and collective bargaining. AP&S has successfully represented clients before all federal and state labor and employment agencies, including the EEOC, NLRB, OSHA and the US Department of Labor.
**Business & Corporate:** The Business and Corporate Group is committed to understanding each client's business, offering solutions for executing business plans and proactively addressing all legal needs, including the organization and structuring of shareholder relations, securities, tax planning, bank and venture capital financing, protection and licensing of intellectual property, product distribution, employee relations, acquisitions, succession planning, execution of exit strategies and resolution of shareholder disputes.
**Healthcare:** The Healthcare Group serves as counsel to New England's premier hospitals and healthcare facilities, including freestanding surgi-centers and nursing homes. The firm's attorneys also represent regional and national hospital networks on interstate healthcare acquisitions as well as provide defense to healthcare providers on compliance and fraud investigations.
**Environmental:** The Environmental Group boasts nationally-recognized lawyers who have helped define environmental standards in New England. AP&S has served as lead counsel for many cases with long-term effects on current environmental law - from the defense of multi-million dollar EPA fines and compliance actions to the initiation and management of Superfund cost recovery actions for Fortune 100 companies of over 100 parties.

**Real Estate:** The Real Estate Group represents developers, multi-national corporations, family-owned businesses, contractors and individuals in every aspect of industrial, commercial and residential real estate, including the permitting, financing, leasing, and development of major retail commercial centers, office building, golf courses, assisted living facilities, hotels, apartments and condominiums.

**CLIENTS:** The core of the AP&S approach is the personal attention each client receives. The firm's ability to create and execute winning strategies has earned AP&S national recognition and a growing roster of loyal clients, from publicly-held Fortune 500 and Fortune 100 companies to small businesses, individuals and organizations. The firm represents clients such as The Dow Chemical Company, Atlantic Richfield, Cookson America, Textron Inc., Hasbro, Inc. and Blue Cross/Blue Shield Association among others.

## HEAD OFFICE

### RHODE ISLAND
One Citizens Plaza, 8th Floor, **Providence**, RI 02903-1345
**Tel:** 401 274 7200 **Fax:** 401 751 0604
**Website:** www.apslaw.com

## BRANCH OFFICES

### MASSACHUSETTS
175 Federal Street, **Boston**, MA 02110
**Tel:** 617 482 0600 **Fax:** 617 482 0604

### NEW HAMPSHIRE
800 Lake Street, P.O. Box 536, **Bristol**, NH 03222
**Tel:** 603 744 1021 **Fax:** 603 744 2799

**CONTENTS:** Corporate/M&A p.1775; Employment p.1777; Litigation p.1778; Real Estate p.1780; Individuals' Profiles p.1781; Firm' Profiles p.1786.

## How lawyers are ranked

Every year we carry out thousands of in-depth interviews with clients and lawyers in order to assess the reputations and expertise of business lawyers across the USA. Chambers rankings and editorial are referred to extensively by General Counsel and other purchasers of legal services who look to our recommendations when choosing their lawyers.

# CORPORATE/M&A

## Corporate/M&A
### Leading Firms

**1** HAYNSWORTH SINKLER BOYD PA *Charleston*
MCNAIR LAW FIRM PA *Columbia*
NELSON MULLINS *Columbia*
NEXSEN PRUET, LLC *Columbia*
WYCHE *Greenville*

**2** BUIST MOORE SMYTHE MCGEE PA *Charleston*
LEATHERWOOD WALKER *Greenville*
WARREN & SINKLER LLP *Charleston*
WOMBLE CARLYLE SANDRIDGE & RICE *Greenville*

### Leading Individuals

#### Senior Statesman
SHOEMAKER JR James *Wyche*

**1** CURRIE John Withers *McNair Law Firm PA*
KING JR George *Haynsworth Sinkler Boyd PA*
MENZIE Edward *Nexsen Pruet, LLC*
WARREN III John *Warren & Sinkler LLP*

**2** DIXON Augustus *Nelson Mullins*
HALL JR Cary *Wyche*
HOGUE JR P Mason *Nelson Mullins*
KNIGHT G Marcus *Nexsen Pruet, LLC*

**3** AMSTUTZ Eric *Wyche*
BLAKE JR Joseph *Haynsworth Sinkler Boyd PA*
BOYD William *Haynsworth Sinkler Boyd PA*
DERRICK Elizabeth *Womble Carlyle*
FEW JR Richard *Leatherwood Walker*
FRITZE Daniel *Nelson Mullins*
GRAYSON Neil *Nelson Mullins*
MCKINNEY Kathleen *Haynsworth Sinkler Boyd PA*
MUSSER William *McNair Law Firm PA*

## Band 1

### Haynsworth Sinkler Boyd PA

**The Firm:** Some 60 attorneys are spread across four full-service offices statewide. Their achievements are said to be both "*outstanding and consistent*" and allow the firm to lay claim to a "*highly visible and top-quality reputation*" in corporate and finance matters. The practice encompasses public finance, commercial transactions and M&A, and a range of lending work, including bank formations and regulation. Lawyers have notable experience in all the usual commercial sectors, not least medical research; they have also built up a great deal of experience with nonprofit organizations and are renowned for their securities and corporate governance advice. Recent practice highlights include negotiating the acquisition of a regional bank on behalf of a national financial institution, as well as working on an aggregate of $250 million in various secured loans from institutions across the state.

**The Lawyers:** Group head **George King** is "*an absolute leader in corporate finance*," according to market sources. In addition to his M&A portfolio, he has extensive experience as SEC counsel for a variety of companies, and recently negotiated a $250 million debt offering on a major securities deal. The "*brilliant and innovative*" **Joseph Blake** has worked on several health care ventures, including the development of research complexes. One such ongoing matter relates to the establishment of a medical research and training complex at USC. **William Boyd** has "*decades of experience*" in complex commercial transactions and general business advice. This multiskilled lawyer is also proficient in real estate matters. **Kathy McKinney** is extremely highly regarded for her expertise in public finance matters. She works as bond counsel for leading hospitals, colleges and other nonprofit organisations, and is hailed as "*the dean of tax-exempt financings in the state!*"

**Clients/Work Highlights:** Sonoco Products, Synalloy Corporation and Greenville Hospital System are three of the group's established clients.

### McNair Law Firm PA

**The Firm:** This "*flexible and impressive*" team impressed commentators with its "*deep bench and innovative approach*." The group numbers over 100 attorneys, based in eight offices across the state. They focus primarily on corporate transactions, and have widespread experience in M&A and securities offerings. Of the other strings to the group's bow, the areas of greatest prominence are bankruptcy-related and tax-led restructurings, financing transactions, both bank lending and bond issues, corporate-styled real estate transactions and insurance matters. Away from the deal table, lawyers assist state and federal bodies on compliance issues.

**The Lawyers:** **John Currie** "*possesses an extraordinary knowledge of the law*" and a "*sound business sense.*" His practice is primarily transactional and has included some notable M&A deals. Fellow partner **William Musser** is said to possess "*a meticulous legal mind.*" He focuses on municipal as well as corporate law, and has undertaken a secondment as in-house counsel to a major energy company.

**Clients/Work Highlights:** The team represents clients in health care, utilities and technology, as well as financial institutions and various government bodies.

### Nelson Mullins Riley & Scarborough LLP

See firm details p.1788

**The Firm:** There was plenty of client endorsement for this "*dynamic, broad-based practice,*" which is "*already among the primary groups in the state and continues to grow right across the board.*" The firm has a formidable regional presence due to the sterling efforts of its four South Carolina offices; particular strength lies in the areas of health care, technology and insurance. The team has negotiated a number of M&A for public and private companies, as well as private capital securities offerings. It has additionally acted as underwriter's counsel for public entities and lays claim to one of the most sophisticated venture capital departments in the state, having worked on the investment of some $200 million to date for clients. Its compliance practice is extensive, with lawyers ensuring clients fulfil their state and federal regulatory requirements. It must not be forgotten that the South Carolina lawyers have the ability to call upon the skills of colleagues in four other states, including those in the firm's three North Carolina offices.

**The Lawyers:** **Augustus Dixon**'s wide-ranging practice is served well by his "*great communication skills and highly developed sense of responsibility.*" His technology law and outsourcing expertise helps to define his work, though he is equally adept at corporate finance and M&A, as well as bankruptcy issues. Dixon has a large and enviable corporate clientele. **Mason Hogue** was praised for being "*thorough and diligent;*" commentators clearly respected his good judgment. Like Dixon, he too has developed a niche in technology-related matters. **Daniel Fritze** comes recommended for his breadth of commercial expertise; he handles corporate and securities matters and has an eye for detail. **Neil Grayson** is a popular securities expert, whose practice includes a substantial amount of work for financial institutions and e-commerce companies.

**Clients/Work Highlights:** The team's client roster includes significant companies in the technology, pharmaceutical, health care and manufacturing industries.

### Nexsen Pruet, LLC
See firm details p.1789

**The Firm:** This prominent full-service corporate team was applauded for its *"resourceful and responsive"* working style. Each of Nexsen's seven offices in the Carolinas can call upon an *"extensive network of support,"* prompting clients to view the firm as *"well-equipped to handle the most sophisticated transactions."* It displays a collegiate and versatile approach to complex M&A and securities matters, and is able to access strong litigation support when corporate matters veer towards dispute situations. A clientele of manufacturing, communications, biotechnology and software companies, among others, provides a rich vein of good work. Recent matters include a substantial joint venture involving forestry products, and a number of restructuring and M&A assignments for a major financial services provider.

**The Lawyers:** *"Outstanding"* **Edward Menzie** (see p.1783) maintains an *"exciting corporate practice"* while also excelling in real estate matters, most obviously at the nexus of the two. He is a familiar face on the lecture circuit. **Marcus Knight** (see p.1783) exhibits *"wonderful organizational skills and attention to detail;"* consequently, clients were confident that *"he really knows the law."* His practice is steered towards finance transactions, and he has also recently been involved in two significant forestry products matters.

**Clients/Work Highlights:** Financial institutions, manufacturers and wholesalers join companies in the technology, transport, insurance and forestry industries on the firm's client list.

### Wyche, Burgess, Freeman & Parham, PA
See firm details p.1791

**The Firm:** Portraying it as *"a model of old-school excellence,"* commentators spoke warmly of this Columbia and Greenville firm's *"brilliant attorneys, who shine in sophisticated deals."* One competitor admitted candidly: *"We really want their business!"* As one of the foremost corporate teams in the state, it regularly represents national and multinational companies in some of the East Coast's larger transactions. Traditional corporate and M&A transactions form the backbone of the practice, and this is supple-

mented with public finance and compliance work. Recent highlights include negotiating the acquisition of a hockey team by a group of local investors, and acting for the buyer in a complex acquisition of a distressed private company.

**The Lawyers:** **Cary Hall** (see p.1783) is *"an outstanding tax specialist,"* according to commentators. His profile also extends to general commercial, M&A and securities matters. Ranking as a senior statesman, **James Shoemaker** (see p.1784) was for several interviewees *"the dean of securities law."* He has 40 years of corporate and finance experience and continues to work with the firm's public company clients. Researchers learned that **Eric Amstutz** (see p.1781) is *"knowledgeable, practical, and a pleasure to work with."* He has a strong general corporate practice.

**Clients/Work Highlights:** Bowater Incorporated; Carolina First Bank; Centerplate; Chubb Group; InRe Financial; KEMET Electronics; Michelin North America; Milliken & Company and South Financial Group.

## Band 2

### Buist Moore Smythe McGee PA
See firm details p.1786

**The Firm:** Viewed as *"a great homegrown group,"* the Buist team maintains a well-respected, full-service corporate practice. Based in the Charleston area, but frequently representing clients throughout the region, the team displays an excellent synergy with the banking and real estate departments of the firm. Recent practice highlights include negotiating some significant acquisitions for a state newspaper and a major construction contractor. The team also negotiated a $60 million stock sale on behalf of the owners of a golf course.

**Clients/Work Highlights:** The client list includes regional businesses, financial institutions and real estate developers.

### Leatherwood Walker Todd & Mann PC
See firm details p.1787

**The Firm:** Clients were delighted with the performance of this 12-strong Greenville outfit, saying of the lawyers: *"They're informative, helpful and extremely well-rounded."* In particular, they mentioned the team's younger attorneys, deeming them to be *"a strong and efficient set."* The corporate group offers a comprehensive service, with banking and technology expertise coming to the fore along with solid securities and M&A work. Of late, it has been assisting a southern grocery chain in divestitures involving some $800 million worth of assets. The team also has experience on a wide range of economic development projects and has expanded

its corporate governance capability by way of some interesting lateral hires.

**The Lawyers:** **Richard Few** is the firm's managing director and *"a fantastic corporate attorney."* He is active in a broad range of transactions, and recently negotiated the bank and bond financing for a 400-room student housing facility at a Greenville technical college.

**Clients/Work Highlights:** Banks and financial institutions and manufacturing, construction and real estate companies.

### Warren & Sinkler LLP

**The Firm:** This compact Charleston offering has an impressive bench of attorneys. One client told researchers: *"They're small, but all of the attorneys are senior and extremely experienced at large-scale corporate transactions."* Sarbanes-Oxley compliance, assistance with FCC reviews and general commercial advice sit side-by-side with securities and M&A matters in the team's portfolio of work. The lawyers are particularly recommended to startup businesses and also represent significant financial institutions. The firm continues to provide primary counsel to a significant national aviation client.

**The Lawyers:** Versatile **John Warren** is *"practical, thorough and quick,"* according to commentators who happily recommended him for *"just about any business query you can think of."*

**Clients/Work Highlights:** Clients include insurance companies; property developers; small businesses; major banks and financial institutions.

### Womble Carlyle Sandridge & Rice, PLLC
See firm details p.1589

**The Firm:** Greenville is the location for one of the smaller offices of this significant national firm. The lawyers here offer a full service and have notable experience representing financial institutions in a variety of lending and workout matters. Drawing on the breadth of corporate expertise offered by the firm's extensive regional network, the group provides confident compliance advice in a variety of regulatory forums. Research revealed lawyers described as *"excellent communicators who always follow up"* and whose *"work product is always of the highest standard."* The team recently negotiated the sale of an electrical testing service parts company.

**The Lawyers:** **Betty Derrick** (see p.1782) joins the table following strong client endorsement. Interviewees said that she is *"an impressive all-rounder who particularly understands what motivates businesses and how they look at the world."*

**Clients/Work Highlights:** South Financial Group, Carolina First Bank and ScanSource are three of the team's significant clients.

# EMPLOYMENT

## MAINLY DEFENDANT

## Band 1

### Fisher & Phillips LLP
See firm details p.732

**The Firm:** Commentators felt this streamlined local office of the national employment boutique was "*a deservedly prominent figure in the state's employment market.*" The Columbia group of ten attorneys benefits from the firm's national reputation and the coverage afforded by the network of offices – it acts for clients all over the country as well as throughout the state. It is noted for its significant labor law practice and work on large-scale negotiations between unions and employers. The employment side of the practice has lately featured a number of wage and hour class actions as well as the usual spread of employee benefits, employee discrimination and business immigration matters.

**The Lawyers:** **Daniel Ellzey** (see p.1782) is "*an outstanding font of knowledge,*" according to market sources. He offers years of experience in union matters and the defense of discrimination claims. The managing partner, "*bright and focused*" **Jonathan Pearson** (see p.1784), won acclaim for his litigation prowess. He represents employers in wrongful discharge claims and advises on health and safety matters and union contracts. **Michael Carrouth** (see p.1781) is a respected labor law specialist, particularly noted for his achievements in union negotiations. On the employment law side, his services – both contentious and advisory – are sought by employer clients of all kinds.

**Clients/Work Highlights:** Employers in manufacturing; technology; banking; health care and insurance.

### Ogletree, Deakins, Nash, Smoak & Stewart, PC
See firm details p.738

**The Firm:** "*Their hard work and attention to detail means they always deliver:*" so said one source of the 85-attorney, three-office South Carolina group at this national labor and employment law firm. Another remarked on this worthy occupant of the top band: "*I've used them for 25 years and they've helped work some real miracles.*" With assistance from the rest of the extensive national network, the group offers employers a full service in labor and employment law, plus advice on business, immigration, health care and benefits. Lawyers have taken on a notable amount of civil rights-related employment litigation and recently defended an employer in a wage and hour class action involving 11,000 employees. The active labor practice encompasses preventative counseling and the resolution of complex union disputes.

**The Lawyers:** **Charles Speth** (see p.1785) was widely acknowledged as "*a brilliant and very experienced employment litigator.*" Clients billed him as "*the go-to person for complex disputes*" and noted his track record in large class actions. **Hamilton Stewart** (see p.1785) is "*an outstanding strategist,*" both in traditional labor matters and employment law. He has been advising clients in the automotive industry and recently represented a national company in a complex government-related union matter. "*Creative thinker*" **Lewis Smoak** (see p.1784) was recommended for his employment litigation defense work, especially that done in the field of class actions. **Fred Suggs** (see p.1785) has a broad advisory practice, including assistance to clients on employee contracts and noncompete agreements as well as negotiating collective bargaining agreements. He is thought to be "*extremely knowledgeable and very comfortable litigating before any court.*" Indeed, he has represented clients before the NLRB and EEOC, as well as state and federal courts and the US Courts of Appeal.

**Clients/Work Highlights:** GE; Milliken; Fluor; Michelin North America; SCANA Corporation and Duke Energy.

## Band 2

### Gignilliat, Savitz & Bettis LLP

**The Firm:** This Columbia employment boutique is viewed as a "*fine firm with a long history and a good stable of lawyers.*" The ten attorneys attend to the needs of "*an impressive list of clients*" from throughout the state, including public sector clients such as hospitals and municipalities. They are perhaps best-known for their defense of complex employment cases but also perform well in the area of employee benefits.

**The Lawyers:** The "*eminent*" **Vance Bettis** "*really knows employment law*" and has vast expertise of municipal and other state work. Fellow name partner **Stephen Savitz** is recommended both for his employment and labor counseling and his disputes practice.

**Clients/Work Highlights:** Many of the firm's clients are public entities, including hospitals and government departments.

### Nelson Mullins Riley & Scarborough LLP
See firm details p.1788

**The Firm:** The capability of the employment team at this state heavyweight is greatly enhanced by the presence of an exceptional general litigation group. Accordingly, market sources say the team delivers "*the same kind of all-around excellence that you expect from the rest of the firm,*" remarking in particular on the quality of its employment defense work. Lawyers represent management from a variety of industries.

**The Lawyers:** **Sue Harper** is a "*fantastic all-rounder*" who ably provides general commercial advice as well as assisting clients on specific employment problems. She has a successful track record in the defense of discrimination claims. "*Knowledgable and capable*" **Kenneth Young** leads the team, which also includes **Andreas Satterfield**, who has a broad advisory and litigation practice in this area of law.

**Clients/Work Highlights:** The client list includes companies in the manufacturing, health care and industrial sectors.

### Nexsen Pruet, LLC
See firm details p.1789

**The Firm:** The employment group at this South Carolina juggernaut is known for its "*timely and professional demeanour.*" Some 30 attorneys work in five of the firm's South Carolina offices, of whom clients report: "*They're accurate, responsive, and always know what they're doing.*" Their work encompasses general employment litigation and advice, traditional labor law, ERISA concerns and business immigration. The team represents both plaintiffs and defendants at trial, and recently negotiated a wage and hour class action involving several hundred employees for a significant international client. It is working on an ongoing collective bargaining matter for an international chemical manufacturer.

**The Lawyers:** **David Dubberly** (see p.1782) was widely praised as a "*solid and intelligent attorney.*" He divides his time between employment and traditional labor law, and recently defended a major state hospital in a breach of contract suit filed by a former physician. **Susi McWilliams** (see p.1783) is a "*responsive and knowledgeable source of advice.*" She maintains a broad commercial practice in addition to her complex employment litigation caseload.

**Clients/Work Highlights:** Orient Express; Verizon Wireless; Ryan's Restaurant; Tuomey Hospital and Honda of South Carolina Manufacturing.

## Band 3

### Jackson Lewis

**The Firm:** This is a national workplace law firm with a 15-lawyer employment group in Greenville. Interviewees viewed it as "*a solid statewide player*" and praised its extensive practice. In addition to employment litigation, employee benefits and health and safety matters, the team also advises on labor relations and force reduction. The firm takes on international work, provides immigration counseling and has a growing expertise in trade secrets agreements.

**The Lawyers:** "*Responsive and helpful*" managing partner **Steve Warren** (see p.1785) concentrates on labor relations and management training.

**Clients/Work Highlights:** The group represents public and private companies as well as nonprofit organizations.

# LITIGATION

| Litigation: General Commercial |
| --- |
| **Leading Firms** |

| 1 | HAYNSWORTH SINKLER BOYD PA *Charleston* |
|---|---|
| | NELSON MULLINS *Columbia* |
| | NEXSEN PRUET, LLC *Columbia* |
| | WYCHE *Greenville* |
| 2 | BUIST MOORE SMYTHE MCGEE PA *Charleston* |
| | LEATHERWOOD WALKER *Greenville* |
| | MCNAIR LAW FIRM PA *Columbia* |
| | OGLETREE, DEAKINS *Greenville* |
| | PRATT-THOMAS, EPTING & WALKER *Charleston* |
| | SOWELL GRAY STEPP & LAFFITTE LLC *Columbia* |
| | YOUNG, CLEMENT & RIVERS LLP *Charleston* |

| Leading Individuals |
| --- |

| | **Senior Statesman** |
|---|---|
| | OXNER Dewey *Haynsworth Sinkler Boyd PA* |
| 1 | DUKES David *Nelson Mullins* |
| | LINTON John *Haynsworth Sinkler Boyd PA* |
| | MORRISON Stephen *Nelson Mullins* |
| 2 | EPTING Andrew *Pratt-Thomas, Epting & Walker* |
| | HOWE JR Gedney *Gedney M Howe III PA* |
| | LIGHTSEY Wallace *Wyche* |
| | SOWELL Thornwell *Sowell Gray Stepp & Laffitte* |
| | STEPHENSON Thomas *Nexsen Pruet, LLC* |
| 3 | CLEVELAND III William *Buist Moore Smythe McGee* |
| | COCKRILL Donald *Ogletree, Deakins* |
| | HALL Kevin *Nelson Mullins* |
| | JONES Celeste *McNair Law Firm PA* |
| | MAJOR Joseph *Leatherwood Walker* |
| | MCWILLIAMS Susan *Nexsen Pruet, LLC* |
| | PARR Henry *Wyche* |
| | TATE Simmons *Haynsworth Sinkler Boyd PA* |
| | TESSIER Troy *Wyche* |
| | TISDALE Thomas *Nexsen Pruet, LLC* |
| | WALKER Trenholm *Pratt-Thomas, Epting & Walker* |
| | YOUNG JR Rutledge *Young, Clement & Rivers LLP* |

## Band 1

### Haynsworth Sinkler Boyd PA

**The Firm:** This South Carolina stalwart "*never fails to meet expectations.*" Forty attorneys offer a full service in litigation and dispute resolution, covering everything from antitrust and environmental disputes to health care and product liability. The firm's success rests on "*a deep bench of all-around excellent lawyers and a great client base.*" The firm has lately represented cellular phone dealers in a series of unfair trade and commercial tort actions. Other highlights include defending major health care providers in a series of ongoing class actions, and successfully representing Green Diamond Development in a federal court matter concerning a 2,000-acre development in the Columbia area.

**The Lawyers:** The "*outstanding*" **John Linton** was praised as an "*honorable, wise and reliable*" lawyer. He works generally in the field of commercial litigation and recently advised other attorneys, outside the firm, on certain internal disputes. **Simmons Tate** has a wealth of knowledge drawn from decades of appearing in state and federal courts. He is also a frequent and well-respected speaker on civil proceedings. **Dewey Oxner** has over 40 years' experience as a medical malpractice and product liability expert; he continues to be active in state and federal trials.

**Clients/Work Highlights:** Financial institutions; accounting firms; cellular phone companies; real estate developers and manufacturers are all on the client list.

### Nelson Mullins Riley & Scarborough LLP

See firm details p.1788

**The Firm:** Clients told researchers that this large team of litigators "*inspires the highest level of confidence in trial matters.*" The firm's size and its presence right across the state mean it has few true rivals for litigation; as one commentator put it: "*They can really pull in the manpower for major cases.*" Drawing strength from an outstanding corporate practice, the team offers an impressive spread of litigation expertise, acting most recently for hefty clients in the financial, pharmaceutical and chemical sectors. In addition to its cornerstone defense practice, the team also offers a highly regarded pre-litigation counseling and dispute resolution service. Ongoing work includes national pharmaceutical liability cases and product liability cases relating to automobiles and agricultural equipment.

**The Lawyers:** Managing partner **David Dukes** is "*a consistent and outstanding trial expert,*" according to market sources, who noted his vast experience in relation to pharmaceutical matters. He was recently elected head of the National Defense Attorney Association. **Stephen Morrison** is the department chair and was praised for his "*able mind and great experience.*" This includes handling numerous matters before the FTC. **Kevin Hall** comes recommended for his work in complex class actions and has expertise in technology and utiltities cases.

**Clients/Work Highlights:** Clients include financial institutions and government agencies, plus insurance, pharmaceutical and industrial companies.

# GENERAL COMMERCIAL

### Nexsen Pruet, LLC

See firm details p.1789

**The Firm:** Numbering almost 100 attorneys, the litigation group is very much the heart of the firm and was hailed as "*one of the premier groups in the state*" by clients and peers. They cited the team's "*remarkable scope and experience,*" and agreed that it was "*a go-to group for complex litigation.*" It has a broad commercial outlook and represents clients from all industries. Practice highlights include acting on behalf of a trust foundation in a complex boundary dispute, as well as representing significant insurance companies.

**The Lawyers:** One competitor said of **Thomas Stephenson** (see p.1785): "*He is someone we'd want at our firm!*" His is a general commercial and appellate practice, and he is highly rated for his skills as a mediator. **Thomas Tisdale** (see p.1785) is "*just excellent in a courtroom,*" according to his clients. His practice includes estate management disputes as well as general commercial matters. **Susi McWilliams** (see p.1783) "*never drops the ball.*" She exhibits "*a succinct approach and attention to detail*" in complex litigation matters.

**Clients/Work Highlights:** Banks and financial institutions, as well as insurance, accountancy, pharmaceutical and technology companies are all on the client list.

### Wyche, Burgess, Freeman & Parham, PA

See firm details p.1791

**The Firm:** This "*wonderful blue-chip firm,*" based in Greenville and Columbia, employs "*some of the brightest attorneys in the state,*" researchers learned. It drew plaudits for its lawyers' "*responsiveness, professionalism and knowledge,*" as well as for its continued interest in the local market despite having a regional and national profile. "*It is very involved in the Greenville community – I really like that,*" reported one client. Litigation matters are central to the firm's business, and the team has real breadth of experience: antitrust, employment, First Amendment, real estate, product liability and media litigation supplement a vast general commercial caseload. There is a niche in design and architectural copyright matters, and the firm recently settled a copyright infringement dispute concerning a residential development project on behalf of an architect client. It is presently handling numerous ongoing medical malpractice and employment disputes, as well as an antitrust matter for Hillenbrand relating to hospital equipment purchases.

**The Lawyers:** *"Forthright"* **Wallace Lightsey** (see p.1783) is *"a brilliant communicator"* with particular expertise in First Amendment matters. **Troy Tessier** (see p.1785) has a product liability and IP caseload and *"fantastic knowledge of insurance matters."* **Henry Parr** (see p.1784) joins the tables following strong client endorsement. Commentators felt him to be *"a brilliant trial attorney with an encyclopedic knowledge of the law."* His general commercial litigation practice includes antitrust matters.

**Clients/Work Highlights:** Bowater Incorporated; Carolina First Bank; Centerplate; Chubb Group; InRe Financial; KEMET Electronics; Michelin North America; Milliken & Company and South Financial Group.

## Band 2

### Buist Moore Smythe McGee PA
See firm details p.1786

**The Firm:** This is a *"professional and diligent team"* with a particular forte in banking and financial matters. It has represented financial institutions in a range of lender liability cases and employee fraud matters. On the agenda, too, are creditor rights representations, and residential and commercial foreclosure matters. The group has also represented clients from the tobacco, energy, telecom, insurance and real estate sectors.

**The Lawyers:** Group head **William Cleveland** (see p.1781) is *"an excellent and meticulous adviser."* While he maintains a diverse portfolio of business litigation matters, he is also recommended as a trained dispute mediator.

**Clients/Work Highlights:** Banks; financial institutions; individual stockholders and private companies make up the client roster.

### Leatherwood Walker Todd & Mann PC
See firm details p.1787

**The Firm:** This *"knowledgeable and detail-oriented"* group is *"not just an excellent legal team but also delightfully nonantagonistic."* It comprises a dozen litigators whose practice portfolio includes IP and business fraud in addition to general commercial trial matters. It has an unusual specialty – the defense of claims relating to tractor-trailers – and one recent highlight was the defense of a mobile home manufacturer in a significant product liability claim. The team is ongoing trial counsel for Chubb

Group and frequently represents pharmaceutical companies and financial institutions. Several medical malpractice suits have been settled before trial in the past year.

**The Lawyers:** Clients reported that **Joseph Major** is *"a pleasure to work with,"* and were particularly impressed with his *"wide experience and excellent connections."* Major concentrates on medical malpractice, fraud and product liability cases. He is additionally appellate counsel for an underwriters' association.

**Clients/Work Highlights:** Clients include insurance companies, financial institutions and manufacturers, including the producers of tractors and mobile homes.

### McNair Law Firm PA

**The Firm:** The *"astute"* Columbia litigation team at this national player has developed *"an enviable health care practice."* Many members of the 35-strong team have particular specialisms, not only related to health care and pharmaceuticals but also in the areas of regulatory law, insurance and corporate and bond litigation.

**The Lawyers:** **Celeste Jones** (see p.179643) has an impressive health care portfolio, which sees her representing hospitals, pharmaceutical companies and medical suppliers.

### Ogletree, Deakins, Nash, Smoak & Stewart, PC
See firm details p.738

**The Firm:** The national labor and employment firm has an *"impressive"* team of 22 litigators who not only dominate the employment disputes scene in the state but also represent clients in general commercial matters. Product liability, environmental and business contract disputes are important aspects of the practice.

**The Lawyers:** **Donald Cockrill** (see p.1782) is *"bright, knowledgeable and successful,"* according to enthusiastic clients. He focuses on environmental and toxic tort claims, as well as employment and labor law.

### Pratt-Thomas, Epting & Walker PA

**The Firm:** There was effusive praise for this *"outstanding and highly visible litigation boutique,"* which competes well with the larger firms. The Charleston-based team has broad experience, including expertise in IP and municipal liability matters, and is noted for its *"innovative and fresh"* approach to complex business disputes. It has an impressive civil litigation practice, featuring PI, product liability and workers' compensation disputes.

**The Lawyers:** Interviewees praised **Andrew Epting** for his *"diligence and keen legal mind."* **Trenholm**

**Walker** is billed as *"one of the most diverse trial attorneys around."* Clients say, *"he's a wonderful mediator and good to have in a tight spot."*

**Clients/Work Highlights:** The firm's corporate clients include a number of insurance companies and health care organizations.

### Sowell Gray Stepp & Laffitte LLC
See firm details p.1790

**The Firm:** Some 20 Columbia-based attorneys offer a full litigation service. Clients noted the *"high quality of their work,"* particularly in medical malpractice and other professional and general liability, employment law and probate litigation. The firm also has a proven track record in regulatory and compliance advice, plus plenty of experience of mediation and pretrial dispute resolution. The client base extends to government bodies and financial institutions as well as prominent private companies.

**The Lawyers:** Commentators were delighted with **Thornwell Sowell**'s (see p.1784) *"extraordinary ability and ease in trial proceedings."* His practice encompasses a wide range of commercial proceedings, representing clients from the media, financial services and other commercial sectors.

**Clients/Work Highlights:** Investment banks, financial institutions and government bodies are among those that turn to the firm.

### Young, Clement & Rivers LLP

**The Firm:** A more compact outfit than most in this table, this Charleston firm is a respected player in the state. It has a strong focus on IP and its most prominent clients include technology, telecom and software companies.

**The Lawyers:** The *"excellent"* **Rutledge Young** is a great choice for health care matters, according to interviewees. His practice also includes product liability and complex commercial disputes in both state and federal courts.

**Clients/Work Highlights:** The clientele includes media, manufacturing, telecom and software companies.

### Other Notable Practitioners

**Gedney Howe** of Gedney M Howe III PA is highly recommended for PI and product liability claims, representing primarily plaintiffs. Commentators noted his *"extraordinary courtroom presence"* and were particularly impressed with his *"unwavering client focus and dedication to the job."*

# REAL ESTATE

### Real Estate
#### Leading Firms

1. **BUIST MOORE SMYTHE MCGEE PA** *Charleston*
   **MCNAIR LAW FIRM PA** *Columbia*
   **NEXSEN PRUET, LLC** *Columbia*
2. **GOTTLIEB & SMITH PA** *Columbia*
   **HAYNSWORTH SINKLER BOYD PA** *Charleston*
   **NELSON MULLINS** *Columbia*
3. **JEFFCOAT PIKE & NAPPIER LLC** *Myrtle Beach*
   **LEATHERWOOD WALKER** *Greenville*
   **WARREN & SINKLER LLP** *Charleston*
   **WOMBLE CARLYLE** *Greenville*

#### Leading Individuals

★ **MENZIE Edward** *Nexsen Pruet, LLC*

1. **BOONE JR Sidney** *McNair Law Firm PA*
   **ESTRIDGE Larry** *Womble Carlyle*
   **GAILLARD W Foster** *Buist Moore Smythe McGee*
   **GOTTLIEB Joel** *Gottlieb & Smith PA*
   **WARREN III John** *Warren & Sinkler LLP*
2. **BOYD William** *Haynsworth Sinkler Boyd*
   **ELLEFSON Anne** *Haynsworth Sinkler Boyd*
   **ELLISON Morris** *Buist Moore Smythe McGee*
   **ROBINSON JR Neil** *Nexsen Pruet, LLC*
   **SWANSON David** *Haynsworth Sinkler Boyd*
3. **BOBO JR William** *Nelson Mullins*
   **GOSSETT David** *Nexsen Pruet, LLC*
   **JEFFCOAT III Otis** *Jeffcoat Pike & Nappier LLC*
   **MCINNIS Judith** *McNair Law Firm PA*
   **QUATTLEBAUM Marvin** *Leatherwood Walker*
   **SMITH W Lindsay** *Womble Carlyle*
   **SMYTHE Susan** *Buist Moore Smythe McGee*

## Band 1

### Buist Moore Smythe McGee PA

See firm details p.1786

**The Firm:** This *"outstanding"* team was highly praised for its *"visibility and professionalism"* across the full spectrum of real estate matters. Based in Charleston, the eight-strong group is an integral part of the state's booming industry, acting for developers and owners of commercial and residential projects. It has prowess in complex zoning and land conservation matters, as well as its experience in sophisticated real estate financing. Lawyers have advised significant clients in resort and tourist developments, negotiating over golf courses and marine complexes among other recreational ventures. Recent highlights include refinancing a series of luxury hotels across three states, and negotiating with conservationists on the sale of 4,000 acres of land close to an urban area.

**The Lawyers: Foster Gaillard** (see p.1782) is *"diligent and accommodating," "I'd always recommend him,"* one satisfied client told researchers. He focuses on hotel and condominium development, and also represents institutional lenders in real estate financings. **Morris Ellison** (see p.1782) brings *"all-around excellence"* to his work. A skilled real estate transactionalist, he is also excellent in banking and finance matters and is a respected litigator. **Susan Smythe** (see p.1784) *"has phenomenal intellectual ability and energy, and is one of the best problem solvers in town."* Her conservation and development expertise are of especial interest to clients planning residential and resort complexes. She recently worked on a further phase of a large development at Daniel Island on behalf of a major client.

**Clients/Work Highlights:** Banks; financial institutions; developers and tract builders.

### McNair Law Firm PA

**The Firm:** This Carolinas stalwart has 30 real estate attorneys working from seven offices across the state; it is particularly strong along the coast. Interviewees called the group *"able and extremely professional"* and were particularly impressed with its achievements in zoning matters. Other areas of expertise for this versatile group include residential, office and industrial development, construction and environmental concerns. It performs well in finance, advising on construction and long-term lending.

**The Lawyers:** Well-known **Sidney Boone** was labeled *"an outstanding transactional attorney."* Although active in a wide range of real estate matters, residential developments take prominence. **Judith McInnis** was singled out for her real estate finance advice; she commonly works for lenders but also acts for developers involved in complex commercial projects.

**Clients/Work Highlights:** Developers; financial institutions; manufacturing and industrial concerns.

### Nexsen Pruet, LLC

See firm details p.1789

**The Firm:** The real estate team at this regional heavyweight is consistently praised for the breadth and scope of its practice. There is a substantive operation in each of its seven offices across the state, each benefiting from the current development boom. Work ranges from cell phone tower construction to the redevelopment of former ports and naval bases, and securing land for golf courses and marina construction. Recent highlights include negotiating a $40 million acquisition for a resort developer, as well as handling entitlement matters for a remediated former industrial site prior to its sale.

**The Lawyers:** Vastly experienced, **Edward Menzie** (see p.1783) is *"a whirlwind of brilliance"* and ideal for *"the most unique and innovative deals."* He is a frequent speaker at South Carolina Bar Association seminars. *"A stalwart for complex deals,"* **Neil Robinson** (see p.1784) advises large developers on permitting, zoning and regulatory issues. He has recently worked on developments of former landfill sites. Commentators say the *"outstanding"* **David Gossett** (see p.1783) is a true authority on real estate finance. He has lately served as lead counsel on significant real estate secured financings, including one in Florida

that totaled $170 million.

**Clients/Work Highlights:** The team represents lenders, developers and construction companies across the region, as well as manufacturers and utilities.

## Band 2

### Gottlieb & Smith PA

**The Firm:** Interviewees sang the praises of this compact team, whose reputation for quality commercial, residential and retail real estate work easily matches some of the state's largest players. One client told us: *"They know exactly what an entrepreneur needs – I have no reason to go anywhere else."* Based in Columbia, the team offers a full service with particular emphasis on major retail developments. It has represented some of the country's largest developers of shopping malls in more than 15 states, and has also acted for domestic and international timberland investors and forestry products companies. Other areas of expertise include title insurance matters and extensive residential and condominium developments and resort complexes.

**The Lawyers: Joel Gottlieb** is *"active, capable and the first name for complex retail matters,"* according to interviewees. In addition to retail development and acquisition, he also represents office and residential developers.

**Clients/Work Highlights:** Retail, residential and office developers.

### Haynsworth Sinkler Boyd PA

**The Firm:** Of this *"excellent and efficient"* group, clients said: *"They're the people to go to with a complicated transaction."* The real estate department operates from all four of the firm's offices across the state, offering a full service that caters for residential, commercial and industrial developers. There is particular experience in large and complex real estate projects, such as major office parks and shopping centers. Lawyers are familiar with all the usual real estate investment and financing deals, as well as zoning and land use issues. The team recently handled several title insurance matters for federal agencies and has frequently represented a significant regional bank in real estate financings.

**The Lawyers: William Boyd** is *"extremely knowledgeable and highly recommended"* for finance deals and large-scale property acquisitions. His clients also benefit from his significant corporate knowledge. **David Swanson** *"does a precise and impressive job,"* according to those familiar with his work. His practice centers on retail and office development work, as well as complex real estate financing, where he frequently advises Bank of America and Wachovia among others. Interviewees described **Anne Ellefson** as *"diligent and first-class."* She represents commercial developers as well as owners in complex commercial transactions and a number of REITs.

**Clients/Work Highlights:** Liberty Property Trust,

Lazarus Shouse and SunTrust are among the group's most important clients.

## Nelson Mullins Riley & Scarborough LLP

See firm details p.1788

**The Firm:** Nelson Mullins has "*a strong group who pull well together.*" Fourteen real estate attorneys across the state provide a full service, including lender and developer representation as well as construction and title insurance counsel. Other strong suits are federal and state environmental permit negotiations concerning wetland issues and, in conjunction with the firm's bankruptcy department, workout agreements and loan transactions. Clients come from all industries, among them forestry and paper companies, resort developers and major title insurance companies.

**The Lawyers:** **William Bobo** is "*a really creative thinker*" whose work centers on commercial and residential development. He is an active member of the local and national Bar associations.

**Clients/Work Highlights:** Developers; insurance companies; financial institutions and construction companies are among the firm's clients.

## Band 3

### Jeffcoat Pike & Nappier LLC (Myrtle Beach)

**The Firm:** This smaller firm with a sizable coastal presence continues to make waves in the commercial and residential markets: researchers were told that "*any list of the best real estate groups should include this one.*" Seven lawyers take on real estate matters,

covering construction, planning disputes, title insurance and environmental concerns as well as all the usual types of commercial transactions.

**The Lawyers:** **Otis Allen Jeffcoat** is widely thought to be "*capable of handling any deal.*" He represents developers and lenders right across the market, is a member of the Freshwater Wetland Forum and has acted as an expert witness in state and federal courts.

**Clients/Work Highlights:** Lenders; developers; realtors; government agencies and homeowners' associations.

### Leatherwood Walker Todd & Mann PC

See firm details p.1787

**The Firm:** This is an "*impressive, substantial group,*" according to market sources, who deemed the attorneys to be "*technical and experienced.*" Noted for its excellent zoning practice, the team also tackles a wide range of real estate financings and sophisticated corporate transactions. Ample experience in the residential, retail, office and industrial markets has been built up by lawyers who cater to lenders, developers and sellers, as well as significant financial institutions.

**The Lawyers:** There was enthusiastic support for **Marvin Quattlebaum:** clients said he is "*just fantastic*" and "*always the first person we call with a problem.*" He has plenty of experience with financial institutions and government agencies.

### Warren & Sinkler LLP

**The Firm:** This "*highly respected and versatile*" group is said to show "*innovation and quality.*" Four real estate attorneys represent developers and lenders in complex commercial, residential and resort projects; they are currently engaged in a joint venture between

a private developer and the City of Charleston. The team has increased involvement in timberlands and conservation matters.

**The Lawyers:** **John Warren**'s real estate portfolio is just one element of his broad commercial practice. The "*professional and competent*" attorney is particularly known for high-value real estate finance transactions.

**Clients/Work Highlights:** Banks, developers and investors all use the firm.

### Womble Carlyle Sandridge & Rice, PLLC

See firm details p.1589

**The Firm:** The Greenville office of this regional heavyweight includes a respected and growing real estate team that offers a full service to clients from all industries. "*They have great resources and accessible, knowledgeable attorneys,*" commentators confirmed. Particular areas of expertise include lending, zoning, commercial leasing and real estate litigation.

**The Lawyers:** **Larry Estridge** (see p.1782) is "*a business-oriented attorney*" whose commercial acumen is matched by excellent connections in the community. "*He's the one to go to for major projects,*" one client assured researchers. **Lindsay Smith** (see p.1784) was recommended for inclusion in the tables this year as "*one of the best real estate lenders' lawyers in the state.*" Smith also advises borrowers and has acted on an extensive range of residential, retail and office developments.

# Leaders in South Carolina

**AMSTUTZ, Eric B**
Wyche, Burgess, Freeman & Parham, PA, Greenville 864 242 8201
eamstutz@wyche.com
*Recommended in Corporate/M&A*
**Practice Areas:** Mergers and acquisitions; securities; contracts; corporate; public-private development. Eric Amstutz concentrates his practice in the representation of publicly traded companies and the negotiation and drafting of complex agreements, including business mergers; acquisitions; dispositions and spin-offs; securities offerings of debt and equity securities; tender offers; proxy contests; public company board governance; government-private sector transactions. He is admitted to practice in South Carolina State and Federal Courts, the United States Court of Appeals for the Fourth Circuit, and the United States Supreme Court.
**Prof. Memberships:** District of Columbia Bar Association since 1980; South

Carolina Bar Association since 1981.
**Career:** Law clerk to the Honorable Gerhard A Gesell, United States District Court for the District of Columbia, 1978-79; law clerk to the Honorable Potter Steward, associate Justice, United States Supreme Court, 1979-80. Associate, Wyche Burgess Freeman & Parham, P.A. 1981-84. Member of the Wyche law firm from 1984 to present.
**Personal:** Swarthmore College (BA, with highest honors,1975); Phi Beta Kappa; Yale University (JD, 1978). Listed in 'The Best Lawyers In America'.

**BETTIS, Vance**
Gignilliat, Savitz & Bettis LLP, Columbia
803 799 9311
*Recommended in Employment*

**BLAKE JR, Joseph**
Haynsworth Sinkler Boyd PA, Greenville
864 240 3200
*Recommended in Corporate/M&A*

**BOBO JR, William**
Nelson Mullins Riley & Scarborough LLP, Columbia 803 799 2000
*Recommended in Real Estate*

**BOONE JR, Sidney**
McNair Law Firm PA, Columbia
803 799 9800
*Recommended in Real Estate*

**BOYD, William**
Haynsworth Sinkler Boyd PA, Charleston
843 722 3366
*Recommended in Corporate/M&A, Real Estate*

**CARROUTH, Michael**
Fisher & Phillips LLP, Columbia
803 255 0000
mcarrouth@laborlawyers.com
*Recommended in Employment*
**Practice Areas:** Mike Carrouth is certified as a specialist in employment and labor law by the South Carolina Supreme Court. Carrouth represents management only in a wide array of employment,

labor, and litigation matters. He practices before the state and federal courts, the National Labor Relations Board, and state and federal administrative agencies in the areas of union avoidance, union campaigns, labor relations, employment litigation, discrimination cases, non-compete agreements, and wrongful discharge cases. He received his JD from the University of South Carolina School of Law in 1988.

**CLEVELAND III, William**
Buist Moore Smythe McGee P.A.,
Charleston 843 722 3400
wcleveland@bmsmlaw.com
*Recommended in Litigation*
**Practice Areas:** Head of the firm's Business and Commercial Litigation Group. Handles a broad range of business disputes including those involing intellectual property, securities, lender liability and corporate control issues.
**Prof. Memberships:** Has just completed his service as President of the Interna-

tional Association of Defense Counsel (IADC), an invitation-only association of approximatley 2200 lawyers who represent corporations and insurers. In 1999, served as Director of the Defense Counsel Trial Academy, a week-long school for young lawyers conducted every summer at the University of Colorado in Boulder. Is currently a Member of the American Board of Trial Advocates, the Board of Directors of the Defense Research Institute and the Board of Directors of Lawyers for Civil Justice.

**Career:** Admitted to the Bar of California in 1975 and South Carolina in 1979. After finishing law school, practiced with the firm of Bronson, Bronson & McKinnon in San Francisco before moving back to his home state of South Carolina.

**Publications:** Has a special interest in the use of technology in the courtroom and is a frequent speaker on the topic at continuing legal education seminars.

**Personal:** Received a JD from the Univeristy of Virginia in 1975 and a BA from Yale University in 1972.

### COCKRILL, Donald A
Ogletree, Deakins, Nash, Smoak & Stewart, PC, Greenville 864 271 1300
donald.cockrill@ogletreedeakins.com
*Recommended in Litigation*

**Practice Areas:** Labor and employment, civil litigation (products liability, business torts, commercial disputes, class actions), environmental and toxic tort litigation.

**Prof. Memberships:** District of Columbia Bar Association, South Carolina Bar Association, American Bar Association.

**Career:** Admitted to practice in South Carolina, District of Columbia, US Supreme Court, and US Court of Appeals (Fourth and Eleventh Circuits).

**Personal:** Vanderbilt University (BA, 1965), University of Virginia Law School (LLB, 1968).

### CURRIE, John
McNair Law Firm PA, Columbia
803 799 9800
*Recommended in Corporate/M&A*

### DERRICK, Elizabeth O
Womble Carlyle Sandridge & Rice, PLLC, Greenville 864 255 5415
BDerrick@wcsr.com
*Recommended in Corporate/M&A*

**Practice Areas:** Betty concentrates in securities and corporate law, including advising issuers and underwriters in connection with public offerings and private placements of securities. She represents public and private companies in a variety of merger and acquisition transactions. A significant portion of her practice involves providing general corporate and securities counsel on matters such as SEC compliance, securities and disclosure issues and corporate governance matters.

**Personal:** JD, 1989, University of North Carolina School of Law; editor, Journal of International Law and Commercial Regulation; Joyner Award For Legal Writing. BA, 1986, University of North Carolina at Chapel Hill.

### DIXON, Augustus
Nelson Mullins Riley & Scarborough LLP, Columbia 803 799 2000
*Recommended in Corporate/M&A*

### DUBBERLY, David E
Nexsen Pruet, LLC, Columbia
803 253 8281
ddubberly@nexsenpruet.com
*Recommended in Employment*

**Practice Areas:** Member of Employment and International Practice Groups. Certified by the South Carolina Supreme Court as a Specialist in Employment and Labor Law since 1993. Mr Dubberly has successfully defended companies in employment lawsuits in several federal and state courts. He has also helped clients negotiate international joint venture, distribution, and licensing agreements, and set up sales offices and distribution centers in the US and approximately 10 countries in Latin America, Europe, and Asia. Fluent in Spanish.

**Prof. Memberships:** Admitted in South Carolina; US Court of International Trade; US Courts of Appeals for the Fourth, Sixth, and Federal Circuits. Vice-Chair, International Employment Law Committee, ABA (2004-present); Chair, Foreign Investment in the US Committee, ABA (2001-04). Member of the SC Supreme Court's Employment and Labor Specialization Advisory Board (1995-98). Chairman of the SC Bar's Employment and Labor Law Section (1992-93) and of the International Law Committee (1998-2001).

**Career:** Law clerk to the Honorable Curtis G Shaw, Associate Justice, SC Court of Appeals (1984-85).

**Publications:** 'New Military Leave Regulations Clarify National Guard and Reserve Obligations', South Carolina Business Journal (March 2006); 'Federal Appeals Court Rejects Private Releases Of FMLA Claims', South Carolina Lawyers Weekly (October 2005); 'Sarbanes-Oxley Update: Whistleblower Wins Reinstatement', South Carolina Business Journal (May 2005).

**Personal:** JD, University of South Carolina, 1984; BA, cum laude, Bob Jones University, 1981.

### DUKES, David
Nelson Mullins Riley & Scarborough LLP, Columbia 803 799 2000
*Recommended in Litigation*

### ELLEFSON, Anne
Haynsworth Sinkler Boyd PA, Greenville
864 240 3200
*Recommended in Real Estate*

### ELLISON, Morris
Buist Moore Smythe McGee P.A., Charleston 843 720 4614
mellison@bmsmlaw.com
*Recommended in Real Estate*

**Practice Areas:** Practice includes commercial transactions and litigation, banking law and commercial real estate. Also an arbitrator for the American Arbitration Association and a Circuit Court approved mediator.

**Prof. Memberships:** Fellow of the American College of Mortgage Attorneys, Fellow of the American College of Real Estate Lawyers, Co-Chairman, American Bar Association Hotels, Resorts and Tourism Committee, Past Chairman, Real Estate Council of the South Carolina Bar, Member, Real Estate and Business Law Sections of the American Bar Association and the South Carolina Bar, South Carolina Law Institute, Member, Advisory Committee for Article 2A of the Uniform Commercial Code, Associate Member, South Carolina Bankers Association.

**Career:** Admitted to South Carolina Bar (1982). Law clerk to the Honorable James C Hill, Circuit Judge for the United States Court of Appeals for the Eleventh Circuit, Atlanta, Georgia, 1982-83. Listed in a leading legal publication.

**Publications:** Contributing author, 'Foreclosure Law & Related Remedies, A State-by-State Digest', (ABA 1995).

**Personal:** Received JD from Duke University School of Law in 1982 and a BA, magna cum laude, from Yale University in 1979.

### ELLZEY, Daniel
Fisher & Phillips LLP, Columbia
803 255 0000
dellzey@laborlawyers.com
*Recommended in Employment*

**Practice Areas:** Dan Ellzey is certified as a specialist in employment and labor law by the South Carolina Supreme Court. In the employment area, Ellzey counsels clients on and litigates discrimination, retaliation, wrongful discharge, non-compete, wage and hour, plant closure, OSHA, and other employment issues. In the labor area, he is extensively involved in preventive union avoidance work and has participated in some of the highest profile union campaigns in the United States. Co-author of the South Carolina Employers Reference Manual, Ellzey received his JD from the University of South Carolina and an MBA from the University of Utah.

### EPTING, Andrew
Pratt-Thomas, Epting & Walker PA, Charleston 843 727 2200
*Recommended in Litigation*

### ESTRIDGE, Larry D
Womble Carlyle Sandridge & Rice, PLLC, Greenville 864 255 5401
lestridge@wcsr.com
*Recommended in Real Estate*

**Practice Areas:** Larry Estridge has 35 years of experience in all facets of real estate acquisition, finance and development, including zoning and other land use and regulation issues. He represents buyers, sellers, lenders, brokers, developers, lessors and lessees.

**Prof. Memberships:** South Carolina Bar Association; Georgia Bar Association.

**Career:** US Army, 1969-71, served in Vietnam as battalion defense counsel for courts martial, awarded Bronze Star. JD, 1969, Harvard University; BA, 1966, Furman University, 'cum laude', Student Body President, Blue Key, History Award, Hughes Trophy (Outstanding Army ROTC Graduate in US).

### FEW JR, Richard
Leatherwood Walker Todd & Mann PC, Greenville 864 242 6440
*Recommended in Corporate/M&A*

### FRITZE, Daniel
Nelson Mullins Riley & Scarborough LLP, Columbia 803 799 2000
*Recommended in Corporate/M&A*

### GAILLARD, W Foster
Buist Moore Smythe McGee P.A., Charleston 843 720 4610
fgaillard@bmsmlaw.com
*Recommended in Real Estate*

**Practice Areas:** Head of the Commercial Real Estate Department of his firm, he routinely handles complex commercial real estate transactions, banking law and business law matters. He has extensive experience in representing corporate and individual clients in all aspects of real estate law, including contract negotiations, zoning and land use issues, financing, regulatory matters and closing the transaction. Clients include owners and developers of shopping centers, office buildings, industrial facilities, apartment complexes, hotels, retail and mixed use developments, and planned unit developments. His practice also includes the representation of various banks and other institutional lenders in all aspects of real estate lending.

**Prof. Memberships:** South Carolina and American Bar Associations, Immediate Past Chair of the South Carolina Bar Real Estate Practices Section, Member of ABA Books/Media Committee, American College of Real Estate Lawyers.

**Career:** Admitted to South Carolina Bar (1973). A Principal in Buist Moore Smythe & McGee, PA since joining firm in 1986. Listed in a leading legal publication.

**Publications:** Contributing Author, 'Foreclosure and Related Remedies: A State by State Digest', (ABA 1995).

**Personal:** Received BA from Washington & Lee University in 1970 and JD from the University of South Carolina School of Law in 1973.

**GOSSETT, David**
Nexsen Pruet, LLC, Greenville
864 370 2211
dgossett@nexsenpruet.com
*Recommended in Real Estate*
**Practice Areas:** David Gossett concentrates his practice in economic development, real estate and lending, and includes extensive experience representing a wide variety of banking and financial institutions on complex real estate, asset-based, commercial, construction and development loan transactions, as well as workouts and debt restructuring. He is also regularly involved in financing some of the larger agribusinesses in the country. Mr Gossett is also active in economic development, representing new and expanding businesses in the Upstate of South Carolina in all phases of their projects.
**Prof. Memberships:** Upstate Alliance, (Board of Directors); South Carolina Economic Developers Alliance; National Council of Farmer Cooperatives (Legal, Tax and Accounting Subcommittee); South Carolina Bar; North Carolina Bar Association.
**Personal:** University of South Carolina, JD, 1986; Columbia Bible College, BS, 1979; South Carolina Honors College.

**GOTTLIEB, Joel**
Gottlieb & Smith PA, Columbia
803 765 9291
*Recommended in Real Estate*

**GRAYSON, Neil**
Nelson Mullins Riley & Scarborough LLP, Greenville 864 250 2300
*Recommended in Corporate/M&A*

**HALL, Kevin**
Nelson Mullins Riley & Scarborough LLP, Columbia 803 799 2000
*Recommended in Litigation*

**HALL JR, Cary H**
Wyche, Burgess, Freeman & Parham, PA, Greenville 864 242 8255
chall@wyche.com
*Recommended in Corporate/M&A*
**Practice Areas:** Certified specialist in taxation law. Corporate, mergers and acquisitions. Cary Hall's practice is equally divided between general corporate representation and tax matters.
**Prof. Memberships:** South Carolina Bar Association since 1975.
**Career:** Associate, Wyche Burgess Freeman & Parham, P.A. 1975-80. Member of the Wyche law firm from 1980 to present.
**Personal:** Princeton University (AB, with honors in Economics, 1969); Harvard University (JD, cum laude, 1975); Harvard Journal on Legislation (editor; 1973-74, managing editor, 1974-75). Listed in the past 10 consecutive issues of 'The Best Lawyers In America'.

**HARPER, Sue Erwin**
Nelson Mullins Riley & Scarborough LLP, Columbia 803 799 2000
*Recommended in Employment*

**HOGUE JR, P Mason**
Nelson Mullins Riley & Scarborough LLP, Columbia 803 799 2000
*Recommended in Corporate/M&A*

**HOWE JR, Gedney**
Gedney M Howe III PA, Charleston
843 722 8048
*Recommended in Litigation*

**JEFFCOAT III, Otis**
Jeffcoat Pike & Nappier LLC (Myrtle Beach), Myrtle Beach 843 626 9000
*Recommended in Real Estate*

**JONES, Celeste**
McNair Law Firm PA, Columbia
803 799 9800
*Recommended in Litigation*

**KING JR, George**
Haynsworth Sinkler Boyd PA, Charleston
843 722 3366
*Recommended in Corporate/M&A*

**KNIGHT, G Marcus**
Nexsen Pruet, LLC, Columbia
803 253 8245
mknight@nexsenpruet.com
*Recommended in Corporate/M&A*
**Practice Areas:** More than 20 years' experience practicing in the securities, mergers and acquisitions, corporate, LLC and partnership areas.
**Prof. Memberships:** A past Chairman of the SC Bar's Corporation, Banking and Securities Section, he also chaired the section's Securities, Partnership, Securities Legislative Study Committees, and continues to lead legislative activities involving limited liability company and securities laws. He is the SC liaison for the ABA Business Section's Corporate Committee.
**Career:** Knight was twice published in the law review as a student at the USC Law School. A frequent speaker on various M&A, securities, and corporate topics, Knight also published a leading article on limited partnerships in the USC Law Review in 1985. Two leading legal publications have named Knight among the best SC lawyers practicing in corporate, M&A and securities law. Knight served as a special hearing officer for the SC Securities Commission in 2003-04. He is a Founding Member and President of the Executive Committee of the SC Investor Network and serves on the 2005 Executive Committee as Legal Chair for InnoVenture, an important Southeastern US venture capital conference.
**Personal:** JD, cum laude, University of South Carolina, 1981; BA, summa cum laude, Furman University, 1978.

**LIGHTSEY, Wallace K**
Wyche, Burgess, Freeman & Parham, PA, Greenville 864 242 8207
wlightsey@wyche.com
*Recommended in Litigation*
**Practice Areas:** Litigation; media and communications; constitutional law; intellectual property. Wallace Lightsey has a diverse litigation practice involving complex securities, corporate, and intellectual property cases, as well as personal injury, news media, and construction litigation. Mr Lightsey is an experienced trial attorney, with well over 50 jury trials in his career, and has argued numerous appeals in the South Carolina Appellate Courts and the United States Court of Appeals for the Fourth Circuit. Mr Lightsey also advises clients on matters involving copyright, trademark and trade secret issues.
**Prof. Memberships:** South Carolina Bar Association since 1986. Chairman, South Carolina Commission on Lawyer Conduct, 1997-2004. Member, South Carolina Fee Disputes Resolution Board; Member, South Carolina Board of Commissioners on Grievances; Member South Carolina Secretary of State Blue Ribbon Committee on Corporations (1998). Fellow, American College of Trial Lawyers.
**Career:** Law clerk to the Honorable John Minor Wisdom, United States Court of Appeals for the Fifth Circuit, 1983-84; Law Clerk to the Honorable Warren E Burger, Chief Justice of the United States, 1984-85. Associate, Wyche Burgess Freeman & Parham, P.A., 1986-89. Member of the Wyche law firm from 1989 to present.
**Publications:** Author, 'Defamation and Invasion of Privacy', South Carolina Law of Damages (2004); author, South Carolina chapter of '50-State Survey: Media Libel Law' (Libel Defense Resource Center/Media Law Resource Center ed, 2001, 2002, 2003, 2004, 2005); author, South Carolina chapter of '50-State Survey: Media Privacy and Related Law' (Libel Defense Resource Center/Media Law Resource Center ed., 2001, 2002, 2003, 2004, 2005); Chairman and contributing author, 'Libel and Slander', South Carolina Jurisprudence (1993); contributing author, 'Appeal and Error', South Carolina Jurisprudence (1992); author, 'A Critique of the Promise Model of Contract', 26 William & Mary Law Review 45 (1984); author, Note, 'Disengaging Sales Law from the Sales Construct: A Proposal to Extend the Scope of Article 2 of the UCC', 96 Harvard Law Review 470 (1982).
**Personal:** Duke University (AB, summa cum laude, 1979; Phi Beta Kappa; Harvard University (JD, cum laude, 1983); Harvard Law Review (editor, 1981-82; Executive Editor, 1982-83). Listed in the past 10 consecutive issues of the 'The Best Lawyers In America'.

**LINTON, John**
Haynsworth Sinkler Boyd PA, Charleston
843 722 3366
*Recommended in Litigation*

**MAJOR, Joseph**
Leatherwood Walker Todd & Mann PC, Greenville 864 242 6440
*Recommended in Litigation*

**MCINNIS, Judith**
McNair Law Firm PA, Columbia
803 799 9800
*Recommended in Real Estate*

**MCKINNEY, Kathleen**
Haynsworth Sinkler Boyd PA, Greenville
864 240 3200
*Recommended in Corporate/M&A*

**MCWILLIAMS, Susan**
Nexsen Pruet, LLC, Columbia
803 253 8221
smcwilliams@nexsenpruet.com
*Recommended in Employment, Litigation*
**Practice Areas:** Susi McWilliams is a trial lawyer with experience in complex litigation, including products liability, employment, business litigation, malpractice defense, securities, and lender liability.
**Prof. Memberships:** Fellow, American College of Trial Lawyers; American Board of Trial Advocates; South Carolina and Georgia Bars; Richland County Bar Association (President, 1998-99); American Bar Association; Federation of Defense and Corporate Counsel; Defense Research Institute; and South Carolina Defense Trial Lawyers Association.
**Career:** Certified Specialist in Labor and Employment Law, South Carolina Supreme Court; In 2005 appointed to the South Carolina Ethics Commission by SC's Governor; 2006 ed 'Best Lawyers in America'; recipient, Columbia YMCA's Tribute to Women and Industry Award.
**Personal:** Mercer University, JD, magna cum laude, 1982; Agnes Scott College, BA, high honors, 1977.

**MENZIE, Edward G**
Nexsen Pruet, LLC, Columbia
803 771 8900
emenzie@nexsenpruet.com
*Recommended in Corporate/M&A, Real Estate*
**Practice Areas:** Ed Menzie combines extensive corporate, finance, real estate and securities experience in the representation of a variety of clients, including major real estate developers.
**Prof. Memberships:** South Carolina Bar (past Chairman, Building Committee and the Unauthorized Practice of Law Committee); American Bar Association (Former SC Liaison, State Regulation of Securities Committee); listed in the Corporate Law and Real Estate Law sections of a leading US legal publication.
**Career:** Board of Directors, Burroughs & Chapin Company, Inc. (Myrtle Beach).

**Personal:** University of South Carolina, JD, magna cum laude,1971; University of South Carolina, BS,1968.

### MORRISON, Stephen
Nelson Mullins Riley & Scarborough LLP, Columbia 803 799 2000
*Recommended in Litigation, Products Liability*

### MUSSER, William
McNair Law Firm PA, Columbia
803 799 9800
*Recommended in Corporate/M&A*

### OXNER, Dewey
Haynsworth Sinkler Boyd PA, Greenville 864 240 3200
*Recommended in Litigation*

### PARR, Henry L
Wyche, Burgess, Freeman & Parham, PA, Greenville 864 242 8209
hparr@wyche.com
*Recommended in Litigation*
**Practice Areas:** Antitrust and trade regulation; corporate; trade secrets; intellectual property; litigation; healthcare; certified mediator; American Arbitration Association Arbitrator. Henry Parr's practice focuses on antitrust counseling and litigation as well as other types of complex litigation. Henry has handled both civil and criminal antitrust matters, as well as cases involving complex commercial disputes for clients involved in textiles, apparel, high-tech industries, chemicals, gearing, tires, paper, education, insurance, paving, communications, shipping, and healthcare. Henry has served as lead counsel in cases before South Carolina's appellate courts, the Fourth Circuit Court of Appeals, the United States Supreme Court, and arbitration panels. Henry also regularly advises clients regarding trade secret protection and distribution arrangements.
**Prof. Memberships:** South Carolina Bar Association since 1976; District of Columbia Bar since 1977. Member, American Health Lawyers Association; American Law Institute; Consultative Group Restatement of Law of Unfair Competition, Fourth Circuit Judicial Conference.
**Career:** Law clerk to the Honorable Clement F Haynsworth, Jr, Chief Judge, United States Court of Appeals for the Fourth Circuit, 1976-77; law clerk to the Honorable Warren E Burger, Chief Justice, United States Supreme Court, 1977-78. Associate, Wyche Burgess Freeman & Parham, P.A. 1979-82. Member of the Wyche law firm from 1982 to present.
**Publications:** Co-author, 'Intellectual Property', South Carolina Jurisprudence (1993).
**Personal:** Furman University (BA, summa cum laude, 1973); University of Virginia (JD, 1976); Order of the Coif; Virginia Law Review (Editorial Board, 1974-75; notes editor, 1975-76). Listed in

'The Best Lawyers In America'.

### PEARSON, Jonathan
Fisher & Phillips LLP, Columbia
803 255 0000
*Recommended in Employment*
**Practice Areas:** Jonathan Pearson is a Partner in the Columbia office of the national labor and employment law firm of Fisher & Phillips LLP. His practice emphasizes traditional labor law, as well as a wide range of employment litigation including Title VII, ADA, ADEA, FMLA and FLSA. He also frequently assists employers in union contract negotiations and in dealing with strike-related issues. Pearson is certified as a specialist in labor and employment law by the South Carolina Supreme Court and is past Chairman of the Labor and Employment Section of the South Carolina Bar.

### QUATTLEBAUM, Marvin
Leatherwood Walker Todd & Mann PC, Greenville 864 242 6440
*Recommended in Real Estate*

### ROBINSON JR, Neil C
Nexsen Pruet, LLC, Charleston
843 720 1723
nrobinson@nexsenpruet.com
*Recommended in Real Estate*
**Practice Areas:** Extensive experience: complex real estate transactions; administrative and regulatory law, including permitting, zoning and property rights; condominium, commercial and resort real estate development.
**Prof. Memberships:** President, Southeastern Wildlife Exposition; President, Clemson University Advancement Foundation; President, Hibernian Society; President, Coastal Properties Institute; V-Pres., South Carolina Tourism Council; serves on Recreation Development Council, Urban Land Institute; Governor's Quality of Life Task Force; College of Charleston Advisory Board; and Charleston Education Network. (Founder and past President); South Carolina Education Oversight Committee.
**Career:** 1973, Assistant Dean, USC Law School; 1974-76 judicial clerkship with Honorable Charles E Simons, Jr; Chief Judge, US District Court, District of SC; 1974, Grimball & Cabaniss in Charleston; 1980-84 Partner in Grimball Cabaniss Vaughan & Robinson; 1984 started Robinson Wall & Hastie, PA. 1991 firm merged with Nexsen Pruet, LLC. Member, Board of Directors, Manager, Charleston, SC office. Awarded the Order of the Palmetto by Governor David Beasley. Recommended in various leading legal publications.
**Personal:** University of South Carolina, JD, 1973; Clemson University, BS, 1966.

### SATTERFIELD JR, Andreas
Nelson Mullins Riley & Scarborough LLP, Greenville 864 250 2300
*Recommended in Employment*

### SAVITZ, Stephen
Gignilliat, Savitz & Bettis LLP, Columbia 803 799 9311
*Recommended in Employment*

### SHOEMAKER JR, James M
Wyche, Burgess, Freeman & Parham, PA, Greenville 864 242 8200
jshoemaker@wyche.com
*Recommended in Corporate/M&A*
**Practice Areas:** Securities; commercial transactions; corporate; mergers and acquisitions. Jim Shoemaker's practice focuses on corporate and securities law with an emphasis on representing publicly traded companies. He is a Member of the Board of Directors of a public company. Together with other members of the firm, he advises corporate clients on the full range of corporate activities engaged in by privately and publicly held companies.
**Prof. Memberships:** South Carolina Bar Association since 1965.
**Career:** United States Marine Corps, 1955-72, Major (Retired). Foreign Service Officer, Department of State, 1958-62. Asssociate, Wyche Burgess Freeman & Parham, PA, 1965-70. Member of the Wyche firm 1970 to present.
**Personal:** University of Virginia (AB, 1955; LLB, 1965); Phi Alpha Delta; Lyle Moot Court Competition Winner, 1965; Virginia Law Review (Board of Editors, 1963-65). Listed in the past 10 consecutive issues of 'The Best Lawyers In America'.

### SMITH, W Lindsay
Womble Carlyle Sandridge & Rice, PLLC, Greenville 864 255 5403
lsmith@wcsr.com
*Recommended in Real Estate*
**Practice Areas:** Lindsay has a broad range of experience in commercial real estate transactions, real estate finance and secured transactions. He represents borrowers and lenders, landlords and tenants in real estate acquisitions and dispositions, financing, development and leasing.
**Prof. Memberships:** South Carolina Bar; Greenville County Bar Association; Fellow, American College of Mortgage Attorneys; Best Lawyers in America, Real Estate Law; International Council of Shopping Centers, Law Division.
**Personal:** JD, 1977, University of South Carolina; BA, 1974, Furman University.

### SMOAK, Lewis T
Ogletree, Deakins, Nash, Smoak & Stewart, PC, Greenville 864 271 1300
lewis.smoak@ogletreedeakins.com
*Recommended in Employment*
**Practice Areas:** Labor and employment.
**Prof. Memberships:** Greenville County, South Carolina, District of Columbia, and American Bar Associations.
**Career:** Admitted to practice in State of South Carolina, District of Columbia, US Supreme Court, and US Courts of Appeal

(various). Founding Partner of Ogletree, Deakins, Nash, Smoak & Stewart. Listed in 'The Best Lawyers in America' and 'Who's Who in American Law'. Fellow of The College of Labor and Employment Lawyers. Member, Fourth Circuit Judicial Conference.
**Publications:** Author of a comprehensive nationwide labor relations study in the construction industry.
**Personal:** Furman University (BA, 1966), University of South Carolina (JD, 1969).

### SMYTHE, Susan
Buist Moore Smythe McGee P.A., Charleston 843 720 4608
ssmythe@bmsmlaw.com
*Recommended in Real Estate*
**Practice Areas:** Head of the firm's Business Department, and the Business and Banking Practice Group. Her practice includes the following concentrations; corporate law: mergers and acquisitions, reorganizations, formation of business entities, structuring of business relationships through buy-sell, employment and other agreements, dispute resolution between minority and majority owners. Real estate law: representation of commercial, industrial, resort and residential developers, commercial leasing, title insurance agent, environmental regulations, conservation and facade easements. Healthcare: hospital and medical group affiliations, consolidations and mergers. Mediator: mediation of commercial, corporate and real estate disputes.
**Prof. Memberships:** Past Chairman of the Real Estate Section of South Carolina Bar, Member of the Real Estate, Antitrust and Business Law Sections of the American Bar Association.
**Career:** Admitted to South Carolina Bar (1977). Principal Drafter of the South Carolina Development Agreement Act, 6-31-10, Code of Laws of South Carolina 1976, as amended. Listed in a leading legal publication.
**Personal:** Received JD from University of Virginia School of Law in 1976 and BA from Brown University in 1972.

### SOWELL, Thornwell F
Sowell Gray Stepp & Laffitte LLC, Columbia 803 929 1400
bsowell@sowell.com
*Recommended in Litigation*
**Practice Areas:** Commercial litigation and corporate counseling.
**Prof. Memberships:** Mr Sowell is a member of the Federation of Defense and Corporate Counsel and the American Board of Trial Advocates. He was a Member of the South Carolina Law Review, has served on the South Carolina Bar's House of Delegates, and is a Fellow of the South Carolina Bar Foundation.
**Personal:** A native of Chesterfield, SC, Mr Sowell practices primarily in the areas of commercial litigation and corporate

counseling. He graduated from Clemson University in 1973 with a BA degree and received his JD in 1976 from the University of South Carolina School of Law, where he was a member of the South Carolina Law Review and President of the Student Bar Association.

### SPETH II, Charles T
Ogletree, Deakins, Nash, Smoak & Stewart, PC, Columbia 803 799 0800
ted.speth@ogletreedeakins.com
*Recommended in Employment*
**Practice Areas:** Employment, class action litigation, healthcare.
**Prof. Memberships:** South Carolina Bar Association (Chair, Employment and Labor Law Section, 1990-91), Richland County Bar Association, American Bar Association, American Board of Trial Advocates (Vice President, South Carolina Chapter, 2006-07), Greater Columbia Chamber of Commerce (General Counsel, 2004-).
**Career:** Admitted to practice in South Carolina, US Supreme Court and US Court of Appeals (Fourth, Fifth and Seventh Circuits). Listed in 2003-04 edition and 2001-02 edition of 'The Best Lawyers in America'.
**Personal:** Duke University (AB, 1973), University of South Carolina School of Law (JD, 1979).

### STEPHENSON, Thomas
Nexsen Pruet, LLC, Greenville
864 370 2211
tstephenson@nexsenpruet.com
*Recommended in Litigation*
**Practice Areas:** Tom Stephenson practices primarily in the areas of labor and employment law, employment-related litigation, mediation and arbitration. Mr Stephenson has authored several books and articles dealing with employment law.
**Prof. Memberships:** Admitted before the state and federal court of South Carolina, the US Court of Appeals Fourth and Sixth Circuits.
**Career:** Litigator, certified mediator; Certified Specialist in Labor and Employment Law, South Carolina Supreme Court; and former adjunct professor in Labor Law at Clemson University. Listed in 'The Best Lawyers in America' 2006.
**Personal:** University of South Carolina, JD, 1979; University of South Carolina, BS, 1976.

### STEWART III, J Hamilton
Ogletree, Deakins, Nash, Smoak & Stewart, PC, Greenville 864 271 1300
jimmie.stewart@ogletreedeakins.com
*Recommended in Employment*
**Practice Areas:** Representing management in labor, employment and litigation. Advising major corporations on positive employee relations and labor matters, corporate campaigns, and class action litigation. Management training.
**Prof. Memberships:** SCBA, TBA, DC Bar, ABA.
**Career:** Founding Shareholder. Admitted in South Carolina (Certified Specialist), Tennessee, Washington, DC, US Supreme Court, US Courts of Appeals (Fourth, Fifth, Eleventh, and District of Columbia Circuits). Listed in 'The Best Lawyers in America'. Fellow, the College of Labor and Employment Lawyers.
**Publications:** Lectured extensively; NLRB Regulations of Election Conduct (1985-97) (Olin Institute).
**Personal:** Presbyterian College (AB, 1965), University of South Carolina (JD, 1969).

### SUGGS JR, Fred W
Ogletree, Deakins, Nash, Smoak & Stewart, PC, Greenville 864 271 1300
fred.suggs@ogletreedeakins.com
*Recommended in Employment*
**Practice Areas:** Labor and employment.
**Prof. Memberships:** American, Alabama, Florida, and South Carolina Bar Associations; Judicial Conference for the Fourth Circuit, Certified Specialist in Labor and Employment Law, and Fellow of the College of Labor and Employment Lawyers.
**Career:** Admitted to practice in US Supreme Court, the Alabama, Florida, and South Carolina Supreme Courts, US District Courts (various), and US Courts of Appeal (various).
**Publications:** 'Employer Liability for Age Discrimination', Institute of Business Law, 1992; 'Advising Your Corporate Client on Avoiding Charges of Sexual Harassment', Alabama Lawyer, July 1985.
**Personal:** Kansas State University (BS, 1970), University of Alabama (JD, 1975).

### SWANSON, David
Haynsworth Sinkler Boyd PA, Charleston
843 722 3366
*Recommended in Real Estate*

### TATE, Simmons
Haynsworth Sinkler Boyd PA, Charleston
843 722 3366
*Recommended in Litigation*

### TESSIER, Troy A
Wyche, Burgess, Freeman & Parham, PA, Greenville
864 242 8219
ttessier@wyche.com
*Recommended in Litigation*
**Practice Areas:** Litigation; products liability; intellectual property; personal injury; construction. Troy Tessier has a diverse litigation practice involving complex commercial disputes, products liability, insurance coverage and intellectual property cases, as well as personal injury and some construction litigation. Mr Tessier is an experienced trial attorney, with well over 30 jury trials, both civil and criminal, in his career.
**Prof. Memberships:** New Hampshire Bar Association since 1993; South Carolina Bar Association since 1997; Georgia Bar Association since 2005. South Carolina Trial Lawyers Association.
**Career:** Judge Advocate, United States Marine Corps, 1993-97. Associate, Wyche, Burgess, Freeman & Parham, PA, 1997-2000. Assistant United States attorney, District of South Carolina, November 2000-April 2001. Member of the Wyche law firm from 2001 to present.
**Personal:** St Lawrence University (BA, summa cum laude, 1990); Phi Beta Kappa; Harvard University (JD, cum laude, 1993).

### TISDALE, Thomas S
Nexsen Pruet, LLC, Charleston
843 577 9440
ttisdale@nexsenpruet.com
*Recommended in Litigation*
**Practice Areas:** General commercial litigation; communications law; products liability law; intellectual property litigation; first amendment law.
**Prof. Memberships:** South Carolina Bar (Board of Governors, 1975; Secretary, 1976; Treasurer, 1979; President-Elect, 1980; President, 1981-82); Charleston Lawyers Club (President, 1970).
**Career:** Assistant solicitor, 9th Judicial Circuit, 1969-70; Associate Judge, Municipal Court, City of Charleston, 1970-72; Supreme Court Commission on Grievances and Discipline, 1977-80; Supreme Court Commission on Continuing Lawyer Competency, 1984-87; South Carolina Law Institute; CPR Institute for Dispute Resolution, 2002-present. Mr Tisdale was a Founding Partner of Young, Clement, Rivers and Tisdale in Charleston, SC. He has served on the Board of Regents of the University of the South and the Board of Trustees of Voorhees College; as Chairman of the Board of Trustees of Porter-Gaud School; and on the boards of the South Carolina Aquarium and Spoleto Festival USA. Mr

Tisdale was also chancellor of the Episcopal Diocese of South Carolina from 1975-85.
**Personal:** University of South Carolina, JD, 1964; University of the South, BA, 1961.

### WALKER, Trenholm
Pratt-Thomas, Epting & Walker PA, Charleston 843 727 2200
*Recommended in Litigation*

### WARREN, J Steve
Jackson Lewis, Greenville
864 232 7000
warrens@jacksonlewis.com
*Recommended in Employment*
**Practice Areas:** Labor law, collective bargaining, union organizing and management training. Managing Partner of Greenville office.
**Prof. Memberships:** South Carolina Bar Association; Mauldin Chamber of Commerce; Upstate Alliance of South Carolina; Greenville Area Development Corporation; South Carolina Chamber of Commerce.
**Career:** Joined Jackson Lewis in 1983. Has practiced labor and employment law exclusively since 1975. Experience includes representation of companies before the National Labor Relations Board, Equal Employment Opportunity Commission, and Federal and State courts and administrative agencies.
**Publications:** Co-authored 'Winning NLRB Elections: Management's Strategy and Preventive Programs', 3d edition.
**Personal:** University of South Carolina, JD, 1975; Furman University, BA, 1972.

### WARREN III, John
Warren & Sinkler LLP, Charleston
843 577 0660
*Recommended in Corporate/M&A, Real Estate*

### YOUNG, Kenneth
Nelson Mullins Riley & Scarborough LLP, Greenville 864 250 2300
*Recommended in Employment*

### YOUNG JR, Rutledge
Young, Clement & Rivers LLP, Charleston 843 577 4000
*Recommended in Litigation*

# BUIST MOORE SMYTHE MCGEE P.A.

## THE FIRM

**Managing Director:** Henry B Smythe Jr

**Number of Principals:** 23
**Number of other lawyers:** 17

**FIRM OVERVIEW:** Buist Moore Smythe McGee P.A. is one of the largest business law firms in the Charleston, South Carolina area. The firm's 40 attorneys provide services to domestic and international clients in the areas of admiralty and aviation, bankruptcy and creditors' rights, business and banking, captive insurance, civil and commercial litigation, construction, employment, environmental, health insurance coverage and defense, media, mergers and acquisitions, products liability, real estate, taxation and trusts and estates. The firm's attorneys represent financial institutions, corporations, partnerships and limited liability companies in all aspects of commercial and litigation services. The firm also offers arbitration and mediation services and has a thriving appellate practice.

## MAIN AREAS OF PRACTICE:

**Business & Banking:** For decades, the diverse and complex field of business law has been an integral feature of the firm. It represents financial institutions, corporations, partnerships, limited partnerships, limited liability companies, captive insurance companies, and other business associations in all aspects of commercial activity, including entity selection, business formation, mergers and acquisitions, dissolutions, and creditors' rights. The Business and Banking Practice Group and the Taxation and Real Estate Practice Groups often work together, using their lawyers' years of experience in these fields to provide synergistic representation to clients. The attorneys in these practice groups collectively possess a wide variety of skills in the area of business law, which are brought to bear on the client's behalf. The attorneys in the groups have represented local, regional, and national clients within South Carolina and throughout the region. Attorneys in the Business and Banking Practice Group have years of experience in the creation of corporate entities, including corporations, partnerships, limited partnerships, limited liability companies, and other business associations. By understanding their clients' goals, the firm's lawyers are able to assist clients in attaining the best use of their existing resources while preparing for their growth. The transactions with which the firm's attorneys have been involved cover the full range of modern acquisition techniques and structures. These include mergers and acquisitions, sales of assets, statutory share exchanges, exchange offers, hostile and friendly tender offers, proxy contests, and leveraged buyout techniques. The firm has represented both sellers and buyers in these transactions and has provided advice on a wide array of issues including, tax, environmental, antitrust and securities, and copyright issues arising from the transactions. Members of the practice group have negotiated, reviewed, and drafted a variety of commercial and business agreements, including purchase and sale, franchise, consulting, supply, purchase, trademark usage, and licensing. In addition, the attorneys in the group have dealt with a vast array of banking and other creditor issues, beginning with the drafting of the initial loan documents through collection and bankruptcy. The firm's lawyers have represented numerous banks and other institutional lenders in loan transactions involving real property and asset-based transactions located in South Carolina and beyond. The group's attorneys also have experience with various collection situations. These include fraudulent transfers; preferences; insider transactions; piercing the corporate veil; sales and dispositions of collateral; actions to set aside foreclosure sales; marshaling; landlord and tenant matters; landlords' liens; bank deposits and collections; bulk sales; letters of credit; actions to recover collateral; attachments; enforcement of judgments; garnishments; levies on real and personal property; and mechanics' liens.

## HEAD OFFICE

**SOUTH CAROLINA**
5 Exchange St, **Charleston**, 29401
**Tel:** 843 722 3400   **Fax:** 843 723 7398
**Website:** www.bmsmlaw.com

## CONTACTS

| | |
|---|---|
| Business & Banking | Susan M Smythe |
| Business Litigation | William C Cleveland III |
| Real Estate | W Foster Gaillard |
| | Morris A Ellison |

**Business Litigation:** The Business Litigation Department handles a broad range of business and commercial matters, including contract disputes, construction litigation, bankruptcy, health care, unfair competition, business torts, employment litigation, insurance disputes, environmental litigation, real estate litigation, corporate and partnership disputes and securities litigation. It typically defends South Carolina businesses; however, the firm also initiate suits on behalf of its clients. In the area of creditors' rights and bankruptcy the Business Litigation Department handles all phases of creditors' rights representation, including workouts, pretrial litigation, trials, appeals, pre and post judgment remedies and bankruptcy. The firm also has experience in all forms of alternative dispute resolution, encompassing arbitration and mediation. The Business Litigation Department represents clients throughout the State of South Carolina foreclosing mortgages, judgment liens, construction liens or other security interests against both real and personal property. Representation ranges from simple residential mortgage foreclosures to complex commercial foreclosures. Both attorneys and staff are well versed in the applicable laws affecting priorities and perfection of security interests. Attorneys provide creditor clients with a problem solving approach that enables clients to enforce their rights quickly and economically. The firm represents lenders and borrowers in restructurings of corporate and real estate transactions that are designed to avoid bankruptcy. The firm's ability to negotiate restructurings that are fair and realistic for its clients is enhanced by its strong Corporate and Real Estate Practice. The firm's business litigation attorneys are leaders in Bar organizations such as the American Bar Association, the South Carolina Bar and the International Association of Defense Counsel at all levels. Many of the attorneys are recognized as preeminent in their areas of practice and are often invited to speak and publish in forums such as the South Carolina Bar Journal, the ABA annual meetings, seminars, national trial advocacy schools and various law schools and their publications.

**Real Estate:** The firm provides legal services for all aspects of real estate transactions, including contract negotiations, zoning and permitting issues, financing, title insurance issues, and other matters related to closing the transaction. The firm's attorneys have extensive experience in closing complex commercial transactions as well as residential transactions. The firm's commercial clientele includes owners and developers of office buildings, shopping centers, industrial facilities, apartment complexes, hotels and motels, and planned unit developments.

Buist · Moore · Smythe · McGee · P.A.

# LEATHERWOOD WALKER TODD & MANN, P.C.

## THE FIRM

**Managing Partner:** Richard L Few, Jr

**Number of partners:** 36
**Number of other lawyers:** 22

**FIRM OVERVIEW:** Since its founding in 1945, Leatherwood has focused on providing its clients with high quality legal services to meet their business needs. Over 50 attorneys with varied skills and experience in both business and litigation matters serve a diverse client base throughout the state and region in over 30 areas of practice.

## MAIN AREAS OF PRACTICE:

**Corporate/Mergers & Acquisitions:** The Business Transactions Group handles a variety of business transactions, including formation of business entities, business acquisitions, dispositions and reorganizations, from traditional stock and asset sales to mergers, leveraged buyouts, and going-private and going-public transactions. The attorneys also assist businesses in raising debt and equity capital in compliance with federal and state securities laws.

**Financing & Commercial Transactions:** Attorneys in this practice area represent businesses, individuals, banks, venture capital firms and other financial institutions in a broad range of matters. These attorneys have significant experience in arranging and negotiating secured and unsecured financing and leveraged leasing transactions, collection and enforcement of loan and security instruments, handling creditor claims in bankruptcy proceedings, and advising on compliance with various lending and other regulations. The firm has extensive experience in innovative financing arrangements involving joint participation by the public and private sectors and in matters involving government bond financing and other forms of public finance. The firm also assists new or existing businesses in securing state and local government economic development incentives for facility relocations and expansions.

**Litigation:** The Litigation Groups support all of the firm's practice areas by handling both business and personal injury litigation for the firm's clients. The South Carolina attorneys enjoy a reputation as respected advocates and negotiators in all state, federal, and appellate courts, as well as in mediation and arbitration proceedings. The Litigation Groups handle all forms of complex litigation in many areas, including antitrust and unfair trade practices, construction, contracts, creditor's rights and bankruptcy, environmental, healthcare, intellectual property, employment, professional malpractice and products liability.

**Real Estate:** Leatherwood's Real Estate Group focuses primarily on handling complex issues relating to real estate investment and development. Attorneys in this group represent developers, lenders, sellers, purchasers and both national and local financial institutions in the development, financing, sale, purchase and lease of commercial, industrial, and residential properties throughout the Southeast. The Real Estate Group helps clients with contract negotiation, arrangements for financing, leasing, management and sale of office buildings, shopping centers, apartments, and other commercial and industrial properties, title examination and certification, zoning and permitting, subdivision regulations, and compliance with federal, state, and local regulations affecting property development.

**Tax & Employee Benefits:** Attorneys in this practice area include certified specialists in taxation and estate planning who assist businesses and individuals with an extensive variety of tax and wealth transfer planning matters, including business disposition planning, business owner buyout arrangements, deferred compensation programs, employee benefit plans, retirement plans, stock and other option plans, tax audits and controversies, and charitable gift planning. The firm's tax attorneys also assist other attorneys in other practice areas with tax issues arising in their matters.

## HEAD OFFICE

**SOUTH CAROLINA**
300 East McBee Avenue, Suite 500, **Greenville**, SC 29601
**Tel:** 864 242 6440   **Fax:** 864 240 2474
**Email:** leatherwood@lwtm.com
**Website:** www.lwtm.com

## CONTACTS

| | |
|---|---|
| **Corporate/Mergers & Acquisitions** | Richard L Few, Jr |
| **Financing & Commercial Transactions** | Frank C Williams, Jr |
| **Litigation** | Steven E Farrar |
| **Real Estate** | Harvey G Sanders, III (Bert) |
| **Tax & Employee Benefits** | William L Dennis |
| **Transportation** | Robert D Moseley, Jr |
| **International** | James L Rogers |

**Transportation:** The Transportation Group represents both large and small trucking companies as insureds on behalf of numerous national insurance companies and as self-insureds. The attorneys in this group are experienced in all aspects of transportation law including issues involving federal and state statutes and regulations promulgated by the former Interstate Commerce Commission (ICC), the successor Surface Transportation Board, the Department of Transportation (DOT) and the Public Service Commission. The Transportation Group has been involved in many truck accident litigation scenarios, including trailer underrides, multiple tractor accidents, environmental spills and saddlebag fuel tank explosions. The attorneys also handle commercial subrogation matters and assist insurance clients in recovering first party claims expenditures, defend and prosecute cargo claims and conduct audits to insure compliance with DOT and safety regulations.

**INTERNATIONAL WORK:** Leatherwood's International Practice Group handles a variety of legal issues which may arise in the course of international business transactions, including creation and modification of cross-border business entity structures, asset transfers, economic and local tax incentive planning, immigration, intellectual property, customs, international tax considerations, commercial agreements and compliance with the Foreign Corrupt Practices Act. Attorneys in this group also speak Spanish, French and Portuguese.

# NELSON MULLINS RILEY & SCARBOROUGH, LLP

## THE FIRM

**Managing Partner:** David E Dukes
**Marketing Partner:** James K Lehman

**Number of partners:** 182
**Number of other lawyers:** 171

## AREAS OF PRACTICE:

| | |
|---|---|
| Corporate Finance | 30% |
| Business Litigation | 20% |
| Pharmaceuticals & Medical Devices | 13% |
| Healthcare | 12% |
| Labor & Employment | 10% |
| Mass Tort Litigation | 10% |
| Government Relations | 5% |

**FIRM OVERVIEW:** Founded in 1897, Nelson Mullins maintains offices in Georgia, North Carolina, South Carolina and Washington, DC. With more than 350 attorneys practicing in nine offices, the firm has more than 40 diversified practice areas and represents a wide variety of clients that range in size from start-up technology companies to Fortune 500 corporations.

## MAIN AREAS OF PRACTICE:

**Corporate Finance:** Firm attorneys handle a broad range of securities, finance and regulatory matters for development stage private companies and large publicly held companies in a wide range of industries.

**Business Litigation:** Attorneys in this group provide counsel throughout the United States in the areas of business, securities and financial fraud, business torts, antitrust matters, lending liability claims, contract disputes, and other areas.

**Mass Tort Litigation:** Firm attorneys are equipped to handle or coordinate the defense of mass tort claims on an individual, regional or national basis, and serve as national trial and coordinating counsel for leading US companies.

**Pharmaceuticals & Medical Devices:** Firm attorneys have extensive knowledge in many areas of science and technology and effectively handle claims regarding clients' products and services. The attorneys have experience with mass torts and multi-district litigation, requiring coordination with attorneys from across the United States.

**Healthcare:** Firm attorneys are capable of providing comprehensive client services. They have experience providing services to healthcare clients in corporate transactions, regulatory and governmental affairs, litigation, finance and tax.

**Labor & Employment:** This diverse group of attorneys defends companies in all facets of labor and employment disputes.

**Government Relations:** These attorneys have extensive experience with a wide range of clients in many areas of lobbying and legislative analysis.

**CLIENTS:** Nelson Mullins clients include leading manufacturers, Fortune 500 companies, commercial banks and other financial institutions, public utilities, venture capital and private equity firms, industrial and service corporations, partnerships, profit and non-profit organizations, government agencies, entrepreneurs and individuals.

**INTERNATIONAL WORK:** The Nelson Mullins International Practice Group serves clients around the world in international business, commercial and trade matters, business immigration, and matters before federal courts, international agencies, and tribunals.

## HEAD OFFICE

**SOUTH CAROLINA**
Meridian, 17th Floor, 1320 Main Street,
**Columbia**, SC 29201
**Tel:** 803 799 2000 **Fax:** 803 256 7500
**Website:** www.nelsonmullins.com

## BRANCH OFFICES

**DISTRICT OF COLUMBIA**
101 Constitution Avenue, NW, Suite 900,
**Washington**, DC 20001
**Tel:** 202 712 2800 **Fax:** 202 712 2862

**GEORGIA**
999 Peachtree Street, NE, Suite 1400,
**Atlanta**, GA 30309-3964
**Tel:** 404 817 6000 **Fax:** 404 817 6050

**NORTH CAROLINA**
Bank of America Corporate Center, Suite 2400,
100 North Tryon Street, **Charlotte**, NC 28202-4007
**Tel:** 704 417 3000 **Fax:** 704 377 4814

GlenLake One, Suite 200, 4140 Parklake Avenue,
**Raleigh**, NC 27612
**Tel:** 919 877 3800 **Fax:** 919 877 3799

The Knollwood, Suite 530, 380 Knollwood Street,
**Winston-Salem**, NC 27103
**Tel:** 336 774 3300 **Fax:** 336 774 3299

**SOUTH CAROLINA**
Liberty Center, Suite 600, 151 Meeting Street,
**Charleston**, SC 29401-2239
**Tel:** 843 853 5200 **Fax:** 843 722 8700

Poinsett Plaza, Suite 900, 104 South Main Street, **Greenville**, SC 29601
**Tel:** 864 250 2300 **Fax:** 864 232 2925

Founders Centre, Suite 301, 2411 North Oak Street,
**Myrtle Beach**, SC 29577-3165
**Tel:** 843 448 3500 **Fax:** 843 448 3437

## CONTACTS

| | |
|---|---|
| Business Litigation | Stephen G Morrison |
| Corporate Finance | John T Moore |
| Government Relations | Edward E Poliakoff |
| Healthcare | Stuart M Andrews |
| Labor & Employment | Kenneth E Young |
| Mass Tort Litigation | R Bruce Shaw |
| Pharmaceuticals & Medical Devices | David E Dukes |

Nelson
Mullins

# NEXSEN PRUET, LLC

## THE FIRM

**Managing Partner:** Wm Leighton Lord III

**Number of partners:** 101
**Number of other lawyers:** 79

**FIRM OVERVIEW:** Nexsen Pruet has earned a reputation for professional, principled service. Nexsen Pruet's team of more than 175 attorneys work out of seven offices in two states: North and South Carolina. The regional locations help make Nexsen Pruet one of the Carolinas' truly comprehensive law firms, and a preferred choice for companies and individuals seeking exceptional legal representation. Nexsen Pruet has addressed the demands of an increasingly diverse client base, serving individuals, institutions, and businesses of all types and sizes by hiring attorneys whose skill and expertise covers a comprehensive range of nearly 30 areas of practice.

## MAIN AREAS OF PRACTICE:

**Real Estate:** Nexsen Pruet's Real Estate Group represents one of the most experienced and diversified teams of real estate attorneys in the southeastern United States, with attorneys in the firm actively engaged in virtually all types of real estate investment and development. The firm's Real Estate Practice includes representation of buyers, sellers, landlords, tenants, lenders, borrowers, developers, investors, as well as all types of businesses needing real estate counseling. The Real Estate Group works closely with the firm's Corporate, Securities, Healthcare, Environmental, Tax and Bankruptcy Groups to provide seamless one-stop service.

**Litigation:** Nexsen Pruet's Litigation Group devotes a great deal of time to resolving its clients' legal disputes. Nexsen Pruet's attorneys combine trial advocacy with well-honed negotiating skills to aggressively seek the outcome desired by its clients. Areas of significant experience include: antitrust and unfair trade practices, aviation, civil rights defense, construction, contracts, creditor's rights and bankruptcy, environmental, health care, intellectual property, international arbitrations, labor and employment, maritime, products liability, professional malpractice, public utilities, securities, tax and worker's compensation.

**Mergers & Acquisitions:** Nexsen Pruet's mergers and acquisitions attorneys utilize the Corporate, Tax, Real Estate, Environmental, Labor and Employment, Securities, Finance and Litigation Practices within the firm to enhance representation, providing clients with direct access to the depth and scope of legal experience necessary to accomplish desired objectives. Along with a results-oriented philosophy, the attorneys in this practice have extensive experience in structuring complex and multi-faceted business transactions, drafting and negotiating comprehensive documents and handling the regulatory and logistical steps required to achieve closing.

**Healthcare:** Nexsen Pruet has an extensive Healthcare Practice which represents several hundred physicians and more than 20 hospitals on an on-going basis throughout South Carolina and North Carolina. The Healthcare Group is managed by eight full-time attorneys who have significant experience and a deep understanding of laws concerning the regulation, delivery, and financing of healthcare services.

**Construction:** Nexsen Pruet is involved in all areas of construction law and related activities, including planning, advice and contract review and preparation in the architectural, engineering and construction areas. The firm's practice includes multi-party and complex construction and construction-related litigation in state and federal courts, and mediation and arbitration proceedings.

**Intellectual Property:** Nexsen Pruet's Intellectual Property Group represents clients with a broad range of intellectual property issues. The attorneys who practice in this area include patent, trademark and copyright attorneys with a broad range of technical backgrounds and experience, intellectual property litigation attorneys and dispute resolution, and transactional attorneys experienced in licensing, technology transfer, employer/employee rights in intellectual property, due diligence and valuation issues.

## HEAD OFFICE

**SOUTH CAROLINA**
1441 Main Street, Suite 1500, **Columbia**, SC 29201
**Tel:** 803 771 8900   **Fax:** 803 253 8277
**Email:** hmatthews@nexsenpruet.com
**Website:** www.nexsenpruet.com

## BRANCH OFFICES

**NORTH CAROLINA**
201 South Tryon Street, Suite 1200, **Charlotte**, NC 28202
**Tel:** 704 339 0304   **Fax:** 704 338 5377

701 Green Valley Road, Suite 100 **Greensboro**, NC 27408
**Tel:** 336 373 1600   **Fax:** 336 273 5357

**SOUTH CAROLINA**
205 King Street, Suite 400, **Charleston**, SC 29401
**Tel:** 843 577 9440   **Fax:** 843 720 1777

201 West McBee Avenue, Suite 400, **Greenville**, SC 29601
**Tel:** 864 370 2211   **Fax:** 864 282 1177

400 Main Street Office Campus, Suite 100A, **Hilton Head**, SC 29926
**Tel:** 843 689 6277   **Fax:** 843 682 1577

2411 North Oak Street, Suite 105, **Myrtle Beach**, SC 29577
**Tel:** 843 445 9688   **Fax:** 843 443 8147

## CONTACTS

| | |
|---|---|
| **Real Estate** | Wm Leighton Lord III |
| **Litigation** | Val A Stieglitz |
| **Mergers & Acquisitions** | G Marcus Knight |
| **Healthcare** | Timothy Hewson |
| **Construction** | David Senter |
| **Intellectual Property** | William Y Klett III |
| **Labor & Employment** | David E Dubberly |

**Labor & Employment:** Nexsen Pruet's Labor and Employment Group represents management in every area of labor and employment law, including employee benefits, business immigration, trade secrets and workers' compensation. The attorneys represent both private and public sector employers in non-union and union settings. Several attorneys are Certified Specialists in Labor and Employment by the South Carolina Supreme Court.

**NEXSEN|PRUET**
The Carolinas Law Firm

# SOWELL GRAY STEPP & LAFFITTE, LLC

## THE FIRM

**Managing Partner:** Robert E Stepp

**Number of partners:** 8
**Number of other lawyers:** 11

**FIRM OVERVIEW:** Sowell Gray Stepp & Laffitte offers a tailored approach to litigation - whether maximizing recovery, minimizing damage and legal fees, or protecting business practices. Diverse backgrounds, education, and experience promote an open exchange of knowledge and ideas. The client defines the objective; the firm analyzes the options, considers the costs and risks, and recommends approaches so that the client can choose among the alternatives. Serving clients ranging from multi-national corporations to small businesses, the firm delivers respectful service, regardless of client size.

## MAIN AREAS OF PRACTICE:

**Administrative & Regulatory:** Attorneys represent clients before the South Carolina Public Service Commission, Department of Revenue, Department of Insurance, Manufactured Housing Board, Residential Builders Commission, the Board of Financial Institutions, the Contractor's Licensing Board, and the Administrative Law Division in South Carolina. The firm provides advice and counsel on important legal issues such as utility regulation and ratemaking, with clients ranging from utilities to consumers.

**Business Litigation:** The Business Litigation Team provides counsel in all areas of business disputes, litigating cases involving class actions, lender liability, premium fraud, corporate governance, business transactions, securities transactions, disputes, financial fraud, directors' liability and derivative actions. Firm attorneys have considerable experience in diverse areas of business litigation, including insurance coverage, lender liability, real estate, and title insurance.

**Employment & ERISA:** The Employment Law Department provides full service representation of public and private-sector management in all employment law areas. The team regularly represents clients in litigating employment-related civil rights and employment discrimination claims, including Title VII of the Civil Rights Act, the Age Discrimination in Employment Act, the Americans with Disabilities Act, and the Family and Medical Leave Act, before federal and state agencies, including the Equal Employment Opportunity Commission (EEOC) and the South Carolina Human Affairs Commission (SCHAC), as well as state and federal courts. Firm attorneys also regularly provide counseling, advice, and training to management and supervisors on employment regulations.

**Medical Malpractice & Nursing Home Defense:** Sowell Gray's Medical Malpractice and Nursing Home Practice defends a wide variety of claims arising from the delivery of healthcare and nursing home care. The firm represents healthcare providers in the defense of negligence and malpractice claims as well as claims brought against care facilities such as hospitals and nursing homes. Attorneys also work closely with clients to provide counseling as to methods of avoiding claims and lawsuits.

**Probate Litigation:** Jurisdiction frequently is placed initially in the Probate Court, and can involve complex business issues, estates and trusts, and other matters relating to the affairs of decedents and incapacitated persons. Firm lawyers represent individuals and personal representatives in litigation surrounding the estates of family members, inter vivos and testamentary trusts, and powers of attorney with sensitivity and efficacy.

### HEAD OFFICE

**SOUTH CAROLINA**
1310 Gadsden Street, PO Box 11449, **Columbia**, SC 29211
**Tel:** 803 929 1400
**Website:** www.sowell.com

**Products Liability:** The firm's representation has spanned local, regional and national products litigation involving diverse industries chemical, silica, asbestos, nuclear, pharmaceuticals, industrial equipment, and manufacturing, equipping firm attorneys to handle and coordinate the defense of products liability claims which attack a product or product lines of a regional or national scope. Firm attorneys also provide counseling as to methods of avoiding or minimizing potential claims, procedures which will assist in the defense of future claims, and compliance with federal, state and local regulators dealing with the manufacture and sale of potentially hazardous products.

**Professional Liability:** Sowell Gray provides aggressive representation at both the trial and appellate levels, with clients including directors and officers, healthcare professionals, accountants, attorneys, insurance agents and brokers, and engineers. A history of acting successfully on behalf of professionals, corporations and individuals involved in liability disputes has provided firm attorneys with in-depth knowledge and experience in this area.

SOWELL GRAY STEPP & LAFFITTE, LLC
ATTORNEYS AND COUNSELORS AT LAW

*Litigation is our business.*

# WYCHE BURGESS FREEMAN & PARHAM, P.A.

## THE FIRM

**Firm Management:** Executive Committee

**Number of members:** 25
**Number of other lawyers:** 8

**FIRM OVERVIEW:** For generations, the lawyers of Wyche Burgess Freeman & Parham, P.A. have earned the trust and loyalty of their clients. This has occurred in no small part because they have not hesitated to confront difficulty or act upon opportunity, and have been fully engaged with each client in meeting that client's legal needs. The firm's clients are diverse. They include major pharmaceutical companies, multinational corporations, electronics manufacturers, hospitals, real estate developers, engineering and architectural firms, newspapers and television stations, colleges and universities, wealthy and not-so-wealthy individuals and even other lawyers and law firms. Over the years, the firm's lawyers have become trusted advisors and counselors to many of their clients. Whatever the station and circumstance of the client, the firm is attentive to that client. This includes the structure of fee arrangements. The firm finds that clients increasingly prefer alternatives to hourly billing that share risk and reward results. This has always been the firm's preference. Although the firm's practice is concentrated in South Carolina, by its nature it often leads elsewhere. For example, Wyche lawyers have experience in putting together transactions on Wall Street and arguing cases in the United States Supreme Court. Wyche attorneys have law degrees from Harvard, Yale, the University of Virginia, Columbia, and other leading law schools, where many served on Law Review. Collectively, the firm's attorneys have earned a bounty of academic honors. Several have held clerkships in the United States District Court, the Court of Appeals, or the United States Supreme Court. The firm recognizes, however, that such distinctions alone are not enough to be successful in the practice of law; Wyche attorneys have the real-world experience and wisdom that can only be acquired through years of practice. They also recognize that it is essential to be deeply involved in public affairs so that they may better understand and help shape the economic, social and political forces that affect their community. Members of the firm have assumed leadership roles with, and provided major support for, many significant projects that have enhanced the quality of life in South Carolina, e.g., the Greenville Chamber of Commerce, the Greenville Symphony Association, the Community Foundation of Greenville, the Greenville County Museum of Art, the Roper Mountain Science Center, the Peace Center for the Performing Arts, the United Way, the YMCA, the Greenville Little Theatre and many other community organizations. Whether you are a citizen of America or a citizen of the world, the Wyche firm would not expect you to select legal counsel based on a few printed words. The firm invites you to call them, to come to their offices, or invite you to yours. In that way, you and the firm can determine how the firm can be of service and lasting value to you.

## MAIN AREAS OF PRACTICE:

**Corporate:** The Corporate Practice includes leveraged buy-outs, recapitalizations, public and private offerings, securities compliance, debt refinancings, and mergers and acquisitions. These transactions range from relatively small transactions to billion dollar deals.

**Business Litigation:** The firm also engages in complex civil litigation in state and federal courts, including substantial class action work. It regularly handles matters in areas such as antitrust, First Amendment, securities, insurance practices, and patent and trade secrets. In addition to the areas just mentioned, the firm advises and litigates on behalf of clients in numerous areas, including bankruptcy, communications, construction, employment, employee benefits, environmental, financial institutions, healthcare, municipal bonds, probate, commercial real estate, taxation, intellectual property and trade regulation.

## HEAD OFFICE

**SOUTH CAROLINA**
44 East Camperdown Way, **Greenville**, SC 29601
**Tel:** 864 242 8200   **Fax:** 864 235 8900
**Website:** www.wyche.com

## BRANCH OFFICES

**SOUTH CAROLINA**
1122 Lady Street, Suite 810, **Columbia**, SC 29201
**Tel:** 803 254 6542   **Fax:**  803 254 6544

**Employment:** Wyche attorneys handle employment litigation in federal and state courts. They have successfully argued a complex ERISA case on behalf of their client before the United States Supreme Court; persuaded the South Carolina Court of Appeals to affirm summary judgment for a client in an employee handbook case; and obtained favorable interpretations of the South Carolina Payment of Wages Act in the South Carolina Supreme Court. Members of the practice also provide general counseling for human resources personnel and management.

**Intellectual Property:** The Intellectual Property Practice involves both counseling with respect to the protection of intellectual property, as well as representing clients in litigation concerning infringement or misappropriation of intellectual property. Wyche attorneys have litigated virtually every aspect of intellectual property, including copyrights, trademarks, patents, trade secrets, confidentiality agreements, electronic commerce and common law proprietary information.

**Real Estate:** The Real Estate Practice includes commercial development, asset-based lending purchases and sales, construction contracts, leases, and fee-in-lieu of taxes transactions. Through its subsidiary, Camperdown Title Services, Inc., the firm provides title insurance services and acts as agent for four major title insurance companies.

**First Amendment:** The firm offers a great depth of experience in advising and representing media clients in the full range of First Amendment matters, from defamation to freedom of information.

**Trusts & Estates:** The firm provides comprehensive counseling to clients with complex wealth management needs. Its services include setting up gift trusts, insurance trusts, charitable lead and remainder trusts, family partnerships, premarital agreements and personal residence trusts. The firm also assists clients with probate and trust and estate administration issues.

The Wyche firm is the South Carolina member of Lex Mundi, the world's leading association of independent law firms.

W Y C H E

WYCHE BURGESS FREEMAN & PARHAM, P.A.

Attorneys at Law

## How lawyers are ranked

Every year we carry out thousands of in-depth interviews with clients and lawyers in order to assess the reputations and expertise of business lawyers across the USA. Chambers rankings and editorial are referred to extensively by General Counsel and other purchasers of legal services who look to our recommendations when choosing their lawyers.

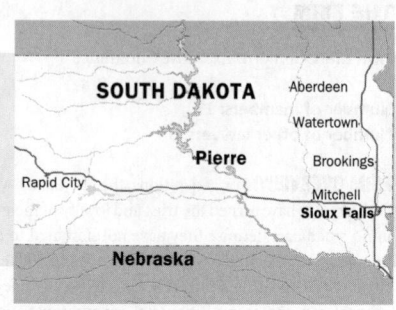

# CORPORATE/COMMERCIAL

### Corporate/Commercial
#### Leading Firms

1. DAVENPORT, EVANS, HURWITZ *Sioux Falls*
   WOODS, FULLER, SHULTZ & SMITH PC *Sioux Falls*
2. CUTLER & DONAHOE LLP *Sioux Falls*
   GUNDERSON, PALMER, GOODSELL *Rapid City*
   MURPHY, GOLDAMMER & PRENDERGAST *Sioux Falls*
3. BANGS, MCCULLEN, BUTLER, FOYE *Rapid City*
   BOYCE, GREENFIELD, PASHBY & WELK *Sioux Falls*
   CADWELL SANFORD DEIBERT & GARRY *Sioux Falls*
   LYNN, JACKSON, SHULTZ & LEBRUN PC *Rapid City*

#### Leading Individuals

1. DAMGAARD Roger *Woods, Fuller, Shultz*
   GOLDAMMER Vance *Murphy, Goldammer*
   GROSSENBURG Bradley *Woods, Fuller, Shultz*
   HAYES Robert *Davenport, Evans, Hurwitz*
   KNUDSON David *Davenport, Evans, Hurwitz*
2. CUTLER Richard *Cutler & Donahoe LLP*
   GOETZINGER Patrick *Gunderson, Palmer, Goodsell*
   GULLICKSON Charles *Davenport, Evans, Hurwitz*
   HAJEK Douglas *Davenport, Evans, Hurwitz*
   KROON David *Woods, Fuller, Shultz*
   WIEDERRICH James *Woods, Fuller, Shultz*
3. ANDERSON Scott *Davenport, Evans, Hurwitz*
   GREENFIELD Gregg *Boyce, Greenfield, Pashby*
   MAGNUSON Lee *Lynn, Jackson, Shultz*
   PERRENOUD Scott *Cadwell Sanford Deibert*
   RAFORTH John *Bangs, McCullen, Butler, Foye*

#### Up-and-coming individuals
   LUST David *Gunderson, Palmer, Goodsell*

### Corporate/Commercial: Bankruptcy
#### Leading Individuals

1. DAMGAARD Roger *Woods, Fuller, Shultz*
   HAYES Robert *Davenport, Evans, Hurwitz*
2. ENTWISTLE Frederick *Woods, Fuller, Shultz*
   GAUER Keith *Davenport, Evans, Hurwitz*

## Band 1

### Davenport, Evans, Hurwitz & Smith LLP

**The Firm:** This firm is regarded as "*among the best in South Dakota*" for the breadth of its corporate and financial expertise. Clients lauded the firm as a "*valuable asset for our company and an integral part of our whole business model.*" Financial institutions and healthcare organizations remain among the firm's core client base and the team handles matters such as securitization, tax credit transactions, bankruptcy and M&A on their behalf. The firm acts as lead counsel on a large railroad construction project and counts several spin-off transactions resulting from this representation.

**The Lawyers:** The "*outstanding*" **Robert Hayes** is "*all-around an extremely knowledgeable attorney who sees the bigger picture.*" He acts for creditors in the form of local and national institutional lenders and juggles this work alongside an active real estate practice. "*He has a calming way of getting things done,*" clients stated. The "*classy*" **David Knudson** provides "*creative and imaginative*" advice on corporate and financial matters. He represents a raft of important clients in the railroad, banking and healthcare sectors. A revered bankruptcy attorney at the firm, **Keith Gauer** gears his practice to helping financial institutions with creditor rights, bankruptcy court representation and foreclosures. Acting for MetaBank in relation to Dan Nelson Automotive Group's bankruptcy counts among his largest recent cases. **Charles Gullickson** impresses with his "*incredibly firm grasp on banking issues.*" His core practice involves advising credit card banks, consumer lending operations and other financial institutions. Highlights have included the structuring of an affinity credit card program for a banking client. He devotes one third of his practice to insurance company insolvencies, with the National Organization of Life & Health Insurance Guaranty Associations counting among his major clients. Former banker **Douglas Hajek** maintains an emphasis on finance-related transactions and has a growing practice in the ethanol industry. He acts as special counsel to a credit card bank and enjoys links with other major financial service institutions. "*A man of high integrity,*" **Scott Anderson** handles corporate finance and M&A matters for an array of clients in the telecom, banking, railroad, hospitality and media sectors. Clients comment that he is "*easy to work with*" and appreciate his "*shrewd business sense.*"

**Clients/Work Highlights:** Citibank; Target National Bank; 1st Financial Bank USA; First PREMIER Bank; Dakota, Minnesota and Eastern Railroad; Sioux Valley Hospitals & Health System and Midcontinent Communications.

### Woods, Fuller, Shultz & Smith PC

**The Firm:** The corporate team here comprises "*top-notch attorneys who work well together.*" The firm stands out as a "*good choice for referrals,*" based on the team's "*considerable experience in specialized transactions.*" Areas of expertise include M&A, regulation and security transactions, as well as bankruptcy, tax and estate planning. Its client base comprises businesses and financial institutions of all shapes and sizes, with particular strength in the banking, agriculture, ethanol and healthcare sectors.

**The Lawyers:** The "*bright, intelligent*" **Roger Damgaard** is admired as a "*bulldog that doesn't back off.*" Acting for regional and national clients on creditor rights cases occupies a large percentage of his time. He is also known for his expertise in the field of banking and financial institutions. "*A key player in corporate law with a strong background in tax and business,*" **Bradley Grossenburg** also comes highly recommended. He is "*responsive and well coordinated.*" Bankruptcy and foreclosure expert **Frederick Entwistle** is "*well regarded for creditor rights issues,*" interviewees report. "*Detail-oriented*" **David Kroon** is "*easy to work with and extremely effective.*" He advises on general corporate matters with a focus on the healthcare sector. **James Wiederrich** received praise for being "*unafraid of complexity*" when it comes to handling corporate and commercial matters.

**Clients/Work Highlights:** Minwest Bank; MetLife; US Bank; Great Plains Ethanol and South Dakota Soybean Processors.

## Band 2

### Cutler & Donahoe LLP

**The Firm:** This firm has a solid reputation for advising local businesses spanning sectors such as telecom, media and banking. In addition, it has a strong client base of larger enterprises including several railroad operators. The attorneys handle a wide variety of commercial and corporate issues and provide strategic advice alongside dealing with transactional matters.

**The Lawyers:** **Richard Cutler** is a *"great businessman"* as much as an *"excellent and experienced attorney."* He underpins the corporate and real estate service offered by the firm, with his expertise in M&A as well as estate and succession planning.

**Clients/Work Highlights:** First American Bank & Trust; Great Western Bank; First National Bank in Sioux Falls; Stan Houston Equipment and Myrl & Roy's Paving.

### Gunderson, Palmer, Goodsell & Nelson LLP

**The Firm:** Hailed by interviewees as coming from the *"number-one law firm in Rapid City,"* the six-strong corporate team covers all aspects of banking law including securitizations, bankruptcies and M&A. It also offers a comprehensive service to business clients on matters such as acquisitions, sales and restructuring.

**The Lawyers:** **Patrick Goetzinger** possesses *"an excellent business mind,"* which he puts to good use as leader of the firm's business and estate planning group. His practice is divided into succession planning, corporate transactions and estate planning, and he acts for family enterprises and wealthy individuals in particular. **David Lust**, who provides ongoing advice to clients on strategic and legal issues, backs him up.

**Clients/Work Highlights:** BankWest; US Bank; Rapid City Telco Federal Credit Union; First PREMIER Bank; Credit Bureau of Rapid City and Wells Fargo.

### Murphy, Goldammer & Prendergast

**The Firm:** The five-strong corporate team advises a range of local and national businesses on transactional matters including sales and acquisitions and stockholder agreements. Creditor bankruptcy is a further area of expertise at the firm.

**The Lawyers:** *"Masterful negotiator"* **Vance Goldammer** is *"skilled at getting great results for clients."* His expertise in corporate and banking matters is well respected and clients *"can always depend on him to do a great job."*

**Clients/Work Highlights:** Furniture Outlets USA, Wells Fargo and Elmen Enterprises are among the firm's clientele.

## Band 3

### Bangs, McCullen, Butler, Foye & Simmons, LLP

**The Firm:** A growing reputation for corporate and commercial work has generated the firm's place in the rankings this year. Split between offices in Rapid City and Sioux Falls, the group advises businesses large and small on corporate matters such as antitrust regulation and stockholder disputes. Assistance is also provided on financial transactions such as sales, acquisitions and restructuring.

**The Lawyers:** **John Raforth** is a *"determined attorney, able to grasp complex issues."* He advises clients on transactional and strategic queries and stands out for his specialization and background knowledge in estate and tax planning.

**Clients/Work Highlights:** These include local businesses of all sizes as well as national and foreign companies.

### Boyce, Greenfield, Pashby & Welk LLP

**The Firm:** Corporate and commercial law is an important focus at this Sioux Falls-based firm. Sales and acquisitions, contracts and stockholder agreements are just some of the matters on which the firm advises. The five attorneys working in this field serve

clients ranging in size and sector, with hospitals and other healthcare organizations being heavily represented.

**The Lawyers:** The *"meticulous and thoughtful"* **Gregg Greenfield** has significant expertise in corporate law. He juggles this work with a busy environmentally focused practice.

**Clients/Work Highlights:** Clients include Harms Oil, Raven Industries and First National Bank in Sioux Falls.

### Cadwell Sanford Deibert & Garry LLP

**The Firm:** The firm's reputation for corporate work comes on the back of its established position in litigation and insurance defense. Clients drawn from across the banking, business and general financial sectors come to the firm for advice on transactional matters and bankruptcy issues in particular.

**The Lawyers:** **Scott Perrenoud** complements his real estate practice with expertise in banking, bankruptcy and consumer regulation. He *"handles sophisticated work with a thorough attention to detail."*

**Clients/Work Highlights:** US Bank; Security Bank; First PREMIER Bank; Security Mortgage; First Midwest Bank; Household Credit Services; Wachovia; Toyota Motor Credit; NationsCredit Commercial; Beneficial and Transamerica Commercial Finance.

### Lynn, Jackson, Shultz & Lebrun PC

**The Firm:** This well-established South Dakota firm has a growing reputation in the corporate arena for the quality of its attorneys. The team advises a variety of clients on transactional matters, as well as tax planning and bankruptcy proceedings.

**The Lawyers:** Founder of the firm's Sioux Falls office and a certified public accountant, **Lee Magnuson** runs a busy general business law practice.

**Clients/Work Highlights:** Black Hills Regional Eye Institute; Rushmore Electric Power Cooperative; Westhills Village; South Dakota School of Mines & Technology; US Bank of South Dakota and Montana-Dakota Utilities.

---

# EMPLOYMENT

# MAINLY DEFENDANT

| Employment: Mainly Defendant |
| Leading Firms |
| [1] BOYCE, GREENFIELD, PASHBY & WELK *Sioux Falls* |
| DAVENPORT, EVANS, HURWITZ & SMITH *Sioux Falls* |
| WOODS, FULLER, SHULTZ & SMITH PC *Sioux Falls* |

## Band 1

### Boyce, Greenfield, Pashby & Welk LLP

**The Firm:** The expanding team of employment law specialists at this firm covers all aspects of discrimination, contractual disputes and workers' compen-

sation. The group successfully defended a local healthcare provider in a claim brought by a doctor for libel, defamation and interference with contract. The team is now handling the case as it goes to the Supreme Court on appeal.

**The Lawyers:** *"The number one in South Dakota for workers' compensation,"* **Michael McKnight** is *"willing to recognize and acknowledge risks for the good of his clients."* He has developed his practice by acting as a mediator on these matters. This skill is in addition to advising on and litigating claims on behalf of defense clients. **Lisa Hansen Marso** yields *"very positive results"* in her civil litigation practice. She places an emphasis on employment and workers' compensation alongside sexual discrimination, FMLA

matters and ERISA litigation.

**Clients/Work Highlights:** The firm represents an array of insurance companies as well as a range of other enterprises.

### Davenport, Evans, Hurwitz & Smith LLP

**The Firm:** The team is rated as a *"key player"* in the South Dakota employment law market, boasting an *"impressive client base and array of files."* The firm provides a comprehensive employment law service and focuses just as squarely on dispute prevention and policy advice as it does on servicing clients' litigation needs. The group handles workers' compensation, discrimination, employee benefits and wage

## Employment: Mainly Defendant
### Leading Individuals

**[1]** HARALDSON Comet *Woods, Fuller, Shultz*
MCKNIGHT Michael *Boyce, Greenfield, Pashby*
ORR Rick *Davenport, Evans, Hurwitz*
SHULTZ Jeff *Woods, Fuller, Shultz*
SIMONS Susan *Davenport, Evans, Hurwitz*

**[2]** ASHMORE Daniel *Gunderson, Palmer, Goodsell*
HOLM Kristi *Davenport, Evans, Hurwitz*
MARSO Lisa *Boyce, Greenfield, Pashby*
SOGN Jon *Lynn, Jackson, Shultz*

and hour work.

**The Lawyers:** Peers enjoy working with "*professional and highly regarded*" civil litigator **Rick Orr** because he "*represents clients' interests without making cases a personal battle.*" **Susan Brunick**

Simons "*consistently gives her best, lending clarity and direction to clients' business.*" She specializes in advising clients pre-litigation on policy issues and the prevention of employment disputes. Clients also rate workers' compensation specialist **Kristi Holm**, who "*leaves no stone unturned and always takes the time to explain issues.*"
**Clients/Work Highlights:** Examples include AIG; Acuity Insurance; St. Paul Travelers; Risk Administration Services and Liberty Mutual.

### Woods, Fuller, Shultz & Smith PC

**The Firm:** The "*successful and respected*" specialists combine to make this firm a "*principal player*" in the state's employment law market. Workers' compensation stands out as one of the firm's main areas of focus, with attorneys having handled a series of successful cases over the last year.
**The Lawyers:** In South Dakota employment law

this firm "*still boasts the two big horses pulling the plow.*" **Comet Haraldson** has "*an ability to handle complex facts and procedures*" while industrial injury and disability expert **Jeff Shultz** is respected for "*winning cases by effective arguing.*" He continues to act for GE and is state counsel for Home Depot.
**Clients/Work Highlights:** The client base comprises large companies in addition to a diverse base of local businesses.

### Other Notable Practitioners

**Daniel Ashmore** of Gunderson, Palmer, Goodsell & Nelson, LLP has a diverse practice. His reputation for work in general employment law and particularly workers' compensation has gained him a place in the rankings this year. **Jon Sogn** of Lynn, Jackson, Schultz & Lebrun, PC is highlighted as a "*quality lawyer*" who deals with a wide range of employment defense cases.

# LITIGATION

## Litigation: General Commercial
### Leading Firms

**[1]** DAVENPORT, EVANS, HURWITZ *Sioux Falls*
WOODS, FULLER, SHULTZ & SMITH PC *Sioux Falls*

**[2]** BANGS, MCCULLEN, BUTLER, FOYE *Rapid City*
BOYCE, GREENFIELD, PASHBY & WELK *Sioux Falls*
CADWELL SANFORD DEIBERT & GARRY *Sioux Falls*
GUNDERSON, PALMER, GOODSELL *Rapid City*
MAY, ADAM, GERDES & THOMPSON, L.L.P. *Pierre*

**[3]** COSTELLO PORTER HILL HEISTERKAMP *Rapid City*
JOHNSON, HEIDEPRIEM, MINER *Sioux Falls*
LYNN, JACKSON, SHULTZ & LEBRUN PC *Rapid City*
SCHAFFER LAW OFFICE *Sioux Falls*

## Band 1

### Davenport, Evans, Hurwitz & Smith LLP

**The Firm:** "*As good as it comes*" is the verdict on the litigation team at this prominent firm where the group of over a dozen attorneys has a "*shrewd sense of which cases should settle and which should be tried.*" Matters handled by the "*excellent*" firm span a broad spectrum of commercial litigation. Insurance defense stands out as a particular area of expertise and the group covers professional and products liability as well as personal injury cases.
**The Lawyers:** Medical malpractice expert **Edwin Evans** is praised as being "*incredibly sharp and hardworking*" and for having "*among the most courtroom experience in South Dakota.*" The "*bright and tenacious*" **Michael Luce** turns his hand to a wide range of trial work including a significant number of insurance defense cases. He has devoted a considerable amount of his time to acting for engineers and architects in construction litigation. "*Upcoming star*" **Mark Haigh** continues to build his expertise in

medical malpractice, with doctors constituting the bulk of his clients. He continues to take on cases of a general commercial nature.
**Clients/Work Highlights:** Sioux Valley Hospitals & Health System; Sioux Falls School District; CNA; Allied Insurance; Liberty Mutual; AIG and Creative Risk Solutions.

### Woods, Fuller, Shultz & Smith PC

**The Firm:** Recognized for its "*considerable strength in business litigation,*" the 15-strong team has earned "*heaps of respect*" within the marketplace. Antitrust, bankruptcy, insurance defense and employment litigation comprise just a small part of the group's business and commercial know-how. The firm also has a considerable reputation for representing lawyers and physicians in professional malpractice cases.
**The Lawyers:** "*Top-notch appellate lawyer*" **James Moore** is the "*complete package*" according to interviewees. "*Not only does he pay incredible attention to detail, he has a great analytical mind and is a skilled writer.*" Products liability and insurance litigation are two of his main areas of focus. **Gary Thimsen** is "*ideal for a case requiring a passionate response,*" according to peers. He has a "*weighty court presence*" and "*such a great memory at trial.*" Aviation, personal injury defense and government liability count among his areas of expertise.
**Clients/Work Highlights:** State of South Dakota; Hy-Vee; Novartis; Tiger Corporation; US Bank and Home Federal Bank.

## Band 2

### Bangs, McCullen, Butler, Foye & Simmons, LLP

**The Firm:** Litigation features heavily at this "*reputable firm,*" which maintains its position as a player in the South Dakota market. The team of 17

attorneys handles a considerable breadth of cases with insurance defense and professional malpractice featuring heavily. General commercial litigation experience includes shareholder and partnership actions, antitrust claims, construction disputes and products liability matters.
**The Lawyers:** **Michael Hickey** enjoys a broad civil practice with minerals, natural resources and water law among his areas of specialization. "*Driven and undoubtedly very bright,*" **Daniel Duffy** has recognized expertise in medical malpractice. He also represents attorneys involved in professional liability claims.
**Clients/Work Highlights:** Clients include Rapid City Regional Hospital, ALPS Corporation and Acuity Insurance.

### Boyce, Greenfield, Pashby & Welk LLP

**The Firm:** "*Always visible and extremely respected,*" this firm has a weighty reputation for litigation and is expanding, with a ninth litigator having joined the ranks this year. As well as handling a broad range of general commercial litigation the firm is able to deal with cases in construction, personal injury, product and professional liability.
**The Lawyers:** **Gary Pashby** "*brings a lot of experience to the table*" and has an "*impressive demeanor in court.*" Architects and engineers involved in construction-related professional malpractice disputes count among his clients. He also handles a wide range of insurance defense and general civil litigation matters. **Roger Sudbeck** is tipped as a "*great young lawyer in the field.*" He mixes general civil litigation with a considerable amount of medical malpractice work and "*takes a common-sense approach to resolving litigation.*" "*Well-regarded*" litigator **Thomas Welk** specializes in general commercial litigation and lawyer malpractice defense. In the healthcare field he handles business-related cases

## Litigation: General Commercial
### Leading Individuals

1  ANDERSON Robert *May, Adam, Gerdes*
   EVANS Edwin *Davenport, Evans, Hurwitz*
   FULLER William *Fuller & Sabers*
   LUCE Michael *Davenport, Evans, Hurwitz*
   MCMAHON James *Murphy, Goldammer*
   MOORE James *Woods, Fuller, Shultz*
   PASHBY Gary *Boyce, Greenfield, Pashby*
   SANFORD Steven *Cadwell Sanford Deibert*
   SCHAFFER Michael *Schaffer Law Office*
   THIMSEN Gary *Woods, Fuller, Shultz*

2  CARPENTER Edward *Costello Porter Hill*
   FRITZ Thomas *Lynn, Jackson, Shultz*
   GARRY William *Cadwell Sanford Deibert*
   GOODSELL Verne *Gunderson, Palmer, Goodsell*
   HICKEY Michael *Bangs, McCullen, Butler, Foye*
   JOHNSON Steven *Johnson, Heidepriem, Miner*
   LANDON Stephen *Cadwell Sanford Deibert*
   PALMER Crisman *Gunderson, Palmer, Goodsell*
   SUDBECK Roger *Boyce, Greenfield, Pashby*
   WELK Thomas *Boyce, Greenfield, Pashby*
   WILBUR Brent *May, Adam, Gerdes*

### Up-and-coming individuals

   HIEB Jack *Richardson, Wyly, Wise*

## Litigation: Healthcare
### Leading Individuals

1  DUFFY Daniel *Bangs, McCullen, Butler, Foye*
   EVANS Edwin *Davenport, Evans, Hurwitz*

2  BRAUN Lonnie *Thomas Nooney Braun Solay*
   GOODSELL Verne *Gunderson, Palmer, Goodsell*
   HAIGH Mark *Davenport, Evans, Hurwitz*
   PALMER Crisman *Gunderson, Palmer, Goodsell*
   RASMUSSEN Reed *Siegel, Barnett & Schutz LLP*
   SUDBECK Roger *Boyce, Greenfield, Pashby*
   WELK Thomas *Boyce, Greenfield, Pashby*

such as physician shareholder disputes. Recent highlights include acting for Avera Health as part of a class action suit.

**Clients/Work Highlights:** Avera Health; Big Stone Project; Wells Fargo; CNA; ConAgra Foods; Swift Beef; XL Design Professional; Raven Industries and Banner Associates.

### Cadwell Sanford Deibert & Garry LLP

**The Firm:** The eight-strong team handles a wide spectrum of litigation matters covering shareholder and stockholder cases, breach of contract and an increasing number of employment disputes. Banking and financial services cases also occupy the team while two attorneys specialize entirely in insurance defense. Highlights of a busy year include settling a regulatory dispute for First PREMIER Bank and defending several large derivative class action cases.

**The Lawyers:** Large, high-risk commercial cases are the domain of **Steven Sanford**, described by interviewees as "*one of the best commercial litigators around*." He impresses clients with his "*incredible

attention to detail.*" Insurance defense specialist **William Garry** takes on cases ranging from workers' compensation to automobile, professional and premises liability. Clients praise him as "*trustworthy and responsive.*" "*Quick-witted*" **Stephen Landon** "*always has an answer to clients' arguments.*" He manages a busy business litigation practice and handles a high volume of employment-related cases.

**Clients/Work Highlights:** First PREMIER Bank; Ronning Enterprises; Hot Stuff Foods; Auto-Owners Insurance; Allied Insurance and EMC Insurance.

### Gunderson, Palmer, Goodsell & Nelson LLP

**The Firm:** Healthcare litigation is a particular forte of this expanding Rapid City firm. The attorneys handle a wide range of cases on behalf of the medical community including medical malpractice. Alongside these healthcare capabilities, insurance defense in its varying guises is a core focus. Personal injury, products liability and banking matters count among the regularly handled cases and an array of insurance companies completes the firm's client roster.

**The Lawyers:** Peers have the "*utmost respect*" for **Verne Goodsell**, a senior partner at the firm whose litigation practice focuses predominantly on medical malpractice, insurance and personal injury. **Crisman Palmer** has an "*engaging personality that suits him well in the courtroom,*" according to interviewees. Many commented on the varied facets of his practice, which includes insurance defense and general commercial litigation.

**Clients/Work Highlights:** American State Bank; Alpha Property & Casualty; American Underwriting Managers; Center Mutual Insurance; Western Dakota Insurers and American Risk Pooling Consultants.

### May, Adam, Gerdes & Thompson, L.L.P.

**The Firm:** The firm comes highly recommended for insurance defense work as well as its expertise in lender and governmental liability litigation. The eight lawyers making up the litigation team at the firm's Pierre office have varied experience in court and tribunals. They regularly undertake litigation at the state and federal level on behalf of clients. The firm takes on a considerable number of personal injury matters on behalf of both plaintiffs and defendants, and has a healthy diet of products liability work.

**The Lawyers:** "*A wonderful lawyer with great jury appeal,*" **Robert Anderson** gained admiration across the board for his expertise as a litigator. He acts for both sides when it comes to personal injury matters and also handles general commercial litigation for a strong client base. "*There is nobody more knowledgeable*" than **Brent Wilbur** when it comes to the litigious aspects of agricultural lending. Among other matters, he acts as lead attorney for American Bank & Trust in a dispute with a livestock owner. Commercial litigation, creditor bankruptcy and lender liability are further facets of his practice.

**Clients/Work Highlights:** South Dakota Public

Entity Pool for Liability; IBM; GM; South Dakota Bankers Association; BankWest South Dakota and Farm Credit Services.

## Band 3

### Costello Porter Hill Heisterkamp Bushnell & Carpenter LLP

**The Firm:** Based in Rapid City, this well-established firm has considerable ability in the field of litigation. In addition to acting on general commercial matters the team attracts a variety of clients on the strength of its professional and products liability expertise. Personal injury and healthcare matters also feature strongly.

**The Lawyers:** "*Fearless*" **Edward Carpenter** impresses by being "*smart and consistently well prepared.*" Insurance defense and construction are core elements of his litigation practice.

**Clients/Work Highlights:** American States Insurance; Prudential Insurance; Continental Loss Adjusting Services and MetLife.

### Johnson, Heidepriem, Miner, Marlow & Janklow, LLP

**The Firm:** This is a specialized civil litigation outfit known for being a leader in plaintiff representation, although the firm does serve a broad array of clients. Operating out of Sioux Falls and Yankton the attorneys handle a range of business and commercial litigation. Personal injury is a core source of work, and on insurance matters the firm represents insurance companies in addition to plaintiffs.

**The Lawyers:** **Steven Johnson** is a man who can be relied upon to "*add value to cases*" and "*build clients' perception of risk.*" He divides his practice between personal injury and business litigation.

**Clients/Work Highlights:** The firm acts for a range of banks, insurance companies, public entities and businesses including First Dakota National Bank, EMC Insurance and a number of individuals.

### Lynn, Jackson, Shultz & Lebrun PC

**The Firm:** Split between offices in Rapid City and Sioux Falls the litigation attorneys at this firm have a solid reputation, particularly in terms of their defense work. The firm engages in general commercial litigation as well as medical malpractice, personal injury, products liability and property cases.

**The Lawyers:** The "*charming*" **Thomas Fritz** is singled out. He is "*not afraid of the courtroom and has a great feel for the jury.*" The trial lawyer's practice includes complex litigation in the commercial field.

**Clients/Work Highlights:** The firm acts for a range of local and national enterprises including a series of insurance companies. Examples include Federated Insurance, Prudential Life Insurance and Transamerica Insurance Group.

### Schaffer Law Office

**The Firm:** Civil litigation is the name of the game at this two-man team based in Sioux Falls. The attorneys tackle insurance defense, personal injury and professional and products liability as well as general commercial litigation matters. The group is known particularly for its trial and appellate capabilities.

**The Lawyers:** **Michael Schaffer**'s style is certainly revered: he is "*the most tenacious lawyer I have ever seen*," claimed one commentator; "*he will not stop until he gets his result.*" Insurance defense and commercial litigation are prominent aspects of his practice.

**Clients/Work Highlights:** Continental Western; American Family Insurance; State Auto Insurance; North Star Mutual Insurance and First Savings Bank.

## Other Notable Practitioners

**William Fuller** left Woods, Fuller, Shultz & Smith PC this year to establish his own firm in Sioux Falls, Fuller & Sabers. Described as "*down to earth with much jury appeal,*" commentators continued to recommend him as a top choice. Professional malpractice and insurance defense are his particular strengths. **James McMahon** of Murphy, Goldammer & Prendergast stands tall for his excellence as a "*forceful but not overly aggressive*" litigator. He acts largely on behalf of plaintiffs and "*comes across to the jury as resolutely strong and solid.*" Medical malprac-

tice defense specialist **Lonnie Braun** of Thomas Nooney Braun Solay & Bernard, LLP is highly respected among peers and clients for his comprehensive practice. Siegel, Barnett & Schutz LLP's **Reed Rasmussen** is well known in the market for his civil and criminal litigation work. Market sources singled out **Jack Hieb** of Richardson, Wyly, Wise, Sauck & Hieb, LLP for his developing expertise as a litigator. His practice covers insurance and general civil litigation.

# REAL ESTATE

## Real Estate
### Leading Firms

1. **BANGS, MCCULLEN, BUTLER, FOYE** *Rapid City*
   **DAVENPORT, EVANS, HURWITZ** *Sioux Falls*
2. **BOYCE, GREENFIELD, PASHBY & WELK** *Sioux Falls*
   **CUTLER & DONAHOE LLP** *Sioux Falls*
   **GUNDERSON, PALMER, GOODSELL** *Rapid City*
   **WOODS, FULLER, SHULTZ & SMITH PC** *Sioux Falls*

### Leading Individuals

#### Senior Statesman
**GREENFIELD** Russell *Boyce, Greenfield, Pashby*

1. **CUTLER** Richard *Cutler & Donahoe LLP*
   **DONOHUE** P Daniel *Davenport, Evans, Hurwitz*
   **FOYE** Thomas *Bangs, McCullen, Butler*
   **RITER** Charles *Bangs, McCullen, Butler*
2. **GOETZINGER** Patrick *Gunderson, Palmer, Goodsell*
   **GOLDAMMER** Vance *Murphy, Goldammer*
   **HAYES** Robert *Davenport, Evans, Hurwitz*
   **JENSEN** Curtis *DeMersseman Jensen Christianson*
   **WIEDERRICH** James *Woods, Fuller, Shultz*

## Band 1

### Bangs, McCullen, Butler, Foye & Simmons, LLP

**The Firm:** The real estate department of this firm contains "*many rising stars,*" according to interviewees. The lawyers provide "*quality, broad-based business advice*" to a clientele that includes landlords and tenants, buyers and sellers, brokers and developers. The department commonly handles commercial as well as residential development and acts on the full spectrum of real estate matters. Its expertise covers transactions, leases, real estate tax and zoning issues.

**The Lawyers:** Clients spoke highly of the service from specialist **Thomas Foye**, with one commenting: "*He always does a marvelous job for us.*" His deep knowledge of real estate sits alongside the business, estate planning, tax and probate elements of his practice. **Charles Riter** is "*one of the best-connected attorneys in the area,*" claimed one client; "*if he doesn't have the answer he'll always know where to find it.*"

The last year has seen this real estate expert handling substantial sales of ranch land of behalf of sellers.

**Clients/Work Highlights:** The firm enjoys a widening client portfolio drawn from within and beyond the state borders. Examples include Crazy Horse Memorial, Corner Construction and Sutton Rodeo.

### Davenport, Evans, Hurwitz & Smith LLP

**The Firm:** The success of this real estate practice is informed by the firm's weighty reputation in corporate law and banking. The team of eight attorneys acts for clients from these areas on a regular basis, dealing with real estate needs that include loans and mortgages. Handling foreclosures for South Dakota Housing Development Authority is a continuing mainstay of the team's work. Some of South Dakota's largest developers and general contractors also benefit from the real estate expertise offered by the firm. As well as managing sales, acquisitions and other development transactions, the lawyers are experienced in providing regulatory representation.

**The Lawyers:** **Daniel Donohue** "*absolutely qualifies for his ranking,*" market sources professed. An acclaimed expert in complex transactions, he handles all aspects of acquisition on behalf of both individuals and companies seeking to develop land. He also advises on a plethora of valuation matters. Highlights this year include advising a contractor on the acquisition of land by Sioux River for a substantial commercial development. Interviewees also singled out the "*outstanding*" **Robert Hayes**. He is known for his expertise in real estate financing and acts as local attorney on multistate lending transactions, usually on behalf of creditors.

**Clients/Work Highlights:** Sioux Valley Hospital; South Dakota Housing Development Authority; Schoeneman Brothers Company; Ronning Companies; First National Bank; Sioux Falls Development Foundation and Children's Care Hospital & School.

## Band 2

### Boyce, Greenfield, Pashby & Welk LLP

**The Firm:** The established real estate practice at this "*top-drawer firm*" is recognized for providing a broad range of advice to clients. The group advises on all aspects of sales, acquisitions and leasing, both commercial and residential. In addition, clients seek out the firm for assistance with property financing and management issues.

**The Lawyers:** Veteran real estate expert **Russell Greenfield** upholds his "*outstanding reputation*" in this field. He has a wealth of experience and connections in such areas as state and municipal bonds. His practice extends to estate planning, real estate financing and development.

**Clients/Work Highlights:** Citibank (South Dakota) and First American Bank & Trust.

### Cutler & Donahoe LLP

**The Firm:** Based in Sioux Falls, this strong player has a well-established reputation in the South Dakota real estate market. Many family businesses head to this firm for advice, where the lawyers handle numerous land transactions on their behalf. Commercial and residential developers, banks and other financial institutions also obtain varied assistance on real estate matters. Financing and acquisitions remain particular areas of expertise for the firm.

**The Lawyers:** **Richard Cutler** "*combines superior legal skills with excellent business knowledge,*" according to interviewees. He is known as an expert in varied aspects of real estate practice, and market sources recognized his business-getting acumen to be a substantial asset to the firm.

**Clients/Work Highlights:** Individuals, developers and banks count among the firm's clients.

### Gunderson, Palmer, Goodsell & Nelson LLP

**The Firm:** Real estate is a core area of practice at this firm and there is no doubt that its reputation in the marketplace is growing. The "*well-versed*" attorneys handle a broad spectrum of real estate deals for residential and commercial developments, from small-scale to complex. Clients can expect to find expertise in such aspects as sales, acquisitions, financing and mortgages.

**The Lawyers:** Corporate and estate planning specialist **Patrick Goetzinger** is held in high regard for real estate work. Commercial developers are the main beneficiaries of his expertise and he advises on all aspects of development, including zoning. He also acts for a swathe of family-run enterprises, farms and ranches, as well as high net worth individuals.

**Clients/Work Highlights:** Eagle Sales of the Black Hills; RCC Western Stores; Stoneridge Development; Rapid City Area School District; Austin Mutual Insurance; CIGNA; Casualty Reciprocal Exchange and American Underwriting Managers.

## Woods, Fuller, Shultz & Smith PC

**The Firm:** Riding on the success of its corporate and litigation work, this firm has a growing reputation in the real estate market. Clients recommended the "*excellent set of lawyers*" that has earned the firm a foothold in the rankings this year. The attorneys act for a wide range of clients on commercial real estate matters. This service is bolstered by the considerable tax, estate planning and regulatory expertise the firm has to offer.

**The Lawyers:** Many commentators highlighted **James Wiederrich**'s skill in the real estate field and this recommendation has earned him a place in the rankings for the first time.

## Other Notable Practitioners

Not only is **Vance Goldammer** of Murphy, Goldammer & Prendergast, LLP a sought-after corporate attorney, he is also "*a sound choice for real estate,*" according to market sources. He manages a busy practice advising real estate clients on a range of concerns. DeMersseman Jensen Christianson Stanton & Huffman LLP's **Curtis Jensen** was singled out as an "*extremely prominent*" figure in the market. He devotes a substantial part of his practice to real estate matters.

# Leaders in South Dakota

**ANDERSON, Robert**
May, Adam, Gerdes & Thompson, L.L.P., Pierre 605 224 8803
*Recommended in Litigation*

**ANDERSON, Scott**
Davenport, Evans, Hurwitz & Smith LLP, Sioux Falls 605 336 2880
*Recommended in Corporate/Commercial*

**ASHMORE, Daniel**
Gunderson, Palmer, Goodsell & Nelson LLP, Rapid City 605 342 1078
*Recommended in Employment*

**BRAUN, Lonnie**
Thomas Nooney Braun Solay & Bernard, LLP, Rapid City 605 348 7516
*Recommended in Litigation*

**CARPENTER, Edward**
Costello Porter Hill Heisterkamp Bushnell & Carpenter LLP, Rapid City 605 343 2410
*Recommended in Litigation*

**CUTLER, Richard**
Cutler & Donahoe LLP, Sioux Falls 605 335 4950
*Recommended in Corporate/Commercial, Real Estate*

**DAMGAARD, Roger**
Woods, Fuller, Shultz & Smith PC, Sioux Falls 605 336 3890
*Recommended in Corporate/Commercial*

**DONOHUE, PDaniel**
Davenport, Evans, Hurwitz & Smith LLP, Sioux Falls 605 336 2880
*Recommended in Real Estate*

**DUFFY, Daniel**
Bangs, McCullen, Butler, Foye & Simmons, LLP, Rapid City 605 343 1040
*Recommended in Litigation*

**ENTWISTLE, Frederick**
Woods, Fuller, Shultz & Smith PC, Sioux Falls 605 336 3890
*Recommended in Corporate/Commercial*

**EVANS, Edwin**
Davenport, Evans, Hurwitz & Smith LLP, Sioux Falls 605 336 2880
*Recommended in Litigation*

**FOYE, Thomas**
Bangs, McCullen, Butler, Foye & Simmons, LLP, Rapid City 605 343 1040
*Recommended in Real Estate*

**FRITZ, Thomas**
Lynn, Jackson, Shultz & Lebrun PC, Rapid City 605 342 2592
*Recommended in Litigation*

**FULLER, William**
Fuller & Sabers, Sioux Falls 605 333 0003
*Recommended in Litigation*

**GARRY, William**
Cadwell Sanford Deibert & Garry LLP, Sioux Falls 605 336 0828
*Recommended in Litigation*

**GAUER, Keith**
Davenport, Evans, Hurwitz & Smith LLP, Sioux Falls 605 336 2880
*Recommended in Corporate/Commercial*

**GOETZINGER, Patrick**
Gunderson, Palmer, Goodsell & Nelson LLP, Rapid City 605 342 1078
*Recommended in Corporate/Commercial, Real Estate*

**GOLDAMMER, Vance**
Murphy, Goldammer & Prendergast, Sioux Falls 605 331 2975
*Recommended in Corporate/Commercial, Real Estate*

**GOODSELL, Verne**
Gunderson, Palmer, Goodsell & Nelson LLP, Rapid City 605 342 1078
*Recommended in Litigation*

**GREENFIELD, Gregg**
Boyce, Greenfield, Pashby & Welk LLP, Sioux Falls 605 336 2424
*Recommended in Corporate/Commercial*

**GREENFIELD , Russell**
Boyce, Greenfield, Pashby & Welk LLP, Sioux Falls 605 336 2424
*Recommended in Real Estate*

**GROSSENBURG, Bradley**
Woods, Fuller, Shultz & Smith PC, Sioux Falls 605 336 3890
*Recommended in Corporate/Commercial*

**GULLICKSON, Charles**
Davenport, Evans, Hurwitz & Smith LLP, Sioux Falls 605 336 2880
*Recommended in Corporate/Commercial*

**HAIGH, Mark**
Davenport, Evans, Hurwitz & Smith LLP, Sioux Falls 605 336 2880
*Recommended in Litigation*

**HAJEK, Douglas**
Davenport, Evans, Hurwitz & Smith LLP, Sioux Falls 605 336 2880
*Recommended in Corporate/Commercial*

**HARALDSON, Comet**
Woods, Fuller, Shultz & Smith PC, Sioux Falls 605 336 3890
*Recommended in Employment*

**HAYES, Robert**
Davenport, Evans, Hurwitz & Smith LLP, Sioux Falls 605 336 2880
*Recommended in Corporate/Commercial, Real Estate*

**HICKEY, Michael**
Bangs, McCullen, Butler, Foye & Simmons, LLP, Rapid City 605 343 1040
*Recommended in Litigation*

**HIEB, Jack**
Richardson, Wyly, Wise, Sauck & Hieb, LLP, Aberdeen 605 225 6310
*Recommended in Litigation*

**HOLM, Kristi**
Davenport, Evans, Hurwitz & Smith LLP, Sioux Falls 605 336 2880
*Recommended in Employment*

**JENSEN, Curtis**
DeMersseman Jensen Christianson Stanton & Huffman LLP, Rapid City 605 342 2814
*Recommended in Real Estate*

**JOHNSON , Steven**
Johnson, Heidepriem, Miner, Marlow & Janklow, LLP, Sioux Falls 605 338 4304
*Recommended in Litigation*

**KNUDSON, David**
Davenport, Evans, Hurwitz & Smith LLP, Sioux Falls 605 336 2880
*Recommended in Corporate/Commercial*

**KROON, David**
Woods, Fuller, Shultz & Smith PC, Sioux Falls 605 336 3890
*Recommended in Corporate/Commercial*

**LANDON, Stephen**
Cadwell Sanford Deibert & Garry LLP, Sioux Falls 605 336 0828
*Recommended in Litigation*

**LUCE, Michael**
Davenport, Evans, Hurwitz & Smith LLP, Sioux Falls 605 336 2880
*Recommended in Litigation*

**LUST, David**
Gunderson, Palmer, Goodsell & Nelson
LLP, Rapid City 605 342 1078
*Recommended in
Corporate/Commercial*

**MAGNUSON, Lee**
Lynn, Jackson, Shultz & Lebrun PC,
Rapid City 605 342 2592
*Recommended in
Corporate/Commercial*

**MARSO, Lisa**
Boyce, Greenfield, Pashby & Welk LLP,
Sioux Falls 605 336 2424
*Recommended in Employment*

**MCKNIGHT, Michael**
Boyce, Greenfield, Pashby & Welk LLP,
Sioux Falls 605 336 2424
*Recommended in Employment*

**MCMAHON, James**
Murphy, Goldammer & Prendergast,
Sioux Falls 605 331 2975
*Recommended in Litigation*

**MOORE, James**
Woods, Fuller, Shultz & Smith PC, Sioux
Falls 605 336 3890
*Recommended in Litigation*

**ORR, Rick**
Davenport, Evans, Hurwitz & Smith LLP,
Sioux Falls 605 336 2880

*Recommended in Employment*

**PALMER, Crisman**
Gunderson, Palmer, Goodsell & Nelson
LLP, Rapid City 605 342 1078
*Recommended in Litigation*

**PASHBY, Gary**
Boyce, Greenfield, Pashby & Welk LLP,
Sioux Falls 605 336 2424
*Recommended in Litigation*

**PERRENOUD, Scott**
Cadwell Sanford Deibert & Garry LLP,
Sioux Falls 605 336 0828
*Recommended in
Corporate/Commercial*

**RAFORTH, John**
Bangs, McCullen, Butler, Foye & Simmons, LLP, Rapid City 605 343 1040
*Recommended in
Corporate/Commercial*

**RASMUSSEN, Reed**
Siegel, Barnett & Schutz LLP, Aberdeen
605 225 5420
*Recommended in Litigation*

**RITER, Charles**
Bangs, McCullen, Butler, Foye & Simmons, LLP, Rapid City
605 343 1040
*Recommended in Real Estate*

**SANFORD, Steven**
Cadwell Sanford Deibert & Garry LLP,
Sioux Falls 605 336 0828
*Recommended in Litigation*

**SCHAFFER, Michael**
Schaffer Law Office, Sioux Falls
605 274 6760
*Recommended in Litigation*

**SHULTZ, Jeff**
Woods, Fuller, Shultz & Smith PC, Sioux
Falls 605 336 3890
*Recommended in Employment*

**SIMONS, Susan**
Davenport, Evans, Hurwitz & Smith LLP,
Sioux Falls 605 336 2880
*Recommended in Employment*

**SOGN, Jon**
Lynn, Jackson, Shultz & Lebrun PC,
Rapid City 605 342 2592
*Recommended in Employment*

**SUDBECK, Roger**
Boyce, Greenfield, Pashby & Welk LLP,
Sioux Falls 605 336 2424
*Recommended in Litigation*

**THIMSEN, Gary**
Woods, Fuller, Shultz & Smith PC, Sioux
Falls 605 336 3890
*Recommended in Litigation*

**WELK, Thomas**
Boyce, Greenfield, Pashby & Welk LLP,
Sioux Falls 605 336 2424
*Recommended in Litigation*

**WIEDERRICH, James**
Woods, Fuller, Shultz & Smith PC, Sioux
Falls 605 336 3890
*Recommended in
Corporate/Commercial, Real Estate*

**WILBUR, Brent**
May, Adam, Gerdes & Thompson, L.L.P.,
Pierre 605 224 8803
*Recommended in Litigation*

## How lawyers are ranked

Every year we carry out thousands of in-depth interviews with clients and lawyers in order to assess the reputations and expertise of business lawyers across the USA. Chambers rankings and editorial are referred to extensively by General Counsel and other purchasers of legal services who look to our recommendations when choosing their lawyers.

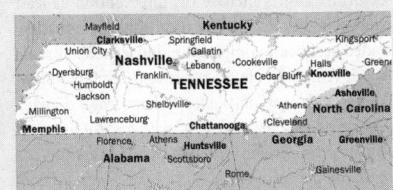

# CORPORATE/M&A

## Corporate/M&A
### Leading Firms

1. **BASS, BERRY & SIMS PLC** *Nashville*
   **WALLER LANSDEN DORTCH & DAVIS** *Nashville*
2. **BAKER, DONELSON** *Memphis*
   **BOULT, CUMMINGS, CONNERS & BERRY** *Nashville*
   **HARWELL HOWARD HYNE GABBERT** *Nashville*
3. **GLANKLER BROWN, PLLC** *Memphis*
   **MILLER & MARTIN PLLC** *Nashville*
   **SHERRARD & ROE PLC** *Nashville*

### Leading Individuals

1. **BRAUN Stephen** *Boult, Cummings, Conners*
   **CHEEK III James** *Bass, Berry & Sims PLC*
   **COLE J Chase** *Waller Lansden Dortch*
   **MANNER Mark** *Harwell Howard Hyne Gabbert*
   **WALTON Leigh** *Bass, Berry & Sims PLC*
2. **BISHOP III George** *Waller Lansden Dortch*
   **COWART Richard** *Baker, Donelson*
   **DAVIS JR Ralph** *Waller Lansden Dortch*
   **GILBERT Paul** *Waller Lansden Dortch*
   **HARDCASTLE Jay** *Boult, Cummings, Conners*
   **HILL J Reginald** *Waller Lansden Dortch*
   **HYNE Ernest** *Harwell Howard Hyne Gabbert*
   **WALKER Mitchell** *Bass, Berry & Sims PLC*
3. **HOLT III Berry** *Boult, Cummings, Conners*
   **LAMAR III Howard** *Bass, Berry & Sims PLC*
   **MITCHELL E Marlee** *Waller Lansden Dortch*
   **SHERRARD III Thomas** *Sherrard & Roe PLC*
   **THOMPSON Bob** *Bass, Berry & Sims PLC*
   **VOIGT John** *Sherrard & Roe PLC*

### Up-and-coming individuals

**BAILEY Roger** *Miller & Martin PLLC*
**COX David** *Harwell Howard Hyne Gabbert*
**METCALF Bryan** *Bass, Berry & Sims PLC*
**ROLAPP Todd** *Bass, Berry & Sims PLC*

## Band 1

### Bass, Berry & Sims PLC

See firm details p.1820

**The Firm:** With four offices statewide, this *"top-notch"* local outfit provides *"as good a service as New York or Washington firms at Nashville prices."* With prominent clients in the healthcare, corporate and financial services industries, the firm's 49-strong team has extensive experience of M&A, public offerings and securities issues. During the past year, for instance, the group has acted as underwriters' counsel on numerous REIT public offerings for a total value of almost $1billion. A further area of expertise lies in corporate governance regulation and the firm advises on a number of corporate boards of directors.

**The Lawyers:** *"First choice for venture capital work,"* **James Cheek** (see p.1811) is *"as good a securities lawyer as you can get in the whole of the USA,"* according to one source. Over the past year, he has been involved in several large acquisitions. Corporate governance represents another focal point of his practice and he is busy developing training schemes for corporate boards of directors. *"Leading securities lawyer"* **Leigh Walton** (see p.1818) has a combination of *"broad technical knowledge"* and *"the ability to find pragmatic, business-minded solutions."* She is also strong on M&A in the healthcare sector. **Mitchell Walker** (see p.1818) has successfully established a niche in acting for publicly traded companies. He recently represented Performance Food Group in the sale of its fresh-cut produce segment to Chiquita Brands International for $855 million. Known for his *"dependable judgment,"* **Bob Thompson**'s (see p.1817) practice focuses on securities regulation, M&A and advice to financial institutions. Recently, he represented Pinnacle Financial Partners in the acquisition of Cavalry Banking. *"Highly intelligent and experienced"* **Howard Lamar** (see p.1815) is very active in the areas of M&A and venture capital financing transactions. Recent highlights include the representation of HealthSpring in an approximately $430 million recapitalization transaction with investors affiliated to GTCR Golder Rauner. **Bryan Metcalf** (see p.1815) enters the tables this year following enthusiastic endorsement by clients and peers. With the *"ability to integrate business, tax and legal concerns,"* he has been busy developing a stock option plan for Jack Daniel's manufacturers Brown-Forman. Also present is **Todd Rolapp** (see p.1816) who has a *"wonderful attitude to service,"* according to sources.

**Clients/Work Highlights:** The firm has advised Gaylord Entertainment on corporate and securities law. It also advised Brown-Forman on securities and corporate governance, and assisted it in the creation of a stock option plan. Genesco; National Health Investors; Greene County Bank and Mid-America Apartment Communities are part of the firm's client roster.

### Waller Lansden Dortch & Davis

See firm details p.1828

**The Firm:** This *"nationally reputed, deal-making firm"* is particularly strong at closing transactions involving regulated sectors such as the financial services, IT and communications industries. Its undoubted strength in healthcare also guarantees it a presence in major deals within that field. By way of example, one recent highlight was the closure of a major transaction involving the acquisition of a hospital formerly owned by the Dona Ana County Health Council in New Mexico. Corporate restructuring proves a further boon to the practice, with its team addressing issues arising from the acquisition or sale of financially troubled companies, and corporate governance is also well to the fore. Clients stressed the group's *"outstanding technical confidence"* and its *"flexibility and honesty"* as its defining features.

**The Lawyers:** *"Terrific"* **Chase Cole** (see p.1811) *"stands out for his corporate governance expertise,"* according to one market source. Recent engagements include representing Capstone Turbine Corporation in a common stock offering and assisting in the sale of KEYS Group Holdings to Universal Health Services. Peers expressed recognition for **George Bishop**'s (see p.1810) vast experience in dealing with sales and acquisitions of investor-owned hospitals and healthcare facilities. Although he usually represents buyers, he recently acted for the seller in the KEYS Group transaction. Chair of the corporate and M&A practice **Ralph Davis** (see p.1812) has been engaged by Thomas Cressey Equity Partners to represent them in a series of acquisitions and investments in the healthcare industry. His other highlights include handling corporate governance, securities and M&A work for BancorpSouth, a financial services holding company. Commentators highlighted Davis' *"supportiveness"* and *"great combination of business judgment and legal knowledge"* as reasons for his continuing success. "*Outstanding*" **Paul Gilbert** (see p.1813) has worked on several high-profile transactions within the healthcare sector. Examples include his intervention as lead counsel in the sale of a Florida hospital by a publicly traded healthcare company headquartered in Brentwood, Tennessee. He offers clients a combination of "*remarkable legal and industry knowledge, disarmingly effective communication skills and an uncanny ability to consistently offer practical solutions to the most complex issues.*" A "*top choice for healthcare matters,*" **Reginald Hill** (see p.1813) brings gravitas to a mix of matters that includes acquisitions and divestitures for hospital companies, IPOs and corporate governance issues. **Marlee Mitchell** (see p.1815) has extensive securities law and corporate finance experience. Mitchell recently represented a national bank holding company, directing the securities work involved in the simultaneous acquisition of two community banks comprised of 15 branches and more than $300 million in deposits.

**Clients/Work Highlights:** The firm represented a behavioral healthcare services provider in a $210 million divestiture recently. Other highlights include the group's representation of the largest hospital corporation in the world; acting in the sale of a national managed care network and in the forming of a joint venture with an oncology company in order to pursue cancer research.

## Band 2

### Baker, Donelson, Bearman, Caldwell & Berkowitz, PC

See firm details p.1819

**The Firm:** With offices in Memphis, Nashville, Knoxville, Chattanooga, Johnson City and Huntsville, this firm benefits from an extensive statewide presence. It boasts a particularly impressive corporate governance team, with some of its members having provided advice on aspects of the Sarbanes-Oxley Act while the Senate debated the legislation. The firm's focus on corporate government is further reflected in its involvement with the Ethics Officer Association. Clients value the firm's size and the fact that it is "*well qualified in many areas.*" These include corporate finance, M&A, venture capital and business structuring and planning.

**The Lawyers:** Chairman of the healthcare department and president of the American Healthcare Lawyers Association **Richard Cowart** (see p.1811) works primarily as board counsel to health service organizations. Sources indicated he is a "*top-notch*" attorney and "*the first choice for the representation of physicians.*"

**Clients/Work Highlights:** The team recently acted for a biomedical foundation in all parts of the process leading to the creation of a research park. Prominent clients include Toyota; Entergy; American Trucking Association and Boeing.

### Boult, Cummings, Conners & Berry, PLC

See firm details p.1821

**The Firm:** The corporate practice at this "*top healthcare firm*" has a slant towards healthcare-related transactions. By way of example, over the past year the team has worked on the restructuring of a specialty hospital and on a number of purchases and sales of businesses within the healthcare sector. It also benefits from the firm's capabilities in other areas such as government relations, tax and intellectual property, with the result that it can provide all-around advice when working on transactions.

**The Lawyers:** "*One of the best for healthcare-related acquisition work,*" **Stephen Braun** (see p.1810) provides counsel to some of the nation's largest hospital systems on transactional, regulatory and operations matters. **Jay Hardcastle** (see p.1813) is "*the go-to guy for regulatory issues,*" according to sources. Over the past year, he has worked on the defense of several whistle-blower claims involving fraud and abuse allegations. **Berry Holt** (see p.1814) has a particularly strong grasp of tax-exempt legislation applicable to nonprofit healthcare organizations. This "*excellent*" attorney has almost 30 years of experience and can cover transactional, regulatory and operational matters.

### Harwell Howard Hyne Gabbert & Manner, PC

See firm details p.1823

**The Firm:** This firm is comparatively small but, nevertheless, is known to handle complex M&A and financing matters. Recent examples include representing three bidders in arranging the financing for the purchase of ten hospitals. The team also assisted two healthcare industry executives in the forming of their own company and in the obtaining of venture capital. Clients expressed their satisfaction with the firm's "*high level of support*" and with its "*quick and timely responses.*"

**The Lawyers:** **Mark Manner** has substantial experience of assisting public companies in dealing with their outside auditors, and advising companies on capital formation and securities offerings. Recently, he has been spending an increasing amount of time working with boards of directors of public companies on corporate governance issues flowing out of the new regulatory environment. Clients keep returning to him because "*he can always provide the exact kind of advice required.*" Sources consider name partner **Ernest Hyne** to be "*excellent, responsive, professional and reliable.*" He has recently represented an independent committee involved in a transaction worth around $1.5 billion. Consistent endorsement from market commentators has propelled **David Cox** into the tables this year. He acts as main adviser to a number of clients in the healthcare and technology sectors and is appreciated by clients for his "*excellent business and legal judgment.*" Interviewees described him as "*a good person to bounce ideas off.*"

**Clients/Work Highlights:** The team represented the shareholders of Triad Mining in the $90 million

sale of the company to James River Coal. Other clients include Berlitz; National Health Investors; American HomePatient; Pinnacle Financial Partners and Advocat.

## Band 3

### Glankler Brown, PLLC

**The Firm:** With a 12-attorney corporate, business and tax team, this firm has significant presence in Memphis. Known to have a core of "*excellent attorneys,*" the group is involved in a considerable number of significant transactions through its representation of a major national bank. The team has acted in debt and equity securities offerings and is particularly renowned for its expertise with respect to federal and state franchise law matters.

**The Lawyers:** **Grattan Brown** is a senior partner at the firm. He represents National Commerce Financial Corporation and is general counsel to Memphis-Shelby County Airport Authority.

### Miller & Martin PLLC

See firm details p.1826

**The Firm:** With more than 170 attorneys housed in its three offices, this leading Southeastern player has "*the strongest presence in Chattanooga.*" The corporate group at the firm has extensive M&A experience, having recently completed both domestic and international acquisitions, valued in excess of $3 billion, for a major corporation. Securities, private equity and venture capital financing constitute further areas of excellence.

**The Lawyers:** "*Great transactional and securities lawyer*" **Roger Bailey** (see p.1810) enters the tables for the first time following strong recommendation from market commentators. Bailey has a collection of clients in the technology sector and also represents a private equity fund that utilizes federal tax credits to make investments.

**Clients/Work Highlights:** The team has an enviable portfolio of large public clients. Its recent highlights include representing a consumer products company in a series of separate transactions relating to the purchase of product lines for a total sum of more than $300 million. It also handled the sale of a publicly held major fast food chain valued at $145 million.

### Sherrard & Roe PLC

**The Firm:** The firm has considerably strengthened its corporate team over the past year with the incorporation of several former Stokes Bartholomew attorneys. The department has had a high volume of M&A work recently, arranging, for instance, the management buy-up of a credit card issuer for more than $60 million. On the advisory side, the team counsels public and private companies on securities compliance issues and corporate governance.

**The Lawyers:** Founding member **Thomas Sherrard** was recommended to researchers for his wide-ranging expertise. He combines his legal practice with a position as adjunct professor at Vanderbilt

University Law School and at Owen Graduate School of Management. Colleague **John Voigt** is also recommended for his corporate work, especially on the healthcare side. "*An attorney with a sensible approach* *to business, he makes the complicated look easy.*" Clients/Work Highlights: During 2005, the team closed a transaction in excess of $25 million for a printing company and negotiated the takeout of a large stockholder from a public company. Signature Health Alliance; UBS Financial Services; Nissan and MarketStreet Equities are part of the firm's long-standing clientele.

# EMPLOYMENT

**Employment: Mainly Defendant**
Leading Firms

1. **BASS, BERRY & SIMS PLC** *Nashville*
   **KIESEWETTER WISE KAPLAN PRATHER** *Memphis*
   **KING & BALLOW** *Nashville*
   **MILLER & MARTIN PLLC** *Chattanooga*
   **WALLER LANSDEN DORTCH & DAVIS** *Nashville*
2. **BOULT, CUMMINGS** *Nashville*
   **CONSTANGY, BROOKS & SMITH, LLC** *Nashville*
   **FORD & HARRISON LLP** *Memphis*
   **KRAMER RAYSON LLP** *Knoxville*
   **LEWIS FISHER HENDERSON** *Memphis*
   **OGLETREE, DEAKINS** *Nashville*

Leading Individuals

1. **BOSTON Robert** *Waller Lansden Dortch*
   **OZIER William** *Bass, Berry & Sims PLC*
   **PRATHER Paul** *Kiesewetter Wise*
2. **BLUE JR William** *Constangy, Brooks*
   **BRIDGESMITH Larry** *Waller Lansden Dortch*
   **ELLIS Karen** *Bass, Berry & Sims PLC*
   **FRAZIER Keith** *Ogletree, Deakins*
   **GARRETT Tim** *Bass, Berry & Sims PLC*
   **GERSON Herb** *Ford & Harrison LLP*
   **KAPLAN Jonathan** *Kiesewetter Wise*
   **KIESEWETTER Jay** *Kiesewetter Wise*
   **LEWIS Frederick** *Lewis Fisher Henderson*
   **LONERGAN Matthew** *Boult, Cummings*
   **PHILLIPS Edward** *Kramer Rayson LLP*
   **PHILLIPS JR John** *Miller & Martin PLLC*
   **WAYLAND R Eddie** *King & Ballow*
3. **CRENSHAW JR Waverly** *Waller Lansden Dortch*
   **KRAMER Steven** *Kramer Rayson LLP*
   **STEGER Christopher** *Miller & Martin PLLC*
   **STEVENS C Eric** *Miller & Martin PLLC*
   **SWAFFORD T Anthony** *Miller & Martin PLLC*

Up-and-coming individuals
   **HATMAKER J Chadwick** *Woolf, McClane, Bright*
   **OLIVER Craig** *Boult, Cummings*

## Band 1

### Bass, Berry & Sims PLC
See firm details p.1820
The Firm: With the addition of three young attorneys, this team has expanded considerably over the past year and now has 12 lawyers within its ranks. This is a reflection of the fact that the group is busy on both the labor and employment fronts. On the employment side, the team has represented healthcare and manufacturing companies in discrimination, retaliation and FLSA compliance issues. When it comes to labor, it has advised local businesses with respect to union arbitration matters. Clients keep returning to the firm because of its "*top service*" and "*excellent value for money.*"
The Lawyers: "*Dean of labor and employment law*" **Bill Ozier** (see p.1812) possesses an extremely "*sharp, quick grasp of issues.*" He commands respect owing to his "*knowledge and experience*" and for "*the excellent work he produces in an incredibly short time.*" **Karen Ellis** (see p.1812) is a fellow at the prestigious American College of Labor and Employment and is known to be "*one of the top trial lawyers in the state.*" One of the major areas of her work and expertise is in the representation of unionized clients, especially within the manufacturing industry, in arbitrations and other labor matters. Chairperson of the department **Tim Garrett** (see p.1812) wins through as a result of his "*thoroughness, experience and practical approach to his cases.*" His practice covers day-to-day advisory work, union arbitration issues and employment discrimination cases.
Clients/Work Highlights: The team recently obtained a significant victory in a religious discrimination class action tried before a grand jury. Other highlights include obtaining summary judgment for a national communications company in a public policy retaliation claim. The group acts for companies in the hospitality, healthcare, communications and manufacturing sectors.

### Kiesewetter Wise Kaplan Prather, PLC
See firm details p.1824
The Firm: This "*premier Memphis boutique*" represents "*a collection of extremely strong lawyers,*" researchers were told. It specializes in the representation of management in all areas of labor relations, employment law and human resources in both union and nonunion environments. With "*a strong local presence*" and a "*solid reputation,*" the team has experience in representing both regional and national companies before the EEOC, the state equal opportunities commission and other human rights commissions.
The Lawyers: **Paul Prather** is "*a great trial lawyer with excellent client relation skills.*" Aside from his extensive litigation experience, he has also represented companies before the National Labor Relations Board and has been instrumental in developing and presenting training programs in key areas of employee relations. "*Experienced and knowledge-*

# MAINLY DEFENDANT

*able,*" **Jonathan Kaplan** specializes in labor/union matters but has also represented clients across the US and Canada in employment litigation and consultation. "*Traditional labor guy*" **Jay Kiesewetter** works with unionized companies to improve union/management relations and further represents management in contract negotiations, arbitrations and labor disputes. He also counsels clients on the implementation of effective initiatives to pre-empt labor relations challenges.
Clients/Work Highlights: The firm represents national and regional companies including many Fortune 500 corporations. These emanate from a range of sectors including the manufacturing, healthcare, telecommunications, hospitality, automotive, petroleum, transportation and chemical industries.

### King & Ballow
The Firm: This seven-strong team negotiates a "*traditional and prestigious labor practice*" but is also proficient at dealing with all types of employment issues including discrimination, wrongful termination, noncompete and wage and hour cases. The firm is a strong proponent of preventive labor relations and frequently presents seminars for management personnel across the country. Sources pointed to the "*forceful and intense*" style of its lawyers as a defining characteristic of the team.
The Lawyers: "*Well-respected*" **Eddie Wayland**'s practice is devoted primarily to the representation of management and companies in all areas of employment law and related litigation at both federal and state level.
Clients/Work Highlights: The group successfully defended a major department store in a wage and hour lawsuit involving more than 1,200 employees. Other highlights include representing a hotel chain in a case involving ADA violation claims and appearing in a number of age, sex and racial discrimination cases. The firm has an impressive roster of media clients featuring, among others, the Chicago Tribune; the St. Louis Post-Dispatch; The Denver Post and The San Diego Union-Tribune. Other prominent clients include BellSouth Mobility; American Airlines; Gaylord Entertainment and Vanderbilt University.

### Miller & Martin PLLC
See firm details p.1826
The Firm: With around 30 labor and employment lawyers, this "*impressive*" Chattanooga player has one of the largest concentrations of experience in this area within a full-service firm in the Southeast. The

team places a great emphasis on preventive work to avoid unnecessary enforcement and regulatory costs, but is nevertheless more than capable of dealing with contentious issues. For instance, the group has experience in handling Title VII, ADA, FMLA and ERISA litigation.

**The Lawyers: John Phillips** (see p.1816) has *"broad experience"* and displays *"good judgment,"* according to sources. One of his areas of expertise is in the coordination of significant downsizings of major corporations, where he advises on overall strategy and the preparation of separation pay plans and severance agreements. Clients also endorsed his work in designing and conducting management training seminars. **Christopher Steger** (see p.1816) is a new entrant to the tables following strong client commendation. Interviewees also endorsed **Eric Stevens** (see p.1816) for his work on labor relations, employment counseling and litigation with a particular focus on the transportation and healthcare industries. Labor specialist **Tony Swafford** (see p.1816) has successfully defended union-organizing attempts in several states and has practiced before the NLRB and the National Mediation Board.

**Clients/Work Highlights:** Coca-Cola is the firm's flagship client. The team also represents regional and national companies from the manufacturing, services and hospitality sectors, as well as foreign corporations doing business in the USA.

### Waller Lansden Dortch & Davis
See firm details p.1828

**The Firm:** This *"first-rate"* team received praise particularly for its *"extremely strong"* ERISA and employee benefits expertise. Aside from counseling work for an impressive array of clients from the entertainment, healthcare and manufacturing sectors, the group's practice has a significant slant toward litigation work involving discrimination and wage and hour claims. Additionally, the team has considerable experience in labor arbitrations under collective bargaining agreements and labor-related litigation. It also deals with OSHA citations and inquiries.

**The Lawyers: Bob Boston** (see p.1810) is *"adept at bringing realistic solutions to the table."* His extensive knowledge of labor and employment law is combined with a *"good business perspective"* and *"outstanding litigation skills"* to make him *"overall, a formidable choice."* **Larry Bridgesmith's** (see p.1810) practices focus on union relations and labor agreements negotiation. Interviewees described him as *"a very knowledgeable, technically minded"* attorney capable of applying his knowledge of labor law to meet the needs of specific business sectors. Also recommended is **Waverly Crenshaw** (see p.1810). Particularly adept at discrimination cases, he *"knows how the system works and displays inherent credibility."*

**Clients/Work Highlights:** The firm has represented employers from the entertainment, pharmaceutical, healthcare and manufacturing sectors in employment disputes in federal and state courts. It has appeared before the EEOC, NLRB, DOL, DOJ

and other state and local agencies across the country. The team is also active in the design and implementation of training programs and other strategies to minimize the risk of disputes.

## Band 2

### Boult, Cummings, Conners & Berry, PLC
See firm details p.1821

**The Firm:** The ten-attorney employment team at this well-respected local firm received endorsement from clients for its *"responsiveness, great client relationships"* and *"ability to satisfy needs quickly and accurately."* The group handles all aspects of labor and employment law including employment discrimination defense work, arbitration in labor disputes, ERISA and benefits counsel and general HR management advice.

**The Lawyers:** *"Well-rounded"* **Matt Lonergan** (see p.1815) chairs the department and is admired for his *"confidence and thoughtfulness,"* as well as for his *"capacity to align legal issues with realities."* Peers highlighted the fact that he is not only a knowledgeable employment attorney but also has broad experience in handling labor matters. **Craig Oliver** (see p.1815) has a very similar practice and, although he lacks the latter's extensive experience, is said to be *"caliber-wise at the same level"* as his mentor.

**Clients/Work Highlights:** The team represents union and nonunion companies, as well as public and privately held businesses. These range from Fortune 500 companies to small, locally owned businesses operating in a wide range of industries.

### Constancy, Brooks & Smith, LLC
**The Firm:** Eight lawyers make up the team at the Nashville office of this nationally renowned management-only labor and employment firm. Satisfied clients appreciate the group's *"cost-effectiveness"* and the manner in which it *"treats every client as an important one."* A particular niche of work for the group lies in counseling Japanese companies with offices in the USA on management skills in order to avoid potential disputes.

**The Lawyers:** Managing member of the Nashville office **Zan Blue** is *"an outstanding litigator with great communication skills,"* researchers were told. With more than 20 years of legal experience, he is a much-respected generalist with extensive knowledge of both labor and employment law.

**Clients/Work Highlights:** AmSouth Bank; Nashville Bar Association; Renfro; Pizza Hut; McDonald's and Highway Transport are some of the prominent names in the team's impressive client portfolio.

### Ford & Harrison LLP
See firm details p.733

**The Firm:** The Memphis branch of this national player combines the advantages of traditional labor boutiques – its size being relatively small, with only 17 attorneys in Tennessee – with the benefits of

nationwide presence and reach that come with a network of more than 150 lawyers in 16 locations. Apart from the traditional fare of discrimination, wage and hour, and labor disputes, the team is experienced in handling matters related to business immigration and other complex employment-related matters.

**The Lawyers: Herb Gerson** (see p.1813) is a respected lawyer who *"knows the business very well,"* partly thanks to his past experience as in-house counsel. His practice is focused on managing all areas related to traditional labor and employment issues, and he devotes much of his practice to counseling clients on avoiding employment discrimination, wage and hour, and labor claims.

**Clients/Work Highlights:** The team has handled several discrimination trial cases on behalf of the City of Memphis. The group also obtained summary judgment for an insurance company in a benefits case. On the advisory side, the Memphis office has a strong clientele within the hospitality sector and represents, for instance, one of the largest restaurant chains in the country.

### Kramer Rayson LLP
See firm details p.1825

**The Firm:** With offices in Knoxville and Oak Ridge, this 32-strong firm with around a dozen labor and employment lawyers has a very strong presence in East Tennessee. The team's practice has an emphasis on discrimination litigation, workers' compensation and FMLA-related matters. Its reputation rests on being adept at accepting and handling difficult cases and the team frequently handles major litigation.

**The Lawyers: Ward Phillips** (see p.1814) is a *"practical and thorough"* attorney who *"listens to clients and responds to their needs."* His practice focuses on discrimination litigation, although he also acts as adviser to major private and public employers in East Tennessee. **Steven Kramer** (see p.1814) concentrates on both traditional labor and employment work and *"exhibits a sure touch in all he does."*

**Clients/Work Highlights:** The group successfully defended Wackenhut Services from a retaliation claim also involving FMLA-related allegations. Other highlights include obtaining dismissal of all claims in an ERISA case brought against the Department of Energy and Lockheed Martin Energy Systems. The firm's healthy client roster further includes Knoxville Utilities Board; Boeing Oak Ridge; Rohm and Haas; Citigroup and Superior Steel.

### Lewis Fisher Henderson Claxton & Mulroy
**The Firm:** This employment boutique has offices in Memphis, Jackson, Mississippi and Los Angeles. It is known to house a core of attorneys experienced in representing clients in proceedings before the EEOC, OFCCP, NLRB and other agencies in all 50 states. *"The best choice boutique-wise,"* according to one market commentator, it elicited praise from clients for its ability to build closer, more direct relationships with clients.

**The Lawyers:** Name partner **Fred Lewis** is "*at the top of the profession,*" peers stated. With more than 30 years' experience, he is regarded as a "*great court performer*" who possesses "*reliable judgment when having to decide whether a case should be tried or settled.*" Clients also value his "*practical approach to problems*" and the fact that he provides "*top-quality service at reasonable cost.*"

**Clients/Work Highlights:** FedEx Express; Bell-South Communication Systems; City of Memphis Credit Union; First Tennessee Bank National Association and Schering-Plough.

## Ogletree, Deakins, Nash, Smoak & Stewart, PC
See firm details p.738

**The Firm:** Despite the relatively small size of the Nashville office of this national powerhouse – the third largest nationally for labor and employment – the Tennessee-based, nine-lawyer team is present in a number of major cases. For instance, the group has been active over the past few years in a wage and hour case involving around 5,000 plaintiffs. The group's practice has a focus on employment litigation and is seeing an increase in the flow of ERISA and discrimination collective cases. Peers consider the firm "*a leading name in Tennessee because of the experience and good judgment of its attorneys.*"

**The Lawyers:** "*Highly qualified and respected*" **Keith Frazier**'s (see p.1812) practice concentrates on employment litigation and on preventive advisory work, although he has also undertaken some labor work in the past. With more than 20 years' experience behind him, he is the "*driving force*" in the team, researchers were told.

**Clients/Work Highlights:** Dollar General; Nissan; Corrections Corporation of America; HCA and Home Depot.

## Other Notable Practitioners

**Chad Hatmaker** of Woolf, McClane, Bright, Allen & Carpenter was described by peers as "*young, good and a rising star.*" He represents clients in proceedings before such organisations as the EEOC, the Tennessee Human Rights Commission and the Department of Labor.

# LITIGATION

| Litigation: General Commercial |
| --- |
| **Leading Firms** |
| 1 BASS, BERRY & SIMS PLC *Nashville* |
| BOULT, CUMMINGS *Nashville* |
| BOWEN RILEY WARNOCK & JACOBSON *Nashville* |
| WALKER, BRYANT, TIPPS & MALONE *Nashville* |
| 2 BAKER, DONELSON *Nashville* |
| HARWELL HOWARD HYNE GABBERT *Nashville* |
| NEAL & HARWELL, PLC *Nashville* |
| WALLER LANSDEN DORTCH & DAVIS *Nashville* |
| 3 ARMSTRONG ALLEN PLLC *Memphis* |
| BURCH, PORTER & JOHNSON PLLC *Memphis* |
| GLANKLER BROWN, PLLC *Memphis* |
| MILLER & MARTIN PLLC *Chattanooga* |
| SHERRARD & ROE PLC *Nashville* |

## Band 1

### Bass, Berry & Sims PLC
See firm details p.1820

**The Firm:** With over 70 litigators, the team at this leading regional outfit qualifies as one of the top three statewide in terms of size. Despite a number of losses in recent years, the group continues to be "*an obvious pick for litigation*" as it has kept "*several aces in its ranks.*" Apart from a steady flow of business litigation arising from the firm's corporate practice, the team is also proficient in other facets of commercial litigation such as healthcare and IP. Clients value the group's "*responsiveness, superior service and excellent value for money.*"

**The Lawyers:** **Lee Barfield** (see p.1810) received warm endorsement from interviewees for his "*absolute integrity.*" Although he handles a varied fare of litigation, his medical malpractice defense work is particularly prestigious. On that front, he has represented a number of major healthcare clients including HCA. Clients defined him as "*the person we pull out of the hat in really difficult cases.*"

**Wally Dietz** (see p.1810) is an "*exceedingly hard-working*" attorney who is particularly gifted at making "*superb court presentations.*" His work varies from business torts and trade secrets to internal investigations and ERISA litigation. **Michael Dagley**'s (see p.1810) main area of interest lies in the securities field. An attorney who has handled securities litigation on a nationwide basis, he is "*a great friend to investment banks.*" "*Bright and experienced,*" **Dale Grimes** (see p.1810) devotes most of his time to antitrust defense work. He recently obtained a favorable jury verdict for Philip Morris in a case involving allegations of Robinson-Patman Act violations. Former US attorney assistant **Nancy Jones** (see p.1810) has extensive experience of healthcare litigation including internal investigations and qui tam defense. Peers referred to her "*sophisticated approach*" as being highly beneficial in complex commercial cases. "*Thoughtful and cautious*" **Overton Thompson** (see p.1810) has the bulk of his work in the field of securities and consumer class actions. His further areas of expertise include breach of contract, business fraud, corporate and partnership dissolutions and franchise disputes. Chair of the litigation and bankruptcy practices **Paul Jennings** (see p.1810) is "*one of the best bankruptcy lawyers in town,*" according to one source. His "*extremely pleasant manner*" helps bring negotiations forward and "*makes things happen,*" clients said. With unmatched experience of Chapter 11 proceedings and bankruptcy class action litigation, he is said to "*get into every big case.*" Sam Felker heads the firm's products liability practice and works in the field of pharmaceutical defense.

**Clients/Work Highlights:** The team was kept busy by several ERISA cases filed against a managed care company. Other significant matters include representing Merrill Lynch in a securities case and acting for a major public national healthcare company in books and records litigation.

# GENERAL COMMERCIAL

## Boult, Cummings, Conners & Berry, PLC
See firm details p.1821

**The Firm:** With a team of around 40 litigators, this strong Nashville player can handle the full fare of commercial litigation from insurance coverage to antitrust and toxic tort matters. The firm also has a robust alternative dispute resolution practice, with over a dozen lawyers trained as mediators and arbitrators. Corporate governance counseling is a further area of expertise for the team, as the increased focus on this issue in recent years has led to an upturn in the group's advisory workload. Sources pointed to the "*high number of excellent attorneys*" as the key to the firm's success overall.

**The Lawyers:** "*Well-rounded*" **Paul Alexis** (see p.1810)' practice focuses primarily on large securities and antitrust class action cases, some of which are national in scope. Head of the firm's environmental law practice, Alexis has experience in the representation of clients in connection with Superfund environmental lawsuits and advises on compliance with environmental regulatory laws and regulations. IP and entertainment specialist **Sam Lipshie** (see p.1810) is an experienced attorney adept at handling copyright, royalty and trade secrets litigation at both trial and appellate levels. He has been rejoined in the team by **Bob Patterson** (see p.1810), who has returned to full practice after a few years as managing director of the firm. This "*fine litigator*" with almost 30 years' experience has acted as lead counsel in cases ranging from products liability to IP and securities. Peers particularly emphasized his "*outstanding knowledge of securities law*" and his "*terrific courtroom skills.*" Additionally, Patterson serves as outside counsel on corporate governance for various clients. Also recommended is **Thor Urness** (see p.1810) who is renowned for his work in the IP and entertainment arena. On the bankruptcy front, **William Norton** (see p.1815) is the toast of many a client. As one stated: "*He has stretched our* *imagination to reach for home runs and ensured we've hit them every time."*

**Clients/Work Highlights:** Within the healthcare industry, the firm recently represented a hospital in a post-closing adjustment case and defended a separate healthcare provider in a PI case. Other representative matters include representing the San Francisco 49ers in a $2.5 million insurance coverage dispute and acting for a hotel in relation to construction litigation in Texas.

## Bowen Riley Warnock & Jacobson, PLC

See firm details p.1822

**The Firm:** This relatively young boutique, founded in 1995 out of a spin-off from Bass, Berry & Sims, earned consistent endorsement from peers for the *"top-quality work and results"* it has produced in a series of prominent cases. The team's reputation rides especially high in IP, entertainment and securi-

ties matters. For instance, over the past year the group has acted in several securities suits involving clients as prominent as HCA and PwC. Aside from its defense work, the group also takes on board a varied diet of plaintiff work for both corporations and individuals.

**The Lawyers:** *"Forceful trial attorney"* **Steve Riley** is the prime mover behind the firm's thriving securities practice. Famed for his *"excellent communication skills,"* he is not only a much admired commercial litigator but also has significant experience as a mediator and a good track record of assisting corporate clients in internal investigation procedures. **Jay Bowen**, a past chair of the ABA's subcommittee on the manufacture and sale of counterfeit copies of audiovisual works and sound recordings, has an *"outstanding reputation for his knowledge of IP and entertainment law."* He is also highly adept at suits with defamation and First Amendment aspects to them. Colleague **John Jacobson** is a *"level-headed and determined"* attorney with *"great potential."* He has proven himself able to handle sophisticated IP and securities effectively and is an experienced mediator.

**Clients/Work Highlights:** The group acted recently in a suit for Qwest involving the installation by that company of fiber-optic cables. Another significant case saw the team representing a local healthcare company in a case brought against a major computer software company arising from allegations of the defective functioning of a software product. Other clients include American Express; Gaylord Entertainment; Coca-Cola; Sony BMG Entertainment and Vanderbilt University.

## Walker, Bryant, Tipps & Malone

See firm details p.1827

**The Firm:** This *"fine litigation shop,"* which came into existence in 2000 out of a spin-off from one of the larger Tennessee firms, attracts much praise and many referrals from peers. Known for its ability to *"tackle all types of litigation confidently and comfortably,"* the 15-attorney team is particularly well known for its medical and legal malpractice work, having represented, among others, Vanderbilt University in several cases over the past five years. Clients appreciate the *"down-to-earth attitude"* and the *"practical, well thought-out approach"* the group of *"great strategists"* at the firm can offer, as well as the *"reasonably priced fees."*

**The Lawyers:** Reputedly *"one of the best trial attorneys in Tennessee,"* **Bob Walker** (see p.1810) is said to offer the *"complete package of experience, brainpower and litigation talent."* In the course of his more than 35 years of practice, he has acted both on the plaintiff and on the defendant side. His work in recent years has concentrated on class action litigation involving commercial and products liability claims. Medical malpractice defense attorney **Steve Anderson** (see p.1810) is an *"excellent litigator at the peak of his career,"* according to market commentators. His *"excellent grasp of technical terms and medical conditions"* stands him in good stead in high-profile cases. Another medical malpractice expert,

**John Bryant** (see p.1810) is *"a great technician"* who is *"highly effective at getting good results,"* clients said. Other members of the team include *"tough and confident"* **Gayle Malone** (see p.1810). Malone represents hospitals in Tennessee in all types of matters, but has a particular area of expertise in the field of PI, representing both plaintiffs and defendants.

**Clients/Work Highlights:** American Healthways Services; BellSouth; IBM Credit; GE Medical Systems; McDonald's; Morgan Stanley and Kraft Foods.

## Band 2

## Baker, Donelson, Bearman, Caldwell & Berkowitz, PC

See firm details p.1819

**The Firm:** With half a dozen offices across Tennessee, this all-service firm has a broader reach than most on a regional level. The different offices vary in size, the Memphis branch providing the highest concentration of litigators. The team is especially renowned for its bankruptcy law expertise, an area in which it received *"a ten out of ten"* from clients. Healthcare law, products liability and automobile and transportation litigation also make up a sizable portion of the team's workload. Interviewees highlighted *"depth and responsiveness"* as two key elements of the firm's success, pointing to the *"excellent quality to price ratio"* the group offers.

**The Lawyers:** Senior attorney **Leo Bearman** (see p.1810) is *"without any doubt one of the leading names"* for commercial litigation in Memphis. His varied practice covers insurance, antitrust, IP and professional malpractice defense. With more than 40 years' trial experience, he is regarded, despite his age, as a *"wonderfully strong and energetic"* litigator. He demonstrated these qualities recently while successfully representing the world's leading medical technology company in the longest trial ever in the Western District of Tennessee. Cochair of the firm's healthcare and medical professional litigation group **John Hicks** (see p.1810) is a *"top-quality litigator"* known to combine an *"aggressive courtroom style"* with *"excellent judgment as to when to go to court and when to settle."* His practice is slanted towards health law and medical malpractice cases, but he is also experienced in the areas of consumer fraud and banking litigation. **Matt Sweeney**'s (see p.1810) litigation practice has its emphasis on securities law including related breach of fiduciary duty and D&O class action litigation. He also has a wide experience of mediation processes. Bankruptcy specialist **Randal Mashburn** (see p.1810) is *"an excellent strategist with an effective negotiating demeanor,"* researchers were told. A veteran of many Chapter 11 bankruptcy cases, lien priority litigations, secured transaction issues and other similar creditors' rights matters, clients describe him as *"the go-to guy if you want to get the job done in an efficient and timely manner."*

**Clients/Work Highlights:** The team has repre-

## Litigation: Bankruptcy
### Leading Individuals

**1** **GABBERT JR Craig** *Harwell Howard Hyne Gabbert*
   **JENNINGS Paul** *Bass, Berry & Sims PLC*
   **MASHBURN Randal** *Baker, Donelson*
   **NORTON III William** *Boult, Cummings*

**2** **AHERN III Lawrence** *Greenebaum Doll*
   **BUCY Rhea** *Gullett, Sanford, Robinson*
   **GONZALES Robert** *MGLAW*
   **KELLEY James** *Neal & Harwell, PLC*
   **ROSE Glenn** *Harwell Howard Hyne Gabbert*

## Litigation: Medical Malpractice Defense
### Leading Individuals

**1** **ANDERSON Steve** *Walker, Bryant, Tipps & Malone*
   **BARFIELD II Lee** *Bass, Berry & Sims PLC*
   **BRYANT John** *Walker, Bryant, Tipps & Malone*
   **GIDEON CJ** *Gideon & Wiseman PLC*
   **NORTH Phillip** *North Pursell Ramos & Jameson*
   **TRENTHAM Robert** *Miller & Martin PLLC*
   **WISEMAN III Thomas** *Gideon & Wiseman PLC*

sented the City of Memphis in several cases alleging interferences with a Mississippi aquifer. Other representative matters include defending healthcare provider LifeCare from abuse and neglect allegations and handling several asbestos cases in Jackson, Mississippi.

## Harwell Howard Hyne Gabbert & Manner, PC
See firm details p.1823

**The Firm:** With the recent addition of former US DOJ attorney David McDowell, this "*extraordinary team*" now counts ten litigators in its ranks. Best known for its lawyers' expertise on bankruptcy and securities matters, the group has, however, established in recent years a reputation for its "*premium trademark and copyright law practice.*" Another blooming area of work for the firm comes in the field of noncompete and trade secrets, where the team is viewed as "*proficient,*" according to sources.

**The Lawyers:** "*Quiet, persuasive and persistent*" is how peers described **Alex Fardon**, a specialist in noncompete and trade secrets with broad experience of all areas of business litigation. His "*exceptional analytical skills*" make him "*a truly brilliant trial attorney.*" Researchers found a general consensus among interviewees that **Craig Gabbert** has "*magnificent trial skills.*" His bankruptcy and business reorganization practice received especially warm accolades, but he is regarded as an "*efficient generalist*" with comprehensive commercial litigation experience. "*Extraordinarily bright*" **Glenn Rose** devotes most of his time to bankruptcy and securities cases. His "*capacity to develop and follow a strategy in a thorough and consistent manner*" helps him achieve "*impressive results,*" according to clients.

**Clients/Work Highlights:** The team represented a corporate client within the healthcare sector in the purchase of several hospitals out of Chapter 11. A

further relevant matter saw the group mediate on behalf of an acute care hospital group in a dispute over insurance coverage. Regal Entertainment Group; Central Parking; MedCap and Pinnacle Financial Services are long-standing clients of the team.

## Neal & Harwell, PLC
**The Firm:** This well-respected boutique has 27 litigation attorneys best known for participating in high-profile, much-publicized civil and criminal litigation. Peers stressed many of these have an "*excellent nationwide reputation.*" Although an important part of the firm's workload is made up of criminal cases involving mainly white-collar crime allegations, it has seen a significant development of its business transactions and bankruptcy practices in recent years.

**The Lawyers:** The most prominent figure at the firm, **Jim Neal** has a "*breathtakingly impressive track record*" of participating in historical cases. For instance, he served as chief trial counsel of the Watergate Special Prosecution Force in 1973 and worked on the Exxon Valdez case. He wins the admiration of peers for his "*intellectual firepower*" and for his "*fine style in court.*" Managing partner **Aubrey Harwell** specializes in white-collar criminal defense work and crisis management, but is also a reputed commercial litigator. Commentators appreciate his "*friendly manner*" and his "*brilliant negotiation skills.*" **Jimmy Sanders** is "*one of the best business attorneys around,*" both for civil and commercial litigation. Sources particularly emphasized his "*ability to handle extremely difficult situations in a calm and effective way.*" **Jim Kelley**'s practice has a focus on tax and bankruptcy cases. He was recommended to researchers as a "*tough and bright*" attorney who "*fights his client's corner.*"

**Clients/Work Highlights:** The team obtained a favorable multimillion-dollar verdict for a former Cambio Health Solutions executive who alleged that Triad Hospitals of Dallas, which had bought Cambio, tortiously interfered with his contract. Other representative clients of the firm include Barclays International; Bridgestone/Firestone; Bank of America; Lloyds TSB; ExxonMobil and Capitol Records.

## Waller Lansden Dortch & Davis
See firm details p.1828

**The Firm:** With around 30 litigators and arbitrators, this prestigious firm, with offices in Nashville, Birmingham and LA, boasts "*unmatched depth and coverage*" and is backed by the "*substantive specialist knowledge*" of its corporate and healthcare departments. Clients told researchers they felt "*in good hands*" because the group is always "*extremely well prepared,*" something which was said to contribute to the team's ability to deliver "*great courtroom performances.*"

**The Lawyers:** **Robert Boston** (see p.1810) is a "*supremely gifted*" litigator who represents the "*complete package for the client.*" "*Extremely competent and knowledgeable in all areas, he has great busi-

ness perspective and always brings realistic solutions to the table.*" Senior attorney **Ames Davis** (see p.1810) divides his time between a varied commercial litigation practice, which includes both plaintiff and defendant work, and an active role as arbitrator. Although his practice has traditionally focused on securities work, in recent times he has worked on an increasing number of bankruptcy and officer liability disputes. **James Doran** (see p.1810) enters this year's tables following strong market recommendation. Doran's work concentrates on the defense of pharmaceutical, medical device and general products liability matters. Described as "*easily the best in the field,*" he has handled very prominent drug cases for pharmaceutical giants such as Merck and Bayer.

**Clients/Work Highlights:** The team represents for-profit healthcare providers, financial institutions and manufacturers from a variety of sectors including the automotive and pharmaceutical industries.

## Band 3

## Armstrong Allen PLLC
**The Firm:** With offices in Mississippi, Arkansas and, of course, Tennessee, this firm is extremely well placed to serve the region. One of the oldest practices around, it has devoted more than 100 years to serving a clientele of national and international corporations and individuals. Today it "*provides as secure a service as it always has done*" and offers advice across a broad canvas. Areas of particular litigation specialty include antitrust, healthcare, products liability and white-collar crime, all handled within the context of a general practice encompassing sophisticated commercial disputes.

**The Lawyers:** James Arthur III is the main contact partner for litigation.

**Clients/Work Highlights:** The firm has a diverse clientele acting for retailers, healthcare companies and local lenders, as well as numerous Fortune 500 companies.

## Burch, Porter & Johnson PLLC
**The Firm:** This local player commands respect from peers for the "*high ethical standards*" of its lawyers. The 25-attorney team covers not only the regular business litigation fare but has further specialties in areas as diverse as agricultural and industrial chemical cases, civil rights, propane gas defense and college and university law matters.

**The Lawyers:** **Jef Feibelman**'s "*sharpness and persuasiveness,*" as well as his ability to produce "*top-quality written work,*" make him "*one of the front-line business litigators*" in Memphis. **Michael Cody** was praised by market commentators for his "*highly ethical*" approach and "*great reputation.*" Arbitration, mediation and alternative dispute resolution are key facets of his practice.

**Clients/Work Highlights:** The team has recently been involved in the defense of several medical malpractice cases. It also intervened in two contested minority/majority shareholder disputes.

## Glankler Brown, PLLC

**The Firm:** This Memphis outfit, with almost one hundred years' history, has succeeded in establishing a "*solid group of talented litigators with an impressive reputation locally.*" The department is known to have the knowledge, resources and experience to handle effectively matters as varied as contractual disputes, broker-dealer regulatory issues, medical malpractice suits, products liability and IP.

**The Lawyers:** **Lee Chase** (see p.1811) is a "*tough and experienced lawyer*" who concentrates his practice in the areas of torts, health and construction litigation.

## Miller & Martin PLLC

See firm details p.1826

**The Firm:** More than 40 attorneys at the Nashville and Chattanooga offices of this much-admired Southeastern operation offer comprehensive advice on commercial and bankruptcy-related contentious matters. Particularly adept at dealing with large and complex class action and products liability cases of national scope, the team attracts an enviable corporate clientele that features Coca-Cola Enterprises.

**The Lawyers:** **Roger Dickson** (see p.1812) is admired by clients for his "*ability to find solutions to extremely complicated problems.*" Always striving to settle before court, he is nevertheless also an "*accomplished performer in court who can consistently pull rabbits out of the hat.*" Colleague **Robert Trentham** (see p.1818) tackles medical malpractice defense. "*A man for the big case,*" he has "*an appealing air which wins over clients and tribunals alike.*"

**Clients/Work Highlights:** Primary outside counsel for Coca-Cola Enterprises since 1992, the team recently represented that client in a dispute over land use and rezoning issues in South Florida.

## Sherrard & Roe PLC

**The Firm:** Although smaller than some of its key rivals, the eight-strong team is seen to be "*very on the ball.*" The group's reputation is especially strong owing to its knowledge of the corporate world and its thriving securities arbitration practice. Further areas of work include estate and trust litigation, employment case and insurance coverage disputes. The firm is comfortable both at trial and appellate level.

**The Lawyers:** "*Effective*" **Webb Campbell** is a "*well-liked, solid young litigator*" who is "*fun to work with.*" An experienced litigator and arbitrator, he has a broad-based practice that includes contract disputes, business torts and employment matters. **Bill Harbison** specializes in litigation related to corporate and estate and trust matters. He is said to be a "*thorough, well-reasoned*" attorney with a "*terrific reputation with the courts.*"

**Clients/Work Highlights:** The team argued before the United States Court of Appeals for the Sixth Circuit regarding an insurer's potential vicarious liability for the alleged misconduct of an attorney engaged to represent the interests of its insured. Other highlights include defending a global financial firm in an arbitration concerning consulting services provided to a pension fund. UBS Financial Services, Vanderbilt University; State Volunteer Mutual Insurance; Renal Care Group and Nashville Predators are amongst the firm's representative clients.

## Other Notable Practitioners

Reputedly the "*best there is for litigation in Chattanooga,*" **Max Bahner** (see p.1810) at Chambliss, Bahner & Stophel, PC has more than 40 years' experience in the field. Apart from his litigation practice,

he is also renowned for his mediation work. Cochair of the litigation department at Wyatt, Tarrant & Combs LLP **Glen Reid** is an "*outstanding attorney*" whose depth of knowledge and experience in the areas of products liability and white-collar crime is widely recognized. New entry to this year's table **CJ Gideon** (see p.1810) of Gideon & Wiseman PLC boasts an impressive nationwide reputation for his "*extraordinary*" medical malpractice work. Peers acknowledged his "*exceptional medical knowledge,*" which, according to one source, "*rivals that of most physicians.*" Partner **Tom Wiseman** (see p.1810) also enjoys widespread market recognition for his work in the field. One of the keys of his success is his "*ability to put complex medical terms in a way a layperson would understand.*" This proves to be of particular use in jury trials. Similarly favored, **Phillip North** of North, Pursell, Ramos & Jameson PLC impresses as a "*bright and talented drafter who is highly effective in front of judges.*" **Rhea Bucy** (see p.1810) of Gullett, Sanford, Robinson & Martin PLLC has more than 25 years' experience in assisting financially troubled companies in bankruptcy, out-of-court financial restructuring, asset sales and debt-related litigation. Member-in-charge at Greenebaum, Doll & McDonald PLLC **Lawrence Ahern** wins the admiration of peers for his "*problem-solving skills.*" Clients also appreciate the fact that he "*fiercely defends*" their interests. Also recommended is **Robert Gonzales** (see p.1813) of MGLAW. Well experienced in representing debtors, creditors, creditors' committees and trustees, he shows "*limitless energy in pursuit of the client's goals.*"

# MEDIA & ENTERTAINMENT

## Media & Entertainment

### Leading Firms

| | |
|---|---|
| [1] | **BASS, BERRY & SIMS PLC** *Memphis* |
| | **LOEB & LOEB LLP** *Nashville* |
| [2] | **ADAMS AND REESE LLP** *Nashville* |
| | **GORDON, MARTIN, JONES, HARRIS** *Nashville* |
| | **RUSH LAW GROUP** *Nashville* |
| | **ZUMWALT, ALMON & HAYES** *Nashville* |

### Leading Individuals

| | |
|---|---|
| [1] | **ALMON** Orville *Zumwalt, Almon & Hayes* |
| | **HOWARD** Linda *Adams and Reese LLP* |
| | **JONES** Russell *Gordon, Martin, Jones* |
| | **KRAUS** Kenneth *Loeb & Loeb LLP* |
| | **MILOM** W Michael *Bass, Berry & Sims PLC* |
| | **RUSH** Stephen *Rush Law Group* |
| | **SULLIVAN** Robert *Loeb & Loeb LLP* |

## Band 1

### Bass, Berry & Sims PLC

See firm details p.1820

**The Firm:** This five-attorney media and entertainment team represents a prestigious roster of recording artists, songwriters, authors, publishers and producers. Clients appreciate the impressive resources on hand and value the support of a "*wonderful full-service team*" that offers advice not only on general media matters but also on ancillary issues such as IP and tax. The bulk of the practice centers on transactional and advisory work for country, religious and pop musicians and their record labels.

**The Lawyers:** "*Unbelievably knowledgeable and creative,*" **Mike Milom** (see p.1815) chairs the entertainment department at the firm. Clients endorsed his "*ability to maintain long-lasting, personable relationships,*" while peers highlighted his "*unmatched experience.*"

**Clients/Work Highlights:** The team has an impressive portfolio of country and pop recording

artists. In recent times, it has been working to combat the challenges that the Internet and globalization pose to individual artists and to music labels.

### Loeb & Loeb LLP

See firm details p.334

**The Firm:** This national player houses five entertainment law specialists at its Nashville office. The team specializes in the representation of recording artists and record labels, with its expertise ranging from advice on domestic and international recording contracts to the overseeing of agreements for the use of recorded material on film and television. Sources indicated the group is "*a clear leader*" due to its "*broad industry reach and the wide-ranging experience of its lawyers.*"

**The Lawyers:** **Ken Kraus** (see p.1814) is famous for his "*entrepreneurial spirit and ability to keep business in perspective.*" The greater part of his practice is on the transactional side and he recently handled all negotiations for the financing, production and exploitation for the television special and DVD 'Elvis by the Presleys'. "*Driving force*" **Robert Sullivan**'s (see p.1817) practice is slanted towards the resolution of contentious copyright matters, although recently he has been active in the sale of a music publishing company. Sources praised the way in which he "*brings his litigation skills to the analysis of problems.*"

**Clients/Work Highlights:** The team negotiated an agreement between BB King and the BB King Museum Foundation regarding the licensing of the Foundation to undertake the financing and construction of a $10 million museum in Mississippi honoring BB King and the blues. The group also handled numerous merchandising agreements between a recent 'American Idol' winner and several companies. BHT Entertainment; Elevation Group; EMI Christian Music Group; John R Cash Estate and Elvis Presley Enterprises are other prominent names that feature in the firm's client roster.

### Band 2

### Adams and Reese LLP
See firm details p.989

**The Firm:** With two offices in Nashville, one of which is on Music Row, this national outfit is particularly strong in IP and trademark matters. The team's practice is divided between purely entertainment work and copyright-related issues. With about 300 lawyers nationwide, the group benefits from the size and reach of the firm and from the fact that clients can find all-around assistance.

**The Lawyers:** **Linda Edell Howard** (see p.1814) is very active representing artists within the country music industry. She is also well known for her unparalleled expertise in copyright law.

**Clients/Work Highlights:** While the entertainment segment of the department's practice has a clear local flavor, with an emphasis on the representation of country musicians, the copyright work of the team covers the whole spectrum of music genres.

### Gordon, Martin, Jones, Harris & Shrum

**The Firm:** This local six-attorney boutique is recognized by peers as "*one of the leading names*" in the market. The team services a broad range of established music industry clients including artists, producers, managers, publishers, songwriters, booking agents and independent record labels. Although the bulk of the group's work is in entertainment, its attorneys have experience in other areas such as civil litigation, estate planning, bankruptcy and trademark law.

**The Lawyers:** **Russell Jones**' experience covers not only entertainment and copyright matters but also corporate issues.

**Clients/Work Highlights:** The team boasts an impressive client portfolio, featuring Garth Brooks and Martina McBride. The group also acts for independent record labels; producers; managers; authors and booking agents.

### Rush Law Group

**The Firm:** This global business and IP protection boutique with offices in Nashville, New York and San Francisco has a particular focus on music publishing. The team has comprehensive catalog management experience, and provides administration and marketing services to owners and publishers of music catalogs.

**The Lawyers:** Founding partner **Stephen Rush** has more than 25 years' experience in IP and entertainment law. His practice has several components, including arranging debt financing for music catalogs and songwriters, dealing with trademark issues and IP safeguard work.

**Clients/Work Highlights:** The team has been advising a portable video player manufacturer on IP-related matters. Other clients include owners and purchasers of national and international music catalogs.

### Zumwalt, Almon & Hayes

**The Firm:** Four partners concentrate solely on the practice of entertainment law, representing, in the main, music industry figures. Members of the team have previously worked for giant entertainment companies, such as EMI or Warner, and therefore know the industry inside out. Sources referred to the presence of such "*outstandingly skilled and experienced*" attorneys as the key to the firm's success.

**The Lawyers:** Peers described **Orville Almon** as a "*master negotiator*" with the "*ability to draft uniquely clear, excellent quality documents.*"

**Clients/Work Highlights:** Creed; Courtney Love and the estate of Kurt Cobain; Kings of Leon; Vertical Horizon; Lonestar and the Neville Brothers.

# REAL ESTATE

| Real Estate |
|---|
| Leading Firms |
| [1] BAKER, DONELSON *Memphis* |
| BASS, BERRY & SIMS PLC *Nashville* |
| BOULT, CUMMINGS, CONNERS & BERRY *Nashville* |
| WALLER LANSDEN DORTCH & DAVIS *Nashville* |
| [2] BURCH, PORTER & JOHNSON PLLC *Memphis* |
| GLANKLER BROWN, PLLC *Memphis* |
| SHERRARD & ROE PLC *Nashville* |
| SHUMACKER WITT GAITHER *Chattanooga* |
| [3] ARMSTRONG ALLEN PLLC *Memphis* |
| HARKAVY SHAINBERG *Memphis* |

### Band 1

### Baker, Donelson, Bearman, Caldwell & Berkowitz, PC
See firm details p.1819

**The Firm:** The team is a "*clear leader*" thanks to its size, its statewide presence and its "*premium lawyers.*" Reflecting the market tendency, the group has lately been particularly active assisting developers across the Southeast in the construction of (or conversion into) apartment condominiums. While the Nashville office focuses on residential, retail and healthcare-related projects, the bulk of the Memphis team's practice concerns developments for large industrial uses. Sources revealed the team has an array of imposing clients because it has "*the size and muscle to handle major deals.*"

**The Lawyers:** Project financing expert **Rob Liddon** (see p.1815) acts for several insurance companies with investments in the commercial real estate sector. His expertise ranges from leasing transactions to advising investment trusts that hold healthcare use properties. One interviewee commented: "*It is hard to think of anyone as good as him.*" "*Superlative*" **John Gupton** (see p.1813) has participated in the development of mixed-use buildings in several states including Tennessee, Florida, Mississippi, Ohio and Alabama. Recently he worked on the conversion of a former Holiday Inn into an apartment condominium in Memphis. Clients appreciate his "*approachability, attentiveness and sense of urgency*" when dealing with a matter. **Mary Aronov** (see p.1810) does a large volume of project financing work and is said to have a "*very sophisticated understanding of real estate and of investor entities.*" She has been busy lately, handling refinancing work for a client with offices across the USA and in the UK. **Kenneth Ezell** (see p.1812) is highly rated for his experience in the areas of commercial real estate and municipal finance. He is part of a team that includes the "*entrepreneurial*" **Laurence Papel** (see p.1816), who has recently been involved in several high-profile developments. An example of this is his representation of Vastland Realty in the development of a shopping center in Hendersonville, Tennessee.

**Clients/Work Highlights:** One of the year's highlights for the team was the acquisition of land for, and involvement in all parts of the process leading to the building of a $70 million high-end residential condominium in midtown Nashville known as Adelicia. The team also worked on the acquisition and renovation of the Union Station Hotel.

### Bass, Berry & Sims PLC
See firm details p.1820

**The Firm:** The 28-strong team at this "*top firm*" represents both developers and real estate lending institutions in all aspects of acquiring, financing, leasing and selling property. It is also expert in litigation resulting from real estate conflicts, including, for instance, eminent domain matters, mechanic's lien suits, quiet title actions and various types of contract disputes. The firm boasts the additional asset of having a commercial lending team that can provide advice on real estate, construction and industrial development loans.

**The Lawyers:** **Dewees Berry** (see p.1810) received fulsome praise from peers, who affirmed that he is a "*first-rate, top-tier*" lawyer. In recent years, his practice has increasingly turned to real estate-related litigation, representing, for instance, insurance companies in title policy disputes and lenders in mortgage challenges related to debtors' filings for bankruptcy. **John Stemmler** (see p.1817) is well respected for his "*character and ability to find consensus.*" The bulk of his work is in the hospitality sector and he has served as counsel to hotel management companies in connection with the acquisition, construction and sale of hotel properties. Department chair **Felix Dowsley** (see p.1812) "*does a tremendous job representing clients,*" according to one source. His practice is primarily transactional and focuses on the negotiation and documentation of real estate transactions including construction loans, leasing and refinancing, and sales and purchases. "*Excellent*" **Michael Peek** (see p.1816) enters the tables for the first time following warm recommen-

dations from market sources. He has acted for a provider of healthcare services in connection with acquisition, development, leasing and disposition of medical facilities throughout the USA. With more than 30 years' experience, he is "*at the top of the profession in terms of experience and reputation.*" "*Credible and honest,*" **Mark Sheets**' (see p.1817) work has a specific emphasis on real estate acquisition and development, as well as tax and accounting-driven lease transactions. **Jim Tate** (see p.1817) is seen as a "*solid lawyer with a strong track record*" in representing developers in a variety of real estate projects. His recent efforts have included developments of an entertainment center, a multitenant office and several retail and residential developments.

## Boult, Cummings, Conners & Berry, PLC
See firm details p.1821

**The Firm:** This "*truly magnificent*" team has developed an interesting niche advising and representing foreign real estate investors – mainly German and Dutch – on all aspects of transactions. The firm's membership of the prestigious Association of Foreign Investors in Real Estate further confirms the group's expertise on cross-border operations. Clients gave the team, whose performance was said to "*match that of New York or Los Angeles firms,*" a "*clear A-plus*" for its work on acquisitions and dispositions. Another area of work for the team lies in the field of healthcare real estate and the group has acted on the sale and purchase of hospitals and other healthcare facilities.

**The Lawyers:** "*Credible and honest,*" **Tom Trent** (see p.1817) represents one of the country's top ten for-profit healthcare organizations on real estate matters. Aside from healthcare-related transactions, he acts for manufacturers, institutional investors and insurance companies in acquisitions, leasing, financing and dispositions. **Anne Cargile** (see p.1811) is a "*bright, organized, experienced and detailed*" attorney able to successfully handle contract, loan and leasing negotiations. She has recently been involved in the acquisition and financing of several shopping centers in Tennessee. "*One of the finest contract attorneys around,*" **John Haynes** (see p.1813) centers much of his work around foreign investment, leading clients to point to his ability to adapt to the peculiarities of cross-border transactions. Endowed with a "*sunny disposition and impeccable Southern style,*" Haynes is said to "*bridge international customs by dint of his personality.*" Name partner **Greer Cummings**' (see p.1811) entrance in this year's tables reflects the dense volume of high-profile transactions he has recently been involved in. His practice is mainly outside Tennessee and focuses on operations for foreign investors seeking to acquire top-quality properties. One of the transactions he closed recently was valued at almost $1 billion. **David Rutter** (see p.1816) has experience in representing developers in all matters relating to retailing including land acquisition, financing and leasing. Also present is "*high-quality*" **Richard Warren** (see p.1818) who "*does a tremendous job,*" according to clients. In recent years,

he has represented Hines Interests in the development and leasing of an office and retail project on the campus of Vanderbilt University. Real estate specialist **Robert Wood** (see p.1818) represents both institutional investors in lending transactions and developers in real estate acquisition and conversion projects.

**Clients/Work Highlights:** The team recently negotiated the setup of a joint venture for the creation of a lifestyle center in Illinois. Other highlights include overseeing industrial office developments in Texas, California and Florida, and assisting a major healthcare company in the acquisition and renovation of a hospital in Nashville.

## Waller Lansden Dortch & Davis
See firm details p.1828

**The Firm:** The presence of 20 attorneys means this team has the "*talent and depth*" to make it "*one of the strongest in the state.*" Although the group's practice has a definite bias toward transactions within the healthcare sector, the department also represents owners, operators, agents and developers of commercial, industrial, retail and residential properties. The team is also known to have extensive experience in the representation of banks and other lending institutions in connection with commercial real estate secured financing transactions. Clients keep returning to the firm because they feel it "*does a heck of a lot to defend business interests.*"

**The Lawyers:** Former Stokes Bartholomew attorney **Robert Campbell**'s (see p.1811) practice focuses on the negotiation of credit and term loan facilities, construction loans and asset-based financing. Clients stated that Campbell's "*warm, respectful manner*" was key during negotiations, while peers reflected a similar view by affirming "*he is able to work out his issues so that a deal can move forward.*" "*Highly skilled*" **Matthew Harris** (see p.1813) manages the department and is respected for being "*a deal-maker.*" He serves as counsel to a leading healthcare company in the acquisition and development of office buildings and is experienced in representing clients in disputes over land use. Sources highlighted his ability to "*spot and resolve potentially problematic issues.*" **Steven Kirkham** (see p.1814) represents several restaurant companies in the acquisition and leasing of unimproved real property for the purpose of building new restaurants throughout the country. He was described to researchers as "*a solid, top-flight*" real estate lawyer.

**Clients/Work Highlights:** The firm represents a national wireless telecommunications company in acquisition transactions across the USA. Further highlights include a role as lead real estate counsel for the world's largest healthcare company in the spin-off of more than 70 hospitals to two publicly traded companies.

## Band 2

### Burch, Porter & Johnson PLLC

**The Firm:** Despite its small size, this "*outstanding*" team received endorsement from peers for its core of lawyers "*capable of dealing with complex matters in a sophisticated way.*" Particular expertise exists in relation to commercial lending, franchising and the financing of hospitality-related projects.

**The Lawyers:** "*Smart, hard-working*" **Thomas Cates** has recently been working on the acquisition of the Crescent Center, a major office building in Memphis. Other highlights include participating in the sale of several large farming properties in the Midsouth. His expertise covers not only purchase, acquisitions and lending agreements, but also land planning issues. **LeeAnn Marshall Cox** has extensive experience in lending transactions and in acquisitions and dispositions related to the hospitality industry.

**Clients/Work Highlights:** The firm advises local authorities on land planning issues and represents life insurance companies and national investors.

### Glankler Brown, PLLC

**The Firm:** This leading Memphis outfit has significant experience in all areas of real estate, including the negotiation of loans and purchase agreements, the structuring of transactions and financing plans and the representation of developers seeking tax freezes and other government development incentives. The 11-lawyer team boasts an impressive cadre of "*talented*" practitioners who offer "*reasonably priced, quality service.*"

**The Lawyers:** **Hunter Humphreys** (see p.1814) continues to elicit praise from peers for his "*ability to work around roadblocks.*" He concentrates his practice around the representation of investors, developers and lenders in real estate and secured lending transactions. "*Bright and effective*" **Doug Earthman** (see p.1812) has a particular niche in the representation of national and regional banks in connection with real estate-based loans and credit facilities. He recently joined the firm from Armstrong Allen.

**Clients/Work Highlights:** The team completed the sale of Crescent Center, one of the largest office buildings in Memphis, for $85 million.

### Sherrard & Roe PLC

**The Firm:** Although lacking the size and presence of the top-tier players, this "*well-respected*" operation manages nonetheless to get into big, juicy deals. Its team of six attorneys is particularly active in the healthcare and hospitality sectors; for instance, the

team took part recently in the development of a full-service hotel in Memphis, partially financed with free market tax credits. This constituted one of the first instances of a hospitality project using that particular type of financing.

**The Lawyers:** **Kim Brown** "*brings a palpable sense of calm to all his dealings,*" according to market commentators. Peers said they would feel "*comfortable*" referring work to him because of the top quality of the service he offers.

**Clients/Work Highlights:** The team has been busy representing both developers and lenders involved in retail and hospitality projects. Chartwell Hospitality, Fidelity Real Estate Group and Nashville Commercial Real Estate Services are part of the group's clientele.

### Shumacker Witt Gaither & Whitaker, PC

**The Firm:** The multistate, 12-attorney real estate group at this Chattanooga firm has a broad-based real estate development practice, representing both developers and lenders. The negotiation and preparation of contracts to purchase and sell real property, loan documentation, leases, operating agreements, use and development restrictions, and cross-easements with major tenants are just some of the areas of the team's expertise. Additionally, the group handles litigation and advises on zoning and land use regulation.

**The Lawyers:** Ron Feldman chairs the firm's team and is well versed in all areas of real estate including acquisitions, secured lending and leasing.

**Clients/Work Highlights:** The group acted recently for an Australian REIT on several acquisitions across the USA. It also handled a major acquisition of a shopping mall package, a sophisticated transaction that required coordinating loans and due diligence matters.

## Band 3

### Armstrong Allen PLLC

**The Firm:** The decision of the six former principals of Harkavy Shainberg to leave and reinstitute their old firm is bound to weaken Armstrong Allen's position. Despite the loss of some of its key attorneys, however, the team is still "*a player to be taken into account,*" according to sources. It represents insurance companies in connection with the disposition of foreclosed properties, and acts for acquirers of credit-tenant leased commercial properties in connection with real estate and commercial loan matters.

**The Lawyers:** **Scott Rowlett** is a "*knowledgeable and experienced*" attorney and "*a great all-rounder.*" His practice covers not only real estate matters but also commercial lending, bankruptcy and business litigation. "*Hardworking and impressive,*" **Jason Yarbro** enters the tables for the first time following strong recommendation from market sources. He has acted for special-purpose entities in connection with the issuance of more than $250 million of commercial mortgage 'pass-through' certificates. He is said to be "*in the process of becoming a rainmaker for the firm.*"

**Clients/Work Highlights:** The firm represents all types of real estate lenders including banks; life insurance companies; pension funds; investment banks and conduits. It also acts for developers, landlords and tenants.

### Harkavy Shainberg Kaplan & Dunstan PLC

**The Firm:** This "*quality boutique*" with an emphasis on real estate has the capability to deal with complex and sophisticated transactions despite its limited size. Nine attorneys band together to form a team that is particularly adept at assisting in the formation of entities that then go on to purchase commercial realty. The group has an enviable client portfolio in the hospitality, banking and retail sectors.

**The Lawyers:** **Ronald Harkavy** is "*an extremely seasoned attorney who has seen and done it all,*" according to one source. He is particularly strong on land use and zoning matters but has a varied practice that also comprises sales, acquisitions and refinancings. New arrival to this year's table **Raymond Shainberg** is an "*experienced and cooperative*" attorney, according to peers. Commentators stressed the "*excellent, unmatched quality*" of his work and his "*great ability to work around and solve problems.*"

**Clients/Work Highlights:** The team participated in all the stages of the development of a twin tower, riverside office complex in Mississippi. Other highlights include handling the sale of a restaurant chain with 45 locations in eight states and advising on a number of planning and zoning projects.

### Other Notable Practitioners

**Woods Weathersby** of Evans & Petree PC is known for his "*very good business judgment*" and "*ability to prioritise matters.*" Peers regularly refer matters to him, a claim that can also be made by **Philip Jones** of Martin, Tate, Morrow & Marston, PC Jones is "*a deft exponent of his art who can always be relied on in a crisis.*"

# Leaders in Tennessee

## AHERN III, Lawrence
Greenebaum Doll & McDonald PLLC,
Nashville 615 760 7100
*Recommended in Litigation*

## ALEXIS, Paul
Boult, Cummings, Conners & Berry, PLC,
Nashville 615 252 2385
palexis@boultcummings.com
*Recommended in Litigation*
**Practice Areas:** Commercial litigation
with special emphasis on antitrust,
telecommunications, environmental,
trade regulation matters (including
trademarks), securities, ERISA litigation
and class action lawsuits.
**Prof. Memberships:** Member of the
Nashville, Tennessee and American Bar
Associations.
**Career:** Joined Boult Cummings in 1986.
Prior to joining Boult Cummings, he was
Deputy General Counsel of Genesco, Inc.
and was previously with the firm of
Donovan Leisure Newton & Irvine in
New York City.
**Personal:** JD, Georgetown University
Law Center (1971); AB, Yale University
(1968).

## ALMON, Orville
Zumwalt, Almon & Hayes, Nashville
615 256 7200
*Recommended in Media &
Entertainment*

## ANDERSON, Steve
Walker, Bryant, Tipps & Malone,
Nashville 615 313 6000
sanderson@walkerbryant.com
*Recommended in Litigation*
**Practice Areas:** Litigation including the
defense of medical malpractice, product
liability, and other catastrophic injury or
death cases, as well as commercial litiga-
tion.
**Prof. Memberships:** Tennessee and
Nashville Bar Association; Defense
Research Institute; International Associa-
tion of Defense Counsel.
**Career:** Partner.
**Publications:** Articles editor of the Van-
derbilt Journal of Transnational Law,
authored law review article 'Intrusive
Border Searches: What Protection
Remains for the International Traveler
Entering the United States After United
States v. Montoya de Hernandez and Its
Progeny?'.
**Personal:** Vanderbilt University (JD
1988); Baylor University (BA, with high-
est honors, 1985).

## ARONOV, Mary L
Baker, Donelson, Bearman, Caldwell &
Berkowitz, PC, Memphis 901 577 2223
maronov@bakerdonelson.com
*Recommended in Real Estate*
**Practice Areas:** Practice concentrated in
commercial real estate and financial

transactions. Extensive experience in real
estate and asset-based loan transactions,
purchases and sale of commercial real
estate, mergers and acquisitions, multi-
state lending transactions, leases, corporate finance operations, loan modifications and workouts, foreclosures and
other commercial transactions.
**Prof. Memberships:** Member of American Bar Association (Commercial Law,
Real Estate and Probate Sections), Tennessee and Memphis Bar Associations.
Member, Leo Bearman Sr Inn of Court.
Former Chairperson, Memphis and Shelby County Air Pollution Control Board.
Authored articles in several legal publications.
**Career:** Licensed in Tennessee since
1984.

## BAHNER, Maxwell
Chambliss, Bahner & Stophel, P.C.,
Chattanooga 423 756 3000
*Recommended in Litigation*

## BAILEY, Roger (Roddy)
Miller & Martin PLLC, Chattanooga
423 785 8366
rbailey@millermartin.com
*Recommended in Corporate/M&A*
**Practice Areas:** Corporate/M&A, secu-
rities. Represents issuers in connections
with the sale of securities in private place-
ments or registered offerings with the
Securities and Exchange Commission.
Represents buyers and sellers in connec-
tion with merger, acquisition or disposi-
tion transactions.
**Prof. Memberships:** Member of the
State Bar of Georgia, Tennessee, and the
District of Columbia.
**Personal:** Born November 17, 1970.
Married. Secretary of Georgia Labrador
Rescue, Inc., a rescue organization for
Labrador Retrievers.

## BARFIELD II, Lee
Bass, Berry & Sims PLC, Nashville
615 742 6202
lbarfield@bassberry.com
*Recommended in Litigation*
**Practice Areas:** Litigation and healthcare law. Handles broad variety of litigation, including business disputes, healthcare fraud, class actions, insurance litigation, commercial law issues, malpractice
defense, professional liability, banking
matters and constitutional law claims.
Counsels healthcare providers on hospital operational issues, child abuse reporting, fraud and abuse and other healthcare
regulatory issues.
**Prof. Memberships:** American, Tennessee and Nashville Bar Associations.
**Career:** Joined the firm in 1974. Served
as President of Board of Law Examiners
for the State of Tennessee, 1986-2000.
**Personal:** BA (1968) and JD (1974),

Vanderbilt University.

## BEARMAN JR, Leo
Baker, Donelson, Bearman, Caldwell &
Berkowitz, PC, Memphis
901 577 2220
lbearman@bakerdonelson.com
*Recommended in Litigation*
**Practice Areas:** 45 years' experience
representing local, regional and national
companies as well as city and county gov-
ernments in class action defense, antitrust
matters, insurance defense litigation,
products liability defense, intellectual
property litigation, professional liability
and general commercial litigation.
**Prof. Memberships:** Fellow, American
College of Trial Lawyers. Member, Ameri-
can Academy of Appellate Lawyers. Life
Member, Fellows of the American Bar
Foundation. Member, Shelby County and
Memphis Bar Associations. Member,
American Board of Trial Advocates.
Adjunct Professor of law, University of
Memphis Cecil C. Humphreys School of
Law.
**Career:** Licensed in Tennessee since 1960
and United States Supreme Court since
1973.

## BERRY IV, C Dewees
Bass, Berry & Sims PLC, Nashville
615 742 6215
cberry@bassberry.com
*Recommended in Real Estate*
**Practice Areas:** Litigates such real estate
conflicts as eminent domain matters,
mechanic's lien and construction suits,
quiet title actions and contract disputes.
Also advises clients concerning zoning,
planning, lease disputes and boundary,
easement, restrictive covenant and land
use issues. Has extensive transactional
experience including purchases and sales,
financings, leasing and all other aspects of
commercial real estate.
**Prof. Memberships:** Rule 31 Listed General Civil Mediator; past President,
Nashville Bar Association.
**Career:** Joined the firm in 1981. Editor,
Tennessee Real Estate Law Letter. Instructor in Real Property Law, Nashville
School of Law.
**Personal:** BA (1973) and JD (1976),
Vanderbilt University.

## BISHOP III, George W
Waller Lansden Dortch & Davis,
Nashville 615 244 6380
george.bishop@wallerlaw.com
*Recommended in Corporate/M&A*
**Practice Areas:** Mergers and acquisitions, particularly those involving hospitals and other healthcare facilities. Securities and offerings, especially syndications
of healthcare facilities and venture capital
financings. Antitrust and regulatory
issues relating to healthcare. Healthcare

service companies with the acquisition
and disposition of healthcare facilities.
Negotiation and documentation of
healthcare transactions.
**Prof. Memberships:** Member of the
Nashville Bar Association, served as the
initial Chairman of the Health Law Com-
mittee in 1989. Member of the Tennessee
Bar Association, served as the founder
and initial Chairman of the Health Law
Section in 1989 and 1990. Served on an
Antitrust Section Task Force on Hospital
Mergers for the American Bar Associa-
tion and on the National Membership
Committee of the National Health
Lawyers Association. Member of the Ten-
nessee Bar Association Ethics and Profes-
sional Responsibility Committee.
**Career:** Practiced law at Waller Lansden
since 1976. Served on the firm's Executive
Committee for over a decade. Past Chair-
man of the firm.

## BLUE JR, William
Constangy, Brooks & Smith, LLC,
Nashville 615 320 5200
*Recommended in Employment*

## BOSTON, Robert E
Waller Lansden Dortch & Davis,
Nashville 615 244 6380
bob.boston@wallerlaw.com
*Recommended in Employment,
Litigation*
**Practice Areas:** Labor and employment
and commercial litigation. Represents
manufacturing, service and commercial
industries in the following areas: employ-
er/employee-related issues including day
to day management advice, labor rela-
tions, business litigation and dispute res-
olution.
**Prof. Memberships:** Member of the
Nashville, Tennessee and American Bar
Associations with memberships in the
Labor and Employment and Litigation
Sections. Fellow of the Nashville Bar
Foundation.
**Career:** Practiced law at Waller Lansden
since 1982. Serves on the firm's Board of
Directors. Manages the firm's Trial and
Appellate Practice Group.

## BOWEN, Jay
Bowen Riley Warnock & Jacobson, PLC,
Nashville 615 320 3700
*Recommended in Litigation*

## BRAUN, Stephen T
Boult, Cummings, Conners & Berry, PLC,
Nashville 615 252 2300
sbraun@boultcummings.com
*Recommended in Corporate/M&A*
**Practice Areas:** Advises hospitals,
surgery centers and other healthcare
providers in transactional, regulatory and
operational matters. Transactional experience includes numerous acquisitions,
dispositions and joint ventures of hospi-

tals, ambulatory surgery centers and insurance companies.

**Career:** Joined Boult Cummings in 2003. Prior to joining Boult Cummings, he was Senior Vice President and General Counsel of HCA, Inc.

**Personal:** JD, University of Notre Dame Law School (1981); BA, St Cloud State University (1978).

### BRIDGESMITH, Larry W
Waller Lansden Dortch & Davis, Nashville 615 244 6380
larry.bridgesmith@wallerlaw.com
*Recommended in Employment*

**Practice Areas:** Employment litigation, including union relations, labor agreement negotiation, alternative dispute resolution and strategic approaches to employee relations. Represents management in numerous industries including, automotive, manufacturing, hospitality, airport, healthcare, transportation, warehousing and distribution.

**Prof. Memberships:** Member of the Tennessee, Michigan and American Bar Associations. Member of the American Employment Law Council and faculty member of the National Institute of Trial Advocacy. Founder of the Human Resources Leadership Forum. Member of the Pepperdine University School of Law Board of Visitors. Member of the Tennessee Business Roundtable and member of the Tennessee Chamber of Commerce and Business.

**Career:** Practiced law since 1978. Prior to joining Waller Lansden in 2000, he was Managing Partner of the Nashville office of Constangy, Brooks and Smith, LLC from 1986 to 2000.

### BROWN, Kim
Sherrard & Roe PLC, Nashville 615 742 4200
*Recommended in Real Estate*

### BRYANT, John
Walker, Bryant, Tipps & Malone, Nashville 615 313 6000
jbryant@walkerbryant.com
*Recommended in Litigation*

**Practice Areas:** Litigation including professional negligence and product liability; Rule 31 listed general civil mediator.

**Prof. Memberships:** Nashville and Tennessee Bar Association; Lawyers-Pilot Bar Association; Defense Research Institute; Fellow American College of Trial Lawyers.

**Career:** Partner.

**Personal:** Vanderbilt University (JD 1973); Davidson College (AB 1970).

### BUCY, Rhea
Gullett, Sanford, Robinson & Martin PLLC, Nashville 615 244 4994
*Recommended in Litigation*

### CAMPBELL II, L Webb
Sherrard & Roe PLC, Nashville 615 742 4200
*Recommended in Litigation*

### CAMPBELL JR, Robert R
Waller Lansden Dortch & Davis, Nashville 615 850 8469
robert.campbell@wallerlaw.com
*Recommended in Real Estate*

**Practice Areas:** Real estate development and corporate and commercial transactions involving banks and financial institutions. Negotiation of credit and term loan facilities, construction loans and asset-based financing.

**Prof. Memberships:** Member, Nashville, Tennessee and American Bar Associations. Chairman, 2002 Large Firm Campaign for Legal Services of Middle Tennessee. Listed in the 2005-06 edition of 'The Best Lawyers in America' (Woodward White, Inc.). Listed in the Nashville Business Journal's 2005 Best of the Bar.

**Career:** Practiced law at Waller Lansden since 2005.

### CARGILE, Ann Peldo
Boult, Cummings, Conners & Berry, PLC, Nashville 615 252 2373
acargile@boultcummings.com
*Recommended in Real Estate*

**Practice Areas:** Represents landlords and tenants in retail, office and industrial leases, and represents local and national lenders and developers in the acquisition, financing and sale of real estate projects, including condominiums, planned unit developments, office buildings and parks, and retail centers.

**Prof. Memberships:** Member of the Nashville, Tennessee and American Bar Associations, International Council on Shopping Centers and Commercial Real Estate Women. Fellow in American College of Real Estate Lawyers.

**Career:** Joined Boult Cummings in 1986.

**Personal:** JD, University of Virginia School of Law (1986); BA, University of Virginia (1982).

### CATES, C Thomas
Burch, Porter & Johnson PLLC, Memphis 901 524 5000
*Recommended in Real Estate*

### CHASE III, Lee James
Glankler Brown, PLLC, Memphis 901 576 1729
lchase@glankler.com
*Recommended in Litigation*

**Practice Areas:** Tort, health and construction law with an emphasis on litigation, concerning personal injuries, medical malpractice, commercial disputes and construction contracting.

**Prof. Memberships:** Journal Club; Tennessee Hospital Association; Director and Vice-Chairman, The Assisi Foundation of Memphis, Inc.; American, Tennessee and Memphis (Director, 1984-85). Bar Associations; Tennessee and Memphis Bar Foundations.

**Career:** Listed, The Best Lawyers in America.

**Personal:** Born 1942; BA, LLB, Vanderbilt University, 1967.

### CHEEK III, James
Bass, Berry & Sims PLC, Nashville 615 742 6223
jcheek@bassberry.com
*Recommended in Corporate/M&A*

**Practice Areas:** Represents public and private companies and investment banking firms in capital raising and merger and acquisition activities. Counsels boards on matters relating to corporate governance and legal compliance. Also serves as the Regulatory Auditor of the NYSE.

**Prof. Memberships:** American Bar Association (past Chair, Section of Business Law and Federal Regulation of Securities Committee); National ABA Task Force on Corporate Responsibility (past Chair); San Diego Securities Regulation Institute (Executive Committee and past Chair).

**Career:** Joined the firm in 1970.

**Personal:** BA, (1964), Duke University; JD, (1967), Vanderbilt University; LLM, (1968), Harvard University.

### CODY, W J Michael
Burch, Porter & Johnson PLLC, Memphis 901 524 5000
*Recommended in Litigation*

### COLE, J Chase
Waller Lansden Dortch & Davis, Nashville 615 244 6380
chase.cole@wallerlaw.com
*Recommended in Corporate/M&A*

**Practice Areas:** Corporate law and governance, securities law, public offerings, mergers and acquisitions, venture capital and financing.

**Prof. Memberships:** Member of the Nashville, Tennessee and American Bar Associations. Member, ABA Committees on Corporate Governance, Negotiated Acquisitions, Federal Regulation of Securities and Venture Capital. Fellow, Nashville Bar Foundation. Member, Dean's Council of the Vanderbilt University School of Law. Member, Society of International Business Fellows. Member, National Association of Corporate Directors. Co-Chair for Host Committee, ABA Section of Business Law 2005 Spring Meeting.

**Career:** Practiced law at Waller Lansden since 1979. Chair of firm's Corporate Governance Task Force.

### COWART, Richard
Baker, Donelson, Bearman, Caldwell & Berkowitz, PC, Nashville 615 726 5660
dcowart@bakerdonelson.com
*Recommended in Corporate/M&A*

**Practice Areas:** Chair of Baker Donelson's Health Law Department and 2004-05 President of the American Health Lawyers Association. Practice concentrated in advising clients regarding legal, regulatory and business issues related to healthcare. Mr Cowart works primarily as Board Counsel to health service organizations (both for-profit and not-for-

profit). He is also a national columnist and frequent speaker on health law topics.

**Prof. Memberships:** 2004-05 President, Board of Directors/Executive Committee, American Health Lawyers Association.

**Career:** Licensed in Mississippi since 1978 and Tennessee since 1999.

**Personal:** University of Southern Mississippi, BA, 1975. University of Mississippi Law School, JD, 1978.

### COX, David
Harwell Howard Hyne Gabbert & Manner, PC, Nashville 615 256 0500
*Recommended in Corporate/M&A*

### CRENSHAW JR, Waverly D
Waller Lansden Dortch & Davis, Nashville 615 244 6380
waverly.crenshaw@wallerlaw.com
*Recommended in Employment*

**Practice Areas:** Labor and employment, all employer/employee-related issues and government regulatory issues.

**Prof. Memberships:** Fellow, Nashville and Tennessee Bar Foundations. Life Member to the Conference of the Sixth Judicial Circuit of the United States. Former Chair, Tennessee Supreme Court's Advisory Committee on the Board of Professional Responsibility. Former Chair, Labor and Employment Section of the Tennessee Bar Association. Charter member, Harry Phillips American Inns of Courts. Member, Board of Trustees of the Napier-Looby Bar Foundation.

**Career:** Practiced law since 1982. Joined Waller Lansden in 1990. Manages firm's Labor and Employment Practice Group.

### CUMMINGS, Greer
Boult, Cummings, Conners & Berry, PLC, Nashville 615 252 2316
gcummings@boultcummings.com
*Recommended in Real Estate*

**Practice Areas:** Commercial real estate transactions, including the acquisition, financing, leasing, management and sale of real estate projects. Represents German institutional investors, syndicators and individuals active in purchasing and financing investment grade properties throughout the United States.

**Prof. Memberships:** Member of the Nashville, Tennessee and American Bar Associations.

**Career:** Joined Boult Cummings in 1973.

**Personal:** JD, Vanderbilt University Law School (1973); BA, Vanderbilt University (1970).

### DAGLEY, Michael L
Bass, Berry & Sims PLC, Nashville 615 742 7729
mdagley@bassberry.com
*Recommended in Litigation*

**Practice Areas:** Practice focuses in the areas of complex commercial, securities and class action litigation. Represents clients in arbitrations, mediations and other means of alternative dispute resolu-

tion. Regularly conducts internal investigations for public company clients with potential accounting or regulatory issues.
**Prof. Memberships:** Nashville, Tennessee and American Bar Associations; Harry Phillips American Inn of Court.
**Career:** Joined the firm in 1999. Served as Chair of the Nashville Bar Association's Federal Court Committee, 2004.
**Personal:** BS (1978), Middle Tennessee State University; JD (1981), Vanderbilt University.

### DAVIS, Ames
Waller Lansden Dortch & Davis, Nashville 615 244 6380
ames.davis@wallerlaw.com
*Recommended in Litigation*
**Practice Areas:** Dispute resolution with an emphasis on complex commercial disputes involving issues of federal and state securities, antitrust and healthcare regulation.
**Prof. Memberships:** Member, Nashville, Tennessee and American Bar Associations. Founder and Fellow, Tennessee Supreme Court Historical Society. Fellow, Nashville and Tennessee Bar Foundation.
**Career:** Practiced law at Waller Lansden since 1971. Past Chairman of the firm.

### DAVIS JR, Ralph W
Waller Lansden Dortch & Davis, Nashville
615 850 8481
rdavis@wallerlaw.com
*Recommended in Corporate/M&A*
**Practice Areas:** Mergers and acquisitions, financial institutions, public and private equity and debt financing and general corporate law.
**Prof. Memberships:** Adjunct Professor of Law, Vanderbilt University, teaching Regulation of Financial Institutions. Listed in 'The Best Lawyers in America' (Woodward/White) in both financial institutions and transactional law, and corporate, mergers and acquisitions and securities law. Member, Nashville, Tennessee, District of Columbia and American Bar Associations. Member, Bank Lawyers Committee of the Tennessee Bankers Association.
**Career:** Practiced law at Waller Lansden since 1992. Serves as the firm's Chairman and on its Board of Directors. Serves as Chair of the firm's Diversity Committee.

### DICKSON, Roger W
Miller & Martin PLLC, Chattanooga
423 785 8330
rdickson@millermartin.com
*Recommended in Litigation*
**Practice Areas:** Commercial litigation, white-collar crime, mass tort defense. Successfully resolved lawsuits filed against Chattem Inc. alleging personal injuries from the ingestion of Dexatrim.
**Prof. Memberships:** Fellow, American College of Trial Lawyers; Fellow, American Bar Association; Fellow, Tennessee Bar Association, Member, Tennessee

Commission on Continuing Legal Education and Specialization.
**Career:** Graduated Order of Coif: University of Tennessee Law School 1971. Private Practice in Chattanooga 1971-79. United States Magistrate, United States District Court for Eastern District of Tennessee 1979-84. Private Practice in Chattanooga 1984-present. Partner, Miller and Martin 1990-present.
**Personal:** Born August 14, 1945. Married, three children.

### DIETZ, Wallace W
Bass, Berry & Sims PLC, Nashville
615 742 6276
wdietz@bassberry.com
*Recommended in Litigation*
**Practice Areas:** Focuses his practice on complex business and commercial litigation, including cases involving business torts, trade secrets, internal investigations, banking and commercial law, media and entertainment law, healthcare law, ERISA and mergers and acquisitions.
**Prof. Memberships:** Nashville Bar Association; past President and Chair, Nashville Pro Bono, Inc.
**Career:** Joined the firm in 1983. Legislative assistant and media aide to former US Senator Jim Sasser, 1977-81.
**Personal:** BA (1977), Emory University; JD (1982), cum laude, Georgetown University.

### DORAN JR, James M
Waller Lansden Dortch & Davis, Nashville
615 850 8843
jim.doran@wallerlaw.com
*Recommended in Litigation*
**Practice Areas:** Defense of pharmaceutical, medical device, and other companies against product liability claims. Liability, toxic injury, and commercial litigation.
**Prof. Memberships:** Member, American Board of Trial Advocates. Emeritus Member, Harry Phillips American Inns of Court. Fellow, American College of Trial Lawyers. Fellow, International Society of Barristers. Member, Tennessee Defense Lawyers Association, where he has served as: Member and President, Board of Directors. Member, American, Tennessee, and Nashville Bar Associations, where he has served as: President, NBA, Member, NBA Board of Directors. Chair, Merit Selection Panel for United States Magistrate Judge. Member, Civil Justice Reform Act Advisory Panel for the Middle District of Tennessee. One of only two attorneys appointed to assist the Tennessee Judicial Conference in rewriting the Tennessee Pattern Jury Instructions-Civil. Member, IADC, where he has served as Member, Executive Committee, Faculty Member and Director of IADC Trial Academy and Chairman, Product Liability Committee. Member, DRI, where he has served as Member, Board of Directors

and Chair, Amicus Curiae Committee.
**Career:** Practiced law at Waller Lansden since 1998.

### DOWSLEY III, Felix R
Bass, Berry & Sims PLC, Nashville
615 742 6228
fdowsley@bassberry.com
*Recommended in Real Estate*
**Practice Areas:** Focuses on commercial lending, secured transactions, real estate and general commercial law. Negotiation and documentation of a variety of financing and real estate transactions, including asset-based financings, syndicated revolving credit and term loan facilities, mezzanine and subordinated loans, construction loans and workouts and restructures of credit facilities, as well as the sale and leasing of commerical real estate.
**Prof. Memberships:** Member of the Board of Directors, Mid-South Commercial Law Institute.
**Career:** Joined the firm in 1984.
**Personal:** BA (1981) and JD (1984), University of Tennessee.

### EARTHMAN, B Douglas
Glankler Brown, PLLC, Memphis
901 576 1707
dearthman@glankler.com
*Recommended in Real Estate*
**Practice Areas:** Real estate and secured lending; municipal bonds and tax-exempt financing; business transactions.
**Prof. Memberships:** Member, American Bar Association (Real Property, Probate and Trust Law Section); Member, Tennessee Bar Association (Real Estate Section, Chairman 1987-88); Member, Memphis Bar Association (Real Estate Section); Member, National Association of Bond Lawyers; Member, International Association of Attorneys and Executives in Corporate Real Estate (Member, 2006 Conference Committee).
**Career:** Admitted to practice in Tennessee; Glankler Brown, PLLC (2006); Armstrong Allen, PLLC (1999-2005); Servicemaster Diversified Health Services, LP (Senior Vice President, Senior Living Services) (1995-99); Waring Cox (1974-94).
**Personal:** Born November 26, 1949, Kingsport, TN; JD, University of Memphis, 1973; BE, cum laude, Vanderbilt University, 1971.

### ELLIS, Karen
Bass, Berry & Sims PLC, Nashville
615 742 6226
kellis@bassberry.com
*Recommended in Employment*
**Practice Areas:** Defends discrimination lawsuits involving age, religion, gender, race, disability, FMLA and sexual harassment claims and employers and providers in denial of benefits claims under ERISA. Defends class action lawsuits involving discrimination and FLSA claims. Prepares affirmative action plans

for government contractors and subcontractors.
**Prof. Memberships:** Fellow, American College of Labor and Employment Lawyers; Lawyers' Association for Women; Nashville Bar Association.
**Career:** Joined the firm in 1981.
**Personal:** BA (1971), with distinction, Transylvania University; MA (1978), Middle Tennessee State University; JD (1980), Order of the Coif, University of Tennessee.

### EZELL JR, Kenneth P (Pete)
Baker, Donelson, Bearman, Caldwell & Berkowitz, PC, Nashville
615 726 5721
pezell@bakerdonelson.com
*Recommended in Real Estate*
**Practice Areas:** Commercial real estate transactions, including portfolio sales and acquisitions, development, leasing and financing. Also engages in conduit tax-exempt financings, serving as bond counsel, underwriter or placement agent counsel and credit provider counsel.
**Prof. Memberships:** Chair, Committee on Legal Opinions in Real Estate Transactions; Real Property, Probate and Trust Section of the American Bar Association (2003-05). ABA Task Force on Tax Shelter Ethical Responsibilities.
**Career:** Licensed in Tennessee since 1979.
**Personal:** BA, The University of the South, 1971; MBA, National University, 1976; JD, Vanderbilt University, 1979.

### FARDON, D Alexander
Harwell Howard Hyne Gabbert & Manner, PC, Nashville
615 256 0500
*Recommended in Litigation*

### FEIBELMAN, Jef
Burch, Porter & Johnson PLLC, Memphis
901 524 5000
*Recommended in Litigation*

### FRAZIER, Keith D
Ogletree, Deakins, Nash, Smoak & Stewart, PC, Nashville
615 254 1900
keith.frazier@ogletreedeakins.com
*Recommended in Employment*
**Practice Areas:** Labor and employment, litigation.
**Prof. Memberships:** American Bar Association (Labor and Employment Section: Co-Chair of Finance, 2004 to present; Fellow of the ABA/YLD), Tennessee Bar Association (Chair, Judiciary Committee, 1999-2000; Member, Jury Reform Task Force, 1998; YLD: President, 1994-95; Fellow of the TBA/YLD), Nashville Bar Association (Federal Court Committee, 2004; Fellow, Nashville Bar Foundation).
**Career:** Admitted to practice in Tennessee, US Court of Appeals (Fifth, Sixth and Eleventh Circuits) and various US District Courts. Listed in 'The Best

Lawyers in America'.

**Personal:** University of Tennessee (BS, 1982), University of Tennessee College of Law (JD, 1985).

### GABBERT JR, Craig
Harwell Howard Hyne Gabbert & Manner, PC, Nashville 615 256 0500
*Recommended in Litigation*

### GARRETT, Tim K
Bass, Berry & Sims PLC, Nashville
615 742 6270
tgarrett@bassberry.com
*Recommended in Employment*
**Practice Areas:** Chairs the Labor and Employment Practice area. Represents employers in all aspects of employment discrimination (both class actions and individual claims) and traditional labor law, including union avoidance, responding to unfair labor practices, grievance and arbitration matters, contract interpretation, wage and hour claims (collective actions and individual claims), ERISA litigation, OSHA/TOSHA proceedings, covenants not to compete, and FMLA.
**Career:** Joined the firm in 1986.
**Personal:** BA (1983), summa cum laude, University of the South; JD (1986), Order of the Coif, Vanderbilt University.

### GERSON, Herb
Ford & Harrison LLP, Memphis
901 291 1530
HGerson@fordharrison.com
*Recommended in Employment*
**Practice Areas:** Herb Gerson represents management with traditional labor and employment issues. His practice is devoted to counseling clients to avoid employment discrimination claims and to develop a positive work environment. Herb is listed in a leading legal publication, has written articles on labor and employment matters, and co-chaired the Labor and Employment Committee of the American Bar Association's Litigation Section. He is editor of the 'Tennessee Employers Desk Manual', and the national version of the same publication. Herb earned his Undergraduate and Law Degrees from Emory University. He is a member of the College of Labor and Employment Lawyers.

### GIDEON, CJ
Gideon & Wiseman PLC, Nashville
615 254 0400
*Recommended in Litigation*

### GILBERT, Paul D
Waller Lansden Dortch & Davis, Nashville 615 244 6380
paul.gilbert@wallerlaw.com
*Recommended in Corporate/M&A*
**Practice Areas:** Securities and mergers and acquisitions, virtually always on behalf of healthcare clients.
**Prof. Memberships:** Member, American Bar Association. Member, Committee on Federal Regulation of Securities and the

Subcommittee on Annual Review of Securities of the American Bar Association. Member of the Committee on Negotiated Acquisitions of the American Bar Association. Member, American Health Lawyers Association.
**Career:** Practiced law since 1991. Joined Waller Lansden in 1996. Serves on the firm's Board of Directors.

### GONZALES, Robert J
MGLAW, Nashville 615 846 9010
rjg@mglaw.net
*Recommended in Litigation*
**Practice Areas:** Representation of debtors, creditors, creditors' committees, preference defendants, trustees and purchasers of assets in business bankruptcy cases and out-of-court restructurings.
**Prof. Memberships:** Board certified in business bankruptcy law by the American Board of Certification; Board Member, Mid-South Commercial Law Institute; Nashville Bar Association (2005 Chair, Bankruptcy Court Committee; past Chair, Corporate and Commercial Practice Committee); Tennessee Bar Association (Member, Bankruptcy Committee); American Bar Association (Member, Business Bankruptcy Section); American Bankruptcy Institute; included in 2006 edition of 'The Best Lawyers in America'; named 'Best of the Bar' in Business Bankruptcy by the Nashville Business Journal in 2003, 2004, 2005.
**Career:** Member.
**Personal:** BA (1990), Louisiana Tech University; JD (1994), Vanderbilt University Law School.

### GRIMES, Dale
Bass, Berry & Sims PLC, Nashville
615 742 6244
dgrimes@bassberry.com
*Recommended in Litigation*
**Practice Areas:** Handles civil litigation matters with a special focus on antitrust, consumer fraud, complex litigation, class actions and telecommunications. Has been Counsel of record for defendants in over 30 class actions. His practice includes antitrust counseling to clients on a variety of merger, distribution, pricing and joint venture issues, as well as government and internal antitrust investigations.
**Prof. Memberships:** Fellow, Nashville Bar Foundation; past Chair, Civil Justice Reform Act Advisory Group of the Middle District of Tennessee.
**Career:** Joined the firm in 1980.
**Personal:** BA (1975), University of the South; JD (1978), University of Tennessee.

### GUPTON III, John A
Baker, Donelson, Bearman, Caldwell & Berkowitz, PC, Nashville
615 726 7351
jgupton@bakerdonelson.com
*Recommended in Real Estate*
**Practice Areas:** Practice concentrated in

commercial real estate and mortgage lending. Represents several life insurance companies, developers, commercial real estate owners, brokers and contractors. Extensive experience in the formation, development, financing, acquisition, disposition and leasing of commercial real estate projects and properties. Chair of the Real Estate Practice Group.
**Prof. Memberships:** Member, American (Real Property Section), Tennessee (Real Property Section) and Nashville Bar Associations. Fellow, American College of Mortgage Attorneys.
**Career:** Licensed in Tennessee since 1976.
**Personal:** University of Virginia, BA University of Memphis Cecil C Humphreys School of Law, JD.

### HARBISON, William
Sherrard & Roe PLC, Nashville
615 742 4200
*Recommended in Litigation*

### HARDCASTLE, Jay
Boult, Cummings, Conners & Berry, PLC, Nashville 615 252 2386
jhardcastle@boultcummings.com
*Recommended in Corporate/M&A*
**Practice Areas:** Advises hospitals, surgery centers, physicians, long-term care providers, imaging centers and other participants in the healthcare industry with joint venture formation, regulatory issues, and the purchase and sale of healthcare facilities.
**Prof. Memberships:** Member of the Nashville, Tennessee and American Bar Associations and American Health Lawyers Association.
**Career:** Joined Boult Cummings in 1987. Currently serves on the firm's Board of Governors.
**Personal:** JD, Vanderbilt University Law School (1987); BA, University of Pennsylvania (1984).

### HARKAVY, Ronald
Harkavy Shainberg Kaplan & Dunstan PLC, Memphis 901 761 1263
*Recommended in Real Estate*

### HARRIS, Matthew T
Waller Lansden Dortch & Davis, Nashville 615 244 6380
matt.harris@wallerlaw.com
*Recommended in Real Estate*
**Practice Areas:** Commercial real estate, land use and zoning and real estate lending. Extensive experience in the acquisition, disposition and leasing of office, industrial and retail properties for public and private companies. Management of multi-state acquisition and financing transactions.
**Prof. Memberships:** Member, Nashville, Tennessee and American Bar Associations.
**Career:** Practiced law since 1984. Joined Waller Lansden in 1997. Manages the firm's Real Estate Practice Group.

### HARWELL JR, Aubrey
Neal & Harwell, PLC, Nashville
615 244 1713
*Recommended in Litigation*

### HATMAKER, J Chadwick
Woolf, McClane, Bright, Allen & Carpenter, PLLC, Knoxville 865 215 1000
*Recommended in Employment*

### HAYNES, John
Boult, Cummings, Conners & Berry, PLC, Nashville 615 252 2343
jhaynes@boultcummings.com
*Recommended in Real Estate*
**Practice Areas:** Development, acquisition, financing, leasing and sale of institutional quality investment properties, with a special emphasis on serving German clients. Experience in the development and financing of affordable and low income housing, including projects financed with bonds, low income housing tax credits and various state and federal grants, including HOME and HOPE VI Revitalization Grants.
**Prof. Memberships:** Member of the Nashville, Tennessee and American Bar Associations, NAIOP, the Association for Commercial Real Estate and the Brentwood Chamber of Commerce.
**Career:** Joined Boult Cummings in 1986.
**Personal:** JD, University of Kentucky College of Law (1986); BA, Transylvania University (1983).

### HICKS, John
Baker, Donelson, Bearman, Caldwell & Berkowitz, PC, Nashville
615 744 7337
jhicks@bakerdonelson.com
*Recommended in Litigation*
**Practice Areas:** Chair, Health Care and Medical Professional Litigation Section. Practice concentrated in health law litigation, medical malpractice defense, class action defense, ADR, insurance coverage, and commercial and banking litigation. Experienced in creditors' rights and business reorganizations.
**Prof. Memberships:** Member, American (Litigation, Health Law, Dispute Resolution, Tort Trial and Insurance Practice sections and The Center for Professional Responsibility), Tennessee (Litigation, Dispute Resolution and Health Care Law sections) and Nashville (Federal Court Practice and Ethics and Professional Service committees) Bar Associations. Member, American Health Lawyers Association, Tennessee Defense Lawyers Association, Defense Research Institute and American Bankruptcy Institute.
**Career:** Tennessee license, 1983.

### HILL, J Reginald
Waller Lansden Dortch & Davis, Nashville
615 244 6380
reggie.hill@wallerlaw.com
*Recommended in Corporate/M&A*
**Practice Areas:** Extensive experience in

the areas of business transaction law, mergers and acquisitions, securities, venture capital financing and health law.

**Prof. Memberships:** Member, Nashville Bar Association and its Health Law Committee. Member, Tennessee Bar Association, serving in its Health Law Section. Member, American Bar Association and its Business Law and Health Law Sections. Member, American Health Lawyers Association.

**Career:** Practiced law at Waller Lansden since 1982. Serves on the firm's Board of Directors.

## HOLT III, Berry

Boult, Cummings, Conners & Berry, PLC, Nashville 615 252 2312
bholt@boultcummings.com
*Recommended in Corporate/M&A*

**Practice Areas:** Practice ranges from general corporate advice to specific healthcare advice regarding transactional, regulatory or operational matters.

**Prof. Memberships:** Tennessee Academy of Hospital Attorneys, Advisory Board of Directors of First Tennessee Bank, NA and Board Member of the Mental Health Cooperative, St Thomas Medical Clinic, Baptist North Tower Surgical Hospital and the St Thomas Outpatient Cath Lab Center.

**Career:** Joined Boult Cummings in 1975.

**Personal:** JD, Vanderbilt University Law School (1976); BA, Vanderbilt University (1973).

## HOWARD, Linda Edell

Adams and Reese LLP, Nashville
615 341 0068
linda.edellhoward@arlaw.com
*Recommended in Media & Entertainment*

**Practice Areas:** Partner: entertainment/new media, intellectual property/technology, e-commerce.

**Prof. Memberships:** Admitted to Tennessee, Nashville, New York, and New Jersey Bar Associations.

**Career:** Entertainment/New Media Practice Team Leader; Partner in Charge Music Row Office. Experienced in all areas of entertainment, new media/technology and domestic/international intellectual property law. Transaction-based practice focuses on entertainment/new technology contracts, advocacy for creators and protection for copyright and other rights holders. Ms Edell Howard has an extensive client list including entertainers, key industry executives, independent publishers, songwriters, producers, authors and related industry players.

**Personal:** JD Seton Hall University School of Law, 1985; BA Rutgers University, 1982.

## HUMPHREYS, Hunter

Glankler Brown, PLLC, Memphis
901 576 1744
hhumphreys@glankler.com
*Recommended in Real Estate*

**Practice Areas:** Real estate and secured lending. Mr Humphreys represents numerous investors, developers, lenders and participants in real estate, secured lending and other business transactions.

**Prof. Memberships:** Admitted to practice in Tennessee. Adjunct Professor, University of Memphis School of Law (Real Estate Transactions). Past President and current Board Member of the University of Memphis Law School Alumni Association. Past Board Member of the Estate Planning Council of Memphis. Board member of the the District Investigating Committee for the Tennessee Bar Association. Member, American Bar Association (Business Law, Real Property, Probate and Trust Sections). Member, Tennessee Bar Association (Real Estate Section). Member, Memphis Bar Association (Former member, CLE Committee, Moral Fitness for Admission to the Bar Committee; Former Chairman, University of Memphis Law School Liaison Committee).

**Career:** Lawler, Humphreys, Dunlap & Wellford (1977-85); Glankler Brown, PLLC (1985-present), Member, Chair of Real Estate Section. Named to Best 101 Lawyers in the State of Tennessee, Best 150 Lawyers in the State of Tennessee and Best 150 Commercial Real Estate (influential individuals in CRE) by Business TN magazine.

**Personal:** Born 24 November 1951, Memphis, TN; JD, University of Memphis, 1977; BA, University of North Carolina (Chapel Hill), 1974.

## HYNE, Ernest

Harwell Howard Hyne Gabbert & Manner, PC, Nashville 615 256 0500
*Recommended in Corporate/M&A*

## JACOBSON, John

Bowen Riley Warnock & Jacobson, PLC, Nashville 615 320 3700
*Recommended in Litigation*

## JENNINGS, Paul G

Bass, Berry & Sims PLC, Nashville
615 742 6267
pjennings@bassberry.com
*Recommended in Litigation*

**Practice Areas:** Commercial litigation, restructuring and bankruptcy law. Represents creditors including institutional creditors in corporate bankruptcies, Counsel to state's largest corporate debtors and Counsel to official unsecured creditors committees.

**Prof. Memberships:** American Bankruptcy Institute; Nashville Bar Association; Tennessee Bar Association (past President of Section of Commercial, Bankruptcy and Banking Law); Mid-South Commercial Law Institute (direc-

tor); Tennessee Chapter Turnaround Management Association (Board Member).

**Career:** Joined the firm in 1990.

**Personal:** BS (1987), Middle Tennessee State University; JD (1990), with high honors, University of Tennessee (Order of the Coif).

## JONES, Nancy S

Bass, Berry & Sims PLC, Nashville
615 742 6239
njones@bassberry.com
*Recommended in Litigation*

**Practice Areas:** Focuses on healthcare litigation, including internal investigations and qui tam defenses, as well as complex federal court commercial and securities litigation.

**Prof. Memberships:** American, Tennessee, New York and Nashville Bar Associations; American Health Lawyers Association; Fellow, Nashville and Tennessee Bar Foundations.

**Career:** Joined the firm in 2004. Assistant US Attorney for the Middle District of Tennessee, 1991-93. Assistant US Attorney for the Western District of Oklahoma, 1987-91; Assistant US Attorney for the Northern District of New York, 1980-87.

**Personal:** BA (1971), with honors, University of Missouri; JD (1978), Syracuse University.

## JONES, Philip

Martin, Tate, Morrow & Marston, P.C., Memphis 901 522 9000
*Recommended in Real Estate*

## JONES, Russell

Gordon, Martin, Jones, Harris & Shrum, Nashville 615 321 5469
*Recommended in Media & Entertainment*

## KAPLAN, Jonathan

Kiesewetter Wise Kaplan Prather, PLC, Memphis 901 795 6695
*Recommended in Employment*

## KELLEY, James

Neal & Harwell, PLC, Nashville
615 244 1713
*Recommended in Litigation*

## KIESEWETTER, Jay

Kiesewetter Wise Kaplan Prather, PLC, Memphis 901 795 6695
*Recommended in Employment*

## KIRKHAM, J Steven

Waller Lansden Dortch & Davis, Nashville 615 244 6380
steve.kirkham@wallerlaw.com
*Recommended in Real Estate*

**Practice Areas:** Commercial real property, business and banking law. Extensive experience in representing developers and end-use retailers in shopping center and regional mall developments and has experience including work with land development companies in financing, purchasing, selling and leasing potential

development sites. Represents clients in acquisition, syndication and financing of multi-family housing complexes, exerpience involves structuring and negotiating complex acquisition and financing vehicles utilizing securitized credit facilities and multi-tiered ownership structures.

**Prof. Memberships:** Member of the Nashville, Tennessee, Kentucky and American Bar Associations.

**Career:** Practiced law since 1989. Joined Waller Lansden in 2001.

## KRAMER, Steven E

Kramer Rayson LLP, Knoxville
865 525 5134
skramer@kramer-rayson.com
*Recommended in Employment*

**Practice Areas:** Mr Kramer's law practice principally involves employment and labor law, corporate law and sports law.

**Prof. Memberships:** He is a Member of the Knoxville (TN), Kingsport (TN), Tennessee, and American Bar Associations. Mr Kramer is a Member of the Regional Board of Directors for First Tennessee Bank. He has served as Chairman of the Kingsport Economic Development Board for the past 10 years and is a member of the Board of Directors for the Northeast State Community College Foundation and the Boys and Girls Club.

**Career:** The law firm of Kramer Rayson LLP named Steven E Kramer 'Of Counsel' with the firm in 2003. Mr Kramer was Vice President of Human Resources and General Counsel for AFG Industries, Inc. from 1990-2003. Prior to joining AFG, Mr Kramer spent 10 years in the private practice of law as a Partner at the Hunter, Smith & Davis and Baker, Donaldson law firms. Steve has been identified as a leading employment lawyer in Tennessee by Chambers USA, The Client's Guide 2004.

**Personal:** Mr Kramer holds an undergraduate degree in business administration from Miami University in Oxford, Ohio. He received his MBA (finance) from the University of Southwestern Louisiana and his JD from the University Of Tennessee College Of Law. Steve and his wife Tina have three children and reside in East Tennessee.

## KRAUS, Kenneth L

Loeb & Loeb LLP, Nashville
615 749 8300
kkraus@loeb.com
*Recommended in Media & Entertainment*

**Practice Areas:** Focuses on entertainment, copyright, trademark, intellectual property law. Primarily on music, but extensive experience in film/television. Has represented major recording artists, songwriters, record companies, music publishers, authors, managers, music executives and others in entertainment industry. Has been involved in numerous start-ups, representing both companies and investors.

**Prof. Memberships:** TN Bar Association; Nashville Bar Association; CA Bar Association; LA County Bar Association.
**Career:** Partner since 2000.
**Publications:** Regularly lectures at Practicing Law Institute, USC Entertainment Law Institute, Nashville Bar Association and other professional organizations.
**Personal:** UCLA School of Law (JD, 1971); Occidental College (BA, 1967).

### LAMAR III, Howard H
Bass, Berry & Sims PLC, Nashville
615 742 6209
hlamar@bassberry.com
*Recommended in Corporate/M&A*
**Practice Areas:** Focuses on complex transactions, such as mergers and acquisitions for public and private companies, public offerings on behalf of issuers and investment banking firms and venture capital and other private financings (equity and subordinated debt) for venture funds and issuers, including venture capital partnership formation. Counsels companies on a variety of corporate and securities matters, including capital formation, corporate governance, public company disclosure matters, strategic analysis and start-up concerns.
**Prof. Memberships:** American and Nashville Bar Associations.
**Career:** Joined the firm in 1989.
**Personal:** BA (1983) and JD (1989), Vanderbilt University.

### LEWIS, Frederick
Lewis Fisher Henderson Claxton & Mulroy, Memphis 901 767 6160
*Recommended in Employment*

### LIDDON, Robert C
Baker, Donelson, Bearman, Caldwell & Berkowitz, PC, Memphis 901 577 2269
rliddon@bakerdonelson.com
*Recommended in Real Estate*
**Practice Areas:** Practice concentrated in lending, financing and real estate. Experience includes multi-state lending transactions, credit and financing, bank regulatory, corporate formation, and acquisition and financing of healthcare facilities. Extensive experience in banking law, credit law, commercial credit, interest and usury, shopping center law, construction contracts, asset based finance, military base closings, and commercial real estate acquisition, finance and leasing.
**Prof. Memberships:** Member, American, Tennessee, Mississippi and Memphis Bar Associations. Member, Phi Beta Kappa.
**Career:** Licensed in Tennessee since 1975 and Mississippi since 1976.
**Personal:** BA, Vanderbilt University, 1972; JD, Columbia University, 1975.

### LIPSHIE, Samuel D
Boult, Cummings, Conners & Berry, PLC, Nashville 615 252 2332
slipshie@boultcummings.com
*Recommended in Litigation*

**Practice Areas:** Entertainment, music, intellectual property and commercial litigation. Experience in acquisition and disposition of media, broadcast and other intellectual property. Litigation involving copyright, royalty, intellectual property, Uniform Commercial Code, trade secrets, covenants not to compete, interference with contractual relations, and other business and commercial issues.
**Prof. Memberships:** Member of the Nashville, Tennessee and American Bar Associations, Association of Trial Lawyers of America, Tennessee Trial Lawyers Association and the Copyright Society of the South.
**Career:** Joined Boult Cummings in 1981. Currently serves on the firm's Board of Governors.
**Personal:** JD, Vanderbilt University Law School (1981); BA, Vanderbilt University (1977).

### LONERGAN, Matthew
Boult, Cummings, Conners & Berry, PLC, Nashville 615 252 2322
mlonergan@boultcummings.com
*Recommended in Employment*
**Practice Areas:** Labor relations and employment law on behalf of management with emphasis in collective bargaining agreement negotiations, grievance and arbitration, employment discrimination litigation in both federal and state courts, the National Labor Relations Act, wrongful discharge, and wage and hour law. Also experienced in ADR and mediation.
**Prof. Memberships:** Member of the Nashville, Tennessee, Texas and American Bar Associations. Fellow of the Nashville Bar Association.
**Career:** Joined Boult Cummings in 1988. Serves as Chair of the firm's Labor and Employment Practice Group.
**Personal:** JD, Southern Methodist University – Dedman School of Law (1983); BS, Denison University (1980).

### MALONE, JR, Gayle
Walker, Bryant, Tipps & Malone, Nashville 615 313 6000
gmalone@walkerbryant.com
*Recommended in Litigation*
**Practice Areas:** Civil trial law; personal injury litigation including medical malpractice; products liability; premises liability and motor vehicle actions; hospital law; Rule 31 listed general civil mediator.
**Prof. Memberships:** American, Tennessee and Nashville Bar Associations; International Academy of Defense Counsel; Tennessee Defense Lawyers Association; Tennessee Trial Lawyers Association; American College of Trial Lawyers.
**Career:** Partner.
**Personal:** Vanderbilt University (JD 1973, BA 1970).

### MANNER, Mark
Harwell Howard Hyne Gabbert & Manner, PC, Nashville 615 256 0500
*Recommended in Corporate/M&A*

### MARSHALL COX, LeeAnne
Burch, Porter & Johnson PLLC, Memphis 901 524 5000
*Recommended in Real Estate*

### MASHBURN, Randal
Baker, Donelson, Bearman, Caldwell & Berkowitz, PC, Nashville 615 726 7336
rmashburn@bakerdonelson.com
*Recommended in Litigation*
**Practice Areas:** Practice concentrated on commercial, business, and bankruptcy disputes. Extensive experience in restructuring and insolvency matters and litigation involving financial transactions, lender liability, UCC, business dissolutions, claims against officers/directors, trustee actions, and debtor-creditor issues. Wide range of representation including creditors, debtors, trustees, creditors' committees, examiners and receivers.
**Prof. Memberships:** Member, American, Tennessee and Nashville Bar Associations. Member, American Bankruptcy Institute. Fellow, Nashville Bar Foundation. Past President, Mid-South Commercial Law Institute.
**Career:** Licensed in Tennessee since 1982. Certified business bankruptcy specialist by the American Board of Certification. Rule 31 certified mediator.

### METCALF, Bryan W
Bass, Berry & Sims PLC, Nashville 615 742 6212
bmetcalf@bassberry.com
*Recommended in Corporate/M&A*
**Practice Areas:** Experience in corporate and partnership taxation and in planning business formations, acquisitions, restructurings and other transactions. Advises clients on a broad range of compensation-related issues in both the corporate and partnership context, including the implementation of executive and equity-based compensation.
**Career:** Joined the firm in 1996.
**Personal:** BA (1992), Furman University; JD (1995), The University of Michigan Law School; LLM (1996), New York University School of Law.

### MILOM, W Michael
Bass, Berry & Sims PLC, Nashville 615 255 6161
mmilom@bassberry.com
*Recommended in Media & Entertainment*
**Practice Areas:** Has practiced entertainment and intellectual property and technology law for more than 30 years. Concentrates his practice in the areas of copyright, literary property and entertainment law.
**Prof. Memberships:** American Bar Association (Copyright Office Commit-

tee of the Intellectual Property Section); Tennessee Bar Association (past Chair, Section on Copyright, Entertainment and Sports Law); Nashville Bar Association (past Chair, Entertainment Law Committee); Past Member, International Copyright Panel of the US State Department Advisory Committee on International Intellectual Property.
**Career:** Joined the firm in 2001.
**Personal:** BS (1964), Middle Tennessee State University; JD (1971), Vanderbilt University.

### MITCHELL, E Marlee
Waller Lansden Dortch & Davis, Nashville 615 244 6380
marlee.mitchell@wallerlaw.com
*Recommended in Corporate/M&A*
**Practice Areas:** Securities law, including underwritten equity and debt public offerings, private placements, joint ventures and venture capital financings, federal and state broker-dealer and investment adviser regulatory compliance matters and Tennessee Securities Division contested case issues. Corporate governance, mergers and acquisitions and intellectual property matters.
**Prof. Memberships:** Member, Committees on Federal Regulation of Securities and State Regulation of Securities, Business Law Section of the American Bar Association. Member, Tennessee Bar Association's Corporation and Business Law Section. Member, Nashville Bar Association's Corporate and Commercial Practice Committee.
**Career:** Practiced law since 1983. Joined Waller Lansden in 1989. Co-manages the firm's Corporate Practice Group. Serves on the firm's Board of Directors.

### NEAL, James
Neal & Harwell, PLC, Nashville 615 244 1713
*Recommended in Litigation*

### NORTH, Phillip
North Pursell Ramos & Jameson, Nashville 615 255 2555
*Recommended in Litigation*

### NORTON III, William L
Boult, Cummings, Conners & Berry, PLC, Nashville 615 252 2397
bnorton@boultcummings.com
*Recommended in Litigation*
**Practice Areas:** Commercial finance dealing primarily in creditors' rights and insolvency.
**Prof. Memberships:** Fellow of the American College of Bankruptcy. President and Board Member of the American Board of Certification. Board Member of Nashville Conflict Resolution Center, Mid-South Commercial Law Institute and Tennessee Turnaround Management Association (Founder). Member of Nashville, Tennessee and American Bar Associations, AAA Commercial Arbitration Panel Commercial Law League of

America and the Downtown Rotary Club of Nashville.

**Career:** Joined Boult Cummings in 1984.
**Personal:** JD, Vanderbilt University Law School (1982); BA, Vanderbilt University (1975).

## OLIVER, Craig
Boult, Cummings, Conners & Berry, PLC, Nashville 615 252 2310
coliver@boultcummings.com
*Recommended in Employment*

**Practice Areas:** Labor relations and employment law on behalf of management with experience in labor relations and union activity issues, Title VII and other employment discrimination litigation, wage and hour laws, alternative dispute resolutions and providing general day to day advice to employers.
**Prof. Memberships:** Member of the Nashville, Tennessee and American Bar Associations.
**Career:** Joined Boult Cummings in 1994.
**Personal:** JD, Harvard University Law School (1994); BA, Duke University (1991).

## OZIER, William
Bass, Berry & Sims PLC, Nashville 615 742 6232
bozier@bassberry.com
*Recommended in Employment*

**Practice Areas:** Represents management in all types of labor and employment matters including union avoidance, union relations, negotiation of union contracts, labor arbitration, defense of age, gender and race discrimination claims, retaliatory discharge, and enforcement and defense of non-compete agreements. Represents academic institutions in employment and student-related litigation.
**Prof. Memberships:** Fellow, American College of Labor and Employment Lawyers; Tennessee Bar Association, Labor Law Committee; Nashville Bar Association, Federal Court Committee.
**Career:** Joined the firm in 1969. Served as Managing Partner, 1987-92.
**Personal:** BA (1966) and JD (1969), Vanderbilt University.

## PAPEL, Laurence M
Baker, Donelson, Bearman, Caldwell & Berkowitz, PC, Nashville
615 726 5656
lpapel@bakerdonelson.com
*Recommended in Real Estate*

**Practice Areas:** Practice concentrated primarily in the areas of real estate and corporate transactions, including the acquisition, leasing, development, financing and disposition of commercial, residential and industrial real estate; and commercial transactions, including entity and capital formation, private offerings, and mergers and acquisitions.
**Prof. Memberships:** Member, American (Corporate and Real Estate Sections), Tennessee and Nashville Bar Associa-

tions.
**Career:** Licensed in Tennessee and federal courts since 1980.
**Personal:** Trinity College, BA, 1977. Vanderbilt University School of Law, JD, 1980.

## PATTERSON, Robert S
Boult, Cummings, Conners & Berry, PLC, Nashville 615 252 2335
bpatterson@boultcummings.com
*Recommended in Litigation*

**Practice Areas:** Commercial litigation with special emphasis in business litigation, class actions, intellectual property litigation, tort litigation and healthcare litigation.
**Prof. Memberships:** Serves on the Board for Vanderbilt Children's Hospital, Junior Achievement and the University School of Nashville. Member of the Nashville, Tennessee and American Bar Associations.
**Career:** Joined Boult Cummings in 1978. Served as the firm's Managing Director from 2000-05.
**Personal:** JD, Vanderbilt University Law School (1978); BA, Rice University (1975).

## PEEK, Michael S
Bass, Berry & Sims PLC, Nashville 615 742 6231
mpeek@bassberry.com
*Recommended in Real Estate*

**Practice Areas:** Practices primarily in the areas of commercial real estate development, banking and commercial lending, tax increment finance and general commercial law. Devotes the majority of professional time to the negotiation and documentation of a variety of commercial lending and real estate transactions, including commercial real estate developments, construction loans, revolving credit and term loan facilities, tax increment financings and corporate financings.
**Prof. Memberships:** Tennessee Bar Association (Condominium Law Committee).
**Career:** Joined the firm in 1974. Former Managing Partner. Former Member of the Vanderbilt Law School Alumni Board.
**Personal:** BA (1970), Murray State University; JD (1974), Vanderbilt University.

## PHILLIPS, Edward G
Kramer Rayson LLP, Knoxville 865 525 5134
ephillips@kramer-rayson.com
*Recommended in Employment*

**Practice Areas:** Mr Phillips practices exclusively representing management in the areas of employment and labor relations law. His practice spans litigation, prospective advice, training, and counseling clients ranging from major corporations to small business, as well as public employers. He has been recognized in a leading legal publication in America in

employment law since 2003.
**Prof. Memberships:** Admitted, Tennessee 1978. Mr Phillips is a member of the Knox and Anderson County Bar Associations, as well as the American and Tennessee Bar Association, where he served as Chairman of the Labor and Employment Section of the Tennessee Bar Association for 1995-96. Mr Phillips was a Member of the Editorial Review Board for The Tennessee Labor Letter, a comprehensive employer information service, from its inception in 1993 through 2000. He has also been elected as a Fellow in both the Tennessee and Knoxville Bar Foundations.
**Career:** Mr Phillips is currently the Managing Partner for Kramer Rayson LLP, with whom he has spent all 27 years in practicing labor and employment law. Judicial clerk for the Honorable Houston Goddard, Tennessee Court of Appeals, Eastern Section (1986-87).
**Personal:** Born December 31, 1953, Knoxville, Tennessee; JD University of Tennessee College of Law, 1978 Order of the Coif; Bachelors in Accounting, East Tennessee State University, 1975.

## PHILLIPS JR, John B
Miller & Martin PLLC, Chattanooga 423 785 8325
jphillips@millermartin.com
*Recommended in Employment*

**Practice Areas:** Represent management in all areas of labor and employment law. Involved in representing Coca-Cola Enterprises Inc. in class actions across USA.
**Prof. Memberships:** Chattanooga Bar Association; Tennessee Bar Association; American Bar Association.
**Career:** Associate Stophel, Caldwell & Heggie from 1974-79; Partner Caldwell, Heggie & Helton from 1979-91; Partner Miller & Martin from 1991-2005 (Managing Partner from 1997-2002).
**Publications:** Editor: Tennessee Employment Law Letter since 1986. Author: 'Tennessee Employment Law'; author: 'Employment Law Desk Book for Tennessee Employers'.
**Personal:** Born January 28, 1947; BS David Lipscomb College, 1969; JD University of Tennessee, 1974; lives in Chattanooga and Atlanta; married.

## PRATHER, Paul
Kiesewetter Wise Kaplan Prather, PLC, Memphis 901 795 6695
*Recommended in Employment*

## REID, JR, Glen G
Wyatt, Tarrant & Combs, LLP, Memphis 901 537 1057
greid@wyattfirm.com
*Recommended in Litigation*

**Practice Areas:** Banking and commercial litigation.
**Prof. Memberships:** He is a member of the Memphis and Tennessee Bar Associations and the Memphis and Tennessee

Bar Foundations.
**Career:** Formerly, Assistant United States Attorney for the Western District of Tennessee. He is a Fellow of the American College of Trial Lawyers, Member of the American Board of Trial Advocates; a Master of the Leo Bearman, Sr American Inn of Court.
**Personal:** Received his BBA cum laude in 1968 from Memphis State University and his JD Degree in 1971 from Memphis State University School of Law.

## RILEY, Steven
Bowen Riley Warnock & Jacobson, PLC, Nashville 615 320 3700
*Recommended in Litigation*

## ROLAPP, Todd J
Bass, Berry & Sims PLC, Nashville 615 742 6288
trolapp@bassberry.com
*Recommended in Corporate/M&A*

**Practice Areas:** Focuses on general corporate and securities law, including representation of issuers, underwriters and investors in public and private securities offerings and the representation of both public and private buyers and sellers in M&A transactions. Regularly counsels clients on matters of corporate governance and heads the firm's Executive Compensation Group.
**Career:** Joined the firm in 1996.
**Personal:** BA (1991), Brigham Young University; JD (1994), Duke University.

## ROSE, Glenn
Harwell Howard Hyne Gabbert & Manner, PC, Nashville 615 256 0500
*Recommended in Litigation*

## RUSH, Stephen
Rush Law Group, Nashville 615 327 7370
*Recommended in Media & Entertainment*

## RUTTER, David
Boult, Cummings, Conners & Berry, PLC, Nashville 615 252 2346
drutter@boultcummings.com
*Recommended in Real Estate*

**Practice Areas:** Practices in the areas of commercial leasing, development of residential and industrial projects, real estate acquisitions and due diligence. Represents large retail companies in lease negotiations throughout the United States.
**Prof. Memberships:** Member of the Nashville, Tennessee and American Bar Associations.
**Career:** Joined Boult Cummings in 1993. Currently serves as Section Leader of the firm's Real Estate and Finance area.
**Personal:** JD, Vanderbilt University Law School (1993); BA, Oberlin College (1990).

## SANDERS, James
Neal & Harwell, PLC, Nashville 615 244 1713
*Recommended in Litigation*

## SCOTT, W Rowlett
Armstrong Allen PLLC, Memphis
901 523 8211
*Recommended in Real Estate*

## SHAINBERG, Raymond
Harkavy Shainberg Kaplan & Dunstan
PLC, Memphis 901 761 1263
*Recommended in Real Estate*

## SHEETS, D Mark
Bass, Berry & Sims PLC, Nashville
615 742 6258
msheets@bassberry.com
*Recommended in Real Estate*
**Practice Areas:** Focuses on commercial
real estate, commercial lending and general commercial law. Areas of representation include acquisition and development, leasing, sale – leasebacks, synthetic
leases, tax-free exchanges, loss allocation
vehicles, commercial financing and resi-
dential/golf course development.
**Prof. Memberships:** Nashville Bar Association; International Council of Shopping Centers.
**Career:** Joined the firm in 1990.
**Personal:** BA (1987), Centre College; JD
(1990), with honors, University of Kentucky.

## SHERRARD III, Thomas
Sherrard & Roe PLC, Nashville
615 742 4200
*Recommended in Corporate/M&A*

## STEGER, Christopher
Miller & Martin PLLC, Nashville
423 785 8314
csteger@millermartin.com
*Recommended in Employment*
**Practice Areas:** Employment and civil
litigation. Represented national, international, corporations in defense of various
employment discrimination lawsuits.
Counsels clients with respect to employment decisions including hiring, termination, reductions in force, disciplinary
actions, separation agreements, unemployment compensation claims and
employment contracts.
**Prof. Memberships:** Member of the
American, Tennessee, Georgia, and Federal Bar Associations. Active participant
on the Criminal Justice Advisory Panel.
Serves on the Tennessee Board of Law
Examiners.
**Personal:** BA in 1979 and a JD in 1983,
both from Baylor University.

## STEMMLER, John A
Bass, Berry & Sims PLC, Memphis
901 543 5908
jstemmler@bassberry.com
*Recommended in Real Estate*
**Practice Areas:** Has over 30 years of
experience in commercial transactions
and real estate and corporate law. Advises
clients in mergers and acquisitions, commercial and residential real estate development and commercial lending. Extensive experience in the hospitality and
multi-family residential industries. Rep-

resents borrowers in multi-property,
multi-state hotel and apartment commu-
nity financings and acquisitions.
**Prof. Memberships:** American, Ten-
nessee and Memphis Bar Associations.
Former Chair, Corporation and Business
Law Section, Tennessee Bar Association.
**Career:** Joined the firm in 2000. Member
of firm's Executive Committee.
**Personal:** BA (1968) and JD (1971),
Vanderbilt University.

## STEVENS, C Eric
Miller & Martin PLLC, Nashville
615 744 8423
estevens@millermartin.com
*Recommended in Employment*
**Practice Areas:** Primarily focused in the
areas of hospitals/healthcare and financial institutions, covering broad range of
areas including union avoidance/train-
ing, labor negotiations, employment
counseling, litigation and governmental
compliance (OFCCP, EEOC, DOL, etc).
**Prof. Memberships:** Member, Tennessee
and Nashville Bar Associations.
**Career:** Entire career with Miller & Martin and its Nashville predecessor, Trabue,
Sturdivant & DeWitt. Founded the
Employment Practice Group at Trabue,
Sturdivant and DeWitt.
**Personal:** Born June 17, 1958 Carterville,
Illinois. Summa cum laude, Millikin University, 1980 (BS, Accounting). Vanderbilt
University School of Law, 1983. Earned
CPA certification (not currently licensed)
before entering practice of law. Married,
two sons.

## SULLIVAN, Robert L
Loeb & Loeb LLP, Nashville
615 749 8312
rsullivan@loeb.com
*Recommended in Media &
Entertainment*
**Practice Areas:** Focuses on entertain-
ment primarily in music; also litigation
and mediation in entertainment and IP.
Represents major recording artists, song-
writers, publishing and record companies.
**Prof. Memberships:** Certified mediator
– Tennessee Supreme Court; ABA; Ten-
nessee Bar Association; Board of Direc-
tors – Copyright Society of the South;
Leadership Music.
**Career:** Partner.
**Publications:** Adjunct Faculty at Bel-
mont College; Instructor on entertain-
ment law at Nashville Law School.
**Personal:** Vanderbilt University Law
School (JD, 1977) Vanderbilt (BA, 1974,
magna cum laude).

## SWAFFORD, T Anthony
Miller & Martin PLLC, Nashville
615 744 8411
tswafford@millermartin.com
*Recommended in Employment*
**Practice Areas:** Labor and Employment; represents national, regional clients
in traditional labor- and employment-
related matters. Successfully represented

private airport screening company in
union organizational campaign with
ramifications for entire industry.
**Prof. Memberships:** American, Tennessee Bar Associations; Transportation
Lawyers Association; Association for
Transportation Law, Logistics and Policy;
Sports Lawyers Association.
**Career:** Started Labor and Employment
Practice for firm in Nashville, 1998;
became Vice-Chair of Department, January 2005.
**Publications:** Frequent writer, lecturer for
number of bar associations, professional
associations and seminar producers.
**Personal:** Graduated (high honors) Uni-
versity of Tennessee, 1990 (BS, Accounting); cum laude, Case Western Reserve
University, 1995 (JD). Married, three
sons.

## SWEENEY, Matt
Baker, Donelson, Bearman, Caldwell &
Berkowitz, PC, Nashville 615 726 5774
msweeney@bakerdonelson.com
*Recommended in Litigation*
**Practice Areas:** Litigation and ADR.
Extensive experience in franchising, busi-
ness tort, and D&O and securities class
litigation. Former Circuit Court Judge
and Presiding Judge of district's Trial
Courts – Nashville.
**Prof. Memberships:** Fellow, former
Trustee – Nashville Bar Foundation. Fel-
low, Tennessee Bar Foundation. Master,
Executive Committee – Harry Phillips
American Inn of Court. Approved medi-
ator Tennessee Commission on Alterna-
tive Dispute Resolution. Member, Ameri-
can Arbitration Association, Mediation
and Arbitration Panels (Commercial,
Employment, Sports Law). Member,
American, Tennessee and Nashville Bar
Associations and Tennessee Trial Lawyers
Association.
**Career:** Tennessee license, 1976.
**Personal:** Vanderbilt Law School, JD;
National Judicial College, General Juris-
diction Program.

## TATE JR, James S
Bass, Berry & Sims PLC, Nashville
615 742 6235
jtate@bassberry.com
*Recommended in Real Estate*
**Practice Areas:** Focuses on banking and
commercial lending, secured transactions, real estate, creditors', rights and
general commercial law. Represents
clients in the negotiation and documentation of a variety of corporate financing,
commercial lending and real estate transactions including revolving credit and
term loan facilities, secured financings,
construction loans, long-term real estate
loans and real estate development projects.
**Career:** Joined the firm in 1980.
**Personal:** BA (1976), cum laude, and JD
(1980), Order of the Coif, Vanderbilt
University.

## THOMPSON, Bob F
Bass, Berry & Sims PLC, Nashville
615 742 6262
bthompson@bassberry.com
*Recommended in Corporate/M&A*
**Practice Areas:** Focuses on securities
regulation, mergers and acquisitions and
financial institutions. Serves as Principal
Corporate and Securities Counsel for
public companies in the banking, managed care, healthcare information and
small business lending industries. Represents clients in going private transactions,
spin-offs, initial public offerings and venture capital placements.
**Prof. Memberships:** Nashville, Tennessee and American (Banking Law
Committee; Federal Regulation of Securities Committee) Bar Associations; Tennessee Bankers Association (Lawyers
Committee).
**Career:** Joined the firm in 1975. US
Navy, 1969-72.
**Personal:** BA (1969), Princeton University; JD (1975), Harvard.

## THOMPSON III, Overton
Bass, Berry & Sims PLC, Nashville
615 742 7730
othompson@bassberry.com
*Recommended in Litigation*
**Practice Areas:** Focuses practice on
complex corporate, class action and business torts litigation, including cases
involving securities class action defense,
derivative actions, officer and director liability, intellectual property, breach of
contract, business and consumer fraud,
corporate and partnership dissolutions,
lender liability, trust and estates litigation
and bad faith insurance litigation.
**Prof. Memberships:** Tennessee Bar
Association (past Chair of the Litigation
Section).
**Career:** Joined the firm in 1999. Has
practiced litigation exclusively for 21
years in Nashville.
**Personal:** BA (1981), University of the
South; JD (1984), Vanderbilt University.

## TRENT, Tom
Boult, Cummings, Conners & Berry, PLC,
Nashville 615 252 2327
ttrent@boultcummings.com
*Recommended in Real Estate*
**Practice Areas:** Real estate transactions
including industrial development and
economic incentives, leasing, corporate,
joint venture, partnership and limited lia-
bility company law, and tax-exempt
finance.
**Prof. Memberships:** Member of the
Nashville, Tennessee and American Bar
Associations; the National Association of
Bond Lawyers; the Tennessee Industrial
Development Council; International
Association of Attorneys and Executives
in Corporate Real Estate; and the Ten-
nessee-Japan Society. Fellow of the American College of Mortgage Attorneys.
**Career:** Joined Boult Cummings in 1979.

Former Managing Director of the firm and currently serves on the firm's Board of Governors.
**Personal:** JD, Vanderbilt University Law School (1979); AB, Wabash College (1976).

## TRENTHAM, Robert
Miller & Martin PLLC, Nashville
615 744 8417
rtrentham@millermartin.com
*Recommended in Litigation*
**Practice Areas:** Legal-medical malpractice litigation, civil litigation and personal injury litigation, commercial litigation.
**Prof. Memberships:** Nashville, Tennessee and American Bar Associations; Life Member of the Judicial Conference of the Sixth Circuit, US Court of Appeals; Fellow of the American College of Trial Lawyers.
**Personal:** Received a BA in 1969 and a JD in 1972 from Vanderbilt University. Married, one child.

## URNESS, Thor
Boult, Cummings, Conners & Berry, PLC, Nashville 615 252 2384
turness@boultcummings.com
*Recommended in Litigation*
**Practice Areas:** Practices in the areas of alternative dispute resolution, commercial litigation, entertainment, franchise law, intellectual property litigation, insurance law and tort litigation.
**Prof. Memberships:** Member of the Nashville Technology Council, the American Bar Association, the Tennessee Intellectual Property Law Association, the American Intellectual Property Law Association, the Association of Trial Lawyers of America and the International Trademark Association. Board member for the Nashville Pro Bono Program.
**Career:** Joined Boult Cummings in 1988. Serves as the firm's Pro Bono Member.
**Personal:** JD, Indiana University School of Law (1988); BBA, Indiana University (1986).

## VOIGT, John
Sherrard & Roe PLC, Nashville
615 742 4200
*Recommended in Corporate/M&A*

## WALKER, Mitchell
Bass, Berry & Sims PLC, Nashville
615 742 6275
mwalker@bassberry.com
*Recommended in Corporate/M&A*
**Practice Areas:** Represents public companies and underwriters in public offerings and in mergers and acquisitions. Works with issuers and underwriters on public offerings of both equity and debt securities. Advises boards of directors or special committees on corporate governance issues, corporate restructurings, management led buyouts and investigations of accounting irregularities. Counsels clients on acquisitions or divestitures of operating subsidiaries or divisions and often coordinates an acquisition with raising the necessary capital to finance the purchase price.
**Career:** Joined the firm in 1982.
**Personal:** AB (1979), cum laude, Harvard University; JD (1982), Vanderbilt University.

## WALKER, Robert
Walker, Bryant, Tipps & Malone, Nashville 615 313 6005
bwalker@walkerbryant.com
*Recommended in Litigation*
**Practice Areas:** General civil trial practice with significant experience in product liability, medical malpractice and aviation lawsuits; focuses primarily on commercial and business litigation including securites and corporate goverance lawsuits, shareholder and hostile takeover suits, antitrust, consumer protection, business fraud suits, proxy challenges and director and officer liability claims.
**Prof. Memberships:** Tennessee and Nashville Bar Associations; Fellow in American College of Trial Lawyers; Harry Phillips Inns of Court – Emeritus.
**Career:** Partner.
**Personal:** Vanderbilt University (JD 1968, BA 1962).

## WALTON, Leigh
Bass, Berry & Sims PLC, Nashville
615 742 6201
lwalton@bassberry.com
*Recommended in Corporate/M&A*
**Practice Areas:** Concentrates her practice in corporate, securities and healthcare law matters. Represents public companies in securities, mergers and acquisitions, and corporate governance matters. Represents numerous early stage healthcare businesses in connection with securing venture capital funding.
**Prof. Memberships:** American, Tennessee and Nashville Bar Associations; Vice-Chair, ABA Committee on Negotiated Acquisitions; ABA Corporate Practices Committee; American Health Lawyers Association; Fellow, Tennessee Bar Foundation.
**Career:** Joined the firm in 1979.
**Personal:** BA (1973), magna cum laude, Randolph-Macon Woman's College; JD (1979), Order of the Coif, Vanderbilt University.

## WARREN JR, Richard F
Boult, Cummings, Conners & Berry, PLC, Nashville 615 252 2337
rwarren@boultcummings.com
*Recommended in Real Estate*
**Practice Areas:** Acquisition, development and financing of commercial real estate projects and general corporate law. Represents buyers and sellers of downtown and suburban office buildings. Represents clients in acquiring and selling portfolios of apartment and retail projects across the nation and has represented numerous institutional lenders in financing such projects.
**Prof. Memberships:** Member of the Nashville, Tennessee and American Bar Associations. Presently serves as Director and Secretary of Nashville Public Television.
**Career:** Joined Boult Cummings in 1975.
**Personal:** JD, Vanderbilt University Law School (1976); BA, Birmingham Southern College (1973).

## WAYLAND, R Eddie
King & Ballow, Nashville
615 259 3456
*Recommended in Employment*

## WEATHERSBY, E Woods
Evans & Petree PC, Memphis
901 525 6781
*Recommended in Real Estate*

## WISEMAN III, Thomas
Gideon & Wiseman PLC, Nashville
615 254 0400
*Recommended in Litigation*

## WOOD, Robert
Boult, Cummings, Conners & Berry, PLC, Nashville 615 252 2336
bwood@boultcummings.com
*Recommended in Real Estate*
**Practice Areas:** Commercial real estate and commercial lending transactions. Represents institutional lenders, real estate developers and investors in real estate finance, acquisition and development transactions.
**Prof. Memberships:** Member of the Nashville, Tennessee and American Bar Associations; ALTA's Lender's Counsel Group; and the Tennessee Land Title Association. Associate member of the American Land Title Association.
**Career:** Joined Boult Cummings in 1983. Currently serves as Managing Director for the firm and is a Member of the Board of Governors.
**Personal:** JD, Emory University (1983); BA, David Lipscomb College (1980).

## YARBRO, Jason
Armstrong Allen PLLC, Memphis
901 523 8211
*Recommended in Real Estate*

# BAKER, DONELSON, BEARMAN, CALDWELL & BERKOWITZ, PC

## THE FIRM

**Chairman & CEO:** Ben C Adams, Jr
**COO:** Jerry Stauffer
**Shareholders:** 218
**Other lawyers:** 226 (attorneys and public policy advisors)

**FIRM OVERVIEW:** Baker, Donelson, Bearman, Caldwell & Berkowitz, PC was ranked in 2004 as one of the 10 fastest growing law firms in the US and is one of the 100 largest law firms in the country. The firm has more than 440 attorneys and public policy advisors in 11 US markets, as well as a representative office in Beijing, China. Baker Donelson represents local, regional, national and international clients across numerous industries in a myriad of issues. The firm is committed to providing innovative, results-oriented solutions while placing the needs of its clients first. Baker Donelson understands the constantly evolving nature of the law, and provides the necessary continuing education to maintain the thought leadership and sophistication of its attorneys and public policy advisors.

## MAIN AREAS OF PRACTICE:

**Corporate/M&A:** Baker Donelson represents clients in every stage of the business life cycle, including the formation of all types of business entities by negotiating commercial contracts and reorganizing and recapitalizing businesses; the purchase, sale, merger or reorganization of publicly and privately held businesses; corporate conflicts; 'going private' transactions; and public offerings. The Securities Group handles formation transactions, securities offerings and compliance matters under federal and state laws. The Mergers and Acquisitions Group guides clients through asset purchases, statutory mergers, management buyouts and spin-offs.

**Health Law:** The firm delivers corporate, regulatory and financial services with an institutional knowledge of the healthcare industry. The breadth of Baker Donelson's healthcare knowledge and the diversity of its client base enable the department to provide services in commercial and contract matters, antitrust disputes, regulatory and governmental issues, and defense of tort cases in this complex industry.

**Labor & Employment:** Much of the firm's Labor and Employment Practice focuses on litigation avoidance and working with clients to ensure compliance with employment-related laws and regulations, as well as numerous state fair employment practice acts. The firm has developed training programs for client supervisors and managers in union avoidance, workplace harassment prevention, FMLA management and drug-free workplace. When litigation is unavoidable, the firm has extensive experience in state and federal courts throughout the country, defending against a wide range of employment claims.

**Litigation:** Baker Donelson's Litigation Department provides aggressive representation in civil disputes of all kinds and appears in state and federal venues in every region of the country. Trial attorneys are trained to listen first and understand that clients have differing business and legal objectives, from righting a wrong to limiting financial exposure.

**Real Estate:** Baker Donelson's Real Estate Group has a long history in all aspects of real estate development and capital finance, including project financing, syndication and the negotiation of purchase and sale agreements. Firm lawyers have represented clients in major retail developments, office buildings, industrial and business parks and apartment projects.

**Bankruptcy:** Baker Donelson's Bankruptcy and Creditors' Rights Group represents clients in litigation and transactions relating to bankruptcy, insolvency, loan workouts, collections, repossessions, foreclosures, lien disputes and other matters affecting debtor/creditor relationships. The group has extensive experience in both commercial and consumer issues.

**Other Areas of Practice:** Antitrust; construction; ebusiness and technology; eminent domain; employee benefits and executive compensation; environmental, health and safety; equipment leasing; estate planning/probate; financial service and transactions; government investigations and litigation; immigration; intellectual property; international; state and federal public policy; taxation; transportation, and alternative dispute resolution.

## ADMINISTRATIVE OFFICE

### TENNESSEE
165 Madison Avenue, Suite 2000, **Memphis**, TN 38103
**Tel:** 901 526 2000   **Fax:** 901 577 2303
**Website:** www.bakerdonelson.com

## BRANCH OFFICES

### ALABAMA
420 20th Street N, 1600 Wachovia Tower, **Birmingham**, AL 35203
**Tel:** 205 328 0480   **Fax:** 205 322 8007

### GEORGIA
Six Concourse Parkway, Suite 3100, **Atlanta**, GA 30328
**Tel:** 678 406 8700   **Fax:** 678 406 8701

### LOUISIANA
201 St. Charles Ave., Suite 3600, **New Orleans**, LA 70170
**Tel:** 504 566 5200   **Fax:** 504 636 4000

3 Sanctuary Blvd., Suite 201, **Mandeville**, LA 70471
**Tel:** 985 819 8400   **Fax:** 985 819 8484

301 N Main Street, One American Place, Suite 830,
**Baton Rouge**, LA 70825
**Tel:** 225 381 7000   **Fax:** 225 343 3612

### MISSISSIPPI
4268 I-55 North, Meadowbrook Office Park, **Jackson**, MS 39211
**Tel:** 601 351 2400   **Fax:** 601 351 2424

### TENNESSEE
633 Chestnut Street, 1800 Republic Centre, **Chattanooga**, TN 37450
**Tel:** 423 756 2010   **Fax:** 423 756 3447

207 Mockingbird Lane, Suite 300, **Johnson City**, TN 37604
**Tel:** 423 928 0181   **Fax:** 423 928 5694

900 South Gay Street, 2200 Riverview Tower, **Knoxville,** TN 37902
**Tel:** 865 549 7000   **Fax:** 865 525 8569

6060 Poplar Ave., Suite 440, **Memphis**, TN 38119
**Tel:** 901 579 3100   **Fax:** 901 577 2303

211 Commerce Street, Suite 1000, **Nashville**, TN 37201
**Tel:** 615 726 5600   **Fax:** 615 726 0464

### WASHINGTON, DC
Lincoln Square, 6th Floor, 555 Eleventh Street NW,
**Washington**, DC 20004
**Tel:** 202 508 3400   **Fax:** 202 508 3402

## INTERNATIONAL OFFICES

Baker, Donelson, Bearman, Caldwell & Berkowitz, PC also have offices in Beijing, China (representative office), BDBC International, LLC.

1819

# BASS, BERRY & SIMS PLC

## THE FIRM

**Managing Partner:** Keith B Simmons

**Number of partners:** 101
**Number of other lawyers:** 92

**FIRM OVERVIEW:** Bass, Berry & Sims PLC has been recognized for more than 80 years as one of Tennessee's most respected law firms by offering superior client service and unsurpassed legal representation, counseling, guidance and support for its clients in the Southeast and beyond. Firm clients range from Fortune 500 companies to regional and local businesses, including representation of approximately 40 public companies. The firm's affiliation with three legal networks includes the distinction of being a founding member of both Lex Mundi and State Capital Global Law Firm Group, and also a member of Southern Law Network.

## MAIN AREAS OF PRACTICE:

**Bankruptcy:** Offers sophisticated service in workouts, debt restructurings, reorganizations and secured financings, as well as commercial litigation matters and dispute resolution.

**Corporate & Securities:** Extensive experience and depth in mergers, acquisitions, public offerings, securities offerings, regulatory issues, venture capital, corporate governance and Sarbanes-Oxley compliance.

**Commercial Transactions & Real Estate:** Specializes in commercial lending and debt financings, real estate acquisitions, development and leasing, synthetic leases and off-balance sheet financing, equipment financing and leasing and tax-exempt and tax increment financings.

**Entertainment:** Extensive representation in the film, television, music, book publishing and theater industries.

**Environmental:** Litigation, administrative hearings, and counsel on environmental matters, including air and water pollution, hazardous and solid waste, toxic materials, Superfund and NEPA.

**Government Relations:** Highly skilled consulting and lobbying services in areas of administrative rules, attorney general's investigations, legislation and regulatory and administrative hearings.

**Healthcare:** Substantive expertise in all aspects of healthcare law such as licensing and certification, disease management, operational issues, HIPAA, physician self-referral, fraud and abuse, reimbursement, certificate of need, corporate compliance, legislative and regulatory matters and managed care contracting.

**Intellectual Property & Technology:** Protection of trademarks, copyrights, trade secrets and other intellectual property; intellectual property litigation and technology licensing.

**Labor & Employment:** Counsels on employment discrimination litigation (individual and class claims), employee relations, labor management relations, non-compete litigation, wage and hour compliance, workers' compensation and affirmative action plans.

**Litigation:** Specializes in complex business litigation matters such as antitrust, class actions, construction, director liability, securities liability, insurance disputes, intellectual property, professional liability and whistleblower claims, among others.

**Products Liability:** Exceptional capabilities in litigation involving pharmaceuticals, medical devices and consumer goods. Handles a variety of complex mass tort litigation, MDL's, class action cases, as well as serious individual suits alleging personal injury and economic loss against manufacturers.

**Public Finance:** Expertise in governmental bonds, private activity bonds, property tax abatements and pool financings. Also serves as underwriter's counsel, borrower's counsel, credit enhancer's counsel and trustee's counsel.

**Tax:** Comprehensive counseling in transactional tax, state and local tax, business and personal tax planning, estate planning and probate and employee benefits/ERISA.

## HEAD OFFICE

**TENNESSEE**
AmSouth Center, 315 Deaderick Street, Suite 2700, **Nashville**, TN 37238
**Tel:** 615 742 6200   **Fax:** 615 742 6293
**Email:** info@bassberry.com
**Website:** www.bassberry.com

## BRANCH OFFICES

**TENNESSEE**
1700 Riverview Tower, 900 S Gay Street, **Knoxville**, TN 37902
**Tel:** 865 521 6200   **Fax:** 865 521 6234

The Tower at Peabody Place, 100 Peabody Place, Suite 900, **Memphis**, TN 38103
**Tel:** 901 543 5900   **Fax:** 901 543 5999

29 Music Square East, **Nashville**, TN 37203
**Tel:** 615 255 6161   **Fax:** 615 254 4490

## CONTACTS

| | |
|---|---|
| **Bankruptcy** | Paul G Jennings |
| **Corporate & Securities** | J Page Davidson |
| **Commercial Transactions & Real Estate** | D Mark Sheets |
| **Entertainment** | W Michael Milom |
| **Environmental** | J Andrew Goddard |
| **Government Relations** | J Richard Lodge Jr |
| **Healthcare** | T Andrew Smith |
| **Intellectual Property & Technology** | W Michael Milom |
| **Labor & Employment** | Tim K Garrett |
| **Litigation** | Paul G Jennings |
| **Products Liability** | Samuel L Felker |
| **Public Finance** | Charles K Wray |
| **Tax** | Michael D Sontag |

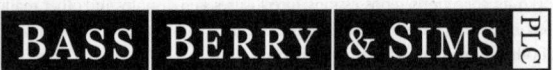

# BOULT, CUMMINGS, CONNERS & BERRY, PLC

## THE FIRM

**Managing Director:** Robert E Wood
**Number of partners:** 59
**Number of other lawyers:** 45

**FIRM OVERVIEW:** Boult Cummings is among the largest law firms in Tennessee. The firm was founded in 1910 and provides broad legal counsel to privately held and publicly traded companies across the country. Clients choose Boult Cummings for specific expertise, excellent value and responsive, individualized service. The firm's attorneys are nationally known for their work in specific industries, such as healthcare and real estate, and for their experience in helping clients meet unique legal challenges. In an effort to meet the expanding needs of clients who are doing business across borders, Boult Cummings is a founding member of one of the world's largest legal networks, TAGLaw, with member firms in more than 70 countries.

## MAIN AREAS OF PRACTICE:

**Corporate/M&A:** Boult Cummings corporate/M&A attorneys provide clients with counsel for their immediate needs and help create long-term strategies to achieve their business goals. The firm's corporate/M&A attorneys combine technical knowledge of the law with many years of business and industry experience to tailor creative solutions to help clients succeed. The corporate/M&A attorneys provide counsel regarding incorporation, buy-sell arrangements, public and private stock offerings, mergers and acquisitions, general corporate operations and governance matters, fiduciary responsibilities, stock option plans, tax issues, and joint ventures.

**Creditors' Rights & Insolvency:** Boult Cummings creditors' rights and insolvency attorneys are experienced in all aspects of insolvency problems, ranging from out-of-court workouts of troubled loans to protecting a client's interest in bankruptcy cases. The firm's creditors' rights and insolvency attorneys have represented both borrowers and financial institutions in complex lending transactions and have the expertise to structure and document all types of workout agreements, including intercreditor agreements, loan modifications, forbearance agreements, subordination agreements and liquidation agreements.

**Employee Benefits & Executive Compensation:** Boult Cummings employee benefits and executive compensation attorneys are experienced in the design, implementation and administration of all types of tax-qualified retirement plans and related Internal Revenue Service, Department of Labor, and Pension Benefit Guaranty Corporation regulatory compliance issues. The firm's employee benefits and executive compensation attorneys handle disputed claims and appeals of denied claims on behalf of both plan administrators and insurance carriers. These attorneys also have experience in representing ERISA fiduciaries in various enforcement actions, including both federal and state court litigation and Department of Labor investigations.

**Entertainment:** Boult Cummings entertainment attorneys provide a full range of legal services to clients in the entertainment industry from the firm's offices in Music City, USA. The firm's entertainment attorneys are not only familiar with the industry's special needs and practices, but also are well-versed in general business and commercial matters. The firm's entertainment clients include management companies, television and radio stations and networks, booking agencies, artists, songwriters, on-air personalities and other talent, producers, music and book publishers, record labels, promoters, and alternative media and communication companies.

**Healthcare:** Boult Cummings healthcare attorneys handle both operational and transactional matters for all types of healthcare providers, with a particular emphasis in three main healthcare segments – hospitals and health systems, long-term care, and outpatient imaging and surgery centers. Headquartered in one of the healthcare capitals of the world, the firm is equally adept at meeting the needs of for-profit and non-profit entities. The firm's client list includes some of the largest and most prestigious healthcare companies and institutions in the country.

**Intellectual Property:** Boult Cummings intellectual property attorneys have a broad range of experience with all types of businesses, handling both 'traditional'

intellectual property issues, such as trademarks, copyrights and patents, and those involving more recent innovations, such as domain names, software and the internet. The firm's intellectual property attorneys help clients realize the value of their intellectual property through transactions such as licensing arrangements, assignments, securitization or outright sales. The intellectual property attorneys understand the complex issues surrounding security interests in intellectual property, and work with lenders and borrowers to leverage these intangible assets.

**Labor & Employment:** Boult Cummings labor and employment attorneys work proactively to protect clients' business interests in this ever-changing legal landscape. The firm's experience includes traditional labor relations, employment discrimination defense work and counseling businesses on state and federal employment laws. The firm's clients include union and non-union companies, as well as public and privately held businesses ranging from Fortune 500 companies to small, locally owned businesses operating in a wide range of industries.

**Litigation:** Boult Cummings has one of the largest litigation practices in Tennessee, with a reputation of effective and efficient client representation. The firm's litigation attorneys are experienced in every phase of trial and appellate litigation, and practice before all state and federal courts and administrative agencies in Tennessee as well as state and federal courts in other jurisdictions throughout the United States. The litigation attorneys also are skilled in all methods of negotiation and alternative dispute resolution, including mediation, arbitration and judicial settlement conferences.

**Real Estate & Finance:** The firm's real estate and finance attorneys are well versed in acquisitions, financing, lending, leasing, construction, regulatory, tax and other real estate matters. The real estate and finance attorneys manage transactions for a variety of clients ranging from those whose primary business is real estate investment or development to those whose corporate existence requires an infrequent, yet significant investment in real estate, including banks, insurance companies and other institutional real estate investors and lenders. The firm represents buyers and sellers, borrowers and lenders, developers and property managers, and landlords and tenants who are continually involved in significant real estate transactions locally, regionally and nationwide.

**Tax:** Boult Cummings tax attorneys provide comprehensive tax services to a diverse client base that includes publicly held corporations, privately held businesses, corporate and individual fiduciaries and individuals. The firm's experience includes taxation of business transactions, partnership and real estate taxation, state and local taxation, estate and gift taxation, taxation of exempt organizations, and controversy resolution.

**CLIENTS:** Boult Cummings provides services to a national client base that comprises both large and small clients and includes financial institutions, privately held enterprises, publicly traded entities, individuals and government agencies. The firm's clients are engaged in diverse activities including healthcare, real estate, banking and finance, manufacturing, construction, technology, telecommunications, lodging, wholesale, retail and entertainment.

# BOWEN RILEY WARNOCK & JACOBSON, PLC

## THE FIRM

**Managing Partner:** John R Jacobson
**Senior Partners:** Jay S Bowen, Steven A Riley

**Number of partners:** 6
**Number of other lawyers:** 14

**FIRM OVERVIEW:** Bowen Riley Warnock & Jacobson, PLC was founded in 1995 by four experienced trial lawyers whose goal was to provide the highest quality legal services in the most responsive and cost effective means available. While the firm limits its practice to civil litigation, it defines 'litigation' broadly to encompass dispute resolution in all forums, whether state or federal courts, appellate courts, arbitration and mediation and, equally as important, resolving problems before they reach those formal processes. Bowen Riley has grown to 20 lawyers in order to provide resources necessary to deal with those complex problems which its clients face. Regardless of the circumstances, the firm's commitment is to design and execute an appropriate strategy to accomplish their clients' goals.

## MAIN AREAS OF PRACTICE:

**Commercial Litigation:** The firm's lawyers have in-depth experience as trial lawyers in complex commercial litigation. These specific areas include antitrust, business torts and unfair competition, copyright, trademark and intellectual property, corporate and securities, employment, entertainment, healthcare, insurance, commercial and banking and shareholder derivative law.

**CLIENTS:** Bowen Riley Warnock & Jacobson, PLC focuses its practice on resolving complex problems for local, regional, national and international clients. The firm represents both corporate and individual clients, and plaintiffs as well as defendants. Many of the nation's major industries have a presence in Tennessee. These include the entertainment industry, healthcare businesses and financial institutions. Their experience includes litigating and resolving issues unique to those industries. Representative clients include American Express Company, Gaylord Entertainment Company, Gibson Guitar Corporation, HCA Inc., Morgan Stanley DW Inc., Sony BMG Entertainment, The Coca-Cola Company, Thomas Nelson, Inc., UnumProvident Corporation, Vanderbilt University, Warner Music Group and an array of other businesses and individuals.

## HEAD OFFICE

**TENNESSEE**
1906 West End Avenue, **Nashville**, TN 37203
**Tel:** 615 320 3700  **Fax:** 615 320 3737
**Website:** www.bowenriley.com

# HARWELL HOWARD HYNE GABBERT & MANNER PC

## THE FIRM

**Managing Partner:** Mark Manner

**Number of partners:** 20
**Number of other lawyers:** 10

**FIRM OVERVIEW:** Recognized for its sophisticated clients and capabilities, 'H3GM' is a boutique business law firm in Nashville, Tennessee with a national reputation for providing superior legal services to emerging private and public growth companies. H3GM applies its experience and expertise by partnering with clients in transactions and events critical to their business success.

## MAIN AREAS OF PRACTICE:

**Mergers & Acquisitions:** Core practice area, having closed over 300 transactions in six years with total deal value approximating $5 billion. Routine acquisitions as well as mergers of public companies, spin-offs, recapitalizations, tender offers, leveraged and management buyouts.

**Commercial Bankruptcy & Reorganization:** Market leader for large, complex cases. Regularly represents debtors and creditors, including official committees, and other interested parties in bankruptcy cases and related lawsuits. Full service representation of lenders with troubled loans. Special expertise acquiring assets from bankrupt entities.

**Venture Capital:** Regular involvement in equity transactions, including assistance with business plans, disclosure documents, stock purchase agreements, registration rights, preferences, anti-dilution provisions, voting rights, shareholders agreements, employment agreements, placement agent agreements, put and call provisions, and co-sale rights.

**Securities:** Extensive experience with initial and secondary public offerings, private placements and venture capital financings; tender offers and going private transactions; periodic reporting and exchange rules and regulations; proxy statements, annual reports and stockholder meetings.

**Litigation & Alternative Dispute Resolution:** Respected practitioners in state and federal courts and alternative dispute resolution proceedings throughout the United States. Handles disputes involving state and federal securities laws, corporate governance, debtor/creditor relations, commercial transactions, state and federal employment laws, non-competition and non-disclosure agreements, trademark and copyright law, healthcare regulations, consumer protection laws, construction issues, attorney-client relations and trusts and estates.

**Healthcare:** Recognized leader representing broad spectrum of healthcare clients on key industry issues. Noted expertise in transactional arena.

**General Business, Corporate & Governance:** Ongoing general business, corporate and governance issues, regularly advising management, boards of directors and investors.

**Going Private/Related Party Transactions:** Noted for representing companies and special committees in related party transactions, going private transactions, leveraged buyouts, management buyouts and tender offers.

**Real Estate:** Represents developers, banks, municipalities, life insurance companies, mezzanine lenders, healthcare companies, and other businesses in a broad spectrum of real estate transactions, including REIT transactions, eminent domain and condemnation disputes.

**Commercial Finance:** Secured and unsecured transactions involving revolving credits, working capital loans, equipment financings, real estate loans, asset based loans, and high yield debt financings. Regular exposure to financial centers throughout the United States and Canada.

## HEAD OFFICE

**TENNESSEE**
315 Deaderick Street, Suite 1800, **Nashville**, TN 37238
**Tel:** 615 256 0500  **Fax:** 615 251 1059
**Website:** www.h3gm.com

## CONTACTS

| | |
|---|---|
| Litigation/ADR | D Alexander Fardon, Glenn B Rose |
| Bankruptcy/Reorganization | Craig V Gabbert Jr, Barbara Holmes |
| General Business, Corporate, M&A | David Cox, Kris Kemp |
| Healthcare | Michael R Hill |
| Healthcare Transactions | Ernest E Hyne, Greg Giffen |
| Real Estate | Jonathan Harwell, John Popham |
| Corporate Finance | Glen Allen Civitts, John M Brittingham |
| E-Commerce/Technology | Curtis Capeling |
| Securities | Susan V Sidwell, Mark Manner |
| Biotechnology/Life Sciences | Mark Manner, David Cox |

**Information Technology:** Assists in commercializing intellectual property assets and capitalizing on business opportunities, primarily in software with commercial applications.

**Biotechnology & Life Sciences:** The leading Tennessee firm representing companies in the biotechnology and life sciences industries.

**Employment Law:** Compliance with federal and state laws and regulations affecting employer-employee relations. Noncompetition disputes.

**Tax:** Structuring advice to transactional clients and federal and state taxation of ongoing client activities. Wealth preservation and estate planning.

For more details, visit www.h3gm.com.

**CLIENTS:** The firm has significant public company experience with NYSE, AMEX, NASDAQ and TSE listed issuers. Clients span the spectrum of commercial entities and include start-up growth ventures, private and public companies, financial institutions, insurers, healthcare providers, private equity and venture capital groups, municipalities, nonprofits and individuals. The firm's bankruptcy/reorganization practice routinely represents creditors, debtors, official committees and other participants. Visit www.h3gm.com for more specifics.

# KIESEWETTER WISE KAPLAN PRATHER, PLC

## THE FIRM

**Chief Executive Member:** Jay W Kiesewetter

**Number of Members:** 10
**Number of other lawyers:** 10

**FIRM OVERVIEW:** Kiesewetter Wise is a leading labor and employment law firm representing management clients exclusively in all areas of labor relations, employment law, and human resource management. In addition to being the largest labor and employment law firm in Memphis, Kiesewetter Wise has an extensive regional and national practice. The geographically central location of the firm's offices in Memphis enables the firm's professionals to reach most business destinations across the United States within a matter of hours.

**Firm Mission & Professionals:** Kiesewetter Wise believes that in labor relations and employment law, it is not sufficient simply to advise clients as to the status of the law. Nor does a client benefit from receiving unengaged, detached legal advice. Rather, the firm takes great pride in partnering with its clients to assist them in addressing and resolving their labor and employment law issues, while meeting their business goals and needs. Preventive education, planning, and proactive advice are key to successful labor and employee relations in today's complex business environment. When conflict or litigation arises, Kiesewetter Wise represents its clients' interests aggressively and creatively, while seeking to resolve controversies as economically as possible. This is achieved through a combination of skill, innovation, and consistency, working together as a team with its clients. The firm's professionals are dedicated to winning, and not afraid to take reasonable risks. All of the firm's team members embody these attributes, and combine their unique talents and diverse backgrounds and experiences to bring a high-energy, team approach to meeting clients' needs.

## MAIN AREAS OF PRACTICE:

**Employment Law:** Kiesewetter Wise represents management in proceedings before the EEOC, state equal employment opportunity and human rights commissions, as well as litigation in federal and state courts involving claims under Title VII of the 1964 Civil Rights Act, Equal Pay Act, ADEA, ADA, FMLA, Pregnancy Discrimination Act, and numerous other federal and state equal employment laws. The firm also assists in preparing and implementing Affirmative Action Plans for clients who are government contractors, and handles audits and proceedings before the OFCCP. The firm represents clients in state court litigation involving workers' compensation claims, as well as claims asserting statutory, contract, and tort theories of wrongful discharge or unjust dismissal. It represents employers in matters before the US Department of Labor, including Wage and Hour cases under the Fair Labor Standards Act, OSHA claims, and ERISA matters. Kiesewetter Wise frequently presents training initiatives in all these areas, and also assists clients in developing and implementing employee handbooks, policy and procedure manuals, substance abuse programs, employee compensation and benefit programs, etc.

**Labor Law:** Kiesewetter Wise provides legal advice to employers in union organizing campaigns and representation elections, and represents clients in election proceedings before the NLRB. It also defends management in unfair labor practice charges and litigation before the NLRB. The firm's attorneys represent management in the negotiation and administration of collective bargaining agreements, as well as in the arbitration of grievances and contract disputes. As part of its strategy to strengthen the human resource environments of its clients, Kiesewetter Wise develops and conducts cutting-edge supervisory leadership training programs, labor relations seminars, and management audits and surveys of human relations issues. The firm frequently assists its clients in maintaining positive relations with their employees and any unions that may represent them.

## HEAD OFFICE

**TENNESSEE**
3725 Champion Hills Drive, Suite 3000, **Memphis**, TN 38125
**Tel:** 901 795 6695   **Fax:** 901 795 1646
**Email:** info@kiesewetterwise.com
**Website:** www.kiesewetterwise.com

**Immigration & International Standards:** Kiesewetter Wise assists clients facing global employment issues with immigration services, expatriate agreements, and the development and execution of comprehensive strategic plans designed to meet sustainable development expectations in the areas of workplace human rights and social accountability. The firm is capable of providing these sustainability services both in the US and in developing countries around the world.

**CLIENTS:** Kiesewetter Wise's clientele includes a broad mix of international, national, and regional companies, including many Fortune 1000 corporations. The firm's diverse client base includes both manufacturing and service companies in healthcare, oil and chemical, transportation, telecommunications, financial, technology, hospitality, automotive, retail, and pharmaceutical industries.

# KRAMER RAYSON LLP

## THE FIRM

**Managing Partner:** Edward G Phillips
**Senior Partner:** E H Rayson

**Number of Attorneys:** 32

**FIRM OVERVIEW:** Since its inception in Knoxville in 1948, Kramer Rayson has dedicated itself to the representation of businesses and business owners in Tennessee. The firm is committed to providing superior, cost-effective legal services covering the gamut of issues its business clients face. Building on its strengths in employment law, general business counseling and litigation, Kramer Rayson has grown to over 30 attorneys. The firm is regularly employed by corporate counsel, government agencies, and public and private entities as well as individuals either doing business or involved in litigation in Tennessee.

## MAIN AREAS OF PRACTICE:

**Labor & Employment Law:** Kramer Rayson represents management in employment discrimination litigation; unfair competition disputes; harassment and whistleblower cases; traditional labor law, including union campaign, collective bargaining, arbitration and NLRB practice; human resources counseling and training; and ADR-mediation processes. The firm has one of the largest management-side employment practices in East Tennessee and has successfully litigated through trial and appeal many high profile matters. Decisions can be reviewed on www.kramer-rayson.com.

**Litigation:** The firm represents a broad array of clients in commercial litigation, unfair competition, construction law, insurance defense, personal injury litigation, condemnation, worker's compensation, product liability litigation, government contract disputes, ERISA litigation, arbitration, mediation and appellate practice, as well as administrative matters including in tax and related forums.

**Corporate/Business:** Kramer Rayson maintains a strong practice in traditional corporate and transactional areas including corporate governance, start-up ventures, purchase, sale, merger or acquisitions, financing and credit arrangements and related commercial transactions, creditor's rights, business planning, zoning, loan workouts and other commercial transaction.

**Government Relations:** Kramer Rayson government relations attorneys have extensive experience representing clients' interests before federal, state and local governmental decision-makers, boards and public bodies.

**Tax:** Kramer Rayson's Tax Practice includes work in the areas of corporate, partnership, estate, gift, state and local tax (including sales, use and property taxes), tax exempt entities, and individuals in their personal tax planning and various other tax issues. One of the firm's partners has a highly regarded reputation representing major businesses in ad valorem, property and sales and use tax planning and litigation.

**Estate/Planning/Probate:** The firm provides a full range of estate planning services and advises clients with respect to succession issues and closely held businesses.

**Healthcare:** Kramer Rayson has successfully represented and counseled clients ranging from major hospitals and practice groups to independent practitioners on a complete range of matters spanning business-related issues, licensing, certificates of need, compliance plans/audits, Medicare reimbursement, HIPPA compliance, fraud/abuse, Stark, anti-kickback and false claims.

## HEAD OFFICE

**TENNESSEE**
First Tennessee Plaza, Suite 2500, P.O. Box 629, Gay Street, **Knoxville**, 37901
**Tel:** 865 525 5134   **Fax:** 865 522 5723
**Website:** www.kramer-rayson.com

## BRANCH OFFICES

**TENNESSEE**
105 Donner Drive, Suite B, **Oak Ridge**, TN 37830
**Tel:** 865 220 5134   **Fax:** 865 220 5132

## CONTACTS

| | |
|---|---|
| **Labor & Employment** | Edward G Phillips, Steven E Kramer |
| **Litigation** | John T Johnson, Jr |
| **Corporate/Tax/Estate** | Wayne R Kramer |
| **Healthcare/Government Relations** | Warren L Gooch |
| **Dispute Resolution** | Robert P Murrian |
| **Municipal & Local Government** | Thomas M Hale |

**CLIENTS:** The firm represents a variety of clients from closely held corporations and start up ventures to Fortune 500 companies and multinational corporations; public entities, including cities, counties, public utilities; and individuals. The diverse client base includes manufacturing and service companies, retail establishments, utilities, banks and financial institutions, health care institutions, telecommunications, technology companies, institutions of higher learning, a national laboratory, a nuclear weapons complex, and insurance companies. Visit www.kramer-rayson.com for more specifics.

# MILLER & MARTIN PLLC

## THE FIRM

**Chairman:** Howard Levine

**Number of members:** 123
**Number of other lawyers:** 49
**Website:** www.millermartin.com

**FIRM OVERVIEW:** Miller & Martin lawyers are dedicated to knowing and understanding the industries and clients they represent. Their commitment is to provide quality legal services for their regional, national and international clients.

## MAIN AREAS OF PRACTICE:

**Labor & Employment:** Miller & Martin's labor and employment attorneys represent a broad range of businesses from multi-national corporations with thousands of employees to small, family-owned businesses with only a few employees. Its lawyers have expertise in the issues that can confront today's employer, including all aspects of traditional labor, employment, wage and hour, OSHA, and employee benefits law. The firm's lawyers have defeated various union organizing attempts in campaigns across the country including recent victories in Arizona, California, Georgia, Illinois, Maryland, Minnesota, Missouri, South Carolina, Tennessee, Texas, and Wisconsin. The firm successfully represented a national client in opposing an application for class certification in a class action involving 20, 000 potential claimants.

**Corporate:** Miller & Martin's corporate attorneys are knowledgeable in structuring and planning transactions, including acquisitions and divestitures of public and private companies, debt and equity investments, and public offerings. Its attorneys have handled more than $5 billion of public debt and equity offering for a corporation with operations in the US and international markets. They have completed domestic and international acquisitions valued in excess of $3 billion.

**Financial Services:** Miller & Martin's financial services attorneys serve the legal needs of financial institutions ranging from community banks to major international lenders. Services include compliance management, filing applications with state and federal regulators, forming non-bank subsidiaries, establishing complex business structures, and handling securities issues. The firm's attorneys have represented a publicly traded bank in its sale of merchant credit card processing portfolio valued at $206 million and represented an international bank in a $2 billion commercial loan securitization.

**Litigation:** Miller & Martin's litigation attorneys are able to handle any civil dispute arising in state or federal courts as well as white collar criminal matters and internal corporate investigations. Members of the department also have significant expertise in alternative dispute resolutions as advocates, arbitrators, and mediators. The firm served as national coordinating counsel for a publicly traded consumer products company in defense of pharmaceutical products liability claims in multiple jurisdictions including federal multi-district litigation.

**Real Estate:** Miller & Martin's real estate attorneys can handle the issues that arise in any commercial real estate transaction: tax, zoning, financing, and environmental. Its attorneys represent owners, developers and/or investors in all projects, including manufacturing facilities, warehouses, office buildings, shopping centers, recreation property developments and residential developments. The firm has served as lead counsel for a $400 million mixed-use project including a regional mall site, power centers and offices and represented a publicly traded REIT which owns, manages, and redevelops properties in 29 major markets.

## OFFICES

**GEORGIA**
Suite 800, 1170 Peachtree Street, N.E. **Atlanta**, GA 30309-7706
**Tel:** 404 962 6100  **Fax:** 404 962 6300

**TENNESSEE**
Suite 1000, Volunteer Building, 832 Georgia Avenue
**Chattanooga**, TN 37402-2289
**Tel:** 423 756 6600  **Fax:** 423 785 8480

1200 One Nashville Place, 150 Fourth Avenue, North
**Nashville**, TN 37219-2433
**Tel:** 615 244 9270  **Fax:** 615 256 8197

## CONTACTS

**Labor & Employment** ........................................................John R Bode
**Corporate** ...................................................................Jonathan F Kent
**Financial Services** .......................................................Kathryn R Edge
**Litigation** ...................................................................W Randy Wilson
**Real Estate** ..................................................................R Grant Dobson

**CLIENTS:** Fast food restaurants, insurance companies, financial institutions, pharmaceutical manufacturer, soft drink bottler, and telecommunications companies.

**INTERNATIONAL WORK:** Miller & Martin's clients benefit the firm's membership of the World Law Group, an international network of more than 51 law firms representing 39 different countries. The firm's lawyers regularly secure incentives and abatements for international companies establishing operations in the US as well as assist companies seeking to do business overseas and represent clients in international litigation.

# WALKER, BRYANT, TIPPS & MALONE

## THE FIRM

**Managing Partner:** J Mark Tipps
**Senior Partner:** Robert J Walker

**Number of lawyers:** 15

## AREAS OF PRACTICE:

Commercial Litigation . . . . . . . . . . . . . . . . . . . . . . . . . . . . . . . . . . . . . . 70%
Personal Injury/Professional Liability, Defense . . . . . . . . . . . . . . . 20%
Personal Injury/Plaintiff . . . . . . . . . . . . . . . . . . . . . . . . . . . . . . . . . . . 10%

**FIRM OVERVIEW:** Walker, Bryant, Tipps & Malone is a law firm located in Nashville, Tennessee, focusing exclusively on civil litigation. The firm was originally formed as Walker, Bryant & Tipps on January 1, 2000, by eight attorneys who formerly practiced in the litigation department of Nashville's Bass, Berry & Sims and who desired to continue their well-developed civil litigation practices in a smaller law firm, focusing exclusively on trial work. On May 1, 2002, the law firm became Walker, Bryant, Tipps & Malone when Gayle Malone, a senior partner in the litigation group of another prominent Tennessee law firm, joined the firm. WBTM represents individual, corporate, and institutional clients in Tennessee and throughout the Southeastern United States. The firm's attorneys regularly practice before federal and state courts in both jury and non-jury trials and at appellate levels. They have extensive experience in all forms of alternative dispute resolution, including arbitration and mediation. WBTM attorneys also represent clients in administrative matters before federal and state departments, agencies, boards, and commissions. The attorneys at WBTM concentrate their law practices in civil litigation and dispute resolution. Three of the firm's attorneys are Fellows in the American College of Trial Lawyers and are also listed in a leading American publication as among the top attorneys in America. WBTM attorneys have served as judicial clerks to federal district and appellate court judges and as counsel to congressional investigative committees. WBTM has grown from the initial eight attorneys to 15 and has assembled an outstanding staff of support personnel. WBTM has earned a reputation as a quality litigation boutique whose attorneys hold their clients' interest paramount while providing efficient and effective representation.

## MAIN AREAS OF PRACTICE:

**Commercial Litigtion:** The firm's commercial litigation includes defense of class action and non-class action suits in securities, private and public corporate governance (including proxy fights and takeover litigation), products liability defense, complex commercial and business disputes, and other commercial matters.
**Personal Injury:** The firm is well-known for its abilities in the defense of medical malpractice litigation, but also defends personal injury suits in other areas. Additionally, WBTM has developed a plaintiff's personal injury practice in selected cases and has recovered several multi-million-dollar results for its clients.
**Dispute Resolution:** Two of the firm's partners are Rule 31-listed Civil Mediators.

**CLIENTS:** The firm's clients include individuals, teaching hospitals, commercial banks, insurance and other financial institutions, venture capital and private equity firms, industrial and service corporations, partnerships, and myriad businesses clients in the fields of health care, private prison management and ownership, accounting, and other service industries.

**INTERNATIONAL WORK:** The firm has represented a number of international companies engaged in civil litigation in the United States.

## HEAD OFFICE

**TENNESSEE**
2300 One Nashville Place, **Nashville**, TN 37219
**Tel:** 615 313 6000   **Fax:** 615 313 6001
**Email:** info@walkerbryant.com

## CONTACTS

Complex Business Litigation . . . . . . . . . .Bob Walker, Mark Tipps, John Hayworth
Dispute Resolution . . . . . . . . . . . . . . . . . . . . . . .Gayle Malone, John Bryant
Financial Institutions/Insurance . . . . . . . . . . . . . . . .Mark Tipps, Joe Welborn
Governmental Relations (federal) . . . . . . . . . . . . . . . . . . . . . . .Mark Tipps
Personal Injury/Defense. . . . . . . . . . . . . . . . . . . . . .John Bryant, Steve Anderson
Personal Injury/Plaintiff. . . . . . . . . . . . . . . . . . . . . .Gayle Malone, Joe Welborn
Product Liability . . . . . . . . . . . . . . . . . . . . . . . .Gayle Malone, Clisby Barrow
Securities & Corporate Governance . . . . . . . .Bob Walker, John Hayworth
Prisoner Rights Litigation . . . . . . . . . . . . . . . . . . . . . . . . . . . . .Joe Welborn

# WALLER LANSDEN DORTCH & DAVIS, LLP

## THE FIRM

**Chairman:** Ralph W Davis
**Number of partners:** 105
**Number of other lawyers:** 83

**FIRM OVERVIEW:** Founded in Nashville in 1905, Waller Lansden Dortch & Davis is one of the oldest law firms headquartered in Tennessee. Waller Lansden's attorneys take pride in their ability to understand and respond to the specific needs and business goals of each of the firm's clients. The firm understands that a client wants more in its outside legal counsel than just attorneys that can solve legal problems - clients want a business partner.

Waller Lansden's goal is to achieve the highest level of service by creating and maintaining the depth, resources, and experience necessary to meet the diverse needs of its clients in today's evolving business and legal environment. In 2006, Waller Lansden was ranked by general counsel of Fortune 1000 companies among the leading law firms in the country for delivery of superior client service according to an independent study conducted by the research firm BTI Consulting Group. No other law firm in Tennessee was named in the study.

A work environment that facilitates a free and robust exchange of ideas is essential to the way Waller Lansden provides exceptional legal services. The entire firm, from its leadership and across the board, respects and values the approach to issues that comes from people with diverse life experiences and backgrounds. It is the firm's diversity and basic respect for these differences that makes the whole greater than the individual parts. Waller Lansden's firm-wide commitment to diversity through hiring, training and retention practices enhances the service provided to clients through the recruitment and retention of highly qualified attorneys, paralegals and staff.

**MAIN AREAS OF PRACTICE:** Alternative dispute resolution, aviation/aerospace, bankruptcy, business transactions, corporate restructuring, dispute resolution, electronic transactions, environmental, executive and employee benefits/ERISA, financial services, franchising, government relations, healthcare, immigration, intellectual property, labor and employment, land use planning, zoning and eminent domain, mergers and acquisitions, real estate, relocating and expanding businesses, securities and corporate finance, tax, state and local government, state and local tax, trial and appellate, trusts and estates, utilities, venture capital and emerging business.

## HEAD OFFICE

**TENNESSEE**
511 Union Street, Suite 2700, **Nashville**, TN 37219
**Tel:** 615 244 6380   **Fax:** 615 244 6804
**Website:** www.wallerlaw.com

## BRANCH OFFICES

**CALIFORNIA**
520 South Grand Avenue, Suite 800, **Los Angeles**, CA 90071
**Tel:** 213 362 3680   **Fax:** 213 362 3679

**ALABAMA**
1901 Sixth Avenue North, Suite 1400, **Birmingham**, AL 35203
**Tel:** 205 216 6380   **Fax:** 205 214 8787

**TENNESSEE**
809 South Main Street, **Columbia**, TN 38402
**Tel:** 931 388 6031   **Fax:** 931 381 7317

**Waller Lansden** Dortch & Davis
www.wallerlaw.com

## How lawyers are ranked

Every year we carry out thousands of in-depth interviews with clients and lawyers in order to assess the reputations and expertise of business lawyers across the USA. Chambers rankings and editorial are referred to extensively by General Counsel and other purchasers of legal services who look to our recommendations when choosing their lawyers.

# ANTITRUST

## Antitrust
### Leading Firms

1. **HAYNES AND BOONE LLP** *Dallas*
   **SUSMAN GODFREY LLP** *Houston*
   **VINSON & ELKINS LLP** *Houston*
2. **BAKER BOTTS LLP** *Houston*
   **FULBRIGHT & JAWORSKI L.L.P.** *Houston*
3. **ANDREWS KURTH LLP** *Dallas*
   **CARRINGTON, COLEMAN** *Dallas*
   **COX SMITH MATTHEWS INC** *San Antonio*
   **GARDERE WYNNE SEWELL LLP** *Dallas*
   **GIBSON, DUNN & CRUTCHER LLP** *Dallas*
   **THOMPSON & KNIGHT LLP** *Dallas*

### Leading Individuals

1. **GODFREY** Lee *Susman Godfrey LLP*
   **MCNEIL** Barry *Haynes and Boone LLP*
   **SUSMAN** Stephen *Susman Godfrey LLP*
2. **BEANE** Jerry *Andrews Kurth LLP*
   **CARRELL** Richard *Fulbright & Jaworski L.L.P.*
   **FRISBIE JR** Curtis *Gardere Wynne Sewell LLP*
   **HUFFMAN** Gregory *Thompson & Knight LLP*
   **KRUSE** Layne *Fulbright & Jaworski L.L.P.*
   **OLIVER III** Rufus *Baker Botts LLP*
   **REASONER** Harry *Vinson & Elkins LLP*
   **ROYALL M** Sean *Gibson, Dunn & Crutcher LLP*
   **SMITH** Alison *Haynes and Boone LLP*
   **WALTERS** Robert *Vinson & Elkins LLP*
3. **BREAUX** Ronald *Haynes and Boone LLP*
   **JOHN** Philip *Baker Botts LLP*
   **KAISER** Keith *Cox Smith Matthews Incorporated*
   **OXFORD** Terrell *Susman Godfrey LLP*
   **SPIVEY** James *Cox Smith Matthews Incorporated*
   **VAN FLEET** Allan *Vinson & Elkins LLP*

### Up-and-coming individuals

   **BAYER** Mark *Gardere Wynne Sewell LLP*
   **HARRISON** Lauren *Vinson & Elkins LLP*
   **SUSMAN** Harry *Susman Godfrey LLP*

## Band 1

### Haynes and Boone LLP

**The Firm:** This developing group has joined the top band of antitrust firms on the back of client admiration for its *"total commitment to antitrust,"* *"key lateral recruits"* and *"a long track record"* in the defense and prosecution of competition cases. The 20-lawyer Texas team will benefit from the DC office's hiring of Jim Wade and Veronica Kayne, who will bring merger guidance expertise to the firm. Wade was formerly with the DOJ; Kayne came from the much-respected international firm WilmerHale. In addition to commendations for its work on domestic civil and criminal antitrust matters, researchers learnt of the firm's potency on international cartels. The team has been representing Cheil Jedang Corporation, a Korean company, in antitrust litigation throughout the USA. The case began with a criminal price-fixing grand jury investigation and expanded into a federal court class action and over 20 state court class actions. This was followed by an EU investigation, a Canadian Competition Bureau investigation and foreign purchaser litigation.

**The Lawyers:** Considerable experience, amassed while at the DOJ, underpins the practice of *"absolutely terrific"* **Barry McNeil**, whose greatest strength lies in his canny defense of criminal antitrust litigation. *"One of the best lawyers in the state,"* and with substantial experience of price-fixing, grand jury and trial work, lately McNeil has spent much of his time on SEC and fraud investigations. The group further beefed up its antitrust expertise with the hire in September 2005 of *"thoroughly prepared and bright"* **Alison Smith**, *"a very good addition"* from Dewey Ballantine. Clients profit from Smith's experience as deputy assistant attorney at the DOJ antitrust division, where she was in charge of antitrust enforcement in the nation's regulated industries, including energy, transportation and healthcare. In addition to antitrust counseling, her general business litigation practice encompasses federal securities litigation. She advised incumbent local exchange carrier, SBC, in a federal antitrust case brought by a competitive local exchange carrier (CLEC). Seeking $2 billion in damages, the CLEC claimed SBC failed to provide it with elements of its telephone network that were essential for it to compete against SBC. Cartel-related work features in the caseload of *"solid, thoughtful and very bright"* **Ron Breaux**, who also counsels companies and individuals on government investigations and SEC enforcement requirements.

**Clients/Work Highlights:** Dynegy; Bank of America; PepsiCo; SBC; Commercial Metals; ExxonMobil; Harley-Davidson; Ryder Systems; Nortel; Tandy and Waste Management.

### Susman Godfrey LLP

**The Firm:** *"Aggressive, efficient and among the smartest attorneys around."* These were the words used to describe this nationally admired litigation boutique. *"There are no other antitrust plaintiff firms of that caliber in the state,"* noted one observer, who underlined the lawyers' *"immense preparation"* as a key contribution to the group's success. In September 2005, it finalized the settlement of the $250 million antitrust claim brought by ChoiceParts against GM, Ford, DaimlerChrysler and OEConnection. Market sources lavished praise on the firm's contingency work in both commercial and antitrust litigation.

**The Lawyers:** There was widespread recognition for the *"almost unmatchable talents"* of **Lee Godfrey**, deemed *"one of the most brilliant attorneys at trial,"* and a man with *"charisma that fills the room."* Also on the team is *"wonderfully accomplished"* **Stephen Susman**, a *"tremendously gifted"* national icon in commercial and antitrust litigation, especially on the plaintiff side. Interviewees appreciated the *"work ethic and lateral thinking"* of **Terrell Oxford**, and there was similar praise for *"splendid litigator"* **Harry Susman**, whose *"smartness, confidence and boldness"* greatly benefited clients. His input into the ChoiceParts case is said to have been invaluable.

**Clients/Work Highlights:** Medtronic; Barr Laboratories; Little Caesar Enterprises; Novell and Clear Channel Communications.

### Vinson & Elkins LLP

See firm details p.1938

**The Firm:** In light of a reduction in the number of lawsuits, this legal giant's *"strength in court"* and *"impressive record of trial results"* is especially commendable. A *"well-connected group of attorneys"* make up a strong commercial litigation team that contains a number of "*real antitrust scholars.*" It is replete with attorneys who "*know how to talk to the agencies and commissions*" and the firm boasts genuine expertise in the energy, healthcare and airline sectors. As further evidence of the firm's prominent position in this area, V&E has produced four past chairs of the ABA's Antitrust Section.

**The Lawyers:** A multitude of superlatives were used to describe legend **Harry Reasoner** (see p.1911), who spends much of his time on business development and shepherding cases. Peers have "*tremendous respect*" for his "*great mind*" and the fact that he retains "*a great passion*" for antitrust litigation. Reasoner has recently defended American National Insurance Company and American National Property And Casualty Company in multijurisdiction lawsuits. Among the plaintiffs' grievances were allegations of market conspiracy and the fixing of commission rates. There was also widespread admiration for "*a true star in the Dallas market*" – **Rob Walters** (see p.1918). Walters earned praise for his "*energy and effectiveness,*" as well as his "*quick thinking on his feet.*" He is acting for a major insurer in an MDL class action through the New Jersey federal court, and secured a trial verdict in nationally recognized antitrust litigation brought by independent video retailers against Blockbuster. Commentators applauded "*smart generalist litigator*" **Allan Van Fleet**, who also cochairs the firm's antitrust practice group. He is defending SBC in a $2 billion case brought by Premiere Network Services, which has alleged restraint of competition and other violations of antitrust and telecommunications laws. Up-and-coming **Lauren Harrison** (see p.1896) is given credit for her "*constant availability*" and "*ability to fill a courtroom.*" She recently obtained summary judgment for one of the largest commercial air carriers in an antitrust case.

**Clients/Work Highlights:** Belo Corp; Blockbuster; Continental Airlines; Froup 1 Automotive; Liberty Mutual Group; Novation; SBS; Southwest Airlines and VHA Inc.

## Band 2

### Baker Botts LLP
See firm details p.1922

**The Firm:** Strong corporate and litigation departments, a healthy reputation in the energy sector and tremendous backup from around the firm combine to help the dozen "*smart and talented*" antitrust practitioners at this Texas colossus achieve a leading position in the tables. Called on by clients for being trial attorneys, the team handles litigation for companies and individuals in civil and criminal investigations and adversary proceedings involving the entire spectrum of antitrust and competition issues. The team represented Reliant Energy in a series of cases brought by competing electric service providers in allegations of price-fixing electricity prices in the state.

**The Lawyers:** The market considered "*top flight*" **Rufus Oliver** (see p.1908) a "*perennial pick,*"

respected as a "*very careful, hands-on and smart*" attorney, whose practice is evenly split between antitrust and commercial litigation. He spends significant time providing merger guidance and is advising on a merger under review for a pharmaceutical manufacturer client, which is in dispute with a competing manufacturer over a branded product. The bulk of his practice is spent undertaking commercial litigation but **Philip John** (see p.1898) also offers particular antitrust expertise. He has been advising SBC, which often faces challenges to its lead role on a changing telecommunications stage.

**Clients/Work Highlights:** HomeTeam Pest Defense, Hydril Company and Reliant Energy are a sample of the firm's clients.

### Fulbright & Jaworski L.L.P.
See firm details p.1928

**The Firm:** The firm's strength and long track record in commercial litigation lends weight to its well-respected antitrust litigation practice. Indeed, the firm places a great deal of emphasis on this area of work, with around 30 of the firm's 46 attorneys having expertise in a range of conspiracy, dealer termination, monopolization, price-fixing and discrimination issues. Historical connections to the energy and healthcare sectors sees the team advising hospital chains and healthcare facilities on related antitrust issues, for example on the exclusivity of contracts. Similarly, the firm enjoys a good profile in criminal antitrust and white-collar crime, an area of its work that will profit from the arrival in June 2005 of corporate fraud expert Mike Shelby, the former US Attorney for the Southern District of Texas.

**The Lawyers:** Commentators praised **Rick Carrell** (see p.1885) for his "*thoughtful and studious*" approach; for antitrust matters he was considered "*an outstanding referral.*" Although it represents just one part of his litigation practice, Carrell has a standing in the market that has warranted a term as chair of the Antitrust and Trade Regulation Section for the State Bar of Texas. He recently acted as lead counsel for The Home Insurance Company in the Voluntary Market Premium litigation, and as defense attorney for Viacom in a multidefendant alleged price-fixing case. Great respect was paid to **Layne Kruse** (see p.1901), who chairs the firm's nationwide antitrust, marketing and trade regulation practice group. His "*sound analysis*" and "*approachable way with clients*" made him a force to be reckoned with. On the one hand driven by antitrust compliance and counseling, his practice also contains a good measure of white-collar crime investigations and civil antitrust litigation. Kruse acted as lead counsel for an offshore petroleum drilling company following plaintiff allegations of a conspiracy to suppress wages paid to workers.

**Clients/Work Highlights:** Sony; PwC; Shell; ConocoPhillips; Duke Energy; The Association of American Medical Colleges; Farmers; Coral Energy and Mitsui & Co.

## Band 3

### Andrews Kurth LLP
See firm details p.1921

**The Firm:** A respected team of a dozen attorneys, and experience of both antitrust counseling and litigation, have placed this respected Houston-born firm in the rankings. The group earned praise for its advice to clients on a range of merger, joint venture and distribution issues, as well as for guiding transactions through the Hart-Scott-Rodino (HSR) review process at the FTC and DOJ. Its trial success in an antitrust price-fixing case against more than 52,000 class members highlights its expertise in handling civil and criminal investigations and trials.

**The Lawyers:** Market acclaim for "*smart, comfortable and hands-on*" **Jerry Beane** bordered on unanimous. "*Unafraid to try lawsuits,*" he "*rolls his sleeves up;*" his intellect and experience as a first-chair trial lawyer made him a top choice. His antitrust representations span a range of industries from food, healthcare and transportation to manufacturing and telecommunications. He represents Coca-Cola Enterprises against Harmar Bottling in litigation which is pending in the Texas Supreme Court.

**Clients/Work Highlights:** National Dairy Holdings, KoSa and Tempur-Pedic are among the firm's clients.

### Carrington, Coleman, Sloman & Blumenthal, LLP

**The Firm:** Respect for the litigation and bankruptcy prowess of this much-admired Dallas firm of nearly 100 lawyers extends into the area of antitrust disputes and has continued despite senior specialist Tyler Baker's move to California in 2003. A handful of attorneys conducts a mostly regional antitrust litigation practice. Their civil antitrust work covers conspiracy claims, price-fixing and discrimination, market division, boycotts and attempted monopolization.

**The Lawyers:** Ken Carroll is a point of contact for antitrust litigation and other commercial disputes.

**Clients/Work Highlights:** Among the firm's clients are Realm Business Solutions, EDS and AT&T Wireless.

### Cox Smith Matthews Incorporated
See firm details p.1926

**The Firm:** This firm is the product of a 2004 merger between Cox & Smith and Matthews and Branscomb. Operating from three other offices in Texas, with headquarters in San Antonio, this fast-expanding firm enters the rankings through the efforts of its small team of four antitrust practitioners. They take on price-fixing, tying arrangements and group boycotts as well as DOJ/FTC investigations. Competitors say it is developing a name as "*the premier law firm in south Texas.*"

**The Lawyers:** Table newcomer **Keith Kaiser** (see p.1899) is "*a very impressive trial lawyer*" with "*long experience*" in general practice and a leading position on the San Antonio stage. He represents national and international clients on antitrust, securities and other complex commercial litigation, as well as providing counseling on antitrust, trade regulation and licensing issues pertaining to the telecom, computer, software and medical device industries. Interviewees continue to be impressed by San Antonio business litigator **James Spivey** (see p.1915). His diverse industry experience comes from representing clients in various sectors; latterly this has included representing a healthcare system in its dispute with a software provider and a wireless phone network in antitrust litigation.

**Clients/Work Highlights:** City of San Antonio; Clear Channel Communications; Eye Care Centers of America; San Antonio Federal Credit Union; Sirius Computer Solutions and Southwest Foundation for Biomedical Research.

### Gardere Wynne Sewell LLP

See firm details p.1931

**The Firm:** Five partners and six associates make up the antitrust team of this "*established, well-known and well-respected*" Texas general practice firm. The group is working on a number of antitrust, class action and RICO matters filed in several states. For example, it acts for Pennsylvania-headquartered General Nutrition Company in a variety of suits or matters involving trade regulation and antitrust claims brought by franchisees across the country.

**The Lawyers:** "*A sense of organization, an incisive and in-depth knowledge, and an ability to lead*" are the hallmarks of "*thorough and tenacious*" **Curt Frisbie** (see p.1891). This former president of the Dallas Bar Antitrust Section is "*a devoted antitrust lawyer*" who spends more than two thirds of his time litigating antitrust cases or providing counseling in this area. Frisbie, who heads the firm's trial department, also

received compliments for his class action expertise. He has been acting as outside counsel to the Dallas-headquartered Brook Mays Music Company, a chain of national retail music stores, in a range of litigation including antitrust. Joining the elite is the "*up-and-coming, solid*" **Mark Bayer** (see p.1882), who "*hits all the right cylinders*," according to one interviewee. Antitrust is only one feature of a diverse practice for this former chair of the Dallas Bar Association's Antitrust and Trade Regulation Law Section. In a major case recently he successfully defended a large scrap metal dealer against predatory pricing claims brought in El Paso.

**Clients/Work Highlights:** SBC Corporation; CompUSA; Allied Waste Systems; Kalmar Industries USA; Clear Channel Entertainment; Global 360 and The National Association for the Self-Employed.

### Gibson, Dunn & Crutcher LLP

See firm details p.328

**The Firm:** The firm's long-standing national reputation in civil and criminal antitrust litigation arises from "*a deep well of talent*" and involvement in high-profile assignments. The six antitrust attorneys in Dallas – and their clients – greatly benefit from "*seamless access to the firm's highly demanded resources,*" including high-level government regulatory expertise. The team is acting in a number of ongoing cartel and antitrust grand jury investigations, both at home and abroad.

**The Lawyers:** There was considerable market approval for the "*smart*" cochair of the antitrust and trade regulation practice group, **Sean Royall** (see p.1912). Fresh out of the DOJ, he offers clients "*tailored advice, business pragmatism and sound risk assessment.*" Interviewees admired this "*very capable*

*and well-connected quick study*" for his experience "*in and outside government.*" Royall's time is split between Dallas and DC, and he represents clients from a diverse range of industries. Lately he has been providing high-level strategic advice to BMC Software, The Williams Companies and Allergan. While serving in his own senior FTC post, Royall was also the lead official responsible for the government review of several mergers, including Pepsi/Quaker Oats, General Mills/Pillsbury and Chevron/Texaco.

**Clients/Work Highlights:** Dell; CoStar Group; Atlantic Coast Airlines; American Airlines; Intel; Ticketmaster and Hewlett-Packard.

### Thompson & Knight LLP

See firm details p.1936

**The Firm:** The trial department at this old-line Texas firm has around 14 attorneys with experience of antitrust cases in federal and state courts as well as before the FTC. The firm also advises on the range of statutes, including the Sherman, Clayton and Robinson-Patman Acts. It recently defended the nation's leading manufacturer of tortillas against charges that it had monopolized shelf space through the use of slotting allowances.

**The Lawyers:** The firm's antitrust capability currently depends in large part on the "*very smart, analytical and methodical*" **Greg Huffman** (see p.1898), who undertakes both advisory work and litigation. Considered "*a great academic,*" "*a fantastic oral advocate,*" and "*a sound brief-writer,*" he also runs general commercial cases.

**Clients/Work Highlights:** Chaparral Steel and Gruma both feature on the group's client list.

# BANKING & FINANCE

| Banking & Finance<br>Leading Firms | |
|---|---|
| 1 | VINSON & ELKINS LLP *Houston* |
| 2 | BRACEWELL & GIULIANI LLP *Houston* |
| 3 | ANDREWS KURTH LLP *Dallas* |
| | BAKER BOTTS LLP *Houston* |
| | MAYER, BROWN, ROWE & MAW LLP *Houston* |
| 4 | HAYNES AND BOONE LLP *Dallas* |
| | JENKENS & GILCHRIST PC *Dallas* |
| | JONES DAY *Dallas* |
| | PORTER & HEDGES, LLP *Houston* |
| | THOMPSON & KNIGHT LLP *Dallas* |
| | WEIL, GOTSHAL & MANGES LLP *Dallas* |
| | WINSTEAD SECHREST & MINICK P.C. *Dallas* |

### Band 1

### Vinson & Elkins LLP

See firm details p.1938

**The Firm:** Commentators believed that "*strong relationships with money center banks*" and "*a big repu-*

*tation in energy*" were among reasons why this "*premier Texas firm*" with "*enormous expertise*" stood out. "*When a financial transaction involves an energy company, either seeking or providing finance, they are almost always there,*" noted one client. Such transactions provide both the staple and the highlights of V&E's practice, and in such instances the firm competes head on with New York outfits.

**The Lawyers:** "*Confident, outgoing and highly skilled*" **Larry Barbour** (see p.1882) has an established lending practice and significant experience of mezzanine finance transactions. At home on large and complex transactions, he represented Spinnaker Exploration as lessee of a long-term operating lease of an undivided interest in an offshore production platform. Bank of America was the lessor. He also acted for Wachovia Bank, National Association as arranger and administrative agent of a $650 million financing for Universal Compression. Sources heaped praise on the "*professorial and bright*" **David Keyes** (see p.1900), who "*never trips up a transaction.*" In a gradual two-year phase-down he increasingly takes on a consulting role; for example, he has

been working closely with the National Clearing House Association, a trade organization for US banks. The popularity of "*very talented*" **Ken Anderson** (see p.1881) owes much to his "*ability to find the middle ground in a transaction, which keeps both sides happy.*" Chairing the syndicated finance practice, he acts for domestic and foreign banks as arrangers and agents in syndicated finance transactions. "*Transactions always go smoothly*" with "*smart and egoless*" senior finance attorney **Craig Murray** (see p.1907), who is deemed a strong lawyer with significant experience on both sides of a deal. He undertakes a large number of VPP and MLP financings. There was widespread praise for **Billy Young** (see p.1920) and his Dallas group, who were considered excellent on structured and energy finance matters. Young earned most recognition for his international structured finance work, and many of his recent deals have had Japanese, German or Taiwanese components. He has been acting for Lone Star Funds in connection with a JPY110 billion structured bond financing of investment in Tokyo Star Bank. He acted for a joint venture between two US-based real estate private

## Banking & Finance
### Leading Individuals

**1**
- **BARBOUR Larry** *Vinson & Elkins LLP*
- **GOYNE Roderick** *Baker Botts LLP*
- **HAYES William** *Bracewell & Giuliani LLP*
- **NIEBRUEGGE Michael** *Mayer, Brown, Rowe & Maw*

**2**
- **EVANS Mark** *Bracewell & Giuliani LLP*
- **KEYES David** *Vinson & Elkins LLP*

**3**
- **ANDERSON Kenneth** *Vinson & Elkins LLP*
- **FONTANA Angela** *Weil, Gotshal & Manges LLP*
- **HILLIARD Michael** *Winstead Sechrest & Minick P.C.*
- **MILES Robin** *Bracewell & Giuliani LLP*
- **MURRAY Craig** *Vinson & Elkins LLP*
- **PERICH Thomas** *Andrews Kurth LLP*

**4**
- **BARBOUR David** *Andrews Kurth LLP*
- **BOREN Alison** *Baker Botts LLP*
- **GILLESPIE Thomas** *Jones Day*
- **GONSOULIN JR Dewey** *Bracewell & Giuliani LLP*
- **LITTLEJOHN James** *Winstead Sechrest & Minick P.C.*
- **MALONEY Marilyn** *Liskow & Lewis*
- **MCKELLAR James** *Thompson & Knight LLP*
- **RAIN John** *Thompson & Knight LLP*
- **VILARDO Terry** *Mayer, Brown, Rowe & Maw*
- **YOUNG William** *Vinson & Elkins LLP*

### Up-and-coming individuals
- **KAMINSKY Neal** *Porter & Hedges, LLP*
- **MARCUS Courtney** *Weil, Gotshal & Manges LLP*
- **RABALAIS Robert** *Vinson & Elkins LLP*

equity funds in connection with a $200 million structured CMBS financing for a portfolio of eight hotel properties. "*Terrific and bright up-and-comer*" **Robert Rabalais** (see p.1911) represents corporate borrowers, issuers, investors, insurance companies, commercial banks and underwriters in commercial and capital market finance transactions. "*He is about the best lawyer I work with, period,*" noted one impressed client.

**Clients/Work Highlights:** Wachovia Bank, National Association; JPMorgan Chase; Deutsche Bank and BNP Paribas are some of the firm's key lender clients.

## Band 2

### Bracewell & Giuliani LLP
See firm details p.1924

**The Firm:** "*Their experience of the market and the quality of their work*" make this old-line Texas firm "*a major force*" in the banking world in Texas. A team of "*responsive*" lawyers impresses the domestic and international banking community with its "*fast work to tight time frames.*" Energy remains the cornerstone of the practice, and the firm has considerable expertise in term loans, revolvers, volumetric production payment (VPP) deals and special purpose entities. Clients consider the firm's exposure to both sides of transactions, acting for banks and underwriters as well as borrowers, to be its greatest strength, and it was considered "*big enough to be up-to-date with all*

the latest developments" yet "*not too big that the client doesn't matter.*"

**The Lawyers:** There was considerable praise for "*incredibly honest, forthright and talented*" **Bill Hayes** (see p.1896), whose "*thorough, meticulous analysis*" shines through in his representation of bank syndicates. As well as advising Citibank in a $1.3 billion syndicated secured credit facility to The Williams Companies, he has also been acting for EPCO as borrower in a $2.4 billion syndicated secured-credit facility. Another name at the forefront of the group is the "*intelligent, creative and pragmatic*" **Mark Evans** (see p.1890), whose "*to-the-point, real-world and pro-business style*" make him incredibly easy to work with. "*His sympathetic ear to borrowers*" ensures deals go smoothly, researchers were told. Lately, he has been involved in various different types of energy finance, including a $500 million credit facility in favor of National Oilwell Varco, with an accordion feature up to $750 million, as arranged by Wells Fargo. The transaction additionally involved the merger of two large oilfield service companies. There was much praise for "*smart*" **Robin Miles** (see p.1906), who "*does not miss a beat.*" Although he has left Texas to expand the firm's energy and finance base in its New York office, for now he still retains strong Texas links. Miles has been acting for Reliant Energy in a $299 million secured-term loan; he also advised BNP Paribas on a $300 million secured oil and gas loan to Belden & Blake. Interviewees admired the "*cooperative, up-to-date and responsive*" **Dewey Gonsoulin**'s (see p.1893) real estate, energy finance practice. He closed a $175 agented loan transaction between Union Bank of California and borrower Mariner Energy, the transaction being a senior, unsecured oil and gas borrowing base facility. He also handled all the financing transactions for Ferrellgas, the second largest retail propane distribution company in North America. He helped them close their $330 million revolving credit facility with a syndicate of banks led by Bank of America.

**Clients/Work Highlights:** Citibank; JPMorgan Chase; Reliant Energy and Dynegy.

## Band 3

### Andrews Kurth LLP
See firm details p.1921

**The Firm:** This Texas stalwart has "*a sound and consistent banking practice.*" The 30 or so "*reliable*" business attorneys were praised for their transactional capacity and history of representing major financial institutions in syndicated loans. The firm is strong in the public-debt, high-yield and securitization markets.

**The Lawyers:** "*Talented and organized*" **Tom Perich** earned commendations for his "*natural ability to move the deal along and get it completed.*" Under the umbrella of a private bank and syndicated loans practice, he has been acting for borrowers in debt and equity transactions as well as several institutions in energy-related deals. Also recommended is **David Barbour**, who is "*easy to deal with and very sharp.*"

He is admired for his "*technical proficiency*" and "*trusted intelligence.*" Blessed with a "*highly personable manner*" with clients, Barbour tends to be known for asset securitization and intellectually challenging finance matters.

**Clients/Work Highlights:** JPMorgan Chase; Wachovia; Bank of America and Wells Fargo.

### Baker Botts LLP
See firm details p.1922

**The Firm:** Clients appreciated the "*effectiveness and practicality*" of this group of about 12 "*professional and well-trained*" banking and finance attorneys. As well as a "*diversity of experience and technical competence*" within the group, one client felt there was more consistency at partner level than at some rival firms. Although recognized in the technology and energy sectors, specifically downstream, the firm was acknowledged to be highly competent in representing banks and insurance companies in the private-placement and public-debt markets.

**The Lawyers:** Clients enjoyed working with the "*thorough and forthright*" chair of the firm's finance section, **Rick Goyne** (see p.1894). "*He is one of the best corporate finance attorneys around Dallas, and in the state,*" noted one client, impressed by his "*very good judgment*" and "*logic and ability to rationally negotiate a transaction and not bluster his way around.*" Goyne represented Pogo Producing in a $750 million revolving credit facility (since increased to $1 billion) that closed in December 2004, and also advised Pogo in connection with the financing of its $1.8 billion acquisition of Northrock Resources, Unocal's largest Canadian subsidiary. He additionally acted for Marathon Ashland Petroleum in connection with its securitization of commercial and industrial receivables. Entering the tables this year is the "*very responsive and smart*" **Alison Boren** (see p.1883), an adviser to both lenders and borrowers. She has been representing Martin Midstream Partners in its planned $100 million acquisition of Prism Gas Systems I. She also represents Martin Midstream in its $225 million revolving line of credit and term-loan facilities.

**Clients/Work Highlights:** Marathon Ashland Petroleum; Encore Acquisition Company; Hines Interests; Pride Offshore; JPMorgan Chase; ConocoPhillips; Halliburton and Equistar Chemical.

### Mayer, Brown, Rowe & Maw LLP
See firm details p.876

**The Firm:** Mayer Brown has a "*small, smart and committed*" team of around 12 attorneys. As part of an international firm, the Texas team has access to a far greater pool of resources, and certainly benefits from the firm's global reputation in syndicated finance. Typically acting for the lender, the group has experienced a spike in its representation of UK banks and is noticeably involved in energy finance. The transfer of Kevin Shaw from the LA office has brought further energy finance expertise to Houston.

**The Lawyers:** "*Pleasant, honest and totally reliable*" **Michael Niebruegge** (see p.1907) combines his "*extensive knowledge*" with "*a constructive and help-*

ful attitude." This "*gem of a gentleman*" has wide transactional experience and undertakes significant work for a number of Canadian banks, whose various relationships with Mayer Brown stem from the firm's Chicago origins. Despite occupying a managerial position at the firm, he recently found time to lead the team representing Barclays Bank, as agent and arranger, in a $300 million VPP financing for Wolfcamp Oil and Gas Trust. He also led the team acting for Tesoro, one of the largest independent refiners in the country, in a transaction to secure a $275 million letter of credit facility agented by RBS. Commentators admired **Terry Vilardo**'s (see p.1917) "*attention to detail*" and her considerable experience of large and complex project finance transactions. She was lead counsel for ConocoPhillips, as lead senior secured lender in a construction and term financing for the Freeport LNG project. She also acted for Wachovia Capital Markets in the acquisition and financing of oil properties in Texas and the acquisition and financing of natural gas properties in Kansas.

**Clients/Work Highlights:** CIBC, RBS and Bank of Montreal are all on the client roster.

## Band 4

### Haynes and Boone LLP

**The Firm:** Labeled a "*good, solid and careful*" practice, Haynes and Boone's banking and finance group is recommended for the work carried out by its Houston office in the middle-market banking sector. This respected regional firm has built its reputation on the representation of mezzanine lenders; however, the group of around 40 lawyers advises domestic and foreign borrowers, lenders and vendors in a range of secured and unsecured credit transactions.

**The Lawyers:** Former banker Joe Vilardo is a senior member of the finance practice in Houston. He negotiates and documents complex financing transactions of various types.

**Clients/Work Highlights:** Bank of America; Bank of Scotland; Crédit Lyonnais; Deutsche Bank; Highland Capital; JP Morgan Chase and Société Générale.

### Jenkens & Gilchrist PC

**The Firm:** The market considered this newly ranked Dallas-born firm to have a great name in midmarket banking deals. These are carried out by a team of "*good, practical and responsive*" lawyers whose "*solid market knowledge*" enables them to do "*a fine job*" in a range of commercial areas, including asset-based and secured lending as well as revolving, term and other commercial lending.

**The Lawyers:** Daniel Garner serves as manager of the firm's business and financial services groups.

**Clients/Work Highlights:** The group acts for banks, finance companies and other institutions in a range of commercial lending and credit activities.

### Jones Day

See firm details p.570

**The Firm:** This firm retains its place in the Texas tables for its enthusiasm and drive in the local market and access to significant resources, not only across the country but also internationally. It represents a number of large institutional clients, such as Bank of America; the Dallas office has been representing Bank of America/Banc of America Securities with respect to due diligence and bids for 12 commercial aircraft. In November 2005, the team advised The Frost National Bank in connection with a $20 million revolving and term loan facility provided to a franchising/restaurant company.

**The Lawyers:** Overseeing the firm's lending/structured finance and derivatives practice in the Dallas office, **Tom Gillespie** (see p.1893) emerges as a "*quiet but smart, thoughtful and collegiate lawyer.*" Clients considered him "*extremely helpful, deliberate and measured*" on aircraft leasings and other finance transactions. He and the team acted for The Neiman Marcus Group in providing secured financing to fund the buyout of assets of companies located in Italy, France, the UK and the USA.

**Clients/Work Highlights:** ANZ; Bank of America; Dow Chemical; Frost National Bank; Morgan Stanley Real Estate Funds; Novelis; Regions Bank and Washington Mutual.

### Porter & Hedges, LLP

**The Firm:** Regional firm Porter & Hedges' "*small but solid and competent*" banking and finance team joins the rankings this year as a result of its good performance in the middle market. In particular the group represents banks in a range of real estate transactions.

**The Lawyers:** **Neal Kaminsky** earned client praise for his "*broad knowledge*" and the "*value he added as a business consultant.*" Said to be "*always willing and ready*" to assist on a transaction from the outset, "*he is not just a drafter; he is someone you can bounce ideas off.*" Project finance and major lines of credit form just part of his broad commercial lending and corporate finance practice. He has represented banks, as agents, as well as borrowers, in syndicated revolving and term loan credit facilities.

**Clients/Work Highlights:** Bank of America; Compass Bank; International Bank of Commerce; Main Street Mezzanine Fund and Whitney National Bank

### Thompson & Knight LLP

See firm details p.1936

**The Firm:** A small team of "*careful, meticulous and professional lawyers*" shines at this old-line Dallas firm. Energy finance is the main activity and the firm, which has further offices in Texas and other parts of the country, is very active in the senior bank credit market. Interestingly, the firm has lawyers working in Brazil, Mexico, Europe and North Africa.

**The Lawyers:** Making his debut in the tables is "*excellent, bright and tenacious energy lawyer*" **James McKellar** (see p.1905); he regularly works for Bank of America and Wachovia and has a specialty in

senior bank lending and restructuring. McKellar recently represented a public company in the restructuring of $150 million of debt, and a private company in the restructuring of $65 million of existing debt and the creation of $70 million of new financing. There was nothing but praise for top Dallas lawyer **John Rain** (see p.1911), who earned compliments for his "*thorough knowledge of the oil and gas industry*" and his work on private debt and investment transactions. His practice encompasses the structuring and negotiation of VPP-related deals, and during 2005 he represented sellers and buyers of VPPs in transactions totaling over $1 billion. Rain also represented a manufacturing company in four integrated bank loans and note issuances totaling $900 million.

**Clients/Work Highlights:** The firm advises banks, insurance companies, pension fund managers, savings and loan associations and factoring companies.

### Weil, Gotshal & Manges LLP

See firm details p.1565

**The Firm:** This national private equity powerhouse with three offices in the state is well deserving of its place in the Texas table. Of note is a "*seamless relationship with New York,*" a long track record in complex finance transactions and an ability to move work around its extensive network. Although many interviewees considered the firm's biggest pull to be bankruptcy, its representation of Hicks Muse Tate & Furst is also seen as key to its involvement in a range of interesting financial transactions. The national team additionally carries out significant work for Citibank, Lehman Brothers and Wachovia.

**The Lawyers:** Undertaking significant private equity finance and debt restructurings, Dallas partner **Angela Fontana** (see p.1891) is admired for her "*broad understanding and in-depth knowledge of complex financial transactions.*" She represented the agents and lead arrangers on Kmart's exit financing and acted for Hicks, Muse, Tate and Furst in financing the acquisition of Persona Communications cable network. Interviewees appreciated the skills of senior associate **Courtney Marcus** (see p.1903), whose practice contains considerable experience of investment and refinancing. She represented Southwest Sports Group in connection with its refinance of various subsidiaries including the Dallas Stars and the Texas Rangers. She also represented Thomas H Lee Partners, Monitor Clipper Partners, Genstar Capital and The Sterling Group in various high-value investments.

**Clients/Work Highlights:** Thomas H Lee Partners, DLJ Merchant Banking Partners and The Blackstone Group are among the clientele.

### Winstead Sechrest & Minick P.C.

See firm details p.1939

**The Firm:** This 32-year-old firm garnered respect for a developing team of 25 lending lawyers in a banking and credit transactions group which offers special expertise in asset-based, commercial and energy lending as well as mezzanine, project and real estate finance. The group earned special recognition for its syndicated and asset-based lending in the upper-middle market. In August 2001, the firm was boosted by the acquisition of the respected Dallas banking and finance boutique Donohoe, Jameson and Carroll.

**The Lawyers:** A former head of group, "*hard-working and practical*" **Michael Hilliard** applies "*an effective working style*" to syndicated and asset-based lending. He has recently been involved in matters which fall outside the mainstream of traditional banking work, for example being involved in a

complex $400 million transaction that provides currency for use in a large ATM network. A number of commentators had enjoyed very good professional experiences with **James Littlejohn**, who "*always keeps the deal moving.*" His 30 years of experience in a range of corporate and commercial lending transactions have stood him in good stead, and he advises agents, bank groups, individual lenders and borrowers on the structuring and documenting of a variety of secured and unsecured commercial credit facilities.

**Clients/Work Highlights:** This group represents

the interests of regional, national and international financial institutions, as well as assisting corporate clients to establish and maintain credit facilities.

### Other Notable Practitioners

There was much praise for **Marilyn Maloney**, the "*sound and thorough*" head of the Houston office of New Orleans-headquartered Liskow & Lewis. This experienced transaction attorney represents borrowers and lenders on energy loans for the construction of pipelines, platforms and other facilities.

# BANKRUPTCY/RESTRUCTURING

| Bankruptcy/Restructuring |
| --- |
| Leading Firms |
| ① HAYNES AND BOONE LLP *Dallas* |
| ② FULBRIGHT & JAWORSKI L.L.P. *Dallas* |
|    VINSON & ELKINS LLP *Dallas* |
|    WEIL, GOTSHAL & MANGES LLP *Dallas* |
| ③ AKIN GUMP STRAUSS HAUER & FELD LLP *Dallas* |
|    ANDREWS KURTH LLP *Houston* |
|    BAKER BOTTS LLP *Dallas* |
|    GARDERE WYNNE SEWELL LLP *Dallas* |
|    NELIGAN TARPLEY ANDREWS & FOLEY LLP *Dallas* |
|    THOMPSON & KNIGHT LLP *Dallas* |
|    WINSTEAD SECHREST & MINICK P.C. *Dallas* |
| ④ BRACEWELL & GIULIANI LLP *Houston* |
|    CARRINGTON, COLEMAN *Dallas* |
|    COX SMITH MATTHEWS INC *San Antonio* |
|    GREENBERG TRAURIG LLP *Dallas* |
|    MUNSCH HARDT KOPF & HARR, P. C. *Dallas* |
|    PORTER & HEDGES, LLP *Houston* |

## Band 1

### Haynes and Boone LLP

**The Firm:** Researchers were unsurprised to learn that with "*one of the largest and deepest bankruptcy practices*" in the state, this "*excellent and talented*" group was on virtually every interviewee's shortlist. It retains its place at the head of the pack due to the efforts of the "*solution-oriented and consistent*" team of around 30 attorneys. The team is replete with seasoned experts and earns top marks for its "*almost constant involvement*" in the biggest bankruptcies. For example, it acted for the debtors in the scene-stealing Mirant and Schlotzsky's bankruptcies. In the former, it provides co-counsel for a Chapter 11 debtor with electric generating facilities in North America, the Caribbean and the Philippines and claims against it worth over $12 billion. At the same time, the firm's experience acting for creditors and committees was not lost on the market; it is much admired for its role advising the creditors' committee in Romacorp (Tony Roma's restaurants) and for advice given to the parent of Mesaba Airlines.

**The Lawyers:** Most peers would happily refer work

to the "*preeminent*" **Bob Albergotti** "*in a heartbeat;*" indeed there was an abundance of positive feedback for the "*smart, flamboyant and courteous*" lawyer. Clients admired his "*very honest approach and fast-thinking ability,*" which make working with him "*a true pleasure.*" Since wrapping up the National Benevolent Association and Schlotzsky's cases in 2005, he has been litigating claims on behalf of American Airlines in the United Airlines and Hawaiian Airlines bankruptcies. Well known as an "*experienced and knowledgeable*" bankruptcy expert, both in Texas and nationally, **Robin Phelan** "*does a very good job of keeping up with the latest cases, orders and rulings.*" For one client, "*knowledge is definitely power*" when it comes to Phelan, who can be asked "*oddball questions and will give you an immediate reply.*" He has been instrumental in the Mirant and Adelphia Communications confirmations. The team also counsels Bank of America, the agent for the Century Communications lenders in the Adelphia Chapter 11. Clients admired "*ethical, creative and driven*" **Charles Beckham**, who divides his time between the representation of creditors, debtors and several French banks. **Stacey Jernigan** has been well received by in-house legal departments; her "*detail-oriented and thorough approach,*" combined with her "*sharpness,*" has proved to be very attractive.

**Clients/Work Highlights:** The firm has a wide selection of clients including Bank of America, American Airlines and Crédit Lyonnais.

## Band 2

### Fulbright & Jaworski L.L.P.

See firm details p.1928

**The Firm:** This established Texas firm's bankruptcy reputation goes hand in hand with its prowess in litigation. There was widespread commendation for the lead partners as well as "*an extremely strong supporting cast.*" Earning specific praise for their creditor representations, the 34 Texas-based bankruptcy lawyers also act for debtors in restructuring, refinance and insolvency litigation. The team assisted creditors in the Mirant case, while also impressing sources with their representation of YUKOS in its Chapter 11 proceedings. The arrival in June 2004 of

former bankruptcy judge Bill Greendyke was considered "*an excellent coup*" for the group.

**The Lawyers:** "*Outstanding*" **Lou Strubeck**'s (see p.1916) "*first-rate reputation*" owes much to his long trial experience and his handling some of the larger creditors in high-profile bankruptcies such as Mirant. Commentators rated practice head **Evelyn Biery** (see p.1883) for her "*impressive communication skills;*" she acts for creditors and creditors' committees in major bankruptcies, and has been acting for the Southern Company, former parent of Mirant, in the multilayered bankruptcy. Biery is also on the creditors' committee in the ASARCO case. A "*considerable amount of large company debtor work*" drives the "*remarkable and polished*" **Zack Clement** (see p.1886) into the tables. His "*business-oriented approach*" and "*courageous manner*" greatly assist him in his work, which recently included the representation of YUKOS. Sources also admired the "*very savvy, top-drawer*" **Toby Gerber** (see p.1892), who has been lead bankruptcy counsel for numerous bank groups in major cases, as well as representing the International Air Transport Association in major airline bankruptcies. After joining the firm's Houston office, the "*amazing and devoted*" **Bill Greendyke** (see p.1894), a former bankruptcy judge, has shown that he has "*the maturity, experience and ability to bring people together and make his points adroitly.*"

**Clients/Work Highlights:** The group mostly represents creditors in bankruptcy, but also counts various debtors among its clientele.

### Vinson & Elkins LLP

See firm details p.1938

**The Firm:** This well-established Texas group rides high in the market on the back of the achievements of its "*experienced*" attorneys. Commentators say this "*very good team of lawyers*" is a familiar sight in high-profile bankruptcies, be these larger regional cases or national matters. The team enjoys an especially strong reputation for creditor and committee representations.

**The Lawyers:** Researchers learned much about seasoned practitioner **Dan Stewart** (see p.1915), who has been leading the group since 1999. His own practice has included representations of major creditors, debtors and bankruptcy trustees in numerous Chapter 7 and Chapter 11 cases. Both Stewart and the immensely respected **James Lee** (see p.1902) have been co-representing debtors in the complex VarTec Telecom Chapter 11 proceedings in the US Bankruptcy Court for the Northern District of Texas. Meanwhile, sources described **Bill Wallander** (see p.1918) as *"a relentless advocate for his clients."* Some 20 years of experience have enabled him to build a good reputation in a range of areas, including reorganization plans. For example, he acted recently for the debtor, transportation leasing company Action Auto Rental, in bankruptcy proceedings. Commentators were also impressed with the *"intelligence and diversity"* of **Josiah Daniel** (see p.1888), who advised

the parent and affiliates in the mass tort Chapter 11 case of A.G. Financial Service Center. He also represented the lender group in a prenegotiated Chapter 11 case for HealthCare America.

**Clients/Work Highlights:** Daisytek International; GE Commercial Finance; Lone Star Bank; Société Générale and CIBC.

## Weil, Gotshal & Manges LLP
See firm details p.1565

**The Firm:** Expertise in restructuring public companies combines with an almost unmatched national debtor reputation and *"the respect of the Bar and the judges"* ensure this New York powerhouse's position in the Texas table. The market identified the firm's core competencies as *"extensive bankruptcy litigation experience;"* exposure to *"all issues imaginable;"* and a track record representing massive debtors as well as creditors. A team of 16 attorneys was praised for being *"very good at transactions with distressed companies, both outside and inside bankruptcy."*

**The Lawyers:** Described as *"a consummate gentleman,"* the *"technically proficient"* **Alfredo Perez** (see p.1909) spent part of his time last year buying a fleet of vessels from a New Orleans-based company. The *"smart and creative"* **Martin Sosland** (see p.1914) is admired as *"effective in court"* and having *"impeccable integrity."* He acted for Tejas Securities Group in connection with its acquisition of Trenwick America in a Chapter 11 case. He also served as counsel to Lehman Brothers, as agent for the bank group in the Mirant case.

**Clients/Work Highlights:** The firm remains involved as a principal partner in the Enron litigation following the confirmed plan in late 2004. The team acts too for MCI as a creditor in a number of smaller telecoms cases. Other clients include GE Capital; Lehman Brothers; Tejas Securities Group; International Wire Group; Viasystems Group; Resurgence Asset Management; Leucadia National and Omnicare.

## Akin Gump Strauss Hauer & Feld LLP
See firm details p.559

**The Firm:** As well as an ovation for its national work, Akin Gump collected accolades for the *"reliable expertise"* in its Dallas and Houston offices. Although clearly leaning towards creditor and committee representations, the firm undertakes debtor work too. Its capability is boosted by the corporate, M&A and project finance expertise available to companies in distress, and there is an impressive depth of understanding of the oil, gas and real estate sectors regionally. The team of 15 attorneys is strong, but the market believes the loss of Henry Kaim to Bracewell & Giuliani must have been a blow. Russell Reid has moved to the firm's New York office.

**The Lawyers:** Interviewees applauded the *"effective, experienced and persuasive"* **Charles Gibbs** (see p.1892) for *"his ability to facilitate negotiations."* He represents Gadzooks, a mall-based retail store, which filed its Chapter 11 bankruptcy petition in 2004. In

early 2005 Gadzooks sold substantially all of its assets to Gadzooks 21, a wholly-owned subsidiary of Forever 21. The $33 million sale closed in March 2005. Gibbs has also been instrumental in the representation of Skin Nuvo, which filed Chapter 11 bankruptcy petitions in Nevada. An impressive bankruptcy career behind him, *"long-time dean of debtor bankruptcy work"* **Myron Sheinfeld** (see p.1914) has shifted towards advising boards of directors on Sarbanes-Oxley, corporate governance and related bankruptcy issues. Commentators were also impressed by the former head of the firmwide restructuring group, **Rey Stroube** (see p.1916), who has 30 years' experience. He has been advising creditors in dispute with Enron, and on suits related to energy and derivative contracts. Texas Petrochemicals sought his advice in relation to the acquisition and financing of a reorganized debtor company.

**Clients/Work Highlights:** This group represents large business entities across the USA, including Gadzooks, CHI-CHI'S and CEI Roofing.

## Andrews Kurth LLP
See firm details p.1921

**The Firm:** This firm has *"a deep, talented pool"* of over 30 attorneys, and an impressive track record in bankruptcy litigation. Despite a good deal of work for Deutsche Bank and JPMorgan Chase, there has been a notable shift from representing secured creditors to large trustee, official committee and debtor cases. This has left the group with an ability to *"run tough cases effectively from either side."* Clients recommended Andrews Kurth as *"a very aggressive local counsel"* and were clearly impressed by its *"local finesse, knowledge and connections."*

**The Lawyers:** Both peers and clients regarded **John Lee** as *"an experienced key player"* in bankruptcy litigation. He represents one of the largest creditor groups in the Mirant case. Clients recommended the head of the national bankruptcy practice, *"Texas good ol' boy"* **Hugh Ray**, as *"a very appealing advocate"* with many talents and connections. He represents all parties in bankruptcy proceedings; for example, he acted for the debtor in the Physicians Resource Group, and for the unsecured creditors' committee of Flagstar Corporation. Meanwhile, *"tireless lawyers' lawyer"* **Jeff Spiers** applies *"a deft touch to sensitive cases,"* frequently representing official committees in Chapter 11 cases. Both Ray and Spiers worked as co-counsel for Deutsche Bank in late 2004 and early 2005 in the YUKOS bankruptcy case filed in Houston. They succeeded in obtaining a dismissal of the bankruptcy case and related proceedings. Spiers was also an integral part of the team which acted as special debtors' counsel to Enron during its bankruptcy proceedings. That team provided advice in coordination with Weil Gotshal during the early months of the case, and also served as bankruptcy and transactional counsel with respect to a number of asset dispositions. Lastly, observers pointed out that *"hard-working, aggressive and savvy"* ex-New York lawyer **Jason Brookner** remains one to watch in Texas.

**Clients/Work Highlights:** Ranging across the creditor and debtor fields, other clients include Vlasic Foods International, Mobile Energy Services and Crown Pacific Partners.

## Baker Botts LLP

See firm details p.1922

**The Firm:** The bankruptcy work of this "*clearly excellent firm*" has often been overshadowed by that done in other well-recognized practice areas; however, the firm seems to be "*moving very much in the right direction*" with regard to its Texas practice group. Clients paid tribute to a "*sharp*" group of "*mental powerhouses and creative thinkers,*" who offered "*great-quality service*" and "*lack any weak link in the chain.*" The team advised Gazpromneft in the high-profile YUKOS bankruptcy and also acted for ASARCO, one of the largest producers of copper in the USA in connection with its asbestos-impacted subsidiaries, as well as in its own bankruptcy proceedings.

**The Lawyers:** Researchers learned that **Jack Kinzie** (see p.1900) is viewed as "*a good strategist and court performer.*" Interviewees enjoyed working with the leader of the Dallas office, remarking on his "*guidance through problems*" and a "*nonconfrontational*" style which "*does not bottleneck deals.*" He advised Halliburton and its subsidiaries on one of the largest mass tort restructurings in 2005. The firm helped create and fund two settlement trusts that will be responsible for the companies' asbestos and silica liabilities on a going-forward basis. The arrival of "*smart and experienced*" former Thompson & Knight attorney **Judy Ross** (see p.1912) has further raised the team's profile. With expertise in all aspects of bankruptcy, she has been acting for the creditors' committee in the bankruptcy of a plastics manufacturer.

**Clients/Work Highlights:** With the help of Baker Botts lawyers, Halliburton and its subsidiaries completed a significant mass tort restructuring in January 2005. Other clients include Gazpromneft; ASARCO; Ultimate Electronics; Corban Communications and NextStage.

## Gardere Wynne Sewell LLP

See firm details p.1931

**The Firm:** This "*reliable and effective*" operation of around 16 mostly Dallas-based lawyers impresses with its "*immediate responsiveness and targeted advice*" on bankruptcy and Chapter 11 matters. The regional firm has a full docket of debtor and creditor committee work.

**The Lawyers:** The team includes **Richard Roberson** (see p.1912), a "*highly skilled, likable and informed*" frontrunner. His "*courtroom performance and behind-the-scenes efforts*" make him an invaluable addition to any client's team of advisers. With a debtor or trustee-leaning practice, his diverse experience and background as a litigator serves him well, and he has been acting for the examiner in the mammoth Mirant bankruptcy. "*One of the most talented people at the firm*" is **Dee Ruckman** (see p.1912), whose "*true knowledge, direct honesty and professionalism*" clearly impressed clients. With the

majority of her experience on the company side, lately she has been undertaking an increasing number of out-of-court restructurings. Ruckman was involved in the successful Chapter 11 reorganization of American Pad & Paper. **Holly O'Neil** (see p.1908) came under the spotlight for her experience of complex bankruptcies, workouts and private acquisitions. A good example of her work is the representation of CoServ Electric and its telecom, real estate and related affiliates in the restructuring of $1 billion of debt.

**Clients/Work Highlights:** The team advises secured lenders, debtors, trustees and creditors' committees.

## Neligan Tarpley Andrews & Foley LLP

**The Firm:** This "*pretty darned decent*" nine-lawyer Dallas boutique received high marks for its representation of debtors in smaller Chapter 11 assignments, commercial bankruptcies and corporate restructurings. Although lacking the resources of many of its larger rivals, this unique outfit boasts an abundance of bankruptcy expertise and can staff cases "*leanly and meanly*" in the middle market.

**The Lawyers:** The firm's founder, **Pat Neligan**, has picked up "*a sound market reputation*" for his debtor representation and his "*driven and conscientious*" work ethic. Recently the firm represented Minorplanet Systems in its restructuring.

## Thompson & Knight LLP

See firm details p.1936

**The Firm:** The bankruptcy group at this veteran Texas firm is highly regarded as "*a quality practice.*" The depth of associate talent is considered a key asset of the "*solid and steady*" group of around 14 lawyers, which is closely allied to the firm's excellent energy practice. It is known for its role as counsel to creditors and official committees and for the lawyers' expertise in energy-related bankruptcy litigation and restructuring.

**The Lawyers:** "*Bright as can be, scholar*" **Rhett Campbell** (see p.1885) has unquestioned "*technical strength and oil and gas experience.*" Researchers learned that Campbell's "*intellectual honesty*" is admired as much as his "*strategic thinking.*" He recently helped settle a major piece of Enron-related litigation involving Noble Energy. Boasting both energy and telecom expertise is **David Bennett** (see p.1882), who has acted for the agents for Mirant bank groups. His diverse practice also saw him representing the creditor/telecommunication contract counterparty (the incumbent local exchange carrier) in the Chapter 11 case of VarTec Telecom.

**Clients/Work Highlights:** The firm acts for the full range of bankruptcy participants.

## Winstead Sechrest & Minick P.C.

See firm details p.1939

**The Firm:** This outfit retains market respect for its historical connections to big banks, particularly Bank of America. However, over time the group of around 18 attorneys has sought and achieved greater diversity in its work and is now acting for trustees, secured

and unsecured creditors, official unsecured creditors' committees and debtors.

**The Lawyers:** Former bankruptcy judge **Mike McConnell** "*knows the system*" and brings "*a unique perspective*" to clients requiring arbitration, mediation and advocacy services. He has been involved in the defense of an action brought by a Securities Investor Protection Act trustee seeking over $25 million damages from a Texas bank. He is also currently involved in an attempt to purchase a significant package of assets in a pending Chapter 11 case. Sources admired "*top-notch and intelligent*" attorney **Berry Spears** for being "*skilled at finding solutions*" and bringing parties together. He and the team acted for the unsecured creditors' committee in the Chapter 11 case of Schlotzsky's, the Austin-based national restaurant chain.

**Clients/Work Highlights:** The team has been representing Oregon Arena Corporation, the owner of the Rose Garden Arena, home of the NBA Portland Trail Blazers, in its Chapter 11 case. Other clients include American Plumbing & Mechanical; WebLink Wireless; Classic Communications; Senior Living Properties and Stonebridge Technologies.

## Band 4

### Bracewell & Giuliani LLP

See firm details p.1924

**The Firm:** Although capable of advising all parties in bankruptcy issues, this impressive Texas firm earned most recognition for its representation of distressed companies in Chapter 11 and bankruptcy proceedings. Some 13 lawyers are active in a range of industries such as energy, retail, and restaurants. For example, the group represented restaurant chain Souper Salad in its bankruptcy proceedings.

**The Lawyers:** "*Skilled problem solver*" and section head **Henry Kaim** (see p.1899) is one of a team of lawyers with a "*genuine ability to tackle complex problems.*" Backed by more than 25 years' experience acting for all parties, he has lately been shepherding Souper Salad through its bankruptcy. Another admired lawyer is "*likable consensus builder*" **Sam Stricklin** (see p.1915), who acts for creditors' committees as well as distressed companies. Sources warn: "*He is not afraid to fight in court for what he could not get in negotiations.*"

**Clients/Work Highlights:** The firm caters for clients ranging from large secured creditors to bank agents in syndicated credits, unsecured creditors, institutional noteholders, purchasers of assets and debtors.

### Carrington, Coleman, Sloman & Blumenthal, LLP

**The Firm:** This "*terrific*" 100-lawyer Dallas litigation firm gained good marks for "*its strategic ability and careful preparation of companies for reorganization.*" A "*small and talented*" bankruptcy group has built a good name for lesser roles in major bankruptcies. Working on all sides of the docket, the group has acted as debtor counsel for First City Bancorporation of Texas, for the unsecured creditors' committee in VarTec Telecom, and for one of the secured creditors in the ASARCO litigation. A large proportion of its work is for secured creditors, among them foreign and specialty banks such as Mitsui or RBS.

**The Lawyers:** Sources applauded the "*great judgment, ability and experience*" of "*smart gent*" and one-time Vinson & Elkins attorney **Mike Sutherland**. He joined the firm in March 2005 from Winstead Sechrest & Minick.

### Cox Smith Matthews Incorporated
See firm details p.1926

**The Firm:** This leading San Antonio law firm with offices in Austin, Dallas and McAllen became a dominant player in southern Texas when Cox Smith merged with Matthews and Branscomb in 2004. Having recently welcomed David Bryant to its Dallas office, it now fields ten lawyers who advise secured creditors, debtors, trustees and committees in bankruptcy litigation and reorganizations.

**The Lawyers:** Head of the firm's creditors' rights, corporate restructuring and bankruptcy department is **Deborah Williamson** (see p.1919), the "*knowledgeable and well-connected*" former chair and past president of the American Bankruptcy Institute. She is considered by many to be "*at the top of her game.*" Energy-related bankruptcies remain key in a year in which she also represented MBIA, a worldwide financial guarantor, in connection with the wind-down of a hospital in Fort Worth.

**Clients/Work Highlights:** The clientele is drawn from debtors, trustees, committees and purchasers, plus secured and unsecured creditors.

### Greenberg Traurig LLP
See firm details p.664

**The Firm:** Entering the Texas bankruptcy tables is Greenberg Traurig, an international law firm which is expanding in the state through lateral hires. The opening of its Dallas office in late 2003 pulled in lawyers from firms such as Andrews Kurth, Patton Boggs and Larson King. Able to call upon a national team of almost 60 attorneys, some seven specialists in Dallas undertake complex Chapter 11 restructurings and smaller, creditor-related assignments.

**The Lawyers:** The 2004 recruitment of the "*wonderful but still underrated*" **Clifton Jessup** (see p.1898) has served the firm well. According to interviewees, "*he does not make rookie mistakes,*" and is considered "*an articulate courtroom performer who never loses his cool.*" He has taken the role of liquidating trustee in the case of Baptist Foundation of America, one of the largest nonprofits to file for bankruptcy.

**Clients/Work Highlights:** A range of debtors, secured and unsecured creditors, investors and boards of directors use the firm.

### Munsch Hardt Kopf & Harr, P. C.
**The Firm:** This 20-year-old Texas firm employs a group of 24 reorganization and creditors' rights lawyers in its three offices in Dallas, Houston and Austin. Considered by the market as "*experts in smaller and more routine bankruptcy cases,*" a "*sound and competent team*" advises on all aspects of reorganization but gained particular acclaim for its knowledge of restructuring distressed companies, and its representation of financial institutions and other secured lenders.

**The Lawyers:** Heading the bankruptcy group is "*wise, creative and experienced*" **Russ Munsch** (see p.1907), who acts for major creditors, bank groups and financial institutions in large loan workouts and bankruptcies. Significant cases have included Enron, Coho Energy and Dow Chemical. Commentators also heaped praise on "*smart and savvy*" **Joseph Wielebinski** (see p.1919) for his caseload of loan workouts and restructurings. He played a key role in the formation of the official committee of franchisees in the Color Tile bankruptcy in Delaware, serving as its lead counsel.

**Clients/Work Highlights:** The group primarily represents financial institutions and banks. It has significant experience in the real estate and oil and gas industries.

### Porter & Hedges, LLP
**The Firm:** This group's small size does not detract from the "*fine reputation*" it has earned while representing both debtors and creditors. A team of around ten attorneys enters the tables after earning top marks from those who have encountered it. Clients include those seeking to acquire oil and gas properties, refining operations, real estate, manufacturing facilities, and other assets and operations from bankruptcy estates.

**The Lawyers:** At the forefront of the bankruptcy and litigation practices is **John Higgins**, whose "*precise methodology, responsiveness and coherent advice*" have shaped his diverse 20-year bankruptcy practice. Higgins has been representing Concert Capital Resources in the Dunhill Resources case. His team was successful in taking over operating oil and gas properties in Texas, California and offshore. The case was rare in that it was among the first known foreclosures of offshore properties. He proceeded to assist Concert in the sale of the properties.

**Clients/Work Highlights:** The team has advised Bridgeline Holdings in Enron cases. Enron, a 40% owner of Bridgeline, was a counterparty to numerous contracts. Other clients include financial institutions and commercial credit organizations.

### Other Notable Practitioners
An "*easy style and great sense of humor*" plus more than 25 years of experience make **Buzz Rochelle** of the eight-lawyer Dallas boutique Rochelle, Hutcheson & McCullough, LLP a top choice for clients. Commentators say he has "*an ability to get to the meat of an issue.*"

# CONSTRUCTION

## Band 1

### Canterbury, Stuber, Elder, Gooch & Surratt, PC
See firm details p.1925

**The Firm:** This boutique firm has focused its practice on the construction industry. Celebrating its 25th anniversary in 2006, the firm has been dubbed by clients the "*best of the best*" in its chosen sector. According to one client, the firm is "*professional, client-oriented and we are just thankful that they are our lawyers.*" The group is praised as "*terrific and they do a great job for their clients.*" It represents owners, contractors and subcontractors and handled both contentious and transactional work. Among recent matters, the group has handled a large construction dispute concerning a power plant. An international and domestic mediation and arbitration specialty also distinguishes this firm.

**The Lawyers:** A "*premier construction lawyer,*" **Joe Canterbury** is involved in a wide spectrum of construction law matters. He has arbitrated a dispute involving contractors and subcontractors in the northeast of Texas and mediated a number of complex multiparty cases. Sources described his "*dedication to his clients and his practical approach to litigation.*" He is also well known for writing the "*most definitive book on construction law.*" **Kyle Gooch** (see p.1893) impresses as "*a knowledgeable and effective litigator who gets to the point.*" He has a broad construction practice with particular expertise in handling insurance-related construction disputes. Gooch represented the contractor in a major piece of litigation involving the Dallas Convention Center and advised on a dispute over underground conditions in a construction project.

### Cokinos, Bosien and Young
**The Firm:** This excellent boutique firm has grown to become one of the largest construction groups in Texas, with five attorneys dedicated to transactional matters and 22 specialist litigators. Clients spoke of their confidence in the firm's handling of significant matters, praising these "*talented and diligent attorneys*" for providing a "*good product at the right price.*" The firm represents contractors, owners and engineers, and its workload of late has included advice on the construction of processing and power plants. Insurance coverage issues affecting parties involved in the industry are a further string to the firm's bow. Attorneys have successfully defended the suppliers of EIFS (exterior insulation and finish systems) products in litigation.

**The Lawyers:** **Gregory Cokinos** is "*a bright attorney with an outstanding personality.*" He primarily

## Construction

### Leading Firms

1. CANTERBURY, STUBER, ELDER, GOOCH *Dallas*
   COKINOS, BOSIEN AND YOUNG *Houston*
2. ALLENSWORTH AND PORTER, L.L.P *Austin*
   ANDREWS MYERS COULTER & COHEN PC *Houston*
   COATS ROSE YALE RYMAN LEE *Houston*
   FORD NASSEN & BALDWIN *Dallas*
3. FISK & FIELDER *Dallas*
   GARDERE WYNNE SEWELL LLP *Dallas*
   GRIFFITH & NIXON, P.C. *Dallas*
   JENKENS & GILCHRIST *Houston*
   JONES DAY *Dallas*
   PORTER & HEDGES, LLP *Houston*
   PRATT & SANDERFORD *Temple*
   WINSTEAD SECHREST & MINICK P.C. *Dallas*

### Leading Individuals

1. CANTERBURY JR Joe *Canterbury, Stuber, Elder*
2. COATS William *Coats Rose Yale Ryman Lee*
   COKINOS Gregory *Cokinos, Bosien and Young*
3. ALLENSWORTH William *Allensworth and Porter, LLP*
   ANDREWS William *Andrews Myers Coulter*
   BASS JR Robert *Winstead Sechrest & Minick PC*
   FISK Hollye *Fisk & Fielder*
   FLAKE Richard *Cokinos, Bosien and Young*
   FORD Jeffrey *Ford Nassen & Baldwin*
   GOOCH W Kyle *Canterbury, Stuber, Elder*
   MEYERS III Robert *Jones Day*
   PEDEN David *Porter & Hedges, LLP*
   PRATT Donald *Pratt & Sanderford*
4. ALBERS Michael *Jenkens & Gilchrist PC*
   BALDWIN George *Ford Nassen & Baldwin*
   CAPSHAW Richard *Capshaw, Goss & Bowers LLP*
   GREER Scott *King & Spalding LLP*
   GRIFFITH Scott *Griffith & Nixon, PC*
   HENRY D Steven *Gardere Wynne Sewell LLP*
   MERWIN Bruce *Haynes and Boone LLP*
   RIEGER Michelle *Winstead Sechrest & Minick PC*
   SHORT JR William *William B Short Jr, PC*
   SNYDER Allison *Porter & Hedges, LLP*
   UNDERKOFLER Paul *Goins, Underkofler, Crawford*
   YUNGBLUT Stephen *Pratt & Sanderford*

### Up-and-coming individuals

COHEN Eric *Andrews Myers Coulter*

---

focuses on construction litigation although he is also involved in negotiating contracts on behalf of owners and general contractors. He possesses the ability to "*mitigate the circumstances and work towards solutions*" for his clients. "*He has a winning combination of likability, intelligence and thorough preparation.*" Cokinos successfully defended a $24 million claim against an owner of a gas pipeline being constructed in east Texas, and negotiated agreements concerning work on the Texas Medical Center. The "*wonderful*" **Richard Flake** is a "*phenomenal construction mediator – as good as they get.*" He is often the first choice to mediate and arbitrate difficult cases, and advises contractors in contract negotiations and drafting.

## Band 2

### Allensworth and Porter, L.L.P

**The Firm:** A mere ten years after this boutique firm was founded it has earned a statewide reputation for its excellence construction practice representing architects and engineers. The team has the experience to advise on both transaction matters and to resolve construction disputes, either through litigation or arbitration. Its lawyers also serve as arbitrators and mediators, which gives them a broader perspective into dispute resolution.

**The Lawyers:** The "*scholarly*" **William Allensworth** combines his legal practice with his teaching duties at The University of Texas. Sources commended his ability to effectively represent architects and engineers in large, complex cases. He is a "*top professional who plays fair and knows his business.*"

### Andrews Myers Coulter & Cohen PC

**The Firm:** This ten-lawyer team devotes its practice to the whole range of issues arising out of the construction industry. It has developed a "*strong group of attorneys having a vast array of expertise who work well together.*"

**The Lawyers:** **William Andrews** litigates and arbitrates complex construction disputes and acts as a mediator. He is a "*real mover and shaker among the Texas construction Bar,*" reported interviewees. His "*experience and ability to analyze in the construction field*" is widely recognized. Among his recent caseload, Andrews settled a pipeline case that involved multiple issues relating to increased cost, performance and delays. **Eric Cohen** is a highly professional attorney and a "*fine trial lawyer*" who impresses sources with his solution-focused attitude and ability to get the deal done.

### Coats Rose Yale Ryman Lee

**The Firm:** Market commentators "*recommend this firm without reservation*" because of the specialist expertise of its attorneys and their ability to handle complex cases. Its dedicated litigators handle defect, liability and mass tort defense work. In addition to its broad construction practice, this firm has developed a major surety practice.

**The Lawyers:** **William Coats** has carved out a great reputation in the industry for his experience, expertise and success as a trial lawyer. He is "*one of the most knowledgeable and effective lawyers around.*" He heads up the construction and surety section of the firm and advises on all aspects of document preparation and interpretation as well as litigating disputes. He is a "*skilled and tireless advocate for his clients.*"

### Ford Nassen & Baldwin

**The Firm:** This well-known firm also represents contractors and major suppliers in both the public and private sectors. The lawyers here are described by clients as "*first-class, professional and competent.*"

Despite the fact that it is a smaller firm, it has the experience and technical skills to handle major construction matters.

**The Lawyers:** Founding shareholder **Jeffrey Ford** is a "*smart attorney who knows his way around complex matters.*" He represents parties involved in the construction and government contracts industry and "*does a great job protecting his clients' interests.*" Austin-based **George Baldwin** represents public and private owners, commercial general contractors, specialty subcontractors and suppliers.

## Band 3

### Fisk & Fielder

**The Firm:** This six-lawyer team represents architects and engineers in construction disputes relating to performance, delay and liability issues. The industrial experience of the lawyers sets this firm apart. Registered architects and certified construction specialists are found among the ranks and provide a valuable in-depth knowledge of the industry.

**The Lawyers:** **Hollye Fisk** is renowned for defending design professionals. "*He leaves no stone unturned, is calm, to the point and absolutely on top of strategy.*" His highlights include winning a $6 million suit for a geotechnical engineer, and he has advised an architecture firm that was joined in an action concerning the Fort Worth Water Gardens drowning case. "*One of the best cross-examiners in the courtroom,*" he combines his litigation practice with work evaluating new legislation for clients.

### Gardere Wynne Sewell LLP

See firm details p.1931

**The Firm:** This firm wins approval for its "*responsiveness, ability to look at the big picture and close attention*" it pays to its clients' business needs. According to one client, the firm "*believes in becoming part of the client's family – they know everything about us and our strategies.*" Attorneys represent commercial contractors and national homebuilders, and the group has, of late, worked on a number of high-rise residential projects. This team is able to "*create the feeling of a small firm with large-firm resources.*"

**The Lawyers:** **Steven Henry** (see p.1896) has developed a national construction practice, serving as national counsel for a number of large residential home-building companies and large commercial construction companies. He handles environmental issues, IP litigation and contract drafting that can be used across the USA for his client Lennar. A skilled litigator, he recently won a $40 million verdict for a homebuilder company in Texas. He has been working on the Notice and Opportunity to Repair (NOR) initiative for the National Association of Home Builders, seeking to get legislation passed in all states to allow builders the right to make repairs to alleged defects before claims are made. Clients consider him to be a "*valued member of the team.*" Another stated that he is "*head and shoulders above any other attorney I deal with around the country.*"

## Griffith & Nixon, P.C.

**The Firm:** This firm is home to 15 lawyers who practice exclusively in commercial construction and real estate law. The team undertakes construction contract negotiation and dispute resolution. Its expanding client base includes subcontractors and general contractors. It recently advised a developer of student housing with six developments.

**The Lawyers:** **Scott Griffith** (see p.1894) represents general contractors on all aspects of their business including the resolution of disputes. He is "*personable, attentive and responds quickly,*" reported sources. Among his recent cases, Griffith had a two-week oral commercial contract jury trial where he obtained a judgment for over $7 million. He has also been involved in the development of a 200-acre mixed-use project in Dallas.

## Jenkens & Gilchrist

**The Firm:** This firm's construction practice is predominately owner-oriented and transactions-based: it is involved in residential, commercial and industrial projects. The construction specialists here also draw an advantage from their close working relationship with the real estate practice, which provides clients with a broad understanding of the market.

**The Lawyers:** **Michael Albers** is "*always prepared, personable, business-minded and highly responsive,*" agree clients. He principally represents owners in industrial and large commercial transactions. He recently advised the US Federal Reserve Bank in its construction of a new facility in Houston. He is "*adept at developing concepts and is a great problem solver.*"

## Jones Day

See firm details p.570

**The Firm:** This full-service, multidisciplinary firm is capable of handling contentious and transactional matters. It principally represents owners, lenders and contractors but also advises a number of architects. The team has represented two of the biggest builders in Dallas on several condominium and multi storey residential projects.

**The Lawyers:** **Robert Meyers** (see p.1906) is considered to be the "*ultimate owners' lawyer*" because of his long experience in the sector and his success in attracting an enviable client base of leading owners. He "*can do everything you expect a lawyer to do – draft, negotiate and resolve disputes at a very high level.*" He represented the designer of a power plant in litigation and advised on the Dallas Center for the Performing Arts construction project.

## Porter & Hedges, LLP

**The Firm:** This firm serves its clients on a national basis from its office in Houston. It has been involved in complex litigation in Mexico, Maryland and Florida. The team has a broad client base, representing developers, contractors, design professionals and subcontractors. The firm's high reputation is appreciated by clients because "*when you say this firm is defending or representing you, you win the respect of all parties right away.*"

**The Lawyers:** The "*outstanding* **David Peden** *is one of the best in his field.*" He spends the majority of his time arbitrating or litigating construction delay and defect cases, and recently tried a three-week multimillion-dollar arbitration involving construction defects. He also negotiated a $145 million project in Florida. His clients value him because he "*totally understands construction details right down to the finest point and so can deal easily with sophisticated issues.*" **Allison Snyder** "*gets right to the point*" in her negotiations. Commentators also endorsed her skill and knowledge in both arbitration and litigation. In the past year she has successfully tried three construction defect and delay cases. She is an excellent trial lawyer and is "*able to grasp the situation and evaluate it quickly.*"

## Pratt & Sanderford

**The Firm:** This Arlington-based boutique specializes in construction law, representing clients in a broad array of dispute resolution. According to sources, "*it knows the industry so well that nothing is missed.*" It also has an office in Temple.

**The Lawyers:** **Donald Pratt** represented a church in a dispute with a construction manager concerning defective work and misrepresentation. From the standpoint of expertise, knowledge and ethics, he is "*head and shoulders above anyone else in the construction industry.*" He is able to "*manage different personalities and can resolve issues effectively.*" **Stephen Yungblut** is a talented litigator and a well-respected member of the construction Bar.

## Winstead Sechrest & Minick P.C.

See firm details p.1939

**The Firm:** This excellent regional law firm, headquartered in Dallas, fields 18 lawyers from its construction group who work closely with the firm's litigation, real estate and corporate lawyers. Its ability to provide expertise in certain niches such as franchise taxes has been "*extremely valuable,*" said clients. The team provides a full service to its construction clients, mainly contractors, owners, developers and subcontractors.

**The Lawyers:** **Robert Bass** is a transactional lawyer who specializes in complex stadium contract work. He represented the Dallas Cowboys in the financing, design and construction of the new Cowboys stadium in Arlington. He is "*knowledgeable in the architect and design field, friendly and quick to respond*

*to questions.*" He also served as underwriter's counsel on four military housing projects for the departments of the Navy, Army and Air Force. He is also the go-to lawyer for construction law legislative issues in Texas, and has lobbied in favor of legislation providing for blanket waiver of sovereign immunity for all breach of contract claims against local governmental entities in Texas. **Michelle Rieger** is an "*absolutely outstanding lawyer because she handles herself well and can think on her feet.*" Her practice comprises litigation and contract drafting, particularly that arising out of the condominium sector. A respected trial lawyer, she is "*practical, good with clients and respected by opposing counsel.*"

**Clients/Work Highlights:** The firm represented Carter & Burgess in resolving claims asserted by Granite Construction regarding the Las Vegas Monorail project, and assisted the same client in litigation with Tex Mall relating to a mall redevelopment. The team also advised Gilbert Southern in the negotiation of a close-out agreement on a Louisiana power project and assisted Bibb and Associates in an arbitration claim and collection of over $1 million in unpaid fees for engineering services on the Boston, MA area power project.

## Other Notable Practitioners

**Richard Capshaw** of Capshaw, Goss & Bowers LLP was singled out for his experience in representing design professionals, primarily architects. **Scott Greer** (see p.1894) of King & Spalding LLP primarily represents owners and developers, negotiating agreements and handling disputes during projects. He is a "*tough negotiator and extremely hard-working.*" He was a structural engineer prior to practicing law, which means he "*knows all the ins and outs of the construction business and how to protect his clients.*" His highlights include drafting and negotiating engineering, procurement and construction (EPC) agreements for offshore oil and gas platforms in the Gulf of Mexico and a petrochemical facility in the Middle East. He also acted for Cheniere Energy in its EPC agreement to design and construct natural gas terminals. **Bruce Merwin** of Haynes & Boone LLP has a dynamic transactional practice advising on real estate and construction contracts. **William Short** of William B Short Jr, PC is an excellent construction lawyer and a skilled mediator. According to interviewees, he is especially "*good at helping confrontational parties to work out their differences.*" **Paul Underkofler** of Goins, Underkofler, Crawford & Langdon LLP is recognized for his surety and insurance work. He is a respected senior member of the construction Bar and is admired for his "*impeccable integrity.*" His expertise in the construction field means "*he knows the ins and outs of plans and specifications,*" making him an efficient and effective mediator.

# CORPORATE/M&A

## Band 1

### Baker Botts LLP

See firm details p.1922

**The Firm:** Almost inexhaustible resources and enormous transactional experience virtually guarantee Baker Botts' place at the top of the tree in Texas. Certainly the size and sophistication of its corporate clientele are a testimony to the team's talents. In the lively technology and energy sectors – where the firm excels – there are teams of "*excellent securities attorneys,*" "*very good corporate finance players*" and "*several M&A experts.*" It must be pointed out, however, that while clients greatly admired the lawyers' "*professionalism and thoroughness*" on oil and gas-related transactions, they also have proficiency in other sectors.

**The Lawyers:** Senior figure **Stephen Massad** (see p.1904) has "*incredible wisdom, market knowledge and an ability to see the woods for the trees.*" Last year he advised Pogo Producing in its $1.7 billion acquisition of Northrock Resources, Unocal's largest Canadian subsidiary. He also advised the same client in its $820 million sale of Thaipo, its Thai subsidiary, to PTTEP Offshore Investment and Mitsui Oil Exploration. There was just as much admiration for "*savvy, thoughtful and careful*" **Joel Swanson** (see p.1916), whose deep corporate knowledge was of great assistance in Valero's $30 million sale of Colorado Refining to Suncor Energy, a Canadian integrated-energy company. The "*efficient go-to lawyer*" **Josh Davidson** (see p.1888) has a diverse corporate/M&A practice with specific MLP expertise. He represented LB Pacific in its $340 million acquisition of a general partner interest in Pacific Energy Partners. The seller was The Anschutz Corporation. Sources identified "*very bright*" **David Kirkland** (see p.1900) in the energy and oil field services sector. He drew praise for being "*conversant with all the technicalities of a deal*" and recently acted for GlobalSantaFe in the repurchase of 23.5 million shares of company stock from Kuwait Petroleum for $810 million in cash. Rig operator GlobalSantaFe has drilling activities in most of the world's major oil-producing regions. **Joe Poff** (see p.1910) advised the owners of Zilkha Renewable Energy in the sale of ZRE to The Goldman Sachs Group for an undisclosed amount. ZRE, now known as Horizon Wind Energy, is a wind energy development company with wind projects in development throughout the USA. Commentators appreciated the "*good business head*" of **Charles Szalkowski** (see p.1916), whose "*very good common sense*" and "*practical responses*" enhance his reputation as "*the small-company leader.*" He represents financial investors in private equity and venture capital transactions. Researchers learned of the talents of "*business-getter and deal-doer*" **Andrew Baker** (see p.1881), a lead attorney in Dallas, and "*organized and thorough*" **Ted Paris** (see p.1908), who heads the corporate practice in Houston. Working on many private placements and public offerings, Paris represents clients such as Dynegy and Marathon Oil on investment-grade debt offerings.

**Clients/Work Highlights:** Mariner Energy; Martin Midstream Partners; Pogo Producing; Energy Spectrum Partners; Valero; GlobalSantaFe; Affiliated Computer Services; Lyondell Chemical; CenterPoint Energy; Sarofim Realty Advisors; Texas Pacific Group Ventures; Evergreen Resources; Dynergy and Marathon Oil.

### Vinson & Elkins LLP

See firm details p.1938

**The Firm:** The market remains impressed by the depth of resources and spread of talent at both partner and associate level at this "*first-rate*" Texas giant. A "*good range of attorneys*" has earned statewide and nationwide admiration for their expertise in M&A, securities and capital markets. Commentators underlined the large group's particular strength in IPOs, private equity transactions and MLPs. "*Energy and Vinson & Elkins are flip sides of the same coin,*" noted one interviewee, adding that: "*They can always find a specialized attorney for complex energy deals.*" Clients thought them to be "*technically as good as anyone we know*" and able to assemble teams from a wide range of supporting disciplines.

**The Lawyers:** Department head **Mark Kelly** (see p.1900), whose practice mixes capital markets and M&A, is renowned for being "*very good with developing relationships.*" Clients admired his "*superior judgment and diplomatic approach;*" they say "*his feathers are impossible to ruffle.*" Kelly's "*focus on the important issues*" has come to the fore on deals such as Seabulk International's $1 billion acquisition by SEACOR Holdings. Described as an "*exquisite counselor,*" **Michael Wortley** (see p.1919) earned plaudits as "*one of the most knowledgeable corporate M&A attorneys around.*" Of particular note is his "*ability to identify a problem before it arises*" and his "*great analytical skills;*" clients like the fact that his availability is never a problem and peers admire his knack of "*resolving issues in minutes.*" Wortley represented LifeCare Holdings in its sale to an affiliate of The Carlyle Group for approximately $550 million. The strong corporate generalist **Scott Wulfe** (see p.1920) utilizes his "*creativity and nonconfrontational style*" in private equity and M&A transactions, where his "*proactive attitude*" always "*gets it right for clients.*" He was part of the team that represented Targa Resources in its acquisition of Dynegy's midstream natural gas business for $2.3 billion. There was ample praise too for **Alan Bogdanow** (see p.1883), who has been spending significant time on M&A transactions in the energy industry, and making his debut in the table is "*practical and technical*" **Jeff Chapman** (see p.1885), whose reputation owes much to his "*attention to detail and responsiveness.*" Chapman represented Republic Companies Group in its $84 million IPO of six million common shares. Sources say **Bill Finnegan** (see p.1890) is "*just great;*" they like the way he combines broad expertise with a special understanding of MLPs. He represented

Sunoco Logistics Partners in its $104 million offering of common units, where he represented limited partner interests. **Michael Harrington** (see p.1895) undertakes significant corporate finance and M&A transactions and is especially talented in the high-yield debt area. "*He is the most thorough individual I ever met,*" noted one client of this "*direct*" attorney. One of his latest deals involved the debt aspects of the takeover of GulfTerra Energy Partners by client Enterprise Products Partners in a deal valued at $14 billion. Finally among the Baker Botts A-listers, "*great client skill*" is the calling card of up-and-coming **David Oelman** (see p.1908), who represented The Shaw Group in its $274 million offering of common stock.

**Clients/Work Highlights:** Riverstone Holdings; EDS; Blockbuster; Hicks, Muse, Tate & Furst; Goldman Sachs; Crow Holdings; Pioneer Natural Resources; SCF Partners; Forest Oil; Occidental Petroleum; Complete Energy Holdings; LifeCare Holdings; Targa Resources; U.S. Shipping Partners; Seaspan Corporation and Lehman Brothers.

## Band 2

### Andrews Kurth LLP
See firm details p.1921

**The Firm:** Market leaders would not hesitate to work with this excellent, established, full-service firm. Its "*continued and consistent development of its corporate expertise*" rests on more than 100 years of history in the state and around 100 corporate and securities attorneys. The Houston-born outfit with three other offices in the state, three others nationally and outposts in London and Beijing, enjoys an "*excellent energy presence, practice and background,*" although its transactional prowess extends to many other industry sectors. In July 2005, the Dallas office welcomed Dudley Murrey from Hughes & Luce LLP, where he headed up the corporate practice.

**The Lawyers:** At the forefront of this practice are "*pragmatic*" **Bob Jewell** and "*solution-driven*" **Michael O'Leary**, both trusted to deliver results and capable of inspiring client confidence. Commentators admired the "*always professional*" Jewell for his "*get-the-transaction-done approach.*" His corporate and securities practice sees him acting for issuers and underwriters in public and private offerings of equity and debt securities. O'Leary, meanwhile, represents public and private companies as well as investment banks; his financing transactions include public offerings and private placements of equity and debt. He played a significant role in representing El Paso in the acquisition of a privately held exploration and production acquisition in east Texas for approximately $179 million

**Clients/Work Highlights:** Public and private companies, investment banks, REITs and private equity houses comprise the clientele.

### Fulbright & Jaworski L.L.P.
See firm details p.1928

**The Firm:** Fulbright & Jaworski has a corporate,

securities and transactions group numbering around 80 lawyers in Texas, and together they "*meet and exceed client expectations,*" according to those who use them. The clients range from startups to large multinationals, and use the firm on all manner of corporate transactions, not least M&A and IPOs. For example, in 2005 the team acted for Clear Channel Communication, the global outdoor advertising giant, in its equity carve-out IPO of its worldwide outdoor advertising business.

**The Lawyers:** Admired for his "*practical and quality advice,*" the "*sage and wise*" joint partner in charge of the Houston office, **Michael Conlon** (see p.1886), goes about transactions in a "*quietly effective*" way. Clients admired his "*superb integrity, cost effectiveness and responsiveness.*" His general corporate practice involves the representation of a number of publicly held corporations on securities offerings, disclosure issues, corporate governance, M&A and borrowing, and last year he advised Pulse EFT Association in connection with its merger with a subsidiary of Morgan Stanley, a deal valued at more than $300 million. The former head of the firmwide corporate department, **Hank Still** (see p.1915) "*knows the law and can explain it clearly.*" He advises on corporate finance and securities and has been involved in the acquisition of US Oncology by Welsh, Carson, Anderson & Stowe, and the disposal by Stewart & Stevenson Services of its engineered products division. Dallas partner **William McCormack** (see p.1904) earned commendations for his advice to clients on domestic and international M&A, divestitures and financings. He has represented a leading NYSE food and beverage company in more than $10 billion-worth of transactions, including a $2.6 billion acquisition of a food company in a stock and cash deal.

**Clients/Work Highlights:** Freebird Partners; Grant Prideco; Luby's; Oyo Geospace; Simmons & Company International and Stewart & Stevenson Services.

### Weil, Gotshal & Manges LLP
See firm details p.1565

**The Firm:** Although the heart of this international giant lies in New York, there is a strong pulse in Texas. Here, the Dallas office shows itself to be "*particularly well attuned to both the legal and business issues,*" with "*deep corporate and M&A knowledge*" permeating the team. An "*impressive team of acquisition finance attorneys*" operates in conjunction with the NY office and, unsurprisingly, it also scooped plaudits for its high-quality private equity work. "*They don't just tell you what the law is, they give you practical advice,*" noted clients.

**The Lawyers:** Described as "*an efficient and effective class act,*" the managing partner of the Dallas office, **Glenn West** (see p.1918), is "*a gifted jack-of-all-trades.*" Having opened the office almost 20 years ago, he now has diverse corporate experience including significant private equity matters; for example, he was instrumental in Koch Industries' $1.3 billion sale of its natural gas liquids business to ONEOK, and Hicks, Muse, Tate & Furst's purchase of Swett &

Crawford from Aon Corporation. Commentators admired the "*low-key yet can-do approach*" of **Scott Cohen** (see p.1886), who enjoys a reputation among clients as "*a no-nonsense and creative type with a strong grasp of the legal issues.*" Regarded as "*one of the most technical attorneys around,*" he has a practice encompassing both M&A and securities. He acted for Viasystems Group throughout its acquisition program, its IPO and its prepackaged bankruptcy structuring. He has also served as principal M&A attorney for Texas Instruments for over ten years. Market acclaim, too, for **Gilbert Friedlander** (see p.1891), formerly general counsel with EDS. He is renowned for his corporate governance and compliance expertise. **Jeffrey Hitt** (see p.1897) centers his practice on private equity and fund formation work, with debt and equity finance also key. **Mary Korby** (see p.1900), meanwhile, is a good choice for high-profile M&A; "*awfully good at tough acquisition-related issues,*" she has lately been representing ENSR International in its sale to AECOM, and Invensys in the $150 million sale to Schneider Electric of its advanced building systems operations in Europe and the Middle East. **Michael Saslaw** (see p.1913) is a worthy inclusion in the table. His diverse work is characterized by "*a consensus-building and nonconfrontational approach.*" This "*bright and energetic*" lawyer has been advising 7-Eleven in connection with the $1.2 billion going-private tender offer launched by Seven-Eleven Japan. Completing the roll-call is "*one of the best M&A attorneys,*" **Jay Tabor** (see p.1916), who represented Great Lakes Chemical in its merger with Crompton Corporation. The combined entity became Chemtura, the world's largest plastics additives company.

**Clients/Work Highlights:** American Airlines; Koch Industries; Greyhound Lines; Hicks, Muse, Tate & Furst; Ewing Management Group; Crestview Capital Funds; Lindsay Goldberg & Bessemer; GE; Activant Solutions; Texas Instruments; Southwest Sports Group (owner of the Texas Rangers and the Dallas Stars); Home Interiors & Gifts and NextMedia Group.

## Band 3

### Akin Gump Strauss Hauer & Feld LLP
See firm details p.559

**The Firm:** Although commentators emphasized the firm's strength in DC and New York, this "*well-connected*" international operation enjoys a "*seamless cooperation between multiple offices,*" considerable trans-industry experience and a growing pool of resources in the Texas market. Securities and M&A are among the corporate transactions offered by an 80-lawyer group. The October 2005 arrival of Barry Greenberg to the Dallas office adds weight to an impressive investment funds practice. He served as vice president at American Beacon Advisors.

**The Lawyers:** Devoted to the full range of energy transactions is "*smart, bright and energetic*" **Chris Lafollette** (see p.1901), whose 25-plus years of experience and expertise in project development, M&A

and compliance stand her in good stead. She advised Bill Barrett Corporation, a Denver-headquartered energy company, in its $375 million IPO. There was also acclaim for table newcomer **Michael Dillard** (see p.1888), who *"leads corporate charges from the front."* This experienced Dallas heavyweight has been advising Kerr-McGee in its agreement to sell all of its interest in oil and natural gas properties on the Gulf of Mexico shelf for approximately $1.3 billion in cash, closure of the transaction being expected in the first half of 2006.

Clients/Work Highlights: Anadarko; Ashford Hospitality Trust; Bill Barrett Corporation; Bronco Drilling; Caris; Comsys Holding; Dynegy; Friedman Billings Ramsey; Ocean Rig ASA; Petroleum Helicopters (PHI) and Alliance Data Systems.

## Bracewell & Giuliani LLP
See firm details p.1924

The Firm: Considered by many to have one of the best banking and finance practices in the state, this 60-year-old Houston-headquartered firm offers *"a sound team"* of corporate and M&A attorneys from its four Texas offices. Serving *"an enviable client list,"* especially in the regional and middle market, the group inspires confidence in others, who say it does *"a reliable and safe job"* and ensures that clients are always *"well cared for."* Possessing a strong energy base, the firm was often mentioned alongside Kinder Morgan, one of its key clients.

The Lawyers: Sources described *"seasoned corporate veteran"* **Edgar Marston** (see p.1903) as *"wonderfully bright and experienced"* and *"a real pistol."* With 40 years of deals behind him, he acted for Goodman Global Holdings in its acquisition by an affiliate of the Apollo Management private equity group for approximately $1.4 billion. He has also been representing Norsk Hydro in its purchase of Spinnaker Exploration for approximately $2.4 billion.

Clients/Work Highlights: Time Warner; Kinder Morgan Energy Partners; San Antonio Spurs; Reliant Energy; Goodman Global Holdings; Bechtel; AKQA; Valero and Bank of America.

## Gardere Wynne Sewell LLP
See firm details p.1931

The Firm: Rooted in Dallas, this corporate team is staffed by some 75 high-caliber attorneys with *"a strong reputation in the midmarket."* Having grown up as a corporate securities firm, it earned particularly warm praise for its corporate governance, SEC, private equity and general securities advice to major investment groups. From three Texas offices, the latest one having opened in Austin in 2002, attorneys frequently serve as outside counsel to respected middle-market clients.

The Lawyers: More than 30 years' experience of corporate, securities and M&A transactions lead **Larry Schoenbrun** (see p.1913) to be referred to as *"one of the corporate deans."* A *"professional but personal"* attorney, he *"commands the respect of the local business community,"* and his *"incredible smartness and practicality"* undoubtedly help transactions go smoothly. Interviewees considered him one of the

top public-company attorneys in Dallas; as a case in point, he represented Charlesbank Capital Partners and an investor group in the $400 million sale of Regency Gas Services to an affiliate of Hicks, Muse, Tate & Furst. He also acted for the stockholders of Minyard Food Stores, a 72-store supermarket chain, in the auction of the company to an investor group.

Clients/Work Highlights: The firm represents various Fortune 500 clients in matters across Texas and beyond.

## Gibson, Dunn & Crutcher LLP
See firm details p.328

The Firm: The impressive resources offered by a large national firm, a sound local M&A practice, and the ability to tap into the expertise of *"former SEC gurus"* in DC make this firm a growing force in Texas. A *"small and talented"* group of around 14 attorneys brings expertise in complex federal securities matters, and has been busy with a good number of financings and M&A transactions, many referred from other offices in the network. The firm's capabilities in private equity and corporate governance matters are clearly not underestimated by competitors.

The Lawyers: Clients admired the *"thorough and technically excellent"* **Irwin Sentilles** (see p.1913) for his *"thinking outside the box and anticipation of problems."* He has significant experience in securities, M&A, capital markets and corporate governance, and acted in the secondary offering of Halliburton stock for the DII trust and additional debt offerings for DR Horton. Sentilles also represented Atmos Energy in its $1.9 billion acquisition of the operations of TXU Gas and related public debt and equity financings.

Clients/Work Highlights: Del Monte Foods; JPMorgan Chase; Atmos Energy; National Petcare and Union Pacific.

## Haynes and Boone LLP

The Firm: *"A large local presence and a robust standing in the community"* ensure this firm's position in the table. There are around 65 attorneys in the corporate practice, covering M&A, asset dispositions, recapitalizations and reorganizations of public and private companies. The firm has earned recognition for its advice to venture capital businesses, and is also developing an active hedge funds practice.

The Lawyers: There was widespread respect for the firm's founder **Michael Boone**, considered by the market to be *"a terrific public M&A attorney"* and *"a very experienced all-round senior corporate attorney"* who *"knows and does all the right things."* He acted for Texas Genco Holdings Special Board Committee in an auction process resulting in its $2.8 billion acquisition by a group of private funds.

Clients/Work Highlights: Callon Petroleum; Harken Energy; Landry's Restaurants; Prudential Securities; RadioShack and Trilogy.

## Jones Day
See firm details p.570

The Firm: Traditionally seen carrying out national work from its Texas offices, this major international player is *"trying to make a local run,"* according to commentators. Its reputation lies in corporate and M&A work, for which it fields around 40 *"very solid attorneys."* *"They do an excellent job in corporate and securities,"* clients pointed out, adding that their knowledge of corporate governance issues was also excellent. The lawyers are thought to benefit from a *"broad base of skills which many local players do not have."*

The Lawyers: Co-heading the Dallas office is the *"highly talented, responsive and technical"* **Mark Betzen** (see p.1882), who, after 20 years in practice, has become known for his *"good conceptual and commercial view."* He is advising Albertsons, one of the world's largest food and drug retailers, in its $17.4 billion acquisition by a consortium of investors.

Clients/Work Highlights: The team advised JC Penney Company in the sale of its Eckerd drug store operations to the Jean Coutu Group and CVS for $4.5 billion. Other clients include Alderwoods Group; BP; Bay Harbour Management; CenterPoint Energy; Foster's Brewing Group; JC Penney Company; Kaiser Aluminum; Morgan Stanley Real Estate Funds; SKM Growth Investors (now called Parallel Investment Partners) and The Shansby Group (now called TSG Consumer Partners).

## King & Spalding LLP
See firm details p.1938

The Firm: This Atlanta-headquartered firm has begun to reenergize its corporate practice following some lateral moves to Akin Gump Strauss Hauer & Feld in June 2004. Its reputation in energy projects and transactions and a strong Latin America practice ensure that the firm remains visible in the Texas marketplace. A lateral hire in project finance has added to the strength of the Houston office, while a team of 26 attorneys has been active in the oil and gas sector.

The Lawyers: Bill Parish and Carlos Treistman are key points of contact in the corporate team, which has handled a number of transactions in 2005. For example, in July the team closed Arcapita Bank's acquisition of Houston-based Falcon Gas Storage from Energy Spectrum Partners, a Dallas-based private equity firm.

Clients/Work Highlights: UPS; Coca-Cola; Shell Oil; GE; Arcapita Bank; AMB Property; Friedman Billings Ramsey and Seabord Corporation.

## Mayer, Brown, Rowe & Maw LLP
See firm details p.876

The Firm: International colossus Mayer Brown joins the corporate tables in Texas this year. Traditionally a banking finance player in this part of the country, its Houston team has certainly been working to capture greater market share and raise its profile in the corporate, securities and M&A market. Last year, the team represented Precision Drilling in the sale of its energy services and international contract drilling divisions to Weatherford International of Houston.

**The Lawyers:** Clients admired "*excellent,*" ex-Fulbright & Jaworski attorney **Bob Gray** (see p.1894), not least because, after almost 30 years working on corporate, securities and M&A matters, he is vastly experienced. Highlighted was his "*ability to explain legalese to business people in a straightforward and modest way*" and his "*constant and reliable input and advice to boards and committees.*"

**Clients/Work Highlights:** The team acted for Bindview Development, a regulatory and compliance-software company, in its $209 million acquisition by Symantec. Precision Drilling is another key client.

## Thompson & Knight LLP
See firm details p.1936

**The Firm:** Said to be "*a great tradition in Dallas,*" this respected Texas firm with overseas offices and a valued client base earns a place in the rankings. It maintains a great name for capital formation, IPOs and private placements of debt and equity securities. Highlighting its M&A expertise, the team acted for Magnum Hunter Resources in its $4.5 billion merger with Cimarex Energy.

**The Lawyers:** Fred Fulton is a key player in the team.

**Clients/Work Highlights:** The firm advises a diverse clientele made up of public and private companies, partnerships and LLPs as well as insurance companies, financial institutions and investment advisers.

## Other Notable Practitioners
Clients admired the "*good, solid, friendly and efficient*" **Charles Harrell** (see p.1895) of Duane Morris LLP for his "*knowledge and understanding*" of clients' businesses. The former Weil, Gotshal & Manges lawyer carries out a range of debt and equity securities offerings and corporate finance transactions, concentrating in the middle market.

# EMPLOYMENT

# MAINLY DEFENDANT

### Employment: Mainly Defendant
**Leading Firms**

1. **BAKER BOTTS LLP** *Houston*
   **VINSON & ELKINS LLP** *Houston*
2. **AKIN GUMP STRAUSS HAUER & FELD LLP** *Dallas*
   **FULBRIGHT & JAWORSKI L.L.P.** *Houston*
   **OGLETREE, DEAKINS** *Houston*
3. **HAYNES AND BOONE LLP** *Dallas*
   **JENKENS & GILCHRIST PC** *Dallas*
   **LITTLER MENDELSON, PC** *Dallas*
4. **BAKER & HOSTETLER LLP** *Houston*
   **BRACEWELL & GIULIANI LLP** *Houston*
   **HUGHES & LUCE LLP** *Dallas*
   **JONES DAY** *Dallas*
   **KEMP SMITH LLP** *El Paso*
   **LOCKE LIDDELL & SAPP LLP** *Dallas*
   **NEEL, HOOPER & BANES, P.C.** *Houston*

## Band 1

## Baker Botts LLP
See firm details p.1922

**The Firm:** The depth of experience and "*dogged enthusiasm*" of this large bench combine to ensure the front-running position of this Texas stalwart. Clients were full of praise for the team's "*emphasis on responsiveness and strategy*" resulting in an "*impressive work product.*" While remaining highly active in the areas of wage and hour collective actions, the team also advises employers on trade secret/employment issues and the more exotic ERISA and benefits cases.

**The Lawyers:** Commentators underlined the "*natural-born instincts*" of **Richard Brann** (see p.1884), whose "*ton of high-profile trial work, tactfulness and around 30 years' experience,*" set him apart as "*one of the deans of employment law*" in the state. Peers praised his representation of clients as if they were "*the only client in the world.*" He secured a summary judgment for Omega Protein on the employment claims of a former executive, who sued after his termination for poor work performance. He

had alleged age discrimination and a violation of ERISA. There was widespread praise for the "*academic, creative and effective*" **Tony Rosenstein** (see p.1912), whose "*statistical knowledge and sensitivity*" and "*assertive but not aggressive style*" benefited clients in a wide range of cases, earning recognition especially for employment-related collective and class actions across the USA. He was instrumental in getting the class action certification denied for the Federal Deposit Insurance Corporation (FDIC) where former employees alleged a decade-long scheme of age discrimination. The "*fast-rising*" **Teresa Valderrama** (see p.1917) has been involved in employment cases where there has been an intersection of statutes, including race discrimination cases with FLSA issues, where she is considered a leader. She was also noted for her experience of traditional labor and arbitrations. She won summary judgment for Goodyear on claims asserted by three current and former employees who were seeking overtime wages under the FLSA. There was respect for **Dan Hartsfield** (see p.1896), who chairs the Dallas labor and employment practice and boasts significant experience in traditional labor, employment discrimination and wrongful discharge litigation. Entering the tables is **Chapman Smith** (see p.1914), whose "*direct and tough approach*" and "*respected trial skills*" fitted well with his union-focused practice. He counts Reliant Energy as one of his key clients.

**Clients/Work Highlights:** FDIC; Goodyear; Omega Protein; Reliant Energy; Continental Airlines; Exxon Mobil Corporation and Hines Interests.

## Vinson & Elkins LLP
See firm details p.1938

**The Firm:** This Texas giant boasts a "*terrific pool of smart and experienced attorneys*" and has a reputation among clients for its "*first-rate accessibility, thoroughness and accountability.*" Peers too admired the breadth and scope of the employment group of this national and state player, whose expertise includes race, age and gender-related class actions alongside a traditional labor practice. The group's involvement in the BP explosion case in Texas City is evidence of its recognized and fast-growing OSHA expertise.

**The Lawyers:** The well-respected labor and employment team can draw on the strengths of two of the state's most seasoned and experienced attorneys, its own joint heads of department. The "*excellent*" **Doug Hamel** (see p.1895) garnered praise for his expertise in difficult collective bargaining issues and executive employment matters, as well as general labor and union-related advice. He is also renowned for his handling of large exposure and class action litigation. For example, he has defended an oil field equipment manufacturing company in cross-appeals from a trial judgment in a 1000-member class action race discrimination case. There was national recognition for the "*brilliant, impressive and aggressive*" **Carl Jordan** (see p.1899), who earned praise for his "*effective strategy*", "*quality leadership*" and his expertise in major complex employment class action, FLSA and ERISA-related litigation. He has defended age discrimination claims, including class action claims, for a consulting and software firm which serviced the energy industry. The redundancies of 25 individuals were made as part of a global restructuring. He has also been acting for a national chemical manufacturer in connection with adverse determinations by the EEOC of class-based gender discrimination. Commendations came in for **Christopher Bacon** (see p.1881), whose growing reputation builds on trial experience gained at the public defender's office. He was instrumental in obtaining summary judgment for Norwegian Cruise Line after five former passengers alleged that NCL had discriminated against them because of their disabilities. **Tom Wilson** (see p.1919) is a new entry in the tables whose "*impressive listening abilities*" marry with his specialized skills and level of expertise to ensure his understanding of his clients' needs.

**Clients/Work Highlights:** Abitibi-Consolidated; Amerada Hess; BP; Dell; Grupo Bimbo; Halliburton; Koch Industries; NCI Building Systems; Norwegian Cruise Line; Plains All American Pipeline; Rhodia; Shell and Swift & Company.

## Band 2

### Akin Gump Strauss Hauer & Feld LLP
See firm details p.559

**The Firm:** *"The willingness to go the extra mile"* delighted clients of this legal giant, which enjoys an elevated position in the rankings this year. Thirty-six attorneys operate in Texas, where the group has a *"tremendous"* presence in Dallas. In addition to FLSA litigation, this respected team has a strong reputation in defending employers against large collective and class actions, including national origin and ADA allegations.

**The Lawyers:** Chairing both the Texas and Califor-

nia labor and employment sections at the firm, **Laura Franze** (see p.1891) enjoys a *"wonderful reputation,"* based on her depth of knowledge and her *"immediate responsiveness."* Clients praised former chair **John Jansonius** (see p.1898), a *"bright and creative writer,"* for having *"all the tools a lawyer should have."* Involved in significant ERISA litigation and wrongful discharge disputes, the *"highly reliable"* attorney gained acknowledgment for his noncompete expertise. The *"very direct and straightforward"* litigator **Holly Williamson** (see p.1919) drew praise from clients for her *"methodical, organized and thorough approach."* Although having a recognized forte in sexual harassment cases, her practice runs the full gamut of employment litigation. She recently defended Anadarko in sex and age discrimination and retaliation claims made by female plaintiffs after Anadarko's recruitment of crew members to operate a platform in the Gulf of Mexico. Commentators appreciated the *"high intellect and quieter manner"* of **Fraser McAlpine** (see p.1904), who handles highly sensitive executive compensation issues. He deals with disputes between executives and directors over employment contract and stock option agreements.

**Clients/Work Highlights:** In January 2005 the firm's Dallas attorneys secured the affirmation of a defense judgment for Tyco Electronics in two lawsuits brought by the Communications Workers of America (CWA), concerning plant closure benefits. In the same month, the team also secured an arbitration award in Washington, DC for AT&T in a labor arbitration case also brought by the CWA. Other clients include Cinemark USA, Valero Energy and UPS.

### Fulbright & Jaworski L.L.P.
See firm details p.1928

**The Firm:** *"Watch this expanding group,"* advised a number of commentators on this much-admired firm, which earns its elevated position in the tables for a sound traditional labor base and a recognized litigation capacity. The team of 30 attorneys in its four Texas offices includes newcomers like Bill Finegan, who moved from Haynes and Boone in late 2005. The firm's defense of management in a wide variety of employment disputes builds on its 80 years of labor and employment experience and an active trial reputation.

**The Lawyers:** Sources identified the *"creativity, experience and lateral thinking"* of the *"top-notch"* **Brian Greig** (see p.1894), who manages the Austin group and is considered *"one of the best in the city."* Well known in legal circles for his union prevention work, he has also been advising in Silicon Laboratories' theft of trade secrets and patent case in the US District Court for the Western District of Texas. Many observers viewed the seasoned practice head **A J Harper** (see p.1895), a long-standing and much-admired player, to be increasingly selective in the cases he takes on. Clients have benefited from his quick grasp and in-depth understanding of complex issues. With arbitrations a core part of his recent workload, he handled an arbitration for Western Union concerning the issue of actual disability for a

long-term disability plan. He also secured summary judgment for TransWestern Publishing against plaintiff claims of ADA and intentional infliction of emotional distress. Considered a frontrunner in the state for traditional labor and employment is the *"approachable and practical"* **Philip Pfeiffer** (see p.1910). Running the San Antonio office occupies a significant amount of his time but this *"first-rate"* practitioner is also involved in the mediation and arbitration of employment disputes. Clients appreciated *"his business knowledge, commercial astuteness and responsiveness."* *"A good handling of clients"* and *"a nurturing manner"* assist **Carter Crow**'s (see p.1887) growing reputation in a wide range of litigation and arbitration matters. Co-chair of the firm's unfair competition practice group, his more general practice includes executive contract and compensation disputes, retaliation and discrimination claims, and the protection of trade secrets. He also advises clients on the Sarbanes-Oxley Act, including retaliation claims and a wide variety of corporate investigations.

**Clients/Work Highlights:** Dell; Motorola; AMD; Freescale Semiconductor; Silicon Laboratories; National Western Life Insurance and Titus Electrical Contracting.

### Ogletree, Deakins, Nash, Smoak & Stewart, PC
See firm details p.738

**The Firm:** Market observers cited the *"talented attorneys and high level of consistency"* as key reasons for the lofty position of this specialist boutique. The ability to call on its national resources is deemed invaluable to its four Texas offices, where more than 40 attorneys have been active in the litigation and arbitration of a range of employment disputes. These include retaliation, discrimination, harassment and wage and hour collective actions. With an additional focus on labor issues, the team has been advising employers on preventive measures and union avoidance campaigns. The firm developed a presence in Kansas and Missouri during 2005.

**The Lawyers:** Clients enjoyed working with the *"hands-on and creative"* **Jeff Londa** (see p.1902), who drew plaudits for his *"natural ability to relate well to clients"* and to *"cut through the fluff to get to the real issues."* He has served as chief negotiator for Houston's Metropolitan Transit Authority (Metro) in labor negotiations with the Transport Workers Union. A precedent-setting agreement was reached in July 2005. He is also currently engaged in labor negotiations for StarTran with the Amalgamated Transit Union. StarTran is the transit system operator for Capital Metro in Austin. Peers admire the strong practice of **Tom Melo** (see p.1905), formerly of Bracewell & Giuliani, due to his *"broad range of capabilities"* and ability to apply *"the right touch to handle unions."* Interviewees were forthcoming in their praise for the *"deeply knowledgeable"* **Michael Fox** (see p.1891), described as *"a real scholar, always up to date on key legal issues."* He impressed peers and clients alike with his *"great business sense"* and *"presence before juries"*, as well as an increasingly national practice following his arrival at the firm a couple of years ago. A popular choice with clients who praised her *"thoroughness"*, **Ethel Johnson** (see p.1898) enters the tables this year. **Bryant McFall** (see p.1905) gained recognition for the *"very strong counseling skills"* he employs in his up-and-coming litigation practice. He has recently tried and achieved a no-liability jury verdict in a multiple plaintiff sexual harassment case in Dallas, where he also manages the office.

**Clients/Work Highlights:** Metropolitan Transit Authority of Harris County; Capital Metropolitan Transit Authority; Washington Mutual; ARAMARK; SavaSeniorCare; Tokyo Electron; Dell; Mariner healthcare; Tyco International; CVS; Wyndham and Sanderson Farms.

## Band 3

### Haynes and Boone LLP

**The Firm:** The rapid growth of this Dallas-born firm has not escaped the attention of the market. Almost 20 lawyers enjoy a diverse labor and employment practice, including a specialty in unfair competition and noncompete agreements, and they have been busy in FLSA collective actions. Following Bill Finegan's move to Fulbright, Jon Wilson heads the firm's traditional labor practice, which has solid experience in defeating union drives. For example, the team acted for Ben E. Keith Company in successfully resisting a union drive by the Teamsters.

**The Lawyers:** The market admired the *"knowledgeable, talented and trusted"* senior litigator **Bill Strock**, who has been handling several affirmative action compliance reviews by the OFCCP. His litigation docket has also been active: he has, for example, successfully defended a large national technology employer in a contractual dispute with a former president of one of its subsidiaries. **Laura O'Donnell**'s practice emphasizes her experience in the defense of sexual harassment lawsuits as well as workers' compensation retaliatory claims and government investigations. For example, she acted for a national specialty maintenance contractor in 2005 in the company's compliance with immigration laws and hiring of undocumented workers. She also obtained summary judgment in a case against a major financial institution alleging reverse race discrimination for failure to promote and retaliation for reporting race discrimination.

**Clients/Work Highlights:** Bank of America; Hanson Building Products North America; Dynegy and American Airlines feature in the firm's clientele.

### Jenkens & Gilchrist PC

**The Firm:** At around 20 lawyers, this *"strong regional player"* with its *"stable of academic attorneys"* benefits from experience in the traditional labor and employment domains, with a particular knowledge of employment benefit class actions. The group defended WorldCom in a nationwide class action where the plaintiffs alleged a denial of benefits due to a policy change regarding absenteeism. The

Federal Court for the Southern District of Texas granted summary judgment on all counts and denied class certification.

**The Lawyers:** Leaning towards employment litigation, **Bob Sheeder** also counsels employers on union avoidance issues, especially in the hotel and healthcare industries. The team has also been involved in handling a series of individual and collective actions, which have challenged the large reduction in force by a media company in Texas.

**Clients/Work Highlights:** MCI; Vought Aircraft Industries; PwC; Belo and CompuCom Systems.

### Littler Mendelson, PC
See firm details p.333

**The Firm:** The market considers this 40-strong and *"highly capable legal outfit"* to be a key player in the field and *"one of the better boutiques in Houston."* Clients always feel *"kept in the loop on legal updates and changes"* in the employment field. Particular strength in the coastal offices and the firm's national scope compensate for some attrition from the Houston and Dallas offices. Moreover, the clear focus on employment means *"there is little the firm has not done"* and the group has developed expertise in specific areas including OSHA, noncompete and employment discrimination.

**The Lawyers:** The market offered nothing but praise for the *"talented and bright"* **Linda Headley** (see p.1896). Considered to be one of the elite women attorneys, she can offer clients a diverse range of litigation and counseling experience, with a special forte in sexual harassment defense cases. Commentators spoke highly of the *"aggressive, sharp and extremely knowledgeable"* **Steven McCown** (see p.1904), whose practice has afforded him an impressive OSHA and high-stakes litigation expertise. Considered by some clients to be a *"great first port of call for quick questions,"* he also commanded the respect of the judiciary. Managing the Dallas office is the *"very talented and impressive"* **Scott McDonald** (see p.1905), who is a *"master at unfair competition issues."* While the market admired this niche expertise, he also earned praise for his experience of high-level executive wrongful termination.

**Clients/Work Highlights:** The firm acts for a diverse range of clients in their employment needs.

## Band 4

### Baker & Hostetler LLP

**The Firm:** This 90-year-old national firm offers up a respected Houston employment team of 11 attorneys, who act for management in a range of matters, including employment litigation, class actions and collective bargaining agreements. The group has handled negotiations with significant unions including the Teamsters, machinists, autoworkers and Service Employees International Union (SEIU), the latter increasingly active in Texas in recent years.

**The Lawyers:** There was significant positive feedback on the *"tenacious and highly reliable"* **Nancy Patterson**. Described as *"one of the most consummate

*trial attorneys in this field,"* she earned praise for her success in complex employment litigation cases.

**Clients/Work Highlights:** Bayer; Case Credit; Chevron; Fisher Scientific International; Hitachi Construction Machinery and Shell.

### Bracewell & Giuliani LLP
See firm details p.1924

**The Firm:** This team of around 30 experienced attorneys drew admiration from commentators and was considered *"the right fit for the right employment case."* The firm is beefing up its existing employment counseling and litigation expertise following the departure of Tom Melo to Ogletree Deakins. The group commands respect for its representation of public and private employers in certain industry sectors including airline, transportation and oil and gas.

**The Lawyers:** There was confident market feedback that the *"extremely pleasant and very capable"* **Amy Halevy** (see p.1895) will do a fine job of *"steadying the ship."* Drawing acclaim for her *"responsiveness and client focus,"* she heads the practice section and leads by example. With a national and diverse practice, she was successful in obtaining the dismissal of an FLSA collective action before certification for a US subsidiary of an international company. She also acted successfully for a national retail chain in a two-party race discrimination case dismissed in the Federal Court.

**Clients/Work Highlights:** Schlumberger; Hanover Compressor; Target; SYSCO Corporation; Adventist Health System; San Antonio Spurs; Levi Strauss and Southwest Airlines.

### Hughes & Luce LLP

**The Firm:** A track record in employment and a range of employment expertise push this 32-year-old Dallas-born law firm into the rankings. A *"small but respected"* employment group of 11 attorneys advises employers on all aspects of the employer-employee relationship from its three Texas offices. The former Austin mayor and respected litigator Kirk Watson joined the Austin office as a partner in August 2005, while key hires have bolstered the Fort Worth office.

**The Lawyers:** Employment discrimination and retaliation cases feature in the diverse docket of **Mark Shank**, a key player at the firm. Typically he acts for management and executives in disputes and transactions involving executive compensation and related issues. He obtained summary judgment in a multimillion-dollar gender discrimination claim for a national brokerage firm and has handled numerous internal investigations, involving alleged wrongful conduct by employees and former employees.

**Clients/Work Highlights:** The firm acts for a range of corporate clients in labor and employment issues.

### Jones Day
See firm details p.570

**The Firm:** Eleven of the firm's 15 employment attorneys in Texas operate from Dallas although the firm acts as a single unit nationally. Both the Dallas and Houston offices have been an instrumental part of the national handling of FLSA collective action litigation for JPMorgan Chase and Verizon Wireless. For JPMorgan, the case involved allegations that employees at call centers nationwide had performed off-the-clock work. Both cases involve company-wide, nationwide challenges involving over 20,000 employees.

**The Lawyers:** The reputation of the Houston office is closely connected with the "*absolutely consummate professionalism*" of **Ted Meyer** (see p.1906), who according to clients offers them "*unquestionable knowledge*" on local, state and federal employment issues. This former Seyfarth Shaw managing partner has been advising clients on employment issues in the homebuilding, technology and energy sectors.

**Clients/Work Highlights:** JPMorgan Chase and Verizon Wireless are among a long list of clients.

## Kemp Smith LLP

**The Firm:** This El Paso leader's five employment attorneys are considered to be the "*first and foremost*" in the region. The team boasts diverse experience in retaliation, wrongful discharge and discrimination claims as well as wage and hour violations. The team is "*unafraid of taking cases to trial*" and has recently successfully defended PJS in Fondren v PJS of El Paso in an action for breach of an employment contract filed by a former employee of PJS.

**The Lawyers:** The most senior lawyer is the "*excellent, very smart*" **Charlie High**, whom some commentators believed to be "*vastly underrated.*" With considerable trial experience, he offers clients expertise in union avoidance, alongside traditional employment discrimination litigation and OSHA advice.

**Clients/Work Highlights:** IMC Potash Carlsbad; 3M; The Toro Company; Border Steel; dmDickason Personnel Services; Western Refining and Pizza Properties.

## Locke Liddell & Sapp LLP

**The Firm:** Across three of the firm's five Texas offices is a team of 22 attorneys, whose "*aggressive litigation culture*" earned respect for "*delivering results.*" The team's experience of a range of employment litigation includes specialties such as unfair competition, OSHA and ADA cases and a breadth of knowledge in dealing with unions.

**The Lawyers:** Clients appreciated the "*fantastic expertise*" of the "*precise and personable*" **Ed Friedman** in noncompete disputes across the USA. He successfully defended the general counsel of a Fortune 100 company in an action filed by the former associate general counsel of the company alleging breach of legal ethics, sexual harassment and constructive termination. There was respect for the "*very courteous*" **Larry McNamara**, who garnered client praise for his "*presentation and analytical skills*" as well as his "*overall professionalism.*" His ability to "*drill down to the key issues*" was particularly useful in a practice that covers a range of litigation.

**Clients/Work Highlights:** neopost; Goodrich; Greyhound Lines; Sally Beauty; Mary Kay; Microsoft; Vetco Gray; Disney; Acme Brick; Wyndham; Southern Methodist University; Capital One; Guidant; Ernst & Young and ABB Lummus Global.

## Neel, Hooper & Banes, P.C.

See firm details p.1935

**The Firm:** This "*small, lean and old-line*" five-lawyer team was widely acknowledged by the Houston market as having considerable experience in all aspects of traditional labor law. Although the firm's expertise is heavily weighted towards contract negotiations and arbitration agreements, the team also adopted a "*very solid approach*" to employment and Title VII litigation. Commentators had faith that clients' cases would be treated "*soundly and competently.*"

**The Lawyers:** Researchers learned of the admiration for the experience of **Sam Hooper** (see p.1897), who has been undertaking contract negotiations for a significant printing company as well as unfair labor challenges and Title VII cases for a number of

employers. The "*fearless, quick and intellectually driven*" **Jim Neel** (see p.1907) is especially talented in contract negotiations and pure labor work. He has been advising the same printing company, with offices across the USA, on day-to-day employment issues.

**Clients/Work Highlights:** amco Insurance Group, FedEx Kinko's and Texas Petrochemicals are among the clients.

## Other Notable Practitioners

Interviewees admired **Hershell Barnes** for his comprehensive traditional labor expertise. The former Haynes and Boone star, who had spent 20 years directing the employment section of the regional firm, now runs his own boutique, The Barnes Law Firm PC. Focusing on union prevention, he has been negotiating three different sets of contracts for employers who are already unionized. "*The strong advocate*" **Stephen Fink** (see p.1890) at Thompson & Knight LLP joins the rankings and is well thought of as an "*excellent trial attorney,*" who has been "*around the block*" in labor and employment issues. Commentators admired his ability to "*build consensus among the parties.*" The "*bright and moderately aggressive*" **Ron Manthey** (see p.1903) of Baker & McKenzie drew praise for his class action and employment litigation practice. He defended Sabre in a gender discrimination case and BHP Billiton in an age discrimination case. The "*very knowledgeable and tough*" **Neil Martin** (see p.1903) of Gardere Wynne Sewell LLP joins the tables for his impressive handling of management's labor and employment issues. Interviewees described him as "*master at witness examination and forensics*" and an expert in noncompete and traditional labor advice. Ford & Harrison LLP's **Mike Maslanka** (see p.1904) retains his place in the rankings for his "*high level of commerciality*" and "*conciliatory approach.*" Having opened the Atlanta firm's Texas office in January 2005, he is aiming to build up the employment team, which boasts expertise in the airline and healthcare sectors.

# ENERGY & NATURAL RESOURCES

## Band 1

### Baker Botts LLP

See firm details p.1922

**The Firm:** Riding high on the firm's resurgent international profile, this group cruises into the top tier on the strength of its "*extraordinary capabilities.*" The breadth and depth of the Houston team is "*hard to match,*" and commentators do not begrudge success to an outfit that displays such "*extraordinary commitment*" to this sector: it is particularly renowned for upstream oil and gas work, and continues its involvement in "*cutting-edge*" LNG deals. The team advises prominent clients on corporate, commercial, regulatory, litigation and, of course, project finance issues. Headline deals of late include counseling Hallibur-

ton in its divestiture of exploration and production assets in Indonesia and Bangladesh. CenterPoint Energy employed the team's power sector talents in the sale of Texas Genco. Attorneys also recently represented major clients ExxonMobil and Anadarko on property divestitures.

**The Lawyers:** The "*erudite*" **David Asmus** (see p.1881) is a globally recognized name in this sector. Clients extol his "*affable style*" and knack for relating legal issues to a commercial context. **George Goolsby** (see p.1893) heads the Russia practice and is rated for his knowledge of emerging markets. He is "*the one you want for any pipeline matter,*" say clients. The versatile **Michael Darden** (see p.1888) is "*a thoroughly dependable lawyer,*" say clients, and can turn his hand to anything.

**Clients/Work Highlights:** The team advised Marathon Oil and GEPetrol in the sale of equity interests in Equatorial Guinea. Other clients include BP; Pogo Producing; Energy Spectrum Partners; Valero Energy; GlobalSantaFe; LB Pacific; Enterprise Products Operating; Evergreen Resources and AES.

### Vinson & Elkins LLP

See firm details p.1938

**The Firm:** This firm is "*a force to be reckoned with,*" offering a large team of specialists with an industry reputation that is simply unsurpassed anywhere in the world. Clients are drawn by the team's long reach and "*legal dexterity,*" and above all by its sheer versatility: there is not an area of energy law in which it does not excel. In line with market developments, it

## Energy & Natural Resources
### Leading Firms

1. **BAKER BOTTS LLP** *Houston*
   **VINSON & ELKINS LLP** *Houston*
2. **FULBRIGHT & JAWORSKI L.L.P.** *Houston*
3. **AKIN GUMP STRAUSS HAUER & FELD LLP** *Houston*
   **KING & SPALDING LLP** *Houston*
4. **ANDREWS KURTH LLP** *Houston*
   **BRACEWELL & GIULIANI LLP** *Houston*
   **SKADDEN, ARPS** *Houston*
5. **LOCKE LIDDELL & SAPP LLP** *Dallas*
   **THOMPSON & KNIGHT LLP** *Dallas*

### Leading Individuals

★ **DILG Joseph** *Vinson & Elkins LLP*
1. **ASMUS David** *Baker Botts LLP*
   **BILGER Bruce** *Vinson & Elkins LLP*
   **COGAN JR John** *Akin Gump*
2. **ALE John** *Skadden, Arps*
   **CULOTTA Ken** *King & Spalding LLP*
   **GOOLSBY George** *Baker Botts LLP*
   **KUTZSCHBACH George** *Fulbright & Jaworski L.L.P.*
   **WEEMS Philip** *King & Spalding LLP*
3. **KELLEY Jay** *Vinson & Elkins LLP*
   **UNGER Timothy** *Andrews Kurth LLP*
4. **BACKUS Marcia** *Vinson & Elkins LLP*
   **BLAND Douglas** *Vinson & Elkins LLP*
   **GITOMER Deborah** *Fulbright & Jaworski L.L.P.*
   **GREMILLION L Todd** *Akin Gump*
   **IRVIN Michael** *Fulbright & Jaworski L.L.P.*
   **LANGLOIS Jack** *Akin Gump*
   **RAFTE Alan** *Bracewell & Giuliani LLP*
   **THURBER Mark** *Andrews Kurth LLP*
5. **CUCLIS James** *Vinson & Elkins LLP*
   **DARDEN Michael** *Baker Botts LLP*
   **MOORE Thomas** *LeBoeuf, Lamb*
   **PATTON David** *Locke Liddell & Sapp LLP*
   **ROGERS Daniel** *King & Spalding LLP*
   **THOMPSON Dahl** *Andrews Kurth LLP*

### Up-and-coming individuals
**STEPHENS Robert** *Bracewell & Giuliani LLP*

offers deep LNG and renewables expertise as well as oil and gas; there is also a strong projects practice acting for sponsors. Clients report top-shelf M&A, regulatory and corporate services, and an admired niche in MLPs. Houston is the undoubted hub of the firm's energy offering, with powerful finance-focused input from New York and regulatory input from DC. The team acted for BP Pipelines (Alaska) in various regulatory proceedings connected with the Trans Alaska Pipeline System (TAPS). It advised Occidental Petroleum and Statoil on various oil and gas production acquisitions of late. The firm also acts for a healthy finance clientele, and recently represented Goldman Sachs in its purchase of wind power generation facilities across North America. **The Lawyers:** Managing partner **Joseph Dilg** (see p.1888) is the dynamic and visionary engine of the

team, according to sources: "*If anyone can keep the firm moving forward, it's him.*" His practice consists mainly of providing strategic advice to clients. **Bruce Bilger** (see p.1883) is one of the most respected transactional lawyers in the market, and clients report: "*He knows how to get deals done and that's what we look for.*" **Jay Kelley** (see p.1900) brings "*incredible experience and strategic understanding of the deal process*" to the table. He is credited with spearheading the firm's phenomenal foray into the LNG market. **Marcia Backus** (see p.1881) has a strong M&A background and "*the right mix of diplomacy and aggression,*" say sources. **Douglas Bland** (see p.1883) attracts high praise, with sources avowing: "*There are very few true energy experts, and he is one of them.*" The internationally active **James Cuclis** (see p.1887) "*has tremendous understanding of not just the legal, but the financial and political elements of a deal,*" according to clients.
**Clients/Work Highlights:** JPMorgan Chase; The Blackstone Group; Entergy-Koch; Reliant Energy; BG Group; Chevron Phillips Chemical; WestLB; AES; PSEG Global; Bank of Nova Scotia; Bonus Energy; AIG; El Paso and Shell.

## Band 2

### Fulbright & Jaworski L.L.P.
See firm details p.1928

**The Firm:** This team is a byword for oil and gas expertise, particularly upstream, and clients confirm that the lawyers are "*beyond technically proficient: their understanding of the industry and the commercial environment is second to none.*" The group offers first-rate corporate and M&A services, which keep anchor clients returning for advice on acquisitions and divestitures. It also specializes in deepwater exploration, which is a real draw according to clients. Recently the team represented Anadarko in its $1.312 billion disposition of oil and gas properties in the Gulf of Mexico. Another highlight for the team was advising Kaneb in its $2.8 billion merger with Valero Energy.
**The Lawyers:** **George Kutzschbach** (see p.1901) is an expert in oil and gas drilling and exploration contracts, and clients aver: "*He is our go-to guy – down to earth and solves issues quickly.*" **Deborah Gitomer** (see p.1893) attracts praise for her "*professionalism and common sense.*" She recently represented Enbridge in its $613 million acquisition from Shell of offshore gas pipeline interests in the Gulf of Mexico. Clients "*can't speak highly enough of*" **Michael Irvin** (see p.1898), who advises on transactions across the business, from upstream to downstream: he is "*sharp, always available and knows the business.*"
**Clients/Work Highlights:** BG Group; Blackstone Capital Partners; AEP; Calpine; Magnum Hunter Resources; Crown Central Petroleum; Petro-Canada; El Paso; Sempra Energy; Total; Forest Oil; Cabot Oil & Gas; EOG Resources and TEPPCO Partners.

## Band 3

### Akin Gump Strauss Hauer & Feld LLP
See firm details p.559

**The Firm:** The attorneys here serve clients in key global markets across the oil and gas, electricity and nuclear industries. The team has seen action in the Middle East, Latin America, Asia, Australia and Europe, and has handled a number of deals in Russia. Domestically, highlights have included handling the $900 million sale of El Paso's nonregulated midstream assets. For Anadarko, attorneys recently advised on credit facility financings and LNG developments. The group is sharpening its focus on the LNG sector, and it acted for Repsol in its recent acquisition and development of interests in the Camisea gas fields.
**The Lawyers:** The "*internationally accomplished*" **John Cogan** (see p.1886) is widely acknowledged to be a key player in LNG. **Todd Gremillion** (see p.1894) focuses on oil and gas industry clients. He is adept at domestic and overseas transactions, particularly acquisitions and financings. Energy projects specialist **Jack Langlois** (see p.1901) also acts for domestic and international players in oil and gas, including LNG.
**Clients/Work Highlights:** Dynegy and Targa Resources are significant clients of the group.

### King & Spalding LLP
See firm details p.1938

**The Firm:** This firm has established a dominant position in the LNG markets. Sources point to the attorneys' comprehensive knowledge of all facets of the LNG industry, including shipping, receiving terminals and foreign production developments. LNG project companies figure heavily in the client roster, but the firm is attracting a growing number of finance sources, too.
**The Lawyers:** Clients appreciate **Ken Culotta's** (see p.1887) "*shrewd commercial sense,*" and recommend him for his international transactions expertise. **Philip Weems** (see p.1918) focuses squarely on LNG matters, and **Daniel Rogers** (see p.1912) enters the rankings this year thanks to testimonials to his expertise in energy.
**Clients/Work Highlights:** The group represents a number of LNG project developers.

## Band 4

### Andrews Kurth LLP
See firm details p.1921

**The Firm:** According to commentators, this outfit's strong domestic oil and gas team is "*increasingly competitive.*" Attorneys also offer specialty expertise in renewable energy sources, including thermal and wind power, and have acted on five wind projects over the past year. The LNG practice is notable, too, and the team acted for Cheniere on the financing of LNG import terminals. The firm's international energy practice centers largely on Latin America. Sources have been impressed with the team's foray into the coal-to-liquid market.

**The Lawyers:** Clients agree that the attorneys know what it takes to get a deal done *"even if it means breaking the mold."* **Tim Unger** has a mainly domestic practice that is focused on complex energy transactions and project development and financing. **Mark Thurber** has a broad energy transactions practice and represents clients in the conventional and alternative energy sectors. **Dahl Thompson** advises on all aspects of energy infrastructure projects, including electricity and LNG matters.

**Clients/Work Highlights:** DrKW; Wachovia; Bank One; RBS; Duke Energy; ConocoPhillips and CapRock.

## Bracewell & Giuliani LLP

See firm details p.1924

**The Firm:** Commentators recommend this firm for its standout energy finance expertise. Attorneys assist energy companies and financial institutions in acquisitions. These recognized oil and gas specialists negotiate agreements of all types for clients in this industry as well as for electric businesses. Restructuring transactions play an increasingly central role in the firm's energy practice.

**The Lawyers:** **Alan Rafte** (see p.1911) is highly respected for his domestic M&A work in the energy sector, and his practice encompasses varied transactional matters for oil, gas and electric pipeline clients. Energy financing and contract specialist **Robert Stephens** (see p.1915) also enjoys a worthy reputation for being a player in the Texas market.

**Clients/Work Highlights:** Valero Energy; El Paso; BC Hydro; Powerex; McDermott International; Kinder Morgan; ONEOK; Bechtel; Shell Nigeria; Stone Energy and Intratex Gas.

## Skadden, Arps, Slate, Meagher & Flom LLP & Affiliates

See firm details p.1557

**The Firm:** The Houston office of this global transactional heavyweight attracts a healthy proportion of the firm's oil, gas and LNG work. Its fêted prowess in corporate transactions draws clients from around the world; the Middle East is a particularly valuable source of work. LNG acquisitions and developments form the bulk of the team's workload, but renewables are making steady headway on the deal list: the team has been involved in wind, ethanol and biomass deals recently. Clients report quality at every level of the bench, noting the *"fiercely capable senior associates"* that back up the *"highly responsive"* partners.

**The Lawyers:** Houston chief **John Ale** (see p.1880) is described as *"an amazing lawyer"* and he is especially recommended for acquisitions work.

**Clients/Work Highlights:** NRG; Wisconsin Energy; ITC Holdings; Mirant and CSFB.

## Band 5

## Locke Liddell & Sapp LLP

**The Firm:** Energy is a core practice area for this Texas and Louisiana-based firm. It handles transactions ranging from acquisitions to energy trading, acting for a clientele that includes independent and alternative energy producers. Sources extol the levels of service delivered here, noting that the lawyers *"remain focused on what the client is trying to accomplish."*

**The Lawyers:** **David Patton** is an oil and gas specialist, and regularly handles upstream and downstream transactions.

**Clients/Work Highlights:** Amerada Hess; Black Stone Minerals; BP America; Calpine; Centrica; ChevronTexaco; Comstock Resources; ConocoPhillips; Coral Energy; Devon Energy; Dynegy; El Paso; Energen Resources; Entergy; Genesis Energy; GlobalSantaFe; Kinder Morgan; Marathon Oil; Shell; Southwestern Energy and Total Exploration & Production USA.

## Thompson & Knight LLP

See firm details p.1936

**The Firm:** Restructuring, acquisitions and divestitures have put this firm on the Texas energy transactions map. With offices in Dallas and Houston, it is well placed to serve its varied clientele, which is heavy with independent oil and gas companies. The team represented several companies following Enron's bankruptcy, consolidating its reputation for restructuring within the energy sector.

**The Lawyers:** John Rain and Arthur Wright are key contacts.

**Clients/Work Highlights:** Clients include multinational, independent and host government oil and gas companies, utilities, private power plants, refineries, petrochemical companies, contractors and financial institutions.

## Other Notable Practitioners

M&A specialist **Thomas Moore** (see p.1906) of LeBoeuf, Lamb, Greene & MacRae LLP is *"the best of the bunch"* for energy transactions, according to commentators. He advised Eastern Petrochemical on the expansion of its petrochemical facilities in Saudi Arabia.

# ENERGY & NATURAL RESOURCES

| Energy & Natural Resources: Dispute Resolution Leading Firms |
|---|
| [1] FULBRIGHT & JAWORSKI L.L.P. *Houston* |
| VINSON & ELKINS LLP *Dallas* |
| [2] BAKER BOTTS LLP *Houston* |
| GIBBS & BRUNS, LLP *Houston* |
| KING & SPALDING LLP *Houston* |
| [3] BEIRNE MAYNARD & PARSONS, LLP *Houston* |
| BRACEWELL & GIULIANI LLP *Houston* |
| JONES DAY *Houston* |
| LEBOEUF, LAMB, GREENE & MACRAE LLP *Houston* |
| MCDADE FOGLER LLP *Houston* |
| SUSMAN GODFREY LLP *Houston* |

## Band 1

## Fulbright & Jaworski L.L.P.

See firm details p.1928

**The Firm:** This team offers a core of *"bright and business-focused"* litigators of great experience, backed up by an effective global network. The attorneys handle a broad and impressive caseload and *"leave no stone unturned"* in the service of upstream and downstream oil and gas enterprises and companies in the pipeline, electricity, nuclear, geothermal, coal and cogeneration sectors. Clients note that the team's deep resources make it an ideal choice for complex litigation, representing both plaintiffs and defendants in varied energy-related disputes. Recent highlights include obtaining the dismissal of a suit filed against Automated Power Exchange for alleged violations of federal and state antitrust laws. The team also successfully defended Sasol in a case filed by injured employees in New York. The distinguished international arbitration group handles disputes from all corners of the globe. It successfully represented UEG Araucária in an $875 million contract dispute with Brazil's Petrobras.

**The Lawyers:** The *"extremely clever"* **Jeff Dykes** (see p.1889) has a broad litigation practice that includes energy expertise. He is particularly recommended for pipeline work, and clients value his ability to *"bring himself up to speed on a case almost instantly."*

# DISPUTE RESOLUTION

**William Wood**'s (see p.1919) energy expertise is complemented by his experience in environmental and toxic torts. He handled a substantial litigation load arising out of the Californian energy crisis, and clients report that *"he handles a jury exceptionally well."* Commercial litigator and securities guru **Gerald Pecht** (see p.1909) attracts praise for his *"remarkable work"* in the energy sector. **John Bowman** (see p.1884) offers *"extremely detailed"* knowledge of the energy industry, and interviewees agree that *"he's done a brilliant job"* of promoting the firm's international arbitrations practice. Clients extol accomplished arbitrator **Mark Baker** (see p.1881) for his work in alternative dispute resolution.

**Clients/Work Highlights:** UEG Araucária; Enbridge, The Williams Companies and Northville Industries; the YUKOS bankruptcy case; Nigerian National Petroleum; Storm Water Joint Appeals Group; Verizon Capital; Automated Power Exchange (APX); SPA Pipe; Weatherford International and Devon Canada.

## Vinson & Elkins LLP

See firm details p.1938

**The Firm:** An avalanche of client recommendations for this "*set of superb litigators*" and regulatory experts confirms its position at the top of the table. The team is a regular feature in weighty and high-profile cases, and is especially rated for royalty cases. It is involved in complex royalty cases on behalf of US companies holding an oil concession in the Democratic Republic of Congo. On the domestic front, the team obtained a favorable settlement for BP in a class action brought by its royalty owners in Wyoming. The group is also litigating for oil companies facing similar claims in Kansas and New Mexico. The international arbitration practice here is an undoubted draw, and a team of lawyers from Houston, Washington and London recently obtained an interim

measures award of almost $200 million for El Paso companies involved in a dispute with Petrobras.

**The Lawyers:** **Harry Reasoner** (see p.1911) "*can juggle all the components of a complex case,*" report sources that add: "*He may well be the finest strategic lawyer in Texas.*" He is a veteran civil litigator with a largely appellate practice and is well known for his deep involvement in Enron litigation. **Harrell Feldt** (see p.1890) is an accomplished litigator with an exclusively oil and gas-focused practice. **David Harvin** (see p.1896) is an antitrust expert and "*really fine trial attorney.*" The "*superb*" **Phillip Dye**'s (see p.1889) caseload includes representing multinationals involved in litigation resulting from oil well blowouts and tanker explosions, as well as a series of jurisdiction cases on behalf of foreign companies sued in US courts. The "*bright and articulate*" litigator and arbitrator **Guy Lipe** (see p.1902) is praised as a man who "*remains cool under pressure.*" Domestic oil and gas specialist **Andrew McCollam** (see p.1904) has a geology background which, clients perceive, "*gives him a real advantage*" in energy matters. The firm has an impressive four regulatory specialists in the tables this year. **Henry May** (see p.1904) is a much-admired FERC specialist, and leading the work on Alaskan pipeline cases is **Bert Tabor** (see p.1916), who maintains his status as "*the dean of pipelines.*" **Charles Caldwell**'s (see p.1885) recent successes before FERC include defending Calnev Pipeline against challenges to its inflation-based rate increases. **John Kennedy**'s (see p.1900) regulatory expertise is also brought to bear in Alaskan pipeline litigation.

**Clients/Work Highlights:** Unocal; Shell; Kinder Morgan; Amerada Hess; China Oil & Gas Pipeline Bureau; BP America Production Company; Perenco; Royal Dutch Petroleum; Shell Transport and Trading; El Paso Rio Claro; FW Oil Interests; NRG Energy; Cairn Energy India; Ravva Oil Singapore; Trigeant; Devon Energy and MarkWest Energy Partners.

## Band 2

## Baker Botts LLP

See firm details p.1922

**The Firm:** This leading national firm offers deep expertise in all aspects of energy dispute resolution, and sources report it is building up both its international arbitration and domestic mediation capability. Based in Dallas and Houston, lawyers here handle oil, gas and coal disputes on behalf of industry clients including producers, processors, transporters, distributors and companies providing support services. As part of a thriving royalty practice, the firm has represented majors including Marathon Oil and Chevron in federal Qui Tam lawsuits. Exxon-Mobil is a key client, for which the firm has handled an energy trading arbitration as well as contract and regulatory disputes.

**The Lawyers:** According to sources, **Gregory Copeland** (see p.1887) demonstrates "*real mastery*" of oil and gas litigation. He also undertakes a considerable amount of mediation and arbitration. **Mark**

Robeck's (see p.1912) clients include producers, utilities and independent power generators, and he appears before an array of courts and regulatory commissions.

**Clients/Work Highlights:** API; BP; ExxonMobil; Fina; Marathon Oil; Pennzoil; Chevron; Wagner & Brown; Entergy; Texas Genco; Reliant Energy; Guardian Pipeline; Transocean and Baker Hughes.

## Gibbs & Bruns, LLP

See firm details p.1932

**The Firm:** This commercial litigation boutique is "*top notch*" for energy work, say sources, and the expertise on offer enables the firm to handle a varied caseload of disputes. Recent highlights include landing a favorable settlement on appeal for a plaintiff claiming breach of a joint venture agreement to develop cogeneration projects. The team advises on contractual matters and regularly handles oil company royalty disputes and wrongful death cases.

**The Lawyers:** **Robin Gibbs** (see p.1892) "*has a razor-sharp mind and knows the energy business inside out,*" agree commentators, and **Phillip Bruns** (see p.1885) is recognized for his handling of complex commercial litigation. Oil and gas specialist **Chris Reynolds** (see p.1911) enjoys a solid reputation as a trial attorney.

**Clients/Work Highlights:** Boyce Engineering International; The Coastal Corporation; MW Kellogg; Stone Energy; Sunrise Gas Marketing and Pennzoil.

## King & Spalding LLP

See firm details p.1938

**The Firm:** This firm offers a strong team of trial attorneys and is deemed capable of handling "*any type of energy dispute that comes their way.*" Oil and gas royalty litigation is a key strength, but the team also advises producers, refiners, contractors and service companies in disputes arising from agreements. Attorneys are perfectly at home with electricity regulatory and nuclear-related matters. Sources also single out the firm's growing international arbitration practice.

**The Lawyers:** **Robert Meadows**' (see p.1905) reputation as a leading litigator goes before him. He acts for some seriously heavyweight clients including Chevron and Halliburton. The "*first rate*" **Adam Schiffer** (see p.1913) acted for Shell in a solo arbitration regarding an investor power trading agreement. Internationally acclaimed arbitrator **Doak Bishop** (see p.1883) is described as a "*worthy advocate.*"

**Clients/Work Highlights:** Chevron; Amerada Hess; Ocean Energy; Shell; Halliburton and Exxon-Mobil.

## Band 3

## Beirne Maynard & Parsons, LLP

See firm details p.1923

**The Firm:** This litigation firm attracts clients' praise for its "*big-picture approach and excellent problem-solving skills.*" The team appears before state and federal courts across the full range of industry issues, including oil field injury cases, construction litigation, contracts, employment and IP. Interviewees commend the team's track record at securing injunctions and note the group's significant regulatory and arbitration expertise.

**The Lawyers:** Clients report that the team is "*very effective at achieving results,*" and declare the attorneys' industry knowledge to be "*almost unsurpassed.*"

**Clients/Work Highlights:** ConocoPhillips; BP; ATP Oil and Gas and Chevron Phillips Chemical.

## Bracewell & Giuliani LLP

See firm details p.1924

**The Firm:** This firm has a trial team of impressive size and stature, and attorneys handle a broad spectrum of energy disputes in the oil, gas and electricity sectors. Recent highlights include defending Kinder Morgan against claims in contract and tort by ExxonMobil relating to gas processing at the Bushton Gas Plant. The team serves a broad spectrum of clients ranging from large publicly traded companies down to small privately owned enterprises. It also engages in alternative dispute resolution and offers considerable expertise in international arbitration.

**The Lawyers:** **Clifford Gunter** (see p.1895) heads the trial group and is acclaimed as an "*outstanding*" generalist with an impressive record in energy disputes. He handles take-or-pay and pricing cases, as well as issues relating to natural gas and electricity trading.

**Clients/Work Highlights:** Kinder Morgan; BC Hydro; Valero and Bechtel.

## Jones Day

See firm details p.570

**The Firm:** The Houston outpost of this national powerhouse focuses on oil and gas disputes. The team has had notable successes in both domestic litigation and international arbitration. The team is particularly adept at handling royalty, valuation and take-or-pay matters. Recent highlights include obtaining summary judgment for Chevron USA,

thwarting a claim to cap its rent revenue for lessee gas stations in Hawaii. Pipeline issues in Alaska provide a considerable flow of work and attorneys represent Unocal and BP in numerous regulatory proceedings. The team represents oil and gas majors in disputes arising from domestic and international development projects, and is increasing its focus on the burgeoning LNG sector.

**The Lawyers:** Senior litigation partner **Tom Bayko** (see p.1882) has a formidable reputation in trials and international arbitrations. Clients value his "*excellent leadership skills.*" **Brad Keithley** (see p.1899) is recommended by his clients as a lawyer who "*can handle anything*" in the oil and gas regulatory arena. Much of his time is spent advising BP and Unocal.

**Clients/Work Highlights:** Halliburton; BP; Chevron and Unocal.

## LeBoeuf, Lamb, Greene & MacRae LLP

See firm details p.1540

**The Firm:** The litigation and arbitration expertise here is embedded within an integrated energy group that handles a broad spectrum of transactional and regulatory matters. The Houston attorneys represent clients in all sectors of the oil and natural gas industry and a number of electricity companies. The team has provided litigation and regulatory expertise to Enron.

**The Lawyers:** **Charles Moore** (see p.1906) is an adept litigator, but is best known as an expert in international energy regulation. He has decades of FERC experience under his belt, both as general counsel and in representing companies such as Enron.

**Clients/Work Highlights:** The firm represents publicly traded and independent companies across the oil and gas industry.

## McDade Fogler LLP

**The Firm:** Energy-related disputes constitute the bulk of the work handled by attorneys at this respected litigation boutique. The firm handles regu-

latory disputes on behalf of both plaintiffs and defendants. Expertise covers oil and gas royalty cases as well as contract disputes, and the team is currently handling several arbitrations relating to contractual disputes arising out of the recent hurricanes in the Southern states.

**The Lawyers:** "*Commanding all-rounder*" **Thomas McDade** undertakes complex litigation in the oil and gas market, acting for clients such as El Paso. **Murray Fogler** receives "*high marks across the board*" from commentators for his handling of energy disputes. His workload includes the defense of legal malpractice suits.

**Clients/Work Highlights:** El Paso; Transocean; Duke Energy; Ocean Energy and Osborn Oil & Gas Operations.

## Susman Godfrey LLP

**The Firm:** The "*refreshingly enthusiastic team*" at this litigation boutique handles a healthy energy workload in the oil and gas and electricity industries. Interviewees point out that the firm is lucky to have a number of younger lawyers coming through the ranks. Plaintiff representation includes oil royalties, take-or-pay and contractual matters. The firm also acts for defendants in construction and contract disputes.

**The Lawyers:** **Lee Godfrey** is a "*superb*" plaintiff's counsel, according to commentators, and "*brilliant in front of a jury.*"

**Clients/Work Highlights:** Southern Natural Gas; Unocal; Seagull Energy; El Paso Energy; Tenneco and Texas-New Mexico Power.

## Other Notable Practitioners

The "*wonderful*" **David Beck** of Beck Redden & Secrest LLP is hailed by market sources as a "*superb lawyer who can get up to speed on anything.*" **Dick Watt** of Watt Beckworth Thompson & Henneman LLP has a substantial reputation in oil and gas litigation and is best known for representing plaintiffs.

# ENVIRONMENT

## Band 1

### Baker Botts LLP

See firm details p.1922

**The Firm:** Acting for a "*formidable client base,*" this group of "*highly energized lawyers*" delivers "*consistent quality at the highest level,*" according to commentators; in short, it offers both "*mass and class.*" Attorneys have been involved in some of the most spectacular cases of 2005, and recently represented ExxonMobil in the review, permitting and authorization of three LNG terminals in onshore Texas and offshore Louisiana. The team also acted for the BCCA Appeal Group in litigation, negotiations

and advocacy regarding the requirements of the Houston/Galveston/Brazoria air quality plan under the federal CAA. It is also experienced in stormwater permitting. Another recent highlight was the representation of a global aluminum producer in federal and state claims for response actions and natural resource damages arising out of the alleged discharge of hazardous substance into a Texas bay.

**The Lawyers:** According to interviewees, **Pam Giblin** (see p.1892) "*deserves a lifetime achievement award for the extraordinary things she's done.*" She draws praise for her "*quick wit, great knowledge and incredible lobbying experience.*" She is an authority on EPA matters, and is especially recommended for air

regulation issues. **Sara Burgin** (see p.1885) is commended as "*a supreme water rights lawyer.*" Clients value her "*global perspective*" and the "*fantastic technical insight*" she offers as a trained biologist. She recently represented Texan industry in relation to stormwater matters. **Jennifer Keane** (see p.1899) "*knows her air regulation stuff inside out,*" say clients, who also praise her "*exemplary work ethic.*" She recently obtained an air permit for a major oil and gas facility and achieved a successful settlement of state air enforcement issues in west Texas. She is "*a definite rising star,*" and recognized for her work in multistate matters. Clients recommend her as a "*formidable expert*" in CWA issues. **Matthew Kuryla** (see p.1901) is described as "*a strong public speaker.*" **Derek McDonald** (see p.1905) works night and day, say clients who regard him as a strong up-and-comer. **Walter Conrad** (see p.1886) is described as a "*superb litigator with great technical virtuosity.*" He is particularly renowned for his toxic tort practice.

**Clients/Work Highlights:** ExxonMobil; CenterPoint Energy; Huntsman; Valero; BASF; Union Pacific; Halliburton and Marathon Ashland Petroleum.

## Vinson & Elkins LLP
See firm details p.1938
**The Firm:** Clients praise this group's "*high visibility and top-notch regulatory advice.*" The 24 lawyers are often found on headline-grabbing cases, and the team houses some of the most accomplished litigators in the field. It is particularly noted for its strength in the cleanup of contaminated properties, and handles all related investigation, regulatory and permitting issues. There has been a resurgence of Superfund work and lawyers have been involved in the acquisition of a number of sites across Texas. Lawyers advise the firm's long-standing energy clients, such as BP, on transactional and regulatory issues as they arise. The team has been advising on new pipeline projects and is negotiating permits for the regeneration of facilities. It recently advised a London-based energy major in relation to an explosion at one of its factories in Texas, which included the assessment of management and health and safety systems.
**The Lawyers:** **Christopher Amandes** (see p.1881) is described as "*a worldly lawyer to whom you would refer all of your most pressing business needs.*" His recent workload has been dominated by the resolution of the lawsuit that resulted from a factory explosion, with much of his time taken up by permitting matters and investigations. The "*tenacious and gutsy litigator*" **Molly Cagle** (see p.1885) stands out for her courtroom skills, especially in water rights and permitting matters. As one client observes: "*Any*

woman who wants to prove herself in Texas needs to be bold, and she most certainly is.*" **Carol Dinkins** (see p.1889) is "*competitive, engaging and dynamic in all aspects of her work,*" according to sources. She works closely with government regulators and is regarded by many as "*a real superstar.*" **Sharon Mattox** (see p.1904) is "*the best there is on wetlands matters.*" She is renowned for her litigation skills and brings "*a great deal of energy to cases.*" **Eric Groten** (see p.1894) is an expert on air law and emission matters, and is a recent arrival from Bracewell & Giuliani. Regarded as "*one of the smartest lawyers on technical issues,*" he has conducted several important proceedings for mineral extraction and smelting operators. Clients praise **Larry Nettles** (see p.1907)' "*great analytical skills and high degree of credibility.*" He also wins for his "*spectacular drafting,*" producing documents that are a model of clarity and concision. **John Howard** (see p.1897) brings "*top governmental lobbying skills and formidable political connections*" to the table.
**Clients/Work Highlights:** The firm's clientele includes major energy companies, such as Shell, and leaders in the chemical, transportation and oil businesses. The team also acts for commercial developers and investment banks.

## Bracewell & Giuliani LLP
See firm details p.1924
**The Firm:** Lawyers at this "*well-rounded environmental practice staffed with high-quality people*" focus on regulatory compliance, corporate and risk management matters. The team also handles criminal defense, enforcement and investigations work. Over the past year, it was involved in two major criminal prosecutions and has also handled several wastewater matters. Hazardous and toxic substance cases are another mainstay of the practice.
**The Lawyers:** The "*brilliantly smart*" **Tracy Hester** (see p.1896) is praised as a "*highly conscientious*" lawyer with an outstanding knowledge of hazardous waste matters. He has long-established relations with regulators and has increasingly been involved in criminal prosecutions. **Timothy Wilkins** (see p.1919) stays "*ahead of the game*" on developments in the field, and enjoys close relations with regulators. He advises companies on corporate environmental governance, management and auditing matters.
**Clients/Work Highlights:** The client base is made up of energy, refinery, chemical and technology companies, among which Chevron, Shell and Goodyear are prominent.

## Fulbright & Jaworski L.L.P.
See firm details p.1928
**The Firm:** This is one of the largest environmental practices in the state. Clients praise its highly experienced lawyers, who "*know the ropes of the business inside-out.*" The group enjoys great visibility and a reputation for quality, and clients cite its "*superb*

client services" as a significant draw. The team is experienced in litigation, permitting and approvals, enforcement actions and Superfund actions, and regularly provides environmental auditing services. Clients range from chemical and petrochemical manufacturers to refineries and pipeline facilities. The team recently acted for the Texas Independent Producers and Royalty Owners Association to challenge an EPA ruling requiring permits for small oil and gas reconstruction facilities. Lawyers also represented a large foreign oil refiner in Toxic Substances Control Act (TOSCA) matters, and acted for LS Power in obtaining raw water and reclaimed water supplies for a power plant in central Texas. Other matters in the lawyers' workload this year have included merger and insurance work, as well as offshore, emission and air pollution matters and the defense of companies accused of criminal conduct.
**The Lawyers:** **Patricia Finn Braddock** (see p.1890) receives unanimous praise for her waste management, plant permitting and tax benefit work. She regularly deals with the EPA, the DOJ, the Texas Commission on Environmental Quality and the Texas Railroad Commission, counseling clients on regulatory programs and business transactional issues. **Eva Fromm O'Brien** (see p.1891) is "*a technically impressive lawyer*" with "*great public speaking skills*" and a "*tremendous personality,*" say commentators. She handles property and toxic tort litigation, and assists firms with the environmental aspects of mergers and acquisitions and problems that arise from the management of contaminated properties. **Janet McQuaid** (see p.1905) impresses clients with her "*strategic acumen and powers of persuasion.*" She has an impressive record as a litigator in state and federal courts, and regularly handles waste management, site remediation, wastewater and stormwater management and toxic substance control and reporting matters. Newcomer **Heather Corken** (see p.1887) is a definite one-to-watch, and clients are confident that "*this highly dedicated lawyer will only get better and better with time.*" **Edward Lewis** (see p.1902) is an adroit litigator and admired for his permitting work. Clients extol his combination of "*great technical skills and a top personality.*"
**Clients/Work Highlights:** Texas Eastern Products Pipeline; Union Pacific; Goldston Oil; Dominion Exploration & Production; Alamo Cement; Solvay America; Weatherford International; Stewart & Stevenson and Duke Energy.

## Haynes and Boone LLP
**The Firm:** "*Brimming with high-quality lawyers,*" this environmental powerhouse wins acclaim for its wide-ranging practice. The group has been active on the transactional side and handled a range of property deals for developers. The lawyers have extensive experience of Superfund cases, offshore permitting and LNG matters. The group offers extensive litigation capacity, particularly in toxic tort and criminal defense. The team also obtained a favorable verdict for a client in a Superfund case.
**The Lawyers:** Commentators aver that **Jeff Civins** "*deserves a category of his own for the kind of fabulous*

| Environment |
| --- |
| Leading Individuals |

**Senior Statesman**

GOLEMON Kinnan *Brown McCarroll LLP*

★ CIVINS Jeff *Haynes and Boone LLP*

GIBLIN Pamela *Baker Botts LLP*

[1] AMANDES Christopher *Vinson & Elkins LLP*

CAGLE Molly *Vinson & Elkins LLP*

DINKINS Carol *Vinson & Elkins LLP*

DUTTON Diana *Akin Gump*

FINN BRADDOCK Patricia *Fulbright & Jaworski L.L.P.*

FROMM O'BRIEN Eva *Fulbright & Jaworski L.L.P.*

PHILLIPS Frances *Gardere Wynne Sewell*

[2] BRADDOCK James *Haynes and Boone LLP*

BURGIN Sara *Baker Botts LLP*

HESTER Tracy *Bracewell & Giuliani LLP*

MATTOX Sharon *Vinson & Elkins LLP*

MORRISS James *Thompson & Knight LLP*

RAMIREZ Kenneth *Brown McCarroll LLP*

SEALS Paul *Akin Gump*

SLAVICH John *Guida, Slavich & Flores, P.C.*

STEWART Robert *Kelly, Hart & Hallman*

[3] AXE Albert *Jenkens & Gilchrist*

BOHANNON Paul *Andrews Kurth LLP*

GROTEN Eric *Vinson & Elkins LLP*

HARRIS James *Thompson & Knight LLP*

HOPSON Keith *Brown McCarroll LLP*

MCQUAID Janet *Fulbright & Jaworski L.L.P.*

NETTLES Larry *Vinson & Elkins LLP*

PELS Gerald *Locke Liddell & Sapp LLP*

[4] BAKER Debra *Connelly Baker Wotring Jackson LLP*

COOKE Gregg *Guida, Slavich & Flores, P.C.*

FLORES Jean *Guida, Slavich & Flores, P.C.*

GOSSELINK Paul *Lloyd Gosselink*

HEAD J *Fritz, Byrne, Head & Harrison*

HOWARD JR John *Vinson & Elkins LLP*

KEANE Jennifer *Baker Botts LLP*

KURYLA Matthew *Baker Botts LLP*

ROSS Jerry *Pillsbury Winthrop Shaw Pittman LLP*

THOMAS John *Hicks, Thomas, Lillienstern LLP*

VAY John *Kelly, Hart & Hallman*

WILKINS Timothy *Bracewell & Giuliani LLP*

WORRELL Danny *Brown McCarroll LLP*

**Up-and-coming individuals**

MCDONALD Derek *Baker Botts LLP*

MENDOZA Mary *Haynes and Boone LLP*

NASI Michael *Lloyd Gosselink*

**Associates to watch**

CORKEN Heather *Fulbright & Jaworski L.L.P.*

*work he is doing.*" An expert on contaminated property cases and regulatory issues, he is recognized as "*a major force in the business, with outstanding advocacy skills and an incredible ability to communicate with expert witnesses.*" He recently represented an energy client in issues related to an offshore general discharge permit. **James Braddock** is "*firmly in the super league*" of air lawyers in the state. Sources commend his "*encyclopedic knowledge*" of the area.

Newcomer **Mary Mendoza** achieves recognition for her strong wastewater work and her "*hard-nosed attitude in transactions.*" Clients praise litigator **John Eldridge**'s "*fantastic regulatory background.*"

**Clients/Work Highlights:** BP; El Paso; Sun Refining and Marketing Company; Elk; Shell and Amerada Hess.

## Band 3

### Akin Gump Strauss Hauer & Feld LLP
See firm details p.559

**The Firm:** This is one of the most developed and well-resourced environmental practices in the state, and commentators particularly laud the team's "*superb knowledge of local government regulatory issues.*" Clients are attracted by its capacity in environmental litigation and toxic tort, and the team is making headway in transactional work for clients in the real estate and energy sectors. Lawyers recently advised Agrifos Fertilizer on the operation of a fertilizer plant located on the Houston Ship Channel, which involved siting, permitting, operation and maintenance issues. In another highlight, attorneys advised El Paso in the construction of an LNG terminal in the Gulf of Mexico, which entailed one of the first licenses issued under the Deep Water Port Act. The team also served as litigation counsel for Abitibi's paper manufacturing and recycling facilities in Texas, and counseled Lehman Brothers on the public offering of Kerr-McGee's former chemical business, Tronox.

**The Lawyers:** Sources praise **Diana Dutton** (see p.1889) for her "*incredible thoroughness*" and the "*incredible energy she puts into all of her work.*" Hers is a first-rate regulatory practice, and she recently advised Agrifos Fertilizer on one of its fertilizer operations in Texas. The "*exceptionally talented*" **Paul Seals** (see p.1913) impresses clients with his "*practical interpretation*" of their needs. He acted as environmental regulatory and litigation counsel for Abitibi's manufacturing and recycling facilities in Texas.

**Clients/Work Highlights:** Novartis; Abitibi-Consolidated; Texas Association of Dairymen; Western Refining Company; CITGO Petroleum and Enterprise Products.

### Brown McCarroll LLP

**The Firm:** This Austin-based outfit is commended for its "*thoughtful negotiators.*" After a period of losses, it has recently attracted market attention with a number of high-profile lateral hires, and the arrival of Ken Ramirez from Bracewell & Giuliani is seen as a welcome boost. The firm plays an active role in environmental legislation matters and lawyers regularly represent clients before the Texas legislature, the US Congress and various Texas municipalities. It also has a strong tradition of representing clients in permitting and compliance matters. Increasingly, lawyers are called on to handle issues associated with the acquisition or sale of property and construction facilities. The firm offers a vibrant litigation practice

and lawyers frequently appear before administrative agencies.

**The Lawyers:** Newly arrived from Bracewell & Giuliani, **Ken Ramirez** is described as "*an outstanding lawyer with some of the best connections in the state.*" He is "*a born rainmaker*" and particularly well versed in water rights issues. He currently serves on the EPA's federal advisory committee concerned with the USA's border with Mexico. **Keith Hopson** is a "*bright and energetic*" attorney with wide-ranging expertise in environmental law. His practice includes Superfund, litigation, permitting and auditing. **Danny Worrell** focuses on permitting and enforcement matters, and advises on Superfund and regulatory compliance issues involving hazardous and municipal waste. **Kinnan Golemon** is "*a key player*" who brings "*unmatched experience*" to the table. Though less active these days, he still represents clients in matters involving federal, state and local regulation of air pollutants, wastewater discharges and hazardous substance spills.

**Clients/Work Highlights:** Shell; Devon Energy; DuPont; Gulf Coast Waste Disposal Authority; Texas Chemical Council and Serco.

### Connelly Baker Wotring Jackson LLP

**The Firm:** This relatively new boutique has achieved "*fantastic growth*" and has assembled a bevy of "*top-tier lawyers who have made quite an impact on the market.*" The firm has a particularly active Superfund workload and regularly investigates contamination issues and coordinates regulatory requirements. The team includes polished litigators and defends companies on issues such as contaminated waterways.

**The Lawyers:** **Debra Baker** has a long and "*exemplary track record*" in Superfund recovery cases. Litigator **Michael Connelly** possesses "*all the skills it takes in the courtroom,*" according to sources. Newcomer **Dan Vineyard** enjoys a strong reputation as a litigator, and has made a name for himself in multiparty actions.

**Clients/Work Highlights:** The client roster includes Chevron, Union Pacific and Arco/Lyondell. The firm also represents a number of municipal authorities such as the Port of Texas City.

### Guida, Slavich & Flores, P.C.

**The Firm:** This traditional and effective boutique fields "*capable and skilled lawyers*" on environmental transactions throughout the state. Advising the refinery industry on permitting for new environmental plants is a mainstay of the practice. The team has been busy advising Kimco Realty on the redevelopment of a 42-acre site into a mixed-use development including condominium, office and retail facilities. It has also advised clients on environmental cleanups and municipal setting designations, and was involved in a high-profile brownfield development in Dallas.

**The Lawyers:** Practice head **John Slavich** is admired for taking on "*cases that others are afraid to touch.*" He advises on both transactional and regulatory matters, and was the key figure on the Kimco Realty deal. **Gregg Cooke** is portrayed as "*a confident* *player who is completely at ease with major environmental agencies."* Newcomer **Jean Flores** catches commentators' eyes with his *"energetic approach and strategic thinking."* In the words of one source: *"You will never see him take a stupid position."*

**Clients/Work Highlights:** International and local developers, financial institutions, industrial enterprises and commercial and retail businesses.

## Kelly, Hart & Hallman, A Professional Corporation

**The Firm:** This *"small but high-quality"* boutique is firmly in the spotlight for its multifaceted environmental and administrative law practice. The team offers environmental litigation, compliance counseling and transactional advice, and the Austin office is dedicated to regulatory issues. The substantial clientele includes large chemical companies, and attorneys are well versed in trying enforcement cases. The team represents clients in judicial challenges to agency decisions and rulemakings in courts all the way up to the Supreme Court of Texas.

**The Lawyers:** **Robert Stewart** is an *"old and trusted hand,"* and especially recommended for his Superfund work. He has extensive experience in white-collar proceedings and is an accomplished court performer. Practice head **John Vay** is *"one of the best-kept secrets in the state,"* according to sources. With a background at the Texas Water Commission, he has extensive experience dealing with regulatory bodies. **Susan Zachos** is recognized as *"a very sharp lawyer with a superb knowledge of waste contamination issues."*

**Clients/Work Highlights:** Bridgestone/Firestone; XTO Energy; Kawasaki and GM.

## Thompson & Knight LLP

See firm details p.1936

**The Firm:** This sizable team handles enforcement work and advises clients on the development of compliance policies. Lawyers offer niche expertise in sustainable energy projects and projects related to

the protection of rare species and wildlife in the USA, including creating safe harbors for endangered species.

**The Lawyers:** Clients commend **James Morriss'** (see p.1907) *"strong advocacy skills mixed with a detail-orientated approach."* His work includes permitting, compliance counseling and administrative and judicial litigation. Acknowledging **James Harris** (see p.1895) as *"one of the pioneers"* of environmental law, sources *"would put him right up there for his ability to handle regulatory as well as litigious matters."* **Scott Deatherage** (see p.1888) has an excellent reputation in air emissions, wastewater and hazardous waste litigation.

**Clients/Work Highlights:** The firm's clientele consists of steel, cement, refining, petrochemical, building materials and quarrying companies. The team also provides regular advice to public agencies and ecological funds.

## Band 4

## Fritz, Byrne, Head & Harrison

**The Firm:** This Austin-based team handles an impressive volume of environmental transactions, given its comparatively modest size. Lawyers act for defendants as well as plaintiffs, and are respected for their innovative work. Recent highlights include the representation of an applicant for a new municipal landfill, and advising another client on a new renewable hazardous waste permit. The team is experienced in compliance issues and regularly works on water rights and municipal solid waste matters.

**The Lawyers:** Group chief **JD Head** is *"highly efficient and always dynamic."* His practice includes enforcement work and he is recommended for groundwater rights issues: he regularly defends water supply clients in court.

**Clients/Work Highlights:** The clientele includes insurance companies, financial institutions, government bodies, commercial entities and healthcare organizations.

## Hicks, Thomas, Lillienstern LLP

**The Firm:** This compact group's clients describe it as *"the best environmental boutique one could possibly imagine."* The team is particularly recommended for contamination issues, and lawyers are praised for being *"not only superb in court but also knowing how to deal properly with government bodies."* Formed as a spin-off from Andrews Kurth in 1997, the team now houses 18 lawyers focused on environmental litigation. In City of Modesto v Dow Chemical, attorneys obtained a pretrial ruling that the City of Modesto could not recover the costs of the remediation of soil and groundwater.

**The Lawyers:** **John Thomas** is described as an *"exceptional litigator – aggressive, diligent and vigorous."* He recently argued on behalf of clients before the Texas Supreme Court.

**Clients/Work Highlights:** RR Street; Gulf States Laundry Machinery; SUEZ Energy Generation; Reichhold and a number of chemical industry

clients.

## Jenkens & Gilchrist

**The Firm:** Observers praise this firm's busy Austin office for its expertise in solid waste and landfill matters. The group combines its environmental practice with an administrative advocacy law practice. Lawyers regularly handle compliance issues and defend clients against claims in court. They are also experienced in Superfund issues. Other specialties include advising on air and water quality matters, environmental audits, hazardous waste generation, toxic substances and criminal investigations.

**The Lawyers:** **Albert Axe** does *"great work – consistently,"* and regularly advises on regulatory and transactional matters.

**Clients/Work Highlights:** The clientele includes clients from the mining, chemical, electronic, paper and forestry industries.

## Lloyd Gosselink Blevins Rochelle & Townsend, P.C.

**The Firm:** Sources recommend this boutique for its *"superior regulatory practice"* and its frequent representation of government entities. The lawyers also advise public utilities and regularly undertake construction-related litigation work. Other focal points of the team are administrative and municipal law, and attorneys represent a variety of coalmines, coal-fired electric power plants and steel mills. The team provides permitting, enforcement defense and compliance counseling services in the areas of municipal and industrial hazardous and nonhazardous solid waste management, disposal and remediation.

**The Lawyers:** **Paul Gosselink** is *"one of the most rigorous lawyers we have ever come across,"* say clients. He is expert in waste and landfill matters, and experienced in air permitting issues. Sources regard *"highly dynamic"* **Michael Nasi** as the spearhead of *"the next generation of leaders."* He advises clients on all areas of air quality, waste permitting, remediation and surface mining.

**Clients/Work Highlights:** Manufacturing companies, municipal governments, utilities, and mining entities and developers are all clients.

## Locke Liddell & Sapp LLP

**The Firm:** This firm is home to *"some of the most skilled negotiators in town"* and is renowned for private party litigation, risk management and compliance issues. Two projects have dominated the workload over the past year. Firstly, lawyers represented two entities seeking to recover costs associated with the cleanup of 13 chemical facilities around the country. Secondly, the team represented MI Drilling Fluids against real estate developers in a case concerning a contaminated site in Houston. The lawyers regularly work on redevelopment issues with the EPA.

**The Lawyers:** **Gerry Pels** possesses a *"great business sense."* Speaking of his litigation skills, admiring peers admit: *"You just pray you don't get him opposite you."* His practice increasingly involves private party litigation.

**Clients/Work Highlights:** Nabors Industries; Cypress Real Estate Advisors; Riviana Foods; Tyco International and various regulators.

## Pillsbury Winthrop Shaw Pittman LLP

See firm details p.1550

**The Firm:** Clients come to this *"first-rate environmental litigation practice"* for its *"particularly strongly regulatory counseling."* The good-sized team has been involved in a number of significant environmental litigation cases over the past year, including ongoing representation of Chevron in administrative proceedings and litigation regarding soil and groundwater contamination at refineries and petrochemical facilities in five states. In another matter, attorneys secured a no-liability determination from the EPA on behalf of Avista with respect to sediment contamination at its Noxon Rapids Hydroelectric Project in Montana. The team regularly represents national and international clients in international,

federal and state environmental regulatory matters. **The Lawyers:** Lead partner **Jerry Ross** (see p.1912) *"inspires confidence,"* and clients declare him *"extremely quick, with a great understanding of state business and federal laws."* He is representing Chevron in administrative proceedings and groundwater contamination lawsuits.

## Other Notable Practitioners

The *"highly skilled and multifaceted"* **Paul Bohannon** of Andrews Kurth LLP is strongly endorsed by clients for his Superfund work, especially in relation to chemical and pipeline companies. He also regularly handles environmental litigation and contested regulatory matters with a particular focus on groundwater, surface water and sediment issues. *"Formidable litigator"* **Jim Smith** (see p.1914) of Beirne Maynard & Parsons LLP is recommended for his *"stellar Superfund work."* Gardere Wynne Sewell LLP's **Frances Phillips** is described as *"one of the best envi-*

*ronmental lawyers one could wish for,"* and is endorsed for her transactional work and inside knowledge of the workings of the EPA. Her stable mate, **Richard Faulk** (see p.1890), is a respected litigator with a long track record before appellate courts. **Tom Fennell** (see p.1890) of Jones Day's Dallas office is commended for his *"outstanding court demeanor and laid-back style with clients."* He has been involved in a number of class actions involving port and public nuisance claims, and has been advising industrial clients on global warming issues. **Tracie Renfroe** (see p.1911) has recently joined King & Spalding LLP from Bracewell & Giuliani. She is dedicated to litigation and served a large clientele in the chemical and refining industries at her previous firm. Commentators portray her as *"a careful and analytical lawyer"* who is good at sifting through evidence and is *"always well prepared in court."*

# HEALTHCARE

## Healthcare
### Leading Firms

1 **FULBRIGHT & JAWORSKI L.L.P.** *Houston*
  **VINSON & ELKINS LLP** *Houston*

2 **BROWN MCCARROLL LLP** *Austin*
  **DAVIS & WILKERSON, PC** *Austin*

3 **BAKER & MCKENZIE** *Dallas*
  **HAYNES AND BOONE LLP** *Dallas*
  **JACKSON WALKER LLP** *Dallas*
  **JENKENS & GILCHRIST** *Houston*
  **STRASBURGER & PRICE LLP** *Dallas*

## Band 1

## Fulbright & Jaworski L.L.P.

See firm details p.1928

**The Firm:** This firm is the clients' choice for *"superb breadth and depth of experience"* in representing healthcare providers. The practice splits into three divisions: litigation, transactional and regulatory, the latter based in DC. Lawyers handle volumes of nursing home litigation as well as the defense of medical malpractice and professional liability cases. Praising the transactional practice, clients appreciate the team's ability to *"close complex deals on good terms."* Joint ventures between physicians and hospitals remain popular, and the team offers compliance advice on federal and state Medicare and Medicaid regulations. The firm has received increased instructions from pharmaceutical and medical device manufacturers, especially with regard to new drug applications and protecting the IP rights of providers and medical schools.

**The Lawyers:** **Jerry Bell** (see p.1882) impresses clients with his *"common-sense solutions"* to diverse

health law issues. Recent work includes representing Baylor College of Medicine in a dispute and in mediation before the Texas attorney general. **Tony Patterson**'s (see p.1909) practice centers on business and operational matters and commentators particularly admire his regulatory expertise. He acted recently for hospitals and healthcare systems in physician/hospital joint ventures. The *"personable and responsive"* **Yvonne Puig** (see p.1910) has represented hospital systems, manufacturers and retailers of medical devices in various litigation matters, and her regulatory work includes credentialing and Emergency Medical Treatment and Active Labor Act (EMTALA) issues. **Terry Tottenham** (see p.1917) is regarded as *"incredibly bright and down to earth,"* and he takes on healthcare litigation in both state and federal courts.

**Clients/Work Highlights:** Baylor College of Medicine; Memorial Hermann Baptist Beaumont Hospital; Seton Medical Center; Scott & White Healthcare System and CHRISTUS Health.

## Vinson & Elkins LLP

See firm details p.1938

**The Firm:** Clients turn to this 79-strong national healthcare team for its *"consummate capability"* in regulatory matters, investigations and transactions. It complements this with services in litigation and labor law. Clients hold that its Medicare and Medicaid reimbursement practice is *"impeccable,"* and lawyers recently represented a medical school in a Medicare Part B administrative hearing on overpayments. On the transactional side, the team advises on joint ventures for profit-making and nonprofit organizations and represents clients on the acquisition and disposal of hospitals. Attorneys also offer peer review and staff credentialing services. Drug litiga-

tion volumes are up, and the group has attracted high-profile instructions from Wyeth and represented Purdue Pharma in all its OxyContin litigation in Texas. Attorneys offer IP advice to healthcare clients in relation to patent prosecutions and trade secrets.

**The Lawyers:** Practice co-head **Gary Eiland** (see p.1889) is *"second to none"* in the field and specializes in defending clients against false claims and investigations. He offers unrivaled expertise in Medicare and Medicaid compliance and reimbursement matters. Recent highlights include preparing a request before the Office of Inspector General (OIG) for the donation of a building to a medical school. **Dennis Dunn** (see p.1889) is recommended for his transactional work and recently completed the merger of the operations of one hospital into a healthcare system. He also advises on joint ventures between hospitals, surgery centers and diagnostic imaging centers. **Debbi Johnstone** (see p.1899) is *"a real problem solver"* with both transactional and regulatory expertise. She recently advised on a joint venture between a multihospital nonprofit system and a profit-making oncologist to form a radiation therapy center. **Brenda Strama** (see p.1915) is commended for her *"strong management skills."* She is expert in operational and regulatory matters such as peer reviews, medical staff credentialing, surveys and certification. Recent work includes advising organ procurement organizations. **J D Epstein** (see p.1889) co-heads the practice and has been involved recently in the reorganization of troubled hospitals and in advising clients on compliance matters.

**Clients/Work Highlights:** The Methodist Hospital (Houston); University of Texas, Parkland Memorial Hospital; MD Anderson Cancer Center and University of Oklahoma.

| Healthcare |
| --- |
| Leading Individuals |
| **Senior Statesman** |
| EPSTEIN Jon *Vinson & Elkins LLP* |
| [1] BELL Jerry *Fulbright & Jaworski L.L.P.* |
| EILAND Gary *Vinson & Elkins LLP* |
| [2] DARLING William *Strasburger & Price LLP* |
| DUNN Dennis *Vinson & Elkins LLP* |
| ELTING Kimberley *Jones Day* |
| FOUST Lawrence *Jenkens & Gilchrist* |
| GORDON R Kenneth *Baker & McKenzie* |
| HILGERS David *Brown McCarroll LLP* |
| JOHNSTONE Debbi *Vinson & Elkins LLP* |
| MORRISON Edgar *Jackson Walker LLP* |
| PATTERSON JR J *Fulbright & Jaworski LLP* |
| PUIG Yvonne *Fulbright & Jaworski L.L.P.* |
| REED Kevin *Davis & Wilkerson, PC* |
| STRAMA Brenda *Vinson & Elkins LLP* |
| TOTTENHAM Terry *Fulbright & Jaworski L.L.P.* |
| WOOD Ivan *Strasburger & Price LLP* |
| **Up-and-coming individuals** |
| BROWN Fletcher *Davis & Wilkerson, PC* |
| **Associates to watch** |
| GERACI Joseph *Brown McCarroll LLP* |

## Band 2

### Brown McCarroll LLP

**The Firm:** Clients beat a path to this practice's door because of its "*professionalism and ethics.*" A dedicated team of 19 lawyers offers a comprehensive range of services to providers including hospitals, managed care organizations, long-term care facilities and government entities. Recent highlights include physician joint ventures and other organizational and transactional matters. Reimbursement and regulatory issues regarding long-term care and assisted living provide a steady flow of instructions. The firm also handles litigation, such as, disputes between physicians and health plans, and has an active lobbying arm.

**The Lawyers:** "*Visionary thinker*" **David Hilgers** has an excellent track record defending physicians in complex cases. Clients appreciate his thoroughness and organizational abilities. He recently represented a physician-owned hospital following attacks from health plans and competitors. Observers will be watching **Joe Geraci**'s career with great interest; he specializes in managed care and reimbursement.

**Clients/Work Highlights:** Clients include hospitals and healthcare providers.

### Davis & Wilkerson, PC

**The Firm:** This team has a solid reputation for its work with community and regional hospitals. The practice covers the main areas of transactions, regulations, litigation (including medical malpractice)

and general advice. Sources flag up the team's experience in medical staff credentialing, forming managed care networks and advising on retirement and congregate housing matters. The firm is general counsel to several rural hospital and clinic associations and also represents a large nonprofit retirement center.

**The Lawyers:** **Kevin Reed** wins fans with his ability to assimilate information quickly and "*translate legalese into sense.*" Sources commend his clear and balanced opinions on senior living issues and medical staff relations. He handles both contentious and noncontentious matters. **Fletcher Brown** acts for government boards and hospitals and impresses clients with his "*attention to detail and smart approach.*" His portfolio includes fraud and abuse, hospital contracts and medical staff matters.

**Clients/Work Highlights:** Texas Organization of Rural & Community Hospitals; Hospital Based Rural Health Clinic Association of Texas; RCH Protect; Westminster Manor and more than 60 individual hospitals.

## Band 3

### Baker & McKenzie

See firm details p.866

**The Firm:** This is part of a nationwide practice that spans transactions, regulatory and compliance work, litigation and IP matters. The team has seen an increase in investigations into alleged fraud and abuse and in managing and responding to government subpoenas. It continues to uphold its fine reputation in the medical and pharmaceutical devices arena.

**The Lawyers:** Dallas-based **Ken Gordon** (see p.1893) heads the firm's sizable North American health law group. Clients value his "*ability to address potential obstacles before they become problematic.*" He recently handled the financing of a hospital construction project and various hospital acquisitions.

**Clients/Work Highlights:** Novation; HCA; Triad Hospitals; VHA Southwest; Schering-Plough and Abbott Laboratories.

### Haynes and Boone LLP

**The Firm:** Best known for representing healthcare clients in business transactions such as financings, acquisitions and joint ventures, this practice also offers regulatory, compliance and operational advice. Commentators also recommend the stellar healthcare litigation practice here. The client base includes healthcare systems, hospitals, nursing homes and research facilities.

**Clients/Work Highlights:** HCA; Memorial Hermann Healthcare System; Southwest Physician Associates; Tenet HealthSystem Medical; Triad Hospitals and Hospice Austin.

### Jackson Walker LLP

**The Firm:** This group of "*personable and efficient attorneys*" provides advice to a range of healthcare clients on transactions, Health Insurance Portability and Accountability Act (HIPAA) issues, litigation, regulation and compliance. Attorneys are also experienced in administrative and operational matters.

**The Lawyers:** **Jed Morrison** delivers regulatory and transactional advice, and also handles fraud, abuse and managed care matters.

### Jenkens & Gilchrist

**The Firm:** The clients of this comparatively compact group range from emerging enterprises to large healthcare providers. Lawyers offer expertise in compliance and regulatory matters, HIPAA and transaction finance, and regularly deal with managed care litigation. The group also advises on contracts and employment issues. It recently acted for a healthcare provider in the sale of a nursing home system.

**The Lawyers:** "*Managed care guru*" **Lawrence Foust** is noted for his skilled negotiations with insurance companies. An experienced player in M&A, he deals with a variety of complex cases for hospital systems, such as joint ventures with multiple faculties and hospital systems.

**Clients/Work Highlights:** Clients include East Texas Medical Center and CHRISTUS Health.

### Strasburger & Price LLP

**The Firm:** Interviewees particularly rate this group's transactional capability, and the team is experienced in the representation of hospitals and physicians in the financing and construction of hospitals. Clients also praise the firm's litigation and regulatory expertise. The recent proliferation of ambulatory surgery centers has provided a steady flow of instructions.

**The Lawyers:** The arrival of **Bill Darling** from Brown McCarroll adds depth to the well-established healthcare team. "*Responsive, articulate and thorough,*" his practice spans regulatory and transactional matters. He frequently advises hospital systems on improving their organizational structure and in strategic planning matters. **Ivan Wood** is an acknowledged medical malpractice expert who can "*handle complex joint ventures creatively.*"

### Other Notable Practitioners

**Kimberley Elting** (see p.1889) leads the charge for Jones Day's healthcare practice. Clients appreciate her "*circumspect*" approach to problems and her "*unrivaled responsiveness.*" Her experience includes joint ventures, acquisitions and disposals, both in Texas and beyond.

# IMMIGRATION

## Band 1

### Jenkens & Gilchrist PC

**The Firm:** Breaking the rule that immigration is the preserve of boutiques, this team is "*astonishingly good for a big firm.*" Lawyers earn respect for their "*consistency, integrity and willingness to go the extra mile.*" A large support staff and "*electronic and technical sophistication*" drive a significant practice in Dallas. Skilled at representing large companies, the team advises on a range of employment-based immigrant and nonimmigrant visas to secure skilled foreign professionals, managers and executives.

**The Lawyers:** "*Rainmaker*" **Harry Joe** offers polished general counsel services and expertise in business-related immigration litigation, such as removal proceedings. The "*no-nonsense, creative and direct*" **Steven Ladik** garners praise for his ability to "*reach right into the heart of the issue.*" He has a niche representing professional entertainers and athletes, especially on the PGA golf circuit, and also acts for multinational corporations on issues including due diligence, Sarbanes-Oxley compliance and visa transfer.

**Clients/Work Highlights:** Clients range from high-profile individuals to large companies, including oil businesses.

### Quan, Burdette & Perez, PC

**The Firm:** This "*pleasant and capable*" 20-strong team earns respect for its corporate immigration, family and litigation expertise. It is a sizable boutique with growing offices in San Antonio, Mexico City and Houston. Attorneys advise clients on business immigration, deportation and family visa issues. Clients admire the team's "*efforts to completely understand the nature of the business*" and the lawyers' "*appropriately cautious approach.*" Mexican and Latin American business immigration work has been thriving lately, including work on the NAFTA-created investor visa.

**The Lawyers:** **Brian Bates** is hailed as "*the big player,*" and is involved in national immigration litigation in the federal courts. For example, he argued Zhu v Ashcroft before the Fifth Circuit Court of Appeals. Clients appreciate the "*responsive, amiable and bright*" **Kelly Cobb**, whose practice includes permanent residency visas for university academics. **Judy Lee**'s "*accuracy, responsiveness and professionalism*" draws the praise of clients. She handles H1-B visas, among other things. **Gordon Quan** is a "*sound strategist and plum draw for the firm,*" admired for his connections and lobbying on border issues. He is an experienced performer before the Board of Immigration Appeals and the Board of Alien Labor Certification Appeals.

**Clients/Work Highlights:** Clients include Fortune 500 companies, small startups and midsize enterprises. These include the American Bureau of Shipping; Air Liquide; ConocoPhillips; National Instruments; Smith International and Wood Group.

### Tindall & Foster PC

**The Firm:** The combination of significant lobbying expertise, a nationwide reputation and a glittering track record in the field guarantees a top slot for this group. One of the largest employment-based immigration firms in the Southwest, it is a strong contender in the Houston and Austin markets and "*demands to be taken seriously.*" The team advises companies such as Schlumberger on the employment of foreign nationals, and acts for individuals such as former officials of foreign governments. Attorneys also work with members of the legislature on immigration laws.

**The Lawyers:** The "*terrific and influential*" **Charlie Foster** is a "*landmark*" of the Texas marketplace.

**Clients/Work Highlights:** Clients include individuals and companies.

## Band 2

### Kemp Smith LLP

**The Firm:** This significant player is especially rated in the western part of the state. Though smaller than many of its rivals, it wins fans with its "*extremely ethical and conservative*" approach. Interviewees admire the "*readily available and dependable attorneys,*" rating them particularly for homeland security and inspections-related work as well as a traditional diet of advice to multinationals and families on transfers and visas. Clients are also drawn by the team's "*unique understanding of cross-border procedures*" between the USA and Mexico.

**The Lawyers:** **Kathleen Walker** "*always has the answers at her fingertips*" and has the kind of "*high-level contacts*" that oil the wheels of a top-notch practice. She carries out legislative and lobbying work in Washington, DC and is expert in consular, advocacy, national inspections and cross-border issues. She recently advised a Swedish company on its creation of a plant in Mexico, and a Japanese corporation on employment transfer issues in the USA.

**Clients/Work Highlights:** The team acts for a range of domestic and international corporate clients.

### Law Offices of Richard A Gump Jr PC

**The Firm:** This boutique houses four attorneys who handle employment-related immigrant and nonimmigrant visas for visitors, employees, students, investors and families. The team is adept at complex citizenship matters and removal proceedings. It also handles worksite compliance investigations and audits, and offers training to clients.

**The Lawyers:** **Richard Gump** earns the sort of praise that is reserved for those that have "*struck out alone and become a great success.*" He has over three decades of experience under his belt and concentrates on strategic planning for businesses and personal visas for international personnel. He is expert in the structuring of international joint ventures and compliance issues.

**Clients/Work Highlights:** The team acts for small and large companies, investors, athletes, medical personnel, families and individuals in a range of immigration work.

### Miley & Brown PC

**The Firm:** This small 20-year-old boutique is acknowledged statewide for "*punching above its weight*" in immigration matters for individuals. The team handles residency, citizenship and employment visa matters, and is experienced in exclusion and deportation proceedings.

**Clients/Work Highlights:** The group advises Dallas-based corporations and individual clients from around the world on immigration and nationality law.

### Paul Parsons PC

**The Firm:** **Paul Parsons** is an Austin-based sole practitioner who offers "*tremendous knowledge and overwhelming experience.*" His practice includes business counseling, but it is for family cases that he is best known.

**Clients/Work Highlights:** The office represents a range of individuals, families and companies.

### Reina & Associates

**The Firm:** **Joe Reina** heads this boutique and enjoys a reputation as *"one of Dallas' finest attorneys."* Backed by a respected team of eight, he advises individuals and families on temporary and permanent visas, including student, work and visitor visas. The team is developing its business immigration practice nicely and offers advice on citizenship and deportation cases. Reina recently litigated several cases for aliens resisting deportation, including the precedent-setting case of Deanda-Romo.

**Clients/Work Highlights:** The team acts for business clients as well as individuals and families.

### Shivers & Shivers

**The Firm:** The San Antonio pairing of **Nancy Shivers** and **Bob Shivers** draws praise for successfully straddling the line between business and family immigration advice. Nancy is recommended for her business-related expertise, while husband Bob is the man to see for federal litigation.

**Clients/Work Highlights:** The team acts for corporate and individual clients.

### Winstead Sechrest & Minick P.C.

See firm details p.1939

**The Firm:** This small but experienced business immigration team is thriving on a varied diet that includes obtaining nonimmigrant and immigrant visas for individuals ranging from athletes and entertainers to professionals and executives. The team is particularly noted for its services to the skills economy, helping technology businesses recruit and retain experts from overseas.

**The Lawyers:** The arrival of **Brian Graham** from Jenkens & Gilchrist *"really puts them on the map."* He specializes in the relocation of skilled workers to the USA.

# INSURANCE

| Insurance |
| --- |
| Leading Firms |
| [1] FULBRIGHT & JAWORSKI L.L.P. *Houston* |
| HAYNES AND BOONE LLP *Dallas* |
| MARTIN, DISIERE, JEFFERSON & WISDOM *Houston* |
| THOMPSON, COE, COUSINS & IRONS, LLP *Dallas* |
| [2] AKIN GUMP STRAUSS HAUER & FELD LLP *Austin* |
| GARDERE WYNNE SEWELL LLP *Houston* |
| NICKENS KEETON LAWLESS FARRELL *Austin* |
| VINSON & ELKINS LLP *Houston* |
| YORK, KELLER & FIELD *Austin* |
| [3] BEIRNE MAYNARD & PARSONS, LLP *Houston* |
| COOK & ROACH, L.L.C. *Houston* |
| COOPER & SCULLY PC *Dallas* |
| GRAVES, DOUGHERTY, HEARON & MOODY *Austin* |
| STRASBURGER & PRICE LLP *Dallas* |

## Band 1

### Fulbright & Jaworski L.L.P.

See firm details p.1928

**The Firm:** With four offices in Texas and a sizable team of *"fantastically talented lawyers,"* this group has significant reach across the state. The practice has a credible international element, which is reinforced by its office in London. Attorneys represent insurance industry and corporate clients in litigation, transactional and regulatory matters. Commentators note the team's coverage disputes work in particular. The team was recently appointed by AIG to handle matters in the wake of Hurricane Katrina.

**The Lawyers:** **Reagan Brown** (see p.1885) is experienced in jury trial and appellate litigation, and practices in state and national arenas. He is particularly recommended for his defense work against class actions. **Steve Pate** (see p.1909) is *"one of the finest first-party insurance lawyers in the state"* and also handles commercial coverage, extracontractual, bad faith and construction litigation. **Arno Krebs** (see p.1900) is a specialist in third-party insurance coverage and extracontractual liability defense. He advises insurance companies on coverage issues and declara-

tory judgments and defends them against extracontractual liability claims.

**Clients/Work Highlights:** AIG; Progressive Casualty Insurance; Amica Mutual Insurance; Gray Insurance; MetLife; National Western Life; Texas Mutual Insurance; Commonwealth Insurance and St. Paul Travelers.

### Haynes and Boone LLP

**The Firm:** This firm is *"the cream of the crop"* when it comes to representing corporate policyholders. It specializes in complex coverage litigation, and is also recommended for coverage analysis, advice and auditing. The dedicated team of lawyers is recognized in such fields as marine, aviation, business interruption and general liability.

**The Lawyers:** **Ernest Martin** is a coverage litigator par excellence. He represents clients on major property damage and professional liability claims and was recently engaged to deal with hurricane coverage claims and potential claims against large brokers following an investigation by Eliot Spitzer. **Werner Powers** also handles coverage litigation and brings to the table additional muscle in torts, securities and contract disputes.

**Clients/Work Highlights:** Texas Health Resources; ExxonMobil; CellStar; Shell; Dynegy; Correctional Services Corporation; Ericsson; Frost Bank; JPI; Crow Holdings; Pioneer Natural Resources; Warrantech and Trinity Industries.

### Martin, Disiere, Jefferson & Wisdom LLP

**The Firm:** Representing major insurance carriers, this team is rated for its expertise in mold and homeowners cases. Many of the lawyers have valuable in-house experience at insurance companies. The recent workload has included increasing volumes of construction defect litigation, and lawyers act as coordinating counsel in a number of claims stemming from the hurricanes of 2005. A recent highlight was Republic Underwriters Insurance Co v Mex-Tex before the Supreme Court of Texas, which reversed a lower court decision on late payment penalties. The

recent addition of a Dallas office boosts the firm's coverage in Texas.

**The Lawyers:** Commentators enthuse that **Chris Martin** *"cannot be ranked highly enough."* He takes great pains to remain *"ahead of the game"* on market developments, and is sought out for sophisticated cases for prestigious clients such as Farmers and St. Paul Travelers. He recently represented the carrier in Fiess v State Farm Lloyds, a high-profile mold case.

**Clients/Work Highlights:** ACE USA; Farmers; The Hartford; Prudential Property & Casualty; Royal & SunAlliance; State Farm; St. Paul Travelers; Zurich and American Honda Motor Company.

### Thompson, Coe, Cousins & Irons, LLP

See firm details p.1937

**The Firm:** This 50-strong group is omnipresent in Texas, and regarded as *"at the top of the game"* for carrier-side coverage issues. Sources report a potent regulatory and lobbying practice and *"well-delivered"* services in bad faith, first-party and corporate matters.

**The Lawyers:** Clients describe **Brian Martin** as a *"model attorney."* His recent workload has included toxic tort, environmental and construction cases. A potent litigator, *"he is like a pit bull in court yet charms the jury at the same time."* **Roger Higgins** is one of the best class action attorneys in the state. He advises on regulatory, coverage and extracontractual matters, and recently handled Texas' first major credit scoring case for a carrier client. *"Capable and articulate"* **Jay Thompson** focuses on regulatory, legislative and litigation matters. Clients value his connections and his knowledge of the public policy considerations underlying these areas. His recent caseload has included life and health insurance lobbying as well as hurricane insurance matters. **Diego Garcia** is a *"smart lawyer gifted with excellent analysis skills."* He handles coverage and environmental liability matters. Of counsel **Richard Geiger's** wealth of experience earns him the respect of industry players. He represents industry and trade association clients before the legislature.

**Clients/Work Highlights:** The firm has well-established relationships with several major insurance industry clients.

## Band 2

### Akin Gump Strauss Hauer & Feld LLP
See firm details p.559

**The Firm:** This prestigious insurance group advises on transactions, regulations and legislative policy, and attorneys are praised for their litigation and advocacy work. The team takes on a varied workload that includes M&A, reinsurance arbitration and investigations into insurance broking.

**The Lawyers:** **Tom Bond** (see p.1883) is renowned for his regulatory and lobbying work and frequently represents clients in the managed care industry. He also earns praise for his advice on the insurance and regulatory implications of mergers and acquisitions.

**Clients/Work Highlights:** Allstate; Marsh & McLennan; The Hartford; AIG and Liberty Mutual.

### Gardere Wynne Sewell LLP
See firm details p.1931

**The Firm:** The attorneys here impress clients with their service skills and practical approach to solving problems. The team fixes its attention on complex insurance coverage and litigation work. It enjoys a strong reputation among homebuilders, for which it acts on construction defect matters. Its portfolio also extends to D&O liability, marine and oil insurance.

**The Lawyers:** **Jim Cooper**'s (see p.1886) clients value his "*practical and reliable*" approach and the speed with which he "*gets on top of the needs of the company*" he is representing. He recently successfully represented a debtor to recover on professional liability policies following a nursing home bankruptcy. **John Pearson** (see p.1909) is "*prompt, conscientious and very effective with both counsel and the opposition.*" He handles coverage, commercial disputes, maritime and oilfield matters.

**Clients/Work Highlights:** Schlumberger; Baker Hughes; Pilgrim's Pride; Lennar and McDermott International.

### Nickens Keeton Lawless Farrell & Flack LLP

**The Firm:** Clients avow that this group is "*truly one of the best*" for representing policyholders. It often deals with complex coverage cases against insurance companies, with an emphasis on construction, products liability and toxic torts. Clients find the firm "*very ethical and reasonable*" and seek it out for "*the expertise of some of the best attorneys around.*"

**The Lawyers:** **Mark Lawless**' policyholder practice focuses on clients in coverage disputes with carriers. He specializes in environment and toxic tort cases. "*Bona fide star*" **Lee Shidlofsky** is described as an excellent problem solver who is "*totally conversant with the law.*" He frequently represents construction industry clients on complex coverage matters, and recently represented a home-building company in a landmark case before the Texas Supreme Court regarding construction coverage.

**Clients/Work Highlights:** S&B Engineers and Constructors; Temple-Inland; Swinerton Builders; J.T. Thorpe & Son; Comfort Systems USA; Total Petrochemicals USA; Tyler Technologies; Genmar Holdings and CITGO.

### Vinson & Elkins LLP
See firm details p.1938

**The Firm:** Offering "*uniformly great lawyers,*" this firm delivers a full range of services clustered around a deep-rooted litigation practice handling arbitration and appeal proceedings. The practice is divided into two areas: the first, headed by David Brown in Houston, deals with claims brought by policyholders; and the second, headed by Russell Yager in Dallas, focuses on defending class actions brought against insurance industry clients. An excellent portfolio of sophisticated insurance coverage cases particularly impresses commentators.

**The Lawyers:** **David Brown** (see p.1884) works extensively in business interruption cases following Tropical Storm Allison and was recently engaged to deal with similar cases stemming from the hurricanes of 2005. He also handles D&O and errors and omissions (E&O) liability matters. **Scott Statham** (see p.1915) is "*tirelessly hard-working with a brilliant legal mind,*" according to sources, and regularly takes on litigation and arbitration cases concerning business interruption and other coverage issues. Dallas chief **Russell Yager** (see p.1920) earns acclaim for his commercial litigation, class action and antitrust work. Clients praise his lucidity when explaining complex issues.

**Clients/Work Highlights:** Southwest Airlines; Reliant Energy; Memorial Hermann; CEMEX and one of the nation's largest property and casualty insurers.

### York, Keller & Field

**The Firm:** This four-lawyer team is celebrated for its appearances before the state Department of Insurance and for the attorneys' impressive "*political problem-solving*" capabilities. The group is especially recommended for its regulatory expertise, and also undertakes transactional work with a reinsurance and insurance element.

**The Lawyers:** **Mary Keller** is one of the state's top regulatory lawyers. She is well connected and offers previous experience in the Texas Attorney General's office and the Texas Department of Insurance. The "*massively experienced*" **Larry York** acts on a variety of commercial litigation and Insurance Code issues, and is comfortable working with the state legislature.

**Clients/Work Highlights:** State Farm; CIGNA; ACE; Affiliated Computer Services and Washington Mutual.

## Band 3

### Beirne Maynard & Parsons, LLP
See firm details p.1923

**The Firm:** This is a traditional litigation powerhouse, and enters the insurance table this year as commentators acknowledge its "*consistent efforts in this area.*" Around 20 lawyers work on coverage and bad faith disputes for carriers. They counsel clients at pretrial as well as in arbitration and mediation. D&O liability, environmental and construction insurance are further areas of specialization.

**The Lawyers:** "*Knowledgeable, pragmatic and methodical,*" **Jay Brown** (see p.1884) is especially admired for his commercial property coverage opinions and defense and bad faith litigation. His clients appreciate his "*even temper,*" which is an asset in scenarios from mediation to the courtroom.

**Clients/Work Highlights:** Clients include large carriers such as AIG, ACE USA and RSUI Group.

### Cook & Roach, L.L.P.

**The Firm:** This team of seven lawyers offers a polished insurance coverage practice for policyholders. Its wider expertise encompasses appellate and litigation matters, with specific experience in the areas of products liability, construction and environment.

The Lawyers: **Bob Cunningham** is always "*100% up to date,*" and focuses on matters such as insurance analysis and complex commercial litigation. The "*intelligent, superbly well-connected and extraordinarily creative*" **Randy Roach** is acclaimed for his analysis, dispute and litigation work and his extensive appellate experience. He is accustomed to appearing before the Texas Supreme Court on cutting-edge matters, and recently conducted a case of first impression regarding the admissibility of evidence extrinsic to policies. He has also been handling a case to determine whether punitive damages are coverable by insurance.

Clients/Work Highlights: Waste Management; Sulzer; Temple-Inland; Chicago Bridge & Iron; Cyberonics; Volvo; ConocoPhillips; KB Home; Odfjell; Air Liquide; Alcoa; Product Liability Advisory Council; Raytheon; Stryker; J T Thorpe Company; Tyler Technologies; Vopak and Shell.

## Cooper & Scully PC

The Firm: This team is seasoned in litigation and regulation cases including bad faith, professional liability, toxic torts and mass torts. Representing insurers and policyholders, it is also equipped to handle reinsurance cases.

The Lawyers: **Brent Cooper** is "*at the forefront*" of the field and regularly appears before the Texas Supreme Court and the court of appeal. Sources commend his medical malpractice work, and he is also experienced in insurance defense coverage work representing carriers.

Clients/Work Highlights: Clients include insurance and reinsurance companies.

## Graves, Dougherty, Hearon & Moody, P.C.

The Firm: Around ten lawyers focus on insurance matters, drawing on support from the firm's substantial network of litigators. The team's reputation is particularly strong in insurance regulation and litigation, with class actions and administrative work being active areas. Over the past year it has experienced a flurry of activity in representing homeowner and workers' compensation insurance carriers.

The Lawyers: **Susan Conway** is a veteran regulatory litigator. Recent experience includes homeowners' rate regulation at both administrative and district court levels and a variety of insurance-related litigation.

Clients/Work Highlights: Clients include large insurance carriers such as State Farm and Texas Mutual Insurance.

## Strasburger & Price LLP

The Firm: This group of more than 40 lawyers covers insurance matters including arbitration and litigation. The portfolio includes drafting policies, ensuring compliance and evaluating coverage. As well as complex first and third-party insurance claims, the team handles reinsurance and excess issues and defends parties covered by liability insurance.

The Lawyers: Michael Keeley's specialty is defending coverage disputes.

Clients/Work Highlights: Allianz; The Hartford; Everest Re Group and Zurich.

## Other Notable Practitioners

**Mike Huddleston** at Shannon, Gracey, Ratliff & Miller LLP represents corporate policyholders and insurance companies in coverage disputes and bad faith litigation. **Scott Hoyt** (see p.1897) at Gibson, Dunn & Crutcher LLP impresses clients with his expertise in coverage matters. He has heaps of experience in asbestos and silicosis matters, and is expert in bad faith and products liability cases. Construction insurance coverage specialist **Pat Wielinski** of Cokinos, Bosien and Young handles sophisticated work "*with fantastic results.*" He has established a national practice in construction defect work for policyholder clients such as American Contractors Insurance Group. **Burnie Burner** at Long, Burner, Parks & DeLargy is described as "*probably the best reinsurance lawyer in the state.*" **Jim Cornell** is a founding partner of the recently established civil litigation and family law boutique Cornell & Pardue LLP. He is "*willing to steam in and fight*" for his policyholder clients and his practice extends to first and third-party work as well as bad faith and coverage matters. "*A pillar of regulatory work,*" **Will Davis** at Heath, Davis & McCalla is a "*formidable political problem solver*" especially recommended for lobbying work. **James Moody** of Quilling, Selander, Cummiskey & Lownds, P.C. is an excess insurance expert whose practice includes insurance defense, reinsurance, bad faith and environmental insurance coverage matters. **Vince Morgan** (see p.1907) at Pillsbury Winthrop Shaw Pittman LLP is a "*brilliant rising star,*" according to commentators. His practice includes sophisticated litigation and arbitration for policyholders.

# INTELLECTUAL PROPERTY

## Band 1

### Baker Botts LLP

See firm details p.1922

The Firm: This large, well-established team strikes sources across the country as "*a strong and truly excellent regional group.*" Clients described the group of more than 100 IP specialists as "*stellar people with brilliant intellectual and strategic approaches to IP law.*" Of its performance in litigation, one client told researchers: "*They are absolutely first-rate and the go-to people for trial matters.*" In addition to the litigation practice, the team excels in patent procurement, licensing deals and due diligence for corporate transactions. The Texas IP lawyers operate from offices in Houston, Austin and Dallas, handling oil-based caseloads, medical, pharmaceutical and electronics-related matters. Recent practice highlights include representing an international information resource in an ongoing patent enforcement matter, and worldwide trademark portfolio management for Computer Associates. The team acts as primary counsel to a number of international hi-tech manufacturers and other corporations.

The Lawyers: **Scott Partridge** (see p.1909) heads the Houston group and was praised as "*an outstanding authority on IP matters.*" He has been busy with several trials before the Eastern District Court of Texas and recently represented an IT management software company in a successful settlement and countersuit. **Jerry Mills** (see p.1906) is the firmwide IP chair and a widely acknowledged "*leader in technology law.*" He focuses on patents and licensing and recently managed the sale of several significant patent portfolios. **Thomas Felger** (see p.1890) is another "*patent portfolio expert,*" admired for his "*breadth of knowledge and exceptional focus.*" He advises multinational corporations on licensing and due diligence matters. "*Rising star*" **Carey Jordan** (see p.1899) maintains a broad IP practice with particular emphasis on patent portfolio advisory work for large energy and technology companies. Meanwhile, **Mitch Lukin** (see p.1903) is the general IP counsel for Halliburton Energy Services and is additionally experienced in media and medical device issues. **Luke Pedersen** (see p.1909) continues to be regarded as "*one to watch*" in the IP market. He recently completed a fruitful secondment with Computer Associates and continues to advise on patent portfolio management for the company, in

## Intellectual Property
### Leading Individuals

addition to his work elsewhere in patent prosecution and litigation. Clients picked out **Barton Showalter** (see p.1914) as an *"exceptional attorney,"* noted for the breadth of his IP practice. He is currently involved in strategy formulation and other counseling for Cisco Systems and Fujitsu, as well as complex patent litigation for a multinational information resource. **Gene Spears** (see p.1914) was strongly recommended for inclusion in this year's tables by both peers and clients, who identified him as *"a notable and excellent IP lawyer."* His recent caseload includes representing Applica Incorporated in a complex ITC investigation that eventually settled in the company's favor.

**Clients/Work Highlights:** Aventis Pharmaceuticals; Halliburton; i2 Technologies; Raytheon; Texas Instruments; Trinity Industries; Cisco Systems and Dell.

## Fulbright & Jaworski L.L.P.
See firm details p.1928

**The Firm:** A major player across the region, this 100-strong group won effusive praise from clients, who said that it offered *"fantastic client awareness and a creative approach to strategy, as well as a really solid understanding of the law."* The group was also singled out for its *"expertise and aggression in oral arguments,"* which interviewees felt *"they always deliver beautifully."* The team maintains a wide platform, representing clients in patent prosecution as well as litigation, and is particularly skilled in biotech and hi-tech computer matters. Practice highlights include representing a variety of inventors in the fields of Internet service provision and online music distribution, and acting for Mars in a patent infringement case that resulted in a $4.2 million judgment for the company.

**The Lawyers: Louis Pirkey** (see p.1910), who is for some *"the leading trademark specialist in the state,"* garnered praise for his *"experience and outstanding trial management."* He is currently involved in a series of patent infringement and unfair competition matters for several multinational IT and communications companies, both in Texas and throughout the South. **Brett Govett** (see p.1893) is *"a real force to reckon with,"* according to his clients. Highly recommended for litigation, he successfully represented PepsiCo in a product labeling matter and acts as regular counsel for Citigroup. **Bill Barber** (see p.1882) debuts in the rankings following enthusiastic endorsement by clients: *"He gives excellent advice and is a top-notch litigator."* Group head **Paul Krieger** (see p.1901) is *"a senior guy with fantastic client relationship skills."* He is currently running several significant federal circuit court appeals and recently oversaw a number of large settlements in favor of major corporate clients. **David Parker** (see p.1908) heads the Austin IP team and has broad experience as a patent litigator, prosecutor and adviser. An expert in pharmaceutical and biotech matters, he is currently helping to manage the patent portfolios of leading gene therapy companies.

**Clients/Work Highlights:** The team advises a range of multinational biotech and manufacturing companies and other corporations, including PepsiCo; Weatherford International; Starbucks; Transocean; Schlumberger; ROHM; Aerobus International; Harris; Infowave Software; ExxonMobil; Home Depot; LexisNexis and 3M.

## Vinson & Elkins LLP
See firm details p.1938

**The Firm:** This *"superb"* IP group enjoys an outstanding reputation based on *"years of wisdom and excellence."* It is composed of more than 50 specialists based in three offices statewide and benefits from the support of lawyers across a national and international network. Interviewees called the team *"client-centric and responsive,"* citing *"a cornucopia of experience and strategic skills."* Patent litigation is central to the practice, but the team also has vast experience in patent prosecution and trademark matters, as well as licensing and trade secrets. Recent highlights include successfully defending a landmark fuel cell patent matter, and obtaining a motion to dismiss a trade secrets claim brought against a multinational energy company. The team also provides ongoing support in corporate transactions, licensing deals and IP protection, primarily for clients in the software and technology industries.

**The Lawyers:** A past chair of the ABA's IP Section, **William LaFuze** (see p.1901) is *"extremely knowledgeable, reliable and all-around excellent,"* according to interviewees. They were particularly impressed with his expertise in technology and computer-related matters, although he also counsels a range of manufacturers and other types of company. **Willem Schuurman** (see p.1913) has earned a reputation as *"one of the foremost and most experienced IP litigators in the state."* He is currently involved in several key patent and trade secrets trials and has been successful in a series of Markman hearings. **Adam Floyd** (see p.1891) continues to be known as a skilled patent litigator with particular knowledge of medical device technologies, as well as the electronic, mechanical and chemical industries. **Clark Martin** (see p.1903) emerged from the research process as *"infinitely recommendable,"* with interviewees admiring both his breadth of experience and his specific expertise in matters affecting the construction industry.

**Clients/Work Highlights:** Lutron Electronics; Core Laboratories; Continental Airlines; Prodigy Communications; Dynegy; Textron; Kearney & Trecker and Dow Chemical.

## Band 2

## Akin Gump Strauss Hauer & Feld LLP
See firm details p.559

**The Firm:** This *"exceptional"* international firm has four offices in Texas, each with an experienced IP practice group that has *"responded really well to the lively Texas market."* One interviewee said: *"They're ethical and principled, but what really stands out is their responsiveness."* The main thrust of the group's work is patent litigation and prosecution, but it also offers trademark expertise to clients in a variety of industries. It has successfully defended several matters in the Eastern District of Texas, most recently on behalf of a liquid crystal display manufacturer and an international boat builder. The clientele includes a large number of electronics, telecom and Internet-based companies.

**The Lawyers: David Clonts** (see p.1886) is *"sharp and effective,"* according to market sources. He concentrates on patent litigation for software and other hi-tech companies, and recently successfully represented Lowe's in a lighting fixtures infringement matter. Houston IP head and firmwide IP cochair **Lester Hewitt** (see p.1897) is *"professional, knowledgeable and an undisputed leader in this area."* He focuses on patent matters, as well as writing and speaking extensively on IP law. One recent case saw him defending AOL in a patent infringement matter filed in the Southern District of Texas. **Randall Sarosdy** (see p.1913) is highly recommended for his litigation experience and his capacity to handle complex commercial IP issues. He is adept at handling electronic trading, securities trading and Internet access cases, and most recently represented AT&T in a long-running Internet access protocol dispute.

**Clients/Work Highlights:** ArvinMeritor; Bausch & Lomb; AT&T; Samsung; Lufkin Industries; Kinetic Concepts; NBC and IQ Products.

## Bracewell & Giuliani LLP
See firm details p.1924

**The Firm:** In the area of IP law, this *"fine Texas-grown practice"* has *"impressive, dedicated attorneys."* According to one satisfied client, *"they're great communicators and really understand the technical elements of IP; I find myself using this firm more and more."* Cross-disciplinary working and easy communication between practice areas are said to be a real draw for clients, and the effect within the firm appears to be an informed and broadly focused IP group. It operates primarily from the Houston office but also maintains a presence in Austin and Dallas. Lawyers represent companies in software, food and waste management as well as the energy sector.

**The Lawyers: Albert Kimball** (see p.1900) is *"a stalwart of the Texas IP Bar"* and has deep knowledge of the petroleum products and refinery market. Proving his experience extends to other areas, he recently asserted multiple patents for a multinational cell phone company. Market sources described **Ben Tobor** (see p.1917) as *"a formidable source of knowledge,"* praising the breadth of his experience. He divides his time between patent and trademark matters, litigating and counseling as his clients require. Tobor continues to act as primary IP counsel for an international waste management company. **Constance Rhebergen** (see p.1911) is *"a top-notch attorney with broad technical and legal expertise."* She does major work for an international software corporation.

**Clients/Work Highlights:** Waste Management; Goodman Global Holdings; Farouk Systems and other national and international electrical, software and technology-related clients.

## Haynes and Boone LLP

**The Firm:** This Dallas-born outfit was warmly recommended by market sources as one of the *"major players"* in IP law. *"When it comes to breadth, quality and lawyers, these guys have few competitors,"* researchers were told. It operates from six offices across the state, offering some 30 IP lawyers, mostly litigators. In patent disputes, the firm has represented national telecom and communications companies, as well as various Internet service providers. The full-service team also offers patent prosecution and trademark services to a client base of regional and national electrical, energy and medical supplies companies. The firm recently secured successful outcomes for musicians and songwriters in copyright disputes, and advised a national telecom corporation on a trademark policing and enforcement initiative.

**The Lawyers:** Praise for *"outstanding and well-versed patent lawyer"* **David McCombs** was unanimous. He has built a fine reputation for his patent portfolio management advice to clients in the electronics, software and communications sectors. **Jeffrey Becker** maintains a full-service IP practice and lectures widely, in particular on Internet disputes. He has also negotiated trademark licensing and merchandise agreements on behalf of companies such as Microsoft and Warner Bros. **Donald Templin** heads the firm's business litigation team and conducts IP litigation. He has represented software, semiconductor and musical equipment manufacturers in patent and trademark infringement cases.

**Clients/Work Highlights:** RadioShack; Siemens; Cisco Systems; Dell; Hitachi; Tristar Products; Halliburton; Novell and Acutex.

## Howrey LLP

**The Firm:** Clients continue to be impressed by the *"fine and focused"* Texas branch of this international firm: *"They're top-notch litigators and general all-stars."* Competitors agreed, saying: *"We'd want them representing us."* The Houston office has around 60 IP attorneys, most of whom concentrate on patent litigation, patent prosecution and trademark disputes. The firm represents clients in many areas of business, not least the Internet and telecom sectors, and it also has a particularly well-regarded team of biotech attorneys. Lawyers additionally advise on patent portfolio drafting and management. Recent highlights include victory for Monsanto in two extensive patent infringement matters involving crop technology and herbicide resistant products, and defending Shell in an alleged trade secret and misappropriation dispute.

**The Lawyers:** Litigator **Nick Barzoukas** is a *"smart and impressive"* adviser with ample exposure to pharmaceutical matters, including representing Merck in a series of patent infringement claims. In a similar vein, **Susan Knoll** is *"a fantastic trial attorney with a solid reputation in pharmaceuticals."* Her skills are additionally applied to a broader clientele of computer, oil and biotech companies. She led the team that acted for Monsanto in its recent patent

infringement disputes and successfully represented Kemin Foods in a patent infringement case. **John Lynch** is *"a jewel,"* according to market sources, who cited his years of experience of patent litigation and *"exceptional"* counseling skills. Lynch advises on portfolio management and is a renowned speaker. **John Norris** was commended as a *"very fine"* trial attorney with valuable know-how relating to chemical and petrochemical technologies. His achievements include defending Shell in a patent infringement involving an ethylene oxide process. *"Vastly experienced"* **Floyd Nation** carries out impressive patent litigation work in the mechanical and electro-mechanical industries, and recently defended Sun Microsystems in a computer technology patent infringement case.

**Clients/Work Highlights:** Coca-Cola; Merck; Xerox; Caterpillar; Dana; Quantum; Weatherford International; Sun Microsystems and 3M.

## Jones Day
See firm details p.570

**The Firm:** The international behemoth has a group of 22 patent litigators and IP consultants in its two Texas offices. Commentators spoke of a growing, *"top of the line"* team, impressed that *"the sizable Dallas office is handling some of the biggest cases around."* The patent trial attorneys have been busy in the Eastern District of Texas and were also successful in recent matters before the ITC. Highlights include the defense of two multinational computer corporations in alleged patent infringement cases, as well as ongoing support to cell phone manufacturers. Anticipating growth, the Houston team is concentrating efforts in the oil and energy technology sectors.

**The Lawyers: Robert Turner** (see p.1917) is *"an excellent trial lawyer"* with decades of trial experience across a broad spectrum of IP law. He is judged to be particularly effective in the cell phone industry, and also gives patent portfolio advice to Texas Instruments. **Ken Adamo** (see p.1880) is recommended for the first time in the tables; he is *"definitely a patent litigator I'd want on my side,"* one source reported. Adamo's time is divided between Cleveland and Dallas, and he works on the full gamut of patent, trademark and copyright disputes. According to one client, **Hilda Galvan** (see p.1892) is *"just outstanding and beyond all praise."* Her litigation practice centers on computer software and telecom, including cell phones. She recently led a team that secured a favorable settlement for Texas Instruments in a patent infringement matter.

**Clients/Work Highlights:** The MathWorks; Texas Instruments; Dell; Apple; Nokia and Motorola.

## McKool Smith
See firm details p.1934

**The Firm:** This 80-strong litigation boutique has offices in Dallas, Austin and, the hive of patent activity, Marshall. It has an enviable reputation in IP law, having distinguished itself as *"a fine and very competent litigation firm."* Clients were impressed with the group's *"concentration and finesse"* and noted many *"significant wins"* by McKool attorneys. Many in the

IP practice group are geared towards the computer software industry and have earned well-deserved successes in patent infringement matters for Plano, American Video Graphics and Microsoft, among others. The team also has a good name in the cell phone and telecom sectors, recently securing a trial victory for Ericsson in a patent dispute relating to subscriber line interface circuits.

**The Lawyers:** *"Talented"* **Douglas Cawley**'s (see p.1885) broad practice includes plaintiff and defendant representation in software and computer patent disputes. He recently acted for IEX against Blue Pumpkin Software in a patent infringement of IEX scheduling call center software. Founding partner **Mike McKool** (see p.1905) is *"a highly effective patent litigator."* He recently won a victory for Austin-based National Instruments in an appeal in the US Court of Appeals in Washington, DC brought by The Mathworks, concerning a 2003 software patent infringement verdict. Managing partner **Gordon White** (see p.1919) earns plaudits for his work in the electrical, semiconductor and telecom industries. He is primary counsel for American Video Graphics in a series of patent infringement claims against multinational software corporations.

**Clients/Work Highlights:** Ericsson; Lockheed Martin; National Instruments; EDS; Samsung Electronics; Taiwan Semiconductor and Excel Communications.

## Sidley Austin LLP
See firm details p.883

**The Firm:** Interviewees were confident of the abilities of this *"established solid group,"* saying that *"they're consistent and always focused on the job."* The Dallas office of this international player numbers about 20 attorneys and offers a full service in IP matters. It caters to a diverse clientele and has a particular interest in the chemical and software industries. In addition to extensive trial experience, lawyers have a good deal of experience in copyright licensing and trade secrets, advising leading names in the literary, music, architectural and visual arts media.

**The Lawyers:** **Bryan Medlock** (see p.1905) was commended as *"a first-class member of the patent Bar."* He has regularly been special master and expert witness in patent matters, and also maintains an active litigation and advisory practice. Managing partner **James Bradley** (see p.1884) joins the tables following positive market feedback. His practice centers on patent litigation in the electrical, semiconductor and oil industries. **Charles Cotropia** (see p.1887) comes *"most highly recommended,"* and commentators cited his expertise in trademark and patent litigation as his strong point. He concentrates on clothing and restaurant clients, and is a long-time adviser to Justin Brands.

**Clients/Work Highlights:** Ciba Specialty Chemicals; Kimberly-Clark; Microsoft; Delphion; MicroPatent; Litex Industries; TGI Friday's; Fuddruckers; Holiday Retirement Corporation and Justin Brands.

## Band 3

## Davis Munck Butrus PC
See firm details p.1927

**The Firm:** This Dallas-based outfit of 20 IP attorneys drew effusive praise from across the market. Commentators were impressed with the firm's *"consistent quality and expertise"* and determined that it is *"definitely a star on the horizon."* The team has expanded through the incorporation of eight attorneys from commercial and IP litigation boutique Butrus Khoshbin Wilson Vogt, LLP. This has not only enhanced the firm's all-around litigation capability but has also added an office in Charlotte, North Carolina. The team offers a full sweep of IP services, although it has a particular focus on the technology sector. Recent highlights include handling procurements, enforcement and patent defense pertaining to hardware and software, as well as acting for significant international clients in telecom and medical devices.

**The Lawyers:** **William Munck** (see p.1907) is *"one to watch,"* according to his clients, who made much of his *"diligence and superb focus."* Munck's practice centers on IT advisory work, both at home and overseas.

**Clients/Work Highlights:** The firm represents a broad US and international clientele.

## Dewey Ballantine LLP
See firm details p.1530

**The Firm:** Dewey Ballantine's standing in the IP arena rests on the talents of its Austin office, opened in 2002. Here, ten specialists combine to form *"a solid team of experienced patent litigators"* whose telecom and computer industry work is especially well regarded. *"Almost all of those attorneys have technical degrees and it really shows,"* one client revealed. The team has resolved several matters for Intel lately, and also acts as primary counsel for Gateway in ongoing suits. In addition, it works on behalf of several technology-based clients, including pharmaceutical and biotech companies. Further highlights include representing Edwards Life Science in a $30 million patent infringement dispute.

**The Lawyers:** Darryl Adams spearheads the Austin team.

**Clients/Work Highlights:** Microsoft; Gateway; Intel and Brother International.

## Locke Liddell & Sapp LLP

**The Firm:** A 35-strong IP team operates from three cities across the state, where they are commended as an *"active, interesting group with an excellent reputation."* Market sources praised the group's diversity and innovation, saying that they were *"just terrific and responded really well to changing client needs."* Many of the group hold technical degrees in subjects as diverse as aeronautical engineering and organic chemistry. Patent litigation is at the core of the team's work and attorneys also handle patent prosecution and trade dress litigation. There is also a good volume of licensing work for multinational energy companies, software corporations, restaurant chains

and furnishing companies. Recent highlights include successfully asserting two patents for an inventor against Gerber Products, and obtaining a favorable settlement for Tyco Industries in a trademark action. The group also won a series of trade dress infringement suits for subsidiaries of Emerson.

**The Lawyers:** **Robert McAughan** is known as *"a fantastic general IP lawyer."* He divides his time between patent and trademark matters, taking on litigation as well as transactional and counseling roles. He recently acted for Ridge Tools in a multipatent case.

**Clients/Work Highlights:** Compaq; Microsoft; Hewlett-Packard; Baker Hughes; Emerson; Acuity Brands; Varco International; Mary Kay Cosmetics; Gerber Products; BP and Technip.

## Thompson & Knight LLP
See firm details p.1936

**The Firm:** Interviewees praised this Dallas-led team for its *"excellent IP prowess"* and the fact that *"they're always a pleasure to work with."* It has around 20 attorneys, half of whom concentrate on patent, trademark and copyright litigation. The group also includes experienced patent prosecutors and a group of niche technology rights attorneys. Thomson & Knight has been active in several matters brought in the Eastern District of Texas, including a significant dispute between two national semiconductor manufacturers. The team offers advisory and counseling services to a disparate client base, though it has an especially strong profile in e-commerce, Internet patents, cell phones and medical software.

**The Lawyers:** **Bruce Sostek** (see p.1914) is widely acclaimed as *"a superb attorney with enormous experience across the board."* He maintains a broad practice, and regularly represents software, telecom and media companies in patent litigation, trademark and copyright proceedings. Clients view **Herb Hammond** (see p.1895) as *"a really good litigator who always knows what he's doing."* He takes on patent, trademark and copyright matters and is renowned for his mediation of complex disputes.

**Clients/Work Highlights:** CompUSA, STMicroelectronics and Hewlett-Packard are among the group's major clients.

## Band 4

## Conley Rose, PC

**The Firm:** This 50-strong team, the largest boutique in Texas, continues to impress commentators with its *"solid history and broad range of IP services."* Operating from three offices across the state, it is particularly commended for its patent prosecution work and demonstrates expertise in e-commerce matters. Many of its clients are to be found in the digital media, software, energy, medical device and information industries.

**The Lawyers:** **David Rose** was noted as much for his *"sharp and able mind"* as for his long experience. He handles dispute resolution, IP regulation and patent portfolio maintenance.

Clients/Work Highlights: ATI Technologies; Centerpulse Dental; Chevron Phillips Chemical; ConocoPhillips; Cooper Cameron; Daniel Industries; Halliburton; Hewlett-Packard; Nortel Networks; Rice University; Sprint and Texas Instruments.

## Cox Smith Matthews Incorporated
See firm details p.1926
**The Firm:** The IP department of this San Antonio-based regional player comprises nine attorneys. It works seamlessly with the firm's general litigators and its commercial lawyers, offering the full gamut of IP expertise, ranging from patent litigation to trademark and copyright commercial advice. Lawyers have a great deal of experience in the software, medical device, energy and telecom sectors.
**The Lawyers:** Gale Peterson, a highly respected patent litigator, now spends much of his time acting as a special master.
Clients/Work Highlights: Cancer Therapy & Research Center; Clear Channel Communications; Eye Care Centers of America; Sirius Computer Solutions; Southwest Foundation for Biomedical Research and Trinity University.

## Fish & Richardson PC
See firm details p.1113
**The Firm:** This national IP and litigation specialist has offices in Austin and Dallas, where some 60 attorneys together represent "*a growing force in the region.*" The team includes patent litigators and patent prosecutors, as well as trademark specialists. It also caters to clients' transactional needs, advising on due diligence and patent portfolio management. Work highlights include representing a regional airline in a patent infringement dispute over electronic data systems, and defending a national financial institution in an infringement claim relating to electronic check processing.
**The Lawyers:** Experienced Kevin Gray is assistant managing principal of the Dallas office.
Clients/Work Highlights: The group's clientele includes regional and national corporate and financial institutions; tobacco companies; print media and cell phone companies.

## Gardere Wynne Sewell LLP
See firm details p.1931
**The Firm:** Clients strongly endorsed this regional team of "*experienced and aggressive litigators who get results.*" The growing IP group currently comprises 18 attorneys in the Dallas and Houston offices,

where they offer a full range of IP services. The team recently defended LandAmerica Financial Group on a business method patent infringement matter, and also achieved the dismissal of patent claims brought against a national client involved in highway safety.
**The Lawyers:** Department chair **Ken Glaser** (see p.1893) is "*all-around great,*" according to interviewees. His practice encompasses both transactions and litigation, and in the latter sphere, he recently met with success when defending a major cable and wire manufacturer from a patent infringement claim brought by a competitor.
Clients/Work Highlights: The team represents clients in many industry sectors.

## Slusser, Wilson & Partridge LLP
**The Firm:** This Houston-based IP and litigation boutique earned praise disproportionate to its compact size. Commentators were adamant that "*it's just a terrific team,*" pointing to its "*wide-lens focus.*" Extensive patent litigation and trademark expertise enables lawyers to advise a variety of clients, including several in the energy, electrical and petroleum industries. Cases of note include a significant patent infringement matter in the Eastern District of Texas for Smith International, and a complex patent dispute involving multiple energy companies in which it represented Shell.
**The Lawyers:** Founding partner **William Slusser** is admired for his "*breadth, depth and brilliance.*" His IP practice centers on patent litigation, in which he offers decades of trial experience.
Clients/Work Highlights: Shell; Smith International; BJ Services and Exxon Mobil Corporation are among the group's significant clients.

## Weil, Gotshal & Manges LLP
See firm details p.1565
**The Firm:** This international group now has three offices in Texas, which market sources deem "*certainly up-and-coming.*" The IP department of 15 lawyers works closely with the firm's national IP practice on out-of-state and federal trials. Closer to home, the lawyers offer a full service including licensing and transactional support to clients, many of which are in the electrical, hi-tech and information industries. In the Eastern District of Texas, lawyers recently defended Microsoft in a video games patent infringement suit. Additional highlights include representing a multinational computer manufacturer in a trade secrets matter in California, and

successfully asserting the heart pacemaker patents of a prominent cardiologist.
**The Lawyers:** **David Healey** (see p.1896) was recommended as "*a fantastic litigator.*" He concentrates on patent disputes and successfully defended Samsung in a series of cases brought by a competitor. He is also counsel to Microsoft in several ongoing patent infringement matters. Following his recent move from Dewey Ballantine, **Kevin Kudlac** (see p.1901) continues to impress competitors. His work incorporates disputes relating to information software and other computer-related technologies, both in the USA and overseas.
Clients/Work Highlights: SAMSUNG; Lexar Media; Microsoft and Oracle are among the group's significant clients.

## Other Notable Practitioners
**Margaret Boulware** (see p.1883) of Baker & McKenzie is a "*prominent figure*" on the Houston IP scene, according to interviewees. She has experience in the chemicals and biotech patent fields and also takes on trademark matters, focusing on international and domestic portfolio management. **Andrew Dillon** of Dillon & Yudell LLP has "*a top-notch patent prosecution practice.*" He also offers trademark and general IP litigation services to clients in the electronics and software industries. "*Smart and reliable*" **Michael Heim**, who recently moved from Conley Rose to form Heim, Payne & Chorush LLP, specializes in hi-tech and electronics matters; he also offers vast experience in antitrust and trademark disputes relating to brand-name pharmaceutical products. At Mayer, Brown, Rowe & Maw LLP, **Sharon Israel** (see p.1898) has earned a name as "*a highly responsive and outstanding appellate lawyer.*" She recently represented various customers of the Zi Corporation in a patent infringement matter in the Western District of Texas, and also acted for a client in the oil services industry in an infringement suit. **Jerry Selinger** (see p.1913) of Morgan, Lewis & Bockius LLP has "*a terrific reputation in Dallas,*" where he focuses on patent and trademark litigation. He acted for Quick Systems in a business method patent infringement case that ended in a favorable settlement for his client. Sellinger also works as ongoing counsel for Ericsson. Lastly, **Molly Richard** of Richard Law Group has a stellar reputation as "*an outstanding trademark specialist.*" Her clients benefit from her extensive knowledge of domain names and other copyright problems.

# LITIGATION

## Band 1

### Gibbs & Bruns, LLP

See firm details p.1932

**The Firm:** This "*phenomenal and strategic*" Texas litigation boutique continues out in front thanks to "*its second to none preparation*" and team of around 30 "*brilliant trial attorneys, who love trial work and business litigation.*" Its state and national trial track record includes representing plaintiff and defendants in a variety of disputes, including substantial securities, construction and Houston-centric energy litigation. The firm has also been a key player in legal and professional malpractice and has been kept on its toes by the hot IP and patent litigation, with east Texas a key venue for the rocket docket.

**The Lawyers:** The well-known name of **Robin Gibbs** (see p.1892) is associated with "*immense thoroughness and first-class ethics.*" Even with his extensive litigation experience, a "*lack of complacency*" is another bonus for this highly effective trial attorney. He has been wrapping up the representation of former Enron directors as well as defending a lender liability case. Commentators felt entirely comfortable with the "*very gifted*" **Phil Bruns** (see p.1885), a generalist litigator with a broad docket of experience. Sources highlighted his strength in patent infringement, IP and oil and gas litigation. With a mixture of defense and plaintiff work, the "*impressive*" **Jean Frizzell** (see p.1891) earned commendations for a practice that encompasses commercial, IP and partnership disputes. The "*incredibly talented, principled and consistent*" **Chris Reynolds** (see p.1911) impressed clients with his experience, "*intense focus*" and ability to "*sift rapidly through masses of information.*" He has been advising former directors of Peregrine Systems in a securities fraud

and breach of fiduciary case. A "*laid-back style*" marries well with the "*extremely smart and professional approach*" of **Barrett Reasoner** (see p.1911), who enters this year's tables. This top-notch attorney and son of the Vinson & Elkins legend is very much making his own name on the back of "*superb cross-examining skills, which can make witnesses fall apart,*" according to one client. He has been acting for the plaintiffs in a breach of contract case concerning three apartment complexes. In the wake of Enron, there has been a spate of securities litigation in the state, helping to keep busy the "*extremely accomplished and tough*" **Kathy Patrick** (see p.1909), who joins the new securities litigation table. Admired for her securities and financial litigation expertise and a "*never say die attitude,*" she has achieved outstanding results on behalf of officers and directors sued in securities fraud cases.

**Clients/Work Highlights:** Unocal; Pennzoil; Fidelity Management; Coastal Corporation and Stone Energy.

### Susman Godfrey LLP

**The Firm:** Interviewees were unanimous in their praise for this "*nationally renowned litigation powerhouse,*" which has offices in Houston and Dallas as well as Seattle and Los Angeles. The market admired the firm for its recruitment of "*top talent from all over the USA,*" emphasizing its "*identical caliber to top New York firms.*" There are more than 70 "*tough-as-nails, smart*" attorneys who are "*chomping at the bit for success.*" A long track record in the highest-profile antitrust, IP and securities cases has served the firm well in the current climate. Impressive for its experience and understanding of the plaintiff's side, this proactive firm earned respect for remaining "*totally in sync with its clients*" and for its successful reputation in taking cases on contingency and at the last minute.

**The Lawyers:** Clients and peers considered the "*extremely cerebral*" **Lee Godfrey** to be the "*supreme trial lawyer*" and "*brilliantly effective in front of a jury.*" He defended ConocoPhillips and Rio Grande Resources against claims that the defendants' Karnes County uranium mining and milling operations caused cancer and other ailments. **Steve Susman** is admired by commentators for his "*high energy, commitment and intelligence,*" qualities that combine to produce an attorney who is "*as good as they come.*" He was instrumental on behalf of Novamedix in reaching the settlement of its patent infringement lawsuit against KCI after more than a 13-year battle for the company. He and the team finalized the settlement of the $250 million antitrust claim brought by firm client ChoiceParts against the big three automakers, GM, Ford and DaimlerChrysler. The case alleged that the automakers conspired to refuse to license parts data to ChoiceParts' electronic parts locating service. Clients consider the "*passionate and thoughtful*" **Neal Manne** "*one of the finest commercial litigators around*" due to his "*astute, incisive and nimble mind.*" Interviewees underlined his

"*rare gift of penetrating dense rhetoric and complex facts*" to get quickly to the heart of the matter. In spring 2005, he was brought in by Wal-Mart as lead counsel in a massive statewide class action, containing more than 115,000 hourly employees in California. He has also been serving as co-lead counsel for Huntleigh Security in PI litigation and property damage cases arising from the 9/11 terrorist attacks on the World Trade Center. The superb **Mark Wawro** earned compliments for his "*thorough preparation and excellent presentational skills*" in a broad litigation practice, which recently saw him act for Amazon.com. The case was brought by Soverain Software in January 2004, alleging that the website infringed patents covering e-commerce technology. **Ken Marks** earned praise for an enviably broad practice, with notable expertise in securities litigation.

**Clients/Work Highlights:** Nokia; Hertz; Conoco-Phillips; Apache Corporation; Novell; Amazon.com; Universal Studios and Texas Instruments.

### Vinson & Elkins LLP

See firm details p.1938

**The Firm:** This Texan giant featured strongly in local, national and international litigation, according to commentators. A deep bench of "*strong, strategic and talented*" trial attorneys elicited praise for its ability to handle complex commercial litigation, being described as the first port of call for oil and gas and energy-related litigation. The sheer number of attorneys and their breadth of expertise enable the group to handle many complex matters simultaneously, including mass and toxic tort litigation, IP, securities and antitrust disputes. An impressive reputation in domestic and international arbitrations is particularly useful in the current climate and is equally matched by the firm's status in appellate work, carried out by at least 20 attorneys on a regular basis.

**The Lawyers:** Maintaining a very active docket is the "*outstanding lawyers' lawyer*" **Harry Reasoner** (see p.1911), who earned much admiration from the market for his expertise in complex commercial and antitrust litigation and his firm management skills. Prolific in Texas, he has served as lead trial counsel for ETSI Pipeline Project, a joint venture attempting to build a coal slurry pipeline, in a suit brought against various western railroads. Another trial attorney is the "*savvy and knowledgeable*" co-section head **David Harvin** (see p.1896), whose tremendous corporate and securities litigation practice has spanned more than 30 years to date. More than 20 years' experience in a range of commercial and antitrust disputes boosts the "*top-shelf litigator*" **Rob Walters** (see p.1918) into the rankings. Interviewees admired the co-head of the Dallas office for a broad and high-profile litigation practice. For example, he represented Blockbuster in national antitrust litigation brought by independent video retailers, and acted for officers and directors of Alamosa Holdings against a securities fraud class action filed in the Northern District of Texas. Interviewees admired the "*well-seasoned and hard-working*" **Bill Dawson** (see p.1888) as a top choice for legal and accounting professionals facing malpractice claims. The co-section head in Dallas has also been involved in patent infringement cases on both sides of the docket. Having obtained a significant settlement for client Unocal in a contract dispute with Nuevo Energy, which had bought almost all of Unocal's California oilfields in 1996, **Phillip Dye** (see p.1889) earned commendations for his expertise in domestic and international energy litigation. An additional forte is his representation of clients in major casualty litigation. Commentators praised the "*terrific, common-sense approach*" of **Ferguson McNiel** (see p.1905), who enjoys a broad commercial, tort, energy and construction litigation workload. He has recently been acting for the owner in a dispute with the general contractor in the Hobby Center case. The Hobby Center is a new state of the art performing arts center built in downtown Houston. He also represented Pogo Producing Company in a case filed by a landowner seeking damages for alleged surface contamination. Interviewees were highly enthusiastic about the "*extremely talented and trial-experienced*" **Bob Schick** (see p.1913), who boasted extensive products liability and mass toxic tort defense expertise. He and the team have been acting for Wyeth in the massively high-profile diet drug litigation. Although he continues to act for Fluor in most of their construction-related litigation in the Southwest, **Gib Walton** (see p.1918) also garnered praise for his general trial skills, which recently saw him involved in trade secrets and products liability work. In one of the largest and strongest appellate groups in the state, clients admired "*the extremely smart*" **Marie Yeates** (see p.1920) for her "*intense dedication*" to her national appellate practice. With the firm retained by Shell, she defended Equilon Enterprises and other individuals against claims of fraud and breach of contract in the State of California Court of Appeals. Her expertise was also called upon in her defense of Waste Management in two securities fraud and negligence cases brought by a significant former shareholder. In a securities litigation and enforcement group of more than 40 attorneys, **Scott Fletcher** (see p.1891) stands out to commentators. He has acted for individuals and entities in investigations, class actions and shareholder derivative cases. The "*very driven and eloquent*" **Karen Hirschman** (see p.1897) represents accounting firms in many pending securities investigations regarding the financial statements of their audit clients.

**Clients/Work Highlights:** AG Financial Service Center; Equilon Enterprises; Waste Management; UBS Financial Services; Wyeth; Bridgestone/Firestone; Blockbuster; Port of Houston Authority; Shell; HCA; Trammell Crow and Continental Airlines.

## Band 2

### Baker Botts LLP

See firm details p.1922

**The Firm:** Market commentators praised this Texas juggernaut for its diverse and deep pool of litigation expertise, especially among its seasoned jury trial attorneys. The group is seen to have particular expertise in securities litigation, corporate governance and white-collar crime, where the team was deemed strong in its "*guidance of management through the thicket of complex investigations.*" The addition of Seth Taube in New York further enhances this strength. The firm is at the forefront of products liability, IP and oil and gas litigation. In the latter domain, the group recently acted for Shell Oil in the appeal of HRN v Shell, a suit brought by independent service station dealers challenging the pricing system used by Shell and other major gasoline refiners.

**The Lawyers:** Clients and peers admired "*fantastic leader*" **Daryl Bristow** for his "*tireless preparation and cross-examining skills.*" His credibility with the courts and peers owes much to decades of experience in a range of complex litigation. He recently represented CenterPoint Energy in its post-electric deregulation true-up proceeding before the Public Utility Commission fo Texas. The market endorsed the "*tremendous and fierce*" **Irv Terrell** (see p.1916), whose high national profile, like that of Bristow, has been based on long-standing experience and a wide array of complex cases. In New York, he has been representing a high-ranking executive against the SEC's allegations of self-dealing. Interviewees agreed that the "*intense dedication and quick mind*" of **Rod Phelan** (see p.1910) would ensure his place on any shortlist for the defense of legal and accounting malpractice claims. Interviewees considered the "*bright intellect, confidence and photographic memory*" of **Richard Josephson** to be just part of an impressive and underestimated package for clients. A new entry in the rankings this year, he has been acting for Merck in drug litigation and also boasts significant mass tort expertise. Heading the firm's trial department is **Robb Voyles** (see p.1918), whose comprehensive knowledge of securities and professional malpractice litigation served him and clients well in 2005. He successfully represented Deloitte & Touche in a professional negligence case and has also been representing Halliburton in significant commercial litigation. In September 2005, the appellate group was significantly boosted by the arrival of former Chief Justice **Thomas Phillips** (see p.1910), who is credited with the reform of the Texas Supreme Court. Returning to private practice, Phillips is based in Austin and is working closely with Houston, Dallas and Washington, DC attorneys in appellate, trial and alternative dispute resolution work. Blessed with significant experience and an excellent reputation in financial and securities litigation, **David Sterling** (see p.1915) enters the tables due to his substantive knowledge and work for clients such as Morgan Stanley, Prudential Financial and Banc of America Securities. Up-and-coming

## Litigation: Appellate
### Leading Individuals

**1** FROST Claudia *Mayer, Brown, Rowe & Maw*
SIMPSON Reagan *King & Spalding LLP*
YEATES Marie *Vinson & Elkins LLP*

**2** BOYCE William *Fulbright & Jaworski L.L.P.*
COLEMAN Gregory *Weil, Gotshal & Manges LLP*
CORTELL Nina *Haynes and Boone LLP*
GUNN David *Beck, Redden & Secrest LLP*
HATCHELL Mike *Locke Liddell & Sapp LLP*
LIBERATO Lynne *Haynes and Boone LLP*

**3** COHEN Murry *Akin Gump Strauss Hauer & Feld LLP*
DUBOSE Kevin *Alexander Dubose Jones*
HARRIS Warren *Bracewell & Giuliani LLP*
HOLMAN David *Godwin Pappas Langley Ronquillo, LLP*
KELTNER David *Jose, Henry, Brantley & Keltner*
PHILLIPS Thomas *Baker Botts LLP*
TOWNSEND Roger *Alexander Dubose Jones*

## Litigation: Securities
### Leading Individuals

**1** FLETCHER N Scott *Vinson & Elkins LLP*
HARRISON III Orrin *Akin Gump*
HENSLEY Noel *Haynes and Boone LLP*
HIRSCHMAN Karen *Vinson & Elkins LLP*
PATRICK Kathy *Gibbs & Bruns, LLP*
SCHWARTZ Charles *Skadden, Arps*
STERLING David *Baker Botts LLP*
VILLAREAL Patricia *Jones Day*

### Up-and-coming individuals
COOPER Samuel *Baker Botts LLP*

**Sam Cooper** (see p.1887) also enters the securities litigation table and is described by the market as *"very bright, talented, impressive and diligent."* His practice consists of business disputes over contracts and fraudulent and anticompetitive conduct, as well as securities and antitrust lawsuits.

**Clients/Work Highlights:** Alcoa; Exxon Mobil Corporation; Dr Pepper/Seven Up; Hispanic Broadcasting; Alcatel; Deloitte & Touche and CenterPoint Energy.

## Beck, Redden & Secrest LLP

**The Firm:** *"They are not afraid to take the case to trial,"* warned commentators on this much admired 13-year-old Texas litigation boutique. Typically acting for defendants, the 32-strong group of *"terrific and high-flying"* attorneys enjoys considerable experience in a range of high-profile commercial litigation, especially in the realms of mass tort and products liability. The firm defended a multinational corporation from products liability claims, where the plaintiffs alleged defectively designed, manufactured and marketed respiratory equipment had failed to protect them from exposure to silica dust.

**The Lawyers:** The cream of a well-respected crop is *"the outstanding and brave"* **David Beck**, who impressed peers and clients for *"getting in there and shaking things up with an appropriately aggressive*

*approach."* Peers acknowledged a *"very strong trial background"* and a *"folksy approach to jurors,"* which make him a *"formidable opponent."* Praise also rained down on the *"top-notch"* **Joe Redden**, who earned plaudits for his quality practice and expertise in products liability, PI and business litigation. The vice chair of the Litigation Section of the State Bar of Texas, **Alistair Dawson** consolidated his place as a *"sharp up-and-comer,"* according to interviewees. He has been defending Exxon Mobil Corporation in a multimillion-dollar breach of contract claim by a distributor and has acted for Triumph HealthCare against claims of fraud. The *"low-key and incredibly efficient"* **Eric Nichols** enters the tables as a *"superb newcomer"* with *"excellent judgment,"* growing experience and enhanced visibility in oil and gas, IP and securities litigation. *"An excellent memory"* and a distinctive writing style ensure the high profile of the *"highly effective and experienced"* **David Gunn** as a top appellate lawyer.

**Clients/Work Highlights:** 3M; Allied Waste Industries; Becton, Dickinson and Company; Central Parking; GE and Wyeth.

## Fulbright & Jaworski L.L.P.
See firm details p.1928

**The Firm:** This *"excellent"* Houston-based firm has a deep tradition of advocacy and strong arbitration expertise. With more than 300 litigation attorneys in Texas, clients praised the *"well-organized"* team for their *"brilliant execution in court"* and value the firm's expertise in products liability, IP, securities and general commercial litigation. The team has been boosted by the arrival of securities expert Hal Degenhardt, who headed the SEC office in Fort Worth, and former US attorney Mike Shelby, who heads the white-collar crime practice. In a significant IP litigation case, the team emerged victorious for its client Mars after a three-year patent battle with HJ Heinz and Del Monte Foods.

**The Lawyers:** The *"fiercely devoted strategist"* **Linda Addison** (see p.1880) earned compliments for her brilliant legal advice and her *"openness"* with clients. As one of the top female litigators in Texas, her broad commercial litigation practice has seen her acting for the former directed trustee of the Enron 401k program in consolidated Enron employee benefit cases, set for trial in October 2006. She has also been acting for Mars in a patent infringement case against HJ Heinz and Del Monte Foods. There was market praise for **Reagan Brown** (see p.1885), described as *"one of the best legal writers around"* due to his *"persuasiveness and amazing ability to distill arguments."* While heading up the insurance group, Brown has also worked on legal malpractice and arbitrations. *"Seasoned professional"* **Frank Jones** (see p.1899) commands respect for his long-standing experience, assuring his continuing status as a major player in the commercial litigation field. He recently acted for U-Haul International in a wrongful death case. The *"immensely likeable, smart and credible"* **Otway Denny** (see p.1888) enjoys a great reputation in high-profile tort cases, due to his ability to *"make corporate clients look incredibly human,"* according to

one interviewee. He has been acting for BP Products North America regarding an explosion that occurred at the BP plant in Texas City in March 2005. He also represents Shell in cases involving alleged environmental contamination throughout Louisiana. Heading up the litigation department is the well-regarded **Steve Dillard** (see p.1888), who enjoys a sound reputation for products liability and toxic tort litigation. Another highly respected member of the team is **Dudley Oldham** (see p.1908), who has been acting for Tantivy Communications in its patent infringement dispute against Lucent Technologies. Clients attributed the superb appellate reputation of **Bill Boyce** (see p.1884) to his *"great grasp of the law and fast reading of the facts."* *"Honest ethics"* also helped to ensure a great reputation with the fifth Circuit Court of Appeals. Among many cases, he has argued for Continental Airlines in multidistrict litigation proceedings arising from claims of injuries to passengers, which were attributed to the development of blood clots during flight.

**Clients/Work Highlights:** GE; Mars; Continental Airlines; Anadarko Petroleum; Shell; BP America; Bayer and PepsiCo feature in an extensive client roster.

## Band 3

## Carrington, Coleman, Sloman & Blumenthal, LLP

**The Firm:** The market had nothing but praise for this Dallas firm, which is home to many skilled trial attorneys. An *"impeccable level of professionalism, integrity and work ethic"* pervades this almost 100-strong firm, which is renowned for both a strong mix of commercial litigation and transactional work. The influx of new associates in late 2005 combined with the presence of seasoned veteran litigators bolstered the team's presence in the Texas market. Acting on a range of commercial litigation, the team attracted particular praise for legal, accounting and medical malpractice as well as products liability and securities litigation. Sources acknowledged that a number of the state's judges have come from this firm.

**The Lawyers:** A *"long-time lion"* of the Dallas Bar, **Jim Coleman** was awarded the Outstanding 50-Year Lawyer Award by the Texas Bar Foundation in June 2005 and maintains an active litigation caseload. Joining the rankings is the well-regarded trial lawyer **Fletcher Yarbrough**, cited as the *"local dean of complex commercial litigation."* Observers praised the *"responsive and proactive"* **Tim Gavin** for his superb cross-examining skills. In a diverse practice, he recently acted for a private Dallas-based oil and gas company in a right of first refusal case and advised a telecom industry entrepreneur accused of breach of fiduciary duty. He has also defended a law firm in a professional malpractice claim.

**Clients/Work Highlights:** Clients include leading private and public corporations in the state and across the USA.

## Haynes and Boone LLP

**The Firm:** Clients appreciated the manner in which this "*very quick and responsive*" firm is focused on its clients' needs. The business litigation group of more than 200 attorneys is recognized for a range of commercial litigation, and the 60 or so attorneys based in Houston and Dallas earn praise for disputes, including environment, white-collar and securities litigation. Clients also recommended a talented appellate section of 17 attorneys, who recently persuaded the Texas Supreme Court to strike down the Texas public school finance system on constitutional grounds.

**The Lawyers:** Interviewees admired the "*extremely experienced and go-getting*" **Lynne Liberato**, who earned significant kudos as a strong appellate attorney. She obtained a reversal of class certification for BMG Direct Marketing in a suit brought by a class of hundreds of thousands of Texas-based music club members. They sought recovery of the late fees they had paid on their compact disc purchases. She is complemented by Dallas colleague **Nina Cortell**, whose clients are appreciative of her "*nurturing manner*" and ability to empathize with them. The "*very professional, responsive and pragmatic*" Cortell has a strong reputation in appellate work, recently defending Siemens in a $7.5 million appeal by a widow in a fatal design defect case. She also affirmed the nationwide injunction for Exxon Mobil Corporation against Greenpeace. Entering this year's new securities litigation table is the "*detail-oriented*" **Noel Hensley**, who has been involved in significant securities class action litigation and internal investigations. A "*good listener,*" he is recommended by clients for his dedication to finding them workable solutions.

**Clients/Work Highlights:** American Airlines; El Paso; Siemens; Bank of America; Blockbuster; Dynegy; Waste Management; HCA; Toshiba America and Viacom International.

## King & Spalding LLP

See firm details p.1938

**The Firm:** This widely respected, 50-strong commercial litigation team earned widespread plaudits as "*arguably the place to go to*" for major environmental and tort litigation. The entrepreneurial firm has been acting for Chevron in their defense of claims of pesticide and radiation litigation. The team also serves as lead trial counsel for welding rod manufacturers Lincoln Electric Company, Hobart Brothers and Teledyne McKay in significant national litigation, in which welders are claiming injury through exposure to the manganese in welding rod fumes.

**The Lawyers:** Commercial, royalty and environmental contamination litigation are the backbone of "*consummate trial attorney*" **Bobby Meadows'** (see p.1905) practice. His excellent judgment commands the respect of an equally impressive clientele, including Chevron, Shell, Halliburton and Oxydental Petroleum, who entrust him with bet-the-company cases. The "*straight-shooting*" **Adam Schiffer** (see p.1913) relates well to clients and boasts great advocacy skills and trial experience. He

has been involved in significant matters for both Shell Trading and Halliburton KBR. The Shell Trading case centered on a breach of agreement dispute with a power plant owner over the recall rights to electric generation capacity. The former Vinson & Elkins attorney also continues to work on the $200 million defective engineering design and construction dispute for KBR. Joining this year's tables is another former Vinson & Elkins attorney, the "*steady, seasoned and tough*" practitioner **Mark Glasser** (see p.1893), who enjoys a strong counseling and commercial, securities and oil and gas litigation practice. There was much market admiration for **Reagan Simpson**'s (see p.1914) long-time appellate practice, general trial experience and "*incredibly calming influence and style.*" The former leader of the Fulbright & Jaworski appellate section has been instrumental in the growth of this firm's expertise, bringing in a lateral hire from Jackson Walker in early 2005. Simpson played a key role in the reversal of a $122 million jury verdict against client Coastal Refining and Marketing. Plaintiffs were three workers who suffered serious burn injuries in an explosion at a refinery operated by a subsidiary of the client.

**Clients/Work Highlights:** In a significant antitrust suit in federal court in New York, the team also acted for Home Depot as the plaintiff in a billion-dollar suit against Visa and MasterCard. International arbitrations play a massive role in the firm's reputation across the USA. Other clients include Chevron; Shell; Halliburton; Miller Brewing; ExxonMobil; KPMG; Dow Chemical and Home Depot.

## Mayer, Brown, Rowe & Maw LLP

See firm details p.876

**The Firm:** Approaching 40 litigators in Houston, this international giant commands respect on the Texas scene for a range of litigation, appellate cases and international arbitrations. Its ability to tap into the resources of a legal goliath was among the significant advantages described by commentators. Clients appreciated a "*uniformly excellent*" team of appellate lawyers and litigators, renowned for being "*superb strategists and writers*" with a "*direct, to-the-point style.*"

**The Lawyers:** Clients admired the "*highly responsive and fabulous strategist*" **Claudia Frost** (see p.1892) for her powers of "*brilliant analysis.*" She has a trial background and a depth of appellate experience, with a particular niche in patent infringement. In Freedom Wireless v Boston Communications Group, she has been representing Cingular Wireless in a patent infringement case, which at the time of writing is on appeal to the US Court of Appeals. Under Frost's stewardship, the team is going from strength to strength with a group of attorneys to watch. Bill Knull features prominently in international arbitrations.

**Clients/Work Highlights:** Dow Chemical; Marathon Oil; Equistar; Agrium; Ameritrade; Apache Corporation and Government of Turkmenistan

## McDade Fogler LLP

**The Firm:** "*Small, selective and efficient*" were the words of one commentator on this "*market-respected and cost-conscious*" litigation boutique. The 13-year-old firm earned commendations for its four talented attorneys and its civil litigation practice, with particular emphasis on insurance coverage, antitrust and legal malpractice.

**The Lawyers:** Praise was forthcoming for the "*very smart brains behind the outfit,*" **Murray Fogler**, for his "*persuasiveness, thoughtfulness and sense of humor.*" An ability to "*cut through the unnecessary to get to the bigger picture*" benefits a diverse commercial litigation practice, specifically focused recently on oil and gas, legal malpractice and insurance litigation. For example, he assisted in a successful motion to dismiss Andrews & Kurth from the Enron shareholder litigation. He also acted for Service Corporation International (SCI) in a large insurance coverage dispute. SCI is the largest funeral home and cemetery corporation in the USA. This dispute arises out of a $100 million settlement of a class action in Florida.

**Clients/Work Highlights:** Bridas; Cardinal Health; Coastal Corporation; Transocean; Andrews & Kurth; SCI; Duke Energy; Field Services and El Paso.

## Band 4

## Akin Gump Strauss Hauer & Feld LLP

See firm details p.559

**The Firm:** With more than 100 lawyers in the team, interviewees underlined the growing presence of this mammoth firm in commercial litigation in the Texas market. Four offices in the state give the firm a good base, from where many significant cases are handled, including white-collar, commercial, securities and litigation and appellate work. For example, the team acted for Bank of America in litigation brought by Nitla, alleging aiding and abetting of fraud and breach of fiduciary duties.

**The Lawyers:** Sources expected the "*instincts of a judge*" to stand **Murry Cohen** (see p.1886) in good stead as he makes the transition from the bench to private practice. Since his August 2004 move, the former Court of Appeals judge has been heading the appellate practice. Clients appreciated his "*unique perspective as to what judges are looking for,*" as well as his connections. Cohen argued and won a reversal for BNSF Railway in the Court of Appeals for the 14th District of Texas. Entering the tables for securities litigation is **Orrin Harrison** (see p.1896), who has been advising Waddell & Reed Financial Services in its investigation by the NASD's Department of Enforcement. The NASD filed the suit alleging claims of unsuitability and failure to supervise in the exchange of variable annuity products and seeking approximately $50 million in damages.

**Clients/Work Highlights:** Nokia; RSC Investments; Waddell & Reed Financial Services and CenterPoint Energy.

## Bracewell & Giuliani LLP

See firm details p.1924

**The Firm:** Commentators point out the advantages of the lean staffing approach and collegial group of smart lawyers at this much-admired firm, which has lately seen an increase in corporate investigations and Sarbanes-Oxley work. The recruitment of several well-known attorneys has enhanced the firm's glossy reputation, which continues to shine in the local market for its expertise in commercial, energy, securities and antitrust litigation.

**The Lawyers:** There was much praise for the "*savvy and fearless*" **Cliff Gunter** (see p.1895) for his "*effective and low-key*" approach to cases, which have spanned the full range of commercial litigation. Lately, he has been working in antitrust, securities and oil and gas litigation. He acted for Kinder Morgan in contract and tort claims by Exxon Mobil Corporation concerning gas processing at the Bushton gas plant – one of the largest and oldest gas processing plants in the USA. Exxon Mobil Corporation had alleged breach of contract and conversion of liquids extracted from gas for a period covering more than 15 years. Gunter has been acting for the world's largest funeral and cemetery operator in antitrust matters in Texas and California. Clients appreciated the "*really good bedside manner*" of **Warren Harris** (see p.1895), who cultivated close client relationships as well as a well-respected rapport with the judiciary. Harris is chair-elect of the Texas State Bar Appellate Section.

**Clients/Work Highlights:** BP; Apple; Bank of America; San Antonio Spurs; Houston Livestock Show and Rodeo; Coral Energy and Kinder Morgan.

## Jones Day

See firm details p.570

**The Firm:** Bolstered by the resources of its multiple offices, this national player is making a push in the Texas litigation market, earning particular commendations for IP, products liability and securities litigation. The litigation team contains almost 140 cost-conscious lawyers in Dallas and Houston, with both offices involved in litigation for Dole Food Company brought by thousands of foreign banana workers who alleged injuries caused by chemical exposure.

**The Lawyers:** Entering the tables for securities litigation is the "*very talented, no-nonsense and calm*" **Patricia Villareal** (see p.1917). Clients considered her "*practical and constructive advice*" invaluable. She was part of a large team acting for EDS and certain of its officers and directors in several matters arising out of disclosure that its earnings would be lower than anticipated. She also acted for Dell in a separate patent infringement dispute with Intergraph.

**Clients/Work Highlights:** Bayer; BP America; Chevron; Dell; Dole Food Company; EDS; Halliburton and Texas Instruments.

## Locke Liddell & Sapp LLP

**The Firm:** Market respect continued for this Texas-born stalwart, which offers a range of litigation advice from its three state offices of more than 150

litigation lawyers. The team, whose litigation experience spans multimillion-dollar class action litigation, business, contract and tort disputes, was praised for its "*effective grasp of both the law and clients' business objectives.*"

**The Lawyers:** The market was impressed by the "*seasoned and smart*" **Mike Powell**, who joins this year's tables having been recommended for his "*strategic thinking.*" The "*highly academic and studious*" **Mike Hatchell** combined teaching, analysis and advocacy with "*wonderful and effective talent.*" The long-standing appellate expert commanded the respect of the judiciary and peers, being described as the "*dean of the appellate Bar*" and a "*tremendous drawing card.*" Attracting a number of fans is **James Leahy**, who recently joined from Thompson & Knight. He has represented American National Petroleum in a claim against Transcontinental Gas Pipe Line Corporation over take-or-pay and pricing disputes in an interstate gas sales contract.

**Clients/Work Highlights:** The firm's client roster includes the Houston Astros.

## McKool Smith

See firm details p.1934

**The Firm:** This well-staffed, Dallas-based trial firm of 80 "*particularly effective and active trial lawyers*" was noted for a range of commercial litigation, especially IP and securities litigation.

**The Lawyers:** There was widespread praise for the "*exceptionally talented and experienced*" **Lewis LeClair** (see p.1902), who enters this year's rankings. Approaching almost 30 years' experience, his broad docket includes a range of commercial and IP litigation as well as arbitrations. He has acted for Pioneer Natural Resources in partnership, securities and contract claims and Texas Rangers Baseball Club in a trade secrets dispute. The firm was founded by the "*first-class*" **Mike McKool** (see p.1905), a "*smart and aggressive*" attorney who gained particular respect and an increased profile for his work on behalf of clients such as Ericsson and EDS.

**Clients/Work Highlights:** A wide gamut of clients includes massive names, such as Excel Communications; National Instruments; Parental Guide; Southwest Sports Group and Trilogy.

## Smyser Kaplan & Veselka LLP

**The Firm:** This "*talented and aggressive*" litigation boutique enters the tables for its growing presence on the Texas stage. The ten-year-old Houston-based firm boasts a stable of highly skilled trial attorneys, formerly of the super firms, and a diverse range of trial experience drives its promising reputation forward. The 12-strong team represents plaintiffs and defendants in multimillion-dollar lawsuits, including class actions. The team won $9 million in damages and a permanent injunction in a patent infringement case involving drag-reducing agents in pipelines.

**The Lawyers:** **Craig Smyser** commanded respect for his great trial skills and his willingness to go the extra mile for clients. His broad litigation docket has included the defense of officers and directors in

major securities class action and derivative cases. Achieving great results for his clients is the "*very smart and tenacious*" **Lee Kaplan**, who "*quickly gets to the heart of the matter,*" according to interviewees. He enjoys a strong reputation in commercial litigation, especially patent and trademark litigation, and has represented plaintiffs and defendants in state and federal courts. He recently represented a Fortune 20 company as lead plaintiff counsel in a patent infringement trial.

**Clients/Work Highlights:** The firm acts for a range of Fortune 20, 100 and 500 companies.

## Thompson & Knight LLP

See firm details p.1936

**The Firm:** With its roots in Dallas, this long-standing Texas firm continues to blossom in commercial litigation. From four offices in the state, its team of almost 130 lawyers offers an extensive trial practice, including specialist advice in antitrust, energy, toxic tort, IP, products liability and securities litigation. The market endorsed the firm's reputation for "*in-depth analysis and impressive trial preparation.*"

**The Lawyers:** The market agreed that **Tim McCormick** (see p.1904) is "*one very fine business litigator*" whose practice continues to prosper. Spending time in both the Dallas and New York offices, his areas of expertise include securities and corporate governance litigation as well as internal corporate investigations. The team recorded the departure of the much-admired James Leahy, who recently moved to Locke Liddell.

**Clients/Work Highlights:** American National Petroleum; Frio Exploration; TOTAL Minatome; Nicor Petroleum and Total Oil Marine.

## Weil, Gotshal & Manges LLP

See firm details p.1565

**The Firm:** This international giant has established a strong Texas presence through its involvement in bet-the-company and high-stakes commercial litigation. The market considers the firm's strength to lie in a Dallas office, where a team of around 30 litigators are involved in a variety of litigation, earning particular credit for its class action and multiple jurisdiction litigation. Renowned for its bankruptcy litigation expertise, the firm also earned commendations for its IP and products liability work.

**The Lawyers:** Co-heading the litigation practice is **Ralph Miller** (see p.1906), whose trial practice includes a strong securities litigation flavor. He has been involved in the representation of Motient in several high-profile lawsuits adverse to one of the company's largest shareholders, Highland Capital Management. Praise also fell heavily on **Greg Coleman** (see p.1886), who is seen to be quickly developing the seeds of a national practice. He and the team represented Exxon Mobil Corporation, Exxon Chemical Arabia and Mobil Yanbu Petrochemical Company in related appeals before the Delaware and US Supreme Courts. The team also handled a major appeal for Hyundai Mipo Dockyard and Hyundai Corporation, reversing the district court's liability finding and dismissing the $100 million in claims against them.

**Clients/Work Highlights:** The Dallas office successfully defended Prudential Securities in two lawsuits involving the company's former client Epic Resorts, and successfully defended MasterCard in three putative class action lawsuits involving MasterCard's currency conversion process. Additional clients include ExxonMobil; and STMicroelectronics.

## Other Notable Practitioners

Described as a "*first-rate trial lawyer who can try any commercial case,*" **Chip Babcock** of Jackson Walker LLP earned most plaudits for his media and First Amendment expertise. The Houston-based attorney enjoys a national practice, boosted by more than 25 years' experience and his representation of Oprah Winfrey in high-profile litigation in the 1990's. There was much praise for the "*unbelievably intense and*

*smart*" **Bruce Golden** (see p.1893) from Golden & Owens LLP. Golden shines in a small yet fierce litigation boutique, possessing a "*voice perfect for the courtroom*" coupled with a "*level of preparation to terrify opposing counsel.*" There was widespread acclaim for the long track record of senior Dallas trial lawyer **Bob Mow** of Hughes & Luce LLP. More than 35 years' experience in a diverse array of litigation placed him on most peers' shortlists. Entering the securities litigation table is the "*tremendous*" **Charles Schwartz** (see p.1913) of Skadden, Arps, Slate, Meagher & Flom LLP. A former Vinson & Elkins specialist in corporate governance, he boasts "*an encyclopedic knowledge of case law*" and has been representing KMPG-TCI in litigation in Houston, as well as French client Virbac, a defendant in securities and derivative actions pending in Texas.

## Other Notable Appellate Experts

There was market admiration for the "*smart, ethical and trustworthy*" appellate specialists **Kevin Dubose** and **Roger Townsend** of Alexander Dubose Jones & Townsend. Dubose earned commendations for the "*easy organization and readability of his briefs,*" while Townsend, the former leader of Fulbright & Jaworski's appellate practice, drew praise for his "*brilliant, articulate and measured*" approach to the law. Peers respected the "*tremendous oral advocacy skills*" of **David Holman** of Godwin Pappas Langley Ronquillo LLP, while **David Keltner** of Jose, Henry, Brantley & Keltner remains a main player on the strength of his reputation and background knowledge. The "*excellent strategist*" also earned compliments for having enough energy and enthusiasm "*to wake up a courtroom.*"

# PROJECTS

| Projects |
|---|
| **Leading Firms** |
| **1** BAKER BOTTS LLP *Houston* |
| VINSON & ELKINS LLP *Houston* |
| **2** AKIN GUMP STRAUSS HAUER & FELD *Houston* |
| **3** ANDREWS KURTH LLP *Houston* |
| KING & SPALDING LLP *Houston* |
| **4** BRACEWELL & GIULIANI LLP *Houston* |
| PILLSBURY WINTHROP SHAW PITTMAN *Houston* |
| SKADDEN, ARPS *Houston* |

| Leading Individuals |
|---|
| **1** ASMUS David *Baker Botts LLP* |
| BILGER Bruce *Vinson & Elkins LLP* |
| COGAN JR John *Akin Gump* |
| **2** ALE John *Skadden, Arps* |
| BLAND Douglas *Vinson & Elkins LLP* |
| CULOTTA Ken *King & Spalding LLP* |
| GOOLSBY George *Baker Botts LLP* |
| KELLEY Jay *Vinson & Elkins LLP* |
| UNGER Timothy *Andrews Kurth LLP* |
| WEEMS Philip *King & Spalding LLP* |
| **3** KREBS Stephen *Baker Botts LLP* |
| MAUEL John *Pillsbury Winthrop* |
| PINKERTON Glenn *Vinson & Elkins LLP* |
| THURBER Mark *Andrews Kurth LLP* |
| **4** ARRINGTON Scott *Akin Gump* |
| BACKUS Marcia *Vinson & Elkins LLP* |
| CULWELL Todd *Pillsbury Winthrop* |
| EVANS Mark *Bracewell & Giuliani LLP* |
| RAFTE Alan *Bracewell & Giuliani LLP* |
| ROGERS Daniel *King & Spalding LLP* |
| SCHUMACHER David *Chadbourne & Parke LLP* |
| THOMPSON Dahl *Andrews Kurth LLP* |

| Up-and-coming individuals |
|---|
| BRADSHAW Brian *Skadden, Arps* |

## Band 1

### Baker Botts LLP
See firm details p.1922

**The Firm:** According to commentators, this firm has really gained momentum in the projects arena, and a quick scan of its deal list makes it obvious why. The firm has been involved in most of the major LNG projects in recent years in both the domestic and international markets. Clients report that while the partners here are "*technically excellent and business-minded,*" it is the strength of the associates supporting them that distinguishes this firm from its competitors. Internationally, the team has impressed with its penetration into not just the busy Middle East market, but also into Asia and the emerging markets. The group is advising on the Tangguh project in Indonesia and was instructed by Petronet on the development of two receiving terminals in India. It is also working for Marathon as principal sponsor of the Equatorial Guinea LNG project. This "*efficient operation*" also advised ConocoPhillips on the purchase of LNG in relation to the Qatargas III development.

**The Lawyers:** **David Asmus** (see p.1881) is "*probably one of the best project finance lawyers in the world,*" said clients. He continues to impress with his practical approach to deal negotiations born out of a wealth of experience. **George Goolsby** (see p.1893) is rated highly for his pipeline work, and brings to the deal table a significant international experience, having worked in Russia and the emerging markets. **Stephen Krebs** (see p.1901) heads the project finance practice and he is "*thorough, precise and strategic*" in his advice.

**Clients/Work Highlights:** Hunt Oil Company; Repsol LNG; Brass LNG; Dahej LNG project; Kochi LNG project and BP.

### Vinson & Elkins LLP
See firm details p.1938

**The Firm:** This Texas stalwart has established a robust projects practice that is nimble enough to track market trends. It is growing from its historical energy roots into the power and renewables sector, prompting commentators to remark that it has "*adjusted remarkably well to the post-Enron landscape.*" Traditionally viewed as a sponsors' practice, the firm's lenders work is steadily increasing and clients report that "*the technical knowledge of the lawyers there is hard to beat.*" Illustrating this technical ability, the team advised the Bank of Nova Scotia on a highly structured project financing of the Medusa Spar in the Gulf of Mexico, a region spawning a significant level of work. There is a high degree of integration between the Houston office and its New York and DC colleagues, and the team has been instrumental in advising Complete Energy Holdings in the financing of its acquisition of La Paloma Generating Company, which owns the 1000 MW project.

**The Lawyers:** **Bruce Bilger** (see p.1883) is a big draw for clients, bringing extensive domestic and international projects expertise. He is "*fast, sharp and knows the ins and outs of getting the deal done,*" said clients. **Douglas Bland** (see p.1883) "*is a true energy expert,*" and advises international oil majors as well as finance source clients. **Jay Kelley** (see p.1900) is recommended for his partnership expertise and LNG know-how, while **Glenn Pinkerton** (see p.1910) stands out for his expertise in international matters. His project finance experience is supplemented by a broader base of transactional work. **Marcia Backus** (see p.1881) has a wide-ranging energy transactional practice and is applauded for her "*first-class negotiation skills.*"

**Clients/Work Highlights:** The team was involved in the project financing of the pipeline that connects to the Atlantic LNG facility for the National Gas

Company of Trinidad and Tobago, marking the first project financing in Trinidad. Other clients include BG Group; Chevron Phillips Chemical; JPMorgan Chase; WestLB; AES; PSEG Global; Bank of Nova Scotia; Shell; Occidental Petroleum and Hunt Oil.

## Band 2

### Akin Gump Strauss Hauer & Feld LLP
See firm details p.559

**The Firm:** This team is really making its mark on the Texan, national and international projects markets. Energy is the focus here, with LNG a particular specialty. The firm is advising on a range of projects from upstream to downstream, with a very healthy midstream practice that includes an impressive maritime group, which is currently advising the Qatari ship acquisition team. The Middle East has been a key focus of activity of late, and in the last year the group has been involved in Qatargas II and III and RasGas II and III. Central Europe and Latin America have also been busy areas for the firm, with advice to Repsol YPF in its acquisition and development of interests in the Camisea field gas project with Hunt Oil. Sources admired the recent push the firm has made into the projects sector, commenting: *"They're out there doing the deals, and doing them well."*

**The Lawyers:** *"Superstar"* **John Cogan** (see p.1886) is an internationally recognized projects lawyer. Clients were quick to praise his *"great interpersonal style"* and the fact that he *"manages his team well and staffs transactions effectively – you can trust his judgment."* **Scott Arrington** (see p.1881) is another highly regarded attorney, commended for his expertise in the international sector. He speaks Mandarin and Spanish fluently and clients particularly appreciate his in-depth understanding of state oil companies.

**Clients/Work Highlights:** The firm is representing Anadarko in the development of an LNG receiving terminal in Nova Scotia and related activities. Dynegy and El Paso are additional clients of the team.

## Band 3

### Andrews Kurth LLP
See firm details p.1921

**The Firm:** Market sources report that this firm is making a significant push into the projects sphere, and this strategy is bearing fruit, with the firm being involved in a healthy workload of domestic deals. While the team has been involved in a number of LNG deals, it is the renewables sector where it is particularly distinguishing itself, having completed a number of wind projects, including representing the developer of the Sweetwater 135 MW WPP in Texas. The firm is also making a foray into the coal-to-liquid arena, ideally positioning itself to benefit from renewed interest in this industry.

**The Lawyers:** **Timothy Unger** is *"a subtle negotiator,"* say clients who praise his *"personable manner*

*and ability to keep deals moving forward."* **Mark Thurber** works across the full range of the power and energy sectors and is *"very bright and always ahead of the game."* **Dahl Thompson** represents both sponsors and lenders and is always *"technically astute and business-minded."*

**Clients/Work Highlights:** DKRW; Wachovia; Bank One; RBS; Duke Energy; ConocoPhillips and CapRock are among the firm's clients.

### King & Spalding LLP
See firm details p.1938

**The Firm:** This firm is dominating the domestic LNG projects market, fielding a team of *"sharp and savvy"* lawyers from its Houston office. It is currently representing eight LNG terminal developers in the USA, including acting as project counsel to the Freeport LNG terminal, and Cheniere Energy in the construction of an LNG receiving facility in Sabine Pass, Louisiana. While it grabs the headlines in the energy sector, the firm covers the market from soup to nuts, with a growing niche in transportation projects. Internationally, the firm has turned its attention to Latin America, representing Chevron in various gas developments in Venezuela. In addition to developers, the firm's profile is rising among finance clients, particularly private equity funds such as Haddington Ventures.

**The Lawyers:** The firm fields a very strong team of lawyers with expertise across all energy areas, and particularly in the LNG field. **Ken Culotta** (see p.1887) is an esteemed international projects attorney and clients report he is *"so easy to work with – he is practical and solutions-focused and pays a lot of attention to detail."* **Philip Weems**'s (see p.1918) understanding of the LNG field has led clients to remark: *"He is someone I would trust implicitly."* **Daniel Rogers** (see p.1912) has joined the team from Chadbourne & Parke; a prescient hire, according to commentators, as he brings a strong lender experience to the group.

**Clients/Work Highlights:** The group represents Woodside in its LNG transportation operations between Australia and the USA.

## Band 4

### Bracewell & Giuliani LLP
See firm details p.1924

**The Firm:** This firm has a strong domestic presence, advising on power and oil and gas projects. Restructurings have been the focus of the group in recent times, and its strong finance practice ensures a mixed client base of financial institutions as well as key industry clients. Sources report that the team has a high degree of industry knowledge and that their responsiveness to clients is a key draw.

**The Lawyers:** **Mark Evans** (see p.1890) represents commercial banks and lenders in a range of finance transactions **Alan Rafte** (see p.1911) garnered praise for his work across the power and oil and gas industries and his ability to handle a wide range of transactions.

**Clients/Work Highlights:** InterGen; Calpine; Reliant; Plains Exploration & Production; JPMorgan Chase; Citibank; Bank One; Calyon; Société Générale; BNP Paribas; Wells Fargo and Union Bank of California.

### Pillsbury Winthrop Shaw Pittman LLP
See firm details p.1550

**The Firm:** The firm is making a concerted push into the projects market, bringing key lateral hires and clients into the fold. John Mauel and Todd Culwell have joined the team from Baker & McKenzie, and bring with them a wealth of industry experience. They have continued to advise as project counsel to the Tractebel Bahamas LNG project, and have solid ties with the power industry, assisting SunCoke in their development of integrated coke and power projects. Harnessing the synergies provided by the firm's recent merger, these moves complement the enhanced energy and projects practice of the firm on each coast of the USA. Notably, the strong finance and regulatory capability in New York and Washington, DC provides a valuable set of resources.

**The Lawyers:** These lateral hires are seen as *"a very smart move"* by commentators who predict that the projects practice here will be worth watching in the year ahead. **John Mauel** (see p.1904) now leads the local finance practice and is *"very talented with a knack for driving deals forward,"* say clients. **Todd Culwell** (see p.1888) is noted for his lenders practice and is *"extremely savvy."*

**Clients/Work Highlights:** RBS; JPMorgan Chase; SUEZ Energy North America; Entre Energy; Macquarie Securities (USA); DZ Bank; Wells Fargo HSBC Trade Bank; Atlas Methanol Company; Econo-Power International.

### Skadden, Arps, Slate, Meagher & Flom LLP & Affiliates
See firm details p.1557

**The Firm:** The Houston office of this international projects powerhouse continues to drive the team's domestic and international energy practice forward, working closely with its New York and Washington, DC counterparts. The office is feted for its transactional capabilities across all projects sectors. While oil and gas are a natural focus for the Texas team, its attorneys are also striding ahead in the power arena, representing NRG Energy in its acquisition of Texas Genco. Sources report the Texas market can be a difficult one for the top-drawer New York firms. However, this team performed admirably in developing the depth of its team. This has allowed it to weather the departure of Lyndon Taylor – who has gone in-house to Devon Energy – with relative ease. The team is home, not only to respected senior partners, but also a promising stable of juniors and associates.

**The Lawyers:** **John Ale** (see p.1880), by all accounts, is a *"great guy, a trusted business adviser and a great lawyer."* His projects experience extends to both the domestic and international markets and clients report that he lends his *"creative insight"* to the deals he works on. Sources also highlighted the practice of

**Brian Bradshaw** (see p.1884): "*He knows what he is doing and is definitely one to watch in the LNG sector.*" Clients/Work Highlights: Other clients include Goldman Sachs, Sumitomo Mitsui Banking and BHP Billiton.

## Other Notable Practitioners

**David Schumacher** (see p.1913) is the driving force behind Chadbourne & Parke LLP's Houston office. Having recently relocated from Washington, DC, he brings his oil and gas expertise – which includes a valuable understanding of the regulatory scene – to the deal table. He has recently advised the IFC on the financing of a natural gas pipeline owned and operated by Transierra SA in Bolivia.

# REAL ESTATE

| Real Estate |
| --- |
| Leading Firms |
| [1] **BAKER BOTTS LLP** Houston |
| **HAYNES AND BOONE LLP** Dallas |
| **VINSON & ELKINS LLP** Houston |
| **WINSTEAD SECHREST & MINICK P.C.** Dallas |
| [2] **AKIN GUMP STRAUSS HAUER & FELD LLP** Dallas |
| **ANDREWS KURTH LLP** Houston |
| **BRACEWELL & GIULIANI LLP** Dallas |
| **FULBRIGHT & JAWORSKI L.L.P.** Houston |
| **LOCKE LIDDELL & SAPP LLP** Houston |
| **MAYER, BROWN, ROWE & MAW LLP** Houston |
| **WEIL, GOTSHAL & MANGES LLP** Dallas |
| [3] **GARDERE WYNNE SEWELL LLP** Dallas |
| **JACKSON WALKER LLP** Houston |
| **JENKENS & GILCHRIST PC** Dallas |
| **THOMPSON & KNIGHT LLP** Houston |

## Band 1

### Baker Botts LLP

See firm details p.1922

The Firm: "*A major force in the real estate sector,*" this top-drawer firm is continuously involved in some of the most high-profile transactions in the field. It has a wide-ranging blue-chip clientele that encompasses a host of major developers and institutional lenders in the state. The team regularly handles complex projects including acquisition, development, leasing, financing and debt restructuring work. In recent times, the lawyers have been involved in a large number of sales transactions and have increasingly worked with asset management funds. One of its ongoing highlights involves working for Hines Interests on a project in Shanghai relating to a high-level mixed-use project consisting of retail and office space and state-of-the-art residential living. In another important transaction, the lawyers handled the acquisition of 650,000 sq ft of office space in Houston for Marathon Oil. Additionally, the team represented a family fund that is heavily investing in residential and retail properties across Mexico. It is also assisting with the development of medical facilities across Texas.

The Lawyers: Clients and peers emphatically commended **Fred Dunlop** (see p.1889) for his "*great intelligence mixed with formidable integrity.*" Having won a great degree of acclaim for his role in the Galleria project, he is currently heavily involved in the mixed-use project in Shanghai on behalf of Heinze. The "*highly energetic and responsive*"

**Robert Wright** (see p.1920) was praised by those peers who had acted opposite him for his ability to "*filter out easily what is important and what isn't.*" He "*always makes sure that he retains a personable approach and lets the client know where he stands.*" Wright does a lot of work with the energy industry and also tackles a considerable amount of environmental work. The "*very talented*" **Jon Dunlay** (see p.1889) is "*good to work with*" and has extensive experience working on residential and leisure developments across Texas. He continues to represent various lending institutions across the USA. "*A favorite choice of major clients,*" **Marley Lott** (see p.1902) has "*a real voice as the sole woman in a team of heavyweight male lawyers.*" Known as being "*very thorough,*" she regularly represents Hines Interests in its major projects and frequently works on joint ventures. Praised as "*a strategic thinker who always makes sure things are thought through to the smallest detail,*" **Mark Van Kirk** (see p.1917) predominantly advises sellers, buyers and investment funds on financing matters, especially in regard to retail projects.

Clients/Work Highlights: Hines Interests; Kellogg Brown & Root; Marathon Oil; BP and a number of major developers nationwide.

### Haynes and Boone LLP

The Firm: One of the most prominent real estate practices around, this firm has a "*stellar real estate tax practice and an incredible breadth of experience.*" Clients pointed to the emergence of "*young lawyers who are already doing a superb job*" as a key factor in its success. With 35 lawyers, of whom 12 are partners, in six offices across Texas, the firm offers in-depth real estate advice on a raft of topics. It tackles commercial and industrial lease work for a range of clients and has experienced an upsurge of transactional work over the past year, much in line with overall market trends. At present, the lawyers are involved in two major joint venture developments in the downtown Houston area and are handling various major real estate projects in California, Texas and New Jersey. They are also heavily engaged in the Regency project, a matter entailing the acquisition and development of shopping centers across the Midwest.

The Lawyers: **Robert Wilson** is "*worth a mint to clients*" due to the fact that he "*represents their views extremely well and provides careful advice.*" His major highlights include working on the Regency project across the Midwest, as well as advising on various residential developments in Florida, California and Illinois. "*Well on her way to becoming one of the top

lawyers in the field,*" **Ann Saegert** has "*excellent contacts in the enforcement industry.*" Her client portfolio includes publicly traded real estate companies, lenders and corporate users. Praised for his "*highly innovative advice and thinking outside the box,*" **Steve Jenkins** is "*the most technology-oriented lawyer of the team.*" A frequent speaker on environmental matters, he focuses his work on land use regulatory issues and the negotiation of complex leases. Market sources were also impressed with newcomer **Walter Miller**'s work, calling him "*a terrific lawyer who truly strives to get the best results for clients.*" Recently made partner, he primarily handles complex real estate transactions, in particular acquisitions, leasing and development.

Clients/Work Highlights: Archon Group; Crescent Real Estate Equities; Hillwood Development; Heitman Capital Management; American Airlines; Ericsson and Wal-Mart.

### Vinson & Elkins LLP

See firm details p.1938

The Firm: The plaudits came fast and furious for this heavyweight, with clients extolling its "*tremendous acuity in all areas of the law.*" According to several clients, this is "*the top firm – we choose them because they offer a great balance between dollars and services.*" The firm offers advice on all aspects of real estate law, ranging from transactional work to corporate governance advice. In recent times, the lawyers have spent a substantial amount of time advising private investors and have worked increasingly on loan financings and shopping center developments. The Tenance Group is one of the biggest clients, and the team advised it on a six-unit apartment development and several real estate projects nationwide. The lawyers have also handled several securitized loan financings and list among their portfolio a number of lending institutions. Increasingly, the team is involved in the construction of medical facilities and the selling of medical buildings in the state. In a recent highlight, the lawyers worked on the acquisition of a 1.2 million sq ft dormitory in Houston, that was bought by its client, a family-owned business. It has also worked on the development and financing of shopping centers nationwide, worth between $600 - 700 million.

The Lawyers: "*Always spot-on in his legal advice,*" **Randy Jurgensmeyer** (see p.1899) is superb at protracted negotiations with investors, great at closings and "*extremely responsive to clients' needs.*" He "*gets to the bottom of every deal*" and has been heavily involved in loan financings and shopping center

## Real Estate
### Leading Individuals

**1**
DOW Melvin *Winstead Sechrest*
DUNLOP Fred *Baker Botts LLP*
JURGENSMEYER Randy *Vinson & Elkins LLP*
KATZ M Marvin *Mayer, Brown*
ROBERTS Harry *Thompson & Knight LLP*
WALLENSTEIN Jim *Jenkens & Gilchrist PC*
WEINER Sanford *Vinson & Elkins LLP*
WELLER Phillip *Vinson & Elkins LLP*
WILSON Robert *Haynes and Boone LLP*
WRIGHT Robert *Baker Botts LLP*

**2**
DUNLAY Jon *Baker Botts LLP*
ERWIN Greg *Winstead Sechrest*
FELDMAN Robert *Weil, Gotshal & Manges LLP*
HOLLYFIELD John *Fulbright & Jaworski L.L.P.*
JACOBS Stephen *Locke Liddell & Sapp LLP*
LEE Carl *Akin Gump*
LOTT Marley *Baker Botts LLP*
NEWSOME J Kent *Fulbright & Jaworski L.L.P.*
PETERSON Edward *Winstead Sechrest*
ROSS Joel *Vinson & Elkins LLP*
SAEGERT Ann *Haynes and Boone LLP*
THOMPSON JR Clark *Bracewell & Giuliani LLP*

**3**
BANTA Robert *Locke Liddell & Sapp LLP*
BOULDEN Michael *Vinson & Elkins LLP*
CAMPBELL Andrew *Andrews Kurth LLP*
DOW T Andrew *Winstead Sechrest*
FIELDS Jack *Andrews Kurth LLP*
HICKS JR M Lawrence *Thompson & Knight LLP*
JENKINS Steve *Haynes and Boone LLP*
KELLEY Kevin *Gardere Wynne Sewell LLP*
KUHN Michael *Jackson Walker LLP*
MARTIN Paul *Vinson & Elkins LLP*
NONDORF Kurt *Jackson Walker LLP*
RATNER Randall *Akin Gump*
VAN KIRK Mark *Baker Botts LLP*

### Up-and-coming individuals
ALESSIO Michael *Winstead Sechrest*
MILLER Walter *Haynes and Boone LLP*

developments. Currently, he is representing a nationwide engineering firm in the process of acquiring millions of square feet of office space in Dallas. **Sandy Weiner** (see p.1918) "*cuts right through to the heart of an issue and approaches deals with a good dose of attitude.*" "*Straightforward, practical and strategic,*" he recently worked on the acquisition of a large dormitory in Houston and has also handled several financings for office space in New Jersey, worth $180 million. Financings of power plants are another mainstay of his practice. The "*very efficient and extremely knowledgeable*" **Phillip Weller** is "*fair and thoughtful to his clients*" and has "*a client roster that is the envy of every lawyer in town.*" He is extensively involved in real estate financings and won the enthusiastic backing of clients, as did **Joel Ross** (see p.1912), one of the most experienced partners in the team. His "*terrific insider knowledge of the real estate industry*" serves him well and he concentrates heavily

on the finance side. Interviewees described him as "*responsive, practical, great at negotiations and always well-informed.*" "*Multifaceted*" **Michael Boulden** (see p.1883) was commended for his wide-ranging expertise, which includes commercial lending, acquisitions, joint ventures and development matters, while the "*technically terrific*" **Paul Martin** (see p.1903) received accolades for his office leasing work. He "*brings points across convincingly in every situation.*"

**Clients/Work Highlights:** JMI Realty; Crow Holdings; Cockrell Interests; Greystar Capital Partners; Archon Group; Trammell Crow Company; General Investment & Development; Clarion; Triton Energy; Dell and Dow Chemical.

## Winstead Sechrest & Minick P.C.
See firm details p.1939

**The Firm:** "*A big pool of high-quality lawyers who do a great job*" band together to form one of the most consistent real estate teams in the state. Especially strong in Houston, the firm has a broad real estate practice that takes in such areas as construction, corporate facilities management, real estate restructuring and lending. Its team is at the forefront of the latest developments and offers a full service to clients both in-state and nationwide. Its independent condominium practice generates a good deal of work with advice being regularly proferred to developers, lenders and owners in residential, commercial and multiuse condominium projects. Conduit lending and structured finance also form two key struts to the practice and the team has closed more than 3,000 conduit loans in recent times. Finally, the lawyers further regularly engage in real estate lending and restructuring transactions and frequently undertake long-term portfolio transactions.

**The Lawyers:** According to a number of market sources, **Melvin Dow** is "*one of the finest lawyers we have ever come across – he is still in top form, despite having been around forever.*" An "*excellent draftsman who has a good judgment of situations and never talks about unimportant things,*" he has continued to be highly active for key client Weingarten, advising it on acquisitions in the retail sector primarily. He has also worked on student accommodation projects and large residential projects. "*A very careful lawyer who is also thorough and a real pleasure to work with,*" **Greg Erwin** is well-known for his work on the leasing and financing of shopping centers. He is part of a team that includes **Ed Peterson**, "*a very affable lawyer who is direct to the core,*" and tackles lending and finance work. He has experience advising pension plan banks, life insurance companies and several other institutional clients. The "*energetic*" **Andrew Dow** has significant experience working with hotel developers, owners of pension funds and other investors in all stages of development. Praised for offering "*the best value for money,*" **Michael Alessio** enters the table for his multisite and multijurisdictional portfolio acquisition work and his frequent debt and equity structuring on behalf of pension plans.

**Clients/Work Highlights:** GE Capital; Baylor Healthcare System; Crow Holdings and various major real estate investors.

## Band 2

## Akin Gump Strauss Hauer & Feld LLP
See firm details p.559

**The Firm:** This firm benefits from "*fantastic connections with regulators and the wider business community.*" It covers all facets of real estate work including financing, acquisition, development and joint venture mandates. In recent times, the firm has seen an upsurge in multifamily developments in particular and the lawyers have also spent an increasing portion of their time working on various financings involving student housing developments, high-rise condominiums and office sales. Most recently, it handled the purchase by a major property developer of land to be used for a modern mixed-use development in Las Vegas. The team also has special expertise in servicing complex conduit loans and representing investors in the hospitality industry. It was involved in the financing of a large $70 million hotel development in Orlando, Florida on behalf of Diamond Rock Hospitality.

**The Lawyers:** "*Ultrasuccessful lawyer*" **Carl Lee** (see p.1902) has long-standing experience of representing some of the largest hotel chains on major developments. Most recently, he worked on two large portfolio and mezzanine financings for a brace of hotels. He also continues to be heavily engaged in projects for Wyndham International. **Randy Ratner** (see p.1911) does "*exemplary work on securitisations*" and is renowned for his "*detail-oriented*" practice. He represents a large proportion of private clients and has lately worked heavily on multifamily developments.

**Clients/Work Highlights:** Wyndham International; JF Capital Advisors; Apollo Real Estate Advisors; Diamond Rock Hospitality, CAPSTAR Commercial Real Estate Services and Centex Destination Properties.

## Andrews Kurth LLP
See firm details p.1921

**The Firm:** With nearly 30 real estate attorneys in its Dallas and Houston offices, this firm was especially commended for its "*fantastic lending practice run by some of the most experienced attorneys in the field.*" Its lawyers are renowned for their expertise in oil and gas acquisitions and these are handled in close conjunction with real estate deals. The firm also regularly tackles all aspects of construction, environmental and tax law. It is currently involved in one of the largest real estate developments in Texas, as part of which it regularly deals with the most prominent lenders in the state.

**The Lawyers:** The "*very pleasant and highly skilled*" **Andrew Campbell** is currently working on a major mixed-use development in the state. He is particularly well versed in handling leasing developments and multistate acquisitions and regularly advises large institutional clients. Described as "*an efficient lawyer who always has an open ear for his clients,*" **Jack Fields** has extensive experience advising large shopping retailers on real estate investments across the country.

**Clients/Work Highlights:** Hilton Hotels; Citigroup; Archon Group; Wal-Mart; Wells Fargo; JPMorgan Chase and GE Capital.

## Bracewell & Giuliani LLP
See firm details p.1924

**The Firm:** This "*well-connected firm*" has "*highly energetic lawyers who are willing to go the extra mile for their clients.*" With a total of six offices across the state, the firm is able to provide wide-ranging services on complex asset-based financings, structured financings, land development work and synthetic leases. The lawyers regularly advise clients from the pension fund, insurance, banking and mortgage industries.

**The Lawyers: Clark Thompson** (see p.1917) is "*an astute, smart, highly energetic and analytical lawyer.*" "*A great negotiator,*" he focuses on the finance and divestiture of commercial and industrial projects and regularly handles renewable energy matters including wind farm projects and power plant constructions. Additionally, leasing work in relation to office developments takes up a material amount of his time.

**Clients/Work Highlights:** Louisiana-Pacific; FPL Energy; Coral Energy and HNG Storage.

## Fulbright & Jaworski L.L.P.
See firm details p.1928

**The Firm:** This firm has experienced another busy year, particularly in relation to real estate projects for the electronics and telecom industries. Currently, the team is working on a $25 million project for a semiconductor plant in Texas and is extensively advising Samsung on its plant projects in the state. Often privy to the largest transactions, it is also working on the conversion of a natural wildlife reserve on Texas' North Padre Island into a luxurious leisure complex including top hotels, a marina and residential units. Other matters handled by the eight-member team include working on the implementation of the spin-off by Motorola of its headquarters in Austin. Market sources cited the firm as "*one of the very best when it comes to client service.*"

**The Lawyers:** "*A low-key lawyer who enjoys a lot of respect in the field,*" **John Hollyfield** (see p.1897) is "*highly practical in all his dealings.*" Colleague **Kent Newsome** (see p.1907) has extensive experience of leasing and lending work. He also garners a lot of respect for his permitting work and has recently handled several mortgage financings in the Houston area.

**Clients/Work Highlights:** The clientele comprises of office, retail and residential developers, electronics giants, owners, tenants and developers.

## Locke Liddell & Sapp LLP
**The Firm:** Interviewees complimented this firm for its "*extremely busy Austin and Dallas offices, which have managed to put the group firmly on the map for institutional investors and developers.*" The group has experienced another busy year and has reinforced its strength in condominium, retail and leisure projects. Its heavy institutional investor workload encom-

passes regular acquisition financings, mortgage financings and developments in the healthcare and retail sectors. Recently, the team has worked on various mixed-use developments around the state.

**The Lawyers:** "*A very pleasant lawyer to work with,*" **Stephen Jacobs** is "*detail-oriented, practical and smart as a whip in his dealings with clients.*" As one of the best-known partners at the firm, he regularly handles developments of leisure resorts and multi-family residential projects. An "*extremely thoughtful lawyer who is thorough and knowledgeable,*" **Robert Banta** regularly handles acquisitions, dispositions, leasings and financings in commercial lending transactions.

**Clients/Work Highlights:** The bulk of the clientele consists of leading Fortune 500 companies, entrepreneurs and leading institutional investors.

## Mayer, Brown, Rowe & Maw LLP
See firm details p.876

**The Firm:** Boasting "*a stable of several very well-connected individuals,*" this national heavyweight is appreciated for its "*outstanding high-investment real estate work.*" In line with a strong push for office development in the state, the lawyers have worked on two prime real estate acquisitions in Houston involving the construction of large shopping centers. They also generally work heavily with regulatory agencies and are currently in the process of developing a 700,000 sq ft mixed-use facility in a prime downtown location. The team is also involved in a high-rise condominium project. Most recently, it advised a number of local developers on large property developments between Monterrey and Mexico City.

**The Lawyers:** "*One of the top lawyers in the field who represents clients in difficult negotiations to the highest standard and employs a great degree of precision in all his transactions,*" **Marvin Katz** (see p.1899) has an impressive track record. In one of his recent deals, he represented a number of developers investing in high-profile projects in Mexico and worked on the finalization of a 100-year lease for an insurance company associated with Bank of America. Aside from his busy practice, he also spends 25% of his time as a university lecturer.

**Clients/Work Highlights:** Clients include Cockrell Interests, Teachers Insurance and Annuity Association – College Retirement Equities Fund, and major financial institutions, lenders, borrowers and banks.

## Weil, Gotshal & Manges LLP
See firm details p.1565

**The Firm:** This insolvency powerhouse also has a "*first-class real estate team.*" Its one partner and six associates are based in Houston and have experienced an active year. Involved in some of the largest transactions of the year, they have become the envy of the market. In one of its major highlights, the team assisted Lehman Brothers in its acquisition of the MetLife Building in the heart of Manhattan at a value of $1.8 billion. The lawyers have also advised the same client in its $2.4 billion acquisition of Gables Residential. Another important deal was the acquisition of a shopping district and marina in the

Lido section of Newport Beach, California by Wasserman Vornado Real Estate. The lawyers have also been highly active in the hotel and leisure sector, advising Starwood Hotels & Resorts on the acquisition of a European resort development company and resort properties.

**The Lawyers:** "*A very sophisticated lawyer who has built a small but highly successful real estate practice,*" **Robert Feldman** (see p.1890) was widely complimented for his work in the sector. He acted as lead advisor to Lehman Brothers in its acquisition of the MetLife Building and has recently worked on the development of a large resort in Florida, a condominium project in Boston and the development of a large shopping complex between the Dallas Cowboys and Texas Rangers stadiums.

**Clients/Work Highlights:** Starwood Vacation Ownership; Wasserman Real Estate Capital; Six Flags Theme Parks; Lehman Brothers Global Real Estate and Southwest Sports Realty.

## Band 3

## Gardere Wynne Sewell LLP
See firm details p.1931

**The Firm:** "*A traditionally well-established Dallas house,*" this firm retains a foothold in the market due to a slew of real estate transactions covering a variety of areas. With a team of well over 20 lawyers spread across its Dallas and Houston offices, its attorneys are known for providing advice to a wide-ranging clientele that includes institutional lenders, national development firms, financial institutions, pension funds and their advisers, REITs and Fortune 500 companies. With its broad geographic scope, the group handles projects throughout the USA, Canada, Mexico and the Caribbean. In addition to regularly handling acquisitions, development and disposition matters, it also tackles debt and equity financings and landlord and tenant representations. A number of the lawyers have also developed a special expertise in the setting up of complex joint ventures and the development of specialized resort and entertainment facilities such as hotels and golf courses.

**The Lawyers:** The "*highly skilled*" **Kevin Kelley** (see p.1900) has over 20 years of experience and is known for his work with residential developers and hotel chains. He continues to be heavily involved in the restructuring of portfolios for a large hotel chain.

**Clients/Work Highlights:** Koll Development Company (KDC); Vail Resorts; MacFarlane Real Estate Investment Management; Lehman Brothers and Gaylord Entertainment.

## Jackson Walker LLP
**The Firm:** "*Very strong in Houston and almost as formidable in Dallas,*" this firm has around 30 professionals who specialize in land use matters and cover a wide gamut of real estate transactional work. It received ample praise for its leasing work and its representation of landowners, developers, tenants and lending institutions in their drafting engagements and

negotiations. The lawyers have a strong niche on the development side and tackle questions of zoning, declaration of covenants and long-term ground leases and construction contracts. The team has also increasingly taken on high-rise condominium projects and regularly negotiates contracts for the building of hotels, shopping centers and resort developments.

**The Lawyers:** A "*capable and effective lawyer,*" **Michael Kuhn** is best known for his commercial lending and corporate finance practice. He also frequently handles traditional purchases and sales, and leases and financings involving office buildings. **Kurt Nondorf** was similarly warmly received as an attorney who is "*perceptive and a pleasure to work with.*" He has long-standing expertise advising clients in relation to commercial condominiums and acquisitions of new office facilities.

**Clients/Work Highlights:** Clients include pension funds, individual investors, banks and medical facilities such as the Texas Medical Center.

## Jenkens & Gilchrist PC

**The Firm:** With a "*consistently strong presence in Houston,*" the 12-partner, nine-associate and five-of counsel team has experienced an active year, with refinancings especially dominating the workload. Its lawyers have been heavily engaged in representing developers and lenders in relation to office building

work and residential projects. They have also been engaged in joint venture projects and have boosted their litigation practice with a string of important cases.

**The Lawyers:** **Jim Wallenstein** is "*an absolutely superb lawyer who is head and shoulders above many in the field.*" He "*works extremely well under pressure*" and regularly handles land use matters and apartment development work.

**Clients/Work Highlights:** The firm's extensive client portfolio includes government agencies, developers, individual investors and REITs.

## Thompson & Knight LLP
See firm details p.1936

**The Firm:** With more than 40 lawyers across its four Texas offices, this team has the resources to take on the best. "*Strategically impressive,*" it handles the entire range of real estate matters and has been involved in a slew of lending and purchasing transactions. Its workload in relation to downtown development in the Dallas area has picked up of late and it has advised a number of large institutions locally on complex investments. In one of the highlights of the year, the team is working on an ongoing transaction concerning a $133 million loan for several real estate projects between Dallas and Houston. The team also regularly prepares partnership documents for large

corporate entities across the USA.

**The Lawyers:** **Harry Roberts** (see p.1912) enjoys a strong reputation for his work with developers and lenders. He is "*a highly intelligent strategist who has a top knowledge of relevant law.*" He works intensively with major client MetLife, administering its client portfolio and regularly preparing partnership documents for large corporate entities. The "*highly intelligent, practical and responsive*" **Larry Hicks** (see p.1897) is best known for his work with clients in the insurance industry and also boasts extensive experience in multistate real estate lending transactions.

**Clients/Work Highlights:** The firm advises MetLife, as well as a range of industrial and residential developers and nationwide lessors and lessees.

# TAX

| Tax |
|-----|
| Leading Firms |

| | |
|---|---|
| 1 | **VINSON & ELKINS LLP** *Dallas* |
| 2 | **BAKER BOTTS LLP** *Houston* |
| | **BRACEWELL & GIULIANI LLP** *Houston* |
| | **FULBRIGHT & JAWORSKI L.L.P.** *Houston* |
| | **LOCKE LIDDELL & SAPP LLP** *Dallas* |
| | **THOMPSON & KNIGHT LLP** *Dallas* |
| 3 | **AKIN GUMP STRAUSS HAUER & FELD LLP** *Dallas* |
| | **BAKER & MCKENZIE** *Dallas* |
| | **GARDERE WYNNE SEWELL LLP** *Dallas* |
| | **MEADOWS, OWENS** *Dallas* |
| | **TOWNSEND & JONES** *Houston* |
| | **WINSTEAD SECHREST & MINICK P.C.** *Dallas* |

## Band 1

## Vinson & Elkins LLP
See firm details p.1938

**The Firm:** "*Outstanding technical competence*" is matched by a "*practical real-world approach to business transactions*" at this national powerhouse. Researchers learned that its "*top-notch product*" owed much to the presence of a strong, talented group of attorneys. This unit tackles an "*almost unparalleled breadth of transactional work*" and, with it, the associated "*cutting-edge tax issues.*" In addition to strong domestic and international tax planning, the group

serves clients on a federal, state and local level. Matters handled include issues stemming from the active energy-related M&A market, as well as other corporate, joint venture and MLP tax issues. In one significant energy-related transaction, the group advised Statoil on the tax aspects of its $2 billion acquisition of oil and gas interests in the deepwater Gulf of Mexico.

**The Lawyers:** The "*always up-to-speed and highly skilled*" **Ed Osterburg** (see p.1908) can always be counted on for his "*long experience*" and "*in-depth analysis of the law.*" This "*easy to work with*" traditional corporate tax lawyer earned specific credit for his expertise in corporate, partnership and international tax issues. Recently, he has been acting for a Chinese company in relation to its acquisition of a US company with operations in Asia. Considered a national expert in the formation of MLPs and royalty trusts, **Barry Miller** (see p.1906) has advised Goldman Sachs on federal income tax matters in connection with its public sale of approximately $1.1 billion of institutionally oriented securities. Also present is the "*smart and considerably experienced*" **Judy Blissard** (see p.1883), who advises on note offerings and stock purchase agreements while also boasting expertise in international tax as well. Further market acclaim came for the leader of the firm's 12-lawyer federal tax controversy and litigation practice, **George Gerachis** (see p.1892). Sources viewed him as "*exceptional,*" due to his "*technical proficiency and practical solutions.*" In addition to his knowledge of

international transfer pricing issues and corporate tax shelters, he has represented several Fortune 500 companies in tax court cases involving hundreds of millions of dollars in proposed adjustments.

**Clients/Work Highlights:** AIG; Dow Chemical; Duke Energy; TEPPCO Partners and Dell are just a few of the firm's many clients.

## Band 2

## Baker Botts LLP
See firm details p.1922

**The Firm:** This "*very strong group with a broad skill set and a creative business-oriented approach*" is a major force in the tax arena. The team boasts a "*good depth of expertise*" regarding the state and federal income tax aspects of M&As, offerings and financings. Almost 30 attorneys band together to form a sound US and international practice that offers advice on cross-border transactions, domestic investments, public offerings and MLPs.

**The Lawyers:** "*Long experience, broad corporate tax expertise and an involvement in truly complex issues*" all ensure that the "*very smart*" **Ben Wells** (see p.1918) remains ahead of the pack. In a practice that includes cross-border M&A and international tax advice, he has represented Lyondell in its acquisition of Millennium Chemicals. He also advised TransMontaigne Partners, a Delaware MLP, on its $83 million IPO. Joining the tables is the "*excellent and

## Tax
### Leading Individuals

**Senior Statesman**

HUGHES Vester *Hughes & Luce LLP*

1. KALTEYER Ronald *Locke Liddell & Sapp LLP*
   OSTERBERG Edward *Vinson & Elkins LLP*
   WELLS Benjamin *Baker Botts LLP*

2. ALLISON Christopher *Locke Liddell & Sapp LLP*
   ASOFSKY Paul *Weil, Gotshal & Manges LLP*
   BOWERS William *Fulbright & Jaworski L.L.P.*
   HARDIE Thornton *Thompson & Knight LLP*
   HELFAND Thomas *Winstead Sechrest*

3. ALLENDER John *Fulbright & Jaworski L.L.P.*
   CRAIG III Allen *Gardere Wynne Sewell LLP*
   FORD JR Thomas *Andrews Kurth LLP*
   MICCICHE Daniel *Akin Gump*
   MILLER Barry *Vinson & Elkins LLP*
   SALCH Steven *Fulbright & Jaworski L.L.P.*
   WHEAT David *Thompson & Knight LLP*

4. AKSAMIT Roger *Bracewell & Giuliani LLP*
   BLISSARD Judith *Vinson & Elkins LLP*
   CLIFTON R Brent *Locke Liddell & Sapp LLP*
   FIJOLEK Richard *Haynes and Boone LLP*
   HULL Robert *Bracewell & Giuliani LLP*
   JENNINGS Gray *Baker Botts LLP*
   MOOREFIELD G Crawford *Akin Gump*
   SINAK David *Gibson, Dunn & Crutcher LLP*
   STONE Susan *Baker & McKenzie*

## Tax: Litigation
### Leading Individuals

**Senior Statesman**

HALL Charles *Fulbright & Jaworski L.L.P.*

1. TAYLOR Jasper *Fulbright & Jaworski L.L.P.*

2. ALBRIGHT Val *Gardere Wynne Sewell LLP*
   GERACHIS George *Vinson & Elkins LLP*
   LEE William *Fulbright & Jaworski L.L.P.*
   LOWELL Cym *Gardere Wynne Sewell LLP*
   MEADOWS Charles *Meadows, Owens*
   PARKER Emily *Thompson & Knight LLP*
   SALCH Steven *Fulbright & Jaworski L.L.P.*
   TOWNSEND John *Townsend & Jones*

*extremely smart*" **Gray Jennings** (see p.1898). He represented Evergreen Resources in its $2.1 billion acquisition by Pioneer Natural Resources. Evergreen was an independent energy company that explored for methane gas in coalbed deposits.

Clients/Work Highlights: CenterPoint Energy; Halliburton; Lyondell; NCI Building Systems; Pogo Producing Company; Teekay LNG Partners; Crosstex Energy; Link Energy; Encore Acquisition; Evergreen Resources; Enterra Energy Trust; Oceaneering International and GlobalSantaFe.

### Bracewell & Giuliani LLP
See firm details p.1924
The Firm: The market applauded this "*personable, timely and responsive*" group for its ability to "*explain*

issues in layman's terms rather than complex legalese.*" The firm's areas of specific tax expertise include domestic and international business transactions, benefit plans and tax controversy. The group has particular forte in the energy domain and has added several key wind power clients in recent times. These join an existing client base comprising domestic and multinational concerns, partnerships and MLPs. Clients admired the lawyers for their "*business-savvy attitude and understanding of complex issues,*" stating that they are "*very easy to work with.*"

The Lawyers: Chairman of the tax group is **Roger Aksamit** (see p.1880), a generalist tax attorney with a strong energy bent. "*Very experienced and quick on the ball,*" he has a strong background in M&A and has been advising on $1 billion acquisition of a portfolio of electrical generation assets. Other work undertaken includes the establishment of an offshore captive insurance company for a publicly traded client. **Joe Hull** (see p.1898) earned market acclaim as a "*positive, can-do guy*" who is especially good on state tax matters. His varied workload includes M&A, partnerships and real estate work. Recently, he has been advising American Plumbing and Mechanical on the tax aspects of its reorganization.

Clients/Work Highlights: Dynegy; Hillenbrand; Coral Energy; Calpine; GE; Eaton; PG&E Gas Transmission-Texas; Apple and SYSCO.

### Fulbright & Jaworski L.L.P.
See firm details p.1928
The Firm: Although this well-known and admired firm earned client admiration for its "*ability to answer technical questions on partnerships and Joint Ventures,*" the heart of its reputation lies in tax litigation and controversy work. Clients noted: "*It is definitely an excellent go-to group if you have a problem with the IRS or are getting ready for trial.*" A team of around 50 tax attorneys in Texas advise on corporate tax, regulatory issues and individual tax matters, as well as tax litigation. Clients welcome its "*comprehensive understanding of tax laws and administrative procedures.*"

The Lawyers: An expert in partnership tax, **William Bowers** (see p.1884) acted on the combination of Kaneb Pipeline Partners, one of the largest pipeline companies in the USA, with Valero LP. In what has been a busy year, he has also acted on the reorganization of a real estate investment partnership with a portfolio in excess of $500 million. The "*totally sound*" **John Allender** (see p.1880) undertakes all aspects of traditional M&A transactions, working closely with privately held companies and wealthy owners in industries as varied as the communications and oil services sectors. Clients admired the "*well-prepared and sharp*" **Steven Salch** (see p.1912) for his wide-ranging tax practice. Possessed of an "*array of expertise,*" he has the "*ability to master the complex intricacies of any business.*" Both an attorney and certified public accountant, **Jack Taylor** (see p.1916) earned compliments for his representation of taxpayers in administrative proceedings and litigation. He was a lead participant in cases alleging that large energy companies,

including Shell, were guilty of fraudulent acts in connection with determinations of Texas property tax liability. Commentators respect **William Lee** (see p.1902) for his exhaustive knowledge of federal tax controversy, while **Charles Hall** (see p.1895) enters *Chambers'* tables as a senior statesman, honored for his "*long commitment to the field*" and reputation in the market as "*one of the finest tax litigators around.*" His practice takes in expertise from the full length and breadth of the tax field at the local, state and federal level. Some of his key tax matters relate to Shell, Schering-Plough, Texas Medical Center and several Ernst & Young tax shelter matters.

Clients/Work Highlights: American Bureau of Shipping; Bank of New York; Baker Hughes; Baylor health Care System; El Paso; Memorial Hermann Hospital and SEMATECH.

### Locke Liddell & Sapp LLP

The Firm: Possessing "*one of the deepest tax benches in Dallas,*" this much-admired, old-line Texas firm also has state offices in Austin and Houston. Commentators point out that the group of 40 attorneys is "*often a lot more practical and creative than some of its larger rivals.*" The group spends a significant portion of its time on the tax aspects of corporate and M&A transactions, with specialties in real estate and partnership tax. In May 2005, the Dallas office welcomed Garry Miles and Geoffrey Polma from Vinson & Elkins, adding further local, state and multistate tax expertise.

The Lawyers: The "*extremely impressive reputation*" of **Ron Kalteyer** owes much to his being particular strength in partnership and bankruptcy tax. Researchers were informed of his "*excellence on the tax implications for REITs*" and his "*calm and methodical style,*" which make him a "*pleasure to deal with.*" There was also widespread respect for the "*trusted and willing*" **Christopher Allison**. Head of the tax group, he has over 20 years of experience and is a "*good project manager who always keeps clients in the loop.*" He is considered by clients to be an expert on partnership issues but he further interests himself in the tax implications of corporate and M&A transactions, tax issues related to investments by tax-exempt entities, and tax controversy matters. A recent highlight saw him advising a publicly held client on the tax aspects of a transaction that included the formation of a limited liabilty company and its conversion into a corporation. Joining the ranks is **Brent Clifton**, who is "*very practical and has a fine sense of where the lines are drawn.*" His "*aggressive but within bounds*" representation of his clients makes him a "*formidable opponent.*" His workload includes counseling and developing tax strategies for M&As and debt and equity placements, particularly in the real estate sphere.

Clients/Work Highlights: INVESCO; Service Corporation International; Crescent Real Estate Equities; JPMorgan Chase; Carlson Companies; Dell; JC Penney Company and Sabre Holdings.

### Thompson & Knight LLP
See firm details p.1936
The Firm: Yet another top-notch quality practice in

Dallas earned widespread commendations from the Texas market for its "*real tax capability*." Owing to its long history in the field, the team enjoys a "*national reputation in oil and gas-related transactions as well as tax controversy.*" Around 40 tax attorneys offer advice on federal, state and local tax compliance, as well as planning matters. Other areas of specialty include corporate issues, exempt organisations, partnership and real estate.

**The Lawyers:** "*Outstanding*" in oil and gas-related transactions, **Thornton Hardie** (see p.1895) garnered admiration from the market for his "*thoroughness and professionalism*" and his ability to "*run rings around the competition.*" "*So smart it's scary,*" he has a practice geared towards oil and gas and partnership tax matters. Interviewees respected the "*bright, careful and straightforward*" **David Wheat** (see p.1919) as a "*fine, energetic corporate tax attorney*" who works on corporate transactions and some tax controversy issues. Having completed the chairmanship of the corporate tax committee at the ABA, he is now free to devote yet more time to his busy practice. In the energy field, for example, he has been working on the sale of $2 billion worth of oil and gas properties in the Gulf of Mexico by a public energy company. He has also advised on the new spin-off of a steel business for Texas Industries. Entering the tax litigation tables is "*absolute rising star*" **Emily Parker** (see p.1908), who drew praise for her "*integrity and effectiveness at settling cases.*" She is considered a "*great addition*" to the team after joining from the IRS Office of Chief Counsel. Her practice involves representing taxpayers in IRS audits and appeals proceedings, Texas tax audits and hearings, and federal and state tax refund and deficiency litigation.

**Clients/Work Highlights:** Clients include individuals and all types of business entities and organizations.

## Band 3

### Akin Gump Strauss Hauer & Feld LLP
See firm details p.559

**The Firm:** Although only a small team of tax experts work from its Dallas office, this giant can draw on the resources of multiple offices across the USA. The "*sound group*" enjoys a "*recognized ability to plan and strategize a range of transactions,*" such as oil and gas, partnership, and international structures. There was particular acclaim for the firm's public funds practice and its strength in state, local and franchise taxation.

**The Lawyers:** The "*really responsive and insightful*" **Dan Micciche** (see p.1906) scooped plaudits among clients for his "*reliable, general business advice*" and "*complete understanding of the Texas Tax Code.*" "*A preeminent expert on state and local tax controversy,*" he is good on transactions too and represented Cinemark in a merger valued at approximately $1.5 billion. He also represented Westport Resources in a strategic merger with Kerr-McGee for $2.5 billion in stock and $900 million in assumed debt. Interviewees respected the "*smart and excellent*" **Crawford Moorefield** (see p.1906), whose tax expertise lies in M&A, private equity investments and publicly

traded partnership work. Clients admire his "*confident, responsive and friendly manner and advice.*" He was instrumental in AIG's purchase of Utilicorp from Nuon, and the acquisition by a US private equity fund of a US water treatment holding company from a Dutch conglomerate.

**Clients/Work Highlights:** Clear Channel Communications; Westport Resources; EEX Corporation and Cinemark.

### Baker & McKenzie
See firm details p.866

**The Firm:** This worldwide giant is considered to be developing its reputation in Texas for tax transactional work. After the loss of Val Albright to Gardere Wynn Sewell, the team contains four attorneys in Houston and six in Dallas who have been undertaking a great deal of acquisitions, restructurings and deals in the energy sector. According to the market, the firm's reputation is among the very best for international tax transactions.

**The Lawyers:** Having started the Houston practice in 2001, the "*very business-like and driven*" **Susan Stone** (see p.1915) was an expert in international tax before it ever came into vogue. Over 20 years' experience and a comprehensive understanding of the oil, gas and energy sector continue to make her a force to be reckoned with.

**Clients/Work Highlights:** US and foreign multinationals feature among the firm's client roster.

### Gardere Wynne Sewell LLP
See firm details p.1931

**The Firm:** Around 25 attorneys earn market respect for a broad range of tax transactional and controversy work. The team advises on a range of M&A and income tax work, with transfer pricing proving an additional area of expertise. Having added a lateral hire from KPMG, the firm also obtained the services of Daniel Leightman in the Houston office in December 2005. These hires bring further international tax expertise to a group already strong in M&A, global tax planning and federal and foreign income tax issues.

**The Lawyers:** The "*bright and solution-driven*" **Allen Craig**'s (see p.1887) practice includes M&A, corporate reorganization, partnership and limited liability company planning issues. "*Highly experienced in tax controversy and transfer pricing,*" **Val Albright** (see p.1880) has "*good judgment and credibility.*" With 15 years' experience at the office of chief counsel for the IRS, he was "*involved in anything the IRS did for a long time*" and, consequently, is able to advise clients regarding US federal tax matters before the IRS. Joining the elite is **Cym Lowell** (see p.1902), who is considered a "*total expert*" in international tax transfer pricing and controversy work. He has handled cases ranging from $10 million to over $1 billion in proposed adjustments and advanced pricing agreements with the US and foreign tax authorities.

**Clients/Work Highlights:** The firm serves Fortune 500 companies, private clients and governmental entities.

### Meadows, Owens, Collier, Reed, Cousins & Blau

**The Firm:** With its roots long planted in tax litigation and planning, this respected, smaller Dallas boutique has expanded its services to also include white-collar and commercial litigation. Its areas of expertise range from federal income and wealth transfer litigation to general business planning advice. Commentators consider the group to be a "*good place to go*" for individuals in need of tax shelter and litigation matters.

**The Lawyers:** The "*very strong*" **Charlie Meadows** has more than 25 years' experience of acting for public and private companies in tax litigation and white-collar defense matters. "*Well-known around town,*" he is a "*very well-rounded attorney.*"

**Clients/Work Highlights:** Clients include Fortune 100 corporations, private corporations, nonprofit entities, individuals, and estates and trusts.

### Townsend & Jones

**The Firm:** Earning referrals from many top players are the pair of partners at this Texas boutique, who specialize in all matters related to tax litigation, including IRS audits and appeals. Operating at all stages of proceedings, the team employs two assistants to help in matters including criminal tax issues, civil and criminal litigation.

**The Lawyers:** "*The expert*" **Jack Townsend** commands market respect as a former trial attorney in the Tax Division at the DOJ. His extensive tax litigation practice includes federal income tax controversy matters while he also teaches classes on tax procedure, fraud and money laundering to University of Houston law students.

**Clients/Work Highlights:** Corporations and individuals form constituents of the firm's client base.

### Winstead Sechrest & Minick P.C.
See firm details p.1939

**The Firm:** A team of seven tax practitioners earned commendations for expertise in general corporate, real estate and partnership work, especially in the energy and technology sectors. The "*responsive and keenly alert*" team advises on corporation, partnership, Limited Liability Companies, joint ventures, REITs and tax-exempt organizations.

**The Lawyers:** Interviewees underlined **Thomas Helfand** as an "*outstanding tax attorney*" with expertise in real estate and partnership transactions. He has been doing more tax controversy work of late but is considered to be predominantly a transactional lawyer. Helfand has served as special tax counsel for the owners of multiple resort properties in the consolidation of all their operations into a group of entities.

**Clients/Work Highlights:** Clients include publicly traded and private companies operating in a range of business sectors including banking, construction, energy, healthcare and real estate.

## Other Notable Practitioners

Sources informed researchers that **Paul Asofsky** (see p.1881) of Weil, Gotshal & Manges LLP "*can handle any tax matter.*" He does his best work, however, in the bankruptcy and insolvency spheres while also being a dab hand at private equity tax matters. Having headed the tax group since 1990, he enjoys a national reputation as one of the premier bankruptcy tax attorneys. The "*talented and knowledgeable*" **Thomas Ford** stands out in Houston at Andrews Kurth LLP due to his "*immense expertise*" in MLPs. His diverse practice also takes in federal income taxation, advising clients and structuring transactions based on Section 29 of the Internal Revenue Code. Cochairing the investment fund practice group of Haynes and Boone LLP, **Richard Fijolek**'s practice focuses on partnership and international tax. In addition to real estate, Venture Capital and hedge funds, he has a "*sound grasp*" of private equity and energy funds as well. Interviewees saluted him for his representation of investment funds, high net worth individuals and real estate companies. **David Sinak** (see p.1914) of Gibson, Dunn & Crutcher LLP is "*very bright and deal-focused.*" He shows "*great creativity*" in proffering tax structure advice to a client base of corporations, partnerships and limited liability companies. "*Deal and solution-focused,*" he has been providing ongoing tax advice for traded construction products manufacturer, Eagle Materials. Also recommended is seasoned veteran tax attorney **Vester Hughes** of Hughes & Luce LLP. Hughes "*has seen and done all manner of transactions*" and is "*something of a legend in Texas.*" "*One of the deans of taxation,*" he has a "*wealth of expertise,*" especially in federal taxation, income, estate, gift and excise matters.

# TECHNOLOGY & IT OUTSOURCING

## Band 1

### Baker Botts LLP

See firm details p.1922

**The Firm:** This "*fabulous*" firm enjoys a great reputation. Its technology practice has three facets – IP, transactional work and IT outsourcing. "*Its excellent lawyers prove responsive to the client's needs and constitute a very strong presence in the state.*" These attorneys represent an entire spectrum of concerns from emerging entities to Fortune 500 technology firms such as EDS. Of late, they have spent much of their time assisting companies in the restructuring of their capital with a view to acquiring other emerging concerns in the technology sector.

**The Lawyers:** "*Highly regarded*" **John Martin** (see p.1903) leads the firm's IT outsourcing practice. He is an outstanding lawyer as he is "*approachable, practical and a good influence in moving a deal forward.*" Recently, he closed an outsourcing deal for a global management-consulting firm relating to its end user computing, help desk, asset management and procurement needs. He also represented Affiliated Computer Services in connection with the $405 million acquisition of Mellon Financial. **David Monk** (see p.1906) has "*a foot in both the M&A and the technology world.*" "*A sharp lawyer with a pleasant persona,*" he has acted on behalf of an international investment company in an outsourcing regarding its managed reference data service needs. **Don McDermett** (see p.1904) is experienced in representing software companies, taking them public, raising capital and guiding them through M&A transactions. He has "*a quick grasp of the issues and a business sense often lacking in outside general counsel.*" He advised General Bandwidth in its seventh round of venture capital financing and advised Motive on its IPO and securities work. "*Deal-doer*" **Charles Szalkowski** (see p.1916) is "*very well connected with technology.*" He completed several rounds of financing for MircoMed and took the company public through a reverse merger. When he is negotiating, "*he will do anything to protect the client and get the deal done without being disagreeable.*" He has also acted for Knowledge Systems in raising capital from a private equity fund based in Norway and selling the company's common stock. An attorney with an excellent head for business, "*he can look past the pure technical legal aspects of a matter and get to the right answer from a commercial perspective.*"

**Clients/Work Highlights:** The lawyers have represented MicroMed in its acquisition of Salmon Express; Microtune in its acquisition of Three-Five Systems Pacific, a company based in the Philippines; S2 Systems when it sold its company to Transaction Systems Architects; i2 Technologies in the private placement of its common stock to Q Investments; Liberty Media International in its planned acquisition of Telenet, a Belgian cable TV operator; SourceNet in its merger with Mellon Financial; and the special committee of National Processing in the $1.4 billion sale to Bank of America. The firm has also completed IT outsourcing agreements in connection with an international investment company.

### Hughes & Luce LLP

**The Firm:** This "*terrific firm*" grew up with technology and outsourcing work. It is admired by its peers for the deals it wins and by clients for its "*flexible approach to transactions combined with its ability to keep risks bottled up.*" Although strictly a Texas firm, it has a renowned national IT outsourcing practice. It is also involved in sophisticated deals with international companies. In the past year, it has completed deals for large companies based in California, New York and Washington, DC. Clients rely on and trust its lawyers and are very pleased with its "*professionalism, responsiveness and good value.*"

**The Lawyers:** "*Thoughtful, thorough and knowledgeable,*" **Chad King** primarily focuses on technology licensing, advertising and marketing deals, with a particular emphasis on the retail and transportation industries. He has been involved in completing licensing agreements relating to homeland security and encryption. A good technician when it comes to drafting, he has a "*quiet and methodical way of negotiating that is very effective.*" Clients praise him for being "*extremely responsive*" and having the ability to "*translate technology speak into easy-to-understand business terms.*" He helped Blockbuster launch its DVD mail subscription service and was involved in all legal work related to the design, creation and licensing of the infrastructure. "*Super lawyer*" **John Howell** is respected by both competitors and clients. "*One of the pillars of the outsourcing world,*" he is often called upon to handle major deals for prominent technology clients. Not only is he extremely experienced in this area, he is very responsive and thorough – "*he will meet deadlines no matter what.*" Commentators were enthusiastic in recommending **Todd Fisher** as he has the "*right temperament to navigate issues and work with business people and*" *lawyers.*" He represented EDS in the structuring and negotiating of its IT outsourcing agreement and Enterprise Resource Planning (ERP) implementation with Allegheny Energy. He also acted as lead counsel for a network security company in the structuring and negotiating of three data and voice transport agreements. Clients have a high degree of confidence in his abilities and tout him as "*diligent and good at understanding the nature of risk.*"

**Clients/Work Highlights:** Blockbuster; American Airlines; McAfee; EDS; Wal-Mart; Worldspan; Rent-A-Center and JiWire.

## Jones Day
See firm details p.570

**The Firm:** This outsourcing powerhouse has significantly increased its capability with the arrival of David Guedry from Hughes & Luce and Shawn Helms from Sprint. Its global reach and worldwide resources prove a major attraction to clients, who claim it provides "*superior market information and knowledge.*" It has both customer and vendor teams working across all industries, with particular expertise in the financial services industry. It also has an "*extremely deep competence in the outsourcing space.*" Its success, in some part, is attributed to the collaborative approach its lawyers take when negotiating deals. This positive approach is particularly appealing to clients, as is the fact that it represents "*tremendous value per hour*" when it comes to fees.

**The Lawyers:** "*One of the top five outsourcing lawyers in the country,*" **David Guedry** (see p.1894) is just "*fantastic.*" He focuses on representing vendors on IT outsourcing deals and has top clients such as CGI and Hewitt. "*Extremely professional, creative and with a strong business sense,*" he was involved in transactions for EDS relating to the renegotiation and restructuring of several of its customer relationships. His work also entails advising smaller startups on appropriate business models, revenue sources and licensing agreements. Clients value his ability to get "*consensus and*

cooperation from others while he is negotiating deals.*" **Jason Krieser** (see p.1901) continues to shine in the technology transactions field. He closed 25 IT services and software development deals for Hotels.com and his other highlights include completing an IT outsourcing deal worth $500 million per year. Clients are impressed with his "*skill, knowledge and ability to relate legal issues to business,*" with one saying that "*he is the best attorney we have ever worked with and, if he left, I would go wherever he went.*" Global team leader **John Funk** (see p.1892) is "*often involved in front-page world-class deals.*" He works almost exclusively on the customer side in IT outsourcing deals in a variety of industries and has a "*good understanding of both sides of a deal.*" He closed a major transaction for Nokia and has been advising on a large offshore technology outsourcing transaction. He also represented a privately held Swiss company in an 80-country desktop support deal. Having worked on many major outsourcing deals, he is felt to have an "*irresistible combination of subject matter expertise, negotiating prowess and client management skills.*"

**Clients/Work Highlights:** The team assisted EDS in the renegotiation of an IT outsourcing deal with the Federal Reserve Bank, completed two IT outsourcing deals for Washington Mutual and counts CGI and Hewitt among its clients.

## Vinson & Elkins LLP
See firm details p.1938

**The Firm:** This firm has 40 lawyers in its technology team. It is "*one of the finest energy firms around*" and also focuses on corporate transactional and more traditional technology work. Its global reach and large resources mean it can staff cases at a very short notice. In a recent highlight, the lawyers represented a local company in Dubai in connection with the commodities exchange. It also has a policy of putting the client first, which seems to be reaping dividends. Those interviewed by researchers praised the firm for its "*professionalism, intelligence and accessibility,*" with one commenting: "*We are paying premium prices but there's no doubt we are receiving premium value.*"

**The Lawyers:** "*Very responsive and knowledgeable,*" **Dean Harvey** (see p.1896) is valued by his clients for his ability to pick up issues and actually "*talk the lingo with the IT personnel and point out issues that even they have not recognized.*" With a computer science background, he is well placed to complete IT-related transactions. He is involved in a wide range of technology transactions, including licensing, IT-related agreements, regulatory work and outsourcing. "*Just fantastic at protecting his client's interests,*" he recently helped an energy company complete a $300 million outsourcing transaction and also advised a Fortune 100 company in dealing with its security breaches. **Edward Stockbridge** (see p.1915) is "*very service-oriented and hands-on.*" He has an engineering background and "*is knowledgeable in the areas of computer software, hardware and intellectual property.*" He was lead counsel in IT outsourcing deals in Moscow, India and China, coordinating with local counsel on localization issues. He also represented a private equity company in buying royalty interests on drugs

from universities and biotech companies. Interviewees observed that he is "*very detail-minded*" and "*takes a business approach to solving problems.*" **Nixon Fox** (see p.1891) represented Cadent Energy Partners in closing a private equity fund and handled all its portfolio investments. He is "*especially pragmatic and creative,*" qualities he displayed recently when he assisted a client in a $650 million acquisition by a foreign company. "*Able to complete the work well without too much friction with the other side, he knows when to push and when not to push.*" Interviewees enthusiastically recommended **William Volk** (see p.1918) as "*one of the most prominent lawyers in Austin.*" He has developed an "*outstanding*" practice in representing early-stage technology companies and venture capital firms in the formation of funds.

**Clients/Work Highlights:** Clients include Perficient; Toppan Photomask; Austin Ventures; EDS; BearingPoint USA; Halliburton; BMC Software; Worldspan; Capital Royalty and eOriginal.

## Band 2

## Andrews Kurth LLP
See firm details p.1921

**The Firm:** This "*tremendous*" 100-year-old Houston-based firm focuses on the energy, healthcare and technology industries and enjoys significant relationships with underwriters, venture capital and private equity firms. Clients appreciate the support and resources the lawyers provide, describing them as "*readily available and always eager to oblige.*" The firm's technology practice is split into three distinct groups: venture capital and emerging companies, IP, and technology transactions. It is further supported by the firm's renowned corporate finance and "*superior securities*" practices. Observers ascribe much of the team's success to the fact that it hires "*young and talented attorneys.*"

**The Lawyers:** **Jeff Dodd** specializes in counseling companies on the legal issues associated with having computer systems and the legal requirements for maintaining safe networks. He is also involved in the commercialization of IP and handles licensing, outsourcing and other technology-related transactions. **Robert Jewell** is "*one of the great lawyers of the firm.*" He is particularly known for his work in the energy industry and has a significant corporate practice, handling M&A and public offerings. He represents a range of Limited Liability Companies, utilities and service companies. "*Exceptional transaction attorney*" **Matthew Lyons**' practice is built around representing emerging growth and technology companies throughout their life cycle. He is involved in the formation of companies, financing, M&As, IPOs and SEC filings. Clients comment that he is "*extremely thorough, hard-working and consistent in focusing on the right issues.*" He has been involved in a number of venture capital transactions and a public equity financing.

## Fulbright & Jaworski L.L.P.

See firm details p.1928

**The Firm:** This full-service law firm has a distinguished patent prosecution, technology litigation and life sciences practice. From this they have built up a substantial technology transactional practice. It has "*top-quality lawyers at reasonable prices*" and has benefited recently from the arrival of Michael Brito from Munsch Hardt Kopf & Harr. He has added to the firm's capability for handling IT outsourcing deals. Clients are impressed with the firm's "*responsiveness, professionalism, great resources and knowledge.*"

**The Lawyers:** **David Peterman** (see p.1910) is involved in the whole spectrum of work for technology companies, from the formulation of public companies to the completion of complicated transactions. He is praised for being "*very strategic and able to dovetail the legal world with the business world.*" Based in Houston, he spends a considerable amount of his time working for energy companies but also handles matters for retail and manufacturing concerns. Clients are impressed with his business mind and "*capacity for understanding the trade-off between taking risks and protecting the interests of a company.*" Recently, he acted as coordinating legal counsel in Asia in relation to a number of acquisition deals in Indonesia.

**Clients/Work Highlights:** Houston Technology Center, University of Texas Health Science Center and MD Anderson Cancer Center.

## Haynes and Boone LLP

**The Firm:** This "*fabulous firm has a terrific name when it comes to technology deals.*" It is highly involved in the venture capital world and has proved successful in its attempts to expand its telecom and biomedicine practices. It has also started to advise companies on obtaining a listing on the London AIM as an alternative source of finance. On top of this, it has strong involvement in the energy sector and is "*regularly involved in the cream of the deals.*"

**The Lawyers:** **Charles Powell** heads the firm's technology practice in Houston. He continues to enjoy an excellent reputation and is "*definitely one of the most technology-oriented lawyers in the state.*" A venture capital specialist, he is renowned for representing early-stage technology companies due to his "*innate understanding of the entrepreneurial spirit of his clients.*" He was lead counsel in a venture capital-backed acquisition of a group of UK-based companies, and has represented Crown Castle in a $150 million investment of a telecom company.

## Wilson Sonsini Goodrich & Rosati

See firm details p.344

**The Firm:** This firm divides its technology practice into three areas: representing technology clients in raising capital, technology litigation and technology transactions. Building on its West Coast reputation as a technology expert, it has become one of the leaders in Austin in this field. Able to provide "*quality service and in-depth advice,*" it focuses on representing technology and high growth companies. Clients

have been impressed with its "*ability to bring in the right kind of expertise and effectively coordinate its lawyers and support staff.*"

**The Lawyers:** **Brian Beard** (see p.1882) is "*business-oriented and levelheaded.*" He represents public and private technology and high-growth companies and has a strong venture capital client base that includes Austin Ventures, CenterPoint Ventures and Trellis Partners. The size of his venture deals ranges from $2 million to $40 million and in the past year he has closed about 35 of these. He is also general counsel to private companies of various sizes including Vignette Corporation and Pervasive Software. His business understanding combined with his legal knowledge is something his high-growth clients appreciate highly. **Paul Tobias** (see p.1917) "*focuses on the right issues and gets transactions done.*" He represented Spatial Wireless in its acquisition by Alcatel; TrueTech in its acquisition of Computas and Neon Systems in its acquisition of a Florida-based company. He is also involved in venture capital deals and represents underwriters in IPOs. Clients describe him as their "*rock,*" as he is "*focused on structuring a proper deal and is a real problem solver.*"

## Band 3

### Bracewell & Giuliani LLP

See firm details p.1924

**The Firm:** This significant corporate finance player is based in Houston. Its lawyers are known to be involved in high-quality work and, as many of them hold engineering and other technical degrees, are well placed to serve entrepreneurs, investors, and established companies in the technology space. The firm has specialist groups who deal with the bioscience, nanotechnology, software and telecom industries.

**The Lawyers:** **Thomas Manford** (see p.1903) has a general corporate practice and is well known for representing early stage startup companies. He is an "*outstanding adviser and professional*" who also handles venture capital transactions and LBOs. He is rated as "*a very skillful architect of deals.*"

### DLA Piper Rudnick Gray Cary US LLP

See firm details p.870

**The Firm:** With 34 lawyers highly focused on emerging technology companies, this firm is recognized as "*one of the venture capital leaders in Austin.*" Since the merger with DLA Piper Rudnick, there is an increased commitment to pro bono activities and diversity within the firm. It has now achieved full-service capability and can offer clients resources on an impressive scale. The firm holds a significant market share of the technology work in Austin and caters to a client base heavily drawn from the semiconductor and software industries. Its lawyers have handled a series of acquisitions for SigmaTel and a number of deals for United Devices.

**The Lawyers:** Austin-based Paul Hurdlow is a key figure in the venture capital and emerging companies group.

## Gardere Wynne Sewell LLP

See firm details p.1931

**The Firm:** This full-service firm is "*comprehensive, large and expert in many areas.*" The technology team is primarily involved in the Internet and computer technology market and also has a niche practice in the healthcare industry. In addition, it boasts a significant corporate technology practice, representing the oil and gas exploration industry. The client's specific need is at the heart of the firm's technology practice and it is able to assemble multidisciplinary teams as and when the need arises.

**The Lawyers:** **Frank Putman** (see p.1910) is involved in M&A, international transactions and the counseling of entrepreneurial businesses in their growth period. For the most part, he represents clients from the medical and energy industries eager to benefit from his "*undoubted knowledge of his sector.*" In the past year, he has been working on the technology, development and contracting needs of offshore drilling platforms. He is described as "*creative, savvy and an attorney well able to get to the economic heart of any transaction.*" **Peter Vogel** (see p.1917) has "*always been the expert's expert in the field of computer law.*" With his computer science background, he has developed a niche in representing the buyers and sellers of computer technology and Internet services. Admired for his "*ability to resolve issues,*" he "*can work with different types of people, always in a refreshingly candid manner.*" He represented various chip manufacturers in the global sale and distribution of chips embedded in new technology, primarily in telecom and personal computers. He is also a well-known litigator and continues to be heavily involved in litigation on failed computer implementation projects for public utilities and county and city governments.

## Jenkens & Gilchrist PC

**The Firm:** This is "*one of the oldest and most prestigious firms in Dallas.*" It has 70 lawyers involved in technology work and assembles teams from multiple practice disciplines depending on the client's needs. The firm enjoys good brand recognition and is seen as a "*very worthy opponent.*" Clients appreciate the fact that, as an old-line firm, it has put a lot of effort into creating long-term relationships. Its lawyers are "*very sharp and on the cutting edge of the law.*"

**The Lawyers:** **John Holzgraefe** "*has a great business mind, a solid understanding of finance and is able to use his legal training to blend business and legal strategy.*" He represents a major advertising agency in licensing out its technology, and has been closing venture capital transactions for technology companies. "*Strong in investment documentation for finance and equity capital,*" he is "*always available and easily accessible.*" Clients consider him to be a "*valuable and dependable business partner.*"

**Clients/Work Highlights:** The firm represented a video game development company in its development, licensing and distribution agreements. It has also acted for a Finnish company in the $40 million acquisition of a US technology company and has advised various venture capital firms regarding investment transactions.

## Locke Liddell & Sapp LLP

**The Firm:** This large Texas-based firm has six lawyers who make up the core of its commercial and technology transactions group. It has continued to increase its presence and reputation in the industry and has "*quality lawyers*" dedicated to assisting emerging companies in the technology sector. It is praised for its "*breadth of knowledge and superior business acumen.*"

**The Lawyers:** Head of the team **Rick Bays** is "*thoughtful and someone who takes a careful approach to issues.*" He has been representing a public company licensing SAT software and has completed a number of telecom license agreements for the owners of the land and facilities. He also represents vendors and licensees of new technology and is an active member of the Computer Law Section of the State Bar of Texas.

**Clients/Work Highlights:** The firm's clients are drawn from the media, financial services, electronic, energy and industrial sectors. It also represents Web site owners.

## Mayer, Brown, Rowe & Maw LLP

See firm details p.876

**The Firm:** This international firm has a significant presence in each of the money centers of the world and is rapidly expanding its office in Texas. Clients were impressed with its "*enormous global footprint combined with its strong local presence.*" As a global firm with deep expertise, "*it has the size and substance to meet the needs of any client, however large.*" The arrival of Bob Gray has further enhanced its standing as "*a fully-fledged player in the technology field.*"

**The Lawyers:** **Bob Gray** (see p.1894) is involved in the whole spectrum of corporate technology business, from early-stage financing to taking companies public and selling them. He represents Tyrell, BindView and Symantec. He is a "*sophisticated legal thinker,*" able to be a business partner for his clients. He is also valued for his entrepreneurial nature combined with his "*wonderful grasp of the law.*"

## Thompson & Knight LLP

See firm details p.1936

**The Firm:** This solid Texas firm is renowned for its energy practice and has a strong international presence. Highly regarded in the emerging technology sector, it has an excellent group of lawyers experienced in counseling technology-oriented entities from startups to multinationals and research institutions. Its attorneys are admired for their "*powerful legal minds and tremendous business insights.*"

**The Lawyers:** Houston-based **Dallas Parker** (see p.1908) is a sharp securities lawyer. He "*knows how to complete transactions quickly, negotiates well and understands technology.*" Recognized as one of the state's leading technology and acquisition finance lawyers, his strengths lie in representing emerging growth companies and completing early-stage corporate financing transactions.

# Leaders in Texas

### ADAMO, Ken
Jones Day, Cleveland
216 586 3939
*Recommended in Intellectual Property*
**Practice Areas:** Complex IP litigation matters. He has extensive lead trial counsel experience in jury and nonjury matters before state and federal courts and before the International Trade Commission, as well as ex parte and inter partes experience in the US Patent and Trademark Office. He also has extensive appellate experience before the US Court of Appeals for the Federal Circuit, having appeared in 30 appeals, most of which he has argued himself.
**Publications:** Written and lectured extensively on intellectual property law and trial advocacy for US and non-US publications and organizations.

### ADDISON, Linda L
Fulbright & Jaworski L.L.P., Houston
713 651 5628
laddison@fulbright.com
*Recommended in Litigation*
**Practice Areas:** Complex commercial litigation, intellectual property litigation, international litigation, business litigation, arbitration and ADR, ERISA litigation.
**Prof. Memberships:** American Board of Trial Advocates (ABOTA); American Law Institute (ALI); Houston and American Bar Associations, State Bar of Texas; Life Fellow: American Bar Foundation, Texas Bar Foundation, Houston Bar Foundation; Life Member, Texas Law Review Ex-

Editors' Association; Federal Judicial Evaluation Committee of United States Senators Hutchison and Cornyn.
**Career:** Named one of America's Top 50 Women Litigators (National Law Journal, 2001); named by Texas Lawyer as one of Texas' top five lawyers to defend civil cases (Texas Lawyer 'Go-To' Guide 2002) and one of Texas Super Lawyers (2003-04). Has tried over 50 cases. Admitted to practice: Texas, 1976; United States Supreme Court; United States Court of Appeals for the Fifth Circuit; United States District Court (Northern, Southern, and Eastern Districts of Texas); joined Fulbright & Jaworski in 1976; admitted to partnership, 1984 (Executive Committee, Technology Partner, heads one of firm's litigation teams).
**Personal:** University of Texas, 1973 (BA cum laude in Plan II Honors Program); University of Texas School of Law, JD 1976 (Managing Editor, Texas Law Review).

### AKSAMIT, Roger D
Bracewell & Giuliani LLP, Houston
713 221 1591
roger.aksamit@bracewellgiuliani.com
*Recommended in Tax*
**Practice Areas:** Board certified in tax law and estate planning and probate by the Texas Board of Specialization, he has extensive experience in a wide variety of national and state energy, partnership corporate tax issues, with emphasis in the areas of power and energy tax credits. Recognized in his practice by regional

legal publication for the last three years.
**Personal:** LLM, Taxation, Southern Methodist University Dedman School of Law, 1987; JD, The University of Texas School of Law, 1978; BBA, Accounting, Southern Methodist University, 1975.

### ALBERGOTTI, Robert
Haynes and Boone LLP, Dallas
214 651 5000
*Recommended in Bankruptcy*

### ALBERS, Michael
Jenkens & Gilchrist PC, Dallas
214 855 4500
*Recommended in Construction*

### ALBRIGHT, Val
Gardere Wynne Sewell LLP, Dallas
214 999 4825
valbright@gardere.com
*Recommended in Tax*
**Practice Areas:** Tax, tax litigation, transfer pricing.
**Prof. Memberships:** State Bar of Texas (Taxation Section); Tax Controversy Subcommittee (State Bar of Texas); American Bar Association (Taxation Section); Dallas Bar Association (Taxation Section, Council).
**Career:** Albright represents clients in US federal tax matters before the IRS and in federal courts. He also advises clients concerning domestic and international tax planning. Previously he worked for the Office of Chief Counsel for the IRS (Chicago and Dallas).
**Personal:** LLM, Southern Methodist University School of Law, 1986; JD, Uni-

versity of Arkansas School of Law, 1977; BA, University of Arkansas-Monticello, 1971.

### ALE, John C
Skadden, Arps, Slate, Meagher & Flom LLP & Affiliates, Houston
713 655 5263
jale@skadden.com
*Recommended in Energy, Projects*
**Practice Areas:** Concentrates in US and international energy, infrastructure, finance, and corporate matters. Represents clients in the development, financing and acquisition of energy and water infrastructure projects; privatizations; and acquisitions and divestitures. Has experience in MLPs and other equity structures.
**Career:** JD, University of Virginia, 1979 (Order of the Coif; Executive Director, Virginia Law Review); BA, University of Virginia, 1976.
**Publications:** Author, 'Partnership Law for Securities Practitioners' (The West Group).

### ALESSIO, Michael
Winstead Sechrest & Minick P.C., Dallas
214 745 5400
*Recommended in Real Estate*

### ALLENDER, John R
Fulbright & Jaworski L.L.P., Houston
713 651 5664
jallender@fulbright.com
*Recommended in Tax*
**Practice Areas:** Taxation.
**Prof. Memberships:** Mr Allender is a

former Chair of the Section of Taxation of the State Bar of Texas and the Houston Bar Association. Mr Allender is a Member of the State Bars of Texas (1977) and California (1976).

**Career:** Mr Allender joined the firm in 1976 and heads the firm's Tax Department. His practice focuses on taxation and corporate matters emphasizing federal income taxation. Mr Allender is often involved in the negotiation and planning of complex transactions, often related to the firm's substantial mergers and acquisition practice. In addition, Mr Allender is frequently involved in tax and business matters for wealthy individuals and their closely held businesses. He has been named in 'Texas Super Lawyers', 'The Best Lawyers in America' in tax law, 'Who's Who in America', and 'Top 100 Houston Region Super Lawyers'. Mr Allender is a frequent speaker on complex taxation topics.

**Personal:** BS, Iowa State University (1972); JD, cum laude, University of San Diego (1975); LLM, New York University School of Law. A long-term member of Ronald McDonald House-Houston's Board of Directors, he served as President from 2003-05. Mr Allender is also an Advisory Director of Catholic Charities-Galveston/Houston and trustee of the Southwest Research Institute.

**ALLENSWORTH, William**
Allensworth and Porter, L.L.P, Austin
512 708 1250
*Recommended in Construction*

**ALLISON, Christopher**
Locke Liddell & Sapp LLP, Dallas
214 740 8000
*Recommended in Tax*

**AMANDES, Christopher B**
Vinson & Elkins LLP, Houston
713 758 1146
camandes@velaw.com
*Recommended in Environment*
**Practice Areas:** Principal area of practice is environmental law, with emphasis on compliance counseling, enforcement defense, transactional environmental issues, and cost-recovery litigation. Listed: in a leading legal publication in America in environmental law, since 1995.
**Prof. Memberships:** Co-Chair: City of Houston's Brownfield Redevelopment Committee, 1996-2000; ABA Annual Conference on Environmental Law (Keystone), 2004-present. Air and Waste Management Association.
**Career:** Admitted to practice: Texas, 1985. Joined Vinson & Elkins, 1986; admitted to partnership, 1994. Registered Professional Engineer, Texas, 1983-present.
**Personal:** Rice University, BA, 1976; Masters of Environmental Engineering, 1978; University of California at Los Angeles, JD, 1985.

**ANDERSON, Kenneth M**
Vinson & Elkins LLP, Houston
713 758 2444
kanderson@velaw.com
*Recommended in Banking & Finance*
**Practice Areas:** Chair of Vinson & Elkins' Syndicated Finance Practice Group. Extensive syndicated finance experience including private equity, project, structured and energy financings. Representative clients include JPMorgan Chase Bank, Deutsche Bank AG and Hicks Muse Tate & Furst.
**Prof. Memberships:** Admitted to practice in Texas (1982). Member of Texas Association of Bank Counsel and American Bar Association, Business Law Section. Appointments: Chair, Syndicated Finance Subcommittee (Developments in Business Finance Committee, Business Law Section, ABA).
**Career:** Joined Vinson & Elkins LLP, 1982; became Partner, 1992.
**Personal:** BYU, BS, accounting, 1979; BYU Law School, JD, cum laude, 1982 (Associate Editor, Law Review).

**ANDREWS, William**
Andrews Myers Coulter & Cohen PC, Houston 713 850 4200
*Recommended in Construction*

**ARRINGTON, Scott J**
Akin Gump Strauss Hauer & Feld LLP, Houston 713 220 5845
sarrington@akingump.com
*Recommended in Projects*
**Practice Areas:** Focuses on infrastructure development, acquisitions, dispositions and financings in the oil, gas, petrochemical and power industries, particularly those involving cross-border transactions and negotiation, documentation and administration of engineering, procurement and construction contracts. Speaks Mandarin Chinese and Spanish.
**Prof. Memberships:** Member, Houston Bar Association and State Bar of Texas; 2004-05 Chair, International Law Section, Houston Bar Association; Fellow, Houston Bar Foundation and Texas Bar Foundation; Member, Association of International Petroleum Negotiators, Houston World Affairs Council and the Asia Society.
**Personal:** BA (cum laude), Rice University (1990); JD, University of Texas (1995).

**ASMUS, David**
Baker Botts LLP, Houston
713 229 1539
david.asmus@bakerbotts.com
*Recommended in Energy, Projects*
**Practice Areas:** Practice focuses on oil and gas development projects (including LNG projects, FPSO and platform-based offshore developments, and integrated field development, pipeline, and processing projects); acquisitions and divestitures (including auction and negotiated sales and property exchanges); and ener-

gy-based financings (including reserve-based loans, project financings, and production payments).
**Prof. Memberships:** Past President of Association of International Petroleum Negotiators (AIPN); Chairman of Oil and Gas Committee of International Bar Association; Houston Producer's Forum; Houston Bar Association; State Bar of Texas.
**Career:** Head of firmwide Oil and Gas Practice.
**Personal:** JD from Harvard Law School, 1985; BS from Yale University, 1981.

**ASOFSKY, Paul**
Weil, Gotshal & Manges LLP, Houston
713 546 5118
paul.asofsky@weil.com
*Recommended in Tax*
**Practice Areas:** Paul Asofsky's Tax Practice includes investment partnerships, mergers and acquisitions, and bankruptcy and debt restructuring. He heads the Private Equity Group within the firm's Tax Department, structuring private equity, real estate and hedge funds, structuring acquisitions and dispositions of portfolio investments and structuring general partner and manager compensation arrangements. He is Chairman of the Private Equity Subcommittee of the American Bar Association Section of Taxation's Committee on Partnerships. He is a Conferee of the National Bankruptcy Conference, where for many years he chaired the Committee on Tax Matters.
**Personal:** Columbia University, AB, 1962; Harvard Law School, LLB, 1965.

**AXE, Albert**
Jenkens & Gilchrist, Austin
512 499 3800
*Recommended in Environment*

**BABCOCK, Charles**
Jackson Walker LLP, Dallas
214 953 6000
*Recommended in Litigation*

**BACKUS, Marcia E**
Vinson & Elkins LLP, Houston
713 758 1101
mbackus@velaw.com
*Recommended in Energy, Projects*
**Practice Areas:** Domestic and international acquisition, divestiture and project finance and project development transactions, corporate law, power-related transactions and other energy-related transactions. Is Co-Administrative Head of the Houston office, a member of the firm's Management Committee, the Energy Practice Group, and Chair of the Partner Admissions Committee.
**Prof. Memberships:** Fellow: Houston Bar Association; Keeton Fellow, The University of Texas.
**Career:** Came to the firm in 1983 and was admitted to the partnership in 1991.
**Personal:** Attended Georgetown University and graduated from The University

of Texas, BA in 1976 and JD in 1983 (Order of the Coif).

**BACON, Christopher V**
Vinson & Elkins LLP, Houston
713 758 1148
cbacon@velaw.com
*Recommended in Employment*
**Practice Areas:** Chris's practice is primarily devoted to the litigation of civil rights and employment matters on behalf of public and private employers.
**Career:** Admitted to practice: Texas, 1990; United States Supreme Court; US Courts of Appeal for the Fifth and District of Columbia Circuits; US District Courts for the Northern, Southern, Eastern, and Western Districts of Texas.
**Personal:** University of Houston, BA summa cum laude, in 1979 and MEd in mathematics education, 1982; Harvard School of Law, JD cum laude, 1990.

**BAKER, Andrew M**
Baker Botts LLP, Dallas
214 953 6735
andrew.baker@bakerbotts.com
*Recommended in Corporate/M&A*
**Practice Areas:** Chair: Dallas Corporate Section. Principal practice areas: general corporate, mergers, acquisitions, corporate finance/securities and government and internal investigations. Practice emphasizes development of close, long-term, value-added relationships with public and private entities. Counseled with senior management/boards of directors/audit and compensation committees on numerous matters, and led transaction teams in complex mergers and acquisitions and corporate finance transactions involving a variety of industries around the world.
**Personal:** BA, summa cum laude, State University of New York at Albany, 1976; JD, magna cum laude, Cornell Law School, 1979.

**BAKER, Debra**
Connelly Baker Wotring Jackson LLP, Houston 713 980 1700
*Recommended in Environment*

**BAKER, Mark**
Fulbright & Jaworski L.L.P., Houston
713 651 7708
mbaker@fulbright.com
*Recommended in Energy, International Arbitration*
**Practice Areas:** Arbitration, mediation, and litigation.
**Prof. Memberships:** Mr Baker has arbitrated before most of the world's arbitral bodies and has been involved in numerous alternative dispute resolution procedures. In every year since 1998, he has chaired at least eight significant arbitration cases while acting as lead counsel in dozens more on five continents. He is a Fellow of the Chartered Institute of Arbitrators; a Director and arbitrator for numerous panels of the AAA and ICDR;

a court member and arbitrator for the LCIA; an arbitrator for CPR, WIPO, CAM, CAS; and a mediator for CEDR and the Texas courts. He is also a member of the ICC Commission.

**Career:** Mr Baker is a Co-Head of Fulbright's 13-office International Department and also Co-Head of the firm's Arbitration and ADR Practice Group. He has also represented numerous clients in international and domestic energy contracts, power purchase and sale agreements, construction contracts, joint ventures, and project finance and development agreements.

**Personal:** BA, summa cum laude Yale University (1981); JD, with high honors, Duke University School of Law (1984). Before joining Fulbright, Mr Baker was a law clerk to the Honorable John R Brown, Chief Judge of the US Fifth Circuit.

### BALDWIN, George
Ford Nassen & Baldwin, Dallas
214 523 5100
*Recommended in Construction*

### BANTA, Robert
Locke Liddell & Sapp LLP, Dallas
214 740 8000
*Recommended in Real Estate*

### BARBER, Bill
Fulbright & Jaworski L.L.P., Austin
512 536 3028
bbarber@fulbright.com
*Recommended in Intellectual Property*
**Practice Areas:** Intellectual property; trademark litigation.
**Prof. Memberships:** State Bar of Texas; American Intellectual Property Law Association; Austin Intellectual Property Law Association; Travis County Bar Association; Federal Bar Association and Austin Young Lawyers Association.
**Career:** Admitted to practice in Texas, US District Courts, US Court of Appeals, US Supreme Court and US Patent and Trademark Office. Listed on 'The International Who's Who of Trademark Lawyers' (2005).
**Publications:** 'A 'Rational' Approach for Analyzing Dilution Claims: The Three Hallmarks of True Trademark Dilution', AIPLA Quarterly Journal, Vol 33, No 1, at 25-72 (Winter 2005).
**Personal:** Received JD, high honors, University of Texas School of Law (1997); BS, highest honors, Chemical Engineering, University of Texas (1984).

### BARBOUR, David
Andrews Kurth LLP, Dallas
214 659 4400
*Recommended in Banking & Finance*

### BARBOUR, Larry G
Vinson & Elkins LLP, Houston
713 758 2126
lbarbour@velaw.com
*Recommended in Banking & Finance*
**Practice Areas:** Business transactions,

finance, including project and structured finance, and mergers and acquisitions. Has extensive experience in international transactions and complex syndicated bank transactions, representing either the lenders or the borrower. Worked on all aspects of energy finance.
**Career:** Came to the firm in 1977 and was admitted to the partnership in October 1985.
**Personal:** Graduated from Princeton University, AB in Economics with honors in 1972, New York University, MBA in Finance in 1974, and The University of Texas, JD with high honors, in 1977. (Chancellors; Order of the Coif).

### BARNES JR, Hershell
The Barnes Law Firm PC, Dallas
214 615 7920
*Recommended in Employment*

### BARZOUKAS, Nicolas
Howrey LLP, Houston
713 787 1400
*Recommended in Intellectual Property*

### BASS JR, Robert
Winstead Sechrest & Minick P.C., Austin
512 370 2800
*Recommended in Construction*

### BATES, Brian
Quan, Burdette & Perez, PC, Houston
713 625 9200
*Recommended in Immigration*

### BAYER, Mark W
Gardere Wynne Sewell LLP, Dallas
214 999 4521
mbayer@gardere.com
*Recommended in Antitrust*
**Practice Areas:** Antitrust, securities, intellectual property, class actions, complex litigation.
**Prof. Memberships:** State Bar of Texas (Antitrust and Litigation Sections); American Bar Association (Antitrust and Litigation Sections); Fellow, Texas Bar Foundation; Fellow, Dallas Bar Foundation; Former Chair, Dallas Bar Association Antitrust Section.
**Career:** Mark Bayer has more than two decades of major case litigation experience. His emphasis is on antitrust, distribution issues, securities, theft of trade secrets, intellectual property, class actions and other complex litigation.
**Publications:** '2004 Annual Survey of Texas Class Action Cases', Texas Business Litigation, Winter 2005.
**Personal:** JD, Columbia Law School, 1981; AB, Bowdoin College, 1981.

### BAYKO, Tom
Jones Day, Houston
832 239 3700
tbayko@jonesday.com
*Recommended in Energy*
**Practice Areas:** His international litigation and arbitration experience includes successfully defending claims involving offshore blowouts, tortious interference

with contractual and prospective contractual relationships, construction claims, production sharing agreements, joint operating agreements, participation agreements, area of mutual interest agreements, transportation agreements, take or pay agreements, theft of technology and trade secrets, and other commercial disputes. He has tried cases or arbitrations under the applicable laws of more than 25 countries and is admitted to practice before numerous US courts. He is a featured speaker at conferences on international litigation and arbitration, including 'The Asian M&A Forum 2005' held in Hong Kong.

### BAYS, Richard
Locke Liddell & Sapp LLP, Houston
713 226 1200
*Recommended in Technology*

### BEANE, Jerry
Andrews Kurth LLP, Dallas
214 659 4400
*Recommended in Antitrust*

### BEARD, Brian
Wilson Sonsini Goodrich & Rosati, Austin
512 338 5400
bbeard@wsgr.com
*Recommended in Technology*
**Practice Areas:** Specializes in areas of corporate and securities law with a focus on representation of start-up and growth companies, representation of issuers and underwriters involved in public offerings, and representation of companies involved in merger and acquisition transactions.
**Prof. Memberships:** Admitted to practice in Illinois, California and Texas.
**Career:** Joined WSGR as Partner, 2002. Former Partner, Austin office of Gunderson Dettmer Stough Villeneuve Franklin & Hachigian, LLP (which he co-founded in 1997).
**Personal:** JD, 1990, University of Iowa and BA (Economics), 1987, University of Illinois.

### BECK, David
Beck, Redden & Secrest LLP, Houston
713 951 3700
*Recommended in Energy, Litigation*

### BECKER, Jeffrey
Haynes and Boone LLP, Dallas
214 651 5000
*Recommended in Intellectual Property*

### BECKHAM JR, Charles
Haynes and Boone LLP, Houston
713 547 2000
*Recommended in Bankruptcy*

### BELL, Jerry
Fulbright & Jaworski L.L.P., Houston
713 651 8482
jbell@fulbright.com
*Recommended in Healthcare*
**Practice Areas:** Health law.
**Prof. Memberships:** Board certified by

the Texas Board of Legal Specialization, Health Law Examination Commission (2003-05); Chair, Managed Care and Integrated Delivery Systems Committee, American Academy of Hospital Attorneys (1993-95); Chair, Health Law Section of the State Bar of Texas (1994-95); Board of Directors, American Health Lawyers Association (1997-2001); Board of Directors, American Academy of Healthcare Attorneys (1995-97); Member, Texas Board of Legal Specialization, Health Law Examination Commission, 2003-05.
**Career:** Mr Bell is Head of Fulbright & Jaworski L.L.P's Health Law Business and Regulatory Department and practices in the Houston office. He practices exclusively in the healthcare area. Mr Bell is also an Adjunct Professor at the The University of Texas Law School where he teaches the course Business and Regulatory Aspects of Health Law.
**Personal:** BA, University of Texas (1974); JD, University of Texas School of Law (1977).

### BENNETT, David
Thompson & Knight LLP, Dallas
214 969 1486
David.Bennett@tklaw.com
*Recommended in Bankruptcy*
**Practice Areas:** Mr Bennett's expertise includes both transactions and litigation involving troubled and insolvent businesses. His clients include debtors, creditors, capital providers, as well as other counter-parties in reorganization and liquidation bankruptcy cases. Mr Bennett has been named as a 'Top Bankruptcy Lawyer' in Texas Lawyer (2002) and as a Texas 'Super Lawyer' (Texas Monthly, 2003 -05).
**Prof. Memberships:** State Bar of Texas, Dallas Bar Association, American Bankruptcy Institute, Turnaround Managers' Association.
**Career:** Partner since 1992.
**Personal:** The University of Texas School of Law (JD, with high honors, 1986); University of Texas at Austin (BA, with high honors, 1983).

### BETZEN, Mark E
Jones Day, Dallas
214 969 3704
mbetzen@jonesday.com
*Recommended in Corporate/M&A*
**Practice Areas:** Co-chairs Jones Day's Mergers and Acquisitions Practice in the Texas Region. Extensive experience in mergers, acquisitions, and dispositions involving publicly traded and closely held companies and in public offerings and private placements of equity and debt securities. Also counsels clients with respect to corporate governance, fiduciary duties and securities law compliance.
**Prof. Memberships:** State Bar of Texas; Dallas Bar Association.
**Career:** Partner since 1993.

**Publications:** Member of the Editorial Board of The Corporate Compliance and Regulatory Newsletter.
**Personal:** Texas Tech University (National Merit Scholar; BBA 1981); University of Texas School of Law (JD with honors 1984).

### BIERY, Evelyn H
Fulbright & Jaworski L.L.P., Houston
713 651 5544
ebiery@fulbright.com
*Recommended in Bankruptcy*
**Practice Areas:** Bankruptcy, reorganization and international insolvency matters.
**Prof. Memberships:** Chair of the Board of Directors, American College of Bankruptcy; President, Miller Foltz Inn of Court; past Chair, Business Law Section and Bankruptcy Law Committee, the State Bar of Texas; past Director, Texas Association of Bank Counsel; Past Texas Chair, Society of International Business Fellows; Director, International Insolvency Institute; Diplomat, World Affairs Council.
**Career:** As a Partner with over 32 years of experience, Ms Biery heads Fulbright's Bankruptcy, Reorganization and Creditors' Rights Department.
**Personal:** BA, summa cum laude, Abilene Christian University (1968); JD, Southern Methodist University School of Law (1973).

### BILGER, Bruce R
Vinson & Elkins LLP, Houston
713 758 2614
bbilger@velaw.com
*Recommended in Energy, Projects*
**Practice Areas:** Chair of the firm's Energy Practice Group and Co-Head of the firm's Business and International Section. Practice consists primarily of domestic and international business transactions, including mergers and acquisitions, international infrastructure development projects, project finance, and other corporate transactions, particularly in the energy industry.
**Prof. Memberships:** Member and Former Trustee: American College of Investment Counsel.
**Career:** Lecturer and author: programs and articles on partnership law, corporate law, mergers and acquisitions, project finance, and international law topics.
**Personal:** Graduated from Dartmouth College, BA in 1973, and the University of Virginia, MBA and JD in 1977.

### BISHOP, Doak
King & Spalding LLP, Houston
713 751 3205
dbishop@kslaw.com
*Recommended in Energy, International Arbitration*
**Practice Areas:** Litigation with 29 years of experience focusing on international arbitration and litigation of oil and gas, energy, construction, environmental and foreign investment disputes. Board Certi-

fied in Civil Trial Law by the Texas Board of Legal Specialization.
**Prof. Memberships:** American Bar Association; Dallas Bar Association; State Bar of Texas; Vice Chairman of the Institute of Transnational Arbitration (1990-present); Member of the US delegation to the NAFTA Advisory Committee on Private Commercial Disputes.
**Personal:** BA, Southern Methodist University, 1973; JD, University of Texas, 1976.

### BLAND, Douglas S
Vinson & Elkins LLP, Houston
713 758 2498
dbland@velaw.com
*Recommended in Energy, Projects*
**Practice Areas:** Partner in Business and International Section. Has a domestic and international Business Transactions Practice focusing on the development, acquisition, divestiture, and financing of energy-related projects. Co-Head of Project Finance and Development Practice Group and Member of Merger and Acquisitions and Electric Power Practice Groups.
**Prof. Memberships:** Houston Bar Association.
**Career:** Admitted to Texas Bar in 1984. Joined Vinson & Elkins in 1984; admitted to the partnership in January 1992.
**Personal:** Graduated from the University of Virginia, BA with high honors, 1981 (Phi Beta Kappa), and the University of Michigan, JD cum laude, in 1984 (Order of the Coif).

### BLISSARD, Judith M
Vinson & Elkins LLP, Houston
713 758 2374
jblissard@velaw.com
*Recommended in Tax*
**Practice Areas:** Judith's principal areas of practice are business transactions and domestic and international tax planning.
**Prof. Memberships:** American Bar Association, Taxation Section; Committee on US Activities of Foreigners and Tax Treaties; Co-Chair: Subcommittee on Current Developments; State Bar of Texas; Houston Bar Association; International Fiscal Association; Houston International Tax Forum; Houston Tax Roundtable.
**Career:** Admitted to practice: Texas, 1987; United States Tax Court.
**Personal:** University of Houston, BBA summa cum laude, 1984 (Beta Alpha Psi); University of Houston Law Center, JD cum laude, 1987 (Order of the Barons; Order of the Coif).

### BOGDANOW, Alan J
Vinson & Elkins LLP, Dallas
214 220 7857
abogdanow@velaw.com
*Recommended in Corporate/M&A*
**Practice Areas:** Primary areas of practice are mergers and acquisitions, public and private financings, and corporate

control and governance matters. Represents public and private acquirers, targets, sellers, special committees, and investment bankers in a broad range of merger and acquisition transactions.
**Career:** Admitted to New York Bar in 1972 and Texas Bar in 1977. Came to the firm as a Partner in 2001.
**Personal:** Graduated cum laude from Brown University, AB in 1968 and Columbia Law School, JD in 1971, served as editor of the Columbia Law Review.

### BOHANNON, Paul
Andrews Kurth LLP, The Woodlands
713 220 4801
*Recommended in Environment*

### BOND, Thomas J
Akin Gump Strauss Hauer & Feld LLP, Austin 512 499 6217
tbond@akingump.com
*Recommended in Insurance*
**Practice Areas:** Chair, firmwide Insurance Practice. Represents holding, life insurance, and property and liability companies; trade associations; reinsurers; HMOs; e-commerce insurance ventures; title underwriters and agencies; prepaid legal entities; agents; large insureds; insurance departments of other states. Has been involved in rehabilitation and liquidation of troubled companies, hostile and negotiated acquisitions and mergers, regulatory approval projects, investment decisions, and design and approval of new coverages.
**Prof. Memberships:** Founding Board Member, Federation of Regulatory Counsel; State Bars of Texas and Colorado.
**Career:** Texas Commissioner of Insurance, 1982-85.
**Personal:** BA, Baylor University; MFA, Bowling Green State University; JD (honors), University of Texas.

### BOONE, Michael
Haynes and Boone LLP, Dallas
214 651 5000
*Recommended in Corporate/M&A*

### BOREN, Alison
Baker Botts LLP, Dallas
214 953 6827
alison.boren@bakerbotts.com
*Recommended in Banking & Finance*
**Practice Areas:** Financing transactions and debt restructurings, including investment grade lending, acquisition financing, debtor-in-possession financing, exit financing, letter of credit facilities, cash flow lending, asset-based lending, bridge financing, equity and subordinated debt financing, and workouts and restructurings. She represents both borrowers and financial institutions, and has been involved in a wide variety of financing transactions in both the United States and abroad.
**Personal:** SMU Dedman School of Law (JD, 1983); S.M.U. (BA, 1980 and BBA, 1980).

### BOULDEN, Michael R
Vinson & Elkins LLP, Dallas
214 220 7840
mboulden@velaw.com
*Recommended in Real Estate*
**Practice Areas:** Experience includes construction and permanent lending on commercial real estate; joint ventures and equity participations involving the formation of partnerships and limited liability companies; participating mortgages; real estate debt and partnership workouts; representing institutional lenders and equity investors; real estate outsourcing, and US and foreign investment by private equity funds.
**Prof. Memberships:** American Bar Association; State Bar of Texas; Dallas Bar Association; Dallas Real Estate Council.
**Career:** Admitted to Texas Bar, 1977. Came to the firm as a Partner, 1994.
**Personal:** Graduated from Rice University, BA in 1973, and Southern Methodist University, JD in 1977.

### BOULWARE, Margaret
Baker & McKenzie, Houston
713 427 5003
meg.boulware@bakernet.com
*Recommended in Intellectual Property*
**Practice Areas:** Ms Boulware's IP Practice includes patent, with a chemistry and biotechnology emphasis; trademark, particularly international portfolios; and domestic copyright issues.
**Prof. Memberships:** Patent Public Advisory Committee, First Chair; American Intellectual Property Law Association, President (1998-99); State Bar of Texas, IP Section, past Chair; Texas Bar Foundation, Life Fellow; Houston Bar Foundation, Life Fellow; Houston IP Law Association, past President; University of Houston Law Alumni Board, Director; Copyright Society of the USA., Trustee (1996-98); National Inventor 'Hall of Fame', Secretary (1994-95); Foundation for a Creative America Board Member; International Trademark Association, Panel of Neutrals.
**Career:** Ms Boulware was selected one of The Best IP Lawyers in America by IP Law and Business, and included in The American and International 'Who's Who' of Business Lawyers. She also serves on the Clemson University Foundation Board; served as Officer and Director of the University of Houston Law Center Alumni Board (1982-87); was appointed by Secretary of Commerce to serve as inaugural Chair of the Patent Public Advisory Committee for the US Patent and Trademark Office; and was founding Chair of the University of Houston Law Center IP Law Program Advisory Board.
**Publications:** Ms Boulware has been and continues to be a frequent publisher of articles and lecturer for various IP-related publications and organizations.
**Personal:** JD, University of Houston Law Center (1975); MS, Clemson University

(1970); BS, University of Georgia (1969). Admitted to practice: Texas; United States Patent and Trademark Office.

## BOWERS, William
Fulbright & Jaworski L.L.P., Dallas
214 855 8219
bbowers@fulbright.com
*Recommended in Tax*

**Practice Areas:** Tax.
**Prof. Memberships:** Mr Bowers teaches partnership tax at the University of Texas School of Law, and has taught taxation of property transactions at the Southern Methodist University School of Law. He is Chair of the State Bar of Texas' Tax Section and has formerly chaired the Tax Section of the Dallas Bar Association, as well as the ABA Committee on Tax Accounting Problems. Mr Bowers was certified as a public accountant in Maryland in 1978.
**Career:** Mr Bowers joined the Dallas office of Fulbright & Jaworski L.L.P. as a Partner in 2003. A member of the Fulbright Tax Practice Group, his practice focuses on tax planning in complex transactions. His practice concentration is federal income tax planning for complex business transactions involving corporations, partnerships and real estate investment trusts.
**Personal:** Mr Bowers received a Bachelor of Business Administration in accounting, with honors, in 1972 from Texas A&M University; a Master of Law Taxation in 1979 from Georgetown University Law Center and a Juris Doctor in 1975 from the Southern Methodist University School of Law.

## BOWMAN, John
Fulbright & Jaworski L.L.P., Houston
713 651 3732
jbowman@fulbright.com
*Recommended in Energy, International Arbitration*

**Practice Areas:** Energy and petrochemicals, arbitration and litigation.
**Prof. Memberships:** Fellow of the College of Commercial Arbitrators and of The Chartered Institute of Arbitrators; member of Association of International Petroleum Negotiators; International Arbitration Club, London; International Arbitration Institute, Paris; Advisory Board of the Institute for Transnational Arbitration; Panel of International Centre for Dispute Resolution; CPR Institute Oil and Gas Panel; LCIA; Lawdragon 500 Leading Lawyers in America (2005); and Houston International Arbitration Club; Board of Directors, Houston World Affairs Council.
**Career:** Today his practice focuses on representation of IOC's and service companies in international oil and gas disputes in arbitration and litigation and on acting as an arbitrator in international and domestic upstream disputes.
**Publications:** The Panama Convention

and Its Implementation under the Federal Arbitration Act (Kluwer 2002).
**Personal:** Married to Katie-Pat Bowman. He received a BA in 1974 and a JD in 1980 from the University of Kansas, where he was Editor-in-Chief of the Kansas Law Review. He is licensed to practice law in Texas.

## BOYCE, William J
Fulbright & Jaworski L.L.P., Houston
713 651 5313
wboyce@fulbright.com
*Recommended in Litigation*

**Practice Areas:** Commercial, constitutional, and libel law; appellate practice.
**Prof. Memberships:** Mr Boyce is a Member of the Appellate Practice Section of both the State Bar of Texas and the Houston Bar Association. He is also a fellow of the Texas Bar Foundation and the past Chair of the Civil Appellate Law Examination Committee of the Texas Board of Legal Specialization.
**Career:** A Board Certified appellate specialist and Partner, Mr Boyce joined the Houston office of Fulbright & Jaworski L.L.P. in 1989. Texas Monthly recognized him as a Texas Super Lawyer in 2003, 2004 and 2005; Texas Lawyer listed him as '40 Under 40' in 2001.
**Personal:** BS, Highest Distinction, Northwestern University (1985); JD, cum laude, Northwestern University School of Law. He was admitted to practice law in Texas in 1989.

## BRADDOCK, James
Haynes and Boone LLP, Austin
512 867 8400
*Recommended in Environment*

## BRADLEY, James P
Sidley Austin LLP, Dallas
214 981 3306
jbradley@Sidley.com
*Recommended in Intellectual Property*

**Practice Areas:** Managing Partner of Sidley's Dallas office. Mr Bradley has over 30 years of experience in trying intellectual property cases in district courts and before the International Trade Commission. He focuses his litigation practice on patents. Mr Bradley's litigated patent cases have involved a variety of technologies, including semiconductor devices, semiconductor process technology, telecommunications, oil drilling apparatus, metal detectors and medical devices.
**Prof. Memberships:** State Bar of Texas; State Bar of California (inactive); Texas Bar Foundation – Life Fellow; Dallas Bar Foundation – Fellow; The Center for American and International Law – Research Fellow; Grievance Committee for the State Bar of Texas for the Sixth Bar District (1979-88); American Inn of Court LVI at Dallas, Texas – Charter Barrister Member (1988-90); Fellow Institute of Electrical and Electronics Engineers.
**Career:** Texas Monthly Magazine's 'Texas Super Lawyer' for 2005 (top 5% of his

profession).
**Publications:** Annual Institute on Patent Law, 'Obtaining Advice of Counsel to Avoid Infringement, Willful Infringement and Increased Damages', Bradley, Chibib and Jones, November, 1998; Annual Institute on Patent Law, 'Issue Preclusion Regarding Claim Interpretation', Bradley and Lively, October, 2001; Texas Intellectual Property Law Journal, 'Issue Preclusion As It Applies To Claim Interpretation', Bradley and Kubasta, February, 2002.

## BRADSHAW, Brian A
Skadden, Arps, Slate, Meagher & Flom LLP & Affiliates, Houston
713 655 5141
bbradsha@skadden.com
*Recommended in Projects*

**Practice Areas:** Concentrates in the area of domestic and international project finance with particular emphasis on the development and financing of LNG liquefaction and regasification terminals and other energy infrastructure projects. Has advised project developers, commodity purchasers, commercial lenders, investment banks and equity investors regarding the development, financing, acquisition and sale of numerous energy infrastructure projects, including electric power facilities, natural gas pipelines, gas exploration programs, LNG liquefaction facilities and LNG regasification facilities.
**Career:** JD, University of Houston School of Law, 1995; MBA, University of Houston, 1995; AB, Washington University, 1991.

## BRANN, Richard
Baker Botts LLP, Houston
713 229 1563
richard.brann@bakerbotts.com
*Recommended in Employment*

**Practice Areas:** Represents management in all aspects of labor and employment law. Defends collective actions under the Fair Labor Standards Act and class actions alleging employment discrimination, plus individual lawsuits and agency proceedings. Represents employers in disputes under the National Labor Relations Act, the Railway Labor Act, and Occupational Safety and Health Act. Counsels employers on managing workplace legal issues and lawsuit prevention.
**Career:** 30+ years of practice. Chairs firm's Labor and Employment Law Practice.
**Personal:** JD, magna cum laude, University of Texas School of Law, 1968; Order of the Coif BA, magna cum laude, Mississippi State University, 1965.

## BREAUX, Ronald
Haynes and Boone LLP, Dallas
214 651 5000
*Recommended in Antitrust*

## BRISTOW, Daryl
Baker Botts LLP, Houston
713 229 1234
*Recommended in Litigation*

## BROOKNER, Jason
Andrews Kurth LLP, Dallas
214 659 4400
*Recommended in Bankruptcy*

## BROWN, David H
Vinson & Elkins LLP, Houston
713 758 2098
dbrown@velaw.com
*Recommended in Insurance*

**Practice Areas:** Principal area of practice is the representation of policyholders in insurance coverage disputes. Has represented a variety of business enterprises, including energy and transportation companies, and healthcare providers, in insurance litigation and arbitration matters under both first party and liability policies. Represents the Port of Houston Authority in litigation matters.
**Prof. Memberships:** Member: Houston Bar Association; Texas Association of Defense Counsel; Texas Bar Foundation; Maritime Law Association.
**Career:** Admitted to practice: Texas, 1976. Joined Vinson & Elkins, 1977; admitted to partnership, 1984.
**Personal:** Northwestern University, BS, 1972; The University of Texas School of Law, JD with honors, 1975.

## BROWN, Fletcher
Davis & Wilkerson, PC, Austin
512 482 0614
*Recommended in Healthcare*

## BROWN, Jay W
Beirne Maynard & Parsons, LLP, Houston 713 960 7306
jbrown@bmpllp.com
*Recommended in Insurance*

**Practice Areas:** Jay Brown's litigation practice includes contract disputes, fraud, wrongful death, energy, insurance bad faith, insurance contract, deceptive trade practices, civil rights, product liability, toxic tort, catastrophic accidents, and other cases. Mr Brown is Board Certified in Civil Trial Law and Personal Injury Trial Law by the Texas Board of Legal Specialization.
**Prof. Memberships:** State Bar of Texas, Litigation Section; American Bar Association, Litigation Section; Houston Bar Association, Litigation Section; State Bar College; Texas Association of Defense Counsel; Univ. of Houston Law Foundation Faculty.
**Career:** Admitted in all Texas courts; US District Courts for the Northern, Southern, Eastern and Western Districts of Texas; and US Court of Appeals or the 5th Circuit. Co-Chair of the firm's Insurance Litigation/Coverage Section; has served as Hiring Partner for the firm; presently serves on the firm's Executive Committee. Named a 'Texas Super

Lawyer' by Texas Monthly and named as one of 'Houston's Top Lawyers' by H Magazine.
**Personal:** BA with high honors and special honors, Phi Beta Kappa, The University of Texas, 1981; JD with honors, The University of Texas School of Law, Austin, Texas, 1984.

## BROWN, Reagan
Fulbright & Jaworski L.L.P., Houston
713 651 5469
rbrown@fulbright.com
*Recommended in Insurance, Litigation*
**Practice Areas:** Trial and appellate litigation, insurance, legal malpractice, ERISA and products liability.
**Prof. Memberships:** Member of the American Board of Trial Advocates. Admitted to practice before the United States Supreme Court, the United States Court of Appeals for the Fifth Circuit.
**Career:** Admitted to the Texas Bar (1981). A Partner of Fulbright & Jaworski LLP since 1990. Has tried over 85 cases and arbitration proceedings with over 50 jury cases to verdict. Certified by the Texas Board of Legal Specialization in Civil Trial Law, Civil Appellate Law and Personal Injury Trial Law.
**Personal:** Received a BS and BA, summa cum laude, (1978) from Southern Methodist University and a JD, with honors, in 1981 from the University of Texas.

## BRUNS, Phillip T
Gibbs & Bruns, LLP, Houston
713 650 8805
pbruns@gibbs-bruns.com
*Recommended in Energy, Litigation*
**Practice Areas:** Full range of commercial and business litigation and arbitration, both plaintiff and defendant. Has extensive experience with intellectual property disputes, including trade secrets, patent infringement and non-competition, and construction and engineering disputes.
**Prof. Memberships:** Admitted to practice in Texas in 1981 and admitted to various federal district courts, as well as the Fifth Circuit Court of Appeals and the Third Circuit Court of Appeals. Member American Bar Association, Section of Litigation, Houston Bar Association and Houston Bar Foundation.
**Career:** Joined Wood, Campbell, Moody & Gibbs in Houston in 1981. Founding Partner in Gibbs & Ratliff, LLP in 1983, which became Gibbs & Bruns, LLP in 1994.
**Personal:** Born January 24, 1956 in Bartlesville, Oklahoma. JD with honors, University of Texas 1981. Chancellors and Order of Coif; BA University of Oklahoma, 1978.

## BURGIN, Sara
Baker Botts LLP, Austin
512 322 2649
sara.burgin@bakerbotts.com
*Recommended in Environment*

**Practice Areas:** Practice includes all water matters and solid and hazardous waste.
**Prof. Memberships:** State Bar of Texas – Environmental and Natural Resources Section; American Bar Association – Environment, Energy and Resources Section; Water Quality Committee.
**Career:** JD, University of Houston Law Center (1982), associate editor, Houston Law Review, MS, Texas A&M University (1977), BS, The University of Texas (1973).
**Personal:** Recognized as The Best Lawyers in America; 'Go-To Lawyer in Environmental Law', Texas Lawyer; 'Best in Bar' by the Austin Business Journal, 'Texas Super Lawyer' by Texas Monthly and Law and Politics Magazine.

## BURNER, Burnie
Long, Burner, Parks & DeLargy, Austin
512 474 1587
*Recommended in Insurance*

## CAGLE, Molly
Vinson & Elkins LLP, Austin
512 542 8552
mcagle@velaw.com
*Recommended in Environment*
**Practice Areas:** Administrative and environmental law.
**Career:** Admitted to Texas Bar in 1981. Joined Vinson & Elkins in 1981 and was admitted to the partnership in January 1989.
**Personal:** Attended the University of Southwestern Louisiana and graduated from Texas Tech, BS magna cum laude in 1978, and The University of Texas, JD with honors in 1981.

## CALDWELL, Charles
Vinson & Elkins LLP, Houston
713 758 4518
ccaldwell@velaw.com
*Recommended in Energy*
**Practice Areas:** Partner in the firm's Energy Regulatory Practice and Member of executive committee of Energy Practice Group. Practice consists primarily of representation of oil and gas pipelines before regulatory authorities, regulatory compliance counseling, and energy transactions involving regulatory assets.
**Prof. Memberships:** Member, Energy Bar Association; past President, Energy Bar Association – Houston Chapter.
**Career:** Regular speaker: continuing education and client compliance programs on energy regulatory law. Law clerk to Hon George P Kazen, US District Court, Southern District of Texas (1990-91).
**Publications:** Co-Editor, Gas Regulation 2003 (Global Competition Review).
**Personal:** Rice University, BA 1985; University of Virginia, JD 1990.

## CAMPBELL, Andrew
Andrews Kurth LLP, Dallas
214 659 4400
*Recommended in Real Estate*

## CAMPBELL, Rhett
Thompson & Knight LLP, Houston
713 653 8660
Rhett.Campbell@tklaw.com
*Recommended in Bankruptcy*
**Practice Areas:** Mr Campbell represents clients in corporate reorganization and business and commercial litigation, with a special emphasis on creditors' rights and bankruptcy matters. He is experienced in all aspects of business bankruptcy and particularly in energy bankruptcies, in which he represents public and private companies, creditors' committees, bondholders, service companies, individual working interest owners and operators, exploration, and production companies. He is Board Certified in Business Bankruptcy Law and Civil Trial Law by the Texas Board of Legal Specialization.
**Personal:** SMU Dedman School of Law (JD, 1973); Southern Methodist University (BA, 1970).

## CANTERBURY JR, Joe F
Canterbury, Stuber, Elder, Gooch & Surratt, PC, Dallas
972 239 7493
jcanterbury@canterburylaw.com
*Recommended in Construction*
**Practice Areas:** Construction and labor and employment law; domestic and international arbitration and mediation of construction disputes.
**Prof. Memberships:** Member, Dallas, Texas and American Bar Associations; Fellow and President Elect of, American College of Construction Lawyers; Founding Member and past Chairman, Construction Law Sections of Dallas and Texas Bar Associations; past Chairman, Labor and Employment Lawyers Council, Associated General Contractors of America; Member, American Arbitration Association National Construction Dispute Resolution Committee; Board Member and Arbitrator, American Arbitration Association; Member, Board of Directors, Dallas Chapter, Associated General Contractors of America (1997-98).
**Career:** Construction work, United States Navy, followed by college and law school. Active practice of law since 1967, with emphasis on employment and labor law and construction law. Founding Member and majority shareholder of Canterbury, Stuber, Elder, Gooch & Surratt, PC.
**Publications:** 'Texas Construction Law Manual', West Group (1st ed 1981, 2nd ed 1993, 3rd ed 2006, co-authored with Robert J Shapiro); Annual Supplements Thesis 2004 (West); 'Construction Law Handbook', contributing author, Aspen Law & Business (1999-2002); 'Construction Business Handbook', contributing author, McGraw-Hill (1st ed 1978, 2nd ed 1984); 'Wiley Construction Law Update', contributing author (1994-2004). Author of numerous articles,

speeches and papers on construction law delivered to legal community and industry groups.
**Personal:** BA, University of Dallas, 1963; JD, Southern Methodist University School of Law, 1966 (Phi Delta Phi); United States Navy 1956-59. Married to the former Patricia Ferguson since 1963; they maintain homes in Dallas, Texas and County Tipperary, Ireland. They have four grown children and five grandchildren. His hobbies include grandchildren, fly fishing and travel.

## CAPSHAW, Richard
Capshaw, Goss & Bowers LLP, Dallas
214 761 6610
*Recommended in Construction*

## CARRELL, Richard
Fulbright & Jaworski L.L.P., Houston
713 651 5447
rcarrell@fulbright.com
*Recommended in Antitrust*
**Practice Areas:** Antitrust, business litigation, securities litigation, contracts, and oil and gas litigation.
**Prof. Memberships:** The Houston and the American Bar Associations and the State Bar of Texas. Trustee of Baylor College of Medicine and the Kelsey Foundation for Research.
**Career:** Admitted Texas Bar (1970). A Partner of Fulbright & Jaworski L.L.P. which he joined in 1970. Served as a member of the firm's Executive and Policy Committees.
**Personal:** Received a BA from Washington & Lee University in 1965 and a JD from the University of Virginia in 1970.

## CAWLEY, Douglas
McKool Smith, Dallas
214 978 4000
dcawley@mckoolsmith.com
*Recommended in Intellectual Property*
**Practice Areas:** Intellectual property litigation for US and international corporations, including patent litigation, patent licensing, and appeals, with an emphasis on patent and software copyright litigation.
**Prof. Memberships:** ABA, American Intellectual Property Law Association, Federal Circuit Bar Association, Dallas Bar Association.
**Career:** Principal in Dallas since 2001.
**Personal:** University of Texas School of Law (JD, with honors, 1975); University of Texas (BA, with honors, 1972); Texas Super Lawyer (Law and Politics Magazine, 2003-05).

## CHAPMAN, Jeffrey A
Vinson & Elkins LLP, Dallas
214 220 7797
jchapman@velaw.com
*Recommended in Corporate/M&A*
**Practice Areas:** Represents publicly and privately held corporations in wide variety of merger and acquisition transactions. Represents issuers, underwriters

and investors in numerous public and private securities transactions, including equity and debt offerings. Extensive experience in corporate reorganizations. Advises executives and boards of directors regarding sensitive corporate matters and transactions, including takeover defenses, acquisition inquiries, fiduciary duties, and disclosure obligations.
**Career:** Admitted to Texas Bar, 1983. Came to firm as Partner, 1995.
**Personal:** Graduated from University of Iowa, BBA with highest distinction, 1979, and Harvard Law School, JD cum laude, 1983.

**CIVINS, Jeff**
Haynes and Boone LLP, Austin
512 867 8400
*Recommended in Environment*

**CLEMENT, Zack**
Fulbright & Jaworski L.L.P., Houston
713 651 5434
zclement@fulbright.com
*Recommended in Bankruptcy*
**Practice Areas:** Bankruptcy, reorganization and creditor's rights.
**Prof. Memberships:** American College of Bankruptcy; International Insolvency Institute; American Bar Association; American Bankruptcy Institute; State Bar of Texas and Houston Bar Association.
**Career:** Zack is licensed to practice law in Texas, the District of Columbia, Virginia, and Illinois. He is also admitted to practice in the US District Courts in Texas, the US Courts of Appeal for the Third, Fifth, Eleventh, and DC Circuits, and the US Supreme Court.
**Publications:** 'Corporate Finance in Bankruptcy', June 2004.
**Personal:** JD, University of Virginia School of Law (1975); US Navy Air Intelligence Officer (1972); AB, cum laude, Public and International Affairs (Economics), Princeton University (1970).

**CLIFTON, R Brent**
Locke Liddell & Sapp LLP, Dallas
214 740 8000
*Recommended in Tax*

**CLONTS, David R**
Akin Gump Strauss Hauer & Feld LLP, Houston 713 220 5886
dclonts@akingump.com
*Recommended in Intellectual Property*
**Practice Areas:** A member of Akin Gump's Patent Litigation Practice Group, Mr Clonts focuses on patent litigation and intellectual property counseling for large US and international companies in electronics, software, medical device and business method fields.
**Personal:** BSEE, Georgia Institute of Technology (1987); JD, University of Texas (1991).

**COATS, William M**
Coats Rose Yale Ryman Lee, Houston
713 651 0111
*Recommended in Construction*

**COBB, Kelly**
Quan, Burdette & Perez, PC, Houston
713 625 9200
*Recommended in Immigration*

**COGAN JR, John P**
Akin Gump Strauss Hauer & Feld LLP, Houston 713 220 5885
jcogan@akingump.com
*Recommended in Energy, Projects*
**Practice Areas:** Focuses on international energy, financial, shipping and commercial transactions, particularly involving projects for international exploration, extraction, processing, transportation and sale of hydrocarbons. Named one of the top five international lawyers in Texas.
**Prof. Memberships:** Corresponding Editor, 'International Legal Materials'; Member – Association of International Petroleum Negotiators; frequent lecturer on international energy matters.
**Personal:** BA, 1965, JD, 1968, University of Texas. Attended Universidad Autnoma de Guanajuato, Mexico, Escuela de Derecho, 1968; Universidad Nacional Autnoma de Mexico, Instituto de Derecho Comparativo, 1967; Bucknell University, 1961-62. Work/study program at Université de Nantes, France, 1964.

**COHEN, Eric**
Andrews Myers Coulter & Cohen PC, Houston 713 850 4200
*Recommended in Construction*

**COHEN, Murry B**
Akin Gump Strauss Hauer & Feld LLP, Houston
713 220 5866
mcohen@akingump.com
*Recommended in Litigation*
**Practice Areas:** Justice Cohen served for 20 years on the Court of Appeals for the First District of Texas before joining Akin Gump Strauss Hauer & Feld as Head of its Texas Appellate Practice Group. He is a board certified specialist in civil appeals and in criminal law, has been an Adjunct Professor at two law schools, and regularly argues before Texas and federal trial and appellate courts.
**Career:** Judge, Court of Appeals for the First District of Texas (1982-2002); Life Fellow, Texas Bar Foundation and Houston Bar Foundation.
**Personal:** BA, George Washington University; JD, University of Texas.

**COHEN, R Scott**
Weil, Gotshal & Manges LLP, Dallas
214 746 7738
scott.cohen@weil.com
*Recommended in Corporate/M&A*
**Practice Areas:** R Scott Cohen has practiced in the area of corporate and securities law for over 25 years. Mr Cohen's practice concentrates on domestic and international mergers and acquisitions, restructurings and public and private offerings of debt and equity securities. Mr Cohen has led acquisition and financ-

ing transactions for such clients as Texas Instruments Incorporated, Viasystems Group, Inc., Thermadyne Holdings Corporation, Berg Electronics, Inc., International Wire Group, Inc., Dr Pepper/Seven-Up Companies, Inc., Dr Pepper/Seven-Up Bottling Group, Inc., The Morningstar Group, Inc., and Inet Technologies, Inc.
**Personal:** University of Texas, BBA, 1976; Southern Methodist University School of Law, JD, 1979.

**COKINOS, Gregory**
Cokinos, Bosien and Young, Houston
713 535 5500
*Recommended in Construction*

**COLEMAN, Gregory S**
Weil, Gotshal & Manges LLP, Austin
512 349 1937
greg.coleman@weil.com
*Recommended in Litigation*
**Practice Areas:** Gregory S Coleman heads Weil Gotshal's Supreme Court and Appellate Litigation Practice Group. He has experience in numerous areas of appellate litigation, including complex business torts, class actions, white-collar criminal defense, securities, products liability, insurance, bankruptcy, telecommunications, intellectual property, accounting malpractice, constitutional litigation, and governmental representation. Mr Coleman has successfully represented clients before the US Supreme Court, the US Courts of Appeals, and numerous state supreme courts and intermediate courts of appeals. He previously served as Solicitor General for the State of Texas and has taught as an Adjunct Professor at the University of Texas School of Law and South Texas College of Law.
**Personal:** Texas A&M University, BS, 1987; Texas A&M University, MBA, 1989; University of Texas School of Law, JD, 1992.

**COLEMAN, James**
Carrington, Coleman, Sloman & Blumenthal, LLP, Dallas
214 855 3000
*Recommended in Litigation*

**CONLON, Michael W**
Fulbright & Jaworski L.L.P., Houston
713 651 5427
mconlon@fulbright.com
*Recommended in Corporate/M&A*
**Practice Areas:** Corporate Securities and M&A.
**Prof. Memberships:** State Bar of Texas; Houston and American Bar Associations.
**Career:** He is Co-Partner in charge of Fulbright & Jaworski LLP's Houston office, and Co-Head of its Corporation, Business and Banking Practice. His general corporate practice primarily involves the representation of publicly held corporations in matters involving securities offerings and routine reporting, corporate governance and compliance matters,

disclosure issues, secured and unsecured borrowing, mergers, acquisitions and dispositions. He has represented special committees of boards of directors connected with takeover offers and corporate restructurings.
**Personal:** He received a BA (magna cum laude and Phi Beta Kappa) from Catholic University of America in 1968 and his JD (Order of Coif) from Duke University in 1971.

**CONNELLY, Michael**
Connelly Baker Wotring Jackson LLP, Houston 713 980 1700
*Recommended in Environment*

**CONRAD, Walter**
Baker Botts LLP, Houston
713 229 1230
walter.conrad@bakerbotts.com
*Recommended in Environment*
**Practice Areas:** Expert in toxic tort and environmental litigation. Represents corporations in suits brought by individual plaintiffs, groups of plaintiffs, government agencies and nonprofit organizations. Nationally recognized practice focuses on trials in both state and federal courts. Extensive experience in administrative litigation. Develops innovative group defense strategies that provide significant savings in legal fees for clients.
**Career:** 38 years of practice.
**Personal:** LLB, The University of Texas School of Law, 1964; Member, Texas Law Review Phi Alpha Delta; BA, Princeton University, 1961.

**CONWAY, Susan**
Graves, Dougherty, Hearon & Moody, P.C., Austin 512 480 5600
*Recommended in Insurance*

**COOKE, Gregg**
Guida, Slavich & Flores, P.C., Dallas
214 692 0009
*Recommended in Environment*

**COOPER, Brent**
Cooper & Scully PC, Dallas
214 712 9500
*Recommended in Insurance*

**COOPER, James**
Gardere Wynne Sewell LLP, Houston
713 276 5884
jcooper@gardere.com
*Recommended in Insurance*
**Practice Areas:** Insurance coverage, commercial litigation, maritime, trial.
**Prof. Memberships:** Co-Chair, ABA Insurance Coverage Litigation Committee, Products Liability Subcommittee; Board of Directors, American Inns of Court, Houston Chapter; Proctor Member, Maritime Law Association of the United States.
**Career:** Jim Cooper has 20 years of experience handling a wide variety of commercial litigation and insurance matters. He primarily represents policyholders in the resolution of multi-million dollar

insurance coverage disputes. He also handles a wide variety of commercial litigation matters, including breach of contract cases, maritime liens, and litigation arising out of damage to international shipments of cargo. Mr Cooper is a frequent speaker at the Texas Insurance Law Conference, and has authored insurance coverage articles for the Journal of Texas Insurance Law and University of Houston International Law Journal.
**Publications:** 'The Rising Price of Declining Coverage in the Construction Industry', Mealey's 4th Annual Advanced Insurance Coverage Conference: Top 10 Issues (2006); 'Fielder Road and the Future of the Eight Corners Rule', Texas Insurance Law Symposium (2006); 'Maximizing Insurance Coverage for Pre-Suit Settlements of Construction Defect Claims', Journal of Texas Insurance Law, 2004 (Special Construction Coverage Issue); 'Recovery of Economic Damages for Delayed Offshore Production', J Maritime Law and Commerce, 1997; 'Weathering the Storm: International Loss of Hire Policies and the Problem of Unchartered Rigs', University of Houston International Law Journal, 1994.
**Personal:** JD, Tulane University School of Law, cum laude, 1984; BA, Wabash College, 1981.

### COOPER, Samuel W
Baker Botts LLP, Houston
713 229 1834
samuel.cooper@bakerbotts.com
*Recommended in Litigation*
**Practice Areas:** Commercial trial lawyer focusing on securities and antitrust litigation and government investigations. Has tried cases to decision before juries, judges and arbitrators. Represents audit committees and corporate boards conducting internal investigations.
**Prof. Memberships:** ABA; SBOT; HBA.
**Career:** Partner since 2001.
Publications: Note, 'Considering "Power" in Separation of Powers', 46 Stan L Rev 361 (1994).
**Personal:** Stanford Law School (JD 1993, Order of the Coif); Harvard College (AB 1990, summa cum laude, Phi Beta Kappa); Managing Editor Stanford Law Review (1992-93); Law Clerk to the Honorable J Harvie Wilkinson III, US Court of Appeals for the Fourth Circuit (1993-94).

### COPELAND, Gregory
Baker Botts LLP, Houston
713 229 1301
greg.copeland@bakerbotts.com
*Recommended in Energy*
**Practice Areas:** Represents clients in the energy industry in complex litigation, covering an expansive array of matters involving the production, transmission and sale of electricity, oil, gas, lignite, coal and nuclear fuels. Represents clients in state and federal courts throughout the

United States, and in arbitration proceedings, mediations and administrative hearings.
**Career:** 30+ years of practice. Serves on the Executive Committee for the firm. Member of the CPR Panel of Neutrals on Energy.
**Personal:** JD, The University of Texas School of Law, 1972; Phi Delta Phi; BA, University of Oklahoma, 1970.

### CORKEN, Heather M
Fulbright & Jaworski L.L.P., Houston
713 651 8386
hcorken@fulbright.com
*Recommended in Environment*
**Practice Areas:** Environmental law; litigation.
**Prof. Memberships:** Houston Bar Association; State Bar of Texas; American Bar Association.
**Career:** For more than 10 years, Heather Corken has practiced all aspects of environmental law advising clients on regulatory requirements, assisting them in the evaluation and negotiation of corporate and real estate transactions, and representing them in environmental litigation and criminal defense matters. A major focus of her practice is representing clients in state and federal Superfund matters. Heather advises clients on a range of environmental issues impacting the oil and gas, petrochemical and pipeline industries. In addition, she counsels corporations on compliance with the Sarbanes-Oxley Act and disclosure of environmental matters in public filings.
**Publications:** Contributing author and editor of the 'Texas Environmental Law Handbook', which is published by Government Institutes.
**Personal:** 1994, JD, Vanderbilt University; 1991, BA, cum laude, History and International Studies, Rhodes College.

### CORNELL, James
Cornell & Pardue LLP, Houston
713 526 0500
*Recommended in Insurance*

### CORTELL, Nina
Haynes and Boone LLP, Dallas
214 651 5000
*Recommended in Litigation*

### COTROPIA, Charles S
Sidley Austin LLP, Dallas
214 981 3305
ccotropia@sidley.com
*Recommended in Intellectual Property*
**Practice Areas:** Handles cases involving trademarks, service marks, copyrights and patents and has represented clients in diverse areas, including wearing apparel, consumer products, hi-tech products and restaurants and building design. He handles infringement issues involving trademarks/service marks, copyrights, unfair competition, product trade dress and building decor. He represents Justin

Brands, Inc., handling all litigation and registration of trademarks, copyrights and patents and trade dress infringement for the company. He has 30 years' experience dealing with the US Patent and Trademark Office, and has registered more than 800 trademarks and has obtained more than 600 patents.
**Prof. Memberships:** Served as Chairman of the Intellectual Property Law Section of the State Bar of Texas, served as a Director of the Dallas Bar Association, of the Intellectual Property Law Section of the Dallas Bar Association and as an Officer of the Dallas-Fort Worth Intellectual Property Law Section. He is a Fellow of the Dallas and Texas Bar Foundations.
**Personal:** Cornell Law School, JD, 1973; University of Texas – Austin, BS in Aerospace Engineering, 1968. Admissions: Texas, 1973; US Patent and Trademark Office, 1973.

### CRAIG III, Allen
Gardere Wynne Sewell LLP, Houston
713 276 5570
acraig@gardere.com
*Recommended in Tax*
**Practice Areas:** Tax, tax litigation, trusts and estates.
**Prof. Memberships:** Board Certified, Taxation Law, Texas Board of Legal Specialization; American Bar Association; Member, State Bar of Texas (Tax Section); current Council Member, Tax Section of the State Bar of Texas; Houston Bar Association; Texas Representative, Internal Revenue Service Liaison Council.
**Career:** Allen Craig is board certified as a specialist in taxation law. His practice includes merger and acquisitions, corporate reorganizations, partnership and limited liability company planning, state tax planning, and international inbound and outbound transactions. He is additionally involved in income and estate planning for individuals and closely held businesses, in audit and compliance matters before the IRS and state taxing authorities and has experience in obtaining private letter rulings from the IRS.
**Publications:** 'American Jobs Creation Act of 2004', Lone Star Network, 2005; KTRH (Radio), Business Law Brief, Succession Planning, 2004; 'A Guide to Potential Tax Shelter Transactions', State Bar of Texas, Corporate Committee, 2002; 'A Guide to Potential Tax Shelter Transactions', Houston Tax Roundtable, 2002.
**Personal:** JD, University of Texas School of Law, 1971; BS, Washington & Lee University, with special attainments, 1968.

### CROW, Carter
Fulbright & Jaworski L.L.P., Houston
713 651 5218
mcrow@fulbright.com
*Recommended in Employment*
**Practice Areas:** Labor and employment, commercial litigation, oil and gas.
**Prof. Memberships:** Mr Crow is a Mem-

ber of both the Labor and Employment, and Commercial Litigation Sections of the American Bar Association. He is a past President of the Houston Management Lawyers Forum.
**Career:** Mr Crow joined Fulbright's Houston office in 1991. As Partner, he co-chairs the firm's Unfair Competition Practice Group. He is listed in the Best Lawyers in America and Texas Lawyer Rising Stars publications.
**Personal:** BS, Oklahoma State University, accounting (1988); JD, University of Oklahoma College of Law (1991). Mr Crow is a member of the Children's Fund, a charity for children's causes.

### CUCLIS, James
Vinson & Elkins LLP, Houston
713 758 3415
jcuclis@velaw.com
*Recommended in Energy*
**Practice Areas:** Coordinator of the firm's International Practice. Practice consists of international mergers and acquisitions and project development and finance, primarily in the energy industry. Represented clients in over 50 countries throughout the Americas, Europe, Asia, the Middle East, and Africa.
**Prof. Memberships:** International Bar Association, Association of International Petroleum Negotiators.
**Career:** Frequent lecturer/author on international energy topics.
**Publications:** 'Key Legal Issues in International M&A Transactions', Texas Lawyer, April 2004; 'Capitalism Behind the Iron Curtain', Houston Business Review, Spring 1997; 'Bringing Capitalist Ways to Russia', National Law Journal, August 1996.
**Personal:** University of Texas, JD 1981. Working knowledge of Russian.

### CULOTTA, Ken
King & Spalding LLP, Houston
713 276 7374
kculotta@kslaw.com
*Recommended in Energy, Projects*
**Practice Areas:** Advises US and non-US clients in domestic and international oil, gas, LNG, power and natural resources transactions, including mergers and acquisitions, joint ventures, project development and finance, energy management services and other direct and indirect investment transactions. Experienced with industry documentation, including concession, production sharing, joint operating, power purchase, tolling, fuel supply, O&M, construction, gas and electricity transportation and distribution, marketing and other agreements. Languages: German; Spanish.
**Prof. Memberships:** Association of International Petroleum Negotiators; Houston Bar Association; State Bar of Texas.
**Personal:** BA University of Texas 1979; JD 1985; Albert Ludwigs-Universität, Freiburg, Germany (DAAD Fellow 1980-81).

**CULWELL, Todd**
Pillsbury Winthrop Shaw Pittman LLP,
Houston 713 425 7392
todd.culwell@pillsburylaw.com
*Recommended in Projects*
**Practice Areas:** Domestic and international (Latin America, Middle East and Asia) project development and project financings for power plants, LNG facilities and petrochemical facilities; corporate financing activities; and acquisition and disposition of a variety of energy-related assets.
**Prof. Memberships:** State Bar of Texas, Houston Bar Association, American Bar Association (International Law Section, Business Law Section and Oil, Gas and Mineral Law Section), Texas Association of Bank Counsel and Rocky Mountain Mineral Law Foundation.
**Career:** Admitted to practice: Texas.
**Personal:** South Texas College of Law (JD, magna cum laude, 1993, Order of Lytae); University of Texas at Austin (BA, Economics, 1990).

**CUNNINGHAM, Robert**
Cook & Roach, L.L.P., Houston
713 652 2939
*Recommended in Insurance*

**DANIEL, Josiah**
Vinson & Elkins LLP, Dallas
214 220 7718
jdaniel@velaw.com
*Recommended in Bankruptcy*
**Practice Areas:** Represents lenders, debtors, creditors committees, trustees, and unsecured creditors in Chapter 11 cases, including: plan formulation and confirmation; fraudulent transfer, preference, and other bankruptcy litigation; mass torts; resolution of secured and unsecured claims; Section 363 asset acquisitions; postpetition financing and cash collateral; leases and executory contracts; bankruptcy settlements.
**Prof. Memberships:** Business Bankruptcy Committee, American Bar Association; Bankruptcy Law Section, State Bar of Texas; Texas Association of Bank Counsel.
**Career:** Admitted to Texas Bar, 1978. Came to firm as Partner, 1999.
**Personal:** University of the South, BA, 1973; University of Texas School of Law, JD, 1978.

**DARDEN, Michael P**
Baker Botts LLP, Houston
713 229 1559
mike.darden@bakerbotts.com
*Recommended in Energy*
**Practice Areas:** Practice focuses on international and US oil and gas ventures, LNG projects, international and US infrastructure projects, multijurisdictional business transactions, and asset acquisitions and divestitures. Board certified in oil and gas law by the Texas Board of Legal Specialization.
**Prof. Memberships:** State Bar of Texas;

American Association of Professional Landmen; Association of International Petroleum Negotiators (AIPN); Houston Bar Association.
**Personal:** MBA from Rice University in 2002; JD from the University of Houston Law Center in 1986; BBA in Petroleum Land Management from The University of Texas in 1980.

**DARLING, William Duane**
Strasburger & Price LLP, Austin
512 499 3600
*Recommended in Healthcare*

**DAVIDSON, Joshua**
Baker Botts LLP, Houston
713 229 1527
joshua.davidson@bakerbotts.com
*Recommended in Corporate/M&A*
**Practice Areas:** Concentrates on a wide range of corporate and securities work; nationally recognized for expertise in master limited partnership (MLP) transactions. In the past 12 years he has participated in over 90 public offerings of MLPs, including 30 initial public offerings. Represents companies, particularly energy companies, in acquisitions, dispositions and joint ventures. Also advises special committees of boards of directors on such matters as asset dropdowns, mergers and reorganizations.
**Personal:** JD, cum laude, Harvard Law School, 1985; BA, summa cum laude, history, Yale University, 1981.

**DAVIS, Will**
Heath, Davis & McCalla, Austin
512 478 5671
*Recommended in Insurance*

**DAWSON, Alistair**
Beck, Redden & Secrest LLP, Houston
713 951 3700
*Recommended in Litigation*

**DAWSON, William B**
Vinson & Elkins LLP, Dallas
214 220 7926
bdawson@velaw.com
*Recommended in Litigation*
**Practice Areas:** Defends professionals, lawyers and auditors in malpractice actions (eg tried to take nothing jury verdict August 2004 audit malpractice case filed by public company in bankruptcy). Leads trial teams in significant patent infringement cases on both sides of the docket (eg currently lead plaintiff's counsel in patent case against Gillette involving its Mach3 razor blades). Defends securities actions. Continues to try oil and gas cases and is expert in matters involving pipeline safety. Transplants trial techniques from one area of trial practice to others.
**Prof. Memberships:** Fellow, The American College of Trial Lawyers (past Chair and Member of its Science and Technology in the Courts Committee); Fifth Circuit Bar Association; American Law Institute (consultative group on Restatement

of the Law Governing Lawyers).
**Career:** Admitted to Texas Bar in 1975.
**Personal:** Graduated from Texas Tech University, BBA, 1972 and JD with highest honors, 1975.

**DEATHERAGE, Scott**
Thompson & Knight LLP, Dallas
214 969 1206
Scott.Deatherage@tklaw.com
*Recommended in Environment*
**Practice Areas:** Mr Deatherage focuses his practice on compliance, transactions, administrative law, and judicial litigation in air emissions, wastewater discharges, hazardous waste and substances. He has worked on the development of significant environmental legislation and regulations. He advises clients in environmental financial disclosure/reporting issues generally and as they relate to the Sarbanes-Oxley Act.
**Prof. Memberships:** Member of the State Bar of Texas, and the American and Dallas Bar Associations; Vice-Chair for Newsletters of the ABA Special Committee on Environmental Disclosure.
**Publications:** Published on a variety of environmental issues.
**Personal:** Harvard Law School (JD, 1987); University of Oklahoma (BA, 1984).

**DENNY, Otway**
Fulbright & Jaworski L.L.P., Houston
713 651 5588
odenny@fulbright.com
*Recommended in Litigation, Products Liability*
**Practice Areas:** Product liability, personal injury, commercial, and professional liability litigation; mass and toxic tort litigation.
**Prof. Memberships:** Mr Denny is past President of the Houston Bar Association, and past Chair of the Board of Directors of both the State Bar of Texas, and the Houston Bar Foundation. Mr Denny is a Fellow of the American College of Trial Lawyers, an advocate of the American Board of Trial Advocates, and a Member of the International Association of Defense Counsel, the Defense Research Institute and the Texas Association of Defense Counsel. He has been selected for Texas Super Lawyers, the 'International Who's Who of Product Liability Defense Lawyers' and other leading legal publications.
**Career:** Partner in the Houston office since 1981. He has litigated numerous cases in state and federal courts, including products liability cases involving chemicals, automobiles and other vehicles and construction equipment. He has extensive experience in the defense of personal injury claims and other tort matters, and has handled matters involving plant and refinery explosions. He has also handled cases involving professional liability litigation and commercial litigation.

**Personal:** BA – Texas A&M University (1971); JD – cum laude, Baylor University (1973).

**DILG, Joseph C**
Vinson & Elkins LLP, Houston
713 758 2062
jdilg@velaw.com
*Recommended in Energy*
**Practice Areas:** Practice focuses on domestic and international business transactions, including acquisitions, divestitures, joint ventures, and financings. Well-versed in all aspects of the domestic and international energy business.
**Career:** Currently serves as Managing Partner of Vinson & Elkins. Director: The Business Committee for the Arts, Inc.; and the Greater Houston Partnership. Trustee: The University of Texas Law School Foundation.
**Personal:** Graduated from Southern Methodist University, BA in economics in 1973, and The University of Texas School of Law, JD with high honors in 1976; Chancellors Society; Note Editor, Texas Law Review.

**DILLARD, Michael E**
Akin Gump Strauss Hauer & Feld LLP,
Houston 713 220 5821
mdillard@akingump.com
*Recommended in Corporate/M&A*
**Practice Areas:** Heads Akin Gump's Corporate Energy and Emerging Markets practice group. Focuses on mergers and acquisitions and securities matters with emphasis in the energy industry. Involved in M&A transactions valued in excess of $50 billion ($16.5 billion in the energy industry).
**Prof. Memberships:** Texas Bar Association.
**Personal:** BA (1979) and JD (1982), Southern Methodist University.

**DILLARD, Stephen**
Fulbright & Jaworski L.L.P., Houston
713 651 5507
sdillard@fulbright.com
*Recommended in Litigation*
**Practice Areas:** Mr Dillard's concentration in the litigation practice area includes environmental, mass and toxic tort, product liability, and complex civil litigation.
**Prof. Memberships:** Mr Dillard is a Fellow of the American College of Trial Lawyers, an advocate of the American Board of Trial Advocates and a Life Fellow of the Texas Bar Foundation. He has held leadership positions as a Member of the State Bar of Texas Pattern Jury Charge Committee, the Houston and American Bar Associations, and the State Bar of Texas. Mr Dillard is also a member of the Defense Research Institute, the International Association of Defense Counsel, and the Texas Association of Defense Counsel.
**Career:** Mr Dillard has been a Partner in

the Houston office of Fulbright & Jaworski L.L.P. since 1978, and he currently serves as Chair of the firm's worldwide Litigation Department. He has been selected by his peers as one of 'The Best Lawyers in America' as published in 'Who's Who in American Law'. In 2003, 2004 and 2005 he was recognized as a Texas Super Lawyer.
**Personal:** Mr Dillard received a BA in 1968 and a JD, cum laude, in 1971 from Baylor University.

### DILLON, Andrew
Dillon & Yudell LLP, Austin
512 343 6116
*Recommended in Intellectual Property*

### DINKINS, Carol
Vinson & Elkins LLP, Houston
713 758 2528
cdinkins@velaw.com
*Recommended in Environment*
**Practice Areas:** Chairs Vinson & Elkins' Administrative and Environmental Law Practice. Practice includes client counseling on business transactions and regulatory matters; civil litigation, mediation, and criminal defense.
**Prof. Memberships:** Board of Governors, American Bar Association.
**Career:** Admitted to practice: Texas, 1971. Joined Vinson & Elkins, 1973; admitted to partnership, 1980. Served as: Assistant Attorney General in charge of the Environment and Natural Resources Division of the Department of Justice, 1981-83; Deputy Attorney General of the United States, 1984-85.
**Personal:** The University of Texas, BS, 1968; University of Houston, JD, 1971.

### DODD, Jeff
Andrews Kurth LLP, Houston
713 225 7000
*Recommended in Technology*

### DOW, Melvin
Winstead Sechrest & Minick P.C., Houston 713 650 8400
*Recommended in Real Estate*

### DOW, T Andrew
Winstead Sechrest & Minick P.C., Dallas
214 745 5400
*Recommended in Real Estate*

### DUBOSE, Kevin
Alexander Dubose Jones & Townsend, Austin 512 482 9300
*Recommended in Litigation*

### DUNLAY, Jon
Baker Botts LLP, Dallas
214 953 6711
jon.dunlay@bakerbotts.com
*Recommended in Real Estate*
**Practice Areas:** Practice focuses on commercial real estate transactions, with significant involvement in the acquisition, financing, including debt and equity, leasing and disposition of shopping centers, hotels, office buildings, apartments and land in Texas and other parts

of the country.
**Prof. Memberships:** State Bar of Texas.
**Personal:** JD, with honors, from the University of Maryland School of Law, 1982; AB, cum laude, from Princeton University, 1979.

### DUNLOP, Fred
Baker Botts LLP, Houston
713 229 1273
fred.dunlop@bakerbotts.com
*Recommended in Real Estate*
**Practice Areas:** Represents clients in complex commercial real estate transactions for major developers, institutional lenders and investors. Works with insurance companies and other institutional investors to structure their investments, including long-term mortgage loans for apartment, office, hotel, and shopping center projects; and represents clients in workouts, foreclosures, and a variety of restructurings.
**Prof. Memberships:** American College of Real Estate Lawyers; State Bar of Texas.
**Personal:** JD from Vanderbilt University School of Law, 1971; BA from Vanderbilt University, 1968.

### DUNN, Dennis C
Vinson & Elkins LLP, Houston
713 758 3478
ddunn@velaw.com
*Recommended in Healthcare*
**Practice Areas:** Dennis's principal areas of practice are transactional, financing, and business matters within the healthcare industry.
**Prof. Memberships:** American Health Lawyers Association; Health Law and Business Law Sections, State Bar of Texas.
**Career:** Admitted to practice: Texas, 1982, Wood, Lucksinger & Epstein, 1982-85, 1987-91, Associate General Counsel for a publicly traded healthcare management corporation, 1985-87; Vinson & Elkins, 1992-present.
**Personal:** Dickinson College, BA in economics and political science magna cum laude, 1979; University of Houston Law Center, JD magna cum laude, 1982.

### DUTTON, Diana C
Akin Gump Strauss Hauer & Feld LLP, Dallas 214 969 2855
ddutton@akingump.com
*Recommended in Environment*
**Practice Areas:** Focuses on all areas of environmental law, including Comprehensive Environmental Response, Compensation and Liability Act (Superfund); Resource Conservation and Recovery Act; Clean Water Act; Clean Air Act; other state/federal environmental statutes and related legislation, eg Deep Water Port Act.
**Prof. Memberships:** Former Chair, Environmental Section, State Bar of Texas, Dallas Bar Environmental Section, Greater Dallas Chamber's Environmental Committee; Board of Directors, Girls Inc. Dallas; Mental Health Association of Dal-

las; University of Texas Law School Dean's Roundtable.
**Career:** Regional Counsel and Director, Enforcement Division, US Environmental Protection Agency, Region 6 (1976-81).
**Personal:** BS, Georgetown University; JD, University of Texas.

### DYE, Phillip
Vinson & Elkins LLP, Houston
713 758 2048
pdye@velaw.com
*Recommended in Energy, Litigation*
**Practice Areas:** Complex civil litigation and arbitration practice, with a particular expertise in representing non-US based corporations who are sued in the Courts of the United States; in the handling of matters in which foreign governments or their institutions are involved; and in the law of personal jurisdiction.
**Prof. Memberships:** ABA, International Bar Association, International Association of Defense Counsel, Maritime Law Association. Licensed: Texas and Louisiana.
**Career:** Partner since 1993.
**Publications:** Has lectured extensively on the law of personal jurisdiction and transnational litigation.
**Personal:** Louisiana State University (BS, 1982; JD with honors, 1986).

### DYKES, Jeff
Fulbright & Jaworski L.L.P., Houston
713 651 5545
jdykes@fulbright.com
*Recommended in Energy*
**Practice Areas:** Energy, environmental, tort, construction, and contracts.
**Prof. Memberships:** Mr Dykes has been certified since 1979 as a specialist in Civil Trial Law by the Texas Board of Legal Specialization. He holds the rank of advocate in the American Board of Trial Advocates, and is a Director and past President of The Texas Association of Civil Trial and Appellate Specialists. He is Secretary of the Federal Bar Association (South Texas Chapter) and a Member of the Houston and American Bar Associations; Bar Association of the Fifth Federal Circuit; Independent Petroleum Association of America; Rocky Mountain Mineral Law Foundation. He is a Life Fellow of the Houston, Texas, and American Bar Foundations.
**Career:** Jeff Dykes is a Senior Litigation Partner in Fulbright & Jaworski L.L.P.'s Houston office where he is Co-Chair of the firm's Energy Practice Group. His practice as a trial lawyer covers a wide range of cases, including energy, tort, contract, construction and antitrust matters. He has tried over 60 cases to jury verdict and has been named as a 'Texas Super Lawyer' by Texas Monthly magazine.
**Personal:** BA – Stanford University (1966); MA – Stanford University (1968); JD – University of Texas School of Law (1972).

### EILAND, Gary
Vinson & Elkins LLP, Houston
713 758 3474
geiland@velaw.com
*Recommended in Healthcare*
**Practice Areas:** Co-Section Head of Health Industry Group. Represents healthcare providers, academic medical centers, and pharmaceutical and medical device manufacturers in handling fraud and abuse, Stark, and False Claims Act matters; compliance matters; business transactions; Medicare and Medicaid and other federal and state regulatory issues.
**Prof. Memberships:** State Bar of Texas (Former Chair, Health Law Section); Charter Member, Health Law Exam Commission, Texas Board of Legal Specialization; AHLA (former President), Recipient of AHLA's David J Greenburg Award.
**Career:** Admitted to practice: Texas, 1976.
**Personal:** The University of Texas, BBA with honors, 1973, JD with honors, 1976.

### ELDRIDGE, John
Haynes and Boone LLP, Houston
713 547 2000
*Recommended in Environment*

### ELTING, Kimberley A
Jones Day, Dallas
214 969 2925
kelting@jonesday.com
*Recommended in Healthcare*
**Practice Areas:** Health law and general corporate law, counseling clients in the healthcare industry. Represents public and private investor-owned, governmental, and tax-exempt entities in acquisitions, dispositions, joint ventures, restructurings, and private placements. Counsels clients on Medicare fraud and abuse, Stark law, HIPAA, and other federal and state health law compliance issues.
**Prof. Memberships:** State Bars of Texas, Colorado and Illinois; American Health Lawyers Association; Dallas Bar Association (Vice-Chair Health Law Section).
**Career:** Partner since 2002, leads Jones Day's Healthcare Transactions Team.
**Publications:** Lecturer and author of numerous articles and commentary on health law matters.

### EPSTEIN, Jon David
Vinson & Elkins LLP, Houston
713 758 3468
jepstein@velaw.com
*Recommended in Healthcare*
**Practice Areas:** Co-Chair Health Industry Group. Represented healthcare providers throughout the country for over 30 years, including representation before administrative boards and federal courts; consulting and negotiating third-party payor contract disputes; illegal remuneration, Stark, and federal FCA matters; and structuring and contracting for integrated delivery systems.
**Prof. Memberships:** AAHA (Fellow and

past President); Health Law and Policy Institute, University of Houston Law Center (Board Member).
**Career:** Admitted to practice: Illinois, 1970; Texas, 1974; DC, 1978.
**Publications:** Numerous articles on subjects ranging from fraud and abuse to capital financing.
**Personal:** University of Illinois, BS, 1965; JD, 1967.

## ERWIN, Greg
Winstead Sechrest & Minick P.C., Houston 713 650 8400
*Recommended in Real Estate*

## EVANS, Mark C
Bracewell & Giuliani LLP, Houston
713 221 1300
mark.evans@bracewellgiuliani.com
*Recommended in Banking & Finance, Projects*
**Practice Areas:** Represents domestic and international lenders in complex financing transactions, such as syndicated loans, revolving credit and term 'B' loans, leveraged transactions, structured transactions, subordinated and mezzanine investments and project finance. Heads Bracewell's finance team, which has been ranked among the nation's leaders for handling syndicated loans.
**Career:** Has practiced finance law for over 28 years and represented numerous agents in large syndicated bank credit facilities. Clients include Societe Generale, Calyon, BNP Paribas, ABN AMRO and JPMorgan Chase Bank.
**Personal:** JD, The University of Texas School of Law, 1977; BBA, The University of Texas at Austin, 1974.

## FAULK, Richard
Gardere Wynne Sewell LLP, Houston
713 276 5651
rfaulk@gardere.com
*Recommended in Environment*
**Practice Areas:** Environmental, personal injury defense, class action defense, products liability, appellate.
**Prof. Memberships:** Board Certified, Civil Appellate Law, Texas Board of Legal Specialization; American Bar Association; State Bar of Texas; Houston Bar Association; Texas Association of Civil Trial and Appellate Specialists.
**Career:** Richard Faulk has served as lead counsel for toxic tort and environmental litigation in Texas and other jurisdictions, including class actions and other 'mass tort' cases, in almost 30 years of practice. He has significant expertise in cases with international implications and comparative mass tort procedures. Mr Faulk is experienced in environmental litigation, including groundwater contamination cases, cost recovery and contribution actions under CERCLA and state environmental laws, and 'neighborhood' exposure cases alleging residential toxic exposures and property value diminution from alleged pollution released by manu-

facturing facilities.
**Publications:** 'Dispelling the Myths of Asbestos Litigation: Solutions for Common Law Courts', South Texas Law Review, October 2003; 'Armageddon Through Aggregation: The Use and Abuse of Class and Group Actions in International Dispute Resolution', 10 MSU-DCL International Law Journal 205, 2002.
**Personal:** JD, Southern Methodist University Dedman School of Law, 1977; leading articles editor, Journal of Air Law and Commerce, Symposium Scholar. BA, University of North Texas, 1974.

## FELDMAN, Robert C
Weil, Gotshal & Manges LLP, Dallas
214 746 7744
robert.feldman@weil.com
*Recommended in Real Estate*
**Practice Areas:** Robert C Feldman's practice focuses on secured finance, real estate finance transactions and execution of business transactions involving partnerships, limited liability companies and private equity funds. Mr Feldman also has extensive experience in out-of-court and court-supervised restructurings, representing lenders and debtors in a variety of industries, including retail, real estate, mining and energy. Mr Feldman's representative clients include Citibank, GE Capital, Lehman Bros., Commercial Metals Company, Hicks Muse Tate & Furst, Olympus Real Estate Fund, Olympia & York, Martin Marietta Materials, and Starwood Hotels.
**Personal:** Duke University, BA, 1970; University of Texas School of Law, JD, 1973.

## FELDT, Harrell
Vinson & Elkins LLP, Houston
713 756 3868
hfeldt@velaw.com
*Recommended in Energy*
**Practice Areas:** Harrell has tried cases in New Mexico, Oklahoma, Louisiana, and more than 50 Texas counties (with jury trials in more than 25 of these counties). He has appeared before ad valorem taxing authorities, conducted Texas Water Commission hearings, and handled zoning matters before municipal authorities.
**Prof. Memberships:** American College of Trial Lawyers; American Law Institute; International Association of Insurance Counsel; Texas Association of Defense Counsel; American Board of Trial Advocacy (ABOTA); Fellow, American Bar Foundation; International Association of Defense Counsel.
**Career:** Partner since 1986.
**Personal:** University of Texas (BBA 1961); University of Texas School of Law (JD 1963).

## FELGER, Thomas
Baker Botts LLP, Austin
*Recommended in Intellectual Property*
**Practice Areas:** Partner Austin Intellectual Property. 25+ years' experience managing IP and related disputes. Current work – technology licensing and manufacturing joint ventures in China. Clients – medical device/biotechnology, oil/gas service industry, computer manufacturing, telecommunications. Arbitrator – IP disputes. Lead counsel for strategic alliances, joint technology development agreements
**Prof. Memberships:** Texas Business Law Section, Council Member; Texas Intellectual Property Section, Chair IP Opinion Committee; American Arbitration Association, Commercial Arbitration Panel; Registered Texas Professional Engineer.
**Career:** US Navy – Nuclear Submarine Officer; University of Texas Law School; Otis Engineering Corporation Assistant General Counsel and Manager IP Group; Baker Botts.

## FENNELL, Thomas E
Jones Day, Dallas 214 969 5130
tefennell@jonesday.com
*Recommended in Environment*
**Practice Areas:** Manages the product liability/toxic tort group in the Dallas office. He has extensive experience serving as national/regional counsel in complex product liability/toxic tort matters, including in connection with the new wave of public entity cost recovery litigation. He has argued appeals in state intermediate appellate and supreme courts and in various US federal courts of appeal. His participation in the highly publicized NAACP gun trial in New York was recognized as one of the 10 Top Defense Verdicts in 2003. In the prestigious AmLaw competition, Jones Day's Products Group won best group in 2003 and finalist in 2005.

## FIELDS, Jack
Andrews Kurth LLP, Houston
713 225 7000
*Recommended in Real Estate*

## FIJOLEK, Richard
Haynes and Boone LLP, Dallas
214 651 5000
*Recommended in Tax*

## FINK, Stephen F
Thompson & Knight LLP, Dallas
214 969 1120
Stephen.Fink@tklaw.com
*Recommended in Employment*
**Practice Areas:** Mr Fink represents management in all aspects of labor and employment law, including jury and non-jury trials, appeals, mediations and arbitrations, administrative proceedings, advice and counseling, training, drafting, and investigations.
**Prof. Memberships:** Certified in Labor and Employment Law by the Texas Board

of Legal Specialization; Member, the American Law Institute; Member, the American Society of Writers on Legal Topics.
**Personal:** University of Texas School of Law (JD, 1974, with honors); Pennsylvania State University (BA, 1971, with high distinction); Phi Beta Kappa.

## FINN BRADDOCK, Patricia
Fulbright & Jaworski L.L.P., Austin
512 536 4547
pbraddock@fulbright.com
*Recommended in Environment*
**Practice Areas:** Toxic tort; environmental law.
**Prof. Memberships:** Member of the American Bar Association; the Texas Bar Association; Travis County Bar Association; Air and Waste Management Association; Texas Water Pollution Control Association; Board of Directors for Voluntary Legal Services in Central Texas and Fellow of the State Bar of Texas.
**Career:** Admitted to Texas Bar (1974). A Partner in Fulbright's Austin office since 1992. Prior to joining the firm, she worked for Texas' environmental regulatory agencies for almost 15 years.
**Personal:** Received a BA (1971) from the American University in Washington, DC and a JD (1974) from St. Mary's University College of Law in San Antonio, Texas. Certified in Administrative Law by the Texas Board of Legal Specialization.

## FINNEGAN IV, William N
Vinson & Elkins LLP, Houston
713 758 3704
bfinnegan@velaw.com
*Recommended in Corporate/M&A*
**Practice Areas:** Practice is focused on various corporate and securities transactions on both a national and international basis, including: representing issuers and underwriters in public and private offerings of equity and debt securities, including MLPs; negotiating and structuring asset and stock acquisitions; the formation and financing of joint venture and partnership transactions; and advising on general corporate and securities matters.
**Prof. Memberships:** American Bar Association; Houston Bar Association; Houston Bar Foundation.
**Career:** Admitted to Texas Bar in 1981. Joined the firm in 2000 as a Partner.
**Personal:** The University of Texas, BBA, 1978; University of Houston, JD, 1981.

## FISHER, Todd A.
Hughes & Luce LLP, Dallas
214 939 5500
*Recommended in Technology*

## FISK, Hollye
Fisk & Fielder, Dallas
214 638 3744
*Recommended in Construction*

**FLAKE, Richard**
Cokinos, Bosien and Young, Houston
713 535 5500
*Recommended in Construction*

**FLETCHER, N Scott**
Vinson & Elkins LLP, Houston
713 758 3234
sfletcher@velaw.com
*Recommended in Litigation*
**Practice Areas:** Co-Chair of Securities
Litigation and Enforcement Group and
focuses practice on securities, commer-
cial, and intellectual property litigation.
**Prof. Memberships:** Texas Bar Associa-
tion; Houston Bar Association; Texas Bar
Foundation; Houston Bar Foundation;
Director: Houston Volunteer Lawyers
Program Board.
**Career:** Law clerk to the Honorable Jus-
tice Andrew G T Moore II, Delaware
Supreme Court, 1989-90. Admitted to
practice: Pennsylvania, 1990; Delaware,
1991; District of Columbia, 1991; Texas,
1994; United States Supreme Court;
United States Court of Appeals for the
Fifth Circuit and District of Columbia
Circuit; various federal district courts.
**Personal:** Harvard College, AB with
honors, 1984; Tulane Law School, JD
with honors, 1989 (Order of the Coif;
notes and comments editor, Tulane Law
Review).

**FLORES, Jean**
Guida, Slavich & Flores, P.C., Dallas
214 692 0009
*Recommended in Environment*

**FLOYD, Adam**
Vinson & Elkins LLP, Austin
*Recommended in Intellectual Property*
**Practice Areas:** Intellectual property.
Specifically patent litigation.
**Prof. Memberships:** Federal Circuit Bar
Association, AIPLA, ABA, ATLA.
**Career:** Partner since 2003.
**Publications:** Legal Research Guide to
Mechanical Patent litigation, Hein Pub-
lishing Company (1994).
**Personal:** Texas A&M University, BS in
Aerospace Engineering summa cum
laude, 1991 (Engineering Scholars Pro-
gram; All-American Scholar; National
Dean's List; Sigma Gamma Tau Honor
Society); Tau Beta Pi Honor Society; Har-
vard Law School, JD cum laude, 1994
(Journal of Law and Technology); Recipi-
ent: National Science Foundation Fellow-
ship; Garland Coker Endowed Scholar-
ship; JG McGuire Engineering Scholarship; Admitted to practice: Texas, 1994;
United States Patent and Trademark
Office.

**FOGLER, Murray**
McDade Fogler LLP, Houston
713 654 4300
*Recommended in Energy, Litigation*

**FONTANA, Angela**
Weil, Gotshal & Manges LLP, Dallas
214 746 7895
angela.fontana@weil.com
*Recommended in Banking & Finance*
**Practice Areas:** Angela Fontana's practice consists of a broad spectrum of
financing transactions and debt restructurings including cash-flow and asset-
based lending, leveraged acquisitions,
recapitalizations, bridge and mezzanine
financing, and workouts and restructurings, both domestic and cross-border. She
represents private equity funds including
Berkshire Partners, DLJ Merchant Banking, Diamond Castle, Ewing Management, Hicks, Muse, Tate & Furst, Providence Equity Partners, Summit Partners
and Thomas H. Lee Partners, and lead
arrangers, including GE Capital.
**Personal:** University of Iowa, BBA, 1987;
University of Iowa College of Law, JD,
1989.

**FORD, Jeffrey**
Ford Nassen & Baldwin, Dallas
214 523 5100
*Recommended in Construction*

**FORD JR, Thomas**
Andrews Kurth LLP, Houston
713 220 4200
*Recommended in Tax*

**FOSTER, Charles**
Tindall & Foster PC, Houston
713 229 8733
*Recommended in Immigration*

**FOUST, Lawrence**
Jenkens & Gilchrist, Houston
713 951 3300
*Recommended in Healthcare*

**FOX, J Nixon**
Vinson & Elkins LLP, Austin
*Recommended in Technology*
**Practice Areas:** Corporate and securi-
ties law, including public offerings, private placements, mergers and acquisitions, joint ventures and strategic
alliances, licensing and other technology-
related business transactions and international business transactions.
**Prof. Memberships:** Texas Bar Association; the Bar Association of the District of
Columbia.
**Career:** Partner since joining the firm in
2001. Co-Chairs the firm's Technology
Practice Group. Has practiced in Austin,
Washington, DC and Hong Kong.
**Personal:** Southern Methodist University, BA magna cum laude, 1981; The University of Texas School of Law, JD with
honors, 1984; New York University
School of Law, LLM (in taxation), 1985.

**FOX, Michael W**
Ogletree, Deakins, Nash, Smoak &
Stewart, PC, Austin 512 344 4711
michael.fox@ogletreedeakins.com
*Recommended in Employment*
**Practice Areas:** Employment litigation.

**Prof. Memberships:** American Bar
Association, Society for Human Resource
Management, Management Labor and
Employment Roundtable.
**Career:** Fellow, College of Labor and
Employment Lawyers. Listed in 'The Best
Lawyers in America' and named as a
Texas Monthly 'Super Lawyer' in employ-
ment litigation.
**Publications:** First employment law
weblog, Jottings By An Employer's
Lawyer. 'Piercings, Makeup and Appear-
ance: The Changing Face of Discrimina-
tion Law', Texas State Bar (2006);
'Whistleblowers and Retaliation', Univer-
sity of Texas School of Law (2005).
**Personal:** Stephen F Austin State Univer-
sity (BA, with honors, 1972), University
of Texas (JD, with high honors, 1975).

**FRANZE, Laura M**
Akin Gump Strauss Hauer & Feld LLP,
Dallas 214 969 2779
lfranze@akingump.com
*Recommended in Employment*
**Practice Areas:** Chair of Akin Gump's
Texas and California Labor Practices,
Laura Franze leads one of the region's
most respected employment practices,
representing leading employers including
Cinemark USA, Fujitsu Network,
Hotels.com, AMC Entertainment, Inc.,
Wyndham Hotels and Pier 1. Board Cer-
tified and named to numerous national
and state best lawyer lists, including 'Best
Lawyers in America' and 'Texas Super
Lawyers'. Franze has been elected to the
Texas and Dallas Bar Foundations and
serves on the firm's management com-
mittee.
**Publications:** Texas Employment Law
(1998-2005); 'Risky Business', HR Magazine (November 2005); 'The Wages of
Sex', The Metropolitan Corporate Counsel (November 2004).

**FRIEDLANDER, D Gilbert**
Weil, Gotshal & Manges LLP, Dallas
214 746 8178
gil.friedlander@weil.com
*Recommended in Corporate/M&A*
**Practice Areas:** Gilbert Friedlander's
practice focuses on corporate, securities
and general business law. Prior to joining
Weil Gotshal, Mr Friedlander was Executive Vice President, General Counsel and
Secretary at Electronic Data Systems Corporation (EDS). In these roles, he had
oversight responsibilities for all aspects of
EDS' legal activities on a global basis and
was responsible for EDS' Office of Ethics
and Business Conduct, as well as coordination of Board of Directors meetings
and activities.
**Personal:** University of Texas, BS; University of Texas School of Law, JD.

**FRIEDMAN, Edward**
Locke Liddell & Sapp LLP, Houston
713 226 1200
*Recommended in Employment*

**FRISBIE JR, Curtis L**
Gardere Wynne Sewell LLP, Dallas
214 999 4757
cfrisbie@gardere.com
*Recommended in Antitrust*
**Practice Areas:** Trial Section Chair,
antitrust and trade regulation, class
action defense, commercial and IP litiga-
tion.
**Prof. Memberships:** American Bar
Association; State Bar of Texas; past
Chair, Antitrust and Business Litigation
Section; past President, Dallas Bar Associ-
ation Section on Antitrust and Trade
Regulation Law; Selected for 'Best
Lawyers in America', 'Texas Super
Lawyers' and 'Best Lawyers in Dallas'.
**Career:** Frisbie has more than 30 years of
trial experience handling major antitrust
and other commercial litigation matters.
He has substantial experience defending
class action cases involving antitrust,
RICO, usury and other claims.
**Personal:** JD, St. Mary's University
School of Law, 1971; BS, University of
Alabama, 1966. US Marine Corps (1966-
69), Bronze Star with V and Purple Heart.
Trial attorney, US Department of Justice
Antitrust Division (Special Achievement
Award).

**FRIZZELL, Jean C**
Gibbs & Bruns, LLP, Houston
713 650 8805
jfrizzell@gibbs-bruns.com
*Recommended in Litigation*
**Practice Areas:** Practice is complex
commercial and business litigation for
both plaintiffs and defendants, including
breach of contract, securities, environmental, trade secret, trademark, copyright, oil and gas, director liability, and
partnership disputes in both state and
federal courts.
**Prof. Memberships:** Admitted to practice in the State of Texas in 1990 and
admitted before the United States District
Courts for the Eastern, Northern, and
Southern Districts of Texas, District of
Colorado, and Federal District, and United States Court of Appeals for the Fifth
Circuit. A Member of the State Bar of
Texas, American Bar Association, Texas
Bar Foundation (Fellow), Houston Bar
Association, Houston Bar Foundation
(Fellow).
**Career:** Joined Gibbs & Bruns, LLP in
1990.
**Personal:** Born in New Jersey, October 6,
1965; Rice University (BA, 1987); Univer-
sity of Texas (JD, honors, 1990); Member,
Texas Law Review.

**FROMM O'BRIEN, Eva**
Fulbright & Jaworski L.L.P., Houston
713 651 5321
eobrien@fulbright.com
*Recommended in Environment*
**Practice Areas:** Environmental law,
crimes and litigation; enforcement controversies, mergers and acquisitions, per-

mits, and property damage litigation.
**Prof. Memberships:** Included in a leading legal publication. Past secretary, Vice-Chair and Chair of the Houston Bar Association's Environmental Law Section. Former Chair of the American Bar Association's Real Estate and Probate Section's RCRA and Underground Storage Tank Committee.
**Career:** Admitted to Texas Bar (1985). Partner at Fulbright & Jaworski L.L.P. joining the firm in 1986. Heads the Environmental Law Department.
**Personal:** Received a BS in Chemical Engineering in 1978 from Syracuse University and a JD in 1985 from the University of Houston.

### FROST, Claudia Wilson
Mayer, Brown, Rowe & Maw LLP,
Houston 713 547 9636
cfrost@mayerbrownrowe.com
*Recommended in Litigation*
**Practice Areas:** Specializes in appellate litigation and civil trial law. Briefed and argued cases in the Texas Supreme Court and intermediate Texas appellate courts. Significant appearances before United States Courts of Appeals including in the Fifth, Federal and DC Circuits. Merits and amicus briefs in the United States Supreme Court. Handled numerous civil trials and provided appellate and error preservation assistance in complex litigation in federal and state courts in Texas, Delaware, California, Colorado, Louisiana and Alabama, among others. Board Certified by the Texas Board of Legal Specialization in both Civil Appellate and Civil Trial law. Areas of expertise include general commercial litigation, oil and gas, products liability and torts, intellectual property, ERISA, securities law and class actions.
**Prof. Memberships:** Admitted: Texas, 1982; US Court of Appeals, Fifth and Federal Circuits; Texas and US District Court, Southern, Northern and Eastern Districts; US Supreme Court.
**Career:** Joined Mayer, Brown, Rowe & Maw LLP as Partner, 2003. Slusser & Frost, LLP, 1999-July 2003. BakerBotts, LLP, 1982-98.
**Personal:** JD, magna cum laude, University of Houston Law Center, 1982; Editor-in-Chief, Houston Law Review; Order of the Barons and The Advocates; Teaching Assistant. MA, University of Houston, 1979. BA, University of Texas at Austin, 1975.

### FUNK, John A
Jones Day, Dallas
214 969 2981
jafunk@jonesday.com
*Recommended in Business Process Outsourcing, Technology*
**Practice Areas:** Oversees Jones Day's Global Outsourcing Practice. Focuses on representing customers in complex outsourcing transactions. He has over 25

years' experience representing clients in information technology outsourcing transactions, including the first European outsourcing transaction over $1 billion. Since its inception in the mid-90s, he has worked on business process outsourcing transactions, including customer care, finance and accounting, human resource administration, logistics, procurement and other back- and mid-office functions. Many of his transactions present multi-country scope, including a recent engagement with a geographic scope of 80 countries, and include offshore delivery solutions.
**Publications:** Frequent lecturer and author on outsourcing topics.

### GALVAN, Hilda
Jones Day, Dallas
214 969 4556
hcgalvan@jonesday.com
*Recommended in Intellectual Property*
**Practice Areas:** Practices in the area of patent, trademark, copyright, trade secret, and unfair competition. Has substantial litigation experience, particularly in patent litigation matters in federal and appellate courts, including the International Trade Commission. She has a growing practice in trademark litigation, with an emphasis on domestic and foreign protection. She also has an active Transactional and Counseling Practice and advises clients in intellectual property matters, particularly in the computer software and telecommunication fields. She has been a speaker at a number of seminars on topics relating to protection of software and the use of experts in patent litigation.

### GARCIA, Rodrigo
Thompson, Coe, Cousins & Irons, LLP,
Dallas 214 871 8200
*Recommended in Insurance*

### GAVIN, Tim
Carrington, Coleman, Sloman & Blumenthal, LLP, Dallas
214 855 3000
*Recommended in Litigation*

### GEIGER, Richard S
Thompson, Coe, Cousins & Irons, LLP,
Dallas 214 871 8200
*Recommended in Insurance*

### GERACHIS, George Matthew
Vinson & Elkins LLP, Houston
713 758 1056
ggerachis@velaw.com
*Recommended in Tax*
**Practice Areas:** Co-Chair of the firm's Taxation Practice and leader of the firm's Tax Controversy and Litigation Group. Member of firm's Management Committee. Practice consists primarily of business tax planning and resolution of complex tax disputes for individuals and businesses. Also counsels multinational companies on 'inbound' and 'outbound' tax issues, including transfer pricing.

**Prof. Memberships:** American Bar Association, Section of Taxation; International Fiscal Association.
**Career:** Admitted to practice US Tax Court, US District Court for the Southern District of Texas; frequent lecturer.
**Personal:** Graduated from University of Virginia, BA 1979, JD 1983. Languages: German and Spanish.

### GERACI, Joseph V
Brown McCarroll  LLP, Austin
512 472 5456
*Recommended in Healthcare*

### GERBER, Toby L
Fulbright & Jaworski L.L.P., Dallas
214 855 7171
tgerber@fulbright.com
*Recommended in Bankruptcy*
**Practice Areas:** Bankruptcy and transportation.
**Prof. Memberships:** Mr Gerber is a Member of the Dallas and American Bar Associations, the State Bar of Texas, the Texas Association of Bank Counsel, and the American Bankruptcy Institute.
**Career:** Mr Gerber regularly represents financial institutions in troubled loans and insolvencies across all industries throughout the US. He also represents the International Air Transport Association and its air carrier members in insolvency matters throughout the world. Gerber has been named one of the 'Best Lawyers in Dallas' by D Magazine and was named a 'Texas Super Lawyer' and one of the 'Top 100 Dallas/Fort Worth Region Super Lawyers' by Texas Monthly and Law and Politics Magazine.
**Personal:** Mr Gerber received his AB, and BJ, with honors, from the University of Missouri-Columbia in 1972, and in 1975 he earned his JD from Georgetown University Law Center.

### GIBBS, Charles R
Akin Gump Strauss Hauer & Feld LLP,
Dallas 214 969 4710
cgibbs@akingump.com
*Recommended in Bankruptcy*
**Practice Areas:** Represents secured and unsecured creditors in complex restructurings, frequently advising unsecured creditor committees, banks and nonbank lenders, and special servicers of commercial mortgage securitized trusts. Experienced particularly in real estate, oil and gas, textiles, retail and restaurant industries. Has represented several private investment funds that provide rescue equity and reorganization services to troubled real estate syndications and ventures, and has acted as lead debtor's counsel in several significant Chapter 11 proceedings.
**Prof. Memberships:** American Bankruptcy Institute (Business Reorganization Committee, Chapter 11 and Secured Creditor Subcommittees); Texas Bar Foundation.
**Personal:** BA, Duke University; MBA and JD, Southern Methodist University.

### GIBBS, Robin C
Gibbs & Bruns, LLP, Houston
713 751 5217
rgibbs@gibbs-bruns.com
*Recommended in Energy, Litigation*
**Practice Areas:** Mr Gibbs' practice includes the representation of plaintiffs and defendants in significant contract, securities, trade secret, intellectual property, patent, insurance, antitrust, lender liability, oil and gas, director liability, copyright, and partnership disputes in Texas, throughout the United States, and in various courts and tribunals outside the United States.
**Prof. Memberships:** Fellow, American College of Trial Lawyers. Advocate, American Board of Trial Advocates. Fellow, International Academy of Trial Lawyers. Member, The American Law Institute. Member, Texas Bar Association. Fellow, Texas Bar Foundation. Member, American Bar Association. Fellow, American Bar Foundation. Member, Harris County Bar Association.
**Career:** Upon graduation from law school in 1971, Mr Gibbs joined Vinson & Elkins as an associate in its Insurance Defense Group. In 1974, he left to form a full-service law firm, Wood, Campbell, Moody & Gibbs, P.C., in which Mr Gibbs undertook to develop a general litigation practice and career. In 1983, Mr Gibbs and the litigation attorneys formed Gibbs & Bruns, L.L.P. (formerly known as Gibbs & Ratliff, L.L.P.), a firm which limits its practice to all forms of commercial litigation. Mr Gibbs was ranked among the top 15 commercial trial lawyers in the United States in a survey conducted by 'International Commercial Litigation' magazine. In September 1999, the National Law Journal ranked Mr Gibbs as one of the top trial lawyers in Texas. Mr Gibbs was recently selected by the Texas Lawyer as the 'go to' lawyer in securities litigation in Texas and was also listed among America's leading business lawyers in 'Chambers USA, America's Leading Business Lawyers'. Mr Gibbs was recognized as one of the 'Top 100 Texas Super Lawyers' in 2003 and 2004.

### GIBLIN, Pamela
Baker Botts LLP, Austin
512 322 2509
pam.giblin@bakerbotts.com
*Recommended in Environment*
**Practice Areas:** Environmental; permitting, acquisitions, enforcement under state and federal laws.
**Prof. Memberships:** Board Certified Administrative Law; Texas Bar; First woman recipient Travis County Bar Association's Distinguished Lawyer Award.
**Career:** General Counsel Texas Air Control Board; former Chair Austin Commission on Electric Rates, currently Chair Baker Botts, Environmental Department
**Personal:** University of Texas, BA, with

honors, JD, 1970; fluent in Spanish; frequent seminar and conference speaker Best Lawyers in America; Chambers' USA; 'Texas Super Lawyer'; 'Top 50 Regional/West Texas Region'; 'Top 50 Female Lawyers', Texas Monthly and Law and Politics; Environmental Protection Agency's Federal Clean Air Act Advisory Committee member.

### GILLESPIE, Thomas
Jones Day, Dallas
214 969 5076
tgillespie@jonesday.com
*Recommended in Banking & Finance*
**Practice Areas:** Oversees Jones Day's Lending/Structured Finance and Derivatives Practice in the Dallas Office. Specializes in the representation of financial institutions and corporations in complex domestic and international financial transactions. He also has considerable experience working in specific industry areas, including healthcare, energy, private equity, and transportation (aircraft, railcars, and vessels).
**Publications:** Co-editor and contributing author of 'The Commercial Finance Guide'. Contributing author of 'NAFTA and Beyond – A New Framework for Doing Business in the Americas'. A frequent speaker on banking and finance topics, he has prepared programs on loan and collateral documentation and leasing and leveraged leasing.

### GITOMER, Deborah
Fulbright & Jaworski L.L.P., Houston
713 651 3636
dgitomer@fulbright.com
*Recommended in Energy*
**Practice Areas:** Oil, gas and energy transactions.
**Prof. Memberships:** Ms Gitomer is a Member of the Houston Bar Association and the State Bar of Texas.
**Career:** Deborah Gitomer joined Fulbright & Jaworski L.L.P.'s Houston office in 1982, and has been a Partner since 1991. Her practice is concentrated in transactions related to the acquisition, and disposition of oil and gas reserves, pipelines, gas processing plants, refineries, petrochemical facilities and storage facilities, whether structured as asset or entity acquisitions as well as joint ventures, partnerships and other joint ownership or participation arrangements in the oil, gas and energy areas.
**Personal:** BA, Trinity University (1979); JD, St. Mary's University (1982). She was admitted to practice in Texas in 1982.

### GLASER, Kenneth
Gardere Wynne Sewell LLP, Dallas
214 999 4352
kglaser@gardere.com
*Recommended in Intellectual Property*
**Practice Areas:** Intellectual property, intellectual property litigation.
**Prof. Memberships:** State Bar of Texas; President, Dallas-Fort Worth Patent Law Association; Dallas Bar Association; AIPLA; IHTA; and ABA.
**Career:** Glaser has represented clients worldwide in patent, trademark, copyright and other intellectual property matters for more than 30 years. He has held a variety of positions, including Division Patent Counsel for Texas Instruments, Partner and Founding Partner of Dallas, Texas-based intellectual property firms, and Chair of the Intellectual Property Practices of Akin Gump Strauss Hauer & Feld and Gardere Wynne Sewell. Mr Glaser has taught intellectual property law at The University of Texas and Southern Methodist University.
**Personal:** JD, University of Texas School of Law, 1964, with honors; BSEE, University of Texas at Austin, 1962.

### GLASSER, Mark K
King & Spalding LLP, Houston
713 751 3212
mkglasser@kslaw.com
*Recommended in Litigation*
**Practice Areas:** Litigation focusing on complex commercial litigation, energy litigation and arbitration.
**Prof. Memberships:** State Bar of Texas and a Fellow of the Texas Bar Foundation.
**Personal:** BA, with honors, Columbia University, 1973; JD, University of Texas, 1976.

### GODFREY, Lee
Susman Godfrey LLP, Houston
713 651 9366
*Recommended in Antitrust, Energy, Litigation*

### GOLDEN, H Bruce
Golden & Owens LLP, Houston
713 223 2600
golden@goldenowens.com
*Recommended in Litigation*
**Practice Areas:** Mr Golden represents a diverse array of plaintiffs and defendants in significant disputes relating to contracts, warranties, securities, commercial real estate, oil and gas, premises liability, trade secrets, intellectual property, antitrust, partnerships, business torts, employment and other matters.
**Prof. Memberships:** Admitted to practice before Texas Supreme Court, United States Supreme Court, United States Courts of Appeals for the Fifth, Tenth, and Eleventh Circuits and federal district courts in Texas; State Bar of Texas; American and Houston Bar Associations.
**Career:** In addition to being listed in 'Chambers USA, America's Leading Business Lawyers', Mr Golden was named a Texas Super Lawyer by Texas Monthly Magazine in 2005 and was recognized as one of Houston's Top Lawyers by H Texas Magazine in 2005.
**Personal:** JD, Emory University School of Law, 1974; BA, Indiana University, 1971.

### GOLEMON, Kinnan
Brown McCarroll LLP, Austin
512 472 5456
*Recommended in Environment*

### GONSOULIN JR, Dewey J
Bracewell & Giuliani LLP, Houston
713 221 1110
dewey.gonsoulin@bracewellgiuliani.com
*Recommended in Banking & Finance*
**Practice Areas:** Focuses on representation of domestic and foreign lending institutions in all types of financing transactions ranging from basic forms of lending such as corporate and other working capital loans, to complex financing structures including acquisition loans, energy securitizations and project finance. Extensive knowledge in energy lending with emphasis on upstream oil and gas loans, midstream pipeline loans, and loans to energy service companies. Serves as borrower's counsel for many of firm's corporate clients in various financing transactions.
**Personal:** JD, The University of Texas School of Law, 1991; BBA Finance, with honors, The University of Texas at Austin, 1988.

### GOOCH, W Kyle
Canterbury, Stuber, Elder, Gooch & Surratt, PC, Dallas 972 239 7493
kgooch@canterburylaw.com
*Recommended in Construction*
**Practice Areas:** Construction litigation and arbitration; construction insurance (builder's risk, commercial general liability, errors and omissions).
**Prof. Memberships:** Admitted to the Texas and Dallas Bar Associations; Construction Law Section of the Texas Bar (immediate past Chairman, past Council Member); American Arbitration Association (arbitrator); and Fellow, American College of Construction Lawyers.
**Career:** Following graduation from Baylor Law School, he commenced law practice in Dallas, Texas and has practiced consistently in the field of construction and insurance. He has been a member and shareholder of Canterbury, Stuber, Elder, Gooch & Surratt since 1981.
**Publications:** 'Builder's Risk: The Forgotten Insurance', 1999; 'Builder's Risk: The Devil is in the Exclusions', 2003; and other articles on construction and insurance issues.
**Personal:** Born Greenville, Texas, November 14, 1952; Bachelor of Science – Texas A & M University; JD Baylor University. Married to the former Suzy Davis, they have three children.

### GOOLSBY, George
Baker Botts LLP, Houston
713 229 1416
george.goolsby@bakerbotts.com
*Recommended in Energy, Projects*
**Practice Areas:** Practice includes oil and gas ventures and pipeline projects. Regularly consults with project sponsors and lenders on LNG, and has a wide range of regulatory, transactional, trial, and dispute resolution experience representing producers, marketers, transporters and distributors of oil, gas, and refined petroleum products.
**Prof. Memberships:** State Bar of Texas; Energy Bar Association; Institute for Energy Law, Advisory Board.
**Career:** Partner-in-Charge of the Moscow Office.
**Personal:** JD from The University of Texas School of Law, 1974; BA from The University of Texas, 1971.

### GORDON, R Kenneth
Baker & McKenzie, Dallas
214 978 3002
kenneth.gordon@bakernet.com
*Recommended in Healthcare*
**Practice Areas:** Significant experience with a wide variety of issues facing healthcare providers, pharma and device companies, and others involved in the healthcare industry. Regularly works with both the laws and practical considerations involved with strategic planning; fraud and abuse compliance and investigation response and defense; hospital operations; joint ventures; HIPAA privacy and security; pharmaceutical regulation; medical staff relations; physician, hospital and other provider integration; group medical practices; DME suppliers; group purchasing; joint ventures; mergers and acquisitions; third-party reimbursement; FHA-insured financings; and managed care organizations.
**Prof. Memberships:** Health Law Legal Specialization Exam Commission (Founding Chair 2002-present); State Bar of Texas (Health Law Section; Chair 2004-05); Health Industry Council of Dallas-Fort Worth (Board of Directors; Chair-Elect 2006-present); American College of Healthcare Executives (Member).
**Career:** Admitted in Texas and Illinois; Baker & McKenzie LLP North America Pharma and Healthcare Industry Group Chair; Baker & McKenzie Pharm & Healthcare Industry Group Steering Committee Member.
**Publications:** Presenter and author of 100+ live and audio presentations and articles on various health law and related issues, including fraud and abuse matters.
**Personal:** Married with two children.

### GOSSELINK, Paul
Lloyd Gosselink Blevins Rochelle & Townsend, P.C., Austin
512 322 5800
*Recommended in Environment*

### GOVETT, Brett C
Fulbright & Jaworski L.L.P., Dallas
214 855 8118
bgovett@fulbright.com
*Recommended in Intellectual Property*
**Practice Areas:** Commercial litigation, patent infringement litigation, personal

injury defense litigation.

**Prof. Memberships:** American Bar Association, State Bar of Texas, Dallas Bar Association, American Chemical Society.

**Career:** Brett Govett, a Partner, has been with the Dallas office of Fulbright & Jaworski LLP since 1991 and practices in the firm's Litigation Department. He is Board Certified in Civil Trial Law by the Texas Board of Legal Specialization and is a registered patent attorney. In 2003, he completed his term as a barrister in The Patrick E Higginbotham American Inn of Court. Some of his trial wins have been featured in the National Law Journal, Texas Lawyer, Dallas Business Journal, Dallas Morning News and numerous other daily and weekly publications. Mr Govett is also experienced in the defense and handling of mass toxic tort lawsuits representing multiple defendants in claims brought by multiple plaintiffs. His representation is responsible for over $100 million in jury verdicts and client recoveries.

**Personal:** Mr Govett received a BA in Chemistry, with honors, from The Citadel in 1987. He continued his education at Texas Tech University, where he received a JD, with honors, in 1990.

### GOYNE, Roderick
Baker Botts LLP, Dallas
214 953 6527
rick.goyne@bakerbotts.com
*Recommended in Banking & Finance*

**Practice Areas:** Chair: Finance Section (firmwide). Concentrates on private placements, primarily on behalf of institutional purchasers, and has broad experience in transactions involving senior secured and unsecured debt, mezzanine investments, subordinated debt, acquisition and MLP financings, financing leases, and a variety of structured securities and debt restructurings. Additionally handles asset securitizations and other structured financings in the oil, gas, petrochemicals, computers, information technology and consumer products industries. Represents agent lenders/borrowers in acquisitions, margin credits, debt restructurings and other financings.

**Personal:** JD, cum laude, Harvard Law School, 1974; BA, with highest honors, history, The University of Texas at Arlington, 1971.

### GRAHAM, F Brian
Winstead Sechrest & Minick P.C., Austin
512 370 2800
*Recommended in Immigration*

### GRAY, Robert F
Mayer, Brown, Rowe & Maw LLP, Houston 713 546 0522
rgray@mayerbrownrowe.com
*Recommended in Corporate/M&A, Technology*

**Practice Areas:** Corporate and securities laws representation, public and private mergers and acquisitions, public

offerings (issuers and underwriters/placement agents/dealer managers), private placements and private equity financings.

**Prof. Memberships:** Admitted to California Bar (1977); Texas Bar (1978); and District of Columbia Bar (1979). Chairman, Business Law Section of the State Bar of Texas (1995-96); Texas State Liaison, ABA Committee on Corporate Laws (1990-98); and Fellow, Texas Business Law Foundation.

**Career:** Fulbright & Jaworski LLP, 1978-2005, Partner 1985; Mayer, Brown, Rowe & Maw LLP, 2005-present, Partner 2005.

**Publications:** Co-author of 'Annual Survey of Texas Law: Corporations' – Southwest Law Journal Articles, 1988, 1989, 1990, 1991, 1992 and 1993.

**Personal:** BBA (1972) and MBA (1974), University of Michigan. JD (1977), University of San Diego; LLM (1978), New York University.

### GREENDYKE, William
Fulbright & Jaworski L.L.P., Houston
713 6515193
wgreendyke@fulbright.com
*Recommended in Bankruptcy*

**Practice Areas:** Bankruptcy, reorganization and creditor's rights.

**Prof. Memberships:** Federal Bar Association; State Bar of Texas; Houston Bar Association and National Conference of Bankruptcy Judges.

**Career:** Prior to joining Fulbright, Mr Greendyke served as Chief Judge of the United States Bankruptcy Court for the Southern District of Texas sitting in Houston. He was appointed to the bankruptcy bench in Houston by the Fifth Circuit on September 1, 1987.

**Personal:** BS, Baylor University, (1976); JD, Baylor Law School with honors, (1979).

### GREER, Scott
King & Spalding LLP, Atlanta
404 572 4600
*Recommended in Construction*

**Practice Areas:** Focuses on practice of construction law and construction litigation. Represents clients in all aspects of a construction project, including structuring, drafting, modifying and negotiating of construction, engineering, architectural and development agreements, and negotiating, mediating, arbitrating and litigating claims on construction defects, delay, design deficiencies, wrongful termination, non-payment and surety bonds. Focuses on the representation of owners and developers. Extensive experience in LNG matters.

**Prof. Memberships:** American Bar Association; American Concrete Institute; Atlanta Bar Association; State Bar of Georgia.

**Personal:** 5) BS, Oklahoma State University, 1987; MS, University of Illinois, Champaign-Urbana, 1988; JD, Emory University, 1995.

### GREIG, Brian
Fulbright & Jaworski L.L.P., Austin
512 536 4510
bgreig@fulbright.com
*Recommended in Employment*

**Practice Areas:** Labor and employment law, trade secrets, technology litigation, federal practice, commercial litigation and construction litigation.

**Prof. Memberships:** Travis County Bar Association, Federal Bar Association, American Bar Associations and the State Bar of Texas.

**Career:** Partner since 1983, practices in Fulbright & Jaworski L.L.P.'s Austin office, where he heads the office's Labor and Employment Practice.

**Publications:** Editor-in-Chief, 'Texas Employment Law Handbook – A Guide for Employers', published annually by the Texas Association of Business; contributor, 'The Developing Labor Law', Labor and Employment Law Section of the ABA.

**Personal:** Received his BA in Economics from Washington & Lee University (1972) and a JD from The University of Texas School of Law (1975).

### GREMILLION, L Todd
Akin Gump Strauss Hauer & Feld LLP, Houston 713 220 5875
tgremillion@akingump.com
*Recommended in Energy*

**Practice Areas:** Handles international and domestic oil, gas and related energy transactions. Experienced in hydrocarbons exploration and production joint ventures; liquified natural gas commercialization; acquisition and sale of hydrocarbons properties and companies; contractual arrangements and related economic issues regarding transportation, marketing and distribution of hydrocarbons; gas-fired electric generation projects and related power distribution and marketing; and equity and debt financing relating to the foregoing. Is involved extensively with oil and gas exploration and production operations in the Russian Federation, Kazakhstan and other Central Asian Republics of the former Soviet Union and the Caspian Region.

**Personal:** BA, JD, Louisiana State University.

### GRIFFITH, Scott
Griffith & Nixon, P.C., Dallas
972 386 8988
sgriffith@griffithnixon.com
*Recommended in Construction*

**Practice Areas:** Construction law and commercial real estate.

**Prof. Memberships:** Vice-Chairman of the Construction Law Section of the Dallas Bar Association; Member of the Construction Law and Real Estate Law Sections of the Texas State Bar; Member of Associated Builders and Contractors; Member of Texas Real Estate Council; Member of Associated General Contrac-

tors (Quoin).

**Career:** Scott is a Founding Partner of Griffith & Nixon, P.C. and has served as its Managing Partner since its formation. He has established himself as one of the leading construction lawyers in the State. Named a Texas Super Lawyer for the past three consecutive years, Scott is a dynamic leader in his field.

**Publications:** Scott is a frequent speaker at various industry and community functions. He has spoken on a variety of construction and real estate topics and has been published in multiple industry journals.

**Personal:** Scott is very active in community charity and church activities. He has been married many years to his wife, Kasey, and is the father of five children.

### GROTEN, Eric
Vinson & Elkins LLP, Austin
*Recommended in Environment*

**Practice Areas:** Serves industrial, manufacturing, utility and municipal clients in managing their environmental issues, principally air quality, including representation in permit application proceedings, defense of enforcement actions, environmental audits and investigations, compliance counseling, transaction of emission rights, advocacy in state and federal rulemakings and related litigation. Specially recognized by Texas Lawyer as one of the State's leading 'legal innovators' for facilitating the first-ever air emissions trading program across the Texas/Mexico border. Other career firsts include the first single-property designations and first contested air permit renewal proceedings under the Texas Clean Air Act, and the first audits under the Texas audit statutes.

**Career:** JD, The University of Texas School of Law, 1985; BA, Chemistry and Environmental Studies, Baylor University, 1981.

### GUEDRY, David N
Jones Day, Dallas
214 969 5190
dnguedry@jonesday.com
*Recommended in Business Process Outsourcing, Technology*

**Practice Areas:** Nationally recognized for nearly 20 years of leadership at structuring outsourcing relationships, joint ventures, mergers and acquisitions, and other complex business arrangements. He advises technology-based businesses engaged in these transactions and helps them develop their overall legal and business strategies. He excels at giving his clients strategic advise on the structuring of business relationships, then translating strategy into the practical negotiation and documentation of the deal. Significant experience includes information management, telecommunication, and human resource outsourcing agreements; licensing arrangements; and joint ven-

tures, strategic alliances, and teaming relationships.
**Prof. Memberships:** ABA; State Bar of Texas.

### GUMP JR, Richard
Law Offices of Richard A Gump Jr PC, Dallas 972 386 9544
*Recommended in Immigration*

### GUNN, David
Beck, Redden & Secrest LLP, Houston
713 951 3700
*Recommended in Litigation*

### GUNTER, Clifford
Bracewell & Giuliani LLP, Houston
713 221 1213
clifford.gunter@bracewellgiuliani.com
*Recommended in Energy, Litigation*
**Practice Areas:** Maintains extensive commercial litigation background with client roster listing some of the nation's largest energy companies. Experience includes cases involving fraud, theft of trade secrets, breach of contract, construction litigation, antitrust litigation, securities fraud litigation, special matters and investigations, international dispute resolution, arbitrations of transnational gas sales contracts, and take-or-pay and pricing disputes. Has tried several international corporate project finance issues cases to verdict. Heads firmwide Trial Section.
**Career:** Listed in Euromoney's '2005 Guide to the Leading US Litigation Lawyers'.
**Personal:** LLB, The University of Texas School of Law, 1967; BA, The University of Texas at Austin, 1965.

### HALEVY, Amy Karff
Bracewell & Giuliani LLP, Houston
713 221 1329
amy.halevy@bracewellgiuliani.com
*Recommended in Employment*
**Practice Areas:** Head of the firm's nationally regarded Labor and Employment Section. Represents employers in all areas of employment law, including litigation in state and federal court and complaints before the Equal Employment Opportunity Commission and the Texas Commission on Human Rights. Provides advice to employers regarding the preparation and application of employment policies, including sexual harassment policies. Board Certified in labor and employment law, she is also a prolific legal writer, editor and speaker. Recognized in her practice by other legal publications.
**Personal:** JD, University of Houston Law Center, 1987; BA, with honors, Wesleyan University, 1984.

### HALL, Charles
Fulbright & Jaworski L.L.P., Houston
713 651 5268
chall@fulbright.com
*Recommended in Tax, Tax Litigation*
**Practice Areas:** Tax litigation; tax law;

corporate law.
**Prof. Memberships:** American Bar Association; State Bar of Texas and Houston Bar Association.
**Personal:** LLM, Taxation, Southern Methodist University (1959); JD, Southern Methodist University School of Law (1954); BA, University of the South (1951).

### HAMEL, Douglas
Vinson & Elkins LLP, Houston
713 758 2036
dhamel@velaw.com
*Recommended in Employment*
**Practice Areas:** Representing management in labor and employment law, civil rights law, ERISA litigation and related issues. Represented clients in connection with numerous class action employment discrimination lawsuits involving issues of disparate treatment and disparate impact. Also regularly appears before federal and state agencies including NLRB, EEOC and OFCCP.
**Career:** Partner since 1983; Section Head, Employment Litigation and Labor, and chairs firm's Benefits and Compensation Committee.
**Publications:** Planning Committee and Faculty, University of Texas Annual Employment Law Conference since 1996 and speaker at University of Texas Corporate Counsel Institute.
**Personal:** University of Virginia, (BA, 1972; JD, 1976).

### HAMMOND, Herbert
Thompson & Knight LLP, Dallas
214 969 1607
Herbert.Hammond@tklaw.com
*Recommended in Intellectual Property*
**Practice Areas:** Mr Hammond represents clients in intellectual property matters. He focuses his practice on litigation, licensing, and counseling in patent, trademark, copyright, trade secret, computer, and entertainment matters. Mr Hammond also acts as an arbitrator and mediator in intellectual property and hi-tech cases.
**Prof. Memberships:** State Bar of Texas; Dallas Bar Association; American Intellectual Property Law Association.
**Career:** Partner since 1995.
**Publications:** Texas Intellectual Property Handbook (LexisNexis 2005) and numerous chapters and articles.
**Personal:** New York University (JD, 1976), University of New Mexico (BS, 1973).

### HARDIE, Thornton
Thompson & Knight LLP, Dallas
214 969 1504
Thornton.Hardie@tklaw.com
*Recommended in Tax*
**Practice Areas:** Mr Hardie focuses his practice on taxation of business transactions, oil and gas taxation and energy finance, and tax and business planning for individuals, partnerships, and corpo-

rations. He has significant involvement in structuring oil and gas debt and equity financing transactions including public and private offerings and privately negotiated transactions, representing both industry parties and institutional investors.
**Prof. Memberships:** Member of the State Bar of Texas, American and Dallas Bar Associations, Texas Bar Foundation.
**Career:** Partner since 1981.
**Personal:** University of Texas School of Law (JD, 1975); Washington and Lee University (BS, 1973).

### HARPER, A J
Fulbright & Jaworski L.L.P., Houston
713 651 5442
ajharper@fulbright.com
*Recommended in Employment*
**Practice Areas:** Labor and Employment law.
**Prof. Memberships:** Member of the State Bar of Texas, the Houston Bar Association and the American Bar Association. Fellow in the College of Labor and Employment Lawyers and is included in a leading legal publication.
**Career:** Admitted to the Texas Bar (1967). Admitted before the United States Court of Appeals for the First, Second, Fifth, Sixth, Eighth, Ninth, Tenth and Eleventh Circuits. Admitted to practice before the United States Supreme Court. Admitted to the US District Courts for the Eastern, Northern, Southern and Western Districts of Texas, and District of Nebraska. Partner since 1975 and currently heads the firm's Labor and Employment Law Department. Certified by the Texas Board of Legal Specialization in Labor and Employment Law.
**Personal:** Received a BA (1964) from North Texas State University and an LLB, cum laude, (1967) from Southern Methodist University.

### HARRELL, Charles E
Duane Morris LLP, Houston
713 402 3916
ceharrell@duanemorris.com
*Recommended in Corporate/M&A*
**Practice Areas:** Charles E Harrell is the Managing Partner of Duane Morris' Houston office. Mr Harrell practices in the area of corporate law with a focus on corporate transactions, mergers and acquisitions, capital markets and structured finance. Mr Harrell represents a number of Fortune 100 companies as well as middle-market companies, startups, joint ventures and partnerships. He also handles offerings of debt and equity securities and he regularly advises clients with respect to reporting and disclosure issues and corporate governance.
**Prof. Memberships:** American Bar Association – Section of Corporation – Banking and Business Law; The State Bar of Texas; Houston Bar Association; American Institute of Certified Public

Accountants; National Association of Corporate Directors – Houston Chapter (President).
**Career:** Admitted to practice in Texas.
**Personal:** St. Mary's University School of Law, JD, 1981; University of Texas, BBA, 1976.

### HARRINGTON, C Michael
Vinson & Elkins LLP, Houston
713 758 2148
charrington@velaw.com
*Recommended in Corporate/M&A*
**Practice Areas:** Corporate finance, mergers and acquisitions law. Corporate Finance Practice emphasizes high-yield debt. Industry experience includes energy companies, beer wholesalers, and airlines.
**Prof. Memberships:** State Bar of Texas, Houston Bar Association, and Texas Business Law Foundation.
**Career:** Admitted to practice: Texas, 1973. Came to V&E in 1973; admitted to partnership in 1980.
**Personal:** Graduated from Yale College, BA in 1969 (Phi Beta Kappa), Cambridge University, Diploma in Development Economics in 1970, and Harvard University, JD in 1973.

### HARRIS, James
Thompson & Knight LLP, Dallas
214 969 1102
James.Harris@tklaw.com
*Recommended in Environment*
**Practice Areas:** Mr Harris represents clients who are suing or have been sued by the government. He has tried and appealed cost recovery actions; successfully defended in court and before agencies air, water, and hazardous waste enforcement actions, including citizen suits, obtained acquittals in regulatory crimes cases, handled contested environmental cases in bankruptcy proceedings, and obtained judicial invalidation of regulations.
**Publications:** 'Divisible Injuries and Arbitrary Remedies After Sequa', 26 Chemical Waste Litigation Report 1075, October 1993, November 1993.
**Personal:** University of Texas School of Law (JD, with honors, 1978); Southern Methodist University (BAS (Environmental Systems), with high honors, 1975).

### HARRIS, Warren W
Bracewell & Giuliani LLP, Houston
713 221 1490
warren.harris@bracewellgiuliani.com
*Recommended in Litigation*
**Practice Areas:** Board certified in civil appellate law, he serves as Head of the firm's Appellate Group. He has handled hundreds of appeals and original proceedings in the Texas Supreme Court, US Supreme Court, and state and federal courts of appeals, including cases that were originally tried by other law firms. He also assists in pretrial and trial strategy, preservation of error at trial, prepara-

tion of and arguing jury charges, post-verdict proceedings in trial courts, and analysis of the trial record for appellate potential.

**Personal:** JD, cum laude, University of Houston Law Center, 1988; BBA, The University of Houston, 1985.

## HARRISON, Lauren
Vinson & Elkins LLP, Houston
713 758 4430
lharrison@velaw.com
*Recommended in Antitrust*

**Practice Areas:** Lauren is a commercial litigator with a nationwide practice. She handles complex commercial cases before judges, juries, and arbitrators. Her clients include companies in aviation, rail transportation, energy, entertainment, technology leasing, and diverse manufacturing industries.

**Prof. Memberships:** American Bar Association; Houston Bar Association.

**Career:** Partner since 2005. Admitted to practice: Washington State, 1996; Texas, 2000; United States Supreme Court; US District Courts for the Southern, Eastern and Western District of Texas.

**Personal:** Dartmouth College, (BA 1990); Cornell Law School, JD, 1995 (Order of the Coif; Articles Editor, Cornell Law Review, 1994-95).

## HARRISON III, Orrin L
Akin Gump Strauss Hauer & Feld LLP, Dallas 214 969 2860
oharrison@akingump.com
*Recommended in Litigation*

**Practice Areas:** Practice focuses principally on complex business litigation, usually involving energy, securities, antitrust and director/officer issues, on behalf of utility companies, accounting and investment banking firms, and oil and gas companies.

**Prof. Memberships:** President, Dallas Bar Association (1992); President, Dallas Chapter, American Board of Trial Advocates (1990); Director, State Bar of Texas (1993-96), Life Fellow, Dallas Bar Foundation, Southwestern Legal Foundation, Texas Bar Foundation and American Bar Foundation; State Bar Commission on Lawyer Discipline (2003-06); International Society of Barristers.

**Personal:** BA (cum laude), University of the South (1971); JD (cum laude), Southern Methodist University School of Law (1974).

## HARTSFIELD, Dan
Baker Botts LLP, Dallas
214 953 6575
dan.hartsfield@bakerbotts.com
*Recommended in Employment*

**Practice Areas:** Represents management in individual and class action employment discrimination, wage and hour collective action, wrongful discharge and other employment-related litigation and in union organizational efforts and collective bargaining. Defends

clients against federal and state administrative charges and represents government contractors before the Office of Federal Contract Compliance Programs (OFCCP). Exclusive representation of management in matters brought before the NLRB, EEOC, US Department of Labor, OFCCP, and other state and federal agencies.

**Career:** Chairs Labor and Employment Practice Group in Dallas. Serves on firm's Client Development Committee.

**Personal:** JD, Southern Methodist University, 1982; Phi Delta Phi; BA, magna cum laude, The University of Texas, 1979.

## HARVEY, Dean William
Vinson & Elkins LLP, Dallas
214 220 7815
dharvey@velaw.com
*Recommended in Technology*

**Practice Areas:** Practice focuses on technology and communications-related business transactions such as outsourcing, licensing, and joint ventures. Counsels clients on communications and technology-related legal issues such as privacy and security, and assists clients in protecting, acquiring and developing technology.

**Prof. Memberships:** Licensing Executives Society.

**Career:** Admitted to Texas Bar, 1997. Came to firm, 1997. Admitted to partnership, January 2001.

**Publications:** Special Member HIPAA Briefing Collection: Section IV – Security Standards, 'American Health Lawyers Association', October 2004.

**Personal:** Graduated from West Virginia University, BS summa cum laude, 1986 and The University of Texas, JD, Order of the Coif, 1997.

## HARVIN, David
Vinson & Elkins LLP, Houston
713 758 2368
dharvin@velaw.com
*Recommended in Energy, Litigation*

**Practice Areas:** Principal areas of practice include energy litigation, business litigation, class actions, securities, corporate and antitrust litigation.

**Prof. Memberships:** Fellow of the American College of Trial Lawyers; listed since 1987 in the area of Business Litigation in a leading legal US publication.

**Career:** Admitted to Texas Bar in 1970. Joined Vinson & Elkins in 1971; admitted to partnership, 1977. Served on Management Committee, 2000-05; Chair, Litigation Section.

**Personal:** Yale University, BA magna cum laude, 1967 (Phi Beta Kappa); University of Texas School of Law, JD, high honors, 1970 (Chancellors; Order of the Coif; Articles Editor, Texas Law Review).

## HATCHELL, Mike A
Locke Liddell & Sapp LLP, Austin
512 305 4700
*Recommended in Litigation*

## HAYES, William
Bracewell & Giuliani LLP, Houston
713 221 1333
bill.hayes@bracewellgiuliani.com
*Recommended in Banking & Finance*

**Practice Areas:** Focuses on structuring, drafting and negotiating a wide variety of financing transactions, including secured and unsecured credit facilities, acquisition financings, borrowing base financings, insured credit facilities, subordinated debt, workouts of troubled credits, sales of accounts receivable, letters of credit and interest rate and commodity derivatives.

**Career:** Has practiced finance law for more than 25 years and has represented a number of agents in significant syndicated bank credit facilities. Clients include Citibank NA and JPMorgan Chase Bank.

**Personal:** JD, Harvard Law School, 1974; BSEE, University of Arkansas, 1970.

## HEAD, J D
Fritz, Byrne, Head & Harrison, Austin
512 476 2020
*Recommended in Environment*

## HEADLEY, Linda
Littler Mendelson, PC, Dallas
713 951 9400
lheadley@littler.com
*Recommended in Employment*

**Practice Areas:** Focus includes labor and employment litigation and administrative proceedings before the NLRB, EEOC and OSHA. Represents employers in disputes alleging discrimination, and litigates cases involving workers' compensation, breach of employment contract, covenants-not-to-compete, and other workplace claims.

**Prof. Memberships:** Member, Employee Rights and Responsibilities Committee of the Labor and Employment Section of ABA; serves on the Council for the State Bar Labor and Employment Section of the Texas State Bar; Co-Chair, Human Resources and Employment Law Committee for Associated General Contractors.

**Personal:** University of Houston Law Center, (JD, cum laude, 1982); University of Houston (BFA, 1972).

## HEALEY, David J
Weil, Gotshal & Manges LLP, Houston
713 546 5111
david.healey@weil.com
*Recommended in Intellectual Property*

**Practice Areas:** David Healey's experience is in intellectual property and complex commercial litigation. His practice includes trials, appeals, pre-litigation analyses, and counseling on litigation strategy, including the use of alternative dispute resolution proceedings. He has extensively litigated cases involving semiconductors, telecommunications and software. Mr Healey is recognized for his experience handling antitrust issues in intellectual property matters involving

trade secrets and covenants not to compete. Mr Healey also has experience handling patent issues involving trade associations and standard-setting groups. Mr Healey has extensive experience in patent cases in Marshall, Texas, and is active in the Eastern District of Texas Bar Association.

**Personal:** Brown University, BA, 1982; University of Texas School of Law, JD, with honors, 1985.

## HEIM, Michael
Heim, Payne & Chorush LLP, Houston
713 221 2000
*Recommended in Intellectual Property*

## HELFAND, Thomas
Winstead Sechrest & Minick P.C., Dallas
214 745 5400
*Recommended in Tax*

## HENRY, D Steven
Gardere Wynne Sewell LLP, Dallas
214 999 4838
shenry@gardere.com
*Recommended in Construction*

**Practice Areas:** Construction, trial.

**Prof. Memberships:** State Bar of Texas, Dallas Bar Association, National Association of Homebuilders, Texas Association of Builders, Association of General Contractors.

**Career:** Henry chairs Gardere's Construction Practice Group, and has built it into one of the largest multi-disciplinary construction sections in the US. His practice is divided between the commercial and residential construction industries and he specializes in litigation, lobbying, contracting, policies and procedures, environmental, mold, mass tort and IP matters arising from the construction industry. Henry is national Coordinating Counsel for the National Association of Homebuilder's Notice and Opportunity to Repair Legislation Initiative.

**Personal:** JD, Texas Tech University School of Law, with honors, 1984; BS, Texas A&M University, with honors, 1981.

## HENSLEY, Noel MB
Haynes and Boone LLP, Dallas
214 651 5000
*Recommended in Litigation*

## HESTER, Tracy
Bracewell & Giuliani LLP, Houston
713 221 1407
tracy.hester@bracewellgiuliani.com
*Recommended in Environment*

**Practice Areas:** Counsels on regulatory compliance, enforcement defense, permitting, cost recovery litigation, environmental aspects of corporate transactions, emergency response planning and security assurance legal requirements. Industrial clients include petrochemicals, petroleum and natural gas pipelines, refineries, utilities, local governments, nanomaterial producers, renewable energy developers, hazardous waste disposal operations and financial institutions.

**Career:** Elected to American Law Institute; recognized by Best Lawyers in America as outstanding in his field. Adjunct Professor, University of Houston Law Center.

**Personal:** JD, Stone Scholar, Columbia University, 1986; BA, Plan II Honors Program, The University of Texas at Austin, 1983.

### HEWITT, Lester L
Akin Gump Strauss Hauer & Feld LLP, Houston 713 220 5851
lhewitt@akingump.com
*Recommended in Intellectual Property*
**Practice Areas:** Co-Chair, firmwide Intellectual Property Practice. Has served as lead counsel in numerous complex lawsuits, including proceedings related to patents and trademarks. Counsels clients on broad range of IP issues in antitrust law. Often involved in patent/antitrust issues in litigation, eg standard-setting, patent and antitrust cases.
**Prof. Memberships:** Past President, Houston Intellectual Property Law Association; past Secretary, Board Member, Houston Bar Association; former Director, State Bar of Texas and Texas Young Lawyers Association; American Intellectual Property Law Association; American Bar Association, Intellectual Property Law Section.
**Personal:** BS (Mechanical Engineering) and JD, University of Houston. 'Best Lawyers in America', 2001-present.

### HICKS JR, M Lawrence
Thompson & Knight LLP, Dallas
214 969 1627
Larry.Hicks@tklaw.com
*Recommended in Real Estate*
**Practice Areas:** Mr Hicks' practice encompasses multi-state real estate lending transactions, purchases and sales, ground leases, workouts, foreclosures, conveyances, leases, reciprocal easements, operating agreements, management agreements, and loan documents. Mr Hicks has been selected for listing in 'The Best Lawyers in America' (Real Estate and Banking Law, 1995-present); Texas Monthly's Texas Super Lawyers (2003-present); and D Magazine's Best Lawyers in Dallas.
**Prof. Memberships:** Regent and State Chair, American College of Mortgage Attorneys.
**Personal:** University of Texas School of Law (JD, with honors,1970); Duke University (BA, 1967); Articles Editor, Texas Law Review; law clerk, US Court of Appeals, Ninth Circuit.

### HIGGINS, John
Porter & Hedges, LLP, Houston
713 226 6000
*Recommended in Bankruptcy*

### HIGGINS, Roger
Thompson, Coe, Cousins & Irons, LLP, Dallas 214 871 8200
*Recommended in Insurance*

### HIGH JR, Charles
Kemp Smith LLP, El Paso
915 533 4424
*Recommended in Employment*

### HILGERS, David
Brown McCarroll LLP, Austin
512 472 5456
*Recommended in Healthcare*

### HILLIARD, Michael
Winstead Sechrest & Minick P.C., Dallas
214 745 5400
*Recommended in Banking & Finance*

### HIRSCHMAN, Karen L
Vinson & Elkins LLP, Dallas
214 220 7795
khirschman@velaw.com
*Recommended in Litigation*
**Practice Areas:** Specializes in large, complex business disputes including accounting and legal malpractice, securities, and civil RICO. Expertise in all aspects of expert testimony. Trial experience in state courts in Texas, federal courts in Texas and other states, and in adversary proceedings in US bankruptcy courts.
**Prof. Memberships:** American Law Institute; American Bar Association; University of Texas Law School Alumni Executive Committee; Texas Bar Foundation.
**Career:** Admitted to Texas Bar, 1983. Came to firm as Partner, 1999.
**Personal:** Graduated from University of Delaware, BA with high honors, 1973, and The University of Texas, MA, 1980, JD with honors, 1983.

### HITT, Jeffrey
Weil, Gotshal & Manges LLP, Dallas
214 746 7702
jeffrey.hitt@weil.com
*Recommended in Corporate/M&A*
**Practice Areas:** Jeffrey Hitt's practice primarily focuses on private equity, M&A, and securities matters. His range of experience includes representation of private equity firms and their portfolio companies with public and private acquisitions, divestitures, and recapitalization transactions; representation of issuers in public and private placements of debt and equity; and representation of fund sponsors with the formation of private equity and other pooled investment vehicles. Representative clients include Hicks, Muse, Tate & Furst, Brazos Investment Partners, Ewing Management, and Activant Solutions.
**Career:** Licensed in Texas and New York.
**Personal:** Colgate University, BA, 1985; Boston University School of Law, JD, 1988.

### HOLLYFIELD, John S
Fulbright & Jaworski L.L.P., Houston
713 651 3717
jhollyfield@fulbright.com
*Recommended in Real Estate*
**Practice Areas:** Real estate.
**Prof. Memberships:** Mr Hollyfield is included in multiple leading legal US publications. He is a Member of the Houston Bar Association, where he was a past Chair of the Real Estate Law Section; the American Bar Association, where he is a past Chair of Real Property, Probate and Trust Law Section; the State Bar of Texas; a past President of the American College of Real Estate Lawyers; and past President of the Anglo-American Real Property Institute. He is a former Member of the House of Delegates of the American Bar Association.
**Career:** Mr Hollyfield focuses his legal practice on real estate matters, including mortgage lending, leasing (landlord and tenant), real estate development, construction (owner, contractor, lender and architect), sale and purchase of raw land, commercial and industrial properties, real estate brokerage and management, joint venture partnerships, mortgage foreclosures and loan workouts.
**Personal:** Mr Hollyfield received a BBA in 1961 and an LLB, with honors, in 1968 from The University of Texas.

### HOLMAN, David
Godwin Pappas Langley Ronquillo, LLP, Dallas 214 939 4400
*Recommended in Litigation*

### HOLZGRAEFE, John
Jenkens & Gilchrist PC, Dallas
214 855 4500
*Recommended in Technology*

### HOOPER, Samuel E
Neel, Hooper & Banes, P.C., Houston
713 629 1800
shooper@neelhooper.com
*Recommended in Employment*
**Practice Areas:** Represents management in labor and employment law matters before administrative agencies as well as state and federal courts.
**Career:** Mr Hooper has defended Title VII class actions as well as individual discrimination and wrongful termination actions in the trial court and in appeals. He has also litigated administrative claims before the NLRB and DOL brought under the NLRA, OSHA, ERA and Sarbanes-Oxley Act.
**Personal:** JD from the University of Oklahoma College of Law, 1967; Order of Coif; Contributing Editor, Oklahoma Law Review; BBA, University of Oklahoma, 1964; Board Certified – Labor and Employment – Texas Board of Legal Specialization, 1975-2010.

### HOPSON, Keith
Brown McCarroll LLP, Austin
512 472 5456
*Recommended in Environment*

### HOWARD, JR, John L
Vinson & Elkins LLP, Austin
512 542 8564
jhoward@velaw.com
*Recommended in Environment*
**Practice Areas:** State and federal environmental, natural resource and energy matters, including complex public policy and legislation. Has represented major corporations, associations, and local governments.
**Prof. Memberships:** Chairman, National Environmental Council for Environmental Policy and Technology; State Bar of Texas Environmental and Natural Resources Section.
**Career:** Partner since 2004; Federal Environmental Executive (appointed by President Bush, 2002-04); Senior Associate Director, White House Council on Environmental Quality (2001-02); Bush-Cheney Environmental Transition Team Director (2000-01); Environment and Natural Resources Policy Director to Governor Bush (1996-2000).
**Publications:** Has lectured and written extensively on environmental policy.
**Personal:** University of Texas School of Law (JD, 1988, Texas Law Review); Baylor University (BA, 1985, Phi Beta Kappa).

### HOWELL, John
Hughes & Luce LLP, Dallas
214 939 5500
*Recommended in Business Process Outsourcing, Technology*

### HOYT, Scott R
Gibson, Dunn & Crutcher LLP, Dallas
214 698 3265
shoyt@gibsondunn.com
*Recommended in Insurance*
**Practice Areas:** Commercial litigation, focus on insurance, telecommunications, accounting malpractice defense, intellectual property and products liability defense. Experience defending environmental, asbestos bodily injury/property damage, defective products, advertising and intellectual property coverage cases and insurance bad faith cases. Fluent in Spanish and has developed an expertise in defending Mexican companies in cases involving Mexican law.
**Prof. Memberships:** State Bars of Texas and California, J Reuben Clark Law Society.
**Publications:** Numerous articles in Mealey's Litigation, Insurance Reports, Insurance Journals.
**Personal:** JD, University of California Hastings College of Law, 1983, Order of the Coif and Hastings Law Review; California Supreme Court law clerk.

## HUDDLESTON, Michael
Shannon, Gracey, Ratliff & Miller LLP, Dallas 214 245 3090
*Recommended in Insurance*

## HUFFMAN, Gregory
Thompson & Knight LLP, Dallas
214 969 1144
Gregory.Huffman@tklaw.com
*Recommended in Antitrust*
**Practice Areas:** Mr Huffman focuses his practice on antitrust, complex commercial litigation, and criminal investigations. He has tried numerous cases to a successful conclusion.
**Prof. Memberships:** State Bar of Texas, American and Dallas Bar Associations, Texas and Dallas Bar Foundations.
**Career:** Partner since 1980.
**Publications:** Mr Huffman is a frequent speaker and writer on antitrust, litigation, and professional topics.
**Personal:** Harvard Law School (JD, 1973); Stanford University (BA, 1969).

## HUGHES, Vester
Hughes & Luce LLP, Dallas
214 939 5500
*Recommended in Tax*

## HULL, Robert J
Bracewell & Giuliani LLP, Houston
713 221 1589
joe.hull@bracewellgiuliani.com
*Recommended in Tax*
**Practice Areas:** Has represented clients in diverse industries, including real estate (development and finance, syndications and REITs); oil and gas, financial, aerospace, equipment leasing, hi-tech and telecommunications. Expertise includes partnerships and limited liability companies; business planning and formation, acquisitions and reorganizations; and executive compensation. Has handled matters of corporate income and franchise taxes, including unitary, allocation and apportionment issues; property taxes; sales and use taxes; city taxes; utility taxes; environmental taxes; transfer taxes; and unclaimed property and escheat laws.
**Personal:** JD, The University of Texas School of Law, 1969; BA, The University of Texas at Austin, 1966.

## IRVIN, Michael P
Fulbright & Jaworski L.L.P., Houston
713 651 3705
mirvin@fulbright.com
*Recommended in Energy*
**Practice Areas:** Oil, gas and energy transactions, project finance, real estate.
**Prof. Memberships:** Mr Irvin is a Member of the Houston and American Bar Associations and the State Bar of Texas. While in law school, he was Editor-in-Chief of the Houston Law Review and a member of Phi Delta Phi.
**Career:** Mr Irvin heads the firm's Energy and Real Property Department. His practice focuses on domestic and international oil, gas and energy transactions related to the acquisition and disposition of oil and gas exploration and producing properties, pipelines, gas processing plants, petrochemical facilities and oil and gas companies, whether accomplished through asset or stock acquisitions; the exploration, development, project finance, construction and operation of oil and gas properties, pipelines, gas processing plants, petrochemical and LNG facilities or projects; joint ventures, partnerships and other joint ownership or participation arrangements in the energy area; mortgage and asset-based financing relating to oil, gas and petrochemical related properties, pipelines, plants and other assets; and other areas of oil and gas practice, including production sales, storage, processing and transportation agreements.
**Personal:** Mr Irvin received a BA in 1972 from The University of Texas and a JD in 1975 from the University of Houston.

## ISRAEL, Sharon
Mayer, Brown, Rowe & Maw LLP, Houston 713 546 0575
sisrael@mayerbrownrowe.com
*Recommended in Intellectual Property*
**Practice Areas:** Specializes in intellectual property law with an emphasis in patent litigation, opinion work, and client counseling. Served as counsel in cases involving patent infringement, trademark infringement, copyright infringement, trade secret misappropriation, unfair competition, and infringement under the Plant Variety Protection Act. Has litigated patents relating to a variety of technologies, including telecommunications, electrical devices, chemical compositions, medical devices, mechanical devices, and oilfield equipment.
**Career:** Mayer, Brown, Rowe & Maw LLP, Houston, 2005 to date. Jenkens & Gilchrist, P.C., Houston, 1998-2005. Fish & Richardson, P.C., 1993-98. Law clerk to the Honorable Alan D Lourie, United States Court of Appeals for the Federal Circuit, 1991-93.
**Personal:** Emory University School of Law, JD, 1991. Emory University School of Business Administration, MBA, 1991. Massachusetts Institute of Technology, SBEE, 1986. American Intellectual Property Law Association (Board of Directors). Federal Circuit Bar Association (Board of Governors). President's Award, Houston Intellectual Property Law Association (2005). Texas SuperLawyers (2003-present). Admissions: Texas, Georgia, and United States Patent and Trademark Office.

## JACOBS, Stephen
Locke Liddell & Sapp LLP, Houston
713 226 1200
*Recommended in Real Estate*

## JANSONIUS, John V
Akin Gump Strauss Hauer & Feld LLP, Dallas 214 969 4770
jjansonius@akingump.com
*Recommended in Employment*
**Practice Areas:** Board Certified in Labor and Employment Law, Texas Board of Legal Specialization. Defends employment discrimination claims, wrongful discharge claims, unfair labor practice claims under National Labor Relations Act, plan administration and denial of benefits claims under Employee Retirement Income Security Act, and collective and individual actions under Fair Labor Standards Act. Has represented the defense in jury and non-jury trials in state/federal court and presented oral arguments to US Supreme Court and several federal courts of appeals.
**Prof. Memberships:** Chair, Labor and Employment Law Section, State Bar of Texas, 2004-05.
**Personal:** BA, Drake University; JD, Southern Methodist University.

## JENKINS, Steve
Haynes and Boone LLP, Dallas
214 651 5000
*Recommended in Real Estate*

## JENNINGS, Gray
Baker Botts LLP, Houston
713 229 1640
Gray.Jennings@bakerbotts.com
*Recommended in Tax*
**Practice Areas:** US federal and state tax matters (domestic and international) including transactions, financings and other capital flows for corporations, partnerships, other business organizations and high net worth individuals; administrative practice before the IRS and tax-related controversies.
**Prof. Memberships:** ABA, State Bar of Texas, Houston Bar Association, American College of Tax Counsel, International Fiscal Association.
**Career:** Partner since 1984.
**Publications:** Frequent speaker; adjunct faculty University of Houston Law Center.
**Personal:** JD (with high honors) University of Texas; PhD, MS NYU (Mathematics), BS (with honors), California Institute of Technology.

## JERNIGAN, Stacey
Haynes and Boone LLP, Dallas
214 651 5000
*Recommended in Bankruptcy*

## JESSUP JR, Clifton R
Greenberg Traurig LLP, Dallas
972 419 9113
jessup@gtlaw.com
*Recommended in Bankruptcy*
**Practice Areas:** Bankruptcy.
**Prof. Memberships:** Served on the North Texas Regional Mental Health Board; currently serves on the Board of Trustees of Oakwood College; Member, Texas State Bar; Member, American Bar Association.
**Career:** Recognized, one of America's Top Black Lawyers in Black Enterprise Magazine, November 2003; recognized, one of the Texas Super Lawyers by Texas Monthly, 2003 and 2004; listed, 'Best Lawyers in America'; Master in the John C Ford American Inns of Court.
**Personal:** JD, University of Michigan Law School, 1978; BA, summa cum laude, Oakwood College, 1976.

## JEWELL, Robert
Andrews Kurth LLP, Houston
713 220 4200
*Recommended in Corporate/M&A, Technology*

## JOE, Harry
Jenkens & Gilchrist PC, Dallas
214 855 4500
*Recommended in Immigration*

## JOHN, Philip
Baker Botts LLP, Houston
713 229 1215
Philip.john@bakerbotts.com
*Recommended in Antitrust*
**Practice Areas:** John has a diverse commercial litigation practice. He has headed litigation efforts for clients involved in prosecuting or defending hostile acquisition attempts and successfully defended a number of class action suits. He also represents clients before the Securities and Exchange Commission. He has tried a number of lawsuits to a jury verdict, including antitrust claims.
**Prof. Memberships:** Texas State Bar; Houston Bar Association.
**Career:** 38+ years of practice.
**Personal:** JD (with honors), The University of Texas School of Law, 1967, Order of the Coif, Chancellors, Associate Editor, Texas Law Review; BA (with honors), The University of Texas, 1965.

## JOHNSON, Ethel J
Ogletree, Deakins, Nash, Smoak & Stewart, PC, Houston
713 655 0855
ethel.johnson@ogletreedeakins.com
*Recommended in Employment*
**Practice Areas:** Management representation in labor and employment law, employment litigation, benefits litigation, and arbitrations. Counsels on discipline, discharge, wage and hour, investigations, handbooks, employment agreements (including non-compete and non-disclosure), and policies and practices.
**Prof. Memberships:** Houston Bar, American Bar, State Bar of Texas.
**Career:** Board Certified – labor and employment law. Texas 'Super Lawyer' (2004, 2005); 'The Best of the Best', Jan/Feb 2006 edition of Diversity and The Bar Magazine.
**Personal:** University of Texas (JD, 1991); Siena Heights College (BS, 1987).

## JOHNSTONE, Debbi M
Vinson & Elkins LLP, Houston
713 758 3420
djohnstone@velaw.com
*Recommended in Healthcare*

**Practice Areas:** Specializes in representation of healthcare entities on transactional and regulatory matters, and third party reimbursement, including coverage and payment under Medicare and Medicaid, anti-kickback, physician self-referral, false claims, and civil monetary penalties.

**Prof. Memberships:** American Health Lawyers Association; ABA, Health Law Section; Houston Bar Association, Health Law Section (Chair 2004-05); Healthcare Financial Management Association.

**Career:** Admitted to practice: Indiana, 1980; Texas, 1982; Board Certified in Health Law by the Texas Board of Legal Specialization.

**Publications:** Various articles on health law issues.

**Personal:** Northwestern University, BA, 1977; Indiana University School of Law, JD, cum laude, 1980.

## JONES, Frank G
Fulbright & Jaworski L.L.P., Houston
713 651 5473
fjones@fulbright.com
*Recommended in Litigation*

**Practice Areas:** Mr Jones has tried over 100 jury cases and has particular experience in product liability, securities, construction, and professional liability litigation.

**Prof. Memberships:** Mr Jones has been certified in Civil Trial Law by the Texas Board of Legal Specialization, elected to membership in the American College of Trial Lawyers, the American Board of Trial Advocates and the International Academy of Trial Lawyers, and is a Member of The Chartered Institute of Arbitrators.

**Career:** Mr Jones has been a Partner in the Houston office of Fulbright & Jaworski L.L.P. since 1974, and is Co-Partner-in-Charge of the Houston office.

**Personal:** BS, History, Rice University (1963); LLB, The University of Texas (1966).

## JORDAN, Carey
Baker Botts LLP, Houston
713 229 1233
carey.jordan@bakerbotts.com
*Recommended in Intellectual Property*

**Practice Areas:** Experienced in patent and trade secret litigation. Has expertise in advising clients on creating and managing patent portfolios to offensively protect technology, asserting patent rights when appropriate, and recognizing competitive advantages and licensing opportunities. Often provides counsel on competitive intelligence management, freedom to operate analyses, and joint development programs. Experienced with technologies including developments in

the downstream energy industry; chemical refining processes such as catalysis and polymerization; alternative fuel technologies such as fuel cells; and products like films, laminates, paints, carpets, diapers, and other personal care products. Also works on prosecution and litigation involving business methods.

## JORDAN, Carl
Vinson & Elkins LLP, Houston
713 758 2258
cjordan@velaw.com
*Recommended in Employment*

**Practice Areas:** Practice focuses on representing management in labor, ERISA, and employment-related trial work and counseling. Certified in labor and employment law by the Texas Board of Legal Specialization.

**Prof. Memberships:** Member: Labor and Employment Section and Section's Committee on Equal Employment Opportunity Law, American Bar Association. General Counsel: Texas Employment Law Council. Fellow: American College of Labor and Employment Lawyers.

**Career:** Admitted to practice: Texas, 1974. Joined Vinson & Elkins, 1974; admitted to partnership, 1981.

**Personal:** Baylor University, BA, 1971; Harvard Law School, JD, 1974.

## JOSEPHSON, Richard
Baker Botts LLP, Houston
713 229 1234
*Recommended in Litigation*

## JURGENSMEYER, Randy R
Vinson & Elkins LLP, Dallas
214 220 7790
rjurgensmeyer@velaw.com
*Recommended in Real Estate*

**Practice Areas:** Practice areas include business and finance, concentrating on real estate transactions. Randy has extensive involvement representing private equity funds, investors and REITs in forming joint ventures and strategic alliances and acquiring, selling, developing, financing, restructuring and leasing shopping centers, office buildings, hotels, industrial parks and apartment complexes.

**Prof. Memberships:** American Bar Association; Texas Bar Association; Dallas Bar Association.

**Career:** Admitted Texas Bar in 1986. Came to the firm as Partner in 1996.

**Personal:** Graduated from University of Missouri, BA magna cum laude, 1982; and Southern Methodist University School of Law, JD, 1985. Member of Phi Beta Kappa.

## KAIM, Henry
Bracewell & Giuliani LLP, Houston
713 221 1204
henry.kaim@bracewellgiuliani.com
*Recommended in Bankruptcy*

**Practice Areas:** Heads firm-wide Bank-

ruptcy Section. Experienced in all aspects of Chapter 11 reorganizations, including negotiation of complex plans of reorganization and the litigation of contested matters and adversary proceedings. Represented Chapter 11 debtors-in-possession, creditors committees, secured creditors, landlords and acquirers in bankruptcy in a variety of industries in major Chapter 11 cases nationwide.

**Prof. Memberships:** Fellow, American College of Bankruptcy.

**Career:** Listed in Euromoney's '2005 Guide to the World's Leading Insolvency and Restructuring Lawyers'. Adjunct Professor, University of Houston Law Center, Chapter 11 bankruptcy.

**Personal:** JD, University of Houston Law Center, 1977; BA, Southern Methodist University, 1974.

## KAISER, Keith
Cox Smith Matthews Incorporated, San Antonio 210 554 5281
kekaiser@coxsmith.com
*Recommended in Antitrust*

**Practice Areas:** Keith is a shareholder and the Department Leader for the firm's Litigation Department. His practice is concentrated in the areas of antitrust, securities and other forms of complex commercial litigation for domestic and international clients in a wide variety of industries.

**Prof. Memberships:** Fellow, American College of Trial Lawyers; Sustaining Life Fellow, Texas Bar Foundation; Former Director, San Antonio Bar Association; Former Director, Defense Counsel of San Antonio; Former Adjunct Professor, St. Mary's University School of Law; Past President and former Member of the Board of Directors, St. Mary's Law Alumni Association.

**Career:** Licensed to practice in all Texas state courts, the United States Supreme Court, the United States Courts of Appeals for the Fifth, Ninth, Tenth and Eleventh Circuits, and the United States District Courts for the Northern, Southern and Western Districts of Texas, Keith argued Group Life and Health Insurance Co. v Royal Drug Co., 440 US 205 before the United States Supreme Court. He was named in The Best Lawyers In America, 1995-present, and a 'Texas Super Lawyer', by Texas Monthly in 2003, 2004 and 2005.

**Personal:** St. Mary's University School of Law, JD, 1971; Texas Tech University, BA, 1966.

## KALTEYER, Ronald
Locke Liddell & Sapp LLP, Dallas
214 740 8000
*Recommended in Tax*

## KAMINSKY, Neal
Porter & Hedges, LLP, Houston
713 226 6000
*Recommended in Banking & Finance*

## KAPLAN, Lee
Smyser Kaplan & Veselka LLP, Houston
713 221 2300
*Recommended in Litigation*

## KATZ, M Marvin
Mayer, Brown, Rowe & Maw LLP, Houston 713 546 0513
mkatz@mayerbrown.com
*Recommended in Real Estate*

**Practice Areas:** Real estate, estate planning, probate, corporate.

**Prof. Memberships:** Admitted in Texas, 1958. US District Court for the Southern District of Texas, 1959. US Court of Appeals for the Fifth Circuit, 1961. US Supreme Court, 1972. American College of Real Estate Lawyers. Real Estate Roundtable. Board Certified, Commercial Real Estate Law, Texas Board of Legal Specialization; former Adjunct Professor of Law, University of Houston School of Law, Real Estate Transfers and Finance; City of Houston Planning Commission from 1980 to present (served as Chairman from 1991-2005 and as Vice-Chairman from 1984-91).

**Career:** Joined Mayer, Brown, Rowe & Maw LLP as Partner, 1989. De Lange, Hudspeth, Pitman & Katz, Houston, 1959-89. United States Air Force, 1955-57.

**Personal:** University of Texas School of Law, LLB with honors, 1959; Order of the Coif; Article Editor, Texas Law Review. Texas A&M University, BBA, 1954. Speaks Spanish.

## KEANE, Jennifer
Baker Botts LLP, Austin
512 322 2594
jennifer.keane@bakerbotts.com
*Recommended in Environment*

**Practice Areas:** Practice focuses on the regulatory aspects of environmental law, particularly Clean Air Act issues. Counsels industrial clients throughout the United States on permitting, enforcement, and compliance matters, and participates in state and federal rulemakings aimed at establishing equitable environmental standards for industry.

**Career:** Admitted to Texas Bar, 1990. Baker Botts Partner since 1999.

**Personal:** JD (with honors), The University of Texas School of Law (1989), Order of the Coif, Phi Delta Phi; MS, BS, BA, University of South Carolina (1986, 1984).

## KEITHLEY, Bradford G
Jones Day, Dallas
214 969 2920
bgkeithley@jonesday.com
*Recommended in Energy*

**Practice Areas:** Matters affecting companies involved in the oil and natural gas industry, particularly upstream and midstream-related litigation and regulation. Responsible also for structuring a number of complex industry-related commercial transactions. For the past five years, engaged primarily in matters related to Alaska (North Slope and Cook Inlet), LNG and US upstream and midstream operations. Appears regularly before federal and state commissions and courts, and speaks frequently on industry matters.

**Prof. Memberships:** ABA; Virginia, District of Columbia and Oklahoma State Bars; RMMLF; Institute for Energy Law (Member, Advisory Board).
**Personal:** University of Virginia (JD, 1976); University of Tulsa (BS, 1973).

### KELLER, Mary
York, Keller & Field, Austin
512 867 1616
*Recommended in Insurance*

### KELLEY, Jay D
Vinson & Elkins LLP, Houston
713 758 4838
jkelley@velaw.com
*Recommended in Energy, Projects*
**Practice Areas:** Commercial practice, with an emphasis on project development and finance in the energy sector, particularly gas-fired and renewable power projects and LNG liquefaction and receiving projects.
**Prof. Memberships:** Member: State Bar of Texas, New York State Bar Association, International Bar Association, and College of the State Bar of Texas.
**Career:** Admitted to practice law in Texas (1985) and New York (1995).
**Personal:** Graduated from The University of Texas, BBA (Accounting) in 1981, and the University of Houston, JD summa cum laude in 1985.

### KELLEY, Kevin
Gardere Wynne Sewell LLP, Dallas
214 999 4503
kkelley@gardere.com
*Recommended in Real Estate*
**Practice Areas:** Financial services, real estate.
**Prof. Memberships:** American Bar Association, State Bar of Texas, Dallas Bar Association, DBA Real Estate Council.
**Career:** Kelley heads Gardere's Real Estate Practice and advises owners, investors, developers, landlords and lenders, both domestic and foreign, on matters relating to resort properties, hotels, golf courses, office and industrial buildings, and retail and multi-family projects. Clients range from Fortune 500 companies, institutional lenders, equity funds and REITS, to private businesses and individuals.
**Personal:** JD, St Mary's University School of Law, 1985; Articles Editor, St Mary's Law Journal; BBA, Texas Christian University, with honors, 1981.

### KELLY, T Mark
Vinson & Elkins LLP, Houston
713 758 4592
mkelly@velaw.com
*Recommended in Corporate/M&A*

**Practice Areas:** Partner and Co-Chair of the firm's Corporate Practice, which focuses on mergers and acquisitions and public and private offerings. Serves as principal outside counsel to several public and private companies in the exploration and production, oilfield service, insurance and manufacturing industries, and also represents a number of major investment banks. Extensive experience in merger and acquisition transactions, representing clients in transactions totaling over $6 billion in the last two years. Has represented clients in over 100 domestic and cross-border debt and equity offerings since 2002.
**Prof. Memberships:** Director, Houston Bar Association; Chairman, Board of Trustees, Houston Lawyer Referral Service; past Chair, Houston Bar Foundation; past President, Houston Young Lawyers Association; past Director, Texas Young Lawyers Association; past Vice-Chair, Center for Hearing and Speech.
**Career:** Joined Vinson & Elkins in May 1981 and admitted to partnership in January 1989. Recognized as one of 12 corporate lawyers in the United States as Dealmaker of the Year for 2003 by a leading legal publication. Also listed: Texas Lawyer 'Go To' Lawyer in corporate law, 2002-05; Texas Monthly's Top 100 Lawyers, 2003-05.
**Personal:** Texas A&M University, BBA, magna cum laude, 1978; Southern Methodist University, JD, 1981. Editor of SMU Law Review.

### KELTNER, David
Jose, Henry, Brantley & Keltner, Fort Worth 817 877 3303
*Recommended in Litigation*

### KENNEDY, John
Vinson & Elkins LLP, Houston
713 758 2550
jkennedy@velaw.com
*Recommended in Energy*
**Practice Areas:** Practice consists primarily of representing oil pipelines in proceedings before the Federal Energy Regulatory Commission and state commissions and appeals from decisions of these commissions and providing regulatory advice to oil pipelines and in connection with acquisitions of oil pipelines.
**Prof. Memberships:** Energy Bar Association; American Bar Association; Houston Bar Association.
**Career:** Admitted to practice: Texas, 1971; United States Supreme Court; US Court of Appeals for the Fifth Circuit; US Court of Appeals for the District of Columbia Circuit.
**Personal:** Graduated from Harvard College, AB cum laude in 1968; Harvard Law School, JD magna cum laude in 1971.

### KEYES, David
Vinson & Elkins LLP, Houston
713 758 2418
dkeyes@velaw.com

*Recommended in Banking & Finance*
**Practice Areas:** Structured, secured and commercial finance; Uniform Commercial Code; Bank-payments systems. Clients include large banks, corporations and clearing-house organizations.
**Prof. Memberships:** ABA, State Bar of Texas, Houston Bar Association (Fellow in each). Chairman of State Bar Business Law Section Legal Opinions Committee.
**Career:** Admitted to Texas Bar in 1968. Joined the firm in 1969 and admitted to Partner in 1975.
**Publications:** Articles on legal opinions, secured transactions, and conflicts of law.
**Personal:** Graduated from Princeton University, 1965 and The University of Texas Law School with high honors, 1968.

### KIMBALL, Albert
Bracewell & Giuliani LLP, Houston
713 223 2900
albert.kimball@bracewellgiuliani.com
*Recommended in Intellectual Property*
**Practice Areas:** Represents US and multinational clients in IP litigation, and in acquiring and transferring rights in IP and technology. Has participated on behalf of an international company entering US operations in the transfer of IP rights required for US operations of a petroleum refinery.
**Prof. Memberships:** Presently serving as elected officer of local IP Bar Association; previously served as Member of Council of the IP Law Section of the American Bar Association.
**Personal:** LLM, The George Washington University Law School, 1972; LLB, The University of Texas at Austin, 1968; BSEE, The University of Texas at Austin, 1962.

### KING, Chad
Hughes & Luce LLP, Dallas
214 939 5500
*Recommended in Technology*

### KINZIE, Jack L
Baker Botts LLP, Dallas
214 953 6727
jack.kinzie@bakerbotts.com
*Recommended in Bankruptcy*
**Practice Areas:** Partner in Charge of Dallas Office; Chair: Bankruptcy Section (firmwide). Represents a diverse range of institutional lenders, asset acquirers, creditors, debtors, officers and directors, and parent companies in virtually every aspect of complex Chapter 11 cases, as well as out-of-court workouts. He has particular experience in prepackaged mass tort bankruptcies.
**Career:** Prior to joining Baker Botts in 1988, he worked for an Oklahoma City law firm and previously served as Adjunct Professor of Oil and Gas Law at Oklahoma City University.
**Personal:** JD, University of Oklahoma College of Law, 1975; BS, Psychology, Oklahoma State University, 1971.

### KIRKLAND, David
Baker Botts LLP, Houston
713 229 1101
david.kirkland@bakerbotts.com
*Recommended in Corporate/M&A*
**Practice Areas:** Chair: Corporate Department (firmwide); Member: Executive Committee. Concentrates on mergers and acquisitions, securities offerings and corporate control and governance issues. Represents parties and investment bankers in mergers and acquisitions, including negotiated acquisitions and dispositions, controlled auctions, tender offers and related financings. Involved in many of the largest mergers in the oilfield service sector and participates in numerous contested takeovers and proxy fights. Represents issuers, underwriters and shareholders in registered public offerings, Rule 144A transactions and private placements.
**Personal:** JD, Yale Law School, 1983; BA, summa cum laude, economics, Yale College, 1980.

### KNOLL, Susan
Howrey LLP, Houston
713 787 1400
*Recommended in Intellectual Property*

### KORBY, Mary
Weil, Gotshal & Manges LLP, Dallas
214 746 7864
mary.korby@weil.com
*Recommended in Corporate/M&A*
**Practice Areas:** Mary Korby's practice focuses on mergers and acquisitions, including complex cross-border public and private transactions. She regularly represents private equity investors in acquisitions, dispositions and public and private debt and equity offerings. She also advises in restructurings and acquisitions relating to companies in bankruptcy. Ms Korby regularly works with the offshore exploration and production, chemicals, aviation and manufacturing industries. She represented Millennium Chemicals in its $3.6 billion stock-for-stock disposition to Lyondell Chemicals, and Enron in the $3 billion disposition of its online energy trading business.
**Personal:** Baylor University, BA, 1965; Southern Methodist University School of Law, JD, 1984.

### KREBS, Arno
Fulbright & Jaworski L.L.P., Houston
713 651 5522
akrebs@fulbright.com
*Recommended in Insurance*
**Practice Areas:** Extracontractual liability and insurance coverage.
**Prof. Memberships:** Listed in a leading legal US publication. Member of the Houston, State Bar of Texas, and the American Board of Trial Advocates.
**Career:** Admitted to Texas Bar (1967). Admitted to the United States Court of Appeals for the Fifth and Eleventh Circuits. Partner in Fulbright & Jaworski

L.L.P.'s Houston office.
**Personal:** Received a BA (1964) from Texas A&M University and an LLB (1967) from the University of Texas.

### KREBS, Stephen
Baker Botts LLP, Houston
713 229 1467
stephen.krebs@bakerbotts.com
*Recommended in Projects*
**Practice Areas:** Practice focuses on infrastructure projects and complex financings. He has broad expertise in project development and capital market, bank, lease, and private placement financings involving power plants, renewables projects, petrochemical and LNG facilities, refineries, rigs, drillships, FPSOs, pipelines, and oil and gas projects.
**Prof. Memberships:** State Bar of Texas; State Bar of Georgia.
**Career:** Head of firm's Project Development and Finance Practice.
**Publications:** Frequent speaker at industry conferences on LNG, gas storage and renewable and other power projects.
**Personal:** JD, cum laude, from the University of Georgia School of Law, 1985; BS from Georgia Institute of Technology, 1978.

### KRIEGER, Paul
Fulbright & Jaworski L.L.P., Houston
713 651 5167
pkrieger@fulbright.com
*Recommended in Intellectual Property*
**Practice Areas:** Intellectual property, litigation, and licensing.
**Prof. Memberships:** Mr Krieger is a Life Fellow of the American Bar Foundation, the Houston Bar Foundation, and the Texas Bar Foundation. He also serves as a Member of the American Bar Association, the American Intellectual Property Law Association, the International Association of Defense Counsel, and the State Bar of Texas.
**Career:** As a Partner in the Houston office of Fulbright & Jaworski L.L.P, Mr Krieger heads the Intellectual Property and Technology Department. He also mentors students at the University of Houston Law Center where he has taught trademark and trade secret law courses for 20 years. Mr Krieger has been recognized by 'Who's Who in American Law', 'Who's Who in America', and 'Who's Who in the World'. His career has centered on litigating and counseling in patent, trademark, copyright and trade secret matters. He has lectured on these topics in the US, Europe, People's Republic of China, South Korea, Republic of China (Taiwan) and India.
**Personal:** BS, University of Pittsburgh (1964); LLB, University of Maryland (1968); LLM, George Washington University (1971). Mr Krieger was admitted to practice law in Maryland (1968) and Texas (1980).

### KRIESER, Jason D
Jones Day, Dallas
214 969 4865
jdkrieser@jonesday.com
*Recommended in Technology*
**Practice Areas:** Represents companies in technology transactions and general corporate matters. These technology transactions include information technology outsourcing, business process outsourcing, licensing, distribution arrangements for software and hardware, joint ventures, strategic alliances, and technology service arrangements. General corporate practice includes mergers and acquisitions and corporate finance matters. He also represents clients in IP asset transfers, evaluations of IP rights portfolios, and in service arrangements relating to mergers and acquisitions. Counsels clients on day-to-day operational issues, such as advice on strategic customer and supplier relationships, privacy issues, data security issues, product distribution channels, software development, and software implementation.

### KRUSE, Layne
Fulbright & Jaworski L.L.P., Houston
713 651 5194
lkruse@fulbright.com
*Recommended in Antitrust*
**Practice Areas:** Antitrust, marketing and trade regulation; securities litigation; international litigation and arbitration; intellectual property litigation; class actions; government investigations and energy.
**Prof. Memberships:** Chair, Fuel and Energy Committee and former Chair, Ethics and Professional Responsibility and Exemption and Immunities Committees, ABA Antitrust Section; Board Certified in Civil Trial Law, Texas Board of Legal Specialization; former Chair, Antitrust and Business Litigation Section, Texas State Bar; former President, Texas Association of Civil Trial Specialists; member of ABA Antitrust and Litigation Sections.
**Career:** Partner since 1986. Former judicial clerk, Chief Judge John Brown, US Court of Appeals, Fifth Circuit. Co-Chair of Fulbright's Antitrust, Marketing and Trade Regulation Practice Group; Member of Firm Policy Committee and Litigation Committee.
**Personal:** JD, Yale Law School (1977); MSc, London School of Economics (1974); BA (Economics), Texas A&M University (1973).

### KUDLAC, Kevin
Weil, Gotshal & Manges LLP, Austin
512 349 1885
kevin.kudlac@weil.com
*Recommended in Intellectual Property*
**Practice Areas:** Kevin Kudlac specializes in litigating patent disputes concerning a wide variety of technologies, particularly those involving complex electrical

and computer-related (both hardware and software) technology. He has handled cases involving operating system software, telecommunications software and hardware, financial transaction software, microprocessors, PC chipsets, computer memory, semiconductor processing technology, analog-to-digital converters and video software. Mr Kudlac has extensive experience with litigating intellectual property matters in Asia and Europe. Prior to becoming an attorney, he was a software engineer at Schlumberger Industries.
**Personal:** University of Dayton, BS, 1987; Georgia State University College of Law, JD, 1991.

### KUHN, Michael
Jackson Walker LLP, Houston
713 752 4200
*Recommended in Real Estate*

### KURYLA, Matthew
Baker Botts LLP, Houston
713 229 1114
matthew.kuryla@bakerbotts.com
*Recommended in Environment*
**Practice Areas:** Environmental regulatory litigation, compliance counseling, project authorization and permitting.
**Prof. Memberships:** State Bar of Texas, Houston Bar Association, Houston Bar Foundation (Fellow), Houston/Galveston Air Quality Leadership Group, Greater Houston Partnership Environment Committee.
**Career:** JD, University of Virginia School of Law (1989), Executive Editor, Virginia Environmental Law Journal, BA (with highest distinction), University of Virginia (1986), Phi Beta Kappa; named a 'Texas Rising Star' by Texas Monthly and Law and Politics Magazine (July 2004).

### KUTZSCHBACH, George
Fulbright & Jaworski L.L.P., Houston
713 651 3702
gkutzschbach@fulbright.com
*Recommended in Energy*
**Practice Areas:** Energy.
**Prof. Memberships:** Houston and American Bar Associations and the State Bar of Texas.
**Career:** He is a Partner in the firm's Houston office and Co-Chairman of the firm's Energy Practice Group. He focuses his practice on domestic and international transactions related to the exploration, acquisition, disposition, development and financing of (and joint venture, operational, transportation and marketing activities concerning) oil, gas, petrochemical and energy properties, pipelines, plants, refineries and other energy assets and companies.
**Personal:** He received a BBA in 1969 and a JD in 1972 from The University of Texas at Austin.

### LADIK, Steven
Jenkens & Gilchrist PC, Dallas
214 855 4500
*Recommended in Immigration*

### LAFOLLETTE, Chris B
Akin Gump Strauss Hauer & Feld LLP, Houston 713 220 5896
clafollette@akingump.com
*Recommended in Corporate/M&A*
**Practice Areas:** Represents issuers and underwriters in public offerings and private placements of equity and debt securities, restructurings and financings, including master limited partnerships, and federal and state securities law matters. Represents clients in public and private M&A and disposition transactions, particularly in the energy industry. Has represented boards of directors in securities-related and corporate governance matters.
**Prof. Memberships:** Sustaining Fellow, Houston Bar Association and former Chair, Corporate Counsel Section; Fellow, Texas Bar Foundation; Director, Houston World Affairs Council; Member, National Association of Corporate Directors (Houston Chapter).
**Personal:** BS (highest honors), University of Texas; JD (honors), Loyola University.

### LAFUZE, William L
Vinson & Elkins LLP, Houston
713 758 2595
blafuze@velaw.com
*Recommended in Intellectual Property*
**Practice Areas:** Practices in most areas of intellectual property law, with emphasis on electronics, oilfield equipment, and computer-related patent litigation.
**Prof. Memberships:** Former Member: Patent Public Advisory Committee, United States Patent and Trademark Office. Past Chair: American Bar Association, Section of Intellectual Property Law. Former President: American Intellectual Property Law Association.
**Career:** Admitted to practice: Texas, 1973. Joined Vinson & Elkins, 1973; admitted to partnership, 1980.
**Publications:** Authored over 100 articles on IP Law.
**Personal:** University of Texas, BS, 1969; Southern Methodist University, MS in Applied Science, 1971; University of Texas School of Law, JD, 1973.

### LANGLOIS, Jack J
Akin Gump Strauss Hauer & Feld LLP, Houston 713 220 5857
jlanglois@akingump.com
*Recommended in Energy*
**Practice Areas:** Focuses on domestic and international energy law. Is experienced in mergers, acquisitions, dispositions and privatizations of assets and stock of energy companies, joint ventures, investments in and financings of energy projects and acquisitions of exploration rights from sovereigns. Also handles acquisitions and dispositions of

interstate natural gas pipelines, gathering systems and other midstream assets, as well as power plants and other downstream assets. Is involved in North America, Russia, Latin America and Europe. **Personal:** BA (honors), University of Southwestern Louisiana; JD, Louisiana State University.

## LAWLESS, J Mark
Nickens Keeton Lawless Farrell & Flack LLP, Austin 512 472 3067
*Recommended in Insurance*

## LEAHY, James
Locke Liddell & Sapp LLP, Houston
713 226 1200
*Recommended in Litigation*

## LECLAIR, Lewis
McKool Smith, Dallas
214 978 4000
lleclair@mckoolsmith.com
*Recommended in Litigation*
**Practice Areas:** Complex commercial litigation for US and international corporations, including intellectual property, partnership agreements, securities, contracts, trade secrets, antitrust, bankruptcy, and patent claims.
**Prof. Memberships:** State Bar of Texas, Dallas Bar Association, Texas Bar Foundation.
**Career:** Principal in Dallas since 1997.
**Personal:** University of Texas School of Law (JD, with honors, 1976); University of Texas (BBA, with honors, 1973).

## LEE, Carl B
Akin Gump Strauss Hauer & Feld LLP, Dallas 214 969 2726
clee@akingump.com
*Recommended in Real Estate*
**Practice Areas:** Chair, firmwide Real Estate and Finance Practice; Chair, firmwide Hospitality practice. Extensive experience in real estate finance, including securitizations, portfolio financings, workouts and restructurings, representing lenders and borrowers. Has handled many significant acquisitions and dispositions of real estate, including large portfolios of office buildings and hotels, and sale/leasebacks.
**Prof. Memberships:** Texas Academy of Real Estate, Probate and Trust Lawyers; Real Estate Council; American, Texas, Dallas Bar Associations (Real Property Sections); Fellow, Texas and Dallas Bar Associations; Past President – Dallas Bar Association Real Property Section.
**Personal:** AB (cum laude), Harvard; JD, University of Chicago (Order of the Coif).

## LEE, James J
Vinson & Elkins LLP, Dallas
214 220 7744
jimlee@velaw.com
*Recommended in Bankruptcy*
**Practice Areas:** Complex commercial and bankruptcy litigation; reorganizations. Board Certified in Civil Trial Law,

Texas Board of Legal Specialization. Litigation experience includes creditors' rights, lender liability, securities fraud, class actions, and business torts. Substantial experience in reorganizations, loan restructures, and workouts. Has litigated a broad range of matters in large, complex bankruptcy cases on behalf of secured lenders, debtors, creditors' committees, and trustees.
**Prof. Memberships:** American Bar Association.
**Career:** Admitted to Texas Bar, 1976. Came to firm as Partner, 2000.
**Personal:** Tulane University, BA, 1973; University of Virginia School of Law, JD, 1976.

## LEE, John
Andrews Kurth LLP, Houston
713 220 4200
*Recommended in Bankruptcy*

## LEE, Judy
Quan, Burdette & Perez, PC, Houston
713 625 9200
*Recommended in Immigration*

## LEE, William S
Fulbright & Jaworski L.L.P., Houston
713 651 5633
wlee@fulbright.com
*Recommended in Tax*
**Practice Areas:** Tax.
**Career:** Bill Lee has been a Partner since 1985 in Fulbright's Houston office. He concentrates his practice on all phases of federal tax controversy, including representation of individual taxpayers, partnerships, estates, and corporations in a wide range of industries before the Appeals Office of the IRS, and in litigation in the United States Tax Court, the Court of Federal Claims, United States District Court, and the Courts of Appeals. He has spoken at programs sponsored by the Tax Executives Institute, the American Bar Association Section of Taxation, the Texas State Bar Association, the Texas Society of Certified Public Accountants, and various tax institutes. Mr Lee served as a faculty member at the week-long program, 'Litigating in the US Tax Court', sponsored by the National Institute for Trial Advocacy. Before joining Fulbright, Mr Lee practiced as a certified public accountant in the Tax Department of the Houston office of Arthur Andersen & Co.
**Personal:** BA – The University of Texas at Austin (1972); LLB – The University of Texas Law School (1975); LLM – Taxation, New York University School of Law (1979).

## LEWIS, Edward
Fulbright & Jaworski L.L.P., Houston
713 651 3760
elewis@fulbright.com
*Recommended in Environment*
**Practice Areas:** Environmental law.
**Prof. Memberships:** State Bar of Texas;

Houston Bar Association; American Bar Association.
**Career:** Admitted to practice law in Texas. Prior to joining the firm, Mr Lewis served as a judicial intern to the Texas Supreme Court Justice Lloyd Doggett.
**Publications:** Contributing author, Texas Environmental Law Handbook (3rd, 4th, and 5th eds); 'Environmental Considerations in the Acquisition of Producing Properties', Oil, Gas and Energy Resources, (Mar 2003); 'Recent EPA Enforcement Initiatives Under the Clean Air Act: The Any Credible Evidence and Compliance Assurance Monitoring Rules', The National Law Journal (April 1998); 'Allocating Environmental Liabilities in Acquisitions', Journal of Corporation Law (Spring 1997); 'Senate Bill No 1126 – Implementing the Qualified Facility Flexibility and the Flexibile Permitting Program', Texas Environmental Law Journal (Summer 1996).
**Personal:** JD, with honors, University of Texas (1992); BS, Texas A & M University (1988).

## LIBERATO, Lynne
Haynes and Boone LLP, Houston
713 547 2000
*Recommended in Litigation*

## LIPE, Guy
Vinson & Elkins LLP, Houston
713 758 1109
glipe@velaw.com
*Recommended in Energy*
**Practice Areas:** Guy engages in a Litigation and Arbitration Practice, primarily representing energy clients, with an emphasis on international matters. He has particular expertise in representing non-US parties sued in the United States, in handling matters involving foreign governments, and in compelling arbitration and enforcing domestic and foreign arbitral awards.
**Prof. Memberships:** Vice-Chair, International Litigation Committee, ABA Section of International Law.
**Career:** Partner since 1991.
**Personal:** Texas A&M University (BBA 1980); University of Texas School of Law (JD 1983).

## LITTLEJOHN, James
Winstead Sechrest & Minick P.C., Dallas
214 745 5400
*Recommended in Banking & Finance*

## LONDA, Jeffrey C
Ogletree, Deakins, Nash, Smoak & Stewart, PC, Houston
713 655 5750
jeffrey.londa@ogletreedeakins.com
*Recommended in Employment*
**Practice Areas:** Labor and employment.
**Prof. Memberships:** Texas Association of Business (Chair, State Employment Relations Committee), American Arbitration Association (Panel of Arbitra-

tors), American Public Transit Association Legal Affairs/13(c) Committee.
**Career:** Listed, The Best Lawyers in America, Fellow, the College of Labor and Employment Lawyers. Adjunct Professor at Thurgood Marshall School of Law, TSU.
**Publications:** Author, 'O'Connor's Texas Employment Codes Plus' (Jones McClure Pub.); author, 'O'Connor's Federal Employment Codes Plus' (Jones McClure Pub.); Executive Editor, Texas Labor Letter (1991-2000).
**Personal:** University of Texas at Austin (BA with honors, 1972), SMU (JD, 1975).

## LOTT, Marley
Baker Botts LLP, Houston
713 229 1666
marley.lott@bakerbotts.com
*Recommended in Real Estate*
**Practice Areas:** Practice focus in commercial real estate transactions, with emphasis on structuring, development, and equity financing. Ms Lott has devoted substantial time to international transactions and to representing sponsors in the formation of funds for real estate investment.
**Prof. Memberships:** Houston Bar Association; American Bar Association, Real Property, Probate and Trust Law Section; Contemporary Arts Museum of Houston, Executive Committee; Hermann Park Conservancy, Executive Committee and Vice-Chairman of Projects.
**Career:** Head of firmwide Real Estate Practice.
**Personal:** JD (cum laude) from Harvard Law School in 1977; BA (with honors) from Hollins College in 1969.

## LOWELL, Cym
Gardere Wynne Sewell LLP, Dallas
214 999 4239
clowell@gardere.com
*Recommended in Tax*
**Practice Areas:** Federal, state and international tax, global projects, tax, transfer pricing.
**Prof. Memberships:** American Bar Association (Taxation Section); ABA Committee on Committees; ABA Committee on the US Tax Problem of Foreign Persons; American Tax Law Institute; ATLI Tax Treaty Advisory Group; ATLI Subchapter C Advisory Group; International Chamber of Commerce (Taxation Committee); International Fiscal Association; US Council of Business (Business and Industry Advisory Council to Organization for Economic Cooperation and Development); Editorial Board (The International Journal of Taxation and Journal of Entity Taxation).
**Career:** Lowell is an international transfer pricing expert who handles a wide range of planning and controversy matters for US and foreign-based multinational companies and wealthy individuals. He also serves as a consultant to leg-

islative bodies, counsels OECD member countries, and leads workshops on the conduct of transfer pricing examinations for national tax authority officials. He has handled transfer pricing cases from $10 million to over $1 billion in proposed adjustments and has structured advance pricing agreements with the US and foreign tax authorities.
**Publications:** Lowell, Cym, 'US International Transfer Pricing' (Boston: Warren Gorham & Lamont, 1998).
**Personal:** JD, Duke Law School, 1972. BS, Indiana University, 1969.

### LUKIN, Mitch
Baker Botts LLP, Houston
713.229.1733
mitch.lukin@bakerbotts.com
*Recommended in Intellectual Property*
**Practice Areas:** Primary expertise in intellectual property litigation, representing both plaintiffs and defendants. Counsels clients on intellectual property asset management, including implementation of protection programs, transaction due diligence, evaluation of intellectual property assets and minimization of litigation risks. Represents clients in licensing and other intellectual property transactions.
**Prof. Memberships:** Houston, Texas and American Bar Associations.
**Personal:** JD, with high honors, University of Houston Law Center, 1982; Bachelor of Electrical Engineering (1972) and MSEE (1976), Georgia Tech.

### LYNCH, John
Howrey LLP, Houston 713 787 1400
*Recommended in Intellectual Property*

### LYONS, J Matthew
Andrews Kurth LLP, Austin
512 320 9200
*Recommended in Technology*

### MALONEY, Marilyn
Liskow & Lewis, Houston
713 651 2900
*Recommended in Banking & Finance*

### MANFORD III, Thomas D
Bracewell & Giuliani LLP, Houston
713 221 1303
tom.manford@bracewellgiuliani.com
*Recommended in Technology*
**Practice Areas:** Emphasizes acquisitions; mergers; private placements of securities; management and leveraged buyout transactions; debt and equity financings; venture capital transactions; and negotiation and preparation of a broad variety of commercial agreements, including preparation of general and limited partnership agreements and limited liability company agreements. Has represented early-stage companies in connection with their organization, structuring and seed and other private financings.
**Career:** Former Chairman, Venture Capital Committee, Business Law Section, State Bar of Texas and former Chairman, MIT Enterprise Forum of Texas.

**Personal:** JD, The University of Texas School of Law, 1970; BA, The University of Texas at Austin, 1966.

### MANNE, Neal
Susman Godfrey LLP, Houston
713 651 9366
*Recommended in Litigation*

### MANTHEY, Ron
Baker & McKenzie, Dallas
214 978 3030
ron.manthey@bakernet.com
*Recommended in Employment*
**Practice Areas:** Employment Litigation and advice and counseling on US employment laws, special emphasis on Class Actions, Discrimination and Civil Rights, employment law torts, privacy, defamation, wage-hour disputes, and unfair competition. Represents management clients in trial and administative proceedings and has successfully argued before numerous Federal Circuit Courts of Appeals.
**Prof. Memberships:** ABA; State Bar of Texas; ABA Subcommittee on Individual Rights and Responsibilities in the Workplace; admitted in 4th, 5th, 10th, and 11th US Circuit Courts of Appeals, and the US Supreme Court.
**Career:** Principal Shareholder of Baker McKenzie, LLP and Head of Labor Section in Dallas (2004 to present); Littler Mendelson and Chair of Class Action group (1992-2004); Jenkens and Gilchrist (1983-92); USAF JAG officer: Chief of the Labor and General Law Division for HQ SAC (1979-83). Mr Manthey has tried nearly 30 cases with an over 95% success rate.
**Publications:** Numerous papers on discrimination laws, class actions, privacy, remedies for employment law claims, electronic discovery, and new common law employment torts for ABA subcommittee and other legal publications.
**Personal:** University of Virginia School of Law (JD; Earle K. Shawe Labor Relations Award 1979); University of Southern Mississippi (BA 1976); spouse: Donna Lewis Manthey; daughters: Katharine and Alison.

### MARCUS, Courtney
Weil, Gotshal & Manges LLP, Dallas
214 746 8127
courtney.marcus@weil.com
*Recommended in Banking & Finance*
**Practice Areas:** Courtney Marcus' practice focuses on corporate finance and restructuring transactions including the representation of borrowers and financial institutions in acquisition financing, asset-based financing, mezzanine and subordinated debt financing, debtor-in-possession financing, real estate financing and restructurings and workouts. Recent matters include acquisitions and other corporate finance transactions for the following clients: Airborne, Inc., Darling International, General Electric Capital

Corporation, Genstar Capital, Hicks, Muse, Tate & Furst, Isola GmbH, Monitor Clipper Partners, Panolam Industries, Providence Equity Partners, Lehman Brothers, Southwest Sports Group, Summit Partners and Thomas H Lee Partners.
**Personal:** Vanderbilt University, BA, 1995; St Mary's University, JD, 1998.

### MARKS, Kenneth
Susman Godfrey LLP, Houston
713 651 9366
*Recommended in Litigation*

### MARSTON, Edgar
Bracewell & Giuliani LLP, Houston
713 221 1315
edgar.marston@bracewellgiuliani.com
*Recommended in Corporate/M&A*
**Practice Areas:** Expertise includes asset acquisitions, business combinations and divestitures, securities offerings and contests for corporate control. Has represented clients in various industries, including oil and gas, cement production, computer manufacturing, telecommunications, biotech, heating and air conditioning manufacturing and retail sales businesses. Has served as counsel to special committees of boards of directors and controlling stockholders in public companies.
**Career:** Recognized in 'Chambers Global' 2003 and 2004.
**Personal:** LLB, The University of Texas School of Law, 1964; BA, Brown University, 1961.

### MARTIN, Brian
Thompson, Coe, Cousins & Irons, LLP, Houston 713 403 8210
*Recommended in Insurance*

### MARTIN, Christopher
Martin, Disiere, Jefferson & Wisdom LLP, Houston 713 632 1700
*Recommended in Insurance*

### MARTIN, Clark
Vinson & Elkins LLP, Houston
713 758 2490
cmartin@velaw.com
*Recommended in Intellectual Property*
**Practice Areas:** Clark practices in all areas of intellectual property law and has represented firm clients in litigation involving such matters as trade secret disputes; contract disputes involving technology; and patent, trademark, and copyright infringement.
**Career:** Partner since 1975.
**Personal:** Louisiana State University, BSEE, 1963; JD, 1966.

### MARTIN, Ernest
Haynes and Boone LLP, Dallas
214 651 5000
*Recommended in Insurance*

### MARTIN, John
Baker Botts LLP, Dallas
214 953 6757
john.martin@bakerbotts.com
*Recommended in Business Process Outsourcing, Technology*

**Practice Areas:** Mergers and acquisitions, corporate finance/securities, outsourcing, and joint ventures. Represents purchasers and sellers in complex M&A transactions, acquisitions, divestitures, leveraged buyouts, and spin-offs. Represents issuers and underwriters in public offerings. Extensive experience with venture capital and private equity fund transactions. Represents industry leaders in wide variety of technology transactions, including complex BPO/ITO outsourcings. Counsels senior management, boards of directors and special committees on corporate governance, disclosure, Sarbanes Oxley and compliance issues. Significant client concentration in technology sector.
**Personal:** JD, with honors, The University of Texas School of Law, 1984; BA, summa cum laude, political science, Baylor University, 1981.

### MARTIN, Neil
Gardere Wynne Sewell LLP, Dallas
713 276 5678
nmartin@gardere.com
*Recommended in Employment*
**Practice Areas:** Employment litigation, labor and employment.
**Prof. Memberships:** American Bar Association; Texas State Bar; Texas Labor and Employment Law Advisory Commission; Houston Bar Foundation.
**Career:** Martin represents employers in labor, civil rights, contract negotiations, non-competition covenants, arbitration, OSHA, wage and hour, age discrimination, ERISA, FMLA and equal credit matters before the US Supreme Court, National Labor Relations Board, EEOC, OSHA, US Department of Labor and other appellate and district courts and agency boards. He is Board Certified in Labor Law by the Texas Board of Legal Specialization.
**Personal:** JD, Baylor Law School, 1967; BBA, Baylor University, 1964.

### MARTIN, Paul
Vinson & Elkins LLP, Dallas
214 220 7875
pmartin@velaw.com
*Recommended in Real Estate*
**Practice Areas:** Experience includes representation of a wide variety of clients engaged in many types of real estate, financing and other business transactions, as well as institutional lenders in the sale of commercial property and the restructuring of existing credit facilities. Experience in commercial leasing, lease disputes, and general corporate representation.
**Prof. Memberships:** American Bar Association; Real Property, Probate, and Trust Section, the Texas Bar Association and the Dallas Bar Association.
**Career:** Admitted to Texas Bar in 1991.
**Personal:** Graduated from Stanford University, BA with highest honors, 1988;

and The University of Texas School of Law, JD with honors, 1991.

## MASLANKA, Michael
Ford & Harrison LLP, Dallas
214 256 4702
mmaslanka@fordharrison.com
*Recommended in Employment*

**Practice Areas:** Mike Maslanka works with employers to simplify their issues; to quickly understand their options; and to effectively manage their workforces. He is Editor of the Texas Employment Law Letter, founded in 1990, and subscribed to by over 1,800 Texas employers. Mike has tried a number of cases to verdict, including four in 2005, on issues ranging from employee raiding to fraudulent inducement, across Texas, and has tried 11 age discrimination cases to verdict as well. He is Board Certified in labor and employment law by the Texas board of legal specialization.

## MASSAD, Stephen A
Baker Botts LLP, Houston
713 229 1475
stephen.massad@bakerbotts.com
*Recommended in Corporate/M&A*

**Practice Areas:** Chair: Houston Corporate Department (1994-2002); Member: Executive Committee (1995-2001). Concentrates practice in general corporate, securities, mergers, acquisitions and joint ventures. Has substantial experience in M&A transactions and related financings, including negotiated acquisitions, tender offers, proxy contests and takeover defense. Much of his practice has involved representing major participants in the restructuring and consolidation of the oil and gas, power and chemicals sectors. Additional areas of emphasis include underwritten public offerings, Rule 144A transactions, and audit committee and other internal investigations.
**Personal:** JD, cum laude, Harvard Law School, 1975; AB, summa cum laude, Princeton University, 1972.

## MATTOX, Sharon
Vinson & Elkins LLP, Houston
713 758 4598
smattox@velaw.com
*Recommended in Environment*

**Practice Areas:** Principal areas of practice are administrative and environmental law. Is a Fellow of the Texas Bar Foundation and is listed in a leading legal US publication in environmental law.
**Career:** Admitted to Texas Bar in 1981. Joined Vinson & Elkins in 1981; admitted to the partnership in 1990.
**Personal:** Graduated from Emporia State University, BA in 1974, The University of Texas, PhD in 1978, and The University of Texas School of Law, JD in 1981 (Order of Barristers, Order of the Coif).

## MAUEL, John G
Pillsbury Winthrop Shaw Pittman LLP, Houston 713 425 7391
john.mauel@pillsburylaw.com
*Recommended in Projects*

**Practice Areas:** Local section leader, Finance Practice. Mr Mauel focuses his practice on domestic and international energy projects, oil and gas transactions, major projects and project finance. His practice encompasses the financing, development, acquisition and sale of domestic and international electric power projects, oil and gas reserves, pipelines, processing plants, LNG receiving and regasification terminals, and LNG tankers. He has worked on energy project bids, developments and financings in the United States and abroad.
**Prof. Memberships:** State Bar of Texas, American Bar Association, Houston Bar Association.
**Personal:** BA, Harvard University,1983 (cum laude); JD, Notre Dame University, 1986.

## MAY, JR, Henry S
Vinson & Elkins LLP, Houston
713 758 2554
hmay@velaw.com
*Recommended in Energy*

**Practice Areas:** Extensive experience in the regulatory, policy and transactional aspects of the natural gas and electric industries. Has represented clients before federal and state agencies and courts, and assisted in the development of energy policy initiatives, and participated in the structuring and negotiation of domestic and international energy transactions.
**Career:** Attended: The University of Texas (BA with honors, 1969); The University of Texas School of Law (JD with honors 1971); Admitted to practice (Texas, 1972; US Supreme Court; Court of Appeals of the District of Columbia; Fifth Circuit and Eleventh Circuit.)

## MCALPINE, Fraser A
Akin Gump Strauss Hauer & Feld LLP, Houston 713 220 8129
fmcalpine@akingump.com
*Recommended in Employment*

**Practice Areas:** Board Certified in Labor and Employment Law, Texas Board of Legal Specialization. Focuses on complex employment disputes involving class actions, collective actions, and claims by former executives and managers involving stock options and other incentive compensation arrangements. Has represented employers in state and federal cases involving employee raiding, misappropriation of trade secrets and restrictive covenants. Handles federal and state court cases alleging discrimination, retaliation and harassment, and federal court litigation alleging violations of ERISA or FLSA.
**Personal:** BA, Colorado College; JD, University of Toledo; Clerk, Woodrow B

Seals, US District Court for the Southern District of Texas.

## MCAUGHAN JR, Robert
Locke Liddell & Sapp LLP, Houston
713 226 1200
*Recommended in Intellectual Property*

## MCCOLLAM, Andrew
Vinson & Elkins LLP, Houston
713 758 1004
DMcCollam@velaw.com
*Recommended in Energy*

**Practice Areas:** Commercial litigation. Drew is a trial lawyer specializing in energy-related matters for plaintiffs and defendants. He has been involved in the resolution of cases and administrative proceedings in Alaska, the District of Columbia, in 10 states in the lower-48, before the US Tax Court, and in the Louisiana and Texas Supreme Courts and the Fifth, Eighth, and Tenth federal circuit courts.
**Prof. Memberships:** ABA; Louisiana State Bar (1983); Texas State Bar (1990).
**Career:** Partner since 1993; Energy Trial Practice in New Orleans, Louisiana, 1983-90.
**Personal:** Louisiana State University (JD, 1983); Washington & Lee University (BA, 1980).

## MCCOMBS, David
Haynes and Boone LLP, Dallas
214 651 5000
*Recommended in Intellectual Property*

## MCCONNELL, Mike
Winstead Sechrest & Minick P.C., Fort Worth 817 420 8200
*Recommended in Bankruptcy*

## MCCORMACK, William A
Fulbright & Jaworski L.L.P., Dallas
214 855 7433
wmccormack@fulbright.com
*Recommended in Corporate/M&A*

**Practice Areas:** Corporate, securities.
**Prof. Memberships:** State Bar of Texas; American Bar Association; District of Columbia Bar Association; Dallas Bar Association.
**Career:** Admitted to practice in Texas. Bill has represented numerous Fortune 500 companies in mergers, acquisitions, divestitures and financings. He also has substantial experience in corporate governance, securities, private equity and international business. He has been recommended by clients and opposing counsel as a leading corporate and securities attorney in many independent 'Best Lawyers' publications.
**Personal:** 1977 – JD, Georgetown University (1977); Certificate, Sorbonne (1974); AB, magna cum laude, St Louis University (1973).

## MCCORMICK, Timothy R
Thompson & Knight LLP, Dallas
214 969 1103
Timothy.Mccormick@tklaw.com

*Recommended in Litigation*

**Practice Areas:** Mr McCormick focuses his litigation practice on corporate governance, securities, shareholder rights, and mergers and acquisitions. He chairs the firm's Securities and Corporate Governance Litigation Group and has been involved in a number of Sarbanes-Oxley internal investigations, as well as investigations under the Foreign Corrupt Practices Act.
**Prof. Memberships:** State Bar of Texas, New York, and DC, American College of Trial Lawyers.
**Personal:** SMU Dedman School of Law (JD, 1975); University of Texas Arlington (BA, 1973).

## MCCOWN, Steven R
Littler Mendelson, PC, Dallas
214 880 8100
smccown@littler.com
*Recommended in Employment*

**Practice Areas:** Focuses on employment discrimination, class action defense, wrongful discharge litigation, traditional labor law, and occupational safety and health law. Defends complex employment law class actions. Nationally recognized for his expertise in defense of employers in proceedings brought under the Occupational Safety and Health Act.
**Prof. Memberships:** Certified in labor and employment law by the State Bar of Texas Board of Legal Specialization; involved in community activities including delivery of pro bono labor and employment legal services to charitable and civic organizations.
**Personal:** Southern Methodist University School of Law (JD, 1975); University of Texas at Austin, (Bachelor's, 1972).

## MCDADE, Thomas
McDade Fogler LLP, Houston
713 654 4300
*Recommended in Energy*

## MCDERMETT JR, Don J
Baker Botts LLP, Dallas
214 953 6454
don.mcdermett@bakerbotts.com
*Recommended in Technology*

**Practice Areas:** Securities, mergers and acquisitions, corporate finance, capital markets, IT/BPO outsourcing. Significant client concentration in the information technology and software industries.
**Prof. Memberships:** ABA, State Bar of Texas, American Society of Corporate Secretaries, Texas Business Law Foundation.
**Publications:** 'Corporate Governance Update', Practising Law Institute/Bowne Seminar, Dallas, December 2005; 'Due Diligence in a Post-Enron World: Accounting Practices Take Center Stage', Texas Lawyer, April 2002;
**Personal:** JD, with honors, University of Texas School of Law, 1984 (Texas Law Review, Order of the Coif); BBA, with high honors, finance, University of Texas 1981.

### MCDONALD, Derek
Baker Botts LLP, Austin
512 322 2667
derek.mcdonald@bakerbotts.com
*Recommended in Environment*
**Practice Areas:** Focuses practice in the areas of environmental law and litigation, concentrating on federal and state permitting and remediation projects.
**Prof. Memberships:** Member, State Bar of Texas; Member, Austin Bar Association.
**Career:** Admitted to Texas Bar in 1993. Joined Baker Botts in 1994; admitted to partnership 2001.
**Personal:** University of Texas, BA, with honors, 1989; JD, with honors, 1992.

### MCDONALD, Scott
Littler Mendelson, PC, Dallas
214 8808100
*Recommended in Employment*
**Practice Areas:** Practice focuses on representing employers in employment and labor law matters including employment contracts, wrongful termination litigation, mandatory arbitration programs, and consulting on litigation prevention. A core member and past Co-Chair of Littler's National Unfair Competition and Trade Secrets Practice Group.
**Prof. Memberships:** Board Certified in Labor and Employment Law by the Texas Board of Legal Specialization. Past Chair, Dallas Bar Association Employment Law Section; serves on committees for ABA; active in Texas Association of Business and the Metro Dallas YMCA.
**Personal:** University of Texas School of Law (JD, 1987); University of Texas at El Paso (BA, 1984).

### MCFALL, Bryant S
Ogletree, Deakins, Nash, Smoak & Stewart, PC, Dallas 214 987 3800
bryant.mcfall@ogletreedeakins.com
*Recommended in Employment*
**Practice Areas:** Labor and employment. Board Certified in labor and employment law by the Texas Board of Legal Specialization.
**Prof. Memberships:** State Bar of Texas (Labor and Employment Section), Dallas Bar Association (Labor and Employment Section), American Inns of Court (William 'Mac' Taylor Chapter).
**Career:** Shareholder since 1998. Admitted in all Texas state and federal courts. Former law clerk to A Joe Fish, Chief Judge, USDC Northern District of Texas. Consistently recognized by Texas Monthly magazine as a 'Texas Super Lawyer' in employment litigation.
**Personal:** Emory University (BA, summa cum laude, 1989), University of Texas (JD, cum laude, 1992).

### MCKELLAR, James W
Thompson & Knight LLP, Dallas
214 969 1605
James.Mckellar@tklaw.com
*Recommended in Banking & Finance*

**Practice Areas:** James W McKellar advises clients in structuring, negotiating, and documenting business transactions with an emphasis on capital markets, energy, and financing transactions. His experience also includes counseling clients in connection with workouts, restructurings, and bankruptcy. He has significant experience in acquisition and buyout financing, venture capital transactions, energy commodity purchases and derivative transactions, and general corporate matters.
**Prof. Memberships:** State Bar of Texas, American College of Investment Counsel, and Texas Association of Bank Counsel.
**Career:** Partner since 1985.
**Personal:** SMU Dedman School of Law (JD, 1978); Southern Methodist University (BS, 1975).

### MCKOOL JR, Mike
McKool Smith, Dallas
214 978 4002
mmckool@mckoolsmith.com
*Recommended in Intellectual Property, Litigation*
**Practice Areas:** Intellectual property litigation for US and international corporations, including patent infringement, patent licensing, and appeals. He also handles complex commercial litigation for a variety of corporations, including major airlines, energy companies, telecommunications firms and investment banking houses.
**Prof. Memberships:** ABA; State Bar of Texas; Dallas Bar Association.
**Career:** Founding Partner and Chairman since 1991.
**Personal:** University of Texas School of Law (JD, with honors, 1974); University of Notre Dame (BA, magna cum laude, 1971); Best Lawyers in Dallas (D Magazine); Best Lawyers in America (2003-04); Texas Super Lawyer (Law and Politics Magazine, 2003-05).

### MCNAMARA, Lawrence
Locke Liddell & Sapp LLP, Dallas
214 740 8000
*Recommended in Employment*

### MCNEIL, Barry
Haynes and Boone LLP, Dallas
214 651 5000
*Recommended in Antitrust*

### MCNIEL, D Ferguson
Vinson & Elkins LLP, Houston
713 758 3882
fmcniel@velaw.com
*Recommended in Litigation*
**Practice Areas:** Represents clients in various types of litigation. Practice concentrates on toxic tort, product liability, professional malpractice, construction, and commercial litigation. Certified: civil trial law and personal injury trial law by Texas Board of Legal Specialization.
**Prof. Memberships:** International Soci-

ety of Barristers; American Board of Trial Advocates; International Association of Defense Counsel; Defense Research Institute; American Bar Association; Texas Association of Defense Counsel; Houston Bar Association. Fellow: Texas Bar Foundation; Houston Bar Foundation.
**Career:** Admitted to practice: Texas, 1980. Joined Vinson & Elkins, 1980; admitted to partnership, 1990.
**Personal:** University of Arkansas, BSBA, 1977; University of Arkansas, JD, 1980.

### MCQUAID, Janet
Fulbright & Jaworski L.L.P., Austin
512 536 2429
jmcquaid@fulbright.com
*Recommended in Environment*
**Practice Areas:** Environmental regulations, water law, contested permits, property and environmental litigation.
**Prof. Memberships:** Ms McQuaid is a Member of the Environmental, Real Estate, Construction, and Administrative Law Sections of the State Bar of Texas and the Travis County Bar Association. She is a Member of the Section on Environment, Energy and Resources, in which she is Co-Vice-Chair of the Water Quality and Wetlands Newsletter, as well as the Construction Law Forum and the Administrative Law Section of the American Bar Association, along with the Texas Water Conservation Association and the Society of Women Engineers.
**Career:** Janet McQuaid, a Partner, joined Fulbright's Austin office in 1992. Prior to attending law school she worked for 11 years for a major oil company, where she designed, built, and operated oil and gas production and oil refining facilities.
**Personal:** BSChE, University of Pittsburgh (1978); MBA, Houston Baptist University (1989); JD, The University of Texas (1992).

### MEADOWS, Charles
Meadows, Owens, Collier, Reed, Cousins & Blau, Dallas 214 7443700
*Recommended in Tax*

### MEADOWS, Robert E
King & Spalding LLP, Houston
713 276 7370
rmeadows@kslaw.com
*Recommended in Energy, Litigation*
**Practice Areas:** Extensive trial experience in general commercial litigation and defense of corporations including oil/gas companies, construction/engineering companies, and product manufacturers in tort litigation. Oil/gas litigation includes lease and royalty disputes, offshore property evaluation and contract disputes arising under operating agreements. Tort litigation includes defense of corporations confronted with multi-plaintiff environmental claims.
**Prof. Memberships:** American Board of Trial Advocates (ABOTA); American College of Trial Lawyers; Connecticut State Bar; Houston Bar Foundation; State Bar

of Texas; Texas Association of Defense Counsel; Texas Supreme Court Advisory Committee.
**Personal:** BA, University of Texas, 1971; JD, University of Houston, Order of the Barons, 1977.

### MEDLOCK, V Bryan
Sidley Austin LLP, Dallas
214 981 3302
bmedlock@sidley.com
*Recommended in Intellectual Property*
**Practice Areas:** V Bryan Medlock, Jr has 35 years of experience trying patent cases. He has served as special master, arbitrator, mediator and expert witness in numerous patent cases.
**Prof. Memberships:** Mr Medlock served as Chairman of the Patent, Trademark and Copyright Law Section of the Texas State Bar, and received the Chairman's Award in 1993. He also served as Chairman of the American Bar Association's Committee on Patent Litigation, Litigation Section. He is a Member of the American Intellectual Property Law Association.
**Publications:** Mr Medlock was a guest lecturer on Trade Secret Law at Southern Methodist University and has served as Chairman of the annual Southwestern Legal Foundation Institute on Patent Law.

### MELO, Thomas M
Ogletree, Deakins, Nash, Smoak & Stewart, PC, Houston 713 655 5752
tom.melo@ogletreedeakins.com
*Recommended in Employment*
**Practice Areas:** Employment discrimination, employment litigation, traditional labor, workplace safety and health, unfair competition, and executive employment.
**Prof. Memberships:** American, Federal, Texas, and Houston Bar Associations, Houston Bar Foundation, Houston Management Lawyers' Forum, Texas Association of Business, Texas Lyceum Association, and Houston Human Resource Management Association.
**Career:** Listed, The Best Lawyers in America; Fellow, College of Labor and Employment Lawyers. Named as a Houston Super Lawyer in 2003 and 2004.
**Publications:** 'Texas Employment Law Handbook' (Editor and chapter author), BNA's Occupational Safety and Health Law (contributing author).
**Personal:** University of Georgia (BBA, 1974), University of Virginia Law School (JD, 1977).

### MENDOZA, Mary
Haynes and Boone LLP, Austin
512 867 8400
*Recommended in Environment*

### MERWIN, Bruce
Haynes and Boone LLP, Houston
713 547 2000
*Recommended in Construction*

### MEYER, Theodore D
Jones Day, Houston
832 239 3616
tdmeyer@jonesday.com
*Recommended in Employment*

**Practice Areas:** Has broad-based, multistate experience in labor and employment law and is Board Certified in labor and employment law by the Texas Board of Legal Specialization. He handles a wide variety of employment litigation, counseling, and training matters, including multiplaintiff cases, discrimination and contract matters, ADA/FMLA/Workers' Comp matters, ERISA litigation, wage and hour litigation, and training and counseling/advice involving all levels throughout organizations. He is a frequent speaker at labor and employment seminars and has been recognized by Texas Lawyer and Texas Monthly as one of the 'Texas Super Lawyers' in labor and employment law.

### MEYERS III, Robert L
Jones Day, Dallas
214 969 4829
rlmeyers@jonesday.com
*Recommended in Construction*

**Practice Areas:** His worldwide practice is concentrated on design, construction, and related transactional areas, and dispute resolution including construction litigation, arbitration, and mediation.
**Prof. Memberships:** ABA; Texas Bar; Dallas Bar. Board member of the Center for American and International Law and chairman of the Research Fellows. Founding member and past President of the American College of Construction Lawyers.
**Publications:** Authored articles and book chapters on various aspects of construction law. Frequent speaker and panelist at the Construction Litigation Superconference, the Global Construction Superconference, the Texas Bar Annual Construction Seminar, and other industry group presentations on construction law and related topics.

### MICCICHE, Daniel J
Akin Gump Strauss Hauer & Feld LLP, Dallas 214 969 2797
dmicciche@akingump.com
*Recommended in Tax*

**Practice Areas:** Has extensive experience in tax and business planning for acquisitions, divestitures and specialized capital structure planning, as well as in the formation and operation of corporations, partnerships and limited liability companies. Also represents clients in federal and state tax controversy matters.
**Prof. Memberships:** Chair, State Taxation Committee of the State Bar of Texas; Appointed by Texas Comptroller of Public Accounts, Carole Keeton Strayhorn, to the Comptroller's Tax Advisory Group; past Chair, Dallas Bar Association Tax Section (2001); past Chair, Corporate

Taxation Committee of the State Bar of Texas (1998-99).
**Personal:** BA, SUNY Stony Brook; JD, University of Chicago.

### MILES, Robin
Bracewell & Giuliani LLP, New York
212 508 6100
*Recommended in Banking & Finance*

**Practice Areas:** Extensive experience in representing lenders and borrowers in bank and capital markets debt transactions, including syndicated loans, secured notes offerings, asset securitizations, structured financings, lease financings, project and acquisition financings, tax-exempt bond financings, private debt placements, restructuring of problem credits, subordinated debt offerings, leveraged buyouts, recapitalizations and hedge arrangements. Major clients include Reliant Energy, Inc., Dynegy Inc., Credit Suisse, and Societe Generale.
**Personal:** JD, The University of Kansas School of Law, 1986. BS, University of Colorado, 1978.

### MILLER, Barry
Vinson & Elkins LLP, Houston
713 758 4438
brmiller@velaw.com
*Recommended in Tax*

**Practice Areas:** Nationally recognized authority on taxation and formation of publicly traded partnerships (MLPs) and royalty trusts. Practice includes all aspects of federal income taxation and state tax (Texas) with emphasis in asset monetization, REITs, natural resource taxation, partnership taxation, and mergers and acquisitions.
**Prof. Memberships:** American Bar Association; Houston Bar Association.
**Career:** Speaker and author: numerous conferences and publications and MLPs, royalty trusts and income taxation.
**Personal:** Graduated from University of Illinois School of Commerce, BS (highest honors), 1967 and University of Illinois School of Law, JD, 1970 (honors).

### MILLER, Ralph I
Weil, Gotshal & Manges LLP, Dallas
214 746 7756
ralph.miller@weil.com
*Recommended in Litigation*

**Practice Areas:** Ralph Miller has had more than 29 years of substantial experience in antitrust law, arbitrations, business tort cases, contract disputes, insurance coverage actions, professional malpractice matters, purchase price disputes, securities class actions, successor liability, and general commercial litigation. He regularly speaks at professional education programs on numerous trial-related topics, such as litigation management, simulation techniques, and courtroom technology. Mr Miller's representative clients include American Airlines, CSFB, Exxon Mobil, and UICI Corp.
**Personal:** University of Texas, BA, 1969;

University of Texas School of Law, JD, 1972.

### MILLER, Walter
Haynes and Boone LLP, Richardson
972 739 6900
*Recommended in Real Estate*

### MILLS, Jerry
Baker Botts LLP, Dallas
214 953 6665
jerry.mills@bakerbotts.com
*Recommended in Intellectual Property*

**Practice Areas:** Chairman of the Baker Botts Intellectual Property Department, which numbers over 115 attorneys. Has extensive experience preparing and prosecuting electronic and software patent applications and designing and managing corporate intellectual property protection programs. Has been involved in complex patent and trademark litigation, including the Texas Instruments DRAM litigation and conducted numerous successful licensing programs for patents involving, for example, voice mail, automated attendant PBX systems, electronic learning aids and semiconductor portfolios. Worked two years as patent examiner in the electronics arts in the USPTO in Washington, DC. Practiced patent, trademark and copyright law in Dallas since 1967.

### MONK, David
Baker Botts LLP, Dallas
214 953 6591
david.monk@bakerbotts.com
*Recommended in Technology*

**Practice Areas:** Technology and business process outsourcing transactions; mergers and acquisitions; corporate securities; venture capital and private equity investments.
**Prof. Memberships:** State Bar of Texas; American Bar Association; Dallas Bar Association; Dallas Association of Young Lawyers.
**Career:** Partner since 2001.
**Publications:** 'Self Contol Issues: Special Concerns of Outsourcing Providers and Customers in Light of Section 404 of the Sarbanes-Oxley Act' (November 2005); 'Sarbanes-Oxley: Effects of the Corporate Governance Statute on Private Companies' (March 2005).
**Personal:** Southern Methodist University School of Law (JD, 1992); Texas A&M University (BBA in Finance, 1989).

### MOODY III, James
Quilling, Selander, Cummiskey & Lownds, P.C., Dallas
214 871 2100
*Recommended in Insurance*

### MOORE, Charles A
LeBoeuf, Lamb, Greene & MacRae LLP, Houston
713 287 2086
cmoore@llgm.com
*Recommended in Energy*

**Practice Areas:** Internationally recog-

nized authority in the field of energy industry regulation and litigation. He has held a number of high-level government positions in this field. In private practice, he has been involved in numerous international and domestic transactions in the energy sector.
**Prof. Memberships:** American Bar Association (Litigation Section); Energy Bar Association; Maritime Law Association of the United States.
**Career:** Joined LeBoeuf in 2002; Chairman, Energy and Converging Industries, Akin, Gump, Strauss, Hauer & Feld, LLP; General Counsel, US Federal Energy Regulatory Commission (1981-83).
**Personal:** University of Houston (JD magna cum laude) 1975; University of Houston (BA) 1972.

### MOORE, Thomas J
LeBoeuf, Lamb, Greene & MacRae LLP, Houston 713 287 2066
tmoore@llgm.com
*Recommended in Energy*

**Practice Areas:** Lead role in national energy mergers and acquisitions practice and international projects practice. Representation of high-profile clients in areas that include mergers and acquisitions and power, pipeline, petrochemical and LNG projects. He has a strong presence in the international arena, leading the firm's representation in client development of foreign investment initiatives and natural gas-based economic expansion.
**Prof. Memberships:** Colorado Bar; Texas Bar.
**Career:** Joined LeBoeuf Lamb in 1994; Faegre & Benson (1974-77, 1979-94); University of Minnesota, Associate Professor of Law (1977-79).
**Personal:** University of Minnesota Law School (JD) 1974; University of California at Berkeley (AB) 1971.

### MOOREFIELD, G Crawford
Akin Gump Strauss Hauer & Feld LLP, Houston 713 220 5884
cmoorefield@akingump.com
*Recommended in Tax*

**Practice Areas:** Practice encompasses all aspects of US federal income tax planning for business transactions, including acquisitions, divestitures and specialized capital structure planning, taxation of partnerships, and limited liability companies, with a particular emphasis on energy and natural resource industries. Extensive experience in the area of publicly traded partnerships, as well as tax issues related to bankruptcy and troubled corporations.
**Prof. Memberships:** State Bar of Texas, Section of Taxation; Houston Bar Association, Taxation Section.
**Personal:** AB (cum laude), Woodrow Wilson School of Public and International Affairs, Princeton University (1984); JD, Harvard Law School (1987).

**MORGAN, Vincent E**
Pillsbury Winthrop Shaw Pittman LLP,
Houston 713 425 7325
vincent.morgan@pillsburylaw.com
*Recommended in Insurance*
**Practice Areas:** Mr Morgan represents
corporate policyholders through litigation and arbitration in a wide range of
insurance coverage matters involving
both first party and third party policies.
As part of his practice, he also advises
clients on insurance and risk management issues before losses occur. Mr Morgan currently serves on the Council of the
State Bar of Texas Insurance Law Section
and as a member of the Editorial Board
of West's 'Insurance Litigation Reporter'.
**Personal:** JD, The University of Texas
School of Law, 2000 (with honors); BA,
Economics and Finance, The University
of Texas at Dallas, 1995 (summa cum
laude).

**MORRISON, Edgar**
Jackson Walker LLP, Dallas
214 953 6000
*Recommended in Healthcare*

**MORRISS, James**
Thompson & Knight LLP, Austin
512 469 6130
James.Morriss@tklaw.com
*Recommended in Environment*
**Practice Areas:** Mr Morriss focuses his
practice on environmental permitting,
compliance counseling, legislative affairs,
and administrative and judicial litigation
before local state and federal environmental agencies and courts. He has extensive
experience in counseling clients in managing environmental risks both in operations and transactions, including the
design and implementation of due diligence and auditing procedures and environmental management systems, and in
the investigation and disclosure of environmental liabilities and contingencies.
**Prof. Memberships:** State Bar of Texas,
Austin and American Bar Associations.
**Career:** Partner since 1982.
**Personal:** University of Texas School of
Law (JD, 1976); Southern Methodist University (BS, 1973).

**MOW JR, Robert**
Hughes & Luce LLP, Dallas
214 939 5500
*Recommended in Litigation*

**MUNCK, William A**
Davis Munck Butrus PC, Dallas
972 628 3630
wamunck@davismunck.com
*Recommended in Intellectual Property*
**Practice Areas:** Domestic and foreign
intellectual property (IP) procurement,
exploitation, enforcement and counseling. Practice focus on development of
market-focused offensive and defensive
IP portfolios in hardware, firmware, software, communications and medical
device industries (pre- and post-FDA

approval). Practice emphasis on long-
range corporate strategies for the domestic and foreign enforcement and defense
of IP rights, rendering legal opinions, IP
licensing negotiation, prosecution of
reexamination proceedings, and counseling on IP issues associated with private
and public financings, mergers, acquisitions and establishing market leadership.
**Prof. Memberships:** State Bar of Texas,
New York State Bar, USPTO, ABA, DBA,
AIPLA, DFW IPLA.
**Career:** Chairman of Davis Munck
Butrus P.C. since 2002; Shareholder since
1997.
**Publications:** Frequent media source for
commentary and analysis on technology-
related legal issues, particularly IP issues
in the fields of hardware, software,
telecommunications, medical devices,
motion pictures and entertainment, and
global convergence of technology.
**Personal:** Hofstra University School of
Law (JD 1992, highest honors, List Distinction), and Hofstra University (MS
Computer Science 1989 – highest honors;
BS Computer Science (Electrical Engineering and Mathematics) 1987).

**MUNSCH, Russell**
Munsch Hardt Kopf & Harr, P. C., Austin
512 391 6104
rmunsch@munsch.com
*Recommended in Bankruptcy*
**Practice Areas:** Reorganization, creditors' rights, corporate finance, bankruptcy, international insolvency and commercial litigation. Represents financial institutions, bank groups and significant
creditors, debtors, and creditors' committees and entities acquiring assets from
troubled organizations. Served as bankruptcy trustee and examiner in both
Chapter 11 and Chapter 7 cases.
**Prof. Memberships:** American Bankruptcy Institute; American Bar Association; State Bar of Texas (Business Bankruptcy Section); Dallas Bar Association;
Travis County Bar Association.
**Career:** Founding Shareholder of Munsch Hardt Kopf & Harr, P.C..
**Publications:** Frequent speaker and
author on various bankruptcy and creditors' rights issues.
**Personal:** University of Houston (JD,
with honors, 1980); The University of
Texas (BA, with honors, 1977).

**MURRAY, Craig**
Vinson & Elkins LLP, Houston
713 758 2008
cmurray@velaw.com
*Recommended in Banking & Finance*
**Practice Areas:** Business transactions,
finance, including structured and project
finance and mergers and acquisitions.
Has extensive experience in complex syndicated bank transactions, representing
either the lenders or the borrower. Has
worked on all aspects of energy finance
and commercial finance.

**Career:** Came to the firm in 1976 and
was admitted to the Partnership in October 1983.
**Personal:** Graduated from Rhodes College, BA in English, 1969 and Louisiana
State University, JD with high honors in
1976. (Order of the Coif; Managing Editor, Louisiana Law Review).

**NASI, Michael**
Lloyd Gosselink Blevins Rochelle &
Townsend, P.C., Austin
512 322 5800
*Recommended in Environment*

**NATION, Floyd**
Howrey LLP, Houston
713 787 1400
*Recommended in Intellectual Property*

**NEEL, James M**
Neel, Hooper & Banes, P.C., Houston
713 629 1800
jneel@neelhooper.com
*Recommended in Employment*
**Practice Areas:** Exclusively represents
management in all phases of labor and
employment matters including union
avoidance training and election campaigns; collective bargaining; arbitration
cases; unfair labor practice trials; claims
of race, age, sex, disability and other types
of employment discrimination under
state and federal civil rights laws; wage
and hour, equal pay and federal contract
claims investigated by government agencies or tried in federal and state courts.
**Personal:** LLB with honors, University of
Texas School of Law, 1962; Texas Law
Review; BA University of Texas, 1960;
Board Certified – Labor and Employment – Texas Board of Legal Specialization, 1975-2010.

**NELIGAN JR, Patrick**
Neligan Tarpley Andrews & Foley LLP,
Dallas 214 840 5300
*Recommended in Bankruptcy*

**NETTLES, Larry**
Vinson & Elkins LLP, Houston
713 758 4586
lnettles@velaw.com
*Recommended in Environment*
**Practice Areas:** Extensive experience in
all areas of environmental law, including
site remediation, facility permitting, civil
and criminal enforcement defense, land
development, environmental due diligence for transactions, and dispute resolution. Has successfully defended clients
in more than three dozen criminal
enforcement proceedings.
**Prof. Memberships:** Life Fellow, Texas
Bar Foundation; Fellow, Houston Bar
Foundation; Founder, Houston Bar Association Environmental Law Section.
**Career:** Admitted to practice, Texas;
Joined V&E, 1981; admitted to partnership, 1990.
**Publications:** 'Conservation and Land
Use Statutes', Texas Environmental Law
Handbook (West 1997).

**Personal:** Rice University, BS Civil Engineering,1978; University of Texas School
of Law, JD with honors, 1981.

**NEWSOME, J Kent**
Fulbright & Jaworski L.L.P., Houston
713 651 3659
kent@fulbright.com
*Recommended in Real Estate*
**Practice Areas:** Commercial real estate,
real estate development, hospital acquisitions and development, entertainment
law, general business law, and internet-
related transactions.
**Prof. Memberships:** Member, Houston
and American Bar Associations and the
State Bar of Texas; Fellow, Houston Bar
Foundation and member of the American College of Real Estate Lawyers; Voting member, National Academy of
Recording Arts and Sciences.
**Career:** Admitted to practice in Texas
(1985). Joined the firm in 1985, is a Partner in Fulbright's Houston office.
**Personal:** BA, cum laude, in 1982 from
Wake Forest University; JD in 1985 from
Vanderbilt University.

**NICHOLS, Eric**
Beck, Redden & Secrest LLP, Houston
713 951 3700
*Recommended in Litigation*

**NIEBRUEGGE, Michael E**
Mayer, Brown & Maw LLP,
Houston 713 546 0507
mniebruegge@mayerbrownrowe.com
*Recommended in Banking & Finance*
**Practice Areas:** Represents lenders and
arrangers in negotiating and documenting
secured lending and securitization agreements with corporations, general partnerships, limited partnerships, individuals,
and trusts engaged in energy, mining,
transportation and manufacturing. Represents creditors in negotiating and documenting debt restructurings; disputes with
other creditors and debtors. Represents oil
and gas producers in a variety of onshore
matters. Represents corporations engaged
principally in service businesses and
extractive businesses on acquisitions and
general corporate matters.
**Prof. Memberships:** State Bar of Texas.
Texas Association of Bank Counsel.
Admitted in Texas, 1981. Illinois, 1977.
US District Court for the Southern Dis-
trict of Texas, 1988. US District Court for
the Northern District of Illinois, 1977.
**Career:** Joined Mayer, Brown, Rowe &
Maw LLP, 1982; became Partner, 1984.
Partner-in-charge of Houston office,
1995 to date. Formerly with Gulf Coast
Royalty Co., Vice President and General
Counsel, Houston, 1981-82. Mayer,
Brown, Rowe & Maw LLP, Chicago, 1977-
81. Northwestern University, Lecturer in
Business Law, Chicago, 1979-80.
**Personal:** Cornell University, JD, 1977;
Note and Comment Editor, Cornell Law
Review. Harvard College, AB, cum laude,
1974.

**NONDORF, Kurt**
Jackson Walker LLP, Dallas
214 953 6000
*Recommended in Real Estate*

**NORRIS, John**
Howrey LLP, Houston
713 787 1400
*Recommended in Intellectual Property*

**O'DONNELL, Laura**
Haynes and Boone LLP, San Antonio
210 978 7000
*Recommended in Employment*

**OELMAN, David**
Vinson & Elkins LLP, Houston
713 758 3708
doelman@velaw.com
*Recommended in Corporate/M&A*
**Practice Areas:** Focuses on corporate
and securities transactions, including
representation of public and private
companies and investment banking
firms; advising boards on corporate governance matters; public offerings and private placements of equity and debt; publicly traded limited partnerships and limited liability companies; mergers and
acquisitions; venture capital and private
equity investments; issuance of high yield
debt securities; redemptions and
exchanges of preferred equity and debt.
**Career:** Admitted to Texas Bar in 1991.
Joined the firm as a Partner in 2000.
**Personal:** Graduated from Princeton
University, Woodrow Wilson School of
Public and International Affairs, BA
(summa cum laude, Phi Beta Kappa),
1987; The University of Texas School of
Law, JD (Chancellors, Order of the Coif),
1990.

**OLDHAM, Dudley**
Fulbright & Jaworski L.L.P., Houston
713 651 5397
doldham@fulbright.com
*Recommended in Litigation*
**Practice Areas:** Complex commercial
and business litigation.
**Prof. Memberships:** Fellow, the American College of Trial Lawyers; the Ameri-
can Board of Trial Advocates; Former
Chair, the American Bar Association
Standing Committee on Independence of
the Judiciary, the ABA Standing Commit-
tee on Federal Judicial relations; the Advi-
sory Council of the National Judicial Col-
lege; Chairman of the Board and past
President, the Federation of Defense and
Corporate Counsel, one of the three
major defense trial organizations in the
United States; Board of the Defense
Research Institute; and President,
Lawyers for Civil Justice, a national orga-
nization of corporations and corporate
counsel.
**Career:** Senior Partner. Resident in the
Houston office. Member firm's Executive
Committee over 25 years and former
Chairman, firm's Litigation Management
Committee. Practice consists of complex

litigation primarily in the areas of energy,
intellectual property, commercial and
business litigation, class actions, arbitration, securities, insurance disputes and
mass torts. Certified mediator and arbitrator, member of the AAA Texas Large
Complex Case Panel and CPR.
**Personal:** BA, the University of Texas
(1964); JD, UT School of Law (1966).
Admitted in Texas (1966), the US
Supreme Court, all US District Courts in
Texas and the US Courts of Appeals for
the Third, Fifth and Eleventh Circuits.

**O'LEARY, Michael**
Andrews Kurth LLP, Houston
713 220 4200
*Recommended in Corporate/M&A*

**OLIVER III, Rufus W**
Baker Botts LLP, Houston
713 229 1366
Rufus.oliver@bakerbotts.com
*Recommended in Antitrust*
**Practice Areas:** Concentrates on
antitrust law, with extensive experience in
class action and other complex litigation
and in government review of mergers
and acquisitions. Matters involving a
variety of industries including steel; oil
and gas; petrochemicals; offshore drilling
and other oilfield services; automotive
products; electric utilities; airlines; pharmaceuticals; data processing.
**Career:** Chairs firm's Antitrust Section.
Has served in leadership positions in
American and Houston Bar Associations
and State Bar of Texas.
**Personal:** JD, honors, The University of
Texas School of Law, 1972; Research Editor, Texas Law Review; Phi Delta Phi; BA,
high honors, Plan II, The University of
Texas, 1969.

**O'NEIL, Holland**
Gardere Wynne Sewell LLP, Dallas
214 999 4961
honeil@gardere.com
*Recommended in Bankruptcy*
**Practice Areas:** Bankruptcy, financial
services.
**Prof. Memberships:** State Bar of Texas;
State Bar of Arizona; Texas Turnaround
Management Association; Dallas Bar
Association; American Bar Association;
American Bankruptcy Institute.
**Career:** Holly O'Neil's practice focuses
on complex bankruptcies, workouts, purchases of distressed assets and debt, and
bankruptcy litigation. In her 19 years of
practice, Ms O'Neil's clients have included debtors-in-possession, creditors' committees, secured creditors, trustees, examiners, as well as those who wish to acquire
assets from troubled companies. Ms
O'Neil has been recognized by Chambers
in 2004-06, has been recognized among
2006's 'The Best Lawyers in America', has
been named as a 'Texas Super Lawyer' by
Law and Politics magazine for 2003-05,
and 'The Best Lawyers in Dallas' by D
Magazine in 2005.

**Personal:** JD, Texas Tech University
School of Law, 1987; BBA-Finance, University of Texas at Austin, 1983.

**OSTERBERG, Edward**
Vinson & Elkins LLP, Houston
713 758 2192
eosterberg@velaw.com
*Recommended in Tax*
**Practice Areas:** Federal income taxation
with emphasis on international transac-
tions, mergers and acquisitions, and part-
nerships and joint ventures.
**Prof. Memberships:** Vice-President,
International Fiscal Association USA
Branch; President, International Tax
Forum of Houston.
**Publications:** 'Using the Brown Group
Regulations to Minimize Subpart F
Income', Journal of Taxation of Global
Transactions, Summer 2003; 'Basic US
Tax Considerations in Buying or Selling a
Non-US Business', Tax Notes, June 2,
2003; 'International Joint Ventures: Basis
Tax Goals and Structures', Tax Notes,
April 23, 2001.
**Personal:** BA, JD cum laude, Northwest-
ern University; LLM in Taxation, South-
ern Methodist University.

**OXFORD, Terrell**
Susman Godfrey LLP, Dallas
214 754 1900
*Recommended in Antitrust*

**PARIS, Theodore W**
Baker Botts LLP, Houston
713 229 1838
ted.paris@bakerbotts.com
*Recommended in Corporate/M&A*
**Practice Areas:** Deputy Department
Head: Corporate (Houston). Mergers,
acquisitions, securities offerings, corporate control and governance issues and
joint ventures. Represents parties in
negotiated acquisitions and dispositions,
controlled auctions, tender offers and
related financings. Also represents
domestic and foreign issuers, underwriters and selling shareholders in public
offerings and in Rule 144A transactions
and other private placements. Substantial
experience in a wide variety of industries,
including oil and gas, oilfield services,
shipping, manufacturing, industrial services and consumer products and services.
**Personal:** JD with honors, The University of Texas School of Law, 1988; MBA
and BBA-Accounting, Texas A&M University – Corpus Christi, 1983.

**PARKER, Dallas**
Thompson & Knight LLP, Houston
713 951 5800
Dallas.Parker@tklaw.com
*Recommended in Technology*
**Practice Areas:** Mr Parker is the leader
of the firm's International Practice. He
represents clients in corporate and securities law matters, with extensive experience in the areas of mergers, acquisitions,

takeovers, proxy contests, public and private offerings of equity and debt securities, corporate governance, independent
committees, and related matters. Mr
Parker represents US-based clients wishing to do business around the globe, as
well as international clients wishing to
conduct business in the United States.
**Prof. Memberships:** State Bar of Texas,
Houston, Texas, and American Bar Associations.
**Personal:** University of Texas School of
Law (JD, 1972); Vanderbilt University
(BA, 1969).

**PARKER, David**
Fulbright & Jaworski L.L.P., Austin
512 536 3055
dparker@fulbright.com
*Recommended in Intellectual Property*
**Practice Areas:** Litigation, prosecution,
licensing, and biotechnology.
**Prof. Memberships:** Member of the
American Bar Association, the American
Intellectual Property Law Association, the
Austin Intellectual Property Law Associa-
tion, the Travis County Bar Association
and the Association of the University
Technology Managers.
**Career:** Dr David Parker is Head of the
Intellectual Property and Technology
Group in the firm's Austin office. In addi-
tion to his law practice, he serves as the
Vice President of Intellectual Property for
Introgen Therapeutics, a gene therapy
company involved in clinical trials of
genetic based anti-cancer therapies. Dr
Parker is admitted to the US Court of
Appeals for the Federal Circuit, the US
Supreme Court, and the US Patent and
Trademark Office.
**Personal:** JD, The University of Texas
(1986); PhD, Molecular Pharmacology
and Genetic Engineering, Baylor College
of Medicine (1981); BA, The University
of Texas (1976).

**PARKER, Emily A**
Thompson & Knight LLP, Dallas
214 969 1502
Emily.Parker@tklaw.com
*Recommended in Tax*
**Practice Areas:** Emily A Parker represents taxpayers in IRS audits and appeals
proceedings, state tax audits and hearings, and federal and state tax refund and
deficiency litigation. She also advises on
federal income tax and Texas franchise
tax planning, with special expertise in
taxation of natural resources and partnership and corporate transactions
involving the petroleum industry. Ms
Parker was previously Acting Chief
Counsel and Deputy Chief Counsel for
the IRS. She is Board Certified in Tax Law
by the Texas Board of Legal Specialization.
**Personal:** SMU Dedman School of Law
(JD, 1973); Stephen F. Austin State (BA,
1970).

## PARSONS, Paul
Paul Parsons PC, Austin
512 477 7887
*Recommended in Immigration*

## PARTRIDGE, Scott
Baker Botts LLP, Houston
713 229 1569
scott.partridge@bakerbotts.com
*Recommended in Intellectual Property*
**Practice Areas:** Chairs Houston Office Intellectual Property Department. Expertise in litigation and counseling involving patents, trade secrets, copyrights, trademarks and unfair competition. Represented clients in bench and jury trials in federal and state courts throughout the US and before International Trade Commission.
**Prof. Memberships:** American Bar Association, House of Delegates; past Chair, Science and Technology Section; Section Officers Conference, Executive Committee. International Trade Commission Trial Lawyers Association, Executive Council and past President. Admitted in DC, Virginia, Texas. Frequent lecturer on IP law in US and internationally.
**Personal:** JD, Georgetown University, 1974; BS, electrical engineering, University of Cincinnati, 1969.

## PATE, Stephen
Fulbright & Jaworski L.L.P., Houston
713 651 5132
spate@fulbright.com
*Recommended in Insurance*
**Practice Areas:** First-party insurance, commercial insurance, coverage, extra-contractual and bad faith litigation, and construction litigation.
**Prof. Memberships:** Pate is a Member of the American Board of Trial Advocates and a Faculty Member of The Litigation Management College. He is a past Chair of the Property Insurance Committee of the TIPS Section of the ABA. He is also a past Chair of the Property Insurance Section of the Federation of Defense and Corporate Counsel. The Federation of Defense and Corporate Counsel awarded him the prestigious 2004 John S Appleman Award. Pate has served as Director of both the Texas and Houston Young Lawyers Associations. He is a Fellow of the Texas and Houston Bar Foundations.
**Career:** Pate has been a Partner in the Houston office of Fulbright since 1994. He appears in 'Who's Who in America', 'Who's Who in American Law', 'Who's Who in the South and Southwest', and 'Who's Who in the World'.
**Publications:** Pate is a frequent speaker at seminars on bad faith and property insurance issues. He has spoken before the DRI, ABA, Mealy's and other groups. He has authored several articles and books. He is an Editor of the Bad Faith Litigation Reporter and has co-authored 'Toxic Mold Litigation' (Lawyers and Judges Publishing Co. 2005) and 'Law

and Practice of Insurance Covered Litigations' (2000).
**Personal:** Pate received his BA, magna cum laude, in 1980 from Vanderbilt University, and his JD, from Vanderbilt in 1983. He was admitted to practice law in Texas in 1984. He is a member of Phi Beta Kappa.

## PATRICK, Kathy
Gibbs & Bruns, LLP, Houston
713 650 8805
kpatrick@gibbs-bruns.com
*Recommended in Litigation*
**Practice Areas:** Ms Patrick's practice is in commercial litigation, large-scale securities litigation, and securities arbitration on both sides of the docket. She represents institutional investors, governmental entities, banks and mutual funds in actions to recover their capital. She also represents investment management firms in the defense of investor complaints, and corporate directors in the defense of litigation and investigations arising from some of the most notable corporate collapses in history.
**Prof. Memberships:** Admitted to practice, Texas and District of Columbia, 1985. Also admitted to practice in various federal trial and appellate courts. Member, Texas, American, and Houston Bar Associations.
**Career:** Ms Patrick received her law degree from Harvard Law School in 1985. She served as a law clerk to the Hon John R Brown, United States Court of Appeals for the Fifth Circuit, from 1985-86. She then joined the predecessor firm to Gibbs & Bruns, LLP, and has practiced with the firm for the past 20 years. She was made a Partner in the firm in 1991. Ms Patrick has spoken at seminars and symposia throughout the United States on topics such as the cross-examination of experts, pretrial discovery, damage models, liability under the securities laws, and class actions.
**Publications:** Author, 'The Liability of Lawyers for Fraud Under the Federal and State Securities Laws', 34 St. Mary's L. J. 915 (2003); 'Private Securities Litigation Reform Act: Ease Burden on Plaintiffs', National Law Journal, June 20, 2005.
**Personal:** Born 1960. BA with highest honors, University of Texas at El Paso, 1982 (Major: Soviet and East European Studies); JD Harvard Law School, 1985. Legal Methods Instructor, Harvard Law School. Married, with two children.

## PATTERSON, Nancy
Baker & Hostetler LLP, Houston
713 751 1600
*Recommended in Employment*

## PATTERSON, JR, J A 'Tony'
Fulbright & Jaworski L.L.P., Dallas
214 855 8036
japatterson@fulbright.com
*Recommended in Healthcare*
**Practice Areas:** Health law and business

organizations.
**Prof. Memberships:** Mr Patterson is an Adjunct Professor at the University of Iowa College of Law, and a former Adjunct Professor at the Southern Methodist Univeristy Law School. He is also a Member of the Health Law Section of the State Bar of Texas and American Bar Assocaiton and is the Chair of the American Bar Association Health Law Section and is currently Chair of the American Bar Association Officers Conference Section.
**Career:** Having been a Partner in the Dallas office of Fulbright & Jaworski L.L.P since 1988, Tony Patterson heads the firm's Health Law Practice in Dallas. He is certified in Health Law by the Texas Board of Legal Specialization.
**Personal:** BA, Coe College (1970); JD, cum laude, Southern Methodist University (1973). Mr Patterson has served as a Trustee for Coe College since 1974. He is also involved with the Dallas-Fort Worth Health Industry Council and other industry and civic associations.

## PATTON, David
Locke Liddell & Sapp LLP, Houston
713 226 1200
*Recommended in Energy*

## PEARSON, John R
Gardere Wynne Sewell LLP, Houston
713 276 5782
jpearson@gardere.com
*Recommended in Insurance*
**Practice Areas:** Insurance, oil and gas litigation, commercial litigation and arbitration, personal injury defense, trial.
**Prof. Memberships:** State Bar of Texas.
**Career:** John Pearson is a litigator with over 35 years' experience handling commercial disputes, including maritime and oilfield matters and insurance coverage. Mr Pearson represents policyholders and brokers in insurance litigation and arbitration. Mr Pearson represents several oil field service companies. Mr Pearson also handles a wide variety of maritime disputes, including charter party disputes, maritime liens, personal injury/death, and indemnity.
**Personal:** JD, University of Texas School of Law, 1968; BE, Chemical Engineering, Vanderbilt University, 1965.

## PECHT, Gerald
Fulbright & Jaworski L.L.P., Houston
713 651 5243
gpecht@fulbright.com
*Recommended in Energy*
**Practice Areas:** Energy, business, and international litigation; class actions and intellectual property.
**Prof. Memberships:** Mr Pecht is a Member of both the Houston and the American Bar Associations, and is a Fellow of the Texas Bar Foundation and and a Life Fellow of the Houston Bar Association. He is a Council Member of the Antitrust and Business Litigation Section of the

State Bar of Texas.
**Career:** Gerry Pecht, a Partner in Fulbright & Jaworski L.L.P.'s Houston office, practices in the firm's Litigation Section. He regularly represents investment banking firms, energy companies, healthcare institutions, broker dealers, and numerous other types of companies, individuals, and institutions. Mr Pecht was named as a 'Texas Super Lawyer' in business litigation law in the November 2003 issue of Texas Monthly.
**Personal:** Mr Pecht received a BA from Georgetown University in 1975 and a JD, with honors, from the University of Cincinnati in 1978.

## PEDEN, David
Porter & Hedges, LLP, Houston
713 226 6000
*Recommended in Construction*

## PEDERSEN, Luke
Baker Botts LLP, Dallas
214 953 6655
luke.pedersen@bakerbotts.com
*Recommended in Intellectual Property*
**Practice Areas:** Intellectual property law with an emphasis on patent prosecution, litigation, technology transfers, and licensing involving complex and emerging technologies. Develops and monitors comprehensive intellectual property protection programs that allow organizations to identify, protect, manage and exploit intellectual property assets. Significant patent prosecution experience with various technologies including telecommunications, Internet infrastructure, software, oil and gas production, and medical equipment. Counsels clients regarding priority of invention and initiation of interference proceedings. Drafts and negotiates license and technology transfer agreements. Litigation experience includes misappropriation of trade secrets, patent infringement, and breach of agreements governing intellectual property assets.

## PELS, Gerald
Locke Liddell & Sapp LLP, Houston
713 226 1200
*Recommended in Environment*

## PEREZ, Alfredo R
Weil, Gotshal & Manges LLP, Houston
713 546 5040
alfredo.perez@weil.com
*Recommended in Bankruptcy*
**Practice Areas:** Alfredo Pérez has practiced in the areas of business reorganizations, debtors' and creditors' rights and insolvency since 1980. He concentrates his practice in the representation of Chapter 11 debtors and other diverse claimants, including secured creditors and committees in all aspects of corporate restructurings, formal bankruptcy proceedings and out-of-court workouts. He has also represented statutory and ad hoc bondholder committees, agent banks

in syndicated credit transactions, secured and unsecured creditors, as well as litigants, in adversary proceedings involving alleged preferences, fraudulent conveyances and other avoidance claims. **Personal:** Haverford College, BA, 1977; University of Chicago Law School, JD, 1980.

## PERICH, Thomas
Andrews Kurth LLP, Houston
713 225 7000
*Recommended in Banking & Finance*

## PETERMAN, David
Fulbright & Jaworski L.L.P., Houston
713 651 3635
dpeterman@fulbright.com
*Recommended in Technology*
**Practice Areas:** Corporate, securities and transactions.
**Prof. Memberships:** Mr Peterman is a Member of the Texas and Houston Bar Associations.
**Career:** Mr Peterman has successfully represented clients in numerous corporate, securities and business law matters. He joined Fulbright & Jaworski as a Partner in 2003. His experience includes representing a broad range of domestic and international buyers, sellers, issuers, underwriters and investors in a number of substantial acquisitions and corporate finance transactions, including acquisitions and dispositions of stock, assets and business divisions, and public and private securities transactions. He has represented clients in industries including energy, telecom, automobile, technology, hospitality and staffing.
**Personal:** 1982 – BBA, Finance, the University of Texas-Austin; 1985 – JD, with honors, the University of Texas School of Law, Austin.

## PETERSON, Edward
Winstead Sechrest & Minick P.C., Dallas
214 745 5400
*Recommended in Real Estate*

## PFEIFFER, Philip J
Fulbright & Jaworski L.L.P., San Antonio
210 270 7117
ppfeiffer@fulbright.com
*Recommended in Employment*
**Practice Areas:** Labor and employment law.
**Prof. Memberships:** Mr Pfeiffer is a Member of the San Antonio Bar Association, the San Antonio Bar Foundation and the Texas Bar Foundation; and a Member of the American Bar Association's Equal Employment Opportunity Committee. He served as Co-Chair of the ABA's EEO Liaison Committee for the South Texas area. He also served as Editor-in-Chief of the Second Supplement to Lindemann and Grossman, Employment Discrimination Law. He has been elected by his peers to membership in the College of Labor and Employment Lawyers.

**Career:** Mr Pfeiffer focuses his legal practice on labor and employment matters, with particular emphasis on complex civil rights and employment discrimination cases; employment torts, including wrongful discharge and defamation; alternative dispute resolution, including arbitration programs; employment contracts, including restrictive covenants; and Employment Retirement Income Security Act litigation. In addition, Mr Pfeiffer has with increasing frequency, served as a mediator in employment and civil rights cases, including class actions and has completed the approved mediator training program of the A.A. White Dispute Resolution Institute.
**Personal:** Mr Pfeiffer received a BS in 1969 from Sam Houston State University and a JD in 1972 from Southern Methodist University.

## PHELAN, Robin
Haynes and Boone LLP, Dallas
214 651 5000
*Recommended in Bankruptcy*

## PHELAN, Rod
Baker Botts LLP, Dallas
214 953 6609
rod.phelan@bakerbotts.com
*Recommended in Litigation*
**Practice Areas:** Commercial litigation, primarily defending claims of professional malpractice (against accountants, lawyers, architects, and engineers), representing parties on both sides of cases involving oil and gas, partnerships, intellectual property, antitrust, securities, tax and corporate governance. Clients are professional service firms, national and local business entities, and their principals.
**Career:** 30+ years of experience. Member, American College of Trial Lawyers, International Academy of Trial Lawyers, American Board of Trial Advocates.
**Personal:** JD, cum laude, Duke University School of Law, 1973; Order of the Coif; Editorial Board, Duke Law Journal; BA, cum laude, Vanderbilt University, 1970.

## PHILLIPS, Frances
Gardere Wynne Sewell LLP, Dallas
214 999 3000
*Recommended in Environment*

## PHILLIPS, Thomas R
Baker Botts LLP, Austin
512 322 2565
tom.phillips@bakerbotts.com
*Recommended in Litigation*
**Practice Areas:** General litigation, appellate and alternate dispute resolution.
**Prof. Memberships:** Board Certified Trial Law; American Law Institute; CPR Texas Panel of Distinguished Neutrals; Conference of Chief Justices.
**Career:** State District Judge, 1981-88; Chief Justice, Supreme Court of Texas,

1988-2004; Visiting Professor, South Texas College of Law, Houston, 2004; SMU School of Law, Dallas, 2004-05.
**Publications:** 'The Constitutional Right to a Remedy', 78 N.Y.U. L.Rev. 1309 (2003); 'State Supreme Courts: Local courts in a Global World', 38 Tex. Int'l L.J. 557 (2003); 'Electoral Accountability and Judicial Independence', 64 Ohio State L.J. 137 (2003).
**Personal:** BA, Baylor 1971; JD, Harvard, 1974.

## PINKERTON, Glenn
Vinson & Elkins LLP, Houston
713 758 2701
gpinkerton@velaw.com
*Recommended in Projects*
**Practice Areas:** Member of the firm's Private Equity Practice Group, Project Finance and Development Practice Group, and International Practice Group. Has extensive experience in mergers and acquisitions, project development and finance, and international transactions.
**Career:** Admitted to Texas Bar, 1986. Came to the firm, 1986 and was admitted to the partnership, January 1995.
**Personal:** Graduated from The University of Texas at Austin, BBA in 1981, and Columbia University, JD in 1986.

## PIRKEY, Louis
Fulbright & Jaworski L.L.P., Austin
512 536 3001
lpirkey@fulbright.com
*Recommended in Intellectual Property*
**Practice Areas:** Trademark litigation and counseling.
**Prof. Memberships:** Past President of the American Intellectual Property Law Association, past Chairman of the Intellectual Property Law Section of the State Bar of Texas, and was the charter President of the Austin Intellectual Property Law Association.
**Career:** Represented clients in over 300 trademark and unfair competition litigations in federal district and appellate courts across the country.
**Personal:** Received a BSChE (1960) from The University of Texas at Austin and a JD, with honors, (1964) from The George Washington University Law School.

## POFF, Joe
Baker Botts LLP, Houston
713 229 1410
joe.poff@bakerbotts.com
*Recommended in Corporate/M&A*
**Practice Areas:** Corporate finance, securities, and mergers and acquisitions, especially in energy and telecommunications. Handles US and international M&As and represents US and non-US issuers, underwriters, and investment banking firms in public, private, Rule 144A, and Regulation S offerings, as well as specialized financings including offerings of American Depositary Receipts, interests in master limited partnerships and trust preferred securities. Counsels

clients in financings, general corporate matters and corporate governance issues and special investigations.
**Personal:** JD, with high honors, The University of Texas School of Law, 1979; BS, summa cum laude, economics, Texas A&M University, 1976.

## POWELL, Charles
Haynes and Boone LLP, Houston
713 547 2000
*Recommended in Technology*

## POWELL, Michael
Locke Liddell & Sapp LLP, Dallas
214 740 8000
*Recommended in Litigation*

## POWERS, Werner
Haynes and Boone LLP, Dallas
214 651 5000
*Recommended in Insurance*

## PRATT, Donald
Pratt & Sanderford, Temple
254 773 8311
*Recommended in Construction*

## PUIG, Yvonne Karen
Fulbright & Jaworski L.L.P., Austin
512 474 5201
ypuig@fulbright.com
*Recommended in Healthcare*
**Practice Areas:** Health law.
**Prof. Memberships:** Ms Puig is currently a Council Member and past Chair of the Health Law Section of the State Bar of Texas. She is also a member of the American Board of Trial Advocates, the American Health Lawyers Association, and the Texas Association of Defense Counsel.
**Career:** Yvonne Puig joined the Austin office of Fulbright as a Partner with over 24 years of experience. She has extensive experience in a variety of health law regulatory matters, such as EMTALA, JCAHO accreditation, credentialing, and due process hearings.
**Personal:** BA, high honors, University of Texas (1975); JD, University of Texas School of Law (1978). Ms Puig was admitted to practice in Texas in (1978).

## PUTMAN, Frank
Gardere Wynne Sewell LLP, Houston
713 276 5777
fputman@gardere.com
*Recommended in Technology*
**Practice Areas:** Corporate, securities, M&A, energy and energy services, global projects.
**Prof. Memberships:** American Bar Association; State Bar of Texas; Houston Bar Association.
**Career:** Over the last 30 years, Frank Putman has developed a comprehensive national and international business practice focusing on corporate and securities work and general business matters. He also offers a particular expertise in energy-related companies, financial institutions and manufacturing companies. Earlier in his career, Mr Putman pio-

neered the development and implementation of creative financing strategies utilizing investment tax credits in public and private partnerships to finance offshore drilling rig construction projects.

**Personal:** LLB, University of Texas School of Law, 1965; BS, University of Texas, 1962.

## QUAN, Gordon
Quan, Burdette & Perez, PC, Houston
713 625 9200
*Recommended in Immigration*

## RABALAIS, Robert René
Vinson & Elkins LLP, Houston
713 758 4526
RRabalais@velaw.com
*Recommended in Banking & Finance*

**Practice Areas:** Co-Chair of the firm's Financial Institutions Practice Group, his practice consists of secured and unsecured syndicated finance transactions, capital markets and privately placed debt securities.

**Personal:** Louisiana State University, BS, 1986; Louisiana State University, JD, 1989.

## RAFTE, Alan
Bracewell & Giuliani LLP, Houston
713 221 1411
alan.rafte@bracewellgiuliani.com
*Recommended in Energy, Projects*

**Practice Areas:** Handles diverse commercial transactions involving energy industries such as electric power, oil and gas exploration and production, gas and liquid pipeline facilities. Has represented project sponsors, equity investors and credit providers in transactions which included acquisitions and divestitures of assets and companies, structured and commercial finance and project development and project finance.

**Career:** Recognized by Project Finance magazine with 'Deal of the Year' honors for innovative work on a power generation project. Listed in Euromoney's '2005 Guide to the World's Leading Energy and Natural Resources Lawyers'.

**Personal:** JD, Emory University School of Law, 1979; BA, Syracuse University, 1976.

## RAIN, John W
Thompson & Knight LLP, Dallas
214 969 1644
John.Rain@tklaw.com
*Recommended in Banking & Finance*

**Practice Areas:** Represents capital providers and capital users in private debt or investment transactions, with an emphasis on the energy industry. Has special experience in structuring and negotiating volumetric production payments and other deals involving the combination of property or commodity sales with derivative contracts.

**Prof. Memberships:** State Bar of Texas, State Bar of New York, American College of Investment Counsel, Texas Association

of Bank Counsel, Dallas Bar Association, Dallas Bar Foundation.

**Career:** Partner since 1983.

**Personal:** University of Texas Law School (JD, 1978); Gordon-Conwell Theological Seminary (graduate study, 1974-75); Amherst College (BA, 1973).

## RAMIREZ, Kenneth
Brown McCarroll LLP, Austin
512 472 5456
*Recommended in Environment*

## RATNER, Randall M
Akin Gump Strauss Hauer & Feld LLP, Dallas 214 969 2893
rratner@akingump.com
*Recommended in Real Estate*

**Practice Areas:** Extensive experience in office, hotel, industrial, apartment and retail projects development, including negotiation of partnerships, joint ventures, LLC agreements with public companies, national and regional developers, insurance companies, pension funds. Has represented clients in acquisition and disposition of real estate portfolios, including portfolios of office and industrial buildings, hotels and closed retail stores, and borrowers in all aspects of financings (securitized loans, loans secured by portfolio of buildings, construction loans, permanent loans, lines of credit financings).

**Prof. Memberships:** Texas Academy of Real Estate, Probate and Trust Lawyers.

**Personal:** BS (high distinction), Indiana University; JD (honors), University of Texas.

## RAY, Hugh
Andrews Kurth LLP, Houston
713 225 7000
*Recommended in Bankruptcy*

## REASONER, Barrett
Gibbs & Bruns, LLP, Houston
713 751 5244
breasoner@gibbs-bruns.com
*Recommended in Litigation*

**Practice Areas:** Practice consists of representing plaintiffs and defendants in business litigation matters including breach of contract, securities, oil and gas, construction, intellectual property, officer and director liability, professional liabilty and partnership disputes.

**Prof. Memberships:** Admitted to the Texas Bar in 1990. Admitted to all federal districts in Texas as well as the Fifth Circuit Court of Appeals and the United States Supreme Court. Member of the American Law Institute and has served on the Board of the American Judicature Society. Has been active in Bar service, currently serving as First Vice President of the Houston Bar Association and Chair of the Board of the Houston Volunteer Lawyers Program. Has received three Bar Presidents' awards for ouanding service in chairing Bar Committees.

**Career:** Upon graduation in 1990, was

an Assistant District Attorney for Harris County (Houston), Texas. Joined Gibbs & Bruns, LLP in 1992 and made Partner in 1996. Has been recognized in the Best Lawyers in America, Who's Who in American Law, Texas Super Lawyers and H Texas Magazine.

**Personal:** Born in Houston, Texas on April 16, 1964. BA cum laude from Duke University in 1986. Graduate Diploma in International and Comparative Politics from the London School of Economics in 1987. JD with honors from the University of Texas School of Law in 1990. Named to the Order of Barristers.

## REASONER, Harry
Vinson & Elkins LLP, Houston
713 758 2358
hreasoner@velaw.com
*Recommended in Antitrust, Energy, Litigation*

**Practice Areas:** Complex civil litigation. Served as lead counsel in trials, arbitrations, and appeals involving antitrust, securities, energy, insurance, contract, and tort claims.

**Prof. Memberships:** Fellow: American College of Trial Lawyers; International Academy of Trial Lawyers; International Society of Barristers; American Law Institute; American Board of Trial Advocates. Chair, ABA Section of Antitrust Law.

**Career:** Admitted: Texas; District of Columbia; New York. Law clerk, USCA, 2d Cir. Partner, Vinson & Elkins LLP.

**Publications:** With C A Wright, 'Procedure: The Handmaid of Justice'.

**Personal:** Rice University, BA; The University of Texas Law School, JD; Rotary Foundation Fellow, University of London.

## REDDEN, Joe
Beck, Redden & Secrest LLP, Houston
713 951 3700
*Recommended in Litigation*

## REED, Kevin
Davis & Wilkerson, PC, Austin
512 482 0614
*Recommended in Healthcare*

## REINA, Joseph
Reina & Associates, Dallas
214 905 9100
*Recommended in Immigration*

## RENFROE, Tracie
King & Spalding LLP, Houston
713 751 3200
trenfroe@kslaw.com
*Recommended in Environment*

**Practice Areas:** Maintains national practice focusing on environmental and toxic tort litigation and product liability disputes, including federal and state class actions and multi-district litigation. Has significant experience in contaminated groundwater and drinking water cases. Serves as national coordinating counsel for several oil companies in MTBE contamination litigation. Has handled cases involving petroleum hydrocarbons, sol-

vents, chlorinated compounds, oxygenates and radioactive materials. Has litigated actions under CERCLA, RCRA, Safe Drinking Water Act and state and local statutes. Has litigated deep injection well disputes, personal injury and chemical exposure suits.

**Personal:** JD, Baylor University School of Law; BA, Baylor University.

## REYNOLDS, Chris
Gibbs & Bruns, LLP, Houston
713 751 5214
jreynolds@gibbs-bruns.com
*Recommended in Energy, Litigation*

**Practice Areas:** Practice consists of commercial litigation, with an emphasis on intellectual property and energy-related litigation.

**Prof. Memberships:** Fellow in the Texas Bar Foundation, and a Member of Tau Beta Pi and Chi Epsilon, each of which is an engineering honor society.

**Career:** Started with Wood, Campbell, Moody & Gibbs, PC (a predecessor firm), in March of 1983; joined Gibbs & Ratliff in the fall of 1983; and has been with it (the name changed to Gibbs & Bruns LLP in 1993) ever since. Became a full Partner in October of 1987.

**Publications:** Has written and presented seminar papers on the following topics: i) the use of statistics in litigation; ii) piercing the corporate veil; and iii) how lawyers can avoid liability when deals 'go bad'.

**Personal:** Married with two children and loves deep sea fishing and fox hunting.

## RHEBERGEN, Constance Gall
Bracewell & Giuliani LLP, Houston
713 221 3306
constance.rhebergen@bracewellgiuliani.com
*Recommended in Intellectual Property*

**Practice Areas:** Focuses on all aspects of intellectual property law, including patents, trademarks and copyrights as well as litigation. In addition to traditional patent, trademark and copyright infringement cases, her litigation experience includes Internet domain name cases, international law issues, trade secrets and unfair competition as well as bankruptcy issues related to intellectual property judgments. She also advises private businesses and government agencies in Latin America, Europe and elsewhere on intellectual property matters.

**Personal:** JD, University of Houston Law Center, 1994; MBA, The University of Houston, 1994; BS, Northwestern University, 1986.

## RICHARD, Molly
Richard Law Group, Dallas
214 206 4300
*Recommended in Intellectual Property*

## RIEGER, Michelle
Winstead Sechrest & Minick P.C., Dallas
214 745 5400
*Recommended in Construction*

## ROACH JR, Robert
Cook & Roach, L.L.P., Houston
713 652 2939
*Recommended in Insurance*

## ROBECK, Mark
Baker Botts LLP, Houston
713 229 2071
mark.robeck@bakerbotts.com
*Recommended in Energy*

**Practice Areas:** Represents energy industry members in complex litigation, arbitrations and mediations, and criminal and administrative investigations before state and federal courts and regulatory agencies throughout the country.
**Prof. Memberships:** State Bar of Texas; American Bar Association; Houston Bar Association; Texas Bar Foundation; Houston Bar Foundation; Institute for Energy Law, Advisory Board.
**Publications:** 'Power and Gas Trading Litigation and Investigations Update', American Bar Association, Section of Environment, Energy and Resources, September 2005.
**Personal:** JD (with honors), The University of Texas School of Law, 1989; BS (cum laude), Texas A&M University, 1982.

## ROBERSON, Richard
Gardere Wynne Sewell LLP, Dallas
214 999 4955
rroberson@gardere.com
*Recommended in Bankruptcy*

**Practice Areas:** Bankruptcy, financial services.
**Prof. Memberships:** American Bar Association; State Bar of Texas; Dallas Bar Association; American Bankruptcy Institute; Turnaround Management Association; Honorable John C Ford American Inn of Court.
**Career:** Richard Roberson represents secured lenders, debtors, trustees, examiners and creditors' committees, primarily in large, complex corporate reorganizations. He also handles all litigation arising from his bankruptcy and creditors' rights matters. Mr Roberson has been recognized by Chambers in 2004-06, has been recognized among 'The Best Lawyers in America' 2006, and has been named as a 'Texas Super Lawyer' by Law and Politics magazine published by Texas Monthly magazine for 2005. Additionally, Mr Roberson is a regular lecturer on bankruptcy and creditors' rights topics at continuing education seminars, both legal and financial, as well as a guest lecturer at Columbia University's School of Business.
**Personal:** JD, St Mary's University School of Law, with honors, 1978; BBA, Southern Methodist University, cum laude, 1975.

## ROBERTS, Harry
Thompson & Knight LLP, Dallas
214 969 1616
Harry.Roberts@tklaw.com
*Recommended in Real Estate*

**Practice Areas:** Mr Roberts' practice focuses primarily on real estate transactions including permanent and construction loan work, purchase and sale of commercial real estate, development of real property, leasing, loan servicing including modification agreements and assumption agreements, management agreements, reciprocal and other easements, limited partnership and limited liability company agreements, local counsel opinions, loan workouts, foreclosure, and usury analysis.
**Prof. Memberships:** American College of Real Estate Lawyers, State Bar of Texas, Dallas Bar Association, American, Texas, and Dallas Bar Foundations.
**Publications:** Mr Roberts is an active author and speaker.
**Personal:** Harvard Law School (JD, 1963); Southern Methodist University (BBA, 1960).

## ROCHELLE, Michael
Rochelle, Hutcheson & McCullough, LLP, Dallas 214 953 0182
*Recommended in Bankruptcy*

## ROGERS, Daniel R
King & Spalding LLP, Houston
713 751 3204
drogers@kslaw.com
*Recommended in Energy, Projects*

**Practice Areas:** Represents sponsors, lenders, suppliers, transporters, operators, and marketers in all aspects of gas-related energy infrastructure projects. Extensive experience in the development and financing of Liquefied Natural Gas production.
**Prof. Memberships:** American Bar Association, State Bar of Texas, Houston Bar Association.
**Personal:** BS, University of California at Irvine, 1988; JD, Southern Methodist University School of Law, 1991.

## ROSE, David
Conley Rose, PC, Houston
713 238 8000
*Recommended in Intellectual Property*

## ROSENSTEIN, Tony P
Baker Botts LLP, Houston
713 229 1582
tony.rosenstein@bakerbotts.com
*Recommended in Employment*

**Practice Areas:** Specializes in labor and employment litigation matters in state and federal court. Represents employers before the Equal Employment Opportunity Commission, National Labor Relations Board, the Occupational Safety and Health Review Commission, the Department of Labor, and related administrative agencies. Board Certified in labor and employment law, Texas Board of Legal

Specialization. Represents major national oil and gas, insurance, and banking companies.
**Career:** 27+ years in practice.
**Personal:** JD, cum laude, University of Houston, 1976; MA, clinical psychology, Memphis State University, 1969; BS, Rensselaer Polytechnic Institute, 1967.

## ROSS, Jerry W
Pillsbury Winthrop Shaw Pittman LLP, Houston 713 425 7320
Jerry.Ross@pillsburylaw.com
*Recommended in Environment*

**Practice Areas:** Mr Ross has handled numerous complex rulemaking and adjudicatory regulatory proceedings, as well as private party litigation. These matters include significant cost recovery actions, challenges to government clean-up orders, regulatory enforcement actions, citizen suits, piercing the corporate veil claims and bankruptcy matters. Mr Ross also has extensive experience handling environmental issues associated with mergers and acquisitions.
**Personal:** JD, University of Notre Dame Law School, 1978; MS, University of Notre Dame, 1977; BS, Stanford University, 1973.

## ROSS, Joel L
Vinson & Elkins LLP, Dallas
214 220 7769
Jross@velaw.com
*Recommended in Real Estate*

**Practice Areas:** Joel practices in the areas of business and finance, with emphasis in real estate transactions. He has been involved in all facets of the real estate industry, including acquisitions, dispositions, equity arrangements, partner buyouts, debt/equity workouts, development, leasing, and management. Real estate clients include both local and national developers, private equity sources, and real estate investment trusts.
**Career:** Admitted to Texas Bar, 1979. Came to firm as Partner, 1996.
**Personal:** Graduated from The University of Texas of the Permian Basin, BS with highest honors, 1976, and Texas Tech University, JD with honors, 1979.

## ROSS, Judith
Baker Botts LLP, Dallas
214 953 6605
judith.ross@bakerbotts.com
*Recommended in Bankruptcy*

**Practice Areas:** Partner. Represents a diverse range of asset acquirers, lenders, creditors, debtors, officers and directors in virtually every aspect of complex chapter 11 cases, as well as out-of-court workouts. She has particular experience in bankruptcy litigation.
**Career:** Prior to joining Baker Botts in 2004, she was a Partner at Thompson & Knight L.L.P.
**Personal:** JD, The University of Texas School of Law, 1985; BA, Miami University, 1979.

## ROYALL, M Sean
Gibson, Dunn & Crutcher LLP, Dallas
214 698 3256
sroyall@gibsondunn.com
*Recommended in Antitrust*

**Practice Areas:** Co-Chair, Antitrust Practice Group. Litigates complex antitrust matters; represents firms before federal/international antitrust agencies; antitrust counseling in M&A, joint venture, distribution, and IP contexts; litigates other commercial disputes, including IP, securities, false advertising.
**Prof. Memberships:** Vice-Chair, FTC Committee, ABA Section of Antitrust Law; Chair, Dallas Bar Antitrust Section.
**Career:** Deputy Director, FTC Bureau of Competition (2001-03); Clerk, Hon Patrick Higginbotham, Fifth Circuit Court of Appeals.
**Publications:** Editor, Von Kalinowski Antitrust Treatise; Chair, Antitrust Law Journal (1997-2000). Numerous articles on antitrust issues.
**Personal:** JD, University of Chicago, with honors, 1990; Managing Editor, University of Chicago Law Review.

## RUCKMAN, Deirdre
Gardere Wynne Sewell LLP, Dallas
214 999 4250
druckman@gardere.com
*Recommended in Bankruptcy*

**Practice Areas:** Bankruptcy, financial services.
**Prof. Memberships:** State Bar of Texas; American Bar Association; Master, American Inns of Court; Delegate, Fifth Circuit Judicial Conference.
**Career:** Deirdre Ruckman has more than three decades of experience in the financial services sector. She specializes in representation of both debtors and creditors in business reorganizations involving private and/or public debt in court proceedings and out-of-court workouts. She is also the section Head for Gardere's Creditors Rights and Business Reorganization Group and a member of the firm's Partners' Board.
**Personal:** JD, Southern Methodist University Dedman School of Law, 1975; BS, Chestnut Hill College, 1970.

## SAEGERT, Ann
Haynes and Boone LLP, Dallas
214 651 5000
*Recommended in Real Estate*

## SALCH, Steven
Fulbright & Jaworski L.L.P., Houston
713 651 5433
ssalch@fulbright.com
*Recommended in Tax*

**Practice Areas:** Tax controversy, state and federal tax planning, multinational tax and business law, mediation, arbitration, expert witness, administrative agency determinations and rulemaking, legislation, antiboycott compliance, foreign asset controls, and export administration.

**Prof. Memberships:** Listed in 'Who's Who in America'; Past Chair, Section of Taxation, American Bar Association; Secretary-Treasurer, American College of Tax Counsel; Member, American Law Institute, the International Fiscal Association, the American Bar Foundation, and the Houston Bar Foundation.
**Career:** Admitted to Texas Bar (1968). Partner in the Houston office of Fulbright since 1975.
**Personal:** BBA, Accounting (1965) and JD, (1968) from Southern Methodist University.

### SAROSDY, Randall L
Akin Gump Strauss Hauer & Feld LLP, Austin 512 499 6225
rsarosdy@akingump.com
*Recommended in Intellectual Property*
**Practice Areas:** Mr Sarosdy focuses on patent litigation and complex commercial litigation. He represents clients in and has tried to judgment numerous patent infringement and complex commercial litigation matters, including multistate class actions, in federal district and appellate courts throughout the nation.
**Prof. Memberships:** Adjunct Professor, George Mason University School of Law, Fall 2000; Member, Intellectual Property Section, State Bar of Texas; Member, Civil Litigation Section, Austin Bar Association; Life Fellow, Texas Bar Foundation.
**Personal:** AB (high honors), College of William and Mary (1974); JD, University of Texas School of Law (1977) (Associate Editor, Texas Law Review).

### SASLAW, Michael A
Weil, Gotshal & Manges LLP, Dallas 214 746 8117
michael.saslaw@weil.com
*Recommended in Corporate/M&A*
**Practice Areas:** Michael Saslaw's primary practice areas include mergers and acquisitions, securities offerings, financings, restructurings and corporate counseling. He has extensive experience counseling businesses in a variety of industries, including media, real estate, retail, consumer products and manufacturing. Mr Saslaw's representative clients include Bell Helicopter Textron, Inc., Citigroup, Covad Communications Group, Inc., Crestview Capital Partners, LP, Electronic Data Systems Corporation (EDS), General Electric Company, General Motors Corporation, J.C. Penney Company, Inc., Lone Star Funds and 7-Eleven, Inc.
**Personal:** Miami University, BS Accounting, 1979; University of Pennsylvania Law School, JD, 1982.

### SCHICK, Robert M
Vinson & Elkins LLP, Houston 713 758 4582
rschick@velaw.com
*Recommended in Litigation*
**Practice Areas:** Over 20 years of experience in all aspects of products liability, environmental and toxic tort litigation,

representing domestic and foreign corporations throughout Texas and in eight other states.
**Prof. Memberships:** American College of Trial Lawyers; American Board of Trial Advocates; Product Liability Advisory Council; IADC; DRI.
**Career:** Partner since 1989. Texas Board certified since 1987 in Civil Trial Law and Personal Injury Law. Listed, Best Lawyers in America, 2003-06.
**Publications:** Co-author: Hampton, Schick & McGehee's Texas Civil Practice and Remedies Code Annotated, Thompson West 2002-04.
**Personal:** Princeton University (AB 1976), University of Houston (JD 1981).

### SCHIFFER, Adam P
King & Spalding LLP, Houston 713 751 3234
aschiffer@kslaw.com
*Recommended in Energy, Litigation*
**Practice Areas:** Extensive experience representing both plaintiffs and defendants in complex business and construction litigation and arbitrations involving a wide variety of contract and tort claims. Has tried over 30 commercial cases throughout Texas (state and federal courts), Pennsylvania (federal court) and Delaware (Chancery Courts). Has arbitrated disputes in Texas, Nevada, Geneva, Switzerland and London, England under AAA, JAMS, UNCITRAL, LCIA and ICC rules.
**Prof. Memberships:** Texas Bar Association.
**Personal:** BA, Dickenson College,1983; JD, University of Houston, 1986.

### SCHOENBRUN, Larry
Gardere Wynne Sewell LLP, Dallas 214 999 4703
lschoenbrun@gardere.com
*Recommended in Corporate/M&A*
**Practice Areas:** Corporate, M&A, securities.
**Prof. Memberships:** Dallas Bar Association; American Bar Association; Former Chairman, Securities Committee of the Council of the Business Law Section of the State Bar of Texas; Former Chairman, Texas Business Law Foundation; Former Chairman, Council of the Business Law Section of the State Bar of Texas.
**Career:** Larry Schoenbrun has served as the coordinator of legal activities for large and medium-sized corporations for more than 30 years. He has represented corporations in their initial public offerings, corporate reorganizations, re-incorporations, roll-ups and structuring of employee benefit plans. Schoenbrun has also represented underwriters in public offerings, buyers and sellers in various corporate acquisitions and dispositions and venture capitalists in their investments. He has served as counsel for special committees of boards of directors dealing with affiliate transactions and

conflict situations and for audit committees dealing with various corporate governance and fiduciary issues.
**Personal:** LLB, University of Texas School of Law, 1965; BA, University of Texas at Austin, 1962.

### SCHUMACHER, David
Chadbourne & Parke LLP, Houston 713 571 5961
dschumacher@chadbourne.com
*Recommended in Projects*
**Practice Areas:** David Schumacher is Managing Partner of the Houston office and is a member of the energy project finance practice. He represents lenders to and developers of oil and gas projects and independent power projects developed worldwide. In this regard, he has advised lenders and investors in commercial bank and capital markets debt financings of energy projects and has drafted, negotiated, reviewed and analyzed project documents necessary for energy project construction and operation. He also advises clients on the impact of utility regulatory regimes on project development and financing.
**Prof. Memberships:** District of Columbia and Virginia State Bars.

### SCHUURMAN, Willem
Vinson & Elkins LLP, Austin 512 542 8663
bschuurman@velaw.com
*Recommended in Intellectual Property*
**Practice Areas:** Partner, Co-Section Head at Vinson & Elkins, Intellectual Property Section, Austin Texas. Practice is devoted to patent law with emphasis on patent litigation. Technical background in the chemical and chemical engineering fields. Also handles matters in the electrical, mechanical, biotechnology, and computer fields. Author of several journal articles.
**Prof. Memberships:** US Patent and Trademark Office, and the South African Patent Office; American, Federal, Travis County and Federal Circuit Bar Associations; International, American, and Austin Intellectual Property Law Associations.
**Career:** South Texas College of Law, JD, magna cum laude, 1981; University of Cape Town, LLB (1964) and BS (1962).

### SCHWARTZ, Charles
Skadden, Arps, Slate, Meagher & Flom LLP & Affiliates, Houston 713 655 5160
schwartz@skadden.com
*Recommended in Litigation*
**Practice Areas:** Has extensive experience in all aspects of business litigation. His principal areas of focus include defending companies and their directors and officers in securities and fiduciary duty cases, principally in securities fraud and takeover situations, environmental, consumer, and other class actions, antitrust cases, and commercial disputes.

He is the former Chairman of the Board of the State Bar of Texas.
**Career:** LLM, Harvard University, Cambridge, Massachusetts, 1980; MA, University of Texas, Austin, Texas, 1980; JD, University of Texas, Austin, Texas, 1977 (with honors); BS, University of Texas, Austin, Texas, 1975 (with highest honors).

### SEALS, Paul
Akin Gump Strauss Hauer & Feld LLP, Austin 512 499 6203
pseals@akingump.com
*Recommended in Environment*
**Practice Areas:** Paul Seals has more than 30 years of experience in environmental regulatory matters, focusing on environmental licensing and compliance matters as well as public policy issues. He provides environmental and natural resource counseling on project development issues in the energy, paper, petroleum refining and waste management industries. His experience includes both administrative and judicial litigation and appeals.
**Prof. Memberships:** Environmental and Natural Resources Law Section, Texas State Bar (former Chairman).
**Career:** Regional Counsel, US Environmental Protection Agency, Dallas (1982-86); Assistant General Counsel, Texas Department of Water Resources (1977-82).
**Personal:** BA, St. Edwards University; JD, University of Texas.

### SELINGER, Jerry
Morgan, Lewis & Bockius LLP, Dallas 214 438 1569
jselinger@morganlewis.com
*Recommended in Intellectual Property*
**Practice Areas:** Jerry R Selinger is a Partner in the Litigation Practice. Mr Selinger's practice focuses on litigation of intellectual property and related matters. He has tried cases in federal and state courts and appeared before various appellate courts and agencies, including the International Trade Commission. He has handled patent litigation in an extensive range of technical disciplines, including computer science technology, electrical devices, chemical processes and mechanical devices.

### SENTILLES III, Irwin F
Gibson, Dunn & Crutcher LLP, Dallas 214 698 3119
isentilles@gibsondunn.com
*Recommended in Corporate/M&A*
**Practice Areas:** Extensive experience in corporate and securities law. Practice encompasses mergers and acquisitions, debt and equity financings, restructurings, joint ventures, securities law compliance, corporate governance and general corporate advice for both publicly and privately held companies. Industry experience includes energy, healthcare, homebuilding, manufacturing, retail, technology, transportation and utilities.

**Prof. Memberships:** Admitted before New York and Texas Bars.
**Publications:** Frequent speaker on corporate and securities law topics.
**Personal:** JD, Yale Law School, 1972.

### SHANK, Mark
Hughes & Luce LLP, Dallas
214 939 5500
*Recommended in Employment*

### SHEEDER, Robert
Jenkens & Gilchrist PC, Dallas
214 855 4500
*Recommended in Employment*

### SHEINFELD, Myron M
Akin Gump Strauss Hauer & Feld LLP, Houston 713 220 5801
msheinfeld@akingump.com
*Recommended in Bankruptcy*
**Practice Areas:** Focuses on reorganization and bankruptcy law, bankruptcy tax, creditors' rights, workout matters, commercial litigation, business transactions. Has 40+ years of experience in all aspects of Chapter 11 reorganizations, including negotiation of complex plans of reorganization and litigation of contested matters and adversary proceedings. Has been involved in many of the major bankruptcy reorganizations or business problems in the United States.
**Prof. Memberships:** Chair, American Bar Association Standing Committee on Specialization; Member, National Bankruptcy Conference and American College of Bankruptcy; past President, current Director, National Association of Corporate Directors (Houston Chapter).
**Personal:** BA, Tulane University; JD, University of Michigan.

### SHIDLOFSKY, Lee
Nickens Keeton Lawless Farrell & Flack LLP, Austin 512 472 3067
*Recommended in Insurance*

### SHIVERS, Nancy
Shivers & Shivers, San Antonio
210 226 9725
*Recommended in Immigration*

### SHIVERS, Robert
Shivers & Shivers, San Antonio
210 226 9725
*Recommended in Immigration*

### SHORT JR, William
William B Short Jr, PC, Dallas
214 523 5100
*Recommended in Construction*

### SHOWALTER, Barton E
Baker Botts LLP, Dallas
214 953 6509
bart.showalter@bakerbotts.com
*Recommended in Intellectual Property*
**Practice Areas:** Partner focused on patent procurement, litigation, licensing and counseling for high technology companies. Significant experience litigating and licensing patents in a variety of fields, including telecommunications, electron-

ics, software, semiconductors, wireless technology, computers, and medical devices. Also provides strategic counseling to maximize research and development investments. Develops and implements innovative processes and tools for patent portfolio management, enforcement, licensing, and IP risk mitigation.
**Personal:** BS and MS in Aerospace Engineering, MIT; Adjunct Professor, SMU School of Law; Chair, State Bar of Texas IP Section; Executive Committee, Institute of Law and Technology; Governing Board, Dallas Museum of Natural History.

### SIMPSON, Reagan
King & Spalding LLP, Houston
713 751 3229
RSimpson@kslaw.com
*Recommended in Litigation*
**Practice Areas:** Handles a wide variety of trial and appellate matters, including litigation involving personal injury, commercial torts, mass torts, media law and defamation, and products liability. Has active appellate and trial practice in both state and federal courts.
**Prof. Memberships:** American Board of Trial Advocates; American College of Trial Lawyers; Federation of Insurance and Corporate Counsel; Houston Bar Association; State Bar of Texas.
**Personal:** BA, highest honors, University of Texas, 1974; JD, high honors, University of Texas, 1977.

### SINAK, David
Gibson, Dunn & Crutcher LLP, Dallas
214 698 3100
dsinak@gibsondunn.com
*Recommended in Tax*
**Practice Areas:** Focuses on federal income taxation of corporations, partnerships, limited liability companies, investment securities, and Texas franchise taxation. Involved in tax planning for private equity funds and their institutional investors, (specializing in oil and gas funds), corporate and partnership M&A, financings, solvent/insolvent restructurings, tax free spin-offs, tax free corporate reorganizations, partnership structuring and reorganizations, debt/equity offerings, and foreign investments in US. Experienced in obtaining private letter rulings from IRS and handling IRS audit appeals.
**Prof. Memberships:** American Bar Association, State Bar of Texas, Dallas Bar Association.
**Personal:** JD, cum laude, Boston College, 1979; Articles Editor, Boston College Law Review.

### SLAVICH, John
Guida, Slavich & Flores, P.C., Dallas
214 692 0009
*Recommended in Environment*

### SLUSSER, William
Slusser, Wilson & Partridge LLP, Houston 713 860 3300
*Recommended in Intellectual Property*

### SMITH, Alison
Haynes and Boone LLP, Houston
713 547 2000
*Recommended in Antitrust*

### SMITH, James E
Beirne Maynard & Parsons, LLP, Houston 713 963 7348
jsmith@bmpllp.com
*Recommended in Environment*
**Practice Areas:** Environmental enforcement; environmental permitting; toxic torts; natural resources (gas and electricity); patent and related intellectual property litigation. Mr Smith has tried civil cases in state and federal court, and before arbitration panels.
**Prof. Memberships:** Texas State Bar – Litigation; Environmental and Natural Resources; Intellectual Property; American Bar Association – Litigation; Natural Resources and Environmental; Intellectual Property; Houston Bar Association – Litigation; Environmental; Intellectual Property.
**Career:** Admitted to Bar, 1982, Texas; also admitted to practice before US Court of Appeals, Fifth Circuit and Federal Circuit; US District Court, Northern, Southern, Eastern and Western Districts of Texas; and United States Patent and Trademark Office. Selected by a leading US legal publication for environmental litigation in Texas.
**Publications:** 'Fundamentals of Environmental Enforcement'; 'Suggestions on Dealing With Agency Investigations'.
**Personal:** BS Chemical Engineering, 1978, University of Kansas, Tau Beta Pi (Engineering Honor Society), Phi Lambda Upsilon (Chemistry Honor Society); JD, 1982, University of Texas, with honors.

### SMITH, L Chapman
Baker Botts LLP, Houston
713 229 1546
chapman.smith@bakerbotts.com
*Recommended in Employment*
**Practice Areas:** Labor and employment.
**Prof. Memberships:** Board Certified in Labor and Employment Law; Texas Board of Legal Specialization; State Bar of Texas Professional Ethics Committee; Woodward/White's Best Lawyers in America; Texas Monthly's 'Texas Super Lawyers'; Inside Houston's 'Super Lawyers'; Who's Who Legal USA; City of Houston Civil Service Commission, Chairman; South Texas College of Law Visitors' Committee; United Way Texas Gulf Coast Human Resources Committee.
**Publications:** The Employment Law Handbook; Texas Association of Business; The Developing Labor Law; American Bar Association; Section of Labor Relations Law.
**Personal:** Southern Methodist University, JD, 1968; BBA 1966.

### SMYSER, Craig
Smyser Kaplan & Veselka LLP, Houston
713 221 2300
*Recommended in Litigation*

### SNYDER, Allison
Porter & Hedges, LLP, Houston
713 226 6000
*Recommended in Construction*

### SOSLAND, Martin
Weil, Gotshal & Manges LLP, Dallas
214 746 7730
martin.sosland@weil.com
*Recommended in Bankruptcy*
**Practice Areas:** Martin Sosland's practice focuses on business reorganization, debtors' and creditors' rights, refinancings, and acquisitions of troubled companies. He was a Lead Partner in Weil Gotshal's representation of Enron Corp. in its Chapter 11 case, Sulzer Orthopedics in its class-action product liability settlement, and Tejas Securities and other bondholders in Trenwick America. His other representative clients include Home Interiors Group, GE Capital, and Lehman.
**Personal:** Rice University, BA, 1976; University of Texas School of Law, JD, 1983.

### SOSTEK, Bruce
Thompson & Knight LLP, Dallas
214 969 1237
Bruce.Sostek@tklaw.com
*Recommended in Intellectual Property*
**Practice Areas:** Mr Sostek's practice focuses on intellectual property and complex litigation, technology, and business counseling, primarily in the areas of semiconductors, telecommunications, hardware, software, the Internet, sports, media, and entertainment. In addition to patent litigation, he also tries cases involving trademark and copyright infringement; theft of trade secrets; and other intellectual property claims in state and federal courts in Texas and across the United States.
**Prof. Memberships:** Texas, Massachusetts, and Washington, DC Bar Associations and the Federal Circuit Bar Association.
**Personal:** Emory University (JD, 1981); State University of New York at Albany (MA, 1977); Union College (BA, 1975).

### SPEARS, Berry
Winstead Sechrest & Minick P.C., Austin
512 370 2800
*Recommended in Bankruptcy*

### SPEARS, L Gene
Baker Botts LLP, Houston
713 229 1590
gene.spears@bakerbotts.com
*Recommended in Intellectual Property*
**Practice Areas:** Patent enforcement and counselling; trade secret and copyright litigation. Has represented clients in federal courts throughout the United States and before the International Trade Commission.

## SPIERS, Jeffrey
Andrews Kurth LLP, Houston
713 220 4200
*Recommended in Bankruptcy*

## SPIVEY, James K
Cox Smith Matthews Incorporated, San
Antonio 210 554 5218
jkspivey@coxsmith.com
*Recommended in Antitrust*
**Practice Areas:** Jim is a shareholder in
the firm's Litigation Department. Jim has
represented clients in a variety of business disputes, including disputes involving claims brought under the Texas and
federal antitrust laws. He has advised
clients on all aspects of business litigation
and has represented clients from a number of industries.
**Prof. Memberships:** Former Chair, State
Bar of Texas, Antitrust and Business Litigation Section; Former Director, Defense
Counsel of San Antonio; Former Director, San Antonio Young Lawyers Association; Member, San Antonio Bar Association, Fifth Circuit Bar Association; Member, William S. Sessions American Inn of
Court; Member, American Bar Association, Litigation and Antitrust Sections
and Business Torts Litigation Committee.
**Career:** Jim has been licensed to practice
law in the State of Texas since 1995. He is
also licensed to practice before all Texas
state courts, the United States Court of
Appeals for the Fifth Circuit and the
United States District Courts for the
Northern, Southern, Eastern, and Western Districts of Texas. In both 2003 and
2004, Jim was named a 'Texas Super
Lawyer' by Texas Monthly.
**Personal:** University of Texas School of
Law, JD, 1995; Texas A&M University, BS,
Economics, magna cum laude, 1992.

## STATHAM, Kenneth Scott
Vinson & Elkins LLP, Houston
713 758 2878
sstatham@velaw.com
*Recommended in Insurance*
**Practice Areas:** Scott's Trial Practice is
focused on product liability, toxic tort,
insurance law and alternative dispute res-
olution.
**Career:** Partner, Vinson & Elkins LLP
since 1997.
**Publications:** 'Restatement by Design: A
Survey of the Impact of the Restatements
Second and Third on Design Defect
Claims Involving Prescription Drugs', RX
for the Defense (Winter 2004).
**Personal:** The University of Texas, BBA,
1984 (Beta Gamma Sigma); University of
Houston School of Law, JD with highest
honors, 1987 (Order of the Coif).

## STEPHENS, Robert
Bracewell & Giuliani LLP, Houston
713 221 1202
robert.stephens@bracewellgiuliani.com
*Recommended in Energy*
**Practice Areas:** Expertise in representing energy companies, financial institu-

tions, and private investors in domestic
and international energy and energy
finance transactions. Has handled multi-
billion dollar secured financings involving public and private secured debt,
bankruptcy remote structured transactions, international project financings,
long-term trading, netting, and supply
contracts, and asset acquisition and disposition transactions.
**Personal:** JD, with honors, The University of Texas School of Law, 1990; MBA,
Finance, University of Wisconsin School
of Business, 1987; BBA, Marketing and
Management Information Systems, University of Wisconsin School of Business,
1985.

## STERLING, David
Baker Botts LLP, Houston
713 229 1946
david.sterling@bakerbotts.com
*Recommended in Litigation*
**Practice Areas:** Broker-dealers in securities suits, arbitrations, and investigations; companies and their directors in
class action securities fraud claims, derivative actions, and breach of fiduciary
suits; corporate boards in investigations;
and other major commercial litigation.
**Prof. Memberships:** Securities Industry
Association; State Bar of Texas.
**Career:** Mr Sterling is a Senior Partner at
Baker Botts, LLP.
**Publications:** Mr Sterling frequent
speaks on securities litigation and arbitration.
**Personal:** Mr Sterling graduated from
Williams College in 1980 and The University of Texas Law School in 1984. He
and his wife, Kimberly, who heads a consulting firm for nonprofit institutions,
have three children.

## STEWART, Dan
Vinson & Elkins LLP, Dallas
214 220 7761
dstewart@velaw.com
*Recommended in Bankruptcy*
**Practice Areas:** Practice spans all
aspects of debtor/creditor relationships.
Major creditor representations include
agent banks, bank groups, and creditor
committee representations in connection
with bankruptcy proceedings for major
corporations. Served as lead counsel for
borrowers in some of the largest workouts and reorganizations in Texas for over
25 years. Served as Bankruptcy Trustee in
hundreds of Chapter 7 and Chapter 11
cases under the Bankruptcy Act and
Code.
**Prof. Memberships:** Dallas Bar Association.
**Career:** Admitted to Texas Bar, 1972.
Came to firm as Partner, 1999.
**Personal:** Graduated from Brown University, BA (1969), and Duke University
School of Law, JD (1972).

## STEWART, Robert
Kelly, Hart & Hallman, A Professional
Corporation, Austin 512 495 6400
*Recommended in Environment*

## STILL, Charles
Fulbright & Jaworski L.L.P., Houston
713 651 5270
cstill@fulbright.com
*Recommended in Corporate/M&A*
**Practice Areas:** Corporate law; securi-
ties law; mergers and acquisitions; board
and corporate governance.
**Prof. Memberships:** American Law
Institute; American Bar Association; State
Bar of Texas; Life Fellow, Texas and
American Bar Foundations; Fellow,
Houston Bar Foundation; Clark Fellow,
University of Texas School of Law; and
Board Member, Texas Business Law
Foundation.
**Career:** Mr Still has been a Partner in
Fulbright's Houston office since 1975. He
has served as Head of the Corporate
Department and as a member of the
firm's Executive Committee. Among
other honors, Mr Still has been recog-
nized in An International Who's Who of
Merger and Acquisition Lawyers; Ameri-
ca's Leading Business Lawyers; The Best
Lawyers in America; and Super Lawyers
as published in Texas Monthly magazine.
His practice includes corporate finance
and securities law, M&A, and other corporate specialty areas, including general
corporate governance matters, Sarbanes-
Oxley Act matters, legal compliance programs and Foreign Corrupt Practices Act
matters.
**Personal:** BBA – Texas Tech University
(1965); JD – with honors, University of
Texas (1968).

## STOCKBRIDGE, Edward T
Vinson & Elkins LLP, Houston
713 758 1032
tstockbridge@velaw.com
*Recommended in Technology*
**Practice Areas:** Focus on various types
of technology-related business transactions: information technology outsourcing transactions; offshore outsourcing;
business process outsourcing (including
human resource BPO and billing and
account service BPO); technology and
software licensing; e-commerce and
internet matters; international licensing;
structured purchase of royalty payments
derived from licenses of IP rights and
acquisition and divestitures of technology
companies.
**Career:** Admitted to practice: Texas 1982
and Florida 1983. Attorney at V&E since
1982.
**Personal:** Duke University, BSE,
mechanical engineering magna cum
laude (1976); University of Florida, JD
high honors (1982) (Phi Kappa Phi;
Order of the Coif; University of Florida
Law Review).

## STONE, Susan
Baker & McKenzie, Houston
713 427 5008
n.susan.stone@bakernet.com
*Recommended in Tax*
**Practice Areas:** International tax and
business transactions, including structuring inbound/outbound transactions for
US and foreign clients, implementing
global/regional tax minimization strategies, tax structuring of foreign oil, gas,
energy and related infrastructure projects, transfer pricing planning and controversy, including competent authority
proceedings and advance pricing agreements.
**Prof. Memberships:** American Bar
Association, Council Director and immediate past Secretary for the Section of
Taxation; State Bar of Texas; Houston Bar
Association.
**Career:** Admitted to Bar, Texas, 1982.
**Publications:** Frequent speaker; including, 'Using Partnerships Affirmatively in
International Tax Transactions', Tax Executives Institute, November 2003.
**Personal:** 2003: Named in various lead-
ing US legal publications.

## STRAMA, Brenda
Vinson & Elkins LLP, Austin
512 542 8544
bstrama@velaw.com
*Recommended in Healthcare*
**Practice Areas:** Healthcare. Peer review
and credentialing, health information
privacy, health facility licensure, and
Medicare survey and certification.
**Prof. Memberships:** ABA; TBA; AHLA;
Texas Attorney General's Task Force on
HIPAA Preemption; Health Law Exam
Commission, Texas Board of Legal Spe-
cialization.
**Career:** Partner since 1993.
**Publications:** Author: 'The AIDS Epi-
demic and Local Government Liability'
(ABA); 'The National Practitioner Data
Bank: Has it Accomplished its Objec-
tives?' Health Lawyers News, February
2002 (AHLA); Editor: Vinson & Elkins
Healthcare Legal Update; TBA; AHLA.
**Personal:** Georgetown University School
of Foreign Service, BA 1962; University of
Houston Law Center, JD cum laude,
1984.

## STRICKLIN, Samuel M
Bracewell & Giuliani LLP, Dallas
214 758 1095
sam.stricklin@bracewellgiuliani.com
*Recommended in Bankruptcy*
**Practice Areas:** Board certified in business bankruptcy law by the Texas Board
of Legal Specialization, he has extensive
trial and courtroom experience on a wide
variety of commercial bankruptcy issues,
including contested hearings before 37
bankruptcy judges in 17 states. Recognized in his practice by regional legal
publication for the last three years.
**Personal:** JD, University of Houston Law

Center, 1987; BA, Texas A&M University, 1984.

## STROCK, William
Haynes and Boone LLP, Dallas
214 651 5000
*Recommended in Employment*

## STROUBE III, H Rey
Akin Gump Strauss Hauer & Feld LLP, Houston 713 220 5858
rstroube@akingump.com
*Recommended in Bankruptcy*
**Practice Areas:** Focuses on debt restructurings and business reorganizations, representing debtors, secured creditors (individually and as participant groups), unsecured creditors, committees of creditors and equity holders and equity interest committees. Experience includes serving as primary debtor's counsel in major national cases and leading the representation of various formal and informal creditor committee constituencies. Also represents clients acquiring interests in financially distressed entities.
**Prof. Memberships:** Texas Bar Foundation; State Bar of Texas; American Bar Association; American Bankruptcy Institute.
**Personal:** AB, Yale University; JD, University of Texas; Clerk, Ben C Connally, US District Court for the Southern District of Texas.

## STRUBECK, Lou
Fulbright & Jaworski L.L.P., Dallas
214 855 8040
lstrubeck@fulbright.com
*Recommended in Bankruptcy*
**Practice Areas:** Bankruptcy law and debtor/creditors' rights, with emphasis on representation of financial institutions, institutional lenders, investors and creditors in complex workouts and Chapter 11 bankruptcy reorganization cases.
**Prof. Memberships:** Member, American Bankruptcy Institute; Inns of Court; Dallas and American Bar Associations; State Bar of Texas, Fee Dispute and Judiciary Subcommittee of the Dallas Bar Association (Officer) and the Dallas and Tarrant County Bankruptcy Bar Associations.
**Career:** Admitted to Texas Bar (1983). Partner in Dallas office of Fulbrights since 1992. Former panel bankruptcy trustee in the Northern District of Texas.
**Personal:** BA, College of Charleston (1980); JD, Temple University (1983).

## SUSMAN, Harry
Susman Godfrey LLP, Houston
713 651 9366
*Recommended in Antitrust*

## SUSMAN, Stephen
Susman Godfrey LLP, Houston
713 651 9366
*Recommended in Antitrust, Litigation*

## SUTHERLAND, J Michael
Carrington, Coleman, Sloman & Blumenthal, LLP, Dallas 214 855 3000
*Recommended in Bankruptcy*

## SWANSON, Joel
Baker Botts LLP, Houston
713 229 1330
joel.swanson@bakerbotts.com
*Recommended in Corporate/M&A*
**Practice Areas:** Partner in Corporate Department. Practice focuses on securities, mergers and acquisitions and joint ventures. In the past several years, he has participated in more than 30 public offerings of all types of securities, representing both issuers and underwriters and handled numerous acquisitions and divestitures. He has represented many energy companies, particularly those in the refining industry.
**Career:** Worked for Exxon as a chemical engineer prior to law school.
**Personal:** JD, cum laude, Harvard Law School, 1972; MBA, Harvard Business School, 1972; BS, chemical engineering, The University of Texas, 1967, highest ranking engineering graduate.

## SZALKOWSKI, Charles
Baker Botts LLP, Houston
713 229 1480
charles.szalkowski@bakerbotts.com
*Recommended in Corporate/M&A, Technology*
**Practice Areas:** Mergers, acquisitions, general corporate, public and private financings, venture capital, private equity transactions. Represents emerging growth and small public companies, venture capitalists, investment bankers, and investors in such companies, private equity funds, hedge funds, institutional investors, insurance companies, universities and endowments. Representation of software and telecommunications companies, consumer and industrial products manufacturers, oil, gas and energy service companies, consolidators in various industries and other ventures with prospects embodied in intellectual property, including biotechnology, medical devices, internet content and e-commerce.
**Personal:** JD, cum laude, and MBA, Harvard University, 1975; BA, cum laude, and BS Accounting, Rice University, 1971.

## TABOR, Bert
Vinson & Elkins LLP, Houston
713 758 2620
btabor@velaw.com
*Recommended in Energy*
**Practice Areas:** Broad-based practice counseling clients in the energy and transportation industries mainly related to the formation, construction, acquisition, financing, sale, regulation, and operation of oil pipelines and products pipelines, and representing clients in administrative litigation before the Federal Energy Regulatory Commission and

state regulatory agencies. He has represented clients in pipeline ventures throughout the United States, including extensive experience in Alaska.
**Prof. Memberships:** Member: Energy Bar Association (Served, Executive Committee; past Chair; Oil Pipeline Committee).
**Career:** Joined the firm in 1973; admitted to the partnership in January 1976.
**Personal:** Ohio State University, BS, 1961; JD, 1964 (Phi Delta Phi).

## TABOR, Jay
Weil, Gotshal & Manges LLP, Dallas
214 746 7889
jay.tabor@weil.com
*Recommended in Corporate/M&A*
**Practice Areas:** Mr Tabor handles complex corporate transactions for clients in a variety of industries. His experience includes representing Great Lakes Chemical Corporation in its $1.8 billion merger with Crompton Corporation, and representing Enron in its contract to sell Portland General Electric Company in a $2.35 billion transaction. He has represented American Airlines in its airline industry acquisitions, and Wal-Mart in its acquisition of a grocery chain. Mr Tabor also represents a number of private equity funds in transactions in various industries.
**Personal:** Oklahoma Christian University, BS, 1986; Harvard Law School, JD, magna cum laude, 1990.

## TAYLOR, Jasper
Fulbright & Jaworski L.L.P., Houston
713 651 5670
jtaylor@fulbright.com
*Recommended in Tax, Tax Litigation*
**Practice Areas:** Tax litigation and tax controversies.
**Prof. Memberships:** Mr Taylor has been a member of the American Bar Association's Section of Taxation for over 20 years and has served as Chair of the Section's Committee on Court Procedure. He has also served as Chair of the Texas State Bar's Section of Taxation.
**Career:** Jack Taylor, an attorney and certified public accountant, has an active practice in tax controversy, including representation of taxpayers in both administrative proceedings and litigation. A Partner with Fulbright & Jaworski LLP since 1985, Mr Taylor has served a wide range of clients. He has actively litigated in Texas district courts, federal district courts, the US Tax Court, the US Court of Federal Claims and predecessors, and respective appeals courts. He is also a frequent speaker at Bar Association and tax professional meetings, most recently on the economic substance doctrine and representing participants in transactions alleged to be abusive tax shelters. His professional background includes Big 8 accounting firm experience prior to attending law school.

**Personal:** Mr Taylor received a BBA in 1973 from the University of Florida and a JD in 1978 from Duke University.

## TEMPLIN, Donald
Haynes and Boone LLP, Dallas
214 651 5000
*Recommended in Intellectual Property*

## TERRELL, Irv
Baker Botts LLP, Houston
713 229 1231
irv.terrell@bakerbotts.com
*Recommended in Litigation*
**Practice Areas:** Trial practice concerning business litigation in Texas, Arizona, California, Delaware, Florida, Illinois, New Mexico, Louisiana, New York, and Pennsylvania: takeover suits, contract disputes, intellectual property claims, and business torts, including such matters as tortious interference, antitrust, fiduciary duty, and securities fraud. Trial counsel for President Bush in the 2000 Florida election contest against Vice-President Gore.
**Career:** National Law Journal's Co-Lawyer of The Year in 2000; 33 years in practice.
**Personal:** JD, cum laude, The University of Texas School of Law, 1972; Order of the Coif; Phi Delta Phi; BA, cum laude, The University of Texas, 1968.

## THOMAS, John B
Hicks, Thomas, Lillienstern LLP, Houston
713 547 9106
jthomas@hicks-thomas.com
*Recommended in Environment*
**Practice Areas:** Commercial litigation with extensive experience in environmental, natural resources and energy law.
**Prof. Memberships:** State Bar of Texas; Houston Bar Association, Environmental Section; American Bar Association.
**Career:** A Founding Partner of the litigation firm Hicks Thomas & Lilienstern, John Thomas represents clients in complex commercial litigation matters and has in-depth experience handling environmental, natural resources and energy law cases. He has argued environmental cases in state and federal courts in Texas, California and Louisiana. Recent accomplishments include obtaining a favorable verdict for a client in a ten-week trial in case of first impression under the Texas Solid Waste Disposal Act. Mr Thomas also utilizes his knowledge of environmental litigation to proactively advise clients on environmental planning, strategy, indemnity and insurance matters. Mr Thomas has been named among Texas' best attorneys in Business Litigation by Texas Monthly magazine and 'Texas Super Lawyers' magazine in 2003, 2004 and 2005. He has also been recognized as one of the best attorneys in Environmental Law by 'Inside Houston' magazine.
**Personal:** BS, Western Michigan University, 1983; JD, The University of Michigan

Law School, 1986; Judicial Clerkship, Honorable Edith H Jones, United States Court of Appeals for the Fifth Circuit.

**THOMPSON, Dahl**
Andrews Kurth LLP, Houston
713 225 7000
*Recommended in Energy, Projects*

**THOMPSON, Jay**
Thompson, Coe, Cousins & Irons, LLP, Austin 512 708 8200
*Recommended in Insurance*

**THOMPSON, JR, Clark**
Bracewell & Giuliani LLP, Houston
713 221 1477
clark.thompson@bracewellgiuliani.com
*Recommended in Real Estate*
**Practice Areas:** Represents a variety of clients in the acquisition, development, finance and divestiture of commercial and industrial projects, ranging from complex office, industrial, residential and retail developments to power plants, pipelines, terminals and other energy related facilities. Has a particular expertise in large corporate relocations, having been personally involved in leasing transactions totaling in excess of 5,000,000 square feet over the past few years. Recognized in his practice by national and regional legal publications for the last five years.
**Personal:** JD, with honors, The University of Texas at Austin, 1980; BA, magna cum laude, Washington and Lee University, 1977.

**THURBER, Mark**
Andrews Kurth LLP, Houston
713 220 4200
*Recommended in Energy, Projects*

**TOBIAS, Paul R**
Wilson Sonsini Goodrich & Rosati, Austin 512 338 5401
ptobias@wsgr.com
*Recommended in Technology*
**Practice Areas:** Practice focuses on helping technology and growth companies form and operate businesses, raise capital through private and public offerings, and buy and sell companies.
**Prof. Memberships:** Admitted to practice in Texas and California. Member, American Bar Association; Austin Bar Association; Board of Directors, Texas Exes Alumni Association, University of Texas.
**Career:** Managing Partner of Wilson Sonsini Goodrich & Rosati's Austin office.
**Personal:** JD and BA, University of Texas, Austin.

**TOBOR, Ben D**
Bracewell & Giuliani LLP, Houston
713 221 1352
ben.tobor@bracewellgiuliani.com
*Recommended in Intellectual Property*
**Practice Areas:** Recognized by IP Worldwide in 2001 in 'Patent Plums' for

the 'most valuable US patents and the lawyers who nurtured them' and again in 2002 among the lawyers who obtained one of the '10 Patents That Changed The World'. Experience includes acquisition of intellectual property rights, including copyrights, US and international patents and trademarks, intellectual property licensing and litigation concerning patents and trade secrets. Represents clients in many technologies including medical equipment and devices, oil and gas field equipment, air conditioning and heating equipment, waste treatment, chemicals and chemical processing, beauty care products and computer software.

**TOTTENHAM, Terry O**
Fulbright & Jaworski L.L.P., Austin
512 536 4555
ttottenham@fulbright.com
*Recommended in Healthcare*
**Practice Areas:** Healthcare.
**Prof. Memberships:** American Board of Trial Advocates (President, Austin chapter); American College of Trial Lawyers (fellow); International Academy of Trial Lawyers (fellow); International Society of Barristers (fellow).
**Career:** Terry heads the firm-wide Pharmaceutical and Medical Device Litigation Practice Group, and is Partner-in-Charge of the Austin office. Terry is certified in Personal Injury and Civil Trial Law by the Texas Board of Legal Specialization. He is also certified in Civil Trial Advocacy by the National Board of Trial Advocacy.
**Personal:** LLM, George Washington University (1973); JD, with honors, The University of Texas School of Law (1970); Registered Pharmacist (1967); BS, magna cum laude, Pharmacy, The University of Texas (1967).

**TOWNSEND, John**
Townsend & Jones, Houston
713 521 9773
*Recommended in Tax*

**TOWNSEND, Roger**
Alexander Dubose Jones & Townsend, Austin 512 482 9300
*Recommended in Litigation*

**TURNER, Robert**
Jones Day, Dallas
214 969 2984
rwturner@jonesday.com
*Recommended in Intellectual Property*
**Practice Areas:** His primary emphasis is in intellectual property litigation. He has been lead trial counsel in numerous complex patent, trade secret, trademark, and copyright matters for a number of Fortune 500 companies and has tried nonjury and jury cases as well as International Trade Commission and arbitration cases. He is an Adjunct Professor of Law at The University of Texas and is on the faculty of the Patent Resources Group providing CLE to attorneys throughout the US.

**Prof. Memberships:** ABA; State Bar of Texas; Dallas Bar Association; Dallas-Fort Worth Intellectual Property Law Association.

**UNDERKOFLER, Paul**
Goins, Underkofler, Crawford & Langdon LLP, Dallas 214 969 5454
*Recommended in Construction*

**UNGER, Timothy**
Andrews Kurth LLP, Houston
713 220 4200
*Recommended in Energy, Projects*

**VALDERRAMA, Teresa S**
Baker Botts LLP, Houston
*Recommended in Employment*
**Practice Areas:** Represents management in all aspects of labor and employment-related trial work and preventative counseling. Practice includes workplace investigations, individual/class-based discrimination and harassment, wage/overtime collective actions, whistleblowers, noncompete/trade secret disputes, and defending employers before federal/state courts and agencies in all aspects of employment law (eg, SOx, NLRA, RLA, Title VII, FLSA, ADEA, ERISA, ADA, OSHA, Texas Codes). Represents major national oil and gas, retail, transportation industry companies and emerging enterprises.
**Career:** 17 years in practice. Board certified, Labor/Employment law, Texas Board of Legal Specialization.
**Personal:** JD, summa cum laude, University of Houston Law Center, 1988; BA, Rice University, 1983.

**VAN FLEET, Allan**
Vinson & Elkins LLP, Houston
713 758 2222
*Recommended in Antitrust*

**VAN KIRK, Mark**
Baker Botts LLP, Dallas
214 953 6593
mark.vankirk@bakerbotts.com
*Recommended in Real Estate*
**Practice Areas:** Practice focuses on representing developers, investors and other privately held buyers, sellers, and lenders in connection with development, acquisition, debt and equity financing, and sale of major retail, office, hotel, multifamily, industrial, resort, assisted living, and mixed-use projects; complex lease arrangements; private real estate equity funds; and workouts and restructurings.
**Prof. Memberships:** State Bar of Texas; Dallas Bar Association.
**Personal:** JD from University of Chicago Law School in 1982; MBA from University of Chicago in 1982; BA (magna cum laude) from Duke University in 1978.

**VAY, John**
Kelly, Hart & Hallman, A Professional Corporation, Austin 512 495 6400
*Recommended in Environment*

**VILARDO, Terry Otero**
Mayer, Brown, Rowe & Maw LLP, Houston 713 546 0509
tvilardo@mayerbrownrowe.com
*Recommended in Banking & Finance*
**Practice Areas:** Represents lenders and developers in domestic, emerging markets and cross-border and international transactions including acquisitions, cross-border investments, green field projects, project finance including construction and term financings, joint ventures, and privatizations; represents lenders in securitizations, including structuring of cross-border multiseller vehicles and sales of receivables resulting from the sale and transportation of oil and gas; represents lenders in structured and secured financings, including synthetic leasing, production payments, financings of oil and gas onshore and offshore properties including methane gas financings, financings of pipelines, power plants, chemical plants, airplanes, refineries and shipping financings.
**Prof. Memberships:** Texas, 1984 Hispanic Bar Association. American Bar Association, Section of Corporation, Business and Banking Law. Houston Bar Association.
**Career:** Joined Mayer, Brown, Rowe & Maw LLP, Houston, 1984; Partner, 1992.
**Personal:** University of Houston, JD cum laude, 1984. Georgetown University, Washington, DC, BSFS, 1979. Speaks Spanish (native); knowledge of French and Italian.

**VILLAREAL, Patricia J**
Jones Day, Dallas 214 969 2973
pjvillareal@jonesday.com
*Recommended in Litigation*
**Practice Areas:** Co-Chair of the Securities and Shareholder Litigation and SEC Enforcement Practice. She has been with the firm for over 24 years, specializing in securities and complex litigation and corporate governance. She has been highly successful in winning securities cases – in motions to dismiss under the Private Securities Litigation Reform Act, in motions for summary judgment and in Daubert motions. Her practice includes defense of public companies and directors and officers in securities and derivative actions, representation of boards and board committees, and corporate governance counseling. She is also an expert on director and officer indemnification and insurance.

**VINEYARD, Dan**
Connelly Baker Wotring Jackson LLP, Houston 713 980 1700
*Recommended in Environment*

**VOGEL, Peter**
Gardere Wynne Sewell LLP, Dallas
214 999 4422
pvogel@gardere.com
*Recommended in Technology*
**Practice Areas:** Internet and computer

technology, intellectual property, outsourcing, and trial.

**Prof. Memberships:** Chair, Texas Supreme Court Judicial Committee on Information Technology; Founding Chair, Computer and Technology Section of the State Bar of Texas; Texas Task Force for Uniform Electronic Transaction Act (UETA).

**Career:** Peter Vogel's involvement with the computer industry began in 1967. For nearly 30 years of legal practice, Peter has drawn on his Masters in Computer Science and his experience as a mainframe programmer, systems analyst, and management consultant. In addition to litigating disputes, Peter offers practical advice on technology related business issues and negotiates complex agreements. Areas include ERP implementation projects, Internet security, software patents, copyrights, trade secret protection, website business management, and outsourcing. As an Adjunct Professor in the Law of eCommerce at SMU, Peter stays on the leading edge of emerging Internet law (See smu-ecommerce.gardere.com). Peter is often appointed as an Arbitrator, Court Ordered Mediator, and Special Master in internet, intellectual property, and computer technology litigation and heads the firm's Electronic Discovery and Document Retention Practice Group.

**Publications:** 'Due Diligence and Don't Be Sorry – Absolute Rules of Computer Contracts', www.watchIT.com, January 2002; 'Limiting Liability Exposure of the IT Manager', www.watchIT.com, February 2003.

**Personal:** MS, Computer Science, American University, 1972; JD, St Mary's University School of Law, 1976; BBA, University of Texas at Austin, 1969.

### VOLK, William R
Vinson & Elkins LLP, Austin
512 542 8609
wvolk@velaw.com
*Recommended in Technology*

**Practice Areas:** Partner, Co-Section Head of Corporate Finance and Securities Section. Practice includes venture capital and private equity financing, public offerings, mergers and acquisitions, joint ventures and strategic alliances and general corporate counseling and advice.

**Prof. Memberships:** State Bar of Texas (Venture Capital Committee, Section of Business Law); American Bar Association; Life Fellow, Texas Bar Foundation.

**Career:** Vanderbilt University, BA, 1972; The University of Texas School of Law, JD, with honors, 1975.

### VOYLES, Robb L
Baker Botts LLP, Austin
512 322 2500
robb.voyles@bakerbotts.com
*Recommended in Litigation*

**Practice Areas:** Mr Voyles is Chair of

Baker Botts' worldwide Litigation Practice. He has represented US accounting firms regarding accountants' liability and securities actions and has counseled law firms in professional liability actions. He has also represented high technology companies in disputes involving trade secrets, noncompetition agreements, computer software and the performance of computer systems, and other high-tech products and services.

**Career:** 23+ years of practice. Partner-in-Charge of the Austin office (1994-2005). Member of the firm's Executive Committee.

**Personal:** JD (magna cum laude), University of Michigan Law School, 1982 (summa cum laude); Business Administration in Accounting, University of Dayton, 1979.

### WALKER, Kathleen
Kemp Smith LLP, El Paso
915 533 4424
*Recommended in Immigration*

### WALLANDER, William
Vinson & Elkins LLP, Dallas
214 220 7905
bwallander@velaw.com
*Recommended in Bankruptcy*

**Practice Areas:** Experience includes representation of creditors, committees, trustees, and debtors in restructuring, exchange offers, remedies enforcement, prepackaged plans, and bankruptcy cases.

**Prof. Memberships:** American Bar Association; Dallas Bar Association; Dallas Bankruptcy Bar Association; Texas Banker's Association; American Bankruptcy Institute; Turnaround Management Association; Keeton Fellow, University of Texas School of Law; Dean's Roundtable, University of Texas School of Law.

**Career:** Admitted to Texas Bar, 1984. Came to firm as Partner, 1999.

**Personal:** University of Pittsburgh, BA magna cum laude, 1981; The University of Texas School of Law, JD, 1984; and University of Phoenix, MBA summa cum laude, 2001.

### WALLENSTEIN, Jim
Jenkens & Gilchrist PC, Dallas
214 855 4500
*Recommended in Real Estate*

### WALTERS, Robert
Vinson & Elkins LLP, Dallas
214 220 7704
rwalters@velaw.com
*Recommended in Antitrust, Litigation*

**Practice Areas:** Trial of antitrust, securities, technology, class action, and business controversies in federal and state courts. Counsels clients on the antitrust implications of business transactions, including mergers and acquisitions.

**Prof. Memberships:** Texas Bar Foundation; The Center for American and International Law; Dallas Citizens Council;

The Dallas Assembly; Dallas Council on World Affairs.

**Career:** Admitted to Texas Bar, 1983. Admitted to partnership, 1990. Serves on firm's Management Committee.

**Personal:** Graduated from The University of Texas, BA with highest honors, 1980; and The University of Texas School of Law, JD with honors, 1983. Texas Law Review.

### WALTON, Gibson
Vinson & Elkins LLP, Houston
713 758 2026
gwalton@velaw.com
*Recommended in Litigation*

**Practice Areas:** Civil trial work; represents both plaintiffs and defendants in commercial, corporate, securities, fiduciary, construction, professional liability, probate, and energy litigation.

**Prof. Memberships:** International Society of Barristers; ABOTA; IADC; Houston Bar Association (former President); Houston Bar Foundation (former Chair); Fellow, American Bar Foundation; American Inn of Court; Board Certified, 1981.

**Career:** Partner since 1982.

**Publications:** Numerous papers and speeches on trial advocacy, evidence, procedure, construction law, and other litigation topics for various professional organizations.

**Personal:** University of Virginia, BA 1972 (Pi Beta Kappa); The University of Texas School of Law, JD 1975 (Order of the Coif, Texas Law Review).

### WATT, Dick
Watt, Beckworth, Thompson & Henneman, Houston 713 650 8100
*Recommended in Energy*

### WAWRO, Mark
Susman Godfrey LLP, Houston
713 651 9366
*Recommended in Litigation*

### WEEMS, Philip R
King & Spalding LLP, Houston
713 276 7373
pweems@kslaw.com
*Recommended in Energy, Projects*

**Practice Areas:** Practice includes structuring, negotiating and documenting projects involving the international exploration, production, processing, transportation and sale of oil and gas and the acquisition and disposition of energy-related assets. Extensive energy company experience. Possesses special expertise in legal aspects of developing, marketing, constructing and operating LNG and natural gas projects.

**Prof. Memberships:** Association of International Petroleum Negotiators; California Bar Association; International Bar Association; Texas State Bar.

**Personal:** BA, Texas Tech University, 1979; JD, cum laude, Texas Tech University, 1982.

### WEINER, Sanford A
Vinson & Elkins LLP, Houston
713 758 2558
sweiner@velaw.com
*Recommended in Real Estate*

**Practice Areas:** Real estate transactions and finance law. Co-Head of National Real Estate Practice.

**Prof. Memberships:** Member: American College of Real Estate Lawyers (President 2003); Anglo-Amercian Real Property Institute.

**Career:** Admitted to Texas Bar, 1971. Joined Vinson & Elkins, LLP 1971, became Partner in 1978.

**Publications:** Introduction: 'Making Choice of Law a Contact Sport: Contractual Choices of Law in Texas', 54 Texas Bar Journal 262 (1991).

**Personal:** Born August 21, 1946. Graduated The University of Texas, BA in 1968 (cum laude, Phi Beta Kappa), and Harvard University, JD in 1971 (cum laude).

### WELLER, Phillip
Vinson & Elkins LLP, Houston
713 758 2222
*Recommended in Real Estate*

### WELLS, Benjamin
Baker Botts LLP, Houston
713 229 1210
benjamin.wells@bakerbotts.com
*Recommended in Tax*

**Practice Areas:** Chair: Tax Department (firmwide). Concentration: cross-border transactions, tax planning for American companies operating abroad, structuring 'inbound' investments by investors in other countries, other acquisitions and joint ventures, debt and stock offerings, and other tax planning.

**Prof. Memberships:** ABA Tax Section (Chair, Corporate Tax Committee, 2001-02); American College of Tax Counsel.

**Career:** Captain in US Army in the Judge Advocate General's Corp 1969-72.

**Publications:** Articles on international tax, corporate tax, and other tax subjects.

**Personal:** JD, cum laude, Harvard Law School, 1968; BA, magna cum laude, Latin, Amherst College, 1965.

### WEST, Glenn D
Weil, Gotshal & Manges LLP, Dallas
214 746 7780
glenn.west@weil.com
*Recommended in Corporate/M&A*

**Practice Areas:** Glenn West's practice focuses on private equity, mergers and acquisitions, and corporate finance. He represents leading private equity and venture firms in acquiring and investing in public and private companies in the US and Europe. He has led public and private acquisition and corporate finance transactions for clients including Ewing Management Group, HM Capital Partners LLC, Lindsay, Goldberg & Bessemer, Koch Industries, American Airlines, Greyhound Lines, Inc., Six Flags, Inc., Home Interiors & Gifts, Inc., LIN Television Corporation, Blockbuster, Inc. and Brazos Equity Partners. He also led the project finance for the new American Airlines Center in Dallas. Mr West is a member of the Board of Directors of United Way of Metropolitan Dallas and a member of the Finance Committee and Board of Directors of the Vogel Alcove Childcare Center for the Homeless in Dallas, Texas.

**Personal:** Tarleton State, BA, 1975; Texas Tech University School of Law, JD, 1978.

### WHEAT, David
Thompson & Knight LLP, Dallas
214 969 1468
David.Wheat@tklaw.com
*Recommended in Tax*

**Practice Areas:** Mr Wheat focuses his practice on corporate tax, mergers and acquisition tax, transactions involving partnerships and LLCs, state tax, and tax controversies. He provides clients with transactional planning and advice, document preparation, and preparation of tax opinions on federal and state tax implications of business transactions, including corporate mergers and acquisitions and the formation and operation of partnerships and limited liability companies.

**Prof. Memberships:** Member of the State Bars of Texas and Louisiana, American and Dallas Bar Associations, Dallas Bar Foundation.

**Personal:** New York University (Master of Laws in Taxation, 1989); Louisiana State University (JD, 1988; BS, 1985).

### WHITE, T Gordon
McKool Smith, Austin
512 692 8700
gwhite@mckoolsmith.com
*Recommended in Intellectual Property*

**Practice Areas:** Intellectual property litigation for US and international corporations, including patent litigation, patent licensing, and appeals, particularly in cases involving complex electrical technology and telecommunications, including computer hardware and software.

**Prof. Memberships:** State Bar of Texas; American Intellectual Property Law Association; Austin Bar Association.

**Career:** Managing principal in Austin since 2000.

**Personal:** University of Houston Law Center (JD, 1976); University of Texas (MSEE, with honors, 1967); University of Texas (BSEE, with honors, 1965); Texas Super Lawyer (Law and Politics Magazine, 2003-04).

### WIELEBINSKI, Joseph
Munsch Hardt Kopf & Harr, P. C., Dallas
214 855 7561
jwielebinski@munsch.com
*Recommended in Bankruptcy*

**Practice Areas:** All aspects of reorganization, creditors' rights and corporate finance. Practice includes loan workouts and restructures, bankruptcy litigation, and representation of Committees (both

official and ad hoc) and Trustees. Currently serves as Federal Court Receiver.

**Prof. Memberships:** American Bankruptcy Institute; American Bar Association; Turnaround Management Association (past President, Dallas/Ft Worth Chapter); and Dallas Bar Association (past President, Commercial Law Section).

**Career:** Shareholder (since 1987) and Chairman of the Reorganization/Corporate Finance Practice Group.

**Publications:** Frequent speaker and author on various bankruptcy, creditors' rights and litigation issues.

**Personal:** Syracuse University College of Law (JD, 1983); Syracuse University Maxwell School (MBA, 1983); Temple University (BA, magna cum laude, 1980).

### WIELINSKI, Patrick
Cokinos, Bosien and Young, Houston
713 535 5500
*Recommended in Insurance*

### WILKINS, Timothy A
Bracewell & Giuliani LLP, Houston
713 221 1136
timothy.wilkins@bracewellgiuliani.com
*Recommended in Environment*

**Practice Areas:** Assists companies in identifying and addressing environmental issues; advises on environmental management systems and auditing programs; defends administrative, civil, and criminal environmental enforcement actions; helps resolve contaminated property issues; and counsels on environmental aspects of transactions, project siting and development. Clients include power, energy, cement, chemicals, telecommunications, and real estate businesses.

**Career:** Heads firm's Environmental Practice. Former Editor-in-Chief, Harvard Environmental Law Review. Adjunct Professor, University of Houston Law Center.

**Personal:** JD, cum laude, Harvard Law School, 1993; MPP, John F Kennedy School of Government, Harvard University, 1993; BA, magna cum laude, Phi Beta Kappa, Trinity University, 1988.

### WILLIAMSON, Deborah
Cox Smith Matthews Incorporated, San Antonio 210 554 5275
ddwilliamson@coxsmith.com
*Recommended in Bankruptcy*

**Practice Areas:** Deborah is a shareholder and the Department Leader for the firm's Creditor's Rights, Restructuring and Bankruptcy Department and is Board Certified by the Texas Board of Legal Specialization and by the American Bankruptcy Board of Certification in Business Bankruptcy Law. Deborah advises clients on all aspects of business bankruptcy, including pre-bankruptcy strategic planning, fraudulent conveyances, acquisitions, lending, and complex issues in real estate and commercial transactions.

**Prof. Memberships:** Past President, American Bankruptcy Institute; Former Executive Editor and Author of Bench Notes Column, ABI Journal; Vice Chair, State Bar of Texas, Bankruptcy Section; Chair, Examination Committee for Texas Board of Legal Specialization (Bankruptcy); Chair, San Antonio Bar Association, Bankruptcy Subcommittee of Federal Courts Committee; Director, American Board of Certification; Former Vice President, San Antonio Bankruptcy Bar Association.

**Career:** Deborah has testified before the United States Senate Judiciary Committee Subcommittee on Administrative Oversight and the Courts and was selected by Texas Monthly as one of the Top 50 Women Lawyers in Texas and as an Outstanding National Bankruptcy Attorney in 1998.

**Personal:** University Of Houston Law Center, JD, cum laude, 1981. Order of the Coif; Order of the Barons; Director, Board of Advocates; Phi Delta Phi. University of Texas at El Paso, BA, Political Science, 1977.

### WILLIAMSON, Holly H
Akin Gump Strauss Hauer & Feld LLP, Houston
713 220 8136
hwilliamson@akingump.com
*Recommended in Employment*

**Practice Areas:** Represents corporations in the chemical, transportation, oil and gas production, retailing and servicing, and telecommunications industries in complex litigation and appeals involving trade secrets, unfair competition, discrimination and harassment claims, benefits, and wage and hour issues. Practice includes federal, state employment matters involving ADA, ADEA and laws prohibiting discrimination, harassment and retaliation under Title VII of the Civil Rights Act of 1964.

**Prof. Memberships:** Fellow, Texas and Houston Bar Foundations.

**Personal:** BBA (honors), Southwest Texas State University; JD (magna cum laude), South Texas College of Law; Clerk, Edith Hollan Jones, US Court of Appeals for the 5th Circuit.

### WILSON, Robert
Haynes and Boone LLP, Dallas
214 651 5000
*Recommended in Real Estate*

### WILSON, Thomas H
Vinson & Elkins LLP, Houston
713 758 2042
twilson@velaw.com
*Recommended in Employment*

**Practice Areas:** Tom's area of practice is labor and employment law and includes labor/employment issues in business transactions, traditional labor matters, ERISA, international employment issues, employment litigation, drafting and litigation of non-competition agreements,

and OSHA issues.

**Prof. Memberships:** American Bar Association, Committees on International Labor and Employment Law and OSHA, Labor Relations Advisory Committee; American Health Lawyers Association; Interamerican Bar Association.

**Publications:** 'OSHA Guide for Healthcare Facilities', Thompson Publishing; Norwegian labor law chapter of ABA International Labor Law Treatise, to be published 2006.

**Personal:** Drake University, BA in journalism cum laude1982; University of Tennessee, JD with high honors, 1985.

### WOOD, Ivan
Strasburger & Price LLP, Dallas
214 651 4300
*Recommended in Healthcare*

### WOOD, William
Fulbright & Jaworski L.L.P., Houston
713 651 5537
wwood@fulbright.com
*Recommended in Energy*

**Practice Areas:** Litigation and arbitration, domestic and international.

**Prof. Memberships:** Mr Wood is a Member of the State Bar of Texas, and the Houston, American, and International Bar Associations. He is a fellow of the Houston Bar Foundation, past President of The University of Houston Law Alumni Association, and a current Board Member of the University of Houston Law Foundation. A skilled trial advocate, Mr Wood is an elected member of the American Board of Trial Advocates.

**Career:** As a Partner in the Houston office of Fulbright & Jaworski L.L.P., Mr Wood holds leadership roles in the firm's Energy, Energy Litigation, and Latin America Practice Groups and has an active trial and arbitration practice. He concentrates his practice on the defense and prosecution of business litigation matters with an emphasis on energy industry controversies.

**Personal:** BBA (Accounting), Texas A&M, (1981); JD, University of Houston Law Center (1984), Associate Editor of the Houston Law Review.

### WORRELL, Danny
Brown McCarroll LLP, Austin
512 472 5456
*Recommended in Environment*

### WORTLEY, Michael
Vinson & Elkins LLP, Dallas
214 220 7732
mwortley@velaw.com
*Recommended in Corporate/M&A*

**Practice Areas:** Primary area of practice is corporate and securities law. Experience in the food, telecommunications, oil and gas, REITs, manufacturing, healthcare, biotechnology, and high technology industries. Clients include issuers, underwriters, and private equity and other investors in public and private securities and M&A transactions.

**Prof. Memberships:** American Bar Association and Dallas Bar Association.
**Career:** Admitted to Texas Bar, 1978. Came to the firm as a Partner, 1995.
**Personal:** Graduated from Southern Methodist University, BA with highest honors, 1970, the University of North Carolina at Chapel Hill, Masters of Regional Planning, 1973, and Southern Methodist University, JD with honors,1978.

## WRIGHT, Robert
Baker Botts LLP, Houston
713 229 1237
bob.wright@bakerbotts.com
*Recommended in Real Estate*

**Practice Areas:** Represents clients in Texas and multi-state acquisitions and divestitures, financing, workouts, development, and leasing of real estate and energy projects. Counsels clients on environmental issues including investigations, remediation, voluntary cleanup programs, public disclosure requirements, and environmental claims involving real estate projects.
**Prof. Memberships:** American College of Real Estate Lawyers (former member of Board of Governors); Houston Real Estate Lawyers Council; State Bar of Texas (former section chair); Houston Bar Association (former section Chair).
**Personal:** JD from Columbia University School of Law, 1975 (Harlan Fiske Stone Scholar, Phi Delta Phi); AB, magna cum laude, from Princeton University, 1972.

## WULFE, Scott
Vinson & Elkins LLP, Houston
713 758 2750
swulfe@velaw.com
*Recommended in Corporate/M&A*

**Practice Areas:** Concentrates on public and private mergers and acquisitions, securities offerings and corporate control and governance issues. Has extensive experience representing private equity funds and public companies.
**Career:** Admitted to Texas Bar, 1983; joined Vinson & Elkins, 1983; admitted to the partnership, January 1991.
**Personal:** Graduated from The University of Texas, Plan II BA with highest honors in 1979 (Phi Beta Kappa) and JD in 1983 with high honors (Chancellors).

## WYATT, William
Vinson & Elkins LLP, Dallas
214 220 7700
*Recommended in Real Estate*

## YAGER, Russell
Vinson & Elkins LLP, Dallas
214 220 7820
ryager@velaw.com
*Recommended in Insurance*

**Practice Areas:** Russ handles antitrust and general business litigation at both trial and appellate levels, with an emphasis on defending class actions. He has defended cases involving issues of antitrust conspiracy, securities fraud, RICO, trademark infringement, federal taxation and insurance coverage. His clients have included companies in the chemical, insurance, accounting, transportation, healthcare and entertainment industries.
**Prof. Memberships:** American Bar Association and Dallas Bar Association.
**Career:** Admitted to Texas Bar, 1992. Came to firm in 1992.
**Personal:** Graduated from the University of California, Berkeley, AB with high distinction and highest honors, 1985, and Yale Law School, JD, 1988.

## YARBROUGH, Fletcher
Carrington, Coleman, Sloman & Blumenthal, LLP, Dallas 214 855 3000
*Recommended in Litigation*

## YEATES, Marie
Vinson & Elkins LLP, Houston
713 758 4576
myeates@velaw.com
*Recommended in Litigation*

**Practice Areas:** Chairs V&E Appellate Practice; concentrates on civil appeals. Certified in civil appellate law by Texas Board of Legal Specialization. Named by National Law Journal as one of top 50 women litigators in US.
**Prof. Memberships:** American Academy of Appellate Lawyers, American Bar Association; American Law Institute.
**Career:** Admitted to practice: Louisiana, 1980; Texas, 1982. Joined Vinson & Elkins: 1981; admitted to partnership: 1988.
**Personal:** Louisiana State University, BS, 1977 (summa cum laude); Louisiana State University School of Law, JD, 1980 (first in class); Editor-in-Chief, Louisiana Law Review; clerk to US Fifth Circuit Judge Alvin Rubin, 1980-81.

## YORK, Larry
York, Keller & Field, Austin
512 867 1616
*Recommended in Insurance*

## YOUNG, William
Vinson & Elkins LLP, Dallas
214 220 7994
byoung@velaw.com
*Recommended in Banking & Finance*

**Practice Areas:** Represents US and international private investment funds, commercial banks and corporations in private debt transactions, including syndicated credits, asset based loans, real estate finance and mezzanine debt. Significant emphasis on international financings, and particularly, securitized financing of Asian and European distressed debt and real estate portfolios.
**Prof. Memberships:** Section on Business Law, American Bar Association, International Law Section, and Dallas Bar Association.
**Career:** Admitted to Texas Bar, 1985. Came to firm as Partner, 1998.
**Personal:** University of Mississippi BBA (1982), JD (1984); Managing Editor, Mississippi Law Journal; married, three children.

## YUNGBLUT, Stephen
Pratt & Sanderford, Temple
254 773 8311
*Recommended in Construction*

## ZACHOS, Susan
Kelly, Hart & Hallman, A Professional Corporation, Fort Worth
817 332 2500
*Recommended in Environment*

# ANDREWS KURTH LLP

## THE FIRM

**Managing Partner:** Howard Ayers

**Number of partners:** 192
**Number of other lawyers:** 224

### AREAS OF PRACTICE:

| | |
|---|---|
| Litigation | 25.8% |
| Business Transactions | 19.3% |
| Corporate & Securities | 28.2% |
| Bankruptcy | 12.5% |
| Public Law | 7.4% |
| Tax | 1.8% |
| Environmental | 1.5% |
| Labor & Employment | 0.9% |
| Intellectual Property | 2.5% |

**FIRM OVERVIEW:** A prominent participant in the early commercial development of the Southwest region of the US, Andrews Kurth today is a nationally ranked and recognized firm that handles the vital interests of established companies and emerging businesses around the globe. Founded in 1902, the firm has an international client base and has experience in all major industries and areas of business law and litigation. The result is the consistent delivery of efficient, effective and valuable legal services. Andrews Kurth enjoys an international presence, providing legal services worldwide from offices in major corporate and government centers on two continents.

## MAIN AREAS OF PRACTICE:

**Corporate & Securities:** Andrews Kurth is recognized as having one of the most effective corporate and securities departments, representing many of the Fortune 500 companies. Since the inception of the firm more than 100 years ago, Andrews Kurth has maintained the focus of practicing quality law. The firm's lawyers serve public and private corporations, partnerships, joint ventures, national and regional investment banks, merchant banks, and other financial institutions, venture capital firms, capital market groups of commercial banks and individual clients. The firm is recognized as a leading securites firm for the energy industry. Areas of practice include all types of corporate finance transactoins, joint venture transactions, mergers and acquisitions, and complex, tax-sensitive financings. In addition, the firm created the master limited partnership, and has been involved in establishing more than 70% of the MLPs in existence.

**Business Transactions:** Lawyers in this practice counsel to a far-ranging client base, with specific emphasis on transactional matters related to energy, banking, public and private financing and real estate. These involve work in project and structured finance, syndicated lending, leasing, swaps and loan workouts, and restructuring, and in the real estate area, acquisition and development and the financing of a wide array of commercial, industrial and public projects. In addition, the firm's work includes representation to all aspects of the energy industry.

**Litigation:** With trial lawyers in Houston, Dallas, New York, Austin, Washington, DC and Los Angeles, the firm offers coast to coast experience in jury and bench trials in state and federal courts and other tribunals. The majority of the firm's lawyers concentrate on general corporate and business litigation, handling a variety of complex cases for companies in virtually every industry.

**Bankruptcy:** The firm offers a sophisticated insolvency practice, representing clients nationwide in large, complex bankruptcies under both Chapter 11 and Chapter 7. Currently, Andrews Kurth ranks among the country's seven largest bankruptcy practices. The firm enjoys a large, diverse client base, representing debtors, creditors, trustees, creditors' committees, and institutional lenders. Bankruptcy issues are handled out of all the firm's offices. Firm lawyers also handle a significant volume of out of court restructurings and workouts, and Houston and New York lawyers handle the regulatory aspects of financial institution insolvency work.

## HEAD OFFICE

**TEXAS**
600 Travis, Suite 4200, **Houston**, Texas 77002
**Tel:** 713 220 4200   **Fax:** 713 220 4285
**Email:** webmaster@andrewskurth.com
**Website:** www.andrewskurth.com

## BRANCH OFFICES

**TEXAS**
111 Congress Ave, Suite 1700, **Austin**, Texas 78701
**Tel:** 512 320 9200   **Fax:** 512 320 9292

1717 Main Street, Suite 3700, **Dallas**, Texas 75201
**Tel:** 214 659 4400   **Fax:** 214 659 4401

Waterway Plaza Two, 10001 Woodloch Forest Drive, Suite 200
**The Woodlands**, Texas 77380
**Tel:** 713 220 4801   **Fax:** 713 220 4815

**CALIFORNIA**
601 South Figueroa, Suite 3700, **Los Angeles**, California 90017
**Tel:** 213 896 3100   **Fax:** 213 896 3137

**NEW YORK**
450 Lexington Avenue, **New York**, New York 10017
**Tel:** 212 850 2800   **Fax:** 212 850 2929

**WASHINGTON**
1350 I Street, NW, Suite 1100, **Washington**,
District of Columbia 20005
**Tel:** 202 662 2700   **Fax:** 202 662 2739

## INTERNATIONAL OFFICES

The firm also has offices in London, England and Beijing, China.

## CONTACTS

| | |
|---|---|
| Corporate & Securities | Robert V Jewell |
| Business Transactions | Thomas J Perich |
| Litigation | Rosemarie Donnelly |
| Bankruptcy | Hugh M Ray |

# ANDREWS
ATTORNEYS   KURTH LLP

# BAKER BOTTS LLP

## THE FIRM

**Managing Partner:** Walter J Smith

**Number of partners worldwide:** 263
**Number of other lawyers worldwide:** 426

**FIRM OVERVIEW:** Baker Botts is a leading international law firm, recognized for its energy, intellectual property, corporate, litigation, tax and environmental practices. This depth of knowledge enables the firm to work in partnership with its clients to deliver the right solution. Founded in Houston, Texas in 1840, Baker Botts has a network of offices in the US, Europe, Russia, and the Middle East, advising clients in over 100 countries around the world. Baker Botts ranks among the largest law firms in the United States and conducts operations on a basis that is global in scope and influence. Baker Botts also has one of the largest IP practices in the US for a general service firm, with IP Law & Business recognizing Baker Botts as one of the leading firms to represent IP America.

**CLIENTS:** Baker Botts is legal and business counsel to many of the world's leading companies, including nearly every major oil company in the United States, as well as numerous international companies. The firm's clients include private and public companies, banks, insurance companies, investment banking and venture capital firms, nonprofit organizations, individuals, estates, partnerships and government agencies. Its lawyers work with clients in almost every area of the law, including international and domestic corporate and financial matters, corporate governance, technology, intellectual property, business litigation, appellate matters, white collar criminal defense, government contracts, federal and state legislative matters, energy and oil and gas matters, real estate, administrative and regulatory matters involving energy, environmental and international trade.

## WORLDWIDE OFFICES

### DUBAI

In 2005, the firm expanded its presence in the region by opening an office in Dubai to complement its existing office in Riyadh, Saudi Arabia. Baker Botts' Dubai office provides service to clients in a number of sectors in the energy industry, including oil and gas exploration and development, oil field services, electric power, LNG, petrochemicals, pipelines, and gas-to-liquids. The firm's energy-related project development and finance work is enhanced by their experience with the complex issues faced in financing these projects under local law, which is largely founded on the *shari'a* or Islamic law. In addition to work across the broad spectrum of the energy sector, the Dubai office serves clients with their corporate, banking, finance (including Islamic finance), capital markets, telecommunications, government contracts and dispute resolution matters.

### SAUDI ARABIA

The firm's Riyadh office operates in association with the law office of Mohammed bin Saud Al-Rasheed. It is acknowledged as one of the leading practices it the region and advises clients in Saudi Arabia and throughout the Middle East on a broad range of commercial, banking, project finance, telecoms, oil and gas matters, as well as litigation and arbitration.

### EUROPE

The London office plays a pivotal role in the firm's international activity; serving clients in the UK, continental Europe, and beyond. It handles market leading energy, finance, corporate/M&A, TMT, chemicals and dispute resolution matters, and has both UK and US law capabilities.

## HEAD OFFICE

**TEXAS**
One Shell Plaza, 910 Louisiana Street, **Houston** TX 77002-4995
**Tel:** 713 229 1234  **Fax:** 713 229 1522
**Email:** greg.nelson@bakerbotts.com
**Website:** www.bakerbotts.com

## BRANCH OFFICES

**NEW YORK**
30 Rockefeller Plaza, **New York** NY 10112-4998
**Tel:** 212 408 2500  **Fax:** 212 408 2501
**Email:** lee.charles@bakerbotts.com

**TEXAS**
1500 San Jacinto Center, 98 San Jacinto Blvd, **Austin** TX 78701-4039
**Tel:** 512 322 2500  **Fax:** 512 322 2501
**Email:** jim.cannon@bakerbotts.com

2001 Ross Avenue, **Dallas** TX 75201-2980
**Tel:** 214 953 6500  **Fax:** 214 953 6503
**Email:** jack.kinzie@bakerbotts.com

**DISTRICT OF COLUMBIA**
The Warner, 1299 Pennsylvania Avenue, NW,
**Washington** DC 20004-2400
**Tel:** 202 639 7700  **Fax:** 202 639 7890
**Email:** jamie.baker@bakerbotts.com

## INTERNATIONAL OFFICES

The firm also has offices in Dubai; Hong Kong; Moscow, Russia; Riyadh, Saudi Arabia; and London, United Kingdom.

### RUSSIA

Baker Botts' Moscow office, with its growing portfolio of Russian work, advises on energy, mining, corporate/M&A, intellectual property, dispute resolution, real estate, finance, and investment funds. In its most recent survey, the firm was acclaimed by the Petroleum Economist magazine as having 'Best Knowledge of Energy Law and Transaction in the CIS'.

### HONG KONG

Baker Botts has represented clients involved in major energy projects in Asia for more than three decades. In 2005, the firm decided to cement its practice in Asia by establishing an office in Hong Kong. The Asian market's rapid economic development has brought about a tremendous rise in the demand for energy, with China now the world's second largest energy consumer. Baker Botts' Hong Kong office is well-suited to assist energy sector clients with their business and investment needs in Asia. In addition to the firm's emphasis on the energy industry, the Hong Kong office provides corporate and private equity clients with cross-border mergers and acqusitions capabilities throughout Asia, with an emphasis on China.

# BEIRNE, MAYNARD & PARSONS, L.L.P.

## THE FIRM

**Managing Partner:** Martin D Beirne
**Number of partners:** 40
**Number of other lawyers:** 80 (include of counsels as well as associates)

### AREAS OF PRACTICE:

Civil Trials, Appellate & Arbitration . . . . . . . . . . . . . . . . . . . . . . . . . 100%

**FIRM OVERVIEW:** Founded in 1987, Beirne, Maynard & Parsons, L.L.P. has become a nationally significant force in civil trial and appellate work. Now the largest firm in Texas dedicated solely to litigation, the firm has pursued a growth path based on general litigation and industry specialization. As specialists, the firm has developed one of the nation's leading life sciences and pharmaceutical litigation practices, along with prestigious national practice teams serving the energy and transportation industries. As generalists, the firm serves a diverse range of Fortune 500 companies locally, nationally, and internationally. Because the firm specializes in winning trials, all its lawyers are trained to practice in court, which has enabled Beirne, Maynard & Parsons to attract attorneys who might not otherwise obtain courtroom experience working at larger firms. The firm's arbitration specialists have vast experience before national and international tribunals. The Arbitration/Alternative Dispute Resolution Group (AADR) has successfully resolved disputes through mediation, national and international arbitration and other resolution forums. Beirne, Maynard & Parsons understands that going to court may not always be in the client's best interest and that there are many avenues for dispute resolution. Thus, the firm's trial lawyers are also trained to recognize when matters are best resolved through other mechanisms.

### MAIN AREAS OF PRACTICE:

**Civil Trials, Appeals & Arbitration:** As one of the nation's leading litigation firms, Beirne, Maynard & Parsons is distinguished for both breadth and depth. Beirne, Maynard & Parsons represents hundreds of diverse corporations and other clients in cases ranging from product liability defense to anti-counterfeiting to representation of sovereign states. The firm's biomedical litigation specialty is supported by a network of MDs, PhD pathologists, and nurse paralegals. In addition to life sciences, energy, and transportation, the firm continues its significant practices in aviation, intellectual property, coverage, mass tort litigation, and computer sciences. Because Texas is a plaintiff-friendly jurisdiction, Fortune 500 companies throughout the country retain the firm when they are sued in the state.

**CLIENTS:** Clients are often national and international companies seeking outside litigation counsel in capacities ranging from local or regional counsel to national coordinating counsel, from individual cases to dockets involving thousands of plaintiffs. The firm's fabled transportation client list includes such companies as American Suzuki Motor Corporation; Associated Aviation Underwriters; Aviation Office of America; The Cessna Aircraft Company; Freightliner, LLC; Hyundai North America; Mazda North America; Mercedes-Benz Truck Company; Mitsubishi Motor Sales of American, Inc; Orion Bus Industries; Porsche Cars North America; Pratt & Whitney of Canada, Inc; Subaru of America, Inc; Toyota Motor Sales, USA, Inc; Union Tank Car Company; and Volvo North American Corporation. Energy clients include BP; Conoco Phillips; ATP Oil & Gas Corporation; Schlumberger Technology Corporation, and Brazos Electric Power Cooperative, Inc. Chemical company clients include Air Liquide Corporation and Chevron Phillips Chemical Company. In Life Sciences, the firm represents drug maker Wyeth and has also represented Pfizer Inc. as regional counsel in major litigation; Tanox, a biopharmaceutical company; and Baylor College of Medicine, an internationally respected medical institution. Among the many prominent insurance companies represented are: AIG Companies; ACE USA; Chubb Group of Insurance Companies; CNA Insurance; Fireman's Fund Insurance Companies; Global Aerospace Underwriting Managers Ltd.; Lloyd's of London; Royal & SunAlliance; and The Travelers Insurance Companies. International sovereign state clients include the People's Republic of China and the Republic of Estonia. Other client companies from various industries

## HEAD OFFICE

**TEXAS**
1300 Post Oak Boulevard, Suite 2500, **Houston**, TX 77056
**Tel:** 713 623 0887 **Fax:** 713 960 1527
**Email:** info@bmpllp.com
**Website:** www.bmpllp.com

## BRANCH OFFICES

**TEXAS**
1700 Pacific Avenue, Suite 4400, **Dallas**, TX 75201
**Tel:** 214 237 4300 **Fax:** 214 237 4340

## CONTACTS

| | |
|---|---|
| General Litigation/Commercial | Martin D Beirne |
| Life Sciences & Pharmaceutical | Joseph S Cohen |
| | Thomas Sartwelle |
| | Sawnie A McEntire |
| Energy/Utilities | Martin D Beirne |
| | Brit T Brown |
| | Sawnie A McEntire |
| | Wm Bruce Stanfill |
| Transportation | Brit T Brown |
| | Martin D Beirne |
| Intellectual Property | William Norvell |
| | Scott D Marrs |
| Toxic Tort | Timothy Hogan |
| | Jeffrey R Parsons |
| | Stephen L Russell |
| Environmental | James Smith |
| Aviation | William L Maynard |
| | Ron E Frank |
| Appellate | Jeffery Nobles |
| | Terry Adams |
| Product Liability | Sawnie A McEntire |
| | Roger L McCleary |
| | Mark A Waite |
| Coverage/Reinsurance Bad Faith | Jeffrey R Parsons |
| | Jay W Brown |
| | David A Clark |
| Labor & Employment | Benjamin A Escobar |
| | Danya W Blair |

include Corrections Corporation of America; David Weekley Homes; Marriott Corporation; Newell Rubbermaid, Inc.; Procter & Gamble; United Technologies Corporation; and U.S. Silica Company.

**INTERNATIONAL WORK:** Beirne, Maynard & Parson's has represented numerous Fortune 500 companies in foreign disputes. In addition, the firm has been retained by sovereign nations like the People's Republic of China and the Republic of Estonia to litigate on their behalf. In one major case, Beirne, Maynard & Parsons represented the Republic of Estonia in a bilateral investment treaty issue. The Arbitration of the case was conducted under the auspices of the International Center for the Settlement of Investment Disputes (ICSID). The case was arbitrated in Switzerland, the UK and Washington, DC, with a final decision rendered on behalf of the Republic of Estonia.

# BRACEWELL & GIULIANI LLP

## THE FIRM

**Managing Partner:** Patrick C Oxford

**Number of partners:** 113
**Number of other lawyers:** 248

**FIRM OVERVIEW:** A new chapter in a 60-year history of global excellence began during 2005, as Bracewell & Patterson became Bracewell & Giuliani. Former New York Mayor Rudolph W Giuliani joined the firm as a name partner and brought his international reputation to its newly established New York office. With a presence in the world's financial capitals of New York and London, at the heart of political and regulatory leadership in Washington, DC, throughout the important international energy and trade centers of Texas, and in the rapidly expanding economy of Kazakhstan, Bracewell is strategically positioned to serve the commercial law needs of its worldwide client base. Symbolizing this client service effectiveness, Bracewell received high praise in 2006 from The Survey of Client Service Performance for Law Firms: The BTI Client Service A-Team. Among the firm's strengths cited in the survey were the ability to understand the client's business, advise on business issues, coordinate national resources and international capability, and offer wide-ranging services. Throughout the United States and around the world, Fortune 500 companies, major financial institutions, and leading government and public entities depend on Bracewell & Giuliani for practical solutions and creative advice spanning law, business and public policy.

## MAIN AREAS OF PRACTICE:

**Energy:** Bracewell & Giuliani and the international oil and gas industry have grown together since 1945. Bracewell handles matters related to corporate finance and restructuring, federal and state government regulations, tax, environment, corporate governance, litigation, labor and employment, and strategic communications. The firm represents operators and suppliers in the deregulated US electric energy industry. Its lawyers represent clients engaged in upstream and downstream energy transactions across the US as well as in Europe, the North and Caspian Sea Regions and Latin America, and provide commentary and insight on the global energy industry on their Energy Legal Blog at www.energylegalblog.com. Bracewell's regulatory attorneys bring extensive experience in the development of gas pipeline, electric transmission infrastructure projects and telecommunications. Among this group are former top officials with FERC as well as former top administrators with Texas agencies that regulate public utilities and oil and gas industries. Canada's leading legal business magazine, *Lexpert: The Business Magazine for Lawyers*, ranked a Bracewell & Giuliani multi-billion-dollar transaction on behalf of one of North America's largest pipeline companies among its Top 10 Corporate Deals of 2005. In the 2006 Chambers Global, Bracewell's Energy Practice was ranked as one of the US leaders in oil and gas work. *Euromoney Institutional Investor's* 2005 *Guide to the World's Leading Energy and Natural Resources Lawyers* recognized four firm energy partners. Since 2003, Bracewell has been named annually as a leading firm in energy matters by the Chambers USA: America's Leading Lawyers for Business. In the *National Law Journal's* 2005 'Who Represents Corporate America,' two Fortune 500 energy clients listed Bracewell & Giuliani as their go-to legal resource.

**Banking & Corporate Finance:** Bracewell & Giuliani represents some of the world's largest lending institutions, corporate industry leaders and institutional investors in high-end and complex transactions. Bracewell's finance lawyers structure documents and negotiate financing arrangements, including syndicated loan transactions, capital markets finance, bilateral financing, project finance, specialized financing such as securitizations, restructuring and workouts, and trade finance. The firm also serves as transactional counsel on a diverse range of matters including mergers, acquisitions and dispositions, capital markets, corporate governance issues, and partnership and joint venture matters. *The Euromoney Guide to the World's Leading Project Finance Lawyers* named two Bracewell partners to its book of experts. Since 2003, Chambers USA: America's Leading Lawyers for Business has cited Bracewell & Giuliani as a leading law firm

## HEAD OFFICE

### TEXAS
711 Louisiana, Ste. 2300, **Houston**, TX 77002-2770
**Tel:** 713 223 2300 **Fax:** 713 221 1212
**Website:** www.bracewellgiuliani.com

## BRANCH OFFICES

### NEW YORK
1177 Avenue of the Americas, **New York**, NY 10036-2714
**Tel:** 212 508 6100 **Fax:** 212 508 6101

### DISTRICT OF COLUMBIA
2000 K St. NW, Ste. 500, **Washington**, DC 20006-1872
Tel: 202 828 5800 Fax: 202 223 1225

### TEXAS
111 Congress Ave., Ste. 2300, **Austin**, TX 78701-4061
**Tel:** 512 472 7800 **Fax:** 512 472 9123

500 N Akard St., Ste. 4000, **Dallas**, TX 75201-3387
**Tel:** 214 758 1000 **Fax:** 214 758 1010

800 One Alamo Center, **San Antonio**, TX 78205-3603
**Tel:** 210 226 1166 **Fax:** 210 226 1133

## INTERNATIONAL OFFICES

Kazakhstan and London.

in Banking & Finance and Corporate/M&A. *American Banker* ranked Bracewell within the top five every year since 1999 for the number of mergers that the firm handled for financial institutions. *Project Finance* magazine listed the firm among the Top 10 legal advisors in North America, and *Bank Director* magazine named Bracewell among the 10 most-active bank legal advisers in the country.

**Bankruptcy & Corporate Restructuring:** Bracewell & Giuliani's Debt Restructuring and Corporate Finance Group participated in nearly every major energy industry restructuring deal in Texas during the past five years. The firm has extensive experience representing both secured and unsecured creditors, committees, debtors, and trustees in formal bankruptcy proceedings, out-of-court workouts and loan restructures. The *2005 Euromoney Guide to the World's Leading Insolvency and Restructuring Lawyers* named the head of the firm's Bankruptcy Section to its elite list. The firm's Bankruptcy Practice has also been lauded as a leading firm by Chambers USA since 2004.

**Caspian Region:** Established in 1994, Bracewell's presence in the Republic of Kazakhstan has helped clients capture significant opportunities in the Caspian Region. The firm's energy and finance attorneys provided groundbreaking guidance to create the legal and financial infrastructure in that emerging nation and today actively advise energy and financial companies in the region and the government of Kazakhstan. In *Euromoney's 2005 IFLR 1000: The Guide to the World's Leading Financial Law Firms*, Bracewell was recommended among Kazakhstan firms for maintaining a 'strong niche advising on Eurobond issues.' Since 2003, Chambers Global has noted the firm and the managing partner of its Kazakhstan offices as the Caspian Region's leaders in corporate/commercial work.

**Trial:** The firm's litigation attorneys have extensive experience arguing commercial and complex tort contingency cases in federal and state courts. The addition of four former federal prosecutors in Bracewell's New York office has added greater depth to the firm's defense capabilities in securities fraud, class action and shareholder derivative claims and white collar crime. Among Bracewell's other premier practice areas are energy litigation, toxic tort/environmental defense and international dispute resolution. Bracewell's Trial Section head was listed in the *2005 Euromoney Guide to the Leading U.S. Litigation Lawyers*.

# CANTERBURY, STUBER, ELDER, GOOCH & SURRATT, P.C.

## THE FIRM

**Managing Committee:** Robert C Elder, W Kyle Gooch, David G Surratt

**Number of partners:** 9
**Number of other lawyers:** 6

### AREAS OF PRACTICE:

| | |
|---|---|
| Construction | 70% |
| Labor & Employment | 15% |
| Corporate & Real Estate | 15% |

**FIRM OVERVIEW:** The firm has an emphasis on construction law and labor and employment law related to the construction industry. The firm's practice has expanded into the areas of real estate, corporate, public construction law, personal injury law and insurance law; however, the mainstay is the construction industry. Three members of the firm are also active in arbitration and mediation of construction disputes.

## MAIN AREAS OF PRACTICE:

**Construction:** The firm has expertise and extensive experience in the construction industry. Members of the firm have represented developers, owners, contractors, subcontractors and suppliers in construction disputes and other legal problems of construction and development, including commercial, industrial, highway, power plant and pipeline projects.

**Labor & Employment:** The firm represents employers in labor and employment matters. Specifically, the firm handles defense of discrimination and other claims arising under the State and Federal Equal Employment Opportunity law, Occupational Safety and Health Act, and the National Labor Relations Act. The firm has extensive experience in advising clients regarding union-related matters, personnel situations, harassment situations and wage and hour claims. It will review and prepare, where appropriate, personnel manuals and handbooks on behalf of clients.

**Corporate/Real Estate:** The firm provides corporate services in entity organization and corporate reorganizations such as mergers and conversions by analyzing innovative business solutions that serve the firm's clients' best interest. The firm represents sellers and purchasers of asset and stock purchase transactions. The firm serves as counselors and negotiators for developers, buyers, sellers, landlords and tenants in office and industrial properties. The firm counsels borrowers in construction financing and analyzes a wide variety of construction issues for commercial developments.

**CLIENTS:** Clients include Carter & Burgess, Inc.; Centex Construction Co.; Charter Builders; Clark Contractors, Inc.; Dee Brown Masonry, Inc.; douglas e. barnhart, inc.; Driver Pipeline Company; Federal Reserve Bank of Dallas; Gilbane Building Company; GLF Construction Corporation; Granite Construction Co.; Haws & Tingle, Ltd., Hensel-Phelps Construction; Independent Electrical Contractors Association; JPI Companies; L.H. Lacy Company; Linbeck Construction; Lloyd Plyler Construction, Inc.; Manhattan Construction; Marek Companies; Sundt Corporation; Morgan Buildings; Prudential Insurance Company; Roy Anderson Corporation; Sunmount Corp.; TAC Americas, Inc.; Tellepsen Builders, L.P.; S&B Constructors and Engineers; Walker Engineering, Inc.; Zachry Construction Company.

# COX SMITH MATTHEWS INCORPORATED

## THE FIRM

**FIRM OVERVIEW**: Cox Smith Matthews Incorporated is the leading San Antonio commercial law firm with expertise ranging from sophisticated corporate transactions to complex litigation to personal estate planning. Headquartered in San Antonio, Texas with offices in Austin, Dallas and McAllen, the firm employs 120 attorneys with diverse experience in 19 primary practice areas and more than 25 areas of specialization. This depth of experience enables Cox Smith Matthews to deliver exceptional legal services and the best in client service to regional, national and international clients.

## MAIN AREAS OF PRACTICE:

**Appellate:** The firm advises general counsel and trial lawyers to supply immediate and ongoing support relating to appellate issues. Additionally, the firm provides representation from entry of verdict through briefing and argument in federal and state appellate courts, including the Fifth Circuit and the Texas Supreme Court.

**Business Litigation:** The firm's Litigation Practice focuses primarily on business-related disputes and issues. Additionally, the firm provides counseling before problems arise on how best to structure business operations to avoid unnecessary risk of litigation.

**Corporate & Securities:** The firm provides counseling on mergers and acquisitions, public and private offerings of securities, corporate governance, partnerships, joint ventures and strategic alliances, and technology contracting.

**Creditors' Rights, Corporate Restructuring & Bankruptcy:** The firm advises on all aspects of business bankruptcy, including representation of debtors, trustees, committees, acquirers, secured and unsecured creditors, lenders and other parties-in-interest. The firm advises clients in connection with restructuring; lending issues and maximization of realization on extended credit; pre-bankruptcy strategic planning; issues involving preferences and fraudulent conveyances under both state and federal law; and a multiplicity of bankruptcy issues in real estate and other commercial transactions.

**Employee Benefits:** The firm advises on a variety of employee benefit matters, including qualified and non-qualified retirement and deferred compensation plans, health plans, executive compensation and a broad range of tax and ERISA matters.

**Energy & Natural Resources:** The firm's Natural Resources Department provides legal counseling, structuring of transactions and litigation services to companies involved in the development, operation and marketing of natural and mineral resources. The firm also provides legal advice to clients relating to environmental compliance and environmental issues in structuring acquisition and disposition transactions.

**Estate Planning, Probate & Wealth Transfer:** The firm advises on the preparation of wills, life insurance trusts, educational trusts, powers of attorney, strategies for tax advantaged charitable giving, life insurance, tax minimization and pre-marital agreements.

**Healthcare:** The firm's healthcare attorneys work with a full range of providers in business formation and restructuring, healthcare transactions, general healthcare law and regulatory matters, and dispute resolution.

**Intellectual Property:** The firm's intellectual property attorneys assist clients with domestic and international trademark prosecution and licensing; domestic and international franchising formation and evaluation; registration and enforcement of copyright prosecution; licensing and enforcements of patents; and trademark, copyright and patent litigation.

**Labor & Employment:** The firm advises on personnel policies, discrimination claims, employee contracts, COBRA, ERISA, ERISA Litigation, class actions, alternate dispute resolution, labor/union issues, wage and hour claims and employment litigation.

**Public Law:** The firm counsels on matters including elections; annexation; condemnation and land use; water rights and service; depository and investment issues; and organizational and governance issues.

## HEAD OFFICE

**TEXAS**
112 East Pecan Street, Suite 1800, **San Antonio**, TX 78205
**Tel:** 210 554 5500  **Fax:** 210 226 8395
**Website:** www.coxsmith.com

## BRANCH OFFICES

**TEXAS**
111 Congress, Suite 2800, **Austin**, TX 78701
**Tel:** 512 703 6300  **Fax:** 512 703 6399

1201 Elm Street, Suite 4242 **Dallas**, TX 75270
**Tel:** 214 698 7800  **Fax:** 214 698 7899

801 East Fern, Suite 112, **McAllen**, Texas 78501
**Tel:** 956 984 7400  **Fax:** 956 984 7499

## CONTACTS

| | |
|---|---|
| Appellate | Renée F McElhaney |
| Business Litigation | Keith E Kaiser |
| Corporate & Securities | Steven A Elder |
| Creditors' Rights, Corporate Restructuring & Bankruptcy | Deborah D Williamson |
| Employee Benefits | Mary M Potter |
| Energy & Natural Resources | John R Ray |
| Estate Planning, Probate & Wealth Transfer | Allan G Patterson |
| Healthcare | James A Gilman |
| Intellectual Property | Pamela B Huff |
| Labor & Employment | Donna K McElroy |
| Public Law | Howard D Bye |
| Real Estate | John B Stewart |
| Tax | Bill Lester |

Additionally, the firm advises on matters related to franchise work for public utilities; condemnations; sales tax and other taxation issues; cable television and fiber optics infrastructure; construction contracts; and public utility litigation.

**Real Estate:** The firm advises on matters related to real estate acquisition, development and finance, environmental and land-use planning issues, lease agreements, landlord/tenant issues, workout and commercial construction.

**Tax:** The firm advises on matters related to tax strategies, tax controversies, tax planning, business succession planning, Texas franchise tax planning and international tax planning.

**CLIENTS:** The firm provides a wide variety of services to clients ranging from entrepreneurs and family business owners to Fortune 100 public companies and represents some of the region's largest businesses, including SBC Communications, Clear Channel Communications, International Bancshares Corporation, Valero Energy Corporation and City Public Service.

**INTERNATIONAL WORK:** The firm advises clients on international acquisitions and investments; the formation of offshore corporations; structuring international joint ventures; international tax planning; international patent, trademark and copyright protection; and the implications of the North American Free Trade Agreement (NAFTA).

# DAVIS MUNCK BUTRUS, P.C.

## THE FIRM

**Chairman:** William A Munck

**Number of shareholders:** 14
**Number of other lawyers:** 17

**FIRM OVERVIEW:** Davis Munck Butrus is a technology-focused boutique law firm headquartered in Dallas, Texas, with a second office in Charlotte, North Carolina. The firm's focus is on complex trial work, transactions and intellectual property with a passion and expertise in providing full-service counsel to technology-focused companies.

## MAIN AREAS OF PRACTICE:

**Intellectual Property:** In addition to traditional trademark, copyright and patent preparation and prosecution, Davis Munck Butrus has extensive experience in the development of comprehensive corporate IP strategies. Through technology assessment techniques and applied research, Davis Munck Butrus helps clients improve business performance and institute organizational and strategic change for competitive advantage.

**IP Licensing, Audits & Legal Opinions:** Davis Munck Butrus represents domestic, foreign and multi-national companies in developing and executing offensive and defensive licensing strategies. The firm routinely performs intellectual property audits on specific licenses, trademarks, patents or technologies to determine whether any rights are being or could be protected or exploited. The firm also investigates the validity of letters patent, registrations, contracts, designs and filings to be certain all avenues are explored and all proper precautions are in effect. The firm's attorneys often are engaged to investigate enforcement and validity issues, develop and render legal opinions and offer testimony regarding the same.

**Complex Litigation & Dispute Resolution:** Davis Munck Butrus maintains a nationwide Complex Commercial Litigation and Arbitration Practice. The firm's trial lawyers have expertise in a wide variety of legal disputes including: intellectual property and trade secrets, system procurement, complex commercial disputes, large property subrogation, insurance coverage, construction claims, product liability, corporate, contract and employment disputes. The Litigation Practice is focused on clients' business objectives. Through intelligent case development and pre-trial preparation, Davis Munck Butrus attorneys provide legal strategies that are most likely to yield maximum value to clients.

**Corporate/Mergers & Acquisitions/Private Equity:** Davis Munck Butrus provides counsel on entity formations, venture and other finance transactions, mergers and acquisitions, and business restructuring. Davis Munck Butrus attorneys negotiate and prepare a wide variety of technology and other agreements, including licensing, employment, development and distribution agreements.

**Employment:** Davis Munck Butrus' Employment Practice focuses on preventing disputes by ensuring that employer policies are in compliance with discrimination, safety and other laws and that the policies are consistently applied. The firm has extensive experience with policies and procedures that protect a company's intellectual property. The firm's attorneys also counsel businesses on employment disputes through arbitration and litigation.

## HEAD OFFICE

**TEXAS**
900 Three Galleria Tower, 13155 Noel Road, **Dallas**, TX 75240
**Tel:** 972 628 3600  **Fax:** 972 628 3616
**Email:** info@davismunck.com
**Website:** www.davismunckbutrus.com

## BRANCH OFFICES

**NORTH CAROLINA**
11520 North Community House Road Suite 200, **Charlotte**, NC 28277
**Email:** info@davismunck.com
**Website:** www.davismunckbutrus.com

## CONTACTS

| | |
|---|---|
| **Intellectual Property** | William Munck |
| | Robert McCutcheon |
| **IP Licensing, Audits & Legal Opinions** | William Munck |
| | Daniel Venglarik |
| **Complex Litigation** | John Butrus |
| | James Davis |
| **Corporate Transactions** | Larry Mandala |
| **Employment** | Audrey Mross |
| **International Business & Trade** | James Chester |

**International Business & Trade:** Whether assisting clients in global expansion, helping resolve transnational commercial disputes, counseling on the international transfer of technology or working on import or customs issues, Davis Munck Butrus provides legal counsel to meet the challenges of the global economy.

**CLIENTS:** The firm's clients range from start-ups to Fortune 50 international technology companies. The firm also works with foreign associate firms in the areas of patent preparation and prosecution.

**INTERNATIONAL WORK:** Davis Munck Butrus routinely represents domestic, foreign and multi-national companies in all areas of intellectual property and technology.

DAVISMUNCKBUTRUS
Trials. Transactions. Technology.

# FULBRIGHT & JAWORSKI L.L.P.

## THE FIRM

**Managing Partner:** Steven B Pfeiffer
**Number of partners:** 359
**Number of other lawyers:** 615

**FIRM OVERVIEW:** Founded in 1919, Fulbright & Jaworski L.L.P is a leading full-service international law firm, with more than 940 lawyers in 13 locations in Houston, New York, Washington DC, Austin, Dallas, Los Angeles, Minneapolis, San Antonio, Dubai, Hong Kong, London, Munich and Riyadh. Fulbright provides a full range of legal services to both domestic and foreign clients worldwide. The 2005 BTI survey of *Fortune* 1000 general counsel chose Fulbright as a 'Power Elite Law Firm', *Corporate Board Member* magazine named Fulbright among the top 20 corporate law firms in the US in their survey of board members of public companies, and *International Law Office*, based on survey responses received from international corporate counsel, awarded Fulbright the '2005 Client Choice Award' as the top law firm for client service in the United States.

## MAIN AREAS OF PRACTICE:

**Arbitration/ADR:** Fulbright & Jaworski's Arbitration and ADR Practice Group move easily between traditional litigation, arbitration and ADR, and the firm's excellence in this area has grown to match its renowned courtroom capabilities. There are many potential remedies for disputes, and the firm's Arbitration Group develops the best solution for each client and each dispute. Fulbright & Jaworski's long-standing commitment to resolve disputes efficiently is accomplished through the four strong building blocks of its Arbitration and Alternative Dispute Resolution (ADR) Practice Group: mediation, domestic arbitration, international arbitration and the other ADR practices. Reflecting its experience and dedication in this area of law, Fulbright has significant affiliations with virtually all ADR institutions, several of which the firm was instrumental in organizing. Additionally, Chamber & Partners, USA ranked Fulbright as one of the top national firms for International Arbitration and *The American Lawyer* included Fulbright in a list of 17 firms in the world named as the 'Arbitration Elite.' Fulbright is the only Texas-based law firm included in the list.

**Corporate:** Fulbright & Jaworski provides a broad array of corporate legal services to a diverse client base that ranges from start-up ventures to large multi-national companies. The firm carefully guides its clients through the legal issues that affect not only their ability to obtain financing, but also to maintain their operations in today's highly competitive, high-speed business environment. The firm's skill and commitment to service span many industries including energy, healthcare, media, financial services, insurance software and hardware, biotechnology, telecommunications, information technology, transportation, business services, manufacturing, retail, ecommerce and consumer products. For the fourth year in a row, Fulbright was named one of the nation's best corporate law firms according to a survey published in the July/August 2005 issue of *Corporate Board Member* magazine identifying the top 20 firms nationally.

**Energy:** Fulbright & Jaworski is recognized as a premier energy firm with a diversified practice that serves the needs of the global energy industry. With over 50 years of experience in energy matters, the firm has accumulated a wealth of experience and valuable knowledge. The firm's attorneys are regularly involved in both international and domestic energy matters and are highly skilled in energy litigation, transactions, regulatory matters and dispute resolution. In the transaction area, Fulbright attorneys are well versed in the development, financing and construction of energy projects, as well as acquisitions and dispositions. Fulbright regulatory attorneys serve the needs of clients engaged in the pipeline, oil and gas production, and electric power industries. The firm provides a full range of services in federal and state regulatory matters. In addition, the firm is ranked internationally among the best in litigation and arbitration. That ranking stems in large part from the experience and successes of the firm's energy litigation and arbitration attorneys.

**Healthcare:** Fulbright & Jaworski's Healthcare Practice Group is widely known

## HEAD OFFICE

### TEXAS
1301 Fulbright Tower, Suite 5100, **Houston**, TX 77010-3095
**Tel:** 713 651 5151   **Fax:** 713 651 5246
**Email:** info@fulbright.com
**Website:** www.fulbright.com

## BRANCH OFFICES

### NEW YORK
666 Fifth Avenue, **New York**, NY 10103-3198
**Tel:** 212 318 3000   **Fax:** 212 318 3400
**Email:** info@fulbright.com

### DISTRICT OF COLUMBIA
801 Pennsylvania Avenue, NW, Market Square,
**Washington**, DC 20004-2623
**Tel:** 202 662 0200   **Fax:** 202 662 4643
**Email:** info@fulbright.com

### CALIFORNIA
865 South Figueroa, Twenty-Ninth Floor, **Los Angeles**, CA 90017-2571
**Tel:** 213 892 9200   **Fax:** 213 680 4518
**Email:** info@fulbright.com

### MINNESOTA
2100 IDS Center, 80 South Eighth Street, **Minneapolis**, MN 55402
**Tel:** 612 321 2800   **Fax:** 612 321 9600
**Email:** info@fulbright.com

### TEXAS
600 Congress Avenue, Suite 2400, **Austin**, TX 78701-3271
**Tel:** 512 474 5201   **Fax:** 512 536 4598
**Email:** info@fulbright.com

2200 Ross Avenue, Suite 2800, **Dallas**, TX 75201-2748
**Tel:** 214 855 8000   **Fax:** 214 855 8200
**Email:** info@fulbright.com

300 Convent Street, Suite 2200, **San Antonio**, TX 78205-3792
**Tel:** 210 224 5575   **Fax:** 210 270 7205
**Email:** info@fulbright.com

## CONTACTS

| | |
|---|---|
| **Arbitration & ADR** | Mark Baker, John Bowman |
| **Bankruptcy** | Evelyn H Biery |
| **Corporate** | Mike W Conlon, Paul Jacobs |
| **Energy** | Jeff Dykes, Poe Leggette, George Kutzschbach |
| **Energy & Real Property** | Michael P Irvin |
| **Environmental** | Eva Fromm O'Brien |
| **Family Law** | Stewart W Gagnon |
| **Healthcare** | Jerry A Bell, Robert J Swift, Terry O Tottenham |
| **Intellectual Property & Technology** | Paul Krieger |
| **International** | Mark Baker, Jeff Blount |
| **Labor & Employment Law** | AJ Harper II |
| **Litigation** | Steve Dillard |
| **Middle East** | John Lonsberg, Mark Bisch, Johen Boehm |
| **Public Finance** | Fredric A Weber |
| **Tax** | John R Allender |
| **Technology & Emerging Companies** | John C Boehm |
| | Merrill M Kraines |

for strengths in transactional practice, professional liability and medical malpractice, general tort and commercial litigation, and administration and regulatory representation. Fulbright has more than 50 years of experience, representing healthcare clients in a wide range of issues, including tax matters, federal compli-

# FULBRIGHT & JAWORSKI L.L.P. CONT'D

ance issues, and commercial and professional malpractice claims. The firm has been deeply involved in the development of both large and small healthcare providers as well as community health clinics ever since Fulbright attorneys helped establish the Texas Medical Center.

**INTERNATIONAL WORK:** Fulbright & Jaworski's International Practice Group, made up of more than 130 lawyers, provides a range of services on international transactional, commercial, financial, investment and dispute resolution matters. Attorneys in the group are strategically located in Dubai, Hong Kong, London, Munich and Riyadh, as well as the firm's US offices. The firm's international clients represent a broad cross-sector of industry groups, including energy, manufacturing, mining, information and communications technologies, telecommunications, banking and financial services and insurance. To meet the diversity of clients' needs, Fulbright & Jaworski's international attorneys are drawn from throughout the firm and work closely with attorneys in all areas of practice. Many of the firm's international lawyers are multilingual, have lived and worked outside of the United States and are intimately familiar with different legal and business cultures. As a complement to Fulbright & Jaworski's capabilities, the firm has developed an extensive network of relationships with law firms throughout the world that provide expert assistance with respect to various 'host' nation legal issues that arise in international investments, transactions and disputes. In addition, *International Law Office*, based on survey responses received from international corporate counsel, awarded Fulbright the '2005 Client Choice Award' as the top law firm for client service in the United States. **International Offices:** Fulbright and Jaworski has offices in Dubai, Hong Kong, London, Munich and Riyadh.
**Languages:** Afrikaans, Arabic, Bengali, Cantonese, Chinese, Croatian, Dutch, French, German, Hebrew, Hindu, Italian, Japanese, Korean, Mandarin Chinese, Polish, Portuguese, Romanian, Russian, Spanish, Tagalog, Taiwanese, Urdu, Vietnamese and Yugoslavian.
**Middle East:** Fulbright & Jaworski's Middle East Practice supports its many clients who have businesses, investments, construction and development projects, offices and other interests throughout the Middle East. Fulbright maintains offices in Dubai, United Arab Emirates and Riyadh, Saudi Arabia. The activities of the firm's clients are supported by the firm's domestic United States, as well as its London and Hong Kong locations. The deep and longstanding diplomatic, commercial and personal ties between nations, companies and individuals from the Middle East and Houston, Washington, DC, London and New York are well known. As international commerce has grown, many close attorney-client relationships have evolved naturally in parallel, providing a solid foundation for Fulbright's Middle East Practice. The firm's attorneys resident in the Middle East locations have decades of experience living and advising clients in the region. Various members of the firm's Middle East Practice Group are fluent in Arabic and other languages that are relevant to the firm's work Middle East.

## HEAD OFFICE

### TEXAS

1301 McKinney, Suite 5100, Houston, TX 77010
**Partners in charge:** Michael W Conlon, Frank G Jones
**Number of lawyers:** 335

**Office Profile:** Founded on October 1, 1919, Fulbright & Jaworski's Houston office is its largest. The combined creativity, commitment and experience of its attorneys produces prompt, innovative solutions to both routine and complex legal problems. Its highly trained and motivated attorneys understand the needs of the firm's clients in today's global community and are committed to playing a meaningful, efficient and effective role in their growth and success. As a full-service, international law firm at the forefront of the evolving legal marketplace,

Fulbright is well positioned to assist its clients, as they move into the new millennium, in the following areas: admiralty, alternative dispute resolution, appellate, bankruptcy, reorganization and creditors' rights, corporate, securities and transactions, employee benefits, environmental, energy, family law, healthcare, intellectual property and technology, international, labor and employment, litigation, project finance, public finance, real estate, tax, technology and emerging companies, trusts and estates.

## US OFFICES

### NEW YORK

666 Fifth Avenue, New York, NY 10103-3198
**Partner in charge:** William Bush
**Number of lawyers:** 137

**Office Profile:** Formed over 65 years ago, the New York office serves a broad client base including large publicly-held corporations, investment banking and brokerage firms, venture capital and leveraged buy-out firms, investment funds, private equity and institutional investors, life science, high-technology and other emerging growth companies, privately-held companies, partnerships, individuals, estates and charitable organizations and foundations.

### WASHINGTON, DC

801 Pennsylvania Avenue, NW, Market Square, Washington, DC 20004-2623
**Partner in charge:** Joseph T Small, Jr
**Number of lawyers:** 92

**Office Profile:** Since its founding in 1927, Fulbright & Jaworski's Washington, DC office has grown from a few lawyers providing federal agency representation in support of the firm's practice, to a full-service office of more than 90 lawyers handling litigation, business and regulatory matters for a national and international clientele.

### CALIFORNIA

865 South Figueroa, Twenty-Ninth Floor, Los Angeles, CA 90017-2571
**Partner in charge:** Peter H Mason
**Number of lawyers:** 77

**Office Profile:** Fulbright & Jaworski's growing Los Angeles office is full-service, with a diverse litigation and sophisticated business practice that includes: appellate; corporate, securities and transactions; banking and business; bankruptcy, reorganization and creditors' rights; environmental; healthcare; intellectual property and technology; international; labor and employment law; litigation; public finance; real estate; tax; trusts and estates; venture capital.

### MINNESOTA

2100 IDS Center, 80 South Eighth Street, Minneapolis, MN 55402
**Partner in charge:** Ronn B Kreps
**Number of lawyers:** 22

**Office Profile:** The Minneapolis office of Fulbright opened in February 2000 and has grown rapidly over the past four years to serve a broad client base both in the

# FULBRIGHT & JAWORSKI L.L.P. CONT'D

Midwest and throughout the United States. The Minneapolis team remains focused on the ever-changing needs of clients who face a broad range of issues involving intellectual property, commercial litigation and products liability.

## TEXAS

600 Congress Avenue, Suite 2400, Austin, TX 78701-3271
**Partner in charge:** Terry O Tottenham
**Number of lawyers:** 86

**Office Profile:** Opened in January 1978, Fulbright & Jaworski's Austin Office is a full-service presence with more than 85 lawyers. In 2000 alone it added more than 35 patent, trademark and technology attorneys and scientific advisors in Austin, many of whom joined the firm from the IP specialty firm Arnold, White & Durkee, and several of whom have served as senior in-house counsel. Integrating that in-house experience with the firm's practice reflects Fulbright & Jaworski's commitment to deliver prompt and practical solutions to its clients.

2200 Ross Avenue, Suite 2800, Dallas, TX 75201-2748
**Partner in charge:** Kenneth L Stewart
**Number of lawyers:** 128

**Office Profile:** Fulbright & Jaworski's Dallas office opened in 1981 by merging with the bond firm of Dumas, Huguenin, Boothman & Morrow. For several years, the firm's Dallas attorneys focused on municipal finance transactions, then expanded to a full-service office to include: appellate; bankruptcy, reorganization and creditors' rights; corporate, securities, and transactions; healthcare; intellectual property and technology; international; labor and employment law; litigation; public finance; real estate; tax.

300 Convent Street, Suite 2200, San Antonio, TX 78205-3792
**Partner in charge:** George W Scofield
**Number of lawyers:** 62

**Office Profile:** Fulbright & Jaworski opened its San Antonio office in 1980, which has since grown to a full-service office with more than 60 attorneys to include: appellate; bankruptcy, reorganization and creditors' rights; corporate, securities and transactions; environmental; healthcare; labor and employment law; litigation; public finance; real estate; tax and employee benefits; trusts and estates.

**FULBRIGHT**
**&** *Jaworski L.L.P.*
*Attorneys at Law*

# GARDERE WYNNE SEWELL LLP

## THE FIRM

**Managing Partner:** Stephen D Good

**Number of partners:** 158
**Number of other lawyers:** 123

### AREAS OF PRACTICE:

| | |
|---|---|
| Trial | 33% |
| Corporate | 26% |
| Financial Services | 19% |
| Labor & Employment | 7% |
| Environmental | 6% |
| Tax | 8% |
| Intellectual Property | 6% |

**FIRM OVERVIEW:** Gardere is one of the preeminent full-service law firms in the Southwest. With approximately 290 lawyers and more than 40 practice areas to serve its clients, Gardere is strong and diverse, combining the comprehensive resources of a large firm with an interdisciplinary approach to providing clients with effective counsel in terms of time, cost, and results. This approach creates a team-based professional service environment in which attorneys experienced in specific areas of law and particular industries are available to provide effective, timely counsel according to specific client and case needs. The firm provides solutions to complicated legal matters to achieve its client's goals - Gardere's primary objective.

## MAIN AREAS OF PRACTICE:

**Corporate:** Counsels companies on strategic planning, outsourcing and a full range of issues involving business operations. Attorneys are recognized for their aggressive approach to finding meaningful solutions for the companies they represent, and not only provide general counsel but specialized expertise in areas such as investment partnerships, major business transactions, partnership interests, public and private offerings, start-up ventures, and venture capital.

**Environmental:** Covers a breadth of issues including high-stakes complex litigation involving multiple parties, regulatory rulemaking, transactions and compliance assistance for ongoing operations. This national practice includes team members from diverse backgrounds including federal and state environmental agencies, the judiciary, Fortune 500 companies and academia.

**Financial Services:** Serves both public and private as well as regulated and unregulated entities and institutions in a variety of issues including regulatory matters, financing transactions, development transactions and restructurings. Attorneys have experience with virtually every form of commercial financing, both secured and unsecured, and handle transactions involving all types of assets, including real estate, mineral interests, inventory, accounts receivable, factoring and various forms of intangible properties. Attorneys are particularly experienced in the special issues involved in the financing and operation of hotels and resorts, ships, and energy assets, such as drilling rigs and production platforms.

**Intellectual Property:** Focuses on patent, trademark, copyright, trade secret and unfair competition law and the antitrust aspects of intellectual property law, with significant expertise in trademark and patent prosecution, licensing, IPOs, and related litigation. Clients range between individual inventors, artists and authors, universities and large multinational corporations.

**Labor & Employment:** Provides counsel and representation for employers in decision making and litigation involving the National Labor Relations Act, the Fair Labor Standards Act, and individual and class action employment discrimination matters. Representative matters include wrongful discharge claims, such as workers compensation retaliation, negligent hiring or retention, implied contract, acquisition-related, and those pendant to employment claims (libel, slander, infliction of emotional distress, fraud). Matters also include Executive Order 11246 affirmative action plans and audits, Occupational Safety and Health Act matters, government contractor employment issues, and immigration and naturalization matters.

## HEAD OFFICE

**TEXAS**
3000 Thanksgiving Tower, 1601 Elm Street, **Dallas**, TX 75201-4761
**Tel:** 214 999 3000  **Fax:** 214 999 4667
**Website:** www.gardere.com

## BRANCH OFFICES

**TEXAS**
3000 One American Center,  600 Congress Avenue,
**Austin**, TX 78701-2978
**Tel:** 512 542 7000  **Fax:** 512 542 7100

1000 Louisiana, Suite 3400, **Houston**, Texas 77002-5011
**Tel:** 713 276 5500  **Fax:** 713 276 5555

## INTERNATIONAL OFFICES

Gardere, Arena y Robles, S.C. is based in **Mexico City**.

## CONTACTS

| | |
|---|---|
| Corporate | Larry Stevens |
| Environmental | Richard Faulk |
| Financial Services | Clifford Risman |
| Intellectual Property | Kenneth Glaser |
| Labor & Employment | Ronald Gaswirth |
| Tax | Suzan Fenner |
| Trial | Curtis Frisbie, Jr |

**Tax:** Consists of several practice specialties including federal income taxation, state and local taxation, international taxation, estate planning and administration, employee benefits and executive compensation.

**Trial:** Focuses on trials in United States District Courts and all State courts, and appellate matters in both federal and state courts of appeals and the US Supreme Court as well as representation before various state, national and international arbitration boards.  Practice areas within the section include admiralty, antitrust, appellate, aviation litigation, class action, computer technology, construction, environmental/toxic tort, government contracts, medical malpractice, securities, and tort defense/insurance litigation.

**INTERNATIONAL WORK:** Provides a comprehensive range of legal services to both Mexican and foreign clients. The office of Gardere, Arena y Robles, S.C. (GAR) in Mexico City is a civil partnership formed by Mexican and US attorneys. GAR has developed a special focus on assisting Mexican and foreign clients in acquisitions, joint ventures, and other investments; the development of infrastructure projects with the Mexican government and private sector entities involving the privatization or operations of public assets, e.g., tollroads, potable water and water treatment facilities, airports, seaports, drilling contracts and electrical energy projects; and representing clients generally in the energy, manufacturing, technology, telecommunications, financial and environmental sectors.

# GARDERE

*attorneys and counselors*

# GIBBS & BRUNS, LLP

## THE FIRM

**Managing Partner:** Robin C Gibbs

**Number of partners:** 18
**Number of other lawyers:** 15

### AREAS OF PRACTICE:
Commercial Litigation....................................90%
Appellate................................................10%

**FIRM OVERVIEW:** Gibbs & Bruns, LLP engages exclusively in a commercial litigation practice in Texas, throughout the United States, and in various courts and tribunals outside the United States. The firm practices in a broad range of business-related complex litigation, and has been involved in much of the major litigation in the region since the firm's inception in 1983. The firm prides itself on its ability to handle difficult and novel legal problems and routinely represents plaintiffs and defendants in significant contract, securities, trade secret, intellectual property, patent, class action, antitrust, insurance, construction, lender liability, energy, director liability, copyright, and partnership disputes.

## MAIN AREAS OF PRACTICE:

**Commercial Litigation:** The firm prides itself on its ability to handle all types of complex and high-stakes commercial litigation for both plaintiffs and defendants. They handle every aspect of the most complicated commercial disputes, from discovery through trials and on to appeal, and they are committed to winning. In 2004, the National Law Journal included Gibbs & Bruns on its short-list of 'Hot' Plaintiff's firms – signifying the top 20 go-to firms in the country; seven of its partners have been designated among the state's 'Super Lawyers', eight of its lawyers were cited as 'Rising Stars', and four have made the 'Best' of Houston list.
**Appellate:** The firm's appellate attorneys prosecute and defend appeals in a variety of jurisdictions and at all levels of the appellate process. Gibbs & Bruns' appellate work arises from litigation work performed by the firm as well as cases in which other counsel have handled the case in the lower courts.

**CLIENTS:** The firm's clients include many of the world's largest industrial companies, banks, brokerage firms, and professional firms. Representative clients are Conoco Phillips, Merrill Lynch Investment Managers, Franklin Templeton Funds, Fidelity Management & Research, the outside directors of Enron Corporation, certain officers of Dynegy, Hermann Hospital, John J. Moores (owner of the San Diego Padres), Preussag AG, Saipem SpA, Zachry Construction Corporation and Unocal Corporation.

**INTERNATIONAL WORK:** In addition to its nationwide practice, the firm has been called upon to represent parties in international courts and tribunals. The firm has handled litigation in the courts of the United Kingdom, and to arbitration panels in the United Kingdom and Kuala Lumpur. The firm has also been called upon to handle multi-jurisdictional litigation that involves simultaneous proceedings in the United States and other countries. Recently, the firm has handled such litigation involving disputes addressed jointly by the courts of the United States and the courts of Norway and the United Kingdom.

### HEAD OFFICE

**TEXAS**
1100 Louisiana, Suite 5300, **Houston**, TX 77002
**Tel:** 713 650 8805   **Fax:** 713 750 0903

### CONTACTS
**Commercial Litigation** ................................Robin C Gibbs
**Appellate**...........................................Jennifer Horan Greer

# KING & SPALDING LLP

## THE FIRM

**Chairman:** Robert D Hays
**Managing Partner, Atlanta:** Mason W Stephenson
**Managing Partner, Houston:** Robert E Meadows
**Managing Partner, London:** John L Keffer
**Managing Partner, New York:** Michael J O'Brien
**Managing Partner, Washington:** J Sedwick Sollers

**Number of partners:** 240
**Number of other lawyers:** 560

**FIRM OVERVIEW:** King & Spalding LLP is an international law firm with more than 800 lawyers in Atlanta, Houston, London, New York, and Washington, DC. The firm represents more than 250 public companies, including over half of the *Fortune* 100.

## MAIN AREAS OF PRACTICE:

**Antitrust:** King & Spalding's antitrust lawyers are trial lawyers who know how to litigate in 'bet the company' situations. The firm has been counsel for clients in numerous antitrust litigation settings, ranging from class actions and multi-district litigation to disputes between particular suppliers and their customers or competitors.

**Financial Transactions:** The practice group provides legal services for domestic and non-US banks and other financial institutions. It handles all aspects of credit-facilities and financial products.

**Construction:** Today, the Construction and Procurement Practice Group represents some of the world's largest organizations involved in global construction projects. King & Spalding was one of the first large, general practice firms in the nation to establish a practice devoted to construction and procurement law.

**Corporate/M&A:** Consistently ranks among the leading M&A practices in the United States in terms of aggregate deal value and total number of transactions handled.

**Corporate Finance:** The firm represents issuers, underwriters, investors, and other corporate finance participants, and provides corporate advice to public and private companies.

**Employment & Labor Law:** The firm defends *Fortune* 500 corporate defendants against complex claims of unlawful employment policies and conduct involving allegations of discrimination under federal and state non-discrimination statutes.

**Energy:** The firm's energy attorneys have been involved in transactions throughout the world related to energy and natural resources. King & Spalding's experience includes developing project structures as well as the drafting and negotiating of project agreements, contracts and documentation. Additionally, King & Spalding lawyers have been active advisors to the Liquefied Natural Gas (LNG) marketplace for the last 30 years. As pioneers on this legal scene, the internationally recognized group of lawyers have been key participants in LNG export, transport, and import projects . Today, King & Spalding's team is sought after by LNG players worldwide owing to depth of experience, knowledge, skill, and determination.

**Environment:** King & Spalding is recognized as one of the leading environmental firms and combines substantive expertise, technical knowledge and litigation experience on numerous environmental issues.

**Insolvency/Corporate Recovery:** The Financial Restructuring Group at King & Spalding provides valuable knowledge and experience in the areas of corporate reorganizations, commercial debt restructuring, workouts, bankruptcy, and insolvency litigation.

**Intellectual Property:** The firm's IP lawyers concentrate on acquiring, creating, licensing, protecting, and litigating intellectual property rights, both domestically and internationally.

## HEAD OFFICE

### GEORGIA
1180 Peachtree Street, **Atlanta**, GA 30309-3521
**Tel:** 404 572 4600 **Fax:** 404 572 5100
**Email:** kingspalding@kslaw.com
**Website:** www.kslaw.com

## BRANCH OFFICES

### NEW YORK
1185 Avenue of the Americas, **New York**, NY 10036-4003
**Tel:** 212 556 2100 **Fax:** 212 556 2222
**Email:** kingspalding@kslaw.com

### TEXAS
1100 Louisiana, Suite 4000, **Houston**, TX 77002-5213
**Tel:** 713 751 3200 **Fax:** 713 751 3290
**Email:** kingspalding@kslaw.com

### DISTRICT OF COLUMBIA
1700 Pennsylvania Avenue, N.W., **Washington**, DC 200006-4706
**Tel:** 202 737 0500 **Fax:** 202 626 3737
**Email:** kingspalding@kslaw.com

## INTERNATIONAL OFFICES

King & Spalding International LLP, London.

**Litigation & Arbitration:** The firm provides litigation services in the areas of antitrust, appellate, class action, commercial disputes, product liability, shareholder and securities litigation, trade and customs, and toxic tort. The firm also has a substantial international arbitration practice.

**Real Estate:** The firm's real estate practice includes acquisition, development, financing and leasing of commercial real estate primarily for nationally recognized developers, and non-US institutional and private investors.

**Tax:** The firm works with clients on the planning and execution of business transactions of all sizes and types arising in domestic and cross border settings, including acquisitions, disposition, joint ventures, and financing transactions.

**CLIENTS:** 3M, Brown & Williamson Tobacco Corporation, Chevron Corporation, The Coca-Cola Company, Credit Suisse First Boston LLC, The Dow Chemical Company, Ernst & Young LLP, ExxonMobil Corporation, General Electric Company, General Motors Corporation, Georgia-Pacific Corporation, GlaxoSmithKline, Goldman Sachs & Company, The Home Depot, Inc., Honeywell International Inc., KPMG LLP, Lehman Brothers Inc., Lockheed Martin Corporation, Merrill Lynch & Co., Inc., Morgan Stanley Capital Group, Inc., Purdue Pharma L.P., Scientific-Atlanta, Inc., Shell Oil Company, Sprint Nextel Corporation, SunTrust Banks Inc., Turner Broadcasting System, Inc., UCB Inc., UPS.

# KING & SPALDING

# McKOOL SMITH, P.C.

## THE FIRM

**Chairman:** Mike McKool Jr

**Number of partners:** 22
**Number of other lawyers:** 60

## AREAS OF PRACTICE:

Intellectual Property Litigation................................55%
Complex Commercial Litigation.............................45%

**FIRM OVERVIEW:** Since the firm was founded in 1991, McKool Smith, PC, has grown to become one of the largest law firms in the US devoted exclusively to intellectual property litigation and commercial litigation. By maintaining such a clear focus, McKool Smith's attorneys have been responsible for obtaining verdicts and settlements worth billions of dollars to clients. The firm employs more than 80 attorneys in Dallas, Austin and Marshall, Texas, home to one of the most active intellectual property jurisdictions in the US. McKool Smith's attorneys focus exclusively on commercial, civil and appellate litigation in state and federal courts. The firm's Litigation Practice encompasses a broad range of commercial actions, including intellectual property, technology, antitrust, class action, environmental, securities and business tort litigation.

## MAIN AREAS OF PRACTICE:

**Intellectual Property Litigation:** The firm represents US and international clients in all aspects of intellectual property litigation, including patent infringement, trademarks, trade secrets, patent licensing, and copyright matters. McKool Smith employs skilled and experienced trial attorneys who have the legal and technical expertise to persuade judges and juries deciding technologically complex issues. Several firm attorneys also hold technical degrees and have worked as engineers themselves, providing clients with an enhanced level of experience in complex intellectual property matters. McKool Smith also assists intellectual property clients in appeals before the US Court of Appeals for the Federal Circuit.

**Complex Commercial Litigation:** McKool Smith represents US and international clients in all facets of complex commercial litigation. The firm's expertise includes cases involving breach of contract, merger disputes, antitrust claims, class actions, business torts, franchisor/franchisee claims, royalty disagreements, and securities litigation. McKool Smith attorneys have represented clients in virtually every type of complex commercial litigation in every available forum, including state and federal trials and appeals, and domestic and international mediations and arbitrations.

**CLIENTS:** McKool Smith clients have included Ericsson; Infineon Technologies; Electronic Data Systems Corp. (EDS); National Instruments; Motorola; American Airlines; Hunt Oil; BDO Seidman; El Paso Natural Gas; Nortel; BearingPoint; American Video Graphics; Lockheed Martin; Medtronic; Hicks Muse Tate & Furst; and Cisco.

**INTERNATIONAL WORK:** McKool Smith represents international clients in US courts and international arbitration proceedings. The firm has represented international businesses in Germany, Sweden, Switzerland and the United Kingdom.

## HEAD OFFICE

**TEXAS**
300 Crescent Court, Suite 1500, **Dallas**, TX 75201
**Tel:** 214 978 4000   **Fax:** 214 978 4044
**Email:** gweden@mckoolsmith.com
**Website:** www.mckoolsmith.com

## BRANCH OFFICES

**TEXAS**
300 W 6th Street, Suite 1700, **Austin**, TX 78701
**Tel:** 512 692 8700   **Fax:** 512 692 8744

505 E Travis, Suite 105, **Marshall**, TX 75670
**Tel:** 903 927 2111   **Fax:** 903 927 2622

## CONTACTS

**Executive Director** ...........................................Gary Eden

**McKOOL SMITH**
A PROFESSIONAL CORPORATION • ATTORNEYS
Complex Business Litigation · Intellectual Property Litigation

# NEEL, HOOPER & BANES, P.C.

## THE FIRM

**Founding Partners:** James M Neel, Samuel E Hooper

**Number of partners:** 3
**Number of other lawyers:** 4

## AREAS OF PRACTICE
**Labor & Employment Law & Government Contracts** . . . . . . . . . . . 100%

**FIRM OVERVIEW:** Since being established in 1972, the firm has focused on the exclusive representation of management in all aspects of labor and employment law. The firm prides itself on providing individualized, cost-effective legal services. Four of the firm's attorneys are Board Certified in labor and employment law by the Texas Board of Legal Specialization. The depth of knowledge and experience covers virtually every aspect of labor and employment law arising under the National Labor Relations Act, Title VII of the Civil Rights Act of 1964, the ADA, FMLA, ADEA, FLSA, OSHA, WARN, Sarbanes-Oxley retaliatory provisions, Drug-Free Workplace Act, Rehabilitation Act, HIPAA, and COBRA, as well as equivalents arising under Texas law. In addition, the firm assists employers in securing and administering government contracts in compliance with applicable regulations.

## MAIN AREAS OF PRACTICE:

**Traditional Labor:** The firm's Traditional Labor Practice assists non-union clients in remaining union free, advises and counsels employers that are the subject of union organizing drives, and represents unionized clients in collective bargaining negotiations, arbitration proceedings and unfair labor practice cases.
**Employment Litigation:** The firm represents clients, at both trial and appellate levels, cases involving alleged sex, age, race, national origin, disability and retaliation discrimination; alleged breaches of employment contracts created by oral promises and/or handbooks or other written pronouncements; alleged discriminatory treatment because of an employee's filing of a workers' compensation claim or complaining about unsafe practices; slander, libel, blacklisting; claimed breaches of covenants not-to-compete; and alleged tortious interference with contractual relationships.
**Administrative Agency Representation:** Neel, Hooper & Banes, P.C. has considerable experience representing employers in discrimination, harassment and retaliation charges brought before the Equal Employment Opportunity Commission and other state fair employment practice agencies. The firm also has ample experience handling claims brought before other administrative agencies such as the Department of Labor, National Labor Relations Board, Occupational Safety and Health Administration and Texas Workforce Commission. In addition, the firm has significant experience before the Government Accountability Office, Small Business Administration and Office of Federal Contract Compliance.
**Wage & Hour:** The firm assists clients to achieve compliance with the minimum wage, overtime and recordkeeping requirements of all federal and state wage and hour laws. The firm also assists clients in complying with state wage payment laws involving vacation pay, deductions, commissions, etc, and reviews and designs pay plans. The firm conducts preventive audits, as well as represents clients in investigations conducted by the US Department of Labor's Wage and Hour Division and similar state agencies. It also defends wage and hour lawsuits in court, including representative actions.
**Government Contracts:** Neel, Hooper & Banes, P.C. has an extensive practice in government contracts. This practice includes business and proposal development, teaming arrangements and strategic partnerships, contract and subcontract management, contract and federal acquisition regulation compliance issues, and relations with government officials. The firm also represents clients in litigation arising from government contract awards and performance, including protests and disputes pursuant to the Contract Disputes Act before the Court of Federal Claims, the US Court of Appeals for the Federal Circuit and various federal and state boards and decision authorities.

## HEAD OFFICE

**TEXAS**
1700 West Loop South, Suite 1400, **Houston**, TX 77027-3008
**Tel:** 713 629-1800 **Fax:** 713 629-1812
**Website:** www.neelhooper.com

## BRANCH OFFICES

Neel, Hooper & Banes is a member of the Worklaw Network. Consequently, the firm works with over 25 firms with offices throughout the US so that it may further service clients with diverse geographical needs.

**Training & Counseling:** The firm's attorneys counsel employers on compliance strategies and the prevention of litigation, including issues on the hiring and termination of employees in both union and non-union settings. Similarly, the firm regularly conducts reviews of employee handbooks and personnel policies for both legal compliance and completeness. The firm also conducts training encompassing such subjects as harassment in the workplace, union avoidance, proper record keeping, and effective disciplinary counseling. Finally, the firm drafts and reviews employment agreements, including covenants not-to-compete and severance agreements.

**Industries Served:** Neel, Hooper & Banes, P.C. represents clients involved in a wide range of industries including: aerospace, petrochemical, restaurant and food service, banking and finance, retail, construction, insurance, manufacturing, property management, healthcare, printing and publishing, telecommunications, steel erection, municipal government, auto service, consumer products, employee providers, oil and gas, engineering and parcel carriers.

**worklaw® network.**
worklaw network affiliate

# THOMPSON & KNIGHT LLP

## THE FIRM

**Managing Partner:** Peter J Riley
**Number of attorneys:** 420

**FIRM OVERVIEW:** Since 1887, Thompson & Knight attorneys have been anticipating clients' needs and striving to exceed expectations. With an emphasis on international energy, litigation, tax, and insolvency matters, the firm's attorneys provide clients with innovative, cost-effective legal and business solutions to their issues. Thompson & Knight's experience in these areas establishes it as a leading international energy law firm, with more than two-thirds of its practice relating to the energy industry.

## MAIN AREAS OF PRACTICE:

**Corporate & Securities:** Thompson & Knight's corporate and securities attorneys serve as outside general counsel and as advisors on day-to-day operational matters for a diverse range of corporations, partnerships, limited liability companies, and other business entities. They provide similar counsel to investment banking firms, investment advisors, financial institutions, and insurance companies, and are particularly adept at public offerings and private placements of debt and equity securities.

**Corporate Reorganization & Creditors' Rights:** The firm's attorneys represent trade creditors, lien claimants, and large and small creditor and debtor companies in all aspects of bankruptcy litigation and take a leading role in corporate reorganizations, both in and out of court, and in bankruptcy proceedings of all types throughout the country. They often serve as special litigation counsel in extremely complex cases, and excel at conceptualizing and negotiating innovative business finance solutions.

**Energy:** Thompson & Knight attorneys counsel oil, gas, and energy industry clients worldwide – those who explore, develop, produce, store, market, transport, and process energy resources. The firm's client roster is a 'who's who' of the industry and includes many of the largest publicly traded energy companies and a host of oil and gas exploration, production, refining, pipeline, marketing, and investment businesses.

**Environmental:** For nearly half a century, the firm's environmental attorneys have been assisting clients in all aspects of federal, state, and local environmental laws, from their development to their application. Thompson & Knight's practice includes permitting, environmental auditing, administrative and judicial proceedings, environmental tort litigation, and rulemaking and legislative lobbying.

**Finance:** Thompson & Knight's finance attorneys are experienced in all types of domestic and international private debt and equity finance transactions, as well as public offerings and commercial finance transactions. The firm's clients include banks, insurance companies, pension fund managers, savings and loan associations, factoring companies, and other lenders located around the world.

**Government Relations & Public Policy:** With expertise gained through years of regulatory counsel in major industries and legislative lobbying at all levels of government, Thompson & Knight attorneys guide clients' participation in the lawmaking process. The firm's attorneys assist in negotiating with governmental and quasi-governmental entities and represent clients' interests in regulatory, legislative, and administrative rulemaking and licensing matters.

**Health:** The attorneys in Thompson & Knight's Health Law Practice Group routinely deal with complex issues that arise from the maze of laws, rules, and public policy imposed on healthcare providers by the government and private insurers. The firm has a thorough understanding of the legal issues faced by institutional and professional healthcare providers (including, but not limited to, hospitals, physicians, nursing homes, nurses, ICF/MR facilities and ambulatory surgery centers), helping these clients interface with governmental entities at both the state and federal level. In addition, the firm is in frequent contact with key personnel in state and federal regulatory agencies.

**Intellectual Property & Technology:** Thompson & Knight attorneys counsel clients in the development, protection, licensing, valuation, and enhancement of their technology, ideas, and goodwill. The firm's core practice includes client counseling, applications and registrations, prosecution, licensing, technology transfer, corporate advisory work, and litigation in the areas of patents, trademarks, copyrights, trade dress, and common-law rights.

**Labor & Employment:** The firm's attorneys counsel and represent private and public employers in all aspects of the employment relationship. Their practice encompasses defending employers against all types of labor- or employment-related claims, as well as counseling employers on compliance strategies and the prevention of litigation.

**Real Estate:** Thompson & Knight's real estate attorneys have an innovative, multi-state, and international practice. They structure and document numerous matters, including the purchase, sale, development, leasing, and financing of properties used for multi-family housing, retail shopping centers, research facilities, mixed use industrial warehouses, distribution centers, and manufacturing and office buildings.

**Tax:** Thompson & Knight offers comprehensive federal, state, and local tax compliance and tax planning advice to individuals and all types of business entities and organizations. With extensive experience in federal and state tax matters, the firm's tax attorneys resolve clients' tax law challenges by creatively applying current and comprehensive knowledge of tax law and best practices to their needs.

**Trial & Appellate:** Thompson & Knight has an extensive trial practice worldwide, combining keen analysis, careful preparation, practical skills, and comprehensive experience to represent clients effectively before judges and juries, and in alternative dispute resolution forums. The team includes more than 170 skilled trial and appellate lawyers, staff attorneys, and legal assistants who work resolutely to resolve the issues in dispute and achieve clients' objectives.

**INTERNATIONAL WORK:** The firm's attorneys work with clients worldwide in connection with a variety of transactions, particularly legal matters related to energy, litigation, tax, and creditors' rights. In the realm of global energy, the firm offers a full range of legal and commercial services including advice on host government contracts; joint operating, study, and bidding agreements; service contracts; regulatory matters; tax; corporate structure; arbitration; mergers and acquisitions; financings; pipeline and refinery projects; and other numerous matters.

## HEAD OFFICE

**TEXAS**
1700 Pacific Avenue, Suite 3300, **Dallas**, TX 75201
**Tel:** 214 969 1700 **Fax:** 214 969 1751
**Website:** www.tklaw.com

## BRANCH OFFICES

**NEW YORK**
919 Third Avenue, 39th Floor, **New York**, NY 10022-3915
**Tel:** 212 751 3001 **Fax:** 212 751 3113

**TEXAS**
98 San Jacinto Boulevard, Suite 1900, **Austin**, TX 78701
**Tel:** 512 469 6100 **Fax:** 512 469 6180

801 Cherry Street, Unit 1, Burnett Plaza, Suite 1600,
**Fort Worth**, TX 76102
**Tel:** 817 347 1700 **Fax:** 817 347 1799

333 Clay Street, Suite 3300, **Houston**, TX 77002
**Tel:** 713 654 8111 **Fax:** 713 654 1871

## INTERNATIONAL OFFICES

The firm has offices in Algiers, Algeria; London, England; Monterrey and Mexico City, Mexico; Paris, France; Rio de Janeiro and Vitória, Brazil.

Thompson & Knight | Impact
ATTORNEYS AND COUNSELORS

# THOMPSON, COE, COUSINS & IRONS, LLP

## THE FIRM

**Managing Partner:** Jack M Cleaveland Jr

**FIRM OVERVIEW:** Founded in 1951, Thompson Coe has roots in the earliest days of the 20th century legal practice in Texas. The founding partners had extensive knowledge of the insurance business and quickly built a reputation unparalleled for experience in areas unique to insurance. Today the firm is recognized nationally as not only a preeminent insurance firm, but also as a provider of a wide range of legal services to clients in many industries. The firm spans the state of Texas with offices in Austin, Dallas and Houston and has now expanded further, establishing an office in Saint Paul, Minnesota.

## MAIN AREAS OF PRACTICE:

**Insurance Law:** Given that Thompson Coe is recognized as a national authority on insurance law, the firm's clients depend on its broad insurance background and knowledge to provide reliable and efficient legal advice and assistance for all insurance business and regulatory matters. Whether giving advice pertaining to insurance laws, representing a client before an insurance regulator, handling mergers and acquisitions or formations of insurance companies and agencies, or drafting or reviewing documents needed for insurance-related transactions, this practice group brings extensive experience to areas of law that are unfamiliar to many.

**Insurance Litigation & Coverage:** This practice group provides counsel to insurance companies through a broad range of insurance-related litigation, coverage disputes, bad faith and other extra-contractual liabilities litigation. Drawing upon the firm's experience in the administrative and regulatory arena, the firm represents carriers facing complex corporate, regulatory and class action litigation.

**Casualty & Tort Litigation:** The firm's casualty and tort attorneys have been recognized for their proficiency in the trial and defense of personal injury cases involving premises liability, products liability, medical malpractice, mass tort litigation, negligence and other tort-related claims. They are committed to excellence in trial advocacy and pride themselves in responding to litigation needs with practical, creative solutions.

**Commercial Litgation:** This practice group has handled every type of commercial dispute ranging from simple contract matters to complex international disputes. The attorneys share a commitment to do whatever it takes in terms of preparation and development of innovative strategies to ensure the best possible results for its business litigation clients - including trying cases to a conclusion with successful results.

**Governmental & Legislative Advocacy:** The firm's attorneys help clients achieve legislative initiatives and resolve regulatory issues. Their involvement and experience in the legislative and governmental process enables them to provide clients with efficient and effective representation and advocate their positions before the legislature and other governmental agencies.

**General Litigation:** This practice group represents clients in mass tort litigation, nursing home negligence cases, healthcare regulatory matters, and medical products/device litigation. These successful litigators are adept at handling high-profile clients and are experienced at allocating resources in terms of personnel, time, database management and preparation to ensure the best possible results for their clients.

**Labor & Employment:** The firm's attorneys counsel both private and public sector management in connection with all employment-related matters, including compliance with the FLSA, Title VII, ADEA, ADA, WARN, OHSA and other federal, state and local laws regulating employment. They have an active labor litigation practice defending management against EEO claims, wrongful termination, workers' compensation retaliation, civil rights and other employment-related claims. The firm handles employment and non-competition agreements, as well as collective bargaining, grievance-arbitrations, unfair labor practice proceedings, and other labor-management relations issues.

## HEAD OFFICE

**TEXAS**
700 N Pearl Street, Twenty-fifth Floor, **Dallas**, TX 75201-2832
**Tel:** 214 871 8200   **Fax:** 214 871 8209
**Website:** www.thompsoncoe.com

## BRANCH OFFICES

**MINNESOTA**
The Historic Hamm Building, 408 St. Peter Street, Suite 510
**Saint Paul**, MN 55102
**Tel:** 651 389 5000   **Fax:** 651 389 5059

**TEXAS**
701 Brazos, Suite 1500, **Austin**, TX 78701
**Tel:** 512 708 8200   **Fax:** 512 708 8777

One Riverway, Suite 1600, **Houston**, TX 77056
**Tel:** 713 403 8210   **Fax:** 713 403 8299

## CONTACTS

| | |
|---|---|
| Austin | Jay Thompson |
| Dallas | Roger Higgins |
| Houston | Brian Martin |
| St Paul | Lynn Meyer |

**Professional Liability:** Lawsuits involving malpractice claims against attorneys, accountants, insurance agents and brokers, corporate directors and officers and other business professionals are being asserted at an increasing rate. The attorneys draw upon years of hands-on experience in dealing with claims to provide the firm's professional clients with the finest quality legal representation.

**Business Transactions:** This practice group encompasses everything from contractual relationships, including mergers and acquisitions, sales and purchases of ownership interests, shareholder agreements, management compensation arrangements, entity formation and financing, to bankruptcy, real estate transactions, estate planning and tax issues.

**CLIENTS:** Association of Fire and Casualty Companies in Texas (AFACT); Progressive Insurance Company; All American Life Insurance Company; Zurich; Allstate; 3M; Employers General Insurance Company and Texas Medical Liability Insurance Underwriting Association.

THOMPSON
COE

# VINSON & ELKINS

## THE FIRM

**Managing Partner:** Joseph C Dilg

**Number of partners worldwide:** 322
**Number of other lawyers worldwide:** 399

**FIRM OVERVIEW:** For almost a century, Vinson & Elkins lawyers have provided innovative business solutions for clients whose needs are as diverse as the entities they represent. In today's challenging environment of global markets, volatile economies and complex human and environmental issues, the firm's time-tested role as trusted advisor has become even more critical. The depth and breadth of its lawyers' experience, combined with the responsiveness and efficiencies of the firm's global reach, enable Vinson & Elkins to serve clients from start-up, to the negotiating table and boardroom, before legislative and regulatory bodies in the courtroom, and beyond.

**Diversity:** At Vinson & Elkins, the approach to diversity is driven by core values, which stress the firm's commitment to hiring and developing the best legal talent; providing excellence in service to their clients; and creating an environment of 'shared values of civility, compassion and respect for one another.' These core values of individuality and innovation are factors that have driven the firm's success for nearly 90 years and are the basis upon which it builds its diversity efforts. It is the firm's hope that its efforts will lead it to be not only the law firm of choice for its clients, but also the employer of choice for top lawyers.

**MAIN AREAS OF PRACTICE:** Core practice areas include admiralty; antitrust; bankruptcy; business transactions; capital markets; communications; contracts; e-commerce; eminent domain; employee benefits (ERISA) and executive compensation; energy and electric power regulation; environmental; finance; financial institutions; government and international procurement; health law; intellectual property; international arbitration; international law; internet; labor and employment relations; litigation; mergers and acquisitions; oil and gas; outsourcing; private equity; project finance and development; public finance; public policy; real estate; securities; structured finance; syndicated finance; taxation; technology; trusts and estates; and white collar criminal defense. At Vinson & Elkins, their approach to diversity is driven by their core values, which stress their commitment to hiring and developing the best legal talent; providing excellence in service to the firm's clients; and creating an environment of 'shared values of civility, compassion and respect for one another.' These core values of individuality and innovation are factors that have driven the firm's success for nearly 90 years and are the basis upon which they build their diversity efforts. It is their hope that their efforts will lead them to be not only the law firm of choice for their clients, but also the employer of choice for top lawyers.

**CLIENTS:** Since the firm was founded in 1917, it has attracted an outstanding and diverse group of lawyers who serve an international clientele. Clients include the governments of sovereign nations and of North American states, cities and municipalities, public and private companies, domestic and international financial institutions, new entities, joint ventures, project companies, and individuals and families.

## US OFFICES

**NEW YORK**
666 Fifth Ave., 26th Floor, **New York**, NY 101031-0040
**Tel:** 212 237 0000  **Fax:** 212 237 0100
**Email:** wstuart@velaw.com

**TEXAS**
2801 Via Fortuna, Suite 100, **Austin**, TX 78746-7568
**Tel:** 512 542 8400  **Fax:** 512 542 8612
**Email:** dwood@velaw.com

3700 Trammell Crow Center, 2001 Ross Avenue, **Dallas**, TX 75201-2975
**Tel:** 214 220 7700  **Fax:** 214 220 7716
**Email:** mwortley@velaw.com

First City Tower, 1001 Fannin, Suite 2300, **Houston**, TX 77002-6760
**Tel:** 713 758 2222  **Fax:** 713 758 2346
**Email:** jdilg@velaw.com

**DISTRICT OF COLUMBIA**
The Willard Office Building, 1455 Pennsylvania Avenue NW,
**Washington**, DC 20004-1008
**Tel:** 202 639 6500  **Fax:** 202 639 6604
**Email:** jherbert@velaw.com

## INTERNATIONAL OFFICES

The firm also has offices in Beijing and Shanghai, China; Dubai, United Arab Emirates; Moscow, Russia; Tokyo, Japan; and London, United Kingdom.

**INTERNATIONAL WORK:** Eleven offices worldwide allow Vinson & Elkins' lawyers to work efficiently across time zones, as well as with local lawyers in foreign jurisdictions to accomplish the client's objectives. In addition to legal experience, the firm has strong personal relationships with business people and other professionals that offer significant benefits to the client including broad experience in transactions spanning multiple jurisdictions, cultures and languages. The firm efficiently guides its clients through a wide range of transactions, such as mergers and acquisitions, joint ventures and strategic alliances, public and private offerings of securities in the developed and emerging capital markets, as well as development and financing of a variety of projects.

## Vinson&Elkins LLP

# WINSTEAD SECHREST & MINICK P.C.

## THE FIRM

**Chairman, CEO:** W Mike Baggett

**Number of shareholders in US:** 165
**Number of other lawyers in US:** 138

**FIRM OVERVIEW:** Winstead Sechrest & Minick P.C. has grown steadily since it was founded as a four-attorney practice in Dallas in 1973. The firm's initial period of growth was organic, but in the last few years it has expanded by merging with small firms that specialize in its traditional strengths of litigation, banking, real estate and corporate law. In 2001, the firm bucked the industry-wide trend for downsizing by acquiring three Texas boutique firms in the space of five months, and now employs more than 300 attorneys in seven locations across the US. The political consulting practice of Winstead Sechrest & Minick P.C., Winstead Consulting Group, LLC, provides local, state and federal government relations and strategic services throughout the United States.

## MAIN AREAS OF PRACTICE:

**Banking & Credit Transactions:** The firm advises regional, national, and international financial institutions, financial services companies, and other lending organizations in virtually all aspects of their business activities. Attorneys represent and counsel lenders, agents, participants, and borrowers in single-lender and syndicated credit facilities of all types and complexities. Winstead also represents the firm's corporate clients in establishing and maintaining credit facilities. Attorneys have extensive experience in restructurings of troubled credits, debtor-in-possession financing, post-confirmation financing, and other workout matters. The firm regularly advises financial services clients who seek counsel on mergers and acquisitions, the development of new products and services, regulatory matters, enforcement actions, litigation, and other financial services issues.

**Business Restructuring/Bankruptcy:** Winstead's Business Restructuring/Bankruptcy Practice is one of the largest in Texas and the southwestern United States. This cross-sectional practice involves not only the traditional bankruptcy practice, but also attorneys from banking, corporate, securities, tax, real estate and other areas, who all have extensive experience in both operational and financial restructurings. The practice is national in scope and focuses on nonjudicial workouts and restructures, as well as the traditional bankruptcy court process. This unique focus, combined with the substantial experience of the firm's Business Restructuring Practice, provides clients with the ability to analyze all of the possible options in a workout, from the inception. The practice covers representation of debtors, creditors, committees, and other parties in interest in all aspects of financial restructurings, including out-of-court restructurings, prebankruptcy negotiation and strategy, the bankruptcy process itself, and all types of litigation arising out of, or related to, bankruptcy and insolvency matters. Given their broad diversity of experience, Winstead's business restructuring professionals are able to provide a keen understanding of the business goals of all interested parties, to any transaction, along with the ability to craft solutions that will achieve those goals in a manner that is consistent with the client's goals and expectations.

**Corporate, Securities & Taxation:** Winstead attorneys are experienced in corporate finance, securities regulation, tax matters related to federal, state, and local governments, insurance regulation, asset securitization, and investment management. Attorneys also provide specialized counsel and insight with respect to the successful operation of both public and private businesses. The firm represents clients in connection with the offering and sale of public and private equity, public and private debt, mortgage and asset-backed securities, and tax-exempt public bond issuances. Winstead provides counsel to both mature and start-up businesses with respect to corporate governance, public and private financing, mergers, acquisitions and divestitures, antitrust issues, shareholder disputes and agreements, adoption of employee incentive and stock option plans, implementation of anti-takeover defenses, noncompetition agreements, and protection and exploitation of intellectual property and other proprietary information.

**Government Relations:** Winstead operates a local, state and federal Government Relations Practice supported by Winstead Consulting Group, LLC, the

## HEAD OFFICE

**TEXAS**
5400 Renaissance Tower, 1201 Elm Street, **Dallas**, TX 75270
**Tel:** 214 745 5400 **Fax:** 214 745 5390
**Website:** www.winstead.com

## BRANCH OFFICES

**DISTRICT OF COLUMBIA**
1850 M Street NW, Suite 800, **Washington**, DC 20036
Tel: 202 572 8000 Fax: 202 572 8001

**TEXAS**
401 Congress Avenue, Suite 2100, **Austin**, TX 78701
**Tel:** 512 370 2800 **Fax:** 512 370 2850

2100 McKinney Avenue, Suite 1501, **Dallas**, TX 75201
**Tel:** 214 745 5400 **Fax:** 214 745 5883

777 Main Street, Suite 1100, **Fort Worth**, TX 76102
**Tel:** 817 420 8200 **Fax:** 817 420 8201

2400 Bank One Center, 910 Travis Street, **Houston**, TX 77002
**Tel:** 713 650 8400 **Fax:** 713 650 2400

700 North St. Mary's Street, Suite 1900, **San Antonio**, TX 78205
**Tel:** 210 277 6800 **Fax:** 210 277 6810

600 Town Center One, 1450 Lake Robbins Drive,
**The Woodlands**, TX 77380
**Tel:** 281 681 5900 **Fax:** 281 681 5901

## CONTACTS

| | |
|---|---|
| **Banking & Credit** | T Randall Matthews |
| **Bankruptcy** | Mark Brannum |
| **Corporate** | Bruce A Cheatham |
| **Government Relations** | Paul N Wageman |
| **Intellectual Property** | Ross Spencer Garsson |
| **Labor & Employment** | Dan C Dargene |
| **Litigation** | Wayne W Bost |
| **Real Estate** | T Andrew Dow |

firm's wholly owned, political consulting subsidiary. Attorneys and consultants represent a wide range of corporate clients, associations and large public entities before all levels of government. Winstead's government relations practice in the Washington, DC office focuses on federal and national government relations. Each of the firm's Texas offices handles state and local government matters working with the Governor's office, the Texas Legislature and state agencies as well as municipal governments. Attorneys' and consultants' experience includes, but is not limited to, condemning authority in condemnation litigation matters, healthcare, energy, telecommunications, financial institutions, transportation including public-private partnerships, government procurement and contracting, sports authorities and facilities, international trade, high technology, land use, environment and natural resources, public finance and real estate.

**Intellectual Property:** The firm's IP lawyers seek to identify, exploit, and protect a client's intellectual property by a wide variety of techniques, beginning with the protection of trade secrets and know-how, to the preparation and prosecution of patents, copyrights, trademarks, to the negotiation of related technology agreements and licenses, to the enforcement and/or defense of such rights, in all forums, i.e., mediation, arbitration, various state and US District/Appellate Courts, and the International Trade Commission. Clients are drawn from diverse sciences and technologies, ranging from oilfield, display signage, highway safety, and medical devices to nanotechnology and biotechnology.

Labor & Employment: Winstead represents employers across the spectrum of the employment relationship. The firm's representation includes traditional union-management disputes before labor arbitrators and administrative law judges, as well as the needs of management in the multifaceted and complex area

# WINSTEAD SECHREST & MINICK P.C.

of employees' individual rights. Attorneys provide comprehensive advice to employers faced with restrictions on the exercise of their business judgment in dealing with employees, and counsel employers so they may act in a manner that is lawful, yet consistent with their business objectives. Winstead also offers advice and training programs aimed at preventing employment-related complaints and lawsuits. The Labor and Employment Group has substantial experience defending all forms of workplace litigation, including defense of claims under virtually every federal and state fair employment practices statute, governmental entities against whistleblower claims, substantive and procedural due process claims, and other state and federal constitutional and statutory claims unique to the public employment sector. Winstead's employment litigators are also experienced in the defense of labor arbitrations, administrative proceedings before state and federal agencies, and all forms of alternate dispute resolution.

**Litigation:** When it is reasonably possible and consistent with the firm's clients' objectives, Winstead initially strives to resolve a dispute without resorting to litigation. In this regard, negotiation, arbitration, and mediation are viable alternatives. When litigation is unavoidable, however, the firm provides analysis, advice, and representation that enables its clients to properly evaluate, manage, and control the risks, costs, and uncertainties associated with litigation. Attorneys enforce or defend clients' rights wherever disputes arise, in Texas or elsewhere, and whether in court (state or federal) or an arbitration organization. From massive class actions for publicly traded entities to simple commercial disputes for small businesses, Winstead represents clients from numerous industries in a wide variety of cases, and in many different venues.

**Real Estate:** Winstead's Real Estate Group includes more than 60 full-time real estate attorneys and more than 20 paralegals. The depth and breadth of Winstead's real estate expertise gives its clients access to real estate professionals with experience in virtually every type of real estate and every transaction structure, anywhere in the US and in any stage of the real estate cycle. For example, Winstead has successfully represented Fortune 500 retailers in the rapid roll-out of new retail concepts during periods of economic expansion. Yet at the same time, Winstead enjoys, as a result of the significant size of its Real Estate Group, a national reputation in the field of real estate restructuring. Winstead's client list includes many of the largest and most active real estate development companies, institutional investors, mortgage lenders and loan servicers in the United States,

as well as individual investors and entrepreneurs. The firm's attorneys achieve desired results across the full real estate spectrum, including the development of all property types in mixed-use configurations and common ownership structures, acquisition and disposition of all property types, zoning and land use, construction, environmental, corporate facilities management, development and private investment, real estate finance (including new construction, mezzanine, portfolio, and CMBS debt and structured leases), loan servicing, restructuring and workouts, REITs and REMICs, sports and public facilities, taxation issues (from TIF districts to 1031 exchanges), leasing and asset management, portfolio acquisitions and dispositions, and institutional equity and mortgage investments.

**INTERNATIONAL WORK:** Group attorneys have experience in more than 30 foreign jurisdictions and have represented US and foreign clients engaged in international business throughout the world and in a variety of industries. The firm is particularly experienced at handling large, high-profile mergers and acquisitions, energy projects and new investments abroad. Winstead is a member of both the Interlex Group and The Bridge Group, which are associations of leading law firms serving international clients.

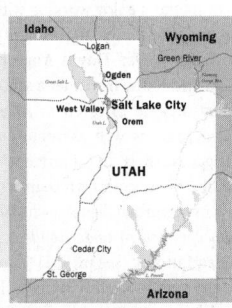

## How lawyers are ranked

Every year we carry out thousands of in-depth interviews with clients and lawyers in order to assess the reputations and expertise of business lawyers across the USA. Chambers rankings and editorial are referred to extensively by General Counsel and other purchasers of legal services who look to our recommendations when choosing their lawyers.

# CORPORATE/M&A

### Corporate/M&A
### Leading Firms

1. **STOEL RIVES LLP** *Salt Lake City*
   **WILSON SONSINI** *Salt Lake City*
2. **HOLLAND & HART LLP** *Salt Lake City*
   **JONES WALDO** *Salt Lake City*
   **PARR WADDOUPS** *Salt Lake City*
   **SNELL & WILMER LLP** *Salt Lake City*
3. **DORSEY & WHITNEY LLP** *Salt Lake City*
   **HOLME ROBERTS & OWEN LLP** *Salt Lake City*
4. **BALLARD SPAHR** *Salt Lake City*
   **DURHAM JONES & PINEGAR** *Salt Lake City*
   **PARSONS BEHLE & LATIMER PC** *Salt Lake City*
   **RAY, QUINNEY & NEBEKER PC** *Salt Lake City*

### Leading Individuals

1. **BONHAM Mark** *Wilson Sonsini*
   **LLOYD Brian** *Parr Waddoups*
   **LOVELESS Scott** *Parr Waddoups*
   **O'CONNOR Robert** *Wilson Sonsini*
   **TAYLOR Nolan** *Dorsey & Whitney LLP*
2. **ANDERSON Chris** *Snell & Wilmer LLP*
   **FREDMAN Stuart** *Holme Roberts & Owen LLP*
   **MOFFITT Ronald** *Stoel Rives LLP*
   **POELMAN Ronald** *Jones Waldo*
   **STEVENSON Brent** *Parr Waddoups*
   **TOPHAM Reed** *Stoel Rives LLP*
3. **ANGERBAUER David** *Holland & Hart LLP*
   **JONES Nathan** *Stoel Rives LLP*
   **LINDLEY Greg** *Holland & Hart LLP*
   **LITTLE David** *Holme Roberts & Owen LLP*
   **MANGUM Geoffrey** *Parsons Behle & Latimer PC*
   **RUDD David** *Ballard Spahr*
   **TAYLOR Tom** *Holme Roberts & Owen LLP*
   **WESTON John** *Snell & Wilmer LLP*
   **WILSON Randon** *Jones Waldo*
   **WINGER Gary** *Ray, Quinney & Nebeker PC*
   **YOUNG Howard** *Jones Waldo*

### Up-and-coming individuals

**GARDINER Samuel** *Dorsey & Whitney LLP*
**JACOBSEN Brad** *Holme Roberts & Owen LLP*

## Band 1

### Stoel Rives LLP

**The Firm:** This Portland, Oregon-based firm provides a full service, with "*people on the ground to cover all areas.*" It has, however, been particularly busy on M&A and financing transactions in the hi-tech, mining and manufacturing sectors. The firm has also developed a niche in venture capital, in no small part due to its Silicon Valley connections. Despite the departure of Brian Lloyd to his old firm Parr Waddoups Brown Gee & Loveless, the team retains its dominant position in Salt Lake City, representing the largest local companies including Huntsman Corporation. Stoel Rives lawyers are active internationally, having recently helped a client with its negotiations in the UK.

**The Lawyers:** **Ron Moffitt** "*would go the extra mile to get things done on time and achieve what his clients want.*" This "*levelheaded*" lawyer not only has an accounting and tax background but in-house experience as a former general counsel for Huntsman, all of which make him "*a great business adviser.*" Lately he has worked on a number of transactions for RDO Properties, and continues to act as general counsel for companies owned by Sorenson and AlphaGraphics. The "*phenomenal*" **Reed Topham** applies his "*tremendous intellect and skill set*" to often-complicated deals. His general pragmatism helps him to "*wade through a forest of issues to find the trees that his clients should be concerned about.*" Representative clients include Weider Nutrition and GE Capital. **Nathan Jones** has an unusually deep in-house perspective and continues to work extensively for Huntsman Corporation. He assists with most of Huntsman's SEC reporting requirements and advises on the corporate restructuring matters. In addition to his work for this valuable client, Jones is involved in joint venture formations and financing projects. Interviewees liked the fact that he can "*put aside his ego to get deals done.*"

**Clients/Work Highlights:** AlphaGraphics; PSC Military Housing; KF Holdings; Precision Cast Parts; MK Resources; Sorenson and RDO Properties. The firm also acted on the sale on Envirocare.

### Wilson Sonsini Goodrich & Rosati

See firm details p.344

**The Firm:** "*The 900-pound gorilla for hi-tech work*" dominates the startup market in Utah and has an abundance of "*experts in venture capital.*" The Salt Lake City team is trusted implicitly by its clients; they confirmed that with the Wilson team on their side they have "*never felt disadvantaged.*" Indeed, one deemed their chosen advisers to be "*awesome.*" This firm is handling an increased number of national transactions for energy companies. For example, it advised solar power company Q-Cells in a $79 million public offering and a $90 million convertible debt offering.

**The Lawyers:** "*Bright and talented*" **Robert O'Connor** (see p.1952) really "*knows what he is doing.*" Clients appreciate his "*high ethical standards and trustworthiness.*" Highlights include working on a $70 million acquisition by Altiris and advising a client on a $20 million acquisition of a French software company. **Mark Bonham** (see p.1950) has a "*creative and unique way of problem solving*" and genuine expertise in the hi-tech area, where he represents startups and midsized public companies such as Sonic innovations and Nu Skin. Bonham is known as "*a smart guy and an outstanding lawyer*" because he "*really understands his clients' business needs.*"

**Clients/Work Highlights:** Chase Manhattan Mortgage; Delta Air Lines; Honda; Questar; Qwest; Lockheed Martin; Visa; Altiris; vSpring Capital; UV Partners; MyFamily.com; LANDesk; Evergreen Solar; Solaria; JPMorgan; SG Cowen & Co; Avinti and Backcountry.com.

## Band 2

### Holland & Hart LLP

See firm details p.369

**The Firm:** This firm enjoys "*a strong reputation in the Salt Lake City legal and business community*" because it "*provides a wide range of legal expertise at a fair price.*" The firm enjoys client loyalty. One told researchers: "*I still use Holland & Hart even though I have relocated.*" Four partners lead the corporate team and, as part of a large full-service regional firm, they can call upon employment, benefits and tax specialists, among others, to assist in transactions. Competitors enjoy working with them on transactions as they know "*the deal will get done.*"

**The Lawyers: David Angerbauer** (see p.1949) returned to the firm after a sabbatical and immediately became involved in a large acquisition for MedQuest as well as venture capital financings. Angerbauer is the President of MountainWest Venture Group and is recognized as one of the leaders in this area. Clients say he "*understands business concepts and so understands how to advise them.*" **Greg Lindley** (see p.1951) "*knows which issues are important and which are not.*" He advised Eastern Sports on several acquisitions and closed three private placements of securities deals, one for an oil and gas company and another for a water treatment recycling company. Researchers learned that Lindley has "*that rare combination of legal and business common sense that makes him almost a business partner rather than just another legal consultant.*"

## Jones Waldo Holbrook & McDonough PC

**The Firm:** "*Probably one of the best local firms in Utah,*" this 12-lawyer team is involved in general M&A, corporate governance counseling, securities issues and venture capital. Of particular interest to some clients is the firm's niche expertise in relation to agricultural co-op business. The office has been expanding its corporate practice and has hired a number of lawyers.

**The Lawyers:** Former member of the board of directors of USANA Health Science, **Ron Poelman** has "*great corporate sense.*" He has deep roots in the community and is well regarded by his peers. "*Solutions-oriented*" **Howard Young** has been involved in more private equity deals of late and has excellent knowledge of the medical devices industry. A previous role as an in-house counsel is said to help him better understand his role as outside counsel. One of his highlights saw him advising Kiddie Candid in a $40 million investment. **Randon Wilson** is the key figure in the firm's national agricultural co-op practice. Having managed numerous significant finance deals and acquisitions in this area, his reputation is unquestioned. Competitors describe him as "*easy to work with.*"

**Clients/Work Highlights:** The Salt Lake City team was involved in a $26 million financing of a TV network deal, and for client Numaco it advised on a ten-year strategic alliance enabling distribution of products in Europe. Clients include ZEVEX International; Q-Comm; USTV and Agilix.

## Parr Waddoups Brown Gee & Loveless

**The Firm:** This Salt Lake City-based outfit is deeply rooted in the commercial and business activities of the state, as well as the local community. Client feedback confirms the popularity of the lawyers here, not least among them Brian Lloyd, who recently returned to the firm last year after time spent at Stoel Rives LLP. Utah clients form the backbone of the corporate practice; one recent highlight was the representation of St George-based SkyWest Airlines in its acquisition of Atlantic Southeast Airlines from Delta Air Lines, making SkyWest the largest Delta Connection provider.

**The Lawyers:** "*Outstanding*" **Brian Lloyd** has "*a sensible and practical approach to dealing with issues and clients.*" He has three main areas of expertise – technology, healthcare and aviation – and since his return has been involved in several portfolio company acquisitions and investments for DW Healthcare Partners, as well as being instrumental in the SkyWest deal. Known to be thorough and a good negotiator, **Scott Loveless** is "*excellent in protecting the client from any unforeseen matters after a deal is done.*" He has been successful in representing mid-level companies, and closed several major transactions for Sports West. "*Accessible*" **Brent Stevenson**, "*goes the extra mile to get things done.*" As a former president of the Huntsman Holdings Corporation, he has a business-minded approach to his work. Described as "*extremely talented and bright,*" he is involved in international acquisitions and dispositions. For example, he represents the Japanese company Arysta Life Science Corporation and continues to advise Huntsman.

**Clients/Work Highlights:** The firm counts the Workers Compensation Fund of Utah, Zions Bank and Tandem Laboratories among its clients.

## Snell & Wilmer LLP
See firm details p.200

**The Firm:** This regional firm bases a core M&A team in Salt Lake City. Its work overlaps with that of the banking and finance group, and together these "*outstanding lawyers with great credentials*" can meet the requirements of clients on larger projects. Although the firm's fees are on the high end for Salt Lake City, the quality of service and effective staffing of deals means that it is said to be "*worth every penny.*" Many clients are Utah-based but some come from California and throughout the Midwest.

**The Lawyers: Chris Anderson** (see p.1949) has completed a number of deals in the biotech field, including financing and licensing. He is regarded as "*a strong player*" by his peers and has acted as expert witness in court cases concerning venture capital. Involved in resolving stockholder disputes, his negotiation skills are said to be "*invaluable,*" and clients praise him for his ability to handle difficult situations "*beautifully.*" "*Energetic and capable*" **John Weston** (see p.1953) focuses on M&A and securities. One of the first things researchers learned about this industrious lawyer was that "*his turnaround time is phenomenal.*" Weston represented TruVision in its disposition and the Officia Group in various acquisitions.

**Clients/Work Highlights:** Accuride; Officia Group; OGIO International; TruVision and GH Peterson Holdings.

## Band 3

## Dorsey & Whitney LLP
See firm details p.1169

**The Firm:** Dorsey's Salt Lake City office is well known for its venture capital practice and its significant experience in M&A, capital markets, securities, private equity and fund formation. There is also an interesting niche in mutual and hedge fund work. Although the corporate team is smaller than some of its competitors, it has access to significant resources elsewhere in the international firm. This fact is not lost on clients, who appreciate the firm's "*national footprint and international reputation.*" The Utah group has built an impressive client following due to its "*responsive staff and quick turnaround in producing high-quality work.*" Major highlights include the $46 million underwritten secondary offering for Ladish Co and the recapitalization of Franklin Covey. The team also advised on a debt offering for Unicity International; ten private equity transactions for Wasatch Advisors; 25 144A and PIPE financing transactions for Wasatch Advisors; and Matsushita Electric's acquisition of emWare.

**The Lawyers:** Sources have "*total confidence*" in **Nolan Taylor** (see p.1952), who is praised for his "*competence, professionalism and excellent judgment.*" Taylor, who was further described as "*extremely diplomatic and effective in negotiations,*" takes on a wide variety of corporate work, including the $102 million IPO of Volcom on which he represented Wachovia Securities, Piper Jaffray and DA Davidson, the underwriters of the offering. He also represented Cornerstone Nutritional Labs in its sale to Mitsui USA. **Samuel Gardiner** (see p.1951) was singled out as "*an extremely competent younger lawyer.*" His practice encompasses many areas of corporate finance, securities and M&A, and his recent experience includes advising Peterson Partners on its acquisition of True North AR.

**Clients/Work Highlights:** Nu Skin Enterprises; Franklin Covey; SCO Group; Arch Coal; Piper Jaffray; Roth Capital; vSpring Capital; Morinda Holdings; Basic Research; Peterson; Lehman Brothers; Goldman Sachs; Merrill Lynch; St. Paul Travelers and Wells Fargo.

## Holme Roberts & Owen LLP
See firm details p.370

**The Firm:** The Denver-headquartered firm receives a "*gold standard for client service.*" The eight-lawyer Utah team is mostly involved in midsized M&A and refinancing work and is well connected with its counterparts in other parts of the Holme Roberts' network. Several of the lawyers have previously worked in out-of-state law firms and thus the breadth and depth of expertise is almost unique in Utah. Holme Roberts is a well-networked firm where lawyers can draw from the resources of the whole firm and they work closely on a regular basis. There is a "*professional presence among employees and staff who are also extremely helpful.*" Questar is one of its biggest clients and last year the team helped them sell Consonus, one of its subsidiaries. The firm also represented Equity Oil in a merger worth $90 million.

The Lawyers: Chair of the corporate group **Stuart Fredman** "*cuts to the chase and gets to the issue.*" He is "*responsive and offers practical solutions.*" His highlights include working on a merger of two public companies and acting as local counsel in a $640 million financing project. He also has a "*great instinct when it comes to negotiating.*" **Tom Taylor** is "*level-headed with solid experience.*" He represents both private and public companies and has particular expertise in venture capital and private equity work. Clients appreciate his timeliness with his work and his ability to "*anticipate the issues and incorporate those issues clearly in the documents.*" He represented US Bank on a large transaction with a London-based firm in a $553 million acquisition and on a loan to the purchaser of Utah Blaze. "*Analytical*" **Brad Jacobsen** was singled out as "*definitely a rising star.*" He has particular expertise in corporate and venture capital transactions and is described as having "*strong deal skills.*" **David Little** boasts Intermountain Power Agency as one of his biggest clients. He does the Agency's financing work and advises it on its corporate governance issues as well as ongoing work for it in connection with adding three generating units. Little is described as "*hard-working, honest, bright-understands the issues and is good to work with.*" He also does corporate work for his real estate clients: for instance he closed a $40 million acquisition of a major shopping mall.

Clients/Work Highlights: The firm has represented CORDA Technologies in connection with a venture capital financing; Supersonic Car Wash in connection with its restructuring; Wencor West; and English Language Learning and Instruction System on a deregistration and going-private transaction.

### Band 4

### Ballard Spahr Andrews & Ingersoll LLP
See firm details p.1746

The Firm: Although headquartered in Philadelphia, this national firm has local lawyers doing local work. Interviewees are impressed with this well-networked firm's ability to draw on expertise from its domestic and international affiliates. The firm was described as "*professional, yet personable and client service-*

*oriented.*" This eight-attorney Salt Lake City group "*dominates the bond market*" and is also praised for "*getting deals done.*" 1-800 Contacts continues to be one of the group's main clients.

The Lawyers: Lead partner **David Rudd** (see p.1952) is "*always willing to listen and help.*" This "*hard-working, conscientious and detailed*" lawyer has been busy with large private equity deals for emerging biotech companies and is also involved in ongoing acquisition work for publicly traded companies such as Nature's Sunshine Products. Rudd has experience of international transactions; one client confirmed him to be "*outstanding at handling our domestic and international needs.*" He represented Flying J Inc on a project in Mexico, and worked on an international joint venture for Kennecott Utah Copper.

Clients/Work Highlights: 1-800 Contacts; Wasatch Venture Fund; Kennecott Utah Copper; TechniScan; SonoSite and ZARS.

### Durham Jones & Pinegar, A Professional Corporation

The Firm: This firm has rapidly expanded its corporate team through lateral hires from major law firms around the country. Clients like the fact that the lawyers "*really understand our business,*" and confirm also that support staff are "*extremely responsive.*" The firm represents businesses at all stages of development plus venture capital funds based in California and Texas. It provided counsel on an M&A transaction valued at nearly $1 billon, advising a 50% stockholder of an international privately held enterprise. Lawyers also worked on the formation of Accent Texas Fund I, a $23 million venture capital fund organized as a Texas certified capital company.

The Lawyers: Jeffrey Jones spearheads the corporate team and is a well-regarded litigator. Russell Smith and Todd Leishman further enhance the team with their understanding of the commercial needs of clients.

Clients/Work Highlights: The firm negotiated a $70 million acquisition for Quest Software, and was involved in financing deals for American Institutional Partners and Fonix. Other representative clients include Nanocoats, Adam Aircraft Industries and Brightsmile.

### Parsons Behle & Latimer PC
See firm details p.1956

The Firm: This well-established Utah outfit enjoys a "*stellar*" reputation among its clients. The corporate and tax department consists of 15 lawyers, 12 of them partners. Interviewees would recommend the firm "*without hesitation or qualification,*" confident in the knowledge that the lawyers help them "*get the deal closed at the best price.*" The firm assisted Barrick Goldstrike Mines in issues relating to the company's energy plant, and represented the purchaser of four automobile dealerships. The firm is praised for its "*responsiveness*" and for "*making sure they meet clients' tight deadlines.*"

The Lawyers: Chair of the corporate group **Geoff Mangum** (see p.1952) is "*a man to get deals done.*" He advised ClearOne Communications in connection with the sale of its teleconferencing division to American Teleconferencing Services. He also represented a foreign purchaser of a US software company.

Clients/Work Highlights: Intermountain Healthcare sought the firm's advice on a multiyear software development and licensing agreement with GE Healthcare, and UCN used it in the acquisition of TelAmerica.

### Ray, Quinney & Nebeker PC

The Firm: This firm has expanded its business and commercial transactions practice to complement its highly regarded litigation practice. As one of the largest Utah firms, it fielded an impressive team to work on a $270 million transaction. Efficiency and cost-effectiveness are at the heart of its work ethic, and clients told researchers: "*We feel like we get high quality at substantially less cost than in other states.*" The firm services a number of technology clients as well as financial institutions.

The Lawyers: Clients are very happy with the advice of corporate finance lawyer **Gary Winger**; he is an able negotiator who is "*attuned to detail and very creative.*"

Clients/Work Highlights: United Subcontractors; Set Point; Market Star; Headwaters and Mining Services International.

# EMPLOYMENT

# MAINLY DEFENDANT

### Band 1

### Jones Waldo Holbrook & McDonough PC

The Firm: This well-established 130-year-old Utah firm has a ten-lawyer group with an exceptional reputation, acting for management across the spectrum of labor and employment issues. Clients speak of an "*extremely professional*" firm and feel well served by lawyers who "*really have their clients' interests at heart.*" From client audits, HR policy drafting

and training to due diligence, contract drafting and pre-litigation counseling, the noncontentious side of the practice performs to a high standard. On the litigation front, there is a full caseload and, due to the increased workload in such matters, a subpractice group has been created to handle trade secrets and noncompete cases. Again, on the labor side, the lawyers have broad experience; the firm recently represented Ballet West on collective bargaining agreements. Employee benefits advice is dispensed by a specialist adviser. The group is particularly active

for the Society for Human Resource Management, with lawyers serving on the Board of the Northern Utah Chapter.

The Lawyers: **Michael O'Brien** (see p.1952) is "*smart, practical and litigates tough cases without being uncivil.*" He had some significant early victories representing a major hospital in the region, a large department store chain and a large farmers co-op. Commentators commend him for being "*marvelous to work with*" because he is "*a reasonable and decent person with a great deal of experience.*" He chairs the employment group and also has a keen interest in media law matters. The "*efficient and well-prepared*" **Ali Levin** (see p.1951) is "*practical and looks for the best solutions.*" She has been involved in two large noncompete cases, defending a large Internet company in federal court. Levin is judged by others to be someone who "*will continue to have an impact on the market.*"

**Clients/Work Highlights:** Utah Society for Human Resource Management (SHRM); Salt Lake Tribune; Zions Bank and Bonneville International.

## Ray, Quinney & Nebeker PC

**The Firm:** This large, 90-lawyer Utah firm has two offices in the state and ample bench strength in other commercial areas to back up its respected employment law group. Clients reported favorably on "*highly responsive, talented and efficient*" attorneys who together comprise a "*firm of the highest order providing top-quality legal services at competitive prices in a cooperative and effective style.*" The team has specialists in areas such as ERISA litigation and FLSA and FMLA matters, as well as the capacity to handle the more usual requirements of its employer clients, both advisory and litigious.

**The Lawyers:** **Jan Smith** is "*exceptionally knowledgeable*" and "*argues persuasively in court.*" She has been involved in a multitude of employment matters, including race and sex discrimination, harassment cases and a number of noncompete cases requiring temporary restraining orders. Smith is admired for her overall guidance and supervision of younger attorneys in the group.

**Clients/Work Highlights:** The firm's clients include Kennecott Utah Copper; Delta Air Lines; Target and Home Depot.

## Band 2

### Holme Roberts & Owen LLP
See firm details p.370

**The Firm:** The "*terrific lawyers*" in this five-person Salt Lake City team are involved in all aspects of workplace counseling and litigation and, in conjunction with the firm's European offices, service a clientele with an international dimension. One key matter involved the transfer of personal data to the USA by a major nonprofit organization with affiliates in the EU. An increasing amount of the team's domestic work involves enforcing or defeating noncompete and confidentiality provisions in employment contracts. Also significant to the practice is a regular stream of discrimination defense, covering issues of age, sex, race and national origin.

**The Lawyers:** The "*extremely professional and tenacious*" **Elizabeth Dunning** is heavily engaged in noncompete and confidentiality matters, though she continues her discrimination defense work. She is described as "*dogged and determined,*" someone who "*works hard, gets results and has a real appreciation of her client's standpoint.*" Clients are loyal to her, with one confirming that "*when she transferred firms, we transferred with her.*" The "*energetic*" **Carolyn Cox** is expert in benefits plans, pensions and healthcare. "*An excellent communicator and drafter,*" she is also "*good at giving practical advice and dealing with thorny problems.*" Cox presents seminars for clients on a variety of employment law issues and is involved in the defense of employers on a range of claims.

**Clients/Work Highlights:** Boede + Partners; Huish Detergents; Questar and Wasatch Academy.

### Manning Curtis Bradshaw & Bednar LLC

**The Firm:** Between them, the eight experienced trial lawyers who make up the Salt Lake City employment group are involved in the full spectrum of employment-related litigation. They represent employers in dealings with state and federal administrative agencies and provide training on employee benefits, including ERISA issues. Clients remarked that the firm is "*very cost and client-conscious.*" Highlight achievements include obtaining summary judgments in federal court actions in five cases involving such issues as FLMA leave, sexual harassment and workplace retaliation.

**The Lawyers:** **Steven Bednar** works "*extremely well with corporate clients to understand their businesses.*" This "*good writer, thinker and communicator*" defends employers when they become embroiled in litigation and provides counseling and training to help them avoid it. At the heart of his success lies "*an ability to see the potential turning points in a case and an uncanny knack for steering a case down the correct path.*"

**Clients/Work Highlights:** Franklin Covey; Intermountain Healthcare; Smith's Food & Drug Stores; Sinclair Oil; Stein Eriksen Lodge; RC Willey Home Furnishings; Wal-Mart and XanGo.

### Parsons Behle & Latimer PC
See firm details p.1956

**The Firm:** One of the oldest in the intermountain region, this firm has expanded its regional presence by opening an office in Las Vegas. In Utah, the "*highly responsive*" Salt Lake City team offers advice on employment issues, traditional labor law and employee benefits. One recent highlight involved a multistate ERISA issue, acting for Alliant Techsystems; the team also obtained summary judgment on a race and gender-based hostile work environment claim. It distinguishes itself through the efforts of a very healthy number of ranked individuals.

**The Lawyers:** **David Anderson**'s (see p.1949) practice encompasses classic labor law and employment discrimination cases. Described as "*one of the smartest lawyers in town,*" he is also an ERISA specialist. Anderson's clients are drawn from the manufacturing, retail and technology sectors. **Mark Gavre** (see p.1951) "*even-tempered and calming*" nature renders him "*a steady hand to work through emotional problems.*" He has a full general discrimination and ERISA caseload and serves as national ERISA counsel to Albertsons and its subsidiaries. "*Responsive and smart,*" **Michael Zody** (see p.1953) is a man who "*gets results.*" He is increasingly involved in counseling companies on the enforceability of noncompete clauses throughout the country, and combines an environmental caseload with employment litigation, including an emerging specialism in whistle-blowing. Interviewees were enthusiastic about "*articulate and responsive*" **Elisabeth Blattner-Thompson** (see p.1950), who chairs the employment group and offers clients "*good judgment tempered by common sense.*" She recently won a case for Novell and was involved in the Alliant ERISA matter.

## Band 3

### Holland & Hart LLP
See firm details p.369

**The Firm:** This sizable firm has developed a noteworthy profile throughout the region, and although its employment practice is smaller than some other competitors, its stock has risen since the arrival of Lois Baar. Interviewees sense the importance placed on "*solving the employer's problem rather than going straight to litigation;*" indeed, these lawyers are deemed to show "*sensitivity while meeting clients' needs.*" Employer training and preventative counseling are important elements, although the lawyers are more than competent in court when defending claims. Recent litigation has covered wage and hour class action, potentially dealing with 500 plaintiffs.

**The Lawyers:** The "*brilliant*" **Lois Baar** (see p.1949) is "*a gracious litigator with a great bedside manner.*" She divides her time between litigation, mediation and counseling, with a growing emphasis on whistle-blowing cases. "*Great at communicating with the other side,*" Baar "*really sees through the eyes of her clients, bringing a business perspective as well as a legal one.*" **Bryan Benard** (see p.1949) is an "*honest, straight-up guy*" who epitomizes the word "*reasonable.*" The focus of his work is defending wrongful termination, harassment and discrimination claims, and he has obtained a number of successful summary judgments for his clients in the past year. Another major part of his work is the presentation of seminars, including specialized training on military, family and disability leave.

## Stoel Rives LLP

**The Firm:** This expansive Western states firm has a compact employment practice in Salt Lake City. The team works closely with the corporate practice, often assisting them on due diligence. In terms of litigation, the team handles all the usual discrimination and harassment cases and, increasingly, noncompete and nondisclosure cases.

**The Lawyers:** The "*responsive*" **Matthew Durham** "*anticipates his clients' needs, has good ideas and plans ahead.*" In a recent case he obtained injunctive relief against an individual who had sold a business and

signed a noncompete agreement with his client, and then set up a competing business.

## Other Notable Practitioners

**Carol Clawson** of Clawson & Falk LLC represents mainly plaintiffs but is increasingly advising defendants. "*No scorched-earth litigator,*" she is highly respected by her peers; clients, meanwhile, "*count on her to do the right thing from both a legal, moral and ethical perspective.*"

# LITIGATION

## Litigation: General Commercial

### Leading Firms

[1] **BURBIDGE & MITCHELL** *Salt Lake City*
**HOLME ROBERTS & OWEN LLP** *Salt Lake City*
**HOWREY LLP** *Salt Lake City*
**PARSONS BEHLE & LATIMER PC** *Salt Lake City*
**RAY, QUINNEY & NEBEKER PC** *Salt Lake City*
**SNELL & WILMER LLP** *Salt Lake City*

[2] **PARR WADDOUPS** *Salt Lake City*
**STOEL RIVES LLP** *Salt Lake City*

[3] **FABIAN & CLENDENIN** *Salt Lake City*
**VAN COTT** *Salt Lake City*

### Leading Individuals

[1] **BENDINGER Gary** *Howrey LLP*
**BURBIDGE Richard** *Burbidge & Mitchell*
**HALEY George** *Holme Roberts & Owen LLP*
**JARDINE James** *Ray, Quinney & Nebeker PC*
**JORDAN David** *Stoel Rives LLP*
**SULLIVAN Alan** *Snell & Wilmer LLP*

[2] **BILLINGS JR Peter** *Fabian & Clendenin*
**BLACK Kenneth** *Stoel Rives LLP*
**CAMPBELL JR Robert** *Van Cott*
**CLARK Robert** *Parr Waddoups*
**ETCHEVERRY Raymond** *Parsons Behle & Latimer PC*
**GREENWOOD David** *Howrey LLP*
**KARRENBERG Thomas** *Anderson & Karrenberg*
**WADDOUPS Clark** *Parr Waddoups*
**WIKSTROM Francis** *Parsons Behle & Latimer PC*

[3] **HUNT Jeffrey** *Parr Waddoups*
**SAVAGE Greggory** *Holme Roberts & Owen LLP*

### Up-and-coming individuals

**BENARD Blaine** *Holme Roberts & Owen LLP*
**GROSS Jefferson** *Burbidge & Mitchell*

## Band 1

## Burbidge & Mitchell
See firm details p.1954

**The Firm:** This small litigation boutique has a strong track record in both jury trials and appellate work.

Its lawyers litigate complex disputes, including antitrust, securities fraud, IP and catastrophic personal injury cases. Clients praise the firm's "*professionalism and efficiency*" and appreciate that these lawyers pay great attention to detail. They are "*so well prepared that there are never surprises in the courtroom.*"

**The Lawyers:** "*One of the best advocates in the state,*" **Richard Burbidge** (see p.1950) is a popular port of call because he displays the "*highest professional and ethical standards.*" He has secured a summary judgment to save a multimillion-dollar development project. He has experience of trying complex cases and has one of the "*brightest and quickest minds,*" agree clients. Clients are comfortable letting **Jefferson Gross** (see p.1951) handle complex, high-value matters. His commercial litigation practice includes expertise in patent and IP matters, aviation and products liability.

## Holme Roberts & Owen LLP
See firm details p.370

**The Firm:** This Denver-based firm operates offices across three states and has two overseas offices. The nine-partner Salt Lake City team utilizes this depth of expertise in handling complex matters such as the Visa antitrust case. "*Every one of the lawyers is outstanding*" and provides "*incredible client service*" and a high standard of professional advice. These lawyers "*do not miss deadlines and keep clients informed.*" Highlights include representing Delta Air Lines in a class action case, and litigation for Questar, which resulted in an early settlement.

**The Lawyers:** The "*phenomenal*" **George Haley** has developed a general commercial litigation practice that features disputes arising out of the energy sector. One recent highlight for him was obtaining summary judgment and dismissal of a case on behalf of a law firm involved in the oil and gas industry. Clients appreciated his responsiveness and strategic advice. **Blaine Benard** is an "*excellent litigator and a methodological thinker.*" He has developed a niche practice in representing hospitals and acts for Rolls-Royce. **Greggory Savage** has a clear eye for detail and thorough preparation that means he "*does not miss anything – he's wholeheartedly trusted.*"

# GENERAL COMMERCIAL

## Howrey LLP

**The Firm:** Formerly Bendinger, Crockett, Peterson, Greenwood & Casey, this Salt Lake City-based group has joined forces with the broad-based national and international firm Howrey LLP. Its increased breadth and sizable supporting resources has led to an increased caseload in securities and antitrust matters. The group has also developed significant expertise in the accounting malpractice arena. The team obtained a summary judgment for one of Utah's biggest healthcare providers, which was sued for antitrust violations after an eight-day evidential hearing.

**The Lawyers:** **Gary Bendinger**'s style is not to everyone's taste but he "*gets results and has the highest professional and ethical standards,*" agree interviewees. He is "*accustomed to the courtroom and is an articulate trial lawyer.*" He has built up significant expertise in the accounting malpractice area and is skilled in antitrust and securities litigation. **David Greenwood** has recently acted in a number of cases involving allegations of violations of securities law, including investigations conducted by the SEC. He is "*smart and capable*" and is experienced in running complex cases.

**Clients/Work Highlights:** Bridgestone/Firestone; Deloitte & Touche; Ernst & Young; Farmers; Grant Thornton; Intermountain Healthcare; KPMG and Lockheed Martin.

## Parsons Behle & Latimer PC
See firm details p.1956

**The Firm:** This top-notch litigation group is home to over 60 attorneys, one of the biggest litigation teams in the Intermountain West region. Clients appreciate the "*strong representation and good value for money*" they receive from the firm's "*responsive and efficient lawyers.*" The team has cultivated a broad range of expertise, including IP litigation. It recently completed a trade secrets case for a manufacturer of shuttle rockets. The firm is developing its Qui Tam litigation work, and this expertise complements an already thriving environmental practice. Antitrust and tax litigation are further strings to this firm's bow.

**The Lawyers:** **Francis Wikstrom** (see p.1953) is a

*"respected trial lawyer and effective negotiator – professional, very prepared and articulate."* He represented a major corporation involved in a nationwide environmental case brought by the US DOJ and settled a large insurance case linked to an environmental cleanup in Montana. He also advised an international gold mining company on its EPCM (Engineering, Procurement, Construction Management) contracts. The *"bright and organized"* **Raymond Etcheverry** (see p.1950) is involved in antitrust, IP litigation, environmental cases and large business disputes. He has worked on a multidistrict antitrust class action in the medical waste industry for Stericycle. He also advised on an investigation related to misrepresentation in financial statements. Clients spoke of his *"tremendous reputation for being a problem solver."*

**Clients/Work Highlights:** The firm represented GE in a patent infringement suit and secured a summary judgment of invalidity of the patents. It obtained a summary judgment for Baker Hughes in a patent infringement action, where the jury awarded damages in excess of $1 million, and represented Savage Industries in a matter concerning allegations of toxic air emissions.

## Ray, Quinney & Nebeker PC

**The Firm:** A skilled trial firm group is split into three main practice areas: general commercial, tort and IP. Clients appreciate the *"strong leadership and awareness of our needs"* and highlight the depth of the practice that has allowed lawyers to work in specialist areas. Among its recent caseload, the firm represented an officer of a publicly traded company in a civil fraud action filed by the SEC – the claims were dropped before the trial.

**The Lawyers:** Managing partner **James Jardine** advises clients on business disputes, antitrust, securities and construction matters. He is well respected for his trial skills and wealth of experience and is described as a *"gentleman with an impeccable reputation who is very good with juries and judges."* He is also an effective negotiator who can *"make things happen."*

**Clients/Work Highlights:** The firm's clients include CR England; Allied Waste; Huntsman; Goldman Sachs and Microsoft.

## Snell & Wilmer LLP

See firm details p.200

**The Firm:** This 35-strong team has attracted plaudits for its consistency and high quality of lawyers. Amid its broad litigation practice, the firm has established a separate products liability group and recently been engaged in high-profile IP cases. Attorneys have been involved in the ongoing case concerning the carrying of concealed weapons on property belonging to the University of Utah.

**The Lawyers:** **Alan Sullivan** (see p.1952) is a talented trial lawyer who wins respect because of his *"high professional standards"* and is *"smart, well-prepared and articulate"* in court. His practice of late features an increased level of technology, technology transfer and IP litigation. He has represented The

Church of Jesus Christ of Latter-day Saints in a high-profile free speech case regarding a piece of land, which was later affirmed by the Court of Appeal.

## Band 2

### Parr Waddoups Brown Gee & Loveless

**The Firm:** This long-established Utah firm fields high-quality lawyers who have cultivated a broad-based litigation expertise. This strategy has impressed clients who spoke of the effective staffing of cases and *"the great quality and broad scope that exceeds many of its competitors."* The firm represents significant institutional clients such as Brigham Young University, SkyWest and the fast-growing XanGo Company. Attorneys handle general corporate litigation, contract disputes and securities litigation.

**The Lawyers:** **Clark Waddoups** is a *"smart lawyer and good communicator."* He has a broad commercial litigation practice, handling everything from construction to intellectual property matters. Of late, he has been heavily engaged in a construction dispute in Wyoming and has acted in an arbitration concerning a manufacturing agreement. According to sources, his wealth of experience means he *"handles complex matters with ease."* **Robert Clark** has earned the confidence of his clients and the respect of his peers for his efficient handling of difficult litigation and his strong courtroom presence. He handles corporate governance issues and securities disputes and has recently advised a client on a dispute with the SEC. He was involved in IP litigation for Nu Skin Enterprises and completed a three-week arbitration in California for a real estate company. *"Highly confident"* **Jeffrey Hunt** has developed a niche practice in media and First Amendment law. He forges a strong relationship with his clients through his proactive service; he is *"decent and reasonable and always gets great results."* He represents two national TV networks, the Utah Press Association and the Society of Professional Journalists. In a recent highlight, Hunt assisted reporters in gaining access to the court proceedings of a high-profile kidnapping case.

**Clients/Work Highlights:** Deseret Morning News, SkyWest Airlines and Brigham Young University.

### Stoel Rives LLP

**The Firm:** This Northwest regional firm fields a team of 20 lawyers, who combine their general commercial litigation practice with a specialism in products liability issues for pharmaceutical companies. The firm is praised for its *"high-quality advice and scope of services."* The team focuses on business disputes including antitrust and trademark matters, as well as contract disputes and administrative law. Clients also value the cost-efficient case management and dedicated service provided by the attorneys.

**The Lawyers:** The *"outstanding trial lawyer"* **David Jordan** is *"very organized in how he puts a case together."* According to sources, his courtroom pres-

ence is impressive; he is *"very articulate – from appearance to tone of voice to his command of the English language."* He is *"like a chess player when negotiating – he's half a dozen moves ahead of the opposition."* **Kenneth Black** is *"attuned to crafting and creating solutions."* His practice is focused on IP, trademark, patent and copyright matters and he was also involved in a complete dismissal of a 95-plaintiff fraud and breach of duty case in the Ninth Circuit Court of Appeals.

**Clients/Work Highlights:** The firm continues to handle litigation concerning Deseret Morning News and Las Vegas Sun over the partnership agreement that exists between newspapers.

## Band 3

### Fabian & Clendenin

**The Firm:** A sizable litigation group, its experience spans the breadth of corporate litigation, with particular expertise in bankruptcy, tax and water resources law. The firm has been involved in a major natural resources lawsuit involving roads being built in wilderness areas. PacifiCorp is a key client of the group and attorneys have advised it on antitrust, utilities and natural resources disputes.

**The Lawyers:** **Peter Billings** is a *"smart guy and effective in getting results."* He is particularly experienced in Chapter 11 proceedings and related litigation, and has acted on antitrust and professional malpractice matters both in Utah and across the state borders.

### Van Cott, Bagley, Cornwall & McCarthy

**The Firm:** This full-service firm has significantly increased its litigation capability through successful lateral hires. The growing team concentrates on commercial disputes in state and federal courts and administrative tribunals. Commentators say that the firm definitely *"deserves recognition for its strong trial skills."*

**The Lawyers:** **Robert Campbell** is well-versed in complex commercial disputes, and has a particular expertise in condemnation litigation. A skilled trial lawyer, he successfully reinstated an antitrust case for Summit Water Distribution, where the Supreme Court reversed the trial court judgment and sent the case back for retrial.

### Other Notable Practitioners

*"Tenacious"* **Thomas Karrenberg** of Anderson & Karrenberg represents a broad range of commercial clients including national computer software companies. He is bullish in the courtroom, and described as *"effective – he fights for his clients."*

# REAL ESTATE

## Band 1

### Parr Waddoups Brown Gee & Loveless

**The Firm:** Sources endorsed the broad coverage of the real estate practice group and its success in developing a strong focus on the sector. It is "*an outstanding firm with a number of excellent lawyers and a good client base.*" A team of six partners is supported by water and environmental law experts as well as related groups across the firm. Mixed-use developments have been at the top of the agenda of late, as well as ski resorts and healthcare projects. Clients are attracted to the firm because its lawyers "*provide value beyond their fees*" and are "*ready and willing to*

put in long hours on short notice to become prepared for whatever matter that may arise.*"

**The Lawyers:** "*Top-flight lawyer*" **Charles Maak** is well respected in the industry. Having practiced for many years, he has built up considerable expertise, which has proved valuable in negotiations. He possesses "*a calm temperament that makes him capable of getting the job done for his clients.*" **David Gee** is "*bright, responsive and his work is of the highest caliber,*" reported clients. He has attracted an impressive client base, representing Tegra Healthcare, Washington Capital and Wal-Mart on zoning and land use issues. He is "*practical and sensitive to the realities of the marketplace, the kind of attorney who works well with business people.*" He is also flexible in how he approaches negotiations: he "*can be tenacious and a real pit bull, or diplomatic and conciliatory depending on the needs of the client.*" **Robert McConnell** has developed a broad real estate practice including leases and financing issues. He is skilled in technical documentation and brings an awareness of business needs to the deal table. According to sources, "*he pays great attention to detail, yet sees the big picture.*" He has been working on the housing component of a military privatization.

**Clients/Work Highlights:** The firm has been engaged in financing a low level radioactive waste facility, as well as a mixed-use project valued at $200 million and the sale of a number of properties in the $50 million plus price range.

### Stoel Rives LLP

**The Firm:** Already a force in its own right, this Salt Lake team can also draw on the resources of the firm's network of offices in its most complex multi-state transactions. The firm has a significant institutional practice and represents industrial as well as resort and community developer clients. Its service is responsive and focused on the business needs of its clients: these attorneys "*treat every matter importantly, no matter how small,*" reported sources. Environmental and tax experts work closely with the real estate group, and the team continues to grow in strength at the associate level. The firm's experience is amplified by its regular interface with city official planners and engineers.

**The Lawyers:** The "*stellar*" **Thomas Ellison** has devoted much of his recent practice to a southern Utah-based project developing a ski and golf resort community. For this, he has been integrating project planner engineers, advising on ordinances and planning the development. He is a "*negotiator and facilitator*" who combines his land use and development work with a lender practice. He represents JPMorgan Chase and continues to work on the privatization of the US Air Force housing. **Ervin Holmes** is "*an experienced and honorable attorney.*" He has recently been advising on acquisitions related to industrial properties and has been involved in an 800-acre mixed-use commercial and industrial development. **Guy Kroesche** is "*conscientious about doing what is right – he carefully considers his clients' interests.*" He repre-

sents lenders, healthcare concerns and industrial clients in the acquisition and development of sites. He successfully completed an acquisition of a 100-acre medical campus and was advised on a project for an industrial client involving the establishment of a cement plant in Nevada.

## Band 2

### Ballard Spahr Andrews & Ingersoll LLP

See firm details p.1746

**The Firm:** Headquartered in Philadelphia, the Salt Lake City office fields seven attorneys who focus on resort development, supported by smaller teams that specialize in land use, finance and general development issues. The firm has particular expertise in the timeshare industry, and its attorneys have advised on timeshare issues for private president clubs. Commentators also spoke of the firm's outstanding municipal bond finance department.

**The Lawyers:** **Thomas Bennett** (see p.1950) has a "*unique base of knowledge devoted to resort real estate projects*" and is therefore on peers' referrals list. His practice is divided into two areas: localized ski and golf course resort development work and a regional practice representing international hospitality companies engaged in the timeshare industry. He has worked on two large resort master plan developments of ski resorts in Utah and a condominium hotel project that spans Western states.

### Jones Waldo Holbrook & McDonough PC

**The Firm:** Clients endorsed this proactive real estate practice for its ability to handle complex deal negotiations: "*Absolutely dollar for dollar, an extremely efficient firm.*" By way of illustration, the 21-lawyer team represents Lowe's in its efforts to acquire sites. Its attorneys possess a wealth of development and financing experience and have recently advised on a $25 million mixed-use project involving offices and 120 condominium units with a parking structure and a resort development in Deer Valley.

**The Lawyers:** Clients described **Tom Berggren** (see p.1950) as "*absolutely irreplaceable as our guy on the ground who gets things done.*" He is often referred to for leasing issues or advice on complex documentation because he is "*detail-oriented, has good judgment and can foresee the issues.*" He acted on a $15 million historic tax credit project, which involved residential and retail properties and assisted in the acquisition of a 180,000 sq ft office building. **Keven Rowe** (see p.1952) is "*attentive and often meets short deadlines.*" He has particular expertise in mortgage lending and has assisted Wells Fargo in a $20 million financing of a golf course resort. He takes a "*collaborative approach*" to his work and so "*does not waste time and money arguing about unimportant details.*" "*Extremely decisive*" **Paul Harman** (see p.1951) "*grasps situations and understands complex real estate*" transactions." He was involved in Extra Space's purchase of 61 properties in 24 states. Clients also highlighted his "*understanding of the legal ramifications and good business sense.*" **Glen Watkins** (see p.1952) uses his "*natural skill and great demeanor very effectively in negotiations, resolving conflict and keeping the transaction going,*" reported clients.

Clients/Work Highlights: Extra Space Storage; Tesoro; Lowe's; Bridge Investment Group; Albertson's and Browning.

## Snell & Wilmer LLP

See firm details p.200

**The Firm:** This sizable regional firm is home to a talented group of real estate attorneys. The 14-strong team advises developers, lenders and borrowers in a wide range of development and acquisition issues. Using its extensive network of offices, the real estate team has been involved in projects in Arizona, Nevada, California and Colorado.

**The Lawyers:** **Cary Jones**'s (see p.1951) approach is direct and to the point: "*He does not waste time and is focused on the completion of a deal.*" He primarily represents developers involved in the hotel and resort business. He has completed transactions for two developers in the acquisition, zoning and development of two 5-star hotels. Jones has cultivated a national practice and has been involved in a number of mixed-use projects in San Diego and San Francisco.

Clients/Work Highlights: Park City Mountain Resort, Santa Fe Partners and SITLA are clients of the firm.

## Band 3

## Fabian & Clendenin

**The Firm:** This long-established Utah firm is held in very high esteem. It has been "*an excellent partner in preparing documentation and completing transactions,*" reported clients. Due to the expansion of its transactional work, the firm has established a dedicated real estate group of eight lawyers. Clients agree that "*we have access to the full resources of the firm and the right people on projects.*" The firm successfully defended a $147 million claim in a dispute between two developers regarding zoning issues and the purchase of three office buildings in Las Vegas.

**The Lawyers:** **Diane Banks** is an "*excellent negotiator and drafter of documents for nonstandard transactions.*" Clients feel comfortable with her business-savvy advice: "*She's really great and knows what works in a deal.*" She has advised on the leasings, acquisitions and the financings of mixed-use developments. She recently advised on the sale of 190,000 sq ft of office space. **Rosemary Beless** has been defending litigation arising out of the construction industry and acted on a $46 million claim related to the environmental aspect of a real estate matter. Her experience is highly valued by clients: "*She brings her real-world environmental experience in advising her client,*" and her work is "*efficient and timely.*"

Clients/Work Highlights: The firm represents title

insurance underwriters such as Fidelity National Title, Chicago Title and Ticor Title Insurance Company. Other representative clients include PacifiCorp; Barnes Bank; Wasatch Constructors; Granite Construction; Talisker Resort Development Company/United Park City Mines Company; Psomas Engineering; Motion Picture Association of America; Aflac-American Family Life Assurance of Columbus; Re/Max; Anesta Corporation; Cephalon; eBay and PayPal.

## Holland & Hart LLP

See firm details p.369

**The Firm:** This firm has 12 offices in the Rocky Mountain region. The Salt Lake office fields highly professional attorneys who have attracted an enviable client base. According to one client, "*the long-term value and strength gained from their counsel is worth its weight in gold.*" The firm enjoys the loyalty of its clients as one explained: "*The service, accuracy and confidence they illicit will always keep you home at Holland & Hart.*" The firm also has a specialist environmental team to deal with issues such as regulations related to wetlands.

**The Lawyers:** "*Reliable and bright,*" **David Broadbent** (see p.1950) represents major title insurance companies and has been busy in developing a Superfund site for a multiuse project involving high-level commercial retail, office, housing and open space. He is "*persuasive in gentle ways that really work.*" The "*charismatic*" **Carl Barton** (see p.1949) is "*dedicated, organized and absolutely thorough in every regard,*" say clients. He has negotiated 60 retail leases for a national tenant and represented a client in the development of two large condominium resorts worth $350 million.

Clients/Work Highlights: The firm has been negotiating the refinancing of assisted homes, representing a company in acquiring a power plant in Idaho and involved in acquiring a large waste treatment facility. The team represents landowners, developers and financial institutions.

## Kirton & McConkie

See firm details p.1955

**The Firm:** This is one of Utah's largest firms and it provides a full range of services to clients. An expanding department of 15 lawyers handles all of the real estate needs of the Church of Jesus Christ of Latter-day Saints in North America, a substantial and significant client that ensures this firm a high-profile in the market. The firm has experience in all aspects of the purchase and sale, financing, development, and management of real property.

**The Lawyers:** Chair of the property group **Robert Hyde** (see p.1951) is often referred to because of his financing expertise. He is a "*fantastic lawyer – he really knows the ins and outs of the market.*" He represents Bonneville Mortgage Company and has been busy with commercial retail and financing transactions. **Read Hellewell** is a "*deal-maker – experienced and able to negotiate effectively.*"

## Parsons Behle & Latimer PC

See firm details p.1956

**The Firm:** This well-established Utah firm has cultivated a solid practice of traditional real estate lawyers who work alongside specialists in environmental, water and air regulation. The real estate practice has been engaged in redevelopment projects that feature an element of environmental cleanup. Attorneys have also represented major ski resorts in the Salt Lake metropolitan area and have played a part in key retail developments. The firm has been representing American Skiing Company in its development activities, particularly in the Canyons Resort. The firm also has a great natural resources practice to complement its real estate work.

**The Lawyers:** **Shawn Ferrin** (see p.1951) has a "*great personality and works well with clients and lawyers.*" Sources also appreciated that he is "*very straightforward and able to keep deals going.*" He has represented Home Depot in its acquisition and development work throughout Utah, Colorado, Idaho and Nevada. He also represents two of the major national homebuilders in their acquisition and development activities in Utah.

Clients/Work Highlights: The firm has been representing Howa Properties in a lease and build-to-suit transaction. It has also assisted Paladin Development Partners in the development of the Silver Star at Park City commercial condominium project with ski access to the Park City Mountain Resort, and advises DR Horton in all of its real estate development work within Utah.

## Ray, Quinney & Nebeker PC

**The Firm:** This six-lawyer group is involved in real estate litigation as well as transactional work. This balanced approach ensures that the firm is alert to potentially relevant issues that may arise later in litigation when structuring transactions. The firm has particular expertise in representing institutional lenders. It has also recently advised a commercial developer who has undertaken a major urban redevelopment project and worked with city government to revitalize a downtown retail area.

**The Lawyers:** **Larry Moore** is "*an incredibly smart and effective attorney.*" He has been representing a bank in its real estate activities, buying properties to open new branches and negotiating ground leases. He is also active in litigating cases connected to boundary lines, adverse possession, title insurance and partition. **Ira Rubinfeld** is a "*deal-maker who gets results.*" He has a national practice and has represented the Utah Retirement Fund, completing transactions all over the country.

Clients/Work Highlights: The client base includes Solitude Ski Resort, Wells Fargo and Washington Mutual.

## Van Cott, Bagley, Cornwall & McCarthy

**The Firm:** This 131-year-old Intermountain West law firm has the capacity to provide a full service to its real estate clients. Clients were impressed with the diversity and level of service they received. Although a smaller team, it contains some "*talented and highly capable real estate lawyers.*"

**The Lawyers:** Chair of the real estate group **Gregory Williams** is "*easy to deal with, honorable, intelligent and conscientious.*" His practice focuses on transactional matters for oil and gas, and mining as well as a broader base of business clients. He also has an excellent understanding of municipal entitlements. **Rand Cook** possesses "*an encyclopedic knowledge of real estate law and is a great drafter with common sense.*" He is primarily involved in commercial transactions and has particular expertise in commercial lending. **Clients/Work Highlights:** The firm's clients are drawn from a range of industries including ski resorts; pension funds; developers and management companies; banks; title insurance companies; healthcare companies; industrial, sand and gravel operations and insurance companies.

**Other Notable Practitioners**

Interviewees recommended **Stephen Christensen** of Nelson, Christensen & Helsten PC. He impresses sources as a confident attorney, who "*gets deals done and doesn't over-lawyer things.*"

# Leaders in Utah

## ANDERSON, Chris
Snell & Wilmer LLP, Salt Lake City
801 257 1997
canderson@swlaw.com
*Recommended in Corporate/M&A*
**Practice Areas:** Practices primarily in the areas of business, securities and international law. Extensive background in venture capital transactions for emerging growth companies, and in the representation of high technology companies in the initial stages of development. Mr Anderson represents more mature companies in public and private financings, acquisitions, dispositions, recapitalizations, mergers, and other complex commercial transactions and agreements. He assists with matters related to corporate structuring, establishment of commercial and strategic relationships, international expansion and franchising. Also works with non-profits, and on Utah business legislation.
**Prof. Memberships:** Utah and California Bar Associations and ABA.
**Personal:** Speaks Spanish.

## ANDERSON, David A
Parsons Behle & Latimer PC, Salt Lake City 801 532 1234
DAnderson@parsonsbehle.com
*Recommended in Employment*
**Practice Areas:** Employment law; employee benefits; collective bargaining, grievance arbitration and National Labor Relations Act matters; discrimination; wrongful discharge and employment-at-will counsel and litigation.
**Prof. Memberships:** Member, American Bar Association: Labor and Employment Law Section, Employee Benefits and Litigation Section.
**Career:** Past Chairman, Utah Bar Section, Labor and Employment Law. Adjunct Professor, University of Utah College of Law, Pension and Employee Benefits Law. Frequent speaker at employer conferences and seminars on employment law topics.
**Personal:** JD, Cornell University, 1979. Master of Industrial and Labor Relations, Cornell University, 1980. BA, University of Utah, 1976.

## ANGERBAUER, David G
Holland & Hart LLP, Salt Lake City
801 595 7808
dangerbauer@hollandhart.com
*Recommended in Corporate/M&A*
**Practice Areas:** Partner practicing in securities, venture capital, technology, and M&A. Represents a wide range of clients, including start-ups, emerging growth businesses, and public companies. Counseled both issuers and underwriters in more than two billion dollars of public and private equity and debt offerings, including US and international financings. Works with regional and national investment banking and venture capital firms in venture capital financings, initial public offerings, secondary offerings, mergers, and acquisitions. Industries include life sciences, information technology, computer hardware and software, financial services, communications, healthcare, medical products, manufacturing, transportation and mining.
**Prof. Memberships:** Member of the Utah State Bar, Sections on Business Law (past President) and Securities Law; National Association of Stock Plan Professionals, Utah Chapter (past President); and the American Bar Association, Section of Business Law. Appointments: past Chairman and President, MountainWest Capital Network; Alumni Board Member, SJ Quinney School of Law, University of Utah.
**Career:** Admitted to the Utah Bar (1986).
**Personal:** Received a JD from the University of Utah (1986, Order of the Coif, William H Leary Scholar), an MBA (1986) and a BA from the University of Utah (Finance, 1982).

## BAAR, Lois A
Holland & Hart LLP, Salt Lake City
801 799 5929
labaar@hollandhart.com
*Recommended in Employment*
**Practice Areas:** Employment litigation, training and mediation.
**Prof. Memberships:** American Bar Association, Labor and Employment Law Section, Committee on Alternative Dispute Resolution; Utah State Bar, Ethics and Discipline Committee, Employment Law Section, Alternative Dispute Resolution Committee; SJ Quinney College of Law Alumni Board 2002-05; President of Legal Aid Society 1999; Utah Employment Lawyer of the Year 1999; Board of Directors of Utah Nonprofits Association 2001-03; State of Utah Labor Commission Antidiscrimination Advisory Council 1998-2003; Sutherland Inn of Court 1991-98; Utah Task Force on Gender and Justice 1989-91.
**Publications:** Frequent speaker on avoiding employment claims and on good management practices.
**Personal:** University of Utah College of Law (JD 1982); Drexel University (MBA 1973); Drexel University (BS 1968).

## BANKS, Diane
Fabian & Clendenin, Salt Lake City
801 531 8900
*Recommended in Real Estate*

## BARTON, Carl
Holland & Hart LLP, Salt Lake City
801 595 7831
cbarton@hollandhart.com
*Recommended in Real Estate*
**Practice Areas:** Mr Barton's practice focuses on real estate acquisitions, sales, leasing, options, finance, development, and 1031 tax-deferred exchanges. Projects include the development and financing of golf course and luxury condominium resorts, hotels, shopping malls and strip centers, business and industrial parks, large ranches, power plants and energy facilities, national restaurants, office buildings and condominiums, and multi-family residential ventures in all regions of the United States. He specializes in leasing, representing both landlords and tenants in retail, office, industrial, agricultural, and ground leases. His practice also involves real estate loans and other financial transactions on behalf of developers and owners, banks, insurance companies, and private lenders. Transactions include real estate and asset-based loans, tenant-in-common loans, construction loans, conduit loans, lines of credit, mezzanine loans, energy project financing, and sale/leaseback financing.

Mr Barton is also experienced in obtaining rights of way, in land-use planning and zoning, and in the purchase, sale, and financing of water rights.
**Prof. Memberships:** Real Property and Business Law Sections, Utah State Bar; Honorary French Consul, State of Utah (1988-2001).
**Career:** Admitted to the Utah State Bar (1986).
**Personal:** Received a JD (1986) and two BA Degrees (1982) from the University of Utah.

## BEDNAR, Steven
Manning Curtis Bradshaw & Bednar LLC, Salt Lake City
801 363 5678
*Recommended in Employment*

## BELESS, Rosemary
Fabian & Clendenin, Salt Lake City
801 531 8900
*Recommended in Real Estate*

## BENARD, Blaine
Holme Roberts & Owen LLP, Salt Lake City 801 521 5800
*Recommended in Litigation*

## BENARD, Bryan
Holland & Hart LLP, Salt Lake City
801 595 7833
bbenard@hollandhart.com
*Recommended in Employment*
**Practice Areas:** Partner focusing on labor and employment counseling and litigation, commercial litigation. Regularly represents both private and public clients in wrongful termination, harassment, and discrimination claims in both federal and state courts, as well as in administrative proceedings before federal and state agencies. Counsels clients regarding employee relations, employee and non-compete agreement, and employee handbooks. Represents employers in matters related to discrimination statutes, the Family and Medical Leave Act, the Uniformed Services Employment and Re-employment Rights Act, the Americans with Disabilities Act, and the Fair Labor Standards Act, including administrative investigations into wage and hour complaints as well as

defending against collective actions. Broad experience in appellate matters and intellectual property and complex litigation.

**Prof. Memberships:** American Bar Association; California State Bar Association; Utah State Bar Association; Salt Lake County Bar Association.

**Career:** Admitted to California Bar and US District Courts for Central and Southern Districts of California (1997); Utah State Bar and US District Court, District of Utah (2001); US Court of Appeals, Tenth Circuit and US Supreme Court (2004).

**Personal:** Received a JD (1997) from the University of Utah and a BA (1994) from Weber State University.

### BENDINGER, Gary
Howrey LLP, Salt Lake City
801 533 8383
*Recommended in Litigation*

### BENNETT, Thomas G
Ballard Spahr Andrews & Ingersoll LLP, Salt Lake City 801 531 3060
bennett@ballardspahr.com
*Recommended in Real Estate*

**Practice Areas:** Focuses on development of commercial and resort properties, with an emphasis on property acquisition, community structuring, financing, zoning and entitlements, construction, state and federal regulatory compliance, and sales of planned communities, condominiums, timeshares, fractional ownership, private residence clubs, golf courses, condominium hotels, office buildings, and shopping centers.

**Prof. Memberships:** Member, American Resort Development Association (ARDA) serving on ARDA's State Legislative Committee. Member, Editorial Board of the Timeshare Law Compendium being prepared as a joint effort between ARDA and the American Bar Association.

**Career:** Admitted to the Utah Bar (1981).

**Personal:** JD, cum laude, J Reuben Clark Law School, Brigham Young University (1981); BS, cum laude, Brigham Young University (1976).

### BERGGREN, Tom
Jones Waldo Holbrook & McDonough PC, Salt Lake City
801 521 3200
tberggren@joneswaldo.com
*Recommended in Real Estate*

**Practice Areas:** Practice includes the purchase and sale, leasing, financing, development and entitlement of commercial office buildings, retail space, industrial parks, professional buildings and multi-family complexes. Has extensive experience in assisting national retailers acquire property for stores in the West, by both purchase and ground lease. Represented several Fortune 500 companies in connection with negotiating gov-

ernmental incentive packages, including for regional distribution centers. Acts as local counsel for out-of-state real property lenders and borrowers.

**Prof. Memberships:** ICSC, NAIOP, ABA's Committee on Legal Opinions and SLC Board of Adjustment for Zoning Appeals.

**Career:** First four years with Morrison & Foerster (San Francisco and London). Practicing in Utah since 1983. Chair of Real Estate Department and Member of Opinion Letter Committee.

**Personal:** Harvard (College 1974, Law 1978).

### BILLINGS JR, Peter
Fabian & Clendenin, Salt Lake City
801 531 8900
*Recommended in Litigation*

### BLACK, Kenneth
Stoel Rives LLP, Salt Lake City
801 328 3131
*Recommended in Litigation*

### BLATTNER-THOMPSON, Elisabeth
Parsons Behle & Latimer PC, Salt Lake City 801 532 1234
EBlattner@parsonsbehle.com
*Recommended in Employment*

**Practice Areas:** Employment law: defending and counseling management on breach of contract, discrimination, harassment, employee medical issues, OSHA, retaliation, wage and hour, workers' compensation and wrongful discharge; handbook reviews; training programs; workplace investigations.

**Prof. Memberships:** Member: American Bar Association; Utah and California State Bars; Salt Lake County Bar Association; Women Lawyers of Utah; Women Presidents Organization.

**Career:** Shareholder and Chair, Employment Law Department, Parsons Behle & Latimer. Frequent trainer and speaker on employment law topics.

**Personal:** JD, Order of the Coif, University of Utah, 1988. BS, cum laude, University of Utah 1985. Trustee, past Secretary: Park City Jazz Foundation.

### BONHAM, Mark E
Wilson Sonsini Goodrich & Rosati, Salt Lake City 801 993 6400
mbonham@wsgr.com
*Recommended in Corporate/M&A*

**Practice Areas:** Counsels technology-based companies on financing, public offerings, mergers and acquisitions, equity compensation, technology licensing, public company governance and disclosure, structuring of transactions and basic corporate and securities matters.

**Prof. Memberships:** Admitted to practice in California and Utah.

**Career:** Joined WSGR, 1987; became Partner, 1995. Co-Chair of WSGR's Knowledge Management Initiative. He participated in more than 70 merger and

acquisition transactions and public offerings valued at an aggregate of more than $10 billion.

**Personal:** JD, 1987, Harvard Law School. Recipient of the John M Olin Fellowship in Law and Economics; BA (magna cum laude), 1984, Brigham Young University.

### BROADBENT, David K
Holland & Hart LLP, Salt Lake City
801 595 7806
dbroadbent@hollandhart.com
*Recommended in Real Estate*

**Practice Areas:** Mr Broadbent practices primarily in the fields of real estate and corporate law. He represents both developer and lender clients in real estate acquisition, development, leasing and tax-free exchanges, as well as conventional, tax credit, and bond financing. He has helped clients develop and finance shopping center, office building, office park, condominium, hotel, multi-family housing and residential and recreational projects.

**Prof. Memberships:** Member, Real Property, Corporate Counsel and Business Law Sections, Utah State Bar; Member, Business Law and Real Property Sections of the American Bar Association. Mr Broadbent has served as the Chairman of the Real Property Section of the Utah State Bar. Appointments: Board of Directors, Valley Mental Health.

**Career:** Admitted to the Utah State Bar (1979).

**Personal:** Received a JD (1979, Order of the Coif) and a BA (1976, magna cum laude) from the University of Utah.

### BURBIDGE, Richard D
Burbidge & Mitchell, Salt Lake City
801 355 6677
rburbidge@burbidgeandmitchell.com
*Recommended in Litigation*

**Practice Areas:** Trial practice in complex commercial litigation and prosecution of catastrophic injury. Represents a wide range of clients, including emerging and established national and local concerns, governmental entities and prominent individuals. His extensive experience includes a wide range of business claims, including contract disputes, antitrust, securities, intellectual property and national and local class action cases.

**Prof. Memberships:** Fellow, American College of Trial Lawyers; Fellow (State Chair), International Academy of Trial Lawyers; Fellow (State Chair), International Society of Barristers; and Member, American Board of Trial Advocacy; Trial Lawyer of the Year 2002 (ABOTA, Utah Chapter).

**Career:** Over 30 years of litigation and trial practice throughout the United States. Has won numerous jury verdicts for both plaintiffs and defendants in multi-million dollar cases.

**Personal:** Graduated with a Juris Doctor Degree in 1972 from the University of

Utah College of Law; Order of the Coif. Articles Editor, Utah Law Review. Adjunct Professor, Trial Practice, University of Utah College of Law, 1986-93. Listed in leading legal publication.

### CAMPBELL JR, Robert
Van Cott, Bagley, Cornwall & McCarthy, Salt Lake City 801 532 3333
*Recommended in Litigation*

### CHRISTENSEN, Stephen
Nelson, Christensen & Helsten PC, Salt Lake City 801 531 8400
*Recommended in Real Estate*

### CLARK, Robert
Parr Waddoups Brown Gee & Loveless, Salt Lake City 801 532 7840
*Recommended in Litigation*

### CLAWSON, Carol
Clawson & Falk LLC, Salt Lake City
801 322 5000
*Recommended in Employment*

### COOK, Rand
Van Cott, Bagley, Cornwall & McCarthy, Salt Lake City 801 532 3333
*Recommended in Real Estate*

### COX, Carolyn
Holme Roberts & Owen LLP, Denver
303 861 7000
*Recommended in Employment*

### DUNNING, Elizabeth
Holme Roberts & Owen LLP, Salt Lake City 801 521 5800
*Recommended in Employment*

### DURHAM, Matthew
Stoel Rives LLP, Salt Lake City
801 328 3131
*Recommended in Employment*

### ELLISON, Thomas
Stoel Rives LLP, Salt Lake City
801 328 3131
*Recommended in Real Estate*

### ETCHEVERRY, Raymond J
Parsons Behle & Latimer PC, Salt Lake City 801 532 1234
REtcheverry@parsonsbehle.com
*Recommended in Litigation*

**Practice Areas:** Complex business litigation with expertise in antitrust defense including class action defense, intellectual property disputes involving primarily patents and trade secrets, and insurance coverage disputes.

**Prof. Memberships:** Fellow, American Bar Foundation. Member, American Bar Association: Litigation Section; Antitrust Section; Intellectual Property Section. Master of the Bench, American Inns of Court II.

**Career:** President and Chairman of the Board of Directors, Parsons Behle & Latimer, 1992-present.

**Personal:** JD, Duke University, 1976. Honors BS, magna cum laude, University of Utah, 1973.

## FERRIN, Shawn
Parsons Behle & Latimer PC, Salt Lake City 801 532 1234
SFerrin@parsonsbehle.com
*Recommended in Real Estate*
**Practice Areas:** Real property transactions, with an emphasis on retail and resort development, and land use planning. Shawn has handled acquisition, lease and financing transactions throughout the West for numerous clients, including Home Depot, American Skiing Company and Micron Technology, Inc.
**Prof. Memberships:** American Bar Association: Real Estate Section. Utah State Bar: Real Estate Section.
**Career:** Shareholder and former Department Chair, Real Estate & Finance Department, Parsons Behle & Latimer. Executive Committee, Economic Development Corporation of Utah. Advisor to the Governor's Task Force on Economic Development and the Environment.
**Personal:** JD, University of Utah, 1986. BUS, University of Utah, 1982.

## FREDMAN, Stuart
Holme Roberts & Owen LLP, Salt Lake City 801 521 5800
*Recommended in Corporate/M&A*

## GARDINER, Samuel P
Dorsey & Whitney LLP, Salt Lake City 801 933 7362
gardiner.sam@dorsey.com
*Recommended in Corporate/M&A*
**Practice Areas:** Practices in corporate finance, securities and mergers and acquisitions. Extensive experience in venture capital and private equity and debt financing transactions, representing both emerging companies and investors, as well as representing underwriters and companies in public equity offerings. Also substantial experience in M&A transactions involving both public and private companies and in strategic alliances and joint ventures. Significant experience in syndicated debt financings, public company securities law compliance, and general corporate governance matters.
**Prof. Memberships:** Utah Chapter of Association for Corporate Growth.
**Personal:** Brigham Young University, J. Reuben Clark Law School (JD, 1997); Brigham Young University (BA, 1993).

## GAVRE, Mark
Parsons Behle & Latimer PC, Salt Lake City 801 532 1234
MGavre@parsonsbehle.com
*Recommended in Employment*
**Practice Areas:** Employment, labor and benefits law, including ERISA litigation, wrongful discharge, workplace discrimination, sexual and other harassment claims, employee pension and benefits, union relations and whistleblower complaints, and alternative dispute resolution.
**Prof. Memberships:** Member, Utah

State Bar.
**Career:** Shareholder, Parsons Behle & Latimer. Judicial intern for Justice Christine Durham of the Utah Supreme Court. Before becoming an attorney, was professor of political science at the University of Utah, with specialization in political and constitutional theory.
**Personal:** JD, University of Utah, 1985. PhD University of California, Los Angeles, 1978. Fulbright Scholar, University of Madrid. BA, University of California, Berkeley, 1968.

## GEE, David
Parr Waddoups Brown Gee & Loveless, Salt Lake City 801 532 7840
*Recommended in Real Estate*

## GREENWOOD, David
Howrey LLP, Salt Lake City 801 533 8383
*Recommended in Litigation*

## GROSS, Jefferson W
Burbidge & Mitchell, Salt Lake City 801 355 6677
jwgross@burbidgeandmitchell.com
*Recommended in Litigation*
**Practice Areas:** Trial practice for both plaintiffs and defendants in complex commercial litigation and catastrophic injury. Has experience in a range of disputes, including general business litigation, patent infringement, real estate disputes, securities fraud claims and class action lawsuits.
**Personal:** JD, University of Southern California (1993); AB (Economics), University of California, Berkeley (1989).

## HALEY, George
Holme Roberts & Owen LLP, Salt Lake City 801 521 5800
*Recommended in Litigation*

## HARMAN, Paul M
Jones Waldo Holbrook & McDonough PC, Salt Lake City 801 521 3200
pharman@joneswaldo.com
*Recommended in Real Estate*
**Practice Areas:** Practices in the area of commercial real estate development, focusing in the representation of national retail 'Big Box' companies in transactions throughout the United States. Extensive experience in negotiating acquisition documents, leases, development agreements, restrictive covenants and governmental incentive packages. In 2005, represented a client in conjunction with a $2.3 billion real estate asset acquisition involving 320 separate properties in 24 states.
**Prof. Memberships:** International Council of Shopping Centers (ICSC), National Association of Industrial & Office Properties (NAIOP).
**Personal:** J Reuben Clark Law School, Brigham Young University (JD, 1983, Cum Laude), Brigham Young University, (BA, 1980, Magna Cum Laude).

## HELLEWELL, Read
Kirton & McConkie, Salt Lake City
801 328 3600
*Recommended in Real Estate*

## HOLMES, Ervin
Stoel Rives LLP, Salt Lake City
801 328 3131
*Recommended in Real Estate*

## HUNT, Jeffrey
Parr Waddoups Brown Gee & Loveless, Salt Lake City 801 532 7840
*Recommended in Litigation*

## HYDE, Robert C
Kirton & McConkie, Salt Lake City
801 323 5915
rhyde@kmclaw.com
*Recommended in Real Estate*
**Practice Areas:** Robert Hyde specializes in real estate and land use law, as well as real estate lending. He is heavily involved in the representation of developers of commercial real estate properties. He also has a substantial practice in representing mortgage lenders and borrowers.
**Career:** After graduating from BYU's law school, Robert Hyde practiced from 1979 to 2000 with Parsons Behle & Latimer in Salt Lake City, Utah. After taking a three-year leave of absence to serve a mission for his church, he resumed his career with Kirton & McConkie in 2003.

## JACOBSEN, Brad
Holme Roberts & Owen LLP, Denver
303 861 7000
*Recommended in Corporate/M&A*

## JARDINE, James
Ray, Quinney & Nebeker PC, Salt Lake City 801 532 1500
*Recommended in Litigation*

## JONES, Cary
Snell & Wilmer LLP, Salt Lake City
801 257 1811
cjones@swlaw.com
*Recommended in Real Estate*
**Practice Areas:** Real estate transactions, focusing in resort, hotel, retail, office and industrial development and disposition; office/retail leasing; zoning and land use; joint ventures.
**Prof. Memberships:** Admitted Utah Supreme Court; Supreme Court of Arizona; Utah State Bar, Former Chairman, Real Property Section; American Bar Association.
**Career:** Representative cases include: lead counsel for Utah Transit Authority on all real estate and land use matters for $200 million acquisition of Union Pacific facilities for 175-mile Wasatch Front Commuter Rail Project.
**Personal:** Adjunct Professor, University of Utah S J Quinney College of Law, 2004-present; Executive Committee, Salt Lake Convention and Visitors Bureau, 2004-present.

## JONES, Nathan
Stoel Rives LLP, Salt Lake City
801 328 3131
*Recommended in Corporate/M&A*

## JORDAN, David
Stoel Rives LLP, Salt Lake City
801 328 3131
*Recommended in Litigation*

## KARRENBERG, Thomas
Anderson & Karrenberg, Salt Lake City
801 534 1700
*Recommended in Litigation*

## KROESCHE, Guy
Stoel Rives LLP, Salt Lake City
801 328 3131
*Recommended in Real Estate*

## LEVIN, Ali
Jones Waldo Holbrook & McDonough PC, Salt Lake City 801 521 3200
alevin@joneswaldo.com
*Recommended in Employment*
**Practice Areas:** Counsels employers in all aspects of labor and employment law and represents employers in employment litigation. Negotiates, drafts and litigates employment contracts, confidentiality and non-competition agreements, collective bargaining agreements and severance packages. Provides in-house unlawful harassment training, investigations and drafts employee policies and handbooks. Frequent speaker and contributor on employment law topics. Listed in Utah Business Legal Elite.
**Prof. Memberships:** Society for Human Resource Management (SHRM).
**Career:** Admitted to practice in Massachusetts (1997), Colorado (1991) and Utah since 2002.
**Personal:** University of California Santa Cruz (1992); Northeastern University School of Law (1997).

## LINDLEY, Greg
Holland & Hart LLP, Salt Lake City
801 595 7829
glindley@hollandhart.com
*Recommended in Corporate/M&A*
**Practice Areas:** Corporate law, securities law, mergers and acquisitions, and franchise law. Mr Lindley has represented numerous companies with their bank financings, joint ventures and strategic alliances, distributorship and licensing agreements, and general contractual matters. He has worked on numerous public and private offerings of securities for a wide variety of clients. He also represents public companies in the compliance work required by the Securities and Exchange Act of 1934, including the preparation of Forms 10-K, 10-Q, and 8-K and proxy statements, and the Sarbanes-Oxley Act. He has represented both buyers and sellers in many mergers and acquisitions in a variety of industries, including food manufacture and distribution, banking, printing and publishing, insurance, mine drill bit manufacturing

and servicing, and medical diagnostics. Mr Lindley has also counseled many companies with organizational, executive compensation, and fundraising issues.

**Prof. Memberships:** Utah State Bar and the State Bar of Texas.
**Career:** Admitted to Utah Bar (1988) and Texas Bar (1983).
**Personal:** Received a JD from Duke University (1983), an MBA (1981) and a BS (1978) from Utah State University.

**LITTLE, David**
Holme Roberts & Owen LLP, Salt Lake City 801 521 5800
*Recommended in Corporate/M&A*

**LLOYD, Brian**
Parr Waddoups Brown Gee & Loveless, Salt Lake City 801 532 7840
*Recommended in Corporate/M&A*

**LOVELESS, Scott**
Parr Waddoups Brown Gee & Loveless, Salt Lake City 801 532 7840
*Recommended in Corporate/M&A*

**MAAK, Charles**
Parr Waddoups Brown Gee & Loveless, Salt Lake City 801 532 7840
*Recommended in Real Estate*

**MANGUM, Geoffrey W**
Parsons Behle & Latimer PC, Salt Lake City 801 532 1234
GMangum@parsonsbehle.com
*Recommended in Corporate/M&A*
**Practice Areas:** Corporate and commercial real estate, with an emphasis on negotiating and structuring complex business transactions, including mergers and acquisitions, joint ventures and commercial real estate financing arrangements. Also has extensive experience on co-branding identity issues, including co-branded credit and loyalty card programs.
**Prof. Memberships:** Utah State Bar Association; American Bar Association.
**Career:** Currently, shareholder and Chair of Corporate and Tax Department, Parsons Behle & Latimer; 1996-99: Vice President of Corporate Transactions for American Stores Company; 1979-96: Associate and shareholder, Prince Yeates & Geldzahler.
**Personal:** JD, Georgetown University Law Center, 1979. BA, magna cum laude, University of Utah, 1976.

**MCCONNELL, Robert**
Parr Waddoups Brown Gee & Loveless, Salt Lake City 801 532 7840
*Recommended in Real Estate*

**MOFFITT, Ronald**
Stoel Rives LLP, Salt Lake City 801 328 3131
*Recommended in Corporate/M&A*

**MOORE, Larry**
Ray, Quinney & Nebeker PC, Salt Lake City 801 532 1500
*Recommended in Real Estate*

**O'BRIEN, Michael**
Jones Waldo Holbrook & McDonough PC, Salt Lake City 801 521 3200
mobrien@joneswaldo.com
*Recommended in Employment*
**Practice Areas:** Practice includes counseling businesses and employers on how to minimize and manage risks in all aspects of labor and employment law and representing employers in employment-related litigation. Has extensive experience assisting news and publishing organizations in obtaining access to places and records, and in minimizing risks and responding to claims of defamation, invasion of privacy, tort and other matters related to publishing. Serves as an arbitrator and mediator in employment law disputes. Utah Employment Lawyer of the Year. Listed in Utah Business Legal Elite.
**Prof. Memberships:** Works with the local and national Society for Human Resource Management (SHRM) and serves as the legal and legislative director for Utah SHRM and Salt Lake SHRM.
**Career:** Practicing in Utah since 1986. Chair of Litigation Department and Employment Group.
**Personal:** University of Notre Dame (1983); University of Utah College of Law (1986).

**O'CONNOR, Robert**
Wilson Sonsini Goodrich & Rosati, Salt Lake City 801 993 6400
roconnor@wsgr.com
*Recommended in Corporate/M&A*
**Practice Areas:** Advises technology and growth companies, organizes and capitalizes businesses, raises capital through private and public debt and equity financings, and buys/sells companies and technologies. Also represents a number of venture capital investors in connection with investments in their portfolio companies.
**Prof. Memberships:** Admitted to practice in California and Utah. Member, Westminster College's Technology Commercialization and Entrepreneurship Program Advisory Board and Utah Information Technology Association Board of Trustees. Director, Utah Life Science Association.
**Career:** Managing Partner, Salt Lake City office. Became Partner, 2002.
**Personal:** JD, 1993, Loyola Law School; BA, 1990, University of California (Los Angeles).

**POELMAN, Ronald**
Jones Waldo Holbrook & McDonough PC, Salt Lake City 801 521 3200
*Recommended in Corporate/M&A*

**ROWE, Keven**
Jones Waldo Holbrook & McDonough PC, Salt Lake City 801 521 3200
krowe@joneswaldo.com
*Recommended in Real Estate*
**Practice Areas:** Partner and Head of the

firm's Real Estate Finance Group and practices in the areas of complex real estate and asset-based lending for institutional and governmental clients, including construction, permanent and securitized financings, complex real estate transactions including shopping center, apartment, residential and resort developments (including negotiation of acquisition documents, leases, development agreements and restrictive covenants), office and commercial building acquisition and leasing. Also handles business acquisitions and divestures involving real estate and non-real estate assets.
**Prof. Memberships:** ICSC, NAIOP.
**Career:** Admitted to practice in the State of Utah, Jones, Waldo, Holbrook & McDonough, P.C.; Partner, 1986-present; President, 2003-present; Executive Committee Member, 1996-present.
**Personal:** University of Utah (JD, 1986, Order of the Coif, William H Leary Scholar), University of Utah (BA, 1983).

**RUBINFELD, Ira**
Ray, Quinney & Nebeker PC, Salt Lake City 801 532 1500
*Recommended in Real Estate*

**RUDD, David R**
Ballard Spahr Andrews & Ingersoll LLP, Salt Lake City 801 517 6829
rudd@ballardspahr.com
*Recommended in Corporate/M&A*
**Practice Areas:** Focuses on complex domestic and international business transactions in a wide variety of legal fields and industrial sectors.
**Prof. Memberships:** Member, US Senator Orrin G Hatch's Trade Advisory Group, advising on NAFTA and GATT; Co-Chair, International Special Interest Group, Utah Information Technology Association; Member, Utah Life Sciences Association; Chairman ex officio, Board of Trustees of the Mexico Utah Business Council; Member, State of Utah Securities Advisory Committee; Officer, Mountain West Venture Group; past Chairman, Utah State Bar Business Law Section; Member, American Bar Association, Inter-American Bar Association, Utah State Bar Association, and District of Columbia Bar Association.
**Career:** Admitted to the Utah Bar (1982); admitted to the District of Columbia Bar (1989); joined as Partner (2001).
**Personal:** JD, Pepperdine University School of Law (1982); BA, Brigham Young University (1979).

**SAVAGE, Greggory**
Holme Roberts & Owen LLP, Denver 303 861 7000
*Recommended in Litigation*

**SMITH, Janet**
Ray, Quinney & Nebeker PC, Salt Lake City 801 532 1500
*Recommended in Employment*

**STEVENSON, Brent**
Parr Waddoups Brown Gee & Loveless, Salt Lake City 801 532 7840
*Recommended in Corporate/M&A*

**SULLIVAN, Alan**
Snell & Wilmer LLP, Salt Lake City 801 257 1955
asullivan@swlaw.com
*Recommended in Litigation*
**Practice Areas:** Representation of clients in litigation relating to healthcare, intellectual property, natural resources development, manufacturing, and finance. Frequent representation of lawyers and law firms in relation to ethical issues pending before courts and disciplinary boards.
**Prof. Memberships:** American College of Trial Lawyers (Fellow 1996-present, State Chair 2000-02); American Bar Foundation (Fellow 1998-present); Utah Constitutional Revision Commission (Chair 1987-99); Salt Lake County Bar Association (past President).

**TAYLOR, Nolan S**
Dorsey & Whitney LLP, Salt Lake City 801 933 7360
taylor.nolan@dorsey.com
*Recommended in Corporate/M&A*
**Practice Areas:** Extensive experience representing underwriters and issuers in initial public offerings and registered follow-on and secondary offerings. Also extensive experience representing clients in mergers, acquisitions, and divestitures, private equity and venture capital transactions, securities law compliance, NYSE and Nasdaq compliance and corporate governance.
**Prof. Memberships:** USBA; ABA (Business Law Section Committees: Federal Regulation of Securities, Negotiated Acquisitions, Venture Capital and Private Equity, Business Finance); American Society of Governance Professionals (Public Company Affairs Committee).
**Personal:** University of Utah College of Law (JD, 1986); Brigham Young University (BA, 1983).

**TAYLOR, Tom**
Holme Roberts & Owen LLP, Salt Lake City 801 521 5800
*Recommended in Corporate/M&A*

**TOPHAM, Reed**
Stoel Rives LLP, Salt Lake City 801 328 3131
*Recommended in Corporate/M&A*

**WADDOUPS, Clark**
Parr Waddoups Brown Gee & Loveless, Salt Lake City 801 532 7840
*Recommended in Litigation*

**WATKINS, Glen**
Jones Waldo Holbrook & McDonough PC, Salt Lake City 801 521 3200
gwatkins@joneswaldo.com
*Recommended in Real Estate*
**Practice Areas:** Practice includes the

acquisition, financing, development and sale of commercial properties and resort properties; land use and regulatory matters; unique corporate and corporate governance matters involving owners and developers associations; and development of resort infrastructure. Extensive experience in connection with multi-state business acquisitions, including real estate assets.
**Prof. Memberships:** Advisory Board Member, University of Utah College of Social and Behavioral Science; Technology and Business Advisory Board of Westminster College; Trustee of the Utah Information Technology Association.
**Career:** Served as Jones Waldo's Board Chair since 2001; presently serves as Chair of the firm's Resort and Leisure Practice Group; served as resident managing shareholder of firm's Washington, DC office (1981-86); admitted to practice in Utah and the District of Columbia.
**Personal:** JD (University of Utah, 1975); BA magna cum laude (Stanford University/University of Utah, 1972).

### WESTON, John
Snell & Wilmer LLP, Salt Lake City
801 257 1931
jweston@swlaw.com
*Recommended in Corporate/M&A*
**Practice Areas:** Areas of concentration include securities regulation, private placements, public offerings, mergers, acquisitions, consolidations, joint ventures and partnerships, commercial loans and other financings, venture capital financing, and general corporate law.
**Prof. Memberships:** Utah State Bar Association; California State Bar Association; American Bar Association.
**Career:** Partner, Snell & Wilmer L.L.P., Salt Lake City, Utah; Associate, Andrews and Kurth, L.L.P., Los Angeles, California (1995-96).

### WIKSTROM, Francis M
Parsons Behle & Latimer PC, Salt Lake City 801 532 1234
FWikstrom@parsonsbehle.com
*Recommended in Litigation*
**Practice Areas:** Complex civil litigation, white collar criminal defense, environmental and intellectual property litigation.
**Prof. Memberships:** Fellow, American College of Trial Lawyers. International Association of Defense Counsel. Fellow, American Bar Foundation (State Chair). National Association of Former US Attorneys. Chair, Utah Supreme Court Advisory Committee on the Rules of Civil Procedure. Utah Representative, Tenth Circuit Advisory Committee (1997-2004). Program Chair, 2004 Tenth Circuit Judicial Conference. Master of the Bench, American Inns of Court II.
**Career:** Shareholder, Parsons Behle & Latimer since 1981. Former US attorney and assistant US attorney.
**Personal:** JD, Yale University, 1974. BS, Weber State College, 1971.

### WILLIAMS, Gregory
Van Cott, Bagley, Cornwall & McCarthy, Salt Lake City 801 532 3333
*Recommended in Real Estate*

### WILSON, Randon
Jones Waldo Holbrook & McDonough PC, Salt Lake City 801 521 3200
*Recommended in Corporate/M&A*

### WINGER, Gary
Ray, Quinney & Nebeker PC, Salt Lake City 801 532 1500
*Recommended in Corporate/M&A*

### YOUNG, Howard
Jones Waldo Holbrook & McDonough PC, Salt Lake City 801 521 3200
*Recommended in Corporate/M&A*

### ZODY, Michael A
Parsons Behle & Latimer PC, Salt Lake City 801 532 1234
MZody@parsonsbehle.com
*Recommended in Employment*
**Practice Areas:** Environmental litigation, including defense of civil and criminal enforcement actions, citizens' suits, landfill litigation, environmental disputes arising from the sale of land and CERCLA cases. Employment law, including ADA (also public accommodation/access barrier cases), ADEA, Title VII, Fair Housing, employment contracts (including non-compete clauses) and OSHA. Whistleblower/retaliation cases, including environmental and Sarbanes-Oxley whistleblower cases.
**Prof. Memberships:** American Bar Association: Natural Resources, Energy and Environmental Law Section; Tort Trial and Insurance Practice Section, Toxic Torts and Environmental Law Committee; Employment Law Section.
**Career:** Shareholder, Parsons Behle & Latimer.
**Personal:** JD, cum laude, Indiana University, 1990. BA, Purdue University, 1987.

# BURBIDGE & MITCHELL

## THE FIRM

**Managing Partner:** Richard D Burbidge

**Number of partners:** 3
**Number of other lawyers:** 3

**FIRM OVERVIEW:** Since its founding in 1976, Burbidge & Mitchell has emphasized excellence in litigation and trial practice. The firm's consistent success in all phases of litigation and trial practice is founded on the philosophy that the best results for its clients are achieved by thoroughly assessing and preparing each case as though it were going to be tried. The activities of the firm are strategically and purposefully directed to achieve maximum result and value for its clients. The firm has successfully applied its extensive litigation and trial experience in a wide range of complex business disputes, including contract, antitrust, securities, intellectual property and class action litigation. Small by design, the firm has the talent and flexibility to direct the considerable energies of its trial attorneys and experienced staff to quickly and efficiently respond to the needs of its clients. Although based in Utah, the firm includes attorneys licensed to practice in California and has experience in federal and state courts throughout the United States.

## MAIN AREAS OF PRACTICE:

**Trial Practice:** Litigation and trial practice are hallmarks of the firm. Unlike some law firms devoted to commercial litigation, the firm's lawyers have extensive trial experience. This experience translates into an ability to analyze, create and employ intelligent trial strategies and assess risks and potential benefits of trial. By virtue of its reputation and experience in the trial setting, the firm has represented national and local commercial interests and individuals in a wide range of complex litigation. In addition to commercial litigation, the firm has extensive experience in the prosecution and defense of catastrophic personal injury and product liability claims.

**Antitrust Litigation:** Clients interested in protecting and advancing their competitive positions in the marketplace will find that the firm provides litigation support in areas such as antitrust and competition law.

**Securities & Corporate Litigation:** The firm offers its corporate and individual clients representation on issues related to securities and corporate governance, including securities fraud and shareholder derivative claims.

**Intellectual Property Litigation:** As the importance of intellectual property in the modern economy has increased, the firm has become extensively involved in prosecuting and defending claims of patent infringement and trade secret theft. In addition to securing and successfully defending a $31 million jury verdict in a recent patent infringement case, the firm has secured the successful resolution of numerous other intellectual property cases for its clients. Firm lawyers have degrees in engineering and information technology.

**Class Actions & Mass Torts:** The firm has extensive experience in class actions, in both state and federal courts. The firm's extensive experience in prosecuting and defending national and local class actions aids it in developing successful strategies for its clients.

**CLIENTS:** The firm's clients include emerging businesses and established corporations, corporate executives and directors, public and governmental entities, entrepreneurs, and individuals. Burbidge & Mitchell represents clients in a broad range of businesses and industries, including energy, healthcare, medicine and medical products, computers and information technology, telecommunications, real estate, manufacturing, banking and finance. References are available upon request.

## HEAD OFFICE

**UTAH**
215 South State Street, Suite 920, **Salt Lake City**, UT 84111
**Tel:** 801 355 6677　**Fax:** 801 355 2341
**Email:** rburbidge@burbidgeandmitchell.com
**Website:** www.burbidgeandmitchell.com

## CONTACTS

**Antitrust Litigation** .................Richard D Burbidge, Jefferson W Gross
**General Litigation & Trial Practice** ..Richard D Burbidge, Jefferson W Gross
**Class Action & Mass Torts** ....................................Richard D Burbidge
**Securities & Corporate Litigation** .........................Jefferson W Gross
**Intellectual Property Litigation** ...........................Richard D Burbidge

**BURBIDGE & MITCHELL**
TRIAL ATTORNEYS

# KIRTON & MCCONKIE

## THE FIRM

**President:** Berne S Broadbent
**Vice President:** Lorin C Barker
**Secretary/Treasurer:** William A Meaders

**HEAD OFFICE**

**UTAH**
60 East South Temple, Suite 1800, **Salt Lake City**, UT 84111
**Tel:** 801 328 3600   **Fax:** 801 321 4893
**Website:** www.kmclaw.com

**FIRM OVERVIEW:** Kirton & McConkie's 80 plus attorneys provide proven expertise and practical experience in a broad spectrum of legal services in essential practice areas including real estate, finance, business taxation, intellectual property, international law, business litigation, immigration, employment, bankruptcy, appellate work and healthcare. Since being founded in 1964, Kirton & McConkie's client base has permitted it to develop extensive worldwide contacts and expertise as reflected in the firm's slogan of having 'local roots' and a 'global reach'. Many of the firm's lawyers have practiced and/or lived throughout the world, including lawyers native to China, Japan, and Mexico. In addition, the lawyers of Kirton & McConkie collectively speak 21 languages. Kirton & McConkie is recognized as one of the "preeminent law firms" in the nation by the prestigious Bar Register and is the recipient of the highest rating for professional and ethical standards by Martindale-Hubbell. The experience of the attorneys permits the firm to meet the needs of its clients, whether a complex, multifaceted entity, a smaller entrepreneurial company, or an individual.

## MAIN AREAS OF PRACTICE:

**Real Property & Land Use Development:** Kirton & McConkie's broad real estate experience includes acquisition and disposition, financing, development, commercial leasing, entitlement, zoning and land use planning and management of real property. The firm's Real Estate Section is one of the largest in the state of Utah and its client base includes the largest and second largest commercial mortgage brokers in Utah, leading real estate development and ownership firms, several life insurance companies, and the largest independent supermarket chain in the west.

**Intellectual Property:** Kirton & McConkie's intellectual property lawyers are all registered patent attorneys and constitute the largest intellectual property section in Utah for a general practice firm. The firm represents clients ranging from start-ups to large international entities with intellectual property interests in over one hundred countries. Clients such as The Olympic Organizing Committee, Fanny May Chocolates and other such clients owning long-established trademarks have turned to Kirton & McConkie to protect their valuable assets.

**Corporate & Taxation:** The firm's Corporate and Tax Section has experience in mergers and acquisitions, entity formation and governance for all types of entities. This practice group also assists clients with tax planning, tax controversies, personal tax, estate planning, wills, charitable donations, IRS representation, retirement plans, and administrative practice benefits.

**Business Litigation:** The firm's Business Litigation Section represents a variety of clients ranging from Fortune 100 companies to individuals with complex problems requiring alternative dispute resolution, litigation and related appeals in federal and state courts. The firm's attorneys have experience in the following types of cases: business tort, construction, shareholder derivative, lender liability, securities, healthcare, environmental, labor and employment, creditor rights, qui tam and constitutional claims.

**Constitution, Appellate & Religious:** With one of its largest clients being a prominent religious organization, the firm has extensive experience in First Amendment and other constitutional issues, trial and appellate litigation, amicus briefs, and legislative services.

**Risk Management:** The firm's services include insurance defense litigation, construction defects, tort claims, malpractice, automobile accidents, commercial liability, PIP claims, declaratory actions, and statements under oath. The firm also offers coverage opinions, coverage analysis, and alternative dispute resolution.

**Construction & Surety Bonds:** The firm offers expert legal assistance on every phase of construction from the initial concept and design through post-substantial completion matters. It is regularly involved with many aspects of contractor defaults, claims defense, indemnity/salvage, license and other bonds. The firm expeditiously resolves payment bond claims and successfully mediates, arbitrates, and litigates various construction disputes, including Miller Act, Little Miller Act, and claims for bad faith. The firm has drafted construction contracts for worldwide use and for many of the major buildings in downtown Salt Lake City. The firm advises clients on construction issues in all 50 states, most Canadian provinces, Europe, Asia, Latin America, and Africa.

**Healthcare & Risk Management:** For over three decades, Kirton & McConkie has provided a broad range of healthcare related services, including risk management, quality assurance, medical malpractice defense, corporate and financial issues, Medicare/Medicaid representation, bioethical legal issues, consent policies and procedures, death and dying, taxation and emergency medicine.

**Immigration:** The firm handles the full spectrum of immigration cases including employment and family based immigration, asylum, naturalization, compliance, employer sanctions, removal defense and all non-immigrant matters, such as issuance of visas and changes of status.

**Employment:** The firm's Employment Section has broad experience with federal and state employment matters including compensation, liability, audits, agreements, training procedures, claims, and litigation.

**CLIENTS:** 3Com; Morinda, Inc.; Ogio; Cephalon, Inc.; Sharp Labs, Inc.; Xactware, Inc.; In2M Corporation; The Church of Jesus Christ of Latter-day Saints; Property Reserve, Inc.; Brigham Young University; University of Utah; General Growth Properties; Bonneville Mortgage Co.; Johanson Thackeray Real Estate Commercial Services; International Development Group/Affordable Housing Partners; Jiangsu Easthigh International Group; and Zions Securities Corp.

**INTERNATIONAL WORK:** The firm represents not only local clients doing business abroad, but also works for a variety of non-foreign and foreign clients with activities throughout the United States. The firm can help determine the optimal structure for international transactions, including technology transfers, licensing arrangements, joint ventures, manufacturing contracts and distribution agreements, acquisitions and joint ventures. The firm works closely with an established network of law firms and legal professionals in all 50 states and throughout the world as it represents one of the nation's largest multinational corporations. Kirton & McConkie can leverage this worldwide relationship to assist clients in selecting local counsel.

KIRTON &
McCONKIE
ATTORNEYS AT LAW

# PARSONS BEHLE & LATIMER

## THE FIRM

**Chairman:** Raymond J Etcheverry
**Senior Shareholder:** James B Lee
**Number of shareholders:** 81
**Number of other lawyers:** 34

## AREAS OF PRACTICE:

Litigation . . . . . . . . . . . . . . . . . . . . . . . . . . . . . . . . . . . . . . . . . . . . 50%
Environmental – Natural Resources. . . . . . . . . . . . . . . . . . . . . . . 30%
Corporate, Tax & Technology . . . . . . . . . . . . . . . . . . . . . . . . . . . . 20%

**FIRM OVERVIEW:** Parsons Behle & Latimer was founded in 1882 and is one of the oldest and best known law firms offering litigation and business law services in the intermountain region. The firm's first clients were in the business of mining - one of the major industries that helped fuel the growth of the area. Over time, its reputation and client base has grown with the dynamic intermountain region. The firm offers clients the resources and capabilities of a large and diverse firm, coupled with the highest levels of accessibility and responsiveness. With more than 100 attorneys, it brings a depth and range of experience to six major practice areas: litigation; environmental, energy and natural resources; corporate and tax; intellectual property and technology; real estate, banking and finance; and employment.

## MAIN AREAS OF PRACTICE:

**Litigation:** The firm has one of the largest litigation departments in the Intermountain West. Its trial lawyers take an interdisciplinary approach. They assemble appropriate teams for each client need, allowing them to address a client's concerns in the most efficient manner possible. And, it gives clients the benefits of multiple, informed viewpoints based on years of business acumen. They practice before federal and state courts, administrative agencies, and arbitration panels. Representative areas of trial practice are: commercial litigation, natural resources and environmental, intellectual property and antitrust, banking, insolvency, personal injury, products liability, mass media and white collar criminal law.

**Employment:** The firm's Labor and Employment Law Practice is the broadest and most extensive in Utah. Many of its attorneys practice exclusively in the labor and employment area. Areas of representation include wrongful discharge and discrimination, sexual harassment, employee benefits and ERISA, workers' compensation, OSHA and MSHA, immigration and National Labor Relations Act.

**Intellectual Property & Technology:** The Intellectual Property and Technology Department is a team of attorneys, patent agents and paralegals who represent the firm's clients in all aspects of intellectual property, technology and computer law, including: representation before the Patent and Trademark Office and the Copyright Office; litigation in state and federal courts throughout the country; contract and other transactional matters; and international intellectual property protection and licensing.

**Corporate & Tax:** Members of the firm's Corporate and Tax Department regularly participate in the negotiation and documentation of complex business transactions furnishing timely advice about securities, tax, natural resources, employment law and other issues. The firm regularly advises clients concerning business, corporate and securities, tax, international business, regulatory and administrative, energy and government relations.

**Real Estate & Finance:** These department members represent commercial banks, mortgage companies and other financial institutions. They also handle all aspects of real estate transactions, including acquisition, finance, development, condominium and PUD documentation, and zoning and land use regulations.

**Environmental, Energy & Natural Resources:** Parsons Behle & Latimer has one of the largest environmental, energy and natural resources practices in the western United States. More than 20 attorneys, many with state and federal regulatory agency backgrounds, including employment with the US Environmental Protection Agency; US Department of Justice; the President's Council on Environmental Quality, and the Utah Department of Natural Resources advise corporate and individual clients on all aspects of environmental, energy and natural resources law. The practice is national and international in scope with particular emphasis on the western United States and Latin America. Areas of practice include mining, oil and gas, water rights, public lands, energy and electrical power, air and water quality, hazardous waste, Superfund and Brownfields, and occupational issues. In these and other areas the firm advises and assist clients with transactions and finance, project development and closure, property acquisition and title, permitting, compliance, enforcement, cost recovery, rate cases, litigation, rulemakings and legislation.

**INTERNATIONAL WORK:** Parsons Behle & Latimer maintains an active and varied practice internationally, in particular in Latin America. Over the years it has assembled teams of attorneys and paralegals who have worked on a wide range of legal and business matters often while working on site in Bolivia, Chile, Colombia, Peru and Venezuela.

## HEAD OFFICE

**UTAH**
201 South Main Street Suite 1800, **Salt Lake City**, UT 84111
**Tel:** 801 532 1234  **Fax:** 801536 6111
**Email:** webmaster@parsonsbehlelaw.com
**Website:**www.parsonsbehlelaw.com

## BRANCH OFFICES

**NEVADA**
333 Holcomb Avenue, Ste. 300, **Reno,** NV 89502
**Tel:** 775 3231601  **Fax:** 775 348 7250

411 E. Bonneville Avenue, Ste. 300, **Las Vegas,** NV 89101
**Tel:** 702 884 3877  **Fax:** 702 599 6023

## CONTACTS

**Chairman** . . . . . . . . . . . . . . . . . . . . . . . .Raymond J Etcheverry (SLC)
**Litigation** . . . . . . . . . . . . . . . . . . . . . . . . . . . .Michael L Larsen (SLC)
**Corporate & Tax** . . . . . . . . . . . . . . . . . . . . .Geoffrey W Mangum (SLC)
**Technology** . . . . . . . . . . . . . . . . . . . . . . . . .Daniel P McCarthy (SLC)
**Employment**. . . . . . . . . . . . . . . . . . . .Elisabeth Blattner-Thompson (SLC)
**Environmental, Energy & Natural Resources** ..Michael J Malmquist (SLC)
**Real Estate & Finance** . . . . . . . . . . . . . . . . . . .Jonathan Butler (SLC)
**Retail**. . . . . . . . . . . . . . . . . . . . . . . . . . . . . . . . . . . . . .Hal J Pos (SLC)
**Mining** . . . . . . . . . . . . . . . . . . . . . . . . . . .Michael J Malmquist (SLC)
**Media** . . . . . . . . . . . . . . . . . . . . . . . . . . . . . . . .Randy Dryer (SLC)
**Energy & Telecommunications** . . . . . . . . . . . . . .Robert Reeder (SLC)
**Sports** . . . . . . . . . . . . . . . . . . . . . . . . . . . . .R Craig Johnson (SLC)

A PROFESSIONAL
LAW CORPORATION

## How lawyers are ranked

Every year we carry out thousands of in-depth interviews with clients and lawyers in order to assess the reputations and expertise of business lawyers across the USA. Chambers rankings and editorial are referred to extensively by General Counsel and other purchasers of legal services who look to our recommendations when choosing their lawyers.

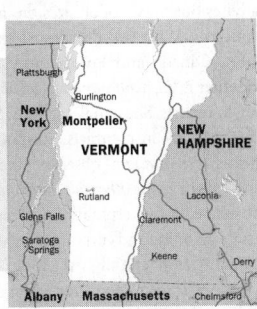

# CORPORATE/COMMERCIAL

### Corporate/Commercial
### Leading Firms

1. **DINSE, KNAPP & MCANDREW PC** *Burlington*
   **DOWNS RACHLIN MARTIN PLLC** *Burlington*
   **GRAVEL AND SHEA** *Burlington*
2. **PAUL, FRANK + COLLINS** *Burlington*
   **PRIMMER PIPER EGGLESTON** *Burlington*
   **SHEEHEY FURLONG & BEHM PC** *Burlington*

### Leading Individuals

1. **ERLY Peter** *Gravel and Shea*
   **FRYE B Michael** *Paul, Frank + Collins*
   **HAEFNER Gail** *Paul, Frank + Collins*
   **KNAPP Spencer** *Dinse, Knapp & McAndrew PC*
   **MCCONAUGHY Stewart** *Gravel and Shea*
   **MOODY Thomas** *Downs Rachlin Martin PLLC*
   **ODE Paul** *Downs Rachlin Martin PLLC*
2. **BOE Kathleen** *English, Carroll & Ritter PC*
   **EGGLESTON Jon** *Primmer Piper Eggleston*
   **MCMAHAN Jeffrey** *Dinse, Knapp & McAndrew PC*
   **MONTGOMERY Margaret** *Gravel and Shea*
   **MURPHY Brian** *Dinse, Knapp & McAndrew PC*
   **PORT Alan** *Paul, Frank + Collins*

## Band 1

### Dinse, Knapp & McAndrew PC

**The Firm:** This *"nimbly staffed"* outfit offers *"a responsive, personal touch,"* report clients. Six attorneys handle a broad range of matters, from negotiating and documenting sales to advising businesses on contractual agreements, executive compensation and tax planning. The group has an impressive roster of clients in the healthcare sector and acts for schools and universities, as well as medium sized businesses in the construction, manufacturing, real estate and service industries. This year's highlights include appointment as corporate counsel to the Vermont Teddy Bear in its take private, and advising on the $25 million sale of Annie's Enterprises.

**The Lawyers:** *"Rainmaker"* **Spencer Knapp** has extensive experience in corporate, healthcare and banking issues, and is sought out for *"more than just legal counsel – he gives outstanding business counsel too."* He is deemed smart, self-confident and *"quick*

to react to evolving circumstances.*"* He continues to act as in-house counsel for Fletcher Allen Hospital. Corporate and IP lawyer **Jeff McMahan** wins praise as an excellent technician who, *"for all his attention to detail, can still think about the big picture."* Clients assert that his personable nature enables him to work well in negotiations. **Brian Murphy** attracts notice by his strong tax background and experience in dealing with nonprofit organizations. He has a general corporate practice that includes contracts and M&A. Sources declare him: *"A real dynamic guy with a good head on his shoulders."*

**Clients/Work Highlights:** The firm's client list includes Fletcher Allen Hospital and Green Mountain College.

### Downs Rachlin Martin PLLC

**The Firm:** The largest firm in Vermont benefits from a statewide presence and *"awesome resources,"* agree commentators. It has more bench strength than most, and the depth of the group allows lawyers to specialize in sub-areas such as IP, tax and environmental law. The team is made up of *"sharp attorneys who have broad expertise and meet just about any legal need,"* report clients. Highlights from the past twelve months include providing local counsel in the $1.2 billion merger of IDX Systems with a subsidiary of GE.

**The Lawyers:** *"Sharp and creative"* lawyer **Paul Ode**'s practice includes startups, large transactions and legislative work. Sources declare him *"thoughtful, considerate and great at reviewing and analyzing issues."* He possesses the rare quality of being *"extremely hard working without wearing it on his sleeve,"* and clients endorse his *"magical ability to make you feel like you're his only client."* Leading the venture capital group, **Tom Moody** is an *"efficient and smart"* corporate and securities lawyer and a talented facilitator. He is best known for representing out-of-state venture capital investors. His unique practice involves carrying out multinational transactions in such places as India, Singapore and Europe.

**Clients/Work Highlights:** Ridgewood Capital; Rural Cellular; Mass. Bay Brewing; Marlboro College; Vermont Gas Systems and Country Home Products.

### Gravel and Shea

**The Firm:** Peers brand this *"the top firm in Vermont for quality and service."* Six *"excellent"* attorneys are skilled at handling business formations, finance, M&A and taxation issues. The group regularly assists newly formed companies and financial institutions in diverse transactions, including investment and securities concerns. It advises a conspicuously loyal stable of buyers and sellers.

**The Lawyers:** **Stewart McConaughy** reigns as *"one of the most revered lawyers in the community."* A veteran in bank financing and an *"excessively hard worker,"* he has a reputation as a nonconfrontational deal-maker. Peers praise his calm and methodical demeanor, describing him as *"creative not combative."* Senior partner **Peter Erly** moves up the tables this year in recognition of his deep corporate and securities experience. A levelheaded and *"clear-thinking"* attorney, he runs a sophisticated operation specializing in securities transactions. Transactional expert **Margaret Montgomery** brings her *"big-city experience"* from DC and New York to the table. She is respected for her expertise in acquisitions and financings.

**Clients/Work Highlights:** Champlain Oil; VELCO; IBM and Merchants Bank.

## Band 2

### Paul, Frank + Collins,
### A Professional Corporation

**The Firm:** This prestigious outfit *"carries a lot of weight in the state"* and offers *"top-notch talent,"* according to sources. Its sizable corporate group houses lawyers representing regional, national and international businesses, as well as individual entrepreneurs and emerging companies. The team advises a number of Canadian businesses on legal issues in the USA. Areas of expertise include business organization, all kinds of commercial transactions, captive insurance and M&A. Franchising, licensing and immigration advice are also offered. As attractive to clients as its cost-efficiency is the firm's willingness to *"bend over backward to meet deadlines."*

**The Lawyers:** *"Steadfast, honest and smart,"* **Michael Frye** is *"just a brilliant corporate lawyer with nifty business sense and on-the-nail judgment,"* report interviewees. He has a strong tax background and advises businesses of all sizes on the range of their concerns. With two decades of experience in the USA, Canada and Europe under her belt, **Gail Haefner** is *"incredibly commercial and quick,"* according to reports. She handles sales, M&A and negotiations of software contracts. Commentators describe her as *"firm but fair,"* observing that when in court she *"often puts the other side to shame."* **Alan Port** has developed a fine reputation for captive insurance, estate planning and corporate tax organization.

**Clients/Work Highlights:** HSBC; Vermont Tubbs; Vermont Information Processing; Magma Design Automation; Bell Helicopter; Unilever; Bank North; Merchants Bank; Ben & Jerry's and Brit Syndicates.

### Primmer Piper Eggleston & Cramer PC

**The Firm:** Following the merger of Burlington firms Eggleston & Cramer and Primmer & Piper, this has become the second largest law firm in Vermont. It fields more than 30 lawyers, offering services more comprehensive than ever to the firm's regulatory and corporate clients. Health sector clients feature strongly on the roster. The Primmer & Piper legacy brings particular strength in government regulations and regulatory law, insurance and banking to the table, while the Eggleston & Cramer contingent delivers healthcare, hospitality, real estate and immigration expertise. The merger has yielded a large and diverse client base that includes many out-of-state businesses as well as regional ones.

**The Lawyers:** Despite the loss of Kathy Boe, the firm has a deep pool of lawyers, among whom **Jon Eggleston** (see p.1962) stands out as a *"really experienced"* tax expert and *"astute"* business lawyer. He focuses on transaction structuring, M&A and estate planning. Sources note his dynamic work for ski companies. Recent work highlights include playing a significant part in the reorganization of several nonprofit, tax-exempt organizations into a single hospital on a tax-free basis.

**Clients/Work Highlights:** Vermont Association of Hospitals and Health Systems; Porter Medical Center; Central Vermont Medical Center; Northeastern Vermont Regional Hospital and University Wholesalers.

### Sheehey Furlong & Behm PC

**The Firm:** This established boutique offers highly regarded litigation and corporate services. Peers describe a happy combination of *"excellent lawyers and loyal clients,"* while clients extol the *"impressive"* level of coordination within the firm. A broad corporate practice includes startup and organizational advice to all types of businesses, as well as counsel on M&A, strategic alliances, financings and commercial contracts. Niche areas of expertise are technology and IP licensing and protection. Ongoing representation of Mt. Mansfield Television involves negotiations with government, real estate agencies and broadcasters. The group also represented two energy companies in the sales of their businesses.

**The Lawyers:** Richard Kozlowski joined the firm in February from Lisman, Webster, Kirkpatrick & Leckerling PC, as managing partner and head of the corporate and business services team.

**Clients/Work Highlights:** Bruegger's Enterprises; Competitive Computing; Hill Associates; Green Mountain Coffee Roasters; Mt. Mansfield Television; SymQuest; GS Blodgett and Twincraft Soap.

### Other Notable Practitioners

**Kathy Boe** left Eggleston & Cramer to become of counsel at Middlebury firm English, Carroll & Ritter, PC. She specializes in general business law and banking, and has cultivated a niche in nonprofit organizations. Clients endorse her responsiveness and user-friendly manner.

# EMPLOYMENT

# MAINLY DEFENDANT

| Employment: Mainly Defendant |
| --- |
| **Leading Firms** |
| **1**   DOWNS RACHLIN MARTIN PLLC *Burlington* |
|     GRAVEL AND SHEA *Burlington* |
| **2**   DINSE, KNAPP & MCANDREW PC *Burlington* |

| Leading Individuals |
| --- |
| **1**   BRIGGS Heather *Gravel and Shea* |
|     ROBB Peter *Downs Rachlin Martin PLLC* |
|     SABALIS Patricia *Downs Rachlin Martin PLLC* |
| **2**   GRANT Elizabeth *The Grant Law Firm* |
|     MAITLAND Johan *Downs Rachlin Martin PLLC* |
|     MCANDREW Karen *Dinse, Knapp & McAndrew PC* |
|     MCKEARIN Robert *Dinse, Knapp & McAndrew PC* |

## Band 1

### Downs Rachlin Martin PLLC

**The Firm:** This *"definite alpha group"* offers a full service and fields eight *"highly accomplished"* attorneys across five offices in Vermont and New Hampshire. While most of the group's work is in Vermont, attorneys benefit from out-of-state labor work. Recent caseload highlights include representing the Elevator Manufacturers Association of New York on a lengthy lockout, and establishing a new ruling in a Boston court.

**The Lawyers:** Star lawyer **Peter Robb** attracts a national clientele and provides *"exceptional expertise"* at the heart of the group. A specialist in organized labor and labor management, he understands the inner workings of the NLRB and is said by sources to be *"very wise,"* candid and unpretentious. His instincts *"set the bar"* in this field. Also nationally active, **Pat Sabalis** is an *"unbelievable resource"* to her clients. Described as *"very helpful"* and *"proactive in keeping things current,"* she divides her time between counseling employers and litigating for clients in crisis. None of her major cases have gone to trial in the past year. The *"approachable"* **Johan Maitland** joins the firm from Gravel and Shea. He focuses on employment counseling in day-to-day human resources management issues, training and litigation. Clients praise his *"thoughtful and conscientious"* style, and for *"bringing a perspective to the table that you just hadn't even thought about."*

**Clients/Work Highlights:** Otis Elevator; Dominion Resources Services; Entenergy and Elevator Manufacturers Association of New York.

### Gravel and Shea

**The Firm:** This boutique fields professional attorneys who are largely focused on counseling employers and avoiding litigation. They represent companies of all sizes, helping them to implement strategies against claims that range from employment discrimination to wrongful discharge and wage and hour issues. The group has extensive experience defeating union-organizing drives. Despite the loss of Johan Maitland to Downs Rachlin Martin, clients remain impressed with the *"broad expertise"* and responsiveness demonstrated by attorneys.

**The Lawyers:** **Heather Briggs** stands out for her *"bright and balanced approach."* She is dedicated to counseling employers in preventive strategies, thus avoiding litigation, and advising on employee benefits. Clients admit they *"would be lost without her"* and cherish her *"remarkable common sense that is grounded in both the law and reality."*

**Clients/Work Highlights:** Merchant Bank; Geiger; IP Capital Group and Concept2.

## Band 2

### Dinse, Knapp & McAndrew PC

**The Firm:** Six *"highly specialized"* attorneys here handle any employment matter for clients on the management side, from litigation and its avoidance to workers' compensation and regulatory and compliance issues. Clients of all sizes are advised on employee benefits and executive compensation, and the team offers specialist expertise in immigration issues affecting foreign employees and recruits. The bulk of the group's work is for colleges and universities, including issues related to faculty tenure, institutional governance and premises liability.

**The Lawyers:** Heading up the firm's litigation and education practice, **Karen McAndrew** acts for colleges and universities throughout the state. She offers ongoing advice on a range of employment matters and provides supervisory training to her clients to prevent claims and litigation. An "*aggressive*" trial lawyer, she has defended employers at trial and appellate level in state and federal courts. Clients remark: "*She has excellent presence in court and knows when it's better to settle than to win.*" **Bob McKearin** leads the employment practice group, representing businesses in diverse employment matters. Commended by peers as "*a skilled litigator,*" he also serves as a mediator and arbitrator in state courts.

**Clients/Work Highlights:** Fletcher Allen Health Care; Vermont Teddy Bear; Greenmount College; Hubbardton Forge; University of Vermont; Middlebury College; OMYA and Bombardier Capital.

### Other Notable Practitioners

**Elizabeth Grant** quit Paul Frank + Collins last year to found The Grant Law Firm in Montpelier. Her practice is exclusively management-oriented in the area of employment law, which includes education law services to public and independent schools and higher education institutions. The core of her clientele comprises entities that have remained loyal to her since she struck out on her own, including a publicly held corporation with operations in over 20 states.

# LITIGATION

## Litigation: General Commercial
### Leading Firms

[1] **DINSE, KNAPP & MCANDREW PC** *Burlington*
**GRAVEL AND SHEA** *Burlington*
**PAUL, FRANK + COLLINS** *Burlington*
**SHEEHEY FURLONG & BEHM PC** *Burlington*
[2] **CLEARY SHAHI & AICHER, PC** *Rutland*
**DOWNS RACHLIN MARTIN PLLC** *Burlington*
**PRIMMER PIPER EGGLESTON** *Burlington*
**SPINK & MILLER PLC** *Burlington*
**THERIAULT & JOSLIN PC** *Montpelier*

### Leading Individuals

#### Senior Statesman
**RACHLIN Robert** *Downs Rachlin Martin PLLC*
[1] **BEHM Jeffrey** *Sheehey Furlong & Behm PC*
**BERGER Ritchie** *Dinse, Knapp & McAndrew PC*
**HEMLEY Robert** *Gravel and Shea*
**MCANDREW Karen** *Dinse, Knapp & McAndrew PC*
[2] **BENNETT II Crocker** *Paul, Frank + Collins*
**CLEARY David** *Cleary Shahi & Aicher, PC*
**HEATH Marc** *Downs Rachlin Martin PLLC*
**MILLER Elizabeth** *Spink & Miller PLC*
**O'NEILL Robert** *Gravel and Shea*
**SARTORE John** *Paul, Frank + Collins*
**SPINK James** *Spink & Miller PLC*
[3] **FRANKLIN Gary** *Primmer Piper Eggleston*
**JOSLIN Peter** *Theriault & Joslin PC*
**MANITSKY Andrew** *Gravel and Shea*
**MONAHAN JR John** *Dinse, Knapp & McAndrew PC*

## Band 1

### Dinse, Knapp & McAndrew PC

**The Firm:** This group "*performs at the highest level*" and "*gives excellent value for each dollar spent,*" clients confirm. A team of "*smart and thoughtful*" lawyers handles all types of commercial and business litigation, as well as employment, construction and domestic matters. The group has cultivated a strong reputation in insurance defense and medical malpractice work. The firm has more than 500 active litigation files, representing local, regional and national clients in state and federal courts in Vermont, New Hampshire and upstate New York. Highlights from 2005 include acting on behalf of AMRESCO Commercial Finance in a four-week federal trial to defeat a debtor claim.

**The Lawyers:** "*Aggressive*" trial lawyer **Ritchie Berger** is "*a zealous advocate*" who "*can keep his adversaries on the run throughout trial.*" Innovative, forceful and "*committed to doing the best job possible,*" he is recognized statewide for his medical malpractice work. **Karen McAndrew** is an "*accomplished and dedicated trial lawyer*" who "*does a tremendous job*" before the courts, according to sources. She is expert in employment matters and commentators admire her "*truly brilliant legal mind*" and "*excellent judgment.*" Seasoned attorney **John Monahan** is "*bright and analytical*" and offers a deep understanding of the medical and insurance defense market. He wins praise for his "*cool and subtle*" approach, and peers look to him to ascertain "*how things would play to the jury.*"

**Clients/Work Highlights:** Green Mountain College; Dartmouth-Hitchcock Medical Center; Middlebury College; IBM; The University of Vermont and Fletcher Allen Health Care.

### Gravel and Shea

**The Firm:** This "*smooth, professional*" firm offers a mature group of litigation specialists that gets "*nothing but the highest marks*" from peers. The "*eminent*" attorneys are experienced in the full gamut of litigation, from general business and complex bankruptcy to IP and products liability. Highlights include representing a leading art expert in complex litigation regarding a fake Georgia O'Keeffe painting, and representing a New York consultancy in a major contract dispute against a law firm in a New York court. Sources observe: "*They're frequently engaged in contentious litigation and they really stand their ground.*"

**The Lawyers:** **Bob Hemley** is respected statewide as a "*savvy, relentless, smart, tenacious and successful*" attorney. Summing up opinion, a source notes: "*He only has one speed, which is full throttle!*" He has a 100% success rate in mediations. **Bob O'Neill** is a quick, effective lawyer who clients describe as "*strong, articulate, very New York*" and "*capable of blowing the other side away.*" Sources endorse his diligence and tenacity, describing him as "*in his element when the stakes are highest.*" **Andrew Manitsky** represents local and national clients in general business disputes, complex commercial litigation and IP matters. Clients find comfort in his "*ability to keep your spirits up,*" adding that he is "*a nice guy, but when it comes down to it he knows how to play hardball.*"

# GENERAL COMMERCIAL

**Clients/Work Highlights:** Middlebury Equity Partners; Independent Wireless One; Amtrak; Burlington Free Press; Rutland Herald; Valley News and The Vermont Country Store.

### Paul, Frank + Collins, A Professional Corporation

**The Firm:** This firm shines as "*perhaps the best medical malpractice firm in Vermont,*" according to sources. Fifteen expert trial attorneys "*cover soup to nuts,*" ranging from complex insurance litigation to medical negligence and products liability cases. They also represent clients in contract and tort disputes. The range and quality of the group's trial experience receives consistent praise, and clients are impressed that lawyers "*do an excellent job of evaluating a case and recommending a course of action.*" A varied caseload includes multimillion-dollar complex litigation for institutional and individual clients, as well as traditional insurance line claims for hospitals and other healthcare providers.

**The Lawyers:** **Crocker Bennett**'s achievements in the medical malpractice arena are widely praised. He is an "*adept and hard-working trial lawyer who delivers excellent results.*" He recently successfully tried two medical negligence cases, one of which was a verdict for the defendant. **John Sartore** is a "*smart and thoughtful lawyer who knows how to capitalize on his broad experience.*" He has an impressive courtroom demeanor and his areas of expertise include commercial and product liability.

**Clients/Work Highlights:** Clients include Fletcher Allen Health Care, Planned Parenthood and Copley Hospital.

### Sheehey Furlong & Behm PC

**The Firm:** This boutique offers four "*very astute lawyers*" who provide litigation and dispute resolution services in civil, administrative and criminal matters. While the team tends to focus on complex litigation, it has seen an increasing amount of healthcare fraud cases over the last few years. Antitrust and patent litigation matters also feature, and sources single out the firm's reputation in white-collar criminal defense work. The team has been defending a doctor in a federal healthcare fraud prosecution and has represented a number of privately and publicly held companies charged by the state with consumer fraud.

**The Lawyers:** **Jeff Behm** is reputed to be a "*top-shelf, tenacious advocate.*" Tough and hard-working, he is best known for representing clients in sophisticated litigation, white-collar trials and business deals. Clients find him *"low-key, competent and effective at whatever he does."*

**Clients/Work Highlights:** Green Mountain Power; Burlington Drug; Shelburne Museum; WCAX; Merchants Bank; Howard Opera House Associates and Bruegger's Enterprises.

## Band 2

### Cleary Shahi & Aicher, PC

**The Firm:** This Rutland boutique houses six PI and insurance defense specialists defending clients in all types of accident, injury, and liability cases. Attorneys offer medical malpractice strength and have a national reputation for defending serious sporting and resort injury claims. Clients agree that the *"diligent"* attorneys respond effectively to their needs.

**The Lawyers:** **David Cleary** is a *"colorful and accomplished lawyer"* with more than three decades of trial experience. Commentators agree that he is entertaining in court and *"unusually eloquent."*

**Clients/Work Highlights:** Dartmouth-Hitchcock Medical Center; Washington County Mental Health Services; Acordia Resort Services; American Skiing; Okemo Mountain Resort and Cumberland Farms.

### Downs Rachlin Martin PLLC

**The Firm:** This full-service firm deploys the largest group of lawyers in the state and has a *"terrific"* reputation for representing corporate interests. Roughly 20 lawyers handle a broad variety of business litigation services in areas including IP, contract disputes, environmental pollution claims and insurance defense. Highlights from the year include representing TransCanada on a matter involving an attempt to force the sale of a hydroelectric dam, and successfully pressing a counterclaim of $300,000 against the plaintiff in a breach of contract claim in the manufacturing industry.

**The Lawyers:** **Bob Rachlin** is a *"brilliant"* and *"very intellectually gifted"* attorney. He recently represented the cotton industry in an appeal against the verdict in a PI claim concerning a girl who got burnt when her t-shirt caught fire. **Marc Heath** is a *"sharp and*

*thoughtful"* litigator who excels in handling complex commercial cases. Clients find him *"receptive to strategic input"* and appreciate his efforts to reach settlement. He is renowned for trademark infringement and antitrust counsel.

**Clients/Work Highlights:** SOPAKCO; Vermont Mutual Insurance; Scott Construction; Home Depot; Country Home Products and Champlain Investment Partners.

### Primmer Piper Eggleston & Cramer PC

**The Firm:** This *"capable and professional"* outfit has spliced Eggleston & Cramer's successful commercial litigation practice with Primmer & Piper's active medical malpractice and insurance defense practice. Following the departure of Scot Kline from Eggleston & Cramer last year, there are three full-time partners engaged in litigation, and the group is looking to expand. On the commercial side, attorneys are largely engaged in matters related to transactions and regulations, as well as creditors' rights and antitrust issues. Sources sum up the offering as *"a niche firm for sophisticated work,"* offering *"smart and well thought-of lawyers."*

**The Lawyers:** **Gary Franklin** has established himself as a *"smart and thorough guy who does his homework and is great to bounce ideas off."* Clients portray him as articulate and studious, and *"able to position himself well without being aggressive."* His varied practice includes IP, banking, commercial real estate and employment disputes. Recent highlights include winning a jury trial on a breach of contract dispute over the sale of a helicopter.

**Clients/Work Highlights:** Mansfield Heliflight; HA Manosh; Corporation; Homebound Mortgage and Country Village Rentals & Real Estate.

### Spink & Miller PLC

**The Firm:** This small, blossoming boutique is *"definitely on the rise,"* agree sources. Four *"very sharp, very focused"* lawyers specialize in complex civil litigation of all kinds, representing clients in commercial and individual matters. The team represents small domestic, national and even Canadian motor carriers in a variety of transportation matters, and is developing a robust mediation and arbitration practice.

**The Lawyers:** The *"academic and hard-working"* **Elizabeth Miller** brings *"raw intellectual horsepower"* to the team, and peers admire her as a *"worthy adversary."* In the course of her varied workload, *"she digs deep into the nitty-gritty of the law."* **James Spink** is an accomplished and practical lawyer whose *"energetic and friendly delivery is attractive to jurors and clients;"* he is also commended for his unimpeachable ethical standards. Focused on transportation, products liability, and professional negligence matters, he regularly serves as a mediator and arbitrator. Sources agree that together Spink and Miller *"make a formidable and scary team."*

**Clients/Work Highlights:** A wide range of businesses and corporate clients, as well as individuals.

### Theriault & Joslin PC

**The Firm:** This Montpelier-based firm has a long and distinguished history in insurance defense work. The *"close-knit"* group of four lawyers (three of which are brothers) enjoys an excellent reputation locally, representing clients in state and federal courts throughout Vermont. The firm's trial practice focuses on civil litigation and emphasizes defense against medical malpractice, products liability, PI and workers' compensation claims. It is also active in a range of real estate and land use matters, and the team offers professional liability advice to its clients.

**The Lawyers:** **Peter Joslin** is a senior defense lawyer, *"a gentleman and a scholar."* He mainly handles medical work and is an experienced mediator.

**Clients/Work Highlights:** Allstate; AIG; Concord Group Insurance; The Hartford; Kaiser Permanente; Lexington Insurance; Medical Mutual Insurance; ProMutual Group; St. Paul Travelers and Western World Insurance Group.

# REAL ESTATE

| Real Estate |
| --- |
| Leading Firms |
| 1 DINSE, KNAPP & MCANDREW PC *Burlington* |
| GRAVEL AND SHEA *Burlington* |
| MURPHY SULLIVAN KRONK *Burlington* |
| 2 DOWNS RACHLIN MARTIN PLLC *Burlington* |
| LANGROCK SPERRY & WOOL, LLP *Burlington* |
| LISMAN, WEBSTER, KIRKPATRICK *Burlington* |
| 3 KENLAN, SCHWIEBERT & FACEY, PC *Rutland* |
| PAUL, FRANK + COLLINS *Burlington* |
| PRIMMER PIPER EGGLESTON *Burlington* |
| SHEMS DUNKIEL KASSEL & SAUNDERS *Burlington* |

| Leading Individuals |
| --- |
| 1 LEBOWITZ Molly *Dinse, Knapp & McAndrew PC* |
| LISMAN Carl *Lisman, Webster, Kirkpatrick* |
| MURPHY Liam *Murphy Sullivan Kronk* |
| RUSHFORD Robert *Gravel and Shea* |
| SCHROEDER William *Downs Rachlin Martin PLLC* |
| 2 CONARD David *Langrock Sperry & Wool, LLP* |
| FARKAS Michelle *Gravel and Shea* |
| HART Austin *Dinse, Knapp & McAndrew PC* |
| 3 FARKAS Jeremy *Murphy Sullivan Kronk* |
| FOLEY Robert *Paul, Frank + Collins* |
| KENLAN Jay *Kenlan, Schwiebert* |
| KNUDSEN Eric *Langrock Sperry & Wool, LLP* |
| KRONK Catherine *Murphy Sullivan Kronk* |
| RILEY Douglas *Lisman, Webster, Kirkpatrick* |
| WHEELWRIGHT Neil *Primmer Piper Eggleston* |

| Real Estate: Zoning/Land Use |
| --- |
| Leading Individuals |
| 1 KENLAN Jay *Kenlan, Schwiebert & Facey, PC* |
| MURPHY Liam *Murphy Sullivan Kronk* |
| 2 HALL Mark *Paul, Frank + Collins* |
| KASSEL John *Shems Dunkiel Kassel* |
| PONSETTO John *Gravel and Shea* |
| REYNES Stephen *Primmer Piper Eggleston* |
| SULLIVAN Brian *Murphy Sullivan Kronk* |

## Band 1

### Dinse, Knapp & McAndrew PC

**The Firm:** Interviewees rate this *"unfailingly thorough and prepared"* group highly. It specializes in representing banks and other lenders in all types of real estate transactions, and offers complementary expertise in local and state land use, zoning and environmental laws. The *"extremely capable and serious"* attorneys serve a loyal client base of developers, owners, financiers and investors.

**The Lawyers:** The *"exceptionally sharp"* **Molly Lebowitz** has *"that great combination of personality and ability to get stuff done and closed,"* according to commentators. Her organizational skills and attention to detail are well known, and sources assert: *"When you've got 20 balls in the air, she won't drop of*

any of them."* Zoning and land use expert **Austin Hart's** practice is envied, replete as it is with *"interesting clients and fascinating transactions."* Clients find him *"prompt and comprehensive."*

**Clients/Work Highlights:** Middlebury College; Pizzagalli Properties; University of Vermont and TD Banknorth.

### Gravel and Shea

**The Firm:** This is a full-service firm in the *"collegial"* style. It offers *"an assortment of truly great people dedicated to client service,"* enthuse sources. While its strength lies in commercial transactional work, the group also advises on matters ranging from the development and disposition of properties to the formation of common interest communities. It recently carried out finance work for a large ski hotel and is active on the Winooski city redevelopment project.

**The Lawyers:** The *"smart and versatile"* **Bob Rushford** offers transactional, land use and development advice. Sources enjoy his sense of humor, and avow: *"You know things will be done right by him."* The *"confident and adroit"* **Michelle Farkas** has a sophisticated practice representing developers and noninstitutional investors in a range of areas. She also handles national leasing for retail clients. **John Ponsetto** is recommended in permitting and land use matters, and is described as *"focused, precise and good at getting things accomplished."*

**Clients/Work Highlights:** The Snyder Group; Sprint; Renaissance Development Corporation; Stewart Title Company and JL Davis Realty.

### Murphy Sullivan Kronk

**The Firm:** This *"remarkable"* boutique is exclusively focused on real estate matters. Founded in 2004 by *"a bunch of deeply experienced lawyers"*, it has carved a reputation in diverse areas of commercial real estate, including transactions, permitting and litigation in development matters. Clients value the group's expertise in land use regulations, zoning, and environmental law, saying: *"They really know their way around the environmental stuff."*

**The Lawyers:** The *"prolific"* **Liam Murphy** is commended as an *"outstanding lawyer."* He handles everything from litigation to transactional work and is considered *"the powerhouse behind the firm."* He represents developers, landowners, and tenants in the course of a varied and busy practice. **Kate Kronk** is *"good at big business deals,"* and has a *"shoot from the hip"* style. **Brian Sullivan** *"really knows his stuff,"* and represents Verizon Wireless as part of a practice that is focused on acquiring land use permits. **Jeremy Farkas'** *"thoughtful approach to problems"* finds favor with sources and propels him into the tables this year. His varied caseload includes real estate transactions, land use counseling and permitting work.

**Clients/Work Highlights:** The firm's clients include the Winooski Community Development Project and Redstone.

## Band 2

### Downs Rachlin Martin PLLC

**The Firm:** This commercial heavyweight has three offices in Vermont and sets *"a gold standard for law firms in a range of areas,"* according to observers. Equipped with 15 attorneys and plentiful resources, the real estate group can focus on complex transactional matters, development and construction contracts. Other areas of interest include leasing and common ownership. The client list is studded with developers, banks, businesses and individuals, which are frequently drawn from outside the state.

**The Lawyers:** Clients prize **Bill Schroeder** as an *"outstanding"* and personable real estate specialist. He boasts an impressive portfolio of national clients whom he represents in complex commercial transactions. Sources observe: *"He stands out as a star, and yet is understated."*

**Clients/Work Highlights:** The team acts for a wide range of clients including banks and financial institutions; developers; contractors and title insurance companies.

### Langrock Sperry & Wool, LLP

**The Firm:** This firm *"does absolutely anything you could imagine,"* according to sources. It worked hard to regroup in the wake of Liam Murphy's departure and recently picked up a number of out-of-state clients. Four attorneys in the Burlington office focus primarily on commercial real estate and residential development financing. The team acted on the lender side for an $8 million refinance and expansion of several gasoline retail stations in the state.

**The Lawyers:** **David Conard** has a healthy transactional and litigation practice. An excellent communicator, he *"takes his work seriously, but doesn't take himself too seriously."* Previously involved in construction litigation counseling, he now works on residential development financing on the lender side. *"Young and smart"* **Eric Knudsen** represents local lenders in commercial real estate matters.

**Clients/Work Highlights:** Chittenden Bank; Merchants Bank; First American Title Insurance; New England Federal Credit Union and TD Banknorth.

### Lisman, Webster, Kirkpatrick & Leckerling, PC

**The Firm:** This 11-strong, *"well-rounded"* firm serves a broad client base of domestic and international businesses, governments, financial institutions and private individuals. The highly regarded real estate practice owes much to Carl Lisman's excellent reputation. It has strong ties with the resort industry and can handle healthy volumes of commercial leases and financings.

**The Lawyers:** **Carl Lisman** is *"dean of the Vermont Bar, period!"* He is expert in common interest communities and, according to interviewees, *"has done more resort development and condominium work than any other lawyer in the state."* Commentators

agree that **Doug Riley**'s profile is on the rise. A transactional lawyer with over 20 years' experience, he is a *"strong technician"* with a varied practice.
Clients/Work Highlights: Local, regional, national and international lenders, mortgage brokers, property managers and developers.

## Band 3

### Kenlan, Schwiebert & Facey, P

**The Firm:** Based in Rutland, this outfit leads the market in representing ski resorts. Seven lawyers offer expertise in complex commercial transactions, from the organization of businesses to financing, permitting and acquisitions. Sources agree: *"They have a lot of good guys over there and deep specialist knowledge."* Recent highlights include representing a major resort client in a joint venture with a developer.
**The Lawyers:** The *"justly famous"* **Jay Kenlan** is credited with trailblazing the ski resort condominiums business with Carl Lisman. He gets involved in the entire scope of transactions and is in his element on the complex financing, land use and zoning side. Peers concur: *"He has an excellent handle on the business side of things."*
Clients/Work Highlights: The firm's clients include American Skiing Company, Killington Ski Area and Mount Snow Ski Area.

### Paul, Frank + Collins, A Professional Corporation

**The Firm:** This real estate practice has been advising on transactional, environmental and land use issues

for decades. The group benefits from a strong litigation background and excels in contested matters. Catherine Kronk's departure to Murphy Sullivan Kronk in 2004 and cofounder Peter Collins' recent semiretirement have impacted on visibility. Nevertheless, the firm still offers a credible practice, particularly where construction matters are concerned, and it remains popular with clients.
**The Lawyers:** **Rob Foley** is a relative newcomer to the group and is *"busily making a name for himself."* His practice focuses on permitting, financing, leasing, disposition and sales. **Mark Hall** is a talented litigator specializing in land use contests. *"He knows his way around the barn,"* agree sources, and was recently involved in the development of 343 houses in South Burlington, including related litigation.
Clients/Work Highlights: Lake Champlain, Retrovest and Champlain College are among the clients.

### Primmer Piper Eggleston & Cramer PC

**The Firm:** The recent merger unites Eggleston & Cramer's specialty in commercial real estate and title work with Primmer & Piper's environment and land use expertise. The attorneys are *"firm and efficient,"* representing lenders, sellers and purchasers in all aspects of real estate transactions from acquisition and finance, through development and leasing. A standout feature of the practice is its extensive title and claims load, which includes title and permit searches and opinions as well as title insurance.
**The Lawyers:** *"Fabulous"* title attorney **Neil Wheelwright** carries out complex title work for clients buying, selling or mortgaging properties, and also

acts for title insurance companies. He *"has the nuts and bolts"* needed for the job, say sources who endorse his thorough and technical approach. **Stephen Raynes'** *"outstanding"* work in land use and development permitting catches the eye of observers. He is popular with clients, who are vocal in their support.
Clients/Work Highlights: Century 21 Jack Associates; Lawyers Title Insurance Corporation; Commonwealth Land Title Insurance; Chicago Title Insurance and First American Corporation.

### Shems Dunkiel Kassel & Saunders PLLC

**The Firm:** This ethically oriented firm is renowned for its niche in environmental, permitting and land use matters. Attorneys engage in regulatory rather than transactional work, and handle large claims for plaintiffs against real estate businesses and developers thought to be harming the environment. The group often represents large environmental groups in permitting and land use battles, but attorneys will act for developers who share the firm's environmentally friendly philosophy. Market observers endorse the firm as *"a leader"* in the permitting and land use arena.
**The Lawyers:** The thoughtful **John Kassel** *"doesn't jump to conclusions and works his way carefully through things."* He has a broad practice but is particularly identified with wind energy work.
Clients/Work Highlights: Businesses; nonprofit corporations; government agencies; cooperatives and individuals.

# Leaders in Vermont

**BEHM, Jeffrey**
Sheehey Furlong & Behm PC, Burlington
802 864 9891
*Recommended in Litigation*

**BENNETT II, Crocker**
Paul, Frank + Collins, A Professional Corporation, Burlington
802 658 2311
*Recommended in Litigation*

**BERGER, Ritchie**
Dinse, Knapp & McAndrew PC, Burlington 802 864 5751
*Recommended in Litigation*

**BOE, Kathleen**
English, Carroll & Ritter PC, Middlebury
802 388 6711
*Recommended in Corporate/Commercial*

**BRIGGS, Heather**
Gravel and Shea, Burlington
802 658 0220
*Recommended in Employment*

**CLEARY, David**
Cleary Shahi & Aicher, P.C., Rutland
802 775 8800
*Recommended in Litigation*

**CONARD, David**
Langrock Sperry & Wool, LLP, Burlington
802 864 0217
*Recommended in Real Estate*

**EGGLESTON, Jon**
Primmer Piper Eggleston & Cramer PC, Burlington 802 864 0880
jeggleston@ecvtlaw.com
*Recommended in Corporate/Commercial*

**ERLY, Peter**
Gravel and Shea, Burlington
802 658 0220
*Recommended in Corporate/Commercial*

**FARKAS, Jeremy**
Murphy Sullivan Kronk, Burlington
802 861 7000
*Recommended in Real Estate*

**FARKAS, Michelle**
Gravel and Shea, Burlington
802 658 0220
*Recommended in Real Estate*

**FOLEY, Robert**
Paul, Frank + Collins, A Professional Corporation, Burlington
802 658 2311
*Recommended in Real Estate*

**FRANKLIN, Gary**
Primmer Piper Eggleston & Cramer PC, Burlington 802 864 0880
*Recommended in Litigation*

**FRYE, B Michael**
Paul, Frank + Collins, A Professional Corporation, Burlington 802 658 2311
*Recommended in Corporate/Commercial*

**GRANT, Elizabeth**
The Grant Law Firm, Montpelier
802 223 0581
*Recommended in Employment*

**HAEFNER, Gail**
Paul, Frank + Collins, A Professional Corporation, Burlington 802 658 2311
*Recommended in Corporate/Commercial*

**HALL, Mark**
Paul, Frank + Collins, A Professional Corporation, Burlington
802 658 2311
*Recommended in Real Estate*

**HART, Austin**
Dinse, Knapp & McAndrew PC, Burlington 802 864 5751
*Recommended in Real Estate*

**HEATH, Marc**
Downs Rachlin Martin PLLC, Burlington
802 863 2375
*Recommended in Litigation*

**HEMLEY, Robert**
Gravel and Shea, Burlington
802 658 0220
*Recommended in Litigation*

**JOSLIN, Peter**
Theriault & Joslin PC, Montpelier
802 223 2381
*Recommended in Litigation*

**KASSEL, John**
Shems Dunkiel Kassel & Saunders
PLLC, Burlington 802 860 1003
*Recommended in Real Estate*

**KENLAN, Jay**
Kenlan, Schwiebert & Facey, P.C.,
Rutland 802 773 3300
*Recommended in Real Estate*

**KNAPP, Spencer**
Dinse, Knapp & McAndrew PC, Burlington
802 864 5751
*Recommended in
Corporate/Commercial*

**KNUDSEN, Eric**
Langrock Sperry & Wool, LLP, Burlington
802 864 0217
*Recommended in Real Estate*

**KRONK, Catherine**
Murphy Sullivan Kronk, Burlington
802 861 7000
*Recommended in Real Estate*

**LEBOWITZ, Molly**
Dinse, Knapp & McAndrew PC, Burlington
802 864 5751
*Recommended in Real Estate*

**LISMAN, Carl**
Lisman, Webster, Kirkpatrick & Leckerling,
P.C., Burlington 802 864 5756
*Recommended in Real Estate*

**MAITLAND, Johan**
Downs Rachlin Martin PLLC, Burlington
802 863 2375
*Recommended in Employment*

**MANITSKY, Andrew**
Gravel and Shea, Burlington
802 658 0220
*Recommended in Litigation*

**MCANDREW, Karen**
Dinse, Knapp & McAndrew PC, Burlington
802 864 5751
*Recommended in Employment,
Litigation*

**MCCONAUGHY, Stewart**
Gravel and Shea, Burlington
802 658 0220
*Recommended in
Corporate/Commercial*

**MCKEARIN, Robert**
Dinse, Knapp & McAndrew PC, Burlington
802 864 5751
*Recommended in Employment*

**MCMAHAN, Jeffrey**
Dinse, Knapp & McAndrew PC, Burlington
802 864 5751
*Recommended in
Corporate/Commercial*

**MILLER, Elizabeth**
Spink & Miller PLC, Burlington
802 864 1100
*Recommended in Litigation*

**MONAHAN JR, John**
Dinse, Knapp & McAndrew PC,
Burlington 802 864 5751
*Recommended in Litigation*

**MONTGOMERY, Margaret**
Gravel and Shea, Burlington
802 658 0220
*Recommended in
Corporate/Commercial*

**MOODY, Thomas**
Downs Rachlin Martin PLLC, Burlington
802 863 2375
*Recommended in
Corporate/Commercial*

**MURPHY, Brian**
Dinse, Knapp & McAndrew PC,
Burlington 802 864 5751
*Recommended in
Corporate/Commercial*

**MURPHY, Liam**
Murphy Sullivan Kronk, Burlington
802 861 7000
*Recommended in Real Estate*

**ODE, Paul**
Downs Rachlin Martin PLLC, Burlington
802 863 2375
*Recommended in
Corporate/Commercial*

**O'NEILL, Robert**
Gravel and Shea, Burlington
802 658 0220
*Recommended in Litigation*

**PONSETTO, John**
Gravel and Shea, Burlington
802 658 0220
*Recommended in Real Estate*

**PORT, Alan**
Paul, Frank + Collins, A Professional
Corporation, Burlington 802 658 2311
*Recommended in
Corporate/Commercial*

**RACHLIN, Robert**
Downs Rachlin Martin PLLC,
Burlington 802 863 2375
*Recommended in Litigation*

**REYNES, Stephen**
Primmer Piper Eggleston & Cramer PC,
Montpelier 802 223 2102
*Recommended in Real Estate*

**RILEY, Douglas**
Lisman, Webster, Kirkpatrick & Leckerling,
P.C.,
Burlington 802 864 5756
*Recommended in Real Estate*

**ROBB, Peter**
Downs Rachlin Martin PLLC, Brattleboro
802 258 3070
*Recommended in Employment*

**RUSHFORD, Robert**
Gravel and Shea, Burlington
802 658 0220
*Recommended in Real Estate*

**SABALIS, Patricia**
Downs Rachlin Martin PLLC, Burlington
802 863 2375
*Recommended in Employment*

**SARTORE, John**
Paul, Frank + Collins, A Professional
Corporation, Burlington 802 658 2311
*Recommended in Litigation*

**SCHROEDER, William**
Downs Rachlin Martin PLLC, Burlington
802 863 2375
*Recommended in Real Estate*

**SPINK, James**
Spink & Miller PLC, Burlington
802 864 1100
*Recommended in Litigation*

**SULLIVAN, Brian**
Murphy Sullivan Kronk, Burlington
802 861 7000
*Recommended in Real Estate*

**WHEELWRIGHT, Neil**
Primmer Piper Eggleston & Cramer PC,
Burlington 802 864 0880
*Recommended in Real Estate*

# PRIMMER PIPER EGGLESTON & CRAMER PC

## THE FIRM

**Chairman:** William B Piper
**President:** Anne E Cramer
**Number of shareholders:** 15
**Number of other lawyers:** 14

**FIRM OVERVIEW:** Combining Primmer & Piper, founded in 1982, with Eggleston & Cramer, founded in 1983, brings together complimentary business law practices resulting in more comprehensive services with added depth and experience. The new firm becomes the second largest firm in the State with offices in Burlington, Montpelier, and St. Johnsbury. With greater resources, personnel and capacity, Primmer Piper Eggleston & Cramer is well positioned to provide its clients with the level of services required in an increasingly complex business environment throughout Vermont as well as the broader New England market. Primmer Piper Eggleston & Cramer continues a long standing commitment to value, responsiveness and integrity as the foundations for providing the highest level of legal services and achieving excellent results for its clients.

## MAIN AREAS OF PRACTICE:

**Accounting Firms:** Primer Piper Eggleston & Cramer represents and advises accounting firms in the areas of loss prevention, malpractice defense and provides consultation on a wide array of matters.

**Bankruptcy:** Primmer Piper Eggleston & Cramer has an active practice in bankruptcy courts in both Vermont and upstate New York, representing both debtors and creditors in Chapter 7, 11, 12 and 13 cases. The firm has extensive experience in structuring complicated workouts and handling complex Chapter 11 cases on behalf of creditors.

**Business Entity/Commercial Law:** Primmer Piper Eggleston & Cramer provides a wide range of legal services to established businesses and new ventures. These services include representation and advice in connection with Business Purchase or Sale Planning, Corporate Planning, Nonprofit Corporation Planning, Securities Law and Antitrust/Trade Regulation.

**Captive Insurance:** Vermont is the preeminent domestic domicile for captive insurers and Primmer Piper Eggleston & Cramer PC is the leading firm representing Vermont captives. The firm represents more than 150 captives, including single parent, industrial insured, association, and sponsored captives, risk retention groups and reciprocals. The firm's Captive Team represents clients during planning and organization, on routine regulatory and corporate matters, as well as on extraordinary legal issues such as major restructurings, mergers and various transactions.

**Environmental & Land Use:** Primmer Piper Eggleston & Cramer represents clients before District Commissions, the Environmental Court and the Vermont Supreme Court, as well as before local land use boards and the Agency of Natural Resources. The firm also represents business clients regarding compliance issues and provides practical and efficient legal representation through the Vermont permitting process.

**Financial Services/Banking:** Primmer Piper Eggleston & Cramer represents both lenders and borrowers in commercial and retail finance matters which range from personal to small business loans or international multi-million dollar transactions. These services include loan transactions, loan restructuring/collections, representing business borrowers, cross border transactions, public finance, general banking, retail banking, acquisition and sale of bank assets, compliance and operations.

**Government Relations:** Primmer Piper Eggleston & Cramer provides a broad range of government relations and legislative services, including lobbying either in support of or against legislation, monitoring the status of legislative efforts, including attendance at hearings and bill-tracking services. The firm also serves as regulatory counsel for many of its government relations clients on a year-round basis.

**Healthcare Law:** Healthcare is a highly regulated industry. Primmer Piper Eggleston & Cramer provides counsel to the Vermont Association of Hospitals and Health Systems and represents a broad array of clients on regulatory, corpo-

## HEAD OFFICE

**VERMONT**
150 South Champlain Street, PO Box 1489, **Burlington**, VT 05402-1489
**Tel:** 802 864 00880   **Fax:** 802 864 0328

## BRANCH OFFICES

**VERMONT**
100 East State Street, PO Box 1309, **Montpelier**, VT 05601-1309
**Tel:** 802 223 2102   **Fax:** 802 223 2628

421 Summer Street, PO Box 159, **St Johnsbury**, VT 05819-0159
**Tel:** 802 748 5061   **Fax:** 802 748 3976

## CONTACTS

| | |
|---|---|
| **Accounting** | Gary H Barnes |
| **Bankruptcy** | Douglas J Wolinsky |
| **Business Entity** | Jon R Eggleston |
| **Captive Insurance** | Jeffrey P Johnson |
| **Environmental** | Stephen A Reynes |
| **Financial Services/Banking** | Denise J Deschenes |
| **Government Relations** | Jeffrey P Johnson |
| **Healthcare Law** | Anne E Cramer |
| **Immigration** | Gary H Barnes |
| **Insurance** | Gary F Karnedy |
| **Intellectual Property** | Victoria J Brown |
| **Litigation** | Gary L Franklin |
| **Mediation & Arbitration** | Gary H Barnes |
| **Public Utilities/Regulatory** | William B Piper |
| **Real Estate** | Neil Wheelwright |
| **Taxation/Estate Planning** | Jon R Eggleston |

rate issues, compliance issues and HIPAA compliance.

**Insurance:** Primmer Piper Eggleston & Cramer's firm represents insurance companies and licensed insurance professionals in connection with their regulatory compliance issues and concerns.

**Litigation:** Primmer Piper Eggleston & Cramer's trial attorneys practice in both state and federal courts, at trial and appeal levels and provide representation with respect to a wide range of commercial litigation issues, in areas including contract and sale, criminal, employment, environmental, insurance, foreclosure, lender liability, bankruptcy adversarial proceedings, franchises, consumer fraud, probate, trademark and copyright, antitrust, accountant liability, and construction litigation.

**Mediation & Arbitration:** Primmer Piper Eggleston & Cramer accepts mediation and arbitration appointments throughout the United States. Members of the firm are appointed as court-appointed mediators in both federal and state courts or may serve as arbitrators on a wide variety of disputes.

**Real Estate:** Primmer Piper Eggleston & Cramer represents lenders, sellers and purchasers with respect to all aspects of real estate transactions from acquisition and finance, though development and leasing, including full title searches.

**Utilities/Regulatory Assistance:** Primmer Piper Eggleston & Cramer have decades of experience in this industry and its legal and regulatory needs. The firm provides a range of services ranging from permit assistance, litigation before administrative boards and courts and resolution of enforcement action.

**Estate Planning & Taxation:** Primmer Piper Eggleston & Cramer represent clients in a wide array of tax matters, tax audits, administrative appeals and tax litigation before federal and state agencies and courts. Its attorneys are admitted to practice before the US Tax Court and the US Claims Court and are familiar with collection matters. The firm also advises on estate planning, probate, state and local taxation, exempt organizations and unincorporated entities.

**CLIENTS:** The firm represents a wide range of local and national businesses, municipalities and private clients.

## How lawyers are ranked

Every year we carry out thousands of in-depth interviews with clients and lawyers in order to assess the reputations and expertise of business lawyers across the USA. Chambers rankings and editorial are referred to extensively by General Counsel and other purchasers of legal services who look to our recommendations when choosing their lawyers.

# CONSTRUCTION

### Construction

#### Leading Firms

1. **WATT, TIEDER, HOFFAR & FITZGERALD** McLean
2. **MOORE & LEE LLP** McLean
   **SMITH PACHTER MCWHORTER PLC** Vienna
   **WICKWIRE GAVIN P.C.** Vienna
3. **HOLLAND & KNIGHT LLP** McLean
   **KRAFTSON CAUDLE LLC** McLean
   **VENABLE LLP** Vienna
   **WRIGHT ROBINSON OSTHIMER** Richmond

#### Leading Individuals

**Senior Statesmen**

**WICKWIRE** Jon *Wickwire Gavin P.C.*
**WRIGHT** Murray *Wright Robinson Osthimer*

1. **BAKER** Lewis *Watt, Tieder, Hoffar*
   **FITZGERALD** Robert *Watt, Tieder, Hoffar*
   **HOFFAR** Julian *Watt, Tieder, Hoffar*
   **LALLE** Wayne *Venable LLP*
   **LOULAKIS** Michael *Wickwire Gavin P.C.*
   **MCWHORTER** Val *Smith Pachter McWhorter PLC*
   **TIEDER** John *Watt, Tieder, Hoffar*
   **WATT** Robert *Watt, Tieder, Hoffar*
2. **ALLEN** Randall *Smith Pachter McWhorter PLC*
   **BROWNELL** Thomas *Holland & Knight LLP*
   **COX** Robert *Watt, Tieder, Hoffar*
   **KRAFTSON** Daniel *Kraftson Caudle LLC*
   **LEE** Charlie *Moore & Lee LLP*
   **MOORE** Robert *Moore & Lee LLP*
   **SGARLATA** Mark *Watt, Tieder, Hoffar*
   **VARELA** Paul *Watt, Tieder, Hoffar*

## Band 1

### Watt, Tieder, Hoffar & Fitzgerald LLP
See firm details p.1990

**The Firm:** Perceived to be one of the highest-quality construction specialists in the industry, clients choose this firm because they *"want to hire the best."* The imposing boutique also gains respect from its competitors, with sources asserting: *"The name alone tends to get people's attention, and has stopped many a lawsuit by itself."* Watt Tieder lawyers distinguish themselves by their *"energy and drive,"* as well as *"keen business judgment – they really know the nuts and bolts of the industry."* The firm handles the entire spectrum of domestic and international construction matters, government contracting and surety transactions and disputes. Its work characteristically relates to heavy industry, infrastructure and homeland security projects, although the firm is currently emerging as a key player in sports stadium projects, and has recently represented Mitsubishi in the mediation and settlement of the Milwaukee Brewers' Miller Park dispute.

**The Lawyers:** *"Cool, calm and collected"* **Lewis Baker** (see p.1981) is celebrated among clients as *"a guy with an air of experience and wisdom,"* as well as *"one of the most knowledgeable construction dispute authorities around."* This *"phenomenal attorney,"* a former civil engineer, impresses clients with his readiness to *"roll up his sleeves and really get involved."* **Robert Fitzgerald**'s (see p.1983) heavy construction contracting and litigation/alternative dispute resolution practice has earned him a prominent US and international reputation in the infrastructure field. Recent matters include the representation of various private and public entities on subway and bridge projects. **Julian Hoffar** (see p.1984) has earned a reputation as one of the most respected arbitrators/mediators in the business, with sources recognizing him as *"a real charmer with a winning personality."* **John Tieder** (see p.1987) is *"an icon in construction litigation,"* having a wealth of experience trying construction cases and advocating before international arbitration committees. Lauded by peers as a power industry expert, this skilled trial lawyer and negotiator is also recognized for his outstanding track record for major clients. **Robert Watt** (see p.1987). During a career spanning more than three decades, and now also taking the role of managing partner, Watt has built an outstanding reputation as one of the top surety experts in the USA. Sources assert that the commanding influence of this *"formidable lawyer"* is one of the reasons why Watt Tieder is shortlisted whenever a major construction project falters. **Robert Cox** (see p.1981) is known as a leader for his work on construction and surety matters, concentrating principally on public projects including the security enhancement of existing buildings. An immense level of technical know-how, along with the ability to *"inject business sense into legal issues,"* are his core strengths. Contract and dispute resolution work on heavy construction projects all over the USA has firmly established **Paul Varela** (see p.1987) as a big player. *"Personality and high intellect"* as well as *"tough and tenacious"* representation define this lawyer in the eyes of clients. The final spot in an impressive lineup is taken by the confident and effective **Mark Sgarlata** (see p.1986), who is recognized as a skilled negotiator.

**Clients/Work Highlights:** ALSTOM; Kiewit; Raytheon; Washington Group International and Zurich North America.

## Band 2

### Moore & Lee LLP

**The Firm:** This emergent McLean-based practice, established in 1998, focuses on government contracts and all facets of surety and construction law. Competitors describe Moore & Lee as small but excellent, while clients appreciate the *"great performance and value for money"* that helps it punch above its weight on complex regional and national matters. The firm has recently represented heavy industry general contractors on default termination cases for power and wastewater treatment plants all over the USA. It has also been active on office and condominium developments within Virginia.

**The Lawyers:** Clients hire **Charlie Lee** for various reasons – his *"creativity and planning,"* his commercial awareness and his tireless work ethic. This *"great communicator"* is a pleasure to work with and always *"on the money"* both inside and outside the courtroom. **Robert Moore** is *"an excellent lawyer and an excellent businessman."* Clients value his diligent and thorough advice and are confident that he is *"truly looking out for our needs."* Fellow attorneys agree, citing his *"passionate and vigorous representation"* of clients as a key attribute.

**Clients/Work Highlights:** Babcock & Wilcox; Bell Corporation; Clark Construction Group; Fru-Con; McNeil Technologies and St. Paul Travelers.

### Smith Pachter McWhorter PLC

**The Firm:** This Vienna-based boutique construction and public procurement firm combines a strong reputation in the Virginia community with visibility at national level. The cornerstone of the practice is the representation of clients in claims against the federal government in relation to large complex infrastructure projects such as dams, tunnels and bridges.

**The Lawyers:** In his 30 years in the areas of construction and government contracts law, **Randall Allen** has become known as an "*excellent lawyer who is respected and trusted.*" He has recently been involved in the negotiation of design-build projects on behalf of municipalities all over Virginia. Sources identified **Val McWhorter** as one of the leaders practicing in Virginia today. With a wealth of experience representing contractors in claims against government and commercial bodies, he has built a strong profile in nationwide civil infrastructure projects.

**Clients/Work Highlights:** Fru-Con; Soletanche; Sundt Construction and Washington Group International.

## Wickwire Gavin P.C.

**The Firm:** Clients commended these "*tactical and strategic*" lawyers, who offer expertise in all elements of the construction process from start to finish. Particular appreciation was shown for the cost-saving emphasis on arbitration and other forms of alternative dispute resolution. Although this big player is chiefly known for its work on projects in the power, petrochemical and refining industries, it also has a growing niche in public sector design-build projects. The firm has recently advised the Virginia Department of Transportation on the drafting and negotiation of sophisticated procurement plans for the $60 million Fairfax County Parkway design-build project.

**The Lawyers:** **Jon Wickwire** (see p.1987) exerts a weighty influence in the construction industry and, as the chairman of the Project Management Institute College of Scheduling, he is widely recognized for his tireless efforts to advance best practice standards. **Michael Loulakis** (see p.1984) "*achieves credibility through his thorough preparation and analysis.*" An

extremely bright lawyer, he has the "*necessary wattage*" to take on any matter. Clients noted his ability to orchestrate agreement between parties, while still knowing how to "*hit the opponent's buttons,*" if necessary.

**Clients/Work Highlights:** AEP; BP; El Paso; Nevada Power and Tractebel.

## Band 3

## Holland & Knight LLP

See firm details p.1534

**The Firm:** With a US-wide footprint, as well as a significant overseas presence, this excellent firm is working on some of the largest construction projects around. An interdisciplinary approach and a focus on industry knowledge provide clients with comprehensive construction services in the areas of public and private contract negotiation and drafting, dispute resolution and project finance.

**The Lawyers:** **Thomas Brownell** (see p.1980) is a member of the firm's mid-Atlantic litigation group and is described by sources as "*a bright, intelligent man and a brilliant lawyer.*" He has recently acted for a leading condominium developer and a custom home builder, as well as on disputes arising from the refurbishment of a major hotel.

## Kraftson Caudle LLC

**The Firm:** This construction boutique is known for its litigation and arbitration expertise relating to complex public and private contracts. Competitors were envious of its client base as well as its high-quality work, including the recent representation of a global engineering and construction company in relation to a $250 million contract for a new Major League Baseball stadium.

**The Lawyers:** **Dan Kraftson**, a "*formidable, impressive and highly effective*" lawyer, is appreciated for his "*honest and trustworthy nature – when he says something, you can really put it in the bank.*" He has a great

depth of experience in drafting and negotiating construction claims and maintains a high visibility in the industry.

## Venable LLP

**The Firm:** The great "*depth and breadth of expertise*" found in the Vienna team of this regional heavyweight inspires "*complete confidence*" from owner, developer, public and private contractor and lender clients. This firm is described by competitors as a "*big mover in the area*" and is known for its quality coverage and real understanding of the construction industry. The firm has recently strengthened its Metropolitan DC lineup with the appointment of a five-strong team of construction specialists, in speedy response to the departure of David Lane.

**The Lawyers:** With his "*focus on the business end game,*" clients believe **Wayne Lalle** is "*always looking for timely solutions.*" This "*exceptional*" attorney brings his "*encyclopedic knowledge of the law and the industry*" to bear in representing clients to the maximum.

## Wright Robinson Osthimer & Tatum

**The Firm:** This highly respected firm with its five-office, coast-to-coast presence is a renowned leader in the US-wide construction market. Although categorized by a broad counseling and dispute resolution practice, the Richmond construction team is noted for its niche expertise in the representation of architects, designers, engineers and their professional liability insurers in contract, tort and alleged design deficiency matters.

**The Lawyers:** Firm founder and chief executive officer **Murray Wright** is a celebrated player within the industry. As "*a smart lawyer who has built up a great practice*" built over a distinguished 30-year career, he has earned a commanding reputation. This widely published expert is well known for his work on some of the most significant construction disputes in the mid-Atlantic region.

# CORPORATE/M&A

# NORTHERN VIRGINIA

| Corporate/M&A: Northern Virginia |
|---|
| Leading Firms |
| 1 HOGAN & HARTSON LLP *McLean* |
| 2 COOLEY GODWARD LLP *Reston* |
| MORRISON & FOERSTER LLP *McLean* |
| PILLSBURY WINTHROP SHAW PITTMAN *McLean* |
| WILMERHALE *McLean* |
| 3 DLA PIPER RUDNICK GRAY CARY US LLP *Reston* |
| VENABLE LLP *Vienna* |

## Band 1

## Hogan & Hartson LLP

See firm details p.568

**The Firm:** Since opening in 1984, the "*prestigious*" McLean branch of this international firm has estab-

lished itself as a powerhouse in the vibrant Northern Virginia marketplace. The lawyers here were highly praised by clients for "*never missing a trick,*" and earned plaudits for the "*outstanding*" quality of their work. Indeed, some clients indicated a preference for this group over New York attorneys, telling researchers that a "*leaner, meaner and fresher*" service is provided "*at a fraction of the cost.*" The 20-strong team handles a diverse range of corporate matters, including M&A, capital markets, securities and private equity. Whether utilizing the worldwide resources of Hogan & Hartson's 23-office network in major cross-border transactional work, or supporting emerging businesses from initial financing and startup, this group possesses the skills and know-how to deliver great results for clients.

**The Lawyers:** "*Amazing*" **Richard Becker** (see p.1980) impresses clients with his "*perfect marriage of*

*detailed and big-picture viewpoints*" and his ability to "*get the deal to the finish line.*" His corporate finance and M&A practice is conducted alongside a variety of commercial transactions. **Richard Horan** (see p.1983), "*one of the most charming guys around,*" is admired by clients for his "*cool, calm and collected*" handling of public and private company M&A transactions. He is particularly strong in broadcasting and the communications sector, where he is prized for his FCC regulatory know-how. Clients view **Brian Lynch** (see p.1984) as "*really special*" with broad and "*phenomenal*" skills in M&A, capital markets, securities and corporate governance. He recently represented Wal-Mart Stores and Wal-Mart International in relation to its joint venture with CARHCO, the largest retailer in Central America. Highly regarded **Richard Parrino** (see p.1985) is recognized as "*a smart lawyer and a tough customer.*" His practice

| Corporate/M&A: Northern Virginia |
| --- |
| Leading Individuals |
| **Senior Statesman** |
| **LEWIS** Jack *Morrison & Foerster LLP* |
| [1] **BECKER** Richard *Hogan & Hartson LLP* |
| **CHASON** Craig *Pillsbury Winthrop* |
| **CONROY** Joseph *Cooley Godward LLP* |
| **HORAN** Richard *Hogan & Hartson LLP* |
| **LINCOLN** Michael *Cooley Godward LLP* |
| **SYLVESTER** David *WilmerHale* |
| [2] **FRANCE** Thomas *Venable LLP* |
| **KNOX** Thomas *Morrison & Foerster LLP* |
| **LYNCH** Brian *Hogan & Hartson LLP* |
| **MELTZER** Steven *Pillsbury Winthrop* |
| **PARRINO** Richard *Hogan & Hartson LLP* |
| **YANOWITCH** Lawrence *Morrison & Foerster LLP* |

covers corporate transactions and securities regulatory matters, and he recently represented ITC^Delta-Com in a $240 million secured debt refinancing and restructuring.

**Clients/Work Highlights:** Clients typically come from the heavily regulated telecom, healthcare and pharmaceutical industries and include DIRECTV; King Pharmaceuticals; Primus Telecommunications; Titan and Trex Company.

## Band 2

### Cooley Godward LLP

**The Firm:** The Reston office of this national firm is recognized as a "*leading*" corporate team, at its best when servicing the fast-moving technology sector. Here it represents Fortune 500 companies, entrepreneurs and innovators, research institutions, venture capitalists and other financiers. This "*talented and sophisticated*" group is commended for its flexibility and track record of supporting clients during every phase of the business cycle, from the initial financing and startup of emerging companies, through to M&A deals and stock market offerings.

**The Lawyers:** The "*real deal*," **Joseph Conroy** represents clients in the life sciences, computer software and telecom industries on a wide range of corporate and finance transactions, and IP and technology procurement and transfer. Cofounder of the Reston office, **Michael Lincoln** works on venture capital, public and private offerings, M&A and IP. He has "*a big following*" among startups and high-growth technology companies, and is considered to be a real expert in venture capital.

**Clients/Work Highlights:** Blackboard; The Carlyle Group; Columbia Capital; iDirect Technologies; GTSI; MCI; mindSHIFT Technologies; Prestwick Pharmaceuticals and Updata Venture.

### Morrison & Foerster LLP

See firm details p.335

**The Firm:** The Northern Virginia corporate group of this global force is well known for its "*high-quality*" work in private equity, venture capital and emerging company matters, capital markets, and M&A and public company transactions. Clients know they are hiring "*the A-team*" when they choose these "*cerebral but business-oriented*" lawyers. The arrival of the highly regarded ex-Shaw Pittman corporate and technology group has bolstered the overall strength of the practice. For larger matters, or those with a multijurisdictional element, clients take advantage of the wealth of resources available through the firm's worldwide network. The McLean team recently represented the computer network security company Sourcefire in its planned acquisition by Check Point Software Technologies.

**The Lawyers:** **Jack Lewis** (see p.1983) has long been recognized as an "*excellent businessman and one of the best deal guys around*." Clients say he does a "*phenomenal*" job in nurturing technology ventures from inception to flotation "*always with an eye on protecting and forwarding the business.*" Clients also admire the way he really "*rolls his sleeves up and gets involved.*" "*Tremendous attorney*" **Thomas Knox** (see p.1983) is co-head of the emerging companies/venture capital group. This leader in the field shows "*wonderful*" insight into client organization and the industry, enabling him to deliver well-balanced business and legal advice. Cochair of the firm's worldwide M&A practice, **Lawrence Yanowitch** (see p.1988) has a very strong legal mind and great knowledge of the commercial marketplace. Known as a great strategist, he "*sees many moves ahead, like a chess master,*" and is "*flexible and nimble*" in addressing business challenges to ensure an M&A plan comes together successfully.

**Clients/Work Highlights:** Acterna; Essex Corporation; SI International; Telarix and webMethods.

### Pillsbury Winthrop Shaw Pittman LLP

See firm details p.1550

**The Firm:** The McLean corporate and securities practice of this national and international firm has a strong Northern Virginia presence as a result of the deep pool of expertise provided by its lawyers. Some market sources were reserved in their assessment of the firm's 2005 merger, preferring to wait and "*see if the chemistry works;*" however, others were sure it was "*a good move that will result in a better, stronger whole.*" It also remains to be seen how the transfer of Jack Lewis and his team to McLean rivals Morrison Foerster will affect the overall character of this corporate practice. The US-wide footprint and international reach of this 16-office firm provides a platform from which approximately 225 corporate and securities lawyers can deliver a complete legal service to clients of all sizes, from startups to publicly traded companies. The firm recently represented Touchstone Consulting Group in its acquisition by SRA International, as well as ObjectVideo in its $8 million Series D Financing.

**The Lawyers:** **Craig Chason**'s (see p.1981) very active practice covers M&A, venture capital financing and securities offerings. He represents clients at various stages of maturity across a variety of industries, and is especially skilled in the representation of emerging hi-tech companies and government IT contractors. "*Top man and great lawyer*" **Steven Meltzer** (see p.1984) is renowned for his work with hi-tech clients. He too is involved in government contracting, commonly in relation to defense and homeland security.

**Clients/Work Highlights:** Applied Bioscience; Dimensions International; Legg Mason Wood Walker; Macquarie Securities; NCI Information Systems; ObjectVideo; Stargazer Foundation and Systems Net Computer Service.

### WilmerHale

See firm details p.580

**The Firm:** The "*formidable*" Northern Virginia corporate practice is comprised of "*talented*" lawyers, able to handle sophisticated and complex deals. The group is famed for its venture capital, private equity, M&A, strategic alliance and corporate governance work for public and private technology and life sciences companies. Whether working with startups or publicly traded corporations, it is known to always "*look out for the clients' interests and find the right solutions.*"

**The Lawyers:** Many commentators select **David Sylvester** for their "*dream team*" of Northern Virginia corporate lawyers. He chiefly represents technology companies in venture capital, M&A, securities, and IP and technology licensing. Peers suggest his reputation rests in large part on the fact that "*he is easy to deal with, and clients love him.*"

**Clients/Work Highlights:** The technology and life sciences sectors feature heavily on a client list that includes NetSec; Network Alliance; TGS Soft and Valhalla Partners.

## Band 3

### DLA Piper Rudnick Gray Cary US LLP

See firm details p.870

**The Firm:** The corporate and finance team in Reston has an established name in corporate and securities, venture capital and emerging companies work. When serving clients with far-reaching or multinational interests, the lawyers are able to unite with colleagues from any number of the firm's 56 other US and overseas offices. As might be expected from an outfit located in the thriving Northern Virginia market, hi-tech clients, including Internet, e-commerce, telecom, IT and biotech ventures, are responsible for a significant proportion of a packed portfolio of work. The group recently represented VeriSign in its acquisition of the INS software division of transaction software company Lightbridge, a deal worth approximately $20 million.

**The Lawyers:** The makeup of this team has altered somewhat in recent times: most notably, "*excellent*" Nancy Spangler and Edwin 'Ned' Martin crossed the Atlantic to reinforce the corporate and finance capability of the firm's London office. Jay Finkelstein remains in Reston as head of the Virginia corporate group, supported by young partners Jeffrey Lehrer and Geoffrey Willard.

**Clients/Work Highlights:** Top clients include

Carlyle Venture Partners; Cendant; Eschelon; PEC; Space Vest III and VeriSign.

## Venable LLP

**The Firm:** The corporate finance and securities practice group at this impressive, full-service firm is recognized as being among the best in Northern Virginia. The compact team is especially good in its delivery of streamlined and cost-efficient corporate advice to small and midmarket businesses; however, clients of all sizes are ably served. This firm is rightly

regarded as something of a one-stop shop, and the corporate lawyers here are often found to be working alongside competitors from the other firms ranked in the Virginia tables, as well as lawyers in other offices up and down Venable's mid-Atlantic network. The team has experience in the representation of national and international clients operating within industries such as hi-tech, life sciences and financial services. It recently assisted an Australian pharmaceutical company with its initial public offering in the USA.

**The Lawyers: Thomas France**'s Recent work includes the representation of the global information security company SafeNet in its $20 million acquisition of MediaSentry, a provider of antipiracy and business management services for the entertainment industry.

**Clients/Work Highlights:** This group works with businesses, nonprofit organizations and individuals throughout the world. Notable clients include Optelecom; Ferris Baker Watt; Dynex Capital and LifeMinders.com.

# CORPORATE/M&A

# SOUTHERN VIRGINIA

### Corporate/M&A: Southern Virginia
#### Leading Firms

| | |
|---|---|
| 1 | **HUNTON & WILLIAMS LLP** Richmond |
| | **MCGUIREWOODS LLP** Richmond |
| 2 | **TROUTMAN SANDERS LLP** Richmond |
| | **WILLIAMS MULLEN** Richmond |
| 3 | **KAUFMAN & CANOLES** Norfolk |
| | **LECLAIR RYAN** Richmond |
| | **WILLCOX & SAVAGE** Norfolk |

#### Leading Individuals

##### Senior Statesmen

| | |
|---|---|
| | **BURRUS** Robert *McGuireWoods LLP* |
| | **GOOLSBY** Allen *Hunton & Williams LLP* |
| | **MOORE** Thurston *Hunton & Williams LLP* |
| 1 | **BUCKLEY** Kevin *Hunton & Williams LLP* |
| | **CUTCHINS IV** Clifford *McGuireWoods LLP* |
| | **JOHNSTON** Jay *Troutman Sanders LLP* |
| 2 | **FRANTZ** Thomas *Williams Mullen* |
| | **GRANDIS** Leslie *McGuireWoods LLP* |
| | **LECLAIR** Gary *LeClair Ryan* |
| | **MASTRACCO** Vincent *Kaufman & Canoles* |
| | **SMITH** Julious *Williams Mullen* |
| | **VAUGHAN III** C Porter *Hunton & Williams LLP* |
| 3 | **INGLIMA** Thomas *Willcox & Savage* |
| | **MCKEE** T Braxton *Kaufman & Canoles* |
| | **MOORE** Justin *Hunton & Williams LLP* |
| | **OLD JR** William *Williams Mullen* |
| | **THOMPSON** Gary *Hunton & Williams LLP* |
| | **WHEATON** James *Troutman Sanders LLP* |
| | **WRIGHT** David *Hunton & Williams LLP* |

## Hunton & Williams LLP

See firm details p.1989

**The Firm:** This full-service heavyweight is roundly praised as an outstanding player in the Virginia corporate market. Clients have come to rely on these "*smart, proactive and top-quality*" lawyers, safe in the knowledge that they will "*always deliver the goods.*" Operating from three cities in the state and multiple offices throughout the USA, Europe and Asia, this "*wonderful*" team manages to measure up to the extensive and diverse requirements of clients rang-

ing from emerging ventures to major international corporations. The firm offers specific industry knowledge and a wealth of technical resources, which together combine into a truly bespoke client service.

**The Lawyers:** "*Corporate guru*" **Allen Goolsby** (see p.1982) is clearly a "*valuable asset*" to his clients. This "*key man*" advises the executive directors of various public and private organizations on corporate governance and strategic issues, and he is still "*the first person to call*" for M&A transactions, securities and financing. Clients appreciate that they are receiving a complete service from a lawyer who knows "*the letter of the law as well as the nature of our business and the industry.*" As managing partner for the past 15 years, **Thurston Moore** (see p.1984) has overseen the development of a firm that has grown into a dominant force in the state. His strengths lie in corporate finance and corporate governance, venture capital, REITs and partnership law. Commentators place "*outstanding*" **Kevin Buckley** (see p.1980) at the cutting edge of asset and mortgage-backed securitizations and structured finance. He has a deep understanding of the law and the market, as well as "*a personal touch that really makes him part of the client's team.*" Buckley represents several major Wall Street banks, as underwriters of mortgage-backed securities offerings by REITs. "*Star of the show,*" **Porter Vaughan** (see p.1987) "*ticks all the right boxes*" with his work in M&A, corporate finance, securities regulation, and Sarbanes-Oxley and corporate governance advice. This "*excellent*" attorney impresses with shrewd strategic advice, great negotiating skills and "*personality in abundance.*" Another clients' favorite, **Justin Moore** (see p.1984) is famed for his wealth of transactional experience and his "*sharp*" legal mind, commercial awareness and well-developed people skills. He covers private equity, venture capital, corporate finance, securities regulation and corporate governance. Clients view **Gary Thompson** (see p.1987) as "*right up there with the top New York City deal lawyers.*" Over the years, Thompson has had notable success in fending off hostile takeovers. **David Wright**'s (see p.1988) REIT practice is considered to be among the best in the USA. He is also sought after for corporate finance, securities offerings and M&A deals.

**Clients/Work Highlights:** Bank of America;

Barclays; Department of Veterans Affairs; Fieldstone Investment; Friedman Billings Ramsey; Genworth; Owens & Minor; Progress Energy; Smithfield Foods and Wells Fargo.

## McGuireWoods LLP

**The Firm:** This firm houses "*clearly one of the leading corporate practices in the region.*" Peers were envious of the "*good work and great clients*" of this 170-year-old firm with 15 offices worldwide. The Virginia corporate services team, operating out of four offices in the state, focuses on corporate finance, technology and IP, venture capital, energy and utilities, and government relations. Clients range from small and midmarket businesses to multinational public corporations. Newer ventures are supported throughout the full business lifecycle: Corporate clients confirm that they benefit from the "*mass of resources,*" both human and technical, offered across the different practice areas at this full-service firm.

**The Lawyers:** Firm chairman **Robert Burrus** is the "*driving force and figurehead*" of the practice. He is considered to be a major advantage in any boardroom, where he counsels clients on corporate governance and fiduciary duties. Although heavily involved in the running of the firm, Burrus is still actively involved in overseeing M&A transactions. Market commentators associate "*wonderful fellow*" **Clifford Cutchins** with some of the firm's top clients. He brings "*great business judgment*" to his counseling practice, in which he advises boards of directors on corporate governance and fiduciary duties. M&A is another of his strengths, as evidenced by his representation of both buyers and sellers in major transactions in the metals, transportation and distribution industries. **Leslie Grandis**' recent work has focused on the structuring, financing, negotiation and execution of transactions in the buoyant energy and natural resources sectors.

**Clients/Work Highlights:** Circuit City; CSX; Dominion; Lockheed Martin and Peoples Energy.

## Troutman Sanders LLP

**The Firm:** The Virginia corporate and securities group attached to this Atlanta-headquartered firm is viewed as an evolving practice that is "*going places.*" Lawyers here represent national and international businesses varying in size and nature from small closely held companies to large publicly traded conglomerates. The "*excellent, communicative and responsive*" attorneys are considered to be "*a cut above*" most practitioners in the M&A, corporate governance and securities regulation fields. Although certainly a big player within the state, the firm has a sweeping eastern US presence, as well as offices in Europe and Asia.

**The Lawyers:** **Jay Johnston** provides "*thoughtful and far-sighted*" advice to public and privately held businesses on, among other issues, M&A and securities offerings. He also counsels boards of directors on corporate governance regulations and duties; clients include a number of securities issuers and underwriters, banks and bank holding companies. Clients can count on **James Wheaton** to "*understand our business dynamics and goals, and successfully navigate a transaction through to completion.*" He recently represented an NYSE-traded company in its recapitalization of preferred stock.

## Williams Mullen

**The Firm:** This firm's corporate finance and securities group, spread across eight regional offices and a London outpost, has recognized skills in the areas of debt and equity securities, IPOs, mortgage and asset-backed securitizations and venture capital financings. An impressive track record in M&A, asset disposition and corporate restructuring is also evident. Clients were impressed by the industry insight of the firm's lawyers, along with the delivery of "*commercial solutions that achieve the best result for the business.*"

**The Lawyers:** **Thomas Frantz**' corporate and tax practice deals with M&A and joint venture transactions involving public and private businesses and tax-exempt organizations. This "*cool-headed businessman*" has personality and a "*refreshing*" negotiating style, both of which he uses to "*protect the client's*

business while getting deals done.*" He recently worked on the $125 million acquisition of CarePlus by NYSE-listed AMERIGROUP, as well as the acquisition of a Puerto Rican television station by CMCG-Puerto Rico. The "*top-class*" **Julious Smith** advises clients on such matters as M&A, corporate governance and Sarbanes-Oxley compliance. **William Old** sits on the board of directors and is vice chair of the firm's business group. His corporate and business law practice is particularly admired in the areas of securities, M&A and taxation.

**Clients/Work Highlights:** CarMax; Dollar Trees Stores; Hilb Rogal and Hobbs; LandAmerica Financial Group and Sentara Healthcare.

## Kaufman & Canoles

**The Firm:** This "*fine*" Southern Virginia player serves clients through a seven-office network spread across the region. "*Solid and creative*" lawyers are frequently seen "*out there in the trenches,*" and clients have no hesitation in calling on them when they need to "*get a deal done.*" This multitalented group represents individuals as well as privately owned, public and foreign business entities on the full range of corporate matters.

**The Lawyers:** "*Deal facilitator*" **Vincent Mastracco** is considered to be among the top corporate lawyers operating in Southern Virginia. This skilled technician and strategist is plugged in to the dynamics of the local marketplace and brings a wealth of experience to the table. Chairman of the healthcare practice group, **Braxton McKee** represents physicians, hospitals, health centers and nursing facilities across 20 states. He is currently utilizing his specialist healthcare expertise and regulatory knowledge on the development and management of physician/hospital joint ventures. Clients turn to this "*outside-the-box thinker and solution finder*" because he has such a keen awareness of, and a "*genuine commitment*" to, their business sector.

## LeClair Ryan, A Professional Corporation

**The Firm:** Founded in 1988 as a securities and venture capital boutique, this firm has developed a real pedigree in the cultivation of emerging businesses – technology enterprises in particular – from the financing and startup stage onward. Now a full-service operation, clients include more mature midmarket and high-end operations, including a number of publicly traded corporations. Private and public debt and equity financings, venture capital, joint ventures, strategic alliances and M&A transactions are all areas in which the corporate and securities team excels. As a major regional player, the firm has the resources and manpower to handle large and complex transactions, some of them international in scope.

**The Lawyers:** **Gary LeClair** (see p.1983) is said to be "*a great lawyer to hire to develop a business.*" This "*brilliant and entrepreneurial*" corporate player is especially well known in the venture capital financing world.

## Willcox & Savage

**The Firm:** Clients see the group here as a "*one-stop shop*" for business startups, venture capital and asset-backed financing, corporate governance, regulatory compliance and business acquisitions. This team also delivers on the requirements of more mature concerns, where M&A, and restructurings are more common methods of facilitating further growth. Cross-disciplinary teams serve clients with wider requirements, ensuring coverage of collateral issues such as labor and employment, tax, real estate and environmental regulations.

**The Lawyers:** "*Excellent young lawyer*" **Thomas Inglima** can be relied upon for his "*crackerjack*" efforts in M&A, venture capital, securities and other transactions. Market commentators point to this rising figure as "*a guy who is probably going to the very top.*"

# EMPLOYMENT

## Band 1

### Hunton & Williams LLP

See firm details p.1989

**The Firm:** The dedicated employment team at this Virginia and US heavyweight works out of offices in Richmond, Norfolk and McLean. It is admired for its "*depth, breadth and history,*" making it the "*first stop*" for a broad range of clients seeking labor and employment counseling and dispute resolution. The firm's capacity to "*attract all the best people*" was not lost on clients, who also noted the "*exceptional*" value of the service on offer. Clients come from a variety of areas including banking and financial services, healthcare, manufacturing and telecom.

**The Lawyers:** As a "*key player*" in Virginia, "*excellent*" **Gregory Robertson** is considered to be "*number one*" for traditional labor law and general employment matters. Recent work includes the

representation of executives and businesses in noncompete and trade secrets disputes, and the successful defense on behalf of a large utility company of an FLSA class action. Practicing in the area for more than 30 years, **Hill Wellford** (see p.1987) is "*universally respected*" as one of the best employment lawyers in Virginia. "*Insight and judgment based on experience, a straight-shooting style, and people skills in spades*" combine to make this lawyer a "*go-to guy.*" He recently defended wage and hour audits by the DOL on behalf of companies in the electric utility industry. With "*depth and breadth of legal capability, and business sense to match,*" **Thomas Murphy** (see p.1984) is much admired by clients in the Metropolitan DC area. An expert in a range of labor and employment issues, he has recently met with success in a number of union-organizing and election campaigns, and wage and hour cases. **Elizabeth Lalik** (see p.1983) is an *"exceptional litigator"* with a background in employment and traditional labor law. Over on the employee benefits and executive compensation side of the practice group, **Mark Dray** (see p.1981) sits *"head and shoulders above the competition."* He recently assisted on several major M&A transactions, including the sale of a large radio and cable company, and is currently advising clients in relation to the new nonqualified deferred compensation rules under IRS Section 409A. Capitalizing on his background as an attorney at the IRS, **David Mustone** (see p.1985) is now firmly established as a highly visible player in the employee benefits arena. Within the past year, this *"excellent communicator and down-to-earth individual"* has advised on the employee benefits issues affecting a client's acquisition of foreign energy facilities from a US publicly traded company. **Clients/Work Highlights:** Bon Secours Richmond Health System; Constellation Energy Group; Honeywell; IBM; Philip Morris and Smithfield Foods.

## McGuireWoods LLP

**The Firm:** The *"excellent"* employment and labor practice group at McGuireWoods is lauded for its *"breadth of experience and bench strength."* The teams in its four Virginia offices received acclaim for their detailed understanding of clients' businesses, along with an *"innovative and creative"* approach to the lawyer/client relationship. Clients also pointed to the lawyers' canny use of technology, particularly in litigation, as a key reason for the cost-efficiency of service. The strong regional practice has expanded into several other parts of the USA and also has involvement in some international matters.

**The Lawyers:** Litigator **Stephen Robinson** *"always makes the shortlist whenever a bet-the-company dispute arises."* In the opinion of clients, his *"wealth of experience and understanding of business translates to genuine cost savings."* The firm has an interesting niche in the representation of professional athletes, including Fred Couples and Michael Johnson. **Carter Younger**'s *"incredible breadth of experience and extensive knowledge in the field"* sets him apart from the majority. An *"excellent resource"* on a full range of labor and employment issues, his *"analytical, creative and practical"* approach has minimized claims against management clients throughout the USA and overseas. Chair of the firm-wide practice group, **Gary Marshall** represents management clients on union discrimination claims, as well as sexual harassment cases. *"Astute"* **Dana Rust** is a skilled trial lawyer with experience defending employers against single-plaintiff and class action discrimination claims. Clients welcomed her *"big-picture"* outlook, along with her *"ability to translate legal requirements into pragmatic business solutions."* Clients additionally highlighted the young but experienced litigator **Jonathan Harmon** as *"a thorough lawyer who is good on his feet."* **James McElligott**'s employment, employee benefits and compensation practice has national reach. This widely published lawyer advises some major Fortune 100 players.

## Band 2

## Kaufman & Canoles

**The Firm:** The *"business-minded employment practitioners"* at this *"power firm"* represent management clients in the complete range of employment and traditional labor matters. The employment team is particularly valued for its client support and *"exceptional"* seminars.

**The Lawyers:** "Quick-witted and good-humored," **John Bredehoft**, newly arrived to the firm from Venable, is *"among the best employment lawyers around and a skilled trial attorney."* This former plaintiff lawyer is valued for the *"fresh perspective he brings to the table."* His general employment law practice includes the drafting and enforcement of covenants not to compete and confidentiality agreements, plus the defense of discrimination and wrongful termination claims. With his *"unrivaled enthusiasm for the subject matter,"* clients' favorite **Burt Whitt** represents management in the full spec-

trum of employer/employee matters. Handling issues with *"absolute finesse,"* he is both *"phenomenal in court"* and highly valued for his ability to keep clients away from litigation through long-term counseling on workplace policy and management training.

**Clients/Work Highlights:** The team acts for Virginia-based companies and national and international clients with a presence in the state. These include Bank of America; CarMax Auto Superstores; Circuit City; Eastern Virginia Medical School; Harbor Group International and SunTrust Banks.

## LeClair Ryan, A Professional Corporation

**The Firm:** The work of the 18-strong employment and labor group of this regional firm centers on the provision of counseling, training and litigation prevention policies to management clients. The dedicated employment lawyers are also well equipped to handle contentious issues as and when they arise, be this through alternative dispute resolution, particularly arbitration, or litigation. The *"cost-conscious and efficient"* team has allowed clients to develop *"a high level of confidence,"* with clients happy to report that *"expectations are always met."*

**The Lawyers:** The *"remarkably talented"* **David Nagle** (see p.1985) is the *"ideal choice"* for matters involving the implementation and enforcement of arbitration programs. On behalf of management clients, he has obtained motions to compel arbitration throughout the USA. The strategic thinker has charmed clients with his ability to *"concentrate on the business endgame"* through the delivery of *"innovative and tailored solutions."* **Clinton Morse** (see p.1984) cochairs the firmwide labor and employment practice group and is widely considered to be an expert in the area of traditional labor relations.

## Troutman Sanders LLP

**The Firm:** Operating out of offices in Norfolk, Richmond, Tysons Corner and Virginia Beach, the labor and employment team of this *"solid"* firm is *"well placed among the top practices in the area."* Management clients are provided with contentious and noncontentious advice on employment, employee benefits and traditional labor issues, and a *"collaborative partnership"* style leads them to confirm their satisfaction with the *"receptive"* team.

**The Lawyers:** Leading the way for the firm in Virginia is **Eugene Webb**, a much-admired litigator in the wider Metropolitan DC market. His broad practice includes federal and state litigation on behalf of management clients, as well as general employment and labor law counseling. **David Constine** is an *"intuitive young lawyer with style and personality."* Known to be *"very bright and strong on his feet,"* recent highlights from his broad caseload include a favorable judgment for a broadcasting company in a collective age discrimination action, and defending a variety of EEOC charges. The *"exemplary"* **Wallace Starke** is *"an incredibly smart, experienced and knowledgeable"* compensation and benefits lawyer.

## Venable LLP

**The Firm:** The Northern Virginia employment and labor group of this regional giant has a commanding presence throughout the Metropolitan DC area. With backup from the rest of the firm, the team is "*a smart choice*" for dispute resolution plus advice on the human resources aspects of corporate transactions, workplace policy drafting and litigation avoidance.

**The Lawyers:** **David Smith**'s successful practice, built on over 30 years' experience, focuses on traditional labor counseling and dispute work.

## Williams Mullen

**The Firm:** This "*substantive and established*" outfit counsels management clients on the implementation of workplace policies relating to training, human resources and litigation avoidance. The team is also equipped to handle contentious employment issues through litigation, arbitration and other forms of alternative dispute resolution. These "*talented*" lawyers work alongside colleagues from other practice disciplines to form dedicated client teams, and are considered to have "*a good sense of how to deal with clients and achieve results.*"

**The Lawyers:** **James Meath** is the "*poised, confident and affable*" vice chairman of the firm. He enjoys a fantastic reputation in Virginia and serves an enviable clientele of national and international organizations. Meath arbitrates and mediates on a variety of labor and employment disputes, recently achieving favorable results when defending employment discrimination claims and resisting unions. **Catherine Marriott** is the chair of the firmwide employee benefits section. Clients value her expertise in designing stock-based compensation plans and departure packages, and for her ERISA-related work.

**Clients/Work Highlights:** The client list includes names from the mining, print, steel, and food and beverage sectors. Key clients include American Standard; Exel Mining Systems; Media General and Yellow Transportation.

## Band 3

### DLA Piper Rudnick Gray Cary US LLP

See firm details p.870

**The Firm:** As part of a firm with an imposing global footprint comprising 57 offices throughout the USA, Asia and Europe, the Northern Virginia branch of DLA Piper is able to count many multinational heavyweights within its impressive client portfolio. The labor and employment group here is noted for its invaluable "*combination of legal expertise and business sense,*" and it works in close collaboration with the firm's DC and Maryland offices in the representation of employer clients on labor management and human resources issues and disputes.

**The Lawyers:** With an eye on litigation avoidance through long-term policy counseling, risk assessment and training, the "*ever-impressive*" **Theresa Connolly** (see p.1981) "*speaks with the voice of experience.*" Employer clients "*could not be as effective without her on board,*" and they enthused about her ability to "*really get inside the employee's head and anticipate their next step.*"

## Hogan & Hartson LLP

See firm details p.568

**The Firm:** The Northern Virginia team of three partners and six associates is the largest of Hogan & Hartson's labor and employment groups worldwide. Management clients are "*attracted by the big-firm profile,*" and are confident that the "*top-notch practitioners*" in Virginia and elsewhere "*can handle any issues which may arise in other related areas.*" Clients seek out these lawyers for their expertise in single-plaintiff and class action defense, trade secrets and noncompete litigation, and advice on the creation and implementation of human resources and training policies.

**The Lawyers:** A director of the firm's labor and employment group, **Stanley Brown** (see p.1980) is "*an excellent and creative strategist*" with a wealth of experience and "*exceptional customer service skills.*" Talented in all areas of employment law and litigation, he is also noted for his expertise in the traditional labor field, and contributes heavily to the overall strength of the firm's Virginia practice.

## Pillsbury Winthrop Shaw Pittman LLP

See firm details p.1550

**The Firm:** With the backing of 15 other offices across the USA and around the world, the team in McLean is noted for its "*deep expertise in all aspects of labor and employment.*" Discrimination, whistleblower and sales commission litigation are all areas of excellence, and many early to midstage technology clients rely on the lawyers' advice concerning trade secrets, stock options and ownership rights. A solid traditional labor element completes the picture.

**The Lawyers:** Utilizing his "*keen intellect*" to defend management clients in court, **Thomas Flaherty** (see p.1982) is deemed to be "*an outstanding and tenacious litigator with superb judgment.*" As an "*excellent communicator,*" he is also recognized for his general employment counsel, particularly in the realm of workplace policy drafting and management training.

## Ray & Isler PC

**The Firm:** Management clients view this "*agile*" employment boutique as a "*fresh alternative*" in a busy marketplace. The "*service-oriented*" lawyers here are expert at building client relationships and consistently deliver "*tremendous value and efficiency.*" Litigation is viewed as a key strength at a firm whose background lies in the defense of discrimination, harassment and wage and hour claims. Also key are disputes involving the enforceability of trade secrets and noncompete agreements.

**The Lawyers:** The embodiment of the firm as a whole, **Eddie Isler** is "*blessed with the talent of practicality.*" This "*energetic, creative and smart guy*" is deemed to be something of "*a hot ticket*" in the employment field right now. Clients welcome an approach that centers on litigation avoidance through an understanding of the business; however, he is considered to be "*great on his feet*" in the courtroom. **Steven Ray** pleases clients by "*moving quickly to the pressure points*" when handling contentious issues. A "*proactive and practical approach to problem solving*" is also evident in his workplace counseling.

**Clients/Work Highlights:** Cable & Wireless US; Enterprise Rent-a-Car; DCI Publishing; Infonet Services and Global Printing.

## Other Notable Practitioners

Reed Smith LLP's Northern Virginia office houses the well-respected employment practice of one of the firm's leading lights, **Mark Dare** (see p.1981). Clients from around the USA choose him for his advice on workplace policy and training, with a view to minimizing employee claims. Dare also has ample experience of defending management in litigation. New arrival at Jackson Lewis in Vienna, **Mark de Bernardo** (see p.1981) is a nationally recognized expert on drug testing and substance abuse in the workplace. Clients praised him as "*a strategist and problem solver, who knows how to contain and resolve an issue.*" He also received ringing endorsements for his "*logical but creative manner and unparalleled expertise.*" **Robert Sparks** of the McLean-based firm Sparks & Craig LLP is considered to be well deserving of his position in the rankings for this competitive area of law.

# ENVIRONMENT

| Environment |
| --- |
| Leading Firms |
| [1] HUNTON & WILLIAMS LLP *Richmond* |
| MCGUIREWOODS LLP *Richmond* |
| [2] TROUTMAN SANDERS LLP *Richmond* |
| WILLIAMS MULLEN *Richmond* |
| [3] AQUALAW PLC *Richmond* |
| ELLIS & THORP PLLC *Richmond* |
| LECLAIR RYAN *Richmond* |

| Leading Individuals |
| --- |
| Senior Statesman |
| GASCH JR Manning *Hunton & Williams LLP* |
| [1] EVANS David *McGuireWoods LLP* |
| FINTO Kevin *Hunton & Williams LLP* |
| HAYES Timothy *Hunton & Williams LLP* |
| MARTIN Channing *Williams Mullen* |
| [2] BUNIVA Brian *LeClair Ryan* |
| CALAMITA Paul *Aqualaw PLC* |
| DANIEL II John *Troutman Sanders LLP* |
| ELLIS William *Ellis & Thorp PLLC* |
| KNAUER Thomas *Williams Mullen* |
| POMEROY Chris *Aqualaw PLC* |
| RYAN JR James *Troutman Sanders LLP* |
| SLONE Daniel *McGuireWoods LLP* |
| SMITH Brooks *Hunton & Williams LLP* |
| THORNHILL James *McGuireWoods LLP* |

## Band 1

### Hunton & Williams LLP

See firm details p.1989

**The Firm:** This established environmental practice is widely recognized as a "*dominant force*" in the USA. It comprises a nationwide team of more than 60 dedicated environmental lawyers, whom clients in Virginia describe as "*top-notch specialists*" with the "*necessary horsepower*" to deal with the analytical, technical and political issues attached to large and complex environmental programs. With clients and projects based throughout the USA, the "*talented and capable*" Virginia team adds value by being able to "*plug into the industry and the regulators.*" It represents companies and private individuals on matters of permitting, natural resources and hazardous materials, but is also heavily involved in the federal regulation of large sections of US industry, where it represents interest groups including the Utility Air Regulatory Group and the Utility Water Act Group. Recent activities include obtaining federal and state environmental permits for a proposed 1,500 MW coal-fueled power station, and the handling of environmental issues associated with a merger between two major steel companies.

**The Lawyers:** "*Big thinker*" **Kevin Finto**'s (see p.1982) highly respected practice currently focuses on energy, electricity generation, heavy manufacturing and agriculture. Clients consider him to speak

with "*a trusted voice of authority,*" and are impressed by his ability to "*immediately relate to the technical issues at hand.*" His internal environmental audit expertise facilitates the avoidance of enforcement actions through the development of sophisticated air and water programs. Clients describe **Timothy Hayes** (see p.1982) as the "*preeminent authority on a variety of environmental issues.*" He is "*able to digest complex regulations and propose high-level but cost-effective business strategies in compliance with the letter of the law.*" He has particular expertise in the areas of project permitting, project management, water quality, solid waste and endangered species. **Brooks Smith**'s (see p.1986) stock has risen consistently over the past few years, leading clients to describe him as "*one of the top environmental lawyers in Virginia.*" This "*upfront and proactive*" character is a "*real problem solver*" in all areas of environmental law, but has gained a great deal of respect for his compliance audit work and CWA advice, chiefly in the complex area of Total Maximum Daily Load (TMDL) regulations. "*Charismatic*" **Manning Gasch** (see p.1982) is one of the founding fathers of the firm's environmental group and has practiced in Virginia for over 30 years. This seasoned veteran has built a commanding reputation as a lawyer of tremendous skill and judgment. He delivers "*a lot of bang for the buck*" in his work on environmental disasters throughout the USA.

**Clients/Work Highlights:** American Water; Bank of America; General Dynamics; Georgia-Pacific; Nortel Networks; Smithfield Foods and Wells Fargo.

### McGuireWoods LLP

**The Firm:** As the name might suggest, the Environmental Solutions Group at McGuireWoods is rated for its ability to achieve results for its clients. The team of "*exceptional lawyers*" is "*always up to speed*" and represents "*great value*" on project development, enforcement defense and permitting. In addition to litigation services, clients are offered general counseling to ensure compliance with federal, state and local regulations. Clients come from all over the USA, and beyond, in recognition of a practice that has "*the potency to handle big pieces of work.*" One recent highlight was the representation of a large municipality in EPA negotiations with regard to the provision of wastewater discharge permits.

**The Lawyers:** According to clients and peers, the "*absolutely excellent*" **David Evans** "*stands head and shoulders above the rest.*" This "*top-notch water guy*" advises clients on their CAA obligations, along with permit acquisition and compliance issues. He has recently appeared before the EPA's Environmental Appeals Board in relation to major storm water and combined sewer overflow permits. With a focus on sustainable and green development projects, **Daniel Slone** represents something of an overlap between the firm's environmental and land use practices. He acts as national counsel for the US Green Building Council and is heavily involved in the emergent areas of 'walkable community' and 'traditional neighbor-

hood' developments. **James Thornhill** is co-leader of the environmental solutions group. He advises clients on all aspects of environmental and land use law, and is particularly recognized for his transactional work with the firm's corporate and real estate teams, where he undertakes due diligence and permitting analysis.

**Clients/Work Highlights:** A diverse client portfolio of businesses, trade organizations, municipalities and client groups includes DuPont, Dominion and the City of Richmond.

## Band 2

### Troutman Sanders LLP

**The Firm:** The "*beefy*" environmental and natural resources practice attached to this distinguished firm is thought to have "*sufficient muscle*" to compete for top environmental work. "*Experienced and talented*" lawyers offer regulatory counseling and litigation expertise in the areas of, among other things, water and air quality, hazardous waste, toxic torts and brownfield development. The natural resources development and management wing of the practice advises clients on issues such as NEPA compliance, protected species, wetlands and water resource and pubic land development.

**The Lawyers:** Former Virginia secretary of natural resources, **John Daniel** is a respected figure in the solid waste and air-permitting spheres, where he carries out state and federal compliance audit work. He also has experience in obtaining the relevant land use permissions and permits for numerous construction projects for clients, including heavy industry companies and municipalities. "*Big player*" **James Ryan** is lauded for his "*true expertise in the environmental area.*" His general environmental practice covers work in the water area, where he has experience of permitting for wetland, heavy industry and municipal water projects.

**Clients/Work Highlights:** Akzo Nobel Chemicals; American Home Products; Cinergy; General Mills; Nuclear Energy Institute and Southern Nuclear.

### Williams Mullen

**The Firm:** The environmental attorneys at Williams Mullen are considered "*among the best in Virginia.*" They deliver expert advice in the areas of environmental compliance auditing, enforcement, permitting and litigation, and support is also provided to the firm's construction, real estate and corporate teams wherever collateral environmental advice can maximize the value of transactions. Clients were more than happy with the service offered, suggesting that the work undertaken represented "*extraordinary*" value.

**The Lawyers:** Chair of the environmental practice group, **Channing Martin** is rated by clients as "*truly one of the best.*" This "*analytical and solution-driven*" adviser facilitates successful client relationships through an understanding of the "*interests and strategic*" goals of a business." His keen appreciation of the regulatory demands of state and federal agencies serves trade associations and construction and heavy industry clients well. The Richmond environmental practice has recently been strengthened as a result of the return to the fold of "outstanding" lawyer **Thomas Knauer**. A celebrated authority on clean air issues, he also has significant know-how in the areas of hazardous and solid waste, and on the provisions of the Emergency Planning and Community Right to Know Act. Clients approved of his ability to "communicate on a business level," as well as the "creative and strategic" manner in which he facilitates compliance.

## Band 3

### Aqualaw PLC

**The Firm:** Since opening its doors on the 30th anniversary of the CWA, this "up-and-coming" water boutique has become an increasingly prominent player in a competitive marketplace. The team boasts "well-established players with demonstrated water law

expertise" on issues including storm water management, wastewater collection and treatment, and water supply and treatment. Experts in compliance counseling, enforcement defense and litigation work closely with those with active involvement in government affairs and rulemaking, and together these attorneys provide municipal and industrial clients with complete coverage.

**The Lawyers:** **Paul Calamita** is recognized both as a leader within Virginia and for his "good reputation throughout the USA." This former McGuireWoods lawyer earned particular recognition for his combined sewer overflow (CSO) work. **Chris Pomeroy**, an emergent force in the Virginia environmental market, is a "bright and personable fellow who is really in tune with clients." Sources singled him out for his ability to "identify issues and formulate solutions."

**Clients/Work Highlights:** Wet Weather Partnership (formerly the CSO Partnership); Maryland Association of Municipal Wastewater Agencies; South Carolina Water Quality Association; Virginia Association of Municipal Wastewater Agencies and West Virginia Municipal Water Quality Association.

### Ellis & Thorp PLLC

**The Firm:** The "expert" lawyers in this esteemed environmental boutique are on hand to represent and advise clients on, among other things, CAA, water pollution, toxic substances and regulatory programs.

**The Lawyers:** According to market sources, **William Ellis**, formerly of Hunton & Williams, is "a fierce advocate who really stands out as a great lawyer."

### LeClair Ryan, A Professional Corporation

**The Firm:** As part of the firm's business litigation practice, the environmental, zoning and land use team of this Virginia and DC heavyweight is considered to be highly capable in the representation of clients on contentious issues. Counseling and negotiation services round off the practice.

**The Lawyers:** The leading light is **Brian Buniva** (see p.1980), an environmental and land use expert who has been "around since the start." This "darned good" lawyer is well known as an "aggressive and highly effective" advocate.

# INTELLECTUAL PROPERTY

| Intellectual Property: Northern Virginia |
|---|
| Leading Firms |
| 1 FINNEGAN HENDERSON *Reston* |
| MORRISON & FOERSTER LLP *McLean* |
| OBLON, SPIVAK, MCCLELLAND *Alexandria* |
| PILLSBURY WINTHROP SHAW PITTMAN *McLean* |
| 2 ARNOLD & PORTER LLP *McLean* |
| BIRCH, STEWART, KOLASCH & BIRCH *Falls Church* |
| BUCHANAN INGERSOLL PC *Alexandria* |
| COOLEY GODWARD LLP *Reston* |
| HOGAN & HARTSON LLP *McLean* |
| MCGUIREWOODS LLP *McLean* |
| NIXON & VANDERHYE P.C. *Arlington* |
| OLIFF & BERRIDGE PLC *Alexandria* |

### Finnegan Henderson Farabow Garrett & Dunner LLP

See firm details p.567

**The Firm:** Since opening its doors in 2002, the Reston office of this "top" IP boutique has built a commanding reputation for excellence. Powered by the "terrifically talented" and experienced lawyers resident here, this group is considered to be one of the best places in Virginia for trademark, copyright, trade secrets and patent work. Various patent teams operate in such fields as biotech, mechanical devices, chemicals, IT and nanotechnology, and they include former patent examiners and qualified patent attorneys with specialist, technical backgrounds. Altogether they make up a "healthy and well-balanced" practice, with IP startup and portfolio management advice, patent drafting and prosecution, as well as complex interference work, all handled with

aplomb. On the disputes side, the Finnegan litigators have become known as "the go-to team when it comes to bet-the-company patent litigation." It recently acted for Eli Lilly in the successful patent defense of ZYPREXA, the $3 billion antipsychotic prescription drug, against generic challengers in the Southern District Court of Indiana. Domestic and international clients are offered complete coverage via the firm's East and West Coast offices plus its outposts in Brussels, Taipei and Tokyo.

**The Lawyers:** Splitting his time between DC and Reston, managing partner **Christopher Foley** (see p.1982) has a "wonderful" client portfolio and handles copyright, trademark and patent matters. An experienced speaker and former patent examiner, IP litigator **Charles Lipsey** (see p.1985) concentrates on disputes, in trial and appeal, and at all courts up to the US Supreme Court. Although his track record in biotech and pharmaceuticals is highly impressive, he is known too for his excellent work on cases concerning mechanical patents and boat design.

### Morrison & Foerster LLP

See firm details p.335

**The Firm:** This "premier" global firm fields more than 300 dedicated IP practitioners throughout the USA, Europe and Asia. The "A-plus" Northern Virginia team is "absolutely doing the top work" on the full spectrum of patent, trademark and copyright matters, including prosecution, litigation and alternative dispute resolution, counseling, portfolio management and licensing transactions. These "masterful" lawyers serve clients ranging from emerging ventures to mature publicly traded companies, across such industries as biotech, healthcare,

electronics, IT, telecom, pharmaceuticals, and media and entertainment. The firm's recognized strength in corporate transactions is seen as a distinct advantage to the department's clients, and certainly the IP lawyers make their contribution to the due diligence process on IP-rich deals.

**The Lawyers:** Patent specialist **Barry Bretschneider** (see p.1980) covers prosecution, interference, licensing and portfolio advice, and in litigation he is "tenacious" in his appearances before district courts and the ITC. Clients praised this responsive lawyer for becoming "totally immersed in the technology and making the effort to really get to know the business." **Clients/Work Highlights:** BEA Systems; Dyson; Johnson & Johnson; Nikon; Siemens; Sanyo Electronic Device; Sprint Nextel and Storm Ventures.

### Oblon, Spivak, McClelland, Maier & Neustadt PC

**The Firm:** Market commentators consider this Alexandria IP boutique to be among the best in the field, and certainly "a powerhouse" in patent procurement, an area in which it holds the record for procuring more US patents than any other organization. The firm's prominence in the market is the result of strong technical skills, aided by the many ex-judges and examiners now on staff and a high proportion of scientific and technically qualified lawyers. The team also has a deep understanding of the patent system, aided by the office's location close to the US Patent & Trademark Office (USPTO). The litigation practice is increasingly recognized and covers patents, copyright and trademarks; unsurprisingly the firm also excels at interference work. The range of the firm's IP activities are as vast as its clients' business activities: current cases cover everything from socks, tequila and the Blue Man Group to electrical products and antibiotics.

**The Lawyers: Charles Gholz** is known nationally as a top litigator and patent interference *"guru."* He has recently extended his impressive track record by representing a major Silicon Valley software company in relation to a digital rights management system. Litigation department head, the esteemed **Arthur Neustadt**, has a distinguished career spanning more than 35 years. He has been a familiar sight in trial and appellate courts at all levels up to and including the US Supreme Court.

**Clients/Work Highlights:** Clients come from throughout the USA, Europe and the Far East, and include universities and research facilities, foreign and US government agencies and business entities ranging in maturity from startups to some of the most established names in the world.

### Pillsbury Winthrop Shaw Pittman LLP
See firm details p.1550

**The Firm:** Market sources responded positively when asked for a prognosis on this recently merged national and international heavyweight. Most asserted that the firm's Northern Virginia IP capability had been strengthened as a result of the convergence of so many *"top people."* Enforcing IP rights through litigation is the bread and butter work; clients thought it *"large enough to easily absorb complex cases and provide timely assistance."* Strength also lies in *"high-end"* counseling, with the *"excellent"* lawyers providing clients with IP, due diligence, and patent prosecution. More than 40 patent prosecution professionals ensure protection for their clients' valuable innovations, and value is added in this regard through a keen understanding of the inner workings of the nearby USPTO – many of the firm's attorneys are former patent examiners. Overall, one of the most appealing elements for clients is *"a focus on customer satisfaction and a desire to ensure that business goals are achieved."*

**The Lawyers:** *"Innovative"* in his counseling, **George Sirilla** (see p.1987) is also an *"excellent litigation strategist."* An eye for detail and sound judgment are the hallmarks of this *"sharp as a whip"* senior statesman. In the past year, he advised Home Depot and American Biophysics. **Jack Barufka** (see p.1979) *"stands out"* from the crowd by virtue of the *"painstaking detail"* of his work. Especially adept at handling opinion and USPTO matters, his clients warmed to his communication skills and pointed to the fact that he offered them advice in a way they could easily understand. This, they said, made him *"an integral part of their business."* *"Shrewd litigator"* **William Atkins** (see p.1979) successfully represented Atlas Copco in a recent trade secrets and patent infringement case, protecting his client from hundreds of millions of dollars in damages. Highly valued by clients for his handling of complex issues, Atkins was described as *"a tiger in the courtroom."* **James Gatto** (see p.1982) performs well in litigation, prosecution and counseling. His recent highlights include cases for Expo Power Systems, for whom he won a summary judgment, and E-centives, whom he represented in an enforcement matter. Clients greatly admired Gatto for his *"resourcefulness and creativity"* at the USPTO. Meanwhile, peers were united in extolling the IP litigation talents of **Lawrence Gotts** (see p.516), whose recent work has included representation of Honeywell in a case against the US government and Lockheed Martin over an alleged infringement of a patent relating to night-vision goggles and instrumentation displays in aircraft cockpits. **Adam Hess** (see p.1982) continues to represent American Biophysics

and has been active for other clients in pursuing trademark infringement. Clients say he is *"good on his feet"* and *"hard to rattle"* in the courtroom; they also appreciated his commitment to understanding their business and technology.

### Arnold & Porter LLP
See firm details p.560

**The Firm:** The IP and technology group operating within this *"powerful"* international firm is deemed *"one of the best in the business"* by the Northern Virginia IP community. The lawyers have demonstrable skill in IP portfolio management, offering advice and representation on the protection, exploitation, enforcement and licensing of all kinds of rights. Clients take advantage of the full-service offered by the firm, and can utilize its overseas capacity where necessary.

**The Lawyers:** Seasoned IP litigator **Charles Ossola** has *"a great courtroom presence and can make a difficult argument seem simple."* He tackles patent, antitrust, copyright, trademark, trade secrets and unfair competition disputes, recently representing GEICO in a trademark dispute with Google.

### Birch, Stewart, Kolasch & Birch, LLP

**The Firm:** For more than 25 years this widely respected boutique has been helping clients protect their IP rights and maximize their commercial value. It excels at patent prosecution, and is consistently positioned near the top of tables identifying leading firms by the number of US patents obtained. A particularly strong overseas profile is in evidence - the firm's many leading international clients, commonly based in the Far East, rely on the experts here to execute their US patent applications. Patent work aside, the group is strong in litigation and alternative dispute resolution, and also well versed in trademark and copyright protection and exploitation.

**The Lawyers:** Senior counsel IP Raymond Stewart has a specialty in organic chemistry.

### Buchanan Ingersoll PC
See firm details p.1749

**The Firm:** At the time of research, commentators felt it was *"just too early to say"* how the chemistry would work between top-120 US firm Buchanan Ingersoll and long-established Virginia and California IP boutique Burns Doane Swecker & Mathis. Their merger was one of the more interesting market developments of 2005, and all eyes will now be on the combined forces in Alexandria as the office moves forward under the Buchanan Ingersoll banner. Working in the IP field *"long before it was cool,"* this deeply experienced and knowledgeable group is historically known for its patent prosecution, litigation and interference practice. Strengths also lie in the areas of licensing, trademarks, copyright and trade secrets. The newly combined firm delivers a full legal service across 15 nationwide offices.

**The Lawyers:** Biotech specialists Susan Dadio and Teresa Stanek Rea are key contacts.

## Cooley Godward LLP

**The Firm:** The Northern Virginia office of this Silicon Valley force is a "*big player*" in the hi-tech arena and has a particular focus on emerging companies. In this regard, the IP team assists new, high-potential technology ventures in safeguarding their valuable IP assets. Counseling and portfolio management, patent prosecution, and enforcement or defense of rights through the courts are all offered. The team is similarly proficient in handling large matters for mature businesses, and many clients are publicly traded and Fortune-listed.

**The Lawyers:** **Frank Pietrantonio** leads the firm's patent counseling and prosecution group. He has notable experience in the drafting and prosecution of patent applications in IT, computing, telecom and business methods.

## Hogan & Hartson LLP

See firm details p.568

**The Firm:** Over the past 15 years this Northern Virginia IP practice has gone from strength to strength. The team presently comprises 16 dedicated practitioners, with a handful more available for litigation matters. It provides a complete package of IP services – trademark and patent prosecution, due diligence, litigation and general counseling. Emphasis is given to the management and exploitation of clients' IP portfolios through acquisitions, assignments and licensing, as well as brand strategy advice and trademark prosecution. International clients take advantage of the breadth of expertise on offer at Hogan & Hartson's other 15 offices across the USA, Europe and Asia.

**The Lawyers:** According to clients, "**Philip Porter**'s (see p.1985) *personality, intelligence, comprehensive IP and technology know-how, and extreme practicality are great assets*" in his provision of "*efficient and cost-effective*" business solutions.

**Clients/Work Highlights:** Lawyers recently worked alongside their corporate counterparts to negotiate software, patent and trademark licensing agreements for Wal-Mart Stores and Wal-Mart International in relation to a joint venture with CARHCO, the largest retailer in Central America.

## McGuireWoods LLP

**The Firm:** This established practice offers solid expertise in corporate IP counseling and litigation over trademarks, trade dress, trade secrets, copyright, licensing and patents. Market sources comment on the "*great team behind the scenes,*" with several agreeing that the lawyers "*will go the extra mile.*" The firm has experienced an increase in computer software and patent infringement cases.

**The Lawyers:** "*Top-notch*" litigator **Brian Riopelle** heads up the department and makes a real impact with his ethical yet tenacious approach. "*His clients are big fans,*" one competitor notes: "*He listens first and talks second.*" With substantial experience in patent infringement, trademark and copyright litigation, this "*calm and courteous*" individual is well regarded in the rocket docket of the Eastern District of Virginia. In one of his biggest recent cases he was

co-counsel for Infineon Technologies and, according to one source, his long-term management of Circuit City's trademark portfolio reveals a unique ability: "*He can find a solution when others cannot.*" **Robert Tyler** is a "*smart, impressive and extremely practical*" litigator in trademark, copyright and software matters. He has acted for RIM in the high-profile BlackBerry case. **Richard Meyer**'s IP asset management practice focuses on the tactical enforcement, defense and development of patent and trademark rights. Technically excellent and personable to boot, this client-sensitive lawyer inspires "*full confidence*" from clients who particularly admire his "*tenacious*" negotiating style.

**Clients/Work Highlights:** The team works for a clientele of retailers, merchandisers, healthcare providers, software developers and advertising agencies. These include Circuit City; Infineon Technologies; Owens & Minor; Markel and Rose & Tuck.

## Nixon & Vanderhye P.C.

**The Firm:** This "*high-impact*" Arlington IP boutique celebrated its 20th anniversary in 2005 and enjoys a long-standing reputation for quality patent, trademark and copyright advice. It is certainly a big name in the patent area, where it is consistently ranked among the top 12 firms for the total number of successful US patent prosecutions per year. "*On-the-ball*" lawyers draw on specialist know-how acquired from technical backgrounds in electrical, chemical and mechanical engineering, chemistry, pharmacy and biochemistry; many also have previous experience on the staff of the USPTO. Foreign-origin patent applications represent a substantial proportion of their business, while the international IP rights of US-based clients are also protected through associations with patent attorneys and IP lawyers around the world. The keen litigation capability of this "*unique shop*" was highlighted as a valuable asset bringing balance to the overall practice.

**The Lawyers:** Clients feel confident that "*excellent*" **Larry Nixon** will always do a "*first-class job*" in litigation and patent prosecution, particularly in the computer software sphere. This engineer blends clear thinking with sound judgment and is considered to be "*one of the very best on intense matters.*"

**Clients/Work Highlights:** The varied clientele includes individuals and entrepreneurial ventures, manufacturers, universities, research facilities and multinational corporations including BT; Eriksson; GE; Nintendo; RIM; Sharp and Toshiba.

## Oliff & Berridge PLC

**The Firm:** Since its inception in 1983, this firm has built a great name as a full-service IP boutique. The 40-strong operation is well established as one of the leading domestic and foreign origin patent prosecution practices in the USA, although full rights protection and exploitation is ensured through litigation where necessary. Indeed, the lawyers here possess a wealth of experience appearing before trial and appellate courts on the federal circuit in DC and district courts all over the USA, particularly the Eastern District of Virginia.

**The Lawyers:** "*Top guy*" **James Oliff** has been a key player in the patent prosecution and litigation area for years. Insight gained from his previous experience working within the USPTO, a strong technical background and "*thorough homework*" in advance combine to produce a high-quality product.

## Hunton & Williams LLP

See firm details p.1989

**The Firm:** Highly regarded by peers, this firm's stock continues to grow at a fast pace. Commentators claim: "*It deserves the top spot*" as the "*biggest player in Southern Virginia*" and "*a truly national practice.*" The Richmond office has now doubled its number of patent, trademark and copyright practitioners to cope with a significant increase in workflow after several high-profile successes with existing and new clients worldwide. Capable of providing the full range of IP protection, the group inspires a high level of trust. Its legal and technical expertise has earned it considerable respect, and there are ample examples of complex patent law preparation, prosecution, interferences and opinion work through which its lawyers have proven their ability. Recent prominent cases include the representation of Internet, telecom and biotech companies.

**The Lawyers:** A "*very proactive*" patent lawyer, **Michael Martinez de Andino** (see p.1984) is someone who "*focuses on the important stuff,*" other attorneys regard him as "*one of the premier patent prosecutors in the area.*" He has the necessary skills to "*manage a large volume of detailed work,*" and proved this while advising InComm on an entire IP portfolio, remaining "*communicative, upbeat and positive*" in the process. He recently negotiated several favorable license deals for both GSSC and E-Vision, filing patent applications, conducting due diligence and preparing the agreements. **Robert Tata** (see p.1987) is a robust general litigator whose IP successes lie in tackling false advertising, patent portfolio conspiracy and trade secrets litigation; indeed he is carving a niche in trade secrets misappropriation. Tata is "*willing to consider unconventional solutions,*" and his strategic approach reaps "*answers not problems.*" Significant work includes co-counseling a leading pharmaceuticals company, acting as lead counsel for X-IT Products, representing a top state university and portfolio patent management for Earl Industries. Another "*superb*" litigator and counselor is **Christopher Campbell** (see p.1982), who impresses clients by creatively pitching his advice at the point where "*technology, business and the law intersect.*" A "*customer-oriented and solution-minded*" approach leads clients to view working with this "*effective and efficient*" attorney as "*a pleasure.*"

**Clients/Work Highlights:** The group represents a full range of clients from fledgling companies to multinational corporations. These include InComm; GSSC; E-Vision; Bank of America; DTE Energy; Earl Industries; General Dynamics; Smithfield Foods and SunTrust.

## Kaufman & Canoles

**The Firm:** This firm has a number of strong individuals in its broad technology ventures team. Solid IP counseling is offered to business clients with trademark, copyright, trade secrets and patent rights to protect. Patent litigation and licensing deals are important to the practice, and in particular the group has been further extending its reach into the hi-tech market. The regional firm makes good use of its local connections but also works with several Fortune 100 companies.

**The Lawyers:** "*Up to date on all the cutting-edge stuff,*" **Christopher Mugel** (known as "*The Professor*" to some) is hailed as "*top tier.*" His practice includes transactional work and litigation, the former involving trademark and licensing work for software and biotech companies, Internet businesses and medical services clients. Competitors observe him to be "*a very bright guy.*" Head of IP litigation at the firm, **Stephen Noona** also "*deserves top ranking.*" Having practiced for 20 years, pure IP litigation now makes up the majority of his caseload. Headline achievements include counseling on a major patent matter for Lubrizol and working for GlaxoSmithKline on an antitrust matter with significant patent issues. Clients appreciate his "*accessibility and responsiveness*" and regard him as an exemplary team player. The depth of Noona's knowledge of the substantive areas of law and his valuable insights into the local judicial system are legendary.

## Williams Mullen

**The Firm:** Situated outside the beltway, this firm distinguishes itself with a significant IP prosecution practice. Peers comment on its "*strong capabilities*" and observe "*a good mix of transaction work and litigation.*" The lawyers counsel clients on the acquisition, disposal and international licensing of rights, and the registration and further protection of trademarked and copyrighted assets. Franchise law is also a forte.

**The Lawyers:** **Ian Titley** is "*highly recommended*" for a mixed practice made up of 40% trademarks, 40% software licensing and 20% general corporate work. His strong background in corporate practice assists

him when negotiating high-pressure deals, such as the recent acquisition of multiple IP assets for a manufacturing client. **Craig Mytelka** is "*good at pulling deals together.*" He is frequently to be found working on licensing deals, acquisitions or disposals, and he also represents defendants in data mining cases.

## Leading-Edge Law Group, PLC

**The Firm:** Dealing in cyber-law, hi-tech issues and all aspects of IP other than patent prosecution, this "*solid IP boutique*" has prompted growing interest from the commercial sector, with US trademark registration activity particularly elevated. It has had cases heard in the federal court and in the Trademark Trial and Appeal Board on a range of issues from infringement to breaches of license terms.

**The Lawyers:** **John Farmer** is "*extremely capable, knowledgeable and effective*" in his field. A "*serious IP lawyer who knows what he is doing,*" he works for clients on both transactions and litigation. His "*devotion to IP*" is well known among peers.

**Clients/Work Highlights:** The client base includes e-commerce, hi-tech and computer sciences businesses; among the ongoing assignments being undertaken by the firm is a large outsourcing project for a public company.

## Troutman Sanders LLP

**The Firm:** While big deals often involve the Atlanta headquarters, this "*growing practice*" in Richmond is sharpening its focus on IP and technology counseling and litigation. This is in response to the burgeoning market for patent infringement litigation, now becoming the "*golden fleece*" for litigators in the Eastern District of Virginia with its rocket docket court attracting ever greater numbers of filings. The practice group has managed more than 10,000 trademarks for clients and can lay claim to both local and national clients. Highlights include representing a large regional chemical distribution company and strengthening a local pharmaceutical company's IP portfolio.

**The Lawyers:** For clients, "*smooth operator*" **Robert Brooke** "*puts legal brilliance into action to meet objectives.*" His IP work divides up as 60% transactional in

trademark, copyright filing and prosecution, and 40% general counseling and litigation. Clients note his candid approach, unsurpassed breadth of knowledge and ability to remain responsive and personable. "*His understanding of the corporate dimension is invaluable.*" Of his advice, clients said his assessment of risk versus opportunity was pragmatic and business-oriented. With Richmond attorney Robert Angle, he helped to bring a patent infringement case for a major military gun manufacturer to a successful resolution. Clients paid tribute to the "*pleasant and responsive*" **John Anderson** for his delivery of "*exceptional*" advice that is "*creative, focused and business-oriented.*" This accomplished litigator is a common sight throughout the courts of Virginia and DC; however, he is especially familiar with the Alexandria division of the Eastern District of Virginia where he deals with patent, trademark and Internet domain name disputes.

**Clients/Work Highlights:** Clients come from a variety of sectors, among them manufacturing, biotech, pharmaceuticals and software. On the books are Atley Pharmaceuticals; Intelliject; Heckler & Koch Defense and SAP.

## Other Notable Practitioners

**Lisa Krizan** (see p.1983) of LMK Associates elicited praise from peers who view her as "*a serious lawyer building a great practice.*" As well as transactional work, she conducts trademark/copyright litigation including domain name protection. She also covers patent licensing, nationally and internationally. A software client told researchers that her work demonstrated "*integrity, efficiency and street-smart intelligence.*" **Dana McDaniel** of Spotts Fain in Richmond is a "*rare asset.*" Distinguished by his expertise in patent infringement litigation and his recent foray into mediation, he is recognized as a "*versatile and tenacious*" attorney. McDaniel's cases include patent, trademark and copyright infringement and business disputes over trade secrets in courts across the USA. He has also served as local counsel for attorneys handling IP in the Eastern and Western Districts of Virginia.

# LITIGATION

## Band 1

### Hunton & Williams LLP

See firm details p.1989

**The Firm:** This "*superior*" full-service firm is renowned for its "*outstanding*" Virginia litigation practice. Clients seek out this team whenever they encounter "*big, ugly matters that need to be addressed quickly,*" and are pleased to work with lawyers of "*consistently high quality across the board.*" An impressive bench of litigators possesses rich trial experience, many of the individuals having earned distinguished track records. The team represents clients on the full range of contentious matters, including corporate/M&A, antitrust, IP, products

liability and employment disputes. The global reach of this firm is also evidenced by its proficiency in international arbitration and dispute resolution, where it represents domestic and foreign clients on cross-jurisdictional disputes. The group is valued for its focus on the specific needs of clients' businesses, and for taking time to develop a customized trial strategy for each. It streamlines its efforts by utilizing sophisticated technology as and when required.

**The Lawyers:** Litigation group co-head **Thomas Slater** (see p.1987) is admired throughout the Virginia Bar. Over the course of a distinguished career he has appeared in more than 60 state and federal jury trials throughout the USA, and has represented clients in actions at all state levels includ-

ing the Virginia Supreme Court. Renowned for his antitrust and IP work, he is also experienced in handling a variety of other complex disputes including products liability and white collar crime. Norfolk office managing partner **Gregory Stillman** (see p.1987) is regarded as a commercial litigator with real courtroom presence and jury appeal. Representing MercExchange, he was recently involved in a US Supreme Court appeal of a decision in a patent infringement case involving eBay and Half.com, Inc. According to clients, the vastly experienced **Joseph Kearfott** (see p.1984) "*never misses a trick.*" "*Flawless*" legal analysis coupled with clarity of thought and communication are highlighted as the key strengths of a man who has the rare ability to "*take*

## Litigation: General Commercial
### Leading Firms

**1** HUNTON & WILLIAMS LLP *Richmond*
MCGUIREWOODS LLP *Richmond*

**2** KAUFMAN & CANOLES *Norfolk*
TROUTMAN SANDERS LLP *Richmond*
WILLCOX & SAVAGE *Norfolk*

**3** CHRISTIAN & BARTON LLP *Richmond*
HIRSCHLER FLEISCHER *Richmond*
HOGAN & HARTSON LLP *McLean*
LATHAM & WATKINS LLP *Reston*
LECLAIR RYAN *Richmond*
MORRIS & MORRIS PC *Richmond*
VENABLE LLP *Vienna*
WILLIAMS MULLEN *Richmond*
WOODS ROGERS PLC *Roanoke*

### Leading Individuals

#### Senior Statesmen

MORRIS III James *Morris & Morris PC*
POFF William *Woods Rogers PLC*
ROBERTS James *Troutman Sanders LLP*

**1** ALLEN Everette *LeClair Ryan*
KING William *McGuireWoods LLP*
SLATER Thomas *Hunton & Williams LLP*
SMITH Michael *Christian & Barton LLP*
STILLMAN Gregory *Hunton & Williams LLP*

**2** BAYLISS William *Williams Mullen*
BISHOP Bruce *Willcox & Savage*
BROADDUS William *McGuireWoods LLP*
CULLEN Richard *McGuireWoods LLP*
HARLESS Warren *Christian & Barton LLP*
HIXON III Samuel *Williams Mullen*
JENNINGS JR James *Woods Rogers PLC*
KEARFOTT Joseph *Hunton & Williams LLP*
NOONA Stephen *Kaufman & Canoles*
PAGE Rosewell *McGuireWoods LLP*
RUDLIN D Alan *Hunton & Williams LLP*
SHUMADINE Conrad *Willcox & Savage*
SIMS Hunter *Kaufman & Canoles*
TATA Robert *Hunton & Williams LLP*
WHITTEMORE Anne *McGuireWoods LLP*
WITTHOEFFT Charles *Hirschler Fleischer*

**3** BURKE JR John *Troutman Sanders LLP*
CHERRY Steven *WilmerHale*
FARNHAM James *Hunton & Williams LLP*
FUHR Edward *Hunton & Williams LLP*
NORTHUP Stephen *Troutman Sanders LLP*
PEARSON JR John *Willcox & Savage*
RAPHAEL Stuart *Hunton & Williams LLP*
SMILAN Laurie *Latham & Watkins LLP*
WILLIAMS Steven *McGuireWoods LLP*

*care of the detail while also developing an overall strategy.*" Considered to be "*one of the finest*" toxic tort lawyers in the country, his practice is also strong in the areas of personal injury and products and premises liability. **Alan Rudlin** (see p.1986) also handles toxic tort cases plus products liability and

various types of class actions. Pharmaceutical and medical device issues are an increasingly common source of work, and he additionally represents clients on First Amendment and constitutional matters. Described as "*articulate and quick on his feet,*" **Robert Tata** (see p.1987) is viewed by clients as "*the first person to call for high-stakes, bet-the-company*" litigation. His caseload has a distinct IP emphasis yet his broad experience extends to all types of complex litigation, not least products liability, employment and personal injury defense. **James Farnham** (see p.1983) works on a wide variety of commercial litigation and alternative dispute resolution cases, with particular emphasis on securities, M&A, corporate governance and stockholder derivative disputes. He is experienced in State Attorney General and other regulatory investigations. Former Department of Justice official **Edward Fuhr** (see p.1984) is a corporate litigator with expertise in M&A, stockholder derivative cases and SEC investigation work. His track record in the defense of securities actions has recently been enhanced by his representation of a major utilities company in a securities fraud claim. Last in the line-up this year is the "*enormously talented*" **Stuart Raphael** (see p.1986), a "*rising star who really influences cases.*" His broad general litigation experience includes a specialism in water rights disputes, an area in which he is chief outside counsel to one of the largest public water utilities in the country. For that client he recently obtained judgment on the merits of a $500,000 construction defect claim after a three-day bench trial.

**Clients/Work Highlights:** A diverse client portfolio includes everything from businesses startups to multinational corporations. Among those on the client roster are Genworth Financial; IMC Global; Koch Industries; Philip Morris and Union Pacific.

## McGuireWoods LLP

**The Firm:** The "*wonderful litigation shop*" attached to this 15-office heavyweight is considered to be a "*key player,*" both in Virginia and throughout the nation. Its lawyers are well known and well respected in this competitive market, not least because they have a wealth of experience in a broad range of contentious issues, including IP, construction, corporate and securities disputes, plus white-collar defense and government investigations. Products liability is recognized as an area of particular strength. Clients benefit from the lawyers' use of advanced IT-driven case/document analysis and management systems, and can also choose to avail themselves of the litigation support services provided by the firm's media and public affairs offshoot, McGuireWoods Consulting.

**The Lawyers:** **William King** is the "*go-to guy*" for products liability, particularly the management of defense at a national level. While he represents clients in suits relating to chemicals and industrial equipment, he is principally recognized for his work with the producers of automobiles and their components. In this sphere, he has counseled and defended several of the world's largest automobile manufacturers. Former Virginia attorney general **William Broaddus**

is one of the first names on people's lips whenever experience is the deciding factor. This "*great*" litigator has appeared in the Virginia Supreme Court, Fourth Circuit and US Supreme Court in commercial disputes ranging from employment and defamation to land use and environmental matters. **Richard Cullen** leads the firm's white collar and government investigations team. "*Few come close*" to this "*politically well-connected*" authority who regularly advises companies and their executives in relation to prosecutions and examination by federal and state government entities. "*Dominant force*" **Rosewell Page** is "*clearly one of the best*" trial lawyers in the state. He is skilled in litigation management, trial and alternative dispute resolution work, and is "*frequently called upon by big clients*" in relation to environmental, products and professional liability matters. **Anne Marie Whittemore** has a fantastic reputation for her counseling and trial work on general corporate, corporate governance and securities matters. She represents clients from the telecommunication, manufacturing and financial and professional services areas. General commercial, environmental and constitutional work makes up the remainder of her practice. Described simply as "*great,*" **Steven Williams** works in the firm's complex products liability and mass tort litigation department, where he defends mass/toxic tort and commercial class/consolidated actions on behalf of major industrial clients. He is currently instructed as national coordinating counsel to a manufacturing defendant in nationwide lead pigment litigation, and also runs the team representing several major automobile manufacturers in asbestos litigation. A "*very experienced*" former federal prosecutor, **Howard Vick** focuses on white-collar criminal defense and internal corporate investigation and compliance matters. He has recently represented major clients with regard to fraud, false claims, environmental crimes and SEC violations.

**Clients/Work Highlights:** The firm's client roster includes DuPont and Ford.

### Band 2

#### Kaufman & Canoles

**The Firm:** According to a number of peers, working with the "*tough competitors*" at this "*fine*" firm is thought to be a "*positive and enjoyable*" experience. The firm's caseload covers the full gamut of general commercial disputes, including environmental, IP, and securities disputes. It is also known and respected for its defense of corporations, executives and employees charged with, or investigated for, alleged white-collar criminal offences.

**The Lawyers:** A former Assistant US Attorney, **Hunter Sims** benefits from the wealth of jury experience built up during his 25 years of trying complex commercial cases and dealing with white-collar prosecutions and government agency investigations. In defining the key to his success, peers pointed to a deep understanding of the law and case material, and the ability to "*make things simple*" for the client.

**Stephen Noona** specializes in trying complex federal cases within the US District Court for the Eastern District of Virginia. Clients view this *"very knowledgeable and efficient"* trial lawyer as *"a practical team player who adds great value to the service."* His ranking in Chambers' IP section reflects the importance of IP matters in his practice; however, he also has a name for First Amendment and media disputes. Noona is a principal of the firm's litigation section and cochairs its technology ventures group.

## Troutman Sanders LLP

**The Firm:** Clients choose this firm for high-stakes cases because of the *"exemplary"* customer service provided by the group's *"dedicated battlers."* The lawyers, who are further described as *"always accessible and very responsive,"* act for clients on a broad spectrum of contentious matters, litigating and pursuing other resolution methods in, for example, the areas of products liability, real estate, corporate and securities, IP, media and entertainment law. An in-house litigation technology team provides sophisticated IT backup.

**The Lawyers:** Outstanding **James Roberts** has long enjoyed a reputation as a dominant force in Virginia courtrooms. He has particular experience representing clients in relation to corporate governance issues, internal investigations and conspiracy and fraud allegations at Virginia's state and federal courts. **John Burke** runs an effective business and commercial litigation practice. Although experienced in a wide array of complex claims, his practice has a real estate flavor. He recently obtained specific performance of a $39 million contract on behalf of a developer client, and achieved a satisfactory outcome for a landowner in an eminent domain appropriation matter. Clients rate **Stephen Northup** as *"an exceptional lawyer who is always on the ball."* This *"straight shooter"* is a *"vigorous and persuasive"* advocate who inspires respect with his willingness to *"dive in and achieve a command and mastery of the facts."*

## Willcox & Savage

**The Firm:** This *"key player"* in the Virginia marketplace impresses clients with its *"hard-working, smart and talented"* litigators; they have real trial know-how. The team represents clients in state and federal courts, and before arbitration panels and governmental bodies. The lawyers take on a variety of general commercial disputes, including issues in the areas of IP, corporate, antitrust, real estate and professional liability, and are also proficient in white-collar crime defense. Particular strength lies in the team's products liability and asbestos defense work, which extends the reach of this practice to a national level. Responsive lawyers and *"fair"* billing rates prompt clients to view working with this team as a wholly positive experience.

**The Lawyers:** *"Loved by jurors all over the USA,"* the *"preeminent"* **Bruce Bishop** has built an imposing reputation for his asbestos defense work. Nonetheless, his reputation is also strong in the area of transportation, especially trucking, aviation and environmental litigation. Clients highlighted a business practicality and the ability to present complex facts to the court in a simple way as his best assets. *"Terrifically bright"* general commercial litigator **Conrad Shumadine**'s name reaches far in the areas of antitrust, trade regulation and First Amendment matters. Blessed with a deep understanding of the subject matter and a wealth of jury experience, this litigator has the rare talent of *"making things simple"* for the client. **John Pearson** is recognized as a skilled general commercial litigator with particular experience in the defense of medical malpractice and other professional liability actions.

**Clients/Work Highlights:** Amron; Dana Corporation; ExxonMobil; Hobart; Honeywell; Lincoln Electric and Volkswagen.

## Band 3

## Christian & Barton LLP

**The Firm:** The litigators at this full-service Richmond firm offer counsel to clients ranging from hi-tech startups to long-established Fortune 500 corporations, public entities, nonprofit organizations and individuals. Courtroom and alternative dispute resolution expertise extends over a swath of commercial and other areas, including construction, insurance, environmental, employment and First Amendment law. The experienced lawyers here have made successful appearances in state, federal and appellate courts as well as at various administrative proceedings.

**The Lawyers:** According to market sources, **Michael Smith**, chairman of the firm's litigation department and executive committee, is a *"savvy"* commercial litigator with a well-deserved reputation in the Virginia Bar. *"Good trial instincts"* and a keen knowledge of the court system have served clients well over the course of his distinguished career. In particular he has experience of products liability, corporate and securities, healthcare, professional liability and insurance disputes. **Warren David Harless** offers litigation and alternative dispute resolution representation and counseling on a variety of general commercial, products liability and constitutional matters. Labor and employment disputes are a key strand of his practice; he defends employers from, among other things, discrimination, wage and hour and wrongful discharge actions in state and federal courts around the USA.

## Hirschler Fleischer

**The Firm:** The litigation team operates out of the firm's offices in Richmond and Fredericksburg. The lawyers are traditionally known for their commercial real estate work, encompassing contentious construction, zoning and land use, landlord and tenant and transaction-based disputes. Over time, their work in other areas, namely labor and employment, corporate and securities, stockholder, bankruptcy, probate and employment litigation, has become more widely recognized. The litigators here appear in the state, federal and appellate courts, and are also familiar with making representations before various administrative authorities and in arbitrations and other forms of alternative dispute resolution.

**The Lawyers:** The *"excellent"* **Charles Witthoeft** (see p.1988), chair of the litigation section, has been trying defendant and plaintiff cases at state and federal levels for more than three decades. Interviewees said he *"gives you great confidence that he is on top of the facts and the law;"* this leaves them certain that they will receive *"sensible"* counsel and representation. His work takes in a multitude of commercial areas, including antitrust, banking, business torts, breach of contract, employment, environmental, insurance and real estate.

## Hogan & Hartson LLP
See firm details p.568

**The Firm:** This 13-lawyer Northern Virginia litigation team has a piece of the action on some of the largest disputes around. The group represents major clients in courtrooms throughout the nation, but has particular knowledge of the Virginia state and federal courts, especially the 'rocket docket' of the Eastern District of Virginia. The disputes handled commonly fall into the areas of complex commercial, technology, IP, media and telecommunications litigation. Currently occupying lawyers is the defense of Blue Cross and Blue Shield Association in a RICO action brought by a nationwide class of healthcare providers, and lawyers have recently met with success in the representation of the Holy See in licensing disputes involving the reproduction rights and counterfeiting of Vatican artifacts. Clients benefit from the intellectual capital and technical resources spread throughout the firm's US, Latin American, European and Asian network.

**The Lawyers:** Northern Virginia managing partner Emily Yinger heads the commercial litigation group.

**Clients/Work Highlights:** College Loan Corporation; Exclusive Resorts; The Fairchild Corporation; Home Shopping Network; InterActiveCorp; L-Soft international; TV Azteca and The Vatican.

## Latham & Watkins LLP

**The Firm:** Working closely with lawyers from the firm's DC outpost and other offices nationally and beyond, this Northern Virginia litigation team has involvement in matters that extend way beyond the state lines. Major Fortune 500 corporations, many from the hi-tech arena, choose the firm for its ability to coordinate national and international disputes. Corporate litigation covers such areas as securities class actions and stockholder derivative actions, SEC enforcement, contested corporate control and white-collar criminal defense.

**The Lawyers:** Clients instruct **Laurie Smilan**, cochair of the securities litigation and professional liability group, for her "*exceptional*" skills and "*ency-clopedic*" knowledge of the law. Her recent experience includes the representation of a leading mechanical and electrical services company, and several of its executives, in a securities class action in which a motion to dismiss was successfully argued, and granted by the court.

**Clients/Work Highlights:** Adecco; Adolor Corporation; The AES Company; Bally Total Fitness; Boeing; The Carlyle Group; Dell and Tyco International.

## LeClair Ryan, A Professional Corporation

**The Firm:** Operating out of three cities within the state, the business litigation practice group of this regional firm represents clients in state and federal courts plus administrative hearings. The team is well known for its expertise in IP, particularly in the hi-tech marketplace. It is also skilled in the areas of antitrust, breach of contract, construction, defamation, employment and noncompete disputes, and has a distinct securities litigation and regulatory practice group which deals with the defense of securities fraud, insider trading, churning, and unsuitable and unauthorized investment actions.

**The Lawyers:** **Everette Allen**'s arrival within the past year as a result of the merger with commercial litigation boutique Allen & Allen has reinforced the firm's trial practice. Market sources described this general commercial authority as someone with "*bags of jury experience who understands the area and makes it simple.*"

## Morris & Morris PC

**The Firm:** This 15-strong litigation boutique houses excellent trial attorneys who practice in the state and federal courts of Virginia and throughout the mid-Atlantic. They take on all areas of general commercial litigation, arbitration and other forms of alternative dispute resolution, including construction, environmental, IP, labor and employment, products liability and transportation disputes. Insurance defense stands out as a key area of expertise.

**The Lawyers:** **James Morris** enjoys a "*supreme*" reputation throughout the region. Over a 30-year career, he has tried over 500 cases to verdict - an impressive achievement recognized by his election as the 55th President of the American College of Trial Lawyers in 2005. He is widely published and is commonly asked to deliver presentations for professional, commercial and educational organizations.

## Venable LLP

**The Firm:** Impressing with its solid litigation expertise and "*seamless*" service, this Virginia litigation group is seen as an ideal place to go "*whenever clients are in a pickle.*" The lawyers are skilled in dealing with general commercial, banking and workout, labor and employment, environmental, government contract, products liability, corporate and securities, tax, and unfair competition disputes in state and federal courts in Virginia, the mid-Atlantic region and all over the USA. The corporate defense and white-collar crime team is experienced at all kinds of government investigations and prosecutions.

**The Lawyers:** **William Dolan** is seen as someone with a "*huge presence*" in both the courtroom and the boardroom, prompting one client to describe him as simply "*the man*" for contentious matters. His work encompasses general commercial and patents disputes plus securities regulation and enforcement. Special praise was reserved for his "*outstanding*" white-collar crime and internal investigations work.

**Clients/Work Highlights:** Kansas-Lincoln, LC; CW Government Travel (Carlson); Anteon; VistaRMS and Ashburn Volunteer Fire and Rescue Department (Loundon County).

## Williams Mullen

**The Firm:** As one of the major practices in this firm, the litigation group is staffed by "*sharp and effective*" lawyers, and involved in some of the best cases around. Said to be "*tough*" opponents, the lawyers focus on cases in Virginia and DC state and federal courts; however, clients are from time to time also represented in other jurisdictions. Clients high-lighted the caliber and depth of the human and technological resources available to them, and welcomed the firm's efforts at achieving cost-efficient and streamlined working practices.

**The Lawyers:** **William Bayliss** conducts general commercial, professional liability, products liability, construction, toxic tort and insurance litigation. This "*great*" advocate "*knows his audience,*" researchers were told. They also learned of Bayliss's ability to develop an overall strategy while concentrating on the minutiae. **Samuel Hixon** is considered to be one of the best litigators in the state. He acts for plaintiffs and defendants on general commercial disputes in state, federal and appellate courts. Former prosecutor and now the head of the white-collar group, "*smart and easygoing*" **David Barger** uses his past experience to great advantage when defending clients in white-collar prosecutions, government investigations, corporate compliance and criminal tax controversies.

## Woods Rogers PLC

**The Firm:** This long-established commercial and civil litigation practice operates out of five statewide locations. According to clients, the litigators "*deserve all the praise in the world.*" Said to be "*always on the ball,*" they often team up with specialists from the firm's many other practice groups to provide an expert service in such issues as antitrust, construction, family, transportation and products and professional liability matters.

**The Lawyers:** The "*godfather*" of litigation in Virginia, according to some commentators, **William Poff** has tried cases at all levels up to and including the US Supreme Court. This "*senior guardsman*" has dominated the area throughout a long and distinguished career and is still considered to be an excellent choice, especially for professional liability, specifically medical malpractice. Another "*great*" trial lawyer, **James Jennings**, is experienced in general commercial litigation plus personal injury, products liability, Federal Employers Liability Act, environmental and land use matters. Clients were impressed by his "*very good courtroom presence and ability to keep the jury interested.*"

**Clients/Work Highlights:** Adams Construction; Carilion Healthcare; MeadWestvaco; Norfolk Southern Railway; Strongwell Corporation and Wachovia.

## Other Notable Practitioners

**Steven Cherry** (see p.278947) of "*premier*" firm WilmerHale is, according to clients, "*just what we're looking for.*" The "*savvy*" litigator is a "*pretty laid-back guy, but aggressive when he needs to be.*" He has litigated in trial and appellate courts throughout the USA, and also has experience of appearing in front of arbitration panels and administrative authorities. Representative clients include the Norwegian shipping company Odfjell ASA, Vie Financial Group and the Danaher Corporation. The "*marvelous*" **Jennifer Short** (see p.1986) of Holland & Knight LLP is well respected for her white-collar defense, government investigation and corporate compliance practice. Building on a background in healthcare, she now deals with such issues as fraud and false claims in heavily regulated industries and government contracting. She is loved by clients for her "*confident and relaxed*" courtroom style and a willingness to "*take the battle to the opponent.*" Proving that she is a complete lawyer, Short is equally impressive with her "*creative and practical*" counseling.

# REAL ESTATE

## Band 1

### Hirschler Fleischer

**The Firm:** This "*preeminent*" firm is considered to be something of a dominant force in the Virginia real estate market and "*may be the best around in zoning and land use.*" Impressing clients with the "*consistently high standard of attorneys throughout,*" this group is "*unique in its understanding of the marketplace, and is genuinely concerned about finding solutions that benefit both client and community.*" The team has carved out a strong profile in the financing and development of large-scale master-planned communities and mixed-use projects, as well as condominium builds and conversions. Lawyers in the REIT practice, although with a lower Virginia visibility, are nationally recognized and thought to be doing a "*super job.*"
**The Lawyers:** Clients admire **Charles Rothenberg**'s (see p.1986) ability to "*view a complicated legal proposal from a business perspective and make the deal*

work for both parties." A broad practice services owners, lenders, developers, builders and commercial landlords and tenants. By "*seeing to a greater depth than most attorneys,*" this detail-oriented lawyer "*never misses a trick.*" Recent activity includes the representation of a group of developers in the financing and execution of a 3,000-acre mixed-use development, and the handling of the zoning and permitting issues for a medical campus project on behalf of a healthcare client. **Mike Terry** (see p.1987), the "*top-shelf businessperson's lawyer,*" represents developers, property owners and tenants on real estate transactions. Lenders and borrowers attached to troubled transactions also turn to his niche practice in workout and reorganization for financial restructuring advice and pre-bankruptcy planning and negotiation. Clients appreciated his focus on "*starting with the commercial goals and then layering in the law afterward, and not vice versa.*" The "*quick-witted*" **James Theobald** (see p.1987) is well known for his "*sharp intellect*" and "*strong technical foundation*" in zoning and land use. Clients benefit from a "*masterful perspective in terms of business issues*" which particularly assists in facilitating agreement between parties with seemingly divergent points of view. This "*creative problem solver*" also undertakes real estate securities work for private REITs throughout the USA. Over a career spanning more than 45 years, **Jay Weinberg** (see p.1988) has built a reputation as a "*preeminent*" zoning, land use and general real estate authority throughout Virginia.
**Clients/Work Highlights:** Atack Properties; Daniel Corporation; Gumenick Properties; HH Hunt; Highwoods Properties; Home Depot and Silver Companies.

### Hunton & Williams LLP

See firm details p.1989
**The Firm:** Clients find value in the services of the Virginia real estate group in its "*commitment to making sure business goals are accomplished.*" A solid grounding in complex transaction, finance and REIT work is complemented by niche expertise in hospitality and leisure, transportation and infrastructure, healthcare, energy and land regeneration sectors. As a result of the firmwide ethos of assigning cross-disciplinary teams to work with clients as a unit, the real estate lawyers here are typically found to be operating alongside specialists from the corporate, securities, tax and environmental areas. Clients responded well to this bespoke delivery of a complete service by highlighting the firm's "*great value and efficiency.*"
**The Lawyers:** **William Walsh** (see p.1988) is considered to be an "*excellent*" lawyer who is leading the way with his transaction and development/redevelopment practice. He has built a particularly strong reputation for his national work in the areas of brownfield redevelopment projects and college/university student accommodation. As a senior member of the firm's multidisciplinary transportation infrastructure group, **Waverly Pulley** (see p.1986) is skilled in the develop-

ment, financing and leasing of transportation facilities and equipment. This "*top guy*" has been involved in some of the biggest projects carried out under Virginia's Public Private Transportation Act. Market sources view **Andrew Tapscott** (see p.1986) as a "*fine lawyer with a precise and professional approach.*" His emergent practice has built a national reputation on the back of an emphasis on the hospitality and leisure market, where he has experience of hotel, lodge, casino and golf course projects as well as in the increasingly popular 'condo hotels' concept. Through a close working relationship, **Daniel Campbell** (see p.1982) acquires an "*inside out*" knowledge of the client's organization and commercial objectives and is "*really willing to roll his sleeves up*" in order to achieve them. His "*technical competence, big-picture viewpoint and great business judgment*" combine to impress clients, who commonly hail from the healthcare and energy industries.
**Clients/Work Highlights:** Fluor; Halliburton; Norfolk State University and Virginia Commonwealth University.

### McGuireWoods LLP

**The Firm:** The "*leading individuals*" practicing here along with the high-profile matters undertaken have pushed the team up among the top players in the area. With a specialist real estate and land use team comprising over 50 attorneys from 15 multijurisdictional offices firmwide, this outfit certainly has the resources to tackle some of the largest and most complex transactions around the USA and the globe. The Virginia team often organizes itself across practice boundaries, adding value by pulling together expertise from the corporate and environmental groups in order to provide complete and seamless coverage on M&As, sales of assets and structured financings. The well-respected zoning and land use arm operates throughout Virginia and the mid-Atlantic region.
**The Lawyers:** The "*truly great*" **Nancy Little** is particularly renowned for real estate financing and development. Commonly found advising on the real estate aspects of corporate and M&A deals, she works closely with colleagues throughout the firm. Power and energy projects have been prominent in her impressive deal list, which also includes large aircraft transactions. **Craig Harmon**'s real estate finance practice stresses the representation of credit tenants, developers/equity participants and lenders on project finance and lease finance transactions. Developers and end users, particularly national retailers, also seek out this top lawyer for his work on acquisitions and lease transactions. A flourishing music industry side practice attracts recording artists, producers, labels, studios and management to his already plump client roster. **John Bates** handles the full sweep of real estate transactions and developments, particularly with respect to office, hotel, shopping center and major mixed-use projects. This "*first-class*" lawyer is considered to be a star in zoning and land use. **John Cogbill** has

worked on zoning and land use as well as general real estate matters throughout his 25 years at the firm. The "*highly thoughtful*" lawyer is a big player in land use and has particular expertise in mixed-use and sustainable/green developments. His reach extends beyond Virginia and, after an appointment by President George W Bush, he is currently engaged as chairman of the DC National Capital Planning Commission.
Clients/Work Highlights: The firm represents developers, REITs, institutional investors and Fortune 100 companies. Clients include CarMax; Circuit City; ConocoPhillips; Dominion Resources; GE Capital; SunTrust Bank and TIAA-CREF Financial Services.

## Troutman Sanders LLP
**The Firm:** This highly visible group, operating out of offices in Norfolk, Richmond, Tysons Corner and Virginia Beach, is recommended by market sources as one of the top real estate teams in Virginia. Interviewees agree it has "*a truly national practice and a great reputation.*" The team is experienced in all areas of real estate finance, acquisition, investment and development, and represents local, national and international developers, financial institutions, insurance companies and investors.
**The Lawyers:** Practicing for over 35 years, enduring Virginia "*icon*" **Philip Bagley** is quite rightly admired by peers for being "*at the top of the game.*" This valuable rainmaker is outstanding in his ability to attract top-quality national work and clients. He is recognized for his expertise in shopping center and office building development, financing and leasing.
Clients/Work Highlights: The team represents national corporations and institutional clients including Daniel Corporation, State Fair of Virginia and Wachovia.

## Band 2
## Holland & Knight LLP
See firm details p.1534
**The Firm:** With the ability to call upon the combined expertise of over 1,200 "*excellent*" lawyers and professionals practicing across the full spectrum of disciplines, this high-quality international firm can offer a comprehensive real estate service. A strong mid-Atlantic group advises clients on the acquisition and disposal of real estate, real estate financing, leasing, workouts, foreclosures and real estate-based bankruptcies. The deep knowledge and experience evident in the land use group is utilized in the representation of developer clients in front of local government regulators and state agencies. Construction and environmental teams are also on hand to collaborate on matters, as and when required.
**The Lawyers:** Renowned expert David Kahn directs the operations of the 60-lawyer real estate practice group from a strategically located DC base.

## Reed Smith LLP
See firm details p.1762
**The Firm:** The Falls Church office of this estimable global player houses a fine commercial real estate practice driven by a group of excellent lawyers. The team is skilled in the areas of commercial and residential acquisitions, finance and development; it acts for developers and builders as well as institutional and commercial lenders and investors. Clients additionally benefit from the firm's experience in the fields of public-private partnership development schemes and with REITs. Peers also pointed to a "*solid*" zoning and land use practice; its lawyers bring their knowledge of the local market to bear in the acquisition of regulatory consents for projects, appearing before government agencies, negotiating with civic action groups and conducting litigation if necessary.
**The Lawyers:** "*Real player*" **James Brennan** (see p.1982) represents lenders and developers on large-

scale commercial real estate transactions. An "*absolute grasp*" of the marketplace enhances his advice on retail, office, industrial and residential projects. Capitalizing on a wealth of government relations and lobbying experience, the "*highly effective*" **Bill Thomas** (see p.1988) appears before regulatory authorities at local and state levels in relation to land use approvals.

## Williams Mullen
**The Firm:** "*The volume of transactions and the high quality of clients*" combine to make this "*solid*" real estate and land use group a key player in Virginia and the wider region. The transactional and leasing expertise underpinning the group is supplemented by experts in land use who advise developers and landowners in planning matters and take cases before local and state authorities. As a further string to the firm's bow, lawyers advise borrower and lender clients associated with troubled projects on loan restructuring and workout schemes.
**The Lawyers:** Moving to Williams Mullen after a distinguished career in the public sector, former Virginia legislator **Ralph Axselle** "*casts a long shadow*" in the area of land use law. Clients seek his counsel in the knowledge that his depth of experience on the regulatory lobbying and administrative front is huge. **Andrew Condlin**'s practice also has a particular emphasis on zoning and land use. Historic preservation and local government law issues are key strengths.

## Other Notable Practitioners
**John Lavoie** (see p.1983) of construction law giant Watt Tieder Hoffar & Fitzgerald LLP was singled out for his regional and nationwide work in the acquisition and disposition, leasing and financing of commercial real estate plus workouts, restructurings and foreclosures. Cooley Godward LLP's **Antonio Calabrese** is considered one of the best land use and zoning lawyers in Northern Virginia. He worked with AOL in relation to its corporate headquarters in Dulles.

# Leaders in Virginia

**ALLEN, Everette**
LeClair Ryan, A Professional Corporation, Richmond 804 545 1500
buddy.allen@leclairryan.com
*Recommended in Litigation*
**Practice Areas:** Civil litigation, real estate development, commercial and professional disputes, securities/finance and debt restructuring.
**Prof. Memberships:** Member and Fellow, American College of Trial Lawyers.
**Career:** Everette G "*Buddy*" Allen, Jr was selected in 2004 Virginia Business' 'Legal Elite' as Virginia's top civil litigator; also selected, The Best Lawyers in America.
**Personal:** University of Virginia, LLB, 1965; Executive Editor, Virginia Law

Review (1964-65); law clerk to Judge Albert V Bryan of the Fourth Circuit US Court of Appeals (1965-66); Randolph-Macon College, BA, 1962. Fomer Member, Board of Trustees of Randolph-Macon College; Trustee, Virginia Student Aid Foundation; board member, other NASDAQ and ASE registered companies as well as real estate investment trusts.

**ATKINS, William P**
Pillsbury Winthrop Shaw Pittman LLP, McLean 703 770 7777
william.atkins@pillsburylaw.com
*Recommended in Intellectual Property*
**Practice Areas:** Mr Atkins is a trial and patent attorney. If the case cannot be settled, he uses the latest trial management software with a trial team carefully select-

ed for their legal/technical skill. His most recent victory was a three week jury trial win where plaintiff sought over $400M. It was just affirmed on appeal. Member, firm's Managing Board; recent Co-Leader, firm's IP Section; and President, Bar Association of DC.
**Prof. Memberships:** ABA; Virginia, Maryland, DC Bar Associations; Federal Circuit Bar Association.
**Personal:** LLM George Washington University, 1996; JD/MBA University of Baltimore, 1992; BS University of Maryland, 1986.

**BAKER, Lewis J**
Watt, Tieder, Hoffar & Fitzgerald LLP, McLean 703 749 1000
lbaker@wthf.com

*Recommended in Construction*
**Practice Areas:** Construction law, suretyship, goverment contracts, international construction.
**Prof. Memberships:** American Bar Association, Fellow - American College of Construction Lawyers, Maryland State Bar Association.
**Career:** Larry's practice involves the preparation, defense and litigation of major construction, surety and architect/engineer claims. He has an active goverment contracts practice and litigates bid protests both in the courts and before state and federal administrative forums.
**Publications:** 'Americans With Disabilities Act: Construction Industry Consid-

erations,' Construction Briefings (Author), 'Ambiguities in Contract Documents,' Construction Briefings (Author), 'Procurement Disputes at the State and Local Level: A Look for Fairness Among the Hodgepodge of Available Remedies,' (Author).

**BARUFKA, Jack S**
Pillsbury Winthrop Shaw Pittman LLP, McLean 703 770 7712
jack.barufka@pillsburylaw.com
*Recommended in Intellectual Property*
**Practice Areas:** Mr Barufka heads the Northern Virginia office Intellectual Property Counseling Practice. His practice includes patent prosecution, dispute resolution, licensing and pre-litigation opinions. He represents technology companies in the areas of electronics, semiconductor manufacturing, medical devices and mechanical technologies. He has served as an expert witness in patent infringement litigation. The 'Legal Times' ranked Mr Barufka as one of the best IP attorneys in the Washington DC area.
**Career:** Adjunct Professor, George Washington University
**Personal:** JD, American University, Washington College of Law (cum laude), 1992; LLM, George Washington University National Law Center, 1996; BS Binghamton University, 1987.

**BECKER, Richard K A**
Hogan & Hartson LLP, McLean 703 610 6123
rkbecker@hhlaw.com
*Recommended in Corporate/M&A*
**Practice Areas:** Mr Becker advises on M&A, private equity and venture capital matters in the information technology, biotechnology, defense, satellite, hospitality and healthcare industries. Recent transactions include advising The DIRECTV Group, Inc. in the sale of its set top box and VSAT businesses.
**Prof. Memberships:** Steering Committee, Corporation, Finance and Securities Law Section, District of Columbia Bar Member, Virginia State Bar Member, Virginia Bar Association.
**Career:** Mr Becker is Administrative Partner of the firm's Northern Virginia office.
**Publications:** 'Focus On Venture Capital: Legal Primer for Emerging Business' (5/1/2004).
**Personal:** Harvard Law School (JD, 1983); Princeton University, (AB, cum laude, 1980).

**BRENNAN, James C**
Reed Smith LLP, Falls Church 703 641 4252
jbrennan@reedsmith.com
*Recommended in Real Estate*
**Practice Areas:** Commercial real estate and business transactions. Represents clients in all aspects of acquisition, development, construction, financing and leasing. Experienced in developing golf

course communities, shopping centers, and air cargo facilities at airports around the country; negotiating long-term ground leases; and providing representation of complex financing transactions through conventional or bond financing.
**Career:** Joined Hazel & Thomas in 1997, which combined with Reed Smith in 1999.
**Personal:** New York Law School (JD, 1992), member of the 'Law Review'; Georgetown University Law Center (LLM, 1998); University of Richmond (1989).

**BRETSCHNEIDER, Barry E**
Morrison & Foerster LLP, McLean 703 760 7743
bbretschneider@mofo.com
*Recommended in Intellectual Property*
**Practice Areas:** Concentrates on patent infringement litigation in district courts and before the International Trade Commission: patent interferences, patent licensing and related transactional work, patent prosecution and trademark litigation and prosecution. Represents US and foreign corporations. Clients cover a wide range of industries, including the medical devices, electronics, polymers, composite materials and consumer products industries, among many others.
**Career:** Admitted to practice in the District of Columbia, Virginia and Texas. Former Chair, Education and Interference Committees, American Intellectual Property Law Association.
**Personal:** AB, Princeton University; JD, University of Iowa College of Law; LLM, The George Washington University Law School.

**BROWN, Stanley**
Hogan & Hartson LLP, McLean 703 610 6150
sjbrown@hhlaw.com
*Recommended in Employment*
**Practice Areas:** Single plaintiff and class action equal employment litigation, wrongful discharge, whistleblower, FLSA and ERISA litigation; trade secrets and non-compete litigation, labor management relations, including collective bargaining arbitration and cases before the NLRB; Employment contracts and employment disputes relating to senior level executives.
**Prof. Memberships:** American Bar Association; Committee on Development of the Law under the National Labor Relations Act; Faculty, Virginia State Bar Professionalism Course; Virginia Bar Association, Labor Relations and Employment Law Section.
**Career:** Partner since 1994. Former attorney, Appellate Litigation Branch, National Labor Relations Board.
**Publications:** 'An Ounce of Prevention Inoculating Your Company Against Sarbanes-Oxley and Whistleblower Threats', Hogan & Hartson L.L.P. Managing Your

People: From Hiring to Firing and Everything in Between., Hogan & Hartson L.L.P. (5/6/2004); Has presented papers at conferences sponsored by the US Department of Labor and received a Certificate of Commendation from that agency for his contributions.
**Personal:** Georgetown University Law Center (JD, 1969); Columbia University (BS, 1966).

**BROWNELL, Thomas**
Holland & Knight LLP, McLean 703 720 8600
thomas.brownell@hklaw.com
*Recommended in Construction*
**Practice Areas:** Partner in the firm's Litigation Section practicing in the areas of intellectual property law, government contracts, construction claims and disputes and real estate and business litigation. He is experienced in the preparation and trial of complex civil cases, and in the counseling and drafting of agreements in the areas of software development, software licensing, construction and real estate. He has significant trial experience in the areas of patent infringement, trade secret, and copyright infringement in the computer software industry, commercial disputes relating to the delivery and installation of integrated computer systems and a wide range of construction disputes.

**BUCKLEY, Kevin J**
Hunton & Williams LLP, Richmond 804 788 8616
kbuckley@hunton.com
*Recommended in Capital Markets, Corporate/M&A*
**Practice Areas:** Mr Buckley is Co-Head of Hunton & Williams' nationally-prominent Asset Securitization Practice. His practice focuses on mortgage and asset-backed securitizations, structured financings, and other capital markets transactions. He represents issuers, underwriters, trustees, master servicers, insurers, and other participants in securitizations and other capital markets transactions. Mr Buckley has served as issuer's counsel in connection with the design and implementation of securitization programs involving unique asset types and innovative securities structures, including the first REMIC program backed by a full faith and credit guarantee of the US and the first public securitization of reperforming government-guaranteed loans.

**BUNIVA, Brian L**
LeClair Ryan, A Professional Corporation, Richmond 804 916 7130
brian.buniva@leclairryan.com
*Recommended in Environment*
**Practice Areas:** Administrative law; environmental; land use and zoning; local government; litigation. Represents public utilities, local governments, publicly traded and privately held companies, developers, manufacturing interests.
**Prof. Memberships:** Past Chair, Virginia

State Bar's Administrative and Environmental Law Sections. Board of Governors, Virginia Bar's Environmental Section (past Chair, Administrative Law Section). Past Chair, Richmond Bar's Environmental Section. Vice-Chair, Solid Waste Committee - ABA's Environmental Section. Member, Virginia State Bar's Bench-Bar Relations Committee.
**Career:** Virginia Assistant Attorney General for Health and Environmental Sections (1979-83), private practice (1983-present). Selected, Virginia Business' 'Legal Elite' - Environmental Law, 2000, 2001 (profiled), 2003, and 2004, Transportation/Admiralty/Intermodal - 2005. Selected, top Environmental Lawyers, Richmond Magazine. Selected, Chambers USA 2004 - 2006 Client's Guide to America's Leading Lawyers for Business for Environmental Law.
**Personal:** University of Richmond Law, JD, 1979; Georgetown University, AB, 1972.

**CAMPBELL, Christopher C**
Hunton & Williams, McLean 703 714 7553
ccampbell@hunton.com
*Recommended in Intellectual Property*
**Practice Areas:** Mr Campbell's practice focuses on intellectual property with emphasis on all aspects of patent law, including patent infringement litigation, client counseling, licensing and transactional matters, patent prosecution and freedom to operate opinions. He also has extensive experience in complex patent practice matters, including patent interference, reissues, reexaminations (including inter partes), appeals and protests, as well as claims relating to trademark and copyright matters, including infringement claims; unfair competition and deceptive trade practices; misappropriation of trade secrets, false advertising; claims relating to licensing, and other contracts relating to intellectual property rights in US district courts.

**CAMPBELL, Daniel M**
Hunton & Williams LLP, Richmond 804 788 8503
dcampbell@hunton.com
*Recommended in Real Estate*
**Practice Areas:** Daniel Campbell focuses on land development, in particular the needs of Hunton & Williams' energy and healthcare clients in addressing the unique development, financing and related regulatory issues facing those industries. He also has substantial experience in the leasing, acquisition, disposition and securitization of real estate assets in the context of real estate investment trusts and mergers, acquisitions and other corporate restructurings.

**CHASON, Craig**
Pillsbury Winthrop Shaw Pittman LLP, McLean 703 770 7947
Craig.Chason@pillsburylaw.com

*Recommended in Corporate/M&A*

**Practice Areas:** Mr Chason has extensive expertise in mergers and acquisitions, venture capital financings and public and private securities offerings. His practice includes advising clients on consolidation strategies, auction sales and public company acquisitions. While he represents a broad range of private and public corporations, a significant number of his clients are high-tech companies and government contractors.

**Prof. Memberships:** Admitted to Practice: District of Columbia, Virginia; American Bar Association Section of Business Law; Northern Virginia Technology Council; Association of Corporate Growth.

**Personal:** University of Virginia School of Law, JD, 1983; University of Virginia, BA, with high honors, 1977.

---

**CHERRY, Steven F**
WilmerHale, McLean 703 251 9770
steven.cherry@wilmerhale.com
*Recommended in Litigation*

**Practice Areas:** Represents a wide range of institutions and individual executives in trial and appellate courts throughout the country before federal and state courts, regulatory agencies and commercial arbitration tribunals. He focuses on complex civil litigation, including antitrust, ERISA, securities class actions, and other corporate and commercial disputes.

**Prof. Memberships:** Member of American Bar Association, District of Columbia Bar Association and Virginia Bar Association, as well as their respective litigation, business law and employment law sections.

**Personal:** JD, cum laude, University of Michigan Law School, 1989, Note Editor, Michigan Law Review; MPA, Indiana University, 1986; BS, Indiana State University, 1983.

---

**CONNOLLY, Theresa**
DLA Piper Rudnick Gray Cary US LLP,
Reston 703 773 4007
theresa.connolly@dlapiper.com
*Recommended in Employment*

**Practice Areas:** Labor and employment.

**Career:** Represents employers in all labor and employment law matters, including litigation in state and federal courts, before arbitration panels and administrative agencies, negotiating employment agreements, drafting employment policies, and compliance with employment-related statutes and regulations. Performs training on human resource management and employment law issues. Handles traditional labor matters including union avoidance, elections, arbitrations and NLRB proceedings. She has written or co-authored numerous articles on employment-related topics, including investigating and resolving harassment complaints, privacy in the workplace, violence in the workplace, union organiz-

ing, and union avoidance.

**Personal:** JD, Fordham University; BS, Cornell University.

---

**COX, Robert K**
Watt, Tieder, Hoffar & Fitzgerald LLP,
McLean 703 749 1000
rcox@wthf.com
*Recommended in Construction*

**Practice Areas:** Construction law, suretyship, government contracts, international construction.

**Prof. Memberships:** AGC of America, Virginia State Bar, Board of Governors - Construction Law and Public Contracts Section (1991-2000, Chair 1999-2000).

**Career:** Bob Cox focuses his practice on construction and suretyship matters, including the negotiation of construction contracts and resolution of construction disputes. Honors include Chambers USA - Top Construction Lawyers in Virginia; Virginia Business Legal Elite; International Who's Who of Construction Lawyers; and International Who's Who of Business Lawyers.

**Publications:** Bob has authored and co-authored numerous articles on construction law and suretyship issues and frequently lectures on these topics.

---

**DARE, Mark**
Reed Smith LLP, Falls Church
703 641 4290
mdare@reedsmith.com
*Recommended in Employment*

**Practice Areas:** Employment litigation and counseling, advising and defending employers faced with employment-related claims, handling counseling and representation before local human rights commissions, the EEOC, and state and federal courts.

**Prof. Memberships:** American, Virginia and Fairfax Bar Associations. Former President, Fairfax Bar Association.

**Publications:** Editor of 'Employment Law in Virginia,' a two-volume reference work. Frequent lecturer and author of written materials on employment issues for Virginia State Bar, and Fairfax and Alexandria Chambers of Commerce, among others.

**Personal:** University of Virginia (JD, 1974); Princeton University (1971); named one of state's 'Legal Elite' by 'Virginia Business' magazine.

---

**DE BERNARDO, Mark A**
Jackson Lewis, Vienna
703 821 4308
debernam@jacksonlewis.com
*Recommended in Employment*

**Practice Areas:** Labor and employment; executive employment termination; employment litigation; drug testing; substance-abuse prevention; class action management.

**Prof. Memberships:** District of Columbia Court of Appeals; US Supreme Court; American Bar Association.

**Career:** Executive Director, Institute for a

Drug-Free Workplace; General Counsel, Council for Employment Law Equity; Director, Labor Law and Special Counsel for Domestic Policy, US Chamber of Commerce; testified 40+ times before Congress and regulatory agencies; wrote 11 amici curiae briefs to US Supreme Court.

**Publications:** Authored 18+ publications on drug testing, plant closings, labor relations, wage-hour and occupational safety.

**Personal:** Georgetown University, JD, 1979; Marquette University, BA, cum laude, 1976.

---

**DRAY, Mark S**
Hunton & Williams LLP, Richmond
804 788 8408
mdray@hunton.com
*Recommended in Employment*

**Practice Areas:** Mark Dray's practice focuses on all areas of ERISA, including the design, implementation and administration of pension and welfare benefits plans for public and private taxable and exempt private sector employers and governmental entities. Mark has significant experience with all types of executive and incentive compensation arrangements, with the fiduciary provisions of Title I of ERISA, in addressing qualified plan compliance problems, and in co-ordinating benefits issues arising in the context of mergers and acquisitions. Mr Dray is a frequent speaker on benefits topics and has long held leadership roles in ABA related and other professional organizations.

---

**FARNHAM, James**
Hunton & Williams LLP, Richmond
804 788 8501
jfarnham@hunton.com
*Recommended in Litigation*

**Practice Areas:** Jim Farnham's practice concentrates on complex business litigation matters in the financial services/securities industries. It includes class actions, derivative actions, multi-party fraud trials, internal investigations and corporate governance matters. In more than 38 years of trial work, he's handled more than 50 significant jury trials/arbitrations through verdict, involving a variety of substantive areas of law.

**Prof. Memberships:** Fellow, American College of Trial Lawyers, 20 years; Fourth Circuit Judicial Conference, 12 years; Best Lawyers in America - Civil Litigation, 23 years; Faculty Member, VBA Professionalism Course; speaker/lecturer - law schools, Bar CLE, Pro-Bono Projects.

---

**FINTO, Kevin**
Hunton & Williams LLP, Richmond
804 788 8568
kfinto@hunton.com
*Recommended in Environment*

**Practice Areas:** Kevin Finto's practice focuses on air and water permitting (electric generation facilities, pulp and paper mills, steel mills and specialty chemical

facilities), enforcement (New Source Review) and permit challenges; wetlands; voluntary remediation; economic development; environmental aspects of business transactions; and environmental management system development. He is listed in Who's Who in Executives and Professionals, has been selected to Virginia's Legal Elite, December 2000-04 and Best Lawyers in America, 2006.

**Career:** Engineer, Chevron USA; Adjunct Professor, Virginia Commonwealth University School of Engineering.

---

**FITZGERALD, Robert M**
Watt, Tieder, Hoffar & Fitzgerald LLP,
McLean 703 749 1000
rfitzger@wthf.com
*Recommended in Construction*

**Practice Areas:** Construction law, suretyship, government contracts, international construction.

**Prof. Memberships:** American Bar Association, New York, Virginia, District of Columbia and Fairfax County Bar Associations, Martindale-Hubbell's Highest Peer Rating, elected to membership in Moles Honorary Underground Construction Society.

**Career:** Bob Fitzgerald's Construction Contract Legal Practice is focused primarily on the preparation and resolution of claims for additional time and money under both public and private construction contracts. His practice is international in scope and he has developed a particular expertise in heavy construction contract disputes relating to dams, canals, powerplants, water and sewage treatment plants, and machine mined tunnels.

---

**FLAHERTY, Thomas**
Pillsbury Winthrop Shaw Pittman LLP,
McLean 703 770 7886
Thomas.Flaherty@pillsburylaw.com
*Recommended in Employment*

**Practice Areas:** Mr Flaherty has a national and local practice encompassing all areas of employment and labor law, including litigation and advice. He has litigated in many jurisdictions and is experienced in federal court class action litigation under the employment discrimination laws and the wage-hour laws, as well as in multi-plaintiff litigation in harassment and downsizing cases. He has also represented management in all aspects of traditional labor relations, including both representation cases and unfair labor practice proceedings before the National Labor Relations Board.

**Personal:** JD, Boston College, 1975; BA, Yale University, 1972.

---

**FOLEY, Christopher**
Finnegan Henderson Farabow Garrett & Dunner LLP, Reston 571 203 2720
christopher.foley@finnegan.com
*Recommended in Intellectual Property*

**Practice Areas:** Practices both trademark and patent law. Trademark practice includes procurement of trademark reg-

istrations, participation in inter partes administrative proceedings, evaluating potentially infringing marks, licensing, and litigation. Has co-ordinated the daily activities of litigations from the initial pleading stage through trials before judges and juries. Has handled patent prosecution and disputes relating to aircraft and automotive parts, packaging designs, injection molding products and equipment, medical products and methods, networking systems, and tools and tooling machinery.
**Prof. Memberships:** District of Columbia Bar; American Intellectual Property Law Association.
**Personal:** United States Naval Academy (BS, 1975); Georgetown University Law Center (JD, 1983).

### FUHR, Edward J
Hunton & Williams LLP, Richmond
804 788 8201
efuhr@hunton.com
*Recommended in Litigation*
**Practice Areas:** Ed Fuhr is Head of the Securities and Corporate Governance Litigation Practice at Hunton & Williams. His practice focuses on corporate governance and securities litigation, mergers and acquisitions, business torts, commercial contract disputes and appellate litigation. He has received recognition in Who's Who in American Lawyers, The Best Lawyers In America - Business Litigation, and Virginia's Legal Elite. Prior to joining the firm, Mr Fuhr served as Attorney-Advisor in the Office of Legal Counsel with the Department of Justice. He received his Law Degree, cum laude, from the University of Chicago.

### GASCH JR, Manning
Hunton & Williams LLP, Richmond
804 788 8342
mgasch@hunton.com
*Recommended in Environment*
**Practice Areas:** Manning Gasch's practice focuses on 'environmental disaster' cases including all phases of CERCLA, general toxics, oil spill and natural resource damages practice, from development of expert reports and testimony to negotiations with various state and federal regulatory, law enforcement and trustee entities, through state and federal litigation.

### GATTO, James
Pillsbury Winthrop Shaw Pittman LLP, McLean 703 770 7754
james.gatto@pillsburylaw.com
*Recommended in Intellectual Property*
**Practice Areas:** Mr Gatto focuses on patents, trade secrets, and open source for computer software, bioinformatics, financial services, business methods and internet-related inventions. Mr Gatto regularly provides strategic counseling for IP portfolio development and enforcement and handles high profile litigation, including: Won patent interference for Nobel Prize

winner; successfully sued the US Government for patent infringement; successfully defended two internet coupon patent lawsuits; successfully enforced coupon patent in a third; and successfully defended against OGT patents and enforced DNA image array analysis software patent for same company.
**Personal:** JD, Georgetown University, 1988; BE Manhattan College (Electrical Engineering; Physics minor), 1984.

### GOOLSBY, Allen
Hunton & Williams LLP, Richmond
804 788 8289
agoolsby@hunton.com
*Recommended in Corporate/M&A*
**Practice Areas:** Allen Goolsby's practice focuses on corporate law, including corporate governance, mergers and acquisitions, and securities and finance.
**Career:** Mr Goolsby has worked on a variety of merger, acquisition and financing transactions involving publicly held corporations. He specializes in advising publicly-held corporations regarding corporate governance. He also served as the princial draftsman of the Virginia Stock Corporation Act.
**Publications:** 'Goolsby on Virginia Corporations' (LexisNexis) (Second Edition); 'Virginia Corporation Law and Practice' (Prentice Hall Law & Business).

### GOTTS, Lawrence
Pillsbury Winthrop Shaw Pittman LLP, Washington, DC 202 663 8000
*Recommended in Intellectual Property*
*Please see District of Columbia for profile*

### HAYES, Timothy G
Hunton & Williams LLP, Richmond
804 788 8244
thayes@hunton.com
*Recommended in Environment*
**Practice Areas:** Timothy Hayes' Environmental Practice focuses on enforcement, permitting, litigation, regulatory counseling, appellate advocacy, project development, land use and government relations.

### HESS, Adam R
Pillsbury Winthrop Shaw Pittman LLP, McLean 703 770 7789
adam.hess@pillsburylaw.com
*Recommended in Intellectual Property*
**Practice Areas:** Mr Hess' practice encompasses all aspects of intellectual property litigation, including Section 337 cases before the US ITC. He also has extensive experience in Intellectual Property Counseling, including patent prosecution; preparation of opinions; licensing; and ADR. He has represented US, European, and Far East clients in a wide range of technologies. He has been consistently recognized by peers as one of the best IP lawyers in Virginia in several polls. Prior to joining the firm, he worked at Hercules Chemicals, Borg Warner Chemicals, and FMC Corporation.

**Personal:** JD, George Washington University, 1992; BS, Lehigh University (Chemical Engineering), 1987.

### HOFFAR, Julian F
Watt, Tieder, Hoffar & Fitzgerald LLP, McLean 703 749 1000
jhoffar@wthf.com
*Recommended in Construction*
**Practice Areas:** Construction law, goverment contracts, international construction.
**Prof. Memberships:** AAA Large Complex Case Panel of Arbitrators, Fellow - American College of Construction Lawyers, Association of Trial Lawyers of America, Virginia Bar Association.
**Career:** Jules has focused on representation of owners, contractors, subcontractors, engineers and owner-developers involved in construction and supply disputes both in the United States and internationally. He has also served as mediator in a wide range of construction disputes. Honors include Chambers USA - Top Construction Lawyers in Virginia; Virginia Business Legal Elite; Best Lawyers in America; Best Lawyers in International Construction and Virginia Super Lawyer 2006.

### HORAN, Richard
Hogan & Hartson LLP, McLean
703 610 6111
rthoran@hhlaw.com
*Recommended in Corporate/M&A*
**Practice Areas:** Mr Horan serves as a Director of the firm's Corporate, Securities and Finance Group and is a Member of the firm's Executive Committee.
**Career:** His practice focuses on mergers and acquisitions. Mr Horan represents public and private companies in strategic transactions in many different industries, including communications and media, technology, energy, pharmaceutical, healthcare and government contracts. He has wide-ranging experience advising clients on various acquisition matters, including public and private mergers, stock and asset purchases, divestitures, spin-offs, and auction transactions.
**Personal:** James Madison University (BA, summa cum laude, 1984); University of Virginia School of Law (JD, 1987).

### KEARFOTT, Joseph C
Hunton & Williams LLP, Richmond
804 788 8446
jkearfott@hunton.com
*Recommended in Litigation*
**Practice Areas:** Joseph Kearfott's practice focuses on all aspects of civil litigation, both state and federal, at the trial and appellate levels, with particular focus on complex product liability and toxic tort litigation. Other areas of practice include premises liability and other personal injury litigation, commercial disputes, business torts and valuation litigation. He is listed in Who's Who in America, Who's Who in American Law, Virginia Business Maga-

zine, 'Legal Elite' in 2001-02 (best civil litigators in Virginia), and the 2005 BTI Client Service All-Star Team for Law Firms.

### KNOX, Thomas J
Morrison & Foerster LLP, McLean
703 760 7317
tknox@mofo.com
*Recommended in Corporate/M&A*
**Practice Areas:** Co-Chair of the firm's Mid-Atlantic Corporate Practice Group. Concentrates on corporate and securities matters, including corporate governance issues, investment transactions and mergers and acquisitions, and technology transactions work, including licensing, channel agreements, technology transfers and related matters. Clients include a wide range of information technology, internet services, telecommunications, life sciences, network security and other companies in the Mid-Atlantic region and elsewhere. Has worked with companies at every stage of development, from Fortune 500 companies to start-ups.
**Career:** Admitted to practice in Virginia, Maryland, and the District of Columbia.
**Personal:** JD, University of Michigan Law School; BA, Middlebury College.

### KRIZAN, Lisa M
LMK Associates, Richmond
804 359 2964
lkrizan@lmkassociates.com
*Recommended in Intellectual Property*
**Practice Areas:** Patent, copyright and trademark licensing, music licensing, national, foreign and international trademark and copyright prosecution, trademark and copyright infringement, employment agreements, intellectual property creation, trade secret protection, advertising law, transactional work.
**Prof. Memberships:** Virginia State Bar Association, INTA, National Association of Women Business Owners (Richmond).
**Career:** Partner since 2001.
**Publications:** Authored The Non-Specialist's Guide to Intellectual Property Law (the Virginia Law Foundation). Author of a column on www.soniccontrol.com 'Krizan on IP'. Author of a column in Average Girl Magazine, 'Women and the Law'.
**Personal:** Catholic University School of Law (JD, 1990); College of William & Mary (BA, 1985).

### LALIK, Elizabeth A
Hunton & Williams, McLean
703 714 7432
elalik@hunton.com
*Recommended in Employment*
**Practice Areas:** Emphasis on litigation of employment-related disputes involving sales commission issues, non-compete/non-solicitation/trade secret claims, discrimination/harassment claims, and wage and hour issues.
**Prof. Memberships:** Past Board Member and Secretary, Women in Technology; past President, Fairfax Bar Employment

Law Section.

**Publications:** Author, Employment Law in Virginia (FMLA chapter); Co-chair, Trade Secret Transactions & Litigation Conference; Presenter, The Employee Whistleblower and Complaint Procedure Provisions of the Sarbanes-Oxley Act; Co-author, 'New Code of Ethics Requirements for All Employees of NYSE and NASDAQ Listed Companies'.

**Personal:** JD, University of Virginia School of Law, 1993; BS, Cornell University, School of Industrial and Labor Relations, 1990.

### LAVOIE, John G
Watt, Tieder, Hoffar & Fitzgerald LLP, McLean 703 749 1000
jlavoie@wthf.com
*Recommended in Real Estate*

**Practice Areas:** Commercial Real Estate.
**Prof. Memberships:** Virginia, Maryland and District of Columbia Bar Associations, GWCAR, NAIOP.
**Career:** Jack focuses his practice on real estate transactions including the acquisition and disposition of commercial real estate. He has substantial experience in the representation of landlords, tenants, lenders and borrowers in the leasing and finance of commercial property. He has represented both institutional and individual landlords and tenants in many lease transactions.
**Publications:** Jack has published several articles and spoken on a range of practical legal topics.
**Personal:** Jack is also a licensed real estate salesperson in Virginia, DC and Massachusetts.

### LECLAIR, Gary D
LeClair Ryan, A Professional Corporation, Richmond 804 783 2003
gleclair@leclairryan.com
*Recommended in Corporate/M&A*

**Practice Areas:** Represents public and privately held companies, Boards of Directors and executives as securities and general counsel. Lead attorney in numerous private and public debt and equity financings, joint ventures, strategic alliances, mergers and acquisitions, and other major domestic and international transactions. Director of various business and civic entities including a bank, a trust company, a real estate development company, a foundation and a university board of visitors.
**Prof. Memberships:** Virginia Bar.
**Career:** Co-founder and Chairman of LeClair Ryan.
**Publications:** Frequent lecturer/author at CLE and industry conferences.
**Personal:** Georgetown University, JD, magna cum laude, 1982. Virginia Business' 'Legal Elite'. Ernst & Young Virginia Entrepreneur of the Year Award, 1997. The Leadership Award by the Greater Richmond Technology Council, 1999.

### LEWIS, Jack L
Morrison & Foerster LLP, McLean 703 760 7322
Jlewis@mofo.com
*Recommended in Corporate/M&A*

**Practice Areas:** Extensive experience helping businesses and entrepreneurs develop effective business strategies, from start-up stage to operation as successful public companies. A pioneer in developing the venture capital/emerging companies practice for technology companies in the Mid-Atlantic region. Counsels clients in the internet, e-commerce, enterprise and other software, and information technology matters. Represents exiting employees forming new businesses and executives joining public and private companies. Experienced in capital raising, employee arrangements, international expansion, buyouts, mergers and acquisitions, and public offerings.
**Career:** Admitted to practice in Virginia and the District of Columbia.
**Personal:** AB, Brown University, 1965; JD, Cornell Law School, 1969.

### LIPSEY, Charles
Finnegan Henderson Farabow Garrett & Dunner LLP, Reston 571 203 2755
charles.lipsey@finnegan.com
*Recommended in Intellectual Property*

**Practice Areas:** Concentrates on intellectual property litigation, particularly patent infringement litigation, in the district courts, the US Court of Appeals for the Federal Circuit, and the US Supreme Court. Has handled cases involving mechanical, chemical, and electrical technologies, with emphasis on biotechnology and pharmaceutical chemistry. Also has handled numerous patent arbitration proceedings and patent interferences.
**Prof. Memberships:** District of Columbia Bar, Virginia State Bar, American Intellectual Property Law Association.
**Personal:** Georgia Institute of Technology (BS, Chemical Engineering, 1972); George Washington University National Law Center (JD, 1977; LLM, Patent and Trademark Regulation Law, 1981).

### LOULAKIS, Michael
Wickwire Gavin P.C., Vienna 703 790 8750
mloulakis@wickwire.com
*Recommended in Construction*

**Practice Areas:** Represents parties in the construction industry, including owners/developers, design-builders, general contractors, and design professionals. Substantial experience representing owners of international power, petrochemical and refinery projects, including the development of risk and claims management programs, and negotiation of EPC contracts. Nationally recognized for advising clients on public sector design-build projects, including development of procurement documents, design-build contracts and teaming agreements. Preparation,

negotiation and defense of contract claims through litigation, arbitration and other ADR methods.
**Prof. Memberships:** Design-Build Institute of America (Member, Board of Directors, 1993-2003); Construction Management Association of America; American Arbitration Association, National Construction Panel.
**Publications:** 'Construction Business Formbook', Aspen Publishers, 2003; 'Design-Build for the Public Sector', Aspen Publishers, 2003, editor; 'Design-Build Lessons Learned', published annually since 1995, A/E/C Training Technologies, LLC; 'Design-Build: Planning Through Development', McGraw-Hill, 2001; 'Design-Build Contracting Handbook', 2nd Edition, Aspen Publishers, 2001; 'Construction Project Delivery Systems: Evaluating the Owner's Alternatives', A/E/C Training Technologies, LLC (1999).

### LYNCH, Brian
Hogan & Hartson LLP, McLean 703 610 6165
BJLynch@hhlaw.com
*Recommended in Corporate/M&A*

**Practice Areas:** Mr Lynch represents a wide range of corporate issuers, directors, investment banks and private equity firms in capital market, private investment and merger and acquisition transactions in the US and internationally.
**Career:** Mr Lynch's career began at the US Securities and Exchange Commission in 1987 and he has maintained an active private practice focus, since 1990, on securities regulation, corporate governance and transactional engagements involving publicly traded corporations, including large multinationals. He serves on firm-wide Capital Markets and Life Sciences leadership groups.
**Personal:** La Salle University (BS, Accounting, cum laude, 1983); Temple University School of Law (JD, 1987).

### MARTINEZ DE ANDINO, J Michael
Hunton & Williams LLP, Richmond 804 788 7216
mmartinez@hunton.com
*Recommended in Intellectual Property*

**Practice Areas:** Patents - prosecution, litigation, licensing, due diligence and transactional work. Counsels clients concerning IP issues in structuring deals and drafting agreements.
**Prof. Memberships:** Virginia, Kansas, Missouri State Bars. US Court of Appeals for the Federal Circuit, US Patent & Trademark Office; ABA, AIPLA.
**Career:** Partner.
**Publications:** 12/01/05 Privilege of IP Opinions Under the Common Interest Doctrine, The Practical Lawyer; 12/01/04 Careers in Intellectual Property Law, Minority Trial Lawyer; 08/01/04 Conducting an Intellectual Property Due Diligence Investigation, Intellectual Prop-

erty & Technology Law Journal.
**Personal:** University of Kansas Law (1991), William & Mary (MBA 1986), University of Virginia (BS 1978).

### MELTZER, Steven
Pillsbury Winthrop Shaw Pittman LLP, McLean 703 770 7950
Steven.Meltzer@pillsburylaw.com
*Recommended in Corporate/M&A*

**Practice Areas:** Mr Meltzer represents numerous private and publicly held businesses in a wide range of transactions including mergers and acquisitions, divestitures, joint ventures, international and domestic licensing and distribution agreements, venture capital financings, public and private securities offerings, 'going private' transactions, and financial restructurings. He counsels companies and investors in capital formation, governance, securities compliance, employment and compensation matters, and shareholder issues. He is a member of Pillsbury's Managing Board.
**Personal:** Brown University (AB Economics, cum laude, 1968), Harvard Business School (MBA with high distinction/Baker Scholar, 1973), Harvard Law School (JD,1973).

### MOORE, Justin
Hunton & Williams LLP, Richmond 804 788 8464
jmoore@hunton.com
*Recommended in Corporate/M&A*

**Practice Areas:** Jay Moore's practice focuses on mergers and acquisitions, corporate finance, corporate governance and securities regulation. He is Co-Head of the firm's Global Capital Markets and Mergers and Acquisitions Team. He is listed in The Best Lawyers in America for corporate, mergers and acquisitions and securities law, Virginia's Legal Elite selected by Virginia Business magazine and Virginia Super Lawyers selected by Richmond magazine.

### MOORE, Thurston R
Hunton & Williams LLP, Richmond 804 788 8295
tmoore@hunton.com
*Recommended in Corporate/M&A*

**Practice Areas:** Thurston Moore's practice focuses primarily on corporate and securities representation with emphasis on corporate financing and governance, venture capital, real estate investment trusts and partnership law. He was Managing Partner of the firm from 1991 to 2006 and Chairman of the firm since 2006.
**Prof. Memberships:** Trustee, Virginia Museum of Fine Arts; immediate past Chairman, The Nature Conservancy of Virginia; Advisor to Special Committee on Uniform Limited Partnership Act of the National Conference of Commissioners on Uniform Laws; Fellow, American Bar Foundation; Fellow, Virginia Bar Foundation; Member of Council, Busi-

ness Law Section, American Bar Association (1999-2003).

## MORSE, Clinton S
LeClair Ryan, A Professional Corporation, Roanoke 540 510 3023
clinton.morse@leclairryan.com
*Recommended in Employment*
**Practice Areas:** Labor and employment; represents unionized companies across the nation (collective bargaining, grievance/arbitrations, NLRB matters). Counsel on union-free management issues (union avoidance strategies, management training, election campaigns); employment litigation and counseling; wage and hour law.
**Prof. Memberships:** Roanoke, Virginia (past Chairman, Labor Relations and Employment Law Section) Bar Associations; State Bar of Texas (Labor Law Section); Virginia State Bar; Member - Board, Executive Committee & Management Relations Committee, Virginia Chamber of Commerce.
**Publications:** National lecturer/author on labor and employment topics. Contributor, Virginia Employment Law Letter.
**Personal:** University of Texas, JD, 1970. Order of the Coif. Texas Law Review. Selected: The Best Lawyers in America; Virginia Business 'Legal Elite'.

## MURPHY, Thomas P
Hunton & Williams, McLean
703 714 7533
tpmurphy@hunton.com
*Recommended in Employment*
**Practice Areas:** Thomas Murphy's practice focuses on all areas of labor and employment law, with particular emphasis on the trial of discrimination cases. He has been listed in The Best Lawyers In America for over 10 years, and listed in The Legal Elite by Virginia Business magazine the last three years.

## MUSTONE , David Albert
Hunton & Williams, McLean
703 714 7509
dmustone@hunton.com
*Recommended in Employment*
**Practice Areas:** US federal tax, ERISA and related labor and securities law aspects of employee benefits law. Clients include for-profit employers (both publicly-traded and privately-held), as well as a wide variety of non-profit and governmental employers.
**Prof. Memberships:** Vice Chairman, Employee Benefits Committee, Tax Section (ABA).
**Career:** Partner since 2000; Reed Smith - 1990-2000; Office of Chief Counsel, IRS (1986-90).
**Publications:** Has spoken and written extensively on employee benefit matters; Member, Advisory Board, BNA's ERISA Compliance and Enforcement Library.
**Personal:** GW Law School (JD, 1977; LLM - Taxation, 1989); University of Notre Dame (BA, 1974).

## NAGLE, David E
LeClair Ryan, A Professional Corporation, Richmond 804 343 4077
dnagle@leclairryan.com
*Recommended in Employment*
**Practice Areas:** Employment and labor law (management). Representation in litigation, and counsel on personnel practices to avoid litigation. Extensive experience enforcing workplace arbitration programs. Substantial appellate practice including Circuit City v Adams, 532 US 105 (2001). Clients include retailers, airlines, local governments, financial institutions and service firms.
**Prof. Memberships:** Virginia, American Bar Associations; American Arbitration Association, Panel of Arbitrators.
**Career:** Practicing since 1981. AV rating (Martindale). Virginia Business 'Legal Elite' 2000-05; Richmond Magazine 'Top Lawyers'; The Best Lawyers in America.
**Publications:** Editor, Virginia Employment Law Letter, 2003-present; columnist, Metro Business (Richmond Times Dispatch), 1986-90; articles in law review, trade publications; 250+ presentations on employment law topics.
**Personal:** Georgetown, LLM (Labor Law), 1983; University of Richmond, JD, 1981; William & Mary, AB, 1976.

## OSSOLA, Charles
Arnold & Porter LLP, Washington, DC
202 942 5000
*Recommended in Intellectual Property*

## PARRINO, Richard
Hogan & Hartson LLP, McLean
703 610 6174
rjparrino@hhlaw.com
*Recommended in Corporate/M&A*
**Practice Areas:** Mr Parrino represents US and international companies in public and institutional securities offerings, mergers and acquisitions, private equity investments, and other corporate transactions. He counsels extensively on corporate governance and securities regulation matters. His clients operate in telecommunications, information technology, manufacturing, consumer products, defense, and other industries.
**Career:** Co-editor of Hogan & Hartson's SEC Update newsletter; Member of Hogan & Hartson's Capital Markets and Corporate Governance Coordinating Groups.
**Personal:** Georgetown University (BSFS, summa cum laude, 1975); University of Virginia School of Law (JD, Managing Editor, Virginia Law Review, 1978); Cambridge University (LLM, first class honors, 1980).

## PORTER, Philip
Hogan & Hartson LLP, McLean
703 610 6108
PDPorter@hhlaw.com
*Recommended in Business Process Outsourcing, Intellectual Property*
**Practice Areas:** Domestic and international IT, telecommunications and business process outsourcing; commercialization of technology and information, including joint ventures, strategic alliances, assignments, licenses and consulting services for computer hardware and software, biotechnology and electronic commerce.
**Prof. Memberships:** ITechLaw; Computer and Telecommunications Law Section, DC Bar; NACUA.
**Publications:** 'Communications Management: An Essential Component for Successful Outsourcing', Bio/Pharmaceutical Outsourcing Report (12/1/2005); co-author, 'Judicial Guidance on Electronic Contracting', IP Update, Hogan & Hartson (10/17/05).
**Personal:** Who's Who in American Law, 2006; Finalist, Washington Business Journal's Top Washington Lawyer, Technology Transactions, 2005; Virginia Business magazine 'The 2004 Legal Elite' for IP Law.

## PULLEY III , J Waverly
Hunton & Williams LLP, Richmond
804 788 8783
wpulley@hunton.com
*Recommended in Real Estate, Transportation*
**Practice Areas:** Waverly Pulley's practice focuses on capital finance and public-private infrastructure projects.

## RAPHAEL, Stuart A
Hunton & Williams, McLean
703 714 7463
sraphael@hunton.com
*Recommended in Litigation*
**Practice Areas:** Complex litigation, products liability, and water rights.
**Prof. Memberships:** Virginia State Bar; District of Columbia Bar.
**Career:** Joined in 1989. Partner since 1997. Clients include multi-national corporations and governmental bodies. Served as Virginia's counsel in the United States Supreme Court, successfully establishing Virginia's right to use the Potomac River. Virginia v Maryland, 540 US 56 (2003).
**Publications:** 'TROs and Preliminary Injunctions, Chancery Practice in Virginia', Virginia CLE (2000); 'Public Employees and the Internet': Vol. IX, No. 3, p.2., Journal of Local Gov't Law (March 1999).
**Personal:** University of Virginia (JD, 1989); Harvard University (BA, Magna Cum Laude, 1986).

## ROTHENBERG, Charles
Hirschler Fleischer, Richmond
804 771 9503
crothenberg@hf-law.com
*Recommended in Real Estate*
**Career:** Chuck is a real estate attorney who represents commercial lenders, developers, builders, commercial landlords and tenants. Chuck routinely negotiates and closes real estate sales and acquisitions for commercial, office, residential and mixed-use projects. Additionally, he assists purchasers in all phases of feasibility studies for acquisitions; represents owners and purchasers on zoning and other matters before planning commissions, boards of supervisors, city councils, and boards of zoning appeals; negotiates, documents, and closes commercial loans, loan modifications, and loan workouts; and prepares integrated project documents for planned unit developments, including declarations of covenants, marketing agreements and form contracts for the sale of lots to builders and consumers.
**Personal:** JD, University of Richmond; BA, State University of New York, Oneonta.

## RUDLIN, D Alan
Hunton & Williams LLP, Richmond
804 788 8459
arudlin@hunton.com
*Recommended in Litigation*
**Practice Areas:** Alan Rudlin's practice focuses on class actions, mass torts, pharmaceutical, product and toxic litigation, as well as commercial, First Amendment, and constitutional litigation. Specialty includes national co-ordinating counsel role in managing complex litigation, and development of expert evidence and medical causation issues for product, pharmaceutical and environmental litigation. Co-Chair of the ABA Litigation Section's Mass Torts Litigation Committee.

## SGARLATA , Mark A
Watt, Tieder, Hoffar & Fitzgerald LLP, McLean 703 749 1000
msgarlat@wthf.com
*Recommended in Construction*
**Practice Areas:** Construction law, suretyship, government contracts, international construction.
**Prof. Memberships:** American Bar Association, Virginia State Bar Association, CMAA, HCAA.
**Career:** Mark Sgarlata represents clients in contract drafting and negotiations, dispute resolution and litigation on a wide range of heavy industrial and commercial construction projects. His projects include tunnels, cable-stayed bridges, mass transit, process, and heavy civil buildings. Mark has extensive claims negotiation and litigation experience on behalf of contractors, owners and sureties. He lectures nationally.
**Publications:** 'Allocation of Risk for Delay and Disruption,' CMAA (Co-Author), 'Successful Projects Through an Understanding of the Law of Lost Productivity,' CMAA (Co-Author).

## SHORT, Jennifer A
Holland & Knight LLP, McLean
703 720 8600
jennifer.short@hklaw.com
*Recommended in Litigation*
**Practice Areas:** Partner in the Litigation

Section, with a practice focusing on complex civil and white collar criminal matters, including healthcare and government contracts fraud. She regularly practices in the federal courts and has particular experience representing individuals and corporations in government investigations of procurement and billing fraud, related qui tam lawsuits, and commercial contract and licensing disputes. She works closely with companies in heavily-regulated industries, and frequently counsels clients on creating and implementing corporate compliance and ethics programs designed to avoid, minimize, or respond to potential litigation and prosecution risks.

### SIRILLA, George M
Pillsbury Winthrop Shaw Pittman LLP, McLean 703 770 7784
george.sirilla@pillsburylaw.com
*Recommended in Intellectual Property*
**Practice Areas:** Mr Sirilla has led teams that successfully upheld as well as invalidated patents in numerous cases, both in the federal courts and before the US International Trade Commission. He has considerable experience in technology licensing, patents and trade secrets, and in litigating disputes over such licenses.
**Personal:** JD, Georgetown University Law Center; BS, Rensselaer Polytechnic Institute (Mechanical Engineering, Tau Beta Pi and Pi Tau Sigma national engineering honor societies).

### SLATER, Thomas
Hunton & Williams LLP, Richmond
804 788 8475
tslater@hunton.com
*Recommended in Litigation*
**Practice Areas:** Tom Slater's practice focuses on complex litigation matters with emphasis on antitrust, intellectual property, trade secrets, unfair trade practices, product liability and white collar criminal defense. He has handled over 60 jury trials in courts throughout the US. Tom Slater has handled dozens of civil antitrust cases, many of which were national in scope, including numerous antitrust class action cases that were consolidated by the Judicial Panel on Multi-district Litigation. He has also handled criminal and civil actions brought by the US Justice Department. In 2005, he was co-lead counsel in a mock jury trial program sponsored by the American Bar Association Antitrust Section.
**Prof. Memberships:** Fellow, American College of Trial Attorneys; Fellow, American Bar Foundation; Fellow, Virginia Law Foundation; Member, Fourth Circuit Judicial Conference; Listed in 'Best Lawyers in America' for over 10 years, antitrust and corporate litigation.
**Career:** Tom Slater has been active in bar and community activities. He is a past President of the Richmond Bar Association and a former Member of the Vir-

ginia State Bar Executive Committee. He currently serves on the Board of Directors of the Central Virginia Legal Aid Society and the Virginia Historical Society.
**Publications:** Co-author, 'Communication Methods and Skills' chapter, 'Successful Partnering Between Inside and Outside Counsel', American Corporate Counsel Association, 2000; author, 'Sentence Yourself' article on federal sentencing guidelines, ABA Journal.

### SMITH, Brooks
Hunton & Williams LLP, Richmond
804 787 8086
bsmith@hunton.com
*Recommended in Environment*
**Practice Areas:** Brooks Smith concentrates on proceedings that arise under the Clean Water Act, including rule, permit, enforcement and TMDL actions. Brooks also counsels clients on a wide range of regulatory compliance issues in voluntary environmental audit, EMS, permit and enforcement proceedings, as well as transactions.

### STILLMAN, Gregory
Hunton & Williams, Norfolk
757 640 5314
gstillman@hunton.com
*Recommended in Litigation*
**Practice Areas:** Gregory Stillman's practice focuses on federal trial and appellate litigation, with emphasis on business torts, intellectual property (copyright and patent), securities and corporate governance. He is Managing Partner of the firm's Norfolk Office.

### SYLVESTER, David
WilmerHale, Washington, DC
202 663 6000
*Recommended in Corporate/M&A*

### TAPSCOTT, Andrew
Hunton & Williams LLP, Richmond
804 788 8620
atapscott@hunton.com
*Recommended in Real Estate*
**Practice Areas:** Andy Tapscott's practice focuses on commercial real estate transactions, including sophisticated finance, development, acquisitions, dispositions, joint ventures, leasing, loan workouts and foreclosures. Mr Tapscott's practice has a special emphasis on the hospitality and leisure industry, as well as the Real Estate Investment Trust (REIT) industry.

### TATA, Robert M
Hunton & Williams, Norfolk
757 640 5328
btata@hunton.com
*Recommended in Intellectual Property, Litigation*
**Practice Areas:** Bob Tata's practice includes complex commercial litigation, intellectual property (copyright, trademark, trade dress, trade secret and patent) litigation, pharmaceutical and other products liability defense, govern-

ment contracts, and other high stakes litigation in federal and state courts. Bob's focus is on results. Bob at one time held the record for the largest jury verdict in the history of Virginia. He has won and recovered seven and eight figure awards for his IP and commercial clients and defeated numerous multi-million dollar claims. Bob has taught, spoken and been quoted extensively on IP and other commercial litigation topics.

### TERRY, Mike
Hirschler Fleischer, Richmond
804 771 9510
mterry@hf-law.com
*Recommended in Real Estate*
**Career:** Mike has assisted the financial restructuring of a wide range of commercial businesses and real estate development companies. He also has represented numerous lenders (inside and outside of bankruptcy) in collecting their credit and realizing upon their collateral from borrowers. Mike's experience in financial workouts/reorganizations has led to a practice consulting with business owners and negotiating on their behalves with respect to organization of assets, general business planning and division/dissolution of business organizations (business divorces). Mike also represents financial institutions and investors in the purchase and sale of loan portfolios and servicing portfolios.
**Personal:** JD, College of William & Mary; BS, University of Richmond.

### THEOBALD, James
Hirschler Fleischer, Richmond
804 771 9513
jtheobald@hf-law.com
*Recommended in Real Estate*
**Career:** Jim has assisted some of the nation's largest developers and retailers in making their projects a reality for over two decades. From contract negotiations through rezoning, licensing and permitting, entity structuring, financing and leasing, Jim brings creative, aggressive advocacy to bear in finding a way to make a deal work. Jim has, among other things, represented one of the nation's largest discount appliance chains in acquiring sites throughout the country. He also has structured sale/lease back transactions, including those with foreign investors, and other financing related to the acquisition and development of store locations. Additionally, Jim has represented Wal-Mart Stores, Inc. and other national retailers in the acquisition, rezoning and approval process in various portions of Virginia.
**Personal:** JD, Cleveland Marshall College of Law; BA College of William & Mary.

### THOMAS, Bill
Reed Smith LLP, Falls Church
703 641 4238
wthomas@reedsmith.com
*Recommended in Real Estate*
**Practice Areas:** Administrative practice before state agencies; legislative practice before the Virginia General Assembly; land use and administrative practice before all Northern Virginia jurisdictions and agencies; and corporate governance practice.
**Prof. Memberships:** American Law Institute, American College of Real Estate Lawyers, member of the Fourth Circuit Judicial Conference.
**Career:** Partner at Hazel & Thomas, which combined with Reed Smith in 1999.
**Publications:** Writes extensively in the condominium field.
**Personal:** University of Richmond (JD, 1963), editor of 'Richmond Law Notes'; served by Governor's appointment to the Board of Directors of The Center for Innovative Technology.

### THOMPSON, Gary
Hunton & Williams LLP, Richmond
804 788 8787
gthompson@hunton.com
*Recommended in Corporate/M&A*
**Practice Areas:** Gary Thompson's practice focuses on mergers and acquisitions, hostile and friendly tender offers, public and private securities offerings, corporate governance issues and a wide range of corporate finance activities. Head of the firm's US Mergers and Acquisitions Group.

### TIEDER, John B
Watt, Tieder, Hoffar & Fitzgerald LLP, McLean 703 749 1000
jtieder@wthf.com
*Recommended in Construction*
**Practice Areas:** Construction law, government contracts, international construction and arbitration.
**Prof. Memberships:** American Bar Association, American College of Construction Lawyers, District of Columbia, New York and Virginia Bar Associations.
**Career:** Jack Tieder concentrates his practice on major construction matters with a particular emphasis on international projects. He represents foreign governments, utilities, oil companies and US and international contractors on infrastructure, industrial, power and commercial projects.
**Publications:** Numerous publications relating to international and domestic construction, arbitration and litigation (eg. 'The Globalization of Construction-Evolving International Standards of Construction Law,' Vol 15, Pt 4, INT'L CONST L REV 500 (Oct 1998).

## VARELA, Paul
Watt, Tieder, Hoffar & Fitzgerald LLP, McLean 703 749 1000
pvarela@wthf.com
*Recommended in Construction*
**Practice Areas:** Construction law, suretyship, government contracts, international construction.
**Prof. Memberships:** ABA Forum on Construction, TIPS.
**Career:** Paul Varela represents clients in contract planning, administration, and dispute resolution matters nationwide. His projects include power, stadium, transportation, pharmaceutical, process, and heavy civil and general building. Paul has extensive claims negotiation and prosecution experience on behalf of private and public entities. He lectures nationally.
**Publications:** 'The Design/Build Process: A Guide to Licensing and Procurement Requirements in the 50 States and Canada,' sections on Virginia and the District of Columbia, ABA (Co-Author), 'Design Defect Liabiltiy Under Design/Build,' Washington Building Congress Bulletin (Co-Author).

## VAUGHAN III, C Porter
Hunton & Williams LLP, Richmond
804 788 8285
pvaughan@hunton.com
*Recommended in Corporate/M&A*
**Practice Areas:** Mr Vaughan's practice focuses on public and private market mergers and acquisitions, corporate financings, corporate governance and securities regulation. He is Co-Head of the firm's Business Practice Group.

## WALSH, William
Hunton & Williams LLP, Richmond
804 788 8378
wwalsh@hunton.com
*Recommended in Real Estate*
**Practice Areas:** Bill Walsh's practice focuses primarily on strategic real estate planning, student housing for colleges and universities, urban redevelopment, private-public ventures and commercial leasing. He is listed in Best Lawyers in America, Who's Who in America and America's Leading Business Lawyers and was named Best Real Estate and Construction Lawyer in Virginia by Virginia Business magazine. Bill is a Member of the American College of Real Estate Lawyers.

## WATT, Robert G
Watt, Tieder, Hoffar & Fitzgerald LLP, McLean 703 749 1000
rwatt@wthf.com
*Recommended in Construction*
**Practice Areas:** Construction Law, suretyship, international construction, government contracts.
**Prof. Memberships:** Virginia and District of Columbia Bar Associations.

**Career:** Bob Watt's highly recognized practice focuses on private and public construction disputes and complex surety matters, both on a national and international level. He has tried cases before various Boards of Contract Appeals, construction arbitration panels, federal and state courts throughout the United States, International Chamber of Commerce Arbitration and London Court of International Arbitration. Honors include Best Lawyers in America, Construction Law; Chambers USA - Top Construction Lawyers in Virginia; Virginia Business Legal Elite; and Virginia Super Lawyer 2006.

## WEINBERG, Jay
Hirschler Fleischer, Fredericksburg
804 771 9533
jlweinberg@hf-law.com
*Recommended in Real Estate*
**Career:** Jay Weinberg is a founding member of the real estate section of Hirschler Fleischer. His practice focuses on sophisticated land use and zoning matters. He has practiced law for over 40 years and has handled virtually all forms of sophisticated real estate matters, including the acquisition, rezoning, financing, syndication, development, adaptive reuse and sale of major residential communities, apartment complexes, shopping centers, industrial parks and office-service buildings. He has had substantial experience in counseling real estate developers in connection with the taxation and structure of legal entities to develop, own and sell real estate projects.
**Personal:** LLB (JD), University of Virginia; BA, University of Virginia.

## WELLFORD, Hill
Hunton & Williams LLP, Richmond
804 788 8518
hwellford@hunton.com
*Recommended in Employment*
**Practice Areas:** Hill Wellford is Head of the Labor and Litigation Group with Hunton & Williams. His practice focuses on equal opportunity law, labor relations, labor arbitrations, collective bargaining, executive employment agreements, covenants not to complete/trade secrets, wage-hour law, occupational safety and health law and litigation of employment claims, including class actions, under federal and state labor and employment statutes. He has been recognized for his expertise in Best Lawyers in America for labor and employment law; Who's Who in America; Who's Who in American Law; and selected to Virginia's Legal Elite Virginia Business magazine, December, 2000-05.

## WICKWIRE, Jon
Wickwire Gavin P.C., Vienna
703 790 8750
jwickwire@wickwire.com
*Recommended in Construction*
**Practice Areas:** Advises clients on the avoidance, evaluation and resolution of performance problems for the construction industry, as well as the preparation of major systems claims. Prepares construction policies and procedures for Fortune 50 corporations. Member of Construction Strategies, Inc., a consulting firm specializing in construction claims review and risk management.
**Prof. Memberships:** American Bar Association; American Arbitration Association, National Panel of Arbitrators; American College of Construction Lawyers (Founding Fellow); Project Management Institute (Founding Chair, College of Scheduling); Associated General Contractors of America.
**Publications:** 'Construction Scheduling: Preparation, Liability and Claims', 2003, Aspen Publishers; 'Drafting Scheduling Specifications, Part One', CMAdvisor (CMAA newsletter), May/June 2003, Part Two, July/August 2003, Part Three October 2003; 'Construction Management: Law and Practice', Wiley Law Publications, 1995; 'The Construction Subcontracting Manual: Practice Guide with Forms', Wiley Law Publications, 1995; 'The Use of Critical Path Method Techniques in Contract Claims', 'Public Contract Law Journal', October 1974; 'Use of Critical Path Method Techniques in Contract Claims: Issues and Developments, 1974 to 1988', 'Public Contract Law Journal', Vol. 18, No. 2, March 1989; 'Use of Critical Path Method on Contract Claims - 2000,' The Construction Lawyer, October 1999.

## WITTHOEFFT, Charles
Hirschler Fleischer, Richmond
804 771 9562
rwitthoefft@hf-law.com
*Recommended in Litigation*
**Career:** Rick Witthoefft is Chair of the firm's Litigation Section and has over 30 years of trial experience in handling a wide variety of commercial disputes in state and federal courts throughout Virginia. He has represented both plaintiffs and defendants in complex, frequently multiparty, commercial cases including contract, business tort, landlord-tenant, land use, professional liability, employment, utilities law, administrative law, antitrust, securities, banking, RICO, construction, trust and estate, environmental, and liability insurance issues. Additionally, Rick is a Fellow of the prestigious American College of Trial Lawyers.
**Personal:** JD, University of Richmond; BA, Hampden-Sydney College.

## WRIGHT, David C
Hunton & Williams LLP, Richmond
804 788 8638
dwright@hunton.com
*Recommended in Corporate/M&A*
**Practice Areas:** Mr Wright's practice focuses on capital markets transactions, and in particular, real estate capital markets transactions for real estate investment trusts, real estate operating companies and companies in the hospitality industry, as well as specialty finance companies. Mr Wright regularly advises companies and leading investment banks on public and private issuances of debt and equity securities and merger and acquisition transactions. He heads the firm's Real Estate Capital Markets Practice Group, which has handled over 70 IPOs and Rule 144A equity offerings and over 300 capital markets transactions for over 100 companies in recent years.

## WRIGHT, Murray
Wright Robinson Osthimer & Tatum, Richmond 804 783 1100
*Recommended in Construction*

## YANOWITCH, Lawrence T
Morrison & Foerster LLP, McLean
703 760 7318
lyanowitch@mofo.com
*Recommended in Corporate/M&A*
**Practice Areas:** Represents emerging companies (private and public), investment banks, special committees and institutional investors. Concentrates on mergers and acquisitions, corporate finance, SEC compliance and corporate counseling. Has successfully completed well over 100 M&A transactions with purchase prices ranging from $5 million to over $5 billion. Also has expertise with registered public offerings of debt and equity, PIPEs, private equity sponsored financings, venture capital financings and corporate restructurings.
**Career:** Admitted to practice in Virginia, New York, and the District of Columbia. Began career at Skadden, Arps, Slate Meagher & Flom.
**Personal:** BA, Georgetown University, cum laude 1984; JD, Georgetown University Law Center, cum laude 1987.

# HUNTON & WILLIAMS LLP

## THE FIRM

**Chairman, Executive Committee:** Thurston R Moore
**Managing Partner:** Walfrido J Martinez
**Number of partners worldwide:** 348
**Number of other lawyers worldwide:** 516

**FIRM OVERVIEW:** Since its establishment in 1901, Hunton & Williams has grown to more than 850 attorneys who have served clients in over 100 countries from 17 offices around the world. The firm has experience in more than 60 separate practice areas.

## MAIN AREAS OF PRACTICE:

**Capital Markets, Mergers & Acquisitions:** The capital markets attorneys at Hunton & Williams have broad experience and insight on initial public and private offerings of equity securities, the issuance of debt securities in foreign and domestic markets, the creation of open and closed-end mutual funds, and public and private partnership offerings. The corporate attorneys counsel clients on domestic and international merger and acquisition transactions. The firm provides guidance in all aspects of contested and negotiated acquisitions, including tender offers, proxy fights, takeover defenses, leveraged buyouts, corporate spin-offs, holding company formations, corporate auctions, mergers of equals, and strategic acquisition and divestiture programs.

**Energy:** Hunton & Williams represents clients involved in the electricity, oil and natural gas industries in the United States and throughout the world. Attorneys in the firm's energy practice advise on a wide range of matters, including project development and acquisition financing, regulatory and legislative issues, market design, environmental matters, financial restructuring, leasing and related corporate transactions, representation of energy marketing and trading companies, corporate and regulatory work associated with the formation and operation of independent system operators and regional transmission organizations, restructuring and privatization of utility assets in Asia, Africa, the Middle East, Europe and Latin America, and the development and financing of energy projects around the world.

**Environmental:** Hunton & Williams' Environmental Practice is among the oldest and largest in the nation. Its attorneys have helped clients navigate every major federal environmental statute, and those of most states and international jurisdictions. The team advises a range of industries on innovative response to environmental compliance, represents companies in litigation and administrative proceedings, and ensures that clients have a voice in shaping policy.

**Labor & Employment:** Hunton & Williams' Labor and Employment Practice covers the entire spectrum of labor and employment litigation; arbitration; administrative practice before the NLRB, EEOC and the Labor Department; federal contract compliance; wage-house standards; Occupational Safety and Health Administration standards; workers' compensation; and client counseling under federal and state labor and employment laws.

**Litigation:** Hunton & Williams' Litigation Team is recognized as one of the premier litigation groups in the country. Its nearly 300 attorneys handle litigation in virtually every area of law including antitrust/global competition, appellate, business crimes defense, corporate governance/mergers and acquisitions, intellectual property and patent, international arbitration/dispute resolution, product liability, securities, telecommunications, toxic tort and workouts/creditors' rights.

**CLIENTS:** Hunton & Williams serves clients in the following industry sectors: associations, biotech and chemical, consumer products, energy, environmental services, financial services, government entities, health care, hospitality, international, manufacturing, professional services, real estate, technology, telecommunications and transportation.

**INTERNATIONAL WORK:** Hunton & Williams has a significant international presence with offices in London, Brussels, Beijing, Singapore and Bangkok. As the firm's clients pursue international opportunities, they appreciate the support of locally experienced lawyers who know the legal and business practices of their region.

## HEAD OFFICE

**VIRGINIA**
Riverfront Plaza, East Tower, 951 East Byrd Street
**Richmond**, VA 23219-4074
**Tel:** 804 788 8200   **Fax:** 804 788 8218
**Email:** info@hunton.com   **Website:** www.hunton.com

## BRANCH OFFICES

**DISTRICT OF COLUMBIA**
1900 K Street, NW, **Washington**, DC 20006-1109
**Tel:** 202 955 1500   **Fax:** 202 778 2201

**FLORIDA**
1111 Brickell Avenue, Suite 2500, **Miami**, FL 33131
**Tel:** 305 810 2500   **Fax:** 305 810 2460

**GEORGIA**
Bank of America Plaza, Suite 4100, 600 Peachtree Street, NE
**Atlanta**, GA 30308-2216
**Tel:** 404 888 4000   **Fax:** 404 888 4190

**NEW YORK**
200 Park Avenue, 52nd Floor, **New York**, NY 10166-0136
**Tel:** 212 309 1000   **Fax:** 212 309 1100

**NORTH CAROLINA**
Bank of America Plaza, Suite 3500, 101 South Tryon Street
**Charlotte**, NC 28280
**Tel:** 704 378 4700   **Fax:** 704 378 4890

One Bank of America Plaza, Suite 1400, 421 Fayetteville Street Mall
**Raleigh**, NC 27601
**Tel:** 919 899 3000   **Fax:** 919 833 6352

**TENNESSEE**
2000 Riverview Tower, 900 South Gay Street
**Knoxville**, TN 37902
**Tel:** 865 549 7700   **Fax:** 865 549 7704

**TEXAS**
Energy Plaza, 30th Floor, 1601 Bryan Street, **Dallas**, TX 75201-3402
**Tel:** 214 979 3000   **Fax:** 214 880 0011

Bank of America Center, Suite 4200, 700 Louisiana Street
**Houston**, Texas 77002
**Tel:** 713 229 5700   **Fax:** 713 229 5750

**VIRGINIA**
1751 Pinnacle Drive, Suite 1700, **McLean**, VA 22102
**Tel:** 703 714 7400   **Fax:** 703 714 7410

SunTrust Center, Suite 1000, 500 East Main Street
**Norfolk**, VA 23510-3889
**Tel:** 757 640 5300   **Fax:** 757 625 7720

Hunton & Williams' international clients include leading US and foreign corporations, governments and governmental entities, financial institutions, commercial and investment banks, multilateral and bilateral lending and guarantee agencies.

# WATT, TIEDER, HOFFAR & FITZGERALD

## THE FIRM

**Managing Partner:** Robert Watt

**Number of partners:** 43
**Number of other lawyers:** 48

**FIRM OVERVIEW:** Watt, Tieder, Hoffar & Fitzgerald is one of the largest construction law firms in the world, with a practice that encompasses all aspects of construction contracting and public procurement. With three offices and nearly 100 professionals devoted to serving public and commercial construction, government supply and service contracting, and real estate industry clients, the firm brings to bear the high level of skill that develops only in an intensely focused practice enabling it to meet the complete n eeds of its clients in a timely and cost-effective manner.

## MAIN AREAS OF PRACTICE:

**Construction:** The firm's attorneys represent clients throughout the world in every phase of development and construction from site acquisition and financing through construction litigation and real estate portfolio management. The firm knows its clients' industries from the inside; several of the firm's attorneys have engineering degrees, others have worked as estimators and construction managers; and every attorney in the firm has years of practical experience solving the problems contractors, engineers, owners, subcontractors, sureties and lenders encounter. The firm is also known for providing strategic counsel to help clients manage their contracts and programs for guarding their interests when disputes arise. The attorneys have experience in virtually every type of construction including heavy civil, transportation, power, industrial, process and general building.

**Commercial Real Estate:** The Real Estate Practice Group plays an integral role in the firm's ability to provide clients with a full range of construction, project finance and transactional legal services. The firm's real estate attorneys represent corporations, developers, lenders, healthcare companies, brokers, entrepreneurs, buyers, sellers, investors, landlords and tenants, assisting them in the acquisition, financing, construction, leasing and sale of all types of commercial property, structuring construction and development agreements, documenting and settling construction, development and real estate disputes and related litigation.

**Government Contracts:** The firm specializes in all facets of government contracting, successfully addressing the increasing pressures on prime contractors and subcontractors in competing for, profitably performing and successfully completing contracts, as well as facing the potential for audit and procurement integrity and compliance risks. The firm also assists public owners in contract administration and dispute resolution.

**International Construction:** Watt, Tieder, Hoffar & Fitzgerald is a major firm in the international construction arena. The firm is engaged in a worldwide practice, with largescale projects and arbitrations throughout Europe, the Middle East, Africa, Asia and Australia, and includes the representation of both US and foreign companies in all phases of the construction process: qualification to do business in foreign countries, arrangement of financing with both private and public lenders, creation of consortia, bidding and negotiation of the prime contract, contract administration and dispute resolution.

**Suretyship:** As part of the firm's dedication to ensuring a competitive edge over other law firms servicing the construction industry, Watt, Tieder, Hoffar & Fitzgerald maintains a robust and vibrant Surety Practice. Although the practice encompasses a broad range of issues, the firm has acquired particular expertise in handling default terminations, affirmative construction claims, surety 'abuse of discretion' cases, government contract disputes, surety bad faith claims and all forms of contract bond defaults. The firm believes that the scope of its Construction Practice gives it a level of experience and insight which offers unique advantages in protecting the interests of the firm's surety clients and in identifying and implementing creative solutions to resolve complex performance and payment bond disputes.

## HEAD OFFICE

### VIRGINIA
8405 Greensboro Drive, Suite 100, **Mclean**, VA 22102
**Tel:** 703 749 1000  **Fax:** 703 893 8029
**Email:** contactus@wthf.com
**Website:** www.wthf.com

## BRANCH OFFICES

### CALIFORNIA
2040 Main Street, Suites 300 & 550, **Irvine**, CA 92614
**Tel:** 949 852 6700  **Fax:** 949 261 0771

Citigroup Center, One Sansome Street, Suite 1050
**San Francisco**, CA 94104
**Tel:** 415 623 7000  **Fax:** 415 623 7001

**CLIENTS:** AIG (American Insurance Group); Alstom Power Inc.; Angelo Iafrate Construction Co.; Baltimore County, Maryland; Barnard Construction Co.; Bilfinger Berger; Bovis Lend Lease; CH2M HILL; Condotte America/Recchi; F.H. Paschen/S.N. Nielsen; Fireman's Fund Insurance Co.; Grupo San José; Josef Gartner USA, Inc.; Kenny Construction Co.; Kiewit Construction Co.; Liberty Mutual Insurance Co.; Mitsubishi Heavy Industries America; Nevada Department of Transportation; P&O Steam Navigation Co.; Permasteelisa Cladding Technologies; The Shaw Group; St. Paul Travelers; Suez Energies North America; Sunrise Senior Living; Washington Group International, Inc.; Weeks Marine, Inc.; WorleyParsons; Zurich North America.

WATT, TIEDER, HOFFAR & FITZGERALD, L.L.P.™

BUILDING SOLUTIONS™

## How lawyers are ranked

Every year we carry out thousands of in-depth interviews with clients and lawyers in order to assess the reputations and expertise of business lawyers across the USA. Chambers rankings and editorial are referred to extensively by General Counsel and other purchasers of legal services who look to our recommendations when choosing their lawyers.

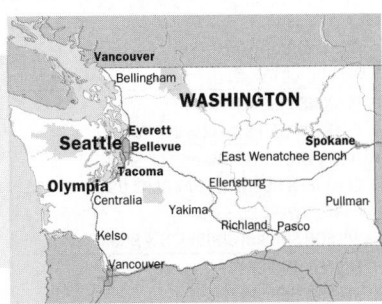

# BANKRUPTCY/RESTRUCTURING

### Bankruptcy/Restructuring

**Leading Firms**

1 **BUSH, STROUT & KORNFELD** *Seattle*
  **DAVIS WRIGHT TREMAINE LLP** *Seattle*
  **FOSTER PEPPER PLLC** *Seattle*
  **LANE POWELL PC** *Seattle*
  **PRESTON GATES & ELLIS LLP** *Seattle*

**Leading Individuals**

1 **ALLRED C Keith** *Davis Wright Tremaine LLP*
  **BUSH Gayle** *Bush, Strout & Kornfeld*
  **CULLEN Jack** *Foster Pepper PLLC*
  **EKBERG Charles** *Lane Powell PC*
  **KORNFELD Armand** *Bush, Strout & Kornfeld*
  **OSENBAUGH Kim** *Preston Gates & Ellis LLP*
  **POWERS Ragan** *Davis Wright Tremaine LLP*

2 **BARRECA Marc** *Preston Gates & Ellis LLP*
  **HESTON Mary** *Lane Powell PC*
  **JACKSON Dillon** *Foster Pepper PLLC*
  **LEAVERTON Bruce** *Lane Powell PC*

## Band 1

### Bush, Strout & Kornfeld

**The Firm:** This seven-strong boutique practice specializes principally in debtor representation, where competitors recommended it as "*probably the leading debtor firm in the area.*" It advises clients on out-of-court workouts, restructurings and Chapter 11 cases and has experience representing companies from various industries including the maritime, technology and real estate sectors. Clients also benefit from the firm's skill in commercial litigation.

**The Lawyers:** Interviewees warmly recommended **Gayle Bush** as a "*top-tier debtor lawyer and excellent litigator.*" He is renowned within the field and has played a leading role in the Catholic Bishop of Spokane bankruptcy case, where he has been appointed as future claims representative. Peers were also impressed by his partner, **Armand Kornfeld**, who they described as "*an outstanding negotiator.*" Rival firms concede that both lawyers are names that "*instantly spring to mind*" in the Washington bankruptcy arena. Together, this pair of "*creative problem solvers*" are renowned for their long-standing representation of debtors.

**Clients/Work Highlights:** Alaska Power & Tele-phone; Fisgard Asset Management; Pacific Realty Advisors and Safeguard Mortgage.

### Davis Wright Tremaine LLP

**The Firm:** This small and efficient team of five partners and two associates has a strong track record representing lenders, such as leasing and credit card companies, but also has expertise in debtor work. Commentators admire the group for its "*ethical, fair and community-minded*" approach and for its success in cutting-edge cases. Recent examples include successfully representing 43 newspapers in the multimillion-dollar Kmart case.

**The Lawyers:** Interviewees highlighted the group for its "*knowledgeable, competent and experienced*" lawyers who have "*accumulated a wealth of experience*" in the field. One of its leading lights is **Keith Allred**, who has lengthy experience acting for lenders in complex cases and is renowned for his creditors' rights expertise. **Ragan Powers** is another leading lawyer who recently advised a company that supplies the International Space Station on the company's emergence from bankruptcy.

**Clients/Work Highlights:** Bank of America; GE Capital; US Bank and Bank of Tokyo.

### Foster Pepper PLLC

**The Firm:** Interviewees rate this group as one of the leading bankruptcy practices in the state. It stands out for its work on behalf of debtors, but also has a following among a range of creditor and trustee clients. This "*creative and well-connected*" boutique is home to around six specialist lawyers who are frequently involved in high-profile cases. Recent examples include advising on the bankruptcy case of a Catholic Church and acting for purchasers of distressed companies and assets.

**The Lawyers:** Clients are attracted to the group thanks to the "*competence and creativity*" of its lawyers. **Jack Cullen** spearheads the practice and is a Chapter 11 specialist, characterized by peers as a "*quick and efficient worker.*" **Dillon Jackson** is another talented member of the team who represents secured creditors or committees. He is well known on a national level and has a long-standing involvement with the American Bankruptcy Institute.

**Clients/Work Highlights:** Paul Allen Companies and Burger King are among the clients.

### Lane Powell PC

See firm details p.2009

**The Firm:** This "*strong and high-caliber*" practice, comprising ten lawyers, is respected for its long-standing expertise in bankruptcy cases. It has an extensive client base ranging from banks and mortgage lenders to insurance companies and a range of debtors. Client satisfaction stems from the consistently accurate advice offered by the strong team of lawyers. Sources praised the "*skilled and capable*" group for its commitment to a spectrum of client requirements.

**The Lawyers:** This impressive group houses some of the top names in the state for bankruptcy and creditors' rights. **Charles Ekberg**'s "*client-oriented approach*" coupled with over three decades of bankruptcy experience makes him one of the most respected players in the field. Clients and peers praise him for his "*outstanding legal mind*" and point to his role in high-profile cases such as the Catholic Bishop of Spokane case. **Mary Jo Heston** is a talented practitioner with a wealth of experience to offer in all areas of bankruptcy. **Bruce Leaverton** has a flair for handling complex cases and wins plaudits for his "*thorough and precise*" work. He has experience in reorganizations, workouts and commercial litigation.

**Clients/Work Highlights:** Wells Fargo; KeyBank; Washington Mutual and Irwin Business Finance.

### Preston Gates & Ellis LLP

**The Firm:** This Seattle-based, sophisticated commercial bankruptcy firm is adept at both debtor and creditor representation. Peers praise the "*excellent, highly effective professionalism*" of the team and believe it has niche strengths in IP matters as they relate to bankruptcies. The group's highlights during 2005 include advising on the Olympic Pipe Line case, which involved the successful reorganization of a fuel supplier that served an international airport.

**The Lawyers:** **Kim Osenbaugh** leads the firm's bankruptcy group and advises clients on commercial litigation and insolvency law. Interviewees declared her a "*leading light*" in the field and recommended her for her excellent communication skills and talented performances in court. **Marc Barreca**'s ability to deal with IP issues relating to bankruptcies has earned him considerable respect from both clients and peers.

**Clients/Work Highlights:** Microsoft; Maryland Aviation Administration; Port of Seattle and Metawave .

## CORPORATE/COMMERCIAL

## Band 1

### Perkins Coie LLP

**The Firm:** This sizable Seattle-based firm is home to around 80 top-quality lawyers and was widely acknowledged by interviewees as the "*leading corporate practice*" in the Northwest. It represents a large percentage of the state's technology companies and has been one of the most active players in the Northwestern IPO market. The group is highly regarded for its representation of public companies, private equity funds and emerging enterprises, which it advises on a range of corporate and M&A deals. In 2005 the group advised on the emergence of a new company headed by two of the founders of Expedia.com. Interviewees believe that the firm is "*ahead of the other Seattle firms*" and praised it for its "*responsiveness to clients' needs.*"

**The Lawyers:** Stewart Landefeld specializes in corporate governance for public companies and larger private companies and also advises on private equity and M&A transactions. Peers commend his "*deep knowledge, strong customer ethos and meticulous attention to detail.*" Clients praised **Andrew Bor** for being a "*responsive and excellent negotiator.*" He acts for an assortment of major Washington companies and handled numerous M&A deals during 2005. **Evelyn Cruz Sroufe** is well respected among peers for her skill in M&A and securities transactions and for her integrity and communication skills. Her highlights include advising a Seattle bank on a major SEC registration project. **David McShea** has been busy advising on the startup of an online real estate company. His clients also rely on him for assistance in M&A and corporate finance deals. **Carl Crow** leads the firm's federal tax practice and is another sought-after adviser at the firm. He advises on the tax aspects of high-profile transactions, such as Coinstar's acquisition of ACMI. His "*committed and results-oriented approach*" instills confidence in clients and respect in peers.

**Clients/Work Highlights:** Microsoft; Expedia.com; Amazon.com; Google and aQuantive.

### Preston Gates & Ellis LLP

**The Firm:** This is a long-standing player in the market, providing "*pragmatic and solution-oriented*" advice in relation to a range of corporate governance and transactional issues. It is a popular choice among clients, who choose it for its "*perfect combination of excellent technical expertise with practical know-how.*" The team frequently acts for Fortune 500 companies such as Microsoft, but its extensive and diverse client base also includes emerging businesses and public entities. It has a string of high-profile, multimillion-dollar transactions under its belt and has expertise in securities offerings, venture capital and private equity deals.

**The Lawyers:** Kent Carlson is "*highly knowledgeable and communicative and has a great depth of expertise in corporate law.*" He specializes in M&A transactions and reorganizations and won praise from interviewees for his exceptional powers of reasoning and his lengthy experience in the field. His headline transactions include advising on the sale of Milgard Manufacturing to Masco. **Stephan Coonrad**'s areas of expertise include acquisitions, equity investments and a range of cross-border deals. He recently advised on the joint venture to create CarPoint.com. **Richard Dodd** is a "*first-rate lawyer*" who is well known for his work on behalf of Microsoft, which he advised on its acquisition of Vicinity. **Scott Greenburg** attracted praise for his "*exceptional understanding of the dynamics of acquisition transactions.*" Interviewees were particularly impressed with his practical approach and up-to-the-minute knowledge of corporate and M&A law. **Gary Kocher** is another esteemed lawyer who specializes in representing technology and biotech companies. Clients confirm that he is an "*excellent and resourceful practitioner*" who is "*extremely pleasant to deal with.*" **Andrew Zuccotti** has an in-depth knowledge of all matters relating to partnership tax and federal income tax. His clients praised him as "*an outstanding tax lawyer with a solid understanding of all the relevant issues.*"

**Clients/Work Highlights:** Microsoft; Starbucks; Western Wireless; Quinton Cardiology Systems and Amazon.com.

## Band 2

### Davis Wright Tremaine LLP

**The Firm:** This firm has enjoyed a stellar year, having advised on some of the most significant deals in the market. Foremost among these was its role as lead counsel to a satellite communications company in its $650 million senior secured convertible bond. The team wins praise for its "*innovative and creative group of conscientious professionals*" and has an impressive stable of clients, including national and international entities, and one of the state's largest newspapers. The group retains a strong focus on large technology companies and emerging company work but is also expanding into the communications and media sectors.

**The Lawyers:** Greg Adams is "*a concise and intelligent practitioner,*" who advises public and large private companies on corporate governance, stockholder rights and M&A transactions. **Joseph Weinstein** has experience in big-ticket M&A deals and recently advised on the multistate sale of a major seafood company. He is held in high esteem among peers and impressed clients with his "*experience and dedication.*" *Chambers'* sources recommended **Joseph Whitford** as a "*quick-thinking and diligent lawyer.*" He has expertise in a range of emerging industries including life sciences and medical devices and brings "*a depth of knowledge*" to the negotiating table. **LaVerne Woods** chairs the firm's tax-exempt organizations department and has a particular focus on nonprofit organizations. Peers widely hold her to be "*the crème de la crème*" thanks to her experience and legal talent. **James Wreggelsworth** has an equally high reputation as a "*fine tax lawyer*" and drew particular praise for his employment and real estate-related tax knowledge. **Martin Morfeld** also caught the attention of interviewees with his "*thorough and efficient work ethos.*" He advises on tax planning issues in relation to the sale and purchase of companies and on obtaining exempt status for healthcare entities.

**Clients/Work Highlights:** Seattle Times Company; Starbucks; Tyson Foods and Orca Bay Capital.

## DLA Piper Rudnick Gray Cary US LLP

See firm details p.870

**The Firm:** This team advises public and private companies of all sizes and advises them on a spectrum of transactions ranging from IPOs to M&A deals. Clients are attracted to the firm's "*attentive, intelligent and practical*" ethos and its practitioners' impressive knowledge of their field. The group also drew praise for its geographical reach, which extends across the USA to Europe and Asia, thanks to the firm's extensive international network of offices. Its extensive client base includes emerging enterprises as well as established companies, all of which call on the team for its wide range of business services.

**The Lawyers:** **John Steel** (see p.1977) is widely recognized as "*one of the top lawyers in the city.*" He is respected among clients for the consistency and reliability of his advice and is "*an outstanding business lawyer*" who often advises boards on corporate governance issues. **Mark Hoffman** (see p.1976) chairs the public company and corporate governance group and is in particular demand among clients for his advice on insider trading and SEC reporting issues. **Laura Treadgold Puckett** (see p.1977) caters for a client base heavy in technology companies. Her expertise lies mainly in the areas of venture capital financings and M&A deals. Sources declared **Steven Yentzer** (see p.1978) "*one of the leading figures in partnership tax*" and believe that he has significantly strengthened the team since his arrival in early 2005.

**Clients/Work Highlights:** Starbucks; Onvia.com; Tegic Communications and Phycom.

## Lane Powell PC

See firm details p.2009

**The Firm:** The Seattle branch of this prestigious firm houses "*some exceptional M&A lawyers*" and continues to go from strength to strength. The full-service department offers specialist expertise in a range of areas including corporate governance and stockholder activism. In 2005 the team, comprising around 40 "*experienced and sharp practitioners,*" successfully negotiated the high-profile sale of a bottled water company. Its broad client base increasingly includes a number of startup companies, and lawyers here have experience in both national and international transactions.

**The Lawyers:** **Mike Morgan** has "*a concise and practical legal mind,*" and broad experience counseling clients such as Java Trading Company and Tully's.

In one of his most important recent deals, he advised United Online on its acquisition of classmates.com. Clients often turn to **Michael Dwyer** for assistance on M&A deals in the healthcare and biotech sectors. He received a flurry of recommendations as a "*thoughtful and careful practitioner.*"

**Clients/Work Highlights:** Nordstrom; Cutter & Buck; ImageX and Advanced H20.

## Wilson Sonsini Goodrich & Rosati

See firm details p.344

**The Firm:** The Seattle office of this West Coast powerhouse is firmly established in the market and is able to take advantage of the resources available to it from the firm's other offices across the USA. It houses "*a group of dedicated and results-oriented*" lawyers who act principally for high-growth public companies in the technology fields. The team took advantage of the resurgence of activity among local venture capitalists in 2005, and has advised on a spate of deals in the biotech sector.

**The Lawyers:** **Patrick Schultheis** (see p.1977) is the managing partner at the Seattle office and represents a spectrum of clients, ranging from startup companies to large, publicly held entities. Sources describe him as a "*relentless adversary,*" who is nevertheless "*highly admired.*" Another key member of the team is **Craig Sherman** (see p.1977), who has extensive experience representing private companies and venture capital investors. He employs a "*results-oriented, can-do attitude*" and recently advised on the sale of 4thpass to Motorola.

**Clients/Work Highlights:** RealNetworks; InfoSpace; Inrix; RadioFrame Networks; Calypso Medical and ePartners.

## Band 3

## Foster Pepper PLLC

**The Firm:** This group of "*solid professionals*" specializes in deals involving emerging companies and venture capital investors. It has a wealth of international deals and expertise in sports franchises, financial institutions and general corporate representation. The team boasts an impressive clientele, drawn from a wide range of industries, particularly the biotechnology and life sciences sectors, and has a strong following among national pension funds.

**The Lawyers:** Interviewees herald **Robert Diercks** as "*an excellent, savvy lawyer.*" He has a flair for business acquisitions and dispositions, but is also a popular choice of counsel for venture capital financings. Another "*fine legal practitioner*" is **Allen Israel**, who acts for a variety of investment and technology businesses.

## Heller Ehrman LLP

See firm details p.329

**The Firm:** This well-established practice specializes in M&A transactions in the life sciences, energy and technology fields. In 2005 the team successfully advised on an acquisition by one of the largest at-sea processing companies in the USA and acted on a

multibillion-dollar acquisition of a credit card business that spanned several US states. Sources praised this highly regarded group for its "*depth of knowledge and familiarity with corporate issues.*"

**The Lawyers:** **Pamela Charles Brown** (see p.1974) has an excellent reputation for her advice on tax planning, tax-exempt organizations and executive compensation matters. Interviewees repeatedly praised her as a "*highly capable and knowledgeable practitioner.*"

**Clients/Work Highlights:** Washington Mutual; Yahoo!; IBM; Nokia; Johnson & Johnson and Microsoft.

## Stoel Rives LLP

**The Firm:** The Seattle branch of this Portland firm acts for midmarket private companies, emerging companies and entrepreneurs, particularly in the fields of technology, software and Internet applications. The group is well known for its thorough, committed and dedicated approach and "*leaves no stone unturned*" in its representation of clients. Recent highlights for the 12-strong corporate group include representing a consulting firm on a major acquisition.

**The Lawyers:** **Carl Lewis** focuses mainly on federal income tax and advises on the planning and execution of sophisticated tax-motivated transactions. He is a "*committed and diligent practitioner*" who has more than two decades' worth of experience in the tax arena. **Duff Bryant** is experienced in M&A deals and corporate law matters. Sources claim he is "*a cut above the rest*" and believe he is someone to watch out for in the future.

**Clients/Work Highlights:** Dairygold; Endeavour Capital; Cobalt Group and Lion, Inc.

## Band 4

## Dorsey & Whitney LLP

See firm details p.1169

**The Firm:** Clients recommended this group for its expertise in a range of M&A and corporate transactions and applauded its "*responsive and knowledgeable practitioners.*" Although this is a relatively small and compact team, many of its deals are often cross-border in nature. Much of the group's time and resources are also devoted to advising emerging companies, often from the technology and life sciences fields, on a range of business law issues.

**The Lawyers:** **Robert Kaplan** (see p.1976) often advises on cross-border matters, including international financings and privatization projects, and has been active advising on several acquisitions in the international seafood industries. Clients are attracted to his "*skilled and informed approach,*" gained from more than three decades of experience in the field.

**Clients/Work Highlights:** The firm serves a range of public and private clients including investment banks and management buyout groups. Key clients include Bell Canada and Carrix.

### Graham & Dunn PC

**The Firm:** This small, regional firm is highly respected by clients and peers for its "*group of top-notch practitioners*," who are renowned for the care and attention they show to their clients. The group is well established in the local market and has a broad practice advising clients on their business structure, M&A and joint venture transactions, and franchising and distribution agreements. It acts for a range of clients, spanning from large corporations to emerging companies and individuals.

**The Lawyers:** Interviewees regard **Jack Strother** as an excellent practitioner who gives "*careful and detailed attention*" to legal problems and who demonstrates excellent communication skills.

**Clients/Work Highlights:** The group's clients include banks, startup entities and established businesses.

### Orrick, Herrington & Sutcliffe LLP

See firm details p.337

**The Firm:** With offices across the USA, Europe and Asia, this group has a depth of resources that allows it to advise on sophisticated national and international transactions. It serves a wide client base ranging from emerging enterprises to Fortune 500 companies and was cited by interviewees as the group that "*springs to mind in the field of biotech.*" Recent highlights include advising on a multimillion-dollar acquisition by a leading research-based pharmaceutical company.

**The Lawyers:** **Stephen Graham** (see p.1975) leads the Seattle corporate department. He is a "*diligent and committed*" practitioner who focuses on corporate finance transactions, including private and public offerings and M&A deals. Sources warmly recommended **Alan Smith** (see p.1977) as "*a fine young lawyer*" who acts for a range of clients.

**Clients/Work Highlights:** The group counsels a wide range of clients including biotech, life sciences, software and technology companies.

### Riddell Williams PS

**The Firm:** This regional firm has been established in Seattle for over a century and has developed "*a firm footprint*" in the corporate law arena. The group is well known for its highly client-oriented service and integrity, and acts for clients ranging from emerging companies to large, established organizations. Lawyers here have experience in all types of corporate and M&A transactions and have recently advised a key client on the successful acquisition of a large technological company.

**The Lawyers:** **Bruce Bjerke** is a "*truly outstanding lawyer*" who excels in all aspects of corporate and M&A work, particularly in the hotel industry.

**Clients/Work Highlights:** Tegic Communications; American Package Express; Biddle & Crowther and Cascadian Fruit Shippers.

# EMPLOYMENT

## MAINLY DEFENDANT

| Employment: Mainly Defendant |
| --- |
| Leading Firms |
| [1] **DAVIS WRIGHT TREMAINE LLP** *Seattle* |
| **PERKINS COIE LLP** *Seattle* |
| [2] **PRESTON GATES & ELLIS LLP** *Seattle* |
| **SEBRIS BUSTO JAMES** *Bellevue* |
| **WINTERBAUER & DIAMOND, P.L.L.C.** *Seattle* |
| [3] **LANE POWELL PC** *Seattle* |
| **RIDDELL WILLIAMS PS** *Seattle* |
| **STOEL RIVES LLP** *Seattle* |

## Band 1

### Davis Wright Tremaine LLP

**The Firm:** This is one of the largest employment groups in the state and is renowned for the quality of its lawyers throughout its ranks. Clients rely on the team to deliver a full employment service. They explained: "*Their work product is always excellent and they make you feel like you're the only client they're dealing with.*" Much of the group's time is devoted to defending clients in employment discrimination suits but it also assigns significant resources to alternative dispute resolution and counseling on litigation avoidance. The team is also well versed in labor law and frequently advises on collective bargaining agreements and union contracts.

**The Lawyers:** This team of "*smart and responsive*" attorneys is home to some of the leading practitioners in the market. They include **Mark Hutcheson**, who particularly impressed commentators with his skill in collective bargaining work. He is renowned among peers as someone who is not afraid to take a "*firm stance*" and whose clients "*think the world of him.*" Arbitration proceedings and negotiations with unions still account for much of his practice, but he has recently been engaged in an increasing amount of litigation. One of his recent highlights includes advising a key client, WestFarm Foods, on a strike threatened by the work force. Within the labor law community, **Robert Blackstone** is regarded as the "*first referral choice in a conflict.*" His practice is divided between noncompete and trade secrets matters and employment law counseling. He also handles traditional labor law, and has recently negotiated a labor contract in which his client was able to rationalize its healthcare provision for approximately 300 employees. **Thomas Lemly** is renowned for his enviable court demeanor. As one commentator put it: "*He's about as smooth and gentlemanly as the day is long – juries always warm to him.*" He undertakes the full range of employment-related litigation, including discrimination cases and wage and hour claims. According to sources, **Michael Reiss** is one of the leading employment litigators in the state. He is renowned for his performance in nationwide race and sex discrimination class actions. Interviewees also singled out **Lawton Humphrey** for his employment litigation and alternative dispute resolution practice. Part of his time is also devoted to counseling clients on employment law compliance and wage and hour matters.

**Clients/Work Highlights:** Bank of America; Seattle Times Company; ConocoPhilips; Virginia Mason Clinic; Boeing; Calpine; adidas America; Comcast; Seattle Opera; Campbells; FedEx and Amgen.

### Perkins Coie LLP

**The Firm:** Researchers heard that this is "*one of the largest and most diverse employment practices in the state.*" Clients appreciate the firm's expansive presence and the range of services it offers. One interviewee said: "*They span such a large geographical area that they meet our needs in a number of venues, and the quality of the practice is consistently high across the board. The results we have had from them over the years have been extraordinary.*" The team has three main focus areas: employment class actions, regional and national employment litigation and traditional labor relations work in both the private and the public sector. It acts for a number of high-profile clients and is particularly well known for its representation of Boeing.

**The Lawyers:** Although the departure of Clemens Barnes is undoubtedly a blow to the group, market commentators continued to point to its impressive roster of lawyers. These include the senior statesman **John Aslin**, who won plaudits as an "*excellent mediator.*" Interviewees regard **Russ Perisho** as "*one hell of a lawyer and a gem of a person to boot.*" He represents employers in a variety of employment and labor litigation and is especially renowned for his representation of hospitals. Perisho continues to enjoy strong client loyalty: "*He is very responsive, knowledgeable and likable – more recently we have used him for mediation and have been very impressed by the outstanding service he and his team have given us,*" said one satisfied customer. **Nancy Williams** is a "*talented and tough lawyer who always does a good job for her clients.*" She has a broad practice encompassing various aspects of employment law, including wrongful discharge and equal employment opportunity. Interviewees identified **Bruce Cross** as the go-to guy in the group for more traditional labor work.

**Clients/Work Highlights:** Boeing; Starbucks; Qwest; UPS; Puget Sound Energy; Amazon.com; Safeco Insurance; InfoSpace; KremeWorks; Swedish Medical Center and Matsushita Avionics Systems.

## Band 2

### Preston Gates & Ellis LLP

**The Firm:** This "*highly able*" firm won recognition for the strength of its one-stop labor and employment practice. It has developed a particularly strong reputation for its top-quality noncompete work but also provides clients with expertise in the fields of ERISA, wage and hour and collective bargaining agreements. Lawyers also act for clients in a full spectrum of employment discrimination suits and counsel companies on the employment aspects of their business transactions and on immigration issues.

**The Lawyers:** Patrick Madden has a "*sterling reputation*" and received plaudits from market commentators for his wage and hour expertise and his work both as a counselor and a litigator.

**Clients/Work Highlights:** The group acts for employers from a range of industries.

### Sebris Busto James

**The Firm:** This boutique firm was a popular choice among interviewees, who praised it for the caliber of its team of nine lawyers. Peers hold it in high esteem, with one competitor remarking: "*When conflicts come up this is the firm I send work to, because although it's smaller, their individuals have real superstar strength.*" The group is especially well known for its traditional labor law expertise but also has strengths in employment litigation. Alternative dispute resolution is also a key feature of the group's workload and clients rely on the team for preventive counseling and assistance on management training.

**The Lawyers:** Interviewees believe that this is "*one of*

the best firms in the state for traditional labor law.*" The group's key lawyer, **Mark Busto**, commands enormous respect among clients and peers alike. He has been involved in several high-profile cases and acted for Spokane City Council in relation to an investigation into the workplace conduct of Mayor James West. He also has a strong background in labor relations issues and advises clients on their human resources policies. **Robert Sebris** has lengthy experience in the field and is in particular demand in the traditional labor law arena. His work here includes advising clients on union elections, strike avoidance and workplace drugs testing.

**Clients/Work Highlights:** Clients are typically, but not exclusively, drawn from the public sector. Lawyers act for entities from the healthcare industry, including hospitals, long-term care institutions and community health organizations, and also represent various cities, counties and public entities. It also has a following among private sector clients from the construction, manufacturing and retail sectors.

### Winterbauer & Diamond, P.L.L.C.

**The Firm:** This boutique firm enters the tables this year following enthusiastic praise from peers for the quality of its attorneys and its strength in litigation. The size of the practice, with its two partners and three associates, belies the group's comprehensive capability across a spectrum of employment and labor law litigation and counseling. "*I happily refer my clients here when I'm conflicted,*" one peer confided. Another remarked that the group is "*definitely punching above its weight.*"

**The Lawyers:** **Steven Winterbauer** is an "*ambitious and able*" attorney whose thriving litigation practice encompasses both employment and labor law. His colleague **Kenneth Diamond** combines his work in the employment field with a busy commercial litigation and insurance practice.

**Clients/Work Highlights:** Costco; Safeway; Les Schwab Tire Centers; Sheraton Seattle Hotel and Towers; Swedish Medical Center; Northwest Airlines; Volkswagen; DeVry and Lee Enterprises.

## Band 3

### Lane Powell PC

See firm details p.2009

**The Firm:** This team provides a full labor and employment service with a particularly notable litigation practice. It handles an array of discrimination and harassment claims and has a busy ERISA litigation component to the practice. The group has witnessed an upsurge in whistle-blower actions and has recently successfully defended a client from the retail sector against a wrongful discharge and retaliation claim. Members of the team have also been selected by the EEOC to train regional employers at the EEOC Training Institute.

**The Lawyers:** Michael Reilly spearheads the firm's labor and employment and employer benefits group. He has experience in a range of employment litigation cases concerning alleged age, religion, sex, disability and race discrimination.

**Clients/Work Highlights:** The group acts for a mix of public and private entities. Key clients include Home Depot; Nordstrom; Cutter & Buck; Wells Fargo; Metropolitan Mortgage; King County; Ferrellgas; Countrywide Home Loans; Kodak and Knowledge Learning.

### Riddell Williams PS

**The Firm:** This group continues to expand and now boasts eight full-time attorneys, who represent national and regional clients throughout the Pacific Northwest. The team's profile has also been boosted by its ability to attract a number of new, high-profile mandates that call on the firm for its advice on employment law compliance and its defense of complex wage and hour and discrimination suits. The group also has a labor relations capability and advises on union-organizing campaigns and collective bargaining agreements.

**The Lawyers:** Praise abounded for the team's star attorney, **Karen Jones**. Clients warmly described her as "*savvy, knowledgeable and tough when necessary.*" One of her peers also tipped her as "*one of the best mediators I have worked with – she has a wonderful ability to make both sides get real about their cases.*" Jones advises HR departments and in-house counsel on the full range of employment compliance issues. She also defends businesses in a range of employment law cases.

**Clients/Work Highlights:** Primera Blue Cross; Philips; Allstate; Redhook Brewing; T-Mobile; AT&T Wireless; DHL and Idaho Power.

### Stoel Rives LLP

**The Firm:** This is a group of "*excellent lawyers*" who represent an enviable list of clients throughout the USA. It advises a wide array of clients on the full gamut of labor and employment, employee benefits and workers' compensation laws. The group is well known for its advocacy skills but also has a successful track record in alternative dispute resolution and is popular among clients for its training and compliance programs. The group has been especially busy on behalf of healthcare providers and entities from the communications industry, but also acts for a range of clients located in the Northwest and the Intermountain West.

**The Lawyers:** With around 30 years' experience in the industry, **Jerome Rubin** was described to researchers as a "*phenomenal lawyer for labor law negotiations.*" He continues to handle contract negotiations for a large healthcare system but also devotes some of his time to counseling on and litigating wage and hour and discrimination disputes. **Margaret Barbier** provides high-level counseling and policy development advice on reductions in the work force, reorganizations and FMLA leave issues. She is also a keen litigator in the ADA arena and defends clients in state and federal courts against sexual harassment suits. **Tim O'Connell**'s practice is evenly weighted between traditional labor law and employment litigation. He continues to advise Verizon on all of its labor and employment law issues in the Pacific Northwest.

**Clients/Work Highlights:** McDonald's; Cray Inc; T-Mobile; Verizon; Casey Family Programs; Good Samaritan Hospital and MultiCare Medical Center.

## Other Notable Practitioners

**Carolyn Cairns** of Stokes Lawrence commands the respect of market commentators, who told us: "*She knows when to be tough and when to be soft. She has a brilliant intellect and a personality to match – all in all she is very effective and a pleasure to work with.*" She is particularly well known for her mediation skills but also represents public and private entities and individuals in the full range of employment litigation. **Clem Barnes** has left Perkins Coie and is now based at Graham & Dunn PC. His peers have such confidence in his abilities that they would "*refer clients to him without hesitation.*" He leads the firm's labor and employment team and is seen acting for clients in a range of employment discrimination and harassment cases. He is also gaining increased recognition for the mediation slant to his practice. At Summit Law Group, **Otto Klein** stood out as a "*very fine employment lawyer*" and a leading authority in labor relations. He counsels, litigates and mediates for a range of public and private sector clients and has recently acted for a public transport company facing allegations of race discrimination, following the dismissal of an employee. *Chambers'* interviewees recommended **Doug Mooney** (see p.1976) as "*one of the state's best traditional labor lawyers.*" He recently joined Littler Mendelson PC from Preston Gates & Ellis and is currently the Seattle office's managing stockholder.

# ENVIRONMENT

| Environment | |
|---|---|
| **Leading Firms** | |
| [1] CASCADIA LAW GROUP *Seattle* | |
| DAVIS WRIGHT TREMAINE LLP *Seattle* | |
| HELLER EHRMAN LLP *Seattle* | |
| PERKINS COIE LLP *Seattle* | |
| PRESTON GATES & ELLIS LLP *Seattle* | |
| STOEL RIVES LLP *Seattle* | |
| SUMMIT LAW GROUP, PLLC *Seattle* | |

| Leading Individuals | |
|---|---|
| [1] BLUMENFELD Chuck *Perkins Coie LLP* | |
| BROWN JR Rodney *Cascadia Law Group* | |
| LEPPO Jeffery *Stoel Rives LLP* | |
| PALUMBO Ralph *Summit Law Group, PLLC* | |
| SCHNEIDER Mark *Perkins Coie LLP* | |
| [2] CHAPMAN William *Preston Gates & Ellis LLP* | |
| COHEN Matthew *Heller Ehrman LLP* | |
| DUNN Loren *Riddell Williams PS* | |
| ELLIOTT Richard *Davis Wright Tremaine LLP* | |
| GINSBERG Beth *Stoel Rives LLP* | |
| MANOLOPOULOS Lynn *Davis Wright Tremaine LLP* | |
| THORP Michael *Heller Ehrman LLP* | |

## Band 1

### Cascadia Law Group

**The Firm:** This environmental law boutique houses eight lawyers who handle the full spectrum of environmental law. It is highly regarded for the skill and experience of its "*fabulous*" lawyers who have expertise in air and water quality issues and endangered species and natural resources law. They also advise on waste management, permitting and reviews, and environmental issues surrounding property development and acquisitions. The group also has a strong environmental litigation capability.

**The Lawyers:** Interviewees recommended **Rodney Brown** as a "*wonderful top-tier lawyer.*" He advises clients on and litigates a range of clean air, water, waste management and endangered species matters. He also has expertise in property development and acquisitions and is an "*excellent lawyer who does a very good job for his clients.*"

### Davis Wright Tremaine LLP

**The Firm:** This national firm represents businesses throughout the USA and around the world. The environmental team counsels on and litigates a wide spectrum of environmental matters, and is known for its "*great depth of expertise.*" It benefits from the experience of its lawyers, many of whom have worked as engineers, consultants and government officials, responsible for environmental policies in their past careers. *Chambers'* researchers also heard that the group is "*responsive to clients and works well as a team.*"

**The Lawyers:** **Richard Elliott** represents clients in the petroleum industry before the federal and state courts and assists them on regulatory compliance with environmental laws. He is "*responsive, hardworking and knows how to deal with in-house counsel.*" Clients also appreciate his commitment to their cause and his efforts to keep them informed of new legal developments. **Lynn Manolopoulos** advises on regulation and compliance and also has a litigation strand to her practice. She has advised a number of clients on the acquisition and development of contaminated properties and has increasingly been involved in environmental cleanups and related cost recovery. She also handles regulatory work under CERCLA and EPCRA (Emergency Planning & Community Right-to-Know Act) and has advised clients on national environmental audits.

### Heller Ehrman LLP

See firm details p.329

**The Firm:** This full-service firm has a well-recognized national environment practice. Its lawyers have been involved in some significant projects in Alaska and advise on a full range of environmental regulatory and compliance issues. They are also well versed in the environmental aspects of transactions and are frequently seen litigating before various courts and agencies. Recent areas of activity for the group include toxic torts, California Proposition 65 and Superfund cleanup issues, natural resources law and permitting.

**The Lawyers:** **Matthew Cohen** (see p.1974) advises on clean air and water compliance and represents manufacturers, electric utilities and power plant project developers. He is an "*extraordinarily good lawyer*" who is acting for BP in litigation concerning the permitting of a dock. He has also been appointed to an advisory committee to the State Department of Ecology and often comments on new legislation and proposed changes to regulations. **Michael Thorp** (see p.1978) is an expert in environmental and natural resources litigation and counseling. He has built up 30 years of experience in natural resources damages, toxic tort suits, class actions and water rights and is "*thoroughly deserving of his strong reputation,*" according to interviewees.

**Clients/Work Highlights:** Ash Grove Cement; Chugach Electric Association; King County and Nucor Steel.

### Perkins Coie LLP

**The Firm:** This top-notch regional firm boasts an environmental group that represents corporations and project owners on a spectrum of compliance and permitting issues. It also handles litigation and has developed a strong Endangered Species Act practice, which continues to expand due to the group's increased activity in the natural resources arena. Its seasoned lawyers won praise for their responsiveness, negotiation skills and ability to work with business people. One interviewee said: "*The work they've done has been exceptional – with them acting for me, I've never felt the need to change outside counsel.*"

**The Lawyers:** **Chuck Blumenfeld** chairs the firm's national environmental practice and works primarily in the environment regulation and project permitting arenas, although he is also renowned for his transactional work. His recent work includes advising Kinross Gold on the permitting of the first significant underground gold mine in Washington for decades. He also handled Dawn Mining's dispute with the government over the cleanup of an old Superfund site and is widely viewed in the market as a "*wonderful and spectacular lawyer.*" *Chambers'* interviewees recommended **Mark Schneider** as a "*first-rate environmental trial lawyer.*" He defended Boeing against an environmental contamination suit relating to the operation of the Larson Air Force Base. He also defended Weyerhaeuser in a natural resources damage matter concerning PCB contamination of the Kalamazoo River. Clients choose him because "*he is extremely bright and highly capable.*"

## Preston Gates & Ellis LLP

**The Firm:** The Seattle office of this national firm fields a team of around 30 lawyers, including some 16 experienced environmental partners. The group has a distinguished track record and is noted for its success in handling a range of projects and transactions. It enjoys a strong reputation in Seattle as "*one of the biggest and deepest environmental practices in the Northwest.*" Its work includes Superfund and environmental criminal defense litigation and a range of permitting and environmental compliance matters relating to CAA, CWA and hazardous waste. **The Lawyers: Bill Chapman** is "*one of the standout environmental lawyers in the state.*" He handles matters at the state and local government level, across a number of jurisdictions, and has particular expertise in land use permitting and litigation and hazardous waste cleanups. Interviewees referred to him as a "*big name*" in the industry and one of the leading lawyers at the firm.

## Stoel Rives LLP

**The Firm:** This large regional firm handles environmental work throughout the west of the USA, including states such as Alaska, Hawaii and Oregon, and continues to build on an enviable reputation in Washington. Interviewees continue to point to its strengths in hydroelectric projects but it is also busy advising on other areas such as environmental compliance and permitting, and litigation including enforcement

actions and the defense of toxic tort suits. This year it has significantly boosted its team with the notable arrival of Steven Thiele, who is the former chief toxics cleanup attorney for the ecology division of the Washington state attorney general's office.

**The Lawyers: Jeffery Leppo**'s highlights include successfully defending PPM Energy in a case in Kansas Federal Court that challenged a wind project based on the Migratory Bird Treaty Act. He is well known for his expertise in federal permitting and endangered species matters, particularly in the context of the fisheries industry in Hawaii. He is also in the oil and gas arena and has handled a variety of projects for ConocoPhillips, BP and Pioneer Resources relating to permitting matters in Alaska. **Beth Ginsberg** concentrates on environmental and natural resources litigation. She represented the BPA Customer Group in a lawsuit brought by the National Wildlife Federation regarding the Columbia hydropower system. In another highlight, she secured a victory for six Washington and Oregon public ports in a case in which an environmental group challenged a project to deepen the Columbia River, in order to allow larger ships to enter the ports.

**Clients/Work Highlights:** The firm represents public ports in Seattle, Portland and Vancouver. Lawyers have handled a number of Endangered Species Act and CWA matters for clients and have been busy advising on an Endangered Species

Act project for the Washington Forest Protection Association.

## Summit Law Group, PLLC

**The Firm:** This innovative firm's emphasis on customer service is obviously paying dividends and it has built up an outstanding reputation for its environmental practice. Its five environmental lawyers have expertise in a range of areas including hazardous waste, land use, zoning and permitting for developments. In one of its most significant recent projects, the group has been working on finalizing the cleanup of a large phosphorus manufacturing plant in Idaho.

**The Lawyers:** Interviewees recommended **Ralph Palumbo** as a "*wonderful lawyer*" who has over 30 years' experience in clean air, water and hazardous waste legislation. He is a talented trial lawyer who is principally involved in a spate of litigation relating to regulatory issues and has been busy working on a Shoreline Management Act case.

## Other Notable Practitioners

**Loren Dunn** of Riddell Williams PS spends much of his time advising on harbor cleanup projects and litigation in the Northwest, where sediment cleanup has become a priority due to concerns for the protection of salmon and orca whales. He is also a board member of and counsel to the Washington Environment Council.

# IMMIGRATION

## Band 1

### Cowan & Miller

**The Firm:** While this practice may still be relatively young, it has flourished rapidly into "*one of the finest and most highly respected immigration groups in the Northwest,*" with a client base to match. The firm represents large organizations such as Microsoft in business immigration matters, its main area of

expertise. Attorneys also service midsized, often expanding, enterprises. The four-strong boutique focuses primarily on biotech, technology and healthcare as well as assisting trade, shipping and transportation companies.

**The Lawyers: Pamela Cowan**, the founder of the firm, specializes in labour certifications and permanent residences; peers describe her as "*an excellent, prominent lawyer.*" The last two decades have seen the "*meticulous and gifted practitioner*" focus her strengths on immigration law, honing her skills to perfection. **Steven Miller** focuses his experience and talent mainly on biotech, medical research and complex financial transactions. He, too, boasts years of specialist experience in the field, making the team the first port of call for clients' needs.

**Clients/Work Highlights:** The group's clientele is extremely diverse and evenly distributed from the likes of Starbucks and Microsoft to the small entrepreneur, including established family businesses. Holland America and Univar are further examples.

### MacDonald Hoague & Bayless

**The Firm:** An "*extremely strong firm*" that houses "*top-notch lawyers,*" is the consensus of interviewees. The team is renowned for its long-standing relationship with hi-tech giant Microsoft. The

attorneys are respected for their provision of business-savvy advice in cases that span the USA. Its workload is also peppered with landmark cases in immigration law. The group has the capacity and commitment to counsel a full spectrum of clients, from individuals and local businesses to the world's largest software company in all areas of immigration law.

**The Lawyers: Daniel Hoyt Smith** specializes in immigration law and has successfully litigated in both criminal and civil cases. He is extremely well versed in complex immigration issues, and is an outstanding and reliable counselor. His "*experienced and communicative nature*" instills confidence into his clients and the results are consistently positive, said sources.

**Clients/Work Highlights:** The firm boasts a range of clients from individuals and families to larger businesses and the software giant Microsoft.

### Perkins Coie LLP

**The Firm:** The four-strong team in Seattle – part of a large national full-service firm – has a strong technological focus, in particular counseling those expanding and startup companies who are looking to recruit new talent among foreign nationals. "*A very knowledgeable, responsive firm – they always get the job done,*" it has attracted an extensive client base that often demands immigration work, such as advice on immigration audits. The group specializes in counseling biotech, hi-tech and electronics industries. It has also successfully obtained visas for a number of basketball players with well-known Seattle teams. Sources praised the firm's consistent quality, classifying them as "*an outstanding counsel and experts in immigration law.*"

**The Lawyers: Gregory McCall** focuses his skills primarily in business immigration. "*A strong lawyer in all aspects of business immigration law,*" McCall is well regarded by clients and peers alike.

**Clients/Work Highlights:** Seattle Mariners, AMI Semiconductor and ICOS.

## Ryan, Swanson & Cleveland, PLLC

**The Firm:** Market commentators place this group among the "*highest-quality firms*" in the region, providing stiff competition for other, larger firms. The group counsels clients ranging from individuals to larger corporate entities in all areas of immigration law, including visas, residences and naturalizations. These attorneys show "*a great depth of knowledge in their field*" and appreciate the need for fast action and broad experience of the legal issued involved.

**The Lawyers:** The firm houses some of the top names in immigration law. **Janet Cheetham,** the chair of the Seattle immigration group, is a highly regarded practitioner. Sources spoke of her "*extensive expertise*" in her field and success in attracting significant clients, including government agencies. She is respected for her experience in nonimmigrant

visas and immigrant visas involving marriage petitions. Clients from a range of industries such as forestry and banking seek her expert counsel. **Joel Paget** oversees a range of immigration matters for clients, centered on business visa and classification work. His provision of "*a reassuringly personal service*" and wealth of experience instills confidence in clients.

**Clients/Work Highlights:** Intrawest Corporation; Premium Brands; Canadian Fishing Company and Nordstrom.

## Other Notable Practitioners

**Carol Edward** at the Law Offices of Carol L Edward & Associates was commended for her diverse immigration practice and real strength in related litigation.

# INTELLECTUAL PROPERTY

### Intellectual Property
**Leading Firms**

1. CHRISTENSEN O'CONNOR JOHNSON *Seattle*
   DAVIS WRIGHT TREMAINE LLP *Seattle*
   DORSEY & WHITNEY LLP *Seattle*
   PERKINS COIE LLP *Seattle*
2. BLACK LOWE & GRAHAM *Seattle*
   HELLER EHRMAN LLP *Seattle*
   PRESTON GATES & ELLIS LLP *Seattle*
   SEED IP LAW GROUP PLLC *Seattle*

### Leading Individuals

1. AL-SALAM Ramsey *Perkins Coie LLP*
   BODINE Brian *Davis Wright Tremaine LLP*
   BULCHIS Ed *Dorsey & Whitney LLP*
   MEIKLEJOHN Paul *Dorsey & Whitney LLP*
   RIEDINGER Jerry *Perkins Coie LLP*
2. BATEMAN David *Preston Gates & Ellis LLP*
   DUNWOODY Stuart *Davis Wright Tremaine LLP*
   FERRON JR William *Seed IP Law Group PLLC*
   GRAHAM Lawrence *Black Lowe & Graham*
   MORGAN Kevan *Christensen O'Connor Johnson*
   NELSON Marshall *Davis Wright Tremaine LLP*
   RHEAUME Warren *Heller Ehrman LLP*
   SIEFERT Richard *Merchant & Gould PC*

## Band 1

### Christensen O'Connor Johnson Kindness, PLLC

**The Firm:** With a tradition that spans more than 70 years, this top-quality IP boutique is an established part of the Seattle Bar. The firm has capability in the full range of work from patent, trademark, copyright and trade secrets, through to unfair competition and litigation. All industries are catered for with an emphasis on the scientific side of the market. The

firm's expertise is such that their work is conducted far beyond state boundaries.

**The Lawyers:** Patent attorney **Kevan Morgan** is the firm's star turn for his patent prosecution practice. As well as conducting patent and trademark registration across the globe, he counsels clients typically drawn from the technological industries: electrical, telecom, software and medical instrumentation.

**Clients/Work Highlights:** Amazon.com; Nintendo; Starbucks; Boston Scientific; Weyerhaeuser and Microsoft.

## Davis Wright Tremaine LLP

**The Firm:** This nine-office firm has considerable presence throughout the states and has an office in Shanghai. As one would expect, the team can offer the full range of services including copyright, trademark, trade secrets and patent work, both at the initial counseling and licensing stage and all the way through to litigation. This is the firm's fastest growing practice group boasting many great attorneys, three of whom are ranked here.

**The Lawyers:** "*Technically very competent,*" **Brian Bodine** can claim much of the success of this firm's patent litigation practice. His expertise is not restricted to patent infringement litigation and recently he has undertaken trademark litigation and licensing disputes. Such work has included a sizable licensing dispute over a software license. Particularly interesting and ongoing patent infringement work includes the case of Forscillo v Le Monde. After filing for summary judgment, the other side moved to dismiss the claims against Bodine's client. The case is currently on appeal. Bodine plays on both sides of the field, representing plaintiffs and defendants. His rank belies his relative youth and his career promises to keep on blooming. **Stuart Dunwoody** has been engaged in notable work of late including attaining a summary judgment of noninfringement for Trinity Glass International. Dunwoody also boasts a good base of media

company clients for whom he undertakes libel, defamation and invasion of privacy work. **Marshall Nelson** possesses a practice that is split between IP, copyright and trademark, and media law. He gains the greatest recognition for his work representing publishers and writers, for instance Nelson undertakes all the licensing for Gary Larson's FarWorks and has had a busy year doing the legal work for the compilation and publication of the complete 'The Far Side'.

**Clients/Work Highlights:** Vermont Fitness; Altair Eyewear; Data Depth; Clearwire; Kaiser Permanente and Scientific Explorer.

## Dorsey & Whitney LLP

See firm details p.1169

**The Firm:** This firm is acknowledged by commentators to boast a well-earned reputation for representing the developers of cutting-edge technology and they have recently been rated in the top ten in terms of quality in 'IP Law and Business' by virtue of their capability and experience in this arena.

**The Lawyers:** Clients trust **Ed Bulchis** (see p.1974) because he is a "*knowledgeable, top-quality attorney with an excellent team around him.*" Bulchis focuses his practice on electronics patent counseling, preparation and prosecution, especially regarding semiconductors and computer systems. He is also a capable litigator when the need arises. Recently he has continued to protect leading edge memory devices for Micron Technology: this is typical of the type of cutting-edge technology work that the team as a whole is famed for. A "*real stalwart*" of the IP Bar, **Paul Meiklejohn** (see p.1976) has a reputation for taking adamant stances during litigation – and sticking to them.

**Clients/Work Highlights:** This firm has a varied client base and accepts instructions from those in the technology, life science and food industries, to name but a few.

## Perkins Coie LLP

**The Firm:** This firm has a large and well-regarded IP practice that covers procurement, litigation and licensing. Clients commended the team to researchers for being a *"full-service firm that is very responsive to our needs."* Moreover, some commentators suggested that it housed the *"most knowledgeable IP lawyers in the state."*

**The Lawyers:** Bearing *"extensive and valuable experience,"* **Jerry Riedinger** was described as being *"extremely technically competent and exceptionally bright."* Riedinger is chair of the firm's national patent litigation practice. **Ramsey Al-Salam** continues to impress peers: *"He has enormous personal poise, he is personable and technically superb – all the hallmarks of being a top-flight litigator."* Recently he obtained a summary judgment of patent noninfringement for Getty Images in a case filed by E-Data. He has also conducted a trademark trial for Blizzard Entertainment with a decision pending.

**Clients/Work Highlights:** Vulcan Companies; Boeing; Blizzard Entertainment; Intel; Microsoft; Micron Technology; Nintendo and Semitool.

## Band 2

## Black Lowe & Graham

**The Firm:** This full-service IP boutique boasts a sterling reputation for patent prosecution work both domestically and internationally. The attorneys here undertake IP law, trademarks, copyrights, trade secrets, unfair competition, computer and Internet law, technology transfer, franchising, and related litigation.

**The Lawyers:** Principally a litigator, **Lawrence Graham** (see p.1975) undertakes a diverse spread of industries from electrical and software to sporting goods. When not litigating, Graham is engaged in an eclectic mix of patent and trademark work. Recent work has included a patent infringement trial for Costco. The client had been accused of selling an

athletic shoe that infringed a patent: there was found to be no infringement. Graham has been teaching at Seattle law school for some time now – this helps to keep him up to date with legal developments in the area.

**Clients/Work Highlights:** Costco; Alaska Airlines; AOL; Honeywell; Progressive International and K2.

## Heller Ehrman LLP

See firm details p.329

**The Firm:** This global law firm boasts offices throughout the states and has a presence in Asia with offices in Beijing, Hong Kong and Singapore. The practice here is split between the firm's IP litigation and IP transaction teams.

**The Lawyers:** The *"impressive"* **Warren Rheaume** (see p.1977) earns particular respect among peers for his courtroom style and the ease with which he communicates legally and factually complex cases to juries and judges. His practice is focused on trademark, copyright and trade secrets litigation, with a little patent litigation as the need arises. Recent work has included representing regular client Philip Morris in groundbreaking litigation against the largest Internet seller of cigarettes. They obtained an injunction that was violated – to further enforce this the court enjoined the domain names of all the websites used to sell the cigarettes despite the fact that they were not in violation. The client also received a court judgment for $173 million.

**Clients/Work Highlights:** Garden Botanika; Philip Morris; Microsoft and the Children's Hospital & Regional Medical Center.

## Preston Gates & Ellis LLP

**The Firm:** From its beginnings as an exclusively Seattle practice, this firm now has 11 offices throughout the states and an international presence with offices in Hong Kong, Beijing and Taipei. Based at the Seattle office, the IP litigation and IP transaction teams have a reputation for representing the software giants, but beyond that they have a

broad client base that includes biotech and pharmaceutical companies.

**The Lawyers:** Partner in the Seattle office, **David Bateman** is a trial lawyer whose practice encompasses a generous helping of high-profile IP litigation and counseling. The possessor of an unmatched expertise in the fields of cyber and technology law, he is the *"undisputed king"* of spamming litigation, having prosecuted more than 100 of these lawsuits.

**Clients/Work Highlights:** Midsized to major companies rely on the firm's specialist expertise.

## Seed IP Law Group PLLC

**The Firm:** This full-service IP practice boasts 30 specialized attorneys supported by a generous team of patent agents and technical advisers. The firm's extensive expertise is divided into finely drawn practice areas, including biotech and chemistry, engineering, electrical engineering, computer science, trademarks and litigation.

**The Lawyers:** **Bill Ferron** has a practice that focuses on counseling, licensing, litigation and dispute resolution in the fields of patent, trademarks and copyright law. In particular he has earned significant market recognition for his trademark practice. His typical clients are based in the Pacific Northwest.

**Clients/Work Highlights:** Red Robin International is a key client for the firm.

## Other Notable Practitioners

**Richard Siefert** at Merchant & Gould PC has earned great respect over the years for his busy patent and trademark practice that takes him all over the country. Recent work has included representing Nisus who brought a biochemical patent case with an antitrust counterclaim. Unlike many of his peers, Siefert comes from a general sophisticated commercial litigation background; this means that he has developed the ability to reduce the message without losing it – an essential skill when dealing with cases that are both legally and factually complex.

# LITIGATION

## Band 1

## Byrnes & Keller

**The Firm:** This small litigation boutique is considered the first stop for tobacco litigation but is gaining a parallel reputation in the arena of professional liability. It is particularly renowned for representing attorneys and, as one peer said: *"Were my firm to find itself in trouble, these are the guys I would have represent me."* The attorneys here are respected for their deep trial experience and determination to go to court when necessary.

**The Lawyers:** **Brad Keller** is considered by commentators to be *"entering the sweet spot of his career."* His complex business litigation practice is focused on professional liability and products liability. In the last year, Keller has successfully defended a

law firm against a $100 million-plus lawsuit brought by a preeminent national law firm. Stablemate **Peter Byrnes** commands enormous respect in the community. One competitor mused: *"You could run a busy and successful practice just on the work that he turns away."* In particular, Byrnes and the firm are currently benefiting from the rise in litigation related to the itinerant nature of today's top executives. For instance, he is currently acting for a top ex-Microsoft executive whose move to Google spawned major litigation. Forty years in the business has earned Byrnes a sagacity that makes him a sought-after mediator and arbitrator.

**Clients/Work Highlights:** Kimberly-Clark; Honeywell; RJ Reynolds; Philips and Clear Channel feature as clients, as do numerous large, regional law firms.

## Litigation: General Commercial
### Leading Individuals

**[1] BURMAN David** *Perkins Coie LLP*

**BYRNES Peter** *Byrnes & Keller*

**HARRIGAN JR Arthur** *Danielson Harrigan Leyh*

**KELLER Brad** *Byrnes & Keller*

**[2] CORR Kelly** *Corr Cronin LLP*

**GORDON Charles** *Gordon Murray Tilden*

**GRAY JR Marvin** *Davis Wright Tremaine LLP*

**KAPLAN Barry** *Wilson Sonsini*

**PALUMBO Ralph** *Summit Law Group, PLLC*

**SCHNEIDER JR Harry** *Perkins Coie LLP*

**[3] CRONIN William** *Corr Cronin LLP*

**DUNNE Daniel** *Heller Ehrman LLP*

**ENGLUND Rudy** *Lane Powell PC*

**GOODNIGHT David** *Stoel Rives LLP*

**GREER George** *Heller Ehrman LLP*

**KEEHNEL Stellman** *DLA Piper*

**MCDONALD David** *Preston Gates & Ellis LLP*

**MCNAUL Jerry** *McNaul Ebel*

**MILLER Craig** *Davis Wright Tremaine LLP*

**RUMMAGE Stephen** *Davis Wright Tremaine LLP*

**SCHWAB Evan** *Dorsey & Whitney LLP*

**SQUIRES III William** *Summit Law Group, PLLC*

**SULKIN Robert** *McNaul Ebel*

**TILDEN Jeffrey** *Gordon Murray Tilden*

## Litigation: White-Collar Crime & Government Investigations
### Leading Individuals

**[1] CALFO Angelo** *Yarmuth Wilsdon Calfo*

**DUBITZKY Dan** *Dubitzky & Zarky PS*

**FINEGOLD Laurence** *Finegold Law Firm*

**SCHWARTZ Irwin** *The Law Office of*

**SIM J Ronald** *Stoel Rives LLP*

**WOLFE John** *Wolfe Leinbach*

## Perkins Coie LLP

**The Firm:** Boasting the largest litigation department in the state, Perkins Coie is acknowledged to be *"unsurpassed in the area of aviation litigation."* It is large enough, however, to deliver a top-class service across the entire plain of commercial litigation, and has particular expertise in IP litigation, commercial class actions and products liability. Clients praise the team for being *"able to sort the wheat from the chaff, looking after our work in a sensible and smart manner."*

**The Lawyers: Dave Burman** is a *"top-notch litigator."* An eclectic mix of work this year has included the continued representation of Costco in an antitrust challenge to Washington wine distribution regulations. He also successfully represented the Washington State Democratic Party in a high-profile case relating to the disputed outcome of the election for governor. Others in the industry make **Harry Schneider** their first choice when conflicted. He possesses a level of trial experience that is near unique among commercial litigators. Much of Schneider's time has been taken up with manage-

ment of the firm, but the balance is swinging quickly and heavily back toward full-time litigation.
**Clients/Work Highlights:** Costco; Washington State Democratic Party; Weyerhaeuser; Wallace Theater; Starbucks and Boeing.

## Band 2

## Corr Cronin LLP

**The Firm:** This is a litigation boutique whose size belies the breadth of its capabilities. Researchers received plenty of endorsements for a practice *"well capable of taking on and beating the best."* Much of the attorneys' time is spent representing large local companies and companies from outside the state that, nevertheless, have a strong Seattle presence.
**The Lawyers:** *"One of the best attorneys you could go to,"* **Kelly Corr** enjoys a hugely varied practice. Highlights of the year have included the continuing representation of Hearst in its ongoing battle with The Seattle Times. Corr was particularly commended for *"conducting a very tight case."* He also represented the former chair and CEO of Metropolitan Mortgages in a class action securities fraud and grand jury investigations. An adept appeal attorney, Corr was also engaged in a significant trade secrets case involving the semiconductor industry where he prevailed in the Ninth Circuit Court of Appeals. **William Cronin's** practice focuses on securities and fiduciary litigation and insurance coverage litigation. Both lawyers are considered to be *"devilishly effective strategists who always keep the goal in sight."*
**Clients/Work Highlights:** Microsoft; Amazon; Cingular Wireless; Alaska Airlines; ExxonMobil; Alamo and other national car rental companies.

## Danielson Harrigan Leyh & Tollefson, LLP

**The Firm:** A litigation boutique whose depth of skill and expertise places it comfortably in our second tier for another year. Particular areas of proficiency include professional negligence, admiralty, aviation, construction and securities litigation.
**The Lawyers:** The *"excellent"* **Arthur Harrigan** is the undoubted star here and received unqualified plaudits from commentators. *"He would be my first choice for any type of litigation,"* said one interviewee.
**Clients/Work Highlights:** AIG Aviation; Associated Aviation Underwriters; BP; AXA Global Risks; Port of Seattle; Lloyd's and Weyerhaeuser.

## Davis Wright Tremaine LLP

**The Firm:** This large full-service law firm has an approach to its general litigation clients that earns it considerable loyalty. One client commented: *"The attorneys understand I'm the client and do everything they possibly can without ever trying to dominate me. They understand the value of our perception by the public and help us keep good face by behaving ethically and fairly."*
**The Lawyers:** *"Standout attorney"* **Marvin Gray** has had a busy year representing a wide variety of clients. Work has included the representation of a large local

financial institution against a multimillion-dollar claim for breach of contract. He also acted for a farm labor contractor in a class action against allegations of discrimination and regulatory violations, and took on a pro bono immigration case on behalf of an individual threatened with deportation. **Stephen Rummage's** practice focuses on consumer class actions, work for financial institutions and general appellate matters. His high-profile work this year has included representing The Seattle Times in its dispute with Hearst, a matter in which Rummage's client prevailed at the Washington Supreme Court. While based largely in Washington, work for clients such as Getty Images takes Rummage all over the country. **Craig Miller** has admirable experience in the areas of lender liability defense, commercial foreclosures and commercial collections. He has recently represented Bank of America on a major trust case and a major securities case. Miller also makes time to continue the pro bono representation of a group from the Marshall Islands who have filed a claim before the Nuclear Claims Tribunal for property damage allegedly caused by a US atomic testing program conducted in the 1950's.
**Clients/Work Highlights:** Bank of America; Banner Bank; James G Murphy Company; Children's Hospital; Oaktree Capital Management; Washington Mutual; Archon Group and Sachs.

## Gordon Murray Tilden

**The Firm:** This boutique firm enters its tenth year with an unchanged diet of civil litigation matters seasoned with some PI litigation, mainly on the defense side. Commentators admire its group of specialist litigators for being *"talented lawyers with tremendous forensic experience who can take a case from beginning to end."* Being a small firm, clients are able to relax in the knowledge that work will not suffer from imprudent delegation.
**The Lawyers: Charles Gordon** is a *"fine courtroom lawyer with a wide range of experience."* His general litigation practice covers many areas including contract dispute work, insurance litigation representing policyholders and environmental insurance coverage. Colleague **Jeffrey Tilden** continues to enjoy a full and varied practice and was described to researchers as *"a good man in a crisis."*
**Clients/Work Highlights:** Puget Sound Energy and Boeing.

## McNaul Ebel Nawrot Helgren & Vance PLLC

**The Firm:** This firm was commended to researchers for *"providing a depth of reliable litigators."* It has notable employment, environment, insurance coverage and real estate litigation practices and is *"a byword for reliability."*
**The Lawyers: Robert Sulkin** is considered to be *"heading fast toward the best part of his career."* With a varied business litigation practice, Sulkin is currently defending two law firms against legal malpractice suits. Other work this year has included representing a football coach in a wrongful termination case against the University of Washington. After a seven-week trial the case settled for $4.5 million in favor of Sulkin's

client. **Jerry McNaul** is esteemed by all for bringing a near unequalled *"sense of creativity and trial experience that only years in the game can provide."*
Clients/Work Highlights: Nordstrom, Albertson's and Cutter & Buck are among the firm's clients.

## Summit Law Group, PLLC
The Firm: Approximately half of the 30 or so lawyers at this outfit are involved in commercial and employment litigation. As a firm, it is famous for its fluid organizational structure. This enables it to offer a truly bespoke service such that *"every client will receive advice exactly tailored to his or her needs."*
The Lawyers: **Ralph Palumbo** is admired by many for a practice that spans both commercial and environmental litigation. He works alongside **William Squires**, who engages in a wide spectrum of business litigation with a particular focus on toxic torts, complex real estate work and some securities matters. Squires was one of the lawyers involved in the infamous Hanford downwinder case, which consisted of 3,000-plus individual suits and has been ongoing for 15 years. The case finally made it to trial this year and Squires received favorable results for both his clients, one of which was DuPont.
Clients/Work Highlights: Clients include Fluor and and Associated University.

## Band 3

## Dorsey & Whitney LLP
See firm details p.1169
The Firm: This firm is a real global giant with a generous spread of 19 offices worldwide. Straddling Asia, Europe, Canada and, of course, the USA, it has the resources to handle matters of some magnitude. Closer to home, the Seattle office has a general commercial litigation group that has antitrust, securities, professional liability and products liability expertise.
The Lawyers: **Evan Schwab** (see p.1977) engages in complex business litigation and has a particular reputation for securities defense and malpractice work for law and accountancy firms. Highlights this year have included obtaining a summary judgment on the eve of trial for Western Wireless over a contract and fraud claim made by minority shareholders. After 40 years of practice, Schwab has a reputation for being *"a smart and tenacious litigator."* He also enjoys a preeminent place in the local legal community and recently received the honor of becoming chairman of the Washington state committee of the Association of Trial Lawyers of America.
Clients/Work Highlights: A diverse client base includes accountancy firms and major concerns such as Western Wireless.

## Heller Ehrman LLP
See firm details p.329
The Firm: This truly full-service law firm offers particular expertise in the areas of securities litigation, real estate, products liability and IP litigation. The Seattle office is just one constituent of a global firm whose presence spans Asia as well as the USA.

The Lawyers: **Daniel Dunne** (see p.1975) chairs the litigation group for the Pacific Northwest offices. His practice focuses on securities, consumer class action and professional liability litigation. Notable engagements have included denial of class certification in a federal case against Household Finance and Beneficial Mortgage, alleging predatory lending. Colleague **George Greer** (see p.1975) focuses his practice on securities, accountant liability and D&O liability. He represents individuals in SEC investigations and enforcement proceedings.
Clients/Work Highlights: Clients range in size from startups to Fortune 500 companies. Industries catered to include software, Internet, retail, telecom, financial institutions and energy concerns.

## Lane Powell PC
See firm details p.2009
The Firm: This is a true Pacific Northwest law firm with offices in Seattle, Portland, Olympia, Tacoma and Anchorage. It also has a European presence courtesy of its office in England. Rudy Englund is director of litigation and is in overall control of specialty subgroups that have expertise in securities, products liability, gas and oil issues, and work relating to financial institutions.
The Lawyers: **Rudy Englund** has a complex business litigation practice that is directed toward class actions, wage and hour issues, and securities-related matters. Work has included being engaged by Wells Fargo in a substantial wage and hour class action; through Englund's defense of the case, the opposition was persuaded to enter into mediation and a very favorable settlement was obtained. RBC Dain Rauscher has entered the client books this year, having engaged the team in a successful arbitration against allegations of breach of fiduciary duty, negligence and failure to supervise properly.
Clients/Work Highlights: Wal-Mart and Cutter & Buck figure in an impressive client base.

## Preston Gates & Ellis LLP
The Firm: Primarily known as IP litigators, the firm also has a very strong reputation for more general commercial litigation. Particular areas of expertise include antitrust, healthcare and environmental litigation.
The Lawyers: **David McDonald** enjoys a practice that spans both IP litigation and more general commercial litigation. Two of McDonald's most high-profile clients are Microsoft and the Washington State Democratic Party. Microsoft has engaged him for software-related disputes for some 20 years while, acting for the Democratic Party, he led the successful defense of its constitutional right to determine its nominees and candidates.
Clients/Work Highlights: Microsoft; Verizon; Seagate Technology; State of Alaska; Nike and Premera Blue Cross.

## Stoel Rives LLP
The Firm: The firm has a capability across the range of commercial litigation and has particular expertise in the fields of products liability, contract, conspir-

acy, trade secrets, technology, and D&O liabilities issues. The team works dynamically with attorneys from their Salt Lake City, San Francisco and Portland offices.
The Lawyers: *"Great attorney"* **David Goodnight** has had a particularly good year being engaged in back-to-back top-end business litigation. Perhaps the biggest of these cases was the representation of Toys 'R' Us in a dispute with Amazon. The companies had entered into a ten-year strategic alliance agreement that prevented Amazon from selling other companies' toys through their website. After the breach of this agreement Toys 'R' Us filed a lawsuit to terminate the agreement in 2004 and enjoined Amazon to prevent them from selling their products on the site. Goodnight took the matter to the New Jersey Court of Appeal and won on all the issues. The win received worldwide coverage.
Clients/Work Highlights: Clients include Weyerhaeuser and Qwest.

## Litigation: General Commercial
## Other Notable Practitioners
**Barry Kaplan** (see p.1976) at Wilson Sonsini Goodrich & Rosati continues to focus his practice on securities litigation and is recognized by peers as the *"go-to guy for this type of work."* Representative work of late has included engagement by OfficeMax in multiple shareholder derivative litigation in Chicago, and the representation of the board of a major Northwest public company in an internal investigation regarding allegations of the board's breach of fiduciary duties over the sale of a line of business. Of late, Kaplan has been engaged in an increasing amount of internal investigations. One satisfied customer referred to **Stellman Keehnel** (see p.1976) as *"the top litigator in Washington."* Practicing from DLA Piper Rudnick Gray Cary US LLP, Keehnel, too, has earned a great reputation for his aptitude in securities cases – you would be hard pushed to find any major securities litigation in the Northwest that he hadn't been engaged in. Conclusive victories recently have included the summary dismissal of two parallel federal class actions brought against Keehnel's client Shurgard Storage Centers.

## Litigation: White-Collar Crime
## Notable Practitioners
*"Bearer of an excellent reputation for being very smart, always prepared and easy to work with,"* **Angelo Calfo** of Yarmuth Wilsdon Calfo PLLC was a federal prosecutor for nearly 12 years. In that time, he focused on complex tax and fraud cases and gained experience that has informed his present practice, one which encompasses some of the most complex white-collar cases around. Calfo is famed throughout the Bar for his *"determination to defend his client's position vehemently."* *"Smart, likable and at the forefront of the profession,"* **Dan Dubitzky** of Dubitzky & Zarky PS is, according to one commentator, *"one of the best lawyers in town – were anyone close to me in trouble, this is the man I would call."* Dubitzky is another practitioner who spent valuable time earning his stripes at the US attorney's office. One commentator

suggested that his preeminence in the field can, in part, be attributed to his "*tremendous mastery of both the big and the little picture. He has a unique ability to work compassionately with clients of all types and get them to understand the process of a criminal investigation and consequently the import of his legal advice.*" Recent high-profile work includes the defense of the University of Washington in a very large healthcare investigation. Similarly lauded was "*icon in the community*" **Laurence Finegold** of Finegold Law Firm. "*A tremendous fine-tuner of a case,*" he is "*a superlative lawyer who can make any defense case concept better. He tweaks and approaches things differently and every time the product is better for it.*"

Researchers received universal praise for "*dean of the defense Bar*" **Irwin Schwartz** of The Law Office of Irwin Schwartz. As one peer stated: "*He is just a superb criminal trial lawyer. He can do by himself what it would take three other lawyers to do – he is quickwitted, has a keen intellect, is a brilliant strategist and has the kind of enviable memory that allows him to recall facts and put them into legal and factual context instantly.*" Schwartz' extensive history in the field affords him the very finest of contacts. Practicing at Stoel Rives LLP, "*class act*" **Ronald Sim** has earned the strongest reputation as a white-collar defense lawyer since leaving the US attorney's office in 1980. Currently, Sim is benefiting from the upsurge in the

prosecution of healthcare and securities fraud, and has represented a number of physicians against allegations involving the University of Washington School of Medicine. **John Wolfe** practices from the two-man boutique Wolfe Leinbach. Highly visible in the market, he "*seems to be acting for one of the defendants in every major criminal case that comes up.*" Commentators agreed that he engenders respect from both sides of the fence: "*He is always reasonable and never belligerent, meaning that he is trusted and respected by defendant and attorney's office alike.*"

# REAL ESTATE

## Band 1

### Alston Courtnage & Bassetti LLP

**The Firm:** The fortunes of this Seattle boutique march on and the team makes it into *Chambers'* top tier this year thanks to significant transactional presence in a number of industries. The practice "*leads the way*" in both strength and vision, according to commentators, and offers an unbeatable stable of elite lawyers. The team recently represented a bank in the acquisition financing of a historic register building in Seattle. Lawyers here are not limited to the local stage: they recently represented several German investment funds in the acquisition of properties across the country. The group acts for a client base that includes large financial institutions.

**The Lawyers:** **Andrew Bassetti** has a "*practical attitude and the ability to get the job done.*" Sources admire his "*efficient business sense,*" which he brings to bear on a range of commercial real estate transactions. He is especially noted for secured financing, leasing and acquisition work. **Michael Courtnage** represents developers in the commercial, industrial and retail sectors in all their real estate needs. His "*commitment and positive attitude*" attract warm praise from commentators who extol his long track record in multibillion-dollar deals. **Parker Mason** is a "*practical problem solver*" with a flair for retail projects. He represents both lenders and borrowers in real estate secured finance transactions.

**Clients/Work Highlights:** Bank of America, Metzler Real Estate and Powell Development Company are some of the clients.

### Buck & Gordon LLP

**The Firm:** This bunch of "*fine, dedicated*" practitioners brings a wealth of experience to the table. Lawyers offer polished skills in all manner of high-end commercial real estate transactions, but it is for zoning and land use matters that they are most celebrated. The team's transactional expertise spans development, financing and leasing, for both public and private clients, and it is well supported by colleagues in ancillary disciplines such as environment. The year's highlights include defending Kitsap County in the State Supreme Court against a class

action brought by developers challenging its collection of land use fees. The team also acted on two wind farm developments for a public utility.

**The Lawyers:** The "*creative*" **Peter Buck** "*shines in an adversarial context,*" observe sources. His practice centers on land use and environment work and includes a range of real estate and general litigation matters. The departure of Bill Block throws the spotlight squarely onto **Joel Gordon**, who is now the primary contact for wider real estate enquiries. He represents corporate clients in land use permit, acquisition and development matters.

**Clients/Work Highlights:** Amazon.com; Starbucks; Skagit County; University of Washington; Puget Sound Energy; McDonald's; Gull Industries and Connecticut General Life Insurance Company.

### Foster Pepper PLLC

**The Firm:** This muscular practice is home to "*a spectacular group of lawyers*" and "*clearly stands out*" for its consistency and "*superb*" results. Described as a "*responsive, loyal and high-quality firm,*" it counsels private and public companies in just about any area of the real estate market and at every stage of transactions and negotiations. Lawyers acted recently for the Washington State Investment Board on matters concerning a multibillion dollar fund, and advised a notable development company on its redevelopment of a large chunk of Seattle.

**The Lawyers:** **Gary Fluhrer** is a big player in this field and acts for clients around the globe. His practice encompasses development, leasing, finance, acquisitions and workouts. **Michael Kuntz**'s "*great breadth of knowledge and superb global contacts*" win him both praise and clients. He comes highly recommended for development work and complex transactions, and sources suggest: "*He can dip his toe in any area of real estate law and produce stunning results.*" **Gary Ackerman** is "*experienced and diligent*" and specializes in homeowner association and condominium law. He advises clients on both commercial and residential projects. Of counsel **Judith Runstad** is a senior and much-respected figure in land use matters. **Thomas Walsh** is another land use "*heavyweight*" and sources praise his "*nuanced understanding of both the law and politics –*"

| Real Estate: Zoning/Land Use |
| --- |
| Leading Individuals |
| **Senior Statesman** |
| RUNSTAD Judith *Foster Pepper PLLC* |
| [1] BUCK Peter *Buck & Gordon LLP* |
| MARCY Donald *Cairncross & Hempelmann* |
| MCCULLOUGH Jack *McCullough Hill PS* |
| [2] AMSTER Glenn *Lane Powell PC* |
| GOELTZ Thomas *Davis Wright Tremaine LLP* |
| HEMPELMANN John *Cairncross & Hempelmann* |
| HILL Richard *McCullough Hill PS* |
| WALSH Thomas *Foster Pepper PLLC* |
| WILSON Richard *Hillis Clark Martin & Peterson* |

*he can get a complex public project done."*

Clients/Work Highlights: Amazon.com; Northwest Hospital & Medical Center; ODS Tower; Colman Building and Safeway.

## Perkins Coie LLP

The Firm: Scion of a national powerhouse, this is one of the largest operators in the Northwest. The team serves a diverse clientele and advises on the financing, acquisition, development and disposition of major projects. It also advises high-profile corporate clients on the lease and sublease of commercial space. The group is studded with experts and the *"proactive practitioners are accomplished negotiators."* Recent matters include securing a multibillion-dollar credit facility for a major storage company and ongoing transactional advice to educational clients.

The Lawyers: **Mike Barrett** works principally on complex real estate finance and investment issues. He has been active in large property sales for Boeing, along with the restructuring and creation of joint venture agreements across other states. The *"versatile and adept"* **Ellen Dial** has worked on a number of projects for retirement communities and assisted living centers. **William Green** lately handled the lease and development of the Cobb Building, converting it from office to luxury residential space. He does volumes of work for the University of Washington.

Clients/Work Highlights: Adobe Systems; Boeing; Costco; Starbucks and Microsoft.

## Preston Gates & Ellis LLP

The Firm: This firm abounds with *"prominent and gifted lawyers"* and carries real cachet on the real estate finance side. It is one of the longest-established practices in Seattle and is a vibrant presence in Washington's real estate market. The team acts for an impressive mix of financial institutions and local companies. Recent highlights include representing the Seattle Art Museum in its facilities expansion project, including a joint development with a Washington bank.

The Lawyers: **Scott Osborne**'s clients include developers, investors and lenders, and he is an acknowledged expert in municipal finance. He is known in certain circles as the *"professor"* in tribute to his long and distinguished track record in multi-

million-dollar deals. **Robert Neugebauer** has a broad real estate practice and is particularly recommended for complex commercial transactions and developments. **Shannon Skinner** shows *"seemingly endless capabilities"* and works in all areas of real estate for a diverse client base. She is an adroit finance specialist and played a key role in the Seattle Art Museum case.

Clients/Work Highlights: John Hancock; Nationwide Insurance; MetLife; Teachers Insurance and Annuity Associaton; BlackRock; US Bank; Microsoft; Merrill Gardens and Simon Property Group.

## Band 2

## Cairncross & Hempelmann, A Professional Service Corporation

The Firm: This *"busy and well-regarded"* team offers a broad range of real estate services and is renowned for providing bespoke solutions to thorny transactional problems. It achieves particular recognition for its land use practice, where it combines technical virtuosity with strong connections to the regulatory community.

The Lawyers: **Donald Marcy** has *"genuine depth"* in land use matters, and sources commend his *"thoughtful demeanor"* and efficiency. He also handles a transactional workload. **John Hempelmann**'s *"strategic approach to projects"* wins him fans in the land use, natural resources and real estate development fields.

Clients/Work Highlights: Clients include American Capital Development and Capital One.

## Davis Wright Tremaine LLP

The Firm: This is a strong transactional outfit that offers expertise in office, retail and leasing matters as well as development projects. These *"masters of real estate law"* are attuned to both business and legal issues. Interviewees spoke of the firm's strength in acquisitions and dispositions and an impressive flow of office and residential developments.

The Lawyers: Clients praise **Dennis McLean** as a *"careful yet confident"* lawyer who always keeps a clear goal in mind. He *"embodies the knowledgeable, succinct ethos of the firm."* **Thomas Goeltz** is an *"outstanding and focused lawyer,"* say sources. He acts for giants such as Microsoft and for clients in the construction and hotel sectors. He has a respected land use practice. **Warren Koons** is a technical and meticulous practitioner with extensive experience in transactions and real estate loans.

Clients/Work Highlights: Hines Interests; Bank of America; Port Blakely Communities; Children's Hospital & Regional Medical Center; Virginia Mason Medical Center; Seattle Biomedical Research Institute; PEMCO Insurance and Flynn Properties.

## Fikso Kretschmer Smith Dixon PS

The Firm: Newly spun out of a larger entity, this *"intimate"* practice attracts clients with *"good communication, consistent availability and outstanding personal service."* It is a respected real estate

boutique with a strong niche in land use. The varied client base includes a healthy number of public sector clients.

The Lawyers: **Robert Fikso**'s *"focused, no-fuss approach"* is coupled with polished deal-closing skills to provide smooth transactional advice.

## Jameson Babbitt Stites & Lombard

The Firm: Clients are impressed with the *"positive attitude"* of the capable and versatile lawyers here. The firm's twin pillars of commercial real estate and litigation support a team that serves clients on the full range of transactions and disputes. Peers are suitably envious of the firm's close ties with Schnitzer Northwest and Larry Benaroya's real estate empire.

The Lawyers: The *"ever fine"* **Jennifer Cobb** is a highly efficient practitioner and a *"vibrant"* member of the team. Her clients range from developers to institutional lenders. The *"thorough, efficient and dependable"* **David Lombard** is an adaptable business attorney with a strong real estate investment and financing practice.

Clients/Work Highlights: Cosmos Development; The Benaroya Companies; Schnitzer Northwest; University of Washington and Central Pacific Bank.

## Lane Powell PC

See firm details p.2009

The Firm: This full-service group garners praise for a solid, general real estate practice and is particularly recommended for its financing expertise. The team acts for a mix of clients, especially in the retail industry, and over the past year it has advised a key home improvements client on the opening and construction of new stores.

The Lawyers: **Jane Nelson** is a familiar figure in the retail sector and acts for high-profile clients such as Nordstrom and Home Depot. **Glenn Amster** is an expert in real estate development and a noted authority on environment and land use issues.

Clients/Work Highlights: Home Depot; Nordstrom; United Dominion Real Estate Trust and Chelsea Property Group.

## McCullough Hill PS

The Firm: One of the products of McCullough Hill Fikso Kretschmer Smith's split, this boutique focuses on environment, land use and zoning matters alongside a smaller volume of general real estate transactions. The offering includes urban, shoreline and mixed-use developments and redevelopments, and lawyers are expert in the rehabilitation of landmark buildings. The team acts mainly for private developers. Highlights include advising The Bill and Melinda Gates Foundation on obtaining permits for a facility in Seattle.

The Lawyers: **Jack McCullough** is regarded as *"one of the most prominent land use lawyers in town right now."* **Richard Hill** also enjoys a strong profile in the land use and zoning area.

Clients/Work Highlights: Fred Hutchinson Cancer Research Center; Schnitzer Northwest; Southwest Airlines and Downtown Seattle Association.

## Real Property Law Group PLLC

**The Firm:** This small but potent Seattle outfit guides clients through all stages of transactions and offers *"surprising depth."* The *"devoted"* client base includes buyers, sellers, investors and lenders. Sources note useful capabilities in tax and land use.

**The Lawyers:** Cynthia Thomas is a *"high-energy, bright, thorough and responsive lawyer"* whose attentiveness to her clients' needs impresses all who see her in action.

## Stoel Rives LLP

**The Firm:** This *"fine and reliable"* team advises clients across the region on real estate financing, leasing and sales and acquisitions. It offers a solid core real estate service and important auxiliary capabilities in areas such as construction, land use and design. The group is particularly well known for its expertise in condominium law. Lawyers recently handled the sale of an office building in Seattle for Casey Family Programs.

**The Lawyers:** David Rockwell's *"effortlessly clear and concise drafting"* is a hit with clients, and he is a power in the world of condominium law. Sources commend **Gordon Tanner**'s *"positive and hard-working attitude"* and capable contract work and knowledge of finance.

**Clients/Work Highlights:** Kemper Freeman; Continental Properties; Pure One; Casey Family Programs; AEGON USA Realty advisors and Genworth Financial.

## Other Notable Practitioners

**Richard Wilson** of Hillis Clark Martin & Peterson, A Professional Service Corporation, is a *"high-caliber"* attorney who is useful in *"all elements of getting controversial projects accomplished,"* according to commentators. Pepple Johnson Cantu & Schmidt's **Daniel Pepple** is sought after for his knowledge of real estate finance and leasing. Clients value him as *"a deal-maker – we have a common goal and he never hinders its achievement."*

# Leaders in Washington

**ACKERMAN, Gary**
Foster Pepper PLLC, Seattle
206 447 4400
*Recommended in Real Estate*

**ADAMS, Greg**
Davis Wright Tremaine LLP, Seattle
206 622 3150
*Recommended in Corporate/Commercial*

**ALLRED, Keith**
Davis Wright Tremaine LLP, Seattle
206 622 3150
*Recommended in Bankruptcy*

**AL-SALAM, Ramsey**
Perkins Coie LLP, Seattle
206 583 8888
*Recommended in Intellectual Property*

**AMSTER, Glenn**
Lane Powell PC, Seattle 206 223 7000
*Recommended in Real Estate*

**ASLIN, John**
Perkins Coie LLP, Seattle 206 583 8888
*Recommended in Employment*

**BARBIER, Margaret Louise**
Stoel Rives LLP, Seattle 206 624 0900
*Recommended in Employment*

**BARNES, Clemens**
Graham & Dunn PC, Seattle
206 624 8300
*Recommended in Employment*

**BARRECA, Marc**
Preston Gates & Ellis LLP, Seattle
206 623 7580
*Recommended in Bankruptcy*

**BARRETT, Michael**
Perkins Coie LLP, Seattle 206 583 8888
*Recommended in Real Estate*

**BASSETTI, Andrew**
Alston Courtnage & Bassetti LLP, Seattle
206 623 7600
*Recommended in Real Estate*

**BATEMAN, David**
Preston Gates & Ellis LLP, Seattle
206 623 7580
*Recommended in Intellectual Property*

**BJERKE, Bruce**
Riddell Williams PS, Seattle
206 624 3600
*Recommended in Corporate/Commercial*

**BLACKSTONE, Robert**
Davis Wright Tremaine LLP, Seattle
206 622 3150
*Recommended in Employment*

**BLUMENFELD, Chuck**
Perkins Coie LLP, Seattle 206 583 8888
*Recommended in Environment*

**BODINE, Brian**
Davis Wright Tremaine LLP, Seattle
206 622 3150
*Recommended in Intellectual Property*

**BOR, Andrew**
Perkins Coie LLP, Seattle 206 583 8888
*Recommended in Corporate/Commercial*

**BROWN, Pamela Charles**
Heller Ehrman LLP, Seattle
206 389 6110
pamela.charles@hellerehrman.com
*Recommended in Corporate/Commercial*
**Practice Areas:** Tax.
**Prof. Memberships:** Former Chair of Tax Section of the Washington State Bar Association; Tax Section, American Bar Association; King County Bar Association; Washington Research Council Board of Trustees (Member of Executive Committee).
**Career:** Ms Charles practices federal and Washington State tax law. She provides transactional tax planning advice in domestic and international business transactions with an emphasis on mergers and acquisitions. She also advises tax-exempt organizations on exemption and unrelated business taxable income issues and represents taxpayers in Washington Department of Revenue proceedings.
**Personal:** Stanford Law School (JD, 1992); Order of the Coif.

**BROWN, Rodney**
Cascadia Law Group, Seattle
206 292 6300
*Recommended in Environment*

**BRYANT, Duff**
Stoel Rives LLP, Seattle 206 624 0900
*Recommended in Corporate/Commercial*

**BUCK, Peter**
Buck & Gordon LLP, Seattle
206 382 9540
*Recommended in Real Estate*

**BULCHIS, Ed**
Dorsey & Whitney LLP, Seattle
206 903 8785
bulchis.ed@dorsey.com
*Recommended in Intellectual Property*
**Practice Areas:** Practices in all areas of intellectual property law with emphasis on patent prosecution and counseling in complex electrical technologies and patent litigation.
**Prof. Memberships:** Washington State Bar Association; American Intellectual Property Law Association; Washington State Patent Law Association (past President).
**Personal:** Georgetown University Law Center (JD, 1974); Northeastern University (BSEE, 1970).

**BURMAN, David**
Perkins Coie LLP, Seattle 206 583 8888
*Recommended in Litigation*

**BUSH, Gayle**
Bush, Strout & Kornfeld, Seattle
206 292 2110
*Recommended in Bankruptcy*

**BUSTO, Mark**
Sebris Busto James, Bellevue
425 454 4233
*Recommended in Employment*

**BYRNES, Peter**
Byrnes & Keller, Seattle 206 622 2000
*Recommended in Litigation*

**CAIRNS, Carolyn**
Stokes Lawrence, PS, Seattle
206 626 6000
*Recommended in Employment*

**CALFO, Angelo**
Yarmuth Wilsdon Calfo PLLC, Seattle
206 516 3800
*Recommended in Litigation*

**CARLSON, Kent**
Preston Gates & Ellis LLP, Seattle
206 623 7580
*Recommended in Corporate/Commercial*

**CHAPMAN, William**
Preston Gates & Ellis LLP, Seattle
206 623 7580
*Recommended in Environment*

**CHEETHAM, Janet**
Ryan, Swanson & Cleveland, PLLC, Seattle 206 464 4224
*Recommended in Immigration*

**COBB, Jennifer Dunn**
Jameson Babbitt Stites & Lombard, Seattle 206 516 3202
*Recommended in Real Estate*

**COHEN, Matthew**
Heller Ehrman LLP, Seattle
206 389 6024
matthew.cohen@hellerehrman.com
*Recommended in Environment*
**Practice Areas:** Environmental litigation and counseling; energy.
**Prof. Memberships:** Air Quality Committee, Association of Washington Business; Western States Petroleum Association Associates Committee, Washington

Water Quality Partnership; Air and Waste Management Association; Washington State Bar Association.

**Career:** Mr Cohen represents manufacturers, electric utilities and independent power project developers in legislative, rulemaking, permitting and enforcement matters arising under state and federal environmental laws. He represents coalitions of industries and trade associations in the development of state rules to implement the 1990 Clean Air Act Amendments.

**Personal:** Amherst College (BA, magna cum laude, Phi Beta Kappa, 1976); Yale Law School (JD, 1979).

**COONROD, Stephan**
Preston Gates & Ellis LLP, Seattle
206 623 7580
*Recommended in Corporate/Commercial*

**CORR, Kelly**
Corr Cronin LLP, Seattle 206 625 8600
*Recommended in Litigation*

**COURTNAGE, Michael**
Alston Courtnage & Bassetti LLP, Seattle
206 623 7600
*Recommended in Real Estate*

**COWAN, Pamela**
Cowan & Miller, Seattle 206 340 1033
*Recommended in Immigration*

**CRONIN, William**
Corr Cronin LLP, Seattle 206 625 8600
*Recommended in Litigation*

**CROSS, Bruce Michael**
Perkins Coie LLP, Seattle 206 583 8888
*Recommended in Employment*

**CROW, Carl**
Perkins Coie LLP, Seattle 206 583 8888
*Recommended in Corporate/Commercial*

**CULLEN, Jack**
Foster Pepper PLLC, Seattle
206 447 4400
*Recommended in Bankruptcy*

**DIAL, Ellen**
Perkins Coie LLP, Seattle 206 583 8888
*Recommended in Real Estate*

**DIAMOND, Kenneth**
Winterbauer & Diamond, P.L.L.C., Seattle
206 676 8440
*Recommended in Employment*

**DIERCKS, Robert**
Foster Pepper PLLC, Seattle
206 447 4400
*Recommended in Corporate/Commercial*

**DODD, Richard**
Preston Gates & Ellis LLP, Seattle
206 623 7580
*Recommended in Corporate/Commercial*

**DUBITZKY, Dan**
Dubitzky & Zarky PS, Seattle
206 467 6709
*Recommended in Litigation*

**DUNN, Loren**
Riddell Williams PS, Seattle
206 624 3600
*Recommended in Environment*

**DUNNE, Daniel**
Heller Ehrman LLP, Seattle
206 389 6026
daniel.dunne@hellerehrman.com
*Recommended in Litigation*
**Practice Areas:** Securities litigation; consumer litigation.
**Prof. Memberships:** Trustee, Antitrust and Unfair Business Practices Section, Washington State Bar Association; American Bar Association; former Chair, Community Legal Services Committee, King County Bar Association; Trustee, King County Bar Foundation.
**Career:** Mr Dunne's Litigation Practice has focused on defense of technology companies, financial institutions, and directors and officers in complex litigation in federal and state courts. He has represented parties in securities, consumer class action, professional liability, corporate governance, patent, and intellectual property cases.
**Personal:** University of Virginia (BA, with distinction, 1980); Virginia Law School (JD, 1985).

**DUNWOODY, Stuart**
Davis Wright Tremaine LLP, Seattle
206 622 3150
*Recommended in Intellectual Property*

**DWYER, Michael**
Lane Powell PC, Seattle
206 223 7000
*Recommended in Corporate/Commercial*

**EDWARD, Carol**
Law Offices of Carol L Edward & Associates, Seattle 206 956 9556
*Recommended in Immigration*

**EKBERG, Charles**
Lane Powell PC, Seattle
206 223 7000
*Recommended in Bankruptcy*

**ELLIOTT, Richard**
Davis Wright Tremaine LLP, Bellevue
425 646 6100
*Recommended in Environment*

**ENGLUND, Rudy**
Lane Powell PC, Seattle
206 223 7000
*Recommended in Litigation*

**FERRON, William**
Seed IP Law Group PLLC, Seattle
206 622 4900
*Recommended in Intellectual Property*

**FIKSO, Robert**
Fikso Kretschmer Smith Dixon PS, Seattle
206 448 1818
*Recommended in Real Estate*

**FINEGOLD, Laurence**
Finegold Law Firm, Seattle
206 682 1116
*Recommended in Litigation*

**FLUHRER, Gary**
Foster Pepper PLLC, Seattle
206 447 4400
*Recommended in Real Estate*

**GINSBERG, Beth**
Stoel Rives LLP, Seattle 206 624 0900
*Recommended in Environment*

**GOELTZ, Thomas**
Davis Wright Tremaine LLP, Seattle
206 622 3150
*Recommended in Real Estate*

**GOODNIGHT, David**
Stoel Rives LLP, Seattle 206 624 0900
*Recommended in Litigation*

**GORDON, Charles**
Gordon Murray Tilden, Seattle
206 467 6477
*Recommended in Litigation*

**GRAHAM, Lawrence**
Black Lowe & Graham, Seattle
206 381 3300
graham@blacklaw.com
*Recommended in Intellectual Property*
**Practice Areas:** Patent, trademark, trade secret, and related IP litigation; patent and trademark procurement; intellectual property counseling.
**Prof. Memberships:** Washington State Patent Law Association, AIPLA, Federal Bar Association; Adjunct Professor of Law for patent litigation and patent prosecution at Seattle University Law School.
**Career:** Founded Black Lowe & Graham in 1999. Named a Washington Super Lawyer, 2006.
**Publications:** 'Legal Battles that Shaped the Software Industry' (Greenwood Press, 1999). Numerous law review articles and publications as legal column editor for IEEE Software journal.
**Personal:** JD, University of Washington, 1995; MBA, Pepperdine University, 1990; BSEE, Air Force Academy, 1987.

**GRAHAM, Stephen**
Orrick, Herrington & Sutcliffe LLP, Seattle
206 839 4320
sgraham@orrick.com
*Recommended in Corporate/Commercial*
**Practice Areas:** Focuses on securities law compliance, mergers and acquisitions, public offerings, private placements, and general corporate matters. Represents emerging and established technology and life science companies, as well as major investment banking and venture capital firms in IPOs, M&A transactions, and private debt and equity offerings.

**Prof. Memberships:** Board of Directors and Executive Committee of the WSA; Board of Directors of Washington Biotechnology and Biomedical Association; Board of Trustees of Fred Hutchinson Cancer Research Center; Board of Directors of Friends of the Children of King County.
**Personal:** JD, Yale University, 1973; BA, Iowa State University, 1976.

**GRAY, Marvin**
Davis Wright Tremaine LLP, Seattle
206 622 3150
*Recommended in Litigation*

**GREEN, William**
Perkins Coie LLP, Seattle 206 583 8888
*Recommended in Real Estate*

**GREENBURG, Scott**
Preston Gates & Ellis LLP, Seattle
206 623 7580
*Recommended in Corporate/Commercial*

**GREER, George E**
Heller Ehrman LLP, Seattle
206 389 6006
george.greer@hellerehrman.com
*Recommended in Litigation*
**Practice Areas:** Securities litigation; corporate governance.
**Prof. Memberships:** American Bar Association; Washington State Bar Association; King County Bar Association.
**Career:** Mr Greer has extensive experience in complex commercial litigation with an emphasis on securities, accountant liability, and officer and director liability. He has represented issuers, officers, directors, accountants, and underwriters in class action securities litigation and in SEC investigations and enforcement proceedings. Mr Greer's practice also includes representation of companies, Special Litigation Committees, and individuals in corporate governance disputes.
**Personal:** University of Virginia (BA, with highest distinction, Phi Beta Kappa, 1977); Stanford Law School (JD, 1980).

**HARRIGAN, Arthur**
Danielson Harrigan Leyh & Tollefson, LLP, Seattle 206 623 1700
*Recommended in Litigation*

**HEMPELMANN, John**
Cairncross & Hempelmann,
A Professional Service Corporation,
Seattle 206 587 0700
*Recommended in Real Estate*

**HESTON, Mary Jo**
Lane Powell PC, Seattle 206 223 7000
*Recommended in Bankruptcy*

**HILL, Richard**
McCullough Hill PS, Seattle
206 812 3388
*Recommended in Real Estate*

**HOFFMAN, Mark F**
DLA Piper Rudnick Gray Cary US LLP,
Seattle 206 839 4823
mark.hoffman@dlapiper.com
*Recommended in
Corporate/Commercial*
**Practice Areas:** Corporate and securities; mergers and acquisitions.
**Career:** He concentrates on corporate finance, securities, and general corporate law.
**Personal:** JD, University of Michigan; AB, Princeton University.

**HUMPHREY, Lawton**
Davis Wright Tremaine LLP, Seattle
206 622 3150
*Recommended in Employment*

**HUTCHESON, Mark**
Davis Wright Tremaine LLP, Seattle
206 622 3150
*Recommended in Employment*

**ISRAEL, Allen**
Foster Pepper PLLC, Seattle
206 447 4400
*Recommended in
Corporate/Commercial*

**JACKSON, Dillon**
Foster Pepper PLLC, Seattle
206 447 4400
*Recommended in Bankruptcy*

**JONES, Karen**
Riddell Williams PS, Seattle
206 624 3600
*Recommended in Employment*

**KAPLAN, Barry**
Wilson Sonsini Goodrich & Rosati,
Seattle 206 883 2500
bkaplan@wsgr.com
*Recommended in Litigation*
**Practice Areas:** Securities and corporate governance litigation, class action defense, SEC and internal corporate investigations, complex commercial litigation including international disputes.
**Prof. Memberships:** Admitted in Washington and before the US Court of Appeals for the Ninth Circuit; US District Courts for the Western and Eastern Districts of Washington; and the US Tax Court. Member, American Bar Association, Washington Bar Association, King County Bar Association, and Federal Bar Association for the Western District of Washington.
**Career:** Joined WSGR as Partner, 2005. Former Partner, Seattle office of Perkins Coie LLP.
**Personal:** JD, (cum laude) University of Michigan,1976; BA, Colgate University, 1973.

**KAPLAN, Robert D**
Dorsey & Whitney LLP, Seattle
206 903 8810
kaplan.robert@dorsey.com
*Recommended in
Corporate/Commercial*
**Practice Areas:** Practice focuses on international financing, privatization projects, and general business matters across all continents. Familiar with federal income taxation of nonresident aliens, foreign corporations, partnerships, and real estate transactions - knowledge vital to US companies venturing or operating overseas.
**Prof. Memberships:** Washington State Bar Assocation (Business Law and Tax Section); ABA (Tax Section, Business Law Section, Real Property Probate Section and International Law Section).
**Personal:** University of Washington School of Law (JD, 1969); Brown University (AB, International Relations, 1961).

**KEEHNEL, Stellman**
DLA Piper Rudnick Gray Cary US LLP,
Seattle 206 839 4888
stellman.keehnel@dlapiper.com
*Recommended in Litigation*
**Practice Areas:** Securities litigation; intellectual property litigation; class action defense.
**Career:** His practice focuses on defense of securities class actions and shareholder derivative/fiduciary breach actions. He has a record of securing pre-discovery dismissals of securities and derivative lawsuits using Rule 12(b)(6) motions. He represents public companies and directors/officers in SEC and SRO proceedings and in corporate governance litigation. He defends and prosecutes lawsuits involving patent infringement, trademark, copyright and trade secrets. He defends consumer class actions and high-stakes commercial and real estate lawsuits.
**Personal:** JD, Yale Law School; AB, Stanford University.

**KELLER, Brad**
Byrnes & Keller, Seattle 206 622 2000
*Recommended in Litigation*

**KLEIN, Otto**
Summit Law Group, PLLC, Seattle
206 676 7000
*Recommended in Employment*

**KOCHER, Gary**
Preston Gates & Ellis LLP, Seattle
206 623 7580
*Recommended in
Corporate/Commercial*

**KOONS, Warren**
Davis Wright Tremaine LLP, Bellevue
425 646 6100
*Recommended in Real Estate*

**KORNFELD, Armand**
Bush, Strout & Kornfeld, Seattle
206 292 2110
*Recommended in Bankruptcy*

**KUNTZ, Michael**
Foster Pepper PLLC, Seattle
206 447 4400
*Recommended in Real Estate*

**LANDEFELD, Stewart**
Perkins Coie LLP, Seattle 206 583 8888
*Recommended in
Corporate/Commercial*

**LEAVERTON, Bruce**
Lane Powell PC, Seattle 206 223 7000
*Recommended in Bankruptcy*

**LEMLY, Thomas**
Davis Wright Tremaine LLP, Seattle
206 622 3150
*Recommended in Employment*

**LEPPO, Jeffery**
Stoel Rives LLP, Seattle 206 624 0900
*Recommended in Environment*

**LEWIS, Carl**
Stoel Rives LLP, Seattle 206 624 0900
*Recommended in
Corporate/Commercial*

**LOMBARD, David**
Jameson Babbitt Stites & Lombard,
Seattle 206 516 3202
*Recommended in Real Estate*

**MADDEN, Patrick**
Preston Gates & Ellis LLP, Seattle
206 623 7580
*Recommended in Employment*

**MANOLOPOULOS, Lynn**
Davis Wright Tremaine LLP, Bellevue
425 646 6100
*Recommended in Environment*

**MARCY, Donald**
Cairncross & Hempelmann,
A Professional Service Corporation,
Seattle 206 587 0700
*Recommended in Real Estate*

**MASON, Parker**
Alston Courtnage & Bassetti LLP,
Seattle 206 623 7600
*Recommended in Real Estate*

**MCCALL, Gregory**
Perkins Coie LLP, Seattle 206 583 8888
*Recommended in Immigration*

**MCCULLOUGH, Jack**
McCullough Hill PS, Seattle
206 812 3388
*Recommended in Real Estate*

**MCDONALD, David**
Preston Gates & Ellis LLP, Seattle
206 623 7580
*Recommended in Litigation*

**MCLEAN, Dennis**
Davis Wright Tremaine LLP, Seattle
206 622 3150
*Recommended in Real Estate*

**MCNAUL, Jerry**
McNaul Ebel Nawrot Helgren & Vance
PLLC, Seattle 206 467 1816
*Recommended in Litigation*

**MCSHEA, David**
Perkins Coie LLP, Seattle
206 583 8888
*Recommended in
Corporate/Commercial*

**MEIKLEJOHN, Paul**
Dorsey & Whitney LLP, Seattle
206 903 8746
meiklejohn.paul@dorsey.com
*Recommended in Intellectual Property*
**Practice Areas:** Practice focuses on intellectual property litigation.
**Prof. Memberships:** American Bar Association.
**Career:** Adjunct Professor at the University of Washington.
**Publications:** 'Supreme Court's ruling restores patent protection', American City Business Journals, Inc., November 2002.
**Personal:** Georgetown University (MS, Inorganic Chemistry, 1983); American University - Washington College of Law (JD, 1975); Allentown College (BS, Chemistry, 1969).

**MILLER, Craig**
Davis Wright Tremaine LLP, Seattle
206 622 3150
*Recommended in Litigation*

**MILLER, Steven**
Cowan & Miller, Seattle 206 340 1033
*Recommended in Immigration*

**MOONEY, Douglas G**
Littler Mendelson, PC, Seattle
206.623.3300
dmooney@littler.com
*Recommended in Employment*
**Practice Areas:** Area of practice encompasses all aspects of employment and labor law. Counsels employers on employment, traditional labor and strategic management issues. Extensive experience assisting executive management in reorganizations, succession planning, management development, managing agency and internal investigations, and litigation. Repeatedly selected for inclusion in The Best Lawyers in America, repeatedly listed as a Washington Super Lawyer by Washington Law and Politics. Martindale-Hubbell Law Directory has awarded 'AV' rating.
**Prof. Memberships:** Board of Evergreen Safety Council; Commissioner appointed by Governor to Public Employment Relations Commission.
**Personal:** Washington University, St Louis, Missouri (JD, 1975); Stanford University (BA, with honors, 1972).

**MORFELD, Martin**
Davis Wright Tremaine LLP, Seattle
206 622 3150
*Recommended in
Corporate/Commercial*

**MORGAN, Kevan**
Christensen O'Connor Johnson Kindness,
PLLC, Seattle 206 682 8100
*Recommended in Intellectual Property*

**MORGAN, Mike**
Lane Powell PC, Seattle 206 223 7000
*Recommended in*
*Corporate/Commercial*

**NELSON, Jane**
Lane Powell PC, Seattle 206 223 7000
*Recommended in Real Estate*

**NELSON, Marshall**
Davis Wright Tremaine LLP, Seattle
206 622 3150
*Recommended in Intellectual Property*

**NEUGEBAUER, Robert**
Preston Gates & Ellis LLP, Seattle
206 623 7580
*Recommended in Real Estate*

**O'CONNELL, Timothy**
Stoel Rives LLP, Seattle 206 624 0900
*Recommended in Employment*

**OSBORNE, Scott**
Preston Gates & Ellis LLP, Seattle
206 623 7580
*Recommended in Real Estate*

**OSENBAUGH, Kim**
Preston Gates & Ellis LLP, Seattle
206 623 7580
*Recommended in Bankruptcy*

**PAGET, Joel**
Ryan, Swanson & Cleveland, PLLC,
Seattle 206 464 4224
*Recommended in Immigration*

**PALUMBO, Ralph**
Summit Law Group, PLLC, Seattle
206 676 7000
*Recommended in Environment,*
*Litigation*

**PEPPLE, Daniel**
Pepple Johnson Cantu & Schmidt, PLLC,
Seattle 206 625 1711
*Recommended in Real Estate*

**PERISHO, Russell**
Perkins Coie LLP, Seattle
206 583 8888
*Recommended in Employment*

**POWERS, Ragan**
Davis Wright Tremaine LLP, Seattle
206 622 3150
*Recommended in Bankruptcy*

**PUCKETT, Laura Treadgold**
DLA Piper Rudnick Gray Cary US LLP,
Seattle 206 839 4822
laura.puckett@dlapiper.com
*Recommended in*
*Corporate/Commercial*
**Practice Areas:** Corporate and securities; emerging growth and venture capital; mergers and acquisitions.
**Career:** She has extensive experience in
corporate matters, venture capital financings, and mergers and acquisitions. She
works with companies in diverse industries with a focus on software, internet,
wireless and medical device companies.
**Personal:** JD, University of Washington;
AB, Stanford University.

**REISS, Michael**
Davis Wright Tremaine LLP, Seattle
206 622 3150
*Recommended in Employment*

**RHEAUME, Warren J**
Heller Ehrman LLP, Seattle
206 389 4226
warren.rheaume@hellerehrman.com
*Recommended in Intellectual Property*
**Practice Areas:** Intellectual property litigation.
**Prof. Memberships:** Washington State
Bar Association; American Bar Association; Federal Bar Association, Western
District of Washington;
ICANN@LARGE.
**Career:** Mr Rheaume is a prominent
Seattle-based litigator with over 21 years
of legal experience. His practice is
focused on intellectual property litigation
with particular emphasis on copyright,
trademark and trade secret issues. He also
has extensive experience in general commercial litigation.
**Personal:** Gonzaga University (BA, cum
laude, 1978); Georgetown University Law
Center (JD, 1983).

**RIEDINGER, Jerry**
Perkins Coie LLP, Seattle 206 583 8888
*Recommended in Intellectual Property*

**ROCKWELL, David**
Stoel Rives LLP, Seattle 206 624 0900
*Recommended in Real Estate*

**RUBIN, Jerome**
Stoel Rives LLP, Seattle 206 624 0900
*Recommended in Employment*

**RUMMAGE, Stephen**
Davis Wright Tremaine LLP, Seattle
206 622 3150
*Recommended in Litigation*

**RUNSTAD, Judith**
Foster Pepper PLLC, Seattle
206 447 4400
*Recommended in Real Estate*

**SCHNEIDER, Mark**
Perkins Coie LLP, Seattle 206 583 8888
*Recommended in Environment*

**SCHNEIDER, Harry**
Perkins Coie LLP, Seattle 206 583 8888
*Recommended in Litigation*

**SCHULTHEIS, Patrick J**
Wilson Sonsini Goodrich & Rosati,
Seattle 425 576 5800
pschultheis@wsgr.com
*Recommended in*
*Corporate/Commercial*
**Practice Areas:** Specializes in the corporate representation of technology, life
science and other growth companies
(start-ups to large public companies) in
the Pacific Northwest. Regularly represents underwriters and venture capital
investors. Has extensive transactional
experience in public offerings, mergers
and acquisitions and private financings.

**Prof. Memberships:** Admitted to practice
in Washington and California, USDC for
the Northern District of California and US
Court of Appeals for the Ninth Circuit.
Member, ABA (Business Law Section).
**Career:** Managing Partner, Kirkland
office. Joined WSGR, 1989; became Partner, 1997.
**Personal:** JD, 1989, University of Chicago; AB, 1986 (with distinction, departmental honors), Stanford University.

**SCHWAB, Evan L**
Dorsey & Whitney LLP, Seattle
206 903 8858
schwab.evan@dorsey.com
*Recommended in Litigation*
**Practice Areas:** Practice is focused
upon complex commercial cases, with
emphasis on securities litigation, class
action litigation, and defense of legal and
accounting firms.
**Prof. Memberships:** Washington State
Bar Association; Seattle-King County Bar
Association; ABA (Litigation Section);
Federal Bar Association for the Western
District of Washington; Fellow, American
College of Trial Lawyers (Chair, 2005;
Committee on Federal Rules of Civil Pro-
cedure, 1985-98, 1999-2005).
**Personal:** University of Washington
School of Law (JD, 1963); University of
Washington (BA, Business Administra-
tion, 1961).

**SCHWARTZ, Irwin**
The Law Office of Irwin Schwartz,
Seattle 206 623 5084
*Recommended in Litigation*

**SEBRIS, Robert**
Sebris Busto James, Bellevue
425 454 4233
*Recommended in Employment*

**SHERMAN, Craig E**
Wilson Sonsini Goodrich & Rosati,
Seattle 206 833 2500
csherman@wsgr.com
*Recommended in*
*Corporate/Commercial*
**Practice Areas:** Focuses on corporate
and securities laws, representing compa-
nies, venture capital firms and invest-
ments banks in private placements and
public offerings. Also has extensive expe-
rience in mergers and acquisitions, tech-
nology licensing, and domestic and inter-
national joint ventures.
**Career:** Joined WSGR as Partner, 2002.
Managing Director of Venture Law
Group's Kirkland office from May 2000 -
August 2002.
**Personal:** JD, 1989, Harvard Law School
(cum laude). Articles editor, Harvard
Human Rights Yearbook, 1988-89. AB
(with honors), and MA from Stanford
University, 1985.

**SIEFERT, Richard**
Merchant & Gould PC, Seattle
206 342 6200
*Recommended in Intellectual Property*

**SIM, Ronald**
Stoel Rives LLP, Seattle 206 624 0900
*Recommended in Litigation*

**SKINNER, Shannon**
Preston Gates & Ellis LLP, Seattle
206 623 7580
*Recommended in Real Estate*

**SMITH, Alan C**
Orrick, Herrington & Sutcliffe LLP,
Seattle 206 839 4322
asmith@orrick.com
*Recommended in*
*Corporate/Commercial*
**Practice Areas:** Focuses his practice on
technology, life sciences, internet and
other high growth companies, with an
emphasis on public and private securities
offerings, mergers and acquisitions, venture capital financings, corporate formation, public company reporting and disclosure, and general corporate matters.
Frequent speaker on corporate finance
topics, including the initial public offering process, venture and angel financing
and mergers and acquisitions.
**Prof. Memberships:** State Bars of Washington and Oregon; Board Member,
Social Venture Partners; Co-Chair,
Coaching Committee, Early State Investment Forum.
**Personal:** JD with distinction, Stanford
University, 1996; BA with honors, 1993.

**SMITH, Daniel Hoyt**
MacDonald Hoague & Bayless, Seattle
206 622 1604
*Recommended in Immigration*

**SQUIRES, William**
Summit Law Group, PLLC, Seattle
206 676 7000
*Recommended in Litigation*

**SROUFE, Evelyn Cruz**
Perkins Coie LLP, Seattle 206 583 8888
*Recommended in*
*Corporate/Commercial*

**STEEL, John M**
DLA Piper Rudnick Gray Cary US LLP,
Seattle 206 839 4833
john.steel@dlapiper.com
*Recommended in*
*Corporate/Commercial*
**Practice Areas:** Corporate and securities; emerging growth and venture capital; mergers and acquisitions; public
company and corporate governance.
**Career:** He concentrates in structuring
and negotiating a wide range of financing
transactions, acquistions, and strategic
alliances. He has managed hundreds of
private equity financings for issuers and
investors and served as lead counsel on
approximately 30 public offerings. He is
experienced in a broad variety of commercial transactions including commercial finance, licensing, and distribution
arrangements.
**Personal:** JD, University of Washington;
BA, Stanford University.

**STROTHER, Jack**
Graham & Dunn PC, Seattle
206 624 8300
*Recommended in*
*Corporate/Commercial*

**SULKIN, Robert**
McNaul Ebel Nawrot Helgren & Vance
PLLC, Seattle 206 467 1816
*Recommended in Litigation*

**TANNER, Gordon**
Stoel Rives LLP, Seattle 206 624 0900
*Recommended in Real Estate*

**THOMAS, Cynthia**
Real Property Law Group PLLC, Seattle
206 625 1717
*Recommended in Real Estate*

**THORP, Michael**
Heller Ehrman LLP, Seattle
206 389 6200
michael.thorp@hellerehrman.com
*Recommended in Environment*
**Practice Areas:** Environmental litigation and counseling; energy.
**Prof. Memberships:** Washington State Bar Association; American Bar Association.
**Career:** For more than 29 years, Mr Thorp has represented clients in a wide range of environmental and natural resource matters, including natural resource damages, toxic tort suits including class actions, state and federal Superfund, RCRA, Clean Water Act, Clean Air Act, water rights and issues dealing with natural resources owned or claimed by Indian tribes.
**Personal:** University of Washington (BA, History, 1968); Gonzaga University School of Law (JD, magna cum laude, 1974).

**TILDEN, Jeffrey**
Gordon Murray Tilden, Seattle
206 467 6477
*Recommended in Litigation*

**WALSH, Thomas**
Foster Pepper PLLC, Seattle
206 447 4400
*Recommended in Real Estate*

**WEINSTEIN, Joseph**
Davis Wright Tremaine LLP, Seattle
206 622 3150
*Recommended in*
*Corporate/Commercial*

**WHITFORD, Joseph**
Davis Wright Tremaine LLP, Seattle
206 622 3150
*Recommended in*
*Corporate/Commercial*

**WILLIAMS, Nancy**
Perkins Coie LLP, Seattle 206 583 8888
*Recommended in Employment*

**WILSON, Richard**
Hillis Clark Martin & Peterson,
A Professional Service Corporation,
Seattle 206 623 1745
*Recommended in Real Estate*

**WINTERBAUER, Steven**
Winterbauer & Diamond, P.L.L.C.,
Seattle 206 676 8440
*Recommended in Employment*

**WOLFE, John**
Wolfe Leinbach, Seattle 206 467 9088
*Recommended in Litigation*

**WOODS, LaVerne**
Davis Wright Tremaine LLP, Seattle
206 622 3150
*Recommended in*
*Corporate/Commercial*

**WREGGELSWORTH, James**
Davis Wright Tremaine LLP, Seattle
206 622 3150
*Recommended in*
*Corporate/Commercial*

**YENTZER, Steven R**
DLA Piper Rudnick Gray Cary US LLP,
Seattle 206 839 4836
steven.yentzer@dlapiper.com
*Recommended in*
*Corporate/Commercial*
**Practice Areas:** Corporate and securities; international tax; real estate capital markets; emerging growth and venture capital; fund formation and operations.
**Career:** His practice focuses on corporate finance, tax, and investment entities. He has been involved in the formation of venture capital, buyout, and other private equity funds, as well as real estate investment partnerships. His experience also includes real estate transactions, debt restructurings, and M&A transactions. He has represented both large and small clients, from venture-backed start-ups and venture capital investors to publicly traded companies.
**Personal:** JD, Marquette University School of Law; BA, Gonzaga University.

**ZUCCOTTI, Andrew**
Preston Gates & Ellis LLP, Seattle
206 623 7580
*Recommended in*
*Corporate/Commercial*

# LANE POWELL PC

## THE FIRM

**President:** Mark Rossi
**Vice President:** Lewis Horowitz

**Number of partners in the US:** 121
**Number of other lawyers in the US:** 50

**FIRM OVERVIEW:** Lane Powell, *Your Pacific Northwest Law Firm®*, provides legal solutions for businesses and individuals. Its business, employment and litigation attorneys help companies manage growth, build workforces and capitalize on creativity. Founded more than 130 years ago, the firm has more than 170 attorneys and is a member of both the US Law Firm Group and World Law Group.

## MAIN AREAS OF PRACTICE:

**Business:** Lane Powell provides a full range of services to emerging and established businesses and individuals on a regional, national and international level. The business services the firm provides include administrative law, banking and financial services, construction, corporate finance, securities, mergers and acquisitions, initial public offerings, emerging companies and venture investment, environmental, franchise and dealership, healthcare, intellectual property and Internet, international business and investment, international tax, natural resources and forest products, real estate, retail distribution and trade regulation, tax and estate planning, and transportation and utilities.

**Labor & Employment:** Lane Powell represents management in the entire range of labor and employment matters and issues. It serves clients in virtually every industry in both the private and public sectors. Lane Powell advises clients with matters relating to labor relations, employment discrimination, wrongful discharge, civil rights, employee benefits (ERISA, COBRA, etc.) immigration in state and federal courts, and before the NLRB, OFCCP, EEOC and all other state and federal agencies involved in employment matters. The firm frequently arbitrates or represents clients in employment-related jury trials. Lane Powell's attorneys have designed ERISA plans for some of America's best known companies, and many smaller companies. The firm regularly advises plan administrators and plan fiduciaries on administrative compliance with state and federal law. With many published and unpublished court opinions, Lane Powell is one of the leading firms representing clients in litigated ERISA matters involving breach of fiduciary duty, plan benefits, and many other related claims.

**Litigation:** The firm represents clients in all aspects of commercial litigation, including trials and appeals in all state and federal courts; and federal, state and self regulatory administrative proceedings and arbitrations/mediations under alternative dispute resolution procedures. The broad range of litigation matters that Lane Powell handles includes complex litigation, securities, commercial cases, creditors' rights and bankruptcy, labor and employment, antitrust, healthcare, franchise/dealership law, software licensing, intellectual property and internet.

**CLIENTS:** Aramark Corporation; AT&T Corporation; Callison Architecture, Inc.; ChevronTexaco Corp.; Coffman Engineers, Inc.; Con-Agra Inc.; CNF, Inc.; Cutter & Buck, Inc.; Eagle River; Equilon; Enterprises LLC; ERA Aviation, Inc.; Exxon Mobil Corporation; The Fishing Company of Alaska; Fred Hutchinson Cancer Research Center; Frito-Lay, Inc.; General Electric Capital Corporation; Georgia-Pacific Corporation; Home Depot U.S.A., Inc.; IBP, Inc.; ImageX, Inc.; KeyBank; Les Schwab Tire Centers; Monsanto Company; The Mony Group, Inc.; Morgan Stanley Dean Witter & Co.; Mowat Construction Company; Nike, Inc.; Nordstrom, Inc.; Norm Thompson Outfitters, Inc.; Northwest Biotherapeutics, Inc.; Oregon Public Employees Retirement Fund; Oremet-Wah Chang; Premera Blue Cross; Quinton Inc.; Shell Oil; Simpson Investment Company; Sound Transit; T-Mobile; Tokai Carbon Co., Ltd.; TransAlta Corporation; Triad Hospitals Inc.; Tri-County Metropolitan Transportation District of Oregon (Tri-Met); Underwriters at Lloyd's; Union Pacific Railroad Corp.; Verisign, Inc.; Wal-Mart Stores, Inc.; Wells Fargo & Company; Weyerhaeuser Company; White Consolidated Industries, Inc.

## HEAD OFFICE

**WASHINGTON**
1420 Fifth Avenue, Suite 4100, **Seattle,** WA 98101-2338
**Tel:** 206 223 7000   **Fax:** 206 223 7107
**Email:** info@lanepowell.com
**Website:** www.lanepowell.com

## BRANCH OFFICES

**ALASKA**
301 West Northern Lights Boulevard, Suite 301, **Anchorage,** AK 99503-2648
**Tel:** 907 277 9511   **Fax:** 907 276 2631

**OREGON**
601 SW Second Avenue, Suite 2100, **Portland,** OR 97204-3158
**Tel:** 503 778 2100   **Fax:** 503 778 2200

**WASHINGTON**
111 Market Street, Suite 360, **Olympia,** WA 98501
**Tel:** 360 764 6001   **Fax:** 360 754 1605

## INTERNATIONAL OFFICES

The firm also has an office in London, UK

## CONTACTS

| | |
|---|---|
| **Appellate** | Thomas Sondag |
| **Aviation** | Kit Narodick |
| **Complex Litigation** | Charles Huber, Randall Beighle |
| | Vicki Smith, Barbara Duffy |
| **Construction** | Grant Degginger |
| **Creditors' Rights and Bankruptcy** | Charles Ekberg |
| **Environmental** | Donald Pyle |
| **Employee Benefits & Executive Compensation** | Jack Walsh |
| **Estate Planning** | Chuck Riley |
| **Immigration** | Diane Butler |
| **Insurance Litigation** | Cathy Spicer |
| **Intellectual Property (Business)** | Anne Glazer |
| **Intellectual Property (Litigation)** | Craig Bachman |
| **Labor and Employment** | Gail Mautner |
| **Mergers & Acquisitions/Finance** | Tom Grohman |
| **Real Estate** | Jane Rakay Nelson, Brian Powell |
| **Tax** | Gary Tober |

**INTERNATIONAL WORK:** Lane Powell's international practice includes business, insurance, maritime, aviation and international trade. Some areas in which the firm has provided legal representation include: independent sales representative agreements; joint ventures; strategic alliances; licensing and other forms of proprietary protection; distribution arrangements; establishment, financing and operation of foreign branches and subsidiaries; international business negotiations; structuring, acquisition and disposition of real estate investments; handling of international disputes; trade regulation; compliance with US securities and export laws; immigration matters; trademark, copyright and other intellectual property matters; and all aspects of international and domestic tax law matters.

CONTENTS: Corporate/Commercial p.2010; Employment p.2011; Litigation p.2012; Real Estate p.2014;
Individuals' Profiles p.2015; Firms' Profiles p.2019.

## How lawyers are ranked

Every year we carry out thousands of in-depth interviews with clients and lawyers in order to assess the reputations and expertise of business lawyers across the USA. Chambers rankings and editorial are referred to extensively by General Counsel and other purchasers of legal services who look to our recommendations when choosing their lawyers.

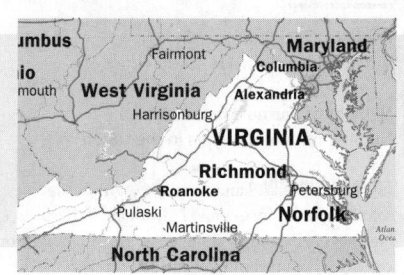

# CORPORATE/COMMERCIAL

### Corporate/Commercial
### Leading Firms

1. **BOWLES RICE MCDAVID GRAFF** *Charleston*
   **JACKSON KELLY PLLC** *Charleston*
2. **STEPTOE & JOHNSON PLLC** *Clarksburg*
3. **HUDDLESTON BOLEN LLP** *Huntington*
   **KAY CASTO & CHANEY PLLC** *Charleston*
   **ROBINSON & MCELWEE PLLC** *Charleston*
   **SPILMAN THOMAS & BATTLE, PLLC** *Charleston*

### Leading Individuals

1. **ALBERT Michael** *Jackson Kelly PLLC*
   **CAPPELLANTI Ellen** *Jackson Kelly PLLC*
   **HEYWOOD Thomas** *Bowles Rice McDavid Graff*
   **SOUTHWORTH II Louis** *Jackson Kelly PLLC*
2. **DEEM Patrick** *Steptoe & Johnson PLLC*
   **GRAFF JR F Thomas** *Bowles Rice McDavid Graff*
   **KING JR Evans** *Steptoe & Johnson PLLC*
   **MURRAY Thomas** *Huddleston Bolen LLP*
3. **BASILE Michael** *Spilman Thomas & Battle, PLLC*
   **HIGGINS David** *Robinson & McElwee PLLC*
   **KONRAD Daniel** *Huddleston Bolen LLP*
   **LORD Elizabeth** *Jackson Kelly PLLC*
   **STUMP John** *Steptoe & Johnson PLLC*

### Up-and-coming individuals
**CALLAS Chris** *Jackson Kelly PLLC*

## Band 1

### Bowles Rice McDavid Graff & Love LLP
See firm details p.2020

**The Firm:** This group is a dominant player in terms of both volume and size of deals in West Virginia and across the region. The driving force behind the practice's success is its *"excellent transactional depth and strength in energy and real estate."* Commentators also note the firm's finance expertise and close links with state regulators. For out-of-state clients wanting to break into the local market, this firm, with its *"diversity of pleasant attorneys,"* is an obvious place to start.
**The Lawyers:** The *"quietly competent and clever"* **Thomas Heywood** gives the impression of being *"involved in everything."* He is an acclaimed health-

care specialist with strong regulatory and lobbying capabilities. Managing partner **Thomas Graff** is a hugely respected business lawyer with top-shelf clients. He is particularly noted for his energy expertise. Banking and finance specialist **Sandra Murphy** is a favorite with financial institutions for her regulatory and transactional advice; her engagement with the industry's legislative agenda is ongoing. Former West Virginia Tax Commissioner **Michael Caryl** now leads the tax practice group.
**Clients/Work Highlights:** United Bankshares; Bright Enterprises; Acordia; McJunkin; West Virginia Media Holdings and Caterpillar.

### Jackson Kelly PLLC
See firm details p.2023

**The Firm:** West Virginia's most venerable firm *"absolutely stands out,"* according to clients, for its *"well-rounded traditional approach,"* deep expertise and the breadth and depth of its attorneys. The group offers general corporate and business structuring services and specialty expertise in areas such as public utility regulation. Attorneys represent Bluefield Gas in its West Virginia Public Service Commission affairs, including its 2005 general rate case and purchased gas cost adjustment proceeding.
**The Lawyers:** **Michael Albert** (see p.2015) *"knows what it takes"* to win cases for public utility companies. A direct and forceful player, *"he gives his honest opinion and doesn't sugarcoat anything."* His business advice extends to regulatory issues and clients value his *"industry contacts and ethical approach."* **Ellen Cappellanti** (see p.2016) is *"a magnificent corporate lawyer"* who represents some of the state's largest developers in creating condominium and planned communities. The *"godfather of tax,"* **Louis Southworth** (see p.2018) has a well-balanced commercial practice. When dealing with **Charles Dunbar** (see p.2016) *"it's impossible not to conclude that he's one of the finest lawyers on the block,"* say commentators. **Robert Tweel** (see p.2018) handles federal tax issues with an emphasis on transactional tax planning and analysis, while corporate authority **Elizabeth Osenton Lord** (see p.2018) is renowned for her securities work. **Chris Callas** (see p.2016), is seen as an excellent foil to Michael Albert: he is *"hard working, hands-on and aggressive"* and together they make a formidable pair.

**Clients/Work Highlights:** The firm represents businesses of all sizes from big international companies to small, family-owned outfits. These include Allegheny Energy; West Virginia-American Water; Cabela; Centra Bank; Snowshoe Mountain ski resort; Potomac Edison and Bright Enterprises.

## Band 2

### Steptoe & Johnson PLLC

**The Firm:** This *"competitive"* practice delivers transactional and corporate governance services from six offices throughout West Virginia. Alongside general business advice, the department offers expertise in bankruptcy, taxation and IP, and commentators identify a *"deep synergy with the business litigation practice."*
**The Lawyers:** The *"personable and intelligent"* **Patrick Deem** heads the business group and focuses on M&A and real estate. **Evans King**'s experience includes M&A and all aspects of commercial banking, and he is a polished adviser on tax issues. The prominent **John Stump** has a reputation for his public finance and utility regulation work.
**Clients/Work Highlights:** AEP Service Corporation; AIG Risk Management; Armstrong Wood Products; Bank One; The Huntington National Bank; Intrawest; NiSource; Ogden Newspapers; Pratt & Whitney and PPG Industries.

## Band 3

### Huddleston Bolen LLP

**The Firm:** This team holds a commanding position in Huntington thanks to its *"cosmopolitan"* style, the expertise of its lawyers and an impressive client roster. Six partners advise local, national and international clients on business issues in the south of the state. The group's expertise includes securities, successor management and ownership and M&A.
**The Lawyers:** Peers love to cross swords with the *"incredibly talented and pleasant"* **Thomas Murray**. Commending his promptness clients observe: *"He gets back to you so quickly you are lucky if you have two hours breathing space after hanging up."* **Daniel Konrad** is a *"committed and hard-working"* attorney.

| Corporate/Commercial: |
|---|
| **Banking & Finance** |
| Leading Individuals |
| [1] **BOOKER** William *Kay Casto & Chaney PLLC* |
| **MURPHY** Sandra *Bowles Rice McDavid Graff* |
| [2] **DUNBAR** Charles *Jackson Kelly PLLC* |
| **GARDILL** James *Phillips Gardill Kaiser & Altmeyer* |

| Corporate/Commercial: Tax |
|---|
| Leading Individuals |
| [1] **LORENSEN** Charles *George & Lorensen* |
| **SOUTHWORTH II Louis** *Jackson Kelly PLLC* |
| [2] **CARYL** Michael *Bowles Rice McDavid Graff* |
| **KAY** Craig *Kay Casto & Chaney PLLC* |
| **KING JR** Evans *Steptoe & Johnson PLLC* |
| **TWEEL** Robert *Jackson Kelly PLLC* |

His *"affable and laid-back approach"* stands him in good stead in his litigation practice.

**Clients/Work Highlights:** Allied Worldwide; Applied Card Systems; CSX; Norfolk Southern; Rubberlite; St. Mary's Medical Center; Western Pocahontas Properties Limited Partnership; White Consolidated Industries; First Sentry Bank and Merrill Lynch Credit Corporation.

### Kay Casto & Chaney PLLC

**The Firm:** This outfit maintains a modest profile in the general commercial market, but it is a popular choice with clients looking for added value in the tax and banking arenas. It fields 11 *"sound attorneys"* with experience in such areas as M&A, business reorganization and debt collection.

**The Lawyers:** **William Booker** has a healthy business practice and is particularly noted for his banking expertise. **Craig Kay** is a specialist in federal and state taxation.

**Clients/Work Highlights:** Clients include EquiFirst; First National Bank; Intrawest and Westfield Insurance.

### Robinson & McElwee PLLC

**The Firm:** The cornerstones of this midsized practice are quality, service and efficiency. With offices in Charleston and Clarksburg, the team offers advice on a full range of business issues including state and federal tax assessment, due diligence and M&A. It is experienced in handling the transactional needs of financial institutions.

**The Lawyers:** The *"bright and straightforward"* **David Higgins** has a rounded commercial practice that includes litigation, taxation and securities issues.

**Clients/Work Highlights:** AEP; Food Lion; Koch Industries; Pilot Travels Centers; Kaiser Aluminum and Chicago Title.

### Spilman Thomas & Battle, PLLC

See firm details p.2024

**The Firm:** With 40 *"dedicated"* attorneys this is one of the biggest groups in West Virginia. Attorneys offer experience in corporate governance, board and stockholder issues, and liquidation and dissolution. It has a strong track record acting for financial institutions in acquisitions and is noted for its politically adroit approach.

**The Lawyers:** **Michael Basile** focuses on M&A, state tax and government relations issues.

**Clients/Work Highlights:** Clients range from individual entrepreneurs to Fortune 500 companies and financial institutions.

### Other Notable Practitioners

George & Lorensen's **Charles Lorensen** is regarded as *"the tax man – the authority,"* while **James Gardill** from Philips Gardill Kaiser & Altmeyer in Wheeling is *"the complete banking expert."*

# EMPLOYMENT

# MAINLY DEFENDANT

| Employment: Mainly Defendant |
|---|
| Leading Firms |
| [1] **STEPTOE & JOHNSON PLLC** *Clarksburg* |
| [2] **BOWLES RICE MCDAVID GRAFF** *Charleston* |
| **DINSMORE & SHOHL LLP** *Charleston* |
| **SPILMAN THOMAS & BATTLE, PLLC** *Charleston* |
| [3] **JACKSON KELLY PLLC** *Charleston* |
| **JENKINS FENSTERMAKER, PLLC** *Huntington* |
| **ROBINSON & MCELWEE PLLC** *Charleston* |

## Band 1

### Steptoe & Johnson PLLC

**The Firm:** Operating out of six offices across the state, this large team *"sets the standard"* for employment and labor matters. In addition to general avoidance and compliance advice, attorneys offer expertise in litigation, OSHA and FMLA. There is also a strong line in workers' compensation. The group has successfully targeted the insurance market, which yields a steady flow of cases instructions.

**The Lawyers:** The *"meticulous"* **Bryan Cokeley** *"leaves no stone unturned"* and is famed for his hard graft. He is an accomplished trial lawyer and defends employers in protected class litigation. **Robert Steptoe** is regarded as *"pretty much the dean around these parts."* **David Dick** is *"as good as it comes"* in labor matters and brings prior HR experience to the table. **David Morrison** is an *"all-rounder"* with significant experience in employment counseling and training. Appellate group chief **Rodney Bean** has a broad

employment litigation practice. Researchers were encouraged to *"keep an eye out"* for **Christopher Slaughter,** who wins praise for his *"incredible intellect and excellent research skills."*

**Clients/Work Highlights:** AEP Service Corporation; AIG Risk Management; Armstrong Wood Products; The Hartford; Intrawest; Lowe's Companies; NiSource; Ogden Newspapers; Pratt & Whitney; PPG Industries and West Virginia University.

## Band 2

### Bowles Rice McDavid Graff & Love LLP

See firm details p.2020

**The Firm:** This team offers *"everything you could expect"* to clients across the region. The Charleston-based group has an impressive track record in preventive counseling and litigation before administrative agencies and state and federal courts. The firm also has a discrete workers' compensation group.

**The Lawyers:** Sources warned researchers not to be fooled by **Ricklin Brown's** *"disarmingly charming personality,"* as he can be *"tough as anything"* when he needs to be and this wins him an extremely loyal client base. **Elizabeth Walker** brings *"hard work and balanced judgment"* to a practice that covers both labor and employment issues.

**Clients/Work Highlights:** West Virginia Media Holdings; Verizon; FMC; Community Bank of Parkersburg; NGK Spark Plugs; Allegheny Wood Products and Century Aluminum.

### Dinsmore & Shohl LLP

See firm details p.1645

**The Firm:** With seven offices throughout the USA, this firm serves national and international clients on all their employment concerns. The attorneys are especially noted for their labor expertise and are respected in disputes including arbitrations. The team is expanding rapidly on the strength of *"high-quality work, reasonable rates and a competitive attitude."*

**The Lawyers:** **Mark Carter** (see p.2016) has a national reputation and clients report that he is *"user-friendly, hands-on and well connected."* Sources commend the quality and lucidity of his documents and opinions. The *"tenacious and authoritative"* **Forrest Roles** (see p.2018) is the attorney to call for labor issues in the coal industry. **Anna Dailey's** (see p.2016) practice includes defeating union organizing campaigns, contract negotiations, strikes and successorship matters.

**Clients/Work Highlights:** Wal-Mart; Coca-Cola Bottling; Rite Aid; Amazon.com; Peabody Energy; Matanuska Electric Association; Foundation Coal Holdings and ResCare.

### Spilman Thomas & Battle, PLLC

See firm details p.2024

**The Firm:** This firm helps clients with a range of challenges, notably union issues, class actions and disability discrimination. Attorneys are also expert in ERISA and managed care matters. The group has a regional footprint that takes in Pennsylvania and Southeast Ohio as well as West Virginia.

**The Lawyers:** **Charles Woody** chairs the litigation group and is as active as ever. His practice includes

## Employment: Mainly Defendant

### Leading Individuals

[1]
- **BROWN** Ricklin *Bowles Rice McDavid Graff*
- **CARTER** Mark *Dinsmore & Shohl LLP*
- **COKELEY** Bryan *Steptoe & Johnson PLLC*
- **ROLES** Forrest *Dinsmore & Shohl LLP*
- **STEPTOE JR** Robert *Steptoe & Johnson PLLC*
- **WOLFE** Roger *Jackson Kelly PLLC*
- **WOODY** Charles *Spilman Thomas & Battle*

[2]
- **CARR** Kevin *Spilman Thomas & Battle*
- **DAILEY** Anna *Dinsmore & Shohl LLP*
- **DICK** David *Steptoe & Johnson PLLC*
- **ISKRA** Eric *Spilman Thomas & Battle*
- **KRIEGER** Thomas *Jenkins Fenstermaker*
- **LEDBETTER** Cheryl *Jackson Kelly PLLC*
- **MORRISON** David *Steptoe & Johnson PLLC*
- **PAUL** Niall *Spilman Thomas & Battle*
- **PRICE** Joseph *Robinson & McElwee PLLC*
- **SURBER** Charles *Jackson Kelly PLLC*
- **WALKER** Elizabeth *Bowles Rice McDavid Graff*

### Up-and-coming individuals

- **BEAN** Rodney *Steptoe & Johnson PLLC*
- **SLAUGHTER** Christopher *Steptoe & Johnson PLLC*

organizational campaigns and elections and the defense against unfair labor practice charges. The *"young and intelligent big hitter"* **Kevin Carr** heads the labor and employment practice group. **Eric Iskra** has an excellent track record in employment litigation, which encompasses *"great expertise in employee*

*benefits."* **Niall Paul** is regarded as the heir presumptive to Charles Woody's throne thanks to his increasing engagement in litigation matters. He chairs the ERISA/employee benefits litigation group.
**Clients/Work Highlights:** DuPont; Coventry Health Care; Acordia and Coca-Cola Bottling.

## Band 3

### Jackson Kelly PLLC
See firm details p.2023
**The Firm:** This group wins clients' approval for *"consistently sound legal work, accessibility, quick responses and favorable geographic locations."* It has seven offices in the state. Beyond its traditional labor practice, the team offers management advice regarding nonunion environments and opposing organizational campaigns. It also represents employers in the defense against civil rights and discrimination claims.
**The Lawyers:** Clients love **Roger Wolfe**'s (see p.2018) *"ability to make you feel like the most important thing in the world."* He is a *"bright and tough"* litigator hailed for his *"methodical and analytical approach."* The hard-working **Cheryl Ledbetter** (see p.2017) has extensive experience in discrimination and sexual harassment cases. The *"charming"* all-around labor and employment lawyer **Charles Surber** (see p.2018) *"knows what it takes to convince a jury."*
**Clients/Work Highlights:** Bank One; IntraWest; EquiFirst and First National Bank.

### Jenkins Fenstermaker, PLLC
**The Firm:** This polished, midsized team is admired for handling matters in *"a moral and ethical way"* and for keeping grateful clients *"on the straight line."* It is celebrated particularly for its excellence in traditional labor work.
**The Lawyers:** Sources commend the *"gentlemanly and personable"* **Thomas Krieger** for his *"great discipline and sense of humor."*
**Clients/Work Highlights:** Clients include Cabell Huntington Hospital, Steel of West Virginia and ACF Industries.

### Robinson & McElwee PLLC
**The Firm:** This group is a significant presence in the healthcare industry, where it offers clients strength in traditional labor law as well as broader employment issues. Sources commend the attorneys' ability to *"guide clients through cases at the complex end of the spectrum."* The team also undertakes a degree of plaintiff work.
**The Lawyers:** Clients praise **Joseph Price** for his *"integrity and performance in court,"* noting: *"He is always well prepared and communicates well."* He has many strings to his bow but focuses on administrative and trial court litigation.
**Clients/Work Highlights:** Columbia Gas Transmission; AEP; Virginia Manufacturers Association; Marathon Ashland Petroleum; Georgia-Pacific and Koch Industries.

# LITIGATION

## Band 1

### Allen Guthrie McHugh & Thomas PLLC
**The Firm:** This respected Charleston boutique's reputation is equally impressive in civil and criminal matters. Attorneys are thoroughly at home in any court and also excel in mediation and arbitration. The team broke new ground in state litigation involving the trading of government securities, and handled a federal case regarding the alleged contraction of HIV through blood transfusion.
**The Lawyers:** **Robert Allen** is *"the absolute top in criminal defense litigation,"* according to interviewees, and **David Thomas** has a high profile assisting pharmaceutical companies in tort litigation and products liability defense. **Rebecca Betts** handles civil criminal and appellate law cases.
**Clients/Work Highlights:** 3M; Aegis Mortgage; Bear Stearns; Bluefield Regional Medical Center; GlaxoSmithKline; The Greenbrier Clinic; Lehman Brothers; Philip Morris; Realco Limited Liability; Transamerica Mortgage Company; Trinity Health System and Yamaha Motor.

### Bowles Rice McDavid Graff & Love LLP
See firm details p.2020
**The Firm:** The attorneys here, in the words of one client, have *"been around the block"* and offer a wealth of hard-won experience. The team's diverse caseload includes insurance, toxic tort and construction litigation through all available procedures.
**The Lawyers:** Sources regard **Charles Love** as *"the grand old man of litigation in West Virginia."* He is the first stop for complex cases and sources commend his *"thorough and practical approach"* and demeanor in court. Sources praise *"easygoing"* **Gerard Stowers'** *"thorough and low-key approach"* to a practice that includes PI, legal malpractice and business litigation.
**Clients/Work Highlights:** Clients include Exxon Mobil Corporation, Verizon and Bridgestone/Firestone.

### Jackson Kelly PLLC
See firm details p.2023
**The Firm:** Commentators acknowledge this firm's wealth of *"exceptionally strong individuals with good reputations and academic profiles."* The group offers

a full suite of dispute resolution services at state and national levels. Corporate and private clients benefit from the group's expertise in complex litigation, mass tort cases and class actions of all stamps. Attorneys are closely identified with the natural resources industry, though this is by no means the extent of their expertise. They are highly regarded for medical malpractice work.
**The Lawyers:** **Alvin Emch** (see p.2016) specializes in PI, products liability and toxic torts. The *"technically exemplary"* **Michael Cimino**'s (see p.2016) practice emphasizes premises liability, medical professional liability, products liability and deliberate intent cases. **Thomas Hurney** (see p.2017) and his team represent healthcare providers throughout West Virginia. **Stephen LaCagnin** (see p.2017) focuses on labor and employment matters, though he also handles defense work in wrongful death, products liability and aviation accident cases.
**Clients/Work Highlights:** The clientele includes businesses of all sizes, healthcare providers and energy corporations such as Massey Coal, CONSOL Energy and Consolidation Coal.

## Litigation: General Commercial

### Leading Firms

**1**  ALLEN GUTHRIE MCHUGH *Charleston*
BOWLES RICE MCDAVID GRAFF *Charleston*
JACKSON KELLY PLLC *Charleston*
SPILMAN THOMAS & BATTLE, PLLC *Charleston*
STEPTOE & JOHNSON PLLC *Clarksburg*

**2**  BAILEY & GLASSER LLP *Charleston*
DINSMORE & SHOHL LLP *Charleston*
DITRAPANO, BARRETT & DIPIERO, PLLC *Charleston*
FARMER, CLINE & CAMPBELL PLLC *Charleston*

**3**  CAREY, SCOTT & DOUGLAS, PLLC *East Charleston*
FLAHERTY, SENSABAUGH & BONASSO *Charleston*
GOODWIN & GOODWIN, LLP *Charleston*
HENDRICKSON & LONG, PLLC *Charleston*
JENKINS FENSTERMAKER, PLLC *Huntington*
THE TINNEY LAW FIRM *Charleston*

### Leading Individuals

#### Senior Statesman

ALLEN Robert *Allen Guthrie McHugh*

**1**  BAILEY Benjamin *Bailey & Glasser LLP*
EMCH A L *Jackson Kelly PLLC*
FARMER Stephen *Farmer, Cline & Campbell PLLC*
JERNIGAN JR W Henry *Dinsmore & Shohl LLP*
LOVE III Charles *Bowles Rice McDavid Graff*
THOMAS David *Allen Guthrie McHugh*
TINNEY John *The Tinney Law Firm*

**2**  BARRETT Joshua *DiTrapano, Barrett & DiPiero*
BETTS Rebecca *Allen Guthrie McHugh*
CAREY Michael *Carey, Scott & Douglas, PLLC*
CIMINO Michael *Jackson Kelly PLLC*
GALEOTA William *Steptoe & Johnson PLLC*
GEORGE Shawn *George & Lorensen*
GLASSER Brian *Bailey & Glasser LLP*
GOODWIN Thomas *Goodwin & Goodwin, LLP*
HENDRICKSON David *Hendrickson & Long, PLLC*
LACAGNIN Stephen *Jackson Kelly PLLC*
LONG Scott *Hendrickson & Long, PLLC*
PAUL Niall *Spilman Thomas & Battle*
SCARR Thomas *Jenkins Fenstermaker, PLLC*
STOWERS Gerard *Bowles Rice McDavid Graff*
SWEENEY Robert *Jenkins Fenstermaker, PLLC*

## Litigation: Healthcare

### Leading Individuals

**1**  FLAHERTY Thomas *Flaherty, Sensabaugh*
SENSABAUGH Don *Flaherty, Sensabaugh*

**2**  BREWER Susan *Steptoe & Johnson PLLC*
HURNEY JR Thomas *Jackson Kelly PLLC*
LUSK Neva *Spilman Thomas & Battle*

## Litigation: Mass Tort

### Leading Individuals

**1**  FIFE Randolph *Steptoe & Johnson PLLC*
GIFFORD Robert *Steptoe & Johnson PLLC*
HENDRICKSON David *Hendrickson & Long*

### Spilman Thomas & Battle, PLLC

See firm details p.2024

**The Firm:** This group is a compelling presence in the markets of West Virginia and enjoys a sterling reputation for its litigation capability. The team handles business disputes of all kinds for clients from industries including chemical, coal, banking, insurance healthcare and construction. With a reach throughout the state and in Pittsburgh, the group engages in toxic tort, IP, white-collar crime and real estate litigation.

**The Lawyers:** **Neva Lusk** is an acknowledged authority in consolidated products liability matters. She is also expert in healthcare and defends hospitals, individuals and corporations in healthcare litigation both in civil and criminal matters, and has a solid knowledge of Medicare and Medicaid fraud and abuse. Labor and employment specialist **Niall Paul** is making a name for himself in complex cases. He recently defeated the West Virginia attorney general's effort to obtain an injunction against a leading check guarantee company.

**Clients/Work Highlights:** Clients are a quality mix of small and large businesses from across the state.

### Steptoe & Johnson PLLC

**The Firm:** This is an *"undoubted leader"* in the litigation market and acts for nearly every major insurance company and their insureds, in part thanks to its reputation for keeping cases out of court. The team fields a wealth of established players and also houses an impressive array of younger talent. Attorneys advise clients in areas such as products liability, governmental liability, medical malpractice, insurance coverage and bad faith, automobile liability and toxic torts.

**The Lawyers:** **Susan Brewer** is the *"absolute top"* in healthcare, according to commentators. She is expert in medical professional liability and legal malpractice. The *"aggressive and capable"* **William Galeota** concentrates on PI and commercial litigation. Products liability chief **Robert Gifford** is a key figure in the mass tort arena and defends cases involving organic and inorganic substances such as asbestos, silica, benzene, vinyl chloride, manganese and mold. **Randolph Fife** is recommended for his work in toxic tort, defending asbestos, hearing loss and breast implant claims.

**Clients/Work Highlights:** The firm's client list includes Marshall University; Mylan Pharmaceuticals; NiSource; West Virginia University and St. Paul Travelers.

## Band 2

### Bailey & Glasser LLP

See firm details p.2019

**The Firm:** This *"up-and-coming litigation boutique"* has earned a distinguished reputation in both civil and criminal defense cases. The lawyers *"shine in the courtroom,"* say clients. The team has been active in a variety of areas including oil and gas contracts, antitrust violations, employment matters and PI cases.

**The Lawyers:** The *"witty and engaging"* **Benjamin Bailey** (see p.2015) is adept at complex litigation, in which he represents both plaintiffs and defendants; while *"aggressive, he is never over the top."* Commentators also single him out for his white-collar criminal defense skills. **Brian Glasser** (see p.2017) is expert in trial and appeals work.

**Clients/Work Highlights:** The firm acts for commercial and plaintiff clients.

### Dinsmore & Shohl LLP

See firm details p.1645

**The Firm:** This team earns high marks for its expertise in mass tort products liability. It offers deep multidisciplinary capability and a network that spans Ohio, Kentucky and Pennsylvania as well as West Virginia. The lawyers are experienced in business, finance, medical, scientific and engineering matters. They are also skilled in mediation and commercial arbitration proceedings.

**The Lawyers:** The *"effective and diligent"* **Henry Jernigan** (see p.2017) is a *"knowledgeable and confident litigator,"* known in some circles as *"Mr. Steady."* His practice includes pharmaceutical litigation.

**Clients/Work Highlights:** The group has been representing commercial and medical companies in a number of class actions including Purdue Pharma and OxyContin.

### DiTrapano, Barrett & DiPiero, PLLC

**The Firm:** The bulk of this *"talented"* team's work is plaintiff litigation. Its varied caseload includes death claims, medical malpractice, defective product injuries, business torts and criminal defense cases. Based in Charleston, the team tries cases throughout West Virginia.

**The Lawyers:** **Joshua Barrett** (see p.2016) is identified as the *"brains behind the group's success."* He works *"tirelessly"* on contract disputes and cases involving claims of fraud, negligent misrepresentation and tortious interference. He is also experienced in coal mining and related injuries cases.

**Clients/Work Highlights:** The client roster includes oil and gas companies and The Charleston Gazette.

### Farmer, Cline & Campbell PLLC

**The Firm:** This young firm has a growing reputation in the litigation sector handling both plaintiff and defense work. The team of nine engages in PI, products liability and medical malpractice cases and also has substantial expertise in pharmaceutical litigation and toxic tort defense.

**The Lawyers:** Peers single out **Stephen Farmer** as a litigator in products liability and commercial disputes.

**Clients/Work Highlights:** The firm's clients include pharmaceutical companies and corporations.

## Band 3

### Carey, Scott & Douglas, PLLC

**The Firm:** These lawyers impress onlookers with their extensive trial experience in business disputes. The team has been going strong since 1999 and the caseload includes products liability, both plaintiff and defendant PI and wrongful death, asbestos, natural resources and white-collar criminal cases.

**The Lawyers:** **Michael Carey** is recommended for his white-collar crime defense work.

**Clients/Work Highlights:** The clients are a mixture of small to midsize corporations and professional individuals.

### Flaherty, Sensabaugh & Bonasso PLLC

**The Firm:** Eager sources aver: *"Overall, this firm is probably the best in the state, top to bottom, for medical malpractice and hospital liability."* It offers a consistently high-quality staff and a thoroughly convincing local presence. Working out of offices in Morgantown, Wheeling and Charleston, the team has an enviable record at trial and an instinct for knowing when to settle.

**The Lawyers:** *"Charismatic and dynamic"* healthcare specialist **Thomas Flaherty** is reassuringly *"on his toes, professional and always prepared."* Meanwhile, his colleague, **Don Sensabaugh**, is declared the *"king of medical malpractice."* Observers endorse his *"easygoing and likable style, impressive network and up-to-date knowledge."*

**Clients/Work Highlights:** Clients include individuals, corporations and a number of healthcare organizations such as the West Virginia Physicians' Mutual Insurance Company.

### Goodwin & Goodwin, LLP

**The Firm:** Clients turn to this versatile group for advice on a melting pot of commercial disputes, insurance coverage problems and employment law issues. A family firm of three generations, it is regarded as *"well connected and active on the political front."*

**The Lawyers:** Litigation chief **Thomas Goodwin** is adept in toxic torts and the representation of clients in civil litigation through West Virginia's state and federal courts.

**Clients/Work Highlights:** This outlet represents a range of corporate clients.

### Hendrickson & Long, PLLC

See firm details p.2022

**The Firm:** This sizable litigation boutique handles matters before state and federal courts, from smaller cases for individual clients through to complex business disputes. The practice is especially noted for asbestos and toxic contamination work, and its reputation rests squarely on the shoulders of its founding partners.

**The Lawyers:** The *"easygoing"* **Scott Long** has a broad litigation practice that includes products liability, PI, medical malpractice, toxic tort and asbestos defense. Interviewees admire the *"alert and quick"* mass tort specialist **David Hendrickson** for his *"energetic approach and superb cross-examination skills."* He specializes in chemical cases including acrylamide, benzene, PCB and multichemical sensitivities, and recently acted in a major asbestos case.

**Clients/Work Highlights:** The client base includes individuals, local businesses and national and international companies.

### Jenkins Fenstermaker, PLLC

**The Firm:** This Huntington-based outfit regularly engages in state and federal litigation in West Virginia, Kentucky and Ohio. A group of 19 lawyers handles a caseload that includes insurance defense and coverage analysis, PI and healthcare. Sources flag up the attorneys' experience in mediation and arbitration.

**The Lawyers:** **Thomas Scarr**'s practice emphasizes general civil litigation and labor and employment law. **Robert Sweeney**'s similarly broad practice offers niche expertise in asbestos, lead and toxic tort litigation.

**Clients/Work Highlights:** Clients range from smaller local entities to Fortune 500 companies. The firm also represents individuals.

### The Tinney Law Firm

**The Firm:** This *"aggressive litigation boutique"* is a byword for quality, and the team specializes in trials and appeals in state and federal courts throughout the state. Peers remark on the attorneys' advocacy skills, observing: *"They definitely know their way around the courtroom."*

**The Lawyers:** The firm's rainmaker, **John Tinney**, remains active and is hailed as a worthy opponent by his competitors, who appreciate the *"touch of flamboyance"* he brings to a case.

**Clients/Work Highlights:** The firm acts on behalf of a variety of clients including drug manufacturers; financial institutions; municipalities and individuals.

### Other Notable Practitioners

The *"sharp and aggressive"* **Shawn George** at George & Lorensen receives accolades for his work in commercial disputes, industrial accidents, toxic torts and products liability.

# REAL ESTATE

## Band 1

### Bowles Rice McDavid Graff & Love LLP

See firm details p.2020

**The Firm:** This is an *"outstanding shop"* and one of the most prominent players in West Virginia real estate. It also offers deep energy and natural resources expertise, which makes it a perfect choice for the coal, minerals, oil and natural gas clients that are ubiquitous in the region. Lawyers work on major commercial sales and acquisitions, minerals leases and contracts. They also offer a comprehensive disputes service as needed.

**The Lawyers:** The *"easygoing"* **Carl Andrews** is particularly known for his commercial real estate work. **Thomas Lane**'s practice is a combination of mineral law and real estate development, frequently in the energy industry. **Charles Dollison** is an expert in coal, oil and gas matters and **Robert Dinsmore** is also recommended for his knowledge of natural resources law.

**Clients/Work Highlights:** The team acts for owners, operators, producers and contractors of all sizes.

### Jackson Kelly PLLC

See firm details p.2023

**The Firm:** This first-rate firm *"leads the charge on complex issues that touch every phase of our business,"* enthuse clients. The Charleston office is backed up by a network throughout the state and further afield, and impressed commentators observe that the large team is well stocked with *"decent honorable lawyers."*

**The Lawyers:** **Ellen Cappellanti**'s (see p.2016) direct style wins applause, and relieved clients agree: *"You don't have to guess what she means."* She represents some of the state's largest developers in creating condominium and planned communities. **Robert Fluharty** (see p.2017) is respected for his expertise in commercial financing and transactional work in energy and natural resources development projects. *"Hard-working"* **Charles Loeb** (see p.2017) is an expert in coal transactions and offers a broad commercial practice. **Eric London** (see p.2017) is a well-regarded commercial real estate lawyer.

**Clients/Work Highlights:** Chicago Title Insurance; Peabody Coal; Bright Enterprises and Foundation Coal Holdings are all on the client roster.

### Steptoe & Johnson PLLC

**The Firm:** This firm offers *"great coverage"* and fields around 30 lawyers in a flourishing and multitalented team that is active in the region. Between them, the lawyers deliver a genuinely diverse commercial service and *"cover absolutely all the bases"* in this sector, notably in the coal, oil and gas industries.

**The Lawyers:** **Patrick Deem**'s broad practice is particularly noted for commercial transactions and business organization matters. Observers admire **James Russell** for his *"invaluable natural resources knowledge."* **Louis Enderle** is recommended for general expertise in real estate and for his specialty mineral resources.

**Clients/Work Highlights:** Penn Virginia; The Huntington National Bank; Chicago Title Insurance;

## Real Estate

### Leading Firms

1. **BOWLES RICE MCDAVID GRAFF** *Charleston*
   **JACKSON KELLY PLLC** *Charleston*
   **STEPTOE & JOHNSON PLLC** *Clarksburg*
2. **HUDDLESTON BOLEN LLP** *Huntington*
   **PILL & PILL** *Martinsburg*
   **REEDER & SHUMAN** *Morgantown*
   **ROBINSON & MCELWEE PLLC** *Charleston*
   **SPILMAN THOMAS & BATTLE, PLLC** *Charleston*

### Leading Individuals

1. **ANDREWS Carl** *Bowles Rice McDavid Graff*
   **DEEM Patrick** *Steptoe & Johnson PLLC*
2. **CAPPELLANTI Ellen** *Jackson Kelly PLLC*
   **DOLLISON Charles** *Bowles Rice McDavid Graff*
   **GILPIN Thomas** *Huddleston Bolen LLP*
   **PLYBON Christopher** *Huddleston Bolen LLP*
   **SHUMAN Stephen** *Reeder & Shuman*
3. **DINSMORE Robert** *Bowles Rice McDavid Graff*
   **ENDERLE JR Louis** *Steptoe & Johnson PLLC*
   **LOEB JR Charles** *Jackson Kelly PLLC*
   **LONDON Eric** *Jackson Kelly PLLC*
   **MCELWEE Douglas** *Robinson & McElwee PLLC*
   **OFSA Joyce** *Spilman Thomas & Battle*
   **PILL Richard** *Pill & Pill*
   **SHUMAN Robert** *Reeder & Shuman*

### Real Estate: Energy & Natural Resources

### Leading Individuals

1. **LANE Thomas** *Bowles Rice McDavid Graff*
2. **DOLLISON Charles** *Bowles Rice McDavid Graff*
   **FLUHARTY Robert** *Jackson Kelly PLLC*
   **RUSSELL James** *Steptoe & Johnson PLLC*
3. **BOLEN Richard** *Huddleston Bolen LLP*
   **MCELWEE Douglas** *Robinson & McElwee PLLC*

Columbia Gas Transmission; Dominion; The Forestland Group; West Virginia University Foundation; US Fish and Wildlife Service; The Greenbrier and Drilling Appalachian.

## Band 2

### Huddleston Bolen LLP

**The Firm:** This small group offers *"remarkable knowledge of the Huntington market."* It handles large transactions for individuals, businesses and financial institutions in West Virginia, eastern Kentucky and southern Ohio. For example, lawyers act as agents for First American Title Insurance and regularly provide legal assistance in zoning representations and appeals.

**The Lawyers:** **Thomas Gilpin** is a *"true all-around attorney"* who represents clients in the fields of healthcare, real estate, banking, bankruptcy and commercial law. He has handled multimillion-dollar loans and acquisitions for a major coal and timberland client. **Christopher Plybon** is particularly well known for his commercial real estate transactions, banking and bankruptcy work. *"Exceptional litigator"* **Richard Bolen** offers expertise in natural resources and is commended for his arbitration work in coal, oil and gas matters.

**Clients/Work Highlights:** Bank One; Tri-State Transit Authority; Natural Resource Partners/Western Pocahontas Properties and a private physicians' practice group.

### Pill & Pill

**The Firm:** With its headquarters in Martinsburg this small outlet is best known for its work in the residential arena, especially in the northern part of the state. Part of the workload is generated from other firms, who avow they are *"always happy to refer to them."*

**The Lawyers:** **Richard Pill** is a residential real estate guru and particularly visible on foreclosures, mortgages and loans.

**Clients/Work Highlights:** Eastern Panhandle Board of REALTORS; Baker & Parkinson Real Estate; Panhandle Homes of Berkeley County; A & A Homes and Tel Builders.

### Reeder & Shuman

**The Firm:** This *"venerable and traditional"* firm is expert in real estate transactions centered on minerals. The flourishing practice *"transcends regional boundaries"* and enjoys a far-flung reputation for its niche.

**The Lawyers:** At the heart of the team is a father and son pairing: **Stephen Shuman** is *"the guy you want on your side"* on any real estate deal in Morgantown, while his *"academic and thoughtful"* son, **Robert Shuman**, is the clear heir apparent.

**Clients/Work Highlights:** The boutique assists a variety of developers and regional owners.

### Robinson & McElwee PLLC

**The Firm:** With offices in Carlsberg and Charleston, the corporate and energy and environment departments here handle real estate and mineral law matters throughout West Virginia. Market commentators emphasize the firm's involvement in title issues.

**The Lawyers:** **Douglas McElwee** handles acquisitions and disposals and the development of large industrial and commercial sites. He is also a noted minerals specialist.

**Clients/Work Highlights:** The firm advises banks; utilities; developers; trust departments; small and large businesses; governmental agencies and individuals.

### Spilman Thomas & Battle, PLLC

See firm details p.2024

**The Firm:** This group ensures client loyalty with its *"great capacity and variety."* Lawyers are experienced at structuring large, multiasset transactions for businesses and lenders in West Virginia. The team acts as local counsel for multistate transactions and manages local matters for developers, lenders, and individuals.

**The Lawyers:** **Joyce Ofsa**'s practice includes commercial, mineral, and residential real estate law. David Hammond has left the firm to pursue a career as an in-house counsel in the coal industry.

**Clients/Work Highlights:** The diverse client base includes local institutions and national and international companies: for example, the University of Charleston, First American Title Insurance and the City of Charleston.

# Leaders in West Virginia

### ALBERT, Michael
Jackson Kelly PLLC, Charleston
304 340 1287
malbert@jacksonkelly.com
*Recommended in*
*Corporate/Commercial*
**Practice Areas:** Administrative, business and commercial, corporate, insurance regulation, public utilities, securities, transportation law.
**Prof. Memberships:** American Bar Association; WV Bar Association; WV State Bar; WVU Alumni Association;

Kanawha County Bar Association.
**Career:** Kanawha County Public Library (President of and Member of the Board of Directors); former Board Member of the Charleston Regional Chamber of Commerce; Former Chairman of the Board of Junior Achievement; former Chairman of the Board of National Institute for Chemical Studies; former Chairman of the Board of the Education Alliance; listed in a leading American legal publication.
**Personal:** BS from West Virginia University, JD from the West Virginia University School of Law.

### ALLEN, Robert
Allen Guthrie McHugh & Thomas PLLC, Charleston 304 345 7250
*Recommended in Litigation*

### ANDREWS, Carl
Bowles Rice McDavid Graff & Love LLP, Charleston 304 347 1100
*Recommended in Real Estate*

### BAILEY, Benjamin
Bailey & Glasser LLP, Charleston
304 345 6555
bbailey@baileyglasser.com
*Recommended in Litigation*
**Practice Areas:** Complex commercial, coal and environmental litigation and white-collar criminal defense.
**Prof. Memberships:** West Virginia State Bar; Fourth Circuit Judicial Conference; American Bar Association; American Inns of Court.

**BARRETT, Joshua**
DiTrapano, Barrett & DiPiero, PLLC,
Charleston
304 342 0133
jbarret@dbdlaw1.com
*Recommended in Litigation*

**Practice Areas:** Lead Counsel in most of DiTrapano, Barrett & DiPiero, PLLC's commercial and complex litigation; also handles plaintiff's personal injury, environmental, and other civil and administrative litigation.

**Prof. Memberships:** Admitted to practice in the West Virginia Supreme Court of Appeals, United States District Courts for the Northern and Southern Districts of West Virginia, United States Court of Appeals for the Fourth Circuit, and the Supreme Court of the United States. Member of Kanawha County and West Virginia State Bar Associations, American Bar Association (Business Law Section and Litigation Section), and Association of Trial Lawyers of America. Current member of the West Virginia State Bar Board of Governors.

**Career:** Founding member, DiTrapano, Barrett & DiPiero, PLLC, 1998; Previously Partner in DiTrapano & Jackson, having joined firm in 1981; law clerk to the Hon K K Hall, United States Circuit Judge for the Court of Appeals for the Fourth Circuit from 1979-80. Adjunct Lecturer of Environmental Law, West Virginia University College of Law, 1996, 2004.

**Personal:** Born 4 September, 1948; JD West Virginia University College of Law (Order of the Coif), 1979; BA Wesleyan University, 1971.

**BASILE, Michael**
Spilman Thomas & Battle, PLLC,
Charleston 304 340 3800
*Recommended in
Corporate/Commercial*

**BEAN, Rodney**
Steptoe & Johnson PLLC, Morgantown
304 598 8000
*Recommended in Employment*

**BETTS, Rebecca**
Allen Guthrie McHugh & Thomas PLLC,
Charleston 304 345 7250
*Recommended in Litigation*

**BOLEN, Richard**
Huddleston Bolen LLP, Charleston
304 344 9869
*Recommended in Real Estate*

**BOOKER, William**
Kay Casto & Chaney PLLC, Charleston
304 345 8900
*Recommended in
Corporate/Commercial*

**BREWER, Susan**
Steptoe & Johnson PLLC, Morgantown
304 598 8000
*Recommended in Litigation*

**BROWN, Ricklin**
Bowles Rice McDavid Graff & Love LLP,
Charleston 304 347 1100
*Recommended in Employment*

**CALLAS, Chris**
Jackson Kelly PLLC, Charleston
304 340 1251
ccallas@jacksonkelly.com
*Recommended in
Corporate/Commercial*

**Practice Areas:** Represents investor-owned utilities and non-utility generators in state regulatory and legislative matters. Frequently advises utilities and utility holding companies, including Allegheny Energy and American Water, on ratemaking issues and the regulatory aspects of financings, acquisitions, corporate restructurings, and transactions between affiliates. Special expertise in power generation siting in West Virginia. Primary drafter of West Virginia's 2005 environmental securitization legislation.

**Prof. Memberships:** ABA, Section of Public Utility, Communications, and Transportation Law.

**Career:** Member since 1999.

**Publications:** Frequent speaker on wind energy siting and development issues in West Virginia.

**Personal:** Vanderbilt University (JD, 1992); Washington & Lee University (BA, 1989).

**CAPPELLANTI, Ellen**
Jackson Kelly PLLC, Charleston
304 340 1277
ecappellanti@jacksonkelly.com
*Recommended in
Corporate/Commercial, Real Estate*

**Practice Areas:** Bankruptcy, real estate development, mergers and acquisitions, general commercial law.

**Prof. Memberships:** Chair of West Virginia Law Institute; American Bar Association; WV State Bar; Master, The Judge John A Field, Jr Inn of Court; Judicial Conference of the United States Court of Appeals for Fourth Circuit.

**Career:** Listed in a leading American legal publication (bankruptcy law); Discover the Real West Virginia Foundation; current Co-Chair, Advantage Valley, Inc.; past Chair and Member of Board of Trustees of the Avampato Discovery Museum; past Vice-Chair and Current Member of Board of Trustees of Clay Center for the Art and Sciences; Member, Board of Directors of Charleston YMCA.

**Personal:** JD, West Virginia University; BA, West Virginia University.

**CAREY, Michael**
Carey, Scott & Douglas, PLLC, East
Charleston 304 345 1234
*Recommended in Litigation*

**CARR, Kevin**
Spilman Thomas & Battle, PLLC,
Charleston 304 340 3800
*Recommended in Employment*

**CARTER, Mark**
Dinsmore & Shohl LLP, Charleston
304 357 0924
mark.carter@dinslaw.com
*Recommended in Employment*

**Practice Areas:** Practice focuses on traditional labor law, employment litigation and Racketeer Influenced Corrupt Organizations Act (RICO). Serves on the Board of Advisors for the Civil RICO Report. Appointed by President George W Bush to serve as a member of the Federal Service Impasses Panel.

**Prof. Memberships:** American Bar Association (Past Labor and Employment Law Section, Management Chair of the Annual Meeting Subcommittee, and Antitrust RICO and Labor Law Committee).

**Career:** Joined firm as Partner in 2003; Heenan, Althen & Roles 1986-2002.

**Personal:** JD, West Virginia University College of Law (1986); BA, University of Michigan (1982).

**CARYL, Michael**
Bowles Rice McDavid Graff & Love LLP,
Charleston 304 347 1100
*Recommended in
Corporate/Commercial*

**CIMINO, Michael**
Jackson Kelly PLLC, Charleston
304 340 1299
mcimino@jacksonkelly.com
*Recommended in Litigation*

**Practice Areas:** Litigation.

**Prof. Memberships:** Kanawha County Bar Association; West Virginia Defense Trial Counsel (Board of Governors); Adjunct Faculty, University of Charleston.

**Publications:** 'Medical and Professional Liability Issues', Workshop for the New River Family Health Center, January 1999; 'Criminal Prosecution of Workplace Safety Violations', 94 W Va Law Review 1007 (Summer 1992); 'Prosecutorial Discretion under the Federal Sentencing Guidelines: Is the Fox Guarding the Henhouse?', 97, W Va Law Review (Spring 1995); West Virginia Law Review (member 1991-92; Student Works Editor 1992-93).

**Personal:** 1993 JD, West Virginia University; 1989 BBA, University of Notre Dame (IN) (Finance).

**COKELEY, Bryan**
Steptoe & Johnson PLLC, Charleston
304 353 8000
*Recommended in Employment*

**DAILEY, Anna M**
Dinsmore & Shohl LLP, Charleston
304 357 0923
anna.dailey@dinslaw.com
*Recommended in Employment*

**Practice Areas:** Practices in labor and employment law. In labor, she assists companies in labor campaigns; defends against unfair labor practices; assists in

violent strike situations; and handles significant arbitration cases. In employment law, represents employers in jury trials involving discrimination claims, conducts sexual harassment investigations and provides supervisory training. Serves on firm's Professional Development Committee.

**Prof. Memberships:** First Chair of Labor and Employment Law Committee of DTCWV; Board of Directors, Leadership West Virginia; Business Development Committee of WV Chamber of Commerce; Trustee of Eastern Mineral Law Foundation; Vice President of Kanawha County Parks and Recreation Commission.

**DEEM, Patrick**
Steptoe & Johnson PLLC, Clarksburg
304 624 8000
*Recommended in
Corporate/Commercial, Real Estate*

**DICK, David**
Steptoe & Johnson PLLC, Morgantown
304 598 8000
*Recommended in Employment*

**DINSMORE, Robert**
Bowles Rice McDavid Graff & Love LLP,
Charleston 304 347 1100
*Recommended in Real Estate*

**DOLLISON, Charles**
Bowles Rice McDavid Graff & Love LLP,
Charleston 304 347 1100
*Recommended in Real Estate*

**DUNBAR, Charles**
Jackson Kelly PLLC, Charleston
304 340 1196
cdunbar@jacksonkelly.com
*Recommended in
Corporate/Commercial*

**Practice Areas:** Banking, business and commercial, contracts, insurance, international, commercial litigation, corporate, securities, technology and computer law.

**Prof. Memberships:** American Bar Association, Section on Corporations; Banking and Business Law; Committees on Banking Law and Consumer Financial Services; Section on International Law; West Virginia State Bar; Kanawha County Bar.

**Career:** Listed in a leading American legal publication (banking law and corporate law).

**Publications:** Interest, Inducements and the IRS, Compliance with Regulations Q and D in the New Competitive Landscape, 'American Banking Association Bank Compliance Magazine', 2001.

**Personal:** JD, West Virginia University; CPA, BS, West Virginia University.

**EMCH, A L**
Jackson Kelly PLLC, Charleston
304 340 1172
aemch@jacksonkelly.com
*Recommended in Litigation*

**Practice Areas:** ADR, aviation, class actions, contracts and business litigation,

personal injury litigation, product liability, toxic, mass tort, other complex litigation.
**Prof. Memberships:** Fellow, American College of Trial Lawyers; American Board of Trial Advocates; International Association of Defense Counsel; Fellow, American Bar Foundation; Fellow, West Virginia Bar Foundation; Mediator, US District Courts, Northern and Southern Districts of West Virginia, state courts; Defense Trial Counsel of West Virginia, Permanent Member, Fourth Circuit Judicial Conference.
**Career:** USAF and WV Air National Guard, Pilot, Lt Col Retired; listed in a leading American legal publication; currently CEO of Jackson Kelly PLLC.
**Personal:** JD University of Virginia, AB West Virginia University.

**ENDERLE JR, Louis**
Steptoe & Johnson PLLC, Clarksburg
304 624 8000
*Recommended in Real Estate*

**FARMER, Stephen**
Farmer, Cline & Campbell PLLC, Charleston 304 346 5990
*Recommended in Litigation*

**FIFE, Randolph**
Steptoe & Johnson PLLC, Charleston
304 353 8000
*Recommended in Litigation*

**FLAHERTY, Thomas**
Flaherty, Sensabaugh & Bonasso PLLC, Charleston 304 345 0200
*Recommended in Litigation*

**FLUHARTY, Robert**
Jackson Kelly PLLC, Charleston
304 340 1174
rfluharty@jacksonkelly.com
*Recommended in Real Estate*
**Practice Areas:** Business and commercial law, commercial and mineral real estate law, natural resources recovery, transportation and sales.
**Prof. Memberships:** West Virginia State Bar; West Virginia Bar Association; Kanawha County Bar Association; American Bar Association; Eastern Mineral Law Foundation, Trustee.
**Personal:** LLM, Cambridge University (England); JD, Rutgers University; BA, Washington & Lee University.

**GALEOTA, William**
Steptoe & Johnson PLLC, Morgantown
304 598 8000
*Recommended in Litigation*

**GARDILL, James**
Phillips Gardill Kaiser & Altmeyer, Wheeling 304 232 6810
*Recommended in Corporate/Commercial*

**GEORGE, Shawn**
George & Lorensen, Charleston
304 343 5555
*Recommended in Litigation*

**GIFFORD, Robert**
Steptoe & Johnson PLLC, Clarksburg
304 624 8000
*Recommended in Litigation*

**GILPIN, Thomas**
Huddleston Bolen LLP, Huntington
304 529 6181
*Recommended in Real Estate*

**GLASSER, Brian**
Bailey & Glasser LLP, Charleston
304 345 6555
bglasser@baileyglasser.com
*Recommended in Litigation*
**Practice Areas:** Coal, environmental and commercial litigation; class action litigation.
**Prof. Memberships:** West Virginia State Bar; American Inns of Court.

**GOODWIN, Thomas**
Goodwin & Goodwin, LLP, Charleston
304 346 7000
*Recommended in Litigation*

**GRAFF JR, F Thomas**
Bowles Rice McDavid Graff & Love LLP, Charleston 304 347 1100
*Recommended in Corporate/Commercial*

**HENDRICKSON, David**
Hendrickson & Long, PLLC, Charleston
304 346 5500
*Recommended in Litigation*

**HEYWOOD, Thomas**
Bowles Rice McDavid Graff & Love LLP, Charleston 304 347 1100
*Recommended in Corporate/Commercial*

**HIGGINS, David**
Robinson & McElwee PLLC, Charleston
304 344 5800
*Recommended in Corporate/Commercial*

**HURNEY JR, Thomas J**
Jackson Kelly PLLC, Charleston
304 340 1346
thurney@jacksonkelly.com
*Recommended in Litigation*
**Practice Areas:** Medical professional liability, personal injury, products liability, healthcare.
**Prof. Memberships:** West Virginia State Bar (Board of Governors 2002-05); Defense Trial Counsel of WVa (Board of Governors 2000-present; Secretary, 2005-present) DRI; ADTA; IADC.
**Career:** Member, Jackson Kelly PLLC 1983-present.
**Publications:** Hurney & Aliff, 'Medical Professional Liability in West Virginia', 105 WVa L Rev 369 (2003); Hurney, Hospital Liability in WVa 95 WVa L Rev 943 (1993).
**Personal:** University of Dayton: BS Business Administration, 1980; JD, cum laude, 1983.

**ISKRA, Eric**
Spilman Thomas & Battle, PLLC, Charleston 304 340 3800
*Recommended in Employment*

**JERNIGAN JR, W Henry**
Dinsmore & Shohl LLP, Charleston
304 357 0901
henry.jernigan@dinslaw.com
*Recommended in Litigation*
**Practice Areas:** Focuses practice in the areas of natural resource litigation, business litigation, and products liability litigation.
**Prof. Memberships:** Defense Research Institute, State Representative; West Virginia State Bar; Kentucky Bar Association; Kanawha County Bar Association; West Virginia Defense Trial Counsel, Past President; and West Virginia Coal Association.
**Career:** Admitted to practice in WV in 1976; Partner in major defense firm from 1981-2002. Joined Dinsmore as Partner in 2002.
**Personal:** JD, Washington and Lee University School of Law, magna cum laude, Order of the Coif (1975); BS, Washington and Lee University, magna cum laude, Phi Beta Kappa (1972).

**KAY, Craig**
Kay Casto & Chaney PLLC, Charleston
304 345 8900
*Recommended in Corporate/Commercial*

**KING JR, Evans**
Steptoe & Johnson PLLC, Clarksburg
304 624 8000
*Recommended in Corporate/Commercial*

**KONRAD, Daniel**
Huddleston Bolen LLP, Huntington
304 529 6181
*Recommended in Corporate/Commercial*

**KRIEGER, Thomas**
Jenkins Fenstermaker, PLLC, Huntington
304 523 2100
*Recommended in Employment*

**LACAGNIN, Stephen**
Jackson Kelly PLLC, Morgantown
304 284 4108
slacagnin@jacksonkelly.com
*Recommended in Corporate/Commercial*
**Practice Areas:** Civil litigation, employment law, products liability, insurance and professional liability.
**Prof. Memberships:** Admitted to practice before the West Virginia and North Carolina State Bars as well as the United States Court of appeals for the Fourth Circuit; Member of the American Bar Association; Defense Research Institute; West Virginia State Bar and North Carolina State Bar.
**Career:** Administrative Manager and head of the Litigation Department of the Morgantown office of Jackson Kelly PLLC.

**Personal:** West Virginia University, JD 1983; West Virginia University BS Journalism, 1975.

**LANE, Thomas**
Bowles Rice McDavid Graff & Love LLP, Charleston
304 347 1100
*Recommended in Real Estate*

**LEDBETTER, Cheryl**
Jackson Kelly PLLC, Charleston
304 340 1107
cledbetter@jacksonkelly.com
*Recommended in Employment*
**Practice Areas:** Employment discrimination with an emphasis on sexual harassment law.
**Prof. Memberships:** Kanawha County Bar Association; West Virginia Bar Association; American Bar Association (Labor Section), Defense Trial Counsel of West Virginia.
**Career:** Ms Ledbetter began with Jackson Kelly in 1980 and has practiced exclusively in the area of labor and employment law. She has defended employers in all forums, both in court and in the administrative arena, such the West Virginia Human Rights Commission. In addition to litigation, Ms Ledbetter also provides advice to employers on various employment issues.
**Personal:** JD, Washington & Lee University; BA, University of Arkansas.

**LOEB JR, Charles W**
Jackson Kelly PLLC, Charleston
304 340 1298
cloeb@jacksonkelly.com
*Recommended in Real Estate*
**Practice Areas:** Corporate law, banking law, mergers and acquisitions.
**Prof. Memberships:** American Bar Association.
**Career:** Clerk, Honorable James M Sprouse, US Court of Appeals for the Fourth Circuit (1982-83); Charleston City Council 1995-present (Majority Leader, 1999-present, Chairman, Rule and Ordinance Committee, 1995-present); Chairman of the Board of the Avampato Discovery Museum, 2005.
**Personal:** Yale University, BA 1979; University of Virginia Law School, JD 1982 (Member, Law Review).

**LONDON, Eric**
Jackson Kelly PLLC, Morgantown
304 284 4109
elondon@jacksonkelly.com
*Recommended in Real Estate*
**Practice Areas:** Banking, business/commercial, contracts, landlord/tenant, leasing, real estate/property law, trusts/estates.
**Prof. Memberships:** West Virginia State Bar Association; Monongalia County Bar Association.
**Career:** Frequent speaker on banking, business and related topics.
**Personal:** JD, University of Pittsburgh

School of Law; BS, Pennsylvania State University.

## LONG, Scott
Hendrickson & Long, PLLC, Charleston
304 346 5500
*Recommended in Litigation*

## LORD, Elizabeth Osenton
Jackson Kelly PLLC, Charleston
304 340 1390
elord@jacksonkelly.com
*Recommended in Corporate/Commercial*
**Practice Areas:** Securities, corporate, homeland security, mergers and acquisitions, technology and emerging companies, white-collar compliance and defense.
**Prof. Memberships:** West Virginia State Bar; Maryland State Bar Association; District of Columbia Bar Association; American Bar Association, US Securities and Exchange Commission Historical Society.
**Career:** 1990-present Jackson Kelly PLLC; 1987-90 US Securities and Exchange Commission, Division of Corporation Finance, attorney.
**Publications:** 'The New Sarbanes-Oxley Attorney Responsibility Standards', Jackson Kelly PLLC, 2003; 'Sarbanes-Oxley – Aftermath of the Perfect Storm', The West Virginia Lawyer, 2003.
**Personal:** JD, The American University; BS, West Virginia University (business administration and accounting).

## LORENSEN, Charles
George & Lorensen, Charleston
304 343 5555
*Recommended in Corporate/Commercial*

## LOVE III, Charles
Bowles Rice McDavid Graff & Love LLP, Charleston 304 347 1100
*Recommended in Litigation*

## LUSK, Neva
Spilman Thomas & Battle, PLLC, Charleston 304 340 3800
*Recommended in Litigation*

## MCELWEE, Douglas
Robinson & McElwee PLLC, Charleston
304 344 5800
*Recommended in Real Estate*

## MORRISON, David
Steptoe & Johnson PLLC, Clarksburg
304 624 8000
*Recommended in Employment*

## MURPHY, Sandra
Bowles Rice McDavid Graff & Love LLP, Charleston 304 347 1100
*Recommended in Corporate/Commercial*

## MURRAY, Thomas
Huddleston Bolen LLP, Huntington
304 529 6181
*Recommended in Corporate/Commercial*

## OFSA, Joyce
Spilman Thomas & Battle, PLLC, Charleston 304 340 3800
*Recommended in Real Estate*

## PAUL, Niall
Spilman Thomas & Battle, PLLC, Charleston 304 340 3800
*Recommended in Employment, Litigation*

## PILL, Richard
Pill & Pill, Martinsburg
304 263 4971
*Recommended in Real Estate*

## PLYBON, Christopher
Huddleston Bolen LLP, Huntington
304 529 6181
*Recommended in Real Estate*

## PRICE, Joseph
Robinson & McElwee PLLC, Charleston
304 344 5800
*Recommended in Employment*

## ROLES, Forrest
Dinsmore & Shohl LLP, Charleston
304 357 0921
forrest.roles@dinslaw.com
*Recommended in Employment*
**Practice Areas:** Practices in the areas of labor and employment law, employment litigation, and natural resources law. Has experience representing employers in significant labor disputes with unions, negotiating collective bargaining agreements, trying NLRB cases, secondary boycotts and union violence damage actions, and negotiating termination of representative agreements. Listed in a leading legal publication.
**Prof. Memberships:** West Virginia State Bar; West Virginia University Law Review, Board of Editors; Concord College Foundation; and Kanawha County Public Defender Corp., Board of Directors.
**Career:** Joined firm as Partner in 2003.
**Personal:** JD, West Virginia University College of Law (1967); BA, Davidson College (1964).

## RUSSELL, James
Steptoe & Johnson PLLC, Morgantown
304 598 8000
*Recommended in Real Estate*

## SCARR, Thomas
Jenkins Fenstermaker, PLLC, Huntington
304 523 2100
*Recommended in Litigation*

## SENSABAUGH, Don
Flaherty, Sensabaugh & Bonasso PLLC, Charleston 304 345 0200
*Recommended in Litigation*

## SHUMAN, Robert
Reeder & Shuman, Morgantown
304 292 8488
*Recommended in Real Estate*

## SHUMAN, Stephen
Reeder & Shuman, Morgantown
304 292 8488
*Recommended in Real Estate*

## SLAUGHTER, Christopher
Steptoe & Johnson PLLC, Clarksburg
304 624 8000
*Recommended in Employment*

## SOUTHWORTH II, Louis S
Jackson Kelly PLLC, Charleston
304 340 1231
lsouthworth@jacksonkelly.com
*Recommended in Corporate/Commercial*
**Practice Areas:** Administrative, legislative services, business and commercial, mergers and acquisitions, business planning, securities, corporate, taxation, leases, trusts and estates.
**Prof. Memberships:** American Bar Association; West Virginia Bar Association; Kanawha County Bar Association; American College of Tax Counsel, Fellow; West Virginia Tax Institute; University of Charleston, Trustee Emeritus; CAMC Foundation, Trustee; Highland Hospital Foundation, Trustee; Clay Foundation, Board Member; West Virginia Bar Foundation, Fellow.
**Career:** Listed in a leading American legal publication (corporate law and tax law).
**Personal:** LLM, New York University; JD, West Virginia University; AB, Marshall University.

## STEPTOE JR, Robert
Steptoe & Johnson PLLC, Clarksburg
304 624 8000
*Recommended in Employment*

## STOWERS, Gerard
Bowles Rice McDavid Graff & Love LLP, Charleston 304 347 1100
*Recommended in Litigation*

## STUMP, John
Steptoe & Johnson PLLC, Charleston
304 353 8000
*Recommended in Corporate/Commercial*

## SURBER, Charles M
Jackson Kelly PLLC, Charleston
304 340 1382
ksurber@jacksonkelly.com
*Recommended in Employment*
**Practice Areas:** Labor and employment, energy and natural resources, litigation, health law, discrimination and harassment, ERISA, Union Organization Campaigns.
**Prof. Memberships:** West Virginia State Bar, West Virginia Human Rights Commission, mediator.
**Career:** Member, Jackson Kelly PLLC 1978-present.
**Publications:** 'Military Leave: What are the Employer's Obligations?', West Virginia Executive, Summer 2003.
**Personal:** West Virginia University, BS

Business Administration 1971; University of Dayton, JD 1978.

## SWEENEY, Robert
Jenkins Fenstermaker, PLLC, Huntington
304 523 2100
*Recommended in Litigation*

## THOMAS, David
Allen Guthrie McHugh & Thomas PLLC, Charleston 304 345 7250
*Recommended in Litigation*

## TINNEY, John
The Tinney Law Firm, Charleston
304 720 3310
*Recommended in Litigation*

## TWEEL, Robert
Jackson Kelly PLLC, Charleston
304 340 1111
rtweel@jacksonkelly.com
*Recommended in Corporate/Commercial*
**Practice Areas:** Federal taxation.
**Prof. Memberships:** American Bar Association (Section of Taxation); West Virginia Bar Association; Kanawha County Bar Association.
**Personal:** 1994 LLM, New York University; 1993 JD, West Virginia University; 1990 BA, Southern Methodist University (TX) (Mathematics/English).

## WALKER, Elizabeth
Bowles Rice McDavid Graff & Love LLP, Charleston 304 347 1100
*Recommended in Employment*

## WOLFE, Roger
Jackson Kelly PLLC, Charleston
304 340 1105
rwolfe@jacksonkelly.com
*Recommended in Employment*
**Practice Areas:** Discrimination, labor and employment, unemployment compensation, wrongful discharge litigation, NLRB proceedings, collective bargaining, class actions, statistics, public sector employment law, alternative dispute resolution.
**Prof. Memberships:** Past Chair of the WV State Bar Employment Law Committee.
**Career:** Listed in a leading American legal publication (labor and employment law); frequent lecturer on various employment law topics; Adjunct Professor of Employment Law for West Virginia University; Member, Governor's Commission on Public Employment and Employee Relations.
**Personal:** JD, West Virginia University; AB, West Virginia University.

## WOODY, Charles
Spilman Thomas & Battle, PLLC, Charleston 304 340 3800
*Recommended in Employment*

# BAILEY & GLASSER LLP

## THE FIRM

**Partners:** Benjamin L Bailey, Brian A Glasser, John W Barrett
**Number of other lawyers:** 6

**FIRM OVERVIEW:** Bailey & Glasser LLP was formed in March of 1999, when Ben Bailey and Brian Glasser left a larger Charleston firm to start their own litigation practice. Both are graduates of the Harvard Law School and served as law clerks to federal judges before entering the private practice of law. The firm has grown from two lawyers, one investigator and a secretary to 27 people today. Virtually all of the firm's practice is trial work. The firm's nine lawyers are assisted by a team of in-house investigators, environmental specialists, and paralegals. The firm has made a substantial investment in the technology of trial lawyering, to enable it to compete with much larger firms. The firm occupies its own building in the center of downtown Charleston, West Virginia, the state's capitol city. For all of its clients, the firm offers either fixed, contingent or standard hourly fees, in an effort to be sure the clients' interests are best served.

**MAIN AREAS OF PRACTICE:** Bailey & Glasser's practice is litigation oriented. Whether aggressively pursuing a commercial claim or vigorously defending business clients, the firm plans and strategizes as if all its cases are going to trial. Though many matters are ultimately resolved through negotiation, the firm firmly believes that no case can be resolved to the maximum benefit of the client unless it is exhaustively investigated, meticulously researched and prepared for courtroom presentation.

**Commercial & General Civil Litigation:** A substantial portion of the firm's practice is commercial litigation, for both plaintiffs and defendants. The firm routinely handles substantial disputes involving sales or acquisitions of businesses, disputes between business clients and their insurance carriers, and disputes involving professional corporations and partnerships. Bailey & Glasser is also heavily involved in litigation involving natural resource issues. In the past five years, its lawyers have handled cases involving coal contracts and leases, natural gas pipelines, oil and gas contracts and leases, lost coal claims and coal and timber waste claims. The firm also does some serious personal injury work, for defendants and plaintiffs. The firm handles these matters in state and federal courts, as well as before arbitrators and mediators. The firm averages four to five major trials per year, and a partner serves as lead counsel in every trial.

**Environmental Litigation:** The firm took a lead role for the State of West Virginia in two landmark environmental cases governing the way all coal mining is conducted and permitted in West Virginia: Bragg v Robertson and OVEC v Castle. Largely as an outgrowth of these cases, the firm has undertaken environmental cases, often for business and individual plaintiffs, in the energy and manufacturing sectors of West Virginia's economy. Those cases have included NEPA, SMCRA, RCRC and CWA challenges. The firm's clients have included coal companies, small businesses, and land owners in disputes with larger coal companies or other manufacturing enterprises.

**Class Action Litigation:** As an outgrowth of its general and environmental litigation, the firm handles class actions, including asbestos and welding rod litigation. The firm successfully represented the State of West Virginia against Microsoft, and litigates some consumer class actions for plaintiffs nationally and in West Virginia.

**White-Collar Criminal Defense:** Bailey & Glasser enjoys an active criminal defense practice. In the last five years, the firm's lawyers have been involved in some of the most high profile cases pending in West Virginia. While most criminal defense work must remain confidential, in cases of public record the firm has represented the Majority Leader of the West Virginia Senate, the Education Committee Chairman of the West Virginia House of Delegates, the Chairman of the West Virginia Republican Party, former gubernatorial candidates, prominent doctors and businessmen. In many of these cases, the firm prevailed at trial. These cases have involved clients accused of murder, attempted murder, wire fraud, mail fraud, vote buying, Medicaid fraud, Medicare fraud, distribution of controlled substances, and medical billing/record keeping violations. In addition to handling the trial of cases, the firm often takes over cases that have been tried to prosecute the appeal. The firm has handled criminal defense matters in West Virginia, Virginia, North Carolina, Pennsylvania, Washington State and Washington, DC.

**CLIENTS:** The firm's clients have included the State of West Virginia, several governors of West Virginia, a major West Virginia-based media holding company, several medium-sized coal companies, major national and international insurance carriers and bonding companies, a national labor union, a railroad parts company, a large regional insurance brokerage firm, and various smaller businesses, lawyers, doctors, commercial landlords, and politicians in West Virginia.

## HEAD OFFICE

**WEST VIRGINIA**
227 Capitol Street, **Charleston**, WV 25301
**Tel:** 304 345 6555   **Fax:** 304 342 1110
**Email:** info@baileyglasser.com
**Website:** www.baileyglasser.com

# BOWLES RICE McDAVID GRAFF & LOVE LLP

## THE FIRM

**Managing Partner:** FT Graff, Jr
**Assistant Managing Partner:** Thomas A Heywood
**Number of partners:** 76
**Number of other lawyers:** 35

**FIRM OVERVIEW:** Bowles Rice is a strong client-focused law firm committed to providing high-quality, effective and efficient legal services. This commitment has contributed to the firm's development since its founding in 1920. Through expansions and mergers, the firm has grown into a major regional firm with six offices with more than 110 attorneys, representing clients throughout West Virginia, Kentucky, Virginia and the surrounding region.

## MAIN AREAS OF PRACTICE:

**Commercial & Financial Services:** Clients receive assistance in the forming of corporations, partnerships and other business entities, negotiating and drafting of contracts, and developing strategies to create, enhance, preserve and dispose of business assets. They work on matters involving partners, shareholders, directors and officers, in mergers and acquisitions, and ensuring compliance with state ethics laws. Firm services include rendering opinions on business matters, bond financing, due diligence investigations, government relations, lobbying and legislative drafting. Bankruptcy lawyers provide counsel concerning bankruptcy and creditors' rights concepts when evaluating a business transaction, or developing business strategy and planning.

**Banking:** The firm serves as general counsel to banks, bank holding companies, and other banking organizations, including the West Virginia Bankers Association, and are active in formations, mergers and acquisitions, branch expansions, de novo banking, and special projects. They regularly draft loan agreements, notes and security instruments, assist clients with lending activities and business workout strategies, and counsel trust officers, plan estates, and design pension plans.

**Education Law:** The firm is a leader in serving West Virginia's school boards, regional educational service agencies, and multi-county vocational centers and universities, and are counsel to the West Virginia School Boards Association.

**Energy:** Energy matters are a significant part of the firm's practice, developed because coal, oil and natural gas are substantial industries in this region. The firm represents owners, operators, producers, and contractors ranging from small, locally owned businesses to international corporations. The practice includes public utility and regulatory law, mineral-related issues, and real estate and land use development.

**Environmental Law:** The firm's environmental representation encompasses commercial transactional structuring, compliance counseling, representation in judicial and administrative proceedings, legislative activity, and technical services. The firm has extensive experience in assisting financial institutions to establish environmental risk management programs, and has the technical knowledge and understanding which impact environmental policy formulation, implementation, interpretation and enforcement.

**Healthcare:** The firm offers assistance to providers, employers and payors in regulatory and contractual matters and are experienced in the business of medicine and health benefits. The healthcare attorneys represent individuals and groups of physicians, hospitals, insurance companies, benefit administrators, associations and companies offering healthcare coverage to employees.

**Intellectual Property Services:** The firm's Intellectual Property Practice encompasses significant experience in a variety of legal matters such as patent, trademark, copyright, unfair competition, and trade secret matters. Related service include client counseling, litigation, drafting and negotiating of agreements related to joint research and development, licensing, employee innovation and trade secret exchanges.

**Labor, Employment & Workers' Compensation Law:** The firm represents clients in employer/employee relations, union organizing attempts, work stoppages, strikes, boycotts and labor arbitrations, negotiation of collective bargaining agreements, wrongful discharge and employment discrimination law, defense of wage and hour investigations, and before labor related federal and state agencies responsible for safety issues. They advise clients on hiring, discipline, discharge, and other personnel issues, preparation of tailored employee handbooks and employment contracts. The firm represents businesses in the defense of workers' compensation claims. The firm's lawyers represent employers in disputes related to workers' compensation rates, industry classifications, and other administrative matters which affect workers' compensation costs.

**Litigation:** Lawyers engaged in trial practice constitute the single largest practice area in the firm. More than 60 lawyers are engaged in litigation on behalf of individuals, businesses, and large multi-national corporations, to achieve favorable verdicts and settlements for clients. The firm prosecutes and defends lawsuits in all federal and state courts and in administrative agencies of all branches of government. The firm's trial lawyers are engaged in the defense of personal injury, occupational and products liability suits; insurance, bond, surety and construction law; environmental and toxic torts; lender liability and complex commercial disputes; RICO; lease, real property and coal, oil and gas matters; medical, legal and other professional malpractice cases; white collar criminal defense and other varied contract and tort cases.

**Real Estate:** The Real Estate Practice includes purchase and sale transactions and related financing, litigation involving real estate and mineral law issues, contract preparation, and title examinations. Individual and real estate developers proposing industrial, commercial and residential projects receive counsel in land use and development law, planning and zoning, compliance with state and federal sales registration requirements and filings, approvals, permits, and other governmental requirements as well as with residential real estate matters.

**Taxation & Estate Planning:** Tax practitioners advise in the formation, purchase and sale, and reorganization of businesses, mergers, acquisitions, property, sale use tax, on issues related to qualified and non-qualified retirement plans, executive compensation, estate planning and administration, on federal, state, and local taxation, and in the ongoing operations of large and small businesses and of non-profit organizations. The firm has wide experience in estate planning and administration. They have experience creating and assisting capital venture companies, and should a dispute with tax authorities arise, represent clients at both the administrative and trial levels.

## HEAD OFFICE

### WEST VIRGINIA
600 Quarrier Street, Post Office Box 1386, **Charleston**, WV 25325
**Tel:** 304 3471100  **Fax:** 304 343 3058
**Website:** www.bowlesrice.com

## BRANCH OFFICES

### WEST VIRGINIA
101 South Queen Street, **Martinsburg**, WV 25401
**Tel:** 304 263 0836

7000 Hampton Center, **Morgantown**, WV 26505
**Tel:** 304 285 2500

501 Avery Street, **Parkersburg**, WV 26102
**Tel:** 304 485 8500

### KENTUCKY
155 East Main Street, **Lexington**, KY 40507
**Tel:** 859 252 2202

### VIRGINIA
19 West Cork Street, **Winchester**, VA 22601
**Tel:** 540 723 8877

# DITRAPANO, BARRETT & DIPIERO, PLLC

## THE FIRM

**Managing Member:** Rudolph L DiTrapano

**Number of Members:** 4
**Number of other Lawyers:** 5

**FIRM OVERVIEW:** The firm's nine lawyers have a combined 187 years of experience in all types of litigation. Their diverse backgrounds and unique talents enable DiTrapano, Barrett, & DiPiero PLLC to handle every client's case with insight, understanding, and preparedness. In addition to their many years representing plaintiffs in serious personal injury and death cases, the firm's lawyers have developed a substantial business and commercial litigation and environmental practice, and have considerable experience in both defending and prosecuting civil and criminal cases, appeals, and administrative proceedings and arbitrations.

**MAIN AREAS OF PRACTICE:** The firm has achieved significant success in death claims, medical malpractice, on-the-job accidents, defective product and other personal injuries, commercial litigation and business torts, environmental litigation, employment discrimination cases, and criminal defense.

**Litigation:** The firm represents clients in civil and criminal matters in state and federal trial and appellate courts, as well administrative tribunals, arbitration and other forms of alternative dispute resolution. The firm's lawyers have litigated matters concerning:

**Business Litigation and Business Torts:** Contracts; product marketing; lender liability; state and federal antitrust; unfair or deceptive trade practices; unfair competition; tortious interference; commercial real estate; coal, oil and gas; environmental liability.

**First Amendment:** Defamation; protection of free speech and press; third party discovery from media; newsgatherers' rights and privileges; access to public records and proceedings.

**Corporate Securities/Governance:** Fraud or negligent misrepresentation in sales of securities or financial statements; shareholder derivative claims; breaches of fiduciary duties of directors, officers and employees and of corporate governance provisions.

**Employment/Discrimination Matters:** Race, sex and age discrimination.

**Class Actions:** Class actions relating to commercial transactions, including oil and gas royalties, transportation, and marketing, securities fraud, and consumer related transactions.

**Criminal Defense:** Criminal defense in state and federal courts.

**Sports Law:** In addition to its litigation practice, the firm also provides sports agency and contract advisory services for professional athletes, including several All-Pro professional football players.

**CLIENTS:** The firm has diverse clients, including a wide variety of commercial and governmental entities. Among its clients are: The State of West Virginia; The Daily Gazette Company; Randy Moss.

## HEAD OFFICE

**WEST VIRGINIA**
604 Virginia Street East, **Charleston**, WV 25301
**Tel:** 304 342 0133   **Fax:** 304 342 4605
**Website:** http://ditrapano.lawoffice.com

## BRANCH OFFICES

**GEORGIA**
4400 Peachtree Street, N.E. **Atlanta**, GA 30319
**Tel:** 404 814 5722   **Fax:** 404 467 1166

## CONTACTS

**Contact** ........................................................................Joshua I Barrett

# HENDRICKSON & LONG, P.L.L.C.

## THE FIRM

**Managing Partner:** David K Hendrickson, R Scott Long

**Number of partners:** 5
**Number of other lawyers:** 5

## AREAS OF PRACTICE:

Toxic Tort Defense . . . . . . . . . . . . . . . . . . . . . . . . . . . . . . . . . . . . . 35%
Product Liability Defense . . . . . . . . . . . . . . . . . . . . . . . . . . . . . 35%
Insurance Law Defense . . . . . . . . . . . . . . . . . . . . . . . . . . . . . 15%
Commercial Law . . . . . . . . . . . . . . . . . . . . . . . . . . . . . . . . . . . . 15%

**FIRM OVERVIEW:** Hendrickson & Long, P.L.L.C. is a general litigation firm, formed in July 1994 by David K Hendrickson and R Scott Long. The firm is counsel for individuals, local West Virginia companies, national and international companies and is recognized as one of the most progressive legal establishments in the state. The law firm's attorneys are supported by paralegals and an administrative and secretarial staff who are afforded the latest state-of-the-art communications and computer technology. The firm's mission is to provide quality legal services in a manner that exceeds clients' expectations.

## MAIN AREAS OF PRACTICE:

**Toxic Tort Defense:** The firm's toxic tort defense includes representing clients in all aspects of litigation. The firm regularly defends manufacturers, distributors, premises owners and/or employers in the glass, chemical, electronics, mining, welding, silica, rubber, automotive and utilities-related industries against individual and mass tort personal injury claims. The firm offers a group of experienced first-chair lawyers who know how to relate to both judge and jury in West Virginia. Lawyers in the firm are especially skilled at developing factual and legal defenses for complex scientific and technical issues.

**Products Liability Defense:** The firm's product liability defense includes representing clients in all aspects of litigation. The firm regularly defends manufacturers and distributors in the medical, chemical, and home products industries against individual and mass tort personal injury claims. The firm offers a group of experienced first-chair lawyers who know how to relate to both judge and jury in West Virginia.

**Insurance Law Defense:** The firm regularly handles insurance defense, including bad faith and direct actions. Lawyers in the firm regularly research, write and deliver coverage opinions. Hendrickson & Long is also adept at handling subrogation issues.

**Commercial Law:** Hendrickson & Long has long represented clients on creditor bankruptcies. Lawyers in this form are adept at retail and healthcare collections.

**CLIENTS:** Range from International conglomerates to individual West Virginia businesses. Routinely represent Fortune 100 companies. Rountinely represent clients in states outside of West Virginia.

## HEAD OFFICE

**WEST VIRGINIA**
214 Capitol Street, **Charleston**, WV 25301
**Tel:** 304 346 5500   **Fax:** 304 346 5515
**Email:** handl@handl.com
**Website:** www.handl.com

Hendrickson & Long PLLC
ATTORNEYS AT LAW

# JACKSON KELLY PLLC

## THE FIRM

**Chief Executive Officer:** AL Emch
**Assistant Managing Member:** Michael D Foster
**Number of members:** 94
**Number of associates:** 52
**Number of counsel:** 14

**FIRM OVERVIEW:** Jackson Kelly PLLC is historically synonymous with the practice of law. The oldest and largest law firm in West Virginia, Jackson Kelly traces its roots back to the early 1800s. In 11 offices across the country, with over 170 lawyers, Jackson Kelly combines diversity and specialization, with a strong commitment to excellence. Although meeting the legal needs of myriad corporate and individual clients effectively and efficiently is of paramount concern, the firm maintains a strong tradition of public involvement through charitable generosity and participation in the arts and education. The tradition that has become the trademark of Jackson Kelly is perhaps exemplified in these areas of support, a dedication that complements the legal services performed for employers, business and commercially-oriented clients.

## MAIN AREAS OF PRACTICE:

**Business & Commercial:** The firm offers services that range from general corporate law and public financing to more specialized areas, such as the formation of banking holding companies and government contracting. Specific areas of practice include: banking and securities, bankruptcy, business and corporate law, casino and gaming law, commercial loans and securitization, commercial real estate, construction law, corporate governance and Sarbanes-Oxley, corporate transactions, economic development, election, campaign, and political law, employee benefits, energy and natural resources, equine, government contracts, immigration, indian law and economic development, intellectual property, legislative services and government affairs, media, mergers and acquisitions, municipal and government law, product safety, public and private financing, public utilities and motor carriers, securities law, state and federal taxation, technology and emerging companies, trade association representation, trusts, estates, and succession planning.

**Labour & Employment:** An employer-oriented firm, Jackson Kelly is dedicated to representing management's interests in all types of employment-related matters, including: labor law, labor management matters, employment litigation, family medical, leave, human resources consulting.

**Environmental Law:** The firm provides assistance in obtaining permits and approvals, and in defending both private and government environmental claims. Specific areas of practice including: air quality and permitting, brownfields, cultural property, endangered species, environmental litigation, facility siting, mining, solid and hazardous waste, water quality and permitting, water rights.

**Litigation:** The firm offers clients experienced representation from advice, planning, and litigation avoidance to case development and trial representation including jury trials and appellate advocacy. Specific areas of practice include: alternative dispute resolution, appellate, business and commercial litigation, class action and other complex litigation, deliberate intent litigation (West Virginia), insurance litigation, mass torts, professional liability, products liability, toxic torts, white collar compliance and defense.

**Occupational Safety & Health Law:** Jackson Kelly's nationally recognized Safety and Health Practice provides a broad spectrum of services to clients, emphasizing matters with the Mine Safety and Health Administration, Occupational Safety and Health Administration, and the Department of Transportation.

### HEAD OFFICE

**WEST VIRGINIA**
1600 Laidley Tower, PO Box 553, **Charleston**, WV 25322
**Tel:** 304 340 1000   **Fax:** 304 340 1033
**Website:** www.jacksonkelly.com

### BRANCH OFFICES

The firm also has offices in Morgantown, WV; Clarksburg, WV; New Martinsville, WV; Martinsburg, WV; Parkersburg, WV; Wheeling, WV; Denver, CO; Lexington, KY; Pittsburgh, PA; Washington, DC.

**Federal & State Workers' Compensation:** A management-oriented firm, Jackson Kelly provides the nation's largest defense practice against claims arising under the Federal Black Lung Act. The firm also has one of the most extensive defense practices under the Kentucky Workers' Compensation Act and the largest workers' compensation practice in West Virginia. Specific areas of practice include: administrative law, administrative litigation, federal black lung legislative drafting, analysis, and review, Longshoreman's Act, self insurance and premium classification, state workers' compensation practice (WV and KY).

**Energy & Natural Resources:** Jackson Kelly has formed a multi-disciplinary team to support the needs of the coal, energy, and natural resource clients. As one of the most comprehensive energy teams in the country, the firm's attorneys represent clients in an array of areas, including business formation and transactions, environmental matters, labor issues, litigation, workers' compensation, and safety and health.

**CLIENTS:** Clients include manufacturing, natural resources, business and commercial, trade associations, medical, retail, transportation, government contractions, utilities, local, state and federal agencies.

# SPILMAN THOMAS & BATTLE, PLLC

## THE FIRM

**Managing Member:** Michael J Basile
**Member in Charge of Lawyer Administration:** David P Ferretti
**Member in Charge of Client Relations:** Eric W Iskra
**Number of members:** 48
**Number of other lawyers:** 45

**FIRM OVERVIEW:** Spilman Thomas & Battle, PLLC was formed in 1864 - one year after West Virginia became a state - and has been serving the legal needs of its clients ever since. Today, the firm has more than 175 attorneys and professional support staff dedicated to providing outstanding legal services and helping clients achieve their business goals. As one of the region's largest law firms, Spilman Thomas & Battle, PLLC offers a full-service legal practice and is proud of the diversity of its client base - one that includes Fortune 500 companies with thousands of employees and family-owned businesses that are just around the corner. The firm's attorneys have been carefully trained to serve as an extension of its clients' management team - working with them as one to prevent problems before they occur and guiding them carefully and successfully through the legal process. That has been the firm's tradition for more than a century and continues to be its guiding force today.

## HEAD OFFICE

**WEST VIRGINIA**
Spilman Center, 300 Kanawha Boulevard, East, **Charleston**, WV 25301
**Tel:** 304 340 3800   **Fax:** 304 340 3801
**Email:** stb@spilmanlaw.com   **Website:** www.spilmanlaw.com

## BRANCH OFFICES

**WEST VIRGINIA**
990 Elmer Prince Drive, Suite 205, **Morgantown**, WV 26505
**Tel:** 304 599 8175   **Fax:** 304 599 8229

333 Penco Road, Suite A, **Weirton**, WV 26062
**Tel:** 304 723 6980   **Fax:** 304 723 6986

**PENNSYLVANIA**
One Oxford Centre, Suite 3440, 301 Grant Street, **Pittsburgh**, PA 15219
**Tel:** 412 325 3301   **Fax:** 412 325 3324

## MAIN AREAS OF PRACTICE:

**Corporate & Business Law:** The firm's business attorneys are skilled in virtually all areas of a commercial business practice and are prepared to meet the needs of multi-million dollar public corporations as well as closely held private entities. Spilman Thomas & Battle, PLLC is proficient in all aspects of corporate governance, including formation, board and shareholder issues, and liquidation and dissolution. The firm also performs work for partnerships, limited liability companies, and limited liability partnerships. In addition, the firm handles all types of corporate issues including banking and finance law, bankruptcy, business expansion and development, consumer debt regulation and collections, federal/state/local taxation, immigration and naturalization, intellectual property, mergers and acquisitions, natural resources, public finance, real estate, securities, and venture capital finance.

**Litigation:** Whether the case is simple or complex, the firm's goal is to manage the litigation as efficiently and effectively as possible. Spilman utilizes an early case assessment (ECA) for virtually every new litigation matter. The ECA reflects the firm's philosophy to proactively identify and quantify the risks in order to ensure that clients achieve their goals. The firm has successfully tried numerous cases to verdict in various jurisdictions and legal avenues, including almost every substantive area of the law. These include antitrust, appellate, asbestos, banking, bankruptcy, commercial and business litigation, construction, creditors' rights and foreclosures, consumer protection, environmental, federal black lung, healthcare, insurance, intellectual property, personal injury, product liability, Public Service Commission, real estate, shareholder and partnership disputes, toxic tort, white collar crime, and workers' compensation.

**Labor & Employment:** The firm's lawyers regularly counsel, advise, and represent clients on every legal issue arising out of the employment relationship. The firm's goal is to work with clients to avoid employment litigation. Nevertheless, the firm's lawyers are often retained to defend employers against an ever increasing array of employment litigation matters. The firm's labor and employment lawyers are trial lawyers who have developed best-in-class strategies, not only for single-plaintiff litigation, but also for class actions and administrative agency maintained actions. Spilman also provides counsel and represents management in connection with union organizing campaigns, salting attacks, collective bargaining negotiations, arbitration pursuant to collective bargaining agreements, representation in unfair labor practice proceedings before the National Labor Relations Board, injunction proceedings to halt unlawful union picketing and violence, and lawsuits in federal and state courts against labor unions based on union member misconduct and damage to the company.

**Energy:** The Spilman Energy Group is comprised of attorneys from varied practice areas. From acquisitions to litigation to government relations, the firm's dedication to providing outstanding legal counsel to the energy industry is founded on a commitment of furthering this growing industry. The Spilman Energy Group is well versed in issues that most impact energy clients, including regulatory issues, contract negotiations, litigation, and labor and employment. The firm's goal is to keep its clients well informed about trends and changes in the industry, and to help clients stay one step ahead of the multitude of other issues that arise in business every day.

**Environmental:** The goal of the firm's Environmental Practice Group is to resolve the environmental challenges that face clients in a cost-effective manner using negotiation, mediation, compliance planning, regulatory or legislative changes, and, where necessary, litigation. Attorneys provide environmental counseling to a wide range of businesses and industries, including manufacturing, mining, oil and gas development and transmission, forestry, banking and lending, and retail establishments.

**Healthcare:** Spilman has a large and diverse practice in the area of healthcare law. During the past 30 years, the firm has represented nearly all of the general acute care hospitals in West Virginia. The firm also represents healthcare systems, nursing homes, home health agencies, physicians, and other healthcare providers. The experienced lawyers that focus on the healthcare industry are continually contacted to serve as speakers, authors, and advisors on a multitude of healthcare issues, including certificates of need, contracts, corporate reorganizations, due diligence investigations, Health Care Quality Improvement Act, integrated delivery systems, internal investigations, Medicare and Medicaid fraud abuse, rate review, and reimbursement issues.

**Government Relations:** Since West Virginia was formed, Spilman has effectively represented clients before the West Virginia Legislature and within state and local government. Numerous Spilman lawyers have held elected and appointed positions within the legislature and state and local government, equipping the firm with the experience and insight to effectively assist clients. And, the firm continues to maintain strong contacts and access with government entities, which are the keys to a successful government relations practice.

SPILMAN THOMAS & BATTLE, PLLC

## How lawyers are ranked

Every year we carry out thousands of in-depth interviews with clients and lawyers in order to assess the reputations and expertise of business lawyers across the USA. Chambers rankings and editorial are referred to extensively by General Counsel and other purchasers of legal services who look to our recommendations when choosing their lawyers.

# CORPORATE/M&A

### Corporate/M&A
### Leading Firms

1 **FOLEY & LARDNER LLP** *Milwaukee*
2 **GODFREY & KAHN, SC** *Milwaukee*
  **QUARLES & BRADY LLP** *Milwaukee*
3 **MICHAEL BEST & FRIEDRICH LLP** *Milwaukee*
  **REINHART BOERNER VAN DEUREN SC** *Milwaukee*

### Leading Individuals

1 **GARMER III Benjamin** *Foley & Lardner LLP*
  **SOMMERHAUSER Peter** *Godfrey & Kahn, SC*
2 **BARTELL Jeff** *Quarles & Brady LLP*
  **BEDORE James** *Reinhart Boerner Van Deuren sc*
  **BUONO Kathryn** *Quarles & Brady LLP*
  **DAVIDSON Bruce** *Quarles & Brady LLP*
  **LINSTROTH Tod** *Michael Best & Friedrich LLP*
  **RYAN Patrick** *Quarles & Brady LLP*
  **SIMS Luke** *Foley & Lardner LLP*
  **TYSON JR Joseph** *Foley & Lardner LLP*
3 **ABRAHAM Bill** *Foley & Lardner LLP*
  **COFFEY Peter** *Michael Best & Friedrich LLP*
  **DICKENS John** *Godfrey & Kahn, SC*
  **EHRMANN Mark** *Quarles & Brady LLP*
  **GOODKIND Conrad** *Quarles & Brady LLP*
  **LUNDGREN K Thor** *Michael Best & Friedrich LLP*
  **NOYES Christopher** *Godfrey & Kahn, SC*
  **PEPKE Michael** *Reinhart Boerner Van Deuren sc*
  **ROBISON John** *Quarles & Brady LLP*
  **ROTHMAN Jay** *Foley & Lardner LLP*
  **SKINDRUD Michael** *Godfrey & Kahn, SC*
  **WAHL Nicholas** *Godfrey & Kahn, SC*
  **WALSH David** *Foley & Lardner LLP*

### Up-and-coming individuals

  **JONES Paul** *Foley & Lardner LLP*
  **QUICK Patrick** *Foley & Lardner LLP*
  **RYBA Russell** *Foley & Lardner LLP*

## Band 1

### Foley & Lardner LLP
See firm details p.2037

**The Firm:** With a strong national focus, this "*firm of choice*" remains "*the one to beat*" in the corporate/M&A sector. The responsiveness and commitment of the team stand out as distinguishing features while an "*extensive table of clients*" means that it inevitably becomes involved in some of the region's most notable transactions. Said to radiate confidence, this highly regarded team has the breadth and depth to handle the most complex cases. **The Lawyers:** The "*bright and confident*" **Benjamin Garmer** (see p.2033) is "*top-notch on both a technical and a business level.*" His practice focuses on acquisitions and financings for public and private companies as well as takeover defense. "*Talented*" **Luke Sims** (see p.2005) concentrates on acquisitions, leveraged buyouts and securities law matters. He is part of a team that includes **Joseph Tyson** (see p.2036). "*Easy to work with,*" Tyson handles acquisitions, financing for public and private companies, UCC matters and general corporate law. He is also the chairman of the business law department. **Bill Abraham** (see p.2001) practices across a broad range of business and real estate matters but has a bias towards securities, acquisitions, leveraged buyouts and finance work. He is known for being "*indefatigable in the client's cause,*" a claim that could also be made of **Jay Rothman** (see p.2035). Rothman, the chairman of the firm's national transactional & securities practice group, practices primarily in the areas of mergers and acquisitions, securities law, takeover defense and general corporate and business law. Clients praised him for being a "*terrifically smart attorney*" with a "*practical and straightforward approach.*" The Madison-based **David Walsh** (see p.2006) has represented communications entities for over 30 years and has developed particular skill in cable television and telecommunications law. He has assisted cable television companies and competitive local exchange carriers in all aspects of their business. A debutant in the *Chambers'* tables, senior counsel **Paul Jones** (see p.2003) represents buyers and sellers in public and private mergers, acquisitions, dispositions and other strategic transactions. Jones won particular backing from clients for being "*business minded and swift in grasping the technical legal aspects of any case.*" **Patrick Quick** (see p.2035) regularly acts for public companies concerning compliance requirements and governance matters and has participated in initial and other public offerings for Wisconsin corporations. Also present is **Russell Ryba** (see p.2005) who is very popular with clients.

He practices in the areas of mergers, acquisitions, divestitures, tender offers and venture capital transactions. He was described to researchers as "*energetic, with a fabulous work ethos.*"

**Clients/Work Highlights:** Foley & Lardner's diverse client base ranges from investment banks such as Goldman Sachs and Lehman Brothers to Fortune 100 companies such as Harley-Davidson. It also represents entrepreneurs and emerging growth companies as well as smaller and midmarket companies.

## Band 2

### Godfrey & Kahn, SC

**The Firm:** This well-established firm is active across the Mid-west and is recommended by clients for its transactional expertise. Its business team fields "*premier practitioners*" renowned for their "*entrepreneurial spirit, goal-oriented attitude and pragmatic approach to legal problems.*" It traditionally focuses on the middle market, assisting clients in every stage of their development.

**The Lawyers:** "*Great strategist*" **Peter Sommerhauser** possesses a "*commanding presence in the local market*" and is widely acclaimed for his "*negotiating skills.*" One client proclaimed that "*he has a Midwest demeanor but can go to New York City and do business there,*" while another said "*he is an astute business person.*" "*Creative*" **John Dickens** "*gets the deal done and never loses track of the greater objective.*" He represents closely held businesses, venture funds and institutional investors. The "*trustworthy*" **Christopher Noyes** is the team leader of the firm's corporate group. He has "*unparalleled knowledge of securities and corporate finance law that he carries very lightly.*" **Michael Skindrud** counsels a wide range of clients from small, emerging technology companies to large integrated healthcare systems while **Nicholas Wahl** deals with a unique mixture of business and real estate law.

**Clients/Work Highlights:** The firm's business practice group has traditionally focused on providing advice for middle market businesses and their owners in Wisconsin. Examples of these businesses include Shopko, Kohl's Corporation, M&I Marshall & Ilsley Bank and The Mark Travel Corporation.

## Quarles & Brady LLP

See firm details p.2039

**The Firm:** This well-respected full-service firm continues to dominate the corporate middle market of Wisconsin. Clients refer to the "*responsiveness*" and "*excellent service*" of the business law group and comment on the breadth of issues covered. The firm maintains solid and enduring relationships with a diversity of clients including publicly and privately held companies of all sizes, traditional industries and cutting-edge technology and biotech firms.

**The Lawyers:** Madison-based **Jeff Bartell** (see p.2031) specializes in corporate and securities, insurance regulatory and administrative law. "*An attorney of integrity*," he recently represented the donor and developer of a $100 million performing and visual arts center in Madison. Chair of the firm's corporate services group, **Kathryn Buono** (see p.2032) handles M&A cases and private equity investments in the context of a general corporate caseload. **Bruce Davidson** (see p.2032), on the other hand, is chair of the corporate finance/securities team. A significant portion of his practice includes the representation of clients subject to regulation by the SEC. **Patrick Ryan** (see p.2035) was characterized as a "*catalyst; he does not throw up roadblocks every step of the way and is creative in coming up with suitable legal solutions*." A managing partner, he has extensive experience in private equity, capital markets transactions, acquisitions, commercial lending and all facets of the paper industry. From Madison, **Mark Ehrmann** (see p.2003) represents companies and investors in domestic and international stock and asset acquisitions, divestitures, mergers and public and private

financings. His "*effulgent mind*" is applied to each of these areas to great effect. Equally bright, the "*extremely intelligent*" **Conrad Goodkind** (see p.2033) focuses on securities and corporate law and specializes in securities and corporate governance. Finally, **John Robison** (see p.2035) specializes in privately held businesses, with the emphasis being on business transactions, taxation and healthcare.

**Clients/Work Highlights:** The team represents companies of all sizes and descriptions ranging from household name multinationals to small local businesses. These are drawn from such sectors as agriculture, energy, financial services, healthcare, insurance, pharmaceuticals and real estate.

## Band 3

### Michael Best & Friedrich LLP

See firm details p.2038

**The Firm:** Interviewees endorsed this firm for its "*knowledge and professionalism*." While the Chicago office has had some ups and downs, the Wisconsin arm continues to flourish and has some quality performers. The team is best known for its corporate finance and securities practice and has made a mark for itself through the representation of clients in the technology sector.

**The Lawyers:** **Tod Linstroth** is the leading light at the firm. "*Efficient, bright, thorough and well connected,*" he is "*not only a big name in the legal field but also in the community.*" He serves as lead corporate counsel to many significant corporate and technology-based clients. **Peter Coffey** won praise for his

financing, acquisition and sale of businesses work. **Thor Lundgren** concentrates on all aspects of corporate law and finance, including domestic and foreign M&A, debt and equity financing and equity restructurings.

**Clients/Work Highlights:** The firm represents clients who vary in type and size. These include Nutra-Park, OpGen, Genomix, Stratatech and Mero Structures.

### Reinhart Boerner Van Deuren sc

See firm details p.2040

**The Firm:** A strong local practice with a "*growing profile,*" the firm has over 50 professionals populating its business law department. Although smaller than other competitors, rivals consider it a serious opponent. Clients benefit from the team's extensive experience in the structuring, negotiation and closure of complicated deals. Business acquisitions, divestitures and strategic combinations prove to be specialties.

**The Lawyers:** **James Bedore** (see p.2031) provides counsel on corporate and securities issues while **Michael Pepke** (see p.2034) advises clients with respect to routine legal and business matters such as banking relationships, owner relationships and strategic planning. Both were described as being "*punctilious in everything they do.*"

**Clients/Work Highlights:** Resolute Systems; Allen Edmonds; Sargento Cheese and Ruud Lighting.

# EMPLOYMENT

| Employment: Mainly Defendant |
|---|
| Leading Firms |
| [1] FOLEY & LARDNER LLP *Madison* |
| MICHAEL BEST & FRIEDRICH LLP *Milwaukee* |
| QUARLES & BRADY LLP *Milwaukee* |
| [2] DAVIS & KUELTHAU, SC *Milwaukee* |
| LINDNER & MARSACK, SC *Milwaukee* |
| MELLI WALKER PEASE & RUHLY SC *Madison* |

## Band 1

### Foley & Lardner LLP

See firm details p.2037

**The Firm:** "*Highly responsive and home to a legion of alert attorneys,*" this firm is geared up to tackle matters on a national level. Its Wisconsin branch is but part of its extensive network but makes a material contribution, proving a force in matters both within and beyond state boundaries. Clients appreciate the firm's vast resource of 75 talented attorneys working from coast to coast, and admire its excellent relationship with the legal world. The labor and employment attorneys here operate as part of the litigation department.

**The Lawyers:** The Madison-based **Michael Auen** (see p.2031) was praised for his "*direct, no-nonsense approach*" and "*refusal to polish the truth.*" One client commented that "*his is the sharpest mind I have ever worked with. He is so up to date with the latest case law.*" Auen's practice focuses on advising and defending employers in labor law, employment and litigation. "*Practical, down-to-earth and bright,*" **Bernard Bobber** (see p.2032) represents employers before federal and state courts and administrative agencies throughout the country. He has a particular focus on employment discrimination, wage and hour, trade secrets and employee benefits matters. The firm's chairman of the labor and employment practice group, **Thomas Pence** (see p.2034), is recognized by market sources as "*a skilled practitioner.*" He represents employers in all aspects of employment and labor law.

**Clients/Work Highlights:** Johnson Controls; SubZero Freezer; The Swiss Colony and Nothelfergilman.

### Michael Best & Friedrich LLP

See firm details p.2038

**The Firm:** Sources identified this "*first-class*" employment relations group for a breadth of coverage that takes in acting for employers in labor, employment and employee benefits issues. An old and substantial Midwest firm, it houses a "*deep bench of extremely professional attorneys*" who focus on litigation prevention and the achievement of strategic objectives.

**The Lawyers:** "*A great thinker who is able to analyze matters from all angles,*" **David Croysdale** is an expert in matters relating to labor law. "*He radiates confidence and has an inexhaustible work ethos.*" "*Analytic and quick,*" **Tom Scrivner** easily adapts to different company cultures. He assists entities within a multitude of industries including construction, healthcare, printing, education, manufacturing and the nonprofit sector. Chairman of the firm's labor and employment practice group **Jonathan Levine** is well respected for his "*up to the minute knowledge*" and has a "*fine ability to think strategically.*" Market observers reported that he "*never causes annoyance because he is, in contrast to other attorneys, not in love with himself.*" **Charles Stevens** is, according to clients, an "*open and humorous attorney who knows*" the legal profession inside out." "*Meticulous in his approach to the detail of a case,*" he specializes in employee benefits law.

Clients/Work Highlights: The team represented the YMCA of Racine in defense of a race discrimination and retaliation action brought by one of its former employees. It also assisted Waukesha County in a group health insurance arbitration. Other clients of the firm include Associated General Contractors of Greater Milwaukee; Bradley Center; Covenant Healthcare System; Cub Foods; Five Star Quality Care; Gehl; JohnsonDiversey; Milwaukee Area Technical College; Procter & Gamble; SUPERVALU and Unilever Bestfoods.

## Quarles & Brady LLP

See firm details p.2039

The Firm: Many clients regard this firm's service-minded attorneys as "*business partners, but above all,*

staunch allies. They listen and deliver consistently high quality work.*" The "*solid*" group represents management in all areas of labor and employment law. It further received many compliments for its ancillary services such as providing free educational programs for clients' staff.

The Lawyers: The "*responsive and flexible*" David Kern (see p.2034) chairs the firm's national labor and employment practice group. Described as "*trustworthy and easy to work with,*" he has a reputation for delivering excellent traditional labor work. The "*organized, result-focused and thorough*" Ely Leichtling (see p.2034) "*will always make time to talk to whoever, whenever,*" and is said to have the "*ability to translate difficult legal decisions and definitions into understandable language for a layman.*" Robert Duffy (see p.2032) provides front-end employment solutions and defends employers from civil rights, wrongful discharge, workers' compensation and union-related litigation. "*Bullet sharp*" Mary Pat Ninneman (see p.2034) is renowned for her employment litigation and counseling, proving particularly adept at discrimination defenses. The "*level-headed and prudent*" Pamela Ploor (see p.2034) also has a reputation for handling discrimination and employment litigation successfully in state and federal courts as well as before the Wisconsin Equal Rights Division and the EEOC. Sean Scullen (see p.2035) is a "*young and sharp attorney*" who advises private and public sector employers in all areas of labor and employment law.

Clients/Work Highlights: The group provides legal support to employers of every size, from every industry across the country. Clients include Journal Communications, Procter & Gamble and Unilever Bestfoods.

## Band 2

### Davis & Kuelthau, SC

The Firm: "*Straightforward, honest lawyers*" work in the Davis & Kuelthau labor and employment group. Within the firm, 30 attorneys handle a variety of employment work from collective bargaining and

contract mediation to subcontracting and strike preparation. The firm has five offices throughout Wisconsin.

The Lawyers: Mark Vetter is the chairman of the Davis & Kuelthau board of directors. "*An attorney with integrity,*" his practice focuses on private and public sector labor and employment law, as well as school law. Spokesmen for school districts reported that he delivers "*tremendous quality work,*" with one tagging him "*the dean of lawyers in southeast Wisconsin.*"

Clients/Work Highlights: The firm serves a diverse group of public and private sector clients nationwide.

### Lindner & Marsack, SC

The Firm: Interviewees commended this Milwaukee-based outlet as a sought-after firm with both a strong labor practice and an established community presence. The boutique practice, established in 1908, represents municipalities, government entities and companies of all sizes in a variety of industries.

The Lawyers: The director of the company, Gary Marsack, is respected for his labor work in particular.

Clients/Work Highlights: The firm's clients include Master Lock, Fortune Brands and Mercury Marine.

### Melli Walker Pease & Ruhly SC

The Firm: Market sources gave positive feedback to a Madison-based firm that specializes in labor and employment, construction, business and school law. "*Always willing to go the extra mile,*" it is always ready to fight but puts a high premium on advising its many clients about litigation prevention.

The Lawyers: Managing partner Tom Crone is a "*thorough litigator*" who has successfully represented a broad range of employers in more than 400 discrimination claims filed at the local, state and federal level.

Clients/Work Highlights: The firm represents clients from the public and private sector.

# INTELLECTUAL PROPERTY

## Band 1

### Boyle Fredrickson Newholm Stein & Gratz SC

The Firm: Acknowledged by peers to be the leading niche firm in Milwaukee, Boyle Fredrickson has an exemplary team providing a diverse clientele with expertise across the full range of IP law. This boutique of 12 "*no-nonsense*" attorneys is primarily known for its outstanding technology litigation.

The Lawyers: James Boyle and John Fredrickson, both "*top-notch*" IP litigators, are the twin figureheads of the practice. Boyle prepares and prosecutes both patent and trademark applications while

Fredrickson has a particular expertise in appellate cases. These have included Serco Services v Kelley and Slowiak v Land O'Lakes.

Clients/Work Highlights: Finite Hone; Prismagraphics; Kelley Company; ProStyle; Scofield Souvenir and Watertower Associates.

### Foley & Lardner LLP

See firm details p.2037

The Firm: This "*resourceful and dynamic practice*" is a frequent participant in larger national cases. Clients were full of praise for the service offered by the team and appreciative of the breadth of knowledge of its counsel. The firm counts 40 dedicated IP attorneys in Wisconsin among its ranks and is a key figure in the

prosecution of both hard and soft IP cases.

The Lawyers: Clients recommend Russell Barron (see p.2001) as a "*true IP trial expert*" with an outstanding record of success in complex cases. He has a wide experience of litigation involving patents, trade secrets, copyrights, trademarks and unfair competition issues. Chair of the IP department Richard Florsheim (see p.2033) has acquired a strong reputation as an "*influential patent trial lawyer.*" He also handles alternative dispute resolution of patent infringement disputes.

Clients/Work Highlights: Mueller Sports Medicine; Hewlett-Packard; Juno Online Services and Rockwell MOCVD.

## Intellectual Property

### Leading Firms

[1] **BOYLE FREDRICKSON NEWHOLM** *Milwaukee*
   **FOLEY & LARDNER LLP** *Milwaukee*
   **HELLER EHRMAN LLP** *Madison*
   **MICHAEL BEST & FRIEDRICH LLP** *Milwaukee*

[2] **ANDRUS, SCEALES, STARKE & SAWALL** *Milwaukee*
   **GODFREY & KAHN, SC** *Milwaukee*
   **QUARLES & BRADY LLP** *Milwaukee*
   **REINHART BOERNER VAN DEUREN** *Milwaukee*
   **WHYTE HIRSCHBOECK DUDEK S.C.** *Milwaukee*

### Leading Individuals

[1] **BARRON Russell** *Foley & Lardner LLP*
   **HARTH David** *Heller Ehrman LLP*
   **MARGOLIES Jonathan** *Michael Best & Friedrich LLP*

[2] **BAKER Jean** *Quarles & Brady LLP*
   **BOYLE James** *Boyle Fredrickson Newholm*
   **CARTER Eugenia** *Whyte Hirschboeck Dudek S.C.*
   **DE BRUIN David** *Michael Best & Friedrich LLP*
   **FLORSHEIM Richard** *Foley & Lardner LLP*
   **FREDRICKSON John** *Boyle Fredrickson Newholm*
   **HANSON David** *Reinhart Boerner Van Deuren sc*
   **SAMMONS Barry** *Quarles & Brady LLP*
   **SOLVESON George** *Andrus, Sceales, Starke*

## Heller Ehrman LLP

See firm details p.329

**The Firm:** A major player in Wisconsin with a growing national and international footprint and a strong client base, Heller Ehrman was praised to researchers for its outstanding IP litigation. One peer reported: "*Everybody who litigates against them will tell you they are the best in the state.*" Competitors admit to "*nothing but respect*" for the firm's expertise in litigating complex patent, software licensing, trade secret, copyright and trademark cases.

**The Lawyers:** The "*flamboyant, reasonable and communicative*" **David Harth** (see p.2003) has a particular expertise in handling high-stakes civil litigation, often involving complex scientific and technical issues. Clients described him as straightforward and down-to-earth, saying: "*He doesn't produce sugar-coated nonsense, only trenchant advice.*"

**Clients/Work Highlights:** The firm has advised Members of Congress (including Senators John McCain and Russell Feingold) in relation to the Bipartisan Campaign Reform Act of 2002. Kohler, Mylan Pharmaceuticals and GE Wind Energy are other key clients of the firm.

## Michael Best & Friedrich LLP

See firm details p.2038

**The Firm:** This IP group is acknowledged to be "*an enormous force*" in the marketplace and is respected for its "*professionalism and strength.*" According to its clients, it is the premier shop in the state for patent prosecution. The firm's attorneys and engineers have practical backgrounds and advanced degrees in a variety of fields. This goes some way to explaining the firm's overall strength in representing clients from the mechanical, biotech and chemical industries.

**The Lawyers:** "*Civilised and smart*" IP litigator **Jonathan Margolies** is appreciated for his "*ability to identify legal problems quickly and to cut to the heart of an issue.*" **David De Bruin** deals with a wide range of disputes, and is noted for his expertise in patent litigation.

**Clients/Work Highlights:** Representative clients include Stoughton Trailers; Morris Material Handling; ACCO Brands and Ingersoll Rand.

## Band 2

### Andrus, Sceales, Starke & Sawall LLP

**The Firm:** This Milwaukee outfit practiced IP law long before it came into fashion. The firm covers the full range of IP matters, including litigation and licensing services. The team consists of 13 attorneys and one patent agent, who serve clients in a variety of technical fields.

**The Lawyers:** With a bachelor degree in science and a doctorate in law, **George Solveson** "*has the right combination of skills to be an excellent patent litigator.*" Peers described him as "*old-school in the best sense of the word. He has an incredible amount of experience and is extremely meticulous.*"

**Clients/Work Highlights:** The firm represents large and small businesses in all areas of IP law.

### Godfrey & Kahn, SC

**The Firm:** Although best known for its outstanding corporate work, this Wisconsin firm also has a technology and IP department that more than holds its own in a competitive market. Around 12 attorneys advise on the full of IP matters. The team serves a varied array of life sciences and chemical clients including universities, corporations and small startup companies.

**The Lawyers:** Nicholas Kees leads the IP practice group.

**Clients/Work Highlights:** Godfrey & Khan's client base includes universities and corporations located throughout the USA and abroad. It also represents small startup companies.

## Quarles & Brady LLP

See firm details p.2039

**The Firm:** This large generalist firm enjoys a dominant place in the Wisconsin IP scene, largely due to the extensive experience of its attorneys. Qualified to advise in many areas, they offer advice on patent, copyright, trademark and trade secret issues. The team is further known for its strength in IP litigation and has a strong client base, acting for universities in particular.

**The Lawyers:** Quite simply "*one of the top practitioners*" in the field, **Jean Baker**'s (see p.2031) skills in drafting and prosecuting chemical and biotechnological patent applications are held in high esteem by commentators. She works alongside **Barry Sammons** (see p.2035), who was described by one client as "*fully tried and tested and someone we always go back to.*" He has a particular expertise in representing universities and educational institution clients in medical imaging and medical device patent-related matters.

**Clients/Work Highlights:** The group serves companies and organizations in a variety of industries. These include traditional manufacturers, advertising agencies and hi-tech research and educational institutions.

## Reinhart Boerner Van Deuren sc

See firm details p.2040

**The Firm:** High-quality work is in evidence here, with clients speaking of a team that "*has obtained great results.*" The department covers a full range of IP cases and also offers a synergistic approach to IP protection and intangible asset management. The team, consisting of experts from different practice groups, is active in a variety of industries including mechanical arts, biological sciences and the e-commerce field.

**The Lawyers:** "*Straightforward*" **David Hanson** (see p.2033) leads the IP litigation group.

**Clients/Work Highlights:** The group represents a diverse range of businesses from multinational corporations to academic institutions.

## Whyte Hirschboeck Dudek S.C.

**The Firm:** Peers view Wisconsin's largest full-service law firm as an "*increasingly important player in the IP field.*" Particularly strong in the IP trial arena, it has attorneys who have acted for both plaintiff and defendant in state and federal trial and appellate courts across the country.

**The Lawyers:** Much of the responsibility for the group's success rests upon the shoulders of **Gina Carter**, who is a "*skilled and trustworthy patent and trademark litigator.*" Peers value her for her "*straightforward approach and confident attitude – when she walks into a room she takes over.*"

**Clients/Work Highlights:** Clients of the IP group include AbsoluteBusiness; BOC; Dow Chemical; Extreme Biotech; JW Winco; Kennecott Utah Copper; Pro Technical Products; RBP Chemical; Standard Process; Tankstar USA and Vilter Manufacturing.

# LITIGATION

# GENERAL COMMERCIAL

| Litigation: General Commercial |
| --- |
| Leading Firms |

| Leading Individuals |
| --- |

## Band 1

### Foley & Lardner LLP
See firm details p.2037

**The Firm:** "*No honest person would dispute that this firm is the best in the state,*" a Wisconsin-based interviewee told researchers. The litigation team is largest department in the firm and covers 13 practice areas. In the Milwaukee office there are ten practicing litigators who handle the full range of litigation. Peers emphasized the firm's strong presence in distribution and franchise law.

**The Lawyers:** The "*responsive and extremely intelligent*" **Michael Bowen** (see p.2032) "*always arrives well prepared.*" One of the big cats in the jungle, he has a strong litigation and arbitration practice, rich in dealer and distributor disputes. He is part of a commercial department whose head is **Jon Christiansen** (see p.2032). Also present is **James Clark** (see p.2002), whose "*thoroughness is daunting,*" according to market sources. He has over 30 years' experience of various types of civil litigation. A "*good theoretician,*" **Thomas Shriner** (see p.2035) concentrates on commercial and public law litigation and is something of an expert in bankruptcy cases. Peers characterized him as "*an intellectual attorney with a profound knowledge of jurisprudence.*" **Brian McGrath's** (see p.2004) forte, meanwhile, centers

more around real estate and dealership litigation. "*Unpretentious and an attorney who cuts to the heart of the issue,*" he enjoys the backing of the market, alongside **Nancy Sennett** (see p.2035). Sennett, the managing partner of Foley & Lardner's Milwaukee office, was also founder and first chair of the securities litigation, enforcement and regulation practice group.

**Clients/Work Highlights:** Clients are drawn from a variety of domestic and international companies.

## Band 2

### Heller Ehrman LLP
See firm details p.329

**The Firm:** This compact offering enjoys an enviable reputation in the Madison area for its IP litigation abilities. Although the firm has a worldwide network with offices in New York, Hong Kong and Beijing, it remains extremely robust locally and can be relied upon to provide "*quality attorneys at every level.*"

**The Lawyers:** "*Gifted legal all-rounder*" **Charles Curtis** (see p.2002) focuses on complex issues at trial and appellate level. Colleague **John Skilton** (see p.2035) has a similarly strong grasp in the IP area and is noted for being a "*seasoned performer with a good business mind.*"

**Clients/Work Highlights:** Microsoft; 3M; Visa and Mylan Laboratories.

### Quarles & Brady LLP
See firm details p.2039

**The Firm:** "*Good solid trial lawyers*" abound at the litigation department of Quarles & Brady. "*It has breadth and depth enough to offer an excellent service,*" due to its impressive network of offices throughout the USA, and can produce teams large enough to tackle the weightiest of matters.

**The Lawyers:** "*Brilliant strategist*" **John Rothstein** (see p.2035) handles business litigation, products liability, probate and real estate matters. One client valued the fact that "*he is not a big guy who sits there and tells you things you know already; he doesn't waste anyone's time.*" Similarly switched on, colleague **Stuart Parsons** (see p.2034) "*doesn't beat around the bush.*" This "*practical and calm*" attorney represents corporate clients in business litigation nationwide and is particularly renowned for his negotiation skills.

**Clients/Work Highlights:** Wisconsin Energy; Harley-Davidson; Briggs & Stratton; Kohler; M&I Bank and Harnischfeger.

## Band 3

### Godfrey & Kahn, SC

**The Firm:** Although this firm is not perceived as one of the state's traditional litigation firms, it won praise for its "*great combination*" of general trial skills and transactional experience. Responsiveness, emphasis

on a workable and pleasant client relationship and reasonable billing rates are all key elements to its success.

**The Lawyers:** The "*smart and effective*" **William Levitt** "*fights hard for his client*" and has done so successfully for decades. Based in Milwaukee, he is a litigator and arbitrator who "*gets things done with the minimum of fuss.*"

**Clients/Work Highlights:** Manpower, Marshall & Ilsley and Toolworks.

### Liebmann, Conway, Olejniczak & Jerry, S.C.

**The Firm:** This outfit, "*the best firm in Green Bay,*" currently employs 22 attorneys, nine of which frequently represent clients in state, federal, and bankruptcy courts and before administrative agencies and arbitrators. The firm handles personal injury, commercial transactions, construction, insurance litigation, and professional malpractice suits.

**The Lawyers:** The "*energetic and articulate*" **Gregory Conway** is popular among his clients owing to his writing and listening skills and extensive legal network. His practice includes counseling corporations on litigation avoidance, as well as the prosecution and defense of business, commercial, and personal injury claims.

### Michael Best & Friedrich LLP
See firm details p.2038

**The Firm:** Clients heaped praise on this "*highly professional and responsive*" market player, commending it for its in-depth knowledge and dedication to the local market. Displaying a reach far beyond Wisconsin, it regularly acts for clients before the state and federal courts across the USA and has an extremely varied client base. Its litigation group is divided into teams of attorneys that focus their practices in specific areas.

**The Lawyers:** **John Busch** is "*extremely knowledgeable technically.*" "*Not only does he understand the law, but he gives straightforward advice which always helps us to prevail,*" revealed one client. Chairman of the litigation group **James Troupis** was described to researchers as a "*thoughtful and solid attorney.*" His primary practice emphasis is on general civil trials, IP and appellate litigation.

**Clients/Work Highlights:** Harley-Davidson; Federal Insurance Company; Milwaukee Electric Tools; University of Wisconsin Medical Foundation and American Appraisal Associates.

### Reinhart Boerner Van Deuren sc
See firm details p.2040

**The Firm:** Commentators were enthusiastic in their praise of the substantial trial experience on offer here. "*It has an excellent mix of academic and street-wise litigators,*" one client said. The firm, with its own hi-tech courtroom, handles a variety of litigation matters from IP and professional malpractice to real estate issues.

**The Lawyers:** Chairman of the litigation department **Scott Hansen** (see p.2033) is *"pragmatic, honest, straightforward and commercially savvy."* Peers confirmed that he *"consistently prevails in litigation cases and is a true trial dog."* He is currently serving as lead counsel for Milwaukee County and the Milwaukee County Pension Board who are wrongfully accused of enacting over $150 million of unconstitutional new benefits.

**Clients/Work Highlights:** Harley-Davidson; JohnsonDiversey; QuadGraphics; Siemens; International

Paper; Blommer Chocolate; Joy Global; Hader-Seitz; Spectral Diagnostics; Weigel Broadcasting; FABCO Equipment and the City and County of Milwaukee.

## Stafford Rosenbaum LLP

**The Firm:** There is a considerable amount of respect in the local market for this *"wonderful"* Madison law firm. Seventeen attorneys represent a variety of clients including insurance companies, businesses, individuals and governments.

**The Lawyers:** One of the market's outstanding figures on the dealership side, **Brian Butler** won praise as a well-respected litigator. *"He has a good jury appeal,"* said one commentator, while another reported: *"He has a down-to-earth approach but can show passion when necessary."*

**Clients/Work Highlights:** Highlights of the litigation team include the recovery of significant damages incurred by three Wisconsin counties following the failure of a waste-to-energy incinerator.

# REAL ESTATE

| Real Estate | |
|---|---|
| **Leading Firms** | |
| [1] FOLEY & LARDNER LLP *Milwaukee* | |
| [2] GODFREY & KAHN, SC *Milwaukee* | |
| QUARLES & BRADY LLP *Milwaukee* | |
| REINHART BOERNER VAN DEUREN *Milwaukee* | |
| [3] MICHAEL BEST & FRIEDRICH LLP *Milwaukee* | |
| WHYTE HIRSCHBOECK DUDEK S.C. *Madison* | |

| Leading Individuals | |
|---|---|
| [1] BLOCK Bruce *Reinhart Boerner Van Deuren sc* | |
| CHERNOF Steve *Godfrey & Kahn, SC* | |
| HATCH Michael *Foley & Lardner LLP* | |
| JOST Lawrence *Quarles & Brady LLP* | |
| LEVIN Jim *Michael Best & Friedrich LLP* | |
| [2] DALTON Larry *Whyte Hirschboeck Dudek S.C.* | |
| DANIELS JR John *Quarles & Brady LLP* | |
| DWYER Michael *Godfrey & Kahn, SC* | |
| ISHIKAWA Jesse *Reinhart Boerner Van Deuren sc* | |
| JELENCIC Sarah *Foley & Lardner LLP* | |
| LEVIN Benjamin *Foley & Lardner LLP* | |
| OSTERMEYER Michael *Quarles & Brady LLP* | |
| PUCHNER Joseph *Quarles & Brady LLP* | |
| TEMKIN Harvey *Reinhart Boerner Van Deuren sc* | |
| ZABROWSKI Patrick *Foley & Lardner LLP* | |

## Band 1

### Foley & Lardner LLP
See firm details p.2037

**The Firm:** The Wisconsin real estate department of this legal powerhouse forms part of a national team of over 100 professionals. Such an abundance of attorneys proves a highly desirable factor to the many clients, large and small, who come to the firm. As one commented: *"If you have a huge matter on, it's reassuring to know that if necessary they can throw bodies at the case."* The Milwaukee-based group tackles a range of matters from major commercial, residential and agricultural developments to medical/healthcare, mining and energy projects. Market sources hold the group in high regards for its *"excellent client relationships, tireless work ethic and unparalleled responsiveness."*

**The Lawyers:** The attorneys here are a natural choice for many developers, financial institutions and real

estate investment trusts. Researchers were told *"there is no major deal in the state of Wisconsin in which* **Michael Hatch** (see p.2033) *is not involved."* Chairman of the firm's real estate group, he is *"well-connected, disciplined, business-minded and easy to deal with."* He has been lead counsel for a number of the biggest real estate transactions around including, for example, the Milwaukee Center, the largest commercial development in the town. **Sarah Jelencic** (see p.2003)is praised for *"her eye for detail, solid advice and ability really to listen to what clients have to say."* She has experience in different fields including retail, office and multifamily development. **Benjamin Levin** (see p.2004) is valued for the high quality and practicality of his work. He is particularly strong in tax and financing matters. **Patrick Zabrowski** (see p.2006), meanwhile, impresses with a wide-ranging practice. *"Smart, practical and always sniffing out solutions,"* he is *"a sophisticated attorney with strong presentational skills."*

**Clients/Work Highlights:** The Milwaukee practice group was involved in the pre-development work on a planned $200 million mixed-use tower development for US Bank. It also provided legal advice in the two-tier refinancing of Yankee Hill Apartments and Coventry Square Apartments. Other matters handled include a tax-exempt refinancing of Dunton Tower for affiliates of Oakbrook Corporation. Other clients include Mandel Group; Interstate Partners; Weas Development and Menomonee Valley Partners.

## Band 2

### Godfrey & Kahn, SC

**The Firm:** Described by market commentators as an *"outstanding shop,"* this team represents financial institutions, owners, developers, contractors, construction managers and brokers. Clients value it because *"it gets deals done and always delivers."* A full range of real estate services is provided.

**The Lawyers:** The *"thoughtful and diligent"* **Steve Chernof** is respected for his *"thorough and practical approach."* Clients said: *"He will always fight our corner but at the same time is not afraid to tell us the sometimes painful truth when appropriate."* He advises on a wide variety of matters acting for developers and others engaged in the subsidized and tax

credit housing market. **Michael Dwyer** heads the group. He is one of the most seasoned real estate lawyers in the state. Clients appreciate his commercial shrewdness and reasonable personality, saying *"his ego will never get in the way of a deal."*

**Clients/Work Highlights:** The team was involved in the 875 East Wisconsin project, a $48 million office building under construction in downtown Milwaukee. Another representative project involved the representation of the developer/landlord of the Midwest Express headquarters building. It also counseled a lender in a $30 million loan to Cathedral Place, LLC for development of the Cathedral Place Condominium, a mixed-use office, residential and retail condominium.

### Quarles & Brady LLP
See firm details p.2039

**The Firm:** This *"excellent all-around firm"* scores highly on the list of the real estate players in Wisconsin due to its broad-based knowledge and entrepreneurial spirit. The group has considerable experience in representing clients regarding acquisition, development, leasing, management and sale of real estate assets matters.

**The Lawyers:** **Lawrence Jost**'s (see p.2034) strength lies in his determination to get a deal done and his dedication to the profession. Clients described him as *"incredibly timely, client-focused and adept at taking the heat out of pressured situations."* Colleague **John Daniels** (see p.2032) is highly regarded for his legal ability, personality and business acumen. The market lavished praise on his *"human compassion and professional attitude."* **Michael Ostermeyer** (see p.2034) has a particular focus on the development and conveyance of industrial, commercial and institutional realty. He counsels UPS and Miller Brewing on real estate matters. **Joseph Puchner**'s (see p.2035) star continues to rise. He earns the respect of peers on account of his work in the areas of immigration and real estate law.

**Clients/Work Highlights:** Quarles & Brady represents buyers, sellers and other parties engaged in a variety of real estate transactions.

## Reinhart Boerner Van Deuren sc

See firm details p.2040

**The Firm:** This top-notch firm stands out from the crowd for the sheer breadth and depth of its real estate practice. The regional giant offers a variety of services across the state from its Milwaukee, Madison and Waukesha offices. Attorneys provide legal counsel in areas including financing, zoning, land use, construction and architects' contracts.

**The Lawyers:** Market sources commended **Bruce Block** (see p.2032) as "*above and beyond everybody in the local real estate arena.*" Clients reported very positive experiences with him, with one claiming: "*He is a delight to work with, is an excellent listener, gives brilliant guidance, has a low-key approach and, above all, has a good sense of humor.*" Peers give him credit for being "*trustworthy, creative and practical.*" The "*thorough and hard-working*" **Jesse Ishikawa** (see p.2033) represents developers, mortgage lenders and businesses in all aspects of real estate law, while **Harvey Temkin** (see p.2006) was described to researchers as "*a pleasant, responsive and intelligent man with a highly approachable demeanor.*" He specializes in the tax aspects of real estate development and investment.

**Clients/Work Highlights:** The team assisted Pabst Farms with its development in Oconomowoc. This development includes approximately 1,600 acres of land in an "*exurban*" area outside Milwaukee. They also led the Summerfest lease negotiations on behalf of the Board of Harbor Commissioners. Other clients include Brewery Works/Schlitz Park; Columbia St. Mary's Hospital; Milwaukee Jewish Federation and Weigel Broadcasting.

### Band 3

## Michael Best & Friedrich LLP

See firm details p.2038

**The Firm:** Despite having experienced vicissitudes in the recent past, this practice remains an important player in the state's real estate market. The practice covers all areas of real estate planning, development and transactions - from zoning applications to sophisticated financing of highly valuable properties.

**The Lawyers:** The "*charming*" **Jim Levin** is "*a dean of the Wisconsin real estate scene who really makes the firm shine.*" Clients described him as a "*smart, efficient deal-maker*" who, despite his many years in the legal world, shows no signs of slowing down.

**Clients/Work Highlights:** Argus of Wisconsin; Associated General Contractors of America; Bryce Styza Properties; Chula Vista; Fiduciary Real Estate Development; LakePointe Development; Metropolitan Builders Association of Greater Milwaukee; Metropolitan Ventures; Payne & Dolan; Spectrum Development Group and Weas Development.

## Whyte Hirschboeck Dudek S.C.

**The Firm:** The corporate prowess of this firm leaves it well positioned to advise on the full range of complex real estate matters. The 22-lawyer team works closely with the firm's construction, environmental, municipal, telecommunications, finance, corporate, tax, bankruptcy, business reorganization and litigation attorneys.

**The Lawyers:** The "*practical and responsive*" **Larry Dalton** has, beside experience in a broad range of real estate matters, a particular knowledge of tax-exempt industrial revenue bond financing for private enterprises and tax-exempt financing for healthcare institutions.

**Clients/Work Highlights:** Clients who have made use of the firm's real estate practice include Acuity Mutual Insurance; Alexian Village of Milwaukee; Independent Physicians Network; Pro Technical Products; Siepmann Realty and UnitedHealthcare of Wisconsin.

# Leaders in Wisconsin

**ABRAHAM, Bill**
Foley & Lardner LLP, Milwaukee
414 297 5667
wabraham@foley.com
*Recommended in Corporate/M&A*
**Career:** A Partner in the Milwaukee office of Foley & Lardner LLP, William J Abraham Jr is former Chair of the Business Law Department and Securities Law Practice Group as well as a former member of the firm's Management Committee. Mr Abraham is a member of the Transactional and Securities Practice Group and deals in a broad range of business and real estate law matters, with an emphasis in securities, acquisitions, leveraged buyouts and finance. He regularly represents growing companies that finance growth through creative use of private and public markets. He graduated from the University of Michigan Law School.

**AUEN, Michael H**
Foley & Lardner LLP, Madison
608 258 4221
mauen@foley.com
*Recommended in Employment*
**Career:** Michael H Auen is a Partner in the Madison office of Foley & Lardner LLP and a member of the Labor and Employment Practice Group. His practice has focused on advising and defending employers for over 25 years in labor law, employment, and litigation. His work involves collective bargaining, arbitration and organizing campaigns, as well as discrimination and wage and hour cases, assistance with individual employment issues and problems, drafting and litigating confidentiality, non-compete and trade secret issues, and ERISA litigation. Mr Auen is an honors (magna cum laude) graduate of the University of Wisconsin Law School.

**BAKER, Jean C**
Quarles & Brady LLP, Milwaukee
414 277 5709
jcb@quarles.com
*Recommended in Intellectual Property*
**Practice Areas:** Intellectual property.
**Prof. Memberships:** State Bar of Wisconsin (elected Board Member of Intellectual Property Section, 2000-present; elected Vice-Chairman, 2002-03, Chairman, 2003-04); Wisconsin Intellectual Property Law Association (Secretary-Treasurer, 1995-97; President, 1997-98).
**Career:** Partner since 1999.
**Personal:** University of Wisconsin (JD, 1990); University of Georgia (PhD, 1987; BS, 1979).

**BARRON, Russell J**
Foley & Lardner LLP, Milwaukee
414 297 5783
rbarron@foley.com
*Recommended in Intellectual Property*
**Career:** Russell J Barron is a Partner in the Milwaukee office of Foley & Lardner LLP. As a member and past Co-Chair of the firm's Intellectual Property Litigation Practice Group, Mr Barron's practice focuses on the business of intellectual assets, and litigation involving patents, trade secrets, copyrights, trademarks, and unfair competition. Mr Barron is the founder of the firm's IP Best Practices Group. He received his Law Degree from New York University where he was the recipient of the Vanderbilt Medal.

**BARTELL, Jeff**
Quarles & Brady LLP, Madison
608 283 2432
jbb@quarles.com
*Recommended in Corporate/M&A*
**Practice Areas:** Corporate services, corporate finance/securities, mergers & acquisitions, insurance regulation.
**Prof. Memberships:** Forward Wisconsin, Inc. (Officer and Director, 1984-present); Wisconsin Memorial Union (Trustee and Council Member, 1984-present); Wisconsin Foundation for the Arts (Chairman, 1990-present); Overture Development Corporation (Director, 1998-present); Meriter Health Services, Inc. and Meriter Hospital, Inc. (Director, 2000-present); State Bar of Wisconsin.
**Career:** Partner since 1979.
**Publications:** What Constitutes a Security? Securities Law Handbook for the Wisconsin Practitioner, 1997; Blue Sky Registration, Securities Law Techniques: The Practitioner's Guide to Transactions and Litigation, 1991.
**Personal:** University of Wisconsin (JD, 1968; BS, 1965).

**BEDORE, James M**
Reinhart Boerner Van Deuren sc, Milwaukee 414 298 8196
jbedore@reinhartlaw.com
*Recommended in Corporate/M&A*
**Practice Areas:** Mergers and acquisitions; securities.
**Prof. Memberships:** State Bar of Wisconsin.
**Career:** Shareholder focuses on mergers and acquisitions and corporate and securities issues including public securities offerings on behalf of issuers and underwriters, private placements and other financing arrangements, takeover defenses, proxy contests, executive compensation, general contract matters, licensing and shareholder matters. Bedore works with corporate clients and in-house counsel to manage corporate and securities law compliance needs, including Sarbanes-Oxley compliance, and preparing and filing quarterly and annual reports, proxy statements and other filings required by the SEC.

**BLOCK, Bruce**
Reinhart Boerner Van Deuren sc,
Milwaukee 414 298 8130
bblock@reinhartlaw.com
*Recommended in Real Estate*
**Practice Areas:** Real estate; government relations.
**Prof. Memberships:** State Bar of Wisconsin; American College of Real Estate Lawyers; Former Advisor to National Trust for Historic Preservation; Member of the Greater Milwaukee Committee.
**Career:** Bruce Block, shareholder and Chair of the firm's Real Estate Department, focuses on land use planning, zoning, tax incremental financing, eminent domain, historic tax credits, multiple and mixed-use ownership structures, leasing and construction and design contracts. He has played an active role in structuring numerous complex financing schemes for public/private developments throughout Wisconsin.

**BOBBER, Bernard J**
Foley & Lardner LLP, Milwaukee
414 297 5803
bbobber@foley.com
*Recommended in Employment*
**Career:** Bernard J Bobber is a Partner with Foley & Lardner LLP in the national Labor and Employment Practice Group. Although he maintains his office in Milwaukee, Mr Bobber represents employers before federal and state courts and administrative agencies throughout the country in all areas of employment law, with particular focus on employment discrimination, wage and hour, trade secrets/noncompete, and employee benefits matters. He also routinely represents clients in labor arbitrations and in unfair labor practice proceedings. He received his JD from Northwestern University School of Law in 1987.

**BOWEN, Michael A**
Foley & Lardner LLP, Milwaukee
414 297 5538
mbowen@foley.com
*Recommended in Litigation*
**Career:** Michael A Bowen, a Partner in the Milwaukee office of Foley & Lardner LLP, is a member of the Distribution and Franchise and Appellate practices. He concentrates on commercial litigation and arbitration at both the trial and appellate levels. Dealer and distributor disputes play an important role in his practice. Other key practice areas include lender liability, constitutional challenges to land use regulation, and original appellate work. Mr Bowen received his JD Degree, cum laude, from Harvard Law School in 1976.

**BOYLE, James**
Boyle Fredrickson Newholm Stein & Gratz SC, Milwaukee
414 225 9755
*Recommended in Intellectual Property*

**BUONO, Kathryn M**
Quarles & Brady LLP, Milwaukee
414 277 5109
kbuono@quarles.com
*Recommended in Corporate/M&A*
**Practice Areas:** Corporate services, commercial financial services, corporate finance/securities, mergers & acquisitions, private equity/venture capital, project finance services.
**Prof. Memberships:** Milwaukee Bar Association; American Bar Association; State Bar of Wisconsin.
**Career:** Partner since 1995.
**Publications:** 'Antitrust Considerations in the M&A Context', presentation to the M&A Forum, February 2004; Panelist at 'Mergers & Acquisitions' seminar sponsored by Marsh, May 2001; 'Private Equity Investing from a Legal, Tax and Business Perspective', presentation at the Corporate Practice Institute, December 1997.
**Personal:** Marquette University (JD, 1986); University of Dayton (BS, 1983).

**BUSCH, John**
Michael Best & Friedrich LLP, Milwaukee
414 271 6560
*Recommended in Litigation*

**BUTLER, Brian**
Stafford Rosenbaum LLP, Madison
608 256 0226
*Recommended in Litigation*

**CARTER, Eugenia**
Whyte Hirschboeck Dudek S.C.,
Madison 608 255 4440
*Recommended in Intellectual Property*

**CHERNOF, Steve**
Godfrey & Kahn, SC, Milwaukee
414 273 3500
*Recommended in Real Estate*

**CHRISTIANSEN, Jon P**
Foley & Lardner LLP, Milwaukee
414 297 5557
jchristiansen@foley.com
*Recommended in Litigation*
**Career:** Jon P Christiansen is a Partner in the Milwaukee office of Foley & Lardner LLP. Mr Christiansen serves as the leader of the firm's Litigation Specialties Group, which includes the following litigation practice areas: antitrust, appellate, construction, distribution and franchise, energy litigation, insurance dispute resolution, family law, tax valuation and fiduciary, and product liability. Mr Christiansen is also a member of the Food Industry Team. His experience includes preliminary injunctions, trials, arbitrations and appeals throughout the United States in commercial and distribution cases. He was awarded his JD Degree in 1975 by Vanderbilt University.

**CLARK, James R**
Foley & Lardner LLP, Milwaukee
414 297 5543
jclark@foley.com
*Recommended in Litigation*

**Career:** James R Clark has over 30 years experience in civil litigation as a Partner in the Milwaukee office of Foley & Lardner LLP. He is a member of the Antitrust Practice. His areas of trial practice include negligence and product liability matters (including drug, medical devices, and toxic torts), professional malpractice defense, construction disputes, condemnation and other real estate litigation, trade secret and non-competition agreements, antitrust, securities, general contract, and other commercial disputes. He received his JD Degree from the University of Wisconsin.

**COFFEY, Peter**
Michael Best & Friedrich LLP, Milwaukee
414 271 6560
*Recommended in Corporate/M&A*

**CONWAY, Gregory**
Liebmann, Conway, Olejniczak & Jerry, S.C., Green Bay 920 437 0476
*Recommended in Litigation*

**CRONE, Tom**
Melli Walker Pease & Ruhly SC, Madison
608 257 4812
*Recommended in Employment*

**CROYSDALE, David**
Michael Best & Friedrich LLP, Milwaukee
414 271 6560
*Recommended in Employment*

**CURTIS, Charles G**
Heller Ehrman LLP, Madison
608 663 7480
charles.curtis@hellerehrman.com
*Recommended in Litigation*
**Practice Areas:** Appeals and strategy, intellectual property litigation, antitrust and trade regulation, consumer litigation.
**Career:** Mr Curtis has more than 20 years experience in counseling and litigating in a diversity of areas, including constitutional, administrative, antitrust, intellectual property, cable and telecommunications, environmental and natural resource, Native American treaty rights, and general commercial law. He specializes in the briefing of complex issues at the trial and appellate levels.
**Publications:** Editor-in-Chief, Volume 49, The University of Chicago Law Review.
**Personal:** The University of Chicago Law School (JD, 1982).

**DALTON, Larry**
Whyte Hirschboeck Dudek S.C.,
Milwaukee 414 273 2100
*Recommended in Real Estate*

**DANIELS JR, John W**
Quarles & Brady LLP, Milwaukee
414 277 5103
jwd@quarles.com
*Recommended in Real Estate*
**Practice Areas:** Real estate, corporate services, corporate finance/securities.
**Prof. Memberships:** National President, American College of Real Estate Lawyers

(1999-present); National Council, Real Property, Probate and Trust Law Section, (Member, 1981-84, 1990-95), (National Secretary 1996-97); State Bar of Wisconsin; Milwaukee Bar Association (Director); American Bar Association.
**Career:** Partner since 1981.
**Publications:** Editor: '1989 Wisconsin Real Estate Cases: Annual Compendium of Decisions', Quarles & Brady, 1990-97; Co-author: 'Real Estate and Economic Development', Quarles & Brady program, 1991.
**Personal:** Harvard University (JD, 1974); University of Wisconsin (MS, 1972); North Central College (BA, 1969).

**DAVIDSON, Bruce C**
Quarles & Brady LLP, Milwaukee
414 277 5115
bcd@quarles.com
*Recommended in Corporate/M&A*
**Practice Areas:** Corporate services, corporate finance/securities, mergers & acquisitions.
**Prof. Memberships:** Securities Law Committee, Society of Corporate Secretaries and Governance Professionals (formerly American Society of Corporate Secretaries), 1994-2001; past President of Milwaukee Chapter; Executive Committee of Milwaukee Chapter; Milwaukee Bar Association; American Bar Association (Business Law Section); State Bar of Wisconsin.
**Career:** Partner since 1977.
**Publications:** Quarles & Brady updates on a variety of corporate, corporate finance and securities law developments.
**Personal:** Harvard University (JD, 1970); Marist College (BA, 1966).

**DE BRUIN, David**
Michael Best & Friedrich LLP, Milwaukee
414 271 6560
*Recommended in Intellectual Property*

**DICKENS, John**
Godfrey & Kahn, SC, Milwaukee
414 273 3500
*Recommended in Corporate/M&A*

**DUFFY, Robert H**
Quarles & Brady LLP, Milwaukee
414 277 5647
rduffy@quarles.com
*Recommended in Employment*
**Practice Areas:** Labor and employment, litigation.
**Prof. Memberships:** American Bar Association, State Bar of Wisconsin, Milwaukee Bar Association (Member, Sections on Litigation and Labor Law), Eastern District of Wisconsin Bar Association. Co-ordinator: Quarles & Brady Milwaukee Office Labor and Employment Group (2001-present).
**Career:** Partner since 1991.
**Publications:** 'Does My Disabled Janitor Have to Mop Yet? 'Reasonable Accommodation' Challenges Facing Wisconsin Employers', SHRM 2004 WI State Con-

ference, 7 October 2004; 'Reasonable Accommodation Under the WFEA: A 2003 Update', Milwaukee Bar Association Continuing Education Program, 24 September 2003.
**Personal:** Marquette University (JD, 1984; BA, 1981).

## DWYER, Michael
Godfrey & Kahn, SC, Milwaukee
414 273 3500
*Recommended in Real Estate*

## EHRMANN, Mark T
Quarles & Brady LLP, Madison
608 283 2479
mehrmann@quarles.com
*Recommended in Corporate/M&A*
**Practice Areas:** Corporate services, mergers & acquisitions, private equity/venture capital.
**Prof. Memberships:** State Bar of Wisconsin; Milwaukee Bar Association; Dane County Bar Association, Chicago Bar Association, American Bar Association (Member, Sections on: Business Law and Health Law); Board of Directors of WIN Foundation of Milwaukee, Officer and Director of Badger Basketball Boosters, Inc.
**Career:** Partner since 1993.
**Personal:** University of Wisconsin (JD, 1985; BS,1982).

## FLORSHEIM, Richard S
Foley & Lardner LLP, Milwaukee
414 297 5515
rflorsheim@foley.com
*Recommended in Intellectual Property*
**Career:** Richard Florsheim is a Partner in the Milwaukee office Foley & Lardner LLP and is the firm's Industry Teams leader. He is also a member of the firm's Management Committee. Mr Florsheim is the former Chair of the firm's Intellectual Property Department, and is currently a member of the Intellectual Property Litigation Practice Group. His practice is devoted exclusively to the litigation and alternative dispute resolution of patent infringement disputes. He received his JD, magna cum laude (first in his class), from Marquette University Law School in 1974.

## FREDRICKSON, John
Boyle Fredrickson Newholm Stein & Gratz SC, Milwaukee
414 225 9755
*Recommended in Intellectual Property*

## GARMER III, Benjamin F
Foley & Lardner LLP, Milwaukee
414 297 5675
bgarmer@foley.com
*Recommended in Corporate/M&A*
**Career:** A Partner in the Milwaukee office of Foley & Lardner LLP, Benjamin F Garmer III is a member of the firm's Transactional and Securities Practice Group and Energy Industry Team. His practice focuses on acquisitions and financings for public and private companies and takeover defense. He has repre-

sented national underwriters, including CS First Boston, Merrill Lynch, and Goldman Sachs, as well as regional underwriters, Robert W Baird, William Blair and others, in financings and other matters. Mr Garmer received his JD, cum laude, from the University of Michigan Law School and an LLM in taxation from New York University.

## GOODKIND, Conrad G
Quarles & Brady LLP, Milwaukee
414 277 5305
cgg@quarles.com
*Recommended in Corporate/M&A*
**Practice Areas:** Corporate services, corporate finance/securities, mergers & acquisitions, private equity/venture capital, commercial financial services.
**Prof. Memberships:** American Bar Association; ABA Federal Regulation of Securities Committee and Subcommittee on Investment Companies and Investment Advisors; ABA State Regulation of Securities Committee; State Bar of Wisconsin Business Law Section; State Bar of Wisconsin Securities Law Committee.
**Career:** Partner since 1981.
**Publications:** Q&B Updates 2003: 'SEC Adopts New Form N-CSR and Related Certification Disclosure and Internal Control Requirements for Mutual Funds'; 'Proposed Rules for Mutual Fund Reports to Shareholders and Quarterly Disclosure'.
**Personal:** University of Wisconsin (JD, 1969; BS, 1966).

## HANSEN, Scott W
Reinhart Boerner Van Deuren sc, Milwaukee 414 298 8123
shansen@reinhartlaw.com
*Recommended in Litigation*
**Practice Areas:** Litigation: complex commercial; competition, distribution and franchise law.
**Prof. Memberships:** Wisconsin, federal and American Bar associations (Antitrust and Franchise sections); Inns of Court, Wisconsin Academy of Trial Lawyers.
**Career:** Litigation Chair; competition law: antitrust, distribution and franchising, trade secrets, unfair competition, and complex commercial disputes. Recent examples: summary judgment dismissing franchisee group's $200m encroachment claim; defense verdict dismissing $250m trade secret claim; summary judgment dismissing class action against public pension system; defense verdict dismissing wrongful termination claim by exclusive Mexican distributor. For sample reported cases, representative clients and more information, visit Mr Hansen's biography at reinhartlaw.com.

## HANSON, David G
Reinhart Boerner Van Deuren sc, Milwaukee 414 298 8324
dhanson@reinhartlaw.com
*Recommended in Intellectual Property*
**Practice Areas:** Litigation, intellectual

property.
**Prof. Memberships:** State Bar of Wisconsin, American Bar Association; United States District Courts for Eastern and Western Districts of Wisconsin; Northern District of Illinois; United States Courts of Appeals for the Federal and Seventh Circuits.
**Career:** Shareholder, leader of the firm's Intellectual Property Litigation Practice Group and is immediate past Chair of the Board of Directors for the Intellectual Property Section of the State Bar of Wisconsin. He is 'AV-rated', the highest quality rating from Martindale-Hubbell, and is recognized as a 2005 'Super Lawyer' by the Wisconsin Super Lawyers publication based on his degree of peer recognition and professional achievement. Adjunct Professor of Law, Marquette University Law School (Copyright Litigation and Trademark Litigation, 1997-2002). For more detailed information, including description of trial work and list of speeches and seminars, please see Mr Hanson's biography at reinhartlaw.com.

## HARTH, David J
Heller Ehrman LLP, Madison
608 663 7470
david.harth@hellerehrman.com
*Recommended in Intellectual Property*
**Practice Areas:** Intellectual property litigation, appeals and strategy.
**Career:** Mr Harth has more than 25 years of experience trying all types of cases, including patent, trademark and copyright, products liability, environmental damage, engineering and accounting malpractice, civil rights, public law, securities fraud, insurance and breach of contract actions. Mr Harth also has considerable experience arguing cases in the federal courts of appeal. For the past 10 years, Mr Harth has focused on intellectual property litigation, including several patent cases involving biotechnology and human genetics.
**Personal:** University of Wisconsin (JD, 1979).

## HATCH, Michael W
Foley & Lardner LLP, Milwaukee
414 297 5706
mhatch@foley.com
*Recommended in Real Estate*
**Career:** Michael W Hatch is a Partner with Foley & Lardner LLP. He is a member of the firm's Real Estate Practice Group, of which he previously served as Chair. Mr Hatch has been with the real estate group in the Milwaukee office since joining the firm in 1974, and he has practiced extensively in the areas of real estate development, finance, restructuring and workouts, brownfields and other urban redevelopment, public/private partnerships, syndication, historic rehabilitation, real estate investment trusts, and investment analysis. Mr Hatch is an honors graduate of Yale Law School.

## ISHIKAWA, Jesse
Reinhart Boerner Van Deuren sc, Madison 608 229 2208
jishikaw@reinhartlaw.com
*Recommended in Real Estate*
**Practice Areas:** Real estate.
**Prof. Memberships:** State Bar of Wisconsin; American College of Real Estate Lawyers.
**Career:** Shareholder and Managing Partner of the firm's Madison office, represents developers, lenders and businesses in real estate purchases, sales, commercial leasing transactions and land development transactions. He has represented developers in a number of tax incremental financing projects, including research parks, distribution centers and downtown developments. He was voted Madison's number one real estate lawyer in Madison Magazine's most recent poll of local attorneys.
**Personal:** Member, Board of Trustees of Madison Museum of Contemporary Art; former member, Madison Board of Parks Commissioners.

## JELENCIC, Sarah O
Foley & Lardner LLP, Milwaukee
414 297 5719
sjelencic@foley.com
*Recommended in Real Estate*
**Career:** Sarah O Jelencic is a Partner in the Real Estate Practice Group in the Milwaukee office of Foley & Lardner LLP. Ms Jelencic has experience in retail, office and multi-family development, including preparation and negotiation of joint venture agreements, leases and financing Milwaukee office documents, condominium and homeowners association documentation, declarations of covenants and restrictions (residential and commercial), acquisition and sales of real estate (developed and undeveloped), construction and architect agreements, leasing (landlord and tenant), management and leasing agreements, and workouts and tax-free exchanges. Ms Jelencic graduated magna cum laude from the University of Michigan Law School.

## JONES, Paul J
Foley & Lardner LLP, Milwaukee
414 297 5553
pjones@foley.com
*Recommended in Corporate/M&A*
**Career:** Paul J Jones is a Partner in the Milwaukee office of Foley & Lardner LLP. As a member of the Transactional and Securities Practice Group, Mr Jones practices corporate law, with an emphasis in mergers and acquisitions, corporate securities and general corporate matters. He has represented buyers and sellers in public and private mergers, acquisitions, dispositions and other strategic transactions, and both underwriters and corporate issuers in public offerings of debt and equity securities. He is also a member of the firm's Sports Industry Team. Mr

Jones received his JD, cum laude, from Georgetown University Law Center.

## JOST, Lawrence J
Quarles & Brady LLP, Milwaukee
414 277 5535
ljj@quarles.com
*Recommended in Real Estate*
**Practice Areas:** Real estate.
**Prof. Memberships:** American College of Real Estate Lawyers; State Chair and Fellow, American College of Mortgage Attorneys; Board of Directors, Wisconsin Chapter of National Association of Industrial and Office Properties; Urban Land Institute; Wisconsin State Bar (Real Property Section); American Bar Association (Real Property, Probate and Trust Law Section); Milwaukee Bar Association.
**Career:** Partner since 1976.
**Personal:** University of Wisconsin (JD, 1969; BS, 1968).

## KERN, David B
Quarles & Brady LLP, Milwaukee
414 277 5653
dbk@quarles.com
*Recommended in Employment*
**Practice Areas:** Labor and employment.
**Prof. Memberships:** State Bar of Wisconsin (Former Member, Board of Directors, Labor and Employment Law Section); American Bar Association (Labor Law Section; Committee on Development of the Law Under the National Labor Relations Act; Committee on Equal Employment Opportunity).
**Career:** Partner since 1986.
**Publications:** 'Employee Handbooks Must Be Carefully Written', Small Business Times, 2005; 'My Employees Can Get Away With What??? The Nature and Scope of Protected Activity Under the Law', Quarles & Brady Program, 2004.
**Personal:** University of Michigan (JD, 1979); Marquette University (BA, 1976).

## LEICHTLING, Ely A
Quarles & Brady LLP, Milwaukee
414 277 5681
eal@quarles.com
*Recommended in Employment*
**Practice Areas:** Labor and employment, litigation.
**Prof. Memberships:** Milwaukee Bar Association (Labor and Employment Section, Chair 1997-99, Vice-Chair 1995-97); American Bar Association (Member, Labor and Employment Law Section, 1979-present); State Bar of Wisconsin (Member, Labor Law Section, 1979-present); Human Resource Management Association of Southeastern Wisconsin, Inc.
**Career:** Partner since 1986.
**Personal:** University of Virginia (JD, 1979); Wesleyan University (BA, 1976).

## LEVIN, Benjamin D
Foley & Lardner LLP, Milwaukee
414 297 5715
blevin@foley.com
*Recommended in Real Estate*
**Career:** Benjamin D Levin is a Partner in the Milwaukee office of Foley & Lardner LLP. He is a member of the Real Estate Practice Group and represents municipalities, underwriters, and businesses in land acquisition, redevelopment, loan, and tax incremental finance transactions. His practice also encompasses annexation and financing via community and redevelopment area borrowing. Mr Levin graduated from Harvard Law School, cum laude, in 1990.

## LEVIN, Jim
Michael Best & Friedrich LLP, Milwaukee
414 271 6560
*Recommended in Real Estate*

## LEVINE, Jonathan
Michael Best & Friedrich LLP, Milwaukee
414 271 6560
*Recommended in Employment*

## LEVIT, William
Godfrey & Kahn, SC, Milwaukee
414 273 3500
*Recommended in Litigation*

## LINSTROTH, Tod
Michael Best & Friedrich LLP, Madison
608 257 3501
*Recommended in Corporate/M&A*

## LUNDGREN, K Thor
Michael Best & Friedrich LLP, Milwaukee
414 271 6560
*Recommended in Corporate/M&A*

## MARGOLIES, Jonathan
Michael Best & Friedrich LLP, Milwaukee
414 271 6560
*Recommended in Intellectual Property*

## MARSACK, Gary
Lindner & Marsack, SC, Milwaukee
414 273 3910
*Recommended in Employment*

## MCGRATH, Brian W
Foley & Lardner LLP, Milwaukee
414 297 5508
bmcgrath@foley.com
*Recommended in Litigation*
**Career:** Brian W McGrath is a Partner in the Milwaukee office of Foley & Lardner LLP, where he specializes in the area of dealership law and litigation. He is a member of the firm's Distribution and Franchise Practice Group and the Food and Automotive Industry Teams. Along with several other attorneys, Mr McGrath created a 50-state computerized database that has been trademarked as NationLink and which the firm uses to advise clients on a nationwide basis regarding the law relating to dealership terminations and related issues. He is a graduate of Harvard Law School.

## NINNEMAN, Mary Pat
Quarles & Brady LLP, Milwaukee
414 277 5153
mpn@quarles.com
*Recommended in Employment*
**Practice Areas:** Labor and employment, litigation.
**Prof. Memberships:** Milwaukee Bar Association (Lead Chair, Labor and Employment Section; past Chair, Judicial Selection Committee and former Member, Judicial Polling Committee and Joint Bench/Bar Committee); State Bar of Wisconsin; American Bar Association; International Association of Defense Counsel.
**Career:** Partner since 1983.
**Publications:** 'Mackenzie v. Miller Brewing Co. – Looking Forward', Quarles & Brady (2001); 'Wisconsin Employment Torts – Successful Defense Strategies', Quarles & Brady (2000).
**Personal:** Marquette University (JD, 1976); University of Illinois (BA, 1973).

## NOYES, Christopher
Godfrey & Kahn, SC, Milwaukee
414 273 3500
*Recommended in Corporate/M&A*

## OSTERMEYER, Michael J
Quarles & Brady LLP, Milwaukee
414 277 5521
mjo@quarles.com
*Recommended in Real Estate*
**Practice Areas:** Real estate, school.
**Prof. Memberships:** American Law Institute; American Bar Association; ABA Section of Real Property, Probate and Trust Law: Standing Committee on Publications (2004-present); Pro bono counsel to Milwaukee Habitat for Humanity, Inc. (1991-present); International Association of Attorneys and Executives in Corporate Real Estate; State Bar of Wisconsin.
**Career:** Partner since 1998.
**Publications:** 'Protect Your Rights and Remedies with Owner Default Clause', Commercial Tenant's Lease Insider (January 2005); 'A Primer on Remedies for Landlord Defaults', The Practical Real Estate Lawyer (May 2004).
**Personal:** Vanderbilt University (JD, 1989); University of Notre Dame (MA, 1984); Luther College (BA, 1983).

## PARSONS, W Stuart
Quarles & Brady LLP, Milwaukee
414 277 5657
wsp@quarles.com
*Recommended in Litigation*
**Practice Areas:** Litigation; commercial transactions litigation; antitrust and trade regulation litigation; financial institutions litigation; insurance coverage litigation; professional liability; securities litigation; antitrust, trade regulation and franchising.
**Prof. Memberships:** Fellow, American College of Trial Lawyers; Management Committee, Quarles & Brady (1987-93); Seventh Circuit Bar Association (President, 1997-99; Board of Governors, 1991-99); State Bar of Wisconsin.

**Career:** Partner since 1974.
**Publications:** Author: 'Civil Procedure', Annual Survey of Wisconsin Law 1984-90.
**Personal:** Harvard University (JD, 1967; BA, 1962).

## PENCE, Thomas C
Foley & Lardner LLP, Milwaukee
414 297 5809
tpence@foley.com
*Recommended in Employment*
**Career:** Thomas C Pence is a Partner in Milwaukee office of Foley & Lardner LLP and leader of the firm's Labor and Employment Practice Group. He handles employment litigation, labor arbitrations, and collective bargaining. Mr Pence counsels employers concerning all aspects of employment and labor law, including the ADA, the FMLA, and workplace harassment. He works with employers to develop problem prevention processes, training programs, and alternative dispute resolution programs. Mr Pence is a frequent speaker on employment and labor law topics. He received his Law Degree from Indiana University.

## PEPKE, Michael T
Reinhart Boerner Van Deuren sc, Milwaukee 414 298 8133
mpepke@reinhartlaw.com
*Recommended in Corporate/M&A*
**Practice Areas:** Business law.
**Prof. Memberships:** State Bars of Wisconsin and Colorado; Member of the Boards of Directors of Children's Service Society of Wisconsin, Inc.; Junior Achievement of Wisconsin, Inc.; Children's Hospital and Health Systems, Inc.; US Bank Championship.
**Career:** Michael Pepke advises businesses primarily with respect to mergers and acquisitions, raising capital and strategic and succession planning. He advises clients with respect to both legal and business matters, including banking relationships, customer and supplier relationship, manufacturing and distribution matters, employee and key executive relationships, executive compensation planning and owner relationships.

## PLOOR, Pamela M
Quarles & Brady LLP, Milwaukee
414 277 5661
pploor@quarles.com
*Recommended in Employment*
**Practice Areas:** Labor and employment.
**Career:** Partner since 2001.
**Publications:** Co-Author, 'When Applicants Apply Through the Internet', Employee Relations Law Journal, vol 30, no 2, 2004; 'Supreme Court Addresses Use of Race in Admissions', Sidebar (published by the Federal Litigation Section of the Federal Bar Association) 2003; 'FMLA Update 2002-03' (MRA's Society of Human Resource Professionals: 6 March 2003; 'How to Write an Electronic Com-

munication System Policy', (HRMA Employment Practices Committee E-Practices Program: 15 May 2002. **Personal:** Harvard University (JD, 1993); University of California, Los Angeles (BA, 1989.)

### PUCHNER, Joseph E
Quarles & Brady LLP, Milwaukee
414 277 5533
jpuchner@quarles.com
*Recommended in Real Estate*
**Practice Areas:** Real estate, international business, immigration.
**Prof. Memberships:** State Bar of California; State Bar of Wisconsin (International Section Board Member); International Young Lawyers Association (Prix des Anciens Presidents, 1994); American Immigration Lawyers Association.
**Career:** Partner since 1999.
**Personal:** Stanford University (JD, 1986); Marquette University (BA, 1983).

### QUICK, Patrick G
Foley & Lardner LLP, Milwaukee
414 297 5678
pgquick@foley.com
*Recommended in Corporate/M&A*
**Career:** Patrick G Quick is a Partner in the Milwaukee office of Foley & Lardner LLP. He is a member of the firm's Transactional and Securities Practice Group and Sports Industry Team. Mr Quick practices corporate law, with an emphasis in securities law compliance, acquisitions, and takeover defense. He participates in many complex acquisition transactions, representing both buying and selling parties, and assists clients doing advance takeover preparedness planning, including those who have received unsolicited takeover proposals or similar overtures. Mr Quick graduated, magna cum laude, from the University of Michigan Law School in 1984.

### ROBISON, John
Quarles & Brady LLP, Madison
608 283 2653
jsr@quarles.com
*Recommended in Corporate/M&A*
**Practice Areas:** Corporate services, corporate finance/securities, mergers & acquisitions, private equity/venture capital, tax, health.
**Prof. Memberships:** State Bar of Wisconsin (Business, Health and Taxation Sections); American Bar Association (Business Law, Health Law and Taxation Sections); Dane County Bar Association; Downtown Madison, Inc. (Board Member, 2001-present).
**Career:** Partner since 1986.
**Personal:** University of Illinois (JD, 1978); University of Michigan (AB, 1974).

### ROTHMAN, Jay O
Foley & Lardner LLP, Milwaukee
414 297 5644
jrothman@foley.com
*Recommended in Corporate/M&A*
**Career:** Jay O Rothman is a Partner in Milwaukee office of Foley & Lardner LLP and a member of the firm's Management Committee. Mr Rothman serves as the leader of the firm's national Transactional & Securities Practice Group and practices primarily in the areas of mergers and acquisitions, securities law, takeover defense, and general corporate and business law. He has structured and negotiated numerous acquisition transactions in various industries and has represented both underwriters and corporate issuers in various public offerings of both debt and equity securities. He graduated, cum laude, from Harvard Law School in 1985.

### ROTHSTEIN, John A
Quarles & Brady LLP, Milwaukee
414 277 5351
jar@quarles.com
*Recommended in Litigation*
**Practice Areas:** Litigation; commercial transactions litigation; construction litigation; insurance coverage Litigation; product liability, toxic tort litigation; real estate, land use and condemnation litigation; trade secrets and unfair competition litigation; financial institutions litigation; intellectual property and technology litigation; professional liability; securities litigation; real estate.
**Prof. Memberships:** State Bar of Wisconsin (Section on Litigation); American Bar Association (Section on Litigation); Milwaukee Bar Association.
**Career:** Partner since 1986.
**Publications:** 'New Directions in Federal Civil Practice and Procedure' (Seminar ALI/ABA, 1996).
**Personal:** Marquette University (JD, 1979; BA, 1976).

### RYAN, Patrick M
Quarles & Brady LLP, Milwaukee
414 277 5181
pmr@quarles.com
*Recommended in Corporate/M&A*
**Practice Areas:** Corporate services, mergers and acquisitions, private equity/venture capital, commercial financial services, financial institutions.
**Prof. Memberships:** Milwaukee and American Bar Associations; State Bar of Wisconsin.
**Career:** Partner since 1976. Chair and Managing Partner of Quarles & Brady LLP.
**Personal:** Marquette University (JD, 1969); St Mary's College (BA, 1966).

### RYBA, Russell E
Foley & Lardner LLP, Milwaukee
414 297 5668
rryba@foley.com
*Recommended in Corporate/M&A*
**Career:** Russell E Ryba is a Partner in the

Milwaukee office of Foley & Lardner LLP and is a member of the Transactional and Securities Practice Group and Energy Industry Team. He practices in the areas of mergers, acquisitions, divestitures, tender offers and venture capital transactions; public and private offerings of debt and equity securities; public company compliance with federal and state securities laws and reporting requirements; joint ventures and strategic alliances; general corporate matters and counseling; and assisting in the organization, development, and financing of startup and development stage companies. Mr Ryba graduated from Duke University School of Law.

### SAMMONS, Barry E
Quarles & Brady LLP, Milwaukee
414 277 5705
bes@quarles.com
*Recommended in Intellectual Property*
**Practice Areas:** Intellectual property.
**Prof. Memberships:** State Bar of Wisconsin; Wisconsin Intellectual Property Law Association; American Intellectual Property Law Association.
**Career:** Partner since 1976.
**Personal:** University of Michigan (JD, 1969; BS, 1965).

### SCRIVNER, Tom
Michael Best & Friedrich LLP, Milwaukee
414 271 6560
*Recommended in Employment*

### SCULLEN, Sean M
Quarles & Brady LLP, Milwaukee
414 277 5421
ss8@quarles.com
*Recommended in Employment*
**Practice Areas:** Labor and employment, litigation.
**Prof. Memberships:** State Bar of Wisconsin (Labor and Employment Section); American Bar Association (Labor and Employment Section). Thomas Fairchild American Inns of Court. Member, HRMA.
**Career:** Associate. Joined Quarles & Brady 1999.
**Publications:** 'Wage/Hour Law Compliance Update', August 2005; 'What Do You Mean I Owe My Lead Worker Overtime?', May 2005; 'E-mails to the Human Resources Department Are Subject to Discovery; They Are Not Privileged', Human Resource Management Associates of Southeastern Wisconsin Newsletter, April 2005; 'Public Sector Wage and Hour Compliance', December 2004.
**Personal:** University of Wisconsin (JD, 1999); Santa Clara University (BS, 1994).

### SENNETT, Nancy J
Foley & Lardner LLP, Milwaukee
414 297 5522
nsennett@foley.com
*Recommended in Litigation*
**Career:** Nancy J Sennett is Managing Partner of the Milwaukee office of Foley

& Lardner LLP. A member of the firm's Management Committee, she also chaired the firm's Strategic Planning Committee. Ms Sennett is a member, founder and first Chair of the Securities Litigation, Enforcement and Regulation Practice Group. She is also a member of the International Industry Team. Ms Sennett's practice includes all aspects of commercial and business litigation. Her practice is focused on securities litigation representing corporations, boards of directors, broker-dealers, investment advisers, law firms and individuals in private securities litigation. She received her JD from Northwestern University.

### SHRINER JR, Thomas L
Foley & Lardner LLP, Milwaukee
414 297 5601
tshriner@foley.com
*Recommended in Litigation*
**Career:** Thomas L Shriner Jr is a Partner in the Milwaukee office of Foley & Lardner LLP. He is a member of the firm's Business Reorganizations, General Commercial Litigation and Appellate Practice Groups. Mr Shriner concentrates his practice in commercial and public law litigation and has an extensive appellate practice in both state and federal courts. He also has substantial experience in the bankruptcy courts and regularly speaks on creditor-debtor law subjects. Mr Shriner's expertise includes disputes over business acquisitions and shareholder disputes. He is a graduate of Indiana University (JD, magna cum laude, 1972).

### SIMS, Luke E
Foley & Lardner LLP, Milwaukee
414 297 5680
lsims@foley.com
*Recommended in Corporate/M&A*
**Career:** Luke E Sims, a Partner in the Milwaukee office of Foley & Lardner LLP, is a member of the firm's Transactional and Securities Practice Group. He is a corporate lawyer with concentrations in acquisitions, leveraged buyouts, and securities law matters. He has extensive experience in all aspects of mergers and acquisitions (and particularly leveraged buyouts), including structuring, negotiating and financing acquisitions and dispositions of private and publicly held companies. He is a frequent lecturer and author on acquisitions, leveraged buyouts, and public offerings. Mr Sims received his JD from Georgetown University in 1976.

### SKILTON, John
Heller Ehrman LLP, Madison
608 663 7474
john.skilton@hellerehrman.com
*Recommended in Litigation*
**Practice Areas:** Intellectual property litigation, patents and trademarks, antitrust and trade regulation, appeals and strategy.
**Career:** In the past 15 years Mr Skilton has concentrated his practice in patent litigation. Mr Skilton has managed com-

plex commercial, antitrust, patent and intellectual property, dealer and distribution, contract, product liability, and constitutional disputes. He has tried more than 30 cases, and has argued more than 20 appeals in state and federal courts around the country.

**Publications:** Articles editor, Wisconsin Law Review.

**Personal:** University of Wisconsin Law School (JD, 1969).

## SKINDRUD, Michael
Godfrey & Kahn, SC, Milwaukee
414 273 3500
*Recommended in Corporate/M&A*

## SOLVESON, George
Andrus, Sceales, Starke & Sawall LLP, Milwaukee 414 271 7590
*Recommended in Intellectual Property*

## SOMMERHAUSER, Peter
Godfrey & Kahn, SC, Milwaukee
414 273 3500
*Recommended in Corporate/M&A*

## STEVENS, Charles
Michael Best & Friedrich LLP, Milwaukee
414 271 6560
*Recommended in Employment*

## TEMKIN, Harvey L
Reinhart Boerner Van Deuren sc, Madison 608 229 2210
htemkin@reinhartlaw.com
*Recommended in Real Estate*

**Practice Areas:** Real estate.

**Prof. Memberships:** American College of Real Estate Lawyers (head of its Title Insurance Coverage Subcommittee); American Bar Association; State Bar of Wisconsin.

**Career:** Shareholder in the firm's Madison office, represents real estate developers and lenders, business clients and healthcare providers since 1978. Areas of concentration include acquisitions, sales, zoning, land division and development, leasing, real estate litigation, commercial finance, business organizations and tax deferred exchanges. Frequently named one of the top real estate lawyers in Madison Magazine's survey of Madison lawyers.

**Personal:** A former law professor, Harvey still enjoys teaching at real estate programs throughout the country.

## TROUPIS, James
Michael Best & Friedrich LLP, Madison
608 257 3501
*Recommended in Litigation*

## TYSON JR, Joseph B
Foley & Lardner LLP, Milwaukee
414 297 5631
jtyson@foley.com
*Recommended in Corporate/M&A*

**Career:** Joseph B Tyson Jr is a Partner in Milwaukee office of Foley & Lardner LLP and Chairman of the Business Law Department. He is a member of the Transactional and Securities, Finance and Financial Institutions, Commercial Transactions and Business Counseling, and Private Equity and Venture Capital Practice Groups. His practice focuses on acquisitions, financing for public and private companies, Uniform Commercial Code matters, and general corporate law. He has over 20 years experience in dealing with the legal issues involving mergers, financing transactions, and business needs. He received his JD Degree from the University of Virginia.

## VETTER, Mark
Davis & Kuelthau, SC, Milwaukee
414 276 0200
*Recommended in Employment*

## WAHL, Nicholas
Godfrey & Kahn, SC, Milwaukee
414 273 3500
*Recommended in Corporate/M&A*

## WALSH, David G
Foley & Lardner LLP, Madison
608 258 4269
dwalsh@foley.com
*Recommended in Corporate/M&A*

**Career:** David G Walsh is a Partner with Foley & Lardner LLP and former Managing Partner of the Madison office. Mr Walsh is a member of the firm's Public Affairs and Government Procurement Practice Group and the Sports Industry Team. He has represented communications entities for over 30 years, developing particular skill in cable television and telecommunications law. Mr Walsh also counsels and represents business clients in all phases of business activity including the restructuring of reorganized entities. His JD Degree was conferred in 1970 by Harvard Law School.

## ZABROWSKI, Patrick M
Foley & Lardner LLP, Milwaukee
414 297 5716
pzabrowski@foley.com
*Recommended in Real Estate*

**Career:** Patrick M Zabrowski, a Partner in the Milwaukee office of Foley & Lardner LLP, has experience in a broad spectrum of real estate matters, such as purchase and sale transactions, construction and development of real estate projects, mortgage loan transactions and commercial leasing matters. He is a member of the firm's Real Estate Practice Group and Energy Industry Team. Mr Zabrowski has developed expertise in title insurance-related legal matters. He received his JD from the University of Wisconsin.

# FOLEY & LARDNER LLP

## THE FIRM

**Chairman & Chief Executive Officer:** Ralf-Reinhard Böer
**Number of partners:** 478
**Number of associates:** 336
**Number of senior counsel:** 90
**Number of special counsel:** 35
**Number of counsel:** 17
**Total number of attorneys:** 956
**Total number of support staff:** 1417
**Website:** www.foley.com

**FIRM OVERVIEW:** For over 160 years, Foley has delivered legal services focused on meeting their clients' business objectives with integrity, insight, and innovation. The firm is a strong and reliable business partner with a culture dedicated to understanding industry issues, government policies, and client goals. This philosophy has led the firm through tremendous growth, and today the firm has emerged as a highly regarded firm with offices across the United States. With more than 60 practice areas encompassing the full range of corporate legal services, their attorneys understand today's most complex business issues. The firm's wealth of experience and knowledge is leveraged to serve their diverse client base, ranging from global multinationals to small entrepreneurial companies.

## MAIN AREAS OF PRACTICE:

**Business Law:** Foley's business lawyers are knowledgeable and experienced in assisting clients with legal issues, bringing solid business judgment to every situation. Since Foley's founding in 1842, business advice and ideas have been mainstays of their service. Business judgment in concert with legal judgment enhances their ability to help you achieve your objectives. The firm's clients range from investment banks and *Fortune* 100 companies to entrepreneurs and emerging growth companies as well as the small and middle market companies in between.

**Litigation:** Foley understands the business side of the challenges and risks posed by potential and actual lawsuits, and has the skills and experience to win cases. With approximately 400 practicing litigators nationwide, the firm has one of the largest and most comprehensive litigation departments in the country. The firm's Litigation Department applies business insight during disputes to reduce client risk. Their attorneys leverage multiple tools and strategies, ranging from jury trials to alternative dispute resolution methods to deliver results that are favorable to their clients. To counsel is a key fundamental in their approach, but to achieve their clients' business goals is the critical component in their strategy.

**Intellectual Property:** In surveys by *IP Law & Business*, Foley ranked among the top five patent litigation firms in the United States (2005), as the number one go-to firm for intellectual property (IP) matters for the *Fortune* Global 100 (2002), and among the top go-to firms for IP counsel in the United States (2003, 2004). With over 150 lawyers, Foley's IP Department delivers an innovative life cycle of IP services to obtain, protect, and add value to their clients' IP. The firm secures high-quality patents, trademarks, and copyrights; provide product clearance opinions; conduct licensing programs; and handle the IP due diligence for corporate transactions. And when and if their clients must litigate to enforce or defend their IP rights, they can call upon their experienced IP trial lawyers who have handled hundreds of patent and IP litigation matters.

**Industry Teams:** Foley's unique industry-focused approach enables them to blend hands-on industry experience with sophisticated legal skills to provide their clients with the most significantly enhanced value-added service. The firm's industry teams include attorneys and related practitioners who have served as industry executives within corporations, associations, and regulatory agencies, among others — many of whom are viewed as industry pioneers and sought out as experts. These teams represent a range of service offerings, enabling them to take a comprehensive view of their clients' industries and bring together the right practitioners and competencies to address their needs. Industries represented include automotive, emerging technologies, energy, entertainment and media, food, golf and resort services, healthcare, insurance, life sciences, nanotechnology, and sports

## US OFFICES

Boston, Chicago, Detroit, Jacksonville, Los Angeles, Madison, Milwaukee, New York, Orlando, Sacramento, San Diego, San Diego/Del Mar, San Francisco, Silicon Valley, Tallahassee, Tampa, Washington, DC

## INTERNATIONAL OFFICES

Brussels, Belgium; Tokyo, Japan.

## CONTACTS

### INDUSTRY TEAMS

| | |
|---|---|
| **Automotive** | Steven H Hilfinger and John R Trentacosta |
| **Emerging Technologies** | Susan E Pravda |
| **Energy Industry** | Allen W Williams, Jr |
| **Entertainment & Media** | James D Nguyen and Miriam Claire Beezy |
| **Food** | Michael D Flanagan |
| **Golf & Resort Services** | Fred S Ridley and Van A Tengberg |
| **Healthcare Industry** | J Mark Waxman |
| **Insurance Industry** | Kevin G Fitzgerald |
| **Life Sciences** | Stephen A Bent, Gabor Garai |
| | David L Rosen and Michael R Scarano, Jr |
| **Nanotechnology** | Stephen B Maebius |
| **Sports** | Mary K Braza |

### LEGAL PRACTICES

| | |
|---|---|
| **Biotechnology & Pharmaceuticals** | Michelle M Simkin |
| **Business Law** | Joseph B Tyson, Jr |
| **Business Reorganizations** | Michael J Small |
| **Chemical & Pharmaceuticals** | Richard C Peet |
| **Commercial Transactions & Business Counseling** | Stephen A Crane |
| **Consumer & Industrial Products** | James G Morrow |
| **E-Business & Information Technology** | James R Kalyvas |
| **Electronics** | Pavan K Agarwal |
| **Finance & Financial Services** | James T Tynion, III |
| **General Commercial Litigation** | Jon M Wilson |
| **Intellectual Property** | Sharon R Barner |
| **IP Litigation** | Larry L Shatzer |
| **Labor & Employment** | Thomas C Pence |
| **Litigation** | Jon M Wilson |
| **Private Equity & Venture Capital** | Gabor Garai |
| **Public Affairs & Government Procurement** | George W Ash |
| **Real Estate** | Elizabeth L Corey |
| **Securities Litigation** | Gregory S Bruch |
| **Tax & Individual Planning** | David W Reinecke |
| **Trademark & Copyright** | Miriam Claire Beezy |
| **Transactional & Securities** | Jay O Rothman |
| **White Collar Defense & Corporate Compliance** | Sharie A Brown |

**Award Winning Technology Trendsetter:** The firm is exceedingly proud of their commitment to innovation and technology, which has earned the firm accolades from industry experts. For instance, in 2001, 2002, 2004 and 2005 *CIO* magazine recognized the firm as one of 100 global companies demonstrating innovation in improving products, services, and relationships with clients. As well, Foley was named to BTI Consulting Group's 2003 Tech-Savvy Team for providing "technological prowess" in serving their clients. In October 2004, Foley was awarded a Legal IT Award, given annually by *Legal IT* magazine. The publication honors law firms worldwide for exceptional strategic vision and innovation in information technology initiatives. *CIO* Magazine named Foley the 2005 recipient of the CIO Enterprise Value Award in the management services category for the development of cutting-edge information technology capabilities in response to the needs of their clients.

**FOLEY & LARDNER LLP**

# MICHAEL BEST & FRIEDRICH LLP

## THE FIRM

**Managing Partner:** Thomas E Obenberger
**Chair of the Management Committee:** David A Krutz
**Number of partners:** 155
**Number of attorneys:** 260
**Website:** www.michaelbest.com

**FIRM OVERVIEW:** Michael Best & Friedrich LLP was founded in 1848. Clients range in size from one-person start-up ventures to Fortune 500 companies. As a broad-based business law firm, Michael Best is able to offer the experience needed to handle a complete range of business legal matters.

## MAIN AREAS OF PRACTICE:

**Corporate & Business Law:** Corporate and business law is a core competency of the firm. The range of services involves individuals, partnerships, limited liability companies and corporations and includes assisting in the organization, financing and operation of business ventures, through and including mergers, acquisitions, divestitures and joint ventures. Experience in corporate finance has resulted in representation of venture capital investors through the firm's VentureBest Group, mezzanine lenders, and start-up and later-phase companies in all facets of business, including distribution, manufacturing and emerging technology.

**Employment Law:** Michael Best's 50 labor and employment attorneys and professionals work on the leading edge of labor and employment law, representing some of the most innovative and ground breaking businesses, public sector, and non-profit organizations in the nation. The attorneys continually strive to develop close partnerships with clients, focusing on litigation prevention and the achievement of strategic objectives through human resources counseling, planning, and training in order to cultivate the client's superior labor force. The attorneys are recognized by their clients and peers as among the best and most respected management-side labor, employment, and employee benefits attorneys in the Midwest, providing legal defense in all aspects of labor and employment litigation; union organizing, collective bargaining, and grievance arbitration; wage-hour issues; safety and workers compensation; employee benefits; and immigration. They have decades of experience practicing in state and federal trial courts, appellate and Supreme courts, administrative agencies and arbitrators, and designing compensation, retirement, pension, stock, and health plans.

**Healthcare:** Michael Best's Healthcare Practice Group has earned a national reputation for its healthcare practice. Michael Best provides counsel to a wide variety of healthcare clients, including hospitals and health systems, academic medical centers, physician groups, clinical laboratories, skilled nursing facilities, community residential facilities, home health agencies, hospices, health maintenance organizations, health insurance carriers, healthcare associations, and pharmaceutical and medical device manufacturers. Services provided for clients range from acting as general counsel for health systems, to representing healthcare providers in complex transactional, regulatory and litigation matters.

**Intellectual Property Law & IP Litigation:** Michael Best has one of the nation's leading intellectual property practices. Nearly 100 professionals offer a complete range of services to clients throughout the nation and around the world. Michael Best offers legal and technical experience in areas such as patent, trademark and copyright prosecution and counseling; all types of intellectual property litigation; internet and e-commerce; technology transfer and joint venture agreements; computer software and system acquisition agreements; M&A due diligence; and trade secrets. Nationally, the firm ranks high among the top trademark law firms, and among the top intellectual property litigation practice groups. When clients choose litigation as the right strategy for a given situation, the firm offers them a roster of experienced litigators whose practices are dedicated to intellectual property. Michael Best was recently ranked by IP Worldwide as one of the top IP defense firms in the nation. In addition, IP Law & Business, which ranks law firms by those who filed the most IP suits, placed Michael Best among the nation's top 25 law firms.

**Land & Resources:** The attorneys in Michael Best's Land and Resources Group practice in all areas of environmental, construction, development and real estate law, serving property owners, developers, all types of manufacturers and industrial operations, public utilities, construction and agribusiness companies.

**Litigation:** Michael Best's Litigation Practice Group has an unmatched depth of experience and success with more than 150 published cases at every level of State and Federal Courts in the recent years. Its members include a host of former judicial law clerks, law review editors, a former Wisconsin Supreme Court Justice and board members and officers of local, state and national bar associations. The attorneys have been consistently honored by publications as among the best counsel in their fields. More than 70 members strong, Michael Best is equipped to provide clients with first class representation in any type of litigation.

**Tax Law:** Michael Best's Tax Group is comprised of some of the most prominent practitioners in the Midwest. Attorneys include former trial lawyers with the Tax Division of the US Department of Justice, the former chairperson of the Wisconsin Tax Appeals Commission, and a founding member of the American Property Tax Counsel. In the tax planning area, attorneys advise organizations with respect to the federal, state and international tax aspects of structuring acquisitions, reorganizations, real estate developments, exchanges and related transactions. In the tax controversy area, members of the group appear regularly in federal and state trial and appellate courts, litigating all aspects of income taxes, excise taxes, sales and use taxes and property taxes. The firm's tax attorneys teach and write frequently on a wide variety of tax subjects. One of the group's publications is 'The Complete Guide to Wisconsin Sales and Use Taxes,' a 350-page treatise that is widely considered the definitive work on the subject.

**Wealth Plannng Services:** Michael Best provides high quality, cost effective and innovative services regarding business succession planning, financial planning, asset protection planning, retirement planning, estate litigation and family counseling. The attorneys in this group consult with clients to determine short-term and long-term objectives regarding asset protection and management, minimization of taxes and disposition of wealth.

**INTERNATIONAL WORK:** Through various international legal alliances, Michael Best has the ability to bring global resources to clients. Michael Best is the exclusive Wisconsin member of Lex Mundi ('Law of the World'), enabling the firm to arrange effective representation for clients around the world. The China Alliance is a unique arrangement allowing the member firms to enhance their ability to serve the needs of clients in the rapidly developing China market.

# QUARLES & BRADY LLP

## THE FIRM

**Managing Partner:** Patrick M Ryan
**Number of partners:** 259
**Number of other lawyers:** 151

**FIRM OVERVIEW:** Quarles & Brady LLP provides broad-based, national-level legal services through a strong network of regional practices and local offices. In the firm's more than 100 year history, it has grown from a small, well-respected local Milwaukee law firm to a place among the Am Law 200, building a national practice and earning a comparable reputation throughout the United States. The firm's lawyers (more than 400) practice from offices in Chicago, Illinois; Madison and Milwaukee, Wisconsin; Naples, Florida; and Phoenix and Tucson, Arizona. Through all the changes, one attribute has remained constant: Quarles & Brady brings a common-sense, solution-oriented approach to its clients' complicated legal problems. The firm's success has been based on the strength of its client relationships. It is the firm's philosophy that it has reached its goals only when their clients' objectives have been met and exceeded.

## MAIN AREAS OF PRACTICE:

**Business Law:** The Business Law Group at Quarles & Brady is composed of teams of experienced attorneys with deep knowledge of a multitude of business and transactional areas such as antitrust and trade regulation, bankruptcy, e-commerce, immigration, labor and employment, mergers and acquisitions and project finance services. While these attorneys are well versed in business law as a whole, each core member also has specific industry knowledge, enabling them to assign attorneys to client matters in a way that maximizes success.

**Intellectual Property:** The Intellectual Property Law Group of Quarles & Brady encompasses some of the best legal minds available, many of whom are highly trained scientists and engineers. The firm's IP attorneys have decades of experience in tackling every sort of patent, copyright, trademark and trade secret issue, as well as IP litigation. The firm's attorneys include former in-house counsel with experience in negotiating major technology agreements and managing global technology licensing and distribution programs.

**Litigation:** The seasoned attorneys of Quarles & Brady's Litigation Group have the legal knowledge and national experience to help clients, as plaintiffs or defendants, determine their objectives, identify appropriate options and pursue positive results with all of the tools and knowledge at their disposal. The firm's skilled litigation attorneys have the judgment, experience and resources to make candid assessments of their various clients' circumstances and needs, to recommend appropriate courses of action and to maximize every opportunity for successful results.

**Real Estate:** Quarles & Brady's Real Estate Group understands that, just as no two real estate transactions are alike, their clients come to the negotiating table from many different perspectives. Quarles & Brady is dedicated to providing responsive and pragmatic solutions that meet real-world needs, working side-by-side with their clients to better understand their unique challenges and opportunities.

**Regulated Business:** Quarles & Brady's Regulated Business Group has extensive experience in handling issues that arise in the electric power, financial institution, gas distribution, health and telecommunication industries. Additionally, be it environmental, government relations, or school law, Quarles & Brady possesses the depth and breadth of legal knowledge to provide their clients with efficient solutions to increasingly complex legal problems.

**Tax & Personal Services:** The Tax and Personal Service Group of Quarles & Brady are sophisticated, experienced attorneys with an extensive history of providing effective legal counsel to high-net-worth individuals and their families in the areas of estate planning, and family and domestic relations. Furthermore, their attorneys encompass all areas of federal, state and local taxation. The firm works with clients to clarify their own unique circumstances and help set a finan-

### HEAD OFFICE

**WISCONSIN**
411 East Wisconsin Avenue, Suite 2040, **Milwaukee**, 53202-4497
**Tel:** 414 277 5000   **Fax:** 414 271 3552
**Website:** www.quarles.com

### OTHER OFFICES

**ARIZONA**
One Renaissance Square, Two North Central Avenue,
**Phoenix**, 85004-2391
**Tel:** 602 229 5200   **Fax** 602 229 5690

One South Church Avenue, Suite 1700, **Tucson**, 85701-1621
**Tel:** 520 770 8700   **Fax:** 520 623 2418

**FLORIDA**
1395 Panther Lane, Suite 300, **Naples**, 34109-7874
**Tel:** 239 262 5959   **Fax:** 239 434 4999

**ILLINOIS**
Citicorp Center, 500 West Madison Street, Suite 3700,
**Chicago**, 60661-2511
**Tel:** 312 715 5000   **Fax:** 312 715 5155

**WISCONSIN**
One South Pinckney Street, Suite 600, **Madison**, 53702-2808
**Tel:** 608 251 5000   **Fax:** 608 251 9166

### CONTACTS

| | |
|---|---|
| **Bankruptcy** | John J Dawson |
| **Commercial Litigation** | Eric J Van Vugt |
| **Corporate Services** | Michael H Lappin |
| **Employee Benefits** | J Paul Jacobson |
| **Environmental** | Michael S McCauley |
| **Financial Institutions** | James D Friedman |
| **Government Relations** | Anthony H Driessen |
| **Hospital & Health** | Roger N Morris |
| **Indian Law** | James K LeValley |
| **Intellectual Property** | Barry E Sammons |
| **International/Immigration** | Joseph E Puchner |
| **Labor & Employment** | David B Kern |
| **Product Liability** | Patrick W Schmidt |
| **Public Finance** | Julianna Ebert |
| **Real Estate & Land Use** | Lawrence J Jost |
| **School Law** | Gary M Ruesch |
| **Taxation** | David D Wilmoth |
| **Tax-Exempt Organizations** | Janice E Rodgers |
| **Trust & Estates** | Kathleen A Gray |
| **White Collar Criminal & Governmental Investigations** | Edward F Novak |

cial and legal course that enables individuals and families to more effectively direct their own futures via the firm's deep personal commitment to obtaining the best possible result for their clients. Whether in trial, negotiating a settlement or addressing the wealth preservation needs of clients, the firm's attorneys and their colleagues at Quarles & Brady bring a depth of creativity and understanding unmatched elsewhere.

# REINHART BOERNER VAN DEUREN S.C.

## THE FIRM

**Chairman Emeritus:** Robert E Bellin
**Chairman, President & Chief Executive Officer:** Richard W Graber
**Number of partners:** 112
**Number of associates:** 84
**Total number of attorneys:** 201
**Total number of support staff:** 234

**FIRM OVERVIEW:** Reinhart Boerner Van Deuren s.c. serves business needs with innovation, focus and commitment. The firm's attorneys are dedicated to providing service efficiently and cost-effectively throughout their offices in Milwaukee, Madison and Waukesha, Wisconsin and Rockford, Illinois. Founded in 1894, the firm's total commitment to clients and to innovation has allowed it to grow to over 200 attorneys. Reinhart serves as attorneys and business counselors to public and privately held corporations, financial institutions, family-owned businesses, retirement plans, exempt organizations and individuals.

## MAIN AREAS OF PRACTICE:

**Banking & Finance:** Reinhart's Banking and Finance Department brings projects to life. The firm's attorneys go beyond counseling banks and financial institutions on state and federal regulatory compliance. It also brings together lenders and borrowers to meet the needs of business or help municipalities finance memorable projects.

**Bankruptcy & Creditors' Rights:** Reinhart's Bankruptcy Department has taken the lead role in virtually every major bankruptcy in Milwaukee and throughout Wisconsin. Representing debtors, creditors, trustees or creditors' committees, its attorneys have produced exceptional outcomes in an area where good results don't come easily.

**Business Law:** The firm's staff of more than 40 professionals tailors innovative solutions to the complex needs of corporate clients. Partnered with in-house counsel, they create a team with the depth and experience to tackle any issue cost efficiently and effectively.

**Employment Benefits:** Highly respected, Reinhart's Employee Benefits Department is one of the largest in the country with clients in almost every state .As one of the first law firms to represent employee benefit plans more than 40 years ago, Reinhart is large enough to offer clients the advantage of working with sub-specialists in every field as employee benefits laws expand.

**Environment Law:** Reinhart's environmental attorneys aren't just experts in the law, they're experts in science, too. With credentials in a number of scientific and technical fields, Reinhart's Environmental Law Department provides one-stop shopping for resolution of environmental problems.

**Estate Planning:** Because the only certainties in life are death and taxes, Reinhart's Estate Planning Department helps clients preserve wealth when it passes to the next generation. Many of Wisconsin's most successful family-owned businesses rely on Reinhart estate planning attorneys for tax planning and estate/trust administration.

**Government Relations:** Reinhart's Government Relations Department is unique in its ability to get attention on both sides of the aisle. Its attorneys include the chairman of the Wisconsin Republican Party as well as a long-time activist for Wisconsin Democrats.

**Healthcare:** With several attorneys who have worked inside the healthcare system, Reinhart's Healthcare Department offers experience unmatched by any other law firm in Wisconsin. Its attorneys understand first-hand the intricate network of legal relationships that bind patients, physicians, hospitals, and third party payers.

**Intellectual Property:** Reinhart's Intellectual Property Department understands how businesses maintain a competitive edge. The firms IP attorneys identify, establish, expand, and enforce intellectual property portfolios domestically and internationally. Often in conjunction with the Litigation and Business Law Departments, Reinhart's IP attorneys make sure clients have all the tools they need to compete.

## HEAD OFFICE

**WISCONSIN**
1000 North Water Street Suite 2100, **Milwaukee** WI 53202
**Tel:** 414 298 1000   **Fax:** 414 298 8097
**Website:** www.reinhartlaw.com

W233 N2080 Ridgeview Parkway, **Waukesha**, WI 53187
**Tel:** 262 951 4500   **Fax:** 262 951 4690

22 East Mifflin Street Suite 600, **Madison**, WI 53701
**Tel:** 608 229 2200   **Fax:** 608 229 2100

**ILLINOIS**
483 North Muford Road Suite Seven, **Rockford**, IL 61107
**Tel:** 815 484 1900   **Fax:** 815 484 1032

**International:** Reinhart's International Law Department attorneys are not only up to date on business laws around the world, they have the connections to compete in any foreign political or economic system. Whether it's helping a US company do business away from home, or helping a foreign business succeed in the US, Reinhart's International Department has the experience needed for today's global business world.

**Labor & Employment:** Reinhart's labor and employment attorneys are proactive in approach minimizes employment law violations for both public and private sector employers. When litigation does occur, they are experienced at representing management before federal and state courts or administrative agencies.

**Litigation:** Reinhart's Litigation Department includes former assistant US attorneys, former assistant district attorneys, and several attorneys who have clerked for federal, appellate, or Wisconsin Supreme Court justices. The firm has experienced practice teams that focus on key areas including products liability, sales and distribution, intellectual property, healthcare and financial professional liability defense. Its litigation attorneys have more trial experience than their counterparts in most firms this size. Reinhart's attorneys test cases in their own state-of-the-art, high-tech courtroom.

**Real Estate:** With the largest Real Estate Department of any law firm in Wisconsin, Reinhart offers clients custom-tailored expertise. Attorneys form groups of subspecialties so that its broad range of expertise and depth of experience apply to every matter.

**Securities:** Efficiency, responsiveness, and the ability to get involved in the early stages of financing are what set apart Reinhart's Securities Department. Its attorneys do more than just structure and negotiate financial transactions. They're experienced at raising capital by locating the right source.

**Tax:** Attorneys in Reinhart's Tax Department are dedicated to saving clients money. The firms Tax Controversy Group is the largest in Wisconsin, enjoying a reputation for winning large reductions from tax agencies. Four of its attorneys are former IRS or Department of Revenue trial attorneys. Moreover, most of its lawyers teach or have taught other tax practitioners in the University of Wisconsin- Milwaukee Master of Tax Program.

**Telecommunications & Energy:** Reinhart's Telecommunications and Energy Department helps clients compete successfully in the complex world of heavily regulated industries. Listed among the state's top public policy lawyers by Madison Magazine, the firm understands the unique needs of telecommunications providers and power generators facing close scrutiny by government agencies. Reinhart's reputation for innovative problem solving and efficiency is highly regarded by businesses in these two competitive industries.

**CONTENTS:** Corporate/M&A p.2041; Employment p.2042; Litigation p.2043; Real Estate p.2045; Individuals' Profiles p.2047; Firm's Profiles' p.2049.

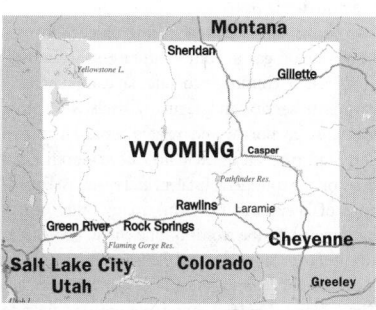

## How lawyers are ranked

Every year we carry out thousands of in-depth interviews with clients and lawyers in order to assess the reputations and expertise of business lawyers across the USA. Chambers rankings and editorial are referred to extensively by General Counsel and other purchasers of legal services who look to our recommendations when choosing their lawyers.

# CORPORATE/M&A

**Corporate/M&A**
Leading Firms

**1** BROWN, DREW & MASSEY LLP *Casper*
DRAY, THOMSON & DYEKMAN PC *Cheyenne*
HIRST & APPLEGATE, PC *Cheyenne*
HOLLAND & HART LLP *Cheyenne*
THOMAS N LONG PC *Cheyenne*

Leading Individuals

**1** BARBE J Kenneth *Brown, Drew & Massey LLP*
DRAY W Perry *Dray, Thomson & Dyekman PC*
LONG Thomas *Thomas N Long PC*
**2** BELCHER James *Holland & Hart LLP*
BUFFINGTON Teresa *Holland & Hart LLP*
COTTAM Dale *Hirst & Applegate, PC*
DYEKMAN Gregory *Dray, Thomson & Dyekman PC*
MCCALL Donn *Brown, Drew & Massey LLP*
METZKE John *Hirst & Applegate, PC*
REED Randall *Dray, Thomson & Dyekman PC*
TONER Tom *Yonkee & Toner LLP*

## Band 1

### Brown, Drew & Massey LLP
See firm details p.2049
**The Firm:** With offices in Casper and Sheridan, this outfit offers the full range of legal services to international, national and local clients. Two attorneys focus on corporate matters supported by a team that divides its time between corporate and other areas, acting on acquisitions, sales and financings and providing support to the business litigation department. The firm boasts particular expertise in banking, creditors' rights, bankruptcy and oil and gas law.
**The Lawyers:** Co-managing partner **Donn McCall** "*has a wealth of experience in sophisticated commercial and bankruptcy matters,*" according to market commentators. With an emphasis on banking, bankruptcy and business law, he "*knows the bankruptcy code inside and out,*" and represents banks and other lending institutions in oil, gas and asset-based financings as well as consumer loan financings. Peers agree that **Ken Barbe** "*enjoys a good general reputation as a very capable attorney with good knowledge in his areas of expertise.*" His corpo-

rate practice ranges from incorporating LLCs and other corporations to acting on M&A matters, which has taken up an increasing amount of time during the past year. For example, he advised on the sale of various businesses to public companies for more than $48 million in aggregate. Recent examples of his banking work include representing both Bank of the West and the Wyoming Industrial Development Corporation (WIDC) in various loan transactions.
**Clients/Work Highlights:** Bank of the West, Greiner Ford Lincoln Mercury and White's Mountain Motors are some of the clients.

### Dray, Thomson & Dyekman PC
**The Firm:** What characterizes this premier Wyoming firm is the breadth and depth of the service it offers clients. With a very broad-based corporate practice, the group advises on M&A, corporate governance and compliance issues, and employment and workers' compensation matters. Expertise in bankruptcy, creditors' rights, securities law, tax, consumer and commercial lending and regulatory issues bolster the corporate team's position. The firm serves as general counsel to some of the state's largest corporations and business litigation services are also on offer to a roster of clients that includes major financial institutions.
**The Lawyers:** The "*informed and knowledgeable*" founding partner **Perry Dray** has a practice that includes corporate transactions and litigation, estate planning and real estate, although his main focus is on healthcare law. He has an enviably top-level clientele and, according to commentators, what sets him apart is his "*great deal of experience when it comes to judging a business deal.*" **Gregory Dyekman** is "*technically very sound*" and sought after for his "*particular expertise with respect to financial institutions and bankruptcy law.*" His multifaceted practice encompasses creditors' rights, banking, litigation and real estate. His recent work includes corporate sales and acquisitions, several significant estate and trust administrations and acting for borrowers and lenders in a number of substantial loan negotiations. As a member of the firm's government relations practice, he has also represented many national and international companies in administrative law matters, such as tax disputes with the state, and he is

an active lobbyist. Managing partner **Randall Reed**'s eclectic practice runs the gamut from general business law, litigation, real estate and healthcare to natural resource and mineral tax matters, an area in which he particularly skilled.
**Clients/Work Highlights:** The team represents a wide variety of international, national and local clients from a broad range of industry sectors including oil, gas and energy companies; financial institutions; healthcare providers and insurance companies.

### Hirst & Applegate, PC
**The Firm:** Clients appreciate the high-quality corporate services provided by the firm's two corporate partners. Their practice has a strong emphasis on advising clients on the sale of company assets and on the formation of entities such as partnerships, LLCs and other corporations, with particular expertise in the area of continuances into and transfers out of Wyoming. The firm possesses a substantial corporate litigation capacity and related specialist knowledge on employment, energy, public utilities and creditors' rights.
**The Lawyers:** With an emphasis on business organization, public utilities, creditors' rights issues and real estate, clients were full of praise for **Dale Cottam**'s practice and particularly valued his "*astuteness and technical legal expertise as well as his levelheadedness.*" His corporate practice has a regulatory bent and he represents the utility regulatory interests of many energy companies in front of the Wyoming Public Service Commission; a recent appearance being in connection with the acquisition of Kaneb Pipe Line's assets by Rocky Mountain Pipeline System. He acts for various nonprofit organizations and assisted Cheyenne LEADS in bringing a Wal-Mart distribution facility to the Cheyenne area. "*Experienced business lawyer*" **John Metzke** has extensive experience in the areas of estate planning and trusts. While also acting on corporate matters for his estate planning clients, Metzke recently advised on four business disposals, including the sale of two large ranches.
**Clients/Work Highlights:** AARP; Cheyenne LEADS; Liquid Cognition; Pacific Energy Partners and Wyoming Bank & Trust.

## Holland & Hart LLP

See firm details p.369

**The Firm:** This firm's Wyoming practice focuses heavily on oil, gas and other natural resources work. However, it continues to offer a comprehensive corporate service and regularly deals with more specialist corporate and related issues. The two corporate partners based in the Cheyenne office can draw on the considerable talent and specialist knowledge of lawyers in the firm's many other offices nationwide. In the words of one client: "*Whenever you deal with Buffington and Belcher, they have a team of one hundred partners standing right behind them.*"

**The Lawyers:** Market commentators were glowing in their praise for "*the conscientious and hard-working*" **James Belcher** (see p.2047), whose expertise incorporates general corporate work, finance and bankruptcy law. While he regularly advises on entity formation, M&A, and continuances into and transfers out of Wyoming, he also has an impressive list of oil and gas companies as clients. Moreover, his experience as a commercial banker gives him a notable edge, providing him with a "*strong, practical background in deal negotiations.*" The "*knowledgeable and reliable*" **Teresa Buffington** (see p.2047) has a broad commercial practice covering entity formation, M&A and corporate financing work. She represents businesses in all commercial areas, with particular emphasis on the energy and resources sectors and related real estate transactional work. Clients particularly value her "*strong analytical abilities and practical advice.*"

**Clients/Work Highlights:** As the largest firm in the Rocky Mountain region, the firm has a very diverse client base ranging from individuals to companies of all sizes, including large national and international corporations.

## Thomas N Long PC

**The Firm:** Observers consider this small Cheyenne practice to be a leader in its field in Wyoming. The five-attorney team acts on a variety of transactional matters, business formations and reorganizations. Recent examples include advising on the corporate division of a ranch and representing the purchaser in the acquisition of a Colorado golf course and country club business. Clients also take advantage of the firm's expertise in real estate, tax-related estate planning and employment benefit matters.

**The Lawyers:** Commentators bestowed extensive praise on "*terrific attorney*" **Thomas Long**, highlighting his "*marvelous tax background and great experience.*" As the firm's leading individual, his practice reflects that of his firm and includes general business, estate planning, real estate and employment matters. In all these areas the focus is firmly on the tax aspects of the transactions. Over the past year, Long acted on the reorganization of two partnerships, settled several large estates and established two sizable foundations, one of which was designed to receive an estate worth $100 million.

**Clients/Work Highlights:** Clients include Cheyenne Radiology Group and Federal National Mortgage Association.

### Other Notable Practitioners

**Tom Toner** of Yonkee & Toner LLP is "*one of the brightest attorneys in Wyoming*" and is widely recognized for his expertise in a number of areas. While he is primarily a litigator with a focus on the oil and gas sector, he also undertakes transactional work in the lending, general commercial and real estate arenas.

# EMPLOYMENT

# MAINLY DEFENDANT

### Employment: Mainly Defendant

**Leading Firms**

**1**
DAVIS & CANNON *Cheyenne*
HOLLAND & HART LLP *Cheyenne*
WILLIAMS, PORTER, DAY & NEVILLE PC *Casper*
YONKEE & TONER LLP *Sheridan*

**2**
HIRST & APPLEGATE, PC *Cheyenne*
MURANE & BOSTWICK LLC *Casper*
SCHWARTZ, BON, WALKER & STUDER LLC *Casper*

**Leading Individuals**

**1**
CAVE Bradley *Holland & Hart LLP*
DAVIS Michael *Yonkee & Toner LLP*
FOX Kate *Davis & Cannon*
ORTIZ Scott *Williams, Porter, Day & Neville*
SCOTT Gary *Hirst & Applegate, PC*

**2**
SHUMATE Roger *Murane & Bostwick LLC*
STUDER Judith *Schwartz, Bon, Walker & Studer*

## Band 1

### Davis & Cannon

**The Firm:** This ten-attorney generalist practice has offices in Cheyenne and Sheridan that provide effective coverage for clients across the whole state. With a wide and varied stable of clients including large national corporations, the firm enjoys a diverse diet of business and administrative law and litigation. The team handles a broad range of litigation matters, including employment and discrimination law claims and defense.

**The Lawyers:** **Kate Fox**'s eclectic practice includes general civil litigation, with particular focus on water law issues, and additional expertise in employment matters, including employment litigation.

**Clients/Work Highlights:** Clients include First Interstate Bank, Marion Merrell Dow and Memorial Hospital of Sheridan County.

### Holland & Hart LLP

See firm details p.369

**The Firm:** With the largest labor and employment defense practice in the region, this firm can also draw on the extensive resources of its other 11 offices across six states and "*is always well prepared for its cases.*" The firm's attorneys defend employers in discrimination, wrongful discharge and wage and hour claims. Experience in labor matters, including union-organizing campaigns and collective bargaining agreements, is complemented by expertise in noncompete covenants and employee benefits, health and safety and immigration matters.

**The Lawyers:** With his focus firmly on employment, **Bradley Cave**'s (see p.2047) peers are full of admiration for his expertise: "*If had to name one attorney in Wyoming for employment law, I would name him.*" He defends employers in wrongful discharge, discrimination, harassment and wage and hour disputes, as well as defamation and employment-related tort actions. He also counsels and trains employers on policy issues and compliance with regulations.

**Clients/Work Highlights:** Chevron; Kennecott Energy; Triton Coal and United Medical Center.

### Williams, Porter, Day & Neville PC

**The Firm:** The "*professional and dedicated*" five-attorney team counsels employers and defends them in a range of employment litigation matters. In view of the favorable economic climate in Wyoming and in line with the national trend towards more counseling, the team has been busy reviewing employment policies and handbooks for many corporate clients drawn from various industry sectors.

**The Lawyers:** The "*ethical, dependable and personable*" **Scott Ortiz** is "*thorough and always well prepared.*" His practice covers employment as well as labor issues and his clients include private and public employers with a particular focus on the energy sector. A recent example of his work is his successful representation of Pacific Power & Light in multiple termination cases that went to arbitration and defense of a number of employment cases that were dismissed at the administrative level. Clients were full of praise for his responsiveness, reliability and integrity.

**Clients/Work Highlights:** BP Amico; Casper College; City of Casper; Devon Energy; Little America Hotels; PacifiCorp; Scottish Power; Sinclair Oil Corporation and Wyoming Medical Center.

### Yonkee & Toner LLP

**The Firm:** This six-attorney Sheridan outfit advises clients on a wide range of transactional and litigation issues, including corporate and commercial, estate planning, insurance defense, environmental, PI and medical malpractice defense law. The firm has a good reputation with respect to general litigation matters and two of its attorneys have specific expertise in a range of employment matters.

The Lawyers: **Michael Davis** draws admiration from his peers for being *"very well experienced"* and *"great to work with."* This *"hard-working"* attorney can be relied on to *"always come up with a creative application of the law,"* said one commentator. He has a diverse practice that encompasses general litigation, PI, medical malpractice and insurance defense and employment law.

Clients/Work Highlights: Metropolitan Life Insurance; Mountain West Farm Bureau; North Big Horn Hospital District; Ohio Hospital Insurance and Wyeth.

## Band 2

### Hirst & Applegate, PC

The Firm: This Cheyenne-based outfit has a general practice but is better known for its litigation expertise and its employment practice is very much litigation-oriented. The two employment attorneys have defended employers in relation to harassment, discrimination, breach of contract and wrongful discharge claims. The firm was recently appointed as Wyoming counsel in a class action suit against a large national discount store alleging wage payment discrepancies. Another string to the team's bow is training and counseling employers on matters such as employee policies and hiring and firing practices.

The Lawyers: *"Well-reputed"* **Gary Scott** is among *"the highest caliber of legal competence in Wyoming."* His is a diverse practice, most of which is centered on a variety of litigation matters including products liability and PI disputes. Employment matters make up about a quarter of his litigation practice and he almost exclusively acts on the defense side. Cases current at the time of writing include defending three school districts against allegations of gender and disability discrimination made by former teachers. Peers particularly admired his *"ease in mastering complex litigation."*

Clients/Work Highlights: AIG; GM; Sutherlands; Wal-Mart and Wells Fargo.

### Murane & Bostwick LLC

The Firm: This full-service law firm has offices in Casper and Cheyenne, with an employment practice that covers all employment issues other than labor law. The small team acts on a range of employment litigation, including state and federal discrimination claims, workers' compensation and employers' compensation claims. The team's workload also includes business formation, writing employment manuals and conducting seminars for employers.

The Lawyers: **Roger Shumate**'s civil litigation practice is focused mainly on employment litigation, and he has extensive experience of acting for both plain-tiff and defense sides. Recent successes include settling various sexual harassment claims out of court and defending several state law discrimination cases. He counsels employers on compliance with federal and state law and assists them in drafting personnel policies, procedures and employee handbooks. He has additional expertise in the areas of workers' compensation and ERISA law. Observers point towards his solid client base and *"deep understanding of the law."*

Clients/Work Highlights: The team has a diverse stable of clients including individuals, local and multinational businesses and insurance companies.

### Schwartz, Bon, Walker & Studer LLC

The Firm: This Casper-based firm has a general civil and trial practice. The seven-attorney team advises clients in corporate, environmental, oil and gas, administrative, banking, insurance and employment law.

The Lawyers: **Judith Studer**'s practice encompasses a variety of litigation ranging from general commercial, oil and gas, insurance defense work and employment litigation. Observers commented that they frequently see her in the courtroom. One of her peers noted: *"She does a lot and does it well."*

Clients/Work Highlights: The firm acts for a variety of clients including many insurance companies.

# LITIGATION

# GENERAL COMMERCIAL

## Band 1

### Davis & Cannon

The Firm: This seven-attorney litigation team has a significant statewide practice and is often involved in complex litigation, which has recently involved commercial and natural resources law. The firm has also benefited from an increase in litigation activity as a result of the coal bed methane development, particularly in the eastern part of the state. The team has also advised national companies on litigation before the Wyoming state and federal courts, including the team's representation of Wyeth in the fenfluramine mass torts litigation in which the plaintiffs alleged that the diet drug caused heart damage. The firm also acted for Eli Lilly in the Zyprexa litigation in Wyoming.

The Lawyers: *"Hard-worker"* **Kate Fox** is heavily involved in employment litigation and often defends large self-insured pharmaceutical companies in products liability actions. She has also advised on cutting-edge water quality issues and observers noted her proficiency in complicated matters. **Kim Cannon** deals with a variety of litigation such as securities, natural resource and products liability defense matters. He recently advised in securities litigation against Merrill Lynch, which resulted in a confidential settlement. He has also represented a number of plaintiffs in securities litigation arising out of the dot.com bubble burst. He moreover defended Rockwell Automation in a products liability matter involving the explosion of a gas regulator. Clients above all appreciate his *"ability to simplify complex matters."*

Clients/Work Highlights: The team advised a diverse client base of insurance companies, banks, healthcare providers and businesses from the natural resources and energy sectors. Clients include Eli Lilly; First Interstate Bank; Laramie County; St. Paul Travelers and Wyeth.

### Hirst & Applegate, PC

The Firm: This seven-strong team of *"straight-up folks whose word you can count on"* advises on general civil litigation, products liability, creditors' rights and foreclosure, and professional malpractice law, representing individual insured defendants and insurance companies in breach of contract and bad faith actions. The firm also boasts experience in the various alternative dispute resolution mechanisms and has particular expertise in multiparty and multiforum litigation. The *"real depth in highly complex multiparty litigation"* is complemented by specialist experience in public utilities and energy law.

The Lawyers: The *"very experienced and hard-working"* **Thomas Nicholas** commands the respect of judges and peers alike *"because of his strong coordination skills and excellence in the courtroom."* His litigation practice encompasses PI, wrongful death, insurance defense and environmental and commercial matters, including oil and gas royalty cases. Commentators were impressed with his ability to *"shed more light than heat on everything he touches."*

Clients/Work Highlights: Aetna; AT&T; Bank of America; Ford; Simon Contractors and Wells Fargo.

### Holland & Hart LLP

See firm details p.369

The Firm: With its litigation focus firmly on complex commercial and energy-related litigation, the Cheyenne office of eight talented attorneys primarily represents energy companies involved in oil and gas production, transportation and pipelines. The team also maintains a strong labor litigation practice and is heavily involved in the litigation

## Litigation: General Commercial
Leading Individuals

### Senior Statesman
DAY Richard *Williams, Porter, Day*

**[1]** NICHOLAS Thomas *Hirst & Applegate, PC*
REEVES Weston *The Law Offices of Weston Reeves*
SCHULTZ Donald *Holland & Hart LLP*
TONER Tom *Yonkee & Toner LLP*

**[2]** BRINKERHOFF Jeffrey *Brown, Drew & Massey LLP*
CANNON Kim *Davis & Cannon*
FOX Kate *Davis & Cannon*
GIFFORD Mark *Sole Practitioner*
MACKEY Terry *Moriarity, Gooch, Badaruddin*
MURPHY Patrick *Williams, Porter, Day & Neville*
NEVILLE Frank *Williams, Porter, Day & Neville*
RUTLEDGE Kent *Lathrop & Rutledge*
STUDER Judith *Schwartz, Bon, Walker & Studer*
SUNDAHL John *Sundahl, Powers, Kapp*

**[3]** HICKEY Paul *Hickey & Evans LLP*
POWERS JR George *Sundahl, Powers, Kapp & Martin*

relating to water rights and access to coal bed methane, which flows from the increase in energy exploration and development in Wyoming.

**The Lawyers:** The "*exemplary, extraordinarily diligent, bright and hard-working*" **Donald Schultz** (see p.2048) is described by his clients as "*one of the very best trial lawyers in Wyoming or anywhere else.*" Engaged mainly in litigation for natural gas pipeline and natural gas production companies, he continues to be kept busy by his role as coordinated counsel in a series of 72 consolidated cases relating to the False Claims Act. Peers recognize him as "*a great lawyer*" and he is so admired by his clients that they "*can't say enough good things about him.*"

**Clients/Work Highlights:** Burlington Resources; EOG Resources; ExxonMobil; Questar Pipeline and The Williams' Companies.

### Williams, Porter, Day & Neville PC

**The Firm:** Most of this firm's 14 attorneys are litigators with a practice covering almost every area of litigation, including in particular, insurance defense, both insurance coverage and bad faith, professional malpractice, PI and some tax litigation. The firm also has an active business practice with a focus on the energy sector. Clients were appreciative of its "*knowledge of the territory and its good business presence in Wyoming.*"

**The Lawyers:** **Frank Neville** is "*a thoughtful lawyer who preserves his credibility in all situations.*" His practice concentrates on medical malpractice defense but also includes defending PI claims on behalf of energy companies. He is "*an extremely professional and conscientious lawyer*" who inspires "*high trust and confidence levels*" in his clients. **Patrick Murphy** is "*well liked by colleagues and judges.*" His practice has always focused almost entirely on insurance defense work and he still spends most of his time defending death and injury cases, much of this relating to carbon monoxide. In recent years, he has been more

involved in business litigation. More than 40 years of experience means **Richard Day** has "*a wealth of industry knowledge and a terrific rapport with the courts and judges.*" Recently he has taken a step back and now primarily focuses on energy-related matters, oil and gas royalty litigation and some county malpractice litigation.

**Clients/Work Highlights:** The firm represents energy and insurance companies such as AIG, CNA Insurance Companies and The Hartford Financial Services Group. Other clients include BP America; Casper College; Devon Energy; Helmerich & Payne; Marathon Oil; PacifiCorp; the True companies; USAviation and the Wyoming Medical Center.

### Yonkee & Toner LLP

**The Firm:** This Sheridan-based firm of six attorneys undertakes a wide range of general civil litigation, environmental, insurance defense, PI and medical malpractice defense, and employment litigation for major insurers, healthcare providers and the energy and natural resource sectors. The six-attorney team also advises on trusts and estate planning as well as general corporate and commercial law.

**The Lawyers:** "*Admired by everyone he practices with,*" **Tom Toner** has "*great people skills*" and "*may be the smartest Wyoming lawyer there is,*" according to peers. He is "*certainly one of the very best*" and maintains a broad practice while having a special focus on natural resources and water rights. This "*thoughtful and hard-working lawyer*" impresses with his "*really strong strategy skills.*"

**Clients/Work Highlights:** Memorial Hospital of Sheridan County; Metropolitan Life Insurance; Mountain West Farm Bureau; North Big Horn Hospital District; Ohio Hospital Insurance Company and State Farm.

## Band 2

### Hickey & Evans LLP

**The Firm:** This 12-attorney Cheyenne practice advises individuals and corporate clients on civil and criminal matters. The team has particular expertise in business and commercial litigation, especially with respect to public utility regulation and environmental law.

**The Lawyers:** **Paul Hickey** is a "*very bright and experienced lawyer.*" His has a general trial practice spanning 30 years and including energy, utilities and natural resource law, PI litigation, employment and trusts and estate matters. With education law an additional specialty, he has particular expertise in school litigation, representing the large school districts in Wyoming.

**Clients/Work Highlights:** The firm has represented Kinder Morgan; Laramie County Schools District 2; PacifiCorp and Qwest.

### Lathrop & Rutledge

**The Firm:** This five-partner general civil practice has specific expertise in products liability, PI and professional liability litigation, representing various busi-

ness entities, insurance companies, physicians and hospitals. The team also advises on civil litigation, including employment, insurance coverage, bad faith, commercial, real estate and bankruptcy matters, and has significant experience with alternative dispute resolution mechanisms.

**The Lawyers:** **Kent Rutledge**'s litigation expertise has a particular focus on medical malpractice defense, but he also has a good reputation for commercial, insurance and products liability work. Observers describe him as "*a very likable man with a more subdued approach that is very effective with a jury.*"

**Clients/Work Highlights:** Continental General Insurance; Omaha Property & Casualty Insurance; The Doctors Company; United States Life Insurance and the Wyoming Hospital Association.

### Schwartz, Bon, Walker & Studer LLC

**The Firm:** Based in Casper, this general civil and trial practice offers a broad range of litigation services with seven attorneys regularly advising on corporate, employment, environmental, oil and gas, banking and insurance litigation.

**The Lawyers:** A "*strong and uncompromising advocate,*" **Judith Studer**'s practice encompasses commercial litigation, insurance defense, oil and gas and labor and employment matters in particular. Observers depict her as "*a very thoughtful, analytical lawyer who is super prepared and really understands tactics very well.*"

**Clients/Work Highlights:** Community First National Bank; Hilltop Shopping Center; ITT Hartford Insurance Group; Komatsu Equipment Company; St. Paul Travelers; Union Carbide and the Wyoming Association of Municipalities.

### Sundahl, Powers, Kapp & Martin LLC

**The Firm:** This Cheyenne practice services clients throughout Wyoming, and some of its attorneys are also licensed to practice in Colorado and Nebraska. The firm concentrates on general civil litigation with a focus on medical malpractice, insurance defense and administrative law. The attorneys also advise clients on construction, real estate, tax, employment, products liability, public utility, environmental and oil and gas law.

**The Lawyers:** "*Thinking-man's lawyer*" **George Powers** "*always brings a view to a case that has not been thought of before.*" The practice of this "*bright and very prepared*" attorney covers litigation as well as insurance and railroad law. **John Sundahl** advises on professional malpractice, products liability and insurance issues. Commentators particularly admire his expertise in brain injury defense cases, an area about which he knows more than anyone else in Wyoming: "*He knows so much, he is almost a subspecialist in neuropsychological brain matters,*" acknowledged one commentator.

**Clients/Work Highlights:** The team represents a variety of clients, among which insurance companies and healthcare providers feature prominently.

## The Spence Law Firm LLC

**The Firm:** Commentators have described this practice as the "*leading plaintiff firm in Wyoming.*" The eight-attorney team services clients from its main office in Jackson, but the firm also has affiliated offices in Idaho and New Mexico. The attorneys advise on a range of litigation including plaintiff PI and wrongful death actions, toxic torts and malpractice matters, criminal defense, and general business and employment litigation.

**The Lawyers:** Gerry Spence is the leading individual at the firm.

**Clients/Work Highlights:** The firm represents individuals in their suits against other individuals or business entities.

## Other Notable Practitioners

Now a sole practitioner, **Weston Reeves** has a general litigation practice with a focus on complex commercial, PI and medical malpractice matters. Observers describe him as both "*brilliant in the law, persuasive and good at framing the issues,*" possessing "*the ability to get to the point quickly.*" **Jeffrey Brinkerhoff** of Brown, Drew & Massey LLP is a "*strong, intelligent and hard-working advocate.*" His practice spans a variety of civil litigation, with particular expertise in the areas of medical malpractice defense, insurance defense and PI litigation. Representing both defendants and plaintiffs, he is recommended by peers as "*perhaps the best medical malpractice defense lawyer in the state.*" Although

now mostly focused on mediation, **Mark Gifford** has broad litigation experience in areas including PI, malpractice, family as well as labor and employment law. He is "*an extremely fair, balanced and somewhat understated presenter,*" qualities from which his mediation work benefits. "*He is gifted verbally and as a writer and has tremendous people skills that earn him the admiration of everyone he meets,*" explained one commentator. **Terry Mackey**, who is now of counsel with Moriarity, Gooch, Badaruddin & Booke LLC, is "*an extremely engaging lawyer with a fertile imagination and a great deal of energy.*" He concentrates his practice on plaintiff PI and death cases as well as some criminal defense work.

# REAL ESTATE

## Band 1

### Dray, Thomson & Dyekman PC

**The Firm:** This firm offers the full range of real estate services. It represents both buyers and sellers of commercial, agricultural and residential real estate and acts on behalf of developers, municipalities and realtors. Alongside the purchase, sale and development of real estate, the attorneys also advise on annexation, zoning, planning, land use and condo-

minium projects, and mineral and water rights. An active finance and lending practice overlaps and complements the real estate team's work.

**The Lawyers:** Peers commend the commercially minded **Gregory Dyekman** for his "*sophisticated transaction experience*" and his "*interest in completing the deal.*" Besides his broad general commercial practice, he has expertise in a variety of real estate and lending work. On his recent deal list are the sale of several significant commercial properties, including development and operating business property and several transactions involving rural agricultural property, a hot commodity in Wyoming. Founding partner **Perry Dray**'s practice is predominantly commercial and healthcare, but he also advises on real estate law. He is currently representing a major affordable housing developer that is developing statewide.

**Clients/Work Highlights:** The firm has a diverse client bass of large corporations and municipalities as well as small, family-owned businesses from a wide variety of business sectors.

### Mullikin, Larson & Swift

**The Firm:** With the addition of two more "*young, bright and talented attorneys,*" this seven-strong outfit is described as the state's premier real estate firm by certain market commentators. Four of the team members advise on the whole range of real estate matters and represent an enviably broad client base on many larger transactions due to the firm's great depth of resources.

**The Lawyers:** **David Larson** is considered to be the "*wise old man of real estate in Wyoming.*" His extensive involvement in real estate matters evolved, to a large degree, from his representation of many of the local real estate developers, and now "*he has more political and business connections than any other real estate lawyer in Jackson.*" Thanks to his time as Jackson town attorney, he has significant expertise in land use and zoning law and is currently involved in a project in southern Utah involving land use entitlements for a 690-acre mixed-use development. Larson has also been

working on a significant expansion of a resort district in Jackson Hole for Snake River Associates and assisted the Snake River Sporting Club with a private golf course and real estate development. With a practice similar to that of his partner, **Phelps Swift** practices in the areas of real estate and commercial law, though he is increasingly selective about the transactions he takes on. Observers describe this "*very competent real estate and transactional attorney*" as one of the easiest attorneys to work with in Jackson: "*He has great knowledge and gets a project done at a very high level of quality without adversity or over complication.*"

**Clients/Work Highlights:** The Jackson State Bank & Trust, Teton County School District and Teton Pines Resort and Country Club are among the firm's clients.

## Band 2

### Brown, Drew & Massey LLP

See firm details p.2049

**The Firm:** This firm offers a range of corporate and commercial legal services and acts on sale, purchase, leasing, development and financing aspects of real estate transactions. The three attorneys extensively involved in real estate matters advise on commercial, agricultural and residential transactions and represent clients of all types and sizes. Several attorneys have specific expertise with regard to title work, an area particularly important in oil and gas extraction. The firm boasts further extensive experience with water and mineral rights, environmental and planning issues.

**The Lawyers:** Renowned for his high-quality advice, **Kenneth Barbe**'s real estate practice focuses on the transactional and development aspects and overlaps with his commercial practice, as he often sets up the LLC that will own the property to be developed. At the time of writing, Barbe was busy representing a developer in Casper in various projects and assisting various realtors with their commercial real estate developments.

Clients/Work Highlights: Citation Oil & Gas; JPMorgan Chase; Marathon Oil and Wells Fargo.

## Davis & Cannon

The Firm: This general Wyoming practice maintains two offices to better serve clients from every part of the state. The real estate team assists landowners and business people with the sale and purchase of real estate and represent municipalities in land use and eminent domain matters. The firm has particular experience in the areas of mineral leasing, water and access issues, which is complemented by particular expertise in title problems, mortgages and liens.

The Lawyers: As "one of the old lions of the Bar," Richard Davis has a "sterling reputation" and is well established in northern Wyoming and well respected around the state. His practice encompasses real estate as well as general commercial matters.

Clients/Work Highlights: Clients have included Hawkins & Powers Aviation; Life Care Centers of America; Memorial Hospital of Sheridan County; Padlock Ranch and Peter Kiewit Sons'.

## Holland & Hart LLP

See firm details p.369

The Firm: This regional firm runs a two-attorney general real estate practice out of Jackson, representing both buyers and sellers in residential and commercial transactions. The team advises on acquisitions and sales, leasing, development, subdivisions, financing, covenants, zoning and condominiumization, often representing high-end clients in substantial transactions, such as on the recent sale of two large ranches. Litigious real estate matters are also handled from time to time, with the firm advising on easements, breaches of covenants and disputed real estate contracts.

The Lawyers: The "detail-oriented and methodical" John Gallinger (see p.2047) has broad-based commercial experience, which "gives him a lot of insight into how deals work and how they can be put together." He represents buyers and sellers both on residential and commercial developments, particularly in regards to planning and zoning issues, land exchanges and 1031 exchanges. Recent examples of his work include advising on the development of various golf courses and other large commercial developments. Clients rate this "fabulous lawyer" for his depth of knowledge.

Clients/Work Highlights: The firm represents a variety of clients including sellers and purchasers of real estate and some realtors, such as Sotheby's International Realty.

## Williams, Porter, Day & Neville PC

The Firm: This 14-attorney Casper firm is first and foremost a trial practice. However, the team had the benefit of working with the late Barry Williams, a leading real estate attorney, and continues to advise on a variety of general business and real estate matters. The group's work is complemented by its particular strength in environmental and natural resource law.

The Lawyers: The attorneys to go to for real estate work are Kevin Huber, Margo Harlan Sabec and Nicol Thompson Kramer.

Clients/Work Highlights: AIG; BP Amoco; Crum & Forster; Farmers Union Central Exchange; Marathon Oil; Pacific Power & Light and True Industries.

## Band 3

## Lonabaugh and Riggs

The Firm: This "absolutely wonderful" Sheridan-based general practice has a strong real estate team that acts on major real estate transactions, representing both buyers and sellers in transactional matters and also advising on litigation issues. With particular expertise in mineral leasing, water and access issues, the attorneys are well placed to advise on title issues as well as on mortgages and liens.

The Lawyers: The market recommends "confident all-around attorney" Dan Riggs alongside Haultain Corbett and up-and-comer Lori McMullen.

Clients/Work Highlights: The team services a broad range of clients from various industry sectors.

## MacPherson Kelly & Thompson

The Firm: Situated in the small community of Rawlins, this outstanding firm has developed an extensive real estate practice. The firm's two real estate attorneys have a particular focus on ranching transactions, especially the sale and purchase of large ranches. With attorneys licensed in both Wyoming and Colorado, clients in both states can utilize the firm's services.

The Lawyers: John MacPherson's real estate practice is mostly devoted to transactions involving ranches or other agricultural land. He recently assisted Elk Mountain Ranch in selling a significant portion of its Wyoming ranch holdings and helped it invest the proceeds in other real estate throughout the Midwest. Clients rate him as "an outstanding upright guy" whose "judgment they can always trust, who is extremely prompt in his responses and consistently meets their needs."

Clients/Work Highlights: The Anschutz Corporation; Carbon County; Silver Spur Land & Cattle and the State of Wyoming.

## Phibbs Law Office PC

The Firm: This Jackson practice has a reputation for acting on the sophisticated Jackson real estate transactions and, in particular, ranch acquisitions and sales.

The Lawyers: The knowledgeable Henry Phibbs is a "sophisticated real estate practitioner who often has simple solutions to complicated problems." He is very well connected locally due to his Wyoming background.

Clients/Work Highlights: The firm represents a variety of clients including owners and purchasers of land as well as developers.

## Thomas N Long PC

The Firm: The firm undertakes a variety of real estate work, with particular emphasis on the tax planning issues involved therein. The firm represents clients in buying and selling large ranches and assists developers in subdivision issues, preparation of covenants and tax planning for real estate development. The team also acts in connection with 1031 exchanges.

The Lawyers: Thomas Long is a "hard-working attorney who does quality real estate work." His main practice focus is on tax and estate planning matters and his expertise in tax law is a major drawing point for clients.

Clients/Work Highlights: The team represents a broad range of clients, including many developers.

## Yonkee & Toner LLP

The Firm: This Sheridan based firm has a general civil and trial practice. The six-attorney team also acts on general corporate and commercial as well as real estate matters and has particular expertise in environmental, oil and gas, mineral and water rights, and land use issues.

The Lawyers: Tom Toner's practice revolves around oil, gas and other natural resource matters, an area in which he has "more knowledge than anyone." He undertakes a great deal of litigation but also acts on all natural resource-related transactional work, including real estate matters. Observers describe him as "one of brightest guys I know who, no doubt, will do a good job at whatever he sets his mind to." He garnered praise from his peers for being a "very passionate guy who represents his clients very zealously and well."

Clients/Work Highlights: The firm represents a variety of insurance companies as well as the Memorial Hospital of Sheridan County; Mountain West Farm Bureau and Sheridan County School Districts 1, 2 and 3.

## Other Notable Practitioners

With a focus on real estate foreclosure, the "competent and technically astute" Dale Cottam of Hirst & Applegate, PC has represented creditors and mortgagees and played an instrumental part in recent changes to Wyoming's foreclosure laws. He assists developers in converting agricultural land into residential and commercial property by zoning and redivision. He also advised on real estate disputes, counseling utilities and pipeline companies on eminent domain issues. Christopher Hawks of Christopher Hawks PC concentrates on resort, hospitality and commercial mixed-use real estate developments. Recent examples include acting on a significant number of golf resort and ski area developments and several large masterplanned communities with 160 slot divisions for mixed-use development. He has also advised the Jackson Hole Mountain Resort and the Vail Resorts on their real estate and development work. Clients portray him as "knowledgeable and thorough" and have confidence in his ability "to make sure he gets matters right first time." Hard-working Andrea Leah Richard of The

Richard Law Firm PC is a "*forceful advocate*" who practices business and general commercial litigation alongside real estate law. She is "*a good, detail-* *oriented attorney*" who is very strong on land use planning issues and "*brings muscle to a development team to get things approved.*"

# Leaders in Wyoming

### BARBE, J Kenneth
Brown, Drew & Massey LLP, Casper
307 234 1000
*Recommended in Corporate/M&A, Real Estate*

### BELCHER, James
Holland & Hart LLP, Cheyenne
307 778 4200
jbelcher@hollandhart.com
*Recommended in Corporate/M&A*
**Practice Areas:** Partner practicing in all areas of financial and corporate business matters. Works with corporations, limited partnerships and limited liability companies in formation, merger, continuance into Wyoming, and transfer from Wyoming to another jurisdiction. Has also assisted clients with securities matters. Assists clients with energy development and transmission, including wind energy projects, natural gas gathering and pipelines, and electrical transmission, including project development and finance, right-of-way acquisition and condemnation and related advice. In his financial and corporate practice, has assisted both borrowers and lenders with UCC, real estate, mortgage, and loan documentation, and has extensive experience in issuing opinions for business and secured transactions.
**Prof. Memberships:** Wyoming Bar Association, Business Law Section (Past Chairman), Wyoming Bar Foundation (Director and past President).
**Career:** Admitted to the Wyoming (1988) and Colorado (1989) Bar. Commercial Finance (1972-85); Attorney (1988-present).
**Publications:** Editor, 'The Wyoming Law of Mortgages' (2d ed. 1993).
**Personal:** Received a JD (with honors) from the University of Wyoming (1988) and a BS from the University of Colorado (1972).

### BRINKERHOFF, Jeffrey
Brown, Drew & Massey LLP, Casper
307 234 1000
*Recommended in Litigation*

### BUFFINGTON, Teresa
Holland & Hart LLP, Cheyenne
307 778 4237
tbuffington@hollandhart.com
*Recommended in Corporate/M&A*
**Practice Areas:** A Partner practicing in all areas of commercial transactions throughout the state of Wyoming, including real estate, business, finance, and construction. Her practice includes acquisitions and sales, contract preparation and negotiation, energy project transactions, rights of way for gathering and pipelines, commercial financing, entity planning, formation and continuation, design, engineering and construction, transactional due diligence, and legal opinions. She has assisted clients in a variety of industries, projects, and businesses.
**Prof. Memberships:** Member of the Laramie County Bar Association; Wyoming Bar Association; Colorado Bar Association; and the American Bar Association.
**Career:** Admitted to the Colorado (1985) and Wyoming Bar (1991). Administrative Partner of Holland & Hart's Cheyenne office since January 2003. Formerly Manager of the firm's Business Entities and Transactions Practice Group.
**Personal:** Received a JD from the University of Colorado (1985) and a BA (with highest honors) from Ohio University (1977).

### CANNON, Kim
Davis & Cannon, Cheyenne
307 643 3210
*Recommended in Litigation*

### CAVE, Bradley
Holland & Hart LLP, Cheyenne
307 778 4210
bcave@hollandhart.com
*Recommended in Employment*
**Practice Areas:** A Partner practicing employment law and litigation, he represents employers in matters involving discrimination, harassment, wage and hour disputes, defamation, wrongful discharge, breach of contract and employment-related torts. Also advises employers on issues related to employee handbooks and personnel policies, compliance with federal and state statutes and regulations and employee investigations, discipline and termination. Regularly conducts training sessions for employers, managers and supervisors in areas such as investigations, discipline and termination, harassment, discrimination, disability accommodation and supervisory responsibilities.
**Prof. Memberships:** Member of the American Bar Association; Wyoming Bar Association; Colorado Bar Association; Defense Lawyers Association of Wyoming; Defense Research Institute; and the Society of Human Resource Management.
**Career:** Admitted to the Colorado (1988) and Wyoming (1991) Bar. Editor of the Wyoming Employment Law Letter.
**Personal:** Received a JD (with honors) from George Washington University (1988) and a BS from the University of Wyoming (1985).

### COTTAM, Dale
Hirst & Applegate, PC, Cheyenne
307 632 0541
*Recommended in Corporate/M&A, Real Estate*

### DAVIS, Michael
Yonkee & Toner LLP, Sheridan
307 674 7451
*Recommended in Employment*

### DAVIS JR, Richard
Davis & Cannon, Sheridan
307 672 7491
*Recommended in Real Estate*

### DAY, Richard
Williams, Porter, Day & Neville PC, Casper 307 265 0700
*Recommended in Litigation*

### DRAY, W Perry
Dray, Thomson & Dyekman PC, Cheyenne 307 634 8891
*Recommended in Corporate/M&A, Real Estate*

### DYEKMAN, Gregory
Dray, Thomson & Dyekman PC, Cheyenne 307 634 8891
*Recommended in Corporate/M&A, Real Estate*

### FOX, Kate
Davis & Cannon, Cheyenne
307 643 3210
*Recommended in Employment, Litigation*

### GALLINGER, John
Holland & Hart LLP, Jackson
307 734 4505
jgallinger@hollandhart.com
*Recommended in Real Estate*
**Practice Areas:** Substantial experience in real estate and natural resources law. Real estate practice involves both residential and commercial developments including planning and zoning issues, land exchanges, 1031 exchanges, and representation of both sellers and buyers.
**Career:** Admitted to the Montana (1971), Wyoming (1975), and District of Columbia Bar (1975). Prior to joining Holland & Hart, Mr Gallinger worked with the Office of Legal Counsel, US Department of Justice, and served as a special assistant to the general counsel for the Federal Trade Commission.
**Publications:** Mr Gallinger has published several articles about natural resources law and has given several presentations on various aspects of real estate transactions.
**Personal:** Received a JD (1971, with Honors) and a BA (1968) from the University of Wyoming.

### GIFFORD, Mark
Mark W. Gifford, Casper
307 265 3265
*Recommended in Litigation*

### HAWKS, Christopher
Christopher Hawks PC, Jackson
307 733 9437
*Recommended in Real Estate*

### HICKEY, Paul
Hickey & Evans LLP, Cheyenne
307 634 1525
*Recommended in Litigation*

### LARSON, David
Mullikin, Larson & Swift, Jackson
307 733 3923
*Recommended in Real Estate*

### LONG, Thomas
Thomas N Long PC, Cheyenne
307 635 0710
*Recommended in Corporate/M&A, Real Estate*

### MACKEY, Terry
Moriarity, Gooch, Badaruddin & Booke LLC, Cheyenne 307 635 7517
*Recommended in Litigation*

### MACPHERSON, John
MacPherson Kelly & Thompson, Rawlins
307 324 2713
*Recommended in Real Estate*

### MCCALL, Donn
Brown, Drew & Massey LLP, Casper
307 234 1000
*Recommended in Corporate/M&A*

### METZKE, John
Hirst & Applegate, PC, Cheyenne
307 632 0541
*Recommended in Corporate/M&A*

### MURPHY, Patrick
Williams, Porter, Day & Neville PC, Casper 307 265 0700
*Recommended in Litigation*

**NEVILLE, Frank**
Williams, Porter, Day & Neville PC,
Casper
307 265 0700
*Recommended in Litigation*

**NICHOLAS, Thomas**
Hirst & Applegate, PC, Cheyenne
307 632 0541
*Recommended in Litigation*

**ORTIZ, Scott**
Williams, Porter, Day & Neville PC,
Casper 307 265 0700
*Recommended in Employment*

**PHIBBS, Henry**
Phibbs Law Office PC, Jackson
307 733 5004
*Recommended in Real Estate*

**POWERS JR, George**
Sundahl, Powers, Kapp & Martin LLC,
Cheyenne 307 632 6421
*Recommended in Litigation*

**REED, Randall**
Dray, Thomson & Dyekman PC,
Cheyenne 307 634 8891
*Recommended in Corporate/M&A*

**REEVES, Weston**
The Law Offices of Weston Reeves,
Casper 307 265 3843
*Recommended in Litigation*

**RICHARD, Andrea**
The Richard Law Firm PC, Jackson
307 732 6680
*Recommended in Real Estate*

**RUTLEDGE, Kent**
Lathrop & Rutledge, Cheyenne
307 632 0554
*Recommended in Litigation*

**SCHULTZ, Donald I**
Holland & Hart LLP, Cheyenne
307 778 4217
dschultz@hollandhart.com
*Recommended in Litigation*
**Practice Areas:** A Partner practicing in commercial litigation, primarily in the oil and gas and construction industries. Serves as court-appointed Liaison Counsel to coordinate among hundreds of defendants in nearly 75 MDL-consolidated gas measurement and gas valuation lawsuits. Has jury trial and appellate experience in gas measurement disputes, gas contract pricing and take-or-pay disputes, JOA disputes, and gas balancing claims. Represents owners in litigation of construction disputes involving pipelines, gas plants, refineries, coal mines, trona mines, and resort properties. Substantial experience in defense of class actions, False Claims Act actions, and in gas royalty and accounting cases. Leads firm's Oil and Gas Service Group to enhance service to industry across Rocky Mountain regional network of offices.
**Prof. Memberships:** Member of the American Bar Association, Forum of the Construction Industry; Wyoming Bar Association; and the Defense Lawyers Association of Wyoming.
**Career:** Admitted to the Colorado (1982) and Wyoming (1985) Bar.
**Personal:** Received a JD from Harvard University (1982) and a BA from the University of Wyoming (1979).

**SCOTT, Gary**
Hirst & Applegate, PC, Cheyenne
307 632 0541
*Recommended in Employment*

**SHUMATE, Roger**
Murane & Bostwick LLC, Casper
307 234 9345
*Recommended in Employment*

**STUDER, Judith**
Schwartz, Bon, Walker & Studer LLC,
Casper 307 235 6681
*Recommended in Employment,
Litigation*

**SUNDAHL, John**
Sundahl, Powers, Kapp & Martin LLC,
Cheyenne 307 632 6421
*Recommended in Litigation*

**SWIFT, Phelps**
Mullikin, Larson & Swift, Jackson
307 733 3923
*Recommended in Real Estate*

**TONER, Tom**
Yonkee & Toner LLP, Sheridan
307 674 7451
*Recommended in Corporate/M&A,
Litigation, Real Estate*

# BROWN, DREW & MASSEY, LLP

## THE FIRM

**Managing Partner:** J Kenneth Barbe

**Number of partners:** 11
**Number of other lawyers:** 5

**FIRM OVERVIEW:** Tracing its roots back to 1936, Brown, Drew & Massey, LLP (Brown & Drew) is one of Wyoming's oldest and largest law firms. The firm's principal office is in Casper, Wyoming, and it has a branch office in Sheridan, Wyoming. Brown & Drew is Wyoming's only representative in Lex Mundi, a world-wide alliance of prestigious law firms, and is the reviser of the Martindale-Hubbell Wyoming Law Digest. The firm has the distinction of being listed in the Martindale-Hubbell Bar Register of Preeminent Attorneys in all of its primary practice areas. Members of the firm have contributed to treatises on oil and gas law, trial practice, mortgage lending law, and construction law and have acted as counsel in numerous count cases of significance in the development of oil and gas law in Wyoming. Four of the current members of the firm have also been recognized by their listing in The Best Lawyers in America in the areas of corporate law, bankruptcy law, medical malpractice and healthcare law, natural resources law, and real estate law. Firm attorneys have been selected by their peers for membership in honorary legal organizations such as the American Academy of Appellate Lawyers, the American College of Mortgage Attorneys, and the Federation of Insurance and Corporate Counsel. Former members of the firm have received judicial appointments to both the federal and state district courts in Wyoming, and one member was elected and served two terms as Governor of the state and later as US Ambassador to Ireland.

**MAIN AREAS OF PRACTICE:** Brown & Drew operates statewide, offering a full range of legal services that are concentrated in the areas of oil and gas, mining, energy, and natural resources; banking and finance; bankruptcy and creditor's rights; business transactions; corporations and business organizations; intellectual property; real estate; construction; healthcare; medical malpractice, products liability, tort claims, and insurance defense; employment and labor; environment; regulatory and administrative; probate and estate planning; and alternative dispute resolution. The firm also specializes in civil litigation and appellate practice incidental to its main practice areas.

**CLIENTS:** Brown & Drew is a full legal resource for its diverse national and Wyoming-based clientele, which includes oil and gas companies, state and national banking and financial institutions, commercial, consumer, and mortgage lenders, private corporations and other business organizations, physicians and other healthcare providers, casualty and liability insurers, small businesses, construction firms, utility companies, railroads, ranchers, and professionals. The firm frequently acts as Wyoming counsel for money center banking and financial institutions and other commercial and mortgage lenders in major mult-state financing transactions. Brown & Drew is employed to represent its clients in substantial litigation matters as well as by corporate counsel or other law firms to represent corporate entities and individuals in substantial, non-recurring litigation. The firm's corporate clients include Wells Fargo Bank, JP Morgan Chase Bank, Bank of the West, First Interstate Bank, ChevronTexaco Company, ConocoPhillips Company, Cabot Oil & Gas Corp., Duke Energy Companies, Kerr-McGee Companies, Marathon Oil Company, Bituminous Insurance Companies, The Doctor's Company, ITT Hartford Insurance Company, Protective Life Insurance Co., The CIT Group, Chase Manhattan Mortgage Corp., and Wells Fargo Home Mortgage Corp., among others.

**INTERNATIONAL WORK:** Brown & Drew advises a number of international clients in the formation of a variety of business organizations under Wyoming's favorable business laws. The firm also has represented a number of foreign clients in litigation within the United States.

## HEAD OFFICE

**WYOMING**
Suit 200, 159 North Wolcott Street, **Casper**, WY 82601
**Tel:** 307 234 1000   **Fax:** 307 265 8025
**Email:** bdm@browndrew.com
**Website:** www.browndrew.com

## BRANCH OFFICES

**WYOMING**
248 West Brundage, **Sheridan,** WY 82801
**Tel:** 307 673 8565   **Fax:** 307 673 6612

## CONTACTS

| Practice Area | Contact |
| --- | --- |
| **Alternative Dispute Resolution** | Rex O Arney |
| **Appellate** | Morris R Massey |
| **Banking & Finance** | Donn J McCall |
| **Bankruptcy & Creditor's Rights** | Donn J McCall |
| **Business Transactions** | Donn J McCall |
| **Commercial Litigation** | Donn J McCall |
| **Construction** | Thomas F Reese |
| **Energy** | Thomas F Reese |
| **Environmental** | Drake D Hill |
| **Healthcare** | Jeffrey C Brinkerhoff |
| **Intellectual Property** | J Kenneth Barbe |
| **Insurance Defense** | Jeffrey C Brinkerhoff |
| **Labor & Employment** | J Kenneth Barbe |
| **Medical Malpractice & Products Liability** | Jeffrey C Brinkerhoff |
| **Mining** | Harry B Durham III |
| **Oil & Gas** | Thomas F Reese |
| **Probate & Estate Planning** | J Kenneth Barbe |
| **Regulatory & Administrative** | Drake D Hill |
| **Real Estate** | J Kenneth Barbe |
| **Torts & Insurance** | Jeffrey C Brinkerhoff |

BROWN ┃ DREW & MASSEY LLP

ATTORNEYS AT LAW

# FIRM INDEX

**PROFILE:** CONTACT DETAILS AT THE END OF EVERY STATE  **TABLE:** REFERS TO THE SPECIALIST LISTS IN WHICH THE FIRM APPEARS

2053

Corporate/M&A p.1840, Employment:
Mainly Defendant p.1843, Energy &
Natural Resources p.1847, Energy &
Natural Resources: Dispute Resolution
p.1848, Energy: Electricity p.444,
Energy: Oil & Gas p.441, Environment
p.450, Intellectual Property p.1859,
Intellectual Property: Patent p.1383,
Litigation p.470, Litigation: General
Commercial p.1864, Projects p.56, Real
Estate p.1871, Tax p.1874, Technology &
IT Outsourcing p.1877

### Baker & Daniels
Profile: p.902
Tables: Corporate/M&A p.887,
Employment: Mainly Defendant p.889,
Litigation: General Commercial p.890,
Real Estate p.892

### Baker, Donelson, Bearman, Caldwell & Berkowitz, PC
Profile: p.1819
Tables: Corporate/Commercial p.148,
Corporate/M&A p.1799, Employment:
Mainly Defendant p.149, Litigation:
General Commercial p.972, Real Estate
p.153

### Baker & Hostetler LLP
Tables: Bankruptcy/Restructuring
p.1600, Construction p.589,
Corporate/M&A p.1604, Employee
Benefits & Executive Compensation
p.1606, Employment: Mainly Defendant
p.596, Environment p.1610, Litigation:
General Commercial p.1616, Media &
Entertainment p.476, Real Estate p.1620

### Baker & McKenzie
Profile: p.866
Tables: Antitrust p.766, Banking &
Finance p.770, Business Process
Outsourcing p.1, Corporate/M&A &
Private Equity p.780, Healthcare p.1854,
Immigration p.459, International
Arbitration p.35, Litigation: General
Commercial p.801, Tax p.273,
Technology & IT Outsourcing p.813

### Balch & Bingham
Profile: p.161
Tables: Banking & Finance p.147,
Corporate/Commercial p.148,
Employment: Mainly Defendant p.149,
Litigation: General Commercial p.151,
Real Estate p.153

### Bales Weinstein
Table: Environment p.600

### Ballard Spahr Andrews & Ingersoll LLP
Profile: p.1746
Tables: Banking & Finance p.1694,
Corporate/M&A p.1700, Employment:
Mainly Defendant p.1282, Environment
p.1284, Intellectual Property p.1710,
Litigation: General Commercial p.352,
Real Estate p.354

### Ball Janik LLP
Table: Real Estate p.1676

### Bangs, McCullen, Butler, Foye & Simmons, LLP
Tables: Corporate/Commercial p.1792,
Litigation: General Commercial p.1794,
Real Estate p.1796

### Bankston, Gronning, O'Hara, PC
Table: Litigation: General Commercial
p.171

### Banner & Witcoff Ltd
Tables: Intellectual Property p.466

### Banta Immigration Law Ltd
Table: Immigration p.694

### Barack Ferrazzano Kirschbaum Perlman & Nagelberg
Table: Real Estate p.808

### Barger & Wolen
Table: Insurance: Insurer Firms p.242

### Barnes & Thornburg LLP
Profile: p.903
Tables: Corporate/M&A p.887,
Employment: Mainly Defendant p.889,
Litigation: General Commercial p.890,
Real Estate p.892

### Barnett, Bolt, Kirkwood, Long & McBride
Table: Tax p.622

### Barran Liebman LLP
Profile: p.1686
Table: Employment: Mainly Defendant
p.1669

### Barrasso Usdin Kupperman Freeman & Sarver LLC
Profile: p.990
Table: Litigation: General Commercial
p.972

### Barris, Sott, Denn & Driker, PLLC
Tables: Litigation: General Commercial
p.1128, Real Estate p.1130

### Barst & Mukamal LLP
Table: Immigration p.1376

### Bartlit Beck Herman Palenchar & Scott
Tables: Corporate/M&A p.346,
Litigation: General Commercial p.352

### Bass, Berry & Sims PLC
Profile: p.1820
Tables: Corporate/M&A p.1799,
Employment: Mainly Defendant p.1801,
Litigation: General Commercial p.1803,
Media & Entertainment p.1806, Real
Estate p.1807

### Bassford Remele, A Professional Association
Table: Litigation: General Commercial
p.1156

### Bateman Seidel Miner Blomgren Chellis & Gram, P.C.
Table: Real Estate p.1676

### Bates & Carey
Table: Insurance: Coverage Litigation
p.795

### The Bayard Firm
Profile: p.417
Tables: Bankruptcy/Restructuring p.388,
Chancery p.391, Intellectual Property
p.397, Real Estate p.399

### Bays Deaver Lung Rose Baba
Tables: Litigation: General Commercial
p.745, Real Estate p.747

### Beasley, Allen, Crow, Methvin, Portis & Miles, PC
Table: Litigation: General Commercial
p.151

### Beck, Redden & Secrest LLP
Table: Litigation: General Commercial
p.1864

### Beck, De Corso, Daly, Kreindler & Harris
Profile: p.324
Table: Litigation: Specialist Firms in
White-Collar Crime & Government
Investigations p.255

### Becker & Poliakoff PA
Table: Construction p.589

### Bedell, Dittmar, DeVault, Pillans & Coxe
Tables: Litigation: General Commercial
p.608, Litigation: White-Collar Crime &
Government Investigations p.610

### Beirne Maynard & Parsons, LLP
Profile: p.1923
Tables: Energy & Natural Resources:
Dispute Resolution p.1848, Insurance
p.1857

### Belin Lamson McCormick Zumbach Flynn, PC
Tables: Corporate/M&A p.909,
Employment: Mainly Defendant p.911,
Litigation: General Commercial p.913,
Real Estate p.917

### Bell, Boyd & Lloyd LLC
Tables: Antitrust p.766, Construction
p.433, Corporate/M&A & Private Equity
p.780, Environment p.790, Healthcare
p.793, Real Estate p.808

### Belles Graham Proudfoot and Wilson
Table: Land Use p.743

### Bello, Black & Welsh LLP
Table: Employment: Mainly Defendant
p.1065

### Benesch, Friedlander, Coplan & Aronoff LLP
Profile: p.1643
Tables: Banking & Finance p.1598,
Construction p.1602, Real Estate
p.1620

### Bercow & Radell PA
Profile: p.659
Table: Real Estate: Zoning/Land Use
p.620

### Berens & Tate PC
Table: Employment: Mainly Defendant
p.1238

### Berger Singerman
Tables: Bankruptcy/Restructuring p.585,
Litigation: General Commercial p.608

### Berger & Montague PC
Table: Antitrust p.1692

### Berkes Crane Robinson & Seal, LLP
Table: Insurance: Insurer Firms p.242

### Berkowitz Oliver Williams Shaw & Eisenbrandt LLP
Table: Litigation: General Commercial
p.1197

### Berman DeValerio Pease Tabacco Burt & Pucillo
Table: Antitrust p.581

### Berman & Simmons
Table: Litigation: General Commercial
p.1005

### Bernard P Wolfsdorf PC
Table: Immigration p.241

### Bernstein Shur
Profile: p.1018
Tables: Corporate/M&A p.1000,
Employment: Mainly Defendant p.1002,
Environment p.1004, Litigation: General
Commercial p.1005, Real Estate p.1008

### Bernstein, Cushner & Kimmell PC
Table: Environment p.1068

### Bernstein Litowitz Berger & Grossmann LLP
Profile: p.1519
Table: Litigation: Securities Mainly
Plaintiff p.1390

### Berry Appleman & Leiden LLP
Table: Immigration p.241

### Betzer Roybal & Eisenberg PC
Table: Corporate/Commercial p.1320

### Beus Gilbert PLLC
Table: Real Estate: Zoning/Land Use
p.186

### Beveridge & Diamond PC
Profile: p.562
Tables: Environment p.450

### Bierce & Kenerson, P.C.
Tables: Business Process Outsourcing
p.1, Technology & IT Outsourcing p.1428

### Bilzin Sumberg Baena Price & Axelrod LLP
Profile: p.660
Tables: Bankruptcy/Restructuring p.585,
Construction p.589, Environment p.600,
Litigation: General Commercial p.608,
Real Estate p.616, Real Estate:
Zoning/Land Use p.620, Tax p.622

### Bingham McCutchen LLP
Profile: p.1110
Tables: Antitrust p.215, Banking &
Finance p.218, Bankruptcy/Restructuring
p.1343, Construction p.224,
Corporate/M&A p.1060, Energy &
Natural Resources p.233, Environment
p.235, Litigation: General Commercial
p.255, Private Equity: Buyouts & Venture
Capital Investment p.1077, Projects
p.1412, Real Estate p.380, Sports Law
p.59, Tax p.1084, Telecom, Broadcast &
Satellite: Regulatory p.491

**Bingham McHale LLP**
Tables: Litigation: General Commercial
p.890, Real Estate p.892

**Birch, Horton, Bittner & Cherot**
Tables: Corporate/M&A p.168, Litigation:
General Commercial p.171

**Birch, Stewart, Kolasch
& Birch, LLP**
Table: Intellectual Property: Northern
Virginia p.1974

**Bird, Marella, Boxer
& Wolpert PC**
Table: Litigation: Specialist Firms in
White-Collar Crime & Government
Investigations p.255

**Black Lowe & Graham**
Table: Intellectual Property p.1998

**Black, Srebnick, Kornspan &
Stumpf PA**
Table: Litigation: White-Collar Crime &
Government Investigations p.610

**Blackwell Sanders Peper
Martin LLP**
Profile: p.1212
Tables: Corporate/M&A p.924,
Employment: Mainly Defendant p.1195,
Litigation: General Commercial p.1197,
Real Estate p.1200

**Blank Rome LLP**
Profile: p.1747
Tables: Banking & Finance p.1694,
Bankruptcy/Restructuring p.388,
Corporate/M&A p.1700, Employment:
Mainly Defendant p.1703, Government:
Government Relations p.32, Litigation:
General Commercial p.1713, Real Estate
p.1717, Transportation: Shipping (outside
New York) p.78, Wealth Management p.80

**Blecher & Collins**
Profile: p.325
Table: Antitrust p.215

**Blish & Cavanagh, LLP**
Table: Litigation: General Commercial
p.1768

**Bloom, Hergott and Diemer LLP**
Table: Media & Entertainment:
Transactional p.265

**Bodman LLP**
Profile: p.1141
Tables: Banking & Finance p.1120,
Corporate/M&A p.1121, Litigation:
General Commercial p.1128

**Boehl Stopher & Graves, LLP**
Profile: p.953
Table: Litigation: General Commercial
p.942

**Boies, Schiller & Flexner LLP**
Profile: p.1520
Tables: Antitrust p.425, International
Arbitration p.35, Litigation: General
Commercial p.1387

**Bond, Schoeneck & King, PLLC**
Table: Employment: Mainly Defendant
p.1364

**Bondurant, Mixson & Elmore, LLP**
Profile: p.731
Tables: Antitrust p.675, Litigation:
General Commercial p.697

**Boone, Karlberg PC**
Tables: Corporate/M&A p.1222,
Litigation: General Commercial p.1225,
Real Estate p.1230

**Boose Casey Ciklin Lubitz
Martens McBane & O'Connell**
Table: Construction p.589

**Bose McKinney & Evans LLP**
Tables: Corporate/M&A p.887,
Employment: Mainly Defendant p.889,
Litigation: General Commercial p.890,
Real Estate p.892

**Bouchard Margules &
Friedlander PA**
Table: Chancery p.391

**Boult, Cummings, Conners
& Berry, PLC**
Profile: p.1821
Tables: Corporate/M&A p.1799,
Employment: Mainly Defendant p.1801,
Litigation: General Commercial p.1803,
Real Estate p.1807

**Bowditch & Dewey LLP**
Table: Environment p.1068

**Bowen Riley Warnock &
Jacobson, PLC**
Profile: p.1822
Table: Litigation: General Commercial
p.1803

**Bowles Rice McDavid Graff &
Love LLP**
Profile: p.2020
Tables: Corporate/Commercial p.2010,
Employment: Mainly Defendant p.2011,
Litigation: General Commercial p.2013,
Real Estate p.2015

**Boyce, Greenfield, Pashby
& Welk LLP**
Tables: Corporate/Commercial p.1792,
Employment: Mainly Defendant p.1793,
Litigation: General Commercial p.1794,
Real Estate p.1796

**Boyle Fredrickson Newholm
Stein & Gratz SC**
Table: Intellectual Property p.2028

**Bracewell & Giuliani LLP**
Profile: p.1924
Tables: Banking & Finance p.1831,
Bankruptcy/Restructuring p.1834,
Corporate/M&A p.1840, Employment:
Mainly Defendant p.1843, Energy &
Natural Resources p.1847, Energy &
Natural Resources: Dispute Resolution
p.1848, Energy: Electricity p.444,
Energy: Oil & Gas p.441, Environment
p.1851, Intellectual Property p.1859,
Litigation: General Commercial p.1864,
Projects p.1869, Real Estate p.1871, Tax
p.1874, Technology & IT Outsourcing
p.1877

**Bradley Arant Rose & White LLP**
Profile: p.162

**Tables**: Banking & Finance p.147,
Construction p.433,
Corporate/Commercial p.148,
Employment: Mainly Defendant p.149,
Litigation: General Commercial p.151,
Real Estate p.153

**Bradley & Riley, PC**
Tables: Corporate/M&A p.909,
Employment: Mainly Defendant p.911,
Litigation: General Commercial p.913,
Real Estate p.917

**Bradshaw, Fowler, Proctor &
Fairgrave, PC**
Tables: Corporate/M&A p.909,
Employment: Mainly Defendant p.911,
Litigation: General Commercial p.913,
Real Estate p.917

**Brady Hathaway Brady & Bretz**
Profile: p.1142
Table: Employment: Mainly Defendant
p.1125

**Brault Graham Scott & Brault LLC**
Table: Litigation: General Commercial
p.1032

**Breazeale, Sachse & Wilson, LLP**
Table: Employment: Mainly Defendant
p.967

**Bricker & Eckler LLP**
Tables: Construction p.1602,
Environment p.1610, Real Estate p.1620

**Bricklemyer Smolker & Bolves PA**
Table: Real Estate: Zoning/Land Use
p.620

**Briggs and Morgan, Professional
Association**
Tables: Corporate/M&A p.1151,
Employment: Mainly Defendant p.1154,
Litigation: General Commercial p.1156,
Real Estate p.1159

**Brinks Hofer Gilson & Lione**
Profile: p.867
Table: Intellectual Property p.798

**Broad and Cassel**
Tables: Construction p.589, Healthcare
p.603, Insurance p.606, Real Estate
p.616

**Bronstein, Carlson, Gleim &
Smith, PA**
Table: Tax p.622

**Brooks, Pierce, McLendon,
Humphrey & Leonard LLP**
Tables: Antitrust p.1568,
Corporate/M&A p.1571, Employment:
Mainly Defendant p.1573, Environment
p.1574, Litigation: General Commercial
p.1577

**Brooks Tom Porter Quitiquit**
Table: Real Estate p.747

**Brown, Drew & Massey LLP**
Profile: p.2049
Tables: Corporate/M&A p.2041, Real
Estate p.2045

**Browning, Kaleczyc, Berry
& Hoven PC**
Profile: p.1233
Tables: Litigation: General Commercial
p.1225, Natural Resources &
Environment p.1228

**Brown Law Firm PC**
Tables: Employment: Mainly Defendant
p.1223, Litigation: General Commercial
p.1225

**Brown McCarroll LLP**
Tables: Environment p.1851, Healthcare
p.1854

**Brown Raysman Millstein Felder
& Steiner LLP**
Profile: p.1521
Tables: Business Process Outsourcing
p.1, Construction p.1350,
Corporate/M&A p.374, Employment:
Mainly Defendant p.376, Intellectual
Property: Trademark & Copyright
p.1384, Litigation: General Commercial
p.378, Real Estate p.380, Technology &
IT Outsourcing p.1428

**Brown Rudnick Berlack
Israels LLP**
Tables: Bankruptcy/Restructuring
p.1057, Environment p.1068, Healthcare
p.1070, Real Estate p.380

**Brownstein Hyatt & Farber PC**
Profile: p.368
Tables: Corporate/Commercial p.1320,
Corporate/M&A p.346, Employment:
Mainly Defendant p.348, Real Estate
p.354

**Brown, Winick, Graves, Gross,
Baskerville and Schoenebaum
PLC**
Profile: p.923
Tables: Corporate/M&A p.909,
Litigation: General Commercial p.913,
Real Estate p.917

**Bruder Gentile & Marcoux LLP**
Table: Energy: Electricity p.444

**Brunini, Grantham, Grower &
Hewes, PLLC**
Profile: p.1188
Tables: Corporate/Commercial p.1174,
Litigation: General Commercial p.1178,
Real Estate p.1181

**Bryan Cave LLP**
Tables: Corporate/M&A p.175,
Corporate/M&A: Mid-Tier Firms p.1359,
Employment: Mainly Defendant p.784,
Environment p.1370, Environment
(including water rights) p.179, Litigation:
General Commercial p.1197, Real Estate
p.1200

**Buchalter Nemer Fields & Younger**
Table: Banking & Finance p.218

**Buchanan Ingersoll PC**
Profile: p.1749
Tables: Corporate/M&A p.1700,
Employment: Mainly Defendant p.1703,
Healthcare p.603, Intellectual Property
p.1710, Intellectual Property: Northern
Virginia p.1974, Litigation: General
Commercial p.1713

**C**

**Clarence & Dyer LLP**
Table: Litigation: Specialist Firms in White-Collar Crime & Government Investigations p.255

**Clark, Atcheson & Reisert**
Table: Transportation: Shipping (New York) p.73

**Clark Hill PLC**
Profile: p.1144
Tables: Corporate/M&A p.1121, Employment: Mainly Defendant p.1125, Real Estate p.1130

**Cleary Gottlieb Steen & Hamilton LLP**
Profile: p.1525
Tables: Antitrust p.425, Bankruptcy/Restructuring p.1343, Capital Markets: CDOs, Repackaging & Other Synthetic Products p.12, Capital Markets: Debt & Equity (excludes West Coast) p.6, Capital Markets: Derivatives p.14, Capital Markets: Securitisation p.17, Corporate/M&A p.1353, Employee Benefits & Executive Compensation p.1361, Financial Services: Financial Institutions M&A p.23, Litigation: General Commercial p.1387, Litigation: Securities p.1389, Private Fund Formation p.1409, Real Estate p.1416, Tax p.1422

**Cleary Shahi & Aicher, P.C.**
Table: Litigation: General Commercial p.1959

**Clifford Chance LLP**
Profile: p.1526
Tables: Capital Markets: CDOs, Repackaging & Other Synthetic Products p.12, Insurance: Dispute Resolution p.1378, Insurance: Transactional & Regulatory p.1380, International Arbitration p.35, Litigation: Securities p.1389, Projects p.479

**Cline, Williams, Wright, Johnson & Oldfather LLP**
Tables: Corporate/M&A p.1236, Litigation: General Commercial p.1239

**Coats Rose Yale Ryman Lee**
Table: Construction p.1838

**Coblentz, Patch, Duffy & Bass LLP**
Table: Real Estate p.269

**Coffman, Coleman, Andrews & Grogan**
Table: Employment: Mainly Defendant p.596

**Cohen & Grigsby PC**
Table: Employment: Mainly Defendant p.1703

**Cohn Whitesell & Goldberg LLP**
Profile: p.1111
Table: Bankruptcy/Restructuring p.1057

**Cokinos, Bosien and Young**
Table: Construction p.1838

**Cole, Raywid, Braverman LLP**
Table: Telecom, Broadcast & Satellite: Regulatory p.491

**Cole, Schotz, Meisel, Forman & Leonard PA**
Tables: Litigation: General Commercial p.1289, Real Estate p.1293

**Collier Shannon Scott PLLC**
Table: International Trade p.41

**Colson Hicks Eidson**
Profile: p.662
Tables: Litigation: General Commercial p.608, Litigation: White-Collar Crime & Government Investigations p.610

**Comiter, Singer & Baseman, LLP**
Table: Tax p.622

**Commercial Law Group**
Table: Corporate/Commercial p.1653

**Condon & Forsyth LLP**
Table: Transportation: Aviation: Regulatory & Litigation p.67

**Conklin, Jenke & Woodcock PC**
Table: Employment: Mainly Defendant p.1321

**Conley Rose, P.C.**
Table: Intellectual Property p.1859

**Conmy Feste Ltd**
Tables: Corporate/Commercial p.1590, Employment: Mainly Defendant p.1592, Real Estate p.1595

**Connelly Baker Wotring Jackson LLP**
Table: Environment p.1851

**Conner & Winters, PC**
Tables: Corporate/Commercial p.1653, Employment: Mainly Defendant p.1654

**Connolly Bove Lodge & Hutz LLP**
Profile: p.418
Table: Intellectual Property p.397

**Connolly, O'Malley, Lillis, Hansen & Olson LLP**
Table: Real Estate p.917

**Conrad O'Brien Gellman & Rohn PC**
Profile: p.1751
Table: Litigation: General Commercial p.1713

**Constangy, Brooks & Smith, LLC**
Tables: Employment: Mainly Defendant p.149

**Conway & Mrowiec**
Profile: p.869
Table: Construction p.778

**Cook, Little, Rosenblatt & Manson PLLC**
Profile: p.1275
Tables: Corporate/Commercial p.1263, Litigation: General Commercial p.1267

**Cook & Roach, L.L.P.**
Table: Insurance p.1857

**Cooley Godward LLP**
Tables: Antitrust p.215, Capital Markets:

Debt & Equity (West Coast) p.8, Corporate/M&A p.346, Corporate/M&A: Northern California p.226, Corporate/M&A: Northern Virginia p.1967, Intellectual Property p.247, Intellectual Property: Northern Virginia p.1974, IT & IT Outsourcing p.253, Litigation: General Commercial p.255, Tax p.273

**Cooper & Scully PC**
Table: Insurance p.1857

**Corr Cronin LLP**
Table: Litigation: General Commercial p.1999

**Correro Fishman Haygood Phelps Walmsley & Casteix LLP**
Profile: p.992
Tables: Banking & Finance p.963, Corporate/M&A p.964, Litigation: General Commercial p.972

**Corretti, Newsom & Hawkins**
Table: Real Estate p.153

**Costello Porter Hill Heisterkamp Bushnell & Carpenter LLP**
Table: Litigation: General Commercial p.1794

**Cotchett, Pitre, Simon & McCarthy**
Table: Litigation: General Commercial p.255

**Cotsirilos Tighe & Streicker Ltd**
Table: Litigation: White-Collar Crime & Government Investigations p.801

**Couch White, LLP**
Table: Energy: Upstate New York p.1370

**Covington & Burling**
Profile: p.563
Tables: Bankruptcy/Restructuring p.431, Corporate/Commercial p.435, Employee Benefits & Executive Compensation p.437, Environment p.450, Financial Services: Regulatory Compliance p.23, Financial Services: Regulatory Enforcement & Investigations p.28, Government: Government Relations p.32, Healthcare: Pharmaceutical/Medical Products Regulatory p.455, Insurance: Policy Holder p.244, International Trade p.41, Litigation p.470, Litigation: White-Collar Crime & Government Investigations p.1391, Media & Entertainment p.476, Real Estate p.481, Securities p.485, Sports Law p.59, Telecom, Broadcast & Satellite: Regulatory p.491, Transportation: Rail p.68

**Cowan & Miller**
Table: Immigration p.1997

**Cowan, Liebowitz & Latman**
Tables: Intellectual Property: Trademark & Copyright p.1384, Media & Entertainment: Litigation p.1404

**Cox Castle & Nicholson LLP**
Tables: Construction p.224, Real Estate p.269

**Cox Smith Matthews Incorporated**
Profile: p.1926
Tables: Antitrust p.1829, Bankruptcy/Restructuring p.1834, Intellectual Property p.1859

**Cozen O'Connor**
Tables: Bankruptcy/Restructuring p.388, Corporate/M&A p.1700

**Cravath, Swaine & Moore LLP**
Profile: p.1527
Tables: Antitrust p.1334, Banking & Finance p.1339, Capital Markets: Debt & Equity (excludes West Coast) p.6, Capital Markets: Securitisation p.17, Corporate/M&A p.1353, Energy & Natural Resources p.1367, Environment: Mainly Transactional p.1372, Intellectual Property: Patent p.1383, Intellectual Property: Trademark & Copyright p.1384, Litigation: General Commercial p.1387, Litigation: Securities p.1389, Media & Entertainment p.1402, Media & Entertainment: Litigation p.1404, Tax p.1422, Transportation: Shipping (New York) p.73

**Croker, Huck, Kasher, DeWitt, Anderson & Gonderinger, P.C.**
Table: Real Estate p.1241

**Cross, Gunter, Witherspoon & Galchus, PC**
Profile: p.211
Table: Employment: Mainly Defendant p.202

**Crowe & Dunlevy, PC**
Profile: p.1662
Tables: Corporate/Commercial p.1653, Employment: Mainly Defendant p.1654, Litigation: General Commercial p.1656, Real Estate p.1657

**Crowell & Moring LLP**
Profile: p.564
Tables: Antitrust p.425, Energy: Electricity p.444, Energy: Oil & Gas p.441, Environment p.450, Government: Government Contracts p.29, Healthcare p.455, Insurance: Insurer Firms p.461, Transportation: Aviation: Regulatory & Litigation p.67

**Crowley, Haughey, Hanson, Toole & Dietrich, PLLP**
Profile: p.553, 1234
Tables: Corporate/M&A p.1222, Employment: Mainly Defendant p.1223, Litigation: General Commercial p.1225, Natural Resources & Environment p.1228, Real Estate p.1230

**Cunningham, Bounds, Yance, Crowder & Brown, LLC**
Table: Litigation: General Commercial p.151

**Curran & Parry**
Profile: p.1261
Table: Gaming & Licensing p.1250

**Cutler & Donahoe LLP**
Tables: Corporate/Commercial p.1792, Real Estate p.1796

**Cyrus D Mehta & Associates PLLC**
Table: Immigration p.1376

## D

**Dale M Schwartz & Associates LLP**
Table: Immigration p.694

**D'Amante Couser Steiner Pellerin, P.A.**
Tables: Litigation: General Commercial p.1267, Real Estate p.1269

**Daniels, Kashtan, Downs, Robertson & Magathan**
Table: Construction p.589

**Danielson Harrigan Leyh & Tollefson, LLP**
Table: Litigation: General Commercial p.1999

**Dann Pecar Newman & Kleiman, PC**
Table: Real Estate p.892

**Davenport, Evans, Hurwitz & Smith LLP**
Tables: Corporate/Commercial p.1792, Employment: Mainly Defendant p.1793, Litigation: General Commercial p.1794, Real Estate p.1796

**Davis & Kuelthau, SC**
Table: Employment: Mainly Defendant p.2026

**Davis Munck Butrus PC**
Profile: p.1927
Table: Intellectual Property p.1859

**Davis & Boghigian, PC**
Table: Real Estate p.1269

**Davis, Brown, Koehn, Shors & Roberts, PC**
Tables: Corporate/M&A p.909, Employment: Mainly Defendant p.911, Litigation: General Commercial p.913, Real Estate p.917

**Davis & Cannon**
Tables: Employment: Mainly Defendant p.2042, Litigation: General Commercial p.2043, Real Estate p.2045

**Davis & Gilbert**
Table: Media & Entertainment: Advertising p.1399

**Davis Graham & Stubbs LLP**
Tables: Corporate/M&A p.346, Employment: Mainly Defendant p.348, Environment p.349, Litigation: General Commercial p.352, Real Estate p.354

**Davis Polk & Wardwell**
Profile: p.1528
Tables: Antitrust p.1334, Banking & Finance p.1339, Bankruptcy/Restructuring p.1343, Capital Markets: Debt & Equity (excludes West Coast) p.6, Capital Markets: Debt

& Equity (West Coast) p.8, Capital Markets: Derivatives p.14, Corporate/M&A p.1353, Corporate/M&A: Northern California p.226, Employee Benefits & Executive Compensation p.1361, Energy & Natural Resources p.1367, Environment: Mainly Transactional p.1372, Financial Services: Financial Institutions M&A p.23, International Trade p.41, Litigation: General Commercial p.1387, Litigation: Securities p.1389, Litigation: White-Collar Crime & Government Investigations p.1391, Media & Entertainment: Corporate p.1402, Private Equity: Buyouts & Venture Capital Investment p.1406, Private Fund Formation p.1409, Projects p.1412, Tax p.1422

**Davis & Wilkerson, PC**
Table: Healthcare p.1854

**Davis Wright Tremaine LLP**
Tables: Bankruptcy/Restructuring p.167, Corporate/Commercial p.1992, Corporate/M&A p.168, Energy & Natural Resources p.233, Energy: Electricity p.444, Environment p.1672, Healthcare p.238, Intellectual Property p.1998, Litigation: General Commercial p.1674, Media & Entertainment p.476, Media & Entertainment: Litigation p.262, Real Estate p.172

**Dawda, Mann, Mulcahy & Sadler PLC**
Table: Real Estate p.1130

**Day, Berry & Howard LLP**
Profile: p.386
Tables: Corporate/M&A p.374, Employment: Mainly Defendant p.376, Litigation: General Commercial p.378, Real Estate p.380

**Day Casebeer Madrid & Batchelder LLP**
Table: Intellectual Property p.247

**Deacy & Deacy LLP**
Table: Litigation: General Commercial p.1197

**Deaner, Deaner, Scann, Malan & Larsen**
Table: Real Estate p.1255

**Dean, Mead, Egerton, Bloodworth, Capouano & Bozarth PA**
Tables: Litigation: General Commercial p.608, Real Estate p.616, Tax p.622

**Debevoise & Plimpton LLP**
Profile: p.1529
Tables: Antitrust p.1334, Banking & Finance p.1339, Bankruptcy/Restructuring p.1343, Capital Markets: Debt & Equity (excludes West Coast) p.6, Corporate/M&A p.1353, Employee Benefits & Executive Compensation p.1361, Energy & Natural Resources p.1367, Environment: Mainly Transactional p.1372, Financial Services: Regulatory Compliance p.23, Insurance: Dispute Resolution p.1378, Insurance: Transactional & Regulatory p.1380, Intellectual Property: Trademark & Copyright p.1384, Litigation: General Commercial p.1387, Litigation: Securities

p.1389, Litigation: White-Collar Crime & Government Investigations p.1391, Media & Entertainment: Corporate p.1402, Media & Entertainment: Litigation p.1404, Private Equity: Buyouts & Venture Capital Investment p.1406, Private Fund Formation p.1409, Projects p.1412, Real Estate p.1416, Sports Law p.59, Tax p.1422

**Dechert LLP**
Profile: p.1752
Tables: Antitrust p.1692, Capital Markets: Securitisation p.17, Corporate/M&A p.1700, Corporate/M&A: Mid-Tier Firms p.1359, Employment: Mainly Defendant p.1703, Environment p.1706, Financial Services: Regulatory Compliance p.23, Intellectual Property p.247, Investment Management p.468, Litigation: General Commercial p.1713, Litigation: Products Liability p.1292, Products Liability p.49, Real Estate p.269, Securities p.485

**Denlinger, Rosenthal & Greenberg LPA**
Table: Employment: Mainly Defendant p.1608

**Dennis, Corry, Porter & Smith LLP**
Table: Transportation: Road (Carriage/Commercial) p.71

**DeOrchis & Partners LLP**
Tables: Transportation: Rail p.68, Transportation: Road (Carriage/Commercial) p.71, Transportation: Shipping (New York) p.73, Transportation: Shipping (outside New York) p.78

**Devine Millimet & Branch PA**
Tables: Corporate/Commercial p.1263, Employment: Mainly Defendant p.1265, Litigation: General Commercial p.1267, Real Estate p.1269

**Dewey Ballantine LLP**
Profile: p.1530
Tables: Antitrust p.1334, Capital Markets: Debt & Equity (excludes West Coast) p.6, Capital Markets: Securitisation p.17, Corporate/M&A p.1353, Energy & Natural Resources p.1367, Energy: Electricity p.444, Energy: Oil & Gas p.441, Insurance: Dispute Resolution p.1378, Insurance: Transactional & Regulatory p.1380, Intellectual Property p.247, Litigation: General Commercial p.1387, Media & Entertainment: Corporate p.1402, Private Fund Formation p.1409, Projects p.1412, Sports Law p.59, Tax p.487, Transportation: Aviation: Finance p.64

**Dickinson, Mackaman, Tyler & Hagen, PC**
Tables: Employment: Mainly Defendant p.911, Real Estate p.917

**Dickinson Wright PLLC**
Profile: p.1145
Tables: Banking & Finance p.1120, Corporate/M&A p.1121, Employment: Mainly Defendant p.1125, Litigation: General Commercial p.1128, Real Estate p.1130

**Dickstein Shapiro Morin & Oshinsky LLP**
Profile: p.565
Tables: Bankruptcy/Restructuring p.431, Corporate/Commercial p.435, Employment: Mainly Defendant p.439, Energy: Electricity p.444, Government: Government Relations p.32, Insurance: Dispute Resolution p.1378, Insurance: Policy Holder p.244, Litigation p.470, Securities p.485

**Dilworth Paxson LLP**
Table: Bankruptcy/Restructuring p.1696

**Dinse, Knapp & McAndrew PC**
Tables: Corporate/Commercial p.1957, Employment: Mainly Defendant p.1958, Litigation: General Commercial p.1959, Real Estate p.1961

**Dinsmore & Shohl LLP**
Profile: p.1645
Tables: Banking & Finance p.1598, Bankruptcy/Restructuring p.1600, Corporate/M&A p.1604, Employee Benefits & Executive Compensation p.1606, Employment: Mainly Defendant p.939, Environment, Natural Resources & Regulated Industries p.940, Intellectual Property p.1614, Litigation: General Commercial p.942

**DiTrapano, Barrett & DiPiero, PLLC**
Table: Litigation: General Commercial p.2013

**DLA Piper Rudnick Gray Cary US LLP**
Profile: p.870
Tables: Banking & Finance p.218, Bankruptcy/Restructuring p.774, Construction p.433, Corporate/Commercial p.1992, Corporate/M&A p.1025, Corporate/M&A & Private Equity p.780, Corporate/M&A: Northern California p.226, Corporate/M&A: Northern Virginia p.1967, Employee Benefits & Executive Compensation p.1026, Employment: Mainly Defendant p.1028, Energy & Natural Resources p.789, Environment p.450, Government: Government Contracts p.29, Government: Government Relations p.32, Insurance: Reinsurance Litigation p.795, Intellectual Property p.247, IT & IT Outsourcing p.253, Litigation: General Commercial p.1032, Media & Entertainment: Litigation p.262, Products Liability p.49, Real Estate p.269, Technology & IT Outsourcing p.813

**Doerner, Saunders, Daniel & Anderson, LLP**
Table: Employment: Mainly Defendant p.1654

**Doffermyre, Shields, Canfield, Knowles & Devine**
Table: Litigation: General Commercial p.697

**Donahue, Tucker & Ciandella**
Table: Real Estate p.1269

**F**

**Doney, Crowley, Bloomquist, Payne & Uda, P.C.**
Table: Natural Resources & Environment p.1228

**Donovan Parry McDermott & Radzik**
Table: Transportation: Shipping (New York) p.73

**Dorsey & Whitney LLP**
Profile: p.1169
Tables: Bankruptcy/Restructuring p.167, Corporate/Commercial p.1590, Corporate/M&A p.168, Environment, Natural Resources & Regulated Industries p.169, Intellectual Property p.1998, Litigation: General Commercial p.171, Native American Law p.47, Real Estate p.172

**Dover Dixon Horne**
Table: Real Estate p.206

**Dow, Lohnes & Albertson, PLLC**
Profile: p.566
Table: Telecom, Broadcast & Satellite: Regulatory p.491

**Downey, Brand, Seymour & Rohwer LLP**
Table: Energy & Natural Resources p.233

**Downs Rachlin Martin PLLC**
Tables: Corporate/Commercial p.1957, Employment: Mainly Defendant p.1958, Litigation: General Commercial p.1959, Real Estate p.1961

**Dray, Thomson & Dyekman PC**
Tables: Corporate/M&A p.2041, Real Estate p.2045

**Drinker Biddle & Reath LLP**
Tables: Antitrust p.1692, Banking & Finance p.1694, Bankruptcy/Restructuring p.1696, Corporate/M&A p.1278, Environment p.1284, Insurance: Insurer Firms p.461, Intellectual Property p.1710, Litigation: General Commercial p.1289, Litigation: Products Liability p.1292, Real Estate p.1293

**Drummond Woodsum & MacMahon**
Tables: Corporate/M&A p.1000, Employment: Mainly Defendant p.1002, Real Estate p.1008

**Duane Morris LLP**
Profile: p.1753
Tables: Antitrust p.1692, Banking & Finance p.770, Bankruptcy/Restructuring p.1057, Corporate/M&A p.1700, Energy & Natural Resources p.689, Healthcare p.603, Immigration p.459, Insurance: Dispute Resolution p.1378, Insurance: Insurer Firms p.242, Intellectual Property p.1710, Litigation: General Commercial p.1289

**Duffy, Sweeney & Scott Ltd**
Tables: Corporate/Commercial p.1766, Litigation: General Commercial p.1768

**Dunn Carney Allen Higgins & Tongue LLP**
Profile: p.1688
Tables: Litigation: General Commercial p.1674, Real Estate p.1676

**Durant, Nichols, Houston, Hodgson & Cortese-Costa, P.C.**
Table: Employment: Mainly Defendant p.376

**Durham Jones & Pinegar, A Professional Corporation**
Table: Corporate/M&A p.1941

**Durrell Law Group, PC**
Table: Corporate/M&A p.168

**Dutton, Braun, Staack & Hellman PLC**
Table: Litigation: General Commercial p.913

**Duvin, Cahn & Hutton**
Profile: p.1646
Table: Employment: Mainly Defendant p.1608

**Dykema Gossett PLLC**
Tables: Corporate/M&A p.1121, Employee Benefits & Executive Compensation p.1124, Employment: Mainly Defendant p.1125, Litigation: General Commercial p.1128, Real Estate p.1130

**E**

**Earl, Curley & Lagarde, PC**
Table: Real Estate: Zoning/Land Use p.186

**Eastman & Smith Ltd**
Table: Environment p.1610

**Eaton Peabody**
Profile: p.1020
Tables: Corporate/M&A p.1000, Employment: Mainly Defendant p.1002, Environment p.1004, Litigation: General Commercial p.1005, Real Estate p.1008

**Eaves & Mendenhall PA**
Table: Litigation: General Commercial p.1324

**Eberle, Berlin, Kading, Turnbow & McIlveen, Chartered**
Table: Litigation: General Commercial p.760

**Edwards Angell Palmer & Dodge LLP**
Profile: p.1112
Tables: Antitrust p.1053, Banking & Finance p.1055, Corporate/Commercial p.1766, Corporate/M&A p.374, Employment: Mainly Defendant p.1767, Insurance: Dispute Resolution p.1378, Insurance: Transactional & Regulatory p.1380, Litigation: General Commercial p.1768, Private Equity: Buyouts & Venture Capital Investment p.1077, Real Estate p.1081

**Edwards Frickle Anner-Hughes & Cook**
Table: Litigation: Mainly Plaintiff p.1227

**Eimer Stahl Klevorn & Solberg LLP**
Profile: p.871
Table: Antitrust p.766

**Elam & Burke PA**
Table: Litigation: General Commercial p.760

**Elarbee, Thompson, Sapp & Wilson, LLP**
Tables: Employment: Mainly Defendant p.686, Immigration p.694

**Elderkin & Pirnie PLC**
Table: Litigation: General Commercial p.913

**Eldridge Cooper Steichen & Leach PLLC**
Table: Employment: Mainly Defendant p.1654

**Ellis & Thorp PLLC**
Table: Environment p.1972

**Ellison Schneider & Harris**
Table: Energy & Natural Resources p.233

**Ellis & Winters LLP**
Tables: Antitrust p.1568, Litigation: General Commercial p.1577

**Elsaesser Jarzabek Anderson Marks Elliott & McHugh, Chartered**
Table: Bankruptcy/Restructuring p.758

**Epstein Becker & Green PC**
Tables: Employment: Mainly Defendant p.596, Environment p.690, Healthcare p.455

**Erickson & Sederstrom, PC**
Tables: Corporate/M&A p.1236, Litigation: General Commercial p.1239

**Everett Law Firm**
Table: Litigation: General Commercial p.204

**F**

**Fabian & Clendenin**
Tables: Litigation: General Commercial p.1945, Real Estate p.1947

**Fabyanske, Westra & Hart PA**
Table: Real Estate p.1159

**Faegre & Benson LLP**
Profile: p.1170
Tables: Construction p.345, Corporate/M&A p.346, Employment: Mainly Defendant p.348, Environment p.349, Intellectual Property p.351, Litigation: General Commercial p.352, Real Estate p.354

**Farella Braun & Martel LLP**
Tables: Construction p.224, Environment p.235, Insurance: Policy Holder p.244, Intellectual Property p.247, Litigation: General Commercial p.255

**Farer Fersko**
Tables: Environment p.1284, Real Estate p.1293

**Farmer, Cline & Campbell PLLC**
Table: Litigation: General Commercial p.2013

**Farr & Taranto**
Table: Litigation: Appellate p.474

**Faruki Ireland & Cox PLL**
Table: Litigation: General Commercial p.1616

**Fay Sharpe Fagan Minnich & McKee LLP**
Profile: p.1647
Table: Intellectual Property p.1614

**Feldman Orlansky & Sanders**
Table: Litigation: General Commercial p.171

**Felhaber, Larson, Fenlon & Vogt, PC**
Tables: Employment: Mainly Defendant p.1154, Real Estate p.1159

**Fellers, Snider, Blankenship, Bailey & Tippens, A Professional Corporation**
Profile: p.1663
Table: Litigation: General Commercial p.1656

**Fennemore Craig**
Profile: p.197
Tables: Corporate/M&A p.175, Employment: Mainly Defendant p.177, Environment (including water rights) p.179, Litigation: General Commercial p.181, Litigation: White-Collar Crime & Government Investigations p.182, Real Estate p.183, Real Estate: Zoning/Land Use p.186

**Fenwick & West LLP**
Profile: p.326
Tables: Corporate/M&A: Northern California p.226, Intellectual Property p.247, IT & IT Outsourcing p.253, Tax p.273

**Ferencik, Libanoff, Brandt, Bustamante & Williams**
Table: Construction p.589

**Fikso Kretschmer Smith Dixon PS**
Table: Real Estate p.2002

**Fine, Kaplan and Black, RPC**
Table: Antitrust p.1692

**Finley, Alt, Smith, Scharnberg, Craig, Hilmes & Gaffney PC**
Table: Litigation: General Commercial p.913

**Finn Dixon & Herling LLP**
Profile: p.387
Table: Corporate/M&A p.374

**Finnegan Henderson Farabow Garrett & Dunner LLP**
Profile: p.567
Tables: Intellectual Property p.247, Intellectual Property: Northern Virginia p.1974

**Fish & Richardson P.C.**
Profile: p.1113
Tables: Intellectual Property p.247, Intellectual Property: Patent p.1383

**Fisher & Phillips LLP**
Profile: p.732
Tables: Employment: Mainly Defendant p.596, Immigration p.694

**Fisk & Fielder**
Table: Construction p.1838

**Fitzpatrick, Cella, Harper & Scinto**
Profile: p.1531
Table: Intellectual Property: Patent p.1383

**Flaherty, Sensabaugh & Bonasso PLLC**
Table: Litigation: General Commercial p.2013

**Fleck, Mather & Strutz, Ltd.**
Table: Litigation: General Commercial p.1593

**Fleeson, Gooing, Coulson & Kitch, LLC**
Tables: Corporate/M&A p.924, Real Estate p.929

**Flygare Schwarz & Closson PLLC**
Table: Employment: Mainly Defendant p.1265

**Foley & Lardner LLP**
Profile: p.2037
Tables: Antitrust p.581, Bankruptcy/Restructuring p.585, Construction p.589, Corporate/M&A p.593, Employment: Mainly Defendant p.596, Energy & Natural Resources p.789, Environment p.450, Healthcare p.238, Insurance p.606, Insurance: Transactional & Regulatory p.795, Intellectual Property p.2028, Litigation: General Commercial p.1074, Media & Entertainment: Litigation p.805, Real Estate p.616, Real Estate: Zoning/Land Use p.620, Telecom, Broadcast & Satellite: Regulatory p.815

**Foley Hoag LLP**
Tables: Antitrust p.1053, Banking & Finance p.1055, Bankruptcy/Restructuring p.1057, Corporate/M&A p.1060, Employment: Mainly Defendant p.1065, Environment p.1068, Intellectual Property p.1072, Litigation: General Commercial p.1074, Private Equity: Buyouts & Venture Capital Investment p.1077, Tax p.1084

**Ford & Harrison LLP**
Profile: p.733
Tables: Employment: Mainly Defendant p.596, Immigration p.694

**Ford Nassen & Baldwin**
Table: Construction p.1838

**Forizs and Dogali PL**
Table: Construction p.589

**Forman Perry Watkins Krutz & Tardy LLP**
Profile: p.1190
Table: Litigation: General Commercial p.1178

**Foster Pepper PLLC**
Tables: Bankruptcy/Restructuring p.1991, Corporate/Commercial p.1992, Real Estate p.2002

**Foulston Siefkin LLP**
Profile: p.935
Tables: Corporate/M&A p.924, Employment: Mainly Defendant p.925, Litigation: Environmental p.928, Litigation: General Commercial p.927, Real Estate p.929

**Fowler White Boggs Banker**
Tables: Employment: Mainly Defendant p.596, Healthcare p.603, Immigration p.606, Real Estate: Zoning/Land Use p.620, Tax p.622

**Fowler White Burnett PA (FowlerWhite)**
Table: Transportation: Shipping (outside New York) p.78

**Fox Rothschild LLP**
Profile: p.1755
Tables: Environment p.1706, Litigation: General Commercial p.1713, Tax p.622

**Fragomen, Del Rey, Bernsen & Loewy, LLP**
Tables: Immigration p.241

**Franczek Sullivan**
Table: Employment: Mainly Defendant p.784

**Frankfurt Kurnit Klein & Selz**
Tables: Media & Entertainment: Advertising p.1399, Media & Entertainment: Commercial p.1401

**Franklin, Weinrib, Rudell & Vassallo**
Table: Media & Entertainment: Commercial p.1401

**Frantz Ward LLP**
Tables: Construction p.1602, Employment: Mainly Defendant p.1608

**Fraser Stryker Law Firm**
Profile: p.1245
Tables: Corporate/M&A p.1236, Employment: Mainly Defendant p.1238, Litigation: General Commercial p.1239, Real Estate p.1241

**Fredrikson & Byron PA**
Tables: Corporate/M&A p.1151, Employment: Mainly Defendant p.1154, Litigation: General Commercial p.1156, Real Estate p.1159

**Freeborn & Peters**
Tables: Antitrust p.766, Litigation:

General Commercial p.801, Media & Entertainment: Transactional p.806

**Freedman Boyd Daniels Hollander Goldberg & Cline PA**
Table: Litigation: General Commercial p.1324

**Freehill Hogan & Mahar LLP**
Table: Transportation: Shipping (New York) p.73

**Freeman, Freeman & Salzman**
Table: Antitrust p.766

**Freshfields Bruckhaus Deringer**
Tables: Antitrust p.425, Capital Markets: CDOs, Repackaging & Other Synthetic Products p.12, International Arbitration p.35, Projects p.1412, Tax p.487

**Friday, Eldredge & Clark**
Tables: Corporate/Commercial p.201, Employment: Mainly Defendant p.202, Litigation: General Commercial p.204, Real Estate p.206

**Fried, Frank, Harris, Shriver & Jacobson LLP**
Profile: p.1532
Tables: Antitrust p.425, Banking & Finance p.1339, Bankruptcy/Restructuring p.1343, Capital Markets: Debt & Equity (excludes West Coast) p.6, Corporate/M&A p.1353, Employee Benefits & Executive Compensation p.1361, Financial Services: Regulatory Compliance p.23, Financial Services: Regulatory Enforcement & Investigations p.28, Government: Government Contracts p.29, Insurance: Transactional & Regulatory p.1380, Intellectual Property: Patent p.1383, Litigation p.470, Litigation: General Commercial p.1387, Litigation: Securities p.1389, Litigation: White-Collar Crime & Government Investigations p.1391, Media & Entertainment: Corporate p.1402, Private Equity: Buyouts & Venture Capital Investment p.1406, Real Estate p.1416, Securities p.485, Tax p.487

**Frilot, Partridge, Kohnke & Clements LC**
Tables: Employment: Mainly Defendant p.967, Litigation: General Commercial p.972

**Fritz, Byrne, Head & Harrison**
Table: Environment p.1851

**Fross Zelnick Lehrman & Zissu PC**
Table: Intellectual Property: Trademark & Copyright p.1384

**Frost Brown Todd LLC**
Profile: p.954
Tables: Banking & Finance p.1598, Bankruptcy/Restructuring p.1600, Construction p.1602, Corporate/M&A p.937, Employee Benefits & Executive Compensation p.1606, Employment: Mainly Defendant p.939, Environment p.1610, Environment, Natural Resources & Regulated Industries p.940, Intellectual Property p.1614, Litigation: General Commercial p.942, Real Estate p.943

**Fruth, Jamison & Elsass**
Table: Litigation: General Commercial p.1156

**Fulbright & Jaworski L.L.P.**
Profile: p.1928
Tables: Antitrust p.1829, Bankruptcy/Restructuring p.1834, Corporate/M&A p.1840, Employment: Mainly Defendant p.1843, Energy & Natural Resources p.1847, Energy & Natural Resources: Dispute Resolution p.1848, Energy: Oil & Gas p.441, Environment p.1851, Healthcare p.238, Insurance p.1857, Intellectual Property p.1859, International Arbitration p.35, Litigation: General Commercial p.255, Products Liability p.49, Projects p.479, Real Estate p.1871, Tax p.1874, Technology & IT Outsourcing p.1877, Transportation: Aviation: Finance p.64

**Fullenkamp, Doyle & Jobeun**
Table: Real Estate p.1241

**Gable & Gotwals**
Profile: p.1664
Table: Litigation: General Commercial p.1656

**Gadsby Hannah LLP**
Table: Bankruptcy/Restructuring p.1057

**Gainsburgh, Benjamin, David, Meunier & Warshauer**
Table: Litigation: General Commercial p.972

**Gallagher, Callahan and Gartrell, PC**
Tables: Banking & Finance p.1055, Employment: Mainly Defendant p.1265, Litigation: General Commercial p.1267, Real Estate p.1269

**Gallagher, Evelius & Jones, LLP**
Tables: Healthcare p.1030, Real Estate p.1035

**Gallagher & Kennedy PA**
Tables: Environment (including water rights) p.179, Litigation: General Commercial p.181, Litigation: White-Collar Crime & Government Investigations p.182, Real Estate p.183, Real Estate: Zoning/Land Use p.186

**Gallegos Law Firm PC**
Tables: Environment, Natural Resources & Regulated Industries p.1322, Litigation: General Commercial p.1324

**Gamble, Rosenberger & Joswick LLP**
Table: Employee Benefits & Executive Compensation p.1124

**Gammage & Burnham, PLC**
Table: Real Estate: Zoning/Land Use p.186

**Gang Tyre Ramer & Brown**
Table: Media & Entertainment: Transactional p.265

**Gardere Wynne Sewell LLP**
Profile: p.1931
Tables: Antitrust p.1829,
Bankruptcy/Restructuring p.1834,
Construction p.1838, Corporate/M&A
p.1840, Insurance p.1857, Intellectual
Property p.1859, Real Estate p.1871,
Tax p.1874, Technology & IT Outsourcing
p.1877

**Gardner Carton & Douglas LLP**
Profile: p.872
Tables: Corporate/M&A & Private Equity
p.780, Employment: Employee Benefits
p.784, Environment p.790, Healthcare
p.455, Technology & IT Outsourcing
p.813

**Garfunkel, Wild & Travis PC**
Table: Healthcare p.1374

**Garlington, Lohn &
Robinson, PLLP**
Tables: Corporate/M&A p.1222,
Employment: Mainly Defendant p.1223,
Litigation: General Commercial p.1225,
Natural Resources & Environment
p.1228, Real Estate p.1230

**Garofalo Goerlich Hainbach PC**
Table: Transportation: Aviation:
Regulatory & Litigation p.67

**Garvey Schubert Barer**
Table: Transportation: Shipping (outside
New York) p.78

**Gelber, Gelber, Ingersoll &
Klevansky, A Law Corporation**
Tables: Bankruptcy/Restructuring p.739,
Corporate/Commercial p.740

**Genova, Burns & Vernoia**
Table: Employment: Mainly Defendant
p.1282

**Genovese Joblove & Battista, PA**
Profile: p.663
Table: Bankruptcy/Restructuring p.585

**George & Titus PA**
Table: Litigation: White-Collar Crime &
Government Investigations p.610

**Gibbons, Del Deo, Dolan,
Griffinger & Vecchione**
Profile: p.1310
Tables: Environment p.1284, Healthcare
p.1287, Litigation: General Commercial
p.1289, Litigation: White-Collar Crime &
Government Investigations p.1292, Real
Estate p.1293

**Gibbs & Bruns, LLP**
Profile: p.1932
Tables: Energy & Natural Resources:
Dispute Resolution p.1848, Litigation:
General Commercial p.1864

**Gibbs, Giden, Locher & Turner**
Profile: p.327
Table: Construction p.224

**Gibson, Dunn & Crutcher LLP**
Profile: p.328
Tables: Antitrust p.215, Banking &
Finance p.218, Bankruptcy/Restructuring
p.221, Construction p.433,
Corporate/Commercial p.435,

Corporate/M&A p.346, Corporate/M&A:
Northern California p.226, Employee
Benefits & Executive Compensation
p.437, Employment: Mainly Defendant
p.230, Environment p.235, Government:
Government Contracts p.29, Insurance:
Insurer Firms p.242, Intellectual Property
p.247, International Trade p.41, Litigation:
Appellate p.474, Litigation: General
Commercial p.255, Litigation: Securities
p.1389, Media & Entertainment: Litigation
p.262, Media & Entertainment:
Transactional p.265, Private Equity:
Buyouts & Venture Capital Investment
p.1406, Private Fund Formation p.1409,
Products Liability p.49, Real Estate
p.269, Securities p.485, Tax p.273

**Gignilliat, Savitz & Bettis LLP**
Table: Employment: Mainly Defendant
p.1777

**Gilbert Heintz & Randolph LLP**
Table: Insurance: Policy Holder p.464

**Gilker and Jones PA**
Table: Employment: Mainly Defendant
p.202

**Gilkey & Stephenson PA**
Profile: p.1331
Table: Employment: Mainly Defendant
p.1321

**Gilmartin, Poster & Shafto**
Table: Transportation: Shipping (New
York) p.73

**Giordano Halleran & Ciesla PC**
Tables: Corporate/M&A p.1278,
Environment p.1284, Healthcare p.1287,
Real Estate p.1293

**Givens Pursley LLP**
Tables: Employment: Mainly Defendant
p.759, Natural Resources & Environment
p.761, Real Estate p.762

**Glankler Brown, PLLC**
Tables: Corporate/M&A p.1799,
Litigation: General Commercial p.1803,
Real Estate p.1807

**Glenn Rasmussen Fogarty &
Hooker**
Tables: Bankruptcy/Restructuring p.585,
Corporate/M&A p.593

**Godfrey & Kahn, SC**
Tables: Corporate/M&A p.2025,
Intellectual Property p.2028, Litigation:
General Commercial p.2029, Real Estate
p.2030

**Goetz Fitzpatrick LLP**
Table: Construction p.1350

**Goetz, Gallik & Baldwin, PC**
Table: Litigation: Mainly Plaintiff p.1227

**Goldberg Godles Weiner & Wright**
Table: Telecom, Broadcast & Satellite:
Regulatory p.491

**Goldberg, Kohn, Bell, Black,
Rosenbloom & Moritz, Ltd**
Tables: Banking & Finance p.770,
Bankruptcy/Restructuring p.774, Real
Estate p.808

**Gonzalez & Harris PC**
Table: Immigration p.241

**Goodell, DeVries, Leech
& Dann, LLP**
Profile: p.1047
Tables: Healthcare p.1030, Litigation:
General Commercial p.1032

**Goodin MacBride Squeri
Ritchie & Day LLP**
Table: Energy & Natural Resources
p.233

**Goodsill Anderson Quinn & Stifel**
Tables: Corporate/Commercial p.740,
Employment: Mainly Defendant p.742,
Land Use p.743, Litigation: General
Commercial p.745, Real Estate p.747

**Goodwin & Goodwin, LLP**
Table: Litigation: General Commercial
p.2013

**Goodwin Procter LLP**
Profile: p.1114
Tables: Banking & Finance p.1055,
Bankruptcy/Restructuring p.1057,
Corporate/M&A p.1060, Employee
Benefits & Executive Compensation
p.1063, Employment: Mainly Defendant
p.1065, Environment p.1068, Intellectual
Property p.1072, Intellectual Property:
Patent p.1383, Litigation p.470,
Litigation: General Commercial p.1074,
Private Equity: Buyouts & Venture Capital
Investment p.1077, Private Fund
Formation p.1079, Real Estate p.1081,
Tax p.1084

**Goold Patterson Ales & Day**
Table: Real Estate p.1255

**Gordon Murray Tilden**
Table: Litigation: General Commercial
p.1999

**Gordon, Arata, McCollam,
Duplantis & Eagan LLP**
Tables: Energy & Natural Resources
p.969, Litigation: General Commercial
p.972

**Gordon, Feinblatt, Rothman,
Hoffberger & Hollander, LLC**
Tables: Employment: Mainly Defendant
p.1028, Healthcare p.1030, Litigation:
General Commercial p.1032, Real Estate
p.1035

**Gordon, Martin, Jones, Harris
& Shrum**
Table: Media & Entertainment p.1806

**Gordon & Silver Ltd**
Table: Gaming & Licensing p.1250

**Gottlieb & Smith PA**
Table: Real Estate p.1780

**Gough, Shanahan, Johnson &
Waterman**
Profile: p.1235
Tables: Employment: Mainly Defendant
p.1223, Litigation: General Commercial
p.1225, Natural Resources &
Environment p.1228

**Goulston & Storrs**
Tables: Banking & Finance p.1055,
Bankruptcy/Restructuring p.1057,
Corporate/M&A p.1060, Environment
p.1068, Litigation: General Commercial
p.1074, Real Estate p.481

**Graham & Dunn PC**
Table: Corporate/Commercial p.1992

**Grant & Eisenhofer PA**
Table: Chancery p.391

**Gravel and Shea**
Tables: Corporate/Commercial p.1957,
Employment: Mainly Defendant p.1958,
Litigation: General Commercial p.1959,
Real Estate p.1961

**Graves, Dougherty, Hearon
& Moody, P.C.**
Table: Insurance p.1857

**Gray, Plant, Mooty, Mooty
& Bennett, PA**
Tables: Corporate/M&A p.1151,
Employment: Mainly Defendant p.1154,
Litigation: General Commercial p.1156,
Real Estate p.1159

**Gray Robinson PA**
Tables: Construction p.589, Real Estate
p.616, Real Estate: Zoning/Land Use
p.620

**Greenbaum, Rowe, Smith
& Davis LLP**
Profile: p.1311
Tables: Corporate/M&A p.1278,
Environment p.1284, Litigation: General
Commercial p.1289, Real Estate p.1293

**Greenberg Glusker Fields Claman
Machtinger & Kinsella LLP**
Table: Media & Entertainment: Litigation
p.262

**Greenberg Traurig LLP**
Profile: p.664
Tables: Antitrust p.581, Banking &
Finance p.583, Bankruptcy/Restructuring
p.585, Construction p.589,
Corporate/M&A p.175, Corporate/M&A &
Private Equity p.780, Corporate/M&A:
Latin American Investment p.595,
Employment: Mainly Defendant p.177,
Environment p.349, Government:
Government Relations p.32, Healthcare
p.603, Immigration p.459, International
Arbitration p.35, Litigation: General
Commercial p.608, Litigation: White-
Collar Crime & Government Investigations
p.610, Media & Entertainment:
Commercial p.1401, Real Estate p.183,
Real Estate: Zoning/Land Use p.620, Tax
p.622

**Greenebaum Doll &
McDonald PLLC**
Profile: p.955
Tables: Corporate/M&A p.937,
Employment: Mainly Defendant p.939,
Environment, Natural Resources &
Regulated Industries p.940, Intellectual
Property p.1614, Litigation: General
Commercial p.942, Real Estate p.943

**PROFILE:** CONTACT DETAILS AT THE END OF EVERY STATE   **TABLE:** REFERS TO THE SPECIALIST LISTS IN WHICH THE FIRM APPEARS

2061

**Hirst & Applegate, PC**
Tables: Corporate/M&A p.2041,
Employment: Mainly Defendant p.2042,
Litigation: General Commercial p.2043

**Hite, Fanning & Honeyman LLP**
Table: Litigation: General Commercial p.927

**Hodge Dwyer Zeman**
Table: Environment p.790

**Hodgson Russ LLP**
Table: Healthcare p.1374

**Hoffman Reilly Pozner & Williamson**
Table: Litigation: General Commercial p.352

**Hogan & Hartson LLP**
Profile: p.568
Tables: Antitrust p.425,
Bankruptcy/Restructuring p.431,
Corporate/Commercial p.435,
Corporate/M&A p.346, Corporate/M&A:
Latin American Investment p.595,
Corporate/M&A: Northern Virginia
p.1967, Employee Benefits & Executive
Compensation p.437, Employment:
Mainly Defendant p.348, Energy:
Electricity p.444, Energy: Oil & Gas
p.441, Environment p.349, Government:
Government Contracts p.29,
Government: Government Relations
p.32, Healthcare p.455, Immigration
p.459, Insurance: Insurer Firms p.461,
Intellectual Property p.351, Intellectual
Property: Northern Virginia p.1974,
Litigation p.470, Litigation: General
Commercial p.608, Litigation: White-
Collar Crime & Government Investigations
p.352, Media & Entertainment: Corporate
p.1402, Media & Entertainment: Litigation
p.262, Projects p.479, Real Estate
p.481, Securities p.485, Telecom,
Broadcast & Satellite: Regulatory p.491,
Transportation: Road
(Carriage/Commercial) p.71

**Hogan Marren Ltd**
Table: Healthcare p.793

**Holland & Hart LLP**
Profile: p.369
Tables: Bankruptcy/Restructuring p.758,
Construction p.345, Corporate/M&A
p.346, Employment: Mainly Defendant
p.348, Environment p.349, Environment,
Natural Resources & Regulated Industries
p.1322, Intellectual Property p.351,
Litigation: General Commercial p.352,
Native American Law p.47, Natural
Resources & Environment p.761, Real
Estate p.354

**Holland & Knight LLP**
Profile: p.1534
Tables: Antitrust p.581, Banking &
Finance p.583, Bankruptcy/Restructuring
p.585, Construction p.433,
Corporate/M&A p.593, Corporate/M&A:
Latin American Investment p.595,
Employment: Mainly Defendant p.596,
Environment p.600, Government:
Government Contracts p.29,
Government: Government Relations
p.32, Healthcare p.603, Immigration
p.606, Litigation: General Commercial
p.608, Litigation: White-Collar Crime &
Government Investigations p.610, Media

& Entertainment p.476, Media &
Entertainment: Transactional p.806,
Products Liability p.49, Real Estate
p.481, Real Estate: Zoning/Land Use
p.620, Tax p.622, Transportation:
Aviation: Finance p.64, Transportation:
Aviation: Regulatory & Litigation p.67,
Transportation: Shipping (New York)
p.73, Transportation: Shipping (outside
New York) p.78

**Holme Roberts & Owen LLP**
Profile: p.370
Tables: Corporate/M&A p.346,
Employment: Mainly Defendant p.348,
Environment p.349, Litigation: General
Commercial p.352, Real Estate p.354

**Honigman Miller Schwartz
and Cohn LLP**
Profile: p.1146
Tables: Corporate/M&A p.1121,
Employee Benefits & Executive
Compensation p.1124, Employment:
Mainly Defendant p.1125, Litigation:
General Commercial p.1128, Real Estate
p.1130

**Hooper Lundy & Bookman Inc**
Table: Healthcare p.238

**Hopping Green & Sams, PA**
Profile: p.665
Tables: Environment p.600, Real Estate:
Zoning/Land Use p.620, Tax p.622

**Howard, Rice, Nemerovski,
Canady, Falk & Rabkin**
Table: Bankruptcy/Restructuring p.221

**Howrey LLP**
Tables: Antitrust p.215, Insurance: Policy
Holder p.244, Intellectual Property
p.247, Litigation p.470, Litigation: General
Commercial p.255

**Hoyt & Blewett**
Table: Litigation: Mainly Plaintiff p.1227

**Huddleston Bolen LLP**
Tables: Corporate/Commercial p.2010,
Real Estate p.2015

**Hughes & Luce LLP**
Tables: Business Process Outsourcing
p.1, Employment: Mainly Defendant
p.1843, Technology & IT Outsourcing
p.1877

**Hughes Bauman Pfiffner Gorski
& Seedorf LLC**
Tables: Corporate/M&A p.168,
Environment, Natural Resources &
Regulated Industries p.169

**Hughes, Kellner, Sullivan & Alke**
Tables: Employment: Mainly Defendant
p.1223, Litigation: General Commercial
p.1225

**Hughes Hubbard & Reed LLP**
Profile: p.1535
Tables: Corporate/M&A: Mid-Tier Firms
p.1359, Native American Law p.47,
Products Liability p.49, Transportation:
Aviation: Finance p.64

**Hunter, Maclean, Exley
& Dunn, PC**
Table: Environment p.690

**Hunton & Williams LLP**
Profile: p.1989
Tables: Antitrust p.581, Banking &
Finance p.583, Bankruptcy/Restructuring
p.585, Capital Markets: Securitisation
p.17, Corporate/M&A p.1571,
Corporate/M&A: Latin American
Investment p.595, Corporate/M&A:
Southern Virginia p.1967, Employment:
Mainly Defendant p.686, Energy:
Electricity p.444, Environment p.450,
Insurance: Insurer Firms p.461,
Intellectual Property p.696, Intellectual
Property: Southern Virginia p.1974,
Litigation: General Commercial p.608,
Projects p.479, Real Estate p.1977

**Hurley Toevs Styles Hamblin
& Panter PA**
Table: Real Estate p.1326

**Hurwitz & Sagarin LLC**
Table: Litigation: General Commercial
p.378

**Husch & Eppenberger, LLC**
Tables: Corporate/M&A p.1192,
Litigation: General Commercial p.1197,
Real Estate p.1200

**Hyman Phelps & McNamara**
Table: Healthcare:
Pharmaceutical/Medical Products
Regulatory p.455

**I**

**Ice Miller LLP**
Profile: p.904
Tables: Corporate/M&A p.887,
Employment: Mainly Defendant p.889,
Litigation: General Commercial p.890,
Real Estate p.892

**Imanaka Kudo & Fujimoto**
Tables: Employment: Mainly Defendant
p.742, Land Use p.743, Real Estate
p.747

**Irell & Manella LLP**
Tables: Bankruptcy/Restructuring p.221,
Corporate/M&A: Southern California
p.226, Intellectual Property p.247,
Litigation: General Commercial p.255,
Media & Entertainment: Litigation p.262,
Media & Entertainment: Transactional
p.265, Tax p.273

**Isaacson Rosenbaum PC**
Tables: Litigation: White-Collar Crime &
Government Investigations p.352, Real
Estate p.354

**Iseman Cunningham Riester
& Hyde LLP**
Table: Healthcare p.1374

**Ivener & Fullmer LLP**
Table: Immigration p.241

**Ivins, Phillips & Barker**
Table: Tax p.487

**J**

**Jack, Lyon & Jones, PC**
Table: Corporate/Commercial p.201

**Jackson Kelly PLLC**
Profile: p.2023
Tables: Corporate/Commercial p.2010,
Employment: Mainly Defendant p.2011,
Litigation: General Commercial p.2013,
Real Estate p.2015

**Jackson Lewis LLP**
Tables: Employment: Mainly Defendant
p.376

**Jackson Walker LLP**
Tables: Healthcare p.1854, Real Estate
p.1871

**Jacobs, Chase, Frick, Kleinkopf &
Kelley**
Tables: Litigation: General Commercial
p.352, Real Estate p.354

**Jacobs, Grudberg, Belt & Dow PC**
Table: Litigation: General Commercial
p.378

**Jaffe, Raitt, Heuer & Weiss, PC**
Tables: Corporate/M&A p.1121, Real
Estate p.1130

**Jameson Babbitt Stites &
Lombard**
Table: Real Estate p.2002

**Janis Schuelke & Wechsler**
Table: Litigation: Specialist Firms in
White-Collar Crime & Government
Investigations p.471

**Jeffcoat Pike & Nappier LLC
(Myrtle Beach)**
Table: Real Estate p.1780

**Jenkens & Gilchrist PC**
Tables: Banking & Finance p.1831,
Construction p.1838, Employment:
Mainly Defendant p.1843, Environment
p.1851, Healthcare p.1854, Immigration
p.1856, Real Estate p.1871, Technology
& IT Outsourcing p.1877

**Jenkins Fenstermaker, PLLC**
Tables: Employment: Mainly Defendant
p.2011, Litigation: General Commercial
p.2013

**Jenner & Block LLP**
Profile: p.873
Tables: Antitrust p.766,
Bankruptcy/Restructuring p.774,
Corporate/M&A & Private Equity p.780,
Employment: Mainly Defendant p.784,
Environment p.790, Government:
Government Contracts p.29, Insurance:
Coverage Litigation p.795, Intellectual
Property p.798, Litigation: Appellate
p.474, Litigation: General Commercial
p.801, Media & Entertainment p.476,
Media & Entertainment: Litigation p.805,
Real Estate p.808, Tax p.811, Telecom,
Broadcast & Satellite: Regulatory p.491

**Jennings, Strouss & Salmon, PLC**
Table: Corporate/M&A p.175

M

Tables: Corporate/M&A p.1151, Litigation: General Commercial p.1156, Real Estate p.1159

**LePatner & Associates LLP**
Profile: p.1541
Table: Construction p.1350

**Lerach Coughlin Stoia Geller Rudman & Robbins LLP**
Table: Litigation: General Commercial p.255

**Lerner David Littenberg Krumholz & Mentlik, LLP**
Profile: p.1312
Table: Intellectual Property p.1288

**Levene, Neale, Bender, Rankin & Brill**
Table: Bankruptcy/Restructuring p.221

**Leventhal Senter & Lerman PLLC**
Table: Telecom, Broadcast & Satellite: Regulatory p.491

**Leventhal & Slaughter PA**
Table: Litigation: White-Collar Crime & Government Investigations p.610

**Levine, Blaszak, Block & Boothby LLP**
Profile: p.573
Table: Telecom, Broadcast & Satellite: Regulatory p.491

**Levine Sullivan Koch & Schulz LLP**
Tables: Media & Entertainment p.476, Media & Entertainment: Litigation p.1404

**Levy, Ram & Olson**
Table: Media & Entertainment: Litigation p.262

**Lewis and Roca**
Tables: Corporate/Commercial p.1320, Corporate/M&A p.175, Employment: Mainly Defendant p.177, Environment (including water rights) p.179, Gaming & Licensing p.1250, Litigation: General Commercial p.181, Litigation: White-Collar Crime & Government Investigations p.182, Real Estate p.183, Real Estate: Zoning/Land Use p.186

**Lewis Fisher Henderson Claxton & Mulroy**
Tables: Employment: Mainly Defendant p.1176

**Lewis, Longman & Walker PA**
Table: Environment p.600

**Lewis, Rice & Fingersh, L.C.**
Profile: p.1215
Tables: Litigation: General Commercial p.1197, Real Estate p.1200

**Lewis & Slovak PC**
Table: Litigation: Mainly Plaintiff p.1227

**Leydig, Voit & Mayer, Ltd**
Table: Intellectual Property p.798

**Lichter Grossman Nicholas Adler & Goodman**
Table: Media & Entertainment:

Transactional p.265

**Liebert Cassidy Whitmore**
Table: Employment: Mainly Defendant p.230

**Liebmann, Conway, Olejniczak & Jerry, S.C.**
Table: Litigation: General Commercial p.2029

**Lightfoot, Franklin & White, LLC**
Table: Litigation: General Commercial p.151

**Lightfoot, Vandevelde, Sadowsky, Medvene & Levine**
Table: Litigation: Specialist Firms in White-Collar Crime & Government Investigations p.255

**Lindner & Marsack, SC**
Table: Employment: Mainly Defendant p.2026

**Lindquist & Vennum PLLP**
Profile: p.1171
Tables: Corporate/M&A p.1151, Litigation: General Commercial p.1156, Real Estate p.1159

**Linklaters**
Profile: p.1542

**Linowes and Blocher LLP**
Profile: p.1049
Table: Real Estate p.1035

**Lionel Sawyer & Collins**
Tables: Corporate/Commercial p.1246, Employment: Mainly Defendant p.1247, Environment p.1249, Gaming & Licensing p.1250, Litigation: General Commercial p.1252, Real Estate p.1255

**Liskow & Lewis PLC**
Tables: Banking & Finance p.963, Corporate/M&A p.964, Energy & Natural Resources p.969, Environment p.970, Litigation: General Commercial p.972, Real Estate p.975

**Lisman, Webster, Kirkpatrick & Leckerling, P.C.**
Table: Real Estate p.1961

**Little, Medeiros, Kinder, Bulman & Whitney PC**
Tables: Employment: Mainly Defendant p.1767, Litigation: General Commercial p.1768

**Littler Mendelson, PC**
Profile: p.333
Tables: Employment: Mainly Defendant p.230

**Litwin & Associates**
Table: Immigration p.241

**Lloyd Gosselink Blevins Rochelle & Townsend, P.C.**
Table: Environment p.1851

**Locke Liddell & Sapp LLP**
Tables: Employment: Mainly Defendant p.1843, Energy & Natural Resources

p.1847, Environment p.1851, Intellectual Property p.1859, Litigation: General Commercial p.1864, Real Estate p.1871, Tax p.1874, Technology & IT Outsourcing p.1877

**Locke Reynolds LLP**
Table: Litigation: General Commercial p.890

**Loeb & Loeb LLP**
Profile: p.334
Tables: Media & Entertainment p.1806, Media & Entertainment: Advertising p.1399, Media & Entertainment: Commercial p.1401, Media & Entertainment: Litigation p.262, Media & Entertainment: Transactional p.265, Tax p.273

**Lonabaugh and Riggs**
Table: Real Estate p.2045

**Lord, Bissell & Brook**
Tables: Insurance: Coverage Litigation p.795, Transportation: Aviation: Regulatory & Litigation p.67

**Lottner Rubin Fishman Brown & Saul, PC**
Table: Real Estate p.354

**Lovells**
Profile: p.1543
Tables: Insurance: Reinsurance Litigation p.795, Insurance: Transactional & Regulatory p.1380

**Lowenstein Sandler PC**
Profile: p.1313
Tables: Corporate/M&A p.1278, Employee Benefits & Executive Compensation p.1281, Employment: Mainly Defendant p.1282, Environment p.1284, Intellectual Property p.1288, Litigation: General Commercial p.1289, Litigation: Products Liability p.1292

**Lowndes Drosdick Doster Kantor & Reed, PA**
Tables: Real Estate p.616, Real Estate: Zoning/Land Use p.620

**Lueders, Robertson & Konzen**
Table: Energy & Natural Resources p.789

**Lum, Danzis, Drasco & Positan, LLC**
Profile: p.1314
Table: Employment: Mainly Defendant p.1282

**Luskin, Stern & Eisler LLP**
Table: Bankruptcy/Restructuring p.1343

**Lyman & Nielsen**
Table: Construction p.778

**Lynn, Jackson, Shultz & Lebrun PC**
Tables: Corporate/Commercial p.1792, Litigation: General Commercial p.1794

M

**MacDonald Hoague & Bayless**
Table: Immigration p.1997

**Macfarlane Ferguson & McMullen PA**
Table: Employment: Mainly Defendant p.596

**MacPherson Kelly & Thompson**
Table: Real Estate p.2045

**Maddin, Hauser, Wartell, Roth & Heller PC**
Table: Real Estate p.1130

**Madison Harbour Mroz & Brennan PA**
Table: Litigation: General Commercial p.1324

**Maggio & Kattar PC**
Table: Immigration p.459

**Manatt Phelps & Phillips LLP**
Tables: Banking & Finance p.218, Healthcare p.238, Media & Entertainment: Advertising p.1399, Media & Entertainment: Transactional p.265

**Mancini Welch & Geiger LLP**
Tables: Land Use p.743, Real Estate p.747

**Manko, Gold, Katcher & Fox LLP**
Table: Environment p.1706

**Manning Curtis Bradshaw & Bednar LLC**
Table: Employment: Mainly Defendant p.1944

**Manning Fulton & Skinner PA**
Table: Real Estate p.1579

**Maring Williams Law Office PC**
Table: Litigation: General Commercial p.1593

**Mariscal, Weeks, McIntyre & Friedlander PA**
Tables: Litigation: General Commercial p.181, Real Estate p.183

**Markowitz, Herbold, Glade & Mehlhaf PC**
Table: Litigation: General Commercial p.1674

**Marr Hipp Jones & Wang**
Profile: p.756
Table: Employment: Mainly Defendant p.742

**Marshall, Gerstein & Borun**
Table: Intellectual Property p.798

**Martin & Churchill Chartered**
Table: Employment: Mainly Defendant p.925

**Martin, Disiere, Jefferson & Wisdom LLP**
Table: Insurance p.1857

**Martin, Pringle, Oliver, Wallace & Bauer, L.L.P.**
Table: Employment: Mainly Defendant p.925

**Maslon Edelman Borman & Brand, LLP**
Table: Litigation: General Commercial p.1156

**Matkov Salzman Madoff & Gunn**
Table: Employment: Mainly Defendant p.784

**Maupin Taylor, PA**
Tables: Employment: Mainly Defendant p.1573, Environment p.1574, Real Estate p.1579

**Mautino & Mautino**
Table: Immigration p.241

**May, Adam, Gerdes & Thompson, L.L.P.**
Table: Litigation: General Commercial p.1794

**Mayer, Brown, Rowe & Maw LLP**
Profile: p.876
Tables: Antitrust p.425, Banking & Finance p.218, Bankruptcy/Restructuring p.774, Capital Markets: CDOs, Repackaging & Other Synthetic Products p.12, Capital Markets: Debt & Equity (excludes West Coast) p.6, Capital Markets: Derivatives p.14, Capital Markets: Securitisation p.17, Corporate/M&A p.1840, Corporate/M&A & Private Equity p.780, Corporate/M&A: Mid-Tier Firms p.1359, Employment: Employee Benefits p.784, Energy & Natural Resources p.789, Environment p.790, Financial Services: Regulatory Compliance p.23, Government: Government Contracts p.29, Government: Government Relations p.32, Insurance: Coverage Litigation p.795, Intellectual Property p.466, International Trade p.41, Investment Management p.468, Litigation: Appellate p.474, Litigation: General Commercial p.801, Private Fund Formation p.1409, Products Liability p.49, Projects p.479, Real Estate p.269, Tax p.811, Technology & IT Outsourcing p.490, Telecom, Broadcast & Satellite: Regulatory p.815, Transportation: Road (Carriage/Commercial) p.71

**Maynard, Cooper & Gale, P.C.**
Profile: p.165
Tables: Banking & Finance p.147, Corporate/Commercial p.148, Employment: Mainly Defendant p.149, Litigation: General Commercial p.151, Real Estate p.153

**Mazur, Carp & Rubin PC**
Table: Construction p.1350

**McAfee & Taft A Professional Corporation**
Profile: p.1666
Tables: Corporate/Commercial p.1653, Employment: Mainly Defendant p.1654,

Litigation: General Commercial p.1656, Real Estate p.1657

**McAndrews, Held & Malloy, Ltd**
Profile: p.877
Table: Intellectual Property p.798

**McCarter & English, LLP**
Tables: Corporate/M&A p.1278, Employee Benefits & Executive Compensation p.1281, Employment: Mainly Defendant p.376, Environment p.1284, Intellectual Property p.1288, Litigation: General Commercial p.378, Litigation: Products Liability p.1292, Real Estate p.1293

**McConn & Rindy**
Table: Real Estate p.1595

**McCorriston Miller Mukai MacKinnon LLP**
Profile: p.757
Tables: Corporate/Commercial p.740, Litigation: General Commercial p.745, Real Estate p.747

**McCullough Hill PS**
Table: Real Estate p.2002

**McDade Fogler LLP**
Tables: Energy & Natural Resources: Dispute Resolution p.1848, Litigation: General Commercial p.1864

**McDermott Will & Emery**
Profile: p.878
Tables: Antitrust p.425, Banking & Finance p.218, Bankruptcy/Restructuring p.774, Corporate/M&A p.1060, Corporate/M&A & Private Equity p.780, Corporate/M&A: Mid-Tier Firms p.1359, Employee Benefits & Executive Compensation p.437, Employment: Employee Benefits p.784, Employment: Electricity p.444, Environment p.1068, Government: Political Law p.34, Healthcare p.238, Healthcare: Pharmaceutical/Medical Products Regulatory p.455, Immigration p.1376, Insurance: Policy Holder p.464, Intellectual Property p.247, International Trade p.41, Litigation: General Commercial p.255, Private Equity: Buyouts & Venture Capital Investment p.1077, Products Liability p.49, Tax p.273

**McDonald Carano Wilson McCune Bergin Frankovich & Hicks LLP**
Tables: Environment p.1249, Gaming & Licensing p.1250, Litigation: General Commercial p.1252, Real Estate p.1255

**McDonald Hopkins Co**
Tables: Banking & Finance p.1598, Bankruptcy/Restructuring p.1600

**McDonnell Boehnen Hulbert & Berghoff LLP**
Profile: p.879
Table: Intellectual Property p.798

**McDowell Knight Roedder & Sledge LLC**
Table: Litigation: General Commercial p.151

**McElroy, Deutsch, Mulvaney & Carpenter, LLP**
Profile: p.1315
Table: Employment: Mainly Defendant p.1282

**McEwen Gisvold LLP**
Table: Real Estate p.1676

**McGee Hankla Backes & Dobrovolny P.C.**
Table: Litigation: General Commercial p.1593

**McGlinchey Stafford**
Profile: p.996
Tables: Banking & Finance p.963, Corporate/Commercial p.1174, Corporate/M&A p.964, Employment: Mainly Defendant p.967, Gaming & Licensing p.971, Real Estate p.975

**McGrath North Mullin & Kratz PC**
Tables: Corporate/M&A p.1236, Employment: Mainly Defendant p.1238, Litigation: General Commercial p.1239, Real Estate p.1241

**McGuireWoods LLP**
Tables: Corporate/M&A: Southern Virginia p.1967, Employment: Employee Benefits p.784, Environment p.790, Healthcare p.793, Intellectual Property: Northern Virginia p.1974, Real Estate p.1977, Technology & IT Outsourcing p.813, Transportation: Road (Carriage/Commercial) p.71, Wealth Management p.80

**McKee Nelson LLP**
Profile: p.574
Tables: Capital Markets: CDOs, Repackaging & Other Synthetic Products p.12, Capital Markets: Securitisation p.17, Tax p.487

**McKenna Long & Aldridge LLP**
Profile: p.737
Tables: Bankruptcy/Restructuring p.679, Corporate/M&A p.683, Energy & Natural Resources p.689, Environment p.450, Government: Government Contracts p.29, Real Estate p.700

**McKool Smith**
Profile: p.1934
Tables: Intellectual Property p.1859, Litigation: General Commercial p.1864

**McLane, Graf, Raulerson & Middleton Professional Association**
Profile: p.1276
Tables: Corporate/Commercial p.1263, Employment: Mainly Defendant p.1265, Litigation: General Commercial p.1267, Real Estate p.1269

**McLaughlin & McCaffrey, LLP**
Table: Litigation: General Commercial p.1616

**McMahon DeGulis LLP**
Table: Environment p.1610

**McMahon Berger Hanna Linihan Cody & McCarthy, A Professional Corporation**
Profile: p.1216

Table: Employment: Mainly Defendant p.1195

**McManus Schor Asmar & Darden, L.L.P.**
Table: Construction p.433

**McNair, Larson & Carlson Ltd**
Tables: Corporate/Commercial p.1590, Litigation: General Commercial p.1593

**McNair Law Firm PA**
Tables: Corporate/M&A p.1775, Litigation: General Commercial p.1778, Real Estate p.1780

**McNaul Ebel Nawrot Helgren & Vance PLLC**
Table: Litigation: General Commercial p.1999

**McTurnan & Turner**
Profile: p.905
Table: Litigation: General Commercial p.890

**Meadows, Owens, Collier, Reed, Cousins & Blau**
Table: Tax p.1874

**Meardon, Sueppel & Downer**
Table: Real Estate p.917

**Meckler Bulger & Tilson LLP**
Table: Employment: Mainly Defendant p.784

**Meland Russin Hellinger & Budwick**
Table: Bankruptcy/Restructuring p.585

**Mendes & Mount LLP**
Table: Insurance: Dispute Resolution p.1378

**Meuleman Mollerup LLP**
Table: Real Estate p.762

**Meyer Capel, PC**
Table: Telecom, Broadcast & Satellite: Regulatory p.815

**Michael Best & Friedrich LLP**
Profile: p.2038
Tables: Corporate/M&A p.2025, Employment: Mainly Defendant p.2026, Intellectual Property p.2028, Litigation: General Commercial p.2029, Media & Entertainment: Transactional p.806, Real Estate p.2030

**Michael Critchley & Associates**
Table: Litigation: White-Collar Crime & Government Investigations p.1292

**Middleton Reutlinger PSC**
Profile: p.956
Table: Litigation: General Commercial p.942

**Milbank, Tweed, Hadley & McCloy LLP**
Tables: Banking & Finance p.218, Bankruptcy/Restructuring p.221, Capital Markets: CDOs, Repackaging & Other Synthetic Products p.12, Employee Benefits & Executive Compensation

p.1361, Energy & Natural Resources
p.233, Litigation: Securities p.1389,
Projects p.56, Tax p.1422, Technology &
IT Outsourcing p.490, Transportation:
Aviation: Finance p.64, Transportation:
Road (Carriage/Commercial) p.71,
Wealth Management p.80

**Milberg Weiss Bershad &
Schulman LLP**
Table: Litigation: Securities Mainly
Plaintiff p.1390

**Miles & Stockbridge PC**
Profile: p.1050
Tables: Corporate/M&A p.1025,
Employee Benefits & Executive
Compensation p.1026, Employment:
Mainly Defendant p.1028, Litigation:
General Commercial p.1032

**Miley & Brown PC**
Table: Immigration p.1856

**Miller Johnson**
Tables: Corporate/M&A p.1121,
Employment: Mainly Defendant p.1125,
Litigation: General Commercial p.1128

**Miller, Balis & O'Neil, PC**
Table: Energy: Electricity p.444

**Miller, Canfield, Paddock
and Stone, P.L.C.**
Profile: p.1148
Tables: Banking & Finance p.1120,
Corporate/M&A p.1121, Employee
Benefits & Executive Compensation
p.1124, Employment: Mainly Defendant
p.1125, Litigation: General Commercial
p.1128, Native American Law p.47, Real
Estate p.1130, Sports Law p.59,
Transportation: Aviation: Regulatory &
Litigation p.67

**Miller & Chevalier Chartered**
Profile: p.575
Tables: International Trade p.41, Tax
p.487

**Miller Hamilton Snider &
Odom LLC**
Table: Banking & Finance p.147

**Miller & Martin PLLC**
Profile: p.1826
Tables: Corporate/M&A p.1799,
Employment: Mainly Defendant p.1801,
Litigation: General Commercial p.1803

**Miller, Morton, Caillat & Nevis**
Table: Construction p.224

**Miller Nash LLP**
Profile: p.1690
Tables: Corporate/M&A p.1667,
Employment: Mainly Defendant p.1669,
Litigation: General Commercial p.1674,
Real Estate p.1676

**Miller Stratvert PA**
Table: Litigation: General Commercial
p.1324

**Millisor & Nobil Co LPA**
Table: Employment: Mainly Defendant
p.1608

**Mintz Levin Cohn Ferris Glovsky
and Popeo PC**
Tables: Bankruptcy/Restructuring
p.1057, Corporate/M&A p.1060,
Employee Benefits & Executive
Compensation p.1063, Employment:
Mainly Defendant p.1065, Environment
p.1068, Healthcare p.1070, Litigation:
General Commercial p.1074, Telecom,
Broadcast & Satellite: Regulatory p.491

**Mitchell, McNutt & Sams PA**
Table: Litigation: General Commercial
p.1178

**Mitchell, Silberberg & Knupp LLP**
Table: Media & Entertainment: Litigation
p.262

**Mitchell, Williams, Selig, Gates
Woodyard, PLLC**
Tables: Corporate/Commercial p.201,
Employment: Mainly Defendant p.202,
Litigation: General Commercial p.204,
Real Estate p.206

**Mock, Schwabe, Waldo, Elder,
Reeves & Bryant**
Table: Real Estate p.1657

**Modrall, Sperling, Roehl, Harris
& Sisk, PA**
Tables: Corporate/Commercial p.1320,
Environment, Natural Resources &
Regulated Industries p.1322, Litigation:
General Commercial p.1324, Native
American Law p.1326

**Moehrke, Mackie & Shea, P.C.**
Table: Environment p.1068

**Moffatt Thomas Barrett Rock
& Fields**
Tables: Bankruptcy/Restructuring p.758,
Employment: Mainly Defendant p.759,
Litigation: General Commercial p.760,
Real Estate p.762

**Monteleone & McCrory, LLP**
Table: Construction p.224

**Montgomery & Andrews, PA**
Profile: p.1333
Tables: Environment, Natural Resources
& Regulated Industries p.1322, Litigation:
General Commercial p.1324

**Montgomery, McCracken, Walker
& Rhoads, LLP**
Tables: Antitrust p.1692, Environment
p.1706, Litigation: General Commercial
p.1713

**Moody & Warner PC**
Table: Employment: Mainly Defendant
p.1321

**Moon, Moss & Shapiro, P.A.**
Profile: p.1021
Table: Employment: Mainly Defendant
p.1002

**Moore & Lee LLP**
Table: Construction p.1965

**Moore, O'Connell & Refling PC**
Table: Real Estate p.1230

**Moore & Van Allen PLLC**
Tables: Banking & Finance p.1569,
Bankruptcy/Restructuring p.1570,
Corporate/M&A p.1571, Litigation:
General Commercial p.1577, Real Estate
p.1579

**Morgan, Brown and Joy LLP**
Profile: p.1116
Table: Employment: Mainly Defendant
p.1065

**Morgan & Finnegan, LLP**
Profile: p.1544
Table: Intellectual Property: Patent
p.1383

**Morgan, Lewis & Bockius LLP**
Profile: p.1758
Tables: Antitrust p.425, Banking &
Finance p.1694,
Bankruptcy/Restructuring p.1343,
Corporate/M&A p.1278, Corporate/M&A:
Mid-Tier Firms p.1359, Corporate/M&A:
Northern California p.226, Employment:
Mainly Defendant p.230, Energy:
Electricity p.444, Energy: Nuclear p.448,
Energy: Oil & Gas p.441, Environment
p.235, Financial Services: Regulatory
Enforcement & Investigations p.28,
Healthcare: Pharmaceutical/Medical
Products Regulatory p.455, Immigration
p.459, Insurance: Coverage Litigation
p.795, Insurance: Policy Holder p.244,
Investment Management p.468,
Litigation: General Commercial p.1713,
Media & Entertainment: Corporate
p.1402, Private Equity: Buyouts & Venture
Capital Investment p.1406, Private Fund
Formation p.1409, Projects p.268, Real
Estate p.1717, Tax p.487, Technology &
IT Outsourcing p.1428

**Morris, Nichols, Arsht &
Tunnell LLP**
Profile: p.420
Tables: Bankruptcy/Restructuring p.388,
Chancery p.391, Corporate/M&A p.394,
Intellectual Property p.397, Real Estate
p.399

**Morris, James, Hitchens &
Williams LLP**
Profile: p.419
Tables: Bankruptcy/Restructuring p.388,
Chancery p.391, Corporate/M&A p.394,
Employment: Mainly Defendant p.396

**Morris, Laing, Evans, Brock &
Kennedy, Chartered**
Tables: Employment: Mainly Defendant
p.925, Real Estate p.929

**Morris, Manning & Martin, LLP**
Tables: Bankruptcy/Restructuring p.679,
Environment p.690, Real Estate p.700,
Tax p.702

**Morris & Morris PC**
Table: Litigation: General Commercial
p.1977

**Morrison & Foerster LLP**
Profile: p.335
Tables: Antitrust p.215, Banking &
Finance p.218, Capital Markets:
Derivatives p.14, Corporate/M&A p.346,
Corporate/M&A: Northern California
p.226, Corporate/M&A: Northern Virginia
p.1967, Employment: Mainly Defendant

p.230, Energy & Natural Resources
p.233, Environment p.235, Financial
Services: Regulatory Enforcement &
Investigations p.28, Intellectual Property
p.247, Intellectual Property: Northern
Virginia p.1974, Investment Management
p.468, IT & IT Outsourcing p.253,
Litigation: General Commercial p.255,
Litigation: Securities p.1389, Real Estate
p.269, Tax p.273, Technology & IT
Outsourcing p.1428, Telecom, Broadcast
& Satellite: Regulatory p.491

**Morris Pickering & Sanner**
Table: Litigation: General Commercial
p.1252

**Morse, Barnes-Brown &
Pendleton PC**
Table: Private Equity: Buyouts & Venture
Capital Investment p.1077

**Morvillo, Abramowitz, Grand,
Iason & Silberberg, PC**
Table: Litigation: Specialist Firms in
White-Collar Crime & Government
Investigations p.1392

**Moscowitz, Moscowitz &
Magolnick PA**
Table: Litigation: White-Collar Crime &
Government Investigations p.610

**Moseley Prichard Parrish
Knight & Jones**
Table: Transportation: Shipping (outside
New York) p.78

**Moseley Biehl Tsugawa
Lau & Muzzi**
Table: Bankruptcy/Restructuring p.739

**Moses & Singer LLP**
Table: Wealth Management p.80

**Moulton, Bellingham,
Longo & Mather, PC**
Table: Real Estate p.1230

**Mound Cotton Wollan &
Greengrass**
Profile: p.1545
Tables: Insurance: Dispute Resolution
p.1378, Insurance: Transactional &
Regulatory p.1380

**Moye, O'Brien, O'Rourke,
Pickert & Martin, LLP**
Profile: p.669
Table: Construction p.589

**Moyer & Bergman, PLC**
Tables: Corporate/M&A p.909, Real
Estate p.917

**Moyes Storey**
Table: Environment (including water
rights) p.179

**Much Shelist Freed Denenberg
Ament & Rubenstein, PC**
Tables: Antitrust p.766, Construction
p.778

**Mullikin, Larson & Swift**
Table: Real Estate p.2045

**Munger & Stone**
Table: Employment: Mainly Defendant p.686

**Munger, Tolles & Olson LLP**
Tables: Antitrust p.215, Corporate/M&A: Southern California p.226, Employment: Mainly Defendant p.230, Energy & Natural Resources p.233, Insurance: Policy Holder p.244, Litigation: General Commercial p.255, Media & Entertainment: Litigation p.262, Real Estate p.269, Tax p.273

**Munsch Hardt Kopf & Harr, P. C.**
Table: Bankruptcy/Restructuring p.1834

**Murane & Bostwick LLC**
Table: Employment: Mainly Defendant p.2042

**Murphy, Goldammer & Prendergast**
Table: Corporate/Commercial p.1792

**Murphy & Shaffer**
Table: Litigation: General Commercial p.1032

**Murphy Sullivan Kronk**
Table: Real Estate p.1961

**Murtha Cullina LLP**
Tables: Corporate/M&A p.374, Employment: Mainly Defendant p.376, Litigation: General Commercial p.378

**Myers Oliver & Price**
Table: Real Estate p.1326

## N

**Nagin Gallop Figueredo PA**
Table: Antitrust p.581

**Neal, Gerber & Eisenberg LLP**
Profile: p.880
Tables: Banking & Finance p.770, Employment: Mainly Defendant p.784, Real Estate p.808, Tax p.811, Technology & IT Outsourcing p.813

**Neal & Harwell, PLC**
Table: Litigation: General Commercial p.1803

**Needle & Rosenberg, P.C**
Table: Intellectual Property p.696

**Neel, Hooper & Banes, P.C.**
Profile: p.1935

**Neligan Tarpley Andrews & Foley LLP**
Table: Bankruptcy/Restructuring p.1834

**Nelson Kinder Mosseau & Saturley PC**
Table: Litigation: General Commercial p.1267

**Nelson Mullins Riley & Scarborough LLP**
Profile: p.1788
Tables: Corporate/M&A p.1775,

Employment: Mainly Defendant p.1777, Healthcare p.693, Litigation: General Commercial p.1778, Products Liability p.49, Real Estate p.1780

**Neubert, Pepe & Monteith PC**
Table: Real Estate p.380

**Nexsen Pruet, LLC**
Profile: p.1789
Tables: Corporate/M&A p.1775, Employment: Mainly Defendant p.1777, Litigation: General Commercial p.1778, Real Estate p.1780

**Nichols, Wolfe, Stamper, Nally, Fallis & Robertson Inc**
Table: Employment: Mainly Defendant p.1654

**Nickens Keeton Lawless Farrell & Flack LLP**
Table: Insurance p.1857

**Nicoletti Hornig Campise and Sweeney**
Table: Transportation: Shipping (New York) p.73

**Nilles, Hansen & Davies Ltd**
Tables: Corporate/Commercial p.1590, Litigation: General Commercial p.1593, Real Estate p.1595

**Niro, Scavone, Haller & Niro**
Table: Intellectual Property p.798

**Nixon Peabody LLP**
Profile: p.1546
Tables: Bankruptcy/Restructuring p.1057, Corporate/Commercial p.1263, Employment: Mainly Defendant p.1364, Energy: Upstate New York p.1370, Healthcare p.1374, Litigation: General Commercial p.1267, Media & Entertainment p.476, Real Estate p.481

**Nixon & Vanderhye P.C.**
Table: Intellectual Property: Northern Virginia p.1974

**Norman, Hanson & DeTroy, LLC**
Table: Litigation: General Commercial p.1005

**Norris, McLaughlin & Marcus, PA, A Professional Corporation**
Table: Corporate/M&A p.1278

**Nourse & Bowles LLP**
Table: Transportation: Shipping (New York) p.73

**Nutter, McClennen & Fish, LLP**
Tables: Antitrust p.1053, Banking & Finance p.1055, Environment p.1068, Litigation: General Commercial p.1074, Real Estate p.1081

**Nyemaster, Goode, West, Hansell, and O'Brien**
Tables: Corporate/M&A p.909, Employment: Mainly Defendant p.911, Litigation: General Commercial p.913, Real Estate p.917

## O

**Ober Kaler Grimes & Shriver**
Tables: Corporate/M&A p.1025, Employee Benefits & Executive Compensation p.1026, Employment: Mainly Defendant p.1028, Healthcare p.455

**Oblon, Spivak, McClelland, Maier & Neustadt PC**
Table: Intellectual Property: Northern Virginia p.1974

**Oertel, Fernandez, Cole & Bryant, PA**
Table: Environment p.600

**Ogletree, Deakins, Nash, Smoak & Stewart, PC**
Profile: p.738
Tables: Construction p.778, Employment: Mainly Defendant p.149, Immigration p.694, Litigation: General Commercial p.1778

**Ohnstad Twichell PC**
Table: Real Estate p.1595

**Oliff & Berridge PLC**
Table: Intellectual Property: Northern Virginia p.1974

**Olson Burns Lee PC**
Table: Corporate/Commercial p.1590

**O'Melveny & Myers LLP**
Profile: p.336
Tables: Antitrust p.215, Banking & Finance p.218, Bankruptcy/Restructuring p.221, Corporate/M&A: Mid-Tier Firms p.1359, Corporate/M&A: Northern California p.226, Employee Benefits & Executive Compensation p.437, Employment: Mainly Defendant p.230, Insurance: Insurer Firms p.242, Intellectual Property p.247, Intellectual Property: Trademark & Copyright p.1384, International Trade p.41, IT & IT Outsourcing p.253, Litigation: General Commercial p.255, Media & Entertainment: Litigation p.262, Media & Entertainment: Transactional p.265, Products Liability p.49, Real Estate p.269, Tax p.273

**Oppenheimer Wolff & Donnelly LLP**
Tables: Corporate/M&A p.1151, Real Estate p.1159

**Orloff, Lowenbach, Stifelman & Siegel**
Table: Corporate/M&A p.1278

**Orrick, Herrington & Sutcliffe LLP**
Profile: p.337
Tables: Banking & Finance p.218, Bankruptcy/Restructuring p.221, Capital Markets: CDOs, Repackaging & Other Synthetic Products p.12, Capital Markets: Securitisation p.17, Corporate/Commercial p.1992, Employment: Mainly Defendant p.230, Energy & Natural Resources p.233, Intellectual Property p.247, Intellectual Property: Patent p.1383, Litigation: General Commercial p.255, Products

Liability p.49, Projects p.268, Real Estate p.269, Tax p.273, Transportation: Road (Carriage/Commercial) p.71

**Orr & Reno PA**
Tables: Corporate/Commercial p.1263, Employment: Mainly Defendant p.1265, Litigation: General Commercial p.1267

**Osborn Maledon PA**
Profile: p.198
Tables: Corporate/M&A p.175, Litigation: General Commercial p.181, Litigation: White-Collar Crime & Government Investigations p.182, Real Estate p.183

**Otten, Johnson, Robinson, Neff + Ragonetti, PC**
Profile: p.371
Table: Real Estate p.354

**Otterbourg, Steindler, Houston & Rosen**
Table: Bankruptcy/Restructuring p.1343

## P

**Pachulski, Stang, Ziehl, Young, Jones & Weintraub P.C.**
Profile: p.338
Tables: Bankruptcy/Restructuring p.221

**Packman, Neuwahl & Rosenberg**
Table: Tax p.622

**Page Law Firm LLC**
Table: Employment: Mainly Defendant p.1592

**Pansing Hogan Ernst & Bachman LLP**
Table: Real Estate p.1241

**Paparelli & Partners LLP**
Table: Immigration p.241

**Pappas Metcalf Jenks and Miller**
Table: Real Estate: Zoning/Land Use p.620

**Parker & Brown**
Table: Employee Benefits & Executive Compensation p.1063

**Parker, Hudson, Rainer & Dobbs LLP**
Tables: Banking & Finance p.677, Bankruptcy/Restructuring p.679, Corporate/M&A p.683, Healthcare p.693

**Parker, Poe, Adams & Bernstein LLP**
Tables: Banking & Finance p.1569, Environment p.1574, Litigation: General Commercial p.1577

**Parr Waddoups Brown Gee & Loveless**
Tables: Corporate/M&A p.1941, Litigation: General Commercial p.1945, Real Estate p.1947

**Parsons Behle & Latimer PC**
Profile: p.1956

**PROFILE:** CONTACT DETAILS AT THE END OF EVERY STATE    **TABLE:** REFERS TO THE SPECIALIST LISTS IN WHICH THE FIRM APPEARS

2069

**P**

Tables: Corporate/M&A p.1941,
Employment: Mainly Defendant p.1944,
Environment p.1249, Litigation: General
Commercial p.1945, Real Estate p.1947

**Partridge Snow & Hahn LLP**
Tables: Corporate/Commercial p.1766,
Employment: Mainly Defendant p.1767,
Litigation: General Commercial p.1768

**Patterson, Belknap,
Webb & Tyler LLP**
Profile: p.1547
Tables: Intellectual Property: Patent
p.1383, Intellectual Property: Trademark
& Copyright p.1384, Media &
Entertainment: Advertising p.1399,
Media & Entertainment: Litigation p.1404

**Pattishall, McAuliffe, Newbury,
Hilliard & Geraldson LLP**
Table: Intellectual Property p.798

**Patton Boggs LLP**
Tables: Environment, Natural Resources
& Regulated Industries p.169,
Government: Government Relations
p.32, Government: Political Law p.34,
Litigation: General Commercial p.171

**Paul Parsons PC**
Table: Immigration p.1856

**Paul, Weiss, Rifkind, Wharton &
Garrison LLP**
Profile: p.1548
Tables: Antitrust p.425,
Bankruptcy/Restructuring p.1343,
Capital Markets: Debt & Equity (excludes
West Coast) p.6, Corporate/M&A
p.1353, Employee Benefits & Executive
Compensation p.1361, Litigation:
General Commercial p.1387, Litigation:
Securities p.1389, Litigation: White-
Collar Crime & Government Investigations
p.1391, Media & Entertainment:
Commercial p.1401, Media &
Entertainment: Corporate p.1402, Media
& Entertainment: Litigation p.1404, Real
Estate p.1416, Tax p.1422, Telecom,
Broadcast & Satellite: Regulatory p.491,
Wealth Management p.80

**Paul, Frank + Collins, A
Professional Corporation**
Tables: Corporate/Commercial p.1957,
Litigation: General Commercial p.1959,
Real Estate p.1961

**Paul, Hastings, Janofsky &
Walker LLP**
Profile: p.339
Tables: Antitrust p.675, Banking &
Finance p.218, Bankruptcy/Restructuring
p.221, Corporate/M&A p.374,
Corporate/M&A: Mid-Tier Firms p.1359,
Corporate/M&A: Southern California
p.226, Employment: Mainly Defendant
p.230, Environment p.235, Healthcare
p.238, Immigration p.459, Intellectual
Property p.247, Intellectual Property:
Trademark & Copyright p.1384, Litigation:
International Trade p.41, Litigation:
General Commercial p.255, Projects
p.268, Real Estate p.269, Tax p.273,
Transportation: Aviation: Finance p.64

**Paul, Johnson, Park & Niles,
Attorneys At Law, A Law
Corporation**
Table: Litigation: General Commercial
p.745

**Pearce & Durick**
Table: Litigation: General Commercial
p.1593

**Pearl Law Group**
Table: Immigration p.241

**Pearson Christensen Cahill &
Clapp, PLLP**
Tables: Corporate/Commercial p.1590,
Litigation: General Commercial p.1593

**Peckar & Abramson PC**
Profile: p.1549
Tables: Construction p.433

**Peifer, Hanson & Mullins PA**
Table: Litigation: General Commercial
p.1324

**Peitzman, Weg & Kempinsky LLP**
Table: Bankruptcy/Restructuring p.221

**Pennington, Moore, Wilkinson,
Bell & Dunbar, PA**
Table: Insurance p.606

**Pepper Hamilton LLP**
Profile: p.1760
Tables: Antitrust p.1692,
Bankruptcy/Restructuring p.388,
Corporate/M&A p.1700, Employment:
Mainly Defendant p.1703, Litigation:
General Commercial p.1713, Products
Liability p.49

**Perkins Coie LLP**
Tables: Corporate/Commercial p.1992,
Corporate/M&A p.175, Employment:
Mainly Defendant p.168, Environment
p.1672, Environment, Natural Resources
& Regulated Industries p.169,
Government: Political Law p.34,
Immigration p.1997, Intellectual Property
p.1998, Litigation: General Commercial
p.181, Natural Resources & Environment
p.761, Real Estate p.183

**Perkins, Thompson,
Hinckley & Keddy, P.A.**
Table: Real Estate p.1008

**Pettiette, Armand, Dunkelman,
Woodley, Byrd & Cromwell LLP**
Table: Banking & Finance p.963

**Phelps Dunbar LLP**
Profile: p.997
Tables: Banking & Finance p.963,
Corporate/Commercial p.1174,
Corporate/M&A p.964, Employment:
Mainly Defendant p.967, Energy &
Natural Resources p.969, Environment
p.970, Gaming & Licensing p.971,
Litigation: General Commercial p.972,
Real Estate p.975, Transportation:
Shipping (outside New York) p.78

**Phibbs Law Office PC**
Table: Real Estate p.2045

**Phillips McFall McCaffrey
McVay & Murrah, P.C.**
Table: Real Estate p.1657

**Piccarreta & Davis PC**
Table: Litigation: White-Collar Crime &
Government Investigations p.182

**Pierce Atwood LLP**
Profile: p.1022
Tables: Corporate/M&A p.1000,
Employment: Mainly Defendant p.1002,
Environment p.1004, Litigation: General
Commercial p.1005, Real Estate p.1008

**Pill & Pill**
Table: Real Estate p.2015

**Pillsbury Winthrop Shaw
Pittman LLP**
Profile: p.1550
Tables: Banking & Finance p.218,
Corporate/Commercial p.435,
Corporate/M&A: Northern California
p.226, Corporate/M&A: Northern Virginia
p.1967, Employee Benefits & Executive
Compensation p.1361, Employment:
Mainly Defendant p.1970, Energy &
Natural Resources p.233, Energy:
Nuclear p.448, Environment p.235,
Financial Services: Regulatory
Enforcement & Investigations p.28,
Government: Political Law p.34, Intellectual
Property: Northern Virginia p.1974, IT &
IT Outsourcing p.253, Litigation: General
Commercial p.255, Projects p.1869,
Real Estate p.269, Tax p.273,
Technology & IT Outsourcing p.490,
Telecom, Broadcast & Satellite:
Regulatory p.491, Transportation:
Aviation: Finance p.64, Wealth
Management p.80

**Pircher, Nichols & Meeks**
Table: Real Estate p.269

**Pitney Hardin LLP**
Profile: p.1316
Tables: Corporate/M&A p.1278,
Employee Benefits & Executive
Compensation p.1281, Employment:
Mainly Defendant p.1282, Environment
p.1284, Litigation: General Commercial
p.1289, Real Estate p.1293

**Plank & Brahm**
Table: Real Estate: Zoning/Land Use
p.1622

**Podhurst Orseck P.A.**
Profile: p.670
Tables: Litigation: General Commercial
p.608, Litigation: White-Collar Crime &
Government Investigations p.610

**Polsinelli Shalton Welte
Suelthaus PC**
Profile: p.1217
Tables: Corporate/M&A p.924,
Litigation: General Commercial p.1197,
Real Estate p.929

**Poore, Roth & Robinson, P.C.**
Table: Litigation: General Commercial
p.1225

**Porter & Hedges, LLP**
Tables: Banking & Finance p.1831,

Construction p.1838

**Porter Wright Morris & Arthur LLP**
Profile: p.1648
Tables: Banking & Finance p.1598,
Bankruptcy/Restructuring p.1600,
Employee Benefits & Executive
Compensation p.1606, Employment:
Mainly Defendant p.1608, Environment
p.1610, Litigation: General Commercial
p.1616, Real Estate p.1620, Real Estate:
Zoning/Land Use p.1622

**Porzio, Bromberg & Newman, P.C.**
Profile: p.1317
Table: Environment p.1284

**Potter Anderson & Corroon LLP**
Profile: p.421
Tables: Bankruptcy/Restructuring p.388,
Chancery p.391, Corporate/M&A p.394,
Employment: Mainly Defendant p.396,
Intellectual Property p.397

**Powell Goldstein LLP**
Tables: Antitrust p.675, Banking &
Finance p.677, Bankruptcy/Restructuring
p.679, Corporate/M&A p.683, Healthcare
p.693, Immigration p.694, Litigation:
General Commercial p.697, Real Estate
p.700, Tax p.702

**Powers Pyles Sutter & Verville PC**
Table: Healthcare p.455

**Poyner & Spruill LLP**
Table: Environment p.1574

**Pratt & Sanderford**
Table: Construction p.1838

**Pratt-Thomas, Epting & Walker PA**
Table: Litigation: General Commercial
p.1778

**Preston Gates & Ellis LLP**
Tables: Bankruptcy/Restructuring
p.1991, Corporate/Commercial p.1992,
Corporate/M&A p.168, Environment
p.1996, Intellectual Property p.1998,
Litigation: General Commercial p.1999,
Real Estate p.172, Telecom, Broadcast &
Satellite: Regulatory p.491

**Preti Flaherty Beliveau &
Pachios, LLP**
Profile: p.1023
Tables: Corporate/M&A p.1000,
Employment: Mainly Defendant p.1002,
Environment p.1004, Litigation: General
Commercial p.1005, Real Estate p.1008

**Prickett, Jones & Elliott PA**
Table: Corporate/M&A p.394

**Primmer Piper Eggleston &
Cramer PC**
Profile: p.1964
Tables: Corporate/Commercial p.1957,
Litigation: General Commercial p.1959,
Real Estate p.1961

**Proctor Heyman LLP**
Profile: p.422
Table: Chancery p.391

**Proskauer Rose LLP**
Profile: p.1551
Tables: Bankruptcy/Restructuring

Litigation: General Commercial p.927, Real Estate p.1200

**Shulman, Rogers, Gandal, Pordy & Ecker, PA**
Table: Real Estate p.1035

**Shults Law Firm, LLP**
Table: Litigation: General Commercial p.204

**Shumacker Witt Gaither & Whitaker, PC**
Table: Real Estate p.1807

**Shumaker Loop & Kendrick LLP**
Tables: Corporate/M&A p.593, Environment p.1610

**Shuttleworth & Ingersoll PLC**
Tables: Corporate/M&A p.909, Employment: Mainly Defendant p.911, Litigation: General Commercial p.913, Real Estate p.917

**Shutts & Bowen LLP**
Profile: p.673
Tables: Banking & Finance p.583, Corporate/M&A p.593, Real Estate p.616, Real Estate: Zoning/Land Use p.620

**Sidley Austin LLP**
Profile: p.883
Tables: Antitrust p.766, Banking & Finance p.770, Bankruptcy/Restructuring p.221, Capital Markets: CDOs, Repackaging & Other Synthetic Products p.12, Capital Markets: Debt & Equity (West Coast) p.8, Capital Markets: Derivatives p.14, Capital Markets: Securitisation p.17, Corporate/M&A & Private Equity p.780, Corporate/M&A: Southern California p.226, Employment: Employee Benefits p.784, Energy & Natural Resources p.789, Energy: Oil & Gas p.441, Environment p.450, Environment: Mainly Transactional p.1372, Financial Services: Regulatory Compliance p.23, Healthcare: Pharmaceutical/Medical Products Regulatory p.455, Insurance: Coverage Litigation p.795, Intellectual Property p.466, Intellectual Property: Patent p.1383, International Arbitration p.35, Litigation p.470, Litigation: Appellate p.474, Litigation: General Commercial p.255, Media & Entertainment: Litigation p.805, Products Liability p.49, Real Estate p.808, Tax p.811, Telecom, Broadcast & Satellite: Regulatory p.491, Transportation: Aviation: Finance p.64, Transportation: Rail p.68

**Siegel, O'Connor, O'Donnell & Beck PC**
Table: Employment: Mainly Defendant p.376

**Siegfried, Rivera, Lerner, De La Torre & Sobel, PA**
Table: Construction p.589

**Sills Cummis Epstein & Gross PC**
Profile: p.1319
Tables: Corporate/M&A p.1278, Healthcare p.1287, Litigation: General Commercial p.1289, Real Estate p.1293

**Simmons Perrine Albright & Ellwood PLC**
Tables: Employment: Mainly Defendant p.911, Litigation: General Commercial p.913, Real Estate p.917

**Simpson Thacher & Bartlett LLP**
Profile: p.1555
Tables: Antitrust p.1334, Banking & Finance p.1339, Bankruptcy/Restructuring p.1343, Capital Markets: Debt & Equity (excludes West Coast) p.6, Capital Markets: Debt & Equity (West Coast) p.8, Capital Markets: Securitisation p.17, Corporate/M&A p.1353, Corporate/M&A: Northern California p.226, Employee Benefits & Executive Compensation p.1361, Energy & Natural Resources p.1367, Environment: Mainly Transactional p.1372, Financial Services: Financial Institutions M&A p.23, Insurance: Dispute Resolution p.1378, Insurance: Transactional & Regulatory p.1380, Intellectual Property p.247, Litigation: General Commercial p.1387, Litigation: Securities p.1389, Private Equity: Buyouts & Venture Capital Investment p.1406, Private Fund Formation p.1409, Products Liability p.49, Projects p.1412, Real Estate p.1416, Tax p.1422, Transportation: Aviation: Finance p.64

**Sirote & Permutt PC**
Tables: Corporate/Commercial p.148, Real Estate p.153

**Sive Paget & Riesel PC**
Profile: p.1556
Table: Environment p.1370

**Skadden, Arps, Slate, Meagher & Flom LLP & Affiliates**
Profile: p.1557
Tables: Antitrust p.425, Banking & Finance p.218, Bankruptcy/Restructuring p.221, Capital Markets: CDOs, Repackaging & Other Synthetic Products p.12, Capital Markets: Debt & Equity (excludes West Coast) p.6, Capital Markets: Derivatives p.14, Capital Markets: Securitisation p.17, Chancery p.391, Corporate/Commercial p.394, Corporate/M&A p.394, Corporate/M&A & Private Equity p.780, Corporate/M&A: Northern California p.1361, Employee Benefits & Executive Compensation p.1361, Energy & Natural Resources p.1367, Energy: Electricity p.444, Energy: Oil & Gas p.441, Environment p.450, Financial Services: Financial Institutions M&A p.23, Government: Political Law p.34, Insurance: Dispute Resolution p.1378, Insurance: Transactional & Regulatory p.1380, Intellectual Property p.247, Intellectual Property: Patent p.1383, Litigation p.470, Litigation: General Commercial p.255, Litigation: Securities p.1389, Litigation: White-Collar Crime & Government Investigations p.1391, Media & Entertainment: Advertising p.1399, Media & Entertainment: Corporate p.1402, Products Liability p.49, Projects p.56, Real Estate p.1416, Securities p.485, Sports Law p.59, Tax p.487, Technology & IT Outsourcing p.1428, Telecom, Broadcast & Satellite: Regulatory p.491

**Slover & Loftus**
Table: Transportation: Rail p.68

**Slusser, Wilson & Partridge LLP**
Table: Intellectual Property p.1859

**Smith & Hale**
Table: Real Estate: Zoning/Land Use p.1622

**Smith Pachter McWhorter PLC**
Tables: Construction p.1965, Government: Government Contracts p.29

**Smith, Currie & Hancock LLP**
Table: Construction p.681

**Smith, Anderson, Blount, Dorsett, Mitchell & Jernigan, LLP**
Profile: p.1588
Tables: Corporate/M&A p.1571, Employment: Mainly Defendant p.1573, Litigation: General Commercial p.1577, Real Estate p.1579

**Smith Bakke Oppegard Porsborg & Wolf**
Table: Litigation: General Commercial p.1593

**Smith Gambrell & Russell LLP**
Tables: Antitrust p.675, Banking & Finance: Mainly Regulatory p.677, Construction p.681, Environment p.690, Intellectual Property p.696, Litigation: General Commercial p.697, Real Estate p.616

**Smith Hulsey & Busey**
Tables: Bankruptcy/Restructuring p.585, Real Estate p.616

**Smith & Kotchka Ltd**
Table: Employment: Mainly Defendant p.1247

**Smith Mackinnon PA**
Table: Banking & Finance p.583

**Smith Moore LLP**
Profile: p.1587
Tables: Employment: Mainly Defendant p.1573, Environment p.1574, Litigation: General Commercial p.1577, Real Estate p.1579

**Smith & Smith Attorneys**
Profile: p.958
Table: Employment: Mainly Defendant p.939

**Smyser Kaplan & Veselka LLP**
Table: Litigation: General Commercial p.1864

**Snell & Wilmer LLP**
Profile: p.200
Tables: Corporate/M&A p.175, Employment: Mainly Defendant p.177, Environment (including water rights) p.179, Litigation: General Commercial p.181, Real Estate p.183, Real Estate: Zoning/Land Use p.186

**Sommer Barnard PC**
Profile: p.906
Tables: Corporate/M&A p.887, Litigation:

General Commercial p.890, Real Estate p.892

**Sommer, Udall, Hardwick, Ahern & Hyatt LLP**
Table: Real Estate p.1326

**Sonnenschein Nath & Rosenthal LLP**
Profile: p.884
Tables: Antitrust p.766, Bankruptcy/Restructuring p.774, Business Process Outsourcing p.1, Corporate/M&A p.1192, Corporate/M&A & Private Equity p.780, Employment: Employee Benefits p.784, Energy & Natural Resources p.789, Environment p.790, Government: Government Relations p.32, Healthcare p.238, Insurance: Coverage Litigation p.795, Insurance: Dispute Resolution p.1378, Insurance: Insurer Firms p.242, Litigation: General Commercial p.1197, Media & Entertainment: Litigation p.805, Real Estate p.808, Technology & IT Outsourcing p.813

**Sowell Gray Stepp & Laffitte LLC**
Profile: p.1790
Table: Litigation: General Commercial p.1778

**Spencer Fane Britt & Browne LLP**
Tables: Corporate/M&A p.1192, Employment: Mainly Defendant p.1195, Litigation: Environmental p.928, Litigation: General Commercial p.927

**Sperling & Slater**
Table: Antitrust p.766

**Spieth Bell McCurdy & Newell Co LPA**
Table: Employment: Mainly Defendant p.1608

**Spilman Thomas & Battle, PLLC**
Profile: p.2024
Tables: Corporate/Commercial p.2010, Employment: Mainly Defendant p.2011, Litigation: General Commercial p.2013, Real Estate p.2015

**Spink Butler, LLP**
Table: Real Estate p.762

**Spink & Miller PLC**
Table: Litigation: General Commercial p.1959

**Spradling, Kennedy & McPhail LLP**
Table: Real Estate p.1657

**Spriggs & Hollingsworth**
Table: Insurance: Policy Holder p.464

**Squire, Sanders & Dempsey LLP**
Profile: p.1650
Tables: Banking & Finance p.1598, Bankruptcy/Restructuring p.1600, Construction p.1602, Corporate/M&A p.175, Employee Benefits & Executive Compensation p.1606, Employment: Mainly Defendant p.1608, Environment p.1610, Environment (including water rights) p.179, Real Estate p.183, Tax p.622

**PROFILE:** CONTACT DETAILS AT THE END OF EVERY STATE · **TABLE:** REFERS TO THE SPECIALIST LISTS IN WHICH THE FIRM APPEARS

2073

**T**

**Thompson Hine LLP**
Profile: p.1651
Tables: Banking & Finance p.1598,
Bankruptcy/Restructuring p.1600,
Construction p.1602, Corporate/M&A
p.1604, Employee Benefits & Executive
Compensation p.1606, Environment
p.1610, Intellectual Property p.1614,
Litigation: General Commercial p.1616,
Real Estate p.1620, Transportation: Rail
p.68, Transportation: Road
(Carriage/Commercial) p.71

**Thompson & Knight LLP**
Profile: p.1936
Tables: Banking & Finance p.1831,
Bankruptcy/Restructuring p.1834,
Corporate/M&A p.1840, Environment
p.1851, Intellectual Property p.1859,
Litigation: General Commercial p.1864,
Tax p.1874

**Thompson, Sizemore & Gonzalez**
Table: Employment: Mainly Defendant
p.596

**Thorp Reed & Armstrong**
Table: Litigation: General Commercial
p.1713

**Tindall Bennett & Shoup PC**
Tables: Employment: Mainly Defendant
p.168, Real Estate p.172

**Tindall & Foster PC**
Table: Immigration p.1856

**Tinnin Law Firm**
Table: Employment: Mainly Defendant
p.1321

**Titus, Brueckner & Berry PC**
Table: Corporate/M&A p.175

**Todd & Weld LLP**
Table: Litigation: General Commercial
p.1074

**Tonkon Torp LLP**
Profile: p.1691
Tables: Corporate/M&A p.1667,
Litigation: General Commercial p.1674,
Real Estate p.1676

**Topel & Goodman PC**
Table: Litigation: Specialist Firms in
White-Collar Crime & Government
Investigations p.255

**Torkildson, Katz, Fonseca, Jaffe,
Moore & Hetherington Attorneys
At Law, A Law Corporation**
Table: Employment: Mainly Defendant
p.742

**Townsend and Townsend
and Crew LLP**
Tables: Antitrust p.215, Intellectual
Property p.247

**Townsend & Jones**
Table: Tax p.1874

**Trenam, Kemker, Scharf, Barkin,
Frye, O'Neill & Mullis PA**
Tables: Bankruptcy/Restructuring p.585,
Corporate/M&A p.593, Real Estate
p.616

**Triplett, Woolf & Garretson LLC**
Tables: Corporate/M&A p.924, Real
Estate p.929

**Trout Cacheris PLLC**
Table: Litigation: Specialist Firms in
White-Collar Crime & Government
Investigations p.471

**Troutman Sanders LLP**
Tables: Antitrust p.675, Banking &
Finance p.677, Bankruptcy/Restructuring
p.679, Corporate/M&A p.683,
Corporate/M&A: Southern Virginia
p.1967, Employment: Mainly Defendant
p.686, Energy & Natural Resources
p.689, Energy: Electricity p.444, Energy:
Oil & Gas p.441, Environment p.690,
Immigration p.694, Intellectual Property
p.696, Intellectual Property: Southern
Virginia p.1974, Litigation: General
Commercial p.697, Real Estate p.700,
Transportation: Shipping (outside New
York) p.78

**Tschider & Smith**
Table: Corporate/Commercial p.1590

**Tsukazaki Yeh & Moore**
Table: Land Use p.743

**Tucker Ellis & West LLP**
Table: Litigation: General Commercial
p.1616

**Turner & Mede, PC**
Table: Employment: Mainly Defendant
p.168

**Tyler Cooper & Alcorn LLP**
Table: Employment: Mainly Defendant
p.376

# U

**Ugrin, Alexander, Zadick
& Higgins, PC**
Tables: Employment: Mainly Defendant
p.1223, Litigation: General Commercial
p.1225

**Ulmer & Berne LLP**
Tables: Construction p.1602, Employee
Benefits & Executive Compensation
p.1606, Employment: Mainly Defendant
p.1608, Litigation: General Commercial
p.1616, Real Estate p.1620

**Ungaretti & Harris**
Table: Healthcare p.793

**Upton and Hatfield LLP**
Tables: Litigation: General Commercial
p.1267, Real Estate p.1269

# V

**Van Kley & Walker**
Table: Environment p.1610

**Van Cott, Bagley, Cornwall
& McCarthy**
Tables: Litigation: General Commercial
p.1945, Real Estate p.1947

**Van Hoy Reutlinger
Adams & Dunn**
Table: Employment: Mainly Defendant
p.1573

**Van Ness Feldman PC**
Tables: Energy: Electricity p.444,
Energy: Oil & Gas p.441, Environment
p.450

**Varnum, Riddering, Schmidt
& Howlett LLP**
Profile: p.1149
Tables: Banking & Finance p.1120,
Corporate/M&A p.1121, Employment:
Mainly Defendant p.1125, Litigation:
General Commercial p.1128

**Vaughan & Murphy**
Table: Antitrust p.675

**Vedder, Price, Kaufman
& Kammholz**
Profile: p.885
Tables: Banking & Finance p.770,
Bankruptcy/Restructuring p.774,
Employment: Employee Benefits p.784,
Transportation: Aviation: Finance p.64

**Venable LLP**
Tables: Construction p.1965,
Corporate/M&A p.1025, Corporate/M&A:
Northern Virginia p.1967, Employee
Benefits & Executive Compensation
p.1026, Employment: Mainly Defendant
p.1028, Environment p.450,
Government: Government Contracts
p.29, Healthcare p.1030, Litigation:
General Commercial p.1032, Real Estate
p.481

**Vercruysse Murray & Calzone, PC**
Profile: p.1150
Table: Employment: Mainly Defendant
p.1125

**Verrill Dana, LLP**
Profile: p.1024
Tables: Corporate/M&A p.1000,
Employment: Mainly Defendant p.1002,
Environment p.1004, Litigation: General
Commercial p.1005, Real Estate p.1008

**Vezina Lawrence & Piscitelli PA**
Table: Construction p.589

**Vickers Madsen & Goldman**
Table: Tax p.622

**Vinson & Elkins LLP**
Profile: p.1938
Tables: Antitrust p.1829, Banking &
Finance p.1831,
Bankruptcy/Restructuring p.1834,
Capital Markets: Debt & Equity (excludes
West Coast) p.6, Corporate/M&A
p.1840, Employment: Mainly Defendant
p.1843, Energy & Natural Resources
p.1367, Energy & Natural Resources:
Dispute Resolution p.1848, Energy:
Electricity p.444, Energy: Oil & Gas
p.441, Environment p.450, Healthcare
p.455, Insurance p.1857, Intellectual
Property p.1859, International Arbitration
p.35, Litigation p.470, Litigation: General
Commercial p.1864, Projects p.56, Real
Estate p.1871, Tax p.1874, Technology &
IT Outsourcing p.1877, Telecom,
Broadcast & Satellite: Regulatory p.491

**Vogel Campbell & Blueher PC**
Table: Real Estate p.1326

**Vogel Law Firm**
Tables: Corporate/Commercial p.1590,
Employment: Mainly Defendant p.1592,
Litigation: General Commercial p.1593,
Real Estate p.1595

**Vorys, Sater, Seymour
and Pease LLP**
Profile: p.1652
Tables: Banking & Finance p.1598,
Bankruptcy/Restructuring p.1600,
Corporate/M&A p.1604, Employee
Benefits & Executive Compensation
p.1606, Employment: Mainly Defendant
p.1608, Environment p.1610, Litigation:
General Commercial p.1616, Real Estate
p.1620, Real Estate: Zoning/Land Use
p.1622

# W

**Wachtell, Lipton, Rosen & Katz**
Profile: p.1561
Tables: Antitrust p.1334,
Bankruptcy/Restructuring p.1343,
Corporate/M&A p.1353, Employee
Benefits & Executive Compensation
p.1361, Energy & Natural Resources
p.1367, Financial Services: Financial
Institutions M&A p.23, Insurance:
Dispute Resolution p.1378, Insurance:
Transactional & Regulatory p.1380,
Litigation: General Commercial p.1387,
Litigation: Securities p.1389, Litigation:
White-Collar Crime & Government
Investigations p.1391, Real Estate
p.1416, Tax p.1422

**Wadleigh, Starr & Peters PLLC**
Tables: Litigation: General Commercial
p.1267, Real Estate p.1269

**Wagner Choi Evers**
Table: Bankruptcy/Restructuring p.739

**Walder, Hayden & Brogan P.A.**
Table: Litigation: White-Collar Crime &
Government Investigations p.1292

**Walker, Bryant, Tipps & Malone**
Profile: p.1827
Table: Litigation: General Commercial
p.1803

**Wallack Somers & Haas PC**
Table: Real Estate p.892

**Waller Lansden Dortch & Davis**
Profile: p.1828
Tables: Corporate/M&A p.1799,
Employment: Mainly Defendant p.1801,
Litigation: General Commercial p.1803,
Real Estate p.1807

**Walter & Haverfield LLP**
Table: Environment p.1610

**Warner Norcross & Judd LLP**
Tables: Banking & Finance p.1120,
Corporate/M&A p.1121, Employee
Benefits & Executive Compensation
p.1124, Employment: Mainly Defendant
p.1125, Litigation: General Commercial
p.1128

**Warren & Sinkler LLP**
Tables: Corporate/M&A p.1775, Real
Estate p.1780

**Watanabe Ing & Komeiji**
Tables: Land Use p.743, Litigation:
General Commercial p.745

**Watkins & Eager PLLC**
Profile: p.1191
Tables: Corporate/Commercial p.1174,
Employment: Mainly Defendant p.1176,
Litigation: General Commercial p.1178,
Real Estate p.1181

**Watkins Ludlam Winter &
Stennis, P.A**
Tables: Corporate/Commercial p.1174,
Employment: Mainly Defendant p.1176,
Litigation: General Commercial p.1178,
Real Estate p.1181

**Watson, Farley & Williams**
Profile: p.1564
Table: Transportation: Shipping (New
York) p.73

**Watt, Tieder, Hoffar &
Fitzgerald LLP**
Profile: p.1990
Table: Construction p.1965

**Weil, Gotshal & Manges LLP**
Profile: p.1565
Tables: Antitrust p.425, Banking &
Finance p.1339,
Bankruptcy/Restructuring p.1343,
Capital Markets: Debt & Equity (excludes
West Coast) p.6, Capital Markets:
Securitisation p.17, Corporate/M&A
p.1060, Employment: Mainly Defendant
p.1364, Environment p.450, Intellectual
Property p.247, Intellectual Property:
Patent p.1383, International Arbitration
p.35, International Trade p.41, Litigation:
General Commercial p.1387, Litigation:
Securities p.1389, Media &
Entertainment: Litigation p.1404, Private
Equity: Buyouts & Venture Capital
Investment p.1077, Private Fund
Formation p.1079, Real Estate p.1416,
Sports Law p.59, Tax p.1422,
Technology & IT Outsourcing p.1428,
Wealth Management p.80

**Weinberg, Wheeler, Hudgins,
Gunn & Dial, LLC**
Table: Construction p.681

**Weinberg Richmond LLP**
Table: Real Estate p.808

**Weissmann, Wolff, Bergman,
Coleman, Grodin & Evall, LLP**
Table: Media & Entertainment:
Transactional p.265

**Welbaum, Guernsey, Hingston,
Greenleaf & Gregory LLP**
Table: Construction p.589

**Welsh & Katz Ltd**
Table: Intellectual Property p.798

**Weston Benshoof Rochefort
Rubalcava MacCuish LLP**
Profile: p.343
Table: Environment p.235

**Wheeler Trigg Kennedy LLP**
Tables: Litigation: General Commercial
p.352, Products Liability p.49

**White & Case LLP**
Profile: p.1566
Tables: Antitrust p.425, Banking &
Finance p.218, Bankruptcy/Restructuring
p.221, Corporate/M&A p.1353,
Corporate/M&A: Latin American
Investment p.595, Employee Benefits &
Executive Compensation p.1361, Energy
& Natural Resources p.233, Environment
p.600, Environment: Mainly Transactional
p.1372, Financial Services: Regulatory
Enforcement & Investigations p.28,
Intellectual Property p.247, Intellectual
Property: Patent p.1383, Intellectual
Property: Trademark & Copyright
p.1384, International Trade p.41,
Litigation: General Commercial p.255,
Private Equity: Buyouts & Venture Capital
Investment p.1406, Projects p.56, Real
Estate p.616, Tax p.622, Technology &
IT Outsourcing p.1428, Telecom,
Broadcast & Satellite: Regulatory p.491,
Transportation: Aviation: Finance p.64,
Wealth Management p.80

**Whiteford, Taylor & Preston LLP**
Profile: p.1052
Tables: Corporate/M&A p.1025,
Employee Benefits & Executive
Compensation p.1026, Employment:
Mainly Defendant p.1028, Healthcare
p.1030, Litigation: General Commercial
p.1032, Real Estate p.1035

**White Goss Bowers March
Schulte & Weisenfels, A
Professional Corporation**
Table: Real Estate p.1200

**Whiteman Osterman & Hanna LLP**
Table: Environment p.1370

**White O'Connor Curry
& Avanzado LLP**
Table: Media & Entertainment: Litigation
p.262

**Whitfield & Eddy, PLC**
Tables: Employment: Mainly Defendant
p.911, Litigation: General Commercial
p.913

**Whyte Hirschboeck Dudek S.C.**
Tables: Intellectual Property p.2028,
Real Estate p.2030

**Wickwire Gavin P.C.**
Table: Construction p.1965

**Wiggin and Dana LLP**
Tables: Corporate/M&A p.374,
Employment: Mainly Defendant p.376,
Litigation: General Commercial p.378,
Real Estate p.380

**Wiggin & Nourie**
Table: Litigation: General Commercial
p.1267

**Wildes & Weinberg PC**
Table: Immigration p.1376

**Wilentz Goldman & Spitzer, P.A.**
Table: Real Estate p.1293

**Wiley Rein & Fielding LLP**
Profile: p.579
Tables: Government: Government
Contracts p.29, Government: Political
Law p.34, Insurance: Insurer Firms
p.461, International Trade p.41, Media &
Entertainment p.476, Telecom,
Broadcast & Satellite: Regulatory p.491

**Wilkinson Barker Knauer LLP**
Table: Telecom, Broadcast & Satellite:
Regulatory p.491

**Willcox & Savage**
Table: Corporate/M&A: Southern Virginia
p.1967

**Williams & Anderson PLC**
Profile: p.213
Tables: Corporate/Commercial p.201,
Litigation: General Commercial p.204

**Williams & Connolly LLP**
Tables: Financial Services: Regulatory
Enforcement & Investigations p.28,
Healthcare: Pharmaceutical/Medical
Products Regulatory p.455, Litigation
p.470, Media & Entertainment p.476,
Products Liability p.49

**Williams & Jensen PLLC**
Table: Government: Government
Relations p.32

**Williams Mullen**
Tables: Corporate/M&A: Southern
Virginia p.1967, Employment: Mainly
Defendant p.1970, Environment p.1972,
Intellectual Property: Southern Virginia
p.1974, Real Estate p.1977

**Williams, Porter, Day & Neville PC**
Tables: Employment: Mainly Defendant
p.2042, Litigation: General Commercial
p.2043, Real Estate p.2045

**Williams, Zografos & Peck**
Table: Employment: Mainly Defendant
p.1669

**Willkie Farr & Gallagher LLP**
Profile: p.1567
Tables: Antitrust p.1334,
Bankruptcy/Restructuring p.1343,
Corporate/M&A p.1353, Environment
p.450, Financial Services: Regulatory
Compliance p.23, Insurance: Dispute
Resolution p.1378, Insurance:
Transactional & Regulatory p.1380,
International Trade p.41, Investment
Management p.468, Litigation: General
Commercial p.1387, Litigation: Securities
p.1389, Private Equity: Buyouts & Venture
Capital Investment p.1406, Real Estate
p.1416, Technology & IT Outsourcing
p.1428, Telecom, Broadcast & Satellite:
Regulatory p.491

**WilmerHale**
Profile: p.580, 1119
Tables: Antitrust p.425,
Bankruptcy/Restructuring p.431,
Corporate/Commercial p.435,
Corporate/M&A p.1025, Corporate/M&A:
Northern Virginia p.1967, Employee
Benefits & Executive Compensation
p.1063, Employment: Mainly Defendant
p.1065, Environment p.450, Financial
Services: Regulatory Compliance p.23,
Financial Services: Regulatory

Enforcement & Investigations p.28,
Healthcare: Pharmaceutical/Medical
Products Regulatory p.455, Insurance:
Insurer Firms p.461, Intellectual Property
p.1072, Intellectual Property: Patent
p.1383, International Trade p.41,
Investment Management p.468,
Litigation p.470, Litigation: Appellate
p.474, Litigation: General Commercial
p.1074, Litigation: Securities p.1389,
Media & Entertainment p.476, Private
Equity: Buyouts & Venture Capital
Investment p.1077, Private Fund
Formation p.1079, Real Estate p.1035,
Securities p.485, Tax p.487, Telecom,
Broadcast & Satellite: Regulatory p.491

**Wilson, Elser, Moskowitz,
Edelman & Dicker LLP**
Table: Insurance: Dispute Resolution
p.1378

**Wilson Sonsini Goodrich & Rosati**
Profile: p.344
Tables: Antitrust p.215, Capital Markets:
Debt & Equity (West Coast) p.8,
Corporate/Commercial p.1992,
Corporate/M&A p.1941, Corporate/M&A:
Northern California p.226, Employment:
Mainly Defendant p.230, Intellectual
Property p.247, IT & IT Outsourcing
p.253, Litigation: General Commercial
p.255, Tax p.273, Technology & IT
Outsourcing p.1877

**Winer & Bennett LLP**
Table: Real Estate p.1269

**Winn & Alexander LLP**
Table: Media & Entertainment: Litigation
p.262

**Winstead Sechrest & Minick P.C.**
Profile: p.1939
Tables: Bankruptcy/Restructuring
p.1834, Immigration p.1856, Real Estate
p.1871

**Winston & Strawn LLP**
Profile: p.886
Tables: Antitrust p.766, Banking &
Finance p.770, Bankruptcy/Restructuring
p.221, Corporate/M&A & Private Equity
p.780, Employment: Mainly Defendant
p.784, Energy: Electricity p.444, Energy:
Nuclear p.448, Environment p.790,
International Arbitration p.35, Litigation:
General Commercial p.801, Media &
Entertainment: Transactional p.806,
Products Liability p.49, Projects p.479,
Real Estate p.808, Tax p.811

**Winterbauer & Diamond, P.L.L.C.**
Table: Employment: Mainly Defendant
p.1994

**Winthrop & Weinstine, A
Professional Association**
Profile: p.1173
Table: Litigation: General Commercial
p.1156

**Wise Carter Child & Caraway,
Professional Association**
Tables: Corporate/Commercial p.1174,
Employment: Mainly Defendant p.1176,
Litigation: General Commercial p.1178

**Withers LLP**
Table: Wealth Management p.80

**Withey Anderson & Morris PLC**
Table: Real Estate: Zoning/Land Use
p.186

**Witman, Stadtmauer
& Michaels PA**
Table: Employee Benefits & Executive
Compensation p.1281

**Wold Johnson PC**
Tables: Employment: Mainly Defendant
p.1592, Real Estate p.1595

**Wolf, Greenfield & Sacks PC**
Table: Intellectual Property p.1072

**Wolf, Block, Schorr and
Solis-Cohen LLP**
Profile: p.1764
Tables: Banking & Finance p.1694,
Bankruptcy/Restructuring p.1696,
Corporate/M&A p.1700, Environment
p.1706, Real Estate p.1717

**Wolff & Samson, A Professional
Corporation**
Table: Employee Benefits & Executive
Compensation p.1281

**Womble Carlyle Sandridge
& Rice, PLLC**
Profile: p.1589
Tables: Antitrust p.1568, Banking &
Finance p.1569, Banking & Finance:
Mainly Regulatory p.677, Corporate/M&A
p.1571, Employment: Mainly Defendant
p.1573, Environment p.1574, Litigation:
General Commercial p.1577, Real Estate
p.1579

**Woodburn and Wedge**
Tables: Corporate/Commercial p.1246,
Environment p.1249

**Woodcock Washburn LLP**
Profile: p.1765
Table: Intellectual Property p.1710

**Wooden & McLaughlin LLP**
Profile: p.908
Table: Real Estate p.892

**Wood, Herron & Evans, LLP**
Table: Intellectual Property p.1614

**Woods & Aitken LLP**
Table: Corporate/M&A p.1236

**Woods, Fuller, Shultz & Smith PC**
Tables: Corporate/Commercial p.1792,
Employment: Mainly Defendant p.1793,
Litigation: General Commercial p.1794,
Real Estate p.1796

**Woods Rogers PLC**
Table: Litigation: General Commercial
p.1977

**Woodward, Hobson & Fulton LLP**
Tables: Employment: Mainly Defendant
p.939, Litigation: General Commercial
p.942

**Worden Thane PC**
Tables: Employment: Mainly Defendant
p.1223, Real Estate p.1230

**Wormser, Kiely, Galef
& Jacobs LLP**
Table: Immigration p.1376

**Wright, Henson, Somers,
Clark & Bake LLP**
Table: Litigation: General Commercial
p.927

**Wright, Lindsey & Jennings LLP**
Profile: p.214
Tables: Corporate/Commercial p.201,
Employment: Mainly Defendant p.202,
Litigation: General Commercial p.204,
Real Estate p.206

**Wright Robinson Osthimer
& Tatum**
Table: Construction p.1965

**Wright & Talisman PC**
Tables: Energy: Electricity p.444,
Energy: Oil & Gas p.441

**Wyatt, Tarrant & Combs, LLP**
Profile: p.962
Tables: Corporate/M&A p.937,
Employment: Mainly Defendant p.939,
Environment, Natural Resources &
Regulated Industries p.940, Litigation:
General Commercial p.942, Real Estate
p.943

**Wyche, Burgess, Freeman
& Parham, PA**
Profile: p.1791
Tables: Corporate/M&A p.1775,
Litigation: General Commercial p.1778

**Wyrsch Hobbs & Mirakian PC**
Table: Litigation: General Commercial
p.1197

## Y

**Yonkee & Toner LLP**
Tables: Employment: Mainly Defendant
p.2042, Litigation: General Commercial
p.2043

**York, Keller & Field**
Table: Insurance p.1857

**Young, Clement & Rivers LLP**
Table: Litigation: General Commercial
p.1778

**Young Conaway Stargatt
& Taylor LLP**
Profile: p.424
Tables: Bankruptcy/Restructuring p.388,
Chancery p.391, Corporate/M&A p.394,
Employment: Mainly Defendant p.396,
Intellectual Property p.397, Real Estate
p.399, Real Estate: Zoning/Land Use
p.400

**Young, Sommer, Ward,
Ritzenberg, Wooley, Baker &
Moore LLC**
Table: Environment p.1370

**Young & Susser PC Attorneys
and Counselors**
Table: Litigation: General Commercial
p.1128

## Z

**Zeiger, Tigges, Little
& Lindsmith LLP**
Table: Litigation: General Commercial
p.1616

**Zetlin & De Chiara LLP**
Table: Construction p.1350

**Ziffren Brittenham Branca Fischer
Gilbert-Lurie & Stiffelman LLP**
Table: Media & Entertainment:
Transactional p.265

**Zimney Foster PC**
Table: Corporate/Commercial p.1590

**Zinober & McCrea, P.A.**
Table: Employment: Mainly Defendant
p.596

**Zuckerman Spaeder LLP**
Tables: Antitrust p.581,
Bankruptcy/Restructuring p.431,
Insurance: Insurer Firms p.461, Litigation:
General Commercial p.608, Litigation:
Specialist Firms in White-Collar Crime &
Government Investigations p.471,
Litigation: White-Collar Crime &
Government Investigations p.610

**Zuckert, Scoutt
& Rasenberger, LLP**
Tables: Transportation: Aviation:
Regulatory & Litigation p.67,
Transportation: Rail p.68

**Zuger Kirmis & Smith**
Tables: Employment: Mainly Defendant
p.1592, Litigation: General Commercial
p.1593

**Zumwalt, Almon & Hayes**
Table: Media & Entertainment p.1806

**PROFILE:** CONTACT DETAILS AT THE END OF EVERY STATE  **TABLE:** REFERS TO THE SPECIALIST LISTS IN WHICH THE FIRM APPEARS

2077

# LEADING LAWYERS INDEX

Sidebar tab: A

A

**A**

**Aube, John R** (Hawaii)
Real Estate **Band** 3
Table: p.748

**Aucutt, Ronald D**
(National)
Wealth Management **Band** 3
Table: p.81

**Auen, Michael H**
(Wisconsin)
Profile: p.2031
Employment **Band** 1
Table: p.2027

**Auerbach, Dennis B**
(District of Columbia)
Profile: p.498
Bankruptcy **Up and coming**
Table: p.432

**Auerbach, Reed** (New York)
Profile: p.86
Capital Markets **Band** 2
Table: p.18

**Aughtry, David D** (Georgia)
Tax **Band** 1
Table: p.703

**August, Jerald David**
(Florida)
Tax **Band** 1
Table: p.623

**Ausherman, Larry P**
(New Mexico)
Environment **Band** 1
Table: p.1323

**Auslander, Charles**
(Florida)
Profile: p.627
Litigation **Band** 1
Table: p.615

**Auspitz, Jack** (New York)
Profile: p.1434
Litigation **Band** 3
Table: p.1390

**Austin, Brad** (Iowa)
Real Estate **Band** 4
Table: p.917

**Austin, Cathy Kiselyak**
(Illinois)
Profile: p.818
Technology **Band** 3
Table: p.814

**Austin, Jesse** (Georgia)
Profile: p.705
Banking & Finance **Band** 3
Table: p.677
Bankruptcy **Band** 1
Table: p.679

**Avil, Richard**
(District of Columbia)
Profile: p.498
Energy **Band** 4
Table: p.441

**Avila, Alcides** (Florida)
Profile: p.627
Banking & Finance **Band** 1
Table: p.583
Corporate/M&A **Band** 1
Table: p.595

**Avitabile, Scott D** (New York)
Profile: p.1434
Insurance **Band** 3
Table: p.1380

**Aviv, Joseph** (Michigan)
Profile: p.1132
Litigation **Band** 2
Table: p.1128

**Awner, Jonathan L** (Florida)
Profile: p.627
Corporate/M&A **Band** 1
Table: p.594

**Axe, Albert** (Texas)
Environment **Band** 3
Table: p.1852

**Axelberg, Tracy** (Montana)
Litigation **Band** 3
Table: p.1225

**Axelrod, Alan D** (Florida)
Profile: p.627
Corporate/M&A **Band** 4
Table: p.594

**Axelrod, David W** (Oregon)
Litigation **Band** 3
Table: p.1674

**Axelroth, Lynn R**
(Pennsylvania)
Profile: p.1721
Real Estate **Band** 2
Table: p.1718

**Axinn, Stephen** (New York)
Profile: p.1434
Antitrust **Band** 2
Table: p.1335

**Axselle, Ralph** (Virginia)
Real Estate **Band** 1
Table: p.1978

**Ayers, David** (Mississippi)
Litigation **Band** 3
Table: p.1179

**Ayres, Jeffrey** (Maryland)
Employment **Band** 1
Table: p.1028

**Azoff, Elliot S** (Ohio)
Employment **Band** 3
Table: p.1609

**Azzollini, Phillip** (National)
Profile: p.86
Capital Markets
**Up and coming**
Table: p.13

## B

**Baach, Martin**
(District of Columbia)
Insurance **Band** 2
Table: p.461

**Baader, Michael**
(Maryland)
Corporate/M&A **Band** 2
Table: p.1025

**Baar, Lois A** (Utah)
Profile: p.1949
Employment **Band** 1
Table: p.1944

**Babbe, David B** (California)
Profile: p.277
Insurance **Band** 2
Table: p.243

**Babcock, Charles** (Texas)
Litigation **Band** 3
Table: p.1865

**Babcock, Kathleen**
(Kansas)
Profile: p.931
Employment **Band** 1
Table: p.926

**Baber, Bruce** (Georgia)
Profile: p.705
Intellectual Property **Band** 2
Table: p.696

**Babst III, Chester**
(Pennsylvania)
Environment **Band** 1
Table: p.1707

**Baca, David C** (Oregon)
Corporate/M&A **Band** 3
Table: p.1667

**Bach, Robert H** (Colorado)
Real Estate **Band** 3
Table: p.355

**Bachelder, Stephen G**
(Maine)
Profile: p.1010
Employment **Band** 1
Table: p.1002

**Bacheller, Chester E**
(Florida)
Profile: p.627
Corporate/M&A **Band** 4
Table: p.594

**Bachman, Gary**
(District of Columbia)
Energy **Band** 4
Table: p.445

**Bachman, John Q**
(Nebraska)
Real Estate **Band** 1
Table: p.1242

**Bachman, Katharine E**
(Massachusetts)
Profile: p.1086
Real Estate **Band** 2
Table: p.1081

**Backus, Marcia E** (Texas)
Profile: p.1881
Energy **Band** 4
Table: p.1847
Projects **Band** 4
Table: p.1869

**Bacon, Christopher V**
(Texas)
Profile: p.1881
Employment **Band** 3
Table: p.1844

**Bacon, J Douglas** (Illinois)
Bankruptcy **Band** 3
Table: p.775

**Badgerow, J Nick** (Kansas)
Litigation **Band** 2
Table: p.927

**Baecher, John** (New York)
Profile: p.1435
Projects **Band** 2
Table: p.1413

**Baechtold, Robert**
(New York)
Profile: p.1435
Intellectual Property ✪
Table: p.1384

**Baena, Scott L** (Florida)
Profile: p.627
Bankruptcy **Band** 1
Table: p.586

**Baer, Gregory A** (National)
Profile: p.86
Financial Services **Band** 3
Table: p.24

**Baer, Teresa D**
(District of Columbia)
Telecom, Broadcast & Satellite
**Band** 4
Table: p.492

**Baer, William**
(District of Columbia)
Profile: p.498
Antitrust **Band** 1
Table: p.426

**Bagley, Philip** (Virginia)
Real Estate **Band** 1
Table: p.1978

**Bagnall, Robert G**
(District of Columbia)
Profile: p.499
Investment Management **Band** 3
Table: p.469

**Bahner, Maxwell**
(Tennessee)
Litigation **Band** 3
Table: p.1804

**Baier, Kelly** (Iowa)
Employment **Band** 1
Table: p.912

**Bail, Lisa A** (Hawaii)
Land Use **Band** 2
Table: p.744

**Bailey, Benjamin** (West Virginia)
Profile: p.2015
Litigation **Band** 1
Table: p.2013

**Bailey, Burck** (Oklahoma)
Litigation **Band** S
Table: p.1656

**Bailey, Roger (Roddy)**
(Tennessee)
Profile: p.1810
Corporate/M&A
**Up and coming**
Table: p.1799

**Baine, Kevin T**
(District of Columbia)
Media & Entertainment **Band** 1
Table: p.477

**Bains, Kay K** (Alabama)
Profile: p.154
Banking & Finance **Band** 2
Table: p.147
Real Estate **Band** 2
Table: p.153

**Bains, Jr, Lee E** (Alabama)
Profile: p.155
Litigation **Band** 3
Table: p.152

**Baird, Joseph H** (Idaho)
Natural Resources **Band** 2
Table: p.761

**Baird, Peter** (Arizona)
Litigation **Band** 1
Table: p.181

**Baker, Andrew M** (Texas)
Profile: p.1881
Corporate/M&A **Band** 4
Table: p.1840

**Baker, Bruce** (Illinois)
Profile: p.818
Banking & Finance **Band** 3
Table: p.771

**Baker, Constance H**
(Maryland)
Healthcare **Band** 2
Table: p.1031

**Baker, D J (Jan)** (New York)
Profile: p.1435
Bankruptcy **Band** 1
Table: p.1344

**Baker, David** (Ohio)
Real Estate **Band** 2
Table: p.1621

**Baker, Debra** (Texas)
Environment **Band** 4
Table: p.1852

**Baker, Douglas**
(New Mexico)
Litigation **Band** 4
Table: p.1324

**Baker, James P** (National)
Profile: p.86
Erisa Litigation **Band** 3

**Baker, Jean C** (Wisconsin)
Profile: p.2031
Intellectual Property **Band** 2
Table: p.2028

**Baker, Kristine G**
(Arkansas)
Profile: p.208
Litigation **Up and coming**
Table: p.205

**Baker, Lewis J** (Virginia)
Profile: p.1979
Construction **Band** 1
Table: p.1965

**Baker, Mark** (Texas)
Profile: p.1881

Energy Band 1
Table: p.1849
International Arbitration Band 2
Table: p.36

**Baker, Pamela** (Illinois)
Profile: p.818
Employment Band 1
Table: p.786

**Baker, Tyler A** (California)
Profile: p.277
Antitrust Band 3
Table: p.216

**Baker III, Frank Lewis**
(Connecticut)
Real Estate Band 2
Table: p.380

**Baker Jr, William T**
(New York)
Profile: p.1435
Energy Band 1
Table: p.1367

**Bakke, Randall J**
(North Dakota)
Litigation Band 2
Table: p.1593

**Balabanian, David M**
(California)
Profile: p.277
Litigation Band 4
Table: p.257

**Baldia, Sonia**
(District of Columbia)
Profile: p.499
Business Process Outsourcing
Associate to watch
Table: p.2
Technology Associate to watch
Table: p.490

**Baldiga, William R**
(Massachusetts)
Bankruptcy Band 3
Table: p.1058

**Baldwin, Charles B**
(Indiana)
Profile: p.894
Employment Band 3
Table: p.889

**Baldwin, George** (Texas)
Construction Band 4
Table: p.1838

**Baldwin III, Garza**
(North Carolina)
Profile: p.1580
Corporate/M&A Band 2
Table: p.1571

**Balick, Steven J** (Delaware)
Profile: p.401
Intellectual Property Band 4
Table: p.397

**Balis, Stanley**
(District of Columbia)
Energy Band 3
Table: p.445

**Ball, Corinne** (New York)
Profile: p.1435
Bankruptcy Band 2
Table: p.1344

**Ball, Dan H** (Missouri)
Litigation Band 2
Table: p.1198

**Ball, Robert** (Oregon)
Real Estate Band S
Table: p.1677

**Ballantine, Douglas C**
(Kentucky)
Profile: p.944
Litigation Band 4
Table: p.942

**Ballantine, Frank D**
(Illinois)
Corporate/M&A: Private Equity
Band 3
Table: p.782

**Ballantine, John T**
(Kentucky)
Profile: p.944
Litigation Band S
Table: p.942

**Ballard, Brian** (Idaho)
Real Estate Band 1
Table: p.762

**Ballati, Deborah**
(California)
Profile: p.277
Construction Band 2
Table: p.225

**Ballis, Jon A** (Illinois)
Profile: p.818
Corporate/M&A: Private Equity
Band 2
Table: p.782

**Balotti, R Franklin**
(Delaware)
Profile: p.401
Chancery Band S
Table: p.392
Corporate/M&A Band S
Table: p.394

**Baltz, Raymond E**
(Georgia)
Profile: p.705
Corporate/M&A
Up and coming
Table: p.684

**Band, Ian P**
(District of Columbia)
Profile: p.499
Immigration Band 3
Table: p.459

**Banducci, Thomas** (Idaho)
Profile: p.763
Litigation Band 2
Table: p.760

**Bangs, Frank** (Arizona)
Real Estate Band 2
Table: p.186

**Bankoff, Joseph R**
(Georgia)
Profile: p.705

Intellectual Property Band 2
Table: p.696

**Banks, David F E** (Hawaii)
Employment Band 2
Table: p.742

**Banks, Diane** (Utah)
Real Estate Band 2
Table: p.1947

**Banks, Jim**
(District of Columbia)
Profile: p.499
Environment Band 4
Table: p.451

**Banks, Michael L**
(Pennsylvania)
Profile: p.1721
Employment Band 4
Table: p.1703

**Banks, Robert S** (Oregon)
Litigation Band 3
Table: p.1674

**Banks Jr, Fred L**
(Mississippi)
Profile: p.1182
Litigation Band 2
Table: p.1179

**Bankston, William M**
(Alaska)
Litigation Band 2
Table: p.171

**Banner, Mark T** (Illinois)
Intellectual Property Band 2
Table: p.799

**Bannon, Eileen** (National)
Profile: p.86
Capital Markets Band 4
Table: p.18

**Banoff, Sheldon I** (Illinois)
Profile: p.819
Tax Band 2
Table: p.812

**Banta, Robert** (Georgia)
Immigration Band 1
Table: p.694

**Banta, Robert J** (Texas)
Real Estate Band 3
Table: p.1872

**Baptista, Robert C**
(Illinois)
Profile: p.819
Banking & Finance Band 1
Table: p.771

**Barad, Edward N**
(Colorado)
Profile: p.357
Real Estate Band 1
Table: p.355

**Barajas, Dino** (California)
Profile: p.277
Projects Band 3
Table: p.268

**Baran, Jan W** (National)
Profile: p.86
Government: Political Law

Band 1
Table: p.34

**Barancik, Tia** (New York)
Profile: p.1435
Energy Band 2
Table: p.1367

**Barbash, Barry**
(District of Columbia)
Profile: p.499
Investment Management Band 1
Table: p.469

**Barbe, J Kenneth**
(Wyoming)
Corporate/M&A Band 1
Table: p.2041
Real Estate Band 2
Table: p.2045

**Barber, Bill** (Texas)
Profile: p.1882
Intellectual Property Band 3
Table: p.1860

**Barber, Steven K** (Florida)
Tax Band 2
Table: p.624

**Barber, Timothy G**
(North Carolina)
Profile: p.1580
Litigation Band 3
Table: p.1577

**Barbier, Margaret Louise**
(Washington)
Employment Band 3
Table: p.1995

**Barbiere, Janet A**
(National)
Profile: p.87
Capital Markets
Up and coming
Table: p.18

**Barbin, Jeffrey M**
(Louisiana)
Profile: p.977
Gaming & Licensing
Up and coming
Table: p.971

**Barbour, David** (Texas)
Banking & Finance Band 4
Table: p.1832

**Barbour, Larry G** (Texas)
Profile: p.1882
Banking & Finance Band 1
Table: p.1832

**Barbuti, Thomas**
(Maryland)
Profile: p.1037
Real Estate Band 4
Table: p.1035

**Barcan, Stephen E**
(New Jersey)
Real Estate Band 2
Table: p.1293

**Barcella Jr, E Lawrence**
(District of Columbia)
Litigation Band 3
Table: p.471

**Barclay, James M** (Florida)
Healthcare Band 2
Table: p.604

**Bardacke, Paul**
(New Mexico)
Litigation Band 1
Table: p.1324

**Bardenwerper, William B**
(Kentucky)
Real Estate Band 1
Table: p.944

**Barfield II, Lee** (Tennessee)
Profile: p.1810
Litigation Band 2
Table: p.1804
Litigation Band 1
Table: p.1805

**Barford, George** (Florida)
Profile: p.627
Employment Band 3
Table: p.597

**Barger, David G** (Virginia)
Profile: p.1981
Litigation Band 1
Table: p.1978

**Barghols, Steven L**
(Oklahoma)
Profile: p.1658
Litigation Band 2
Table: p.1656

**Barker, Christopher B**
(Massachusetts)
Profile: p.1086
Real Estate Band 2
Table: p.1081

**Barker, James H**
(District of Columbia)
Telecom, Broadcast & Satellite
Band 3
Table: p.492

**Barker, John** (National)
Profile: p.87
International Trade Band 2
Table: p.41

**Barker, Scott** (Colorado)
Profile: p.357
Litigation Band 2
Table: p.353

**Barkett, John** (Florida)
Profile: p.627
Environment Band 1
Table: p.601

**Barliant, Ronald** (Illinois)
Bankruptcy Band 2
Table: p.775

**Barlow, Richard**
(New Mexico)
Corporate/Commercial Band 3
Table: p.1320

**Barmeyer, Patricia**
(Georgia)
Profile: p.705
Environment ✪
Table: p.691

**Barnard, Gregg** (Nevada)
Corporate/Commercial Band 3
Table: p.1246

**Barnard, Kevin** (New York)
Profile: p.87
Financial Services Band 2
Table: p.28

**Barnard, Thomas H** (Ohio)
Employment ✪
Table: p.1609

**Barnes, Clemens H**
(Washington)
Employment Band 2
Table: p.1995

**Barnes, Geoffrey K** (Ohio)
Profile: p.1623
Environment Band 2
Table: p.1612

**Barnes, Mark** (New York)
Profile: p.1435
Healthcare Band 1
Table: p.1374

**Barnes, Thomas J**
(Michigan)
Profile: p.1132
Employment Band 2
Table: p.1125

**Barnes Jr, Hershell L**
(Texas)
Employment Band 3
Table: p.1844

**Barnett, Bonnie Allyn**
(Pennsylvania)
Environment Band 1
Table: p.1707

**Barnett, Gary** (National)
Profile: p.87
Capital Markets Band 2
Table: p.13

**Barnett, Leslie** (Florida)
Tax Band 4
Table: p.623

**Barnett, Robert B**
(District of Columbia)
Media & Entertainment Band 2
Table: p.477

**Baron, Robert** (New York)
Profile: p.1435
Litigation Band 2
Table: p.1390

**Baronsky, Kenneth**
(National)
Capital Markets Band 3
Table: p.8

**Barr, Lynne B**
(Massachusetts)
Profile: p.1086
Banking & Finance Band 1
Table: p.1055

**Barr, Michael H** (New York)
Profile: p.1436
Insurance Band 2
Table: p.1379

**Barr, Michael R** (California)
Profile: p.277
Environment Band 1
Table: p.236

**Barragate, Brett** (Ohio)
Profile: p.1623
Banking & Finance
Up and coming
Table: p.1598

**Barrall, James** (California)
Employment Band 2
Table: p.232

**Barran, Paula** (Oregon)
Employment Band 1
Table: p.1670

**Barrasso, Judy Y**
(Louisiana)
Profile: p.977
Litigation Band 1
Table: p.973

**Barreca, Marc**
(Washington)
Bankruptcy Band 2
Table: p.1991

**Barrett, Gayle** (Oklahoma)
Profile: p.1658
Employment Band 1
Table: p.1654

**Barrett, Joshua** (West
Virginia)
Profile: p.2016
Litigation Band 2
Table: p.2013

**Barrett, Michael A**
(Washington)
Real Estate Band 2
Table: p.2002

**Barrett, Patrick** (Nebraska)
Employment Band 2
Table: p.1238

**Barrier, W Christopher**
(Arkansas)
Real Estate Band 1
Table: p.207

**Barriere, Brent B**
(Louisiana)
Profile: p.977
Corporate/M&A Band 2
Table: p.965
Litigation Band 1
Table: p.973

**Barringer, William H**
(District of Columbia)
Profile: p.87
International Trade Band 2
Table: p.42

**Barris, William G**
(Michigan)
Real Estate Band 2
Table: p.1130

**Barron, Russell J**
(Wisconsin)
Profile: p.2031
Intellectual Property Band 1
Table: p.2028

**Barrow, Peter** (Illinois)
Profile: p.819
Banking & Finance Band 3
Table: p.771

**Barry, Dennis M**
(District of Columbia)
Profile: p.499
Healthcare Band 1
Table: p.456

**Barry, James R** (Illinois)
Profile: p.819
Tax Band 3
Table: p.812

**Barry Jr, Desmond T**
(National)
Profile: p.87
Transportation Band 1
Table: p.67

**Barsamian, Bonnie A**
(National)
Profile: p.88
Capital Markets Band 4
Table: p.7

**Barshak, Edward**
(Massachusetts)
Litigation Band 3
Table: p.1074

**Barshay, Scott** (New York)
Profile: p.1436
Corporate/M&A Band 3
Table: p.1354

**Barshefsky, Charlene**
(District of Columbia)
Profile: p.88
International Trade Band 1
Table: p.42

**Barsky, Wayne** (California)
Profile: p.277
Intellectual Property Band 4
Table: p.248

**Barson, Leon R**
(Pennsylvania)
Bankruptcy Band 3
Table: p.1697

**Bartel II, Paul W** (New
York)
Profile: p.1436
Antitrust Band 4
Table: p.1335

**Bartell, Jeff** (Wisconsin)
Profile: p.2031
Corporate/M&A Band 2
Table: p.2025

**Bartelsmeyer, Fred W**
(Missouri)
Corporate/M&A Band 3
Table: p.1193

**Bartfeld, Daniel D**
(New York)
Projects Band 4
Table: p.1413

**Bartine, William** (Iowa)
Real Estate Band 1
Table: p.917

**Bartlit Jr, Fred** (Colorado)
Litigation Band 1
Table: p.353
Litigation Band 2
Table: p.802

**Bartner, Douglas** (New
York)
Profile: p.1436
Bankruptcy Band 2
Table: p.1344

**Barton, Bernard** (Florida)
Profile: p.627
Tax Band 1
Table: p.623

**Barton, Carl** (Utah)
Profile: p.1949
Real Estate Band 3
Table: p.1947

**Bartz Jr, David F** (Oregon)
Environment Band 2
Table: p.1672

**Barufka, Jack S** (Virginia)
Profile: p.1979
Intellectual Property Band 1
Table: p.1975

**Barzoukas, Nicolas G**
(Texas)
Intellectual Property Band 2
Table: p.1860

**Bash, Brian A** (Ohio)
Bankruptcy Band 3
Table: p.1600

**Bash, Roy** (Missouri)
Profile: p.1203
Litigation Band 3
Table: p.1198

**Basich, Anthony M**
(California)
Profile: p.278
Media & Entertainment Band 3
Table: p.263

**Basile, Edward**
(District of Columbia)
Profile: p.499
Healthcare Band 2
Table: p.456

**Basile, Michael**
(West Virginia)
Corporate/Commercial Band 3
Table: p.2010

**Basile, Michael** (Florida)
Banking & Finance Band 2
Table: p.583

**Baskin, Stuart** (New York)
Profile: p.1436
Litigation Band 2
Table: p.1390

**Bason Jr, George R**
(New York)
Profile: p.1436
Corporate/M&A Band 3
Table: p.1354
Private Equity Band 1
Table: p.1407

**Bass, Fred** (National)
Profile: p.88
Transportation Band 3
Table: p.64

**Bass, Hilarie** (Florida)
Profile: p.628
Litigation Band 3
Table: p.609

**Bass, Jo** (Nebraska)
Corporate/M&A Band 3
Table: p.1236

**Bass Jr, Robert C** (Texas)
Construction Band 3
Table: p.1838

**Bass Jr, Ross F**
(Mississippi)
Profile: p.1182
Litigation Band 2
Table: p.1179

**Bassett, David**
(Massachusetts)
Profile: p.1086
Intellectual Property Band 2
Table: p.1072

**Bassett, Peter Q** (Georgia)
Profile: p.706
Litigation Band 2
Table: p.698

**Bassetti, Andrew B**
(Washington)
Real Estate Band 2
Table: p.2002

**Basta, Paul M** (New York)
Profile: p.1436
Bankruptcy Up and coming
Table: p.1344

**Bastianelli, Adrian**
(District of Columbia)
Profile: p.499
Construction Band 1
Table: p.433

**Bateman, David A**
(Washington)
Intellectual Property Band 2
Table: p.1998

**Bateman, Randall** (Oregon)
Real Estate Band 2
Table: p.1677

**Bates, Brian K** (Texas)
Immigration Band 1
Table: p.1856

**Bates, Jeffrey**
(Massachusetts)
Profile: p.1086
Environment Band 1
Table: p.1068

**Bates, John** (Virginia)
Real Estate Band 1
Table: p.1978

**Bates, Robert** (Arizona)
Profile: p.187
Real Estate Band 4
Table: p.184

**B**

**Bates, Walter** (Alabama)
Profile: p.155
Litigation Band 2
Table: p.152

**Bates Jr, Robert J** (Illinois)
Insurance Band 3
Table: p.795
Insurance Band 2
Table: p.796

**Bath, Thomas J** (Kansas)
Litigation Band 2
Table: p.927

**Batson, R Neal** (Georgia)
Profile: p.706
Bankruptcy Band S
Table: p.679

**Battcher, Frederick R**
(Nevada)
Corporate/Commercial
Up and coming
Table: p.1246

**Batten, Fred** (Michigan)
Employment Band 3
Table: p.1125

**Batter III, John F**
(Massachusetts)
Profile: p.1086
Litigation Band 1
Table: p.1075

**Batterman, Robert**
(National)
Profile: p.88
Sport Band 3
Table: p.59

**Battista, Gregory J**
(New York)
Profile: p.1436
Environment Band 2
Table: p.1373

**Battista, Paul J** (Florida)
Profile: p.628
Bankruptcy Band 1
Table: p.586

**Batty, Jerome** (Rhode
Island)
Real Estate Band 2
Table: p.1770

**Bauer, Robert F** (National)
Government: Political Law
Band 1
Table: p.34

**Bauer, Steven M**
(Massachusetts)
Profile: p.1086
Intellectual Property Band 1
Table: p.1072

**Bauer, Steven M**
(California)
Litigation Band 3
Table: p.258

**Bauman, Carl** (Alaska)
Environment Band 2
Table: p.170

**Bauman, Todd** (Oregon)
Corporate/M&A Band 2

**Baumann, Frederick J**
(Colorado)
Profile: p.357
Litigation Band 1
Table: p.353
Litigation Band 2
Table: p.353

**Baumbusch, Peter L**
(District of Columbia)
Profile: p.500
Tax Band 4
Table: p.488

**Baumgarten, Jon**
(District of Columbia)
Profile: p.500
Intellectual Property Band 3
Table: p.466

**Baumgartner, Bruce O**
(Ohio)
Intellectual Property Band 3
Table: p.1614

**Bausch, James** (Nebraska)
Litigation Band 1
Table: p.1239

**Baxa Jr, Edmund T**
(Florida)
Profile: p.628
Construction Band 3
Table: p.590

**Baxley, C William**
(Georgia)
Profile: p.706
Corporate/M&A Band 2
Table: p.684

**Baxter, Jeffrey C** (Georgia)
Healthcare Band 2
Table: p.693

**Baxter, John B** (Indiana)
Profile: p.894
Real Estate Up and coming
Table: p.892

**Baxter, Michael St
Patrick**
(District of Columbia)
Profile: p.500
Bankruptcy Band 2
Table: p.432

**Bayer, Mark W** (Texas)
Profile: p.1882
Antitrust Up and coming
Table: p.1829

**Bayko, Tom** (Texas)
Profile: p.1882
Energy Band 3
Table: p.1849

**Bayliss, William D**
(Virginia)
Profile P.1981
Litigation Band 2
Table: p.1977

**Bays, Richard** (Texas)
Technology Band 2
Table: p.1877

**Baysinger, Kara** (California)
Profile: p.278
Insurance Band 3
Table: p.243

**Bayt, Phillip** (Indiana)
Profile: p.894
Real Estate Band 1
Table: p.892

**Beach, Peter**
(New Hampshire)
Corporate/Commercial Band 2
Table: p.1264

**Beale Jr, Walter M**
(Alabama)
Profile: p.155
Corporate/Commercial Band 2
Table: p.148

**Beall, George** (Maryland)
Profile: p.1037
Litigation Band S
Table: p.1032

**Bean, Rodney L**
(West Virginia)
Employment Up and coming
Table: p.2012

**Beane, Jerry** (Texas)
Antitrust Band 2
Table: p.1829

**Beard, Brian** (Texas)
Profile: p.1882
Technology Band 2
Table: p.1878

**Beard, James** (Illinois)
Profile: p.819
Real Estate Band 2
Table: p.809

**Beard III, RT** (Arkansas)
Litigation Band 1
Table: p.205

**Bearman Jr, Leo**
(Tennessee)
Profile: p.1810
Litigation Band 2
Table: p.1804

**Beasley, Jere L** (Alabama)
Litigation Band 2
Table: p.152

**Beaton, Glenn K** (Colorado)
Profile: p.357
Intellectual Property Band 1
Table: p.351

**Beaton, Kevin** (Idaho)
Natural Resources Band 1
Table: p.761

**Beattie, Richard I** (New
York)
Profile: p.1436
Corporate/M&A Band S
Table: p.1354
Private Equity Band S
Table: p.1407

**Beaudoin, Thomas A**
(Massachusetts)
Profile: p.1087
Private Equity Band 2

**Beaudrot Jr, Charles R**
(Georgia)
Tax Band 2
Table: p.703

**Beavers, Jr, Charles AJ**
(Alabama)
Profile: p.155
Real Estate Band 1
Table: p.153

**Bebawy, Adel F** (California)
IT Outsourcing
Up and coming
Table: p.253

**Becerra, Jacqueline**
(Florida)
Profile: p.628
Litigation Band 4
Table: p.609

**Beck, David** (Texas)
Energy Band 1
Table: p.1849
Litigation Band 1
Table: p.1865

**Beck, Joseph** (Georgia)
Profile: p.706
Intellectual Property Band 2
Table: p.696

**Beck, Mark** (California)
Litigation Band 1
Table: p.258

**Beck, Paul** (Pennsylvania)
Intellectual Property Band 3
Table: p.1711

**Beck, Philip** (Illinois)
Litigation Band 1
Table: p.802

**Beck, Philip** (Georgia)
Construction Band 1
Table: p.682

**Beck, Thomas H** (New
York)
Profile: p.1436
Intellectual Property Band 3
Table: p.1384

**Beck, William G** (Missouri)
Profile: p.1203
Litigation Band 3
Table: p.1198

**Beck Jr, Robert M**
(Kentucky)
Profile: p.944
Corporate/M&A Band 3
Table: p.937

**Becker, Brandon**
(District of Columbia)
Profile: p.500
Investment Management Band 2
Table: p.469

**Becker, Jeffrey** (Texas)
Intellectual Property Band 3
Table: p.1860

**Becker, Jeffrey H**
(New York)
Profile: p.1437
Healthcare Band 1
Table: p.1374

**Becker, Richard K A**
(Virginia)
Profile: p.1980
Corporate/M&A Band 1
Table: p.1967

**Becker, Scott** (Illinois)
Healthcare Band 1
Table: p.793

**Becker, Walter F.**
(Louisiana)
Litigation Band 1
Table: p.973

**Becker, Wendy** (Kentucky)
Employment Band 3
Table: p.939

**Beckerman, Lisa G**
(New York)
Profile: p.1437
Bankruptcy Band 4
Table: p.1344

**Beckham Jr, Charles**
(Texas)
Bankruptcy Band 2
Table: p.1835

**Beckman, David**
(Kentucky)
Profile: p.945
Corporate/M&A Band 3
Table: p.937

**Bednar, Steven C** (Utah)
Employment Band 2
Table: p.1944

**Bedore, James M**
(Wisconsin)
Profile: p.2031
Corporate/M&A Band 2
Table: p.2025

**Bedree, Melvin** (Ohio)
Profile: p.1624
Banking & Finance Band 2
Table: p.1598

**Been, Carol Anne** (Illinois)
Profile: p.819
Intellectual Property Band 3
Table: p.799

**Beer, Steven C** (New York)
Profile: p.1437
Media & Entertainment Band 2
Table: p.1401

**Beeson, Christopher**
(Idaho)
Real Estate Band 1
Table: p.762

**Behm, Jeffrey** (Vermont)
Litigation Band 1
Table: p.1959

**Behnia, Hatef** (California)
Profile: p.278
Tax Band 3
Table: p.274

**Behrend, Andrew** (Alaska)
Profile: p.173
Employment Band 2
Table: p.169

**Behrends IV, Samuel**
(District of Columbia)
Profile: p.500
Energy Band 4
Table: p.445

**Beisner, John** (National)
Profile: p.88
Products Liability Band 2
Table: p.50

**Belanger, James J**
(Arizona)
Litigation Band 2
Table: p.182

**Belcher, Dennis I**
(National)
Wealth Management Band 2
Table: p.81

**Belcher, James** (Wyoming)
Profile: p.2047
Corporate/M&A Band 2
Table: p.2041

**Beless, Rosemary J** (Utah)
Real Estate Up and coming
Table: p.1947

**Belisario, Martin G**
(Pennsylvania)
Profile: p.1722
Intellectual Property Band 4
Table: p.1711

**Bell, Jerry** (Texas)
Profile: p.1882
Healthcare Band 1
Table: p.1855

**Bell, Joseph C**
(District of Columbia)
Profile: p.500
Energy Band 4
Table: p.445

**Bell, Robert B**
(District of Columbia)
Profile: p.500
Antitrust Band 5
Table: p.426

**Bell, Rodney H** (Florida)
Profile: p.628
Corporate/M&A Band 3
Table: p.594

**Bell, Stephen** (Illinois)
Real Estate Band 3
Table: p.809

**Bell, Suzanne Y** (California)
Profile: p.278
IT Outsourcing Band 1
Table: p.253

**Bell, Thomas** (New York)
Profile: p.1437
Private Equity Band 1
Table: p.1410

**Bell Jr, Albert R**
(North Carolina)
Employment Band 2

Table: p.1573

**Bellah Maguire, Jennifer**
(California)
Profile: p.278
Corporate/M&A Band 3
Table: p.227

**Bellamy, Fredric D**
(Arizona)
Profile: p.187
Environment Up and coming
Table: p.179

**Beller, Daniel J** (New York)
Profile: p.1437
Litigation Band 3
Table: p.1388

**Beller, Herbert N**
(District of Columbia)
Profile: p.501
Tax Band 3
Table: p.488

**Belles, Michael J** (Hawaii)
Land Use Band 1
Table: p.744

**Bello, Kenneth**
(Massachusetts)
Employment Band 4
Table: p.1065

**Belnavis, Clarence**
(Oregon)
Profile: p.1679
Employment Band 3
Table: p.1670

**Belt, David L** (Connecticut)
Litigation Band 2
Table: p.378

**Beltzer, Howard S**
(New York)
Profile: p.1437
Bankruptcy Band 4
Table: p.1344

**Belzer, Irvin** (Missouri)
Litigation Band 2
Table: p.1198

**Bemis, Kenneth E** (Oregon)
Profile: p.1680
Employment Band 3
Table: p.1670

**Benach, Andres**
(District of Columbia)
Immigration Up and coming
Table: p.459

**Ben-Ami, Leora** (New York)
Profile: p.1437
Intellectual Property Band 1
Table: p.1384

**Benard, Blaine** (Utah)
Litigation Up and coming
Table: p.1945

**Benard, Bryan** (Utah)
Profile: p.1949
Employment Up and coming
Table: p.1944

**Bender, Jack** (Kentucky)
Environment Band 1

Table: p.941

**Bender, Jeanne
Matthews** (Montana)
Profile: p.1231
Employment Band 1
Table: p.1223

**Bender, Lawrence**
(North Dakota)
Litigation Band 1
Table: p.1593

**Bender Jr, Albert E**
(Georgia)
Profile: p.706
Real Estate Band 3
Table: p.700

**Bendicksen, Perry**
(New Mexico)
Profile: p.1328
Corporate/Commercial Band 2
Table: p.1320

**Bendinger, Gary F** (Utah)
Litigation Band 1
Table: p.1945

**Benedict, James** (New
York)
Litigation Band 2
Table: p.1390

**Benedict, James E**
(Oregon)
Environment Band 3
Table: p.1672

**Benham III, Paul B**
(Arkansas)
Corporate/Commercial Band 2
Table: p.201

**Benjamin, Alan** (California)
Profile: p.278
Banking & Finance Band 1
Table: p.218

**Benjamin, William**
(Massachusetts)
Profile: p.1087
Tax Band 2
Table: p.1084

**Benner, C Jonathan**
(District of Columbia)
Transportation Band 1
Table: p.78

**Benner, Michael B**
(New York)
Profile: p.1437
Real Estate Band 5
Table: p.1417

**Bennett, Alan**
(District of Columbia)
Profile: p.501
Healthcare Band 2
Table: p.456

**Bennett, Blake** (Louisiana)
Energy Band 1
Table: p.969
Gaming & Licensing Band 3
Table: p.971

**Bennett, Bruce S**
(California)
Bankruptcy Band 3
Table: p.222

**Bennett, David** (Texas)
Profile: p.1882
Bankruptcy Band 4
Table: p.1835

**Bennett, J David** (Oregon)
Real Estate Band 2
Table: p.1677

**Bennett, Jackie** (Indiana)
Profile: p.894
Litigation Band 3
Table: p.890

**Bennett, James P**
(California)
Profile: p.278
Litigation Band 4
Table: p.257

**Bennett, Peter** (Maine)
Employment Band 3
Table: p.1002

**Bennett, Robert S**
(District of Columbia)
Profile: p.501
Litigation Band 1
Table: p.471

**Bennett, Thomas G** (Utah)
Profile: p.1950
Real Estate Band 3
Table: p.1947

**Bennett, Wilfred** (Alaska)
Employment Band 2
Table: p.169

**Bennett II, Crocker**
(Vermont)
Litigation Band 2
Table: p.1959

**Bennett Jr, Charles R**
(Massachusetts)
Profile: p.1087
Bankruptcy Band 2
Table: p.1058

**Benoit, Wilfred J**
(Massachusetts)
Profile: p.1087
Employment Band 2
Table: p.1065

**Benson, Matthew H**
(New Hampshire)
Profile: p.1271
Corporate/Commercial
Associate to watch
Table: p.1263

**Benson, Robert E**
(Colorado)
Profile: p.358
Construction Band 1
Table: p.345

**Benudiz, P Peter**
(California)
Profile: p.278
Real Estate Up and coming
Table: p.270

**Benvenutti, Peter J**
(California)
Profile: p.278
Bankruptcy Band 2
Table: p.222

**Beranek, John R** (Florida)
Litigation Band 1
Table: p.615

**Berberian, H Nicholas**
(Illinois)
Profile: p.819
Litigation Band 4
Table: p.802

**Berchem, Kerry E**
(New York)
Profile: p.1437
Corporate/M&A Band 2
Table: p.1359

**Berchild, John** (California)
Banking & Finance Band 3
Table: p.218

**Bercow, Jeffrey** (Florida)
Real Estate Band 2
Table: p.621

**Berenstein, Marvin** (Iowa)
Corporate/M&A Band 3
Table: p.909

**Berenter, Steven** (Idaho)
Employment Band 1
Table: p.759

**Bereveskos, Spiro**
(Indiana)
Litigation Band 3
Table: p.891

**Berg, Andrew** (New York)
Tax Band 3
Table: p.1423

**Berg, Eric** (Illinois)
Profile: p.819
Construction Band 3
Table: p.778

**Berg, Eric L** (New York)
Profile: p.1438
Banking & Finance Band 1
Table: p.1339

**Berg, Gracia M** (National)
Profile: p.88
International Trade Band 4
Table: p.42

**Berg, Timothy J** (Arizona)
Profile: p.187
Litigation Band 4
Table: p.181

**Berger, Don I** (California)
Real Estate Band 3
Table: p.270

**Berger, Lawrence H**
(Pennsylvania)
Profile: p.1722
Banking & Finance Band 1
Table: p.1695

**Berger, Max** (New York)
Profile: p.1438
Litigation Band 1

B

Table: p.1390

**Berger, Ritchie** (Vermont)
Litigation Band 1
Table: p.1959

**Bergère, Timothy**
(Pennsylvania)
Environment Band 2
Table: p.1707

**Bergeson, Donna** (Georgia)
Profile: p.706
Healthcare Band 2
Table: p.693

**Bergeson, Lynn**
(District of Columbia)
Profile: p.501
Environment Band 3
Table: p.451

**Berggren, Tom** (Utah)
Profile: p.1950
Real Estate Band 2
Table: p.1947

**Berghoff, John C** (Illinois)
Profile: p.820
Environment Band 3
Table: p.791

**Bergin, Leo** (Nevada)
Real Estate Band 3
Table: p.1255

**Bergman, Michael**
(California)
Media & Entertainment Band 4
Table: p.263

**Bergmann, Peter G**
(New York)
Profile: p.1438
Healthcare Band 1
Table: p.1374

**Bergtraum, Howard M**
(New York)
Profile: p.1438
Private Equity Band 3
Table: p.1410

**Berkeley, Jill B** (Illinois)
Profile: p.820
Insurance Band 2
Table: p.796

**Berkes, Robert H**
(California)
Insurance Band 3
Table: p.243

**Berkley, Peter L** (New
Jersey)
Profile: p.1296
Real Estate Band 2
Table: p.1293

**Berkman, Jerome**
(Connecticut)
Profile: p.382
Real Estate Band 2
Table: p.380

**Berkoff, Mark** (Illinois)
Profile: p.820
Bankruptcy Band 3
Table: p.775

**Berkowitz, Alan D**
(Pennsylvania)
Profile: p.1722
Employment Band 2
Table: p.1703

**Berkowitz, Alan R**
(California)
Profile: p.278
Employment Band 4
Table: p.231

**Berkowitz, Lawrence**
(Missouri)
Litigation Band S
Table: p.1198

**Berkowitz, Paul** (Florida)
Profile: p.628
Corporate/M&A Band 4
Table: p.594

**Berkowitz, Philip M**
(New York)
Profile: p.1438
Employment Band 3
Table: p.1365

**Berlack, Evan R** (National)
Profile: p.88
International Trade Band 1
Table: p.41

**Berlin, Howard J** (Florida)
Profile: p.628
Bankruptcy Band 2
Table: p.586

**Berlin, Kenneth**
(District of Columbia)
Profile: p.501
Environment Band 1
Table: p.450

**Berlin, Stephen R**
(North Carolina)
Profile: p.1581
Environment Band 2
Table: p.1575

**Berman, Barry D**
(Maryland)
Employee Benefits Band 1
Table: p.1027

**Berman, David**
(Massachusetts)
Banking & Finance Band 3
Table: p.1055

**Berman, Debbie** (Illinois)
Profile: p.820
Media & Entertainment Up
and coming
Table: p.806

**Berman, Garry C**
(Connecticut)
Profile: p.382
Real Estate Band 2
Table: p.380

**Berman, Jeffrey** (California)
Profile: p.279
Employment Band 4
Table: p.231

**Berman, Kenneth J**
(District of Columbia)
Investment Management Band 3

Table: p.469

**Berman, Mark N**
(Massachusetts)
Profile: p.1087
Bankruptcy Band 2
Table: p.1058

**Berman, Michael P**
(Arizona)
Employment Band 4
Table: p.178

**Bermann, George A**
(New York)
Arbitration Band 1
Table: p.37

**Bernard, J Michael**
(Michigan)
Corporate/M&A Band 3
Table: p.1122

**Bernard, John M**
(Pennsylvania)
Profile: p.1722
Employment Band 1
Table: p.1704

**Berne, Gary** (Oregon)
Litigation Band 2
Table: p.1674

**Berner, Frederic**
(District of Columbia)
Profile: p.501
Energy Band 4
Table: p.441

**Bernick, Carol** (Oregon)
Employment Band 3
Table: p.1670

**Bernick, David M** (Illinois)
Profile: p.820
Litigation Band 1
Table: p.802
Products Liability ✪
Table: p.50

**Bernius, Robert**
(District of Columbia)
Profile: p.501
Media & Entertainment Band 2
Table: p.477

**Bernstein, Alan**
(Pennsylvania)
Profile: p.1722
Intellectual Property Band 3
Table: p.1711

**Bernstein, David** (New
York)
Intellectual Property Band 2
Table: p.1385

**Bernstein, Donald S**
(New York)
Profile: p.1438
Bankruptcy Band 1
Table: p.1344

**Bernstein, Greg** (Maryland)
Litigation Band 2
Table: p.1032

**Bernstein, H Bruce**
(Illinois)
Profile: p.820

Banking & Finance Band S
Table: p.771

**Bernstein, Howard** (Illinois)
Profile: p.820
Employment Band 2
Table: p.785

**Bernstein, Jonathan K**
(National)
Profile: p.88
Sport Band 3
Table: p.59

**Bernstein, Leonard A**
(Pennsylvania)
Profile: p.1722
Banking & Finance Band 3
Table: p.1695

**Bernstein, Michael**
(New York)
Profile: p.1438
Employment Band 2
Table: p.1365

**Bernstein, Michael**
(District of Columbia)
Profile: p.501
Bankruptcy Band 3
Table: p.432

**Bernstein, Stephen W**
(Massachusetts)
Profile: p.1087
Healthcare Band 2
Table: p.1071

**Bernstein, William S**
(New York)
Healthcare Band 2
Table: p.1374

**Berry, Andrew T** (New
Jersey)
Litigation Band 1
Table: p.1289
Litigation Band 1
Table: p.1292

**Berry, Charles** (Arizona)
Corporate/M&A Band 4
Table: p.176

**Berry, David P** (California)
Immigration Band 3
Table: p.241

**Berry, John V** (Arizona)
Real Estate Band 1
Table: p.186

**Berry, Leo** (Montana)
Natural Resources Band 1
Table: p.1228

**Berry IV, C Dewees**
(Tennessee)
Profile: p.1810
Real Estate Band 1
Table: p.1808

**Bershad, David** (New York)
Litigation Band 1
Table: p.1390

**Bertelsen, Mark A**
(California)
Profile: p.279
Corporate/M&A Band 4

Table: p.227

**Berz, David**
(District of Columbia)
Profile: p.501
Environment Band 2
Table: p.450

**Beshar, Sarah** (National)
Profile: p.88
Capital Markets Band 4
Table: p.7

**Bessette-Smith, Suzanne**
(Illinois)
Real Estate Band 4
Table: p.809

**Best, Edward S** (Illinois)
Profile: p.820
Corporate/M&A Band 4
Table: p.781

**Betensky, Steven** (New
York)
Profile: p.1438
Technology Band 3
Table: p.1428

**Bettencourt, Mark T**
(Massachusetts)
Profile: p.1087
Corporate/M&A
Up and coming
Table: p.1061

**Better, Herbert** (Maryland)
Litigation Band 3
Table: p.1032

**Bettinger, Carl J**
(New Mexico)
Litigation Band 1
Table: p.1324

**Bettis, Vance J**
(South Carolina)
Employment Band 1
Table: p.1777

**Betts, Rebecca A**
(West Virginia)
Litigation Band 2
Table: p.2013

**Betzen, Mark E** (Texas)
Profile: p.1882
Corporate/M&A Band 4
Table: p.1840

**Betzer, Stan**
(New Mexico)
Corporate/Commercial Band 3
Table: p.1320

**Beus, Leo R** (Arizona)
Litigation Band 4
Table: p.181

**Bevan III, William**
(Pennsylvania)
Profile: p.1722
Employment Band 2
Table: p.1703

**Beveridge, Cathy** (Florida)
Employment Band 4
Table: p.597

**Bevilacqua, Louis** (New York)
Profile: p.1439
Corporate/M&A Band 4
Table: p.1354

**Beyda, Richard**
(District of Columbia)
Real Estate Band 2
Table: p.482

**Beyer, Ruth** (Oregon)
Corporate/M&A Band 2
Table: p.1667

**Bialecki, Gregory P**
(Massachusetts)
Profile: p.1087
Real Estate Band 1
Table: p.1081

**Bialkin, Kenneth J**
(New York)
Profile: p.1439
Corporate/M&A Band S
Table: p.1354

**Bianchi, Alden J**
(Massachusetts)
Employee Benefits Band 2
Table: p.1063

**Bianchi, Jaime A** (Florida)
Profile: p.628
Litigation Band 4
Table: p.609

**Bice, Todd L** (Nevada)
Litigation Band 3
Table: p.1252

**Bick, John** (New York)
Profile: p.1439
Private Equity Band 2
Table: p.1407

**Bickel, John M** (Iowa)
Litigation Band 3
Table: p.914

**Bickford IV, Warren F**
(Oklahoma)
Litigation Band 3
Table: p.1656

**Bicks, Peter A** (National)
Profile: p.89
Products Liability Band 3
Table: p.50

**Bidart, Michael J**
(California)
Insurance Band 2
Table: p.245

**Bieke, James R**
(District of Columbia)
Profile: p.502
Environment Band 4
Table: p.451

**Bienenfeld, Morris**
(New Jersey)
Healthcare Band 2
Table: p.1287

**Bienenstock, Martin**
(New York)
Profile: p.1439
Bankruptcy Band 1

Table: p.1344

**Bierce, William B** (New York)
Business Process Outsourcing Band 3
Table: p.2
Technology Band 3
Table: p.1428

**Bierig, Jack R** (Illinois)
Profile: p.820
Antitrust Band 3
Table: p.767

**Biery, Evelyn H** (Texas)
Profile: p.1883
Bankruptcy Band 3
Table: p.1835

**Bigler, C Stephen**
(Delaware)
Profile: p.402
Corporate/M&A Band 3
Table: p.394

**Biles, Blake A**
(District of Columbia)
Profile: p.502
Environment Band 2
Table: p.451

**Bilger, Bruce R** (Texas)
Profile: p.1883
Energy Band 1
Table: p.1847
Projects Band 1
Table: p.56
Projects Band 1
Table: p.1869

**Bilkis, David** (New York)
Profile: p.1439
Banking & Finance Band 4
Table: p.1339

**Billings Jr, Peter W** (Utah)
Litigation Band 2
Table: p.1945

**Bilzin, Brian L** (Florida)
Profile: p.628
Real Estate Band 1
Table: p.617

**Binnig, Christian F**
(Illinois)
Profile: p.820
Telecom, Broadcast & Satellite Band 3
Table: p.816

**Birchfield, Thomas J**
(Kentucky)
Employment Band 2
Table: p.939

**Bird, Paul S** (New York)
Corporate/M&A Band 3
Table: p.1354
Private Equity Band 2
Table: p.1407

**Bird, Terry W** (California)
Litigation Band 2
Table: p.258

**Birnbaum, Gary** (Arizona)
Litigation Band 1
Table: p.181

**Birnbaum, Sheila L**
(New York)
Profile: p.1439
Insurance Band 3
Table: p.1379
Products Liability ✪
Table: p.50

**Biron, Thomas E**
(Pennsylvania)
Profile: p.1722
Bankruptcy Band 2
Table: p.1697

**Bishop, Doak** (Texas)
Profile: p.1883
Energy Band 1
Table: p.1849
International Arbitration Band 2
Table: p.36

**Bishop, Timothy S** (Illinois)
Profile: p.821
Environment Band 2
Table: p.791

**Bishop III, George W** (Tennessee)
Profile: p.1810
Corporate/M&A Band 2
Table: p.1799

**Biskind, Neil** (Arizona)
Real Estate Band 2
Table: p.184

**Bissinger, Mark C** (Ohio)
Profile: p.1624
Construction Band 4
Table: p.1603

**Bissoon, Cathy**
(Pennsylvania)
Profile: p.1723
Employment Band 4
Table: p.1703

**Bithell, Walter** (Idaho)
Profile: p.763
Litigation Band 1
Table: p.760

**Bivens, Donald** (Arizona)
Litigation Band 2
Table: p.181

**Bixler, Albert G**
(Pennsylvania)
Litigation Band 3
Table: p.1714

**Bizar, Steven E**
(Pennsylvania)
Profile: p.1723
Antitrust Band 3
Table: p.1692

**Bjerke, Bruce** (Washington)
Corporate/Commercial Band 3
Table: p.1992

**Black, Allen** (Pennsylvania)
Antitrust Band 2
Table: p.1692
Litigation Band 2
Table: p.1714

**Black, Bruce** (Colorado)
Litigation Band 1

Table: p.353

**Black, Kathryn** (Alaska)
Corporate/M&A Band 1
Table: p.168

**Black, Kenneth** (Utah)
Litigation Band 2
Table: p.1945

**Black, Margaret F**
(New Jersey)
Profile: p.1296
Real Estate Band 3
Table: p.1293

**Black, Roy** (Florida)
Litigation Band 1
Table: p.610

**Black Jr, Lewis S**
(Delaware)
Profile: p.402
Corporate/M&A Band S
Table: p.394

**Black, Jr, Creed C**
(Pennsylvania)
Profile: p.1723
Litigation Band 2
Table: p.1715

**Blackburn, Frank D**
(Louisiana)
Gaming & Licensing Band 2
Table: p.971

**Blackburn, Thomas**
(District of Columbia)
Energy Band 5
Table: p.445

**Blackburn, W Stanley**
(Georgia)
Profile: p.706
Corporate/M&A Band 4
Table: p.684

**Blackhurst, Steven**
(Oregon)
Profile: p.1680
Litigation Band 2
Table: p.1674

**Blackman, Jana Cohen**
(Illinois)
Profile: p.821
Real Estate Band 3
Table: p.809

**Blackmer, Jill**
(New Hampshire)
Employment Band 3
Table: p.1265

**Blackstock, Jerry** (Georgia)
Profile: p.706
Intellectual Property Band 2
Table: p.696
Litigation Band 2
Table: p.698

**Blackstone, Robert A**
(Washington)
Employment Band 1
Table: p.1995

**Blain, Russell** (Florida)
Profile: p.628
Bankruptcy Band 2

Table: p.586

**Blair, Andrew** (Colorado)
Profile: p.358
Corporate/M&A Band 3
Table: p.346

**Blair, Mitchell G** (Ohio)
Profile: p.1624
Litigation Band 3
Table: p.1617

**Blake, Jonathan D**
(District of Columbia)
Profile: p.502
Telecom, Broadcast & Satellite Band 1
Table: p.492

**Blake Jr, Joseph**
(South Carolina)
Corporate/M&A Band 3
Table: p.1775

**Blanchard, Kimberly S**
(New York)
Profile: p.1439
Tax Band 3
Table: p.1423

**Blanchard, Timothy P**
(California)
Profile: p.279
Healthcare Band 3
Table: p.238

**Bland, Douglas S** (Texas)
Profile: p.1883
Energy Band 4
Table: p.1847
Projects Band 2
Table: p.1869

**Blaney, Brian H** (Arizona)
Profile: p.187
Corporate/M&A Band 3
Table: p.176

**Blaser, Michael R** (Iowa)
Profile: p.919
Corporate/M&A Band 4
Table: p.909

**Blashek, Robert D**
(California)
Profile: p.279
Tax Band 4
Table: p.274

**Blass, Michael S** (New York)
Profile: p.1439
Healthcare Band 3
Table: p.1374

**Blassberg, Franci J**
(New York)
Private Equity Band 1
Table: p.1407

**Blaszak, James S**
(District of Columbia)
Profile: p.502
Telecom, Broadcast & Satellite Band 4
Table: p.492

**Blattmachr, Jonathan G**
(National)
Wealth Management Band 1

B

Table: p.81

**Blattner, J Wray** (Ohio)
Profile: p.1624
Environment **Band** 2
Table: p.1612

**Blattner-Thompson, Elisabeth** (Utah)
Profile: p.1950
Employment **Up and coming**
Table: p.1944

**Blau, Michael L**
(Massachusetts)
Profile: p.1087
Healthcare **Band** 1
Table: p.1071

**Blauch, Kevin C** (National)
Capital Markets **Band** 3
Table: p.18

**Blears, Norman J**
(California)
Profile: p.279
Litigation **Band** 4
Table: p.257

**Blecha, Kirk** (Nebraska)
Litigation **Band** 2
Table: p.1239

**Blecher, Maxwell M**
(California)
Profile: p.279
Antitrust **Band** 1
Table: p.216
Litigation **Band** 2
Table: p.257

**Blechman, Bill** (Florida)
Profile: p.629
Antitrust **Band** 1
Table: p.581

**Bleck, Daniel**
(Massachusetts)
Profile: p.1087
Bankruptcy **Band** 2
Table: p.1058

**Bledsoe, David** (Oregon)
Environment **Band** 2
Table: p.1672

**Blessing, Peter H** (New York)
Profile: p.1439
Tax **Band** 1
Table: p.1423

**Blewett III, Alexander**
(Montana)
Litigation **Band** 2
Table: p.1225

**Bley, Kenneth B** (California)
Real Estate **Band** 2
Table: p.270

**Blissard, Judith M** (Texas)
Profile: p.1883
Tax **Band** 4
Table: p.1875

**Blittner, David** (New York)
Profile: p.1439
Private Equity **Up and coming**
Table: p.1407

**Bloch, Robert E**
(District of Columbia)
Profile: p.502
Antitrust **Band** 5
Table: p.426

**Block, Bruce** (Wisconsin)
Profile: p.2032
Real Estate **Band** 1
Table: p.2030

**Block, David** (Florida)
Profile: p.629
Employment **Band** 4
Table: p.597

**Block, Dennis** (New York)
Profile: p.1440
Corporate/M&A **Band** 1
Table: p.1354

**Block, Joseph G**
(District of Columbia)
Environment **Band** 4
Table: p.451

**Bloodworth, Darryl**
(Florida)
Profile: p.629
Litigation **Band** 3
Table: p.609

**Bloom, Herschel** (Georgia)
Profile: p.706
Tax **Band** 1
Table: p.703

**Bloom, Jacob A** (California)
Media & Entertainment **Band** 2
Table: p.266

**Bloom, Jerry** (California)
Profile: p.279
Energy **Band** 1
Table: p.233

**Bloom, Mark D** (Florida)
Profile: p.629
Bankruptcy **Band** 1
Table: p.586

**Bloom, Michael**
(Pennsylvania)
Profile: p.1723
Bankruptcy **Band** 3
Table: p.1697

**Bloom, Myron A**
(Pennsylvania)
Profile: p.1723
Bankruptcy **Band** 2
Table: p.1697

**Bloom, Warren S** (Florida)
Profile: p.629
Banking & Finance **Band** 2
Table: p.583

**Bloomberg, Mitchell R**
(Florida)
Litigation **Band** 4
Table: p.609

**Blount, David L** (Oregon)
Environment **Band** 2
Table: p.1672

**Blue Jr, William A**
(Tennessee)
Employment **Band** 2

Table: p.1801

**Bluedorn II, Donald C**
(Pennsylvania)
Environment **Band** 3
Table: p.1707

**Blume, Fred** (Pennsylvania)
Profile: p.1723
Corporate/M&A **Band** 3
Table: p.1700

**Blumen, Rick D** (Georgia)
Profile: p.706
Banking & Finance **Band** 3
Table: p.677

**Blumenfeld, Chuck**
(Washington)
Environment **Band** 1
Table: p.1996

**Blumenfeld, Jack B**
(Delaware)
Profile: p.402
Intellectual Property **Band** 1
Table: p.397

**Blumstein, Philip** (Alaska)
Corporate/M&A **Band** 1
Table: p.168

**Boardman, Richard**
(Idaho)
Litigation **Band** 3
Table: p.760

**Boast, Molly S** (New York)
Antitrust **Band** 4
Table: p.1335

**Bobber, Bernard J**
(Wisconsin)
Profile: p.2032
Employment **Band** 1
Table: p.2027

**Bobo Jr, William**
(South Carolina)
Real Estate **Band** 3
Table: p.1780

**Bodine, Brian** (Washington)
Intellectual Property **Band** 1
Table: p.1998

**Boe, Kathleen M** (Vermont)
Corporate/Commercial **Band** 2
Table: p.1957

**Boe, Tim** (Arkansas)
Employment **Band** 1
Table: p.203

**Boeglin, Daniel L** (Indiana)
Profile: p.894
Corporate/M&A **Band** 2
Table: p.887

**Boehnen, Daniel A** (Illinois)
Profile: p.821
Intellectual Property **Band** 2
Table: p.799

**Boehrer, Charles B**
(Illinois)
Profile: p.821
Banking & Finance **Band** 3
Table: p.771

**Bogaard, Jonathan H**
(National)
Transportation **Band** 3
Table: p.64

**Bogdanoff, Lee R**
(California)
Profile: p.279
Bankruptcy **Band** 2
Table: p.222

**Bogdanow, Alan J** (Texas)
Profile: p.1883
Corporate/M&A **Band** 4
Table: p.1840

**Bogdonoff, Michael A**
(Pennsylvania)
Profile: p.1723
Environment **Band** 3
Table: p.1707

**Bogen, Andrew E**
(California)
Profile: p.279
Corporate/M&A **Band** 1
Table: p.227

**Boggs, Jack** (Florida)
Tax **Band** S
Table: p.623

**Boggs Jr, Thomas Hale**
(National)
Profile: p.89
Government Relations **Band** 1
Table: p.32

**Bogue, Stevenson**
(Nebraska)
Employment **Band** 2
Table: p.1238

**Bohannon, Paul** (Texas)
Environment **Band** 3
Table: p.1852

**Bohler, William J**
(California)
Intellectual Property **Band** 4
Table: p.248

**Bohm, Richard D** (New York)
Media & Entertainment **Band** 2
Table: p.1403
Private Equity **Band** 2
Table: p.1407

**Bohrer, Barry A** (New York)
Litigation **Band** 3
Table: p.1391

**Boice, William** (Georgia)
Profile: p.706
Employment **Band** 3
Table: p.687
Litigation **Band** 2
Table: p.698

**Boies, Bill** (Illinois)
Profile: p.821
Employment **Band** 2
Table: p.786

**Boies, David** (New York)
Profile: p.1440
Antitrust **Band** 2
Table: p.1335
Litigation **Band** 1

Table: p.1388

**Boise, April V** (Ohio)
Profile: p.1624
Corporate/M&A
**Up and coming**
Table: p.1605

**Boisseau, Jane** (New York)
Profile: p.1440
Insurance **Band** 3
Table: p.1380

**Boisseau, Richard**
(Georgia)
Profile: p.707
Employment **Band** 2
Table: p.687

**Bokor, Bruce** (Florida)
Tax **Band** 2
Table: p.623

**Bolding, Grady** (California)
Profile: p.279
Tax **Band** 3
Table: p.274

**Boldt, Michael** (Indiana)
Profile: p.894
Employment **Band** 2
Table: p.889

**Bolen, Richard J**
(West Virginia)
Real Estate **Band** 3
Table: p.2015

**Boles, H Hampton**
(Alabama)
Profile: p.155
Banking & Finance **Band** 1
Table: p.147

**Bolstein, Joel**
(Pennsylvania)
Environment **Band** 2
Table: p.1707

**Bolton, Richard M**
(Michigan)
Profile: p.1132
Corporate/M&A **Band** 3
Table: p.1122

**Bomse, Stephen**
(California)
Profile: p.280
Antitrust **Band** 1
Table: p.216
Litigation **Band** 4
Table: p.257

**Bonano, William E**
(National)
Profile: p.89
Tax Litigation **Band** 2
Table: p.62

**Bond, Thomas J** (Texas)
Profile: p.1883
Insurance **Band** 2
Table: p.1858

**Bond, W Michael** (New York)
Profile: p.1440
Real Estate **Band** 5
Table: p.1417

**Bondurant, Emmet J**
(Georgia)
Profile: p.707
Antitrust Band S
Table: p.675
Litigation Band S
Table: p.698

**Bonham, Mark E** (Utah)
Profile: p.1950
Corporate/M&A Band 1
Table: p.1941

**Bonifay, Cecelia** (Florida)
Profile: p.629
Real Estate Band 2
Table: p.621

**Bonner, Michael J**
(Nevada)
Profile: p.1257
Corporate/Commercial Band 1
Table: p.1246

**Booe, Mike**
(North Carolina)
Bankruptcy Band 1
Table: p.1570

**Booker, Daniel I**
(Pennsylvania)
Profile: p.1723
Antitrust Band 2
Table: p.1692

**Booker, William**
(West Virginia)
Corporate/Commercial Band 1
Table: p.2010

**Bookin, Daniel** (California)
Litigation Band 1
Table: p.258

**Bookman, Lloyd A**
(California)
Healthcare Band 2
Table: p.238

**Boone, Michael** (Texas)
Corporate/M&A Band 1
Table: p.1840

**Boone, Thomas** (Montana)
Corporate/M&A Band 1
Table: p.1222
Real Estate Band 2
Table: p.1230

**Boone Jr, Sidney**
(South Carolina)
Real Estate Band 1
Table: p.1780

**Booth, Brian** (Oregon)
Profile: p.1680
Corporate/M&A Band S
Table: p.1667

**Booth, Rebecca L**
(Pennsylvania)
Profile: p.1723
Bankruptcy Band 3

**Booth, William** (California)
Energy Band 3
Table: p.233

**Boothby, Colleen**
(District of Columbia)
Profile: p.502
Telecom, Broadcast & Satellite
Band 4
Table: p.492

**Bopp III, Fred W** (Maine)
Corporate/M&A Band 2
Table: p.1000

**Bor, Andrew** (Washington)
Corporate/Commercial Band 2
Table: p.1992

**Borden, Mark**
(Massachusetts)
Profile: p.1088
Corporate/M&A Band 1
Table: p.1061
Private Equity Band 1
Table: p.1078

**Borders, Sarah** (Georgia)
Profile: p.707
Bankruptcy Band 2
Table: p.679

**Borders, Thomas** (Illinois)
Profile: p.821
Tax Band 3
Table: p.812

**Boren, Alison** (Texas)
Profile: p.1883
Banking & Finance Band 4
Table: p.1832

**Born II, Samuel** (Indiana)
Profile: p.894
Employment Band 1
Table: p.889

**Borowitz, Peter L** (New
York)
Bankruptcy Band 3
Table: p.1344

**Borun, Michael F** (Illinois)
Intellectual Property Band 2
Table: p.799

**Boshkoff, Ellen** (Indiana)
Profile: p.894
Employment Band 3
Table: p.889

**Bossert, Terry**
(Pennsylvania)
Environment Band 2
Table: p.1707

**Bostelman, John T**
(New York)
Profile: p.89
Capital Markets Band 2
Table: p.7

**Boston, Robert E**
(Tennessee)
Profile: p.1810
Employment Band 1
Table: p.1801
Litigation Band 2
Table: p.1804

**Bostwick, Gary** (California)
Media & Entertainment Band 2
Table: p.263

**Bothwick, Jay**
(Massachusetts)
Profile: p.1088
Corporate/M&A Band 3
Table: p.1061

**Botica, Matthew J** (Illinois)
Profile: p.821
Bankruptcy Band 3
Table: p.775

**Bottrell, Lowell**
(North Dakota)
Corporate/Commercial Band 1
Table: p.1590

**Bouchard, Andre G**
(Delaware)
Chancery Band 3
Table: p.392

**Boulden, Michael R**
(Texas)
Profile: p.1883
Real Estate Band 3
Table: p.1872

**Boulet, Virginia** (Louisiana)
Profile: p.977
Corporate/M&A Band 4
Table: p.965

**Boulware, Margaret**
(Texas)
Profile: p.1883
Intellectual Property Band 3
Table: p.1860

**Bouma, John J** (Arizona)
Profile: p.188
Litigation Band 1
Table: p.181

**Bourdeau, Karl S**
(District of Columbia)
Profile: p.503
Environment Band 3
Table: p.451

**Boutrous Jr, Theodore J**
(California)
Profile: p.280
Media & Entertainment Band 3
Table: p.263
Products Liability Band 3
Table: p.50

**Bowden, William P**
(Delaware)
Profile: p.402
Bankruptcy Band 4
Table: p.389

**Bowe Jr, James F**
(District of Columbia)
Profile: p.503
Energy Band 5
Table: p.441

**Bowen, Jay S** (Tennessee)
Litigation Band 3
Table: p.1804

**Bowen, Michael A**
(Wisconsin)
Profile: p.2032
Litigation Band 1
Table: p.2029

**Bowen, Stephen S** (Illinois)
Tax Band 1
Table: p.812

**Bowers, James** (Missouri)
Real Estate Band 2
Table: p.1201

**Bowers, William** (Texas)
Profile: p.1884
Tax Band 2
Table: p.1875

**Bowers, William C**
(National)
Profile: p.89
Transportation Band 2
Table: p.64

**Bowie, Scott O** (New York)
Profile: p.1440
Private Equity Band 3
Table: p.1410

**Bowman, Everett J**
(North Carolina)
Antitrust Band 1
Table: p.1568

**Bowman, John** (Texas)
Profile: p.1884
International Arbitration
Band 3
Table: p.36

**Bowman, Linda A** (Nevada)
Environment Band 2
Table: p.1249

**Bowman, Philip L** (Kansas)
Real Estate Band S
Table: p.930

**Bowman, William**
(District of Columbia)
Profile: p.503
Insurance Band 1
Table: p.461
Litigation Band 3
Table: p.471

**Bowser, William W**
(Delaware)
Profile: p.402
Employment Band 3
Table: p.396

**Boxer, Leonard** (New York)
Real Estate Band S
Table: p.1417

**Boxer, Mark H** (California)
Profile: p.280
Employment Band 4
Table: p.232

**Boyajian, Victor** (New
Jersey)
Profile: p.1296
Corporate/M&A Band 1
Table: p.1278

**Boyce, William J** (Texas)
Profile: p.1884
Litigation Band 2
Table: p.1866

**Boyd, David R** (Alabama)
Profile: p.155
Litigation Band 3

Table: p.152

**Boyd, Eric E** (Illinois)
Environment Band 4
Table: p.791

**Boyd, Paul** (Idaho)
Corporate/Commercial Band 1
Table: p.759

**Boyd, William**
(South Carolina)
Corporate/M&A Band 3
Table: p.1775
Real Estate Band 2
Table: p.1780

**Boyken, Quentin** (Iowa)
Corporate/M&A Band 3
Table: p.909

**Boyle, James F** (Wisconsin)
Intellectual Property Band 2
Table: p.2028

**Bozarth, Stephen J**
(Florida)
Profile: p.629
Real Estate Band 1
Table: p.617

**Brach, Richard** (New York)
Projects Band 2
Table: p.56
Projects Band 3
Table: p.1413

**Bradbury, Steve** (Idaho)
Real Estate Band 2
Table: p.762

**Braddock, James D**
(Texas)
Environment Band 2
Table: p.1852

**Braden, Gregory C**
(National)
Profile: p.89
Erisa Litigation Band 2
Table: p.21

**Bradley, Craig C** (Illinois)
Profile: p.822
Corporate/M&A: Private Equity
Band 2
Table: p.782

**Bradley, James P** (Texas)
Profile: p.1884
Intellectual Property Band 3
Table: p.1860

**Bradley, Wayne N**
(Georgia)
Profile: p.707
Corporate/M&A Band 4
Table: p.684

**Bradley Jr, Craig C**
(Kentucky)
Profile: p.945
Corporate/M&A Band 1
Table: p.937

**Bradshaw, Brian A** (Texas)
Profile: p.1884
Projects Up & Coming

B

B

**Bradshaw, Penni Pearson**
(North Carolina)
Employment Band 2
Table: p.1573

**Bradshaw II, Jean Paul**
(Missouri)
Profile: p.1203
Litigation Band 1
Table: p.1198

**Brady, Christopher J**
(North Carolina)
Profile: p.1581
Capital Markets Band 2
Table: p.18

**Brady, Francis**
(Connecticut)
Litigation Band 1
Table: p.378

**Brady, Patrick G**
(New Jersey)
Employment Band 3
Table: p.1282

**Brady, Robert P**
(District of Columbia)
Profile: p.503
Healthcare Band 2
Table: p.456

**Brady, Robert S** (Delaware)
Profile: p.402
Bankruptcy Band 2
Table: p.389

**Braemer, Richard J**
(Pennsylvania)
Profile: p.1724
Corporate/M&A Band 4
Table: p.1700

**Brahm, Richard** (Ohio)
Real Estate Band 1
Table: p.1622

**Brainard, Barbara A**
(Oregon)
Employment Band 3
Table: p.1670

**Brakke, Jon**
(North Dakota)
Corporate/Commercial Band 1
Table: p.1590

**Braley, Bruce L** (Iowa)
Litigation Band 4
Table: p.914

**Bramlett, Jeffrey** (Georgia)
Profile: p.707
Litigation Band 3
Table: p.698

**Bramnick, James** (Florida)
Profile: p.629
Employment Band 2
Table: p.597

**Bran, Paul Bennett**
(District of Columbia)
Profile: p.503
Bankruptcy Band 3
Table: p.432

**Branca, John G** (California)
Media & Entertainment Band 2

**Braun, Stephen T**
(Tennessee)
Profile: p.1810
Corporate/M&A Band 1
Table: p.1799

**Bray, John**
(District of Columbia)
Profile: p.503
Litigation Band 2
Table: p.471

**Braza, Mary K** (National)
Profile: p.90
Sport Band 3
Table: p.59

**Breaux, Ronald W** (Texas)
Antitrust Band 3
Table: p.1829

**Breay, James** (Michigan)
Banking & Finance Band 2
Table: p.1120

**Bredehoft, John M**
(Virginia)
Employment Band 1
Table: p.1971

**Breedlove, Gregory B**
(Alabama)
Litigation Band 3
Table: p.152

**Breglio, John F** (New York)
Profile: p.1441
Media & Entertainment Band 1
Table: p.1401

**Brenna, Nathan**
(Minnnesota)
Profile: p.1162
Litigation Band 2

**Brennan, Daniel** (Illinois)
Profile: p.822
Construction Band 2
Table: p.778

**Brennan, James C**
(Virginia)
Profile: p.1980
Real Estate Band 3
Table: p.1978

**Brennan, Matthew J**
(New York)
Profile: p.1441
Environment Band 2
Table: p.1373

**Brennan, Maureen A**
(Ohio)
Environment Band 4
Table: p.1612

**Brennan Jr, John T**
(District of Columbia)
Profile: p.503
Healthcare Band 1
Table: p.456

**Brent, Douglas F**
(Kentucky)
Profile: p.945
Environment Up and coming
Table: p.941

**Brescher, John B**
(New Jersey)
Employee Benefits Band 2
Table: p.1281

**Breslow, Stephanie**
(New York)
Private Equity Band 2
Table: p.1410

**Bretschneider, Barry E**
(Virginia)
Profile: p.1980
Intellectual Property Band 1
Table: p.1975

**Bretz, Daniel** (Michigan)
Profile: p.1132
Employment Band 1
Table: p.1125

**Breuer, Lanny A**
(District of Columbia)
Profile: p.503
Litigation Band 3
Table: p.471

**Brewer, Susan Slenker**
(West Virginia)
Litigation Band 2
Table: p.2013

**Brewer Jr, Robert S**
(California)
Profile: p.280
Litigation Band 3
Table: p.258

**Brewster, William H**
(Georgia)
Profile: p.707
Intellectual Property Band 4
Table: p.696

**Breyfogle, Jon W**
(District of Columbia)
Employee Benefits Band 3
Table: p.437

**Brian, Brad** (California)
Litigation Band 1
Table: p.257
Litigation Band 1
Table: p.258

**Bricklemyer, Keith**
(Florida)
Real Estate Band 3
Table: p.621

**Brickman, Steven A**
(Alabama)
Real Estate Band 3
Table: p.153

**Bridge, Catherine** (Indiana)
Profile: p.895
Corporate/M&A Band 2
Table: p.887

**Bridges, Andrew**
(California)
Profile: p.280
Intellectual Property Band 4
Table: p.248

**Bridgesmith, Larry W**
(Tennessee)
Profile: p.1811
Employment Band 2

**Brandel, Roland E**
(National)
Profile: p.89
Financial Services Band S
Table: p.24

**Brandes, Lawrence**
(New York)
Profile: p.1440
Insurance Band 2
Table: p.1379

**Brandow, John M** (New
York)
Profile: p.89
Capital Markets Band 1
Table: p.15

**Brands, Henk**
(District of Columbia)
Profile: p.503
Telecom, Broadcast & Satellite
Band 3
Table: p.492

**Brandt, A Peter** (Florida)
Construction Band 1
Table: p.590

**Brann, Richard** (Texas)
Profile: p.1884
Employment Band 1
Table: p.1844

**Brannan, William**
(New York)
Profile: p.1440
Tax Band 3
Table: p.1423

**Brannon, Jeanna** (Georgia)
Real Estate Band 3
Table: p.700

**Branzburg, Morton R**
(Pennsylvania)
Bankruptcy Band 3
Table: p.1697

**Brasher, Lance**
(District of Columbia)
Profile: p.503
Projects Band 3
Table: p.479

**Brault, Albert D** (Maryland)
Litigation Band 1
Table: p.1032

**Braun, Bruce R** (Illinois)
Litigation Band 4
Table: p.802

**Braun, Lawrence M**
(California)
Corporate/M&A Band 4
Table: p.227

**Braun, Lonnie R**
(South Dakota)
Litigation Band 2
Table: p.1795

**Braun, Peter**
(Massachusetts)
Profile: p.1088
Healthcare Band 2
Table: p.1071

**Table: p.1801**

**Bridston, Kevin** (Colorado)
Profile: p.358
Construction Band 2
Table: p.345

**Briggs, Heather** (Vermont)
Employment Band 1
Table: p.1958

**Brigham, Johan V**
(Massachusetts)
Profile: p.1088
Corporate/M&A Band 3
Table: p.1061

**Bright Jr, William H**
(Connecticut)
Litigation Band 2
Table: p.378

**Brignone, Andrew**
(Nevada)
Employment Band 1
Table: p.1248

**Brincks, Lon** (Missouri)
Profile: p.1204
Real Estate Band 2
Table: p.1201

**Brindell, James** (Florida)
Real Estate Band 3
Table: p.621

**Brinkerhoff, Jeffrey C**
(Wyoming)
Litigation Band 2
Table: p.2044

**Brinkman, David** (Ohio)
Intellectual Property Band 2
Table: p.1614

**Brinkmann, Beth**
(District of Columbia)
Profile: p.504
Litigation Band 2
Table: p.475

**Brinkmann, Karen**
(District of Columbia)
Telecom, Broadcast & Satellite
Band 4
Table: p.492

**Bristow, Daryl** (Texas)
Litigation Band 1
Table: p.1865

**Brito, Michael James**
(National)
Profile: p.90
Business Process Outsourcing
Band 4
Table: p.2

**Brittain, David R** (Florida)
Real Estate Band 3
Table: p.617

**Brittain, Max** (Illinois)
Profile: p.822
Employment Band 1
Table: p.785

**Brittenham, David**
(New York)
Banking & Finance Band 3

Table: p.1339
Capital Markets Band 3
Table: p.7

**Brittenham, Harry M**
(California)
Media & Entertainment Band 1
Table: p.266

**Bro, Ruth Hill** (Illinois)
Profile: p.822
Technology Band 2
Table: p.814

**Broadbent, David K** (Utah)
Profile: p.1950
Real Estate Band 2
Table: p.1947

**Broaddus, William**
(Virginia)
Profile: p.1981
Litigation Band 2
Table: p.1401

**Broccolo, Bernadette**
(Illinois)
Profile: p.822
Healthcare Band 1
Table: p.793

**Brockland, John P**
(California)
IT Outsourcing
Up and coming
Table: p.253

**Brockman, Richard J**
(Alabama)
Corporate/Commercial Band 2
Table: p.148

**Brod, Craig B** (National)
Profile: p.90
Capital Markets Band 3
Table: p.7

**Broderick, David F**
(New Jersey)
Corporate/M&A Band 3
Table: p.1278

**Broderick, JJ** (Pennsylvania)
Profile: p.1724
Real Estate Band 3
Table: p.1718

**Broders, John J** (Louisiana)
Profile: p.977
Energy Band 1
Table: p.969

**Brodsky, David M**
(New York)
Litigation Band 3
Table: p.1390
Litigation Band 3
Table: p.1391

**Brody, Lawrence** (National)
Wealth Management Band 3
Table: p.81

**Brody, Sara** (California)
Profile: p.280
Litigation Band 3
Table: p.257

**Brogan, James P**
(Colorado)
Intellectual Property Band 2
Table: p.351

**Brogan, Stephen J**
(District of Columbia)
Profile: p.504
Litigation Band 3
Table: p.471

**Bromberg, Lisa** (New Jersey)
Profile: p.1296
Environment Band 2
Table: p.1285

**Bromberg, Stephen A**
(Michigan)
Profile: p.1133
Real Estate Band 1
Table: p.1130

**Bromley, James L**
(New York)
Profile: p.1441
Bankruptcy Band 4
Table: p.1344

**Bronis, Stephen** (Florida)
Litigation Band 1
Table: p.610

**Bronson, Jill E.**
(Pennsylvania)
Banking & Finance Band 2
Table: p.1695

**Bronstein, Joel** (Florida)
Tax Band 3
Table: p.623

**Brooke, Robert** (Virginia)
Intellectual Property Band 2
Table: p.1975

**Brookner, Jason S** (Texas)
Profile: p.1884
Bankruptcy Up & coming

**Brooks, Robert**
(Rhode Island)
Profile: p.1771
Employment Band 1
Table: p.1768

**Brooman, David**
(Pennsylvania)
Environment Band 1
Table: p.1707

**Brophy, James E** (Arizona)
Profile: p.188
Corporate/M&A Band 3
Table: p.176

**Brophy, Michael J** (Arizona)
Profile: p.188
Environment Band 1
Table: p.179

**Brose, Steven**
(District of Columbia)
Profile: p.504
Energy Band 1
Table: p.441

**Brosnahan, James**
(California)
Profile: p.280

Litigation Band 1
Table: p.257
Litigation Band 1
Table: p.258

**Broth, Mark T**
(New Hampshire)
Employment Band 1
Table: p.1265

**Broude, Mark A** (New York)
Bankruptcy Band 4
Table: p.1344

**Brower, Charles N**
(London)
Arbitration Band 1
Table: p.37

**Brower, John E** (Minnesota)
Corporate/M&A Band 3
Table: p.1152

**Brown, Alan** (Indiana)
Litigation Band 2
Table: p.890

**Brown, Arthur**
(District of Columbia)
Investment Management Band 2
Table: p.469

**Brown, Barbara B**
(District of Columbia)
Profile: p.504
Employment Band 1
Table: p.439

**Brown, Bowman** (Florida)
Profile: p.629
Banking & Finance Band 1
Table: p.583

**Brown, Christopher**
(Florida)
Profile: p.629
Litigation Band 4
Table: p.609

**Brown, Daniel** (Florida)
Profile: p.630
Insurance Band 1
Table: p.607

**Brown, David** (Iowa)
Litigation Band 2
Table: p.914

**Brown, David B** (Delaware)
Profile: p.402
Corporate/M&A Band 3
Table: p.394

**Brown, David C** (Kentucky)
Profile: p.945
Environment Band 1
Table: p.941

**Brown, David H** (Texas)
Profile: p.1884
Insurance Band 2
Table: p.1858

**Brown, Dickson G**
(New York)
Profile: p.1441
Tax Band 1
Table: p.1425

**Brown, Donald J** (Iowa)
Corporate/M&A Band S
Table: p.909

**Brown, Donald W**
(California)
Profile: p.280
Insurance Band 1
Table: p.245

**Brown, Duane**
(New Mexico)
Corporate/Commercial Band 1
Table: p.1320

**Brown, Elliot H** (New York)
Media & Entertainment Band 1
Table: p.1401

**Brown, Fletcher** (Texas)
Healthcare Up and coming
Table: p.1855

**Brown, Frank E** (Florida)
Employment Band 3
Table: p.597

**Brown, Harald A**
(California)
Media & Entertainment Band 3
Table: p.266

**Brown, J Jeffrey** (Indiana)
Profile: p.895
Corporate/M&A Band 2
Table: p.887

**Brown, James** (Florida)
Profile: p.630
Employment Band 3
Table: p.597

**Brown, James** (Louisiana)
Litigation Band 2
Table: p.973

**Brown, James B**
(Pennsylvania)
Employment Band 2
Table: p.1703

**Brown, Jay W** (Texas)
Profile: p.1884
Insurance Band 3
Table: p.1858

**Brown, Jay Ward**
(District of Columbia)
Media & Entertainment Band 3
Table: p.477

**Brown, Jeffrey** (Ohio)
Real Estate Band 2
Table: p.1622

**Brown, Jeffrey H** (Illinois)
Media & Entertainment Band 2
Table: p.807

**Brown, Jessica** (Colorado)
Profile: p.358
Employment Band 3
Table: p.348

**Brown, John S**
(Massachusetts)
Profile: p.1088
Tax Band 1
Table: p.1084

**Brown, Kim** (Tennessee)
Real Estate Band 2
Table: p.1808

**Brown, Margaret A**
(Massachusetts)
Profile: p.1088
Corporate/M&A Band 3
Table: p.1061

**Brown, Michael K**
(National)
Profile: p.90
Products Liability Band 3
Table: p.50

**Brown, Nicholas A**
(California)
Profile: p.281
Intellectual Property Associate to watch
Table: p.248

**Brown, Pamela Charles**
(Washington)
Profile: p.2004
Corporate/Commercial Band 1
Table: p.1993

**Brown, Reagan** (Texas)
Profile: p.1885
Insurance Band 1
Table: p.1858
Litigation Band 2
Table: p.1865

**Brown, Ricklin** (West Virginia)
Employment Band 1
Table: p.2012

**Brown, Robert** (Colorado)
Profile: p.358
Real Estate Band 1
Table: p.355

**Brown, Spencer** (Missouri)
Litigation Band 1
Table: p.1198

**Brown, Stanley** (Virginia)
Profile: p.1980
Employment Band 3
Table: p.1971

**Brown, Stephen D**
(Pennsylvania)
Profile: p.1724
Antitrust Band 3
Table: p.1692
Litigation Band 3
Table: p.1715

**Brown, Stephen E**
(Alabama)
Profile: p.155
Employment Band 3
Table: p.150

**Brown, Stephen Ross**
(Montana)
Natural Resources Band 1
Table: p.1228

**Brown, Ted** (Florida)
Profile: p.630
Real Estate Band 3
Table: p.621

B

**B**

**Brown, Timothy R** (Ohio)
Profile: p.1624
Employee Benefits **Band 1**
Table: p.1607

**Brown, Walt** (California)
Profile: p.281
Litigation **Band 1**
Table: p.258

**Brown, William** (Iowa)
Profile: p.920
Corporate/M&A **Band 3**
Table: p.909

**Brown II, C David** (Florida)
Real Estate **Band 2**
Table: p.617

**Brown, Jr., Rodney L.**
(Washington)
Environment **Band 1**
Table: p.1996

**Browne, Juliet T** (Maine)
Profile: p.1010
Environment **Band 2**
Table: p.1004

**Browne, Robert E** (Illinois)
Profile: p.822
Intellectual Property **Band 3**
Table: p.799

**Browne, Steven C**
(Massachusetts)
Profile: p.1088
Corporate/M&A **Band 2**
Table: p.1061

**Brownell, Thomas**
(Virginia)
Profile: p.1980
Construction **Band 2**
Table: p.1965

**Brownell, William**
(District of Columbia)
Profile: p.504
Environment **Band 2**
Table: p.451

**Brownrigg, John**
(Nebraska)
Litigation **Band 2**
Table: p.1239

**Brownstein, Andrew R**
(New York)
Profile: p.1441
Corporate/M&A **Band 2**
Table: p.1354

**Brozman, Tina L** (New York)
Profile: p.1441
Bankruptcy **Band 3**
Table: p.1344

**Brubaker, Robert** (Ohio)
Profile: p.1624
Environment **Band 1**
Table: p.1612

**Bruch, Gregory S**
(District of Columbia)
Profile: p.504
Securities **Band 2**
Table: p.485

**Bruemmer, Russell**
(National)
Profile: p.90
Financial Services **Band 2**
Table: p.24

**Bruen, James** (California)
Environment **Band 1**
Table: p.236

**Brumbaugh, John M**
(Florida)
Litigation **Band 3**
Table: p.609

**Brunner, Thomas W**
(District of Columbia)
Profile: p.504
Insurance **Band 2**
Table: p.461

**Bruno, Mary E** (Arizona)
Profile: p.188
Employment **Band 4**
Table: p.178

**Bruns, Phillip T** (Texas)
Profile: p.1885
Energy **Band 2**
Table: p.1849
Litigation **Band 2**
Table: p.1865

**Brunts, Eve M**
(Massachusetts)
Profile: p.1088
Healthcare **Band 3**
Table: p.1071

**Brustad, Orin D** (Michigan)
Profile: p.1133
Employee Benefits **Band 1**
Table: p.1124

**Bruton, Burt** (Florida)
Profile: p.630
Real Estate **Band 2**
Table: p.617

**Bryan, Charles E** (National)
Profile: p.90
Capital Markets **Band 4**
Table: p.18

**Bryan, Karen** (California)
Tax **Band 3**
Table: p.274

**Bryant, David** (Illinois)
Profile: p.822
Real Estate **Band 3**
Table: p.809

**Bryant, Duff** (Washington)
Corporate/Commercial
Associate to watch
Table: p.1992

**Bryant, John** (Tennessee)
Profile: p.1811
Litigation **Band 3**
Table: p.1804
Litigation **Band 1**
Table: p.1805

**Bryant, L Edward** (Illinois)
Profile: p.822
Healthcare ✪
Table: p.793

**Bryant, Timothy** (Illinois)
Profile: p.822
Corporate/M&A: Private Equity
**Band 3**
Table: p.782

**Bryson, Susan J**
(Connecticut)
Profile: p.382
Real Estate **Band 1**
Table: p.380

**Buchanan, John**
(District of Columbia)
Profile: p.504
Insurance **Band 2**
Table: p.464

**Buchanan, Paul** (Oregon)
Employment **Band 2**
Table: p.1670

**Buchanan Jr, Robert**
(Massachusetts)
Antitrust **Band 2**
Table: p.1053

**Buchenroth, Stephen**
(Ohio)
Profile: p.1624
Real Estate **Band 1**
Table: p.1621

**Buchholtz, David**
(New Mexico)
Profile: p.1328
Corporate/Commercial **Band 1**
Table: p.1320

**Buck, Charles**
(Massachusetts)
Profile: p.1088
Healthcare **Up and coming**
Table: p.1071

**Buck, Frank W** (Ohio)
Profile: p.1624
Employment **Band 3**
Table: p.1609

**Buck, Peter** (Washington)
Real Estate **Band 1**
Table: p.2003

**Buck, Peter**
(North Carolina)
Banking & Finance **Band 2**
Table: p.1569
Corporate/M&A **Band 1**
Table: p.1571

**Buck, Willis** (National)
Profile: p.90
Capital Markets **Band 4**
Table: p.18

**Buckholz Jr, Robert E**
(New York)
Profile: p.90
Capital Markets **Band 2**
Table: p.7

**Bucking, James W**
(Massachusetts)
Employment **Band 3**
Table: p.1065

**Buckler, Robert H**
(Georgia)
Employment **Band 2**

Table: p.687

**Buckley, Daniel J** (Ohio)
Profile: p.1624
Litigation **Band 3**
Table: p.1617

**Buckley, Joseph L**
(New Jersey)
Profile: p.1296
Litigation **Band 3**
Table: p.1289

**Buckley, Kevin J** (Virginia)
Profile: p.1980
Capital Markets **Band 2**
Table: p.18
Corporate/M&A **Band 1**
Table: p.1968

**Buckley, Mert** (Kansas)
Real Estate **Band 1**
Table: p.930

**Buckley, Michael** (Nevada)
Real Estate **Band 1**
Table: p.1255

**Buckley Jr, Christopher**
(District of Columbia)
Profile: p.504
Environment **Band 2**
Table: p.451

**Bucy, Rhea** (Tennessee)
Litigation **Band 2**
Table: p.1804

**Budny, Terrence** (Illinois)
Real Estate **Band 4**
Table: p.809

**Budoff, Marc** (Arizona)
Litigation **Band 3**
Table: p.182

**Budofsky, Daniel** (National)
Profile: p.90
Capital Markets **Band 2**
Table: p.15

**Budwick, Michael** (Florida)
Bankruptcy **Band 4**
Table: p.586

**Bueide, Daniel**
(North Dakota)
Real Estate **Band 1**
Table: p.1595

**Buente, David**
(District of Columbia)
Profile: p.504
Environment **Band 1**
Table: p.451

**Buffenstein, Daryl**
(Georgia)
Profile: p.707
Immigration **Band 1**
Table: p.694

**Buffington, Teresa**
(Wyoming)
Profile: p.2047
Corporate/M&A **Band 2**
Table: p.2041

**Buford Jr, C Douglas**
(Arkansas)
Corporate/Commercial **Band 1**
Table: p.201

**Buhle, Warren** (New York)
Profile: p.1441
Banking & Finance **Band 4**
Table: p.1339

**Bulchis, Ed** (Washington)
Profile: p.2004
Intellectual Property **Band 1**
Table: p.1998

**Bulger, Brian** (Illinois)
Employment **Band 1**
Table: p.785

**Bull, Edwin** (Arizona)
Real Estate **Band 2**
Table: p.186

**Bulleit Jr, Thomas N**
(District of Columbia)
Profile: p.505
Healthcare **Band 2**
Table: p.456

**Bullen, Linda M** (Nevada)
Environment **Band 2**
Table: p.1249

**Bullock, Brentley** (Oregon)
Corporate/M&A **Band 3**
Table: p.1667

**Bulman, John** (Rhode
Island)
Litigation **Band 3**
Table: p.1769

**Bumpass, T Merritt** (Ohio)
Employment **Band 3**
Table: p.1609

**Bumpers, Heidi**
(District of Columbia)
Profile: p.505
Environment **Band 4**
Table: p.451

**Bumpers, William**
(District of Columbia)
Profile: p.505
Environment **Band 4**
Table: p.451

**Bundy, David H** (Alaska)
Bankruptcy **Band 1**
Table: p.167

**Bundy, Robert C** (Alaska)
Profile: p.173
Litigation **Band 1**
Table: p.171

**Buniva, Brian L** (Virginia)
Profile: p.1980
Environment **Band 2**
Table: p.1973

**Bunsow, Henry** (California)
Intellectual Property **Band 2**
Table: p.248

**Buoncristiani, David**
(California)
Profile: p.281
Construction **Band 1**

Table: p.225

**Buono, Kathryn M**
(Wisconsin)
Profile: p.2032
Corporate/M&A Band 2
Table: p.2025

**Burbidge, Richard D**
(Utah)
Profile: p.1950
Litigation Band 1
Table: p.1945

**Burch Jr, Francis B**
(Maryland)
Profile: p.1037
Litigation Band S
Table: p.1032

**Burchfield, Bobby R**
(District of Columbia)
Profile: p.505
Government: Political Law
Band 2
Table: p.34
Litigation Band 2
Table: p.471

**Buresh, James** (New York)
Profile: p.1441
Banking & Finance Band 4
Table: p.1339

**Burg, Michael S**
(Pennsylvania)
Profile: p.1724
Real Estate Band 3
Table: p.1718

**Burger, Peter**
(New Hampshire)
Corporate/Commercial Band 3
Table: p.1263

**Burger, Sharon**
(Massachusetts)
Employment Band 3
Table: p.1065

**Burgess, Rick** (Florida)
Environment Band 2
Table: p.601

**Burgin, Sara** (Texas)
Profile: p.1885
Environment Band 2
Table: p.1852

**Burke, Carl** (Idaho)
Profile: p.763
Litigation Band S
Table: p.760

**Burke, David** (Florida)
Profile: p.630
Tax Band 2
Table: p.623

**Burke, James** (Ohio)
Litigation Band 4
Table: p.1617

**Burke, Kim** (Ohio)
Environment Band 2
Table: p.1612

**Burke, Lawrence B**
(Oregon)
Environment Band 3

Table: p.1672

**Burke, P John** (California)
Profile: p.281
Media & Entertainment Band 2
Table: p.266

**Burke, Robert**
(Massachusetts)
Profile: p.1088
Tax Band 3
Table: p.1084

**Burke, Steven M**
(New Hampshire)
Profile: p.1271
Corporate/Commercial Band 2
Table: p.1263
Corporate/Commercial Band 1
Table: p.1264

**Burke, Ted** (New York)
Projects Band 2
Table: p.56
Projects Band 2
Table: p.1413

**Burke, Thomas** (California)
Media & Entertainment Band 3
Table: p.263

**Burke, Jr, John K** (Virginia)
Profile: p.1981
Litigation Band 3
Table: p.19977

**Burke Jr, Raymond J**
(New York)
Transportation Band 2
Table: p.74

**Burleigh, Jennifer J**
(New York)
Private Equity Band 3
Table: p.1410

**Burling, James**
(Massachusetts)
Profile: p.1089
Antitrust Band 1
Table: p.1053

**Burman, David J**
(Washington)
Litigation Band 1
Table: p.2000

**Burmeister, Edward**
(California)
Profile: p.281
Employment Band 3
Table: p.232

**Burner, Burnie** (Texas)
Insurance Band 3
Table: p.1858

**Burnham, Beckey** (Arizona)
Profile: p.188
Real Estate Band 3
Table: p.184

**Burns, Stephen** (National)
Profile: p.91
Capital Markets Band 4
Table: p.7

**Burns, Timothy W** (Illinois)
Profile: p.823
Insurance Band 3

Table: p.796

**Burrage, Michael**
(Oklahoma)
Litigation Band 2
Table: p.1656

**Burrell, Lizabeth L**
(National)
Transportation Band 3
Table: p.74

**Burruezo, Carlos** (Florida)
Profile: p.630
Employment Band 4
Table: p.597

**Burrus, Robert** (Virginia)
Corporate/M&A Band S
Table: p.1968

**Bursky, Daniel** (National)
Profile: p.91
Capital Markets Band 3
Table: p.7

**Burstein, Richard**
(Michigan)
Profile: p.1133
Real Estate Band 2
Table: p.1130

**Burt, Antony** (Illinois)
Profile: p.823
Insurance Band 3
Table: p.795

**Burt, Donald** (Nebraska)
Corporate/M&A Band 2
Table: p.1236

**Burt, Laurie**
(Massachusetts)
Environment Band 1
Table: p.1068

**Busch, John** (Wisconsin)
Litigation Band 1
Table: p.2029

**Busch, William** (Minnesota)
Profile: p.1162
Corporate/M&A Band 2
Table: p.1152

**Buser, James D** (Nebraska)
Real Estate Band 2
Table: p.1242

**Busey, Roxane C** (Illinois)
Profile: p.823
Antitrust Band 2
Table: p.767

**Busey, Stephen D** (Florida)
Bankruptcy Band 1
Table: p.586

**Bush, Christine K**
(Rhode Island)
Litigation Up and coming
Table: p.1769

**Bush, Derek M** (National)
Profile: p.91
Financial Services
Up and coming
Table: p.24

**Bush, Gayle** (Washington)
Bankruptcy Band 1
Table: p.1991

**Bush, John K** (Kentucky)
Litigation Band 4
Table: p.942

**Bush III, F M** (Mississippi)
Profile: p.1182
Corporate/Commercial Band 2
Table: p.1174

**Busis, Richard J**
(Pennsylvania)
Corporate/M&A Band 4
Table: p.1700

**Bussard, Donald A**
(Delaware)
Profile: p.402
Corporate/M&A Band 1
Table: p.394

**Busto, Mark** (Washington)
Employment Band 1
Table: p.1995

**Butcher, David** (Indiana)
Corporate/M&A Band 3
Table: p.887

**Butler, Brian** (Wisconsin)
Litigation Band 1
Table: p.2029

**Butler, Christopher**
(Illinois)
Profile: p.823
Banking & Finance Band 3
Table: p.771

**Butler, James** (Georgia)
Construction Band 2
Table: p.682

**Butler, JoAnn** (Idaho)
Real Estate Band 1
Table: p.762

**Butler III, A Bates**
(Arizona)
Profile: p.188
Litigation Band 2
Table: p.182

**Butler Jr, John Wm
(Jack)** (Illinois)
Profile: p.823
Bankruptcy Band 1
Table: p.775

**Butler Jr, Patrick J**
(Louisiana)
Profile: p.977
Corporate/M&A Band 4
Table: p.965

**Butt, Layne J** (Nevada)
Real Estate Band 3
Table: p.1255

**Buzzell, David W**
(Pennsylvania)
Environment Band 3
Table: p.1707

**Byowitz, Michael H**
(New York)
Profile: p.1442

Antitrust Band 3
Table: p.1335

**Byrd, Robert A**
(Mississippi)
Corporate/Commercial Band 1
Table: p.1175

**Byrne, Lawrence** (New York)
Profile: p.1442
Litigation Band 3
Table: p.1388

**Byrne, Richard L**
(Pennsylvania)
Intellectual Property Band 3
Table: p.1711

**Byrnes, Peter** (Washington)
Litigation Band 1
Table: p.2000

## C

**Caballero, Michael J**
(District of Columbia)
Profile: p.505
Tax Up and coming
Table: p.488

**Cable, Franklin** (Oregon)
Profile: p.1680
Corporate/M&A Band 2
Table: p.1667

**Cable, Stuart M**
(Massachusetts)
Profile: p.1089
Corporate/M&A Band 1
Table: p.1061

**Cabot, Anthony N**
(Nevada)
Gaming & Licensing Band 1
Table: p.1251

**Cabot, Howard Ross**
(Arizona)
Litigation Band 2
Table: p.181

**Cacciabeve, Charles**
(Florida)
Profile: p.630
Construction Band 2
Table: p.590

**Cacciatore, Ronald K**
(Florida)
Litigation Band 2
Table: p.610

**Cacheris, Plato**
(District of Columbia)
Litigation Band 2
Table: p.471

**Cadwallader, John I** (Ohio)
Profile: p.1625
Real Estate Band 3
Table: p.1621

**Cadwallader, John I** (Ohio)
Profile: p.1625
Real Estate Band 3
Table: p.1621

C

**Caen, Mellissa** (Georgia)
Profile: p.707
Energy & Natural Resources
Up & coming

**Cagney, Lawrence K**
(New York)
Employee Benefits Band 2
Table: p.1362

**Cahan, James N** (Illinois)
Profile: p.823
Environment Band 4
Table: p.791

**Cahill Jr, Elwood**
(Louisiana)
Real Estate Band 2
Table: p.975

**Cahoon, Susan** (Georgia)
Profile: p.707
Litigation Band 2
Table: p.698

**Cairns, Carolyn**
(Washington)
Employment Band 1
Table: p.1995

**Cairns, James** (California)
Profile: p.281
Banking & Finance Band 3
Table: p.218

**Calabrese, Antonio J**
(Virginia)
Real Estate Band 1
Table: p.1978

**Calabrese, Joseph**
(California)
Profile: p.281
Media & Entertainment Band 2
Table: p.266

**Calamita, Paul** (Virginia)
Environment Band 2
Table: p.1973

**Caldwell, Charles** (Texas)
Profile: p.1885
Energy Band 2
Table: p.1849

**Caldwell, Stokely**
(North Carolina)
Banking & Finance Band 3
Table: p.1569

**Calfo, Angelo J**
(Washington)
Litigation Band 1
Table: p.2000

**Callahan, Michael R**
(New Hampshire)
Profile: p.1271
Litigation Band 2
Table: p.1267

**Callahan, Michael R**
(Illinois)
Healthcare Band 1
Table: p.793

**Callahan, Timothy P**
(Illinois)
Profile: p.823
Energy Band 1

Table: p.789

**Calland, Dean**
(Pennsylvania)
Environment Band 1
Table: p.1707

**Callas, Chris** (West Virginia)
Profile: p.2016
Corporate/Commercial Up
and coming
Table: p.2010

**Calvin, Charles** (Colorado)
Profile: p.358
Real Estate Band 2
Table: p.355

**Calzacorta, Carmen**
(Oregon)
Corporate/M&A Band 3
Table: p.1667

**Calzone, David B**
(Michigan)
Profile: p.1133
Employment Band 2
Table: p.1125

**Camahort, Steve L**
(California)
Profile: p.282
Corporate/M&A Band 3
Table: p.227

**Cameron, Streetar** (Iowa)
Real Estate Band 4
Table: p.917

**Cameron Jr, Donald B**
(District of Columbia)
Profile: p.91
International Trade Band 2
Table: p.42

**Camp, Leo** (Kentucky)
Real Estate Band 2
Table: p.944

**Campbell, Andrew** (Texas)
Real Estate Band 3
Table: p.1872

**Campbell, Bruce I** (Iowa)
Corporate/M&A Band 3
Table: p.909

**Campbell, Charles E**
(Georgia)
Profile: p.707
Bankruptcy Band 1
Table: p.679

**Campbell, Christopher C**
(Virginia)
Profile: p.1980
Intellectual Property Band 2
Table: p.1975

**Campbell, Daniel M**
(Virginia)
Profile: p.1981
Real Estate Band 3
Table: p.1978

**Campbell, David** (Indiana)
Litigation Band 1
Table: p.890

**Campbell, David S**
(New Mexico)
Real Estate Band 1
Table: p.1327

**Campbell, Donald** (Nevada)
Litigation Band 1
Table: p.1252

**Campbell, Douglas A**
(Pennsylvania)
Bankruptcy Band 3
Table: p.1697

**Campbell, Lawrence**
(Michigan)
Profile: p.1133
Litigation Band 1
Table: p.1128

**Campbell, Margaret
Claiborne** (Georgia)
Environment Band 2
Table: p.691

**Campbell, Margaret H**
(Georgia)
Profile: p.708
Employment Band 3
Table: p.687

**Campbell, Michael**
(New Mexico)
Profile: p.1328
Environment Band 1
Table: p.1323

**Campbell, Michael R**
(Oregon)
Environment Band 3
Table: p.1672

**Campbell, Rhett** (Texas)
Profile: p.1885
Bankruptcy Band 3
Table: p.1835

**Campbell, Roy** (Mississippi)
Profile: p.1183
Litigation Band 2
Table: p.1179

**Campbell, Scott** (Idaho)
Natural Resources Band 1
Table: p.761

**Campbell, Thomas** (Illinois)
Antitrust Band 3
Table: p.767

**Campbell, William**
(Oregon)
Profile: p.1680
Corporate/M&A Band 1
Table: p.1667

**Campbell, William J**
(Colorado)
Profile: p.358
Corporate/M&A Band 3
Table: p.346

**Campbell II, L Webb**
(Tennessee)
Litigation Band 3
Table: p.1804

**Campbell Jr, Boyd**
(North Carolina)
Banking & Finance Band 3

Table: p.1569
Corporate/M&A Band 2
Table: p.1571

**Campbell Jr, John**
(Louisiana)
Corporate/M&A Band 4
Table: p.965

**Campbell Jr, Robert R**
(Tennessee)
Profile: p.1811
Real Estate Band 2
Table: p.1808

**Campbell Jr, Robert S**
(Utah)
Litigation Band 2
Table: p.1945

**Campbell Jr, Woodrow W**
(New York)
Private Equity Band S
Table: p.1410

**Campion, Thomas**
(New Jersey)
Litigation Band 1
Table: p.1289

**Canan, Michael J** (Florida)
Tax Band 2
Table: p.624

**Candler, James** (Michigan)
Profile: p.1133
Real Estate Band 2
Table: p.1130

**Cane, Paul** (California)
Employment Band 2
Table: p.231

**Canellos, Peter C** (New
York)
Profile: p.1442
Tax Band 1
Table: p.1423

**Cannada, Barry**
(Mississippi)
Profile: p.1183
Corporate/Commercial Band 1
Table: p.1174

**Cannada, Don** (Mississippi)
Profile: p.1183
Real Estate Band 1
Table: p.1181

**Cannon, Kim D.** (Wyoming)
Litigation Band 2
Table: p.2044

**Cannon III, L Kinder**
(Florida)
Profile: p.630
Corporate/M&A Band S
Table: p.594

**Cannon Jr, George D**
(District of Columbia)
Energy Band 5
Table: p.445

**Canny, Joan M** (Florida)
Employment Band 4
Table: p.597

**Canoni, John** (New York)
Profile: p.1442
Employment Band 3
Table: p.1365

**Canterbury Jr, Joe F**
(Texas)
Profile: p.1885
Construction Band 1
Table: p.1838

**Cantlin, Richard** (Oregon)
Real Estate Band 1
Table: p.1677

**Canton, Doreen** (Ohio)
Employment Band 3
Table: p.1609

**Cantor, Matthew**
(New York)
Profile: p.1442
Bankruptcy Band 3
Table: p.1344

**Capel, Christopher**
(North Carolina)
Profile: p.1581
Corporate/M&A Band 3
Table: p.1571

**Capers, John** (Georgia)
Profile: p.708
Corporate/M&A Band 3
Table: p.684

**Caplan, David L** (New York)
Profile: p.1442
Corporate/M&A Band 4
Table: p.1354

**Caplan, Gordon** (New York)
Profile: p.1442
Technology Band 3
Table: p.1428

**Caplan, Stuart A** (New
York)
Profile: p.1442
Energy Band 3
Table: p.1367

**Caporizzo, A William**
(Massachusetts)
Profile: p.1089
Employee Benefits Band 2
Table: p.1063

**Cappellanti, Ellen** (West
Virginia)
Profile: p.2016
Corporate/Commercial Band 1
Table: p.2010
Real Estate Band 2
Table: p.2015

**Capraro Jr, Joseph A**
(Massachusetts)
Profile: p.1089
Intellectual Property Band 3
Table: p.1072

**Capshaw, Richard A**
(Texas)
Construction Band 4
Table: p.1838

**Carbino, Jeffrey M**
(Pennsylvania)
Profile: p.1724

**Casserly, James L**
(District of Columbia)
Profile: p.506
Telecom, Broadcast & Satellite
Band 4
Table: p.492

**Cassidy, Bart**
(Pennsylvania)
Environment Band 2
Table: p.1707

**Cassidy Jr, Robert C**
(National)
Profile: p.91
International Trade Band 4
Table: p.42

**Cassis, Charles** (Kentucky)
Profile: p.945
Litigation Band 3
Table: p.942

**Castaldo, Neil**
(New Hampshire)
Corporate/Commercial Band 2
Table: p.1263

**Caster, Lauren** (Arizona)
Profile: p.188
Environment Band 2
Table: p.179

**Cates, C Thomas**
(Tennessee)
Real Estate Band 2
Table: p.1808

**Cathcart, Patrick**
(California)
Profile: p.282
Insurance Band 1
Table: p.243

**Catillaz, Margaret A**
(New York)
Immigration Band 3
Table: p.1376

**Caulkins, Charles** (Florida)
Profile: p.631
Employment Band 3
Table: p.597

**Cavalieri, Nick V** (Ohio)
Bankruptcy Band 3
Table: p.1600

**Cavanagh, Rita A**
(District of Columbia)
Tax Band 4
Table: p.488

**Cavanagh Jr, Joseph V**
(Rhode Island)
Litigation Band 1
Table: p.1769

**Cave, Bradley** (Wyoming)
Profile: p.2047
Employment Band 1
Table: p.2042

**Caverly, Joseph L**
(Louisiana)
Profile: p.978
Corporate/M&A Band 3
Table: p.965

**Cawley, Douglas** (Texas)
Profile: p.1885
Intellectual Property Band 3
Table: p.1860

**Cederoth, Richard A**
(Illinois)
Profile: p.824
Intellectual Property Band 2
Table: p.799

**Celebrezze, Bruce**
(California)
Insurance Band 3
Table: p.243

**Cendali, Dale** (New York)
Profile: p.1443
Intellectual Property Band 1
Table: p.1385
Media & Entertainment Band 1
Table: p.1404

**Cerabino, Thomas M** (New York)
Profile: p.1443
Corporate/M&A Band 4
Table: p.1354

**Cerasia, Edward** (New Jersey)
Profile: p.1296
Employment Band 3
Table: p.1282

**Ceriani, Gary** (Colorado)
Litigation Band 1
Table: p.353

**Cerone, Rudy** (Louisiana)
Profile: p.978
Corporate/M&A Band 2
Table: p.965

**Chadakoff, Richard** (New York)
Real Estate Band 5
Table: p.1417

**Chadwick, James**
(California)
Profile: p.282
Media & Entertainment Band 4
Table: p.263

**Chaffetz, Peter** (New York)
Profile: p.1443
Insurance Band 2
Table: p.1379

**Chalk, Wm David**
(Maryland)
Profile: p.1038
Corporate/M&A
Up and coming
Table: p.1025

**Chambers, Robert C**
(Georgia)
Construction Band 2
Table: p.682

**Chamlin, Marc** (New York)
Profile: p.1443
Media & Entertainment Band 2
Table: p.1401

**Champoux, David** (Maine)
Profile: p.1011
Corporate/M&A Band 2

Table: p.1000

**Chandler, John A** (Georgia)
Profile: p.708
Litigation Band 1
Table: p.698

**Chang, Corlis J** (Hawaii)
Litigation Band 1
Table: p.745

**Chang, Leo** (New York)
Profile: p.91
Transportation Band 2
Table: p.74

**Chang, Wesley Y S**
(Hawaii)
Real Estate Band 3
Table: p.748

**Chanin, Jeffrey R**
(California)
Profile: p.282
Intellectual Property Band 4
Table: p.248

**Chapin, David C**
(Massachusetts)
Profile: p.1089
Corporate/M&A Band 2
Table: p.1061
Private Equity Band 1
Table: p.1078

**Chapman, Jeffrey A**
(Texas)
Profile: p.1885
Corporate/M&A Band 4
Table: p.1840

**Chapman, William**
(Washington)
Environment Band 2
Table: p.1996

**Chapman, William L**
(New Hampshire)
Litigation Band 3
Table: p.1267

**Charbonneau, Robert P**
(Florida)
Profile: p.631
Bankruptcy Band 2
Table: p.586

**Charkoudian, Stephen G**
(Massachusetts)
Profile: p.1089
Intellectual Property Band 3
Table: p.1072

**Charles, Scott K** (New York)
Profile: p.1443
Bankruptcy Band 3
Table: p.1344

**Charness, Michael**
(National)
Profile: p.91
Government Contracts Band 3
Table: p.30

**Charney, Steven M**
(New York)
Profile: p.1444
Construction Band 2
Table: p.1351

**Chase, Jeffrey** (Colorado)
Litigation Band 1
Table: p.353

**Chase III, Lee James**
(Tennessee)
Profile: p.1811
Litigation Band 3
Table: p.1804

**Chason, Craig** (Virginia)
Profile: p.1981
Corporate/M&A Band 1
Table: p.1967

**Chason, James R.**
(Maryland)
Profile: p.1038
Litigation Band 3
Table: p.1032

**Chatfield, Andrea G**
(New Hampshire)
Profile: p.1271
Employment Band 3
Table: p.1265

**Chatham, Henry**
(Mississippi)
Corporate/Commercial Band 1
Table: p.1174

**Chatilovicz, Peter**
(District of Columbia)
Employment Band 2
Table: p.439

**Chatterjee, I Neel**
(California)
Profile: p.282
Intellectual Property Up and coming
Table: p.248

**Chatzinoff, Howard**
(New York)
Profile: p.1444
Corporate/M&A Band 4
Table: p.1354

**Chaves, Robert** (Florida)
Tax Band 4
Table: p.623

**Chaykin, Steven E**
(Florida)
Litigation Band 1
Table: p.610

**Cheatham, Richard R**
(Georgia)
Profile: p.708
Banking & Finance Band 2
Table: p.677

**Cheatham, Robin B**
(Louisiana)
Profile: p.978
Corporate/M&A Band 3
Table: p.965

**Cheatwood, Roy C**
(Louisiana)
Profile: p.978
Litigation Band 1
Table: p.973

**Check, Raymond B**
(National)
Profile: p.91

Capital Markets Band 2
Table: p.13
Capital Markets Band 3
Table: p.18

**Checov, Martin S**
(California)
Profile: p.282
Insurance Band 2
Table: p.243

**Cheek III, James**
(Tennessee)
Profile: p.1811
Corporate/M&A Band 1
Table: p.1799

**Cheetham, Janet**
(Washington)
Immigration Band 1
Table: p.1997

**Chefitz, Joel** (Illinois)
Antitrust Band 2
Table: p.767

**Chehi, Mark S** (Delaware)
Profile: p.402
Bankruptcy Band 2
Table: p.389

**Cheng, Loyti** (New York)
Profile: p.1444
Environment Band 3
Table: p.1373

**Chepiga, Michael J**
(New York)
Profile: p.1444
Litigation Band 1
Table: p.1390

**Cherken Jr, Harry S**
(Pennsylvania)
Real Estate Band 3
Table: p.1718

**Chernekoff, Michael A**
(Louisiana)
Profile: p.978
Environment Band 1
Table: p.970

**Chernof, Steve** (Wisconsin)
Real Estate Band 1
Table: p.2030

**Cherot, Suzanne** (Alaska)
Real Estate Band 1
Table: p.172

**Cherry, Steven F** (Virginia)
Profile: p.1982
Litigation Band 3
Table: p.1977

**Chertok, Mark** (New York)
Profile: p.1444
Environment Band 2
Table: p.1371

**Chesler, Evan** (New York)
Profile: p.1444
Antitrust Band 3
Table: p.1335
Intellectual Property Band 2
Table: p.1384
Intellectual Property Band 1
Table: p.1385
Litigation Band 1

Table: p.1388

**Chesler, Robert D**
(New Jersey)
Profile: p.1297
Litigation **Band 1**
Table: p.1289

**Chesshire, Mary Claire**
(Maryland)
Profile: p.1038
Employee Benefits **Band 3**
Table: p.1027

**Chester, Charles L (Rusty)** (Arizona)
Profile: p.188
Employment **Band 4**
Table: p.178

**Chestler, Stuart** (Oregon)
Corporate/M&A **Band 3**
Table: p.1667

**Chiappari, Ted** (New York)
Immigration **Band 3**
Table: p.1376

**Chida, Junaid H** (New York)
Profile: p.1444
Projects **Band 4**
Table: p.1413

**Chierichella, John W**
(National)
Government Contracts **Band 2**
Table: p.30

**Child, Ralph**
(Massachusetts)
Profile: p.1089
Environment **Band 1**
Table: p.1068

**Childress, Tyrone R**
(California)
Insurance **Band 3**
Table: p.245

**Childs, Linton J** (Illinois)
Profile: p.824
Litigation **Up and coming**
Table: p.802

**Chiles IV, EB (Chip)**
(Arkansas)
Profile: p.208
Litigation **Band 4**
Table: p.205

**Chilton, Frederick**
(California)
Profile: p.282
Tax **Band 3**
Table: p.274

**Chinn, Adam D** (New York)
Profile: p.1445
Employee Benefits **Band 2**
Table: p.1362

**Chisholm, David** (Montana)
Corporate/M&A **Band 1**
Table: p.1222

**Chittick, Michael D**
(Rhode Island)
Profile: p.1771
Employment **Up and coming**
Table: p.1768

**Chlebus, Andrew J**
(Rhode Island)
Profile: p.1771
Corporate/Commercial **Band 1**
Table: p.1766

**Choi, Chuck C** (Hawaii)
Bankruptcy **Band 1**
Table: p.739

**Choi, Paul** (Illinois)
Profile: p.824
Corporate/M&A **Band 3**
Table: p.781

**Chory, John**
(Massachusetts)
Profile: p.1089
Private Equity **Band 3**
Table: p.1078

**Chriss, Timothy** (Maryland)
Real Estate **Band 2**
Table: p.1035

**Christaldi, Ronald A**
(Florida)
Healthcare **Band 3**
Table: p.604

**Christensen, Amy D**
(Montana)
Employment **Band 3**
Table: p.1223

**Christensen, Craig W**
(Idaho)
Bankruptcy **Band 2**
Table: p.758

**Christensen, Dana**
(Montana)
Litigation **Band 1**
Table: p.1225

**Christensen, Douglas**
(North Dakota)
Corporate/Commercial **Band 2**
Table: p.1590

**Christensen, Douglas R**
(Minnesota)
Profile: p.1162
Employment **Band 2**
Table: p.1154

**Christensen, Stephen K**
(Utah)
Real Estate **Band 3**
Table: p.1947

**Christensen, Wallace A**
(District of Columbia)
Insurance **Band 4**
Table: p.461

**Christensen III, Henry**
(New York)
Profile: p.92
Wealth Management **Band 1**
Table: p.81

**Christian, Betty Jo**
(National)
Profile: p.92
Transportation **Band 3**
Table: p.69

**Christian, Joseph J**

(Massachusetts)
Profile: p.1089
Real Estate **Band 3**
Table: p.1081

**Christian, Thomas W**
(Alabama)
Profile: p.155
Litigation **Band 3**
Table: p.152

**Christiansen, Jon P**
(Wisconsin)
Profile: p.2032
Litigation **Band 1**
Table: p.2029

**Christianson, Cabot**
(Alaska)
Bankruptcy **Band 1**
Table: p.167

**Christy, Angela** (Minnesota)
Profile: p.1162
Real Estate **Band 2**
Table: p.1160

**Chu, Morgan** (California)
Intellectual Property **✪**
Table: p.248

**Chumrau, Gary B**
(Montana)
Corporate/M&A **Band 2**
Table: p.1222

**Chun, Deborah** (Hawaii)
Profile: p.750
Real Estate **Band 1**
Table: p.748

**Churchill, David A**
(National)
Profile: p.92
Government Contracts **Band 2**
Table: p.30

**Churchill, Stanley** (Kansas)
Employment **Band 2**
Table: p.926

**Chused, Wesley S**
(National)
Transportation **Band 2**
Table: p.71

**Ciabarra, Laura G**
(Connecticut)
Profile: p.1445
Real Estate **Band 5**
Table: p.1417

**Cicarella, Thomas** (Ohio)
Profile: p.1625
Banking & Finance **Band 2**
Table: p.1598

**Cicero Jr, Frank** (Illinois)
Profile: p.824
Litigation **Band 4**
Table: p.802

**Cieri, Richard** (New York)
Profile: p.1445
Bankruptcy **Band 1**
Table: p.1344

**Ciesla, Frank R** (New Jersey)
Healthcare **Band 1**

Table: p.1287

**Cifelli, James** (Georgia)
Bankruptcy **Band 2**
Table: p.679

**Cifu, Douglas A** (New York)
Profile: p.1445
Private Equity **Band 3**
Table: p.1407

**Cimino, Michael** (West Virginia)
Profile: p.2016
Litigation **Band 2**
Table: p.2013

**Ciresi, Michael V**
(Minnesota)
Profile: p.1162
Litigation **Band 1**
Table: p.1156
Litigation **Band 1**
Table: p.1157

**Ciriaco, Anthony C** (Ohio)
Profile: p.1625
Employee Benefits **Band 3**
Table: p.1607

**Civins, Jeff** (Texas)
Environment **✪**
Table: p.1852

**Clair, John** (California)
Tax **Band 1**
Table: p.274

**Clancy, Patrick L**
(Maryland)
Employment **Band 3**
Table: p.1028

**Clarence, Nanci L**
(California)
Litigation **Band 2**
Table: p.258

**Clark, Anthony W**
(Delaware)
Profile: p.402
Bankruptcy **Band 3**
Table: p.389
Chancery **Band 3**
Table: p.392

**Clark, Bruce F** (Kentucky)

**Clark, Donald** (Mississippi)
Profile: p.1183
Corporate/Commercial **Band 3**
Table: p.1174

**Clark, Glenn A** (New Jersey)
Profile: p.1297
Litigation **Band 2**
Table: p.1289

**Clark, Harry L** (National)
Profile: p.92
International Trade **Band 5**
Table: p.42

**Clark, James** (New York)
Capital Markets **Band 3**
Table: p.7

**Clark, James** (Illinois)
Profile: p.824
Banking & Finance **Band 1**

Table: p.771

**Clark, James P** (California)
Profile: p.283
Litigation **Band 4**
Table: p.257

**Clark, James R** (Wisconsin)
Profile: p.2032
Litigation **Band 1**
Table: p.2029

**Clark, John** (California)
Profile: p.283
Construction **Band 1**
Table: p.225

**Clark, Kenneth A**
(California)
Profile: p.283
Corporate/M&A **Band 4**
Table: p.227

**Clark, Matthew J**
(District of Columbia)
Profile: p.92
International Trade **Band 3**
Table: p.42

**Clark, Merlyn** (Idaho)
Litigation **Band 2**
Table: p.760

**Clark, Peter** (Pennsylvania)
Profile: p.1724
Bankruptcy **Band 3**
Table: p.1697

**Clark, Peter D** (National)
Transportation **Band 4**
Table: p.74

**Clark, Reginald J** (Georgia)
Profile: p.708
Tax **Band 3**
Table: p.703

**Clark, Reuben G**
(North Carolina)
Real Estate **Band 3**
Table: p.1579

**Clark, Robert** (Utah)
Litigation **Band 2**
Table: p.1945

**Clark, Ronald** (Arkansas)
Corporate/Commercial **Band 1**
Table: p.201
Corporate/Commercial **Band 2**
Table: p.201

**Clark, Thomas C**
(Alabama)
Profile: p.156
Real Estate **Band 3**
Table: p.153

**Clark Jr, Blane** (Louisiana)
Profile: p.978
Corporate/M&A **Band 4**
Table: p.965

**Clark Jr, D Lewis** (Ohio)
Profile: p.1625
Employment **Up and coming**
Table: p.1609

**Clark Jr, L Jude** (Kentucky)
Profile: p.945

**C**

Real Estate Band 2
Table: p.944

**Clarke, Donald**
(District of Columbia)
Energy Band 5
Table: p.445

**Clarke, Shaun G**
(Louisiana)
Litigation Band 1
Table: p.973

**Clary, Richard W** (New York)
Profile: p.1445
Litigation Band 3
Table: p.1388

**Claster, William D**
(California)
Profile: p.283
Employment Band 4
Table: p.231

**Claverie Sr, Philip deV**
(Louisiana)
Profile: p.978
Banking & Finance Band 1
Table: p.963
Real Estate Band 1
Table: p.975

**Clawson, Carol** (Utah)
Employment Band 2
Table: p.1944

**Clay, A Stephens** (Georgia)
Profile: p.708
International Arbitration
Band 4
Table: p.36
Litigation Band 2
Table: p.698

**Clay, Richard H C**
(Kentucky)
Litigation Band 3
Table: p.942

**Clayton, Yvonne Lee**
(Pennsylvania)
Profile: p.1724
Real Estate Up and coming
Table: p.1718

**Clayton III, Walter J (Jay)**
(National)
Profile: p.92
Capital Markets
Up and coming
Table: p.7

**Cleary, David L** (Vermont)
Litigation Band 2
Table: p.1959

**Cleary, John J**
(Massachusetts)
Profile: p.1090
Employee Benefits Band 1
Table: p.1063

**Cleary, Richard S**
(Kentucky)
Employment Band 1
Table: p.939

**Clees, Joseph T** (Arizona)
Profile: p.189

Employment Band 2
Table: p.178

**Cleland, A Craig** (Georgia)
Profile: p.709
Employment Band 4
Table: p.687

**Clemens, Steven E**
(New York)
Profile: p.1445
Tax Up and coming
Table: p.1423

**Clement, Zack** (Texas)
Profile: p.1886
Bankruptcy Band 4
Table: p.1835

**Clement Jr, Roger A**
(Maine)
Profile: p.1011
Corporate/M&A Band 1
Table: p.1000

**Clement Jr, W Rodney**
(Mississippi)
Profile: p.1183
Real Estate Band 2
Table: p.1181

**Clements, William L**
(National)
Profile: p.92
International Trade Band 2
Table: p.41

**Clemow, Brian**
(Connecticut)
Employment Band 2
Table: p.376

**Cleveland III, William**
(South Carolina)
Profile: p.1781
Litigation Band 3
Table: p.1778

**Clifton, R Brent** (Texas)
Tax Band 4
Table: p.1875

**Climan, Richard** (California)
Corporate/M&A Band 2
Table: p.227

**Clinton, William J**
(National)
Profile: p.92
International Trade Band 5
Table: p.42

**Cloherty, Thomas**
(Connecticut)
Employment Band 1
Table: p.376

**Clonts, David R** (Texas)
Profile: p.1886
Intellectual Property Band 2
Table: p.1860

**Closson, Tom**
(New Hampshire)
Employment Band 3
Table: p.1265

**Cloud, Douglas** (Georgia)
Profile: p.709
Environment Band 3

Table: p.691

**Cloutier, Andrew J**
(New Mexico)
Profile: p.1328
Environment Band 2
Table: p.1323

**Clowdus, W Michael**
(Colorado)
Profile: p.358
Real Estate Band 1
Table: p.355

**Coalson Jr, John L**
(Georgia)
Profile: p.709
Tax Band 1
Table: p.703

**Coats, William M** (Texas)
Construction Band 2
Table: p.1838

**Coats, William S**
(California)
Profile: p.283
Intellectual Property Band 4
Table: p.248

**Cobb, Jennifer Dunn**
(Washington)
Real Estate Band 3
Table: p.2002

**Cobb, Kelly** (Texas)
Immigration Band 2
Table: p.1856

**Coben, Jerome L**
(California)
Profile: p.283
Corporate/M&A Band 2
Table: p.227

**Cochran, Eric L** (New York)
Profile: p.1445
Corporate/M&A Band 4
Table: p.1354

**Cockrell, Dale R** (Montana)
Natural Resources Band 1
Table: p.1228

**Cockrill, Donald A**
(South Carolina)
Profile: p.1782
Litigation Band 3
Table: p.1778

**Cockrum, James**
(Kentucky)
Profile: p.945
Employment Band 1
Table: p.939

**Cody, W J Michael**
(Tennessee)
Litigation Band 3
Table: p.1804

**Coffey, John** (New York)
Profile: p.1445
Litigation Band 1
Table: p.1390

**Coffey, Peter L** (Wisconsin)
Corporate/M&A Band 3
Table: p.2025

**Cogan, J Kevin** (Ohio)
Profile: p.1625
Litigation Band 4
Table: p.1617

**Cogan Jr, John P** (Texas)
Profile: p.1886
Energy Band 1
Table: p.1847
Projects Band 1
Table: p.56
Projects Band 1
Table: p.1869

**Cogbill III, John V** (Virginia)
Real Estate Band 1
Table: p.1978
Transportation Band 2
Table: p.71

**Cogen, Douglas N**
(California)
Profile: p.283
Corporate/M&A Band 4
Table: p.227

**Coggeshall, Christopher J W** (Maine)
Profile: p.1011
Real Estate Band 2
Table: p.1008

**Coglianese, Matthew**
(Florida)
Profile: p.631
Environment Band 2
Table: p.601

**Cogut, Charles 'Casey'**
(New York)
Profile: p.1445
Corporate/M&A Band 1
Table: p.1354
Private Equity Band 1
Table: p.1407

**Cohen, Abbi L**
(Pennsylvania)
Profile: p.1724
Environment Band 2
Table: p.1707

**Cohen, Ben** (New York)
Tax Band 2
Table: p.1423

**Cohen, Bret A**
(Massachusetts)
Profile: p.1090
Employment Band 3
Table: p.1065

**Cohen, Charles**
(District of Columbia)
Profile: p.506
Employment Band 2
Table: p.439

**Cohen, David** (Maryland)
Profile: p.1038
Real Estate Band 4
Table: p.1035

**Cohen, David**
(District of Columbia)
Profile: p.506
Energy Band 5
Table: p.441

**Cohen, Eric M** (Texas)
Construction Up and coming
Table: p.1838

**Cohen, Ezra H** (Georgia)
Bankruptcy Band 2
Table: p.679

**Cohen, H Rodgin** (New York)
Profile: p.1446
Corporate/M&A Band 1
Table: p.1354
Financial Services ✪
Table: p.24

**Cohen, Harry P** (New York)
Profile: p.1446
Insurance Band 3
Table: p.1379

**Cohen, Jerold** (Georgia)
Profile: p.709
Tax Band 1
Table: p.703

**Cohen, Joel** (New York)
Profile: p.1446
Employment Band 3
Table: p.1365

**Cohen, Joel M** (New York)
Profile: p.1446
Antitrust Band 4
Table: p.1335

**Cohen, Jon** (Arizona)
Profile: p.189
Corporate/M&A Band 2
Table: p.176

**Cohen, Jules** (Florida)
Profile: p.631
Bankruptcy Band 2
Table: p.586

**Cohen, Marc S** (California)
Profile: p.283
Bankruptcy Band 4
Table: p.222

**Cohen, Matthew**
(Washington)
Profile: p.2004
Environment Band 2
Table: p.1996

**Cohen, Michael Marks**
(New York)
Transportation Band 3
Table: p.74

**Cohen, Murry B** (Texas)
Profile: p.1886
Litigation Band 3
Table: p.1866

**Cohen, Nancy** (California)
Profile: p.284
Insurance Band 3
Table: p.245

**Cohen, R Scott** (Texas)
Profile: p.1886
Corporate/M&A Band 4
Table: p.1840

**Cohen, Richard** (Arizona)
Employment Band 1
Table: p.178

**Cohen, Robin L** (New York)
Profile: p.1446
Insurance Band 3
Table: p.1379

**Cohen, Stanley H**
(Pennsylvania)
Profile: p.1724
Intellectual Property Band 2
Table: p.1711

**Cohen, Stephen M L**
(Massachusetts)
Private Equity Band 3
Table: p.1078

**Cohen, Steven** (New Jersey)
Profile: p.1297
Corporate/M&A Band 2
Table: p.1278

**Cohen, Steven**
(New Hampshire)
Corporate/Commercial Band 2
Table: p.1263
Corporate/Commercial Band 1
Table: p.1264

**Cohen, Steven N**
(North Carolina)
Profile: p.1581
Capital Markets Band 3
Table: p.18

**Cohn, Daniel**
(Massachusetts)
Profile: p.1090
Bankruptcy Band 1
Table: p.1058

**Cohn, Joel M**
(District of Columbia)
Profile: p.506
Employment Band 3
Table: p.439

**Cohn, Joshua** (New York)
Profile: p.93
Capital Markets Band 2
Table: p.15

**Cohn, Robert** (National)
Profile: p.93
Transportation Band 2
Table: p.67

**Coil, James** (Georgia)
Profile: p.709
Employment Band 3
Table: p.687

**Cokeley, Bryan**
(West Virginia)
Employment Band 1
Table: p.2012

**Cokinos, Gregory** (Texas)
Construction Band 2
Table: p.1838

**Colacino, Antonio** (Iowa)
Real Estate Band 1
Table: p.917

**Colbo, Kimberlee A**
(Alaska)
Employment Band 2
Table: p.169

**Cole, Alexandra** (Illinois)
Construction Band 3
Table: p.778

**Cole, Howard** (Nevada)
Employment Band 1
Table: p.1248

**Cole, J Chase** (Tennessee)
Profile: p.1811
Corporate/M&A Band 1
Table: p.1799

**Cole, Terry** (Florida)
Environment Band 2
Table: p.601

**Cole, Thomas A** (Illinois)
Profile: p.824
Corporate/M&A Band 1
Table: p.781

**Cole, William** (California)
Employment Band 4
Table: p.231

**Cole III, Kenneth M**
(Maine)
Real Estate Band 2
Table: p.1008

**Coleman, Aubrey L**
(Georgia)
Construction Band 2
Table: p.682

**Coleman, Gregory S**
(Texas)
Profile: p.1886
Litigation Band 2
Table: p.1866

**Coleman, Ira** (Florida)
Profile: p.631
Healthcare Band 1
Table: p.604

**Coleman, James** (Texas)
Litigation Band 2
Table: p.1865

**Coleman, John** (Alabama)
Employment Band 3
Table: p.150

**Coleman, Kathryn A**
(California)
Profile: p.284
Bankruptcy Band 4
Table: p.222

**Coleman, Lynn R**
(District of Columbia)
Profile: p.506
Energy Band 3
Table: p.445

**Coleman, Patrick D**
(Florida)
Employment Band S
Table: p.597

**Coleman, Payson**
(National)
Profile: p.93
Transportation Band 2
Table: p.64

**Coleman, Thomas**
(California)
Profile: p.284
Banking & Finance Band 3
Table: p.218

**Coleman, Tony C**
(Kentucky)
Profile: p.945
Employment Band 3
Table: p.939

**Coleman, W Chris**
(Oklahoma)
Corporate/Commercial Band 2
Table: p.1653

**Colen, Frederick**
(Pennsylvania)
Profile: p.1724
Intellectual Property Band 2
Table: p.1711

**Coletti, Robert E** (Ohio)
Corporate/M&A Band 3
Table: p.1605

**Colleran, Kevin** (Nebraska)
Litigation Band 3
Table: p.1239

**Colletta, Anthony J**
(New York)
Profile: p.1446
Real Estate Band 4
Table: p.1417

**Collier, Philip W** (Kentucky)
Profile: p.945
Litigation Band 2
Table: p.942

**Collings, Robert L**
(Pennsylvania)
Environment Band 2
Table: p.1707

**Collins, Brendan K**
(Pennsylvania)
Profile: p.1725
Environment Band 3
Table: p.1707

**Collins, Dennis G**
(Missouri)
Employment Band 3
Table: p.1195

**Collins, John** (New York)
Profile: p.1446
Antitrust Band 4
Table: p.1335

**Collins, Joseph P** (Illinois)
Profile: p.93
Capital Markets Band 2
Table: p.15

**Collins, Kevin H** (Iowa)
Litigation Band 2
Table: p.914

**Collins, Mark D** (Delaware)
Profile: p.403
Bankruptcy Band 1
Table: p.389

**Collins, W Dale** (New York)
Profile: p.1446
Antitrust Band 3

Table: p.1335

**Collins Jr, P Clarkson**
(Delaware)
Profile: p.403
Chancery Band 4
Table: p.392

**Colodny, Michael** (Florida)
Insurance Band 2
Table: p.607

**Colson, Dean** (Florida)
Profile: p.631
Litigation Band 2
Table: p.609

**Colton, Neal** (Pennsylvania)
Bankruptcy Band 2
Table: p.1697

**Colton, Roberta** (Florida)
Bankruptcy Band 1
Table: p.586

**Colvin, R Keith** (Louisiana)
Profile: p.978
Real Estate Band 2
Table: p.975

**Comerford, David L**
(Pennsylvania)
Profile: p.1725
Litigation Up and coming
Table: p.1715

**Comiter, Richard** (Florida)
Tax Band 2
Table: p.623

**Commander III, Charles E** (Florida)
Profile: p.631
Real Estate Band 3
Table: p.617

**Compton, Charles T**
(California)
Profile: p.284
Antitrust Band 3
Table: p.216

**Compton, Paul** (Alabama)
Profile: p.156
Banking & Finance Band 1
Table: p.147

**Conard, David** (Vermont)
Real Estate Band 2
Table: p.1961

**Conde, Kathryn Keough**
(Massachusetts)
Antitrust Band 3
Table: p.1053

**Condlin, Andrew** (Virginia)
Real Estate Band 1
Table: p.1978

**Condo, James** (Arizona)
Profile: p.189
Litigation Band 4
Table: p.181

**Condon, Creighton**
(New York)
Profile: p.1446
Corporate/M&A Band 2
Table: p.1354

**Confalone, Perry W**
(Hawaii)
Employment Band 3
Table: p.742

**Conklin, Robert**
(New Mexico)
Employment Band 1
Table: p.1321

**Conlan, James F** (Illinois)
Profile: p.824
Bankruptcy Band 3
Table: p.775

**Conley, Cristin A** (Florida)
Profile: p.631
Tax Associate to watch
Table: p.623

**Conlon, Michael W** (Texas)
Profile: p.1886
Corporate/M&A Band 2
Table: p.1840

**Conlon, William** (Illinois)
Profile: p.825
Litigation Band 2
Table: p.802

**Connelly, Michael** (Texas)
Environment Band 1
Table: p.1853

**Connelly, Vincent J**
(Illinois)
Profile: p.825
Litigation Band 1
Table: p.802
Litigation Band 1
Table: p.803

**Connelly, Warren E**
(District of Columbia)
Profile: p.93
International Trade Band 3
Table: p.42

**Conner, Stewart** (Kentucky)
Profile: p.945
Corporate/M&A Band 1
Table: p.937

**Connery, Robert T**
(Colorado)
Profile: p.358
Environment Band 2
Table: p.350

**Conniff, Dennis J**
(Kentucky)
Profile: p.945
Environment Band 2
Table: p.941

**Connolly, Annemargaret**
(District of Columbia)
Profile: p.506
Environment Band 2
Table: p.450

**Connolly, Dennis J**
(Georgia)
Profile: p.709
Bankruptcy Band 1
Table: p.679

**Connolly, Michael J**
(New Hampshire)
Litigation Band 4

**C**

Table: p.1267

**Connolly, Robert M**
(Kentucky)
Profile: p.946
Litigation Band 3
Table: p.942

**Connolly, Theresa** (Virginia)
Profile: p.1981
Employment Band 2
Table: p.1971

**Connolly Jr, Arthur G**
(Delaware)
Profile: p.403
Intellectual Property Band 3
Table: p.397

**Connor, Terence** (Florida)
Profile: p.631
Employment Band 1
Table: p.597

**Connors, Eugene**
(Pennsylvania)
Profile: p.1725
Employment Band 2
Table: p.1703

**Conrad, Albert H** (Georgia)
Profile: p.709
Banking & Finance Band 1
Table: p.677

**Conrad, David** (Ohio)
Real Estate Band 2
Table: p.1621

**Conrad, Walter** (Texas)
Profile: p.1886
Environment Band 1
Table: p.1853

**Conrad Jr, Winthrop B**
(New York)
Profile: p.93
Capital Markets Band 3
Table: p.7

**Conroy, Joseph W** (Virginia)
Corporate/M&A Band 1
Table: p.1967

**Constantine, Lloyd**
(New York)
Antitrust Band 2
Table: p.1335

**Constine III, David E**
(Virginia)
Employment Band 3
Table: p.1971

**Contratto, Dana**
(District of Columbia)
Profile: p.506
Energy Band 4
Table: p.445

**Conway, Gregory B**
(Wisconsin)
Litigation Band 2
Table: p.2029

**Conway, Michael M**
(Illinois)
Profile: p.825
Media & Entertainment Band 1
Table: p.806

**Conway, Susan** (Texas)
Insurance Band 3
Table: p.1858

**Conway, Timothy R**
(Illinois)
Profile: p.825
Construction Band 3
Table: p.778

**Coogan, Peter**
(Massachusetts)
Banking & Finance Band 2
Table: p.1055

**Cook, Bryson** (Maryland)
Corporate/M&A Band 1
Table: p.1025

**Cook, Guy** (Iowa)
Litigation Band 2
Table: p.914

**Cook, James G**
(New Hampshire)
Profile: p.1271
Corporate/Commercial Band 2
Table: p.1263

**Cook, Jay** (Minnesota)
Profile: p.1162
Real Estate Band 1
Table: p.1160

**Cook, Melanie K**
(California)
Media & Entertainment Band 3
Table: p.266

**Cook, Michael** (Colorado)
Profile: p.359
Construction Band 1
Table: p.345

**Cook, Michael L** (New
York)
Profile: p.1446
Bankruptcy Band 4
Table: p.1344

**Cook, Philip C** (Georgia)
Profile: p.709
Tax Band 2
Table: p.703

**Cook, Rand** (Utah)
Real Estate Band 3
Table: p.1947

**Cook Bush, Antoinette**
(District of Columbia)
Profile: p.506
Telecom, Broadcast & Satellite
Band 4
Table: p.492

**Cooke, Gregg** (Texas)
Environment Band 4
Table: p.1852

**Cooke, Susan**
(Massachusetts)
Profile: p.1090
Environment Band 1
Table: p.1068

**Cooney, J Gordon**
(Pennsylvania)
Profile: p.1725
Litigation Band 2

Table: p.1714

**Cooney, John R**
(New Mexico)
Environment Band 1
Table: p.1323

**Cooney III, James P**
(North Carolina)
Profile: p.1581
Litigation Band 2
Table: p.1577

**Cooney Jr, Robert L**
(Pennsylvania)
Profile: p.1725
Real Estate Band 3
Table: p.1718

**Coonrod, Stephan**
(Washington)
Corporate/Commercial Band 2
Table: p.1992

**Cooper, Bo**
(District of Columbia)
Profile: p.506
Immigration Band 3
Table: p.459

**Cooper, Brent** (Texas)
Insurance Band 1
Table: p.1858

**Cooper, James** (New York)
Profile: p.1447
Banking & Finance Band 1
Table: p.1339

**Cooper, James** (Texas)
Profile: p.1886
Insurance Band 3
Table: p.1858

**Cooper, Jay L** (California)
Profile: p.284
Media & Entertainment Band 2
Table: p.266

**Cooper, John H** (Alabama)
Corporate/Commercial Band 2
Table: p.148

**Cooper, John L** (California)
Intellectual Property Band 4
Table: p.248

**Cooper, Marc** (Florida)
Profile: p.632
Litigation Band 2
Table: p.615

**Cooper, Richard**
(District of Columbia)
Healthcare Band 2
Table: p.456

**Cooper, Robert E**
(California)
Profile: p.284
Antitrust ✪
Table: p.216
Litigation Band 2
Table: p.257

**Cooper, Ronald**
(District of Columbia)
Profile: p.507
Employment Band 3
Table: p.439

**Cooper, Samuel W** (Texas)
Profile: p.1887
Litigation Up & Coming

**Cooperman, Harriet E**
(Maryland)
Profile: p.1038
Employment Band 3
Table: p.1028

**Copeland, Gregory** (Texas)
Profile: p.1887
Energy Band 2
Table: p.1849

**Copen, Robert A** (New
York)
Profile: p.1447
Banking & Finance Up and
coming
Table: p.1339

**Copenhaver, W Andrew**
(North Carolina)
Profile: p.1581
Antitrust Band 1
Table: p.1568
Litigation Band 2
Table: p.1577

**Coran, Michael**
(Pennsylvania)
Litigation Band 2
Table: p.1715

**Corash, Michèle B**
(California)
Profile: p.284
Environment Band 1
Table: p.236

**Corbett, Sherrill A**
(Oregon)
Profile: p.1680
Corporate/M&A Band 3
Table: p.1667

**Corbin, Robert L**
(California)
Litigation Band 2
Table: p.258

**Corbyn, George** (Oklahoma)
Litigation Band 1
Table: p.1656

**Cordell, David R**
(Oklahoma)
Employment Band 1
Table: p.1654

**Cordell, Ruffin**
(District of Columbia)
Profile: p.507
Intellectual Property Band 3
Table: p.466

**Cordero, Frank** (Florida)
Profile: p.632
Tax Band 4
Table: p.623

**Cordero, Luis** (Florida)
Profile: p.632
Immigration Band 1
Table: p.606

**Corgan, Brian** (Georgia)
Profile: p.709
Construction Band 2

Table: p.682

**Corken, Heather M** (Texas)
Profile: p.1887
Environment Band 3
Table: p.1852

**Corlew, John** (Mississippi)
Litigation Band 1
Table: p.1179

**Cornell, James L** (Texas)
Insurance Band 3
Table: p.1858

**Cornett, J Gregory**
(Kentucky)
Profile: p.946
Environment Up and coming
Table: p.941

**Corn-Revere, Robert**
(District of Columbia)
Media & Entertainment Band 1
Table: p.477

**Corr, Christopher F**
(National)
Profile: p.93
International Trade Band 4
Table: p.42

**Corr, Kelly** (Washington)
Litigation Band 2
Table: p.2000

**Corrales, Carmen Amalia**
(National)
Profile: p.93
Capital Markets Band 4
Table: p.7

**Correro III, Anthony J**
(Louisiana)
Profile: p.978
Corporate/M&A Band 1
Table: p.965

**Corretti, Douglas P**
(Alabama)
Real Estate Band S
Table: p.154

**Cortell, Nina** (Texas)
Litigation Band 2
Table: p.1866

**Cortesio, John** (Iowa)
Corporate/M&A Band 2
Table: p.909

**Coruzzi, Laura A** (New York)
Profile: p.1447
Intellectual Property Band 2
Table: p.1384

**Coryell II, Cornelius E**
(Kentucky)
Litigation Band 3
Table: p.942

**Costello, Frank J** (National)
Transportation Band 3
Table: p.67

**Costello, Joseph J**
(Pennsylvania)
Profile: p.1725
Employment Band 3
Table: p.1703

KEY TO RANKINGS: ✪ = STAR INDIVIDUAL   S = SENIOR STATESMAN

**Crost, Katharine I**
(National)
Profile: p.94
Capital Markets Band 3
Table: p.18

**Crough, Maureen** (New York)
Profile: p.1447
Environment Band 3
Table: p.1373

**Crow, Carl** (Washington)
Corporate/Commercial Band 2
Table: p.1993

**Crow, Carter** (Texas)
Profile: p.1887
Employment Up and coming
Table: p.1844

**Crow, William** (Oregon)
Litigation Band 2
Table: p.1674

**Crowe, Austin** (Oregon)
Litigation Band 2
Table: p.1674

**Crowley, Frank** (Montana)
Natural Resources Band 2
Table: p.1228

**Crowley, Lisanne**
(District of Columbia)
Energy Band 4
Table: p.441

**Croysdale, David**
(Wisconsin)
Employment Band 2
Table: p.2027

**Crumbaugh, David G**
(Illinois)
Banking & Finance Band 1
Table: p.771

**Crutcher Jr, Pepper**
(Mississippi)
Profile: p.1183
Employment Band 2
Table: p.1177

**Cruz-Brown, Kelly A**
(Florida)
Profile: p.632
Insurance Band 2
Table: p.607

**Cryder, Bruce E** (Kentucky)
Environment Band 1
Table: p.940
Environment Band 1
Table: p.941

**Crystal, Jules I** (Illinois)
Employment Band 3
Table: p.785

**Cubell, Howard A**
(Massachusetts)
Profile: p.1090
Tax Band 1
Table: p.1084

**Cuclis, James** (Texas)
Profile: p.1887
Energy Band 5
Table: p.1847

**Cudkowicz, Ariel D**
(Massachusetts)
Employment Band 4
Table: p.1065

**Cudney, Kevin** (Colorado)
Corporate/M&A Band 3
Table: p.346

**Cuff, Terence** (California)
Profile: p.284
Tax Band 1
Table: p.274

**Culbertson, Robert E**
(District of Columbia)
Profile: p.507
Tax Band 2
Table: p.488

**Culhane, James** (Colorado)
Real Estate Band 2
Table: p.355

**Culhane, Stephen**
(New York)
Profile: p.1447
Private Equity Band 3
Table: p.1410

**Culhane, Thomas**
(Nebraska)
Litigation Band 1
Table: p.1239

**Cullen, Gary P** (Illinois)
Profile: p.826
Corporate/M&A Band 3
Table: p.781

**Cullen, Jack** (Washington)
Bankruptcy Band 1
Table: p.1991

**Cullen, William J** (National)
Profile: p.94
Capital Markets Band 2
Table: p.18

**Cullen, Richard** (Virginia)
Profile: p.1982
Litigation Band 2
Table: p.1978

**Culley, Peter** (Maine)
Profile: p.1011
Litigation Band 2
Table: p.1006

**Culotta, Ken** (Texas)
Profile: p.1887
Energy Band 2
Table: p.1847
Projects Band 2
Table: p.1869

**Culpepper, Bruce** (Florida)
Profile: p.632
Insurance Band 1
Table: p.607

**Culwell, Todd** (Texas)
Profile: p.1888
Projects Band 4
Table: p.1869

**Cummings, Greer**
(Tennessee)
Profile: p.1811
Real Estate Band 3

Table: p.1808

**Cummings, Stephen**
(Montana)
Real Estate Band 1
Table: p.1230

**Cummings, William**
(Alaska)
Real Estate Band 2
Table: p.172

**Cummins, Guylyn**
(California)
Media & Entertainment Band 2
Table: p.263

**Cundiff, Victoria** (New York)
Profile: p.1447
Intellectual Property Band 2
Table: p.1385

**Cunningham, Daniel**
(New York)
Profile: p.94
Capital Markets Band 1
Table: p.15

**Cunningham, Malcolm**
(Florida)
Construction Band 3
Table: p.590

**Cunningham, Peter C**
(Florida)
Profile: p.632
Environment Band 3
Table: p.601

**Cunningham, Richard**
(District of Columbia)
Profile: p.94
International Trade Band 1
Table: p.42

**Cunningham, Robert**
(Alabama)
Litigation Band 1
Table: p.152

**Cunningham, Robert J**
(Texas)
Insurance Band 3
Table: p.1858

**Cunningham, Thomas**
(Iowa)
Employment Band 3
Table: p.912

**Cupps, David** (Ohio)
Profile: p.1626
Litigation Band 1
Table: p.1617

**Curbow, William** (New York)
Profile: p.1448
Corporate/M&A
Up and coming
Table: p.1354

**Curley, James M**
(Massachusetts)
Profile: p.1090
Private Equity Up and coming
Table: p.1078

**Curley, Michael** (New York)
Profile: p.1448
Employment Band 1

Table: p.1365

**Curnin, Paul C** (New York)
Profile: p.1448
Litigation Band 2
Table: p.1390

**Curran, Bob** (Maryland)
Profile: p.1038
Corporate/M&A Band 3
Table: p.1025

**Curran, Gregory S**
(Alabama)
Profile: p.156
Corporate/Commercial Band 1
Table: p.148

**Curran, William P** (Nevada)
Gaming & Licensing Band 2
Table: p.1251

**Currault II, Douglas N**
(Louisiana)
Profile: p.979
Corporate/M&A
Up and coming
Table: p.965

**Currie, John Withers**
(South Carolina)
Corporate/M&A Band 1
Table: p.1775

**Currie, Michael** (Ohio)
Profile: p.1626
Construction Band 2
Table: p.1603

**Currier, Douglas P** (Maine)
Profile: p.1011
Employment Band 3
Table: p.1002

**Currier, Maria** (Florida)
Profile: p.632
Healthcare Band 3
Table: p.604

**Curry, J Stanton** (Arizona)
Environment Band 2
Table: p.179

**Curry, Michael** (Nebraska)
Real Estate Band 2
Table: p.1242

**Curtin, Lawrence** (Florida)
Profile: p.632
Environment Band 2
Table: p.601

**Curtin, Neal J**
(Massachusetts)
Profile: p.1091
Banking & Finance Band 1
Table: p.1055

**Curtin Jr, John J**
(Massachusetts)
Profile: p.1091
Antitrust Band S
Table: p.1053

**Curtis, Charles G**
(Wisconsin)
Profile: p.2032
Litigation Band 2
Table: p.2029

**Curtis, George B**
(Colorado)
Profile: p.359
Litigation Band 3
Table: p.353

**Curtis, J Vaughan**
(Georgia)
Profile: p.710
Corporate/M&A Band 4
Table: p.684

**Curtis, Patricia** (Nevada)
Profile: p.1257
Real Estate Band 2
Table: p.1255

**Curtis, Susan M** (New York)
Profile: p.94
Capital Markets Band 2
Table: p.13

**Curtiss, Catherine**
(National)
Profile: p.94
International Trade Band 5
Table: p.42

**Curtiss, James**
(District of Columbia)
Profile: p.507
Energy Band 2
Table: p.449

**Curtner, Gregory L**
(New York)
Profile: p.1133
Litigation Band 3
Table: p.1128
Sport Band 3
Table: p.59

**Curtz, Chauncey SR**
(Kentucky)
Profile: p.946
Environment Band 1
Table: p.940

**Curzon, Thomas H**
(Arizona)
Profile: p.189
Corporate/M&A Band 1
Table: p.176

**Cushing, Paul M** (Georgia)
Profile: p.710
Banking & Finance Band 1
Table: p.677

**Cusick, Michael** (New York)
Profile: p.1448
Energy Band 3
Table: p.1367

**Cutchins IV, Clifford A**
(Virginia)
Corporate/M&A Band 1
Table: p.1968

**Cutler, Kenneth**
(Minnesota)
Profile: p.1162
Corporate/M&A Band 2
Table: p.1152

**Cutler, Richard A**
(South Dakota)
Corporate/Commercial Band 2
Table: p.1792

**D**

**Davis, Lee** (Georgia)
Profile: p.710
Construction **Band** 1
Table: p.682

**Davis, Mark** (Mississippi)
Real Estate **Band** 2
Table: p.1181

**Davis, Michael**
(Massachusetts)
Tax **Band** 2
Table: p.1084

**Davis, Michael** (Wyoming)
Employment **Band** 1
Table: p.2042

**Davis, Oscar** (Arkansas)
Employment **Band** 3
Table: p.203

**Davis, R Eberley**
(Kentucky)
Profile: p.946
Environment **Band** 2
Table: p.940

**Davis, Robert P**
(District of Columbia)
Profile: p.507
Employee Benefits **Band** 3
Table: p.437
Employment **Band** 2
Table: p.439

**Davis, Scott J** (Illinois)
Profile: p.826
Corporate/M&A **Band** 2
Table: p.781

**Davis, Steven C**
(Oklahoma)
Profile: p.1659
Corporate/Commercial **Band** 1
Table: p.1653

**Davis, Steven H** (New York)
Profile: p.1448
Energy **Band** 2
Table: p.1367

**Davis, Thomas A**
(Alabama)
Employment **Band** 3
Table: p.150

**Davis, Will** (Texas)
Insurance **Band** 3
Table: p.1858

**Davis, William**
(North Carolina)
Litigation **Band** 1
Table: p.1577

**Davis Jones, Laura**
(Delaware)
Bankruptcy **Band** 2
Table: p.389

**Davis Jr, Ralph W**
(Tennessee)
Profile: p.1812
Corporate/M&A **Band** 2
Table: p.1799

**Davis Jr, Richard M**
(Wyoming)
Real Estate **Band** 2

**Davis Jr, William C**
(Nevada)
Real Estate **Band** 3
Table: p.1255

**Dawahare, Debra**
(Kentucky)
Profile: p.946
Employment **Band** 3
Table: p.939

**Dawda, Edward C**
(Michigan)
Real Estate **Band** 1
Table: p.1130

**Dawes, Paul** (California)
Litigation **Band** 4
Table: p.257

**Dawson, Alistair** (Texas)
Litigation Up and coming
Table: p.1865

**Dawson, Amos C**
(North Carolina)
Environment **Band** 2
Table: p.1575

**Dawson, James**
(Minnesota)
Employment **Band** 2
Table: p.1154

**Dawson, Jon S** (Alaska)
Bankruptcy **Band** 2
Table: p.167
Corporate/M&A **Band** 1
Table: p.168

**Dawson, Stephen E**
(Michigan)
Profile: p.1134
Real Estate **Band** 2
Table: p.1130

**Dawson, William B** (Texas)
Profile: p.1888
Litigation **Band** 3
Table: p.1865

**Dax, John** (New York)
Energy **Band** 1
Table: p.1370

**Day, Barton** (Arizona)
Environment **Band** 3
Table: p.179

**Day, Lloyd R** (California)
Intellectual Property **Band** 1
Table: p.248

**Day, Michael** (California)
Energy **Band** 2
Table: p.233

**Day, Richard** (Wyoming)
Litigation **Band** S
Table: p.2044

**Dayan, Michael D**
(New York)
Profile: p.95
Capital Markets **Band** 2
Table: p.15

**Dayanim, Behnam**
(National)
Profile: p.95
International Trade Up and
coming
Table: p.41

**de Alcuaz, Anthony**
(California)
Profile: p.285
Intellectual Property **Band** 4
Table: p.248

**de Armas, Luis** (Florida)
Profile: p.633
Corporate/M&A **Band** 3
Table: p.594
Corporate/M&A **Band** 2
Table: p.595

**de Bernardo, Mark**
(Virginia)
Profile: p.1981
Employment **Band** 3
Table: p.1971

**De Bruin, David L.**
(Wisconsin)
Intellectual Property **Band** 2
Table: p.2028

**De Buys Jr, John** (Alabama)
Real Estate **Band** 1
Table: p.154

**De Chiara, Michael**
(New York)
Construction **Band** 3
Table: p.1351

**de Groot, Steven** (National)
Profile: p.95
Business Process Outsourcing
**Band** 4
Table: p.2

**de Lipkau, Ross E**
(Nevada)
Profile: p.1257
Environment **Band** 1
Table: p.1249

**De Sear, Edward** (New
York)
Profile: p.95
Capital Markets **Band** 1
Table: p.18

**De Vore, Bradford A**
(North Carolina)
Profile: p.1582
Environment **Band** 2
Table: p.1575

**de Wied, Warren**
(New York)
Profile: p.1449
Corporate/M&A **Band** 4
Table: p.1354

**Deakins Jr, Homer L**
(Georgia)
Profile: p.710
Employment **Band** 1
Table: p.687

**Dean, Cathy J** (Missouri)
Profile: p.1204
Litigation **Band** 2
Table: p.1198

**Deane Jr, Richard H**
(Georgia)
Profile: p.710
Litigation **Band** 1
Table: p.698

**Deaner, Charles W**
(Nevada)
Real Estate **Band** S
Table: p.1255

**Deatherage, Scott** (Texas)
Profile: p.1888
Environment **Band** 2
Table: p.1853

**deBeers, Kimberly A**
(Illinois)
Profile: p.826
Corporate/M&A: Private Equity
**Band** 3
Table: p.782

**Debruge, Marcel**
(Alabama)
Employment **Band** 3
Table: p.150

**Dee, David** (Florida)
Environment **Band** 2
Table: p.601

**Dee, Francis X** (New
Jersey)
Employment **Band** 1
Table: p.1282

**Deem, Patrick D**
(West Virginia)
Corporate/Commercial **Band** 2
Table: p.2010
Real Estate **Band** 1
Table: p.2015

**Deeny, Raymond**
(Colorado)
Profile: p.359
Employment **Band** 2
Table: p.348

**Deere, Beth M** (Arkansas)
Profile: p.208
Litigation **Band** 4
Table: p.205

**Dees, C Stanley** (National)
Profile: p.95
Government Contracts
**Band** S
Table: p.30

**DeFranceschi, Daniel J**
(Delaware)
Profile: p.403
Bankruptcy **Band** 3
Table: p.389

**Degnan, Peter** (Georgia)
Profile: p.711
Energy **Band** 2
Table: p.689

**DeGrandis, William D**
(District of Columbia)
Profile: p.507
Projects **Band** 4
Table: p.479

**DeHihns III, Lee A**
(Georgia)
Profile: p.711
Environment **Band** 1
Table: p.691

**Dehney, Robert J**
(Delaware)
Profile: p.403
Bankruptcy **Band** 2
Table: p.389

**Deitch, Laurence B**
(Michigan)
Profile: p.1134
Corporate/M&A **Band** 2
Table: p.1122

**DeJong, Ralph E** (Illinois)
Profile: p.826
Healthcare **Band** 3
Table: p.793

**del Calvo, Jorge** (California)
Profile: p.285
Capital Markets **Band** 2
Table: p.8
Corporate/M&A **Band** 3
Table: p.227

**Delaney, John** (New York)
Profile: p.1449
Business Process Outsourcing
**Band** 4
Table: p.2
Technology **Band** 2
Table: p.1428

**Delegal, Mark** (Florida)
Insurance **Band** 1
Table: p.607

**Delegal, Susan F** (Florida)
Profile: p.633
Real Estate **Band** 2
Table: p.621

**Delikat, Michael** (New
York)
Profile: p.1449
Employment **Band** 1
Table: p.1365

**Dellinger, Walter**
(District of Columbia)
Profile: p.508
Litigation **Band** 1
Table: p.475

**DeLucia, Richard L**
(New York)
Profile: p.1449
Intellectual Property **Band** 2
Table: p.1384

**DeMarco, Daniel A** (Ohio)
Bankruptcy **Band** 3
Table: p.1600

**DeMaria, Gerald C**
(Rhode Island)
Litigation **Band** 2
Table: p.1769

**DeMars, David**
(North Dakota)
Corporate/Commercial **Band** 1
Table: p.1590

**DeMarte, Luke W** (Illinois)
Media & Entertainment Band 2
Table: p.807

**DeMeo, Ralph** (Florida)
Profile: p.633
Environment Band 3
Table: p.601

**Demerath, Jeffrey**
(Missouri)
Litigation Band 1
Table: p.1198

**Demetriou, Andrew James** (California)
Profile: p.285
Healthcare Band 1
Table: p.238

**deMeza Jr, William B**
(Florida)
Profile: p.633
Employment Band 2
Table: p.597

**Dempsey, Kevin M**
(National)
Profile: p.95
International Trade Band 3
Table: p.42

**Dempster, Hazen H**
(Georgia)
Banking & Finance Band 3
Table: p.677

**DeMuro, Paul R** (California)
Healthcare Band 2
Table: p.238

**Denenberg, Alan**
(California)
Profile: p.95
Capital Markets Band 2
Table: p.8

**Denger, Michael L**
(District of Columbia)
Profile: p.508
Antitrust Band 3
Table: p.426

**Denham, Robert E**
(California)
Corporate/M&A Band 4
Table: p.227

**DeNinno, David L**
(Pennsylvania)
Profile: p.1726
Corporate/M&A Band 4
Table: p.1700

**Denis, Paul T**
(District of Columbia)
Profile: p.508
Antitrust Band 5
Table: p.426

**Denitzio Jr, Thomas J**
(New Jersey)
Profile: p.1297
Real Estate Band 3
Table: p.1293

**Denmon, Richard A**
(Florida)
Profile: p.634
Corporate/M&A Band 4

Table: p.594

**Dennis, Patrick W**
(California)
Profile: p.285
Environment Band 2
Table: p.236

**Dennison, Karen D**
(Nevada)
Real Estate Band 2
Table: p.1255

**Denny, Otway** (Texas)
Profile: p.1888
Litigation Band 3
Table: p.1865
Products Liability Band 4
Table: p.50

**Densborn, Donald** (Indiana)
Profile: p.895
Corporate/M&A Band 3
Table: p.887

**Dent, Leslie** (Georgia)
Profile: p.711
Employment Band 3
Table: p.687

**DeOrchis, Vincent M**
(New York)
Profile: p.95
Transportation Band 3
Table: p.74

**DePaoli, Gordon** (Nevada)
Environment Band 1
Table: p.1249

**DePrez, Anne** (Indiana)
Profile: p.895
Litigation Band 2
Table: p.890

**DePuy, Jacques B**
(District of Columbia)
Real Estate Band 3
Table: p.482

**DeRosa, Franca L**
(Connecticut)
Real Estate Band 2
Table: p.380

**DeRosa, Frank J** (New York)
Profile: p.1449
Intellectual Property Band 4
Table: p.1384

**Derosby, Anthony R**
(Maine)
Profile: p.1011
Employment Band 3
Table: p.1002

**Derouin, James** (Arizona)
Profile: p.189
Environment Band 1
Table: p.179

**Derrick, Elizabeth O**
(South Carolina)
Profile: p.1782
Corporate/M&A Band 3
Table: p.1775

**Derrick, Gary** (Oklahoma)
Corporate/Commercial Band 2

Table: p.1653

**DeSanctis, Michael**
(District of Columbia)
Profile: p.508
Telecom, Broadcast & Satellite Band 4
Table: p.492

**DeSantis, Victor J**
(District of Columbia)
Profile: p.508
Projects Band 1
Table: p.56
Projects Band 1
Table: p.479

**Desmarais, John M** (New York)
Profile: p.1449
Intellectual Property Band 3
Table: p.248
Intellectual Property Band 2
Table: p.1384

**Despins, Luc A** (New York)
Bankruptcy Band 1
Table: p.1344

**DeStefano, William**
(Pennsylvania)
Profile: p.1726
Litigation Band 3
Table: p.1715

**Detherage, Andrew**
(Indiana)
Profile: p.895
Litigation Band 3
Table: p.890

**DeTroy, Peter** (Maine)
Litigation Band 1
Table: p.1006

**Dettmann, David** (Iowa)
Real Estate Band 1
Table: p.917

**Dettmer, Scott** (California)
Corporate/M&A Band 4
Table: p.227

**Detzel, Lauren** (Florida)
Profile: p.634
Tax Band 1
Table: p.624
Wealth Management Band 2
Table: p.81

**Deutsch, Edward B** (New Jersey)
Litigation Band 3
Table: p.1289

**DeVault, John** (Florida)
Litigation Band 1
Table: p.609

**DeVecchio, Jay W**
(National)
Profile: p.96
Government Contracts Band 3
Table: p.30

**Devine III, Francis P**
(Pennsylvania)
Profile: p.1726
Litigation Band 3
Table: p.1714

Litigation Band 2
Table: p.1715

**Devlin, Patricia** (Hawaii)
Real Estate Band 2
Table: p.748

**DeWald, Scott** (Arizona)
Corporate/M&A Band 4
Table: p.176

**Di Croce, Camille Holton**
(New Hampshire)
Corporate/Commercial Band 1
Table: p.1263
Corporate/Commercial Band 3
Table: p.1263

**Di Massa Jr, Rudolph J**
(Pennsylvania)
Profile: p.1726
Bankruptcy Band 3
Table: p.1697

**Di Rosa, Paolo**
(District of Columbia)
Profile: p.96
International Arbitration Up and coming
Table: p.36

**Dial, David** (Georgia)
Construction Band 2
Table: p.682

**Dial, Ellen** (Washington)
Real Estate Band 2
Table: p.2002

**Diamond, Brian** (New York)
Real Estate Band 3
Table: p.1417

**Diamond, Ivan M**
(Kentucky)
Corporate/M&A Band 3
Table: p.937

**Diamond, Kenneth J**
(Washington)
Employment Band 3
Table: p.1995

**Diamond, Susan**
(California)
Profile: p.286
Real Estate Band 2
Table: p.270

**Diaz Jr, Victor** (Florida)
Profile: p.634
Litigation Band 3
Table: p.609

**Diaz-Silveira, Jorge**
(Florida)
Profile: p.634
Construction Band 3
Table: p.590

**DiBernardo, S James**
(California)
Profile: p.286
Employment Band 1
Table: p.232

**DiBlasi, Gandolfo V**
(New York)
Profile: p.1449
Litigation Band 1

Table: p.1390

**Dicanio, Jack P** (California)
Profile: p.286
Litigation Band 3
Table: p.258

**Dicharry, Paul** (Louisiana)
Environment Band 1
Table: p.970

**Dichiara, Peter M**
(Massachusetts)
Profile: p.1091
Intellectual Property Band 2
Table: p.1072

**Dichter, Mark**
(Pennsylvania)
Profile: p.1726
Employment Band 1
Table: p.1703

**Dichter, Stephen M**
(Arizona)
Litigation Band 3
Table: p.182

**DiCicco, Susan F** (New York)
Profile: p.1449
Litigation Band 3
Table: p.1390

**Dick, David** (West Virginia)
Employment Band 2
Table: p.2012

**Dickens, John A**
(Wisconsin)
Corporate/M&A Band 3
Table: p.2025

**Dickerson Jr, W Brinkley**
(Georgia)
Corporate/M&A Band 4
Table: p.684

**Dickhaus Agnant, Linda**
(Florida)
Construction Up and coming
Table: p.590

**Dickinson, Christopher C**
(Illinois)
Profile: p.826
Insurance Band 3
Table: p.796

**Dickinson, John** (Florida)
Employment Band 1
Table: p.597

**Dickinson, Mark** (Iowa)
Corporate/M&A Band 2
Table: p.909

**Dickson, Andrea Roumell**
(Michigan)
Profile: p.1134
Employment Band 2
Table: p.1125

**Dickson, Robert J** (Alaska)
Litigation Band 1
Table: p.171
Litigation Band 3
Table: p.171

**Dickson, Roger W**
(Tennessee)
Profile: p.1812
Litigation Band 2
Table: p.1804

**Diehl Jr, Robert J**
(Michigan)
Profile: p.1134
Banking & Finance Band 1
Table: p.1120

**Diehl Jr, William K**
(North Carolina)
Litigation Band 4
Table: p.1577

**Diekmann Jr, Gilmore F**
(California)
Employment Band 3
Table: p.231

**Dietz, Wallace W**
(Tennessee)
Profile: p.1812
Litigation Band 2
Table: p.1804

**DiGiorgio, Valentino F**
(Pennsylvania)
Banking & Finance Band 3
Table: p.1695

**DiGiovanni, Nick J** (Illinois)
Insurance Band 1
Table: p.795

**DiGiovanni, Peter**
(Missouri)
Profile: p.1204
Real Estate Band 1
Table: p.1201

**DiLeo, Anthony M**
(Louisiana)
Corporate/M&A Band 4
Table: p.965

**Dilg, Joseph C** (Texas)
Profile: p.1888
Energy ✪
Table: p.1847

**Dillard, Michael E** (Texas)
Profile: p.1888
Corporate/M&A Band 4
Table: p.1840

**Dillard, Stephen** (Texas)
Profile: p.1888
Litigation Band 3
Table: p.1865

**Diller, Edward D** (Ohio)
Real Estate Band 3
Table: p.1621

**Dilloff, Neil** (Maryland)
Profile: p.1038
Litigation Band 2
Table: p.1032

**Dillon, Andrew J** (Texas)
Intellectual Property Band 3
Table: p.1860

**Dillon, Sean M** (Florida)
Profile: p.634
Construction Associate to watch
Table: p.590

**Dillon, Sheri A**
(District of Columbia)
Profile: p.508
Tax Associate to watch
Table: p.488

**Dillow, John** (National)
Transportation Band 2
Table: p.67

**DiLorenzo, Louis P**
(New York)
Profile: p.1449
Employment Band 2
Table: p.1365

**DiMatteo, John** (New York)
Profile: p.1450
Intellectual Property Band 4
Table: p.1384

**DiMichael, Nicholas**
(National)
Profile: p.96
Transportation Band 2
Table: p.69
Transportation Band 2
Table: p.71

**DiMickele, Susan M**
(Ohio)
Profile: p.1626
Employment Up and coming
Table: p.1609

**Dimling, Robert A** (Ohio)
Profile: p.1626
Employment Band 3
Table: p.1609

**Dimon, Samuel** (New York)
Profile: p.1450
Tax Band 1
Table: p.1425

**DiNardo, Lawrence**
(Illinois)
Profile: p.826
Employment Band 3
Table: p.785

**Dingel, Allyn** (Idaho)
Litigation Band S
Table: p.760

**Dinkins, Carol** (Texas)
Profile: p.1889
Environment Band 2
Table: p.451
Environment Band 1
Table: p.1852

**Dinsmore, Robert** (West Virginia)
Real Estate Band 3
Table: p.2015

**Dintzer, Jeffrey D**
(California)
Profile: p.286
Environment Up and coming
Table: p.236

**Dinwiddie, Thomas**
(Indiana)
Profile: p.895
Real Estate Band 2
Table: p.892

**DiPrinzio, Eugene A**
(Delaware)
Profile: p.403
Real Estate Band 2
Table: p.399

**DiSalvatore, William P**
(New York)
Intellectual Property Band 3
Table: p.1384

**Diskant, Gregory L**
(New York)
Profile: p.1450
Intellectual Property Band 2
Table: p.1384

**DiStefano, Joseph R**
(Rhode Island)
Profile: p.1771
Real Estate Band 2
Table: p.1770

**Dittmar, James S**
(Massachusetts)
Profile: p.1091
Litigation Band 1
Table: p.1075

**Dittrick, William**
(Nebraska)
Litigation Band 1
Table: p.1239

**Diviney, Craig** (Minnesota)
Profile: p.1163
Litigation Band 1
Table: p.1157

**DiVita, Robert R** (New Jersey)
Profile: p.1297
Real Estate Band 3
Table: p.1293

**Divola, Julie** (California)
Profile: p.286
Tax Band 2
Table: p.274

**Dix, Martin R** (Florida)
Profile: p.634
Healthcare Band 3
Table: p.604

**Dixon, Augustus M**
(South Carolina)
Corporate/M&A Band 2
Table: p.1775

**Dixon, Brett W**
(Connecticut)
Profile: p.382
Corporate/M&A Band 2
Table: p.374

**Dixon, Gary**
(District of Columbia)
Insurance Band 2
Table: p.461

**Dixon, Joyce A** (Nebraska)
Profile: p.1243
Corporate/M&A Band 1

Table: p.1236

**Dixon, Sharon Quinn**
(Florida)
Tax Band 1
Table: p.624

**Dobbs, C Edward** (Georgia)
Banking & Finance Band 1
Table: p.677
Bankruptcy Band 1
Table: p.679

**Dobbs, Tammy L** (Alabama)
Employment Band 3
Table: p.150

**Dockery, Michael**
(Montana)
Real Estate Band 1
Table: p.1230

**Docksey, Ross** (Illinois)
Profile: p.826
Business Process Outsourcing Band 1
Table: p.2
Technology Band 1
Table: p.814

**Dodd, Jeff** (Texas)
Technology Band 2
Table: p.1878

**Dodd, Richard** (Washington)
Corporate/Commercial Band 2
Table: p.1992

**Dodds, John C**
(Pennsylvania)
Profile: p.1726
Litigation Up and coming
Table: p.1715

**Dodson, Gerald** (California)
Profile: p.286
Intellectual Property Band 3
Table: p.248

**Doerr, Brian** (Kansas)
Real Estate Band 2
Table: p.930

**Doetsch, Douglas A**
(Illinois)
Profile: p.826
Banking & Finance Band 2
Table: p.771

**Dogali, Andy** (Florida)
Construction Band 3
Table: p.590

**Doheny Jr, Frank P**
(Kentucky)
Litigation Band 3
Table: p.942

**Doke Jr, Marshall J**
(National)
Profile: p.96
Government Contracts Band S
Table: p.30

**Dokos, Daniel S** (New York)
Profile: p.1450
Banking & Finance Band 3
Table: p.1339

**Dolan, Colleen A** (Nevada)
Corporate/Commercial Band 3
Table: p.1246

**Dolan, Edward**
(District of Columbia)
Profile: p.508
Bankruptcy Band 3
Table: p.432

**Dolan, William** (Virginia)
Profile: p.1982
Litigation Band 3
Table: p.1978

**Dolin, Kenneth R** (Illinois)
Employment Band 3
Table: p.785

**Dolin, Mitchell F**
(District of Columbia)
Profile: p.508
Insurance Band 1
Table: p.464
International Arbitration Band 4
Table: p.36

**Doliner, Nathaniel** (Florida)
Profile: p.634
Corporate/M&A Band 1
Table: p.594

**Dollinger, Martin E** (New Jersey)
Profile: p.1297
Real Estate Band 1
Table: p.1293

**Dollison, Charles** (West Virginia)
Real Estate Band 2
Table: p.2015
Real Estate Band 2
Table: p.2015

**Dolson, Scott** (Kentucky)
Profile: p.946
Corporate/M&A Band 3
Table: p.937

**Domby, Arthur H** (Georgia)
Environment Band 3
Table: p.691

**Domina, David A**
(Nebraska)
Litigation Band 2
Table: p.1239

**Donadio, Donald A**
(North Carolina)
Profile: p.1582
Real Estate Band 2
Table: p.1579

**Donarski, Michelle**
(North Dakota)
Employment Band 1
Table: p.1592

**Donati, Donna J** (Michigan)
Profile: p.1134
Employment Band 3
Table: p.1125

**Donnelly, Dennis C**
(Missouri)
Employment Band 2
Table: p.1195

**Donnelly, Paul** (Missouri)
Profile: p.1204
Employment Band 2
Table: p.1195

**Donoghue, Laurence J**
(Massachusetts)
Employment Band 4
Table: p.1065

**Donohue, John**
(Pennsylvania)
Profile: p.1726
Intellectual Property Band 2
Table: p.1711

**Donohue, P Daniel**
(South Dakota)
Real Estate Band 1
Table: p.1796

**Donovan, Donald Francis**
(New York)
Arbitration Band 1
Table: p.37
International Arbitration
Band 1
Table: p.36

**Donovan, John D**
(Massachusetts)
Profile: p.1091
Litigation Band 1
Table: p.1074
Litigation Band 1
Table: p.1075

**Donovan, Joseph E**
(Illinois)
Telecom, Broadcast & Satellite
Up and coming
Table: p.816

**Donovan, Richard T**
(Arkansas)
Litigation Band 4
Table: p.205

**Donovan, Thomas J**
(New Hampshire)
Profile: p.1271
Litigation Band 4
Table: p.1267

**Donovan Jr, Lawrence**
(Colorado)
Real Estate Band 3
Table: p.355

**Doran, James** (Illinois)
Banking & Finance Band 2
Table: p.771

**Doran, John Alan** (Arizona)
Profile: p.189
Employment Band 3
Table: p.178

**Doran, Scott** (Ohio)
Profile: p.1626
Environment Band 2
Table: p.1612

**Doran Jr, James M**
(Tennessee)
Profile: p.1812
Litigation Band 2
Table: p.1804

**Dore, Michael** (New Jersey)
Profile: p.1297
Environment Band 2
Table: p.1285

**Dorn, Joseph W**
(District of Columbia)
Profile: p.96
International Trade Band 4
Table: p.42

**Dornak, David B** (Nevada)
Employment Up and coming
Table: p.1248

**Dorris, Malcolm S**
(National)
Profile: p.96
Capital Markets Band 4
Table: p.18

**Dorris, William** (Georgia)
Profile: p.711
Construction Band 1
Table: p.682

**Dorsey, Rufus Thomas**
(Georgia)
Bankruptcy Band 2
Table: p.679

**Dorton, David**
(North Carolina)
Real Estate Band 3
Table: p.1579

**Dost, Patricia** (Oregon)
Environment Band 2
Table: p.1672

**Dougherty, Charles R**
(Massachusetts)
Profile: p.1091
Bankruptcy Band 3
Table: p.1058

**Dougherty, Lucia** (Florida)
Profile: p.634
Real Estate Band 3
Table: p.621

**Dougherty, Thomas J**
(Massachusetts)
Profile: p.1091
Litigation Band 1
Table: p.1075

**Douglas, Charles W**
(Illinois)
Profile: p.827
Litigation Band 3
Table: p.802

**Douglas, James M**
(New York)
Profile: p.1450
Banking & Finance Band 1
Table: p.1339

**Douglas, John L** (Georgia)
Profile: p.711
Banking & Finance Band 1
Table: p.677
Financial Services Band 2
Table: p.24

**Douglas, John R**
(Nebraska)
Litigation Band 2
Table: p.1240

**Douglas, Robert J** (Iowa)
Real Estate Band 2
Table: p.917

**Dove, Luke** (Mississippi)
Litigation Band 2
Table: p.1179

**Dover, Darrell** (Arkansas)
Real Estate Band 2
Table: p.207

**Dow, Melvin** (Texas)
Real Estate Band 1
Table: p.1872

**Dow, Robert M** (Illinois)
Profile: p.827
Telecom, Broadcast & Satellite
Band 2
Table: p.816

**Dow, T Andrew** (Texas)
Real Estate Band 3
Table: p.1872

**Dowd, Martin F** (New
Jersey)
Real Estate Band 2
Table: p.1293

**Dowd, Mary Joanne**
(District of Columbia)
Profile: p.509
Bankruptcy Band 3
Table: p.432

**Dowd Jr, Edward** (Missouri)
Litigation Band 1
Table: p.1198

**Dowdy, L Craig** (Georgia)
Profile: p.711
Energy Band 2
Table: p.689

**Downer, Robert** (Iowa)
Real Estate Band 4
Table: p.917

**Downes, Robert W**
(National)
Profile: p.96
Capital Markets Band 4
Table: p.7

**Downey, Alicia L**
(Massachusetts)
Profile: p.1091
Antitrust Up and coming
Table: p.1053

**Downey III, Charles J**
(Connecticut)
Profile: p.382
Corporate/M&A Band 2
Table: p.374

**Downs, Clark Evans**
(District of Columbia)
Profile: p.509
Energy Band 1
Table: p.445

**Downs, J Anthony**
(Massachusetts)
Profile: p.1091
Litigation Band 3
Table: p.1074

**Downs, Joe** (Florida)
Construction Band 1
Table: p.590

**Dowsley III, Felix R**
(Tennessee)
Profile: p.1812
Real Estate Band 3
Table: p.1808

**Doyle, David P** (New Jersey)
Profile: p.1298
Employee Benefits Band 2

**Doyle, Katherine R**
(Pennsylvania)
Intellectual Property Band 4
Table: p.1711

**Doyle, Thomas R** (Maine)
Profile: p.1011
Environment Band 1
Table: p.1004

**Doyle Jr, John**
(North Carolina)
Employment Band 1
Table: p.1573

**Dozeman, Douglas A.**
(Michigan)
Litigation Band 3
Table: p.1128

**Dragna, James J**
(California)
Profile: p.286
Environment Band 3
Table: p.236

**Drake, Denise K** (Missouri)
Employment Band 3
Table: p.1195

**Drake, Stuart AC**
(District of Columbia)
Profile: p.509
Environment Band 4
Table: p.451

**Dranoff, David** (Illinois)
Banking & Finance Band 2
Table: p.771

**Draper, Douglas S**
(Louisiana)
Corporate/M&A Band 1
Table: p.965

**Draper, Hayward L** (Iowa)
Litigation Band 3
Table: p.914

**Draper, John B**
(New Mexico)
Environment ✪
Table: p.1323

**Draper, Thomas B**
(Massachusetts)
Profile: p.1092
Banking & Finance Band 2
Table: p.1055

**Drapkin, Steven** (California)
Employment Band 3
Table: p.231

**Drasco, Dennis J**
(New Jersey)
Profile: p.1298
Litigation Band 3
Table: p.1289

**Draucker, Carl A** (Ohio)
Profile: p.1626
Employee Benefits Band 3
Table: p.1607

**Dray, Mark S** (Virginia)
Profile: p.1981
Employment Band 1
Table: p.1971

**Dray, W Perry** (Wyoming)
Corporate/M&A Band 1
Table: p.2041
Real Estate Band 2
Table: p.2045

**Dreher, Nicholas C**
(Hawaii)
Bankruptcy Band 1
Table: p.739

**Dreitler, Joseph R** (Ohio)
Profile: p.1626
Intellectual Property Band 1
Table: p.1614

**Dresher, J David** (Alabama)
Profile: p.156
Banking & Finance Band 2
Table: p.147
Real Estate Band 3
Table: p.153

**Drew, Mark** (Alabama)
Profile: p.156
Corporate/Commercial Band 2
Table: p.148

**Dreyfus, James K**
(New York)
Profile: p.1450
Tax Band 4
Table: p.1423

**Driggs, J Douglas** (Nevada)
Real Estate Band 3
Table: p.1255

**Driker, Eugene** (Michigan)
Litigation ✪
Table: p.1128

**Drinkwater, Robert**
(Mississippi)
Profile: p.1183
Corporate/Commercial Band 1
Table: p.1174

**Drinkwater, Wayne**
(Mississippi)
Profile: p.1183
Litigation ✪
Table: p.1179
Litigation Band 1
Table: p.1179

**Driscoll, Kevin J** (Iowa)
Litigation Band 4
Table: p.914

**Drivas, Dimitrios**
(New York)
Profile: p.1450
Intellectual Property Band 2

**D**

Table: p.1384

**Drooff, Michael J**
(New Hampshire)
Corporate/Commercial Band 3
Table: p.1263

**Drury, Mary J** (Nevada)
Corporate/Commercial Band 3
Table: p.1246

**Dryden, William** (Idaho)
Litigation Band 3
Table: p.760

**Dubberly, David E**
(South Carolina)
Profile: p.1782
Employment Band 2
Table: p.1777

**Dube, Monte I** (Illinois)
Profile: p.827
Healthcare Band 1
Table: p.793

**Dubitzky, Dan** (Washington)
Litigation Band 1
Table: p.2000

**Dubose, Kevin** (Texas)
Litigation Band 3
Table: p.1866

**Dubreuil, Francis W**
(National)
Profile: p.97
Wealth Management Band 3
Table: p.81

**Duca, James N** (Hawaii)
Bankruptcy Band 2
Table: p.739

**Duchelle, John W**
(District of Columbia)
Insurance Band 4
Table: p.461

**Duck, John M** (Louisiana)
Profile: p.979
Corporate/M&A Band 3
Table: p.965

**Duedall, Mark I** (Georgia)
Profile: p.711
Bankruptcy Up and coming
Table: p.679

**Duffie, L Traywick**
(Georgia)
Profile: p.711
Employment Band 4
Table: p.687

**Duffy, Daniel F**
(South Dakota)
Litigation Band 1
Table: p.1795

**Duffy, Don** (Florida)
Profile: p.634
Tax Band 3
Table: p.623

**Duffy, Pamela S** (California)
Real Estate Band 1
Table: p.270

**Duffy, Robert** (Rhode

Island)
Litigation Band 2
Table: p.1769

**Duffy, Robert H** (Wisconsin)
Profile: p.2032
Employment Band 3
Table: p.2027

**Dugan, Christopher F**
(National)
Profile: p.97
International Arbitration Band
4
Table: p.36

**Duhon, Gary W** (Nevada)
Real Estate Band 3
Table: p.1255

**Dukes, David E**
(South Carolina)
Litigation Band 1
Table: p.1778

**Dulcich, Thomas** (Oregon)
Litigation Band 2
Table: p.1674

**DuMouchel, David F**
(Michigan)
Profile: p.1134
Litigation Band 1
Table: p.1128

**Dunagan, Sidney G**
(Oklahoma)
Profile: p.1659
Litigation Band 3
Table: p.1656

**Dunbar, Charles** (West
Virginia)
Profile: p.2016
Corporate/Commercial Band 2
Table: p.2010

**Duncan, Alan W**
(North Carolina)
Profile: p.1582
Litigation Band 4
Table: p.1577

**Duncan, Helen Lalich**
(California)
Profile: p.286
Litigation Band 4
Table: p.257

**Duncan, J Kelly** (Louisiana)
Profile: p.979
Gaming & Licensing Band 1
Table: p.971

**Duncan, Margaret M**
(Illinois)
Profile: p.827
Intellectual Property Band 3
Table: p.799

**Duncan III, Brooke**
(Louisiana)
Profile: p.979
Employment Band 2
Table: p.967

**Dunham, Edward Wood**
(Connecticut)
Profile: p.382
Litigation Band 1

Table: p.378

**Dunham Jr, Wolcott B**
(New York)
Insurance ✪
Table: p.1380

**Dunkle, Mark F** (Delaware)
Real Estate Band 3
Table: p.400

**Dunlay, Jon** (Texas)
Profile: p.1889
Real Estate Band 2
Table: p.1872

**Dunlevie, Steven S**
(Georgia)
Profile: p.711
Banking & Finance Band 3
Table: p.677

**Dunlop, Fred** (Texas)
Profile: p.1889
Real Estate Band 1
Table: p.1872

**Dunn, Christopher A**
(National)
Profile: p.97
International Trade Band 5
Table: p.42

**Dunn, Daniel** (Colorado)
Environment Band 1
Table: p.350

**Dunn, Daniel J**
(North Dakota)
Litigation Band 2
Table: p.1593

**Dunn, Dennis C** (Texas)
Profile: p.1889
Healthcare Band 2
Table: p.1855

**Dunn, Glenn H**
(North Carolina)
Environment Band 2
Table: p.1575

**Dunn, Loren R** (Washington)
Environment Band 2
Table: p.1996

**Dunn, M Douglas** (New
York)
Energy Band 1
Table: p.1367

**Dunn, Matthew S** (New
York)
Profile: p.1450
Immigration Up and coming
Table: p.1376

**Dunn, William** (Michigan)
Real Estate Band 1
Table: p.1130

**Dunn Jr, J Thomas**
(North Carolina)
Banking & Finance Band 3
Table: p.1569

**Dunne, Carey R** (New York)
Profile: p.1450
Litigation Band 2
Table: p.1391

**Dunne, Daniel J**
(Washington)
Profile: p.2005
Litigation Band 3
Table: p.2000

**Dunne, Dennis** (New York)
Bankruptcy Band 2
Table: p.1344

**Dunner, Donald**
(District of Columbia)
Profile: p.509
Intellectual Property ✪
Table: p.466

**Dunning, Elizabeth** (Utah)
Employment Band 2
Table: p.1944

**Dunwoody, Stuart R**
(Washington)
Intellectual Property Band 2
Table: p.1998

**Duplantis, BJ** (Louisiana)
Energy Band 1
Table: p.969

**Dupler, Mitchell S**
(National)
Profile: p.97
Capital Markets Band 2
Table: p.13
Capital Markets Band 3
Table: p.18

**Durant, E Terry**
(Connecticut)
Employment Band 2
Table: p.376

**Durchslag, Stephen P**
(Illinois)
Media & Entertainment Band 1
Table: p.807

**Durham, Matthew M**
(Utah)
Employment Band 3
Table: p.1944

**Durham, Thomas C**
(National)
Profile: p.97
Tax Litigation Band 3

**Durick, Patrick**
(North Dakota)
Litigation Band 2
Table: p.1593

**Durie, Daralyn J** (California)
Profile: p.286
Intellectual Property Band 3
Table: p.248

**Durkin, Denis** (Florida)
Construction Band 2
Table: p.590

**Durkin, Thomas M** (Illinois)
Profile: p.827
Litigation Band 3
Table: p.802

**Durling, James P**
(District of Columbia)
Profile: p.97
International Trade Band 4

Table: p.42

**Durrell, Brian** (Alaska)
Corporate/M&A Band 1
Table: p.168

**Dutton, David J** (Iowa)
Litigation ✪
Table: p.914

**Dutton, Diana C** (Texas)
Profile: p.1889
Environment Band 1
Table: p.1852

**Duvin, Robert P** (Ohio)
Profile: p.1626
Employment Band S
Table: p.1609

**Dworetzky, Joseph A**
(Pennsylvania)
Profile: p.1727
Bankruptcy Band 1
Table: p.1697

**Dwyer, Jeffry**
(District of Columbia)
Profile: p.509
Real Estate Band 3
Table: p.482

**Dwyer, Maureen**
(District of Columbia)
Profile: p.509
Real Estate Band 2
Table: p.482

**Dwyer, Michael**
(Washington)
Corporate/Commercial Band 3
Table: p.1992

**Dwyer, Michael** (Wisconsin)
Real Estate Band 2
Table: p.2030

**Dye, Alan L**
(District of Columbia)
Profile: p.509
Securities Band 1
Table: p.485

**Dye, Alexander M** (New
York)
Profile: p.1450
Insurance Band 1
Table: p.1380

**Dye, Phillip** (Texas)
Profile: p.1889
Energy Band 3
Table: p.1849
Litigation Band 3
Table: p.1865

**Dye, Scott** (Nebraska)
Real Estate Band 1
Table: p.1242
Real Estate Band 1
Table: p.1242

**Dyekman, Donald** (Arizona)
Real Estate Band 4
Table: p.184

**Dyekman, Gregory C**
(Wyoming)
Corporate/M&A Band 2
Table: p.2041

E

**Erickson, David** (Missouri)
Profile: p.1205
Litigation Band 1
Table: p.928

**Erly, Peter** (Vermont)
Corporate/Commercial Band 1
Table: p.1957

**Ernst, Andrew** (Georgia)
Environment Band 2
Table: p.691

**Erspamer, Gordon**
(California)
Profile: p.287
Energy Band 3
Table: p.233

**Ervin, James M** (Florida)
Profile: p.635
Tax Band 3
Table: p.623

**Erwin, Greg** (Texas)
Real Estate Band 2
Table: p.1872

**Erwin, James R** (Maine)
Profile: p.1011
Employment Band 2
Table: p.1002

**Erwin, Martin N**
(North Carolina)
Profile: p.1582
Employment Band 1
Table: p.1573

**Eschels, Philip** (Kentucky)
Employment Band 3
Table: p.939

**Esposito, Grant J**
(New York)
Profile: p.1452
Litigation Up and coming
Table: p.1388

**Esserman, Susan**
(District of Columbia)
Profile: p.98
International Trade Band 2
Table: p.42

**Estes III, John N**
(District of Columbia)
Profile: p.510
Energy Band 1
Table: p.445

**Estevez, Anne M** (Florida)
Profile: p.635
Employment Up and coming
Table: p.597

**Estrada, Miguel A**
(District of Columbia)
Profile: p.510
Litigation Band 1
Table: p.475

**Estridge, Larry D**
(South Carolina)
Profile: p.1782
Real Estate Band 1
Table: p.1780

**Etcheverry, Raymond J**
(Utah)
Profile: p.1950
Litigation Band 2
Table: p.1945

**Etem, Craig E** (Nevada)
Corporate/Commercial Band 3
Table: p.1246

**Eth, Jordan** (California)
Profile: p.287
Litigation Band 3
Table: p.257

**Ettelson, Bruce** (Illinois)
Profile: p.828
Corporate/M&A: Private Fund
Formation Band 1
Table: p.782

**Ettinger, John R** (New York)
Profile: p.1452
Private Equity Band S
Table: p.1407

**Eurich, Gregory** (Colorado)
Profile: p.359
Employment Band 1
Table: p.348

**Evanich, Kevin R** (Illinois)
Profile: p.828
Corporate/M&A Band 2
Table: p.781
Corporate/M&A: Private Equity
Band 1
Table: p.782

**Evans, Brian P**
(North Carolina)
Real Estate Band 2
Table: p.1579

**Evans, Craig** (Missouri)
Profile: p.1205
Corporate/M&A Band 2
Table: p.1193

**Evans, David E** (Virginia)
Environment Band 1
Table: p.1973

**Evans, Edwin E**
(South Dakota)
Litigation Band 1
Table: p.1795
Litigation Band 1
Table: p.1795

**Evans, George Q**
(Mississippi)
Litigation Band 3
Table: p.1179

**Evans, Kevin D** (Colorado)
Profile: p.359
Litigation Band 1
Table: p.353

**Evans, Mark**
(District of Columbia)
Telecom, Broadcast & Satellite
Band 4
Table: p.492

**Evans, Mark C** (Texas)
Profile: p.1890
Banking & Finance Band 2
Table: p.1832

Projects Band 4
Table: p.1869

**Evans, William J** (Alaska)
Profile: p.173
Employment Band 2
Table: p.169

**Evans III, Robert** (New
York)
Profile: p.98
Capital Markets Band 2
Table: p.7

**Evanusa, Michel S**
(New York)
Real Estate Band 5
Table: p.1417

**Everett, Carl B**
(Pennsylvania)
Profile: p.1727
Environment Band 3
Table: p.1707

**Everett, John** (Arkansas)
Litigation Band 1
Table: p.205

**Everroad, John** (Arizona)
Profile: p.189
Litigation Band 3
Table: p.181

**Everson, David** (Missouri)
Profile: p.1205
Litigation Band 1
Table: p.1198

**Ewart, Lani** (Hawaii)
Real Estate Band 1
Table: p.748

**Ewing, Jim** (Georgia)
Profile: p.712
Intellectual Property Band 2
Table: p.696

**Ey Jr, Douglas W**
(North Carolina)
Litigation Band 3
Table: p.1577

**Ezell Jr, Kenneth P
(Pete)** (Tennessee)
Profile: p.1812
Real Estate Band 3
Table: p.1808

**Fabiano, John G**
(Massachusetts)
Profile: p.1092
Litigation Band 3
Table: p.1074

**Fackler, Stephen W**
(California)
Profile: p.287
Employment Band 2
Table: p.232

**Factor, Jason R** (New York)
Profile: p.1452
Tax Up and coming
Table: p.1423

**Fadil, Adeeb** (New York)
Profile: p.1453
Environment Band 2
Table: p.1373

**Fagan, Christopher** (Ohio)
Profile: p.1626
Intellectual Property Band S
Table: p.1614

**Fagen, Leslie Gordon**
(New York)
Profile: p.1453
Litigation Band 3
Table: p.1388

**Fagin, Allen** (New York)
Profile: p.1453
Employment Band 1
Table: p.1365

**Fagone, Michael A**
(Maine)
Profile: p.1012
Corporate/M&A
Up and coming
Table: p.1000

**Fahey, Richard** (Ohio)
Profile: p.1626
Environment Band 2
Table: p.1612

**Fahey, Thomas M** (Illinois)
Healthcare Band 2
Table: p.793

**Fahleson, Mark A**
(Nebraska)
Employment Band 3
Table: p.1238

**Fair, George** (Mississippi)
Corporate/Commercial Band 2
Table: p.1174

**Faiss, Robert D** (Nevada)
Gaming & Licensing Band 1
Table: p.1251

**Fala, Herman C**
(Pennsylvania)
Profile: p.1727
Real Estate Band 1
Table: p.1718

**Falck, David** (New York)
Profile: p.1453
Energy Band 2
Table: p.1367

**Falk, R Scott** (Illinois)
Profile: p.828
Corporate/M&A Band 3
Table: p.1977

**Falstad, Daniel T** (Georgia)
Profile: p.712
Corporate/M&A
Up and coming
Table: p.684

**Fantaci, James** (Louisiana)
Profile: p.979
Corporate/M&A Band 4
Table: p.965

**Fanter, Robert** (Iowa)
Litigation Band 1
Table: p.914

**Farabow, Ford F**
(District of Columbia)
Profile: p.511
Intellectual Property Band 1
Table: p.466

**Farber, Michael** (New York)
Profile: p.1453
Tax Up and coming
Table: p.1425

**Fardon, D Alexander**
(Tennessee)
Litigation Band 2
Table: p.1804

**Farer, David** (New Jersey)
Environment Band 2
Table: p.1285

**Fargotstein, Phillip F**
(Arizona)
Profile: p.190
Environment Band 2
Table: p.179

**Farkas, Jeremy I** (Vermont)
Real Estate Band 3
Table: p.1961

**Farkas, Michelle** (Vermont)
Real Estate Band 2
Table: p.1961

**Farley, Donald J** (Idaho)
Litigation Band 3
Table: p.760

**Farmer, John B** (Virginia)
Intellectual Property Band 2
Table: p.1975

**Farmer, Scott**
(District of Columbia)
Profile: p.511
Tax Band 3
Table: p.488

**Farmer, Stephen** (West
Virginia)
Litigation Band 1
Table: p.2013

**Farmer III, Guy O** (Florida)
Profile: p.635
Employment Band 2
Table: p.597

**Farmer III, Malcom**
(Rhode Island)
Corporate/Commercial Band 2
Table: p.1766

**Farnham, James** (Virginia)
Profile: p.1983
Litigation Band 3

**Farolino, Shane A** (Ohio)
Environment Band 2
Table: p.1612

**Farquhar, Michele C**
(District of Columbia)
Profile: p.511
Telecom, Broadcast & Satellite
Band 4
Table: p.492

**Farr, Bartow**
(District of Columbia)
Litigation Band 1
Table: p.475

**Farr, Thomas A**
(North Carolina)
Profile: p.1582
Employment Band 2
Table: p.1573

**Farrar, Stanley F**
(California)
Profile: p.288
Banking & Finance Band S
Table: p.218
Financial Services Band S
Table: p.24

**Farrell, Margaret**
(Rhode Island)
Corporate/Commercial Band 2
Table: p.1766

**Farris Jr, James G**
(Georgia)
Profile: p.712
Real Estate Band 3
Table: p.700

**Faruki, Charles** (Ohio)
Profile: p.1627
Litigation Band 1
Table: p.1617

**Fasman, Zachary D**
(New York)
Profile: p.1453
Employment Band 3
Table: p.1365

**Fastow, Jay N** (New York)
Profile: p.1453
Antitrust Band 4
Table: p.1335

**Fatell, Bonnie Glantz**
(Delaware)
Profile: p.403
Bankruptcy Band 2
Table: p.389

**Fathe, Fred C** (Arizona)
Real Estate Band 2
Table: p.184

**Faulk, Richard** (Texas)
Profile: p.1890
Environment Band 2
Table: p.1853

**Faulkner, Andrew M**
(National)
Profile: p.98
Capital Markets Band 3
Table: p.18

**Favretto, Richard J**
(District of Columbia)
Profile: p.511
Antitrust Band 4
Table: p.426

**Fay, Richard E**
(North Carolina)
Environment Band 2
Table: p.1575

**Fay, Terrence M** (Ohio)
Profile: p.1627

Environment Band 4
Table: p.1612

**Fayne, Steve** (California)
Profile: p.288
Media & Entertainment Band 3
Table: p.266

**Feder, Philip** (California)
Profile: p.288
Real Estate Band 1
Table: p.270

**Federhar, Andrew M**
(Arizona)
Profile: p.190
Litigation Band 4
Table: p.181

**Fee, Michael K**
(Massachusetts)
Profile: p.1092
Litigation Band 1
Table: p.1075

**Feeney, James** (Michigan)
Litigation Band 3
Table: p.1128

**Feeney, Matthew** (Arizona)
Profile: p.190
Corporate/M&A Band 2
Table: p.176

**Feese, Suzanne** (Georgia)
Profile: p.712
Tax Band 3
Table: p.703

**Feheley, Lawrence F**
(Ohio)
Employment Band 2
Table: p.1609

**Feher, David G** (National)
Profile: p.99
Sport Band 2
Table: p.59

**Feibelman, Jef** (Tennessee)
Litigation Band 2
Table: p.1804

**Fein, Scott N** (New York)
Environment Band 3
Table: p.1371

**Feinstein, Deborah**
(District of Columbia)
Profile: p.511
Antitrust Band 4
Table: p.426

**Feinstein, Fred I** (Illinois)
Profile: p.828
Real Estate Band 4
Table: p.809

**Feirson, Steven B**
(Pennsylvania)
Profile: p.1727
Litigation Band 3
Table: p.1714
Litigation Band 1
Table: p.1715
Litigation Band 2
Table: p.1715

**Felcher, Peter L** (New York)
Profile: p.1453

Media & Entertainment Band 2
Table: p.1403

**Feldberg, Michael** (New York)
Profile: p.1453
Litigation Band 3
Table: p.1388

**Feldman, Boris** (California)
Profile: p.288
Litigation Band 2
Table: p.257

**Feldman, Elliott J**
(National)
International Trade Band 4
Table: p.42

**Feldman, Jeffrey M**
(Alaska)
Litigation Band 1
Table: p.171

**Feldman, Larry** (California)
Profile: p.288
Litigation Band 3
Table: p.257
Media & Entertainment Band 3
Table: p.263

**Feldman, Lewis G**
(California)
Profile: p.288
Real Estate Band 3
Table: p.270

**Feldman, Mark I** (Illinois)
Profile: p.828
Intellectual Property Band 3
Table: p.799

**Feldman, Matthew A**
(New York)
Profile: p.1453
Bankruptcy Band 3
Table: p.1344

**Feldman, Murray** (Idaho)
Profile: p.764
Natural Resources Band 1
Table: p.761

**Feldman, Robert C** (Texas)
Profile: p.1890
Real Estate Band 2
Table: p.1872

**Feldman, Robert P**
(California)
Profile: p.288
Intellectual Property Band 4
Table: p.248
Litigation Band 4
Table: p.257

**Feldman, Roger D**
(Massachusetts)
Profile: p.1092
Corporate/M&A Band 3
Table: p.1061

**Feldstein, Hydee R**
(California)
Profile: p.288
Banking & Finance Band 2
Table: p.218
Bankruptcy Band 3
Table: p.222

**Feldt, Harrell** (Texas)
Profile: p.1890
Energy Band 2
Table: p.1849

**Felger, Mark E** (Delaware)
Bankruptcy Band 3
Table: p.389

**Felger, Thomas** (Texas)
Profile: p.1890
Intellectual Property Band 3
Table: p.1860

**Felix II, H Thomas**
(Pennsylvania)
Profile: p.1727
Employment Band 2
Table: p.1703

**Fellas, John** (New York)
Profile: p.99
International Arbitration Band 4
Table: p.36

**Fellner, Baruch A**
(District of Columbia)
Profile: p.511
Employment Band 3
Table: p.439

**Felman, David** (Florida)
Corporate/M&A Band 3
Table: p.594

**Felmly, Bruce W**
(New Hampshire)
Profile: p.1271
Litigation Band 1
Table: p.1267

**Felsenthal, David**
(National)
Profile: p.99
Capital Markets Band 3
Table: p.13

**Feltenstein, Martha**
(New York)
Profile: p.1454
Real Estate Band 3
Table: p.1417

**Felter, John Kenneth**
(Massachusetts)
Profile: p.1092
Litigation Band 2
Table: p.1074

**Felton, W Raymond** (New Jersey)
Profile: p.1298
Corporate/M&A Band 2
Table: p.1278

**Fenley, David A** (Missouri)
Profile: p.1205
Real Estate Band 1
Table: p.1201

**Fennell, Thomas E** (Texas)
Profile: p.1890
Environment Band 2
Table: p.1853

**Fenton, Kathryn M**
(District of Columbia)
Profile: p.511
Antitrust Band 5

Table: p.426

**Fenzel, Mark S** (Kentucky)
Profile: p.946
Litigation Band 4
Table: p.942

**Feo, Edwin** (California)
Energy Band 1
Table: p.233
Projects Band 1
Table: p.56
Projects Band 1
Table: p.268
Transportation Band 1
Table: p.71

**Feola, Phil**
(District of Columbia)
Real Estate Band 2
Table: p.482

**Feore, John R**
(District of Columbia)
Profile: p.512
Telecom, Broadcast & Satellite Band 4
Table: p.492

**Ferdinands, Paul** (Georgia)
Profile: p.712
Bankruptcy Band 2
Table: p.679

**Fereday, Jeffrey** (Idaho)
Natural Resources Band 1
Table: p.761

**Ferenbach, Cam** (Nevada)
Litigation Band 2
Table: p.1252

**Ferencik, Robert E**
(Florida)
Construction Band 2
Table: p.590

**Ferguson, James R**
(Illinois)
Profile: p.829
Litigation Band 4
Table: p.802

**Ferland, Roger** (Arizona)
Profile: p.190
Environment Band 1
Table: p.179

**Fernandez, Michael**
(National)
Profile: p.99
Transportation Band 4
Table: p.74

**Ferrara, Ralph C**
(District of Columbia)
Profile: p.512
Securities Band 2
Table: p.485

**Ferrario, Mark E** (Nevada)
Profile: p.1258
Litigation Band 3
Table: p.1252

**Ferrazzano, Dennis**
(Illinois)
Real Estate Band 2
Table: p.809

**Ferrell, Charles**
(Minnesota)
Profile: p.1163
Real Estate Band 1
Table: p.1160

**Ferrer, Eugene** (National)
Profile: p.99
Capital Markets
Up and coming
Table: p.13

**Ferrera, Tess**
(District of Columbia)
Profile: p.512
Employee Benefits Band 3
Table: p.437

**Ferrin, Shawn** (Utah)
Profile: p.1951
Real Estate Band 2
Table: p.1947

**Ferris, Charles**
(District of Columbia)
Telecom, Broadcast & Satellite
Band 4
Table: p.492

**Ferron Jr, William O**
(Washington)
Intellectual Property Band 2
Table: p.1998

**Fersko, Jack** (New Jersey)
Real Estate Band 1
Table: p.1293

**Fessler, Daniel W**
(California)
Profile: p.288
Energy Band 3
Table: p.233

**Fetscher, Candace**
(Montana)
Employment Band 1
Table: p.1223

**Feuerstein, Howard**
(Oregon)
Real Estate Band 1
Table: p.1677

**Few Jr, Richard L**
(South Carolina)
Corporate/M&A Band 3
Table: p.1775

**Fickle, Stanley** (Indiana)
Profile: p.896
Litigation ✪
Table: p.890

**Field, Andrea Bear**
(District of Columbia)
Profile: p.512
Environment Band 2
Table: p.451

**Field, Lawrence**
(Minnesota)
Litigation Band 3
Table: p.1156

**Fields, Bertram** (California)
Media & Entertainment Band 1
Table: p.263

**Fields, Henry M** (National)
Profile: p.99
Financial Services Band 2
Table: p.24

**Fields, Jack** (Texas)
Real Estate Band 3
Table: p.1872

**Fields, Leslie** (Colorado)
Profile: p.359
Real Estate Band 2
Table: p.355

**Fields, Richard** (New York)
Profile: p.1454
Insurance Band 3
Table: p.1379

**Fife, Lori R** (New York)
Profile: p.1454
Bankruptcy Band 3
Table: p.1344

**Fife, Randolph W** (West
Virginia)
Litigation Band 1
Table: p.2013

**Fifer, Sam** (Illinois)
Profile: p.829
Media & Entertainment Band 1
Table: p.806

**Figenshaw, Michael H**
(Iowa)
Litigation Band 1
Table: p.914

**Fijolek, Richard M** (Texas)
Tax Band 4
Table: p.1875

**Fikso, Robert** (Washington)
Real Estate Band 3
Table: p.2002

**Filardi, Edward V** (New
York)
Profile: p.1454
Intellectual Property Band 2
Table: p.1384

**Fildes, Richard J** (Florida)
Real Estate Band 3
Table: p.617

**Fileti, Thomas** (California)
Profile: p.288
Real Estate Band 3
Table: p.270

**Fine, Drew S** (National)
Transportation Band 1
Table: p.64

**Finegold, Laurence B**
(Washington)
Litigation Band 1
Table: p.2000

**Fink, Stephen F** (Texas)
Profile: p.1890
Employment Band 3
Table: p.1844

**Finke, Robert F** (Illinois)
Profile: p.829
Antitrust Band 3
Table: p.767

**Finkel, Robert** (New York)
Business Process Outsourcing
Band 3
Table: p.2
Technology Band 3
Table: p.1428

**Finkelman, Daniel P**
(Massachusetts)
Profile: p.1092
Private Equity Band 2
Table: p.1080

**Finkelson, Allen** (New York)
Profile: p.1454
Corporate/M&A Band 1
Table: p.1354

**Finkelstein, Jesse A**
(Delaware)
Profile: p.404
Chancery ✪
Table: p.392
Corporate/M&A Band 2
Table: p.394

**Finkelstein, Stuart M**
(New York)
Profile: p.1454
Tax Band 4
Table: p.1423

**Finley, John G** (New York)
Profile: p.1454
Corporate/M&A Band 2
Table: p.1354

**Finley, Joseph** (Minnesota)
Real Estate Band 3
Table: p.1160

**Finley, Thomas A** (Iowa)
Litigation Band 1
Table: p.914

**Finn, Terrence** (Ohio)
Environment Band 4
Table: p.1612

**Finn Braddock, Patricia**
(Texas)
Profile: p.1890
Environment Band 1
Table: p.1852

**Finn III, Harold B**
(Connecticut)
Profile: p.382
Corporate/M&A Band 1
Table: p.374

**Finnegan, Sheila M**
(Illinois)
Profile: p.829
Litigation Band 4
Table: p.802

**Finnegan IV, William N**
(Texas)
Profile: p.1890
Corporate/M&A Band 4
Table: p.1840

**Finto, Kevin J** (Virginia)
Profile: p.1982
Environment Band 1
Table: p.1973

**Finucane, Brian J**
(Missouri)
Profile: p.1205
Employment Band 1
Table: p.1195

**Fiorentino, Mark H**
(Nevada)
Profile: p.1258
Real Estate Band 1
Table: p.1255

**Fischer, A Robert**
(Connecticut)
Profile: p.383
Employment Band 3
Table: p.376

**Fischer, Gordon** (Iowa)
Employment Band 3
Table: p.912

**Fischer, L Richard**
(National)
Profile: p.99
Financial Services Band 1
Table: p.24

**Fischer, Matthew E**
(Delaware)
Profile: p.404
Corporate/M&A
Up and coming
Table: p.395

**Fischer, Rebecca**
(Colorado)
Profile: p.359
Real Estate Band 1
Table: p.355

**Fischer, Ronald**
(North Dakota)
Litigation Band 1
Table: p.1593

**Fischer, Samuel N**
(California)
Media & Entertainment Band 2
Table: p.266

**Fish, Ronald** (Maryland)
Profile: p.1038
Real Estate Band 2
Table: p.1035

**Fishbein, Matthew E** (New
York)
Litigation Band 3
Table: p.1391

**Fisher, Morton** (Maryland)
Profile: p.1038
Real Estate Band 1
Table: p.1035

**Fisher, Robert** (Missouri)
Profile: p.1205
Corporate/M&A Band 1
Table: p.1193

**Fisher, Todd A.** (Texas)
Technology Up and coming
Table: p.1877

**Fishman, David** (Maryland)
Real Estate Band 1
Table: p.1035

**Fishman, Louis Y**
(Louisiana)
Profile: p.980
Corporate/M&A Band 1
Table: p.965

**Fishman, Michael T**
(Illinois)
Profile: p.829
Real Estate Up and coming
Table: p.809

**Fishman, Robert A**
(Massachusetts)
Real Estate Band 1
Table: p.1081
Real Estate Band 1
Table: p.1081

**Fishman, Robert M**
(Illinois)
Bankruptcy Band 3
Table: p.775

**Fisk, Hollye** (Texas)
Construction Band 3
Table: p.1838

**Fiske, Robert** (New York)
Profile: p.1454
Litigation Band S
Table: p.1388
Litigation Band S
Table: p.1391

**Fitch, Stephen** (Ohio)
Litigation Band 3
Table: p.1617

**Fitz, William A**
(District of Columbia)
Profile: p.512
Telecom, Broadcast & Satellite
Band 4
Table: p.492

**Fitzgerald, Anthony**
(Connecticut)
Litigation Band 1
Table: p.378

**FitzGerald, Brian T**
(New York)
Profile: p.1454
Energy Band 1
Table: p.1370

**FitzGerald, Edmond** (New
York)
Profile: p.1454
Employee Benefits Band 3
Table: p.1362

**Fitzgerald, James**
(Nebraska)
Litigation Band 2
Table: p.1239

**Fitzgerald, Kevin M**
(New Hampshire)
Profile: p.1272
Litigation Band 3
Table: p.1267

**Fitzgerald, Mark R**
(District of Columbia)
Profile: p.512
Healthcare Band 2
Table: p.456

**Fitzgerald, Miranda**
(Florida)
Real Estate Band 1
Table: p.621

**Fitzgerald, Peter F**
(London)
Profile: p.512
Projects Band 1
Table: p.56
Projects Band 1
Table: p.479

**Fitzgerald, Robert M**
(Virginia)
Profile: p.1982
Construction Band 1
Table: p.1965

**Fitzgerald Jr, Robert E**
(Missouri)
Profile: p.1205
Corporate/M&A Band 3
Table: p.1193
Real Estate Band 2
Table: p.1201

**FitzMaurice, Daniel L**
(Connecticut)
Profile: p.383
Litigation Band 3
Table: p.378

**FitzPatrick Jr, James A**
(New York)
Profile: p.1455
Insurance Band 3
Table: p.1380

**Fitzpatrick Jr, Michael F**
(New York)
Profile: p.1455
Energy Band 3
Table: p.1367

**FitzPatrick Jr, Vincent R**
(New York)
Profile: p.1455
Litigation Band 3
Table: p.1388

**Fjelstad, Eric B** (Alaska)
Environment Band 1
Table: p.170

**Flagel, Mark A** (California)
Intellectual Property Band 3
Table: p.248

**Flaherty, Thomas** (West Virginia)
Litigation Band 1
Table: p.2013

**Flaherty, Thomas** (Virginia)
Profile: p.1982
Employment Band 2
Table: p.1971

**Flake, Richard** (Texas)
Construction Band 3
Table: p.1838

**Flanagan, Peter L**
(National)
Profile: p.99
International Trade Band 1
Table: p.41

**Flanders Jr, Robert G**
(Rhode Island)
Litigation Band 2
Table: p.1769

**Flanigan, Daniel J**
(Missouri)
Profile: p.1205
Real Estate Band 3
Table: p.1201

**Flaum, Douglas H**
(New York)
Profile: p.1455
Litigation Band 3
Table: p.1388

**Flaum, Keith** (California)
Corporate/M&A Band 4
Table: p.227

**Fleder, Robert C** (New York)
Profile: p.1455
Employee Benefits Band 2
Table: p.1362

**Fleischaker, Jon** (Kentucky)
Profile: p.947
Employment Band 2
Table: p.939

**Fleischer Jr, Arthur** (New York)
Profile: p.1455
Corporate/M&A Band S
Table: p.1354

**Fleming, John H** (Georgia)
Profile: p.712
Litigation Band 2
Table: p.698

**Fleming, Joseph** (Florida)
Profile: p.635
Employment Band 2
Table: p.597

**Fleming, Joycelyn L**
(Georgia)
Profile: p.712
Immigration Band 2
Table: p.694

**Fleming, Terrence**
(Minnesota)
Profile: p.1163
Litigation Band 2
Table: p.1156

**Fleming Jr, Peter** (New York)
Profile: p.1455
Litigation Band S
Table: p.1391

**Flesher, Gail** (New York)
Profile: p.1455
Environment Band 1
Table: p.1373

**Fletcher, Jennifer** (Georgia)
Profile: p.713
Construction Band 1
Table: p.682

**Fletcher, John** (Arkansas)
Corporate/Commercial Band 2
Table: p.201

**Fletcher, N Scott** (Texas)
Profile: p.1891
Litigation Band 1
Table: p.1866

**Fletcher, PK** (Florida)
Profile: p.636
Real Estate Band 2
Table: p.617

**Flexner, Donald L**
(District of Columbia)
Profile: p.512
Antitrust Band 3
Table: p.426

**Flick II, Lawrence**
(Pennsylvania)
Profile: p.1727
Banking & Finance Band 1
Table: p.1695

**Flics, Martin** (New York)
Profile: p.1455
Bankruptcy Band 4
Table: p.1344

**Flinn, Patrick J** (Georgia)
Profile: p.713
Intellectual Property Band 1
Table: p.696

**Flom, Joseph H** (New York)
Profile: p.1455
Corporate/M&A Band S
Table: p.1354

**Florack, James A** (New York)
Profile: p.1456
Banking & Finance Band 4
Table: p.1339

**Flores, Jean M.** (Texas)
Environment Band 4
Table: p.1852

**Florie, Michael A**
(Alabama)
Profile: p.156
Litigation Band 2
Table: p.152

**Florsheim, Richard S**
(Wisconsin)
Profile: p.2033
Intellectual Property Band 2
Table: p.2028

**Flowe Jr, Benjamin H**
(National)
Profile: p.99
International Trade Band 1
Table: p.41

**Floyd, Adam** (Texas)
Profile: p.1891
Intellectual Property Band 3
Table: p.1860

**Floyd, John** (Georgia)
Profile: p.713
Litigation Band 3
Table: p.698

**Fluharty, Robert** (West Virginia)
Profile: p.2017
Real Estate Band 2
Table: p.2015

**Fluhrer, Gary** (Washington)
Real Estate Band 1
Table: p.2002

**Flumenbaum, Martin**
(New York)
Profile: p.1456
Litigation Band 3
Table: p.1388

**Flygare, Thomas**
(New Hampshire)
Employment Band 1
Table: p.1265

**Flynn, Christopher** (Illinois)
Profile: p.829
Energy Band 2
Table: p.789

**Flynn III, William J**
(Florida)
Immigration Band 1
Table: p.606

**Focht, Jack** (Kansas)
Profile: p.931
Litigation Band 2
Table: p.927

**Fodor, Susanna Serena**
(New York)
Profile: p.1456
Real Estate Band 5
Table: p.1417

**Fogarty, James**
(Connecticut)
Litigation Band 3
Table: p.378

**Fogarty, Robert J** (Ohio)
Litigation Band 4
Table: p.1617

**Foggan, Laura**
(District of Columbia)
Profile: p.512
Insurance Band 2
Table: p.461

**Fogler, Murray** (Texas)
Energy Band 3
Table: p.1849
Litigation Band 2
Table: p.1865

**Fognani, John D** (Colorado)
Environment Band 2
Table: p.350

**Foley, Christopher**
(Virginia)
Profile: p.1982
Intellectual Property Band 2
Table: p.1975

**Foley, Mark** (Pennsylvania)
Profile: p.1728
Employment Band 2
Table: p.1703

**Foley, Robert J** (Vermont)
Real Estate Band 3
Table: p.1961

**Foley, Thomas** (Iowa)
Employment Band 2
Table: p.912

**Foltyn, David** (Michigan)
Profile: p.1134
Corporate/M&A Band 1
Table: p.1122

**Fontaine, Mary C**
(National)
Profile: p.100
Capital Markets Band 4
Table: p.18

**Fontana, Angela** (Texas)
Profile: p.1891
Banking & Finance Band 3
Table: p.1832

**Fontham, Michael R**
(Louisiana)
Profile: p.980
Energy Band 1
Table: p.969

**Foradas, Michael P**
(Illinois)
Profile: p.829
Insurance Band 1
Table: p.796

**Forbes, Amy R** (California)
Profile: p.289
Real Estate Band 2
Table: p.270

**Forcade, Bill S** (Illinois)
Profile: p.829
Environment Band 3
Table: p.791

**Ford, Barry W** (Mississippi)
Profile: p.1184
Litigation Band 2
Table: p.1179

**Ford, Christopher D**
(National)
Profile: p.100
Business Process Outsourcing
Band 2
Table: p.2

**Ford, Debra Weiss**
(New Hampshire)
Employment Band 1
Table: p.1265

**Ford, Gary M**
(District of Columbia)
Employee Benefits Band 2
Table: p.437

**Ford, Jeffrey** (Texas)
Construction Band 3
Table: p.1838

**Ford, John M**
(District of Columbia)
Profile: p.513
Investment Management Band 3
Table: p.469

**Ford Jacob, Valerie**
(New York)
Profile: p.100
Capital Markets Band 3
Table: p.7

**Ford Jr, Thomas W** (Texas)
Tax Band 3
Table: p.1875

**Ford Jr, William F**
(Missouri)
Profile: p.1205
Litigation Band 1
Table: p.928

**Fore, John A** (National)
Profile: p.100
Capital Markets Band 2
Table: p.8

**Foreman, Lee** (Colorado)
Litigation Band 1
Table: p.353

**Forman, Adam**
(Massachusetts)
Profile: p.1092
Employment Band 3
Table: p.1065

**Forman, Harvey**
(Pennsylvania)
Profile: p.1728
Banking & Finance Band 2
Table: p.1695

**Forman, Wayne F**
(Colorado)
Profile: p.360
Real Estate Band 1
Table: p.355

**Fornaris, Carl A** (Florida)
Profile: p.636
Banking & Finance Band 2
Table: p.583

**Forrest, Katherine B**
(New York)
Profile: p.1456
Antitrust Band 4
Table: p.1335
Intellectual Property Band 2
Table: p.1385

**Forrester, J Paul** (Illinois)
Profile: p.830
Banking & Finance Band 2
Table: p.771

**Forry, Robert H** (Georgia)
Energy Band 1
Table: p.689

**Forst, David** (California)
Profile: p.289
Tax Up and coming
Table: p.274

**Forsten, Richard**
(Delaware)
Profile: p.404
Real Estate Band 2
Table: p.400

**Forsyth, J David**
(Louisiana)
Corporate/M&A Band 2
Table: p.965

**Fort, Jeffrey** (Illinois)
Profile: p.830
Environment Band 2
Table: p.791

**Forte, Joseph Philip**
(New York)
Profile: p.1456
Real Estate Band 3

**Table: p.1417**

**Forte, Stephen M**
(Georgia)
Litigation Band 3
Table: p.698

**Forti, David W**
(Pennsylvania)
Profile: p.1728
Real Estate Band 2
Table: p.1718

**Fortino, Paul** (Oregon)
Litigation Band 1
Table: p.1674

**Fortney, David**
(District of Columbia)
Employment Band 2
Table: p.439

**Foss, Marilyn**
(North Dakota)
Corporate/Commercial Band 2
Table: p.1590

**Foster, Charles C** (Texas)
Immigration Band 1
Table: p.1856

**Foster, John S**
(North Dakota)
Corporate/Commercial Band 1
Table: p.1590

**Foster, Joseph E** (Florida)
Profile: p.636
Litigation Band 4
Table: p.609

**Foster, Murphy** (Louisiana)
Employment Band 3
Table: p.967

**Foster, Stephen H**
(Montana)
Profile: p.1231
Natural Resources Band 1
Table: p.1228

**Fournier, David M**
(Delaware)
Profile: p.404
Bankruptcy Band 4
Table: p.389

**Foust, Lawrence L** (Texas)
Healthcare Band 2
Table: p.1855

**Fowler, Jay** (Kansas)
Profile: p.931
Litigation Band 2
Table: p.927

**Fowler, John** (Nevada)
Corporate/Commercial Band 1
Table: p.1246

**Fowler, Lynn E** (Georgia)
Profile: p.713
Tax Band 3
Table: p.703

**Fox, Allen H**
(District of Columbia)
Profile: p.513
Real Estate Band 4
Table: p.482

**Fox, David** (New York)
Profile: p.1456
Corporate/M&A Band 3
Table: p.1354

**Fox, J Nixon** (Texas)
Profile: p.1891
Technology Band 3
Table: p.1878

**Fox, Kate** (Wyoming)
Employment Band 1
Table: p.2042
Litigation Band 2
Table: p.2044

**Fox, Michael W** (Texas)
Profile: p.1891
Employment Band 2
Table: p.1844

**Fox, Robert** (Pennsylvania)
Environment Band 2
Table: p.1707

**Fox, Steven F** (Georgia)
Corporate/M&A Band 4
Table: p.684

**Fox, Thomas**
(District of Columbia)
Profile: p.513
Healthcare Band 2
Table: p.456

**Fox-Isicoff, Tammy**
(Florida)
Immigration Band 1
Table: p.606

**Foy, Stacey W E** (Hawaii)
Profile: p.751
Real Estate Band 3
Table: p.748

**Foye, Thomas H**
(South Dakota)
Real Estate Band 1
Table: p.1796

**Frackman, Russell**
(California)
Media & Entertainment Band 2
Table: p.263

**Fragomen Jr, Austin T**
(New York)
Immigration Band S
Table: p.1376

**Fraidin, Stephen**
(New York)
Profile: p.1456
Corporate/M&A Band 3
Table: p.1354
Private Equity Band 1
Table: p.1407

**Fram, Robert** (California)
Profile: p.289
Intellectual Property Band 4
Table: p.248

**France, Lucy T** (Montana)
Employment Band 3
Table: p.1223

**France, Thomas W**
(Virginia)
Corporate/M&A Band 2

**Table: p.1967**

**France II, William N**
(New York)
Profile: p.100
Transportation Band 4
Table: p.74

**Francescani, David**
(New York)
Profile: p.1456
Intellectual Property Band 3
Table: p.1384

**Franchina, David A**
(North Carolina)
Environment Band 2
Table: p.1575

**Francis, Jane** (Colorado)
Profile: p.360
Employment Band 1
Table: p.348

**Franczek, James** (Illinois)
Employment Band 1
Table: p.785

**Frandsen, Nancy R**
(Pennsylvania)
Intellectual Property Band 4
Table: p.1711

**Frank, Ian H** (Ohio)
Construction Up and coming
Table: p.1603

**Frank, Robert**
(Massachusetts)
Intellectual Property Band 1
Table: p.1072

**Frank, Robert** (Maine)
Litigation Band 1
Table: p.1006

**Frank, Steven J**
(Massachusetts)
Profile: p.1092
Intellectual Property Band 3
Table: p.1072

**Frankel, Roger**
(District of Columbia)
Profile: p.513
Bankruptcy Band 1
Table: p.432

**Frankenheimer, John T**
(California)
Profile: p.289
Media & Entertainment Band 3
Table: p.266

**Franklin, Gary L** (Vermont)
Litigation Band 3
Table: p.1959

**Franklin, Jonathan S**
(District of Columbia)
Profile: p.513
Litigation Band 2
Table: p.475

**Franklin, Samuel H**
(Alabama)
Litigation Band 1
Table: p.152

**Frankovich, John** (Nevada)
Real Estate Band 2
Table: p.1255

**Franse, R Nelson**
(New Mexico)
Litigation Band 2
Table: p.1324
Litigation Band 2
Table: p.1324

**Franson, Marc P** (Illinois)
Banking & Finance Band 3
Table: p.771

**Frantz, Mary Ann** (Oregon)
Profile: p.1681
Corporate/M&A Band 3
Table: p.1667

**Frantz, Michael** (Ohio)
Employment Band 1
Table: p.1609

**Frantz, Steven**
(District of Columbia)
Profile: p.513
Energy Band 3
Table: p.449

**Frantz, Thomas R** (Virginia)
Corporate/M&A Band 2
Table: p.1968

**Frantze, David** (Missouri)
Profile: p.1206
Real Estate Band 1
Table: p.1201

**Franze, Laura M** (Texas)
Profile: p.1891
Employment Band 2
Table: p.1844

**Franzetti, Susan M**
(Illinois)
Environment Band 2
Table: p.791

**Fraser, Thomas**
(Minnesota)
Litigation Band 2
Table: p.1156

**Fratianni, Constance A**
(New York)
Profile: p.1456
Bankruptcy Band 4
Table: p.1344

**Frawley, Alfred** (Maine)
Profile: p.1012
Litigation Band 3
Table: p.1006

**Frazen, Laurence**
(Missouri)
Litigation Band 3
Table: p.1198

**Frazier, Keith D**
(Tennessee)
Profile: p.1812
Employment Band 2
Table: p.1801

**Frazier, Randal B**
(Arkansas)
Profile: p.209
Real Estate Band 1

Table: p.742

**Fulkerson, Sam**
(Oklahoma)
Employment Band 2
Table: p.1654

**Fullenkamp, John**
(Nebraska)
Real Estate Band 1
Table: p.1242

**Fuller, Gary** (Oklahoma)
Corporate/Commercial
Band S
Table: p.1653

**Fuller, James** (California)
Profile: p.289
Tax Band 1
Table: p.274

**Fuller, Robert**
(North Carolina)
Litigation Band 3
Table: p.1577

**Fuller, William P**
(South Dakota)
Litigation Band 1
Table: p.1795

**Fuller III, William H**
(North Carolina)
Banking & Finance Band 2
Table: p.1569

**Fulton, Charles**
(North Carolina)
Real Estate Band S
Table: p.1579

**Funk, John A** (Texas)
Profile: p.1892
Business Process Outsourcing
Band 1
Table: p.2
Technology Band 1
Table: p.1877

**Funk, Mary E** (Iowa)
Employment Up and coming
Table: p.912

**Fuqua, James A** (Delaware)
Real Estate Band 3
Table: p.400

**Furci, Peter** (New York)
Tax Up and coming
Table: p.1423

**Furey, Michael K**
(New Jersey)
Profile: p.1298
Employment Band 2
Table: p.1282

**Furr, Jeffrey L**
(North Carolina)
Profile: p.1583
Litigation Band 4
Table: p.1577

**Fussell, Herman L**
(Georgia)
Construction Band 3
Table: p.682

---

## G

**Gabay, Donald** (New York)
Insurance Band 2
Table: p.1380

**Gabbert Jr, Craig V**
(Tennessee)
Litigation Band 1
Table: p.1804
Litigation Band 2
Table: p.1804

**Gabric, Ralph J** (Illinois)
Profile: p.830
Intellectual Property Band 3
Table: p.799

**Gabrio, Gino L** (Hawaii)
Real Estate Band 1
Table: p.748

**Gade, Mary A** (Illinois)
Profile: p.830
Environment Band 3
Table: p.791

**Gaffney, John T** (New York)
Profile: p.1457
Media & Entertainment Band 1
Table: p.1403

**Gaffney, Todd** (Iowa)
Litigation Band 3
Table: p.914

**Gage, Robert J**
(District of Columbia)
Profile: p.514
Real Estate Band 4
Table: p.482

**Gagliano, Bill** (Ohio)
Real Estate Band 4
Table: p.1621

**Gagliardo, Joseph M**
(Illinois)
Employment Band 2
Table: p.785

**Gagnon, Bruce** (Alaska)
Litigation Band 1
Table: p.171

**Gaillard, W Foster**
(South Carolina)
Profile: p.1782
Real Estate Band 1
Table: p.1780

**Gainor, Edward E**
(National)
Profile: p.100
Capital Markets Band 4
Table: p.18

**Galainena, M David**
(National)
Profile: p.101
Capital Markets Band 4
Table: p.18

**Galardi, Gregg M**
(Delaware)
Profile: p.404
Bankruptcy Band 1
Table: p.389

**Galati, Vito** (Hawaii)
Corporate/Commercial Band 2
Table: p.741

**Galchus, Donna Smith**
(Arkansas)
Employment Band 3
Table: p.203

**Gale, Kelley** (California)
Projects Band 3
Table: p.268

**Galeota, William** (West
Virginia)
Litigation Band 2
Table: p.2013

**Gall, John R** (Ohio)
Profile: p.1627
Litigation Band 3
Table: p.1617

**Gall, Phillip J** (New York)
Tax Up and coming
Table: p.1423

**Gallagher, James J**
(National)
Profile: p.101
Government Contracts Band 2
Table: p.30

**Gallagher, Patrick C**
(New York)
Profile: p.1457
Tax Band 3
Table: p.1423

**Gallagher, Robert**
(District of Columbia)
Employee Benefits Band S
Table: p.437

**Gallagher, Sean** (Colorado)
Profile: p.360
Employment Band 2
Table: p.348

**Gallegos, J E**
(New Mexico)
Environment Band 1
Table: p.1323
Litigation Band 3
Table: p.1324

**Gallinger, John** (Wyoming)
Profile: p.2047
Real Estate Band 2
Table: p.2045

**Gallion, Theresa M**
(Florida)
Profile: p.636
Employment Band 2
Table: p.597

**Gallo, Barbara** (Georgia)
Profile: p.713
Environment Band 2
Table: p.691

**Gallo, Greg** (California)
Profile: p.289

Corporate/M&A Band 2
Table: p.227

**Gallo, John N** (Illinois)
Profile: p.831
Litigation Band 4
Table: p.802

**Gallo, Joie Marie**
(California)
Media & Entertainment Band 4
Table: p.263

**Gallo, Kenneth A**
(District of Columbia)
Profile: p.514
Antitrust Band 5
Table: p.426

**Galloway, Robert**
(Mississippi)
Profile: p.1184
Litigation Band 2
Table: p.1179

**Galvan, Hilda** (Texas)
Profile: p.1892
Intellectual Property Band 3
Table: p.1860

**Galvani, Paul B**
(Massachusetts)
Profile: p.1093
Litigation Band S
Table: p.1074

**Galvis, Sergio J** (New York)
Profile: p.1458
Projects Band 2
Table: p.56
Projects Band 2
Table: p.1413

**Gamboli, Michael**
(Rhode Island)
Employment Band 1
Table: p.1768

**Gambro, Michael S**
(National)
Profile: p.101
Capital Markets Band 3
Table: p.18

**Gammage Jr, Grady**
(Arizona)
Real Estate Band 1
Table: p.186

**Gandhi, Samir A** (National)
Profile: p.101
Capital Markets
Up and coming
Table: p.13

**Gangemi Jr, Columbus R**
(Illinois)
Profile: p.831
Employment Band 1
Table: p.785

**Gannett, William B**
(National)
Capital Markets Band 4
Table: p.7

**Gansberg, Andrew**
(New York)
Profile: p.1458
Energy Band 1

Table: p.1370

**Ganske, Lyle** (Ohio)
Profile: p.1627
Corporate/M&A Band 1
Table: p.1605

**Ganz, Howard** (New York)
Profile: p.1458
Employment Band 2
Table: p.1365
Sport Band 1
Table: p.59

**Garber, Kevin J**
(Pennsylvania)
Environment Band 2
Table: p.1707

**Garcia, Brian** (Florida)
Profile: p.636
Immigration Band 1
Table: p.606

**Garcia, David A** (Nevada)
Corporate/Commercial Band 2
Table: p.1246

**Garcia, Rodrigo** (Texas)
Insurance Band 3
Table: p.1858

**Gardill, James** (West
Virginia)
Corporate/Commercial Band 2
Table: p.2010

**Gardiner, John L** (New York)
Profile: p.101
International Arbitration
Band 3
Table: p.36

**Gardiner, Samuel P** (Utah)
Profile: p.1951
Corporate/M&A
Up and coming
Table: p.1941

**Gardner, Price** (Arkansas)
Corporate/Commercial Band 2
Table: p.201
Real Estate Band 2
Table: p.207

**Gardner, Russell H**
(Maryland)
Profile: p.1039
Employment Band 2
Table: p.1028

**Gardner, Stephen D**
(National)
Tax Litigation Band 1

**Gardner, William** (Alabama)
Employment Band S
Table: p.150

**Garfinkel, Barry H**
(New York)
Profile: p.101
Arbitration Band 1
Table: p.37
International Arbitration
Band 2
Table: p.36

---

G

**Garfunkel, David**
(New Hampshire)
Profile: p.1272
Litigation Band 4
Table: p.1267

**Garibaldi, Oscar M**
(District of Columbia)
Profile: p.101
International Arbitration
Band 2
Table: p.36

**Garland, David W** (New
Jersey)
Profile: p.1298
Employment Band 2
Table: p.1282

**Garmer III, Benjamin F**
(Wisconsin)
Profile: p.2033
Corporate/M&A Band 1
Table: p.2025

**Garner, James** (Louisiana)
Profile: p.980
Litigation Band 2
Table: p.973

**Garnsey Jr, Walter W**
(Colorado)
Profile: p.360
Litigation Band 3
Table: p.353

**Garofalo, Beverly W**
(Connecticut)
Profile: p.383
Employment Band 2
Table: p.376

**Garofalo, Gary B** (National)
Profile: p.101
Transportation Band 3
Table: p.67

**Garon, Philip S** (Minnesota)
Profile: p.1163
Corporate/M&A Band 1
Table: p.1152

**Garone, Michael** (Oregon)
Employment Band 3
Table: p.1670

**Garretson, Thomas P**
(Kansas)
Corporate/M&A Band 2
Table: p.924

**Garrett, G Lee** (Georgia)
Profile: p.713
Litigation Band 3
Table: p.698

**Garrett, Theodore**
(District of Columbia)
Profile: p.514
Environment Band S
Table: p.451

**Garrett, Tim K** (Tennessee)
Profile: p.1813
Employment Band 2
Table: p.1801

**Garrity, James** (New York)
Profile: p.1458
Bankruptcy Band 4

Table: p.1344

**Garry, William C**
(South Dakota)
Litigation Band 2
Table: p.1795

**Gart, Brian** (Florida)
Profile: p.636
Bankruptcy Band 2
Table: p.586

**Gartman, John** (California)
Profile: p.289
Intellectual Property Band 3
Table: p.248

**Gartner, Steven** (New York)
Profile: p.1458
Private Equity Band 2
Table: p.1407

**Garton, Thomas W**
(Minnesota)
Corporate/M&A Band 3
Table: p.1152

**Gartrell, Donald E**
(New Hampshire)
Profile: p.1272
Real Estate Band 2
Table: p.1270

**Garvin, Anthony O**
(California)
Profile: p.290
Environment Band 4
Table: p.236

**Garvin, Michele M**
(Massachusetts)
Profile: p.1093
Healthcare Band 1
Table: p.1071

**Garwood, Thomas** (Florida)
Profile: p.636
Employment Band 1
Table: p.597

**Garza, Deborah**
(District of Columbia)
Profile: p.514
Antitrust Band 5
Table: p.426

**Garza, Oscar** (California)
Profile: p.290
Bankruptcy Band 4
Table: p.222

**Gasch Jr, Manning**
(Virginia)
Profile: p.1982
Environment Band S
Table: p.1973

**Gaskins Jr, Richard C**
(North Carolina)
Environment Band 2
Table: p.1575

**Gately, Mark** (Maryland)
Profile: p.1039
Litigation Band 2
Table: p.1032

**Gates, Allan** (Arkansas)
Litigation Band 1
Table: p.205

**Gates, Martin S** (Ohio)
Profile: p.1627
Banking & Finance Band 2
Table: p.1598

**Gathright Jr, Joseph R**
(Kentucky)
Real Estate Band 2
Table: p.944

**Gatto, James** (Virginia)
Profile: p.1982
Intellectual Property Band 2
Table: p.1975

**Gaudreau Jr, Russell A**
(Massachusetts)
Profile: p.1093
Employee Benefits Band 2
Table: p.1063

**Gauer, Keith A**
(South Dakota)
Corporate/Commercial Band 2
Table: p.1792

**Gault, Robert M**
(Massachusetts)
Profile: p.1093
Employment Band 3
Table: p.1065

**Gaunt, Karen Kreider**
(Ohio)
Intellectual Property
Up and coming
Table: p.1614

**Gavin, Tim** (Texas)
Litigation Band 3
Table: p.1865

**Gavre, Mark** (Utah)
Profile: p.1951
Employment Band 3
Table: p.1944

**Gay, Faith Elizabeth**
(New York)
Profile: p.1458
Litigation Band 3
Table: p.1391

**Gaynor, Bruce** (Ohio)
Profile: p.1627
Real Estate Band 3
Table: p.1621

**Gaynor, Kevin**
(District of Columbia)
Profile: p.514
Environment Band 2
Table: p.451

**Geanacopoulos, Steve**
(Rhode Island)
Profile: p.1772
Corporate/Commercial Band 3
Table: p.1766

**Gearen, John J** (Illinois)
Profile: p.831
Real Estate Band 1
Table: p.809

**Geary Jr, Francis B**
(Florida)
Healthcare Band 2
Table: p.604

**Gee, David E** (Utah)
Real Estate Band 1
Table: p.1947

**Gee, William S** (Delaware)
Profile: p.404
Real Estate Band 2
Table: p.399

**Gehring, Stephen**
(Nebraska)
Corporate/M&A Band 2
Table: p.1236

**Geiger, Glenn C**
(New Jersey)
Profile: p.1299
Real Estate Band 1
Table: p.1293

**Geiger, Kathleen W**
(Delaware)
Profile: p.404
Intellectual Property Band 3
Table: p.397

**Geiger, Richard S** (Texas)
Insurance Band S
Table: p.1858

**Geister III, Charles E**
(Oklahoma)
Profile: p.1659
Litigation Band 3
Table: p.1656

**Gelber, Don** (Hawaii)
Bankruptcy Band 1
Table: p.739

**Gelber, Stephen M**
(Hawaii)
Corporate/Commercial Band 2
Table: p.740
Corporate/Commercial Band 2
Table: p.741

**Gelblum, Seth D**
(New York)
Profile: p.1458
Media & Entertainment Band 1
Table: p.1401

**Gelfand, David I**
(District of Columbia)
Profile: p.514
Antitrust Band 4
Table: p.426

**Geller, Kenneth S**
(District of Columbia)
Profile: p.514
Litigation Band 1
Table: p.475

**Gellman, Nancy**
(Pennsylvania)
Profile: p.1728
Litigation Band 2
Table: p.1714

**Gelman, Bruce L** (Illinois)
Profile: p.831
Tax Band 3
Table: p.812

**Gelston, Philip** (New York)
Profile: p.1458
Corporate/M&A Band 3
Table: p.1354

**Genberg, Ira** (Georgia)
Construction Band 1
Table: p.682

**Genet, Chava** (Florida)
Real Estate Band 3
Table: p.617

**Geno, Craig M** (Mississippi)
Corporate/Commercial Band 1
Table: p.1175

**Genova, Angelo** (New
Jersey)
Employment Band 1
Table: p.1282

**Genovese, John H** (Florida)
Profile: p.636
Bankruptcy Band 2
Table: p.586

**Genth, Geoffrey H**
(Maryland)
Profile: p.1039
Litigation Up and coming
Table: p.1032

**Gentile, Carmen**
(District of Columbia)
Energy Band 4
Table: p.445

**Gentile, Mark J** (Delaware)
Profile: p.404
Corporate/M&A Band 2
Table: p.394

**Gentile, Melinda S**
(Florida)
Profile: p.637
Construction Band 3
Table: p.590

**Gentner, Joshua D**
(National)
Transportation Up and coming
Table: p.64

**Genz, Peter** (Georgia)
Profile: p.713
Tax Band 2
Table: p.703

**Geoghegan, Patricia**
(New York)
Profile: p.1458
Tax Band 4
Table: p.1423

**George, Peter** (Illinois)
Profile: p.831
Business Process Outsourcing
Up and coming
Table: p.2
Technology Band 3
Table: p.814

**George, Peter E** (Florida)
Litigation Band 2
Table: p.610

**George, Shawn P**
(West Virginia)
Litigation Band 2
Table: p.2013

**Gerachis, George
Matthew** (Texas)
Profile: p.1892

G

Tax Band 2
Table: p.1875

**Geraci, Joseph V** (Texas)
Healthcare Associate to
watch
Table: p.1855

**Geraghty, William P**
(Florida)
Profile: p.637
Litigation Up and coming
Table: p.609

**Gerakitis, Richard**
(Georgia)
Employment Band 3
Table: p.687

**Gerber, Dean N** (Illinois)
Banking & Finance Band 3
Table: p.771
Transportation Band 1
Table: p.64

**Gerber, Toby L** (Texas)
Profile: p.1892
Bankruptcy Band 4
Table: p.1835

**Gergen, Michael**
(District of Columbia)
Energy Band 4
Table: p.445

**Germain, Kenneth** (Ohio)
Profile: p.1628
Intellectual Property Band 1
Table: p.1614

**German, Charles** (Missouri)
Litigation Band 1
Table: p.1198
Litigation Band 1
Table: p.1198

**Germann, Hans J** (Illinois)
Profile: p.831
Telecom, Broadcast & Satellite
Up and coming
Table: p.816

**Gerrard, Michael** (New
York)
Profile: p.1458
Environment Band 1
Table: p.1371

**Gersch, David P**
(District of Columbia)
Profile: p.514
Litigation Band 3
Table: p.471

**Gerson, Herb** (Tennessee)
Profile: p.1813
Employment Band 2
Table: p.1801

**Gerstein, Mark D** (Illinois)
Corporate/M&A Band 2
Table: p.781
Corporate/M&A: Private Equity
Band 3
Table: p.782

**Gerstell, Glenn S**
(District of Columbia)

Telecom Broadcast & Sattelte

**Gerstenzang, Michael A**
(New York)
Profile: p.1459
Private Equity Band 3
Table: p.1410

**Gettleman, Chad H**
(Illinois)
Profile: p.831
Bankruptcy Band 3
Table: p.775

**Gewin, James** (Alabama)
Profile: p.156
Litigation Band 1
Table: p.152

**Gewirtz, Elliot** (New York)
Transportation Band 1
Table: p.64

**Gherlein, John M** (Ohio)
Corporate/M&A Band 3
Table: p.1605

**Gholz, Charles** (Virginia)
Intellectual Property Band 1
Table: p.1975

**Gianoulakis, John**
(Missouri)
Litigation Band 2
Table: p.1198

**Gibbens, Ray** (Alabama)
Banking & Finance Band 2
Table: p.147

**Gibbons, 3** (New Jersey)
Profile: p.1299
Litigation Band S
Table: p.1289

**Gibbons, Colette** (Ohio)
Profile: p.1628
Bankruptcy Band 3
Table: p.1600

**Gibbons, Robert J** (New
York)
Projects Band 4
Table: p.1413

**Gibbs, Charles R** (Texas)
Profile: p.1892
Bankruptcy Band 2
Table: p.1835

**Gibbs, Kenneth C**
(California)
Profile: p.290
Construction Band 2
Table: p.225

**Gibbs, Lawrence**
(District of Columbia)
Profile: p.514
Tax Band 3
Table: p.488

**Gibbs, Robert** (Mississippi)
Profile: p.1184
Litigation Band 2
Table: p.1179

**Gibbs, Robin C** (Texas)
Profile: p.1892
Energy Band 1

Table: p.1849
Litigation Band 1
Table: p.1865

**Gibby, Darin J** (Colorado)
Profile: p.360
Intellectual Property Band 1
Table: p.351

**Giblin, Pamela** (Texas)
Profile: p.1892
Environment ✪
Table: p.1852

**Giblin Jr, Thomas P**
(New York)
Profile: p.1459
Energy Band 2
Table: p.1367

**Gibson, Douglas G**
(National)
Profile: p.102
Sport Band 3
Table: p.59

**Gideon, CJ** (Tennessee)
Litigation Band 1
Table: p.1805

**Gideon, Kenneth W**
(District of Columbia)
Profile: p.515
Tax Band 2
Table: p.488

**Gidley, J Mark**
(District of Columbia)
Profile: p.515
Antitrust Band 4
Table: p.426

**Gidley, James** (Oregon)
Litigation Band 2
Table: p.1674

**Giesel, James A** (Kentucky)
Profile: p.947
Corporate/M&A Band 3
Table: p.937

**Gifford, David**
(Pennsylvania)
Profile: p.1728
Real Estate Band 2
Table: p.1718

**Gifford, Mark** (Wyoming)
Litigation Band 2
Table: p.2044

**Gifford, Robert E**
(West Virginia)
Litigation Band 1
Table: p.2013

**Gilberg, David J** (New York)
Profile: p.102
Capital Markets Band 2
Table: p.15

**Gilbert, Donald R** (Arizona)
Profile: p.190
Employment Band 4
Table: p.178

**Gilbert, Leonard H**
(Florida)
Profile: p.637
Bankruptcy Band 2

Table: p.586

**Gilbert, Paul D** (Tennessee)
Profile: p.1813
Corporate/M&A Band 2
Table: p.1799

**Gilbert, Paul E** (Arizona)
Real Estate Band 1
Table: p.186

**Gilbert, Richard** (New York)
Profile: p.1459
Employee Benefits Band 2
Table: p.1362

**Gilbert, Robert** (Florida)
Profile: p.637
Bankruptcy Band 3
Table: p.586

**Gilbert, Scott**
(District of Columbia)
Insurance Band 1
Table: p.464

**Gilden, David M.** (Rhode
Island)
Corporate/Commercial Band 3
Table: p.1766

**Gilford, Steven R** (Illinois)
Profile: p.831
Insurance Band 3
Table: p.795
Insurance Band 1
Table: p.796

**Gilkey, Duane C**
(New Mexico)
Employment Band 1
Table: p.1321

**Gill, Richard** (Alabama)
Litigation Band 3
Table: p.152

**Gillece Jr, James P**
(Maryland)
Profile: p.1039
Employment Band 3
Table: p.1028

**Gillen, Craig A** (Georgia)
Litigation Band 1
Table: p.698

**Gillen, Stephen E** (Ohio)
Intellectual Property Band 3
Table: p.1614

**Gillespie, Michael J**
(New York)
Media & Entertainment Band 2
Table: p.1403

**Gillespie, Thomas** (Texas)
Profile: p.1893
Banking & Finance Band 4
Table: p.1832

**Gillette, Patricia**
(California)
Profile: p.290
Employment Band 3
Table: p.231

**Gilliam, James H** (Iowa)
Profile: p.920
Employment Band 3

Table: p.912

**Gillies Jr, John J**
(Connecticut)
Profile: p.383
Real Estate Band 2
Table: p.380

**Gillis, Theresa** (New York)
Profile: p.1459
Intellectual Property Band 3
Table: p.1384

**Gilmore, Patrick** (Alaska)
Litigation Band 2
Table: p.171

**Gilpin, Thomas** (West
Virginia)
Real Estate Band 2
Table: p.2015

**Gilson, Gary** (Missouri)
Profile: p.1206
Corporate/M&A Band 1
Table: p.1193

**Gilson, Jerome** (Illinois)
Profile: p.832
Intellectual Property Band S
Table: p.799

**Ginn, Gregg H** (Maine)
Profile: p.1012
Employment Band 1
Table: p.1002

**Ginos, Geoffrey** (New York)
Transportation Band 4
Table: p.74

**Ginsberg, Benjamin L**
(National)
Profile: p.102
Government: Political Law
Band 2
Table: p.34

**Ginsberg, Beth**
(Washington)
Environment Band 2
Table: p.1996

**Ginsburg, Dennis** (Florida)
Tax Band 3
Table: p.623

**Ginsburg, Roy** (Minnesota)
Profile: p.1163
Employment Band 3
Table: p.1154

**Giordano, P Gregory**
(Nevada)
Gaming & Licensing Band 2
Table: p.1251

**Giotto, Thomas**
(Pennsylvania)
Profile: p.1728
Employment Band 1
Table: p.1703

**Giove, Stephen** (National)
Profile: p.102
Capital Markets Band 4
Table: p.7

**Girard, Robert D**
(California)
Profile: p.290
Healthcare Band 2
Table: p.238

**Gische, David**
(District of Columbia)
Insurance Band 3
Table: p.461

**Gisvold, Dean P** (Oregon)
Real Estate Band 2
Table: p.1677

**Gitomer, Deborah** (Texas)
Profile: p.1893
Energy Band 4
Table: p.1847

**Gitter, Max** (New York)
Profile: p.1459
Litigation Band 3
Table: p.1388
Litigation Band 3
Table: p.1390

**Gittes, Franklin M**
(New York)
Profile: p.1459
Corporate/M&A Band 3
Table: p.1354

**Gittler, Amy J** (Arizona)
Employment Band 4
Table: p.178

**Giuffra Jr, Robert J**
(New York)
Profile: p.1459
Litigation Band 3
Table: p.1390
Litigation Band 3
Table: p.1391

**Giuliani, Richard**
(Massachusetts)
Profile: p.1093
Tax Band 3
Table: p.1084

**Giunco Jr, John A** (New Jersey)
Real Estate Band 2
Table: p.1293

**Giunta, Joseph J**
(California)
Profile: p.290
Corporate/M&A Band 4
Table: p.227

**Givens, Leonard D**
(Michigan)
Profile: p.1134
Employment Band 1
Table: p.1125

**Glad, Paul E B** (California)
Profile: p.290
Insurance Band 1
Table: p.243

**Glade, Peter** (Oregon)
Litigation Band 2
Table: p.1674

**Glahn III, Wilbur A**
(New Hampshire)
Profile: p.1272

Litigation Band 2
Table: p.1267

**Glancz, Ronald R**
(National)
Financial Services Band 2
Table: p.28

**Glascock, Thomas B**
(California)
Profile: p.290
Projects Band 3
Table: p.268

**Glaser, D Louis** (Illinois)
Profile: p.832
Healthcare Band 2
Table: p.793

**Glaser, Kenneth** (Texas)
Profile: p.1893
Intellectual Property Band 3
Table: p.1860

**Glaser, Patricia** (California)
Litigation Band 4
Table: p.257
Media & Entertainment Band 1
Table: p.263

**Glasgow, Jr, Norman**
(District of Columbia)
Profile: p.515
Real Estate Band 2
Table: p.482

**Glass, Adam W** (National)
Profile: p.102
Capital Markets Band 2
Table: p.13

**Glasscock, C Edward**
(Kentucky)
Profile: p.947
Corporate/M&A Band 1
Table: p.937

**Glasser, Brian** (West Virginia)
Profile: p.2017
Litigation Band 2
Table: p.2013

**Glasser, Mark K** (Texas)
Profile: p.1893
Litigation Band 3
Table: p.1865

**Glassman, Neil** (Delaware)
Profile: p.404
Bankruptcy Band 3
Table: p.389

**Glasspiegel, Harry**
(District of Columbia)
Profile: p.515
Technology Band 3
Table: p.490

**Glazer, Dennis** (New York)
Profile: p.1459
Litigation Band 3
Table: p.1388

**Glazer, Michael H**
(Massachusetts)
Profile: p.1093
Real Estate Band 1
Table: p.1081

**Glazer, Ronald B**
(Pennsylvania)
Profile: p.1728
Real Estate Band 2
Table: p.1718

**Glazer, Steven D** (New York)
Profile: p.1459
Intellectual Property Band 3
Table: p.1384

**Glazier, Robert** (Florida)
Profile: p.637
Litigation Band 2
Table: p.615

**Gleason, Daniel J**
(Massachusetts)
Litigation Band 3
Table: p.1074

**Gleason, Kathryn L**
(District of Columbia)
Profile: p.515
Healthcare Band 2
Table: p.456

**Gleklen, Jonathan**
(District of Columbia)
Profile: p.515
Antitrust Up and coming
Table: p.426

**Glenn, Robert** (Florida)
Bankruptcy Band 2
Table: p.586

**Glerum, Charles L**
(Massachusetts)
Bankruptcy Band 1
Table: p.1058

**Gliatta, Stephen** (New York)
Profile: p.1459
Real Estate Band 5
Table: p.1417

**Glick, Anna** (New York)
Profile: p.102
Capital Markets Band 1
Table: p.18

**Glick, Rick** (Washington)
Environment Band 3
Table: p.1672

**Glickstein, David** (Illinois)
Profile: p.832
Real Estate Band 3
Table: p.809

**Glickstein, Steven**
(National)
Profile: p.102
Products Liability Band 2
Table: p.50

**Glosband, Daniel M**
(Massachusetts)
Profile: p.1093
Bankruptcy Band 1
Table: p.1058

**Glotzer, Paul E** (National)
Profile: p.102
Financial Services Band 3
Table: p.24

**Glover, Stephen I**
(District of Columbia)
Profile: p.515
Corporate/Commercial Band 1
Table: p.435

**Godby, Herbert R** (Ohio)
Profile: p.1628
Real Estate Band 4
Table: p.1621

**Godfrey, Lee** (Texas)
Antitrust Band 1
Table: p.1829
Energy Band 1
Table: p.1849
Litigation Band 1
Table: p.1865

**Godfrey, Richard C**
(Illinois)
Profile: p.832
Litigation Band 2
Table: p.802

**Godiner, Clifford A**
(Missouri)
Profile: p.1206
Employment Band 3
Table: p.1195

**Godshall, Brad** (California)
Bankruptcy Band 4
Table: p.222

**Goebel, Monica** (Arizona)
Profile: p.190
Employment Band 3
Table: p.178

**Goeltz, Thomas**
(Washington)
Real Estate Band 3
Table: p.2002
Real Estate Band 2
Table: p.2003

**Goering, Gail** (Illinois)
Profile: p.832
Insurance Band 2
Table: p.795

**Goering, Kevin W** (New York)
Media & Entertainment Band 2
Table: p.1404

**Goetz, James** (Montana)
Litigation Band 1
Table: p.1225

**Goetz, Peter** (New York)
Construction Band 3
Table: p.1351

**Goetzinger, Patrick**
(South Dakota)
Corporate/Commercial Band 2
Table: p.1792
Real Estate Band 2
Table: p.1796

**Goggin, James G** (Maine)
Profile: p.1012
Litigation Band 3
Table: p.1006

**Gold, Brian J** (Illinois)
Profile: p.832
Employment Band 3

Table: p.785

**Gold, Marc** (Pennsylvania)
Environment Band 2
Table: p.1707

**Gold, Michael** (Illinois)
Profile: p.832
Banking & Finance Band 2
Table: p.771

**Gold, Ronald** (Ohio)
Profile: p.1628
Bankruptcy Band 2
Table: p.1600

**Goldammer, Vance RC**
(South Dakota)
Corporate/Commercial Band 1
Table: p.1792
Real Estate Band 2
Table: p.1796

**Goldberg, Catherine**
(New Mexico)
Real Estate Band 2
Table: p.1327

**Goldberg, Charles**
(Colorado)
Profile: p.360
Litigation Band 3
Table: p.353

**Goldberg, Daniel L**
(Massachusetts)
Profile: p.1093
Antitrust Band 1
Table: p.1053
Sport Band 2
Table: p.59

**Goldberg, Donald J**
(Pennsylvania)
Profile: p.1729
Litigation Band 1
Table: p.1715

**Goldberg, Henry**
(District of Columbia)
Telecom, Broadcast & Satellite Band 3
Table: p.492

**Goldberg, Joseph**
(New Mexico)
Litigation Band 2
Table: p.1324

**Goldberg, Louis L**
(New York)
Profile: p.1460
Private Equity Band 3
Table: p.1407

**Goldberg, Michael**
(Florida)
Profile: p.637
Bankruptcy Band 2
Table: p.586

**Goldberg, Michael**
(Massachusetts)
Profile: p.1093
Bankruptcy Band 3
Table: p.1058

**Goldberg, Morton David**
(New York)
Intellectual Property Band 1

Table: p.1385

**Goldberg, Phillip**
(California)
Healthcare Band 3
Table: p.238

**Goldberg, Richard R**
(Pennsylvania)
Profile: p.1729
Real Estate Band 1
Table: p.1718

**Goldberg, Stephen**
(California)
Profile: p.290
Insurance Band 2
Table: p.245

**Goldberg Jr, Fred T**
(District of Columbia)
Profile: p.515
Tax Band 1
Table: p.488

**Goldblatt, Craig**
(District of Columbia)
Profile: p.515
Bankruptcy Band 3
Table: p.432

**Goldblatt, Stanford J**
(Illinois)
Corporate/M&A: Private Equity
Band 2
Table: p.782

**Golden, Arthur F** (New
York)
Profile: p.1460
Antitrust Band 3
Table: p.1335

**Golden, Daniel H** (New
York)
Profile: p.1460
Bankruptcy Band 1
Table: p.1344

**Golden, Gerald** (Illinois)
Profile: p.832
Employment Band 2
Table: p.785

**Golden, H Bruce** (Texas)
Profile: p.1893
Litigation Band 3
Table: p.1865

**Golden, Jonathan** (Georgia)
Profile: p.713
Corporate/M&A Band 3
Table: p.684

**Golden, Matthew T**
(New York)
Real Estate Band 5
Table: p.1417

**Goldfein, Shepard**
(New York)
Profile: p.1460
Antitrust Band 3
Table: p.1335
Sport Band 1
Table: p.59

**Goldman, Donald**
(California)
Profile: p.291

Healthcare Band 2
Table: p.238

**Goldman, Matthew R**
(Ohio)
Bankruptcy Band 3
Table: p.1600

**Goldman, Melvin**
(California)
Profile: p.291
Antitrust Band 3
Table: p.216
Litigation Band 2
Table: p.257

**Goldman, Michael**
(New York)
Profile: p.1460
Banking & Finance Band 3
Table: p.1339

**Goldman, Michael**
(Delaware)
Profile: p.405
Chancery Band 2
Table: p.392
Corporate/M&A Band 2
Table: p.394

**Goldman, Michael P**
(Illinois)
Profile: p.832
Insurance Band 1
Table: p.796

**Goldman, Robert J**
(California)
Profile: p.291
Intellectual Property Band 3
Table: p.248

**Goldman, Robert S**
(Florida)
Tax Band 2
Table: p.623

**Goldman, Roger**
(District of Columbia)
Healthcare Band 2
Table: p.456

**Goldring, Stuart** (New York)
Profile: p.1460
Tax Band 3
Table: p.1423

**Goldschmidt, David J**
(National)
Profile: p.102
Capital Markets Band 3
Table: p.7

**Goldsmith, Robert S**
(New Jersey)
Profile: p.1299
Real Estate Band 2
Table: p.1293

**Goldsmith, Willis J**
(District of Columbia)
Profile: p.515
Employment Band 1
Table: p.439

**Goldstein, Andrew** (Illinois)
Media & Entertainment Band 2
Table: p.807

**Goldstein, Andrew M.**

(Maryland)
Profile: p.1039
Real Estate Band 4
Table: p.1035

**Goldstein, Arthur S**
(New Jersey)
Litigation Band 3
Table: p.1289

**Goldstein, Bruce** (New
Jersey)
Litigation Band 3
Table: p.1289

**Goldstein, Bruce**
(District of Columbia)
Bankruptcy Band 3
Table: p.432

**Goldstein, Jorge A**
(District of Columbia)
Profile: p.516
Intellectual Property Band 4
Table: p.466

**Goldstein, Joseph** (Florida)
Profile: p.637
Real Estate Band 2
Table: p.621

**Goldstein, Linda A**
(New York)
Media & Entertainment Band 2
Table: p.1400

**Goldstein, Marcia**
(New York)
Profile: p.1460
Bankruptcy Band 1
Table: p.1344

**Goldstein, Mark** (Nevada)
Corporate/Commercial Band 2
Table: p.1246
Real Estate Band 3
Table: p.1255

**Goldstein, Marvin**
(National)
Capital Markets Band 2
Table: p.15

**Goldstein, Marvin M**
(New Jersey)
Profile: p.1299
Employment Band 3
Table: p.1282

**Goldstein, Richard M**
(Florida)
Profile: p.637
Tax Band 4
Table: p.623

**Goldstein, Steven J** (Ohio)
Profile: p.1628
Intellectual Property Band 1
Table: p.1614

**Goldstein, Stuart N**
(North Carolina)
Profile: p.1583
Capital Markets Band 2
Table: p.18

**Goldstein, Thomas C**
(District of Columbia)
Profile: p.516
Litigation Band 2

Table: p.475

**Golemon, Kinnan** (Texas)
Environment Band S
Table: p.1852

**Gonchar, Meryl A G**
(New Jersey)
Profile: p.1299
Real Estate Band 2
Table: p.1293

**Gonsoulin Jr, Dewey J**
(Texas)
Profile: p.1893
Banking & Finance Band 4
Table: p.1832

**Gonzales, Robert J**
(Tennessee)
Profile: p.1813
Litigation Band 2
Table: p.1804

**Gonzalez, Cecilia H**
(District of Columbia)
Intellectual Property Band 3
Table: p.466

**Gonzalez, Eduardo W**
(Florida)
Profile: p.637
Litigation Associate to watch
Table: p.609

**Gonzalez, Edward E**
(New York)
Profile: p.1460
Tax Band 4
Table: p.1423

**Gonzalez, Enrique** (Florida)
Immigration Band 1
Table: p.606

**Gonzalez, Ervin** (Florida)
Profile: p.638
Litigation Band 2
Table: p.609

**Gonzalez, Josie** (California)
Immigration Band 2
Table: p.241

**Gonzalez, Thomas M**
(Florida)
Employment Band 1
Table: p.597

**González, Arturo J**
(California)
Profile: p.291
Litigation Band 4
Table: p.257

**González, Daniel E**
(Florida)
Profile: p.103
International Arbitration
Band 4
Table: p.36

**González, Daniel E**
(Florida)
Profile: p.638
Litigation Band 4
Table: p.609

**Gooch, W Kyle** (Texas)
Profile: p.1893

Construction Band 3
Table: p.1838

**Goodell, Gerald** (Kansas)
Real Estate Band 2
Table: p.930

**Goodell Jr, Charles P**
(Maryland)
Profile: p.1039
Litigation Band 3
Table: p.1032

**Goodheart, Lisa**
(Massachusetts)
Environment Band 2
Table: p.1068

**Gooding, Douglas R**
(Massachusetts)
Bankruptcy Band 2
Table: p.1058

**Goodkind, Conrad G**
(Wisconsin)
Profile: p.2033
Corporate/M&A Band 3
Table: p.2025

**Goodkind, Jim** (California)
Profile: p.291
Media & Entertainment Band 4
Table: p.263

**Goodling, Jonathon L**
(Oregon)
Profile: p.1681
Real Estate Band 2
Table: p.1677

**Goodman, Alan** (Louisiana)
Corporate/M&A Band 3
Table: p.965

**Goodman, Lisa** (Delaware)
Profile: p.405
Real Estate Band 1
Table: p.400

**Goodman, Louis A**
(Massachusetts)
Profile: p.1093
Corporate/M&A Band 1
Table: p.1061

**Goodman, Mark** (Illinois)
Insurance Band 1
Table: p.796

**Goodman, Robert D**
(New York)
Insurance Band 3
Table: p.1379

**Goodman, Ronald**
(District of Columbia)
International Arbitration
Band 3
Table: p.36

**Goodman, Saul**
(District of Columbia)
Profile: p.516
Insurance Band 4
Table: p.464

**Goodman, Stephen**
(Pennsylvania)
Profile: p.1729
Corporate/M&A Band 1

G

**Grandison, W George**
(District of Columbia)
Profile: p.103
International Trade Band 2
Table: p.42

**Granfield, Lindsee P**
(New York)
Profile: p.1461
Bankruptcy Band 4
Table: p.1344

**Grant, Elizabeth** (Vermont)
Employment Band 2
Table: p.1958

**Grant, Eugene L** (Oregon)
Real Estate Band 2
Table: p.1677

**Grant, Stuart M** (Delaware)
Chancery Band 1
Table: p.392

**Granwell, Alan Winston**
(District of Columbia)
Tax Band 3
Table: p.488

**Graves, Judson** (Georgia)
Profile: p.714
Litigation Band 1
Table: p.698

**Graves, Kathlyn** (Arkansas)
Employment Band 1
Table: p.203

**Graw, Andrew E** (New Jersey)
Profile: p.1299
Employee Benefits Band 1
Table: p.1281

**Gray, James** (Maryland)
Litigation Band 2
Table: p.1032

**Gray, Robert F** (Texas)
Profile: p.1894
Corporate/M&A Band 4
Table: p.1840
Technology Band 1
Table: p.1878

**Gray, Tracy** (Colorado)
Profile: p.360
Intellectual Property Up and coming
Table: p.351

**Gray Jr, Marvin L**
(Washington)
Litigation Band 2
Table: p.2000

**Grayson, E Lynn** (Illinois)
Profile: p.833
Environment Band 2
Table: p.791

**Grayson, Neil E**
(South Carolina)
Corporate/M&A Band 3
Table: p.1775

**Greaney, William**
(District of Columbia)
Profile: p.516
Insurance Band 1

**Greeley, Jack** (Florida)
Banking & Finance Band 2
Table: p.583

**Green, Barry D**
(Massachusetts)
Real Estate Band 3
Table: p.1081

**Green, Daniel C** (Idaho)
Bankruptcy Band 3
Table: p.758

**Green, David W** (Oregon)
Real Estate Band 1
Table: p.1677

**Green, Douglas G**
(District of Columbia)
Profile: p.516
Energy Band 2
Table: p.445

**Green, Frederick**
(New York)
Profile: p.1461
Corporate/M&A Band 4
Table: p.1354

**Green, Jonathan**
(New York)
Projects Band 1
Table: p.56
Projects Band 1
Table: p.1413

**Green, Jonathan S**
(Michigan)
Profile: p.1134
Banking & Finance Band 2
Table: p.1120

**Green, Jordan** (Arizona)
Profile: p.190
Litigation Band 1
Table: p.182

**Green, Josh** (California)
Profile: p.291
Corporate/M&A Band 4
Table: p.227

**Green, Karen F**
(Massachusetts)
Profile: p.1094
Litigation Band 1
Table: p.1075

**Green, Mike** (Iowa)
Profile: p.920
Real Estate Band 4
Table: p.917

**Green, Ronald** (New York)
Profile: p.1461
Employment Band 3
Table: p.1365

**Green, Thomas C**
(District of Columbia)
Profile: p.516
Litigation Band 2
Table: p.471

**Green, William** (Florida)
Profile: p.638
Environment Band 1
Table: p.601

**Green, William**
(Washington)
Real Estate Band 3
Table: p.2002

**Greenbaum, Jack A** (New York)
Profile: p.103
Transportation Band 3
Table: p.74

**Greenbaum, Jeffrey J**
(New Jersey)
Profile: p.1299
Litigation Band 3
Table: p.1289

**Greenberg, Barry C.**
(Maryland)
Real Estate Band 3
Table: p.1035

**Greenberg, Bennett D**
(District of Columbia)
Construction Band 4
Table: p.433

**Greenberg, Eric Dodson**
(District of Columbia)
Profile: p.517
Telecom, Broadcast & Satellite Band 4
Table: p.492

**Greenberg, Gary** (Ohio)
Employment Band 3
Table: p.1609

**Greenberg, Gordon A**
(California)
Profile: p.292
Litigation Band 1
Table: p.258

**Greenberg, Jeffrey**
(California)
Projects Band 3
Table: p.268
Projects Band 5
Table: p.1413

**Greenberg, Joel I**
(New York)
Profile: p.1462
Corporate/M&A Band 1
Table: p.1359

**Greenberg, Marilynn R**
(New Jersey)
Profile: p.1299
Environment Band 2
Table: p.1285

**Greenberg, Mark I**
(National)
Profile: p.103
Capital Markets
Up and coming
Table: p.13

**Greenburg, G Scott**
(Washington)
Corporate/Commercial Band 2
Table: p.1992

**Greendyke, William**
(Texas)
Profile: p.1894
Bankruptcy Band 4
Table: p.1835

**Greene, Kenneth**
(North Carolina)
Banking & Finance Band 2
Table: p.1569

**Greene, Kevin C** (Georgia)
Energy Band 1
Table: p.689

**Greener, Richard** (Idaho)
Profile: p.764
Litigation Band 1
Table: p.760

**Greenfield, Andrew B**
(District of Columbia)
Immigration Band 2
Table: p.459

**Greenfield, Gregg S**
(South Dakota)
Corporate/Commercial Band 3
Table: p.1792

**Greenfield, Robert A**
(California)
Bankruptcy Band 2
Table: p.222

**Greenfield, Russell R**
(South Dakota)
Real Estate Band S
Table: p.1796

**Greengrass, Lawrence S**
(New York)
Profile: p.1462
Insurance Band 3
Table: p.1379
Insurance Band 3
Table: p.1380

**Greenman, Ronald L**
(Oregon)
Profile: p.1681
Corporate/M&A Band 2
Table: p.1667

**Greenspan, Eric** (California)
Media & Entertainment Band 4
Table: p.263

**Greenspan, Steven M**
(Connecticut)
Profile: p.383
Litigation Band 2
Table: p.378

**Greenstein, Abraham**
(District of Columbia)
Real Estate Band 2
Table: p.482

**Greenthal, John** (New York)
Profile: p.1462
Environment Band 3
Table: p.1371

**Greenwald, John D**
(District of Columbia)
Profile: p.103
International Trade Band 3
Table: p.42

**Greenwald, Steven**
(California)
Energy Band 2
Table: p.233

**Greenwell, Charles D**
(Kentucky)
Profile: p.947
Litigation Band 4
Table: p.942

**Greenwood, David A**
(Utah)
Litigation Band 2
Table: p.1945

**Greer, Alan** (Florida)
Litigation Band 1
Table: p.609

**Greer, David** (Ohio)
Litigation Band 2
Table: p.1617

**Greer, George E**
(Washington)
Profile: p.2005
Litigation Band 3
Table: p.2000

**Greer, Scott** (Georgia)
Profile: p.1894
Construction Band 4
Table: p.1838

**Gregg, Joseph** (Ohio)
Environment Band 4
Table: p.1612

**Gregorie Jr, Isaac McPherson** (Louisiana)
Profile: p.980
Real Estate Band 3
Table: p.975

**Gregory, Donald** (Ohio)
Construction Band 2
Table: p.1603

**Gregory, H Watt** (Arkansas)
Corporate/Commercial Band 1
Table: p.201

**Greig, Brian** (Texas)
Profile: p.1894
Employment Band 1
Table: p.1844

**Greising, Robert** (Indiana)
Corporate/M&A Band 3
Table: p.887

**Gremillion, L Todd** (Texas)
Profile: p.1894
Energy Band 4
Table: p.1847

**Grenier, John B** (Alabama)
Profile: p.157
Corporate/Commercial Band 1
Table: p.148

**Grice, Richard** (Georgia)
Profile: p.714
Banking & Finance Band 2
Table: p.677

**Griffey, Linda** (California)
Profile: p.292
Employment Band 2
Table: p.232

**Griffin, James** (Missouri)
Profile: p.1206
Litigation Band 1

G

Table: p.1198

**Griffin, John W** (Georgia)
Real Estate Band 1
Table: p.700

**Griffin III, Thomas N**
(North Carolina)
Environment Band 3
Table: p.1575

**Griffinger, Michael R**
(New Jersey)
Profile: p.1299
Litigation Band 1
Table: p.1289

**Griffith, Richard** (Kentucky)
Profile: p.947
Employment Band 1
Table: p.939

**Griffith, Robert W**
(Kentucky)
Profile: p.947
Litigation Band 4
Table: p.942

**Griffith, Scott** (Texas)
Profile: p.1894
Construction Band 4
Table: p.1838

**Griffith, Spencer S**
(National)
Profile: p.103
International Trade Band 3
Table: p.42

**Grigera Naón, Horacio A**
(District of Columbia)
Arbitration Band 1
Table: p.37

**Grimes, Dale** (Tennessee)
Profile: p.1813
Litigation Band 3
Table: p.1804

**Grimm, Thomas C**
(Delaware)
Profile: p.405
Intellectual Property Band 3
Table: p.397

**Grimm, William R** (Rhode Island)
Litigation Band 2
Table: p.1769

**Grimmer, Gary** (Hawaii)
Litigation Band 3
Table: p.745

**Grimshaw, Thomas T**
(Colorado)
Real Estate Band 1
Table: p.355

**Grindstaff, Michael J**
(Florida)
Profile: p.638
Real Estate Band 2
Table: p.621

**Grinfas, Dan** (Washington)
Employment Band 3
Table: p.1670

**Grishman, David**
(Mississippi)
Corporate/Commercial Band 2
Table: p.1174

**Groark Jr, Thomas J**
(Connecticut)
Profile: p.383
Litigation Band S
Table: p.378

**Grogan, Michael K**
(Florida)
Employment Band 2
Table: p.597

**Groll, Michael** (New York)
Profile: p.1462
Insurance Band 2
Table: p.1380

**Gromacki, Joseph P**
(Illinois)
Profile: p.833
Corporate/M&A Band 4
Table: p.781

**Grooms, Timothy**
(Arkansas)
Profile: p.209
Real Estate Band 1
Table: p.207

**Groskaufmanis, Karl**
(District of Columbia)
Profile: p.517
Securities Band 2
Table: p.485

**Gross, David** (Minnesota)
Profile: p.1163
Litigation Band 1
Table: p.1157

**Gross, Doug** (Iowa)
Profile: p.920
Corporate/M&A Band 4
Table: p.909

**Gross, Jefferson W** (Utah)
Profile: p.1951
Litigation Up and coming
Table: p.1945

**Gross, John** (New York)
Profile: p.1462
Insurance Band 2
Table: p.1379

**Gross, Kenneth A**
(National)
Profile: p.104
Government: Political Law
Band 2
Table: p.34

**Gross, Michael J**
(New Jersey)
Environment Band 1
Table: p.1285

**Gross, Steven E** (New Jersey)
Profile: p.1299
Corporate/M&A Band 3
Table: p.1278

**Gross, Steven R** (New York)
Bankruptcy Band 3
Table: p.1344

**Grossbauer, John**
(Delaware)
Profile: p.405
Corporate/M&A Band 3
Table: p.394

**Grossenburg, Bradley C**
(South Dakota)
Corporate/Commercial Band 1
Table: p.1792

**Grosser, Theodore D**
(Ohio)
Profile: p.1628
Corporate/M&A Band 3
Table: p.1605

**Grosshandler, Seth**
(New York)
Profile: p.104
Capital Markets Band 1
Table: p.15

**Grossi, Peter** (National)
Profile: p.104
Products Liability Band 2
Table: p.50

**Grossman, Marshall**
(California)
Profile: p.292
Litigation Band 2
Table: p.257
Media & Entertainment Band 2
Table: p.263

**Grossman, Paul** (California)
Profile: p.292
Employment Band 1
Table: p.231

**Grossman, Robert L**
(Florida)
Profile: p.638
Corporate/M&A Band 4
Table: p.594

**Grossman, Theodore**
(Ohio)
Profile: p.1628
Litigation Band 2
Table: p.1617

**Groten, Eric** (Texas)
Profile: p.1894
Environment Band 3
Table: p.1852

**Grout, Robert W** (Georgia)
Corporate/M&A Band 4
Table: p.684

**Grove, Barry** (New York)
Profile: p.1462
Construction Band 2
Table: p.1351

**Grover, Parry** (Alaska)
Employment Band 1
Table: p.169

**Grovier, Tina M** (Alaska)
Environment Band 3
Table: p.170

**Grubbs, R Howard**
(North Carolina)
Profile: p.1583
Environment Band 2
Table: p.1575

**Grubman, Allen** (New York)
Media & Entertainment Band 1
Table: p.1401

**Grunblatt, David** (New Jersey)
Immigration Band 2
Table: p.1376

**Grundfest, Jack D**
(Arkansas)
Corporate/Commercial Band 1
Table: p.201

**Guattery, Peter** (Maryland)
Profile: p.1040
Employment Band 3
Table: p.1028

**Guben, Jan K** (Maryland)
Real Estate Band 4
Table: p.1035

**Guben, Jerrold K** (Hawaii)
Bankruptcy Band 1
Table: p.739

**Guedry, David N** (Texas)
Profile: p.1894
Business Process Outsourcing
Band 2
Table: p.2
Technology Band 1
Table: p.1877

**Guerra, Michael** (Illinois)
Profile: p.833
Energy Band 3
Table: p.789

**Guerrera, Sal** (New York)
Profile: p.1462
Banking & Finance Up and
coming
Table: p.1339

**Gugelyk, Carolyn K**
(Hawaii)
Employment Up and coming
Table: p.742

**Guinasso, John** (Oregon)
Real Estate Band 2
Table: p.1677

**Guinn, Guy** (Ohio)
Profile: p.1628
Banking & Finance Band 1
Table: p.1598

**Gulland, Eugene D**
(District of Columbia)
Profile: p.104
International Arbitration
Band 3
Table: p.36

**Gullickson, Charles D**
(South Dakota)
Corporate/Commercial Band 2
Table: p.1792

**Gullickson, Randy**
(Minnesota)
Litigation Band 3
Table: p.1156

**Gullikson, Rosemary L**
(Illinois)
Profile: p.833

Business Process Outsourcing
Band 3
Table: p.2
Technology Band 3
Table: p.814

**Gump Jr, Richard** (Texas)
Immigration Band 1
Table: p.1856

**Gundersen, Glenn A**
(Pennsylvania)
Profile: p.1729
Intellectual Property Band 3
Table: p.1711

**Gunderson, Bob** (California)
Corporate/M&A Band 3
Table: p.227

**Gunderson, Joseph R**
(Iowa)
Litigation Band 3
Table: p.914

**Gunn, David M** (Texas)
Litigation Band 2
Table: p.1866

**Gunn, Paul** (Mississippi)
Real Estate Band 2
Table: p.1181

**Gunnell, Bret** (Colorado)
Profile: p.360
Construction Band 1
Table: p.345

**Gunsett, Daniel** (Ohio)
Environment Band 2
Table: p.1612

**Gunter, Clifford** (Texas)
Profile: p.1895
Energy Band 2
Table: p.1849
Litigation Band 3
Table: p.1865

**Gunter, Russell** (Arkansas)
Employment Band 1
Table: p.203

**Gupta, Paul R** (New York)
Profile: p.1463
Intellectual Property Band 3
Table: p.1384

**Gupta, Shilpi** (Illinois)
Profile: p.833
Corporate/M&A
Up and coming
Table: p.781

**Gupton III, John A**
(Tennessee)
Profile: p.1813
Real Estate Band 2
Table: p.1808

**Gurley, David** (Florida)
Construction Band 3
Table: p.590

**Gurney, Scott** (Ohio)
Profile: p.1628
Construction Band 3
Table: p.1603

**Guso, Jordi** (Florida)
Bankruptcy Band 1
Table: p.586

**Gussack, Nina M**
(National)
Profile: p.104
Products Liability Band 2
Table: p.50

**Gustafson, Karna R**
(Oregon)
Real Estate Up and coming
Table: p.1677

**Guthman, Jack** (Illinois)
Real Estate Band 1
Table: p.809

**Gutierrez, Jay**
(District of Columbia)
Profile: p.517
Energy Band 2
Table: p.449

**Gutmacher, Norman** (Ohio)
Profile: p.1629
Real Estate Band 4
Table: p.1621

**Gutowski, Peter** (New York)
Profile: p.104
Transportation Band 1
Table: p.74

**Gutter, Marvin** (Florida)
Tax Band 2
Table: p.623

**Guy III, G Hopkins**
(California)
Profile: p.292
Intellectual Property Band 3
Table: p.248

**Guynn, Randall** (National)
Profile: p.104
Financial Services Band 2
Table: p.24

**Gwynne, Kurt F** (Delaware)
Profile: p.405
Bankruptcy Band 4
Table: p.389

---

**H**

**Haab, Eric** (Illinois)
Profile: p.833
Insurance Band 2
Table: p.795

**Haag, Melinda** (California)
Profile: p.292
Litigation Band 3
Table: p.258

**Haarlow, John** (Illinois)
Insurance Band 1
Table: p.796

**Haas, Karl P** (Indiana)
Profile: p.896
Real Estate Band 1
Table: p.892

**Habbart, Ellisa Opstbaum** (Delaware)
Profile: p.405
Corporate/M&A Band 3
Table: p.395

**Habel, Christopher S**
(Ohio)
Profile: p.1629
Environment Up and coming
Table: p.1612

**Hable, Kevin J** (Kentucky)
Profile: p.947
Corporate/M&A Band 3
Table: p.937

**Hack, Randall A** (Illinois)
Antitrust Band 3
Table: p.767

**Hackett, Robert J**
(Arizona)
Corporate/M&A Band 3
Table: p.176

**Hackman, Stephen**
(Indiana)
Profile: p.896
Corporate/M&A Band 2
Table: p.887

**Hackney, Hamilton**
(Massachusetts)
Profile: p.1094
Environment Band 2
Table: p.1068

**Haddon, Harold** (Colorado)
Litigation Band 1
Table: p.353

**Haden Jr, William H**
(Kentucky)
Profile: p.947
Real Estate Band 1
Table: p.944

**Hadjis, Alexander J**
(District of Columbia)
Profile: p.517
Intellectual Property Band 3
Table: p.466

**Hadley, Joseph P** (New York)
Profile: p.1463
Projects Band 3
Table: p.1413

**Haefner, Gail** (Vermont)
Corporate/Commercial Band 1
Table: p.1957

**Hafer, Randall F** (Georgia)
Profile: p.714
Construction Band 2
Table: p.682

**Hafets, Richard J**
(Maryland)
Profile: p.1040
Employment Band 1
Table: p.1028

**Hafetz, Fred** (New York)
Litigation Band 3
Table: p.1391

**Haffey, Dennis** (Michigan)
Litigation Band 2
Table: p.1128

**Hafter, Jerome C**
(Mississippi)
Profile: p.1184
Corporate/Commercial Band 2
Table: p.1174

**Hagen, Daniel C** (Ohio)
Profile: p.1629
Employee Benefits Band 1
Table: p.1607

**Hagen, Paul**
(District of Columbia)
Profile: p.517
Environment Band 2
Table: p.451

**Hager, Ashley Z** (Georgia)
Employment Up and coming
Table: p.687

**Hagerott, Edward C**
(California)
Real Estate Band 2
Table: p.270

**Haggart, Todd**
(North Dakota)
Litigation Band 2
Table: p.1593

**Haggerty, John J** (Ohio)
Litigation Up and coming
Table: p.1617

**Haglund, Michael E**
(Oregon)
Profile: p.1681
Litigation Band 3
Table: p.1674

**Hahn, Arthur** (Illinois)
Corporate/M&A Band 4
Table: p.781

**Hahn, James H**
(Rhode Island)
Corporate/Commercial Band 2
Table: p.1766

**Hahn, Richard** (New York)
Bankruptcy Band 3
Table: p.1344

**Hahn, Robert J**
(North Carolina)
Profile: p.1583
Capital Markets Band 3
Table: p.18

**Haigh, Mark W**
(South Dakota)
Litigation Band 2
Table: p.1795

**Haight, Catherine L**
(California)
Immigration Band 3
Table: p.241

**Haims, Bruce D** (New York)
Tax Band 3
Table: p.1423

**Haines, Lisa** (Missouri)
Profile: p.1206

**Real Estate Band 2**
Table: p.1201

**Haines, Rush T**
(Pennsylvania)
Real Estate Band 3
Table: p.1718

**Hainline Jr, Theodore**
(Florida)
Real Estate Band 3
Table: p.621

**Hajek, Douglas J**
(South Dakota)
Corporate/Commercial Band 2
Table: p.1792

**Halbreich, David M**
(California)
Profile: p.292
Insurance Band 1
Table: p.245

**Hale, Ben W** (Ohio)
Real Estate Band 1
Table: p.1622

**Hale, David J** (Kentucky)
Profile: p.947
Litigation Band 4
Table: p.942

**Hale, Russell** (Florida)
Profile: p.638
Tax Band 3
Table: p.623

**Halevy, Amy Karff** (Texas)
Profile: p.1895
Employment Band 3
Table: p.1844

**Haley, George M** (Utah)
Litigation Band 1
Table: p.1945

**Haley, Joseph W**
(Massachusetts)
Profile: p.1094
Real Estate Band 1
Table: p.1081

**Haley III, Raymond**
(Kentucky)
Employment Band 2
Table: p.939

**Haley Jr, James F** (New York)
Profile: p.1463
Intellectual Property Band 3
Table: p.1384

**Hall, Alan**
(New Mexico)
Corporate/Commercial Band 1
Table: p.1320

**Hall, Bruce**
(New Mexico)
Litigation Band 1
Table: p.1324

**Hall, Charles** (Texas)
Profile: p.1895
Tax Band S
Table: p.1875

**Hall, Donald** (Florida)
Real Estate Band 2
Table: p.621

**Hall, Gregory** (Arizona)
Profile: p.190
Corporate/M&A
Up and coming
Table: p.176

**Hall, Helena** (Alaska)
Employment Band 2
Table: p.169

**Hall, Kevin A**
(South Carolina)
Litigation Band 3
Table: p.1778

**Hall, Mark** (Vermont)
Real Estate Band 2
Table: p.1961

**Hall, Michael W** (California)
Corporate/M&A Band 4
Table: p.227

**Hall, Richard** (New York)
Profile: p.1463
Corporate/M&A Band 3
Table: p.1354

**Hall, Richard E** (Idaho)
Litigation Band 3
Table: p.760

**Hall, Thomas Jay**
(New Jersey)
Profile: p.1299
Real Estate Band 2
Table: p.1293

**Hall Jr, Cary H**
(South Carolina)
Profile: p.1783
Corporate/M&A Band 2
Table: p.1775

**Hall Jr, Ridgway M**
(District of Columbia)
Profile: p.517
Environment Band 4
Table: p.451

**Haller, Anthony**
(Pennsylvania)
Profile: p.1729
Employment Band 3
Table: p.1703

**Haller, Diane** (Arizona)
Profile: p.190
Real Estate Band 2
Table: p.184

**Halliday, Joseph W**
(New York)
Profile: p.1463
Banking & Finance Band S
Table: p.1339

**Halling, Gary L** (California)
Antitrust Band 3
Table: p.216

**Hallman, Robert**
(New York)
Environment Band 2
Table: p.1373

Tax Band 1
Table: p.1425

**Harkavy, Ronald**
(Tennessee)
Real Estate Band 2
Table: p.1808

**Harkins, Deborah**
(Louisiana)
Profile: p.981
Gaming & Licensing Band 2
Table: p.971

**Harkins Jr, John G**
(Pennsylvania)
Profile: p.1730
Litigation Band S
Table: p.1714

**Harkrider, John D**
(New York)
Profile: p.1463
Antitrust Up and coming
Table: p.1335

**Harless, Warren David**
(Virginia)

**Harman, Paul M** (Utah)
Profile: p.1951
Real Estate Up and coming
Table: p.1947

**Harman, Thomas**
(District of Columbia)
Profile: p.518
Investment Management Band 2
Table: p.469

**Harmon, Christopher B**
(Alabama)
Profile: p.157
Corporate/Commercial Band 2
Table: p.148

**Harmon, Jason C**
(Maryland)
Profile: p.1040
Corporate/M&A
Up and coming
Table: p.1025

**Harmon, Jonathan P**
(Virginia)
Employment Up and coming
Table: p.1971

**Harmon, T Craig** (Virginia)
Real Estate Band 3
Table: p.1978

**Harms, David B** (New York)
Profile: p.105
Capital Markets Band 3
Table: p.7

**Harnden, Edwin** (Oregon)
Employment Band 2
Table: p.1670

**Harnden, Ronald** (Kansas)
Real Estate Band 1
Table: p.930

**Harner, Paul E** (Illinois)
Profile: p.834
Bankruptcy Band 3
Table: p.775

**Haroz, Michael**
(Massachusetts)
Real Estate Band 2
Table: p.1081

**Harper, A J** (Texas)
Profile: p.1895
Employment Band 2
Table: p.1844

**Harper, Sue Erwin**
(South Carolina)
Employment Band 2
Table: p.1777

**Harrell, Charles E** (Texas)
Profile: p.1895
Corporate/M&A Band 4
Table: p.1840

**Harrell, Michael P**
(New York)
Private Equity Band 1
Table: p.1410

**Harrigan, Kenneth**
(New Mexico)
Litigation Band 1
Table: p.1324

**Harrigan Jr, Arthur W**
(Washington)
Litigation Band 1
Table: p.2000

**Harrington, C Michael**
(Texas)
Profile: p.1895
Corporate/M&A Band 4
Table: p.1840

**Harrington, Carol A**
(National)
Profile: p.105
Wealth Management Band 1
Table: p.81

**Harrington, David J**
(National)
Profile: p.105
Transportation
Associate to watch
Table: p.67

**Harrington, James** (Illinois)
Environment Band 3
Table: p.791

**Harrington, John R**
(Illinois)
Profile: p.834
Telecom, Broadcast & Satellite
Band 2
Table: p.816

**Harris, Adam** (New York)
Profile: p.1464
Bankruptcy Band 4
Table: p.1344

**Harris, Alan** (California)
Construction Band 1
Table: p.225

**Harris, Dale** (Colorado)
Litigation Band 1
Table: p.353
Litigation Band 3
Table: p.353

**Harris, David L** (New Jersey)
Profile: p.1300
Intellectual Property Band 2
Table: p.1288
Litigation Band 1
Table: p.1289

**Harris, Edward W** (Indiana)
Profile: p.896
Litigation Band 2
Table: p.890

**Harris, Gregg**
(District of Columbia)
Profile: p.518
Projects Band 4
Table: p.479

**Harris, James** (Texas)
Profile: p.1895
Environment Band 3
Table: p.1852
Environment Band 2
Table: p.1853

**Harris, Jonathan R**
(Massachusetts)
Profile: p.1094
Banking & Finance Band 3
Table: p.1055

**Harris, Judith E**
(Pennsylvania)
Profile: p.1730
Employment Band 4
Table: p.1703

**Harris, Kenneth L** (Illinois)
Profile: p.834
Tax Band 3
Table: p.812

**Harris, L Douglas** (New York)
Projects Band 2
Table: p.56
Projects Band 2
Table: p.1413

**Harris, Larry D**
(District of Columbia)
Profile: p.518
Construction Band 2
Table: p.433

**Harris, Marc S** (California)
Litigation Band 3
Table: p.258

**Harris, Matthew T**
(Tennessee)
Profile: p.1813
Real Estate Band 2
Table: p.1808

**Harris, Morton A** (Georgia)
Tax Band 3
Table: p.703

**Harris, Robert J** (Illinois)
Construction Band 3
Table: p.778

**Harris, Scott Blake**
(District of Columbia)
Telecom, Broadcast & Satellite
Band 2
Table: p.492

**Harris, Warren W** (Texas)
Profile: p.1895
Litigation Band 3
Table: p.1866

**Harris Jr, H Stephen**
(Georgia)
Profile: p.714
Antitrust Band 2
Table: p.675

**Harrison, Bruce S**
(Maryland)
Profile: p.1040
Employment Band 2
Table: p.1028

**Harrison, Ellen K** (National)
Profile: p.105
Wealth Management Band 2
Table: p.81

**Harrison, Kirk R** (Nevada)
Litigation Band 1
Table: p.1253

**Harrison, Lauren** (Texas)
Profile: p.1896
Antitrust Up and coming
Table: p.1829

**Harrison, Louis S**
(National)
Wealth Management Band 3
Table: p.81

**Harrison, Mark I** (Arizona)
Profile: p.191
Litigation Band 3
Table: p.181

**Harrison, Sylvia** (Nevada)
Environment Band 2
Table: p.1249

**Harrison III, Orrin L** (Texas)
Profile: p.1896
Litigation Band 1
Table: p.1866

**Harrison, Jr, Joseph**
(Illinois)
Profile: p.105
Capital Markets Band 2
Table: p.15

**Hart, Austin** (Vermont)
Real Estate Band 2
Table: p.1961

**Hart, Gordon E** (California)
Environment Band 4
Table: p.236

**Hart, J Steven** (National)
Government Relations Band 1
Table: p.32

**Hart, John** (New York)
Profile: p.1464
Tax Band 3
Table: p.1423

**Harth, David J** (Wisconsin)
Profile: p.2033
Intellectual Property Band 1
Table: p.2028

**Hartig, Lawrence** (Alaska)
Environment Band 2

Table: p.170

**Hartigan, John F**
(California)
Profile: p.293
Corporate/M&A Band 4
Table: p.227

**Hartley, James E**
(Colorado)
Profile: p.361
Litigation Band 1
Table: p.353

**Hartmann, H Michael**
(Illinois)
Profile: p.834
Intellectual Property Band 2
Table: p.799

**Hartmann, Melanie**
(Louisiana)
Profile: p.981
Employment Band 3
Table: p.967

**Hartnett, William M**
(New York)
Capital Markets Band 1
Table: p.7

**Hartquist, David A**
(District of Columbia)
International Trade Band 4
Table: p.42

**Hartsfield, Dan** (Texas)
Profile: p.1896
Employment Band 3
Table: p.1844

**Hartsfield, Shannon**
(Florida)
Profile: p.639
Healthcare Up and coming
Table: p.604

**Hartstein, Barry A** (Illinois)
Profile: p.835
Employment Band 2
Table: p.785

**Harty, Frank** (Iowa)
Employment Band 1
Table: p.912

**Harty, Ronan** (New York)
Profile: p.1464
Antitrust Band 1
Table: p.1335

**Harvell, Michael**
(New Hampshire)
Litigation Band 2
Table: p.1267

**Harvey, Charles** (Maine)
Litigation Band 1
Table: p.1006

**Harvey, Dean William**
(Texas)
Profile: p.1896
Technology Band 2
Table: p.1877

**Harvey, James A** (National)
Profile: p.105
Business Process Outsourcing
Band 3

**H**

**H**

Table: p.2

**Harvin, David** (Texas)
Profile: p.1896
Energy Band 2
Table: p.1849
Litigation Band 2
Table: p.1865

**Harwell Jr, Aubrey B**
(Tennessee)
Litigation Band 3
Table: p.1804

**Harwood, Bruce**
(New Hampshire)
Corporate/Commercial Band 1
Table: p.1263

**Haskell, Mark**
(District of Columbia)
Profile: p.518
Energy Band 3
Table: p.441

**Haslam, Robert** (California)
Profile: p.293
Intellectual Property Band 3
Table: p.248

**Hasson Jr, James K**
(Georgia)
Profile: p.714
Tax Band 2
Table: p.703

**Hastie, John** (Oklahoma)
Real Estate Band S
Table: p.1658

**Hastings, Douglas**
(District of Columbia)
Profile: p.518
Healthcare Band 1
Table: p.456

**Hastings, Susan C** (Ohio)
Profile: p.1629
Employment Band 3
Table: p.1609

**Hatch, Michael W**
(Wisconsin)
Profile: p.2033
Real Estate Band 1
Table: p.2030

**Hatchell, Mike A** (Texas)
Litigation Band 2
Table: p.1866

**Hatcher, Julia**
(District of Columbia)
Environment Band 3
Table: p.451

**Hatfield, C Kent** (Kentucky)
Profile: p.948
Environment Band 1
Table: p.941

**Hathaway, Thomas M J**
(Michigan)
Profile: p.1135
Employment Band 3
Table: p.1125

**Hatley, Joseph** (Kansas)
Profile: p.931
Litigation Band 2

Table: p.927

**Hatmaker, J Chadwick**
(Tennessee)
Employment Up and coming
Table: p.1801

**Hattersley III, Thomas E**
(Montana)
Employment Band 2
Table: p.1223

**Hauber, Catherine**
(Missouri)
Profile: p.1206
Real Estate Band 3
Table: p.1201

**Haubert, William J**
(Delaware)
Profile: p.405
Corporate/M&A
Up and coming
Table: p.394

**Hauck, Terry** (Oregon)
Real Estate Band 1
Table: p.1677

**Haughey, Stephen N**
(Ohio)
Profile: p.1629
Environment Band 4
Table: p.1612

**Hauser III, Wade** (Iowa)
Litigation Band 3
Table: p.914

**Havel, Richard W**
(California)
Profile: p.293
Bankruptcy Band 3
Table: p.222

**Havlick, Scott** (Colorado)
Profile: p.361
Intellectual Property Band 2
Table: p.351

**Hawk, Barry E** (New York)
Profile: p.1464
Antitrust Band S
Table: p.1335

**Hawke Jr, John D**
(National)
Profile: p.106
Financial Services Band 1
Table: p.28

**Hawkins, Barry**
(Connecticut)
Real Estate Band 1
Table: p.380

**Hawkins, Holmes** (Georgia)
Profile: p.714
Intellectual Property Band 3
Table: p.696

**Hawkins, John**
(Connecticut)
Profile: p.383
Corporate/M&A Band 2
Table: p.374

**Hawkins, Michael** (Ohio)
Profile: p.1629
Employment Band 3

Table: p.1609

**Hawks, Christopher H.**
(Wyoming)
Real Estate Band 2
Table: p.2045

**Haworth, Gregory R**
(New Jersey)
Profile: p.1300
Litigation Band 3
Table: p.1289

**Hayden, Jan M** (Louisiana)
Corporate/M&A Band 2
Table: p.965

**Hayden, Joseph** (New
Jersey)
Litigation Band 1
Table: p.1292

**Hayden, Raymond P**
(New York)
Transportation Band 2
Table: p.74

**Hayden, William** (Arizona)
Profile: p.191
Employment Band 3
Table: p.178

**Hayes, David**
(District of Columbia)
Environment Band 1
Table: p.451

**Hayes, David L** (California)
Profile: p.293
Intellectual Property Band 3
Table: p.248
IT Outsourcing Band 2
Table: p.253

**Hayes, James P** (Iowa)
Litigation Band 2
Table: p.914

**Hayes, Robert E**
(South Dakota)
Corporate/Commercial Band 1
Table: p.1792
Real Estate Band 2
Table: p.1796

**Hayes, Timothy G** (Virginia)
Profile: p.1982
Environment Band 1
Table: p.1973

**Hayes, William** (Texas)
Profile: p.1896
Banking & Finance Band 1
Table: p.1832

**Hayes, William D** (Ohio)
Profile: p.1629
Environment Band 2
Table: p.1612

**Haygood, Paul M**
(Louisiana)
Profile: p.981
Corporate/M&A Band 2
Table: p.965

**Hayhurst, Matthew B**
(Montana)
Litigation Up and coming
Table: p.1225

**Haynam, Douglas** (Ohio)
Environment Band 3
Table: p.1612

**Haynes, Greg** (Kentucky)
Profile: p.948
Litigation Band 1
Table: p.942

**Haynes, John** (Tennessee)
Profile: p.1813
Real Estate Band 2
Table: p.1808

**Haynes, Joseph B**
(Georgia)
Profile: p.715
Litigation Band 3
Table: p.698

**Haynor, Charles**
(Minnesota)
Real Estate Band 2
Table: p.1160

**Hays, Robert D** (Georgia)
Profile: p.715
Litigation Band 3
Table: p.698

**Hazan, Scott L** (New York)
Bankruptcy Band 3
Table: p.1344

**Hazlett, Mark** (Hawaii)
Real Estate Band 1
Table: p.748

**Hazlett, Richard**
(North Carolina)
Banking & Finance Band 1
Table: p.1569
Corporate/M&A Band 3
Table: p.1571

**Head, J D** (Texas)
Environment Band 4
Table: p.1852

**Headley, Linda** (Texas)
Profile: p.1896
Employment Band 2
Table: p.1844

**Healey, David J** (Texas)
Profile: p.1896
Intellectual Property Band 2
Table: p.1860

**Healy, Kevin** (New York)
Environment Band 2
Table: p.1371

**Healy, Martin R**
(Massachusetts)
Profile: p.1094
Real Estate Band 1
Table: p.1081

**Heaphey, Christopher**
(Alaska)
Real Estate Band 2
Table: p.172

**Heard, Keith W** (New York)
Transportation Band 2
Table: p.74

**Heard, Richard W**
(Montana)
Real Estate Band 2
Table: p.1230

**Heard III, F Lane** (National)
Products Liability Band 4
Table: p.50

**Hearing, Gregory A**
(Florida)
Employment Band 4
Table: p.597

**Hearn, Curtis R** (Louisiana)
Profile: p.981
Corporate/M&A Band 2
Table: p.965

**Heath, Marc** (Vermont)
Litigation Band 2
Table: p.1959

**Heaven Jr, Lewis** (Kansas)
Profile: p.932
Real Estate Band 1
Table: p.930

**Hecht, Philip H**
(District of Columbia)
Insurance Band 3
Table: p.464

**Heckler, Douglas** (Indiana)
Profile: p.896
Employment Band 2
Table: p.889

**Hedican, Chris** (Nebraska)
Employment Band 1
Table: p.1238

**Heeter, James** (Missouri)
Profile: p.1206
Corporate/M&A Band 2
Table: p.1193

**Heffernan, Barbara**
(District of Columbia)
Profile: p.518
Energy Band 5
Table: p.441

**Hefflinger, David**
(Nebraska)
Corporate/M&A Band 1
Table: p.1236

**Heftler, Thomas E**
(New York)
Capital Markets Band 2
Table: p.15

**Heidelberger, Brian L**
(Illinois)
Profile: p.835
Media & Entertainment Band 2
Table: p.807

**Heidt, Jeffrey L**
(Massachusetts)
Profile: p.1094
Healthcare Band 1
Table: p.1071

**Heihre, Michael** (Hawaii)
Litigation Band 2
Table: p.745

**Heil, Joseph B** (California)
Profile: p.293
Real Estate Band 2
Table: p.270

**Heim, Michael F** (Texas)
Intellectual Property Band 3
Table: p.1860

**Heim, Robert C**
(Pennsylvania)
Profile: p.1730
Litigation Band 1
Table: p.1714

**Heiman, David G** (Ohio)
Profile: p.1629
Bankruptcy Band 1
Table: p.1600

**Hein, Laura** (Minnesota)
Litigation Band 1
Table: p.1157

**Heinke, Rex S** (California)
Profile: p.293
Media & Entertainment Band 2
Table: p.263

**Heintz, John**
(District of Columbia)
Insurance Band 2
Table: p.464

**Heinz, Von S** (Nevada)
Litigation Band 2
Table: p.1252

**Heinzelman, Kris**
(New York)
Profile: p.106
Capital Markets Band 1
Table: p.7

**Heisler, Quentin G**
(National)
Profile: p.106
Wealth Management Band 3
Table: p.81

**Heiss, Howard E** (New York)
Profile: p.1464
Litigation Band 3
Table: p.1391

**Heisse II, John R**
(California)
Profile: p.293
Construction Band 3
Table: p.225

**Heist, Dale** (Pennsylvania)
Profile: p.1730
Intellectual Property Band 1
Table: p.1711

**Heitner, Kenneth H**
(New York)
Profile: p.1464
Tax Band 1
Table: p.1423

**Hejmanowski, Paul**
(Nevada)
Litigation Band 2
Table: p.1252

**Held, Jerry** (Alabama)
Real Estate Band 3

Table: p.153

**Helfand, Thomas** (Texas)
Tax Band 2
Table: p.1875

**Heller, David** (Illinois)
Bankruptcy Band 1
Table: p.775

**Heller, Mark A**
(District of Columbia)
Profile: p.518
Healthcare Band 2
Table: p.456

**Heller, Richard B**
(New York)
Profile: p.1464
Media & Entertainment Band 1
Table: p.1401

**Heller, Ron** (Hawaii)
Corporate/Commercial Band 1
Table: p.741

**Heller, William J** (New Jersey)
Intellectual Property Band 1
Table: p.1288

**Heller, William P** (Florida)
Profile: p.639
Litigation Band 3
Table: p.609

**Hellewell, Read** (Utah)
Real Estate Band 3
Table: p.1947

**Hellow, John R** (California)
Healthcare Band 2
Table: p.238

**Helm, Robert W**
(District of Columbia)
Profile: p.518
Investment Management Band 1
Table: p.469

**Helm III, Kennedy**
(Kentucky)
Profile: p.948
Corporate/M&A Band 1
Table: p.937

**Helman, Robert A** (Illinois)
Profile: p.835
Corporate/M&A Band S
Table: p.781

**Helmreich, Richard J**
(Ohio)
Profile: p.1629
Employee Benefits Band 2
Table: p.1607

**Helmsing, Frederick G**
(Alabama)
Litigation Band 3
Table: p.152

**Heltzer, Harold J** (National)
Profile: p.106
Tax Litigation Band 3

**Hemley, Robert** (Vermont)
Litigation Band 1
Table: p.1959

**Hemminger, Pamela L**
(California)
Profile: p.294
Employment Band 3
Table: p.231

**Hemminger, Steven D**
(California)
Profile: p.294
Intellectual Property Band 4
Table: p.248

**Hempelmann, John**
(Washington)
Real Estate Band 2
Table: p.2003

**Henchey, Brian** (National)
Profile: p.106
Business Process Outsourcing
Up and coming
Table: p.2

**Henderson, Douglas A**
(Georgia)
Environment Band 3
Table: p.691

**Henderson, Thomas**
(Florida)
Real Estate Band 2
Table: p.617

**Henderson Jr, Donald B**
(New York)
Profile: p.1464
Insurance Band 2
Table: p.1380

**Hendler, Clifford B**
(District of Columbia)
Profile: p.519
Insurance Band 3
Table: p.461

**Hendren, Jennifer B**
(Arkansas)
Litigation Band 4
Table: p.205

**Hendrick, David R**
(Georgia)
Construction Band 1
Table: p.682

**Hendricks, Sharon J**
(California)
Profile: p.294
Employment Band 4
Table: p.232

**Hendricks Sr, Ed** (Arizona)
Litigation Band 2
Table: p.181

**Hendrickson, David** (West Virginia)
Litigation Band 1
Table: p.2013
Litigation Band 2
Table: p.2013

**Henegan, John** (Mississippi)
Profile: p.1184
Litigation Band 2
Table: p.1179
Litigation Band 2
Table: p.1179

**Hengen, Nancy** (New York)
Profile: p.106
Transportation Band 1
Table: p.74

**Henlein, Carl** (Kentucky)
Profile: p.948
Litigation Band 2
Table: p.942

**Henneburg, Frank H**
(District of Columbia)
Profile: p.519
Real Estate Band 3
Table: p.482

**Hennessey, Gilbert**
(Massachusetts)
Profile: p.1094
Intellectual Property Band 3
Table: p.1072

**Henney, Raymond W**
(Michigan)
Profile: p.1135
Litigation Band 3
Table: p.1128

**Hennigan, Brian J**
(California)
Litigation Band 1
Table: p.258

**Hennigan, J Michael**
(California)
Litigation Band 2
Table: p.257

**Henning, Mark G** (Illinois)
Profile: p.835
Real Estate Band 4
Table: p.809

**Henrie, Michelle**
(New Mexico)
Profile: p.1329
Environment Band 1
Table: p.1323

**Henry, D Steven** (Texas)
Profile: p.1896
Construction Band 4
Table: p.1838

**Henry, Roxann E**
(District of Columbia)
Antitrust Band 5
Table: p.426

**Hensel, Donald** (Georgia)
Profile: p.715
Tax Band 3
Table: p.703

**Hensler, David**
(District of Columbia)
Profile: p.519
Insurance Band 3
Table: p.461
Litigation Band 2
Table: p.471

**Hensley, Noel MB** (Texas)
Litigation Band 1
Table: p.1866

**Hensley Jr, Harold** (Texas)
Profile: p.1329
Environment Band 2
Table: p.1323

**Henze, Tom** (Arizona)
Litigation Band 1
Table: p.182

**Henze II, William F**
(New York)
Profile: p.1464
Energy Band 2
Table: p.1367

**Herald, J Patrick** (Illinois)
Profile: p.835
Litigation Band 4
Table: p.802

**Herbert, John S** (New York)
Profile: p.1464
Private Equity Band 3
Table: p.1407

**Herdzina, John W**
(Nebraska)
Corporate/M&A Band 3
Table: p.1236

**Herf, Charles** (Arizona)
Profile: p.191
Employment Band 3
Table: p.178

**Hering, Louis G** (Delaware)
Profile: p.405
Corporate/M&A Band 1
Table: p.395

**Heringer, Michael**
(Montana)
Employment Band 2
Table: p.1223

**Herlihy, Edward D**
(New York)
Profile: p.1465
Corporate/M&A Band 1
Table: p.1354
Financial Services Band 1
Table: p.24

**Herling, Michael J**
(Connecticut)
Profile: p.383
Corporate/M&A Band 2
Table: p.374

**Herman, John** (Minnesota)
Profile: p.1164
Real Estate Band 1
Table: p.1160

**Herman, Philip**
(Massachusetts)
Banking & Finance Band 2
Table: p.1055

**Herman, Russ M**
(Louisiana)
Profile: p.981
Litigation Band 1
Table: p.973

**Herman, Sarah Andrews**
(North Dakota)
Profile: p.1596
Employment ✪
Table: p.1592

**Hermann, Kristin A**
(Michigan)
Profile: p.1135
Banking & Finance Up and

coming
Table: p.1120

**Hermes, John N**
(Oklahoma)
Litigation Band 1
Table: p.1656

**Hermes, Robert N** (Illinois)
Profile: p.835
Insurance Band 2
Table: p.795

**Hermle, Lynne** (California)
Profile: p.294
Employment Band 2
Table: p.231

**Hernandez, Eugenio**
(Florida)
Profile: p.639
Immigration Band 1
Table: p.606

**Hernandez, Gary A**
(California)
Profile: p.294
Insurance Band 3
Table: p.243

**Hernandez, Jennifer L**
(California)
Profile: p.294
Environment Band 2
Table: p.236

**Heroy, David F** (Illinois)
Bankruptcy Band 3
Table: p.775

**Herr, David** (Minnesota)
Litigation Band 1
Table: p.1157

**Herr, Robert** (California)
Profile: p.294
Real Estate Band 3
Table: p.270

**Herrington, Daniel**
(Arkansas)
Employment Band 3
Table: p.203

**Herschman, Gary W** (New Jersey)
Profile: p.1300
Healthcare Band 1
Table: p.1287

**Hershman, Douglas M**
(Delaware)
Profile: p.406
Real Estate Band 3
Table: p.399

**Hertz, Mitch**
(District of Columbia)
Profile: p.519
Energy Band 4
Table: p.445

**Heryford, Craig**
(Pennsylvania)
Profile: p.1730
Banking & Finance Band 2
Table: p.1695

**Herzberg Esq, Peter J**
(New Jersey)
Environment Band 2
Table: p.1285

**Herzeca, Lois F** (New York)
Profile: p.1465
Insurance Band 3
Table: p.1380

**Herzog, David K** (Indiana)
Profile: p.896
Litigation Band 2
Table: p.890

**Hess, Adam R** (Virginia)
Profile: p.1982
Intellectual Property Band 2
Table: p.1975

**Hession, John**
(Massachusetts)
Profile: p.1094
Private Equity Band 2
Table: p.1078

**Hester, Tracy** (Texas)
Profile: p.1896
Environment Band 2
Table: p.1852

**Heston, Mary Jo**
(Washington)
Bankruptcy Band 2
Table: p.1991

**Heusel, Cornelius**
(Louisiana)
Profile: p.982
Employment Band 3
Table: p.967

**Hewey, Melissa** (Maine)
Profile: p.1012
Employment Band 3
Table: p.1002

**Hewitt, Christopher J**
(Ohio)
Profile: p.1629
Corporate/M&A
Up and coming
Table: p.1605

**Hewitt, Henry** (Oregon)
Corporate/M&A Band S
Table: p.1667

**Hewitt, Lester L** (Texas)
Profile: p.1897
Intellectual Property Band 2
Table: p.1860

**Hewitt, William J**
(New York)
Profile: p.1465
Private Equity Band 2
Table: p.1410

**Heyman, Kurt** (Delaware)
Profile: p.406
Chancery Band 3
Table: p.392

**Heyman, Robert**
(New Mexico)
Corporate/Commercial Band 2
Table: p.1320

**Heywood, Thomas A**
(West Virginia)
Corporate/Commercial Band 1
Table: p.2010

**Hibbs, Carol Dey** (Oregon)
Profile: p.1681
Corporate/M&A Band 3
Table: p.1667

**Hickey, Kathleen O'Callaghan** (Michigan)
Profile: p.1135
Banking & Finance Band 2
Table: p.1120

**Hickey, Michael**
(South Dakota)
Litigation Band 2
Table: p.1795

**Hickey, Paul** (Wyoming)
Litigation Band 3
Table: p.2044

**Hickey Jr, John T** (Illinois)
Profile: p.835
Litigation Band 3
Table: p.802

**Hickok, Arthur** (National)
Profile: p.106
Capital Markets Band 4
Table: p.18

**Hickok, Robert L**
(Pennsylvania)
Profile: p.1730
Litigation Band 2
Table: p.1714
Litigation Band 1
Table: p.1715

**Hicks, Alvin J** (Nevada)
Gaming & Licensing Band 2
Table: p.1251

**Hicks, John** (Tennessee)
Profile: p.1813
Litigation Band 2
Table: p.1804

**Hicks, Patrick H** (Nevada)
Profile: p.1258
Employment Band 2
Table: p.1248

**Hicks, Robert J** (Indiana)
Profile: p.896
Corporate/M&A Band 2
Table: p.887

**Hicks Jr, M Lawrence**
(Texas)
Profile: p.1897
Real Estate Band 3
Table: p.1872

**Hieb, Jack H**
(South Dakota)
Litigation Up and coming
Table: p.1795

**Higer, Dale G** (Idaho)
Real Estate Band S
Table: p.762

**Higgins, Daniel B**
(California)
Healthcare Band 1

Table: p.238

**Higgins, David K** (West Virginia)
Corporate/Commercial Band 3
Table: p.2010

**Higgins, James E**
(New Hampshire)
Litigation Band 3
Table: p.1267

**Higgins, John** (Texas)
Bankruptcy Band 4
Table: p.1835

**Higgins, Keith F**
(Massachusetts)
Profile: p.1095
Corporate/M&A Band 1
Table: p.1061

**Higgins, Roger** (Texas)
Insurance Band 2
Table: p.1858

**High, Mark R** (Michigan)
Profile: p.1135
Corporate/M&A Band 3
Table: p.1122

**High, Michael E** (Maine)
Profile: p.1012
Corporate/M&A Band 1
Table: p.1000

**High Jr, Charles** (Texas)
Employment Band 2
Table: p.1844

**Hiler, Bruce A** (National)
Profile: p.106
Financial Services Band 3
Table: p.28

**Hilgers, David W** (Texas)
Healthcare Band 2
Table: p.1855

**Hill, Donald** (Kansas)
Employment Band 3
Table: p.926

**Hill, Earl M** (Nevada)
Profile: p.1258
Environment Band 2
Table: p.1249

**Hill, Eva H** (Maryland)
Profile: p.1040
Corporate/M&A
Up and coming
Table: p.1025

**Hill, Frank** (Oklahoma)
Real Estate Band 1
Table: p.1658

**Hill, J Reginald** (Tennessee)
Profile: p.1813
Corporate/M&A Band 2
Table: p.1799

**Hill, James**
(North Dakota)
Litigation Band 1
Table: p.1593

**Hill, Lawrence** (National)
Profile: p.106

Tax Litigation Band 3

**Hill, Richard** (Washington)
Real Estate Band 2
Table: p.2003

**Hill, Robert F** (Colorado)
Profile: p.361
Litigation Band 1
Table: p.353
Litigation Band 1
Table: p.353

**Hill, Stephen L** (Missouri)
Profile: p.1206
Litigation Band 2
Table: p.1198

**Hill, Thomas** (Ohio)
Profile: p.1630
Litigation Band 3
Table: p.1617

**Hill, William K** (Florida)
Profile: p.639
Litigation Band 3
Table: p.609

**Hill III, Benjamin** (Florida)
Litigation Band 1
Table: p.609

**Hillenbrand, Hyman**
(Florida)
Transportation Band 3
Table: p.69
Transportation Band 2
Table: p.71

**Hiller, David P** (Ohio)
Employment Band 3
Table: p.1609

**Hilliard, David** (Illinois)
Intellectual Property Band 2
Table: p.799

**Hilliard, Michael** (Texas)
Banking & Finance Band 3
Table: p.1832

**Hilliard, Russell**
(New Hampshire)
Litigation Band 1
Table: p.1267

**Hillman, Robert**
(Massachusetts)
Profile: p.1095
Intellectual Property Band 1
Table: p.1072

**Hilmes, Jack** (Iowa)
Litigation Band 2
Table: p.914

**Hilson, John F** (California)
Profile: p.294
Banking & Finance Band 1
Table: p.218

**Hilton, Paul** (Colorado)
Profile: p.361
Corporate/M&A Band 1
Table: p.346

**Himeles, Martin** (Maryland)
Litigation Band 2
Table: p.1032

**Himmel, Michael B** (New Jersey)
Profile: p.1300
Litigation Band 1
Table: p.1292

**Hinchey, John** (Georgia)
Profile: p.715
Construction Band 1
Table: p.682

**Hinderks, Mark** (Kansas)
Profile: p.932
Litigation Band 1
Table: p.927

**Hinerman, Philip L** (Pennsylvania)
Environment Band 3
Table: p.1707

**Hines, Barry A** (Kentucky)
Profile: p.948
Real Estate Band 1
Table: p.944

**Hingle, Charles** (Montana)
Profile: p.1231
Corporate/M&A Band 2
Table: p.1222

**Hink, John** (Arizona)
Profile: p.191
Real Estate Band 4
Table: p.184

**Hinkle IV, Samuel D** (Kentucky)
Profile: p.948
Litigation Band 1
Table: p.942

**Hinkley, Gerry** (California)
Healthcare Band 2
Table: p.238

**Hinman Jr, William** (California)
Profile: p.107
Capital Markets Band 1
Table: p.8

**Hinson, Bobby D** (North Carolina)
Profile: p.1583
Real Estate Band 3
Table: p.1579

**Hinson, H Douglas** (National)
Profile: p.107
Erisa Litigation Band 3

**Hinson, Robin L** (North Carolina)
Corporate/M&A Band S
Table: p.1571

**Hintze, John** (Iowa)
Corporate/M&A Band 4
Table: p.909

**Hintze, Russell P** (Florida)
Profile: p.639
Tax Up and coming
Table: p.623

**Hipp, Kenneth B** (Hawaii)
Profile: p.751
Employment Band 1

Table: p.742

**Hirsch, Barry L** (California)
Media & Entertainment Band 2
Table: p.266

**Hirsch, Jeffrey L** (Massachusetts)
Employment Band 2
Table: p.1065

**Hirsch, Reece** (California)
Profile: p.295
Healthcare Band 3
Table: p.238

**Hirsch, Stephen** (Arizona)
Real Estate Band 3
Table: p.184

**Hirschberg, William E** (New York)
Profile: p.1465
Banking & Finance Band 1
Table: p.1339

**Hirschfeld, Michael** (Ohio)
Corporate/M&A Band 3
Table: p.1605

**Hirschman, Karen L** (Texas)
Profile: p.1897
Litigation Band 1
Table: p.1866

**Hise, Daniel G** (Mississippi)
Profile: p.1184
Corporate/Commercial Band 1
Table: p.1174

**Hisert, George A** (California)
Profile: p.295
Banking & Finance Band 2
Table: p.218

**Hishon, Robert H** (Georgia)
Tax Band 3
Table: p.703

**Hite, Richard** (Kansas)
Litigation Band 1
Table: p.927

**Hitselberger, Carol A** (Illinois)
Profile: p.107
Capital Markets Band 3
Table: p.18

**Hitt, Jeffrey** (Texas)
Profile: p.1897
Corporate/M&A Band 4
Table: p.1840

**Hixon III, Samuel W** (Virginia)
Litigation Band 2
Table: p.1977

**Hluchan, Richard M** (New Jersey)
Profile: p.1300
Environment Band 1
Table: p.1285
Real Estate Band 2
Table: p.1293

**Hobbins, Robert** (Minnesota)
Profile: p.1164
Employment Band 1
Table: p.1154

**Hobbs, James R** (Missouri)
Litigation Band 1
Table: p.1198

**Hobbs Jr, Michael D** (Georgia)
Intellectual Property Band 4
Table: p.696

**Hobby, Scott M** (National)
Profile: p.107
Business Process Outsourcing Band 3
Table: p.2

**Hobel, Lawrence** (California)
Profile: p.295
Insurance Band 2
Table: p.245

**Hoberg, Timothy E** (Ohio)
Corporate/M&A Band 2
Table: p.1605

**Hochberg, Jeffrey D** (New York)
Profile: p.1465
Tax Up and coming
Table: p.1425

**Hochberg, Kevin J** (National)
Profile: p.107
Capital Markets Band 4
Table: p.18

**Hochberg, Sheldon** (National)
Profile: p.107
International Trade Band 5
Table: p.42

**Hochstetler, William S** (Iowa)
Corporate/M&A Band 4
Table: p.909

**Hockeimer, Henry** (Pennsylvania)
Profile: p.1730
Litigation Up and coming
Table: p.1715

**Hockett, Christopher** (California)
Profile: p.295
Antitrust Band 2
Table: p.216

**Hodara, Fred S** (New York)
Profile: p.1465
Bankruptcy Band 3
Table: p.1344

**Hodes, Scott** (Illinois)
Media & Entertainment ✪
Table: p.807

**Hodess, Ronald E** (Michigan)
Profile: p.1135
Real Estate Band 2
Table: p.1130

**Hodge, Katherine D** (Illinois)
Environment Band 3
Table: p.791

**Hodge Jr, E Clifton** (Mississippi)
Profile: p.1184
Corporate/Commercial Band 2
Table: p.1174
Litigation Band 2
Table: p.1179

**Hodges, Charles** (Georgia)
Tax Up and coming

**Hodges Taylor, Laura C** (Massachusetts)
Profile: p.1095
Private Equity Band 2
Table: p.1078

**Hodgson Jr, C Clark** (Pennsylvania)
Litigation Band 3
Table: p.1714

**Hoeflich, Adam** (Illinois)
Litigation Band 4
Table: p.802

**Hofer, Roy** (Illinois)
Profile: p.835
Intellectual Property Band S
Table: p.799

**Hoffar, Julian F** (Virginia)
Profile: p.1982
Construction Band 1
Table: p.1965

**Hoffman, D Bruce** (Florida)
Profile: p.639
Antitrust Band 2
Table: p.581

**Hoffman, Daniel** (Colorado)
Litigation Band S
Table: p.353

**Hoffman, Jerome** (Florida)
Profile: p.640
Antitrust Band 2
Table: p.581

**Hoffman, Kenneth R** (Maryland)
Employee Benefits Band 2
Table: p.1027

**Hoffman, Mark F** (Washington)
Profile: p.2006
Corporate/Commercial Band 3
Table: p.1992

**Hoffman, William** (National)
Profile: p.107
International Trade Band 1
Table: p.41

**Hoffmann, Christian** (Arizona)
Profile: p.191
Corporate/M&A Band 3
Table: p.176

**Hoffmann, Warren** (Kentucky)
Profile: p.948
Environment Band 1
Table: p.940

**Hofstetter, Richard** (New York)
Profile: p.1465
Media & Entertainment Band 2
Table: p.1401

**Hogan, Adele** (National)
Profile: p.107
Capital Markets Band 4
Table: p.7

**Hogan, Edward** (New Jersey)
Environment Band 2
Table: p.1285

**Hogan, John M** (Florida)
Profile: p.640
Litigation Band 1
Table: p.610

**Hogan, Patricia B** (Ohio)
Intellectual Property Band 3
Table: p.1614

**Hogan III, Dennis P** (Nebraska)
Real Estate Band 1
Table: p.1242

**Hogfoss, Robert** (Georgia)
Profile: p.715
Environment Band 1
Table: p.691

**Hogue Jr, P Mason** (South Carolina)
Corporate/M&A Band 2
Table: p.1775

**Hokanson, Jeffrey** (Indiana)
Profile: p.896
Litigation Band 3
Table: p.890

**Holbreich, Curt** (National)
Sport Band 2
Table: p.59

**Holcomb, James M** (Iowa)
Real Estate Band 1
Table: p.917

**Holcomb, Mark E** (Florida)
Profile: p.640
Tax Band 2
Table: p.623

**Holden, G Graham** (Georgia)
Profile: p.715
Environment Band 3
Table: p.691

**Holden, Robert E** (Louisiana)
Environment Band 1
Table: p.970

**Holden Jr, Frederick D** (California)
Profile: p.295
Bankruptcy Band 4

**H**

KEY TO RANKINGS: ✪ = STAR INDIVIDUAL   S = SENIOR STATESMAN

Table: p.1428

**Howard, Robert** (California)
Environment Band 4
Table: p.236

**Howard, Theodore A**
(District of Columbia)
Profile: p.519
Insurance Band 3
Table: p.461

**Howard Jr, George S**
(California)
Profile: p.295
Employment Band 3
Table: p.231

**Howard Jr, John L** (Texas)
Profile: p.1897
Environment Band 4
Table: p.1852

**Howe Jr, Gedney M**
(South Carolina)
Litigation Band 2
Table: p.1778

**Howell, John E** (Texas)
Business Process Outsourcing
Band 1
Table: p.2
Technology Band 1
Table: p.1877

**Howitt, John P** (National)
Profile: p.108
Transportation Band 3
Table: p.64

**Howlett, Timothy**
(Michigan)
Profile: p.1135
Employment Band 2
Table: p.1125

**Hoyns, John K** (National)
Profile: p.108
Transportation Band 3
Table: p.64

**Hoyt, Scott R** (Texas)
Profile: p.1897
Insurance Band 2
Table: p.1858

**Hubbard, Paul**
(North Dakota)
Real Estate Band 1
Table: p.1595

**Huber, John**
(District of Columbia)
Securities Band 1
Table: p.485

**Huber, Karen A.** (Maine)
Profile: p.1012
Real Estate Band 2
Table: p.1008

**Huck, L Francis** (New York)
Profile: p.1466
Banking & Finance Band 1
Table: p.1339

**Huck, Robert** (Nebraska)
Real Estate Band 2
Table: p.1242
Real Estate Band 2

Table: p.1242

**Hudanish, David M**
(New York)
Profile: p.1466
Business Process Outsourcing
Band 2
Table: p.2
Technology Band 2
Table: p.1428

**Huddleston, Michael**
(Texas)
Insurance Band 1
Table: p.1858

**Hudson, Paul** (Georgia)
Corporate/M&A Band 4
Table: p.684
Healthcare Band 2
Table: p.693

**Hudson, Robert** (Florida)
Profile: p.640
Tax Band 1
Table: p.623

**Huebner, Marshall S**
(New York)
Profile: p.1466
Bankruptcy Band 2
Table: p.1344

**Huey-Burns, Paul**
(District of Columbia)
Profile: p.519
Securities Band 2
Table: p.485

**Huffman, Fordham** (Ohio)
Profile: p.1630
Litigation Band 3
Table: p.1617

**Huffman, Gregory** (Texas)
Profile: p.1898
Antitrust Band 2
Table: p.1829

**Hugg, Joseph A**
(Massachusetts)
Profile: p.1095
Employee Benefits Band 2
Table: p.1063

**Hughes, Christopher**
(New York)
Profile: p.1466
Intellectual Property Band 3
Table: p.1384

**Hughes, Frank J**
(California)
Construction Band 3
Table: p.225

**Hughes, Randall** (Georgia)
Healthcare Band 1
Table: p.693

**Hughes, Vester** (Texas)
Tax Band S
Table: p.1875

**Hughes III, Hunter R**
(Georgia)
Employment Band 1
Table: p.687

**Hughes Jr, William H**
(Georgia)
Profile: p.715
Construction Band 2
Table: p.682

**Hughey, Roger** (Kansas)
Real Estate Band 2
Table: p.930

**Hughey Jr, James F**
(Alabama)
Profile: p.157
Corporate/Commercial Band 1
Table: p.148

**Hugi, Robert F** (Illinois)
Profile: p.109
Capital Markets Band 1
Table: p.18

**Hull, Robert J** (Texas)
Profile: p.1898
Tax Band 4
Table: p.1875

**Hull Jr, Gerald** (New Jersey)
Real Estate Band 1
Table: p.1293

**Humes, Gary**
(District of Columbia)
Profile: p.519
Real Estate Band 2
Table: p.482

**Humke, Steven** (Indiana)
Profile: p.896
Corporate/M&A Band 1
Table: p.887

**Humphrey, Andrew**
(Minnesota)
Profile: p.1164
Corporate/M&A Band 2
Table: p.1152

**Humphrey, Lawton**
(Washington)
Employment Band 3
Table: p.1995

**Humphrey, Thomas P**
(National)
Profile: p.109
Government Contracts Band 4
Table: p.30

**Humphreys, Hunter**
(Tennessee)
Profile: p.1814
Real Estate Band 2
Table: p.1808

**Humphreys, Ivan H**
(California)
Profile: p.295
Tax Band 1
Table: p.274

**Hunt, James L** (California)
Profile: p.295
Antitrust Band 3
Table: p.216

**Hunt, Jeffrey** (Utah)
Litigation Band 3
Table: p.1945

**Hunt, Paul J**
(District of Columbia)
Projects Band 4
Table: p.479

**Hunt, Peter J** (New York)
Profile: p.1467
Employee Benefits Band 3
Table: p.1362

**Hunt, Stephen** (Ohio)
Real Estate Band 4
Table: p.1621

**Hunt, William S** (Hawaii)
Profile: p.751
Litigation Band 3
Table: p.745

**Hunter, Forrest** (Georgia)
Profile: p.715
Employment Band 4
Table: p.687

**Hunter, Jerry** (Missouri)
Employment Band 2
Table: p.1195

**Hunter, Jonathon**
(Louisiana)
Energy Band 1
Table: p.969

**Hunter, Margaret Adams**
(Michigan)
Employee Benefits Band 2
Table: p.1124

**Hunter, Robert** (Missouri)
Profile: p.1207
Corporate/M&A Band 2
Table: p.1193

**Huntington, Danny**
(District of Columbia)
Profile: p.519
Intellectual Property Band 4
Table: p.466

**Huntrods, Ann** (Minnesota)
Employment Band 2
Table: p.1154

**Hurley,**
(New Mexico)
Real Estate Band 1
Table: p.1327

**Hurley, Cynthia A** (Iowa)
Real Estate Up and coming
Table: p.917

**Hurley, Timothy J** (Ohio)
Bankruptcy Band 3
Table: p.1600

**Hurney Jr, Thomas J** (West
Virginia)
Profile: p.2017
Litigation Band 2
Table: p.2013

**Husband, John** (Colorado)
Profile: p.361
Employment Band 1
Table: p.348

**Husid, Douglas M**
(Massachusetts)
Real Estate Band 1

Table: p.1081

**Hutcheon, Peter**
(New Jersey)
Corporate/M&A Band 3
Table: p.1278

**Hutcheson, Mark A**
(Washington)
Employment Band 1
Table: p.1995

**Hutchings, Stephen H**
(Alaska)
Litigation Band 1
Table: p.171
Litigation Band 3
Table: p.171

**Hutchings Reed, Mary**
(Illinois)
Media & Entertainment Band 1
Table: p.807

**Hutchinson Jr, Joseph F**
(Ohio)
Bankruptcy Band 3
Table: p.1600

**Hutson, Benne C**
(North Carolina)
Environment Band 2
Table: p.1575

**Hutt, Peter Barton**
(District of Columbia)
Profile: p.520
Healthcare Band 1
Table: p.456

**Hutton III, John B** (Florida)
Profile: p.640
Bankruptcy Band 4
Table: p.586

**Hutz, Rudolf E** (Delaware)
Profile: p.406
Intellectual Property Band 1
Table: p.397

**Huvelle, Jeffrey** (National)
Profile: p.109
Erisa Litigation

**Hyatt, Townsend** (National)
Profile: p.109
Native Law Band 1
Table: p.47

**Hyatt, William** (New Jersey)
Environment Band 1
Table: p.1285

**Hyde, Kevin E** (Florida)
Profile: p.640
Employment Band 1
Table: p.597

**Hyde, Robert C** (Utah)
Profile: p.1951
Real Estate Band 2
Table: p.1947

**Hyde, Terrill**
(District of Columbia)
Profile: p.520
Tax Band 4
Table: p.488

**H**

**Hyman, Alan** (New York)
Profile: p.1467
Bankruptcy Band 3
Table: p.1344

**Hyman, Milt** (California)
Tax Band 1
Table: p.274

**Hyman, Paul M**
(District of Columbia)
Healthcare Band 2
Table: p.456

**Hyne, Ernest E** (Tennessee)
Corporate/M&A Band 2
Table: p.1799

## I

**Icard, Thomas** (Florida)
Construction Band 2
Table: p.590

**Ichel, David** (New York)
Profile: p.1467
Litigation Band 3
Table: p.1388

**Ihrig, Richard** (Minnesota)
Profile: p.1164
Litigation Band 3
Table: p.1156

**Ilvedson, Duane**
(North Dakota)
Litigation Band 2
Table: p.1593

**Imanaka, Mitchell M**
(Hawaii)
Real Estate Band 3
Table: p.748

**Immelt, Stephen**
(Maryland)
Profile: p.1040
Healthcare Band 2
Table: p.1031
Litigation Band 2
Table: p.1032

**Imperato, Gabriel L**
(Florida)
Healthcare Band 1
Table: p.604

**Imse, Peter**
(New Hampshire)
Real Estate Band 1
Table: p.1270

**Imus, Neil W**
(District of Columbia)
Profile: p.520
Antitrust Band 5
Table: p.426

**Indoe, William F** (New York)
Profile: p.1467
Tax Band 4
Table: p.1423

**Indursky, Arthur I** (New York)
Media & Entertainment Band 1
Table: p.1401

**Ing, J Douglas** (Hawaii)
Land Use Band 1
Table: p.744

**Ingersoll, Josy W**
(Delaware)
Profile: p.406
Intellectual Property Band 4
Table: p.397

**Ingersoll, Richard K**
(Hawaii)
Corporate/Commercial Band 2
Table: p.740
Corporate/Commercial Band 2
Table: p.741

**Inglima, Thomas** (Virginia)
Corporate/M&A Band 3
Table: p.1968

**Ingram, Fredric** (Alabama)
Employment Band S
Table: p.150

**Ingram Jr, Lindsey W**
(Kentucky)
Profile: p.948
Environment Band 1
Table: p.940
Environment Band 1
Table: p.941

**Insolia, Robert S** (New York)
Profile: p.1467
Private Equity Band 3
Table: p.1410

**Intihar, Steve** (Ohio)
Real Estate Band 4
Table: p.1621

**Ippolito, Peter J** (California)
Profile: p.296
Construction Band 3
Table: p.225

**Ipsen, Henry** (Colorado)
Environment Band 2
Table: p.350

**Irby, Peyton** (Mississippi)
Employment Band 3
Table: p.1177

**Iredale, Nancy L**
(California)
Profile: p.296
Tax Band 3
Table: p.274

**Ireland, D Jeffrey** (Ohio)
Profile: p.1630
Litigation Band 4
Table: p.1617

**Ireland, Oliver I** (National)
Profile: p.109
Financial Services Band 2
Table: p.24

**Irmscher, David** (Indiana)
Profile: p.897
Litigation Band 2
Table: p.891

**Irvin, Michael P** (Texas)
Profile: p.1898
Energy Band 4

**Irwin, Kevin** (Ohio)
Bankruptcy Band 3
Table: p.1600

**Irwin, Peter J** (New York)
Real Estate Up and coming
Table: p.1417

**Isaacson, Andrew**
(Maryland)
Profile: p.1041
Real Estate Band 4
Table: p.1035

**Isaacson, Laurence B**
(New York)
Profile: p.109
Capital Markets Band 1
Table: p.13

**Isaacson, William**
(District of Columbia)
Profile: p.109
International Arbitration Band 4
Table: p.36

**Isackson, Robert M**
(New York)
Profile: p.1467
Intellectual Property Band 4
Table: p.1384

**Isaia, Russell E**
(Massachusetts)
Profile: p.1095
Employee Benefits Band 1
Table: p.1063

**Iseman, Robert H** (New York)
Healthcare Band 3
Table: p.1374

**Ishikawa, Jesse S**
(Wisconsin)
Profile: p.2033
Real Estate Band 2
Table: p.2030

**Isken, Donald N** (Delaware)
Profile: p.406
Real Estate Band 1
Table: p.399

**Iskra, Eric W** (West Virginia)
Employment Band 2
Table: p.2012

**Isler, Edward** (Virginia)
Employment Band 1
Table: p.1971

**Isom, Chervis** (Alabama)
Profile: p.157
Real Estate Band 1
Table: p.153

**Ison, Eric** (Kentucky)
Litigation Band 3
Table: p.942

**Israel, Allen D** (Washington)
Corporate/Commercial Band 3
Table: p.1992

**Israel, Sharon** (Texas)
Profile: p.1898

Intellectual Property Band 3
Table: p.1860

**Ivanhoe, Robert** (New York)
Profile: p.1467
Real Estate Band 4
Table: p.1417

**Ivener, Mark** (California)
Immigration Band 3
Table: p.241

**Ivester, Eric** (Illinois)
Profile: p.836
Bankruptcy Band 3
Table: p.775

**Iwamoto, Raymond S**
(Hawaii)
Real Estate Band 2
Table: p.748

**Jack, Andrew**
(District of Columbia)
Profile: p.520
Corporate/Commercial Band 3
Table: p.435

**Jack Jr, Donald** (Arkansas)
Corporate/Commercial Band 2
Table: p.201

**Jackoway, James R**
(California)
Media & Entertainment Band 2
Table: p.266

**Jackson, Charles C**
(Illinois)
Profile: p.836
Employment Band 2
Table: p.785

**Jackson, Dillon**
(Washington)
Bankruptcy Band 2
Table: p.1991

**Jackson, Reginald W**
(Ohio)
Profile: p.1630
Bankruptcy Band 3
Table: p.1600

**Jackson, Thomas C**
(District of Columbia)
Profile: p.520
Environment Band 4
Table: p.451

**Jackson, William Stuart**
(Arkansas)
Profile: p.209
Employment Up and coming
Table: p.203

**Jacob, Clyde** (Louisiana)
Profile: p.982
Employment Band 2
Table: p.967

**Jacob, Cynthia M** (New Jersey)
Profile: p.1301
Employment Band 1

Table: p.1282

**Jacobs, Bruce D**
(District of Columbia)
Profile: p.520
Telecom, Broadcast & Satellite Band 3
Table: p.492

**Jacobs, Charles P** (New York)
Profile: p.1467
Private Equity Band 4
Table: p.1410

**Jacobs, Gina** (Mississippi)
Corporate/Commercial Band 3
Table: p.1174

**Jacobs, Matthew L**
(District of Columbia)
Profile: p.520
Insurance Band 3
Table: p.464

**Jacobs, Michael A**
(California)
Profile: p.296
Intellectual Property Band 2
Table: p.248

**Jacobs, Neil**
(Massachusetts)
Profile: p.1095
Employment Band 2
Table: p.1065

**Jacobs, Paul** (Colorado)
Real Estate Band 2
Table: p.355

**Jacobs, Paul** (New York)
Profile: p.1468
Private Equity Band 3
Table: p.1407

**Jacobs, Peter** (Maine)
Profile: p.1012
Employment Band 2
Table: p.1002

**Jacobs, Stephen C** (Texas)
Real Estate Band 2
Table: p.1872

**Jacobsen, Brad** (Utah)
Corporate/M&A
Up and coming
Table: p.1941

**Jacobsen Jr, Raymond A**
(District of Columbia)
Profile: p.520
Antitrust Band 5
Table: p.426

**Jacobs-Meadway, Roberta** (Pennsylvania)
Profile: p.1731
Intellectual Property Band 1
Table: p.1711

**Jacobson, Craig** (California)
Media & Entertainment Band 3
Table: p.266

**Jacobson, Fruman** (Illinois)
Profile: p.836
Bankruptcy Band 2
Table: p.775

**Jacobson, John R**
(Tennessee)
Litigation Band 3
Table: p.1804

**Jacobson, Kenneth M**
(Illinois)
Profile: p.836
Real Estate Band 3
Table: p.809

**Jacobson, Marc** (New York)
Profile: p.1468
Media & Entertainment Band 2
Table: p.1401

**Jacobson, Martin D**
(New York)
Profile: p.1468
Projects Band 3
Table: p.1413
Transportation Band 2
Table: p.64

**Jacobson, Michael A**
(Illinois)
Profile: p.836
Banking & Finance Up and
coming
Table: p.771

**Jacobson, Michele L**
(New York)
Insurance Band 3
Table: p.1379

**Jacobson, Ronald H**
(Illinois)
Profile: p.836
Banking & Finance Band 3
Table: p.771

**Jacover, Jerold A** (Illinois)
Profile: p.836
Intellectual Property Band 2
Table: p.799

**Jaffe, Helene D** (New York)
Profile: p.1468
Antitrust Band 4
Table: p.1335

**Jaffe, Ira** (Michigan)
Corporate/M&A Band 2
Table: p.1122

**Jaffe, Kenneth G**
(District of Columbia)
Profile: p.520
Energy Band 2
Table: p.445

**Jaffe, Marc D** (National)
Capital Markets Band 3
Table: p.7

**Jaffe, Michael E**
(District of Columbia)
Profile: p.520
Construction Band 2
Table: p.433

**Jaffe, Seth D**
(Massachusetts)
Environment Band 1
Table: p.1068

**Jahn, Paul E** (California)
Profile: p.296
IT Outsourcing Band 3

Table: p.253

**Jahnke, Mark J** (Ohio)
Corporate/M&A Band 2
Table: p.1605

**Jakubowicz, Janet P**
(Kentucky)
Litigation Band 3
Table: p.942

**Jakubowski, Paul**
(Massachusetts)
Profile: p.1095
Real Estate Band 3
Table: p.1081

**James, Bruce A** (Colorado)
Profile: p.362
Real Estate Band 2
Table: p.355

**James, Dwight W** (Iowa)
Litigation Band S
Table: p.914

**James, Eric A** (Hawaii)
Real Estate Band 3
Table: p.748

**Jamieson, Brewster**
(Alaska)
Litigation Band 3
Table: p.171

**Jamison, Tom** (Minnesota)
Litigation Band 3
Table: p.1156

**Janik, Stephen** (Oregon)
Real Estate ✪
Table: p.1677

**Janis, Ronald H** (New
Jersey)
Profile: p.1301
Corporate/M&A Band 2
Table: p.1278

**Janka, John**
(District of Columbia)
Telecom, Broadcast & Satellite
Band 3
Table: p.492

**Janke, Ronald R** (Ohio)
Profile: p.1630
Environment Band 2
Table: p.1612

**Jankowsky, Joel** (National)
Profile: p.109
Government Relations Band 1
Table: p.32

**Janove, Jathan W** (Oregon)
Profile: p.1681
Employment Band 3
Table: p.1670

**Janowitz, Robert** (Missouri)
Employment Band 2
Table: p.1195

**Jansonius, John V** (Texas)
Profile: p.1898
Employment Band 2
Table: p.1844

**Jarboe, Mark A** (National)
Profile: p.109
Native Law Band 1
Table: p.47

**Jardine, James S** (Utah)
Litigation Band 1
Table: p.1945

**Jarin, Kenneth M**
(Pennsylvania)
Profile: p.1731
Employment Band 3
Table: p.1703

**Jarman, William** (Louisiana)
Profile: p.982
Litigation Band 3
Table: p.973

**Jarrell, Brenda H**
(Massachusetts)
Intellectual Property Band 3
Table: p.1072

**Jaudes, Richard E**
(Missouri)
Profile: p.1207
Employment Band 3
Table: p.1195

**Jedrey, Christopher M**
(Massachusetts)
Profile: p.1095
Healthcare Band 1
Table: p.1071

**Jeffcoat III, Otis Allen**
(South Carolina)
Real Estate Band 3
Table: p.1780

**Jeffery, D Ethan**
(Massachusetts)
Profile: p.1095
Bankruptcy Band 3
Table: p.1058

**Jeffress, William**
(District of Columbia)
Profile: p.521
Litigation Band 1
Table: p.471

**Jeffrey, Sheri** (California)
Profile: p.296
Media & Entertainment Band 3
Table: p.266

**Jeffries, M Hill** (Georgia)
Profile: p.715
Corporate/M&A Band 2
Table: p.684

**Jelencic, Sarah O**
(Wisconsin)
Profile: p.2033
Real Estate Band 2
Table: p.2030

**Jenett, Bruce** (California)
Profile: p.296
Corporate/M&A Band 4
Table: p.227

**Jenkins, John** (Ohio)
Profile: p.1630
Corporate/M&A Band 3
Table: p.1605

**Jenkins, Stephen E**
(Delaware)
Profile: p.406
Chancery Band 4
Table: p.392

**Jenkins, Steve** (Texas)
Real Estate Band 3
Table: p.1872

**Jenkins III, Robert M**
(National)
Profile: p.110
Transportation Band 2
Table: p.69

**Jenks, Carrie F**
(District of Columbia)
Profile: p.521
Environment Up and coming
Table: p.451

**Jenner, Jesse J** (New York)
Profile: p.1468
Intellectual Property Band 1
Table: p.1384

**Jennings, Gray** (Texas)
Profile: p.1898
Tax Band 4
Table: p.1875

**Jennings, Paul G**
(Tennessee)
Profile: p.1814
Litigation Band 1
Table: p.1804

**Jennings Jr, James W**
(Virginia)
Litigation Band 2
Table: p.1977

**Jensen, Curtis S**
(South Dakota)
Real Estate Band 2
Table: p.1796

**Jensen, Garth** (Colorado)
Corporate/M&A Band 2
Table: p.346

**Jensen, J Christopher**
(New York)
Intellectual Property Band 2
Table: p.1385

**Jensen, Patricia R.**
(Missouri)
Real Estate Up and coming
Table: p.1201

**Jepson Jr, Edward C**
(Illinois)
Employment Band 1
Table: p.785

**Jernigan, John L**
(North Carolina)
Profile: p.1583
Corporate/M&A Band 1
Table: p.1571

**Jernigan, Stacey G C**
(Texas)
Bankruptcy Band 4
Table: p.1835

**Jernigan Jr, W Henry**
(West Virginia)
Profile: p.2017
Litigation Band 1
Table: p.2013

**Jernstedt, Kenneth**
(Oregon)
Profile: p.1682
Employment Band 2
Table: p.1670

**Jessen, Paul** (Nebraska)
Corporate/M&A Band 2
Table: p.1236

**Jessup Jr, Clifton R** (Texas)
Profile: p.1898
Bankruptcy Band 4
Table: p.1835

**Jewell, Robert V** (Texas)
Corporate/M&A Band 1
Table: p.1840
Technology Band 2
Table: p.1878

**Jewell, Ronald R** (New
York)
Profile: p.1468
Corporate/M&A Band 1
Table: p.1359

**Jewett, Steve** (Colorado)
Intellectual Property Band 2
Table: p.351

**Jobeun, Larry** (Nebraska)
Real Estate Band 2
Table: p.1242

**Jocelyn, Richard L E**
(Rhode Island)
Employment Band 2
Table: p.1768

**Joe, Harry** (Texas)
Immigration Band 1
Table: p.1856

**Joffe, Robert D** (New York)
Profile: p.1468
Antitrust Band 1
Table: p.1335

**John, Philip** (Texas)
Profile: p.1898
Antitrust Band 3
Table: p.1829

**Johnsen, Diane M**
(Arizona)
Profile: p.191
Litigation Up and coming
Table: p.181

**Johnson, Carmen** (Florida)
Profile: p.640
Employment Band 4
Table: p.597

**Johnson, Charles E**
(North Carolina)
Employment Band 3
Table: p.1573

**Johnson, Christopher D**
(Arizona)
Profile: p.192
Corporate/M&A Band 1

Table: p.176

**Johnson, David L**
(North Dakota)
Corporate/Commercial Band 1
Table: p.1590

**Johnson, Dennis** (Indiana)
Profile: p.897
Real Estate Band 3
Table: p.892

**Johnson, Dixie**
(District of Columbia)
Profile: p.521
Securities Band 1
Table: p.485

**Johnson, Donald** (Michigan)
Profile: p.1135
Banking & Finance Band 2
Table: p.1120
Corporate/M&A Band 3
Table: p.1122

**Johnson, Edward D**
(California)
Profile: p.296
Litigation Band 4
Table: p.257

**Johnson, Ethel J** (Texas)
Profile: p.1898
Employment Band 3
Table: p.1844

**Johnson, Garrett B**
(Illinois)
Profile: p.836
Litigation Band 4
Table: p.802

**Johnson, James** (Georgia)
Profile: p.715
Intellectual Property Band 4
Table: p.696

**Johnson, Linda S**
(New Hampshire)
Profile: p.1272
Employment Band 2
Table: p.1265

**Johnson, Philip**
(North Dakota)
Real Estate Band S
Table: p.1595

**Johnson, Philip McBride**
(National)
Profile: p.110
Capital Markets Band 3
Table: p.15

**Johnson, Randal A**
(Oregon)
Profile: p.1682
Real Estate Band 3
Table: p.1677

**Johnson, Richard** (Indiana)
Profile: p.897
Real Estate Band 2
Table: p.892

**Johnson, Robert C** (Illinois)
Profile: p.837
Insurance Band 3
Table: p.796

**Johnson, Robert N**
(Georgia)
Profile: p.716
Immigration Band 2
Table: p.694

**Johnson, Steven**
(North Dakota)
Corporate/Commercial Band 1
Table: p.1590

**Johnson, Steven**
(South Dakota)
Litigation Band 2
Table: p.1795

**Johnson, Thomas**
(Nebraska)
Litigation Band 2
Table: p.1240

**Johnson, V Duncan**
(Rhode Island)
Profile: p.1772
Corporate/Commercial Band 1
Table: p.1766

**Johnson, W Stanfield**
(National)
Profile: p.110
Government Contracts
Band S
Table: p.30

**Johnson, Weyman**
(Georgia)
Profile: p.716
Employment Band 2
Table: p.687

**Johnson, William**
(Nebraska)
Litigation Band 2
Table: p.1240

**Johnson Jr, Daniel**
(California)
Profile: p.296
Intellectual Property Band 3
Table: p.248

**Johnson Jr, John H**
(Georgia)
Environment Band 1
Table: p.691

**Johnson Jr, O Thomas**
(District of Columbia)
Profile: p.110
International Arbitration
Band 3
Table: p.36

**Johnston, George**
(Maryland)
Employment Band 2
Table: p.1028

**Johnston, Jay** (Virginia)
Corporate/M&A Band 1
Table: p.1968

**Johnston, John F**
(Delaware)
Profile: p.406
Corporate/M&A Band 2
Table: p.394

**Johnston, M Elaine**
(New York)
Profile: p.1468

Antitrust Band 3
Table: p.1335

**Johnston, Mark G**
(District of Columbia)
Profile: p.521
Telecom, Broadcast & Satellite
Band 4
Table: p.492

**Johnston, Mike** (Georgia)
Profile: p.716
Employment Band 2
Table: p.687

**Johnston, Ronald L**
(California)
Profile: p.297
Intellectual Property Band 3
Table: p.248
Litigation Band 4
Table: p.257

**Johnston, Susan A**
(Massachusetts)
Profile: p.1095
Tax Band 2
Table: p.1084

**Johnston, Thomas** (Maine)
Profile: p.1013
Employment Band 2
Table: p.1002

**Johnstone, Andrea**
(New Hampshire)
Profile: p.1272
Employment Band 1
Table: p.1265

**Johnstone, Debbi M**
(Texas)
Profile: p.1899
Healthcare Band 2
Table: p.1855

**Jolley, R Gardner** (Nevada)
Litigation Band 2
Table: p.1252

**Jones, Cary** (Utah)
Profile: p.1951
Real Estate Band 3
Table: p.1947

**Jones, Celeste**
(South Carolina)
Litigation Band 3
Table: p.1778

**Jones, Christopher** (Ohio)
Profile: p.1630
Environment Band 4
Table: p.1612

**Jones, Christy** (Mississippi)
Profile: p.1185
Litigation Band 2
Table: p.1179
Products Liability Band 3
Table: p.50

**Jones, David F**
(Pennsylvania)
Profile: p.1731
Employment Band 2
Table: p.1704

**Jones, Erika Z** (National)
Profile: p.110

Transportation Band 1
Table: p.71

**Jones, Frank G** (Texas)
Profile: p.1899
Litigation Band 2
Table: p.1865

**Jones, Haskins W**
(Alabama)
Banking & Finance Band 2
Table: p.147

**Jones, J Randall** (Nevada)
Litigation Band 1
Table: p.1252

**Jones, John** (Montana)
Real Estate Band 2
Table: p.1230

**Jones, Joseph E** (Nebraska)
Litigation Band 2
Table: p.1240

**Jones, Karen** (Washington)
Employment Band 2
Table: p.1995

**Jones, Leslie Terry**
(Nevada)
Corporate/Commercial Band 2
Table: p.1246
Real Estate Band 1
Table: p.1255

**Jones, Lewis B** (Georgia)
Profile: p.716
Environment Up and coming
Table: p.691

**Jones, Linda B** (Idaho)
Profile: p.764
Corporate/Commercial Band 3
Table: p.759
Natural Resources Band 1
Table: p.761

**Jones, Michael R**
(Arkansas)
Employment Band 1
Table: p.203

**Jones, Nancy S**
(Tennessee)
Profile: p.1814
Litigation Band 3
Table: p.1804

**Jones, Nathan W** (Utah)
Corporate/M&A Band 3
Table: p.1941

**Jones, Patrick H** (Hawaii)
Profile: p.751
Employment Band 3
Table: p.742

**Jones, Paul J** (Wisconsin)
Profile: p.2033
Corporate/M&A
Up and coming
Table: p.2025

**Jones, Philip** (Tennessee)
Real Estate Band 3
Table: p.1808

**Jones, Reginald M**
(Georgia)

Construction

**Jones, Richard D**
(Pennsylvania)
Profile: p.1731
Real Estate Band 2
Table: p.1718

**Jones, Robert** (California)
Corporate/M&A Band 4
Table: p.227

**Jones, Rod** (Florida)
Profile: p.640
Banking & Finance Band 2
Table: p.583

**Jones, Roger J** (Illinois)
Tax Band 3
Table: p.812

**Jones, Russell A**
(Tennessee)
Media & Entertainment Band 1
Table: p.1806

**Jones, Steve** (Missouri)
Corporate/M&A Band 2
Table: p.1193

**Jones, Thomas J** (Florida)
Profile: p.641
Insurance Band 2
Table: p.607

**Jones, Walker** (Mississippi)
Profile: p.1185
Litigation Band 2
Table: p.1179

**Jones, William Evan**
(Montana)
Litigation Band S
Table: p.1225

**Jones Jr, Philip K**
(Louisiana)
Corporate/M&A Band 2
Table: p.965

**Jones Jr, Stanley S**
(Georgia)
Healthcare Band 2
Table: p.693

**Jones Van Buren, Carolyn A**
(North Carolina)
Environment Band 2
Table: p.1575

**Jontz, Dennis**
(New Mexico)
Corporate/Commercial Band 3
Table: p.1320
Real Estate Band 3
Table: p.1327

**Jordan, Carey** (Texas)
Profile: p.1899
Intellectual Property Band 3
Table: p.1860

**Jordan, Carl** (Texas)
Profile: p.1899
Employment Band 1
Table: p.1844

**Jordan, David J** (Utah)
Litigation Band 1
Table: p.1945

**Jordan, Hilary P** (Georgia)
Profile: p.716
Banking & Finance Band 2
Table: p.677

**Jordan, James B** (Georgia)
Profile: p.716
Real Estate Band 1
Table: p.700

**Jorgensen, Thomas A**
(Ohio)
Profile: p.1631
Employee Benefits Band 3
Table: p.1607

**Jorgenson, Mary Ann**
(Ohio)
Profile: p.1631
Corporate/M&A Band 2
Table: p.1605

**Jorissen, Paul A** (National)
Profile: p.110
Capital Markets Band 3
Table: p.18

**Joscelyn, Alan L** (Montana)
Natural Resources Band 1
Table: p.1228

**Josefsberg, Robert**
(Florida)
Profile: p.641
Litigation Band 1
Table: p.609
Litigation Band 1
Table: p.610

**Joseph, Allan J** (National)
Government Contracts Band 1
Table: p.30

**Joseph, Gregory P**
(New York)
Litigation Band 2
Table: p.1388

**Joseph, Robert** (Illinois)
Profile: p.837
Antitrust Band 2
Table: p.767

**Joseph III, Alfred S**
(Kentucky)
Profile: p.949
Real Estate Band S
Table: p.944

**Josepher, Richard** (Florida)
Tax Band 3
Table: p.623

**Josephson, Richard**
(Texas)
Litigation Band 3
Table: p.1865

**Joslin, Peter B** (Vermont)
Litigation Band 3
Table: p.1959

**Jospin, Walter** (Georgia)
Profile: p.716
Corporate/M&A Band 3
Table: p.684

**Jost, Lawrence J**
(Wisconsin)
Profile: p.2034

Real Estate Band 1
Table: p.2030

**Joswick, David D**
(Michigan)
Profile: p.1136
Corporate/M&A Band 1
Table: p.1122

**Joswick, Theresa C**
(Michigan)
Employee Benefits Band 2
Table: p.1124

**Joy, Robert** (Massachusetts)
Employment Band 2
Table: p.1065

**Joy, William**
(Massachusetts)
Employment Band 3
Table: p.1065

**Joyce, Edward M**
(New York)
Profile: p.1468
Insurance Band 3
Table: p.1379

**Judge, John P**
(Pennsylvania)
Environment Band 3
Table: p.1707

**Judlowe, Stephen B**
(New York)
Profile: p.1468
Intellectual Property Band 3
Table: p.1384

**Juliussen, James H**
(Alaska)
Employment Band 2
Table: p.169

**Junewicz, James J** (Illinois)
Profile: p.837
Corporate/M&A Band 3
Table: p.781

**Jung, William F** (Florida)
Litigation Band 2
Table: p.610

**Jurgensmeyer, Randy R**
(Texas)
Profile: p.1899
Real Estate Band 1
Table: p.1872

**Juska, William L** (National)
Profile: p.110
Transportation Band 3
Table: p.74

**Justice, Gary L** (California)
Profile: p.297
Insurance Band 3
Table: p.243

## K

**Kabnick, Lisa D**
(Pennsylvania)
Profile: p.1731
Banking & Finance Band 3
Table: p.1695

**Kaden, Alan**
(District of Columbia)
Profile: p.521
Tax Band 4
Table: p.488

**Kadet, Samuel** (New York)
Profile: p.1469
Litigation Band 3
Table: p.1390

**Kadlick, Richard F**
(National)
Profile: p.110
Capital Markets Band 4
Table: p.18

**Kadue, David** (California)
Employment Band 3
Table: p.231

**Kadzielski, Mark A**
(California)
Profile: p.297
Healthcare Band 1
Table: p.238

**Kaempfer, Christopher**
(Nevada)
Profile: p.1259
Real Estate Band 1
Table: p.1255

**Kafin, Robert** (New York)
Profile: p.1469
Environment Band 2
Table: p.1371
Environment Band 2
Table: p.1373

**Kafka, Gerald A** (National)
Tax Litigation Band 1
Table: p.62

**Kahan, Jonathan S**
(District of Columbia)
Profile: p.521
Healthcare Band 2
Table: p.456

**Kahn, Adam**
(Massachusetts)
Environment Band 2
Table: p.1068

**Kahn, David S**
(District of Columbia)
Profile: p.521
Real Estate Band 3
Table: p.482

**Kahn, Henry** (Maryland)
Profile: p.1041
Corporate/M&A Band 1
Table: p.1025

**Kahn, Richard R** (New
Jersey)
Real Estate Band 3
Table: p.1293

**Kahn, Ronald L** (Ohio)
Employee Benefits Band 3
Table: p.1607

**Kahnke, Randall**
(Minnesota)
Profile: p.1164
Litigation Up and coming
Table: p.1157

**Kaim, Henry** (Texas)
Profile: p.1899
Bankruptcy Band 2
Table: p.1835

**Kaiser, Keith** (Texas)
Profile: p.1899
Antitrust Band 3
Table: p.1829

**Kaiser Jr, Gordon S** (Ohio)
Profile: p.1631
Corporate/M&A Band 2
Table: p.1605

**Kalb, Paul E**
(District of Columbia)
Profile: p.521
Healthcare Band 2
Table: p.456

**Kaleczyc, Stanley**
(Montana)
Litigation Band 2
Table: p.1225

**Kalik, Mildred** (National)
Profile: p.111
Wealth Management Band 1
Table: p.81

**Kalish, Paul W**
(District of Columbia)
Profile: p.521
Insurance Band 2
Table: p.461

**Kalkines, George**
(New York)
Healthcare Band 1
Table: p.1374

**Kallas, Hani R** (Ohio)
Profile: p.1631
Banking & Finance Band 2
Table: p.1598

**Kallon, Abdul** (Alabama)
Profile: p.157
Employment Up and coming
Table: p.150

**Kallstrom, D Ward**
(National)
Profile: p.111
Erisa Litigation Band 2

**Kalteyer, Ronald** (Texas)
Tax Band 1
Table: p.1875

**Kamantauskas-Holder,
Katrina** (Maryland)
Employee Benefits Band 3
Table: p.1027

**Kamer, Gregory** (Nevada)
Employment Band 1
Table: p.1248

**Kamikawa, Ray K** (Hawaii)
Corporate/Commercial Band 1
Table: p.741

**Kamin, Chester T** (Illinois)
Profile: p.837
Telecom, Broadcast & Satellite
Band 3
Table: p.816

**Kaminsky, Neal** (Texas)
Banking & Finance
Up and coming
Table: p.1832

**Kamp, David** (Ohio)
Litigation Band 4
Table: p.1617

**Kanan, Gregory B**
(Colorado)
Profile: p.362
Litigation Band 1
Table: p.353

**Kane, Ivan P** (Illinois)
Profile: p.837
Real Estate Band 1
Table: p.809

**Kane, Jonathan**
(Pennsylvania)
Profile: p.1732
Employment Band 3
Table: p.1703

**Kane, Meredith J**
(New York)
Profile: p.1469
Real Estate Band 4
Table: p.1417

**Kannel, William**
(Massachusetts)
Profile: p.1096
Bankruptcy Band 3
Table: p.1058

**Kant, Robert** (Arizona)
Profile: p.192
Corporate/M&A Band 2
Table: p.176

**Kanter, Jane A**
(District of Columbia)
Profile: p.522
Investment Management Band 2
Table: p.469

**Kanter, Stacy J** (National)
Profile: p.111
Capital Markets Band 4
Table: p.7

**Kanter, Stanley**
(Rhode Island)
Profile: p.1772
Real Estate Band 2
Table: p.1770

**Kantor, Hal** (Florida)
Real Estate Band 1
Table: p.621

**Kantor, Michael**
(District of Columbia)
Profile: p.111
International Trade Band 2
Table: p.42

**Kaywood, Sam K** (Georgia)
Profile: p.717
Tax Band 2
Table: p.703

**Kazmarek, Edward 'Skip'**
(Georgia)
Profile: p.717
Environment Band 2
Table: p.691

**Keach, Robert J** (Maine)
Profile: p.1013
Corporate/M&A Band 1
Table: p.1000

**Keane, Jennifer** (Texas)
Profile: p.1899
Environment Band 4
Table: p.1852

**Keane, Paul** (National)
Transportation Band 3
Table: p.74

**Kearfott, Joseph C**
(Virginia)
Profile: p.1983
Litigation Band 2
Table: p.1977

**Kearney, Esq, Dennis T**
(New Jersey)
Profile: p.1301
Litigation Band 2
Table: p.1292

**Kearns, Ellen**
(Massachusetts)
Profile: p.1096
Employment Band 4
Table: p.1065

**Keating, Geoffrey T**
(District of Columbia)
Construction Band 3
Table: p.433

**Keating, Gregory C**
(Massachusetts)
Profile: p.1096
Employment Band 4
Table: p.1065

**Keating, Jennifer L**
(Illinois)
Profile: p.838
Corporate/M&A
Up and coming
Table: p.781

**Keating, Michael**
(Massachusetts)
Litigation Band 1
Table: p.1074

**Kee, Conrad** (Connecticut)
Profile: p.383
Employment Band 3
Table: p.376

**Keefe, Robert D**
(Massachusetts)
Profile: p.1096
Litigation Band 1
Table: p.1075

**Keehnel, Stellman**
(Washington)
Profile: p.2006

**Keleher, William**
(New Mexico)
Real Estate Band S
Table: p.1327

**Kelleher, Rory** (National)
Profile: p.112
Transportation Band 3
Table: p.64

**Kelleher, Thomas** (Georgia)
Construction Band 1
Table: p.682

**Keller, Brad** (Washington)
Litigation Band 1
Table: p.2000

**Keller, Bruce P** (New York)
Intellectual Property Band 1
Table: p.1385
Media & Entertainment Band 1
Table: p.1404

**Keller, Don** (California)
Profile: p.297
Corporate/M&A Band 4
Table: p.227

**Keller, Edwin A** (Nevada)
Employment Up and coming
Table: p.1248

**Keller, Kent** (California)
Insurance Band 3
Table: p.243

**Keller, Mary** (Texas)
Insurance Band 2
Table: p.1858

**Keller, Stanley**
(Massachusetts)
Profile: p.1096
Corporate/M&A Band S
Table: p.1061

**Kelley, Bernard J**
(Delaware)
Profile: p.407
Corporate/M&A Band 2
Table: p.395

**Kelley, David** (Minnesota)
Real Estate Band 1
Table: p.1160

**Kelley, James J**
(District of Columbia)
Profile: p.522
Employment Band 3
Table: p.439

**Kelley, James R**
(Tennessee)
Litigation Band 2
Table: p.1804

**Kelley, Jay D** (Texas)
Profile: p.1900
Energy Band 3
Table: p.1847
Projects Band 2
Table: p.1869

**Kelley, Jeffrey W** (Georgia)
Bankruptcy Band 3
Table: p.679

**Kelley, John** (Georgia)
Profile: p.717
Corporate/M&A Band 4
Table: p.684

**Kelley, Kevin** (Texas)
Profile: p.1900
Real Estate Band 3
Table: p.1872

**Kelley, Timothy** (Illinois)
Media & Entertainment Band 2
Table: p.807

**Kellner, Leon B**
(District of Columbia)
Profile: p.522
Insurance Band 2
Table: p.464

**Kellner, Robert** (Maryland)
Employment Band 2
Table: p.1028

**Kellner, Stuart** (Montana)
Litigation Band 3
Table: p.1225

**Kellogg, Michael**
(District of Columbia)
Telecom, Broadcast & Satellite
Band 1
Table: p.492

**Kelly, Andrew P** (Arizona)
Profile: p.192
Corporate/M&A
Up and coming
Table: p.176

**Kelly, Christopher** (Ohio)
Profile: p.1631
Corporate/M&A Band 3
Table: p.1605

**Kelly, Deborah**
(District of Columbia)
Profile: p.522
Employment Band 2
Table: p.439

**Kelly, Henry** (Illinois)
Telecom, Broadcast & Satellite
Band 2
Table: p.816

**Kelly, Joseph A**
(Rhode Island)
Litigation Band S
Table: p.1769

**Kelly, Michael J** (New York)
Profile: p.1470
Bankruptcy Band 4
Table: p.1344

**Kelly, Shawn L** (New Jersey)
Profile: p.1301
Litigation Band 1
Table: p.1289

**Kelly, T Mark** (Texas)
Profile: p.1900
Corporate/M&A Band 1
Table: p.1840

**Kelly, Thomas M** (New
York)
Insurance Band 2
Table: p.1380

**Kelly, Timothy** (Minnesota)
Litigation Band 1
Table: p.1156

**Kelly, William** (California)
Profile: p.298
Corporate/M&A Band 4
Table: p.227

**Kelsen, Peter Foster**
(Pennsylvania)
Profile: p.1732
Real Estate Band 2
Table: p.1718

**Kelso, Linda Y** (Florida)
Profile: p.641
Corporate/M&A Band 3
Table: p.594

**Keltner, David** (Texas)
Litigation Band 3
Table: p.1866

**Kemp, Hal** (Arkansas)
Real Estate Band 1
Table: p.207

**Kendall, David**
(District of Columbia)
Litigation Band 3
Table: p.471
Media & Entertainment Band 2
Table: p.477

**Kendall, Michael J**
(Massachusetts)
Profile: p.1096
Private Equity Up and coming
Table: p.1078

**Kendall, Richard B**
(California)
Media & Entertainment Band 2
Table: p.263

**Kendig-Schrader, Julie**
(Florida)
Profile: p.641
Real Estate Band 3
Table: p.621

**Kendrick, Edmund H**
(New Mexico)
Environment Band 2

**Kenlan, Jay** (Vermont)
Real Estate Band 1
Table: p.1961
Real Estate Band 3
Table: p.1961

**Kennedy, Dennis** (Nevada)
Litigation Band 1
Table: p.1252

**Kennedy, Donald J**
(New York)
Transportation Band 3
Table: p.74

**Kennedy, Elizabeth Gregg**
(Iowa)
Employment Band 1
Table: p.912

**Kennedy, John** (Texas)
Profile: p.1900
Energy Band 2

**Keeler, Dennis C** (Maine)
Profile: p.1013
Real Estate Band 1
Table: p.1008

**Keen, C Matthew**
(North Carolina)
Profile: p.1584
Employment Band 2
Table: p.1573

**Keenan, Robert** (Georgia)
Profile: p.717
Healthcare Up and coming

**Keene, Thomas** (Alabama)
Litigation Band 1
Table: p.152

**Keener, Mark P.** (Maryland)
Real Estate Band 4
Table: p.1035

**Keeney, Jeffrey H** (Oregon)
Profile: p.1682
Real Estate Band 3
Table: p.1677

**Keeney, Regina**
(District of Columbia)
Telecom, Broadcast & Satellite
Band 3
Table: p.492

**Keesal Jr, Samuel A**
(California)
Transportation Band 1
Table: p.78

**Keeton, Charles R**
(Kentucky)
Profile: p.949
Corporate/M&A Band 3
Table: p.937

**Keim, Robert** (Missouri)
Corporate/M&A Band 3
Table: p.1193

**Keiner, Jeffrey** (Florida)
Construction Band 3
Table: p.590

**Keiner Jr, R Bruce**
(National)
Profile: p.112
Transportation Band 1
Table: p.67

**Keith, Calvin L** (Oregon)
Employment Band 2
Table: p.1670

**Keithley, Bradford G**
(Texas)
Profile: p.1899
Energy Band 2
Table: p.1849

**Keker, John** (California)
Profile: p.297
Intellectual Property Band 1
Table: p.248
Litigation Band 1
Table: p.257
Litigation ✪
Table: p.258

**Kelley, Jeffrey W** (Georgia)
Litigation Band 3
Table: p.2000

**Kennedy, John B**
(New York)
Profile: p.1470
Technology Band 2
Table: p.1428

**Kennedy, Michael** (Arizona)
Litigation Band 3
Table: p.181

**Kennedy, Mike** (California)
Profile: p.298
Corporate/M&A Band 3
Table: p.227

**Kennedy, Robert**
(New York)
Private Equity Band 3
Table: p.1407

**Kennedy, Steven**
(Minnesota)
Profile: p.1164
Corporate/M&A Band 3
Table: p.1152

**Kennedy, Thomas H**
(New York)
Profile: p.1470
Corporate/M&A Band 3
Table: p.1354

**Kennedy III, James J**
(Florida)
Profile: p.641
Healthcare Band 2
Table: p.604

**Kenney, John A** (Oklahoma)
Litigation Band 2
Table: p.1656

**Kenny, Michael** (Georgia)
Profile: p.717
Litigation Band 3
Table: p.698

**Kent, Christopher H**
(Oregon)
Litigation Band 3
Table: p.1674

**Kent, Ronald D** (California)
Profile: p.298
Insurance Band 3
Table: p.243

**Kenyon, Charity** (California)
Media & Entertainment Band 3
Table: p.263

**Kenyon, Douglas W**
(North Carolina)
Profile: p.1584
Antitrust Band 1
Table: p.1568

**Keogh, Kevin** (National)
Profile: p.112
Capital Markets Band 4
Table: p.7

**Keppelman, Nancy**
(Michigan)
Employee Benefits Band 1
Table: p.1124

**Kepple, Lloyd** (Minnesota)
Real Estate Band 2
Table: p.1160

**Kerger, Richard** (Ohio)
Litigation Band 4
Table: p.1617

**Kerl, Ron** (Idaho)
Bankruptcy Band 3
Table: p.758

**Kern, David B** (Wisconsin)
Profile: p.2034
Employment Band 1
Table: p.2027

**Kerr, John** (New York)
Profile: p.112
International Arbitration
Band 2
Table: p.36

**Kerrick, Robert** (Arizona)
Real Estate Band 2
Table: p.186

**Kerrigan Jr, Robert E**
(Louisiana)
Litigation Band 3
Table: p.973

**Kerwin, Brian P** (Illinois)
Profile: p.838
Banking & Finance Band 3
Table: p.771

**Kesslen, Mark** (New Jersey)
Profile: p.1301
Intellectual Property Band 2
Table: p.1288

**Kessler, Jeffrey L**
(New York)
Profile: p.1470
Antitrust Band 4
Table: p.1335
Sport Band 1
Table: p.59

**Kessler, Mark K**
(Pennsylvania)
Profile: p.1732
Corporate/M&A Band 4
Table: p.1700

**Kessler, Philip J** (Michigan)
Profile: p.1136
Litigation Band 1
Table: p.1128

**Kestner, R Steven** (Ohio)
Corporate/M&A Band 3
Table: p.1605

**Keyes, David** (Texas)
Profile: p.1900
Banking & Finance Band 2
Table: p.1832

**Keyes, Jeffrey** (Minnesota)
Litigation Band 2
Table: p.1156

**Keyes, Judith Droz**
(California)
Profile: p.298
Employment Band 4
Table: p.231

**Keyes, Kevin M**
(District of Columbia)
Profile: p.523
Tax Band 4

Table: p.488

**Keyser, Denise M**
(New Jersey)
Profile: p.1301
Employment Band 2
Table: p.1282

**Khorey, David E** (Michigan)
Profile: p.1136
Employment Band 3
Table: p.1125

**Khoury, Joseph S**
(District of Columbia)
Energy Band 5
Table: p.441

**Kiefer, Matthew J**
(Massachusetts)
Real Estate Band 1
Table: p.1081

**Kiel, Donald W** (New
Jersey)
Litigation Band 1
Table: p.1289

**Kiely, Bruce**
(District of Columbia)
Profile: p.523
Energy Band 3
Table: p.441

**Kienbaum, Thomas G**
(Michigan)
Profile: p.1136
Employment ✪
Table: p.1125

**Kiernan, David C** (National)
Products Liability Band 2
Table: p.50

**Kiernan, John S** (New York)
Litigation Band 3
Table: p.1388

**Kieselstein, Marc** (Illinois)
Profile: p.838
Bankruptcy Band 2
Table: p.775

**Kiesewetter, Jay W**
(Tennessee)
Employment Band 2
Table: p.1801

**Kiessling, B Robbins**
(New York)
Profile: p.1470
Banking & Finance Band 1
Table: p.1339

**Kiggans, Thomas H**
(Louisiana)
Profile: p.982
Employment Band 2
Table: p.967

**Kikoler, Stephen P** (Illinois)
Construction Band 2
Table: p.778

**Kilb, Brian D** (California)
Profile: p.298
Banking & Finance Band 2
Table: p.218
Capital Markets Band 2
Table: p.8

**Kilbane, Thomas S** (Ohio)
Profile: p.1631
Litigation Band 1
Table: p.1617

**Kilberg, William J**
(District of Columbia)
Profile: p.523
Employee Benefits Band 3
Table: p.437
Employment Band 1
Table: p.439

**Kilbreth, James** (Maine)
Profile: p.1013
Environment Band 2
Table: p.1004
Litigation Band 3
Table: p.1006

**Kilgore III, Cada T**
(Georgia)
Profile: p.717
Energy Band 1
Table: p.689

**Kilgore III, Leonard L**
(Louisiana)
Profile: p.982
Environment Band 1
Table: p.970

**Killworth, Richard** (Ohio)
Profile: p.1631
Intellectual Property Band S
Table: p.1614

**Kilmer, Jeffrey M** (Oregon)
Litigation Band 3
Table: p.1674

**Kilpatrick, J Thomas**
(Georgia)
Profile: p.717
Employment Band 3
Table: p.687

**Kim, Gregory R** (Hawaii)
Corporate/Commercial Band 1
Table: p.740

**Kim, Richard K** (National)
Profile: p.113
Financial Services Band 3
Table: p.24

**Kim, Robert C** (Nevada)
Profile: p.1259
Corporate/Commercial Band 3
Table: p.1246

**Kimball, Albert** (Texas)
Profile: p.1900
Intellectual Property Band 2
Table: p.1860

**Kimball, Christian** (Illinois)
Profile: p.838
Tax Band 3
Table: p.812

**Kimball, David** (Arizona)
Environment Band 1
Table: p.179

**Kimball, George** (California)
Profile: p.298
Business Process Outsourcing
Band 2
Table: p.2

IT Outsourcing Band 1
Table: p.253

**Kimball, John D** (New York)
Profile: p.113
Transportation Band 1
Table: p.74

**Kimbol, Paul S**
(Pennsylvania)
Profile: p.1732
Employment Band 2
Table: p.1704

**Kimerer, Mike** (Arizona)
Litigation Band 3
Table: p.182

**Kimmell, Kenneth L**
(Massachusetts)
Environment Band 3
Table: p.1068

**Kimmelman, Louis B**
(New York)
Profile: p.113
International Arbitration
Band 3
Table: p.36

**Kinder, Daniel K** (Rhode
Island)
Employment Band 1
Table: p.1768

**King, Bruce** (Florida)
Profile: p.641
Construction Band 2
Table: p.590

**King, Bruce A** (National)
Transportation Band 1
Table: p.78

**King, Carol Weld**
(District of Columbia)
Profile: p.523
Real Estate Band 4
Table: p.482

**King, Chad W** (Texas)
Technology Band 2
Table: p.1877

**King, David** (Florida)
Litigation Band 2
Table: p.609

**King, David C.** (Maine)
Litigation Band 2
Table: p.1006

**King, G Roger** (Ohio)
Profile: p.1631
Employment Band 1
Table: p.1609

**King, Henry A.** (Louisiana)
Energy Band 1
Table: p.969

**King, June N** (Kentucky)
Corporate/M&A Band 3
Table: p.937

**King, Katherine** (Louisiana)
Profile: p.982
Energy Band 1
Table: p.969

**King, Kenton J** (California)
Profile: p.298
Corporate/M&A Band 2
Table: p.227

**King, Richard A** (Missouri)
Profile: p.1207
Real Estate Band 1
Table: p.1201

**King, W Gregory**
(Kentucky)
Profile: p.949
Litigation Band 2
Table: p.942

**King, William** (Virginia)
Litigation Band 1
Table: p.1977

**King Jr, Evans** (West
Virginia)
Corporate/Commercial Band 2
Table: p.2010
Corporate/Commercial Band 2
Table: p.2011

**King Jr, George S**
(South Carolina)
Corporate/M&A Band 1
Table: p.1775

**Kingham, Richard F**
(District of Columbia)
Profile: p.523
Healthcare Band 2
Table: p.456

**Kinney, Michael F**
(Nebraska)
Litigation Band 2
Table: p.1240

**Kinsella, Dale F** (California)
Media & Entertainment Band 4
Table: p.263

**Kinsella, Peter** (Colorado)
Profile: p.362
Intellectual Property Band 2
Table: p.351

**Kinsolving, Ruth Barnes**
(Florida)
Profile: p.641
Real Estate Band 2
Table: p.617

**Kinzie, Jack L** (Texas)
Profile: p.1900
Bankruptcy Band 2
Table: p.1835

**Kipnees, Robert J** (New
Jersey)
Profile: p.1301
Litigation Band 2
Table: p.1292

**Kirby, Matthew T**
(California)
Profile: p.298
Banking & Finance Band 1
Table: p.218

**Kirchhoefer, Gregg**
(Illinois)
Profile: p.838
Business Process Outsourcing
Band 3

Table: p.2
Technology Band 1
Table: p.814

**Kiriakos, Thomas S**
(Illinois)
Profile: p.838
Bankruptcy Band 3
Table: p.775

**Kirk, James** (Oklahoma)
Litigation Band 2
Table: p.1656

**Kirk, Michael K** (Kentucky)
Profile: p.949
Employment Band 3
Table: p.939

**Kirk, Richard D** (Delaware)
Profile: p.407
Intellectual Property Band 4
Table: p.397

**Kirkham, J Steven**
(Tennessee)
Profile: p.1814
Real Estate Band 3
Table: p.1808

**Kirkland, Byron B**
(North Carolina)
Profile: p.1584
Corporate/M&A Band 2
Table: p.1571

**Kirkland, David** (Texas)
Profile: p.1900
Corporate/M&A Band 2
Table: p.1840

**Kirkman, David**
(Minnesota)
Real Estate Band 3
Table: p.1160

**Kirkwood, Peter** (Florida)
Tax Band 2
Table: p.624

**Kirmis, Lyle**
(North Dakota)
Litigation Band 2
Table: p.1593

**Kirpalani, Susheel**
(New York)
Bankruptcy Band 4
Table: p.1344

**Kirsch, Robert**
(Massachusetts)
Profile: p.1096
Environment Band 1
Table: p.1068

**Kirschbaum, Howard**
(Illinois)
Real Estate Band 3
Table: p.809

**Kirschbaum, Thomas**
(California)
Employment Band 3
Table: p.232

**Kirschner, Kenneth**
(Florida)
Corporate/M&A Band 4
Table: p.594

**Kirwin, Brian P** (Florida)
Construction Band 3
Table: p.590

**Kisch, Victor J** (Oregon)
Employment Band 2
Table: p.1670

**Kishner, Joanna S**
(Nevada)
Profile: p.1259
Employment Band 3
Table: p.1248

**Kislin, Scott A** (New York)
Profile: p.1470
Corporate/M&A Band 4
Table: p.1354

**Kissel, Richard J** (Illinois)
Profile: p.839
Environment Band S
Table: p.791

**Kitchel, Chris** (Oregon)
Employment Band 2
Table: p.1670

**Kitchen, F Damon** (Florida)
Employment Band 4
Table: p.597

**Kitslaar, Libby** (Illinois)
Profile: p.839
Corporate/M&A Band 4
Table: p.781

**Klaper, Martin** (Indiana)
Profile: p.897
Employment Band 3
Table: p.889

**Klauberg, John G** (New
York)
Profile: p.1470
Energy Band 2
Table: p.1367

**Klawiter, Donald**
(District of Columbia)
Profile: p.523
Antitrust Band 2
Table: p.426

**Kleban, Barry**
(Pennsylvania)
Bankruptcy Band 1
Table: p.1697

**Klee, Kenneth N**
(California)
Profile: p.298
Bankruptcy Band 1
Table: p.222

**Klegerman, Neal** (Nevada)
Profile: p.1259
Corporate/Commercial Band 3
Table: p.1246

**Klein, Allen**
(District of Columbia)
Business Process Outsourcing
Band 2
Table: p.2
Technology Band 2
Table: p.490

**Klein, Anthony** (California)
IT Outsourcing Band 2

Table: p.253

**Klein, Daniel L** (Delaware)
Profile: p.407
Real Estate Band 2
Table: p.399

**Klein, David F**
(District of Columbia)
Profile: p.523
Insurance Band 4
Table: p.464

**Klein, Deborah** (California)
Media & Entertainment Band 3
Table: p.266

**Klein, Frederick**
(District of Columbia)
Profile: p.523
Real Estate Band 2
Table: p.482

**Klein, Jeffrey** (New York)
Profile: p.1471
Employment Band 3
Table: p.1365

**Klein, Justin P**
(Pennsylvania)
Profile: p.1732
Corporate/M&A Band 1
Table: p.1700

**Klein, Kenneth**
(District of Columbia)
Profile: p.523
Tax Band 4
Table: p.488

**Klein, Michael**
(District of Columbia)
Litigation Band 3
Table: p.471

**Klein, Randall** (Illinois)
Bankruptcy Band 3
Table: p.775

**Klein, Steven** (Louisiana)
Corporate/M&A Band 4
Table: p.965

**Klein, Steven D** (New York)
Profile: p.1471
Real Estate Band 4
Table: p.1417

**Klein III, Otto G**
(Washington)
Employment Band 2
Table: p.1995

**Kleinbard, Edward D** (New
York)
Profile: p.1471
Tax Band 1
Table: p.1425

**Kleinberg, Kenneth A**
(California)
Media & Entertainment Band 3
Table: p.266

**Kleinberg, Norman**
(National)
Profile: p.113
Products Liability Band 4
Table: p.50

**Kleinkopf, David** (Colorado)
Real Estate Band 1
Table: p.355

**Klenk, James** (Illinois)
Profile: p.839
Media & Entertainment Band 1
Table: p.806

**Klenk, Timothy C** (Illinois)
Employment Band 3
Table: p.785

**Klepper, Martin**
(District of Columbia)
Profile: p.524
Projects Band 2
Table: p.56
Projects Band 1
Table: p.479
Sport Band 3
Table: p.59

**Klevansky, Simon** (Hawaii)
Bankruptcy Band 2
Table: p.739

**Klevorn, Andrew G** (Illinois)
Profile: p.839
Antitrust Band 2
Table: p.767

**Klimko, Justin** (Michigan)
Profile: p.1136
Corporate/M&A Band 1
Table: p.1122

**Kline, Douglas J**
(Massachusetts)
Profile: p.1096
Intellectual Property Band 2
Table: p.1072

**Kling, Lou R** (New York)
Profile: p.1471
Corporate/M&A Band 2
Table: p.1354

**Kling, Neal** (Louisiana)
Real Estate Band 3
Table: p.975

**Klinger, Edward F.**
(North Dakota)
Litigation Band S
Table: p.1593

**Klinghoffer, Teddy D**
(Florida)
Profile: p.642
Corporate/M&A Band 2
Table: p.594

**Kluttz, Joseph B C**
(North Carolina)
Banking & Finance Band 3
Table: p.1569
Bankruptcy Band 1
Table: p.1570

**Klyman, Robert** (California)
Bankruptcy Band 4
Table: p.222

**Knapp, Spencer** (Vermont)
Corporate/Commercial Band 1
Table: p.1957

**K**

**Knauer, Thomas E**
(Virginia)
Environment Band 2
Table: p.1973

**Knauss, Charles**
(District of Columbia)
Profile: p.524
Environment Band 2
Table: p.451

**Knauss, Robert B**
(California)
Corporate/M&A Band 4
Table: p.227

**Knebel, Donald** (Indiana)
Profile: p.897
Litigation Band 1
Table: p.891

**Knee, Stephen H**
(New Jersey)
Profile: p.1301
Corporate/M&A Band 3
Table: p.1278

**Kneip, Frederick**
(New York)
Employee Benefits Band 2
Table: p.1362

**Knetsch, Jeffrey** (Colorado)
Profile: p.362
Corporate/M&A Band 3
Table: p.346

**Knight, G Marcus**
(South Carolina)
Profile: p.1783
Corporate/M&A Band 2
Table: p.1775

**Knight, James T** (New York)
Profile: p.1471
Banking & Finance Band 2
Table: p.1339

**Knight, John H** (Delaware)
Profile: p.407
Bankruptcy Band 4
Table: p.389

**Knight, Michael** (Alabama)
Litigation Band 3
Table: p.152

**Knight, Robert** (Montana)
Real Estate Band 1
Table: p.1230

**Knipe, Quentin M** (Idaho)
Real Estate Band 2
Table: p.762

**Knoll, Susan** (Texas)
Intellectual Property Band 2
Table: p.1860

**Knorek, John** (Hawaii)
Employment Band 2
Table: p.742

**Knowles, Leo** (Nebraska)
Litigation Band 2
Table: p.1239

**Knowlton, William A**
(Massachusetts)
Profile: p.1097

Healthcare Band 2
Table: p.1071

**Knox, Daniel** (Oregon)
Litigation Band 3
Table: p.1674

**Knox, Thomas J** (Virginia)
Profile: p.1983
Corporate/M&A Band 2
Table: p.1967

**Knudsen, Eric** (Vermont)
Real Estate Band 3
Table: p.1961

**Knudson, David L**
(South Dakota)
Corporate/Commercial Band 1
Table: p.1792

**Knudson, Kathryn L**
(Georgia)
Banking & Finance Band 2
Table: p.677

**Knull, William H** (National)
Profile: p.113
International Arbitration
Band 4
Table: p.36

**Kobak, Scott M** (New York)
Profile: p.1471
Real Estate Band 5
Table: p.1417

**Kobayashi Jr, Bert T**
(Hawaii)
Litigation Band 2
Table: p.745

**Kobert, Roy** (Florida)
Bankruptcy Band 3
Table: p.586

**Kochanek, Joseph J**
(Michigan)
Profile: p.1136
Banking & Finance Band 2
Table: p.1120

**Kochanski, David**
(Maryland)
Real Estate Band 3
Table: p.1035

**Kocher, Gary J**
(Washington)
Corporate/Commercial Band 2
Table: p.1992

**Kociubes, Joseph L**
(Massachusetts)
Profile: p.1097
Litigation Band 2
Table: p.1074

**Koenigsberg, I Fred**
(New York)
Profile: p.1471
Intellectual Property Band 1
Table: p.1385

**Koestler, Mark D** (New
York)
Profile: p.1471
Immigration Band 3
Table: p.1376

**Koffel, William B**
(Massachusetts)
Employment Band 2
Table: p.1065

**Kofman, Robert** (Florida)
Employment Band 1
Table: p.597

**Kohn, Alan C** (Missouri)
Litigation Band 2
Table: p.1198

**Kohn, Arthur H** (New York)
Profile: p.1471
Employee Benefits Band 2
Table: p.1362

**Kohn, Jeffrey** (New York)
Profile: p.1472
Employment Band 3
Table: p.1365

**Kohn, Joseph**
(Pennsylvania)
Antitrust Band 2
Table: p.1692

**Kohn, Richard** (Illinois)
Banking & Finance Band 2
Table: p.771

**Kohnke IV, Edward F**
(Louisiana)
Litigation Band 3
Table: p.973

**Kokoruda, Thomas G**
(Missouri)
Profile: p.1207
Litigation Band 3
Table: p.1198

**Kolasky, William J**
(District of Columbia)
Profile: p.524
Antitrust Band 2
Table: p.426

**Kolb, Daniel** (New York)
Profile: p.1472
Litigation Band 2
Table: p.1390

**Kolb, William R**
(Massachusetts)
Corporate/M&A Band 3
Table: p.1061

**Kolesar, Andrew** (Ohio)
Profile: p.1631
Environment Band 3
Table: p.1612

**Koltun, Timothy** (Michigan)
Real Estate Band 3
Table: p.1130

**Kolyer, Steve** (National)
Profile: p.113
Capital Markets Band 2
Table: p.13

**Komeiji, John T** (Hawaii)
Litigation Band 2
Table: p.745

**Koneck, John** (Minnesota)
Real Estate Band 1
Table: p.1160

**Konrad, Daniel J** (West
Virginia)
Corporate/Commercial Band 3
Table: p.2010

**Koob, Charles E** (New York)
Profile: p.1472
Antitrust Band 3
Table: p.1335
Litigation Band 2
Table: p.1388

**Koons, Warren**
(Washington)
Real Estate Band 3
Table: p.2002

**Koons Jr, Robert A**
(Pennsylvania)
Intellectual Property Band 4
Table: p.1711

**Korando, Kimberly J**
(North Carolina)
Profile: p.1584
Employment Band 3
Table: p.1573

**Korb, Philip** (Pennsylvania)
Profile: p.1732
Real Estate Band 1
Table: p.1718

**Korby, Mary** (Texas)
Profile: p.1900
Corporate/M&A Band 4
Table: p.1840

**Koren, Edward** (National)
Profile: p.113
Wealth Management Band 2
Table: p.81

**Korff, Phyllis G** (New York)
Profile: p.113
Capital Markets Band 2
Table: p.7

**Korman, Martin W**
(California)
Profile: p.298
Corporate/M&A Band 3
Table: p.227

**Kornberg, Alan W** (New
York)
Profile: p.1472
Bankruptcy Band 2
Table: p.1344

**Kornfeld, Armand J**
(Washington)
Bankruptcy Band 1
Table: p.1991

**Kornreich, David** (Florida)
Profile: p.642
Employment Band 3
Table: p.597

**Kornreich, Edward S**
(New York)
Profile: p.1472
Healthcare Band 1
Table: p.1374

**Kornstein, Alan F** (New
Jersey)
Corporate/M&A Band 2
Table: p.1278

**Kosacz, Barbara**
(California)
Corporate/M&A Band 4
Table: p.227

**Koschik, David N** (New
York)
Profile: p.1472
Banking & Finance Band 4
Table: p.1339

**Kotchka, Malani** (Nevada)
Employment Band 3
Table: p.1248

**Kotler, Lawrence J**
(Pennsylvania)
Profile: p.1732
Bankruptcy Band 3
Table: p.1697

**Kotovsky, Stanley**
(New Mexico)
Employment Band 3
Table: p.1321

**Kotran, Stephen M**
(New York)
Profile: p.1472
Corporate/M&A
Up and coming
Table: p.1354

**Kovner, Victor A** (New York)
Media & Entertainment Band 1
Table: p.1404

**Kozak, John** (Illinois)
Intellectual Property Band 2
Table: p.799

**Kozlowski, Holly D** (Ohio)
Profile: p.1631
Intellectual Property Band 3
Table: p.1614

**Kozyak, John W** (Florida)
Profile: p.642
Bankruptcy Band 1
Table: p.586

**Kraft, Barbara Simpson**
(Alaska)
Corporate/M&A Band 1
Table: p.168

**Krafte, Lori E** (Ohio)
Intellectual Property
Up and coming
Table: p.1614

**Kraftson, Daniel** (Virginia)
Construction Band 2
Table: p.1965

**Krakauer, Bryan** (Illinois)
Profile: p.839
Bankruptcy Band 3
Table: p.775

**Krakoff, David S**
(District of Columbia)
Profile: p.524
Litigation Band 3
Table: p.471

**Krambeck, James** (Iowa)
Corporate/M&A Band 1
Table: p.909

**Kramer, Andrew**
(District of Columbia)
Profile: p.524
Employment Band 2
Table: p.439

**Kramer, Daniel J** (New York)
Profile: p.1472
Litigation Band 3
Table: p.1390

**Kramer, J Scott**
(Pennsylvania)
Profile: p.1733
Intellectual Property Band 4
Table: p.1711

**Kramer, Jay** (Arizona)
Profile: p.192
Real Estate Band 2
Table: p.184

**Kramer, Kenneth M**
(New York)
Profile: p.1472
Antitrust Band 4
Table: p.1335

**Kramer, Merrill**
(District of Columbia)
Profile: p.524
Energy Band 5
Table: p.445

**Kramer, Morris J** (New York)
Profile: p.1472
Corporate/M&A Band 1
Table: p.1354

**Kramer, Myron** (Georgia)
Immigration Band 1
Table: p.694

**Kramer, Samuel** (Illinois)
Profile: p.839
Business Process Outsourcing Band 4
Table: p.2
Technology Band 3
Table: p.814

**Kramer, Steven E**
(Tennessee)
Profile: p.1814
Employment Band 3
Table: p.1801

**Kramer, Thomas I** (Oregon)
Profile: p.1682
Employment Band 3
Table: p.1670

**Krapf, Daniel H** (Delaware)
Profile: p.407
Real Estate Band 2
Table: p.399

**Krapf, Robert J** (Delaware)
Profile: p.407
Real Estate Band 1
Table: p.399

**Krasnow, Jordan**
(Massachusetts)
Real Estate Band 1
Table: p.1081

**Krasnow, Richard P**
(New York)
Profile: p.1473
Bankruptcy Band 4
Table: p.1344

**Krasow, Herbert**
(Connecticut)
Real Estate Band 2
Table: p.380

**Kratz Jr, John E** (Maryland)
Profile: p.1041
Employee Benefits Band 1
Table: p.1027

**Krauland, Edward**
(National)
Profile: p.114
International Trade Band 1
Table: p.41

**Kraus, Alan E** (New Jersey)
Litigation Band 2
Table: p.1289

**Kraus, Bruce R** (New York)
Profile: p.1473
Technology Band 1
Table: p.1428

**Kraus, Kenneth L**
(Tennessee)
Profile: p.1814
Media & Entertainment Band 1
Table: p.1806

**Krause, Cheryl A**
(Pennsylvania)
Profile: p.1733
Litigation Up and coming
Table: p.1715

**Krauss, Joseph G**
(District of Columbia)
Profile: p.524
Antitrust Band 5
Table: p.426

**Kravitt, Jason H P**
(New York)
Profile: p.114
Capital Markets Band S
Table: p.18

**Krebs, Arno** (Texas)
Profile: p.1900
Insurance Band S
Table: p.1858

**Krebs, Michael**
(Massachusetts)
Banking & Finance Band 3
Table: p.1055

**Krebs, Stephen** (Texas)
Profile: p.1901
Projects Band 3
Table: p.1869

**Kreger, Michael E** (Alaska)
Litigation Band 1
Table: p.171

**Kreider, Gary** (Ohio)
Corporate/M&A Band S
Table: p.1605

**Kreiger, Arthur**
(Massachusetts)
Environment Band 2
Table: p.1068

**Kreisler, David**
(Massachusetts)
Profile: p.1097
Private Equity Band 3
Table: p.1080

**Kreitzer, Michael N**
(Florida)
Profile: p.642
Litigation Band 4
Table: p.609

**Kreller, Thomas R**
(California)
Bankruptcy Band 4
Table: p.222

**Krendl, Cathy S** (Colorado)
Corporate/M&A Band 2
Table: p.346

**Kress, Alan** (New York)
Media & Entertainment Band 1
Table: p.1401

**Kreusler-Walsh, Jane**
(Florida)
Litigation Band 1
Table: p.615

**Krevans, Rachel**
(California)
Profile: p.299
Intellectual Property Band 4
Table: p.248

**Krieger, Paul** (Texas)
Profile: p.1901
Intellectual Property Band 3
Table: p.1860

**Krieger, Thomas**
(West Virginia)
Employment Band 2
Table: p.2012

**Krieser, Jason D** (Texas)
Profile: p.1901
Technology Band 2
Table: p.1877

**Krischer, Gordon**
(California)
Profile: p.299
Employment Band 3
Table: p.231

**Kristol, Daniel M**
(Delaware)
Profile: p.407
Real Estate Band 2
Table: p.399

**Kritenbrink, Lawrence E**
(Nebraska)
Real Estate Band 2
Table: p.1242

**Krizan, Lisa M** (Virginia)
Profile: p.1983
Intellectual Property Band 2
Table: p.1975

**Kroesche, Guy** (Utah)
Real Estate Band 2

Table: p.1947

**Kronk, Catherine** (Vermont)
Real Estate Band 3
Table: p.1961

**Kronk, Edward M**
(Michigan)
Profile: p.1136
Litigation Band 3
Table: p.1128

**Kroon, David**
(South Dakota)
Corporate/Commercial Band 2
Table: p.1792

**Krouse Jr, George R**
(New York)
Profile: p.114
Capital Markets Band 4
Table: p.7

**Krovatin, Gerald**
(New Jersey)
Litigation Band 1
Table: p.1292

**Krueger, Herbert W**
(Illinois)
Profile: p.839
Corporate/M&A: Private Fund Formation Band 1
Table: p.782
Employment Band 1
Table: p.786

**Krugman, Edward P**
(New York)
Insurance Band 2
Table: p.1379

**Krugman Beinecke, Candace** (New York)
Profile: p.1473
Corporate/M&A Band 1
Table: p.1359

**Krumholz, Dennis J**
(New Jersey)
Profile: p.1301
Environment Band 1
Table: p.1285

**Krupka, Robert G**
(California)
Profile: p.299
Intellectual Property Band 1
Table: p.248

**Krupp, Peter C** (Illinois)
Profile: p.839
Corporate/M&A: Private Equity Band 2
Table: p.782

**Krupsky, Kenneth J**
(District of Columbia)
Profile: p.524
Tax Band 4
Table: p.488

**Kruse, Layne** (Texas)
Profile: p.1901
Antitrust Band 3
Table: p.1829

**Krutz, Fred** (Mississippi)
Profile: p.1185
Litigation Band 2

Table: p.1179

**Kubetz, Bernard J** (Maine)
Profile: p.1013
Litigation Band 3
Table: p.1006

**Kubicek, David W** (Iowa)
Real Estate Band 1
Table: p.917

**Kuck, Charles H** (Georgia)
Profile: p.717
Immigration Band 2
Table: p.694

**Kudenholdt, Stephen S**
(New York)
Profile: p.114
Capital Markets Band 2
Table: p.18

**Kudlac, Kevin** (Texas)
Profile: p.1901
Intellectual Property Band 3
Table: p.1860

**Kudo, Benjamin** (Hawaii)
Land Use Band 1
Table: p.744

**Kuehne, Benedict P**
(Florida)
Litigation Band 2
Table: p.610

**Kuehnle, Kenton** (Ohio)
Real Estate Band 3
Table: p.1621

**Kuhn, Michael** (Texas)
Real Estate Band 3
Table: p.1872

**Kummer, Thomas F**
(Nevada)
Profile: p.1259
Litigation Band 2
Table: p.1252

**Kumpe, Peter G** (Arkansas)
Profile: p.209
Litigation Band 3
Table: p.205

**Kuney, David**
(District of Columbia)
Profile: p.524
Bankruptcy Band 2
Table: p.432

**Kunkel, Daniel H** (Florida)
Employment Band 4
Table: p.597

**Kunkel, William R** (Illinois)
Profile: p.839
Corporate/M&A Band 2
Table: p.781

**Kuntz, Michael**
(Washington)
Real Estate Band 1
Table: p.2002

**Kunz, C Thomas** (New York)
Profile: p.114
Capital Markets Band 1
Table: p.18

K

**L**

**Kunz, Donald** (Michigan)
Profile: p.1136
Corporate/M&A Band 1
Table: p.1122

**Kupec, Christopher C**
(North Carolina)
Profile: p.1584
Banking & Finance Band 1
Table: p.1569

**Kupietzky, Moshe J**
(California)
Profile: p.299
Corporate/M&A Band 4
Table: p.227

**Kurnit, Rick** (New York)
Profile: p.1473
Media & Entertainment Band 1
Table: p.1400

**Kurtzon, Michael S**
(Illinois)
Real Estate Band 3
Table: p.809

**Kuryla, Matthew** (Texas)
Profile: p.1901
Environment Band 4
Table: p.1852

**Kurz, Theodore A**
(National)
Wealth Management Band S
Table: p.81

**Kurzban, Ira J** (Florida)
Immigration Band 1
Table: p.606

**Kurzweil, David** (Georgia)
Profile: p.717
Bankruptcy Band 3
Table: p.679

**Kurzweil, Harvey** (New
York)
Profile: p.1473
Insurance Band 3
Table: p.1379
Litigation Band 3
Table: p.1388

**Kushner, Harold** (Alabama)
Profile: p.157
Corporate/Commercial Band 1
Table: p.148

**Kutler, Marilyn**
(Pennsylvania)
Real Estate Band 3
Table: p.1718

**Kutzschbach, George**
(Texas)
Profile: p.1901
Energy Band 2
Table: p.1847

**Kwasnick, Raymond**
(Massachusetts)
Real Estate Band 2
Table: p.1081

**Kyle, Amy L**
(Massachusetts)
Profile: p.1097
Banking & Finance Band 2
Table: p.1055

**Kyper, James R**
(Pennsylvania)
Profile: p.1733
Intellectual Property Band 3
Table: p.1711

**La Suer, Gene** (Iowa)
Employment Band 2
Table: p.912

**Labate, Robert J** (Illinois)
Profile: p.840
Media & Entertainment Band 1
Table: p.807

**LaCagnin, Stephen** (West
Virginia)
Profile: p.2017
Litigation Band 2
Table: p.2013

**Lacy, John R** (Hawaii)
Litigation Band 3
Table: p.745

**Lacy Jr, Peyton** (Alabama)
Profile: p.157
Employment Band 3
Table: p.150

**Ladd, Jeffrey R** (Illinois)
Healthcare Band 3
Table: p.793

**Ladik, Steven** (Texas)
Immigration Band 1
Table: p.1856

**Ladner, Gregory W**
(Delaware)
Profile: p.407
Corporate/M&A
Up and coming
Table: p.395

**Ladov, Donald**
(Pennsylvania)
Employment Band 2
Table: p.1703

**Lafferty, William M**
(Delaware)
Profile: p.407
Chancery Band 3
Table: p.392

**Lafiandra, Aldo L** (Georgia)
Profile: p.718
Banking & Finance
Up and coming
Table: p.677

**Lafitte, Gene W** (Louisiana)
Litigation Band 2
Table: p.973

**LaFiura, Esq, Dennis R**
(New Jersey)
Profile: p.1302
Litigation Band 3
Table: p.1289

**LaFollette, Chris B** (Texas)
Profile: p.1901
Corporate/M&A Band 3

Table: p.1840

**LaFuze, William L** (Texas)
Profile: p.1901
Intellectual Property Band 1
Table: p.1860

**Laird, Michael S**
(Oklahoma)
Profile: p.1660
Real Estate Band 2
Table: p.1658

**Lake, William T**
(District of Columbia)
Profile: p.525
Telecom, Broadcast & Satellite
Band 2
Table: p.492

**Lalik, Elizabeth A** (Virginia)
Profile: p.1983
Employment Up and coming
Table: p.1971

**Lalle, Wayne** (Virginia)
Construction Band 1
Table: p.1965

**Lamar III, Howard H**
(Tennessee)
Profile: p.1815
Corporate/M&A Band 3
Table: p.1799

**Lamb, Christopher J**
(Delaware)
Profile: p.407
Real Estate Band 2
Table: p.399

**Lamb, William S** (New York)
Profile: p.1473
Energy Band 1
Table: p.1367

**Lambert, LeRoy** (New York)
Profile: p.114
Transportation Band 3
Table: p.74

**Lamdin III, William**
(Montana)
Corporate/M&A Band 1
Table: p.1222

**Lamken, Jeffrey A**
(District of Columbia)
Profile: p.525
Litigation Band 2
Table: p.475

**Lamm, Carolyn**
(District of Columbia)
Profile: p.114
International Arbitration
Band 2
Table: p.36

**Lamon, Bruce** (Hawaii)
Litigation Band 2
Table: p.745

**Lampe, Donald C**
(North Carolina)
Profile: p.1584
Banking & Finance Band 3
Table: p.1569

**Lampe, Matthew W** (Ohio)
Profile: p.1632
Employment Band 3
Table: p.1609

**Lamson, Jeffrey** (Iowa)
Corporate/M&A Band 3
Table: p.909

**Lamson, William**
(Nebraska)
Litigation Band 1
Table: p.1240

**Landa, Leor** (New York)
Profile: p.1473
Private Equity Band 3
Table: p.1410

**Landefeld, Stewart**
(Washington)
Corporate/Commercial Band 1
Table: p.1992

**Landis, Adam G.**
(Delaware)
Bankruptcy Band 3
Table: p.389

**Landis, James M** (Florida)
Profile: p.642
Antitrust Band 3
Table: p.581

**Landon, Stephen**
(South Dakota)
Litigation Band 2
Table: p.1795

**Landry, Charles** (Louisiana)
Profile: p.983
Real Estate Band 2
Table: p.975

**Landsberg, Barry S**
(California)
Healthcare Band 2
Table: p.238

**Landsman, Stephen A**
(Illinois)
Profile: p.840
Corporate/M&A Band 4
Table: p.781

**Lane, Brian**
(District of Columbia)
Profile: p.525
Securities Band 1
Table: p.485

**Lane, Joe** (Florida)
Construction Band 3
Table: p.590

**Lane, Michael L** (Maine)
Profile: p.1013
Real Estate Up and coming
Table: p.1008

**Lane, Roger**
(Massachusetts)
Profile: p.1097
Litigation Band 3
Table: p.1074

**Lane, Thomas** (West
Virginia)
Real Estate Band 1
Table: p.2015

**Langan, J Andrew** (Illinois)
Profile: p.840
Antitrust Band 2
Table: p.767

**Langdon, Larry R**
(California)
Profile: p.299
Tax Band 4
Table: p.274

**Lange, Cynthia J**
(California)
Immigration Band 2
Table: p.241

**Lange, Mark S** (Georgia)
Profile: p.718
Tax Band 3
Table: p.703

**Langel, John B**
(Pennsylvania)
Profile: p.1733
Employment Band 2
Table: p.1703

**Langer, Howard**
(Pennsylvania)
Antitrust Band 3
Table: p.1692

**Langevin, Judith Bevis**
(Minnesota)
Employment Band 2
Table: p.1154

**Langlois, Jack J** (Texas)
Profile: p.1901
Energy Band 4
Table: p.1847

**Laniado, Sam** (New York)
Energy Band 1
Table: p.1370

**Lanier, Randolph H**
(Alabama)
Profile: p.157
Real Estate Band 2
Table: p.153

**Lansky, David** (Arizona)
Real Estate Band 1
Table: p.184

**Lanza, John D**
(Massachusetts)
Intellectual Property Band 3
Table: p.1072

**Lapidus, Steve** (Florida)
Profile: p.642
Tax Band 1
Table: p.624

**Laporte, Claire**
(Massachusetts)
Intellectual Property Band 3
Table: p.1072

**Lapowsky, Robert**
(Pennsylvania)
Bankruptcy Band 3
Table: p.1697

**Larcombe, Valerie G**
(Florida)
Profile: p.642
Healthcare Band 3

Table: p.604

**Laria, Jon M** (Maryland)
Profile: p.1041
Real Estate Up and coming
Table: p.1035

**Larkin, Terrence B**
(Michigan)
Profile: p.1137
Corporate/M&A Band 2
Table: p.1122

**LaRose, Robert M**
(Missouri)
Profile: p.1207
Corporate/M&A Band 3
Table: p.1193

**Larrabee, Peter** (California)
Immigration Band 2
Table: p.241

**Larsen, Paul E** (Nevada)
Gaming & Licensing Band 2
Table: p.1251

**Larsen, Tracy T** (Michigan)
Profile: p.1137
Corporate/M&A Band 2
Table: p.1122

**Larson, David** (Wyoming)
Real Estate Band 1
Table: p.2045

**Larson, John** (California)
Profile: p.299
Corporate/M&A Band 3
Table: p.227

**Larson, Joseph D**
(New York)
Profile: p.1473
Antitrust Up and coming
Table: p.1335

**Larson, Mary Jo** (Michigan)
Profile: p.1137
Employee Benefits Band 2
Table: p.1124

**LaRue, James D** (Idaho)
Litigation Band 3
Table: p.760

**LaSala, Joseph P**
(New Jersey)
Litigation Band 3
Table: p.1289

**LaSala, Todd A** (Missouri)
Profile: p.1207
Real Estate Up and coming
Table: p.1201

**Lasater Jr, W Robert**
(New Mexico)
Litigation Band 1
Table: p.1324

**Lascher, Alan** (New York)
Profile: p.1474
Real Estate Band 4
Table: p.1417

**Laseter, Scott** (Georgia)
Profile: p.718
Environment Band 3
Table: p.691

**Lassar, Scott R** (Illinois)
Profile: p.840
Litigation Band 2
Table: p.803

**Lassiter, Donnell**
(North Carolina)
Banking & Finance Band 3
Table: p.1569

**Laster, J Travis** (Delaware)
Profile: p.407
Chancery Band 2
Table: p.392

**Latham, William Larry**
(Mississippi)
Litigation Band 3
Table: p.1179

**Lathrop, Alex**
(District of Columbia)
Profile: p.525
Insurance Up and coming
Table: p.464

**Latimer, Kenneth A**
(Illinois)
Profile: p.840
Banking & Finance Band 3
Table: p.771

**LaTour, Randall D** (Ohio)
Profile: p.1632
Bankruptcy Band 3
Table: p.1600

**Latza, William** (New York)
Insurance Band 3
Table: p.1380

**Laughlin, Gerald P**
(Nebraska)
Litigation Band 3
Table: p.1239

**Laughlin, Mark C**
(Nebraska)
Litigation Band 2
Table: p.1240

**Laupheimer, Ann Blair**
(Pennsylvania)
Profile: p.1733
Litigation Band 3
Table: p.1714
Litigation Band 2
Table: p.1715

**Lauria, Thomas** (Florida)
Profile: p.642
Bankruptcy Band 1
Table: p.586

**Laurie, Ty D** (Illinois)
Profile: p.840
Construction Band 1
Table: p.778

**Lause, Christopher A**
(Arizona)
Corporate/M&A Band 3
Table: p.176

**Lause, Michael F**
(Missouri)
Profile: p.1207
Corporate/M&A Band 2
Table: p.1193

**Lavelle Jr, John P**
(Pennsylvania)
Profile: p.1733
Litigation Up and coming
Table: p.1714

**Lavely Jr, John H**
(California)
Media & Entertainment Band 2
Table: p.263

**Lavey, Stewart E**
(New Jersey)
Corporate/M&A Band 3
Table: p.1278

**Lavey, Warren G** (Illinois)
Profile: p.840
Telecom, Broadcast & Satellite
Band 3
Table: p.816

**Lavey, Wendlene M** (Ohio)
Profile: p.1632
Environment Up and coming
Table: p.1612

**Lavoie, John G** (Virginia)
Profile: p.1983
Real Estate Band 3
Table: p.1978

**Lavoie, Mark G** (Maine)
Litigation Band 2
Table: p.1006

**Lavorgna, Gregory J**
(Pennsylvania)
Intellectual Property Band 2
Table: p.1711

**Law, David M**
(New Hampshire)
Corporate/Commercial Band 2
Table: p.1264

**Law, Rhea** (Florida)
Real Estate Band 2
Table: p.621

**Lawall, Francis J**
(Pennsylvania)
Profile: p.1733
Bankruptcy Band 3
Table: p.1697

**Lawler, Andrew** (New York)
Litigation Band 3
Table: p.1391

**Lawler, Kathy A**
(New Jersey)
Profile: p.1302
Employee Benefits Band 1
Table: p.1281

**Lawler, Martin J** (California)
Immigration Band 3
Table: p.241

**Lawless, J Mark** (Texas)
Insurance Band 1
Table: p.1858

**Lawlor, William G**
(Pennsylvania)
Profile: p.1733
Corporate/M&A Band 2
Table: p.1700

**Lawniczak, James** (Ohio)
Profile: p.1632
Bankruptcy Band 3
Table: p.1600

**Lawrence, Adam** (Florida)
Litigation Band 2
Table: p.615

**Lawrence, James K L**
(Ohio)
Profile: p.1632
Employment Band 2
Table: p.1609

**Lawrence, Robert**
(Colorado)
Environment Band 1
Table: p.350

**Lawrence III, Robert C**
(New York)
Profile: p.114
Wealth Management Band 2
Table: p.81

**Lawson, David L**
(District of Columbia)
Profile: p.525
Telecom, Broadcast & Satellite
Band 3
Table: p.492

**Lawson, Jack** (Indiana)
Real Estate Band 3
Table: p.892

**Lawson, Michael**
(California)
Profile: p.299
Employment Band 2
Table: p.232

**Laxalt, Bruce** (Nevada)
Litigation Band 2
Table: p.1252

**Layne, Jonathan K**
(California)
Profile: p.299
Corporate/M&A Band 3
Table: p.227

**Layson, Frank** (Georgia)
Profile: p.718
Corporate/M&A Band 4
Table: p.684

**Laytin, Daniel E** (Illinois)
Profile: p.840
Antitrust Band 3
Table: p.767

**Lazarow, Warren T**
(California)
Profile: p.299
Corporate/M&A Band 4
Table: p.227

**Lazarus, Larry S** (Arizona)
Real Estate Band 2
Table: p.186

**Lazarus, Lewis H**
(Delaware)
Profile: p.408
Chancery Band 3
Table: p.392

**Lazarus, Robert**
(Mississippi)
Corporate/Commercial Band 2
Table: p.1174

**Lazarus, Scott R**
(New York)
Media & Entertainment Band 2
Table: p.1401

**Leace, Benjamin**
(Pennsylvania)
Profile: p.1734
Intellectual Property Up and
coming
Table: p.1711

**Leach, Donald** (Ohio)
Construction Band 2
Table: p.1603

**Leach Jr, John N** (Alabama)
Litigation Band 3
Table: p.152

**Leachman, Tamsen L**
(Idaho)
Employment Band 2
Table: p.759

**Leahy, James R** (Texas)
Litigation Band 3
Table: p.1865

**Leake, Paul** (New York)
Profile: p.1474
Bankruptcy Band 3
Table: p.1344

**Leaverton, Bruce**
(Washington)
Bankruptcy Band 2
Table: p.1991

**Leavitt, Jeffrey S** (Ohio)
Profile: p.1632
Employee Benefits Band 2
Table: p.1607

**Lebowitz, Molly** (Vermont)
Real Estate Band 1
Table: p.1961

**Leccese, Joseph M**
(National)
Profile: p.115
Sport Band 1
Table: p.59

**LeClair, Gary D** (Virginia)
Profile: p.1983
Corporate/M&A Band 2
Table: p.1968

**LeClair, Lewis** (Texas)
Profile: p.1902
Litigation Band 3
Table: p.1865

**LeClaire, John R**
(Massachusetts)
Profile: p.1097
Private Equity Band 1
Table: p.1078

**Ledbetter, Cheryl**
(West Virginia)
Profile: p.2017
Employment Band 2
Table: p.2012

L

L

**Leddy, Mark**
(District of Columbia)
Profile: p.525
Antitrust Band 1
Table: p.426

**Lederer, Gregory** (Iowa)
Litigation Band 2
Table: p.914

**Lederman, Alan** (Florida)
Profile: p.642
Tax Band 1
Table: p.623

**LeDuc, André** (Illinois)
Profile: p.840
Tax Band 2
Table: p.812

**Lee, Carl B** (Texas)
Profile: p.1902
Real Estate Band 2
Table: p.1872

**Lee, Carolyn Joy** (New York)
Tax Band 2
Table: p.1423

**Lee, Charlie** (Virginia)
Construction Band 2
Table: p.1965

**Lee, James J** (Texas)
Profile: p.1902
Bankruptcy Band 2
Table: p.1835

**Lee, Jeffrey** (Alabama)
Profile: p.158
Employment Band 2
Table: p.150

**Lee, John** (Texas)
Bankruptcy Band 1
Table: p.1835

**Lee, John R** (Montana)
Natural Resources Band 2
Table: p.1228

**Lee, Judy J** (Texas)
Immigration Band 2
Table: p.1856

**Lee, Paul L** (National)
Financial Services Band 3
Table: p.24

**Lee, Robert C** (Illinois)
Profile: p.841
Real Estate Band 3
Table: p.809

**Lee, Stephen W** (Indiana)
Profile: p.897
Real Estate Band 2
Table: p.892

**Lee, Steven J** (New York)
Profile: p.1474
Intellectual Property Band 3
Table: p.1384

**Lee, William F**
(Massachusetts)
Profile: p.1097
Intellectual Property ✪
Table: p.1072

**Lee, William S** (Texas)
Profile: p.1902
Tax Band 1
Table: p.1875

**Leet, Alan C** (Georgia)
Corporate/M&A Band 4
Table: p.684

**Leet, Byron E** (Kentucky)
Profile: p.949
Litigation Band 4
Table: p.942

**Lefeber, Peter J**
(Connecticut)
Profile: p.383
Employment Band 2
Table: p.376

**Leff, Philip** (Iowa)
Real Estate Band 2
Table: p.917

**Lefkowitz, David** (National)
Profile: p.115
Capital Markets Band 4
Table: p.7

**Lefkowitz, Ken** (New York)
Profile: p.1474
Corporate/M&A Band 1
Table: p.1359

**Lefkowitz, Stephen**
(New York)
Profile: p.1474
Real Estate Band 1
Table: p.1418

**Leggette, Poe**
(District of Columbia)
Profile: p.525
Energy Band 3
Table: p.441

**Legler, Mitchell** (Florida)
Corporate/M&A Band 3
Table: p.594

**LeGros, Susan P**
(Pennsylvania)
Environment Band 3
Table: p.1707

**Lehman, Michael P**
(New Hampshire)
Litigation Band 1
Table: p.1268

**Lehman, Steven** (Montana)
Employment Band 1
Table: p.1223

**Lehr, Richard** (Alabama)
Employment Band 1
Table: p.150

**Leibenluft, Robert F**
(District of Columbia)
Profile: p.525
Healthcare Band 2
Table: p.456

**Leibensperger, Edward P**
(Massachusetts)
Profile: p.1097
Litigation Band 2
Table: p.1074

**Leibowitz, Hal J**
(Massachusetts)
Profile: p.1097
Corporate/M&A Band 3
Table: p.1061

**Leibowitz, Lewis E**
(District of Columbia)
Profile: p.115
International Trade Band 3
Table: p.42

**Leiby, Larry R** (Florida)
Construction Band 1
Table: p.590

**Leich, Christopher M**
(Massachusetts)
Profile: p.1097
Tax Band 3
Table: p.1084

**Leichtling, Ely A**
(Wisconsin)
Profile: p.2034
Employment Band 2
Table: p.2027

**Leiden, Warren R**
(California)
Immigration Band 1
Table: p.241

**Leisner, Richard** (Florida)
Corporate/M&A Band 3
Table: p.594

**Leitch, Brian** (Colorado)
Profile: p.525
Bankruptcy Band 2
Table: p.432

**Lelong, Rivers** (Louisiana)
Profile: p.983
Banking & Finance
Up and coming
Table: p.963

**Lemein, Gregg D** (Illinois)
Profile: p.841
Tax Band 2
Table: p.812

**Lemly, Thomas A**
(Washington)
Employment Band 1
Table: p.1995

**Lenhard, Kirk** (Nevada)
Litigation Band 3
Table: p.1252

**Lenihan, Brian**
(Massachusetts)
Private Equity Band 3
Table: p.1078

**Lennon, Daniel**
(District of Columbia)
Corporate/Commercial Band 2
Table: p.435

**Lennon, J Patrick**
(Michigan)
Profile: p.1137
Real Estate Up and coming
Table: p.1130

**Lennon, Maureen**
(Montana)
Employment Band 2
Table: p.1223

**Lennox, Heather** (Ohio)
Profile: p.1632
Bankruptcy Band 3
Table: p.1600

**Lents, Donald** (Missouri)
Corporate/M&A Band 2
Table: p.1193

**Leo, Thomas Glen**
(California)
Media & Entertainment Band 3
Table: p.266

**Leon, Christopher E**
(North Carolina)
Profile: p.1584
Banking & Finance Band 3
Table: p.1569

**Leon, Michael**
(Massachusetts)
Environment Band 2
Table: p.1068

**Leonard, Stephen**
(Massachusetts)
Environment Band 2
Table: p.1068

**Leonard III, Edward D**
(Maine)
Profile: p.1013
Real Estate Band 2
Table: p.1008

**Leonetti, Kenneth**
(Massachusetts)
Bankruptcy Band 3
Table: p.1058

**Leong, Alvin K** (National)
Transportation Up and coming
Table: p.64

**Leong, Donna Y L** (Hawaii)
Land Use Band 1
Table: p.744
Real Estate Band 1
Table: p.748

**Leong, Ronald Y K**
(Hawaii)
Employment Band 2
Table: p.742

**Leonhardt, Frederick**
(Florida)
Real Estate Band 3
Table: p.621

**LePage, Margaret**
**Coughlin** (Maine)
Profile: p.1013
Employment Band 2
Table: p.1002

**LePatner, Barry** (New York)
Construction Band 4
Table: p.1351

**Lepene, Alan** (Ohio)
Profile: p.1632
Bankruptcy Band 1
Table: p.1600

**Leppo, Jeffery W.**
(Washington)
Environment Band 1
Table: p.1996

**Lerach, William S**
(California)
Litigation Band 2
Table: p.257

**Lerman, Bradley** (Illinois)
Profile: p.841
Litigation Band 3
Table: p.802

**Lerman, Cary** (California)
Insurance Band 1
Table: p.245

**Lerman, Steven A**
(District of Columbia)
Telecom, Broadcast & Satellite
Band 3
Table: p.492

**Lerner, Arthur N**
(District of Columbia)
Profile: p.525
Healthcare Band 2
Table: p.456

**Lerner, Jonathan J**
(New York)
Profile: p.1474
Litigation Band 2
Table: p.1388
Litigation Band 2
Table: p.1390

**Lerner, Stephen D** (Ohio)
Profile: p.1632
Bankruptcy Band 1
Table: p.1600

**Lesnewich, Alan G**
(New Jersey)
Profile: p.1302
Employment Band 3
Table: p.1282

**Lesser, Bruce**
(Pennsylvania)
Profile: p.1734
Banking & Finance Band 1
Table: p.1695

**Lesser, Henry** (California)
Profile: p.300
Corporate/M&A Band 4
Table: p.227

**Lesser, Steven** (Florida)
Construction Band 1
Table: p.590

**Lester, David** (Kentucky)
Profile: p.949
Corporate/M&A Band 2
Table: p.937

**Lester Jr, Edgel** (Florida)
Profile: p.643
Real Estate Band 3
Table: p.617

**Letscher, Tom** (Minnesota)
Corporate/M&A Band 3
Table: p.1152

**Letzler, Kenneth**
(District of Columbia)
Profile: p.526
Antitrust Band 5
Table: p.426

**Leukart, Barbara** (Ohio)
Profile: p.1632
Employment Band 2
Table: p.1609

**Leukart II, Richard** (Ohio)
Employment Band 3
Table: p.1609

**Levander, Andrew J**
(New York)
Profile: p.1474
Litigation Band 2
Table: p.1391

**LeVee, Jeffrey A**
(California)
Profile: p.300
Antitrust Band 2
Table: p.216

**Leventhal, Robert A**
(Florida)
Litigation Band 2
Table: p.610

**Levi, Stuart D** (New York)
Profile: p.1474
Business Process Outsourcing
Band 4
Table: p.2
Technology Band 2
Table: p.1428

**Levin, Ali** (Utah)
Profile: p.1951
Employment Up and coming
Table: p.1944

**Levin, Barry S** (California)
Profile: p.300
Insurance Band 2
Table: p.245

**Levin, Benjamin D**
(Wisconsin)
Profile: p.2034
Real Estate Band 2
Table: p.2030

**Levin, Christine C**
(Pennsylvania)
Profile: p.1734
Antitrust Band 3
Table: p.1692

**Levin, Edward J** (Maryland)
Profile: p.1041
Real Estate Band 1
Table: p.1035

**Levin, Jack S** (Illinois)
Profile: p.841
Corporate/M&A Band S
Table: p.781
Corporate/M&A: Private Equity
Band S
Table: p.782
Tax Band S
Table: p.812

**Levin, Jay J** (Georgia)
Real Estate Band 2
Table: p.700

**Levin, Jim** (Wisconsin)
Real Estate Band 1
Table: p.2030

**Levin, Matthew W**
(Georgia)
Profile: p.718
Bankruptcy Band 3
Table: p.679

**Levin, Oscar** (Florida)
Profile: p.643
Immigration Band 1
Table: p.606

**Levin, Peter** (New York)
Profile: p.1474
Banking & Finance Band 2
Table: p.1339

**Levine, A Kenneth**
(Florida)
Insurance Band 2
Table: p.607

**Levine, Alan** (New York)
Litigation Band 2
Table: p.1388
Litigation Band 3
Table: p.1391

**Levine, Arthur N**
(District of Columbia)
Profile: p.526
Healthcare Band 2
Table: p.456

**Levine, David J** (National)
Profile: p.115
International Trade Band 2
Table: p.41
International Trade Band 5
Table: p.42

**Levine, Harvey R**
(California)
Insurance Band 2
Table: p.245

**Levine, Henry D**
(District of Columbia)
Profile: p.526
Telecom, Broadcast & Satellite
Band 2
Table: p.492

**Levine, Janet** (California)
Litigation Band 1
Table: p.258

**Levine, Jerome L** (National)
Profile: p.115
Native Law Band 1
Table: p.47

**Levine, Jonathan O**
(Wisconsin)
Employment Band 3
Table: p.2027

**Levine, Lee**
(District of Columbia)
Media & Entertainment Band 1
Table: p.477

**Levine, Richard E**
(Maryland)
Profile: p.1041
Real Estate Band 3
Table: p.1035

**Levine, Richard L**
(Massachusetts)
Bankruptcy Band 3
Table: p.1058

**Levine, Ronald** (Colorado)
Corporate/M&A Band 1
Table: p.346

**Levine, Steve J** (Louisiana)
Profile: p.983
Environment Band 1
Table: p.970

**Levinstein, Mark S**
(National)
Sport Band 3
Table: p.59

**Levit, William** (Wisconsin)
Litigation Band 1
Table: p.2029

**Levitas, Steven J**
(North Carolina)
Profile: p.1584
Environment Band 2
Table: p.1575

**Levy, Charles S** (National)
Profile: p.115
International Trade Band 4
Table: p.42

**Levy, Gregg** (National)
Profile: p.115
Sport Band 1
Table: p.59

**Levy, Jay M** (Florida)
Litigation Band 2
Table: p.615

**Levy, Joshua S**
(Massachusetts)
Profile: p.1098
Litigation Up and coming
Table: p.1075

**Levy, Lisa** (New York)
Profile: p.1474
Tax Band 4
Table: p.1423

**Levy, Mark** (Colorado)
Profile: p.362
Corporate/M&A Band 2
Table: p.346

**Levy, Mark P** (Ohio)
Profile: p.1632
Intellectual Property Band 3
Table: p.1614

**Levy, Neil L**
(District of Columbia)
Profile: p.526
Energy Band 4
Table: p.445

**Levy, Richard A** (Illinois)
Bankruptcy Band 3
Table: p.775

**Levy, William A** (Illinois)
Profile: p.841
Tax Band 3
Table: p.812

**Lewand, F Thomas**
(Michigan)
Profile: p.1137
Corporate/M&A Band 3
Table: p.1122

**Lewin, Robert** (New York)
Insurance Band 3
Table: p.1379

**Lewis, Carl** (Washington)
Corporate/Commercial Band 2
Table: p.1993

**Lewis, Charles** (Illinois)
Construction Band 2
Table: p.778

**Lewis, Daniel**
(District of Columbia)
Profile: p.526
Bankruptcy Band S
Table: p.432

**Lewis, David**
(District of Columbia)
Profile: p.526
Energy Band 2
Table: p.449

**Lewis, Denise** (Michigan)
Profile: p.1137
Real Estate Band 3
Table: p.1130

**Lewis, Edward** (Texas)
Profile: p.1902
Environment Band 2
Table: p.1853

**Lewis, Frederick**
(Tennessee)
Employment Band 2
Table: p.1801

**Lewis, Jack L** (Virginia)
Profile: p.1983
Corporate/M&A Band S
Table: p.1967

**Lewis, John Alan**
(Arkansas)
Real Estate Up and coming
Table: p.207

**Lewis, John B** (Ohio)
Employment Band 2
Table: p.1609

**Lewis, Kim Martin** (Ohio)
Bankruptcy Band 2
Table: p.1600

**Lewis, Mark**
(District of Columbia)
Profile: p.526
Energy Band 5
Table: p.441

**Lewis, Sidney** (Louisiana)
Profile: p.983
Employment Band 2
Table: p.967

**Lewis, Steve** (Florida)
Environment Band 3
Table: p.601

**Lewis, Terry** (Florida)
Environment Band 1

Table: p.601

**Lewis, Thomas B**
(Maryland)
Real Estate Band 4
Table: p.1035

**Lewis, Tom** (Montana)
Litigation Band 1
Table: p.1225

**Lewis, William**
(District of Columbia)
Profile: p.526
Environment Band 2
Table: p.451

**Lewkow, Victor I**
(New York)
Profile: p.1475
Corporate/M&A Band 1
Table: p.1354

**Leyden, James G**
(Delaware)
Profile: p.408
Corporate/M&A Band 2
Table: p.395

**Leyens, Jon** (Louisiana)
Real Estate Band 3
Table: p.975

**Li, Christine F** (New Jersey)
Profile: p.1302
Real Estate Band 3
Table: p.1293

**Liaskos, Peter S** (National)
Profile: p.115
Products Liability Band 3
Table: p.50

**Liazos, Andrew C**
(Massachusetts)
Profile: p.1098
Employee Benefits Band 2
Table: p.1063

**Libanoff, Ira L** (Florida)
Construction Band 2
Table: p.590

**Libbey, Keith** (Minnesota)
Corporate/M&A Band S
Table: p.1152

**Liberato, Lynne** (Texas)
Litigation Band 2
Table: p.1866

**Libin, Jerome**
(District of Columbia)
Profile: p.526
Tax Band 2
Table: p.488

**Lichtenbaum, Greta**
(National)
Profile: p.116
International Trade Band 2
Table: p.41

**Lichtenstein, Robert J**
(Pennsylvania)
Profile: p.1734
Employment Band 1
Table: p.1704

L

KEY TO RANKINGS: ✪ = STAR INDIVIDUAL    S = SENIOR STATESMAN

Table: p.439

**Livingston, Theodore A**
(Illinois)
Profile: p.841
Telecom, Broadcast & Satellite
Band 1
Table: p.816

**Lizotte, Andrew G**
(Massachusetts)
Profile: p.1098
Bankruptcy Band 3
Table: p.1058

**Llorens Jr, Hector E**
(Georgia)
Profile: p.718
Banking & Finance Band 3
Table: p.677

**Lloyd, Brian G** (Utah)
Corporate/M&A Band 1
Table: p.1941

**Lobb, James T** (Kentucky)
Real Estate Band 2
Table: p.944

**Lobel, William N**
(California)
Bankruptcy Band 4
Table: p.222

**Lobo, Glyndwr P** (New York)
Profile: p.1476
Corporate/M&A Band 1
Table: p.1359

**Lobrano, John D** (National)
Profile: p.116
Capital Markets Band 3
Table: p.7

**Lockett, Laurel** (Florida)
Profile: p.643
Environment Band 3
Table: p.601

**Loeb, Christopher**
(North Carolina)
Real Estate Band 3
Table: p.1579

**Loeb Jr, Charles W** (West
Virginia)
Profile: p.2017
Real Estate Band 3
Table: p.2015

**Loeffler, Robert H**
(District of Columbia)
Profile: p.527
Energy Band 4
Table: p.441

**Loftis, James** (Texas)
Profile: p.116
International Arbitration
Band 3
Table: p.36

**Loftis III, James R**
(District of Columbia)
Profile: p.527
Antitrust Band 3
Table: p.426

**Loftis Jr, W Randolph**
(North Carolina)
Employment Band 1
Table: p.1573

**Loftus, C Michael**
(National)
Transportation Band 2
Table: p.69

**Logan, Holly M** (Iowa)
Employment Up and coming
Table: p.912

**Logan, Kenneth** (New York)
Profile: p.1476
Antitrust Band 2
Table: p.1335

**Logan III, Ben H**
(California)
Profile: p.301
Bankruptcy Band 3
Table: p.222

**LoGiudice, Susan E**
(Maine)
Profile: p.1013
Corporate/M&A Band 3
Table: p.1000

**Lohmann, Walter H**
(District of Columbia)
Profile: p.527
Environment Band 2
Table: p.450
Environment Band 4
Table: p.451

**Lohr Jr, Walter** (Maryland)
Profile: p.1041
Corporate/M&A Band S
Table: p.1025

**Lokey Jr, James** (Georgia)
Profile: p.718
Tax Band 3
Table: p.703

**Lombard, David**
(Washington)
Real Estate Band 3
Table: p.2002

**Lombardi, Dennis M**
(Hawaii)
Profile: p.752
Real Estate Band 1
Table: p.748

**Londa, Jeffrey C** (Texas)
Profile: p.1902
Employment Band 1
Table: p.1844

**London, Eric** (West Virginia)
Profile: p.2017
Real Estate Band 3
Table: p.2015

**London, Martin** (New York)
Profile: p.1476
Litigation Band S
Table: p.1388

**Lonergan, James**
(California)
Real Estate Band 3
Table: p.270

**Lonergan, Matthew**
(Tennessee)
Profile: p.1815
Employment Band 2
Table: p.1801

**Long, Christine** (Indiana)
Profile: p.897
Corporate/M&A
Up and coming
Table: p.887

**Long, Clay C** (Georgia)
Profile: p.718
Corporate/M&A Band 2
Table: p.684

**Long, Scott** (West Virginia)
Litigation Band 2
Table: p.2013

**Long, Thomas** (Wyoming)
Corporate/M&A Band 1
Table: p.2041
Real Estate Band 2
Table: p.2045

**Long Jr, Robert A**
(District of Columbia)
Profile: p.527
Litigation Band 2
Table: p.475

**Looman, James** (Illinois)
Profile: p.841
Banking & Finance Band 2
Table: p.771

**Lopatka, Kenneth T**
(Illinois)
Employment Band 2
Table: p.785

**Lopes, James** (California)
Bankruptcy Band S
Table: p.222

**Lopez-Castro, Corali**
(Florida)
Profile: p.643
Bankruptcy Band 4
Table: p.586

**Lord, Craig** (Pennsylvania)
Profile: p.1734
Real Estate Band 2
Table: p.1718

**Lord, Elizabeth Osenton**
(West Virginia)
Profile: p.2018
Corporate/Commercial Band 3
Table: p.2010

**Lord, Michael C**
(North Carolina)
Employment Band 3
Table: p.1573

**Lorensen, Charles** (West
Virginia)
Corporate/Commercial Band 1
Table: p.2011

**Lorig, Frederick** (California)
Profile: p.301
Intellectual Property Band 3
Table: p.248

**Loss, Lewis K**
(District of Columbia)
Insurance Band 3
Table: p.461

**Lotstein, James I**
(Connecticut)
Profile: p.384
Corporate/M&A Band 1
Table: p.374

**Lott, Marley** (Texas)
Profile: p.1902
Real Estate Band 2
Table: p.1872

**Lottner, Alan B** (Colorado)
Real Estate Band 3
Table: p.355

**Louden, Karen Jacobs**
(Delaware)
Profile: p.408
Intellectual Property Band 4
Table: p.397

**Loudon, Timothy D**
(Nebraska)
Employment Band 2
Table: p.1238

**Loulakis, Michael** (Virginia)
Profile: p.1984
Construction Band 1
Table: p.1965

**Loumiet, Carlos** (Florida)
Profile: p.643
Banking & Finance Band 1
Table: p.583
Corporate/M&A Band 1
Table: p.595

**Love III, Charles M**
(West Virginia)
Litigation Band 1
Table: p.2013

**Loveland, Joseph** (Georgia)
Profile: p.718
Litigation Band 3
Table: p.698

**Loveless, Scott** (Utah)
Corporate/M&A Band 1
Table: p.1941

**Lovett, John T** (Kentucky)
Profile: p.949
Employment Band 3
Table: p.939

**Lowe, Ronald E** (Arizona)
Real Estate Band 4
Table: p.184

**Lowell, Cym** (Texas)
Profile: p.1902
Tax Band 2
Table: p.1875

**Lowell, Frederick K**
(National)
Profile: p.116
Government: Political Law
Band 3
Table: p.34

**Lowenfeld, Andreas**
(National)
Arbitration Band 1
Table: p.37

**Lowenthal, Mitchell A**
(New York)
Profile: p.1476
Litigation Band 2
Table: p.1390

**Lowinger, Frederick C**
(Illinois)
Profile: p.842
Corporate/M&A Band 1
Table: p.781

**Lowry, Leslie** (Maine)
Real Estate Band 3
Table: p.1008

**Lowry, Patricia E** (Florida)
Profile: p.643
Litigation Band 4
Table: p.609

**Lowther Jr, Edwin L**
(Arkansas)
Profile: p.209
Litigation Band 2
Table: p.205

**Lozow, Gary** (Colorado)
Litigation Band 1
Table: p.353

**Lubin, Andrew R**
(Connecticut)
Real Estate Band 2
Table: p.380

**Lubin, Donald G** (Illinois)
Profile: p.842
Corporate/M&A Band 2
Table: p.781

**Lucas, Edwin F**
(North Carolina)
Banking & Finance Band 2
Table: p.1569

**Lucas, Michael L**
(Alabama)
Employment Band 3
Table: p.150

**Lucas, Roger S** (Illinois)
Profile: p.842
Tax Band 3
Table: p.812

**Luce, Gregory**
(District of Columbia)
Profile: p.527
Healthcare Band 1
Table: p.456

**Luce, Michael L**
(South Dakota)
Litigation Band 1
Table: p.1795

**Lucero, Gene** (California)
Environment Band 1
Table: p.236

**Luchs, Richard W**
(District of Columbia)
Real Estate Band 4
Table: p.482

Table: p.2045

**Macpherson, Robert J**
(New York)
Profile: p.1476
Construction Band 4
Table: p.1351

**Madan, Raj**
(District of Columbia)
Profile: p.528
Tax Band 4
Table: p.488

**Madden, John J** (New York)
Profile: p.1477
Corporate/M&A Band 2
Table: p.1354

**Madden, Patrick M**
(Washington)
Employment Band 3
Table: p.1995

**Madden, Paul W**
(Maryland)
Profile: p.1041
Employee Benefits Band 2
Table: p.1027

**Madden, Thomas J**
(National)
Government Contracts Band 2
Table: p.30

**Madden, William**
(District of Columbia)
Energy Band 5
Table: p.445

**Maddin, Michael**
(Michigan)
Real Estate Band 2
Table: p.1130

**Maddock, Patrick J**
(North Dakota)
Litigation Band 1
Table: p.1594

**Madison, William**
(New Mexico)
Litigation Band 2
Table: p.1324

**Madsen, Marcia G**
(National)
Profile: p.117
Government Contracts Band 2
Table: p.30

**Magaziner, Fred T**
(Pennsylvania)
Profile: p.1734
Litigation Band 3
Table: p.1714

**Magee, John B**
(District of Columbia)
Profile: p.528
Tax Band 2
Table: p.488

**Maggio, Michael**
(District of Columbia)
Immigration Band 1
Table: p.459

**Magnuson, Lee A**
(South Dakota)
Corporate/Commercial Band 3

Table: p.1792

**Magnuson, Roger**
(Minnesota)
Profile: p.1165
Litigation Band 1
Table: p.1156

**Maguire, William R** (New York)
Litigation Band 3
Table: p.1390

**Maguire Jr, Charles D**
(Colorado)
Corporate/M&A Band 3
Table: p.346

**Mahoney, Colleen P**
(District of Columbia)
Profile: p.529
Securities Band 1
Table: p.485

**Mahoney, Maureen**
(District of Columbia)
Litigation Band 1
Table: p.475

**Mahoney, Sean** (Maine)
Profile: p.1014
Environment Band 2
Table: p.1004

**Mahony, Gael**
(Massachusetts)
Profile: p.1098
Litigation Band S
Table: p.1074

**Maida, Thomas J** (Florida)
Profile: p.643
Insurance Band 2
Table: p.607

**Mailman, Stanley** (New York)
Immigration Band S
Table: p.1376

**Maiman, Earle Jay** (Ohio)
Profile: p.1633
Litigation Band 4
Table: p.1617

**Mair, George P**
(Massachusetts)
Profile: p.1098
Tax Band 3
Table: p.1084

**Maitland, Johan W E**
(Vermont)
Employment Band 2
Table: p.1958

**Maizel, Jonathan**
(District of Columbia)
Projects Band 3
Table: p.479

**Major, Joseph E**
(South Carolina)
Litigation Band 3
Table: p.1778

**Makadon, Arthur**
(Pennsylvania)
Profile: p.1734
Litigation Band 3

Table: p.1714

**Makens, Hugh H**
(Michigan)
Corporate/M&A Band 3
Table: p.1122

**Makley, Roger J** (Ohio)
Litigation Band S
Table: p.1618

**Makoulian, Tina R**
(Pennsylvania)
Profile: p.1735
Real Estate Up and coming
Table: p.1718

**Maledon, William J**
(Arizona)
Profile: p.192
Litigation Band 1
Table: p.181

**Malefatto, Alfred J**
(Florida)
Profile: p.644
Environment Band 2
Table: p.601

**Malester, Ann**
(District of Columbia)
Profile: p.529
Antitrust Band 3
Table: p.426

**Malheiro, Sharon** (Iowa)
Employment Band 3
Table: p.912

**Malkerson, Bruce**
(Minnesota)
Real Estate Band 1
Table: p.1160

**Malkin, Joseph** (California)
Profile: p.301
Energy Band 1
Table: p.233

**Mallery, Mark** (Louisiana)
Profile: p.983
Employment Band 3
Table: p.967

**Mallory, Richard C**
(California)
Real Estate Band 1
Table: p.270

**Mallory, Robert P**
(California)
Profile: p.301
Litigation Band 4
Table: p.257

**Mallow, Matthew J** (New York)
Profile: p.117
Capital Markets Band S
Table: p.7

**Malloy, Elizabeth A**
(Pennsylvania)
Profile: p.1735
Employment Band 4
Table: p.1703

**Malloy, Timothy J** (Illinois)
Profile: p.843
Intellectual Property Band 1

Table: p.799

**Malone, Judith**
(Massachusetts)
Profile: p.1098
Employment Band 2
Table: p.1065

**Malone, Raymond M**
(Ohio)
Employee Benefits Band 2
Table: p.1607

**Malone Jr, Ernest**
(Louisiana)
Employment Band 1
Table: p.967

**Malone Jr, Gayle**
(Tennessee)
Profile: p.1815
Litigation Band 3
Table: p.1804

**Maloney, Marilyn** (Texas)
Banking & Finance Band 4
Table: p.1832

**Maloy, Bruce** (Georgia)
Litigation Band 1
Table: p.698

**Malt, R Bradford**
(Massachusetts)
Profile: p.1098
Corporate/M&A Band 2
Table: p.1061
Private Equity Band 2
Table: p.1078
Private Equity Band 1
Table: p.1080

**Maltz, Gerald** (Arizona)
Litigation Band 2
Table: p.181

**Manchester, Susan A**
(New Hampshire)
Real Estate Band 1
Table: p.1270

**Mancini, Paul** (Hawaii)
Land Use Band 1
Table: p.744
Real Estate Band 2
Table: p.748

**Mancino, Douglas M**
(California)
Profile: p.301
Healthcare Band 1
Table: p.238

**Mandel, David S** (Florida)
Profile: p.644
Litigation Band 2
Table: p.610

**Mandel, Gary B** (New York)
Profile: p.1477
Tax Band 4
Table: p.1423

**Mandel, Jeffrey E** (Florida)
Profile: p.644
Employment Band 4
Table: p.597

**Mandel, Reid A** (Illinois)
Tax Band 3

Table: p.812

**Mandelbaum, David G**
(Pennsylvania)
Profile: p.1735
Environment Band 1
Table: p.1707

**Mandell, Floyd A** (Illinois)
Intellectual Property Band 2
Table: p.799

**Manford III, Thomas D**
(Texas)
Profile: p.1903
Technology Band 3
Table: p.1878

**Mangan, John J** (National)
Profile: p.117
International Trade Band 5
Table: p.42

**Mangum, Geoffrey W**
(Utah)
Profile: p.1952
Corporate/M&A Band 3
Table: p.1941

**Manheimer, Jacob A**
(Maine)
Profile: p.1014
Corporate/M&A Band 1
Table: p.1000

**Manitsky, Andrew D**
(Vermont)
Litigation Band 3
Table: p.1959

**Manko, Joseph M**
(Pennsylvania)
Environment ✪
Table: p.1707

**Mann, Christopher L** (New York)
Profile: p.1477
Projects Band 3
Table: p.1413

**Mann, Phillip L**
(District of Columbia)
Profile: p.529
Tax Band 4
Table: p.488

**Mann, Terry** (Kansas)
Employment Band 1
Table: p.926

**Manne, Neal** (Texas)
Litigation Band 2
Table: p.1865

**Manner, Mark** (Tennessee)
Corporate/M&A Band 1
Table: p.1799

**Manning, John** (Montana)
Profile: p.1232
Corporate/M&A Band 1
Table: p.1222

**Manning, William E**
(Delaware)
Profile: p.408
Real Estate Band 2
Table: p.400

**M**

**Mannino, Edward F**
(Pennsylvania)
Profile: p.1735
Litigation Band 3
Table: p.1714
Litigation Band 2
Table: p.1715

**Manolopoulos, Lynn T**
(Washington)
Environment Band 2
Table: p.1996

**Manos, Karen** (National)
Profile: p.117
Government Contracts Band 3
Table: p.30

**Mansfield, Edward** (Iowa)
Litigation Band 3
Table: p.914

**Mansfield, Stephen A**
(California)
Profile: p.301
Litigation Band 3
Table: p.258

**Manson, Thomas P**
(New Hampshire)
Profile: p.1272
Corporate/Commercial Band 2
Table: p.1263

**Manthey, Ron** (Texas)
Profile: p.1903
Employment Band 3
Table: p.1844

**Manulik, Mark** (Oregon)
Real Estate Band 3
Table: p.1677

**Marcello III, Matthew T**
(Rhode Island)
Corporate/Commercial Band 3
Table: p.1766

**March, Aaron** (Missouri)
Real Estate Band 2
Table: p.1201

**March, Jon G** (Michigan)
Employment Band 2
Table: p.1125

**Marchetta, Anthony J**
(New Jersey)
Profile: p.1302
Litigation Band 3
Table: p.1289

**Marcil, Jack**
(North Dakota)
Litigation Band 2
Table: p.1594

**Marco, Frank J**
(Connecticut)
Profile: p.384
Corporate/M&A Band 2
Table: p.374

**Marcu, Aaron R** (New York)
Profile: p.1477
Litigation Band 2
Table: p.1391

**Marcus, Benjamin E**
(Maine)
Profile: p.1014
Corporate/M&A Band 1
Table: p.1000

**Marcus, Courtney** (Texas)
Profile: p.1903
Banking & Finance Up and
coming
Table: p.1832

**Marcus, George J** (Maine)
Corporate/M&A Band 1
Table: p.1000

**Marcus, Kenneth B**
(Hawaii)
Real Estate Band 2
Table: p.748

**Marcy, Donald**
(Washington)
Real Estate Band 1
Table: p.2003

**Marella, Vincent J**
(California)
Litigation Band 1
Table: p.258

**Marenberg, Steven**
(California)
Media & Entertainment Band 3
Table: p.263

**Marett, Louis J**
(Massachusetts)
Tax Band 3
Table: p.1084

**Margo, Roderick D**
(National)
Transportation Band 3
Table: p.67

**Margolies, Jonathan H.**
(Wisconsin)
Intellectual Property Band 1
Table: p.2028

**Mariani, Richard C** (New
Jersey)
Profile: p.1302
Employment Band 2
Table: p.1282

**Maring, David**
(North Dakota)
Litigation Band 1
Table: p.1593

**Marino, Kevin** (New Jersey)
Litigation Band 2
Table: p.1292

**Marion, David H**
(Pennsylvania)
Litigation Band 2
Table: p.1714

**Mark, Wayne J** (Nebraska)
Litigation Band 2
Table: p.1239

**Markel, Gregory** (New York)
Profile: p.1477
Litigation Band 2
Table: p.1390

**Markham, Jesse W**
(California)
Profile: p.302
Antitrust Band 2
Table: p.216

**Markowitz, David** (Oregon)
Litigation ✪
Table: p.1674

**Marks, Allan T** (California)
Projects Band 3
Table: p.268
Transportation Band 2
Table: p.71

**Marks, Jeffrey A** (Ohio)
Profile: p.1633
Bankruptcy Band 3
Table: p.1600

**Marks, Kenneth S** (Texas)
Litigation Band 3
Table: p.1865

**Marlowe, Deborah**
(Georgia)
Profile: p.719
Immigration Band 1
Table: p.694

**Marmaduke, Don H**
(Oregon)
Profile: p.1682
Litigation Band S
Table: p.1674

**Marmaro, Richard**
(California)
Profile: p.302
Litigation Band 2
Table: p.258

**Marmorstein, Vicki E**
(California)
Banking & Finance Band 3
Table: p.218

**Marovitz, Andrew S**
(Illinois)
Profile: p.843
Antitrust Band 2
Table: p.767

**Marr, Barry W** (Hawaii)
Profile: p.752
Employment Band 1
Table: p.742

**Marren, John P** (Illinois)
Healthcare Band 3
Table: p.793

**Marrinson, Thomas A**
(Illinois)
Profile: p.843
Insurance Band 3
Table: p.796

**Marriott, Catherine M**
(Virginia)
Employment Band 2
Table: p.1971

**Marsack, Gary** (Wisconsin)
Employment Band 3
Table: p.2027

**Marsden Jr, William**
(Delaware)
Profile: p.408
Intellectual Property Band 2
Table: p.397

**Marsh, David** (Alabama)
Litigation Band 1
Table: p.152

**Marsh, Gary W** (Georgia)
Profile: p.719
Bankruptcy Band 3
Table: p.679

**Marshall, Alison**
(District of Columbia)
Profile: p.529
Employment Band 3
Table: p.439

**Marshall, Gary** (Virginia)
Employment Band 2
Table: p.1971

**Marshall, John**
(Pennsylvania)
Intellectual Property Band 2
Table: p.1711

**Marshall, John T** (Georgia)
Antitrust Band 3
Table: p.675
Litigation Band 2
Table: p.698

**Marshall Cox, LeeAnne**
(Tennessee)
Real Estate Band 3
Table: p.1808

**Marso, Lisa Hansen**
(South Dakota)
Employment Band 2
Table: p.1794

**Marston, Edgar** (Texas)
Profile: p.1903
Corporate/M&A Band 4
Table: p.1840

**Martens, Don** (California)
Intellectual Property Band 3
Table: p.248

**Martin, Alan J** (Illinois)
Profile: p.843
Insurance Band 3
Table: p.796

**Martin, Brian** (Texas)
Insurance Band 1
Table: p.1858

**Martin, Channing J**
(Virginia)
Environment Band 1
Table: p.1973

**Martin, Christopher W**
(Texas)
Insurance Band 1
Table: p.1858

**Martin, Chrys** (Oregon)
Employment Band 2
Table: p.1670

**Martin, Clark** (Texas)
Profile: p.1903

Intellectual Property Band 3
Table: p.1860

**Martin, David** (Arkansas)
Employment Band 3
Table: p.203

**Martin, David B H**
(District of Columbia)
Profile: p.529
Securities Band 1
Table: p.485

**Martin, David L**
(Mississippi)
Corporate/Commercial Band 3
Table: p.1174

**Martin, Ernest** (Texas)
Insurance Band 1
Table: p.1858

**Martin, Gerard P.**
(Maryland)
Litigation Band 2
Table: p.1032

**Martin, Gregory S** (Florida)
Profile: p.644
Construction Band 2
Table: p.590

**Martin, John** (Texas)
Profile: p.1903
Business Process Outsourcing
Band 2
Table: p.2
Technology Band 1
Table: p.1877

**Martin, Keith**
(District of Columbia)
Profile: p.529
Projects Band 2
Table: p.56
Projects Band 2
Table: p.479

**Martin, Laura Keidan**
(Illinois)
Antitrust Band 3
Table: p.767

**Martin, Neil** (Texas)
Profile: p.1903
Employment Band 3
Table: p.1844

**Martin, Paul** (Texas)
Profile: p.1903
Real Estate Band 3
Table: p.1872

**Martin, Raymond**
(Colorado)
Employment Band 3
Table: p.348

**Martin, Renwick**
(New York)
Profile: p.117
Capital Markets Band 1
Table: p.13
Capital Markets Band 1
Table: p.18

**Martin, Scott** (New York)
Profile: p.1477
Antitrust Up and coming
Table: p.1335

**Martin, Thene M**
(Maryland)
Profile: p.1041
Corporate/M&A
Up and coming
Table: p.1025

**Martin, Timothy** (Kentucky)
Profile: p.949
Real Estate Band 1
Table: p.944

**Martinez, Roberto**
(Florida)
Profile: p.644
Litigation Band 2
Table: p.609
Litigation Band 1
Table: p.610

**Martinez de Andino, J Michael** (Virginia)
Profile: p.1984
Intellectual Property Band 1
Table: p.1975

**Martinez-Fraga, Pedro J**
(Florida)
Profile: p.117
International Arbitration
Band 4
Table: p.36

**Martini, John D**
(Pennsylvania)
Profile: p.1735
Employment Up and coming
Table: p.1704

**Martland, David A**
(Massachusetts)
Profile: p.1099
Antitrust Band 3
Table: p.1053

**Martson Jr, William F**
(Oregon)
Profile: p.1682
Litigation Band 2
Table: p.1674

**Martucci, William**
(Missouri)
Profile: p.1208
Employment Band 1
Table: p.1195

**Martzell, Jack** (Louisiana)
Litigation Band 3
Table: p.973

**Marvin, Jack** (Kansas)
Profile: p.932
Corporate/M&A Band 1
Table: p.924
Real Estate Band 2
Table: p.930

**Marvin, John** (Missouri)
Profile: p.1208
Corporate/M&A Band 2
Table: p.1193

**Marx, David** (Illinois)
Profile: p.843
Antitrust Band 2
Table: p.767

**Marzetti, Phil** (Georgia)
Profile: p.719

Tax Band 2
Table: p.703

**Maser, Joel** (Florida)
Profile: p.644
Tax Band 1
Table: p.623

**Mashburn, Randal**
(Tennessee)
Profile: p.1815
Litigation Band 1
Table: p.1804

**Maslanka, Michael** (Texas)
Profile: p.1904
Employment Band 3
Table: p.1844

**Mason, Andrew S**
(New York)
Profile: p.1477
Tax Band 3
Table: p.1423

**Mason, C Steven**
(North Carolina)
Profile: p.1584
Real Estate Band 3
Table: p.1579

**Mason, David** (Illinois)
Banking & Finance Band 2
Table: p.771

**Mason, David** (New York)
Employee Benefits Band 3
Table: p.1362

**Mason, J Cheney** (Florida)
Litigation Band 2
Table: p.610

**Mason, J Parker**
(Washington)
Real Estate Band 3
Table: p.2002

**Mason, Richard G**
(New York)
Profile: p.1477
Bankruptcy Band 3
Table: p.1344

**Mason III, Julian L** (Alaska)
Environment Band S
Table: p.170

**Masotti, Marco** (New York)
Profile: p.1478
Private Equity Band 4
Table: p.1410

**Massad, Stephen A**
(Texas)
Profile: p.1904
Corporate/M&A Band 1
Table: p.1840

**Massey, Raymond L**
(Missouri)
Profile: p.1208
Litigation Band 3
Table: p.1198

**Massopust, Richard**
(Minnesota)
Real Estate Band 2
Table: p.1160

**Massouh, Jennifer F**
(New York)
Projects Band 5
Table: p.1413

**Mast, Gregory** (Arizona)
Real Estate Band 1
Table: p.184

**Master, Geofrey L**
(National)
Profile: p.117
Business Process Outsourcing
Band 4
Table: p.2

**Masters, Lori**
(District of Columbia)
Profile: p.529
Insurance Band 2
Table: p.464

**Masters, William B**
(Louisiana)
Profile: p.983
Corporate/M&A Band 3
Table: p.965

**Mastracco, Vincent**
(Virginia)
Corporate/M&A Band 2
Table: p.1968

**Mastriani, Louis S**
(National)
Profile: p.117
International Trade Band 4
Table: p.42

**Mastro, Randy** (New York)
Profile: p.1478
Litigation Band 2
Table: p.1388

**Masur, Daniel A**
(District of Columbia)
Profile: p.529
Business Process Outsourcing
Band 1
Table: p.2
Technology Band 1
Table: p.490

**Matava, George G**
(Colorado)
Profile: p.363
Intellectual Property Band 2
Table: p.351

**Matchett, Sam** (Georgia)
Profile: p.719
Employment Band 4
Table: p.687

**Mather, Barbara W**
(Pennsylvania)
Profile: p.1735
Antitrust Band 2
Table: p.1692
Litigation Band 1
Table: p.1714

**Matheson, David S**
(Oregon)
Corporate/M&A
Up and coming
Table: p.1667

**Mathews, Daniel A**
(National)
Profile: p.118
Transportation Band 1
Table: p.71

**Mathias, Robert**
(Maryland)
Profile: p.1042
Litigation Band 1
Table: p.1032

**Mathias Jr, John H** (Illinois)
Profile: p.843
Insurance Band 1
Table: p.796

**Mathiason, Garry G**
(California)
Profile: p.302
Employment Band 4
Table: p.231

**Matichak, Jill** (California)
Profile: p.302
Banking & Finance Band 2
Table: p.218

**Matkins, Michael L**
(California)
Real Estate Band 1
Table: p.270

**Matkov, George** (Illinois)
Employment Band S
Table: p.785

**Matour, James M**
(Pennsylvania)
Profile: p.1735
Bankruptcy Band 3
Table: p.1697

**Matricciani, Rose M**
(Maryland)
Profile: p.1042
Healthcare Band 3
Table: p.1031

**Mattei, Andrew** (New York)
Profile: p.1478
Banking & Finance Band 3
Table: p.1339

**Mattei, Ivan E** (New York)
Projects Band 4
Table: p.1413

**Matthews, Christopher T**
(Oregon)
Real Estate Band 3
Table: p.1677

**Matthews, Frank** (Florida)
Profile: p.644
Environment Band 1
Table: p.601

**Matthews, Joseph M**
(Florida)
Profile: p.644
Litigation Band 2
Table: p.609

**Matthews, Philip R**
(California)
Profile: p.302
Insurance Band 1
Table: p.243

**Mattingly, Bryan K**
(Kentucky)
Profile: p.950
Corporate/M&A
Up and coming
Table: p.937

**Mattingly, Patrick W**
(Kentucky)
Profile: p.950
Corporate/M&A Band 2
Table: p.937

**Mattox, Sharon** (Texas)
Profile: p.1904
Environment Band 2
Table: p.1852
Environment Band 1
Table: p.1853

**Matyas, David E**
(District of Columbia)
Profile: p.530
Healthcare Band 2
Table: p.456

**Mauel, John G** (Texas)
Profile: p.1904
Projects Band 3
Table: p.1869

**Mautino, Robert A**
(California)
Immigration Band 3
Table: p.241

**Maxey, JoAnn** (Arkansas)
Employment Band 2
Table: p.203

**May, Arnold P**
(Massachusetts)
Profile: p.1099
Tax Band 3
Table: p.1084

**May, Bruce** (Arizona)
Real Estate Band 3
Table: p.184

**May, Gregory**
(District of Columbia)
Tax Band 2
Table: p.488

**May, James** (Alabama)
Profile: p.158
Employment Band 1
Table: p.150

**May Jr, Henry S** (Texas)
Profile: p.1904
Energy Band 1
Table: p.1849

**Mayer, Patricia V**
(California)
Media & Entertainment Band 4
Table: p.263

**Mayer, Theodore VH**
(National)
Profile: p.118
Products Liability Band 3
Table: p.50

**Mayer, Thomas Moers**
(New York)
Profile: p.1478
Bankruptcy Band 3

M

KEY TO RANKINGS: ✪ = STAR INDIVIDUAL   S = SENIOR STATESMAN

**Mechanick, Maury J**
(District of Columbia)
Profile: p.531
Telecom, Broadcast & Satellite
Band 4
Table: p.492

**Medaglia, Anthony J**
(Massachusetts)
Profile: p.1099
Private Equity Band 3
Table: p.1078

**Mede, William** (Alaska)
Employment Band 2
Table: p.169

**Medlock, V Bryan** (Texas)
Profile: p.1905
Intellectual Property Band 1
Table: p.1860

**Medow, Jonathan C**
(Illinois)
Profile: p.845
Litigation Band 4
Table: p.802

**Medved, Joseph W**
(Missouri)
Profile: p.1208
Corporate/M&A Band 1
Table: p.1193

**Meehan, Michael** (Arizona)
Litigation Band 3
Table: p.181

**Meehan, Wayne D**
(New York)
Profile: p.120
Transportation Band 2
Table: p.74

**Meeks, Thomas** (Florida)
Litigation Band 3
Table: p.609

**Meeks, William** (Ohio)
Litigation Band 1
Table: p.1618

**Meenan, Timothy J**
(Florida)
Insurance Band 2
Table: p.607

**Mehlman, Mark** (Illinois)
Profile: p.845
Real Estate Band 2
Table: p.809

**Mehta, Cyrus D** (New York)
Immigration Band 3
Table: p.1376

**Mehta, Kiran H**
(North Carolina)
Litigation Band 3
Table: p.1577

**Meier, Joseph M** (Idaho)
Bankruptcy Band 1
Table: p.758

**Meiklejohn, Paul**
(Washington)
Profile: p.2006
Intellectual Property Band 1
Table: p.1998

**Meir, Dennis** (Georgia)
Profile: p.719
Bankruptcy Band 2
Table: p.679

**Meiser, Kenneth E**
(New Jersey)
Real Estate Band 2
Table: p.1293

**Meisinger, Louis M**
(California)
Media & Enterrtainment
Litigation Band 3
Table: p.230

**Meister, Margaret L**
(New Mexico)
Real Estate Up and coming
Table: p.1327

**Melamed, A Douglas**
(District of Columbia)
Profile: p.532
Antitrust Band 1
Table: p.426

**Meland, Creighton** (Illinois)
Profile: p.845
Banking & Finance Band 3
Table: p.771

**Melbinger, Michael S**
(Illinois)
Profile: p.845
Employment Band 2
Table: p.786

**Melby, Barbara Murphy**
(National)
Profile: p.120
Business Process Outsourcing
Band 2
Table: p.2

**Mele, Dennis** (Florida)
Real Estate Band 2
Table: p.621

**Melo, Thomas M** (Texas)
Profile: p.1905
Employment Band 1
Table: p.1844

**Meloy, Michael M**
(Pennsylvania)
Environment Band 2
Table: p.1707

**Meltzer, Steven** (Virginia)
Profile: p.1984
Corporate/M&A Band 2
Table: p.1967

**Melwani, Vivek** (New York)
Profile: p.1479
Bankruptcy Up and coming
Table: p.1344

**Memel, Sherwin L**
(California)
Healthcare Band S
Table: p.238

**Mencio Jr, George** (Florida)
Profile: p.645
Corporate/M&A Band 2
Table: p.595

**Mendeloff, Scott T**
(Illinois)
Profile: p.845
Litigation Band 4
Table: p.802

**Mendelsohn, David**
(Illinois)
Profile: p.845
Insurance Band 1
Table: p.796

**Mendelson, Alan C**
(California)
Corporate/M&A Band 1
Table: p.227

**Mendelson, Richard C**
(California)
Profile: p.303
Real Estate Band 3
Table: p.270

**Mendelson, Robert C**
(National)
Profile: p.120
Financial Services Band 3
Table: p.28

**Mendenhall, William**
(Mississippi)
Profile: p.1185
Corporate/Commercial Band 3
Table: p.1174

**Mendez, John E** (California)
Banking & Finance Band 2
Table: p.218

**Mendoza, Julie C**
(District of Columbia)
Profile: p.120
International Trade Band 3
Table: p.42

**Mendoza, Mary S** (Texas)
Environment Up and coming
Table: p.1852

**Menendez Cambo,
Patricia** (Florida)
Profile: p.645
Corporate/M&A Band 2
Table: p.595

**Menna, Gilbert G**
(Massachusetts)
Profile: p.1099
Corporate/M&A Band 2
Table: p.1061

**Menotti, David E**
(District of Columbia)
Profile: p.532
Environment Band 2
Table: p.451

**Mensch, Linda** (Illinois)
Media & Entertainment Band 1
Table: p.807

**Mensik, Michael S**
(Illinois)
Profile: p.845
Business Process Outsourcing
Band 3
Table: p.2
Technology Band 1
Table: p.814

**Menson, Richard L**
(Illinois)
Employment Band 2
Table: p.786

**Menting, Mark J** (National)
Profile: p.120
Financial Services Band 3
Table: p.24

**Mentlik, William** (New
Jersey)
Profile: p.1303
Intellectual Property Band 1
Table: p.1288

**Menzie, Edward G**
(South Carolina)
Profile: p.1783
Corporate/M&A Band 1
Table: p.1775
Real Estate ✪
Table: p.1780

**Mercer, John T W**
(Georgia)
Energy Band 2
Table: p.689

**Meredith, Stephen**
(Massachusetts)
Profile: p.1099
Private Equity Band 2
Table: p.1078

**Merkle, Craig** (Maryland)
Profile: p.1042
Healthcare Band 2
Table: p.1031
Litigation Band 3
Table: p.1032

**Mermelstein, Joshua** (New
York)
Profile: p.1479
Real Estate Band 2
Table: p.1417

**Merriam, Dwight**
(Connecticut)
Real Estate Band 1
Table: p.380

**Merrigan, John A**
(National)
Profile: p.121
Government Relations Band 1
Table: p.32

**Merrill, Frank** (Ohio)
Environment Band 3
Table: p.1612

**Merritt, Keith J**
(North Carolina)
Litigation Band 4
Table: p.1577

**Merritt, Mark**
(North Carolina)
Antitrust Band 1
Table: p.1568
Litigation Band 2
Table: p.1577

**Mersol, Gregory V** (Ohio)
Employment Band 2
Table: p.1609

**Merwin, Bruce** (Texas)
Construction Band 4
Table: p.1838

**Messana, Thomas M**
(Florida)
Bankruptcy Band 4
Table: p.586

**Messerschmidt, Michael**
(Maine)
Profile: p.1014
Employment Band 2
Table: p.1002

**Metcalf, Bryan W**
(Tennessee)
Profile: p.1815
Corporate/M&A
Up and coming
Table: p.1799

**Metcalf, Slade R**
(New York)
Profile: p.1479
Media & Entertainment Band 2
Table: p.1404

**Metropoulos, Demetrios
G** (Illinois)
Profile: p.845
Telecom, Broadcast & Satellite
Band 3
Table: p.816

**Metropoulos, Jon**
(Montana)
Natural Resources Band 2
Table: p.1228

**Metzger Jr, Richard A**
(District of Columbia)
Telecom, Broadcast & Satellite
Band 2
Table: p.492

**Metzke, John** (Wyoming)
Corporate/M&A Band 2
Table: p.2041

**Meunier, Gerald E**
(Louisiana)
Litigation Band 1
Table: p.973

**Meusey, Joseph K**
(Nebraska)
Litigation Band 1
Table: p.1239

**Meyer, Andrew C** (Ohio)
Profile: p.1634
Employment Band 3
Table: p.1609

**Meyer, Christopher** (Idaho)
Natural Resources Band 1
Table: p.761

**Meyer, David L** (National)
Profile: p.121
Transportation Band 2
Table: p.69

**Meyer, Dianne A**
(Pennsylvania)
Profile: p.1736
Banking & Finance Band 3
Table: p.1695

M

**M**

**Meyer, G Christopher**
(Ohio)
Profile: p.1634
Bankruptcy Band 1
Table: p.1600

**Meyer, George** (Florida)
Profile: p.645
Construction Band 1
Table: p.590

**Meyer, Michael E**
(California)
Profile: p.303
Real Estate Band 1
Table: p.270

**Meyer, Paul** (New York)
Profile: p.1479
Insurance Band 3
Table: p.1380

**Meyer, Richard S** (Virginia)
Intellectual Property Band 2
Table: p.1975

**Meyer, Theodore D** (Texas)
Profile: p.1906
Employment Band 3
Table: p.1844

**Meyer Jr, Robert A** (Ohio)
Profile: p.1634
Real Estate Band 2
Table: p.1622

**Meyers, Kent** (Oklahoma)
Profile: p.1660
Litigation Band 1
Table: p.1656

**Meyers, Michael**
(New York)
Profile: p.1479
Projects Band 4
Table: p.1413

**Meyers, Todd** (Georgia)
Profile: p.720
Bankruptcy Band 2
Table: p.679

**Meyers III, Robert L**
(Texas)
Profile: p.1906
Construction Band 3
Table: p.1838

**Meyerson, Lee** (New York)
Profile: p.1479
Corporate/M&A Band 4
Table: p.1354
Financial Services Band 2
Table: p.24

**Mezzullo, Louis A**
(National)
Wealth Management Band 3
Table: p.81

**Miano, Steven T**
(Pennsylvania)
Profile: p.1736
Environment Band 2
Table: p.1707

**Micciche, Daniel J** (Texas)
Profile: p.1906
Tax Band 3
Table: p.1875

**Michaels, Jane** (Colorado)
Profile: p.363
Intellectual Property Band 1
Table: p.351

**Michaels, Joel**
(District of Columbia)
Profile: p.532
Healthcare Band 1
Table: p.456

**Michalopoulos, Pantelis**
(District of Columbia)
Profile: p.532
Telecom, Broadcast & Satellite
Band 4
Table: p.492

**Michalski, Paul** (National)
Profile: p.121
Capital Markets Band 4
Table: p.7

**Michetti, Michael E**
(National)
Capital Markets Band 4
Table: p.7

**Middlebrooks, David J**
(Alabama)
Employment Band 1
Table: p.150

**Middleton, Jack B**
(New Hampshire)
Profile: p.1273
Litigation Band S
Table: p.1267

**Mierzewski, Michael B**
(National)
Profile: p.121
Financial Services Band 3
Table: p.28

**Mihlsten, George**
(California)
Real Estate Band 1
Table: p.270

**Mikels, Richard**
(Massachusetts)
Profile: p.1099
Bankruptcy Band 1
Table: p.1058

**Milam, Kenneth E**
(Mississippi)
Employment Band 1
Table: p.1177

**Milch, Thomas**
(District of Columbia)
Profile: p.532
Environment Band 2
Table: p.451

**Milenkovski, Katerina
Eftimoff** (Ohio)
Profile: p.1634
Environment Band 4
Table: p.1612

**Miles, John J**
(District of Columbia)
Healthcare Band 2
Table: p.456

**Miles, Robin J** (New York)
Profile: p.1906
Banking & Finance Band 3
Table: p.1832

**Miles, Steven**
(District of Columbia)
Profile: p.532
Projects Band 3
Table: p.479

**Milkman, Ruth**
(District of Columbia)
Telecom, Broadcast & Satellite
Band 4
Table: p.492

**Millard, David** (Indiana)
Profile: p.898
Corporate/M&A Band 2
Table: p.887

**Millen, Pressly M**
(North Carolina)
Profile: p.1585
Litigation Band 2
Table: p.1577

**Miller, Alan S**
(Pennsylvania)
Environment Band 2
Table: p.1707

**Miller, Barry** (Ohio)
Profile: p.1634
Construction Band 2
Table: p.1603

**Miller, Barry** (Texas)
Profile: p.1906
Tax Band 3
Table: p.1875

**Miller, Bradley** (Oregon)
Real Estate Band 1
Table: p.1677

**Miller, Camille**
(Pennsylvania)
Intellectual Property Up and
coming
Table: p.1711

**Miller, Charles E** (Maine)
Profile: p.1014
Real Estate Band 1
Table: p.1008

**Miller, Charles F** (Missouri)
Profile: p.1208
Real Estate Band 1
Table: p.1201

**Miller, Clifford** (Hawaii)
Real Estate Band 1
Table: p.748

**Miller, Craig** (Washington)
Litigation Band 3
Table: p.2000

**Miller, Craig** (Ohio)
Real Estate Band 2
Table: p.1622

**Miller, David S** (New York)
Profile: p.1479
Tax Band 2
Table: p.1425

**Miller, David W** (Indiana)
Profile: p.898
Employment Band 1
Table: p.889

**Miller, Elizabeth H**
(Vermont)
Litigation Band 2
Table: p.1959

**Miller, Evan**
(District of Columbia)
Profile: p.532
Employee Benefits Band 2
Table: p.437

**Miller, Gale T** (Colorado)
Litigation Band 1
Table: p.353

**Miller, George** (New York)
Profile: p.1479
Projects Band 5
Table: p.1413

**Miller, George** (Kentucky)
Profile: p.950
Employment Band 3
Table: p.939

**Miller, Henry** (Pennsylvania)
Profile: p.1736
Real Estate Band S
Table: p.1718

**Miller, J Gregg**
(Pennsylvania)
Profile: p.1736
Bankruptcy Band 3
Table: p.1697

**Miller, Kenneth W** (Illinois)
Profile: p.846
Corporate/M&A: Private Equity
Band 3
Table: p.782

**Miller, Laura B** (Illinois)
Profile: p.846
Intellectual Property Band 3
Table: p.799

**Miller, Lawrence**
(District of Columbia)
Profile: p.532
Energy Band 5
Table: p.441

**Miller, Lawrence A**
(District of Columbia)
Real Estate Band 4
Table: p.482

**Miller, Michelle**
(Massachusetts)
Profile: p.1100
Antitrust Band 1
Table: p.1053

**Miller, Morris H** (Florida)
Profile: p.645
Healthcare Band 1
Table: p.604

**Miller, Nicholas** (Idaho)
Corporate/Commercial Band 1
Table: p.759

**Miller, O'Malley** (California)
Real Estate Band 2
Table: p.270

**Miller, Peter A** (New York)
Profile: p.1480
Real Estate Band 4
Table: p.1417

**Miller, Ralph I** (Texas)
Profile: p.1906
Litigation Band 3
Table: p.1865

**Miller, Ranne B**
(New Mexico)
Litigation Band S
Table: p.1324

**Miller, Rick** (Georgia)
Corporate/M&A Band 4
Table: p.684

**Miller, Robert** (California)
Profile: p.303
Corporate/M&A Band 4
Table: p.227

**Miller, Roger** (Nebraska)
Employment Band 1
Table: p.1238

**Miller, Stephen D**
(California)
Litigation Band 2
Table: p.258

**Miller, Stephen M**
(Delaware)
Profile: p.409
Bankruptcy Band 4
Table: p.389

**Miller, Steven S**
(Washington)
Immigration Band 1
Table: p.1997

**Miller, Van A**
(District of Columbia)
Profile: p.532
Technology Associate to
watch
Table: p.490

**Miller, W Timothy** (Ohio)
Bankruptcy Up and coming
Table: p.1600

**Miller, Walter** (Texas)
Real Estate Up and coming
Table: p.1872

**Miller, Winston** (Kentucky)
Profile: p.950
Litigation Band 2
Table: p.942

**Miller, Zach** (Colorado)
Environment Band 2
Table: p.350

**Miller Jr, Ben R** (Louisiana)
Profile: p.984
Corporate/M&A Band 3
Table: p.965

**Miller Jr, John C H**
(Alabama)
Banking & Finance Band 2

Table: p.147

**Miller Jr, Max M** (Oregon)
Profile: p.1682
Environment Band 3
Table: p.1672

**Millet, Craig H** (California)
Profile: p.303
Bankruptcy Band 4
Table: p.222

**Millikan, Michael E**
(Indiana)
Profile: p.898
Corporate/M&A
Up and coming
Table: p.887

**Milliman, James E**
(Kentucky)
Profile: p.950
Litigation Band 4
Table: p.942

**Millisor, Kenneth** (Ohio)
Employment Band S
Table: p.1609

**Millner, Robert** (Illinois)
Profile: p.846
Bankruptcy Band 2
Table: p.775

**Millock, Peter J** (New York)
Profile: p.1480
Healthcare Band 3
Table: p.1374

**Mills, Gail L** (Alabama)
Banking & Finance Band 2
Table: p.147
Real Estate Band 3
Table: p.153

**Mills, Jerry** (Texas)
Profile: p.1906
Intellectual Property Band 2
Table: p.1860

**Mills, Michael** (Alaska)
Bankruptcy Band 1
Table: p.167

**Mills, Phillip R** (New York)
Profile: p.1480
Corporate/M&A Band 4
Table: p.1354

**Mills Jr, Osborne** (Ohio)
Profile: p.1634
Banking & Finance Band 1
Table: p.1598

**Millspaugh, Thomas E D**
(Maryland)
Profile: p.1042
Real Estate Band 3
Table: p.1035

**Millstein, Julian** (New York)
Profile: p.1480
Business Process Outsourcing
Band 2
Table: p.2
Technology Band 2
Table: p.1428

**Millstone, David J** (Ohio)
Profile: p.1634

Employment Band 3
Table: p.1609

**Milmed, Paul K** (New York)
Profile: p.1480
Environment Band 3
Table: p.1373

**Milmoe, J Gregory**
(New York)
Profile: p.1480
Bankruptcy Band 1
Table: p.1344

**Milner, Ann L**
(Massachusetts)
Profile: p.1100
Private Equity Band 3
Table: p.1080

**Milom, W Michael**
(Tennessee)
Profile: p.1815
Media & Entertainment Band 1
Table: p.1806

**Minch, Roger J**
(North Dakota)
Corporate/Commercial Band 1
Table: p.1590

**Minchella, Michael F**
(California)
Construction Band 2
Table: p.225

**Mindlin, Philip** (New York)
Profile: p.1480
Bankruptcy Band 3
Table: p.1344

**Minion, Robert G** (New
Jersey)
Profile: p.1303
Corporate/M&A Band 2
Table: p.1278

**Minisman Jr, B G**
(Alabama)
Profile: p.158
Corporate/Commercial Band 2
Table: p.148

**Minkus, Daniel H**
(Michigan)
Corporate/M&A Band 2
Table: p.1122

**Minogue, Thomas J**
(Missouri)
Profile: p.1208
Corporate/M&A Band 3
Table: p.1193

**Minton, Michael D**
(Florida)
Profile: p.645
Tax Band 4
Table: p.623

**Minuti, Mark** (Delaware)
Profile: p.409
Bankruptcy Band 3
Table: p.389

**Miraldi, Leslee** (Ohio)
Profile: p.1634
Banking & Finance Band 1
Table: p.1598

**Mirvis, Theodore N**
(New York)
Profile: p.1480
Litigation Band 2
Table: p.1390

**Miscimarra, Philip A**
(Illinois)
Profile: p.846
Employment Band 2
Table: p.785

**Mishkin, Jeffrey A**
(National)
Profile: p.121
Sport Band 1
Table: p.59

**Missner, David** (Illinois)
Profile: p.846
Bankruptcy Band 2
Table: p.775

**Mitchell, Barry D** (Arizona)
Litigation Up and coming
Table: p.182

**Mitchell, Beth H**
(Massachusetts)
Real Estate Band 3
Table: p.1081

**Mitchell, Chris** (Alabama)
Profile: p.158
Employment Band 2
Table: p.150

**Mitchell, David S**
(New York)
Profile: p.121
Capital Markets Band 2
Table: p.15

**Mitchell, E Marlee**
(Tennessee)
Profile: p.1815
Corporate/M&A Band 3
Table: p.1799

**Mitchell, H Maurice**
(Arkansas)
Real Estate Band S
Table: p.207

**Mitchell, Marvin** (Indiana)
Litigation Band 2
Table: p.890

**Mitchell, Michael H**
(National)
Profile: p.121
Capital Markets Band 4
Table: p.18

**Mitchell, Michael S**
(Louisiana)
Profile: p.984
Employment Band 3
Table: p.967

**Mitchell, Nancy** (Illinois)
Profile: p.846
Bankruptcy Band 3
Table: p.775

**Mitchell, Stephen J**
(Florida)
Profile: p.645
Real Estate Band 2
Table: p.617

**Mitchell Jr, Burley B**
(North Carolina)
Profile: p.1585
Litigation Band 3
Table: p.1577

**Mitchelson Jr, William
(Mitch) R** (Georgia)
Profile: p.720
Litigation Band 1

**Mitzner, David** (Colorado)
Employment Band 1
Table: p.348

**Mix, Kristen L** (Colorado)
Profile: p.363
Employment Band 3
Table: p.348

**Mixson, Dwight** (Alabama)
Banking & Finance Band 2
Table: p.147
Real Estate Band 2
Table: p.153

**Mixson, H Lamar** (Georgia)
Profile: p.720
Litigation Band 2
Table: p.698

**Mixter, Stephen** (Ohio)
Profile: p.1634
Real Estate Band 4
Table: p.1621

**Miziolek, Aleksandra A**
(Michigan)
Corporate/M&A Band 3
Table: p.1122

**Moates, G Paul** (National)
Profile: p.121
Transportation Band 1
Table: p.69

**Moberly, Michael D**
(Arizona)
Profile: p.192
Employment Band 2
Table: p.178

**Mock, Randall D**
(Oklahoma)
Corporate/Commercial Band 2
Table: p.1653

**Mockbee, David**
(Mississippi)
Litigation Band 1
Table: p.1179

**Moeckel, Jennifer Shea**
(New Hampshire)
Employment Band 2
Table: p.1265

**Moeling, Walter G**
(Georgia)
Banking & Finance Band 1
Table: p.677

**Moellenberg, Dalva**
(Arizona)
Environment Band 3
Table: p.179

**Moeller Jr, Armin J**
(Mississippi)
Profile: p.1185

Employment Band 2
Table: p.1177

**Moffatt, Maura Griffith**
(Massachusetts)
Profile: p.1100
Real Estate Band 3
Table: p.1081

**Moffitt, Ronald** (Utah)
Corporate/M&A Band 2
Table: p.1941

**Molen, Chris D** (Georgia)
Profile: p.720
Banking & Finance Band 1
Table: p.677

**Molitor, Steven J** (National)
Profile: p.121
Capital Markets Band 4
Table: p.18

**Mollen, Neal D**
(District of Columbia)
Profile: p.533
Employment Band 3
Table: p.439

**Mollerup, Richard W**
(Idaho)
Real Estate Band 2
Table: p.762

**Mollerus, Michael**
(New York)
Profile: p.1480
Tax Band 4
Table: p.1423

**Molo, Steven F** (New York)
Profile: p.846
Litigation Band 3
Table: p.802

**Moltenbrey, MJ**
(District of Columbia)
Antitrust Band 5
Table: p.426

**Monaco, Daniel A**
(Pennsylvania)
Intellectual Property Band 4
Table: p.1711

**Monaco, Stephanie**
(District of Columbia)
Profile: p.533
Investment Management Band 2
Table: p.469

**Monaghan, John J**
(Massachusetts)
Profile: p.1100
Bankruptcy Band 2
Table: p.1058

**Monahan Jr, John**
(Vermont)
Litigation Band 3
Table: p.1959

**Monk, David** (Texas)
Profile: p.1906
Technology Up & Coming

**Monk, Stephen** (Alabama)
Profile: p.158
Real Estate Band 2
Table: p.153

M

M

**N**

Table: p.1961

**Murphy, Marc S** (Kentucky)
Profile: p.950
Litigation Band 4
Table: p.942

**Murphy, Mary** (California)
Real Estate Band 2
Table: p.270

**Murphy, Michael**
(California)
Profile: p.304
Business Process Outsourcing
Band 3
Table: p.2
IT Outsourcing Band 2
Table: p.253

**Murphy, Patrick A**
(California)
Profile: p.304
Bankruptcy Band S
Table: p.222

**Murphy, Patrick J**
(Wyoming)
Litigation Band 2
Table: p.2044

**Murphy, Paul G**
(North Carolina)
Capital Markets Band 4
Table: p.18

**Murphy, Paul J** (Georgia)
Profile: p.720
Litigation Band 3
Table: p.698

**Murphy, Sandra** (West
Virginia)
Corporate/Commercial Band 1
Table: p.2010

**Murphy, Sean M** (New York)
Litigation Band 3
Table: p.1390

**Murphy, Terrence**
(Pennsylvania)
Profile: p.1737
Employment Band 2
Table: p.1703

**Murphy, Thomas P**
(Virginia)
Profile: p.1984
Employment Band 3
Table: p.1971

**Murphy, William** (Maryland)
Litigation Band 2
Table: p.1032

**Murphy Jr, Charles C**
(Georgia)
Antitrust Band 2
Table: p.675

**Murphy Jr, John C**
(National)
Profile: p.122
Financial Services Band 1
Table: p.24

**Murphy, Jr., William**
(Maryland)
Litigation Band 2

Table: p.1032

**Murray, Christopher**
(California)
Profile: p.304
Media & Entertainment Band 2
Table: p.266

**Murray, Craig** (Texas)
Profile: p.1907
Banking & Finance Band 3
Table: p.1832

**Murray, George E**
(Missouri)
Real Estate Band 2
Table: p.1201

**Murray, Gregory S** (Illinois)
Profile: p.847
Banking & Finance Band 1
Table: p.771

**Murray, Gregory V**
(Michigan)
Profile: p.1138
Employment Band 2
Table: p.1125

**Murray, Thomas**
(West Virginia)
Corporate/Commercial Band 2
Table: p.2010

**Murray Jr, William G**
(California)
Profile: p.304
Real Estate Band 3
Table: p.270

**Murtaugh, Christopher D**
(Illinois)
Profile: p.847
Real Estate Band 3
Table: p.809

**Musil, Greg L** (Kansas)
Profile: p.932
Litigation Band 2
Table: p.927

**Musser, William**
(South Carolina)
Corporate/M&A Band 3
Table: p.1775

**Mustone, David Albert**
(Virginia)
Profile: p.1985
Employment Band 2
Table: p.1971

**Mutchnik, James** (Illinois)
Profile: p.847
Antitrust Band 2
Table: p.767

**Muth, Jon R** (Michigan)
Litigation Band 2
Table: p.1128

**Muto, Fred** (California)
Corporate/M&A Band 4
Table: p.227

**Mutryn, William J**
(District of Columbia)
Profile: p.533
Corporate/Commercial Band 3
Table: p.435

**Muzzi, Christopher J**
(Hawaii)
Bankruptcy Band 2
Table: p.739

**Myers, Donald J**
(District of Columbia)
Profile: p.533
Employee Benefits Band 3
Table: p.437

**Myers, John**
(New Mexico)
Real Estate Band 1
Table: p.1327
Real Estate Band 1
Table: p.1327

**Myers, Marlee**
(Pennsylvania)
Profile: p.1737
Corporate/M&A Band 2
Table: p.1700

**Myers, Roger** (California)
Profile: p.304
Media & Entertainment Band 4
Table: p.263

**Myers, William** (Idaho)
Profile: p.764
Natural Resources Band 1
Table: p.761

**Myerson, Toby S**
(New York)
Profile: p.1481
Corporate/M&A Band 4
Table: p.1354

**Mytelka, Craig L** (Virginia)
Intellectual Property Band 2
Table: p.1975

**N**

**Nachbar, Kenneth J**
(Delaware)
Profile: p.409
Chancery Band 2
Table: p.392

**Nachwalter, Michael**
(Florida)
Profile: p.646
Antitrust Band 2
Table: p.581
Litigation Band 1
Table: p.609

**Nadel, Alan S**
(Pennsylvania)
Profile: p.1737
Intellectual Property Band 2
Table: p.1711

**Nadel, Peter F** (New York)
Profile: p.1482
Healthcare Band 1
Table: p.1374

**Naeve, Clifford M**
(District of Columbia)
Profile: p.534
Energy Band 1
Table: p.441
Energy ✪
Table: p.445

**Naftalis, Gary P** (New York)
Profile: p.1482
Litigation Band 2
Table: p.1388
Litigation Band 2
Table: p.1391

**Nagel, Trevor** (National)
Profile: p.123
Business Process Outsourcing
Band 3
Table: p.2

**Nagelberg, Howard**
(Illinois)
Real Estate Band 3
Table: p.809

**Nager, Glen**
(District of Columbia)
Profile: p.534
Litigation Band 1
Table: p.475

**Nagin, Stephen** (Florida)
Antitrust Band 2
Table: p.581

**Nagle, David** (Virginia)
Profile: p.1985
Employment Band 2
Table: p.1971

**Nagle, James W**
(Massachusetts)
Profile: p.1101
Employment Band 2
Table: p.1065

**Nagy, Tibor** (Arizona)
Profile: p.193
Employment Up and coming
Table: p.178

**Nakahata, John T**
(District of Columbia)
Telecom, Broadcast & Satellite
Band 2
Table: p.492

**Nakashima, David A**
(Hawaii)
Profile: p.752
Litigation Band 3
Table: p.745

**Nakashima, Steven M**
(Hawaii)
Profile: p.752
Employment Band 2
Table: p.742

**Nannes, John M**
(District of Columbia)
Profile: p.534
Antitrust Band 3
Table: p.426

**Napolitano, Steven V**
(Illinois)
Corporate/M&A Band 4
Table: p.781
Corporate/M&A: Private Equity
Band 2
Table: p.782

**Narducci, Lucas** (Arizona)
Environment Band 1
Table: p.179

**Nash, David** (Ohio)
Environment Band 2
Table: p.1612

**Nash, Glenn** (California)
IT Outsourcing Band 2
Table: p.253

**Nasi, Michael** (Texas)
Environment Up and coming
Table: p.1852

**Nassau, Henry N**
(Pennsylvania)
Profile: p.1737
Corporate/M&A Band 2
Table: p.1700

**Natale, Andrew** (Ohio)
Construction Band 2
Table: p.1603

**Nathan, Charles** (New York)
Corporate/M&A Band 3
Table: p.1354

**Nathan, Irvin B**
(District of Columbia)
Profile: p.534
Litigation Band 2
Table: p.471

**Nation, Floyd** (Texas)
Intellectual Property Band 3
Table: p.1860

**Natsis, Anton N** (California)
Real Estate Band 2
Table: p.270

**Naugle, Louis**
(Pennsylvania)
Profile: p.1737
Environment Band 3
Table: p.1707

**Naylor, Greg A** (Iowa)
Employment Band 3
Table: p.912

**Naylor, John M** (Nevada)
Litigation Band 1
Table: p.1253

**Neaher Jr, Edward R**
(District of Columbia)
Profile: p.534
Projects Band 2
Table: p.479

**Neal, Austin** (Florida)
Profile: p.646
Insurance Up and coming
Table: p.607

**Neal, James F** (Tennessee)
Litigation Band 2
Table: p.1804

**Neal, Kathy R** (Oklahoma)
Employment Band 1
Table: p.1654

**Neal, Stephen C**
(California)
Intellectual Property Band 4
Table: p.248
Litigation Band 2
Table: p.257

KEY TO RANKINGS: ✪ = STAR INDIVIDUAL   S = SENIOR STATESMAN

**Neckles, Peter J** (New York)
Profile: p.1482
Banking & Finance Band 3
Table: p.1339

**Nedzbala, Michael**
(North Carolina)
Profile: p.1585
Capital Markets Band 4
Table: p.18

**Needell, Benjamin F**
(New York)
Profile: p.1482
Real Estate Band 1
Table: p.1417

**Needle, William** (Georgia)
Intellectual Property Band 1
Table: p.696

**Neel, James M** (Texas)
Profile: p.1907
Employment Band 3
Table: p.1844

**Neely, Sally S** (California)
Profile: p.304
Bankruptcy Band 3
Table: p.222

**Neff, Daniel A** (New York)
Profile: p.1482
Corporate/M&A Band 3
Table: p.1354

**Neighbours, John T**
(Indiana)
Profile: p.898
Employment Band 2
Table: p.889

**Neill, David S** (New York)
Profile: p.1482
Antitrust Band 4
Table: p.1335

**Neligan Jr, Patrick** (Texas)
Bankruptcy Band 2
Table: p.1835

**Nellis, Noel W** (California)
Profile: p.304
Real Estate Band S
Table: p.270

**Nelson, Carol Sue**
(Alabama)
Profile: p.159
Employment Band 3
Table: p.150

**Nelson, Jane** (Washington)
Real Estate Band 3
Table: p.2002

**Nelson, Mark W**
(District of Columbia)
Profile: p.534
Antitrust Up and coming
Table: p.426

**Nelson, Marshall J**
(Washington)
Intellectual Property Band 2
Table: p.1998

**Nelson, Stephen** (Iowa)
Real Estate Band 2

Table: p.917

**Nelson, William F**
(District of Columbia)
Profile: p.534
Tax Band 2
Table: p.488

**Neppl, William** (Iowa)
Real Estate Band 4
Table: p.917

**Nesgos, Peter** (New York)
Technology Band 1
Table: p.1428

**Ness, Andrew D**
(District of Columbia)
Profile: p.534
Construction Band 1
Table: p.433

**Nessim, Ronald J**
(California)
Litigation Band 2
Table: p.258

**Nester, Daniel C** (Missouri)
Real Estate Band 2
Table: p.1201

**Nestor, Michael R**
(Delaware)
Profile: p.409
Bankruptcy Up and coming
Table: p.389

**Nestrud, Charles**
(Arkansas)
Litigation Band 1
Table: p.205

**Nettles, Larry** (Texas)
Profile: p.1907
Environment Band 3
Table: p.1852

**Neugebauer, Robert**
(Washington)
Real Estate Band 3
Table: p.2002

**Neuhaus, Joseph E**
(New York)
Profile: p.123
International Arbitration
Band 2
Table: p.36

**Neumann, Gordon** (Iowa)
Corporate/M&A Band 2
Table: p.909

**Neuner, Robert** (New York)
Profile: p.1483
Intellectual Property Band 3
Table: p.1384

**Neupert, John** (Oregon)
Profile: p.1683
Litigation Band 3
Table: p.1674

**Neustadt, Arthur I**
(Virginia)
Intellectual Property Band 1
Table: p.1975

**Neveloff, Jay A** (New York)
Profile: p.1483

Real Estate Band 3
Table: p.1417

**Neville, Drew** (Oklahoma)
Profile: p.1660
Litigation Band 1
Table: p.1656

**Neville, Frank D** (Wyoming)
Litigation Band 2
Table: p.2044

**Nevins, Patrick**
(District of Columbia)
Profile: p.535
Energy Band 5
Table: p.441

**Newberg, Joseph H**
(Massachusetts)
Profile: p.1101
Tax Band 3
Table: p.1084

**Newbold, J William**
(Missouri)
Profile: p.1209
Litigation Band 3
Table: p.1198

**Newborn, Steven A**
(District of Columbia)
Profile: p.535
Antitrust Band 2
Table: p.426

**Newcom, Charles W**
(Colorado)
Profile: p.364
Employment Band 3
Table: p.348

**Newcombe, George**
(California)
Profile: p.305
Intellectual Property Band 3
Table: p.248

**Newell, Francis Patrick**
(Pennsylvania)
Antitrust Band 3
Table: p.1692

**Newell, Richard F**
(Kentucky)
Profile: p.950
Environment Band S
Table: p.941

**Newell, Robert D** (Oregon)
Litigation Band 2
Table: p.1674

**Newman, Bradford K**
(California)
Profile: p.305
Employment Up and coming
Table: p.231

**Newman, James** (Nevada)
Corporate/Commercial Band 3
Table: p.1246

**Newman, Jeanne**
(California)
Media & Entertainment Band 3
Table: p.266

**Newman, Jeffrey H** (New

Jersey)
Profile: p.1303
Real Estate Band 1
Table: p.1293

**Newman, Karol Lyn**
(District of Columbia)
Profile: p.535
Energy Band 4
Table: p.441

**Newman, Lawrence W**
(New York)
International Arbitration
Band 3
Table: p.36

**Newman, Margery** (Illinois)
Profile: p.847
Construction Band 3
Table: p.778

**Newman, Mark J** (Georgia)
Immigration Band 1
Table: p.694

**Newman, Richard**
(District of Columbia)
Profile: p.535
Real Estate Band 3
Table: p.482

**Newman, Thomas R** (New
York)
Profile: p.1483
Insurance Band 3
Table: p.1379

**Newman Jr, John (Jack)
M** (Ohio)
Profile: p.1635
Litigation Band 1
Table: p.1617

**Newsome, J Kent** (Texas)
Profile: p.1907
Real Estate Band 2
Table: p.1872

**Newton, Robert O** (Maine)
Profile: p.1015
Litigation Band 2
Table: p.1006

**Newton, Trammell**
(Georgia)
Profile: p.720
Antitrust Band 3
Table: p.675

**Nibert, Gregory J**
(New Mexico)
Profile: p.1329
Environment Band 1
Table: p.1323

**Nibley, Stuart B** (National)
Profile: p.123
Government Contracts Band 3
Table: p.30

**Nicely, Matthew R**
(National)
Profile: p.123
International Trade Up and
coming
Table: p.42

**Nicely, Philip** (Indiana)
Real Estate Band 1

Table: p.892

**Nicholas, Thomas**
(Wyoming)
Litigation Band 1
Table: p.2044

**Nicholls III, Malcolm B**
(Massachusetts)
Profile: p.1101
Private Equity Band 3
Table: p.1080

**Nichols, Eric** (Texas)
Litigation Up and coming
Table: p.1865

**Nichols, Phillip** (California)
Real Estate Band 2
Table: p.270

**Nichols, Tracy A** (Florida)
Profile: p.646
Litigation Band 3
Table: p.609

**Nicholson, Penn** (Georgia)
Bankruptcy Band 3
Table: p.679

**Nicholson, Phillip R**
(California)
Real Estate Band S
Table: p.270

**Nickel, Henry**
(District of Columbia)
Profile: p.535
Environment Band 2
Table: p.451

**Nicklin, Emily** (Illinois)
Profile: p.847
Litigation Band 3
Table: p.802

**Niebruegge, Michael E**
(Texas)
Profile: p.1907
Banking & Finance Band 1
Table: p.1832

**Niehans, Daniel** (California)
Employment Band 3
Table: p.232

**Niehoff, Leonard M**
(Michigan)
Profile: p.1138
Employment Band 3
Table: p.1125

**Nields, John W**
(District of Columbia)
Litigation Band 3
Table: p.471

**Nielsen, Jennifer A**
(Illinois)
Construction Up and coming
Table: p.778

**Niemuth, Nathan R**
(Arizona)
Profile: p.193
Employment Band 3
Table: p.178

**Nierman, Todd** (Indiana)
Profile: p.898

N

Employment Band 3
Table: p.889

**Nigon, Kenneth**
(Pennsylvania)
Profile: p.1737
Intellectual Property Band 3
Table: p.1711

**Nijenhuis, Erika W**
(New York)
Profile: p.1483
Tax Band 2
Table: p.1425

**Nijman, Jennifer T** (Illinois)
Profile: p.848
Environment Band 2
Table: p.791

**Nilson, George** (Maryland)
Profile: p.1043
Litigation Band 2
Table: p.1032

**Nims, Barbara** (New York)
Profile: p.1483
Employee Benefits Band 3
Table: p.1362

**Ninneman, Mary Pat**
(Wisconsin)
Profile: p.2034
Employment Band 3
Table: p.2027

**Nirenberg, David Z**
(New York)
Profile: p.1483
Tax Band 1
Table: p.1425

**Niro, Raymond** (Illinois)
Intellectual Property Band 1
Table: p.799

**Nisbet, A Wyckliff**
(Arkansas)
Employment Band 1
Table: p.203

**Nishimoto, John S** (Hawaii)
Litigation Band 3
Table: p.745

**Nix II, Robert** (Michigan)
Real Estate Band 3
Table: p.1130

**Nixon, Larry S** (Virginia)
Intellectual Property Band 1
Table: p.1975

**Nixon, Richard** (Missouri)
Profile: p.1209
Corporate/M&A Band S
Table: p.1193

**Nixon, Sunny**
(New Mexico)
Environment Band 1
Table: p.1323

**Nobil, Steven M** (Ohio)
Employment Band 3
Table: p.1609

**Noble, Ron** (Florida)
Environment Band 3
Table: p.601

**Nocco, Frank** (New York)
Profile: p.123
Capital Markets Band 4
Table: p.18

**Nochimson, David**
(California)
Media & Entertainment Band 3
Table: p.266

**Nodine, Larry** (Georgia)
Intellectual Property Band 2
Table: p.696

**Noe, Elizabeth H** (Georgia)
Profile: p.721
Corporate Up and coming

**Noecker, Kathlyn E**
(Minnesota)
Profile: p.1165
Employment Band 3
Table: p.1154

**Noell, John W** (Illinois)
Profile: p.848
Corporate/M&A: Private Equity
Band 3
Table: p.782

**Nokes, Gregory**
(Connecticut)
Employment Band 3
Table: p.376

**Nolan, Thomas J**
(California)
Profile: p.305
Antitrust Band 3
Table: p.216
Litigation Band 1
Table: p.257

**Nolan, William A** (Ohio)
Profile: p.1635
Employment Band 3
Table: p.1609

**Nondorf, Kurt** (Texas)
Real Estate Band 3
Table: p.1872

**Nonna, John M** (New York)
Profile: p.1483
Insurance Band 1
Table: p.1379

**Noona, Stephen E**
(Virginia)
Intellectual Property Band 1
Table: p.1975

**Noonan, Elizabeth**
(Rhode Island)
Profile: p.1772
Real Estate Band 2
Table: p.1770

**Nordahl, Stephen D**
(New York)
Technology Up and coming
Table: p.1428

**Nordhaus, Robert**
(District of Columbia)
Energy Band 3
Table: p.445

**Noreika, Maryellen**
(Delaware)
Profile: p.409
Intellectual Property Band 3
Table: p.397

**Norman, Mark A** (Ohio)
Profile: p.1635
Environment Band 3
Table: p.1612

**Norman, Stephen C**
(Delaware)
Profile: p.409
Chancery Band 3
Table: p.392

**Norris, Bruce** (Florida)
Construction Band 3
Table: p.590

**Norris, Daniel J**
(New Hampshire)
Profile: p.1273
Corporate/Commercial
Up and coming
Table: p.1263

**Norris, John** (Texas)
Intellectual Property Band 2
Table: p.1860

**Norris, Megan P** (Michigan)
Profile: p.1138
Employment Band 2
Table: p.1125

**Norris, Trenton H**
(California)
Profile: p.305
Environment Up and coming
Table: p.236

**North, John L** (Georgia)
Profile: p.721
Intellectual Property Band 4
Table: p.696

**North, Phillip** (Tennessee)
Litigation Band 1
Table: p.1805

**Northam, Patrick**
(Kentucky)
Corporate/M&A Band 2
Table: p.937
Environment Band 1
Table: p.940
Environment Band 1
Table: p.941

**Northup, Douglas C**
(Arizona)
Profile: p.193
Litigation Band 4
Table: p.181

**Northup, Stephen A**
(Virginia)
Litigation Band 3
Table: p.1977

**Nortman, William** (Florida)
Profile: p.646
Litigation Band 2
Table: p.610

**Norton, William N**
(Louisiana)
Profile: p.984

Corporate/M&A Band 4
Table: p.965

**Norton III, William L**
(Tennessee)
Profile: p.1815
Litigation Band 1
Table: p.1804

**Norton IV, Floyd L**
(District of Columbia)
Profile: p.535
Energy Band 3
Table: p.445

**Norwich, Donald**
(Minnesota)
Real Estate Band 2
Table: p.1160

**Nosewicz, Thomas**
(Louisiana)
Profile: p.984
Environment Band 1
Table: p.970

**Noteboom, Todd**
(Minnesota)
Litigation Band 3
Table: p.1156

**Notkin, Deborah** (New York)
Immigration Band 2
Table: p.1376

**Noto, Margaret Hill**
(Oregon)
Corporate/M&A Band 2
Table: p.1667

**Nourse, David A** (New York)
Transportation Band 2
Table: p.74

**Nouss, James** (Missouri)
Corporate/M&A Band 2
Table: p.1193

**Novacek, Stephen V**
(Nevada)
Real Estate Band 2
Table: p.1255

**Novack, Stephen** (Illinois)
Litigation Band 4
Table: p.802

**Novak, Edward F** (Arizona)
Profile: p.193
Litigation Band 3
Table: p.182

**Novak, Tabor** (Alabama)
Litigation Band 2
Table: p.152

**Novak, Theodore** (Illinois)
Profile: p.848
Real Estate Band 1
Table: p.809

**Novick, Robert T**
(District of Columbia)
Profile: p.124
International Trade Band 2
Table: p.42

**Novikoff, Harold S**
(New York)
Profile: p.1484

Bankruptcy Band 1
Table: p.1344

**Noyes, Christopher**
(Wisconsin)
Corporate/M&A Band 3
Table: p.2025

**Nuechterlein, Jonathan**
(District of Columbia)
Profile: p.535
Telecom, Broadcast & Satellite
Band 3
Table: p.492

**Nuechterlein, Mike**
(Florida)
Profile: p.646
Construction Band 1
Table: p.590

**Nugent, Eileen T**
(New York)
Profile: p.1484
Corporate/M&A Band 4
Table: p.1354

**Null, Amy A**
(Massachusetts)
Profile: p.1101
Employee Benefits Band 2
Table: p.1063

**Nurik, Marc S** (Florida)
Litigation Band 2
Table: p.610

**Nurkin, Sidney J** (Georgia)
Profile: p.721
Corporate/M&A Band 1
Table: p.684

**Nusbaum, Jack H**
(New York)
Profile: p.1484
Corporate/M&A Band S
Table: p.1354

**Nussbaum, Bernard W**
(New York)
Profile: p.1484
Litigation Band 1
Table: p.1388

**Nussbaum, Martin**
(New York)
Profile: p.1484
Corporate/M&A Band 2
Table: p.1359

**Nussdorf, Melanie**
(District of Columbia)
Profile: p.535
Employee Benefits Band 1
Table: p.437

**Nutt, Robert L**
(Massachusetts)
Profile: p.1101
Corporate/M&A Band 2
Table: p.1061

**Nyhan, Christopher D**
(Maine)
Profile: p.1015
Litigation Band 2
Table: p.1006

**Nyhan, Lawrence** (Illinois)
Profile: p.848

Bankruptcy Band 2
Table: p.775

**Nylen Jr, Richard A**
(Massachusetts)
Real Estate Band 1
Table: p.1081

**Page, Michael** (California)
Profile: p.306
Intellectual Property Band 3
Table: p.248

**Page, Rosewell** (Virginia)
Litigation Band 2
Table: p.1977

**Page, Thomas** (Oregon)
Real Estate Band 1
Table: p.1677

**Pagel, Martha O** (Oregon)
Environment Band 2
Table: p.1672

**Pagel Serebransky,
Elizabeth** (New York)
Employee Benefits Band 3
Table: p.1362

**Paget, David** (New York)
Profile: p.1486
Environment Band 2
Table: p.1371

**Paget, Joel** (Washington)
Immigration Band 1
Table: p.1997

**Painter, Robin A**
(Massachusetts)
Profile: p.1101
Private Equity Band 1
Table: p.1080

**Painter, William S**
(Mississippi)
Profile: p.1186
Corporate/Commercial Band 2
Table: p.1174

**Paisley, Bonnie**
(New Mexico)
Profile: p.1329
Corporate/Commercial Band 2
Table: p.1320

**Pakenham, Kathleen M**
(National)
Profile: p.124
Tax Litigaion Up & Coming

**Pakenham, Timothy J**
(Georgia)
Profile: p.721
Real Estate Band 2
Table: p.700

**Palenchar, James**
(Colorado)
Corporate/M&A Band 1
Table: p.346

**Paley, Alan** (New York)
Capital Markets Band 4
Table: p.7
Corporate/M&A Band 4
Table: p.1354

**Palma, Laura** (New York)
Profile: p.124
Capital Markets Band 2
Table: p.18

**Palmer, Crisman**
(South Dakota)
Litigation Band 2
Table: p.1795

**Palmer, Scott** (Florida)
Antitrust Band 2
Table: p.581

**Palmer, Thomas** (Oregon)
Profile: p.1683
Corporate/M&A Band 3
Table: p.1667

**Paltell, Eric** (Maryland)
Employment Band 2
Table: p.1028

**Palumbo, Ralph H**
(Washington)
Environment Band 1
Table: p.1996
Litigation Band 2
Table: p.2000

**Panagakis, George N**
(Illinois)
Profile: p.849
Bankruptcy Band 3
Table: p.775

**Panitch, Ronald L**
(Pennsylvania)
Profile: p.1738
Intellectual Property Band 1
Table: p.1711

**Pannone, Gary R**
(Rhode Island)
Corporate/Commercial Band 2
Table: p.1766

**Panoff, Robert** (Florida)
Tax Band 2
Table: p.623

**Panovka, Robin** (New York)
Profile: p.1486
Real Estate Band 4
Table: p.1417

**Pantaleo, Peter** (New York)
Profile: p.1486
Bankruptcy Band 1
Table: p.1344

**Pantano, Paul**
(District of Columbia)
Profile: p.537
Energy Band 5
Table: p.445

**Pantel, Glenn S** (New
Jersey)
Real Estate Band 1
Table: p.1293

**Papa, Ronald** (New York)
Profile: p.1486
Corporate/M&A Band 2
Table: p.1359

**Paparelli, Angelo**
(California)
Immigration Band 1
Table: p.241

**Papavizas, Constantine G**
(District of Columbia)
Profile: p.124
Transportation Band 1
Table: p.78

**Papel, Laurence M**
(Tennessee)
Profile: p.1816
Real Estate Band 3
Table: p.1808

**Pappas, Edward H**
(Michigan)
Profile: p.1138
Litigation Band 3
Table: p.1128

**Pappas, George F**
(District of Columbia)
Profile: p.537
Intellectual Property Band 2
Table: p.466

**Pappas, Lynn** (Florida)
Real Estate Band 1
Table: p.621

**Pappone, Michael J**
(Massachusetts)
Profile: p.1101
Bankruptcy Band 1
Table: p.1058

**Paradee, John W**
(Delaware)
Real Estate Band 2
Table: p.400

**Pardo Jr, James** (Georgia)
Profile: p.721
Bankruptcy Band 1
Table: p.679

**Paré, Jay** (New York)
Transportation Band 3
Table: p.74

**Pari, Joseph**
(District of Columbia)
Profile: p.537
Tax Band 2
Table: p.488

**Paris, Theodore W** (Texas)
Profile: p.1908
Corporate/M&A Band 4
Table: p.1840

**Paris, Zachary** (Ohio)
Profile: p.1635
Real Estate Band 2
Table: p.1621

**Parise, Michael J** (Alaska)
Bankruptcy Band 1
Table: p.167

**Park, William W**
(Massachusetts)
Profile: p.124
Arbitration Band 1
Table: p.37

**Parker, C Allen** (New York)
Profile: p.1486
Banking & Finance Band 1
Table: p.1339

**Parker, Dallas** (Texas)
Profile: p.1908
Technology Band 2
Table: p.1878

**Parker, David** (Texas)
Profile: p.1908

**Parker, Douglas S** (Alaska)
Employment Band 1
Table: p.169

**Parker, Emily A** (Texas)
Profile: p.1908
Tax Band 2
Table: p.1875

**Parker, Gilbert E** (Oregon)
Profile: p.1683
Real Estate Band 2
Table: p.1677

**Parker, James**
(New Mexico)
Corporate/Commercial Band 2
Table: p.1320
Employment Band 1
Table: p.1322

**Parker, John** (Georgia)
Healthcare Band 1
Table: p.693

**Parker, Richard G**
(District of Columbia)
Profile: p.537
Antitrust Band 2
Table: p.426

**Parkhurst, Janet**
(New York)
Technology Associate to
watch
Table: p.1428

**Parks, John R** (Georgia)
Real Estate Band 3
Table: p.700

**Parks, Randall S** (National)
Profile: p.125
Business Process Outsourcing
Band 4
Table: p.2

**Parks, Timothy M** (Oregon)
Real Estate Band 3
Table: p.1677

**Parliman, Gregory C**
(New Jersey)
Profile: p.1303
Employment Band 2
Table: p.1282

**Parmley, Bruce**
(District of Columbia)
Profile: p.537
Real Estate Band 2
Table: p.482

**Parobek, Drew** (Ohio)
Profile: p.1635
Bankruptcy Band 3
Table: p.1600

**Parr, Henry L**
(South Carolina)
Profile: p.1784
Litigation Band 3
Table: p.1778

**Parrino, Richard** (Virginia)
Profile: p.1985
Corporate/M&A Band 2

Intellectual Property Band 3
Table: p.1860

**Parrish, Theresa**
(New Mexico)
Employment Band 3
Table: p.1321

**Parsigian, David N**
(Michigan)
Profile: p.1138
Corporate/M&A Band 3
Table: p.1122

**Parsigian, Kenneth J**
(Massachusetts)
Profile: p.1101
Litigation Band 3
Table: p.1074

**Parsonage, Ronald K**
(Nebraska)
Corporate/M&A Band 3
Table: p.1236

**Parsons, Chuck**
(Minnesota)
Real Estate Band 3
Table: p.1160

**Parsons, David** (Illinois)
Profile: p.849
Employment Band 2
Table: p.785

**Parsons, Paul** (Texas)
Immigration Band 1
Table: p.1856

**Parsons, Philip S** (Florida)
Environment Band 1
Table: p.601

**Parsons, W Stuart**
(Wisconsin)
Profile: p.2034
Litigation Band S
Table: p.2029

**Partridge, John J**
(Rhode Island)
Corporate/Commercial Band 2
Table: p.1766

**Partridge, Scott** (Texas)
Profile: p.1909
Intellectual Property Band 1
Table: p.1860

**Parvis, Peter P** (Maryland)
Healthcare Band 3
Table: p.1031

**Parzen, Stanley J** (Illinois)
Profile: p.849
Litigation Band 4
Table: p.802

**Pasahow, Lynn H**
(California)
Profile: p.306
Intellectual Property Band 2
Table: p.248

**Pasano, Michael S**
(Florida)
Litigation Band 1
Table: p.610

P

P

**Pharris, Charles A**
(New Mexico)
Litigation Band 2
Table: p.1324

**Phelan, Jeanne** (Maryland)
Profile: p.1043
Employment Band 2
Table: p.1028

**Phelan, Robin** (Texas)
Bankruptcy Band 1
Table: p.1835

**Phelan, Rod** (Texas)
Profile: p.1910
Litigation Band 2
Table: p.1865

**Phibbs, Henry** (Wyoming)
Real Estate Band 2
Table: p.2045

**Philips, Harry** (Louisiana)
Litigation Band 3
Table: p.973

**Phillips, Bradley S**
(California)
Antitrust Band 2
Table: p.216

**Phillips, Carter**
(District of Columbia)
Profile: p.538
Litigation Band 1
Table: p.475

**Phillips, Edward G**
(Tennessee)
Profile: p.1816
Employment Band 2
Table: p.1801

**Phillips, Greer L** (New York)
Profile: p.1487
Tax Band 3
Table: p.1423

**Phillips, James E** (Ohio)
Profile: p.1636
Litigation Band 3
Table: p.1618

**Phillips, Jim W**
(North Carolina)
Litigation Band 2
Table: p.1577

**Phillips, John R** (Missouri)
Profile: p.1209
Employment Band 1
Table: p.1195

**Phillips, Lee** (California)
Media & Entertainment Band 2
Table: p.266

**Phillips, Paul D** (Colorado)
Profile: p.364
Environment Band 1
Table: p.350

**Phillips, Penny** (Minnesota)
Employment Band 3
Table: p.1154

**Phillips, Stephen** (Georgia)
Construction Band 2
Table: p.682

**Phillips, Thomas R** (Texas)
Profile: p.1910
Litigation Band 3
Table: p.1866

**Phillips, William M** (Ohio)
Profile: p.1636
Real Estate Band 3
Table: p.1621

**Phillips IV, Barnet** (New York)
Profile: p.1488
Tax Band 3
Table: p.1423

**Phillips Jr, John B**
(Tennessee)
Profile: p.1816
Employment Band 2
Table: p.1801

**Philp, Mary Susan**
(District of Columbia)
Profile: p.538
Healthcare Band 2
Table: p.456

**Philpot, Susan C**
(California)
Tax Band 2
Table: p.274

**Phipps, David** (Iowa)
Litigation Band 1
Table: p.914

**Piccarreta, Michael L**
(Arizona)
Litigation Band 2
Table: p.182

**Picco, Steven J**
(New Jersey)
Profile: p.1304
Environment Band 3
Table: p.1285

**Pickens, Scott E** (Illinois)
Profile: p.850
Banking & Finance Band 3
Table: p.771

**Pickert, Stephen W**
(Florida)
Profile: p.647
Construction Band 2
Table: p.590

**Pickett, Andrew**
(Massachusetts)
Profile: p.1102
Employment Band 3
Table: p.1065

**Pickett, Donn P** (California)
Profile: p.307
Antitrust Band 2
Table: p.216

**Pidgeon, Steven** (Arizona)
Profile: p.194
Corporate/M&A Band 2
Table: p.176

**Piels, William** (California)
Profile: p.125
Transportation Band 2
Table: p.64

**Pierce, John V H** (New York)
Profile: p.125
International Arbitration Up and coming
Table: p.36

**Pierce, Kenneth J**
(District of Columbia)
Profile: p.125
International Trade Band 4
Table: p.42

**Pierce, Kenneth R**
(New York)
Profile: p.1488
Insurance Band 3
Table: p.1379

**Pierce, Morton A**
(New York)
Profile: p.1488
Corporate/M&A Band 2
Table: p.1354

**Pierce, Robert** (Florida)
Tax Band 3
Table: p.623

**Pierce, Rudolph**
(Massachusetts)
Litigation Band 2
Table: p.1074

**Pietrantonio, Frank**
(Virginia)
Intellectual Property Band 2
Table: p.1975

**Pietropaoli, Paul D**
(Maine)
Real Estate Band 3
Table: p.1008

**Pietrzak, Robert**
(New York)
Profile: p.1488
Litigation Band 3
Table: p.1390

**Piggott, Cameron**
(Michigan)
Real Estate Band 3
Table: p.1130

**Pigman, Jack R** (Ohio)
Profile: p.1636
Bankruptcy Band 3
Table: p.1600

**Pignatelli, Michael A**
(New Hampshire)
Litigation Band 1
Table: p.1268

**Pigsley, Jerry L** (Nebraska)
Employment Band 3
Table: p.1238

**Pilie, Glen** (Louisiana)
Profile: p.984
Environment Band 1
Table: p.970

**Pill, Richard** (West Virginia)
Real Estate Band 3
Table: p.2015

**Pillans III, Charles P**
(Florida)
Litigation Band 3
Table: p.609

**Pillion, Michael L**
(National)
Profile: p.125
Business Process Outsourcing Band 4
Table: p.2

**Pimstone, Gregory N**
(California)
Healthcare Band 3
Table: p.238

**Pincus, Andrew J**
(District of Columbia)
Profile: p.538
Litigation Band 2
Table: p.475

**Pincus, Robert B**
(Delaware)
Profile: p.410
Corporate/M&A Band 3
Table: p.394

**Pinedo, Anna** (National)
Profile: p.126
Capital Markets Band 3
Table: p.15

**Pinheiro, Brian M**
(Pennsylvania)
Profile: p.1738
Employment Band 2
Table: p.1704

**Pinkerton, Glenn** (Texas)
Profile: p.1910
Projects Band 3
Table: p.1869

**Pinney Jr, Willard F**
(Connecticut)
Corporate/M&A Band 2
Table: p.374

**Pinover, Eugene** (New York)
Profile: p.1488
Real Estate Band 2
Table: p.1417

**Piper, Alika** (Hawaii)
Bankruptcy Up and coming
Table: p.739

**Piper, Jeffrey Scott**
(Hawaii)
Corporate/Commercial Band 2
Table: p.741

**Piper, Jonathan S** (Maine)
Profile: p.1015
Litigation Band 2
Table: p.1006

**Pircher, Leo** (California)
Real Estate Band S
Table: p.270

**Pirkey, Louis** (Texas)
Profile: p.1910
Intellectual Property Band 1
Table: p.1860

**Pisa, Regina M**
(Massachusetts)
Profile: p.1102
Banking & Finance Band 2
Table: p.1055

**Pisanelli, James** (Nevada)
Litigation Band 2
Table: p.1252

**Pisano, Vincent** (National)
Profile: p.126
Capital Markets Band 3
Table: p.7

**Piscitelli, Michael A**
(Florida)
Construction Band 2
Table: p.590

**Pishny, Lyle D** (Kansas)
Profile: p.932
Corporate/M&A Band 2
Table: p.924

**Piskorski, Thomas** (Illinois)
Employment Band 2
Table: p.785

**Pitcairn Jr, Robert** (Ohio)
Litigation Band 3
Table: p.1617

**Pitt, M Stephen** (Kentucky)
Litigation Band 3
Table: p.942

**Pittler, Alan M**
(Pennsylvania)
Profile: p.1738
Employment Up and coming
Table: p.1703

**Pittman, Alisa** (Georgia)
Employment Band 4
Table: p.687

**Pitts, Andrew J** (National)
Profile: p.126
Capital Markets
Up and coming
Table: p.7

**Pitts, Deborah A**
(California)
Profile: p.307
Insurance Band 3
Table: p.243

**Placenti, Frank** (Arizona)
Corporate/M&A Band 3
Table: p.176

**Plaine, Daniel**
(District of Columbia)
Profile: p.126
International Trade Band 4
Table: p.42

**Plaine, Lloyd Leva**
(National)
Profile: p.126
Wealth Management Band 2
Table: p.81

**Plambeck, Stephen**
(North Dakota)
Litigation Band 2
Table: p.1593

**Plank, Don** (Ohio)
Real Estate Band 2
Table: p.1622

**Planning, Anne K**
(District of Columbia)
Profile: p.539
Real Estate Band 4
Table: p.482

**Plant, David W** (National)
Arbitration Band 1
Table: p.37

**Platt, Charles C** (New York)
Profile: p.1488
Litigation Band 3
Table: p.1388

**Platt, Warren** (Arizona)
Profile: p.194
Litigation Up and coming
Table: p.181
Products Liability Band 3
Table: p.50

**Plaut, Christopher R** (New York)
Banking & Finance Band 4
Table: p.1339

**Plevan, Bettina** (New York)
Profile: p.1488
Employment Band 1
Table: p.1365

**Plevan, Kenneth A** (New York)
Profile: p.1489
Media & Entertainment Band 1
Table: p.1400

**Plevin, Mark**
(District of Columbia)
Profile: p.539
Bankruptcy Band 3
Table: p.432
Insurance Band 4
Table: p.461

**Plonsker, Michael**
(California)
Profile: p.307
Media & Entertainment Band 4
Table: p.263

**Ploor, Pamela M**
(Wisconsin)
Profile: p.2034
Employment Band 3
Table: p.2027

**Plotkin, Mark E** (National)
Profile: p.126
Financial Services Band 3
Table: p.28

**Plum, Bernard** (New York)
Profile: p.1489
Employment Band 3
Table: p.1365

**Plumb, Charles** (Oklahoma)
Employment Band 1
Table: p.1654

**Plumer, Mark J**
(District of Columbia)
Profile: p.539
Insurance Band 3

**Plumridge, Richard**
(Colorado)
Corporate/M&A Band 3
Table: p.346

**Plybon, Christopher** (West Virginia)
Real Estate Band 2
Table: p.2015

**Podhurst, Aaron S** (Florida)
Profile: p.647
Litigation Band 1
Table: p.609

**Poelman, Ronald** (Utah)
Corporate/M&A Band 2
Table: p.1941

**Poff, Joe** (Texas)
Profile: p.1910
Corporate/M&A Band 3
Table: p.1840

**Poff, William** (Virginia)
Litigation Band S

**Pogue, Mark** (Rhode Island)
Profile: p.1773
Employment Band 2
Table: p.1768
Litigation Band 2
Table: p.1769

**Pohl, Timothy R** (Illinois)
Profile: p.850
Bankruptcy Band 2
Table: p.775

**Pohlen, Patrick A**
(National)
Capital Markets Band 2
Table: p.8

**Pokempner, Joseph**
(Maryland)
Profile: p.1043
Employment Band 3
Table: p.1028

**Pokorski, Jody** (Arizona)
Profile: p.194
Real Estate Band 1
Table: p.184

**Pokotilow, Manny D**
(Pennsylvania)
Profile: p.1738
Intellectual Property Band 1
Table: p.1711

**Polebaum, Elliot E**
(District of Columbia)
Profile: p.126
International Arbitration Band 4
Table: p.36

**Polevoy, Martin D** (New York)
Profile: p.1489
Real Estate Band 5
Table: p.1417

**Poliakoff, Abba** (Maryland)
Corporate/M&A Band 3
Table: p.1025

**Policastro, Marc D** (New Jersey)
Profile: p.1304
Real Estate Band 2
Table: p.1293

**Polkes, Jonathan** (New York)
Profile: p.1489
Litigation Band 3
Table: p.1388

**Pollack, Martin** (New York)
Profile: p.1489
Tax Band 3
Table: p.1423

**Pollak, Mark** (Maryland)
Profile: p.1043
Real Estate Band 1
Table: p.1035

**Polon, Ira H**
(District of Columbia)
Profile: p.539
Corporate/Commercial Band 3
Table: p.435

**Polsinelli, James A**
(Missouri)
Profile: p.1209
Corporate/M&A Band 3
Table: p.1193

**Pomerantz, Glenn D**
(California)
Antitrust Band 3
Table: p.216
Media & Entertainment Band 3
Table: p.263

**Pomerantz, Harold B**
(Illinois)
Profile: p.850
Real Estate Band 4
Table: p.809

**Pomerantz, Mark F**
(New York)
Profile: p.1489
Litigation Band 1
Table: p.1391

**Pomeroy, Chris** (Virginia)
Environment Band 2
Table: p.1973

**Ponader, Erick** (Indiana)
Profile: p.899
Real Estate Band 3
Table: p.892

**Ponda, Ameek Ashok**
(Massachusetts)
Tax Up and coming
Table: p.1084

**Pongrace, Donald R**
(National)
Profile: p.126
Native Law Band 1
Table: p.47

**Ponikvar, Dale L** (New York)
Tax Band 4
Table: p.1423

**Ponsetto, John** (Vermont)
Real Estate Band 2
Table: p.1961

**Pontone, Kathleen**
(Maryland)
Profile: p.1043
Employment Band 1
Table: p.1028

**Pooley, James** (California)
Profile: p.308
Intellectual Property Band 3
Table: p.248

**Poonja, Zaitun** (California)
Profile: p.308
Employment Band 3
Table: p.232

**Pope, David** (Georgia)
Environment Band 3
Table: p.691

**Pope, Michael** (Illinois)
Profile: p.850
Litigation Band 4
Table: p.802
Products Liability Band 3
Table: p.50

**Pope, Nicholas A** (Florida)
Real Estate Band 2
Table: p.617

**Popeo, R Robert**
(Massachusetts)
Profile: p.1102
Litigation Band S
Table: p.1074

**Popofsky, Laurence**
(California)
Profile: p.308
Antitrust Band S
Table: p.216
Litigation Band S
Table: p.257

**Popofsky, Mark**
(District of Columbia)
Profile: p.539
Antitrust Up and coming
Table: p.426

**Porcelli, Frank P**
(Massachusetts)
Profile: p.1102
Intellectual Property Band 1
Table: p.1072

**Porges, Amelia** (National)
Profile: p.126
International Trade Band 5
Table: p.42

**Porrino, Christopher** (New Jersey)
Profile: p.1304

**Port, Alan D** (Vermont)
Corporate/Commercial Band 2
Table: p.1957

**Port, Gail** (New York)
Profile: p.1489
Environment Band 2
Table: p.1373

**Porter, Amy** (Arizona)
Environment Band 1
Table: p.179

**Porter, Daniel L** (National)
Profile: p.126
International Trade Band 5
Table: p.42

**Porter, David** (Ohio)
Profile: p.1636
Corporate/M&A Band 2
Table: p.1605

**Porter, Jeffrey R**
(Massachusetts)
Profile: p.1102
Environment Band 2
Table: p.1068

**Porter, Philip** (Virginia)
Profile: p.1985
Business Process Outsourcing Band 4
Table: p.2
Intellectual Property Band 2
Table: p.1975

**Porter, R Clay** (National)
Transportation Band 2
Table: p.71

**Porter, Stephen**
(District of Columbia)
Profile: p.539
Real Estate Band 3
Table: p.482

**Porterfield, Curtis D**
(California)
Insurance Band 3
Table: p.245

**Portnoy, Jeffrey** (Hawaii)
Litigation Band 1
Table: p.745

**Portnoy, Lawrence**
(New York)
Profile: p.1489
Litigation Band 3
Table: p.1390

**Pose, Christopher** (Iowa)
Real Estate Band 2
Table: p.917

**Posen, Richard** (New York)
Profile: p.1489
Litigation Band 3
Table: p.1390

**Positan, Wayne J**
(New Jersey)
Profile: p.1304
Employment Band 1
Table: p.1282

**Poss, Stephen D**
(Massachusetts)
Profile: p.1103
Litigation Band 3
Table: p.1074
Litigation Band 1
Table: p.1075

**Poster, Robert L**
(New York)
Profile: p.127
Transportation Band 2
Table: p.74

**P**

**P**

KEY TO RANKINGS: ✪ = STAR INDIVIDUAL   S = SENIOR STATESMAN

Table: p.24

**Pulley III, J Waverly**
(Virginia)
Profile: p.1985
Real Estate Band 2
Table: p.1978
Transportation Band 1
Table: p.71

**Pultman, Jacob** (New York)
Profile: p.1490
Litigation Band 3
Table: p.1388

**Purdy, William R**
(Mississippi)
Litigation Band 2
Table: p.1179

**Puretz, Jeffrey S**
(District of Columbia)
Profile: p.539
Investment Management Band 2
Table: p.469

**Pursley, Kenneth** (Idaho)
Real Estate Band 2
Table: p.762

**Putman, Frank** (Texas)
Profile: p.1910
Technology Band 2
Table: p.1878

**Putziger, Myrna**
(Massachusetts)
Real Estate Band 1
Table: p.1081

**Pyburn Jr, Keith M**
(Louisiana)
Profile: p.985
Employment Band 2
Table: p.967

**Qasim, Imad** (Illinois)
Profile: p.850
Corporate/M&A Band 3
Table: p.781

**Quail, Beverly J** (Colorado)
Profile: p.364
Real Estate Band 2
Table: p.355

**Quale, John C**
(District of Columbia)
Profile: p.540
Telecom, Broadcast & Satellite
Band 3
Table: p.492

**Quan, Gordon J** (Texas)
Immigration Band 2
Table: p.1856

**Quander, Don** (Montana)
Profile: p.1232
Natural Resources Band 1
Table: p.1228

**Quarles, John**
(District of Columbia)
Profile: p.540

Environment Band S
Table: p.451

**Quattlebaum, Marvin**
(South Carolina)
Real Estate Band 3
Table: p.1780

**Quattlebaum, Steven**
(Arkansas)
Profile: p.210
Litigation Band 1
Table: p.205

**Quesenberry, Kathryn A**
(Kentucky)
Employment Band 3
Table: p.939

**Quick, Patrick G**
(Wisconsin)
Profile: p.2035
Corporate/M&A
Up and coming
Table: p.2025

**Quin, Whayne**
(District of Columbia)
Profile: p.540
Real Estate Band 1
Table: p.482

**Quinn, James W** (New York)
Profile: p.1490
Litigation Band 3
Table: p.1388
Sport Band 2
Table: p.59

**Quinn, John** (California)
Profile: p.309
Litigation Band S
Table: p.257

**Quinn, John B** (California)
Profile: p.309
Intellectual Property Band 2
Table: p.248
Litigation Band 2
Table: p.257
Media & Entertainment Band 3
Table: p.263

**Quinn, Kenneth P**
(National)
Profile: p.127
Transportation Band 1
Table: p.67

**Quinn, Patrick T** (National)
Profile: p.128
Capital Markets
Up and coming
Table: p.18

**Quinn, Yvonne S** (New
York)
Profile: p.1490
Antitrust Band 4
Table: p.1335

**Quiñon, Jose** (Florida)
Litigation Band 2
Table: p.610

**Quint, Arnold**
(District of Columbia)
Profile: p.540
Energy Band 4
Table: p.445

**Raab, David S** (New York)
Tax Band 4
Table: p.1423

**Raattama, Henry** (Florida)
Profile: p.648
Tax Band 2
Table: p.623

**Rabalais, Robert René**
(Texas)
Profile: p.1911

**Rabinovitz, Bruce H**
(National)
Profile: p.128
Transportation Band 3
Table: p.67

**Rabinovitz, Joel** (California)
Tax Band 2
Table: p.274

**Rabinowitz, David J**
(New York)
Profile: p.1304
Real Estate Band 2
Table: p.1293

**Rabinowitz, Mark I**
(Pennsylvania)
Profile: p.1738
Banking & Finance Band 3
Table: p.1695

**Rabinowitz, Stephen S**
(New York)
Profile: p.1490
Intellectual Property Band 4
Table: p.1384

**Rachlin, Robert** (Vermont)
Litigation Band S
Table: p.1959

**Racioppi Jr, Nicholas**
(New Jersey)
Profile: p.1304
Real Estate Band 3
Table: p.1293

**Raciti-Knapp, Melissa**
(New York)
Projects Band 4
Table: p.1413

**Rackow, Julian**
(Pennsylvania)
Profile: p.1739
Real Estate Band 2
Table: p.1718

**Radcliffe, Mark F**
(California)
Profile: p.309
IT Outsourcing Band 1
Table: p.253

**Rademaker, Randall J**
(Illinois)
Profile: p.851
Banking & Finance Band 3
Table: p.771

**Rader, Kermit L**
(Pennsylvania)
Profile: p.1739
Environment Band 2

Table: p.1707

**Radke, Kirk** (New York)
Profile: p.1490
Private Equity Band 1
Table: p.1407
Private Equity Band 4
Table: p.1410

**Radler, Barbara** (Oregon)
Real Estate Band 1
Table: p.1677

**Radovich, Scott D** (Hawaii)
Profile: p.753
Real Estate Band 2
Table: p.748

**Radzely, Edward S**
(New Jersey)
Real Estate Band 2
Table: p.1293

**Radzik, Edward C**
(National)
Transportation Band 4
Table: p.74

**Rae, Mark N** (National)
Capital Markets Band 3
Table: p.13

**Raff, Joshua E** (New York)
Profile: p.128
Capital Markets Band 1
Table: p.13

**Rafferty, Thomas G**
(New York)
Intellectual Property Band 3
Table: p.1384

**Raforth, John H**
(South Dakota)
Corporate/Commercial Band 3
Table: p.1792

**Rafte, Alan** (Texas)
Profile: p.1911
Energy Band 4
Table: p.1847
Projects Band 4
Table: p.1869

**Rafuse, Nancy** (Georgia)
Profile: p.722
Employment Band 3
Table: p.687

**Ragalevsky, Stanley V**
(Massachusetts)
Banking & Finance Band 3
Table: p.1055

**Ragland Jr, William M**
(Georgia)
Profile: p.722
Intellectual Property Band 3
Table: p.696

**Ragonetti, Thomas J**
(Colorado)
Profile: p.364
Real Estate Band 1
Table: p.355
Real Estate Band 1
Table: p.355

**Raher, Patrick M**
(District of Columbia)
Profile: p.540
Environment Band 3
Table: p.451
Transportation Band 2
Table: p.71

**Raim, David**
(District of Columbia)
Profile: p.540
Insurance Band 3
Table: p.461

**Rain, John W** (Texas)
Profile: p.1911
Banking & Finance Band 4
Table: p.1832

**Rainey, Richard L**
(North Carolina)
Profile: p.1585
Employment Band 2
Table: p.1573

**Raisch, Jerry W** (Colorado)
Environment Band 2
Table: p.350

**Raish, David L**
(Massachusetts)
Profile: p.1103
Employee Benefits Band 2
Table: p.1063

**Raisler, Kenneth M**
(New York)
Profile: p.128
Capital Markets Band 1
Table: p.15

**Rakusin, Steve** (Florida)
Construction Band 2
Table: p.590

**Ramer, Bruce** (California)
Media & Entertainment Band 1
Table: p.266

**Ramirez, Kenneth R**
(Texas)
Environment Band 2
Table: p.1852

**Ramis, Timothy V** (Oregon)
Real Estate Band 1
Table: p.1677

**Ramos, Carey R** (New York)
Profile: p.1490
Media & Entertainment Band 3
Table: p.1404

**Rance, Brian** (National)
Capital Markets Band 2
Table: p.13

**Rand, Richard M** (Hawaii)
Employment Band 2
Table: p.742

**Randall, Benjamin J**
(Illinois)
Real Estate Band 2
Table: p.809

**Randall, Jeff G** (California)
Profile: p.309
Intellectual Property Band 4
Table: p.248

**R**

R

**Randall, Ryan**
(New Mexico)
Employment Band 3
Table: p.1321

**Rang, Kevin A** (National)
Profile: p.128
Business Process Outsourcing
Up and coming
Table: p.2

**Raper, William C**
(North Carolina)
Profile: p.1585
Litigation Band 3
Table: p.1577

**Raphael, Bruce W**
(Massachusetts)
Profile: p.1103
Banking & Finance Band 3
Table: p.1055

**Raphael, Stuart A**
(Virginia)
Profile: p.1985
Litigation Band 3

**Raphan, Melissa**
(Minnesota)
Profile: p.1166
Employment Band 2
Table: p.1154

**Rapisardi, John** (New York)
Profile: p.1490
Bankruptcy Band 4
Table: p.1344

**Rappaport, Linda E**
(New York)
Profile: p.1491
Employee Benefits Band 1
Table: p.1362

**Rasile, Craig** (Florida)
Profile: p.648
Bankruptcy Band 2
Table: p.586

**Raskin, David**
(District of Columbia)
Profile: p.540
Energy Band 2
Table: p.445

**Raskin, Jane** (Florida)
Litigation Band 1
Table: p.610

**Raskin, Kenneth A**
(New York)
Profile: p.1491
Employee Benefits Band 3
Table: p.1362

**Raskin, Martin R** (Florida)
Litigation Band 1
Table: p.610

**Raskopf, Robert** (New York)
Profile: p.1491
Media & Entertainment Band 3
Table: p.1404

**Rasmussen, Reed**
(South Dakota)
Litigation Band 2
Table: p.1795

**Rasmussen, Robert**
(Florida)
Corporate/M&A Band 2
Table: p.594

**Rassel, Richard E**
(Michigan)
Profile: p.1138
Litigation Band 2
Table: p.1128

**Rath, Thomas D**
(New Hampshire)
Corporate/Commercial Band 1
Table: p.1264

**Rather Jr, Gordon S**
(Arkansas)
Profile: p.210
Litigation Band 1
Table: p.205

**Ratliff, Reeder E**
(Oklahoma)
Profile: p.1660
Corporate/Commercial Band 2

**Ratner, Randall M** (Texas)
Profile: p.1911
Real Estate Band 3
Table: p.1872

**Rattigan, John**
(Massachusetts)
Profile: p.1103
Real Estate Band 2
Table: p.1081

**Rauch, David** (Arizona)
Profile: p.194
Litigation Band 4
Table: p.181

**Rauh, Carl S**
(District of Columbia)
Profile: p.540
Litigation Band 2
Table: p.471

**Ravich, Paul** (Minnesota)
Real Estate Band 3

**Ravikoff, Ronald B**
(Florida)
Antitrust Band 3
Table: p.581
Litigation Band 4
Table: p.609

**Rawlinson, Dennis P**
(Oregon)
Profile: p.1683
Litigation Band 2
Table: p.1674

**Rawson, Rachel** (Ohio)
Profile: p.1636
Banking & Finance Band 1
Table: p.1598

**Ray, Ellen** (National)
Profile: p.128
Business Process Outsourcing
Band 3
Table: p.2

**Ray, Hugh M** (Texas)
Bankruptcy Band 2
Table: p.1835

**Ray, Stephen E** (Illinois)
Construction Band 3
Table: p.778

**Ray, Steven** (Virginia)
Employment Band 3
Table: p.1971

**Raymond, James F**
(New Hampshire)
Real Estate Band 3
Table: p.1270

**Raymond, Robert J**
(New York)
Employee Benefits Band 3
Table: p.1362

**Raymond III, F Douglas**
(Pennsylvania)
Corporate/M&A Band 2
Table: p.1700

**Raysman, Richard**
(New York)
Profile: p.1491
Business Process Outsourcing
Band 3
Table: p.2
Technology Band 3
Table: p.1428

**Re, Donald** (California)
Litigation Band 3
Table: p.258

**Read, Sarah** (Illinois)
Profile: p.851
Energy Band S
Table: p.789

**Reade, Claire E**
(District of Columbia)
Profile: p.128
International Trade Band 3
Table: p.42

**Reamer, David C**
(California)
Profile: p.309
Banking & Finance Band 3
Table: p.218

**Reames, Wayne E** (Iowa)
Corporate/M&A
Up and coming
Table: p.909

**Reardon, Marc A**
(Massachusetts)
Profile: p.1491
Projects Band 4
Table: p.1413

**Reardon, Roy** (New York)
Profile: p.1491
Litigation Band S
Table: p.1388
Products Liability Band S
Table: p.50

**Reaser, Dan R** (Nevada)
Gaming & Licensing Band 2
Table: p.1251

**Reasoner, Barrett** (Texas)
Profile: p.1911
Litigation Up & Coming

**Reasoner, Carroll J** (Iowa)
Corporate/M&A Band 2
Table: p.909

**Reasoner, Harry** (Texas)
Profile: p.1911
Antitrust Band 2
Table: p.1829
Energy Band 1
Table: p.1849
Litigation Band 1
Table: p.1865

**Rebein, David** (Kansas)
Profile: p.932
Litigation Band 1
Table: p.927

**Rebein, Joseph** (Missouri)
Profile: p.1209
Litigation Band 3
Table: p.1198

**Reber, David J** (Hawaii)
Corporate/Commercial Band 1
Table: p.740

**Reck, Joel M**
(Massachusetts)
Real Estate Band 3
Table: p.1081

**Reck, Michael** (Iowa)
Employment Band 3
Table: p.912

**Reckmeyer, Peter R**
(Alaska)
Profile: p.174
Corporate/M&A Band 2
Table: p.168

**Rector, Richard** (National)
Profile: p.128
Government Contracts Band 3
Table: p.30

**Redd, Charles A** (National)
Profile: p.128
Wealth Management Band 3
Table: p.81

**Redden, Joe** (Texas)
Litigation Band 2
Table: p.1865

**Reddin, Jane E** (Arizona)
Employment Band 4
Table: p.178

**Reder, Henry** (Ohio)
Construction Band 4
Table: p.1603

**Reding, John A** (California)
Profile: p.309
Litigation Band 4
Table: p.257

**Redlick, David**
(Massachusetts)
Profile: p.1103
Corporate/M&A Band 1
Table: p.1061

**Redmond, Patricia**
(Florida)
Bankruptcy Band 2
Table: p.586

**Reece, Joseph** (Alaska)
Corporate/M&A Band 2
Table: p.168
Real Estate Band 2
Table: p.172

**Reed, Glen** (Georgia)
Profile: p.722
Healthcare Band 1
Table: p.693

**Reed, John L** (Delaware)
Profile: p.410
Chancery Band 3
Table: p.392

**Reed, John S** (Kentucky)
Profile: p.950
Litigation Band 1
Table: p.942

**Reed, Kevin A** (Texas)
Healthcare Band 2
Table: p.1855

**Reed, Kevin F**
(District of Columbia)
Profile: p.540
Telecom, Broadcast & Satellite
Band 3
Table: p.492

**Reed, Lucy** (New York)
International Arbitration
Band 1
Table: p.36

**Reed, Margery N**
(Pennsylvania)
Profile: p.1739
Bankruptcy Band 3
Table: p.1697

**Reed, Matthew** (Maryland)
Profile: p.1043
Real Estate Band 4
Table: p.1035

**Reed, Michael H**
(Pennsylvania)
Profile: p.1739
Bankruptcy Band 3
Table: p.1697

**Reed, Randall B** (Wyoming)
Corporate/M&A Band 2
Table: p.2041

**Reed, Steven**
(District of Columbia)
Profile: p.540
Energy Band 3
Table: p.441

**Reed, Walter G D**
(Rhode Island)
Profile: p.1773
Corporate/Commercial Band 2
Table: p.1766

**Reed, Wendy N**
(District of Columbia)
Energy Band 5
Table: p.445

**Reed, William N (Bill)**
(Mississippi)
Profile: p.1186
Litigation Band 3
Table: p.1179

**Reeder III, Robert W**
(National)
Profile: p.129
Capital Markets Band 3
Table: p.15

**Reese, Cathy L** (Delaware)
Profile: p.410
Chancery Band 4
Table: p.392

**Reeves, Edward** (Oregon)
Employment Band 3
Table: p.1670

**Reeves, James N** (Alaska)
Profile: p.174
Environment Band 1
Table: p.170

**Reeves, Susan** (Alaska)
Environment Band 2
Table: p.170

**Reeves, Weston** (Wyoming)
Litigation Band 1
Table: p.2044

**Regan, Andrew W**
(National)
Profile: p.129
Wealth Management Band 3
Table: p.81

**Reger, Robert** (New York)
Profile: p.1491
Energy Band 2
Table: p.1367

**Reges, Robert** (Alaska)
Environment Band 3
Table: p.170

**Reich, Judith E.**
(Pennsylvania)
Banking & Finance Band 3
Table: p.1695

**Reich, William Z**
(New York)
Immigration Band 3
Table: p.1376

**Reich, Yaron Z** (New York)
Profile: p.1491
Tax Band 3
Table: p.1423

**Reich Esq, Abraham C**
(Pennsylvania)
Litigation Band 3
Table: p.1714

**Reid, Benjamine** (Florida)
Profile: p.648
Litigation Band 2
Table: p.609

**Reid, Spencer**
(New Mexico)
Litigation Band 3
Table: p.1324

**Reid, Jr, Glen G**
(Tennessee)
Profile: p.1816
Litigation Band 3
Table: p.1804

**Reider, Alan E**
(District of Columbia)
Profile: p.541
Healthcare Band 2
Table: p.456

**Reidy, Daniel** (Illinois)
Profile: p.851
Litigation Band 1
Table: p.802
Products Liability Band 2
Table: p.50

**Reidy, James P**
(New Hampshire)
Employment Band 2
Table: p.1265

**Reidy, Joseph M** (Ohio)
Profile: p.1636
Environment Band 4
Table: p.1612

**Reiff, Laura F**
(District of Columbia)
Profile: p.541
Immigration Band 1
Table: p.459

**Reilly, Daniel** (Colorado)
Litigation Band 2
Table: p.353

**Reilly, Gregory B**
(New Jersey)
Profile: p.1305
Litigation Band 2
Table: p.1289

**Reilly, Kenneth J** (Florida)
Profile: p.648
Litigation Band 3
Table: p.609

**Reilly, Lawrence F**
(New Jersey)
Profile: p.1305
Real Estate Band 3
Table: p.1293

**Reimer, Eric R** (California)
Profile: p.310
Banking & Finance Band 3
Table: p.218

**Reina, Joseph** (Texas)
Immigration Band 1
Table: p.1856

**Reines, Edward R**
(California)
Profile: p.310
Intellectual Property Band 3
Table: p.248

**Reinhardt, Daniel S**
(Georgia)
Litigation Band 3
Table: p.698

**Reinhart, Joe**
(Pennsylvania)
Environment Band 3
Table: p.1707

**Reinhart, Robert**
(Minnesota)
Profile: p.1166
Employment Band 1
Table: p.1154

**Reinhold, Richard L**
(New York)
Profile: p.1491
Tax Band 2
Table: p.1423

**Reisch, Scott H** (Colorado)
Profile: p.364
Environment Band 2
Table: p.350

**Reische, Alan L**
(New Hampshire)
Corporate/Commercial Band 1
Table: p.1263

**Reisman, Ellen** (National)
Profile: p.129
Products Liability Band 4
Table: p.50

**Reisman, Sharyl A**
(New York)
Profile: p.1492
Environment Band 3
Table: p.1371

**Reisman, Stephen H**
(Florida)
Profile: p.648
Construction Band 1
Table: p.590

**Reisman, Steven J**
(New York)
Profile: p.1492
Bankruptcy Band 4
Table: p.1344

**Reisman, W Michael**
(Connecticut)
Arbitration Band 1
Table: p.37

**Reisner, Jeffrey M**
(California)
Bankruptcy Band 4
Table: p.222

**Reisner, Lorin L** (New York)
Media & Entertainment Band 3
Table: p.1404

**Reiss, John** (New York)
Profile: p.1492
Corporate/M&A Band 4
Table: p.1354
Private Equity Band 2
Table: p.1407

**Reiss, Michael**
(Washington)
Employment Band 1
Table: p.1995

**Reiter, Glenn M** (New York)
Profile: p.129
Capital Markets Band 2
Table: p.7

**Remar, Robert** (Georgia)
Litigation Band 3
Table: p.698

**Remele Jr, Lewis A**
(Minnesota)
Profile: p.1166
Litigation Band 1
Table: p.1156

**Remington, Royce** (Ohio)
Construction Band 3
Table: p.1603

**Remsburg, Edward W**
(Iowa)
Litigation Band 2
Table: p.914

**Renehan, Richard**
(Massachusetts)
Litigation Band S
Table: p.1074

**Renfroe, Tracie** (Texas)
Profile: p.1911
Environment Band 2
Table: p.1853

**Reno, Russell** (Maryland)
Real Estate Band 2
Table: p.1035

**Rentenbach, Paul**
(Michigan)
Corporate/M&A Band 3
Table: p.1122

**Repka, David A**
(District of Columbia)
Profile: p.541
Energy Band 2
Table: p.449

**Reppert, Richard L** (Ohio)
Profile: p.1636
Real Estate Band 1
Table: p.1621

**Reschly, Jason** (Missouri)
Profile: p.1209
Corporate/M&A Band 3
Table: p.1193

**Resnick, Donald I** (Illinois)
Profile: p.851
Real Estate Band 4
Table: p.809

**Resnik, Peter L** (National)
Profile: p.129
Products Liability Band 4
Table: p.50

**Ressa, Gregory J** (New York)
Profile: p.1492
Real Estate Band 5
Table: p.1417

**Ressler, Alison S**
(California)
Profile: p.310
Capital Markets Band 2
Table: p.8
Corporate/M&A Band 4
Table: p.227

**Rester, Daniel K**
(Louisiana)
Profile: p.985
Gaming & Licensing Band 3
Table: p.971

**Reuben, Catherine E**
(Massachusetts)
Employment Up and coming
Table: p.1065

**Reymond Jr, Leon J**
(Louisiana)
Real Estate Band 1
Table: p.975

**Reynes, Stephen A**
(Vermont)
Real Estate Band 2
Table: p.1961

**Reynolds, Chris** (Texas)
Profile: p.1911
Energy Band 3
Table: p.1849
Litigation Band 3
Table: p.1865

**Reynolds, Christopher**
(New York)
Profile: p.1492
Employment Band 2
Table: p.1365

**Reynolds, Kevin** (Iowa)
Litigation Band 4
Table: p.914

**Reynolds, Nicholas S**
(District of Columbia)
Profile: p.541
Energy Band 1
Table: p.449

**Reynolds, Robert C**
(National)
Profile: p.129
Business Process Outsourcing
Band 3
Table: p.2

**Reynolds, Timothy G**
(New York)
Profile: p.1492
Insurance Band 3
Table: p.1379

**Reynolds III, John B**
(National)
Profile: p.129
International Trade Band 1
Table: p.41

**Rheaume, Warren J**
(Washington)
Profile: p.2007
Intellectual Property Band 2
Table: p.1998

**Rhebergen, Constance
Gall** (Texas)
Profile: p.1911
Intellectual Property Band 3
Table: p.1860

**Rhodes, Thomas** (Georgia)
Antitrust Band 2
Table: p.675

**Rhodunda Jr, William J**
(Delaware)
Real Estate Band 3
Table: p.400

**Rhorer, John R** (Kentucky)
Profile: p.951
Environment Band 1
Table: p.940

**R**

**R**

**Rhyne, Katherine L**
(District of Columbia)
Profile: p.541
Environment Band 3
Table: p.451

**Riback, Ronald H**
(Michigan)
Profile: p.1139
Banking & Finance Band 2
Table: p.1120

**Ricci, Richard F** (New Jersey)
Profile: p.1305
Environment Band 3
Table: p.1285

**Ricciardi, Mark J** (Nevada)
Profile: p.1260
Employment Band 2
Table: p.1248

**Rice, Arthur Halsey**
(Florida)
Bankruptcy Band 3
Table: p.586

**Rice, Emily G**
(New Hampshire)
Employment Band 3
Table: p.1265
Litigation Band 3
Table: p.1267

**Rice, Gary** (National)
Profile: p.129
Financial Services Band 3
Table: p.24

**Rice, Glenn** (New York)
Bankruptcy Band 4
Table: p.1344

**Rice, Stephen M** (Nevada)
Real Estate Band 3
Table: p.1255

**Rich, Chris W** (Oregon)
Environment Band 2
Table: p.1672

**Rich, Frederic C** (New York)
Profile: p.1492
Projects Band 1
Table: p.56
Projects Band 1
Table: p.1413

**Rich, R Bruce** (New York)
Profile: p.1492
Media & Entertainment Band 1
Table: p.1404

**Richard, Andrea Leah**
(Wyoming)
Real Estate Band 2
Table: p.2045

**Richard, Barry** (Florida)
Profile: p.648
Litigation Band 1
Table: p.609
Litigation Band 2
Table: p.615

**Richard, Molly** (Texas)
Intellectual Property Band 2
Table: p.1860

**Richards, Russell** (Georgia)
Profile: p.722
Corporate/M&A Band 2
Table: p.684

**Richards III, Lee S**
(New York)
Litigation Band 3
Table: p.1391

**Richardson, Joseph**
(Arizona)
Corporate/M&A Band 2
Table: p.176

**Richardson, Julia**
(District of Columbia)
Energy Band 5
Table: p.441

**Richardson, Susan**
(Georgia)
Profile: p.723
Environment Up and coming

**Richardson, Todd**
(Nebraska)
Profile: p.1244
Corporate/M&A Band 2
Table: p.1236

**Richilano, John M**
(Colorado)
Litigation Band 1
Table: p.353

**Richman, Gerald** (Florida)
Profile: p.648
Litigation Band 3
Table: p.609

**Richman, Hershel J**
(Pennsylvania)
Profile: p.1739
Environment Band S
Table: p.1707

**Richman, Lawrence I**
(National)
Profile: p.129
Wealth Management Band 3
Table: p.81

**Richter, Peter** (Oregon)
Profile: p.1683
Litigation Band 2
Table: p.1674

**Riddell, Stephen** (Georgia)
Employment Band 3
Table: p.687

**Ridgley, Thomas** (Ohio)
Profile: p.1636
Litigation Band 4
Table: p.1617

**Ridley, Fred S** (Florida)
Profile: p.648
Real Estate Band 2
Table: p.617

**Ridley, John** (New Jersey)
Employment Band 2
Table: p.1282
Litigation Band 3
Table: p.1289

**Riedel, Harley E** (Florida)
Profile: p.648
Bankruptcy ✪
Table: p.586

**Riedinger, Jerry**
(Washington)
Intellectual Property Band 1
Table: p.1998

**Riedy, James**
(District of Columbia)
Profile: p.541
Tax Band 4
Table: p.488

**Rieger, Michelle I** (Texas)
Construction Band 4
Table: p.1838

**Rieke, Robert** (Nebraska)
Real Estate Band 1
Table: p.1242

**Riesel, Daniel** (New York)
Profile: p.1492
Environment Band 1
Table: p.1371

**Riffel, Jerome** (Missouri)
Profile: p.1209
Real Estate Band 2
Table: p.1201

**Riggs, Kendrick R**
(Kentucky)
Profile: p.951
Environment Band 1
Table: p.941

**Riggs, Richard** (Oklahoma)
Real Estate Band 2
Table: p.1658

**Rigot, Joseph M** (Ohio)
Profile: p.1637
Corporate/M&A Band 3
Table: p.1605

**Rikard, William L**
(North Carolina)
Litigation Band 4
Table: p.1577

**Rikleen, Lauren Stiller**
(Massachusetts)
Environment Band 3
Table: p.1068

**Riley, Byron** (Iowa)
Corporate/M&A Band S
Table: p.909

**Riley, Douglas K** (Vermont)
Real Estate Band 3
Table: p.1961

**Riley, Richard A** (Idaho)
Corporate/Commercial Band 3
Table: p.759

**Riley, Shawn** (Ohio)
Bankruptcy Band 2
Table: p.1600

**Riley, Steven A**
(Tennessee)
Litigation Band 1
Table: p.1804

**Riley Jr, James B** (Illinois)
Healthcare Band 3
Table: p.793

**Rill, James F**
(District of Columbia)
Antitrust Band 2
Table: p.426

**Rillstone, Douglas** (Florida)
Environment Band 3
Table: p.601

**Rindy, Dean**
(North Dakota)
Real Estate Band 2
Table: p.1595

**Ringel, Dean** (New York)
Media & Entertainment Band 2
Table: p.1404

**Riopelle, Brian C** (Virginia)
Intellectual Property Band 1
Table: p.1975

**Rippie, E Glenn** (Illinois)
Profile: p.851
Energy Band 1
Table: p.789

**Rishwain, James**
(California)
Profile: p.310
Real Estate Band 2
Table: p.270

**Ritchie, Stephen L** (Illinois)
Profile: p.851
Corporate/M&A: Private Equity Band 3
Table: p.782

**Riter, Charles**
(South Dakota)
Real Estate Band 1
Table: p.1796

**Ritok, Joseph** (Michigan)
Employment Band 1
Table: p.1125

**Ritt, Roger M**
(Massachusetts)
Profile: p.1103
Tax Band 2
Table: p.1084

**Ritts, Leslie Sue**
(District of Columbia)
Profile: p.541
Environment Band 3
Table: p.451

**Rivera, Henry M**
(District of Columbia)
Profile: p.541
Telecom, Broadcast & Satellite Band 3
Table: p.492

**Rivkin, David W** (New York)
Arbitration Band 1
Table: p.37
International Arbitration Band 1
Table: p.36

**Rizzi, Robert**
(District of Columbia)
Profile: p.310
Tax Band 4
Table: p.274

**Rizzotti, Anthony D**
(Massachusetts)
Profile: p.1103
Employment Band 2
Table: p.1065

**Roach, Gerald F**
(North Carolina)
Profile: p.1586
Corporate/M&A Band 2
Table: p.1571

**Roach, Steven A**
(Michigan)
Profile: p.1139
Banking & Finance Band 2
Table: p.1120

**Roach Jr, Robert M**
(Texas)
Insurance Band 3
Table: p.1858

**Roach Jr, William H**
(Illinois)
Profile: p.851
Healthcare Band 2
Table: p.793

**Roady, Celia**
(District of Columbia)
Profile: p.541
Tax Band 4
Table: p.488

**Robb, Peter** (Vermont)
Employment Band 1
Table: p.1958

**Robbins, Lawrence**
(District of Columbia)
Litigation Band 2
Table: p.471
Litigation Band 1
Table: p.475

**Robbins, Robert B**
(District of Columbia)
Profile: p.541
Corporate/Commercial Band 3
Table: p.435

**Robeck, Mark** (Texas)
Profile: p.1912
Energy Band 3
Table: p.1849

**Robenalt, James** (Ohio)
Profile: p.1637
Construction Band 3
Table: p.1603
Litigation Band 4
Table: p.1617

**Roberson, Richard** (Texas)
Profile: p.1912
Bankruptcy Band 1
Table: p.1835

**Roberson, Jr, Thomas Y**
(Louisiana)
Profile: p.985
Banking & Finance Band 3
Table: p.963

**R**

**Roberts, Harry** (Texas)
Profile: p.1912
Real Estate Band 1
Table: p.1872

**Roberts, James** (Virginia)
Litigation Band S

**Roberts, Kenneth M**
(Illinois)
Profile: p.851
Construction Band 3
Table: p.778

**Roberts, Michele**
(District of Columbia)
Profile: p.542
Litigation Band 2
Table: p.471

**Roberts, Richard**
(District of Columbia)
Profile: p.542
Energy Band 2
Table: p.445

**Roberts, Thomas A**
(New York)
Profile: p.1493
Corporate/M&A Band 3
Table: p.1354
Private Equity Band 1
Table: p.1407

**Robertson, Allen K**
(North Carolina)
Banking & Finance Band 3
Table: p.1569

**Robertson, Elihu** (New York)
Transportation Band 2
Table: p.64

**Robertson, Eric** (Illinois)
Energy Band 2
Table: p.789

**Robertson, Gregory**
(Virginia)
Employment Band 1
Table: p.1971

**Robertson, Jean R** (Ohio)
Bankruptcy Band 3
Table: p.1600

**Robertson, Robert** (Illinois)
Profile: p.852
Antitrust Band 2
Table: p.767

**Robertson, Thomas D**
(Oklahoma)
Employment Band 2
Table: p.1654

**Robertson Jr, James K**
(Connecticut)
Litigation Band 2
Table: p.378

**Robfogel, Susan S**
(New York)
Profile: p.1493
Healthcare Band 2
Table: p.1374

**Robiner, Susan** (Minnesota)
Litigation Band 1

Table: p.1157

**Robins, Andrew S** (Florida)
Real Estate Band 3
Table: p.617

**Robinson, Brent T** (Idaho)
Bankruptcy Band 2
Table: p.758

**Robinson, Donald C**
(Montana)
Employment Band 3
Table: p.1223
Litigation Band 1
Table: p.1225

**Robinson, Frank L**
(Colorado)
Profile: p.365
Real Estate Band 1
Table: p.355

**Robinson, Frederick**
(District of Columbia)
Profile: p.542
Healthcare Band 1
Table: p.456

**Robinson, John** (Florida)
Employment Band 1
Table: p.597

**Robinson, Marcia C**
(Massachusetts)
Profile: p.1103
Real Estate Band 3
Table: p.1081

**Robinson, Michael C**
(Oregon)
Real Estate Band 1
Table: p.1677

**Robinson, Robert J**
(National)
Profile: p.130
Capital Markets Band 2
Table: p.13

**Robinson, Robert P**
(Arizona)
Profile: p.194
Real Estate Band 3
Table: p.184

**Robinson, Spencer**
(Arkansas)
Employment Band 1
Table: p.203

**Robinson, Stephen W**
(Virginia)
Employment Band 1
Table: p.1971

**Robinson II, Russell M**
(North Carolina)
Corporate/M&A Band S
Table: p.1571

**Robinson III, Wm T**
(Kentucky)
Litigation Band 4
Table: p.942

**Robinson Jr, Neil C**
(South Carolina)
Profile: p.1784
Real Estate Band 2

Table: p.1780

**Robison, John** (Wisconsin)
Profile: p.2035
Corporate/M&A Band 3
Table: p.2025

**Robison, Kent** (Nevada)
Litigation Band 3
Table: p.1252

**Robison, Reid** (Oklahoma)
Litigation Band 2
Table: p.1656

**Robitzek, William** (Maine)
Litigation Band 2
Table: p.1006

**Roble, Daniel T**
(Massachusetts)
Profile: p.1103
Healthcare Band 2
Table: p.1071

**Roby, Patrick M** (Iowa)
Litigation Band 1
Table: p.914

**Roby, Jr, Joseph J**
(Minnesota)
Employment Band 3
Table: p.1154

**Rocap, Donald** (Illinois)
Profile: p.852
Tax Band 2
Table: p.812

**Rocap III, James**
(District of Columbia)
Profile: p.542
Insurance Band 1
Table: p.461

**Rocci, Steven**
(Pennsylvania)
Profile: p.1739
Intellectual Property Band 3
Table: p.1711

**Rocha, Patricia**
(Rhode Island)
Profile: p.1773
Litigation Band 2
Table: p.1769

**Roche, William G**
(National)
Profile: p.130
Business Process Outsourcing
Band 3
Table: p.2

**Rochelle, Michael** (Texas)
Bankruptcy Band 4
Table: p.1835

**Rock, Andrew** (Florida)
Profile: p.649
Healthcare Band 3
Table: p.604

**Rock, Neil L** (New York)
Profile: p.1493
Real Estate Band 5
Table: p.1417

**Rockett, James M**
(National)
Profile: p.130
Financial Services Band 3
Table: p.24

**Rockman, Jeffrey**
(Maryland)
Employment Band 3
Table: p.1028

**Rockwell, David**
(Washington)
Real Estate Band 2
Table: p.2002

**Rockwell, Sarah M**
(Colorado)
Real Estate Band 1
Table: p.355

**Rockwood, Linda**
(Colorado)
Profile: p.365
Environment Band 1
Table: p.350

**Rod, Jonathan** (New York)
Projects Band 2
Table: p.56
Projects Band 2
Table: p.1413

**Rodburg, Michael L**
(New Jersey)
Profile: p.1305
Environment Band 1
Table: p.1285

**Roddenberry, Stephen**
(Florida)
Profile: p.649
Corporate/M&A Band 1
Table: p.594

**Rodgers, James**
(Pennsylvania)
Antitrust Band 3
Table: p.1692

**Rodgers, W Stanley**
(Alabama)
Litigation Band 3
Table: p.152

**Rodin, Rita A** (New York)
Profile: p.1493
Business Process Outsourcing
Up and coming
Table: p.2
Technology Up and coming
Table: p.1428

**Rodriguez, Denise Rios**
(California)
Profile: p.310
Healthcare Band 2
Table: p.238

**Rodriguez, Wilfredo A**
(Florida)
Profile: p.130
International Arbitration
Band 4
Table: p.36

**Rodriques, Louis A**
(Massachusetts)
Profile: p.1104
Employment Band 3
Table: p.1065

**Roe Jr, Clifford A** (Ohio)
Profile: p.1637
Corporate/M&A Band S
Table: p.1605

**Roeder, Kim H** (Georgia)
Healthcare Band 2
Table: p.693

**Roesch, Lynda E** (Ohio)
Profile: p.1637
Intellectual Property Band 3
Table: p.1614

**Rogan, Michael P**
(District of Columbia)
Profile: p.542
Corporate/Commercial Band 3
Table: p.435

**Rogers, Alan T** (Alabama)
Profile: p.159
Litigation Band 3
Table: p.152

**Rogers, Bruce F** (Alabama)
Litigation Band 3
Table: p.152

**Rogers, CB** (Georgia)
Litigation Band S
Table: p.698

**Rogers, Daniel R** (Texas)
Profile: p.1912
Energy Band 5
Table: p.1847
Projects Band 4
Table: p.1869

**Rogers, E Mabry**
(Alabama)
Profile: p.159
Litigation Band 1
Table: p.152

**Rogers, Ed**
(District of Columbia)
Profile: p.542
Real Estate Band 4
Table: p.482

**Rogers, Guy W** (Montana)
Litigation Band 4
Table: p.1225

**Rogers Chepiga, Pamela**
(New York)
Profile: p.1493
Litigation Band 3
Table: p.1388

**Rogers III, John L** (Illinois)
Profile: p.852
Energy Band 3
Table: p.789

**Rogers Jr, Theodore O**
(New York)
Profile: p.1493
Employment Band 1
Table: p.1365

**Rogovin, John**
(District of Columbia)
Profile: p.542
Telecom, Broadcast & Satellite
Band 4
Table: p.492

**R**

**Rogow, Bruce S** (Florida)
Litigation Band 1
Table: p.615

**Rogowski, Patricia Smink** (Delaware)
Profile: p.411
Intellectual Property Band 4
Table: p.397

**Roh, Charles E** (National)
Profile: p.130
International Trade Band 3
Table: p.42

**Rohlf, Joan** (Alaska)
Employment Band 2
Table: p.169

**Rohn, Frederick** (New York)
Construction Band 4
Table: p.1351

**Rohn, James J**
(Pennsylvania)
Profile: p.1739
Litigation Band 3
Table: p.1715

**Rohrbach, Peter**
(District of Columbia)
Profile: p.542
Telecom, Broadcast & Satellite Band 2
Table: p.492

**Rohyans, John** (Ohio)
Profile: p.1637
Real Estate Band 2
Table: p.1621

**Rokosz, Ronald E** (Illinois)
Banking & Finance Band 2
Table: p.771

**Rolapp, Todd J** (Tennessee)
Profile: p.1816
Corporate/M&A
Up and coming
Table: p.1799

**Roles, Forrest** (West Virginia)
Profile: p.2018
Employment Band 1
Table: p.2012

**Rolfe, Ronald** (New York)
Profile: p.1493
Antitrust Band 3
Table: p.1335

**Rolnick, Lawrence M**
(New Jersey)
Profile: p.1305
Litigation Band 1
Table: p.1289

**Rom, Rebecca L**
(Minnesota)
Profile: p.1166
Real Estate Band 1
Table: p.1160

**Roman, Terry** (Arizona)
Profile: p.194
Corporate/M&A Band 3
Table: p.176

**Román, Marissa J**
(California)
Profile: p.310
Media & Entertainment Band 3
Table: p.266

**Romano, Carmen J**
(Pennsylvania)
Profile: p.1739
Corporate/M&A Band 2
Table: p.1700

**Romano, Robert M**
(National)
Profile: p.130
Financial Services Band 3
Table: p.28

**Rondeau, Patrick J**
(Massachusetts)
Profile: p.1104
Corporate/M&A Band 2
Table: p.1061
Private Equity Band 2
Table: p.1078

**Ronzetti, Tucker** (Florida)
Profile: p.649
Litigation Band 4
Table: p.609

**Rooney, John E** (Illinois)
Profile: p.852
Energy Band 2
Table: p.789
Telecom, Broadcast & Satellite Band 3
Table: p.816

**Rooney, Stephen G**
(New York)
Profile: p.1493
Insurance Band 3
Table: p.1380

**Rooney, William H** (New York)
Profile: p.1493
Antitrust Band 3
Table: p.1335

**Roos, Norman H**
(Connecticut)
Profile: p.384
Real Estate Band 2
Table: p.380

**Root Jr, George L**
(California)
Profile: p.310
Healthcare Band 1
Table: p.238

**Roper, Harry J** (Illinois)
Profile: p.852
Intellectual Property Band 2
Table: p.799

**Ropski, Gary** (Illinois)
Profile: p.852
Intellectual Property Band 1
Table: p.799

**Rosati, Jack** (Ohio)
Construction Band 2
Table: p.1603

**Rosati, Mario** (California)
Profile: p.310
Corporate/M&A Band 3

Table: p.227

**Rose, Alfred O**
(Massachusetts)
Profile: p.1104
Private Equity Band 3
Table: p.1078

**Rose, Beth S** (New Jersey)
Profile: p.1305
Litigation Band 2
Table: p.1292

**Rose, Crystal K** (Hawaii)
Litigation Band 2
Table: p.745

**Rose, David A** (Texas)
Intellectual Property Band 3
Table: p.1860

**Rose, Glenn B** (Tennessee)
Litigation Band 2
Table: p.1804
Litigation Band 3
Table: p.1804

**Rose, Stephen** (California)
Tax Band 2
Table: p.274

**Rose Jr, J William**
(Alabama)
Corporate/Commercial Band 2
Table: p.148

**Rosegay, Margaret**
(California)
Profile: p.310
Environment Band 4
Table: p.236

**Rosen, Arthur R** (New York)
Profile: p.1494
Tax Band 4
Table: p.1423

**Rosen, Barry F** (Maryland)
Healthcare Band 1
Table: p.1031

**Rosen, Burt** (New York)
Tax Band 3
Table: p.1423

**Rosen, Edward J** (New York)
Profile: p.130
Capital Markets Band 1
Table: p.15

**Rosen, J Philip** (New York)
Profile: p.1494
Real Estate Band 3
Table: p.1417

**Rosen, Jeffrey J** (New York)
Corporate/M&A Band 3
Table: p.1354

**Rosen, Matthew A**
(New York)
Profile: p.1494
Tax Band 1
Table: p.1423

**Rosen, Peter K** (California)
Insurance Band 3
Table: p.245

**Rosen, Richard** (New York)
Profile: p.1494
Litigation Band 2
Table: p.1390

**Rosen, Richard L**
(District of Columbia)
Profile: p.542
Antitrust Band 4
Table: p.426

**Rosen, Seth** (New York)
Tax Band 4
Table: p.1423

**Rosen, Stuart M**
(New York)
Profile: p.130
International Trade Band 3
Table: p.42

**Rosenbaum, David**
(Arizona)
Profile: p.194
Litigation Band 2
Table: p.181

**Rosenbaum, Gary B**
(California)
Profile: p.310
Banking & Finance Band 3
Table: p.218

**Rosenbaum, Lois O**
(Oregon)
Litigation Band 2
Table: p.1674

**Rosenbaum, Michael D**
(Illinois)
Profile: p.852
Employment Band 2
Table: p.786

**Rosenbaum, Robert**
(Minnesota)
Profile: p.1166
Corporate/M&A Band 1
Table: p.1152

**Rosenberg, Benjamin**
(Maryland)
Litigation Band S
Table: p.1032

**Rosenberg, Harry**
(Louisiana)
Profile: p.985
Litigation Band 1
Table: p.973
Litigation Band 3
Table: p.973

**Rosenberg, Kenneth**
(Pennsylvania)
Real Estate Band 2
Table: p.1718

**Rosenberg, Marc S**
(National)
Profile: p.130
Capital Markets Band 4
Table: p.7

**Rosenberg, Mark F**
(New York)
Profile: p.1494
Environment Band 3
Table: p.1371
Environment Band 3

Table: p.1373

**Rosenberg, Michael**
(Florida)
Tax Band 2
Table: p.623

**Rosenberg, Robert**
(New York)
Bankruptcy Band 2
Table: p.1344

**Rosenberg, Sumner**
(Georgia)
Intellectual Property Band 4
Table: p.696

**Rosenberg, Thomas L**
(Ohio)
Construction Band 3
Table: p.1603

**Rosenblatt, Arnold**
(New Hampshire)
Profile: p.1273
Litigation Band 3
Table: p.1267

**Rosenblatt, Paul M**
(Georgia)
Profile: p.723
Bankruptcy Band 3
Table: p.679

**Rosenblatt, Richard G**
(New Jersey)
Profile: p.1305
Employment Band 3
Table: p.1282

**Rosenblatt, Stephen W**
(Mississippi)
Profile: p.1186
Corporate/Commercial Band 1
Table: p.1175

**Rosenblatt, William**
(New York)
Insurance Band 1
Table: p.1380

**Rosenbloom, David**
(District of Columbia)
Tax Band 1
Table: p.488

**Rosenbloom, David**
(Illinois)
Profile: p.852
Litigation Band 3
Table: p.802
Litigation Band 2
Table: p.803

**Rosenbloom, James B**
(Illinois)
Real Estate Band 3
Table: p.809

**Rosenbloom, Lewis S**
(Illinois)
Profile: p.852
Bankruptcy Band 3
Table: p.775

**Rosenbloum, Robert**
(Georgia)
Profile: p.723
Intellectual Property Band 4
Table: p.696

**Rosenblum, Carl D**
(Louisiana)
Profile: p.985
Energy Band 1
Table: p.969

**Rosenblum, Jay**
(New Mexico)
Corporate/Commercial Band 2
Table: p.1320

**Rosenblum, Peter**
(Massachusetts)
Corporate/M&A Band 2
Table: p.1061
Private Equity Band 2
Table: p.1078

**Rosenblum, Steve A**
(New York)
Profile: p.1494
Corporate/M&A Band 3
Table: p.1354

**Rosenfeld, Jonathan**
(Massachusetts)
Profile: p.1104
Employment Band 4
Table: p.1065

**Rosenfeld, Lawrence**
(Arizona)
Profile: p.194
Employment Band 4
Table: p.178

**Rosenfeld, Robert**
(California)
Profile: p.311
Antitrust Band 2
Table: p.216

**Rosenstein, Tony P** (Texas)
Profile: p.1912
Employment Band 2
Table: p.1844

**Rosenthal, Barry P**
(District of Columbia)
Profile: p.543
Real Estate Band 1
Table: p.482

**Rosenthal, Daniel G** (Ohio)
Employment Band 2
Table: p.1609

**Rosenthal, Michael D**
(Illinois)
Profile: p.852
Corporate/M&A: Private Equity
Band 3
Table: p.782

**Rosenthal, Paul C**
(District of Columbia)
International Trade Band 2
Table: p.42

**Rosenthal, Stephen F**
(Florida)
Profile: p.649
Litigation Associate to watch
Table: p.609

**Rosenthal, Steven M**
(District of Columbia)
Profile: p.543
Tax Band 4
Table: p.488

**Rosenwasser, Michael**
(New York)
Profile: p.1494
Energy Band 3
Table: p.1367

**Rosini, Neil** (New York)
Media & Entertainment Band 2
Table: p.1401

**Rosner, David S** (New York)
Bankruptcy Band 4
Table: p.1344

**Rosner, Douglas**
(Massachusetts)
Bankruptcy Band 2
Table: p.1058

**Rosner, Richard** (Ohio)
Profile: p.1637
Real Estate Band 1
Table: p.1621

**Ross, Allen** (New York)
Profile: p.1494
Construction Band 2
Table: p.1351

**Ross, Barry** (New York)
Real Estate Band 4
Table: p.1417

**Ross, Bruce S** (National)
Wealth Management Band 3
Table: p.81

**Ross, David L** (Florida)
Profile: p.649
Antitrust Band 3
Table: p.581
Litigation Band 2
Table: p.609

**Ross, Jerry W** (Texas)
Profile: p.1912
Environment Band 4
Table: p.1852

**Ross, Joel L** (Texas)
Profile: p.1912
Real Estate Band 2
Table: p.1872

**Ross, John Walker**
(Montana)
Natural Resources Band 2
Table: p.1228

**Ross, Judith** (Texas)
Profile: p.1912
Bankruptcy Band 3
Table: p.1835

**Ross, Lauri Waldman**
(Florida)
Litigation Band 2
Table: p.615

**Ross, Nancy** (Illinois)
Profile: p.853
Employment Band 2
Table: p.786

**Ross, Richard** (Minnesota)
Employment Band 2
Table: p.1154

**Rossiter, Robert**
(Nebraska)
Employment Band 1
Table: p.1238

**Rosston, Richard** (Alaska)
Profile: p.174
Corporate/M&A Band 1
Table: p.168
Real Estate Band 1
Table: p.172

**Roston, Carl D** (Florida)
Profile: p.649
Corporate/M&A Band 4
Table: p.594

**Rotatori, Robert J** (Ohio)
Litigation Band 2
Table: p.1618

**Rotch, Peter B**
(New Hampshire)
Profile: p.1273
Real Estate Band 1
Table: p.1270

**Roth, Andrew B** (New York)
Profile: p.1495
Healthcare Band 2
Table: p.1374

**Roth, Stephen E**
(District of Columbia)
Profile: p.543
Investment Management Band 3
Table: p.469

**Rothauge, Renée** (Oregon)
Litigation Band 3
Table: p.1674

**Rothenberg, Charles**
(Virginia)
Profile: p.1985
Real Estate Band 2
Table: p.1978

**Rothenberg, Laraine S**
(New York)
Profile: p.1495
Employee Benefits Band 2
Table: p.1362

**Rothermel, Sarah**
(Massachusetts)
Profile: p.1104
Private Equity Band 2
Table: p.1080

**Rothman, Jay O**
(Wisconsin)
Profile: p.2035
Corporate/M&A Band 3
Table: p.2025

**Rothpletz Jr, Michael E**
(New Jersey)
Real Estate Band 3
Table: p.1293

**Rothschild, Gideon**
(National)
Wealth Management Band 1
Table: p.81

**Rothschild, Gita F**
(New Jersey)
Litigation Band 3
Table: p.1289

Litigation Band 2
Table: p.1292

**Rothstein, John A**
(Wisconsin)
Profile: p.2035
Litigation Band 2
Table: p.2029

**Rothwell, James T**
(National)
Profile: p.131
Capital Markets Band 3
Table: p.15

**Rottenberg, Alan**
(Massachusetts)
Real Estate Band 1
Table: p.1081

**Rounsaville, Keith** (Florida)
Profile: p.649
Antitrust Band 1
Table: p.581

**Rousseau, Dionne M**
(Louisiana)
Profile: p.985
Corporate/M&A
Up and coming
Table: p.965

**Roussel, James H**
(Louisiana)
Profile: p.985
Energy Band 1
Table: p.969

**Roussel, Randy P.**
(Louisiana)
Profile: p.986
Real Estate Band 3
Table: p.975

**Rovner, Jack A** (Illinois)
Profile: p.853
Healthcare Band 3
Table: p.793

**Rovner, Philip A** (Delaware)
Profile: p.411
Intellectual Property Band 4
Table: p.397

**Rowe, Jack D** (Missouri)
Profile: p.1209
Employment Band 1
Table: p.1195

**Rowe, Keven** (Utah)
Profile: p.1952
Real Estate Band 2
Table: p.1947

**Rowe, Larry Jordan**
(Massachusetts)
Profile: p.1104
Private Equity Band 1
Table: p.1080

**Rowe, Paul A** (New Jersey)
Profile: p.1306
Litigation Band 1
Table: p.1289

**Rowen, Andrew S**
(New York)
Profile: p.1495
Insurance Band 2
Table: p.1380

**Roy, Paul J N** (Illinois)
Profile: p.853
Business Process Outsourcing
Band 2
Table: p.2
Technology Band 1
Table: p.814

**Royall, M Sean** (Texas)
Profile: p.1912
Antitrust Band 2
Table: p.1829

**Royall Smith, Thomas**
(Massachusetts)
Profile: p.1104
Employment Band 4
Table: p.1065

**Royse, David T** (Kentucky)
Profile: p.951
Litigation Band 4
Table: p.942

**Rozell, William** (Alaska)
Environment Band 2
Table: p.170

**Rozmarin, George**
(Nebraska)
Employment Band 1
Table: p.1238

**Rubalcava, Sharon**
(California)
Profile: p.311
Environment Band 2
Table: p.236

**Rubenstein, Joshua**
(National)
Profile: p.131
Wealth Management Band 1
Table: p.81

**Rubenstein, William S**
(National)
Profile: p.131
Financial Services Band 3
Table: p.24

**Rubin, David** (Rhode Island)
Real Estate Band 2
Table: p.1770

**Rubin, Howard** (Oregon)
Employment Band 3
Table: p.1670

**Rubin, James** (Illinois)
Profile: p.853
Insurance Band 1
Table: p.795

**Rubin, Jerome L**
(Washington)
Employment Band 2
Table: p.1995

**Rubin, Joel D** (Illinois)
Real Estate Band 2
Table: p.809

**Rubin, Michael H**
(Louisiana)
Profile: p.986
Banking & Finance Band 3
Table: p.963

R

KEY TO RANKINGS: ✪ = STAR INDIVIDUAL   S = SENIOR STATESMAN

Real Estate Band 3
Table: p.1718

**Scott, Ami G** (Illinois)
Profile: p.855
Banking & Finance Up and
coming
Table: p.771

**Scott, Craig M**
(Rhode Island)
Litigation Band 3
Table: p.1769

**Scott, Donald E** (Colorado)
Litigation Band 2
Table: p.353

**Scott, Gary** (Wyoming)
Employment Band 1
Table: p.2042

**Scott, John ES** (Michigan)
Profile: p.1139
Litigation Band 2
Table: p.1128

**Scott, Michael T**
(Pennsylvania)
Profile: p.1741
Litigation Band 3
Table: p.1714
Products Liability Band 3
Table: p.50

**Scott, Pamela J** (Delaware)
Profile: p.411
Real Estate Band 1
Table: p.400

**Scott, Thane D**
(Massachusetts)
Profile: p.1105
Antitrust Band 1
Table: p.1053

**Scott, W Rowlett**
(Tennessee)
Real Estate Band 3
Table: p.1808

**Scott, William C**
(New Mexico)
Environment Band 1
Table: p.1323
Native Law Band 1
Table: p.1326

**Scott IV, William M**
(California)
Banking & Finance Band 2
Table: p.218

**Scrivner, Tom** (Wisconsin)
Employment Band 2
Table: p.2027

**Scullen, Sean M**
(Wisconsin)
Profile: p.2035
Employment Up & coming

**Sczudlo, Paul** (California)
Profile: p.313
Tax Band 4
Table: p.274

**Seabaugh, William F**
(Missouri)
Corporate/M&A Band 2

Table: p.1193

**Seabolt, Richard L**
(California)
Profile: p.313
Insurance Band 1
Table: p.243

**Seals, Paul** (Texas)
Profile: p.1913
Environment Band 2
Table: p.1852

**Sears, Barbara** (Maryland)
Profile: p.1044
Real Estate Band 3
Table: p.1035

**Seaton, Doug** (Minnesota)
Employment Band 3
Table: p.1154

**Seay, James E L** (Florida)
Profile: p.651
Real Estate Band 2
Table: p.617

**Sebris, Robert**
(Washington)
Employment Band 2
Table: p.1995

**Secrest III, Lawrence W**
(District of Columbia)
Profile: p.545
Telecom, Broadcast & Satellite
Band 4
Table: p.492

**Sederstrom, Charles**
(Nebraska)
Corporate/M&A Band 3
Table: p.1236

**Sedran, Howard**
(Pennsylvania)
Antitrust Band 3
Table: p.1692

**Seegull, Larry** (Maryland)
Profile: p.1044
Employment Band 3
Table: p.1028

**Segal, Daniel**
(Pennsylvania)
Profile: p.1741
Litigation Band 3
Table: p.1714

**Segal, Michael J** (New
York)
Profile: p.1499
Employee Benefits Band 3
Table: p.1362

**Segal, Mike** (Florida)
Healthcare Band 2
Table: p.604

**Segel, Alvin G** (California)
Corporate/M&A Band 4
Table: p.227

**Sehgal, Zarrar** (National)
Transportation
Associate to watch
Table: p.64

**Seide, Rochelle** (New York)
Profile: p.1499
Intellectual Property Band 3
Table: p.1384

**Seidel, Amy** (Minnesota)
Profile: p.1166
Corporate M&A Up & coming

**Seidel, Arthur**
(Pennsylvania)
Intellectual Property Band S
Table: p.1711

**Seiden, Richard** (California)
Profile: p.313
Healthcare Band 3
Table: p.238

**Seider, Mitchell A**
(California)
Bankruptcy Band 4
Table: p.1344

**Seidman, Steven** (New
York)
Profile: p.1499
Corporate/M&A Band 4
Table: p.1354

**Seiffert, James C**
(Kentucky)
Profile: p.951
Corporate/M&A Band 3
Table: p.937

**Seka, J Georg** (California)
Intellectual Property Band 4
Table: p.248

**Selber Silverstein, Laurie**
(Delaware)
Profile: p.411
Bankruptcy Band 2
Table: p.389

**Selbo, Gregory B**
(North Dakota)
Corporate/Commercial Band 2
Table: p.1590

**Selden, David** (Arizona)
Profile: p.194
Employment Band 2
Table: p.178

**Self, Shannon** (Oklahoma)
Corporate/Commercial Band 2
Table: p.1653

**Selig, John S** (Arkansas)
Corporate/Commercial Band 1
Table: p.201

**Seligman, David R** (Illinois)
Profile: p.855
Bankruptcy Up and coming
Table: p.775

**Selinger, Jerry** (Texas)
Profile: p.1913
Intellectual Property Band 3
Table: p.1860

**Sellergren, David**
(Minnesota)
Real Estate Band 1

**Sellers, Lawrence** (Florida)
Profile: p.651
Environment Band 1
Table: p.601

**Sellers, Randal H**
(Alabama)
Profile: p.159
Litigation Band 1
Table: p.152

**Selman, Russell** (Illinois)
Profile: p.855
Environment Band 4
Table: p.791

**Seltzer, Martin S** (Ohio)
Profile: p.1638
Environment Band 2
Table: p.1612

**Selver, Paul D** (New York)
Profile: p.1499
Real Estate Band 1
Table: p.1418

**Selwyn, Mark D**
(Massachusetts)
Profile: p.1106
Intellectual Property Band 3
Table: p.1072

**Semple, Lloyd** (Michigan)
Corporate/M&A Band S
Table: p.1122

**Seneker, Carl (Kim)**
(California)
Profile: p.313
Real Estate Band 1
Table: p.270

**Senn, Mark** (Colorado)
Real Estate Band 1
Table: p.355

**Sennett, Michael** (Illinois)
Antitrust Band 2
Table: p.767

**Sennett, Nancy J**
(Wisconsin)
Profile: p.2035
Litigation Band 2
Table: p.2029

**Sensabaugh, Don**
(West Virginia)
Litigation Band 1
Table: p.2013

**Sentilles III, Irwin F**
(Texas)
Profile: p.1913
Corporate/M&A Band 3
Table: p.1840

**Serbaroli, Francis J**
(New York)
Profile: p.1500
Healthcare Band 3
Table: p.1374

**Serdahely, Douglas J**
(Alaska)
Profile: p.174
Environment Band 3
Table: p.170
Litigation Band 3
Table: p.171

**Sernau, Ronald D**
(New York)
Profile: p.1500
Real Estate Band 5
Table: p.1417

**Serota, Susan P** (New York)
Profile: p.1500
Employee Benefits Band 1
Table: p.1362

**Serotte, Neal** (Maryland)
Employment Band 2
Table: p.1028

**Servodidio, Thomas G**
(Pennsylvania)
Profile: p.1741
Employment Band 3
Table: p.1703

**Seryak, Richard J**
(Michigan)
Profile: p.1139
Employment Band 2
Table: p.1125

**Settelmayer, Daniel K**
(California)
Healthcare Band 2
Table: p.238

**Setty, Nagendra** (Georgia)
Profile: p.723
Intellectual Property Band 3
Table: p.696

**Seuch, William M**
(Massachusetts)
Environment Band 3
Table: p.1068

**Sexton, Robert** (Alabama)
Profile: p.159
Real Estate Band 2
Table: p.153

**Seyfer, Greg** (Iowa)
Real Estate Band 3
Table: p.917

**Seymon, Pamela S**
(New York)
Profile: p.1500
Corporate/M&A Band 3
Table: p.1354

**Seymour, Karen Patton**
(New York)
Profile: p.1500
Litigation Band 3
Table: p.1391

**Seymour, Samuel W**
(New York)
Profile: p.1500
Litigation Band 2
Table: p.1391

**Sfregola, Michael F**
(California)
Profile: p.313
Real Estate Band 2
Table: p.270

**Sgarlata, Mark A** (Virginia)
Profile: p.1986
Construction Band 2
Table: p.1965

S

**Shachar, Avishai**
(New York)
Profile: p.1500
Tax Band 2
Table: p.1423

**Shackelford, Richard L**
(Georgia)
Profile: p.724
Healthcare Band 1
Table: p.693

**Shadowen, Steve**
(Pennsylvania)
Profile: p.1741
Antitrust Band 3
Table: p.1692

**Shaft, Grant**
(North Dakota)
Real Estate Band 2
Table: p.1595

**Shainberg, Raymond**
(Tennessee)
Real Estate Band 3
Table: p.1808

**Shalton, Lonnie J**
(Missouri)
Profile: p.1210
Real Estate Band 2
Table: p.1201

**Shank, Mark** (Texas)
Employment Band 3
Table: p.1844

**Shanks, Patricia L**
(California)
Profile: p.313
Environment Band 2
Table: p.236

**Shanman, James A**
(Connecticut)
Insurance Band 3
Table: p.1379

**Shannon, Brendan Linehan** (Delaware)
Profile: p.411
Bankruptcy Band 3
Table: p.389

**Shannon, Kevin** (Delaware)
Profile: p.411
Chancery Band 4
Table: p.392

**Shannon, Michael T** (Ohio)
Real Estate Band 2
Table: p.1622

**Shanor, Stuart D**
(New Mexico)
Profile: p.1329
Litigation Band 2
Table: p.1324

**Shapiro, Clifford J** (Illinois)
Construction Band 3
Table: p.778

**Shapiro, Hal S** (National)
Profile: p.134
International Trade
Up and coming
Table: p.42

**Shapiro, Howard** (National)
Profile: p.134
Erisa Litigation Band 1

**Shapiro, Howard**
(District of Columbia)
Profile: p.545
Litigation Band 2
Table: p.471

**Shapiro, Howard**
(District of Columbia)
Energy Band 3
Table: p.445

**Shapiro, J Ben** (Georgia)
Construction Band 2
Table: p.682

**Shapiro, Joel Charles**
(Pennsylvania)
Profile: p.1741
Bankruptcy Band 3
Table: p.1697

**Shapiro, Jonathan** (Maine)
Profile: p.1016
Employment Band 1
Table: p.1002
Employment Band 2
Table: p.1002

**Shapiro, Keith** (Illinois)
Profile: p.856
Bankruptcy Band 3
Table: p.775

**Shapiro, Raymond**
(Pennsylvania)
Profile: p.1741
Bankruptcy Band 1
Table: p.1697

**Shapiro, Robert**
(District of Columbia)
Profile: p.545
Energy Band 4
Table: p.445

**Shapiro, Stephen Brett**
(District of Columbia)
Profile: p.545
Construction Band 4
Table: p.433

**Shapiro, Stephen R**
(Illinois)
Profile: p.856
Litigation Band 2
Table: p.802

**Shapiro, Stuart** (New York)
Litigation Band 3
Table: p.1390

**Shapley, Christopher**
(Mississippi)
Profile: p.1186
Litigation Band 1
Table: p.1179

**Sharbaugh, Charles**
(Georgia)
Profile: p.724
Real Estate Band 2
Table: p.700

**Sharer, Paul L**
(District of Columbia)
Profile: p.545

**Intellectual Property Band 3**
Table: p.466

**Sharf, Jesse** (California)
Profile: p.313
Real Estate Band 1
Table: p.270

**Shargel, Jason M**
(Pennsylvania)
Profile: p.1741
Corporate/M&A Band 4
Table: p.1700

**Sharko, Susan M**
(New Jersey)
Litigation Band 2
Table: p.1292

**Sharp, F DeArmond**
(Nevada)
Real Estate Band 2
Table: p.1255

**Sharpe, Jeremy** (Iowa)
Real Estate Band 1
Table: p.917

**Sharpe, W Smith 'Kris'**
(Minnesota)
Profile: p.1166
Corporate/M&A Band 2
Table: p.1152

**Sharron, Stephanie L**
(California)
Profile: p.313
IT Outsourcing
Up and coming
Table: p.253

**Sharrow, Regina** (Indiana)
Profile: p.899
Corporate/M&A
Up and coming
Table: p.887

**Shaughnessy, Kevin**
(Florida)
Employment Band 2
Table: p.597

**Shaw, John** (Delaware)
Profile: p.412
Intellectual Property Band 4
Table: p.397

**Shaw, Paul W**
(Massachusetts)
Healthcare Band 2
Table: p.1071

**Shaw, Russell C** (Ohio)
Employee Benefits Band 3
Table: p.1607

**Shawe, Stephen D**
(Maryland)
Profile: p.1044
Employment Band 1
Table: p.1028

**Shay, Kathleen M**
(Pennsylvania)
Profile: p.1741
Corporate/M&A Band 3
Table: p.1700

**Shay, Stephen E**
(Massachusetts)
Profile: p.1106
Tax Band 1
Table: p.1084

**Shea, Daniel** (Colorado)
Profile: p.365
Litigation Band 1
Table: p.353

**Shea, James** (Maryland)
Litigation Band 2
Table: p.1032

**Shea, John** (Massachusetts)
Environment Band 3
Table: p.1068

**Shea, Kevin** (Colorado)
Profile: p.365
Litigation Band 1
Table: p.353

**Shearin, James T**
(Connecticut)
Profile: p.384
Litigation Band 2
Table: p.378

**Sheeder, Robert E** (Texas)
Employment Band 1
Table: p.1844

**Sheehan, Michael L**
(Maine)
Profile: p.1016
Real Estate Band 3
Table: p.1008

**Sheeran, Timothy J** (Ohio)
Profile: p.1638
Employment Band 3
Table: p.1609

**Sheets, D Mark**
(Tennessee)
Profile: p.1817
Real Estate Band 3
Table: p.1808

**Sheffield, Jeffrey** (Illinois)
Profile: p.856
Tax Band 1
Table: p.812

**Sheinfeld, Myron M**
(Texas)
Profile: p.1914
Bankruptcy Band 4
Table: p.1835

**Sheley, Raymond** (Georgia)
Real Estate Band 3
Table: p.700

**Sheller, John** (Kentucky)
Employment Band 2
Table: p.939

**Shelley, Patrick M**
(Maryland)
Real Estate Band 4
Table: p.1035

**Shemin, Kenneth R**
(Arkansas)
Litigation Band 1
Table: p.205

**Shenker, Joseph C**
(New York)
Profile: p.1500
Real Estate Band 1
Table: p.1417

**Shepherd, Jay**
(Massachusetts)
Profile: p.1106
Employment Band 3
Table: p.1065

**Shepherd, Kevin**
(Maryland)
Real Estate Band 1
Table: p.1035

**Shepherd III, Thomas B**
(Mississippi)
Corporate/Commercial Band 1
Table: p.1174

**Shepro, Richard Warren**
(Illinois)
Profile: p.856
Corporate/M&A Band 2
Table: p.781
Insurance Band 2
Table: p.796

**Sher, Leopold** (Louisiana)
Profile: p.986
Real Estate Band 1
Table: p.975

**Sher, Stanley O**
(District of Columbia)
Transportation Band 1
Table: p.78

**Sherck, Timothy C** (Illinois)
Profile: p.856
Tax Band 2
Table: p.812

**Sheridan, Mark F**
(New Mexico)
Profile: p.1329
Native Law Band 1
Table: p.47
Native Law Band 1
Table: p.1326

**Sheridan, Robert E**
(Montana)
Litigation Band 2
Table: p.1225

**Sherk, Kenneth J** (Arizona)
Profile: p.195
Litigation Band 1
Table: p.181

**Sherman, Craig E**
(Washington)
Profile: p.2007
Corporate/Commercial Band 3
Table: p.1992

**Sherman, Kyle** (Georgia)
Profile: p.724
Immigration Up and coming

**Sherman, Morris**
(Minnesota)
Corporate/M&A Band 2
Table: p.1152

**Sherman, Robert L**
(New York)
Profile: p.1501
Intellectual Property Band 3
Table: p.1385

**Sherman, Steven E**
(California)
Profile: p.313
Banking & Finance Band 3
Table: p.218

**Sherman, Terry K** (Ohio)
Litigation Band 3
Table: p.1618

**Shernoff, William M**
(California)
Insurance Band S
Table: p.245

**Sherr, Brian J** (Florida)
Profile: p.651
Real Estate Band 3
Table: p.617

**Sherrard III, Thomas J**
(Tennessee)
Corporate/M&A Band 3
Table: p.1799

**Shevin, Maurice L**
(Alabama)
Banking & Finance Band 2
Table: p.147

**Shevnock, Colleen M**
(Michigan)
Profile: p.1139
Banking & Finance Band 2
Table: p.1120

**Shidlofsky, Lee H** (Texas)
Insurance Band 2
Table: p.1858

**Shiekman, Laurence Z**
(Pennsylvania)
Profile: p.1742
Antitrust Band 2
Table: p.1692

**Shield Jr, William P**
(Michigan)
Profile: p.1139
Banking & Finance Band 1
Table: p.1120

**Shields, Thomas C**
(Illinois)
Healthcare Band 2
Table: p.793

**Shiff, Adam L** (New York)
Bankruptcy Up and coming
Table: p.1344

**Shilling, Cameron G**
(New Hampshire)
Profile: p.1273
Employment
Associate to watch
Table: p.1265

**Shim, Paul J** (New York)
Profile: p.1501
Corporate/M&A Band 4
Table: p.1354

**Shimshak, Stephen J**
(New York)
Profile: p.1501
Bankruptcy Band 3
Table: p.1344

**Shinay, Richard** (Maine)
Profile: p.1016
Real Estate Band 2
Table: p.1008

**Shindell, James W**
(Florida)
Profile: p.651
Real Estate Band 3
Table: p.617

**Shipley, Ann** (New York)
Profile: p.1501
Real Estate Band 4
Table: p.1417

**Shipley III, Benjamin H**
(Arkansas)
Employment Up and coming
Table: p.203

**Shirazi, Ray** (National)
Profile: p.134
Capital Markets
Up and coming
Table: p.13

**Shirley, James** (New York)
Profile: p.134
Transportation Band 4
Table: p.74

**Shivel Jr, Charles**
(Kentucky)
Profile: p.951
Litigation Band 3
Table: p.942

**Shively, John D** (Colorado)
Profile: p.365
Litigation Band 1
Table: p.353

**Shivers, Nancy** (Texas)
Immigration Band 1
Table: p.1856

**Shivers, Robert** (Texas)
Immigration Band 1
Table: p.1856

**Shlachter, Robert A**
(Oregon)
Litigation Band 3
Table: p.1674

**Shockley, Steven C**
(Indiana)
Profile: p.899
Litigation Band 2
Table: p.890

**Shockro, Michael J**
(California)
Business Process Outsourcing
Band 3
Table: p.2
IT Outsourcing Band S
Table: p.253

**Shoemaker, Andrew**
(Colorado)
Profile: p.366
Litigation Band 1

Table: p.353

**Shoemaker Jr, James M**
(South Carolina)
Profile: p.1784
Corporate/M&A Band S
Table: p.1775

**Shoemate, Steven R**
(New York)
Profile: p.1501
Corporate/M&A
Up and coming
Table: p.1354

**Shohat, Edward R** (Florida)
Litigation Band 2
Table: p.610

**Shoneman, Charles H**
(District of Columbia)
Profile: p.545
Energy Band 4
Table: p.441

**Shor, Michael T** (National)
Profile: p.134
International Trade Band 5
Table: p.42

**Shors, John** (Iowa)
Corporate/M&A Band 2
Table: p.909

**Short, Andrew** (New York)
Profile: p.1501
Tax Band 4
Table: p.1423

**Short, Barry** (Missouri)
Litigation Band 1
Table: p.1198
Litigation Band 2
Table: p.1198

**Short, Jennifer A** (Virginia)
Profile: p.1986

**Short, Marianne D**
(Minnesota)
Profile: p.1166
Litigation Band 3
Table: p.1156

**Short Jr, Herbert J**
(Georgia)
Profile: p.724
Energy Band 2
Table: p.689

**Short Jr, William B** (Texas)
Construction Band 4
Table: p.1838

**Shortlidge, Neil** (Kansas)
Profile: p.933
Real Estate Band 2
Table: p.930

**Shortz, Richard** (California)
Profile: p.314
Projects Band 2
Table: p.268

**Shoss, Cynthia R**
(New York)
Profile: p.1501
Insurance Band 3
Table: p.1380

**Showalter, Barton E**
(Texas)
Profile: p.1914
Intellectual Property Band 3
Table: p.1860

**Shoyer, Andrew W**
(District of Columbia)
Profile: p.134
International Trade Band 2
Table: p.42

**Shriner Jr, Thomas L**
(Wisconsin)
Profile: p.2035
Litigation Band 1
Table: p.2029

**Shteamer, Michael B**
(Missouri)
Profile: p.1210
Real Estate Band 3
Table: p.1201

**Shube, Eric** (New York)
Profile: p.1501
Corporate/M&A Band 2
Table: p.1359

**Shubin, John** (Florida)
Real Estate Band 3
Table: p.621

**Shugrue, John** (Illinois)
Profile: p.856
Insurance Band 2
Table: p.796

**Shuker, R Scott** (Florida)
Bankruptcy Band 3
Table: p.586

**Shulman, Larry R**
(Michigan)
Profile: p.1139
Banking & Finance Band 1
Table: p.1120

**Shulman, Lawrence A**
(Maryland)
Real Estate Band 2
Table: p.1035

**Shulman, Robert**
(District of Columbia)
Insurance Band 2
Table: p.464

**Shulman, Ron** (California)
Profile: p.314
Intellectual Property Band 3
Table: p.248

**Shulruff, Stuart P** (Illinois)
Profile: p.856
Banking & Finance Band 2
Table: p.771

**Shults, Leigh-Anne**
(Arkansas)
Employment Up and coming
Table: p.203

**Shults, Steven** (Arkansas)
Litigation Band 4
Table: p.205

**Shultz, Jack L** (Nebraska)
Employment Band 3
Table: p.1238

**Shultz, Jeff**
(South Dakota)
Employment Band 1
Table: p.1794

**Shumadine, Conrad**
(Virginia)
Litigation Band 2
Table: p.1977

**Shuman, Robert**
(West Virginia)
Real Estate Band 3

**Shuman, Stephen**
(West Virginia)
Real Estate Band 2
Table: p.2015

**Shumate, Roger** (Wyoming)
Employment Band 2
Table: p.2042

**Shuster, Michael**
(New York)
Profile: p.1501
Litigation Band 3
Table: p.1388

**Shusterman, Carl**
(California)
Immigration Band 2
Table: p.241

**Shutran, Richard**
(New York)
Profile: p.1501
Projects Band 1
Table: p.56
Projects Band 1
Table: p.1413

**Sicalides, Barbara T**
(Pennsylvania)
Profile: p.1742
Antitrust Band 2
Table: p.1692

**Sicilian, James**
(Connecticut)
Profile: p.384
Litigation Band 2
Table: p.378

**Sickle, David B** (Illinois)
Profile: p.856
Real Estate Band 4
Table: p.809

**Sicular, David R** (New York)
Profile: p.1501
Tax Band 3
Table: p.1423

**Sidman, Robert** (Ohio)
Profile: p.1638
Bankruptcy Band 2
Table: p.1600

**Siebert, Sherill** (Michigan)
Profile: p.1139
Employee Benefits Band 1
Table: p.1124

**Siebert, Susan E**
(Massachusetts)
Profile: p.1106
Banking & Finance Band 3
Table: p.1055

**Siebert, W Bernie**
(Colorado)
Profile: p.366
Employment Band 3
Table: p.348

**Siefert, Richard C**
(Washington)
Intellectual Property Band 2
Table: p.1998

**Siegal, Bradley** (Alabama)
Real Estate Band 3
Table: p.153

**Siegal, Don** (Alabama)
Real Estate Band 1
Table: p.153

**Siegel, Bradd N** (Ohio)
Profile: p.1638
Employment Band 1
Table: p.1609

**Siegel, Clark B** (California)
Media & Entertainment Band 3
Table: p.266

**Siegel, David** (California)
Litigation Band 3
Table: p.257

**Siegel, Nathan E**
(District of Columbia)
Media & Entertainment Band 3
Table: p.477

**Siegel, Robert** (California)
Profile: p.314
Employment Band 4
Table: p.231

**Siegel, Stephen H** (Florida)
Healthcare Band 2
Table: p.604

**Siegfried, Steven** (Florida)
Construction Band 1
Table: p.590

**Siemers, John C** (Alaska)
Bankruptcy Band 1
Table: p.167

**Siemon, Charles L** (Florida)
Real Estate Band S
Table: p.621

**Siffert, John S** (New York)
Litigation Band 2
Table: p.1391

**Sigel, John** (Massachusetts)
Profile: p.1106
Bankruptcy Band 3
Table: p.1058

**Sigmund, Rebecca**
(Georgia)
Immigration Band 2
Table: p.694

**Sikora, Clifford S**
(District of Columbia)
Energy Band 4
Table: p.445

**Silberberg, Marc L**
(New York)
Profile: p.1501

**Silberg, Jay**
(District of Columbia)
Profile: p.545
Energy Band 1
Table: p.449

**Silberman, Alan H** (Illinois)
Profile: p.856
Antitrust Band 2
Table: p.767

**Silberstein, Rebecca F**
(New York)
Private Equity Band 3
Table: p.1410

**Silbert, Earl**
(District of Columbia)
Profile: p.546
Litigation Band 1
Table: p.471

**Siler Jr, W Thomas**
(Mississippi)
Profile: p.1186
Employment Band 1
Table: p.1177

**Silin, Steven** (Maine)
Litigation Band 2
Table: p.1006

**Silliman, Todd** (Georgia)
Profile: p.724
Environment Band 3
Table: p.691

**Silver, Jeffrey** (Nevada)
Gaming & Licensing Band 2
Table: p.1251

**Silver, Michael J**
(Maryland)
Profile: p.1044
Corporate/M&A Band 1
Table: p.1025

**Silverman, Eric** (New York)
Projects Band 3
Table: p.1413

**Silverman, Karen E**
(California)
Antitrust Band 3
Table: p.216

**Silverman, Lawrence**
(Florida)
Profile: p.651
Antitrust Band 1
Table: p.581

**Silverman, Leslie N**
(New York)
Profile: p.134
Capital Markets Band 1
Table: p.7

**Silverman, Mark**
(District of Columbia)
Profile: p.546
Tax Band 2
Table: p.488

**Silverman, Moses**
(New York)
Profile: p.1502

**Silverman, Scott** (Florida)
Employment Up and coming
Table: p.597

**Silverman, Steve I**
(Florida)
Profile: p.651
Litigation Band 4
Table: p.609

**Silverstein, Bruce L**
(Delaware)
Profile: p.412
Chancery Band 3
Table: p.392

**Silvestri, Stephen**
(Maryland)
Employment Band 1
Table: p.1028

**Silvestri Jr, Frank J**
(Connecticut)
Profile: p.384
Litigation Band 2
Table: p.378

**Sim, J Ronald** (Washington)
Litigation Band 1
Table: p.2000

**Simkin, Steven** (New York)
Profile: p.1502
Real Estate Band 2
Table: p.1417

**Simmons, Rebecca J**
(National)
Profile: p.134
Capital Markets
Up and coming
Table: p.15

**Simmons, Richard**
(California)
Employment Band 4
Table: p.231

**Simmons, Sherwin**
(Florida)
Profile: p.651
Tax Band S
Table: p.623

**Simmons, Teri A** (Georgia)
Profile: p.724
Immigration Band 2
Table: p.694

**Simms, Marsha E** (New York)
Profile: p.1502
Banking & Finance Band 4
Table: p.1339

**Simon, Cathy A**
(District of Columbia)
Insurance Band 4
Table: p.461

**Simon, Marc** (Arizona)
Profile: p.195
Real Estate Band 2
Table: p.186

**Simon, Mark C** (Illinois)
Profile: p.857

**Simon, Michael H** (Oregon)
Litigation Band 2
Table: p.1674

**Simons, Andrew J**
(New Mexico)
Native Law Band 2
Table: p.1326

**Simons, Joseph J**
(District of Columbia)
Profile: p.546
Antitrust Band 5
Table: p.426

**Simons, Susan Brunick**
(South Dakota)
Employment Band 1
Table: p.1794

**Simons III, Laird H**
(California)
Profile: p.314
Corporate/M&A Band 4
Table: p.227

**Simonson, James S**
(Minnesota)
Litigation Band 2
Table: p.1156

**Simpler, Gary** (Maryland)
Profile: p.1044
Employment Band 2
Table: p.1028

**Simpson, James A**
(Michigan)
Profile: p.1139
Real Estate Band 2
Table: p.1130

**Simpson, Patrick** (Oregon)
Corporate/M&A Band 2
Table: p.1667

**Simpson, Reagan** (Texas)
Profile: p.1914
Litigation Band 1
Table: p.1866

**Simpson, Robert R**
(Connecticut)
Litigation Up and coming
Table: p.378

**Sims, Charles** (New York)
Profile: p.1502
Media & Entertainment Band 2
Table: p.1404

**Sims, Hunter** (Virginia)
Litigation Band 2

**Sims, Joe**
(District of Columbia)
Profile: p.546
Antitrust Band 1
Table: p.426

**Sims, Luke E** (Wisconsin)
Profile: p.2035
Corporate/M&A Band 2
Table: p.2025

**Sims, Roger** (Florida)
Profile: p.651

**Sinak, David** (Texas)
Profile: p.1914
Tax Band 4
Table: p.1875

**Sinatra, Geraldine A**
(Pennsylvania)
Profile: p.1742
Corporate/M&A Band 3
Table: p.1700

**Sinclair, Brad**
(North Dakota)
Litigation Band 2
Table: p.1593

**Sinclair, J Walter** (Idaho)
Litigation Band 1
Table: p.760

**Sinel, Norman**
(District of Columbia)
Profile: p.546
Telecom, Broadcast & Satellite
Band 4
Table: p.492

**Singer, Alan** (Pennsylvania)
Profile: p.1742
Corporate/M&A Band 2
Table: p.1700

**Singer, Brent A** (Maine)
Employment Band 1
Table: p.1002

**Singer, Eric L** (Illinois)
Construction Band 3
Table: p.778

**Singer, Fern H** (Alabama)
Profile: p.159
Employment Band 2
Table: p.150

**Singer, Gary** (California)
Profile: p.314
Corporate/M&A Band 4
Table: p.227

**Singer, Jonathan E**
(Minnesota)
Profile: p.1167
Litigation Band 1
Table: p.1157

**Singer, Leonard** (New York)
Energy Band 1
Table: p.1370

**Singer, Louis H** (New York)
Profile: p.1502
Private Equity Band 2
Table: p.1410

**Singer, Martin D**
(California)
Media & Entertainment Band 1
Table: p.263

**Singer, Paul** (Pennsylvania)
Profile: p.1742
Bankruptcy Band 1
Table: p.1697

**Antitrust Band 4**
Table: p.1335

**Real Estate Band 3**
Table: p.809

**Singer, Robert A**
(North Carolina)
Banking & Finance Band 3
Table: p.1569
Corporate/M&A Band 3
Table: p.1571

**Singer, Steven**
(Massachusetts)
Profile: p.1106
Corporate/M&A Band 1
Table: p.1061

**Singer, Stuart** (Florida)
Profile: p.652
Antitrust Band 2
Table: p.581
Litigation Band 4
Table: p.609

**Singerman, Paul** (Florida)
Bankruptcy ✪
Table: p.586

**Singh, Amy K** (Illinois)
Media & Entertainment Band 2
Table: p.807

**Singleton, Sarah M**
(New Mexico)
Environment Band 1
Table: p.1323
Environment Band 1
Table: p.1323

**Sinha, Pankaj K**
(District of Columbia)
Profile: p.546
Corporate/Commercial Band 3
Table: p.435

**Siniscalco, Gary**
(California)
Profile: p.314
Employment Band 2
Table: p.231

**Sink, Charles** (California)
Construction Band 1
Table: p.225

**Sinkfield, Richard H**
(Georgia)
Litigation Band 1
Table: p.698

**Sipe Jr, Samuel M**
(National)
Profile: p.135
Transportation Band 1
Table: p.69

**Sipiora, David E** (Colorado)
Profile: p.366
Intellectual Property Band 2
Table: p.351

**Sirilla, George M** (Virginia)
Profile: p.1986
Intellectual Property Band 2
Table: p.466
Intellectual Property Band S
Table: p.1975

**Sirkin, Joel** (Massachusetts)
Profile: p.1106
Real Estate Band 1
Table: p.1081

**Sirkin, Michael** (New York)
Profile: p.1502
Employee Benefits Band 2
Table: p.1362

**Sit, Po** (New York)
Profile: p.1502
Tax Band 2
Table: p.1425

**Sitarchuk, Eric W**
(Pennsylvania)
Profile: p.1742
Antitrust Band 3
Table: p.1692
Litigation Band 3
Table: p.1714

**Sitton, Larry B**
(North Carolina)
Profile: p.1586
Litigation Band 2
Table: p.1577

**Skeffington, James**
(Rhode Island)
Profile: p.1773
Corporate/Commercial Band 2
Table: p.1766

**Skelly, Paul**
(District of Columbia)
Profile: p.546
Employment Band 3
Table: p.439

**Skerritt, Daniel** (Oregon)
Profile: p.1684
Litigation Band 1
Table: p.1674

**Skidmore, Jonathan B**
(National)
Profile: p.135
Products Liability Band 3
Table: p.50

**Skilton, John** (Wisconsin)
Profile: p.2035
Litigation Band 2
Table: p.2029

**Skindrud, Michael E.**
(Wisconsin)
Corporate/M&A Band 3
Table: p.2025

**Skinner, Honey J** (Illinois)
Profile: p.857
Healthcare Band 3
Table: p.793

**Skinner, Shannon**
(Washington)
Real Estate Band 3
Table: p.2002

**Skinner, William P**
(District of Columbia)
Profile: p.546
Insurance Band 2
Table: p.464

**Sklar, Daniel W**
(New Hampshire)
Profile: p.1273
Corporate/Commercial Band 1
Table: p.1263
Corporate/Commercial Band 3
Table: p.1263

**Sklar, Stanley P** (Illinois)
Construction Band S
Table: p.778

**Sklaroff, Michael**
(Pennsylvania)
Profile: p.1742
Real Estate Band 1
Table: p.1718
Real Estate Band 1
Table: p.1718

**Sklarsky, Charles B**
(Illinois)
Profile: p.857
Litigation Band 4
Table: p.802

**Skolnick, Holly** (Florida)
Profile: p.652
Litigation Band 2
Table: p.610

**Slade, Georgiana J**
(National)
Wealth Management Band 2
Table: p.81

**Slade, Lynn H**
(New Mexico)
Environment Band 1
Table: p.1323
Native Law Band 1
Table: p.1326

**Slater, James** (Florida)
Real Estate Band 3
Table: p.617
Litigation Band 1

**Slater, Paul** (Illinois)
Antitrust Band 2
Table: p.767

**Slater, Thomas** (Virginia)
Profile: p.1986
Litigation Band 1

**Slater, Valerie A**
(District of Columbia)
Profile: p.135
International Trade Band 3
Table: p.42

**Slaughter, Christopher**
(West Virginia)
Employment Up and coming
Table: p.2012

**Slaughter Jr, Harrison T**
(Florida)
Litigation Band 2
Table: p.610

**Slavich, John** (Texas)
Environment Band 2
Table: p.1852

**Sleeth, Tim E** (Florida)
Environment Band 3
Table: p.601

**Slonaker, Norman**
(New York)
Profile: p.135
Capital Markets Band 2
Table: p.7

**Slone, Daniel K** (Virginia)
Environment Band 2

**Sloss, John** (New York)
Media & Entertainment Band 2
Table: p.1401

**Slotnick, Barry I** (New York)
Profile: p.1502
Media & Entertainment Band 3
Table: p.1404

**Slovek, Robert M**
(Nebraska)
Litigation Band 3
Table: p.1239

**Slusky, Jerry M** (Nebraska)
Real Estate Band 2
Table: p.1242

**Slusser, William C** (Texas)
Intellectual Property Band 1
Table: p.1860

**Slutzky, Steven J** (National)
Capital Markets
Up and coming
Table: p.7

**Small, Andrew** (Illinois)
Profile: p.857
Real Estate Band 3
Table: p.809

**Small, Jeffrey** (New York)
Profile: p.135
Capital Markets Band 2
Table: p.7

**Small, John H** (Delaware)
Corporate/M&A Band 3
Table: p.394
Corporate/M&A Band 2
Table: p.395

**Small, Michael**
(District of Columbia)
Energy Band 3
Table: p.445

**Small, Richard G**
(Rhode Island)
Profile: p.1106
Private Equity Band 3
Table: p.1078

**Smallwood, Mary F**
(Florida)
Environment Band 1
Table: p.601

**Smedinghoff, Thomas J**
(Illinois)
Profile: p.857
Technology Band 1
Table: p.814

**Smilan, Laurie B** (Virginia)
Litigation Band 3
Table: p.1977

**Smit, Robert H** (New York)
Profile: p.135
International Arbitration
Band 2
Table: p.36

**Smith, Alan C** (Washington)
Profile: p.2007

Corporate/Commercial
Up and coming
Table: p.1992

**Smith, Alison** (Texas)
Antitrust Band 2
Table: p.1829

**Smith, Bradford J**
(Massachusetts)
Profile: p.1106
Employment Up and coming
Table: p.1065

**Smith, Bradley Y** (New York)
Profile: p.1503
Banking & Finance Band 1
Table: p.1339

**Smith, Brian D** (California)
Profile: p.314
Real Estate Band 2
Table: p.270

**Smith, Brooks** (Virginia)
Profile: p.1986
Environment Band 2
Table: p.1973

**Smith, Bruce M** (Idaho)
Natural Resources Band 2
Table: p.761

**Smith, Chris M** (New York)
Profile: p.1503
Real Estate Band 2
Table: p.1417

**Smith, Daniel Hoyt**
(Washington)
Immigration Band 1
Table: p.1997

**Smith, David M** (Alabama)
Profile: p.159
Employment Band 2
Table: p.150

**Smith, David S** (Virginia)
Employment Band 3
Table: p.1971

**Smith, Douglas**
(District of Columbia)
Energy Band 5
Table: p.445

**Smith, Douglas D**
(California)
Profile: p.314
Corporate/M&A Band 4
Table: p.227

**Smith, Edwin E**
(Massachusetts)
Profile: p.1106
Banking & Finance Band 1
Table: p.1055

**Smith, Felton W** (Alabama)
Profile: p.159
Real Estate Band 3
Table: p.153

**Smith, George Anthony**
(Georgia)
Profile: p.724
Construction Band 3
Table: p.682

**S**

**Smith, Glenn L** (Iowa)
Litigation Band 4
Table: p.914

**Smith, Gordon** (Georgia)
Profile: p.724
Litigation Band 3
Table: p.698

**Smith, Gregory** (Nevada)
Employment Band 3
Table: p.1248

**Smith, Gregory A**
(National)
Profile: p.135
Government Contracts Band 3
Table: p.30

**Smith, Gregory C**
(California)
Profile: p.314
Corporate/M&A Band 4
Table: p.227

**Smith, Harrison** (Ohio)
Real Estate Band 1
Table: p.1622

**Smith, J Theodore (Ted)**
(Ohio)
Profile: p.1639
Real Estate Band 4
Table: p.1621

**Smith, James** (Georgia)
Corporate/M&A Band 4
Table: p.684

**Smith, James E** (Texas)
Profile: p.1914
Environment Band 1
Table: p.1853

**Smith, Janet Hugie** (Utah)
Employment Band 1
Table: p.1944

**Smith, Jeffrey** (New York)
Profile: p.1503
Environment Band 1
Table: p.1373

**Smith, Jeffrey Q** (New York)
Profile: p.1503
Litigation Band 2
Table: p.1390

**Smith, Jerry** (Georgia)
Profile: p.724
Tax Band 3
Table: p.703

**Smith, Joseph A** (New York)
Profile: p.1503
Private Equity Band 3
Table: p.1410

**Smith, Julious** (Virginia)
Corporate/M&A Band 2
Table: p.1968

**Smith, Kevin** (Kentucky)
Employment Band 2
Table: p.939

**Smith, L Chapman** (Texas)
Profile: p.1914
Employment Band 3
Table: p.1844

**Smith, Laura** (Arkansas)
Litigation Band 1
Table: p.205

**Smith, Lex R** (Hawaii)
Litigation Band 3
Table: p.745

**Smith, Michael** (Virginia)
Litigation Band 1
Table: p.1977

**Smith, Michael W**
(National)
Profile: p.135
Transportation Band 2
Table: p.64

**Smith, Nathan H** (Maine)
Profile: p.1016
Real Estate Band 2
Table: p.1008

**Smith, Neil A** (California)
Intellectual Property Band 4
Table: p.248

**Smith, Paul**
(District of Columbia)
Profile: p.546
Litigation Band 1
Table: p.475
Media & Entertainment Band 1
Table: p.477

**Smith, Paul T** (California)
Healthcare Band 3
Table: p.238

**Smith, Philip J**
(Massachusetts)
Profile: p.1107
Banking & Finance Band 3
Table: p.1055

**Smith, Roger**
(District of Columbia)
Energy Band 3
Table: p.445

**Smith, Scott** (New York)
Profile: p.1503
Corporate/M&A Band 2
Table: p.1359

**Smith, Sean**
(North Dakota)
Corporate/Commercial Band 1
Table: p.1590

**Smith, Sheldon H**
(Colorado)
Profile: p.366
Employment Band 1
Table: p.348

**Smith, Taylor** (Mississippi)
Employment Band 1
Table: p.1177

**Smith, Tefft W**
(District of Columbia)
Profile: p.547
Antitrust Band 4
Table: p.426

**Smith, W Lindsay**
(South Carolina)
Profile: p.1784
Real Estate Band 3

Table: p.1780

**Smith, William P** (Illinois)
Profile: p.857
Bankruptcy Band 3
Table: p.775

**Smith, Wm Randolph**
(District of Columbia)
Profile: p.547
Antitrust Band 4
Table: p.426

**Smith III, Frank G**
(Georgia)
Profile: p.725
Intellectual Property Band 4
Table: p.696

**Smith III, James** (Kentucky)
Employment Band 1
Table: p.939

**Smith III, William C**
(Mississippi)
Real Estate Band 2
Table: p.1181

**Smith Jr, Richard K**
(California)
Profile: p.135
Transportation Band 2
Table: p.64

**Smith Jr, Robert (Jay) W**
(Maryland)
Profile: p.1044
Corporate/M&A ✪
Table: p.1025

**Smith Jr, Turner T**
(District of Columbia)
Profile: p.547
Environment Band 3
Table: p.451

**Smith, III, Henry A.**
(Maryland)
Employee Benefits Band 1
Table: p.1027

**Smoak, Lewis T**
(South Carolina)
Profile: p.1784
Employment Band 3
Table: p.1777

**Smolen, Lee M** (Illinois)
Profile: p.857
Real Estate Band 2
Table: p.809

**Smoyer, Divonne**
(District of Columbia)
Profile: p.547
Insurance Band 3
Table: p.464

**Smulian, Andrew** (Florida)
Profile: p.652
Real Estate Band 2
Table: p.617

**Smutny, Abby Cohen**
(District of Columbia)
Profile: p.135
International Arbitration
Band 2
Table: p.36

**Smyser, Craig** (Texas)
Litigation Band 3
Table: p.1865

**Smythe, Marianne**
(District of Columbia)
Profile: p.547
Investment Management Band 1
Table: p.469

**Smythe, Susan**
(South Carolina)
Profile: p.1784
Real Estate Band 3
Table: p.1780

**Sneed, Spencer** (Alaska)
Profile: p.174
Bankruptcy Band 1
Table: p.167
Litigation Band 2
Table: p.171

**Sneed, William M** (Illinois)
Profile: p.857
Insurance Band 2
Table: p.795

**Sneirson, Marilyn** (New
Jersey)
Employment Band 3
Table: p.1282

**Snell, Virginia** (Kentucky)
Profile: p.951
Litigation Band 3
Table: p.942

**Snider, Jerry W** (Minnesota)
Profile: p.1167
Litigation Band 2
Table: p.1156

**Snow, Ronald**
(New Hampshire)
Litigation Band 1
Table: p.1267
Litigation ✪
Table: p.1268

**Snow, Stephen E** (Rhode
Island)
Litigation Band 1
Table: p.1769

**Snyder, Allison** (Texas)
Construction Band 4
Table: p.1838

**Snyder, Charles** (Louisiana)
Corporate/M&A Band 4
Table: p.965

**Snyder, David R** (California)
Profile: p.315
Capital Markets Band 2
Table: p.8
Corporate/M&A Band 4
Table: p.227

**Snyder, Jeffrey L** (National)
Profile: p.135
International Trade Band 1
Table: p.41

**Snyder, Joan P** (Oregon)
Environment Band 2
Table: p.1672

**Snyder, Lynn Shapiro**
(District of Columbia)
Profile: p.547
Healthcare Band 2
Table: p.456

**Snyder, Orin** (New York)
Profile: p.1503
Litigation Band 3
Table: p.1388

**Snyder, Sheryl** (Kentucky)
Profile: p.951
Litigation Band 1
Table: p.942

**Snyder, Stephen L**
(Maryland)
Litigation Band 2
Table: p.1032

**Sobel, Gerald** (New York)
Profile: p.1503
Intellectual Property Band 2
Table: p.1384

**Sogn, Jon C**
(South Dakota)
Employment Band 2
Table: p.1794

**Sohn, Michael N**
(District of Columbia)
Profile: p.547
Antitrust Band 2
Table: p.426

**Sokol, Jerry J** (Florida)
Profile: p.652
Healthcare Band 2
Table: p.604

**Solada, Mary** (Indiana)
Real Estate Band 2
Table: p.892

**Solimine, Louis F** (Ohio)
Profile: p.1639
Bankruptcy Band 3
Table: p.1600

**Sollins, Howard L**
(Maryland)
Healthcare Band 2
Table: p.1031

**Sollner, Richard** (Florida)
Real Estate Band 2
Table: p.617

**Solomon, Jay** (Georgia)
Immigration Band 1
Table: p.694

**Solomon, Randall** (Ohio)
Litigation Band 3
Table: p.1617

**Solovy, Jerold S** (Illinois)
Profile: p.858
Litigation Band 2
Table: p.802

**Solow, Alan P** (Illinois)
Bankruptcy Band 3
Table: p.775

**Solow, Michael** (Illinois)
Profile: p.858
Bankruptcy Band 2

Table: p.775

**Solow, Sheldon L** (Illinois)
Profile: p.858
Bankruptcy Band 3
Table: p.775

**Solt, Christine G**
(Massachusetts)
Healthcare Band 2
Table: p.1071

**Solveson, George H**
(Wisconsin)
IP Band 2
Table: p.2027

**Somers, George W**
(Indiana)
Profile: p.899
Real Estate Band 1
Table: p.892

**Somerstein, Barry** (Florida)
Real Estate Band 1
Table: p.617

**Sommer, Dean** (New York)
Environment Band 2
Table: p.1371

**Sommerhauser, Peter**
(Wisconsin)
Corporate/M&A Band 1
Table: p.2025

**Sonberg, Steven** (Florida)
Profile: p.652
Corporate/M&A Band 2
Table: p.594

**Sonnenfeld, Marc**
(Pennsylvania)
Profile: p.1742
Litigation Band 2
Table: p.1714
Litigation Band 1
Table: p.1715

**Sonnett, Neal R** (Florida)
Litigation Band 2
Table: p.610

**Sonsini, Larry W**
(California)
Profile: p.315
Corporate/M&A ✪
Table: p.227

**Sopher, Edward D** (New York)
Profile: p.1503
Private Equity Band 2
Table: p.1410

**Sorensen, Harvey** (Kansas)
Profile: p.933
Corporate/M&A Band 1
Table: p.924

**Sorensen, Sharp** (Illinois)
Profile: p.858
Tax Band 3
Table: p.812

**Sorenson, Derek L**
(Arizona)
Profile: p.195
Real Estate Band 3
Table: p.184

**Soriano, Robert** (Florida)
Profile: p.652
Bankruptcy Band 2
Table: p.586

**Sorin, David** (New Jersey)
Profile: p.1306
Corporate/M&A Band 1
Table: p.1278

**Sorin, Robert J** (New York)
Profile: p.1503
Real Estate Band 5
Table: p.1417

**Sorkin, David** (New York)
Profile: p.1504
Corporate/M&A Band 4
Table: p.1354

**Soroko, John J**
(Pennsylvania)
Profile: p.1742
Litigation Band 2
Table: p.1715

**Sorondo Jr, Rodolfo**
(Florida)
Profile: p.652
Litigation Band 1
Table: p.615

**Sosland, Martin** (Texas)
Profile: p.1914
Bankruptcy Band 1
Table: p.1835

**Sosnick, Fredric** (New York)
Profile: p.1504
Bankruptcy Band 4
Table: p.1344

**Sostek, Bruce** (Texas)
Profile: p.1914
Intellectual Property Band 3
Table: p.1860

**Soto, Edward** (Florida)
Profile: p.652
Litigation Band 3
Table: p.609

**Sottile, James**
(District of Columbia)
Insurance Band 2
Table: p.461

**Soussloff, Andrew D**
(National)
Profile: p.136
Capital Markets Band 3
Table: p.7

**Southworth II, Louis S**
(West Virginia)
Profile: p.2018
Corporate/Commercial Band 1
Table: p.2010
Corporate/Commercial Band 1
Table: p.2011

**Sowell, Thornwell F**
(South Carolina)
Profile: p.1784
Litigation Band 2
Table: p.1778

**Sozio, Stephen** (Ohio)
Profile: p.1639
Litigation Band 1

Table: p.1618

**Spaan, Michael** (Alaska)
Profile: p.174
Litigation Band 2
Table: p.171

**Spaanstra, James R**
(Colorado)
Profile: p.366
Environment Band 1
Table: p.350

**Spackman, David G**
(Massachusetts)
Profile: p.1107
Healthcare Band 2
Table: p.1071

**Spak, Gregory J** (National)
Profile: p.136
International Trade Band 5
Table: p.42

**Spak, Walter J**
(District of Columbia)
Profile: p.136
International Trade Band 4
Table: p.42

**Spangler, Georlen** (Nevada)
Litigation Band 1
Table: p.1253

**Spangler III, John I**
(Georgia)
Profile: p.725
Construction Band 1
Table: p.682

**Sparkman, Jon B**
(New Hampshire)
Corporate/Commercial Band 2
Table: p.1264

**Sparks, Stephen S**
(Missouri)
Real Estate Band 2
Table: p.1201

**Sparks III, A Gilchrist**
(Delaware)
Profile: p.412
Chancery ✪
Table: p.392
Corporate/M&A Band 2
Table: p.394

**Sparks Jr, Robert R**
(Virginia)
Employment Band 3
Table: p.1971

**Spartin, Debbie B**
(District of Columbia)
Profile: p.547
Real Estate Band 4
Table: p.482

**Spatt, Robert E** (New York)
Profile: p.1504
Corporate/M&A Band 2
Table: p.1354

**Spears, Berry** (Texas)
Bankruptcy Band 3
Table: p.1835

**Spears, L Gene** (Texas)
Profile: p.1914

Intellectual Property Band 3
Table: p.1860

**Specie, Karen K** (Florida)
Bankruptcy Band 4
Table: p.586

**Spector, Arthur** (Florida)
Bankruptcy Band 3
Table: p.586

**Spector, Barry S**
(District of Columbia)
Energy Band 4
Table: p.445

**Spector, Brian F** (Florida)
Profile: p.652
Litigation Band 3
Table: p.609

**Spector, David** (Illinois)
Profile: p.858
Insurance Band 1
Table: p.795
Insurance Band 2
Table: p.796

**Spector, Scott** (California)
Profile: p.315
Employment Band 2
Table: p.232

**Spencer, Bob** (Louisiana)
Employment Band 3
Table: p.967

**Spergel, Jonathan**
(Pennsylvania)
Environment Up and coming
Table: p.1707

**Sperling, Allan G** (New
York)
Profile: p.136
Capital Markets Band 2
Table: p.7

**Sperling, Robert Y** (Illinois)
Profile: p.858
Litigation Band 3
Table: p.802

**Speth II, Charles T**
(South Carolina)
Profile: p.1785
Employment Band 1
Table: p.1777

**Spiegel, John** (California)
Litigation Band 2
Table: p.257

**Spielberg, David**
(California)
Profile: p.315
Projects Band 2
Table: p.268

**Spiers, Jeffrey E** (Texas)
Bankruptcy Band 4
Table: p.1835

**Spiller, Keith P** (Ohio)
Profile: p.1639
Employment Band 3
Table: p.1609

**Spink, James W** (Vermont)
Litigation Band 2

Table: p.1959

**Spivak, Mark**
(District of Columbia)
Profile: p.547
Projects Band 3
Table: p.479

**Spivey, James K** (Texas)
Profile: p.1915
Antitrust Band 3
Table: p.1829

**Spivey III, John William**
(Arkansas)
Profile: p.210
Real Estate Band 1
Table: p.207

**Spradling, T Scott**
(Oklahoma)
Real Estate Band 2
Table: p.1661

**Sprague, Richard**
(Pennsylvania)
Litigation Band 2
Table: p.1715

**Spraker, Gary** (Alaska)
Bankruptcy Band 2
Table: p.167

**Spratling, Gary R**
(California)
Profile: p.315
Antitrust Band 1
Table: p.216

**Spratt, William** (Florida)
Profile: p.653
Healthcare Band 3
Table: p.604

**Sprayregen, James HM**
(Illinois)
Profile: p.858
Bankruptcy Band 1
Table: p.775

**Springer, Claudia**
(Pennsylvania)
Profile: p.1743
Bankruptcy Band 1
Table: p.1697

**Springer, Felix**
(Connecticut)
Profile: p.384
Employment Band 1
Table: p.376

**Squires III, William R**
(Washington)
Litigation Band 3
Table: p.2000

**Squyres, Newal** (Idaho)
Profile: p.765
Litigation Band 2
Table: p.760

**Srebnick, Howard M**
(Florida)
Litigation Band 2
Table: p.610

**Srebnick, Scott A** (Florida)
Litigation Band 2
Table: p.615

**Sroufe, Evelyn Cruz**
(Washington)
Corporate/Commercial Band 2
Table: p.1992

**St Clair, Jay D** (Alabama)
Profile: p.160
Employment Band 3
Table: p.150

**St Marie, Scott D**
(New York)
Construction Band 4
Table: p.1351

**St Peter, Gary**
(Rhode Island)
Employment Band 1
Table: p.1768

**St. Ville, Thomas J.**
(Maryland)
Employee Benefits Band 3
Table: p.1027

**Stabler, Wendie C**
(Delaware)
Profile: p.412
Real Estate Band 1
Table: p.400

**Stack Jr, Stephen A**
(Pennsylvania)
Profile: p.1743
Antitrust Band 2
Table: p.1692

**Stacy, David H** (Colorado)
Employment Band 3
Table: p.348

**Staffaroni, Robert J**
(New York)
Tax Band 3
Table: p.1423

**Stage, Jon** (Florida)
Employment Band 4
Table: p.597

**Stageberg, Roger**
(Minnesota)
Corporate/M&A Band 3
Table: p.1152

**Stahl, David M** (Illinois)
Profile: p.858
Antitrust Band 3
Table: p.767
Energy Band 3
Table: p.789

**Stahl, Thomas H** (Missouri)
Profile: p.1210
Corporate/M&A Band 3
Table: p.1193

**Stair, Kent** (Georgia)
Construction Band 2
Table: p.682

**Stallings, John** (Kansas)
Real Estate Band 2
Table: p.930

**Stamas, George**
(District of Columbia)
Profile: p.548
Corporate/Commercial Band 2
Table: p.435

**Stamelman, Andrew J**
(New Jersey)
Profile: p.1306
Corporate/M&A Band 3
Table: p.1278

**Stamp, Vincent B** (Ohio)
Profile: p.1639
Environment Band 3
Table: p.1612

**Stanchfield, Mike**
(Minnesota)
Profile: p.1167
Corporate/M&A Band 3
Table: p.1152

**Standish, Daniel J**
(District of Columbia)
Profile: p.548
Insurance Band 2
Table: p.461

**Stanford, Douglas** (Florida)
Real Estate Band 3
Table: p.617

**Stanley, Douglas** (Kansas)
Profile: p.933
Employment Band 1
Table: p.926

**Stanley, Hugh** (Ohio)
Litigation Band 4
Table: p.1617

**Stanley, James T** (Alaska)
Real Estate Band 2
Table: p.172

**Stanley, Robert K** (Indiana)
Profile: p.899
Litigation Band 2
Table: p.890

**Stanton, Patrick M** (New Jersey)
Profile: p.1306
Employment Band 1
Table: p.1282

**Stanton, W Clark**
(California)
Healthcare Band 2
Table: p.238

**Stapleton, Benjamin F**
(New York)
Profile: p.1504
Corporate/M&A Band 2
Table: p.1354

**Stapleton, James F**
(Connecticut)
Profile: p.385
Litigation Band S
Table: p.378

**Starer, Brian** (New York)
Profile: p.136
Transportation Band 3
Table: p.74

**Stark, Stephen** (Kansas)
Real Estate Band 2
Table: p.930

**Starke, Wallace** (Virginia)
Employment Band 2
Table: p.1971

**Starkey, J Shane** (Ohio)
Profile: p.1639
Employee Benefits Band 2
Table: p.1607

**Starling III, M Jefferson**
(Alabama)
Profile: p.160
Employment Band 3
Table: p.150

**Starn, Peter** (Hawaii)
Real Estate Band 2
Table: p.748

**Starnes, Stancil** (Alabama)
Profile: p.160
Litigation Band 1
Table: p.152

**Starr, Judson**
(District of Columbia)
Environment Band 2
Table: p.451

**Starr, Kenneth W**
(California)
Profile: p.548
Litigation Band S
Table: p.475

**Starr, Michael** (New York)
Profile: p.1504
Employment Band 3
Table: p.1365

**Starrett, Cindy** (California)
Real Estate Band 2
Table: p.270

**Statham, Kenneth Scott**
(Texas)
Profile: p.1915
Insurance Band 3
Table: p.1858

**Stayer, Mark** (Oregon)
Real Estate Band 3
Table: p.1677

**Stearns, Eugene** (Florida)
Litigation Band 2
Table: p.609

**Steeg, Robert M**
(Louisiana)
Real Estate Band 1
Table: p.975

**Steel, John M** (Washington)
Profile: p.2007
Corporate/Commercial Band 1
Table: p.1992

**Steel, Michael J**
(California)
Profile: p.315
Environment Band 3
Table: p.236

**Steenrod, Ralston W**
(Kentucky)
Profile: p.952
Corporate/M&A Band 3
Table: p.937

**Stefani, Randall** (Iowa)
Litigation Band 2
Table: p.914

**Stegemoeller, Mark**
(National)
Capital Markets Band 3
Table: p.8

**Steger, Christopher**
(Tennessee)
Profile: p.1817
Employment Band 3
Table: p.1801

**Stein, Craig** (National)
Profile: p.136
Capital Markets Band 2
Table: p.13
Capital Markets Band 3
Table: p.15

**Stein, Grant T** (Georgia)
Profile: p.725
Bankruptcy Band 1
Table: p.679

**Stein, Jeffrey** (Georgia)
Profile: p.725
Corporate/M&A Band 3
Table: p.684

**Stein, Joshua** (New York)
Real Estate Band 3
Table: p.1417

**Stein, Laurence J**
(California)
Tax Band 4
Table: p.274

**Stein, Lee** (Arizona)
Litigation Band 2
Table: p.182

**Stein, Mark** (New York)
Profile: p.1504
Litigation Band 3
Table: p.1391

**Stein, Stanton 'Larry'**
(California)
Profile: p.315
Media & Entertainment Band 1
Table: p.263

**Stein, Steven GM** (Illinois)
Construction Band 1
Table: p.778

**Steinberg, Arthur**
(New York)
Profile: p.1504
Bankruptcy Band 4
Table: p.1344

**Steinberg, Donald R**
(Massachusetts)
Profile: p.1107
Intellectual Property Band 3
Table: p.1072

**Steinberg, James**
(National)
Profile: p.136
Business Process Outsourcing Band 4
Table: p.2

**Steinberg, Jonathan H**
(California)
Intellectual Property Band 3
Table: p.248

**Steinberg, Marty** (Florida)
Profile: p.653
Antitrust Band 3
Table: p.581
Litigation Band 2
Table: p.609
Litigation Band 2
Table: p.610

**Steinberg, Michael W**
(District of Columbia)
Profile: p.548
Environment Band 2
Table: p.451

**Steindler, Howard** (Ohio)
Profile: p.1639
Real Estate Band 3
Table: p.1621

**Steiner, Beat** (Colorado)
Profile: p.366
Real Estate Band 1
Table: p.355

**Steiner, Edward** (Ohio)
Corporate/M&A Band 2
Table: p.1605

**Steiner, Jeffrey** (New York)
Profile: p.1505
Real Estate Band 5
Table: p.1417

**Steiner, Jonathan H**
(Hawaii)
Litigation Up and coming
Table: p.745

**Steinthal, Kenneth**
(California)
Profile: p.316
Media & Entertainment Band 3
Table: p.263

**Stemmler, John A**
(Tennessee)
Profile: p.1817
Real Estate Band 2
Table: p.1808

**Stempel, James A** (Illinois)
Profile: p.859
Bankruptcy Band 3
Table: p.775

**Stengel, James L**
(National)
Profile: p.136
Products Liability Band 2
Table: p.50

**Stenmoe, Gregory**
(Minnesota)
Employment Band 3
Table: p.1154

**Stensland, Dean** (Montana)
Real Estate Band 2
Table: p.1230

**Stepaniak, Mark J** (Ohio)
Employment Band 2
Table: p.1609

**Stephen, John M** (Ohio)
Profile: p.1639
Employment Band 2
Table: p.1609

**Stephens, Kenneth**
(Oregon)
Profile: p.1684
Corporate/M&A Band 2
Table: p.1667

**Stephens, Robert** (Texas)
Profile: p.1915
Energy & Natural Resources
Up & coming

**Stephens, Thomas**
(Colorado)
Corporate/M&A Band 3
Table: p.346

**Stephens, Thomas M**
(Illinois)
Profile: p.859
Tax Band 3
Table: p.812

**Stephenson, Alan**
(New York)
Profile: p.1505
Corporate/M&A Band 2
Table: p.1354

**Stephenson, Andrew W**
(District of Columbia)
Profile: p.548
Construction Band 2
Table: p.433

**Stephenson, Barbara G**
(New Mexico)
Employment Band 2
Table: p.1321

**Stephenson, Jack**
(Alabama)
Corporate/Commercial Band 2
Table: p.148

**Stephenson, Mason W**
(Georgia)
Profile: p.725
Real Estate Band 1
Table: p.700

**Stephenson, Thomas**
(South Carolina)
Profile: p.1785
Litigation Band 2
Table: p.1778

**Stephenson III, Paul H**
(Mississippi)
Litigation Band 2
Table: p.1179

**Steptoe Jr, Robert M**
(West Virginia)
Employment Band 1
Table: p.2012

**Sterling, David** (Texas)
Profile: p.1915
Litigation Band 1
Table: p.1866

**Sterling, Mark** (Florida)
Profile: p.653
Healthcare Band 3
Table: p.604

**Stern, Akiba** (New York)
Profile: p.1505
Business Process Outsourcing
Band 2

Table: p.2
Technology Band 2
Table: p.1428

**Stern, Claude M**
(California)
Profile: p.316
Intellectual Property Band 3
Table: p.248

**Stern, Elizabeth E**
(District of Columbia)
Profile: p.548
Immigration Band 2
Table: p.459

**Stern, Eric L** (Pennsylvania)
Profile: p.1743
Real Estate Band 3
Table: p.1718

**Stern, Gary** (Illinois)
Profile: p.136
Capital Markets Band 1
Table: p.18

**Stern, Joan N**
(Pennsylvania)
Profile: p.1743
Banking & Finance Band 1
Table: p.1695

**Stern, Richard** (New York)
Bankruptcy Band 4
Table: p.1344

**Stern, Roger D** (California)
Profile: p.316
Employment Band 4
Table: p.232

**Stern, William E**
(Massachusetts)
Profile: p.1107
Banking & Finance Up and
coming
Table: p.1055

**Stern III, Walter E**
(New Mexico)
Environment Band 1
Table: p.1323
Native Law Band 1
Table: p.1326

**Sternberg, Daniel S**
(New York)
Profile: p.1505
Corporate/M&A Band 4
Table: p.1354

**Sternberg, John D**
(Colorado)
Profile: p.366
Real Estate Band 1
Table: p.355

**Sterne, Robert**
(District of Columbia)
Profile: p.548
Intellectual Property Band 3
Table: p.466

**Stetler, David J** (Illinois)
Litigation Band 2
Table: p.803

**Stetson, Jim** (Illinois)
Technology Band 3
Table: p.814

**Steuber, David** (California)
Insurance Band 1
Table: p.245

**Steuer, Richard M**
(New York)
Profile: p.1505
Antitrust Band 3
Table: p.1335

**Stevens, C Eric**
(Tennessee)
Profile: p.1817
Employment Band 3
Table: p.1801

**Stevens, Charles J**
(California)
Litigation Band 1
Table: p.258

**Stevens, Charles P**
(Wisconsin)
Employment Band 1
Table: p.2027

**Stevens, Mark A**
(Pennsylvania)
Environment Band 3
Table: p.1707

**Stevens, Mark C**
(California)
Profile: p.316
Corporate/M&A Band 4
Table: p.227

**Stevens, Michael L**
(District of Columbia)
Profile: p.548
Employment Band 3
Table: p.439

**Stevens, Winfred** (Maine)
Real Estate Band 2
Table: p.1008

**Stevenson, Brent** (Utah)
Corporate/M&A Band 2
Table: p.1941

**Stevenson, Randy**
(Nebraska)
Employment Band 2
Table: p.1238

**Stevenson, Robert B**
(Michigan)
Employee Benefits Band 1
Table: p.1124

**Stever, Donald W**
(New York)
Profile: p.1505
Environment Band 2
Table: p.1371
Environment Band 3
Table: p.1373

**Steverson, Randall**
(Hawaii)
Real Estate Band 1
Table: p.748

**Stewart, Carol** (Alabama)
Real Estate Band 3
Table: p.153

**Stewart, Dan** (Texas)
Profile: p.1915

Bankruptcy Band 1
Table: p.1835

**Stewart, David O**
(District of Columbia)
Profile: p.548
Healthcare Band 2
Table: p.456

**Stewart, Mike** (Oklahoma)
Profile: p.1660
Corporate/Commercial Band 1
Table: p.1653

**Stewart, Robert** (Texas)
Environment Band 2
Table: p.1852
Environment Band 2
Table: p.1853

**Stewart, Robert K** (Alaska)
Employment Band 2
Table: p.169

**Stewart, Scott M**
(National)
Profile: p.136
Tax Litigation Band 2

**Stewart, Terence P**
(District of Columbia)
International Trade Band 3
Table: p.42

**Stewart III, J Hamilton**
(South Carolina)
Profile: p.1785
Employment Band 3
Table: p.1777

**Stichter, Don M** (Florida)
Profile: p.653
Bankruptcy Band S
Table: p.586

**Stier Jr, Robert H** (Maine)
Profile: p.1016
Litigation Band 3
Table: p.1006

**Still, Charles** (Texas)
Profile: p.1915
Corporate/M&A Band 2
Table: p.1840

**Stillman, Charles** (New York)
Litigation Band 1
Table: p.1391

**Stillman, Gregory** (Virginia)
Profile: p.1986
Litigation Band 1

**Stillman, Nina G** (Illinois)
Profile: p.859
Employment Band 1
Table: p.785

**Stillwell, R Newcomb**
(Massachusetts)
Profile: p.1107
Private Equity Band 3
Table: p.1078

**Stinson, James R** (Illinois)
Profile: p.859
Insurance Band 1
Table: p.795
Insurance Band 2

Table: p.796

**Stiver, Charles** (Florida)
Profile: p.653
Tax Band 4
Table: p.623

**Stock, Stuart C** (National)
Profile: p.136
Financial Services Band 2
Table: p.24
Financial Services Band 1
Table: p.28

**Stockbridge, Edward T**
(Texas)
Profile: p.1915
Technology Band 2
Table: p.1877

**Stocker, Joel L** (Florida)
Profile: p.653
Healthcare Band 3
Table: p.604

**Stocks, Bruce** (Colorado)
Corporate/M&A Band 2
Table: p.346

**Stockton, David** (Georgia)
Profile: p.725
Corporate/M&A Band 3
Table: p.684

**Stoddard III, John E** (New Jersey)
Corporate/M&A Band 3
Table: p.1278

**Stokes, Randall** (Arizona)
Real Estate Band 3
Table: p.184

**Stolkin, Ronald J** (Arizona)
Profile: p.195
Employment Band 1
Table: p.178

**Stoll, Neal R** (New York)
Profile: p.1505
Antitrust Band 4
Table: p.1335

**Stoll, R Ryan** (National)
Profile: p.137
Products Liability
Up and coming
Table: p.50

**Stoll, Richard G**
(District of Columbia)
Profile: p.549
Environment Band 4
Table: p.451

**Stoll, Robert** (Oregon)
Litigation Band 1
Table: p.1674

**Stoller, Robert** (Alaska)
Environment Band 2
Table: p.170

**Stoltzfus, Robert**
(Pennsylvania)
Environment Band 3
Table: p.1707

S

**Stolzman, Robert** (Rhode Island)
Profile: p.1773
Real Estate Band 2
Table: p.1770

**Stone, Alan J** (Delaware)
Profile: p.412
Chancery Band 3
Table: p.392

**Stone, Benjamin** (Georgia)
Employment Band 2
Table: p.702

**Stone, Jeffrey E** (Illinois)
Profile: p.859
Litigation Band 2
Table: p.802
Litigation Band 2
Table: p.803

**Stone, Steven W**
(District of Columbia)
Profile: p.549
Investment Management Band 2
Table: p.469

**Stone, Susan** (Texas)
Profile: p.1915
Tax Band 4

**Stone, Susan** (Illinois)
Profile: p.859
Insurance Band 2
Table: p.795

**Stoner, Wayne L**
(Massachusetts)
Profile: p.1107
Intellectual Property Band 2
Table: p.1072

**Stopher, Edward H**
(Kentucky)
Profile: p.952
Litigation Band 1
Table: p.942

**Storey, Anne-Marie L**
(Maine)
Employment Up and coming
Table: p.1002

**Storey, Lee** (Arizona)
Environment Band 2
Table: p.179

**Storey, Lesa J** (Arizona)
Profile: p.195
Real Estate Band 1
Table: p.184

**Stork, Anita** (California)
Antitrust Band 3
Table: p.216

**Storslee, Steven**
(North Dakota)
Litigation Band 1
Table: p.1593

**Stout, David J**
(New Mexico)
Litigation Band 4
Table: p.1324

**Stout, Mikel** (Kansas)
Profile: p.933
Litigation Band 1

Table: p.927

**Stoviak, John F**
(Pennsylvania)
Profile: p.1743
Environment Band 3
Table: p.1707

**Stowers, Gerard**
(West Virginia)
Litigation Band 2
Table: p.2013

**Strafer, Richard** (Florida)
Litigation Band 1
Table: p.615

**Strain, James A** (Indiana)
Profile: p.899
Corporate/M&A Band 1
Table: p.887

**Strain, Paul** (Maryland)
Litigation Band 2
Table: p.1032

**Strama, Brenda** (Texas)
Profile: p.1915
Healthcare Band 2
Table: p.1855

**Strand, Margaret**
(District of Columbia)
Environment Band 4
Table: p.451

**Strand, Peter** (Illinois)
Profile: p.859
Media & Entertainment Band 1
Table: p.807

**Strand, Robert** (Hawaii)
Real Estate Band 2
Table: p.748

**Strangis, Ralph**
(Minnesota)
Corporate/M&A Band 1
Table: p.1152

**Strassberg, Richard M**
(New York)
Profile: p.1505
Litigation Band 3
Table: p.1391

**Stratton, David B**
(Delaware)
Profile: p.412
Bankruptcy Band 3
Table: p.389

**Strauch, John L** (Ohio)
Profile: p.1639
Litigation Band 1
Table: p.1617

**Straus, R James**
(Kentucky)
Profile: p.952
Corporate/M&A Band 1
Table: p.937

**Strauss, Audrey** (New York)
Profile: p.1505
Litigation Band 1
Table: p.1391

**Strauss, David** (Ohio)
Real Estate Band 3

Table: p.1621

**Strecker, David** (Oklahoma)
Employment Band 2
Table: p.1654

**Street, Phillip** (Georgia)
Profile: p.725
Healthcare Band 2
Table: p.693

**Streeter, Jon** (California)
Profile: p.316
Intellectual Property Band 4
Table: p.248

**Streff Jr, William A**
(Illinois)
Profile: p.859
Intellectual Property Band 2
Table: p.799

**Streicker, James R**
(Illinois)
Litigation Band 2
Table: p.803

**Streit, Gary J** (Iowa)
Corporate/M&A Band 1
Table: p.909

**Strench, William G**
(Kentucky)
Profile: p.952
Corporate/M&A Band 2
Table: p.937

**Strickland, Kathleen**
(National)
Profile: p.137
Products Liability Band 3
Table: p.50

**Strickland, Tom** (Colorado)
Profile: p.366
Environment Band 1
Table: p.350

**Stricklin, Samuel M**
(Texas)
Profile: p.1915
Bankruptcy Band 4
Table: p.1835

**Striefsky, Linda** (Ohio)
Profile: p.1639
Real Estate Band 1
Table: p.1621

**Strimbu Jr, Victor** (Ohio)
Employment Band 3
Table: p.1609

**Strinden, Jon E**
(North Dakota)
Profile: p.1597
Corporate/Commercial Band 2
Table: p.1590

**Stringer, N Martin**
(Oklahoma)
Corporate/Commercial Band 2
Table: p.1653

**Stringfellow, James S**
(New York)
Profile: p.137
Capital Markets Band 3
Table: p.13

**Strober, Frederick D**
(Pennsylvania)
Profile: p.1743
Real Estate Band 1
Table: p.1718

**Strock, William** (Texas)
Employment Band 2
Table: p.1844

**Stromberg, Ross E**
(California)
Profile: p.316
Healthcare Band 1
Table: p.238

**Stromfeld, Lary** (National)
Profile: p.137
Capital Markets Band 1
Table: p.15

**Strong, Keith** (Montana)
Profile: p.1232
Litigation Band 1
Table: p.1225

**Strother, Jack** (Washington)
Corporate/Commercial Band 3
Table: p.1992

**Strotman, Andrew D**
(Nebraska)
Litigation Band 3
Table: p.1239

**Stroube III, H Rey** (Texas)
Profile: p.1916
Bankruptcy Band 4
Table: p.1835

**Stroup, Robert**
(North Dakota)
Real Estate Band 1
Table: p.1595

**Strubeck, Lou** (Texas)
Profile: p.1916
Bankruptcy Band 2
Table: p.1835

**Strunk, Sarah A** (Arizona)
Profile: p.195
Corporate/M&A Band 3
Table: p.176

**Struxness, Gregory E**
(Oregon)
Profile: p.1684
Corporate/M&A Band 3
Table: p.1667

**Stuart, Glen R**
(Pennsylvania)
Profile: p.1743
Environment Band 3
Table: p.1707

**Stubbs, Sidney** (Florida)
Litigation Band 2
Table: p.609

**Stucker, Robert J** (Illinois)
Employment Band 2
Table: p.786

**Stuckey, James A**
(Louisiana)
Profile: p.987
Banking & Finance Band 1
Table: p.963

**Studer, Judith** (Wyoming)
Employment Band 2
Table: p.2042
Litigation Band 2
Table: p.2044

**Stumo, Mary** (Minnesota)
Profile: p.1167
Employment Band 2
Table: p.1154

**Stump, John C** (West Virginia)
Corporate/Commercial Band 3
Table: p.2010

**Sturdivant, James**
(Oklahoma)
Profile: p.1661
Litigation Band 1
Table: p.1656

**Sturgeon, John A**
(California)
Profile: p.316
Litigation Band 4
Table: p.257

**Sturtz, Craig A** (Ohio)
Profile: p.1639
Environment Up & coming

**Stutts, Charles** (Florida)
Profile: p.653
Banking & Finance Band 2
Table: p.583

**Styles, Mark**
(New Mexico)
Real Estate Band 2
Table: p.1327

**Subin, Ben** (Florida)
Profile: p.653
Construction Band 2
Table: p.590

**Sudbeck, Roger**
(South Dakota)
Litigation Band 2
Table: p.1795
Litigation Band 2
Table: p.1795

**Sudbury, Deborah A**
(Georgia)
Profile: p.725
Employment Band 4
Table: p.687

**Sudell, William H**
(Delaware)
Profile: p.412
Bankruptcy Band 2
Table: p.389

**Suflas, Steven W**
(New Jersey)
Profile: p.1306
Employment Band 1
Table: p.1282

**Sugarman, Myron**
(National)
Wealth Management Band 3
Table: p.81

**Sugarman, Robert G**
(New York)
Profile: p.1506

Media & Entertainment Band 2
Table: p.1404

**Sugerman, David L**
(National)
Profile: p.137
Capital Markets Band 4
Table: p.18

**Suggs Jr, Fred W**
(South Carolina)
Profile: p.1785
Employment Band 3
Table: p.1777

**Sukin, Michael** (New York)
Media & Entertainment Band 1
Table: p.1401

**Sulkin, Robert M**
(Washington)
Litigation Band 3
Table: p.2000

**Sullivan, Alan** (Utah)
Profile: p.1952
Litigation Band 1
Table: p.1945

**Sullivan, Barry** (Illinois)
Profile: p.859
Litigation Band 3
Table: p.802

**Sullivan, Brendan V**
(District of Columbia)
Litigation Band 1
Table: p.471
Litigation Band 1
Table: p.471

**Sullivan, Brian** (Vermont)
Real Estate Band 2
Table: p.1961

**Sullivan, Diane P**
(New Jersey)
Profile: p.1307
Litigation Band 1
Table: p.1292
Products Liability Band 2
Table: p.50

**Sullivan, Edward J**
(Oregon)
Real Estate Band 1
Table: p.1677

**Sullivan, John** (Montana)
Employment Band 1
Table: p.1223

**Sullivan, John L**
(Massachusetts)
Profile: p.1107
Real Estate Band 2
Table: p.1081

**Sullivan, Jon** (Iowa)
Real Estate Band 2
Table: p.917

**Sullivan, Kevin**
(District of Columbia)
Profile: p.549
Antitrust Band 4
Table: p.426

**Sullivan, Marcia W**
(Illinois)
Profile: p.860
Real Estate Band 4
Table: p.809

**Sullivan, Mary Anne**
(District of Columbia)
Profile: p.549
Energy Band 5
Table: p.445

**Sullivan, Michael D**
(District of Columbia)
Media & Entertainment Band 2
Table: p.477

**Sullivan, Peter** (California)
Profile: p.316
Antitrust Band 3
Table: p.216

**Sullivan, Robert** (Montana)
Litigation Band 3
Table: p.1225

**Sullivan, Robert J**
(New York)
Profile: p.1506
Insurance Band 1
Table: p.1380

**Sullivan, Robert L**
(Tennessee)
Profile: p.1817
Media & Entertainment Band 1
Table: p.1806

**Sullivan, Shaun S**
(Connecticut)
Profile: p.385
Litigation Band 1
Table: p.378

**Sullivan, T J**
(District of Columbia)
Profile: p.549
Healthcare Band 1
Table: p.456

**Sullivan, Thomas** (Illinois)
Profile: p.860
Litigation Band S
Table: p.802

**Sullivan, William** (Illinois)
Employment Band 1
Table: p.785

**Sullivan, William F**
(California)
Profile: p.316
Litigation Band 4
Table: p.257

**Sullivan, Zane** (Montana)
Real Estate Band 2
Table: p.1230

**Sullivan Jr, James J**
(Pennsylvania)
Profile: p.1743
Employment Band 4
Table: p.1703

**Sumberg, John C** (Florida)
Profile: p.653
Real Estate Band 1
Table: p.617

**Summers, John**
(Pennsylvania)
Profile: p.1743
Litigation Band 3
Table: p.1714

**Sun, Brian A** (California)
Profile: p.317
Litigation Band 1
Table: p.258

**Sunberg, Randall B**
(New Jersey)
Profile: p.1307
Corporate/M&A Band 3
Table: p.1278

**Sundahl, John Alan**
(Wyoming)
Litigation Band 2
Table: p.2044

**Sundback, Mark**
(District of Columbia)
Energy Band 3
Table: p.441

**Sunshine, Ilene Robinson**
(Massachusetts)
Employment Band 2
Table: p.1065

**Sunshine, Steven C**
(District of Columbia)
Profile: p.549
Antitrust Band 4
Table: p.426

**Suplee, Dennis R**
(Pennsylvania)
Litigation Band 2
Table: p.1714

**Surber, Charles M**
(West Virginia)
Profile: p.2018
Employment Band 2
Table: p.2012

**Surkin, Elliot**
(Massachusetts)
Profile: p.1107
Real Estate Band 1
Table: p.1081

**Susko, A Richard**
(New York)
Profile: p.1506
Employee Benefits ✪
Table: p.1362

**Susman, Harry** (Texas)
Antitrust Up & coming

**Susman, Stephen** (Texas)
Antitrust Band 1
Table: p.1829
Litigation Band 1
Table: p.1865

**Sussman, Robert M**
(District of Columbia)
Environment Band 2
Table: p.451

**Sutherland, J Michael**
(Texas)
Bankruptcy Band 4
Table: p.1835

**Sutherland, Susan J**
(New York)
Profile: p.1506
Insurance Band 3
Table: p.1380

**Sutton, Kathryn M**
(District of Columbia)
Profile: p.549
Energy Band 3
Table: p.449

**Sutton, William** (Arkansas)
Litigation Band S
Table: p.205

**Suydam, John J** (New York)
Corporate/M&A Band 1
Table: p.1359

**Svonkin, Mark**
(Connecticut)
Real Estate Band 2
Table: p.380

**Swafford, T Anthony**
(Tennessee)
Profile: p.1817
Employment Band 3
Table: p.1801

**Swaim, Hall**
(Massachusetts)
Profile: p.1107
Bankruptcy Band 3
Table: p.1058

**Swain, Lawrence A**
(Kansas)
Profile: p.933
Corporate/M&A Band 1
Table: p.924

**Swanger, James R** (Iowa)
Employment Band 1
Table: p.912

**Swanick, Christine L**
(National)
Profile: p.137
Native Law Up and coming
Table: p.47

**Swann, Jerre** (Georgia)
Profile: p.725
Intellectual Property Band 2
Table: p.696

**Swanson, Daniel G**
(California)
Profile: p.317
Antitrust Band 2
Table: p.216

**Swanson, David M**
(South Carolina)
Real Estate Band 2
Table: p.1780

**Swanson, James R**
(Louisiana)
Profile: p.987
Litigation Band 2
Table: p.973

**Swanson, Joel** (Texas)
Profile: p.1916
Corporate/M&A Band 1
Table: p.1840

**Swanson, M Anne**
(District of Columbia)
Profile: p.549
Telecom, Broadcast & Satellite
Band 4
Table: p.492

**Swartz, Linda Z** (New York)
Profile: p.1506
Tax Band 3
Table: p.1423

**Sweeney, Jill K**
(New Mexico)
Profile: p.1330
Corporate/Commercial Band 3
Table: p.1320

**Sweeney, John** (New York)
Profile: p.1506
Intellectual Property Band 2
Table: p.1384

**Sweeney, Kevin R**
(Missouri)
Profile: p.1210
Corporate/M&A
Up and coming
Table: p.1193

**Sweeney, Matt** (Tennessee)
Profile: p.1817
Litigation Band 3
Table: p.1804

**Sweeney, Maureen E**
(Illinois)
Profile: p.860
Banking & Finance Band 3
Table: p.771

**Sweeney, Michael F**
(Rhode Island)
Corporate/Commercial Band 3
Table: p.1766

**Sweeney, Neal** (Georgia)
Profile: p.725
Construction Band 2
Table: p.682

**Sweeney, Robert**
(West Virginia)
Litigation Band 2
Table: p.2013

**Sweeney III, James F**
(New York)
Transportation Band 4
Table: p.74

**Sweet, Julian** (Maine)
Litigation Band 1
Table: p.1006

**Sweet, William J**
(District of Columbia)
Profile: p.137
Financial Services Band 1
Table: p.24

**Swenson, David** (National)
Profile: p.137
Tax Litigation Band 2

**Swenson, Erik** (Georgia)
Profile: p.725
Energy Band 2
Table: p.689

**S**

**T**

**Tracy, Timothy J** (Alabama)
Profile: p.160
Corporate/Commercial Band 2
Table: p.148

**Trafford, Kathleen M**
(Ohio)
Profile: p.1640
Litigation Band 4
Table: p.1617

**Trafford, Robert W** (Ohio)
Profile: p.1640
Litigation Band 2
Table: p.1617

**Trager, Michael D**
(District of Columbia)
Profile: p.551
Securities Band 2
Table: p.485

**Tranter, Jack C** (Maryland)
Healthcare Band 2
Table: p.1031

**Traurig, Robert** (Florida)
Profile: p.654
Real Estate Band S
Table: p.621

**Travis, Norton L** (New York)
Healthcare Band 3
Table: p.1374

**Travostino, Joan** (Alaska)
Bankruptcy Band 2
Table: p.167
Real Estate Band 2
Table: p.172

**Treece, John** (Illinois)
Profile: p.861
Antitrust Band 2
Table: p.767

**Treece, Lawrence**
(Colorado)
Profile: p.367
Litigation Band 3
Table: p.353

**Treesh, Kevin** (New York)
Profile: p.1508
Tax Band 4
Table: p.1423

**Trela Jr, Constantine L**
(Illinois)
Profile: p.861
Litigation Band 4
Table: p.802

**Trenkle, William** (Kansas)
Profile: p.933
Corporate/M&A Band 2
Table: p.924

**Trent, Tom** (Tennessee)
Profile: p.1817
Real Estate Band 1
Table: p.1808

**Trentacosta, John R**
(Michigan)
Profile: p.1140
Litigation Band 3
Table: p.1128

**Trentham, Robert**
(Tennessee)
Profile: p.1818
Litigation Band 1
Table: p.1805

**Trepper, Myron** (New York)
Profile: p.1508
Bankruptcy Band S
Table: p.1344

**Tribush, Bruce I**
(Massachusetts)
Profile: p.1108
Real Estate Up and coming
Table: p.1081

**Trier, Dana L** (New York)
Profile: p.1508
Tax Band 1
Table: p.1423

**Trigg, John** (National)
Products Liability Band 3
Table: p.50

**Trilling, Helen R**
(District of Columbia)
Profile: p.551
Healthcare Band 2
Table: p.456

**Tringali, Joseph** (New York)
Profile: p.1509
Antitrust Band 4
Table: p.1335

**Triplett, Thomas C**
(Kansas)
Corporate/M&A Band 2
Table: p.924

**Triplett, Thomas M**
(Oregon)
Employment Band 3
Table: p.1670

**Tripp, David** (Missouri)
Profile: p.1210
Litigation Band 1
Table: p.928
Litigation Band 2
Table: p.1198

**Tripp, Mark** (Iowa)
Litigation Band 2
Table: p.914

**Tritt, Cheryl**
(District of Columbia)
Profile: p.551
Telecom, Broadcast & Satellite
Band 2
Table: p.492

**Trombley, Gary** (Florida)
Litigation Band 2
Table: p.610

**Trooboff, Peter D**
(National)
Profile: p.138
International Trade Band 1
Table: p.41

**Tropin, Harley S** (Florida)
Profile: p.654
Litigation Band 1
Table: p.609

**Troupe, Warren L**
(Colorado)
Profile: p.367
Corporate/M&A Band 3
Table: p.346

**Truax, Tim** (California)
Construction Band 3
Table: p.225

**Trucker, Lee A** (California)
Employment Band 2
Table: p.232

**Truesdell, Richard**
(National)
Profile: p.138
Capital Markets Band 3
Table: p.7

**Truitt, Raymond** (Maryland)
Profile: p.1045
Real Estate Band 2
Table: p.1035

**Tryniecki, Timothy**
(Missouri)
Real Estate Band 3
Table: p.1201

**Tse, Marian A**
(Massachusetts)
Profile: p.1108
Employee Benefits Band 1
Table: p.1063

**Tsukazaki, Ben** (Hawaii)
Land Use Band 1
Table: p.744

**Tubach, Michael**
(California)
Profile: p.318
Antitrust Band 2
Table: p.216
Litigation Band 3
Table: p.258

**Tubman, Lloyd H** (New
Jersey)
Profile: p.1307
Environment Band 2
Table: p.1285

**Tuchin, Michael L**
(California)
Profile: p.318
Bankruptcy Band 2
Table: p.222

**Tucker, Robert** (Ohio)
Litigation Band 4
Table: p.1617

**Tucker, Roy** (Oregon)
Corporate/M&A Band 1
Table: p.1667

**Tucker, Stefan**
(District of Columbia)
Real Estate Band 3
Table: p.482

**Tucker, William**
(New Hampshire)
Real Estate Band 1
Table: p.1270

**Tull III, John E** (Arkansas)
Profile: p.210

Litigation Band 3
Table: p.205

**Tully, W Bradley** (California)
Healthcare Band 3
Table: p.238

**Tumas, Michael B**
(Delaware)
Profile: p.413
Corporate/M&A Band 2
Table: p.394

**Tumlin, Wayne E** (Maine)
Profile: p.1017
Corporate/M&A Band 3
Table: p.1000

**Tuohey, Mark H**
(District of Columbia)
Profile: p.551
Litigation Band 2
Table: p.471

**Turano, Thomas A**
(Massachusetts)
Intellectual Property Band 3
Table: p.1072

**Turk, Robert** (Florida)
Employment Band 1
Table: p.597

**Turkus, Albert H** (National)
Profile: p.138
Tax Litigation Band 1

**Turnbull, Kenneth J**
(New York)
Profile: p.1509
Employment Band 3
Table: p.1365

**Turner, Mark A** (Oregon)
Profile: p.1684
Litigation Band 3
Table: p.1674

**Turner, Robert** (Texas)
Profile: p.1917
Intellectual Property Band 2
Table: p.1860

**Turner, Scott M** (New York)
Profile: p.1509
Environment Band 3
Table: p.1371

**Turner, Steven C**
(Nebraska)
Corporate/M&A Band 2
Table: p.1236

**Turner, Wayne C** (Indiana)
Profile: p.900
Litigation Band 2
Table: p.890

**Turner III, Glenn E**
(California)
Profile: p.318
Construction Band 2
Table: p.225

**Tussing, James D** (New
York)
Profile: p.138
Transportation Band 2
Table: p.64

**Tuteur, Michael**
(Massachusetts)
Profile: p.1108
Litigation Band 3
Table: p.1074

**Tuthill, Walter C**
(Delaware)
Profile: p.413
Corporate/M&A Band 1
Table: p.395

**Tweel, Robert** (West
Virginia)
Profile: p.2018
Corporate/Commercial Band 2
Table: p.2011

**Twohig, John E**
(Massachusetts)
Real Estate Band 1
Table: p.1081

**Tyler, Paul** (Iowa)
Real Estate Band 1
Table: p.917

**Tyler, Robert** (Virginia)
Intellectual Property
Up and coming
Table: p.1975

**Tyson Jr, Joseph B**
(Wisconsin)
Profile: p.2036
Corporate/M&A Band 2
Table: p.2025

# U

**Ubell, Donald P**
(North Carolina)
Banking & Finance Band 3
Table: p.1569

**Ubinger Jr, John**
(Pennsylvania)
Profile: p.1744
Environment Band 2
Table: p.1707

**Udolf, Bruce** (Florida)
Litigation Band 2
Table: p.610

**Ugrin, Neil** (Montana)
Litigation Band 2
Table: p.1225

**Uhl, Eric J** (Maine)
Profile: p.1017
Employment Band 3
Table: p.1002

**Ullman, Samuel C** (Florida)
Profile: p.654
Tax Band 1
Table: p.623

**Ulman, Lawrence J**
(California)
Profile: p.318
Media & Entertainment Band 3
Table: p.266

U

**W**

**Wahl, Nicholas P**
(Wisconsin)
Corporate/M&A Band 3
Table: p.2025

**Wahle, Karen**
(District of Columbia)
Profile: p.553
Employee Benefits Band 3
Table: p.437

**Wainer, David** (National)
Profile: p.140
Capital Markets Band 2
Table: p.13

**Wajert, Sean P** (National)
Profile: p.140
Products Liability Band 4
Table: p.50

**Wakelin, David** (Maine)
Employment Band 1
Table: p.1002

**Waks, Jay W** (New York)
Profile: p.1510
Employment Band 1
Table: p.1365

**Wakshlag, Stanley**
(Florida)
Profile: p.655
Litigation Band 2
Table: p.609

**Walbolt, Sylvia** (Florida)
Profile: p.655
Litigation Band 1
Table: p.615

**Walch, Greg** (Nevada)
Environment Band 2
Table: p.1249

**Wald, Douglas**
(District of Columbia)
Profile: p.553
Antitrust Band 4
Table: p.426

**Walden, S Calvin** (New York)
Profile: p.1511
Intellectual Property Up and coming
Table: p.1384

**Walder, Justin** (New Jersey)
Litigation Band 1
Table: p.1292

**Waldman, Ira J** (California)
Real Estate Band 2
Table: p.270

**Walker, Christopher A**
(Ohio)
Environment Band 3
Table: p.1612

**Walker, Clarence W**
(North Carolina)
Corporate/M&A Band S
Table: p.1571

**Walker, Elizabeth D**
(West Virginia)
Employment Band 2
Table: p.2012

**Walker, Homer Lee**
(Georgia)
Profile: p.726
Real Estate Band 3
Table: p.700

**Walker, Jeffrey A**
(Mississippi)
Profile: p.1186
Employment Band 3
Table: p.1177

**Walker, John** (National)
Profile: p.140
Financial Services Band 3
Table: p.24

**Walker, Kathleen** (Texas)
Immigration Band 1
Table: p.1856

**Walker, Mitchell**
(Tennessee)
Profile: p.1818
Corporate/M&A Band 2
Table: p.1799

**Walker, Paul** (California)
Profile: p.319
Real Estate Band 1
Table: p.270

**Walker, Robert** (Tennessee)
Profile: p.1818
Litigation Band 1
Table: p.1804

**Walker, Steve** (Florida)
Environment Band 2
Table: p.601

**Walker, Trenholm G**
(South Carolina)
Litigation Band 3
Table: p.1778

**Walker Jr, Alexander J**
(New Hampshire)
Litigation Up and coming
Table: p.1267

**Walker, Jr, H William**
(Florida)
Profile: p.655
Real Estate Band 1
Table: p.617

**Walkowiak, Vincent**
(National)
Profile: p.140
Products Liability Band 4
Table: p.50

**Wall, Christopher**
(National)
Profile: p.140
International Trade Band 1
Table: p.41

**Wall, Daniel** (California)
Antitrust Band 1
Table: p.216

**Wall, Robert F** (Illinois)
Profile: p.862
Corporate/M&A Band 1
Table: p.781

**Wall, Steven R**
(Pennsylvania)
Profile: p.1744
Employment Band 1
Table: p.1703

**Wallace, Barbara**
(Mississippi)
Employment Band 3
Table: p.1177

**Wallace, Brian D**
(Louisiana)
Profile: p.987
Gaming & Licensing Band 3
Table: p.971

**Wallace, David H** (Ohio)
Construction Band 4
Table: p.1603

**Wallace, John A** (National)
Profile: p.140
Wealth Management Band 3
Table: p.81

**Wallace, Michael B**
(Mississippi)
Profile: p.1187
Litigation Band 1
Table: p.1179
Litigation Band 2
Table: p.1179

**Wallace, W Kirk** (New York)
Profile: p.1511
Tax Band 2
Table: p.1425

**Wallach, Mark** (Ohio)
Profile: p.1640
Litigation Band 3
Table: p.1617

**Wallack, Barry Z** (Indiana)
Profile: p.900
Real Estate Band 1
Table: p.892

**Wallack, James F**
(Massachusetts)
Bankruptcy Band 2
Table: p.1058

**Wallander, William** (Texas)
Profile: p.1918
Bankruptcy Band 2
Table: p.1835

**Wallenstein, Jim** (Texas)
Real Estate Band 1
Table: p.1872

**Wall, Christopher**
(National)
Profile: p.140
International Trade Band 1
Table: p.41

**Waller, Michael**
(North Dakota)
Litigation Band 2
Table: p.1594

**Waller Jr, Edward M**
(Florida)
Healthcare Band 2
Table: p.604

**Walli, Karl T**
(District of Columbia)
Profile: p.1511
Tax Band 2
Table: p.1425

**Wallwork, Nicholas J**
(Arizona)
Profile: p.195
Environment Up and coming
Table: p.179

**Walmsley, Robert**
(Louisiana)
Corporate/M&A Band 3
Table: p.965

**Walsh, Christopher J**
(Colorado)
Profile: p.367
Corporate/M&A Band 2
Table: p.346

**Walsh, David G** (Wisconsin)
Profile: p.2036
Corporate/M&A Band 3
Table: p.2025

**Walsh, John F** (Colorado)
Profile: p.367
Litigation Band 1
Table: p.353

**Walsh, Kathleen A**
(New York)
Profile: p.1511
Private Equity Band 3
Table: p.1410

**Walsh, Kevin J**
(Massachusetts)
Profile: p.1108
Bankruptcy Band 3
Table: p.1058

**Walsh, Linda**
(District of Columbia)
Profile: p.553
Energy Band 5
Table: p.445

**Walsh, Michael F** (New York)
Profile: p.1511
Bankruptcy Band 4
Table: p.1344

**Walsh, Thomas**
(Washington)
Real Estate Band 2
Table: p.2003

**Walsh, Thomas** (Missouri)
Litigation Band 2
Table: p.1198

**Walsh, William** (Virginia)
Profile: p.1987
Real Estate Band 1
Table: p.1978

**Walsh Jr, Peter J**
(Delaware)
Profile: p.413
Chancery Band 3
Table: p.392

**Walter, Priscilla A (Pam)**
(Illinois)
Profile: p.862
Technology Band 3
Table: p.814

**Walter, Teri A** (Montana)
Employment Up and coming
Table: p.1223

**Walters, Martha** (Oregon)
Litigation Band 2
Table: p.1674

**Walters, Robert** (Texas)
Profile: p.1918
Antitrust Band 2
Table: p.1829
Litigation Band 2
Table: p.1865

**Walton, Gibson** (Texas)
Profile: p.1918
Litigation Band 3
Table: p.1865

**Walton, Leigh** (Tennessee)
Profile: p.1818
Corporate/M&A Band 1
Table: p.1799

**Wampler, Samuel** (Ohio)
Construction Band 3
Table: p.1603

**Wamsley, James** (Ohio)
Profile: p.1640
Intellectual Property Band 2
Table: p.1614

**Wander, Herbert S** (Illinois)
Profile: p.862
Corporate/M&A Band 1
Table: p.781

**Wang, Annie J** (New York)
Immigration Band 3
Table: p.1376

**Wang, Sarah O** (Hawaii)
Profile: p.753
Employment Band 2
Table: p.742

**Wanner, David**
(North Dakota)
Real Estate Band 2
Table: p.1595

**Ward, Bradford L** (National)
Profile: p.140
International Trade Band 5
Table: p.42

**Ward, Daniel A** (Ohio)
Employment Band 2
Table: p.1609

**Ward, Erica A**
(District of Columbia)
Profile: p.553
Projects Band 2
Table: p.479

**Ward, Patrick**
(North Dakota)
Employment Band 1
Table: p.1592

**Ward, R Lawrence**
(Missouri)
Profile: p.1210
Litigation ✪
Table: p.1198

**Ward, Richard C**
(Kentucky)
Environment Band 1
Table: p.940
Environment Band 2

Table: p.941

**Ward, Richard P**
(Massachusetts)
Profile: p.1108
Employment Band 1
Table: p.1065

**Ward, Sarah M** (New York)
Profile: p.1511
Projects Band 4
Table: p.1413

**Ward Jr, Frank**
(North Carolina)
Employment Band 2
Table: p.1573

**Warden, John L** (New York)
Profile: p.1511
Antitrust Band 3
Table: p.1335

**Ware, Donald**
(Massachusetts)
Intellectual Property Band 1
Table: p.1072

**Ware, Paul** (Alabama)
Profile: p.160
Corporate/Commercial Band 2
Table: p.148

**Ware, Rex D** (Florida)
Tax Band 3
Table: p.623

**Ware Jr, Paul F**
(Massachusetts)
Profile: p.1108
Intellectual Property Band 2
Table: p.1072
Litigation Band 1
Table: p.1074

**Warin, Edward G**
(Nebraska)
Litigation Band 3
Table: p.1239

**Warin, Roger**
(District of Columbia)
Profile: p.553
Insurance Band 1
Table: p.461

**Warnecke, Michael O**
(Illinois)
Profile: p.862
Intellectual Property Band 1
Table: p.799

**Warner, Charles C** (Ohio)
Profile: p.1641
Employment Band 2
Table: p.1609

**Warner, Douglas** (New York)
Profile: p.1511
Private Equity Band 3
Table: p.1407

**Warner, E Waide** (New York)
Profile: p.1511
Projects Band 3
Table: p.1413

**Warner, Jonathan** (Florida)
Tax Band 4
Table: p.623

**Warner, Margaret H**
(District of Columbia)
Profile: p.553
Insurance Band 4
Table: p.464

**Warner, Whitney**
(New Mexico)
Employment Band 2
Table: p.1321

**Warnke, Stephen A**
(New York)
Profile: p.1511
Healthcare Band 2
Table: p.1374

**Warren, Charles** (New York)
Environment Band 2
Table: p.1371

**Warren, Daniel R** (Ohio)
Litigation Band 4
Table: p.1617

**Warren, Edward W**
(District of Columbia)
Profile: p.553
Environment Band S
Table: p.451

**Warren, J Steve**
(South Carolina)
Profile: p.1785
Employment Band 3
Table: p.1777

**Warren, Jeffrey W** (Florida)
Bankruptcy Band 3
Table: p.586

**Warren, Kenneth**
(Pennsylvania)
Profile: p.1744
Environment Band 2
Table: p.1707

**Warren, William L** (New Jersey)
Environment Band 2
Table: p.1285

**Warren III, John**
(South Carolina)
Corporate/M&A Band 1
Table: p.1775
Real Estate Band 1
Table: p.1780

**Warren Jr, Richard F**
(Tennessee)
Profile: p.1818
Real Estate Band 3
Table: p.1808

**Warshauer, David** (Indiana)
Profile: p.900
Real Estate Band 1
Table: p.892

**Warta, Darrell** (Kansas)
Profile: p.933
Litigation Band 2
Table: p.927

**Washburne, Thomas**
(Maryland)
Corporate/M&A Band 2
Table: p.1025

**Wasserman, Craig M**
(New York)
Profile: p.1512
Corporate/M&A Band 2
Table: p.1354
Financial Services Band 2
Table: p.24

**Wasserman, Michael G**
(Georgia)
Tax Band 2
Table: p.703

**Waterman, Ronald F**
(Montana)
Litigation Band 1
Table: p.1225

**Waterman, Thomas D**
(Iowa)
Litigation Band 1
Table: p.914

**Waterman III, Dana** (Iowa)
Corporate/M&A Band 2
Table: p.909

**Waterman Jr, Robert**
(Iowa)
Litigation Band 1
Table: p.914

**Waters, Barry J**
(Connecticut)
Employment Band 2
Table: p.376

**Waters, Jennifer N**
(District of Columbia)
Profile: p.553
Energy Band 4
Table: p.441

**Waters, Paige D** (Illinois)
Profile: p.863
Insurance Band 2
Table: p.796

**Watkins, Glen** (Utah)
Profile: p.1952
Real Estate Up and coming
Table: p.1947

**Watkins, John** (Maryland)
Profile: p.1045
Corporate/M&A Band 1
Table: p.1025

**Watson, David W**
(Massachusetts)
Profile: p.1108
Private Equity Band 2
Table: p.1080

**Watson, Jerome R**
(Michigan)
Profile: p.1140
Employment Band 3
Table: p.1125

**Watson, John W** (Illinois)
Environment Band 4

**Watson, Rom P**
(Massachusetts)
Profile: p.1108
Tax Band 2
Table: p.1084

**Watt, Dick** (Texas)
Energy Band 3
Table: p.1849

**Watt, Robert G** (Virginia)
Profile: p.1987
Construction Band 1
Table: p.1965

**Watt, Robert M** (Kentucky)
Profile: p.952
Environment Band 1
Table: p.941

**Watterson, Paul N**
(National)
Capital Markets Band 1
Table: p.13

**Watts, Grant** (Alaska)
Litigation Band 1
Table: p.171

**Wawro, Mark** (Texas)
Litigation Band 2
Table: p.1865

**Waxenberg, Jay D**
(National)
Profile: p.141
Wealth Management Band 3
Table: p.81

**Waxman, Scott E**
(Delaware)
Profile: p.413
Corporate/M&A Band 1
Table: p.395

**Waxman, Seth**
(District of Columbia)
Profile: p.553
Litigation ✪
Table: p.475

**Wayland, R Eddie**
(Tennessee)
Employment Band 2
Table: p.1801

**Wayte, Alan** (California)
Profile: p.319
Real Estate Band S
Table: p.270

**Weathersby, E Woods**
(Tennessee)
Real Estate Band 2
Table: p.1808

**Weaver, Ronald** (Florida)
Real Estate Band 1
Table: p.621

**Weaver, William N** (Illinois)
Corporate/M&A: Private Equity Band 3
Table: p.782

**Webb, Dan K** (Illinois)
Litigation ✪
Table: p.802
Litigation ✪
Table: p.803

Products Liability Band 2
Table: p.50

**Webb, Eugene** (Virginia)
Employment Band 2
Table: p.1971

**Webb, Thompson**
(Maryland)
Profile: p.1045
Corporate/M&A Band 2
Table: p.1025

**Webber, Charles F**
(Minnesota)
Profile: p.1167
Litigation Band 3
Table: p.1156

**Webber, Walter E** (Maine)
Real Estate Band S
Table: p.1008

**Weber, Roger A** (Ohio)
Employment Band 2
Table: p.1609

**Weber, Victoria** (Florida)
Profile: p.655
Tax Band 1
Table: p.623

**Weber III, Louis J** (Illinois)
Tax Band 3
Table: p.812

**Webster, Robert**
(New York)
Profile: p.141
Financial Services Band 2
Table: p.28

**Weddington, Keith M**
(North Carolina)
Employment Band 3
Table: p.1573

**Weekley, Augustine S**
(Florida)
Profile: p.655
Healthcare Band 3
Table: p.604

**Weems, Philip R** (Texas)
Profile: p.1918
Energy Band 2
Table: p.1847
Projects Band 2
Table: p.1869

**Weems, Walter S**
(Mississippi)
Profile: p.1187
Corporate/Commercial Band 2
Table: p.1174

**Weerasinghe, Rohan**
(New York)
Profile: p.141
Capital Markets Band 3
Table: p.7

**Weese, Charles W**
(Colorado)
Profile: p.367
Employment Band 3
Table: p.348

W

**Wells, Stephen E**
(District of Columbia)
Profile: p.554
Tax Band 4
Table: p.488

**Wells, Jr, Theodore V**
(New York)
Profile: p.1512
Litigation Band 1
Table: p.1388
Litigation Band 1
Table: p.1391

**Welsch, Thomas M**
(Montana)
Litigation Band 2
Table: p.1225

**Welsh, John F**
(Massachusetts)
Employment Band 2
Table: p.1065

**Welsh, W Russell**
(Missouri)
Profile: p.1211
Litigation Band 3
Table: p.1198

**Weltman, Edward S**
(National)
Profile: p.142
Products Liability Band 3
Table: p.50

**Wenick, George D**
(Georgia)
Construction Band 3
Table: p.682

**Wenner, Adam**
(District of Columbia)
Profile: p.554
Energy Band 4
Table: p.445

**Werner, John D** (Louisiana)
Profile: p.987
Corporate/M&A Band 4
Table: p.965

**Werner, Philip** (New York)
Profile: p.1513
Private Equity Band 3
Table: p.1407

**Wertheimer, Robert J**
(New York)
Profile: p.1513
Real Estate Band 3
Table: p.1417

**Werther, Barbara G**
(District of Columbia)
Profile: p.554
Construction Band 2
Table: p.433

**Werts, Dale A** (Missouri)
Profile: p.1211
Corporate/M&A Band 3
Table: p.1193

**Wesely, Marissa C**
(New York)
Profile: p.1513
Banking & Finance Band 4
Table: p.1339

**West, David** (California)
Profile: p.320
Employment Band 2
Table: p.232

**West, Glenn D** (Texas)
Profile: p.1918
Corporate/M&A Band 2
Table: p.1840

**West, Joseph D**
(District of Columbia)
Profile: p.554
Construction Band 1
Table: p.433
Government Contracts Band 3
Table: p.30

**West, Paul** (Louisiana)
Profile: p.988
Gaming & Licensing Band 1
Table: p.971

**West, Philip**
(District of Columbia)
Profile: p.555
Tax Band 3
Table: p.488

**West, Richard A**
(New Jersey)
Profile: p.1307
Employment Up & coming

**West, Ronald**
(Pennsylvania)
Profile: p.1745
Corporate/M&A Band 4
Table: p.1700

**West Jr, William K**
(District of Columbia)
Intellectual Property Band 2
Table: p.466

**Wester, John**
(North Carolina)
Employment Band 3
Table: p.1573
Litigation Band 1
Table: p.1577

**Westerberg, Gary W**
(National)
Transportation Band 3
Table: p.67

**Westesen, Neil G**
(Montana)
Litigation Band 4
Table: p.1225

**Westgate, J Bradford**
(New Hampshire)
Real Estate Band 2
Table: p.1270

**Weston, John** (Utah)
Profile: p.1953
Corporate/M&A Band 3
Table: p.1941

**Weston, Timothy**
(Pennsylvania)
Profile: p.1745
Environment Band 1
Table: p.1707

**Westover, Michael**
(Colorado)
Profile: p.367
Real Estate Band 3
Table: p.355

**Westra, James**
(Massachusetts)
Profile: p.1109
Corporate/M&A Band 2
Table: p.1061
Private Equity Band 1
Table: p.1078

**Westra, Mark W**
(Minnesota)
Real Estate Band 2
Table: p.1160

**Wettach, Thomas**
(Pennsylvania)
Intellectual Property Band 4
Table: p.1711

**Whalen, Thomas J**
(New York)
Transportation Band 2
Table: p.74

**Wheat, David** (Texas)
Profile: p.1919
Tax Band 3
Table: p.1875

**Wheat, James C**
(New Hampshire)
Litigation Band 3
Table: p.1267

**Wheaton, James  J**
(Virginia)
Corporate/M&A Band 3
Table: p.1968

**Wheaton, John** (Minnesota)
Profile: p.1167
Real Estate Band 1
Table: p.1160

**Wheeler, Francis**
(Colorado)
Corporate/M&A Band 1
Table: p.346

**Wheeler, Malcolm**
(Colorado)
Litigation Band 2
Table: p.353
Products Liability Band 1
Table: p.50

**Wheeler, Raymond**
(California)
Profile: p.320
Employment Band 3
Table: p.231

**Wheelwright, Neil D**
(Vermont)
Real Estate Band 3
Table: p.1961

**Whelan, Joseph D** (Rhode Island)
Employment Band 2
Table: p.1768

**Whelan III, William J**
(National)
Profile: p.142

Capital Markets Band 4
Table: p.7

**Whistler, Philip** (Indiana)
Profile: p.900
Litigation Band 1
Table: p.890

**Whitaker, G Warren**
(New York)
Profile: p.142
Wealth Management Band 1
Table: p.81

**Whitaker, Glenn** (Ohio)
Profile: p.1641
Litigation Band 3
Table: p.1618

**White, Algird** (New York)
Energy Band 1
Table: p.1370

**White, Andrew M**
(California)
Media & Entertainment Band 3
Table: p.263

**White, Benjamin T**
(Georgia)
Profile: p.726
Tax Band 2
Table: p.703

**White, Bruce** (Illinois)
Environment Band 2
Table: p.791

**White, Christen** (Oregon)
Real Estate Band 1
Table: p.1677

**White, Debra**
(District of Columbia)
Business Process Outsourcing
Up and coming
Table: p.2
Technology Up and coming
Table: p.490

**White, Dennis J**
(Massachusetts)
Profile: p.1109
Corporate/M&A Band 3
Table: p.1061

**White, Ira** (New York)
Profile: p.1513
Private Equity Band 3
Table: p.1407

**White, Jeffrey M** (Maine)
Profile: p.1017
Litigation Band 3
Table: p.1006

**White, Mary Jo** (New York)
Litigation Band 1
Table: p.1388
Litigation ✪
Table: p.1391

**White, Michael** (Missouri)
Real Estate Band 1
Table: p.1201

**White, Pamela** (Maryland)
Employment Band 2
Table: p.1028

**White, Robert B** (Idaho)
Employment Band 2
Table: p.759

**White, Robert J** (California)
Profile: p.320
Bankruptcy Band 3
Table: p.222

**White, T Gordon** (Texas)
Profile: p.1919
IP Band 3

**White, Todd** (Rhode Island)
Profile: p.1773
Litigation Up and coming
Table: p.1769

**White, W Christopher**
(New York)
Profile: p.1513
Real Estate Band 2
Table: p.1417

**White III, Fred B** (National)
Profile: p.142
Financial Services Band 3
Table: p.24

**White Jr, Jere F** (Alabama)
Litigation Band 2
Table: p.152

**Whitford, Joseph P**
(Washington)
Corporate/Commercial Band 2
Table: p.1992

**Whitham, Michelle A**
(Massachusetts)
Employment Band 4
Table: p.1065

**Whitledge, William H**
(Massachusetts)
Profile: p.1109
Tax Band 2
Table: p.1084

**Whitlock, David C**
(Georgia)
Profile: p.726
Immigration Band 2
Table: p.694

**Whitney, Charles W**
(Georgia)
Profile: p.727
Energy Band 2
Table: p.689

**Whitney, Douglas** (Illinois)
Profile: p.863
Litigation Up and coming
Table: p.802

**Whitt, Burt** (Virginia)
Employment Band 2
Table: p.1971

**Whittaker, Scott T**
(Louisiana)
Profile: p.988
Corporate/M&A Band 3
Table: p.965

W

**W**

**Yuen, Leighton** (Hawaii)
Real Estate Band 2
Table: p.748

**Yuffee, Michael**
(District of Columbia)
Profile: p.556
Energy Band 5
Table: p.445

**Yund, George** (Ohio)
Profile: p.1642
Employment Band 2
Table: p.1609

**Yungblut, Stephen K**
(Texas)
Construction Band 4
Table: p.1838

**Yura, Mark** (Illinois)
Profile: p.864
Real Estate Band 3
Table: p.809

**Z**

**Zabel, Sheldon** (Illinois)
Profile: p.864
Environment Band 1
Table: p.791

**Zabel, William D** (National)
Profile: p.143
Wealth Management Band 1
Table: p.81

**Zabriskie, Wendy L**
(Michigan)
Profile: p.1140
Banking & Finance Band 2
Table: p.1120

**Zabrowski, Patrick M**
(Wisconsin)
Profile: p.2036
Real Estate Band 2
Table: p.2031

**Zachem, Kathryn A**
(District of Columbia)
Telecom, Broadcast & Satellite
Band 3
Table: p.492

**Zacks, David M** (Georgia)
Profile: p.727
Litigation Band 3

**Zadick, Gary M** (Montana)
Employment Band 2
Table: p.1223

**Zagore, David A** (Ohio)
Profile: p.1642
Corporate/M&A Band 3
Table: p.1605

**Zahler, Robert**
(District of Columbia)
Profile: p.557
Business Process Outsourcing ✪
Table: p.2
Technology Band 1
Table: p.490

**Zaiger, Mark L** (Iowa)
Employment Band 1
Table: p.912

**Zakarian, Albert**
(Connecticut)
Profile: p.385
Employment Band 1
Table: p.376

**Zakupowsky, Alex**
(District of Columbia)
Tax Band 4
Table: p.488

**Zaldivar, Miguel A** (Florida)
Profile: p.656
Corporate/M&A Band 1
Table: p.595

**Zalesin, Steven A**
(New York)
Profile: p.1515
Media & Entertainment Band 1
Table: p.1400

**Zalewski, John D** (Hawaii)
Profile: p.753
Litigation Up and coming
Table: p.745

**Zall, Richard J** (New York)
Profile: p.1515
Healthcare Band 3
Table: p.1374

**Zandy, John C** (Connecticut)
Profile: p.385
Employment Band 1
Table: p.376

**Zangari, Ted** (New Jersey)
Profile: p.1308
Real Estate Band 2
Table: p.1293

**Zanic, Michael G**
(Pennsylvania)
Litigation Band 1
Table: p.1715

**Zaragoza, Richard R**
(District of Columbia)
Profile: p.557
Telecom, Broadcast & Satellite
Band 4
Table: p.492

**Zarov, Herbert L** (Illinois)
Profile: p.864
Litigation Band 4
Table: p.802
Products Liability Band 2
Table: p.50

**Zax, Leonard A**
(District of Columbia)
Real Estate Band 4
Table: p.482

**Zazove, Daniel A** (Illinois)
Bankruptcy Band 3
Table: p.775

**Zech, Paul** (Minnesota)
Employment Band 2
Table: p.1154

**Zeglovitch, Robert**
(Minnesota)
Employment Band 3
Table: p.1154

**Zeiger, Alan L**
(Pennsylvania)
Profile: p.1745
Corporate/M&A Band 4
Table: p.1700

**Zeiger, John W** (Ohio)
Litigation Band 2
Table: p.1617

**Zeilinger, John S**
(Nebraska)
Corporate/M&A Band 1
Table: p.1236

**Zelek, Eugene** (Illinois)
Antitrust Band 3
Table: p.767
Media & Entertainment Band 2
Table: p.807

**Zelek, Mark E** (Florida)
Profile: p.656
Employment Band 4
Table: p.597

**Zelenock, Katheryne L**
(Michigan)
Profile: p.1140
Real Estate Up and coming
Table: p.1130

**Zetlin, Michael** (New York)
Construction Band 2
Table: p.1351

**Zevnik, Paul**
(District of Columbia)
Profile: p.557
Insurance Band 3
Table: p.464

**Zewadski, William
Knight** (Florida)
Bankruptcy Band 3
Table: p.586

**Ziffren, Kenneth**
(California)
Media & Entertainment Band 1
Table: p.266

**Ziman, Kenneth S**
(New York)
Profile: p.1515
Bankruptcy Band 3
Table: p.1344

**Zimbler, Jay** (Illinois)
Profile: p.864
Tax Band 2
Table: p.812

**Zimet, Bruce A** (Florida)
Litigation Band 1
Table: p.610

**Zimmerman, Edward M**
(New Jersey)
Profile: p.1308
Corporate/M&A Band 2
Table: p.1278

**Zimmerman, Eric**
(District of Columbia)
Profile: p.557
Healthcare Band 2
Table: p.456

**Zimmerman, Todd E**
(North Dakota)
Profile: p.1597
Litigation Band 2
Table: p.1593

**Zimpritch, James B**
(Maine)
Profile: p.1017
Corporate/M&A ✪
Table: p.1000

**Zimroth, Peter L** (National)
Profile: p.143
Products Liability Band 3
Table: p.50

**Zinober, Peter** (Florida)
Employment ✪
Table: p.597

**Zirinsky, Bruce R**
(New York)
Profile: p.1515
Bankruptcy Band 2
Table: p.1344

**Zischke, Michael H**
(California)
Profile: p.321
Environment Band 2
Table: p.236
Real Estate Band 1
Table: p.270

**Zisser, David A** (Colorado)
Litigation Band 1
Table: p.353

**Zissu, Roger L** (New York)
Intellectual Property Band 1
Table: p.1385

**Zobitz, George E**
(New York)
Profile: p.1515
Banking & Finance
Up and coming
Table: p.1339

**Zody, Michael A** (Utah)
Profile: p.1953
Employment Band 3
Table: p.1944

**Zoli, Elise N**
(Massachusetts)
Profile: p.1109
Environment Band 3
Table: p.1068

**Zonn, Sidney** (Pennsylvania)
Profile: p.1745
Employment Band 4
Table: p.1703

**Zorn, Jonathan M**
(Massachusetts)
Profile: p.1109
Employee Benefits Band 1
Table: p.1063

**Zorn, William V A**
(New Hampshire)
Profile: p.1274
Corporate/Commercial
Band 2
Table: p.1264

**Zornow, David M**
(New York)
Profile: p.1515
Litigation Band 2
Table: p.1391

**Zovickian, Stephen**
(California)
Profile: p.321
Construction Band 3
Table: p.225

**Zuccotti, Andrew**
(Washington)
Corporate/Commercial Band 1
Table: p.1993

**Zucker, Carol** (Nevada)
Employment Band 1
Table: p.1248

**Zucker, Jeffrey** (Nevada)
Corporate/Commercial Band 1
Table: p.1246
Real Estate Band 1
Table: p.1255

**Zuckerman, Richard**
(Michigan)
Profile: p.1140
Litigation Band 1
Table: p.1128

**Zuckerman, Roger E**
(District of Columbia)
Litigation Band 3
Table: p.471

**Zumbach, Steven E** (Iowa)
Corporate/M&A Band 1
Table: p.909

**Zussman, Richard**
(Michigan)
Real Estate Band 2
Table: p.1130

**Zutz, Robert**
(District of Columbia)
Investment Management Band 3
Table: p.469

**Zweifach, Gerson**
(District of Columbia)
Media & Entertainment Band 2
Table: p.477

**Zwisler, Margaret**
(District of Columbia)
Antitrust Band 3
Table: p.426

**Z**

# OTHER RECOMMENDED FIRMS

**Abrahams Kaslow & Cassman LLP**
8712 West Dodge Road, Suite 300, Omaha, NE 68114

**Adams & Jones Chartered**
600 Market Centre, 155 North Market, PO Box 1034, Wichita, KS 67201-1034

**Adelman Lavine Gold and Levin**
Suite 900, Four Penn Center, Philadelphia, PA 19103-2808

**Ahlers & Cooney PC**
100 Court Avenue, Suite 600, Des Moines, IA 50309

**Alan H Kress**
11 West 42nd Street, Suite 900, New York, NY 10036

**Alexander, Baucus, Taleff & Paul PC**
615 2nd Avenue North, Suite 300, Great Falls, MT 59401

**Allen Guthrie McHugh & Thomas PLLC**
500 Lee Street East, Suite 800, PO Box 3394, Charleston, WV 25333

**Allen Law Firm**
212 Center Street, Ninth Floor, Little Rock, AR 72201

**Allensworth and Porter, LLP**
620 Congress Avenue, Suite 100, Austin, TX 78701-3229

**Allison, MacKenzie, Russell, Pavlakis, Wright & Fagan, Ltd**
402 North Division Street, Carson City, NV 89702

**Alston Courtnage & Bassetti LLP**
1000 Second Avenue, Suite 3900, Seattle, WA 98104-1045

**Amburgey & Rubin PC**
Riverplace Office Building, 1750 SW Harbor Way, Suite 450, Portland, OR 97201-0104

**Anderson & Bottrell**
State Bank Center, Suite 302, 3100 13th Avenue Southwest, Fargo, ND 58106-0247

**Anderson & Karrenberg**
700 Bank One Tower, 50 West Broadway, Salt Lake City, UT 84101-2006

**Anderson & Kreiger LLP**
43 Thorndike Street, Cambridge, MA 02141

**Andrew M Lawler PC**
641 Lexington Avenue, 27th Floor, New York, NY 10022

**Andrews Myers Coulter & Cohen PC**
2900 Weslayan, Suite 375, Houston, TX 77027-5109

**Anthony Ostlund & Baer**
90 South Seventh Street, Suite 3600, Minneapolis, MN 55402

**Anthony van Westrum LLC**
621 Seventeenth Street, Suite 1515, Denver, CO 80293-1501

**Aqualaw PLC**
Wytestone Plaza, 801 E Main Street, Suite 1002, Richmond, VA 23219

**Arent Fox PLLC**
1050 Connecticut Avenue NW, Washington, DC 20036

**Arguedas, Cassman & Headley, LLP**
803 Hearst Avenue, Berkeley, CA 94710

**Armstrong Allen PLLC**
Brinkley Plaza, Suite 700, 80 Monroe Avenue, Memphis, TN 38103

**Armstrong Teasdale LLP**
One Metropolitan Square, Suite 2600, St Louis, MO 63102-2740

**Ashburn & Mason, PC**
1130 West 6th Avenue, Suite 100, Anchorage, AK 99501

**Ashford & Wriston**
Alii Place, Suite 1400, 1099 Alakea Street, Honolulu, HI 96810

**Atkinson, Conway & Gagnon**
420 L Street, Suite 500, Anchorage, AK 99501-1989

**Ausley & McMullen**
Washington Square Building, 227 South Calhoun Street, PO Box 391, Tallahassee, FL 32302

**Ayabe, Chong, Nishimoto, Sia & Nakamura**
Pauahi Tower, 1001 Bishop Street, Suite 2500, Honolulu, HI 96813

**Baach Robinson & Lewis PLLC**
One Thomas Circle NW, Suite 200, Washington, DC 20005-5803

**Babst, Calland, Clements and Zomnir, A Professional Corporation**
Two Gateway Center, Pittsburgh, PA 15222

**Badiak Will & Ruddy**
Suite 1040, 120 Broadway, New York, NY 10271

**Bailey Cavalieri**
10 West Broad Street, Columbus, OH 43215

**Bainbridge, Mims, Rogers & Smith, LLP**
The Luckie Building, 600 Luckie Drive, Ste 415, PO Box 530886, Birmingham, AL 35253

**Baird, Holm, McEachen, Pedersen, Hamann & Strasheim LLP**
1500 Woodmen Tower, Omaha, NE 68102

**Baker & Hostetler LLP**
Washington Square, Suite 1100, 1050 Connecticut Avenue, Washington, DC 20036-5304

**Bales Weinstein**
Courthouse Plaza, 625 East Twiggs Street, Suite 100, Tampa, FL 33602

**Ball Janik LLP**
One Main Place, 101 SW Main Street, Suite 1100, Portland, OR 97204

**Ball, Ball, Matthews & Novak**
2000 Interstate Park, Suite 204, PO Box 2148, Montgomery, AL 36102

**Bangs, McCullen, Butler, Foye & Simmons, LLP**
818 St Joseph Street, PO Box 2670, Rapid City, SD 57709

**Banks Law Office**
200 South West Market Street, Suite 1600, Portland, OR 97201

**Bankston, Gronning, O'Hara, PC**
550 West 7th Avenue, Suite 1800, Anchorage, AK 99501

**Banner & Witcoff Ltd**
Ten South Wacker Drive, Chicago, IL 60606-7407

**Barack Ferrazzano Kirschbaum Perlman & Nagelberg**
333 West Wacker, Suite 2700, Chicago, IL 60606-1227

**Bardenwerper & Talbott PLLC**
8311 Shelbyville Road, Louisville, KY 40222

**Barger & Wolen**
515 South Flower Street, 34th Floor, Los Angeles, CA 90071

**Barlow & Wilcox PA**
201 Third Street North West, Suite 1130, Albuquerque, NM 87102

**Barnett, Bolt, Kirkwood, Long & McBride**
601 Bayshore Boulevard, Suite 700, Tampa, FL 33606

**Barris, Sott, Denn & Driker, PLLC**
211 West Fort Street, Fifteenth Floor, Detroit, MI 48226-3281

**Bartlit Beck Herman Palenchar & Scott**
Courthouse Place, 54 West Hubbard Street, Chicago, IL 60610

**Bassford Remele, A Professional Association**
33 South Sixth Street, Suite 3800, Minneapolis, MN 55402-3707

**Bateman Seidel Miner Blomgren Chellis & Gram, PC**
888 SW Fifth Avenue, Suite 1150, Portland, OR 97204

**Bates & Carey**
333 West Wacker Drive, Suite 900, Chicago, IL 60606

**Bath & Edmonds, PA**
Historic Voigts Building, 7944 Santa Fe Drive, Overland Park, KS 66204

**Bays Deaver Lung Rose Baba**
Ali'i Place 1099 Alakea Street, Suite 1600, Honolulu, HI 96813

**Beasley, Allen, Crow, Methvin, Portis & Miles, PC**
218 Commerce Street, PO Box 4160, Montgomery, AL 36104

**Beck, Redden & Secrest LLP**
One Houston Center, 1221 McKinney Street, Suite 4500, Houston, TX 77010-2010

**Becker & Poliakoff PA**
Emerald Lake Corporate Park, 3111 Stirling Road, Fort Lauderdale, FL 33312

**Beckman Lawson, LLP**
800 Standard Federal Plaza, Fort Wayne, IN 46802

**Bedell, Dittmar, DeVault, Pillans & Coxe**
The Bedell Building, 101 East Adams Street, Jacksonville, FL 32202

**Beggs & Lane**
501 Commendencia Street, PO Box 12950, Pensacola, FL 32591-2950

**Belin Lamson McCormick Zumbach Flynn, PC**
The Financial Center, 666 Walnut Street, Suite 2000, Des Moines, IA 50309

**Bell, Boyd & Lloyd LLC**
Three First National Plaza, Suite 3300, 70 West Madison Street, Chicago, IL 60602-4027

**Bell, Davis & Pitt, PA**
Century Plaza, Suite 600, 100 North Cherry Street, Winston-Salem, NC 27101

**Belles Graham Proudfoot and Wilson**
Watumull Plaza, 4334 Rice Street, Suite 202, Lihue, HI 96766-1388

**Bello, Black & Welsh LLP**
535 Boylston Street, Suite 1102, Boston, MA 02116

**Berens & Tate PC**
10050 Regency Circle, Suite 400, Omaha, NE 68114

**Berenstein, Moore, Berenstein, Heffernan & Moeller**
300 Firstarbank Building, 501 Pierce Street, PO Box 3207, Sioux City, IA 51102

**Berger & Montague PC**
1622 Locust Street, Philadelphia, PA 19103

**Berger Singerman**
315 South Calhoun Street, Suite 712, Tallahassee, FL 32301

**Bergeson & Campbell PC**
1203 19th Street NW, Suite 300, Washington, DC 20036

**Berkes Crane Robinson & Seal, LLP**
515 South Figueroa Street, Suite 1500, Los Angeles, CA 90071

**Berkowitz Oliver Williams Shaw & Eisenbrandt LLP**
2 Emanuel Cleaver II Boulevard, Suite 500, Kansas City, MO 64112

**Berliner, Corcoran & Rowe, LLP**
1101 17th Street, NW, Suite 1100, Washington, DC 20036

**Berman & Simmons**
85 Exchange Street, Portland, ME 04101

**Berman DeValerio Pease Tabacco Burt & Pucillo**
Northbridge Centre Suite 1701, West Palm Beach, FL 33401

**Bernstein, Cushner & Kimmell PC**
585 Boylston Street, Suite 400, Boston, MA 02116

**Betzer Roybal & Eisenberg PC**
4900 Lang Avenue NE, Suite 202, Albuquerque, NM 87109-4303

**Beus Gilbert PLLC**
4800 North Scottsdale Road, Suite 6000, Scottsdale, AZ 85251-7630

**Bierce & Kenerson, PC**
420 Lexington Avenue, Suite 2620, New York, NY, 10170-002

**Bierman, Shohat, Loewy & Klein PA**
Penthouse Two, 800 Brickell Avenue, Miami, FL 33131-2914

**Bieser, Greer, & Landis LLP**
400 National City Center, 6 North Main Street, Dayton, OH 45402-1908

**Billing Cochran Heath Lyles Mauro & Anderson**
888 SE 3rd Avenue, Fort Lauderdale, FL 33316

**Bingham McHale LLP**
2700 Market Tower, 10 West Market Street, Indianapolis, IN 46204

**Birch, Horton, Bittner & Cherot**
1127 W 7th Avenue, Anchorage, AK 99501-3399

**Birch, Stewart, Kolasch & Birch, LLP**
8110 Gatehouse Road, Suite 500 East, Falls Church, VA 22040

**Bird, Marella, Boxer & Wolpert PC**
1875 Century Park East, 23rd Floor, Los Angeles, CA 90067-2561

**Biskind, Hunt & Taylor plc**
11201 N Tatum Boulevard, Phoenix, AZ 85028

**Black Lowe & Graham**
701 Fifth Avenue, Suite 4800, Seattle, WA 98104

**Black, Srebnick, Kornspan & Stumpf PA**
201 South Biscayne Boulevard, Suite 1300, Miami, FL 33131

**Blank Rome LLP**
One Logan Square, 18th & Cherry Streets, Philadelphia, PA 19103-6998

**Blish & Cavanagh, LLP**
Commerce Center, 30 Exchange Terrace, Providence, RI 02903

**Bloom, Hergott and Diemer LLP**
150 South Rodeo Drive, Third Floor, Beverly Hills, CA 90212

**Bond, Schoeneck & King, PLLC**
One Lincoln Center, Syracuse, NY 13202-1355

**Boone, Karlberg PC**
201 West Main Street, Suite 300, PO Box 9199, Missoula, MT 59807-9199

**Boose Casey Ciklin Lubitz Martens McBane & O'Connell**
Northbridge Tower 1, Nineteenth Floor, 515 North Flagler Drive, West Palm Beach, FL 33401

**Bose McKinney & Evans LLP**
2700 First Indiana Plaza, 135 North Pennsylvania Street, Indianapolis, IN 46204

**Bouchard Margules & Friedlander PA**
222 Delaware Avenue, Suite 1400, Wilmington, DE 19801

**Bowditch & Dewey LLP**
311 Main Street, PO Box 15156, Worcester, MA 01615-0156

**Boyce, Greenfield, Pashby & Welk LLP**
101 North Phillips Avenue, Suite 600, PO Box 5015, Sioux Falls, SD 57117-5015

**Bradley & Riley, PC**
2007 First Avenue SE, PO Box 2804, Cedar Rapids, IA 52406

**Bradshaw, Fowler, Proctor & Fairgrave, PC**
801 Grand Avenue, Suite 3700, Des Moines, IA 50309

**Brault Graham Scott & Brault LLC**
101 Washington Street, Rockville, MD 20850

**Breazeale, Sachse & Wilson, LLP**
One American Place, Twenty-Third Floor, PO Box 3197, Baton Rouge, LA 70821

**Bricker & Eckler LLP**
100 South Third Street, Columbus, OH 43215

**Briggs and Morgan, Professional Association**
2200 IDS Center, 80 South Eighth Street, Minneapolis, MN 55402

**Broad and Cassel**
One Biscayne Tower, 21st Floor, 2 South Biscayne Boulevard, Miami, FL 33131

**Bronstein, Carlson, Gleim & Smith, PA**
Suite 1100, 150 Second Avenue North, St Petersburg, FL 33701

**Brooks, Pierce, McLendon, Humphrey & Leonard LLP**
2000 Renaissance Plaza, 230 North Elm Street (27401), Greensboro, NC 27420

**Brown Law Firm PC**
315 North 24th Street, PO Drawer 849, Billings, MT 59101

**Brown McCarroll LLP**
111 Congress Avenue, Suite 1400, Austin, TX 78701-4043

**Brown Rudnick Berlack Israels LLP**
One Financial Center, Boston, MA 02111

**Bruce A Zimet PA**
Suite 2612 One Financial Plaza, Fort Lauderdale, FL 33394

**Bruce S. Rogow, PA**
500 East Broward Boulevard, Suite 1930, Fort Lauderdale, FL 33394

**Bruder Gentile & Marcoux LLP**
1701 Pennsylvania Avenue, Suite 900, Washington, DC 20005-5805

**Bryan Cave LLP**
One Metropolitan Square, 211 North Broadway, Suite 3600, St Louis, MO 63102-2750

**Buchalter Nemer Fields & Younger**
601 South Figuerosa Street, Suite 2400, Los Angeles, CA 90017-5704

**Buck & Gordon LLP**
2025 First Avenue, Suite 500, Seattle, WA 98121-3140

**Buckingham Doolittle & Burroughs LLP**
191 West Nationwide Boulevard, Suite 300, PO Box 151120, Columbus, OH 43215-8120

**Budoff & Ross PC**
111 West Monroe, Suite 1212, Phoenix, AZ 85003

**Bullivant Houser Bailey PC**
300 Pioneer Tower, 888 SW Fifth Avenue, Portland, OR 97204

**Burch & Cracchiolo**
702 East Osborn, Suite 200, Phoenix, AZ 85011

**Burch, Porter & Johnson PLLC**
130 North Court, Memphis, TN 38103

**Burke & Parsons**
100 Park Avenue, 30th Floor, New York, NY 10017-5533

**Burr & Forman LLP**
Southtrust Tower, 420 North Twentieth Street, Suite 3100, Birmingham, AL 35203

**Burr, Pease & Kurtz, PC**
810 N Street, Anchorage, AK 99501

**Burrage Law Firm**
First United Center, Suite 100, 115 North Washington, Durant, OK 74702-1727

**Bush Ross Gardner Warren & Rudy, PA**
220 South Franklin Street, PO Box 3913, Tampa, FL 33602-5330

**Bush, Strout & Kornfeld**
5500 Two Union Square, 601 Union Street, Seattle, WA 98101-2373

**Butler Rubin Saltarelli & Boyd**
70 West Madison, Suite 1800, Chicago, IL 60602

**Byrd & Wiser**
145 Main Street, Biloxi, MS 39533

**Byrnes & Keller**
1000 Second Avenue, 38th Floor, Seattle, WA 98104

**Cabaniss, Johnston, Gardner, Dumas & O'Neal**
2001 Park Place North, Suite 700, Birmingham, AL 35203

**Cades Schutte**
Cades Schutte Building, 1000 Bishop Street, Suite 1200, Honolulu, HI 96808

**Cadwell Sanford Deibert & Garry LLP**
River Center, 200 East 10th Street, Suite 200, Sioux Falls, SD 57101-1157

**Cahill Gordon & Reindel LLP**
80 Pine Street, New York, NY 10005-1702

**Cairncross & Hempelmann, A Professional Service Corporation**
524 Second Avenue, Suite 500, Seattle, WA 98104

**Campbell & Williams**
700 South 7th Street, Las Vegas, NV 89101-6908

**Campbell and Wells PA**
2155 Louisiana Boulevard NE, Suite 10300, Albuquerque, NM 87110

**Caplin & Drysdale**
One Thomas Circle NW, Suite 1100, Washington, DC 20005-5802

**Carey, O'Malley, Whitaker & Manson PA**
712 South Oregon Avenue, Tampa, FL 33606

**Carey, Scott & Douglas, PLLC**
1701 Bank One Center, 707 Virginia Street, East Charleston, WV 25301

**Carlock Copeland Semler & Stair, LLP**
2600 Marquis Two Tower, 285 Peachtree Center Avenue, Atlanta, GA 30303

**Carlsmith Ball LLP**
ASB Tower, 1001 Bishop Street, Suite 2200, Post Office Box 656, Honolulu, HI 96813

**Carlson, Caspers, Vandenburgh & Lindquist**
225 South Sixth Street, Suite 3200, Minneapolis, MN 55402

**Carmody & Torrance LLP**
50 Leavenworth Street, PO Box 1110, Waterbury, CT 06721

**Carpenter & Klatskin**
1500 Denver Club Building, Denver, CO 80202

**Carpenter & Lipps LLP**
280 Plaza, Suite 1300, 280 North High Street, Columbus, OH 43215

**Carpenter & Stout Ltd**
1600 University Boulevard NE, Suite A, Albuquerque, NM 87102-1724

**Carr, Tabb & Pope LLP**
10 North Parkway Square, Atlanta, GA 30327

**Carrington, Coleman, Sloman & Blumenthal, LLP**
200 Crescent Court, Suite 1500, Dallas, TX 75201

**Carroll, Kelly & Murphy**
One Turks Head Place, Suite 400, Providence, RI 02903

**Carruthers & Roth PA**
235 North Edgeworth Street, PO Box 540, Greensboro, NC 27402

**Carver Darden Koretzky Tessier Finn Blossman & Areaux LLC**
Attorneys and Counselors at Law, Energy Centre, 1100 Poydras Street, New Orleans, LA 70163

**Cascadia Law Group**
1201 Third Avenue, Suite 320, Seattle, WA 98101

**Cassem Tierney Adams Gotch & Douglas**
Suite 300, 8805 Indian Hills Drive, Omaha, NE 68114

**Cathcart, Collins & Kneafsey LLP**
444 South Flower Street, 42nd Floor, Los Angeles, CA 90071

**Chamberlain, Hrdlicka, White, Williams & Martin**
1200 Smith Street, Suite 1400, Houston, TX 77002

**Chambliss, Bahner & Stophel, PC**
1000 Tallan Building, Two Union Square, Chattanooga, TN 37402

**Charles L Siemon - Sole Practitioner**
Suite 339, 433 Plaza Real, Boca Raton, FL 33432-3945

**Chester, Willcox & Saxbe LLP**
65 East State Street, Suite 1000, Columbus, OH 43215

**Chisenhall, Nestrud & Julian, PA**
400 West Capitol, Suite 2840, Little Rock, AR 72201

**Choate Hall & Stewart**
Two International Place, Boston, MA 02110

**Christensen O'Connor Johnson Kindness, PLLC**
1420 Fifth Avenue, Suite 2800, Seattle, WA 98101

**Christensen, Miller, Fink, Jacobs, Glaser, Weil & Shapiro, LLP**
2121 Avenue of the Stars, 18th Floor, Los Angeles, CA 90067

**Christensen, Moore, Cockrell, Cummings & Axelberg PC**
Two Medicine Building, 160 Heritage Way, PO Box 7370, Kalispell, MT 59904-0370

**Christian & Barton LLP**
909 East Main Street, Suite 1200, Richmond, VA 23219

**Christian, Samson, Jones & Chisholm, PLLC**
310 West Spruce, PO Box 8479, Missoula, MT 59807

**Christianson, Boutin & Spraker**
911 West 8th Avenue, Suite 302, Anchorage, AK 99501

**Christopher Hawks PC**
220 South King Street, PO Box 1495, Jackson, WY 83001

**Chuhak & Tecson PC**
30 South Wacker Drive, 26th Floor, Chicago, IL 60606

**Chun Rair & Yoshimoto LLP**
Davies Pacific Center, Fourth Floor, 841 Bishop Street, Honolulu, HI 96813

**Chun, Kerr, Dodd, Beaman & Wong**
745 Fort Street Mall, Suite 900, Honolulu, HI 96813

**Cichanowicz, Callan, Keane, Vengrow & Textor, LLP**
61 Broadway, 30th Floor, Suite 3000, New York, NY 10006-2802

**Clarence & Dyer LLP**
899 Ellis Street, San Francisco, CA 94109

**Clark, Atcheson & Reisert**
230 Park Avenue, New York, NY 10169

**Clawson & Falk LLC**
2257 South 1100 East, Suite 105, Salt Lake City, UT 84106

**Cleary Shahi & Aicher, PC**
110 Merchants Row, Suite 3, PO Box 6740, Rutland, VT 05702-6740

**Cleveland, Waters and Bass, PA**
Two Capital Plaza, PO Box 1137, Concord, NH 03302

**Cline, Williams, Wright, Johnson & Oldfather LLP**
1900 US Bank Building, 233 South 13th Street, Lincoln, NE 68508

**Clisham, Satriana & Biscan LLC**
1512 Larimer, Suite 400, Denver, CO 80202

**Coats Rose Yale Ryman Lee**
800 First City Tower, 1001 Fannin, Houston, TX 77002-6707

**Coblentz, Patch, Duffy & Bass LLP**
222 Kearny Street, Seventh Floor, San Francisco, CA 94108

**Coffman, Coleman, Andrews & Grogan**
800 West Monroe Street, Jacksonville, FL 32202

**Cohen & Grigsby PC**
11 Stanwix Street, 15th Floor, Pittsburgh, PA 15222

**Cohen Dax and Koening, PC**
90 State Street, Suite 1030, Albany, NY 12207

**Cokinos, Bosien and Young**
2919 Allen Parkway, Suite 1500, Houston, TX 77019

**Cole, Schotz, Meisel, Forman & Leonard PA**
Court Plaza North, 25 Main Street, Hackensack, NJ 07602

**Collier Shannon Scott PLLC**
Washington Harbour, Suite 400, 3050 K Street NW, Washington, DC 20007

**Comiter, Singer & Baseman, LLP**
3801 PGA Boulevard, Suite 802, Palm Beach Gardens, FL 33410

**Commercial Law Group**
2725 Oklahoma Tower, 210 Park Avenue, Oklahoma City, OK 73102-5643

**Condon & Forsyth LLP**
685 Third Avenue, New York, NY 10017

**Conley Rose, PC**
701 Brazos Street, Suite 500, Austin, TX 78701

**Conmy Feste Ltd**
200 Wells Fargo Center, 406 Main Avenue, PO Box 2686, Fargo, ND 58108-2686

**Connelly Baker Wotring Jackson LLP**
700 Louisiana, Suite 1850, Houston, TX 77002

**Conner & Winters, PC**
3700 First Place Tower, 15 East 5th Street, Tulsa, OK 74103-4344

**Connolly, O'Malley, Lillis, Hansen & Olson LLP**
317 Sixth Avenue, Suite 300, Bank of America Building, Des Moines, IA 50309

**Constancy, Brooks & Smith, LLC**
Suite 2400, 230 Peachtree Street North West, Atlanta, GA 30303-1557

**Constantine Cannon PC**
450 Lexington Avenue, 17th Floor, New York, NY 10017

**Cook & Roach, LLP**
ChevronTexaco Heritage Plaza, 1111 Bagby, Suite 2650, Houston, TX 77002

**Cooley Godward LLP**
5 Palo Alto Square, 3000 El Camino Real, Palo Alto, CA 94306-2155

**Cooper & Scully PC**
900 Jackson Street, Suite 900, Dallas, TX 75202

**Copeland, Franco, Screws & Gill**
444 South Perry Street, PO Box 347, Montgomery, AL 36101-0347

**Corbin & Fitzgerald LLP**
601 West Fifth Street, Suite 1150, Los Angeles, CA 90071-2024

**Corbyn Law Firm**
Two Leadership Square, 211 North Robinson, Suite 1120, Oklahoma City, OK 73102

**Corr Cronin LLP**
1001 Fourth Avenue, Suite 3900, Seattle, WA 98154

**Corretti, Newsom & Hawkins**
1804 7th Avenue North, Birmingham, AL 35203

**Cosho Humphrey LLP**
Washington Group Building 4, Suite 790, 800 Park Boulevard, PO Box 9518, Boise, ID 83707-9518

**Costello Porter Hill Heisterkamp Bushnell & Carpenter LLP**
200 Security Building, 704 St Joseph Street, PO Box 290, Rapid City, SD 57709

**Cotchett, Pitre, Simon & McCarthy**
San Francisco Airport Office Center, 840 Malcolm Road, Suite 200, Burlingame, CA 94010

**Cotsirilos Tighe & Streicker Ltd**
Suite 600, 33 North Dearborn Street, Chicago, IL 60602

**Couch White, LLP**
PO Box 22222, Albany, NY 12201

**Cowan, Liebowitz & Latman**
1133 Avenue of the Americas, New York, NY 10036-6799

**Cox Castle & Nicholson LLP**
2049 Century Park East, 28th Floor, Los Angeles, CA 90067

**Cozen O'Connor**
1900 Market Street, Philadelphia, PA 19103

**Creed C Black Jnr - Sole Practitioner**
1700 Market Street, Suite 2632, Philadelphia, PA 19103

**Croker, Huck, Kasher, DeWitt, Anderson & Gonderinger, PC**
The Omaha Tower, Suite 1250, 2120 South 72nd Street, Omaha, NE 68124

**Cunningham Law Firm**
400 Australian Avenue South, Suite 700, West Palm Beach, FL 33401

**Cunningham, Bounds, Yance, Crowder & Brown, LLC**
1601 Dauphin Street, PO Box 66705, Mobile, AL 36660

**Curtis, Mallet-Prevost, Colt & Mosle LLP**
101 Park Avenue, New York, NY 10178-0061

**Cutler & Donahoe LLP**
100 North Phillips Avenue, 9th Floor, Sioux Falls, SD 57104-6725

**D'Amante Couser Steiner Pellerin, PA**
9 Triangle Park Drive, PO Box 2650, Concord, NH 03302-2650

**Daniels, Kashtan, Downs, Robertson & Magathan**
3300 Ponce De Leon Boulevard, Miami, FL 33134

**Danielson Harrigan Leyh & Tollefson, LLP**
999 Third Avenue, Suite 4400, Seattle, WA 98104

**Dann Pecar Newman & Kleiman, PC**
One American Square, Suite 2300, Indianapolis, IN 46282

**Davenport, Evans, Hurwitz & Smith LLP**
206 West 14th Street, PO Box 1030, Sioux Falls, SD 57101-1030

**David D Caron - Sole Practitioner**
School of Law, Boalt Hall, University of California at Berkeley, Berkeley, CA 94720

**David H Bundy PC**
3201 C Street, Suite 301, Anchorage, AK 99503

**Davis & Boghigian, PC**
221 Main Street, Suite 301, PO Box 525, Nashua, NH 03061-0525

**Davis & Cannon**
40 South Main Street, PO Box 728, Sheridan, WY 82801

**Davis & Ceriani**
1350 17th Street, Denver, CO 80202

**Davis & Gilbert**
1740 Broadway, New York, NY 10019

**Davis & Kuelthau, SC**
111 East Kilbourn Avenue, Suite 1400, Milwaukee, WI 53202

**Davis & Wilkerson, PC**
1801 South MoPac, Suite 300, Austin, TX 78746

**Davis Graham & Stubbs LLP**
1550 Seventeenth Street, Suite 500, Denver, CO 80202

**Davis Wright Tremaine LLP**
1501 Fourth Avenue, Suite 2600, Seattle, WA 98101-1688

**Davis, Brown, Koehn, Shors & Roberts, PC**
The Financial Center, 666 Walnut Street, Suite 2500, Des Moines, IA 50309

**Dawda, Mann, Mulcahy & Sadler PLC**
39533 Woodward Ave, Suite 200, Bloomfield Hills, MI 48304-5103

**Day Casebeer Madrid & Batchelder LLP**
20300 Stevens Creek Boulevard, Suite 400, Cupertino, CA 95014

**Deacy & Deacy LLP**
920 Main Street, Suite 1900, Kansas City, MO 64105

**Dean, Mead, Egerton, Bloodworth, Capouano & Bozarth PA**
800 North Magnolia Avenue, Suite 1500, Orlando, FL 32803

**Deaner, Deaner, Scann, Malan & Larsen**
720 South Fourth Street, Suite 300, Las Vegas, NV 89101

**DeLisio Moran Geraghty & Zobel, PC**
943 West Sixth Avenue, Anchorage, AK 99501

**DeMars & Turman Ltd**
15 Broadway, Suite 510, PO Box 110, Fargo, ND 58107

**DeMersseman Jensen Christianson Stanton & Huffman LLP**
516 Fifth Street, PO Box 1820, Rapid City, SD 57709-1820

**Denlinger, Rosenthal & Greenberg LPA**
425 Walnut Street, Suite 2310, Cincinnati, OH 45202-3918

**Dennis, Corry, Porter & Smith LLP**
3535 Piedmont Road, Building 14, Suite 900, Atlanta, GA 30305

**D**

**DeOrchis & Partners LLP**
61 Broadway, 26th Floor, New York, NY 10006

**Derrick & Briggs LLP**
Bank One Center, 20th Floor, 100 North Broadway Avenue, Oklahoma City, OK 73102

**Devine Millimet & Branch PA**
PO Box 719, 111 Amherst Street, Manchester, NH 03105-0719

**Dickinson, Mackaman, Tyler & Hagen, PC**
Suite 1600 Hub Tower, 699 Walnut Street, Des Moines, IA 50309

**Dillon & Yudell LLP**
Building II, Suite 2110, 8911 North Capital of Texas Highway, Austin, TX 78759

**Dilworth Paxson LLP**
3200 Mellon Bank Center, 1735 Market Street, Philadelphia, PA 19103

**Dinse, Knapp & McAndrew PC**
PO Box 988, 209 Battery Street, Burlington, VT 05402-0988

**Doerner, Saunders, Daniel & Anderson, LLP**
320 South Boston Avenue, Suite 500, Tulsa, OK 74103

**Doffermyre, Shields, Canfield, Knowles & Devine**
1355 Peachtree Street 1600, Atlanta, GA 30309 - 3269

**Domina Law plc LLO**
2425 South 144th Street, Omaha, NE 68144-3267

**Donahue, Tucker & Ciandella**
Water Street Professional Building, 225 Water Street, Exeter, NH 03833

**Doney, Crowley, Bloomquist, Payne & Uda, PC**
Diamond Block Building, Suite 200, 44 West 6th Avenue, PO Box 1185, Helena, MT 59624-1185

**Donovan Parry McDermott & Radzik**
Wall Street Plaza, 88 Pine Street, New York, NY 10005-1801

**Dove and Chill**
4266 I-55 North, Suite 108, Jackson, MS 39211

**Dover Dixon Horne**
425 West Capitol, Suite 3700, Little Rock, AR 72201

**Downey, Brand, Seymour & Rohwer LLP**
555 Capitol Mall, Suite 1050, Sacramento, CA 95814

**Downs Rachlin Martin PLLC**
90 Prospect Street, PO Box 99, St Johnsbury, VT 05819

**Dray, Thomson & Dyekman PC**
204 East 22nd Street, Cheyenne, WY 82001

**Drinker Biddle & Reath LLP**
One Logan Square, 18th & Cherry Streets, Philadelphia, PA 19103-6996

**Ducker, Montgomery, Aronstein & Bess PC**
One Civic Center Plaza, 1560 Broadway, Suite 1400, Denver, CO 80202

**Duffy, Sweeney & Scott Ltd**
One Turks Head Place, Suite 1200, Providence, RI 02903

**Duggan, Shadwick, Doerr & Kurlbaum, PC**
11040 Oakmont Park, Overland Park, KS 66210

**Durant, Nichols, Houston, Hodgson & Cortese-Costa, PC**
1057 Broad Street, Bridgeport, CT 06604-4219

**Durham Jones & Pinegar, A Professional Corporation**
111 East Broadway, Suite 900, Salt Lake City, UT 84111

**Durrell Law Group, PC**
1400 West Benson Boulevard, Suite 370, Anchorage, AK 99503

**Dutton, Braun, Staack & Hellman PLC**
3151 Brockway Road, PO Box 810, Waterloo, IA 50704

**Dykema Gossett PLLC**
Third Floor West, Franklin Square, 1300 I Street NW, Washington, DC 20005

**Earl, Curley & Lagarde, PC**
3101 N. Central Avenue, Suite 1000, Phoenix, AZ 85012

**Eastman & Smith Ltd**
One Seagate, Twenty-Fourth Floor, PO Box 10032, Toledo, OH 43699

**Eaves & Mendenhall PA**
6565 Americas Parkway, Suite 950 NE 87110, Albuquerque, NM 87176

**Eberle, Berlin, Kading, Turnbow & McKlveen, Chartered**
Capitol Park Plaza, 300 North Sixth Street, Boise, ID 83701

**Eckert Seamans Cherin & Mellott, LLC**
US Steel Tower, 600 Grant Street, 44th Floor, Pittsburgh, PA 15219-2788

**Edwards Frickle Anner-Hughes & Cook**
1601 Lewis Avenue, Suite206, PO Box 20039, Billings, MT 59104

**Elam & Burke PA**
Key Financial Center, 702 West Idaho Street, Boise, ID 83701

**Elarbee, Thompson, Sapp & Wilson, LLP**
800 International Tower, 229 Peachtree Street NE, Atlanta, GA 30303

**Elderkin & Pirnie PLC**
115 First Avenue South East, PO Box 1968, Cedar Rapids, IA 52406

**Eldridge Cooper Steichen & Leach PLLC**
Suite 200, 110 West Seventh Street, Tulsa, OK 74119

**Ellis & Thorp PLLC**
1406 Confederate Avenue, Richmond, VA 23227

**Ellis & Winters LLP**
1100 Crescent Green, Suite 200, Cary, NC 27511

**Ellison Schneider & Harris**
2015 H Street, Sacramento, CA 95814-3109

**Ellman, Burke, Hoffman & Johnson**
One Ecker Building, Suite 200, Ecker and Stevenson Streets, San Francisco, CA 94105

**Enns & Archer LLP**
939 Burke Street, Winston-Salem, NC 27101

**Epstein Becker & Green PC**
250 Park Avenue, New York, NY 10177-1211

**Erickson & Sederstrom, PC**
Regency Westpointe, 10330 Regency Parkway Drive, Suite 100, Omaha, NE 68114

**Everett Law Firm**
1944 East Joyce Boulevard, Fayetteville, AR 72703

**Fabian & Clendenin**
215 South State Street, 12th Floor, PO Box 510210, Salt Lake City, UT 84111

**Fabyanske, Westra & Hart PA**
800 Lasalle Avenue, Suite 1900, Minneapolis, MN 55402-2037

**Farella Braun & Martel LLP**
Russ Building, 235 Montgomery Street, San Francisco, CA 94104

**Farer Fersko**
600 South Avenue, PO Box 580, Westfield, NJ 07091-0580

**Farmer, Cline & Campbell PLLC**
Postal Address, PO Box 3842, Charleston, WV 25338

**Farr & Taranto**
Suite 800, 1220 19th Street, NW, Washington, DC 20036-2435

**Faruki Ireland & Cox PLL**
500 Courthouse Plaza SW, 10 North Ludlow Street, Dayton, OH 45402

**Feldman Orlansky & Sanders**
500 L Street, Suite 400, Anchorage, AK 99501

**Felhaber, Larson, Fenlon & Vogt, PC**
220 South Sixth Street, Suite 2200, Minneapolis, MN 55402-4504

**Ferencik, Libanoff, Brandt, Bustamante & Williams**
150 South Pine Island Road, Suite 400, Fort Lauderdale, FL 33324

**Fikso Kretschmer Smith Dixon PS**
2025 First Avenue, Suite 1130, Seattle, WA 98121

**Fine, Kaplan and Black, RPC**
1835 Market Street, 28th Floor, Philadelphia, PA 19103

**Finley, Alt, Smith, Scharnberg, Craig, Hilmes & Gaffney PC**
699 Walnut Street, 1900 Hub Tower, Des Moines, IA 50309

**Fisk & Fielder**
2710 Stemmons Fwy # 400, Dallas, TX 75207-2210

**Flaherty, Sensabaugh & Bonasso PLLC**
200 Capitaol Street, PO Box 3843, Charleston, WV 25301

**Fleck, Mather & Strutz, Ltd.**
Norwest Bank Building, Sixth Floor, 400 East Broadway, Bismarck, ND 58502

**Fleeson, Gooing, Coulson & Kitch, LLC**
125 North Market Street, Suite 1600, PO Box 997, Wichita, KS 67201

**Flygare Schwarz & Closson PLLC**
11 Court Street, PO Box 439, Exeter, NH 03833

**Flynn, Gaskins & Bennett**
2900 Metropolitan Center, Minneapolis, MN 55402

**Fogarty, Cohen, Selby & Nemiroff LLC**
88 Field Point Road, Greenwich, CT 06836-2508

**Fognani & Faught, PLLC**
1700 Lincoln Street, Suite 2222, Denver, CO 80203

**Foley Hoag LLP**
155 Seaport Boulevard, Boston, MA 02210-2600

**Ford Nassen & Baldwin**
8080 North Central Expressway, Suite 1600, LB 65, Dallas, TX 75206

**Forizs and Dogali PL**
4301 Anchor Plaza Parkway, Suite 300, Tampa, FL 33634

**Fortney & Scott, LLC**
1050 Conneticut Avenue NW, Suite 1200, Washington, DC 20036

**Foster Pepper PLLC**
1111 Third Avenue, 34th Floor, Seattle, WA 98101

**Fowler White Boggs Banker**
501 East Kennedy Boulevard, Suite 1700, PO Box 1438, Tampa, FL 33602

**Fowler White Burnett PA (FowlerWhite)**
Espirito Santo Plaza, 1395 Brickell Avenue, 14th Floor, Miami, FL 33131-3302

**Franczek Sullivan**
300 South Wacker Drive, Suite 3400, Chicago, IL 60606

**Frank D Blackburn - Sole Practitioner**
5937 Jones Creek Road, Baton Rouge, LA 70817

**Frankfurt Kurnit Klein & Selz**
488 Madison Avenue, New York, NY 10022

**Franklin, Weinrib, Rudell & Vassallo**
488 Madison Avenue, New York, NY 10022

**Frantz Ward LLP**
2500 Key Center, 127 Public Square, Cleveland, OH 44114

**Franzetti Law Firm PC**
10 South LaSalle Street, Suite 3600, Chicago, IL 60603

**Frazer Ryan Goldberg Arnold & Gittler LLP**
3101 N Central Avenue, Suite 1600, Phoenix, AZ 85012-2615

**Fredrikson & Byron PA**
200 South Sixth Street, Suite 4000,
Minneapolis, MN 55402-1425

**Freeborn & Peters**
311 South Wacker Drive, Suite 3000,
Chicago, IL 60606

**Freedman Boyd Daniels Hollander
Goldberg & Cline PA**
20 First Plaza, Suite 700, Albuquerque, NM
87102

**Freehill Hogan & Mahar LLP**
80 Pine Street, New York, NY 10005

**Freeman, Freeman & Salzman**
401 North Michigan Avenue, Suite 3200,
Chicago, IL 60611-4207

**Freshfields Bruckhaus Deringer**
65 Fleet Street, London, EC4Y 1HS

**Freund, Freeze & Arnold**
One Dayton Centre, 1 South Main Street, Suite
1800, Dayton, OH 45402-2017

**Friday, Eldredge & Clark**
2000 Regions Center, 400 West Capitol
Avenue, Little Rock, AR 72201

**Frilot, Partridge, Kohnke
& Clements LC**
1100 Poydras Street, Suite 3600, New Orleans,
LA 70163

**Fritz, Byrne, Head & Harrison**
2000 San Jacinto, 98 San Jacinto Boulevard,
Austin, TX 78701

**Fross Zelnick Lehrman & Zissu PC**
866 UN Plaza, At First Avenue & 48th Street,
New York, NY 10017

**Frost Tamayo Sessums & Aranda PA**
395 South Central Avenue, PO Box 2188,
Bartow, FL 33830

**Fruth, Jamison & Elsass**
80 South Eighth Street, Suite 3902,
Minneapolis, MN 55402-2248

**Fullenkamp, Doyle & Jobeun**
11440 West Center Road, Omaha, NE 68144

**G Richard Strafer PA**
2400 South Dixie Highway, Suite 200, Miami,
FL 33133

**Gadsby Hannah LLP**
225 Franklin Street, Boston, MA 02110-2811

**Gainsburgh, Benjamin, David,
Meunier & Warshauer**
2800 Energy Centre, 1100 Poydras,
New Orleans, LA 70163-2800

**Gallagher & Kennedy PA**
2575 East Camelback Road, Phoenix, AZ
85016-9225

**Gallagher, Callahan and Gartrell, PC**
214 North Main Street, PO Box 1415,
Concord, NH 03302

**Gallagher, Evelius & Jones, LLP**
Park Charles, Suite 400, Baltimore, MD 21201

**Gallegos Law Firm PC**
460 St Michael's Drive, Building 300, Santa Fe,
NM 87505

**Gammage & Burnham, PLC**
One Renaissance Square, Two North Central
Avenue, 18th Floor, Phoenix, AZ 85004

**Gang Tyre Ramer & Brown**
132 South Rodeo Drive, Beverly Hills,
CA 90212

**Garfunkel, Wild & Travis PC**
111 Great Neck Road, Suite 503, Great Neck,
NY 11021

**Garlington, Lohn & Robinson, PLLP**
199 West Pine Street, PO Box 7909, Missoula,
MT 59807

**Garofalo Goerlich Hainbach PC**
1200 New Hampshire Avenure, Washington,
DC 200036-6802

**Garvey Schubert Barer**
Eleventh Floor, 121 SW Morrison Street,
Portland, OR 97204

**Gedney M Howe III PA**
8 Chalmers Street, PO Box 1034, Charleston,
SC 29402

**Gelber, Gelber, Ingersoll &
Klevansky, A Law Corporation**
Topa Financial Center, 745 Fort Street, Suite
1400, West Tower, Honolulu, HI 96813-3823

**Genova, Burns & Vernoia**
Eisenhower Plaza II, 354 Eisenhower Parkway,
Livingston, NJ 07039

**George & Lorensen**
1526 Kanawhwa Boulevard E, Charleston, WV
25311-2413

**George & Titus PA**
100 South Ashley Street, Suite 1290, Tampa, FL
33602-5360

**George A Bermann - Sole
Practitioner**
Columbia University School of Law, 435 West
116 Street, New York, NY 10027

**Gerald Aksen - Sole Practitioner**
1025 5th Avenue, New York, NY 10028

**Gideon & Wiseman PLC**
110 Noel Place, 200 Fourth Avenue North,
Nashville, TN 37219-2144

**Gignilliat, Savitz & Bettis LLP**
900 Elmwood Avenue, Suite 100, Columbia,
SC 29201

**Gilbert Heintz & Randolph LLP**
1100 New York Avenue, Suite 700,
Washington, DC 20005

**Gilchrist & Rutter Professional
Corporation**
1299 Ocean Avenue, Suite 900, Santa Monica,
CA 90401-1000

**Gilker and Jones PA**
9222 North Highway 71, Mountainburg,
AR 72946

**Gillen Parker & Withers LLC**
One Securities Centre, 3490 Piedmont Road,
NE Suite 1050, Atlanta, GA 30305

**Gilmartin, Poster & Shafto**
845 Third Avenue, New York, NY 10012

**Giordano Halleran & Ciesla PC**
125 Half Mile Road, PO Box 190, Middletown,
NJ 07748

**Givens Pursley LLP**
601 W Bannock Street, Boise, ID 83702

**Glankler Brown, PLLC**
One Commerce Square, Suite 1700, Memphis,
TN 38103

**Glenn Rasmussen Fogarty & Hooker**
100 South Ashley Drive, Suite 1300, Tampa,
FL 33601-3333

**Godfrey & Kahn, SC**
780 North Water Street, Milwaukee, WI 53202

**Godwin Pappas Langley
Ronquillo, LLP**
Renaissance Tower, 1201 Elm Street, Suite
1700, Dallas, 75270

**Goetz Fitzpatrick LLP**
One Penn Plaza, New York, NY 10119

**Goetz, Gallik & Baldwin, PC**
35 North Grand Avenue, PO Box 6580,
Bozeman, MT 59771-6580

**Goins, Underkofler, Crawford
& Langdon LLP**
1201 Elm Street, Suite 4800, Dallas, TX 75270

**Goldberg Godles Weiner & Wright**
1229 19th Street NW, Washington, DC 20036

**Goldberg, Kohn, Bell, Black,
Rosenbloom & Moritz, Ltd**
55 East Monroe Street, Suite 3700, Chicago, IL
60603

**Golden & Owens LLP**
One Houston Center, 1221 McKinney Street,
Suite 3150, Houston, TX 77010

**Goodell, Stratton, Edmonds &
Palmer, LLP**
515 South Kansas Avenue, Topeka, KS 66603-
3999

**Goodin MacBride Squeri Ritchie
& Day LLP**
Suite 900, 505 Sansome Street, San Francisco,
CA 94111

**Goodsill Anderson Quinn & Stifel**
Alii Place, Suite 1800, 1099 Alakea Street,
Honolulu, HI 96813

**Goodwin & Goodwin, LLP**
300 Summers Street, Suite 1500, PO Box 2107,
Charleston, WV 25301-1678

**Goold Patterson Ales & Day**
4496 South Pecos Road, Las Vegas, NV 89121

**Gordon & Silver Ltd**
Ninth Floor, 3960 Howard Hughes Parkway,
Las Vegas, NV 89109

**Gordon Murray Tilden**
1325 Fourth Avenue, Suite 1800, Seattle,
WA 98101-2510

**Gordon, Arata, McCollam, Duplantis
& Eagan LLP**
201 St Charles Avenue, Suite 4000,
New Orleans, LA 70170-4000

**Gordon, Feinblatt, Rothman,
Hoffberger & Hollander, LLC**
The Garrett Building, 233 East Redwood
Street, Baltimore, MD 21202

**Gordon, Martin, Jones, Harris & Shrum**
Suite 600, 49 Music Square West, Nashville,
TN 37203

**Goren Cherof Doody & Ezrol PA**
3099 East Commercial Boulevard, Suite 200,
Fort Lauderdale, FL 33308-4311

**Gottlieb & Smith PA**
Bank of America Plaza, Suite 600, 1901 Main
Street, Columbia, SC 29201

**Goulston & Storrs**
400 Atlantic Avenue, Boston, MA 02110

**Graham & Dunn PC**
Pier 70, 2801 Alaskan Way, Suite 300, Seattle,
WA 98121-1128

**Grant & Eisenhofer PA**
1201 North Market Street, Suite 2100,
Wilmington, DE 19801

**Gravel and Shea**
Corporate Plaza, 76 St Paul Street,
PO Box 369, Burlington, VT 05402-0369

**Graves, Dougherty, Hearon
& Moody, PC**
401 Congress Avenue, Suite 2200, Austin,
TX 78701

**Gray Robinson PA**
301 East Pine Street, Suite 1400, Orlando,
FL 32802

**Gray, Plant, Mooty, Mooty &
Bennett, PA**
500 IDS Center, 80 South Eighth Street,
Minneapolis, MN 55402

**Graydon Head & Ritchey LLP**
1900 Fifth Third Center, 511 Walnut Street,
Cincinnati, 45202

**Greenberg Glusker Fields Claman
Machtinger & Kinsella LLP**
1900 Avenue of the Stars, 21st Floor, Century
City, Los Angeles, CA 90067

**Greene Espel PLLP**
200 South Sixth Street, Suite 1200,
Minneapolis, MN 55402-1415

**Greener Banducci Shoemaker**
815 West Washington Street, Boise, ID 83702

**Greensfelder, Hemker & Gale, PC**
2000 Equitable Building, 10 South Broadway,
St Louis, MO 63102

**Greenstein Delorme & Luchs**
1620 L Street Northwest, Suite 900,
Washington, DC 20036-5605

**Grefe & Sidney, PLC**
2222 Grand Avenue, PO Box 10434,
Des Moines, IA 50306

**Gregory P Joseph Law Offices LLC**
805 Third Avenue, 31st Floor, New York,
NY 10022

**Griffith & Nixon, PC**
One Lincoln Centre, 5400 LBJ Freeway, Suite
1025, Dallas, TX 75240

**Grimshaw & Harring PC**
1700 Lincoln Street, Suite 3800, Denver,
CO 80203

**Gronek & Latham**
390 North Orange Avenue, Suite 600, PO Box
3353, Orlando, FL 32802

**Groom Law Group**
1701 Pennsylvania Avenue NW, Washington,
DC 20006

**Grossberg Yochelson Fox & Beyda**
2000 L Street NW, Suite 675, Washington, DC
20036-4907

**G**

**Grotta, Glassman & Hoffman**
75 Livingston Avenue, Roseland, NJ 07068

**Grubman, Indursky & Shire, PC**
152 West 57th Street, New York, NY 10019

**Guess & Rudd PC**
510 L Street, Suite 700, Anchorage, AK 99501

**Guida, Slavich & Flores, PC**
750 North St. Paul Street, Suite 200, Dallas, TX 75201

**Gullett, Sanford, Robinson & Martin PLLC**
315 Deadrick Street, Suite 1100, Nashville, TN 37238

**Gunderson Dettmer Stough Villeneuve Franklin & Hachigian**
155 Constitution Drive, Menlo Park, CA 94025

**Gunderson, Palmer, Goodsell & Nelson LLP**
440 Mount Rushmore Road, 3rd and 4th Floors, Rapid City, SD 57709

**Gunderson, Sharp & Walke**
317 6th Avenue, Suite 600, Des Moines, IA 50309

**Gunster, Yoakley & Stewart PA**
Phillips Point, Suite 500 East, 777 South Flagler Drive, West Palm Beach, FL 33401

**Gurley Dramis**
535 South Palm Avenue, Sarasota, FL 34236

**Haddon, Morgan, Mueller, Jordan, Mackey & Foreman PC**
150 East Tenth Avenue, Denver, CO 80203

**Hafetz & Necheles**
500 Fifth Avenue, 29th Floor, New York, NY 10110

**Haglund Kelley Horngren Jones & Wilder LLP**
One Main Place, 101 South West Main, Suite 1800, Portland, OR 97204

**Hahn Loeser & Parks LLP**
3300 BP Tower, 200 Public Square, Cleveland, OH 44114

**Hal Joseph Kemp PA**
111 Center Street, Suite 1300, Little Rock, AR 72201

**Hale Lane Peek Dennison and Howard**
5441 Kietzke Lane, Second Floor, Reno, NV 89511

**Hall, Estill, Hardwick, Gable, Golden & Nelson, PC**
320 South Boston Avenue, Suite 400, Tulsa, OK 74103

**Hall, Farley, Oberrecht & Blanton, PA**
Key Financial Center, 702 West Idaho Street, Suite 700, Boise, ID 83701

**Hall, Render, Killian, Heath & Lyman Professional Services Corporation**
One American Square, Suite 2000, Box 82064, Indianapolis, IN 46282

**Hamilton Fay Moon Stephens Steele & Martin, PLLC**
2020 Charlotte Plaza, 201 South College Street, Charlotte, NC 28244-2020

**Haney, Woloson & Mullins**
1117 South Rancho Drive, Las Vegas, NV 89102

**Hankins & Hicks**
800 West Fourth Street, PO Box 5670, Little Rock, AR 72119

**Hansen Jacobson Teller Hoberman Newman, Warren, Sloane & Richman, LLP**
450 North Roxbury Drive, 8th Floor, Beverly Hills, CA 90210-4222

**Hansen, McClintock & Riley**
Fleming Building, 8th Floor, 218 6th Avenue, Des Moines, IA 50309-4092

**Hanson, Bridgett, Marcus, Vlahos & Rudy, LLP**
333 Market Street, 23rd Floor, San Francisco, CA 94105

**Haralson, Miller, Pitt, Feldman & McAnally PLC**
One South Church Avenue, Suite 900, Tucson, AZ 85701-1620

**Harding Shultz & Downs**
800 Lincoln Square, 121 South 13th Street, PO Box 82028, Lincoln, NE 68501-2028

**Hare, Wynn, Newell & Newton LLP**
The Historic Massey Building, 2025 Third Avenue North, Suite 800, Birmingham, AL 35203

**Harkavy Shainberg Kaplan & Dunstan PLC**
6060 Poplar Avenue, Suite 140, Memphis, TN 38119

**Harkins Cunningham LLP**
2800 One Commerce Square, Philadelphia, PA 19103 7042

**Harris & Geno PLLC**
111 East Capitol Street, Suite 290, Jackson, MS 39207

**Harris, Wiltshire & Grannis LLP**
1200 Eighteenth Street NW, Suite 1200, Washington, DC 20036-2560

**Harrison & Moberly LLP**
135 North Pennsylvania Street, Suite 2100, Indianapolis, IN 46204

**Harrison, Kemp & Jones, LLP**
3800 Howard Hughes Parkway, Seventeenth Floor, Las Vegas, NV 89109

**Hartig Rhodes Hoge & Lekisch PC**
717 K Street, Anchorage, AK 99501

**Harvey & Frank**
Two City Center, PO Box 126, Portland, ME 04112-0126

**Hassard Bonnington LLP**
Two Embarcadero Center, Suite 1800, San Francisco, CA 94111

**Hatcher, Stubbs, Land, Hollis & Rothschild, LLP**
The Corporate Center, Suite 500, Columbus, GA 31902

**Hawley Troxell Ennis & Hawley LLP**
877 Main Street, Suite 1000, PO Box 1617, Boise, ID 83702

**Hayes Lorenzen Lawyers PLC**
Plaza Centre One, Suite 580, 125 South Dubuque Street, Iowa City, IA 52240

**Haynes and Boone LLP**
901 Main Street, Suite 3100, Dallas, TX 75202

**Haynsworth Sinkler Boyd PA**
160 East Bay Street, PO Box 340, Charleston, SC 29402-0340

**Heard & Howard**
219 North Fourth Street, PO Box 926, Columbus, MT 59019-0926

**Heath, Davis & McCalla**
200 Perry-Brooks Building, 720 Brazous Street, Austin, TX 78701

**Heller, Draper, Hayden, Patrick & Horn, LLC**
650 Poydras Street, Suite 2500, New Orleans, LA 70130

**Helms Mulliss & Wicker PLLC**
201 North Tryon Street, PO Box 31247, Charlotte, NC 28202

**Hendrick, Phillips, Salzman & Flatt PC**
230 Peachtree Street, North West Suite 1800, Atlanta, GA 30303

**Henson & Efron**
220 South Sixth Street, Suite 1800, Minneapolis, MN 55402-4503

**Hickey & Evans LLP**
1800 Carey Avenue, Suite 700, PO Drawer 467, Cheyenne, WY 82003

**Higgins, Cavanagh & Cooney LLP**
The Hay Building, Fourth Floor, 123 Dyer Street, Providence, RI 02903

**Hill & Robbins PC**
1441 18th Street, 100 Blake Street Building, Denver, CO 80202

**Hill Rivkins & Hayden LLP**
45 Broadway, Suite 1500, New York, NY 10006

**Hill Wallack**
202 Carnegie Center CN 5226, Princeton, NJ 08543-5226

**Hill, Ward & Henderson, PA**
101 East Kennedy Boulevard, Suite 3700, PO Box 2231, Tampa, FL 33601

**Hinckley, Allen & Snyder LLP**
28 State Street, 29th Floor, Boston, MA 02109-1775

**Hinkle Elkouri Law Firm LLC**
Suite 2000 Epic Center, 301 North Main Street, Wichita, KS 67202

**Hirschler Fleischer**
The Federal Reserve Bank Building, 701 East Byrd Street, Richmond, VA 23218

**Hirst & Applegate, PC**
1720 Carey Avenue, Suite 200, PO Box 1083, Cheyenne, WY 82003-1083

**Hite, Fanning & Honeyman LLP**
200 West Douglas Avenue, Suite 600, Wichita, KS 67202-3089

**Hodge Dwyer Zeman**
3150 Roland Avenue, PO Box 5776, Springfield, IL 62705-5776

**Hodgson Russ LLP**
One M & T Plaza, Suite 2000, Buffalo, NY 14203

**Hoffman Reilly Pozner & Williamson**
511 Sixteenth Street, Suite 700, Denver, CO 80202

**Hogan Marren Ltd**
180 North Wacker Drive, Suite 600, Chicago, IL 60606

**Holt Ney Zatcoff & Wasserman, LLP**
100 Galleria Parkway, Suite 600, Atlanta, GA 30339

**Hooper Lundy & Bookman Inc**
1875 Century Park East, Suite 1600, Los Angeles, CA 90067

**Howard, Rice, Nemerovski, Canady, Falk & Rabkin**
Three Embarcadero Center, 7th Floor, San Francisco, CA 94111-4065

**Howrey LLP**
1299 Pennsylvania Avenue NW, Washington, DC 20004-2402

**Hoyt & Blewett**
501 Second Avenue North, PO Box 2807, Great Falls, MT 59403

**Huddleston Bolen LLP**
611 Third Avenue, PO Box 2185, Huntington, WV 25722

**Hughes & Luce LLP**
1717 Main Street, Suite 2800, Dallas, TX 75201

**Hughes Bauman Pfiffner Gorski & Seedorf LLC**
3900 C Street, Suite 1001, Anchorage, AK 99503

**Hughes, Kellner, Sullivan & Alke**
40 West Lawrence, PO Box 1166, Helena, MT 59624

**Hunter, Maclean, Exley & Dunn, PC**
200 East Saint Julian Street, PO Box 9848, Savannah, GA 31412

**Hurley Toevs Styles Hamblin & Panter PA**
4155 Montgomery Boulevard NE, Albuquerque, NM 87109

**Hurwitz & Sagarin LLC**
PO Box 112, Milford, CT 06460

**Husch & Eppenberger, LLC**
1200 Main, Suite 1700, Kansas City, MO 63105

**Hyman Phelps & McNamara**
700 Thirteenth Street NW, Suite 1200, Washington, DC 20005

**Icard, Merrill, Cullis, Timm, Furen & Ginsburg PA**
2033 Main Street, Suite 600, Sarasota, FL 34237

**Imanaka Kudo & Fujimoto**
TOPA Financial Center, Fort Street Tower, 745 Fort Street Mall, 17th Floor, Honolulu, HI 96813

**Irell & Manella LLP**
1800 Avenue of the Stars, Suite 900, Los Angeles, CA 90067-4276

**Isaacson Rosenbaum PC**
633 17th Street, Suite 2200, Denver, CO 80202

**Iseman Cunningham Riester & Hyde LLP**
9 Thurlow Terrace, Albany, NY 12203

**H**

If you can't find a firm here, see firm profiles at the end of every state

Ivins, Phillips & Barker
1700 Pennsylvania Avenue NW, Suite 600,
Washington, DC 20006

J Cheney Mason PA
Bank of America Center, 390 North Orange
Avenue, Suite 2100, Orlando, FL 32801

Jack, Lyon & Jones, PC
3400 TCBY Tower, 425 West Capitol Avenue,
Little Rock, AR 72201

Jackoway Tyerman Wertheimer
Austen Mandelbaum & Morris, A
Professional Corporation
Suite 1800, 1888 Century Park East, Century
City, Los Angeles, CA 90067

Jackson Lewis LLP
One Liberty Square, 55 Beattie Place, Suite
800, Greenville, SC 29601

Jackson Walker LLP
901 Main Street, Suite 6000, Dallas,
TX 75202-3797

Jacobs, Chase, Frick, Kleinkopf
& Kelley
1050 17th Street, Suite 1500, Denver,
CO 80265

Jacobs, Grudberg, Belt & Dow PC
350 Orange Street, New Haven, CT 06503

Jaffe, Raitt, Heuer & Weiss, PC
One Woodward Avenue, Suite 2400, Detroit,
MI 48226

James McElroy & Diehl
600 South College Street, Charlotte, NC 28202

Jane Kreusler-Walsh PA
Flagler Center, Suite 503, 501 South Flagler
Drive, West Palm Beach, FL 33401

Jardine, Stephenson, Blewett and
Weaver, PC
US Bank Building, Seventh Floor, 300 Central
Avenue, Great Falls, MT 59403

Jay M Levy PA
Two Datran Center, Suite 1701, 9130 South
Dadeland Boulevard, Miami, FL 33156

Jeffcoat Pike & Nappier LLC
(Myrtle Beach)
2024 Corporate Centre Drive, Suite 206, PO
Box 3678, Myrtle Beach, SC 29578-3678

Jenkens & Gilchrist PC
1445 Ross Avenue, Suite 3200, Dallas, TX
75202-2799

Jenkins Fenstermaker, PLLC
401 Eleventh Street, 1100 Coal Exchange
Building, PO Box 2688, Huntington,
WV 25726-2688

Jennings, Strouss & Salmon, PLC
One Renaissance Square, Two North Central
Avenue, Phoenix, AZ 85004-2385

Jensen Baird Gardner & Henry
Ten Free Street, PO Box 4510, Portland,
ME 04112

Joel S. Perwin, PA
Suite 1422 Alfred I DuPont Building, 169 E
Flagler St, Miami, FL 33131

Johnson Killen & Seiler
800 Wells Fargo Center, 230 West Superior
Street, Duluth, MN 55802

Johnson, Pope, Bokor, Ruppel
& Burns, PA
911 Chestnut Street, PO Box 1368, Clearwater,
FL 33756

Johnston Barton Proctor & Powell LLP
2900 AmSouth/Harbert Plaza, 1901 Sixth
Avenue North, Birmingham, AL 35203-2618

Jolley, Urga, Wirth & Woodbury
3800 Howard Hughes Parkway, 16th Floor,
Las Vegas, NV 89109

Jones Vargas
3773 Howard Hughes Parkway, Third Floor
South, Las Vegas, NV 89109

Jones Waldo Holbrook &
McDonough PC
1500 Wells Fargo Plaza, 170 South Main Street,
Salt Lake City, UT 84101

Jones, Foster, Johnston
& Stubbs, PA
505 Flagler Drive, Suite 1100, West Palm
Beach, FL 33401

Jose M Quiñon - Sole Practitioner
2400 South Dixie Highway, Suite 200, Miami,
FL 33133

Judge Stephen M Schwebel
1501 K Street NW, Washington, DC 20005

Jung & Sisco
First Union Center, Suite 1240, 100 South
Ashley Drive, Tampa, FL 33602

Kahn Kleinman, LPA
2600 Erieview Tower, 1301 East Ninth Street,
Cleveland, OH 44114-1824

Kamer Zucker & Abbott
3000 West Charleston Boulevard, Suite 3, Las
Vegas, NV 89102

Kantrow Spaht Weaver & Blitzer
Suite 300, City Plaza, 445 North Boulevard,
Baton Rouge, LA 70821-2997

Kaplan Kirsch & Rockwell LLP
1675 Broadway, Suite 2300, Denver, CO 80202

Kaplan, Brewer, Maxey & Haralson
415 Main Street, Little Rock, AR 72201

Kaplan, Strangis & Kaplan
5500 Wells Fargo Center, Minneapolis,
MN 55402

Karaganis, White & Magel
414 North Orleans Street, Suite 810, Chicago,
IL 60610

Karp & Genauer PA
2 Alhambra Plaza, Suite 1202, Coral Gables,
FL 33134

Karp, Heurlin & Weiss PC
3060 North Swan Road, Suite 100, Tucson,
AZ 85712-1225

Kasowitz Benson Torres & Friedman
1633 Broadway, New York, NY 10019

Katz, Teller, Brant & Hild
2400 Chemed Center, 255 East Fifth Street,
Cincinnati, OH 45202-4724

Kaufman & Canoles
One Commercial Place, PO Box 3037,
Norfolk, VA 23514

Kay Casto & Chaney PLLC
1600 Bank One Center, PO Box 2031,
Charleston, WV 25327

Keating, Muething & Klekamp, PLL
1400 Provident Tower, One East Fourth Street,
Cincinnati, OH 45202

Keesal, Young & Logan PC
400 Oceangate, PO Box 1730, Long Beach,
CA 90801-1730

Kegler, Brown, Hill & Ritter
Capitol Square, Suite 1800, 65 East State Street,
Columbus, OH 43215-4294

Keleher & McLeod, PA
201 Third Street NW, Twelth Floor,
Albuquerque, NM 87103

Kelley Drye & Warren
101 Park Avenue, 30th Floor, New York,
NY 10178

Kellogg, Huber, Hansen, Todd,
Evans & Figel, PLLC
1615 M Street NW, Suite 400,
Washington, DC 20036

Kelly & Berens PA
Suite 3720 IDS Center, 80 South Eighth Street,
Minneapolis, MN 55402

Kelly Haglund Garnsey + Kahn LLC
1441 Eighteenth Street, 300 Blake Street
Building, Denver, CO 80202

Kelly, Hart & Hallman,
A Professional Corporation
201 Main Street, Suite 2500, Fort Worth,
TX 76102

Kemp Smith LLP
221 North Kansas, Suite 1700, El Paso,
TX 79901

Kenlan, Schwiebert & Facey, PC
71 Allen Street, PO Box 578, Rutland,
VT 05702

Kennedy Covington Lobdell &
Hickman LLP
Hearst Tower, 47th Floor, 214 North Tryon
Street, Charlotte, NC 28202

Kennedy Lillis Schmidt & English
75 Maiden Lane, Suite 402, New York,
NY 10038-4816

Kennedy, Watts, Arellano
& Ricks LLP
2850 Pacwest Center, 1211 South West Fifth
Avenue, Portland, OR 97204

Kent & Johnson, LLP
1500 South West Taylor Street, Portland,
OR 97205

Kerger & Kerger
33 South Michigan Street, Suite 201, Toledo,
OH 43602

Kerr Russell & Weber
Detroit Center, 500 Woodward Avenue, Suite
2500, Detroit, MI 48226-3427

Kevin C Efroymson
2915 West Charleston Boulevard, Las Vegas,
NV 89101

Kilmer Voorhees & Laurick PC
732 North West nineteenth Avenue, Portland,
OR 97209

Kimerer & Derrick, PC
221 East Indianola Avenue, Phoenix, AZ 85012

King & Ballow
1100 Union Street Plaza, 315 Union Street,
Nashville, TN 37201

King, Blackwell & Downs PA
25 East Pine Street, Orlando, FL 32802-1631

Kirk & Chaney
101 Park Avenue, Suite 800, Oklahoma City,
OK 73102

Kirkpatrick & Lockhart Nicholson
Graham LLP
Henry W Oliver Building, 535 Smithfield
Street, Pittsburgh, PA 15222-2312

Kirschner & Legler
300-A Wharfside Way, Jacksonville, FL 32207

Kirwin Norris PA
338 West Morse Boulevard, Suite 150,
Winter Park, FL 32789

Klehr Harrison Harvey Branzberg &
Ellers LLP
260 South Broad Street, Philadelphia,
PA 19102-5003

Kleinberg, Lopez, Lange,
Brisbin & Cuddy
2049 Century Park East, Suite 3180,
Los Angeles, CA 90067

Knobbe Martens Olson & Bear
2040 Main Street, 14th Floor, Irvine, CA 92614

Kobayashi, Sugita & Goda
999 Bishop Street, 26th Floor, Honolulu,
HI 96813

Kohn Swift & Graf
One South Broad Street, Suite 2100,
Philadelphia, PA 19107 3389

Kohn, Shands, Elbert, Gianoulakis &
Giljum, LLP
One US Bank Plaza, Suite 2410, St Louis,
MO 63101

Koley Jessen PC
One Pacific Place, 1125 South 103 Street, Suite
800, Omaha, NE 68124

Kollman & Saucier PA
Sun Life Building, 8th Floor, 20 South Charles
Street, Baltimore, MD 21201-3225

Kraftson Caudle LLC
1650 Tysons Boulevard, Suite 560, McLean,
VA 22102

Krasow, Garlick & Hadley LLC
One State Street, Hartford, CT 06103

Krendl Krendl Sachnoff & Way PC
370 Seventeenth Street, Denver, CO 80202

Krieg DeVault LLP
One Indiana Square, Suite 2800, Indianapolis,
IN 46204

Kronish Lieb Weiner & Hellman LLP
1114 Avenue of the Americas, New York,
NY 10036-7798

Krovatin & Associates LLC
744 Broad Street, Suite 1903, Newark,
NJ 07102

Kunkel Miller & Hament
Magdalene Center, 15438 North Florida
Avenue, Suite 202, Tampa, FL 33613

Kutak Rock LLP
The Omaha Building, 1650 Farnam Street,
Omaha, NE 68102-2186

**K**

**Lamberth, Cifelli, Stokes & Stout, PA**
Atlanta Financial Center, 3343 Peachtree
Road, NE, East Tower, Atlanta, GA 30326-1022

**Lamson, Dugan & Murray, LLP**
Lamson Dugan & Murray Building, 10306
Regency Parkway Drive, Omaha, NE 68114

**Landers & Parsons**
310 West College Avenue, PO Box 271,
Tallahassee, FL 32302

**Landis Rath & Cobb LLP**
919 Market Street, Suite 600, Wilmington,
DE 19801

**Lane & Waterman LLP**
220 North Main Street, Suite 600, Davenport,
IA 52801

**Laner, Muchin, Dombrow, Becker,
Levin, Tominberg**
515 North State Suite, Suite 2800, Chicago,
IL 60610

**Langer & Grogan PC**
1600 Market Street, Suite 2020, Philadelphia,
PA 19103-7218

**Langrock Sperry & Wool, LLP**
111 South Pleasant Street, PO Drawer 351,
Middlebury, VT 05753

**Langsam Stevens & Silver LLP**
1616 Walnut Street, Suite 1700, Philadelphia,
PA 19103-5319

**Lanier Ford Shaver & Payne PC**
200 West Side Square, Suite 5000, Huntsville,
AL 35804

**Lankler Siffert & Wohl LLP**
500 Fifth Avenue, 33rd Floor, New York,
NY 10110-3398

**Latham & Burwell PLLC**
447 Northpark Drive, Ridgeland, MS 39157

**Latham & Watkins LLP**
633 West Fifth Street, Suite 4000, Los Angeles,
CA 90071-2007

**Lathrop & Rutledge**
1920 Thomes Avenue, Suite 500, PO Box 4068,
Cheyenne, WY 82003

**Lau, Lane, Pieper, Conley &
McCreadie**
100 South Ashley Drive, Suite 1700, Tampa, FL
33602

**Lauri Waldman Ross PA**
Two Datran Center, Suite 1612, 9130 South
Dadeland Boulevard, Miami, FL 33156

**Lavely & Singer PC**
2049 Century Park East, Suite 2400,
Los Angeles, CA 90067-2906

**Law Chambers Nicholas Critelli PC**
317 Sixth Avenue, Suite 950, Des Moines, IA
50309-4128

**Law Offices of Charles B Renfrew**
710 Sansome Street, San Francisco,
CA 94111-1704

**Law Offices of GKRSE**
1500 K Street NW, Suite 330, Washington, DC
20005

**Law Offices of James McCollum LLC**
510 L Street, Suite 540, Anchorage,
AK 99501-1959

**Law Offices of Jonathan H (Jason)
Warner, PA**
9400 South Dadeland Boulevard, Suite 600,
Miami, FL 33156

**Law Offices of Steven Drapkin**
11377 West Olympic Boulevard, Los Angeles,
CA 90064

**Law Offices of William H Booth**
1500 Newell Avenue, 5th Floor, Walnut Creek,
CA 94596

**Lawler, Metzger, Milkman
& Keeney, LLC**
2001 K Street NW, Suite 802, Washington, DC
20006

**Lawrence & Daniels**
100 N Biscayne Boulevard, 21st Floor, Miami,
FL 33132

**Laxalt & Nomura**
Bank of America Plaza, 50 West Liberty Street,
Suite 700, Reno, NV 89501

**Lazarus & Associates**
420 West Roosevelt, Phoenix, AZ 85003

**Lea + O'Reilly**
101 West Grand Avenue, Suite 200, Chicago,
IL 60610

**Leading-Edge Law Group, PLC**
Three James Center, 1051 East Cary Street,
Suite 1130, Richmond, VA 23219

**LeClair Ryan, A Professional
Corporation**
Riverfront Plaza, East Tower, 951 East Byrd
Street, 8th Floor, Richmond, VA 23219

**Leff, Haupert, Traw & Willman LLP**
222 South Linn Street, PO Box 2447, Iowa
City, IA 52244 2447

**Lehr Middlebrooks Price
& Vreeland, PC**
2021 Third Avenue North, Suite 300,
Birmingham, AL 35203

**Leiby Stearns and Roberts, PA**
1000 Sawgrass Corporate Parkway, Fort
Lauderdale, FL 33325

**Leitman, Siegal & Payne, PC**
The Land Title Building, 600 North 20th
Street, Suite 400, Birmingham, AL 35203

**Lemle & Kelleher, LLP**
Pan-American Life Center, 21st Floor, 601
Poydras Street, New Orleans, LA 70130

**Lenrow, Kohn & Oliver A
Professional Corporation**
7 St Paul Street, Suite 940, Baltimore,
MD 21202

**Leonard, Street and Deinard
Professional Association**
150 South Fifth Street, Suite 2300,
Minneapolis, MN 55402

**Leopold, Petrich & Smith PA**
2049 Century Park E, Suite 3110, Los Angeles,
CA 90067

**Lerach Coughlin Stoia Geller
Rudman & Robbins LLP**
655 West Broadway, Suite 1900, San Diego, CA
92101

**Leventhal & Slaughter PA**
111 North Orange Avenue, Suite 700,
Orlando, FL 32801

**Leventhal Senter & Lerman PLLC**
Suite 600, 2000 K Street NW, Washington,
DC 20006

**Levett Rockwood PC**
33 Riverside Avenue, PO Box 5116, Westport,
CT 06881

**Levin Fishbein Sedran & Berman**
Suite 500, 510 Walnut Street, Philadelphia, PA
19106-3697

**Levine Sullivan Koch & Schulz LLP**
1050 17th Street, NW, Suite 800, Washington,
DC 20036

**Levine, Steinberg, Miller & Huver**
550 West Central Street, Suite 1810, San Diego,
CA 92101-8596

**Levy Phillips & Konigsberg LLP**
800 Third Avenue, New York, NY 10022

**Levy, Ram & Olson**
639 Front Street, 4th Floor, San Francisco,
CA 94111

**Lewis & Slovak PC**
725 Third Avenue North, PO Box 2325,
Great Falls, MT 59403

**Lewis and Roca**
40 North Central Avenue, Phoenix,
AZ 85004-4429

**Lewis Fisher Henderson Claxton
& Mulroy**
International Place II, 6410 Poplar Avenue,
Suite 300, Memphis, TN 38119

**Lewis, Longman & Walker PA**
1700 Palm Beach Lakes Boulevard, Suite 1000,
West Palm Beach, FL 33401

**Leydig, Voit & Mayer, Ltd**
Two Prudential Plaza, 180 North Stetson
Avenue, Suite 4900, Chicago, IL 60601-6780

**Lichter Grossman Nicholas Adler &
Goodman**
9200 Sunset Boulevard, Suite 1200, Los
Angeles, CA 90069

**Liebert Cassidy Whitmore**
6033 West Century Boulevard, Suite 500, Los
Angeles, CA 90045

**Liebmann, Conway,
Olejniczak & Jerry, SC**
231 South Adams Street, PO Box 23200, Green
Bay, WI 54305

**Lightfoot, Franklin & White, LLC**
The Clark Building, 400 20th Street North,
Birmingham, AL 35203

**Lightfoot, Vandevelde, Sadowsky,
Medvene & Levine**
655 South Hope Street, 13th Floor, Los
Angeles, CA 90017

**Liles, Gavin, Costantino & Murphy**
One Enterprise Center, Suite 1500, 225 Water
Street, Jacksonville, FL 32202

**Linda S Mensch PC - Sole
Practitioner**
200 South Michigan Avenue, Suite 1240,
Chicago, IL 60604

**Lindner & Marsack, SC**
411 East Wisconsin Avenue, Suite 1000,
Milwaukee, WI 53202

**Linowes and Blocher LLP**
7200 Wisconsin Avenue, Suite 800, Bethesda,
MD 20814

**Lionel Sawyer & Collins**
1700 Bank of America Plaza, 300 South Fourth
Street, Las Vegas, NV 89101

**Liskow & Lewis PLC**
One Shell Square, 701 Poydras Street, Suite
5000, New Orleans, LA 70139-5099

**Lisman, Webster, Kirkpatrick
& Leckerling, PC**
84 Pine Street, PO Box 728, Burlington,
VT 05402

**Litchford & Christopher**
Bank of America Center, 390 North Orange
Avenue, PO Box 1549, Orlando, FL 32802

**Little, Medeiros, Kinder, Bulman &
Whitney PC**
72 Pine Street, Providence, RI 02903

**Lloyd Gosselink Blevins Rochelle &
Townsend, PC**
816 Congress Avenue, Suite 1900, Austin,
TX 78701

**LMK Associates**
1805 Monument Avenue, Suite 614,
Richmond, VA 23220

**Locke Liddell & Sapp LLP**
2200 Ross Avenue, Suite 2200, Dallas,
TX 75201-6776

**Locke Reynolds LLP**
201 North Illinois Street, Suite 1000, PO Box
44961, Indianapolis, IN 46244

**Lommen, Nelson, Cole &
Stageberg, PA**
80 South 8th Street, Suite 2000, Minneapolis,
MN 55402-2119

**Lonabaugh and Riggs**
50 East Loucks Street, PO Drawer 5059,
Sheridan, WY 82801

**Long, Burner, Parks & DeLargy**
515 Congress Avenue, Suite 1500, PO Box
2212, Austin, TX 78768-2212

**Looney & Grossman LLP**
101 Arch Street, Boston, MA 02110

**Lord, Bissell & Brook**
111 South Wacker Drive, Chicago, IL 60606

**Lottner Rubin Fishman
Brown & Saul, PC**
633 Seventeenth Street, Suite 2700, Denver,
CO 80202-3635

**Lowndes Drosdick Doster Kantor
& Reed, PA**
215 North Eola Drive, Orlando, FL 32801

**Lueders, Robertson & Konzen**
PO Box 725, 1939 Delmar Avenue, Granite
City, IL 62040

**Luskin, Stern & Eisler LLP**
330 Madison Avenue, New York, NY 10017

**Lyman & Nielsen**
1301 West 22nd Street, Suite 914, Oak Brook,
IL 60523-2018

**Lynch DeSimone & Nylen LLP**
12 Post Office Square, Floor 6, Boston, MA
02109

If you can't find a firm here, see firm profiles at the end of every state

**Lynn, Jackson, Shultz & Lebrun PC**
First National Bank Building, Eighth Floor, PO
Box 8250, Rapid City, SD 57709-8250

**MacPherson Kelly & Thompson**
616 West Buffalo, PO Box 999, Rawlins, WY
82301

**Maddin, Hauser, Wartell,
Roth & Heller PC**
28400 Northwestern Highway, Third Floor
Essex Centre, Southfield, MI 48034-1839

**Madison Harbour Mroz
& Brennan PA**
Suite 1600 Albuquerque Plaza, 201 Third
Street North West, PO Box 25467,
Albuquerque, NM 87102

**Malkerson, Gilliland, Martin**
1750 Pillsbury Center South, 220 South Sixth
Street, Minneapolis, MN 55402

**Maloy & Jenkins**
75 Fourteenth Street NW, 25th Floor, Atlanta,
GA 30309

**Manatt Phelps & Phillips LLP**
11355 West Olymoic Boulevard, Los Angeles,
CA 90064

**Mancini Welch & Geiger LLP**
The Kahului Building, 33 Lono Avenue, Suite
470, Kahului, HI 96732-1681

**Mandel & Mandel LLP**
1200 Alfred I duPont Building, 169 E Flagler
Street, Miami, FL 33131

**Manko, Gold, Katcher & Fox LLP**
401 City Avenue, Suite 500, Bala Cynwyd, PA
19004

**Manning Curtis Bradshaw
& Bednar LLC**
Third Floor, Newhouse Building, 10 Exchange
Place, Salt Lake City, UT 84111

**Manning Fulton & Skinner PA**
PO Box 20389, Raleigh, NC 27619-0389

**Marcus, Clegg & Mistretta PA**
100 Middle Street, East Tower, Portland, ME
04101

**Marilyn Foss - Sole Practitioner**
917 N Washington, Bismarck, ND 58501

**Maring Williams Law Office PC**
1220 Main Avenue, Suite 105, PO Box 2103,
Fargo, ND 58107-2103

**Marino & Associates PC**
One Newark Center, 9th Floor, Newark, NJ
07102-5211

**Mariscal, Weeks, McIntyre &
Friedlander PA**
2901 North Central Avenue, Suite 200,
Phoenix, AZ 85012

**Mark W Gifford**
243 South Park Street, PO Box 2508, Casper,
WY 82602

**Markowitz, Herbold, Glade &
Mehlhaf PC**
3000 Pacwest Center, 1211 South West Fifth
Avenue, Portland, OR 97204-3730

**Marsh, Rickard & Bryan PC**
800 Shades Creek Parkway, Suite 600,
Birmingham, AL 35209-4532

**Marshall, Gerstein & Borun**
6300 Sears Tower, 233 South Wacker Drive,
Chicago, IL 60606-6402

**Martin & Churchill Chartered**
8415 East 21st Street North, Wichita,
KS 67206-2954

**Martin, Disiere, Jefferson
& Wisdom LLP**
808 Travis, Suite 1800, Houston, TX 77002

**Martin, Pringle, Oliver, Wallace &
Bauer, LLP**
100 North Broadway, Suite 500, Wichita,
KS 67202

**Martin, Tate, Morrow & Marston, PC**
The Falls Building, 22 North Front Street,
Suite 1100, Memphis, TN 38103-1182

**Martzell & Bickford, APC**
338 Lafayette Street, New Orleans, LA 70130-
3244

**Maslon Edelman Borman & Brand, LLP**
3300 Wells Fargo Center, 90 South Seventh
Street, Minneapolis, MN 55402

**Mateer & Harbert PA**
Suite 600, Two Landmark Center, 225 East
Robinson Street, PO Box 2854, Orlando, FL
32802-2854

**Matkov Salzman Madoff & Gunn**
55 East Monroe Street, Suite 2900, Chicago, IL
60603-5709

**Maupin Taylor, PA**
Highwoods Tower One, 3200 Beechleaf Court,
Suite 500, Raleigh, NC 27604

**May, Adam, Gerdes
& Thompson, LLP**
503 South Pierre Street, PO Box 160, Pierre,
SD 57501

**Mazur, Carp & Rubin PC**
1250 Broadway, Suite 3800, New York, NY
10001

**McCarter & English, LLP**
Four Gateway Center, 100 Mulberry Street,
Newark, NJ 07102-0652

**McConn & Rindy**
31-37 3rd Avenue, Southwest, Suite 212,
Fargo, ND 58103

**McDade Fogler LLP**
Two Houston Center, 909 Fannin, Suite 1200,
Houston, TX 77010-1006

**McDonald Carano Wilson McCune
Bergin Frankovich & Hicks LLP**
241 Ridge Street, Reno, NV 89501

**McDonald Hopkins Co**
2100 Bank One Center, 600 Superior Avenue
East, Cleveland, OH 44114-2653

**McDowell Knight Roedder
& Sledge LLC**
63 South Royal Street, Suite 900, Mobile,
AL 36602

**McEwen Gisvold LLP**
Suite 1600, 1100 SW 6th Avenue, Portland, OR
97204-1017

**McGee Hankla Backes &
Dobrovolny PC**
Suite 305 Wells Fargo Bank Center, 15 Second
Avenue Southwest, Minot, ND 58702

**McGrath North Mullin & Kratz PC**
Suite 3700 First National Tower, 1601 Dodge
Street, Omaha, NE 68102-1627

**McGuireWoods LLP**
One James Center, 901 East Cary Street,
Richmond, VA 23219-4030

**McLaughlin & McCaffrey, LLP**
Eaton Center, 1111 Superior Avenue East,
Suite 1350, Cleveland, OH 44114-2500

**McLaughlin & Stern LLP**
260 Madison Avenue, New York, NY 10016

**McMahon DeGulis LLP**
The Caxton Building, Suite 650, 812 Huron
Road, Cleveland, OH 44115

**McManus Schor Asmar
& Darden, LLP**
1301 Conneticut Avenue, NW, Sixth Floor,
Washington, DC 20036

**McNair Law Firm PA**
1301 Gervais Street, PO Box 11390,
Columbia, SC 29211

**McNair, Larson & Carlson Ltd**
PO Box 2189, Fargo, ND 58108

**McNaul Ebel Nawrot Helgren &
Vance PLLC**
600 University Street, Suite 2700, Seattle, WA
98101-3143

**Meadows, Owens, Collier, Reed,
Cousins & Blau**
901 Main Street, Suite 3700, Dallas,
TX 75202-3725

**Meardon, Sueppel & Downer**
122 South Linn Street, Iowa City, IA 52240

**Meckler Bulger & Tilson LLP**
8200 Sears Tower, 233 S Wacker Drive,
Chicago, IL 60606 6306

**Meehan LLP**
127 West Franklin Street, Tucson,
AZ 85702-1671

**Meland Russin Hellinger & Budwick**
3000 Wachovia Financial Center, 200 South
Biscayne Boulevard, Miami, FL 33131

**Melli Walker Pease & Ruhly SC**
Ten East Doty, Suite 900, PO Box 1664,
Madison, WI 53701

**Mendes & Mount LLP**
750 Seventh Avenue, New York,
NY 10019-6829

**Merchant & Gould PC**
3200 IDS Centre, 80 South 8th Street,
Minneapolis, MN 55402

**Meuleman Mollerup LLP**
960 Broadway Avenue, Suite 400, Boise, ID
83701

**Meyer Capel, PC**
Athenaeum Building, 306 West Church Street,
PO Box 6750, Champaign, IL 61826-6750

**Michael Critchley & Associates**
354 Main Street, West Orange, NJ 07052-5726

**Milbank, Tweed, Hadley
& McCloy LLP**
One Chase Manhattan Plaza, 47th Floor, New
York, NY 10005

**Milberg Weiss Bershad
& Schulman LLP**
One Pennsylvania Plaza, New York, NY 10119-
0165

**Miller Hamilton Snider & Odom LLC**
254-256 State Street, PO Box 46, Mobile, AL
36601

**Miller Johnson**
Calder Plaza Building, 250 Monroe Avenue
NW, Suite 800, Grand Rapids, MI 49503-2250

**Miller Stratvert PA**
500 Marquette Avenue, Suite 1100,
Albuquerque, NM 87102

**Miller, Balis & O'Neil, PC**
1140 Nineteenth Street NW, Suite 700,
Washington, DC 20036

**Miller, Morton, Caillat & Nevis**
25 Metro Drive, 7th Floor, San Jose, CA 95110

**Milling Benson Woodward LLP**
909 Poydras Street, Suite 2300, New Orleans,
LA 70112-1017

**Millisor & Nobil Co LPA**
9150 South Hills Boulevard, Suite 300,
Cleveland, OH 44147-3599

**Mintz Levin Cohn Ferris Glovsky and
Popeo PC**
One Financial Center, Boston, MA 02111

**Mitchell Hurst Jacobs & Dick**
152 E Washington Street, Indianapolis, IN
46204

**Mitchell, McNutt & Sams PA**
105 South Front Street, PO Box 7120, Tupelo,
MS 38802

**Mitchell, Silberberg & Knupp LLP**
11377 West Olympic Boulevard, Los Angeles,
CA 90064-1683

**Mitchell, Williams, Selig, Gates &
Woodyard, PLLC**
425 West Capitol Avenue, Suite 1800, Little
Rock, AR 72201-3525

**Mock, Schwabe, Waldo, Elder,
Reeves & Bryant**
Fourteenth Floor, Two Leadership Square, 211
North Robinson Avenue, Oklahoma City,
OK 73102

**Mockbee Hall & Drake**
The Lamar Life Building, 10th Floor, 317 East
Capitol Street, Jackson, MS 39201

**Modrall, Sperling, Roehl,
Harris & Sisk, PA**
500 Fourth Street NW, Bank of America
Centre, Suite 1000, Albuquerque, NM 87103

**Moehrke, Mackie & Shea, PC**
137 Newbury Street, Boston, MA 02116

**Moffatt Thomas Barrett Rock & Fields**
101 South Capitol Boulevard, 10th Floor, PO
Box 829, Boise, ID 83701

**Mohan, Alewelt, Prillaman & Adami**
1 North Old Capitol Plaza, Suite 325,
Springfield, IL 62701-1323

**Monteleone & McCrory, LLP**
725 South Figueroa Street, Suite 3750, Los
Angeles, CA 90017-5402

**M**

**Montgomery, Barnett, Brown, Read, Hammond & Mintz LLP**
3200 Energy Centre, 1100 Poydras Street, New Orleans, LA 70163

**Montgomery, McCracken, Walker & Rhoads, LLP**
123 South Broad Street, Philadelphia, PA 19109

**Moody & Warner PC**
4169 Montgomery NE, Albuquerque, NM 87109

**Moore & Lee LLP**
1750 Tysons Boulevard, Suite 1450, McLean, VA 22102-4208

**Moore & Van Allen PLLC**
40 Calhoun Street, Suite 300, Charleston, SC 29401

**Moore, O'Connell & Refling PC**
601 Haggerty Lane, Suite 10, PO Box 1288, Bozeman, MT 59771

**Morley Law Firm Ltd**
1697 South 42nd Street Suite, 200, PO Box 14519, Grand Forks, ND 58208

**Morris & Morris PC**
1200 Wytestone Plaza, 801 East Main Street, PO Box 30, Richmond, VA 23218-0030

**Morris Pickering & Sanner**
900 Bank of America Plaza, 300 South Fourth Street, Las Vegas, NV 89101

**Morris, Laing, Evans, Brock & Kennedy, Chartered**
300 North Mead, Suite 200, Wichita, KS 67202-2745

**Morris, Manning & Martin, LLP**
1600 Atlanta Financial Center, 3343 Peachtree Road NE, Atlanta, GA 30326

**Morse, Barnes-Brown & Pendleton PC**
Reservoir Place, 1601 Trapelo Road, Suite 205, Waltham, MA 02451

**Morvillo, Abramowitz, Grand, Iason & Silberberg, PC**
565 Fifth Avenue, New York, NY 10017

**Moscowitz, Moscowitz & Magolnick PA**
Barclays Financial Center, 1111 Brickell Avenue, Suite 2050, Miami, FL 33131

**Moseley Prichard Parrish Knight & Jones**
501 West Bay Street, Jacksonville, FL 32202

**Moses & Singer LLP**
The Chrysler Building , 405 Lexington Avenue, New York, NY 10174-1299

**Moss & Barnett, A Professional Association**
4800 Wells Fargo Center, 90 South Seventh Street, Minneapolis, MN 55402

**Moulton, Bellingham, Longo & Mather, PC**
Suite 1900 Sheraton Plaza, 27 North 27th Street, Billings, MT 59103

**Moye White LLP**
16 Market Square, 6th Floor, 1400 Sixteenth Street, Denver, CO 80202-1486

**Moyer & Bergman, PLC**
2720 First Avenue NE, Cedar Rapids, IA 52406

**Moyes Storey**
1850 North Central Avenue, Suite 1100, Phoenix, AZ 85004

**Much Shelist Freed Denenberg Ament & Rubenstein, PC**
191 North Wacker Drive, Suite 1800, Chicago, IL 60606

**Mullikin, Larson & Swift**
Suite 200, 155 East Pearl Street, PO Box 4099, Jackson, WY 83001

**Munger & Stone**
999 Peachtree Street NE, 2850 1st Union Plaza, Atlanta, GA 30309

**Munger, Tolles & Olson LLP**
355 South Grand Avenue, 35th Floor, Los Angeles, CA 90071-1560

**Munsch Hardt Kopf & Harr, P. C.**
3800 Lincoln Plaza, 500 N Akard Street, Dallas, TX 75201-6659

**Murane & Bostwick LLC**
201 North Wolcott, Casper, WY 82601

**Murphy & Shaffer**
36 South Charles Street, Suite 1400, Baltimore, MD 21201-3109

**Murphy Sullivan Kronk**
PO Box 4485, 275 College Street, Burlington, VT 05406-4485

**Murphy, Goldammer & Prendergast**
Wells Fargo Building, 101 North Phillips Avenue, Suite 402, PO Box 1728, Sioux Falls, SD 57101-1728

**Murtha Cullina LLP**
CityPlace I, 29th Floor, 185 Asylum Street, Hartford, CT 06103

**Musick Peeler & Garrett**
One Wilshire Boulevard, Los Angeles, CA 90017-3321

**Myers Oliver & Price**
1401 Central North West, Albuquerque, NM 87104

**Myman, Abell, Fineman, Greenspan & Light LLP**
11777 San Vicente Boulevard, Los Angeles, CA 90049-5011

**Nagin Gallop Figueredo PA**
3225 Aviation Avenue, Suite 301, Coconut Grove, FL 33133

**Neal & Harwell, PLC**
Suite 2000, One Nashville Place, 150 Fourth Avenue North, Nashville, TN 37219

**Needle & Rosenberg, P.C**
Suite 1000, 999 Peachtree Street, Atlanta, GA 30309

**Neligan Tarpley Andrews & Foley LLP**
1700 Pacific Avenue, Suite 2600, Dallas, TX 75201-7322

**Nelson Kinder Mosseau & Saturley PC**
99 Middle Street, Manchester, NH 03101

**Neubert, Pepe & Monteith PC**
195 Church Street, 13th Floor, New Haven, CT 06510

**Nichols, Wolfe, Stamper, Nally, Fallis & Robertson Inc**
Old City Hall Building, Suite 400, 124 East Fourth Street, Tulsa, OK 74103-5010

**Nickens Keeton Lawless Farrell & Flack LLP**
327 Congress Avenue, Suite 490, Austin, TX 78701

**Nicoletti Hornig Campise and Sweeney**
Wall Street Plaza, 88 Pine Street, New York, NY 10005-1801

**Nilles, Hansen & Davies Ltd**
1800 Radisson Tower, PO Box 2626, Fargo, ND 58108

**Niro, Scavone, Haller & Niro**
181 West Madison, Suite 4600, Chicago, IL 60602-4515

**Nixon & Vanderhye PC**
8th Floor, 1100 North Glebe Road, Arlington, VA 22201

**Norman, Hanson & DeTroy, LLC**
415 Congress Street, Fifth Floor, PO Box 4600, Portland, ME 04112

**Norris, McLaughlin & Marcus, PA, A Professional Corporation**
721 Route 202-206, PO Box 1018, Bridgewater, NJ 08876

**Nourse & Bowles LLP**
One Exchange Plaza at 55 Broadway, New York, NY 10006

**Nutter, McClennen & Fish, LLP**
World Trade Centre West, 155 Seaport Boulevard, Boston, MA 02110-2604

**Nyemaster, Goode, West, Hansell, and O'Brien**
700 Walnut, Suite 1600, Des Moines, IA 50309

**Ober Kaler Grimes & Shriver**
120 East Baltimore Street, Suite 800, Baltimore, MD 21202-1643

**Oblon, Spivak, McClelland, Maier & Neustadt PC**
1940 Duke Street, Alexandria, VA 22314

**Oertel, Fernandez, Cole & Bryant, PA**
301 South Bronough Street, Fifth Floor, PO Box 1110, Tallahassee, FL 32301-1110

**Ohnstad Twichell PC**
901 Thirteenth Avenue East, Second Floor, PO Box 458, Fargo, ND 58078

**Oliff & Berridge PLC**
277 South Washington Street, Suite 500, Alexandria, VA 22314

**Olson Burns Lee PC**
PO Box 1180, Minot, ND 58702

**Oppenheimer Wolff & Donnelly LLP**
2029 Century Park East, Suite 3800, Los Angeles, CA 90067

**Orloff, Lowenbach, Stifelman & Siegel**
101 Eisenhower Parkway, Roseland, NJ 07068

**Orr & Reno PA**
One Eagle Square, PO Box 3550, Concord, NH 03302

**Otterbourg, Steindler, Houston & Rosen**
230 Park Avenue, New York, NY 10169

**Packman, Neuwahl & Rosenberg**
1500 San Remo Avenue, Suite 125, Coral Gables, FL 33146

**Page Law Firm LLC**
118 Broadway, Suite 200, PO Box 2067, Fargo, ND 58107-2067

**Pansing Hogan Ernst & Bachman LLP**
10250 Regency Circle, Suite 300, Omaha, NE 68114

**Pappas Metcalf Jenks and Miller**
245 Riverside Avenue, Suite 400, Jacksonville, FL 32202-4926

**Parker, Hudson, Rainer & Dobbs LLP**
1500 Marquis Two Tower, 285 Peachtree Center Avenue NE, Atlanta, GA 30303

**Parker, Poe, Adams & Bernstein LLP**
Three Wachovia Center, 401 South Tryon Street, Suite 3000, Charlotte, NC 28202

**Parr Waddoups Brown Gee & Loveless**
Suite 1300, 185 South State Street, Salt Lake City, UT 84111

**Partridge Snow & Hahn LLP**
180 South Main Street, Providence, RI 02903

**Pattishall, McAuliffe, Newbury, Hilliard & Geraldson LLP**
311 South Wacker Drive, Suite 5000, Chicago, IL 60606

**Patton Boggs LLP**
2550 M Street NW, Washington, DC 20037

**Paul A Beck & Associates, PC**
Suite 100, 157 McFarland Road, Pittsburgh, PA 15216

**Paul, Frank + Collins, A Professional Corporation**
One Church Street, PO Box 1307, Burlington, VT 05402

**Paul, Johnson, Park & Niles, Attorneys At Law, A Law Corporation**
American Savings Bank Tower, Suite 1300, 1001 Bishop Street, Honolulu, HI 96813

**Pearce & Durick**
314 East Thayer Avenue, PO Box 400, Bismarck, ND 58502

**Pearson Christensen Cahill & Clapp, PLLP**
24 North Fourth Street, PO Box 5758, Grand Forks, ND 58201

**Peifer, Hanson & Mullins PA**
20 First Plaza Center North West, Suite 725, Albuquerque, NM 87102-3347

**Peitzman, Weg & Kempinsky LLP**
10100 Santa Monica Boulevard, Suite 1450, Los Angeles, CA 90067

**Penland Munther Goodrum**
1161 West River Street, Suite 260, PO Box 199, Boise, ID 83701

**Pennington, Moore, Wilkinson, Bell & Dunbar, PA**
215 South Monroe Street, Second Floor, Tallahassee, FL 32301

**Pepple Johnson Cantu & Schmidt, PLLC**
1218 Third Avenue, Suite 1900, Seattle, WA 98101-3051

**Perkins & Trotter PLLC**
One Information Way, Suite 200, Little Rock, AR 72202

If you can't find a firm here, see firm profiles at the end of every state

**Perkins Coie LLP**
1201 Third Avenue, Suite 4800, Seattle,
WA 98101-3099

**Perkins, Thompson, Hinckley &
Keddy, PA**
One Canal Plaza, PO Box 426, Portland,
ME 04112

**Petruccelli Martin & Haddow LLP**
50 Monument Square, PO Box 17555,
Portland, ME 04112-8555

**Pettiette, Armand, Dunkelman,
Woodley, Byrd & Cromwell LLP**
509 Market Street, Suite 200, PO Box 1786,
Shreveport, LA 71101

**Phibbs Law Office PC**
PO Box 1028, 330 East Snow King Avenue,
Jackson, WY 83001

**Phillips Gardill Kaiser & Altmeyer**
61 Fourteenth Street, Wheeling, WV 26003

**Phillips McFall McCaffrey McVay &
Murrah, PC**
One Leadership Square, 12th Floor, 211 North
Robinson, Oklahoma City, OK 73102

**Picadio Sneath Miller & Norton**
4710 US Steel Tower, 600 Grant Street,
Pittsburgh, PA 15219-2702

**Piccarreta & Davis PC**
145 South Sixth Avenue, Tucson,
AZ 85701-2007

**Pill & Pill**
1444 Edwin Miller Boulevard, Martinsburg,
WV 25401

**Pircher, Nichols & Meeks**
1925 Century Park East, 17th Floor, Los
Angeles, CA 90067

**Poore, Roth & Robinson, PC**
1341 Harrison Avenue, PO Box 2000, Butte,
MT 59702

**Porter & Hedges, LLP**
1000 Main Street, 36th Floor, Houston,
TX 77002

**Post & Schell, PC**
1800 JFK Boulevard, 19th Floor, Philadelphia,
PA 19103

**Powell Goldstein LLP**
Third Floor, 901 New York Avenue, NW,
Washington, DC 20001-4413

**Poyner & Spruill LLP**
3600 Glenwood Avenue, PO Box 10096,
Raleigh, NC 27605

**Pratt & Sanderford**
2114 Birdcreek Drive, Suite 100, Temple,
TX 76502-1020

**Pratt-Thomas, Epting & Walker PA**
16 Charlotte Street, Charleston, SC 29403

**Preston Gates & Ellis LLP**
701 Fifth Avenue, Suite 5000, Seattle,
WA 98104-7078

**Prickett, Jones & Elliott PA**
1310 King Street, PO Box 1328, Wilmington,
DE 19899-1328

**Pryor Cashman Sherman & Flynn**
410 Park Avenue, 10th Floor, New York, NY
10022

**Pullman & Comley LLC**
850 Main Street, PO Box 7006, Bridgeport, CT
06601-7006

**Quilling, Selander, Cummiskey &
Lownds, PC**
2001 Bryan Tower, Suite 1800, Dallas,
TX 75201

**R William Meeks - Sole Practitioner**
511 South High Street, Columbus, OH 43215

**Radey, Thomas, Yon & Clark**
313 North Monroe Street, Suite 200,
Tallahassee, FL 32310

**Ramis Crew Corrigan LLP**
1727 NW Hoyt Street, Portland, OR 97209

**Ramsay, Bridgforth, Harrelson &
Starling LLP**
Simmons First National Building, Eleventh
Floor, 501 Main Street, Pine Bluff,
AR 71611-8509

**Randall & Kenig LLP**
455 North CityFront Plaza, Suite 3160,
Chicago, IL 60611

**Raskin & Raskin PA**
2601 South Bayshore Drive, Suite 600, Miami,
FL 33133

**Rath, Young and Pignatelli PC**
One Capital Plaza, PO Box 1500, Concord,
NH 03302

**Ravich Meyer Kirkman McGrath &
Nauman, PA**
4545 IDS Center, 80 South Eighth Street,
Minneapolis, MN 55402

**Ray & Isler PC**
8245 Boone Boulevard, Suite 402, Tysons
Corner, Vienna, VA 22182-3813

**Ray, Quinney & Nebeker PC**
36 South State Street, Suite 1400,
Salt Lake City, UT 84111

**Read and Laniado**
25 Eagle Street, Albany, NY 12207

**Real Property Law Group PLLC**
1218 Third Avenue, Suite 1900, Seattle,
WA 98101

**Reeder & Shuman**
PO Box 842, Morgantown, WV 26507

**Reges & Boone LLC**
9095 Glacier Highway, Suite 103, Juneau,
AK 99801

**Rendings, Fry & Dennis, LLP**
1 West Fourth Street, Suite 900, Cincinnati,
OH 45202-3688

**Rice Pugatch Robinson & Schiller**
848 Brickell Avenue, Suite 1100, Miami,
FL 33131

**Rice Silbey Reuther & Sullivan LLP**
3960 Howard Hughes Parkway, Suite 700, Las
Vegas, NV 89109

**Richards Spears Kibbe & Orbe**
One World Financial Center, 29th Floor, New
York, NY 10281

**Richilano & Ridley PC**
1800 15th Street, Suite 101, Denver,
CO 80202-1185

**Riddell Williams PS**
1001 Fourth Avenue Plaza, Suite 4500, Seattle,
WA 98154

**Rider, Bennett, Egan & Arundel, LLP**
333 South Seventh Street, Suite 2000,
Minneapolis, MN 55402

**Riegels Campos & Kenyon**
2500 Venture Oaks Way, Suite 220,
Sacramento, CA 95833

**Riemer & Braunstein LLP**
Three Center Plaza, Boston, MA 02108

**Robbins, Russell, Englert,
Orseck & Untereiner LLP**
1801 K Street NW, Suite 411, Washington, DC
20006

**Robert B von Mehren - Sole
Practitioner**
919 3rd Avenue, New York, NY 10022

**Robert E Panoff PA**
9400 South Dadeland Boulevard, Suite 106,
Miami, FL 33156

**Robert Glazier - Sole Practitioner**
540 Brickell Key Drive, Suite C-1, Miami, FL
33131

**Robert M Knight**
526 East Front Street, PO Box 8899, Missoula,
MT 59807-8899

**Robert Stoller - Sole Practitioner**
800 Dimond Boulevard, Suite 3-537,
Anchorage, AK 99515

**Roberts & Holland LLP**
Worldwide Plaza, 825 Eighth Avenue, New
York, NY 10019-7416

**Robinson & Cole LLP**
280 Trumbull Street, Hartford, CT 06103-3597

**Robinson & McElwee PLLC**
600 United Center, 500 Virginia Street East,
Charleston, WV 25326

**Robinson Wolenty & Young, LLP**
8888 Keystone Crossing, Suite 710,
Indianapolis, IN 46240

**Robinson, Bradshaw & Hinson PA**
101 North Tryon Street, Suite 1900, Charlotte,
NC 28246

**Robison, Belaustegui, Sharp & Low**
71 Washington Street, Reno, NV 89503

**Rochelle, Hutcheson
& McCullough, LLP**
325 North St Paul, Suite 4500, Dallas,
TX 75201

**Rodey, Dickason, Sloan,
Akin & Robb, PA**
201 Third Street North West, Suite 2200,
Albuquerque, NM 87102

**Roetzel & Andress, LPA**
222 South Main Street, Akron, OH 44308

**Rogers & Hardin**
2700 International Tower, 229 Peachtree
Street, Atlanta, GA 30303-1601

**Rogers Joseph O'Donnell & Phillips**
311 California Street, 10th Floor, San
Francisco, CA 94104-2695

**Rogers Towers PA**
1301 Riverplace Boulevard, Suite 1500,
Jacksonville, FL 32207

**Ronald K Cacciatore PA**
100 North Tampa Street, Suite 2835, Tampa,
FL 33602

**Rose Law Firm**
120 East Fourth Street, Little Rock,
AR 72201-2893

**Rosenberg, Martin, Funk,
Greenberg, LLP**
25 South Charles Street, Suite 2115, Baltimore,
MD 21201

**Ross Dixon & Bell LLP**
2001 K Street NW, Washington,
DC 20006-1040

**Rotatori, Bender, Gragel, Stoper &
Alexander Co LPA**
800 Leader Building, 526 Superior Avenue
East, Cleveland, OH 44114-1498

**Rouse Hendricks German May PC**
One Petticoat Lane Building, 1010 Walnut
Street, Suite 400, Kansas City, MO 64106

**Rubin and Rudman LLP**
50 Rowes Wharf, Boston, MA 02110

**Ruby & Schofield**
125 South Market Street, Suite 1001, San José,
CA 95113-2285

**Ruden McClosky, SC**
200 East Broward Boulevard, PO Box 1900,
Fort Lauderdale, FL 33302

**Rudman & Winchell LLC**
84 Harlow Street, PO Box 1401, Bangor,
ME 04402-1401

**Rush Law Group**
1209 Sixteenth Avenue South, Nashville,
TN 37212

**Rush Moore LLP**
Pacific Guardian Center, Mauka Tower, 737
Bishop Street, Honolulu, HI 96813

**Rushton, Stakely, Johnston
& Garrett**
184 Commerce Street, Montgomery, AL 36104

**Rusing & Lopez PLLC**
6262 North Swan Road, Suite 200, Tucson,
AZ 85718

**Ryan Whaley Coldiron**
900 Robinson Renaissance, 119 North
Robinson Avenue, Oklahoma City, OK 73102

**Sabo & Zahn**
401 North Michigan, Suite 2050, Chicago,
IL 60611

**Sachnoff & Weaver Ltd**
10 South Wacker Drive, 40th Floor, Chicago,
IL 60606-7507

**Sacks Montgomery PC**
800 Third Avenue, New York, NY 10022

**Sacks Tierney PA**
4250 North Drinkwater Boulevard, 4th Floor,
Scottsdale, AZ 85251

**Saiber Schlesinger Satz
& Goldstein, LLC**
One Gateway Center, Thirteenth Floor,
Newark, NJ 07102-5311

**S**

**Sale & Kuehne PA**
Bank of America Tower, Suite 3550, 100
Southeast Second Street, Miami,
FL 33131-2154

**Samuel B Weiner Co LPA**
743 South Front Street, Columbus, OH 43206

**Sandler, Travis & Rosenberg**
5200 Blue Lagoon Drive, Suite 600, Miami, FL
33126

**Santoro, Driggs, Walch, Kearney,
Johnson & Thompson**
400 South 4th Street, 3rd Floor, Las Vegas,
NV 89101

**Schaffer Law Office**
311 East 14th Street, Sioux Falls,
SD 57104-5022

**Schagrin Associates**
1100 Fifteenth Street, NW Suite 700,
Washington, DC 20005

**Scheuer Yost & Patterson PC**
125 Lincoln Avenue, Suite 223, PO Drawer
9570, Santa Fe, NM 87504-9570

**Schlack Ito & Lockwood Piper &
Elkind, LLC**
Topa Financial Centre, Fort Street Tower, 745
Fort Street, Honolulu, HI 96813

**Schnader Harrison Segal
& Lewis LLP**
1600 Market Street, Suite 3600, Philadelphia,
PA 19103-7286

**Schneider Tanaka Radovich Andrew
& Tanaka, LLLC**
The Topa Financial Center, Bishop Street
Tower, Suite 501, Honolulu, HI 96813

**Schopf & Weiss**
312 West Randolph Street, Suite 300, Chicago,
IL 60606-1721

**Schreck Brignone**
300 South Fourth Street, Suite 1200, Las Vegas,
NV 89101

**Schuler, Messersmith, Daly &
Lansdowne**
2155 Louisiana Boulevard NE, Suite 8500,
Albuquerque, NM 87110-1229

**Schully, Roberts, Slattery,
Jaubert & Marino**
Energy Centre, 1100 Poydras Street, Suite
1800, New Orleans, LA 70163

**Schwabe Williamson & Wyatt PC**
Suites 1600-1900 Pacwest Center, 1211 SW
Fifth Avenue, Portland, OR 97204

**Schwartz, Bon, Walker & Studer LLC**
141 South Center, Suite 505, Casper,
WY 82601

**Schwartz, Cooper, Greenberger &
Krauss, Chartered**
180 North LaSalle Street, Suite 2700, Chicago,
IL 60601

**Scroggins & Williamson**
1500 The Candler Building, 127 Peachtree
Street NE, Atlanta, GA 30303

**Seaton, Beck, Peters,
Bowen & Feuss**
7300 Metro Boulevard, Suite 500,
Minneapolis, MN 55439

**Sebris Busto James**
14205 SE 36th Street, Suite 325, Bellevue,
WA 98006

**Seed IP Law Group PLLC**
701 Fifth Avenue 6300, Seattle, WA 98104

**Senn Lewis & Visciano**
1801 California Street, Suite 4300, Denver,
CO 80205

**Serkland Law Firm, PC**
10 Roberts Street, PO Box 6017, Fargo,
ND 58108

**Serotte, Rockman & Westcott**
409 Washington Avenue, Suite 610, Baltimore,
MD 21204-7913

**Sessions, Fishman & Nathan LLP**
201 St Charles Avenue, Suite 3500, New
Orleans, LA 70170-3500

**Shaft, Reis & Shaft Ltd**
Gate City Federal Building, PO Box 5116,
Grand Forks, ND 58206-5116

**Shannon, Gracey, Ratliff & Miller LLP**
777 Main Street, Suite 3800, Fort Worth,
TX 76102

**Shapiro Bettinger Chase LLP**
4273 Montgomery Boulevard NE, Suite 110-E,
Albuquerque, NM 87109

**Shapiro Forman Allen Sava &
McPherson LLP**
380 Madison Avenue, New York, NY 10017

**Shapiro Fussell**
One Midtown Plaza, Suite 1200, 1360
Peachtree Street, Atlanta, GA 30309-3214

**Shaw Gussis Fishman Glantz
Wolfson & Towbin LLC**
321N Clark Street, Suite 800, Chicago,
IL 60610

**Sheehey Furlong & Behm PC**
Gateway Square, 30 Main Street, Burlington,
VT 05402

**Shefsky & Froelich**
111 East Wacker Drive, Chicago, IL 60601

**Sheley & Hall**
303 Peachtree Street, Suite 4440, Atlanta,
GA 30308

**Shemin & Hendren, PLLC**
One East Center Street, Suite 212, Bank of
America Plaza, Fayetteville, AR 72702

**Shems Dunkiel Kassel
& Saunders PLLC**
91 College Street, Burlington, VT 05401

**Shepherd Law Group, PC**
99 Summer Street, Suite 910, Boston, MA
02110-1248

**Sheppard, Mullin, Richter &
Hampton LLP**
333 South Hope Street, Forty-Eighth Floor,
Los Angeles, CA 90071

**Sher & Blackwell**
Suite 900, 1850 M Street NW, Washington, DC
20036

**Sherin and Lodgen LLP**
100 Summer Street, Boston, MA 02110

**Shernoff, Bidart & Darras LLP**
600 South Indian Hill Boulevard, Claremont,
CA 91711

**Sherrard & Roe PLC**
SunTrust Center, 424 Church Street, Suite
2000, Nashville, TN 37219

**Shipman & Goodwin LLP**
One Constitution Plaza, Hartford,
CT 06103-1919

**Shulman, Rogers, Gandal, Pordy &
Ecker, PA**
11921 Rockville Pike, Third Floor, Rockville,
MD 20852

**Shults Law Firm, LLP**
200 West Capitol Avenue, Suite 1600,
Little Rock, AR 72201-3637

**Shumacker Witt Gaither
& Whitaker, PC**
1100 SunTrust Bank Building, 736 Market
Street, Chattanooga, TN 37402-4856

**Shumaker Loop & Kendrick LLP**
North Courthouse Square, 1000 Jackson,
Toledo, OH 43624

**Shuttleworth & Ingersoll PLC**
115 Third Street South East, Suite 500, PO Box
2107, Cedar Rapids, IA 52406

**Siegel, O'Connor, O'Donnell
& Beck PC**
150 Trumbell Street, Hartford, CT 06103

**Siegfried, Rivera, Lerner, De La Torre
& Sobel, PA**
Suite 1102, 201 Alhambra Circle, Miami,
FL 33134

**Simmons Perrine Albright
& Ellwood PLC**
115 Third Street SE, Suite 1200, Cedar Rapids,
IA 52401

**Sirote & Permutt PC**
2311 Highland Avenue South, PO Box 55727,
Birmingham, AL 35205

**Slover & Loftus**
1224 Seventeenth Street NW, Washington, DC
20036

**Slusser, Wilson & Partridge LLP**
4720 Three Allen Center, 333 Clay Street,
Houston, TX 77002

**Smith & Kotchka Ltd**
317 South Sixth Street, Las Vegas, NV 89101

**Smith Bakke Oppegard
Porsborg & Wolf**
116 North 2nd Street, PO Box 460, Bismarck,
ND 58502-0460

**Smith Gambrell & Russell LLP**
Promenade II, Suite 3100, 1230 Peachtree
Street NE, Atlanta, GA 30309

**Smith Hulsey & Busey**
225 Water Street, Suite 1800, Jacksonville,
FL 32201

**Smith Mackinnon PA**
(Orange Co), Suite 800 Citrus Center
255 South Orange Avenue, Orlando, FL 32801

**Smith Pachter McWhorter PLC**
8000 Towers Crescent Drive, Suite 900, Vienna,
VA 22182

**Smith, Currie & Hancock LLP**
2700 Marquis One Tower, 245 Peachtree
Center Avenue NE, Atlanta, GA 30303-1227

**Sommer, Udall, Hardwick, Ahern &
Hyatt LLP**
200 West Marcy Street, Suite 129, Santa Fe,
NM 87501

**Sparks & Craig LLP**
6862 Elm Street, Suite 360, McLean, VA 22101

**Spencer Fane Britt & Browne LLP**
1000 Walnut Street, Suite 1400, Kansas City,
MO 64106

**Sperling & Slater**
55 West Monroe Street, Suite 3300, Chicago,
IL 60603-5010

**Spieth Bell McCurdy & Newell Co LPA**
2000 Huntington Building, 925 Euclid Avenue,
Cleveland, OH 44115-1496

**Spink & Miller PLC**
One Lawson Lane, Burlington, VT 05401

**Spink Butler, LLP**
PO Box 639, Boise, ID 83701

**Spradling, Kennedy & McPhail LLP**
The Tower, 1601 NW Expressway, Suite 1750,
Oklahoma City, OK 73118

**Sprague & Sprague**
The Wellington Building, Suite 400, 135 South
Nineteenth Street, Philadelphia, PA 19103

**Spriggs & Hollingsworth**
1350 I Street NW, Washington, DC 20005

**St Peter & Kasle**
Four Richmond Square, Providence, RI 02906

**Stafford Rosenbaum LLP**
3 South Pinckney Street, Suite 1000, PO Box
1784, Madison, WI 53701

**Stearns Weaver Miller Weissler
Alhadeff & Sitterson, PA**
Suite 2200 Museum Tower, 150 West Flagler
Street, Miami, FL 33130

**Steese & Evans PC**
6400 South Fiddlers Green Circle, Suite 1820,
Denver, CO 80111

**Stein, Ray & Harris LLP**
222 West Adams Street, Suite 1800, Chicago,
IL 60606

**Stephen E Kaufman, PC**
277 Park Avenue, 47th Floor, New York,
NY 10172

**Stephen Rakusin PA**
One East Broward Bouleard, Suite 1111,
Fort Lauderdale, FL 33301-1843

**Steptoe & Johnson PLLC**
Bank One Center, Sixth Floor, PO Box 2190,
Clarksburg, WV 26302-2190

**Stetler & Duffy Ltd**
140 South Dearborn, Suite 400, Chicago,
IL 60603

**Stevens & Lee PC**
111 North Sixth Street, Reading, PA 19603-0679

**Stevens & O'Connell LLP**
400 Capitol Mall, Suite 1400, Sacramento,
CA 95814-4412

Stewart & Stewart
Suite 200, 2100 M Street NW, Washington, DC
20037-1218

Stillman & Friedman
425 Park Avenue, New York, NY 10022

Stokes Lawrence, PS
800 Fifth Avenue, Suite 4000, Seattle, WA
98104-3179

Stoll Stoll Berne Lokting & Shlachter
209 Southwest Oak Street, Portland, OR 97204

Storslee Law Firm
PO Box 4007, 1802 Allison Drive, Bismarck,
ND 58502-4007

Stradley Ronon Stevens
& Young LLP
2600 One Commerce Square, Philadelphia,
PA 19103

Strasburger & Price LLP
4300 NationsBank Plaza, 901 Main Street,
Dallas, TX 75202

Strecker & Associates
2150 Mid-Continent Tower, 401 South Boston
Avenue, Tulsa, OK 74103-4009

Stroock & Stroock & Lavan LLP
180 Maiden Lane, New York, NY 10038-4982

Sugarman, Rogers, Barshak &
Cohen, PC
101 Merrimac Street, 9th floor, Boston, MA
02114-4737

Sukin Law Group
1501 Broadway, 30th Floor, New York, NY
10036

Sullivan & Worcester LLP
One Post Office Square, Boston, MA 02109

Sullivan Weinstein & McQuay
Two Park Plaza, Boston, MA 02116-3902

Sullivan, Tabaracci and Rhoades PC
1821 South Avenue West, Third Floor,
Missoula, MT 59801

Sulloway & Hollis PLLC
9 Capitol Street, PO Box 1256, Concord,
NH 03302

Summit Law Group, PLLC
315 Fifth Avenue South, Suite 1000, Seattle,
WA 98104

Sundahl, Powers, Kapp
& Martin LLC
1725 Carey Avenue, PO Box 328, Cheyenne,
WY 82001

Susman Godfrey LLP
Suite 5100, 1000 Louisiana Street, Houston,
TX 77002-5096

Sutin, Thayer & Browne
6565 Americas Parkway NE, Two Park Square,
Suite 1000, Albuquerque, NM 87110

Swanson & McNamara LLP
300 Montgomery Street, Suite 1100,
San Francisco, CA 94104

Taft, Stettinius & Hollister LLP
425 Walnut Street, Suite 1800, Cincinnati,
OH 45202

Tarolli, Sundheim, Covell, &
Tummino LLP
1111 Leader Building, 526 Superior Avenue,
Cleveland, OH 44114

Taylor, Porter, Brooks & Phillips, LLP
Bank One Centre, 8th Floor, 451 Florida
Street, Baton Rouge, LA 70821

Temkin Wielga & Hardt LLP
1900 Wazee Street, Suite 303, Denver,
CO 80202

Tescher Gutter Chaves Josepher
Rubin Ruffin & Forman PA
Boca Corporate Center, 2101 Corporate
Boulevard, Suite 107, Boca Raton, FL 33431-
7343

Tew Cardenas LLP
Four Seasons Office Tower, 15th Floor, 1441
Brickell Avenue, Miami, FL 33131

The Barnes Law Firm PC
One Turtle Creek Village, 3878 Oak Lawn,
Suite 400, Dallas, TX 75219

The James Law Firm PC
630 Equitable Building, 604 Locust Street, Des
Moines, IA 50309

The Kullman Firm PLC
1600 Energy Centre, 1100 Poydras Street, PO
Box 60118, New Orleans, LA 70160

The Law Office of Mark J Svonkin PC
18 North Main Street, West Hartford, CT
06107

The Law Offices of Weston Reeves
Park Street Law Office, 119 South Washington,
PO Box 2229, Casper, WY 82602

The Lyon Firm PA
1031 West Morse Boulevard, Suite 170, Winter
Park, FL 32789

The Richard Law Firm PC
350 East Broadway, Jackson, WY 83001

The Steeg Law Firm, LLC
201 St Charles Avenue, Suite 3201, New
Orleans, LA 70170

The Tinney Law Firm
Fourteenth Floor, 707 Virginia Street,
Charleston, WV 25301

The Webb Law Firm
700 Koppers Building, 436 Seventh Ave,
Pittsburgh, PA 15219-1818

Theriault & Joslin PC
141 Main Street, PO Box 249, Montpelier, VT
05602-0249

Thieman & Farrell
Koppers Buildings 436, 7th Avenue,
Pittsburgh, PA 15219

Thomas Kayden Horstemeyer &
Risley LLP
100 Galleria Parkway North West, Suite 1750,
Atlanta, GA 30339

Thomas N Long PC
American National Bank Building, Suite 406,
Cheyenne, WY 82003-0087

Thompson Miller & Simpson PLC
600 West Main Street, Suite 500, Louisville,
KY 40202

Thompson, Sizemore & Gonzalez
501 East Kennedy Boulevard, Suite 1400, PO
Box 639, Tampa, FL 33602

Thomte, Mazour & Niebergall, LLC
2120 South 72nd Street, Suite 1111, Omaha,
NE 68124-2341

Thorp Reed & Armstrong
One Oxford Centre, Fourteenth Floor,
Pittsburgh, PA 15219-1425

Timothy S Kelley - Sole Practitioner
540 N Lake Shore Drive, Suite 204, Chicago,
IL 60611

Tindall Bennett & Shoup PC
508 West 2nd Avenue, Third Floor, Anchorage,
AK 99501

Tinnin Law Firm
500 Marquette NW, Suite 1300, Albuquerque,
NM 87102

Titus, Brueckner & Berry PC
Scottsdale Centre, Suite B-252, 7373 North
Scottsdale Road, Scottsdale, AZ 85253-3527

Todd & Weld LLP
28 State Street, Boston, MA 02109

Topel & Goodman PC
4th Floor, 832 Sansome Street, San Francisco,
CA 94111

Torkildson, Katz, Fonseca, Jaffe,
Moore & Hetherington Attorneys At
Law, A Law Corporation
Amfac Building, 15th Floor, 700 Bishop Street,
Honolulu, HI 96813

Townsend & Jones
5615 Kirby Drive, Suite 830, Houston,
TX 77005

Townsend and Townsend
and Crew LLP
Two Embarcadero Center, Eighth Floor,
San Francisco, CA 94111-3834

Trenam, Kemker, Scharf, Barkin,
Frye, O'Neill & Mullis PA
2700 Bank of America Plaza, 101 East Kennedy
Boulevard, Tampa, FL 33602

Triplett, Woolf & Garretson LLC
2959 North Rock Road, Suite 300, Wichita,
KS 67226

Trombley & Hanes
10th Floor, 707 North Franklin Street, PO Box
3356, Tampa, FL 33602

Troutman Sanders LLP
401 Ninth Street NW, Suite 1000, Washington,
DC 20004-2134

Tschider & Smith
Professional Building, Suite 200, 418 East
Rosser Avenue, Bismarck, ND 58501

Tsukazaki Yeh & Moore
100 Pauahi Street, Suite 204, Honolulu,
HI 96720-3046

Tucker Ellis & West LLP
1100 Huntingdon Building, 925 Euclid
Avenue, Cleveland, OH 44115-1475

Turner & Mede, PC
1500 West 33rd Avenue, Suite 200, Anchorage,
AK 99503-3502

Tyler Cooper & Alcorn LLP
205 Church Street, PO Box 1936, New Haven,
CT 06509

Ugrin, Alexander, Zadick
& Higgins, PC
2 Railroad Square, PO Box 1746, Great Falls,
MT 59403

Ulmer & Berne LLP
Skylight Office Tower, 1660 West 2nd Street,
Suite 1100, Cleveland, OH 44113-1448

Upton and Hatfield LLP
10 Centre Street, PO Box 1090, Concord,
NH 03302

Van Cott, Bagley, Cornwall &
McCarthy
50 South Main Street, Suite 1600, PO Box
45340, Salt Lake City, UT 84145

Van Hoy Reutlinger Adams & Dunn
737 East Boulevard, Charlotte, NC 28203

Van Ness Feldman PC
1050 Thomas Jefferson Street NW, Seventh
Floor, Washington, DC 20007

Vantage Counsel LLC
Pacific Guardian Center, Makai Tower, 733
Bishop Street, Honolulu, HI 96813

Vaughan & Murphy
260 Peachtree Street NW, Suite 1600,
Atlanta, GA 30303

Vezina Lawrence & Piscitelli PA
318 North Calhoun Street, Tallahassee,
FL 32301

Vickers Madsen & Goldman
1705 Metropolitan Boulevard, Suite 101,
Tallahassee, FL 32308-3765

Vogel Campbell & Blueher PC
6100 Uptown Boulevard NE, Suite 500,
Albuquerque, NM 87110-4143

Vogel Law Firm
218 NP Avenue, PO Box 1389, Fargo, ND
58107-1389

Vranesh and Raisch, LLP
1720 14th Street, Suite 200, PO Box 871,
Boulder, CO 80306-0871

W Michael Reisman - Sole
Practitioner
Myres S McDougal Professor of International
Law, Yale Law School, PO Box 208215,
New Haven, CT 06520

Wadleigh, Starr & Peters PLLC
95 Market Street, Manchester, NH 03101

Wagner Choi Evers
745 Fort Street, Suite 1900, Honolulu,
HI 96813

Walder, Hayden & Brogan PA
5 Becker Farm Road, PO Box 901, Roseland,
NJ 07068

Walston, Wells, Anderson & Bains
One Federal Place, 1819 Fifth Ave North, Suite
1100, Birmingham, AL 35203

Walter & Haverfield LLP
The Tower at Erieview, 1301 East Ninth Street,
Suite 3500, Cleveland, OH 44114-1821

Walters Romm Chanti & Dickens
245 East 4th Avenue, Eugene, OR 97401

Ward and Smith PA
1001 College Court, PO Box 867, New Bern,
NC 28563

W

**Warner Norcross & Judd LLP**
900 Old Kent Building, 111 Lyon Street North West, Grand Rapids, MI 49503

**Warren & Sinkler LLP**
171 Church Street, Suite 340, PO Box 1254, Charleston, SC 29402

**Watanabe Ing & Komeiji**
First Hawaiian Center, 999 Bishop Street, Suite 2300, Honolulu, HI 96813

**Watkins Ludlam Winter & Stennis, PA**
633 North State Street (39202), PO Box 427, Jackson, MS 39205-0427

**Watt, Beckworth, Thompson & Henneman**
1010 Lamar, Suite 1600, Houston, TX 77002

**Weinberg Richmond LLP**
333 West Wacker Drive, Suite 1800, Chicago, IL 60606

**Weinberg, Wheeler, Hudgins, Gunn & Dial, LLC**
950 East Paces Ferry Road, Suite 3000, Atlanta, GA 30326

**Weiner & Weltchek**
The Foxleigh Building, Suite 300, 2330 West Joppa Road, Lutherville, MD 21093

**Weissmann, Wolff, Bergman, Coleman, Grodin & Evall, LLP**
Suite 900, 9665 Wilshire Boulevard, Beverly Hills, CA 90212-2345

**Welbaum, Guernsey, Hingston, Greenleaf & Gregory LLP**
Penthouse Suite, 901 Ponce de Leon Boulevard, Miami, FL 33134-3009

**Welsh & Katz Ltd**
120 South Riverside Plaza, 22nd Floor, Chicago, IL 60606

**Wheeler Trigg Kennedy LLP**
1801 California Street, Suite 3600, Denver, CO 80202-2617

**White Goss Bowers March Schulte & Weisenfels, A Professional Corporation**
4510 Belleview Avenue, Suite 300, Kansas City, MO 64111

**White O'Connor Curry & Avanzado LLP**
10100 Santa Monica Boulevard, Twenty-Third Floor, Los Angeles, CA 90067

**White, Getgey & Meyer Co LPA**
1700 Fourth & Vine Tower, 1 West Fourth Street, Cincinnati, OH 45202-3621

**Whiteman Osterman & Hanna LLP**
One Commerce Plaza, Albany, NY 12260

**Whitfield & Eddy, PLC**
317 Sixth Avenue, Suite 1200, Des Moines, IA 50309

**Whyte Hirschboeck Dudek SC**
111 E Wisconsin Avenue, Suite 2100, Milwaukee, WI 53202

**Wickwire Gavin PC**
8100 Boone Boulevard, Suite 700, Vienna, VA 22182

**Wiggin & Nourie**
20 Market Street, PO Box 808, Manchester, NH 03105-0808

**Wiggin and Dana LLP**
One Century Tower, New Haven, CT 06508

**Wildman Harrold**
225 West Wacker Drive, 30th Floor, Chicago, IL 60606

**Wilentz Goldman & Spitzer, PA**
90 Woodbridge Center Drive, Suite 900, Box 10, Woodbridge, NJ 07095

**Wilkinson Barker Knauer LLP**
2300 N Street NW, Suite 700, Washington, DC 20037-1128

**Willcox & Savage**
One Commercial Place, Suite 1800, Norfolk, VA 23510

**William Aaron**
Miami Center, Suite 850, 201 South Biscayne Boulevard, Miami, FL 33131

**William B Short Jr, PC**
8080 N Central Expressway, Suite 1600, LB-65, Dallas, TX 75206

**William D Preston PA**
4832-A Kerry Forest Parkway, Tallahassee, FL 32309

**William Rozell - Sole Practitioner**
617 Willoghby Avenue, Juneau, AK 99801

**William W. Park - Sole Practitioner**
Professor of Law, Boston University Law School, 765 Commonwealth Ave, Boston, MA 02215

**Williams & Connolly LLP**
725 Twelfth Street, Washington, DC 20005

**Williams & Petro Co LLC**
338 South High Street, Columbus, OH 43215

**Williams Bradbury, Attorneys at Law**
1015 W. Hays Street, Boise, ID 83702

**Williams Mullen**
Two James Center, 1021 East Cary Street, Richmond, VA 23218

**Williams, Porter, Day & Neville PC**
159 North Wolcott Street, Suite 400, Casper, WY 82602

**Williams, Zografos & Peck**
334 Third Street, Post Office Box 547, Lake Oswego, OR 97034

**Wilson, Elser, Moskowitz, Edelman & Dicker LLP**
150 East 42nd Street, New York, NY 10017-5639

**Winer & Bennett LLP**
111 Concord Street, PO Box 488, Nashua, NH 03061-0488

**Winn & Alexander LLP**
820 Bay Avenue, Suite 109, Capitola, CA 95010

**Winne Banta Hetherington Basralian & Kahn, PC**
21 Main Street, PO Box 647, Hackensack, NJ 07602

**Winterbauer & Diamond, PLLC**
1200 Fifth Avenue, Suite 1910, Seattle, WA 98101

**Wise Carter Child & Caraway, Professional Association**
401 East Capitol Street, Suite 600, PO Box 651, Jackson, MS 39205

**Withey Anderson & Morris PLC**
2525 East Arizona Biltmore Circle, Suite A-212, Phoenix, AZ 85016

**Wold Johnson PC**
400 Gate City Building, PO Box 1680, Fargo, ND 58107

**Wood, Herron & Evans, LLP**
2700 Carew Tower, Cincinnati, OH 45202

**Woodburn and Wedge**
6100 Neil Road, Suite 500, Reno, NV 89511

**Woods & Aitken LLP**
301 South 13th Street, Suite 500, Lincoln, NE 68508

**Woods Rogers PLC**
Wachovia Tower, Suite 1400, 10 South Jefferson Street, Roanoke, VA 24038

**Woods, Fuller, Shultz & Smith PC**
300 South Phillips Avenue, Suite 300, PO Box 5027, Sioux Falls, SD 57117

**Woodward, Hobson & Fulton LLP**
2500 National City Tower, 101 South Fifth Street, Louisville, KY 40202

**Woolf, McClane, Bright, Allen & Carpenter, PLLC**
Riverview Tower, PO Box 900, Knoxville, TN 37901-0900

**Word & Bogardus**
500 Tijeras NW, Albuquerque, NM 87102

**Worden Thane PC**
111 North Higgins, Suite 600, PO Box 4747, Missoula, MT 59806

**Wright & Talisman PC**
Suite 600, 1200 G Street NW, Washington, DC 20005-3802

**Wright Robinson Osthimer & Tatum**
411 East Franklin Street, Suite 400, Richmond, VA 23219

**Wright, Henson, Somers, Clark & Bake LLP**
Commerce Bank Building, 100 Southeast Ninth Street, 2nd Floor, PO Box 3555, Topeka, KS 66601-3555

**Wyrsch Hobbs & Mirakian PC**
1101 Walnut Suite, Kansas City, MO 64106

**Yonkee & Toner LLP**
319 West Dow Street, PO Box 6288, Sheridan, WY 82801

**York, Keller & Field**
1265 Frost Bank Plaza, 816 Congress Avenue, Austin, TX 78701

**Young & Susser PC Attorneys and Counselors**
Suite 305 Westview Office Center, 26200 American Drive, Southfield, MI 48034

**Young, Clement & Rivers LLP**
28 Broad Street, PO Box 993, Charleston, SC 29402

**Young, Sommer, Ward, Ritzenberg, Wooley, Baker & Moore LLC**
5 Palisades Drive, Executive Woods, Albany, NY 12205

**Zeiger, Tigges, Little & Lindsmith LLP**
3500 Huntington Center, 41 South High Street, Columbus, OH 43215

**Zetlin & De Chiara LLP**
801 Second Avenue, New York, NY 10017

**Ziffren Brittenham Branca Fischer Gilbert-Lurie & Stiffelman LLP**
1801 Century Park West, Los Angeles, CA 90067-6406

**Zimney Foster PC**
3100 Soouth Columbia Road, Suite 200, PO Box 13417, Grand Forks, ND 58208-3417

**Zinober & McCrea, PA**
Southtrust Plaza, 201 East Kennedy Boulevard Suite 800, PO Box 1378, Tampa, FL 33602

**Zuckerman Spaeder LLP**
Miami Center, Suite 900, 201 Biscayne Boulevard, Miami, FL 33131

**Zuckert, Scoutt & Rasenberger, LLP**
888 Seventeenth St. NW, Washington, DC 20006

**Zuger Kirmis & Smith**
316 North Fifth Street, PO Box 1695, Bismarck, ND 58502

**Zumwalt, Almon & Hayes**
Music Row, 1014 Sixteenth Avenue South, Nashville, TN 37212

If you can't find a firm here, see firm profiles at the end of every state